PETERSON'S®
GRADUATE PROGRAMS
IN ENGINEERING & APPLIED
SCIENCES

2018

About Peterson's®

Peterson's®, a Nelnet company, has been your trusted educational publisher for over 50 years. It's a milestone we're quite proud of, as we continue to offer the most accurate, dependable, high-quality educational content in the field, providing you with everything you need to succeed. No matter where you are on your academic or professional path, you can rely on Peterson's for its books, online information, expert test-prep tools, the most up-to-date education exploration data, and the highest quality career success resources—everything you need to achieve your education goals. For our complete line of products, visit www.petersons.com.

For more information, contact Peterson's, 3 Columbia Circle, Suite 205, Albany, NY 12203-5158; 800-338-3282 Ext. 54229; or find us online at **www.petersons.com.**

ISSN 1093-8443
ISBN: 978-0-7689-4169-2

Printed in the United States of America

10 9 8 7 6 5 4 3 2 1   20 19 18

Fifty-second Edition

CONTENTS

A Note from the Peterson's Editors

The six volumes of Peterson's *Graduate and Professional Programs*, the only annually updated reference work of its kind, provide wide-ranging information on the graduate and professional programs offered by accredited colleges and universities in the United States, U.S. territories, and Canada and by those institutions outside the United States that are accredited by U.S. accrediting bodies. More than 44,000 individual academic and professional programs at more than 2,300 institutions are listed. Peterson's *Graduate and Professional Programs* have been used for more than fifty years by prospective graduate and professional students, placement counselors, faculty advisers, and all others interested in postbaccalaureate education.

Graduate & Professional Programs: An Overview contains information on institutions as a whole, while the other books in the series are devoted to specific academic and professional fields:

- *Graduate Programs in the Biological/Biomedical Sciences & Health-Related Medical Professions*

- *Graduate Programs in Business, Education, Information Studies, Law & Social Work*

- *Graduate Programs in Engineering & Applied Sciences*

- *Graduate Programs in the Humanities, Arts & Social Sciences*

- *Graduate Programs in the Physical Sciences, Mathematics, Agricultural Sciences, the Environment & Natural Resources*

The books may be used individually or as a set. For example, if you have chosen a field of study but do not know what institution you want to attend or if you have a college or university in mind but have not chosen an academic field of study, it is best to begin with the Overview guide.

Graduate & Professional Programs: An Overview presents several directories to help you identify programs of study that might interest you; you can then research those programs further in the other books in the series by using the Directory of Graduate and Professional Programs by Field, which lists 500 fields and gives the names of those institutions that offer graduate degree programs in each.

For geographical or financial reasons, you may be interested in attending a particular institution and will want to know what it has to offer. You should turn to the Directory of Institutions and Their Offerings, which lists the degree programs available at each institution. As in the Directory of Graduate and Professional Programs by Field, the level of degrees offered is also indicated.

All books in the series include advice on graduate education, including topics such as admissions tests, financial aid, and accreditation. **The Graduate Adviser** includes two essays and information about accreditation. The first essay, "The Admissions Process," discusses general admission requirements, admission tests, factors to consider when selecting a graduate school or program, when and how to apply, and how admission decisions are made. Special information for international students and tips for minority students are also included. The second essay, "Financial Support," is an overview of the broad range of support available at the graduate level. Fellowships, scholarships, and grants; assistantships and internships; federal and private loan programs, as well as Federal Work-Study; and the GI bill are detailed. This essay concludes with advice on applying for need-based financial aid. "Accreditation and Accrediting Agencies" gives information on accreditation and its purpose and lists institutional accrediting agencies first and then specialized accrediting agencies relevant to each volume's specific fields of study.

With information on more than 40,000 graduate programs in more than 500 disciplines, Peterson's *Graduate and Professional Programs* give you all the information you need about the programs that are of interest to you in three formats: **Profiles** (capsule summaries of basic information), **Displays** (information that an institution or program wants to emphasize), and **Close-Ups** (written by administrators, with more expansive information than the **Profiles**, emphasizing different aspects of the programs). By using these various formats of program information, coupled with **Appendixes** and **Indexes** covering directories and subject areas for all six books, you will find that these guides provide the most comprehensive, accurate, and up-to-date graduate study information available.

Peterson's publishes a full line of resources with information you need to guide you through the graduate admissions process. Peterson's publications can be found at college libraries and career centers and your local bookstore or library—or visit us on the Web at www.petersons.com.

Colleges and universities will be pleased to know that Peterson's helped you in your selection. Admissions staff members are more than happy to answer questions, address specific problems, and help in any way they can. The editors at Peterson's wish you great success in your graduate program search!

THE GRADUATE ADVISER

The Admissions Process

Generalizations about graduate admissions practices are not always helpful because each institution has its own set of guidelines and procedures. Nevertheless, some broad statements can be made about the admissions process that may help you plan your strategy.

Factors Involved in Selecting a Graduate School or Program

Selecting a graduate school and a specific program of study is a complex matter. Quality of the faculty; program and course offerings; the nature, size, and location of the institution; admission requirements; cost; and the availability of financial assistance are among the many factors that affect one's choice of institution. Other considerations are job placement and achievements of the program's graduates and the institution's resources, such as libraries, laboratories, and computer facilities. If you are to make the best possible choice, you need to learn as much as you can about the schools and programs you are considering before you apply.

The following steps may help you narrow your choices.

- Talk to alumni of the programs or institutions you are considering to get their impressions of how well they were prepared for work in their fields of study.
- Remember that graduate school requirements change, so be sure to get the most up-to-date information possible.
- Talk to department faculty members and the graduate adviser at your undergraduate institution. They often have information about programs of study at other institutions.
- Visit the websites of the graduate schools in which you are interested to request a graduate catalog. Contact the department chair in your chosen field of study for additional information about the department and the field.
- Visit as many campuses as possible. Call ahead for an appointment with the graduate adviser in your field of interest and be sure to check out the facilities and talk to students.

General Requirements

Graduate schools and departments have requirements that applicants for admission must meet. Typically, these requirements include undergraduate transcripts (which provide information about undergraduate grade point average and course work applied toward a major), admission test scores, and letters of recommendation. Most graduate programs also ask for an essay or personal statement that describes your personal reasons for seeking graduate study. In some fields, such as art and music, portfolios or auditions may be required in addition to other evidence of talent. Some institutions require that the applicant have an undergraduate degree in the same subject as the intended graduate major.

Most institutions evaluate each applicant on the basis of the applicant's total record, and the weight accorded any given factor varies widely from institution to institution and from program to program.

The Application Process

You should begin the application process at least one year before you expect to begin your graduate study. Find out the application deadline for each institution (many are provided in the **Profile** section of this guide). Go to the institution's website and find out if you can apply online. If not, request a paper application form. Fill out this form thoroughly and neatly. Assume that the school needs all the information it is requesting and that the admissions officer will be sensitive to the neatness and overall quality of what you submit. Do not supply more information than the school requires.

The institution may ask at least one question that will require a three- or four-paragraph answer. Compose your response on the assumption that the admissions officer is interested in both what you think and how you express yourself. Keep your statement brief and to the point, but, at the same time, include all pertinent information about your past experiences and your educational goals. Individual statements vary greatly in style and content, which helps admissions officers differentiate among applicants. Many graduate departments give considerable weight to the statement in making their admissions decisions, so be sure to take the time to prepare a thoughtful and concise statement.

If recommendations are a part of the admissions requirements, carefully choose the individuals you ask to write them. It is generally best to ask current or former professors to write the recommendations, provided they are able to attest to your intellectual ability and motivation for doing the work required of a graduate student. It is advisable to provide stamped, preaddressed envelopes to people being asked to submit recommendations on your behalf.

Completed applications, including references, transcripts, and admission test scores, should be received at the institution by the specified date.

Be advised that institutions do not usually make admissions decisions until all materials have been received. Enclose a self-addressed postcard with your application, requesting confirmation of receipt. Allow at least ten days for the return of the postcard before making further inquiries.

If you plan to apply for financial support, it is imperative that you file your application early.

ADMISSION TESTS

The major testing program used in graduate admissions is the Graduate Record Examinations (GRE®) testing program, sponsored by the GRE Board and administered by Educational Testing Service, Princeton, New Jersey.

The Graduate Record Examinations testing program consists of a General Test and eight Subject Tests. The General Test measures critical thinking, verbal reasoning, quantitative reasoning, and analytical writing skills. It is offered as an Internet-based test (iBT) in the United States, Canada, and many other countries.

The GRE® General Test's questions were designed to reflect the kind of thinking that students need to do in graduate or business school and demonstrate that students are indeed ready for graduate-level work.

- **Verbal Reasoning**—Measures ability to analyze and evaluate written material and synthesize information obtained from it, analyze relationships among component parts of sentences, and recognize relationships among words and concepts.
- **Quantitative Reasoning**—Measures problem-solving ability, focusing on basic concepts of arithmetic, algebra, geometry, and data analysis.
- **Analytical Writing**—Measures critical thinking and analytical writing skills, specifically the ability to articulate and support complex ideas clearly and effectively.

The computer-based GRE® General Test is offered year-round at Prometric™ test centers and on specific dates at testing locations outside of the Prometric test center network. Appointments are scheduled on a first-come, first-served basis. The GRE® General Test is also offered as a paper-based test three times a year in areas where computer-based testing is not available.

You can take the computer-based GRE® General Test once every twenty-one days, up to five times within any continuous rolling twelve-month period (365 days)—even if you canceled your scores on a previously taken test. You may take the paper-based GRE® General Test as often as it is offered.

Three scores are reported on the General Test:

1. A **Verbal Reasoning score** is reported on a 130–170 score scale, in 1-point increments.
2. A **Quantitative Reasoning score** is reported on a 130–170 score scale, in 1-point increments.
3. An **Analytical Writing score** is reported on a 0–6 score level, in half-point increments.

The GRE® Subject Tests measure achievement and assume undergraduate majors or extensive background in the following eight disciplines:

- Biochemistry, Cell and Molecular Biology
- Biology
- Chemistry
- Computer Science
- Literature in English
- Mathematics
- Physics
- Psychology

The Subject Tests are available three times per year as paper-based administrations around the world. Testing time is approximately 2 hours and 50 minutes. You can obtain more information about the GRE® by visiting the ETS website at www.ets.org or consulting the *GRE® Information and Registration Bulletin*. The *Bulletin* can be obtained at many undergraduate colleges. You can also download it from the ETS website or obtain it by contacting Graduate Record Examinations, Educational Testing Service, P.O. Box 6000, Princeton, NJ 08541-6000; phone: 609-771-7670.

If you expect to apply for admission to a program that requires any of the GRE® tests, you should select a test date well in advance of the application deadline. Scores on the computer-based General Test are reported within ten to fifteen days; scores on the paper-based Subject Tests are reported within six weeks.

Another testing program, the Miller Analogies Test® (MAT®), is administered at more than 500 Controlled Testing Centers, licensed by Pearson, in the United States, Canada, and other countries. The MAT® computer-based test is now available. Testing time is 60 minutes. The test consists of 120 partial analogies. You can obtain the *Candidate Information Booklet,* which contains a list of test centers and instructions for taking the test, from http://www.milleranalogies.com or by calling 800-328-5999 (toll-free).

Check the specific requirements of the programs to which you are applying.

How Admission Decisions Are Made

The program you apply to is directly involved in the admissions process. Although the final decision is usually made by the graduate dean (or an associate) or the faculty admissions committee, recommendations from faculty members in your intended field are important. At some institutions, an interview is incorporated into the decision process.

A Special Note for International Students

In addition to the steps already described, there are some special considerations for international students who intend to apply for graduate study in the United States. All graduate schools require an indication of competence in English. The purpose of the Test of English as a Foreign Language (TOEFL®) is to evaluate the English proficiency of people who are nonnative speakers of English and want to study at colleges and universities where English is the language of instruction. The TOEFL® is administered by Educational Testing Service (ETS) under the general direction of a policy board established by the College Board and the Graduate Record Examinations Board.

The TOEFL® iBT assesses the four basic language skills: listening, reading, writing, and speaking. It was administered for the first time in September 2005, and ETS continues to introduce the TOEFL® iBT in selected cities. The Internet-based test is administered at secure, official test centers. The testing time is approximately 4 hours. Because the TOEFL® iBT includes a speaking section, the Test of Spoken English (TSE) is no longer needed.

The TOEFL® is also offered in the paper-based format in areas of the world where Internet-based testing is not available. The paper-based TOEFL® consists of three sections—listening comprehension, structure and written expression, and reading comprehension. The testing time is approximately 3 hours. The Test of Written English (TWE®) is also given. The TWE® is a 30-minute essay that measures the examinee's ability to compose in English. Examinees receive a TWE® score separate from their TOEFL® score. The *Information Bulletin* contains information on local fees and registration procedures.

The TOEFL® paper-based test (TOEFL® PBT) began being phased out in mid-2012. For those who may have taken the TOEFL® PBT, scores remain valid for two years after the test date. The Test of Written English (TWE®) is also given. The TWE® is a 30-minute essay that measures the examinee's ability to compose in English. Examinees receive a TWE® score separate from their TOEFL® score. The Information Bulletin contains information on local fees and registration procedures.

Additional information and registration materials are available from TOEFL® Services, Educational Testing Service, P.O. Box 6151, Princeton, New Jersey 08541-6151. Phone: 609-771-7100. Website: www.toefl.org.

International students should apply especially early because of the number of steps required to complete the admissions process. Furthermore, many United States graduate schools have a limited number of spaces for international students, and many more students apply than the schools can accommodate.

International students may find financial assistance from institutions very limited. The U.S. government requires international applicants to submit a certification of support, which is a statement attesting to the applicant's financial resources. In addition, international students *must* have health insurance coverage.

Tips for Minority Students

Indicators of a university's values in terms of diversity are found both in its recruitment programs and its resources directed to student success. Important questions: Does the institution vigorously recruit minorities for its graduate programs? Is there funding available to help with the costs associated with visiting the school? Are minorities represented in the institution's brochures or website or on their faculty rolls? What campus-based resources or services (including assistance in locating housing or career counseling and placement) are available? Is funding available to members of underrepresented groups?

At the program level, it is particularly important for minority students to investigate the "climate" of a program under consideration. How many minority students are enrolled and how many have graduated? What opportunities are there to work with diverse faculty and mentors whose research interests match yours? How are conflicts resolved or concerns addressed? How interested are faculty in building strong and supportive relations with students? "Climate" concerns should be addressed by posing questions to various individuals, including faculty members, current students, and alumni.

Information is also available through various organizations, such as the Hispanic Association of Colleges & Universities (HACU), and publications such as *Diverse Issues in Higher Education* and *Hispanic Outlook* magazine. There are also books devoted to this topic, such as *The Multicultural Student's Guide to Colleges* by Robert Mitchell.

Financial Support

The range of financial support at the graduate level is very broad. The following descriptions will give you a general idea of what you might expect and what will be expected of you as a financial support recipient.

Fellowships, Scholarships, and Grants

These are usually outright awards of a few hundred to many thousands of dollars with no service to the institution required in return. Fellowships and scholarships are usually awarded on the basis of merit and are highly competitive. Grants are made on the basis of financial need or special talent in a field of study. Many fellowships, scholarships, and grants not only cover tuition, fees, and supplies but also include stipends for living expenses with allowances for dependents. However, the terms of each should be examined because some do not permit recipients to supplement their income with outside work. Fellowships, scholarships, and grants may vary in the number of years for which they are awarded.

In addition to the availability of these funds at the university or program level, many excellent fellowship programs are available at the national level and may be applied for before and during enrollment in a graduate program. A listing of many of these programs can be found at the Council of Graduate Schools' website: http://www.cgsnet.org. There is a wealth of information in the "Programs" and "Awards" sections.

Assistantships and Internships

Many graduate students receive financial support through assistantships, particularly involving teaching or research duties. It is important to recognize that such appointments should not be viewed simply as employment relationships but rather should constitute an integral and important part of a student's graduate education. As such, the appointments should be accompanied by strong faculty mentoring and increasingly responsible apprenticeship experiences. The specific nature of these appointments in a given program should be considered in selecting that graduate program.

TEACHING ASSISTANTSHIPS

These usually provide a salary and full or partial tuition remission and may also provide health benefits. Unlike fellowships, scholarships, and grants, which require no service to the institution, teaching assistantships require recipients to provide the institution with a specific amount of undergraduate teaching, ideally related to the student's field of study. Some teaching assistants are limited to grading papers, compiling bibliographies, taking notes, or monitoring laboratories. At some graduate schools, teaching assistants must carry lighter course loads than regular full-time students.

RESEARCH ASSISTANTSHIPS

These are very similar to teaching assistantships in the manner in which financial assistance is provided. The difference is that recipients are given basic research assignments in their disciplines rather than teaching responsibilities. The work required is normally related to the student's field of study; in most instances, the assistantship supports the student's thesis or dissertation research.

ADMINISTRATIVE INTERNSHIPS

These are similar to assistantships in application of financial assistance funds, but the student is given an assignment on a part-time basis, usually as a special assistant with one of the university's administrative offices. The assignment may not necessarily be directly related to the recipient's discipline.

RESIDENCE HALL AND COUNSELING ASSISTANTSHIPS

These assistantships are frequently assigned to graduate students in psychology, counseling, and social work, but they may be offered to students in other disciplines, especially if the student has worked in this capacity during his or her undergraduate years. Duties can vary from being available in a dean's office for a specific number of hours for consultation with undergraduates to living in campus residences and being responsible for both counseling and administrative tasks or advising student activity groups. Residence hall assistantships often include a room and board allowance and, in some cases, tuition assistance and stipends. Contact the Housing and Student Life Office for more information.

Health Insurance

The availability and affordability of health insurance is an important issue and one that should be considered in an applicant's choice of institution and program. While often included with assistantships and fellowships, this is not always the case and, even if provided, the benefits may be limited. It is important to note that the U.S. government requires international students to have health insurance.

The GI Bill

This provides financial assistance for students who are veterans of the United States armed forces. If you are a veteran, contact your local Veterans Administration office to determine your eligibility and to get full details about benefits. There are a number of programs that offer educational benefits to current military enlistees. Some states have tuition assistance programs for members of the National Guard. Contact the VA office at the college for more information.

Federal Work-Study Program (FWS)

Employment is another way some students finance their graduate studies. The federally funded Federal Work-Study Program provides eligible students with employment opportunities, usually in public and private nonprofit organizations. Federal funds pay up to 75 percent of the wages, with the remainder paid by the employing agency. FWS is available to graduate students who demonstrate financial need. Not all schools have these funds, and some only award them to undergraduates. Each school sets its application deadline and workstudy earnings limits. Wages vary and are related to the type of work done. You must file the Free Application for Federal Student Aid (FAFSA) to be eligible for this program.

Loans

Many graduate students borrow to finance their graduate programs when other sources of assistance (which do not have to be repaid) prove insufficient. You should always read and understand the terms of any loan program before submitting your application.

FEDERAL DIRECT LOANS

Federal Direct Loans. The Federal Direct Loan Program offers a variable-fixed interest rate loan to graduate students with the Department of Education acting as the lender. Students receive a new rate with each new loan, but that rate is fixed for the life of the loan. Beginning with loans made on or after July 1, 2013, the interest rate for loans made each July 1st to June 30th period are determined based on the last 10-year Treasury note auction prior to June 1st of that year, plus an added percentage. The interest rate can be no higher than 9.5%.

Beginning July 1, 2012, the Federal Direct Loan for graduate students is an unsubsidized loan. Under the *unsubsidized* program, the grad borrower pays the interest on the loan from the day proceeds are issued and is responsible for paying interest during all periods. If the borrower chooses not to pay the interest while in school, or during the grace periods, deferment, or forbearance, the interest accrues and will be capitalized.

Graduate students may borrow up to $20,500 per year through the Direct Loan Program, up to a cumulative maximum of $138,500, including undergraduate borrowing. No more than $65,500 of the $138,500 can be from subsidized loans, including loans the grad borrower may have received for periods of enrollment that began before July 1, 2012, or for prior undergraduate borrowing. You may borrow up to the cost of attendance at the school in which you are enrolled or will attend, minus estimated financial assistance from other federal, state, and private sources, up to a maximum of $20,500. Grad borrowers who reach the aggregate loan limit over the course of their education cannot receive additional loans; however, if they repay some of their loans to bring the outstanding balance below the aggregate limit, they could be eligible to borrow again, up to that limit.

For Unsubsidized loans first disbursed on or after July 1, 2016, and before July 1, 2017, the interest rate was 5.31%. For those first disbursed on or after July 1, 2017, and before July 1, 2018, the interest rate is 6%.

A fee is deducted from the loan proceeds upon disbursement. Loans with a first disbursement on or after July 1, 2010 but before July 1, 2012, have a borrower origination fee of 1 percent. For loans disbursed after July 1, 2012, these fee deductions no longer apply. The Budget Control Act of 2011, signed into law on August 2, 2011, eliminated Direct Subsidized Loan eligibility for graduate and professional students for periods of enrollment beginning on or after July 1, 2012, and terminated the authority of the Department of Education to offer most repayment incentives to Direct Loan borrowers for loans disbursed on or after July 1, 2012.

Under the *subsidized* Federal Direct Loan Program, repayment begins six months after your last date of enrollment on at least a half-time basis. Under the *unsubsidized* program, repayment of interest begins within thirty days from disbursement of the loan proceeds, and repayment of the principal begins six months after your last enrollment on at least a half-time basis. Some borrowers may choose to defer interest payments while they are in school. The accrued interest is added to the loan balance when the borrower begins repayment. There are several repayment options.

Federal Perkins Loans. The Federal Perkins Loan is available to students demonstrating financial need and is administered directly by the school. Not all schools have these funds, and some may award them to undergraduates only. Eligibility is determined from the information you provide on the FAFSA. The school will notify you of your eligibility.

Eligible graduate students may borrow up to $8,000 per year, up to a maximum of $60,000, including undergraduate borrowing (even if your previous Perkins Loans have been repaid). The interest rate for Federal Perkins Loans is 5 percent, and no interest accrues while you remain in school at least half-time. Students who are attending less than half-time need to check with their school to determine the length of their grace period. There are no guarantee, loan, or disbursement fees. Repayment begins nine months after your last date of enrollment on at least a half-time basis and may extend over a maximum of ten years with no prepayment penalty.

Federal Direct Graduate PLUS Loans. Effective July 1, 2006, graduate and professional students are eligible for Graduate PLUS loans. This program allows students to borrow up to the cost of attendance, less any other aid received. These loans have a fixed interest rate (7% for the 2017–2018 academic year), and interest begins to accrue at the time of disbursement. Beginning with loans made on or after July 1, 2013, the interest rate for loans made each July 1st to June 30th period are determined based on the last 10-year Treasury note auction prior to June 1st of that year. The interest rate can be no higher than 10.5%. The PLUS loans do involve a credit check; a PLUS borrower may obtain a loan with a cosigner if his or her credit is not good enough. Grad PLUS loans may be deferred while a student is in school and for the six months following a drop below half-time enrollment. For more information, you should contact a representative in your college's financial aid office.

Deferring Your Federal Loan Repayments. If you borrowed under the Federal Direct Loan Program, Federal Direct PLUS Loan Program, or the Federal Perkins Loan Program for previous undergraduate or graduate study, your payments may be deferred when you return to graduate school, depending on when you borrowed and under which program.

There are other deferment options available if you are temporarily unable to repay your loan. Information about these deferments is provided at your entrance and exit interviews. If you believe you are eligible for a deferment of your loan payments, you must contact your lender or loan servicer to request a deferment. The deferment must be filed prior to the time your payment is due, and it must be re-filed when it expires if you remain eligible for deferment at that time.

SUPPLEMENTAL (PRIVATE) LOANS

Many lending institutions offer supplemental loan programs and other financing plans, such as the ones described here, to students seeking additional assistance in meeting their education expenses. Some loan programs target all types of graduate students; others are designed specifically for business, law, or medical students. In addition, you can use private loans not specifically designed for education to help finance your graduate degree.

If you are considering borrowing through a supplemental or private loan program, you should carefully consider the terms and be sure to read the fine print. Check with the program sponsor for the most current terms that will be applicable to the amounts you intend to borrow for graduate study. Most supplemental loan programs for graduate study offer unsubsidized, credit-based loans. In general, a credit-ready borrower is one who has a satisfactory credit history or no credit history at all. A creditworthy borrower generally must pass a credit test to be eligible to borrow or act as a cosigner for the loan funds.

Many supplemental loan programs have minimum and maximum annual loan limits. Some offer amounts equal to the cost of attendance minus any other aid you will receive for graduate study. If you are planning to borrow for several years of graduate study, consider whether there is a cumulative or aggregate limit on the amount you may borrow. Often this cumulative or aggregate limit will include any amounts you borrowed and have not repaid for undergraduate or previous graduate study.

The combination of the annual interest rate, loan fees, and the repayment terms you choose will determine how much you will repay over time. Compare these features in combination before you decide which loan program to use. Some loans offer interest rates that are adjusted monthly, quarterly, or annually. Some offer interest rates that are lower during the in-school, grace, and deferment periods and then increase when you begin repayment. Some programs include a loan origination fee, which is usually deducted from the principal amount you receive when the loan is disbursed and must be repaid along with the interest and other principal when you graduate, withdraw from school, or drop below half-time study. Sometimes the loan fees are reduced if you borrow with a qualified cosigner. Some programs allow you to defer interest and/or principal payments while you are enrolled in graduate school. Many programs allow you to capitalize your interest payments; the interest due on your loan is added to the outstanding balance of your loan, so you don't have to repay immediately, but this increases the amount you owe. Other programs allow you to pay the interest as you go, which reduces the amount you later have to repay. The private loan market is very competitive, and your financial aid office can help you evaluate these programs.

Applying for Need-Based Financial Aid

Schools that award federal and institutional financial assistance based on need will require you to complete the FAFSA and, in some cases, an institutional financial aid application.

If you are applying for federal student assistance, you **must** complete the FAFSA. A service of the U.S. Department of Education, the FAFSA is free to all applicants. Most applicants apply online at www.fafsa.ed.gov. Paper applications are available at the financial aid office of your local college.

After your FAFSA information has been processed, you will receive a Student Aid Report (SAR). If you provided an e-mail address on the FAFSA, this will be sent to you electronically; otherwise, it will be mailed to your home address.

Follow the instructions on the SAR if you need to correct information reported on your original application. If your situation changes after you file your FAFSA, contact your financial aid officer to discuss amending your information. You can also appeal your financial aid award if you have extenuating circumstances.

If you would like more information on federal student financial aid, visit the FAFSA website or download the most recent version of *Funding Education Beyond High School: The Guide to Federal Student Aid* at http://studentaid.ed.gov/students/publications/student_guide/index.html. This guide is also available in Spanish.

The U.S. Department of Education also has a toll-free number for questions concerning federal student aid programs. The number is 1-800-4-FED AID (1-800-433-3243). If you are hearing impaired, call toll-free, 1-800-730-8913.

Summary

Remember that these are generalized statements about financial assistance at the graduate level. Because each institution allots its aid differently, you should communicate directly with the school and the specific department of interest to you. It is not unusual, for example, to find that an endowment vested within a specific department supports one or more fellowships. You may fit its requirements and specifications precisely.

Accreditation and Accrediting Agencies

Colleges and universities in the United States, and their individual academic and professional programs, are accredited by nongovernmental agencies concerned with monitoring the quality of education in this country. Agencies with both regional and national jurisdictions grant accreditation to institutions as a whole, while specialized bodies acting on a nationwide basis—often national professional associations—grant accreditation to departments and programs in specific fields.

Institutional and specialized accrediting agencies share the same basic concerns: the purpose an academic unit—whether university or program—has set for itself and how well it fulfills that purpose, the adequacy of its financial and other resources, the quality of its academic offerings, and the level of services it provides. Agencies that grant institutional accreditation take a broader view, of course, and examine university-wide or college-wide services with which a specialized agency may not concern itself.

Both types of agencies follow the same general procedures when considering an application for accreditation. The academic unit prepares a self-evaluation, focusing on the concerns mentioned above and usually including an assessment of both its strengths and weaknesses; a team of representatives of the accrediting body reviews this evaluation, visits the campus, and makes its own report; and finally, the accrediting body makes a decision on the application. Often, even when accreditation is granted, the agency makes a recommendation regarding how the institution or program can improve. All institutions and programs are also reviewed every few years to determine whether they continue to meet established standards; if they do not, they may lose their accreditation.

Accrediting agencies themselves are reviewed and evaluated periodically by the U.S. Department of Education and the Council for Higher Education Accreditation (CHEA). Recognized agencies adhere to certain standards and practices, and their authority in matters of accreditation is widely accepted in the educational community.

This does not mean, however, that accreditation is a simple matter, either for schools wishing to become accredited or for students deciding where to apply. Indeed, in certain fields the very meaning and methods of accreditation are the subject of a good deal of debate. For their part, those applying to graduate school should be aware of the safeguards provided by regional accreditation, especially in terms of degree acceptance and institutional longevity. Beyond this, applicants should understand the role that specialized accreditation plays in their field, as this varies considerably from one discipline to another. In certain professional fields, it is necessary to have graduated from a program that is accredited in order to be eligible for a license to practice, and in some fields the federal government also makes this a hiring requirement. In other disciplines, however, accreditation is not as essential, and there can be excellent programs that are not accredited. In fact, some programs choose not to seek accreditation, although most do.

Institutions and programs that present themselves for accreditation are sometimes granted the status of candidate for accreditation, or what is known as "preaccreditation." This may happen, for example, when an academic unit is too new to have met all the requirements for accreditation. Such status signifies initial recognition and indicates that the school or program in question is working to fulfill all requirements; it does not, however, guarantee that accreditation will be granted.

Institutional Accrediting Agencies—Regional

MIDDLE STATES ASSOCIATION OF COLLEGES AND SCHOOLS

Accredits institutions in Delaware, District of Columbia, Maryland, New Jersey, New York, Pennsylvania, Puerto Rico, and the Virgin Islands.

Dr. Elizabeth Sibolski, President
Middle States Commission on Higher Education
3624 Market Street, Second Floor West
Philadelphia, Pennsylvania 19104
Phone: 267-284-5000
Fax: 215-662-5501
E-mail: info@msche.org
Website: www.msche.org

NEW ENGLAND ASSOCIATION OF SCHOOLS AND COLLEGES

Accredits institutions in Connecticut, Maine, Massachusetts, New Hampshire, Rhode Island, and Vermont.

Dr. Barbara E. Brittingham, President/Director
Commission on Institutions of Higher Education
3 Burlington Woods Drive, Suite 100
Burlington, Massachusetts 01803-4531
Phone: 855-886-3272 or 781-425-7714
Fax: 781-425-1001
E-mail: cihe@neasc.org
Website: http://cihe.neasc.org

THE HIGHER LEARNING COMMISSION

Accredits institutions in Arizona, Arkansas, Colorado, Illinois, Indiana, Iowa, Kansas, Michigan, Minnesota, Missouri, Nebraska, New Mexico, North Dakota, Ohio, Oklahoma, South Dakota, West Virginia, Wisconsin, and Wyoming.

Dr. Barbara Gellman-Danley, President
The Higher Learning Commission
230 South LaSalle Street, Suite 7-500
Chicago, Illinois 60604-1413
Phone: 800-621-7440 or 312-263-0456
Fax: 312-263-7462
E-mail: info@hlcommission.org
Website: www.hlcommission.org

NORTHWEST COMMISSION ON COLLEGES AND UNIVERSITIES

Accredits institutions in Alaska, Idaho, Montana, Nevada, Oregon, Utah, and Washington.

Dr. Sandra E. Elman, President
8060 165th Avenue, NE, Suite 100
Redmond, Washington 98052
Phone: 425-558-4224
Fax: 425-376-0596
E-mail: selman@nwccu.org
Website: www.nwccu.org

SOUTHERN ASSOCIATION OF COLLEGES AND SCHOOLS

Accredits institutions in Alabama, Florida, Georgia, Kentucky, Louisiana, Mississippi, North Carolina, South Carolina, Tennessee, Texas, and Virginia.

Dr. Belle S. Wheelan, President
Commission on Colleges
1866 Southern Lane
Decatur, Georgia 30033-4097
Phone: 404-679-4500 Ext. 4504
Fax: 404-679-4558
E-mail: questions@sacscoc.org
Website: www.sacscoc.org

WESTERN ASSOCIATION OF SCHOOLS AND COLLEGES

Accredits institutions in California, Guam, and Hawaii.

Dr. Mary Ellen Petrisko, President
Accrediting Commission for Senior Colleges and Universities
985 Atlantic Avenue, Suite 100
Alameda, California 94501
Phone: 510-748-9001
Fax: 510-748-9797
E-mail: wasc@wascsenior.org
Website: http://www.wascsenior.org/

Institutional Accrediting Agencies—Other

ACCREDITING COUNCIL FOR INDEPENDENT COLLEGES AND SCHOOLS
Anthony S. Bieda, Executive in Charge
750 First Street, NE, Suite 980
Washington, DC 20002-4241
Phone: 202-336-6780
Fax: 202-842-2593
E-mail: info@acics.org
Website: www.acics.org

DISTANCE EDUCATION AND ACCREDITING COMMISSION (DEAC)
Accrediting Commission
Leah Matthews, Executive Director
1101 17th Street, NW, Suite 808
Washington, DC 20036-4704
Phone: 202-234-5100
Fax: 202-332-1386
E-mail: info@deac.org
Website: www.deac.org

Specialized Accrediting Agencies

ACUPUNCTURE AND ORIENTAL MEDICINE
Mark S. McKenzie, LAc MsOM DiplOM, Executive Director
Accreditation Commission for Acupuncture and Oriental Medicine
8941 Aztec Drive
Eden Prairie, Minnesota 55347
Phone: 952-212-2434
Fax: 301-313-0912
E-mail: coordinator@acaom.org
Website: www.acaom.org

ALLIED HEALTH
Kathleen Megivern, Executive Director
Commission on Accreditation of Allied Health Education Programs (CAAHEP)
25400 US Hwy 19 North, Suite 158
Clearwater, Florida 33763
Phone: 727-210-2350
Fax: 727-210-2354
E-mail: mail@caahep.org
Website: www.caahep.org

ART AND DESIGN
Karen P. Moynahan, Executive Director
National Association of Schools of Art and Design (NASAD)
Commission on Accreditation
11250 Roger Bacon Drive, Suite 21
Reston, Virginia 20190-5248
Phone: 703-437-0700
Fax: 703-437-6312
E-mail: info@arts-accredit.org
Website: http://nasad.arts-accredit.org

ATHLETIC TRAINING EDUCATION
Micki Cuppett, Executive Director
Commission on Accreditation of Athletic Training Education (CAATE)
6850 Austin Center Blvd., Suite 100
Austin, Texas 78731-3184
Phone: 512-733-9700
E-mail: micki@caate.net
Website: www.caate.net

AUDIOLOGY EDUCATION
Doris Gordon, Executive Director
Accreditation Commission for Audiology Education (ACAE)
11480 Commerce Park Drive, Suite 220
Reston, Virginia 20191
Phone: 202-986-9550
Fax: 202-986-9500
E-mail: info@acaeaccred.org
Website: www.acaeaccred.org

AVIATION
Dr. Gary J. Northam, Executive Director
Aviation Accreditation Board International (AABI)
3410 Skyway Drive
Auburn, Alabama 36830
Phone: 334-844-2431
Fax: 334-844-2432
E-mail: bayenva@auburn.edu
Website: www.aabi.aero

BUSINESS
Robert D. Reid, Executive Vice President and Chief Accreditation Officer
AACSB International—The Association to Advance Collegiate Schools of Business
777 South Harbour Island Boulevard, Suite 750
Tampa, Florida 33602
Phone: 813-769-6500
Fax: 813-769-6559
E-mail: bob@aacsb.edu
Website: www.aacsb.edu

BUSINESS EDUCATION
Dennis N. Gash, President and Chief Executive Officer
International Assembly for Collegiate Business Education (IACBE)
11257 Strang Line Road
Lenexa, Kansas 66215
Phone: 913-631-3009
Fax: 913-631-9154
E-mail:iacbe@iacbe.org
Website: www.iacbe.org

CHIROPRACTIC
Craig S. Little, President
Council on Chiropractic Education (CCE)
Commission on Accreditation
8049 North 85th Way
Scottsdale, Arizona 85258-4321
Phone: 480-443-8877 or 888-443-3506
Fax: 480-483-7333
E-mail: cce@cce-usa.org
Website: www.cce-usa.org

CLINICAL LABORATORY SCIENCES
Dianne M. Cearlock, Ph.D., Chief Executive Officer
National Accrediting Agency for Clinical Laboratory Sciences
5600 North River Road, Suite 720
Rosemont, Illinois 60018-5119
Phone: 773-714-8880 or 847-939-3597
Fax: 773-714-8886
E-mail: info@naacls.org
Website: www.naacls.org

CLINICAL PASTORAL EDUCATION
Trace Haythorn, Executive Director
Association for Clinical Pastoral Education, Inc.
1549 Clairmont Road, Suite 103
Decatur, Georgia 30033-4611
Phone: 404-320-1472
Fax: 404-320-0849
E-mail: acpe@acpe.edu
Website: www.acpe.edu

DANCE
Karen P. Moynahan, Executive Director
National Association of Schools of Dance (NASD)
Commission on Accreditation
11250 Roger Bacon Drive, Suite 21
Reston, Virginia 20190-5248
Phone: 703-437-0700
Fax: 703-437-6312
E-mail: info@arts-accredit.org
Website: http://nasd.arts-accredit.org

DENTISTRY
Dr. Sherin Tooks, Director
Commission on Dental Accreditation
American Dental Association
211 East Chicago Avenue, Suite 1900
Chicago, Illinois 60611
Phone: 312-440-4643 or 800-621-8099
E-mail: accreditation@ada.org
Website: www.ada.org

DIETETICS AND NUTRITION
Mary B. Gregoire, Ph.D., Executive Director; RD, FADA, FAND
Academy of Nutrition and Dietetics
Accreditation Council for Education in Nutrition and Dietetics (ACEND)
120 South Riverside Plaza, Suite 2000
Chicago, Illinois 60606-6995
Phone: 800-877-1600 Ext. 5400 or 312-899-0040
Fax: 312-899-4817
E-mail: acend@eatright.org
Website: www.eatright.org/ACEND

EDUCATION PREPARATION
Christopher Koch, President
Council for the Accreditation of Education Preparation (CAEP)
1140 19th Street NW, Suite 400
Washington, DC 20036
Phone: 202-223-0077
Fax: 202-296-6620
E-mail: caep@caepnet.org
Website: www.caepnet.org

ENGINEERING
Michael Milligan, Ph.D., PE, Executive Director
Accreditation Board for Engineering and Technology, Inc. (ABET)
415 North Charles Street
Baltimore, Maryland 21201
Phone: 410-347-7700
E-mail: accreditation@abet.org
Website: www.abet.org

FORENSIC SCIENCES
Nancy J. Jackson, Director of Development and Accreditation
American Academy of Forensic Sciences (AAFS)
Forensic Science Education Program Accreditation Commission (FEPAC)
410 North 21st Street
Colorado Springs, Colorado 80904
Phone: 719-636-1100
Fax: 719-636-1993
E-mail: njackson@aafs.org
Website: www.fepac-edu.org

FORESTRY
Carol L. Redelsheimer
Director of Science and Education
Society of American Foresters
5400 Grosvenor Lane
Bethesda, Maryland 20814-2198
Phone: 301-897-8720 or 866-897-8720
Fax: 301-897-3690
E-mail: redelsheimerc@safnet.org
Website: www.safnet.org

HEALTHCARE MANAGEMENT
Commission on Accreditation of Healthcare Management Education (CAHME)
Anthony Stanowski, President and CEO
1700 Rockville Pike
Suite 400
Rockville, Maryland 20852
Phone: 301-998-6101
E-mail: info@cahme.org
Website: www.cahme.org

HEALTH INFORMATICS AND HEALTH MANAGEMENT
Claire Dixon-Lee, Executive Director
Commission on Accreditation for Health Informatics and Information Management Education (CAHIIM)
233 North Michigan Avenue, 21st Floor
Chicago, Illinois 60601-5800
Phone: 312-233-1100
Fax: 312-233-1948
E-mail:E-mail: claire.dixon-lee@cahiim.org
Website: www.cahiim.org

HUMAN SERVICE EDUCATION
Dr. Elaine Green, President
Council for Standards in Human Service Education (CSHSE)
3337 Duke Street
Alexandria, Virginia 22314
Phone: 571-257-3959
E-mail: info@cshse.org
Web: http://www.cshse.org

INTERIOR DESIGN
Holly Mattson, Executive Director
Council for Interior Design Accreditation
206 Grandview Avenue, Suite 350
Grand Rapids, Michigan 49503-4014
Phone: 616-458-0400
Fax: 616-458-0460
E-mail: info@accredit-id.org
Website: www.accredit-id.org

JOURNALISM AND MASS COMMUNICATIONS
Susanne Shaw, Executive Director
Accrediting Council on Education in Journalism and Mass Communications (ACEJMC)
School of Journalism
Stauffer-Flint Hall
University of Kansas
1435 Jayhawk Boulevard
Lawrence, Kansas 66045-7575
Phone: 785-864-3973
Fax: 785-864-5225
E-mail: sshaw@ku.edu
Website: http://www2.ku.edu/~acejmc/

LANDSCAPE ARCHITECTURE
Kristopher D. Pritchard, Executive Director
Landscape Architectural Accreditation Board (LAAB)
American Society of Landscape Architects (ASLA)
636 Eye Street, NW
Washington, DC 20001-3736
Phone: 202-216-2359
Fax: 202-898-1185
E-mail: info@asla.org
Website: www.asla.org

LAW
Barry Currier, Managing Director of Accreditation & Legal Education
American Bar Association
321 North Clark Street, 21st Floor
Chicago, Illinois 60654
Phone: 312-988-6738
Fax: 312-988-5681
E-mail: legaled@americanbar.org
Website: http://www.americanbar.org/groups/legal_education/
    resources/accreditation.html

LIBRARY
Karen O'Brien, Director
Office for Accreditation
American Library Association
50 East Huron Street
Chicago, Illinois 60611-2795
Phone: 312-280-2432
Fax: 312-280-2433
E-mail: accred@ala.org
Website: www.ala.org/accreditation/

MARRIAGE AND FAMILY THERAPY
Tanya A. Tamarkin, Director of Educational Affairs
Commission on Accreditation for Marriage and Family Therapy
    Education (COAMFTE)
American Association for Marriage and Family Therapy
112 South Alfred Street
Alexandria, Virginia 22314-3061
Phone: 703-838-9808
Fax: 703-838-9805
E-mail: coa@aamft.org
Website: www.aamft.org

MEDICAL ILLUSTRATION
Kathleen Megivern, Executive Director
Commission on Accreditation of Allied Health Education Programs
    (CAAHEP)
1361 Park Street
Clearwater, Florida 33756
Phone: 727-210-2350
Fax: 727-210-2354
E-mail: mail@caahep.org
Website: www.caahep.org

MEDICINE
Liaison Committee on Medical Education (LCME)
Robert B. Hash, M.D., LCME Secretary
American Medical Association
Council on Medical Education
330 North Wabash Avenue, Suite 39300
Chicago, Illinois 60611-5885
Phone: 312-464-4933
E-mail: lcme@aamc.org
Website: www.ama-assn.org

Liaison Committee on Medical Education (LCME)
Heather Lent, M.A., Director
Accreditation Services
Association of American Medical Colleges
655 K Street, NW
Washington, DC 20001-2399
Phone: 202-828-0596
E-mail: lcme@aamc.org
Website: www.lcme.org

MUSIC
Karen P. Moynahan, Executive Director
National Association of Schools of Music (NASM)
Commission on Accreditation
11250 Roger Bacon Drive, Suite 21
Reston, Virginia 20190-5248
Phone: 703-437-0700
Fax: 703-437-6312
E-mail: info@arts-accredit.org
Website: http://nasm.arts-accredit.org/

NATUROPATHIC MEDICINE
Daniel Seitz, J.D., Ed.D., Executive Director
Council on Naturopathic Medical Education
P.O. Box 178
Great Barrington, Massachusetts 01230
Phone: 413-528-8877
E-mail: www.cnme.org/contact.html
Website: www.cnme.org

NURSE ANESTHESIA
Francis R.Gerbasi, Ph.D., CRNA, COA Executive Director
Council on Accreditation of Nurse Anesthesia Educational Programs
    (CoA-NAEP)
American Association of Nurse Anesthetists
222 South Prospect Avenue, Suite 304
Park Ridge, Illinois 60068-4010
Phone: 847-655-1160
Fax: 847-692-7137
E-mail: accreditation@coa.us.com
Website: http://home.coa.us.com

NURSE EDUCATION
Jennifer L. Butlin, Executive Director
Commission on Collegiate Nursing Education (CCNE)
One Dupont Circle, NW, Suite 530
Washington, DC 20036-1120
Phone: 202-887-6791
Fax: 202-887-8476
E-mail: jbutlin@aacn.nche.edu
Website: www.aacn.nche.edu/accreditation

Marsal P. Stoll, Chief Executive Officer
Accreditation Commission for Education in Nursing (ACEN)
3343 Peachtree Road, NE, Suite 850
Atlanta, Georgia 30326
Phone: 404-975-5000
Fax: 404-975-5020
E-mail: mstoll@acenursing.org
Website: www.acenursing.org

NURSE MIDWIFERY
Heather L. Maurer, M.A., Executive Director
Accreditation Commission for Midwifery Education (ACME)
American College of Nurse-Midwives
8403 Colesville Road, Suite 1550
Silver Spring, Maryland 20910
Phone: 240-485-1800
Fax: 240-485-1818
E-mail: info@acnm.org
Website: www.midwife.org/Program-Accreditation

NURSE PRACTITIONER
Gay Johnson, CEO
National Association of Nurse Practitioners in Women's Health
Council on Accreditation
505 C Street, NE
Washington, DC 20002
Phone: 202-543-9693 Ext. 1
Fax: 202-543-9858
E-mail: info@npwh.org
Website: www.npwh.org

NURSING
Marsal P. Stoll, Chief Executive Director
Accreditation Commission for Education in Nursing (ACEN)
3343 Peachtree Road, NE, Suite 850
Atlanta, Georgia 30326
Phone: 404-975-5000
Fax: 404-975-5020
E-mail: info@acenursing.org
Website: www.acenursing.org

OCCUPATIONAL THERAPY
Heather Stagliano, DHSc, OTR/L, Executive Director
The American Occupational Therapy Association, Inc.
4720 Montgomery Lane, Suite 200
Bethesda, Maryland 20814-3449
Phone: 301-652-6611 Ext. 2682
TDD: 800-377-8555
Fax: 240-762-5150
E-mail: accred@aota.org
Website: www.aoteonline.org

OPTOMETRY
Joyce L. Urbeck, Administrative Director
Accreditation Council on Optometric Education (ACOE)
American Optometric Association
243 North Lindbergh Boulevard
St. Louis, Missouri 63141-7881
Phone: 314-991-4100, Ext. 4246
Fax: 314-991-4101
E-mail: accredit@aoa.org
Website: www.theacoe.org

OSTEOPATHIC MEDICINE
Director, Department of Accreditation
Commission on Osteopathic College Accreditation (COCA)
American Osteopathic Association
142 East Ontario Street
Chicago, Illinois 60611
Phone: 312-202-8048
Fax: 312-202-8202
E-mail: predoc@osteopathic.org
Website: www.aoacoca.org

PHARMACY
Peter H. Vlasses, PharmD, Executive Director
Accreditation Council for Pharmacy Education
135 South LaSalle Street, Suite 4100
Chicago, Illinois 60603-4810
Phone: 312-664-3575
Fax: 312-664-4652
E-mail: csinfo@acpe-accredit.org
Website: www.acpe-accredit.org

PHYSICAL THERAPY
Sandra Wise, Senior Director
Commission on Accreditation in Physical Therapy Education (CAPTE)
American Physical Therapy Association (APTA)
1111 North Fairfax Street
Alexandria, Virginia 22314-1488
Phone: 703-706-3245
Fax: 703-706-3387
E-mail: accreditation@apta.org
Website: www.capteonline.org

PHYSICIAN ASSISTANT STUDIES
Sharon L. Luke, Executive Director
Accredittion Review Commission on Education for the Physician
    Assistant, Inc. (ARC-PA)
12000 Findley Road, Suite 150
Johns Creek, Georgia 30097
Phone: 770-476-1224
Fax: 770-476-1738
E-mail: arc-pa@arc-pa.org
Website: www.arc-pa.org

PLANNING
Ms. Shonagh Merits, Executive Director
American Institute of Certified Planners/Association of Collegiate
    Schools of Planning/American Planning Association
Planning Accreditation Board (PAB)
2334 West Lawrence Avenue, Suite 209
Chicago, Illinois 60625
Phone: 773-334-7200
E-mail: smerits@planningaccreditationboard.org
Website: www.planningaccreditationboard.org

PODIATRIC MEDICINE
Alan R. Tinkleman, M.P.A., Executive Director
Council on Podiatric Medical Education (CPME)
American Podiatric Medical Association (APMA)
9312 Old Georgetown Road
Bethesda, Maryland 20814-1621
Phone: 301-581-9200
Fax: 301-571-4903
Website: www.cpme.org

PSYCHOLOGY AND COUNSELING
Jacqueline Remondet Wall, CEO of the Accrediting Unit,
Office of Program Consultation and Accreditation
American Psychological Association
750 First Street, NE
Washington, DC 20002-4202
Phone: 202-336-5979 or 800-374-2721
TDD/TTY: 202-336-6123
Fax: 202-336-5978
E-mail: apaaccred@apa.org
Website: www.apa.org/ed/accreditation

Carol L. Bobby, Ph.D., Executive Director
Council for Accreditation of Counseling and Related Educational
    Programs (CACREP)
1001 North Fairfax Street, Suite 510
Alexandria, Virginia 22314
Phone: 703-535-5990
Fax: 703-739-6209
E-mail: cacrep@cacrep.org
Website: www.cacrep.org

Richard M. McFall, Executive Director
Psychological Clinical Science Accreditation System (PCSAS)
1101 East Tenth Street
IU Psychology Building
Bloomington, Indiana 47405-7007
Phone: 812-856-2570
Fax: 812-322-5545
E-mail: rmmcfall@pcsas.org
Website: www.pcsas.org

PUBLIC HEALTH
Laura Rasar King, M.P.H., MCHES, Executive Director
Council on Education for Public Health
1010 Wayne Avenue, Suite 220
Silver Spring, Maryland 20910
Phone: 202-789-1050
Fax: 202-789-1895
E-mail: Lking@ceph.org
Website: www.ceph.org

PUBLIC POLICY, AFFAIRS AND ADMINISTRATION
Crystal Calarusse, Chief Accreditation Officer
Commission on Peer Review and Accreditation
Network of Schools of Public Policy, Affairs, and Administration
(NASPAA-COPRA)
1029 Vermont Avenue, NW, Suite 1100
Washington, DC 20005
Phone: 202-628-8965
Fax: 202-626-4978
E-mail: copra@naspaa.org
Website: www.naspaa.org

RADIOLOGIC TECHNOLOGY
Leslie Winter, Chief Executive Officer Joint Review Committee on
Education in Radiologic Technology (JRCERT)
20 North Wacker Drive, Suite 2850
Chicago, Illinois 60606-3182
Phone: 312-704-5300
Fax: 312-704-5304
E-mail: mail@jrcert.org
Website: www.jrcert.org

REHABILITATION EDUCATION
Frank Lane, Ph.D., Executive Director
Council on Rehabilitation Education (CORE)
Commission on Standards and Accreditation
1699 Woodfield Road, Suite 300
Schaumburg, Illinois 60173
Phone: 847-944-1345
Fax: 847-944-1346
E-mail: flane@core-rehab.org
Website: www.core-rehab.org

RESPIRATORY CARE
Thomas Smalling, Executive Director
Commission on Accreditation for Respiratory Care (CoARC)
1248 Harwood Road
Bedford, Texas 76021-4244
Phone: 817-283-2835
Fax: 817-354-8519
E-mail: tom@coarc.com
Website: www.coarc.com

SOCIAL WORK
Dr. Stacey Borasky, Director of Accreditation
Office of Social Work Accreditation
Council on Social Work Education
1701 Duke Street, Suite 200
Alexandria, Virginia 22314
Phone: 703-683-8080
Fax: 703-519-2078
E-mail: info@cswe.org
Website: www.cswe.org

SPEECH-LANGUAGE PATHOLOGY AND AUDIOLOGY
Patrima L. Tice, Accreditation Executive Director
American Speech-Language-Hearing Association
Council on Academic Accreditation in Audiology and Speech-Language
    Pathology
2200 Research Boulevard #310
Rockville, Maryland 20850-3289
Phone: 301-296-5700
Fax: 301-296-8750
E-mail: accreditation@asha.org
Website: http://caa.asha.org

TEACHER EDUCATION
Christopher A. Koch, President
National Council for Accreditation of Teacher Education (NCATE)
Teacher Education Accreditation Council (TEAC)
1140 19th Street, Suite 400
Washington, DC 20036
Phone: 202-223-0077
Fax: 202-296-6620
E-mail: caep@caepnet.org
Website: www.ncate.org

TECHNOLOGY
Michale S. McComis, Ed.D., Executive Director
Accrediting Commission of Career Schools and Colleges
2101 Wilson Boulevard, Suite 302
Arlington, Virginia 22201
Phone: 703-247-4212
Fax: 703-247-4533
E-mail: mccomis@accsc.org
Website: www.accsc.org

TECHNOLOGY, MANAGEMENT, AND APPLIED ENGINEERING
Kelly Schild, Director of Accreditation
The Association of Technology, Management, and Applied Engineering
(ATMAE)
275 N. York Street, Suite 401
Elmhurst, Illinois 60126
Phone: 630-433-4514
Fax: 630-563-9181
E-mail: Kelly@atmae.org
Website: www.atmae.org

THEATER
Karen P. Moynahan, Executive Director
National Association of Schools of Theatre Commission on
    Accreditation
11250 Roger Bacon Drive, Suite 21
Reston, Virginia 20190
Phone: 703-437-0700
Fax: 703-437-6312
E-mail: info@arts-accredit.org
Website: http://nast.arts-accredit.org/

THEOLOGY
Dr. Bernard Fryshman, Executive VP
Emeritus and Interim Executive Director
Association of Advanced Rabbinical and Talmudic Schools (AARTS)
Accreditation Commission
11 Broadway, Suite 405
New York, New York 10004
Phone: 212-363-1991
Fax: 212-533-5335
E-mail: k.sharfman.aarts@gmail.com

Daniel O. Aleshire, Executive Director
Association of Theological Schools in the United States and Canada
    (ATS)
Commission on Accrediting
10 Summit Park Drive
Pittsburgh, Pennsylvania 15275
Phone: 412-788-6505
Fax: 412-788-6510
E-mail: ats@ats.edu
Website: www.ats.edu

Dr. Timothy Eaton, Interim President
Transnational Association of Christian Colleges and Schools (TRACS)
Accreditation Commission
15935 Forest Road
Forest, Virginia 24551
Phone: 434-525-9539
Fax: 434-525-9538
E-mail: info@tracs.org
Website: www.tracs.org

VETERINARY MEDICINE
Dr. Karen Brandt, Director of Education and Research
American Veterinary Medical Association (AVMA)
Council on Education
1931 North Meacham Road, Suite 100
Schaumburg, Illinois 60173-4360
Phone: 847-925-8070 Ext. 6674
Fax: 847-285-5732
E-mail: info@avma.org
Website: www.avma.org

How to Use These Guides

As you identify the particular programs and institutions that interest you, you can use both the *Graduate & Professional Programs: An Overview* volume and the specialized volumes in the series to obtain detailed information.

- *Graduate Programs in the Biological/Biomedical Sciences & Health-Related Professions*
- *Graduate Programs in Business, Education, Information Studies, Law & Social Work*
- *Graduate Programs in Engineering & Applied Sciences*
- *Graduate Programs the Humanities, Arts & Social Sciences*
- *Graduate Programs in the Physical Sciences, Mathematics, Agricultural Sciences, the Environment & Natural Resources*

Each of the specialized volumes in the series is divided into sections that contain one or more directories devoted to programs in a particular field. If you do not find a directory devoted to your field of interest in a specific volume, consult "Directories and Subject Areas" (located at the end of each volume). After you have identified the correct volume, consult the "Directories and Subject Areas in This Book" index, which shows (as does the more general directory) what directories cover subjects not specifically named in a directory or section title.

Each of the specialized volumes in the series has a number of general directories. These directories have entries for the largest unit at an institution granting graduate degrees in that field. For example, the general Engineering and Applied Sciences directory in the *Graduate Programs in Engineering & Applied Sciences* volume consists of **Profiles** for colleges, schools, and departments of engineering and applied sciences.

General directories are followed by other directories, or sections, that give more detailed information about programs in particular areas of the general field that has been covered. The general Engineering and Applied Sciences directory, in the previous example, is followed by nineteen sections with directories in specific areas of engineering, such as Chemical Engineering, Industrial/Management Engineering, and Mechanical Engineering.

Because of the broad nature of many fields, any system of organization is bound to involve a certain amount of overlap. Environmental studies, for example, is a field whose various aspects are studied in several types of departments and schools. Readers interested in such studies will find information on relevant programs in the *Graduate Programs in the Biological/Biomedical Sciences & Health-Related Professions* volume under Ecology and Environmental Biology and Environmental and Occupational Health; in the *Graduate Programs in the Physical Sciences, Mathematics, Agricultural Sciences, the Environment & Natural Resources* volume under Environmental Management and Policy and Natural Resources; and in the *Graduate Programs in Engineering & Applied Sciences* volume under Energy Management and Policy and Environmental Engineering. To help you find all of the programs of interest to you, the introduction to each section within the specialized volumes includes, if applicable, a paragraph suggesting other sections and directories with information on related areas of study.

Directory of Institutions with Programs in Engineering and Applied Sciences

This directory lists institutions in alphabetical order and includes beneath each name the academic fields in which each institution offers graduate programs. The degree level in each field is also indicated, provided that the institution has supplied that information in response to Peterson's Annual Survey of Graduate and Professional Institutions.

An M indicates that a master's degree program is offered; a D indicates that a doctoral degree program is offered; an O signifies that other advanced degrees (e.g., certificates or specialist degrees) are offered; and an * (asterisk) indicates that a **Close-Up** and/or **Display** is located in this volume. See the index, "Close-Ups and Displays," for the specific page number.

Profiles of Academic and Professional Programs in the Specialized Volumes

Each section of **Profiles** has a table of contents that lists the Program Directories, **Displays**, and **Close-Ups**. Program Directories consist of the **Profiles** of programs in the relevant fields, with **Displays** following if programs have chosen to include them. **Close-Ups,** which are more individualized statements, are also listed for those graduate schools or programs that have chosen to submit them.

The **Profiles** found in the 500 directories in the specialized volumes provide basic data about the graduate units in capsule form for quick reference. To make these directories as useful as possible, **Profiles** are generally listed for an institution's smallest academic unit within a subject area. In other words, if an institution has a College of Liberal Arts that administers many related programs, the **Profile** for the individual program (e.g., Program in History), not the entire College, appears in the directory.

There are some programs that do not fit into any current directory and are not given individual **Profiles**. The directory structure is reviewed annually in order to keep this number to a minimum and to accommodate major trends in graduate education.

The following outline describes the **Profile** information found in the guides and explains how best to use that information. Any item that does not apply to or was not provided by a graduate unit is omitted from its listing. The format of the **Profiles** is constant, making it easy to compare one institution with another and one program with another.

A ★ graphic next to the school's name indicates the institution has additional detailed information in a "Premium Profile" on Petersons.com. After reading their information here, you can learn more about the school by visiting www.petersons.com and searching for that particular college or university's graduate program.

Identifying Information. The institution's name, in boldface type, is followed by a complete listing of the administrative structure for that field of study. (For example, University of Akron, Buchtel College of Arts and Sciences, Department of Theoretical and Applied Mathematics, Program in Mathematics.) The last unit listed is the one to which all information in the **Profile** pertains. The institution's city, state, and zip code follow.

Offerings. Each field of study offered by the unit is listed with all postbaccalaureate degrees awarded. Degrees that are not preceded by a specific concentration are awarded in the general field listed in the unit name. Frequently, fields of study are broken down into subspecializations, and those appear following the degrees awarded; for example, "Offerings in secondary education (M.Ed.), including English education, mathematics education, science education." Students enrolled in the M.Ed. program would be able to specialize in any of the three fields mentioned.

Professional Accreditation. Some **Profiles** indicate whether a program is professionally accredited. Because it is possible for a program to receive or lose professional accreditation at any time, students entering fields in which accreditation is important to a career should verify the status of programs by contacting either the chairperson or the appropriate accrediting association.

Jointly Offered Degrees. Explanatory statements concerning programs that are offered in cooperation with other institutions are included in the list of degrees offered. This occurs most commonly on a regional basis (for example, two state universities offering a cooperative Ph.D. in special education) or where the specialized nature of the institutions encourages joint efforts (a J.D./M.B.A. offered by a law school at an institution with no formal business programs and an institution with a business school but lacking a law school). Only programs that are truly cooperative are listed; those involving only limited course work at another institution are not. Interested students should contact the heads of such units for further information.

Program Availability. This may include the following: part-time, evening/weekend, online only, 100% online, blended/hybrid learning, and/or minimal on-campus study. When information regarding the availability of part-time or evening/weekend study appears in the **Profile**, it means that students are able to earn a degree exclusively through such study. Blended/hybrid learning describe those courses in which some traditional in-class time has been replaced by online learning activities. Hybrid courses take advantage of the best features of both face-to-face and online learning.

Postbaccalaureate Distance Learning Degrees. A postbaccalaureate distance learning degree program signifies that course requirements can be fulfilled with minimal or no on-campus study.

Faculty. Figures on the number of faculty members actively involved with graduate students through teaching or research are separated into full- and part-time as well as men and women whenever the information has been supplied.

Students. Figures for the number of students enrolled in graduate and professional programs pertain to the semester of highest enrollment from the 2016–17 academic year. These figures are broken down into full- and part-time and men and women whenever the data have been supplied. Information on the number of matriculated students enrolled in the unit who are members of a minority group or are international students appears here. The average age of the matriculated students is followed by the number of applicants, the percentage accepted, and the number enrolled for fall 2016.

Degrees Awarded. The number of degrees awarded in the calendar year is listed. Many doctoral programs offer a terminal master's degree if students leave the program after completing only part of the requirements for a doctoral degree; that is indicated here. All degrees are classified into one of four types: master's, doctoral, first professional, and other advanced degrees. A unit may award one or several degrees at a given level; however, the data are only collected by type and may therefore represent several different degree programs.

Degree Requirements. The information in this section is also broken down by type of degree, and all information for a degree level pertains to all degrees of that type unless otherwise specified. Degree requirements are collected in a simplified form to provide some very basic information on the nature of the program and on foreign language, thesis or dissertation, comprehensive exam, and registration requirements. Many units also provide a short list of additional requirements, such as fieldwork or an internship. For complete information on graduation requirements, contact the graduate school or program directly.

Entrance Requirements. Entrance requirements are broken down into the four degree levels of master's, doctoral, first professional, and other advanced degrees. Within each level, information may be provided in two basic categories: entrance exams and other requirements. The entrance exams are identified by the standard acronyms used by the testing agencies, unless they are not well known. Other entrance requirements are quite varied, but they often contain an undergraduate or graduate grade point average (GPA). Unless otherwise stated, the GPA is calculated on a 4.0 scale and is listed as a minimum required for admission. Additional exam requirements/recommendations for international students may be listed here. Application deadlines for domestic and international students, the application fee, and whether electronic applications are accepted may be listed here. Note that the deadline should be used for reference only; these dates are subject to change, and students interested in applying should always contact the graduate unit directly about application procedures and deadlines.

Expenses. The typical cost of study for the 2017–2018 academic year (2016–17 if 2017–18 figures were not available) is given in two basic categories: tuition and fees. Cost of study may be quite complex at a graduate institution. There are often sliding scales for part-time study, a different cost for first-year students, and other variables that make it impossible to completely cover the cost of study for each graduate program. To provide the most usable information, figures are given for full-time study for a full year where available and for part-time study in terms of a per-unit rate (per credit, per semester hour, etc.). Occasionally, variances may be noted in tuition and fees for reasons such

as the type of program, whether courses are taken during the day or evening, whether courses are at the master's or doctoral level, or other institution-specific reasons. Respondents were also given the opportunity to provide more specific and detailed tuition and fees information at the unit level. When provided, this information will appear in place of any typical costs entered elsewhere on the university-level survey. Expenses are usually subject to change; for exact costs at any given time, contact your chosen schools and programs directly. Keep in mind that the tuition of Canadian institutions is usually given in Canadian dollars.

Financial Support. This section contains data on the number of awards administered by the institution and given to graduate students during the 2016–17 academic year. The first figure given represents the total number of students receiving financial support enrolled in that unit. If the unit has provided information on graduate appointments, these are broken down into three major categories: fellowships give money to graduate students to cover the cost of study and living expenses and are not based on a work obligation or research commitment, research assistantships provide stipends to graduate students for assistance in a formal research project with a faculty member, and teaching assistantships provide stipends to graduate students for teaching or for assisting faculty members in teaching undergraduate classes. Within each category, figures are given for the total number of awards, the average yearly amount per award, and whether full or partial tuition reimbursements are awarded. In addition to graduate appointments, the availability of several other financial aid sources is covered in this section. Tuition waivers are routinely part of a graduate appointment, but units sometimes waive part or all of a student's tuition even if a graduate appointment is not available. Federal WorkStudy is made available to students who demonstrate need and meet the federal guidelines; this form of aid normally includes 10 or more hours of work per week in an office of the institution. Institutionally sponsored loans are low-interest loans available to graduate students to cover both educational and living expenses. Career-related internships or fieldwork offer money to students who are participating in a formal off-campus research project or practicum. Grants, scholarships, traineeships, unspecified assistantships, and other awards may also be noted. The availability of financial support to part-time students is also indicated here.

Some programs list the financial aid application deadline and the forms that need to be completed for students to be eligible for financial awards. There are two forms: FAFSA, the Free Application for Federal Student Aid, which is required for federal aid, and the CSS PROFILE®.

Faculty Research. Each unit has the opportunity to list several keyword phrases describing the current research involving faculty members and graduate students. Space limitations prevent the unit from listing complete information on all research programs. The total expenditure for funded research from the previous academic year may also be included.

Unit Head and Application Contact. The head of the graduate program for each unit may be listed with academic title, phone and fax numbers, and e-mail address. In addition to the unit head's contact information, many graduate programs also list a separate contact for application and admission information, followed by the graduate school, program, or department's website. If no unit head or application contact is given, you should contact the overall institution for information on graduate admissions.

Displays and Close-Ups

The **Displays** and **Close-Ups** are supplementary insertions submitted by deans, chairs, and other administrators who wish to offer an additional, more individualized statement to readers. A number of graduate school and program administrators have attached a **Display** ad near the **Profile** listing. Here you will find information that an institution or program wants to emphasize. The **Close-Ups** are by their very nature more expansive and flexible than the **Profiles**, and the administrators who have written them may emphasize different aspects of their programs. All of the **Close-Ups** are organized in the same way (with the exception of a few that describe research and training opportunities instead of degree programs), and in each one you will find information on the same basic topics, such as programs of study, research facilities, tuition and fees, financial aid, and application procedures. If an institution or program has submitted a **Close-Up**, a boldface cross-reference appears below its **Profile**. As with the **Displays**, all of the **Close-Ups** in the guides have been submitted by choice; the absence of a **Display** or **Close-Up** does not reflect any type of editorial judgment on the part of Peterson's, and their presence in the guides should not be taken as an indication of status, quality, or approval. Statements regarding a university's objectives and accomplishments are a reflection of its own beliefs and are not the opinions of the Peterson's editors.

Appendixes

This section contains two appendixes. The first, "Institutional Changes Since the 2017 Edition," lists institutions that have closed, merged, or changed their name or status since the last edition of the guides. The second, "Abbreviations Used in the Guides," gives abbreviations of degree names, along with what those abbreviations stand for. These appendixes are identical in all six volumes of *Peterson's Graduate and Professional Programs*.

Indexes

There are three indexes presented here. The first index, "Close-Ups and Displays," gives page references for all programs that have chosen to place **Close-Ups** and **Displays** in this volume. It is arranged alphabetically by institution; within institutions, the arrangement is alphabetical by subject area. It is not an index to all programs in the book's directories of **Profiles**; readers must refer to the directories themselves for **Profile** information on programs that have not submitted the additional, more individualized statements. The second index, "Directories and Subject Areas in Other Books in This Series", gives book references for the directories in the specialized volumes and also includes cross-references for subject area names not used in the directory structure, for example, "Computing Technology (see Computer Science)." The third index, "Directories and Subject Areas in This Book," gives page references for the directories in this volume and cross-references for subject area names not used in this volume's directory structure.

Data Collection Procedures

The information published in the directories and Profiles of all the books is collected through Peterson's Annual Survey of Graduate and Professional Institutions. The survey is sent each spring to nearly 2,300 institutions offering postbaccalaureate degree programs, including accredited institutions in the United States, U.S. territories, and Canada and those institutions outside the United States that are accredited by U.S. accrediting bodies. Deans and other administrators complete these surveys, providing information on programs in the 500 academic and professional fields covered in the guides as well as overall institutional information. While every effort has been made to ensure the accuracy and completeness of the data, information is sometimes unavailable or changes occur after publication deadlines. All usable information received in time for publication has been included. The omission of any particular item from a directory or Profile signifies either that the item is not applicable to the institution or program or that information was not available. Profiles of programs scheduled to begin during the 2017–18 academic year cannot, obviously, include statistics on enrollment or, in many cases, the number of faculty members. If no usable data were submitted by an institution, its name, address, and program name appear in order to indicate the availability of graduate work.

Criteria for Inclusion in This Guide

To be included in this guide, an institution must have full accreditation or be a candidate for accreditation (preaccreditation) status by an institutional or specialized accrediting body recognized by the U.S. Department of Education or the Council for Higher Education Accreditation (CHEA). Institutional accrediting bodies, which review each institution as a whole, include the six regional associations of schools and colleges (Middle States, New England, North Central, Northwest, Southern, and Western), each of which is responsible for a specified portion of the United States and its territories. Other institutional accrediting bodies are national in scope and accredit specific kinds of institutions (e.g., Bible colleges, independent colleges, and rabbinical and Talmudic schools). Program registration by the New York State Board of Regents is considered to be the equivalent of institutional accreditation, since the board requires that all programs offered by an institution meet its standards before recognition is granted. A Canadian institution must be chartered and authorized to grant degrees by the provincial government, affiliated with a chartered institution, or accredited by a recognized U.S. accrediting body. This guide also includes institutions outside the United States that are accredited by these U.S. accrediting bodies. There are recognized specialized or professional accrediting bodies in more than fifty different fields, each of which is authorized to accredit institutions or specific programs in its particular field. For specialized institutions that offer programs in one field only, we designate this to be the equivalent of institutional accreditation. A full explanation of the accrediting process and complete information on recognized institutional (regional and national) and specialized accrediting bodies can be found online at www.chea.org or at www.ed.gov/admins/finaid/accred/index.html.

DIRECTORY OF INSTITUTIONS
AND THEIR OFFERINGS

ACADEMY OF ART UNIVERSITY
Game Design and Development	M

ACADIA UNIVERSITY
Computer Science	M

ADELPHI UNIVERSITY
Biotechnology	M
Health Informatics	M,O

AIR FORCE INSTITUTE OF TECHNOLOGY
Aerospace/Aeronautical Engineering	M,D
Computer Engineering	M,D
Computer Science	M,D
Electrical Engineering	M,D
Engineering and Applied Sciences—General	M,D
Engineering Management	M
Engineering Physics	M,D
Environmental Engineering	M
Management of Technology	M,D
Materials Sciences	M,D
Nuclear Engineering	M,D
Operations Research	M,D
Systems Engineering	M,D

ALABAMA AGRICULTURAL AND MECHANICAL UNIVERSITY
Computer Science	M
Engineering and Applied Sciences—General	M,D
Materials Engineering	M
Materials Sciences	M,D

ALASKA PACIFIC UNIVERSITY
Telecommunications Management	M

ALCORN STATE UNIVERSITY
Computer Science	M
Information Science	M

ALFRED UNIVERSITY
Bioengineering	M,D
Ceramic Sciences and Engineering	M,D
Electrical Engineering	M,D
Engineering and Applied Sciences—General	M,D
Materials Sciences	M,D
Mechanical Engineering	M,D

AMERICAN INTERCONTINENTAL UNIVERSITY ATLANTA
Information Science	M

AMERICAN INTERCONTINENTAL UNIVERSITY ONLINE
Computer and Information Systems Security	M
Information Science	M

AMERICAN PUBLIC UNIVERSITY SYSTEM
Aerospace/Aeronautical Engineering	M
Computer and Information Systems Security	M
Health Informatics	M
Software Engineering	M

AMERICAN SENTINEL UNIVERSITY
Computer Science	M
Health Informatics	M

THE AMERICAN UNIVERSITY IN CAIRO
Artificial Intelligence/Robotics	M,D,O
Biotechnology	M,D,O
Computer Science	M,D,O
Construction Engineering	M,D,O
Electrical Engineering	M,D,O
Engineering and Applied Sciences—General	M,D,O
Environmental Engineering	M,D,O
Mechanical Engineering	M,D,O
Nanotechnology	M,D,O

THE AMERICAN UNIVERSITY IN DUBAI
Construction Management	M

AMERICAN UNIVERSITY OF ARMENIA
Computer Science	M
Energy Management and Policy	M
Industrial/Management Engineering	M
Information Science	M
Manufacturing Engineering	M

AMERICAN UNIVERSITY OF BEIRUT
Biomedical Engineering	M,D
Civil Engineering	M,D
Computer Engineering	M,D
Computer Science	M,D
Electrical Engineering	M,D
Engineering and Applied Sciences—General	M,D
Engineering Management	M,D
Mechanical Engineering	M,D
Water Resources Engineering	M,D

AMERICAN UNIVERSITY OF SHARJAH
Chemical Engineering	M
Civil Engineering	M
Computer Engineering	M
Electrical Engineering	M
Engineering Management	M
Mechanical Engineering	M

APPALACHIAN STATE UNIVERSITY
Computer Science	M
Energy and Power Engineering	M

ARIZONA STATE UNIVERSITY AT THE TEMPE CAMPUS
Aerospace/Aeronautical Engineering	M,D
Bioinformatics	M,D
Biomedical Engineering	M,D
Biotechnology	M,D
Chemical Engineering	M,D
Civil Engineering	M,D
Computer Engineering	M,D
Computer Science	M,D
Construction Engineering	M,D
Construction Management	M,D
Electrical Engineering	M,D,O
Energy and Power Engineering	M,D
Engineering and Applied Sciences—General	M,D
Environmental Engineering	M,D
Ergonomics and Human Factors	M
Geological Engineering	M,D
Industrial/Management Engineering	M,D
Information Science	M
Management of Technology	M
Manufacturing Engineering	M

Materials Engineering	M,D
Materials Sciences	M,D
Mechanical Engineering	M,D
Medical Informatics	M,D
Modeling and Simulation	M,D
Nanotechnology	M,D
Nuclear Engineering	M,D,O
Reliability Engineering	M
Software Engineering	M,D
Systems Engineering	M
Systems Science	M,D
Technology and Public Policy	M
Transportation and Highway Engineering	M,D,O

ARKANSAS STATE UNIVERSITY
Biotechnology	M,O
Computer Science	M
Engineering and Applied Sciences—General	M
Engineering Management	M

ARKANSAS TECH UNIVERSITY
Engineering and Applied Sciences—General	M
Health Informatics	M
Information Science	M

ARMSTRONG STATE UNIVERSITY
Computer and Information Systems Security	M,O
Computer Science	M
Information Science	M

ARTCENTER COLLEGE OF DESIGN
Transportation and Highway Engineering	M

ASPEN UNIVERSITY
Information Science	M,O

ATHABASCA UNIVERSITY
Management of Technology	M,D,O

AUBURN UNIVERSITY
Aerospace/Aeronautical Engineering	M,D
Biosystems Engineering	M,D
Chemical Engineering	M,D
Civil Engineering	M,D
Computer Engineering	M,D
Computer Science	M,D
Construction Engineering	M
Electrical Engineering	M,D
Engineering and Applied Sciences—General	M,D,O
Industrial/Management Engineering	M,D,O
Materials Engineering	M,D
Mechanical Engineering	M,D
Polymer Science and Engineering	M,D
Software Engineering	M,D
Systems Engineering	M,D,O

AUBURN UNIVERSITY AT MONTGOMERY
Computer and Information Systems Security	M
Information Science	M

AUGUSTA UNIVERSITY
Health Informatics	M

AUSTIN PEAY STATE UNIVERSITY
Database Systems	M
Engineering and Applied Sciences—General	M

BALL STATE UNIVERSITY
Computer Science	M
Information Science	M,O
Telecommunications	M

BARRY UNIVERSITY
Health Informatics	O
Information Science	M

BARUCH COLLEGE OF THE CITY UNIVERSITY OF NEW YORK
Financial Engineering	M

BAYLOR COLLEGE OF MEDICINE
Bioengineering	D
Biomedical Engineering	D

BAYLOR UNIVERSITY
Biomedical Engineering	M,D
Computer Engineering	M,D
Computer Science	M,D
Electrical Engineering	M,D
Mechanical Engineering	M,D

BAY PATH UNIVERSITY
Computer and Information Systems Security	M

BELLEVUE UNIVERSITY
Information Science	M

BENEDICTINE UNIVERSITY
Computer and Information Systems Security	M
Health Informatics	M

BENTLEY UNIVERSITY
Ergonomics and Human Factors	M
Information Science	M

BINGHAMTON UNIVERSITY, STATE UNIVERSITY OF NEW YORK
Biomedical Engineering	M,D
Computer Science	M,D
Electrical Engineering	M,D
Engineering and Applied Sciences—General	M,D*
Industrial/Management Engineering	M,D
Materials Engineering	M,D
Materials Sciences	M,D
Mechanical Engineering	M,D
Systems Science	M,D

BOISE STATE UNIVERSITY
Civil Engineering	M
Computer Engineering	M,D
Computer Science	M,O
Electrical Engineering	M,D
Engineering and Applied Sciences—General	M,D,O
Materials Engineering	M,D
Mechanical Engineering	M

BOSTON UNIVERSITY
Bioinformatics	M,D
Biomedical Engineering	M,D
Computer and Information Systems Security	M,D,O
Computer Engineering	M,D,O
Computer Science	M,D,O
Database Systems	M,O
Electrical Engineering	M,D
Energy Management and Policy	M,D
Engineering and Applied Sciences—General	M,D
Health Informatics	M,O

Management of Technology	M
Manufacturing Engineering	M,D
Materials Engineering	M,D
Materials Sciences	M,D
Mechanical Engineering	M,D
Software Engineering	M,O
Systems Engineering	M,D
Telecommunications Management	M,O
Telecommunications	M,O

BOWIE STATE UNIVERSITY

Computer Science	M,D

BOWLING GREEN STATE UNIVERSITY

Computer Science	M
Operations Research	M
Software Engineering	M

BRADLEY UNIVERSITY

Civil Engineering	M
Computer Science	M
Construction Engineering	M
Electrical Engineering	M
Engineering and Applied Sciences—General	M
Industrial/Management Engineering	M
Information Science	M
Manufacturing Engineering	M
Mechanical Engineering	M

BRANDEIS UNIVERSITY

Bioinformatics	M
Biotechnology	M
Computer and Information Systems Security	M
Computer Science	M,D
Health Informatics	M
Human-Computer Interaction	M
Medical Informatics	M
Software Engineering	M

BRIDGEWATER STATE UNIVERSITY

Computer Science	M

BRIGHAM YOUNG UNIVERSITY

Biotechnology	M,D
Chemical Engineering	M,D
Civil Engineering	M,D
Computer Engineering	M,D
Computer Science	M,D
Construction Management	M
Electrical Engineering	M,D
Engineering and Applied Sciences—General	M,D
Information Science	M
Manufacturing Engineering	M
Mechanical Engineering	M,D

BROCK UNIVERSITY

Biotechnology	M,D
Computer Science	M

BROOKLYN COLLEGE OF THE CITY UNIVERSITY OF NEW YORK

Computer Science	M,O
Health Informatics	M,O
Information Science	M,O

BROWN UNIVERSITY

Biochemical Engineering	M,D
Biomedical Engineering	M,D
Biotechnology	M,D
Chemical Engineering	M,D
Computer Engineering	M,D
Computer Science	M,D
Electrical Engineering	M,D
Engineering and Applied Sciences—General	M,D
Materials Sciences	M,D
Mechanical Engineering	M,D
Mechanics	M,D

BUCKNELL UNIVERSITY

Chemical Engineering	M
Civil Engineering	M
Electrical Engineering	M
Engineering and Applied Sciences—General	M
Mechanical Engineering	M

BUFFALO STATE COLLEGE, STATE UNIVERSITY OF NEW YORK

Industrial/Management Engineering	M

CALIFORNIA BAPTIST UNIVERSITY

Civil Engineering	M
Construction Management	M
Mechanical Engineering	M
Software Engineering	M

CALIFORNIA INSTITUTE OF TECHNOLOGY

Aerospace/Aeronautical Engineering	M,D,O
Bioengineering	M,D
Chemical Engineering	M,D
Civil Engineering	M,D,O
Computer Science	M,D
Electrical Engineering	M,D,O
Engineering and Applied Sciences—General	M,D,O
Environmental Engineering	M,D
Materials Sciences	M,D
Mechanical Engineering	M,D,O
Mechanics	M,D
Systems Engineering	M,D

CALIFORNIA LUTHERAN UNIVERSITY

Management of Technology	M,O

CALIFORNIA MIRAMAR UNIVERSITY

Telecommunications Management	M
Telecommunications	M

CALIFORNIA POLYTECHNIC STATE UNIVERSITY, SAN LUIS OBISPO

Aerospace/Aeronautical Engineering	M
Architectural Engineering	M*
Civil Engineering	M
Computer Science	M
Database Systems	M
Electrical Engineering	M
Engineering and Applied Sciences—General	M
Environmental Engineering	M
Industrial/Management Engineering	M
Mechanical Engineering	M
Polymer Science and Engineering	M

CALIFORNIA STATE POLYTECHNIC UNIVERSITY, POMONA

Aerospace/Aeronautical Engineering	M
Civil Engineering	M
Computer Science	M
Electrical Engineering	M
Engineering Management	M
Mechanical Engineering	M
Systems Engineering	M

CALIFORNIA STATE UNIVERSITY CHANNEL ISLANDS

Bioinformatics	M
Biotechnology	M
Computer Science	M

CALIFORNIA STATE UNIVERSITY, CHICO

Computer Engineering	M
Computer Science	M
Construction Management	M
Electrical Engineering	M
Engineering and Applied Sciences—General	M

CALIFORNIA STATE UNIVERSITY, DOMINGUEZ HILLS

Bioinformatics	M
Computer Science	M

CALIFORNIA STATE UNIVERSITY, EAST BAY

Computer Science	M
Construction Management	M
Database Systems	M
Engineering and Applied Sciences—General	M
Engineering Management	M
Industrial/Management Engineering	M

CALIFORNIA STATE UNIVERSITY, FRESNO

Civil Engineering	M
Computer Engineering	M
Computer Science	M
Electrical Engineering	M
Engineering and Applied Sciences—General	M
Industrial/Management Engineering	M
Mechanical Engineering	M

CALIFORNIA STATE UNIVERSITY, FULLERTON

Architectural Engineering	M
Biotechnology	M
Civil Engineering	M
Computer Engineering	M
Computer Science	M
Electrical Engineering	M
Engineering and Applied Sciences—General	M
Environmental Engineering	M
Information Science	M
Mechanical Engineering	M
Software Engineering	M
Systems Engineering	M

CALIFORNIA STATE UNIVERSITY, LONG BEACH

Civil Engineering	M
Computer Engineering	M
Computer Science	M
Electrical Engineering	M
Engineering Management	M,D

Ergonomics and Human Factors	M
Mechanical Engineering	M,D

CALIFORNIA STATE UNIVERSITY, LOS ANGELES

Civil Engineering	M
Computer Science	M
Electrical Engineering	M
Engineering and Applied Sciences—General	M
Management of Technology	M
Mechanical Engineering	M

CALIFORNIA STATE UNIVERSITY MARITIME ACADEMY

Engineering Management	M

CALIFORNIA STATE UNIVERSITY, NORTHRIDGE

Artificial Intelligence/Robotics	M
Civil Engineering	M
Computer Science	M
Construction Management	M
Electrical Engineering	M
Engineering and Applied Sciences—General	M
Engineering Management	M
Industrial/Management Engineering	M
Manufacturing Engineering	M
Materials Engineering	M
Mechanical Engineering	M
Software Engineering	M
Structural Engineering	M
Systems Engineering	M

CALIFORNIA STATE UNIVERSITY, SACRAMENTO

Civil Engineering	M
Computer Science	M
Electrical Engineering	M
Engineering and Applied Sciences—General	M
Mechanical Engineering	M
Software Engineering	M

CALIFORNIA STATE UNIVERSITY, SAN BERNARDINO

Computer and Information Systems Security	M
Computer Science	M

CALIFORNIA STATE UNIVERSITY, SAN MARCOS

Computer Science	M

CAMBRIDGE COLLEGE

Management of Technology	M
Medical Informatics	M

CANISIUS COLLEGE

Health Informatics	M,O

CAPELLA UNIVERSITY

Computer and Information Systems Security	M,D
Health Informatics	M
Management of Technology	M,D
Operations Research	M

CAPITOL TECHNOLOGY UNIVERSITY

Computer and Information Systems Security	M
Computer Science	M
Electrical Engineering	M
Information Science	M

*M—masters degree; D—doctorate; O—other advanced degree; *—Close-Up and/or Display*

Telecommunications
    Management   M

CARLETON UNIVERSITY
Aerospace/Aeronautical
    Engineering   M,D
Biomedical Engineering   M
Civil Engineering   M,D
Computer Science   M,D
Electrical Engineering   M,D
Engineering and Applied
    Sciences—General   M,D
Environmental Engineering   M,D
Information Science   M,D
Management of Technology   M
Materials Engineering   M,D
Mechanical Engineering   M,D
Systems Engineering   M,D
Systems Science   M,D

CARLOW UNIVERSITY
Computer and Information
    Systems Security   M

CARNEGIE MELLON UNIVERSITY
Architectural Engineering   M,D
Artificial Intelligence/Robotics   M,D
Bioengineering   M,D
Biomedical Engineering   M,D
Biotechnology   M
Chemical Engineering   M,D
Civil Engineering   M,D
Computer and Information
    Systems Security   M
Computer Engineering   M,D
Computer Science   M,D
Construction Management   M,D
Electrical Engineering   M,D
Energy and Power
    Engineering   M,D
Environmental Engineering   M,D
Human-Computer Interaction   M,D
Information Science   M,D
Materials Engineering   M,D
Materials Sciences   M,D
Mechanical Engineering   M,D
Mechanics   M,D
Modeling and Simulation   M,D
Nanotechnology   D
Operations Research   D
Polymer Science and
    Engineering   M
Software Engineering   M,D
Systems Engineering   M
Technology and Public Policy   M,D
Telecommunications
    Management   M
Water Resources Engineering   M,D

CARROLL UNIVERSITY
Software Engineering   M

CASE WESTERN RESERVE UNIVERSITY
Aerospace/Aeronautical
    Engineering   M,D
Biomedical Engineering   M,D*
Chemical Engineering   M,D
Civil Engineering   M,D
Computer Engineering   M,D
Computer Science   M,D
Database Systems   M
Electrical Engineering   M,D
Engineering and Applied
    Sciences—General   M,D
Engineering Management   M
Information Science   M,D
Materials Engineering   M,D
Materials Sciences   M,D
Mechanical Engineering   M,D
Operations Research   M,D

Polymer Science and
    Engineering   M,D
Systems Engineering   M,D

THE CATHOLIC UNIVERSITY OF AMERICA
Biomedical Engineering   M,D
Biotechnology   M,D
Civil Engineering   M,D,O
Computer Science   M,D
Electrical Engineering   M,D
Energy and Power
    Engineering   M,D
Engineering and Applied
    Sciences—General   M,D,O
Engineering Management   M,O
Environmental Engineering   M,D
Ergonomics and Human
    Factors   M,D
Management of Technology   M,O
Materials Engineering   M
Materials Sciences   M
Mechanical Engineering   M,D
Systems Engineering   M,O
Transportation and Highway
    Engineering   M,D,O

CENTRAL CONNECTICUT STATE UNIVERSITY
Computer Science   M,O
Construction Management   M,O
Engineering and Applied
    Sciences—General   M
Management of Technology   M,O

CENTRAL EUROPEAN UNIVERSITY
Database Systems   M,D

CENTRAL MICHIGAN UNIVERSITY
Computer and Information
    Systems Security   O
Computer Science   M
Engineering and Applied
    Sciences—General   M
Engineering Management   M,O
Materials Sciences   D

CENTRAL WASHINGTON UNIVERSITY
Engineering and Applied
    Sciences—General   M
Industrial/Management
    Engineering   M

CHAMPLAIN COLLEGE
Computer and Information
    Systems Security   M
Management of Technology   M

CHATHAM UNIVERSITY
Health Informatics   M

CHICAGO STATE UNIVERSITY
Computer Science   M

CHRISTIAN BROTHERS UNIVERSITY
Engineering and Applied
    Sciences—General   M

CHRISTOPHER NEWPORT UNIVERSITY
Computer Science   M

THE CITADEL, THE MILITARY COLLEGE OF SOUTH CAROLINA
Aerospace/Aeronautical
    Engineering   M,O

Civil Engineering   M,O
Computer Engineering   M,O
Electrical Engineering   M,O
Engineering and Applied
    Sciences—General   M,O
Engineering Management   M,O
Geotechnical Engineering   M,O
Information Science   M
Manufacturing Engineering   M,O
Mechanical Engineering   M,O
Structural Engineering   M,O
Systems Engineering   M,O
Transportation and Highway
    Engineering   M,O

CITY COLLEGE OF THE CITY UNIVERSITY OF NEW YORK
Biomedical Engineering   M,D
Chemical Engineering   M,D
Civil Engineering   M,D
Computer Science   M,D
Electrical Engineering   M,D
Engineering and Applied
    Sciences—General   M,D
Mechanical Engineering   M,D

CITY UNIVERSITY OF SEATTLE
Computer and Information
    Systems Security   M,O
Computer Science   M,O
Management of Technology   M,O

CLAFLIN UNIVERSITY
Biotechnology   M

CLAREMONT GRADUATE UNIVERSITY
Computer and Information
    Systems Security   M,D,O
Database Systems   M,D,O
Financial Engineering   M
Health Informatics   M,D,O
Information Science   M,D,O
Operations Research   M,D
Systems Science   M,D,O
Telecommunications   M,D,O

CLARK ATLANTA UNIVERSITY
Computer Science   M
Information Science   M

CLARKSON UNIVERSITY
Biotechnology   D
Chemical Engineering   M,D
Civil Engineering   M,D
Computer Engineering   M,D
Computer Science   M,D
Electrical Engineering   M,D,O
Energy and Power
    Engineering   M,O
Engineering and Applied
    Sciences—General   M,D,O
Engineering Management   M
Environmental Engineering   M,D
Health Informatics   M,O
Information Science   M
Materials Engineering   D
Materials Sciences   D
Mechanical Engineering   M,D
Systems Engineering   M,O

CLARK UNIVERSITY
Database Systems   M
Information Science   M

CLEMSON UNIVERSITY
Automotive Engineering   M,D
Bioengineering   M,D,O
Biomedical Engineering   M,D,O
Biosystems Engineering   M,D

Chemical Engineering   M,D
Civil Engineering   M,D
Computer Engineering   M,D
Computer Science   M,D
Construction Management   M,O
Electrical Engineering   M,D
Engineering and Applied
    Sciences—General   M,D,O
Environmental Engineering   M,D
Ergonomics and Human
    Factors   D
Human-Computer Interaction   D
Industrial/Management
    Engineering   M,D
Manufacturing Engineering   M
Materials Engineering   M,D
Materials Sciences   M,D
Mechanical Engineering   M,D

CLEVELAND STATE UNIVERSITY
Biomedical Engineering   D
Chemical Engineering   M,D
Civil Engineering   M,D
Electrical Engineering   M,D
Engineering and Applied
    Sciences—General   M,D
Environmental Engineering   M,D
Industrial/Management
    Engineering   M,D
Mechanical Engineering   M,D
Software Engineering   M,D

COASTAL CAROLINA UNIVERSITY
Computer Science   M,D,O

COLEMAN UNIVERSITY
Information Science   M
Management of Technology   M

COLLEGE FOR CREATIVE STUDIES
Automotive Engineering   M
Transportation and Highway
    Engineering   M

COLLEGE OF CHARLESTON
Computer Science   M

THE COLLEGE OF SAINT ROSE
Computer Science   M,O
Information Science   M,O

THE COLLEGE OF ST. SCHOLASTICA
Health Informatics   M,O

COLLEGE OF STATEN ISLAND OF THE CITY UNIVERSITY OF NEW YORK
Computer Science   M
Database Systems   O

THE COLLEGE OF WILLIAM AND MARY
Applied Science and
    Technology   M,D
Artificial Intelligence/Robotics   M,D
Computer Science   M,D
Materials Engineering   M,D
Materials Sciences   M,D
Nanotechnology   M,D
Operations Research   M
Polymer Science and
    Engineering   M,D

COLORADO CHRISTIAN UNIVERSITY
Computer and Information
    Systems Security   M

COLORADO MESA UNIVERSITY

Health Informatics	M,D,O

COLORADO SCHOOL OF MINES

Bioengineering	M,D
Chemical Engineering	M,D
Civil Engineering	M,D
Computer Science	M,D
Construction Engineering	M,D
Electrical Engineering	M,D
Electronic Materials	M,D
Engineering and Applied Sciences—General	M,D,O
Engineering Management	M,D
Environmental Engineering	M,D
Geological Engineering	M,D
Management of Technology	M,D
Materials Engineering	M,D
Materials Sciences	M,D
Mechanical Engineering	M,D
Metallurgical Engineering and Metallurgy	M,D
Mineral/Mining Engineering	M,D
Nuclear Engineering	M,D
Operations Research	M,D
Petroleum Engineering	M,D

COLORADO STATE UNIVERSITY

Bioengineering	M,D
Biomedical Engineering	M,D
Chemical Engineering	M,D
Civil Engineering	M,D
Computer Science	M,D
Construction Management	M
Electrical Engineering	M,D
Energy Management and Policy	M
Engineering and Applied Sciences—General	M,D
Ergonomics and Human Factors	M,D
Industrial/Management Engineering	M,D
Mechanical Engineering	M,D
Systems Engineering	M,D

COLORADO STATE UNIVERSITY–PUEBLO

Applied Science and Technology	M
Engineering and Applied Sciences—General	M
Industrial/Management Engineering	M
Systems Engineering	M

COLORADO TECHNICAL UNIVERSITY AURORA

Computer and Information Systems Security	M
Computer Engineering	M
Computer Science	M
Database Systems	M
Electrical Engineering	M
Management of Technology	M
Software Engineering	M
Systems Engineering	M

COLORADO TECHNICAL UNIVERSITY COLORADO SPRINGS

Computer and Information Systems Security	M,D
Computer Engineering	M
Computer Science	M,D
Database Systems	M,D
Electrical Engineering	M
Management of Technology	M,D
Software Engineering	M,D
Systems Engineering	M

COLUMBIA UNIVERSITY

Biomedical Engineering	M,D
Biotechnology	M,D
Chemical Engineering	M,D
Civil Engineering	M,D
Computer Engineering	M,D
Computer Science	M,D
Construction Engineering	M,D
Construction Management	M,D
Database Systems	M
Electrical Engineering	M,D
Engineering and Applied Sciences—General	M,D
Environmental Engineering	M,D
Financial Engineering	M,D
Industrial/Management Engineering	M,D
Management of Technology	M
Materials Engineering	M,D
Materials Sciences	M,D
Mechanical Engineering	M,D*
Mechanics	M,D
Medical Informatics	M,D,O
Operations Research	M,D

COLUMBUS STATE UNIVERSITY

Computer and Information Systems Security	M,O
Computer Science	M,O
Modeling and Simulation	M,O

CONCORDIA UNIVERSITY (CANADA)

Aerospace/Aeronautical Engineering	M
Biotechnology	M,D,O
Civil Engineering	M,D,O
Computer and Information Systems Security	M,D,O
Computer Engineering	M,D
Computer Science	M,D,O
Construction Engineering	M,D,O
Electrical Engineering	M,D
Engineering and Applied Sciences—General	M,D,O
Environmental Engineering	M,D,O
Game Design and Development	M,D,O
Industrial/Management Engineering	M,D,O
Mechanical Engineering	M,D,O
Software Engineering	M,D,O
Systems Engineering	M,D,O
Telecommunications Management	M,D,O

CONCORDIA UNIVERSITY, NEBRASKA

Computer and Information Systems Security	M
Computer Science	M

CONCORDIA UNIVERSITY OF EDMONTON

Computer and Information Systems Security	M

CONCORDIA UNIVERSITY, ST. PAUL

Computer and Information Systems Security	M

COOPER UNION FOR THE ADVANCEMENT OF SCIENCE AND ART

Chemical Engineering	M
Civil Engineering	M
Electrical Engineering	M

Engineering and Applied Sciences—General	M
Mechanical Engineering	M

CORNELL UNIVERSITY

Aerospace/Aeronautical Engineering	M,D
Agricultural Engineering	M,D
Artificial Intelligence/Robotics	M,D
Biochemical Engineering	M,D
Bioengineering	M,D
Biomedical Engineering	M,D
Biotechnology	M,D
Chemical Engineering	M,D
Civil Engineering	M,D
Computer Engineering	M,D
Computer Science	M,D
Electrical Engineering	M,D
Energy and Power Engineering	M,D
Engineering and Applied Sciences—General	M,D
Engineering Management	M,D
Engineering Physics	M,D
Environmental Engineering	M,D
Ergonomics and Human Factors	M
Geotechnical Engineering	M,D
Human-Computer Interaction	M,D
Industrial/Management Engineering	M,D
Information Science	D
Manufacturing Engineering	M,D
Materials Engineering	M,D
Materials Sciences	M,D
Mechanical Engineering	M,D
Mechanics	M,D
Nanotechnology	M,D
Operations Research	M,D
Polymer Science and Engineering	M,D
Structural Engineering	M,D
Systems Engineering	M,D
Textile Sciences and Engineering	M,D
Transportation and Highway Engineering	M,D
Water Resources Engineering	M,D

DAKOTA STATE UNIVERSITY

Computer and Information Systems Security	M,D,O
Computer Science	M,D,O
Health Informatics	M,D,O
Information Science	M,D,O

DALHOUSIE UNIVERSITY

Agricultural Engineering	M,D
Bioengineering	M,D
Bioinformatics	M,D
Biomedical Engineering	M,D
Chemical Engineering	M,D
Civil Engineering	M,D
Computer Engineering	M,D
Computer Science	M,D
Electrical Engineering	M,D
Engineering and Applied Sciences—General	M,D
Environmental Engineering	M,D
Human-Computer Interaction	M
Industrial/Management Engineering	M,D
Materials Engineering	M,D
Mechanical Engineering	M,D
Medical Informatics	M,D
Mineral/Mining Engineering	M,D

DALLAS BAPTIST UNIVERSITY

Engineering Management	M
Management of Technology	M

DARTMOUTH COLLEGE

Biochemical Engineering	M,D
Biomedical Engineering	M,D
Biotechnology	M,D
Computer Engineering	M,D
Computer Science	M,D
Engineering and Applied Sciences—General	M,D
Engineering Management	M
Environmental Engineering	M,D
Materials Engineering	M,D
Materials Sciences	M,D
Mechanical Engineering	M,D

DAVENPORT UNIVERSITY

Computer and Information Systems Security	M

DEPAUL UNIVERSITY

Computer and Information Systems Security	M,D
Computer Science	M,D
Game Design and Development	M,D
Health Informatics	M,D
Human-Computer Interaction	M,D
Information Science	M,D
Management of Technology	M,D
Software Engineering	M,D

DESALES UNIVERSITY

Computer and Information Systems Security	M,O
Database Systems	M,O
Health Informatics	M,O

DIGIPEN INSTITUTE OF TECHNOLOGY

Computer Science	M

DREXEL UNIVERSITY

Architectural Engineering	M,D
Biochemical Engineering	M
Biomedical Engineering	M,D
Chemical Engineering	M,D
Civil Engineering	M,D
Computer Engineering	M
Computer Science	M,D,O*
Construction Management	M
Electrical Engineering	M
Engineering and Applied Sciences—General	M,D,O
Engineering Management	M,O
Environmental Engineering	M,D
Geotechnical Engineering	M,D
Hydraulics	M,D
Information Science	M,D,O
Materials Engineering	M,D
Mechanical Engineering	M,D
Mechanics	M,D
Software Engineering	M,D,O
Structural Engineering	M,D
Telecommunications	M

DRURY UNIVERSITY

Computer and Information Systems Security	O

DUKE UNIVERSITY

Bioinformatics	D,O
Biomedical Engineering	M,D
Civil Engineering	M,D
Computer Engineering	M,D
Computer Science	M,D
Electrical Engineering	M,D*
Energy Management and Policy	M,O

M—masters degree; D—doctorate; O—other advanced degree; *—Close-Up and/or Display

Engineering and Applied Sciences—General	M
Engineering Management	M
Environmental Engineering	M,D
Health Informatics	M
Materials Engineering	M
Materials Sciences	M,D
Mechanical Engineering	M,D

DUQUESNE UNIVERSITY

Biotechnology	M

EAST CAROLINA UNIVERSITY

Biomedical Engineering	M
Biotechnology	M
Computer and Information Systems Security	M,D,O
Computer Engineering	M,D,O
Computer Science	M,D,O
Construction Management	M
Health Informatics	M
Management of Technology	M,D,O
Software Engineering	M
Telecommunications Management	M,D,O

EASTERN ILLINOIS UNIVERSITY

Computer and Information Systems Security	M,O
Computer Science	M
Energy Management and Policy	M
Engineering and Applied Sciences—General	M,O
Systems Science	M,O

EASTERN KENTUCKY UNIVERSITY

Industrial/Management Engineering	M
Manufacturing Engineering	M

EASTERN MICHIGAN UNIVERSITY

Computer and Information Systems Security	O
Computer Science	M,O
Construction Management	M,O
Engineering and Applied Sciences—General	M
Engineering Management	M
Management of Technology	D
Polymer Science and Engineering	M,O
Technology and Public Policy	M

EASTERN VIRGINIA MEDICAL SCHOOL

Biotechnology	M

EASTERN WASHINGTON UNIVERSITY

Computer Science	M

EAST STROUDSBURG UNIVERSITY OF PENNSYLVANIA

Computer Science	M

EAST TENNESSEE STATE UNIVERSITY

Computer Science	M,O
Information Science	M,O
Manufacturing Engineering	M,O

EC-COUNCIL UNIVERSITY

Computer and Information Systems Security	M

ÉCOLE POLYTECHNIQUE DE MONTRÉAL

Aerospace/Aeronautical Engineering	M,D,O
Biomedical Engineering	M,D,O
Chemical Engineering	M,D,O
Civil Engineering	M,D,O
Computer Engineering	M,D,O
Computer Science	M,D,O
Electrical Engineering	M,D,O
Engineering and Applied Sciences—General	M,D,O
Engineering Physics	M,D,O
Environmental Engineering	M,D,O
Geotechnical Engineering	M,D,O
Hydraulics	M,D,O
Industrial/Management Engineering	M,D,O
Management of Technology	M,D,O
Mechanical Engineering	M,D,O
Mechanics	M,D,O
Nuclear Engineering	M,D,O
Operations Research	M,D,O
Structural Engineering	M,D,O
Transportation and Highway Engineering	M,D,O

ELMHURST COLLEGE

Database Systems	M

EMBRY-RIDDLE AERONAUTICAL UNIVERSITY–DAYTONA

Aerospace/Aeronautical Engineering	M,D
Civil Engineering	M
Computer and Information Systems Security	M,D
Computer Science	M,D
Electrical Engineering	M,D
Engineering Physics	M,D
Ergonomics and Human Factors	M,D
Mechanical Engineering	M,D
Software Engineering	M,D
Systems Engineering	M,D

EMBRY-RIDDLE AERONAUTICAL UNIVERSITY–PRESCOTT

Aviation	M
Safety Engineering	M

EMBRY-RIDDLE AERONAUTICAL UNIVERSITY–WORLDWIDE

Aerospace/Aeronautical Engineering	M
Computer and Information Systems Security	M
Engineering Management	M
Management of Technology	M
Systems Engineering	M

EMORY UNIVERSITY

Bioinformatics	M,D
Computer Science	M,D
Health Informatics	M,D

EVERGLADES UNIVERSITY

Aviation	M

EXCELSIOR COLLEGE

Health Informatics	M,O
Management of Technology	M,O
Medical Informatics	M,O

FAIRFIELD UNIVERSITY

Computer and Information Systems Security	M,O
Computer Engineering	M,O
Database Systems	M,O
Electrical Engineering	M,O

Engineering and Applied Sciences—General	M,O
Management of Technology	M,O
Mechanical Engineering	M,O
Software Engineering	M,O
Telecommunications	M,O

FAIRLEIGH DICKINSON UNIVERSITY, COLLEGE AT FLORHAM

Chemical Engineering	M,O
Computer Science	M
Management of Technology	M,O

FAIRLEIGH DICKINSON UNIVERSITY, METROPOLITAN CAMPUS

Computer Engineering	M
Computer Science	M
Electrical Engineering	M
Engineering and Applied Sciences—General	M
Systems Science	M

FERRIS STATE UNIVERSITY

Computer and Information Systems Security	M
Database Systems	M

FITCHBURG STATE UNIVERSITY

Computer Science	M

FLORIDA AGRICULTURAL AND MECHANICAL UNIVERSITY

Biomedical Engineering	M,D
Chemical Engineering	M,D
Civil Engineering	M,D
Electrical Engineering	M,D
Engineering and Applied Sciences—General	M,D
Industrial/Management Engineering	M,D
Mechanical Engineering	M,D
Software Engineering	M

FLORIDA ATLANTIC UNIVERSITY

Bioengineering	M,D
Civil Engineering	M
Computer Engineering	M,D
Computer Science	M,D
Electrical Engineering	M,D
Engineering and Applied Sciences—General	M,D
Environmental Engineering	M
Mechanical Engineering	M,D
Ocean Engineering	M,D

FLORIDA INSTITUTE OF TECHNOLOGY

Aerospace/Aeronautical Engineering	M,D
Aviation	M,D
Biomedical Engineering	M,D
Biotechnology	M,D
Chemical Engineering	M,D
Civil Engineering	M,D
Computer and Information Systems Security	M
Computer Engineering	M,D
Computer Science	M,D
Electrical Engineering	M,D
Engineering and Applied Sciences—General	M,D
Engineering Management	M,D
Ergonomics and Human Factors	M,D
Human-Computer Interaction	M
Information Science	M
Management of Technology	M,D
Mechanical Engineering	M,D
Ocean Engineering	M,D
Operations Research	M,D

Safety Engineering	M
Software Engineering	M,D
Systems Engineering	M,D

FLORIDA INTERNATIONAL UNIVERSITY

Biomedical Engineering	M,D
Civil Engineering	M,D
Computer and Information Systems Security	M,D
Computer Engineering	M,D
Computer Science	M,D
Construction Management	M
Database Systems	M,D
Electrical Engineering	M,D
Engineering and Applied Sciences—General	M,D
Engineering Management	M
Environmental Engineering	M,D
Information Science	M,D
Materials Engineering	M,D
Materials Sciences	M,D
Mechanical Engineering	M,D
Telecommunications	M,D

FLORIDA STATE UNIVERSITY

Biomedical Engineering	M,D
Chemical Engineering	M,D
Civil Engineering	M,D
Computer and Information Systems Security	M,D
Computer Science	M,D
Electrical Engineering	M,D
Energy and Power Engineering	M,D
Engineering and Applied Sciences—General	M,D
Environmental Engineering	M,D
Industrial/Management Engineering	M,D
Manufacturing Engineering	M,D
Materials Engineering	M,D
Materials Sciences	M,D
Mechanical Engineering	M,D

FONTBONNE UNIVERSITY

Computer Science	M

FORDHAM UNIVERSITY

Computer and Information Systems Security	M
Computer Science	M
Database Systems	M

FRANKLIN PIERCE UNIVERSITY

Energy Management and Policy	M,D,O
Telecommunications	M,D,O

FRANKLIN UNIVERSITY

Computer Science	M

FROSTBURG STATE UNIVERSITY

Computer Science	M

FULL SAIL UNIVERSITY

Game Design and Development	M

GANNON UNIVERSITY

Computer Science	M
Electrical Engineering	M
Engineering Management	M
Environmental Engineering	M
Information Science	M
Mechanical Engineering	M
Software Engineering	M

GEORGE MASON UNIVERSITY

Bioengineering	D

Bioinformatics	M,D,O
Civil Engineering	M,D
Computer and Information	
Systems Security	M
Computer Engineering	M,D,O
Computer Science	M,D,O
Construction Engineering	M,D
Electrical Engineering	M,D,O
Engineering and Applied	
Sciences—General	M,D,O
Engineering Physics	M,D
Information Science	M,D,O
Management of Technology	M
Operations Research	M,D,O
Structural Engineering	M,D
Systems Engineering	M,D,O
Transportation and Highway	
Engineering	M,D

GEORGETOWN UNIVERSITY

Bioinformatics	M,O
Computer Science	M,D
Management of Technology	M,D
Materials Sciences	D
Systems Engineering	M,D

THE GEORGE WASHINGTON UNIVERSITY

Aerospace/Aeronautical	
Engineering	M,D,O
Biomedical Engineering	M,D
Biotechnology	M,D,O
Civil Engineering	M,D,O
Computer and Information	
Systems Security	M,D,O
Computer Engineering	M,D,O
Computer Science	M,D,O
Electrical Engineering	M,D,O
Engineering and Applied	
Sciences—General	M,D,O
Engineering Management	M,D,O
Environmental Engineering	M,D,O
Management of Technology	M,D
Materials Sciences	M,D
Mechanical Engineering	M,D,O
Systems Engineering	M,D,O
Technology and Public Policy	M,O
Telecommunications	M,D,O

GEORGIA INSTITUTE OF TECHNOLOGY

Aerospace/Aeronautical	
Engineering	M,D
Artificial Intelligence/Robotics	D
Bioengineering	M,D
Bioinformatics	M,D
Biomedical Engineering	D
Chemical Engineering	M,D
Civil Engineering	M,D
Computer and Information	
Systems Security	M
Computer Engineering	M,D
Computer Science	M,D
Electrical Engineering	M,D
Engineering and Applied	
Sciences—General	M,D
Environmental Engineering	M
Ergonomics and Human	
Factors	M,D
Human-Computer Interaction	M
Industrial/Management	
Engineering	M,D
Materials Engineering	M,D
Mechanical Engineering	M,D
Mechanics	M
Nuclear Engineering	M,D
Operations Research	M,D
Paper and Pulp Engineering	M,D
Systems Engineering	M

GEORGIA SOUTHERN UNIVERSITY

Civil Engineering	M
Computer Science	M
Construction Management	M
Electrical Engineering	M
Energy and Power	
Engineering	M
Engineering and Applied	
Sciences—General	M,O
Engineering Management	M
Manufacturing Engineering	M,O
Mechanical Engineering	M
Systems Engineering	M

GEORGIA SOUTHWESTERN STATE UNIVERSITY

Computer Science	M,O
Health Informatics	M,O

GEORGIA STATE UNIVERSITY

Bioinformatics	M,D
Computer Science	M,D
Health Informatics	M,D,O
Information Science	M,D,O
Operations Research	M,D

GOLDEN GATE UNIVERSITY

Health Informatics	M,D,O
Management of Technology	M,D,O

GONZAGA UNIVERSITY

Engineering and Applied	
Sciences—General	M,O

GOVERNORS STATE UNIVERSITY

Computer Science	M

THE GRADUATE CENTER, CITY UNIVERSITY OF NEW YORK

Biomedical Engineering	D
Chemical Engineering	D
Civil Engineering	D
Computer Science	D
Electrical Engineering	D
Engineering and Applied	
Sciences—General	D
Mechanical Engineering	D

GRAND CANYON UNIVERSITY

Database Systems	D
Health Informatics	M,D,O

GRAND VALLEY STATE UNIVERSITY

Bioinformatics	M
Computer Engineering	M
Computer Science	M
Electrical Engineering	M
Engineering and Applied	
Sciences—General	M
Information Science	M
Manufacturing Engineering	M
Mechanical Engineering	M
Medical Informatics	M
Software Engineering	M

GRANTHAM UNIVERSITY

Engineering and Applied	
Sciences—General	M

HAMPTON UNIVERSITY

Computer and Information	
Systems Security	M
Computer Science	M

HARRISBURG UNIVERSITY OF SCIENCE AND TECHNOLOGY

Computer and Information	
Systems Security	M
Management of Technology	M
Software Engineering	M
Systems Engineering	M
Systems Science	M

HARVARD UNIVERSITY

Applied Science and	
Technology	M,O
Bioengineering	M,D
Biomedical Engineering	D
Biotechnology	M,O
Computer Science	M,D
Electrical Engineering	M,D
Engineering and Applied	
Sciences—General	M,D
Engineering Design	M,D
Environmental Engineering	M,D
Information Science	M,D,O
Management of Technology	D
Materials Sciences	M,D
Mechanical Engineering	M,D

HEC MONTREAL

Financial Engineering	M
Operations Research	M

HERZING UNIVERSITY ONLINE

Management of Technology	M

HOFSTRA UNIVERSITY

Computer and Information	
Systems Security	M
Engineering and Applied	
Sciences—General	M
Health Informatics	M
Internet Engineering	M

HOOD COLLEGE

Bioinformatics	M,O
Biotechnology	M
Computer and Information	
Systems Security	M,O
Computer Science	M,O
Information Science	M,O
Systems Science	M

HOWARD UNIVERSITY

Biotechnology	M,D
Chemical Engineering	M
Civil Engineering	M
Computer Science	M
Electrical Engineering	M,D
Engineering and Applied	
Sciences—General	M,D
Mechanical Engineering	M,D

HUMBOLDT STATE UNIVERSITY

Hazardous Materials	
Management	M

HUNTER COLLEGE OF THE CITY UNIVERSITY OF NEW YORK

Bioinformatics	M

HUSSON UNIVERSITY

Biotechnology	M

IDAHO STATE UNIVERSITY

Civil Engineering	M
Engineering and Applied	
Sciences—General	M,D,O
Environmental Engineering	M

Hazardous Materials	
Management	M
Management of Technology	M
Mechanical Engineering	M
Nuclear Engineering	M,D
Operations Research	M

IGLOBAL UNIVERSITY

Database Systems	M

ILLINOIS INSTITUTE OF TECHNOLOGY

Aerospace/Aeronautical	
Engineering	M,D
Agricultural Engineering	M
Architectural Engineering	M,D
Artificial Intelligence/Robotics	M,D
Bioengineering	M,D
Biomedical Engineering	M,D
Chemical Engineering	M,D
Civil Engineering	M,D
Computer and Information	
Systems Security	M,D
Computer Engineering	M,D
Computer Science	M,D
Construction Engineering	M,D
Construction Management	M,D
Database Systems	M,D
Electrical Engineering	M,D
Engineering and Applied	
Sciences—General	M,D
Environmental Engineering	M,D
Geotechnical Engineering	M,D
Manufacturing Engineering	M,D
Materials Engineering	M,D
Materials Sciences	M,D
Mechanical Engineering	M,D
Software Engineering	M,D
Structural Engineering	M,D
Telecommunications	M,D
Transportation and Highway	
Engineering	M,D

ILLINOIS STATE UNIVERSITY

Biotechnology	M
Industrial/Management	
Engineering	M
Management of Technology	M

INDIANA STATE UNIVERSITY

Computer Engineering	M
Computer Science	M
Engineering and Applied	
Sciences—General	M
Management of Technology	M,D

INDIANA TECH

Engineering Management	M

INDIANA UNIVERSITY BLOOMINGTON

Artificial Intelligence/Robotics	D
Bioinformatics	M,D,O
Biotechnology	M,D
Computer and Information	
Systems Security	M,D
Computer Science	M,D,O
Database Systems	M,O
Energy Management and	
Policy	M,D,O
Ergonomics and Human	
Factors	M,D
Health Informatics	M,D
Human-Computer Interaction	M,D
Information Science	M,D,O
Materials Sciences	M,D
Safety Engineering	M,D
Systems Engineering	D
Water Resources Engineering	M,D,O

M—masters degree; D—doctorate; O—other advanced degree; *—Close-Up and/or Display

INDIANA UNIVERSITY OF PENNSYLVANIA
Nanotechnology	M

INDIANA UNIVERSITY–PURDUE UNIVERSITY FORT WAYNE
Civil Engineering	M
Computer Engineering	M
Computer Science	M
Construction Management	M
Electrical Engineering	M
Engineering and Applied Sciences—General	M,O
Industrial/Management Engineering	M
Information Science	M
Mechanical Engineering	M
Operations Research	M,O
Systems Engineering	M

INDIANA UNIVERSITY–PURDUE UNIVERSITY INDIANAPOLIS
Bioinformatics	M,D
Biomedical Engineering	M,D
Computer and Information Systems Security	M,D,O
Computer Engineering	M,D
Computer Science	M,D,O
Database Systems	M,D,O
Electrical Engineering	M,D
Health Informatics	M
Human-Computer Interaction	M,D
Information Science	M
Management of Technology	M
Mechanical Engineering	M,D
Software Engineering	M,D,O

INDIANA UNIVERSITY SOUTH BEND
Computer Science	M,O

INSTITUTO CENTROAMERICANO DE ADMINISTRACIÓN DE EMPRESAS
Management of Technology	M

INSTITUTO TECNOLOGICO DE SANTO DOMINGO
Construction Management	M,O
Energy and Power Engineering	M,D,O
Energy Management and Policy	M,D,O
Engineering and Applied Sciences—General	M,O
Environmental Engineering	M,O
Industrial/Management Engineering	M,O
Information Science	M,O
Software Engineering	M,O
Structural Engineering	M,O
Telecommunications	M,O

INSTITUTO TECNOLÓGICO Y DE ESTUDIOS SUPERIORES DE MONTERREY, CAMPUS CENTRAL DE VERACRUZ
Computer Science	M

INSTITUTO TECNOLÓGICO Y DE ESTUDIOS SUPERIORES DE MONTERREY, CAMPUS CHIHUAHUA
Computer Engineering	M,O
Electrical Engineering	M,O
Engineering Management	M,O
Industrial/Management Engineering	M,O
Mechanical Engineering	M,O
Systems Engineering	M,O

INSTITUTO TECNOLÓGICO Y DE ESTUDIOS SUPERIORES DE MONTERREY, CAMPUS CIUDAD DE MÉXICO
Computer Science	M,D
Environmental Engineering	M,D
Industrial/Management Engineering	M,D
Telecommunications Management	M

INSTITUTO TECNOLÓGICO Y DE ESTUDIOS SUPERIORES DE MONTERREY, CAMPUS CIUDAD OBREGÓN
Engineering and Applied Sciences—General	M
Telecommunications Management	M

INSTITUTO TECNOLÓGICO Y DE ESTUDIOS SUPERIORES DE MONTERREY, CAMPUS CUERNAVACA
Computer Science	M,D
Information Science	M,D
Management of Technology	M,D

INSTITUTO TECNOLÓGICO Y DE ESTUDIOS SUPERIORES DE MONTERREY, CAMPUS ESTADO DE MÉXICO
Computer Science	M,D
Information Science	M,D
Materials Engineering	M,D
Materials Sciences	M,D
Telecommunications Management	M,D

INSTITUTO TECNOLÓGICO Y DE ESTUDIOS SUPERIORES DE MONTERREY, CAMPUS IRAPUATO
Computer Science	M,D
Information Science	M,D
Management of Technology	M,D
Telecommunications Management	M,D

INSTITUTO TECNOLÓGICO Y DE ESTUDIOS SUPERIORES DE MONTERREY, CAMPUS LAGUNA
Industrial/Management Engineering	M

INSTITUTO TECNOLÓGICO Y DE ESTUDIOS SUPERIORES DE MONTERREY, CAMPUS MONTERREY
Agricultural Engineering	M,D
Artificial Intelligence/Robotics	M,D
Biotechnology	M,D
Chemical Engineering	M,D
Civil Engineering	M,D
Computer Science	M,D
Electrical Engineering	M,D
Engineering and Applied Sciences—General	M,D
Environmental Engineering	M,D
Industrial/Management Engineering	M,D
Information Science	M,D
Manufacturing Engineering	M,D
Mechanical Engineering	M,D
Systems Engineering	M,D

INSTITUTO TECNOLÓGICO Y DE ESTUDIOS SUPERIORES DE MONTERREY, CAMPUS SONORA NORTE
Information Science	M

INTER AMERICAN UNIVERSITY OF PUERTO RICO, BAYAMÓN CAMPUS
Aerospace/Aeronautical Engineering	M
Biotechnology	M
Electrical Engineering	M
Energy and Power Engineering	M
Mechanical Engineering	M

INTER AMERICAN UNIVERSITY OF PUERTO RICO, FAJARDO CAMPUS
Computer Science	M

INTER AMERICAN UNIVERSITY OF PUERTO RICO, GUAYAMA CAMPUS
Computer and Information Systems Security	M
Computer Science	M

INTER AMERICAN UNIVERSITY OF PUERTO RICO, METROPOLITAN CAMPUS
Computer Science	M

INTERNATIONAL TECHNOLOGICAL UNIVERSITY
Computer Engineering	M
Electrical Engineering	M,D
Engineering Management	M
Software Engineering	M

THE INTERNATIONAL UNIVERSITY OF MONACO
Financial Engineering	M

IONA COLLEGE
Computer and Information Systems Security	M,O
Computer Science	M
Game Design and Development	M
Management of Technology	M,O

IOWA STATE UNIVERSITY OF SCIENCE AND TECHNOLOGY
Aerospace/Aeronautical Engineering	M,D
Agricultural Engineering	M,D
Bioinformatics	M,D
Chemical Engineering	M,D
Civil Engineering	M,D
Computer Engineering	M,D
Computer Science	M,D
Construction Engineering	M,D
Database Systems	M
Electrical Engineering	M,D
Environmental Engineering	M,D
Geotechnical Engineering	M,D
Human-Computer Interaction	M,D
Industrial/Management Engineering	M,D
Information Science	M
Materials Engineering	M,D
Materials Sciences	M,D
Mechanical Engineering	M,D
Mechanics	M,D
Operations Research	M,D
Structural Engineering	M,D
Systems Engineering	M
Transportation and Highway Engineering	M,D

JACKSON STATE UNIVERSITY
Civil Engineering	M,D
Computer Science	M
Environmental Engineering	M,D
Materials Sciences	M,D

JACKSONVILLE STATE UNIVERSITY
Computer Science	M
Software Engineering	M

JACKSONVILLE UNIVERSITY
Health Informatics	M

JAMES MADISON UNIVERSITY
Computer and Information Systems Security	M
Computer Science	M
Engineering and Applied Sciences—General	M

JOHNS HOPKINS UNIVERSITY
Aerospace/Aeronautical Engineering	M
Artificial Intelligence/Robotics	M
Bioengineering	M,D
Bioinformatics	M,D
Biomedical Engineering	M,D,O
Biotechnology	M
Chemical Engineering	M,D
Civil Engineering	M,D,O
Computer and Information Systems Security	M,O
Computer Engineering	M,D,O
Computer Science	M,D,O
Electrical Engineering	M,D,O
Energy Management and Policy	M,O
Engineering and Applied Sciences—General	M,D,O
Engineering Management	M
Environmental Engineering	M,D,O
Health Informatics	M,D,O
Management of Technology	M,O
Materials Engineering	M,D
Materials Sciences	M,D
Mechanical Engineering	M,D,O
Mechanics	M
Medical Informatics	M,D,O
Nanotechnology	M
Operations Research	M,D
Systems Engineering	M,O

JOHNSON & WALES UNIVERSITY
Computer and Information Systems Security	M

KANSAS STATE UNIVERSITY
Agricultural Engineering	M,D
Applied Science and Technology	M,O
Architectural Engineering	M
Bioengineering	M,D
Chemical Engineering	M,D,O
Civil Engineering	M,D
Computer Engineering	M,D
Computer Science	M,D
Database Systems	M,O
Electrical Engineering	M,D
Energy and Power Engineering	M,D
Energy Management and Policy	M,D
Engineering and Applied Sciences—General	M,D,O
Engineering Management	M,D
Environmental Engineering	M,D
Geotechnical Engineering	M,D
Industrial/Management Engineering	M,D
Management of Technology	M
Manufacturing Engineering	M,D
Mechanical Engineering	M,D
Nuclear Engineering	M,D
Operations Research	M,D
Structural Engineering	M,D
Transportation and Highway Engineering	M,D
Water Resources Engineering	M,D

KAPLAN UNIVERSITY, DAVENPORT CAMPUS
Computer and Information
   Systems Security   M

KEAN UNIVERSITY
Biotechnology   M

KEISER UNIVERSITY
Computer and Information
   Systems Security   M

KENNESAW STATE UNIVERSITY
Computer and Information
   Systems Security   M,O
Computer Engineering   M
Computer Science   M
Construction Management   M
Electrical Engineering   M
Engineering and Applied
   Sciences—General   M,O
Health Informatics   M,O
Information Science   M,O
Software Engineering   M,O
Systems Engineering   M,O

KENT STATE UNIVERSITY
Computer and Information
   Systems Security   M
Computer Science   M,D
Engineering and Applied
   Sciences—General   M
Health Informatics   M
Information Science   M

KENTUCKY STATE UNIVERSITY
Computer Science   M

KETTERING UNIVERSITY
Electrical Engineering   M
Engineering Management   M
Manufacturing Engineering   M
Mechanical Engineering   M

KNOWLEDGE SYSTEMS INSTITUTE
Computer Science   M
Information Science   M

KUTZTOWN UNIVERSITY OF PENNSYLVANIA
Computer Science   M

LAKEHEAD UNIVERSITY
Computer Engineering   M
Computer Science   M
Electrical Engineering   M
Engineering and Applied
   Sciences—General   M
Environmental Engineering   M

LAMAR UNIVERSITY
Chemical Engineering   M,D
Computer Science   M
Electrical Engineering   M,D
Engineering and Applied
   Sciences—General   M,D
Engineering Management   M,D
Environmental Engineering   M,D
Industrial/Management
   Engineering   M,D
Mechanical Engineering   M,D

LA SALLE UNIVERSITY
Computer Science   M,O
Management of Technology   M,O

LAURENTIAN UNIVERSITY
Engineering and Applied
   Sciences—General   M,D
Mineral/Mining Engineering   M,D

LAWRENCE TECHNOLOGICAL UNIVERSITY
Architectural Engineering   M,D
Automotive Engineering   M,D
Bioinformatics   M,O
Biomedical Engineering   M,D
Civil Engineering   M,D
Computer and Information
   Systems Security   M,O
Computer Engineering   M,D
Computer Science   M,O
Construction Engineering   M,O
Database Systems   M,O
Electrical Engineering   M,D
Engineering and Applied
   Sciences—General   M,D
Engineering Management   M,D
Industrial/Management
   Engineering   M,D
Information Science   M,O
Manufacturing Engineering   M,D
Mechanical Engineering   M,D
Water Resources Engineering   M,D

LEBANESE AMERICAN UNIVERSITY
Computer Science   M

LEHIGH UNIVERSITY
Biochemical Engineering   M,D
Bioengineering   M,D
Chemical Engineering   M,D
Civil Engineering   M,D
Computer Engineering   M,D
Computer Science   M,D
Electrical Engineering   M,D
Energy and Power
   Engineering   M
Engineering and Applied
   Sciences—General   M,D
Engineering Management   M,D
Environmental Engineering   M,D
Industrial/Management
   Engineering   M,D
Information Science   M
Manufacturing Engineering   M
Materials Engineering   M,D
Materials Sciences   M,D
Mechanical Engineering   M,D
Mechanics   M,D
Polymer Science and
   Engineering   M,D
Systems Engineering   M,D

LEHMAN COLLEGE OF THE CITY UNIVERSITY OF NEW YORK
Computer Science   M

LETOURNEAU UNIVERSITY
Engineering and Applied
   Sciences—General   M
Engineering Management   M

LEWIS UNIVERSITY
Aviation   M
Computer and Information
   Systems Security   M
Database Systems   M
Management of Technology   M

LIBERTY UNIVERSITY
Computer and Information
   Systems Security   M,D,O

Engineering and Applied
   Sciences—General   M
Management of Technology   M,D,O

LINDENWOOD UNIVERSITY
Computer and Information
   Systems Security   M,O

LIPSCOMB UNIVERSITY
Computer and Information
   Systems Security   M,O
Database Systems   M
Health Informatics   M,D,O
Management of Technology   M
Software Engineering   M

LOGAN UNIVERSITY
Health Informatics   M,D

LONDON METROPOLITAN UNIVERSITY
Computer and Information
   Systems Security   M,D
Database Systems   M,D
Management of Technology   M,D

LONG ISLAND UNIVERSITY–HUDSON
Biotechnology   M,O

LONG ISLAND UNIVERSITY–LIU BROOKLYN
Computer Science   M,O

LONG ISLAND UNIVERSITY–LIU POST
Engineering Management   M
Game Design and
   Development   M

LOUISIANA STATE UNIVERSITY AND AGRICULTURAL & MECHANICAL COLLEGE
Agricultural Engineering   M,D
Applied Science and
   Technology   M
Bioengineering   M,D
Chemical Engineering   M,D
Civil Engineering   M,D
Computer Engineering   M,D
Computer Science   M,D
Construction Management   M,D
Electrical Engineering   M,D
Engineering and Applied
   Sciences—General   M,D
Environmental Engineering   M,D
Geotechnical Engineering   M,D
Mechanical Engineering   M,D
Mechanics   M,D
Petroleum Engineering   M,D
Structural Engineering   M,D
Systems Science   M,D
Transportation and Highway
   Engineering   M,D
Water Resources Engineering   M,D

LOUISIANA STATE UNIVERSITY IN SHREVEPORT
Computer Science   M
Systems Science   M

LOUISIANA TECH UNIVERSITY
Biomedical Engineering   D
Chemical Engineering   M
Civil Engineering   M
Computer Science   M,D
Electrical Engineering   M,D

Engineering and Applied
   Sciences—General   M,D
Health Informatics   M
Industrial/Management
   Engineering   M
Nanotechnology   M,D

LOYOLA MARYMOUNT UNIVERSITY
Civil Engineering   M
Electrical Engineering   M
Engineering Management
Mechanical Engineering   M
Systems Engineering   M

LOYOLA UNIVERSITY CHICAGO
Computer Science   M
Information Science   M
Software Engineering   M

MAHARISHI UNIVERSITY OF MANAGEMENT
Computer Science   M

MANHATTAN COLLEGE
Chemical Engineering   M
Civil Engineering   M
Computer Engineering   M
Database Systems   M
Electrical Engineering   M
Engineering and Applied
   Sciences—General   M
Environmental Engineering   M
Mechanical Engineering   M

MARIST COLLEGE
Computer Science   M,O
Management of Technology   M,O
Software Engineering   M,O

MARQUETTE UNIVERSITY
Bioinformatics   M,D
Biomedical Engineering   M,D
Civil Engineering   M,D,O
Computer Engineering   M,D,O
Computer Science   M,D
Construction Engineering   M,D,O
Construction Management   M,D,O
Electrical Engineering   M,D,O
Engineering and Applied
   Sciences—General   M,D,O
Engineering Management   M,D,O
Environmental Engineering   M,D,O
Hazardous Materials
   Management   M,D,O
Management of Technology   M,D
Mechanical Engineering   M,D,O
Structural Engineering   M,D,O
Transportation and Highway
   Engineering   M,D,O
Water Resources Engineering   M,D,O

MARSHALL UNIVERSITY
Computer Science   M
Engineering and Applied
   Sciences—General   M
Engineering Management   M
Environmental Engineering   M
Health Informatics   M
Information Science   M
Management of Technology   M
Transportation and Highway
   Engineering   M

MARYMOUNT UNIVERSITY
Computer and Information
   Systems Security   M,O
Health Informatics   M,O
Software Engineering   M,O

*M—masters degree; D—doctorate; O—other advanced degree; *—Close-Up and/or Display*

MARYVILLE UNIVERSITY OF SAINT LOUIS
Computer and Information Systems Security	M,O
Information Science	M,O

MARYWOOD UNIVERSITY
Biotechnology	M
Computer and Information Systems Security	M

MASSACHUSETTS INSTITUTE OF TECHNOLOGY
Aerospace/Aeronautical Engineering	M,D,O
Bioengineering	M,D
Bioinformatics	M,D
Biomedical Engineering	M,D
Chemical Engineering	M,D
Civil Engineering	M,D,O
Computer Engineering	M,D,O
Computer Science	M,D,O
Construction Engineering	M,D,O
Electrical Engineering	M,D,O
Engineering and Applied Sciences—General	M,D,O
Engineering Management	M
Environmental Engineering	M,D,O
Geotechnical Engineering	M,D,O
Information Science	M,D,O
Manufacturing Engineering	M,D,O
Materials Engineering	M,D,O
Materials Sciences	M,D,O
Mechanical Engineering	M,D,O
Nuclear Engineering	M,D,O
Ocean Engineering	M,D,O
Operations Research	M,D
Structural Engineering	M,D,O
Systems Engineering	M,D
Technology and Public Policy	M,D
Transportation and Highway Engineering	M,D,O

MAYO CLINIC GRADUATE SCHOOL OF BIOMEDICAL SCIENCES
Biomedical Engineering	D

MCGILL UNIVERSITY
Aerospace/Aeronautical Engineering	M,D
Agricultural Engineering	M,D
Bioengineering	M,D
Bioinformatics	M,D
Biomedical Engineering	M,D
Biotechnology	M,D,O
Chemical Engineering	M,D
Civil Engineering	M,D
Computer Engineering	M,D
Computer Science	M,D
Electrical Engineering	M,D
Engineering and Applied Sciences—General	M,D,O
Environmental Engineering	M,D
Geotechnical Engineering	M,D
Hydraulics	M,D
Materials Engineering	M,D,O
Mechanical Engineering	M,D
Mechanics	M,D
Mineral/Mining Engineering	M,D,O
Structural Engineering	M,D
Water Resources Engineering	M,D

MCMASTER UNIVERSITY
Chemical Engineering	M,D
Civil Engineering	M,D
Computer Science	M,D
Electrical Engineering	M,D
Engineering and Applied Sciences—General	M,D
Engineering Physics	M,D
Materials Engineering	M,D
Materials Sciences	M,D

Mechanical Engineering	M,D
Nuclear Engineering	M,D
Software Engineering	M,D

MCNEESE STATE UNIVERSITY
Chemical Engineering	M
Civil Engineering	M
Computer Science	M
Electrical Engineering	M
Engineering and Applied Sciences—General	M,O
Engineering Management	M
Mechanical Engineering	M,O

MEMORIAL UNIVERSITY OF NEWFOUNDLAND
Civil Engineering	M,D
Computer Engineering	M,D
Computer Science	M,D
Electrical Engineering	M,D
Engineering and Applied Sciences—General	M,D
Environmental Engineering	M
Mechanical Engineering	M,D
Ocean Engineering	M,D

MERCER UNIVERSITY
Biomedical Engineering	M
Computer Engineering	M
Electrical Engineering	M
Engineering and Applied Sciences—General	M
Engineering Management	M
Environmental Engineering	M
Health Informatics	M,D
Management of Technology	M
Mechanical Engineering	M
Software Engineering	M

MERCY COLLEGE
Computer and Information Systems Security	M

MERCYHURST UNIVERSITY
Computer and Information Systems Security	M

MERRIMACK COLLEGE
Civil Engineering	M
Computer Science	M
Database Systems	M
Engineering and Applied Sciences—General	M
Engineering Management	M
Mechanical Engineering	M

METROPOLITAN STATE UNIVERSITY
Computer and Information Systems Security	M,D,O
Computer Science	M
Database Systems	M,D,O
Health Informatics	M,D,O

MIAMI UNIVERSITY
Chemical Engineering	M
Computer Engineering	M
Electrical Engineering	M
Engineering and Applied Sciences—General	M
Mechanical Engineering	M
Systems Science	M

MICHIGAN STATE UNIVERSITY
Biosystems Engineering	M,D
Chemical Engineering	M,D
Civil Engineering	M,D
Computer Science	M,D
Construction Management	M,D
Electrical Engineering	M,D

Engineering and Applied Sciences—General	M,D
Environmental Engineering	M,D
Game Design and Development	M
Manufacturing Engineering	M,D
Materials Engineering	M,D
Materials Sciences	M,D
Mechanical Engineering	M,D
Mechanics	M,D
Telecommunications	M

MICHIGAN TECHNOLOGICAL UNIVERSITY
Automotive Engineering	M,D,O
Biomedical Engineering	M,D
Biotechnology	M,D
Chemical Engineering	M,D
Computer and Information Systems Security	M,D
Computer Engineering	M,D,O
Computer Science	M,D
Database Systems	M,D,O
Electrical Engineering	M,D,O
Energy Management and Policy	M,D
Engineering and Applied Sciences—General	M,D,O
Environmental Engineering	M,D,O
Ergonomics and Human Factors	M,D,O
Materials Engineering	M,D
Mechanical Engineering	M,D,O
Mechanics	M,D,O
Medical Informatics	M
Metallurgical Engineering and Metallurgy	M,D
Nanotechnology	M,D,O

MIDDLE GEORGIA STATE UNIVERSITY
Computer and Information Systems Security	M
Health Informatics	M

MIDDLE TENNESSEE STATE UNIVERSITY
Aerospace/Aeronautical Engineering	M
Biotechnology	M
Computer Science	M
Engineering Management	M
Medical Informatics	M

MIDWESTERN STATE UNIVERSITY
Computer Science	M
Health Informatics	M,O

MILLENNIA ATLANTIC UNIVERSITY
Health Informatics	M

MILLS COLLEGE
Computer Science	M,O

MILWAUKEE SCHOOL OF ENGINEERING
Architectural Engineering	M
Civil Engineering	M
Construction Management	M
Engineering and Applied Sciences—General	M
Engineering Management	M
Medical Informatics	M

MINNESOTA STATE UNIVERSITY MANKATO
Automotive Engineering	M
Computer Science	M,O
Information Science	M,O
Manufacturing Engineering	M

MISSISSIPPI COLLEGE
Computer Science	M

MISSISSIPPI STATE UNIVERSITY
Aerospace/Aeronautical Engineering	M,D
Bioengineering	M,D
Biomedical Engineering	M,D
Chemical Engineering	M,D
Civil Engineering	M,D
Computer Engineering	M,D
Computer Science	M,D
Electrical Engineering	M,D
Engineering and Applied Sciences—General	M,D
Ergonomics and Human Factors	M,D
Industrial/Management Engineering	M,D
Mechanical Engineering	M,D
Operations Research	M,D
Systems Engineering	M,D

MISSOURI STATE UNIVERSITY
Applied Science and Technology	M
Computer and Information Systems Security	M
Computer Science	M
Construction Management	M
Materials Sciences	M

MISSOURI UNIVERSITY OF SCIENCE AND TECHNOLOGY
Aerospace/Aeronautical Engineering	M,D
Ceramic Sciences and Engineering	M,D
Chemical Engineering	M,D
Civil Engineering	M,D
Computer Engineering	M,D
Computer Science	M,D
Construction Engineering	M,D
Electrical Engineering	M,D
Engineering Management	M,D
Environmental Engineering	M,D
Geological Engineering	M,D
Geotechnical Engineering	M,D
Hydraulics	M,D
Information Science	M
Manufacturing Engineering	M,D
Mechanical Engineering	M,D
Mechanics	M,D
Metallurgical Engineering and Metallurgy	M,D
Mineral/Mining Engineering	M,D
Nuclear Engineering	M,D
Petroleum Engineering	M,D
Systems Engineering	M,D

MISSOURI WESTERN STATE UNIVERSITY
Computer and Information Systems Security	M
Engineering and Applied Sciences—General	M
Ergonomics and Human Factors	M

MONMOUTH UNIVERSITY
Computer Science	M,O
Software Engineering	M,O

MONROE COLLEGE
Computer Science	M
Information Science	M

MONTANA STATE UNIVERSITY
Chemical Engineering	M,D
Civil Engineering	M,D
Computer Engineering	M,D
Computer Science	M,D

Construction Engineering	M,D
Electrical Engineering	M,D
Engineering and Applied Sciences—General	M,D
Environmental Engineering	M,D
Industrial/Management Engineering	M,D
Mechanical Engineering	M,D
Mechanics	M,D

MONTANA TECH OF THE UNIVERSITY OF MONTANA

Electrical Engineering	M
Engineering and Applied Sciences—General	M
Environmental Engineering	M
Geological Engineering	M
Health Informatics	O
Industrial/Management Engineering	M
Materials Sciences	D
Metallurgical Engineering and Metallurgy	M
Mineral/Mining Engineering	M
Petroleum Engineering	M

MONTCLAIR STATE UNIVERSITY

Computer Science	M,O
Database Systems	O

MOREHEAD STATE UNIVERSITY

Industrial/Management Engineering	M

MORGAN STATE UNIVERSITY

Bioinformatics	M
Civil Engineering	M,D
Electrical Engineering	M,D
Engineering and Applied Sciences—General	M,D
Industrial/Management Engineering	M,D
Transportation and Highway Engineering	M

MOUNT ST. MARY'S UNIVERSITY (MD)

Biotechnology	M

MURRAY STATE UNIVERSITY

Management of Technology	M
Safety Engineering	M
Telecommunications Management	M

NATIONAL TEST PILOT SCHOOL

Aviation	M

NATIONAL UNIVERSITY

Computer Science	M

NAVAL POSTGRADUATE SCHOOL

Aerospace/Aeronautical Engineering	M,D,O
Applied Science and Technology	M,D
Computer and Information Systems Security	M,D
Computer Engineering	M,D,O
Computer Science	M,D,O
Electrical Engineering	M,D,O
Engineering Management	M,D,O
Information Science	M,D,O
Mechanical Engineering	M,D,O
Modeling and Simulation	M,D
Operations Research	M,D
Software Engineering	M,D
Systems Engineering	M,D,O

NEW COLLEGE OF FLORIDA

Database Systems	M

NEW ENGLAND INSTITUTE OF TECHNOLOGY

Construction Management	M

NEW JERSEY CITY UNIVERSITY

Computer and Information Systems Security	M,D,O

NEW JERSEY INSTITUTE OF TECHNOLOGY

Bioinformatics	M,D,O
Biomedical Engineering	M,D
Chemical Engineering	M,D
Computer and Information Systems Security	M,D,O
Computer Engineering	M,D
Computer Science	M,D,O
Database Systems	M,D,O
Electrical Engineering	M,D
Energy and Power Engineering	M,D
Engineering and Applied Sciences—General	M,D
Engineering Management	M,D
Environmental Engineering	M,D
Industrial/Management Engineering	M,D
Information Science	M,D,O
Internet Engineering	M,D
Management of Technology	M,D,O
Manufacturing Engineering	M,D
Materials Engineering	M,D,O
Materials Sciences	M,D,O
Mechanical Engineering	M,D
Pharmaceutical Engineering	M,D
Safety Engineering	M,D
Software Engineering	M,D,O
Systems Science	M,D,O
Telecommunications	M,D
Transportation and Highway Engineering	M,D

NEW MEXICO HIGHLANDS UNIVERSITY

Computer Science	M

NEW MEXICO INSTITUTE OF MINING AND TECHNOLOGY

Computer Science	M,D
Electrical Engineering	M
Engineering Management	M
Environmental Engineering	M
Geological Engineering	M
Hazardous Materials Management	M
Materials Engineering	M,D
Mechanical Engineering	M
Mechanics	M
Mineral/Mining Engineering	M
Operations Research	M,D
Petroleum Engineering	M,D
Systems Engineering	M
Water Resources Engineering	M

NEW MEXICO STATE UNIVERSITY

Aerospace/Aeronautical Engineering	M,D
Bioinformatics	M,D
Biotechnology	M,D
Chemical Engineering	M,D
Civil Engineering	M,D
Computer Engineering	M,D,O
Computer Science	M,D
Electrical Engineering	M,D,O
Engineering and Applied Sciences—General	M,D,O
Environmental Engineering	M,D

Geological Engineering	M,D
Industrial/Management Engineering	M,D,O
Mechanical Engineering	M,D
Systems Engineering	M,D,O

THE NEW SCHOOL

Database Systems	M

NEWSCHOOL OF ARCHITECTURE AND DESIGN

Construction Management	M

NEW YORK INSTITUTE OF TECHNOLOGY

Computer and Information Systems Security	M
Computer Engineering	M
Computer Science	M
Electrical Engineering	M
Energy and Power Engineering	M,O
Energy Management and Policy	M,O
Engineering and Applied Sciences—General	M,O
Environmental Engineering	M

NEW YORK UNIVERSITY

Agricultural Engineering	M,D
Bioinformatics	M,D
Biomedical Engineering	M,D
Biotechnology	M
Chemical Engineering	M,D
Civil Engineering	M,D
Computer and Information Systems Security	O
Computer Engineering	M,O
Computer Science	M,D
Construction Management	M,D,O
Database Systems	M,O
Electrical Engineering	M,D
Energy Management and Policy	M,O
Engineering and Applied Sciences—General	M,D,O
Environmental Engineering	M
Ergonomics and Human Factors	M,D
Financial Engineering	M,O
Game Design and Development	M
Industrial/Management Engineering	M
Management of Technology	M,D,O
Manufacturing Engineering	M
Mechanical Engineering	M,D
Software Engineering	O
Systems Engineering	M
Telecommunications Management	M,D,O
Transportation and Highway Engineering	M,D

NORFOLK STATE UNIVERSITY

Computer Engineering	M
Computer Science	M
Electrical Engineering	M
Materials Sciences	M

NORTH CAROLINA AGRICULTURAL AND TECHNICAL STATE UNIVERSITY

Bioengineering	M
Chemical Engineering	M
Civil Engineering	M
Computer Engineering	M,D
Computer Science	M
Construction Management	M
Electrical Engineering	M,D

NORTH CAROLINA STATE UNIVERSITY

Aerospace/Aeronautical Engineering	M,D
Agricultural Engineering	M,D,O
Bioengineering	M,D,O
Bioinformatics	M,D
Biomedical Engineering	M,D
Biotechnology	M
Chemical Engineering	M,D
Civil Engineering	M,D
Computer Engineering	M,D
Computer Science	M,D
Electrical Engineering	M,D
Engineering and Applied Sciences—General	M,D
Ergonomics and Human Factors	D
Financial Engineering	M
Industrial/Management Engineering	M,D
Management of Technology	D
Manufacturing Engineering	M
Materials Engineering	M,D
Materials Sciences	M,D
Mechanical Engineering	M,D
Nuclear Engineering	M,D
Operations Research	M,D
Paper and Pulp Engineering	M,D
Polymer Science and Engineering	D
Textile Sciences and Engineering	M,D

NORTH CENTRAL COLLEGE

Computer Science	M

NORTH DAKOTA STATE UNIVERSITY

Bioinformatics	M,D
Civil Engineering	M,D
Computer Engineering	M,D
Computer Science	M,D,O
Construction Management	M,O
Electrical Engineering	M,D
Engineering and Applied Sciences—General	M,D,O*
Environmental Engineering	M,D
Industrial/Management Engineering	M,D
Manufacturing Engineering	M,D
Materials Sciences	M,D
Mechanical Engineering	M,D
Nanotechnology	M,D
Polymer Science and Engineering	M,D
Software Engineering	M,D,O
Transportation and Highway Engineering	D

NORTHEASTERN ILLINOIS UNIVERSITY

Computer Science	M

NORTHEASTERN UNIVERSITY

Bioengineering	M,D,O
Bioinformatics	M,D
Biotechnology	M,D
Chemical Engineering	M,D,O

M—masters degree; D—doctorate; O—other advanced degree; *—Close-Up and/or Display

Civil Engineering	M,D,O
Computer and Information Systems Security	M,D,O
Computer Engineering	M,D,O
Computer Science	M,D
Database Systems	M,D
Electrical Engineering	M,D,O
Energy and Power Engineering	M,D,O
Engineering and Applied Sciences—General	M,D,O
Engineering Management	M,D,O
Environmental Engineering	M,D,O
Health Informatics	M,D
Industrial/Management Engineering	M,D,O
Mechanical Engineering	M,D,O
Operations Research	M,D,O
Systems Engineering	M,D,O
Telecommunications	M,D,O

NORTHERN ARIZONA UNIVERSITY

Civil Engineering	M
Computer Engineering	M
Computer Science	M
Electrical Engineering	M
Engineering and Applied Sciences—General	M,D,O
Environmental Engineering	M
Mechanical Engineering	M

NORTHERN ILLINOIS UNIVERSITY

Computer Science	M
Electrical Engineering	M
Engineering and Applied Sciences—General	M
Industrial/Management Engineering	M
Mechanical Engineering	M

NORTHERN KENTUCKY UNIVERSITY

Computer and Information Systems Security	M,O
Computer Science	M,O
Health Informatics	M,O
Information Science	M,O
Management of Technology	M
Software Engineering	M,O

NORTHWESTERN POLYTECHNIC UNIVERSITY

Computer Engineering	M,D
Computer Science	M,D
Electrical Engineering	M,D
Engineering and Applied Sciences—General	M,D

NORTHWESTERN UNIVERSITY

Artificial Intelligence/Robotics	M
Bioengineering	D
Biomedical Engineering	M,D
Biotechnology	M,D
Chemical Engineering	M,D
Civil Engineering	M,D
Computer and Information Systems Security	M
Computer Engineering	M,D
Computer Science	M,D
Database Systems	M
Electrical Engineering	M,D
Engineering and Applied Sciences—General	M,D,O
Engineering Design	M
Engineering Management	M
Environmental Engineering	M,D
Geotechnical Engineering	M,D
Health Informatics	D
Industrial/Management Engineering	M,D
Information Science	M
Materials Engineering	M,D,O
Materials Sciences	M,D,O

Mechanical Engineering	M,D
Mechanics	M,D
Medical Informatics	M,D
Software Engineering	M
Structural Engineering	M,D
Transportation and Highway Engineering	M,D

NORTHWEST MISSOURI STATE UNIVERSITY

Computer Science	M

NORWICH UNIVERSITY

Civil Engineering	M
Computer and Information Systems Security	M
Construction Management	M
Energy Management and Policy	M
Environmental Engineering	M
Geotechnical Engineering	M
Structural Engineering	M

NOTRE DAME COLLEGE (OH)

Computer Science	M,O

NOTRE DAME DE NAMUR UNIVERSITY

Management of Technology	M

NOVA SOUTHEASTERN UNIVERSITY

Bioinformatics	M,D,O
Computer and Information Systems Security	M,D
Computer Science	M,D
Health Informatics	M,D,O
Information Science	M,D
Medical Informatics	M,D,O

OAKLAND UNIVERSITY

Computer Engineering	M,D
Computer Science	M,D
Electrical Engineering	M,D
Engineering and Applied Sciences—General	M,D,O
Engineering Management	M,D,O
Mechanical Engineering	M,D
Software Engineering	M,D
Systems Engineering	M,D,O
Systems Science	M,D

OHIO DOMINICAN UNIVERSITY

Database Systems	M
Engineering Design	M

THE OHIO STATE UNIVERSITY

Aerospace/Aeronautical Engineering	M,D
Agricultural Engineering	M,D
Bioengineering	M,D
Biomedical Engineering	M,D
Chemical Engineering	M,D
Civil Engineering	M,D
Computer Engineering	M,D
Computer Science	M,D
Electrical Engineering	M,D
Engineering and Applied Sciences—General	M,D
Industrial/Management Engineering	M,D
Materials Engineering	M,D
Materials Sciences	M,D
Mechanical Engineering	M,D
Metallurgical Engineering and Metallurgy	M,D
Nuclear Engineering	M,D
Operations Research	M
Systems Engineering	M,D

OHIO UNIVERSITY

Biomedical Engineering	M
Chemical Engineering	M,D
Civil Engineering	M,D
Computer Science	M,D
Construction Engineering	M,D
Electrical Engineering	M,D
Engineering and Applied Sciences—General	M,D
Environmental Engineering	M,D
Geotechnical Engineering	M,D
Industrial/Management Engineering	M,D
Mechanical Engineering	M
Mechanics	M,D
Structural Engineering	M,D
Systems Engineering	M
Telecommunications	M
Transportation and Highway Engineering	M,D
Water Resources Engineering	M,D

OKLAHOMA BAPTIST UNIVERSITY

Energy Management and Policy	M

OKLAHOMA CHRISTIAN UNIVERSITY

Computer Engineering	M
Computer Science	M
Electrical Engineering	M
Engineering and Applied Sciences—General	M
Engineering Management	M
Mechanical Engineering	M
Software Engineering	M

OKLAHOMA CITY UNIVERSITY

Computer Science	M
Energy Management and Policy	M

OKLAHOMA STATE UNIVERSITY

Agricultural Engineering	M,D
Bioengineering	M,D
Chemical Engineering	M,D
Civil Engineering	M,D
Computer Engineering	M,D
Computer Science	M,D
Electrical Engineering	M,D
Engineering and Applied Sciences—General	M,D
Environmental Engineering	M,D
Fire Protection Engineering	M,D
Industrial/Management Engineering	M,D
Information Science	M,D
Materials Engineering	M,D
Materials Sciences	M,D
Mechanical Engineering	M,D
Telecommunications Management	M,D,O

OLD DOMINION UNIVERSITY

Aerospace/Aeronautical Engineering	M,D
Biomedical Engineering	M,D
Civil Engineering	M,D
Computer Engineering	M,D
Computer Science	M,D
Electrical Engineering	M,D
Engineering and Applied Sciences—General	M,D
Engineering Management	D
Environmental Engineering	M,D
Ergonomics and Human Factors	D
Geotechnical Engineering	M
Hydraulics	M
Information Science	D
Mechanical Engineering	M,D
Modeling and Simulation	M,D
Structural Engineering	M

Systems Engineering	M,D
Transportation and Highway Engineering	M

OPEN UNIVERSITY

Engineering and Applied Sciences—General	M

OREGON HEALTH & SCIENCE UNIVERSITY

Bioinformatics	M,D,O
Biomedical Engineering	D
Computer Engineering	M,D
Computer Science	M,D
Electrical Engineering	M,D
Environmental Engineering	M,D
Health Informatics	M,D,O
Medical Informatics	M,D,O

OREGON INSTITUTE OF TECHNOLOGY

Manufacturing Engineering	M

OREGON STATE UNIVERSITY

Agricultural Engineering	M,D
Artificial Intelligence/Robotics	M,D
Bioengineering	M,D
Bioinformatics	D
Biotechnology	M,D
Chemical Engineering	M,D
Civil Engineering	M,D
Computer Engineering	M,D
Computer Science	M,D
Construction Engineering	M,D
Electrical Engineering	M,D
Engineering and Applied Sciences—General	M,D
Engineering Management	M,D
Environmental Engineering	M,D
Geotechnical Engineering	M,D
Industrial/Management Engineering	M,D
Manufacturing Engineering	M,D
Materials Sciences	M,D
Mechanical Engineering	M,D
Modeling and Simulation	M,D
Nuclear Engineering	M,D
Ocean Engineering	M,D
Software Engineering	M,D
Structural Engineering	M,D
Systems Engineering	M,D
Transportation and Highway Engineering	M,D
Water Resources Engineering	M,D

OUR LADY OF THE LAKE UNIVERSITY

Computer and Information Systems Security	M

PACE UNIVERSITY

Computer and Information Systems Security	M,D,O
Computer Science	M,D,O
Information Science	M,D,O
Software Engineering	M,D,O
Telecommunications	M,D,O

PACIFIC STATES UNIVERSITY

Computer Science	M
Management of Technology	M,D

PENN STATE ERIE, THE BEHREND COLLEGE

Engineering and Applied Sciences—General	M

PENN STATE GREAT VALLEY

Computer and Information Systems Security	M,O
Database Systems	M,O

Engineering and Applied Sciences—General	M,O
Engineering Management	M,O
Information Science	M,O
Software Engineering	M,O
Systems Engineering	M,O

PENN STATE HARRISBURG

Computer Science	M,O
Electrical Engineering	M,O
Engineering and Applied Sciences—General	M,O
Engineering Management	M,O
Environmental Engineering	M,O
Structural Engineering	M,O

PENN STATE UNIVERSITY PARK

Aerospace/Aeronautical Engineering	M,D
Agricultural Engineering	M,D
Architectural Engineering	M,D
Bioengineering	M,D
Biotechnology	M,D
Chemical Engineering	M,D
Civil Engineering	M,D
Computer Science	M,D
Electrical Engineering	M,D
Engineering and Applied Sciences—General	M,D
Engineering Design	M
Environmental Engineering	M,D
Geotechnical Engineering	M,D
Industrial/Management Engineering	M,D
Information Science	M,D
Materials Engineering	M,D
Materials Sciences	M,D
Mechanical Engineering	M,D
Mechanics	M,D
Mineral/Mining Engineering	M,D
Nuclear Engineering	M,D

PHILADELPHIA UNIVERSITY

Construction Management	M
Modeling and Simulation	M
Textile Sciences and Engineering	M,D

PITTSBURG STATE UNIVERSITY

Construction Engineering	M
Construction Management	M,O
Electrical Engineering	M
Management of Technology	M,O
Manufacturing Engineering	M
Mechanical Engineering	M
Polymer Science and Engineering	M

POINT PARK UNIVERSITY

Engineering Management	M

POLYTECHNIC UNIVERSITY OF PUERTO RICO

Civil Engineering	M
Computer Engineering	M
Computer Science	M
Electrical Engineering	M
Engineering Management	M
Management of Technology	M
Manufacturing Engineering	M
Mechanical Engineering	M

POLYTECHNIC UNIVERSITY OF PUERTO RICO, MIAMI CAMPUS

Construction Management	M
Environmental Engineering	M

POLYTECHNIC UNIVERSITY OF PUERTO RICO, ORLANDO CAMPUS

Construction Management	M
Engineering Management	M
Environmental Engineering	M
Management of Technology	M

PONTIFICAL JOHN PAUL II INSTITUTE FOR STUDIES ON MARRIAGE AND FAMILY

Biotechnology	M,D,O

PONTIFICIA UNIVERSIDAD CATOLICA MADRE Y MAESTRA

Engineering and Applied Sciences—General	M
Structural Engineering	M

PORTLAND STATE UNIVERSITY

Artificial Intelligence/Robotics	M,D,O
Civil Engineering	M,D,O
Computer Engineering	M,D
Computer Science	M,D
Electrical Engineering	M,D
Engineering and Applied Sciences—General	M,D,O
Engineering Management	M,D,O
Environmental Engineering	M,D
Management of Technology	M,D
Manufacturing Engineering	M,D
Mechanical Engineering	M,D,O
Modeling and Simulation	M,D,O
Software Engineering	M,D
Systems Science	M,D,O

PRAIRIE VIEW A&M UNIVERSITY

Computer Science	M,D
Electrical Engineering	M,D
Engineering and Applied Sciences—General	M,D

PRINCETON UNIVERSITY

Aerospace/Aeronautical Engineering	M,D
Chemical Engineering	M,D
Civil Engineering	M,D
Computer Science	M,D
Electrical Engineering	M,D
Electronic Materials	D
Engineering and Applied Sciences—General	M,D
Environmental Engineering	M,D
Financial Engineering	M,D
Materials Sciences	D
Mechanical Engineering	M,D
Ocean Engineering	D
Operations Research	M,D

PURDUE UNIVERSITY

Aerospace/Aeronautical Engineering	D
Agricultural Engineering	M,D
Biomedical Engineering	M,D
Biotechnology	D
Chemical Engineering	M,D
Civil Engineering	M,D
Computer and Information Systems Security	M
Computer Engineering	M,D
Computer Science	M,D
Construction Management	M
Electrical Engineering	M,D
Engineering and Applied Sciences—General	M,D,O
Environmental Engineering	M,D
Ergonomics and Human Factors	M,D
Industrial/Management Engineering	M,D

Management of Technology	M,D
Materials Engineering	M,D
Mechanical Engineering	M,D,O
Nuclear Engineering	M,D

PURDUE UNIVERSITY NORTHWEST

Biotechnology	M
Computer Engineering	M
Computer Science	M
Electrical Engineering	M
Engineering and Applied Sciences—General	M
Mechanical Engineering	M

QUEENS COLLEGE OF THE CITY UNIVERSITY OF NEW YORK

Computer Science	M
Database Systems	M

QUEEN'S UNIVERSITY AT KINGSTON

Chemical Engineering	M,D
Civil Engineering	M,D
Computer Engineering	M,D
Computer Science	M,D
Electrical Engineering	M,D
Engineering and Applied Sciences—General	M,D
Mechanical Engineering	M,D
Mineral/Mining Engineering	M,D

RADFORD UNIVERSITY

Database Systems	M

REGIS COLLEGE (MA)

Biotechnology	M

REGIS UNIVERSITY

Computer and Information Systems Security	M,O
Computer Science	M,O
Database Systems	M,O
Health Informatics	M,O
Information Science	M,O
Medical Informatics	M,O
Software Engineering	M,O
Systems Engineering	M,O

RENSSELAER AT HARTFORD

Computer Engineering	M
Computer Science	M
Electrical Engineering	M
Engineering and Applied Sciences—General	M
Information Science	M
Mechanical Engineering	M
Systems Science	M

RENSSELAER POLYTECHNIC INSTITUTE

Aerospace/Aeronautical Engineering	M,D
Bioengineering	M,D
Biomedical Engineering	M,D
Chemical Engineering	M,D
Civil Engineering	M,D
Computer Engineering	M,D
Computer Science	M,D
Electrical Engineering	M,D
Engineering and Applied Sciences—General	M,D
Engineering Management	M,D
Engineering Physics	M,D
Environmental Engineering	M,D
Financial Engineering	M
Industrial/Management Engineering	M,D
Information Science	M

Management of Technology	M,D
Materials Engineering	M,D
Materials Sciences	M,D
Mechanical Engineering	M,D
Nuclear Engineering	M,D
Systems Engineering	M,D
Technology and Public Policy	M,D
Transportation and Highway Engineering	M,D

RICE UNIVERSITY

Bioengineering	M,D
Bioinformatics	M,D
Biomedical Engineering	M,D
Chemical Engineering	M,D
Civil Engineering	M,D
Computer Engineering	M,D
Computer Science	M,D
Electrical Engineering	M,D
Energy Management and Policy	M,D
Engineering and Applied Sciences—General	M,D
Environmental Engineering	M,D
Materials Sciences	M,D
Mechanical Engineering	M,D

RIVIER UNIVERSITY

Computer Science	M

ROBERT MORRIS UNIVERSITY

Computer and Information Systems Security	M,D
Database Systems	M,D
Engineering and Applied Sciences—General	M
Engineering Management	M
Information Science	M,D

ROBERT MORRIS UNIVERSITY ILLINOIS

Computer and Information Systems Security	M

ROBERTS WESLEYAN COLLEGE

Health Informatics	M

ROCHESTER INSTITUTE OF TECHNOLOGY

Bioinformatics	M
Computer and Information Systems Security	M,O
Computer Engineering	M
Computer Science	M,D
Database Systems	O
Electrical Engineering	M
Engineering and Applied Sciences—General	M,D,O
Engineering Design	M
Engineering Management	M
Game Design and Development	M
Human-Computer Interaction	M
Industrial/Management Engineering	M
Information Science	M,D
Manufacturing Engineering	M
Materials Engineering	M
Materials Sciences	M
Mechanical Engineering	M
Modeling and Simulation	D
Safety Engineering	M
Software Engineering	M
Systems Engineering	M,D
Technology and Public Policy	M
Telecommunications	M

ROCKHURST UNIVERSITY

Database Systems	M,O

ROGER WILLIAMS UNIVERSITY
Computer and Information Systems Security	M

ROLLINS COLLEGE
Management of Technology	M,D

ROOSEVELT UNIVERSITY
Biotechnology	M
Computer Science	M
Telecommunications	M

ROSE-HULMAN INSTITUTE OF TECHNOLOGY
Biomedical Engineering	M
Chemical Engineering	M
Civil Engineering	M
Computer Engineering	M
Electrical Engineering	M
Engineering and Applied Sciences—General	M
Engineering Management	M
Environmental Engineering	M
Mechanical Engineering	M
Software Engineering	M
Systems Engineering	M

ROWAN UNIVERSITY
Bioinformatics	M
Chemical Engineering	M
Civil Engineering	M
Computer and Information Systems Security	O
Computer Science	M
Electrical Engineering	M
Engineering and Applied Sciences—General	M
Mechanical Engineering	M

ROYAL MILITARY COLLEGE OF CANADA
Chemical Engineering	M,D
Civil Engineering	M,D
Computer Engineering	M,D
Computer Science	M
Electrical Engineering	M,D
Engineering and Applied Sciences—General	M,D
Environmental Engineering	M,D
Materials Sciences	M,D
Mechanical Engineering	M,D
Nuclear Engineering	M,D
Software Engineering	M,D

RUTGERS UNIVERSITY–CAMDEN
Computer Science	M

RUTGERS UNIVERSITY–NEWARK
Bioinformatics	M,D
Biomedical Engineering	O
Management of Technology	D
Medical Informatics	M,D,O

RUTGERS UNIVERSITY–NEW BRUNSWICK
Aerospace/Aeronautical Engineering	M,D
Biochemical Engineering	M,D
Biomedical Engineering	M,D
Chemical Engineering	M,D
Civil Engineering	M,D
Computer Engineering	M,D
Computer Science	M,D
Electrical Engineering	M,D
Environmental Engineering	M,D
Hazardous Materials Management	M,D
Industrial/Management Engineering	M,D
Information Science	M
Materials Engineering	M,D
Materials Sciences	M,D
Mechanical Engineering	M,D
Mechanics	M,D
Operations Research	D
Systems Engineering	M,D

RYERSON UNIVERSITY
Management of Technology	M

SACRED HEART UNIVERSITY
Computer and Information Systems Security	M
Computer Science	M
Game Design and Development	M
Health Informatics	M
Information Science	M

SAGINAW VALLEY STATE UNIVERSITY
Engineering and Applied Sciences—General	M

ST. AMBROSE UNIVERSITY
Management of Technology	M

ST. CLOUD STATE UNIVERSITY
Biomedical Engineering	M
Computer and Information Systems Security	M
Computer Science	M
Electrical Engineering	M
Engineering and Applied Sciences—General	M
Engineering Management	M
Mechanical Engineering	M
Technology and Public Policy	M

ST. FRANCIS XAVIER UNIVERSITY
Computer Science	M

ST. JOHN'S UNIVERSITY (NY)
Biotechnology	M
Database Systems	M
Information Science	

ST. JOSEPH'S COLLEGE, LONG ISLAND CAMPUS
Health Informatics	M

ST. JOSEPH'S COLLEGE, NEW YORK
Health Informatics	M

SAINT JOSEPH'S UNIVERSITY
Computer Science	M,O
Health Informatics	M

SAINT LEO UNIVERSITY
Computer and Information Systems Security	M,D,O

SAINT LOUIS UNIVERSITY
Biomedical Engineering	M,D

SAINT MARTIN'S UNIVERSITY
Civil Engineering	M
Engineering Management	M
Mechanical Engineering	M

SAINT MARY'S COLLEGE
Database Systems	M

SAINT MARY'S COLLEGE OF CALIFORNIA
Database Systems	M

SAINT MARY'S UNIVERSITY (CANADA)
Applied Science and Technology	M

ST. MARY'S UNIVERSITY (UNITED STATES)
Computer and Information Systems Security	M
Computer Engineering	M
Computer Science	M
Electrical Engineering	M
Engineering Management	M
Industrial/Management Engineering	M
Information Science	M
Software Engineering	M,O

SAINT MARY'S UNIVERSITY OF MINNESOTA
Telecommunications	M

SAINT PETER'S UNIVERSITY
Database Systems	M

SAINT XAVIER UNIVERSITY
Computer Science	M

SALEM INTERNATIONAL UNIVERSITY
Computer and Information Systems Security	M

SALVE REGINA UNIVERSITY
Computer and Information Systems Security	M,O

SAMFORD UNIVERSITY
Energy Management and Policy	M

SAM HOUSTON STATE UNIVERSITY
Computer and Information Systems Security	M,D
Computer Science	M,D
Information Science	M,D

SAN DIEGO STATE UNIVERSITY
Aerospace/Aeronautical Engineering	M,D
Civil Engineering	M
Computer Science	M
Electrical Engineering	M
Engineering and Applied Sciences—General	M,D
Engineering Design	M,D
Mechanical Engineering	M,D
Mechanics	M,D
Telecommunications Management	M

SAN FRANCISCO STATE UNIVERSITY
Biotechnology	M
Computer Science	M
Electrical Engineering	M
Energy and Power Engineering	M
Engineering and Applied Sciences—General	M

SAN JOSE STATE UNIVERSITY
Biotechnology	M,O
Computer and Information Systems Security	M,O
Computer Science	M,O

SANTA CLARA UNIVERSITY
Bioengineering	M,D,O
Civil Engineering	M,D,O
Computer Engineering	M,D,O
Computer Science	M,D,O
Electrical Engineering	M,D,O
Energy and Power Engineering	M,D,O
Engineering and Applied Sciences—General	M,D,O
Engineering Management	M,D,O
Mechanical Engineering	M,D,O
Software Engineering	M,D,O

SAVANNAH COLLEGE OF ART AND DESIGN
Game Design and Development	M

SCHOOL OF THE ART INSTITUTE OF CHICAGO
Materials Sciences	M

SEATTLE UNIVERSITY
Computer Science	M
Database Systems	M,O
Engineering and Applied Sciences—General	M
Software Engineering	M

SETON HALL UNIVERSITY
Management of Technology	M,O

SHEPHERD UNIVERSITY (CA)
Game Design and Development	M

SHIPPENSBURG UNIVERSITY OF PENNSYLVANIA
Computer and Information Systems Security	M,O
Computer Science	M,O
Information Science	M,O
Software Engineering	M,O

SILICON VALLEY UNIVERSITY
Computer Engineering	M
Computer Science	M

SIMMONS COLLEGE
Information Science	M,D,O

SIMON FRASER UNIVERSITY
Bioinformatics	M,D,O
Biotechnology	M,D,O
Computer Science	M,D
Engineering and Applied Sciences—General	M,D
Management of Technology	M,D,O
Mechanical Engineering	M,D
Operations Research	M,D
Systems Engineering	M,D

SLIPPERY ROCK UNIVERSITY OF PENNSYLVANIA
Database Systems	M
Health Informatics	M

SOFIA UNIVERSITY
Computer Science	M,D

SOUTH CAROLINA STATE UNIVERSITY
Civil Engineering	M
Mechanical Engineering	M
Transportation and Highway Engineering	M

SOUTH DAKOTA SCHOOL OF MINES AND TECHNOLOGY

Artificial Intelligence/Robotics	M
Bioengineering	D
Biomedical Engineering	M,D
Chemical Engineering	M,D
Civil Engineering	M,D
Construction Management	M
Electrical Engineering	M
Engineering and Applied Sciences—General	M,D
Engineering Management	M
Geological Engineering	M,D
Management of Technology	M
Materials Engineering	M,D
Materials Sciences	M,D
Mechanical Engineering	M,D
Mineral/Mining Engineering	M
Nanotechnology	D

SOUTH DAKOTA STATE UNIVERSITY

Agricultural Engineering	M,D
Biosystems Engineering	M,D
Civil Engineering	M
Electrical Engineering	M,D
Engineering and Applied Sciences—General	M,D
Industrial/Management Engineering	M
Mechanical Engineering	M,D

SOUTHEASTERN LOUISIANA UNIVERSITY

Applied Science and Technology	M

SOUTHEASTERN OKLAHOMA STATE UNIVERSITY

Aviation	M
Biotechnology	M

SOUTHEAST MISSOURI STATE UNIVERSITY

Management of Technology	M

SOUTHERN ARKANSAS UNIVERSITY–MAGNOLIA

Computer and Information Systems Security	M
Computer Science	M
Database Systems	M
Information Science	M

SOUTHERN CONNECTICUT STATE UNIVERSITY

Computer Science	M

SOUTHERN ILLINOIS UNIVERSITY CARBONDALE

Biomedical Engineering	M
Civil Engineering	M,D
Computer Engineering	M,D
Computer Science	M,D
Electrical Engineering	M,D
Energy and Power Engineering	D
Engineering and Applied Sciences—General	M,D
Engineering Management	M
Environmental Engineering	D
Mechanical Engineering	M,D
Mechanics	M
Mineral/Mining Engineering	M,D

SOUTHERN ILLINOIS UNIVERSITY EDWARDSVILLE

Civil Engineering	M
Computer Science	M

Electrical Engineering	M
Engineering and Applied Sciences—General	M
Environmental Engineering	M
Geotechnical Engineering	M
Health Informatics	M
Industrial/Management Engineering	M
Mechanical Engineering	M
Operations Research	M
Structural Engineering	M
Transportation and Highway Engineering	M

SOUTHERN METHODIST UNIVERSITY

Applied Science and Technology	M,D
Civil Engineering	M,D
Computer Engineering	M,D
Computer Science	M,D
Database Systems	M
Electrical Engineering	M,D
Engineering and Applied Sciences—General	M,D
Engineering Management	M,D
Environmental Engineering	M,D
Information Science	M,D
Manufacturing Engineering	M,D
Materials Engineering	M,D
Materials Sciences	M,D
Mechanical Engineering	M,D
Operations Research	M,D
Software Engineering	M,D
Structural Engineering	M,D
Systems Engineering	M,D
Systems Science	M,D
Telecommunications	M,D
Water Resources Engineering	M,D

SOUTHERN NEW HAMPSHIRE UNIVERSITY

Health Informatics	M,O

SOUTHERN OREGON UNIVERSITY

Computer Science	M

SOUTHERN UNIVERSITY AND AGRICULTURAL AND MECHANICAL COLLEGE

Computer Science	M
Engineering and Applied Sciences—General	M

SOUTHERN UTAH UNIVERSITY

Computer and Information Systems Security	M

STANFORD UNIVERSITY

Aerospace/Aeronautical Engineering	M,D,O
Bioengineering	M,D
Biomedical Engineering	M,D,O
Chemical Engineering	M,D
Civil Engineering	M,D,O
Computer Science	M,D
Construction Engineering	M,D,O
Electrical Engineering	M,D
Energy and Power Engineering	M,D,O
Engineering and Applied Sciences—General	M,D,O
Engineering Design	M
Engineering Management	M,D
Engineering Physics	M,D
Environmental Engineering	M,D,O
Geotechnical Engineering	M,D,O
Industrial/Management Engineering	M,D
Materials Engineering	M,D,O

Materials Sciences	M,D,O
Mechanical Engineering	M,D,O
Mechanics	M,D,O
Medical Informatics	M,D
Structural Engineering	M,D,O

STATE UNIVERSITY OF NEW YORK AT NEW PALTZ

Computer Science	M
Electrical Engineering	M

STATE UNIVERSITY OF NEW YORK AT OSWEGO

Human-Computer Interaction	M

STATE UNIVERSITY OF NEW YORK COLLEGE OF ENVIRONMENTAL SCIENCE AND FORESTRY

Construction Management	M,D
Environmental Engineering	M,D
Materials Sciences	M,D,O
Paper and Pulp Engineering	M,D,O
Water Resources Engineering	M,D

STATE UNIVERSITY OF NEW YORK DOWNSTATE MEDICAL CENTER

Biomedical Engineering	M,D

STATE UNIVERSITY OF NEW YORK POLYTECHNIC INSTITUTE

Computer and Information Systems Security	M
Computer Science	M
Information Science	M
Management of Technology	M
Nanotechnology	M,D
Telecommunications	M

STEPHEN F. AUSTIN STATE UNIVERSITY

Biotechnology	M
Computer Science	M

STEPHENS COLLEGE

Health Informatics	M,O

STEVENS INSTITUTE OF TECHNOLOGY

Aerospace/Aeronautical Engineering	M,O
Artificial Intelligence/Robotics	M,D,O
Bioinformatics	M,D,O
Biomedical Engineering	M,D,O
Chemical Engineering	M,D,O
Civil Engineering	M,D,O
Computer and Information Systems Security	M,D,O
Computer Engineering	M,D,O
Computer Science	M,D,O
Construction Engineering	M,O
Construction Management	M,O
Database Systems	M,D,O
Electrical Engineering	M,D,O
Engineering and Applied Sciences—General	M,D,O
Engineering Design	M
Engineering Management	M,D,O
Environmental Engineering	M,D,O
Financial Engineering	M,D,O
Health Informatics	M,D,O
Information Science	M,O
Management of Technology	M,D,O
Manufacturing Engineering	M
Materials Engineering	M,D
Materials Sciences	M,D
Mechanical Engineering	M,D,O
Modeling and Simulation	M,D,O

Nanotechnology	D
Nuclear Engineering	M,D,O
Ocean Engineering	M,D
Polymer Science and Engineering	M,D,O
Software Engineering	M,O
Structural Engineering	M,D,O
Systems Engineering	M,D,O
Systems Science	M,D,O
Telecommunications Management	M,D,O
Telecommunications	M,D,O
Transportation and Highway Engineering	M,D,O
Water Resources Engineering	M,D,O

STEVENSON UNIVERSITY

Computer and Information Systems Security	M
Management of Technology	M

STONY BROOK UNIVERSITY, STATE UNIVERSITY OF NEW YORK

Bioinformatics	M,D,O
Biomedical Engineering	M,D,O
Civil Engineering	M,D,O
Computer Engineering	M,D
Computer Science	M,D,O
Electrical Engineering	M,D
Engineering and Applied Sciences—General	M,D,O
Health Informatics	M,D,O
Management of Technology	M
Materials Engineering	M,D
Materials Sciences	M,D
Mechanical Engineering	M,D
Software Engineering	M,D,O
Systems Engineering	M
Technology and Public Policy	D

STRATFORD UNIVERSITY (VA)

Computer and Information Systems Security	M
Computer Science	M
Software Engineering	M
Telecommunications	M

STRAYER UNIVERSITY

Computer and Information Systems Security	M
Information Science	M
Software Engineering	M
Systems Science	M
Telecommunications Management	M

SYRACUSE UNIVERSITY

Aerospace/Aeronautical Engineering	M,D
Bioengineering	M,D
Chemical Engineering	M,D
Civil Engineering	M,D
Computer and Information Systems Security	M,O
Computer Engineering	M,D
Computer Science	M
Database Systems	M
Electrical Engineering	M,D,O
Energy and Power Engineering	M
Engineering and Applied Sciences—General	M,D,O
Engineering Management	M
Environmental Engineering	M
Information Science	M,D
Mechanical Engineering	M,D

TARLETON STATE UNIVERSITY

Engineering Management	M

TÉLÉ-UNIVERSITÉ
Computer Science — M,D

TEMPLE UNIVERSITY
Bioengineering — M,D
Biotechnology — M,D
Civil Engineering — M,D,O
Computer Science — M,D
Electrical Engineering — M,D
Engineering and Applied
   Sciences—General — D*
Engineering Management — M,O
Environmental Engineering — M,D,O
Financial Engineering — M
Health Informatics — M
Information Science — M,D
Mechanical Engineering — M,D

TENNESSEE STATE UNIVERSITY
Biomedical Engineering — M,D
Biotechnology — M,D
Civil Engineering — M,D
Computer Engineering — M,D
Electrical Engineering — M,D
Engineering and Applied
   Sciences—General — M,D
Environmental Engineering — M,D
Manufacturing Engineering — M,D
Mechanical Engineering — M,D
Systems Engineering — M,D

TENNESSEE TECHNOLOGICAL UNIVERSITY
Chemical Engineering — M
Civil Engineering — M
Computer Science — M
Electrical Engineering — M
Engineering and Applied
   Sciences—General — M,D
Mechanical Engineering — M
Software Engineering — M

TEXAS A&M UNIVERSITY
Aerospace/Aeronautical
   Engineering — M,D
Agricultural Engineering — M,D
Bioengineering — M,D
Biomedical Engineering — M,D
Chemical Engineering — M,D
Civil Engineering — M,D
Computer Engineering — M,D
Computer Science — M,D
Construction Management — M
Electrical Engineering — M,D
Engineering Management — M,D
Industrial/Management
   Engineering — M,D
Management of Technology — M
Manufacturing Engineering — M
Materials Engineering — M,D
Materials Sciences — M,D
Mechanical Engineering — M,D
Nuclear Engineering — M,D
Petroleum Engineering — M,D

TEXAS A&M UNIVERSITY–COMMERCE
Management of Technology — M,O

TEXAS A&M UNIVERSITY–CORPUS CHRISTI
Computer Science — M

TEXAS A&M UNIVERSITY–KINGSVILLE
Chemical Engineering — M
Civil Engineering — M
Computer Science — M
Electrical Engineering — M
Energy and Power
   Engineering — D

Engineering and Applied
   Sciences—General — M,D
Environmental Engineering — M,D
Industrial/Management
   Engineering — M
Mechanical Engineering — M
Petroleum Engineering — M
Systems Engineering — D

TEXAS A&M UNIVERSITY–SAN ANTONIO
Computer and Information
   Systems Security — M

TEXAS SOUTHERN UNIVERSITY
Computer Science — M
Industrial/Management
   Engineering — M
Transportation and Highway
   Engineering — M

TEXAS STATE UNIVERSITY
Computer Science — M
Electrical Engineering — M
Engineering and Applied
   Sciences—General — M
Health Informatics — M
Industrial/Management
   Engineering — M
Management of Technology — M
Manufacturing Engineering — M
Materials Engineering — D
Materials Sciences — M,D
Software Engineering — M

TEXAS TECH UNIVERSITY
Bioengineering — M
Biotechnology — M,D
Chemical Engineering — M,D
Civil Engineering — M,D
Computer Science — M,D
Construction Engineering — M,D
Database Systems — M,D
Electrical Engineering — M,D
Energy and Power
   Engineering — M,D
Engineering and Applied
   Sciences—General — M,D
Engineering Management — M,D
Environmental Engineering — M,D
Industrial/Management
   Engineering — M,D
Manufacturing Engineering — M,D
Mechanical Engineering — M,D
Petroleum Engineering — M,D
Software Engineering — M,D
Systems Engineering — M,D

TEXAS TECH UNIVERSITY HEALTH SCIENCES CENTER
Biotechnology — M

TEXAS WOMAN'S UNIVERSITY
Information Science — M

THOMAS EDISON STATE UNIVERSITY
Applied Science and
   Technology — O

THOMAS JEFFERSON UNIVERSITY
Biotechnology — M

TOWSON UNIVERSITY
Computer and Information
   Systems Security — M,D,O
Computer Science — M
Database Systems — M,D,O
Information Science — M,D,O

Management of Technology — M,O
Software Engineering — M,D,O

TOYOTA TECHNOLOGICAL INSTITUTE AT CHICAGO
Computer Science — D

TRENT UNIVERSITY
Computer Science — M
Materials Sciences — M
Modeling and Simulation — M,D

TREVECCA NAZARENE UNIVERSITY
Information Science — M,O

TRIDENT UNIVERSITY INTERNATIONAL
Computer and Information
   Systems Security — M,D
Health Informatics — M,D,O

TROY UNIVERSITY
Computer Science — M

TUFTS UNIVERSITY
Bioengineering — M,D,O
Bioinformatics — M,D
Biomedical Engineering — M,D
Biotechnology — M,D,O
Chemical Engineering — M,D
Civil Engineering — M,D
Computer Science — M,D,O
Electrical Engineering — M,D,O
Engineering and Applied
   Sciences—General — M,D*
Engineering Management — M
Environmental Engineering — M,D
Ergonomics and Human
   Factors — M,D
Geotechnical Engineering — M,D
Hazardous Materials
   Management — M,D
Human-Computer Interaction — O
Manufacturing Engineering — O
Mechanical Engineering — M,D
Structural Engineering — M,D
Water Resources Engineering — M,D

TULANE UNIVERSITY
Biomedical Engineering — M,D
Chemical Engineering — M,D
Energy Management and
   Policy — M,D

TUSKEGEE UNIVERSITY
Computer and Information
   Systems Security — M
Electrical Engineering — M
Engineering and Applied
   Sciences—General — M,D
Materials Engineering — D
Mechanical Engineering — M

UNITED STATES MERCHANT MARINE ACADEMY
Civil Engineering — M

UNIVERSIDAD AUTONOMA DE GUADALAJARA
Computer Science — M,D
Energy and Power
   Engineering — M,D
Manufacturing Engineering — M,D
Systems Science — M,D

UNIVERSIDAD CENTRAL DEL ESTE
Environmental Engineering — M

UNIVERSIDAD DE LAS AMÉRICAS PUEBLA
Biotechnology — M
Chemical Engineering — M
Computer Science — M,D
Construction Management — M
Electrical Engineering — M
Engineering and Applied
   Sciences—General — M,D
Industrial/Management
   Engineering — M
Manufacturing Engineering — M

UNIVERSIDAD DEL ESTE
Computer and Information
   Systems Security — M

UNIVERSIDAD DEL TURABO
Computer Engineering — M
Electrical Engineering — M
Engineering and Applied
   Sciences—General — M
Mechanical Engineering — M
Telecommunications — M

UNIVERSIDAD NACIONAL PEDRO HENRIQUEZ URENA
Environmental Engineering — M

UNIVERSITÉ DE MONCTON
Civil Engineering — M
Computer Science — M,O
Electrical Engineering — M
Engineering and Applied
   Sciences—General — M
Industrial/Management
   Engineering — M
Mechanical Engineering — M

UNIVERSITÉ DE MONTRÉAL
Bioinformatics — M,D
Biomedical Engineering — M,D,O
Computer Science — M,D
Ergonomics and Human
   Factors — O

UNIVERSITÉ DE SHERBROOKE
Chemical Engineering — M,D
Civil Engineering — M,D
Computer and Information
   Systems Security — M
Electrical Engineering — M,D
Engineering and Applied
   Sciences—General — M,D,O
Engineering Management — M,O
Environmental Engineering — M
Information Science — M,D
Mechanical Engineering — M,D

UNIVERSITÉ DU QUÉBEC À CHICOUTIMI
Engineering and Applied
   Sciences—General — M,D

UNIVERSITÉ DU QUÉBEC À MONTRÉAL
Ergonomics and Human
   Factors — O

UNIVERSITÉ DU QUÉBEC À RIMOUSKI
Engineering and Applied
   Sciences—General — M

UNIVERSITÉ DU QUÉBEC À TROIS-RIVIÈRES
Computer Science — M
Electrical Engineering — M,D
Industrial/Management
   Engineering — M,O

UNIVERSITÉ DU QUÉBEC, ÉCOLE DE TECHNOLOGIE SUPÉRIEURE

Engineering and Applied Sciences—General	M,D,O

UNIVERSITÉ DU QUÉBEC EN ABITIBI-TÉMISCAMINGUE

Engineering and Applied Sciences—General	M,O
Mineral/Mining Engineering	M,O

UNIVERSITÉ DU QUÉBEC EN OUTAOUAIS

Computer Science	M,D,O

UNIVERSITÉ DU QUÉBEC, INSTITUT NATIONAL DE LA RECHERCHE SCIENTIFIQUE

Energy Management and Policy	M,D
Materials Sciences	M,D
Telecommunications	M,D

UNIVERSITÉ LAVAL

Aerospace/Aeronautical Engineering	M
Agricultural Engineering	M
Chemical Engineering	M,D
Civil Engineering	M,D,O
Computer Science	M,D
Electrical Engineering	M,D
Engineering and Applied Sciences—General	M,D,O
Environmental Engineering	M,D
Industrial/Management Engineering	O
Mechanical Engineering	M,D
Metallurgical Engineering and Metallurgy	M,D
Mineral/Mining Engineering	M,O
Modeling and Simulation	M,O
Software Engineering	O

UNIVERSITY AT ALBANY, STATE UNIVERSITY OF NEW YORK

Computer and Information Systems Security	M,O
Computer Science	M,D
Engineering and Applied Sciences—General	M,D,O
Information Science	D
Management of Technology	M

UNIVERSITY AT BUFFALO, THE STATE UNIVERSITY OF NEW YORK

Aerospace/Aeronautical Engineering	M,D
Bioengineering	M,D
Bioinformatics	M,D
Biomedical Engineering	M,D
Biotechnology	M
Chemical Engineering	M,D
Civil Engineering	M,D
Computer Science	M,D,O
Electrical Engineering	M,D*
Engineering and Applied Sciences—General	M,D,O
Environmental Engineering	M,D
Industrial/Management Engineering	M,D
Mechanical Engineering	M,D
Medical Informatics	M,D
Modeling and Simulation	M,D
Structural Engineering	M,D

UNIVERSITY OF ADVANCING TECHNOLOGY

Computer and Information Systems Security	M
Computer Science	M
Game Design and Development	M
Management of Technology	M

THE UNIVERSITY OF AKRON

Biomedical Engineering	M,D
Chemical Engineering	M,D
Civil Engineering	M,D
Computer Engineering	M,D
Computer Science	M
Electrical Engineering	M,D
Engineering and Applied Sciences—General	M,D
Geological Engineering	M
Mechanical Engineering	M,D
Polymer Science and Engineering	M,D

THE UNIVERSITY OF ALABAMA

Aerospace/Aeronautical Engineering	M,D
Chemical Engineering	M,D
Civil Engineering	M,D
Computer Engineering	M,D
Computer Science	M,D
Construction Engineering	M,D
Electrical Engineering	M,D
Engineering and Applied Sciences—General	M,D
Environmental Engineering	M,D
Ergonomics and Human Factors	M
Materials Engineering	M,D
Materials Sciences	D
Mechanical Engineering	M,D
Mechanics	M,D
Metallurgical Engineering and Metallurgy	M,D

THE UNIVERSITY OF ALABAMA AT BIRMINGHAM

Bioinformatics	D
Biomedical Engineering	M,D
Biotechnology	M
Civil Engineering	M,D
Computer and Information Systems Security	M
Computer Engineering	M,D
Computer Science	M,D
Construction Engineering	M,D
Electrical Engineering	M,D
Engineering and Applied Sciences—General	M,D
Engineering Management	M
Health Informatics	M
Information Science	M,D
Materials Engineering	M,D
Mechanical Engineering	M
Structural Engineering	M,D

THE UNIVERSITY OF ALABAMA IN HUNTSVILLE

Aerospace/Aeronautical Engineering	M,D
Biotechnology	M,D
Chemical Engineering	M,D
Civil Engineering	M,D
Computer and Information Systems Security	M,D,O
Computer Engineering	M,D
Computer Science	M,D,O
Electrical Engineering	M,D
Engineering and Applied Sciences—General	M,D
Environmental Engineering	M,D

Industrial/Management Engineering	M,D
Management of Technology	M,O
Materials Sciences	M,D
Mechanical Engineering	M,D
Modeling and Simulation	M,D,O
Operations Research	M,D
Software Engineering	M,D,O
Systems Engineering	M,D

UNIVERSITY OF ALASKA ANCHORAGE

Civil Engineering	M,O
Engineering and Applied Sciences—General	M,O
Engineering Management	M
Environmental Engineering	M
Geological Engineering	M
Ocean Engineering	M,O

UNIVERSITY OF ALASKA FAIRBANKS

Civil Engineering	M,D,O
Computer Science	M
Construction Management	M,D,O
Electrical Engineering	M
Engineering and Applied Sciences—General	D
Environmental Engineering	M,D,O
Geological Engineering	M
Mechanical Engineering	M
Mineral/Mining Engineering	M
Petroleum Engineering	M

UNIVERSITY OF ALBERTA

Biomedical Engineering	M,D
Biotechnology	M,D
Chemical Engineering	M,D
Civil Engineering	M,D
Computer Engineering	M,D
Computer Science	M,D
Construction Engineering	M,D
Electrical Engineering	M,D
Energy and Power Engineering	M,D
Engineering Management	M,D
Environmental Engineering	M,D
Geotechnical Engineering	M,D
Materials Engineering	M,D
Mechanical Engineering	M,D
Mineral/Mining Engineering	M,D
Nanotechnology	M,D
Petroleum Engineering	M,D
Structural Engineering	M,D
Systems Engineering	M,D
Telecommunications	M,D
Water Resources Engineering	M,D

THE UNIVERSITY OF ARIZONA

Aerospace/Aeronautical Engineering	M,D
Agricultural Engineering	M,D
Biomedical Engineering	M,D
Biosystems Engineering	M,D
Chemical Engineering	M,D
Computer Engineering	M,D
Computer Science	M,D
Electrical Engineering	M,D
Engineering and Applied Sciences—General	M,D,O
Engineering Management	M,D,O
Environmental Engineering	M,D
Geological Engineering	M,D,O
Industrial/Management Engineering	M,D,O
Materials Engineering	M,D
Materials Sciences	M,D
Mechanical Engineering	M,D
Medical Informatics	M,D,O
Mineral/Mining Engineering	M,D,O
Systems Engineering	M,D,O

UNIVERSITY OF ARKANSAS

Agricultural Engineering	M,D
Bioengineering	M
Biomedical Engineering	M
Chemical Engineering	M,D
Civil Engineering	M,D
Computer Engineering	M,D
Computer Science	M,D
Electrical Engineering	M,D
Electronic Materials	M,D
Engineering and Applied Sciences—General	M,D
Environmental Engineering	M
Industrial/Management Engineering	M,D
Mechanical Engineering	M,D
Operations Research	M,D
Telecommunications	M,D
Transportation and Highway Engineering	M,D

UNIVERSITY OF ARKANSAS AT LITTLE ROCK

Applied Science and Technology	M,D
Bioinformatics	M,D
Computer Science	M,D
Construction Management	M
Information Science	M,D,O
Systems Engineering	M,D,O

UNIVERSITY OF ARKANSAS FOR MEDICAL SCIENCES

Bioinformatics	M,D,O

UNIVERSITY OF BALTIMORE

Human-Computer Interaction	M

UNIVERSITY OF BRIDGEPORT

Biomedical Engineering	M
Computer Engineering	M,D
Computer Science	M,D
Electrical Engineering	M
Engineering and Applied Sciences—General	M,D
Management of Technology	M,D
Mechanical Engineering	M

THE UNIVERSITY OF BRITISH COLUMBIA

Bioengineering	M,D
Bioinformatics	M,D
Chemical Engineering	M,D
Civil Engineering	M,D
Computer Engineering	M,D
Computer Science	M,D
Electrical Engineering	M,D
Engineering and Applied Sciences—General	M,D
Geological Engineering	M,D
Materials Engineering	M,D
Mechanical Engineering	M,D
Mineral/Mining Engineering	M,D
Operations Research	M

UNIVERSITY OF CALGARY

Biomedical Engineering	M,D
Biotechnology	M
Chemical Engineering	M,D
Civil Engineering	M,D
Computer Engineering	M,D
Computer Science	M,D
Electrical Engineering	M,D
Energy and Power Engineering	M,D
Energy Management and Policy	M,D
Engineering and Applied Sciences—General	M,D
Environmental Engineering	M,D

---

*M—masters degree; D—doctorate; O—other advanced degree; *—Close-Up and/or Display*

Geotechnical Engineering	M,D
Manufacturing Engineering	M,D
Materials Sciences	M,D
Mechanical Engineering	M,D
Mechanics	M,D
Petroleum Engineering	M,D
Software Engineering	M,D
Structural Engineering	M,D
Transportation and Highway Engineering	M,D

UNIVERSITY OF CALIFORNIA, BERKELEY

Applied Science and Technology	D
Bioengineering	M,D
Chemical Engineering	M,D
Civil Engineering	M,D
Computer Science	M,D
Construction Management	O
Database Systems	M
Electrical Engineering	M,D
Energy Management and Policy	M,D
Engineering and Applied Sciences—General	M,D,O
Engineering Management	M,D
Environmental Engineering	M,D
Financial Engineering	M
Geotechnical Engineering	M,D
Industrial/Management Engineering	M,D
Materials Engineering	M,D
Materials Sciences	M,D
Mechanical Engineering	M,D
Mechanics	M,D
Nuclear Engineering	M,D
Operations Research	M,D
Structural Engineering	M,D
Transportation and Highway Engineering	M,D
Water Resources Engineering	M,D

UNIVERSITY OF CALIFORNIA, DAVIS

Aerospace/Aeronautical Engineering	M,D,O
Applied Science and Technology	M,D
Bioengineering	M,D
Biomedical Engineering	M,D
Chemical Engineering	M,D
Civil Engineering	M,D,O
Computer Engineering	M,D
Computer Science	M,D
Electrical Engineering	M,D
Engineering and Applied Sciences—General	M,D,O
Environmental Engineering	M,D,O
Materials Engineering	M,D
Materials Sciences	M,D
Mechanical Engineering	M,D,O
Medical Informatics	M
Transportation and Highway Engineering	M,D

UNIVERSITY OF CALIFORNIA, IRVINE

Aerospace/Aeronautical Engineering	M,D
Biochemical Engineering	M,D
Biomedical Engineering	M,D
Biotechnology	M
Chemical Engineering	M,D
Civil Engineering	M,D
Computer Science	M,D
Electrical Engineering	M,D
Engineering and Applied Sciences—General	M,D
Engineering Management	M,D
Environmental Engineering	M,D
Information Science	M,D
Manufacturing Engineering	M,D
Materials Engineering	M,D

Materials Sciences	M,D
Mechanical Engineering	M,D
Transportation and Highway Engineering	M,D

UNIVERSITY OF CALIFORNIA, LOS ANGELES

Aerospace/Aeronautical Engineering	M,D
Bioengineering	M,D
Bioinformatics	M,D
Biomedical Engineering	M,D
Chemical Engineering	M,D
Civil Engineering	M,D
Computer Science	M,D
Electrical Engineering	M,D
Engineering and Applied Sciences—General	M,D
Environmental Engineering	M,D
Financial Engineering	M,D
Management of Technology	M,D
Manufacturing Engineering	M
Materials Engineering	M,D
Materials Sciences	M,D
Mechanical Engineering	M,D

UNIVERSITY OF CALIFORNIA, MERCED

Bioengineering	M,D
Computer Science	M,D
Electrical Engineering	M,D
Engineering and Applied Sciences—General	M,D
Environmental Engineering	M,D
Information Science	M,D
Mechanical Engineering	M,D
Mechanics	M,D
Systems Engineering	M,D

UNIVERSITY OF CALIFORNIA, RIVERSIDE

Artificial Intelligence/Robotics	M,D
Bioengineering	M,D
Bioinformatics	D
Chemical Engineering	M,D
Computer Engineering	M
Computer Science	M,D*
Electrical Engineering	M,D
Environmental Engineering	M,D
Materials Engineering	M
Materials Sciences	M
Mechanical Engineering	M,D
Nanotechnology	M

UNIVERSITY OF CALIFORNIA, SAN DIEGO

Aerospace/Aeronautical Engineering	M,D
Architectural Engineering	M
Artificial Intelligence/Robotics	M,D
Bioengineering	M,D*
Bioinformatics	D
Chemical Engineering	M,D
Computer Engineering	M,D
Computer Science	M,D
Database Systems	M
Electrical Engineering	M,D
Energy Management and Policy	M
Engineering Physics	M,D
Materials Sciences	M,D
Mechanical Engineering	M,D
Mechanics	M,D
Modeling and Simulation	M,D
Nanotechnology	M,D
Ocean Engineering	M,D
Structural Engineering	M,D
Telecommunications	M,D

UNIVERSITY OF CALIFORNIA, SAN FRANCISCO

Bioengineering	D
Bioinformatics	D

UNIVERSITY OF CALIFORNIA, SANTA BARBARA

Bioengineering	M,D
Chemical Engineering	M,D
Computer Engineering	M,D
Computer Science	M,D
Electrical Engineering	M,D
Engineering and Applied Sciences—General	M,D
Management of Technology	M
Materials Engineering	M,D
Materials Sciences	M,D
Mechanical Engineering	M,D

UNIVERSITY OF CALIFORNIA, SANTA CRUZ

Bioinformatics	M,D
Computer Engineering	M,D
Computer Science	M,D
Electrical Engineering	M,D
Engineering and Applied Sciences—General	M,D
Management of Technology	D

UNIVERSITY OF CENTRAL ARKANSAS

Computer Science	M

UNIVERSITY OF CENTRAL FLORIDA

Aerospace/Aeronautical Engineering	M
Biotechnology	M,D
Civil Engineering	M,D,O
Computer Engineering	M,D
Computer Science	M,D
Construction Engineering	M,D,O
Electrical Engineering	M,D
Engineering and Applied Sciences—General	M,D,O
Environmental Engineering	M,D
Game Design and Development	M
Health Informatics	M,O
Industrial/Management Engineering	M,D,O
Materials Engineering	M,D
Materials Sciences	M,D
Mechanical Engineering	M,D
Modeling and Simulation	M,D,O
Nanotechnology	M
Structural Engineering	M,D,O
Transportation and Highway Engineering	M,D,O

UNIVERSITY OF CENTRAL MISSOURI

Aerospace/Aeronautical Engineering	M,D,O
Computer Science	M,D,O
Information Science	M,D,O
Management of Technology	M,D,O

UNIVERSITY OF CENTRAL OKLAHOMA

Biomedical Engineering	M
Computer Science	M
Electrical Engineering	M
Engineering and Applied Sciences—General	M
Engineering Physics	M
Mechanical Engineering	M

UNIVERSITY OF CHICAGO

Bioengineering	M,D
Computer Science	M,D

UNIVERSITY OF CINCINNATI

Aerospace/Aeronautical Engineering	M,D
Bioinformatics	D,O
Biomedical Engineering	M,D

Chemical Engineering	M,D
Civil Engineering	M,D
Computer Engineering	M,D
Computer Science	M,D
Electrical Engineering	M,D
Engineering and Applied Sciences—General	M,D
Environmental Engineering	M,D
Ergonomics and Human Factors	M,D
Health Informatics	M
Industrial/Management Engineering	M,D
Materials Engineering	M,D
Materials Sciences	M,D
Mechanical Engineering	M,D
Mechanics	M,D
Nuclear Engineering	M,D

UNIVERSITY OF COLORADO BOULDER

Aerospace/Aeronautical Engineering	M,D
Architectural Engineering	M,D
Chemical Engineering	M,D
Civil Engineering	M,D
Computer Engineering	M,D
Computer Science	M,D
Electrical Engineering	M,D
Engineering and Applied Sciences—General	M,D
Engineering Management	M
Environmental Engineering	M,D
Information Science	D
Mechanical Engineering	M,D
Telecommunications Management	M
Telecommunications	M

UNIVERSITY OF COLORADO COLORADO SPRINGS

Aerospace/Aeronautical Engineering	M,D
Computer and Information Systems Security	M,D
Computer Science	M
Electrical Engineering	M
Energy and Power Engineering	M,D
Engineering and Applied Sciences—General	M,D
Engineering Management	M,D
Mechanical Engineering	M
Software Engineering	M,D
Systems Engineering	M,D

UNIVERSITY OF COLORADO DENVER

Applied Science and Technology	M
Bioengineering	M,D
Bioinformatics	D
Civil Engineering	M,D
Computer Science	M,D
Electrical Engineering	M,D
Energy Management and Policy	M
Engineering and Applied Sciences—General	M,D
Environmental Engineering	M,D
Geotechnical Engineering	M,D
Hydraulics	M,D
Information Science	M,D
Management of Technology	M
Mechanical Engineering	M
Mechanics	M
Medical Informatics	M,D
Operations Research	M,D
Structural Engineering	M,D
Transportation and Highway Engineering	M,D

UNIVERSITY OF CONNECTICUT

Biomedical Engineering	M,D
Chemical Engineering	M,D
Civil Engineering	M,D
Computer Science	M,D
Electrical Engineering	M,D
Engineering and Applied Sciences—General	M,D
Environmental Engineering	M,D
Materials Engineering	M
Materials Sciences	M,D
Mechanical Engineering	M,D
Metallurgical Engineering and Metallurgy	M
Polymer Science and Engineering	M,D
Software Engineering	M,D

UNIVERSITY OF DALLAS

Computer and Information Systems Security	M,D
Management of Technology	M,D

UNIVERSITY OF DAYTON

Aerospace/Aeronautical Engineering	M,D
Bioengineering	M
Chemical Engineering	M
Civil Engineering	M
Computer and Information Systems Security	M
Computer Engineering	M,D
Computer Science	M
Electrical Engineering	M,D
Engineering Management	M
Environmental Engineering	M
Geotechnical Engineering	M
Materials Engineering	M,D
Mechanical Engineering	M,D
Mechanics	M
Structural Engineering	M
Transportation and Highway Engineering	M
Water Resources Engineering	M

UNIVERSITY OF DELAWARE

Biotechnology	M,D
Chemical Engineering	M,D
Civil Engineering	M,D
Computer Engineering	M,D
Computer Science	M,D
Electrical Engineering	M,D
Energy Management and Policy	M,D
Engineering and Applied Sciences—General	M,D
Environmental Engineering	M,D
Geotechnical Engineering	M,D
Information Science	M,D
Management of Technology	M
Materials Engineering	M,D
Materials Sciences	M,D
Mechanical Engineering	M,D
Ocean Engineering	M,D
Operations Research	M
Structural Engineering	M,D
Transportation and Highway Engineering	M,D
Water Resources Engineering	M,D

UNIVERSITY OF DENVER

Bioengineering	M,D
Computer and Information Systems Security	M,D
Computer Engineering	M,D
Computer Science	M,D
Construction Management	M
Electrical Engineering	M,D
Engineering and Applied Sciences—General	M,D

Engineering Management	M,D
Information Science	M,O
Materials Engineering	M,D
Materials Sciences	M,D
Mechanical Engineering	M,D

UNIVERSITY OF DETROIT MERCY

Architectural Engineering	M
Civil Engineering	M,D
Computer and Information Systems Security	M,D,O
Computer Engineering	M,D
Computer Science	M,D,O
Electrical Engineering	M,D
Engineering and Applied Sciences—General	M,D
Engineering Management	M,D
Environmental Engineering	M,D
Mechanical Engineering	M,D
Software Engineering	M,D

THE UNIVERSITY OF FINDLAY

Health Informatics	M,D

UNIVERSITY OF FLORIDA

Aerospace/Aeronautical Engineering	M,D
Agricultural Engineering	M,D,O
Bioengineering	M,D,O
Biomedical Engineering	M,D,O
Chemical Engineering	M,D,O
Civil Engineering	M,D
Computer Engineering	M,D
Computer Science	M,D
Construction Management	M,D
Electrical Engineering	M,D
Engineering and Applied Sciences—General	M,D,O
Environmental Engineering	M,D,O
Industrial/Management Engineering	M,D,O
Information Science	M,D
Materials Engineering	M,D
Materials Sciences	M,D
Mechanical Engineering	M,D
Nuclear Engineering	M,D
Ocean Engineering	M,D
Systems Engineering	M,D,O
Telecommunications	M,D

UNIVERSITY OF GEORGIA

Artificial Intelligence/Robotics	M
Biochemical Engineering	M
Bioinformatics	M,D
Computer Science	M,D
Environmental Engineering	M

UNIVERSITY OF GUELPH

Bioengineering	M,D
Biotechnology	M,D
Computer Science	M,D
Engineering and Applied Sciences—General	M,D
Environmental Engineering	M,D
Water Resources Engineering	M,D

UNIVERSITY OF HARTFORD

Engineering and Applied Sciences—General	M

UNIVERSITY OF HAWAII AT MANOA

Bioengineering	M
Civil Engineering	M,D
Computer Science	M,D,O
Electrical Engineering	M,D
Engineering and Applied Sciences—General	M,D
Environmental Engineering	M,D

Geological Engineering	M,D
Information Science	M,D
Materials Engineering	M,D
Materials Sciences	M,D
Ocean Engineering	M,D
Telecommunications	O

UNIVERSITY OF HOUSTON

Biomedical Engineering	D
Chemical Engineering	M,D
Civil Engineering	M,D
Computer and Information Systems Security	M
Computer Science	M,D
Construction Management	M
Electrical Engineering	M,D
Engineering and Applied Sciences—General	M,D
Industrial/Management Engineering	M,D
Information Science	M,D
Mechanical Engineering	M,D
Petroleum Engineering	M,D
Telecommunications	M

UNIVERSITY OF HOUSTON–CLEAR LAKE

Biotechnology	M
Computer Engineering	M
Computer Science	M
Information Science	M
Software Engineering	M
Systems Engineering	M

UNIVERSITY OF HOUSTON–DOWNTOWN

Database Systems	M

UNIVERSITY OF HOUSTON–VICTORIA

Computer Science	M

UNIVERSITY OF IDAHO

Bioengineering	M,D
Bioinformatics	M,D
Chemical Engineering	M,D
Civil Engineering	M,D
Computer Engineering	M,D
Computer Science	M,D
Electrical Engineering	M,D
Engineering and Applied Sciences—General	M,D
Engineering Management	M,D
Geological Engineering	M,D
Management of Technology	M,D
Materials Sciences	M,D
Mechanical Engineering	M,D
Metallurgical Engineering and Metallurgy	M,D
Nuclear Engineering	M,D
Water Resources Engineering	M,D

UNIVERSITY OF ILLINOIS AT CHICAGO

Bioengineering	M,D
Bioinformatics	M,D
Biotechnology	M,D
Chemical Engineering	M,D
Civil Engineering	M,D
Computer Engineering	M,D
Computer Science	M,D
Electrical Engineering	M,D
Engineering and Applied Sciences—General	M,D
Health Informatics	M,O
Industrial/Management Engineering	M,D
Materials Engineering	M,D
Mechanical Engineering	M,D
Operations Research	M,D

UNIVERSITY OF ILLINOIS AT SPRINGFIELD

Computer Science	M
Database Systems	M

UNIVERSITY OF ILLINOIS AT URBANA–CHAMPAIGN

Aerospace/Aeronautical Engineering	M,D
Agricultural Engineering	M,D
Bioengineering	M,D
Bioinformatics	M,D,O
Chemical Engineering	M,D
Civil Engineering	M,D
Computer Engineering	M,D
Computer Science	M,D
Electrical Engineering	M,D
Energy and Power Engineering	M,D
Energy Management and Policy	M
Engineering and Applied Sciences—General	M,D
Environmental Engineering	M,D
Financial Engineering	M
Health Informatics	M,D,O
Human-Computer Interaction	M,D,O
Industrial/Management Engineering	M,D
Information Science	M,D,O
Management of Technology	M,D
Materials Engineering	M,D
Materials Sciences	M,D
Mechanical Engineering	M,D
Mechanics	M,D
Medical Informatics	M,D,O
Nuclear Engineering	M,D
Systems Engineering	M,D

THE UNIVERSITY OF IOWA

Biochemical Engineering	M,D
Bioinformatics	M,D,O
Biomedical Engineering	M,D
Chemical Engineering	M,D
Civil Engineering	M,D
Computer Engineering	M,D
Computer Science	M,D
Database Systems	M
Electrical Engineering	M,D
Energy and Power Engineering	M,D
Engineering and Applied Sciences—General	M,D*
Environmental Engineering	M,D
Ergonomics and Human Factors	M,D,O
Health Informatics	M,D,O
Industrial/Management Engineering	M,D
Information Science	M,D,O
Manufacturing Engineering	M,D
Materials Engineering	M,D
Mechanical Engineering	M,D
Operations Research	M,D

THE UNIVERSITY OF KANSAS

Aerospace/Aeronautical Engineering	M,D
Architectural Engineering	M
Bioengineering	M,D
Biotechnology	M
Chemical Engineering	M,D,O
Civil Engineering	M,D
Computer Engineering	M
Computer Science	M,D
Construction Management	M
Electrical Engineering	M,D
Engineering and Applied Sciences—General	M,D,O
Engineering Management	M,O
Environmental Engineering	M,D

*M—masters degree; D—doctorate; O—other advanced degree; *—Close-Up and/or Display*

Health Informatics	M,O
Mechanical Engineering	M,D
Medical Informatics	M,D,O
Petroleum Engineering	M,D,O

UNIVERSITY OF KENTUCKY

Agricultural Engineering	M,D
Biomedical Engineering	M,D
Chemical Engineering	M,D
Civil Engineering	M,D
Computer Science	M,D
Electrical Engineering	M,D
Engineering and Applied Sciences—General	M,D
Information Science	M
Manufacturing Engineering	M
Materials Engineering	M,D
Materials Sciences	M,D
Mechanical Engineering	M,D
Mineral/Mining Engineering	M,D

UNIVERSITY OF LETHBRIDGE

Computer Science	M,D

UNIVERSITY OF LOUISIANA AT LAFAYETTE

Architectural Engineering	M
Chemical Engineering	M
Civil Engineering	M
Computer Engineering	M,D
Computer Science	M,D
Engineering Management	M
Mechanical Engineering	M
Petroleum Engineering	M
Telecommunications	M

UNIVERSITY OF LOUISVILLE

Bioengineering	M
Bioinformatics	M,D
Chemical Engineering	M,D
Civil Engineering	M,D,O
Computer and Information Systems Security	M,D,O
Computer Engineering	M,D,O
Computer Science	M,D,O
Electrical Engineering	M,D
Engineering and Applied Sciences—General	M,D,O
Engineering Management	M,D,O
Environmental Engineering	M,D,O
Industrial/Management Engineering	M,D,O
Mechanical Engineering	M,D

UNIVERSITY OF MAINE

Bioinformatics	M,D
Biomedical Engineering	M,D
Chemical Engineering	M,D
Civil Engineering	M,D
Computer Engineering	M,D
Computer Science	M,D,O
Electrical Engineering	M,D
Engineering and Applied Sciences—General	M,D
Information Science	M,D,O
Mechanical Engineering	M,D

UNIVERSITY OF MANAGEMENT AND TECHNOLOGY

Computer Science	M,O
Engineering Management	M
Software Engineering	M,O

THE UNIVERSITY OF MANCHESTER

Aerospace/Aeronautical Engineering	M,D
Biochemical Engineering	M,D
Bioinformatics	M,D
Biotechnology	M,D
Chemical Engineering	M,D

Civil Engineering	M,D
Computer Science	M,D
Electrical Engineering	M,D
Engineering Management	M,D
Environmental Engineering	M,D
Hazardous Materials Management	M,D
Materials Sciences	M,D
Mechanical Engineering	M,D
Metallurgical Engineering and Metallurgy	M,D
Modeling and Simulation	M,D
Nuclear Engineering	M,D
Paper and Pulp Engineering	M,D
Polymer Science and Engineering	M,D
Structural Engineering	M,D

UNIVERSITY OF MANITOBA

Biosystems Engineering	M,D
Civil Engineering	M,D
Computer Engineering	M,D
Computer Science	M,D
Electrical Engineering	M,D
Engineering and Applied Sciences—General	M,D
Industrial/Management Engineering	M,D
Manufacturing Engineering	M,D
Mechanical Engineering	M,D

UNIVERSITY OF MARY

Energy Management and Policy	M

UNIVERSITY OF MARYLAND, BALTIMORE COUNTY

Biochemical Engineering	M,D,O
Biotechnology	M,O
Chemical Engineering	M,D
Computer and Information Systems Security	M,O
Computer Engineering	M,D
Computer Science	M,D
Electrical Engineering	M,D
Engineering and Applied Sciences—General	M,D,O
Engineering Management	M,O
Environmental Engineering	M,D
Health Informatics	M
Information Science	M,D
Mechanical Engineering	M,D,O
Systems Engineering	M,O

UNIVERSITY OF MARYLAND, COLLEGE PARK

Aerospace/Aeronautical Engineering	M,D
Bioengineering	M,D
Bioinformatics	D
Chemical Engineering	M,D
Civil Engineering	M,D
Computer Engineering	M,D
Computer Science	M,D
Electrical Engineering	M,D*
Engineering and Applied Sciences—General	M
Environmental Engineering	M,D
Fire Protection Engineering	M
Manufacturing Engineering	M,D
Materials Engineering	M,D
Materials Sciences	M,D
Mechanical Engineering	M,D
Mechanics	M,D
Nuclear Engineering	M,D
Reliability Engineering	M,D
Systems Engineering	M
Telecommunications	M

UNIVERSITY OF MARYLAND EASTERN SHORE

Computer Science	M

UNIVERSITY OF MARYLAND UNIVERSITY COLLEGE

Biotechnology	M,O
Computer and Information Systems Security	M,O
Database Systems	M,O
Health Informatics	M
Information Science	M

UNIVERSITY OF MASSACHUSETTS AMHERST

Architectural Engineering	M,D
Biotechnology	M,D
Chemical Engineering	M,D
Civil Engineering	M,D
Computer Engineering	M,D
Computer Science	M,D
Electrical Engineering	M,D
Engineering and Applied Sciences—General	M,D
Environmental Engineering	M,D
Geotechnical Engineering	M,D
Industrial/Management Engineering	M,D
Mechanical Engineering	M,D
Mechanics	M,D
Operations Research	M,D
Polymer Science and Engineering	M,D
Structural Engineering	M,D
Transportation and Highway Engineering	M,D
Water Resources Engineering	M,D

UNIVERSITY OF MASSACHUSETTS BOSTON

Biomedical Engineering	D
Biotechnology	M,D
Computer Science	M,D

UNIVERSITY OF MASSACHUSETTS DARTMOUTH

Biomedical Engineering	M,D
Biotechnology	M,D
Civil Engineering	M
Computer Engineering	M,D,O
Computer Science	M,D,O
Database Systems	M
Electrical Engineering	M,D,O
Engineering and Applied Sciences—General	D
Industrial/Management Engineering	M,D
Information Science	D
Management of Technology	M
Mechanical Engineering	M
Mechanics	D
Software Engineering	M,O
Systems Engineering	M,D
Telecommunications	M,D,O

UNIVERSITY OF MASSACHUSETTS LOWELL

Chemical Engineering	M,D
Civil Engineering	M,D
Computer Engineering	M,D
Computer Science	M,D
Electrical Engineering	M,D
Energy and Power Engineering	M,D
Engineering and Applied Sciences—General	M,D
Environmental Engineering	M,D
Industrial/Management Engineering	D
Mechanical Engineering	M,D
Nuclear Engineering	M,D
Polymer Science and Engineering	M,D

UNIVERSITY OF MASSACHUSETTS MEDICAL SCHOOL

Bioinformatics	M,D

UNIVERSITY OF MEMPHIS

Bioinformatics	M,D
Biomedical Engineering	M,D
Civil Engineering	M,D,O
Computer Engineering	M,D,O
Computer Science	M,D
Electrical Engineering	M,D,O
Energy and Power Engineering	M,D,O
Engineering and Applied Sciences—General	M,D,O
Environmental Engineering	M,D,O
Geotechnical Engineering	M,D,O
Mechanical Engineering	M,D,O
Structural Engineering	M,D,O
Transportation and Highway Engineering	M,D,O
Water Resources Engineering	M,D,O

UNIVERSITY OF MIAMI

Aerospace/Aeronautical Engineering	M,D
Architectural Engineering	M,D
Biomedical Engineering	M,D
Civil Engineering	M,D
Computer Engineering	M,D
Computer Science	M,D
Electrical Engineering	M,D
Engineering and Applied Sciences—General	M,D
Ergonomics and Human Factors	M
Industrial/Management Engineering	M,D
Management of Technology	M,D
Mechanical Engineering	M,D

UNIVERSITY OF MICHIGAN

Aerospace/Aeronautical Engineering	M,D
Artificial Intelligence/Robotics	M,D
Automotive Engineering	M,D
Bioinformatics	M,D
Biomedical Engineering	M,D
Chemical Engineering	M,D,O
Civil Engineering	M,D,O
Computer Engineering	M,D
Computer Science	M,D
Construction Engineering	M,D,O
Database Systems	M,D,O
Electrical Engineering	M,D
Energy and Power Engineering	M,D
Engineering and Applied Sciences—General	M,D,O
Engineering Design	M,D
Environmental Engineering	M,D,O
Health Informatics	M,D
Industrial/Management Engineering	M,D
Information Science	M,D*
Manufacturing Engineering	M,D
Materials Engineering	M,D
Materials Sciences	M,D
Mechanical Engineering	M,D
Nuclear Engineering	M,D,O
Ocean Engineering	M,D,O
Operations Research	M,D
Pharmaceutical Engineering	M,D
Structural Engineering	M,D,O
Systems Engineering	M,D
Systems Science	M,D

UNIVERSITY OF MICHIGAN–DEARBORN

Automotive Engineering	M,D
Bioengineering	M

Computer and Information
   Systems Security — D
Computer Engineering — M,D
Computer Science — D
Database Systems — M,D
Electrical Engineering — M,D
Energy and Power
   Engineering — M
Engineering and Applied
   Sciences—General — M,D
Engineering Management — M
Health Informatics — M
Industrial/Management
   Engineering — M,D
Information Science — M,D
Manufacturing Engineering — M
Mechanical Engineering — M,D
Software Engineering — M,D
Systems Engineering — M,D

UNIVERSITY OF MICHIGAN–FLINT
Computer Science — M
Health Informatics — M
Information Science — M
Mechanical Engineering — M

UNIVERSITY OF MINNESOTA, DULUTH
Computer Engineering — M
Computer Science — M
Electrical Engineering — M
Engineering Management — M
Safety Engineering — M

UNIVERSITY OF MINNESOTA ROCHESTER
Bioinformatics — M,D

UNIVERSITY OF MINNESOTA, TWIN CITIES CAMPUS
Aerospace/Aeronautical
   Engineering — M,D
Biomedical Engineering — M,D
Biosystems Engineering — M,D
Biotechnology — M
Chemical Engineering — M,D
Civil Engineering — M,D,O
Computer and Information
   Systems Security — M
Computer Engineering — M,D
Computer Science — M,D
Database Systems — M
Electrical Engineering — M,D
Engineering and Applied
   Sciences—General — M,D,O
Geological Engineering — M,D,O
Health Informatics — M,D
Industrial/Management
   Engineering — M,D
Management of Technology — M
Materials Engineering — M,D
Materials Sciences — M,D
Mechanical Engineering — M,D
Mechanics — M,D
Paper and Pulp Engineering — M,D
Software Engineering — M
Technology and Public Policy — M

UNIVERSITY OF MISSISSIPPI
Applied Science and
   Technology — M,D
Engineering and Applied
   Sciences—General — M,D

UNIVERSITY OF MISSISSIPPI MEDICAL CENTER
Materials Sciences — M,D

UNIVERSITY OF MISSOURI
Aerospace/Aeronautical
   Engineering — M,D
Agricultural Engineering — M,D
Bioengineering — M,D
Bioinformatics — D
Chemical Engineering — M,D
Civil Engineering — M,D
Computer Science — M,D
Electrical Engineering — M,D
Engineering and Applied
   Sciences—General — M,D,O
Environmental Engineering — M,D
Geotechnical Engineering — M,D
Health Informatics — M,O
Industrial/Management
   Engineering — M,D
Manufacturing Engineering — M,D
Mechanical Engineering — M,D
Nuclear Engineering — M,D,O
Structural Engineering — M,D
Transportation and Highway
   Engineering — M,D
Water Resources Engineering — M,D

UNIVERSITY OF MISSOURI–KANSAS CITY
Bioinformatics — M,D,O
Civil Engineering — M,D,O
Computer Engineering — M,D,O
Computer Science — M,D,O
Construction Engineering — M,D,O
Electrical Engineering — M,D,O
Engineering and Applied
   Sciences—General — M,D,O
Engineering Management — M,D,O
Mechanical Engineering — M,D,O
Polymer Science and
   Engineering — M,D
Software Engineering — M,D,O
Telecommunications — M,D,O

UNIVERSITY OF MISSOURI–ST. LOUIS
Biotechnology — M,D
Computer and Information
   Systems Security — M,D,O
Computer Science — M,D

UNIVERSITY OF MONTANA
Computer Science — M

UNIVERSITY OF NEBRASKA AT OMAHA
Artificial Intelligence/Robotics — M,O
Bioinformatics — M,D
Computer and Information
   Systems Security — M,D,O
Computer Science — M,O
Database Systems — M,D,O
Information Science — M,D,O
Software Engineering — M,O
Systems Engineering — M,O

UNIVERSITY OF NEBRASKA–LINCOLN
Agricultural Engineering — M,D
Architectural Engineering — M,D
Bioengineering — M,D
Bioinformatics — M,D
Biomedical Engineering — M,D
Chemical Engineering — M,D
Civil Engineering — M,D
Computer Engineering — M,D
Computer Science — M,D
Electrical Engineering — M,D
Engineering and Applied
   Sciences—General — M,D
Engineering Management — M,D
Environmental Engineering — M,D

Industrial/Management
   Engineering — M,D
Information Science — M,D
Manufacturing Engineering — M,D
Materials Engineering — M,D
Materials Sciences — M,D
Mechanical Engineering — M,D
Mechanics — M,D
Metallurgical Engineering and
   Metallurgy — M,D

UNIVERSITY OF NEBRASKA MEDICAL CENTER
Bioinformatics — M,D

UNIVERSITY OF NEVADA, LAS VEGAS
Aerospace/Aeronautical
   Engineering — M,D,O
Biomedical Engineering — M,D,O
Civil Engineering — M,D
Computer Engineering — M,D
Computer Science — M,D
Construction Management — M,O
Database Systems — M,O
Electrical Engineering — M,D
Engineering and Applied
   Sciences—General — M,D,O
Environmental Engineering — M,D
Materials Engineering — M,D,O
Mechanical Engineering — M,D,O
Nuclear Engineering — M,D,O
Transportation and Highway
   Engineering — M,D

UNIVERSITY OF NEVADA, RENO
Biomedical Engineering — M,D
Biotechnology — M
Chemical Engineering — M,D
Civil Engineering — M,D
Computer Engineering — M,D
Computer Science — M,D
Electrical Engineering — M,D
Engineering and Applied
   Sciences—General — M,D
Geological Engineering — M,D
Materials Engineering — M,D
Mechanical Engineering — M,D
Metallurgical Engineering and
   Metallurgy — M,D
Mineral/Mining Engineering — M

UNIVERSITY OF NEW BRUNSWICK FREDERICTON
Chemical Engineering — M,D
Civil Engineering — M,D
Computer Engineering — M,D
Computer Science — M,D
Construction Engineering — M,D
Electrical Engineering — M,D
Engineering and Applied
   Sciences—General — M,D,O
Engineering Management — M
Environmental Engineering — M,D
Geotechnical Engineering — M,D
Materials Sciences — M,D
Mechanical Engineering — M,D
Mechanics — M,D
Structural Engineering — M,D
Surveying Science and
   Engineering — M,D
Transportation and Highway
   Engineering — M,D

UNIVERSITY OF NEW ENGLAND
Health Informatics — M,D,O

UNIVERSITY OF NEW HAMPSHIRE
Chemical Engineering — M,D
Civil Engineering — M,D

Computer Science — M,D,O
Electrical Engineering — M,D
Environmental Engineering — M,D
Materials Sciences — M,D
Mechanical Engineering — M,D
Ocean Engineering — M,D,O
Systems Engineering — M,D

UNIVERSITY OF NEW HAVEN
Biomedical Engineering — M
Computer and Information
   Systems Security — M,D,O
Computer Engineering — M
Computer Science — M,D,O
Database Systems — M
Electrical Engineering — M
Engineering and Applied
   Sciences—General — M,O
Engineering Management — M,O
Environmental Engineering — M
Fire Protection Engineering — M,O
Hazardous Materials
   Management — M
Industrial/Management
   Engineering — M,O
Mechanical Engineering — M
Software Engineering — M,O
Water Resources Engineering — M

UNIVERSITY OF NEW MEXICO
Biomedical Engineering — M,D
Chemical Engineering — M,D
Civil Engineering — M,D
Computer and Information
   Systems Security — M
Computer Engineering — M,D
Computer Science — M,D
Construction Management — M,D
Electrical Engineering — M,D
Engineering and Applied
   Sciences—General — M,D
Management of Technology — M
Manufacturing Engineering — M
Mechanical Engineering — M,D
Nanotechnology — M,D
Nuclear Engineering — M,D
Systems Engineering — M,D

UNIVERSITY OF NEW ORLEANS
Computer Science — M
Engineering and Applied
   Sciences—General — M,D
Engineering Management — M
Mechanical Engineering — M

UNIVERSITY OF NORTH ALABAMA
Information Science — M

THE UNIVERSITY OF NORTH CAROLINA AT CHAPEL HILL
Bioinformatics — D
Biomedical Engineering — M,D
Computer Science — M,D
Environmental Engineering — M,D
Operations Research — M,D
Telecommunications — M,D,O

THE UNIVERSITY OF NORTH CAROLINA AT CHARLOTTE
Bioinformatics — M,D,O
Civil Engineering — M,D
Computer and Information
   Systems Security — M,D,O
Computer Engineering — M,D
Computer Science — M,D,O
Construction Management — M,O
Database Systems — M,O
Electrical Engineering — M,D

M—masters degree; D—doctorate; O—other advanced degree; *—Close-Up and/or Display

Energy and Power Engineering	M,O
Engineering and Applied Sciences—General	M,D,O
Engineering Management	M,O
Environmental Engineering	M,D
Fire Protection Engineering	M,O
Game Design and Development	M,O
Health Informatics	M,O
Information Science	M,O
Mechanical Engineering	M,D
Systems Engineering	M,D,O

THE UNIVERSITY OF NORTH CAROLINA AT GREENSBORO
Computer Science	M

THE UNIVERSITY OF NORTH CAROLINA WILMINGTON
Computer Science	M

UNIVERSITY OF NORTH DAKOTA
Aviation	M
Chemical Engineering	M,D
Civil Engineering	M,D
Computer Science	M
Electrical Engineering	M,D
Engineering and Applied Sciences—General	D
Environmental Engineering	M,D
Geological Engineering	M,D
Mechanical Engineering	M,D

UNIVERSITY OF NORTHERN BRITISH COLUMBIA
Computer Science	M,D,O

UNIVERSITY OF NORTH FLORIDA
Civil Engineering	M
Computer Science	M
Construction Management	M
Electrical Engineering	M
Mechanical Engineering	M
Software Engineering	M

UNIVERSITY OF NORTH TEXAS
Biomedical Engineering	M,D,O
Computer Engineering	M,D,O
Computer Science	M,D,O
Electrical Engineering	M,D,O
Energy and Power Engineering	M,D,O
Engineering and Applied Sciences—General	M,D,O
Information Science	M,D,O
Mechanical Engineering	M,D,O

UNIVERSITY OF NORTH TEXAS HEALTH SCIENCE CENTER AT FORT WORTH
Biotechnology	M,D

UNIVERSITY OF NOTRE DAME
Aerospace/Aeronautical Engineering	M,D
Bioengineering	M,D
Chemical Engineering	M,D
Civil Engineering	M,D
Computer Engineering	M,D
Computer Science	M,D
Database Systems	M
Electrical Engineering	M,D
Engineering and Applied Sciences—General	M,D
Environmental Engineering	M,D
Mechanical Engineering	M,D

UNIVERSITY OF OKLAHOMA
Aerospace/Aeronautical Engineering	M,D

Biomedical Engineering	M,D
Chemical Engineering	M,D
Civil Engineering	M,D
Computer Engineering	M,D
Computer Science	M,D
Construction Management	M,D
Database Systems	M,D
Electrical Engineering	M,D
Engineering and Applied Sciences—General	M,D
Engineering Physics	M,D
Environmental Engineering	M,D
Geological Engineering	M,D
Industrial/Management Engineering	M,D
Mechanical Engineering	M,D
Petroleum Engineering	M,D,O
Telecommunications	M

UNIVERSITY OF OREGON
Computer Science	M,D
Information Science	M,D

UNIVERSITY OF OTTAWA
Aerospace/Aeronautical Engineering	M,D
Bioengineering	M,D
Biomedical Engineering	M
Chemical Engineering	M,D
Civil Engineering	M,D
Computer Engineering	M,D
Computer Science	M,D
Electrical Engineering	M,D
Engineering and Applied Sciences—General	M,D,O
Engineering Management	M,O
Information Science	M,O
Mechanical Engineering	M,D
Systems Science	M,D,O

UNIVERSITY OF PENNSYLVANIA
Artificial Intelligence/Robotics	M
Bioengineering	M,D
Biotechnology	M
Chemical Engineering	M,D
Computer Science	M,D
Electrical Engineering	M,D
Engineering and Applied Sciences—General	M,D*
Information Science	M,D
Materials Engineering	M,D
Materials Sciences	M,D
Mechanical Engineering	M,D
Mechanics	M,D
Nanotechnology	M
Systems Engineering	M,D

UNIVERSITY OF PHOENIX–ATLANTA CAMPUS
Management of Technology	M

UNIVERSITY OF PHOENIX–AUGUSTA CAMPUS
Management of Technology	M

UNIVERSITY OF PHOENIX–BAY AREA CAMPUS
Energy Management and Policy	M,D
Management of Technology	M,D

UNIVERSITY OF PHOENIX–CENTRAL VALLEY CAMPUS
Management of Technology	M

UNIVERSITY OF PHOENIX–CHARLOTTE CAMPUS
Health Informatics	M
Management of Technology	M

UNIVERSITY OF PHOENIX–COLORADO CAMPUS
Management of Technology	M

UNIVERSITY OF PHOENIX–COLORADO SPRINGS DOWNTOWN CAMPUS
Management of Technology	M

UNIVERSITY OF PHOENIX–COLUMBUS GEORGIA CAMPUS
Management of Technology	M

UNIVERSITY OF PHOENIX–DALLAS CAMPUS
Management of Technology	M

UNIVERSITY OF PHOENIX–HAWAII CAMPUS
Management of Technology	M

UNIVERSITY OF PHOENIX–HOUSTON CAMPUS
Management of Technology	M

UNIVERSITY OF PHOENIX–JERSEY CITY CAMPUS
Management of Technology	M

UNIVERSITY OF PHOENIX–LAS VEGAS CAMPUS
Management of Technology	M

UNIVERSITY OF PHOENIX–NEW MEXICO CAMPUS
Management of Technology	M

UNIVERSITY OF PHOENIX–ONLINE CAMPUS
Energy Management and Policy	M,O
Health Informatics	M,O
Management of Technology	M,O

UNIVERSITY OF PHOENIX–PHOENIX CAMPUS
Energy Management and Policy	M,O
Management of Technology	M,O
Medical Informatics	M,O

UNIVERSITY OF PHOENIX–SACRAMENTO VALLEY CAMPUS
Management of Technology	M

UNIVERSITY OF PHOENIX–SAN ANTONIO CAMPUS
Management of Technology	M

UNIVERSITY OF PHOENIX–SAN DIEGO CAMPUS
Management of Technology	M

UNIVERSITY OF PHOENIX–SOUTHERN ARIZONA CAMPUS
Management of Technology	M

UNIVERSITY OF PHOENIX–SOUTHERN CALIFORNIA CAMPUS
Energy Management and Policy	M
Management of Technology	M

UNIVERSITY OF PHOENIX–UTAH CAMPUS
Management of Technology	M

UNIVERSITY OF PHOENIX–WASHINGTON D.C. CAMPUS
Health Informatics	M,D

UNIVERSITY OF PITTSBURGH
Artificial Intelligence/Robotics	M,D
Bioengineering	M,D
Bioinformatics	M,D,O
Chemical Engineering	M,D
Civil Engineering	M,D
Computer and Information Systems Security	M,D,O
Computer Engineering	M,D
Computer Science	M,D
Electrical Engineering	M,D
Energy Management and Policy	M
Engineering and Applied Sciences—General	M,D
Environmental Engineering	M,D
Health Informatics	M
Industrial/Management Engineering	M,D
Information Science	M,D,O
Materials Sciences	M,D
Mechanical Engineering	M,D
Modeling and Simulation	D
Petroleum Engineering	M,D
Telecommunications	M,D,O

UNIVERSITY OF PORTLAND
Biomedical Engineering	M
Civil Engineering	M
Computer Science	M
Electrical Engineering	M
Engineering and Applied Sciences—General	M
Management of Technology	M
Mechanical Engineering	M

UNIVERSITY OF PUERTO RICO, MAYAGÜEZ CAMPUS
Aerospace/Aeronautical Engineering	M,D
Bioengineering	M,D
Chemical Engineering	M,D
Civil Engineering	M,D
Computer Engineering	M,D
Computer Science	M,D
Construction Engineering	M,D
Electrical Engineering	M,D
Energy and Power Engineering	M,D
Engineering and Applied Sciences—General	M,D
Engineering Management	M,D
Environmental Engineering	M,D
Geotechnical Engineering	M,D
Industrial/Management Engineering	M
Information Science	M,D
Manufacturing Engineering	M,D
Materials Engineering	M,D
Materials Sciences	M,D
Mechanical Engineering	M,D
Structural Engineering	M,D
Transportation and Highway Engineering	M,D

UNIVERSITY OF PUERTO RICO, MEDICAL SCIENCES CAMPUS
Health Informatics	M

UNIVERSITY OF PUERTO RICO, RÍO PIEDRAS CAMPUS
Information Science	M,O

UNIVERSITY OF REGINA
Computer Engineering	M,D
Computer Science	M,D
Engineering and Applied Sciences—General	M,D
Engineering Management	M,O
Environmental Engineering	M,D
Industrial/Management Engineering	M,D
Petroleum Engineering	M,D
Software Engineering	M
Systems Engineering	M,D

UNIVERSITY OF RHODE ISLAND
Biomedical Engineering	M,D
Biotechnology	M,D
Chemical Engineering	M,D,O
Civil Engineering	M,D
Computer Engineering	M,D
Computer Science	M,D,O
Electrical Engineering	M,D
Engineering and Applied Sciences—General	M,D,O
Environmental Engineering	M,D
Ocean Engineering	M,D

UNIVERSITY OF ROCHESTER
Biomedical Engineering	M,D
Chemical Engineering	M,D*
Computer Engineering	M,D
Computer Science	M,D
Database Systems	M
Electrical Engineering	M,D
Energy and Power Engineering	M
Energy Management and Policy	M
Engineering and Applied Sciences—General	M,D
Materials Sciences	M,D
Mechanical Engineering	M,D

UNIVERSITY OF ST. AUGUSTINE FOR HEALTH SCIENCES
Health Informatics	M

UNIVERSITY OF ST. THOMAS (MN)
Database Systems	M,O
Electrical Engineering	M,O
Engineering and Applied Sciences—General	M,O
Engineering Management	M,O
Information Science	M,O
Management of Technology	M,O
Manufacturing Engineering	M,O
Mechanical Engineering	M,O
Software Engineering	M,O
Systems Engineering	M,O

UNIVERSITY OF SAN DIEGO
Computer and Information Systems Security	M
Computer Engineering	M
Health Informatics	M,D

UNIVERSITY OF SAN FRANCISCO
Biotechnology	M
Computer Science	M
Database Systems	M
Energy Management and Policy	M
Health Informatics	M

UNIVERSITY OF SASKATCHEWAN
Bioengineering	M,D
Biomedical Engineering	M,D
Biotechnology	M
Chemical Engineering	M,D
Civil Engineering	M,D

Computer Science	M,D
Electrical Engineering	M,D,O
Engineering and Applied Sciences—General	M,D,O
Engineering Physics	M,D
Geological Engineering	M,D
Mechanical Engineering	M,D

THE UNIVERSITY OF SCRANTON
Software Engineering	M

UNIVERSITY OF SOUTH AFRICA
Chemical Engineering	M
Engineering and Applied Sciences—General	M
Information Science	M,D
Technology and Public Policy	M,D
Telecommunications Management	M,D

UNIVERSITY OF SOUTH ALABAMA
Chemical Engineering	M
Civil Engineering	M
Computer Engineering	M
Computer Science	M,D
Electrical Engineering	M
Engineering and Applied Sciences—General	M,D
Environmental Engineering	M
Mechanical Engineering	M
Systems Engineering	D

UNIVERSITY OF SOUTH CAROLINA
Chemical Engineering	M,D
Civil Engineering	M,D
Computer Engineering	M,D
Computer Science	M,D
Electrical Engineering	M,D
Engineering and Applied Sciences—General	M,D
Hazardous Materials Management	M,D
Mechanical Engineering	M,D
Nuclear Engineering	M,D
Software Engineering	M,D

UNIVERSITY OF SOUTH CAROLINA UPSTATE
Health Informatics	M
Information Science	M

THE UNIVERSITY OF SOUTH DAKOTA
Computer Science	M
Database Systems	M

UNIVERSITY OF SOUTHERN CALIFORNIA
Aerospace/Aeronautical Engineering	M,D,O
Artificial Intelligence/Robotics	M,D
Bioinformatics	D
Biomedical Engineering	M,D
Biotechnology	M
Chemical Engineering	M,D,O
Civil Engineering	M,D,O
Computer and Information Systems Security	M,D
Computer Engineering	M,D,O
Computer Science	M,D
Construction Management	M,D,O
Electrical Engineering	M,D,O
Engineering and Applied Sciences—General	M,D,O
Engineering Management	M,D,O
Environmental Engineering	M,D,O
Game Design and Development	M,D

Geotechnical Engineering	M,D,O
Hazardous Materials Management	M,D,O
Industrial/Management Engineering	M,D,O
Manufacturing Engineering	M,D,O
Materials Engineering	M,D,O
Materials Sciences	M,D,O
Mechanical Engineering	M,D,O
Mechanics	M,D,O
Modeling and Simulation	M,D
Operations Research	M,D,O
Petroleum Engineering	M,D,O
Safety Engineering	M,D,O
Software Engineering	M,D
Systems Engineering	M,D,O
Telecommunications	M,D,O
Transportation and Highway Engineering	M,D,O

UNIVERSITY OF SOUTHERN INDIANA
Database Systems	M
Engineering and Applied Sciences—General	M
Engineering Management	M
Health Informatics	M

UNIVERSITY OF SOUTHERN MAINE
Computer Science	M,O
Software Engineering	M,O

UNIVERSITY OF SOUTHERN MISSISSIPPI
Computer Science	M,D
Construction Engineering	M
Information Science	M,O
Polymer Science and Engineering	M,D

UNIVERSITY OF SOUTH FLORIDA
Bioinformatics	M,D,O
Biomedical Engineering	M,D,O
Biotechnology	M,D,O
Chemical Engineering	M,D,O
Civil Engineering	M,D,O
Computer and Information Systems Security	M
Computer Engineering	M,D
Computer Science	M,D
Database Systems	M,D
Electrical Engineering	M,D
Engineering and Applied Sciences—General	M,D,O
Engineering Management	M,D
Environmental Engineering	M,D
Geotechnical Engineering	M,D
Health Informatics	M,D,O
Industrial/Management Engineering	M,D,O
Information Science	M,D
Management of Technology	O
Materials Engineering	M,D,O
Materials Sciences	O
Mechanical Engineering	M,D
Nanotechnology	M,D
Structural Engineering	M,D
Systems Engineering	O
Transportation and Highway Engineering	M,D,O
Water Resources Engineering	M,D,O

THE UNIVERSITY OF TENNESSEE
Aerospace/Aeronautical Engineering	M,D
Agricultural Engineering	M
Aviation	M
Biomedical Engineering	M,D
Biosystems Engineering	M,D

Chemical Engineering	M,D
Civil Engineering	M,D
Computer Engineering	M,D
Computer Science	M,D
Electrical Engineering	M,D
Energy and Power Engineering	D
Engineering and Applied Sciences—General	M,D
Engineering Management	M,D
Environmental Engineering	M
Industrial/Management Engineering	M,D
Information Science	M,D
Materials Engineering	M,D
Materials Sciences	M,D
Mechanical Engineering	M,D
Nuclear Engineering	M,D
Polymer Science and Engineering	M,D
Reliability Engineering	M,D

THE UNIVERSITY OF TENNESSEE AT CHATTANOOGA
Automotive Engineering	M
Chemical Engineering	M
Civil Engineering	M
Computer Science	M
Construction Management	M,O
Electrical Engineering	M
Energy and Power Engineering	M,O
Engineering Management	M,O
Industrial/Management Engineering	M
Mechanical Engineering	M
Medical Informatics	M,D,O

THE UNIVERSITY OF TENNESSEE HEALTH SCIENCE CENTER
Biomedical Engineering	M,D
Health Informatics	M,D

THE UNIVERSITY OF TEXAS AT ARLINGTON
Aerospace/Aeronautical Engineering	M,D
Bioengineering	M,D
Civil Engineering	M,D
Computer Engineering	M,D
Computer Science	M,D
Construction Management	M,D
Electrical Engineering	M,D
Engineering and Applied Sciences—General	M,D
Engineering Management	M
Industrial/Management Engineering	M,D
Materials Engineering	M,D
Materials Sciences	M,D
Mechanical Engineering	M,D
Software Engineering	M,D
Systems Engineering	M

THE UNIVERSITY OF TEXAS AT AUSTIN
Aerospace/Aeronautical Engineering	M,D
Architectural Engineering	M
Biomedical Engineering	M,D
Chemical Engineering	M,D
Civil Engineering	M,D
Computer and Information Systems Security	M,D
Computer Engineering	M,D
Computer Science	M,D
Electrical Engineering	M,D
Engineering and Applied Sciences—General	M,D
Environmental Engineering	M,D
Geotechnical Engineering	M,D

---

*M—masters degree; D—doctorate; O—other advanced degree; *—Close-Up and/or Display*

Industrial/Management	
Engineering	M,D
Materials Engineering	M,D
Materials Sciences	M,D
Mechanical Engineering	M,D
Mechanics	M,D
Mineral/Mining Engineering	M
Operations Research	M,D
Petroleum Engineering	M,D
Technology and Public Policy	M
Textile Sciences and	
Engineering	M
Water Resources Engineering	M,D

THE UNIVERSITY OF TEXAS AT DALLAS

Biomedical Engineering	M,D
Biotechnology	M,D
Computer Engineering	M,D
Computer Science	M,D
Database Systems	M,D
Electrical Engineering	M,D
Engineering and Applied	
Sciences—General	M,D
Management of Technology	M
Materials Engineering	M,D
Materials Sciences	M,D
Mechanical Engineering	M,D
Software Engineering	M,D
Systems Engineering	M,D
Telecommunications	M,D

THE UNIVERSITY OF TEXAS AT EL PASO

Bioinformatics	M,D
Biomedical Engineering	M,D,O
Civil Engineering	M,D,O
Computer Engineering	M,D
Computer Science	M,D
Construction Management	M,D,O
Electrical Engineering	M,D
Engineering and Applied	
Sciences—General	M,D,O
Environmental Engineering	M,D,O
Industrial/Management	
Engineering	M,O
Information Science	M,D
Manufacturing Engineering	M,O
Materials Engineering	M,D
Materials Sciences	M,D
Mechanical Engineering	M,D
Metallurgical Engineering and	
Metallurgy	M,D
Software Engineering	M,D,O
Systems Engineering	M,O

THE UNIVERSITY OF TEXAS AT SAN ANTONIO

Biomedical Engineering	M,D
Biotechnology	M,D
Civil Engineering	M,D
Computer and Information	
Systems Security	M,D,O
Computer Engineering	M,D
Computer Science	M,D
Electrical Engineering	M,D
Engineering and Applied	
Sciences—General	M,D
Environmental Engineering	M,D
Information Science	M,D,O
Management of Technology	M,D,O
Manufacturing Engineering	M,D
Materials Engineering	M,D
Mechanical Engineering	M,D

THE UNIVERSITY OF TEXAS AT TYLER

Civil Engineering	M
Computer and Information	
Systems Security	M
Computer Science	M
Electrical Engineering	M

Energy Management and	
Policy	M
Engineering Management	M
Environmental Engineering	M
Mechanical Engineering	M
Structural Engineering	M
Transportation and Highway	
Engineering	M
Water Resources Engineering	M

THE UNIVERSITY OF TEXAS HEALTH SCIENCE CENTER AT HOUSTON

Bioinformatics	M,D,O

THE UNIVERSITY OF TEXAS HEALTH SCIENCE CENTER AT SAN ANTONIO

Biomedical Engineering	M,D

THE UNIVERSITY OF TEXAS MEDICAL BRANCH

Bioinformatics	D

THE UNIVERSITY OF TEXAS OF THE PERMIAN BASIN

Computer Science	M

THE UNIVERSITY OF TEXAS RIO GRANDE VALLEY

Computer Science	M
Electrical Engineering	M
Engineering Management	M
Manufacturing Engineering	M
Mechanical Engineering	M
Systems Engineering	M

THE UNIVERSITY OF TEXAS SOUTHWESTERN MEDICAL CENTER

Biomedical Engineering	M,D

UNIVERSITY OF THE DISTRICT OF COLUMBIA

Computer Science	M
Electrical Engineering	M
Engineering and Applied	
Sciences—General	M

UNIVERSITY OF THE PACIFIC

Engineering and Applied	
Sciences—General	M

UNIVERSITY OF THE SACRED HEART

Information Science	O

UNIVERSITY OF THE SCIENCES

Bioinformatics	M
Biotechnology	M

THE UNIVERSITY OF TOLEDO

Bioengineering	M,D
Bioinformatics	M,O
Biomedical Engineering	D
Chemical Engineering	M,D
Civil Engineering	M,D
Computer Science	M,D
Electrical Engineering	M,D
Engineering and Applied	
Sciences—General	M
Industrial/Management	
Engineering	M,D
Materials Sciences	M,D
Mechanical Engineering	M,D

UNIVERSITY OF TORONTO

Aerospace/Aeronautical	
Engineering	M,D

Biomedical Engineering	M,D
Biotechnology	M
Chemical Engineering	M,D
Civil Engineering	M,D
Computer Engineering	M,D
Computer Science	M,D
Electrical Engineering	M,D
Engineering and Applied	
Sciences—General	M,D
Health Informatics	M
Industrial/Management	
Engineering	M,D
Management of Technology	M
Manufacturing Engineering	M
Materials Engineering	M,D
Materials Sciences	M,D
Mechanical Engineering	M,D

THE UNIVERSITY OF TULSA

Chemical Engineering	M,D
Computer and Information	
Systems Security	M,D
Computer Science	M,D
Electrical Engineering	M,D
Energy Management and	
Policy	M
Engineering and Applied	
Sciences—General	M,D
Engineering Physics	M,D
Financial Engineering	M
Mechanical Engineering	M,D
Petroleum Engineering	M,D

UNIVERSITY OF UTAH

Bioengineering	M,D*
Bioinformatics	M,D,O
Biotechnology	M
Chemical Engineering	M,D
Civil Engineering	M,D
Computer and Information	
Systems Security	M,O
Computer Science	M,D
Electrical Engineering	M,D
Engineering and Applied	
Sciences—General	M,D
Environmental Engineering	M,D
Game Design and	
Development	M
Geological Engineering	M,D
Materials Engineering	M,D
Materials Sciences	M,D
Mechanical Engineering	M,D
Metallurgical Engineering and	
Metallurgy	M,D
Mineral/Mining Engineering	M,D
Nuclear Engineering	M,D
Petroleum Engineering	M,D
Software Engineering	M,O
Systems Engineering	M,O

UNIVERSITY OF VERMONT

Biomedical Engineering	D
Civil Engineering	M,D
Computer Science	M,D
Electrical Engineering	M,D
Engineering and Applied	
Sciences—General	M,D
Environmental Engineering	M,D
Materials Sciences	M,D
Mechanical Engineering	M,D

UNIVERSITY OF VICTORIA

Computer Engineering	M,D
Computer Science	M,D
Electrical Engineering	M,D
Engineering and Applied	
Sciences—General	M,D
Health Informatics	M
Mechanical Engineering	M,D

UNIVERSITY OF VIRGINIA

Aerospace/Aeronautical	
Engineering	M,D

Biomedical Engineering	M,D
Chemical Engineering	M,D
Civil Engineering	M,D
Computer Engineering	M,D
Computer Science	M,D
Construction Engineering	D
Database Systems	M
Electrical Engineering	M,D
Engineering and Applied	
Sciences—General	M,D
Engineering Physics	M,D
Health Informatics	M
Management of Technology	M
Materials Sciences	M,D
Mechanical Engineering	M,D
Systems Engineering	M,D

UNIVERSITY OF WASHINGTON

Aerospace/Aeronautical	
Engineering	M,D
Bioengineering	M,D
Bioinformatics	M,D
Biotechnology	D
Chemical Engineering	M,D
Civil Engineering	M,D
Computer and Information	
Systems Security	M,D
Construction Engineering	M,D
Construction Management	M
Database Systems	M,D
Electrical Engineering	M,D
Engineering and Applied	
Sciences—General	M,D,O
Environmental Engineering	M,D
Geotechnical Engineering	M,D
Health Informatics	M,D
Industrial/Management	
Engineering	M,D
Information Science	M,D
Management of Technology	M,D
Materials Engineering	M,D
Materials Sciences	M,D
Mechanical Engineering	M,D
Mechanics	M,D
Medical Informatics	M,D
Nanotechnology	M,D
Structural Engineering	M,D
Transportation and Highway	
Engineering	M,D

UNIVERSITY OF WASHINGTON, BOTHELL

Computer Engineering	M
Software Engineering	M

UNIVERSITY OF WASHINGTON, TACOMA

Computer Engineering	M
Software Engineering	M

UNIVERSITY OF WATERLOO

Chemical Engineering	M,D
Civil Engineering	M,D
Computer Engineering	M,D
Computer Science	M,D
Electrical Engineering	M,D
Engineering and Applied	
Sciences—General	M,D
Engineering Management	M,D
Environmental Engineering	M,D
Health Informatics	M,D
Information Science	M,D
Management of Technology	M,D
Mechanical Engineering	M,D
Operations Research	M,D
Software Engineering	M,D
Systems Engineering	M,D

THE UNIVERSITY OF WESTERN ONTARIO

Biochemical Engineering	M,D
Chemical Engineering	M,D
Civil Engineering	M,D

Computer Engineering	M,D
Computer Science	M,D
Electrical Engineering	M,D
Engineering and Applied Sciences—General	M,D
Environmental Engineering	M,D
Materials Engineering	M,D
Mechanical Engineering	M,D

UNIVERSITY OF WEST FLORIDA

Biotechnology	M
Computer Science	M
Database Systems	M
Software Engineering	M

UNIVERSITY OF WEST GEORGIA

Computer Science	M,O

UNIVERSITY OF WINDSOR

Civil Engineering	M,D
Computer Science	M,D
Electrical Engineering	M,D
Engineering and Applied Sciences—General	M,D
Environmental Engineering	M,D
Industrial/Management Engineering	M,D
Manufacturing Engineering	M,D
Materials Engineering	M,D
Mechanical Engineering	M,D

UNIVERSITY OF WISCONSIN–LA CROSSE

Database Systems	M
Software Engineering	M

UNIVERSITY OF WISCONSIN–MADISON

Agricultural Engineering	M,D
Automotive Engineering	M,D
Bioinformatics	M
Biomedical Engineering	M,D
Chemical Engineering	D
Civil Engineering	M,D
Computer and Information Systems Security	M
Computer Science	M,D
Electrical Engineering	M,D
Engineering and Applied Sciences—General	M,D
Engineering Physics	M,D
Environmental Engineering	M,D
Ergonomics and Human Factors	M,D
Geological Engineering	M,D
Industrial/Management Engineering	M,D
Management of Technology	M
Manufacturing Engineering	M
Materials Engineering	M,D
Mechanical Engineering	M,D
Mechanics	M,D
Nuclear Engineering	M,D
Systems Engineering	M,D

UNIVERSITY OF WISCONSIN–MILWAUKEE

Biomedical Engineering	M,D
Civil Engineering	M,D
Computer Engineering	M,D
Computer Science	M,D
Electrical Engineering	M,D
Engineering and Applied Sciences—General	M,D
Ergonomics and Human Factors	M
Health Informatics	M,D
Industrial/Management Engineering	M,D
Management of Technology	M,O

Manufacturing Engineering	M,D
Materials Engineering	M,D
Mechanical Engineering	M,D
Mechanics	M,D
Medical Informatics	M

UNIVERSITY OF WISCONSIN–PARKSIDE

Computer Science	M
Information Science	M

UNIVERSITY OF WISCONSIN–PLATTEVILLE

Computer Science	M
Engineering and Applied Sciences—General	M

UNIVERSITY OF WISCONSIN–STOUT

Construction Management	M
Industrial/Management Engineering	M
Information Science	M
Manufacturing Engineering	M
Telecommunications Management	M

UNIVERSITY OF WYOMING

Biotechnology	D
Chemical Engineering	M,D
Civil Engineering	M,D
Computer Science	M,D
Electrical Engineering	M,D
Engineering and Applied Sciences—General	M,D
Environmental Engineering	M
Mechanical Engineering	M,D
Petroleum Engineering	M,D

UTAH STATE UNIVERSITY

Aerospace/Aeronautical Engineering	M,D
Agricultural Engineering	M,D
Civil Engineering	M,D,O
Computer Science	M,D
Electrical Engineering	M,D
Engineering and Applied Sciences—General	M,D,O
Environmental Engineering	M,D,O
Mechanical Engineering	M,D
Water Resources Engineering	M,D

UTAH VALLEY UNIVERSITY

Computer and Information Systems Security	O

UTICA COLLEGE

Computer and Information Systems Security	M

VALPARAISO UNIVERSITY

Computer and Information Systems Security	M
Engineering Management	M,O

VANDERBILT UNIVERSITY

Bioinformatics	M,D
Biomedical Engineering	M,D
Chemical Engineering	M,D
Civil Engineering	M,D
Computer Science	M,D
Electrical Engineering	M,D
Engineering and Applied Sciences—General	M,D
Environmental Engineering	M,D
Materials Sciences	M,D
Mechanical Engineering	M,D

VERMONT LAW SCHOOL

Energy Management and Policy	M

VILLANOVA UNIVERSITY

Artificial Intelligence/Robotics	M,O
Biochemical Engineering	M,O
Chemical Engineering	M,O
Civil Engineering	M
Computer and Information Systems Security	M
Computer Engineering	M,O
Computer Science	M,O
Database Systems	M
Electrical Engineering	M,O
Engineering and Applied Sciences—General	M,D,O
Environmental Engineering	M,O
Manufacturing Engineering	M,O
Mechanical Engineering	M,O
Software Engineering	M
Water Resources Engineering	M,O

VIRGINIA COMMONWEALTH UNIVERSITY

Biomedical Engineering	M,D
Computer Science	M,D
Engineering and Applied Sciences—General	M,D
Mechanical Engineering	M,D
Nanotechnology	M,D
Nuclear Engineering	M,D

VIRGINIA INTERNATIONAL UNIVERSITY

Computer and Information Systems Security	M,O
Computer Science	M,O
Database Systems	M,O
Game Design and Development	M,O
Health Informatics	M,O
Software Engineering	M,O

VIRGINIA POLYTECHNIC INSTITUTE AND STATE UNIVERSITY

Aerospace/Aeronautical Engineering	M,D,O
Agricultural Engineering	M,D
Bioengineering	M,D
Bioinformatics	M,D
Biomedical Engineering	M,D
Biotechnology	M,D
Chemical Engineering	M,D
Civil Engineering	M,D,O
Computer and Information Systems Security	M,O
Computer Engineering	M,D,O
Computer Science	M,D,O
Construction Engineering	M,D,O
Construction Management	M,D,O
Electrical Engineering	M,D,O
Engineering and Applied Sciences—General	M,D
Engineering Management	M,O
Environmental Engineering	M,D,O
Industrial/Management Engineering	M,D,O
Materials Engineering	M,D
Materials Sciences	M,D
Mechanical Engineering	M,D
Mechanics	M,D
Mineral/Mining Engineering	M,D
Nuclear Engineering	M,D
Ocean Engineering	M,D,O
Software Engineering	M,O
Systems Engineering	M,D,O
Transportation and Highway Engineering	M,O

VIRGINIA STATE UNIVERSITY

Computer Science	M

WAKE FOREST UNIVERSITY

Biomedical Engineering	M,D
Computer Science	M
Database Systems	M

WALDEN UNIVERSITY

Computer and Information Systems Security	M,D,O
Health Informatics	M,D,O

WALSH COLLEGE OF ACCOUNTANCY AND BUSINESS ADMINISTRATION

Computer and Information Systems Security	M
Management of Technology	M

WASHINGTON STATE UNIVERSITY

Agricultural Engineering	M,D
Bioengineering	M,D
Chemical Engineering	M,D
Civil Engineering	M,D
Computer Engineering	M,D
Computer Science	M,D
Electrical Engineering	M,D
Energy and Power Engineering	M,D
Engineering and Applied Sciences—General	M,D,O
Engineering Management	M,O
Environmental Engineering	M,D
Management of Technology	M,O
Materials Engineering	M,D
Materials Sciences	M,D
Mechanical Engineering	M,D

WASHINGTON UNIVERSITY IN ST. LOUIS

Aerospace/Aeronautical Engineering	M,D
Biomedical Engineering	M,D
Chemical Engineering	M,D
Computer Engineering	M,D
Computer Science	M,D
Database Systems	M
Engineering and Applied Sciences—General	M,D
Environmental Engineering	M,D
Materials Sciences	M,D
Mechanical Engineering	M,D

WAYNESBURG UNIVERSITY

Energy Management and Policy	M,D

WAYNE STATE UNIVERSITY

Automotive Engineering	M,O
Bioinformatics	M,D
Biomedical Engineering	M,D,O
Biotechnology	M,D
Chemical Engineering	M,D,O
Civil Engineering	M,D
Computer Engineering	M,D
Computer Science	M,D
Database Systems	M,D,O
Electrical Engineering	M,D
Energy and Power Engineering	M,O
Engineering and Applied Sciences—General	M,D,O
Engineering Management	M,D,O
Industrial/Management Engineering	M,D,O
Manufacturing Engineering	M,D,O
Materials Sciences	M,D,O
Mechanical Engineering	M,D

*M—masters degree; D—doctorate; O—other advanced degree; *—Close-Up and/or Display*

Polymer Science and Engineering	M,D,O
Systems Engineering	M,D,O

WEBER STATE UNIVERSITY

Computer Engineering	M

WEBSTER UNIVERSITY

Aerospace/Aeronautical Engineering	M,D,O
Computer and Information Systems Security	M
Computer Science	M
Management of Technology	M,D,O

WEILL CORNELL MEDICINE

Health Informatics	M

WENTWORTH INSTITUTE OF TECHNOLOGY

Civil Engineering	M
Construction Engineering	M
Construction Management	M
Management of Technology	M
Transportation and Highway Engineering	M

WESLEYAN UNIVERSITY

Bioinformatics	D
Computer Science	M,D

WEST CHESTER UNIVERSITY OF PENNSYLVANIA

Computer and Information Systems Security	M,O
Computer Science	M,O

WESTERN CAROLINA UNIVERSITY

Construction Management	M

WESTERN GOVERNORS UNIVERSITY

Computer and Information Systems Security	M
Database Systems	M
Information Science	M

WESTERN ILLINOIS UNIVERSITY

Computer Science	M
Manufacturing Engineering	M

WESTERN KENTUCKY UNIVERSITY

Computer Science	M
Management of Technology	M

WESTERN MICHIGAN UNIVERSITY

Aerospace/Aeronautical Engineering	M,D
Chemical Engineering	M,D
Civil Engineering	M

Computer Engineering	M,D
Computer Science	M,D
Electrical Engineering	M,D
Engineering and Applied Sciences—General	M,D
Engineering Management	M,D
Industrial/Management Engineering	M,D
Manufacturing Engineering	M
Mechanical Engineering	M,D
Paper and Pulp Engineering	M,D

WESTERN NEW ENGLAND UNIVERSITY

Civil Engineering	M
Electrical Engineering	M
Engineering and Applied Sciences—General	M,D
Engineering Management	M,D
Industrial/Management Engineering	M
Manufacturing Engineering	M
Mechanical Engineering	M

WESTERN WASHINGTON UNIVERSITY

Computer Science	M

WEST TEXAS A&M UNIVERSITY

Engineering and Applied Sciences—General	M

WEST VIRGINIA STATE UNIVERSITY

Biotechnology	M

WEST VIRGINIA UNIVERSITY

Aerospace/Aeronautical Engineering	M,D
Chemical Engineering	M,D
Civil Engineering	M,D
Computer Engineering	D
Computer Science	M,D
Electrical Engineering	M,D
Engineering and Applied Sciences—General	M,D,O
Environmental Engineering	M,D
Game Design and Development	O
Industrial/Management Engineering	M,D
Mechanical Engineering	M,D
Mineral/Mining Engineering	M,D
Petroleum Engineering	M,D
Safety Engineering	M
Software Engineering	M

WICHITA STATE UNIVERSITY

Aerospace/Aeronautical Engineering	M,D
Biomedical Engineering	M
Computer Engineering	M,D
Computer Science	M,D
Electrical Engineering	M,D

Engineering and Applied Sciences—General	M,D
Engineering Management	M,D
Industrial/Management Engineering	M,D
Manufacturing Engineering	M,D
Mechanical Engineering	M,D

WIDENER UNIVERSITY

Biomedical Engineering	M
Chemical Engineering	M
Civil Engineering	M
Electrical Engineering	M
Engineering and Applied Sciences—General	M
Engineering Management	M
Mechanical Engineering	M

WILFRID LAURIER UNIVERSITY

Management of Technology	M,D

WILKES UNIVERSITY

Bioengineering	M
Electrical Engineering	M
Engineering and Applied Sciences—General	M
Engineering Management	M
Mechanical Engineering	M

WILLIAM PATERSON UNIVERSITY OF NEW JERSEY

Biotechnology	M,D

WILMINGTON UNIVERSITY

Computer and Information Systems Security	M
Internet Engineering	M

WINSTON-SALEM STATE UNIVERSITY

Computer Science	M

WOODS HOLE OCEANOGRAPHIC INSTITUTION

Ocean Engineering	D

WORCESTER POLYTECHNIC INSTITUTE

Aerospace/Aeronautical Engineering	M,D
Artificial Intelligence/Robotics	M,D
Bioinformatics	M,D
Biomedical Engineering	M,D,O
Biotechnology	M,D
Chemical Engineering	M,D
Civil Engineering	M,D,O
Computer Engineering	M,D,O
Computer Science	M,D,O
Construction Management	M,D,O
Database Systems	M,D,O
Electrical Engineering	M,D,O
Energy and Power Engineering	M,D

Engineering and Applied Sciences—General	M,D,O
Engineering Design	M,D,O
Environmental Engineering	M,D,O
Fire Protection Engineering	M,D,O
Game Design and Development	M
Manufacturing Engineering	M,D
Materials Engineering	M,D
Materials Sciences	M,D
Mechanical Engineering	M,D,O
Modeling and Simulation	M,D
Systems Engineering	M,O
Systems Science	M,D,O

WORCESTER STATE UNIVERSITY

Biotechnology	M

WRIGHT STATE UNIVERSITY

Aerospace/Aeronautical Engineering	M
Biomedical Engineering	M
Computer Engineering	M,D
Computer Science	M,D
Electrical Engineering	M
Ergonomics and Human Factors	M,D
Industrial/Management Engineering	M
Materials Engineering	M
Materials Sciences	M
Mechanical Engineering	M

YALE UNIVERSITY

Bioinformatics	D
Biomedical Engineering	M,D
Chemical Engineering	M,D
Computer Science	M,D
Electrical Engineering	M,D
Engineering and Applied Sciences—General	M,D*
Engineering Physics	M,D
Environmental Engineering	M,D
Mechanical Engineering	M,D

YORK UNIVERSITY

Computer Science	M,D

YOUNGSTOWN STATE UNIVERSITY

Civil Engineering	M
Computer Engineering	M
Computer Science	M
Electrical Engineering	M
Engineering and Applied Sciences—General	M
Environmental Engineering	M
Industrial/Management Engineering	M
Information Science	M
Mechanical Engineering	M

ACADEMIC AND PROFESSIONAL PROGRAMS IN ENGINEERING & APPLIED SCIENCES

Section 1
Engineering and Applied Sciences

This section contains a directory of institutions offering graduate work in engineering and applied sciences, followed by in-depth entries submitted by institutions that chose to prepare detailed program descriptions. Additional information about programs listed in the directory but not augmented by an in-depth entry may be obtained by writing directly to the dean of a graduate school or chair of a department at the address given in the directory.

For programs in specific areas of engineering, see all other sections in this book. In the other guides in this series:

Graduate Programs in the Humanities, Arts & Social Sciences
See *Applied Arts and Design (Industrial Design)* and *Architecture (Environmental Design)*

Graduate Programs in the Biological/Biomedical Sciences & Health-Related Medical Professions
See *Ecology, Environmental Biology,* and *Evolutionary Biology*

Graduate Programs in the Physical Sciences, Mathematics, Agricultural Sciences, the Environment & Natural Resources
See *Agricultural and Food Sciences* and *Natural Resources*

CONTENTS

Engineering and Applied Sciences—General

Air Force Institute of Technology, Graduate School of Engineering and Management, Dayton, OH 45433-7765. Offers MS, PhD. *Accreditation:* ABET (one or more programs are accredited). *Program availability:* Part-time. *Degree requirements:* For master's, thesis; for doctorate, thesis/dissertation. *Entrance requirements:* For master's, GRE General Test, minimum GPA of 3.0; for doctorate, GRE General Test.

Alabama Agricultural and Mechanical University, School of Graduate Studies, College of Engineering, Technology, and Physical Sciences, Huntsville, AL 35811. Offers M Eng, MS, PhD. *Program availability:* Part-time, evening/weekend. *Degree requirements:* For master's, comprehensive exam, thesis optional. *Entrance requirements:* For master's, GRE General Test. Additional exam requirements/recommendations for international students: Required—TOEFL (minimum score 500 paper-based; 61 iBT). *Application deadline:* For fall admission, 5/1 for domestic students. Applications are processed on a rolling basis. Application fee: $25. Electronic applications accepted. *Expenses:* Tuition, nonresident: part-time $826 per credit hour. Full-time tuition and fees vary according to course load and program. *Financial support:* Research assistantships with tuition reimbursements and career-related internships or fieldwork available. Financial award application deadline: 4/1. *Faculty research:* Ionized gases, hypersonic flow phenomenology, robotics systems development. *Unit head:* Dr. Chance M. Glenn, Sr., Dean, 256-372-5560.

Alfred University, Graduate School, College of Ceramics, Inamori School of Engineering, Alfred, NY 14802. Offers biomaterials engineering (MS); ceramic engineering (MS, PhD); electrical engineering (MS); glass science (MS, PhD); materials science and engineering (MS, PhD); mechanical engineering (MS). *Program availability:* Part-time. *Faculty:* 18 full-time (1 woman). *Students:* 26 full-time (6 women), 16 part-time (4 women); includes 1 minority (Hispanic/Latino), 12 international. Average age 27. 14 applicants, 79% accepted, 10 enrolled. In 2016, 13 master's, 5 doctorates awarded. *Degree requirements:* For master's, thesis; for doctorate, thesis/dissertation. *Entrance requirements:* Additional exam requirements/recommendations for international students: Required—TOEFL (minimum score 590 paper-based; 90 iBT), IELTS (minimum score 6.5). *Application deadline:* For fall admission, 3/1 priority date for domestic students, 3/15 for international students; for spring admission, 10/1 priority date for domestic students, 10/1 for international students. Applications are processed on a rolling basis. Application fee: $60. Electronic applications accepted. *Expenses:* Contact institution. *Financial support:* Fellowships with full tuition reimbursements, research assistantships with full tuition reimbursements, teaching assistantships with full tuition reimbursements, tuition waivers (full and partial), and unspecified assistantships available. Financial award application deadline: 8/1; financial award applicants required to submit FAFSA. *Faculty research:* X-ray diffraction, biomaterials and polymers, thin-film processing, electronic and optical ceramics, solid-state chemistry. *Unit head:* Dr. Alistair N. Cormack, Dean, 607-871-2422, E-mail: cormack@alfred.edu. *Application contact:* Sara Love, Coordinator of Graduate Admissions, 607-871-2115, Fax: 607-871-2198, E-mail: gradinquiry@alfred.edu.
Website: http://engineering.alfred.edu/grad/

The American University in Cairo, School of Sciences and Engineering, Cairo, Egypt. Offers biotechnology (MS); chemistry (MS); computer science (MS); computing (M Comp); construction engineering (M Eng, MS); electronics and communications engineering (M Eng); environmental engineering (MS); environmental system design (M Eng); mechanical engineering (M Eng, MS); nanotechnology (MS); physics (MS); robotics, control and smart systems (MS); sciences and engineering (PhD); sustainable development (MS, Graduate Diploma). *Program availability:* Part-time, evening/weekend. *Faculty:* 43 full-time (4 women), 12 part-time/adjunct (1 woman). *Students:* 50 full-time (21 women), 262 part-time (128 women), 13 international. Average age 28. 193 applicants, 46% accepted, 55 enrolled. In 2016, 71 master's, 5 doctorates awarded. *Degree requirements:* For master's, comprehensive exam (for some programs), thesis (for some programs); for doctorate, comprehensive exam (for some programs), thesis/dissertation. *Entrance requirements:* Additional exam requirements/recommendations for international students: Required—TOEFL (minimum score 450 paper-based; 45 iBT), IELTS (minimum score 5). *Application deadline:* For fall admission, 2/1 priority date for domestic and international students; for spring admission, 10/15 priority date for domestic and international students. Applications are processed on a rolling basis. Application fee: $80. Electronic applications accepted. *Expenses:* Contact institution. *Financial support:* Fellowships with partial tuition reimbursements, scholarships/grants, and unspecified assistantships available. Financial award application deadline: 3/10. *Faculty research:* Construction, mechanical and electronics engineering, physics, computer science, biotechnology and nanotechnology. *Unit head:* Dr. Hassan El Fawal, Dean, 20-2-2615-2926, E-mail: hassan.elfawal@aucegypt.edu. *Application contact:* Maha Hegazi, Director for Graduate Admissions, 20-2-2615-1462, E-mail: mahahegazi@aucegypt.edu.
Website: http://www.aucegypt.edu/sse/Pages/default.aspx

American University of Beirut, Graduate Programs, Faculty of Engineering and Architecture, 11-0236, Lebanon. Offers applied energy (ME); civil engineering (PhD); electrical and computer engineering (PhD); energy studies (MS); engineering management (MEM); environmental and water resources (ME); environmental technology (MSES); mechanical engineering (ME, PhD); urban design (MUD); urban planning and policy (MUPP). *Program availability:* Part-time, evening/weekend, 100% online. *Faculty:* 99 full-time (22 women), 1 part-time/adjunct (0 women). *Students:* 308 full-time (143 women), 86 part-time (39 women). Average age 26. 430 applicants, 69% accepted, 125 enrolled. In 2016, 103 master's, 7 doctorates awarded. Terminal master's awarded for partial completion of doctoral program. *Degree requirements:* For master's, comprehensive exam, thesis optional; for doctorate, comprehensive exam, thesis/dissertation. *Entrance requirements:* For doctorate, GRE. Additional exam requirements/recommendations for international students: Required—TOEFL (minimum score 573 paper-based; 88 iBT); Recommended—IELTS (minimum score 7). *Application deadline:* For fall admission, 2/10 priority date for domestic and international students; for spring admission, 11/2 priority date for domestic students, 11/2 for international students. Application fee: $50. Electronic applications accepted. *Expenses:* Contact institution. *Financial support:* In 2016–17, 22 students received support, including 94 fellowships with full tuition reimbursements available (averaging $18,200 per year), 44 research assistantships with full tuition reimbursements available (averaging $7,596 per year), 124 teaching assistantships with full tuition reimbursements available (averaging $1,056 per year); career-related internships or fieldwork, Federal Work-Study, institutionally sponsored loans, scholarships/grants, traineeships, health care benefits, tuition waivers, and unspecified assistantships also available. Support available to part-time students. Financial award application deadline: 12/20. *Total annual research expenditures:* $1.5 million. *Unit head:* Prof. Alan Shihadeh, Interim Dean, 961-1350000 Ext. 3400, Fax: 961-1744462, E-mail: as20@aub.edu.lb. *Application contact:* Dr. Salim Kanaan, Director, Admissions Office, 961-1350000 Ext. 2594, Fax: 961-1750775, E-mail: sk00@aub.edu.lb.
Website: http://www.aub.edu.lb/fea/fea_home/Pages/index.aspx

Arizona State University at the Tempe campus, Ira A. Fulton Schools of Engineering, The Polytechnic School, Mesa, AZ 85212. Offers MS, PhD. *Program availability:* Part-time, evening/weekend. *Degree requirements:* For master's, thesis, interactive Program of Study (iPOS) submitted before completing 50 percent of required credit hours. *Entrance requirements:* For master's, GRE, minimum GPA of 3.0 or equivalent in last 2 years of work leading to bachelor's degree. Additional exam requirements/recommendations for international students: Required—TOEFL, IELTS, or PTE. Electronic applications accepted. *Expenses:* Contact institution.

Arkansas State University, Graduate School, College of Engineering, State University, AR 72467. Offers engineering (MS Eng); engineering management (MEM). *Program availability:* Part-time. *Degree requirements:* For master's, comprehensive exam. *Entrance requirements:* For master's, GRE, appropriate bachelor's degree, official transcript, letters of recommendation, resume, immunization records. Additional exam requirements/recommendations for international students: Required—TOEFL (minimum score 550 paper-based; 79 iBT), IELTS (minimum score 6), PTE (minimum score 56). Electronic applications accepted. *Expenses:* Contact institution.

Arkansas Tech University, College of Engineering and Applied Sciences, Russellville, AR 72801. Offers emergency management (MS); engineering (M Engr); information technology (MS). *Program availability:* Part-time, online learning. *Students:* 59 full-time (15 women), 63 part-time (21 women); includes 22 minority (8 Black or African American, non-Hispanic/Latino; 2 American Indian or Alaska Native, non-Hispanic/Latino; 4 Asian, non-Hispanic/Latino; 4 Hispanic/Latino; 4 Two or more races, non-Hispanic/Latino), 41 international. Average age 31. In 2016, 43 master's awarded. *Degree requirements:* For master's, comprehensive exam (for some programs), thesis (for some programs), internship. *Entrance requirements:* For master's, GRE General Test. Additional exam requirements/recommendations for international students: Required—TOEFL (minimum score 550 paper-based; 79 iBT), IELTS (minimum score 6). *Application deadline:* For fall admission, 3/1 priority date for domestic students, 5/1 priority date for international students; for spring admission, 10/1 priority date for domestic and international students. Applications are processed on a rolling basis. Application fee: $25 ($75 for international students). Electronic applications accepted. *Expenses:* Tuition, state resident: full-time $4932; part-time $274 per credit hour. Tuition, nonresident: full-time $9864; part-time $548 per credit hour. *Required fees:* $513 per semester. Tuition and fees vary according to course load. *Financial support:* In 2016–17, research assistantships with full tuition reimbursements (averaging $4,800 per year), teaching assistantships with full tuition reimbursements (averaging $4,800 per year) were awarded; career-related internships or fieldwork, Federal Work-Study, scholarships/grants, health care benefits, and unspecified assistantships also available. Support available to part-time students. Financial award application deadline: 4/15; financial award applicants required to submit FAFSA. *Unit head:* Dr. Douglas Barlow, Dean, 479-968-0353, E-mail: dbarlow@atu.edu. *Application contact:* Dr. Mary B. Gunter, Dean of Graduate College, 479-968-0398, Fax: 479-964-0542, E-mail: gradcollege@atu.edu.
Website: http://www.atu.edu/appliedsci/

Auburn University, Graduate School, Ginn College of Engineering, Auburn University, AL 36849. Offers M Ch E, M Mtl E, MAE, MCE, MEE, MISE, MME, MS, MSWE, PhD, Graduate Certificate. *Program availability:* Part-time. *Faculty:* 162 full-time (15 women), 16 part-time/adjunct (2 women). *Students:* 565 full-time (141 women), 334 part-time (63 women); includes 56 minority (24 Black or African American, non-Hispanic/Latino; 2 American Indian or Alaska Native, non-Hispanic/Latino; 10 Asian, non-Hispanic/Latino; 16 Hispanic/Latino; 4 Two or more races, non-Hispanic/Latino), 557 international. Average age 27. 1,346 applicants, 46% accepted, 225 enrolled. In 2016, 220 master's, 75 doctorates, 14 other advanced degrees awarded. *Degree requirements:* For master's, thesis (for some programs); for doctorate, thesis/dissertation. *Entrance requirements:* For master's and doctorate, GRE General Test. *Application deadline:* Applications are processed on a rolling basis. Application fee: $50 ($60 for international students). Electronic applications accepted. *Expenses:* Tuition, state resident: full-time $9072; part-time $504 per credit hour. Tuition, nonresident: full-time $27,216; part-time $1512 per credit hour. *Required fees:* $812 per semester. Tuition and fees vary according to degree level and program. *Financial support:* Fellowships, research assistantships, teaching assistantships, and Federal Work-Study available. Support available to part-time students. Financial award application deadline: 3/15; financial award applicants required to submit FAFSA. *Unit head:* Dr. Chris Roberts, Dean, 334-844-2308. *Application contact:* Dr. George Flowers, Dean of the Graduate School, 334-844-2125.
Website: http://www.eng.auburn.edu/

Austin Peay State University, College of Graduate Studies, College of Science and Mathematics, Department of Engineering Technology, Clarksville, TN 37044. Offers MS. *Program availability:* Part-time. *Faculty:* 2 full-time, 1 part-time/adjunct. *Students:* 7 part-time (1 woman); includes 5 minority (1 Black or African American, non-Hispanic/Latino; 1 Asian, non-Hispanic/Latino; 1 Hispanic/Latino; 2 Two or more races, non-Hispanic/Latino). Average age 41. 11 applicants, 91% accepted, 6 enrolled. In 2016, 1 master's awarded. *Entrance requirements:* For master's, minimum GPA of 2.5. Additional exam requirements/recommendations for international students: Required—TOEFL (minimum score 500 paper-based). *Application deadline:* For fall admission, 8/9 for domestic students. Applications are processed on a rolling basis. Application fee: $45 ($50 for international students). Electronic applications accepted. *Expenses:* Tuition, state resident: full-time $8300; part-time $415 per credit hour. Tuition, nonresident: full-time $22,280; part-time $1114 per credit hour. *Required fees:* $1473; $73.65 per credit hour. *Financial support:* Career-related internships or fieldwork, Federal Work-Study, institutionally sponsored loans, scholarships/grants, and unspecified assistantships available. Support available to part-time students. Financial award application deadline: 4/1; financial award applicants required to submit FAFSA. *Unit head:* Dr. John Byrd, Chair/Professor, 931-221-1474, Fax: 931-221-1463, E-mail: byrdjl@apsu.edu. *Application contact:* Brad Averitt, Coordinator of Graduate Admissions, 800-859-4723, Fax: 931-221-7641, E-mail: gradadmissions@apsu.edu.

Binghamton University, State University of New York, Graduate School, Thomas J. Watson School of Engineering and Applied Science, Binghamton, NY 13902-6000. Offers M Eng, MS, PhD. *Program availability:* Part-time, evening/weekend, online learning. *Faculty:* 101 full-time (16 women), 26 part-time/adjunct (3 women). *Students:* 789 full-time (195 women), 416 part-time (91 women); includes 113 minority (31 Black or African American, non-Hispanic/Latino; 51 Asian, non-Hispanic/Latino; 30 Hispanic/Latino; 1 Native Hawaiian or other Pacific Islander, non-Hispanic/Latino), 893 international. Average age 27. 2,243 applicants, 69% accepted, 431 enrolled. In 2016, 385 master's, 32 doctorates awarded. *Degree requirements:* For master's, comprehensive exam (for some programs), thesis (for some programs); for doctorate, comprehensive exam (for some programs), thesis/dissertation. *Entrance requirements:* For master's and doctorate, GRE General Test. Additional exam requirements/recommendations for international students: Required—TOEFL (minimum score 550 paper-based; 80 iBT). *Application deadline:* Applications are processed on a rolling basis. Application fee: $75. Electronic applications accepted. *Expenses:* Contact institution. *Financial support:* In 2016–17, 332 students received support, including 2 fellowships with full tuition reimbursements available (averaging $10,000 per year), 138 research assistantships with full tuition reimbursements available (averaging $16,500 per year), 94 teaching assistantships with full tuition reimbursements available (averaging $16,500 per year); career-related internships or fieldwork, Federal Work-Study, institutionally sponsored loans, scholarships/grants, health care benefits, tuition waivers (full and partial), and unspecified assistantships also available. Financial award application deadline: 2/15; financial award applicants required to submit FAFSA. *Unit head:* Ellen Tilden, Coordinator of Graduate Programs, The Watson School, 607-777-2873, E-mail: etilden@binghamton.edu. *Application contact:* Ben Balkaya, Assistant Dean and Director, 607-777-2151, Fax: 607-777-2501, E-mail: balkaya@binghamton.edu. Website: http://watson.binghamton.edu

See Display below and Close-Up on page 79.

Boise State University, College of Engineering, Boise, ID 83725-2100. Offers M Engr, MS, PhD, Graduate Certificate. *Program availability:* Part-time, online learning. *Faculty:* 78. *Students:* 136 full-time (42 women), 231 part-time (117 women); includes 52 minority (15 Black or African American, non-Hispanic/Latino; 17 Asian, non-Hispanic/Latino; 15 Hispanic/Latino; 5 Two or more races, non-Hispanic/Latino), 78 international. Average age 34. 309 applicants, 51% accepted, 81 enrolled. In 2016, 72 master's, 1 doctorate awarded. *Degree requirements:* For master's, comprehensive exam (for some programs), thesis (for some programs); for doctorate, comprehensive exam, thesis/dissertation. *Entrance requirements:* For master's, GRE General Test, minimum GPA of 3.0. Additional exam requirements/recommendations for international students: Required—TOEFL (minimum score 550 paper-based; 80 iBT), IELTS (minimum score 6). Application fee: $65 ($95 for international students). Electronic applications accepted. *Expenses:* Tuition, state resident: full-time $6058; part-time $358 per credit hour. Tuition, nonresident: full-time $20,108; part-time $608 per credit hour. *Required fees:* $2108. Tuition and fees vary according to program. *Financial support:* In 2016–17, 50 students received support, including 63 research assistantships (averaging $9,326 per year), 7 teaching assistantships with partial tuition reimbursements available (averaging $10,656 per year); scholarships/grants and unspecified assistantships also available. Financial award applicants required to submit FAFSA. *Unit head:* Dr. Amy Moll, Dean, 208-426-5719. *Application contact:* Hao Chen, Program Coordinator, 208-426-1020, E-mail: haochen@boisestate.edu. Website: http://coen.boisestate.edu/

Boston University, College of Engineering, Boston, MA 02215. Offers M Eng, MS, PhD, MD/PhD, MS/MBA. *Program availability:* Part-time, blended/hybrid learning. *Faculty:* 112 full-time (12 women), 9 part-time/adjunct (1 woman). *Students:* 858 full-time (266 women), 183 part-time (48 women); includes 140 minority (6 Black or African American, non-Hispanic/Latino; 85 Asian, non-Hispanic/Latino; 31 Hispanic/Latino; 2 Native Hawaiian or other Pacific Islander, non-Hispanic/Latino; 16 Two or more races, non-Hispanic/Latino), 552 international. Average age 25. 3,089 applicants, 30% accepted, 372 enrolled. In 2016, 283 master's, 62 doctorates awarded. Terminal master's awarded for partial completion of doctoral program. *Degree requirements:* For master's, thesis (for some programs); for doctorate, comprehensive exam, thesis/dissertation. *Entrance requirements:* For master's and doctorate, GRE General Test. Additional exam requirements/recommendations for international students: Required—TOEFL (minimum score 90 iBT), IELTS (minimum score 7). *Application deadline:* For fall admission, 12/15 for domestic and international students; for spring admission, 10/1 for domestic and international students. Application fee: $95. Electronic applications accepted. *Expenses:* $25,490 per semester. *Financial support:* In 2016–17, 458 students received support, including 115 fellowships with full tuition reimbursements available (averaging $33,000 per year), 246 research assistantships with full tuition reimbursements available (averaging $33,000 per year), 7 teaching assistantships with full tuition reimbursements available (averaging $22,000 per year); scholarships/grants and unspecified assistantships also available. Support available to part-time students. Financial award application deadline: 1/15; financial award applicants required to submit FAFSA. *Faculty research:* Photonics, bioengineering, computer and information systems, nanotechnology, materials science and engineering. *Unit head:* Dr. Kenneth R. Lutchen, Dean, 617-353-2800, Fax: 617-358-3468, E-mail: klutch@bu.edu. *Application contact:* Andrew Butler, 617-353-9760, Fax: 617-353-0259, E-mail: enggrad@bu.edu. Website: http://www.bu.edu/eng/

Bradley University, The Graduate School, Caterpillar College of Engineering and Technology, Peoria, IL 61625-0002. Offers MS, MSCE, MSEE, MSME. *Program availability:* Part-time, evening/weekend. *Degree requirements:* For master's, comprehensive exam, thesis optional. *Entrance requirements:* Additional exam requirements/recommendations for international students: Required—TOEFL (minimum score 550 paper-based; 79 iBT), IELTS (minimum score 6.5). *Application deadline:* For fall admission, 5/15 priority date for domestic and international students; for spring admission, 10/15 priority date for domestic and international students. Applications are processed on a rolling basis. Application fee: $40 ($50 for international students). Electronic applications accepted. *Expenses:* Contact institution. *Financial support:* Research assistantships with full and partial tuition reimbursements, teaching assistantships, institutionally sponsored loans, scholarships/grants, tuition waivers (partial), and unspecified assistantships available. Support available to part-time students. Financial award application deadline: 4/1. *Unit head:* Lex Akers, Dean, 309-677-2721, E-mail: lakers@bradley.edu. *Application contact:* Kayla Carroll, Director of International Admissions and Student Services, 309-677-2375, E-mail: klcarroll@fsmail.bradley.edu. Website: http://www.bradley.edu/academic/colleges/egt/

Brigham Young University, Graduate Studies, Ira A. Fulton College of Engineering and Technology, Provo, UT 84602. Offers MS, PhD. *Faculty:* 107 full-time (3 women), 10 part-time/adjunct (2 women). *Students:* 363 full-time (42 women); includes 14 minority (3 American Indian or Alaska Native, non-Hispanic/Latino; 4 Asian, non-Hispanic/Latino; 4 Hispanic/Latino; 3 Native Hawaiian or other Pacific Islander, non-Hispanic/Latino), 56 international. Average age 27. 203 applicants, 63% accepted, 98 enrolled. In 2016, 87 master's, 18 doctorates awarded. *Degree requirements:* For master's, comprehensive exam (for some programs), thesis (for some programs); for doctorate, comprehensive exam (for some programs), thesis/dissertation (for some programs). *Entrance requirements:* For master's and doctorate, GRE, at least 3 letters of recommendation, transcripts from each institution attended, ecclesiastical endorsement, minimum cumulative GPA of 3.0 in last 60 hours of coursework. Additional exam requirements/recommendations for international students: Required—TOEFL (minimum score 580 paper-based; 85 iBT), IELTS (minimum score 7). *Application deadline:* For fall admission, 1/15 for domestic and international students; for winter admission, 6/15 for domestic and international students; for spring admission, 2/5 for domestic and international students; for summer admission, 2/5 for domestic and international students. Application fee: $50. Electronic applications accepted. *Expenses:* Tuition: Full-time $6680; part-time $393 per credit. Tuition and fees vary according to course load, program and student's religious affiliation. *Financial support:* In 2016–17, 475 students received support, including 26 fellowships with full and partial tuition reimbursements available (averaging $22,961 per year), 631 research assistantships with full and partial tuition reimbursements available (averaging $13,681 per year), 138 teaching assistantships with full and partial tuition reimbursements available (averaging

BIOMEDICAL ENGINEERING FOR OUR FUTURE

Whether it's working on artificial joints or bioengineered and 3D-printed organs, graduate students play integral roles on the cutting edge of medical research in the Biomedical Engineering Department within the Thomas J. Watson School of Engineering and Applied Science at Binghamton University.

$10,574 per year); scholarships/grants and health care benefits also available. Financial award application deadline: 3/1; financial award applicants required to submit FAFSA. *Faculty research:* Combustion, microwave remote sensing, structural optimization, biomedical engineering, networking. *Total annual research expenditures:* $12.3 million. *Unit head:* Dr. Michael A. Jensen, Dean, 801-422-5736, Fax: 801-422-0218, E-mail: college@et.byu.edu. *Application contact:* Claire A. DeWitt, Adviser, 801-422-4541, Fax: 801-422-0270, E-mail: gradstudies@byu.edu.
Website: http://www.et.byu.edu/

Brown University, Graduate School, School of Engineering, Providence, RI 02912. Offers biomedical engineering (Sc M, PhD); chemical and biochemical engineering (Sc M, PhD); electrical sciences and computer engineering (Sc M, PhD); fluid and thermal sciences (Sc M, PhD); materials science and engineering (Sc M, PhD); mechanics of solids and structures (Sc M, PhD). *Degree requirements:* For doctorate, thesis/dissertation, preliminary exam.

Bucknell University, Graduate Studies, College of Engineering, Lewisburg, PA 17837. Offers MS Ch E, MSCE, MSEE, MSEV, MSME. *Program availability:* Part-time. *Degree requirements:* For master's, thesis. *Entrance requirements:* For master's, GRE General Test, minimum GPA of 3.0. Additional exam requirements/recommendations for international students: Required—TOEFL (minimum score 600 paper-based).

California Institute of Technology, Division of Engineering and Applied Science, Pasadena, CA 91125. Offers aeronautics (MS, PhD, Engr); applied and computational mathematics (MS, PhD); applied mechanics (MS, PhD); applied physics (MS, PhD); bioengineering (MS, PhD); civil engineering (MS, PhD, Engr); computation and neural systems (MS, PhD); computer science (MS, PhD); control and dynamical systems (MS, PhD); electrical engineering (MS, PhD, Engr); environmental science and engineering (MS, PhD); materials science (MS, PhD); mechanical engineering (MS, PhD, Engr). Terminal master's awarded for partial completion of doctoral program. *Degree requirements:* For doctorate, thesis/dissertation. *Entrance requirements:* For master's and doctorate, GRE (strongly recommended), minimum GPA of 3.5. Additional exam requirements/recommendations for international students: Required—TOEFL; Recommended—TWE (minimum score 5). Electronic applications accepted.

California Polytechnic State University, San Luis Obispo, College of Engineering, Department of Biomedical and General Engineering, San Luis Obispo, CA 93407. Offers MS, MBA/MS, MCRP/MS. *Program availability:* Part-time. *Faculty:* 9 full-time (2 women). *Students:* 56 full-time (17 women), 76 part-time (18 women); includes 42 minority (1 Black or African American, non-Hispanic/Latino; 18 Asian, non-Hispanic/Latino; 17 Hispanic/Latino; 6 Two or more races, non-Hispanic/Latino), 8 international. Average age 27. 111 applicants, 52% accepted, 46 enrolled. In 2016, 61 master's awarded. *Degree requirements:* For master's, thesis. *Entrance requirements:* For master's, GRE. Additional exam requirements/recommendations for international students: Required—TOEFL (minimum score 80 iBT). *Application deadline:* For fall admission, 3/1 for domestic and international students. Applications are processed on a rolling basis. Application fee: $55. Electronic applications accepted. *Expenses:* Tuition, state resident: full-time $6738; part-time $3906 per year. Tuition, nonresident: full-time $15,666; part-time $8370 per year. *Required fees:* $3603; $3141 per unit. $1047 per term. *Financial support:* Fellowships, research assistantships, teaching assistantships, and scholarships/grants available. Financial award application deadline: 3/2; financial award applicants required to submit FAFSA. *Faculty research:* Biomedical engineering, materials engineering, water engineering, stem cell research. *Unit head:* Dr. David Clague, Graduate Coordinator, 805-756-5145, E-mail: dclague@calpoly.edu.
Website: http://bmed.calpoly.edu/

California State University, Chico, Office of Graduate Studies, College of Engineering, Computer Science, and Construction Management, Chico, CA 95929-0722. Offers MS. *Program availability:* Part-time, online learning. *Faculty:* 59 full-time (12 women), 37 part-time/adjunct (4 women). *Students:* 28 full-time (6 women), 47 part-time (13 women); includes 56 minority (55 Asian, non-Hispanic/Latino; 1 Hispanic/Latino). 89 applicants, 74% accepted, 12 enrolled. In 2016, 34 master's awarded. *Degree requirements:* For master's, thesis or project. *Entrance requirements:* For master's, GRE. Additional exam requirements/recommendations for international students: Required—TOEFL (minimum score 550 paper-based; 80 iBT), IELTS (minimum score 6.5), PTE (minimum score 59). *Application deadline:* For fall admission, 3/1 priority date for domestic students, 3/1 for international students; for spring admission, 9/15 priority date for domestic students, 9/15 for international students. Application fee: $55. Electronic applications accepted. *Financial support:* Fellowships, research assistantships, teaching assistantships, career-related internships or fieldwork, Federal Work-Study, scholarships/grants, and traineeships available. Support available to part-time students. Financial award application deadline: 3/1; financial award applicants required to submit FAFSA. *Unit head:* Ricardo Jacquez, Dean, 530-898-5963, Fax: 530-898-4070, E-mail: ecc@csuchico.edu. *Application contact:* Judy L. Rice, Graduate Admissions Counselor, 530-898-5416, Fax: 530-898-3342, E-mail: jlrice@csuchico.edu.
Website: http://www.csuchico.edu/ecc/

California State University, East Bay, Office of Graduate Studies, College of Science, School of Engineering, Hayward, CA 94542-3000. Offers construction management (MS); engineering management (MS). *Students:* 26 full-time (14 women), 108 part-time (26 women); includes 21 minority (5 Black or African American, non-Hispanic/Latino; 8 Asian, non-Hispanic/Latino; 5 Hispanic/Latino; 3 Two or more races, non-Hispanic/Latino), 87 international. Average age 29. 364 applicants, 40% accepted, 35 enrolled. In 2016, 41 master's awarded. *Degree requirements:* For master's, comprehensive exam (for some programs), research project or exam. *Entrance requirements:* For master's, GRE or GMAT, minimum GPA of 2.5; personal statement; 2 letters of recommendation; resume; college algebra/trigonometry or equivalent. Additional exam requirements/recommendations for international students: Required—TOEFL (minimum score 550 paper-based). *Application deadline:* For fall admission, 6/30 for domestic and international students. Application fee: $55. Electronic applications accepted. *Financial support:* Federal Work-Study and institutionally sponsored loans available. Support available to part-time students. Financial award application deadline: 3/2; financial award applicants required to submit FAFSA. *Faculty research:* Operations research, production planning, simulation, human factors/ergonomics, quality assurance, sustainability. *Unit head:* Dr. Saeid Motavalli, Chair/Graduate Advisor, 510-885-4481, E-mail: saeid.motavalli@csueastbay.edu. *Application contact:* Dr. Donna Wiley, Interim Associate Vice President for Academic Programs and Graduate Studies, 510-885-3716, Fax: 510-885-4777, E-mail: donna.wiley@csueastbay.edu.
Website: http://www20.csueastbay.edu/csci/departments/engineering/

California State University, Fresno, Division of Research and Graduate Studies, Lyles College of Engineering, Fresno, CA 93740-8027. Offers MS, MSE. *Program availability:* Part-time, evening/weekend. *Degree requirements:* For master's, thesis or alternative. *Entrance requirements:* For master's, GRE General Test, minimum GPA of 2.7. Additional exam requirements/recommendations for international students: Required—TOEFL. *Application deadline:* For fall admission, 5/1 for domestic and international students; for spring admission, 10/1 for domestic students, 5/1 for international students. Applications are processed on a rolling basis. Application fee: $55. Electronic applications accepted. *Financial support:* Teaching assistantships, career-related internships or fieldwork, Federal Work-Study, scholarships/grants, and unspecified assistantships available. Support available to part-time students. Financial award application deadline: 3/1; financial award applicants required to submit FAFSA. *Faculty research:* Exhaust emission, blended fuel testing, waste management. *Unit head:* Dr. Ram Nunna, Dean, 559-278-2500, Fax: 559-278-4475.
Website: http://www.fresnostate.edu/engineering/

California State University, Fullerton, Graduate Studies, College of Engineering and Computer Science, Fullerton, CA 92834-9480. Offers MS. *Program availability:* Part-time. *Degree requirements:* For master's, comprehensive exam, project or thesis. *Entrance requirements:* For master's, minimum undergraduate GPA of 2.5. Application fee: $55. *Expenses:* Tuition, state resident: full-time $3369; part-time $1953 per unit. Tuition, nonresident: full-time $3915; part-time $2499 per unit. Tuition and fees vary according to course load, degree level and program. *Financial support:* Career-related internships or fieldwork, Federal Work-Study, institutionally sponsored loans, and scholarships/grants available. Support available to part-time students. Financial award application deadline: 3/1; financial award applicants required to submit FAFSA. *Unit head:* Dr. Raman Unnikrishnan, Dean, 657-278-3362. *Application contact:* Admissions/Applications, 657-278-2371.

California State University, Los Angeles, Graduate Studies, College of Engineering, Computer Science, and Technology, Los Angeles, CA 90032-8530. Offers MA, MS. *Program availability:* Part-time, evening/weekend. *Entrance requirements:* Additional exam requirements/recommendations for international students: Required—TOEFL (minimum score 550 paper-based). Electronic applications accepted.

California State University, Northridge, Graduate Studies, College of Engineering and Computer Science, Northridge, CA 91330. Offers MS. *Program availability:* Part-time, evening/weekend. *Faculty:* 64 full-time (14 women), 108 part-time/adjunct (18 women). *Students:* 281 full-time (65 women), 273 part-time (47 women); includes 54 minority (2 Black or African American, non-Hispanic/Latino; 1 American Indian or Alaska Native, non-Hispanic/Latino; 42 Asian, non-Hispanic/Latino; 1 Native Hawaiian or other Pacific Islander, non-Hispanic/Latino; 8 Two or more races, non-Hispanic/Latino), 286 international. Average age 28. 1,195 applicants, 29% accepted, 145 enrolled. *Entrance requirements:* For master's, GRE General Test, minimum GPA of 2.5. Additional exam requirements/recommendations for international students: Required—TOEFL. *Application deadline:* For fall admission, 11/30 for domestic students. Application fee: $55. *Expenses:* Tuition, state resident: full-time $4152. *Financial support:* Teaching assistantships, career-related internships or fieldwork, and Federal Work-Study available. Support available to part-time students. Financial award application deadline: 3/1. *Unit head:* Dr. S. K. Ramesh, Dean, 818-677-4501, E-mail: s.ramesh@csun.edu.
Website: http://www.ecs.csun.edu/ecsdean/index.html

California State University, Sacramento, Office of Graduate Studies, College of Engineering and Computer Science, Sacramento, CA 95819. Offers MS. *Program availability:* Part-time, evening/weekend. *Students:* 161 full-time (54 women), 206 part-time (55 women); includes 273 minority (18 Black or African American, non-Hispanic/Latino; 1 American Indian or Alaska Native, non-Hispanic/Latino; 224 Asian, non-Hispanic/Latino; 29 Hispanic/Latino; 1 Native Hawaiian or other Pacific Islander, non-Hispanic/Latino). Average age 28. 661 applicants, 72% accepted, 139 enrolled. In 2016, 95 master's awarded. *Degree requirements:* For master's, writing proficiency exam. *Entrance requirements:* Additional exam requirements/recommendations for international students: Required—TOEFL (minimum score 550 paper-based; 80 iBT). *Application deadline:* Applications are processed on a rolling basis. Application fee: $55. Electronic applications accepted. *Expenses:* $4,302 full-time tuition and fees per semester, $2,796 part-time. *Financial support:* Research assistantships, teaching assistantships, career-related internships or fieldwork, and Federal Work-Study available. Support available to part-time students. Financial award application deadline: 3/1; financial award applicants required to submit FAFSA. *Unit head:* Dr. Lorenzo M. Smith, Dean, 916-278-6127, Fax: 916-278-5949, E-mail: lsmith@csus.edu. *Application contact:* Jose Martinez, Graduate Admissions Supervisor, 916-278-7871, E-mail: martinj@skymail.csus.edu.
Website: http://www.hera.ecs.csus.edu

Carleton University, Faculty of Graduate Studies, Faculty of Engineering and Design, Ottawa, ON K1S 5B6, Canada. Offers M Arch, M Des, M Eng, M Sc, MA Sc, PhD. *Degree requirements:* For doctorate, thesis/dissertation. *Entrance requirements:* For master's, honors degree; for doctorate, MA Sc or M Eng. Additional exam requirements/recommendations for international students: Required—TOEFL.

Case Western Reserve University, School of Graduate Studies, Case School of Engineering, Cleveland, OH 44106. Offers ME, MEM, MS, PhD, MD/MS, MD/PhD. *Program availability:* Part-time, evening/weekend, 100% online, blended/hybrid learning. *Faculty:* 112 full-time (15 women). *Students:* 632 full-time (173 women), 70 part-time (21 women); includes 75 minority (11 Black or African American, non-Hispanic/Latino; 48 Asian, non-Hispanic/Latino; 11 Hispanic/Latino; 5 Two or more races, non-Hispanic/Latino), 433 international. 1,310 applicants, 48% accepted, 447 enrolled. In 2016, 153 master's, 70 doctorates awarded. Terminal master's awarded for partial completion of doctoral program. *Degree requirements:* For master's, thesis (for some programs); for doctorate, thesis/dissertation, qualifying exam, teaching experience. *Entrance requirements:* For master's and doctorate, GRE General Test. Additional exam requirements/recommendations for international students: Required—TOEFL (minimum score 577 paper-based; 90 iBT), IELTS (minimum score 7). *Application deadline:* Applications are processed on a rolling basis. Application fee: $50. Electronic applications accepted. *Expenses: Tuition:* Full-time $42,576; part-time $1774 per credit hour. *Required fees:* $34. Tuition and fees vary according to course load and program. *Financial support:* In 2016–17, 334 students received support, including 35 fellowships with tuition reimbursements available, 258 research assistantships with tuition reimbursements available, 32 teaching assistantships; career-related internships or fieldwork, Federal Work-Study, and institutionally sponsored loans also available. Support available to part-time students. Financial award applicants required to submit FAFSA. *Faculty research:* Advanced materials, biomedical engineering and human health, electrical engineering and computer science, civil engineering, engineering management. *Total annual research expenditures:* $42.1 million. *Unit head:* Jeffrey L. Duerk, Dean/Professor, 216-368-4436, Fax: 216-368-6939, E-mail: duerk@case.edu. *Application contact:* Dr. Marc Buchner, Associate Dean, Academics, 216-368-4096, Fax: 216-368-6939, E-mail: marc.buchner@case.edu.
Website: http://www.engineering.case.edu

The Catholic University of America, School of Engineering, Washington, DC 20064. Offers MBE, MCE, MEE, MME, MS, MSCS, MSE, PhD, Certificate. *Program availability:* Part-time. *Faculty:* 33 full-time (3 women), 26 part-time/adjunct (2 women). *Students:* 70 full-time (18 women), 104 part-time (28 women); includes 32 minority (13 Black or African American, non-Hispanic/Latino; 4 Asian, non-Hispanic/Latino; 2 Hispanic/Latino; 13 Two or more races, non-Hispanic/Latino), 104 international. Average age 32. 166 applicants, 68% accepted, 48 enrolled. In 2016, 72 master's, 13 doctorates awarded. *Degree requirements:* For master's, thesis optional; for doctorate, comprehensive exam, thesis/dissertation. *Entrance requirements:* For master's and doctorate, statement of purpose, official copies of academic transcripts, three letters of recommendation. Additional exam requirements/recommendations for international students: Required—TOEFL (minimum score 550 paper-based; 80 iBT). *Application deadline:* For fall

admission, 7/15 priority date for domestic students, 7/1 for international students; for spring admission, 11/15 priority date for domestic students, 11/1 for international students. Applications are processed on a rolling basis. Application fee: $55. Electronic applications accepted. *Expenses:* $43,380 per year; $1,170 per credit; $200 per semester part-time fees. *Financial support:* Fellowships, research assistantships, teaching assistantships, Federal Work-Study, scholarships/grants, tuition waivers (full and partial), and unspecified assistantships available. Financial award application deadline: 2/1; financial award applicants required to submit FAFSA. *Faculty research:* Rehabilitation engineering, cardiopulmonary biomechanics, geotechnical engineering, signal and image processing, fluid mechanics. *Total annual research expenditures:* $1.2 million. *Unit head:* Dr. Charles C. Nguyen, Dean, 202-319-5160, Fax: 202-319-4499, E-mail: nguyen@cua.edu. *Application contact:* Director of Graduate Admissions, 202-319-5057, Fax: 202-319-6533, E-mail: cua-admissions@cua.edu.
Website: http://engineering.cua.edu/

Central Connecticut State University, School of Graduate Studies, School of Engineering, Science and Technology, Department of Engineering, New Britain, CT 06050-4010. Offers MS. *Program availability:* Part-time, evening/weekend. *Faculty:* 3 full-time (0 women). *Students:* 1 full-time (0 women), 4 part-time (1 woman), 1 international. Average age 36. In 2016, 6 master's awarded. *Degree requirements:* For master's, thesis or alternative, special project. *Entrance requirements:* For master's, minimum undergraduate GPA of 2.7; four-year BS program in engineering technology, engineering or other programs with specific courses. Additional exam requirements/recommendations for international students: Required—TOEFL (minimum score 550 paper-based; 79 iBT). *Application deadline:* For fall admission, 6/1 for domestic students, 5/1 for international students; for spring admission, 11/1 for domestic and international students. Applications are processed on a rolling basis. Application fee: $50. Electronic applications accepted. *Expenses: Tuition, area resident:* Full-time $6497; part-time $606 per credit. Tuition, state resident: full-time $9748; part-time $622 per credit. Tuition, nonresident: full-time $18,102; part-time $622 per credit. *Required fees:* $4459; $246 per credit. *Financial support:* Application deadline: 3/1. *Unit head:* Dr. Peter Baumann, Chair, 860-832-1815, E-mail: baumannp@ccsu.edu. *Application contact:* Patricia Gardner, Associate Director of Graduate Studies, 860-832-2350, Fax: 860-832-2362.
Website: http://www.ccsu.edu/engineering/

Central Connecticut State University, School of Graduate Studies, School of Engineering, Science and Technology, Department of Technology and Engineering Education, New Britain, CT 06050-4010. Offers STEM education (MS). *Program availability:* Part-time, evening/weekend. *Faculty:* 4 full-time (1 woman). *Students:* 4 full-time (1 woman), 50 part-time (24 women); includes 1 minority (Hispanic/Latino). Average age 36. 17 applicants, 82% accepted, 10 enrolled. In 2016, 4 master's awarded. *Degree requirements:* For master's, thesis or alternative, special project. *Entrance requirements:* For master's, minimum undergraduate GPA of 2.7. Additional exam requirements/recommendations for international students: Required—TOEFL (minimum score 550 paper-based; 79 iBT). *Application deadline:* For fall admission, 6/1 for domestic students, 5/1 for international students; for spring admission, 11/1 for domestic and international students. Applications are processed on a rolling basis. Application fee: $50. Electronic applications accepted. *Expenses: Tuition, area resident:* Full-time $6497; part-time $606 per credit. Tuition, state resident: full-time $9748; part-time $622 per credit. Tuition, nonresident: full-time $18,102; part-time $622 per credit. *Required fees:* $4459; $246 per credit. *Financial support:* In 2016–17, 7 students received support. Career-related internships or fieldwork, Federal Work-Study, and scholarships/grants available. Support available to part-time students. Financial award application deadline: 3/1; financial award applicants required to submit FAFSA. *Faculty research:* Instruction, curriculum development, administration, occupational training. *Unit head:* Dr. James DeLaura, Chair, 860-832-1850, E-mail: delaura@ccsu.edu. *Application contact:* Patricia Gardner, Associate Director of Graduate Studies, 860-832-2350, Fax: 860-832-2362.
Website: http://www.ccsu.edu/teched/

Central Michigan University, College of Graduate Studies, College of Science and Technology, School of Engineering and Technology, Mount Pleasant, MI 48859. Offers industrial management and technology (MA). *Program availability:* Part-time. *Degree requirements:* For master's, thesis or alternative. Electronic applications accepted. *Faculty research:* Computer applications, manufacturing process control, mechanical engineering automation, industrial technology.

Central Washington University, Graduate Studies and Research, College of Education and Professional Studies, Department of Industrial and Engineering Technology, Ellensburg, WA 98926. Offers engineering technology (MS). *Program availability:* Part-time. *Degree requirements:* For master's, thesis or alternative. *Entrance requirements:* For master's, minimum GPA of 3.0. Additional exam requirements/recommendations for international students: Required—TOEFL (minimum score 550 paper-based; 79 iBT), IELTS (minimum score 6.5). Electronic applications accepted.

Christian Brothers University, School of Engineering, Memphis, TN 38104-5581. Offers MEM, MSEM. *Program availability:* Part-time, evening/weekend, online learning. *Degree requirements:* For master's, engineering management project. *Entrance requirements:* For master's, GRE. Additional exam requirements/recommendations for international students: Required—TOEFL.

The Citadel, The Military College of South Carolina, Citadel Graduate College, School of Engineering, Charleston, SC 29409. Offers MS, Graduate Certificate. *Program availability:* Part-time, evening/weekend. *Faculty:* 3 full-time (0 women), 6 part-time/adjunct (0 women). *Students:* 5 full-time (2 women), 98 part-time (38 women); includes 23 minority (11 Black or African American, non-Hispanic/Latino; 1 American Indian or Alaska Native, non-Hispanic/Latino; 3 Asian, non-Hispanic/Latino; 6 Hispanic/Latino; 1 Native Hawaiian or other Pacific Islander, non-Hispanic/Latino; 1 Two or more races, non-Hispanic/Latino), 1 international. 76 applicants, 96% accepted, 43 enrolled. In 2016, 35 master's, 45 other advanced degrees awarded. *Entrance requirements:* Additional exam requirements/recommendations for international students: Required—TOEFL (minimum score 550 paper-based; 79 iBT). *Application deadline:* Applications are processed on a rolling basis. Application fee: $40. Electronic applications accepted. *Expenses:* Tuition, state resident: full-time $5121; part-time $569 per credit hour. Tuition, nonresident: full-time $8613; part-time $957 per credit hour. *Required fees:* $90 per term. *Financial support:* Fellowships and unspecified assistantships available. Support available to part-time students. Financial award application deadline: 7/1; financial award applicants required to submit FAFSA. *Unit head:* Dr. Ronald W. Welch, Dean, 843-953-6588, E-mail: ronald.welch@citadel.edu. *Application contact:* Dr. Tara Hornor, Associate Provost for Planning, Assessment and Evaluation/Dean of Enrollment Management, 843-953-5089, E-mail: cgc@citadel.edu.
Website: http://www.citadel.edu/root/engineering

City College of the City University of New York, Graduate School, Grove School of Engineering, New York, NY 10031-9198. Offers ME, MIS, MS, PhD. *Program availability:* Part-time. Terminal master's awarded for partial completion of doctoral program. *Degree requirements:* For master's, thesis optional; for doctorate, one foreign language, comprehensive exam, thesis/dissertation. *Entrance requirements:* For master's, GRE General Test, minimum B average in undergraduate coursework; for

doctorate, GRE General Test, minimum GPA of 3.5. Additional exam requirements/recommendations for international students: Required—TOEFL (minimum score 500 paper-based; 61 iBT). Tuition and fees vary according to course load, degree level and program. *Faculty research:* Robotics, network systems, structures.

Clarkson University, Wallace H. Coulter School of Engineering, Potsdam, NY 13699. Offers ME, MS, PhD, Advanced Certificate. *Faculty:* 75 full-time (13 women), 31 part-time/adjunct (5 women). *Students:* 172 full-time (37 women), 111 part-time (21 women); includes 27 minority (5 Black or African American, non-Hispanic/Latino; 11 Asian, non-Hispanic/Latino; 10 Hispanic/Latino; 1 Two or more races, non-Hispanic/Latino), 97 international. *Expenses:* Tuition: Full-time $23,400; part-time $1300 per credit hour. Tuition and fees vary according to campus/location and program. *Unit head:* Dr. William Jemison, Dean of Engineering, 315-268-6446, E-mail: wjemison@clarkson.edu. *Application contact:* Dan Capogna, Graduate Admissions Contact, 518-631-9910, E-mail: graduate@clarkson.edu.

Clemson University, Graduate School, College of Education, Department of Teaching and Learning, Program in Teaching and Learning, Clemson, SC 29634. Offers science, technology, engineering, arts and mathematics education (Certificate); teaching and learning (M Ed), including early childhood, instructional coaching, science, technology, engineering, arts and mathematics. *Program availability:* Part-time, evening/weekend, online only, 100% online. *Faculty:* 24 full-time (19 women). *Students:* 19 part-time (17 women); includes 1 minority (Hispanic/Latino). Average age 32. 4 applicants, 50% accepted, 2 enrolled. In 2016, 27 master's awarded. *Entrance requirements:* For master's, GRE General Test, unofficial transcripts, teaching certificate, letters of recommendation. Additional exam requirements/recommendations for international students: Required—TOEFL (minimum score 80 iBT), IELTS (minimum score 7). *Application deadline:* Applications are processed on a rolling basis. Application fee: $80 ($90 for international students). Electronic applications accepted. *Expenses:* $394 per credit hour; $10 per credit hour information technology fee; $17 fee per session for matriculation and software; $22 fee for activities and career services for students taking over 6 credit hours. *Unit head:* Dr. Jeff Marshall, Department Head, Fax: 864-656-0311, E-mail: soedean@clemson.edu. *Application contact:* Julie Jones, Student Services Program Coordinator, 864-656-5096, E-mail: jgambre@clemson.edu.
Website: http://www.clemson.edu/education/academics/masters-specialist-programs/masters-education-teaching-learning/index.html

Clemson University, Graduate School, College of Engineering, Computing and Applied Sciences, Clemson, SC 29634. Offers M Engr, MFA, MS, PhD, Certificate. *Program availability:* Part-time, 100% online. *Faculty:* 273 full-time (55 women), 15 part-time/adjunct (4 women). *Students:* 1,165 full-time (323 women), 250 part-time (52 women); includes 91 minority (26 Black or African American, non-Hispanic/Latino; 25 Asian, non-Hispanic/Latino; 21 Hispanic/Latino; 2 Native Hawaiian or other Pacific Islander, non-Hispanic/Latino; 17 Two or more races, non-Hispanic/Latino), 853 international. Average age 27. 3,474 applicants, 23% accepted, 410 enrolled. In 2016, 460 master's, 101 doctorates, 10 other advanced degrees awarded. Terminal master's awarded for partial completion of doctoral program. *Degree requirements:* For master's, comprehensive exam (for some programs), thesis (for some programs); for doctorate, comprehensive exam (for some programs), thesis/dissertation. *Entrance requirements:* For master's and doctorate, GRE General Test, unofficial transcripts, letters of recommendation; personal statement/portfolio/writing sample (depending on program). Additional exam requirements/recommendations for international students: Required—TOEFL (minimum score 80 iBT), IELTS (minimum score 6.5). *Application deadline:* Applications are processed on a rolling basis. Application fee: $80 ($90 for international students). Electronic applications accepted. *Expenses:* $4,841 per semester full-time resident, $9,640 per semester full-time non-resident, $612 per credit hour part-time resident, $1,223 per credit hour part-time non-resident. *Financial support:* In 2016–17, 908 students received support, including 81 fellowships with partial tuition reimbursements available (averaging $10,920 per year), 428 research assistantships with partial tuition reimbursements available (averaging $19,916 per year), 227 teaching assistantships with partial tuition reimbursements available (averaging $18,618 per year); career-related internships or fieldwork and unspecified assistantships also available. *Faculty research:* Engineering, computing, engineering and science education. *Total annual research expenditures:* $35.3 million. *Unit head:* Dr. Anand Gramopadhye, Dean, 864-656-3200, E-mail: agrampo@clemson.edu. *Application contact:* Dr. Douglas Hirt, Associate Dean for Research and Graduate Studies, 864-656-3201, E-mail: hirtd@clemson.edu.
Website: http://www.clemson.edu/cecas/

Cleveland State University, College of Graduate Studies, Fenn College of Engineering, Cleveland, OH 44115. Offers MS, D Eng. *Program availability:* Part-time, evening/weekend. *Faculty:* 54 full-time (5 women), 12 part-time/adjunct (0 women). *Students:* 389 full-time (75 women), 258 part-time (53 women); includes 37 minority (13 Black or African American, non-Hispanic/Latino; 18 Asian, non-Hispanic/Latino; 5 Hispanic/Latino; 1 Two or more races, non-Hispanic/Latino), 453 international. Average age 26. 1,037 applicants, 48% accepted, 143 enrolled. In 2016, 250 master's, 9 doctorates awarded. *Degree requirements:* For master's, thesis or alternative; for doctorate, thesis/dissertation, candidacy and qualifying exams. *Entrance requirements:* For master's, GRE General Test, BS in engineering, minimum GPA of 3.0 (2.75 for students from ABET-/EAC-accredited programs from the U.S. and Canada); for doctorate, GRE General Test, MS in engineering, minimum GPA of 3.25. Additional exam requirements/recommendations for international students: Required—TOEFL (minimum score 550 paper-based; 78 iBT). *Application deadline:* For fall admission, 7/15 for domestic students, 5/15 for international students; for spring admission, 12/5 for domestic students, 11/1 for international students. Applications are processed on a rolling basis. Application fee: $30. Electronic applications accepted. *Expenses:* Tuition, state resident: full-time $9565. Tuition, nonresident: full-time $17,980. Tuition and fees vary according to program. *Financial support:* In 2016–17, 93 students received support, including 1 fellowship with full tuition reimbursement available, 120 research assistantships with tuition reimbursements available (averaging $8,694 per year), 20 teaching assistantships with tuition reimbursements available (averaging $8,082 per year); career-related internships or fieldwork, institutionally sponsored loans, scholarships/grants, tuition waivers (full and partial), and unspecified assistantships also available. Support available to part-time students. Financial award application deadline: 3/30; financial award applicants required to submit FAFSA. *Faculty research:* Structural analysis and design, dynamic system and controls, applied biomedical engineering, transportation, water resources, telecommunication, power electronics, computer engineering, industrial automation, engineering management, mechanical design, thermodynamics and fluid mechanics, material engineering, tribology. *Total annual research expenditures:* $7.2 million. *Unit head:* Dr. Paul P. Lin, Associate Dean, 216-687-2556, Fax: 216-687-9280, E-mail: p.lin@csuohio.edu. *Application contact:* Deborah L. Brown, Interim Assistant Director, Graduate Admissions, 216-523-7572, Fax: 216-687-9214, E-mail: d.l.brown@csuohio.edu.
Website: http://www.csuohio.edu/engineering/

Colorado School of Mines, Office of Graduate Studies, Golden, CO 80401. Offers ME, MIPER, MP, MS, PMS, PhD, Graduate Certificate. *Program availability:* Part-time. *Faculty:* 408 full-time (119 women), 192 part-time/adjunct (68 women). *Students:* 1,162

full-time (338 women), 159 part-time (44 women); includes 150 minority (10 Black or African American, non-Hispanic/Latino; 3 American Indian or Alaska Native, non-Hispanic/Latino; 33 Asian, non-Hispanic/Latino; 76 Hispanic/Latino; 1 Native Hawaiian or other Pacific Islander, non-Hispanic/Latino; 27 Two or more races, non-Hispanic/Latino), 409 international. Average age 28. 2,204 applicants, 44% accepted, 394 enrolled. In 2016, 388 master's, 115 doctorates awarded. *Degree requirements:* For master's, thesis (for some programs); for doctorate, comprehensive exam, thesis/dissertation. *Entrance requirements:* For master's, doctorate, and Graduate Certificate, GRE General Test. Additional exam requirements/recommendations for international students: Required—TOEFL (minimum score 550 paper-based; 79 iBT). *Application deadline:* For fall admission, 12/15 priority date for domestic and international students; for spring admission, 9/1 priority date for domestic and international students. Application fee: $50 ($70 for international students). Electronic applications accepted. *Expenses:* Tuition, state resident: full-time $15,690. Tuition, nonresident: full-time $34,020. *Required fees:* $2152. Tuition and fees vary according to course load. *Financial support:* In 2016–17, 63 fellowships with full tuition reimbursements, 486 research assistantships with full tuition reimbursements, 154 teaching assistantships with full tuition reimbursements were awarded; career-related internships or fieldwork, Federal Work-Study, institutionally sponsored loans, scholarships/grants, health care benefits, and unspecified assistantships also available. Financial award application deadline: 12/15; financial award applicants required to submit FAFSA. *Faculty research:* Energy, environment, materials, minerals, engineering systems. *Total annual research expenditures:* $51.7 million. *Unit head:* Dr. Tina Voelker, Dean of Graduate Studies, 303-273-3152, E-mail: bvoelker@mines.edu. *Application contact:* Angel Dotson, Graduate Admissions Coordinator, 303-273-3348, Fax: 303-273-3247, E-mail: grad-app@mines.edu.
Website: http://mines.edu/graduate_admissions

Colorado State University, Walter Scott, Jr. College of Engineering, Fort Collins, CO 80523-1301. Offers ME, MS, PhD. *Accreditation:* ABET. *Program availability:* Part-time, evening/weekend, 100% online, blended/hybrid learning. *Faculty:* 170 full-time (37 women), 45 part-time/adjunct (11 women). *Students:* 333 full-time (88 women), 662 part-time (148 women); includes 94 minority (11 Black or African American, non-Hispanic/Latino; 1 American Indian or Alaska Native, non-Hispanic/Latino; 35 Asian, non-Hispanic/Latino; 33 Hispanic/Latino; 14 Two or more races, non-Hispanic/Latino), 388 international. Average age 30. 875 applicants, 66% accepted, 255 enrolled. In 2016, 203 master's, 50 doctorates awarded. Terminal master's awarded for partial completion of doctoral program. *Degree requirements:* For master's, comprehensive exam (for some programs), thesis (for some programs); for doctorate, comprehensive exam, thesis/dissertation. *Entrance requirements:* For master's, GRE General Test, minimum GPA of 3.0, 3 letters of recommendation, transcripts, curriculum vitae; for doctorate, GRE General Test, minimum GPA of 3.0, transcripts, 3 letters of recommendation, statement of purpose with interests, curriculum vitae. Additional exam requirements/recommendations for international students: Required—TOEFL (minimum score 550 paper-based; 80 iBT), IELTS (minimum score 6.5). Application fee: $60 ($70 for international students). Electronic applications accepted. *Expenses:* Contact institution. *Financial support:* In 2016–17, 30 fellowships with full tuition reimbursements (averaging $45,899 per year), 234 research assistantships with tuition reimbursements (averaging $24,506 per year), 65 teaching assistantships with tuition reimbursements (averaging $16,723 per year) were awarded; scholarships/grants, traineeships, health care benefits, and unspecified assistantships also available. Financial award application deadline: 1/15; financial award applicants required to submit FAFSA. *Faculty research:* Atmospheric science; chemical and biological engineering; civil and environmental engineering; electrical and computer engineering; mechanical and biomedical engineering. *Total annual research expenditures:* $67.6 million. *Unit head:* Dr. David McLean, Dean, 970-491-3366, E-mail: david.mclean@colostate.edu. *Application contact:* Dr. Anthony Marchese, Associate Dean of Academic and Student Affairs, 970-491-6220, Fax: 970-491-3429, E-mail: anthony.marchese@colostate.edu.
Website: http://www.engr.colostate.edu/

Colorado State University–Pueblo, College of Education, Engineering and Professional Studies, Pueblo, CO 81001-4901. Offers M Ed, MS. *Program availability:* Part-time, evening/weekend. *Degree requirements:* For master's, thesis optional. *Entrance requirements:* For master's, GRE General Test. Additional exam requirements/recommendations for international students: Required—TOEFL (minimum score 500 paper-based). Electronic applications accepted. *Expenses:* Contact institution. *Faculty research:* Nanotechnology, applied operations, research transportation, decision analysis.

Columbia University, Fu Foundation School of Engineering and Applied Science, New York, NY 10027. Offers MS, Eng Sc D, PhD, MS/MBA. *Program availability:* Part-time, online learning. Terminal master's awarded for partial completion of doctoral program. *Degree requirements:* For master's, comprehensive exam (for some programs), thesis (for some programs); for doctorate, comprehensive exam (for some programs), thesis/dissertation, qualifying exam. *Entrance requirements:* For master's, GRE General Test; for doctorate, GRE General Test, GRE Subject Test (applied physics program only). Additional exam requirements/recommendations for international students: Required—TOEFL (minimum score 590 paper-based; 96 iBT), IELTS (minimum score 6.5), PTE. Electronic applications accepted.

Concordia University, School of Graduate Studies, Faculty of Engineering and Computer Science, Montréal, QC H3G 1M8, Canada. Offers M App Comp Sc, M Comp Sc, M Eng, MA Sc, PhD, Certificate, Diploma. *Degree requirements:* For doctorate, comprehensive exam, thesis/dissertation. *Expenses:* Contact institution.

Cooper Union for the Advancement of Science and Art, Albert Nerken School of Engineering, New York, NY 10003. Offers chemical engineering (ME); civil engineering (ME); electrical engineering (ME); mechanical engineering (ME). *Program availability:* Part-time. *Faculty:* 27 full-time (1 woman), 15 part-time/adjunct (2 women). *Students:* 36 full-time (5 women), 39 part-time (8 women); includes 34 minority (3 Black or African American, non-Hispanic/Latino; 16 Asian, non-Hispanic/Latino; 5 Hispanic/Latino; 10 Two or more races, non-Hispanic/Latino), 3 international. Average age 24. 59 applicants, 75% accepted, 34 enrolled. In 2016, 25 master's awarded. *Degree requirements:* For master's, thesis (for some programs). *Entrance requirements:* For master's, BE or BS in an engineering discipline; official copies of school transcripts including secondary (high school), college and university work; two letters of recommendation; resume. Additional exam requirements/recommendations for international students: Required—TOEFL (minimum score 600 paper-based; 100 iBT). *Application deadline:* For fall admission, 3/31 for domestic and international students. Application fee: $75. Electronic applications accepted. *Expenses: Tuition:* Full-time $16,055; part-time $1235 per credit. *Required fees:* $925 per semester. One-time fee: $250. Tuition and fees vary according to course load. *Financial support:* In 2016–17, 70 students received support, including 4 fellowships with tuition reimbursements available (averaging $11,000 per year); career-related internships or fieldwork, tuition waivers (full and partial), and tuition scholarships offered to exceptional students also available. Support available to part-time students. Financial award application deadline: 5/1; financial award applicants required to submit FAFSA. *Faculty research:* Civil infrastructure, imaging and sensing technology, biomedical engineering, encryption technology, process engineering. *Unit head:* Richard Stock, Acting Dean of Albert Nerken School of Engineering, 212-353-4285, E-mail: stock@cooper.edu. *Application contact:* Chabeli Lajara, Administrative Assistant, 212-353-4120, E-mail: admissions@cooper.edu.
Website: http://cooper.edu/engineering

Cornell University, Graduate School, Graduate Fields of Engineering, Ithaca, NY 14853. Offers M Eng, MPS, MS, PhD, M Eng/MBA. *Degree requirements:* For doctorate, comprehensive exam, thesis/dissertation. *Entrance requirements:* Additional exam requirements/recommendations for international students: Required—TOEFL. Electronic applications accepted.

Dalhousie University, Faculty of Engineering, Halifax, NS B3H 4R2, Canada. Offers M Eng, M Sc, MA Sc, PhD, M Eng/M Plan, MA Sc/M Plan, MBA/M Eng. *Entrance requirements:* Additional exam requirements/recommendations for international students: Required—1 of 5 approved tests: TOEFL, IELTS, CANTEST, CAEL, Michigan English Language Assessment Battery.

Dartmouth College, Thayer School of Engineering, Hanover, NH 03755. Offers M Eng, MEM, MS, PhD, MD/MS, MD/PhD. *Faculty:* 53 full-time (11 women), 9 part-time/adjunct (0 women). *Students:* 213 full-time (61 women); includes 22 minority (3 Black or African American, non-Hispanic/Latino; 14 Asian, non-Hispanic/Latino; 3 Hispanic/Latino; 2 Two or more races, non-Hispanic/Latino), 123 international. Average age 24. 765 applicants, 21% accepted, 87 enrolled. In 2016, 46 master's, 14 doctorates awarded. *Degree requirements:* For doctorate, thesis/dissertation, candidacy oral exam. *Entrance requirements:* For master's and doctorate, GRE General Test. Additional exam requirements/recommendations for international students: Required—TOEFL. *Application deadline:* For fall admission, 1/1 priority date for domestic and international students. Applications are processed on a rolling basis. Application fee: $45. Electronic applications accepted. *Expenses:* Contact institution. *Financial support:* In 2016–17, 195 students received support, including 30 fellowships with full tuition reimbursements available (averaging $26,520 per year), 77 research assistantships with full tuition reimbursements available (averaging $26,520 per year), 21 teaching assistantships with partial tuition reimbursements available (averaging $7,800 per year); career-related internships or fieldwork, institutionally sponsored loans, scholarships/grants, and tuition waivers (full and partial) also available. Financial award application deadline: 2/15; financial award applicants required to submit CSS PROFILE. *Faculty research:* Biomedical engineering, biotechnology and biochemical engineering, electrical and computer engineering, engineering physics, environmental engineering, materials science and engineering, mechanical systems engineering. *Total annual research expenditures:* $21.7 million. *Unit head:* Dr. Joseph J. Helbie, Dean, 603-646-2238, Fax: 603-646-2580, E-mail: joseph.j.helbie@dartmouth.edu. *Application contact:* Candace S. Potter, Graduate Admissions and Financial Aid Administrator, 603-646-3844, Fax: 603-646-1620, E-mail: candace.s.potter@dartmouth.edu.
Website: http://engineering.dartmouth.edu/

Drexel University, College of Engineering, Philadelphia, PA 19104-2875. Offers MS, MSEE, MSSE, PhD, Certificate. *Program availability:* Part-time, evening/weekend. *Faculty:* 151 full-time (29 women), 49 part-time/adjunct (5 women). *Students:* 436 full-time (111 women), 334 part-time (73 women); includes 128 minority (46 Black or African American, non-Hispanic/Latino; 3 American Indian or Alaska Native, non-Hispanic/Latino; 40 Asian, non-Hispanic/Latino; 25 Hispanic/Latino; 14 Two or more races, non-Hispanic/Latino), 284 international. Average age 29. In 2016, 329 master's, 54 doctorates, 12 other advanced degrees awarded. *Degree requirements:* For doctorate, thesis/dissertation. *Entrance requirements:* Additional exam requirements/recommendations for international students: Required—TOEFL. *Application deadline:* For fall admission, 8/21 for domestic students. Applications are processed on a rolling basis. Application fee: $50. Electronic applications accepted. *Expenses: Tuition:* Full-time $32,184; part-time $1192 per credit hour. *Required fees:* $280. Tuition and fees vary according to campus/location and program. *Financial support:* Research assistantships, teaching assistantships, career-related internships or fieldwork, Federal Work-Study, institutionally sponsored loans, tuition waivers (full and partial), and unspecified assistantships available. Support available to part-time students. Financial award application deadline: 2/1. *Total annual research expenditures:* $16.9 million. *Unit head:* Dr. Giuseppe Palmese, Interim Dean, 215-895-2210. *Application contact:* Director of Graduate Admissions, 215-895-6700, Fax: 215-895-5939, E-mail: enroll@drexel.edu.

Drexel University, Goodwin College of Professional Studies, School of Technology and Professional Studies, Philadelphia, PA 19104-2875. Offers construction management (MS); creativity and innovation (MS); engineering technology (MS); food science (MS); hospitality management (MS); professional studies: creativity studies (MS); professional studies: e-learning leadership (MS); professional studies: homeland security management (MS); project management (MS); property management (MS); sport management (MS). *Program availability:* Part-time, evening/weekend. *Faculty:* 37 full-time (14 women). *Students:* 13 full-time, 462 part-time; includes 133 minority (86 Black or African American, non-Hispanic/Latino; 24 Asian, non-Hispanic/Latino; 23 Hispanic/Latino). In 2016, 88 master's awarded. *Entrance requirements:* Additional exam requirements/recommendations for international students: Required—TOEFL, IELTS. *Application deadline:* For fall admission, 9/1 for domestic students; for winter admission, 12/1 for domestic students; for spring admission, 3/1 for domestic students. Applications are processed on a rolling basis. Application fee: $75. Electronic applications accepted. Application fee is waived when completed online. *Expenses: Tuition:* Full-time $32,184; part-time $1192 per credit hour. *Required fees:* $280. Tuition and fees vary according to campus/location and program. *Financial support:* Applicants required to submit FAFSA. *Unit head:* Dr. William F. Lynch, Dean, 215-895-2159, E-mail: goodwin@drexel.edu. *Application contact:* Matthew Gray, Manager, Recruitment and Enrollment, 215-895-6255, Fax: 215-895-2153, E-mail: mdg67@drexel.edu.
Website: http://drexel.edu/grad/programs/goodwin/

Duke University, Graduate School, Pratt School of Engineering, Master of Engineering Program, Durham, NC 27708-0271. Offers biomedical engineering (M Eng); civil engineering (M Eng); electrical and computer engineering (M Eng); environmental engineering (M Eng); materials science and engineering (M Eng); mechanical engineering (M Eng); photonics and optical sciences (M Eng). *Program availability:* Part-time. *Entrance requirements:* For master's, GRE General Test, resume, 3 letters of recommendation, statement of purpose, transcripts. Additional exam requirements/recommendations for international students: Required—TOEFL.

Eastern Illinois University, Graduate School, Lumpkin College of Business and Applied Sciences, School of Technology, Charleston, IL 61920. Offers computer technology (Certificate); quality systems (Certificate); technology (MS); technology security (Certificate); work performance improvement (Certificate); MS/MBA; MS/MS. *Program availability:* Part-time, evening/weekend.

Eastern Michigan University, Graduate School, College of Technology, School of Engineering Technology, Program in Computer Aided Engineering, Ypsilanti, MI 48197. Offers CAD/CAM (MS); computer-aided technology (MS). *Program availability:* Part-time, evening/weekend, online learning. *Students:* 9 full-time (4 women), 8 part-time (1 woman); includes 3 minority (1 Black or African American, non-Hispanic/Latino; 2 Asian, non-Hispanic/Latino), 7 international. Average age 32. 24 applicants, 50% accepted, 2 enrolled. In 2016, 10 master's awarded. *Entrance requirements:* Additional exam requirements/recommendations for international students: Required—TOEFL. *Application deadline:* Applications are processed on a rolling basis. Application fee: $45. *Financial support:* Fellowships, research assistantships with full tuition reimbursements, teaching assistantships with full tuition reimbursements, and tuition waivers (partial) available. Financial award applicants required to submit FAFSA. *Application contact:* Dr. Tony Shay, Program Coordinator, 734-487-2040, Fax: 734-487-8755, E-mail: tshay@emich.edu.

École Polytechnique de Montréal, Graduate Programs, Montréal, QC H3C 3A7, Canada. Offers M Eng, M Sc A, PhD, DESS. *Program availability:* Part-time, evening/weekend. Terminal master's awarded for partial completion of doctoral program. *Degree requirements:* For master's, one foreign language, thesis; for doctorate, one foreign language, thesis/dissertation. *Entrance requirements:* For master's, minimum GPA of 2.75; for doctorate, minimum GPA of 3.0. Electronic applications accepted. *Faculty research:* Chemical engineering, environmental engineering, microelectronics and communications, biomedical engineering, engineering physics.

Fairfield University, School of Engineering, Fairfield, CT 06824. Offers database management (CAS); electrical and computer engineering (MS); information security (CAS); management of technology (MS); mechanical engineering (MS); network technology (CAS); software engineering (MS); Web application development (CAS). *Program availability:* Part-time, evening/weekend. *Faculty:* 7 full-time (1 woman), 15 part-time/adjunct (2 women). *Students:* 104 full-time (31 women), 56 part-time (15 women); includes 17 minority (8 Black or African American, non-Hispanic/Latino; 5 Asian, non-Hispanic/Latino; 4 Hispanic/Latino), 108 international. Average age 28. 193 applicants, 63% accepted, 20 enrolled. In 2016, 173 master's awarded. *Degree requirements:* For master's, capstone course. *Entrance requirements:* For master's, resume, 2 recommendations. Additional exam requirements/recommendations for international students: Required—TOEFL (minimum score 550 paper-based; 80 iBT) or IELTS (minimum score 6.5). *Application deadline:* For fall admission, 5/15 for international students; for spring admission, 10/15 for international students. Applications are processed on a rolling basis. Application fee: $60. Electronic applications accepted. *Expenses:* $800 per credit hour. *Financial support:* In 2016–17, 27 students received support. Scholarships/grants and unspecified assistantships available. Financial award applicants required to submit FAFSA. *Faculty research:* Artificial intelligence and information visualization, natural language processing, thermofluids, microwaves and electromagnetics, micro-/nano-manufacturing. *Unit head:* Dr. Bruce Berdanier, Dean, 203-254-4147, Fax: 203-254-4013, E-mail: bberdanier@fairfield.edu. *Application contact:* Marianne Gumpper, Director of Graduate and Continuing Studies Admission, 203-254-4184, Fax: 203-254-4073, E-mail: gradadmis@fairfield.edu.
Website: http://www.fairfield.edu/soe

Fairleigh Dickinson University, Metropolitan Campus, University College: Arts, Sciences, and Professional Studies, School of Computer Sciences and Engineering, Teaneck, NJ 07666-1914. Offers computer engineering (MS); computer science (MS); e-commerce (MS); electrical engineering (MSEE); management information systems (MS); mathematical foundation (MS).

Florida Agricultural and Mechanical University, Division of Graduate Studies, Research, and Continuing Education, FAMU-FSU College of Engineering, Tallahassee, FL 32307-3200. Offers M Eng, MS, PhD. College administered jointly by Florida State University. *Entrance requirements:* For master's, GRE General Test, minimum GPA of 3.0. Additional exam requirements/recommendations for international students: Required—TOEFL (minimum score 550 paper-based).

Florida Atlantic University, College of Engineering and Computer Science, Boca Raton, FL 33431-0991. Offers MS, PhD. *Program availability:* Part-time, evening/weekend, online learning. *Faculty:* 74 full-time (8 women), 4 part-time/adjunct (0 women). *Students:* 182 full-time (46 women), 200 part-time (39 women); includes 110 minority (20 Black or African American, non-Hispanic/Latino; 17 Asian, non-Hispanic/Latino; 65 Hispanic/Latino; 8 Two or more races, non-Hispanic/Latino), 135 international. Average age 31. 355 applicants, 56% accepted, 148 enrolled. In 2016, 79 master's, 12 doctorates awarded. Terminal master's awarded for partial completion of doctoral program. *Degree requirements:* For master's, thesis optional; for doctorate, thesis/dissertation, qualifying exam. *Entrance requirements:* For master's, GRE General Test, minimum GPA of 3.0; for doctorate, GRE General Test. Additional exam requirements/recommendations for international students: Required—TOEFL (minimum score 500 paper-based; 61 iBT), IELTS (minimum score 6). *Application deadline:* For fall admission, 7/1 for domestic students, 2/15 for international students; for spring admission, 11/1 for domestic students, 7/15 for international students. Applications are processed on a rolling basis. Application fee: $30. *Expenses:* Tuition, state resident: full-time $7392; part-time $369.82 per credit hour. Tuition, nonresident: full-time $19,432; part-time $1024.81 per credit hour. *Financial support:* Fellowships, research assistantships with partial tuition reimbursements, teaching assistantships with partial tuition reimbursements, career-related internships or fieldwork, Federal Work-Study, and unspecified assistantships available. Support available to part-time students. Financial award applicants required to submit FAFSA. *Faculty research:* Automated underwater vehicles, communication systems, computer networks, materials, neural networks. *Unit head:* Mohammad Ilyas, 561-297-3454, E-mail: ilyas@fau.edu.
Website: http://www.eng.fau.edu/

Florida Institute of Technology, College of Engineering, Melbourne, FL 32901-6975. Offers MS, PhD. *Program availability:* Part-time. *Faculty:* 94 full-time (6 women), 19 part-time/adjunct (1 woman). *Students:* 574 full-time (147 women), 313 part-time (58 women); includes 83 minority (20 Black or African American, non-Hispanic/Latino; 21 Asian, non-Hispanic/Latino; 36 Hispanic/Latino; 6 Two or more races, non-Hispanic/Latino), 571 international. Average age 28. 2,952 applicants, 42% accepted, 252 enrolled. In 2016, 412 master's, 25 doctorates awarded. Terminal master's awarded for partial completion of doctoral program. *Degree requirements:* For master's, comprehensive exam (for some programs), thesis (for some programs), thesis or final exam; for doctorate, thesis/dissertation. *Entrance requirements:* For master's, GRE, minimum GPA of 3.0, 3 letters of recommendation, resume, statement of objectives; for doctorate, GRE, minimum GPA of 3.2, 3 letters of recommendation, resume, statement of objectives. Additional exam requirements/recommendations for international students: Required—TOEFL (minimum score 550 paper-based; 79 iBT). *Application deadline:* For fall admission, 4/1 for international students; for spring admission, 9/30 for international students. Applications are processed on a rolling basis. Electronic applications accepted. *Expenses: Tuition:* Full-time $22,338; part-time $1241 per credit hour. *Required fees:* $250. Tuition and fees vary according to degree level, campus/location and program. *Financial support:* In 2016–17, 74 research assistantships with partial tuition reimbursements, 65 teaching assistantships with partial tuition reimbursements were awarded; career-related internships or fieldwork, institutionally sponsored loans, unspecified assistantships, and tuition remissions also available. Support available to part-time students. Financial award application deadline: 3/1; financial award applicants required to submit FAFSA. *Faculty research:* Electrical and computer science and engineering; aerospace, chemical, civil, mechanical, and ocean engineering; environmental science and oceanography. *Unit head:* Dr. Martin Glicksman, Dean, 321-674-8020, Fax: 321-674-7270, E-mail: coe@fit.edu. *Application contact:* Cheryl A. Brown, Associate Director of Graduate Admissions, 321-674-7581, Fax: 321-723-9468, E-mail: cbrown@fit.edu.
Website: http://coe.fit.edu

Florida International University, College of Engineering and Computing, Miami, FL 33175. Offers MS, PMS, PhD. *Program availability:* Part-time, evening/weekend, online learning. *Faculty:* 129 full-time (24 women), 61 part-time/adjunct (7 women). *Students:* 560 full-time (155 women), 324 part-time (69 women); includes 369 minority (57 Black or African American, non-Hispanic/Latino; 2 American Indian or Alaska Native, non-Hispanic/Latino; 22 Asian, non-Hispanic/Latino; 280 Hispanic/Latino; 8 Two or more races, non-Hispanic/Latino), 430 international. Average age 29. 1,247 applicants, 47% accepted, 226 enrolled. In 2016, 322 master's, 45 doctorates awarded. Terminal master's awarded for partial completion of doctoral program. *Degree requirements:* For master's, thesis (for some programs); for doctorate, comprehensive exam, thesis/dissertation. *Entrance requirements:* For master's, GRE (depending on program), minimum GPA of 3.0; for doctorate, GRE General Test, minimum GPA of 3.0. Additional exam requirements/recommendations for international students: Required—TOEFL (minimum score 550 paper-based; 80 iBT). *Application deadline:* For fall admission, 6/1 for domestic students, 4/1 for international students; for spring admission, 10/1 for domestic students, 9/1 for international students. Applications are processed on a rolling basis. Application fee: $30. Electronic applications accepted. *Expenses:* Tuition, state resident: full-time $8912; part-time $446 per credit hour. Tuition, nonresident: full-time $21,393; part-time $992 per credit hour. *Required fees:* $2185; $195 per semester. Tuition and fees vary according to program. *Financial support:* Career-related internships or fieldwork, Federal Work-Study, institutionally sponsored loans, scholarships/grants, and unspecified assistantships available. Financial award application deadline: 3/1; financial award applicants required to submit FAFSA. *Faculty research:* Databases, informatics, computing systems, software engineering, security, biosensors, imaging, tissue engineering, biomaterials and bio nanotechnology, transportation, wind engineering, hydrology, environmental engineering, engineering management, sustainability and green construction, risk management and decision systems, infrastructure systems, digital signal processing, power systems, Nano photonics, embedded systems, image processing, nanotechnology. *Unit head:* Dr. John Volakis, Dean, 305-348-0273, Fax: 305-348-0127, E-mail: grad_eng@fiu.edu. *Application contact:* Sara-Michelle Lemus, Engineering Admissions Officer, 305-348-1890, E-mail: grad_eng@fiu.edu.

Florida State University, The Graduate School, FAMU-FSU College of Engineering, Tallahassee, FL 32310-6046. Offers M Eng, MS, PhD. *Program availability:* Part-time. *Faculty:* 97 full-time (12 women), 10 part-time/adjunct (3 women). *Students:* 329 full-time (66 women); includes 57 minority (32 Black or African American, non-Hispanic/Latino; 1 American Indian or Alaska Native, non-Hispanic/Latino; 7 Asian, non-Hispanic/Latino; 12 Hispanic/Latino; 5 Two or more races, non-Hispanic/Latino), 187 international. Average age 25. 484 applicants, 46% accepted, 89 enrolled. In 2016, 103 master's, 23 doctorates awarded. *Degree requirements:* For master's, comprehensive exam (for some programs), thesis (for some programs); for doctorate, thesis/dissertation, preliminary exam, qualifying exam. *Entrance requirements:* For master's and doctorate, GRE General Test. Additional exam requirements/recommendations for international students: Required—TOEFL (minimum score 550 paper-based; 80 iBT). *Application deadline:* For fall admission, 3/1 for domestic and international students; for spring admission, 11/1 for domestic and international students. Applications are processed on a rolling basis. Application fee: $30. Electronic applications accepted. *Expenses:* Tuition, state resident: full-time $7263; part-time $403.51 per credit hour. Tuition, nonresident: full-time $18,087; part-time $1004.85 per credit hour. *Required fees:* $1365; $75.81 per credit hour. $20 per semester. Tuition and fees vary according to campus/location. *Financial support:* In 2016–17, 202 students received support, including 20 fellowships with full tuition reimbursements available, 123 research assistantships with full tuition reimbursements available, 79 teaching assistantships with full tuition reimbursements available; career-related internships or fieldwork, scholarships/grants, tuition waivers (full), and unspecified assistantships also available. Financial award application deadline: 1/15; financial award applicants required to submit FAFSA. *Faculty research:* Advanced digital signal processing architecture, composite materials, electrochemical engineering, nanomaterial processing, polymer blends. *Total annual research expenditures:* $16.8 million. *Unit head:* Dr. John Murray Gibson, Dean/Professor, 850-410-6161, Fax: 850-410-6546, E-mail: dean@eng.fsu.edu. *Application contact:* Frederika Manciagli, Director, Student Services, 850-410-6361, E-mail: manciagl@eng.famu.fsu.edu.
Website: http://www.eng.fsu.edu/

George Mason University, Volgenau School of Engineering, Fairfax, VA 22030. Offers M Eng, MS, PhD, Certificate. *Program availability:* Part-time, evening/weekend, online learning. *Faculty:* 196 full-time (50 women), 175 part-time/adjunct (20 women). *Students:* 814 full-time (252 women), 943 part-time (233 women); includes 417 minority (85 Black or African American, non-Hispanic/Latino; 224 Asian, non-Hispanic/Latino; 75 Hispanic/Latino; 4 Native Hawaiian or other Pacific Islander, non-Hispanic/Latino; 29 Two or more races, non-Hispanic/Latino), 701 international. Average age 30. 1,661 applicants, 74% accepted, 520 enrolled. In 2016, 484 master's, 38 doctorates, 106 other advanced degrees awarded. *Degree requirements:* For master's, thesis optional; for doctorate, thesis/dissertation, comprehensive oral and written exams. *Entrance requirements:* For master's, minimum GPA of 3.0 in last 60 hours of course work; for doctorate, GRE General Test, minimum graduate GPA of 3.5. Additional exam requirements/recommendations for international students: Required—TOEFL (minimum score 575 paper-based; 88 iBT), IELTS (minimum score 6.5), PTE (minimum score 59). Application fee: $75 ($80 for international students). Electronic applications accepted. *Expenses:* Contact institution. *Financial support:* In 2016–17, 285 students received support, including 8 fellowships (averaging $9,779 per year), 107 research assistantships with tuition reimbursements available (averaging $18,402 per year), 177 teaching assistantships with tuition reimbursements available (averaging $14,732 per year); career-related internships or fieldwork, Federal Work-Study, scholarships/grants, unspecified assistantships, and health care benefits (for full-time research or teaching assistantship recipients) also available. Support available to part-time students. Financial award application deadline: 3/1; financial award applicants required to submit FAFSA. *Faculty research:* Systems management, quality assurance, decision support systems, cognitive ergonomics. *Total annual research expenditures:* $16.8 million. *Unit head:* Kenneth S. Ball, Dean, 703-993-1498, Fax: 703-993-1734, E-mail: vsdean@gmu.edu. *Application contact:* Suddaf Ismail, Director, Graduate Admissions and Recruitment, 703-993-9115, Fax: 703-993-1242, E-mail: sismail@gmu.edu.
Website: http://volgenau.gmu.edu

The George Washington University, School of Engineering and Applied Science, Washington, DC 20052. Offers MS, D Sc, PhD, App Sc, Engr, Graduate Certificate. *Program availability:* Part-time, evening/weekend. *Faculty:* 91 full-time (18 women). *Students:* 758 full-time (191 women), 1,081 part-time (321 women); includes 409 minority (202 Black or African American, non-Hispanic/Latino; 2 American Indian or Alaska Native, non-Hispanic/Latino; 132 Asian, non-Hispanic/Latino; 53 Hispanic/Latino; 5 Native Hawaiian or other Pacific Islander, non-Hispanic/Latino; 15 Two or more races, non-Hispanic/Latino), 812 international. Average age 32. 2,657 applicants, 74%

accepted, 613 enrolled. In 2016, 449 master's, 69 doctorates, 31 other advanced degrees awarded. *Degree requirements:* For master's, thesis optional; for doctorate, thesis/dissertation, qualifying exam. *Entrance requirements:* For master's, appropriate bachelor's degree; for doctorate, GRE (if highest earned degree is BS), appropriate bachelor's or master's degree; for other advanced degree, appropriate master's degree. Additional exam requirements/recommendations for international students: Required—TOEFL or The George Washington University English as a Foreign Language Test. *Application deadline:* For fall admission, 3/1 for domestic students; for spring admission, 10/1 for domestic students. Applications are processed on a rolling basis. Application fee: $75. *Financial support:* In 2016–17, 216 students received support. Fellowships with tuition reimbursements available, research assistantships with tuition reimbursements available, teaching assistantships with tuition reimbursements available, career-related internships or fieldwork, Federal Work-Study, institutionally sponsored loans, and tuition waivers (full and partial) available. Financial award application deadline: 3/1; financial award applicants required to submit FAFSA. *Faculty research:* Fatigue fracture and structural reliability, computer-integrated manufacturing, materials engineering, artificial intelligence and expert systems, quality assurance. *Total annual research expenditures:* $6.3 million. *Unit head:* David S. Dolling, Dean, 202-994-6080, E-mail: dolling@gwu.edu. *Application contact:* Adina Lav, Marketing, Recruiting and Admissions, 202-994-5827, Fax: 202-994-0909, E-mail: engineering@gwu.edu.
Website: http://www.seas.gwu.edu/

Georgia Institute of Technology, Graduate Studies, College of Engineering, Atlanta, GA 30332-0001. Offers MS, MSMP, MSNE, PhD, MD/PhD. *Program availability:* Part-time, online learning. Terminal master's awarded for partial completion of doctoral program. *Degree requirements:* For doctorate, thesis/dissertation. *Entrance requirements:* For master's and doctorate, GRE. Additional exam requirements/recommendations for international students: Required—TOEFL (minimum score 550 paper-based; 79 iBT). Electronic applications accepted.

Georgia Southern University, Jack N. Averitt College of Graduate Studies, Allen E. Paulson College of Engineering and Information Technology, Statesboro, GA 30458. Offers MS, MSAE, Graduate Certificate. *Program availability:* Part-time, online learning. *Faculty:* 54 full-time (5 women), 1 part-time/adjunct (0 women). *Students:* 81 full-time (15 women), 61 part-time (12 women); includes 46 minority (34 Black or African American, non-Hispanic/Latino; 5 Asian, non-Hispanic/Latino; 6 Hispanic/Latino; 1 Two or more races, non-Hispanic/Latino), 42 international. Average age 29. 146 applicants, 77% accepted, 51 enrolled. In 2016, 30 master's awarded. *Degree requirements:* For master's, comprehensive exam, thesis (for some programs). *Entrance requirements:* For master's, GRE, undergraduate major or equivalent in proposed study area. Additional exam requirements/recommendations for international students: Required—TOEFL (minimum score 550 paper-based; 80 iBT), IELTS (minimum score 6). Application fee: $50. *Expenses:* Tuition, state resident: full-time $7236; part-time $277 per semester hour. Tuition, nonresident: full-time $27,118; part-time $1105 per semester hour. *Required fees:* $2092. *Financial support:* In 2016–17, 8 students received support, including 3 research assistantships with full tuition reimbursements available (averaging $7,750 per year), 4 teaching assistantships with full tuition reimbursements available (averaging $7,750 per year); Federal Work-Study, scholarships/grants, tuition waivers (full), and unspecified assistantships also available. Financial award applicants required to submit FAFSA. *Faculty research:* Electromagnetics, biomechatronics, cyber physical systems, big data, nanocomposite material science, renewable energy and engines, robotics. *Total annual research expenditures:* $178,285. *Unit head:* Dr. Mohammad S. Davoud, Dean, 912-478-8046, E-mail: mdavoud@georgiasouthern.edu.
Website: http://ceit.georgiasouthern.edu/

Gonzaga University, School of Engineering and Applied Science, Spokane, WA 99258. Offers transmission and distribution engineering (M Eng, Certificate). *Program availability:* Online only, 100% online. *Faculty:* 1 full-time (0 women), 4 part-time/adjunct (0 women). *Students:* 1 full-time (0 women), 17 part-time (1 woman); includes 3 minority (all Hispanic/Latino), 4 international. Average age 41. In 2016, 9 master's awarded. *Degree requirements:* For master's, project. *Entrance requirements:* For master's, GRE, letter of intent, two letters of recommendation, transcripts, resume/curriculum vitae. Application fee: $50. *Expenses:* $950 per credit. *Financial support:* Available to part-time students. Applicants required to submit FAFSA. *Unit head:* Dr. Stephen E. Silliman, Dean, 509-313-3522, E-mail: silliman@gonzaga.edu. *Application contact:* Jilliene McKinstry, Assistant Director, 509-313-5701, E-mail: mckinstry@gonzaga.edu.
Website: http://www.gonzaga.edu/Academics/Colleges-and-Schools/School-of-Engineering-and-Applied-Science

The Graduate Center, City University of New York, Graduate Studies, Program in Engineering, New York, NY 10016-4039. Offers biomedical engineering (PhD); chemical engineering (PhD); civil engineering (PhD); electrical engineering (PhD); mechanical engineering (PhD). *Degree requirements:* For doctorate, thesis/dissertation. *Entrance requirements:* For doctorate, GRE General Test. Additional exam requirements/recommendations for international students: Required—TOEFL. Electronic applications accepted.

Grand Valley State University, Padnos College of Engineering and Computing, School of Engineering, Allendale, MI 49401-9403. Offers electrical and computer engineering (MSE); manufacturing operations (MSE); mechanical engineering (MSE); product design and manufacturing engineering (MSE). *Program availability:* Part-time, evening/weekend. *Faculty:* 16 full-time (3 women). *Students:* 29 full-time (8 women), 38 part-time (5 women); includes 5 minority (2 Black or African American, non-Hispanic/Latino; 1 Asian, non-Hispanic/Latino; 2 Hispanic/Latino), 37 international. Average age 26. 129 applicants, 58% accepted, 23 enrolled. In 2016, 24 master's awarded. *Degree requirements:* For master's, project or thesis. *Entrance requirements:* For master's, engineering degree, minimum GPA of 3.0, resume, 3 confidential letters of recommendation, 1-2 page essay, base of underlying relevant knowledge/evidence from academic records or relevant wok experience. Additional exam requirements/recommendations for international students: Required—TOEFL (minimum score 80 iBT) or IELTS (6.5). *Application deadline:* Applications are processed on a rolling basis. Application fee: $30. Electronic applications accepted. *Expenses:* $661 per credit hour. *Financial support:* In 2016–17, 32 students received support, including 8 fellowships; career-related internships or fieldwork, Federal Work-Study, institutionally sponsored loans, scholarships/grants, and unspecified assistantships also available. *Faculty research:* Digital signal processing, computer aided design, computer aided manufacturing, manufacturing simulation, biomechanics, product design. *Total annual research expenditures:* $300,000. *Unit head:* Dr. Wael Mokhtar, Director, 616-331-6015, Fax: 616-331-7215, E-mail: mokhtarw@gvsu.edu. *Application contact:* Dr. Shabbir Choudhuri, Graduate Program Director, 616-331-6845, Fax: 616-331-7215, E-mail: choudhus@gvsu.edu.
Website: http://www.engineer.gvsu.edu/

Grantham University, College of Engineering and Computer Science, Lenexa, KS 66219. Offers information management (MS), including project management; information technology (MS). *Program availability:* Part-time, online only, 100% online. *Faculty:* 12 part-time/adjunct. *Students:* 15 full-time (7 women), 244 part-time (56 women); includes 114 minority (81 Black or African American, non-Hispanic/Latino; 4 American Indian or Alaska Native, non-Hispanic/Latino; 8 Asian, non-Hispanic/Latino; 12 Hispanic/Latino; 9 Two or more races, non-Hispanic/Latino). Average age 40. 293 applicants, 96% accepted, 260 enrolled. In 2016, 78 master's awarded. *Degree requirements:* For master's, comprehensive exam (for information management); capstone (for information technology). *Entrance requirements:* For master's, baccalaureate or master's degree with minimum cumulative GPA of 2.5 from institution accredited by agency recognized by U.S. Department of Education or foreign equivalent. Additional exam requirements/recommendations for international students: Required—PTE (minimum score 50), TOEFL (minimum score 530 paper-based, 71 iBT) or IELTS (minimum score 6.5). *Application deadline:* Applications are processed on a rolling basis. Electronic applications accepted. *Expenses:* $325 per credit hour, $45 per 8-week term technology fee. *Financial support:* Scholarships/grants available. Financial award applicants required to submit FAFSA. *Unit head:* Dr. Nancy Miller, Dean of the College of Engineering and Computer Sciences, 913-309-4738, Fax: 855-681-5201, E-mail: nmiller@grantham.edu. *Application contact:* Jared Parlette, Vice President of Student Enrollment, 888-947-2684, Fax: 866-908-2360, E-mail: admissions@grantham.edu.
Website: http://www.grantham.edu/engineering-and-computer-science/

Harvard University, Graduate School of Arts and Sciences, Harvard John A. Paulson School of Engineering and Applied Sciences, Cambridge, MA 02138. Offers applied mathematics (PhD); applied physics (PhD); computational science and engineering (ME, SM); computer science (PhD); design engineering (MDE); engineering science (ME), including electrical engineering (ME, SM, PhD); engineering sciences (SM, PhD), including bioengineering (PhD), electrical engineering (ME, SM, PhD), environmental science and engineering (PhD), materials science and mechanical engineering (PhD). MDE offered in collaboration with Graduate School of Design. *Program availability:* Part-time. *Faculty:* 80 full-time (13 women), 47 part-time/adjunct (10 women). *Students:* 459 full-time (135 women), 19 part-time (7 women); includes 79 minority (2 Black or African American, non-Hispanic/Latino; 49 Asian, non-Hispanic/Latino; 15 Hispanic/Latino; 1 Native Hawaiian or other Pacific Islander, non-Hispanic/Latino; 12 Two or more races, non-Hispanic/Latino), 233 international. Average age 27. 2,486 applicants, 11% accepted, 126 enrolled. In 2016, 37 master's, 48 doctorates awarded. Terminal master's awarded for partial completion of doctoral program. *Degree requirements:* For master's, thesis (for ME); for doctorate, comprehensive exam, thesis/dissertation. *Entrance requirements:* For master's and doctorate, GRE General Test, GRE Subject Test (recommended), 3 letters of recommendation. Additional exam requirements/recommendations for international students: Required—TOEFL (minimum score 80 iBT). *Application deadline:* For fall admission, 12/15 priority date for domestic and international students. Application fee: $105. Electronic applications accepted. *Expenses:* $43,296 full-time tuition, $3,718 fees. *Financial support:* In 2016–17, 394 students received support, including 86 fellowships with full tuition reimbursements available (averaging $26,424 per year), 258 research assistantships with tuition reimbursements available (averaging $35,232 per year), 106 teaching assistantships with tuition reimbursements available (averaging $6,313 per year); health care benefits also available. *Faculty research:* Applied mathematics, applied physics, computer science and electrical engineering, environmental engineering, mechanical and biomedical engineering. *Total annual research expenditures:* $50.1 million. *Unit head:* Francis J. Doyle, III, Dean, 617-495-5829, Fax: 617-495-5264, E-mail: dean@seas.harvard.edu. *Application contact:* Office of Admissions and Financial Aid, 617-495-5315, E-mail: admissions@seas.harvard.edu.
Website: http://www.seas.harvard.edu/

Hofstra University, School of Engineering and Applied Science, Hempstead, NY 11549. Offers computer science (MS), including cybersecurity, Web engineering. *Program availability:* Part-time, evening/weekend, blended/hybrid learning. *Faculty:* 10 full-time (3 women), 6 part-time/adjunct (1 woman). *Students:* 34 full-time (8 women), 20 part-time (5 women); includes 13 minority (1 American Indian or Alaska Native, non-Hispanic/Latino; 6 Asian, non-Hispanic/Latino; 4 Hispanic/Latino; 1 Native Hawaiian or other Pacific Islander, non-Hispanic/Latino; 1 Two or more races, non-Hispanic/Latino), 20 international. Average age 30. 48 applicants, 90% accepted, 15 enrolled. In 2016, 12 master's awarded. *Degree requirements:* For master's, thesis optional, 30 credits, minimum GPA of 3.0. *Entrance requirements:* For master's, GRE, minimum GPA of 3.0. Additional exam requirements/recommendations for international students: Required—TOEFL (minimum score 550 paper-based; 80 iBT). *Application deadline:* Applications are processed on a rolling basis. Application fee: $75. Electronic applications accepted. *Expenses: Tuition:* Full-time $1240. *Required fees:* $970. Tuition and fees vary according to program. *Financial support:* In 2016–17, 24 students received support, including 6 fellowships with full and partial tuition reimbursements available (averaging $2,647 per year); research assistantships with full and partial tuition reimbursements available, career-related internships or fieldwork, Federal Work-Study, institutionally sponsored loans, scholarships/grants, tuition waivers (full and partial), and unspecified assistantships also available. Support available to part-time students. Financial award applicants required to submit FAFSA. *Faculty research:* Data mining; system and network security; cell and tissue engineering; experimental fluid mechanics; stem education. *Total annual research expenditures:* $1.5 million. *Unit head:* Dr. Sina Rabbany, Dean, 516-463-6672, E-mail: sina.y.rabbany@hofstra.edu. *Application contact:* Sunil Samuel, Assistant Vice President of Admissions, 516-463-4723, Fax: 516-463-4664, E-mail: graduateadmission@hofstra.edu.
Website: http://www.hofstra.edu/academics/colleges/seas/

Howard University, College of Engineering, Architecture, and Computer Sciences, School of Engineering and Computer Science, Washington, DC 20059-0002. Offers M Eng, MCS, MS, PhD. *Program availability:* Part-time. Terminal master's awarded for partial completion of doctoral program. *Degree requirements:* For doctorate, one foreign language, thesis/dissertation, preliminary exam. *Entrance requirements:* For master's and doctorate, GRE General Test, minimum GPA of 3.0. Additional exam requirements/recommendations for international students: Required—TOEFL. Electronic applications accepted. *Faculty research:* Environmental engineering, solid-state electronics, dynamics and control of large flexible space structures, power systems, reaction kinetics.

Idaho State University, Office of Graduate Studies, College of Science and Engineering, Pocatello, ID 83209-8060. Offers MA, MNS, MS, DA, PhD, Postbaccalaureate Certificate. *Accreditation:* ABET. *Program availability:* Part-time. *Degree requirements:* For master's, comprehensive exam (for some programs), thesis, thesis project, 2 semesters of seminar; for doctorate, comprehensive exam, thesis/dissertation, oral presentation and defense of research, oral examination; for Postbaccalaureate Certificate, comprehensive exam (for some programs), thesis optional, oral exam or thesis defense. *Entrance requirements:* For master's, GRE General Test, minimum GPA of 3.0 in upper-division undergraduate classes; for doctorate, GRE General Test, master's degree in engineering or physics, 1-page statement of research interests, resume, 3 letters of reference, 1-page statement of career interests; for Postbaccalaureate Certificate, GRE (if GPA between 2.0 and 3.0), bachelor's degree, minimum GPA of 3.0 in upper-division courses. Additional exam requirements/recommendations for international students: Required—TOEFL (minimum score 550 paper-based; 80 iBT). Electronic applications accepted. *Faculty research:* Nuclear engineering, biomedical engineering, robotics, measurement and control, structural systems.

Illinois Institute of Technology, Graduate College, Armour College of Engineering, Chicago, IL 60616. Offers M Arch E, M Env E, M Geoenv E, M Trans E, MAS, MCEM, MGE, MPW, MS, MSE, PhD, MS/MAS, MS/MS. *Program availability:* Part-time, evening/weekend, online learning. Terminal master's awarded for partial completion of doctoral program. *Degree requirements:* For master's, comprehensive exam (for some programs), thesis (for some programs); for doctorate, comprehensive exam, thesis/dissertation. *Entrance requirements:* For master's and doctorate, GRE General Test, minimum undergraduate GPA of 3.0. Additional exam requirements/recommendations for international students: Required—TOEFL (minimum score 550 paper-based; 80 iBT); Recommended—IELTS (minimum score 5.5). Electronic applications accepted.

Indiana State University, College of Graduate and Professional Studies, College of Technology, Terre Haute, IN 47809. Offers MS, MA/MS. *Entrance requirements:* For master's, bachelor's degree in industrial technology or related field. Additional exam requirements/recommendations for international students: Required—TOEFL. Electronic applications accepted.

Indiana University–Purdue University Fort Wayne, College of Engineering, Technology, and Computer Science, Fort Wayne, IN 46805-1499. Offers MS, MSE, Certificate. *Program availability:* Part-time. *Entrance requirements:* For master's, GRE General Test, minimum GPA of 3.0. Additional exam requirements/recommendations for international students: Required—TOEFL (minimum score 550 paper-based; 79 iBT); Recommended—TWE. Electronic applications accepted. *Faculty research:* Software-defined radios, embedded system software, wireless cloud architecture.

Instituto Tecnologico de Santo Domingo, Graduate School, Area of Engineering, Santo Domingo, Dominican Republic. Offers construction administration (MS, Certificate); data telecommunications (M Eng, MS, Certificate); industrial engineering (M Eng, Certificate); industrial management (M Mgmt); information technology (Certificate); maintenance engineering (M Eng); occupational hazard prevention (M Mgmt); production management (Certificate); quantitative methods (Certificate); sanitary and environmental engineering (M Eng); structural engineering (M Eng); systems engineering and electronic data processing (Certificate); transportation (Certificate).

Instituto Tecnológico y de Estudios Superiores de Monterrey, Campus Ciudad Obregón, Program in Engineering, Ciudad Obregón, Mexico. Offers ME.

Instituto Tecnológico y de Estudios Superiores de Monterrey, Campus Monterrey, Graduate and Research Division, Programs in Engineering, Monterrey, Mexico. Offers applied statistics (M Eng); artificial intelligence (PhD); automation engineering (M Eng); chemical engineering (M Eng); civil engineering (M Eng); electrical engineering (M Eng); electronic engineering (M Eng); environmental engineering (M Eng); industrial engineering (M Eng, PhD); manufacturing engineering (M Eng); mechanical engineering (M Eng); systems and quality engineering (M Eng). M Eng program offered jointly with University of Waterloo; PhD in industrial engineering with Texas A&M University. *Program availability:* Part-time, evening/weekend. Terminal master's awarded for partial completion of doctoral program. *Degree requirements:* For master's, one foreign language, thesis; for doctorate, one foreign language, thesis/dissertation. *Entrance requirements:* For master's, EXADEP; for doctorate, GRE, master's degree in related field. Additional exam requirements/recommendations for international students: Required—TOEFL. *Faculty research:* Flexible manufacturing cells, materials, statistical methods, environmental prevention, control and evaluation.

James Madison University, The Graduate School, College of Integrated Science and Engineering, Harrisonburg, VA 22807. Offers MS. *Accreditation:* AOTA. *Program availability:* Part-time, evening/weekend, 100% online, blended/hybrid learning, study abroad. *Faculty:* 52 full-time (14 women), 4 part-time/adjunct (0 women). *Students:* 24 full-time (14 women), 23 part-time (5 women); includes 9 minority (4 Black or African American, non-Hispanic/Latino; 1 Asian, non-Hispanic/Latino; 3 Hispanic/Latino; 1 Two or more races, non-Hispanic/Latino), 6 international. Average age 30. 29 applicants, 97% accepted, 18 enrolled. In 2016, 17 master's awarded. Application fee: $55. Electronic applications accepted. *Financial support:* In 2016–17, 4 students received support. Career-related internships or fieldwork, Federal Work-Study, and 3 assistantships (averaging $7911) available. Financial award application deadline: 3/1; financial award applicants required to submit FAFSA. *Unit head:* Dr. Robert A. Kolvoord, Dean, 540-568-2752, E-mail: kolvoora@jmu.edu. *Application contact:* Lynette D. Michael, Director of Graduate Admissions, 540-568-6395, Fax: 540-568-7860, E-mail: michaeld@jmu.edu.
Website: http://www.jmu.edu/cise/

Johns Hopkins University, Engineering Program for Professionals, Elkridge, MD 21075. Offers M Ch E, M Mat SE, MCE, MEE, MEM, MME, MS, MSE, Graduate Certificate, Post Master's Certificate, Post-Master's Certificate. *Program availability:* Part-time, evening/weekend, 100% online, blended/hybrid learning. *Faculty:* 6 full-time (0 women), 281 part-time/adjunct (45 women). *Students:* 51 full-time (10 women), 2,076 part-time (503 women); includes 396 minority (88 Black or African American, non-Hispanic/Latino; 2 American Indian or Alaska Native, non-Hispanic/Latino; 140 Asian, non-Hispanic/Latino; 136 Hispanic/Latino; 3 Native Hawaiian or other Pacific Islander, non-Hispanic/Latino; 27 Two or more races, non-Hispanic/Latino), 60 international. Average age 30. 1,100 applicants, 51% accepted, 377 enrolled. In 2016, 703 master's, 100 other advanced degrees awarded. *Entrance requirements:* For master's, minimum GPA of 3.0, official transcripts from all college studies. Additional exam requirements/recommendations for international students: Required—TOEFL (minimum score 600 paper-based; 100 iBT). *Application deadline:* Applications are processed on a rolling basis. Application fee: $0. Electronic applications accepted. *Expenses:* Contact institution. *Unit head:* Dr. Daniel Horn, Assistant Dean, 410-516-2300, Fax: 410-579-8049, E-mail: dhorn@jhu.edu. *Application contact:* Doug Schiller, Admissions Director, 410-516-2300, Fax: 410-579-8049, E-mail: schiller@jhu.edu.
Website: http://www.ep.jhu.edu

Johns Hopkins University, G. W. C. Whiting School of Engineering, Baltimore, MD 21218. Offers M Ch E, M Mat SE, MA, MEE, MME, MS, MSE, MSEM, MSSI, PhD, Certificate, Post-Master's Certificate. *Faculty:* 253 full-time (52 women), 96 part-time/adjunct (23 women). *Students:* 1,159 full-time (323 women), 100 part-time (24 women); includes 155 minority (18 Black or African American, non-Hispanic/Latino; 88 Asian, non-Hispanic/Latino; 30 Hispanic/Latino; 19 Two or more races, non-Hispanic/Latino), 802 international. Average age 25. 4,631 applicants, 32% accepted, 552 enrolled. In 2016, 328 master's, 82 doctorates, 12 other advanced degrees awarded. Terminal master's awarded for partial completion of doctoral program. *Degree requirements:* For master's, comprehensive exam (for some programs), thesis (for some programs); for doctorate, comprehensive exam, thesis/dissertation, oral exam. *Entrance requirements:* For master's, GRE General Test, letters of recommendation, transcripts; for doctorate, GRE General Test, letters of recommendation. Additional exam requirements/recommendations for international students: Required—TOEFL (minimum score 600 paper-based; 100 iBT) or IELTS (minimum score 7). Application fee: $75. Electronic applications accepted. *Expenses:* Contact institution. *Financial support:* In 2016–17, 834 students received support, including 196 fellowships with full and partial tuition reimbursements available, 563 research assistantships with full and partial tuition reimbursements available, 75 teaching assistantships with full and partial tuition reimbursements available; Federal Work-Study, institutionally sponsored loans, scholarships/grants, health care benefits, tuition waivers (full and partial), and unspecified assistantships also available. Support available to part-time students. Financial award applicants required to submit FAFSA. *Faculty research:* Biomedical engineering, environmental systems and engineering, materials science and engineering, signal and image processing, structural dynamics and geomechanics. *Total annual research expenditures:* $121.1 million. *Unit head:* Dr. T. E. Schlesinger, Dean, 410-516-8350 Ext. 3, Fax: 410-516-8627. *Application contact:* Richard Helman, Director, Graduate Admissions and Enrollment, 410-516-8174, Fax: 410-516-0780, E-mail: graduateadmissions@jhu.edu.
Website: http://engineering.jhu.edu/

Kansas State University, Graduate School, College of Engineering, Manhattan, KS 66506. Offers MEM, MS, MSE, PhD, Graduate Certificate. *Program availability:* Part-time, online learning. *Faculty:* 123 full-time (20 women), 24 part-time/adjunct (4 women). *Students:* 286 full-time (76 women), 194 part-time (32 women); includes 57 minority (18 Black or African American, non-Hispanic/Latino; 19 Asian, non-Hispanic/Latino; 11 Hispanic/Latino; 9 Two or more races, non-Hispanic/Latino), 220 international. Average age 29. 598 applicants, 37% accepted, 95 enrolled. In 2016, 98 master's, 29 doctorates, 1 other advanced degree awarded. *Degree requirements:* For doctorate, thesis/dissertation. *Entrance requirements:* For master's and doctorate, GRE. Additional exam requirements/recommendations for international students: Required—TOEFL. *Application deadline:* For fall admission, 2/1 priority date for domestic students, 1/1 priority date for international students; for spring admission, 8/1 priority date for domestic and international students. Applications are processed on a rolling basis. Application fee: $50 ($75 for international students). Electronic applications accepted. *Expenses:* Tuition, state resident: full-time $9670. Tuition, nonresident: full-time $21,828. *Required fees:* $862. *Financial support:* In 2016–17, 126 research assistantships (averaging $16,448 per year), 83 teaching assistantships (averaging $14,697 per year) were awarded; career-related internships or fieldwork, Federal Work-Study, institutionally sponsored loans, and scholarships/grants also available. Support available to part-time students. Financial award application deadline: 3/1; financial award applicants required to submit FAFSA. *Total annual research expenditures:* $20.3 million. *Unit head:* Dr. Darren Dawson, Dean, 785-532-5590, E-mail: dmdawson@k-state.edu. *Application contact:* Maureen Lockhart, Administrative Assistant to the Dean, 785-532-5441, E-mail: maureen@k-state.edu.
Website: http://www.engg.k-state.edu/

Kennesaw State University, Southern Polytechnic College of Engineering and Engineering Technology, Kennesaw, GA 30144. Offers MBA, MS, MSA, Graduate Certificate, Graduate Transition Certificate. *Program availability:* Part-time, evening/weekend, online learning. *Degree requirements:* For master's, comprehensive exam (for some programs), thesis. *Entrance requirements:* For master's, GMAT, GRE, references, statement of purpose. Additional exam requirements/recommendations for international students: Required—TOEFL (minimum score 550 paper-based; 79 iBT), IELTS (minimum score 6.5). Electronic applications accepted. *Faculty research:* Ethics, virtual reality, sustainability, management of technology, quality management, capacity planning, human-computer interaction/interface, enterprise integration planning, economic impact of educational institutions, behavioral accounting, accounting ethics, taxation, information security, visualization simulation, human-computer interaction, supply chain, logistics, economics, analog and digital communications, computer networking, analog and low power electronics design.

Kent State University, College of Applied Engineering, Sustainability and Technology, Kent, OH 44242. Offers technology (MTC). *Program availability:* Part-time. *Faculty:* 27 full-time (0 women). *Students:* 144 full-time (34 women), 32 part-time (7 women); includes 7 minority (3 Black or African American, non-Hispanic/Latino; 3 Asian, non-Hispanic/Latino; 1 Hispanic/Latino), 182 international. Average age 27. 306 applicants, 56% accepted, 36 enrolled. In 2016, 23 master's awarded. *Degree requirements:* For master's, thesis (for some programs). *Entrance requirements:* For master's, baccalaureate degree from accredited college or university; minimum undergraduate GPA of 3.0; three letters of recommendation; one-page statement describing background, interests, and goals, and how this program will help to achieve those goals. Additional exam requirements/recommendations for international students: Required—TOEFL (minimum scores of 525 paper-based, 71 iBT), Michigan English Language Assessment Battery (75), IELTS (6.0), or PTE (48). *Application deadline:* For fall admission, 7/12 for domestic students, 5/1 for international students; for spring admission, 11/29 for domestic students, 10/1 for international students. Applications are processed on a rolling basis. Application fee: $45 ($70 for international students). Electronic applications accepted. *Expenses:* Tuition, state resident: full-time $10,864; part-time $495 per credit hour. Tuition, nonresident: full-time $18,380; part-time $837 per credit hour. *Financial support:* Research assistantships with full tuition reimbursements, teaching assistantships with full tuition reimbursements, career-related internships or fieldwork, Federal Work-Study, and unspecified assistantships available. Financial award application deadline: 2/3. *Unit head:* Robert G. Sines, Jr., Interim Dean, 330-672-9780, E-mail: rsines@kent.edu. *Application contact:* Richard Mangrum, Coordinator, Graduate Program, 330-672-1933, E-mail: rmangum@kent.edu.
Website: http://www.kent.edu/caest

Lakehead University, Graduate Studies, Faculty of Engineering, Thunder Bay, ON P7B 5E1, Canada. Offers control engineering (M Sc Engr); electrical/computer engineering (M Sc Engr); environmental engineering (M Sc Engr). *Program availability:* Part-time. *Degree requirements:* For master's, thesis. *Entrance requirements:* For master's, bachelor's degree in chemical, electrical or mechanical engineering, minimum B average. Additional exam requirements/recommendations for international students: Required—TOEFL. *Faculty research:* Pulp and paper, adaptive/process control, robust/interactive learning control, vibration control.

Lamar University, College of Graduate Studies, College of Engineering, Beaumont, TX 77710. Offers ME, MEM, MES, MS, DE, PhD. *Program availability:* Part-time, evening/weekend. *Faculty:* 48 full-time (5 women), 1 part-time/adjunct (0 women). *Students:* 361 full-time (52 women), 190 part-time (24 women); includes 19 minority (3 Black or African American, non-Hispanic/Latino; 1 American Indian or Alaska Native, non-Hispanic/Latino; 11 Asian, non-Hispanic/Latino; 3 Hispanic/Latino; 1 Two or more races, non-Hispanic/Latino), 511 international. Average age 26. 444 applicants, 87% accepted, 109 enrolled. In 2016, 330 master's, 11 doctorates awarded. Terminal master's awarded for partial completion of doctoral program. *Degree requirements:* For doctorate, thesis/dissertation. *Entrance requirements:* For master's and doctorate, GRE General Test. Additional exam requirements/recommendations for international students: Required—TOEFL (minimum score 550 paper-based; 79 iBT), IELTS (minimum score 6.5). *Application deadline:* For fall admission, 8/1 for domestic students, 7/1 for international students; for spring admission, 1/5 for domestic students, 12/1 for international students. Applications are processed on a rolling basis. Application fee: $25 ($50 for international students). Electronic applications accepted. *Expenses:* $8,134 in-state full-time, $5,574 in-state part-time; $15,604 out-of-state full-time, $10,554 out-of-state part-time per year. *Financial support:* Fellowships with partial tuition reimbursements, research assistantships with partial tuition reimbursements, teaching assistantships with partial tuition reimbursements, career-related internships or fieldwork, Federal Work-Study,

institutionally sponsored loans, scholarships/grants, tuition waivers (full and partial), and laboratory assistantships available. Support available to part-time students. Financial award application deadline: 4/1; financial award applicants required to submit FAFSA. *Faculty research:* Energy alternatives; process analysis, design, and control; pollution prevention. *Unit head:* Dr. Srinivas Palanki, Dean, 409-880-8784, Fax: 409-880-2197. *Application contact:* Deidre Mayer, Interim Director, Admissions and Academic Services, 409-880-8888, Fax: 409-880-7419, E-mail: gradmissions@lamar.edu.
Website: http://engineering.lamar.edu

Laurentian University, School of Graduate Studies and Research, School of Engineering, Sudbury, ON P3E 2C6, Canada. Offers mineral resources engineering (M Eng, MA Sc); natural resources engineering (PhD). *Program availability:* Part-time. *Faculty research:* Mining engineering, rock mechanics (tunneling, rockbursts, rock support), metallurgy (mineral processing, hydro and pyrometallurgy), simulations and remote mining, simulations and scheduling.

Lawrence Technological University, College of Engineering, Southfield, MI 48075-1058. Offers architectural engineering (MS); automotive engineering (MS); biomedical engineering (MS); civil engineering (MA, MS, PhD), including environmental engineering (MS), geotechnical engineering (MS), structural engineering (MS), transportation engineering (MS), water resource engineering (MS); construction engineering management (MA); electrical and computer engineering (MS); engineering management (MA); engineering technology (MS); fire engineering (MS); industrial engineering (MS), including healthcare; manufacturing systems (ME); mechanical engineering (MS, DE, PhD), including manufacturing (DE), solid mechanics (MS), thermal-fluids (MS); mechatronic systems engineering (MS). *Program availability:* Part-time, evening/weekend. *Faculty:* 24 full-time (5 women), 26 part-time/adjunct (2 women). *Students:* 22 full-time (7 women), 588 part-time (81 women); includes 23 minority (11 Black or African American, non-Hispanic/Latino; 4 Asian, non-Hispanic/Latino; 7 Hispanic/Latino; 1 Two or more races, non-Hispanic/Latino), 469 international. Average age 27. 1,186 applicants, 39% accepted, 99 enrolled. In 2016, 293 master's, 3 doctorates awarded. Terminal master's awarded for partial completion of doctoral program. *Degree requirements:* For master's, thesis optional; for doctorate, comprehensive exam, thesis/dissertation optional. *Entrance requirements:* Additional exam requirements/recommendations for international students: Required—TOEFL (minimum score 550 paper-based; 79 iBT), IELTS (minimum score 6.5). *Application deadline:* For fall admission, 5/22 for international students; for spring admission, 10/11 for international students; for summer admission, 2/16 for international students. Applications are processed on a rolling basis. Application fee: $50. Electronic applications accepted. *Expenses: Tuition:* Full-time $14,868; part-time $1062 per credit. *Required fees:* $75 per semester. Tuition and fees vary according to campus/location. *Financial support:* In 2016–17, 25 students received support, including 5 research assistantships with full tuition reimbursements available; unspecified assistantships also available. Financial award application deadline: 4/1; financial award applicants required to submit FAFSA. *Faculty research:* Carbon fiber reinforced polymer reinforced concrete structures; low impact storm water management solutions; vehicle battery energy management; wireless communication; entrepreneurial mindset and engineering. *Total annual research expenditures:* $1.7 million. *Unit head:* Dr. Nabil Grace, Dean, 248-204-2500, Fax: 248-204-2509, E-mail: engrdean@ltu.edu. *Application contact:* Jane Rohrback, Director of Admissions, 248-204-3160, Fax: 248-204-2228, E-mail: admissions@ltu.edu.
Website: http://www.ltu.edu/engineering/index.asp

Lehigh University, P.C. Rossin College of Engineering and Applied Science, Bethlehem, PA 18015. Offers M Eng, MS, PhD, MBA/E. *Program availability:* Part-time, 100% online, blended/hybrid learning. *Faculty:* 141 full-time (21 women), 13 part-time/adjunct (3 women). *Students:* 607 full-time (146 women), 139 part-time (39 women); includes 65 minority (9 Black or African American, non-Hispanic/Latino; 28 Asian, non-Hispanic/Latino; 24 Hispanic/Latino; 2 Native Hawaiian or other Pacific Islander, non-Hispanic/Latino; 2 Two or more races, non-Hispanic/Latino), 448 international. Average age 26. 1,925 applicants, 33% accepted, 201 enrolled. In 2016, 224 master's, 66 doctorates awarded. Terminal master's awarded for partial completion of doctoral program. *Degree requirements:* For master's, comprehensive exam (for some programs), thesis (for some programs); for doctorate, comprehensive exam (for some programs), thesis/dissertation. *Entrance requirements:* For master's and doctorate, GRE General Test, BS. Additional exam requirements/recommendations for international students: Required—TOEFL (minimum score 79 iBT), IELTS (minimum score 6.5). *Application deadline:* For fall admission, 7/15 for domestic and international students; for spring admission, 12/1 for domestic and international students. Application fee: $75. Electronic applications accepted. *Expenses:* $1,420 per credit. *Financial support:* In 2016–17, 279 students received support, including 26 fellowships with tuition reimbursements available (averaging $21,105 per year), 185 research assistantships with tuition reimbursements available (averaging $28,140 per year), 68 teaching assistantships with tuition reimbursements available (averaging $21,530 per year); scholarships/grants, tuition waivers (full and partial), and unspecified assistantships also available. Financial award application deadline: 1/15. *Faculty research:* Energy and the environment, health and healthcare, sustainable infrastructure, nanotechnology and high performance computing. *Unit head:* Dr. Stephen P. DeWeerth, Dean, 610-758-5308, Fax: 610-758-5623, E-mail: steve.deweerth@lehigh.edu. *Application contact:* Brianne Lisk, Manager of Graduate Programs, 610-758-6310, Fax: 610-758-5623, E-mail: brie.lisk@lehigh.edu.
Website: http://www.lehigh.edu/engineering/

LeTourneau University, Graduate Programs, Longview, TX 75607-7001. Offers business (MBA); counseling (MA), including licensed professional counselor, marriage and family therapy, school counseling; curriculum and instruction (M Ed); educational administration (M Ed); engineering (ME, MS); engineering management (MEM); health care administration (MS); marriage and family therapy (MA); psychology (MA); strategic leadership (MSL); teacher leadership (M Ed); teaching and learning (M Ed). *Program availability:* Part-time, 100% online, blended/hybrid learning. *Faculty:* 24 full-time (7 women), 40 part-time/adjunct (15 women). *Students:* 82 full-time (48 women), 428 part-time (331 women); includes 234 minority (138 Black or African American, non-Hispanic/Latino; 5 American Indian or Alaska Native, non-Hispanic/Latino; 5 Asian, non-Hispanic/Latino; 50 Hispanic/Latino; 36 Two or more races, non-Hispanic/Latino), 15 international. Average age 37. 257 applicants, 60% accepted, 141 enrolled. In 2016, 136 master's awarded. *Degree requirements:* For master's, thesis (for some programs). *Entrance requirements:* Additional exam requirements/recommendations for international students: Required—TOEFL. *Application deadline:* For fall admission, 8/22 for domestic students, 8/29 for international students; for winter admission, 10/10 for domestic students; for spring admission, 1/2 for domestic students, 1/10 for international students; for summer admission, 5/1 for domestic and international students. Applications are processed on a rolling basis. Electronic applications accepted. *Expenses:* $10,890-$18,450 tuition per year (depending on program). *Financial support:* Research assistantships, institutionally sponsored loans, and unspecified assistantships available. Financial award applicants required to submit FAFSA. *Application contact:* Chris Fontaine, Assistant Vice President for Enrollment Services and Global Admissions, 903-233-4312, E-mail: chrisfontaine@letu.edu.
Website: http://www.letu.edu

Liberty University, School of Engineering and Computational Sciences, Lynchburg, VA 24515. Offers cyber security (MS). *Program availability:* Part-time, online learning. *Students:* 44 full-time (10 women), 145 part-time (18 women); includes 53 minority (38 Black or African American, non-Hispanic/Latino; 1 American Indian or Alaska Native, non-Hispanic/Latino; 6 Asian, non-Hispanic/Latino; 1 Hispanic/Latino; 1 Native Hawaiian or other Pacific Islander, non-Hispanic/Latino; 6 Two or more races, non-Hispanic/Latino), 3 international. Average age 37. 223 applicants, 24% accepted, 24 enrolled. In 2016, 27 master's awarded. *Entrance requirements:* For master's, baccalaureate degree or its equivalent in computer science, information technology, or other technical degree, or baccalaureate degree in any field along with significant technical work experience. *Application deadline:* Applications are processed on a rolling basis. Application fee: $50. Electronic applications accepted. *Financial support:* Applicants required to submit FAFSA. *Unit head:* David Donahoo, Dean, 434-592-7150. *Application contact:* Jay Bridge, Director of Admissions, 800-424-9595, Fax: 800-628-7977, E-mail: gradadmissions@liberty.edu.

Louisiana State University and Agricultural & Mechanical College, Graduate School, College of Engineering, Department of Biological and Agricultural Engineering, Baton Rouge, LA 70803. Offers biological and agricultural engineering (MSBAE); engineering science (MS, PhD).

Louisiana State University and Agricultural & Mechanical College, Graduate School, College of Engineering, Interdepartmental Program in Engineering Science, Baton Rouge, LA 70803. Offers MSES, PhD.

Louisiana Tech University, Graduate School, College of Engineering and Science, Ruston, LA 71272. Offers MS, PhD. *Program availability:* Part-time. Terminal master's awarded for partial completion of doctoral program. *Degree requirements:* For doctorate, thesis/dissertation. *Entrance requirements:* For master's, GRE General Test, minimum GPA of 3.0 in last 60 hours. Additional exam requirements/recommendations for international students: Required—TOEFL. *Application deadline:* For fall admission, 8/1 for domestic students; for spring admission, 2/1 for domestic students. Applications are processed on a rolling basis. Application fee: $20 ($30 for international students). *Financial support:* Fellowships, research assistantships, teaching assistantships, career-related internships or fieldwork, Federal Work-Study, tuition waivers (partial), and unspecified assistantships available. Financial award application deadline: 4/1. *Faculty research:* Trenchless technology, micromanufacturing, radionuclide transport, microbial liquefaction, hazardous waste treatment. *Unit head:* Dr. Hisham Hegab, Dean, 318-257-4647, Fax: 318-257-2562, E-mail: hhegab@latech.edu. *Application contact:* Marilyn J. Robinson, Assistant to the Dean, 318-257-2924, Fax: 318-257-4487.
Website: http://coes.latech.edu/

Manhattan College, Graduate Programs, School of Engineering, Riverdale, NY 10471. Offers chemical engineering (MS), including chemical engineering, cosmetic engineering; civil engineering (MS); computer engineering (MS); electrical engineering (MS); environmental engineering (ME, MS); mechanical engineering (MS). *Program availability:* Part-time, evening/weekend. *Degree requirements:* For master's, thesis or alternative. *Entrance requirements:* For master's, GRE (recommended), minimum GPA of 3.0. Additional exam requirements/recommendations for international students: Required—TOEFL (minimum score 550 paper-based; 80 iBT), IELTS (minimum score 6). *Application deadline:* For fall admission, 8/10 priority date for domestic students, 8/10 for international students; for spring admission, 1/7 for domestic and international students. Applications are processed on a rolling basis. Application fee: $60. *Expenses:* Contact institution. *Financial support:* Fellowships with full tuition reimbursements, research assistantships with full tuition reimbursements, teaching assistantships with partial tuition reimbursements, career-related internships or fieldwork, Federal Work-Study, scholarships/grants, unspecified assistantships, and laboratory assistantships available. Support available to part-time students. Financial award application deadline: 2/1. *Faculty research:* Environmental/water, nucleation, environmental/management, heat transfer. *Unit head:* Dr. Tim J. Ward, Dean, 718-862-7307, Fax: 718-862-8015, E-mail: deanengr@manhattan.edu. *Application contact:* Erica Reubel, Office Manager, 718-862-7281, Fax: 718-862-8015, E-mail: deanengr@manhattan.edu.
Website: https://manhattan.edu/academics/schools-and-departments/school-of-engineering/index.php

Marquette University, Graduate School, College of Engineering, Milwaukee, WI 53201-1881. Offers ME, MS, MSEM, PhD, Certificate. *Program availability:* Part-time, evening/weekend. *Faculty:* 66 full-time (10 women), 18 part-time/adjunct (4 women). *Students:* 113 full-time (26 women), 80 part-time (16 women); includes 24 minority (4 Black or African American, non-Hispanic/Latino; 9 Asian, non-Hispanic/Latino; 8 Hispanic/Latino; 3 Two or more races, non-Hispanic/Latino), 54 international. Average age 27. 312 applicants, 61% accepted, 45 enrolled. In 2016, 49 master's, 15 doctorates awarded. *Degree requirements:* For doctorate, thesis/dissertation. *Entrance requirements:* For master's, minimum GPA of 3.0; for doctorate, GRE General Test, minimum GPA of 3.0. Additional exam requirements/recommendations for international students: Required—TOEFL (minimum score 530 paper-based). *Application deadline:* Applications are processed on a rolling basis. Electronic applications accepted. *Financial support:* Fellowships, research assistantships, teaching assistantships, scholarships/grants, health care benefits, tuition waivers (partial), and unspecified assistantships available. Support available to part-time students. Financial award application deadline: 2/15. *Faculty research:* Urban watershed management, micro sensors for environmental pollutants, orthopedic rehabilitation engineering, telemedicine, ergonomics. *Total annual research expenditures:* $1.3 million. *Unit head:* Dr. Kris Ropella, Dean, 414-288-6591, Fax: 414-288-7082.
Website: http://www.marquette.edu/engineering/grad.shtml

Marshall University, Academic Affairs Division, College of Information Technology and Engineering, Huntington, WV 25755. Offers MS, MSE, MSME. *Program availability:* Part-time, evening/weekend. *Degree requirements:* For master's, final project, oral exam. *Expenses:* Contact institution.

Massachusetts Institute of Technology, School of Engineering, Cambridge, MA 02139. Offers M Eng, SM, PhD, Sc D, CE, EAA, ECS, EE, Mat E, Mech E, NE, Naval E, SM/MBA. *Faculty:* 377 full-time (68 women), 2 part-time/adjunct (0 women). *Students:* 3,112 full-time (914 women), 12 part-time (3 women); includes 661 minority (33 Black or African American, non-Hispanic/Latino; 3 American Indian or Alaska Native, non-Hispanic/Latino; 395 Asian, non-Hispanic/Latino; 154 Hispanic/Latino; 76 Two or more races, non-Hispanic/Latino), 1,380 international. Average age 26. 8,785 applicants, 16% accepted, 929 enrolled. In 2016, 750 master's, 334 doctorates, 10 other advanced degrees awarded. *Degree requirements:* For master's, thesis (for some programs); for doctorate, comprehensive exam, thesis/dissertation; for other advanced degree, thesis. Application fee: $75. Electronic applications accepted. *Expenses: Tuition:* Full-time $46,400; part-time $725 per credit. One-time fee: $312 full-time. Full-time tuition and fees vary according to course load and program. *Financial support:* In 2016–17, 2,537 students received support, including 615 fellowships (averaging $39,100 per year), 1,664 research assistantships (averaging $37,300 per year), 331 teaching assistantships (averaging $37,900 per year); Federal Work-Study, institutionally sponsored loans, scholarships/grants, traineeships, health care benefits, unspecified assistantships, and resident tutors also available. Support available to part-time students. Financial award application deadline: 5/1; financial award applicants required to submit FAFSA. *Total annual research expenditures:* $388.5 million. *Unit head:* Prof. Ian A. Waitz, Dean of Engineering, 617-253-3291, Fax: 617-253-8549. *Application contact:* 617-324-6730, E-mail: gradadmissions@mit.edu. Website: http://engineering.mit.edu/

McGill University, Faculty of Graduate and Postdoctoral Studies, Faculty of Engineering, Montréal, QC H3A 2T5, Canada. Offers M Arch I, M Arch II, M Eng, M Sc, MMM, MUP, PhD, Diploma.

McGill University, Faculty of Graduate and Postdoctoral Studies, Faculty of Science, Department of Mathematics and Statistics, Montréal, QC H3A 2T5, Canada. Offers computational science and engineering (M Sc); mathematics and statistics (M Sc, MA, PhD), including applied mathematics (M Sc, MA), pure mathematics (M Sc, MA), statistics (M Sc, MA).

McMaster University, School of Graduate Studies, Faculty of Engineering, Hamilton, ON L8S 4M2, Canada. Offers M Eng, M Sc, MA Sc, PhD. *Program availability:* Part-time. *Degree requirements:* For doctorate, comprehensive exam, thesis/dissertation. *Entrance requirements:* Additional exam requirements/recommendations for international students: Required—TOEFL (minimum score 550 paper-based). *Faculty research:* Computer process control, water resources engineering, elasticity, flow induced vibrations, microelectronics.

McNeese State University, Doré School of Graduate Studies, College of Engineering and Engineering Technology, Lake Charles, LA 70609. Offers M Eng, Graduate Certificate, Postbaccalaureate Certificate. *Program availability:* Part-time, evening/weekend. *Degree requirements:* For master's, thesis or alternative. *Entrance requirements:* For master's, GRE, minimum undergraduate GPA of 3.0. Additional exam requirements/recommendations for international students: Required—TOEFL (minimum score 560 paper-based; 83 iBT).

Memorial University of Newfoundland, School of Graduate Studies, Faculty of Engineering and Applied Science, St. John's, NL A1C 5S7, Canada. Offers civil engineering (M Eng, PhD); electrical and computer engineering (M Eng, PhD); mechanical engineering (M Eng, PhD); ocean and naval architecture engineering (M Eng, PhD). *Program availability:* Part-time. *Degree requirements:* For master's, thesis; for doctorate, comprehensive exam, thesis/dissertation, oral thesis defense. *Entrance requirements:* For master's, 2nd class degree; for doctorate, master's degree in engineering. Electronic applications accepted. *Faculty research:* Engineering analysis, environmental and hydrotechnical studies, manufacturing and robotics, mechanics, structures and materials.

Mercer University, Graduate Studies, Macon Campus, School of Engineering, Macon, GA 31207. Offers biomedical engineering (MSE); computer engineering (MSE); electrical engineering (MSE); engineering management (MSE); environmental engineering (MSE); environmental systems (MS); mechanical engineering (MSE); software engineering (MSE); software systems (MS); technical communications management (MS); technical management (MS). *Program availability:* Part-time-only, evening/weekend, online learning. *Faculty:* 21 full-time (5 women), 1 part-time/adjunct (0 women). *Students:* 44 full-time (9 women), 60 part-time (12 women); includes 14 minority (3 Black or African American, non-Hispanic/Latino; 1 American Indian or Alaska Native, non-Hispanic/Latino; 4 Asian, non-Hispanic/Latino; 3 Hispanic/Latino; 3 Two or more races, non-Hispanic/Latino), 2 international. Average age 27. In 2016, 64 master's awarded. *Degree requirements:* For master's, thesis or alternative. *Entrance requirements:* For master's, GRE (minimum score 300), minimum undergraduate GPA of 3.0. Additional exam requirements/recommendations for international students: Required—TOEFL (minimum score 550 paper-based; 80 iBT). *Application deadline:* For fall admission, 4/1 priority date for domestic and international students; for spring admission, 11/1 priority date for domestic and international students. Applications are processed on a rolling basis. Application fee: $75. *Expenses:* $865 per credit hour. *Financial support:* Applicants required to submit FAFSA. *Faculty research:* Designing prostheses and orthotics, oxygen transfer and limitations in biological systems, low-cost groundwater development, lung airway and transport, autonomous mobile robots. *Unit head:* Dr. Laura W. Lackey, Dean, 478-301-4106, Fax: 478-301-5593, E-mail: lackey_l@mercer.edu. *Application contact:* Dr. Richard O. Mines, Jr., Program Director, 478-301-2347, Fax: 478-301-5433, E-mail: mines_ro@mercer.edu. Website: http://engineering.mercer.edu/

Merrimack College, School of Science and Engineering, North Andover, MA 01845-5800. Offers athletic training (MS); civil engineering (MS); community health education (MS); computer science (MS); data science (MS); exercise and sport science (MS); health and wellness management (MS); mechanical engineering (MS), including engineering management. *Program availability:* Part-time, evening/weekend, 100% online. *Faculty:* 16 full-time, 2 part-time/adjunct. *Students:* 88 full-time (32 women), 13 part-time (6 women); includes 6 minority (4 Hispanic/Latino; 2 Two or more races, non-Hispanic/Latino), 39 international. Average age 25. 156 applicants, 67% accepted, 59 enrolled. In 2016, 46 master's awarded. *Degree requirements:* For master's, comprehensive exam, thesis optional, internship or capstone (for some programs). *Entrance requirements:* For master's, official college transcripts, resume, personal statement, 2 recommendations. Additional exam requirements/recommendations for international students: Required—TOEFL (minimum score 84 iBT), IELTS (minimum score 6.5), PTE (minimum score 56). *Application deadline:* For fall admission, 8/14 for domestic students, 7/14 for international students; for spring admission, 1/10 for domestic students, 12/10 for international students; for summer admission, 5/10 for domestic students, 4/10 for international students. Applications are processed on a rolling basis. Application fee: $0. Electronic applications accepted. *Expenses:* Contact institution. *Financial support:* Fellowships with full tuition reimbursements, career-related internships or fieldwork, scholarships/grants, and health care benefits available. Support available to part-time students. Financial award application deadline: 5/1; financial award applicants required to submit FAFSA. *Faculty research:* Viral genomics and evolution (biology), robotics (mechanical engineering), knot theory (mathematics), computer graphics and network security (computer science), water management (civil engineering). *Application contact:* Allison Pena, Graduate Admissions Counselor, 978-837-3563, E-mail: penaa@merrimack.edu. Website: http://www.merrimack.edu/academics/graduate/

Miami University, College of Engineering and Computing, Oxford, OH 45056. Offers MCS, MS. *Expenses:* Tuition, state resident: full-time $12,890; part-time $564 per credit hour. Tuition, nonresident: full-time $29,604; part-time $1260 per credit hour. *Required fees:* $638. Part-time tuition and fees vary according to course load and program. *Unit head:* Dr. Marek Dollar, Dean, 513-529-0700, E-mail: cec@miamioh.edu. *Application contact:* Graduate Admission Coordinator, 513-529-3734, E-mail: applygrad@miamioh.edu. Website: http://miamioh.edu/cec/

Michigan State University, The Graduate School, College of Engineering, East Lansing, MI 48824. Offers MS, PhD. *Program availability:* Part-time. Electronic applications accepted.

Michigan Technological University, Graduate School, College of Engineering, Houghton, MI 49931. Offers MS, PhD, Graduate Certificate. *Program availability:* Part-time, 100% online, blended/hybrid learning. *Faculty:* 277 full-time (45 women), 150 part-time/adjunct (14 women). *Students:* 730 full-time (134 women), 184 part-time (37 women); includes 39 minority (7 Black or African American, non-Hispanic/Latino; 9 Asian, non-Hispanic/Latino; 14 Hispanic/Latino; 9 Two or more races, non-Hispanic/Latino), 651 international. Average age 27. 3,452 applicants, 25% accepted, 244 enrolled. In 2016, 295 master's, 34 doctorates, 63 other advanced degrees awarded. Terminal master's awarded for partial completion of doctoral program. *Degree requirements:* For master's, thesis (for some programs), 30 credits; for doctorate, comprehensive exam, thesis/dissertation, 30 credits beyond master's degree. *Entrance requirements:* For master's and doctorate, GRE, statement of purpose, personal statement, official transcripts, 2-3 letters of recommendation; for Graduate Certificate, statement of purpose, personal statement, official transcripts. Additional exam requirements/recommendations for international students: Required—TOEFL or IELTS. *Application deadline:* Applications are processed on a rolling basis. Electronic applications accepted. *Expenses:* Contact institution. *Financial support:* In 2016–17, 614 students received support, including 38 fellowships with tuition reimbursements available (averaging $15,242 per year), 114 research assistantships with tuition reimbursements available (averaging $15,242 per year), 86 teaching assistantships with tuition reimbursements available (averaging $15,242 per year); career-related internships or fieldwork, Federal Work-Study, scholarships/grants, health care benefits, unspecified assistantships, and cooperative program also available. Financial award applicants required to submit FAFSA. *Faculty research:* Engineering, sustainability, energy systems, transportation, health technologies. *Total annual research expenditures:* $16.4 million. *Unit head:* Dr. Wayne D. Pennington, Dean, 906-487-2005, Fax: 906-487-2782, E-mail: wayne@mtu.edu. *Application contact:* Carol T. Wingerson, Administrative Aide, 906-487-2328, Fax: 906-487-2284, E-mail: gradadms@mtu.edu. Website: http://www.mtu.edu/engineering/

Michigan Technological University, Graduate School, College of Sciences and Arts, Department of Computer Science, Houghton, MI 49931. Offers computational science and engineering (PhD); computer science (MS, PhD); cybersecurity (MS). *Program availability:* Part-time. *Faculty:* 21 full-time, 9 part-time/adjunct. *Students:* 41 full-time (13 women), 6 part-time; includes 1 minority (Two or more races, non-Hispanic/Latino), 32 international. Average age 27. 466 applicants, 19% accepted, 15 enrolled. In 2016, 3 master's, 5 doctorates awarded. *Degree requirements:* For master's, comprehensive exam (for some programs), thesis (for some programs); for doctorate, comprehensive exam, thesis/dissertation. *Entrance requirements:* For master's and doctorate, GRE, statement of purpose, personal statement, official transcripts, 3 letters of recommendation. Additional exam requirements/recommendations for international students: Required—TOEFL (recommended minimum score 90 iBT) or IELTS. *Application deadline:* For fall admission, 5/1 priority date for domestic and international students; for spring admission, 9/1 priority date for domestic and international students. Applications are processed on a rolling basis. Electronic applications accepted. *Expenses:* Contact institution. *Financial support:* In 2016–17, 36 students received support, including 4 fellowships (averaging $15,242 per year), 12 research assistantships with tuition reimbursements available (averaging $15,242 per year), 13 teaching assistantships with tuition reimbursements available (averaging $15,242 per year); career-related internships or fieldwork, Federal Work-Study, scholarships/grants, health care benefits, unspecified assistantships, and cooperative program also available. Financial award applicants required to submit FAFSA. *Faculty research:* Artificial intelligence, graphics/visualization, software engineering, architecture and compiler optimization, human computing interaction. *Total annual research expenditures:* $856,922. *Unit head:* Dr. Min Song, Chair, 906-487-2602, Fax: 906-487-2283, E-mail: mins@mtu.edu. *Application contact:* Cheryl Simpkins, Office Assistant, 906-487-2209, Fax: 906-487-2283, E-mail: cisimpki@mtu.edu. Website: http://www.mtu.edu/cs/

Michigan Technological University, Graduate School, Interdisciplinary Programs, Houghton, MI 49931. Offers atmospheric sciences (PhD); biochemistry and molecular biology (PhD); computational science and engineering (PhD); data science (MS, Graduate Certificate); engineering (M Eng); environmental engineering (PhD); international profile (Graduate Certificate); nanotechnology (Graduate Certificate); sustainability (Graduate Certificate); sustainable water resources systems (Graduate Certificate). *Program availability:* Part-time. *Faculty:* 122 full-time (26 women), 13 part-time/adjunct. *Students:* 58 full-time (18 women), 17 part-time (5 women); includes 1 minority (Black or African American, non-Hispanic/Latino), 56 international. Average age 28. 395 applicants, 20% accepted, 22 enrolled. In 2016, 3 master's, 7 doctorates, 8 other advanced degrees awarded. Terminal master's awarded for partial completion of doctoral program. *Degree requirements:* For master's, comprehensive exam (for some programs), thesis (for some programs); for doctorate, comprehensive exam, thesis/dissertation. *Entrance requirements:* For master's, doctorate, and Graduate Certificate, GRE, statement of purpose, personal statement, official transcripts, 2-3 letters of recommendation. Additional exam requirements/recommendations for international students: Required—TOEFL or IELTS. *Application deadline:* Applications are processed on a rolling basis. Electronic applications accepted. *Expenses:* Tuition, state resident: full-time $16,290; part-time $905 per credit. Tuition, nonresident: full-time $16,290; part-time $905 per credit. *Required fees:* $248; $124 per term. Tuition and fees vary according to course load and program. *Financial support:* In 2016–17, 54 students received support, including 7 fellowships with tuition reimbursements available (averaging $15,242 per year), 19 research assistantships with tuition reimbursements available (averaging $15,242 per year), 5 teaching assistantships with tuition reimbursements available (averaging $15,242 per year); career-related internships or fieldwork, Federal Work-Study, scholarships/grants, health care benefits, unspecified assistantships, and cooperative program also available. Financial award applicants required to submit FAFSA. *Faculty research:* Big data, atmospheric sciences, bioinformatics and systems biology, molecular dynamics, environmental studies. *Unit head:* Dr. Pushpalatha Murthy, Dean of the Graduate School/Associate Provost for Graduate Education, 906-487-3007, Fax: 906-487-2284, E-mail: ppmurthy@mtu.edu. *Application contact:* Carol T. Wingerson, Administrative Aide, 906-487-2328, Fax: 906-487-2284, E-mail: gradadms@mtu.edu.

Milwaukee School of Engineering, Department of Electrical Engineering and Computer Science, Program in Engineering, Milwaukee, WI 53202-3109. Offers MS. *Program availability:* Part-time, evening/weekend. *Faculty:* 1 full-time (0 women), 7 part-time/adjunct (3 women). *Students:* 8 full-time (0 women), 26 part-time (3 women); includes 4 minority (1 Black or African American, non-Hispanic/Latino; 1 American Indian or Alaska Native, non-Hispanic/Latino; 2 Asian, non-Hispanic/Latino), 8 international. 32 applicants, 31% accepted, 7 enrolled. In 2016, 15 master's awarded. *Degree requirements:* For master's, thesis, design project or capstone. *Entrance requirements:* For master's, GRE General Test or GMAT if undergraduate GPA less than 2.8, BS in engineering, 2 letters of recommendation. Additional exam requirements/recommendations for international students: Required—TOEFL (minimum score 79 iBT), IELTS (minimum score 6.5). *Application deadline:* Applications are processed on a rolling basis. Application fee: $0. Electronic applications accepted. *Expenses:* Tuition: Full-time $31,440; part-time $655 per credit. *Financial support:* In 2016–17, 3 research assistantships (averaging $8,043 per year) were awarded; career-related internships or fieldwork, institutionally sponsored loans, scholarships/grants, and tuition waivers (partial) also available. Financial award application deadline: 3/15; financial award

applicants required to submit FAFSA. *Faculty research:* Microprocessors, materials, thermodynamics, artificial intelligence, fluid power/hydraulics. *Unit head:* Dr. Subha Kumpaty, Director, 414-277-7466, Fax: 414-277-2222, E-mail: kumpaty@msoe.edu. *Application contact:* Ian Dahlinghaus, Graduate Admissions Counselor, 414-277-7208, E-mail: dahlinghaus@msoe.edu.
Website: http://www.msoe.edu/community/academics/engineering/page/1277/mse-overview

Mississippi State University, Bagley College of Engineering, Mississippi State, MS 39762. Offers M Eng, MS, PhD. *Program availability:* Part-time, 100% online. *Faculty:* 115 full-time (14 women), 8 part-time/adjunct (1 woman). *Students:* 359 full-time (93 women), 306 part-time (61 women); includes 98 minority (41 Black or African American, non-Hispanic/Latino; 19 Asian, non-Hispanic/Latino; 32 Hispanic/Latino; 1 Native Hawaiian or other Pacific Islander, non-Hispanic/Latino; 5 Two or more races, non-Hispanic/Latino), 215 international. Average age 30. 665 applicants, 44% accepted, 161 enrolled. In 2016, 121 master's, 46 doctorates awarded. *Degree requirements:* For master's, comprehensive exam (for some programs), thesis; for doctorate, comprehensive exam (for some programs), thesis/dissertation. *Entrance requirements:* For master's, GRE, minimum GPA of 2.75; for doctorate, GRE. Additional exam requirements/recommendations for international students: Required—TOEFL (minimum score 477 paper-based; 53 iBT); Recommended—IELTS (minimum score 4.5). *Application deadline:* For fall admission, 7/1 for domestic students, 5/1 for international students; for spring admission, 11/1 for domestic students, 9/1 for international students. Applications are processed on a rolling basis. Application fee: $60. Electronic applications accepted. *Expenses:* Tuition, state resident: full-time $7670; part-time $852.50 per credit hour. Tuition, nonresident: full-time $20,790; part-time $2310.50 per credit hour. Part-time tuition and fees vary according to course load. *Financial support:* In 2016–17, 72 research assistantships with full tuition reimbursements (averaging $17,082 per year), 63 teaching assistantships with full tuition reimbursements (averaging $15,709 per year) were awarded; Federal Work-Study, institutionally sponsored loans, scholarships/grants, and unspecified assistantships also available. Financial award application deadline: 4/1; financial award applicants required to submit FAFSA. *Faculty research:* Fluid dynamics, combustion, composite materials, computer design, high-voltage phenomena. *Total annual research expenditures:* $50.9 million. *Unit head:* Dr. Jason Keith, Dean, 662-325-2270, Fax: 662-325-8573, E-mail: keith@bagley.msstate.edu. *Application contact:* Doretta Martin, Senior Admissions Assistant, 662-325-9514, E-mail: dmartin@grad.msstate.edu.
Website: http://www.engr.msstate.edu/

Missouri Western State University, Program in Applied Science, St. Joseph, MO 64507-2294. Offers chemistry (MAS); engineering technology management (MAS); human factors and usability testing (MAS); industrial life science (MAS); sport and fitness management (MAS). *Accreditation:* AACSB. *Program availability:* Part-time. *Students:* 41 full-time (18 women), 27 part-time (11 women); includes 7 minority (6 Black or African American, non-Hispanic/Latino; 1 Two or more races, non-Hispanic/Latino), 15 international. Average age 29. 43 applicants, 88% accepted, 30 enrolled. In 2016, 34 master's awarded. *Entrance requirements:* Additional exam requirements/recommendations for international students: Recommended—TOEFL (minimum score 79 iBT), IELTS (minimum score 6). *Application deadline:* For fall admission, 7/15 for domestic and international students; for spring admission, 10/1 for domestic and international students; for summer admission, 3/15 for domestic students. Applications are processed on a rolling basis. Application fee: $50. Electronic applications accepted. *Expenses:* Tuition, state resident: full-time $6548; part-time $327.39 per credit hour. Tuition, nonresident: full-time $11,848; part-time $592.39 per credit hour. *Required fees:* $542; $99 per credit hour. $176 per semester. One-time fee: $50. Tuition and fees vary according to course load and program. *Financial support:* Scholarships/grants and unspecified assistantships available. Support available to part-time students. *Unit head:* Dr. Benjamin D. Caldwell, Dean of the Graduate School, 816-271-4394, Fax: 816-271-4525, E-mail: graduate@missouriwestern.edu.

Montana State University, The Graduate School, College of Engineering, Department of Chemical and Biological Engineering, Bozeman, MT 59717. Offers chemical engineering (MS); engineering (PhD), including chemical engineering option, environmental engineering option; environmental engineering (MS). *Program availability:* Part-time. *Degree requirements:* For master's, comprehensive exam, thesis (for some programs); for doctorate, comprehensive exam, thesis/dissertation. *Entrance requirements:* For master's and doctorate, GRE General Test. Additional exam requirements/recommendations for international students: Required—TOEFL (minimum score 550 paper-based). Electronic applications accepted. *Faculty research:* Metabolic network analysis and engineering; magnetic resonance microscopy; modeling of biological systems; the development of protective coatings on planar solid oxide fuel cell (SOFC) metallic interconnects; characterizing corrosion mechanisms of materials in precisely-controlled exposures; testing materials in poly-crystalline silicon production environments; environmental biotechnology and bioremediation.

Montana State University, The Graduate School, College of Engineering, Department of Civil Engineering, Bozeman, MT 59717. Offers civil engineering (MS); construction engineering management (MCEM); engineering (PhD), including applied mechanics option, civil engineering option. *Program availability:* Part-time. *Degree requirements:* For master's, comprehensive exam, thesis (for some programs); for doctorate, comprehensive exam, thesis/dissertation. *Entrance requirements:* For master's and doctorate, GRE General Test. Additional exam requirements/recommendations for international students: Required—TOEFL (minimum score 550 paper-based). Electronic applications accepted. *Faculty research:* Snow and ice mechanics, biofilm engineering, transportation, structural and geo materials, water resources.

Montana State University, The Graduate School, College of Engineering, Department of Mechanical and Industrial Engineering, Bozeman, MT 59717. Offers engineering (PhD), including industrial engineering, mechanical engineering; industrial and management engineering (MS); mechanical engineering (MS). *Program availability:* Part-time. *Degree requirements:* For master's, comprehensive exam, thesis, oral exams; for doctorate, comprehensive exam, thesis/dissertation, qualifying exam. *Entrance requirements:* For master's, GRE, official transcript, minimum GPA of 3.0, demonstrated potential for success, statement of goals, three letters of recommendation, proof of funds affidavit; for doctorate, minimum undergraduate GPA of 3.0, 3.2 graduate; three letters of recommendation; statement of objectives. Additional exam requirements/recommendations for international students: Required—TOEFL or IELTS. Electronic applications accepted. *Faculty research:* Human factors engineering, energy, design and manufacture, systems modeling, materials and structures, measurement systems.

Montana Tech of The University of Montana, Department of General Engineering, Butte, MT 59701-8997. Offers MS. *Program availability:* Part-time. *Faculty:* 7 full-time (0 women), 4 part-time/adjunct (0 women). *Students:* 5 full-time (0 women), 2 part-time (0 women); includes 2 minority (both Black or African American, non-Hispanic/Latino). Average age 25. 5 applicants, 60% accepted, 3 enrolled. In 2016, 8 master's awarded. *Degree requirements:* For master's, comprehensive exam (for some programs), thesis optional. *Entrance requirements:* For master's, minimum GPA of 3.0. Additional exam requirements/recommendations for international students: Required—TOEFL (minimum score 545 paper-based; 78 iBT), IELTS (minimum score 6.5). *Application deadline:* For fall admission, 4/1 priority date for domestic students, 3/1 priority date for international students; for spring admission, 10/1 priority date for domestic students, 6/1 priority date for international students. Applications are processed on a rolling basis. Application fee: $50. Electronic applications accepted. *Expenses:* Tuition, state resident: full-time $2901; part-time $1450.68 per degree program. Tuition, nonresident: full-time $8432; part-time $4215.84 per degree program. *Required fees:* $668; $354 per degree program. Tuition and fees vary according to course load and program. *Financial support:* In 2016–17, 9 students received support, including 11 teaching assistantships with partial tuition reimbursements available (averaging $3,500 per year); research assistantships with partial tuition reimbursements available, career-related internships or fieldwork, tuition waivers (full and partial), and unspecified assistantships also available. Financial award application deadline: 4/1; financial award applicants required to submit FAFSA. *Faculty research:* Wind energy and power controls, robotics, concurrent engineering, remotely piloted aircraft, composite materials. *Unit head:* Dr. Bruce Madigan, Department Head, 406-496-4109, Fax: 406-496-4650, E-mail: bmadigan@mtech.edu. *Application contact:* Daniel Stirling, Administrator, Graduate School, 406-496-4304, Fax: 406-496-4710, E-mail: gradschool@mtech.edu.
Website: http://www.mtech.edu/academics/gradschool/degreeprograms/degrees-general-engineering.htm

Morgan State University, School of Graduate Studies, Clarence M. Mitchell, Jr. School of Engineering, Baltimore, MD 21251. Offers civil engineering (M Eng, D Eng); electrical and computer engineering (M Eng, MS, D Eng); industrial and systems engineering (M Eng, D Eng); transportation (MS). *Program availability:* Part-time, evening/weekend. *Degree requirements:* For master's, thesis, comprehensive exam or equivalent; for doctorate, thesis/dissertation, comprehensive exam or equivalent. *Entrance requirements:* For master's, GRE, minimum undergraduate GPA of 2.5; for doctorate, GRE, minimum GPA of 3.0. Additional exam requirements/recommendations for international students: Required—TOEFL (minimum score 550 paper-based).

New Jersey Institute of Technology, Newark College of Engineering, Newark, NJ 07102. Offers biomedical engineering (MS, PhD); chemical engineering (MS, PhD); computer engineering (MS, PhD); electrical engineering (MS, PhD); engineering management (MS); environmental engineering (PhD); healthcare systems management (MS); industrial engineering (MS, PhD); Internet engineering (MS); manufacturing engineering (MS); mechanical engineering (MS, PhD); occupational safety and health engineering (MS); pharmaceutical bioprocessing (MS); pharmaceutical engineering (MS); pharmaceutical systems management (MS); power and energy systems (MS); telecommunications (MS); transportation (MS, PhD). *Program availability:* Part-time, evening/weekend. *Faculty:* 146 full-time (21 women), 119 part-time/adjunct (10 women). *Students:* 804 full-time (191 women), 550 part-time (129 women); includes 357 minority (82 Black or African American, non-Hispanic/Latino; 1 American Indian or Alaska Native, non-Hispanic/Latino; 138 Asian, non-Hispanic/Latino; 114 Hispanic/Latino; 22 Two or more races, non-Hispanic/Latino), 675 international. Average age 27. 2,959 applicants, 51% accepted, 442 enrolled. In 2016, 595 master's, 29 doctorates awarded. Terminal master's awarded for partial completion of doctoral program. *Degree requirements:* For master's, thesis optional; for doctorate, thesis/dissertation. *Entrance requirements:* For master's, GRE General Test; for doctorate, GRE General Test, minimum graduate GPA of 3.5. Additional exam requirements/recommendations for international students: Required—TOEFL (minimum score 550 paper-based; 79 iBT). *Application deadline:* For fall admission, 6/1 priority date for domestic students, 5/1 priority date for international students; for spring admission, 11/15 priority date for domestic and international students. Applications are processed on a rolling basis. Application fee: $75. Electronic applications accepted. *Expenses:* Contact institution. *Financial support:* In 2016–17, 172 students received support, including 1 fellowship (averaging $1,528 per year), 79 research assistantships (averaging $13,336 per year), 92 teaching assistantships (averaging $20,619 per year); scholarships/grants also available. Financial award application deadline: 1/15. *Faculty research:* Nonlinear signal processing, intelligent medical image analysis, calibration issues in coherent localization, computer-aided design, neural network for tool wear measurement. *Total annual research expenditures:* $11.1 million. *Unit head:* Dr. Moshe Kam, Dean, 973-596-5534, E-mail: moshe.kam@njit.edu. *Application contact:* Stephen Eck, Director of Admissions, 973-596-3300, Fax: 973-596-3461, E-mail: admissions@njit.edu.
Website: http://engineering.njit.edu/

New Mexico State University, College of Engineering, Las Cruces, NM 88003-8001. Offers MS Ch E, MS Env E, MSAE, MSCE, MSEE, MSIE, MSME, PhD, Graduate Certificate. *Program availability:* Part-time. *Faculty:* 62 full-time (12 women), 1 part-time/adjunct (0 women). *Students:* 225 full-time (48 women), 172 part-time (40 women); includes 115 minority (16 Black or African American, non-Hispanic/Latino; 5 American Indian or Alaska Native, non-Hispanic/Latino; 5 Asian, non-Hispanic/Latino; 80 Hispanic/Latino; 9 Two or more races, non-Hispanic/Latino), 167 international. Average age 31. 397 applicants, 48% accepted, 98 enrolled. In 2016, 134 master's, 24 doctorates, 2 other advanced degrees awarded. *Degree requirements:* For master's, final examination; for doctorate, comprehensive exam, thesis/dissertation. *Entrance requirements:* Additional exam requirements/recommendations for international students: Required—TOEFL (minimum score 550 paper-based; 79 iBT), IELTS (minimum score 6.5). *Application deadline:* For fall admission, 7/1 priority date for domestic students; for spring admission, 11/1 for domestic students. Applications are processed on a rolling basis. Application fee: $40 ($50 for international students). Electronic applications accepted. *Expenses:* Tuition, state resident: full-time $4086. Tuition, nonresident: full-time $14,254. *Required fees:* $853. Tuition and fees vary according to course load. *Financial support:* In 2016–17, 227 students received support, including 9 fellowships (averaging $3,402 per year), 71 research assistantships (averaging $14,746 per year), 77 teaching assistantships (averaging $12,577 per year); career-related internships or fieldwork, Federal Work-Study, scholarships/grants, traineeships, health care benefits, and unspecified assistantships also available. Support available to part-time students. Financial award application deadline: 3/1. *Faculty research:* Energy, environment, and water research; data and information science including communications and signal processing, machine learning, and sensors and sensing applications; infrastructure and structures including construction materials, nondestructive testing, and structural monitoring. *Total annual research expenditures:* $6.5 million. *Unit head:* Dr. Phillip De Leon, Associate Dean of Research and Graduate Studies, 575-646-3422, Fax: 575-646-3549, E-mail: oer@nmsu.edu. *Application contact:* Graduate Admissions, 575-646-3121, E-mail: admissions@nmsu.edu.
Website: http://engr.nmsu.edu/

New York Institute of Technology, School of Engineering and Computing Sciences, Old Westbury, NY 11568-8000. Offers MS, Advanced Certificate. *Program availability:* Part-time, evening/weekend, 100% online, blended/hybrid learning. *Faculty:* 26 full-time (6 women), 38 part-time/adjunct (3 women). *Students:* 798 full-time (254 women), 320 part-time (77 women); includes 93 minority (25 Black or African American, non-Hispanic/Latino; 1 American Indian or Alaska Native, non-Hispanic/Latino; 41 Asian, non-Hispanic/Latino; 25 Hispanic/Latino; 1 Two or more races, non-Hispanic/Latino), 949 international. Average age 25. 2,577 applicants, 64% accepted, 283 enrolled. In 2016, 614 master's awarded. *Degree requirements:* For master's, thesis (for some programs). *Entrance requirements:* Additional exam requirements/recommendations for

international students: Required—TOEFL (minimum score 79 iBT), IELTS (minimum score 6). *Application deadline:* For fall admission, 7/1 for domestic students, 6/1 for international students; for spring admission, 12/1 for domestic and international students. Applications are processed on a rolling basis. Application fee: $50. Electronic applications accepted. *Expenses:* $1,215 per credit. *Financial support:* Fellowships with partial tuition reimbursements, teaching assistantships with partial tuition reimbursements, career-related internships or fieldwork, Federal Work-Study, scholarships/grants, tuition waivers (full and partial), and unspecified assistantships available. Support available to part-time students. Financial award application deadline: 3/1; financial award applicants required to submit FAFSA. *Unit head:* Dr. Nada Anid, Dean, 516-686-7931, Fax: 516-625-7933, E-mail: nanid@nyit.edu. *Application contact:* Alice Dolitsky, Director, Graduate Admissions, 516-686-7520, Fax: 516-686-1116, E-mail: nyitgrad@nyit.edu.
Website: http://www.nyit.edu/engineering

New York University, Polytechnic School of Engineering, Brooklyn, NY 11201. Offers MS, PhD, Advanced Certificate, Certificate, Graduate Certificate. *Entrance requirements:* Additional exam requirements/recommendations for international students: Required—TOEFL (minimum score 550 paper-based; 80 iBT). Electronic applications accepted.

North Carolina Agricultural and Technical State University, School of Graduate Studies, College of Engineering, Greensboro, NC 27411. Offers MS, MSCE, MSCS, MSE, MSEE, MSIE, MSME, PhD. *Program availability:* Part-time.

North Carolina State University, Graduate School, College of Engineering, Raleigh, NC 27695. Offers M Ch E, M Eng, MC Sc, MCE, MIE, MIMS, MMSE, MNE, MOR, MS, PhD. *Program availability:* Part-time. Terminal master's awarded for partial completion of doctoral program. *Degree requirements:* For doctorate, thesis/dissertation. Electronic applications accepted.

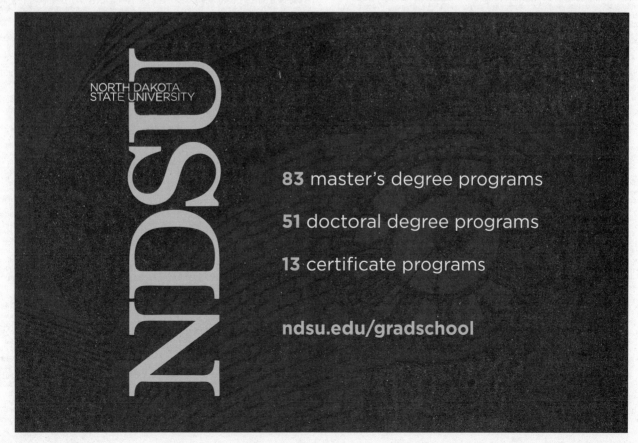

North Dakota State University, College of Graduate and Interdisciplinary Studies, College of Engineering, Fargo, ND 58102. Offers MCM, ME, MS, PhD, Graduate Certificate. *Program availability:* Part-time. Terminal master's awarded for partial completion of doctoral program. *Degree requirements:* For master's, thesis; for doctorate, comprehensive exam, thesis/dissertation. *Entrance requirements:* For master's and doctorate, minimum GPA of 3.0. Additional exam requirements/recommendations for international students: Required—TOEFL. Electronic applications accepted. *Expenses:* Contact institution. *Faculty research:* Theoretical mechanics, robotics, automation, environmental engineering, man-made materials.

See Display below and Close-Up on page 81.

Northeastern University, College of Engineering, Boston, MA 02115-5096. Offers bioengineering (MS, PhD); chemical engineering (MS, PhD); civil engineering (MS, PhD); computer engineering (PhD); computer systems engineering (MS); electrical and computer engineering (MS); electrical and computer engineering leadership (MS); electrical engineering (PhD); energy systems (MS); engineering and public policy (MS); engineering management (MS, Certificate); environmental engineering (MS); industrial engineering (MS, PhD); information assurance (PhD); information systems (MS); interdisciplinary engineering (PhD); mechanical engineering (PhD); operations research (MS); telecommunication systems management (MS). *Program availability:* Part-time, online learning. *Faculty:* 202 full-time (59 women), 53 part-time/adjunct (9 women). *Students:* 2,982 full-time (954 women), 192 part-time (38 women). In 2016, 851 master's, 74 doctorates awarded. Application fee: $75. Electronic applications accepted. *Expenses:* $1,471 per credit. *Financial support:* Fellowships, research assistantships, teaching assistantships, career-related internships or fieldwork, scholarships/grants, health care benefits, tuition waivers, and unspecified assistantships available. Support

available to part-time students. Financial award applicants required to submit FAFSA. *Unit head:* Dr. Nadine Aubry, Dean, College of Engineering. *Application contact:* Jeffery Hengel, Director of Graduate Admissions, 617-373-2711, E-mail: j.hengel@northeastern.edu.
Website: http://www.coe.neu.edu/academics/graduate-school-engineering

Northern Arizona University, Graduate College, College of Engineering, Forestry, and Natural Sciences, Flagstaff, AZ 86011. Offers M Eng, MAST, MAT, MF, MS, MSE, MSF, PhD, Certificate. *Entrance requirements:* For master's, minimum GPA of 3.0 in final 60 hours of undergraduate course work. *Expenses:* Tuition, state resident: full-time $8971; part-time $444 per credit hour. Tuition, nonresident: full-time $20,958; part-time $1164 per credit hour. *Required fees:* $1018; $644 per credit hour. Tuition and fees vary according to course load, campus/location and program.

Northern Illinois University, Graduate School, College of Engineering and Engineering Technology, De Kalb, IL 60115-2854. Offers MS. *Program availability:* Part-time, evening/weekend. *Faculty:* 36 full-time (2 women), 2 part-time/adjunct (0 women). *Students:* 169 full-time (27 women), 143 part-time (21 women); includes 32 minority (8 Black or African American, non-Hispanic/Latino; 7 Asian, non-Hispanic/Latino; 12 Hispanic/Latino; 5 Two or more races, non-Hispanic/Latino), 210 international. Average age 26. 527 applicants, 52% accepted, 68 enrolled. In 2016, 133 master's awarded. *Degree requirements:* For master's, comprehensive exam, thesis optional. *Entrance requirements:* For master's, GRE General Test, minimum GPA of 2.75. Additional exam requirements/recommendations for international students: Required—TOEFL (minimum score 550 paper-based). *Application deadline:* For fall admission, 6/1 for domestic students, 5/1 for international students; for spring admission, 11/1 for domestic students, 10/1 for international students. Applications are processed on a rolling basis. Application fee: $40. Electronic applications accepted. *Financial support:* In 2016–17, 1 research assistantship with full tuition reimbursement, 1 teaching assistantship with full tuition reimbursement were awarded; fellowships with full tuition reimbursements, career-related internships or fieldwork, Federal Work-Study, scholarships/grants, tuition waivers (full), and unspecified assistantships also available. Support available to part-time students. Financial award applicants required to submit FAFSA. *Unit head:* Dr. Omar A. Ghrayeb, Acting Dean, 815-753-1281, Fax: 815-753-1310, E-mail: oghrayeb@niu.edu. *Application contact:* Graduate School Office, 815-753-0395, E-mail: gradsch@niu.edu.
Website: http://www.niu.edu/CEET/

Northwestern Polytechnic University, School of Engineering, Fremont, CA 94539-7482. Offers computer engineering (DCE); computer science (MS); computer systems engineering (MS); electrical engineering (MS). *Program availability:* Part-time, evening/weekend. *Degree requirements:* For master's, thesis optional; for doctorate, thesis/dissertation. *Entrance requirements:* For master's, minimum GPA of 3.0. Additional exam requirements/recommendations for international students: Required—TOEFL (minimum score 550 paper-based; 79 iBT). *Faculty research:* Computer networking, database design, Internet technology, software engineering, digital signal processing.

Northwestern University, McCormick School of Engineering and Applied Science, Evanston, IL 60208. Offers MBA, MEM, MIT, MME, MMM, MPD, MS, PhD, Certificate, MBA/MEM. MS and PhD admissions and degrees offered through The Graduate School. *Program availability:* Part-time, evening/weekend. Terminal master's awarded for partial completion of doctoral program. *Degree requirements:* For master's, comprehensive exam (for some programs), thesis (for some programs); for doctorate, comprehensive exam, thesis/dissertation. *Entrance requirements:* For master's and doctorate, GRE General Test. Additional exam requirements/recommendations for international students: Required—TOEFL (minimum score 577 paper-based; 90 iBT) or IELTS (minimum score 7). Electronic applications accepted.

Engineering and Applied Sciences—General

Oakland University, Graduate Study and Lifelong Learning, School of Engineering and Computer Science, Rochester, MI 48309-4401. Offers MS, PhD, Graduate Certificate. *Program availability:* Part-time, evening/weekend. *Degree requirements:* For doctorate, thesis/dissertation. *Entrance requirements:* For master's and doctorate, minimum GPA of 3.0. Additional exam requirements/recommendations for international students: Required—TOEFL (minimum score 550 paper-based). Electronic applications accepted. *Expenses:* Contact institution.

The Ohio State University, Graduate School, College of Engineering, Columbus, OH 43210. Offers M Arch, M Land Arch, MCRP, MS, PhD. *Program availability:* Part-time, evening/weekend. *Faculty:* 351. *Students:* 1,766 full-time (415 women), 139 part-time (28 women); includes 145 minority (32 Black or African American, non-Hispanic/Latino; 4 American Indian or Alaska Native, non-Hispanic/Latino; 49 Asian, non-Hispanic/Latino; 37 Hispanic/Latino; 23 Two or more races, non-Hispanic/Latino), 1,097 international. Average age 26. In 2016, 523 master's, 166 doctorates awarded. *Degree requirements:* For doctorate, thesis/dissertation. *Entrance requirements:* For master's and doctorate, GRE. Additional exam requirements/recommendations for international students: Required—TOEFL (minimum score 600 paper-based; 100 iBT), Michigan English Language Assessment Battery (minimum score 86); Recommended—IELTS (minimum score 8). *Application deadline:* For fall admission, 11/30 priority date for domestic and international students. Applications are processed on a rolling basis. Application fee: $60 ($70 for international students). Electronic applications accepted. *Financial support:* Fellowships with tuition reimbursements, research assistantships with tuition reimbursements, teaching assistantships with tuition reimbursements, career-related internships or fieldwork, Federal Work-Study, institutionally sponsored loans, and unspecified assistantships available. Support available to part-time students. *Unit head:* Dr. David B. Williams, Dean, 614-292-2836, Fax: 614-292-9615, E-mail: williams.4219@osu.edu. *Application contact:* Graduate and Professional Admissions, 614-292-9444, Fax: 614-292-3895, E-mail: gpadmissions@osu.edu.
Website: http://engineering.osu.edu/

Ohio University, Graduate College, Russ College of Engineering and Technology, Athens, OH 45701-2979. Offers M Eng Mgt, MS, PhD. *Program availability:* Part-time. *Degree requirements:* For master's, comprehensive exam (for some programs), thesis (for some programs); for doctorate, comprehensive exam, thesis/dissertation. *Entrance requirements:* For master's, GRE General Test, BS in engineering or related field; for doctorate, GRE General Test, MS in engineering or related field. Additional exam requirements/recommendations for international students: Required—TOEFL or IELTS. *Application deadline:* Applications are processed on a rolling basis. Application fee: $50 ($55 for international students). Electronic applications accepted. *Expenses:* Contact institution. *Financial support:* Fellowships with full tuition reimbursements, research assistantships with full tuition reimbursements, teaching assistantships with full tuition reimbursements, career-related internships or fieldwork, Federal Work-Study, institutionally sponsored loans, and unspecified assistantships available. Financial award application deadline: 3/15. *Faculty research:* Avionics engineering, coal research, transportation engineering, software systems integration, materials processing. *Unit head:* Dr. Dennis Irwin, Dean, 740-593-1482, Fax: 740-593-0659, E-mail: irwind@ohio.edu. *Application contact:* Dr. Shawn Ostermann, Associate Dean, 740-593-1482, Fax: 740-593-0659, E-mail: ostermann@ohio.edu.
Website: http://www.ohio.edu/engineering/

Oklahoma Christian University, Graduate School of Engineering and Computer Science, Oklahoma City, OK 73136-1100. Offers electrical and computer engineering (MSE); engineering management (MSE); mechanical engineering (MSE); software engineering (MSCS, MSE). *Program availability:* Part-time. *Faculty:* 8 full-time (1 woman), 7 part-time/adjunct (0 women). *Students:* 187 full-time (27 women), 85 part-time (12 women). Average age 25. 255 applicants, 33% accepted, 69 enrolled. In 2016, 188 master's awarded. *Entrance requirements:* Additional exam requirements/recommendations for international students: Required—TOEFL (minimum score 550 paper-based). *Application deadline:* Applications are processed on a rolling basis. Application fee: $25. Electronic applications accepted. *Expenses:* Contact institution. *Unit head:* Mary Ann Brown, Director for Graduate School Engineering, 405-425-5579. *Application contact:* Angie Ricketts, Admissions Counselor, 405-425-5587, E-mail: angie.ricketts@oc.edu.
Website: http://www.oc.edu/academics/graduate/engineering/

Oklahoma State University, College of Engineering, Architecture and Technology, Stillwater, OK 74078. Offers MS, PhD. *Program availability:* Online learning. *Faculty:* 127 full-time (15 women), 5 part-time/adjunct (2 women). *Students:* 251 full-time (45 women), 366 part-time (75 women); includes 50 minority (9 Black or African American, non-Hispanic/Latino; 2 American Indian or Alaska Native, non-Hispanic/Latino; 9 Asian, non-Hispanic/Latino; 12 Hispanic/Latino; 18 Two or more races, non-Hispanic/Latino), 337 international. Average age 28. 1,110 applicants, 21% accepted, 154 enrolled. In 2016, 218 master's, 41 doctorates awarded. *Degree requirements:* For master's, thesis (for some programs); for doctorate, comprehensive exam, thesis/dissertation. *Entrance requirements:* For master's and doctorate, GRE or GMAT. Additional exam requirements/recommendations for international students: Required—TOEFL (minimum score 550 paper-based; 79 iBT). *Application deadline:* For fall admission, 3/1 priority date for domestic and international students; for spring admission, 8/1 priority date for domestic and international students. Applications are processed on a rolling basis. Application fee: $40 ($75 for international students). Electronic applications accepted. *Expenses:* Tuition, state resident: full-time $3775; part-time $209.70 per credit hour. Tuition, nonresident: full-time $14,851; part-time $825.05 per credit hour. *Required fees:* $2027; $112.60 per credit hour. Tuition and fees vary according to campus/location. *Financial support:* In 2016–17, 160 research assistantships (averaging $11,340 per year), 129 teaching assistantships (averaging $7,778 per year) were awarded; career-related internships or fieldwork, Federal Work-Study, scholarships/grants, health care benefits, tuition waivers (partial), and unspecified assistantships also available. Support available to part-time students. Financial award application deadline: 3/1; financial award applicants required to submit FAFSA. *Unit head:* Dr. Paul Tikalsky, Dean, 405-744-5140, E-mail: paul.tikalsky@okstate.edu.
Website: http://www.ceat.okstate.edu

Old Dominion University, Frank Batten College of Engineering and Technology, Norfolk, VA 23529. Offers ME, MS, D Eng, PhD. *Program availability:* Part-time, evening/weekend, 100% online, blended/hybrid learning. *Faculty:* 93 full-time (12 women), 32 part-time/adjunct (5 women). *Students:* 157 full-time (44 women), 569 part-time (125 women); includes 167 minority (72 Black or African American, non-Hispanic/Latino; 36 Asian, non-Hispanic/Latino; 42 Hispanic/Latino; 1 Native Hawaiian or other Pacific Islander, non-Hispanic/Latino; 16 Two or more races, non-Hispanic/Latino), 167 international. Average age 32. 558 applicants, 63% accepted, 144 enrolled. In 2016, 199 master's, 31 doctorates awarded. *Degree requirements:* For master's, comprehensive exam, thesis (for some programs); for doctorate, comprehensive exam, thesis/dissertation, candidacy exam. *Entrance requirements:* For master's, GRE, minimum GPA of 3.0; for doctorate, GRE, minimum GPA of 3.5. Additional exam requirements/recommendations for international students: Required—TOEFL (minimum score 550 paper-based). *Application deadline:* For fall admission, 6/1 for domestic students, 2/15 priority date for international students; for spring admission, 11/1 for domestic students, 10/1 for international students. Applications are processed on a rolling basis. Application fee: $50. Electronic applications accepted. *Expenses:* $478 per credit, in-state full-time tuition. *Financial support:* In 2016–17, 168 students received support, including 8 fellowships with tuition reimbursements available (averaging $15,000 per year), 92 research assistantships with tuition reimbursements available (averaging $15,000 per year), 68 teaching assistantships with tuition reimbursements available (averaging $15,000 per year); career-related internships or fieldwork, Federal Work-Study, institutionally sponsored loans, scholarships/grants, and unspecified assistantships also available. Support available to part-time students. Financial award applicants required to submit FAFSA. *Faculty research:* Physical electronics, computational applied mechanics, structural dynamics, computational fluid dynamics, coastal engineering of water resources, modeling and simulation. *Total annual research expenditures:* $31.8 million. *Unit head:* Dr. Stephanie G. Adams, Dean, 757-683-3789, Fax: 757-683-4898, E-mail: sgadams@odu.edu. *Application contact:* Dr. Rafael E. Landaeta, Associate Dean, 757-683-4478, Fax: 757-683-4898, E-mail: rlandaet@odu.edu.
Website: https://www.odu.edu/eng

Open University, Graduate Programs, Milton Keynes, United Kingdom. Offers business (MBA); education (M Ed); engineering (M Eng); history (MA); music (MA); philosophy (MA).

Oregon State University, College of Engineering, Corvallis, OR 97331. Offers M Eng, MHP, MMP, MS, PhD. *Program availability:* Part-time, 100% online. *Faculty:* 193 full-time (37 women), 12 part-time/adjunct (3 women). *Students:* 1,068 full-time (239 women), 188 part-time (53 women); includes 115 minority (8 Black or African American, non-Hispanic/Latino; 1 American Indian or Alaska Native, non-Hispanic/Latino; 48 Asian, non-Hispanic/Latino; 33 Hispanic/Latino; 1 Native Hawaiian or other Pacific Islander, non-Hispanic/Latino; 24 Two or more races, non-Hispanic/Latino), 700 international. Average age 28. In 2016, 290 master's, 48 doctorates awarded. Terminal master's awarded for partial completion of doctoral program. *Degree requirements:* For doctorate, thesis/dissertation. Application fee: $75 ($85 for international students). *Expenses:* Contact institution. *Financial support:* Fellowships with full tuition reimbursements, research assistantships with full tuition reimbursements, teaching assistantships with full tuition reimbursements, and instructorships available. *Unit head:* Scott Ashford, Dean. *Application contact:* Dr. Dorthe Wildenschild, Associate Dean for Graduate Programs, E-mail: info@engr.oregonstate.edu.
Website: http://engineering.oregonstate.edu/

Penn State Erie, The Behrend College, Graduate School, Erie, PA 16563. Offers accounting (MPAC); business administration (MBA); project management (MPM); quality and manufacturing management (MMM). *Accreditation:* AACSB. *Program availability:* Part-time. *Students:* 28 full-time (9 women), 118 part-time (31 women); includes 11 minority (5 Black or African American, non-Hispanic/Latino; 2 Asian, non-Hispanic/Latino; 1 Hispanic/Latino; 3 Two or more races, non-Hispanic/Latino), 2 international. Average age 32. 91 applicants, 74% accepted, 55 enrolled. In 2016, 59 master's awarded. *Entrance requirements:* Additional exam requirements/recommendations for international students: Required—TOEFL (minimum score 550 paper-based; 80 iBT), IELTS. *Application deadline:* Applications are processed on a rolling basis. Application fee: $65. Electronic applications accepted. *Financial support:* Federal Work-Study available. Financial award application deadline: 3/1; financial award applicants required to submit FAFSA. *Unit head:* Dr. Ralph M. Ford, Chancellor, 814-898-6160, Fax: 814-898-6461. *Application contact:* Ann M. Burbules, Assistant Director, Graduate Admissions, 866-374-3378, Fax: 814-898-6044, E-mail: behrend.admissions@psu.edu.
Website: http://behrend.psu.edu/

Penn State Great Valley, Graduate Studies, Engineering Division, Malvern, PA 19355-1488. Offers engineering management (MEM); software engineering (MSE); systems engineering (M Eng, Certificate). *Unit head:* Dr. James A. Nemes, Chancellor, 610-648-3202 Ext. 610, Fax: 610-725-5296, E-mail: cse1@psu.edu. *Application contact:* JoAnn Kelly, Director of Admissions, 610-648-3315, Fax: 610-725-5296, E-mail: jek2@psu.edu.
Website: http://greatvalley.psu.edu/academics/masters-degrees/systems-engineering

Penn State Harrisburg, Graduate School, School of Science, Engineering and Technology, Middletown, PA 17057. Offers computer science (MS); electrical engineering (M Eng, MS); engineering management (MPS); engineering science (M Eng); environmental engineering (M Eng); environmental pollution control (MEPC, MS); structural engineering (Certificate). *Program availability:* Part-time, evening/weekend. *Unit head:* Dr. Mukund S. Kulkarni, Chancellor, 717-948-6105, Fax: 717-948-6452. *Application contact:* Robert W. Coffman, Jr., Director of Enrollment Management, Admissions, 717-948-6250, Fax: 717-948-6325, E-mail: hbgadmit@psu.edu.
Website: https://harrisburg.psu.edu/science-engineering-technology

Penn State University Park, Graduate School, College of Engineering, University Park, PA 16802. Offers M Eng, MA, MAE, MFR, MS, PhD. *Students:* 1,252 full-time (273 women), 125 part-time (22 women). Average age 26. 4,634 applicants, 23% accepted, 521 enrolled. In 2016, 305 master's, 149 doctorates awarded. *Entrance requirements:* Additional exam requirements/recommendations for international students: Required—TOEFL (minimum score 550 paper-based; 80 iBT), IELTS. *Application deadline:* Applications are processed on a rolling basis. Application fee: $65. Electronic applications accepted. *Financial support:* Fellowships, research assistantships, teaching assistantships, career-related internships or fieldwork, Federal Work-Study, scholarships/grants, traineeships, health care benefits, and unspecified assistantships available. Support available to part-time students. Financial award application deadline: 3/1; financial award applicants required to submit FAFSA. *Unit head:* Dr. Amr S. Elnashai, Dean, 814-865-7537, Fax: 814-863-4749. *Application contact:* Lori Hawn, Director, Graduate Student Services, 814-865-1795, Fax: 814-863-4627, E-mail: l-gswww@lists.psu.edu.
Website: http://www.engr.psu.edu

Pontificia Universidad Catolica Madre y Maestra, Graduate School, Faculty of Engineering Sciences, Santiago, Dominican Republic. Offers earthquake engineering (ME); logistics management (ME).

Portland State University, Graduate Studies, Maseeh College of Engineering and Computer Science, Portland, OR 97207-0751. Offers M Eng, ME, MS, MSE, PhD, Certificate, MS/MBA, MS/MS. *Program availability:* Part-time, evening/weekend. *Faculty:* 103 full-time (16 women), 40 part-time/adjunct (7 women). *Students:* 414 full-time (117 women), 373 part-time (106 women); includes 101 minority (8 Black or African American, non-Hispanic/Latino; 54 Asian, non-Hispanic/Latino; 19 Hispanic/Latino; 20 Two or more races, non-Hispanic/Latino), 409 international. Average age 31. 960 applicants, 40% accepted, 225 enrolled. In 2016, 251 master's, 17 doctorates awarded. *Degree requirements:* For doctorate, one foreign language, thesis/dissertation. *Entrance requirements:* Additional exam requirements/recommendations for international students: Required—TOEFL (minimum score 550 paper-based; 80 iBT). *Application deadline:* For fall admission, 4/1 for domestic students, 3/1 for international students; for winter admission, 9/1 for domestic and international students; for spring admission, 2/1 for domestic and international students. Application fee: $65. *Expenses:* Contact institution. *Financial support:* In 2016–17, 67 research assistantships with tuition

reimbursements (averaging $6,608 per year), 81 teaching assistantships with tuition reimbursements (averaging $3,922 per year) were awarded; career-related internships or fieldwork, Federal Work-Study, scholarships/grants, and unspecified assistantships also available. Support available to part-time students. Financial award application deadline: 3/1; financial award applicants required to submit FAFSA. *Unit head:* Dr. Renjeng Su, Dean, 503-725-8393, Fax: 503-725-2825, E-mail: renjengs@pdx.edu.
Website: http://www.pdx.edu/cecs/

Prairie View A&M University, College of Engineering, Prairie View, TX 77446. Offers computer information systems (MSCIS); computer science (MSCS); electrical engineering (MSEE, PhDEE); general engineering (MS Engr). *Program availability:* Part-time, evening/weekend. *Faculty:* 27 full-time (7 women), 2 part-time/adjunct (both women). *Students:* 171 full-time (45 women), 50 part-time (17 women); includes 89 minority (70 Black or African American, non-Hispanic/Latino; 16 Asian, non-Hispanic/Latino; 3 Hispanic/Latino), 115 international. Average age 30. 155 applicants, 94% accepted, 85 enrolled. In 2016, 43 master's, 3 doctorates awarded. *Degree requirements:* For master's, thesis optional; for doctorate, comprehensive exam, thesis/dissertation. *Entrance requirements:* For master's, GRE General Test (minimum score of 900), bachelor's degree in engineering from ABET-accredited institution; for doctorate, minimum GPA of 3.0. Additional exam requirements/recommendations for international students: Required—TOEFL (minimum score 550 paper-based; 79 iBT). *Application deadline:* For fall admission, 5/1 priority date for domestic and international students; for spring admission, 10/1 priority date for domestic students, 9/1 priority date for international students; for summer admission, 3/1 priority date for domestic students, 2/1 priority date for international students. Applications are processed on a rolling basis. Application fee: $50. Electronic applications accepted. *Expenses:* Tuition, state resident: full-time $4362; part-time $273.48 per credit hour. Tuition, nonresident: full-time $12,390; part-time $534.10 per credit hour. *Required fees:* $2782; $178.26 per credit hour. *Financial support:* In 2016–17, 1 fellowship with full tuition reimbursement (averaging $14,000 per year), 33 research assistantships with full and partial tuition reimbursements (averaging $17,260 per year), 3 teaching assistantships with full and partial tuition reimbursements (averaging $15,000 per year) were awarded; career-related internships or fieldwork, institutionally sponsored loans, scholarships/grants, health care benefits, tuition waivers (full), and unspecified assistantships also available. Financial award application deadline: 4/1; financial award applicants required to submit FAFSA. *Faculty research:* Electrical and computer engineering: big data analysis, wireless communications, bioinformatics and computational biology, space radiation; computer science: cloud computing, cyber security; chemical engineering: thermochemical processing of biofuel, photochemical modeling; civil and environmental engineering: environmental sustainability, water resources, structure; mechanical engineering: thermal science, nanocomposites, computational fluid dynamics. *Unit head:* Dr. Kendall T. Harris, Dean, 936-261-9900, Fax: 936-261-9868, E-mail: tharris@pvamu.edu. *Application contact:* Pauline Walker, Administrative Assistant II, Research and Graduate Studies, 936-261-3521, Fax: 936-261-3529, E-mail: gradadmissions@pvamu.edu.

Princeton University, Graduate School, School of Engineering and Applied Science, Princeton, NJ 08544-1019. Offers M Eng, MSE, PhD. Terminal master's awarded for partial completion of doctoral program. *Degree requirements:* For master's, thesis (for some programs); for doctorate, thesis/dissertation, research, teaching, general exam. *Entrance requirements:* For master's and doctorate, GRE General Test, official transcript(s), 3 letters of recommendation, personal statement. Additional exam requirements/recommendations for international students: Required—TOEFL. Electronic applications accepted.

Purdue University, College of Engineering, West Lafayette, IN 47907-2045. Offers MS, MSABE, MSBME, MSCE, MSChE, MSE, MSECE, MSIE, MSME, MSMSE, MSNE, PhD, Certificate, MD/PhD. *Accreditation:* ABET. *Program availability:* Part-time, 100% online, blended/hybrid learning. *Faculty:* 636. *Students:* 3,463. In 2016, 672 master's, 284 doctorates awarded. Terminal master's awarded for partial completion of doctoral program. *Degree requirements:* For doctorate, thesis/dissertation. *Application deadline:* Applications are processed on a rolling basis. Application fee: $60 ($75 for international students). Electronic applications accepted. *Expenses:* Contact institution. *Financial support:* Fellowships with full and partial tuition reimbursements, research assistantships with full and partial tuition reimbursements, teaching assistantships with full and partial tuition reimbursements, career-related internships or fieldwork, scholarships/grants, health care benefits, and unspecified assistantships available. *Faculty research:* Aerospace, biomed engineering, chemical phenomena and processes, civil infrastructure and the environment, communications, computational science and engineering, computer engineering, computer networks, electrical systems, electronics, energy and power, environment and ecology, human in the loop engineering, imaging, manufacturing and materials processing, materials, measurement, mechanical systems, micro and Nano science and engineering, optics, systems engineering, thermal and transport. *Unit head:* Dr. Audeen Fentiman, Associate Dean, E-mail: engrgrad@purdue.edu. *Application contact:* Dr. Janet Beagle, Director of Graduate Programs, E-mail: engrgrad@purdue.edu.
Website: https://engineering.purdue.edu/Engr

Purdue University Northwest, Graduate Studies Office, School of Engineering, Mathematics, and Science, Department of Engineering, Hammond, IN 46323-2094. Offers computer engineering (MSE); electrical engineering (MSE); engineering (MS); mechanical engineering (MSE). *Program availability:* Evening/weekend. *Entrance requirements:* Additional exam requirements/recommendations for international students: Required—TOEFL.

Purdue University Northwest, Graduate Studies Office, School of Technology, Hammond, IN 46323-2094. Offers MS.

Queen's University at Kingston, School of Graduate Studies, Faculty of Applied Science, Kingston, ON K7L 3N6, Canada. Offers M Eng, M Sc, M Sc Eng, PhD. *Program availability:* Part-time. *Degree requirements:* For doctorate, comprehensive exam, thesis/dissertation. *Entrance requirements:* Additional exam requirements/recommendations for international students: Required—TOEFL. Electronic applications accepted.

Rensselaer at Hartford, Department of Engineering, Hartford, CT 06120-2991. Offers ME, MS. *Program availability:* Part-time, evening/weekend. *Entrance requirements:* For master's, GRE. Additional exam requirements/recommendations for international students: Required—TOEFL (minimum score 600 paper-based; 100 iBT). Electronic applications accepted.

Rensselaer Polytechnic Institute, Graduate School, School of Engineering, Troy, NY 12180-3590. Offers M Eng, MS, D Eng, PhD. *Program availability:* Part-time. Terminal master's awarded for partial completion of doctoral program. *Degree requirements:* For master's, comprehensive exam (for some programs), thesis (for some programs); for doctorate, comprehensive exam (for some programs), thesis/dissertation. *Entrance requirements:* For master's and doctorate, GRE. Additional exam requirements/recommendations for international students: Required—TOEFL (minimum score 570 paper-based; 88 iBT), IELTS (minimum score 6.5), PTE (minimum score 60). Electronic applications accepted. *Expenses: Tuition:* Full-time $49,520; part-time $2060 per credit hour. *Required fees:* $2617. *Faculty research:* Aeronautical, biomedical, chemical, civil, computer and systems, engineering physics, environmental, industrial and management, materials science, mechanical, nuclear, systems engineering and technology management, transportation.

Rice University, Graduate Programs, George R. Brown School of Engineering, Houston, TX 77251-1892. Offers M Ch E, M Stat, MA, MBE, MCAM, MCE, MCS, MEE, MEE, MES, MME, MMS, MS, PhD, MBA/M Stat, MBA/ME, MBA/MEE, MD/PhD. MD/PhD offered jointly with Baylor College of Medicine, The University of Texas Health Science Center at Houston. *Program availability:* Part-time. Terminal master's awarded for partial completion of doctoral program. *Degree requirements:* For master's, comprehensive exam (for some programs), thesis (for some programs); for doctorate, comprehensive exam (for some programs), thesis/dissertation. *Entrance requirements:* For master's and doctorate, GRE General Test. Additional exam requirements/recommendations for international students: Required—TOEFL (minimum score 600 paper-based). Electronic applications accepted. *Faculty research:* Digital signal processing, tissue engineering, groundwater remediation, computational engineering and high performance computing, nanoscale science and technology.

Robert Morris University, School of Engineering, Mathematics and Science, Moon Township, PA 15108-1189. Offers engineering management (MS). *Program availability:* Part-time, evening/weekend. *Faculty:* 7 full-time (1 woman). *Students:* 17 part-time (6 women); includes 2 minority (1 Asian, non-Hispanic/Latino; 1 Hispanic/Latino), 6 international. Average age 36. 40 applicants, 28% accepted, 4 enrolled. In 2016, 20 master's awarded. *Entrance requirements:* For master's, letters of recommendation. Additional exam requirements/recommendations for international students: Required—TOEFL (minimum score 550 paper-based; 79 iBT). *Application deadline:* For fall admission, 7/1 priority date for domestic and international students; for spring admission, 11/1 priority date for domestic and international students. Applications are processed on a rolling basis. Application fee: $35. Electronic applications accepted. *Expenses:* $870 per credit (for master's degree). *Financial support:* Federal Work-Study, institutionally sponsored loans, and unspecified assistantships available. Financial award application deadline: 5/1; financial award applicants required to submit FAFSA. *Unit head:* Dr. Maria V. Kalevitch, Dean, 412-397-4020, Fax: 412-397-2472, E-mail: kalevitch@rmu.edu.
Website: http://www.rmu.edu/web/cms/schools/sems/

Rochester Institute of Technology, Graduate Enrollment Services, Kate Gleason College of Engineering, Rochester, NY 14623-5603. Offers ME, MS, PhD, Advanced Certificate. *Program availability:* Part-time, evening/weekend, 100% online. *Students:* 473 full-time (98 women), 220 part-time (36 women); includes 45 minority (7 Black or African American, non-Hispanic/Latino; 19 Asian, non-Hispanic/Latino; 15 Hispanic/Latino; 4 Two or more races, non-Hispanic/Latino), 393 international. Average age 26. 1,731 applicants, 35% accepted, 193 enrolled. In 2016, 218 master's, 4 doctorates, 1 other advanced degree awarded. Terminal master's awarded for partial completion of doctoral program. *Degree requirements:* For master's, comprehensive exam (for some programs), thesis (for some programs); for doctorate, comprehensive exam, thesis/dissertation. *Entrance requirements:* For master's and doctorate, GRE, minimum GPA of 3.0 (recommended); for Advanced Certificate, minimum GPA of 3.0 (recommended). *Application deadline:* For fall admission, 2/15 priority date for domestic and international students. Applications are processed on a rolling basis. Application fee: $60. Electronic applications accepted. *Expenses:* $1,742 per credit hour. *Financial support:* In 2016–17, 409 students received support. Fellowships with tuition reimbursements available, research assistantships with tuition reimbursements available, teaching assistantships with tuition reimbursements available, career-related internships or fieldwork, scholarships/grants, tuition waivers (full and partial), unspecified assistantships, and health care benefits (for PhD program only) available. Support available to part-time students. Financial award applicants required to submit FAFSA. *Faculty research:* Advanced materials, computer vision, embedded systems and control, high performance computing, operations, photonics, semiconductor processing, supply chain and logistics, sustainability, transportation, energy, communications, and healthcare. *Unit head:* Dr. Doreen Edwards, Dean, 585-475-2145, Fax: 585-475-6879, E-mail: coe@rit.edu. *Application contact:* Diane Ellison, Associate Vice President, Graduate Enrollment Services, 585-475-2229, Fax: 585-475-7164, E-mail: gradinfo@rit.edu.
Website: http://www.rit.edu/kgcoe/

Rose-Hulman Institute of Technology, Faculty of Engineering and Applied Sciences, Terre Haute, IN 47803-3999. Offers M Eng, MS, MD/MS. *Program availability:* Part-time, evening/weekend. *Faculty:* 121 full-time (25 women), 5 part-time/adjunct (1 woman). *Students:* 48 full-time (12 women), 28 part-time (3 women); includes 8 minority (2 Black or African American, non-Hispanic/Latino; 2 Asian, non-Hispanic/Latino; 2 Hispanic/Latino; 2 Two or more races, non-Hispanic/Latino), 36 international. Average age 24. 97 applicants, 75% accepted, 37 enrolled. In 2016, 39 master's awarded. *Degree requirements:* For master's, thesis (for some programs). *Entrance requirements:* For master's, GRE, minimum GPA of 3.0. Additional exam requirements/recommendations for international students: Required—TOEFL (minimum score 580 paper-based; 92 iBT). *Application deadline:* For fall admission, 2/1 priority date for domestic students. Applications are processed on a rolling basis. Application fee: $0. Electronic applications accepted. *Expenses: Tuition:* Full-time $43,122. *Financial support:* In 2016–17, 68 students received support. Fellowships with tuition reimbursements available, research assistantships with tuition reimbursements available, institutionally sponsored loans, scholarships/grants, and tuition waivers (full and partial) available. *Faculty research:* Optical instrument design and prototypes, biomaterials, adsorption and adsorption-based separations, image and speech processing, groundwater, solid and hazardous waste. *Total annual research expenditures:* $534,782. *Application contact:* Dr. Azad Siahmakoun, Associate Dean of the Faculty, 812-877-8400, Fax: 812-877-8061, E-mail: siahmako@rose-hulman.edu.
Website: http://www.rose-hulman.edu

Rowan University, Graduate School, College of Engineering, Program in Engineering, Glassboro, NJ 08028-1701. Offers MSE. *Program availability:* Part-time, evening/weekend. *Degree requirements:* For master's, thesis (for some programs). *Entrance requirements:* For master's, GRE General Test. Additional exam requirements/recommendations for international students: Required—TOEFL. Electronic applications accepted.

Royal Military College of Canada, Division of Graduate Studies and Research, Engineering Division, Kingston, ON K7K 7B4, Canada. Offers M Eng, M Sc, MA Sc, PhD. *Degree requirements:* For master's, thesis; for doctorate, comprehensive exam, thesis/dissertation. *Entrance requirements:* For master's, honours degree with second-class standing; for doctorate, master's degree. Electronic applications accepted.

Saginaw Valley State University, College of Science, Engineering, and Technology, University Center, MI 48710. Offers MS. *Program availability:* Part-time, evening/weekend. *Faculty:* 2 full-time (0 women). *Students:* 1 full-time (0 women), 4 part-time (2 women), 2 international. Average age 31. 33 applicants, 12% accepted, 1 enrolled. *Degree requirements:* For master's, field project or thesis work. *Entrance requirements:* For master's, minimum GPA of 3.0. Additional exam requirements/recommendations for international students: Required—TOEFL (minimum score 550 paper-based; 79 iBT). *Application deadline:* For fall admission, 7/15 for international students; for winter

admission, 11/15 for international students; for spring admission, 4/15 for international students. Applications are processed on a rolling basis. Application fee: $30 ($90 for international students). Electronic applications accepted. *Expenses:* Tuition, state resident: full-time $9652; part-time $536 per credit hour. Tuition, nonresident: full-time $12,259; part-time $1022 per credit hour. *Required fees:* $263; $14.60 per credit hour. Tuition and fees vary according to degree level. *Financial support:* Federal Work-Study and scholarships/grants available. Support available to part-time students. Financial award application deadline: 4/1; financial award applicants required to submit FAFSA. *Unit head:* Dr. Robert Tuttle, Program Coordinator, 989-964-4144, Fax: 989-964-2717. *Application contact:* Jenna Briggs, Director, Graduate and International Admissions, 989-964-6096, Fax: 989-964-2788, E-mail: gradadm@svsu.edu.
Website: http://www.svsu.edu/collegeofscienceengineeringtechnology/

St. Cloud State University, School of Graduate Studies, College of Science and Engineering, St. Cloud, MN 56301-4498. Offers MA, MEM, MS. *Degree requirements:* For master's, thesis or alternative. *Entrance requirements:* For master's, GRE General Test, minimum GPA of 2.75. Additional exam requirements/recommendations for international students: Required—TOEFL (minimum score 550 paper-based). Electronic applications accepted.

San Diego State University, Graduate and Research Affairs, College of Engineering, San Diego, CA 92182. Offers MS, PhD. *Program availability:* Part-time, evening/weekend. Terminal master's awarded for partial completion of doctoral program. *Degree requirements:* For master's, thesis optional; for doctorate, thesis/dissertation. *Entrance requirements:* For master's, GRE General Test; for doctorate, GRE, 3 letters of recommendation. Additional exam requirements/recommendations for international students: Required—TOEFL. Electronic applications accepted.

San Francisco State University, Division of Graduate Studies, College of Science and Engineering, School of Engineering, San Francisco, CA 94132-1722. Offers embedded electrical and computer systems (MS); energy systems (MS); structural/earthquake engineering (MS). *Program availability:* Part-time. *Application deadline:* Applications are processed on a rolling basis. Electronic applications accepted. *Expenses:* Tuition, state resident: full-time $6738. Tuition, nonresident: full-time $15,666. *Required fees:* $1012. Tuition and fees vary according to degree level and program. *Unit head:* Dr. Wenshen Pong, Director, 415-338-7738, Fax: 415-338-0525, E-mail: wspong@sfsu.edu. *Application contact:* Dr. Hamid Shahnasser, Graduate Coordinator, 415-338-2124, Fax: 415-338-0525, E-mail: hamid@sfsu.edu.
Website: http://engineering.sfsu.edu/

Santa Clara University, School of Engineering, Santa Clara, CA 95053. Offers applied mathematics (MS); bioengineering (MS); civil engineering (MS); computer science and engineering (MS, PhD); electrical engineering (MS, PhD); engineering (Engineer); engineering management and leadership (MS); mechanical engineering (MS, PhD); software engineering (MS); sustainable energy (MS). *Program availability:* Part-time, evening/weekend. *Faculty:* 66 full-time (22 women), 59 part-time/adjunct (12 women). *Students:* 449 full-time (188 women), 315 part-time (114 women); includes 197 minority (3 Black or African American, non-Hispanic/Latino; 144 Asian, non-Hispanic/Latino; 33 Hispanic/Latino; 1 Native Hawaiian or other Pacific Islander, non-Hispanic/Latino; 16 Two or more races, non-Hispanic/Latino), 418 international. Average age 28. 1,217 applicants, 45% accepted, 293 enrolled. In 2016, 466 master's awarded. *Entrance requirements:* For master's, GRE, transcript; for doctorate, GRE, master's degree or equivalent, 3 letters of recommendation, statement of purpose; for Engineer, master's degree. Additional exam requirements/recommendations for international students: Required—TOEFL (minimum score 79 iBT) or IELTS (6.5). *Application deadline:* For fall admission, 4/1 for domestic and international students; for winter admission, 9/9 for domestic students, 9/2 for international students; for spring admission, 2/17 for domestic students, 12/9 for international students. Application fee: $60. Electronic applications accepted. *Expenses:* $928 per unit. *Financial support:* Fellowships, research assistantships, teaching assistantships, career-related internships or fieldwork, Federal Work-Study, scholarships/grants, traineeships, health care benefits, tuition waivers, and unspecified assistantships available. Support available to part-time students. Financial award applicants required to submit FAFSA. *Unit head:* Dr. Alfonso Ortega, Dean. *Application contact:* Stacey Tinker, Director of Admissions and Marketing, 408-554-4313, Fax: 408-554-4323, E-mail: stinker@scu.edu.
Website: http://www.scu.edu/engineering/graduate/

Seattle University, College of Science and Engineering, Seattle, WA 98122-1090. Offers MSCS, MSE. *Program availability:* Part-time, evening/weekend. *Faculty:* 11 full-time (5 women), 6 part-time/adjunct (0 women). *Students:* 49 full-time (19 women), 61 part-time (16 women); includes 31 minority (1 Black or African American, non-Hispanic/Latino; 22 Asian, non-Hispanic/Latino; 5 Hispanic/Latino; 3 Two or more races, non-Hispanic/Latino), 31 international. Average age 28. 130 applicants, 52% accepted, 45 enrolled. In 2016, 39 master's awarded. *Degree requirements:* For master's, thesis. *Entrance requirements:* For master's, GRE General Test, 2 years of related work experience. *Application deadline:* For fall admission, 7/1 for domestic students. Application fee: $55. *Expenses:* Contact institution. *Financial support:* In 2016–17, 7 students received support. Career-related internships or fieldwork and Federal Work-Study available. Support available to part-time students. Financial award applicants required to submit FAFSA. *Unit head:* Dr. Michael Quinn, Dean, 206-296-5500, Fax: 206-296-2071. *Application contact:* Janet Shandley, Director of Graduate Admissions, 206-296-5900, Fax: 206-298-5656, E-mail: grad_admissions@seattleu.edu.
Website: https://www.seattleu.edu/scieng/

Simon Fraser University, Office of Graduate Studies and Postdoctoral Fellows, Faculty of Applied Sciences, School of Engineering Science, Burnaby, BC V5A 1S6, Canada. Offers M Eng, MA Sc, PhD. *Program availability:* Part-time. *Faculty:* 27 full-time (6 women). *Students:* 118 full-time (40 women), 5 part-time. 228 applicants, 21% accepted, 19 enrolled. In 2016, 19 master's, 10 doctorates awarded. *Degree requirements:* For master's, thesis (for some programs); for doctorate, thesis/dissertation, qualifying exam, seminar presentations. *Entrance requirements:* For master's, minimum GPA of 3.0 (on scale of 4.33) or 3.33 based on last 60 credits of undergraduate courses; for doctorate, minimum GPA of 3.5 (on scale of 4.33). Additional exam requirements/recommendations for international students: Recommended—TOEFL (minimum score 580 paper-based; 93 iBT), IELTS (minimum score 7), TWE (minimum score 5). *Application deadline:* For fall admission, 1/15 for domestic and international students; for winter admission, 6/14 for domestic and international students; for spring admission, 8/15 for domestic and international students. Applications are processed on a rolling basis. Application fee: $90 ($125 for international students). Electronic applications accepted. *Financial support:* In 2016–17, 51 students received support, including 33 fellowships (averaging $6,500 per year), teaching assistantships (averaging $5,608 per year); research assistantships and scholarships/grants also available. *Faculty research:* Biomedical engineering, communications, microelectronics, systems and robotics. *Unit head:* Dr. Ivan Bajic, Graduate Program Chair, 778-782-7159, Fax: 778-782-4951, E-mail: ensc-grad-chair@sfu.ca. *Application contact:* Kate Crompton, Graduate Program Assistant, 778-782-4923, Fax: 778-782-4951, E-mail: enscgsec@sfu.ca.
Website: http://www.ensc.sfu.ca/

South Dakota School of Mines and Technology, Graduate Division, College of Engineering, Rapid City, SD 57701-3995. Offers MS, PhD. *Program availability:* Part-time, online learning. *Degree requirements:* For doctorate, thesis/dissertation. *Entrance requirements:* For doctorate, minimum graduate GPA of 3.0. Additional exam requirements/recommendations for international students: Required—TOEFL (minimum score 520 paper-based; 68 iBT), TWE. Electronic applications accepted. *Faculty research:* Contaminants in soil, nitrate leaching, environmental changes, fracture formations, greenhouse effect.

South Dakota State University, Graduate School, College of Engineering, Brookings, SD 57007. Offers MS, PhD. *Program availability:* Part-time. *Degree requirements:* For master's, thesis, oral exam; for doctorate, thesis/dissertation, preliminary oral and written exams. *Entrance requirements:* Additional exam requirements/recommendations for international students: Required—TOEFL. *Faculty research:* Process control and management, ground source heat pumps, water quality, heat transfer, power systems.

Southern Illinois University Carbondale, Graduate School, College of Engineering, Carbondale, IL 62901-4701. Offers ME, MS, PhD, JD/MS. *Degree requirements:* For master's, comprehensive exam; for doctorate, thesis/dissertation. *Entrance requirements:* For master's, GRE, minimum GPA of 2.7; for doctorate, GRE General Test, minimum GPA of 3.5. Additional exam requirements/recommendations for international students: Required—TOEFL. *Faculty research:* Electrical systems, all facets of fossil energy, mechanics.

Southern Illinois University Edwardsville, Graduate School, School of Engineering, Edwardsville, IL 62026. Offers MS. *Program availability:* Part-time, evening/weekend. *Degree requirements:* For master's, thesis (for some programs), research paper, final exam. *Entrance requirements:* Additional exam requirements/recommendations for international students: Required—TOEFL (minimum score 550 paper-based; 79 iBT), IELTS (minimum score 6.5). Electronic applications accepted.

Southern Methodist University, Bobby B. Lyle School of Engineering, Dallas, TX 75275. Offers MA, MS, MS Cp E, MSEE, MSEM, MSIEM, MSME, DE, PhD. *Program availability:* Part-time, evening/weekend, online learning. Terminal master's awarded for partial completion of doctoral program. *Degree requirements:* For master's, thesis optional; for doctorate, thesis/dissertation, oral and written qualifying exams. *Entrance requirements:* For master's, GRE General Test, minimum GPA of 3.0 in last 2 years; bachelor's degree in engineering, mathematics, or sciences; for doctorate, bachelor's degree in related field. Additional exam requirements/recommendations for international students: Required—TOEFL (minimum score 550 paper-based). *Expenses:* Contact institution. *Faculty research:* Mobile and fault-tolerant computing, manufacturing systems, telecommunications, solid state devices and materials, fluid and thermal sciences.

Southern University and Agricultural and Mechanical College, Graduate School, College of Engineering, Baton Rouge, LA 70813. Offers ME. *Degree requirements:* For master's, thesis. *Entrance requirements:* For master's, GRE General Test. Additional exam requirements/recommendations for international students: Required—TOEFL (minimum score 525 paper-based).

Stanford University, School of Engineering, Stanford, CA 94305-2004. Offers MS, PhD, Engr. *Degree requirements:* For doctorate, thesis/dissertation; for Engr, thesis. *Entrance requirements:* For master's, doctorate, and Engr, GRE General Test. Additional exam requirements/recommendations for international students: Required—TOEFL. Electronic applications accepted. *Expenses:* Contact institution.

Stevens Institute of Technology, Graduate School, Charles V. Schaefer Jr. School of Engineering and Science, Hoboken, NJ 07030. Offers M Eng, MS, PhD, Certificate, Engr. *Program availability:* Part-time, evening/weekend, online learning. *Faculty:* 173 full-time (36 women), 80 part-time/adjunct (8 women). *Students:* 1,301 full-time (352 women), 331 part-time (76 women); includes 119 minority (28 Black or African American, non-Hispanic/Latino; 1 American Indian or Alaska Native, non-Hispanic/Latino; 72 Asian, non-Hispanic/Latino; 9 Hispanic/Latino; 9 Two or more races, non-Hispanic/Latino), 1,180 international. Average age 26. 4,438 applicants, 54% accepted, 589 enrolled. In 2016, 804 master's, 38 doctorates, 196 other advanced degrees awarded. Terminal master's awarded for partial completion of doctoral program. *Entrance requirements:* Additional exam requirements/recommendations for international students: Required—TOEFL (minimum score 74 iBT). *Application deadline:* For fall admission, 6/1 for domestic students, 4/15 for international students; for spring admission, 11/30 for domestic students, 11/1 for international students. Applications are processed on a rolling basis. Application fee: $65. Electronic applications accepted. *Expenses:* Contact institution. *Financial support:* Fellowships, research assistantships, teaching assistantships, career-related internships or fieldwork, Federal Work-Study, scholarships/grants, and unspecified assistantships available. Financial award application deadline: 2/15; financial award applicants required to submit FAFSA. *Unit head:* Dr. Keith G. Sheppard, Interim Dean, 201-216-5263, E-mail: keith.sheppard@stevens.edu. *Application contact:* Graduate Admissions, 888-783-8367, Fax: 888-555-1306, E-mail: graduate@stevens.edu.
Website: http://www.stevens.edu/ses/

Stony Brook University, State University of New York, Graduate School, College of Engineering and Applied Sciences, Stony Brook, NY 11794-2200. Offers MS, PhD, AGC, Advanced Certificate, Certificate, Graduate Certificate. *Program availability:* Part-time, evening/weekend. *Faculty:* 181 full-time (35 women), 55 part-time/adjunct (15 women). *Students:* 1,226 full-time (356 women), 279 part-time (72 women); includes 154 minority (17 Black or African American, non-Hispanic/Latino; 100 Asian, non-Hispanic/Latino; 31 Hispanic/Latino; 6 Two or more races, non-Hispanic/Latino), 1,140 international. Average age 26. 4,273 applicants, 37% accepted, 459 enrolled. In 2016, 540 master's, 92 doctorates awarded. *Degree requirements:* For doctorate, comprehensive exam, thesis/dissertation. *Entrance requirements:* For doctorate, GRE General Test. Additional exam requirements/recommendations for international students: Required—TOEFL (minimum score 90 iBT). *Application deadline:* For fall admission, 1/15 for domestic students; for spring admission, 10/1 for domestic students. Application fee: $100. *Expenses:* Contact institution. *Financial support:* In 2016–17, 8 fellowships, 167 research assistantships, 201 teaching assistantships were awarded; career-related internships or fieldwork also available. *Total annual research expenditures:* $30.6 million. *Unit head:* Dr. Fotis Sotiropoulos, Dean, 631-632-8380, Fax: 631-632-8205, E-mail: fotis.sotiropoulos@stonybrook.edu. *Application contact:* Melissa Jordan, Assistant Dean for Records and Admission, 631-632-9712, Fax: 631-632-7243, E-mail: gradadmissions@stonybrook.edu.
Website: http://www.ceas.sunysb.edu/

Syracuse University, College of Engineering and Computer Science, Syracuse, NY 13244. Offers MS, PhD, CAS. *Program availability:* Part-time, evening/weekend. *Faculty:* 94 full-time (20 women), 20 part-time/adjunct (2 women). *Students:* 883 full-time (211 women), 207 part-time (40 women); includes 62 minority (17 Black or African American, non-Hispanic/Latino; 32 Asian, non-Hispanic/Latino; 10 Hispanic/Latino; 3 Two or more races, non-Hispanic/Latino), 838 international. Average age 26. 3,045 applicants, 39% accepted, 392 enrolled. In 2016, 453 master's, 24 doctorates, 2 other advanced degrees awarded. *Degree requirements:* For master's, comprehensive exam (for some programs), thesis (for some programs); for doctorate, comprehensive exam, thesis/dissertation. *Entrance requirements:* For master's, doctorate, and CAS, GRE

General Test, resume, official transcripts, personal statement, three letters of recommendation. Additional exam requirements/recommendations for international students: Required—TOEFL, IELTS. *Application deadline:* For fall admission, 7/1 priority date for domestic students, 6/1 priority date for international students; for spring admission, 11/15 priority date for domestic students, 10/15 priority date for international students. Applications are processed on a rolling basis. Application fee: $75. Electronic applications accepted. *Expenses: Tuition:* Full-time $25,974; part-time $1443 per credit hour. *Required fees:* $802; $50 per course. Tuition and fees vary according to course load and program. *Financial support:* Fellowships with full tuition reimbursements, research assistantships with tuition reimbursements, teaching assistantships with tuition reimbursements, scholarships/grants, and tuition waivers (partial) available. Financial award application deadline: 1/1; financial award applicants required to submit FAFSA. *Faculty research:* Environmental systems, information assurance, biomechanics, solid mechanics and materials, software engineering. *Unit head:* Dr. Teresa Dahlberg, Dean, College of Engineering and Computer Science, 315-443-2545, E-mail: dahlberg@syr.edu. *Application contact:* Kathleen Joyce, Assistant Dean, 314-443-2219, E-mail: topgrads@syr.edu. Website: http://eng-cs.syr.edu/

★ **Temple University,** College of Engineering, PhD in Engineering Program, Philadelphia, PA 19122-6096. Offers bioengineering (PhD); civil engineering (PhD); electrical engineering (PhD); environmental engineering (PhD); mechanical engineering (PhD). *Program availability:* Part-time, evening/weekend. *Faculty:* 67 full-time (13 women), 11 part-time/adjunct (1 woman). *Students:* 32 full-time (11 women), 7 part-time (2 women); includes 10 minority (3 Black or African American, non-Hispanic/Latino; 5 Asian, non-Hispanic/Latino; 1 Hispanic/Latino; 1 Two or more races, non-Hispanic/Latino), 19 international. 11 applicants, 64% accepted, 3 enrolled. In 2016, 6 doctorates awarded. *Degree requirements:* For doctorate, thesis/dissertation, preliminary exam, dissertation proposal and defense. *Entrance requirements:* For doctorate, GRE, minimum undergraduate GPA of 3.0; MS in engineering from ABET-accredited or equivalent institution (preferred); resume; goals statement; three letters of reference; official transcripts. Additional exam requirements/recommendations for international students: Required—TOEFL (minimum score 550 paper-based; 79 iBT), IELTS (minimum score 6.5), PTE (minimum score 53). *Application deadline:* For fall admission, 1/15 priority date for domestic and international students; for spring admission, 11/1 priority date for domestic students, 8/1 priority date for international students. Applications are processed on a rolling basis. Application fee: $60. Electronic applications accepted. *Expenses:* $995 per credit hour in-state tuition; $1,319 per credit hour out-of-state. *Financial support:* Fellowships with tuition reimbursements, research assistantships with tuition reimbursements, teaching assistantships with tuition reimbursements, Federal Work-Study, scholarships/grants, health care benefits, and unspecified assistantships available. Financial award application deadline: 3/1; financial award applicants required to submit FAFSA. *Faculty research:* Advanced/computer-aided manufacturing and advanced materials processing; bioengineering; computer engineering; construction engineering and management; dynamics, controls, and systems; energy and environmental science; engineering physics and engineering mathematics; green engineering; signal processing and communication; transportation engineering; water resources, hydrology, and environmental engineering. *Unit head:* Dr. Saroj Biswas, Associate Dean, College of Engineering, 215-204-8403, E-mail: sbiswas@temple.edu. *Application contact:* Leslie Levin, Director, Admissions and Graduate Student Services, 215-204-7800, Fax: 215-204-6936, E-mail: gradengr@temple.edu.
Website: http://engineering.temple.edu/additional-programs/phd-engineering
See Display on this page and Close-Up on page 83.

Tennessee State University, The School of Graduate Studies and Research, College of Engineering, Nashville, TN 37209-1561. Offers biomedical engineering (ME); civil engineering (ME); computer and information systems engineering (MS, PhD); electrical engineering (ME); environmental engineering (ME); manufacturing engineering (ME); mathematical sciences (MS); mechanical engineering (ME). *Program availability:* Part-time, evening/weekend. *Degree requirements:* For master's, project; for doctorate, comprehensive exam, thesis/dissertation. *Entrance requirements:* For doctorate, minimum GPA of 3.3. *Faculty research:* Robotics, intelligent systems, human-computer interaction software systems, biomedical engineering, signal/image processing, probabilistic design, intelligent manufacturing, cooperative mobile robots, condition based maintenance, sensor fusion.

Tennessee Technological University, College of Graduate Studies, College of Engineering, Cookeville, TN 38505. Offers MS, PhD. *Program availability:* Part-time. *Faculty:* 76 full-time (2 women). *Students:* 82 full-time (20 women), 127 part-time (25 women); includes 12 minority (4 Black or African American, non-Hispanic/Latino; 3 Asian, non-Hispanic/Latino; 1 Hispanic/Latino; 1 Native Hawaiian or other Pacific Islander, non-Hispanic/Latino; 3 Two or more races, non-Hispanic/Latino), 110 international. Average age 28. 489 applicants, 45% accepted, 53 enrolled. In 2016, 37 master's, 12 doctorates awarded. *Degree requirements:* For master's, comprehensive exam, thesis; for doctorate, comprehensive exam, thesis/dissertation. *Entrance requirements:* For master's, GRE General Test; for doctorate, GRE, minimum GPA of 3.5. Additional exam requirements/recommendations for international students: Required—TOEFL (minimum score 550 paper-based; 79 iBT), IELTS (minimum score 5.5), PTE (minimum score 53), or TOEIC (Test of English as an International Communication). *Application deadline:* For fall admission, 8/1 for domestic students, 5/1 for international students; for spring admission, 12/1 for domestic students, 10/1 for international students. Applications are processed on a rolling basis. Application fee: $35 ($40 for international students). Electronic applications accepted. *Expenses:* Tuition, state resident: full-time $9375; part-time $534 per credit hour. Tuition, nonresident: full-time $22,443; part-time $1260 per credit hour. *Financial support:* In 2016–17, 3 fellowships (averaging $8,000 per year), 99 research assistantships (averaging $9,293 per year), 80 teaching assistantships (averaging $8,000 per year) were awarded; career-related internships or fieldwork also available. Support available to part-time students. Financial award application deadline: 4/1. *Unit head:* Dr. Joseph Rencis, Dean, 931-372-3172, Fax: 931-372-6172, E-mail: jjrencis@tntech.edu. *Application contact:* Shelia K. Kendrick, Coordinator of Graduate Studies, 931-372-3808, Fax: 931-372-3497, E-mail: skendrick@tntech.edu.

Texas A&M University–Kingsville, College of Graduate Studies, Frank H. Dotterweich College of Engineering, Kingsville, TX 78363. Offers ME, MS, PhD. *Degree requirements:* For master's, variable foreign language requirement, comprehensive exam, thesis (for some programs); for doctorate, variable foreign language requirement, comprehensive exam, thesis/dissertation (for some programs). *Entrance requirements:* For master's and doctorate, GRE, MAT, GMAT. Additional exam requirements/recommendations for international students: Required—TOEFL (minimum score 550 paper-based; 79 iBT). Electronic applications accepted.

Texas State University, The Graduate College, College of Science and Engineering, Program in Engineering, San Marcos, TX 78666. Offers electrical engineering (MS); industrial engineering (MS); manufacturing engineering (MS). *Program availability:* Part-time. *Faculty:* 15 full-time (2 women), 2 part-time/adjunct (0 women). *Students:* 49 full-time (15 women), 10 part-time (3 women); includes 7 minority (3 Asian, non-Hispanic/

Engineering and Applied Sciences—General

Latino; 3 Hispanic/Latino; 1 Two or more races, non-Hispanic/Latino), 45 international. Average age 28. 163 applicants, 43% accepted, 30 enrolled. *Degree requirements:* For master's, comprehensive exam, thesis (for some programs), thesis or research project. *Entrance requirements:* For master's, GRE (minimum preferred scores of 285 overall, 135 verbal, 150 quantitative), baccalaureate degree from regionally-accredited university in engineering, computer science, physics, technology, or closely-related field with minimum GPA of 3.0 on last 60 undergraduate semester hours; resume or curriculum vitae; 2 letters of recommendation; statement of purpose. Additional exam requirements/recommendations for international students: Required—TOEFL (minimum score 550 paper-based; 78 iBT), IELTS (minimum score 6.5). *Application deadline:* For fall admission, 2/15 priority date for domestic students, 2/1 priority date for international students. Application fee: $40 ($90 for international students). Electronic applications accepted. *Expenses:* $4,851 per semester. *Financial support:* In 2016–17, 25 students received support, including 15 research assistantships (averaging $14,047 per year), 19 teaching assistantships (averaging $13,572 per year); Federal Work-Study, institutionally sponsored loans, scholarships/grants, and unspecified assistantships also available. Support available to part-time students. Financial award application deadline: 3/1; financial award applicants required to submit FAFSA. *Faculty research:* Building a regional energy and educational network; recruitment and retention of female undergraduates in engineering and computer science; fostering nanotechnology environment, health, safety awareness; low-cost flexible graphene-based digital beam forming phased-array antennas engaging, sustaining and empowering women and minorities in STEM. *Total annual research expenditures:* $854,198. *Unit head:* Dr. Vishu Viswanathan, Graduate Advisor, 512-245-1826, Fax: 512-245-8365, E-mail: vishu.viswanathan@txstate.edu. *Application contact:* Dr. Andrea Golato, Dean of Graduate School, 512-245-2581, Fax: 512-245-8365, E-mail: gradcollege@txstate.edu. Website: http://www.engineering.txstate.edu/Programs/Graduate.html

Texas Tech University, Graduate School, Edward E. Whitacre Jr. College of Engineering, Lubbock, TX 79409-3103. Offers M Engr, MENVEGR, MS, MS Ch E, MSCE, MSEE, MSIE, MSME, MSPE, MSSEM, PhD, JD/M Engr. *Program availability:* Part-time, evening/weekend, 100% online, blended/hybrid learning. *Faculty:* 176 full-time (30 women), 16 part-time/adjunct (1 woman). *Students:* 663 full-time (162 women), 233 part-time (41 women); includes 102 minority (19 Black or African American, non-Hispanic/Latino; 1 American Indian or Alaska Native, non-Hispanic/Latino; 19 Asian, non-Hispanic/Latino; 54 Hispanic/Latino; 9 Two or more races, non-Hispanic/Latino), 587 international. Average age 29. 1,837 applicants, 34% accepted, 241 enrolled. In 2016, 259 master's, 51 doctorates awarded. *Degree requirements:* For master's, comprehensive exam, thesis (for some programs); for doctorate, comprehensive exam, thesis/dissertation. *Entrance requirements:* For master's, GRE (Verbal and Quantitative), minimum GPA of 3.0. Additional exam requirements/recommendations for international students: Required—TOEFL (minimum score 550 paper-based; 79 iBT), IELTS (minimum score 6.5). *Application deadline:* For fall admission, 6/1 priority date for domestic students, 1/15 priority date for international students; for spring admission, 9/1 priority date for domestic students, 6/15 priority date for international students. Applications are processed on a rolling basis. Application fee: $75. Electronic applications accepted. *Expenses:* $325 per credit hour full-time resident tuition, $733 per credit hour full-time non-resident tuition; $53.75 per credit hour fee plus $608 per term fee. *Financial support:* In 2016–17, 654 students received support, including 574 fellowships (averaging $3,309 per year), 343 research assistantships (averaging $16,212 per year), 209 teaching assistantships (averaging $17,931 per year); health care benefits also available. Financial award application deadline: 4/15; financial award applicants required to submit FAFSA. *Faculty research:* Bioengineering, interdisciplinary studies, health care engineering, intellectual property, law and engineering. *Total annual research expenditures:* $19.2 million. *Unit head:* Dr. Albert Sacco, Jr., Dean, Edward E.

Whitacre Jr. College of Engineering, 806-742-3451, Fax: 806-742-3493, E-mail: al.sacco-jr@ttu.edu. *Application contact:* Dr. Brandon Weeks, Associate Dean of Research and Graduate Programs, Edward E. Whitacre Jr. College of Engineering, 806-834-7450, Fax: 806-742-3493, E-mail: brandon.weeks@ttu.edu. Website: http://www.depts.ttu.edu/coe/

Tufts University, School of Engineering, Medford, MA 02155. Offers ME, MS, MSEM, PhD. *Program availability:* Part-time. Terminal master's awarded for partial completion of doctoral program. *Degree requirements:* For master's, thesis (for some programs); for doctorate, thesis/dissertation. *Entrance requirements:* For master's and doctorate, GRE General Test. Additional exam requirements/recommendations for international students: Required—TOEFL (minimum score 550 paper-based; 80 iBT), IELTS (minimum score 6.5). Electronic applications accepted. *Expenses: Tuition:* Full-time $49,892; part-time $1248 per credit hour. *Required fees:* $844. Full-time tuition and fees vary according to degree level, program and student level. Part-time tuition and fees vary according to course load.
See Display below and Close-Up on page 85.

Tuskegee University, Graduate Programs, College of Engineering, Tuskegee, AL 36088. Offers MSEE, MSME, PhD. *Degree requirements:* For master's, thesis or alternative. *Entrance requirements:* For master's, GRE General Test, GRE Subject Test. Additional exam requirements/recommendations for international students: Required—TOEFL (minimum score 500 paper-based).

Universidad de las Américas Puebla, Division of Graduate Studies, School of Engineering, Puebla, Mexico. Offers M Adm, MS, PhD. *Program availability:* Part-time, evening/weekend. *Degree requirements:* For master's, one foreign language, thesis. *Faculty research:* Artificial intelligence, food technology, construction, telecommunications, computers in education, operations research.

Universidad del Turabo, Graduate Programs, School of Engineering, Gurabo, PR 00778-3030. Offers computer engineering (M Eng); electrical engineering (M Eng); mechanical engineering (M Eng); telecommunications and network systems administration (M Eng). *Students:* 14 full-time (0 women), 46 part-time (7 women); all minorities (all Hispanic/Latino). Average age 34. 74 applicants, 41% accepted, 20 enrolled. In 2016, 13 master's awarded. *Entrance requirements:* For master's, GRE, EXADEP or GMAT, interview, essay, official transcript, recommendation letters. *Application deadline:* Applications are processed on a rolling basis. Application fee: $25. Electronic applications accepted. *Financial support:* Institutionally sponsored loans available. Financial award applicants required to submit FAFSA. *Unit head:* Hector Rodriguez, Dean, 787-743-7979 Ext. 4144. *Application contact:* Diriee Rodriguez, Admissions Director, 787-743-7979 Ext. 4453, E-mail: admisiones-ut@suagm.edu. Website: http://ut.suagm.edu/es/engineering

Université de Moncton, Faculty of Engineering, Moncton, NB E1A 3E9, Canada. Offers civil engineering (M Sc A); electrical engineering (M Sc A); industrial engineering (M Sc A); mechanical engineering (M Sc A). *Degree requirements:* For master's, thesis, proficiency in French. *Faculty research:* Structures, energy, composite materials, quality control, geo-environment, telecommunications, instrumentation, analog and digital electronics.

Université de Sherbrooke, Faculty of Engineering, Sherbrooke, QC J1K 2R1, Canada. Offers M Eng, M Env, M Sc A, PhD, Diploma. *Program availability:* Part-time. *Degree requirements:* For master's, one foreign language, thesis; for doctorate, comprehensive exam, thesis/dissertation. *Entrance requirements:* For master's, bachelor's degree in engineering or equivalent. Electronic applications accepted.

Université du Québec à Chicoutimi, Graduate Programs, Program in Engineering, Chicoutimi, QC G7H 2B1, Canada. Offers M Sc A, PhD. *Program availability:* Part-time.

Degree requirements: For master's, thesis; for doctorate, thesis/dissertation. *Entrance requirements:* For master's, appropriate bachelor's degree, proficiency in French.

Université du Québec à Rimouski, Graduate Programs, Program in Engineering, Rimouski, QC G5L 3A1, Canada. Offers M Sc A. Program offered jointly with Université du Québec à Chicoutimi.

Université du Québec, École de technologie supérieure, Graduate Programs, Montréal, QC H3C 1K3, Canada. Offers M Eng, PhD, Diploma. *Program availability:* Online learning. *Entrance requirements:* For master's and Diploma, appropriate bachelor's degree, proficiency in French; for doctorate, appropriate master's degree, proficiency in French.

Université du Québec en Abitibi-Témiscamingue, Graduate Programs, Program in Engineering, Rouyn-Noranda, QC J9X 5E4, Canada. Offers engineering (ME); mineral engineering (ME); mining engineering (DESS).

Université Laval, Faculty of Sciences and Engineering, Québec, QC G1K 7P4, Canada. Offers M Sc, PhD, Diploma. *Program availability:* Part-time. *Degree requirements:* For doctorate, thesis/dissertation. Electronic applications accepted.

University at Albany, State University of New York, College of Engineering and Applied Sciences, Albany, NY 12222-0001. Offers MS, PhD, CAS. *Accreditation:* ALA (one or more programs are accredited). *Program availability:* Part-time. *Faculty:* 45 full-time (17 women), 36 part-time/adjunct (9 women). *Students:* 177 full-time (64 women), 155 part-time (69 women); includes 35 minority (11 Black or African American, non-Hispanic/Latino; 11 Asian, non-Hispanic/Latino; 11 Hispanic/Latino; 2 Two or more races, non-Hispanic/Latino), 186 international. Average age 27. 563 applicants, 60% accepted, 116 enrolled. In 2016, 131 master's, 8 doctorates awarded. *Degree requirements:* For doctorate, thesis/dissertation. *Entrance requirements:* For doctorate, GRE General Test. Additional exam requirements/recommendations for international students: Required—TOEFL (minimum score 550 paper-based). *Application deadline:* For fall admission, 3/1 for domestic students. Applications are processed on a rolling basis. Application fee: $75. Electronic applications accepted. *Expenses:* Tuition, state resident: full-time $10,870; part-time $453 per credit hour. Tuition, nonresident: full-time $22,210; part-time $925 per credit hour. *International tuition:* $21,550 full-time. *Required fees:* $1864; $96 per credit hour. *Financial support:* Fellowships and Federal Work-Study available. Financial award application deadline: 4/1. *Faculty research:* Human-computer interaction, government information management, library information science, Web development, social implications of technology. *Total annual research expenditures:* $2.5 million. *Unit head:* Kim L. Boyer, Dean, 518-956-8240, Fax: 518-442-5367, E-mail: ceasinfo@albany.edu.
Website: http://www.albany.edu/ceas/

University at Buffalo, the State University of New York, Graduate School, School of Engineering and Applied Sciences, Buffalo, NY 14260. Offers ME, MS, PhD, Certificate. *Program availability:* Part-time, evening/weekend, online learning. Terminal master's awarded for partial completion of doctoral program. *Degree requirements:* For doctorate, thesis/dissertation. *Entrance requirements:* For master's and doctorate, GRE General Test. Additional exam requirements/recommendations for international students: Required—TOEFL (minimum score 550 paper-based; 79 iBT). Electronic applications accepted. *Faculty research:* Bioengineering, infrastructure and environmental engineering, electronic and photonic materials, simulation and visualization, information technology and computing.

The University of Akron, Graduate School, College of Engineering, Akron, OH 44325. Offers MS, PhD. *Program availability:* Part-time, evening/weekend. *Faculty:* 89 full-time (15 women), 25 part-time/adjunct (1 woman). *Students:* 359 full-time (89 women), 75 part-time (14 women); includes 15 minority (7 Asian, non-Hispanic/Latino; 5 Hispanic/Latino; 3 Two or more races, non-Hispanic/Latino), 322 international. Average age 30. 387 applicants, 71% accepted, 99 enrolled. In 2016, 74 master's, 46 doctorates awarded. Terminal master's awarded for partial completion of doctoral program. *Degree requirements:* For master's, thesis optional; for doctorate, one foreign language, thesis/dissertation, candidacy exam, qualifying exam. *Entrance requirements:* For master's, GRE, minimum GPA of 2.75, letters of recommendation, statement of purpose, resume; for doctorate, GRE, minimum GPA of 3.0 with bachelor's degree, 3.5 with master's degree; letters of recommendation; personal statement; resume. Additional exam requirements/recommendations for international students: Required—TOEFL (minimum score 550 paper-based; 79 iBT), IELTS (minimum score 6.5). *Application deadline:* Applications are processed on a rolling basis. Application fee: $45 ($70 for international students). Electronic applications accepted. *Expenses:* Tuition, state resident: full-time $8618; part-time $359 per credit hour. Tuition, nonresident: full-time $17,149; part-time $715 per credit hour. *Required fees:* $1652. *Financial support:* In 2016–17, 1 fellowship with full tuition reimbursement, 150 research assistantships with full tuition reimbursements, 32 teaching assistantships with full tuition reimbursements were awarded; career-related internships or fieldwork, Federal Work-Study, and instructional support assistantships also available. *Faculty research:* Engineering materials, energy research, nano and microelectromechanical systems (NEMS and MEMS), bio-engineering, computational methods. *Total annual research expenditures:* $13.5 million. *Unit head:* Dr. Donald Visco, Interim Dean, 330-972-6978, E-mail: dviscoj@uakron.edu. *Application contact:* Dr. Craig Menzemer, Associate Dean for Graduate Studies and Administration, 330-972-5536, E-mail: ccmenze@uakron.edu.
Website: http://www.uakron.edu/engineering/

The University of Alabama, Graduate School, College of Engineering, Tuscaloosa, AL 35487. Offers MS, MS Ch E, MS Met E, MSAEM, MSCE, PhD. *Program availability:* Part-time, online learning. *Faculty:* 123 full-time (15 women). *Students:* 235 full-time (51 women), 43 part-time (4 women); includes 15 minority (9 Black or African American, non-Hispanic/Latino; 2 Asian, non-Hispanic/Latino; 3 Hispanic/Latino; 1 Two or more races, non-Hispanic/Latino), 152 international. Average age 27. 355 applicants, 45% accepted, 71 enrolled. In 2016, 82 master's, 22 doctorates awarded. Terminal master's awarded for partial completion of doctoral program. *Degree requirements:* For master's, comprehensive exam; for doctorate, thesis/dissertation. *Entrance requirements:* For master's and doctorate, minimum GPA of 3.0. Additional exam requirements/recommendations for international students: Required—TOEFL (minimum score 550 paper-based). *Application deadline:* For fall admission, 7/1 for domestic students, 4/15 for international students; for spring admission, 11/15 for domestic students, 9/1 for international students. Applications are processed on a rolling basis. Application fee: $50 ($60 for international students). Electronic applications accepted. *Expenses:* Tuition, state resident: full-time $10,470. Tuition, nonresident: full-time $26,950. *Financial support:* In 2016–17, 188 students received support, including 23 fellowships with full tuition reimbursements available (averaging $16,022 per year), 85 research assistantships with full tuition reimbursements available (averaging $16,022 per year), 73 teaching assistantships with full tuition reimbursements available (averaging $16,022 per year); career-related internships or fieldwork, Federal Work-Study, and institutionally sponsored loans also available. Financial award application deadline: 2/15. *Faculty research:* Materials and biomaterials networks and sensors, transportation, energy. *Total annual research expenditures:* $31.1 million. *Unit head:* Dr. Charles Karr, Dean, 205-348-6405, Fax: 205-348-8573. *Application contact:* Dr. David A. Francko, Dean, 205-348-8280, Fax: 205-348-0400, E-mail: dfrancko@ua.edu.
Website: http://coeweb.eng.ua.edu/

The University of Alabama at Birmingham, School of Engineering, Birmingham, AL 35294. Offers M Eng, MS Mt E, MSBME, MSCE, MSEE, MSME, PhD. *Program availability:* Part-time, evening/weekend, 100% online, blended/hybrid learning. *Faculty:* 78 full-time (14 women), 19 part-time/adjunct (3 women). *Students:* 131 full-time (25 women), 341 part-time (63 women); includes 132 minority (92 Black or African American, non-Hispanic/Latino; 1 American Indian or Alaska Native, non-Hispanic/Latino; 13 Asian, non-Hispanic/Latino; 13 Hispanic/Latino; 13 Two or more races, non-Hispanic/Latino), 93 international. Average age 33. 278 applicants, 82% accepted, 136 enrolled. In 2016, 150 master's, 19 doctorates awarded. *Degree requirements:* For master's, thesis (for some programs); for doctorate, comprehensive exam, thesis/dissertation. *Entrance requirements:* For master's, GRE General Test. Additional exam requirements/recommendations for international students: Required—TOEFL (minimum score 100 iBT); Recommended—IELTS (minimum score 6.5). *Application deadline:* For fall admission, 7/1 for domestic and international students; for spring admission, 11/1 for domestic and international students; for summer admission, 4/1 for domestic and international students. Applications are processed on a rolling basis. Application fee: $50 ($60 for international students). Electronic applications accepted. *Expenses:* $396 per hour resident tuition; $935 per hour non-resident tuition; $150 per course online course fee. *Financial support:* Fellowships with full tuition reimbursements, research assistantships with full tuition reimbursements, career-related internships or fieldwork, Federal Work-Study, and institutionally sponsored loans available. Support available to part-time students. *Faculty research:* High performance computing/modeling and simulation, sustainable engineering design and construction, composite materials applications and development, metals processing and research, tissue engineering, cardiac rhythm management, biomedical imaging. *Unit head:* Dr. J. Iwan Alexander, Dean, 205-975-5890, Fax: 205-934-8437, E-mail: ialex@uab.edu. *Application contact:* Holly Hebard, Director of Graduate School Operations, 205-934-8227, Fax: 205-934-8413, E-mail: gradschool@uab.edu.
Website: http://www.uab.edu/engineering/

The University of Alabama in Huntsville, School of Graduate Studies, College of Engineering, Huntsville, AL 35899. Offers MS, MSE, MSOR, MSSE, PhD. *Program availability:* Part-time, evening/weekend, online learning. *Degree requirements:* For master's, comprehensive exam, thesis or alternative, oral and written exams; for doctorate, comprehensive exam, thesis/dissertation, oral and written exams. *Entrance requirements:* For master's and doctorate, GRE General Test, minimum GPA of 3.0. Additional exam requirements/recommendations for international students: Required—TOEFL (minimum score 500 paper-based; 80 iBT), IELTS (minimum score 6.5). Electronic applications accepted. *Expenses:* Tuition, state resident: full-time $9834; part-time $600 per credit hour. Tuition, nonresident: full-time $21,830; part-time $1325 per credit hour. *Faculty research:* Transport technology, biotechnology, advanced computer architecture and systems, systems and engineering process, rocket propulsion and plasma engineering.

University of Alaska Anchorage, School of Engineering, Anchorage, AK 99508. Offers M AEST, MCE, MS, Certificate. *Program availability:* Part-time, evening/weekend. *Degree requirements:* For master's, comprehensive exam (for some programs), thesis (for some programs). *Entrance requirements:* For master's, GRE General Test. Additional exam requirements/recommendations for international students: Required—TOEFL (minimum score 550 paper-based).

University of Alaska Fairbanks, College of Engineering and Mines, PhD Programs in Engineering, Fairbanks, AK 99775. Offers PhD. *Program availability:* Part-time. *Faculty:* 43 full-time (7 women), 3 part-time/adjunct (0 women). *Students:* 8 full-time (1 woman), 9 part-time (3 women); includes 3 minority (1 Black or African American, non-Hispanic/Latino; 1 American Indian or Alaska Native, non-Hispanic/Latino; 1 Two or more races, non-Hispanic/Latino), 4 international. Average age 37. 6 applicants, 33% accepted, 1 enrolled. In 2016, 7 doctorates awarded. *Degree requirements:* For doctorate, comprehensive exam, thesis/dissertation, oral defense of dissertation. *Entrance requirements:* For doctorate, GRE General Test, minimum cumulative GPA of 3.0. Additional exam requirements/recommendations for international students: Required—TOEFL (minimum score 550 paper-based; 79 iBT), IELTS (minimum score 6.5). *Application deadline:* For fall admission, 6/1 for domestic students, 3/1 for international students; for spring admission, 10/15 for domestic students, 9/1 for international students. Applications are processed on a rolling basis. Application fee: $60. Electronic applications accepted. *Expenses:* $533 per credit resident tuition, $673 per semester resident fees; $1,088 per credit non-resident tuition, $835 per semester non-resident fees. *Financial support:* In 2016–17, 7 research assistantships (averaging $6,747 per year), 4 teaching assistantships (averaging $5,802 per year) were awarded; career-related internships or fieldwork, Federal Work-Study, scholarships/grants, health care benefits, and unspecified assistantships also available. Support available to part-time students. Financial award application deadline: 7/1; financial award applicants required to submit FAFSA. *Faculty research:* Transportation, energy, housing, and climate change. *Unit head:* Dr. Douglas J. Goering, Dean, 907-474-7730, Fax: 907-474-6994, E-mail: fycem@uaf.edu. *Application contact:* Mary Kreta, Director of Admissions, 907-474-7500, Fax: 907-474-7097, E-mail: admissions@uaf.edu.
Website: http://cem.uaf.edu/

The University of Arizona, College of Engineering, Tucson, AZ 85721. Offers ME, MS, PhD, Certificate. *Program availability:* Part-time, online learning. *Degree requirements:* For doctorate, thesis/dissertation. *Entrance requirements:* Additional exam requirements/recommendations for international students: Required—TOEFL (minimum score 550 paper-based; 79 iBT). Electronic applications accepted.

University of Arkansas, Graduate School, College of Engineering, Fayetteville, AR 72701. Offers MS, MS Cmp E, MS Ch E, MS En E, MS Tc E, MSBE, MSBME, MSCE, MSE, MSEE, MSIE, MSME, MSOR, MSTE, PhD. In 2016, 296 master's, 22 doctorates awarded. *Degree requirements:* For doctorate, one foreign language, thesis/dissertation. *Application deadline:* For fall admission, 4/1 for international students; for spring admission, 10/1 for international students. Applications are processed on a rolling basis. Application fee: $40 ($50 for international students). Electronic applications accepted. *Financial support:* In 2016–17, 198 research assistantships, 21 teaching assistantships were awarded; fellowships with tuition reimbursements, career-related internships or fieldwork, and Federal Work-Study also available. Support available to part-time students. Financial award application deadline: 4/1; financial award applicants required to submit FAFSA. *Unit head:* Dr. John English, Dean, 479-575-4153, Fax: 479-575-4346. *Application contact:* Dr. Norman Dennis, Associate Dean, 479-575-3052, E-mail: ndennis@uark.edu.
Website: http://www.engr.uark.edu/

University of Bridgeport, School of Engineering, Bridgeport, CT 06604. Offers MS, PhD. *Program availability:* Part-time, evening/weekend, online learning. *Degree requirements:* For master's, thesis optional; for doctorate, thesis/dissertation. *Entrance requirements:* Additional exam requirements/recommendations for international students: Recommended—TOEFL (minimum score 550 paper-based; 80 iBT), IELTS (minimum score 6.5). Electronic applications accepted. *Expenses:* Contact institution.

Engineering and Applied Sciences—General

The University of British Columbia, Faculty of Applied Science, Vancouver, BC V6T 1Z4, Canada. Offers M Arch, M Eng, M Sc, M Sc P, MA Sc, MAP, MASA, MASLA, MCRP, MLA, MN, MSN, MUD, PhD, M Arch/MLA. *Program availability:* Part-time. In 2016, 308 master's, 36 doctorates awarded. *Degree requirements:* For master's, comprehensive exam (for some programs), thesis (for some programs); for doctorate, comprehensive exam, thesis/dissertation. *Entrance requirements:* Additional exam requirements/recommendations for international students: Required—TOEFL (minimum score 550 paper-based; 90 iBT), IELTS. Application fee: $102 Canadian dollars ($165 Canadian dollars for international students). Electronic applications accepted. *Expenses:* Contact institution. *Financial support:* Fellowships, research assistantships, teaching assistantships, career-related internships or fieldwork, Federal Work-Study, institutionally sponsored loans, scholarships/grants, health care benefits, tuition waivers (partial), unspecified assistantships, and full-tuition waivers (for all PhD students) available. Financial award application deadline: 9/30. *Faculty research:* Architecture, nursing, engineering, landscape architecture, health leadership and policy. *Unit head:* Dr. Marc Parlange, Dean, Faculty of Applied Science, E-mail: dean@apsc.ubc.ca. Website: https://apsc.ubc.ca/

University of Calgary, Faculty of Graduate Studies, Schulich School of Engineering, Calgary, AB T2N 1N4, Canada. Offers M Eng, M Sc, MPM, PhD. *Program availability:* Part-time, evening/weekend. *Degree requirements:* For doctorate, comprehensive exam, thesis/dissertation. *Entrance requirements:* Additional exam requirements/recommendations for international students: Required—TOEFL, IELTS. Electronic applications accepted. *Faculty research:* Chemical and petroleum engineering, civil engineering, electrical and computer engineering, geomatics engineering, mechanical engineering and computer-integrated manufacturing.

University of California, Berkeley, Graduate Division, College of Engineering, Berkeley, CA 94720-1500. Offers M Eng, MS, MTM, PhD, M Arch/MS, MCP/MS, MPP/MS. *Program availability:* Part-time, 100% online, blended/hybrid learning. *Students:* 1,970 full-time (597 women), 19 part-time (2 women); includes 458 minority (43 Black or African American, non-Hispanic/Latino; 1 American Indian or Alaska Native, non-Hispanic/Latino; 311 Asian, non-Hispanic/Latino; 102 Hispanic/Latino; 1 Native Hawaiian or other Pacific Islander, non-Hispanic/Latino), 866 international. Average age 27. 8,893 applicants, 771 enrolled. In 2016, 548 master's, 204 doctorates awarded. Terminal master's awarded for partial completion of doctoral program. *Degree requirements:* For master's, comprehensive exam (for some programs), thesis (for some programs); for doctorate, thesis/dissertation, qualifying exam. *Entrance requirements:* For master's and doctorate, GRE General Test, minimum GPA of 3.0, 3 letters of recommendation. Additional exam requirements/recommendations for international students: Required—TOEFL (minimum score 570 paper-based; 90 iBT). Application fee: $105 ($125 for international students). Electronic applications accepted. *Financial support:* Applicants required to submit FAFSA. *Unit head:* Dr. Shankar Sastry, Dean, 510-642-5771, E-mail: engineeringdean@berkeley.edu. *Application contact:* 510-642-7594, E-mail: ess@berkeley.edu.
Website: http://www.coe.berkeley.edu

University of California, Berkeley, UC Berkeley Extension, Certificate Programs in Engineering, Construction and Facilities Management, Berkeley, CA 94720-1500. Offers construction management (Certificate); HVAC (Certificate); integrated circuit design and techniques (online) (Certificate). *Program availability:* Online learning.

University of California, Davis, College of Engineering, Davis, CA 95616. Offers M Engr, MS, D Engr, PhD, Certificate, M Engr/MBA. *Program availability:* Part-time. Terminal master's awarded for partial completion of doctoral program. *Degree requirements:* For master's, comprehensive exam (for some programs), thesis (for some programs); for doctorate, comprehensive exam, thesis/dissertation. *Entrance requirements:* For doctorate, GRE. Additional exam requirements/recommendations for international students: Required—TOEFL (minimum score 550 paper-based). Electronic applications accepted.

University of California, Irvine, Henry Samueli School of Engineering, Irvine, CA 92697. Offers MS, PhD. *Program availability:* Part-time. *Students:* 905 full-time (287 women), 55 part-time (16 women); includes 155 minority (8 Black or African American, non-Hispanic/Latino; 1 American Indian or Alaska Native, non-Hispanic/Latino; 106 Asian, non-Hispanic/Latino; 30 Hispanic/Latino; 10 Two or more races, non-Hispanic/Latino), 618 international. Average age 26. 4,165 applicants, 26% accepted, 312 enrolled. In 2016, 336 master's, 63 doctorates awarded. Terminal master's awarded for partial completion of doctoral program. *Degree requirements:* For doctorate, thesis/dissertation. *Entrance requirements:* For master's and doctorate, GRE General Test, minimum GPA of 3.0, 3 letters of recommendation. Additional exam requirements/recommendations for international students: Required—TOEFL (minimum score 550 paper-based). *Application deadline:* For fall admission, 1/15 priority date for domestic students, 1/15 for international students. Applications are processed on a rolling basis. Application fee: $105 ($125 for international students). Electronic applications accepted. *Financial support:* Fellowships with tuition reimbursements, research assistantships with full tuition reimbursements, teaching assistantships with tuition reimbursements, institutionally sponsored loans, traineeships, health care benefits, and unspecified assistantships available. Financial award application deadline: 3/1; financial award applicants required to submit FAFSA. *Faculty research:* Biomedical, chemical and biochemical, civil and environmental, electrical and computer, mechanical and aerospace engineering. *Unit head:* Gregory N. Washington, Dean, 949-824-4333, Fax: 949-824-8200, E-mail: engineering@uci.edu. *Application contact:* Jean Bennett, Director of Graduate Student Affairs, 949-824-6475, Fax: 949-824-8200, E-mail: jean.bennett@uci.edu.
Website: http://www.eng.uci.edu/

University of California, Los Angeles, Graduate Division, Henry Samueli School of Engineering and Applied Science, Los Angeles, CA 90095-1601. Offers MS, PhD, MBA/MS. *Program availability:* Evening/weekend, blended/hybrid learning. *Faculty:* 172 full-time (23 women), 24 part-time/adjunct (1 woman). *Students:* 2,187 full-time (503 women); includes 517 minority (14 Black or African American, non-Hispanic/Latino; 4 American Indian or Alaska Native, non-Hispanic/Latino; 358 Asian, non-Hispanic/Latino; 101 Hispanic/Latino; 1 Native Hawaiian or other Pacific Islander, non-Hispanic/Latino; 39 Two or more races, non-Hispanic/Latino), 1,217 international. 7,218 applicants, 27% accepted, 760 enrolled. In 2016, 639 master's, 163 doctorates awarded. *Degree requirements:* For master's, comprehensive exam or thesis; for doctorate, thesis/dissertation, qualifying exams. *Entrance requirements:* For master's, GRE General Test, minimum GPA of 3.0 depending on department/major; for doctorate, GRE General Test, minimum GPA of 3.25 (depending on department/major). Additional exam requirements/recommendations for international students: Required—TOEFL (minimum score 560 paper-based; 87 iBT), IELTS (minimum score 7). *Application deadline:* For fall admission, 12/1 for domestic and international students. Application fee: $105 ($125 for international students). Electronic applications accepted. *Financial support:* In 2016–17, 740 fellowships, 1,387 research assistantships, 747 teaching assistantships were awarded; career-related internships or fieldwork, Federal Work-Study, institutionally sponsored loans, and tuition waivers (full and partial) also available. Financial award application deadline: 3/2; financial award applicants required to submit FAFSA. *Total annual research expenditures:* $97 million. *Unit head:* Dr. Richard D. Wesel, Associate

Dean, Academic and Student Affairs, 310-825-2942, E-mail: wesel@ee.ucla.edu. *Application contact:* Jan LaBuda, Director, Office of Academic and Student Affairs, 310-825-2514, Fax: 310-825-2473, E-mail: jan@seas.ucla.edu.
Website: http://www.engineer.ucla.edu/

University of California, Merced, Graduate Division, School of Engineering, Merced, CA 95343. Offers biological engineering and small scale technologies (MS, PhD); electrical engineering and computer science (MS, PhD); environmental systems (MS, PhD); mechanical engineering (MS); mechanical engineering and applied mechanics (PhD). *Faculty:* 44 full-time (7 women). *Students:* 170 full-time (52 women), 2 part-time (0 women); includes 34 minority (2 Black or African American, non-Hispanic/Latino; 11 Asian, non-Hispanic/Latino; 14 Hispanic/Latino; 2 Native Hawaiian or other Pacific Islander, non-Hispanic/Latino; 5 Two or more races, non-Hispanic/Latino), 99 international. Average age 28. 307 applicants, 35% accepted, 46 enrolled. In 2016, 15 master's, 12 doctorates awarded. Terminal master's awarded for partial completion of doctoral program. *Degree requirements:* For master's, variable foreign language requirement, comprehensive exam, thesis or alternative; for doctorate, variable foreign language requirement, comprehensive exam, thesis/dissertation. *Entrance requirements:* For master's and doctorate, GRE. Additional exam requirements/recommendations for international students: Required—TOEFL (minimum score 550 paper-based; 80 iBT); Recommended—IELTS (minimum score 7). *Application deadline:* For fall admission, 1/15 priority date for domestic and international students. Applications are processed on a rolling basis. Application fee: $90 ($110 for international students). Electronic applications accepted. *Expenses:* Contact institution. *Financial support:* In 2016–17, 150 students received support, including 16 fellowships with full tuition reimbursements available (averaging $19,088 per year), 45 research assistantships with full tuition reimbursements available (averaging $18,389 per year), 89 teaching assistantships with full tuition reimbursements available (averaging $19,249 per year); scholarships/grants, traineeships, and health care benefits also available. Financial award application deadline: 1/15. *Faculty research:* Water resources, biotechnology, renewable energy, big data, cyber-physical systems. *Total annual research expenditures:* $3.3 million. *Unit head:* Dr. Mark Matsumoto, Dean, Fax: 209-228-4047, E-mail: mmatsumoto@ucmerced.edu. *Application contact:* Tsu Ya, Director of Admissions and Academic Services, 209-228-4521, Fax: 209-228-6906, E-mail: tya@ucmerced.edu.

University of California, Santa Barbara, Graduate Division, College of Engineering, Santa Barbara, CA 93106-5130. Offers MS, MTM, PhD, MS/PhD. Terminal master's awarded for partial completion of doctoral program. *Degree requirements:* For doctorate, thesis/dissertation. *Entrance requirements:* For master's, GRE, 3 letters of recommendation, resume/curriculum vitae; for doctorate, GRE, 3 letters of recommendation, statement of purpose, personal achievements/contributions statement, resume/curriculum vitae, transcripts for post-secondary institutions attended. Additional exam requirements/recommendations for international students: Required—TOEFL, IELTS. Electronic applications accepted.

University of California, Santa Cruz, Jack Baskin School of Engineering, Santa Cruz, CA 95064. Offers MS, PhD. *Program availability:* Part-time. *Students:* 537 full-time (134 women), 53 part-time (11 women); includes 87 minority (6 Black or African American, non-Hispanic/Latino; 3 American Indian or Alaska Native, non-Hispanic/Latino; 45 Asian, non-Hispanic/Latino; 25 Hispanic/Latino; 8 Native Hawaiian or other Pacific Islander, non-Hispanic/Latino), 318 international. 1,804 applicants, 40% accepted, 248 enrolled. In 2016, 116 master's, 35 doctorates awarded. *Entrance requirements:* For master's and doctorate, GRE General Test. Additional exam requirements/recommendations for international students: Required—TOEFL (minimum score 570 paper-based; 89 iBT); Recommended—IELTS (minimum score 8). Application fee: $105 ($125 for international students). Electronic applications accepted. *Financial support:* Fellowships, research assistantships, teaching assistantships, institutionally sponsored loans, traineeships, health care benefits, and tuition waivers available. Financial award applicants required to submit FAFSA. *Unit head:* Dr. Abel Rodriguez, Associate Dean of Graduate Studies, E-mail: abel@soe.ucsc.edu. *Application contact:* BSOE Graduate Advising Office, 831-459-3531, E-mail: bsoe-ga@rt.ucsc.edu.
Website: https://www.soe.ucsc.edu/

University of Central Florida, College of Engineering and Computer Science, Orlando, FL 32816. Offers MS, MS Cp E, MS Env E, MSAE, MSCE, MSEE, MSIE, MSME, MSMSE, PhD, Certificate. *Program availability:* Part-time, evening/weekend. *Faculty:* 175 full-time (27 women), 54 part-time/adjunct (2 women). *Students:* 901 full-time (187 women), 548 part-time (134 women); includes 351 minority (62 Black or African American, non-Hispanic/Latino; 75 Asian, non-Hispanic/Latino; 191 Hispanic/Latino; 23 Two or more races, non-Hispanic/Latino), 623 international. Average age 30. 1,668 applicants, 67% accepted, 459 enrolled. In 2016, 388 master's, 89 doctorates, 22 other advanced degrees awarded. *Degree requirements:* For doctorate, thesis/dissertation, candidacy exam, departmental qualifying exam. *Entrance requirements:* For master's, GRE General Test, minimum GPA of 3.0 in last 60 hours; for doctorate, minimum GPA of 3.5 in last 60 hours, resume. Additional exam requirements/recommendations for international students: Required—TOEFL. *Application deadline:* For fall admission, 7/15 for domestic students; for spring admission, 12/1 for domestic students. Application fee: $30. Electronic applications accepted. *Expenses:* Tuition, state resident: part-time $288.16 per credit hour. Tuition, nonresident: part-time $1071.31 per credit hour. *Financial support:* In 2016–17, 512 students received support, including 127 fellowships with partial tuition reimbursements available (averaging $12,948 per year), 338 research assistantships with partial tuition reimbursements available (averaging $11,586 per year), 190 teaching assistantships with partial tuition reimbursements available (averaging $10,822 per year); career-related internships or fieldwork, Federal Work-Study, institutionally sponsored loans, tuition waivers (partial), and unspecified assistantships also available. Financial award application deadline: 3/1; financial award applicants required to submit FAFSA. *Faculty research:* Electro-optics, lasers, materials, simulation, microelectronics. *Unit head:* Dr. Michael Georgiopoulos, Dean, 407-823-2156, E-mail: michaelg@ucf.edu. *Application contact:* Assistant Director, Graduate Admissions, 407-823-2766, Fax: 407-823-6442, E-mail: gradadmissions@ucf.edu.
Website: http://www.cecs.ucf.edu/

University of Central Oklahoma, The Jackson College of Graduate Studies, College of Mathematics and Science, Department of Engineering and Physics, Edmond, OK 73034-5209. Offers biomedical engineering (MS); electrical engineering (MS); mechanical systems (MS); physics (MS). *Program availability:* Part-time. *Degree requirements:* For master's, thesis optional. *Entrance requirements:* For master's, GRE, 24 hours of course work in physics or equivalent, mathematics through differential equations, minimum GPA of 2.75 overall and 3.0 in last 60 hours attempted. Additional exam requirements/recommendations for international students: Required—TOEFL (minimum score 550 paper-based). Electronic applications accepted.

University of Cincinnati, Graduate School, College of Engineering and Applied Science, Cincinnati, OH 45221. Offers MS, PhD, MBA/MS. *Accreditation:* ABET (one or more programs are accredited). *Program availability:* Part-time, evening/weekend. Terminal master's awarded for partial completion of doctoral program. *Degree requirements:* For master's, thesis or alternative; for doctorate, comprehensive exam, thesis/dissertation. *Entrance requirements:* For master's and doctorate, GRE General

Test. Additional exam requirements/recommendations for international students: Required—TOEFL (minimum score 520 paper-based). *Expenses: Tuition, area resident:* Full-time $12,790; part-time $389 per credit hour. Tuition, state resident: full-time $13,290; part-time $419 per credit hour. Tuition, nonresident: full-time $24,532; part-time $976 per credit hour. *International tuition:* $24,832 full-time. *Required fees:* $3958; $140 per credit hour. Tuition and fees vary according to course load, degree level, program and reciprocity agreements.

University of Colorado Boulder, Graduate School, College of Engineering and Applied Science, Boulder, CO 80309. Offers ME, MS, PhD, JD/MS, MBA/MS. *Faculty:* 208 full-time (38 women). *Students:* 1,729 full-time (475 women), 233 part-time (53 women); includes 214 minority (19 Black or African American, non-Hispanic/Latino; 4 American Indian or Alaska Native, non-Hispanic/Latino; 73 Asian, non-Hispanic/Latino; 74 Hispanic/Latino; 1 Native Hawaiian or other Pacific Islander, non-Hispanic/Latino; 43 Two or more races, non-Hispanic/Latino), 765 international. Average age 28. 3,826 applicants, 40% accepted, 546 enrolled. In 2016, 410 master's, 139 doctorates awarded. *Degree requirements:* For doctorate, thesis/dissertation. *Entrance requirements:* For master's, minimum undergraduate GPA of 2.75. Application fee: $60 ($80 for international students). Electronic applications accepted. Application fee is waived when completed online. *Expenses:* Contact institution. *Financial support:* In 2016–17, 3,133 students received support, including 941 fellowships (averaging $8,707 per year), 537 research assistantships with full and partial tuition reimbursements available (averaging $38,013 per year), 197 teaching assistantships with full and partial tuition reimbursements available (averaging $35,143 per year); institutionally sponsored loans, scholarships/grants, health care benefits, and unspecified assistantships also available. Financial award applicants required to submit FAFSA. *Faculty research:* Chemical engineering, civil engineering, computer science, materials engineering, mechanical engineering. *Total annual research expenditures:* $75.5 million. Website: http://engineering.colorado.edu

University of Colorado Colorado Springs, College of Engineering and Applied Science, Colorado Springs, CO 80918. Offers ME, MS, PhD. *Program availability:* Part-time, evening/weekend. *Faculty:* 33 full-time (7 women), 20 part-time/adjunct (6 women). *Students:* 42 full-time (8 women), 263 part-time (53 women); includes 57 minority (6 Black or African American, non-Hispanic/Latino; 15 Asian, non-Hispanic/Latino; 23 Hispanic/Latino; 13 Two or more races, non-Hispanic/Latino), 96 international. Average age 33. 181 applicants, 68% accepted, 64 enrolled. In 2016, 70 master's, 8 doctorates awarded. *Degree requirements:* For master's, comprehensive exam (for some programs), thesis or alternative; for doctorate, comprehensive exam, thesis/dissertation. *Entrance requirements:* For master's, GRE General Test, minimum GPA of 3.0; for doctorate, GRE General Test, minimum GPA of 3.3. Additional exam requirements/recommendations for international students: Required—TOEFL (minimum score 550 paper-based; 80 iBT), IELTS (minimum score 6.5). *Application deadline:* For fall admission, 6/1 for domestic students, 4/1 for international students; for spring admission, 11/1 for domestic students, 10/1 for international students. Applications are processed on a rolling basis. Application fee: $60 ($100 for international students). *Expenses:* Contact institution. *Financial support:* In 2016–17, 45 students received support. Career-related internships or fieldwork, Federal Work-Study, and scholarships/grants available. Support available to part-time students. Financial award application deadline: 3/1; financial award applicants required to submit FAFSA. *Faculty research:* Synthesis and modeling of digital systems, microelectronics, superconductive thin films, sol-gel processes, linear and nonlinear adaptive filtering, wireless communications networks, computer architecture. *Total annual research expenditures:* $1.6 million. *Unit head:* Dr. Ramaswami Dandapani, Dean, 719-255-3543, Fax: 719-255-3542, E-mail: rdan@cas.uccs.edu. *Application contact:* Ali Langfels, Office of Student Support, 719-255-3544, E-mail: alangfel@uccs.edu. Website: http://eas.uccs.edu/

University of Colorado Denver, College of Engineering and Applied Science, Denver, CO 80217. Offers M Eng, MS, EASPh D, PhD. *Program availability:* Part-time, evening/weekend. *Faculty:* 73 full-time (16 women), 27 part-time/adjunct (4 women). *Students:* 321 full-time (94 women), 138 part-time (31 women); includes 66 minority (10 Black or African American, non-Hispanic/Latino; 1 American Indian or Alaska Native, non-Hispanic/Latino; 23 Asian, non-Hispanic/Latino; 22 Hispanic/Latino; 1 Native Hawaiian or other Pacific Islander, non-Hispanic/Latino; 9 Two or more races, non-Hispanic/Latino), 189 international. Average age 30. 708 applicants, 55% accepted, 98 enrolled. In 2016, 145 master's, 8 doctorates awarded. *Degree requirements:* For master's, comprehensive exam, thesis; for doctorate, comprehensive exam, thesis/dissertation. *Entrance requirements:* For master's, GRE, minimum undergraduate GPA of 2.75; for doctorate, GRE, minimum cumulative GPA of 3.0. Additional exam requirements/recommendations for international students: Required—TOEFL (minimum score 550 paper-based; 79 iBT); Recommended—IELTS (minimum score 6.8). Application fee: $50 ($75 for international students). Electronic applications accepted. *Expenses:* Contact institution. *Financial support:* In 2016–17, 237 students received support. Fellowships, research assistantships, teaching assistantships, Federal Work-Study, institutionally sponsored loans, scholarships/grants, and traineeships available. Financial award application deadline: 4/1; financial award applicants required to submit FAFSA. *Faculty research:* Civil engineering, bioengineering, mechanical engineering, electrical engineering, computer science. *Total annual research expenditures:* $4.4 million. *Unit head:* Dr. Mark Ingber, Dean, 303-556-2870, Fax: 303-556-2511, E-mail: marc.ingber@ucdenver.edu. *Application contact:* Graduate School Admissions, 303-556-2704, E-mail: admissions@ucdenver.edu. Website: http://www.ucdenver.edu/academics/colleges/Engineering/Pages/EngineeringAppliedScience.aspx

University of Connecticut, Graduate School, School of Engineering, Storrs, CT 06269. Offers M Eng, MS, PhD. Terminal master's awarded for partial completion of doctoral program. *Degree requirements:* For master's, comprehensive exam; for doctorate, thesis/dissertation. *Entrance requirements:* For master's and doctorate, GRE General Test. Additional exam requirements/recommendations for international students: Required—TOEFL (minimum score 550 paper-based). Electronic applications accepted.

University of Delaware, College of Engineering, Newark, DE 19716. Offers M Ch E, MAS, MCE, MEM, MMSE, MS, MSECE, MSME, PhD. *Program availability:* Part-time, evening/weekend, online learning. Terminal master's awarded for partial completion of doctoral program. *Degree requirements:* For master's, thesis (for some programs); for doctorate, thesis/dissertation. *Entrance requirements:* For master's and doctorate, GRE General Test. Additional exam requirements/recommendations for international students: Required—TOEFL (minimum score 550 paper-based). Electronic applications accepted. *Faculty research:* Biotechnology, photonics, transportation, composite materials, materials science.

University of Denver, Daniel Felix Ritchie School of Engineering and Computer Science, Denver, CO 80208. Offers MS, PhD. *Faculty:* 38 full-time (4 women), 9 part-time/adjunct (4 women). *Students:* 22 full-time (4 women), 111 part-time (31 women); includes 19 minority (2 Black or African American, non-Hispanic/Latino; 7 Asian, non-Hispanic/Latino; 8 Hispanic/Latino; 2 Two or more races, non-Hispanic/Latino), 65 international. Average age 29. 198 applicants, 64% accepted, 43 enrolled. In 2016, 68 master's, 16 doctorates awarded. *Degree requirements:* For master's, thesis (for some

programs); for doctorate, variable foreign language requirement, comprehensive exam, thesis/dissertation. *Entrance requirements:* For master's, GRE General Test, bachelor's degree, transcripts, three letters of recommendation, personal statement; for doctorate, GRE General Test, master's degree, transcripts, three letters of recommendation, personal statement. Additional exam requirements/recommendations for international students: Required—TOEFL (minimum score 550 paper-based; 80 iBT). *Application deadline:* Applications are processed on a rolling basis. Application fee: $65. Electronic applications accepted. *Expenses:* $29,022 per year full-time. *Financial support:* In 2016–17, 78 students received support, including 14 research assistantships with tuition reimbursements available (averaging $12,410 per year), 14 teaching assistantships with tuition reimbursements available (averaging $14,494 per year); Federal Work-Study, institutionally sponsored loans, scholarships/grants, health care benefits, and unspecified assistantships also available. Financial award application deadline: 2/15; financial award applicants required to submit FAFSA. *Unit head:* JB Holston, Dean, 303-871-3733, Fax: 303-871-2716, E-mail: jb.holston@du.edu. *Application contact:* Information Contact, 303-871-3787, E-mail: ritchieschool@du.edu. Website: http://ritchieschool.du.edu/

University of Detroit Mercy, College of Engineering and Science, Detroit, MI 48221. Offers chemistry (MS); civil and environmental engineering (DE); electrical and computer engineering (ME); electrical engineering (DE); engineering management (M Eng Mgt); environmental engineering (MEE); mechanical engineering (MME, DE); product development (MS); software engineering (MSSE); teaching of mathematics (MATM). *Program availability:* Part-time, evening/weekend. *Degree requirements:* For doctorate, thesis/dissertation. Electronic applications accepted. Application fee is waived when completed online. *Expenses:* Contact institution.

University of Florida, Graduate School, Herbert Wertheim College of Engineering, Gainesville, FL 32611. Offers ME, MS, PhD, Certificate, Engr, JD/MS, MD/PhD, MSM/MS. *Program availability:* Part-time, online learning. *Degree requirements:* For doctorate, thesis/dissertation. *Entrance requirements:* For master's and doctorate, minimum GPA of 3.0; for other advanced degree, GRE General Test. Additional exam requirements/recommendations for international students: Required—TOEFL (minimum score 550 paper-based; 80 iBT), IELTS (minimum score 6). Electronic applications accepted.

University of Guelph, Graduate Studies, College of Physical and Engineering Science, School of Engineering, Guelph, ON N1G 2W1, Canada. Offers biological engineering (M Eng, M Sc, MA Sc, PhD); engineering systems and computing (M Eng, M Sc, MA Sc, PhD); environmental engineering (M Eng, M Sc, MA Sc, PhD); water resources engineering (M Eng, M Sc, MA Sc, PhD). *Program availability:* Part-time. *Degree requirements:* For master's, thesis (for some programs); for doctorate, comprehensive exam, thesis/dissertation. *Entrance requirements:* For master's, minimum B- average during previous 2 years of course work; for doctorate, minimum B average. Additional exam requirements/recommendations for international students: Required—TOEFL (minimum score 550 paper-based; 89 iBT), IELTS (minimum score 6.5). Electronic applications accepted. *Faculty research:* Water and food safety, environmental contaminant fates and mechanisms, computer systems, robotics and mechatronics, waste treatment.

University of Hartford, College of Engineering, Technology and Architecture, Program in Engineering, West Hartford, CT 06117-1599. Offers M Eng. *Entrance requirements:* Additional exam requirements/recommendations for international students: Required—TOEFL.

University of Hawaii at Manoa, Graduate Division, College of Engineering, Honolulu, HI 96822. Offers MS, PhD. *Accreditation:* ABET (one or more programs are accredited). *Program availability:* Part-time. *Entrance requirements:* Additional exam requirements/recommendations for international students: Required—TOEFL or IELTS.

University of Houston, Cullen College of Engineering, Houston, TX 77204. Offers M Pet E, MCE, MCHE, MEE, MIE, MME, MSEE, MSME, PhD. *Program availability:* Part-time. Terminal master's awarded for partial completion of doctoral program. *Degree requirements:* For master's, thesis (for some programs); for doctorate, thesis/dissertation, departmental qualifying exam. *Entrance requirements:* For master's and doctorate, GRE General Test. *Faculty research:* Superconducting materials, microantennas for space packs, direct numerical simulation of pairing vortices.

University of Idaho, College of Graduate Studies, College of Engineering, Moscow, ID 83844. Offers M Engr, MS, PhD. *Faculty:* 71 full-time, 9 part-time/adjunct. *Students:* 132 full-time (21 women), 202 part-time (36 women). Average age 34. In 2016, 92 master's, 13 doctorates awarded. *Degree requirements:* For doctorate, thesis/dissertation. *Entrance requirements:* For master's, minimum GPA of 3.0. Additional exam requirements/recommendations for international students: Required—TOEFL. *Application deadline:* For fall admission, 8/1 for domestic students; for spring admission, 12/15 for domestic students. Applications are processed on a rolling basis. Application fee: $60. Electronic applications accepted. *Expenses:* Tuition, state resident: full-time $6460; part-time $414 per credit hour. Tuition, nonresident: full-time $21,268; part-time $1237 per credit hour. *Required fees:* $2070; $60 per credit hour. Full-time tuition and fees vary according to course load and reciprocity agreements. *Financial support:* Fellowships, research assistantships, teaching assistantships, career-related internships or fieldwork, and Federal Work-Study available. Support available to part-time students. Financial award applicants required to submit FAFSA. *Faculty research:* Robotics, micro-electronic packaging, water resources engineering and science, oscillating flows in macro- and micro-scale methods of mechanical separation, nuclear energy. *Unit head:* Dr. Larry Stauffer, Dean, 208-885-6470, E-mail: deanengr@uidaho.edu. *Application contact:* Sean Scoggin, Graduate Recruitment Coordinator, 208-885-4001, Fax: 208-885-4406, E-mail: graduateadmissions@uidaho.edu. Website: http://www.uidaho.edu/engr/

University of Illinois at Chicago, College of Engineering, Chicago, IL 60607-7128. Offers M Eng, MEE, MS, PhD. *Program availability:* Part-time, evening/weekend. Terminal master's awarded for partial completion of doctoral program. *Degree requirements:* For doctorate, thesis/dissertation. *Entrance requirements:* For doctorate, GRE. Additional exam requirements/recommendations for international students: Required—TOEFL. Electronic applications accepted. *Expenses:* Contact institution.

University of Illinois at Urbana–Champaign, Graduate College, College of Engineering, Champaign, IL 61820. Offers M Eng, MCS, MS, PhD, M Arch/MS, MBA/MS, MCS/JD, MCS/M Arch, MCS/MBA, MS/MBA, PhD/MBA. *Program availability:* Part-time, evening/weekend, online learning. *Expenses:* Contact institution.

The University of Iowa, Graduate College, College of Engineering, Iowa City, IA 52242-1527. Offers MS, PhD. *Faculty:* 93 full-time (12 women), 17 part-time/adjunct (3 women). *Students:* 238 full-time (57 women), 62 part-time (14 women); includes 24 minority (4 Black or African American, non-Hispanic/Latino; 8 Asian, non-Hispanic/Latino; 5 Hispanic/Latino; 7 Two or more races, non-Hispanic/Latino), 143 international. Average age 27. 628 applicants, 18% accepted, 62 enrolled. In 2016, 52 master's, 38 doctorates awarded. *Degree requirements:* For master's, comprehensive exam (for some programs), oral exam and/or thesis; for doctorate, comprehensive exam, thesis/dissertation. *Entrance requirements:* For master's and doctorate, GRE, official academic records/transcripts, 3 letters of

Engineering and Applied Sciences—General

recommendation, resume, statement of purpose. Additional exam requirements/recommendations for international students: Required—TOEFL (minimum score 550 paper-based; 81 iBT), IELTS (minimum score 7). *Application deadline:* For fall admission, 1/15 priority date for domestic and international students; for spring admission, 8/1 priority date for domestic and international students; for summer admission, 1/1 for domestic and international students. Applications are processed on a rolling basis. Application fee: $60 ($100 for international students). Electronic applications accepted. *Expenses:* Contact institution. *Financial support:* In 2016–17, 295 students received support, including 23 fellowships with full and partial tuition reimbursements available (averaging $25,500 per year), 217 research assistantships with full and partial tuition reimbursements available (averaging $22,981 per year), 55 teaching assistantships with full and partial tuition reimbursements available (averaging $18,809 per year); career-related internships or fieldwork, Federal Work-Study, scholarships/grants, traineeships, health care benefits, and unspecified assistantships also available. Financial award application deadline: 1/15; financial award applicants required to submit FAFSA. *Total annual research expenditures:* $44.4 million. *Unit head:* Dr. Alec Scranton, Dean, 319-335-5766, Fax: 319-335-6086, E-mail: alec-scranton@uiowa.edu. *Application contact:* Dr. Brent Gage, Associate Vice President for Enrollment Management, 319-335-1525, Fax: 319-335-1535, E-mail: gradmail@uiowa.edu. Website: http://www.engineering.uiowa.edu/

See Display below and Close-Up on page 87.

The University of Kansas, Graduate Studies, School of Engineering, Lawrence, KS 66045. Offers MCE, MCM, ME, MS, DE, PhD, Certificate. *Program availability:* Part-time, evening/weekend, online learning. *Students:* 398 full-time (99 women), 241 part-time (52 women); includes 59 minority (15 Black or African American, non-Hispanic/Latino; 1 American Indian or Alaska Native, non-Hispanic/Latino; 24 Asian, non-Hispanic/Latino; 8 Hispanic/Latino; 11 Two or more races, non-Hispanic/Latino), 305 international. Average age 29. 847 applicants, 44% accepted, 131 enrolled. In 2016, 155 master's, 31 doctorates awarded. Terminal master's awarded for partial completion of doctoral program. *Entrance requirements:* For master's and doctorate, GRE, minimum GPA of 3.0, 3 letters of recommendation, official transcripts, statement of purpose. Additional exam requirements/recommendations for international students: Required—TOEFL, IELTS. Application fee: $65 ($85 for international students). Electronic applications accepted. *Financial support:* Fellowships, research assistantships, teaching assistantships, career-related internships or fieldwork, Federal Work-Study, scholarships/grants, and unspecified assistantships available. *Faculty research:* Global change, transportation, water, energy, healthcare, information technology, sustainable infrastructure, remote sensing, environmental sustainability, telecommunications, oil recovery, airplane design, structured materials, robotics, sustainable fuels and chemicals, radar systems, composite materials and structures, precision particles, tissue engineering, chemo-enzymatic catalysis, communication systems and networks, intelligent systems, data mining, fuel cells, imaging. *Unit head:* Dr. Michael S. Branicky, Dean, 785-864-2930, E-mail: msb@ku.edu. *Application contact:* Amy Wierman, Assistant to the Dean, 785-864-2930, E-mail: awierman@ku.edu. Website: http://www.engr.ku.edu/

University of Kentucky, Graduate School, College of Engineering, Lexington, KY 40506-0032. Offers M Eng, MCE, MME, MS, MS Ch E, MS Min, MSCE, MSEE, MSEM, MSMAE, MSME, MSMSE, PhD. *Program availability:* Part-time. *Degree requirements:* For master's, comprehensive exam; for doctorate, comprehensive exam, thesis/dissertation. *Entrance requirements:* For master's, GRE General Test, minimum undergraduate GPA of 2.75; for doctorate, GRE General Test, minimum undergraduate GPA of 3.0. Additional exam requirements/recommendations for international students: Required—TOEFL (minimum score 550 paper-based). Electronic applications accepted.

University of Louisville, J. B. Speed School of Engineering, Louisville, KY 40292-0001. Offers M Eng, MS, PhD, Certificate, Graduate Certificate, M Eng/MBA. *Accreditation:* ABET (one or more programs are accredited). *Program availability:* Online learning. *Faculty:* 103 full-time (21 women), 14 part-time/adjunct (4 women). *Students:* 327 full-time (74 women), 302 part-time (49 women); includes 81 minority (22 Black or African American, non-Hispanic/Latino; 1 American Indian or Alaska Native, non-Hispanic/Latino; 22 Asian, non-Hispanic/Latino; 23 Hispanic/Latino; 13 Two or more races, non-Hispanic/Latino), 217 international. Average age 29. 367 applicants, 39% accepted, 98 enrolled. In 2016, 130 master's, 9 doctorates, 2 other advanced degrees awarded. Terminal master's awarded for partial completion of doctoral program. *Degree requirements:* For master's, comprehensive exam (for some programs), thesis optional, minimum GPA of 3.0; for doctorate, comprehensive exam, thesis/dissertation, minimum GPA of 3.0. *Entrance requirements:* For master's and doctorate, GRE, letters of recommendation, final official transcripts; for other advanced degree, undergraduate degree. Additional exam requirements/recommendations for international students: Required—TOEFL (minimum score 550 paper-based, 80 iBT) or IELTS (6.5). *Application deadline:* For fall admission, 6/1 for domestic students, 6/1 priority date for international students; for spring admission, 11/1 for domestic students, 11/1 priority date for international students; for summer admission, 3/1 for domestic students, 4/1 priority date for international students. Application fee: $60. Electronic applications accepted. *Expenses:* Tuition, state resident: full-time $12,246; part-time $681 per credit hour. Tuition, nonresident: full-time $25,486; part-time $1417 per credit hour. *Required fees:* $196. Tuition and fees vary according to program and reciprocity agreements. *Financial support:* In 2016–17, 12 students received support. Fellowships with full tuition reimbursements available, research assistantships with full tuition reimbursements available, teaching assistantships with full tuition reimbursements available, scholarships/grants, health care benefits, and tuition waivers (full) available. Financial award application deadline: 2/1. *Faculty research:* Energy and sustainability; advanced manufacturing and logistics; engineering human health; materials science and engineering, including nanoscience, cyber-enabled discovery. *Total annual research expenditures:* $18.3 million. *Unit head:* Dr. John S. Usher, Dean, 502-852-6281, Fax: 502-852-7033, E-mail: john.usher@louisville.edu. *Application contact:* Dr. Michael Harris, Director of Academic Programs, J. B. Speed School of Engineering, 502-852-6278, Fax: 502-852-7294, E-mail: mharris@louisville.edu. Website: http://louisville.edu/speed/

University of Maine, Graduate School, College of Engineering, Orono, ME 04469. Offers ME, MS, PSM, PhD. *Program availability:* Part-time. *Faculty:* 47 full-time (8 women), 9 part-time/adjunct (1 woman). *Students:* 96 full-time (21 women), 43 part-time (7 women); includes 10 minority (1 Black or African American, non-Hispanic/Latino; 1 American Indian or Alaska Native, non-Hispanic/Latino; 4 Asian, non-Hispanic/Latino; 2 Hispanic/Latino; 2 Two or more races, non-Hispanic/Latino), 60 international. Average age 31. 118 applicants, 69% accepted, 28 enrolled. In 2016, 19 master's, 12 doctorates awarded. Terminal master's awarded for partial completion of doctoral program. *Degree requirements:* For master's, thesis (for some programs); for doctorate, comprehensive exam, thesis/dissertation. *Entrance requirements:* For master's and doctorate, GRE General Test. Additional exam requirements/recommendations for international students: Required—TOEFL. *Application deadline:* For fall admission, 2/1 priority date for domestic students. Applications are processed on a rolling basis. Application fee: $65. Electronic applications accepted. *Expenses:* Tuition, state resident: full-time $7524; part-time $2508 per credit. Tuition, nonresident: full-time $24,498; part-time $8166 per credit. *Required fees:* $1148; $571 per credit. *Financial support:* In 2016–17, 67 students received support, including 3 fellowships (averaging $25,100 per year), 30 research assistantships (averaging $14,600 per year), 22 teaching assistantships (averaging $14,600 per year); Federal Work-Study, institutionally sponsored loans,

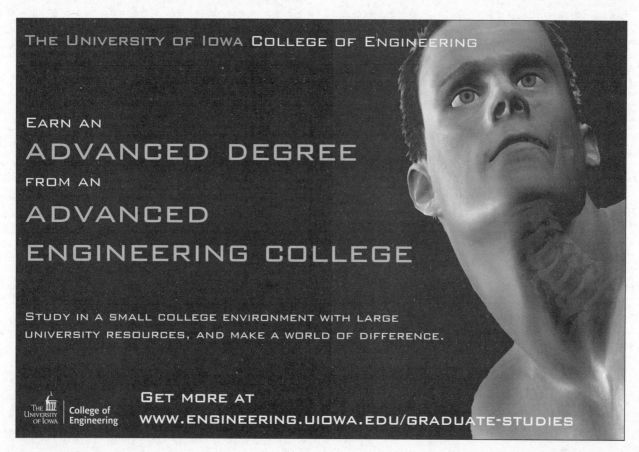

scholarships/grants, tuition waivers (full and partial), and unspecified assistantships also available. Financial award application deadline: 3/1. *Unit head:* Dr. Dana Humphrey, Dean, 207-581-2217, Fax: 207-581-2220, E-mail: dana.humphrey@umit.maine.edu. *Application contact:* Scott G. Delcourt, Assistant Vice President for Graduate Studies and Senior Associate Dean, 207-581-3291, Fax: 207-581-3232, E-mail: graduate@maine.edu.
Website: http://engineering.umaine.edu

University of Manitoba, Faculty of Graduate Studies, Faculty of Engineering, Winnipeg, MB R3T 2N2, Canada. Offers M Eng, M Sc, PhD.

University of Maryland, Baltimore County, The Graduate School, College of Engineering and Information Technology, Baltimore, MD 21250. Offers MPS, MS, PhD, Postbaccalaureate Certificate. *Program availability:* Part-time. *Faculty:* 103 full-time (32 women), 37 part-time/adjunct (7 women). *Students:* 576 full-time (191 women), 604 part-time (175 women); includes 302 minority (130 Black or African American, non-Hispanic/Latino; 3 American Indian or Alaska Native, non-Hispanic/Latino; 106 Asian, non-Hispanic/Latino; 44 Hispanic/Latino; 1 Native Hawaiian or other Pacific Islander, non-Hispanic/Latino; 18 Two or more races, non-Hispanic/Latino), 451 international. Average age 31. 1,435 applicants, 51% accepted, 314 enrolled. In 2016, 343 master's, 27 doctorates, 45 other advanced degrees awarded. Terminal master's awarded for partial completion of doctoral program. *Degree requirements:* For master's, comprehensive exam (for some programs), thesis (for some programs); for doctorate, comprehensive exam, thesis/dissertation. *Entrance requirements:* Additional exam requirements/recommendations for international students: Required—TOEFL (minimum score 550 paper-based; 80 iBT). *Application deadline:* For fall admission, 6/1 for domestic students, 1/1 for international students; for spring admission, 11/1 for domestic students, 6/1 for international students. Applications are processed on a rolling basis. Application fee: $70. Electronic applications accepted. *Expenses:* Contact institution. *Financial support:* In 2016–17, 9 fellowships with full tuition reimbursements (averaging $21,750 per year), 127 research assistantships with full tuition reimbursements (averaging $19,250 per year), 101 teaching assistantships with full tuition reimbursements (averaging $16,750 per year) were awarded; career-related internships or fieldwork, Federal Work-Study, scholarships/grants, health care benefits, tuition waivers (partial), and unspecified assistantships also available. Support available to part-time students. Financial award application deadline: 6/30; financial award applicants required to submit FAFSA. *Faculty research:* Biochemical/biomedical engineering, environmental engineering, computer science/electrical engineering, information systems, mechanical engineering. *Total annual research expenditures:* $14.7 million. *Unit head:* Dr. Julia M. Ross, Dean and Professor, 410-455-3270, Fax: 410-455-3559, E-mail: jross@umbc.edu. *Application contact:* Graduate School, 410-455-2537, E-mail: umbcgrad@umbc.edu.
Website: http://coeit.umbc.edu/

University of Maryland, College Park, Academic Affairs, A. James Clark School of Engineering and School of Public Policy, Program in Engineering and Public Policy, College Park, MD 20742. Offers MS.

University of Massachusetts Amherst, Graduate School, College of Engineering, Amherst, MA 01003. Offers MS, MS Env E, MSCE, MSChE, MSECE, MSEM, MSIE, MSME, PhD. *Program availability:* Part-time. Terminal master's awarded for partial completion of doctoral program. *Degree requirements:* For master's, thesis (for some programs); for doctorate, comprehensive exam, thesis/dissertation. *Entrance requirements:* For master's and doctorate, GRE General Test. Additional exam requirements/recommendations for international students: Required—TOEFL (minimum score 550 paper-based; 80 iBT), IELTS (minimum score 6.5). Electronic applications accepted.

University of Massachusetts Dartmouth, Graduate School, College of Engineering, Program in Engineering and Applied Science, North Dartmouth, MA 02747-2300. Offers applied mechanics and materials (PhD); computational science and engineering (PhD); computer science and information systems (PhD); engineering and applied science (PhD); industrial and systems engineering (PhD). *Program availability:* Part-time. *Students:* 23 full-time (7 women), 8 part-time (3 women); includes 2 minority (both Black or African American, non-Hispanic/Latino), 15 international. Average age 31. 14 applicants, 79% accepted, 7 enrolled. *Degree requirements:* For doctorate, comprehensive exam, thesis/dissertation. *Entrance requirements:* For doctorate, GRE, statement of purpose (minimum of 300 words), resume, 3 letters of recommendation, official transcripts. Additional exam requirements/recommendations for international students: Required—TOEFL (minimum score 550 paper-based; 79 iBT). *Application deadline:* For fall admission, 2/15 priority date for domestic students, 1/15 priority date for international students; for spring admission, 11/15 priority date for domestic students, 10/15 priority date for international students. Application fee: $60. Electronic applications accepted. *Expenses:* Tuition, state resident: full-time $14,994; part-time $624.75 per credit. Tuition, nonresident: full-time $27,068; part-time $1127.83 per credit. *Required fees:* $405; $25.88 per credit. Tuition and fees vary according to course load and reciprocity agreements. *Financial support:* In 2016–17, 11 fellowships (averaging $16,591 per year), 12 research assistantships (averaging $5,160 per year) were awarded; institutionally sponsored loans, scholarships/grants, and doctoral support also available. Support available to part-time students. Financial award application deadline: 3/1; financial award applicants required to submit FAFSA. *Faculty research:* Tissue/cell engineering, bio transport sensors/networks, marine systems biomimetic materials, composite/polymeric materials, resilient infrastructure robotics, renewable energy. *Total annual research expenditures:* $253,000. *Unit head:* Gaurav Khanna, Graduate Program Director, Engineering and Applied Science, 508-910-6605, Fax: 508-999-9115, E-mail: gkhanna@umassd.edu. *Application contact:* Steven Briggs, Director of Marketing and Recruitment for Graduate Studies, 508-999-8604, Fax: 508-999-8183, E-mail: graduate@umassd.edu.
Website: http://www.umassd.edu/engineering/graduate/doctoraldegreeprograms/egrandappliedsciencephd/

University of Massachusetts Lowell, Francis College of Engineering, Lowell, MA 01854. Offers MS, MS Eng, PhD. *Program availability:* Part-time, evening/weekend. Terminal master's awarded for partial completion of doctoral program. *Degree requirements:* For doctorate, thesis/dissertation. *Entrance requirements:* For master's and doctorate, GRE General Test.

University of Memphis, Graduate School, Herff College of Engineering, Memphis, TN 38152. Offers MS, PhD, Graduate Certificate. *Program availability:* Part-time. *Faculty:* 41 full-time (4 women), 2 part-time/adjunct (0 women). *Students:* 88 full-time (29 women), 86 part-time (20 women); includes 33 minority (17 Black or African American, non-Hispanic/Latino; 1 American Indian or Alaska Native, non-Hispanic/Latino; 8 Asian, non-Hispanic/Latino; 3 Hispanic/Latino; 4 Two or more races, non-Hispanic/Latino), 93 international. Average age 32. 183 applicants, 67% accepted, 36 enrolled. In 2016, 30 master's, 18 doctorates, 11 other advanced degrees awarded. *Degree requirements:* For master's, comprehensive exam, thesis optional, 30-36 hours of course work, completion of course work within 6 years, continuous enrollment; for doctorate, comprehensive exam, thesis/dissertation, completion of degree within 12 years, residency, continuous enrollment. *Entrance requirements:* For master's and doctorate, GRE, MAT, GMAT, three letters of recommendation. Additional exam requirements/recommendations for international students: Required—TOEFL (minimum score 550 paper-based; 79 iBT). *Application deadline:* For fall admission, 8/1 for domestic students, 5/1 for international students; for spring admission, 12/1 for domestic students, 9/15 for international students; for summer admission, 5/1 for domestic students. Application fee: $35 ($60 for international students). Electronic applications accepted. *Expenses:* $5,231.50 per semester full-time in-state, $9,623.50 full-time out-of-state. *Financial support:* In 2016–17, 29 students received support, including 12 research assistantships with full tuition reimbursements available (averaging $21,092 per year), 1 teaching assistantship with full tuition reimbursement available (averaging $5,504 per year); fellowships with full tuition reimbursements available, career-related internships or fieldwork, Federal Work-Study, scholarships/grants, tuition waivers (full and partial), and unspecified assistantships also available. Financial award application deadline: 2/1; financial award applicants required to submit FAFSA. *Faculty research:* Medical and biological applications of engineering; infrastructure, including transportation, ground water and GPS studies; computational intelligence and modeling; sensors. *Unit head:* Dr. Richard Joseph Sweigard, Dean, 901-678-4306, Fax: 901-678-4180, E-mail: rjswgard@memphis.edu. *Application contact:* Dr. Warren Haggard, Associate Dean for Research and Graduate Studies, 901-678-4346, Fax: 901-678-5030, E-mail: whaggrd1@memphis.edu.
Website: http://www.memphis.edu/herff/index.php

University of Miami, Graduate School, College of Engineering, Coral Gables, FL 33124. Offers MS, MSAE, MSBE, MSCE, MSECE, MSIE, MSME, MSOES, PhD, MBA/MSIE. *Program availability:* Part-time, evening/weekend. *Degree requirements:* For master's, thesis (for some programs); for doctorate, comprehensive exam, thesis/dissertation. *Entrance requirements:* For master's and doctorate, GRE General Test, minimum GPA of 3.0. Additional exam requirements/recommendations for international students: Required—TOEFL (minimum score 550 paper-based; 59 iBT). Electronic applications accepted.

University of Michigan, College of Engineering, Ann Arbor, MI 48109. Offers M Eng, MS, MSE, D Eng, PhD, CE, Certificate, Ch E, Mar Eng, Nav Arch, Nuc E, M Arch/M Eng, M Arch/MSE, MBA/M Eng, MBA/MS, MBA/MSE, MSE/MS. *Program availability:* Part-time, 100% online. *Faculty:* 409 full-time (82 women). *Students:* 3,248 full-time (794 women), 322 part-time (62 women). 10,718 applicants, 27% accepted, 1198 enrolled. In 2016, 1,088 master's, 255 doctorates awarded. *Application deadline:* Applications are processed on a rolling basis. Electronic applications accepted. *Expenses:* Contact institution. *Financial support:* Fellowships, research assistantships, teaching assistantships, career-related internships or fieldwork, Federal Work-Study, institutionally sponsored loans, scholarships/grants, traineeships, health care benefits, tuition waivers (full and partial), and unspecified assistantships available. Support available to part-time students. Financial award applicants required to submit FAFSA. *Total annual research expenditures:* $295.6 million. *Unit head:* Prof. Alec D. Gallimore, Dean of Engineering, 734-647-7008, Fax: 734-647-7009, E-mail: rasta@umich.edu. *Application contact:* Kim Elliott, Director of Graduate Education, 734-647-7077, Fax: 734-647-7045, E-mail: elliottk@umich.edu.
Website: http://www.engin.umich.edu/

University of Michigan–Dearborn, College of Engineering and Computer Science, Dearborn, MI 48128. Offers MS, MSE, PhD, MBA/MSE. *Program availability:* Part-time, evening/weekend, 100% online. *Faculty:* 73 full-time (10 women), 34 part-time/adjunct (3 women). *Students:* 393 full-time (75 women), 828 part-time (154 women); includes 170 minority (39 Black or African American, non-Hispanic/Latino; 2 American Indian or Alaska Native, non-Hispanic/Latino; 73 Asian, non-Hispanic/Latino; 35 Hispanic/Latino; 1 Native Hawaiian or other Pacific Islander, non-Hispanic/Latino; 20 Two or more races, non-Hispanic/Latino), 580 international. Average age 27. 1,517 applicants, 53% accepted, 444 enrolled. In 2016, 365 master's, 2 doctorates awarded. *Degree requirements:* For master's, thesis optional; for doctorate, comprehensive exam, thesis/dissertation. *Entrance requirements:* For doctorate, GRE. Additional exam requirements/recommendations for international students: Required—TOEFL (minimum score 560 paper-based, 84 iBT), IELTS (minimum score 6.5), or Michigan English Language Assessment Battery (minimum score 80). *Application deadline:* For fall admission, 8/1 priority date for domestic students, 5/1 priority date for international students; for winter admission, 12/1 priority date for domestic students, 9/1 priority date for international students; for spring admission, 4/1 priority date for domestic students, 1/1 priority date for international students. Applications are processed on a rolling basis. Application fee: $60. Electronic applications accepted. *Expenses:* Tuition, state resident: full-time $13,118; part-time $2280 per term. Tuition, nonresident: full-time $21,816; part-time $3771 per term. *Required fees:* $866; $658 per unit. $329 per term. Tuition and fees vary according to program. *Financial support:* Research assistantships, teaching assistantships, career-related internships or fieldwork, scholarships/grants, health care benefits, and non-residential student scholarships available. Financial award application deadline: 3/1; financial award applicants required to submit FAFSA. *Faculty research:* Automotive engineering, power electronics, cyber security, data science and intelligent system, bioengineering. *Total annual research expenditures:* $3.7 million. *Unit head:* Dr. Anthony England, Dean, 313-593-5290, Fax: 313-593-9967, E-mail: england@umich.edu. *Application contact:* Office of Graduate Studies Staff, 313-583-6321, E-mail: umd-graduatestudies@umich.edu.
Website: http://umdearborn.edu/cecs/

University of Minnesota, Twin Cities Campus, College of Science and Engineering, Minneapolis, MN 55455. Offers M Ch E, M Geo E, M Mat SE, MA, MCE, MCS, MFM, MS, MS Ch E, MS Mat SE, MSEE, MSME, MSMOT, MSSE, MSST, PhD, Certificate, MD/PhD. *Program availability:* Part-time, evening/weekend, online learning. Terminal master's awarded for partial completion of doctoral program. *Degree requirements:* For master's, thesis (for some programs); for doctorate, thesis/dissertation. *Entrance requirements:* Additional exam requirements/recommendations for international students: Required—TOEFL (minimum score 550 paper-based; 79 iBT). Electronic applications accepted.

University of Mississippi, Graduate School, School of Engineering, University, MS 38677. Offers MS, PhD. *Faculty:* 61 full-time (50 women), 6 part-time/adjunct (3 women). *Students:* 116 full-time (27 women), 22 part-time (1 woman); includes 14 minority (5 Black or African American, non-Hispanic/Latino; 6 Asian, non-Hispanic/Latino; 2 Hispanic/Latino; 1 Two or more races, non-Hispanic/Latino), 71 international. Average age 27. In 2016, 28 master's, 12 doctorates awarded. *Degree requirements:* For master's, thesis (for some programs); for doctorate, thesis/dissertation. *Entrance requirements:* For master's, GRE General Test, minimum GPA of 3.0; for doctorate, GRE General Test. Additional exam requirements/recommendations for international students: Required—TOEFL. *Application deadline:* For fall admission, 4/1 for domestic students; for spring admission, 10/1 for domestic students. Applications are processed on a rolling basis. Application fee: $40. Electronic applications accepted. *Financial support:* Scholarships/grants available. Financial award application deadline: 3/1; financial award applicants required to submit FAFSA. *Unit head:* Dr. Alexander Cheng, Dean, 662-915-7407, Fax: 662-915-1287, E-mail: engineer@olemiss.edu. *Application contact:* Dr. Christy M. Wyandt, Associate Dean, 662-915-7474, Fax: 662-915-7577, E-mail: cwyandt@olemiss.edu.
Website: https://www.olemiss.edu

Engineering and Applied Sciences—General

University of Missouri, Office of Research and Graduate Studies, College of Engineering, Columbia, MO 65211. Offers ME, MS, PhD, Certificate. *Program availability:* Part-time. *Faculty:* 122 full-time (18 women), 9 part-time/adjunct (3 women). *Students:* 280 full-time (65 women), 307 part-time (65 women); includes 21 minority (6 Black or African American, non-Hispanic/Latino; 5 Asian, non-Hispanic/Latino; 7 Hispanic/Latino; 3 Two or more races, non-Hispanic/Latino), 465 international. Average age 28. *Degree requirements:* For doctorate, thesis/dissertation. *Entrance requirements:* For master's and doctorate, GRE General Test. Additional exam requirements/recommendations for international students: Required—TOEFL (minimum score 550 paper-based; 80 iBT), IELTS (minimum score 6.5). *Application deadline:* Applications are processed on a rolling basis. Application fee: $75 ($90 for international students). *Expenses:* Tuition, state resident: full-time $6347; part-time $352.60 per credit hour. Tuition, nonresident: full-time $17,379; part-time $965.50 per credit hour. *Required fees:* $1035. Tuition and fees vary according to course load, campus/location and program. *Financial support:* Fellowships, research assistantships, teaching assistantships, institutionally sponsored loans, scholarships/grants, traineeships, health care benefits, and unspecified assistantships available. Support available to part-time students. Website: http://engineering.missouri.edu/

University of Missouri–Kansas City, School of Computing and Engineering, Kansas City, MO 64110-2499. Offers civil engineering (MS); computer and electrical engineering (PhD); computer science (MS), including bioinformatics, software engineering, telecommunications networking; computer science and informatics (PhD); computing (PhD); electrical engineering (MS); engineering (PhD); engineering and construction management (Graduate Certificate); mechanical engineering (MS); telecommunications and computer networking (PhD). PhD (interdisciplinary) offered through the School of Graduate Studies. *Program availability:* Part-time. *Faculty:* 45 full-time (6 women), 26 part-time/adjunct (4 women). *Students:* 473 full-time (155 women), 207 part-time (42 women); includes 24 minority (10 Black or African American, non-Hispanic/Latino; 10 Asian, non-Hispanic/Latino; 4 Hispanic/Latino), 581 international. Average age 25. 1,143 applicants, 44% accepted, 227 enrolled. In 2016, 446 master's, 2 other advanced degrees awarded. *Degree requirements:* For doctorate, thesis/dissertation. *Entrance requirements:* For master's, GRE General Test, minimum GPA of 3.0, 3 letters of recommendation from professors; for doctorate, GRE General Test, minimum GPA of 3.5. Additional exam requirements/recommendations for international students: Required—TOEFL (minimum score 550 paper-based; 80 iBT). *Application deadline:* For fall admission, 1/15 priority date for domestic students, 1/15 for international students. Applications are processed on a rolling basis. Application fee: $45 ($50 for international students). *Financial support:* In 2016–17, 37 research assistantships with partial tuition reimbursements (averaging $15,679 per year), 47 teaching assistantships with partial tuition reimbursements (averaging $16,830 per year) were awarded; career-related internships or fieldwork, Federal Work-Study, scholarships/grants, tuition waivers (partial), and unspecified assistantships also available. Support available to part-time students. Financial award application deadline: 3/1; financial award applicants required to submit FAFSA. *Faculty research:* Algorithms, bioinformatics and medical informatics, biomechanics/biomaterials, civil engineering materials, networking and telecommunications, thermal science. *Unit head:* Dr. Kevin Z. Truman, Dean, 816-235-2399, Fax: 816-235-5159. *Application contact:* 816-235-2399, Fax: 816-235-5159. Website: http://sce.umkc.edu/

University of Nebraska–Lincoln, Graduate College, College of Engineering, Lincoln, NE 68588. Offers M Eng, MAE, MEE, MS, PhD. *Degree requirements:* For doctorate, comprehensive exam, thesis/dissertation. *Entrance requirements:* For master's and doctorate, GRE General Test. Additional exam requirements/recommendations for international students: Required—TOEFL. Electronic applications accepted.

University of Nevada, Las Vegas, Graduate College, Howard R. Hughes College of Engineering, Las Vegas, NV 89154-4005. Offers MS, PhD, Certificate, MS/MS, MS/PhD. *Program availability:* Part-time. *Faculty:* 57 full-time (8 women), 6 part-time/adjunct (1 woman). *Students:* 150 full-time (40 women), 95 part-time (19 women); includes 54 minority (3 Black or African American, non-Hispanic/Latino; 1 American Indian or Alaska Native, non-Hispanic/Latino; 22 Asian, non-Hispanic/Latino; 16 Hispanic/Latino; 12 Two or more races, non-Hispanic/Latino), 108 international. Average age 30. 233 applicants, 59% accepted, 53 enrolled. In 2016, 48 master's, 16 doctorates, 6 other advanced degrees awarded. *Degree requirements:* For master's, comprehensive exam (for some programs), thesis (for some programs); for doctorate, comprehensive exam, thesis/dissertation. *Entrance requirements:* For master's, GRE General Test; for doctorate, GRE General Test, 3 letters of recommendation; statement of purpose. Additional exam requirements/recommendations for international students: Required—TOEFL (minimum score 550 paper-based; 80 iBT), IELTS (minimum score 7). Application fee: $60 ($95 for international students). Electronic applications accepted. *Expenses:* $269.25 per credit, $792 per 3-credit course; $9,634 per year resident; $23,274 per year non-resident; $7,094 fees non-resident (7 credits or more); $1,307 annual health insurance fee. *Financial support:* In 2016–17, 2 fellowships with partial tuition reimbursements (averaging $17,500 per year), 49 research assistantships with partial tuition reimbursements (averaging $15,855 per year), 101 teaching assistantships with partial tuition reimbursements (averaging $13,753 per year) were awarded; institutionally sponsored loans, scholarships/grants, health care benefits, and unspecified assistantships also available. Financial award application deadline: 3/15. *Faculty research:* Batteries, big data, biomedical engineering, environmental engineering, water resources, security, renewable energy, transportation, unmanned aerial system. *Total annual research expenditures:* $9.1 million. *Unit head:* Dr. Rama Venkat, Dean, 702-895-3699, Fax: 702-895-4059, E-mail: rama.venkat@unlv.edu. Website: http://engineering.unlv.edu/

University of Nevada, Reno, Graduate School, College of Engineering, Reno, NV 89557. Offers MS, PhD. Terminal master's awarded for partial completion of doctoral program. *Degree requirements:* For master's, thesis optional; for doctorate, thesis/dissertation. *Entrance requirements:* For master's, GRE General Test, minimum GPA of 2.75; for doctorate, GRE General Test, minimum GPA of 3.0. Additional exam requirements/recommendations for international students: Required—TOEFL (minimum score 500 paper-based; 61 iBT), IELTS (minimum score 6). Electronic applications accepted. *Faculty research:* Fabrication, development of new materials, structural and earthquake engineering, computer vision/virtual reality, acoustics, smart materials.

University of New Brunswick Fredericton, School of Graduate Studies, Faculty of Engineering, Fredericton, NB E3B 5A3, Canada. Offers M Eng, M Sc E, PhD, Certificate. *Program availability:* Part-time. *Degree requirements:* For master's, thesis; for doctorate, comprehensive exam, thesis/dissertation, qualifying exam. *Entrance requirements:* For master's, minimum GPA of 3.0. Additional exam requirements/recommendations for international students: Required—TOEFL, TWE. Electronic applications accepted.

University of New Haven, Graduate School, Tagliatela College of Engineering, West Haven, CT 06516. Offers MS, MSIE, Graduate Certificate, MBA/MSIE. *Program availability:* Part-time, evening/weekend. *Students:* 448 full-time (126 women), 167 part-time (32 women); includes 33 minority (12 Black or African American, non-Hispanic/Latino; 2 American Indian or Alaska Native, non-Hispanic/Latino; 15 Asian, non-Hispanic/Latino; 2 Hispanic/Latino; 2 Two or more races, non-Hispanic/Latino), 452 international. Average age 26. 1,982 applicants, 54% accepted, 161 enrolled. In 2016, 333 master's, 24 other advanced degrees awarded. *Degree requirements:* For master's, thesis or alternative. *Entrance requirements:* Additional exam requirements/recommendations for international students: Required—TOEFL (minimum score 75 iBT), IELTS, PTE (minimum score 50). *Application deadline:* Applications are processed on a rolling basis. Application fee: $50. Electronic applications accepted. Application fee is waived when completed online. *Expenses: Tuition:* Full-time $15,660; part-time $870 per credit hour. *Required fees:* $200; $85 per term. Tuition and fees vary according to program. *Financial support:* Research assistantships with partial tuition reimbursements, teaching assistantships with partial tuition reimbursements, career-related internships or fieldwork, Federal Work-Study, scholarships/grants, and unspecified assistantships available. Support available to part-time students. Financial award applicants required to submit FAFSA. *Unit head:* Dr. Ronald Harichandran, Dean, 203-932-7167, E-mail: rharichandran@newhaven.edu. *Application contact:* Michelle Mason, Director of Graduate Enrollment, 203-932-7440, E-mail: mmason@newhaven.edu. Website: http://www.newhaven.edu/engineering/

University of New Mexico, Graduate Studies, School of Engineering, Albuquerque, NM 87131. Offers M Eng, MCM, MEME, MS, MSCE, PhD, MBA/MEME. *Program availability:* Part-time. *Faculty:* 113 full-time (20 women), 14 part-time/adjunct (5 women). *Students:* 363 full-time (71 women), 375 part-time (75 women); includes 154 minority (7 Black or African American, non-Hispanic/Latino; 3 American Indian or Alaska Native, non-Hispanic/Latino; 19 Asian, non-Hispanic/Latino; 111 Hispanic/Latino; 14 Two or more races, non-Hispanic/Latino), 257 international. Average age 30. 798 applicants, 27% accepted, 171 enrolled. In 2016, 142 master's, 53 doctorates awarded. Terminal master's awarded for partial completion of doctoral program. *Degree requirements:* For master's, comprehensive exam, thesis or alternative; for doctorate, comprehensive exam, thesis/dissertation. *Entrance requirements:* For master's, GRE, GMAT, letters of recommendation; letter of intent; for doctorate, GRE, letters of recommendation; letter of intent. Additional exam requirements/recommendations for international students: Required—TOEFL (minimum score 550 paper-based). *Application deadline:* For fall admission, 1/15 priority date for domestic and international students; for spring admission, 7/14 priority date for domestic and international students. Applications are processed on a rolling basis. Application fee: $50. Electronic applications accepted. *Financial support:* Federal Work-Study, scholarships/grants, health care benefits, and unspecified assistantships available. Financial award application deadline: 3/1; financial award applicants required to submit FAFSA. *Faculty research:* Emerging energy technologies, biomedical engineering and biocomputing, water resources and environmental engineering, optical engineering and optoelectronic materials, graphics and digital imaging. *Unit head:* Christos Christodoulou, Dean, 505-277-5522, Fax: 505-277-5521, E-mail: christos@unm.edu. *Application contact:* Deborah Kieltyka, Associate Director, Admissions, 505-277-3140, Fax: 505-277-6686, E-mail: deborahk@unm.edu. Website: http://soe.unm.edu/

University of New Orleans, Graduate School, College of Engineering, New Orleans, LA 70148. Offers MS, PhD. *Program availability:* Part-time. Terminal master's awarded for partial completion of doctoral program. *Degree requirements:* For master's, comprehensive exam, thesis optional; for doctorate, comprehensive exam, thesis/dissertation. *Entrance requirements:* For master's, GRE General Test, minimum GPA of 3.0; for doctorate, GRE General Test. Additional exam requirements/recommendations for international students: Required—TOEFL (minimum score 550 paper-based; 79 iBT). Electronic applications accepted. *Faculty research:* Electrical, civil, environmental, mechanical, naval architecture, and marine engineering.

The University of North Carolina at Charlotte, William States Lee College of Engineering, Charlotte, NC 28223-0001. Offers MS, MSCE, MSE, MSEE, MSEM, MSME, PhD, Graduate Certificate. *Program availability:* Part-time, evening/weekend, blended/hybrid learning. *Faculty:* 122 full-time (15 women), 2 part-time/adjunct (1 woman). *Students:* 446 full-time (93 women), 192 part-time (39 women); includes 45 minority (20 Black or African American, non-Hispanic/Latino; 9 Asian, non-Hispanic/Latino; 15 Hispanic/Latino; 1 Two or more races, non-Hispanic/Latino), 420 international. Average age 27. 1,373 applicants, 57% accepted, 193 enrolled. In 2016, 235 master's, 26 doctorates, 5 other advanced degrees awarded. Terminal master's awarded for partial completion of doctoral program. *Entrance requirements:* For master's, bachelor's degree, or its U.S. equivalent, from regionally-accredited college or university; minimum overall GPA of 3.0 on all previous work beyond high school; statement of purpose (essay); at least three recommendation forms; for doctorate, bachelor's degree (or its U.S. equivalent) from regionally-accredited college or university; minimum overall GPA of 3.5 in master's degree program; for Graduate Certificate, bachelor's degree from regionally-accredited university; minimum GPA of 2.75 on all post-secondary work attempted; transcripts; personal statement outlining why the applicant seeks admission to the program. Additional exam requirements/recommendations for international students: Required—TOEFL (minimum score 523 paper-based, 70 iBT) or IELTS (6.5). *Application deadline:* Applications are processed on a rolling basis. Application fee: $75. Electronic applications accepted. *Expenses:* Tuition, state resident: full-time $4252. Tuition, nonresident: full-time $17,423. *Required fees:* $3026. Tuition and fees vary according to course load and program. *Financial support:* In 2016–17, 239 students received support, including 5 fellowships (averaging $34,552 per year), 129 research assistantships (averaging $9,419 per year), 105 teaching assistantships (averaging $5,996 per year); career-related internships or fieldwork, institutionally sponsored loans, scholarships/grants, and unspecified assistantships also available. Support available to part-time students. Financial award application deadline: 3/1; financial award applicants required to submit FAFSA. *Faculty research:* Environmental engineering, structures and geotechnical engineering, precision engineering and precision metrology, optoelectronics and microelectronics, communications. *Total annual research expenditures:* $9.8 million. *Unit head:* Dr. Robert E. Johnson, Dean, 704-687-8242, E-mail: robejohn@uncc.edu. *Application contact:* Kathy B. Giddings, Director of Graduate Admissions, 704-687-5503, Fax: 704-687-1668, E-mail: gradadm@uncc.edu. Website: http://engr.uncc.edu/

University of North Dakota, Graduate School, School of Engineering and Mines, Program in Engineering, Grand Forks, ND 58202. Offers PhD. *Degree requirements:* For doctorate, comprehensive exam, thesis/dissertation, final exam. *Entrance requirements:* For doctorate, minimum GPA of 3.0. Additional exam requirements/recommendations for international students: Required—TOEFL (minimum score 550 paper-based; 79 iBT), IELTS (minimum score 6.5). *Application deadline:* For fall admission, 8/1 priority date for domestic students, 5/1 priority date for international students; for spring admission, 12/1 priority date for domestic students, 9/1 priority date for international students. Applications are processed on a rolling basis. Application fee: $35. Electronic applications accepted. *Financial support:* In 2016–17, 21 students received support. Fellowships with full and partial tuition reimbursements available, research assistantships with full and partial tuition reimbursements available, teaching assistantships with full and partial tuition reimbursements available, career-related internships or fieldwork, Federal Work-Study, institutionally sponsored loans, scholarships/grants, and tuition waivers (full and partial) available. Support available to

part-time students. Financial award application deadline: 3/15; financial award applicants required to submit FAFSA. *Faculty research:* Combustion science, energy conversion, power transmission, environmental engineering. *Unit head:* Dr. Hossein Salehfar, Graduate Director, 701-777-4331, Fax: 701-777-4838. *Application contact:* Staci Wells, Admissions Associate, 701-777-2945, Fax: 701-777-3619, E-mail: staci.wells@gradschool.und.edu.
Website: http://www.engineering.und.edu/GraduateStudents/index.html#phdprog

University of North Texas, Robert B. Toulouse School of Graduate Studies, Denton, TX 76203-5459. Offers accounting (MS); applied anthropology (MA, MS); applied behavior analysis (Certificate); applied geography (MA); applied technology and performance improvement (M Ed, MS); art education (MA); art history (MA); art museum education (Certificate); arts leadership (Certificate); audiology (Au D); behavior analysis (MS); behavioral science (PhD); biochemistry and molecular biology (MS); biology (MA, MS); biomedical engineering (MS); business analysis (MS); chemistry (MS); clinical health psychology (PhD); communication studies (MA, MS); computer engineering (MS); computer science (MS); counseling (M Ed, MS), including clinical mental health counseling (MS), college and university counseling, elementary school counseling, secondary school counseling; creative writing (MA); criminal justice (MS); curriculum and instruction (M Ed); decision sciences (MBA); design (MA, MFA), including fashion design (MFA), innovation studies, interior design (MFA); early childhood studies (MS); economics (MS); educational leadership (M Ed, Ed D); educational psychology (MS, PhD), including family studies (MS), gifted and talented (MS), human development (MS), learning and cognition (MS), research, measurement and evaluation (MS); electrical engineering (MS); emergency management (MPA); engineering technology (MS); English (MA); English as a second language (MA); environmental science (MS); finance (MBA, MS); financial management (MPA); French (MA); health services management (MBA); higher education (M Ed, Ed D); history (MA, MS); hospitality management (MS); human resources management (MPA); information science (MS); information systems (PhD); information technologies (MBA); interdisciplinary studies (MA, MS); international studies (MA); international sustainable tourism (MS); jazz studies (MM); journalism (MA, MJ, Graduate Certificate), including interactive and virtual digital communication (Graduate Certificate), narrative journalism (Graduate Certificate), public relations (Graduate Certificate); kinesiology (MS); linguistics (MA); local government management (MPA); logistics (PhD); logistics and supply chain management (MBA); long-term care, senior housing, and aging services (MA); management (PhD); marketing (MBA); mathematics (MA, MS); mechanical and energy engineering (MS, PhD); music (MA), including ethnomusicology, music theory, musicology, performance; music composition (PhD); music education (MM Ed, PhD); nonprofit management (MPA); operations and supply chain management (MBA); performance (MM, DMA); philosophy (MA); political science (MA); professional and technical communication (MA); radio, television and film (MA, MFA); rehabilitation counseling (Certificate); sociology (MA); Spanish (MA); special education (M Ed); speech-language pathology (MA); strategic management (MBA); studio art (MFA); teaching (M Ed); MBA/MS. *Program availability:* Part-time, evening/weekend, online learning. Terminal master's awarded for partial completion of doctoral program. *Degree requirements:* For master's, variable foreign language requirement, comprehensive exam (for some programs), thesis (for some programs); for doctorate, variable foreign language requirement, comprehensive exam (for some programs), thesis/dissertation; for other advanced degree, variable foreign language requirement, comprehensive exam (for some programs). *Entrance requirements:* For master's and doctorate, GRE, GMAT. Additional exam requirements/recommendations for international students: Required—TOEFL (minimum score 550 paper-based; 79 iBT). Electronic applications accepted.

University of Notre Dame, Graduate School, College of Engineering, Notre Dame, IN 46556. Offers M Eng, MEME, MS, MS Aero E, MS Bio E, MS Ch E, MS Env E, MSCE, MSCSE, MSEE, MSME, PhD. Terminal master's awarded for partial completion of doctoral program. *Degree requirements:* For master's, comprehensive exam; for doctorate, thesis/dissertation. *Entrance requirements:* For master's and doctorate, GRE General Test. Additional exam requirements/recommendations for international students: Required—TOEFL. Electronic applications accepted.

University of Oklahoma, Gallogly College of Engineering, Department of General Engineering, Norman, OK 73019. Offers MS, PhD. *Program availability:* Part-time. *Faculty:* 3 full-time (2 women). *Students:* 3 full-time (2 women), 7 part-time (1 woman); includes 2 minority (1 American Indian or Alaska Native, non-Hispanic/Latino; 1 Asian, non-Hispanic/Latino), 1 international. Average age 41. 3 applicants, 67% accepted, 2 enrolled. In 2016, 2 master's awarded. Terminal master's awarded for partial completion of doctoral program. *Degree requirements:* For master's, comprehensive exam, thesis optional; for doctorate, comprehensive exam, thesis/dissertation. *Entrance requirements:* For master's and doctorate, GRE. Additional exam requirements/recommendations for international students: Required—TOEFL (minimum score 79 iBT) or IELTS (minimum score 6.5). Application fee: $50 ($100 for international students). Electronic applications accepted. *Expenses:* Tuition, state resident: full-time $4886; part-time $203.60 per credit hour. Tuition, nonresident: full-time $18,989; part-time $791.20 per credit hour. *Required fees:* $3283; $126.25 per credit hour. $126.50 per semester. *Financial support:* In 2016–17, 2 students received support. Fellowships and scholarships/grants available. Financial award application deadline: 6/1; financial award applicants required to submit FAFSA. *Unit head:* Dr. John Antonio, Senior Associate Dean, 405-325-2621, E-mail: antonio@ou.edu. *Application contact:* PJ Meek, Assistant to the Senior Associate Dean, 405-325-4536, E-mail: pjmeek@ou.edu.
Website: http://www.ou.edu/content/coe/academics/graduate/academics/Engineering.html

University of Ottawa, Faculty of Graduate and Postdoctoral Studies, Faculty of Engineering, Ottawa, ON K1N 6N5, Canada. Offers M Eng, MA Sc, MCS, PhD, Certificate. *Degree requirements:* For master's, thesis or alternative; for doctorate, thesis/dissertation. *Entrance requirements:* For master's, honors degree or equivalent, minimum B average. Electronic applications accepted.

★ **University of Pennsylvania,** School of Engineering and Applied Science, Philadelphia, PA 19104. Offers MBT, MCIT, MIPD, MSE, PhD, MSE/MBA, PhD/MD, VMD/PhD. *Program availability:* Part-time. *Faculty:* 115 full-time (18 women), 26 part-time/adjunct (3 women). *Students:* 1,109 full-time (333 women), 301 part-time (102 women); includes 180 minority (13 Black or African American, non-Hispanic/Latino; 116 Asian, non-Hispanic/Latino; 38 Hispanic/Latino; 13 Two or more races, non-Hispanic/Latino), 880 international. Average age 25. 6,263 applicants, 23% accepted, 817 enrolled. In 2016, 581 master's, 78 doctorates awarded. *Degree requirements:* For master's, comprehensive exam, thesis optional; for doctorate, comprehensive exam, thesis/dissertation. *Entrance requirements:* For master's and doctorate, GRE. Additional exam requirements/recommendations for international students: Required—TOEFL (minimum score 100 iBT), IELTS (minimum score 7). *Application deadline:* For fall admission, 3/15 priority date for domestic and international students. Application fee: $80. Electronic applications accepted. *Expenses:* $6,750 per course. *Faculty research:* Robotics, computer and information science, drone development, electrical and system engineering, bioengineering. *Application contact:* William Fenton, Assistant Director of Graduate Admissions, 215-898-4542, Fax: 215-

573-5577, E-mail: gradstudies@seas.upenn.edu.
Website: http://www.seas.upenn.edu
See Display on next page and Close-Up on page 89.

University of Pittsburgh, Katz Graduate School of Business, MBA/Master of Science in Engineering Joint Degree Program, Pittsburgh, PA 15260. Offers MBA/MSE. *Accreditation:* AACSB. *Program availability:* Part-time, evening/weekend. *Faculty:* 88 full-time (27 women), 42 part-time/adjunct (15 women). *Students:* 17 full-time (4 women), 18 part-time (0 women); includes 5 minority (1 Black or African American, non-Hispanic/Latino; 2 Hispanic/Latino; 2 Two or more races, non-Hispanic/Latino), 4 international. Average age 27. 42 applicants, 71% accepted, 18 enrolled. *Entrance requirements:* Additional exam requirements/recommendations for international students: Required—TOEFL (minimum score 100 iBT) or IELTS (minimum score 7.0). *Application deadline:* For fall admission, 4/1 priority date for domestic students, 2/1 priority date for international students. Application fee: $50. Electronic applications accepted. Tuition and fees vary according to program. *Financial support:* Scholarships/grants available. Financial award application deadline: 6/1; financial award applicants required to submit FAFSA. *Faculty research:* Accounting systems/financial reporting, corporate finance, shopper marketing/consumer behavior, management information systems, organizational behavior and entrepreneurship. *Total annual research expenditures:* $493,036. *Unit head:* Dr. Arjang A. Assad, Dean, 412-648-1556, Fax: 412-648-1552, E-mail: aassad@katz.pitt.edu. *Application contact:* Thomas Keller, Director of MBA Admissions, 412-648-1700, Fax: 412-648-1659, E-mail: mba@katz.pitt.edu.
Website: http://www.business.pitt.edu/katz/mba/academics/programs/mba-msengineering.php

University of Pittsburgh, Swanson School of Engineering, Pittsburgh, PA 15260. Offers MS, MS Ch E, MSBENG, MSCEE, MSIE, MSME, MSNE, MSPE, PhD, MD/PhD, MS Ch E/MSPE. *Program availability:* Part-time, 100% online. *Faculty:* 132 full-time (19 women), 102 part-time/adjunct (12 women). *Students:* 722 full-time (200 women), 223 part-time (51 women); includes 106 minority (26 Black or African American, non-Hispanic/Latino; 1 American Indian or Alaska Native, non-Hispanic/Latino; 39 Asian, non-Hispanic/Latino; 23 Hispanic/Latino; 1 Native Hawaiian or other Pacific Islander, non-Hispanic/Latino; 16 Two or more races, non-Hispanic/Latino), 490 international. 2,867 applicants, 37% accepted, 287 enrolled. In 2016, 244 master's, 78 doctorates awarded. Terminal master's awarded for partial completion of doctoral program. *Degree requirements:* For doctorate, comprehensive exam, thesis/dissertation, final oral exams. *Entrance requirements:* For master's and doctorate, minimum GPA of 3.0. Additional exam requirements/recommendations for international students: Required—TOEFL (minimum score 550 paper-based; 80 iBT). *Application deadline:* For fall admission, 3/1 priority date for domestic and international students; for spring admission, 7/1 priority date for domestic and international students. Applications are processed on a rolling basis. Application fee: $50. Electronic applications accepted. *Expenses:* $24,962 full-time per academic year in-state tuition, $41,222 full-time per academic year out-of-state tuition; $830 mandatory fees per academic year. *Financial support:* In 2016–17, 82 fellowships with full tuition reimbursements (averaging $30,720 per year), 229 research assistantships with full tuition reimbursements (averaging $27,396 per year), 137 teaching assistantships with full tuition reimbursements (averaging $26,328 per year) were awarded; scholarships/grants, traineeships, and tuition waivers (full) also available. Financial award application deadline: 3/1. *Faculty research:* Artificial organs, biotechnology, signal processing, construction management, fluid dynamics. *Total annual research expenditures:* $88.2 million. *Unit head:* Dr. Gerald D. Holder, Dean, 412-624-9809, Fax: 412-624-0412, E-mail: holder@engr.pitt.edu. *Application contact:* Rama Bazaz, Director, 412-624-9800, Fax: 412-624-9808, E-mail: ssoeadm@pitt.edu.
Website: http://www.engineering.pitt.edu/

University of Portland, School of Engineering, Portland, OR 97203-5798. Offers biomedical engineering (MBME); civil engineering (ME); computer science (ME); electrical engineering (ME); mechanical engineering (ME). *Program availability:* Part-time, evening/weekend. *Degree requirements:* For master's, thesis optional. *Entrance requirements:* For master's, GRE General Test, minimum GPA of 3.0, 3 letters of recommendation, resume, statement of goals, official transcripts. Additional exam requirements/recommendations for international students: Required—TOEFL (minimum score 550 paper-based; 80 iBT), IELTS (minimum score 7). *Expenses:* Contact institution.

University of Puerto Rico, Mayagüez Campus, Graduate Studies, College of Engineering, Mayagüez, PR 00681-9000. Offers ME, MS, PhD. *Program availability:* Part-time. *Faculty:* 36 full-time (13 women), 7 part-time/adjunct (3 women). *Students:* 33 full-time (10 women), 7 part-time (3 women); includes 32 minority (all Hispanic/Latino), 8 international. Average age 25. 10 applicants, 80% accepted, 3 enrolled. *Degree requirements:* For master's, one foreign language, comprehensive exam, thesis. *Application deadline:* For fall admission, 2/15 for domestic and international students; for spring admission, 9/15 for domestic and international students. Applications are processed on a rolling basis. Application fee: $25. Electronic applications accepted. *Expenses: Tuition, area resident:* Full-time $2466. *International tuition:* $7166 full-time. *Required fees:* $210. One-time fee: $5 full-time. Tuition and fees vary according to course level, campus/location, program and student level. *Financial support:* In 2016–17, 9 students received support, including 6 research assistantships with full and partial tuition reimbursements available (averaging $4,087 per year), 4 teaching assistantships with full and partial tuition reimbursements available (averaging $4,020 per year); unspecified assistantships also available. *Faculty research:* Structural dynamics, plastic materials, fluid mechanics, computer graphics, computer programming. *Unit head:* Dr. Agustin Rullan, Dean, 787-832-4040 Ext. 3822, E-mail: decano.ingenieria@upr.edu. *Application contact:* Lucia Mercado, Administrative Secretary V, 787-832-4040 Ext. 2398, E-mail: lucia.mercado@upr.edu.
Website: http://engineering.uprm.edu/

University of Regina, Faculty of Graduate Studies and Research, Faculty of Engineering and Applied Science, Regina, SK S4S 0A2, Canada. Offers M Eng, MA Sc, PhD. *Program availability:* Part-time. *Faculty:* 43 full-time (4 women), 21 part-time/adjunct (5 women). *Students:* 266 full-time (69 women), 29 part-time (6 women). 500 applicants, 13% accepted. In 2016, 78 master's, 16 doctorates awarded. *Degree requirements:* For master's, thesis, project, report; for doctorate, comprehensive exam, thesis/dissertation. *Entrance requirements:* Additional exam requirements/recommendations for international students: Required—TOEFL (minimum score 550 paper-based; 80 iBT), IELTS (minimum score 6.5), PTE (minimum score 59). *Application deadline:* For fall admission, 3/31 for domestic and international students; for winter admission, 7/31 for domestic and international students; for spring admission, 11/30 for domestic and international students. Application fee: $100. Electronic applications accepted. *Expenses:* Contact institution. *Financial support:* In 2016–17, 60 fellowships (averaging $5,317 per year), 61 teaching assistantships (averaging $2,990 per year) were awarded; career-related internships or fieldwork and scholarships/grants also available. Financial award application deadline: 6/15. *Unit head:* Dr. Esam Hussein, Dean, 306-585-4160, Fax: 306-585-4556, E-mail: esam.hussein@uregina.ca. *Application contact:* Dr. Amr Henni, Associate Dean, Graduate Studies and Research, 306-585-4960, Fax: 306-585-4855, E-mail: amr.henni@uregina.ca.
Website: http://www.uregina.ca/engineering/

University of Rhode Island, Graduate School, College of Engineering, Kingston, RI 02881. Offers MS, PhD, Graduate Certificate, Postbaccalaureate Certificate. *Program availability:* Part-time. *Faculty:* 72 full-time (14 women). *Students:* 125 full-time (29 women), 76 part-time (13 women); includes 22 minority (2 Black or African American, non-Hispanic/Latino; 1 American Indian or Alaska Native, non-Hispanic/Latino; 7 Asian, non-Hispanic/Latino; 10 Hispanic/Latino; 2 Two or more races, non-Hispanic/Latino), 78 international. In 2016, 50 master's, 18 doctorates, 1 other advanced degree awarded. *Entrance requirements:* Additional exam requirements/recommendations for international students: Required—TOEFL. Application fee: $65. Electronic applications accepted. *Expenses:* Tuition, state resident: full-time $11,796; part-time $655 per credit. Tuition, nonresident: full-time $24,206; part-time $1345 per credit. *Required fees:* $1546; $44 per credit. One-time fee: $155 full-time; $35 part-time. *Financial support:* In 2016–17, 25 research assistantships with tuition reimbursements (averaging $9,604 per year), 17 teaching assistantships with tuition reimbursements (averaging $10,217 per year) were awarded. Financial award applicants required to submit FAFSA. *Unit head:* Dr. Raymond Wright, Dean, 401-874-2186, Fax: 401-782-1066, E-mail: dean@egr.uri.edu. *Application contact:* Graduate Admission, 401-874-2872, E-mail: gradadm@etal.uri.edu.
Website: http://www.egr.uri.edu/

University of Rochester, Hajim School of Engineering and Applied Sciences, Rochester, NY 14627. Offers MS, PhD. *Program availability:* Part-time. *Faculty:* 92 full-time (13 women). *Students:* 596 full-time (144 women), 23 part-time (7 women); includes 53 minority (9 Black or African American, non-Hispanic/Latino; 1 American Indian or Alaska Native, non-Hispanic/Latino; 18 Asian, non-Hispanic/Latino; 16 Hispanic/Latino; 9 Two or more races, non-Hispanic/Latino), 382 international. Average age 25. 2,605 applicants, 39% accepted, 259 enrolled. In 2016, 210 master's, 46 doctorates awarded. Terminal master's awarded for partial completion of doctoral program. *Degree requirements:* For doctorate, preliminary and oral exams. *Entrance requirements:* For master's and doctorate, GRE. Additional exam requirements/recommendations for international students: Required—TOEFL (minimum score 600 paper-based; 100 iBT). *Application deadline:* For fall admission, 1/1 for domestic and international students. Application fee: $60. Electronic applications accepted. *Expenses:* $1,538 per credit hour. *Unit head:* Dr. Wendi Heinzelman, Dean, 585-273-3958. *Application contact:* Dr. Margaret Kearney, Dean of Graduate Studies, 585-275-3540, E-mail: margaret.kearney@rochester.edu.
Website: http://www.hajim.rochester.edu/

University of St. Thomas, Graduate Studies, School of Engineering, St. Paul, MN 55105-1096. Offers data science (MS); electrical engineering (MS); information technology (MS); manufacturing engineering (MS); manufacturing systems (Certificate); mechanical engineering (MS); medical device development (Certificate); regulatory science (MS); software engineering (MS); software management (MS); systems engineering (MS); technology leadership (Certificate); technology management (MS). *Accreditation:* ABET (one or more programs are accredited). *Entrance requirements:* For master's, resume, official transcripts. Additional exam requirements/recommendations for international students: Required—TOEFL (minimum score 550 paper-based). *Application deadline:* For fall admission, 8/1 priority date for domestic students; for spring admission, 1/1 priority date for domestic students. Applications are processed on a rolling basis. Application fee: $50. Electronic applications accepted. *Expenses:* Contact institution. *Financial support:* Fellowships, research assistantships, institutionally sponsored loans, and scholarships/grants available. Support available to part-time students. Financial award application deadline: 4/1; financial award applicants required to submit FAFSA. *Unit head:* Don Weinkauf, Dean, 651-962-5760, Fax: 651-962-6419, E-mail: dhweinkauf@stthomas.edu. *Application contact:* Tina M. Hansen, Graduate Program Manager, 651-962-5755, Fax: 651-962-6419, E-mail: tina.hansen@stthomas.edu.
Website: http://www.stthomas.edu/engineering/

University of Saskatchewan, College of Graduate Studies and Research, College of Engineering, Saskatoon, SK S7N 5A9, Canada. Offers M Eng, M Sc, PhD, PGD. *Program availability:* Part-time. *Degree requirements:* For master's, 30 credits (for M Eng); thesis and 12 credits (for MS); for doctorate, comprehensive exam, thesis/dissertation, qualifying exam, 18 credits. *Entrance requirements:* For master's and doctorate, GRE. Additional exam requirements/recommendations for international students: Required—TOEFL, TOEFL (minimum iBT score of 80), IELTS (6.5), CanTEST (4.5), or PTE (59). Electronic applications accepted.

University of South Africa, College of Science, Engineering and Technology, Pretoria, South Africa. Offers chemical engineering (M Tech); information technology (M Tech).

University of South Alabama, College of Engineering, Mobile, AL 36688. Offers MS Ch E, MSCE, MSEE, MSME, D Sc. *Program availability:* Part-time. *Faculty:* 28 full-time (2 women), 2 part-time/adjunct (0 women). *Students:* 92 full-time (21 women), 17 part-time (2 women); includes 9 minority (5 Black or African American, non-Hispanic/Latino; 2 Asian, non-Hispanic/Latino; 1 Native Hawaiian or other Pacific Islander, non-Hispanic/Latino; 1 Two or more races, non-Hispanic/Latino), 58 international. Average age 26. 218 applicants, 50% accepted, 26 enrolled. In 2016, 114 master's awarded. *Degree requirements:* For master's, comprehensive exam, project or thesis; for doctorate, comprehensive exam, thesis/dissertation. *Entrance requirements:* For master's, GRE General Test, BS in engineering, minimum GPA of 3.0; for doctorate, GRE, MS in engineering, minimum graduate GPA of 3.0. Additional exam requirements/recommendations for international students: Required—TOEFL (minimum score 550 paper-based; 79 iBT). *Application deadline:* For fall admission, 7/1 priority date for domestic students, 6/1 priority date for international students; for spring admission, 12/1 priority date for domestic students, 11/1 priority date for international students; for summer admission, 5/1 priority date for domestic students, 4/1 priority date for international students. Applications are processed on a rolling basis. Application fee: $35. Electronic applications accepted. *Expenses:* Contact institution. *Financial support:* Fellowships, research assistantships, teaching assistantships, career-related internships or fieldwork, Federal Work-Study, institutionally sponsored loans, scholarships/grants, and unspecified assistantships available. Support available to part-time students. Financial award application deadline: 5/31; financial award applicants required to submit FAFSA. *Unit head:* Dr. John Steadman, Dean, College of Engineering, 251-460-6140, Fax: 251-460-6343, E-mail: engineering@southalabama.edu. *Application contact:* Brenda Poole, Academic Records Specialist, 251-460-6140, Fax: 251-460-6343, E-mail: engineering@southalabama.edu.
Website: http://www.southalabama.edu/colleges/engineering/index.html

University of South Carolina, The Graduate School, College of Engineering and Computing, Columbia, SC 29208. Offers ME, MS, PhD. *Program availability:* Part-time, evening/weekend, online learning. *Degree requirements:* For master's, thesis (for some programs); for doctorate, thesis/dissertation. *Entrance requirements:* For master's and doctorate, GRE General Test. Additional exam requirements/recommendations for international students: Required—TOEFL. Electronic applications accepted. *Faculty research:* Electrochemical engineering/fuel cell technology, fracture mechanics and nondestructive evaluation, virtual prototyping for electric power systems, wideband-gap electronics materials behavior/composites and smart materials.

University of Southern California, Graduate School, Viterbi School of Engineering, Los Angeles, CA 90089. Offers MCM, ME, MS, PhD, Engr, Graduate Certificate, MS/MBA. *Program availability:* Part-time, online learning. Terminal master's awarded for partial completion of doctoral program. *Degree requirements:* For doctorate, comprehensive exam, thesis/dissertation. *Entrance requirements:* For master's and doctorate, GRE. Additional exam requirements/recommendations for international students: Recommended—TOEFL. Electronic applications accepted. *Expenses:* Contact institution. *Faculty research:* Mechanics and materials, aerodynamics of air/ground vehicles, gas dynamics, aerosols, astronautics and space science, geophysical and microgravity flows, planetary physics, power MEMs and MEMS vacuum pumps, heat transfer and combustion, health systems, transportation and logistics, manufacturing and automation, engineering systems design, risk and economic analysis, electromagnetic devices circuits and VLSI, MEMS and nanotechnology, electromagnetics and plasmas.

University of Southern Indiana, Graduate Studies, Pott College of Science, Engineering, and Education, Evansville, IN 47712-3590. Offers MSE, MSIM, MSSM. *Program availability:* Part-time, evening/weekend. *Faculty:* 22 full-time (11 women), 3 part-time/adjunct (2 women). *Students:* 42 full-time (14 women), 21 part-time (14 women); includes 5 minority (3 Black or African American, non-Hispanic/Latino; 1 Hispanic/Latino; 1 Two or more races, non-Hispanic/Latino), 5 international. Average age 30. In 2016, 21 master's awarded. *Degree requirements:* For master's, project. *Entrance requirements:* For master's, GRE General Test, NTE, PRAXIS I, minimum GPA of 2.5 and BS in engineering or engineering technology (MSIM); minimum GPA of 3.0 and teaching license (MSE). Additional exam requirements/recommendations for international students: Required—TOEFL (minimum score 550 paper-based; 79 iBT), IELTS (minimum score 6). *Application deadline:* For fall admission, 8/15 priority date for domestic students, 3/1 priority date for international students. Applications are processed on a rolling basis. Application fee: $40. Electronic applications accepted. *Expenses:* Tuition, state resident: full-time $8497. Tuition, nonresident: full-time $16,691. *Required fees:* $500. *Financial support:* In 2016–17, 14 students received support. Federal Work-Study, scholarships/grants, tuition waivers (full and partial), and unspecified assistantships available. Financial award application deadline: 3/1; financial award applicants required to submit FAFSA. *Unit head:* Dr. Zane W. Mitchell, Dean, 812-465-7137, E-mail: zwmitchell@usi.edu. *Application contact:* Dr. Mayola Rowser, Director, Graduate Studies, 812-465-7015, Fax: 812-464-1956, E-mail: mrowser@usi.edu.
Website: http://www.usi.edu/science/

University of South Florida, College of Engineering, Tampa, FL 33620-9951. Offers MCE, MEVE, MME, MSBE, MSCE, MSCH, MSCP, MSCS, MSEE, MSEM, MSEV, MSIE, MSIT, MSME, PhD, Graduate Certificate, MSBE/MS. *Program availability:* Part-time, evening/weekend. *Faculty:* 122 full-time (19 women), 1 part-time/adjunct (0 women). *Students:* 915 full-time (211 women), 312 part-time (62 women); includes 141 minority (33 Black or African American, non-Hispanic/Latino; 32 Asian, non-Hispanic/Latino; 68 Hispanic/Latino; 8 Two or more races, non-Hispanic/Latino), 846 international. Average age 27. 2,235 applicants, 47% accepted, 366 enrolled. In 2016, 362 master's, 63 doctorates awarded. Terminal master's awarded for partial completion of doctoral program. *Degree requirements:* For master's, comprehensive exam, thesis (for some programs); for doctorate, comprehensive exam, thesis/dissertation. *Entrance requirements:* For master's, GRE General Test, minimum GPA of 3.0 in last 60 hours of coursework; for doctorate, GRE General Test, minimum GPA of 3.3 in last 60 hours of coursework. Additional exam requirements/recommendations for international students: Required—TOEFL (minimum score 550 paper-based; 79 iBT), IELTS (minimum score 6.5). *Application deadline:* For fall admission, 2/15 for domestic students, 1/2 priority date for international students; for spring admission, 10/15 for domestic students, 6/1 priority date for international students. Applications are processed on a rolling basis. Application fee: $30. Electronic applications accepted. *Expenses:* Tuition, state resident: full-time $7766; part-time $431.43 per credit hour. Tuition, nonresident: full-time $15,789; part-time $877.17 per credit hour. *Required fees:* $37 per term. *Financial support:* In 2016–17, 179 students received support. Career-related internships or fieldwork, Federal Work-Study, scholarships/grants, health care benefits, and unspecified assistantships available. Financial award application deadline: 3/1. *Faculty research:* Biomedical engineering and sustainability, particularly in water resources and energy; electrical engineering; civil/environmental engineering; industrial/management systems engineering; chemical engineering; computer science and engineering; mechanical engineering. *Total annual research expenditures:* $29.5 million. *Unit head:* Dr. Robert Bishop, Dean, 813-974-3864, Fax: 813-974-5094, E-mail: robertbishop@usf.edu. *Application contact:* Dr. Sanjukta Bhanja, Associate Dean for Academic Affairs, 813-974-4755, Fax: 813-974-5094, E-mail: bhanja@usf.edu.
Website: http://www2.eng.usf.edu/

The University of Tennessee, Graduate School, Tickle College of Engineering, Knoxville, TN 37996. Offers MS, PhD, MS/MBA, MS/PhD. *Program availability:* Part-time, online learning. *Faculty:* 233 full-time (35 women), 57 part-time/adjunct (7 women). *Students:* 867 full-time (197 women), 236 part-time (36 women); includes 103 minority (23 Black or African American, non-Hispanic/Latino; 2 American Indian or Alaska Native, non-Hispanic/Latino; 33 Asian, non-Hispanic/Latino; 33 Hispanic/Latino; 12 Two or more races, non-Hispanic/Latino), 413 international. Average age 30. 1,346 applicants, 35% accepted, 263 enrolled. In 2016, 177 master's, 89 doctorates awarded. *Degree requirements:* For master's, thesis or alternative; for doctorate, comprehensive exam, thesis/dissertation. *Entrance requirements:* For master's, GRE General Test (for MS students pursuing research thesis), minimum GPA of 2.7 (for U.S. degree holders), 3.0 (for international degree holders); 3 references; statement of purpose; for doctorate, GRE General Test, minimum GPA of 3.0 on previous graduate course work; 3 references; statement of purpose. Additional exam requirements/recommendations for international students: Required—TOEFL (minimum score 550 paper-based). *Application deadline:* For fall admission, 2/1 priority date for domestic and international students; for spring admission, 6/15 for domestic and international students. Applications are processed on a rolling basis. Application fee: $35. Electronic applications accepted. *Financial support:* In 2016–17, 705 students received support, including 106 fellowships with full tuition reimbursements available (averaging $27,735 per year), 383 research assistantships with full tuition reimbursements available (averaging $23,278 per year), 198 teaching assistantships with full tuition reimbursements available (averaging $20,212 per year); career-related internships or fieldwork, Federal Work-Study, institutionally sponsored loans, health care benefits, and unspecified assistantships also available. Financial award application deadline: 2/1; financial award applicants required to submit FAFSA. *Faculty research:* Chemical and biomolecular engineering; civil and environmental engineering; electrical engineering and computer science; nuclear engineering; materials science and engineering; mechanical, aerospace, and biomedical engineering; industrial and information engineering. *Total annual research expenditures:* $65.4 million. *Unit head:* Dr. Wayne T. Davis, Dean, 865-974-5321, Fax: 865-974-8890, E-mail: wtdavis@utk.edu. *Application contact:* Dr. Masood Parang, Associate Dean of Student Affairs, 865-974-2454, Fax: 865-974-9871, E-mail: mparang@utk.edu.
Website: http://www.engr.utk.edu/

The University of Texas at Arlington, Graduate School, College of Engineering, Arlington, TX 76019. Offers M Engr, MCM, MS, PhD. *Program availability:* Part-time, evening/weekend, online learning. Terminal master's awarded for partial completion of doctoral program. *Degree requirements:* For master's, thesis optional; for doctorate, thesis/dissertation. *Entrance requirements:* For master's, GRE General Test, minimum GPA of 3.0 in last 60 hours of coursework; for doctorate, GRE General Test. Additional exam requirements/recommendations for international students: Required—TOEFL (minimum score 550 paper-based). *Application deadline:* For fall admission, 6/6 for domestic students, 4/4 for international students; for spring admission, 10/15 for domestic students, 9/5 for international students. Applications are processed on a rolling basis. Application fee: $35 ($50 for international students). *Financial support:* Fellowships, research assistantships, teaching assistantships, career-related internships or fieldwork, Federal Work-Study, institutionally sponsored loans, scholarships/grants, and tuition waivers (partial) available. Financial award application deadline: 6/1; financial award applicants required to submit FAFSA. *Faculty research:* Nanotechnology, mobile pervasive computing, bioinformatics intelligent systems. *Unit head:* Dr. Jean-Pierre Bardet, Dean, 817-272-2571, Fax: 817-272-5110, E-mail: bardet@uta.edu. *Application contact:* Dr. Lynn L. Peterson, Associate Dean for Academic Affairs, 817-272-2571, Fax: 817-272-2548, E-mail: peterson@uta.edu.
Website: http://www.uta.edu/engineering/

The University of Texas at Austin, Graduate School, Cockrell School of Engineering, Austin, TX 78712-1111. Offers MA, MS, MSE, PhD, MBA/MSE, MD/PhD, MP Aff/MSE. *Program availability:* Part-time, evening/weekend. *Entrance requirements:* For master's and doctorate, GRE General Test. Additional exam requirements/recommendations for international students: Required—TOEFL (minimum score 550 paper-based). Electronic applications accepted.

The University of Texas at Dallas, Erik Jonson School of Engineering and Computer Science, Richardson, TX 75080. Offers MS, MSEE, MSME, MSTE, PhD. *Program availability:* Part-time, evening/weekend. *Faculty:* 154 full-time (18 women), 17 part-time/adjunct (4 women). *Students:* 1,902 full-time (542 women), 570 part-time (142 women); includes 171 minority (17 Black or African American, non-Hispanic/Latino; 2 American Indian or Alaska Native, non-Hispanic/Latino; 90 Asian, non-Hispanic/Latino; 48 Hispanic/Latino; 14 Two or more races, non-Hispanic/Latino), 2,053 international. Average age 27. 7,329 applicants, 34% accepted, 850 enrolled. In 2016, 989 master's, 70 doctorates awarded. *Degree requirements:* For master's, thesis optional; for doctorate, thesis/dissertation. *Entrance requirements:* For master's, GRE General Test, minimum GPA of 3.0 in related bachelor's course work; for doctorate, GRE General Test, minimum GPA of 3.5. Additional exam requirements/recommendations for international students: Required—TOEFL (minimum score 550 paper-based). *Application deadline:* For fall admission, 7/15 for domestic students, 5/1 priority date for international students; for spring admission, 11/15 for domestic students, 9/1 priority date for international students. Applications are processed on a rolling basis. Application fee: $50 ($100 for international students). Electronic applications accepted. *Expenses:* Tuition, state resident: full-time $12,418; part-time $690 per semester hour. Tuition, nonresident: full-time $24,150; part-time $1342 per semester hour. Tuition and fees vary according to course load. *Financial support:* In 2016–17, 738 students received support, including 37 fellowships (averaging $3,024 per year), 338 research assistantships with partial tuition reimbursements available (averaging $23,853 per year), 225 teaching assistantships with partial tuition reimbursements available (averaging $17,266 per year); career-related internships or fieldwork, Federal Work-Study, institutionally sponsored loans, scholarships/grants, and unspecified assistantships also available. Support available to part-time students. Financial award application deadline: 4/30; financial award applicants required to submit FAFSA. *Faculty research:* Semiconducting materials, nano-fabrication and bio-nanotechnology, biomedical devices and organic electronics, signal processing and language technology, cloud computing and IT security. *Total annual research expenditures:* $33.8 million. *Unit head:* Dr. Mark W. Spong, Dean, 972-883-2974, Fax: 972-883-2813, E-mail: ecsdean@utdallas.edu. *Application contact:* Leiane Davis, Administrative Associate, 972-883-6851, Fax: 972-883-2813, E-mail: leiane.davis@utdallas.edu.
Website: http://ecs.utdallas.edu/

The University of Texas at El Paso, Graduate School, College of Engineering, El Paso, TX 79968-0001. Offers biomedical engineering (PhD); civil engineering (MEENE, MS, MSENE, PhD, Certificate), including civil engineering (MS), civil engineering (PhD), construction management (MS, Certificate), environmental engineering (MEENE, MSENE); computer science (MS, MSIT, PhD), including computer science (MS, PhD), information technology (MSIT); education engineering (M Eng); electrical and computer engineering (MS, PhD), including computer engineering (MS), electrical and computer engineering (PhD), electrical engineering (MS); industrial engineering (MS, Certificate), including industrial engineering (MS), manufacturing engineering (MS), systems engineering; mechanical engineering (MS, PhD), including environmental science and engineering (PhD), mechanical engineering (MS); metallurgical and materials engineering (MS, PhD), including materials science and engineering (PhD), metallurgical and materials engineering (MS); software engineering (M Eng). *Program availability:* Part-time, evening/weekend. *Degree requirements:* For master's, thesis optional; for doctorate, thesis/dissertation. *Entrance requirements:* For master's, GRE, minimum GPA of 3.0, letters of reference; for doctorate, GRE, statement of purpose, letters of reference. Additional exam requirements/recommendations for international students: Required—TOEFL; Recommended—IELTS. Electronic applications accepted. *Expenses:* Contact institution.

The University of Texas at San Antonio, College of Engineering, San Antonio, TX 78249-0617. Offers MCE, MS, MSCE, MSEE, PhD. *Program availability:* Part-time, evening/weekend. *Faculty:* 66 full-time (7 women), 8 part-time/adjunct (0 women). *Students:* 262 full-time (66 women), 228 part-time (54 women); includes 134 minority (15 Black or African American, non-Hispanic/Latino; 28 Asian, non-Hispanic/Latino; 81 Hispanic/Latino; 2 Native Hawaiian or other Pacific Islander, non-Hispanic/Latino; 8 Two or more races, non-Hispanic/Latino), 231 international. Average age 29. 510 applicants, 66% accepted, 115 enrolled. In 2016, 182 master's, 24 doctorates awarded. Terminal master's awarded for partial completion of doctoral program. *Degree requirements:* For master's, variable foreign language requirement, comprehensive exam, thesis optional, completion of all course work requirements within six-year time limit; no courses with grade of less than C; minimum GPA of 3.0; for doctorate, variable foreign language requirement, comprehensive exam, thesis/dissertation, continuous enrollment until time of graduation; all completed coursework included in the final program of study must have been taken within the preceding eight years to include successful completion and defense of the dissertation. *Entrance requirements:* For master's, GRE, baccalaureate degree in related field from regionally-accredited college or university in the U.S. or proof of equivalent training at foreign institution; minimum GPA of 3.0 in last 60 semester credit hours or foreign institution equivalent of coursework taken; for doctorate, GRE, baccalaureate degree or MS in related field from regionally-accredited college or university in the U.S. or proof of equivalent training at foreign institution; minimum GPA of 3.0, 3.3 in upper-division/graduate courses. Additional exam requirements/recommendations for international students: Required—TOEFL (minimum score 550 paper-based; 79 iBT), IELTS (minimum score 6.5). *Application deadline:* For fall admission, 7/1 for domestic students, 4/1 for international students; for spring

admission, 11/1 for domestic students, 9/1 for international students. Application fee: $45 ($80 for international students). *Expenses:* Contact institution. *Financial support:* In 2016–17, 120 students received support. Career-related internships or fieldwork, Federal Work-Study, institutionally sponsored loans, scholarships/grants, health care benefits, unspecified assistantships, and Valero Research Scholar awards available. Financial award application deadline: 9/15. *Faculty research:* Biomedical engineering, civil and environmental science engineering, electrical and computer engineering, advanced materials engineering, mechanical engineering. *Total annual research expenditures:* $10.3 million. *Unit head:* Dr. JoAnn Browning, Dean of Engineering, 210-458-5526, Fax: 210-458-5515, E-mail: joann.browning@utsa.edu. *Application contact:* Monica Rodriguez, Director of Graduate Admissions, 210-458-4331, Fax: 210-458-4332, E-mail: graduateadmissions@utsa.edu.
Website: http://engineering2.utsa.edu/

University of the District of Columbia, School of Engineering and Applied Sciences, Washington, DC 20008-1175. Offers MSCS, MSEE.

University of the Pacific, School of Engineering and Computer Science, Stockton, CA 95211-0197. Offers engineering science (MS). *Students:* 23 full-time (7 women), 40 part-time (14 women); includes 32 minority (4 Black or African American, non-Hispanic/Latino; 16 Asian, non-Hispanic/Latino; 11 Hispanic/Latino; 1 Two or more races, non-Hispanic/Latino), 7 international. Average age 29. 83 applicants, 55% accepted, 31 enrolled. In 2016, 56 master's awarded. *Entrance requirements:* For master's, GRE, three references; official transcripts; personal statement; bachelor's degree in engineering, computer science, or a closely related discipline. Additional exam requirements/recommendations for international students: Required—TOEFL. *Application deadline:* For fall admission, 3/1 for domestic students; for spring admission, 10/1 for domestic students. Electronic applications accepted. *Financial support:* Teaching assistantships available. *Unit head:* Dr. Steve Howell, Dean, 209-946-3068, E-mail: showell@pacific.edu. *Application contact:* Office of Graduate Admissions, 209-946-2011.

The University of Toledo, College of Graduate Studies, College of Engineering, Program in Engineering, Toledo, OH 43606-3390. Offers general engineering (MS). *Entrance requirements:* For master's, GRE General Test, minimum GPA of 2.7, industrial experience.

University of Toronto, School of Graduate Studies, Faculty of Applied Science and Engineering, Toronto, ON M5S 1A1, Canada. Offers M Eng, MA Sc, MH Sc, PhD. *Program availability:* Part-time. *Degree requirements:* For doctorate, thesis/dissertation. *Expenses:* Contact institution.

The University of Tulsa, Graduate School, College of Engineering and Natural Sciences, Tulsa, OK 74104-3189. Offers ME, MS, MSE, MTA, PhD, JD/MS, MBA/MS, MSF/MSAM. *Program availability:* Part-time. *Faculty:* 102 full-time (11 women), 2 part-time/adjunct (1 woman). *Students:* 244 full-time (56 women), 96 part-time (26 women); includes 26 minority (3 Black or African American, non-Hispanic/Latino; 8 American Indian or Alaska Native, non-Hispanic/Latino; 7 Asian, non-Hispanic/Latino; 5 Hispanic/Latino; 1 Native Hawaiian or other Pacific Islander, non-Hispanic/Latino; 2 Two or more races, non-Hispanic/Latino), 184 international. Average age 28. 810 applicants, 27% accepted, 83 enrolled. In 2016, 95 master's, 20 doctorates awarded. Terminal master's awarded for partial completion of doctoral program. *Degree requirements:* For master's, thesis (for some programs); for doctorate, comprehensive exam, thesis/dissertation. *Entrance requirements:* For master's and doctorate, GRE General Test. Additional exam requirements/recommendations for international students: Required—TOEFL (minimum score 550 paper-based), IELTS (minimum score 6). *Application deadline:* Applications are processed on a rolling basis. Application fee: $55. Electronic applications accepted. *Expenses: Tuition:* Full-time $22,230; part-time $1235 per credit hour. *Required fees:* $990 per semester. Tuition and fees vary according to course load. *Financial support:* In 2016–17, 210 students received support, including 80 fellowships with full tuition reimbursements available (averaging $3,515 per year), 168 research assistantships with full tuition reimbursements available (averaging $11,945 per year), 95 teaching assistantships with full tuition reimbursements available (averaging $12,531 per year); career-related internships or fieldwork, Federal Work-Study, scholarships/grants, health care benefits, tuition waivers (full and partial), and unspecified assistantships also available. Support available to part-time students. Financial award application deadline: 2/1; financial award applicants required to submit FAFSA. *Total annual research expenditures:* $17.4 million. *Unit head:* Dr. James Sorem, Dean, 918-631-2288, E-mail: james-sorem@utulsa.edu. *Application contact:* Graduate School, 918-631-2336, Fax: 918-631-2156, E-mail: grad@utulsa.edu.
Website: http://engineering.utulsa.edu/

University of Utah, Graduate School, College of Engineering, Salt Lake City, UT 84112. Offers ME, MEAE, MS, PhD, MS/MBA. *Accreditation:* ABET. *Program availability:* Part-time, evening/weekend. *Faculty:* 146 full-time (22 women), 73 part-time/adjunct (10 women). *Students:* 948 full-time (219 women), 282 part-time (42 women); includes 111 minority (6 Black or African American, non-Hispanic/Latino; 55 Asian, non-Hispanic/Latino; 23 Hispanic/Latino; 1 Native Hawaiian or other Pacific Islander, non-Hispanic/Latino; 26 Two or more races, non-Hispanic/Latino), 560 international. Average age 28. 2,280 applicants, 42% accepted, 418 enrolled. In 2016, 288 master's, 80 doctorates awarded. *Degree requirements:* For master's, comprehensive exam (for some programs), thesis (for some programs); for doctorate, comprehensive exam (for some programs), thesis/dissertation (for some programs). *Entrance requirements:* For master's and doctorate, GRE, minimum GPA of 3.0. Additional exam requirements/recommendations for international students: Required—TOEFL (minimum score 550 paper-based; 80 iBT), IELTS (minimum score 6.5). Application fee: $55 ($65 for international students). Electronic applications accepted. *Expenses:* Contact institution. *Financial support:* Fellowships with full tuition reimbursements, research assistantships with tuition reimbursements, teaching assistantships with tuition reimbursements, career-related internships or fieldwork, Federal Work-Study, institutionally sponsored loans, scholarships/grants, traineeships, health care benefits, tuition waivers (full and partial), and unspecified assistantships available. Support available to part-time students. Financial award applicants required to submit FAFSA. *Faculty research:* Biomaterials, wastewater treatment, computer-aided graphics design, semiconductors, polymers. *Total annual research expenditures:* $40.9 million. *Unit head:* Dr. Richard B. Brown, Dean, 801-585-7498, E-mail: brown@utah.edu. *Application contact:* Megan Shannahan, Direct Admission and Graduate Coordinator, 801-581-8954, Fax: 801-581-8692, E-mail: megan.shannahan@utah.edu.
Website: http://www.coe.utah.edu/

University of Vermont, Graduate College, College of Engineering and Mathematics, Burlington, VT 05405. Offers MS, MST, PhD. *Program availability:* Part-time. *Degree requirements:* For doctorate, thesis/dissertation. *Entrance requirements:* Additional exam requirements/recommendations for international students: Required—TOEFL (minimum score 550 paper-based; 80 iBT). Electronic applications accepted. *Expenses:* Tuition, state resident: full-time $5814. Tuition, nonresident: full-time $14,670.

University of Victoria, Faculty of Graduate Studies, Faculty of Engineering, Victoria, BC V8W 2Y2, Canada. Offers M Eng, M Sc, MA Sc, PhD.

University of Virginia, School of Engineering and Applied Science, Charlottesville, VA 22903. Offers MCS, ME, MEP, MMSE, MS, PhD, ME/MBA. *Program availability:* Part-time, online learning. *Faculty:* 162 full-time (26 women), 4 part-time/adjunct (1 woman). *Students:* 694 full-time (195 women), 49 part-time (13 women); includes 82 minority (8 Black or African American, non-Hispanic/Latino; 46 Asian, non-Hispanic/Latino; 19 Hispanic/Latino; 9 Two or more races, non-Hispanic/Latino), 410 international. Average age 29. 1,816 applicants, 29% accepted, 239 enrolled. In 2016, 136 master's, 57 doctorates awarded. Terminal master's awarded for partial completion of doctoral program. *Degree requirements:* For doctorate, comprehensive exam, thesis/dissertation. *Entrance requirements:* For master's, GRE General Test, 3 letters of recommendation; for doctorate, GRE General Test, 3 letters of recommendation, essay. Additional exam requirements/recommendations for international students: Required—TOEFL (minimum score 600 paper-based; 90 iBT), IELTS (minimum score 7). *Application deadline:* For fall admission, 8/1 for domestic students, 4/1 for international students; for winter admission, 12/1 for domestic students, 8/1 for international students; for spring admission, 5/1 for domestic students, 1/1 for international students. Applications are processed on a rolling basis. Electronic applications accepted. *Expenses:* $15,678 tuition, $2,654 fees in-state; $25,578 tuition, $3,336 fees out-of-state. *Financial support:* Fellowships with full tuition reimbursements, research assistantships with full tuition reimbursements, teaching assistantships with full tuition reimbursements, and career-related internships or fieldwork available. Financial award application deadline: 1/15; financial award applicants required to submit FAFSA. *Unit head:* Craig H. Benson, Dean, 434-924-3593, Fax: 434-924-3555, E-mail: engrdean@virginia.edu. *Application contact:* Pamela M. Norris, Associate Dean for Research and Graduate Programs, 434-243-7683, Fax: 434-982-3044, E-mail: pamela@virginia.edu.
Website: http://www.seas.virginia.edu/

University of Washington, Graduate School, College of Engineering, Seattle, WA 98195-2180. Offers MAB, MAE, MISE, MS, MSAA, MSCE, MSE, MSME, PhD, Certificate. *Program availability:* Part-time, online learning. *Faculty:* 258 full-time (59 women). *Students:* 1,581 full-time (481 women), 834 part-time (218 women); includes 510 minority (26 Black or African American, non-Hispanic/Latino; 1 American Indian or Alaska Native, non-Hispanic/Latino; 303 Asian, non-Hispanic/Latino; 114 Hispanic/Latino; 4 Native Hawaiian or other Pacific Islander, non-Hispanic/Latino; 62 Two or more races, non-Hispanic/Latino), 837 international. 7,119 applicants, 27% accepted, 850 enrolled. In 2016, 562 master's, 131 doctorates awarded. Terminal master's awarded for partial completion of doctoral program. *Degree requirements:* For master's, comprehensive exam (for some programs), thesis (for some programs); for doctorate, comprehensive exam, thesis/dissertation. *Entrance requirements:* Additional exam requirements/recommendations for international students: Required—TOEFL; Recommended—IELTS. *Application deadline:* For fall admission, 12/1 for domestic and international students. Application fee: $85. Electronic applications accepted. *Expenses:* Contact institution. *Financial support:* In 2016–17, 1,065 students received support, including 145 fellowships with full tuition reimbursements available, 660 research assistantships with full tuition reimbursements available, 259 teaching assistantships with full tuition reimbursements available; career-related internships or fieldwork, Federal Work-Study, institutionally sponsored loans, scholarships/grants, traineeships, health care benefits, tuition waivers (full), unspecified assistantships, and stipend supplements also available. Financial award application deadline: 2/28; financial award applicants required to submit FAFSA. *Total annual research expenditures:* $151.2 million. *Unit head:* Dr. Michael B. Bragg, Dean of Engineering, 206-543-0340, Fax: 206-685-0666, E-mail: mbragg@uw.edu. *Application contact:* Scott Winter, Director, Academic Affairs, 206-685-4074, Fax: 206-685-0666, E-mail: swinter@uw.edu.
Website: http://www.engr.washington.edu/

University of Waterloo, Graduate Studies, Faculty of Engineering, Waterloo, ON N2L 3G1, Canada. Offers M Arch, M Eng, MA Sc, MBET, MMS, PhD. *Program availability:* Part-time, evening/weekend, online learning. *Degree requirements:* For master's, research paper or thesis; for doctorate, comprehensive exam, thesis/dissertation. *Entrance requirements:* For master's, honors degree; for doctorate, master's degree, minimum A- average. Additional exam requirements/recommendations for international students: Required—TOEFL, IELTS, PTE. Electronic applications accepted.

The University of Western Ontario, Faculty of Graduate Studies, Physical Sciences Division, Faculty of Engineering, London, ON N6A 5B8, Canada. Offers chemical and biochemical engineering (ME Sc, PhD); civil and environmental engineering (M Eng, ME Sc, PhD); electrical and computer engineering (M Eng, ME Sc, PhD); mechanical and materials engineering (M Eng, ME Sc, PhD). *Program availability:* Part-time. Terminal master's awarded for partial completion of doctoral program. *Degree requirements:* For master's, thesis; for doctorate, thesis/dissertation. *Entrance requirements:* For master's, minimum B average; for doctorate, minimum B+ average. *Faculty research:* Wind, geotechnical, chemical reactor engineering, applied electrostatics, biochemical engineering.

University of Windsor, Faculty of Graduate Studies, Faculty of Engineering, Windsor, ON N9B 3P4, Canada. Offers M Eng, MA Sc, PhD. *Program availability:* Part-time. *Degree requirements:* For doctorate, comprehensive exam, thesis/dissertation. *Entrance requirements:* For master's, minimum B average; for doctorate, master's degree. Additional exam requirements/recommendations for international students: Required—TOEFL. Electronic applications accepted.

University of Wisconsin–Madison, Graduate School, College of Engineering, Madison, WI 53706. Offers MS, PhD. *Program availability:* Part-time, blended/hybrid learning. *Faculty:* 212 full-time (41 women). *Students:* 1,460 full-time (322 women), 361 part-time (83 women); includes 175 minority (22 Black or African American, non-Hispanic/Latino; 3 American Indian or Alaska Native, non-Hispanic/Latino; 62 Asian, non-Hispanic/Latino; 67 Hispanic/Latino; 2 Native Hawaiian or other Pacific Islander, non-Hispanic/Latino; 19 Two or more races, non-Hispanic/Latino), 913 international. Average age 27. 5,562 applicants, 20% accepted, 390 enrolled. In 2016, 473 master's, 169 doctorates awarded. Terminal master's awarded for partial completion of doctoral program. *Degree requirements:* For master's, thesis (for some programs); for doctorate, thesis/dissertation. *Entrance requirements:* For master's and doctorate, GRE. Additional exam requirements/recommendations for international students: Required—TOEFL (minimum score 580 paper-based; 92 iBT), IELTS (minimum score 7). *Application deadline:* Applications are processed on a rolling basis. Application fee: $75 ($81 for international students). Electronic applications accepted. *Expenses:* $13,157 per year in-state tuition and fees; $26,484 per year out-of-state tuition and fees. *Financial support:* In 2016–17, 1,215 students received support, including 68 fellowships with full tuition reimbursements available, 818 research assistantships with full tuition reimbursements available, 282 teaching assistantships with full tuition reimbursements available; career-related internships or fieldwork, Federal Work-Study, institutionally sponsored loans, scholarships/grants, health care benefits, and unspecified assistantships also available. Support available to part-time students. Financial award application deadline: 12/1; financial award applicants required to submit FAFSA. *Total annual research expenditures:* $141.9 million. *Unit head:* Dr. Ian M. Robertson, Dean, 608-262-3482, Fax: 608-262-6400, E-mail: engr-dean_engr@wisc.edu. *Application contact:* Information Contact, 608-262-2433, Fax: 608-265-9505, E-mail: gradadmiss@grad.wisc.edu.
Website: http://www.engr.wisc.edu/

University of Wisconsin–Milwaukee, Graduate School, College of Engineering and Applied Science, Milwaukee, WI 53201. Offers MS, PhD. *Program availability:* Part-time. *Students:* 240 full-time (72 women), 189 part-time (43 women); includes 37 minority (5 Black or African American, non-Hispanic/Latino; 22 Asian, non-Hispanic/Latino; 3 Hispanic/Latino; 7 Two or more races, non-Hispanic/Latino), 285 international. Average age 30. 529 applicants, 54% accepted, 119 enrolled. In 2016, 97 master's, 30 doctorates awarded. *Degree requirements:* For master's, comprehensive exam (for some programs), thesis or alternative; for doctorate, thesis/dissertation, internship. *Entrance requirements:* For master's, GRE, minimum GPA of 2.75; for doctorate, GRE, minimum GPA of 3.5. Additional exam requirements/recommendations for international students: Required—TOEFL (minimum score 550 paper-based; 79 iBT), IELTS (minimum score 6.5). *Application deadline:* For fall admission, 1/1 for domestic students; for spring admission, 9/1 for domestic students. Applications are processed on a rolling basis. Application fee: $56 ($96 for international students). Electronic applications accepted. *Financial support:* Fellowships, research assistantships, teaching assistantships, career-related internships or fieldwork, Federal Work-Study, and unspecified assistantships available. Support available to part-time students. Financial award application deadline: 4/15. *Unit head:* Dr. Brett Peters, Dean, 414-229-4126, E-mail: ceas-deans-office@uwm.edu. *Application contact:* Betty Warras, General Information Contact, 414-229-6169, Fax: 414-229-6958, E-mail: ceas-graduate@uwm.edu.
Website: http://uwm.edu/engineering/

University of Wisconsin–Platteville, School of Graduate Studies, Distance Learning Center, Online Master of Science in Engineering Program, Platteville, WI 53818-3099. Offers MS. *Program availability:* Part-time. *Students:* 8 full-time (1 woman), 139 part-time (19 women); includes 26 minority (11 Black or African American, non-Hispanic/Latino; 2 American Indian or Alaska Native, non-Hispanic/Latino; 3 Asian, non-Hispanic/Latino; 10 Hispanic/Latino). 40 applicants, 78% accepted, 26 enrolled. In 2016, 37 master's awarded. *Degree requirements:* For master's, thesis or alternative. *Entrance requirements:* Additional exam requirements/recommendations for international students: Required—TOEFL (minimum score 550 paper-based; 79 iBT), IELTS (minimum score 6.5). *Application deadline:* For fall admission, 7/1 priority date for domestic students; for spring admission, 11/1 priority date for domestic students. Applications are processed on a rolling basis. Application fee: $56. Electronic applications accepted. *Expenses:* Contact institution. *Financial support:* Scholarships/grants available. Support available to part-time students. *Unit head:* Philip Parker, Coordinator, 608-342-1235, Fax: 608-342-1071, E-mail: disted@uwplatt.edu. *Application contact:* 800-362-5460, Fax: 608-342-1071, E-mail: disted@uwplatt.edu.
Website: http://www.uwplatt.edu/disted/engineering.html

University of Wyoming, College of Engineering and Applied Sciences, Laramie, WY 82071. Offers MS, PhD. *Program availability:* Part-time. *Entrance requirements:* For master's and doctorate, GRE General Test, minimum GPA of 3.0. Additional exam requirements/recommendations for international students: Required—TOEFL. Electronic applications accepted.

Utah State University, School of Graduate Studies, College of Engineering, Logan, UT 84322. Offers ME, MS, PhD, CE. *Program availability:* Part-time, evening/weekend. Terminal master's awarded for partial completion of doctoral program. *Degree requirements:* For master's, thesis (for some programs); for doctorate, thesis/dissertation. *Entrance requirements:* For master's and doctorate, GRE General Test, minimum GPA of 3.0. Additional exam requirements/recommendations for international students: Required—TOEFL. Electronic applications accepted. *Faculty research:* Crop-yield modeling, earthquake engineering, digital signal processing, technology and the public school, cryogenic cooling.

Vanderbilt University, School of Engineering, Nashville, TN 37235. Offers M Eng, MS, PhD, MD/PhD. MS and PhD offered through the Graduate School. *Program availability:* Part-time. Terminal master's awarded for partial completion of doctoral program. *Degree requirements:* For master's, comprehensive exam (for some programs), thesis (for some programs); for doctorate, comprehensive exam (for some programs), thesis/dissertation. *Entrance requirements:* For master's and doctorate, GRE General Test. Additional exam requirements/recommendations for international students: Required—TOEFL. Electronic applications accepted. Application fee is waived when completed online. *Expenses: Tuition:* Part-time $1854 per credit hour. *Faculty research:* Robotics, microelectronics, reliability in design, software engineering, medical imaging.

Villanova University, College of Engineering, Villanova, PA 19085-1699. Offers MSCPE, MSChE, MSEE, MSME, MSWREE, PhD, Certificate. *Program availability:* Part-time, evening/weekend, online learning. Terminal master's awarded for partial completion of doctoral program. *Degree requirements:* For master's, thesis optional; for doctorate, thesis/dissertation. *Entrance requirements:* For master's, GRE General Test (for applicants with degrees from foreign universities), minimum GPA of 3.0; for doctorate, GRE General Test. Additional exam requirements/recommendations for international students: Required—TOEFL (minimum score 600 paper-based; 100 iBT). Electronic applications accepted. *Expenses:* Contact institution. *Faculty research:* Composite materials, economy and risk, heat transfer, signal detection.

Virginia Commonwealth University, Graduate School, School of Engineering, Richmond, VA 23284-9005. Offers MS, PhD. *Degree requirements:* For doctorate, thesis/dissertation, comprehensive oral and written exams. *Entrance requirements:* For master's and doctorate, GRE General Test. Additional exam requirements/recommendations for international students: Required—TOEFL (minimum score 600 paper-based; 100 iBT). *Application deadline:* For fall admission, 2/1 priority date for domestic students; for spring admission, 11/15 for domestic students. Application fee: $50. Electronic applications accepted. *Financial support:* Applicants required to submit FAFSA. *Faculty research:* Artificial hearts, orthopedic implants, medical imaging, medical instrumentation and sensors, cardiac monitoring. *Unit head:* Dr. Rosalyn S. Hobson, Associate Dean for Graduate Affairs, 804-828-3925, E-mail: rhobson@vcu.edu. *Application contact:* Mark D. Meadows, Director of Student Recruitment, 804-827-4005, E-mail: mdmeadows@vcu.edu.
Website: http://www.egr.vcu.edu/

Virginia Polytechnic Institute and State University, Graduate School, College of Engineering, Blacksburg, VA 24061. Offers aerospace engineering (ME, MS, PhD); biological systems engineering (ME, MS, PhD); biomedical engineering (MS, PhD); chemical engineering (ME, MS, PhD); civil engineering (ME, MS, PhD); computer engineering (ME, MS, PhD); computer science (MS, PhD); electrical engineering (ME, PhD); engineering education (PhD); engineering mechanics (ME, MS, PhD); environmental engineering (MS); environmental science and engineering (MS); industrial and systems engineering (ME, MS, PhD); materials science and engineering (ME, MS, PhD); mechanical engineering (ME, MS, PhD); mining and minerals engineering (PhD); mining engineering (ME, MS); nuclear engineering (MS, PhD); ocean engineering (MS); systems engineering (ME, MS). *Faculty:* 400 full-time (73 women), 3 part-time/adjunct (2 women). *Students:* 1,949 full-time (487 women), 393 part-time (69 women); includes 251 minority (56 Black or African American, non-Hispanic/Latino; 3 American Indian or Alaska Native, non-Hispanic/Latino; 87 Asian, non-Hispanic/Latino; 70 Hispanic/Latino; 35 Two or more races, non-Hispanic/Latino), 1,354 international. Average age 27. 4,903 applicants, 19% accepted, 569 enrolled. In

2016, 364 master's, 200 doctorates awarded. *Degree requirements:* For master's, comprehensive exam (for some programs), thesis (for some programs); for doctorate, comprehensive exam (for some programs), thesis/dissertation (for some programs). *Entrance requirements:* For master's and doctorate, GRE/GMAT. Additional exam requirements/recommendations for international students: Required—TOEFL (minimum score 80 iBT). *Application deadline:* For fall admission, 8/1 for domestic students, 4/1 for international students; for spring admission, 1/1 for domestic students, 9/1 for international students. Applications are processed on a rolling basis. Application fee: $75. Electronic applications accepted. *Expenses:* Tuition, state resident: full-time $12,467; part-time $692.50 per credit hour. Tuition, nonresident: full-time $25,095; part-time $1394.25 per credit hour. *Required fees:* $2669; $491.50 per semester. Tuition and fees vary according to course load, campus/location and program. *Financial support:* In 2016–17, 160 fellowships with full tuition reimbursements (averaging $7,387 per year), 872 research assistantships with full tuition reimbursements (averaging $22,329 per year), 313 teaching assistantships with full tuition reimbursements (averaging $18,714 per year) were awarded. Financial award application deadline: 3/1; financial award applicants required to submit FAFSA. *Total annual research expenditures:* $91.8 million. *Unit head:* Dr. Julia Ross, Dean, 540-231-9752, Fax: 540-231-3031, E-mail: deaneng@vt.edu. *Application contact:* Linda Perkins, Executive Assistant, 540-231-9752, Fax: 540-231-3031, E-mail: lperkins@vt.edu.
Website: http://www.eng.vt.edu/

Washington State University, Voiland College of Engineering and Architecture, Pullman, WA 99164-2714. Offers M Arch, METM, MS, PhD, Certificate. Terminal master's awarded for partial completion of doctoral program. *Degree requirements:* For master's, comprehensive exam (for some programs), thesis (for some programs), oral exam; for doctorate, comprehensive exam, thesis/dissertation, oral exam. *Entrance requirements:* For master's, GRE, minimum GPA of 3.0, 3 letters of recommendation; for doctorate, GRE, minimum GPA of 3.4, 3 letters of recommendation. Additional exam requirements/recommendations for international students: Required—TOEFL (minimum score 520 paper-based).

Washington University in St. Louis, School of Engineering and Applied Science, Saint Louis, MO 63130-4899. Offers M Eng, MCE, MCM, MEM, MIM, MPM, MS, MSEE, MSEE, MSI, D Sc, PhD. *Program availability:* Part-time, evening/weekend. Terminal master's awarded for partial completion of doctoral program. *Degree requirements:* For master's, comprehensive exam (for some programs), thesis (for some programs); for doctorate, comprehensive exam, thesis/dissertation. *Entrance requirements:* For master's and doctorate, GRE. Additional exam requirements/recommendations for international students: Required—TOEFL (minimum score 550 paper-based; 90 iBT), IELTS (minimum score 6.5) or TWE. Electronic applications accepted.

Wayne State University, College of Engineering, Detroit, MI 48202. Offers MS, MSET, PhD, Certificate, Graduate Certificate, Postbaccalaureate Certificate. *Program availability:* Part-time, evening/weekend. *Faculty:* 105. *Students:* 1,204 full-time (222 women), 382 part-time (78 women); includes 113 minority (35 Black or African American, non-Hispanic/Latino; 58 Asian, non-Hispanic/Latino; 9 Hispanic/Latino; 1 Native Hawaiian or other Pacific Islander, non-Hispanic/Latino; 10 Two or more races, non-Hispanic/Latino), 1,179 international. Average age 27. 4,150 applicants, 44% accepted, 466 enrolled. In 2016, 448 master's, 42 doctorates, 1 other advanced degree awarded. Terminal master's awarded for partial completion of doctoral program. *Degree requirements:* For master's, thesis (for some programs), project; for doctorate, thesis/dissertation. *Entrance requirements:* For master's and other advanced degree, minimum GPA of 3.0 from ABET-accredited institution and in all upper-division courses; for doctorate, minimum overall GPA of 3.2, 3.5 in last two years as undergraduate student if being admitted directly from a bachelor's program. Additional exam requirements/recommendations for international students: Required—TOEFL (minimum score 550 paper-based; 79 iBT), TWE (minimum score 5.5), Michigan English Language Assessment Battery (minimum score 85); Recommended—IELTS (minimum score 6.5). *Application deadline:* For fall admission, 6/1 priority date for domestic students, 5/1 priority date for international students; for winter admission, 10/1 priority date for domestic students, 9/1 priority date for international students; for spring admission, 2/1 priority date for domestic students, 1/1 priority date for international students. Applications are processed on a rolling basis. Application fee: $50. Electronic applications accepted. *Expenses:* $18,871 per year resident tuition and fees, $36,065 per year non-resident tuition and fees. *Financial support:* In 2016–17, 381 students received support, including 23 fellowships with tuition reimbursements available (averaging $15,878 per year), 69 research assistantships with tuition reimbursements available (averaging $19,550 per year), 114 teaching assistantships with tuition reimbursements available (averaging $19,176 per year); Federal Work-Study, scholarships/grants, tuition waivers (full and partial), and unspecified assistantships also available. Support available to part-time students. Financial award applicants required to submit FAFSA. *Faculty research:* Biomedical research, integrated automotive safety, energy solutions, advanced manufacturing and materials, big data and business analytics. *Total annual research expenditures:* $13.6 million. *Unit head:* Dr. Farshad Fotouhi, Dean, 313-577-3776, E-mail: fotouhi@wayne.edu. *Application contact:* Graduate Program Coordinator, E-mail: engineeringgradadmissions@eng.wayne.edu.
Website: http://engineering.wayne.edu/

Western Michigan University, Graduate College, College of Engineering and Applied Sciences, Kalamazoo, MI 49008. Offers MS, MSE, PhD. *Program availability:* Part-time. *Degree requirements:* For doctorate, thesis/dissertation.

Western New England University, College of Engineering, Springfield, MA 01119. Offers MS, MSEE, MSEM, MSME, PhD, MSEM/MBA. *Program availability:* Part-time, evening/weekend, online learning. *Faculty:* 35 full-time (4 women). *Students:* 123 part-time (17 women); includes 10 minority (1 Black or African American, non-Hispanic/Latino; 2 Asian, non-Hispanic/Latino; 6 Hispanic/Latino; 1 Two or more races, non-Hispanic/Latino), 55 international. Average age 30. 476 applicants, 28% accepted, 33 enrolled. In 2016, 48 master's, 2 doctorates awarded. *Degree requirements:* For master's, comprehensive exam (for some programs), thesis optional; for doctorate, comprehensive exam, thesis/dissertation. *Entrance requirements:* For master's, bachelor's degree in engineering or related field, official transcript, two letters of recommendation, resume; for doctorate, GRE, official transcript, master's or bachelor's degree in engineering or closely-related discipline, two letters of recommendation. Additional exam requirements/recommendations for international students: Required—TOEFL (minimum score 79 iBT). *Application deadline:* For fall admission, 1/15 priority date for domestic students. Applications are processed on a rolling basis. Application fee: $30. Electronic applications accepted. *Expenses:* $32,220 (for master's programs); $1,280 per credit (for PhD). *Financial support:* In 2016–17, 6 fellowships with tuition reimbursements were awarded. Financial award application deadline: 4/15; financial award applicants required to submit FAFSA. *Faculty research:* Fluid mechanics, control systems. *Unit head:* Dr. S. Hossein Cheraghi, Dean, 413-782-1285, E-mail: cheraghi@wne.edu. *Application contact:* Matthew Fox, Director of Admissions for Graduate Students and Adult Learners, 413-782-1410, Fax: 413-782-1777, E-mail: study@wne.edu. Website: http://www1.wne.edu/admissions/graduate/index.cfm

West Texas A&M University, School of Engineering, Computer Science and Mathematics, Program in Engineering Technology, Canyon, TX 79016-0001. Offers MS.

Engineering and Applied Sciences—General

Program availability: Part-time, evening/weekend. *Degree requirements:* For master's, comprehensive exam, thesis optional. *Entrance requirements:* For master's, GRE General Test. Additional exam requirements/recommendations for international students: Required—TOEFL (minimum score 550 paper-based). *Application deadline:* For fall admission, 5/1 for international students; for spring admission, 10/30 for international students. Applications are processed on a rolling basis. Application fee: $40 ($75 for international students). Electronic applications accepted. *Financial support:* Research assistantships, teaching assistantships, career-related internships or fieldwork, Federal Work-Study, institutionally sponsored loans, scholarships/grants, and tuition waivers (partial) available. Support available to part-time students. Financial award applicants required to submit FAFSA. *Faculty research:* Stochastic temporal series, fuzzy network, computer-assisted/introductory physics classes, development of photorefractive polymers, central nervous system. *Application contact:* Dr. Gerald Chen, Graduate Adviser, 806-651-2449, Fax: 806-651-2544, E-mail: gchen@wtamu.edu.
Website: http://www.wtamu.edu/academics/engineering-technology-graduate-program.aspx

West Virginia University, Statler College of Engineering and Mineral Resources, Morgantown, WV 26506-6070. Offers material science and engineering (MSMSE). *Accreditation:* ABET (one or more programs are accredited). *Program availability:* Part-time. Terminal master's awarded for partial completion of doctoral program. *Degree requirements:* For master's, thesis optional; for doctorate, comprehensive exam, thesis/dissertation. *Entrance requirements:* Additional exam requirements/recommendations for international students: Required—TOEFL (minimum score 550 paper-based). Electronic applications accepted. *Expenses:* Contact institution. *Faculty research:* Composite materials, software engineering, information systems, aerodynamics, vehicle propulsion and emission.

Wichita State University, Graduate School, College of Engineering, Wichita, KS 67260. Offers MEM, MS, PhD. *Program availability:* Part-time, evening/weekend. *Unit head:* Dr. Royce O. Bowden, Dean, 316-978-3400, Fax: 316-978-3853, E-mail: royce.bowden@wichita.edu. *Application contact:* Jordan Oleson, Admissions Coordinator, 316-978-3095, Fax: 316-978-3253, E-mail: jordan.oleson@wichita.edu. Website: http://www.wichita.edu/engineering

Widener University, Graduate Programs in Engineering, Chester, PA 19013. Offers M Eng, ME/MBA. *Program availability:* Part-time, evening/weekend. *Faculty:* 18 full-time (2 women), 7 part-time/adjunct (0 women). *Students:* 9 full-time (3 women), 16 part-time (2 women); includes 2 minority (1 Asian, non-Hispanic/Latino; 1 Hispanic/Latino), 8 international. Average age 29. 75 applicants, 19% accepted, 8 enrolled. In 2016, 12 master's awarded. *Degree requirements:* For master's, thesis optional. *Entrance requirements:* Additional exam requirements/recommendations for international students: Required—TOEFL (minimum score 550 paper-based). *Application deadline:* For fall admission, 8/1 priority date for domestic students, 4/1 priority date for international students; for winter admission, 2/1 priority date for international students; for spring admission, 12/1 priority date for domestic students, 9/1 priority date for international students. Applications are processed on a rolling basis. Application fee: $0. Electronic applications accepted. *Expenses:* Contact institution. *Financial support:* In 2016–17, 5 teaching assistantships with partial tuition reimbursements (averaging $8,000 per year) were awarded; research assistantships and unspecified assistantships also available. Financial award application deadline: 3/15. *Faculty research:* Image and signal processing, drug delivery, therapeutics, nanotechnology, brain computer interface, cancer and Alzheimer's research, biomechanics, numerical computation, geotechnics, solid waste disposal, hemodialysis. *Total annual research expenditures:* $490,773. *Unit head:* Rudolph Treichel, Assistant Dean/Director of Graduate Programs, 610-499-1294, Fax: 610-499-4059, E-mail: rjtreichel@widener.edu.
Website: http://www.widener.edu/soe/

Wilkes University, College of Graduate and Professional Studies, College of Science and Engineering, Wilkes-Barre, PA 18766-0002. Offers MS, MSEE. *Program availability:* Part-time. *Students:* 31 full-time (7 women), 27 part-time (5 women); includes 6 minority (1 Black or African American, non-Hispanic/Latino; 1 Asian, non-Hispanic/Latino; 2 Hispanic/Latino; 2 Two or more races, non-Hispanic/Latino), 24 international. Average age 27. In 2016, 23 master's awarded. *Entrance requirements:* Additional exam requirements/recommendations for international students: Required—TOEFL (minimum score 550 paper-based; 79 iBT). *Application deadline:* Applications are processed on a rolling basis. Application fee: $45 ($65 for international students). Electronic applications accepted. Tuition and fees vary according to degree level and program. *Financial support:* Unspecified assistantships available. Financial award application deadline: 3/1; financial award applicants required to submit FAFSA. *Unit head:* Dr. William Hudson, Dean, 570-408-4600, Fax: 570-408-7860, E-mail: william.hudson@wilkes.edu. *Application contact:* Director of Graduate Enrollment, 570-408-4234, Fax: 570-408-7846.Website: http://www.wilkes.edu/academics/colleges/science-and-engineering/index.aspx

Worcester Polytechnic Institute, Graduate Studies and Research, Worcester, MA 01609-2280. Offers M Eng, MBA, ME, MME, MS, PhD, Advanced Certificate, Graduate Certificate. *Program availability:* Part-time, evening/weekend, 100% online, blended/hybrid learning. *Faculty:* 171 full-time (37 women), 92 part-time/adjunct (16 women). *Students:* 1,231 full-time (437 women), 832 part-time (195 women); includes 245 minority (44 Black or African American, non-Hispanic/Latino; 3 American Indian or Alaska Native, non-Hispanic/Latino; 100 Asian, non-Hispanic/Latino; 74 Hispanic/Latino; 1 Native Hawaiian or other Pacific Islander, non-Hispanic/Latino; 23 Two or more races, non-Hispanic/Latino), 900 international. Average age 28. 3,704 applicants, 56% accepted, 772 enrolled. In 2016, 681 master's, 42 doctorates awarded. Terminal master's awarded for partial completion of doctoral program. *Degree requirements:* For master's, thesis (for some programs); for doctorate, thesis/dissertation. *Entrance requirements:* For master's and doctorate, 3 letters of recommendation. Additional exam requirements/recommendations for international students: Required—TOEFL (minimum score 563 paper-based; 84 iBT), IELTS (minimum score 7). *Application deadline:* For fall admission, 1/1 priority date for domestic and international students; for spring admission, 10/1 priority date for domestic and international students. Applications are processed on a rolling basis. Application fee: $70. Electronic applications accepted. *Financial support:* Research assistantships, teaching assistantships, career-related internships or fieldwork, institutionally sponsored loans, scholarships/grants, health care benefits, tuition waivers, and unspecified assistantships available. Financial award application deadline: 1/1; financial award applicants required to submit FAFSA. *Unit head:* Dr. Terri Camesano, Dean, 508-831-5380, E-mail: grad@wpi.edu. *Application contact:* Lynne Dougherty, Administrative Assistant, 508-831-5301, Fax: 508-831-5717, E-mail: grad@wpi.edu. Website: http://grad.wpi.edu/

Yale University, Graduate School of Arts and Sciences, School of Engineering and Applied Science, New Haven, CT 06520. Offers MS, PhD. *Program availability:* Part-time. Terminal master's awarded for partial completion of doctoral program. *Degree requirements:* For doctorate, thesis/dissertation, exam. *Entrance requirements:* For master's and doctorate, GRE General Test. Additional exam requirements/recommendations for international students: Required—TOEFL.
See Display below and Close-Up on page 91.

Youngstown State University, Graduate School, College of Science, Technology, Engineering and Mathematics, Youngstown, OH 44555-0001. Offers MCIS, MSE. *Program availability:* Part-time, evening/weekend. *Degree requirements:* For master's, thesis optional. *Entrance requirements:* For master's, minimum GPA of 2.75 in field. Additional exam requirements/recommendations for international students: Required—TOEFL. *Faculty research:* Structural mechanics, water quality, wetlands engineering, control systems, power systems, heat transfer, kinematics and dynamics.

Applied Science and Technology

The College of William and Mary, Faculty of Arts and Sciences, Department of Applied Science, Williamsburg, VA 23185. Offers accelerator science (PhD); applied mathematics (PhD); applied mechanics (PhD); applied robotics (PhD); applied science (MS); atmospheric and environmental science (PhD); computational neuroscience (PhD); interface, thin film and surface science (PhD); lasers and optics (PhD); magnetic resonance (PhD); materials science and engineering (PhD); mathematical and computational biology (PhD); medical imaging (PhD); nanotechnology (PhD); neuroscience (PhD); non-destructive evaluation (PhD); polymer chemistry (PhD); remote sensing (PhD). *Program availability:* Part-time. *Faculty:* 8 full-time (2 women), 2 part-time/adjunct (0 women). *Students:* 30 full-time (11 women), 4 part-time (0 women); includes 16 minority (2 Black or African American, non-Hispanic/Latino; 12 Asian, non-Hispanic/Latino; 2 Hispanic/Latino), 12 international. Average age 28. 37 applicants, 27% accepted, 7 enrolled. In 2016, 6 doctorates awarded. Terminal master's awarded for partial completion of doctoral program. *Degree requirements:* For master's, comprehensive exam, thesis; for doctorate, comprehensive exam, thesis/dissertation, 4 core courses. *Entrance requirements:* For master's and doctorate, GRE General Test, GRE Subject Test. Additional exam requirements/recommendations for international students: Required—TOEFL, IELTS. *Application deadline:* For fall admission, 2/3 priority date for domestic students, 2/3 for international students; for spring admission, 10/15 priority date for domestic students, 10/14 for international students. Applications are processed on a rolling basis. Application fee: $45. Electronic applications accepted. *Expenses:* Contact institution. *Financial support:* In 2016–17, 7 students received support, including 27 research assistantships (averaging $25,000 per year), 1 teaching assistantship (averaging $9,500 per year); fellowships, scholarships/grants, health care benefits, tuition waivers (full), and unspecified assistantships also available. Financial award application deadline: 4/15; financial award applicants required to submit FAFSA. *Faculty research:* Computational biology, non-destructive evaluation, neurophysiology, laser spectroscopy, nanotechnology. *Total annual research expenditures:* $536,220. *Unit head:* Dr. Christopher Del Negro, Chair, 757-221-7808, Fax: 757-221-2050, E-mail: cadeln@wm.edu. *Application contact:* Lianne Rios Ashburne, Graduate Program Coordinator, 757-221-2563, Fax: 757-221-2050, E-mail: lrashburne@wm.edu. Website: http://www.wm.edu/as/appliedscience

Colorado State University–Pueblo, College of Science and Mathematics, Pueblo, CO 81001-4901. Offers applied natural science (MS), including biochemistry, biology, chemistry. *Program availability:* Part-time, evening/weekend. *Degree requirements:* For master's, comprehensive exam (for some programs), thesis (for some programs), internship report (if non-thesis). *Entrance requirements:* For master's, GRE General Test (minimum score 1000), 2 letters of reference, minimum GPA of 3.0. Additional exam requirements/recommendations for international students: Required—TOEFL (minimum score 500 paper-based), IELTS (minimum score 5). *Faculty research:* Fungal cell walls, molecular biology, bioactive materials synthesis, atomic force microscopy-surface chemistry, nanoscience.

Harvard University, Extension School, Cambridge, MA 02138-3722. Offers applied sciences (CAS); biotechnology (ALM); educational technologies (ALM); educational technology (CET); English for graduate and professional studies (DGP); environmental management (ALM, CEM); information technology (ALM); journalism (ALM); liberal arts (ALM); management (ALM, CM); mathematics for teaching (ALM); museum studies (ALM); premedical studies (Diploma); publication and communication (CPC). *Program availability:* Part-time, evening/weekend. *Degree requirements:* For master's, thesis. *Entrance requirements:* For master's, 3 completed graduate courses with grade of B or higher. Additional exam requirements/recommendations for international students: Required—TOEFL (minimum score 600 paper-based), TWE (minimum score 5). *Expenses:* Contact institution.

Kansas State University, Graduate School, School of Applied and Interdisciplinary Studies, Olathe, KS 66061. Offers applied science and technology (PSM); professional interdisciplinary sciences (Graduate Certificate); professional skills for STEM practitioners (Graduate Certificate). *Program availability:* Part-time, 100% online, blended/hybrid learning. *Faculty:* 22 full-time (16 women), 2 part-time/adjunct (1 woman). *Students:* 8 part-time (2 women); includes 1 minority (Black or African American, non-Hispanic/Latino). Average age 35. 9 applicants, 100% accepted, 8 enrolled. *Degree requirements:* For master's, capstone experience and/or internship. *Entrance requirements:* Additional exam requirements/recommendations for international students: Required—TOEFL (minimum score 550 paper-based; 79 iBT), IELTS (minimum score 6.5), PTE (minimum score 58). *Application deadline:* Applications are processed on a rolling basis. Application fee: $65 ($75 for international students). Electronic applications accepted. *Expenses:* Tuition, state resident: full-time $9670. Tuition, nonresident: full-time $21,828. *Required fees:* $862. *Financial support:* In 2016–17, 8 students received support. Scholarships/grants available. *Faculty research:* Applied and interdisciplinary science, food science, diagnostic medicine and pathobiology, adult education and leadership dynamics, horticulture and urban food systems. *Unit head:* Dr. Ralph Richardson, Dean and CEO, 913-541-1220, Fax: 913-541-1488, E-mail: olatheinfo@ksu.edu. *Application contact:* Dr. Janice Barrow, Associate Dean for Academic Affairs and Executive Education, 913-541-1220, E-mail: jbarrow@k-state.edu. Website: http://olathe.k-state.edu/

Louisiana State University and Agricultural & Mechanical College, Graduate School, College of Science, Master of Natural Sciences Program, Baton Rouge, LA 70803. Offers MNS.

Missouri State University, Graduate College, College of Natural and Applied Sciences, Department of Biology, Springfield, MO 65897. Offers biology (MS); natural and applied science (MNAS), including biology (MNAS, MS Ed); secondary education (MS Ed), including biology (MNAS, MS Ed). *Faculty:* 18 full-time (3 women), 7 part-time/adjunct (2 women). *Students:* 11 full-time (7 women), 30 part-time (22 women); includes 4 minority (1 Asian, non-Hispanic/Latino; 2 Hispanic/Latino; 1 Two or more races, non-Hispanic/Latino), 7 international. Average age 26. 34 applicants, 41% accepted, 10 enrolled. In 2016, 23 master's awarded. *Degree requirements:* For master's, comprehensive exam, thesis or alternative. *Entrance requirements:* For master's, GRE (MS, MNAS), 24 hours of course work in biology (MS); minimum GPA of 3.0 (MS, MNAS); 9-12 teacher certification (MS Ed). Additional exam requirements/recommendations for international students: Required—TOEFL (minimum score 550 paper-based; 79 iBT), IELTS (minimum score 6). *Application deadline:* For fall admission, 7/20 priority date for domestic students, 5/1 for international students; for spring admission, 12/20 priority date for domestic students, 9/1 for international students; for summer admission, 5/20 priority date for domestic students. Applications are processed on a rolling basis. Application fee: $35 ($50 for international students). Electronic applications accepted. *Expenses:* Tuition, state resident: full-time $5830. Tuition, nonresident: full-time $10,708. *Required fees:* $1130. Tuition and fees vary according to class time, course level, course load and program. *Financial support:* In 2016–17, 2 research assistantships with full tuition reimbursements (averaging $10,672 per year), 26 teaching assistantships with full tuition reimbursements (averaging $9,746 per year) were awarded; Federal Work-Study, institutionally sponsored loans, scholarships/grants, and unspecified assistantships also available. Financial award application deadline: 3/31; financial award applicants required to submit FAFSA. *Faculty research:* Hibernation physiology of bats, behavioral ecology of salamanders, mussel conservation, plant evolution and systematics, cellular/molecular mechanisms involved in migraine pathology. *Unit head:* Dr. S. Alicia Mathis, Department Head, 417-836-5126, Fax: 417-836-6934, E-mail: biology@missouristate.edu. *Application contact:* Michael Edwards, Coordinator of Graduate Admissions, 417-836-5330, Fax: 417-836-6200, E-mail: michaeledwards@missouristate.edu. Website: http://biology.missouristate.edu/

Missouri State University, Graduate College, College of Natural and Applied Sciences, Department of Chemistry, Springfield, MO 65897. Offers chemistry (MS); natural and applied science (MNAS), including chemistry (MNAS, MS Ed); secondary education (MS Ed), including chemistry (MNAS, MS Ed). *Program availability:* Part-time. *Faculty:* 15 full-time (2 women). *Students:* 12 full-time (4 women), 7 part-time (1 woman), 4 international. Average age 27. 22 applicants, 18% accepted, 4 enrolled. In 2016, 8 master's awarded. *Degree requirements:* For master's, comprehensive exam, thesis. *Entrance requirements:* For master's, GRE General Test (MS, MNAS), minimum undergraduate GPA of 3.0 (MS and MNAS), 9-12 teacher certification (MS Ed). Additional exam requirements/recommendations for international students: Required—TOEFL (minimum score 550 paper-based; 79 iBT), IELTS (minimum score 6). *Application deadline:* For fall admission, 7/20 priority date for domestic students, 5/1 for international students; for spring admission, 12/20 priority date for domestic students, 9/1 for international students; for summer admission, 5/20 priority date for domestic students. Applications are processed on a rolling basis. Application fee: $35 ($50 for international students). Electronic applications accepted. *Expenses:* Tuition, state resident: full-time $5830. Tuition, nonresident: full-time $10,708. *Required fees:* $1130. Tuition and fees vary according to class time, course level, course load and program. *Financial support:* In 2016–17, 17 teaching assistantships with full tuition reimbursements (averaging $8,772 per year) were awarded; Federal Work-Study, institutionally sponsored loans, scholarships/grants, and unspecified assistantships also available. Financial award application deadline: 3/31; financial award applicants required to submit FAFSA. *Faculty research:* Polyethylene glycol derivatives, electrochemiluminescence of environmental systems, enzymology, environmental organic pollutants, DNA repair via nuclear magnetic resonance (NMR). *Unit head:* Dr. Bryan Breyfogle, Department Head, 417-836-5601, Fax: 417-836-5507, E-mail: chemistry@missouristate.edu. *Application contact:* Michael Edwards, Coordinator of Graduate Admissions, 417-836-5330, Fax: 417-836-6200, E-mail: michaeledwards@missouristate.edu. Website: http://chemistry.missouristate.edu/

Missouri State University, Graduate College, College of Natural and Applied Sciences, Department of Computer Science, Springfield, MO 65897. Offers natural and applied science (MNAS), including computer science. *Program availability:* Part-time. *Faculty:* 6 full-time (1 woman). *Students:* 3 part-time (1 woman), 2 international. Average age 26. 10 applicants, 10% accepted. In 2016, 2 master's awarded. *Degree requirements:* For master's, comprehensive exam, thesis or alternative. *Entrance requirements:* For master's, GRE, minimum GPA of 3.0. Additional exam requirements/recommendations for international students: Required—TOEFL (minimum score 550 paper-based; 79 iBT), IELTS (minimum score 6). *Application deadline:* For fall admission, 7/20 priority date for domestic students, 5/1 for international students; for spring admission, 12/20 priority date for domestic students, 9/1 for international students. Applications are processed on a rolling basis. Application fee: $35 ($50 for international students). Electronic applications accepted. *Expenses:* Tuition, state resident: full-time $5830. Tuition, nonresident: full-time $10,708. *Required fees:* $1130. Tuition and fees vary according to class time, course level, course load and program. *Financial support:* In 2016–17, 1 teaching assistantship with partial tuition reimbursement (averaging $2,150 per year) was awarded; Federal Work-Study, institutionally sponsored loans, scholarships/grants, and unspecified assistantships also available. Financial award application deadline: 3/31; financial award applicants required to submit FAFSA. *Faculty research:* Floating point numbers, data compression, graph theory. *Unit head:* Dr. Jorge Rebaza, Interim Department Head, 417-836-4157, Fax: 417-836-6659, E-mail: computerscience@missouristate.edu. *Application contact:* Michael Edwards, Coordinator of Graduate Admissions, 417-836-5330, Fax: 417-836-6200, E-mail: michaeledwards@missouristate.edu. Website: http://computerscience.missouristate.edu/

Missouri State University, Graduate College, College of Natural and Applied Sciences, Department of Geography, Geology, and Planning, Springfield, MO 65897. Offers natural and applied science (MNAS), including geography, geology and planning; secondary education (MS Ed), including earth science, physical geography. *Program availability:* Part-time, evening/weekend. *Faculty:* 18 full-time (4 women), 1 part-time/adjunct (0 women). *Students:* 18 full-time (6 women), 15 part-time (9 women); includes 2 minority (both Hispanic/Latino), 4 international. Average age 30. 36 applicants, 67% accepted, 19 enrolled. In 2016, 5 master's awarded. *Degree requirements:* For master's, comprehensive exam, thesis (for some programs). *Entrance requirements:* For master's, GRE General Test (MS, MNAS), minimum undergraduate GPA of 3.0 (MS, MNAS), 9-12 teacher certification (MS Ed). Additional exam requirements/recommendations for international students: Required—TOEFL (minimum score 550 paper-based; 79 iBT), IELTS (minimum score 6). *Application deadline:* For fall admission, 7/20 priority date for domestic students, 5/1 for international students; for spring admission, 12/20 priority date for domestic students, 9/1 for international students. Applications are processed on a rolling basis. Application fee: $35 ($50 for international students). Electronic applications accepted. *Expenses:* Tuition, state resident: full-time $5830. Tuition, nonresident: full-time $10,708. *Required fees:* $1130. Tuition and fees vary according to class time, course level, course load and program. *Financial support:* In 2016–17, 3 research assistantships with full tuition reimbursements (averaging $11,574 per year), 15 teaching assistantships with full tuition reimbursements (averaging $9,365 per year) were awarded; career-related internships or fieldwork, Federal Work-Study, institutionally sponsored loans, scholarships/grants, and unspecified assistantships also available. Financial award application deadline: 3/31; financial award applicants required to submit FAFSA. *Faculty research:* Stratigraphy and ancient meteorite impacts, environmental geochemistry of karst, hyperspectral image processing, water quality, small town planning. *Unit head:* Dr. Toby Dogwiler, Department Head, 417-836-5800, Fax: 417-836-6934, E-mail: tobydogwiler@missouristate.edu. *Application contact:* Michael Edwards, Coordinator of Graduate Admissions, 417-836-5330, Fax: 417-836-6200, E-mail: michaeledwards@missouristate.edu. Website: http://geosciences.missouristate.edu/

Missouri State University, Graduate College, College of Natural and Applied Sciences, Department of Mathematics, Springfield, MO 65897. Offers mathematics (MS); natural and applied science (MNAS), including mathematics (MNAS, MS Ed); secondary education (MS Ed), including mathematics (MNAS, MS Ed). *Program availability:* Part-

time. *Faculty:* 21 full-time (4 women). *Students:* 5 full-time (1 woman), 20 part-time (10 women), 7 international. Average age 27. 23 applicants, 43% accepted, 3 enrolled. In 2016, 17 master's awarded. *Degree requirements:* For master's, comprehensive exam, thesis or alternative. *Entrance requirements:* For master's, GRE (MS, MNAS), minimum undergraduate GPA of 3.0 (MS, MNAS), 9-12 teacher certification (MS Ed). Additional exam requirements/recommendations for international students: Required—TOEFL (minimum score 550 paper-based; 79 iBT), IELTS (minimum score 6). *Application deadline:* For fall admission, 7/20 priority date for domestic students, 5/1 for international students; for spring admission, 12/20 priority date for domestic students, 9/1 for international students. Applications are processed on a rolling basis. Application fee: $35 ($50 for international students). Electronic applications accepted. *Expenses:* Tuition, state resident: full-time $5830. Tuition, nonresident: full-time $10,708. *Required fees:* $1130. Tuition and fees vary according to class time, course level, course load and program. *Financial support:* In 2016–17, 11 teaching assistantships with full tuition reimbursements (averaging $10,672 per year) were awarded; Federal Work-Study, institutionally sponsored loans, scholarships/grants, and unspecified assistantships also available. Financial award application deadline: 3/31; financial award applicants required to submit FAFSA. *Faculty research:* Harmonic analysis, commutative algebra, number theory, K-theory, probability. *Unit head:* Dr. William Bray, Department Head, 417-836-5112, Fax: 417-836-6966, E-mail: mathematics@missouristate.edu. *Application contact:* Michael Edwards, Coordinator of Graduate Admissions, 417-836-5330, Fax: 417-836-6200, E-mail: michaeledwards@missouristate.edu.
Website: http://math.missouristate.edu/

Missouri State University, Graduate College, College of Natural and Applied Sciences, Department of Physics, Astronomy, and Materials Science, Springfield, MO 65897. Offers materials science (MS); natural and applied science (MNAS), including physics (MNAS, MS Ed); secondary education (MS Ed), including physics (MNAS, MS Ed). *Program availability:* Part-time. *Faculty:* 9 full-time (0 women). *Students:* 17 full-time (2 women), 3 part-time (0 women), 15 international. Average age 26. 36 applicants, 44% accepted, 7 enrolled. In 2016, 5 master's awarded. *Degree requirements:* For master's, comprehensive exam, thesis. *Entrance requirements:* For master's, GRE (MS, MNAS), minimum undergraduate GPA of 3.0 (MS and MNAS), 9-12 teaching certification (MS Ed). Additional exam requirements/recommendations for international students: Required—TOEFL (minimum score 550 paper-based; 79 iBT), IELTS (minimum score 6). *Application deadline:* For fall admission, 7/20 priority date for domestic students, 5/1 for international students; for spring admission, 12/20 priority date for domestic students, 9/1 for international students. Applications are processed on a rolling basis. Application fee: $35 ($50 for international students). Electronic applications accepted. *Expenses:* Tuition, state resident: full-time $5830. Tuition, nonresident: full-time $10,708. *Required fees:* $1130. Tuition and fees vary according to class time, course level, course load and program. *Financial support:* In 2016–17, 6 research assistantships with full tuition reimbursements (averaging $10,672 per year), 11 teaching assistantships with full tuition reimbursements (averaging $10,672 per year) were awarded; Federal Work-Study, institutionally sponsored loans, scholarships/grants, and unspecified assistantships also available. Financial award application deadline: 3/31; financial award applicants required to submit FAFSA. *Faculty research:* Nanocomposites, ferroelectricity, infrared focal plane array sensors, biosensors, pulsating stars. *Unit head:* Dr. David Cornelison, Department Head, 417-836-4467, Fax: 417-836-6226, E-mail: physics@missouristate.edu. *Application contact:* Michael Edwards, Coordinator of Graduate Admissions, 417-836-5330, Fax: 417-836-6200, E-mail: michaeledwards@missouristate.edu. Website: http://physics.missouristate.edu/

Naval Postgraduate School, Departments and Academic Groups, Department of Operations Research, Monterey, CA 93943. Offers applied science (MS), including operations research; cost estimating analysis (MS); human systems integration (MS); operations research (MS, PhD); systems analysis (MS). Program only open to commissioned officers of the United States and friendly nations and selected United States federal civilian employees. *Program availability:* Part-time. *Degree requirements:* For master's, thesis (for some programs); for doctorate, thesis/dissertation. *Faculty research:* Next generation network science, performance analysis of ground solider mobile ad-hoc networks, irregular warfare methods and tools, human social cultural behavior modeling, large-scale optimization.

Naval Postgraduate School, Departments and Academic Groups, Undersea Warfare Academic Group, Monterey, CA 93943. Offers applied mathematics (MS); applied physics (MS); applied science (MS), including acoustics, operations research, physical oceanography, signal processing; electrical engineering (MS); engineering acoustics (MS, PhD); engineering science (MS), including electrical engineering, mechanical engineering; mechanical engineer (ME); mechanical engineering (MS, MSME); meteorology (MS); operations research (MS); physical oceanography (MS). Program only open to commissioned officers of the United States and friendly nations and selected United States federal civilian employees. *Program availability:* Part-time. *Degree requirements:* For master's, thesis. *Faculty research:* Unmanned/autonomous vehicles, sea mines and countermeasures, submarine warfare in the twentieth and twenty-first centuries.

Saint Mary's University, Faculty of Science, Interdisciplinary Program in Applied Science, Halifax, NS B3H 3C3, Canada. Offers M Sc.

Southeastern Louisiana University, College of Science and Technology, Program in Integrated Science and Technology, Hammond, LA 70402. Offers MS. *Program availability:* Part-time, evening/weekend. *Faculty:* 16 full-time (4 women). *Students:* 14 full-time (5 women), 2 part-time (0 women); includes 2 minority (1 Black or African American, non-Hispanic/Latino; 1 Hispanic/Latino), 11 international. Average age 27. 20 applicants, 35% accepted, 3 enrolled. In 2016, 12 master's awarded. *Degree requirements:* For master's, thesis (for some programs), 33-36 hours. *Entrance requirements:* Additional exam requirements/recommendations for international students: Required—TOEFL (minimum score 500 paper-based; 61 iBT). *Application deadline:* For fall admission, 7/15 priority date for domestic students, 6/1 priority date for international students; for spring admission, 12/1 priority date for domestic students, 10/1 priority date for international students. Applications are processed on a rolling basis. Application fee: $20 ($30 for international students). Electronic applications accepted. *Expenses:* Tuition, state resident: full-time $6540; part-time $465 per credit hour. Tuition, nonresident: full-time $19,017; part-time $1158 per credit hour. *Required fees:* $1829. *Financial support:* In 2016–17, 9 students received support, including 3 research assistantships (averaging $10,100 per year); teaching assistantships, career-related internships or fieldwork, Federal Work-Study, institutionally sponsored loans, scholarships/grants, and unspecified assistantships also available. Support available to part-time students. Financial award application deadline: 5/1; financial award applicants required to submit FAFSA. *Faculty research:* Remote sensing of magnetosphere dynamics, molecular modeling, CAD solid modeling, statistical computational methods, artificial intelligence. *Unit head:* Dr. David Gurney, Program Co-Coordinator, 985-549-3943, E-mail: dgurney@southeastern.edu. *Application contact:* Amanda Harper, Graduate Admissions Analyst, 985-549-5620, Fax: 985-549-5632, E-mail: admissions@southeastern.edu.
Website: http://www.southeastern.edu/acad_research/programs/isat/index.html

Southern Methodist University, Bobby B. Lyle School of Engineering, Department of Electrical Engineering, Dallas, TX 75275-0338. Offers applied science (MS); electrical engineering (MSEE, PhD); telecommunications (MS). *Program availability:* Part-time, evening/weekend, online learning. Terminal master's awarded for partial completion of doctoral program. *Degree requirements:* For master's, thesis optional; for doctorate, thesis/dissertation, oral and written qualifying exams, oral final exam. *Entrance requirements:* For master's, GRE General Test, minimum GPA of 3.0 in last 2 years; bachelor's degree in engineering, mathematics, or sciences; for doctorate, preliminary counseling exam, minimum GPA of 3.0, bachelor's degree in related field. Additional exam requirements/recommendations for international students: Required—TOEFL. Electronic applications accepted. *Faculty research:* Mobile communications, optical communications, digital signal processing, photonics.

Thomas Edison State University, School of Applied Science and Technology, Trenton, NJ 08608. Offers Graduate Certificate. *Program availability:* Part-time, online learning. *Entrance requirements:* Additional exam requirements/recommendations for international students: Required—TOEFL (minimum score 550 paper-based; 79 iBT). Electronic applications accepted.

University of Arkansas at Little Rock, Graduate School, George W. Donaghey College of Engineering and Information Technology, Department of Applied Science, Little Rock, AR 72204-1099. Offers MS, PhD. *Program availability:* Part-time. *Degree requirements:* For master's, comprehensive exam, thesis optional, oral exams; for doctorate, thesis/dissertation, 2 semesters of residency, candidacy exams. *Entrance requirements:* For master's, GRE General Test, interview, minimum GPA of 3.0; for doctorate, GRE General Test, interview, minimum graduate GPA of 3.5. Additional exam requirements/recommendations for international students: Required—TOEFL. *Faculty research:* Particle and powder science and technology, optical sensors, process control and automation, signal and image processing, biomedical measurement systems.

University of California, Berkeley, Graduate Division, College of Engineering, Group in Applied Science and Technology, Berkeley, CA 94720-1500. Offers PhD. *Students:* 47 full-time (9 women); includes 6 minority (all Asian, non-Hispanic/Latino), 20 international. Average age 28. 55 applicants, 7 enrolled. In 2016, 7 doctorates awarded. Terminal master's awarded for partial completion of doctoral program. *Degree requirements:* For doctorate, thesis/dissertation, preliminary exam, qualifying exam. *Entrance requirements:* For doctorate, GRE General Test, BA or BS in engineering, physics, mathematics, chemistry, or related field; minimum GPA of 3.0, 3 letters of recommendation. Additional exam requirements/recommendations for international students: Required—TOEFL (minimum score 570 paper-based; 90 iBT). *Application deadline:* For fall admission, 12/1 for domestic students. Application fee: $105 ($125 for international students). Electronic applications accepted. Application fee is waived when completed online. *Financial support:* Fellowships, research assistantships, teaching assistantships, career-related internships or fieldwork, and unspecified assistantships available. Financial award applicants required to submit FAFSA. *Unit head:* 510-642-0716, Fax: 510-643-5793, E-mail: messa@berkeley.edu. *Application contact:* 510-642-0716, Fax: 510-643-5793, E-mail: messa@berkeley.edu.
Website: http://ast.coe.berkeley.edu/

University of California, Davis, College of Engineering, Program in Applied Science, Davis, CA 95616. Offers MS, PhD. Terminal master's awarded for partial completion of doctoral program. *Degree requirements:* For master's, comprehensive exam (for some programs), thesis (for some programs); for doctorate, thesis/dissertation. *Entrance requirements:* For master's and doctorate, GRE General Test, minimum GPA of 3.3. Additional exam requirements/recommendations for international students: Required—TOEFL (minimum score 550 paper-based). Electronic applications accepted. *Faculty research:* Plasma physics, scientific computing, fusion technology, laser physics and nonlinear optics.

University of Colorado Denver, College of Liberal Arts and Sciences, Program in Integrated Sciences, Denver, CO 80217. Offers applied science (MIS); computer science (MIS); mathematics (MIS). *Program availability:* Part-time, evening/weekend. *Students:* 6 full-time (2 women), 7 part-time (5 women); includes 2 minority (both Hispanic/Latino), 2 international. Average age 35. 8 applicants, 63% accepted, 5 enrolled. In 2016, 2 master's awarded. *Degree requirements:* For master's, 30 credit hours; thesis or project. *Entrance requirements:* For master's, GRE if undergraduate GPA is 3.0 or less, minimum of 40 semester hours in mathematics, computer science, physics, biology, chemistry and/or geology; essay; three letters of recommendation. Additional exam requirements/recommendations for international students: Required—TOEFL (minimum score 537 paper-based; 75 iBT); Recommended—IELTS (minimum score 6.5). *Application deadline:* For fall admission, 4/15 for domestic students, 4/15 priority date for international students; for spring admission, 10/15 for domestic students, 10/15 priority date for international students. Application fee: $50 ($75 for international students). Electronic applications accepted. *Expenses:* Tuition, state resident: full-time $11,006; part-time $474 per credit. Tuition, nonresident: full-time $28,212; part-time $1264 per credit hour. *Required fees:* $256 per semester. One-time fee: $94.32. Tuition and fees vary according to campus/location and program. *Financial support:* In 2016–17, 1 student received support. Fellowships, research assistantships, teaching assistantships, Federal Work-Study, institutionally sponsored loans, scholarships/grants, and traineeships available. Financial award application deadline: 4/1; financial award applicants required to submit FAFSA. *Faculty research:* Computer science, applied science, mathematics. *Unit head:* E-mail: integrated.sciences@ucdenver.edu. *Application contact:* Marissa Tornatore, Graduate School Application Specialist, 303-315-0049, E-mail: marissa.tornatore@ucdenver.edu.
Website: http://www.ucdenver.edu/academics/colleges/CLAS/Programs/MastersofIntegratedSciences/Pages/ProgramOverview.aspx

University of Mississippi, Graduate School, School of Applied Sciences, University, MS 38677. Offers communicative disorders (MS); exercise science (MS); food and nutrition services (MS); health and kinesiology (PhD); health promotion (MS); park and recreation management (MA); social work (MSW). *Faculty:* 68 full-time (29 women), 29 part-time/adjunct (17 women). *Students:* 176 full-time (137 women), 36 part-time (21 women); includes 45 minority (40 Black or African American, non-Hispanic/Latino; 4 Hispanic/Latino; 1 Two or more races, non-Hispanic/Latino), 9 international. Average age 24. *Entrance requirements:* For master's, GRE General Test, minimum GPA of 3.0. Additional exam requirements/recommendations for international students: Required—TOEFL. *Application deadline:* For fall admission, 4/1 for domestic students; for spring admission, 10/1 for domestic students. Applications are processed on a rolling basis. Application fee: $40. Electronic applications accepted. *Financial support:* Scholarships/grants available. Financial award application deadline: 3/1; financial award applicants required to submit FAFSA. *Unit head:* Dr. Velmer Stanley Burton, Dean, 662-915-1081, Fax: 662-915-5717, E-mail: applsci@olemiss.edu. *Application contact:* Dr. Christy M. Wyandt, Associate Dean of Graduate School, 662-915-7474, Fax: 662-915-7577, E-mail: cwyandt@olemiss.edu.
Website: https://www.olemiss.edu

BINGHAMTON UNIVERSITY, STATE UNIVERSITY OF NEW YORK

Thomas J. Watson School of Engineering and Applied Science

BINGHAMTON
UNIVERSITY
STATE UNIVERSITY OF NEW YORK

Thomas J. Watson
School of Engineering
and Applied Science

Programs of Study

Students at the Thomas J. Watson School of Engineering and Applied Science at Binghamton University are the driving force behind innovation. With a real-world approach and dedicated faculty, the Watson School prepares engineering and computer science students to embrace new challenges and create the future.

The Watson School offers graduate programs in biomedical engineering (M.S., Ph.D.), computer science (M.S., Ph.D.), electrical and computer engineering (M.S., Ph.D.), industrial and systems engineering (M.S., Ph.D.), industrial engineering (M.Eng.), materials science and engineering (M.S., Ph.D.), mechanical engineering (M.S., M.Eng., Ph.D.), systems engineering (M.Eng.), and systems science (M.S., Ph.D.).

The M.S. degree programs provide a balance of the advanced theory and practical knowledge necessary to prepare graduates for professional practice and/or for continuation into a Ph.D. program. All M.S. degree programs in the Watson School require that the student completes at least eight courses plus a thesis or, in approved cases, additional course work and a culminating project. The normal period for completion of a master's degree is 18 to 24 months of full-time study.

The M.Eng. is a practice-oriented graduate degree that prepares students for careers in the industry. The degree requirements vary by department, but many are designed as part-time programs for working professionals.

Doctoral programs in the Watson School focus on studies at the forefront of science and technology. The curriculum emphasizes creative approaches to state-of-the-art problems in areas of faculty research interest. Graduation requirements for the Ph.D. degree include satisfactory completion of a comprehensive examination, based on an individual learning contract, and satisfactory defense of a dissertation. There is a 24-credit residence requirement. The normal period for completion of the degree is two years beyond the master's degree. The learning contract permits the development of a highly individualized course of study in close cooperation with senior members of the academic faculty.

Here are additional details about each program and its website:

Biomedical Engineering: A biomedical engineer's primary objective is to improve human health through advances in healthcare and medicine. At Binghamton, the focus is on advancing the understanding of prevention, diagnosis, and treatment of human injury, disease, and the health complications associated with physiologic and sociologic factors such as aging, environment, and diet. The graduate program trains students for leadership positions in biomedical research, education, and entrepreneurship for success in a global environment (binghamton.edu/bme).

Computer Science: Students who are intrigued by solving puzzles, investigating technology, and approaching problems from unusual directions may find that the graduate program in computer science is the right fit for them. The computer science graduate program at Binghamton focuses on design and application of computing systems, ranging from hardware and software components to networking, intelligent systems, and multimedia. Students have access to world-class researchers and can tailor a graduate program to suit individual interests and goals (binghamton.edu/cs).

Electrical and Computer Engineering: Mathematics, science, and engineering are the foundation of the electrical and computer engineering graduate program at Binghamton. The specializations offered include cyber, information, multimedia, and network security; renewable energy; power systems; steganography; photonics and optoelectronics; speech communication; and signal processing, among others. The integration of electrical engineering and computer science lends itself to transdisciplinary areas of research that offer students a superior graduate education with broad employment opportunities (binghamton.edu/ece).

Materials Science and Engineering: Materials science and engineering is an interdisciplinary field that studies solid matter and brings chemistry, physics, and engineering together to look at how materials can be used to advance energy independence, medical devices, and electronic devices. Students can work with the Departments of Chemistry, Geological Sciences, and Physics, as well as all of the departments in the Watson School to investigate scientific issues and take their findings to the next level (binghamton.edu/mse).

Mechanical Engineering: Mechanical engineers really do it all, from modeling, analysis, design, and testing of the very large (aircraft carriers) to the very small (MEMS/NEMS devices). The graduate program at Binghamton offers theoretical to applied topics in transport phenomena, micro/nanofluidics, sensor technology, acoustics, vibrations, reliability, CAD, and biomechanics, among others. The outstanding faculty includes SUNY distinguished professors, NSF Career Awardees, an AFOSR Young Investigator recipient, and an IEEE Fellow (binghamton.edu/me).

Systems Science and Industrial Engineering: SSIE graduate programs focus on how people, equipment, and materials work in industry and life. They study complex systems in industrial and manufacturing settings, healthcare environments, and society and look at intelligent systems, supply chain management, and human factors. SSIE is home to the Watson Institute for Systems Excellence (WISE), one of Binghamton's largest research centers, bringing together graduate students and industry to conduct innovative research that provides funding for graduate students (binghamton.edu/ssie).

Research Facilities

The Small Scale Systems Integration and Packaging (S³IP) Center maintains world-class facilities and infrastructure on the Binghamton University campus and at the Huron Campus in Endicott, New York, devoted to research and development in microelectronics and supporting disciplines. Many of these facilities are available for use by academic, nonprofit, and for-profit communities. More information is available by contacting the Center's Associate Director at 607-777-5314. The facilities and infrastructure include the S³IP Analytical and Diagnostic Laboratory, the Center for Advanced Microelectronics Manufacturing (CAMM) Laboratories, and the Integrated Electronics Engineering Center (IEEC).

The University library system consists of the Glenn G. Bartle Library, housing materials in the social sciences and the humanities, a Science Library, and a Fine Arts/Music Library with a total collection of more than 2 million items. Students also have online access to collections in other State University of New York institutions. Resources are supplemented by membership in academic library consortia, notably the Research Libraries Group, Inc.

Other organized research centers include the Center for Advanced Information Technologies, Center for Computing Technologies, Clinical Science and Engineering Center, Linux Technology Center, and Watson Institute for Systems Excellence.

Financial Aid

Many students hold fellowships, traineeships, or graduate, research, or teaching assistantships. Some awards include a full-tuition scholarship. Other sources of financial aid include the Federal Stafford Student Loan Program, the graduate and professional school Federal College Work-Study Program, and campus jobs.

Cost of Study

Not including student services fees, tuition for full-time matriculated graduate students in 2016–17 was $10,870 per year for New York state residents and $22,210 per year for non–New York state residents.

Living and Housing Costs

Assistance in locating off-campus housing is provided by the listing services of the Off-Campus College at binghamton.edu/occ. For meal plan and dining options, students should explore binghamton. sodexomyway.com.

Student Group

Of the nearly 17,000 students enrolled at Binghamton University, as of fall 2016, almost 3,500 are graduate students. In the Watson School, there are more than 1,000 graduate students. Many students obtain jobs in local high-technology enterprises during their enrollment at the Watson School and after graduation.

Location

The University's 829-acre campus is in a suburban setting just west of Binghamton, ideally situated in the high-tech heart of the state. Industry partnerships, class projects, and internship opportunities provide a wealth of hands-on experience for Watson graduate students. More than 300,000 people live within commuting distance of the campus. Cultural offerings in the community include the museum and programs of the Roberson Center for the Arts and Sciences, as well as performances by the Binghamton Symphony, Tri-Cities Opera, Civic Theater, and other groups. The University's Art Gallery has a permanent collection representing all periods and also displays works from special loan exhibitions. The Anderson Center's annual concert series brings a wide variety of performing artists to campus. The Department of Theater stages more than 25 productions each year.

The University and The School

Binghamton University is one of the four university centers in the State University of New York system. The faculty numbers just under 1,000. Graduate programs were initiated in 1961 with the establishment of Master of Arts programs in English and mathematics.

The Watson School was created in 1983 by combining the established graduate programs in computer science and systems science from the School of Advanced Technology with new programs in electrical, industrial, and mechanical engineering.

Applying

Holders of an appropriate bachelor's degree from any recognized college or university are eligible to apply. Applications should be submitted online to the Graduate School (binghamton.edu/grad-school). Applicants should submit GRE General Test scores. Most international applicants must also submit TOEFL/IELTS/PTE Academic scores and provide immigration and financial documentation. All credentials should be on file at least one month prior to anticipated enrollment. To ensure consideration for assistantship and fellowship awards, the admission application and supporting materials should be received by the dates recommended by each department. These deadlines and other application requirement details can be found at binghamton.edu/grad-school/academic-programs.

Correspondence and Information

Dean's Office
Thomas J. Watson School of Engineering and Applied Science
Binghamton University, SUNY
P.O. Box 6000
Binghamton, New York 13902-6000
United States
Website: binghamton.edu/watson

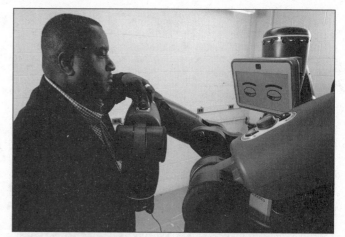

Christopher Greene, Assistant Professor of Systems Science and Industrial Engineering, with his robot in the Engineering Building.

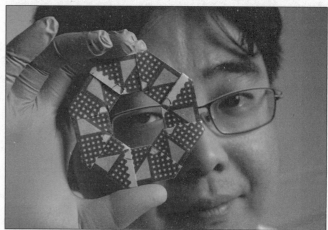

Seokheun Choi, Assistant Professor of Electrical and Computer Engineering, at his laboratory in the Engineering and Science Building at the Innovative Technologies Complex with the origami battery he recently built.

NORTH DAKOTA STATE UNIVERSITY
College of Engineering

NDSU GRADUATE SCHOOL

Programs of Study

Fargo-based North Dakota State University (NDSU) is a public research university with a graduate student enrollment of about 2,100 out of a total enrollment of 14,500 students. NDSU has earned a place on *U.S. News & World Report's* Best National Universities and Top Public Schools lists. *U.S. News & World Report* also ranks the College of Engineering at North Dakota State among the Best Engineering Schools, with recognized programs in agricultural and biological, civil, computer, electrical, industrial and manufacturing, and mechanical engineering. NDSU also offers graduate programs in environmental engineering, construction management and engineering, and biomedical engineering.

The College of Engineering (CoE) is the largest college at North Dakota State. It offers a broad range of graduate-level degree programs, most with both Master of Science and Ph.D. options.

Agricultural and Biosystems Engineering: Students interested in high-level careers in agribusiness, biorenewable energy development, and related fields may choose to earn the M.S. or the Ph.D. in Agricultural and Biosystems Engineering. The master's degree program consists of 30 credits, with up to 24 credit hours earned in the classroom and the remainder in thesis research and writing. The Ph.D. program requires an additional 60 credit hours beyond the M.S., including dissertation research and research publication.

Biomedical Engineering: Biomedical Engineering (BME) is offered jointly by NDSU's College of Engineering and UND's College of Engineering and Mines and School of Medicine and Health Sciences. The interdisciplinary program is designed to meet the needs of regional students interested in biomedical engineering; attract women and under-represented students into a developing field; educate and train students through courses and research focused on biomedical research and device development; advance the biomedical knowledge base through collaborative research; and develop intellectual property to generate company spin-offs, attract new companies, and spur economic development.

Civil and Environmental Engineering: The Department of Civil and Environmental Engineering at NDSU administers four graduate-degree programs. The M.S. in Civil Engineering is intended for students who want to work as planners, consultants, designers, or managers for public and private enterprises. Course work covers the civil engineering sub-fields of environmental, geotechnical, water resource, transportation, and structural engineering.

Course work is also offered in engineering mechanics. The Ph.D. in Civil Engineering gives students the opportunity to delve into a particular sub-field or to develop an interdisciplinary path of study. The M.S. in Environmental Engineering program covers air pollution, wastewater and water quality management, hazardous waste management, and related topics.

Construction Management and Engineering: NDSU offers two master's degree programs in construction management and engineering. The M.S. in Construction Management is a research-oriented program that requires 31 credit hours of work, including a thesis. The Master of Construction Management (M.Cons.M.) program is administered entirely online and is designed for working professionals. This program requires 30 credit hours of course work without a thesis to prepare students for the Associate Constructor and Certified Professional Constructor national exams.

Working students who want a graduate certificate in construction management may apply to NDSU's 9-credit online program, which covers construction cost estimating, construction management, and scheduling and project control. The department also offers supervision for doctoral students in civil engineering who specialize in construction management and engineering.

Industrial and Manufacturing (IME): There are two industrial and manufacturing (IME) master's degree programs at North Dakota State University: the M.S. in Manufacturing Engineering and the M.S. in Industrial Engineering and Management. Each degree program is available with a thesis option or, for working engineers, a project option. The programs are available full- or part-time to accommodate working students. Both the thesis and the project option total 30 credit hours of work, with course topics including engineering economics, logistics and systems engineering and management, quality assurance and control, and supply chain management.

The Ph.D. in Industrial and Manufacturing Engineering requires an additional 60 credit hours; 30 hours of course work and 30 hours of dissertation work.

Mechanical Engineering: Mechanical engineering is critical to a number of industries, and the graduate programs at NDSU are designed to prepare students for engineering and management careers in the public and private sectors. NDSU offers both the M.S. in Mechanical Engineering and the Ph.D. in Mechanical Engineering. The master's program is available with a thesis or a comprehensive study option. Students who hope to obtain an assistantship with the mechanical engineering department must choose the thesis option.

The Ph.D. in Mechanical Engineering may be pursued after completion of the M.S. program or as part of a combined M.S./Ph.D. program for bachelor's degree holders.

Electrical and Computer Engineering (ECE): Students seeking a graduate degree in electrical and computer engineering have three options at NDSU. The M.S. in Electrical and Computer Engineering requires a thesis and is the choice for students seeking an assistantship. The Master of Engineering (M.Engr.) in ECE is a course-only program for students who are not interested in an assistantship position. The Ph.D. in ECE requires a dissertation. Specialized areas of graduate study within the ECE department include: biomedical engineering, communications and signal processing, computer architecture, cyber physical and embedded systems, electromagnetics and optics, power and energy, and very-large scale integration. Prospective students are encouraged to contact NDSU ECE faculty members directly for detailed information on specialized study topics.

Interdisciplinary Graduate Degree Programs: The College of Engineering supports several interdisciplinary graduate degree programs in collaboration with other North Dakota State University colleges. The programs include the M.S. and Ph.D. in Environmental and Conservation Science, the M.S. and Ph.D. in Natural Resources Management, and Ph.D. programs in Materials and Nanotechnology, Transportation and Logistics, and STEM (science, technology, engineering and mathematics) Education.

Research

North Dakota State spends more than $150 million each year on research conducted through government and industry grants and partnerships. Some examples of research topics studied by departments within the College of Engineering include the following:

- the role of precision agricultural technology in reducing energy usage
- the use of nanoparticles for remediation of contaminated soil and water
- the role of RFID technology in leadless cardiac pacemaker electrodes
- ergonomic design

NDSU's Bison Ventures and Bison Microventures elective programs are project-based research efforts that bring together small teams of students and faculty for problem-solving and entrepreneurial development of lab research. Other participants in the Bison Ventures program are NDSU's Department of Architecture and Landscape Architecture, College of Business, and Center for Technical Enterprise.

Financial Aid

Applicants are automatically considered for financial support, such as assistantships that include a full tuition waiver and a stipend. Research and teaching assistantship availability varies by department. Master's degree students should be aware that most programs require them to select the thesis option in order to qualify for an assistantship.

North Dakota State University funds a number of general and departmental scholarships that may be open to graduate engineering students. NDSU also supports educational benefit programs for military veterans and their families, including the Yellow Ribbon program and the G.I. Bill.

Cost of Study

Up-to-date information on costs can be found online at https://www.ndsu.edu/onestop/accounts/tuition/.

Living and Housing Costs

Information about on-campus housing for graduate students can be found at www.ndsu.edu/reslife/general_apartment_information. There is not a specific residence hall for graduate students, but they can live in the University apartments. In addition, there are numerous housing options in the Fargo-Moorhead community.

Location

NDSU is located on the eastern edge of North Dakota in Fargo, the state's largest community. With its sister city, Moorhead, Minnesota, directly across the Red River, Fargo is one of the largest metropolitan centers between Minneapolis and Seattle and offers a family friendly environment with excellent schools, safe neighborhoods, and a low crime rate; an active arts and cultural scene, including a symphony, civic opera company, art museums, and community theater; and many places to shop and eat, including numerous restaurants, coffee shops, and a newly refurbished downtown district.

Applying

Students interested in applying for admission are advised to communicate with the Graduate Program Coordinator(s) and the faculty member(s) with whom they wish to work in the specific department(s) within the College of Engineering. Applicants should visit the NDSU Graduate School website at https://www.ndsu.edu/gradschool/. More information can be obtained from individual CoE academic units.

Correspondence and Information

College of Engineering
North Dakota State University
Graduate School
Dept. 2820, P.O. Box 6050
Fargo, North Dakota 58108-6050
Phone: 701-231-7033
    800-608-6378 (toll-free)
E-mail: ndsu.grad.school@ndsu.edu
Website: www.ndsu.edu/gradschool
    facebook.com/ndsugradschool (Facebook)
    @NDSUGradSchool (Twitter)

The Faculty and their Research

F. Adnan Akyuz, Ph.D., University of Missouri-Columbia, 1994. Applied climatology and microclimatolo-gy/climate-based agriculture.

Allan C. Ashworth, Ph.D., University of Birmingham, 1969. Quaternary Paleoecology, Paleoclimatology

Peter Bergholz, Ph.D.

Michigan State University, 2007. Food Safety and Environmental Microbiology, Landscape Genomics

Achintya Bezbaruah, Ph.D., University of Nebraska-Lincoln, 2002. Nanomaterials for pollution control, recalci-trant and micro pollutants, contaminant fate and transport, small community water and wastewater treatment, environmental sensors, environmental management.

Julia Bowsher, Ph.D., Duke University, 2007. Evolutionary and developmental biology.

Malcolm G. Butler, Ph.D., University of Michigan, 1980. Aquatic invertebrate biology, limnology, wetland ecology.

Patrick M. Carr, Ph.D., Montana State University, 1989. Sustainable Agriculture, Cropping Systems

Frank X. M. Casey, Ph.D., Iowa State University, 2000. Field and laboratory Studies of water flow and chemi-cal transport processes.

Larry Cihacek, Ph.D., Iowa State University, 1979. Carbon sequestration in soils, soil physical properties, soil management for waste disposal.

North Dakota State University

Gary K. Clambey, Ph.D., Iowa State University, 1975. Ecology and biogeography, environmental analysis and planning, structure function relations in the Midwestern ecosystems.

Mark E. Clark, Ph.D., University of Tennessee, 1996. Population ecology, landscape ecology, fish and wildlife ecology, ecological modeling, spatial modeling, species interactions.

Dennis Cooley, Ph.D., University of Rochester, 1995. Ethics of science.

Davis Cope, Ph.D., Vanderbilt University, 1980. Partial differential equations, numerical methods, applied mathematics.

Aaron Daigh, Ph.D., Iowa State University, 2013. Soil physics, transport in soils, soil residue and water man-agement, crop rotations, and nutrient/agrochemical/industrial byproduct soil amendment impacts on soil physical properties.

Stephanie Day, Ph.D., University of Minnesota, 2012. Fluvial geomorphology, slope stability, geospatial scienc-es.

Edward (Shawn) DeKeyser, Ph.D., North Dakota State University, 2000. Wetland ecology, wetland assessment and monitoring, invasive species ecology and management, native prairie restoration.

Anne Denton, Ph.D., University of Mainz, 1996. Data mining, bioinformatics, scientific informatics, educational technology, model building, databases.

Thomas M. DeSutter, Ph.D., Kansas State University, 2004. Trace gas fluxes, inorganic soil chemistry, soil envi-ronmental conditions.

Ned Dochtermann, Ph.D., University of Nevada, Reno, 2009. Ecological and evolutionary causes and conse-quences of phenotypic variation.

Nathan Fisher, Ph.D., University of Michigan, 2006. Ecological and evolutionary of bacterial virulence.

Ann-Marie Fortuna, Ph.D., Michigan State University, 2001. Microbial and soil process regulating nutrient cy-cling, soil health and global climate change, soil health indicators.

Erin Gillam, Ph.D., University of Tennessee, 2007. Behavioral ecology of bats; ecological and evolutionary basis of behavior in all animal groups; behavioral, ecological, and evolutionary factors influence the structure of ani-mal communication signals and wildlife ecology and conservation.

Gary A. Goreham, Ph.D., South Dakota State University, 1985. Rural sociology, community, family research methods, sociology of religion, sociology of agriculture.

Kendra Greenlee, Ph.D., Arizona State University-Tempe, 2004. Environmental and respiratory physiology of insects; insect immunology.

Timothy Greives, Ph.D., Indiana University, 2009. Physiology and behavior of animals in response to environ-mental signals.

James W. Grier, Ph.D., Cornell University, 1975. Animal behavior and ecology, animal population dynamics, applied biostatistics, philosophy of research.

Jason Harmon, Ph.D., University of Minnesota, 2003. Environmental change, ecosystem services, population and community ecology.

Marion O. Harris, Ph.D., Michigan State University, 1986. Insect-pest management, host-plant relationships.

Mark Harvey, Ph.D., University of Wyoming, 1986. American West, environmental history, public history.

Harlene Hatterman-Valenti, Ph.D., Iowa State University, 1993. High-value crop production.

Robert R. Hearne, Ph.D., University of Minnesota, 1995. Economic analysis of emerging environmental and re-source issues in the Northern Great Plains.

Britt Heidinger, Ph.D., Indiana University, 2007. Physiological ecology, senescence, stress physiology.

Linda Helstern, Ph.D., Southern Illinois University-Carbondale, 2001. Writing, literature, and the environment; multicultural literature.

David Hopkins, Ph.D., North Dakota State University, 1997. Soil formation and chemistry.

Tom Isern, Ph.D., Oklahoma State University, 1977. History of agriculture, history of the Great Plains.

Donna Jacob, Ph.D., University College, 2004. Wetland ecology, biogeochemistry, ecophysiology and ecotoxi-cology.

Sivaguru Jayaraman, Ph.D., Tulane University, 2003. Photocatalysis, photochemistry, green chemistry.

Xinhua Jia, Ph.D., University of Arizona, 2004. Evapotranspiration, subsurface drainage and water quality.

Dinesh Katti, Ph.D., University of Arizona, 1991. Geotechnical engineering, constitutive modeling of geologic materials, expansive soils, multiscale modeling, steered molecular dynamics, computational mechanics, nano-composite and bio-nanocomposites, computational biophysics.

Eakalak Khan, Ph.D., University of California Los Angeles, 1997. Water quality, biological process develop-ment for water and wastewater treatment, storm water and non-point source pollution control.

Kenneth E. Lepper, Ph.D., Oklahoma State University, 2001. Quaternary geology and age dating.

Adam R. Lewis, Ph.D., Boston University, 2005. Long-term climate evolution, Antarctic climate evolution, gla-cial geology.

Wei Lin, Ph.D., SUNY at Buffalo, 1992. Water and wastewater treatment, hazardous waste management.

Zhulu Lin, Ph.D., University of Georgia, 2003. Surface and subsurface hydrology and modeling, soil and water resources management, environmental systems analysis, risk identifications and assessment, geostatistics and spatial statistics.

Guodong Liu, Ph.D., Hunan University, 2001. Synthesis of novel nanomaterials, biosensors, bioassays.

John McEvoy, Ph.D., University of Ulster Northern Ireland, 2002. Cryptosporidium virulence factors and mechanisms of pathogenesis.

Mark Meister, Ph.D., University of Nebraska, 1997. Rhetorical and critical theory, environmental communica-tion.

Jennifer Momsen, Ph.D., Rutgers, 2007. Biology education, systems thinking in introductory biology, visualiza-tion, assessing the cognitive level of STEM courses.

Bakr Mourad Aly Ahmed, Ph.D., Virginia Tech., 2001. Sustainability indicators and implementation, carrying capacity measurements, coastal development, built environment and natural resources conservation.

Jack Norland, Ph.D., North Dakota State University, 2008. Restoration ecology, application of remote sensing to natural resource management, study of natural resources management problems in a socioecological setting.

Peter Oduor, Ph.D., University of Missouri–Rolla, 2004. Geographic information systems, groundwater flow modeling, groundwater contamination.

Marinus Otte, Ph.D., Vrije Universiteit, 1991. Wetland ecology, biogeochemistry, ecophysiology and ecotoxi-cology.

G. Padmanabhan, Ph.D., Purdue University, 1980. Hydrology, Water Resources, Hydraulic Engineering.

Birgit Pruess, Ph.D., Ruhr–Universitat Bochum, 1991. Microbial physiology and gene regulation.

Scott Pryor, Ph.D., Cornell University, 2005. Biofuel production from cellulosic feedstocks, biobased chemicals and materials, bioprocess engineering, process optimization, solid state and liquid fermentation systems.

Shafiqur Rahman, Ph.D., University of Manitoba, 2004. Animal waste management, biosolids management, air quality, water quality, composting.

Wendy L. Reed, Ph.D., Iowa State University, 2000. Physiological ecology, wetland and bird ecology, envi-ronmental endocrinology.

David A. Rider, Ph.D., Louisiana State University, 1988. Insect systematics, biodiversity.

David C. Roberts, Ph.D., Oklahoma State University, 2009. Evaluation and design of economically efficient tools and policies for pollution control, economic valuation of environmental and ecological attributes through revealed and stated preference methods, valuation of environmental risk, and low-impact and precision agricul-ture.

Bernhardt Saini-Eidukat, Ph.D., University of Minnesota, 1991. Environmental geochemistry, igneous petrolo-gy, economic geology.

Donald P. Schwert, Ph.D., University of Waterloo, 1978. Quaternary paleoecology, analysis of fossil insects.

Halis Simsek, Ph.D., North Dakota State University, 2012. Bioenvironmental engineering.

Dean D. Steele, Ph.D., University of Minnesota, 1991. Irrigation and environmental engineering.

Craig A. Stockwell, Ph.D., University of Nevada, 1995. Conservation biology, evolutionary ecology of native fishes, human-wildlife interactions.

Steve E. Travers, Ph.D., University of California, 1998. Plant evolutionary ecology.

Cheryl Wachenheim, Ph.D., Michigan State University, 1994. Eliciting perceptions and valuations from con-sumers, firms, students and other stakeholders and decision makers.

Alexander Wagner, Ph.D., Oxford University, 1997. Lattice boltzmann, spinodal decomposition, viscoelasticity, drop deformation and break-up in a shear flow, wetting, non-equilibrium thermodynamics, complex systems.

Dennis Wiesenborn, Ph.D., Rice University, 1989. Refining, fractionation and conversion of fats and oils from plants; process modeling for biofuels and renewable products.

Scott Wood, Ph.D., Princeton University, 1985. Environmental geochemistry, radioactive waste disposal.

George Youngs, Ph.D., University of Iowa, 1981. Perceived ethics of genetically modified organisms, sustaina-ble agriculture.

George M. Linz, Ph.D., North Dakota State University, 1982. Avian ecology.

Brian D. Wisenden, Ph.D., University of Western Ontario, 1993. Behavioral ecology of fishes, chemical ecology of predator-prey interactions, parental care and mating systems.

NDSU's Agricultural and Biosystems Engineering program strives to generate new knowledge in engineering and allied technologies for production agriculture, the food system, and related environmental resources.

NDSU's Electrical and Computer Engineering program offers graduate students the broad education necessary to understand the impact of engineering solutions in a global, economic, environmental, and societal context.

TEMPLE UNIVERSITY
College of Engineering

Programs of Study

The College of Engineering at Temple University has been providing students with a first-rate engineering education for fifty years. The College of Engineering offers Ph.D. and Master of Science degrees, as well as Graduate Certificates in the following areas:
- Bioengineering, M.S. and Ph.D.
- Civil Engineering, M.S. and Ph.D.
- Computer & Systems Security, P.S.M. and Graduate Certificate
- Electrical Engineering, M.S. and Ph.D.
- Engineering, Ph.D.
- Engineering Management, M.S. and Graduate Certificate
- Environmental Engineering, M.S. and Ph.D.
- Mechanical Engineering, M.S. and Ph.D.
- Stormwater Management, Graduate Certificate

Each of the college's Master of Science (M.S.) programs requires 30 semester hours, and can be completed on a part-time or full-time basis. The M.S. programs require some core courses, with the remainder of the program completed with elective course work.

The Ph.D. programs are designed for students who have already have graduate degrees in engineering. The Ph.D. degree requires 30 semester hours beyond the master's degree, of which 15 semester hours are associated with didactic coursework and the remaining 15 semester hours are associated with Ph.D. examinations and dissertation research. The Ph.D. degrees are highly individualized programs; students will work closely with their adviser to discuss their plan of study which outlines required course work. The program will conclude with the dissertation proposal, dissertation writing, and then defense of the dissertation.

Research Facilities

Faculty members, funded by grants through such organizations as the National Institutes of Health, the American Heart Association, the National Science Foundation and PennDOT, are engaging in cutting-edge research. Faculty research is conducted in the college's more than 15 advanced laboratories and centers and is supported by a thriving graduate student population and a team of post-doctoral fellows and research scientists.

Research is critical in graduate-level education. It is through research activities that graduate students can apply what they have learned in their undergraduate- and graduate-level coursework to solve real-world problems. Graduate students have opportunities to participate in research activities using the college's cutting-edge research facilities. In addition, graduate students may conduct interdisciplinary research with departments within other colleges and schools at Temple University, such as the College of Science and Technology and the School of Medicine.

Financial Aid

There are a number of different types of financial assistance opportunities available to incoming students in the College of Engineering. For Ph.D. students, teaching and research assistantships are available. All qualified full-time applicants are automatically reviewed for either a teaching or research assistantship. Students awarded an assistantship receive a stipend, tuition remission, and health insurance. In exchange for this, students are asked to conduct research or assist faculty in the classroom.

Preference is given to those applicants who already have M.S. degrees. In addition, Ph.D. students are eligible for University-wide fellowships, which typically provide a stipend, tuition remission, and health insurance coverage.

For master's students, the College awards merit-based scholarships to the most competitive applicants. Students are automatically considered for these awards when they are reviewed for admission, and will be notified at time of admission if they have received such an award.

All U.S. citizens and permanent residents are eligible to apply for need-based assistance by filling out the Free Application for Federal Student Aid (FAFSA).

Cost of Study

Tuition for the 2017–18 academic year is $1,041 per semester hour for Pennsylvania residents and $1,373 per semester hour for out-of-state residents.

Location

The College of Engineering is located on Temple University's main campus in Philadelphia, less than two miles from the city's center. This location offers easy access to a phenomenal array of employment opportunities throughout the city, an asset for Temple graduate students who are immersed in progressive science and technology. As the second-largest city on the east coast, Philadelphia appeals to graduate students with its numerous music venues, restaurants, theaters, and shopping.

Philadelphia has a full roster of teams: baseball, football, hockey, basketball, soccer, and lacrosse. Students can navigate the neighborhoods using all modes of transportation. Two other major urban areas, New York City and Washington D.C., are within an easy distance.

Philadelphia is a multicultural city, providing numerous opportunities for students to immerse themselves in other cultures and traditions. Moreover, Philadelphia also offers the advantages of a city filled with universities and colleges, including activities and events open to all participants, and a thriving city-wide youth culture. In addition, Philadelphia also offers an affordable cost of living.

The University

Temple University is many things to many people. A place to pursue life's passions. A nurturing learning environment. A hotbed of research. An engine of employment. A melting pot of ideas and innovation. An incubator for tomorrow's leaders.

Temple's 17 schools and colleges, eight campuses, hundreds of degree programs, and more than 38,000 students combine to create one of the nation's most comprehensive and diverse learning environments. In neighborhoods, across disciplines, and on a global stage, members of the Temple community are making things happen.

The Faculty

Graduate-level instruction and research are guided by a talented faculty. College of Engineering graduate faculty members are on the cutting edge of research, publishing in numerous peer-reviewed journals and conference proceedings and receiving grants from prestigious funding sources such as the U.S. Army, the National Science Foundation, the National Institutes of Health, and various private funding sources. Faculty members are engaged in areas of research including, but not limited to, water resources engineering, network securities, artificial intelligence, targeted drug delivery, biomaterials, and remediation of oil spills at sea.

A complete list of faculty members and their areas of research can be found at http://enginering.temple.edu/faculty-staff.

Applying

The College of Engineering at Temple University welcomes applications to its doctoral, master's, and certificate programs. Applications are considered on a rolling basis for both the fall and spring terms. Upon receiving all of the required credentials, the application will be reviewed individually by the appropriate department.

To apply for a Ph.D. or M.S. degree program, students must have:
- an undergraduate degree in engineering from an ABET-accredited or equivalent institution. For applicants to the doctoral program, a master's degree is preferred, though not required.
- A minimum undergraduate GPA of a 3.0 (on a 4.0 scale).
- Minimum GRE scores as follows: Verbal—150, Quantitative—151, Analytical Writing—4.5
- For applicants whose native language is not English, the TOEFL or IELTS exam is required with the following minimum scores: 79 on the internet-based TOEFL or 6.5 on the academic version of the IELTS.

The following credentials must be submitted for doctoral or master's degree programs:
- Completed graduate application and submission of the application fee.
- Official transcripts from all post-secondary institutions attended;
- Three letters of reference
- Statement of Goals
- Resume/CV
- Official GRE score report sent directly from the Educational Testing Agency (ETS). Temple University's institutional code is 2906.
- For applicants whose native language is not English, the TOEFL or the academic-version of the IELTS exam is required. TOEFL scores must be submitted directly from the testing agency.
- The application deadline for the fall term is March 1 for domestic and international students. Ph.D. applicants seeking funding consideration must apply by January 15. The application deadline for the spring term is November 11 for domestic students and August 1 for international students.

Correspondence and Information

Office of Admissions and Graduate Student Services
College of Engineering
Temple University
1947 N. 12th Street
Philadelphia, Pennsylvania 19122
Phone: 215-204-7800
E-mail: gradengr@temple.edu
Website: engineering.temple.edu

TUFTS UNIVERSITY
School of Engineering

 For more information, visit http://petersons.to/tuftsu_engineering

Programs of Study

Tufts School of Engineering offers programs of study leading to the Master of Science (M.S.) and Doctor of Philosophy (Ph.D.) degrees in the Departments of Biomedical Engineering, Chemical and Biological Engineering, Civil and Environmental Engineering, Computer Science, Electrical and Computer Engineering, and Mechanical Engineering. Each department offers a diverse array of concentration areas. Tufts also offers M.S. and Ph.D. degrees in Materials Science and Engineering. Tufts Gordon Institute offers programs of study leading to the Master of Science in Innovation and Management (M.S.I.M.) and Master of Science in Engineering Management (M.S.E.M.).

Applicants for graduate degrees in engineering are required to have a suitable background in mathematics and/or engineering sciences and the prerequisite understanding for the advanced engineering courses to be taken.

Research Facilities

Tufts School of Engineering maintains an environment that makes research attractive and productive by providing a strong infrastructure with modern facilities and instrumentation as well as technical and administrative support. Many of the facilities integrate research with teaching for undergraduates, graduate students, and industry personnel. Each department maintains advanced laboratories related to its field. Moreover, schoolwide collaborative initiatives allow better access to equipment and facilities for multidisciplinary projects. The departments' websites have additional details about labs and facilities.

Financial Aid

Full- and partial-tuition scholarships are available to many Ph.D. students. Provost's and Dean's Fellowships are offered to highly qualified doctoral candidates. Tufts also awards need-based financial aid through the Federal Perkins Loan, Federal Work-Study, and Federal Stafford Student Loan programs. Scholarships and assistantships are not available to M.S. students.

Cost of Study

The cost of graduate education varies, depending on the amount of support a student receives. To learn more about funding packages, students should contact the department to which they are applying. The 2017–18 tuition for M.S. students is $25,260 per semester, charged for two semesters. Tuition for the M.S.I.M. program is $25,000 a semester in 2017–18. Tuition will be charged for two semesters. The 2017–18 tuition for the M.S.E.M. is $13,200 a semester. Tuition for the M.S.E.M. program is charged for four semesters. Doctoral tuition in 2017–18 is $15,578 per semester. Doctoral tuition is charged for nine semesters, unless the student enters the program with an appropriate master's degree, in which case tuition is charged for six semesters.

Living and Housing Costs

Living expenses are estimated at $2,300 per month. There is limited on-campus housing for graduate students. Rent for one-bedroom apartments in Medford and Somerville begins at approximately $1,500 per month. The cost of sharing an apartment averages about $950 per person. A public transportation system serves the greater Boston area and provides transportation to and from the campus.

Student Group

In fall 2016, 686 full- and part-time students were enrolled in Tufts School of Engineering. Approximately 35 percent are women, and there is a diverse group of international students.

Location

Tufts University is located in the Boston suburbs, just 5 miles from the city center and 2 miles from Cambridge. Students with specialized research needs may obtain Boston Library Consortium privileges, enabling them to use the library facilities of other local universities. The area is a center for historic points of interest and cultural offerings.

The University

Since its designation as Tufts College in 1852 and as Tufts University in 1955, Tufts has grown to comprise eight primary faculties, including the School of Engineering. As of 2015, the total enrollment in all schools was about 11,700 students, of whom approximately 5,800 were graduate and professional students.

Applying

For September enrollment, applications should be submitted by December 15. For January enrollment, applications should be submitted by September 15. TOEFL scores are required for international students. Scores on the GRE General Test are required for applicants to biomedical engineering, chemical and biological engineering, computer science, electrical and computer engineering, and mechanical engineering. GRE and GMAT scores are optional for applicants to the Tufts Gordon Institute. GRE requirements are waived for current Tufts undergraduates.

Correspondence and Information

Office of Graduate Admissions
Bendetson Hall
Tufts University
Medford, Massachusetts 02155
United States
Phone: 617-627-3395
Websites: http://engineering.tufts.edu
http://asegrad.tufts.edu

THE FACULTY AND THEIR RESEARCH

SCHOOL OF ENGINEERING
Jianmin Qu, Dean and Karol Family Professor.
James Sarazen, Executive Administrative Dean.
Fiorenzo Omenetto, Dean of Research.

Karen Panetta, Dean of Graduate Education.
Jennifer Stephan, Associate Dean of Undergraduate Advising.
Darryl N. Williams, Dean of Undergraduate Education.

Biomedical Engineering
David Kaplan, Distinguished Professor, Stern Family Professor in Engineering and Chair; Ph.D., Syracuse. Bioengineering, biomaterials, biopolymer engineering, tissue engineering.
Alessandra Balduini, Research Associate Professor; Ph.D., Pavia (Italy). Regulation, environment and pathology of megakarocytes to platelets.
Lauren Black, Associate Professor; Ph.D., Boston University. Cardiovascular tissue engineering, dynamic tissue mechanics and visualization, computational modeling, tissue engineering, regenerative medicine.
Barbara Brodsky, Research Professor; Ph.D., Harvard. Biophysics, collagen, protein structure.
Mark Cronin-Golomb, Professor; Ph.D., Caltech. Optical instrumentation, laser tweezers, atomic-force microscopy, nonlinear optics.
Sergio Fantini, Professor; Ph.D., Florence (Italy). Biomedical optics, near-infrared spectroscopy, diffuse optical imaging.
Irene Georgakoudi, Professor; Ph.D., Rochester. Spectroscopic imaging and characterization, in vivo flow cytometry.
Chiara Ghezzi, Research Assistant Professor; Ph.D., McGill. Tubular tissue models for airway tissue engineering.
Xiaocheng Jiang, Assistant Professor; Ph.D., Harvard. Nanobiotechnology, microfluidic biotechnology, bioelectronics.
Janet Krevolin, Professor of the Practice; Ph.D., Texas at Austin. Medical device design and development.
Chunmei Li, Research Assistant Professor; Ph.D., Tufts. Biomaterials for hard tissue regeneration.
Jean-michel Molenaar, Professor of the Practice; MAT, Utrecht (Netherlands). Digital fabrication, rapid prototyping, additive fabrication.
Zoia Monaco, Research Professor; Ph.D., London (UK). Chromosome biology, genome stability, gene expression, human artificial chromosome.
Daniela Moralli, Research Assistant Professor; Ph.D., Pavia (Italy). Chromosome biology, cytogenetics, human artificial chromosome.
Fiorenzo Omenetto, Frank C. Doble Professor of Engineering; Ph.D., Pavia (Italy). Ultrafast nonlinear optics.
Angelo Sassaroli, Research Assistant Professor; Ph.D., University of Electro-Communications (Tokyo). Infrared spectroscopy, functional magnetic resonance imaging.
Brian Timko, Assistant Professor; Ph.D., Harvard. Nanoelectronics, biosensing, biomaterials, tissue engineering.
Qiaobing Xu, Associate Professor; Ph.D., Harvard. Material science engineering, nanoscience, biomedical application.

Chemical and Biological Engineering
Kyongbum Lee, Professor and Chair; Ph.D., MIT. Metabolic engineering, tissue engineering, systems biology.
Ayse Asatekin, John A. and Dorothy M. Adams Faculty Development Assistant Professor; Ph.D., MIT. Clean water, membranes, polymer science, separations, surface chemistry.
Prashant Deshlahra, Assistant Professor; Ph.D., Notre Dame. Material science, computational catalysis.
Maria Flytzani-Stephanopoulos, Professor; Ph.D., Minnesota. Environmental catalysis, clean energy technologies.
Christos Georgakis, Professor; Ph.D., Minnesota. Modeling, optimization and process control, batch processing.
Derek Mess, Professor of the Practice; Ph.D., MIT. Thermal barrier coating, solid oxide fuel cell ceramics.
Nikhil Nair, Assistant Professor; Ph.D., Illinois at Urbana-Champaign. Synthetic biology, systems bioengineering, protein engineering, metabolic engineering, biocatalysis.
Matthew Panzer, Associate Professor; Ph.D., Minnesota. Sustainable energy, soft electronics, green technologies.
Daniel F. Ryder, Associate Professor; Ph.D., Worcester Polytechnic. Polymer and ceramic materials processing, inorganic/organic nanocomposite materials.
Emmanuel Tzanakakis, Associate Professor; Ph.D., Minnesota. Stem cell and tissue engineering.
James Van Deventer, Assistant Professor; Ph.D., Caltech. Protein engineering, non-canonical amino acids, cancer, directed evolution, yeast display.
Darryl N. Williams, Research Associate Professor; Ph.D., Maryland. Nanobiotechnology, STEM education.
Hyunmin Yi, Associate Professor; Ph.D., Maryland. Nanoarray biosensing, in vitro metabolic engineering platforms.

Civil and Environmental Engineering
Laurie Gaskins Baise, Professor and Chair; Ph.D., Berkeley. Geotechnical earthquake engineering, geohazards.
Linda M. Abriola, University Professor; Ph.D., Princeton. Environmental and water resources engineering.
Jay Borkland, Research Associate Professor; M.A., SUNY at Buffalo. Geophysics, sediments, offshore wind.
Brian Brenner, Professor of the Practice; M.S., MIT. Structural engineering, bridge analysis and design.
Natalie Cápiro, Research Assistant Professor; Ph.D., Rice. Environmental biotechnology and bioremediation applications, fate and transport of persistent organic groundwater contaminants.
Steven C. Chapra, Professor and Louis Berger Chair in Civil and Environmental Engineering; Ph.D., Michigan. Environmental engineering, surface water-quality modeling.
Wayne Chudyk, Associate Professor; Ph.D., Illinois at Urbana-Champaign. Environmental engineering, surface and groundwater monitoring.

Tufts University

Anne Marie Desmarais, Lecturer; M.S.P.H., Massachusetts at Amherst. Environmental health.

Luis Dorfmann, Professor; Ph.D., UCLA. Structural engineering, mathematical models of material behavior, nonlinear interactions.

John Durant, Associate Professor; Ph.D., MIT. Environmental chemistry, air pollution, chemical fate and transport.

John Germaine, Research Professor; Sc.D., MIT. Geotechnical, lab testing, automation, soil behavior, physical properties, mechanical properties.

David M. Gute, Professor; Ph.D., M.P.H., Yale. Environmental and occupational health and safety.

Eric Hines, Professor of the Practice; Ph.D., California at San Diego. Steel design, earthquake engineering, structural systems.

Richard Hooper, Research Professor; Ph.D., Cornell. Hillslope hydrology and catchment biogeochemistry.

Shafiqul Islam, Professor; Sc.D., MIT. Environmental hydrology.

Daniel Kuchma, Professor; Ph.D., Toronto. Design, behavior, and modeling of concrete structures.

Jonathan Lamontagne, Assistant Professor; Ph.D., Cornell. Environmental water resources.

Daniele Lantagne, Associate Professor; Ph.D., P.E., London School of Hygiene and Tropical Medicine. Water treatment, developing countries, emergencies, water quality.

James Limbrunner, Professor of the Practice; Ph.D., Tufts. Hydrology, water resources systems, IWRM.

Kurt Pennell, Professor and Bernard M. Gordon Senior Faculty Fellow in Environmental Engineering; Ph.D., Florida. Contaminant transport, remediation technologies, and environmental toxicology.

Babak Moaveni, Associate Professor; Ph.D., California at San Diego. Structural health monitoring, experimental model analysis, signal processing, uncertainty quantification.

Amy Pickering, Assistant Professor; Ph.D., Stanford University. Water quality, sanitation, developing countries, climate, child health.

C. Andrew Ramsburg, Associate Professor; Ph.D., Georgia Tech. Contaminant fate, transport, and remediation in the subsurface environment.

Masoud Sanayei, Professor; Ph.D., UCLA. Structural engineering, finite element analysis, structural dynamics, earthquake engineering.

Helen Suh, Professor; Sc.D., Harvard. Air pollution health effects, environmental exposure assessment, epidemiology.

Christopher Swan, Associate Professor; Ph.D., MIT. Geoenvironmental engineering, geotechnical engineering.

Robert Viesca, Assistant Professor; Ph.D., Harvard. Applied mathematics and mechanics for geophysical and engineering problems.

Richard M. Vogel, Research Professor; Ph.D., Cornell. Water resource systems, environmental statistics, hydrology.

Mark Woodin, Senior Lecturer; Sc.D., Harvard. Epidemiologypublic health.

Computer Science

Kathleen Fisher, Professor and Chair; Ph.D., Stanford. Programming languages.

Greg Aloupis, Senior Lecturer; Ph.D., McGill. Discrete, combinatorial, and computational geometry.

Anselm C. Blumer, Associate Professor; Ph.D., Illinois at Urbana-Champaign. Data compression, machine learning, artificial intelligence, computational biology.

Remco Chang, Associate Professor; Ph.D., UNC at Charlotte. Visual analytics, information visualization, computer graphics, urban modeling.

Ming Chow, Senior Lecturer; M.S., Tufts. Game development, online game security, web application security, computer science education.

Alva L. Couch, Associate Professor; Ph.D., Tufts. Policy-based languages for system and network administration, support tools for teaching hands-on computer science.

Lenore Cowen, Professor; Ph.D., MIT. Algorithms, graph theory, probabilistic combinatorics.

Jan P. de Ruiter, Bridge Professor; Ph.D., Radboud University (Netherlands). Philosophy of science, artificial intelligence, inferential statistics, social robotics.

Fahad Dogar, Assistant Professor; Ph.D., Carnegie Mellon. Mobile computing, cloud computing, Internet architecture and protocols.

Samuel Guyer, Associate Professor; Ph.D., Texas at Austin. Program analysis and optimization, automatic bug detection, memory management, compiler-based tools to improve software reliability and performance.

Soha Hassoun, Professor; Ph.D., Washington at Seattle. CAD, VLSI design.

Robert J. K. Jacob, Professor; Ph.D., Johns Hopkins. Human-computer interaction.

Roni Khardon, Professor; Ph.D., Harvard. Artificial intelligence.

Susan Landau, Bridge Professor; Ph.D., MIT. Cybersecurity policy, communications surveillance, privacy.

Liping Liu, Assistant Professor; Ph.D., Oregon State. Bayesian modeling, computational sustainability.

Noah Mendelsohn, Professor of the Practice; M.S., Stanford. Distributed systems, operating systems, World Wide Web.

Bruce Molay, Lecturer; Harvard. Computer science education, software design and development, UNIX and Linux programming.

Megan Monroe, Lecturer; Ph.D., Maryland. Interactive event sequence query and transformation.

Norman Ramsey, Associate Professor; Ph.D., Princeton. Programming languages and systems, functional programming.

Matthias Scheutz, Professor and Bernard M. Gordon Senior Faculty Fellow in Computer Science; Ph.D., Indiana. Artificial intelligence, cognitive modeling, human-robot interaction.

Mark Sheldon, Lecturer; Ph.D., MIT. Programming languages, software systems, concurrency, distributed information systems.

Jivko Sinapov, Assistant Professor; Ph.D., Iowa State. Developmental robotics, machine learning, AI.

Donna Slonim, Professor; Ph.D., MIT. Biological and medical information from gene expression.

Diane L. Souvaine, Professor and Chair; Ph.D., Princeton. Computational geometry.

Laney Strange, Lecturer; Ph.D., Dartmouth. Programming, algorithms, data structures, computer architecture.

Electrical and Computer Engineering

Eric L. Miller, Professor and Chair; Ph.D., MIT. Signal processing, image processing.

Shuchin Aeron, Associate Professor; Ph.D., Boston University. Statistical signal processing, machine learning, compressed sensing, information theory.

Mohammed Nurul Afsar, Professor; Ph.D., London. Microwaves and submillimeter waves, design and measurements.

Chorng Hwa Chang, Associate Professor; Ph.D., Drexel. Computer engineering, communication networks, digital systems.

Joel Grodstein, Lecturer; M.S., Utah. Computational design.

Kevin Grossklaus, Research Assistant Professor; Ph.D., Michigan. Optoelectronics, thin film deposition, energy materials.

Mark Hempstead, Associate Professor; Ph.D., Harvard. Computer architecture, computer systems, power-aware computing, embedded systems.

Jeffrey A. Hopwood, Professor; Ph.D., Michigan State. Plasma engineering, microelectronics.

Usman Khan, Associate Professor; Ph.D., Carnegie Mellon. Robotics, signal processing, distributed iterative algorithms in random environments.

Valencia Joyner Koomson, Associate Professor; Ph.D., Cambridge. Optoelectronics, VLSI radiation effects in integrated circuits.

Ronald Lasser, Professor of the Practice; Ph.D., Carnegie Mellon. Product development specialist, innovation and entrepreneurship, image processing, animation.

Nurdan Ozkucur, Research Assistant Professor; Ph.D., Technische Universität Dresden (Germany). Neuroengineering, optoelectronics, developmental neurobiology, pediatric brain tumors.

Karen Panetta, Professor; Ph.D., Northeastern. Digital simulation, multimedia computer architecture.

Douglas Preis, Professor; Ph.D., Utah State. Electromagnetics, signal processing, audio engineering.

Sameer Sonkusale, Professor; Ph.D., Pennsylvania. Mixed-signal VLSI design, sensor electronics.

Aleksandar Stankovic, Alvin H. Howell Endowed Professor in Electrical Engineering; Ph.D., MIT. Electric energy processing, power electrics, power systems, electric drives.

Brian Tracey, Professor of the Practice; Ph.D., MIT. Imaging techniques and image processing, computational acoustics and acoustical signal processing.

Thomas Vandervelde, Associate Professor; Ph.D., Virginia. Sustainable energy, thermal photovoltaics, optoelectronics, semiconductor growth and fabrication.

Mai Vu, Associate Professor; Ph.D., Stanford. Cognitive and cooperative communications, energy-efficient communications, network information theory, statistical signal processing.

Mechanical Engineering

Chris Rogers, Professor and Chair; Ph.D., Stanford. Robotics, musical instrument design, engineering education.

Behrouz Abedian, Associate Professor; Ph.D., MIT. Fluid mechanics, electrokinetics, thermal-fluid systems.

Luisa Chiesa, Associate Professor; Ph.D., MIT. Sustainable energy, superconducting materials.

Jeffrey Guasto, Assistant Professor; Ph.D., Brown. Biophysics and soft matter, cell biomechanics and sensing, microfluidic devices.

Daniel Hannon, Professor of the Practice; Ph.D., Brown. System modeling, human systems integration, simulation and training.

Marc Hodes, Associate Professor; Ph.D., MIT. Sustainable energy, heat transfer.

James Intriligator, Professor of the Practice; Ph.D., Harvard. Human factors, design thinking, marketing.

Mark Kachanov, Professor; Ph.D., Brown. Fracture mechanics, micromechanics of materials.

Erica Cherry Kemmerling, Assistant Professor; Ph.D., Stanford. Medical engineering, fluid mechanics.

Gary Leisk, Senior Lecturer; Ph.D., Tufts. Machine design and nondestructive testing.

Douglas Matson, Associate Professor; Ph.D., MIT. Solidification processes, thermal manufacturing, machine design.

William Messner, John R. Beaver Professor; Ph.D., California at Berkeley. Automatic control systems, data storage systems, robotics, microfluidics.

Pratap Misra, Professor of the Practice; Ph.D., California at San Diego. GPS, emerging satellite navigation systems.

Jianmin Qu, Karol Family Professor and Dean; Ph.D., Northwestern. Micromechanics of composites, interfacial fracture and adhesion, fatigue and creep damage in solder alloys.

Jason Rife, Associate Professor; Ph.D., Stanford. Robotics, dynamics, controls.

Anil Saigal, Professor; Ph.D., Georgia Tech. Materials engineering, manufacturing processes, quality control.

Igor Sokolov, Professor and Bernard M. Gordon Senior Faculty Fellow in Mechanical Engineering; Ph.D., Mendeleev Institute of Metrology (Russia). Photonic sensors, surface science and engineering, nanomechanics of cells, molecules, and polymers.

Kristen Bethke Wendell, McDonnell Family Assistant Professor in Engineering Education; Ph.D., Tufts. Engineering education, design practices, learning sciences.

Robert White, Associate Professor; Ph.D., Michigan. Acoustics, sensors, microelectromechanical systems, cochlear mechanics.

Michael Wiklund, Professor of the Practice; M.S., Tufts. Human factors.

Iryna Zenyuk, Assistant Professor; Ph.D., Carnegie Mellon. Electrochemistry, thermodynamics, fluid mechanics, renewable energy.

Michael Zimmerman, Professor of the Practice; Ph.D., Pennsylvania. Polymer electrolytes for batteries, liquid crystal polymers, composite materials.

Center for Engineering Education and Outreach

Merredith Portsmore, Director and Research Assistant Professor; Ph.D., Tufts. K-12 engineering education.

Ethan Danahy, Research Assistant Professor; Ph.D., Tufts. Educational technology, robotics, makerspaces.

Tufts Gordon Institute

Mark Ranalli, Associate Dean and Executive Director; M.B.A., Dartmouth.

Mary Viola, Program Manager (M.S.E.M.) and Professor of the Practice; Ph.D., Tufts.

Inge Milde, Program Director (E.L.S.) and Senior Lecturer; M.B.A., Babson.

Kevin Oye, Program Director (M.S.I.M.) and Professor of the Practice; M.S., Stanford.

Frank Apeseche, Professor of the Practice; M.B.A., Michigan.

Jack Derby, Professor of the Practice; M.B.A., Chicago.

Gavin Finn, Professor of the Practice; Ph.D., MIT.

Partha Ghosh, Professor of the Practice; M.S., MIT.

Amy Hirschfeld, Senior Lecturer; M.A., Harvard.

Samuel Liggero, Professor of the Practice; Ph.D., Georgetown.

Josh Wiesman, Professor of the Practice; M.S., Tulane.

THE UNIVERSITY OF IOWA

College of Engineering

THE UNIVERSITY OF IOWA
College of Engineering

Programs of Study

The College of Engineering (http://www.engineering.uiowa.edu) at the University of Iowa (http://www.uiowa.edu) offers M.S. and Ph.D. programs in biomedical engineering, chemical and biochemical engineering, civil and environmental engineering, electrical and computer engineering, industrial engineering, and mechanical engineering. The College excels nationally and internationally in several specialty and interdisciplinary research areas, including computer-aided design and simulation, human factors, environmental health solutions, biotechnology, bioinformatics, medical imaging, photopolymerization, hydraulics and water/air resources, and nanotechnology. Master's candidates must maintain at least a 3.0 grade point average and may choose either a thesis or nonthesis program. Students must also successfully complete a minimum of 30 semester hours, 24 of which must be taken at the University of Iowa. Doctoral candidates must complete three years beyond the bachelor's degree, with a minimum of 72 semester hours. One academic year must be in residence. Research tools may be required as specified by the individual program. Those interested should contact the specific department for additional requirements. Graduate students often do interdisciplinary research work in a variety of programs and facilities noted in this description.

Research Facilities

The College of Engineering has twenty research locations in eastern Iowa, covering its six academic programs, four research centers reporting to the College, and interdisciplinary research efforts. IIHR–Hydroscience & Engineering (http://www.iihr.uiowa.edu) is unique for its state-of-the-art in-house capabilities in both computational simulations and laboratory modeling and for field observational research. Today IIHR pioneers high-speed computational analysis and simulation of complex flow phenomena while maintaining exceptional experimental laboratory capabilities and facilities. Observational facilities include a Mississippi River environmental research station (http://www.iihr.uiowa.edu/lacmrers) and a wide range of remote sensing equipment. Experimental facilities include hydraulic flumes, a wave basin facility, sediment labs, and advanced instruments for laboratory and field measurements. Engineers in IIHR's mechanical and electronic shops provide in-house expertise for construction of models and instruments. Active academic and research programs at IIHR are supported by a diverse set of computing resources and facilities. For high-performance computing (HPC) IIHR operates two parallel, distributed-memory computer clusters comprised of more than 10,640 Xeon processor cores, 2,280 Xeon Phi cores, 54 TB memory, and 1.5 PB of scratch space running Linux, MPI, OpenMP, and the Intel and GNU compiler and tool suites. The computing nodes feature InfiniBand and Omnipath interconnects for high-speed, low-latency message passing. Six log-in nodes provide access to the cluster for compiling and launching jobs.

The Center for Computer-Aided Design (http://www.ccad.uiowa.edu) is housed in the Engineering Research Facility and in two buildings located off site, at the Iowa City Regional Airport and the University of Iowa Research Park. The Engineering Research Facility has 7,500 square feet of office space for staff researchers, student assistants, and program administration. Eight on-site laboratories house research facilities for two state-of-the-art motion capture research laboratories, one of which includes a 6-DOF shaker table motion platform, a fully immersive virtual reality environment, robotic systems, materials testing fixtures, and equipment for individual student research in various engineering disciplines. The off-site facility at the Iowa City Regional Airport that includes three flight simulation capabilities (a high-performance, functional Boeing 737-800 mockup for high-workload simulation and analysis as well as functional Boeing 777 and F-15 mock-ups). CCAD's Iowa City airport facility also houses six dedicated research aircraft, including a single-engine Beechcraft A-36 Bonanza aircraft, outfitted to create the CCAD Computerized Airborne Research Platform (CARP) in support of airborne human factors research for advanced flight deck technology; two single-engine tandem seat L-29 jet trainer aircraft, to provide flight testing for additional avionics systems research programs; two Czechoslovakian L-29s; and an MI-2 helicopter. The Iowa City Airport facility also houses a fully instrumented automotive test platform and a recently acquired HMMWV vehicle platform supporting cognitive assessment testing related to ground vehicle human-machine interaction and operation activities at the Operator Performance Laboratory. The center's computer infrastructure incorporates high-performance workstations, servers, and PC network in support of intensive computation, geometric modeling and analysis, software development, and visualization and simulation. The National Advanced Driving Simulator (NADS) is located at the University of Iowa Research Park (https://researchpark.uiowa.edu/). The NADS conducts groundbreaking research and development in the field of driving simulation. Utilizing one of the world's most advanced driving simulator capabilities, researchers at the University have defined the state-of-the-art in driving simulation, vehicle performance, and cognitive systems engineering. The NADS houses the NADS-1 driving simulator as well as several lower-fidelity driving simulators primarily used to support development, testing, and refinement of experimental procedures at lower cost to the client. These include the NADS-2, a static-base simulator with a limited field of view, and several portable PC-based mini-simulators. All simulation platforms at the center share a common software architecture with the NADS-1, ensuring compatibility of scenarios and data across all NADS simulators.

Other engineering research-related facilities include the Engineering Research Facility; Iowa Advanced Technology Laboratories; Iowa Injury Prevention Research Center (http://www.public-health.uiowa.edu/IPRC); University of Iowa Hospitals and Clinics (http://www.uihealthcare.com/uihospitalsandclinics/index.html); National Advanced Driving Simulator (http://www.nads-sc.uiowa.edu); Center for Biocatalysis and Bioprocessing (https://cbb.research.uiowa.edu/); and the chemistry building, which supports laboratories devoted to such areas as biomechanics, biotechnology, molecular and computational biology, bioinformatics, environmental contamination, and remote sensing.

Engineering Technology Center (http://css.engineering.uiowa.edu) provides the curricular and research computing needs of the College through state-of-the-art hardware, the same commercial software used by engineers in the industry, and a dedicated professional support staff. All engineering students receive computer accounts and maintain those accounts throughout their college careers. Full Internet and Web access complement local educational resources, which include enhanced classroom instruction, online classes, engineering design and simulation packages, programming languages, and productivity software. There are twenty-eight Linux and approximately 300 Windows workstations, supported by more than $10-million worth of professional software dedicated for student use 24 hours a day. The H. William Lichtenberger Engineering Library provides Internet access to indexes and abstracts, more than 125,000 volumes, ANSI standards, and electronic access to thousands of engineering and science journals.

Financial Aid

Financial aid is available to graduate students in the form of research and teaching assistantships as well as fellowships from federal agencies and industry. Support includes a competitive stipend reduction in tuition and partial payment of tuition. Specific information is available from individual departments.

Cost of Study

The estimated annual tuition and fee expenses based on 2017–18 for U.S. citizen and permanent resident graduate engineering students enrolled for 9 or more semester hours in the fall and spring semesters (academic year) is $10,836 for Iowa residents and $28,880 for nonresidents. This includes fees for technology, arts and cultural events, student activity, student services, student union, building, recreation, professional enhancement, and health. For international students with 1/4-time or greater graduate assistantships, the estimated annual tuition is $9,078 plus fees. For international students without assistantships, the estimated annual tuition is $27,122 plus fees. Book fees for graduate students are estimated at $1,300. The latest information on engineering cost of study can be found at http://grad.admissions.uiowa.edu/engineering-estimated-costs.

Living and Housing Costs

Housing is available in apartments or private homes within walking distance of the campus. Estimated costs for living and housing can be found online at http://grad.admissions.uiowa.edu/engineering-estimated-costs.

Student Group

Total enrollment at the University for fall 2016 was 33,334 students. Students come from all fifty states, two U.S. possessions, and 113 other countries. Engineering enrollment for fall 2016 was 2,843 undergraduate students and 300 graduate students.

Student Outcomes

Nearly half of the graduates accept positions in Iowa and Illinois, though companies and academic institutions from across the country present offers. Recent graduates have taken positions with companies such as 3M, Accenture, Cargill, Caterpillar, Deere & Company, General Mills, Hewlett-Packard, HNI, Monsanto, Motorola, Pella, and Rockwell Collins.

Location

The University is located in Iowa City, known as the "Athens of the Midwest" because of the many cultural, intellectual, and diverse opportunities available. The Iowa City metropolitan area is a community of 152,600 people, approximately 25 miles from Cedar Rapids, Iowa's second-largest city, with nearly 258,000 people.

The University

The University of Iowa, established in 1847, comprises eleven colleges. The University was the first state university to admit women on an equal basis with men. The University founded the first law school west of the Mississippi River, established one of the first university-based medical centers in the Midwest, and was the first state university in the nation to establish an interfaith school of religion. It was an innovator in accepting creative work—fine art, musical compositions, poetry, drama, and fiction—for academic credit. The University established Iowa City as a national college-prospect testing center. It was a leader in the development of actuarial science as an essential tool of business administration. As a pioneering participant in space exploration, it has become a center for education and research in astrophysical science.

Applying

The application fee is $60 ($100 for international students). Admission requirements differ in each department; students should contact the department in which they are interested for additional requirements.

Correspondence and Information

Admissions
107 Calvin Hall
The University of Iowa
Iowa City, Iowa 52242
Website: http://www.grad.uiowa.edu/ (Graduate College)
http://www.engineering.uiowa.edu/research (College of Engineering)
http://www.engineering.uiowa.edu/graduate-studies (College of Engineering)

DEPARTMENTS, CHAIRS, AND AREAS OF FACULTY RESEARCH

STUDIES BY ENGINEERING DISCIPLINE

Biomedical Engineering (https://bme.engineering.uiowa.edu/). Nicole M. Grosland, Departmental Executive Officer. Biomechanics of the spine, low back pain and scoliosis, articular joint contact mechanics, total joint replacement, computational simulation of artificial heart valve dynamics, hemodynamics of arterial disease, mechanical properties of diseased arteries, biomechanics and

rupture predication of abdominal aorta aneurysms, mechanobiology, control and coordination of the cardiovascular and respiratory systems, controlled drug delivery, medical image acquisition, processing and quantitative analysis, models of cellular processes based on nonequilibrium thermodynamics, tissue-engineered vascular grafts, bioinformatics and computational biology, drug/target discovery, gene therapy, development of genomic resources.

Chemical and Biochemical Engineering (https://cbe.engineering.uiowa.edu/). Allan Guymon, Departmental Executive Officer. Air pollution engineering, atmospheric aerosol particles, atmospheric chemistry, atmospheric radiative transfer, biocatalysis, biochemical engineering, biofilms, biofuels, biomaterials, biotechnological applications of extremophiles, controlled release, drug delivery, electrochemical engineering, energy conversion and storage, engineering education, fermentation, high-speed computing, insect and mammalian cell culture, medical aerosols, microlithography, nanotechnology, oxidative stress in cell culture, photopolymerization, polymer reaction engineering, polymer science, polymer/liquid crystal composites, reversible emulsifiers, satellite remote sensing, spectroscopy, supercritical fluids, surface science, vaccines, virus infection, chemicals from biomass, green chemistry, and sustainable energy.

Civil and Environmental Engineering (https://cee.engineering.uiowa.edu/). Michelle M. Scherer, Departmental Executive Officer. Water sustainability, water quality, flood prediction and mitigation, hydroclimatology, river networks, environmental remediation, air pollution, drinking water quality, bioremediation, biogeochemistry, computational solid mechanics, digital human modeling, design of hydraulics structures, design simulation, hydropower, optimal control of nonlinear systems, optimal design of nonlinear structures, diverse aspects of water resources engineering, rainfall and flood forecasting, wind energy, transportation-infrastructure modeling, highway pavements, winter highway maintenance.

Electrical and Computer Engineering (https://ece.engineering.uiowa.edu/). Er-Wei Bai, Departmental Executive Officer. Big data analytics, Internet of things, sustainable energy, quantitative medical image processing, communication systems and computer networks, sensors and sensor networks, wireless communication, controls, optimization, signal processing, parallel and distributed computing systems, large-scale intelligent systems, database and management, bioinformatics, photonics, photovoltaics, solar systems integration, software engineering, design and testing of very-large-scale integrated circuits, nanotechnology, materials, and devices.

Industrial Engineering (https://mie.engineering.uiowa.edu/graduate/industrial-engineering-graduate-program). Chin-Long Lin, Departmental Executive Officer. Computational intelligence, data analytics, informatics, reliability and quality control, health-care systems, human factors and ergonomics, human-computer interfaces, driving simulation, digital human modeling, engineering design and manufacturing, additive manufacturing, operations research and applied statistics, renewable energy, engineering management, and financial engineering.

Mechanical Engineering (https://mie.engineering.uiowa.edu/graduate/mechanical-engineering-graduate-program). Ching-Long Lin, Departmental Executive Officer. Heat transfer, fluid mechanics, thermal and fluid systems, casting and solidification, combustion, chemically reactive flows, multiphase flow, fluid-structure interactions, manufacturing materials processing and behavior, renewable energy, biorenewable and alternative fuels, wind energy, biomechanics and biofluids, aerodynamics, ship hydrodynamics, computational mechanics, computational thermal and fluid engineering, multiscale modeling and simulation, experimental fluid mechanics, computer-aided analysis and design, reliability-based design, virtual prototyping, dynamics, fatigue and fracture mechanics, composite materials, nanotechnology, structural mechanics, system simulation, vehicle dynamics and simulation, dynamical systems estimation and control, and networked robotic systems.

COLLEGE RESEARCH CENTERS, INSTITUTES, AND LABORATORIES

Center for Bioinformatics and Computational Biology (https://genome.uiowa.edu/home/index.php). Thomas L. Casavant, Director. Catalyzes the development of new areas of study and expanded research opportunities in informatics areas related to the basic biological sciences and applied medical research. Founded in 2002 as a joint enterprise spanning the Colleges of Engineering and Medicine and Science, the center involves faculty from seven colleges, and more than twenty-two departments. It serves as a coordinating home for interdisciplinary research, undergraduate, pre-, and post-doctoral training, as well as faculty recruiting and professional development. At the hub of an inherently interdisciplinary field, the goal of the center is to assist in overcoming traditional disciplinary hurdles to collaboration and assist in utilizing state-of-the-art instrumentation and analysis methods needed by twenty-first century biomedical and basic science research. State-of-the-art practice of bioinformatics involves collection, QC, analysis, archive, and searching of molecular and clinical data. The center has extensive data storage and processing capabilities, as well as a wealth of installed and maintained software analysis tools to enable research and experiment execution at the leading edge of modern biomedical research.

Center for Computer-Aided Design (http://www.ccad.uiowa.edu). Karim Abdel-Malek, Director. National Advanced Driving Simulator (highway safety and transportation efficiency, equipment product development effectiveness enhancement via virtual prototyping, vehicle dynamics and simulation, simulator technology and virtual reality environment and human factors); Virtual Soldier Research (musculoskeletal model, whole body vibration, validation, motion capture, intuitive interface, immersive virtual reality, physiology, standard ergonomic assessments, zone differentiation, posture and motion prediction, hand model, spine modeling, gait: walking and running, predictive dynamics, dynamic strength and fatigue, modeling of clothing, human performance, armor and soldier performance); Operator Performance Laboratory (OPL) [flight test, jet aircraft, turbine helicopter, Opt LiDAR, RADAR, Airborne surveillance, aircraft instrumentation, rotorcraft, Unmanned Aircraft Systems (UAS), Ground Control Station (GCS), GPS Denied Operations, Airborne Data Link, Aerial Combat Training Systems, Live Virtual Constructive, Close Air Support, flight simulation, task analysis, warning-system effectiveness, physiological based workload assessment, cognitive modeling]; Advanced Manufacturing Technology (AMTech) (next-generation manufacturing technologies, model-based manufacturing, bio-manufacturing, electrical engineering, optimization, electronics, digital human modeling, digital manufacturing, simulation and modeling for electronic manufacturing, biomanufactured tissue and organ replacement parts, tissue scaffolds, and medical devices, and cell and organ printing, bio-additive manufacturing platforms.) Musculoskeletal Imaging, Modeling, and Experimentation (MIMX) (Computational modeling of anatomic structures, patient-specific/subject-specific models, imaging and modeling, finite element modeling, software package, orthopaedic-related FE model, patient-specific care, objective analysis-based tools, alternate surgical protocols and treatments.) Reliability and Sensor Prognostic Systems (mesh-free methods for structural analysis and design-sensitivity analysis, composite materials, probabilistic mechanics and reliability, reliability-based design optimization, topology optimization, multidisciplinary design optimization, sensor technologies, sensor-based process monitoring optimization). BioMechanics of Soft Tissues (BioMOST) (Tools for diagnosis and treatment of diseases, modeling of soft tissue structures, biomechanical experimentation, mathematical modeling, computational simulations.

IIHR–Hydroscience and Engineering (http://www.iihr.uiowa.edu). Larry J. Weber, Director. IIHR is one of the world's leading institutes in fundamental and applied fluids-related research. Cutting-edge research activities incorporate computational fluid dynamics with laboratory modeling and field observational studies. Research areas at IIHR include: fluid dynamics (ship hydrodynamics, turbulent flows, biological fluid flow); environmental hydraulics (structures, river and dam hydraulics, fish passage at dams, sediment management, heat dispersal in water bodies, water-quality monitoring); water and air resources (atmospheric boundary layer, hydrology, hydrometeorology, remote sensing); environmental engineering and science (air pollution, water-quality modeling, chemical contamination of aquatic environments, organic contaminant cycling, environmental biotechnology); and water sustainability (actinide chemistry, nanotubes, pollutant fate and transport, water treatment, wastewater nutrient removal, environmental toxicology, human impact on aquatic environments, social vulnerability, catchment science, solute transport and fate). IIHR is also home to the Iowa Flood Center (www.iowafloodcenter.org) and the Iowa Geological Survey (www.iihr.uiowa.edu/igs). Today IIHR pioneers high-speed computational analysis and simulation of complex flow phenomena while maintaining exceptional experimental laboratory capabilities and facilities. Academic and research programs at IIHR are supported by diverse computing resources and facilities. Observational facilities include a Mississippi River environmental research station (www.iihr.uiowa.edu/lacmrers) and a wide range of remote-sensing equipment. Experimental facilities include flumes, a wave basin, sediment labs, and advanced instruments for laboratory and field measurements. Engineers in IIHR's mechanical and electronic shops provide in-house model construction expertise.

Iowa Institute for Biomedical Imaging (http://www.biomed-imaging.uiowa.edu). Milan Sonka, Co-director. Medical image acquisition (MR, CT, ultrasound, X-ray, OCT, and MR spectroscopy). Knowledge-based analysis of biomedical images from a variety of imaging modalities (e.g., X-ray, CT, MR, OCT, IVUS, and ultrasound). Current focus areas include development of computer-aided and automated techniques for quantitative analysis of human, animal, and cellular image data with applications to translational applications in radiology, radiation oncology, cardiology, pulmonology, ophthalmology, and orthopedics, as well as in clinical and epidemiologic trials. Healthcare big data analytics and medical imaging informatics. Development of novel image acquisition approaches with focus on 7T-3T imaging translation, MR-based pH and T1rho imaging, MR spectroscopy, physiologic X-ray CT, and high-value image acquisition strategies.

INTERDISCIPLINARY RESEARCH CENTERS AND INSTITUTES

Medicine and Bioengineering

The Center for Biocatalysis and Bioprocessing (CBB) (https://cbb.research.uiowa.edu/). Mark Arnold, Director. CBB is a microbial pilot plant facility for production of products ranging from ethanol to proteins. Most of the work is focused on therapeutic protein production. CBB also operates a GMP facility for production of therapeutic proteins for human Phase I trials. In addition, CBB also takes on projects such as enzyme/microbe-based production of chemicals from feedstocks, bioprocessing, new biocatalyst discovery, novel biocatalyst applications for chemicals and fuels, biosensing technology, and gene/protein expression and production. Typically CBB operates 10–14 projects on a biweekly basis for biotechnology companies, including several Iowa-based companies.

Center for International Rural and Environmental Health (http://www.public-health.uiowa.edu/cireh). Laurence Fuortes, MD, Director. Rural and environmental health, with special emphasis on adverse health effects that threaten agricultural and other rural populations; promotes greater understanding and awareness of the causes, consequences, and prevention of communicable, chronic, environmental, and occupational diseases in all regions of the globe, focusing on nations with substantial agrarian economies.

Iowa Injury Prevention Research Center (http://www.public-health.uiowa.edu/IPRC). Corinne Peek-Asa, Director. Established in 1990, the University of Iowa Injury Prevention Center (IPRC) aims to use interdisciplinary research to control and prevent injuries, especially in rural communities. The center's activities constitute a broad multidisciplinary and collaborative program in research, training, and outreach. The IPRC has grown to include 66 researchers from twenty-three departments in five colleges, as well as a wide network of community and government collaborators. Six expert research teams are organized around priority research topics: road traffic safety; interpersonal violence; intervention and translation science; rural acute care; global injury and violence, and sports and recreational injury prevention. Teams promote the growth of research within their topic areas by linking researchers to IPRC core services, mentoring students and junior faculty, and engaging with community partners.

Orthopaedic Biomechanics Laboratory (https://uiowa.edu/uiobl/). Donald Anderson, Director. Application of advanced innovative computational formulations and novel experimental approaches to clinically-oriented problems across the diverse spectrum of musculoskeletal biomechanical research; total joint replacement (hip, spine, knee, ankle), posttraumatic arthritis, osteonecrosis of the hip, high-energy limb trauma, carpal tunnel syndrome, and articular contact stresses as they relate to joint degeneration.

Environmental and Hydroscience

NSF Center for Environmentally Beneficial Catalysis (http://cebc.ku.edu/). Tonya Peeples, University of Iowa faculty representative. A multidisciplinary, multi-university research center. Catalyst design, synthesis, and characterization; biocatalyst preparation and characterization; synthesis of catalyst supports with controlled pore structure; benign media, including carbon dioxide–based solvents and ionic liquids; probing reaction mechanisms with advanced analytical tools; advanced molecular modeling of chemical, physical, and thermodynamic properties involving reactions and media; multiphase reactor design and analysis; economic and environmental impact analysis; computational fluid dynamics.

Center for Global and Regional Environmental Research (http://www.cgrer.uiowa.edu). Gregory R. Carmichael and Jerald L. Schnoor, Co-directors. Multiple aspects of global environmental change, including the regional effects on natural ecosystems, environments, and resources and on human health, culture, and social systems.

Center for Health Effects of Environmental Contamination (http://www.cheec.uiowa.edu). Gene F. Parkin, Director. Conducts and supports research on the identification and measurement of environmental toxins, particularly water contaminants, and possible associations between exposure to environmental contaminants and adverse health effects. Provides environmental database design and development and systems support for environmental health research.

Environmental Health Sciences Research Center (https://cph.uiowa.edu/ehsrc/). Peter S. Thorne, Director. Agricultural and rural environmental exposures and health effects, agricultural chemical exposures and health effects.

Science and Technology

Nanoscience and Nanotechnology Institute (http://research.uiowa.edu/nniui). Vicki Grassian, Director. Environment and health (air quality, natural environment, workplace environment, human and animal toxicity, environmental health, drug delivery, disease detection, imaging, bioanalytical assays, environmental remediation and decontamination, green chemistry, fuel cells, energy, sustainability, sensors); nanomaterials (quantum theory, understanding condensed-phase matter at the nanoscale, synthesis and characterization of nanomaterials, defense-related applications).

Optical Science and Technology Center (http://www.ostc.uiowa.edu). Michael Flatté, Director. Laser spectroscopy and photochemistry, photonics and optoelectronics, ultrafast laser development, condensed-matter physics, materials growth techniques, device physics/engineering, surface chemistry, chemical sensors, environmental chemistry, polymer science, plasma physics, nonlinear optics.

Photopolymerization Center (http://user.engineering.uiowa.edu/~cfap/) Allan Guymon, Director. Kinetics and mechanisms of photopolymerizations and their impact on the structure and properties of photopolymerized materials.

Public Policy Center (http://ppc.uiowa.edu). Peter C. Damiano, Director. Transportation, environmental quality, health care, economic growth and development.

Water Sustainability Initiative (http://www.iihr.uiowa.edu/watersustainability/). Jerald Schnoor, Chair, Steering Committee. The University of Iowa has expanded its existing strength in interdisciplinary research on water including its availability, quality, reuse, health impact, and its relationship to a changing climate. Economics, policy, and communications, as well as the natural sciences and engineering, are all engaged to solve the problems of water. The faculty alliance on water sustainability encompasses the Colleges of Liberal Arts and Sciences, Public Health, Engineering, the Graduate College, and the Public Policy Center. Among the various resources already developed to advance the initiative are the Iowa Flood Center and the University of Iowa Office of Sustainability. The Water Sustainability Initiative is housed within IIHR Hydroscience & Engineering.

UNIVERSITY OF PENNSYLVANIA
School of Engineering and Applied Science

 For more information, visit http://petersons.to/upenn-engineering

Programs of Study

Penn Engineering's collaborative research and learning environment truly distinguish the School from its peers, as research and education form its dynamic, creative graduate mission. The excitement and discovery of research is open to all students and is the keystone of the School's world-renowned doctoral programs. These programs are augmented by a diverse array of master's degree offerings.

Students work with and learn from faculty mentors within the core disciplinary programs as well as through scholarly interactions involving the School of Medicine, the School of Arts and Sciences, and the Wharton School, to note a few. This environment is further enriched by Penn's many institutes, centers, and laboratories. For more than 100 years, Penn Engineering has been at the forefront of innovation, just like the University's founder was in his day: Benjamin Franklin, America's first scientist and engineer.

The six Doctor of Philosophy (Ph.D.) programs are research-oriented degree programs for students of superior caliber who will make original contributions to theory and practice in their fields of interest. The programs prepare them for a research career in academe, government, or industry. Curricula are purposely designed to develop the intellectual skills essential for the rapidly changing character of research.

Penn Engineering's sixteen master's programs (Master of Science in Engineering, unless otherwise noted) serve a wide range of highly qualified students such as those expanding on their undergraduate training for professional engineering practice, preparing for doctoral studies, or working toward greater expertise to advance their careers. The School's constantly evolving curricula are grounded in up-to-the-minute research findings and industrial priorities that focus on practical applications of knowledge and responses to career and professional interests, as well as to the needs of today's high-tech society and economy. . These include the M.S.C. in Scientific Computing, added two years ago, and the brand new M.S.E. in Data Science, slated to begin in the fall of 2018.

Research Facilities

Shared research laboratories and facilities are an integral part of research and education at Penn Engineering. The School's collection of labs and facilities share a physical connectivity that enables collaborations with faculty, students, and postdoctoral scholars across Penn. It includes interdisciplinary research centers and institutes, such as the new Pennovation Center, Singh Center for Nanotechnology, GRASP Lab, Nano/Bio Interface Center (NBIC), SIG Center for Computer Graphics, and PRECISE Lab (http://www.seasupenn.edu/research/centers-institutes.php).

Cost of Study

The cost for four courses in the academic year 2017–18 is $27,068. This includes tuition and general and technology fees. Students are charged per registered course unit. Additional information can be found at http://www.seas.upenn.edu/prospective-students/graduate/admissions/pay.php.

Living and Housing Costs

On-campus housing is available for both single and married students. There are also numerous privately-owned apartments for rent in the immediate area. More information can be found on the Graduate Housing website at http://cms.business-services.upenn.edu/residential-services/applications-a-assignments/graduate-students.html.

Student Population

There are approximately 21,000 students at the University, around 11,000 of whom are enrolled in graduate and professional schools. Of these, approximately 1,500 are in graduate engineering programs.

Location

The University of Pennsylvania is located in West Philadelphia, just a few blocks from the heart of the city. Philadelphia is a twenty-first-century city with seventeenth-century origins, a patchwork of distinctive neighborhoods ranging from Society Hill to Chinatown. Renowned museums, concert halls, theaters, and sports arenas provide cultural and recreational outlets for students. Fairmount Park, the largest urban park network in the country, extends through large sections of Philadelphia. Not far away are the Jersey shore to the east, Pennsylvania Dutch country to the west, and the Pocono Mountains to the north. The city is also less than a 3-hour drive from New York City and Washington, D.C.

The School

The School of Engineering and Applied Science has a distinguished reputation for the quality of its programs. The School's alumni have achieved international distinction in research, higher education, management, entrepreneurship and industrial development, and government service. Research is led by faculty members at the forefront of modern technology and makes major contributions in a wide variety of fields.

The University of Pennsylvania was founded in 1740 by Benjamin Franklin. A member of the Ivy League and one of the world's leading universities, Penn is renowned for its graduate schools, faculty, research centers, and institutes. Conveniently situated on a compact and attractive campus, Penn offers an abundance of multidisciplinary educational programs with exceptional opportunities for individually tailored graduate education.

Applying

Candidates may apply directly to the School of Engineering through an online application system. Applicants should visit the admissions website for detailed application requirements and access to the online application system. Ph.D. applications for fall admission must be received by December 15. Master's applications must be received by November 15 or March 15, except for the M.S.E. Robotics and M:IPD/M.S.E. IPD degrees, which are due by February 1. Admission is based on the student's academic record, research, test scores, and letters of recommendation. Scores on the Graduate Record Examinations (GRE) are required. All students whose native language is not English must arrange to take either the Test of English as a Foreign Language (TOEFL) or International English Language Testing System (IELTS) test prior to the application process. The admissions website can be found at http://www.seas.upenn.edu/.

Correspondence and Information

Graduate Admissions
School of Engineering and Applied Science
109 Towne Building
University of Pennsylvania
220 South 33rd Street
Philadelphia, Pennsylvania 19104-6391
Phone: 215-898-4542
E-mail: gradstudies@seas.upenn.edu
Website: http://www.seas.upenn.edu/grad
        @PennEngGradAdm (Twitter)

AREAS OF RESEARCH

Bioengineering: The Master of Science in Bioengineering program has an inter-disciplinary focus on scientific and engineering fundamentals, specifically new developments in bioengineering. The Bioengineering Ph.D. program is designed to train individuals for academic, government, or industrial research careers. Research interests for these programs include: bioengineered therapeutics (device and drug delivery), biomaterials, cardiovascular and pulmonary cell and tissue mechanics, cell mechanics, cellular and molecular imaging, cellular engineering, imaging theory and analysis, injury biomechanics, medical imaging and imagining instrumentation, molecular engineering, neuroengineering, orthopaedic bioengineering, systems and synthetic bioengineering, theoretical and computational bioengineering, and tissue engineering. (http://www.be.seas.upenn.edu)

Biotechnology: The Master of Biotechnology (M.B.) program prepares students for leadership in the critically important and dynamic industries of biotechnology and pharmaceuticals. Strongly interdisciplinary, this program draws its faculty and courses from the Schools of Engineering, Arts and Sciences, and Medicine. Research interests are: biomedical technologies, biopharmaceutical/engineering biotechnology, and molecular biology. (http://www.upenn.edu/biotech)

Chemical and Biomolecular Engineering: The M.S.E. program in Chemical and Biomolecular Engineering (CBE) provides students with the firm theoretical foundation and interdisciplinary skills that are essential in the rapidly-changing field of chemical and biomolecular engineering. The Ph.D. CBE program is a research-oriented degree for students showing exceptional promise for original contributions to the theory and practice of chemical and biomolecular engineering. Research interests are: advanced materials and nanotechnology, catalysis and reaction engineering, cellular and biomolecular engineering, energy and environmental engineering, molecular simulation and thermodynamics, soft matter and complex fluids, and systems engineering. (http://www.cbe.seas.upenn.edu)

Computer Graphics and Game Technology: The M.S.E. program in Computer Graphics and Game Technology is nationally recognized for preparing students for leadership careers as designers, technical animators, directors, and game programmers. Students receive first-hand experience in the latest graphics and animation technologies, interactive media design

University of Pennsylvania

principles, product development methodologies, and entrepreneurship. Courses utilize Penn's Center for Human Modeling and Simulation, internationally recognized for cutting-edge research in 3-D computer graphics, human simulation, and the behavioral animation of embodied intelligent agents. (http://www.cis.upenn.edu/grad)

Computer and Information Science: The M.S.E. program in Computer and Information Science (CIS) is one of the nation's top programs, preparing students to be innovators, leaders, and visionaries. M.S.E. students develop their own advanced study focus and arrange interdisciplinary programs such as CIS and telecommunications, CIS and computational linguistics, CIS and biomedical computation. The Ph.D. CIS program is designed for candidates with strong training in disciplines related to modern information processing, with an emphasis on computer science and mathematics. The curriculum is intended to develop intellectual skills essential for the rapidly changing character of research and to meet the demands of academe and industry. Research interests include: architecture and compilers, artificial intelligence, bioinformatics and computational biology, computational linguistics, databases and data management, embedded and real-time systems, formal methods and software engineering, graphics, machine learning, networks and distributed systems, programming languages, robotics, security and information assurance, theory, and vision. There are also interdisciplinary collaborations with fields such as biology, genetics, linguistics, mathematics, and electrical engineering. (http://www.cis.upenn.edu/grad)

Computer and Information Technology: The master's program in Computer and Information Technology (MCIT) is specifically designed for students and professionals with minimal or no prior computing experience or formal training in computer science. This program gives students the expertise needed to understand and succeed in today's highly innovative and competitive workplace. It benefits students and industry professionals who want to begin or advance a career in information technology or prepare for doctoral studies in computer science. (http://www.cis.upenn.edu/grad)

Electrical and Systems Engineering: The graduate group in electrical and systems engineering offers a Ph.D. in Electrical and Systems Engineering (ESE), an M.S.E. in Electrical Engineering (EE), and an M.S.E. in Systems Engineering (SE). The EE program enables students to tailor their own interests and goals, from electromagnetics and photonics, sensors and MEMS, to VLSI and nanotechnology. It gives students the theoretical foundation and interdisciplinary skills needed to deal with the new ideas and new applications that are the hallmarks of modern electroscience. The SE program, grounded in the intersection of electrical and systems engineering, gives students in-depth theoretical foundation and interdisciplinary skills required by the growing complexity of technological systems. In addition, students are also able to complete a Certificate in Engineering Entrepreneurship, where they take cross degree courses at Wharton, including leadership and Fundamentals of High-Tech Ventures.

The Ph.D. program focuses on the development of research skills to prepare the student for scholarship in their field of interest. These research themes are: circuits and computer engineering, information and decision systems, and nanodevices and nanosystems. (http://www.ese.upenn.edu)

Embedded Systems: The M.S.E. in Embedded Systems (EMBS) is an innovative degree program offered jointly by the departments of Computer and Information Science and Electrical and Systems Engineering and is integrated with the PRECISE Center for Research in Embedded Systems. The program is best for students with either computer science or electrical engineering academic backgrounds who wish to pursue industrial jobs within automotive, aerospace, defense, and consumer electronics, as well as for practicing engineers in the embedded systems industry who want to gain knowledge of state-of-the-art tools and theories. Research interests are: embedded controls, real-time operating systems, model-based design and verification, and implementation of embedded systems. (http://www.cis.upenn.edu)

Integrated Product Design: Two integrated product design degree programs are offered: the Master of Integrated Product Design (M:IPD) and the Master of Science in Engineering in Integrated Product Design (M.S.E. in IPD). The M:IPD is intended for students with a non-engineering background or students with an engineering background who wish to build their skills in other disciplines. Students gain an interdisciplinary perspective of product design, building skills in conceptualization, ideation, manufacturing, marketing, and business planning. The M.S.E. in IPD is intended for students who have an undergraduate degree in engineering. The degree emphasizes technology and manufacturing processes, including coursework in advanced CAD/CAM and mechatronics. (http://ipd.me.upenn.edu)

Materials Science and Engineering: The M.S.E and Ph.D. programs in Materials Science and Engineering prepare students to be leaders, innovators, and visionaries in the materials revolution. Students have access to a broad range of state-of-the-art instrumentation in the department and the Laboratory for Research on the Structure of Matter (LRSM). Research interests include: computational materials science, electronic/optical/magnetic materials, inorganic materials, materials for energy, microscopies/scattering, nano- and low-dimensional materials, and polymers/soft matter/biomaterials. (http://www.mse.seas.upenn.edu)

Mechanical Engineering and Applied Mechanics: The M.S.E in Mechanical Engineering and Applied Mechanics (MEAM) is nationally recognized for its excellence. Research interests are: design and manufacturing, heat transfer/fluid mechanics/energy, mechanics of materials, mechatronic and robotic systems, and micro and nano systems. The MEAM Ph.D. is an interdisciplinary, hands-on, research-focused program that collaborates with

material sciences, computer sciences, electrical and systems engineering, chemical and biomolecular engineering, and the School of Medicine. Research interests are: computational science and engineering, design and manufacturing, energy science and manufacturing, fluid mechanics, mechanics and materials, mechanical engineering in biology and medicine, micro and nano science/technology/devices and systems, robotics and controls, and thermal sciences. (http://www.me.upenn.edu)

Nanotechnology: The M.S.E. program in Nanotechnology prepares students for leadership roles in emerging high-tech industries as well as traditional industries that utilize nanoscale phenomena. Nanotechnology is a highly interdisciplinary field and students are able to take courses from the Schools of Engineering, Arts and Sciences, and Wharton. Technical courses are organized into three research interests: synthesis, materials, and nanofabrication; devices and fundamental properties; and biotechnology. (http://www.masters.nano.upenn.edu/)

Robotics: The M.S.E. program in Robotics is a unique program administered by Penn's General Robotics, Automation, Sensing and Perception (GRASP) Laboratory, recognized as one of the nation's premier robotics research centers. Multidisciplinary in scope, it provides an ideal foundation for what today's experts in robotics and intelligent systems need to know. Research interests are: artificial intelligence, computer vision, control systems, dynamics and machine learning, design, programming, and prototyping of robotic systems. (https://www.grasp.upenn.edu)

Scientific Computing and Data Science: Penn is adding to its cross-disciplinary M.S.E. programs with an M.S.E. in Data Science that is scheduled to have its first incoming class in fall 2018. It will join the M.S.E. in Scientific Computing, which focuses on computational techniques for engineering and the physical sciences, and expects a background in these disciplines. The M.S.E. in Data Science will focus on the use of statistical and data analytics techniques across a variety of disciplines, including business, public policy, medicine, social science, and the humanities, and is aimed at students with a computational, mathematical, or statistical background. Both programs provide graduate training in the fundamentals of computational science, hypothesis testing, data analytics, and machine learning, and they give an opportunity for students to choose a specialization and receive practical experience. (http://www.seas.upenn.edu/prospective-students/graduate/programs/masters/)

Smith Walk in the Penn Engineering Quad.

Dr. George J. Pappas, Joseph Moore Professor and Chair of the Department of Electrical and Systems Engineering, with students.

YALE UNIVERSITY
School of Engineering & Applied Science

Programs of Study

All research and instructional programs in engineering and applied science are coordinated by the School of Engineering & Applied Science (SEAS), which consists of the Departments of Biomedical Engineering, Chemical & Environmental Engineering, Computer Science, Electrical Engineering, and Mechanical Engineering & Materials Science. These five units have autonomous faculty appointments and instructional programs, and students may obtain degrees designated according to different disciplines. A Director of Graduate Studies in each department oversees all graduate student matters. Students have considerable freedom in selecting programs to suit their interests and may choose programs of study that draw upon the resources of departments that are not within the School of Engineering & Applied Science, including the Departments of Applied Physics, Physics, Chemistry, Mathematics, Statistics, Astronomy, Geology and Geophysics, and Molecular Biophysics and Biochemistry, and departments of the School of Medicine and the School of Management.

In most departments within SEAS, the student plans his or her course of study in consultation with faculty advisers (the student's advisory committee). A minimum of ten term courses is required and they must be completed in the first two years. Mastery of the topics is expected, and the core courses, as identified by each department/program, should be taken in the first year. No more than two courses should be Special Investigations, and at least two should be outside the area of the dissertation. Periodically, the faculty reviews the overall performance of the student to determine whether he or she may continue working toward the Ph.D. degree. At the end of the first year, a faculty member typically agrees to accept the student as a research assistant. By December 5 of the third year, an area examination must be passed and a written prospectus submitted before dissertation research is begun. These events result in the student's admission to candidacy. Subsequently, students report orally each year to the full advisory committee on their progress. When the research is nearing completion, but before the thesis writing has commenced, the full advisory committee advises the student on the thesis plan. A final oral presentation of the dissertation research is required during term time. There is no foreign language requirement.

In the Computer Science department, to be admitted to candidacy, a student must (1) pass ten courses (including CPSC 690 and CPSC 691) with at least two grades of honors, the remainder at least high pass, including three advanced courses in an area of specialization; (2) take six advanced courses in areas of general computer science; (3) successfully complete a research project in CPSC 690, 691, and submit a written report on it to the faculty; (4) pass a qualifying examination in an area of specialization; (5) be accepted as a thesis student by a regular department faculty member; (6) serve as a teaching assistant for two terms (four TF units); and (7) submit a written dissertation prospectus, with a tentative title for the dissertation. To satisfy the distribution requirement (item 2 above), the student must take one course in programming languages or systems, one programming-intensive course, two theory courses, and two in application areas. In order to gain teaching experience, all graduate students are required to serve as teaching assistants for two terms during their first three years of study. All requirements for admission to candidacy must be completed prior to the end of the third year. In addition to all other requirements, students must successfully complete CPSC 991, Ethical Conduct of Research, prior to the end of their first year of study. This requirement must be met prior to registering for a second year of study.

M.S. degrees are offered and require the successful completion of at least eight term courses, two of which may be special projects. Although this program can normally be completed in one year of full-time study, a part-time M.S. program is available for practicing engineers and others. Its requirements are the successful completion of eight term courses in a time period not to exceed four calendar years.

Research Facilities

Department facilities are equipped with state-of-the-art experimental and computational equipment in support of the research activity described above. They are centrally located on campus in Mason, Dunham, and Becton Laboratories; the Malone Engineering Center; and the Arthur K. Watson Hall, adjacent to the Department of Mathematics and near the complex of facilities for physics, chemistry, and the biological sciences. The Center for Engineering Innovation and Design is a new 8,500-square-foot area for students to learn, practice, and share engineering design principles in courses, extracurricular activities, and workshops. The Yale West Campus supports research structured around areas of inquiry rather than existing disciplines and hosts five research institutes working on interdisciplinary problems in cancer biology, chemical biology, nanobiology, systems biology, microbial diversity, energy sciences, and the preservation of cultural heritage. The School of Engineering & Applied Science has a rich computing environment, including servers, workstations, and personal computers. High-speed data wired and wireless networks interconnect engineering and extends to the campus network. In addition, advanced instrumentation, computing, and networking are combined in a number of laboratories.

Financial Aid

Almost all first-year Ph.D. students receive a University fellowship paying full tuition and an adjusted stipend. Support thereafter is generally provided by research assistantships, which pay $33,850 plus full tuition in 2017–18. Prize fellowships are available to exceptional students. Fellowship support is not available for master's degree students.

Cost of Study

Tuition is $41,000 for the 2017–18 academic year.

Living and Housing Costs

On-campus graduate dormitory housing units range from $5,010 to $9,084 per academic year. Graduate apartment units range from $528 to $1,336 per month. Additional housing details can be found at http://housing.yale.edu/graduate-housing.

Student Group

Yale has 12,385 students—5,505 are undergraduates and the remainder are graduate and professional students. About 250 graduate students are in engineering, most of them working toward the Ph.D.

Location

Situated on Long Island Sound, among the scenic attractions of southern New England, New Haven provides outstanding cultural and recreational opportunities. The greater New Haven area has a population of more than 350,000 and is only 1½ hours from New York by train or car.

The University

Yale is the third-oldest university in the United States, and its engineering program is also one of the oldest. All programs at the University, including those in the School of Engineering & Applied Science, are structured to give students a high degree of flexibility in arranging their programs, with close interaction between individual students and faculty members.

Applying

Students with a bachelor's degree in any field of engineering or in mathematics, physics, or chemistry may apply for admission to graduate study, as may other students prepared to do graduate-level work in any of the study areas of the chosen department, regardless of their specific undergraduate field. Students are admitted only for the beginning of the fall term. Application should be initiated about a year in advance of desired admission, and the application should be submitted before December 25; the file, including letters of reference, must be completed before January 2. Notifications of admission and award of financial aid are sent by April 1. Applicants must take the General Test of the Graduate Record Examinations; the exam should be taken in October. International applicants must submit scores on the TOEFL unless the undergraduate degree is from an institution in which English is the primary language of instruction.

Correspondence and Information

Office of Graduate Studies
School of Engineering & Applied Science
Yale University
P.O. Box 208267
New Haven, Connecticut 06520-8267
United States
Phone: 203-432-4252
Fax: 203-432-7736
Website: http://www.seas.yale.edu/

Yale University

THE FACULTY AND AREAS OF RESEARCH

APPLIED MECHANICS/MECHANICAL ENGINEERING/MATERIALS SCIENCE: C. Ahn, E. Brown, J. Cha, A. Dollar, J. Fernández de la Mora, A. Gomez, R. Kramer-Bottiglio, M. B Long, C. S. O'Hern, J. Schroers, U. D. Schwarz, M. D. Smooke, M. Venkadesan. Joint appointments (with primary appointment in another department): S. Ismail-Beigi, S.-I. Karato, B. Scassellati. Emeritus faculty: I. B. Bernstein.

Fluids and Thermal Sciences: Suspensions; electrospray theory and characterization; electrical propulsion applications; electrified and magnetized interfaces of electrically conducting liquids and ferrofluids; combustion and flames; computational methods for fluid dynamics and reacting flows; turbulence; laser diagnostics of reacting and nonreacting flows; and magnetohydrodynamics.

Soft matter/complex fluids: Jamming and slow dynamics in gels, glasses, and granular materials; mechanical properties of soft and biological materials; and structure and dynamics of macromolecules.

Materials Science: Studies of thin films; nanoscale effects on electronic properties of two-dimensional layered materials; amorphous metals and nanomaterials including nanocomposites; characterization of crystallization and other phase transformations; nanoimprinting; atomic-scale investigations of surface interactions and properties; classical and quantum nanomechanics; nanotribology; nanostructured energy applications; nanoparticle synthesis for energy applications; combinatorial materials science; and in situ transmission electron and scanning probe microscopy.

Robotics/Mechatronics: Machine and mechanism design; dynamics and control; robotic grasping and manipulation; human-machine interface; rehabilitation robotics; haptics; soft robotics; flexible and stretchable electronics; soft material manufacturing; responsive material actuators; soft-bodied control; electromechanical energy conversion; biomechanics of human movement; human powered vehicles.

BIOMEDICAL ENGINEERING: S. Campbell, R. E. Carson, J. Duncan, T. Fahmy, R. Fan, A. Gonzalez, J. Humphrey, F. Hyder, T. Kyriakides, A. Levchenko, M. Mak, K. Miller-Jensen, M. Murrell, D. Rothman, M. Saltzman, L. Staib, S. Zucker. Joint appointments (with primary appointment in another department): J. Bewersdorf, M. Choma, N. Christakis, R. de Graaf, K. Hirschi, E. Morris, C Liu, L. Niklason, X. Papademetris, M. Schwartz, F. Sigworth, B. Smith, S. Tommasini, H. Tagare, P. Van Tassel, J. Zhou.

Biomedical Imaging and Biosignals: Formation of anatomical and functional medical images; magnetic resonance spectroscopy; analysis and processing of medical image data, including functional MRI (fMRI); diffusion tensor imaging; imaging of brain biochemical processes; image-guided neurosurgery; using biomechanical models to guide recovery of left ventricular strain from medical images; biomedical signal processing; relating EEG and fMRI information.

Biomechanics: Simulation and loading of the lumbar spine in regard to tissue loads during heavy lifting, low-back pain and mechanical instability of the spine, muscle mechanics and electromyography, mechanical performance of implants, microcirculation in skeletal muscle, mechanisms of blood-flow control, cell-to-cell communication in vascular resistance networks.

Biomolecular Engineering and Biotechnology: Drug delivery and tissue engineering, drug delivery systems, polymers as biomaterials, tissue engineering, spinal cord regeneration, drug delivery and repair in retina and optic nerve, new biomaterials for drug delivery and tissue engineering, bioseparations, chromatography and electrophoresis, electrical recording (patch clamp) and signal processing of ion channel currents, studies of structure and function of ion channel proteins, cryoelectron microscopy methods for macromolecular structure determination.

COMPUTER SCIENCE: D. Angluin, J. Aspnes, M. Balakrishnan, J. Dorsey, S. Eisenstat, J. Feigenbaum, M. Fischer, D. Gelernter, R. Manohar, D. McDermott, R. Piskac, D. Radev, M. Raykova, V. Rokhlin, H. Rushmeier, B. Scassellati, Z. Shao, A. Silberschatz, D. Spielman, Y. R. Yang, M. Yu, S. Zucker. Joint appointments (with primary appointment in another department): D. Bergeman, R. Coifman, M. Gerstein, W. Hu, A. Karbasi, S. Krishnaswamy, S. Negahban, F. Shic, J. Szefer, L. Tassiulas. Emeritus faculty: M. Schultz.

Artificial intelligence (vision, robotics, planning, computational neuroscience, knowledge representation, neural networks); programming languages (functional programming, parallel languages and architectures, programming environments, formal semantics, compilation techniques, modern computer architecture, type theory/systems, meta-programming); systems (databases, operating systems, networks, software engineering); scientific computing (numerical linear algebra, numerical solution of partial differential equations, mathematical software, parallel algorithms); theory of computation (algorithms and data structures, complexity, distributed systems, learning, online algorithms, graph algorithms, geometric algorithms, fault tolerance, reliable communication, cryptography, security, electronic commerce); topics of discrete mathematics with application to computer science (combinatorics, graph theory, combinatorial optimization).

CHEMICAL & ENVIRONMENTAL ENGINEERING: E. I. Altman, M. Elimelech, D. Gentner, A. Haji-Akbari, S. Hu, J. Kim, M. Loewenberg, C. Osuji, J. Peccia, L. D. Pfefferle, D. Plata, M. Saltzman, A. D. Taylor, P. Van Tassel, T. K. Vanderlick, M. Zhong, J. Zimmerman. Adjunct faculty: R. McGraw, J. Pignatello. Joint appointments (with primary appointment in another department): M. Bell, R. Blake, E. Kaplan, A. Miranker, U. D. Schwarz. Emeritus faculty: G. L. Haller, D. E. Rosner.

Nanomaterials: Carbon and inorganic nanotubes, nanoscale polymer films, nanoscale devices, nanomaterials and biomolecules in engineered and natural aquatic systems.

Soft Matter and Interfacial Phenomena: Colloidal and interfacial phenomena, surface science, physics of synthetic and biological macromolecules, microfluidic biosensors, self-assembled soft materials for biomedical applications.

Biomolecular Engineering: Biomolecules at interfaces, nanofilm biomaterials, bioaerosol detection and source tracking, microarrays and other high throughput measurements, production of functional binding biomolecules, biological production of sustainable fuels, transport and fate of microbial pathogens in aquatic environments, membrane separations for desalination and water quality control.

Energy: Biofuels, energy extraction from waste materials, efficient water treatment and delivery, integration of science and engineering with economics and policy.

Water: Sustainable and culturally appropriate technologies for low-quality-source water reclamation in the developing world.

Sustainability: Green solvents, bio-based materials, safer nanotechnology and systems optimization for reduced environmental impact and enhanced economic competitiveness.

ELECTRICAL ENGINEERING: J. Han, W. Hu, A. Karbasi, R. Kuc, T. P. Ma, R. Manohar, A. S. Morse, K. S. Narendra, M. A. Reed, J. Szefer, H. Tang, L. Tassiulas, S. Tatikonda, J. R. Vaisnys, F. Xia. Joint appointments (with primary appointment in another department): J. Duncan, L. Staib, R. Yang. Adjunct faculty: R. Lethin. Emeritus faculty: R. C. Barker, P. M. Schultheiss.

Signal, Systems, and Networks: Linear system models, automatic control systems, representation of information in signals, transmission and storage of information, processing information by computers, networking and communication theory. Applications include bioengineering, digital signal processing, image processing, neural networks, robotics, sensors, and telecommunication systems.

Computer Engineering, Sensor Networks, Circuits and Systems: Study and design of digital circuits and computer systems; computer architecture; sensor networks; very-large-scale integrated (VLSI) circuit design, implementation, and testing. Applications include computing networks, computer design, biomedical instrumentation, bio-inspired circuits and systems.

Electronics, Photonics, and Nanodevices: Design, fabrication, and characterization of novel electronic, photonic, and nano devices; study of structure-property relationships in electronic and photonic materials. Applications include chem/bio-sensing, solid-state lighting, solar cells, micro/nano-electromechanical systems, non-volatile memory, and ultrafast devices.

Malone Engineering Center

Section 2
Aerospace/Aeronautical Engineering

This section contains a directory of institutions offering graduate work in aerospace/aeronautical engineering. Additional information about programs listed in the directory may be obtained by writing directly to the dean of a graduate school or chair of a department at the address given in the directory.

For programs offering related work, see also in this book *Engineering and Applied Sciences* and *Mechanical Engineering and Mechanics.* In another guide in this series:

Graduate Programs in the Physical Sciences, Mathematics, Agricultural Sciences, the Environment & Natural Resources
See *Geosciences* and *Physics*

CONTENTS

Program Directories

Aerospace/Aeronautical Engineering

Air Force Institute of Technology, Graduate School of Engineering and Management, Department of Aeronautics and Astronautics, Dayton, OH 45433-7765. Offers aeronautical engineering (MS, PhD); astronautical engineering (MS, PhD); materials science (MS, PhD); space operations (MS); systems engineering (MS, PhD). *Accreditation:* ABET (one or more programs are accredited). *Program availability:* Part-time. *Degree requirements:* For master's, thesis; for doctorate, thesis/dissertation. *Entrance requirements:* For master's and doctorate, GRE General Test, minimum GPA of 3.0, U.S. citizenship. *Faculty research:* Computational fluid dynamics, experimental aerodynamics, computational structural mechanics, experimental structural mechanics, aircraft and spacecraft stability and control.

American Public University System, AMU/APU Graduate Programs, Charles Town, WV 25414. Offers accounting (MBA, MS); applied business analytics (MBA, MS); criminal justice (MA), including business administration, emergency and disaster management, general (MA, MS); educational leadership (M Ed); emergency and disaster management (MA); entrepreneurship (MBA); environmental policy and management (MS), including environmental planning, environmental sustainability, fish and wildlife management, general (MA, MS), global environmental management; finance (MBA); general (MBA); government contracting and acquisition (MBA); health care administration (MBA); health information management (MS); history (MA), including American history, ancient and classical history, European history, global history, public history; homeland security (MA), including business administration, counterterrorism studies, criminal justice, cyber, emergency management and public health, intelligence studies, transportation security; homeland security resource allocation (MBA); humanities (MA); information technology (MS), including digital forensics, enterprise software development, information assurance and security, IT project management; information technology management (MBA); intelligence studies (MA), including criminal intelligence, cyber, general (MA, MS), homeland security, intelligence analysis, intelligence collection, intelligence management, intelligence operations, terrorism studies; international relations and conflict resolution (MA), including comparative and security issues, conflict resolution, international and transnational security issues, peacekeeping; legal studies (MA); management (MA), including strategic consulting; marketing (MBA); military history (MA), including American military history, American Revolution, civil war, war since 1945, World War II; military studies (MA), including joint warfare, strategic leadership; national security studies (MA), including cyber, general (MA, MS), homeland security, regional security studies, security and intelligence analysis, terrorism studies; nonprofit management (MBA); political science (MA), including American politics and government, comparative government and development, general (MA, MS), international relations, public policy; psychology (MA); public administration (MPA), including disaster management, environmental policy, health policy, human resources, national security, organizational management, security management; public health (MPH); reverse logistics management (MA); security management (MA); space studies (MS), including aerospace science, general (MA, MS), planetary science; sports and health sciences (MS); sports management (MBA); teaching (M Ed), including autism spectrum disorder, curriculum and instruction for elementary teachers, elementary reading, English language learners, instructional leadership, online learning, special education, STEAM (STEM plus the arts); transportation and logistics management (MA). *Program availability:* Part-time, evening/weekend, online only, 100% online. *Faculty:* 401 full-time (228 women), 1,678 part-time/adjunct (781 women). *Students:* 378 full-time (184 women), 8,455 part-time (3,484 women); includes 2,972 minority (1,552 Black or African American, non-Hispanic/Latino; 52 American Indian or Alaska Native, non-Hispanic/Latino; 211 Asian, non-Hispanic/Latino; 791 Hispanic/Latino; 70 Native Hawaiian or other Pacific Islander, non-Hispanic/Latino; 296 Two or more races, non-Hispanic/Latino), 109 international. Average age 37. In 2016, 3,185 master's awarded. *Degree requirements:* For master's, comprehensive exam or practicum. *Entrance requirements:* For master's, official transcript showing earned bachelor's degree from institution accredited by recognized accrediting body. Additional exam requirements/recommendations for international students: Required—TOEFL (minimum score 550 paper-based), IELTS (minimum score 6.5). *Application deadline:* Applications are processed on a rolling basis. Application fee: $0. Electronic applications accepted. *Expenses: Tuition:* Part-time $350 per credit hour. *Required fees:* $50 per course. *Financial support:* Scholarships/grants available. Financial award applicants required to submit FAFSA. *Unit head:* Dr. Karan Powell, President, 877-468-6268, Fax: 304-724-3780. *Application contact:* Terry Grant, Vice President of Enrollment Management, 877-468-6268, Fax: 304-724-3780, E-mail: info@apus.edu.
Website: http://www.apus.edu

Arizona State University at the Tempe campus, Ira A. Fulton Schools of Engineering, School for Engineering of Matter, Transport and Energy, Tempe, AZ 85281. Offers aerospace engineering (MS, PhD); chemical engineering (MS, PhD); materials science and engineering (MS, PhD); mechanical engineering (MS, PhD); solar energy engineering and commercialization (PSM). *Program availability:* Part-time, evening/weekend, online learning. Terminal master's awarded for partial completion of doctoral program. *Degree requirements:* For master's, thesis and oral defense (MS); applied project or comprehensive exam (MSE); interactive Program of Study (iPOS) submitted before completing 50 percent of required credit hours; for doctorate, comprehensive exam, thesis/dissertation, interactive Program of Study (iPOS) submitted before completing 50 percent of required credit hours. *Entrance requirements:* For master's, GRE, minimum GPA of 3.0 or equivalent in last 2 years of work leading to bachelor's degree; for doctorate, GRE, minimum GPA of 3.0 in last 2 years of work leading to bachelor's degree. Additional exam requirements/recommendations for international students: Required—TOEFL, IELTS, or PTE. Electronic applications accepted. *Expenses:* Contact institution. *Faculty research:* Electronic materials and packaging, materials for energy (batteries), adaptive/intelligent materials and structures, multiscale fluid mechanics, membranes, therapeutics and bioseparations, flexible structures, nanostructured materials, and micro/nano transport.

Auburn University, Graduate School, Ginn College of Engineering, Department of Aerospace Engineering, Auburn University, AL 36849. Offers MAE, MS, PhD. *Program availability:* Part-time. *Faculty:* 11 full-time (1 woman), 3 part-time/adjunct (0 women). *Students:* 17 full-time (4 women), 28 part-time (5 women); includes 5 minority (2 Black or African American, non-Hispanic/Latino; 1 American Indian or Alaska Native, non-Hispanic/Latino; 2 Hispanic/Latino), 12 international. Average age 26. 52 applicants, 48% accepted, 9 enrolled. In 2016, 9 master's, 3 doctorates awarded. *Degree requirements:* For master's, thesis (MS), exam; for doctorate, thesis/dissertation, exams. *Entrance requirements:* For master's and doctorate, GRE General Test. *Application deadline:* Applications are processed on a rolling basis. Application fee: $50 ($60 for international students). Electronic applications accepted. *Expenses:* Tuition, state resident: full-time $9072; part-time $504 per credit hour. Tuition, nonresident: full-time $27,216; part-time $1512 per credit hour. *Required fees:* $812 per semester. Tuition and fees vary according to degree level and program. *Financial support:* Fellowships, research assistantships, teaching assistantships, and Federal Work-Study available. Support available to part-time students. Financial award application deadline: 3/15; financial award applicants required to submit FAFSA. *Faculty research:* Aerodynamics, flight dynamics and simulation, propulsion, structures and aero elasticity, aerospace smart structures. *Unit head:* Dr. Joe Majdalani, Chair, 334-844-6800. *Application contact:* Dr. George Flowers, Dean of the Graduate School, 334-844-2125.
Website: http://www.eng.auburn.edu/department/ae/

California Institute of Technology, Division of Engineering and Applied Science, Option in Aeronautics, Pasadena, CA 91125-0001. Offers MS, PhD, Engr. Terminal master's awarded for partial completion of doctoral program. *Degree requirements:* For doctorate, thesis/dissertation. *Faculty research:* Computational fluid dynamics, technical fluid dynamics, structural mechanics, mechanics of fracture, aeronautical engineering and propulsion.

California Polytechnic State University, San Luis Obispo, College of Engineering, Department of Aerospace Engineering, San Luis Obispo, CA 93407. Offers MS. *Program availability:* Part-time. *Faculty:* 5 full-time (1 woman). *Students:* 8 full-time (0 women), 8 part-time (0 women); includes 4 minority (all Hispanic/Latino). Average age 25. 37 applicants, 38% accepted, 10 enrolled. In 2016, 22 master's awarded. *Degree requirements:* For master's, thesis. *Entrance requirements:* For master's, GRE. Additional exam requirements/recommendations for international students: Required—TOEFL (minimum score 80 iBT). *Application deadline:* For fall admission, 1/1 for domestic students, 3/1 for international students; for winter admission, 10/1 for domestic students; for spring admission, 1/1 for domestic students. Applications are processed on a rolling basis. Application fee: $55. Electronic applications accepted. *Expenses:* Tuition, state resident: full-time $6738; part-time $3906 per year. Tuition, nonresident: full-time $15,666; part-time $8370 per year. *Required fees:* $3603; $3141 per unit. $1047 per term. *Financial support:* Fellowships, research assistantships, teaching assistantships, career-related internships or fieldwork, scholarships/grants, and unspecified assistantships available. Financial award application deadline: 3/2; financial award applicants required to submit FAFSA. *Faculty research:* Space systems engineering, space vehicle design, aerodynamics, aerospace propulsion, dynamics and control. *Unit head:* Dr. Eric Mehiel, Graduate Coordinator, E-mail: emehiel@calpoly.edu.
Website: http://aero.calpoly.edu

California State Polytechnic University, Pomona, Program in Engineering, Pomona, CA 91768-2557. Offers MSE. *Program availability:* Part-time, evening/weekend. *Students:* 23 part-time (3 women); includes 5 minority (3 Asian, non-Hispanic/Latino; 2 Hispanic/Latino), 2 international. Average age 28. 11 applicants, 100% accepted, 10 enrolled. In 2016, 8 master's awarded. *Entrance requirements:* Additional exam requirements/recommendations for international students: Required—TOEFL. *Application deadline:* Applications are processed on a rolling basis. Application fee: $55. Electronic applications accepted. *Expenses:* Contact institution. *Financial support:* Application deadline: 3/2; applicants required to submit FAFSA. *Unit head:* Dr. Ali R. Ahmadi, Department Chair/Coordinator, 909-869-2470, Fax: 909-869-6920, E-mail: arahmadi@cpp.edu. *Application contact:* Andrew M. Wright, Director of Admissions, 909-869-3130, Fax: 909-869-4529, E-mail: awright@cpp.edu.
Website: http://www.cpp.edu/~engineering/ARO/masters.shtml

Carleton University, Faculty of Graduate Studies, Faculty of Engineering and Design, Department of Mechanical and Aerospace Engineering, Ottawa, ON K1S 5B6, Canada. Offers aerospace engineering (M Eng, MA Sc, PhD); materials engineering (M Eng, MA Sc); mechanical engineering (M Eng, MA Sc, PhD). *Degree requirements:* For master's, thesis optional; for doctorate, thesis/dissertation. *Entrance requirements:* For master's, honors degree; for doctorate, MA Sc or M Eng. Additional exam requirements/recommendations for international students: Required—TOEFL. *Faculty research:* Thermal fluids engineering, heat transfer, vehicle engineering.

Case Western Reserve University, School of Graduate Studies, Case School of Engineering, Department of Mechanical and Aerospace Engineering, Cleveland, OH 44106. Offers MS, PhD, MD/PhD. *Program availability:* Part-time, online learning. *Faculty:* 14 full-time (3 women). *Students:* 91 full-time (16 women), 10 part-time (4 women); includes 8 minority (1 Black or African American, non-Hispanic/Latino; 4 Asian, non-Hispanic/Latino; 3 Hispanic/Latino), 72 international. In 2016, 18 master's, 10 doctorates awarded. *Degree requirements:* For master's, thesis (for some programs); for doctorate, thesis/dissertation, qualifying exam, teaching experience. *Entrance requirements:* For master's and doctorate, GRE General Test. Additional exam requirements/recommendations for international students: Required—TOEFL. *Application deadline:* For fall admission, 7/1 priority date for domestic students. Applications are processed on a rolling basis. Application fee: $50. *Expenses: Tuition:* Full-time $42,576; part-time $1774 per credit hour. *Required fees:* $34. Tuition and fees vary according to course load and program. *Financial support:* In 2016–17, 5 fellowships with tuition reimbursements, 25 research assistantships with tuition reimbursements, 18 teaching assistantships were awarded; institutionally sponsored loans and tuition waivers (full and partial) also available. Financial award application deadline: 3/1; financial award applicants required to submit FAFSA. *Faculty research:* Musculoskeletal biomechanics, combustion diagnostics and computation, mechanical behavior of advanced materials and nanostructures, bio robotics. *Total annual research expenditures:* $5.3 million. *Unit head:* Dr. Robert Gao, Department Chair, 216-368-6045, Fax: 216-368-6445, E-mail: robert.gao@case.edu. *Application contact:* Carla Wilson, Student Affairs Coordinator, 216-368-4580, Fax: 216-368-3007, E-mail: cxw75@case.edu.
Website: http://www.engineering.case.edu/emae

The Citadel, The Military College of South Carolina, Citadel Graduate College, School of Engineering, Department of Mechanical Engineering, Charleston, SC 29409. Offers aeronautical engineering (Graduate Certificate); composites engineering (Graduate Certificate); manufacturing engineering (Graduate Certificate); mechanical engineering (MS); mechatronics engineering (Graduate Certificate); power and energy (Graduate Certificate). *Program availability:* Part-time, evening/weekend. *Students:* 1 part-time; minority (Asian, non-Hispanic/Latino). 1 applicant, 100% accepted, 1 enrolled. *Degree requirements:* For master's, 30 hours of coursework with minimum GPA of 3.0 on hours earned at The Citadel. *Entrance requirements:* For master's, GRE, 2 letters of recommendation; official transcript of baccalaureate degree from an ABET accredited engineering program or approved alternative. Additional exam requirements/recommendations for international students: Required—TOEFL (minimum score 550 paper-based; 79 iBT). *Application deadline:* Applications are processed on a rolling basis. Application fee: $40. Electronic applications accepted. *Expenses:* Tuition, state resident: full-time $5121; part-time $569 per credit hour. Tuition, nonresident: full-time $8613; part-time $957 per credit hour. *Required fees:* $90 per term. *Financial support:* Fellowships and unspecified assistantships available. Support available to part-time students. Financial award application deadline: 7/1; financial award applicants required to submit FAFSA. *Unit head:* Dr. Robert J. Rabb, Department Head, 843-953-0520, E-mail: rrabb@citadel.edu. *Application contact:* Dr. Tara Hornor, Associate Provost for

Planning, Assessment and Evaluation/Dean of Enrollment Management, 843-953-5089, E-mail: cgc@citadel.edu.
Website: http://www.citadel.edu/root/me

Concordia University, School of Graduate Studies, Faculty of Engineering and Computer Science, Program in Aerospace Engineering, Montréal, QC H3G 1M8, Canada. Offers M Eng. Program offered jointly with École Polytechnique de Montréal and McGill University. *Degree requirements:* For master's, thesis or alternative. *Faculty research:* Aeronautics and propulsion avionics and control, structures and materials, space engineering.

Cornell University, Graduate School, Graduate Fields of Engineering, Field of Aerospace Engineering, Ithaca, NY 14853. Offers M Eng, MS, PhD. Terminal master's awarded for partial completion of doctoral program. *Degree requirements:* For master's, thesis (MS); for doctorate, one foreign language, comprehensive exam, thesis/dissertation. *Entrance requirements:* For master's and doctorate, GRE General Test, 3 letters of recommendation. Additional exam requirements/recommendations for international students: Required—TOEFL (minimum score 550 paper-based; 77 iBT). Electronic applications accepted. *Faculty research:* Aerodynamics, fluid mechanics, turbulence, combustion/propulsion, aeroacoustics.

École Polytechnique de Montréal, Graduate Programs, Department of Mechanical Engineering, Montréal, QC H3C 3A7, Canada. Offers aerothermics (M Eng, M Sc A, PhD); applied mechanics (M Eng, M Sc A, PhD); tool design (M Eng, M Sc A, PhD). *Program availability:* Part-time, evening/weekend. *Degree requirements:* For master's, one foreign language, thesis; for doctorate, one foreign language, thesis/dissertation. *Entrance requirements:* For master's, minimum GPA of 2.75; for doctorate, minimum GPA of 3.0. *Faculty research:* Noise control and vibration, fatigue and creep, aerodynamics, composite materials, biomechanics, robotics.

Embry-Riddle Aeronautical University–Daytona, Department of Aerospace Engineering, Daytona Beach, FL 32114-3900. Offers aerodynamics and propulsion (MS, PhD); dynamics and control (MS, PhD); structures and materials (MS, PhD). *Program availability:* Part-time. *Faculty:* 27 full-time (3 women). *Students:* 109 full-time (19 women), 29 part-time (6 women); includes 9 minority (1 Black or African American, non-Hispanic/Latino; 1 American Indian or Alaska Native, non-Hispanic/Latino; 3 Asian, non-Hispanic/Latino; 2 Hispanic/Latino; 2 Two or more races, non-Hispanic/Latino), 102 international. Average age 25. 201 applicants, 26% accepted, 32 enrolled. In 2016, 61 master's awarded. *Degree requirements:* For master's, thesis or alternative; for doctorate, comprehensive exam, thesis/dissertation. *Entrance requirements:* For doctorate, GRE. Additional exam requirements/recommendations for international students: Required—TOEFL (minimum score 550 paper-based, 79 iBT) or IELTS (6). *Application deadline:* For fall admission, 1/15 priority date for domestic students; for spring admission, 9/15 priority date for domestic students; for summer admission, 4/1 priority date for domestic students. Applications are processed on a rolling basis. Application fee: $50. Electronic applications accepted. *Expenses:* Contact institution. *Financial support:* Research assistantships, career-related internships or fieldwork, scholarships/grants, unspecified assistantships, and on-campus employment available. Financial award application deadline: 3/15; financial award applicants required to submit FAFSA. *Faculty research:* Aeroacoustic modeling, rotorcraft aerodynamics, flow control, air breathing hypersonic and rocket propulsion, autonomous unpiloted air and ground vehicles, aircraft and spacecraft guidance, navigation and control, aero elasticity, composites, nanomaterials, smart materials, structural health monitoring, computational structural mechanics and design optimization. *Unit head:* Dr. Anastasios Lyrintzis, Professor/Chair, Aerospace Engineering, 386-226-7007, Fax: 386-226-6747, E-mail: lyrintzi@erau.edu. *Application contact:* Graduate Admissions, 386-226-6176, E-mail: graduate.admissions@erau.edu.
Website: http://daytonabeach.erau.edu/college-engineering/aerospace/index.html

Embry-Riddle Aeronautical University–Daytona, Department of Doctoral and Graduate Studies, Daytona Beach, FL 32114-3900. Offers aeronautics (MSA), including air traffic management, aviation safety management systems, aviation/aerospace education technology, aviation/aerospace management, aviation/aerospace operations, unmanned aircraft systems; aviation (PhD), including aviation safety and human factors, interdisciplinary, operations. Application fee for PhD is $100. *Program availability:* Part-time, primarily online, including three, six-day residencies at designated campuses. *Faculty:* 17 full-time (2 women), 3 part-time/adjunct (0 women). *Students:* 78 full-time (21 women), 46 part-time (16 women); includes 21 minority (5 Black or African American, non-Hispanic/Latino; 8 Asian, non-Hispanic/Latino; 3 Hispanic/Latino; 5 Two or more races, non-Hispanic/Latino), 40 international. Average age 36. 95 applicants, 51% accepted, 26 enrolled. In 2016, 21 master's, 3 doctorates awarded. *Degree requirements:* For master's, thesis; for doctorate, comprehensive exam, thesis/dissertation. *Entrance requirements:* For doctorate, GRE. Additional exam requirements/recommendations for international students: Required—TOEFL (minimum score 550 paper-based, 79 iBT) or IELTS (6). *Application deadline:* For fall admission, 3/1 for domestic students; for spring admission, 11/1 for domestic students; for summer admission, 4/1 for domestic students. Applications are processed on a rolling basis. Application fee: $50. Electronic applications accepted. *Expenses: Tuition:* Full-time $16,296; part-time $1358 per credit hour. *Required fees:* $1294; $647 per semester. One-time fee: $100 full-time. Tuition and fees vary according to course load, degree level and program. *Financial support:* Research assistantships, career-related internships or fieldwork, scholarships/grants, unspecified assistantships, and on-campus employment available. Financial award application deadline: 3/15; financial award applicants required to submit FAFSA. *Unit head:* Dr. Donald Metscher, Professor of Graduate Studies/Program Coordinator, 386-226-6100, E-mail: donald.metscher@erau.edu. *Application contact:* Graduate Admissions, 386-226-6176, E-mail: graduate.admissions@erau.edu.
Website: http://daytonabeach.erau.edu/degrees/master/aeronautics/index.html

Embry-Riddle Aeronautical University–Worldwide, Department of Aeronautics, Graduate Studies, Daytona Beach, FL 32114-3900. Offers aeronautics (MSA); aeronautics and design (MS); aviation maintenance (MAM); aviation/aerospace management (MS); education (MS); human factors (MS, MSHFS), including aerospace (MSHFS), systems engineering (MSHFS); occupational safety management (MS); operations (MS); safety/emergency response (MS); small unmanned aircraft system (SUAS) operation (MS); space systems (MS); unmanned aerospace systems (MS). *Program availability:* Part-time, evening/weekend, 100% online, blended/hybrid learning, EagleVision Classroom (between classrooms), EagleVision Home (faculty and students at home), and a blend of Classroom or Home. *Faculty:* 34 full-time (9 women), 146 part-time/adjunct (20 women). *Students:* 865 full-time (156 women), 998 part-time (163 women); includes 434 minority (179 Black or African American, non-Hispanic/Latino; 7 American Indian or Alaska Native, non-Hispanic/Latino; 65 Asian, non-Hispanic/Latino; 71 Hispanic/Latino; 4 Native Hawaiian or other Pacific Islander, non-Hispanic/Latino; 108 Two or more races, non-Hispanic/Latino), 128 international. Average age 37. In 2016, 572 master's awarded. *Degree requirements:* For master's, comprehensive exam (for some programs), thesis (for some programs), thesis or capstone project. *Entrance requirements:* For master's, GRE (for MSHFS). Additional exam requirements/recommendations for international students: Required—TOEFL (minimum score 550 paper-based, 79 iBT) or IELTS (6). *Application deadline:* Applications are processed on

a rolling basis. Application fee: $50. Electronic applications accepted. *Expenses:* $620 per credit (for civilians), $530 per credit (for military). *Financial support:* Career-related internships or fieldwork and scholarships/grants available. Financial award applicants required to submit FAFSA. *Faculty research:* Aerodynamics statistical design and educational development. *Unit head:* Ian R. McAndrew, PhD, Department Chair, E-mail: ian.mcandrew@erau.edu. *Application contact:* Worldwide Campus, 800-522-6787, E-mail: worldwide@erau.edu.
Website: http://worldwide.erau.edu/colleges/aeronautics/department-aeronautics-graduate-studies/

Embry-Riddle Aeronautical University–Worldwide, Department of Engineering Sciences, Daytona Beach, FL 32114-3900. Offers aerospace engineering (MS); systems engineering (M Sys E), including engineering management, technical. *Program availability:* Part-time, evening/weekend, 100% online, blended/hybrid learning. *Entrance requirements:* For master's, GRE required for MSAE. Additional exam requirements/recommendations for international students: Required—TOEFL (minimum score 550 paper-based; 79 iBT), IELTS (minimum score 6), TOEFL or IELTS accepted. Electronic applications accepted. *Expenses:* Contact institution.

Florida Institute of Technology, College of Aeronautics, Melbourne, FL 32901-6975. Offers airport development and management (MSA); applied aviation safety (MSA); aviation human factors (MS); aviation safety (MSA); aviation sciences (PhD); human factors in aeronautics (MS). *Program availability:* Part-time, evening/weekend, 100% online. *Faculty:* 10 full-time (4 women), 1 part-time/adjunct (0 women). *Students:* 54 full-time (16 women), 67 part-time (13 women); includes 16 minority (6 Black or African American, non-Hispanic/Latino; 1 American Indian or Alaska Native, non-Hispanic/Latino; 2 Asian, non-Hispanic/Latino; 7 Hispanic/Latino), 46 international. Average age 33. 144 applicants, 47% accepted, 42 enrolled. In 2016, 51 master's, 4 doctorates awarded. *Degree requirements:* For master's, thesis (for some programs), thesis or capstone project; for doctorate, thesis/dissertation (for some programs). *Entrance requirements:* For master's, GRE, minimum GPA of 3.0, 3 letters of recommendation, resume, statement of objectives; for doctorate, GRE, minimum GPA of 3.2; master's degree in an aviation field (for international applicants). Additional exam requirements/recommendations for international students: Required—TOEFL (minimum score 550 paper-based; 79 iBT). *Application deadline:* For fall admission, 4/1 for international students; for spring admission, 9/30 for international students. Applications are processed on a rolling basis. Electronic applications accepted. *Expenses: Tuition:* Full-time $22,338; part-time $1241 per credit hour. *Required fees:* $250. Tuition and fees vary according to degree level, campus/location and program. *Financial support:* In 2016–17, 1 research assistantship with partial tuition reimbursement, 2 teaching assistantships with partial tuition reimbursements were awarded; career-related internships or fieldwork, institutionally sponsored loans, tuition waivers (partial), and tuition remissions also available. Support available to part-time students. Financial award application deadline: 3/1; financial award applicants required to submit FAFSA. *Faculty research:* Aircraft cockpit design, medical human factors, operating room human factors, hypobaric chamber operations and effects, aviation professional education. *Unit head:* Dr. Korhan Oyman, Dean, 321-674-8971, Fax: 321-674-7368, E-mail: koyman@fit.edu. *Application contact:* Cheryl A. Brown, Associate Director of Graduate Admissions, 321-674-7581, Fax: 321-723-9468, E-mail: cbrown@fit.edu.
Website: http://coa.fit.edu

Florida Institute of Technology, College of Engineering, Program in Aerospace Engineering, Melbourne, FL 32901-6975. Offers MS, PhD. *Program availability:* Part-time. *Students:* 30 full-time (5 women), 27 part-time (4 women); includes 6 minority (3 Black or African American, non-Hispanic/Latino; 3 Asian, non-Hispanic/Latino), 22 international. Average age 26. 164 applicants, 30% accepted, 14 enrolled. In 2016, 13 master's awarded. *Degree requirements:* For master's, comprehensive exam, 30 credit hours; thesis or additional courses plus final exam; for doctorate, comprehensive exam, thesis/dissertation, 42 credit hours. *Entrance requirements:* For master's, GRE General Test, GRE Subject Test, minimum GPA of 3.0; for doctorate, GRE General Test, GRE Subject Test, minimum GPA of 3.2, resume, 3 letters of recommendation, statement of objectives. Additional exam requirements/recommendations for international students: Required—TOEFL (minimum score 550 paper-based; 79 iBT). *Application deadline:* Applications are processed on a rolling basis. Application fee: $50. Electronic applications accepted. *Expenses: Tuition:* Full-time $22,338; part-time $1241 per credit hour. *Required fees:* $250. Tuition and fees vary according to degree level, campus/location and program. *Financial support:* Research assistantships with tuition reimbursements, teaching assistantships with tuition reimbursements, career-related internships or fieldwork, institutionally sponsored loans, and tuition remissions available. Financial award application deadline: 3/1; financial award applicants required to submit FAFSA. *Faculty research:* Aerodynamics and fluid dynamics, aerospace structures and materials, combustion and propulsion, hydro dynamics stability, computational fluid dynamics. *Unit head:* Dr. Chelakara Subramanian, Program Chair, 321-674-7614, Fax: 321-674-8813, E-mail: subraman@fit.edu. *Application contact:* Cheryl A. Brown, Associate Director of Graduate Admissions, 321-674-7581, Fax: 321-723-9468, E-mail: cbrown@fit.edu.
Website: http://coe.fit.edu

Florida Institute of Technology, College of Engineering, Program in Flight Test Engineering, Melbourne, FL 32901-6975. Offers MS. *Students:* 3 full-time (0 women), 7 part-time (3 women); includes 2 minority (1 Hispanic/Latino; 1 Two or more races, non-Hispanic/Latino). Average age 31. 12 applicants, 67% accepted, 8 enrolled. In 2016, 1 master's awarded. *Degree requirements:* For master's, comprehensive exam (for some programs), thesis optional, 30 credit hours. *Entrance requirements:* For master's, GRE General Test, undergraduate degree in aerospace engineering. Additional exam requirements/recommendations for international students: Required—TOEFL (minimum score 550 paper-based; 79 iBT). *Application deadline:* Applications are processed on a rolling basis. Electronic applications accepted. *Expenses: Tuition:* Full-time $22,338; part-time $1241 per credit hour. *Required fees:* $250. Tuition and fees vary according to degree level, campus/location and program. *Financial support:* Applicants required to submit FAFSA. *Unit head:* Dr. Hamid Hefazi, Department Head, 321-674-7255, E-mail: hhefazi@fit.edu. *Application contact:* Cheryl A. Brown, Associate Director of Graduate Admissions, 321-674-7581, Fax: 321-723-9468, E-mail: cbrown@fit.edu.
Website: http://www.fit.edu/programs/

Florida Institute of Technology, Extended Studies Division, Melbourne, FL 32901-6975. Offers acquisition and contract management (MS); aerospace engineering (MS); business administration (MBA, DBA); computer information systems (MS); computer science (MS); electrical engineering (MS); engineering management (MS); human resources management (MS); logistics management (MS), including humanitarian and disaster relief logistics; management (MS), including acquisition and contract management, e-business, human resources management, information systems, logistics management, management, transportation management; material acquisition management (MS); mechanical engineering (MS); operations research (MS); project management (MS), including information systems, operations research; public administration (MPA); quality management (MS); software engineering (MS); space systems (MS); space systems management (MS); supply chain management (MS); systems management (MS), including information systems, operations research;

technology management (MS). *Program availability:* Part-time, evening/weekend, online learning. *Faculty:* 10 full-time (3 women), 122 part-time/adjunct (29 women). *Students:* 131 full-time (58 women), 997 part-time (348 women); includes 389 minority (231 Black or African American, non-Hispanic/Latino; 9 American Indian or Alaska Native, non-Hispanic/Latino; 26 Asian, non-Hispanic/Latino; 99 Hispanic/Latino; 3 Native Hawaiian or other Pacific Islander, non-Hispanic/Latino; 21 Two or more races, non-Hispanic/Latino), 53 international. Average age 36. 962 applicants, 48% accepted, 323 enrolled. In 2016, 403 master's awarded. *Degree requirements:* For master's, comprehensive exam (for some programs). *Entrance requirements:* For master's, GMAT or resume showing 8 years of supervised experience, minimum GPA of 3.0, 2 letters of recommendation, resume. Additional exam requirements/recommendations for international students: Required—TOEFL (minimum score 550 paper-based; 79 iBT). *Application deadline:* For fall admission, 4/1 for international students; for spring admission, 9/30 for international students. Applications are processed on a rolling basis. Electronic applications accepted. *Expenses:* Contact institution. *Financial support:* Application deadline: 3/1; applicants required to submit FAFSA. *Unit head:* Dr. Theodore R. Richardson, III, Dean, 321-674-8123, Fax: 321-674-7597, E-mail: trichardson@fit.edu. *Application contact:* Carolyn Farrior, Director of Graduate Admissions, Online Learning and Off-Campus Programs, 321-674-7118, Fax: 321-674-8216, E-mail: cfarrior@fit.edu.
Website: http://es.fit.edu

The George Washington University, School of Engineering and Applied Science, Department of Mechanical and Aerospace Engineering, Washington, DC 20052. Offers MS, PhD, App Sc, Engr, Graduate Certificate. *Program availability:* Part-time, evening/weekend. *Faculty:* 22 full-time (4 women). *Students:* 81 full-time (11 women), 71 part-time (10 women); includes 13 minority (2 Black or African American, non-Hispanic/Latino; 4 Asian, non-Hispanic/Latino; 3 Hispanic/Latino; 1 Native Hawaiian or other Pacific Islander, non-Hispanic/Latino; 3 Two or more races, non-Hispanic/Latino), 103 international. Average age 28. 248 applicants, 77% accepted, 42 enrolled. In 2016, 28 master's, 10 doctorates awarded. *Degree requirements:* For master's, thesis optional; for doctorate, thesis/dissertation, final and qualifying exams. *Entrance requirements:* For master's, appropriate bachelor's degree, minimum GPA of 3.0; for doctorate, GRE (if highest earned degree is BS), appropriate bachelor's or master's degree, minimum GPA of 3.4; for other advanced degree, appropriate master's degree, minimum GPA of 3.0. Additional exam requirements/recommendations for international students: Required—TOEFL or The George Washington University English as a Foreign Language Test. *Application deadline:* For fall admission, 3/1 priority date for domestic students; for spring admission, 10/1 for domestic students. Applications are processed on a rolling basis. Application fee: $75. *Financial support:* In 2016–17, 51 students received support. Fellowships with tuition reimbursements available, research assistantships, teaching assistantships with tuition reimbursements available, career-related internships or fieldwork, and institutionally sponsored loans available. Financial award application deadline: 3/1; financial award applicants required to submit FAFSA. *Unit head:* Dr. Michael Plesniak, Chair, 202-994-9800, E-mail: maeng@gwu.edu. *Application contact:* Adina Lav, Marketing, Recruiting and Admissions, 202-994-5827, Fax: 202-994-0909, E-mail: engineering@gwu.edu.

Georgia Institute of Technology, Graduate Studies, College of Engineering, School of Aerospace Engineering, Atlanta, GA 30332-0001. Offers MS, PhD. *Program availability:* Part-time. Terminal master's awarded for partial completion of doctoral program. *Degree requirements:* For master's, thesis optional; for doctorate, thesis/dissertation. *Entrance requirements:* For master's and doctorate, GRE. Additional exam requirements/recommendations for international students: Required—TOEFL (minimum score 550 paper-based; 79 iBT). Electronic applications accepted. *Faculty research:* Structural mechanics and dynamics, fluid mechanics, flight mechanics and controls, combustion and propulsion, system design and optimization.

Illinois Institute of Technology, Graduate College, Armour College of Engineering, Department of Mechanical, Materials and Aerospace Engineering, Chicago, IL 60616. Offers manufacturing engineering (MAS, MS); materials science and engineering (MAS, MS, PhD); mechanical and aerospace engineering (MAS, MS, PhD), including economics (MS), energy (MS), environment (MS). *Program availability:* Part-time, evening/weekend, online learning. Terminal master's awarded for partial completion of doctoral program. *Degree requirements:* For master's, comprehensive exam (for some programs), thesis (for some programs); for doctorate, comprehensive exam, thesis/dissertation. *Entrance requirements:* For master's and doctorate, GRE General Test (minimum score 1000 Quantitative and Verbal, 3.0 Analytical Writing), minimum undergraduate GPA of 3.0. Additional exam requirements/recommendations for international students: Required—TOEFL (minimum score 550 paper-based; 80 iBT). Electronic applications accepted. *Faculty research:* Fluid dynamics, metallurgical and materials engineering, solids and structures, computational mechanics, computer added design and manufacturing, thermal sciences, dynamic analysis and control of complex systems.

Inter American University of Puerto Rico, Bayamón Campus, Graduate School, Bayamón, PR 00957. Offers biology (MS), including environmental sciences and ecology, molecular biotechnology; electrical engineering (ME), including control system, potence system; human resources (MBA); mechanical engineering (ME, MS), including aerospace, energy. *Program availability:* Part-time, evening/weekend. *Faculty:* 12 full-time (5 women), 4 part-time/adjunct (2 women). *Students:* 7 full-time (5 women), 115 part-time (69 women); includes 119 minority (1 Black or African American, non-Hispanic/Latino; 118 Hispanic/Latino). Average age 28. 94 applicants, 72% accepted, 56 enrolled. In 2016, 22 master's awarded. *Degree requirements:* For master's, comprehensive exam, research project. *Entrance requirements:* For master's, EXADEP, GRE General Test, letters of recommendation. *Application deadline:* For fall admission, 7/1 for domestic students, 5/1 priority date for international students; for winter admission, 11/15 priority date for domestic and international students; for spring admission, 2/15 priority date for domestic and international students. Application fee: $31. *Expenses: Tuition:* Part-time $207 per credit. *Required fees:* $328 per semester. *Unit head:* Prof. Juan F. Martinez, Chancellor, 787-279-1200 Ext. 2295, Fax: 787-279-2205, E-mail: jmartinez@bayamon.inter.edu. *Application contact:* Aurelis Baez, Director of Student Services, 787-279-1912 Ext. 2017, Fax: 787-279-2205, E-mail: abaez@bayamon.inter.edu.

Iowa State University of Science and Technology, Department of Aerospace Engineering and Engineering Mechanics, Ames, IA 50011. Offers aerospace engineering (M Eng, MS, PhD); engineering mechanics (M Eng, MS, PhD). *Degree requirements:* For master's, thesis (for some programs); for doctorate, thesis/dissertation. *Entrance requirements:* For master's and doctorate, GRE General Test, resume. Additional exam requirements/recommendations for international students: Required—TOEFL (minimum score 550 paper-based; 80 iBT), IELTS (minimum score 6.5). *Application deadline:* For fall admission, 1/1 priority date for domestic and international students; for spring admission, 9/1 priority date for domestic and international students. Application fee: $60 ($90 for international students). Electronic applications accepted. *Application contact:* Sara Goplin, Application Contact, 515-294-9669, Fax: 515-294-3262, E-mail: aere-info@iastate.edu.
Website: http://www.aere.iastate.edu/

Johns Hopkins University, Engineering Program for Professionals, Part-time Program in Space Systems Engineering, Baltimore, MD 21218. Offers MS. *Program availability:* 100% online, blended/hybrid learning. *Faculty:* 3 part-time/adjunct (0 women). *Students:* 53 part-time (15 women); includes 10 minority (1 Black or African American, non-Hispanic/Latino; 2 Asian, non-Hispanic/Latino; 5 Hispanic/Latino; 2 Two or more races, non-Hispanic/Latino), 2 international. Average age 30. 28 applicants, 79% accepted, 13 enrolled. *Entrance requirements:* For master's, undergraduate degree in a technical discipline; at least two years of experience in the space technology or space science field; minimum of two years of relevant work experience; resume; official transcripts from all college studies. Additional exam requirements/recommendations for international students: Required—TOEFL (minimum score 600 paper-based; 100 iBT). Application fee: $0. Electronic applications accepted. *Unit head:* Dr. Clint Edwards, Program Chair, 240-228-0816, E-mail: clint.edwards@jhuapl.edu. *Application contact:* Doug Schiller, Admissions Director, 410-516-2300, Fax: 410-579-8049, E-mail: schiller@jhu.edu.
Website: http://ep.jhu.edu/graduate-programs/space-systems-engineering

Massachusetts Institute of Technology, School of Engineering, Department of Aeronautics and Astronautics, Cambridge, MA 02139. Offers aeronautics and astronautics (SM, PhD, Sc D, EAA); aerospace computational engineering (PhD, Sc D); air transportation systems (PhD, Sc D); air-breathing propulsion (PhD, Sc D); aircraft systems engineering (PhD, Sc D); autonomous systems (PhD, Sc D); communications and networks (PhD, Sc D); controls (PhD, Sc D); humans in aerospace (PhD, Sc D); materials and structures (PhD, Sc D); space propulsion (PhD, Sc D); space systems (PhD, Sc D); SM/MBA. *Faculty:* 36 full-time (8 women). *Students:* 223 full-time (39 women); includes 37 minority (3 Black or African American, non-Hispanic/Latino; 20 Asian, non-Hispanic/Latino; 9 Hispanic/Latino; 5 Two or more races, non-Hispanic/Latino), 90 international. Average age 26. 618 applicants, 14% accepted, 58 enrolled. In 2016, 58 master's, 28 doctorates, 1 other advanced degree awarded. *Degree requirements:* For master's, thesis; for doctorate, comprehensive exam, thesis/dissertation, minimum cumulative GPA of 4.4 on 5.0 scale; for EAA, comprehensive exam, thesis. *Entrance requirements:* For master's and doctorate, GRE General Test. Additional exam requirements/recommendations for international students: Required—TOEFL, IELTS. *Application deadline:* For fall admission, 12/15 for domestic and international students. Application fee: $75. Electronic applications accepted. *Expenses: Tuition:* Full-time $46,400; part-time $725 per credit. One-time fee: $312 full-time. Full-time tuition and fees vary according to course load and program. *Financial support:* In 2016–17, 188 students received support, including 61 fellowships (averaging $42,500 per year), 137 research assistantships (averaging $36,800 per year), 13 teaching assistantships (averaging $39,600 per year); Federal Work-Study, institutionally sponsored loans, scholarships/grants, traineeships, health care benefits, unspecified assistantships, and resident tutors also available. Support available to part-time students. Financial award application deadline: 5/1; financial award applicants required to submit FAFSA. *Faculty research:* Vehicle design; information sciences; computation; human-system collaboration; atmosphere and space sciences; complex systems. *Total annual research expenditures:* $28.9 million. *Unit head:* Prof. Jaime Peraire, Department Head, 617-258-7537, E-mail: aeroastro-info@mit.edu. *Application contact:* 617-253-0043, E-mail: aagradinfo@mit.edu.
Website: http://aeroastro.mit.edu/

McGill University, Faculty of Graduate and Postdoctoral Studies, Faculty of Engineering, Department of Mechanical Engineering, Montréal, QC H3A 2T5, Canada. Offers aerospace (M Eng); manufacturing management (MMM); mechanical engineering (M Eng, M Sc, PhD).

Middle Tennessee State University, College of Graduate Studies, College of Basic and Applied Sciences, Department of Aerospace, Murfreesboro, TN 37132. Offers aerospace education (M Ed); aviation administration (MS). *Program availability:* Part-time, evening/weekend, online learning. *Degree requirements:* For master's, comprehensive exam, thesis optional. *Entrance requirements:* For master's, GRE General Test or MAT. Additional exam requirements/recommendations for international students: Required—TOEFL (minimum score 525 paper-based; 71 iBT) or IELTS (minimum score 6). Electronic applications accepted.

Mississippi State University, Bagley College of Engineering, Department of Aerospace Engineering, Mississippi State, MS 39762. Offers aerospace engineering (MS); engineering (PhD), including aerospace engineering. *Program availability:* Part-time. *Faculty:* 18 full-time (2 women), 2 part-time/adjunct (1 woman). *Students:* 51 full-time (16 women), 26 part-time (8 women); includes 6 minority (1 Black or African American, non-Hispanic/Latino; 1 Asian, non-Hispanic/Latino; 4 Hispanic/Latino), 45 international. Average age 26. 87 applicants, 55% accepted, 34 enrolled. In 2016, 23 master's awarded. *Degree requirements:* For master's, comprehensive exam, thesis optional, oral exam; for doctorate, comprehensive exam, thesis/dissertation. *Entrance requirements:* For master's, GRE (for graduates from program not accredited by EAC/ABET), bachelor's degree in engineering with minimum GPA of 3.0 from junior and senior years; for doctorate, GRE, bachelor's or master's degree in aerospace engineering or closely-related field. Additional exam requirements/recommendations for international students: Required—TOEFL (minimum score 550 paper-based; 79 iBT); Recommended—IELTS (minimum score 6.5). *Application deadline:* For fall admission, 7/1 for domestic students, 5/1 for international students; for spring admission, 11/1 for domestic students, 9/1 for international students. Applications are processed on a rolling basis. Application fee: $60. Electronic applications accepted. *Expenses:* Tuition, state resident: full-time $7670; part-time $852.50 per credit hour. Tuition, nonresident: full-time $20,790; part-time $2310.50 per credit hour. Part-time tuition and fees vary according to course load. *Financial support:* In 2016–17, 8 research assistantships with partial tuition reimbursements (averaging $15,276 per year), 8 teaching assistantships with partial tuition reimbursements (averaging $15,513 per year) were awarded; Federal Work-Study, institutionally sponsored loans, and unspecified assistantships also available. Financial award application deadline: 4/1; financial award applicants required to submit FAFSA. *Faculty research:* Computational fluid dynamics, flight mechanics, aerodynamics, composite structures, prototype development. *Total annual research expenditures:* $4.8 million. *Unit head:* Dr. Davy Belk, Department Head and Professor, 662-325-3623, Fax: 662-325-7730, E-mail: davy.belk@ae.msstate.edu. *Application contact:* Doretta Martin, Senior Admissions Assistant, 662-325-9514, E-mail: dmartin@grad.msstate.edu.
Website: http://www.ae.msstate.edu/

Missouri University of Science and Technology, Graduate School, Department of Mechanical and Aerospace Engineering, Rolla, MO 65409. Offers aerospace engineering (MS, PhD); mechanical engineering (MS, DE, PhD). *Program availability:* Part-time, evening/weekend. Terminal master's awarded for partial completion of doctoral program. *Degree requirements:* For master's, thesis optional; for doctorate, comprehensive exam, thesis/dissertation. *Entrance requirements:* For master's, GRE General Test (minimum score 1100 verbal and quantitative, writing 3.5), minimum GPA of 3.0; for doctorate, GRE General Test (minimum score: verbal and quantitative 1100, writing 3.5), minimum GPA of 3.5. Additional exam requirements/recommendations for international students: Required—TOEFL (minimum score 550 paper-based). Electronic applications accepted. *Faculty research:* Dynamics and controls, acoustics, computational fluid dynamics, space mechanics, hypersonics.

Naval Postgraduate School, Departments and Academic Groups, Department of Defense Analysis, Monterey, CA 93943. Offers command and control (MS); communications (MS); defense analysis (MS), including astronautics; financial management (MS); information operations (MS); irregular warfare (MS); national security affairs (MS); operations analysis (MS); special operations (MA, MS), including command and control (MS), communications (MS), financial management (MS), information operations (MS), irregular warfare (MS), national security affairs, operations analysis (MS), tactile missiles (MS), terrorist operations and financing (MS); tactile missiles (MS); terrorist operations and financing (MS). Program only open to commissioned officers of the United States and friendly nations and selected United States federal civilian employees. *Program availability:* Part-time. *Degree requirements:* For master's, thesis. *Faculty research:* CTF Global Ecco Project, Afghanistan endgames, core lab Philippines project, Defense Manpower Data Center (DMDC) data vulnerability.

Naval Postgraduate School, Departments and Academic Groups, Department of Mechanical and Aerospace Engineering, Monterey, CA 93943. Offers astronautical engineer (AstE); astronautical engineering (MS); engineering science (MS), including astronautical engineering, mechanical engineering; mechanical and aerospace engineering (PhD); mechanical engineering (MS). Program only open to commissioned officers of the United States and friendly nations and selected United States federal civilian employees. *Accreditation:* ABET (one or more programs are accredited). *Program availability:* Part-time, online learning. *Degree requirements:* For master's, thesis (for some programs), capstone or research/dissertation paper (for some programs); for doctorate, thesis/dissertation; for AstE, thesis. *Faculty research:* Sensors and actuators, new materials and methods, mechanics of materials, laser and material interaction, energy harvesting and storage.

Naval Postgraduate School, Departments and Academic Groups, Space Systems Academic Group, Monterey, CA 93943. Offers applied physics (MS); astronautical engineering (MS); computer science (MS); electrical engineering (MS); mechanical engineering (MS); space systems (Engr); space systems operations (MS). Program only open to commissioned officers of the United States and friendly nations and selected United States federal civilian employees. *Program availability:* Part-time. *Degree requirements:* For master's and Engr, thesis; for doctorate, thesis/dissertation. *Faculty research:* Military applications for space; space reconnaissance and remote sensing; radiation-hardened electronics for space; design, construction and operations of small satellites; satellite communications systems.

New Mexico State University, College of Engineering, Department of Mechanical Engineering, Las Cruces, NM 88003. Offers aerospace engineering (MSAE); mechanical engineering (MSME, PhD). *Program availability:* Part-time. *Faculty:* 16 full-time (1 woman). *Students:* 28 full-time (3 women), 12 part-time (2 women); includes 8 minority (7 Hispanic/Latino; 1 Two or more races, non-Hispanic/Latino), 24 international. Average age 28. 81 applicants, 35% accepted, 10 enrolled. In 2016, 14 master's, 6 doctorates awarded. *Degree requirements:* For master's, thesis (for some programs); for doctorate, comprehensive exam, thesis/dissertation, qualifying exam. *Entrance requirements:* For master's and doctorate, GRE, minimum GPA of 3.0. Additional exam requirements/recommendations for international students: Required—TOEFL (minimum score 550 paper-based; 79 iBT), IELTS (minimum score 6.5). *Application deadline:* For fall admission, 5/1 priority date for domestic students, 3/1 for international students; for spring admission, 11/1 for domestic students, 10/1 for international students. Applications are processed on a rolling basis. Application fee: $40 ($50 for international students). Electronic applications accepted. *Expenses:* Tuition, state resident: full-time $4086. Tuition, nonresident: full-time $14,254. *Required fees:* $853. Tuition and fees vary according to course load. *Financial support:* In 2016–17, 33 students received support, including 6 research assistantships (averaging $17,233 per year), 20 teaching assistantships (averaging $16,199 per year); career-related internships or fieldwork, Federal Work-Study, scholarships/grants, traineeships, health care benefits, and unspecified assistantships also available. Support available to part-time students. Financial award application deadline: 3/1. *Faculty research:* Combustion and propulsion, gas dynamics and supersonic flows; experimental and fluid dynamics; nonlinear dynamics and control; robotics and mechatronics; renewable/alternative energy; smart structure and energy harvesting; experimental and computational mechanics; multiscale modeling and nanosystem; micromechanics of materials; aeroelasticity and flutter; design optimization; heat transfer and energy efficiency; polymer and composite materials; thermal and thermomechanical storage. *Total annual research expenditures:* $741,093. *Unit head:* Dr. Ruey-Hung Chen, Department Head, 575-646-1945, Fax: 575-646-6111, E-mail: chenrh@nmsu.edu. *Application contact:* Dr. Young Ho Park, Graduate Program Director, 575-646-3092, Fax: 575-646-6111, E-mail: ypark@nmsu.edu.
Website: http://mae.nmsu.edu/

North Carolina State University, Graduate School, College of Engineering, Department of Mechanical and Aerospace Engineering, Program in Aerospace Engineering, Raleigh, NC 27695. Offers MS, PhD. *Program availability:* Online learning. *Degree requirements:* For master's, thesis (for some programs), oral exam; for doctorate, thesis/dissertation, oral and preliminary exams. *Entrance requirements:* For master's and doctorate, GRE General Test. Additional exam requirements/recommendations for international students: Required—TOEFL (minimum score 550 paper-based). Electronic applications accepted. *Faculty research:* Aerodynamics, computational fluid dynamics, flight research, smart structures, propulsion.

The Ohio State University, Graduate School, College of Engineering, Department of Mechanical and Aerospace Engineering, Columbus, OH 43210. Offers aerospace engineering (MS, PhD); mechanical engineering (MS, PhD); nuclear engineering (MS, PhD). *Faculty:* 69. *Students:* 374 full-time (60 women), 12 part-time (1 woman); includes 27 minority (5 Black or African American, non-Hispanic/Latino; 9 Asian, non-Hispanic/Latino; 6 Hispanic/Latino; 7 Two or more races, non-Hispanic/Latino), 194 international. Average age 25. In 2016, 98 master's, 35 doctorates awarded. *Degree requirements:* For doctorate, thesis/dissertation. *Entrance requirements:* For master's and doctorate, GRE. Additional exam requirements/recommendations for international students: Required—TOEFL (minimum score 550 paper-based; 79 iBT), Michigan English Language Assessment Battery (minimum score 82); Recommended—IELTS (minimum score 7). *Application deadline:* For fall admission, 11/30 priority date for domestic and international students; for spring admission, 10/1 for domestic and international students. Applications are processed on a rolling basis. Application fee: $60 ($70 for international students). Electronic applications accepted. *Financial support:* Fellowships, research assistantships, teaching assistantships, career-related internships or fieldwork, Federal Work-Study, institutionally sponsored loans, and unspecified assistantships available. Support available to part-time students. *Unit head:* Dr. Vish Subramaniam, Chair, 614-292-6096, E-mail: subramaniam.1@osu.edu. *Application contact:* Janeen Sands, Graduate Program Administrator, 614-247-6605, Fax: 614-292-3656, E-mail: maegradadmissions@osu.edu.
Website: http://mae.osu.edu/

Old Dominion University, Frank Batten College of Engineering and Technology, Programs in Aerospace Engineering, Norfolk, VA 23529. Offers ME, MS, D Eng, PhD. *Program availability:* Part-time, evening/weekend, 100% online, blended/hybrid learning. *Faculty:* 22 full-time (2 women). *Students:* 9 full-time (3 women), 22 part-time (1 woman); includes 5 minority (1 Black or African American, non-Hispanic/Latino; 1 Asian, non-Hispanic/Latino; 3 Hispanic/Latino), 6 international. Average age 29. 50 applicants, 60% accepted, 10 enrolled. In 2016, 10 master's, 4 doctorates awarded. *Degree requirements:* For master's, comprehensive exam, thesis optional, thesis (MS), exam/project (ME); for doctorate, comprehensive exam, thesis/dissertation, candidacy exam, proposal, exam. *Entrance requirements:* For master's, GRE, minimum GPA of 3.0; for doctorate, GRE, minimum GPA of 3.5. Additional exam requirements/recommendations for international students: Required—TOEFL (minimum score 550 paper-based; 79 iBT). *Application deadline:* For fall admission, 7/1 priority date for domestic students, 5/1 priority date for international students; for spring admission, 10/1 priority date for domestic students, 9/1 priority date for international students. Applications are processed on a rolling basis. Application fee: $50. Electronic applications accepted. *Expenses:* $478 per credit, in-state full-time tuition. *Financial support:* In 2016–17, 4 students received support, including 3 fellowships with tuition reimbursements available (averaging $16,000 per year), 30 research assistantships with tuition reimbursements available (averaging $16,000 per year); career-related internships or fieldwork, scholarships/grants, and unspecified assistantships also available. Financial award application deadline: 2/15; financial award applicants required to submit FAFSA. *Faculty research:* Computational fluid dynamics, experimental fluid dynamics, structural mechanics, dynamics and control, microfluidics. *Total annual research expenditures:* $1.8 million. *Unit head:* Dr. Sebastian Bawab, Chair, 757-683-5637, Fax: 757-683-5344, E-mail: sbawab@odu.edu. *Application contact:* Dr. Han Bao, Graduate Program Director, 757-683-4922, Fax: 757-683-3200, E-mail: hbao@aero.odu.edu.
Website: http://www.odu.edu/academics/programs/masters/aerospace-engineering

Penn State University Park, Graduate School, College of Engineering, Department of Aerospace Engineering, University Park, PA 16802. Offers M Eng, MS, PhD. *Unit head:* Dr. Amr S. Elnashai, Dean, 814-865-7537, Fax: 814-863-4749. *Application contact:* Lori Hawn, Director, Graduate Student Services, 814-865-1795, Fax: 814-863-4627, E-mail: l-gswww@lists.psu.edu.
Website: http://aero.psu.edu/

Princeton University, Graduate School, School of Engineering and Applied Science, Department of Mechanical and Aerospace Engineering, Princeton, NJ 08544. Offers M Eng, MSE, PhD. Terminal master's awarded for partial completion of doctoral program. *Degree requirements:* For master's, thesis (MSE); for doctorate, thesis/dissertation, general exam. *Entrance requirements:* For master's, GRE General Test, 3 letters of recommendation; for doctorate, GRE General Test, official transcript(s), 3 letters of recommendation, personal statement. Additional exam requirements/recommendations for international students: Required—TOEFL. Electronic applications accepted. *Faculty research:* Bioengineering and bio-mechanics; combustion, energy conversion, and climate; fluid mechanics, dynamics, and control systems; lasers and applied physics; materials and mechanical systems.

Purdue University, College of Engineering, School of Aeronautics and Astronautics, West Lafayette, IN 47907-2045. Offers PhD. *Program availability:* Part-time, 100% online. *Faculty:* 63. *Students:* 525. In 2016, 28 doctorates awarded. Terminal master's awarded for partial completion of doctoral program. *Degree requirements:* For doctorate, thesis/dissertation. *Entrance requirements:* For doctorate, GRE General Test, minimum GPA of 3.5. *Application deadline:* For fall admission, 1/1 priority date for domestic and international students; for spring admission, 9/15 priority date for domestic and international students. Applications are processed on a rolling basis. Application fee: $60 ($75 for international students). Electronic applications accepted. *Financial support:* Fellowships with full and partial tuition reimbursements, research assistantships with full and partial tuition reimbursements, teaching assistantships with full and partial tuition reimbursements, career-related internships or fieldwork, scholarships/grants, health care benefits, and unspecified assistantships available. *Faculty research:* Aerodynamics, aerospace systems, astrodynamics and space applications, dynamics and control, propulsion, structures and materials. *Unit head:* Dr. Tom Shih, Head/Professor of Aeronautics and Astronautics, E-mail: tomshih@purdue.edu. *Application contact:* Xiaomin Qian, Graduate Program Coordinator, E-mail: xiaomin@purdue.edu.
Website: https://engineering.purdue.edu/AAE

Rensselaer Polytechnic Institute, Graduate School, School of Engineering, Program in Aeronautical Engineering, Troy, NY 12180-3590. Offers M Eng, MS, D Eng, PhD. *Faculty:* 48 full-time (7 women), 1 part-time/adjunct. *Students:* 34 full-time (5 women), 1 part-time. 48 applicants, 23% accepted, 5 enrolled. In 2016, 4 master's, 1 doctorate awarded. *Degree requirements:* For master's, thesis (for some programs); for doctorate, thesis/dissertation. *Entrance requirements:* For master's and doctorate, GRE. Additional exam requirements/recommendations for international students: Required—TOEFL (minimum score 600 paper-based; 100 iBT), IELTS (minimum score 7), PTE (minimum score 68). *Application deadline:* For fall admission, 1/1 priority date for domestic and international students; for spring admission, 8/15 priority date for domestic and international students. Applications are processed on a rolling basis. Application fee: $75. Electronic applications accepted. *Expenses: Tuition:* Full-time $49,520; part-time $2060 per credit hour. *Required fees:* $2617. *Financial support:* In 2016–17, research assistantships with full tuition reimbursements (averaging $22,000 per year), teaching assistantships with full tuition reimbursements (averaging $22,000 per year) were awarded; fellowships also available. Financial award application deadline: 1/1. *Faculty research:* Advanced nuclear materials, aerodynamics, design, dynamics and vibrations, fission systems and radiation transport, fluid mechanics (computational, theoretical, and experimental), heat transfer and energy conversion, manufacturing, medical imaging, health physics, multiscale/computational modeling, nanostructured materials and properties, nuclear physics/nuclear reactor, propulsion. *Total annual research expenditures:* $2 million. *Unit head:* Dr. Theo Borca-Tasciuc, Graduate Program Director, 518-276-2627, E-mail: borcat@rpi.edu. *Application contact:* Office of Graduate Admissions, 518-276-6216, E-mail: gradadmissions@rpi.edu.
Website: http://mane.rpi.edu/

Rutgers University–New Brunswick, Graduate School-New Brunswick, Program in Mechanical and Aerospace Engineering, Piscataway, NJ 08854-8097. Offers design and control (MS, PhD); fluid mechanics (MS, PhD); solid mechanics (MS, PhD); thermal sciences (MS, PhD). *Program availability:* Part-time, evening/weekend. *Degree requirements:* For master's, thesis (for some programs); for doctorate, thesis/dissertation. *Entrance requirements:* For master's, GRE General Test, BS in mechanical/aerospace engineering or related field; for doctorate, GRE General Test, MS in mechanical/aerospace engineering or related field. Additional exam requirements/recommendations for international students: Required—TOEFL. Electronic applications accepted. *Faculty research:* Combustion, propulsion, thermal transport, crystal plasticity, optimization, fabrication, nanoidentation.

San Diego State University, Graduate and Research Affairs, College of Engineering, Department of Aerospace Engineering and Engineering Mechanics, San Diego, CA 92182. Offers aerospace engineering (MS); engineering mechanics (MS); engineering sciences and applied mechanics (PhD); flight dynamics (MS); fluid dynamics (MS). PhD offered jointly with University of California, San Diego and Department of Mechanical Engineering. Terminal master's awarded for partial completion of doctoral program. *Degree requirements:* For master's, comprehensive exam (for some programs), thesis (for some programs); for doctorate, thesis/dissertation. *Entrance requirements:* For master's, GRE General Test; for doctorate, GRE, 3 letters of recommendation. Additional exam requirements/recommendations for international students: Required—TOEFL. Electronic applications accepted. *Faculty research:* Organized structures in post-stall flow over wings/three dimensional separated flow, airfoil growth effect, probabilities, structural mechanics.

Stanford University, School of Engineering, Department of Aeronautics and Astronautics, Stanford, CA 94305-2004. Offers MS, PhD, Eng. Terminal master's awarded for partial completion of doctoral program. *Degree requirements:* For doctorate, thesis/dissertation; for Eng, thesis. *Entrance requirements:* For master's and Eng, GRE General Test, GRE Subject Test; for doctorate, GRE General Test, GRE Subject Test (engineering). Additional exam requirements/recommendations for international students: Required—TOEFL. Electronic applications accepted. *Expenses: Tuition:* Full-time $47,331. *Required fees:* $609.

Stevens Institute of Technology, Graduate School, School of Systems and Enterprises, Program in Space Systems Engineering, Hoboken, NJ 07030. Offers M Eng, Certificate. *Program availability:* Part-time, evening/weekend. *Students:* 3 full-time (0 women), 14 part-time (3 women); includes 3 minority (2 Black or African American, non-Hispanic/Latino; 1 Asian, non-Hispanic/Latino). Average age 30. 8 applicants, 75% accepted, 2 enrolled. In 2016, 41 master's, 20 Certificates awarded. *Degree requirements:* For master's, thesis optional, minimum B average in major field and overall; for Certificate, minimum B average. *Entrance requirements:* Additional exam requirements/recommendations for international students: Required—TOEFL (minimum score 74 iBT), IELTS (minimum score 6). *Application deadline:* For fall admission, 6/1 for domestic students, 4/15 for international students; for spring admission, 11/30 for domestic students, 11/1 for international students. Applications are processed on a rolling basis. Application fee: $65. Electronic applications accepted. *Expenses:* Contact institution. *Financial support:* Fellowships, research assistantships, teaching assistantships, career-related internships or fieldwork, Federal Work-Study, scholarships/grants, and unspecified assistantships available. Financial award application deadline: 2/15; financial award applicants required to submit FAFSA. *Unit head:* Dr. Dinesh Verma, Dean, 201-216-8645, Fax: 201-216-5541, E-mail: dinesh.verma@stevens.edu. *Application contact:* Graduate Admissions, 888-783-8367, Fax: 888-511-1306, E-mail: graduate@stevens.edu.
Website: https://www.stevens.edu/school-systems-enterprises/masters-degree-programs/space-systems-engineering

Syracuse University, College of Engineering and Computer Science, Programs in Mechanical and Aerospace Engineering, Syracuse, NY 13244. Offers MS, PhD. *Program availability:* Part-time. *Students:* Average age 25. In 2016, 55 master's, 8 doctorates awarded. *Degree requirements:* For master's, project or thesis; for doctorate, comprehensive exam, thesis/dissertation. *Entrance requirements:* For master's and doctorate, GRE General Test, official transcripts, personal statement, three letters of recommendation, resume. Additional exam requirements/recommendations for international students: Required—TOEFL (minimum score 100 iBT). *Application deadline:* For fall admission, 7/1 priority date for domestic students, 6/1 priority date for international students; for spring admission, 11/15 priority date for domestic students, 10/15 priority date for international students. Applications are processed on a rolling basis. Application fee: $75. Electronic applications accepted. *Expenses: Tuition:* Full-time $25,974; part-time $1443 per credit hour. *Required fees:* $802; $50 per course. Tuition and fees vary according to course load and program. *Financial support:* Fellowships with full tuition reimbursements, research assistantships with tuition reimbursements, teaching assistantships with tuition reimbursements, scholarships/grants, and tuition waivers (partial) available. Financial award application deadline: 1/1. *Faculty research:* Solid mechanics and materials, fluid mechanics, thermal sciences, controls and robotics. *Unit head:* Dr. John F. Dannenhoffer, III, Associate Professor/Program Director of Aerospace Engineering, 315-443-3340, E-mail: jfdannen@syr.edu. *Application contact:* Kathleen Joyce, Assistant Dean, 315-443-2219, E-mail: topgrads@syr.edu.
Website: http://eng-cs.syr.edu/

Texas A&M University, College of Engineering, Department of Aerospace Engineering, College Station, TX 77843. Offers M Eng, MS, PhD. *Faculty:* 29. *Students:* 106 full-time (16 women), 13 part-time (1 woman); includes 11 minority (1 Black or African American, non-Hispanic/Latino; 1 American Indian or Alaska Native, non-Hispanic/Latino; 2 Asian, non-Hispanic/Latino; 5 Hispanic/Latino; 2 Two or more races, non-Hispanic/Latino), 49 international. Average age 27. 109 applicants, 33% accepted, 26 enrolled. In 2016, 17 master's, 6 doctorates awarded. *Degree requirements:* For master's, thesis (MS); for doctorate, thesis/dissertation. *Entrance requirements:* For master's and doctorate, GRE General Test. Additional exam requirements/recommendations for international students: Required—TOEFL (minimum score 550 paper-based; 80 iBT), IELTS (minimum score 6), PTE (minimum score 53). *Application deadline:* For fall admission, 1/1 priority date for domestic students; for spring admission, 7/1 priority date for domestic students; for summer admission, 12/1 priority date for domestic students. Applications are processed on a rolling basis. Application fee: $50 ($90 for international students). Electronic applications accepted. *Expenses:* Contact institution. *Financial support:* In 2016–17, 98 students received support, including 9 fellowships with tuition reimbursements available (averaging $15,907 per year), 84 research assistantships with tuition reimbursements available (averaging $6,146 per year), 13 teaching assistantships with tuition reimbursements available (averaging $5,931 per year); career-related internships or fieldwork, institutionally sponsored loans, scholarships/grants, traineeships, health care benefits, tuition waivers (full and partial), and unspecified assistantships also available. Support available to part-time students. Financial award application deadline: 3/15; financial award applicants required to submit FAFSA. *Faculty research:* Materials and structures, aerodynamics and computational fluid dynamics (CFD), flight dynamics and control. *Unit head:* Dr. Rodney Bowersox, Department Head, 979-854-4184, E-mail: bowersox@tamu.edu. *Application contact:* Gail Rowe, Senior Academic Advisor II, Graduate Programs, 979-845-5520, Fax: 979-845-6051, E-mail: lgrowe@tamu.edu.
Website: http://engineering.tamu.edu/aerospace

Université Laval, Faculty of Sciences and Engineering, Department of Mechanical Engineering, Program in Aerospace Engineering, Québec, QC G1K 7P4, Canada. Offers M Sc. Program offered jointly with Concordia University, École Polytechnique de Montréal, McGill University, and Université de Sherbrooke. *Program availability:* Part-time. *Entrance requirements:* For master's, knowledge of French and English. Electronic applications accepted.

University at Buffalo, the State University of New York, Graduate School, School of Engineering and Applied Sciences, Department of Mechanical and Aerospace Engineering, Buffalo, NY 14260. Offers aerospace engineering (MS, PhD); mechanical engineering (MS, PhD). *Program availability:* Part-time. Terminal master's awarded for partial completion of doctoral program. *Degree requirements:* For master's, comprehensive exam, project or thesis; for doctorate, thesis/dissertation. *Entrance requirements:* For master's and doctorate, GRE General Test, GRE Subject Test. Additional exam requirements/recommendations for international students: Required—TOEFL (minimum score 79 iBT). Electronic applications accepted. *Faculty research:* Fluid and thermal sciences, systems and design, mechanics and materials.

The University of Alabama, Graduate School, College of Engineering, Department of Aerospace Engineering and Mechanics, Tuscaloosa, AL 35487. Offers aerospace engineering (MSAEM); engineering science and mechanics (PhD). *Program availability:* Part-time, online learning. *Faculty:* 16 full-time (1 woman). *Students:* 34 full-time (2 women), 33 part-time (5 women); includes 6 minority (2 Asian, non-Hispanic/Latino; 4 Hispanic/Latino), 21 international. Average age 27. 70 applicants, 51% accepted, 21 enrolled. In 2016, 24 master's, 2 doctorates awarded. Terminal master's awarded for partial completion of doctoral program. *Degree requirements:* For master's, comprehensive exam (for some programs), thesis (for some programs); for doctorate, comprehensive exam, thesis/dissertation, 1-year residency. *Entrance requirements:* For master's, GRE, BS in engineering or physics; for doctorate, GRE, BS or MS in engineering or physics. Additional exam requirements/recommendations for international students: Required—TOEFL (minimum score 550 paper-based; 79 iBT). *Application deadline:* For fall admission, 7/15 priority date for domestic students, 2/28 priority date for international students; for spring admission, 12/1 priority date for domestic students, 6/30 priority date for international students. Applications are processed on a rolling basis. Application fee: $50 ($60 for international students). Electronic applications accepted. *Expenses:* Tuition, state resident: full-time $10,470. Tuition, nonresident: full-time $26,950. *Financial support:* In 2016–17, 18 students received support, including fellowships with full tuition reimbursements available (averaging $15,000 per year), research assistantships with full tuition reimbursements available (averaging $20,000 per year), teaching assistantships with full tuition reimbursements available (averaging $14,025 per year); Federal Work-Study, institutionally sponsored loans, scholarships/grants, health care benefits, and unspecified assistantships also available. Financial award application deadline: 2/28. *Faculty research:* Aeronautics, astronautics, solid mechanics, fluid mechanics, computational modeling. *Total annual research expenditures:* $1.5 million. *Unit head:* Dr. John Baker, Professor/Department Head, 205-348-4997, Fax: 205-348-7240, E-mail: john.baker@eng.ua.edu. *Application contact:* Dr. James Paul Hubner, Associate Professor, 205-348-1617, Fax: 208-348-7240, E-mail: phubner@eng.ua.edu.
Website: http://aem.eng.ua.edu/

The University of Alabama in Huntsville, School of Graduate Studies, College of Engineering, Department of Mechanical and Aerospace Engineering, Huntsville, AL 35899. Offers aerospace systems engineering (MS, PhD). *Program availability:* Part-time, evening/weekend. *Degree requirements:* For master's, comprehensive exam, thesis or alternative, oral and written exams; for doctorate, comprehensive exam, thesis/dissertation, oral and written exams. *Entrance requirements:* For master's, GRE General Test, BSE, minimum GPA of 3.0; for doctorate, GRE General Test, minimum GPA of 3.0. Additional exam requirements/recommendations for international students: Required—TOEFL (minimum score 500 paper-based; 80 iBT), IELTS (minimum score 6.5). Electronic applications accepted. *Expenses:* Tuition, state resident: full-time $9834; part-time $600 per credit hour. Tuition, nonresident: full-time $21,830; part-time $1325 per credit hour. *Faculty research:* Rocket propulsion and plasma engineering, materials engineering and solid mechanics, energy conversion, transport, and storage.

The University of Arizona, College of Engineering, Department of Aerospace and Mechanical Engineering, Tucson, AZ 85721. Offers aerospace engineering (MS, PhD); mechanical engineering (MS, PhD). *Program availability:* Part-time. *Degree requirements:* For master's, thesis or alternative; for doctorate, thesis/dissertation. *Entrance requirements:* For master's, GRE General Test, 3 letters of recommendation; for doctorate, GRE General Test, 3 letters of recommendation, statement of purpose. Additional exam requirements/recommendations for international students: Required—TOEFL (minimum score 550 paper-based; 79 iBT). Electronic applications accepted.

University of California, Davis, College of Engineering, Program in Mechanical and Aeronautical Engineering, Davis, CA 95616. Offers aeronautical engineering (M Engr, MS, D Engr, PhD, Certificate); mechanical engineering (M Engr, MS, D Engr, PhD, Certificate); M Engr/MBA. *Degree requirements:* For master's, comprehensive exam (for some programs), thesis (for some programs); for doctorate, thesis/dissertation. *Entrance requirements:* For master's and doctorate, GRE General Test, minimum GPA of 3.0. Additional exam requirements/recommendations for international students: Required—TOEFL (minimum score 550 paper-based). Electronic applications accepted.

University of California, Irvine, Henry Samueli School of Engineering, Department of Mechanical and Aerospace Engineering, Irvine, CA 92697. Offers MS, PhD. *Program availability:* Part-time. *Students:* 138 full-time (36 women), 7 part-time (0 women); includes 28 minority (4 Black or African American, non-Hispanic/Latino; 1 American Indian or Alaska Native, non-Hispanic/Latino; 10 Asian, non-Hispanic/Latino; 10 Hispanic/Latino; 3 Two or more races, non-Hispanic/Latino), 84 international. Average age 26. 636 applicants, 20% accepted, 47 enrolled. In 2016, 63 master's, 7 doctorates awarded. Terminal master's awarded for partial completion of doctoral program. *Degree requirements:* For doctorate, thesis/dissertation. *Entrance requirements:* For master's and doctorate, GRE General Test, minimum GPA of 3.0, 3 letters of recommendation. Additional exam requirements/recommendations for international students: Required—TOEFL (minimum score 550 paper-based). *Application deadline:* For fall admission, 1/15 priority date for domestic students, 1/15 for international students. Applications are processed on a rolling basis. Application fee: $105 ($125 for international students). Electronic applications accepted. *Financial support:* Fellowships with tuition reimbursements, research assistantships with full tuition reimbursements, teaching assistantships with tuition reimbursements, institutionally sponsored loans, traineeships, health care benefits, and unspecified assistantships available. Financial award application deadline: 3/1; financial award applicants required to submit FAFSA. *Faculty research:* Thermal and fluid sciences, combustion and propulsion, control systems, robotics, lightweight structures. *Unit head:* Prof. Kenneth Mease, Chair, 949-824-5855, Fax: 949-824-8585, E-mail: kmease@uci.edu. *Application contact:* Prof. Roger Rangel, Graduate Admissions Advisor, 949-824-4033, Fax: 949-824-8585, E-mail: rhrangel@uci.edu.
Website: http://mae.eng.uci.edu/

University of California, Los Angeles, Graduate Division, Henry Samueli School of Engineering and Applied Science, Department of Mechanical and Aerospace Engineering, Program in Aerospace Engineering, Los Angeles, CA 90095-1597. Offers MS, PhD. *Students:* 65 full-time (3 women); includes 30 minority (1 Black or African American, non-Hispanic/Latino; 19 Asian, non-Hispanic/Latino; 8 Hispanic/Latino; 2 Two or more races, non-Hispanic/Latino), 7 international. 180 applicants, 38% accepted, 25 enrolled. In 2016, 12 master's, 6 doctorates awarded. *Degree requirements:* For master's, comprehensive exam or thesis; for doctorate, thesis/dissertation, qualifying exams. *Entrance requirements:* For master's, GRE General Test, minimum GPA of 3.0; for doctorate, GRE General Test, minimum GPA of 3.25. Additional exam requirements/recommendations for international students: Required—TOEFL (minimum score 560 paper-based; 87 iBT), IELTS (minimum score 7). *Application deadline:* For fall admission, 12/1 for domestic and international students. Application fee: $105 ($125 for international students). Electronic applications accepted. *Financial support:* Fellowships, research assistantships, teaching assistantships, Federal Work-Study, institutionally sponsored loans, and tuition waivers (full and partial) available. Financial award application deadline: 12/1; financial award applicants required to submit FAFSA. *Faculty research:* Applied mathematics, applied plasma physics, dynamics, fluid mechanics, heat and mass transfer, design, robotics and manufacturing, nanoelectromechanical/microelectromechanical systems (NEMS/MEMS), structural and solid mechanics, systems and control. *Unit head:* Dr. Christopher S. Lynch, Chair, 310-825-7760, E-mail: cslynch@seas.ucla.edu. *Application contact:* Angie Castillo, Student Affairs Officer, 310-825-7793, Fax: 310-206-4830, E-mail: angie@seas.ucla.edu. Website: http://www.mae.ucla.edu/

University of California, San Diego, Graduate Division, Department of Mechanical and Aerospace Engineering, Program in Aerospace Engineering, La Jolla, CA 92093. Offers MS, PhD. *Students:* 20 full-time (2 women), 6 part-time (1 woman). 117 applicants, 23% accepted, 8 enrolled. In 2016, 9 master's, 1 doctorate awarded. *Degree requirements:* For master's, comprehensive exam (for some programs), thesis (for some programs), comprehensive exam or thesis; for doctorate, comprehensive exam, thesis/dissertation. *Entrance requirements:* For master's and doctorate, GRE General Test, minimum GPA of 3.0. Additional exam requirements/recommendations for international students: Required—TOEFL (minimum score 550 paper-based; 80 iBT), IELTS (minimum score 7). *Application deadline:* For fall admission, 12/14 for domestic students. Application fee: $105 ($125 for international students). Electronic applications accepted. *Expenses:* Tuition, state resident: full-time $11,220. Tuition, nonresident: full-time $26,322. *Required fees:* $1864. *Financial support:* Fellowships, research assistantships, teaching assistantships, scholarships/grants, and unspecified assistantships available. Financial award applicants required to submit FAFSA. *Faculty research:* Aerodynamics, turbulence and fluid mechanics. *Unit head:* Vitali Nesterenko, Chair, 858-534-0113, E-mail: mae-chair-l@ucsd.edu. *Application contact:* Lydia Ramirez, Graduate Coordinator, 858-534-4387, E-mail: mae-gradadm-l@ucsd.edu. Website: http://maeweb.ucsd.edu/

University of Central Florida, College of Engineering and Computer Science, Department of Mechanical and Aerospace Engineering, Program in Aerospace Engineering, Orlando, FL 32816. Offers MSAE. *Students:* 22 full-time (2 women), 18 part-time (1 woman); includes 20 minority (1 Black or African American, non-Hispanic/Latino; 4 Asian, non-Hispanic/Latino; 14 Hispanic/Latino; 1 Two or more races, non-Hispanic/Latino), 3 international. Average age 25. 46 applicants, 65% accepted, 21 enrolled. In 2016, 10 master's awarded. *Degree requirements:* For master's, thesis or alternative. *Entrance requirements:* Additional exam requirements/recommendations for international students: Required—TOEFL. *Application deadline:* For fall admission, 7/15 for domestic students; for spring admission, 12/1 for domestic students. Application fee: $30. Electronic applications accepted. *Expenses:* Tuition, state resident: part-time $288.16 per credit hour. Tuition, nonresident: part-time $1071.31 per credit hour. *Financial support:* In 2016–17, 9 students received support, including 6 research assistantships with partial tuition reimbursements available (averaging $6,078 per year), 9 teaching assistantships with partial tuition reimbursements available (averaging $7,194 per year); fellowships, career-related internships or fieldwork, institutionally sponsored loans, scholarships/grants, tuition waivers (partial), and unspecified assistantships also available. Financial award application deadline: 3/1; financial award applicants required to submit FAFSA. *Unit head:* Dr. Yoav Peles, Chair, 407-823-2416, Fax: 407-823-0208, E-mail: yoav.peles@ucf.edu. *Application contact:* Assistant Director, Graduate Admissions, 407-823-2766, Fax: 407-823-6442, E-mail: gradadmissions@ucf.edu. Website: http://mae.ucf.edu/academics/graduate/

University of Central Missouri, The Graduate School, Warrensburg, MO 64093. Offers accountancy (MA); accounting (MBA); applied mathematics (MS); aviation safety (MA); biology (MS); business administration (MBA); career and technical education leadership (MS); college student personnel administration (MS); communication (MA); computer science (MS); counseling (MS); criminal justice (MS); educational leadership (Ed D); educational technology (MS); elementary and early childhood education (MSE); English (MA); environmental studies (MA); finance (MBA); history (MA); human services/educational technology (Ed S); human services/learning resources (Ed S); human services/professional counseling (Ed S); industrial hygiene (MS); industrial management (MS); information systems (MBA); information technology (MS); kinesiology (MS); library science and information services (MS); literacy education (MSE); marketing (MBA); mathematics (MS); music (MA); occupational safety management (MS); psychology (MS); rural family nursing (MS); school administration (MSE); social gerontology (MS); sociology (MA); special education (MSE); speech language pathology (MS); superintendency (Ed S); teaching (MAT); teaching English as a second language (MA); technology (MS); technology management (PhD); theatre (MA). *Program availability:* Part-time, 100% online, blended/hybrid learning. *Degree requirements:* For master's and Ed S, comprehensive exam (for some programs), thesis (for some programs). *Entrance requirements:* Additional exam requirements/recommendations for international students: Required—TOEFL (minimum score 550 paper-based; 79 iBT). Electronic applications accepted.

University of Cincinnati, Graduate School, College of Engineering and Applied Science, Department of Aerospace Engineering and Engineering Mechanics, Cincinnati, OH 45221. Offers MS, PhD. *Program availability:* Part-time. Terminal master's awarded for partial completion of doctoral program. *Degree requirements:* For master's, project or thesis; for doctorate, thesis/dissertation. *Entrance requirements:* For master's and doctorate, GRE General Test. Additional exam requirements/recommendations for international students: Required—TOEFL (minimum score 550 paper-based). Electronic applications accepted. *Expenses—Tuition, area resident:* Full-time $12,790; part-time $389 per credit hour. Tuition, state resident: full-time $13,290; part-time $419 per credit hour. Tuition, nonresident: full-time $24,532; part-time $976 per credit hour. *International tuition:* $24,832 full-time. *Required fees:* $3958; $140 per credit hour. Tuition and fees vary according to course load, degree level, program and reciprocity agreements. *Faculty research:* Computational fluid mechanics/propulsion, large space structures, dynamics and guidance of VTOL vehicles.

University of Colorado Boulder, Graduate School, College of Engineering and Applied Science, Department of Aerospace Engineering Sciences, Boulder, CO 80309. Offers MS, PhD. *Faculty:* 33 full-time (4 women). *Students:* 259 full-time (49 women), 28 part-time (7 women); includes 36 minority (1 American Indian or Alaska Native, non-Hispanic/Latino; 13 Asian, non-Hispanic/Latino; 16 Hispanic/Latino; 6 Two or more races, non-Hispanic/Latino), 52 international. Average age 26. 304 applicants, 60% accepted, 81 enrolled. In 2016, 86 master's, 28 doctorates awarded. Terminal master's awarded for partial completion of doctoral program. *Degree requirements:* For master's, comprehensive exam, thesis or alternative; for doctorate, comprehensive exam, thesis/dissertation. *Entrance requirements:* For master's, GRE General Test, minimum undergraduate GPA of 3.0; for doctorate, minimum undergraduate GPA of 3.25. *Application deadline:* For fall admission, 1/5 for domestic students, 12/1 for international students; for spring admission, 10/1 for domestic students, 8/1 for international students. Applications are processed on a rolling basis. Application fee: $60 ($80 for international students). Electronic applications accepted. Application fee is waived when completed online. *Financial support:* In 2016–17, 475 students received support, including 138 fellowships (averaging $11,276 per year), 97 research assistantships with full and partial tuition reimbursements available (averaging $40,598 per year), 27 teaching assistantships with full and partial tuition reimbursements available (averaging $39,853 per year); institutionally sponsored loans, scholarships/grants, health care benefits, and unspecified assistantships also available. Financial award application deadline: 2/1; financial award applicants required to submit FAFSA. *Faculty research:* Aeronautical/astronautical engineering, atmospheric sciences, aerospace engineering, earth satellite applications, astronautics. *Total annual research expenditures:* $17.1 million. *Application contact:* E-mail: aerograd@colorado.edu. Website: http://www.colorado.edu/aerospace/

University of Colorado Colorado Springs, College of Engineering and Applied Science, Program in General Engineering, Colorado Springs, CO 80918. Offers energy engineering (ME); engineering management (ME); information assurance (ME); software engineering (ME); space operations (ME); systems engineering (ME). *Program availability:* Part-time, evening/weekend, blended/hybrid learning. *Faculty:* 1 full-time (0 women), 15 part-time/adjunct (6 women). *Students:* 18 full-time (3 women), 166 part-time (34 women); includes 36 minority (6 Black or African American, non-Hispanic/Latino; 8 Asian, non-Hispanic/Latino; 12 Hispanic/Latino; 10 Two or more races, non-Hispanic/Latino), 57 international. Average age 36. 89 applicants, 72% accepted, 41 enrolled. In 2016, 21 master's, 8 doctorates awarded. *Degree requirements:* For master's, thesis, portfolio, or project; for doctorate, comprehensive exam, thesis/dissertation. *Entrance requirements:* For master's, GRE (minimum score of 148 new grading scale on quantitative portion if undergraduate GPA is less than 3.0); for doctorate, GRE (minimum score of 148 new grading scale on the quantitative portion if the applicant has not graduated from a program of recognized standing), minimum GPA of 3.3 in the bachelor's or master's degree program attempted. Additional exam requirements/recommendations for international students: Required—TOEFL (minimum score 80 iBT), IELTS (minimum score 6). *Application deadline:* For fall admission, 7/1 for domestic students, 6/1 for international students; for spring admission, 11/1 for domestic and international students; for summer admission, 4/15 for domestic and international students. Applications are processed on a rolling basis. Application fee: $60 ($100 for international students). Electronic applications accepted. *Expenses:* Contact institution. *Financial support:* In 2016–17, 28 students received support. Federal Work-Study, scholarships/grants, traineeships, and unspecified assistantships available. Support available to part-time students. Financial award application deadline: 3/1; financial award applicants required to submit FAFSA. *Unit head:* Dr. Ramaswami Dandapani, Dean, 719-255-3543, Fax: 719-255-3542, E-mail: rdan@cas.uccs.edu. *Application contact:* Dawn House, Coordinator, 719-255-3246, E-mail: dhouse@uccs.edu.

University of Dayton, Department of Mechanical and Aerospace Engineering, Dayton, OH 45469. Offers aerospace engineering (MSAE, DE, PhD); mechanical engineering (MSME, DE, PhD); renewable and clean energy (MS). *Program availability:* Part-time, blended/hybrid learning. *Faculty:* 17 full-time (3 women), 9 part-time/adjunct (1 woman). *Students:* 143 full-time (19 women), 31 part-time (7 women); includes 14 minority (1 Black or African American, non-Hispanic/Latino; 5 Asian, non-Hispanic/Latino; 4 Hispanic/Latino; 4 Two or more races, non-Hispanic/Latino), 94 international. Average age 28. 432 applicants, 15% accepted. In 2016, 66 master's awarded. *Degree requirements:* For master's, thesis optional; for doctorate, variable foreign language requirement, comprehensive exam, thesis/dissertation, departmental qualifying exam. *Entrance requirements:* For master's, BS in engineering, math, or physics. Additional exam requirements/recommendations for international students: Required—TOEFL (minimum score 550 paper-based; 80 iBT), IELTS (minimum score 6.5). *Application deadline:* Applications are processed on a rolling basis. Application fee: $0 ($50 for international students). Electronic applications accepted. *Expenses:* $890 per credit hour (for MS), $970 per credit hour (for PhD); $25 registration fee. *Financial support:* In 2016–17, 19 research assistantships with full tuition reimbursements (averaging $13,000 per year), 2 teaching assistantships with full tuition reimbursements (averaging $9,150 per year) were awarded; institutionally sponsored loans and health care benefits also available. Support available to part-time students. Financial award application deadline: 3/1; financial award applicants required to submit FAFSA. *Faculty research:* Materials, thermo-fluids, solid mechanics, energy, robotics, design and manufacturing. *Total annual research expenditures:* $1.4 million. *Unit head:* Dr. Kelly Kissock, Chair, 937-229-2999, Fax: 937-229-4766, E-mail: jkissock1@udayton.edu. *Application contact:* Dr. Vinod Jain, Graduate Program Director, 937-229-2992, Fax: 937-229-4766, E-mail: vjain1@udayton.edu. Website: https://www.udayton.edu/engineering/departments/mechanical_and_aerospace/index.php

University of Florida, Graduate School, Herbert Wertheim College of Engineering, Department of Mechanical and Aerospace Engineering, Gainesville, FL 32611. Offers aerospace engineering (ME, MS, PhD); mechanical engineering (ME, MS, PhD). *Program availability:* Part-time, online learning. *Degree requirements:* For master's, thesis (for some programs); for doctorate, comprehensive exam, thesis/dissertation. *Entrance requirements:* For master's and doctorate, minimum GPA of 3.0. Additional exam requirements/recommendations for international students: Required—TOEFL (minimum score 550 paper-based; 80 iBT), IELTS (minimum score 6). Electronic applications accepted. *Faculty research:* Thermal sciences, design, controls and robotics, manufacturing, energy transport and utilization.

University of Illinois at Urbana–Champaign, Graduate College, College of Engineering, Department of Aerospace Engineering, Champaign, IL 61820. Offers MS, PhD. *Program availability:* Part-time, online learning.

The University of Kansas, Graduate Studies, School of Engineering, Program in Aerospace Engineering, Lawrence, KS 66045. Offers ME, MS, DE, PhD. *Program availability:* Part-time. *Students:* 41 full-time (3 women), 4 part-time (0 women), 32 international. Average age 26. 54 applicants, 61% accepted, 9 enrolled. In 2016, 8 master's, 1 doctorate awarded. *Entrance requirements:* For master's, GRE, minimum GPA of 3.0, official transcripts, statement of objectives, three letters of recommendation; Statement of Financial Resources (for international students only); for doctorate, GRE, minimum GPA of 3.5, official transcripts, statement of objectives, three letters of recommendation; Statement of Financial Resources (for international students only). Additional exam requirements/recommendations for international students: Required—TOEFL or IELTS. *Application deadline:* For fall admission, 12/1 for domestic and international students; for spring admission, 9/15 for domestic and international students; for summer admission, 10/15 for domestic students, 9/15 for international students. Application fee: $65 ($85 for international students). Electronic applications accepted. *Financial support:* Fellowships, research assistantships, teaching assistantships, career-related internships or fieldwork, scholarships/grants, tuition waivers (full and partial), and unspecified assistantships available. Financial award application deadline: 12/1. *Faculty research:* Artificial intelligence, composite materials and structures, computational fluid dynamics and computational aeroacoustics, structural vibrations of high performance structures, flight test engineering. *Unit head:* ZJ Wang, Chair, 785-864-2440, E-mail: zjw@ku.edu. *Application contact:* Lesslee Smithhisler, Administrative Assistant, 785-864-2960, E-mail: lksmithh@ku.edu. Website: http://www.ae.engr.ku.edu/

The University of Manchester, School of Materials, Manchester, United Kingdom. Offers advanced aerospace materials engineering (M Sc); advanced metallic systems (PhD); biomedical materials (M Phil, M Sc, PhD); ceramics and glass (M Phil, M Sc,

PhD); composite materials (M Sc, PhD); corrosion and protection (M Phil, M Sc, PhD); materials (M Phil, PhD); metallic materials (M Phil, M Sc, PhD); nanostructural materials (M Phil, M Sc, PhD); paper science (M Phil, M Sc, PhD); polymer science and engineering (M Phil, M Sc, PhD); technical textiles (M Sc); textile design, fashion and management (M Phil, M Sc, PhD); textile science and technology (M Phil, M Sc, PhD); textiles (M Phil, PhD); textiles and fashion (M Ent).

The University of Manchester, School of Mechanical, Aerospace and Civil Engineering, Manchester, United Kingdom. Offers advanced manufacturing technology (M Ent); aerospace engineering (M Phil, M Sc, PhD); civil engineering (M Phil, M Sc, PhD); environmental engineering (M Phil, PhD); management of projects (M Phil, M Sc, PhD); mechanical engineering (M Phil, M Sc, PhD); mechanical engineering design (M Ent); nuclear engineering (M Phil, D Eng, PhD).

University of Maryland, College Park, Academic Affairs, A. James Clark School of Engineering, Department of Aerospace Engineering, College Park, MD 20742. Offers M Eng, MS, PhD. *Program availability:* Part-time, evening/weekend, online learning. *Degree requirements:* For master's, thesis optional; for doctorate, thesis/dissertation. *Entrance requirements:* For master's and doctorate, GRE General Test (recommended), 3 letters of recommendation. Electronic applications accepted. *Faculty research:* Aerodynamics and propulsion, structural mechanics, flight dynamics, rotor craft, space robotics.

University of Miami, Graduate School, College of Engineering, Department of Mechanical and Aerospace Engineering, Coral Gables, FL 33124. Offers MSME, PhD. *Program availability:* Part-time. *Degree requirements:* For master's, thesis (for some programs); for doctorate, comprehensive exam, thesis/dissertation. *Entrance requirements:* For master's and doctorate, GRE General Test, minimum GPA of 3.0. Additional exam requirements/recommendations for international students: Required—TOEFL (minimum score 550 paper-based). Electronic applications accepted. *Faculty research:* Internal combustion engines, heat transfer, hydrogen energy, controls, fuel cells.

University of Michigan, College of Engineering, Department of Aerospace Engineering, Ann Arbor, MI 48109. Offers M Eng, MS, MSE, PhD. *Program availability:* Part-time. *Students:* 201 full-time (31 women), 8 part-time (1 woman). 534 applicants, 36% accepted, 80 enrolled. In 2016, 59 master's, 13 doctorates awarded. *Degree requirements:* For doctorate, thesis/dissertation, oral defense of dissertation, preliminary exams. *Entrance requirements:* For master's, GRE General Test; for doctorate, GRE General Test, master's degree. *Application deadline:* Applications are processed on a rolling basis. Electronic applications accepted. *Expenses:* Tuition, state resident: full-time $21,466; part-time $1152 per credit hour. Tuition, nonresident: full-time $43,346; part-time $2367 per credit hour. Part-time tuition and fees vary according to course load, degree level and program. *Financial support:* Fellowships, research assistantships, teaching assistantships, Federal Work-Study, and tuition waivers (full and partial) available. *Faculty research:* Turbulent flows and combustion, advanced spacecraft control, helicopter aeroelasticity, experimental fluid dynamics, space propulsion, optimal structural design, interactive materials, computational fluid and solid dynamics. *Total annual research expenditures:* $13.4 million. *Unit head:* Dr. Daniel Inman, Department Chair, 734-936-0102, Fax: 734-763-0578, E-mail: daninman@umich.edu. *Application contact:* Denise Phelps, Graduate Admissions Coordinator, 734-615-4406, Fax: 734-763-0578, E-mail: dphelps@umich.edu.
Website: http://www.engin.umich.edu/aero/

University of Michigan, College of Engineering, Department of Climate and Space Sciences and Engineering, Ann Arbor, MI 48109. Offers applied climate (M Eng); atmospheric, oceanic and space sciences (MS, PhD); geoscience and remote sensing (PhD); space and planetary sciences (PhD); space engineering (M Eng). *Program availability:* Part-time. *Students:* 102 full-time (31 women), 1 part-time (0 women). 159 applicants, 21% accepted, 19 enrolled. In 2016, 34 master's, 6 doctorates awarded. Terminal master's awarded for partial completion of doctoral program. *Degree requirements:* For master's, thesis (for some programs); for doctorate, thesis/dissertation, oral defense of dissertation, preliminary exams. *Entrance requirements:* For master's and doctorate, GRE General Test. Additional exam requirements/recommendations for international students: Required—TOEFL. *Application deadline:* Applications are processed on a rolling basis. Electronic applications accepted. *Expenses:* Tuition, state resident: full-time $21,466; part-time $1152 per credit hour. Tuition, nonresident: full-time $43,346; part-time $2367 per credit hour. Part-time tuition and fees vary according to course load, degree level and program. *Financial support:* Fellowships, research assistantships, teaching assistantships, career-related internships or fieldwork, Federal Work-Study, institutionally sponsored loans, and health care benefits available. Support available to part-time students. Financial award applicants required to submit FAFSA. *Faculty research:* Planetary environments, space instrumentation, air pollution meteorology, global climate change, sun-earth connection, space weather. *Total annual research expenditures:* $50.5 million. *Unit head:* Dr. James Slavin, Chair, 734-764-7221, Fax: 734-763-0437, E-mail: jaslavin@umich.edu. *Application contact:* Sandra Pytlinski, Graduate Student Services Coordinator, 734-936-0482, Fax: 734-763-0437, E-mail: sanpyt@umich.edu.
Website: http://clasp.engin.umich.edu/

University of Minnesota, Twin Cities Campus, College of Science and Engineering, Department of Aerospace Engineering and Mechanics, Minneapolis, MN 55455-0213. Offers MS, PhD. *Program availability:* Part-time. *Degree requirements:* For doctorate, thesis/dissertation. *Entrance requirements:* Additional exam requirements/recommendations for international students: Required—TOEFL (minimum score 550 paper-based). Electronic applications accepted. *Faculty research:* Fluid mechanics, solid mechanics and materials, aerospace systems, nanotechnology.

University of Missouri, Office of Research and Graduate Studies, College of Engineering, Department of Mechanical and Aerospace Engineering, Columbia, MO 65211. Offers MS, PhD. *Faculty:* 33 full-time (0 women), 3 part-time/adjunct (1 woman). *Students:* 47 full-time (7 women), 66 part-time (11 women). *Degree requirements:* For master's, thesis; for doctorate, one foreign language, thesis/dissertation. *Entrance requirements:* For master's and doctorate, GRE General Test, minimum GPA of 3.0. Additional exam requirements/recommendations for international students: Required—TOEFL (minimum score 500 paper-based; 61 iBT). *Application deadline:* For fall admission, 5/31 priority date for domestic and international students; for winter admission, 10/31 priority date for domestic and international students; for spring admission, 4/30 priority date for domestic and international students. Applications are processed on a rolling basis. Application fee: $75 ($90 for international students). Electronic applications accepted. *Expenses:* Tuition, state resident: full-time $6347; part-time $352.60 per credit hour. Tuition, nonresident: full-time $17,379; part-time $965.50 per credit hour. *Required fees:* $1035. Tuition and fees vary according to course load, campus/location and program. *Financial support:* Fellowships, research assistantships, teaching assistantships, institutionally sponsored loans, scholarships/grants, health care benefits, and unspecified assistantships available. Support available to part-time students.
Website: http://engineering.missouri.edu/mae/degree-programs/

University of Nevada, Las Vegas, Graduate College, Howard R. Hughes College of Engineering, Department of Mechanical Engineering, Las Vegas, NV 89154-4027. Offers aerospace engineering (MS); biomedical engineering (MS); materials and nuclear engineering (MS); mechanical engineering (MS, PhD); nuclear criticality safety (Certificate); nuclear safeguards and security (Certificate). *Program availability:* Part-time. *Faculty:* 16 full-time (2 women), 3 part-time/adjunct (1 woman). *Students:* 47 full-time (13 women), 21 part-time (4 women); includes 15 minority (1 American Indian or Alaska Native, non-Hispanic/Latino; 6 Asian, non-Hispanic/Latino; 3 Hispanic/Latino; 5 Two or more races, non-Hispanic/Latino), 16 international. Average age 30. 68 applicants, 54% accepted, 15 enrolled. In 2016, 10 master's, 3 doctorates, 4 other advanced degrees awarded. *Degree requirements:* For master's, thesis optional, design project; for doctorate, comprehensive exam, thesis/dissertation. *Entrance requirements:* For master's, GRE General Test, statement of purpose; 2 letters of recommendation; for doctorate, GRE General Test, 3 letters of recommendation; statement of purpose; bachelor's degree with minimum GPA of 3.5/master's degree with minimum GPA of 3.3. Additional exam requirements/recommendations for international students: Required—TOEFL (minimum score 550 paper-based; 80 iBT), IELTS (minimum score 7). *Application deadline:* For fall admission, 8/1 for domestic students, 5/1 for international students; for spring admission, 12/1 for domestic students, 10/1 for international students. Application fee: $60 ($95 for international students). Electronic applications accepted. *Expenses:* $269.25 per credit, $792 per 3-credit course; $9,634 per year resident; $23,274 per year non-resident; $7,094 fees non-resident (7 credits or more); $1,307 annual health insurance fee. *Financial support:* In 2016–17, 1 fellowship with partial tuition reimbursement (averaging $15,000 per year), 13 research assistantships with partial tuition reimbursements (averaging $17,115 per year), 27 teaching assistantships with partial tuition reimbursements (averaging $16,172 per year) were awarded; institutionally sponsored loans, scholarships/grants, health care benefits, and unspecified assistantships also available. Financial award application deadline: 3/15. *Faculty research:* Dynamics and control systems; energy systems including renewable and nuclear; computational fluid and solid mechanics; structures, materials and manufacturing; vibrations and acoustics. *Total annual research expenditures:* $4.5 million. *Unit head:* Dr. Brendan O'Toole, Chair/Professor, 702-895-3885, Fax: 702-895-3936, E-mail: brendan.otoole@unlv.edu. *Application contact:* Dr. Hui Zhao, Graduate Coordinator, 702-895-1463, Fax: 702-895-3936, E-mail: hui.zhao@unlv.edu.
Website: http://me.unlv.edu/

University of Notre Dame, Graduate School, College of Engineering, Department of Aerospace and Mechanical Engineering, Notre Dame, IN 46556. Offers aerospace and mechanical engineering (M Eng, PhD); aerospace engineering (MS Aero E); mechanical engineering (MEME, MSME). Terminal master's awarded for partial completion of doctoral program. *Degree requirements:* For master's, comprehensive exam, thesis or alternative; for doctorate, thesis/dissertation, candidacy exam. *Entrance requirements:* For master's and doctorate, GRE General Test. Additional exam requirements/recommendations for international students: Required—TOEFL (minimum score 600 paper-based; 80 iBT). Electronic applications accepted. *Faculty research:* Aerodynamics/fluid dynamics, design and manufacturing, controls/robotics, solid mechanics or biomechanics/biomaterials.

University of Oklahoma, Gallogly College of Engineering, School of Aerospace and Mechanical Engineering, Program in Aerospace Engineering, Norman, OK 73019. Offers MS, PhD. *Program availability:* Part-time. *Students:* 5 full-time (1 woman), 5 part-time (0 women); includes 1 minority (Black or African American, non-Hispanic/Latino), 3 international. Average age 31. 7 applicants, 57% accepted, 2 enrolled. *Degree requirements:* For master's, comprehensive exam (for some programs), thesis (for some programs); for doctorate, comprehensive exam, thesis/dissertation, general exam. *Entrance requirements:* For master's and doctorate, GRE, letters of reference, resume, statement of purpose. Additional exam requirements/recommendations for international students: Required—TOEFL (minimum score 79 iBT) or IELTS (minimum score 6.5). *Application deadline:* For fall admission, 1/15 for domestic and international students; for spring admission, 9/1 for domestic and international students. Application fee: $50 ($100 for international students). Electronic applications accepted. *Expenses:* Tuition, state resident: full-time $4886; part-time $203.60 per credit hour. Tuition, nonresident: full-time $18,989; part-time $791.20 per credit hour. *Required fees:* $3283; $126.25 per credit hour. $126.50 per semester. *Financial support:* In 2016–17, 6 students received support. Fellowships, research assistantships with full tuition reimbursements available, teaching assistantships with full tuition reimbursements available, and scholarships/grants available. Financial award application deadline: 6/1; financial award applicants required to submit FAFSA. *Faculty research:* Unmanned aerial vehicles; nonlinear aeroelasticity; optimal control theory; turbulence. *Unit head:* Dr. M. Cengiz Altan, Director, 405-325-5011, Fax: 405-325-1088, E-mail: altan@ou.edu. *Application contact:* Kate O'Brien-Hamoush, Student Services Coordinator, 405-325-5013, Fax: 405-325-1088, E-mail: kobrien@ou.edu.
Website: http://www.ou.edu/coe/ame.html

University of Ottawa, Faculty of Graduate and Postdoctoral Studies, Faculty of Engineering, Ottawa-Carleton Institute for Mechanical and Aerospace Engineering, Ottawa, ON K1N 6N5, Canada. Offers M Eng, MA Sc, PhD. MA Sc, M Eng, PhD offered jointly with Carleton University. *Degree requirements:* For master's, thesis or alternative; for doctorate, thesis/dissertation, seminar series, qualifying exam. *Entrance requirements:* For master's, honors degree or equivalent, minimum B average; for doctorate, master's degree, minimum B+ average. Electronic applications accepted. *Faculty research:* Fluid mechanics-heat transfer, solid mechanics, design, manufacturing and control.

University of Puerto Rico, Mayagüez Campus, Graduate Studies, College of Engineering, Department of Mechanical Engineering, Mayagüez, PR 00681-9000. Offers mechanical engineering (ME, MS, PhD), including aerospace and unmanned vehivles (ME), automation/mechatronics, bioengineering, cae and design, fluid mechanics, heat transfer/energy systems, manufacturing, mechanics of materials, micro and nano engineering. *Program availability:* Part-time. *Faculty:* 22 full-time (4 women), 1 part-time/adjunct (0 women). *Students:* 34 full-time (4 women), 8 part-time (2 women); includes 38 minority (all Hispanic/Latino), 3 international. Average age 25. 22 applicants, 100% accepted, 7 enrolled. In 2016, 17 master's awarded. Terminal master's awarded for partial completion of doctoral program. *Degree requirements:* For master's, one foreign language, comprehensive exam, thesis; for doctorate, one foreign language, comprehensive exam, thesis/dissertation. *Entrance requirements:* For master's, BS in mechanical engineering or its equivalent; for doctorate, GRE, BS or MS in mechanical engineering or its equivalent; minimum GPA of 3.0. Additional exam requirements/recommendations for international students: Required—TOEFL (minimum score 80 paper-based; 80 iBT). *Application deadline:* For fall admission, 2/15 for domestic and international students; for spring admission, 9/15 for domestic and international students. Applications are processed on a rolling basis. Application fee: $25. Electronic applications accepted. *Expenses: Tuition, area resident:* Full-time $2466. *International tuition:* $7166 full-time. *Required fees:* $210. One-time fee: $5 full-time. Tuition and fees vary according to course level, campus/location, program and student level. *Financial support:* In 2016–17, 39 students received support, including 26 research assistantships with full and partial tuition reimbursements available (averaging $3,801 per year), 30 teaching assistantships with full and partial tuition reimbursements

available (averaging $3,293 per year); unspecified assistantships also available. *Faculty research:* Computational fluid dynamics, thermal sciences, mechanical design, material health, microfluidics. *Unit head:* Paul Sundaram, Ph.D., Chairperson, 787-832-4040 Ext. 3659, Fax: 787-265-3817, E-mail: paul.sundaram@upr.edu. *Application contact:* Yolanda Perez, Academic Orientation Officer, 787-832-4040 Ext. 2362, Fax: 787-265-3817, E-mail: yolanda.perez4@upr.edu.
Website: https://wordpress.uprm.edu/inme/

University of Southern California, Graduate School, Viterbi School of Engineering, Department of Aerospace and Mechanical Engineering, Los Angeles, CA 90089. Offers aerospace and mechanical engineering: computational fluid and solid mechanics (MS); aerospace and mechanical engineering: dynamics and control (MS); aerospace engineering (MS, PhD, Engr), including aerospace engineering (PhD, Engr); green technologies (MS); mechanical engineering (MS, PhD, Engr), including energy conversion (MS), mechanical engineering (PhD, Engr), nuclear power (MS); product development engineering (MS). *Program availability:* Part-time, evening/weekend, online learning. Terminal master's awarded for partial completion of doctoral program. *Degree requirements:* For master's, thesis optional; for doctorate, thesis/dissertation. *Entrance requirements:* For master's, doctorate, and Engr, GRE General Test. Additional exam requirements/recommendations for international students: Recommended—TOEFL. Electronic applications accepted. *Faculty research:* Mechanics and materials, aerodynamics of air/ground vehicles, gas dynamics, aerosols, astronautics and space science, geophysical and microgravity flows, planetary physics, power MEMs and MEMS vacuum pumps, heat transfer and combustion.

University of Southern California, Graduate School, Viterbi School of Engineering, Division of Astronautics and Space Technology, Los Angeles, CA 90089. Offers astronautical engineering (MS, PhD, Engr, Graduate Certificate). *Program availability:* Part-time, evening/weekend, online learning. Terminal master's awarded for partial completion of doctoral program. *Degree requirements:* For master's, thesis optional; for doctorate, thesis/dissertation; for other advanced degree, comprehensive exam (for some programs). *Entrance requirements:* For master's, doctorate, and other advanced degree, GRE General Test. Additional exam requirements/recommendations for international students: Recommended—TOEFL. Electronic applications accepted. *Faculty research:* Space technology, space science and applications, space instrumentation, advanced propulsion, fundamental processes in gases and plasmas.

The University of Tennessee, Graduate School, Tickle College of Engineering, Department of Mechanical, Aerospace and Biomedical Engineering, Program in Aerospace Engineering, Knoxville, TN 37996. Offers MS, PhD, MS/MBA. *Program availability:* Part-time, online learning. *Faculty:* 6 full-time (1 woman). *Students:* 28 full-time (2 women), 11 part-time (1 woman); includes 5 minority (1 Black or African American, non-Hispanic/Latino; 2 Asian, non-Hispanic/Latino; 1 Hispanic/Latino; 1 Two or more races, non-Hispanic/Latino), 3 international. Average age 28. 41 applicants, 46% accepted, 14 enrolled. In 2016, 8 master's, 1 doctorate awarded. *Degree requirements:* For master's, thesis or alternative; for doctorate, comprehensive exam, thesis/dissertation. *Entrance requirements:* For master's, GRE General Test (for MS students pursuing research thesis), minimum GPA of 2.7 (for U.S. degree holders), 3.0 (for international degree holders); 3 references; statement of purpose; for doctorate, GRE General Test, minimum GPA of 3.0 on previous graduate course work; 3 references; statement of purpose. Additional exam requirements/recommendations for international students: Required—TOEFL (minimum score 550 paper-based). *Application deadline:* For fall admission, 2/1 priority date for domestic and international students; for spring admission, 6/15 for domestic and international students. Applications are processed on a rolling basis. Application fee: $35. Electronic applications accepted. *Financial support:* In 2016–17, 12 students received support, including 2 fellowships with full tuition reimbursements available (averaging $26,471 per year), 2 research assistantships with full tuition reimbursements available (averaging $18,325 per year), 6 teaching assistantships with full tuition reimbursements available (averaging $17,423 per year); career-related internships or fieldwork, Federal Work-Study, institutionally sponsored loans, health care benefits, and unspecified assistantships also available. Financial award application deadline: 2/1; financial award applicants required to submit FAFSA. *Faculty research:* Atmospheric re-entry mechanics, hybrid rocket propulsion, laser-induced plasma spectroscopy, unsteady aerodynamics and aero elasticity. *Unit head:* Dr. Matthew Mench, Head, 865-974-5115, Fax: 865-974-5274, E-mail: mmench@utk.edu. *Application contact:* Dr. Kivanc Ekici, Associate Professor, Graduate Program Director, 865-974-6016, Fax: 865-974-5274, E-mail: ekici@utk.edu.
Website: http://www.engr.utk.edu/mabe/

The University of Tennessee, The University of Tennessee Space Institute, Tullahoma, TN 37388. Offers aerospace engineering (MS, PhD); biomedical engineering (MS, PhD); engineering science (MS, PhD); industrial and systems engineering/engineering management (MS, PhD); mechanical engineering (MS, PhD); physics (MS, PhD). *Program availability:* Part-time, blended/hybrid learning. Terminal master's awarded for partial completion of doctoral program. *Degree requirements:* For doctorate, one foreign language, thesis/dissertation. *Entrance requirements:* Additional exam requirements/recommendations for international students: Required—TOEFL (minimum score 550 paper-based; 80 iBT), IELTS (minimum score 6.5). Electronic applications accepted. *Expenses:* Contact institution. *Faculty research:* Fluid mechanics/aerodynamics, chemical and electric propulsion and laser diagnostics, computational mechanics and simulations, carbon fiber production and composite materials.

The University of Texas at Arlington, Graduate School, College of Engineering, Department of Mechanical and Aerospace Engineering, Program in Aerospace Engineering, Arlington, TX 76019. Offers M Engr, MS, PhD. *Program availability:* Part-time, evening/weekend, online learning. Terminal master's awarded for partial completion of doctoral program. *Degree requirements:* For master's, thesis optional; for doctorate, comprehensive exam, thesis/dissertation. *Entrance requirements:* For master's and doctorate, GRE General Test, minimum GPA of 3.0. Additional exam requirements/recommendations for international students: Required—TOEFL (minimum score 550 paper-based). *Application deadline:* For fall admission, 6/1 for domestic students, 4/1 for international students; for spring admission, 10/15 for domestic students, 9/15 for international students. Applications are processed on a rolling basis. Application fee: $50 ($70 for international students). *Financial support:* Fellowships with partial tuition reimbursements, research assistantships with partial tuition reimbursements, teaching assistantships with partial tuition reimbursements, institutionally sponsored loans, scholarships/grants, health care benefits, and unspecified assistantships available. Financial award application deadline: 6/1; financial award applicants required to submit FAFSA. *Unit head:* Dr. Erian Armanios, Chair, 817-272-2603, Fax: 817-272-5010, E-mail: armanios@uta.edu. *Application contact:* Dr. Kamesh Subbarao, Graduate Advisor, 817-272-7467, Fax: 817-272-2952, E-mail: subbarao@uta.edu.
Website: http://www.mae.uta.edu/

The University of Texas at Austin, Graduate School, Cockrell School of Engineering, Department of Aerospace Engineering and Engineering Mechanics, Program in Aerospace Engineering, Austin, TX 78712-1111. Offers MSE, PhD. *Entrance*

requirements: For master's and doctorate, GRE General Test. Electronic applications accepted.

University of Toronto, School of Graduate Studies, Faculty of Applied Science and Engineering, Institute for Aerospace Studies, Toronto, ON M5S 1A1, Canada. Offers M Eng, MA Sc, PhD. *Program availability:* Part-time. *Degree requirements:* For master's, thesis (for some programs); for doctorate, thesis/dissertation, formal manuscript for publication. *Entrance requirements:* For master's, BA Sc or equivalent in engineering (M Eng); bachelor's degree in physics, mathematics, engineering or chemistry (MA Sc); 2 letters of reference; for doctorate, master's degree in applied science, engineering, mathematics, physics, or chemistry; demonstrated ability to perform advanced research, 2 letters of reference. Additional exam requirements/recommendations for international students: Required—TOEFL (minimum score 580 paper-based), TWE (minimum score 5). Electronic applications accepted.

University of Virginia, School of Engineering and Applied Science, Department of Mechanical and Aerospace Engineering, Charlottesville, VA 22903. Offers ME, MS, PhD. *Program availability:* Online learning. *Faculty:* 22 full-time (5 women). *Students:* 93 full-time (11 women), 2 part-time (0 women); includes 9 minority (1 Black or African American, non-Hispanic/Latino; 5 Asian, non-Hispanic/Latino; 3 Hispanic/Latino), 42 international. Average age 26. 199 applicants, 35% accepted, 30 enrolled. In 2016, 13 master's, 9 doctorates awarded. *Degree requirements:* For master's, thesis (MS); for doctorate, comprehensive exam, thesis/dissertation. *Entrance requirements:* For master's and doctorate, GRE General Test, 3 letters of recommendation. Additional exam requirements/recommendations for international students: Required—TOEFL (minimum score 650 paper-based; 90 iBT), IELTS (minimum score 7). *Application deadline:* For fall admission, 8/1 for domestic students, 4/1 for international students; for winter admission, 12/1 for domestic students, 8/1 for international students; for spring admission, 5/1 for domestic students, 1/1 for international students. Applications are processed on a rolling basis. Application fee: $60. Electronic applications accepted. *Expenses:* Tuition, state resident: full-time $15,026; part-time $834 per credit hour. Tuition, nonresident: full-time $25,168; part-time $1378 per credit hour. *Required fees:* $2654. *Financial support:* Fellowships, research assistantships, and teaching assistantships available. Financial award application deadline: 1/15; financial award applicants required to submit FAFSA. *Faculty research:* Solid mechanics, dynamical systems and control, thermofluids. *Unit head:* Eroc Loth, Chair, 434-924-7424, Fax: 434-982-2037, E-mail: mae-adm@virginia.edu. *Application contact:* Graduate Secretary, 434-924-7425, Fax: 434-982-2037, E-mail: mae-adm@virginia.edu.
Website: http://www.mae.virginia.edu/NewMAE/

University of Washington, Graduate School, College of Engineering, William E. Boeing Department of Aeronautics and Astronautics, Seattle, WA 98195-2400. Offers MAE, MSAA, PhD. *Program availability:* Part-time, online learning. *Faculty:* 19 full-time (2 women). *Students:* 105 full-time (18 women), 130 part-time (25 women); includes 64 minority (4 Black or African American, non-Hispanic/Latino; 29 Asian, non-Hispanic/Latino; 24 Hispanic/Latino; 7 Two or more races, non-Hispanic/Latino), 36 international. 349 applicants, 48% accepted, 76 enrolled. In 2016, 60 master's, 10 doctorates awarded. Terminal master's awarded for partial completion of doctoral program. *Degree requirements:* For master's, thesis optional, completion of all work within 6 years; for doctorate, comprehensive exam, thesis/dissertation, qualifying, general and final exams; completion of all work within 10 years. *Entrance requirements:* For master's and doctorate, GRE General Test, minimum GPA of 3.0, letters of recommendation, statement of objectives, undergraduate degree in aerospace or mechanical engineering. Additional exam requirements/recommendations for international students: Required—TOEFL (minimum score 580 paper-based; 92 iBT); Recommended—IELTS (minimum score 7). *Application deadline:* For fall admission, 12/15 for domestic and international students. Application fee: $85. Electronic applications accepted. *Expenses:* Contact institution. *Financial support:* In 2016–17, 72 students received support, including 4 fellowships (averaging $2,307 per year), 49 research assistantships with full tuition reimbursements available (averaging $2,368 per year), 19 teaching assistantships with full tuition reimbursements available (averaging $2,335 per year); career-related internships or fieldwork, Federal Work-Study, health care benefits, tuition waivers (full), and unspecified assistantships also available. Financial award application deadline: 1/15; financial award applicants required to submit FAFSA. *Faculty research:* Space systems, aircraft systems, energy systems, aerospace control systems, advanced composite materials and structures, fluid mechanics. *Total annual research expenditures:* $11 million. *Unit head:* Dr. Anthony Waas, Professor and Chair, 206-543-1950, Fax: 206-543-0217, E-mail: awass@aa.washington.edu. *Application contact:* Ed Connery, Advisor and Admissions Coordinator, 206-543-6725, Fax: 206-543-0217, E-mail: econnery@aa.washington.edu.
Website: http://www.aa.washington.edu/

Utah State University, School of Graduate Studies, College of Engineering, Department of Mechanical and Aerospace Engineering, Logan, UT 84322. Offers aerospace engineering (MS, PhD); mechanical engineering (ME, MS, PhD). Terminal master's awarded for partial completion of doctoral program. *Degree requirements:* For master's, thesis (for some programs); for doctorate, thesis/dissertation. *Entrance requirements:* For master's, GRE General Test, minimum GPA of 3.0; for doctorate, GRE General Test, minimum GPA of 3.3. Additional exam requirements/recommendations for international students: Required—TOEFL. *Faculty research:* In-space instruments, cryogenic cooling, thermal science, space structures, composite materials.

Virginia Polytechnic Institute and State University, Graduate School, College of Engineering, Blacksburg, VA 24061. Offers aerospace engineering (ME, MS, PhD); biological systems engineering (ME, MS, PhD); biomedical engineering (MS, PhD); chemical engineering (ME, MS, PhD); civil engineering (ME, MS, PhD); computer engineering (ME, MS, PhD); computer science (MS, PhD); electrical engineering (ME, PhD); engineering education (PhD); engineering mechanics (ME, MS, PhD); environmental engineering (MS); environmental science and engineering (MS); industrial and systems engineering (ME, MS, PhD); materials science and engineering (ME, MS, PhD); mechanical engineering (ME, MS, PhD); mining and minerals engineering (PhD); mining engineering (ME, MS); nuclear engineering (MS, PhD); ocean engineering (MS); systems engineering (ME, MS). *Faculty:* 400 full-time (73 women), 3 part-time/adjunct (2 women). *Students:* 1,949 full-time (487 women), 393 part-time (69 women); includes 251 minority (56 Black or African American, non-Hispanic/Latino; 3 American Indian or Alaska Native, non-Hispanic/Latino; 87 Asian, non-Hispanic/Latino; 70 Hispanic/Latino; 35 Two or more races, non-Hispanic/Latino), 1,354 international. Average age 27. 4,903 applicants, 19% accepted, 569 enrolled. In 2016, 364 master's, 200 doctorates awarded. *Degree requirements:* For master's, comprehensive exam (for some programs), thesis (for some programs); for doctorate, comprehensive exam (for some programs), thesis/dissertation (for some programs). *Entrance requirements:* For master's and doctorate, GRE/GMAT. Additional exam requirements/recommendations for international students: Required—TOEFL (minimum score 80 iBT). *Application deadline:* For fall admission, 8/1 for domestic students, 4/1 for international students; for spring admission, 1/1 for domestic students, 9/1 for international students. Applications are processed on a rolling basis. Application fee: $75. Electronic applications accepted. *Expenses:* Tuition, state resident: full-time

Aerospace/Aeronautical Engineering

$12,467; part-time $692.50 per credit hour. Tuition, nonresident: full-time $25,095; part-time $1394.25 per credit hour. *Required fees:* $2669; $491.50 per semester. Tuition and fees vary according to course load, campus/location and program. *Financial support:* In 2016–17, 160 fellowships with full tuition reimbursements (averaging $7,387 per year), 872 research assistantships with full tuition reimbursements (averaging $22,329 per year), 313 teaching assistantships with full tuition reimbursements (averaging $18,714 per year) were awarded. Financial award application deadline: 3/1; financial award applicants required to submit FAFSA. *Total annual research expenditures:* $91.8 million. *Unit head:* Dr. Julia Ross, Dean, 540-231-9752, Fax: 540-231-3031, E-mail: deaneng@vt.edu. *Application contact:* Linda Perkins, Executive Assistant, 540-231-9752, Fax: 540-231-3031, E-mail: lperkins@vt.edu.
Website: http://www.eng.vt.edu/

Virginia Polytechnic Institute and State University, VT Online, Blacksburg, VA 24061. Offers advanced transportation systems (Certificate); aerospace engineering (MS); agricultural and life sciences (MSLFS); business information systems (Graduate Certificate); career and technical education (MS); civil engineering (MS); computer engineering (M Eng, MS); decision support systems (Graduate Certificate); eLearning leadership (MA); electrical engineering (M Eng, MS); engineering administration (MEA); environmental engineering (Certificate); environmental politics and policy (Graduate Certificate); environmental sciences and engineering (MS); foundations of political analysis (Graduate Certificate); health product risk management (Graduate Certificate); industrial and systems engineering (MS); information policy and society (Graduate Certificate); information security (Graduate Certificate); information technology (MIT); instructional technology (MA); integrative STEM education (MA Ed); liberal arts (Graduate Certificate); life sciences: health product risk management (MS); natural resources (MNR, Graduate Certificate); networking (Graduate Certificate); nonprofit and nongovernmental organization management (Graduate Certificate); ocean engineering (MS); political science (MA); security studies (Graduate Certificate); software development (Graduate Certificate). *Expenses:* Tuition, state resident: full-time $12,467; part-time $692.50 per credit hour. Tuition, nonresident: full-time $25,095; part-time $1394.25 per credit hour. *Required fees:* $2669; $491.50 per semester. Tuition and fees vary according to course load, campus/location and program.

Washington University in St. Louis, School of Engineering and Applied Science, Department of Mechanical Engineering and Materials Science, St. Louis, MO 63130-4899. Offers aerospace engineering (MS, PhD); materials science (MS); mechanical engineering (M Eng, MS, PhD). *Program availability:* Part-time. Terminal master's awarded for partial completion of doctoral program. *Degree requirements:* For master's, thesis optional; for doctorate, thesis/dissertation optional. *Entrance requirements:* For master's, GRE; for doctorate, GRE General Test, departmental qualifying exam. *Faculty research:* Aerosols science and technology, applied mechanics, biomechanics and biomedical engineering, design, dynamic systems, combustion science, composite materials, materials science.

Webster University, George Herbert Walker School of Business and Technology, Department of Management, St. Louis, MO 63119-3194. Offers business and organizational security management (MA); digital marketing management (Graduate Certificate); government contracting (Graduate Certificate); health administration (MHA); health care management (MA); health services management (MA); human resources development (MA); human resources management (MA); information technology management (MA, MS); management (D Mgt); management and leadership (MA); marketing (MA); nonprofit leadership (MA); nonprofit revenue development (Graduate Certificate); organizational development (Graduate Certificate); procurement and acquisitions management (MA); public administration (MPA); space systems operations management (MS). *Program availability:* Part-time, evening/weekend, online learning. *Degree requirements:* For master's, thesis (for some programs); for doctorate, thesis/dissertation, written exam. *Entrance requirements:* For doctorate, GMAT, 3 years of work experience, MBA. Additional exam requirements/recommendations for international students: Required—TOEFL. *Application deadline:* Applications are processed on a rolling basis. Application fee: $25 ($50 for international students). *Expenses:* Tuition: Full-time $21,900; part-time $730 per credit hour. Tuition and fees vary according to campus/location and program. *Financial support:* Federal Work-Study available. Support available to part-time students. Financial award application deadline:

4/1; financial award applicants required to submit FAFSA. *Unit head:* Barrett Baebler, Chair, 314-246-7940, E-mail: baeblerb@webster.edu. *Application contact:* Sarah Nandor, Director, Graduate and Transfer Admissions, 314-968-7109, E-mail: gadmit@webster.edu.

Western Michigan University, Graduate College, College of Engineering and Applied Sciences, Department of Mechanical and Aerospace Engineering, Kalamazoo, MI 49008. Offers mechanical engineering (MSE, PhD). *Program availability:* Part-time. *Degree requirements:* For master's, thesis optional; for doctorate, thesis/dissertation.

West Virginia University, Statler College of Engineering and Mineral Resources, Department of Mechanical and Aerospace Engineering, Program in Aerospace Engineering, Morgantown, WV 26506. Offers MSAE, PhD. *Program availability:* Part-time. Terminal master's awarded for partial completion of doctoral program. *Degree requirements:* For master's, thesis; for doctorate, comprehensive exam, thesis/dissertation, qualifying exams, proposal defense. *Entrance requirements:* For master's and doctorate, GRE General Test, minimum GPA of 3.0, 3 reference letters. Additional exam requirements/recommendations for international students: Required—TOEFL (minimum score 550 paper-based; 79 iBT). *Faculty research:* Transonic flight controls and simulations, thermal science, composite materials, aerospace design.

Wichita State University, Graduate School, College of Engineering, Department of Aerospace Engineering, Wichita, KS 67260. Offers MS, PhD. *Program availability:* Part-time. *Unit head:* Dr. L. Scott Miller, Chairperson, 316-978-3410, E-mail: scott.miller@wichita.edu. *Application contact:* Jordan Oleson, Admission Coordinator, 316-978-3095, E-mail: jordan.oleson@wichita.edu.
Website: http://www.wichita.edu/ae

Worcester Polytechnic Institute, Graduate Studies and Research, Program in Aerospace Engineering, Worcester, MA 01609-2280. Offers MS, PhD. *Program availability:* Part-time, evening/weekend. *Students:* 23 full-time (3 women), 2 part-time (0 women); includes 5 minority (1 Black or African American, non-Hispanic/Latino; 2 Asian, non-Hispanic/Latino; 1 Hispanic/Latino; 1 Two or more races, non-Hispanic/Latino), 7 international. 38 applicants, 84% accepted, 12 enrolled. In 2016, 4 master's, 1 doctorate awarded. *Entrance requirements:* For master's and doctorate, 3 letters of recommendation, statement of purpose. Additional exam requirements/recommendations for international students: Required—TOEFL (minimum score 563 paper-based; 84 iBT), IELTS (minimum score 7). *Application deadline:* For fall admission, 1/1 for domestic and international students; for spring admission, 10/1 for domestic and international students. Applications are processed on a rolling basis. Application fee: $70. Electronic applications accepted. *Financial support:* Research assistantships and teaching assistantships available. Financial award application deadline: 1/1; financial award applicants required to submit FAFSA. *Unit head:* Dr. Nikolas Gatsonis, Director, 508-831-5221, Fax: 508-831-5680, E-mail: gatsonis@wpi.edu. *Application contact:* Donna Hughes, Administrative Assistant, 508-831-5221, E-mail: dmhughes@wpi.edu.
Website: http://www.wpi.edu/academics/aero/gradprograms.html

Wright State University, Graduate School, College of Engineering and Computer Science, Department of Mechanical and Materials Engineering, Dayton, OH 45435. Offers aerospace systems engineering (MSE); materials science and engineering (MSE); mechanical engineering (MSE); renewable and clean energy (MSE). *Degree requirements:* For master's, thesis or course option alternative. *Entrance requirements:* Additional exam requirements/recommendations for international students: Required—TOEFL. Application fee: $25. *Expenses:* Tuition, state resident: full-time $9952; part-time $622 per credit hour. Tuition, nonresident: full-time $16,960; part-time $1060 per credit hour. *Financial support:* Fellowships, research assistantships, teaching assistantships, and unspecified assistantships available. Support available to part-time students. Financial award application deadline: 3/15; financial award applicants required to submit FAFSA. *Unit head:* Dr. George P.G. Huang, Chair, 937-775-5040, Fax: 937-775-5009, E-mail: george.huang@wright.edu. *Application contact:* John Kimble, Associate Director of Graduate Admissions and Records, 937-775-2957, Fax: 937-775-2453, E-mail: john.kimble@wright.edu.
Website: https://engineering-computer-science.wright.edu/mechanical-and-materials-engineering

Aviation

Embry-Riddle Aeronautical University–Prescott, Program in Safety Science, Prescott, AZ 86301-3720. Offers aviation safety (MSSS). *Program availability:* Part-time. *Faculty:* 4 full-time (0 women), 1 part-time/adjunct (0 women). *Students:* 27 full-time (7 women); includes 3 minority (1 Black or African American, non-Hispanic/Latino; 2 Two or more races, non-Hispanic/Latino), 9 international. Average age 32. 29 applicants, 69% accepted, 9 enrolled. In 2016, 20 master's awarded. *Degree requirements:* For master's, research project, capstone, or thesis. *Entrance requirements:* For master's, GRE (taken within the last 5 years), transcripts, statement of objectives, references, resume. Additional exam requirements/recommendations for international students: Required—TOEFL (minimum score 550 paper-based, 79 iBT) or IELTS (6). *Application deadline:* For fall admission, 1/15 priority date for domestic students; for spring admission, 11/1 priority date for domestic students; for summer admission, 4/1 priority date for domestic students. Applications are processed on a rolling basis. Application fee: $50. Electronic applications accepted. *Expenses: Tuition:* Full-time $16,296; part-time $1358 per credit hour. *Required fees:* $1234; $617 per semester. One-time fee: $100 full-time. Tuition and fees vary according to course load. *Financial support:* Research assistantships, career-related internships or fieldwork, scholarships/grants, and unspecified assistantships available. Financial award application deadline: 3/15; financial award applicants required to submit FAFSA. *Faculty research:* Wildlife Strike Database, Website maintenance, expansion of graphics applications to Web search for general aviation. *Unit head:* Archie Dickey, PhD, Dean, College of Arts and Sciences, E-mail: archie.dickey@erau.edu. *Application contact:* Graduate Admissions, 928-777-6600, E-mail: prescott@erau.edu.
Website: http://prescott.erau.edu/degrees/master/safety-science/index.html

Everglades University, Graduate Programs, Program in Aviation Science, Boca Raton, FL 33431. Offers aviation operations management (MSA); aviation security (MSA); business administration (MSA). *Program availability:* Part-time, evening/weekend, 100% online. *Entrance requirements:* For master's, GMAT (minimum score of 400) or GRE (minimum score of 290), bachelor's or graduate degree from college accredited by an agency recognized by the U.S. Department of Education; minimum cumulative GPA of 2.0 at the baccalaureate level, 3.0 at the master's level. Additional exam requirements/recommendations for international students: Recommended—TOEFL (minimum score 500 paper-based). Electronic applications accepted. *Expenses:* Contact institution.

Florida Institute of Technology, College of Aeronautics, Program in Applied Aviation Safety, Melbourne, FL 32901-6975. Offers MSA. *Program availability:* Part-time. *Students:* 6 full-time (1 woman), 1 part-time (0 women); includes 1 minority (Hispanic/Latino), 5 international. Average age 26. 10 applicants, 50% accepted, 1 enrolled. In 2016, 2 master's awarded. *Degree requirements:* For master's, thesis, 36 credit hours. *Entrance requirements:* For master's, GRE, 3 letters of recommendation, resume, statement of objectives. Additional exam requirements/recommendations for international students: Required—TOEFL (minimum score 550 paper-based; 79 iBT). *Application deadline:* Applications are processed on a rolling basis. Electronic applications accepted. *Expenses: Tuition:* Full-time $22,338; part-time $1241 per credit hour. *Required fees:* $250. Tuition and fees vary according to degree level, campus/location and program. *Financial support:* Applicants required to submit FAFSA. *Unit head:* Dr. Korhan Oyman, Dean, 321-674-8971, E-mail: koyman@fit.edu. *Application contact:* Cheryl A. Brown, Associate Director of Graduate Admissions, 321-674-7581, Fax: 321-723-9468, E-mail: cbrown@fit.edu.
Website: http://www.fit.edu/programs/8205/msa-aviation-applied-aviation-safety#.VUDm_k10ypo

Florida Institute of Technology, College of Aeronautics, Program in Aviation Safety, Melbourne, FL 32901-6975. Offers MSA. *Program availability:* Part-time-only, evening/weekend, online only, 100% online. *Students:* 1 (woman) full-time, 30 part-time (6 women); includes 6 minority (3 Black or African American, non-Hispanic/Latino; 1 American Indian or Alaska Native, non-Hispanic/Latino; 2 Hispanic/Latino), 3 international. Average age 36. 31 applicants, 26% accepted, 7 enrolled. In 2016, 17 master's awarded. *Degree requirements:* For master's, thesis or alternative, 30 credit hours including capstone course. *Entrance requirements:* For master's, letter of recommendation, resume, statement of objectives, aviation experience or related undergraduate degree or prequisite course. Additional exam requirements/recommendations for international students: Required—TOEFL (minimum score 550 paper-based; 79 iBT). *Application deadline:* Applications are processed on a rolling basis. Electronic applications accepted. *Expenses: Tuition:* Full-time $22,338; part-time $1241 per credit hour. *Required fees:* $250. Tuition and fees vary according to degree level, campus/location and program. *Unit head:* Dr. Korhan Oyman, Dean, 321-674-8971, E-mail: koyman@fit.edu. *Application contact:* Cheryl A. Brown, Associate Director of Graduate Admissions, 321-674-7581, Fax: 321-723-9468, E-mail: cbrown@fit.edu. Website: http://coa.fit.edu.

Florida Institute of Technology, College of Aeronautics, Program in Aviation Sciences, Melbourne, FL 32901-6975. Offers PhD. *Program availability:* Part-time. *Students:* 18 full-time (6 women), 3 part-time (0 women); includes 2 minority (1 Black or African American, non-Hispanic/Latino; 1 Asian, non-Hispanic/Latino), 13 international. Average age 37. 14 applicants, 93% accepted, 9 enrolled. In 2016, 4 doctorates awarded. *Degree requirements:* For doctorate, thesis/dissertation or alternative, 51 semester hours. *Entrance requirements:* For doctorate, 3 letters of recommendation, resume, statement of objectives, minimum GPA of 3.2, three years of work experience in aviation industry. Additional exam requirements/recommendations for international students: Required—TOEFL (minimum score 550 paper-based; 79 iBT). *Application deadline:* Applications are processed on a rolling basis. Electronic applications accepted. *Expenses: Tuition:* Full-time $22,338; part-time $1241 per credit hour. *Required fees:* $250. Tuition and fees vary according to degree level, campus/location and program. *Financial support:* Applicants required to submit FAFSA. *Unit head:* Dr. Korhan Oyman, Dean, 321-674-8971, E-mail: koyman@fit.edu. *Application contact:* Cheryl A. Brown, Associate Director of Graduate Admissions, 321-674-7581, Fax: 321-723-9468, E-mail: cbrown@fit.edu.
Website: http://coa.fit.edu

Lewis University, College of Arts and Sciences, Program in Aviation and Transportation, Romeoville, IL 60446. Offers administration (MS); safety and security (MS). *Program availability:* Part-time, evening/weekend, 100% online, blended/hybrid learning. *Students:* 30 full-time (7 women), 18 part-time (4 women); includes 10 minority (5 Black or African American, non-Hispanic/Latino; 1 Asian, non-Hispanic/Latino; 2 Hispanic/Latino; 2 Two or more races, non-Hispanic/Latino), 9 international. Average age 33. *Entrance requirements:* For master's, bachelor's degree, minimum GPA of 3.0, personal statement, 3 letters of recommendation. Additional exam requirements/recommendations for international students: Required—TOEFL (minimum score 550 paper-based; 80 iBT). *Application deadline:* For fall admission, 5/1 priority date for international students; for spring admission, 11/15 priority date for international students. Applications are processed on a rolling basis. Application fee: $40. Electronic applications accepted. *Expenses: Tuition:* Full-time $13,860; part-time $770 per credit hour. *Required fees:* $75 per semester. Tuition and fees vary according to degree level and program. *Financial support:* Application deadline: 5/1; applicants required to submit FAFSA. *Total annual research expenditures:* $30. *Unit head:* Dr. Randal DeMik, Program Chair, 815-838-0500 Ext. 5559, E-mail: demikra@lewisu.edu. *Application

contact:* Julie Branchaw, Assistant Director, Graduate and Adult Admission, 815-836-5574, E-mail: branchju@lewisu.edu.

National Test Pilot School, National Flight Institute, Mojave, CA 93502-0658. Offers flight test and evaluation (MS); flight test engineering (MS). *Degree requirements:* For master's, final project. *Entrance requirements:* For master's, undergraduate degree in engineering, physical or computer science, mathematics or technical management.

Southeastern Oklahoma State University, Department of Aviation Science, Durant, OK 74701-0609. Offers aerospace administration and logistics (MS). *Program availability:* Part-time, evening/weekend. *Entrance requirements:* For master's, minimum GPA of 3.0 in last 60 hours or 2.75 overall. Additional exam requirements/recommendations for international students: Required—TOEFL (minimum score 550 paper-based; 79 iBT). Electronic applications accepted.

University of North Dakota, Graduate School, John D. Odegard School of Aerospace Sciences, Department of Aviation, Grand Forks, ND 58202. Offers MS. *Program availability:* Part-time, online learning. *Degree requirements:* For master's, comprehensive exam. *Entrance requirements:* For master's, GRE General Test, FAA private pilot certificate or foreign equivalent. Additional exam requirements/recommendations for international students: Required—TOEFL (minimum score 550 paper-based; 79 iBT), IELTS (minimum score 6.5). *Application deadline:* For fall admission, 8/1 priority date for domestic students, 5/1 priority date for international students; for spring admission, 12/1 priority date for domestic students, 9/1 priority date for international students. Applications are processed on a rolling basis. Application fee: $35. Electronic applications accepted. *Financial support:* Fellowships with full and partial tuition reimbursements, research assistantships with full and partial tuition reimbursements, teaching assistantships with full and partial tuition reimbursements, Federal Work-Study, institutionally sponsored loans, scholarships/grants, health care benefits, and unspecified assistantships available. Support available to part-time students. Financial award application deadline: 3/15; financial award applicants required to submit FAFSA. *Unit head:* Dr. Kimberly Kenville, Graduate Director, 701-777-4964, E-mail: kimk@aero.und.edu. *Application contact:* Staci Wells, Admissions Specialist, 701-777-0748, Fax: 701-777-3619, E-mail: staci.wells@gradschool.und.edu.
Website: http://www.aviation.und.edu/

The University of Tennessee, Graduate School, Intercollegiate Programs, Program in Aviation Systems, Knoxville, TN 37996. Offers MS. *Program availability:* Part-time, online learning. *Degree requirements:* For master's, thesis optional. *Entrance requirements:* For master's, minimum GPA of 2.7. Additional exam requirements/recommendations for international students: Required—TOEFL. Electronic applications accepted.

Section 3
Agricultural Engineering and Bioengineering

This section contains a directory of institutions offering graduate work in agricultural engineering and bioengineering, followed by an in-depth entry submitted by an institution that chose to prepare detailed program descriptions. Additional information about programs listed in the directory but not augmented by an in-depth entry may be obtained by writing directly to the dean of a graduate school or chair of a department at the address given in the directory.

For programs offering related work, see also in this book *Biomedical Engineering and Biotechnology; Civil and Environmental Engineering; Engineering and Applied Sciences;* and *Management of Engineering and Technology.* In the other guides in this series:

Graduate Programs in the Biological/Biomedical Sciences & Health-Related Medical Professions

See *Biological and Biomedical Sciences; Ecology, Environmental Biology, and Evolutionary Biology; Marine Biology; Nutrition;* and *Zoology*

Graduate Programs in the Physical Sciences, Mathematics, Agricultural Sciences, the Environment & Natural Resources

See *Agricultural and Food Sciences* and *Natural Resources*

CONTENTS

Agricultural Engineering

Cornell University, Graduate School, Graduate Fields of Agriculture and Life Sciences and Graduate Fields of Engineering, Field of Biological and Environmental Engineering, Ithaca, NY 14853. Offers bioenergy and integrated energy systems (M Eng, MPS, MS, PhD); biological engineering (M Eng, MPS, MS, PhD); bioprocess engineering (M Eng, MPS, MS, PhD); ecohydrology (M Eng, MPS, MS, PhD); environmental engineering (M Eng, MPS, MS, PhD); environmental management (MPS); food engineering (M Eng, MPS, MS, PhD); industrial biotechnology (M Eng, MPS, MS, PhD); nanobiotechnology (M Eng, MPS, MS, PhD); sustainable systems (M Eng, MPS, MS, PhD); synthetic biology (MS); syntheticbiology (M Eng, MPS, PhD). Terminal master's awarded for partial completion of doctoral program. *Degree requirements:* For master's, thesis (MS); for doctorate, comprehensive exam, thesis/dissertation. *Entrance requirements:* For master's, letters of recommendation (3 for MS, 2 for M Eng and MPS); for doctorate, GRE General Test, 3 letters of recommendation. Additional exam requirements/recommendations for international students: Required—TOEFL (minimum score 550 paper-based; 77 iBT). Electronic applications accepted. *Faculty research:* Biological and food engineering, environmental, soil and water engineering, international agricultural engineering, structures and controlled environments, machine systems and energy.

Dalhousie University, Faculty of Engineering, Department of Biological Engineering, Halifax, NS B3J 2X4, Canada. Offers M Eng, MA Sc, PhD. *Degree requirements:* For master's, thesis; for doctorate, thesis/dissertation. *Entrance requirements:* Additional exam requirements/recommendations for international students: Required—TOEFL, IELTS, CANTEST, CAEL, or Michigan English Language Assessment Battery. *Faculty research:* Waste management, energy and environment, bio-machinery and robotics, soil and water, aquacultural and food engineering.

Illinois Institute of Technology, Graduate College, School of Applied Technology, Institute for Food Safety and Health, Bedford Park, IL 60501-1957. Offers food process engineering (MFPE, MS); food safety and technology (MFST, MS). *Program availability:* Part-time. *Degree requirements:* For master's, comprehensive exam (for some programs), thesis (for some programs). *Entrance requirements:* For master's, GRE (minimum score 304), minimum undergraduate GPA of 3.0. Additional exam requirements/recommendations for international students: Required—TOEFL (minimum score 550 paper-based; 80 iBT). Electronic applications accepted. *Faculty research:* Microbial food safety and security, food virology, interfacial colloidal phenomena, development of DNA-based methods for detection, differentiation and tracking of food borne pathogens in food systems and environment, appetite and obesity management and vascular disease.

Instituto Tecnológico y de Estudios Superiores de Monterrey, Campus Monterrey, Graduate and Research Division, Program in Agriculture, Monterrey, Mexico. Offers agricultural parasitology (PhD); agricultural sciences (MS); farming productivity (MS); food processing engineering (MS); phytopathology (MS). *Program availability:* Part-time. *Degree requirements:* For master's, one foreign language, thesis; for doctorate, one foreign language, thesis/dissertation. *Entrance requirements:* For master's, EXADEP; for doctorate, GMAT or GRE, master's degree in related field. Additional exam requirements/recommendations for international students: Required—TOEFL. *Faculty research:* Animal embryos and reproduction, crop entomology, tropical agriculture, agricultural productivity, induced mutation in oleaginous plants.

Iowa State University of Science and Technology, Program in Agricultural and Biosystems Engineering, Ames, IA 50011. Offers M En, MS, PhD. *Students:* 55 full-time (21 women), 21 part-time (7 women); includes 7 minority (3 Black or African American, non-Hispanic/Latino; 1 American Indian or Alaska Native, non-Hispanic/Latino; 2 Asian, non-Hispanic/Latino; 1 Hispanic/Latino), 29 international. *Degree requirements:* For master's, thesis (for some programs); for doctorate, thesis/dissertation. *Entrance requirements:* For master's and doctorate, GRE. Additional exam requirements/recommendations for international students: Required—TOEFL (minimum score 550 paper-based; 79 iBT), IELTS (minimum score 6.5). *Application deadline:* For fall admission, 2/15 priority date for domestic students, 2/1 priority date for international students; for spring admission, 7/1 priority date for domestic and international students. Application fee: $40 ($90 for international students). Electronic applications accepted. *Faculty research:* Grain processing and quality, tillage systems, simulation and controls, water management, environmental quality. *Application contact:* Kris Bell, Graduate Secretary, 515-294-1033, E-mail: kabell@iastate.edu.
Website: http://www.abe.iastate.edu

Kansas State University, Graduate School, College of Agriculture, Department of Grain Science and Industry, Manhattan, KS 66506. Offers MS, PhD. *Program availability:* Part-time. *Faculty:* 19 full-time (5 women), 7 part-time/adjunct (2 women). *Students:* 36 full-time (18 women), 4 part-time (2 women); includes 2 minority (both Hispanic/Latino), 30 international. Average age 26. 15 applicants, 73% accepted, 6 enrolled. In 2016, 11 master's, 4 doctorates awarded. Terminal master's awarded for partial completion of doctoral program. *Degree requirements:* For master's, thesis, oral exam; for doctorate, thesis/dissertation, preliminary exam. *Entrance requirements:* For master's and doctorate, GRE General Test, minimum undergraduate GPA of 3.0. Additional exam requirements/recommendations for international students: Required—TOEFL (minimum score 550 paper-based; 79 iBT), IELTS (minimum score 7). *Application deadline:* For fall admission, 5/1 priority date for domestic students, 2/1 priority date for international students; for spring admission, 10/1 priority date for domestic students, 8/1 priority date for international students. Applications are processed on a rolling basis. Application fee: $50 ($75 for international students). Electronic applications accepted. *Expenses:* Tuition, state resident: full-time $9670. Tuition, nonresident: full-time $21,828. *Required fees:* $862. *Financial support:* In 2016–17, fellowships (averaging $25,000 per year), 35 research assistantships (averaging $20,192 per year), 2 teaching assistantships with partial tuition reimbursements (averaging $16,150 per year) were awarded; Federal Work-Study, institutionally sponsored loans, and scholarships/grants also available. Support available to part-time students. Financial award application deadline: 3/1; financial award applicants required to submit FAFSA. *Faculty research:* Cereal science, bakery science and management, feed science and management, milling science and management. *Total annual research expenditures:* $4.4 million. *Unit head:* Gordon Smith, Head, 785-532-6161, Fax: 785-532-7010, E-mail: glsmith@ksu.edu. *Application contact:* Jon Faubion, Chair, Graduate Admissions, 785-532-5320, Fax: 785-532-7010, E-mail: jfaubion@ksu.edu.
Website: http://www.grains.k-state.edu/

Kansas State University, Graduate School, College of Engineering, Department of Biological and Agricultural Engineering, Manhattan, KS 66506. Offers MS, PhD. *Faculty:* 15 full-time (4 women), 6 part-time/adjunct (0 women). *Students:* 25 full-time (9 women), 11 part-time (4 women); includes 3 minority (2 Black or African American, non-Hispanic/Latino; 1 Asian, non-Hispanic/Latino), 18 international. Average age 29. 22 applicants, 50% accepted, 6 enrolled. In 2016, 7 master's, 2 doctorates awarded. Terminal master's awarded for partial completion of doctoral program. *Degree requirements:* For master's, thesis; for doctorate, thesis/dissertation, preliminary exam. *Entrance requirements:* For master's, GRE, bachelor's degree in biological and agricultural engineering; for doctorate, GRE. Additional exam requirements/recommendations for international students: Required—TOEFL (minimum score 550 paper-based; 79 iBT). *Application deadline:* For fall admission, 2/1 priority date for domestic students, 1/1 priority date for international students; for spring admission, 8/1 priority date for domestic and international students. Applications are processed on a rolling basis. Application fee: $50 ($75 for international students). Electronic applications accepted. *Expenses:* Tuition, state resident: full-time $9670. Tuition, nonresident: full-time $21,828. *Required fees:* $862. *Financial support:* In 2016–17, 2 students received support, including 21 research assistantships (averaging $20,114 per year); fellowships, teaching assistantships, Federal Work-Study, institutionally sponsored loans, and scholarships/grants also available. Support available to part-time students. Financial award application deadline: 3/1; financial award applicants required to submit FAFSA. *Faculty research:* Ecological engineering, watershed modeling, air quality, bioprocessing, biofuel, sensors and controls, 3D engineered biomaterials and biomedical devices, mobile health, point-of-care diagnosis, protein biomarker discovery, cancer early detection. *Total annual research expenditures:* $1.1 million. *Unit head:* Dr. Joseph Harner, Head, 785-532-5580, Fax: 785-532-5825, E-mail: jharner@k-state.edu. *Application contact:* Dr. Naiqian Zhang, Graduate Coordinator, 785-532-2910, Fax: 785-532-5825, E-mail: zhangn@k-state.edu.
Website: http://www.bae.ksu.edu/

Louisiana State University and Agricultural & Mechanical College, Graduate School, College of Engineering, Department of Biological and Agricultural Engineering, Baton Rouge, LA 70803. Offers biological and agricultural engineering (MSBAE); engineering science (MS, PhD).

McGill University, Faculty of Graduate and Postdoctoral Studies, Faculty of Agricultural and Environmental Sciences, Department of Bioresource Engineering, Montréal, QC H3A 2T5, Canada. Offers computer applications (M Sc, M Sc A, PhD); food engineering (M Sc, M Sc A, PhD); grain drying (M Sc, M Sc A, PhD); irrigation and drainage (M Sc, M Sc A, PhD); machinery (M Sc, M Sc A, PhD); pollution control (M Sc, M Sc A, PhD); post-harvest technology (M Sc, M Sc A, PhD); soil dynamics (M Sc, M Sc A, PhD); structure and environment (M Sc, M Sc A, PhD); vegetable and fruit storage (M Sc, M Sc A, PhD).

New York University, Graduate School of Arts and Science, Department of Environmental Medicine, New York, NY 10012-1019. Offers environmental health sciences (MS, PhD), including biostatistics (PhD), environmental hygiene (MS), epidemiology (PhD), ergonomics and biomechanics (PhD), exposure assessment and health effects (PhD), molecular toxicology/carcinogenesis (PhD), toxicology. *Program availability:* Part-time. Terminal master's awarded for partial completion of doctoral program. *Degree requirements:* For master's, thesis or alternative; for doctorate, one foreign language, thesis/dissertation, oral and written exams. *Entrance requirements:* For master's and doctorate, GRE General Test, minimum GPA of 3.0; bachelor's degree in biological, physical, or engineering science. Additional exam requirements/recommendations for international students: Required—TOEFL.

North Carolina State University, Graduate School, College of Agriculture and Life Sciences, Department of Biological and Agricultural Engineering, Raleigh, NC 27695. Offers MBAE, MS, PhD, Certificate. *Program availability:* Part-time, online learning. *Degree requirements:* For master's, thesis (for some programs); for doctorate, thesis/dissertation. *Entrance requirements:* For master's and doctorate, GRE. Additional exam requirements/recommendations for international students: Required—TOEFL. Electronic applications accepted. *Faculty research:* Bioinstrumentation, animal waste management, water quality engineering, machine systems, controlled environment agriculture.

The Ohio State University, Graduate School, College of Food, Agricultural, and Environmental Sciences, Department of Food, Agricultural, and Biological Engineering, Columbus, OH 43210. Offers MS, PhD. Program offered jointly with College of Engineering. *Faculty:* 19. *Students:* 42 full-time (14 women), 5 part-time (1 woman), 24 international. Average age 28. In 2016, 10 master's, 2 doctorates awarded. *Degree requirements:* For master's, thesis optional; for doctorate, thesis/dissertation. *Entrance requirements:* For master's and doctorate, GRE General Test, GRE Subject Test in engineering (recommended). Additional exam requirements/recommendations for international students: Required—TOEFL (minimum score 550 paper-based; 79 iBT), Michigan English Language Assessment Battery (minimum score 82); Recommended—IELTS (minimum score 7). *Application deadline:* For fall admission, 12/13 priority date for domestic students, 11/30 priority date for international students; for spring admission, 12/12 for domestic students, 11/10 for international students; for summer admission, 4/10 for domestic students, 3/13 for international students. Applications are processed on a rolling basis. Application fee: $60 ($70 for international students). Electronic applications accepted. *Financial support:* Fellowships with tuition reimbursements, research assistantships with tuition reimbursements, teaching assistantships with tuition reimbursements, career-related internships or fieldwork, Federal Work-Study, and institutionally sponsored loans available. Support available to part-time students. *Unit head:* Dr. Scott Shearer, Chair, 614-292-7284, E-mail: shearer.95@osu.edu. *Application contact:* Graduate and Professional Admissions, 614-292-9444, Fax: 614-292-3895, E-mail: gpadmissions@osu.edu.
Website: http://fabe.osu.edu/

Oklahoma State University, College of Agricultural Science and Natural Resources, Department of Biosystems and Agricultural Engineering, Stillwater, OK 74078. Offers biosystems engineering (MS, PhD); environmental and natural resources (MS, PhD). *Faculty:* 26 full-time (6 women), 2 part-time/adjunct (0 women). *Students:* 20 full-time (7 women), 11 part-time (3 women); includes 3 minority (2 Hispanic/Latino; 1 Two or more races, non-Hispanic/Latino), 14 international. Average age 29. 21 applicants, 24% accepted, 4 enrolled. In 2016, 9 master's, 8 doctorates awarded. *Degree requirements:* For master's, thesis; for doctorate, comprehensive exam, thesis/dissertation. *Entrance requirements:* For master's and doctorate, GRE or GMAT. Additional exam requirements/recommendations for international students: Required—TOEFL (minimum score 550 paper-based; 79 iBT). *Application deadline:* For fall admission, 3/1 priority date for international students; for spring admission, 8/1 priority date for international students. Applications are processed on a rolling basis. Application fee: $40 ($75 for international students). Electronic applications accepted. *Expenses:* Tuition, state resident: full-time $3775; part-time $209.70 per credit hour. Tuition, nonresident: full-time $14,851; part-time $825.05 per credit hour. *Required fees:* $2027; $112.60 per credit hour. Tuition and fees vary according to campus/location. *Financial support:* In 2016–17, 24 research assistantships (averaging $19,202 per year) were awarded; teaching assistantships, career-related internships or fieldwork, Federal Work-Study, scholarships/grants, health care benefits, tuition waivers (partial), and unspecified assistantships also available. Support available to part-time students. Financial award

application deadline: 3/1; financial award applicants required to submit FAFSA. *Unit head:* Dr. John Veenstra, Department Head, 405-744-5431, Fax: 405-744-6059, E-mail: jveenst@okstate.edu. *Application contact:* Dr. Ning Wang, Professor/Graduate Coordinator, 405-744-2877, E-mail: ning.wang@okstate.edu.
Website: http://bae.okstate.edu/

Oregon State University, College of Agricultural Sciences, Program in Food Science and Technology, Corvallis, OR 97331. Offers brewing (MS, PhD); enology (MS, PhD); flavor chemistry (MS, PhD); food and seafood processing (MS, PhD); food chemistry/biochemistry (MS, PhD); food engineering (MS, PhD); food microbiology/biotechnology (MS, PhD); sensory evaluation (MS, PhD). *Faculty:* 16 full-time (5 women). *Students:* 34 full-time (24 women), 4 part-time (2 women), 17 international. Average age 28. 118 applicants, 13% accepted, 13 enrolled. In 2016, 12 master's, 5 doctorates awarded. *Degree requirements:* For master's, thesis (for some programs); for doctorate, thesis/dissertation. *Entrance requirements:* For master's and doctorate, GRE (minimum Verbal and Quantitative scores of 300), minimum GPA of 3.0 in last 90 hours. Additional exam requirements/recommendations for international students: Required—TOEFL (minimum score 80 iBT), IELTS (minimum score 6.5). *Application deadline:* For fall admission, 4/1 for international students; for winter admission, 7/1 for international students; for spring admission, 10/1 for international students; for summer admission, 1/1 for international students. Application fee: $75 ($85 for international students). *Expenses:* Tuition, state resident: full-time $12,150; part-time $450 per credit. Tuition, nonresident: full-time $21,789; part-time $807 per credit. *Required fees:* $1651; $1507 per credit. One-time fee: $350. Tuition and fees vary according to course load, campus/location and program. *Financial support:* Fellowships, research assistantships, teaching assistantships, career-related internships or fieldwork, Federal Work-Study, and institutionally sponsored loans available. Support available to part-time students. *Unit head:* Dr. Robert McGorrin, Department Head and Professor. *Application contact:* Holly Templeton, Food Science and Technology Advisor, 541-737-6486, E-mail: holly.templeton@oregonstate.edu.
Website: http://oregonstate.edu/foodsci/graduate-program

Penn State University Park, Graduate School, College of Agricultural Sciences, Department of Agricultural and Biological Engineering, University Park, PA 16802. Offers agricultural and biological engineering (MS, PhD); biorenewable systems (MS, PhD). *Unit head:* Dr. Richard T. Roush, Dean, 814-865-2541, Fax: 814-865-3103. *Application contact:* Lori Hawn, Director, Graduate Student Services, 814-865-1795, Fax: 814-863-4627, E-mail: l-gswww@lists.psu.edu.
Website: http://abe.psu.edu/

Purdue University, College of Engineering, School of Agricultural and Biological Engineering, West Lafayette, IN 47907-2093. Offers MS, MSABE, MSE, PhD. *Program availability:* Part-time. *Faculty:* 61. *Students:* 97. In 2016, 8 master's, 21 doctorates awarded. Terminal master's awarded for partial completion of doctoral program. *Degree requirements:* For master's, thesis (for some programs); for doctorate, thesis/dissertation. *Entrance requirements:* For master's and doctorate, GRE General Test, minimum GPA of 3.0. *Application deadline:* For fall admission, 12/1 for domestic and international students; for spring admission, 10/1 for domestic and international students; for summer admission, 12/1 for domestic and international students. Applications are processed on a rolling basis. Application fee: $60 ($74 for international students). Electronic applications accepted. *Financial support:* Fellowships with full and partial tuition reimbursements, research assistantships with full and partial tuition reimbursements, teaching assistantships with full and partial tuition reimbursements, career-related internships or fieldwork, scholarships/grants, health care benefits, unspecified assistantships, and instructorships available. Financial award applicants required to submit FAFSA. *Faculty research:* Agricultural systems management, food process engineering, environmental and natural resources engineering, biological engineering, machine systems engineering. *Unit head:* Dr. Bernard Engel, Department Head/Professor, Agricultural and Biological Engineering, 765-494-1162, E-mail: engrad@purdue.edu. *Application contact:* Daniel Taylor, Assistant to Department Head, 765-494-1181, E-mail: taylordc@purdue.edu.
Website: https://engineering.purdue.edu/ABE

South Dakota State University, Graduate School, College of Engineering, Department of Agricultural and Biosystems Engineering, Brookings, SD 57007. Offers biological sciences (MS, PhD); engineering (MS). PhD offered jointly with Iowa State University of Science and Technology. *Program availability:* Part-time. *Degree requirements:* For master's, thesis (for some programs), oral exam; for doctorate, thesis/dissertation, preliminary oral and written exams. *Entrance requirements:* For master's and doctorate, engineering degree. Additional exam requirements/recommendations for international students: Required—TOEFL (minimum score 550 paper-based; 79 iBT). *Faculty research:* Water resources, food engineering, natural resources engineering, machine design, bioprocess engineering.

Texas A&M University, College of Agriculture and Life Sciences and College of Engineering, Department of Biological and Agricultural Engineering, College Station, TX 77843. Offers agricultural systems management (M Agr, MS); biological and agricultural engineering (M Engr, MS, PhD). *Program availability:* Part-time. *Faculty:* 19. *Students:* 66 full-time (24 women), 24 part-time (9 women); includes 14 minority (3 Black or African American, non-Hispanic/Latino; 1 Asian, non-Hispanic/Latino; 8 Hispanic/Latino; 2 Two or more races, non-Hispanic/Latino), 54 international. Average age 28. 23 applicants, 96% accepted, 17 enrolled. In 2016, 15 master's, 5 doctorates awarded. *Degree requirements:* For master's, thesis (MS), preliminary and final exams; for doctorate, thesis/dissertation, preliminary and final exams. *Entrance requirements:* For master's and doctorate, GRE General Test. Additional exam requirements/recommendations for international students: Required—TOEFL (minimum score 550 paper-based; 80 iBT), IELTS (minimum score 6), PTE (minimum score 53). *Application deadline:* For fall admission, 12/15 priority date for domestic students. Applications are processed on a rolling basis. Application fee: $50 ($90 for international students). Electronic applications accepted. *Expenses:* Contact institution. *Financial support:* In 2016–17, 63 students received support, including 4 fellowships with tuition reimbursements available (averaging $8,642 per year), 37 research assistantships with tuition reimbursements available (averaging $5,471 per year), 11 teaching assistantships with tuition reimbursements available (averaging $9,384 per year); career-related internships or fieldwork, institutionally sponsored loans, scholarships/grants, traineeships, health care benefits, tuition waivers (full and partial), and unspecified assistantships also available. Support available to part-time students. Financial award application deadline: 3/15; financial award applicants required to submit FAFSA. *Faculty research:* Water quality and quantity; air quality; biological, food, ecological engineering; off-road equipment; mechatronics. *Unit head:* Dr. Steve Searcy, Professor and Head, 979-845-3940, Fax: 979-862-3442, E-mail: s-searcy@tamu.edu. *Application contact:* Dr. Sandun Fernando, Director of Graduate Programs, 979-845-9793, E-mail: sfernando@tamu.edu.
Website: http://baen.tamu.edu

Université Laval, Faculty of Agricultural and Food Sciences, Department of Soils and Agricultural Engineering, Programs in Agri-Food Engineering, Québec, QC G1K 7P4, Canada. Offers agri-food engineering (M Sc); environmental technology (M Sc). *Degree requirements:* For master's, thesis (for some programs). *Entrance requirements:* For master's, knowledge of French. Electronic applications accepted.

The University of Arizona, College of Agriculture and Life Sciences, Department of Agricultural and Biosystems Engineering, Tucson, AZ 85721. Offers MS, PhD. Terminal master's awarded for partial completion of doctoral program. *Degree requirements:* For master's, thesis; for doctorate, thesis/dissertation. *Entrance requirements:* For master's, minimum GPA of 3.0 in last 2 years of undergraduate study, 3 letters of recommendation; for doctorate, minimum GPA of 3.0 in last 2 years of undergraduate study, 3 letters of recommendation, statement of purpose. Additional exam requirements/recommendations for international students: Required—TOEFL (minimum score 550 paper-based; 79 iBT). Electronic applications accepted. *Faculty research:* Irrigation system design, energy-use management, equipment for alternative crops, food properties enhancement.

University of Arkansas, Graduate School, College of Engineering, Department of Biological and Agricultural Engineering, Fayetteville, AR 72701. Offers biological and agricultural engineering (MSE, PhD); biological engineering (MSBE); biomedical engineering (MSBME). In 2016, 11 master's, 2 doctorates awarded. *Degree requirements:* For master's, thesis; for doctorate, one foreign language, thesis/dissertation. *Application deadline:* For fall admission, 4/1 for international students; for spring admission, 10/1 for international students. Applications are processed on a rolling basis. Application fee: $40 ($50 for international students). Electronic applications accepted. *Financial support:* In 2016–17, 21 research assistantships, 3 teaching assistantships were awarded; fellowships with tuition reimbursements, career-related internships or fieldwork, and Federal Work-Study also available. Support available to part-time students. Financial award application deadline: 4/1; financial award applicants required to submit FAFSA. *Unit head:* Dr. Lalit Verma, Department Head, 479-575-2351, Fax: 479-575-2846, E-mail: lverma@uark.edu. *Application contact:* Dr. Jin-Woo Kim, Program Coordinator, 479-575-2351, Fax: 479-575-2846, E-mail: jwkim@uark.edu.
Website: http://www.baeg.uark.edu/

University of Florida, Graduate School, Herbert Wertheim College of Engineering and College of Agricultural and Life Sciences, Department of Agricultural and Biological Engineering, Gainesville, FL 32611. Offers agricultural and biological engineering (ME, MS, PhD), including geographic information systems, hydrologic sciences, wetland sciences; biological systems modeling (Certificate). *Program availability:* Part-time. Terminal master's awarded for partial completion of doctoral program. *Degree requirements:* For master's, comprehensive exam, thesis (for some programs); for doctorate, comprehensive exam, thesis/dissertation. *Entrance requirements:* For master's and doctorate, minimum GPA of 3.0, 3 letters of recommendation, statement of purpose. Additional exam requirements/recommendations for international students: Required—TOEFL (minimum score 550 paper-based; 80 iBT), IELTS (minimum score 6). Electronic applications accepted. *Faculty research:* Bioenergy and bioprocessing; hydrological, biological and agricultural modeling; biosensors; precision agriculture and robotics; food packaging and food security.

University of Illinois at Urbana–Champaign, Graduate College, College of Agricultural, Consumer and Environmental Sciences, Department of Agricultural and Biological Engineering, Champaign, IL 61820. Offers agricultural and biological engineering (MS, PhD); technical systems management (MS, PSM).

University of Kentucky, Graduate School, College of Agriculture, Food and Environment, Program in Biosystems and Agricultural Engineering, Lexington, KY 40506-0032. Offers MS, PhD. *Program availability:* Part-time. *Degree requirements:* For master's, comprehensive exam, thesis optional; for doctorate, comprehensive exam, thesis/dissertation. *Entrance requirements:* For master's, GRE General Test, minimum undergraduate GPA of 2.75; for doctorate, GRE General Test, minimum graduate GPA of 3.0. Additional exam requirements/recommendations for international students: Required—TOEFL (minimum score 550 paper-based). Electronic applications accepted. *Faculty research:* Machine systems, food engineering, fermentation, hydrology, water quality.

University of Missouri, Office of Research and Graduate Studies, College of Engineering, Department of Biological Engineering, Columbia, MO 65211. Offers agricultural engineering (MS); biological engineering (MS, PhD). *Faculty:* 9 full-time (3 women), 1 (woman) part-time/adjunct. *Students:* 26 full-time (7 women), 25 part-time (7 women). *Degree requirements:* For master's, thesis; for doctorate, thesis/dissertation. *Entrance requirements:* For master's and doctorate, GRE General Test, minimum GPA of 3.0. Additional exam requirements/recommendations for international students: Required—TOEFL (minimum score 550 paper-based; 80 iBT). *Application deadline:* For fall admission, 4/1 for domestic students. Applications are processed on a rolling basis. Application fee: $75 ($90 for international students). Electronic applications accepted. *Expenses:* Tuition, state resident: full-time $6347; part-time $352.60 per credit hour. Tuition, nonresident: full-time $17,379; part-time $965.50 per credit hour. *Required fees:* $1035. Tuition and fees vary according to course load, campus/location and program. *Financial support:* Fellowships, research assistantships, teaching assistantships, institutionally sponsored loans, scholarships/grants, traineeships, health care benefits, and unspecified assistantships available. Support available to part-time students.
Website: http://bioengineering.missouri.edu/graduate/

University of Nebraska–Lincoln, Graduate College, College of Engineering, Department of Biological Systems Engineering, Interdepartmental Area of Agricultural and Biological Systems Engineering, Lincoln, NE 68588. Offers MS, PhD. *Degree requirements:* For master's, thesis optional. *Entrance requirements:* Additional exam requirements/recommendations for international students: Required—TOEFL (minimum score 550 paper-based). Electronic applications accepted. *Faculty research:* Hydrological engineering, tractive performance, biomedical engineering, irrigation systems.

The University of Tennessee, Graduate School, College of Agricultural Sciences and Natural Resources, Department of Biosystems Engineering and Environmental Science, Program in Biosystems Engineering Technology, Knoxville, TN 37996. Offers MS. *Degree requirements:* For master's, thesis or alternative. *Entrance requirements:* For master's, GRE General Test, minimum GPA of 2.7. Additional exam requirements/recommendations for international students: Required—TOEFL. Electronic applications accepted.

University of Wisconsin–Madison, Graduate School, College of Agricultural and Life Sciences, Department of Biological Systems Engineering, Madison, WI 53706. Offers MS, PhD. *Program availability:* Part-time. Terminal master's awarded for partial completion of doctoral program. *Degree requirements:* For master's, thesis; for doctorate, thesis/dissertation. *Entrance requirements:* Additional exam requirements/recommendations for international students: Required—TOEFL. Electronic applications accepted. *Faculty research:* Biomaterials, biosensors, food safety, food engineering, bioprocessing, machinery systems, natural resources and environment, structures engineering.

Utah State University, School of Graduate Studies, College of Engineering, Department of Biological and Irrigation Engineering, Logan, UT 84322. Offers biological and agricultural engineering (MS, PhD); irrigation engineering (MS, PhD). *Program availability:* Part-time. Terminal master's awarded for partial completion of doctoral program. *Degree requirements:* For master's, thesis (for some programs); for doctorate, thesis/dissertation. *Entrance requirements:* For master's and doctorate, GRE General

Test, minimum GPA of 3.0. Additional exam requirements/recommendations for international students: Required—TOEFL. *Faculty research:* On-farm water management, crop-water yield modeling, irrigation, biosensors, biological engineering.

Virginia Polytechnic Institute and State University, Graduate School, College of Engineering, Blacksburg, VA 24061. Offers aerospace engineering (ME, MS, PhD); biological systems engineering (ME, MS, PhD); biomedical engineering (MS, PhD); chemical engineering (ME, MS, PhD); civil engineering (ME, MS, PhD); computer engineering (ME, MS, PhD); computer science (MS, PhD); electrical engineering (ME, PhD); engineering education (PhD); engineering mechanics (ME, MS, PhD); environmental engineering (MS); environmental science and engineering (MS); industrial and systems engineering (ME, MS, PhD); materials science and engineering (ME, MS, PhD); mechanical engineering (ME, MS, PhD); mining and minerals engineering (PhD); mining engineering (ME, MS); nuclear engineering (MS, PhD); ocean engineering (MS); systems engineering (ME, MS). *Faculty:* 400 full-time (73 women), 3 part-time/adjunct (2 women). *Students:* 1,949 full-time (487 women), 393 part-time (69 women); includes 251 minority (56 Black or African American, non-Hispanic/Latino; 3 American Indian or Alaska Native, non-Hispanic/Latino; 87 Asian, non-Hispanic/Latino; 70 Hispanic/Latino; 35 Two or more races, non-Hispanic/Latino), 1,354 international. Average age 27. 4,903 applicants, 19% accepted, 569 enrolled. In 2016, 364 master's, 200 doctorates awarded. *Degree requirements:* For master's, comprehensive exam (for some programs), thesis (for some programs); for doctorate, comprehensive exam (for some programs), thesis/dissertation (for some programs). *Entrance requirements:* For master's and doctorate, GRE/GMAT. Additional exam requirements/recommendations for international students: Required—TOEFL (minimum score 80 iBT). *Application deadline:* For fall admission, 8/1 for domestic students, 4/1 for international students; for spring admission, 1/1 for domestic students, 9/1 for international students. Applications are processed on a rolling basis. Application fee: $75. Electronic applications accepted. *Expenses:* Tuition, state resident: full-time $12,467; part-time $692.50 per credit hour. Tuition, nonresident: full-time $25,095; part-time $1394.25 per credit hour. *Required fees:* $2669; $491.50 per semester. Tuition and fees vary according to course load, campus/location and program. *Financial support:* In 2016–17, 160 fellowships with full tuition reimbursements (averaging $7,387 per year), 872 research assistantships with full tuition reimbursements (averaging $22,329 per year), 313 teaching assistantships with full tuition reimbursements (averaging $18,714 per year) were awarded. Financial award application deadline: 3/1; financial award applicants required to submit FAFSA. *Total annual research expenditures:* $91.8 million. *Unit head:* Dr. Julia Ross, Dean, 540-231-9752, Fax: 540-231-3031, E-mail: deaneng@vt.edu. *Application contact:* Linda Perkins, Executive Assistant, 540-231-9752, Fax: 540-231-3031, E-mail: lperkins@vt.edu.
Website: http://www.eng.vt.edu/

Washington State University, College of Agricultural, Human, and Natural Resource Sciences, Department of Biological Systems Engineering, Pullman, WA 99164-6120. Offers biological and agricultural engineering (MS, PhD). Program applications must be made through the Pullman campus. *Degree requirements:* For master's, comprehensive exam, thesis (for some programs), written and oral exam; for doctorate, comprehensive exam, thesis/dissertation, written and oral exam. *Entrance requirements:* For master's and doctorate, minimum GPA of 3.0, bachelor's degree in engineering or closely-related subject. Additional exam requirements/recommendations for international students: Required—TOEFL. Electronic applications accepted. *Faculty research:* Agricultural automation engineering; bioenergy and bioproducts engineering; food engineering; land, air, and water resources and environmental engineering.

Bioengineering

Alfred University, Graduate School, College of Ceramics, Inamori School of Engineering, Alfred, NY 14802. Offers biomaterials engineering (MS); ceramic engineering (MS, PhD); electrical engineering (MS); glass science (MS, PhD); materials science and engineering (MS, PhD); mechanical engineering (MS). *Program availability:* Part-time. *Faculty:* 18 full-time (1 woman). *Students:* 26 full-time (6 women), 16 part-time (4 women); includes 1 minority (Hispanic/Latino), 12 international. Average age 27. 14 applicants, 79% accepted, 10 enrolled. In 2016, 13 master's, 5 doctorates awarded. *Degree requirements:* For master's, thesis; for doctorate, thesis/dissertation. *Entrance requirements:* Additional exam requirements/recommendations for international students: Required—TOEFL (minimum score 590 paper-based; 90 iBT), IELTS (minimum score 6.5). *Application deadline:* For fall admission, 3/1 priority date for domestic students, 3/15 for international students; for spring admission, 10/1 priority date for domestic students, 10/1 for international students. Applications are processed on a rolling basis. Application fee: $60. Electronic applications accepted. *Expenses:* Contact institution. *Financial support:* Fellowships with full tuition reimbursements, research assistantships with full tuition reimbursements, teaching assistantships with full tuition reimbursements, tuition waivers (full and partial), and unspecified assistantships available. Financial award application deadline: 8/1; financial award applicants required to submit FAFSA. *Faculty research:* X-ray diffraction, biomaterials and polymers, thin-film processing, electronic and optical ceramics, solid-state chemistry. *Unit head:* Dr. Alistair N. Cormack, Dean, 607-871-2422, E-mail: cormack@alfred.edu. *Application contact:* Sara Love, Coordinator of Graduate Admissions, 607-871-2115, Fax: 607-871-2198, E-mail: gradinquiry@alfred.edu.
Website: http://engineering.alfred.edu/grad/

Baylor College of Medicine, Graduate School of Biomedical Sciences, Program in Translational Biology and Molecular Medicine, Houston, TX 77030-3498. Offers PhD. *Degree requirements:* For doctorate, thesis/dissertation, public defense. *Entrance requirements:* For doctorate, GRE, minimum GPA of 3.0. Additional exam requirements/recommendations for international students: Required—TOEFL. Electronic applications accepted. *Faculty research:* Molecular medicine, translational biology, human disease biology and therapy.

California Institute of Technology, Division of Engineering and Applied Science, Option in Bioengineering, Pasadena, CA 91125-0001. Offers MS, PhD. *Degree requirements:* For master's, thesis; for doctorate, thesis/dissertation. *Faculty research:* Biosynthesis and analysis, biometrics.

Carnegie Mellon University, Carnegie Institute of Technology, Biomedical and Health Engineering Program, Pittsburgh, PA 15213-3891. Offers bioengineering (MS, PhD); MD/PhD. *Degree requirements:* For master's, thesis; for doctorate, thesis/dissertation, qualifying exam. *Entrance requirements:* For master's and doctorate, GRE General Test. Additional exam requirements/recommendations for international students: Required—TOEFL. Electronic applications accepted. *Faculty research:* Cellular and molecular systematics, signal and image processing, materials and mechanics.

Clemson University, Graduate School, College of Engineering, Computing and Applied Sciences, Department of Bioengineering, Clemson, SC 29634-0905. Offers bioengineering (MS, PhD); biomedical engineering (M Engr); medical device recycling and reprocessing (Certificate). *Program availability:* Part-time. *Faculty:* 27 full-time (8 women), 1 (woman) part-time/adjunct. *Students:* 80 full-time (31 women), 12 part-time (5 women); includes 6 minority (1 Black or African American, non-Hispanic/Latino; 2 Asian, non-Hispanic/Latino; 2 Hispanic/Latino; 1 Two or more races, non-Hispanic/Latino), 31 international. Average age 25. 96 applicants, 33% accepted, 18 enrolled. In 2016, 31 master's, 12 doctorates awarded. *Degree requirements:* For master's, thesis optional; for doctorate, comprehensive exam, thesis/dissertation. *Entrance requirements:* For master's and doctorate, GRE General Test, unofficial transcripts, letters of recommendation. Additional exam requirements/recommendations for international students: Required—TOEFL (minimum score 100 iBT), IELTS (minimum score 7). *Application deadline:* For fall admission, 2/15 priority date for domestic students, 1/15 priority date for international students. Applications are processed on a rolling basis. Application fee: $80 ($90 for international students). Electronic applications accepted. *Expenses:* $4,841 per semester full-time resident, $9,640 per semester full-time non-resident, $612 per credit hour part-time resident, $1,223 per credit hour part-time non-resident. *Financial support:* In 2016–17, 69 students received support, including 1 fellowship with partial tuition reimbursement available (averaging $22,667 per year), 29 research assistantships with partial tuition reimbursements available (averaging $19,838 per year), 32 teaching assistantships with partial tuition reimbursements available (averaging $19,151 per year); career-related internships or fieldwork and unspecified assistantships also available. Financial award application deadline: 2/15; financial award applicants required to submit FAFSA. *Faculty research:* Biomaterials, biomechanics, bioinstrumentation, tissue engineering, vascular engineering. *Total annual research expenditures:* $5.1 million. *Unit head:* Dr. Martine LaBerge, Department Chair, 864-656-5557, E-mail: laberge@clemson.edu. *Application contact:* Dr. Agneta Simionescu, Graduate Coordinator, 864-650-2575, E-mail: agneta@clemson.edu.
Website: https://www.clemson.edu/cecas/departments/bioe/

Colorado School of Mines, Office of Graduate Studies, Department of Chemical and Biological Engineering, Golden, CO 80401. Offers MS, PhD. *Program availability:* Part-time. Terminal master's awarded for partial completion of doctoral program. *Degree requirements:* For master's, thesis (for some programs); for doctorate, comprehensive exam, thesis/dissertation. *Entrance requirements:* For master's and doctorate, GRE General Test. Additional exam requirements/recommendations for international students: Required—TOEFL (minimum score 550 paper-based; 80 iBT). Electronic applications accepted. *Expenses:* Tuition, state resident: full-time $15,690. Tuition, nonresident: full-time $34,020. *Required fees:* $2152. Tuition and fees vary according to course load. *Faculty research:* Liquid fuels for the future, responsible management of hazardous substances, surface and interfacial engineering, advanced computational methods and process control, gas hydrates.

Colorado State University, Walter Scott, Jr. College of Engineering, School of Biomedical Engineering, Fort Collins, CO 80523-1376. Offers bioengineering (MS, PhD); biomedical engineering (ME). *Program availability:* Part-time, evening/weekend, 100% online. *Faculty:* 1 (woman) part-time/adjunct. *Students:* 15 full-time (6 women), 20 part-time (11 women); includes 4 minority (2 Asian, non-Hispanic/Latino; 2 Hispanic/Latino), 6 international. Average age 27. 52 applicants, 17% accepted, 7 enrolled. In 2016, 2 master's, 3 doctorates awarded. Terminal master's awarded for partial completion of doctoral program. *Degree requirements:* For master's, thesis (for some programs); for doctorate, thesis/dissertation, qualifying process (minimum B average in core classes); preliminary exam. *Entrance requirements:* For master's and doctorate, GRE General Test, minimum GPA of 3.0, resume, statement of purpose, official transcripts, three letters of recommendation. Additional exam requirements/recommendations for international students: Required—TOEFL (minimum score 550 paper-based; 80 iBT). *Application deadline:* For fall admission, 1/15 priority date for domestic and international students; for spring admission, 9/1 priority date for domestic and international students. Application fee: $60 ($70 for international students). Electronic applications accepted. *Expenses:* Contact institution. *Financial support:* In 2016–17, 18 students received support, including 17 research assistantships with full tuition reimbursements available (averaging $23,940 per year), 2 teaching assistantships with full tuition reimbursements available (averaging $18,000 per year); unspecified assistantships also available. Financial award application deadline: 1/15; financial award applicants required to submit FAFSA. *Faculty research:* Regenerative and rehabilitative medicine, imaging and diagnostics, medical devices and therapeutics. *Unit head:* Dr. Stu Tobet, Director and Professor, 970-491-7157, Fax: 970-491-5569, E-mail: stuart.tobet@colostate.edu. *Application contact:* Sara Mattern, Graduate Academic Adviser, 970-491-7157, Fax: 970-491-5569, E-mail: sara.mattern@colostate.edu.
Website: http://www.engr.colostate.edu/sbme/

Cornell University, Graduate School, Graduate Fields of Agriculture and Life Sciences and Graduate Fields of Engineering, Field of Biological and Environmental Engineering, Ithaca, NY 14853. Offers bioenergy and integrated energy systems (M Eng, MPS, MS, PhD); biological engineering (M Eng, MPS, MS, PhD); bioprocess engineering (M Eng, MPS, MS, PhD); ecohydrology (M Eng, MPS, MS, PhD); environmental engineering (M Eng, MPS, MS, PhD); environmental management (MPS); food engineering (M Eng, MPS, MS, PhD); industrial biotechnology (M Eng, MPS, MS, PhD); nanobiotechnology (M Eng, MPS, MS, PhD); sustainable systems (M Eng, MPS, MS, PhD); synthetic biology (MS); syntheticbiology (M Eng, MPS, PhD). Terminal master's awarded for partial completion of doctoral program. *Degree requirements:* For master's, thesis (MS); for doctorate, comprehensive exam, thesis/dissertation. *Entrance requirements:* For master's, letters of recommendation (3 for MS, 2 for M Eng and MPS); for doctorate, GRE General Test, 3 letters of recommendation. Additional exam requirements/recommendations for international students: Required—TOEFL (minimum score 550 paper-based; 77 iBT). Electronic applications accepted. *Faculty research:* Biological and food engineering, environmental, soil and water engineering, international agricultural engineering, structures and controlled environments, machine systems and energy.

Dalhousie University, Faculty of Engineering, Department of Biological Engineering, Halifax, NS B3J 2X4, Canada. Offers M Eng, MA Sc, PhD. *Degree requirements:* For master's, thesis; for doctorate, thesis/dissertation. *Entrance requirements:* Additional exam requirements/recommendations for international students: Required—TOEFL, IELTS, CANTEST, CAEL, or Michigan English Language Assessment Battery. *Faculty research:* Waste management, energy and environment, bio-machinery and robotics, soil and water, aquacultural and food engineering.

Florida Atlantic University, College of Engineering and Computer Science, Department of Computer and Electrical Engineering and Computer Science, Boca

Raton, FL 33431-0991. Offers bioengineering (MS); computer engineering (MS, PhD); computer science (MS, PhD); electrical engineering (MS, PhD). *Program availability:* Part-time, evening/weekend. *Faculty:* 23 full-time (5 women), 1 part-time/adjunct (0 women). *Students:* 103 full-time (30 women), 127 part-time (30 women); includes 77 minority (15 Black or African American, non-Hispanic/Latino; 10 Asian, non-Hispanic/Latino; 46 Hispanic/Latino; 6 Two or more races, non-Hispanic/Latino), 74 international. Average age 32. 215 applicants, 51% accepted, 85 enrolled. In 2016, 45 master's, 5 doctorates awarded. Terminal master's awarded for partial completion of doctoral program. *Degree requirements:* For master's, thesis optional; for doctorate, thesis/dissertation, qualifying exam. *Entrance requirements:* For master's, GRE General Test, minimum GPA of 3.0; for doctorate, GRE General Test, master's degree, minimum GPA of 3.5. Additional exam requirements/recommendations for international students: Required—TOEFL (minimum score 500 paper-based; 61 iBT), IELTS (minimum score 6). *Application deadline:* For fall admission, 7/1 priority date for domestic students, 2/15 for international students; for spring admission, 11/1 for domestic students, 7/15 for international students. Applications are processed on a rolling basis. Application fee: $30. *Expenses:* Tuition, state resident: full-time $7392; part-time $369.82 per credit hour. Tuition, nonresident: full-time $19,432; part-time $1024.81 per credit hour. *Financial support:* Fellowships, research assistantships with partial tuition reimbursements, teaching assistantships with full tuition reimbursements, career-related internships or fieldwork, and Federal Work-Study available. Support available to part-time students. Financial award application deadline: 4/1; financial award applicants required to submit FAFSA. *Faculty research:* VLSI and neural networks, communication networks, software engineering, computer architecture, multimedia and video processing. *Unit head:* Jean Mangiaracina, 561-297-3855, E-mail: jmangiar@fau.edu.
Website: http://www.ceecs.fau.edu/

George Mason University, Volgenau School of Engineering, Department of Bioengineering, Fairfax, VA 22030. Offers PhD. *Faculty:* 16 full-time (5 women), 6 part-time/adjunct (3 women). *Students:* 12 full-time (5 women), 5 part-time (1 woman); includes 3 minority (1 Black or African American, non-Hispanic/Latino; 1 Asian, non-Hispanic/Latino; 1 Hispanic/Latino), 10 international. Average age 28. 22 applicants, 95% accepted, 8 enrolled. *Entrance requirements:* For doctorate, GRE General Test, two copies of official transcripts; goals statement (1000 words maximum); three letters of recommendation; resume. Additional exam requirements/recommendations for international students: Required—TOEFL (minimum score 575 paper-based; 88 iBT), IELTS (minimum score 6.5), PTE (minimum score 59). *Application deadline:* For fall admission, 1/15 priority date for domestic students. Application fee: $75 ($80 for international students). Electronic applications accepted. *Expenses:* Tuition, state resident: full-time $10,628; part-time $443 per credit. Tuition, nonresident: full-time $29,306; part-time $1221 per credit. *Required fees:* $3096; $129 per credit. Tuition and fees vary according to program. *Financial support:* In 2016–17, 15 students received support, including 7 research assistantships with tuition reimbursements available (averaging $19,714 per year), 8 teaching assistantships with tuition reimbursements available (averaging $18,000 per year); career-related internships or fieldwork, Federal Work-Study, scholarships/grants, unspecified assistantships, and health care benefits (for full-time research or teaching assistantship recipients) also available. Support available to part-time students. Financial award applicants required to submit FAFSA. *Total annual research expenditures:* $1 million. *Unit head:* Brian L. Mark, Acting Chair, 703-993-4069, Fax: 703-993-1601, E-mail: bmark@gmu.edu. *Application contact:* Claudia Borke, Academic Advisor, 703-993-4190, E-mail: cborke@gmu.edu.
Website: http://bioengineering.gmu.edu

Georgia Institute of Technology, Graduate Studies, Multidisciplinary Program in Bioengineering, Atlanta, GA 30332-0001. Offers MS, PhD. Program offered jointly with College of Computing, School of Aerospace Engineering, Wallace H. Coulter Department of Biomedical Engineering, School of Civil and Environmental Engineering, School of Chemical and Biomolecular Engineering, School of Electrical and Computer Engineering, School of Materials Science and Engineering, and George W. Woodruff School of Mechanical Engineering. *Program availability:* Part-time. *Degree requirements:* For master's, thesis; for doctorate, thesis/dissertation. *Entrance requirements:* For master's and doctorate, GRE General Test. Additional exam requirements/recommendations for international students: Required—TOEFL (minimum score 620 paper-based; 105 iBT). Electronic applications accepted.

Harvard University, Graduate School of Arts and Sciences, Harvard John A. Paulson School of Engineering and Applied Sciences, Cambridge, MA 02138. Offers applied mathematics (PhD); applied physics (PhD); computational science and engineering (ME, SM); computer science (PhD); design engineering (MDE); engineering science (ME), including electrical engineering (ME, SM, PhD); engineering sciences (SM, PhD), including bioengineering (PhD), electrical engineering (ME, SM, PhD), environmental science and engineering (PhD), materials science and mechanical engineering (PhD). MDE offered in collaboration with Graduate School of Design. *Program availability:* Part-time. *Faculty:* 80 full-time (13 women), 47 part-time/adjunct (10 women). *Students:* 459 full-time (135 women), 19 part-time (7 women); includes 79 minority (2 Black or African American, non-Hispanic/Latino; 49 Asian, non-Hispanic/Latino; 15 Hispanic/Latino; 1 Native Hawaiian or other Pacific Islander, non-Hispanic/Latino; 12 Two or more races, non-Hispanic/Latino), 233 international. Average age 27. 2,486 applicants, 11% accepted, 126 enrolled. In 2016, 37 master's, 48 doctorates awarded. Terminal master's awarded for partial completion of doctoral program. *Degree requirements:* For master's, thesis (for ME); for doctorate, comprehensive exam, thesis/dissertation. *Entrance requirements:* For master's and doctorate, GRE General Test, GRE Subject Test (recommended), 3 letters of recommendation. Additional exam requirements/recommendations for international students: Required—TOEFL (minimum score 80 iBT). *Application deadline:* For fall admission, 12/15 priority date for domestic and international students. Application fee: $105. Electronic applications accepted. *Expenses:* $43,296 full-time tuition, $3,718 fees. *Financial support:* In 2016–17, 394 students received support, including 86 fellowships with full tuition reimbursements available (averaging $26,424 per year), 258 research assistantships with tuition reimbursements available (averaging $35,232 per year), 106 teaching assistantships with tuition reimbursements available (averaging $6,313 per year); health care benefits also available. *Faculty research:* Applied mathematics, applied physics, computer science and electrical engineering, environmental engineering, mechanical and biomedical engineering. *Total annual research expenditures:* $50.1 million. *Unit head:* Francis J. Doyle, III, Dean, 617-495-5829, Fax: 617-495-5264, E-mail: dean@seas.harvard.edu. *Application contact:* Office of Admissions and Financial Aid, 617-495-5315, E-mail: admissions@seas.harvard.edu.
Website: http://www.seas.harvard.edu/

Illinois Institute of Technology, Graduate College, Armour College of Engineering, Department of Chemical and Biological Engineering, Chicago, IL 60616. Offers biological engineering (MAS); chemical engineering (MAS, MS, PhD); MS/MAS. *Program availability:* Part-time, evening/weekend, online learning. Terminal master's awarded for partial completion of doctoral program. *Degree requirements:* For master's, comprehensive exam (for some programs), thesis (for some programs); for doctorate, comprehensive exam, thesis/dissertation. *Entrance requirements:* For master's, GRE General Test with minimum score of 950 Quantitative and Verbal, 2.5 Analytical Writing (for MAS); GRE General Test with minimum score of 1100 Quantitative and Verbal, 3.0 Analytical Writing (for MS), minimum undergraduate GPA of 3.0; for doctorate, GRE General Test (minimum score 1100 Quantitative and Verbal, 3.0 Analytical Writing), minimum undergraduate GPA of 3.0. Additional exam requirements/recommendations for international students: Required—TOEFL (minimum score 550 paper-based; 80 iBT). Electronic applications accepted. *Faculty research:* Energy and sustainability, biological engineering, advanced materials, systems engineering.

Johns Hopkins University, G. W. C. Whiting School of Engineering and School of Medicine, Department of Biomedical Engineering, Baltimore, MD 21205. Offers bioengineering innovation and design (MSE); biomedical engineering (MSE, PhD). *Faculty:* 21 full-time (4 women), 2 part-time/adjunct (0 women). *Students:* 246 full-time (92 women); includes 85 minority (5 Black or African American, non-Hispanic/Latino; 55 Asian, non-Hispanic/Latino; 14 Hispanic/Latino; 11 Two or more races, non-Hispanic/Latino), 73 international. Average age 25. 312 applicants, 29% accepted, 42 enrolled. In 2016, 33 master's, 29 doctorates awarded. Terminal master's awarded for partial completion of doctoral program. *Degree requirements:* For master's, thesis; for doctorate, comprehensive exam, thesis/dissertation. *Entrance requirements:* For master's and doctorate, GRE General Test, 3 letters of recommendation, statement of purpose, transcripts. Additional exam requirements/recommendations for international students: Required—TOEFL (minimum score 600 paper-based, 100 iBT) or IELTS (7). *Application deadline:* For fall admission, 1/6 for domestic and international students. Application fee: $75. Electronic applications accepted. *Financial support:* In 2016–17, 224 students received support, including 57 fellowships with partial tuition reimbursements available (averaging $30,396 per year), 134 research assistantships with partial tuition reimbursements available (averaging $30,396 per year), 33 teaching assistantships (averaging $8,937 per year); Federal Work-Study, institutionally sponsored loans, scholarships/grants, health care benefits, tuition waivers (full), and unspecified assistantships also available. Financial award application deadline: 1/15. *Faculty research:* Systems neuroscience and neuroengineering, molecular and cellular systems biology, biomedical imaging, cell and tissue engineering, cardiovascular systems engineering. *Total annual research expenditures:* $18.4 million. *Unit head:* Dr. Les Tung, Interim Director, 410-955-3132, Fax: 410-516-4771, E-mail: ltung@jhu.edu. *Application contact:* Samuel Bourne, Academic Program Administrator, 410-516-8482, Fax: 410-516-4771, E-mail: sbourne@jhu.edu.
Website: http://www.bme.jhu.edu/

Johns Hopkins University, G. W. C. Whiting School of Engineering, Department of Chemical and Biomolecular Engineering, Baltimore, MD 21218. Offers MSE, PhD. *Faculty:* 21 full-time (7 women), 2 part-time/adjunct (1 woman). *Students:* 141 full-time (47 women); includes 26 minority (5 Black or African American, non-Hispanic/Latino; 11 Asian, non-Hispanic/Latino; 6 Hispanic/Latino; 4 Two or more races, non-Hispanic/Latino), 70 international. Average age 24. 306 applicants, 56% accepted, 56 enrolled. In 2016, 23 master's, 14 doctorates awarded. Terminal master's awarded for partial completion of doctoral program. *Degree requirements:* For master's, essay presentation; for doctorate, thesis/dissertation, oral exam; thesis presentation. *Entrance requirements:* For master's and doctorate, GRE General Test, 3 letters of recommendation, statement of purpose, transcripts. Additional exam requirements/recommendations for international students: Required—TOEFL (minimum score 600 paper-based, 100 iBT) or IELTS (7). *Application deadline:* For fall admission, 1/5 for domestic and international students. Application fee: $25. Electronic applications accepted. *Financial support:* In 2016–17, 84 students received support, including 9 fellowships with full and partial tuition reimbursements available (averaging $34,008 per year), 75 research assistantships with full tuition reimbursements available (averaging $29,496 per year); teaching assistantships with full and partial tuition reimbursements available, career-related internships or fieldwork, Federal Work-Study, institutionally sponsored loans, scholarships/grants, health care benefits, tuition waivers (partial), and unspecified assistantships also available. Support available to part-time students. Financial award application deadline: 1/15. *Faculty research:* Engineering in health and disease, biomolecular design and engineering, materials by design, micro and nanotechnology, alternative energy and sustainability. *Total annual research expenditures:* $14.7 million. *Unit head:* Dr. Konstantinos Konstantopoulos, Chair and Professor, 410-516-7170, Fax: 410-516-5510, E-mail: kkonsta1@jhu.edu. *Application contact:* Kailey Dille, Academic Program Coordinator, 410-516-4166, Fax: 410-516-5510, E-mail: kdille@jhu.edu.
Website: http://engineering.jhu.edu/chembe/

Kansas State University, Graduate School, College of Engineering, Department of Biological and Agricultural Engineering, Manhattan, KS 66506. Offers MS, PhD. *Faculty:* 15 full-time (4 women), 6 part-time/adjunct (0 women). *Students:* 25 full-time (9 women), 11 part-time (4 women); includes 3 minority (2 Black or African American, non-Hispanic/Latino; 1 Asian, non-Hispanic/Latino), 18 international. Average age 29. 22 applicants, 50% accepted, 6 enrolled. In 2016, 7 master's, 2 doctorates awarded. Terminal master's awarded for partial completion of doctoral program. *Degree requirements:* For master's, thesis; for doctorate, thesis/dissertation, preliminary exam. *Entrance requirements:* For master's, GRE, bachelor's degree in biological and agricultural engineering; for doctorate, GRE. Additional exam requirements/recommendations for international students: Required—TOEFL (minimum score 550 paper-based; 79 iBT). *Application deadline:* For fall admission, 2/1 priority date for domestic students, 1/1 priority date for international students; for spring admission, 8/1 priority date for domestic and international students. Applications are processed on a rolling basis. Application fee: $50 ($75 for international students). Electronic applications accepted. *Expenses:* Tuition, state resident: full-time $9670. Tuition, nonresident: full-time $21,828. *Required fees:* $862. *Financial support:* In 2016–17, 2 students received support, including 21 research assistantships (averaging $20,114 per year); fellowships, teaching assistantships, Federal Work-Study, institutionally sponsored loans, and scholarships/grants also available. Support available to part-time students. Financial award application deadline: 3/1; financial award applicants required to submit FAFSA. *Faculty research:* Ecological engineering, watershed modeling, air quality, bioprocessing, bio-fuel, sensors and controls, 3D engineered biomaterials and biomedical devices, mobile health, point-of-care diagnosis, protein biomarker discovery, cancer early detection. *Total annual research expenditures:* $1.1 million. *Unit head:* Dr. Joseph Harner, Head, 785-532-5580, Fax: 785-532-5825, E-mail: jharner@k-state.edu. *Application contact:* Dr. Naiqian Zhang, Graduate Coordinator, 785-532-2910, Fax: 785-532-5825, E-mail: zhangn@k-state.edu.
Website: http://www.bae.ksu.edu/

Kansas State University, Graduate School, College of Engineering, Department of Electrical and Computer Engineering, Manhattan, KS 66506. Offers electrical engineering (MS), including bioengineering, communication systems, design of computer systems, electrical engineering, energy and power systems, integrated circuits and devices, real time embedded systems, renewable energy, signal processing. *Program availability:* Part-time, evening/weekend, online learning. *Faculty:* 21 full-time (4 women), 1 (woman) part-time/adjunct. *Students:* 47 full-time (11 women), 51 part-time (5 women); includes 13 minority (6 Black or African American, non-Hispanic/Latino; 6 Asian, non-Hispanic/Latino; 1 Two or more races, non-Hispanic/Latino), 40 international. Average age 31. 146 applicants, 29% accepted, 17 enrolled. In 2016, 16 master's, 5 doctorates awarded. *Degree requirements:* For master's, thesis or alternative, final exam; for doctorate, thesis/dissertation, final exam, preliminary exams. *Entrance requirements:* For master's, GRE General Test, bachelor's degree in electrical

engineering or computer science, minimum GPA of 3.0; for doctorate, GRE General Test. Additional exam requirements/recommendations for international students: Required—TOEFL (minimum score 600 paper-based; 85 iBT). *Application deadline:* For fall admission, 1/1 priority date for domestic and international students; for spring admission, 8/1 priority date for domestic and international students. Applications are processed on a rolling basis. Application fee: $50 ($75 for international students). Electronic applications accepted. *Expenses:* Tuition, state resident: full-time $9670. Tuition, nonresident: full-time $21,828. *Required fees:* $862. *Financial support:* In 2016–17, 40 students received support, including 22 research assistantships with tuition reimbursements available (averaging $12,100 per year), 18 teaching assistantships with full tuition reimbursements available (averaging $12,220 per year); career-related internships or fieldwork, institutionally sponsored loans, and scholarships/grants also available. Support available to part-time students. Financial award application deadline: 3/1; financial award applicants required to submit FAFSA. *Faculty research:* Energy systems and renewable energy, computer systems and real time embedded systems, communication systems and signal processing, integrated circuits and devices, bioengineering. *Total annual research expenditures:* $1.3 million. *Unit head:* Dr. Don Gruenbacher, Head, 785-532-5600, Fax: 785-532-1188, E-mail: grue@k-state.edu. *Application contact:* Dr. Andrew Rys, Graduate Program Director, 785-532-4665, Fax: 785-532-1188, E-mail: andrys@k-state.edu.
Website: http://www.ece.k-state.edu/

Lehigh University, P.C. Rossin College of Engineering and Applied Science, Bioengineering Program, Bethlehem, PA 18015. Offers MS, PhD. *Faculty:* 12 full-time (4 women), 1 part-time/adjunct (0 women). *Students:* 16 full-time (8 women); includes 4 minority (2 Asian, non-Hispanic/Latino; 1 Hispanic/Latino; 1 Two or more races, non-Hispanic/Latino), 9 international. Average age 25. 56 applicants, 39% accepted, 3 enrolled. In 2016, 3 master's, 4 doctorates awarded. Terminal master's awarded for partial completion of doctoral program. *Degree requirements:* For master's, thesis; for doctorate, comprehensive exam, thesis/dissertation. *Entrance requirements:* For master's and doctorate, GRE. Additional exam requirements/recommendations for international students: Required—TOEFL (minimum score 79 iBT), IELTS. *Application deadline:* For fall admission, 7/15 for domestic and international students. Applications are processed on a rolling basis. Application fee: $75. Electronic applications accepted. *Expenses:* $42,600 (for MS); $101,000 (for PhD). *Financial support:* In 2016–17, 12 students received support, including 9 research assistantships (averaging $19,000 per year), 10 teaching assistantships (averaging $21,105 per year); fellowships and health care benefits also available. Financial award application deadline: 1/15. *Faculty research:* Biomaterials, biomechanics (biomolecular, cellular, fluid and solid mechanics), BioMEMS Biosensors, bioelectronics/bio photonics, biopharmaceutical engineering. *Unit head:* Dr. Susan Perry, Faculty Graduate Coordinator in Bioengineering, 610-758-4330, E-mail: sup3@lehigh.edu. *Application contact:* Brianne Lisk, Administrative Coordinator of Graduate Studies and Research, 610-758-6310, Fax: 610-758-5623, E-mail: brc3@lehigh.edu.
Website: http://www.lehigh.edu/~inbioe/graduate/index.html

Louisiana State University and Agricultural & Mechanical College, Graduate School, College of Engineering, Department of Biological and Agricultural Engineering, Baton Rouge, LA 70803. Offers biological and agricultural engineering (MSBAE); engineering science (MS, PhD).

Massachusetts Institute of Technology, School of Engineering, Department of Biological Engineering, Cambridge, MA 02139. Offers applied biosciences (PhD, Sc D); bioengineering (PhD, Sc D); biological engineering (PhD, Sc D); biomedical engineering (M Eng); toxicology (SM); SM/MBA. *Faculty:* 34 full-time (5 women). *Students:* 140 full-time (60 women); includes 54 minority (2 Black or African American, non-Hispanic/Latino; 36 Asian, non-Hispanic/Latino; 9 Hispanic/Latino; 7 Two or more races, non-Hispanic/Latino), 24 international. Average age 26. 513 applicants, 8% accepted, 23 enrolled. In 2016, 3 master's, 19 doctorates awarded. Terminal master's awarded for partial completion of doctoral program. *Degree requirements:* For master's, thesis; for doctorate, comprehensive exam, thesis/dissertation. *Entrance requirements:* For master's and doctorate, GRE General Test. Additional exam requirements/recommendations for international students: Required—IELTS. *Application deadline:* For fall admission, 12/15 for domestic and international students. Application fee: $75. Electronic applications accepted. *Expenses: Tuition:* Full-time $46,400; part-time $725 per credit. One-time fee: $312 full-time. Full-time tuition and fees vary according to course load and program. *Financial support:* In 2016–17, 131 students received support, including fellowships (averaging $41,900 per year), 80 research assistantships (averaging $40,900 per year), 1 teaching assistantship (averaging $40,600 per year); Federal Work-Study, institutionally sponsored loans, scholarships/grants, traineeships, health care benefits, unspecified assistantships, and resident tutors also available. Support available to part-time students. Financial award application deadline: 5/1; financial award applicants required to submit FAFSA. *Faculty research:* Biomaterials; biophysics; cell and tissue engineering; computational modeling of biological and physiological systems; discovery and delivery of molecular therapeutics; new tools for genomics; functional genomics; proteomics and glycomics; macromolecular biochemistry and biophysics; molecular, cell and tissue biomechanics; synthetic biology; systems biology. *Total annual research expenditures:* $55 million. *Unit head:* Prof. Douglas A. Lauffenburger, Department Head, 617-452-4086. *Application contact:* 617-253-1712, Fax: 617-253-5208, E-mail: be-acad@mit.edu.
Website: http://be.mit.edu

McGill University, Faculty of Graduate and Postdoctoral Studies, Faculty of Agricultural and Environmental Sciences, Department of Bioresource Engineering, Montréal, QC H3A 2T5, Canada. Offers computer applications (M Sc, M Sc A, PhD); food engineering (M Sc, M Sc A, PhD); grain drying (M Sc, M Sc A, PhD); irrigation and drainage (M Sc, M Sc A, PhD); machinery (M Sc, M Sc A, PhD); pollution control (M Sc, M Sc A, PhD); post-harvest technology (M Sc, M Sc A, PhD); soil dynamics (M Sc, M Sc A, PhD); structure and environment (M Sc, M Sc A, PhD); vegetable and fruit storage (M Sc, M Sc A, PhD).

Mississippi State University, College of Agriculture and Life Sciences, Department of Agricultural and Biological Engineering, Mississippi State, MS 39762. Offers biological engineering (MS, PhD); biomedical engineering (MS, PhD). *Faculty:* 17 full-time (6 women). *Students:* 29 full-time (17 women), 6 part-time (0 women); includes 6 minority (3 Black or African American, non-Hispanic/Latino; 1 Asian, non-Hispanic/Latino; 2 Two or more races, non-Hispanic/Latino), 7 international. Average age 27. 27 applicants, 48% accepted, 9 enrolled. In 2016, 3 master's, 7 doctorates awarded. *Degree requirements:* For master's, thesis (for some programs); for doctorate, thesis/dissertation, preliminary exam. *Entrance requirements:* For master's, GRE General Test, minimum undergraduate GPA of 2.75 (3.0 for biomedical engineering); for doctorate, GRE General Test, minimum GPA of 3.0 (biomedical engineering). Additional exam requirements/recommendations for international students: Required—TOEFL (minimum score 550 paper-based; 79 iBT); Recommended—IELTS (minimum score 6.5). *Application deadline:* For fall admission, 7/1 for domestic students, 5/1 for international students; for spring admission, 11/1 for domestic students, 9/1 for international students. Applications are processed on a rolling basis. Application fee: $60. Electronic applications accepted. *Expenses:* Tuition, state resident: full-time

$7670; part-time $852.50 per credit hour. Tuition, nonresident: full-time $20,790; part-time $2310.50 per credit hour. Part-time tuition and fees vary according to course load. *Financial support:* In 2016–17, 12 research assistantships with partial tuition reimbursements (averaging $15,733 per year) were awarded; Federal Work-Study, institutionally sponsored loans, and unspecified assistantships also available. Financial award application deadline: 4/1; financial award applicants required to submit FAFSA. *Faculty research:* Bioenvironmental engineering, bioinstrumentation, biomechanics/biomaterials, precision agriculture, tissue engineering, ergonomics human factors, biosimulation and modeling. *Total annual research expenditures:* $3.1 million. *Unit head:* Dr. Jonathan Pote, Department Head and Professor, 662-325-3570, Fax: 662-325-3853, E-mail: jpote@abe.msstate.edu. *Application contact:* Marina Hunt, Admissions Assistant, 662-325-5188, E-mail: mhunt@grad.msstate.edu.
Website: http://www.abe.msstate.edu/

North Carolina Agricultural and Technical State University, School of Graduate Studies, College of Engineering, Department of Chemical and Bioengineering, Greensboro, NC 27411. Offers bioengineering (MS); biological engineering (MS); chemical engineering (MS).

North Carolina State University, Graduate School, College of Agriculture and Life Sciences, Department of Biological and Agricultural Engineering, Raleigh, NC 27695. Offers MBAE, MS, PhD, Certificate. *Program availability:* Part-time, online learning. *Degree requirements:* For master's, thesis (for some programs); for doctorate, thesis/dissertation. *Entrance requirements:* For master's and doctorate, GRE. Additional exam requirements/recommendations for international students: Required—TOEFL. Electronic applications accepted. *Faculty research:* Bioinstrumentation, animal waste management, water quality engineering, machine systems, controlled environment agriculture.

Northeastern University, College of Engineering, Boston, MA 02115-5096. Offers bioengineering (MS, PhD); chemical engineering (MS, PhD); civil engineering (MS, PhD); computer engineering (PhD); computer systems engineering (MS); electrical and computer engineering (MS); electrical and computer engineering leadership (MS); electrical engineering (PhD); energy systems (MS); engineering and public policy (MS); engineering management (MS, Certificate); environmental engineering (MS); industrial engineering (MS, PhD); information assurance (PhD); information systems (MS); interdisciplinary engineering (PhD); mechanical engineering (PhD); operations research (MS); telecommunication systems management (MS). *Program availability:* Part-time, online learning. *Faculty:* 202 full-time (59 women), 53 part-time/adjunct (9 women). *Students:* 2,982 full-time (954 women), 192 part-time (38 women). In 2016, 851 master's, 74 doctorates awarded. Application fee: $75. Electronic applications accepted. *Expenses:* $1,471 per credit. *Financial support:* Fellowships, research assistantships, teaching assistantships, career-related internships or fieldwork, scholarships/grants, health care benefits, tuition waivers, and unspecified assistantships available. Support available to part-time students. Financial award applicants required to submit FAFSA. *Unit head:* Dr. Nadine Aubry, Dean, College of Engineering. *Application contact:* Jeffery Hengel, Director of Graduate Admissions, 617-373-2711, E-mail: j.hengel@northeastern.edu.
Website: http://www.coe.neu.edu/academics/graduate-school-engineering

Northwestern University, The Graduate School, Interdisciplinary Biological Sciences Program (IBiS), Evanston, IL 60208. Offers biochemistry (PhD); bioengineering and biotechnology (PhD); biotechnology (PhD); cell and molecular biology (PhD); developmental and systems biology (PhD); nanotechnology (PhD); neurobiology (PhD); structural biology and biophysics (PhD). *Degree requirements:* For doctorate, thesis/dissertation, qualifying exam. *Entrance requirements:* For doctorate, GRE General Test. Additional exam requirements/recommendations for international students: Required—TOEFL (minimum score 600 paper-based). Electronic applications accepted. *Faculty research:* Biophysics/structural biology, cell/molecular biology, synthetic biology, developmental systems biology, chemical biology/nanotechnology.

The Ohio State University, Graduate School, College of Food, Agricultural, and Environmental Sciences, Department of Food, Agricultural, and Biological Engineering, Columbus, OH 43210. Offers MS, PhD. Program offered jointly with College of Engineering. *Faculty:* 19. *Students:* 42 full-time (14 women), 5 part-time (1 woman), 24 international. Average age 28. In 2016, 10 master's, 2 doctorates awarded. *Degree requirements:* For master's, thesis optional; for doctorate, thesis/dissertation. *Entrance requirements:* For master's and doctorate, GRE General Test, GRE Subject Test in engineering (recommended). Additional exam requirements/recommendations for international students: Required—TOEFL (minimum score 550 paper-based; 79 iBT), Michigan English Language Assessment Battery (minimum score 82); Recommended—IELTS (minimum score 7). *Application deadline:* For fall admission, 12/13 priority date for domestic students, 11/30 priority date for international students; for spring admission, 12/12 for domestic students, 11/10 for international students; for summer admission, 4/10 for domestic students, 3/13 for international students. Applications are processed on a rolling basis. Application fee: $60 ($70 for international students). Electronic applications accepted. *Financial support:* Fellowships with tuition reimbursements, research assistantships with tuition reimbursements, teaching assistantships with tuition reimbursements, career-related internships or fieldwork, Federal Work-Study, and institutionally sponsored loans available. Support available to part-time students. *Unit head:* Dr. Scott Shearer, Chair, 614-292-7284, E-mail: shearer.95@osu.edu. *Application contact:* Graduate and Professional Admissions, 614-292-9444, Fax: 614-292-3895, E-mail: gpadmissions@osu.edu.
Website: http://fabe.osu.edu/

Oklahoma State University, College of Agricultural Science and Natural Resources, Department of Biosystems and Agricultural Engineering, Stillwater, OK 74078. Offers biosystems engineering (MS, PhD); environmental and natural resources (MS, PhD). *Faculty:* 26 full-time (6 women), 2 part-time/adjunct (0 women). *Students:* 20 full-time (7 women), 11 part-time (3 women); includes 3 minority (2 Hispanic/Latino; 1 Two or more races, non-Hispanic/Latino), 14 international. Average age 29. 21 applicants, 24% accepted, 4 enrolled. In 2016, 9 master's, 8 doctorates awarded. *Degree requirements:* For master's, thesis; for doctorate, comprehensive exam, thesis/dissertation. *Entrance requirements:* For master's and doctorate, GRE or GMAT. Additional exam requirements/recommendations for international students: Required—TOEFL (minimum score 550 paper-based; 79 iBT). *Application deadline:* For fall admission, 3/1 priority date for international students; for spring admission, 8/1 priority date for international students. Applications are processed on a rolling basis. Application fee: $40 ($75 for international students). Electronic applications accepted. *Expenses:* Tuition, state resident: full-time $3775; part-time $209.70 per credit hour. Tuition, nonresident: full-time $14,851; part-time $825.05 per credit hour. *Required fees:* $2027; $112.60 per credit hour. Tuition and fees vary according to campus/location. *Financial support:* In 2016–17, 24 research assistantships (averaging $19,202 per year) were awarded; teaching assistantships, career-related internships or fieldwork, Federal Work-Study, scholarships/grants, health care benefits, tuition waivers (partial), and unspecified assistantships also available. Support available to part-time students. Financial award application deadline: 3/1; financial award applicants required to submit FAFSA. *Unit head:* Dr. John Veenstra, Department Head, 405-744-5431, Fax: 405-744-6059, E-mail: jveenst@okstate.edu. *Application contact:* Dr. Ning Wang, Professor/Graduate

Coordinator, 405-744-2877, E-mail: ning.wang@okstate.edu.
Website: http://bae.okstate.edu/

Oregon State University, College of Engineering, Program in Bioengineering, Corvallis, OR 97331. Offers biomaterials (M Eng, MS, PhD); biomedical devices and instrumentation (M Eng, MS, PhD); human performance engineering (M Eng, MS, PhD); medical imaging (M Eng, MS, PhD); systems and computation biology (M Eng, MS, PhD). *Faculty:* 2 full-time (0 women). *Students:* 1 full-time (0 women). Electronic applications accepted. *Expenses:* $14,130 resident full-time tuition, $23,769 non-resident. *Faculty research:* Biomaterials, biomedical devices and instrumentation, human performance engineering, medical imaging, systems and computational biology. *Unit head:* Dr. James Sweeney, Head. *Application contact:* Anita Hughes, Graduate Program Coordinator, E-mail: anita.hughes@oregonstate.edu.

Oregon State University, College of Engineering, Program in Biological and Ecological Engineering, Corvallis, OR 97331. Offers bio-based products and fuels (M Eng, MS, PhD); biological systems analysis (M Eng, MS, PhD); bioprocessing (M Eng, MS, PhD); ecosystems analysis and modeling (M Eng, MS, PhD); water quality (M Eng, MS, PhD); water resources (M Eng, MS, PhD). *Faculty:* 8 full-time (1 woman), 2 part-time/adjunct (1 woman). *Students:* 9 full-time (1 woman), 1 part-time (0 women), 6 international. Average age 35. 18 applicants, 17% accepted, 2 enrolled. In 2016, 2 master's, 1 doctorate awarded. Terminal master's awarded for partial completion of doctoral program. *Degree requirements:* For master's, thesis or alternative; for doctorate, thesis/dissertation. *Entrance requirements:* For master's and doctorate, GRE, minimum GPA of 3.0 in last 90 hours. Additional exam requirements/recommendations for international students: Required—TOEFL (minimum score 80 iBT), IELTS (minimum score 6.5). *Application deadline:* For fall admission, 1/3 for domestic students. Application fee: $75 ($85 for international students). *Expenses:* $14,130 resident full-time tuition, $23,769 non-resident. *Financial support:* Fellowships with full tuition reimbursements, research assistantships with full tuition reimbursements, teaching assistantships, Federal Work-Study, and institutionally sponsored loans available. Support available to part-time students. *Faculty research:* Bioengineering, water resources engineering, food engineering, cell culture and fermentation, vadose zone transport. *Unit head:* Dr. John P. Bolte, Head, 541-737-2041, E-mail: info-bee@engr.orst.edu. *Application contact:* Ganti Murthy, Biological and Ecological Engineering Advisor, 541-737-6291, E-mail: info-bee@engr.orst.edu.
Website: http://bee.oregonstate.edu/programs/graduate

Penn State University Park, Graduate School, College of Agricultural Sciences, Department of Agricultural and Biological Engineering, University Park, PA 16802. Offers agricultural and biological engineering (MS, PhD); biorenewable systems (MS, PhD). *Unit head:* Dr. Richard T. Roush, Dean, 814-865-2541, Fax: 814-865-3103. *Application contact:* Lori Hawn, Director, Graduate Student Services, 814-865-1795, Fax: 814-863-4627, E-mail: l-gswww@lists.psu.edu.
Website: http://abe.psu.edu/

Penn State University Park, Graduate School, Intercollege Graduate Programs, Intercollege Graduate Program in Bioengineering, University Park, PA 16802. Offers MS, PhD. *Unit head:* Dr. Regina Vasilatos-Younken, Dean, 814-865-2516, Fax: 814-863-4627. *Application contact:* Lori Hawn, Director, Graduate Student Services, 814-865-1795, Fax: 814-863-4627, E-mail: l-gswww@lists.psu.edu.
Website: http://www.bioe.psu.edu/

Rensselaer Polytechnic Institute, Graduate School, School of Engineering, Program in Chemical Engineering, Troy, NY 12180-3590. Offers M Eng, MS, D Eng, PhD. *Faculty:* 15 full-time (2 women). *Students:* 65 full-time (25 women), 3 part-time. 176 applicants, 21% accepted, 14 enrolled. In 2016, 8 master's, 14 doctorates awarded. Terminal master's awarded for partial completion of doctoral program. *Entrance requirements:* For master's and doctorate, GRE. Additional exam requirements/recommendations for international students: Required—TOEFL (minimum score 570 paper-based; 88 iBT), IELTS (minimum score 6.5), PTE (minimum score 60). *Application deadline:* For fall admission, 1/1 priority date for domestic and international students; for spring admission, 8/15 priority date for domestic and international students. Applications are processed on a rolling basis. Application fee: $75. Electronic applications accepted. *Expenses: Tuition:* Full-time $49,520; part-time $2060 per credit hour. *Required fees:* $2617. *Financial support:* In 2016–17, research assistantships with full tuition reimbursements (averaging $22,000 per year), teaching assistantships with full tuition reimbursements (averaging $22,000 per year) were awarded; fellowships also available. Financial award application deadline: 1/1. *Faculty research:* Advanced materials, biochemical engineering; biomedical engineering; biotechnology; drug delivery; energy; fluid mechanics; interfacial phenomena; mass transport; molecular simulations; molecular thermodynamics; nanotechnology; polymers; process control, design, and optimization; separation and bio separation processes; systems biology; systems engineering; transport phenomena. *Total annual research expenditures:* $5.3 million. *Unit head:* Dr. Cynthia Collins, Graduate Program Director, 518-276-4178, E-mail: ccollins@rpi.edu. *Application contact:* Office of Graduate Admissions, 518-276-6216, E-mail: gradadmissions@rpi.edu.
Website: http://cbe.rpi.edu/graduate

Rice University, Graduate Programs, George R. Brown School of Engineering, Department of Bioengineering, Houston, TX 77251-1892. Offers MBE, MS, PhD, MD/PhD. Terminal master's awarded for partial completion of doctoral program. *Degree requirements:* For master's, thesis; for doctorate, thesis/dissertation, qualifying exam, internship. *Entrance requirements:* For master's and doctorate, GRE General Test. Additional exam requirements/recommendations for international students: Required—TOEFL (minimum score 600 paper-based; 90 iBT). Electronic applications accepted. *Faculty research:* Biomaterials, tissue engineering, laser-tissue interactions, biochemical engineering, gene therapy.

Rice University, Graduate Programs, George R. Brown School of Engineering, Department of Electrical and Computer Engineering, Houston, TX 77251-1892. Offers bioengineering (MS, PhD); circuits, controls, and communication systems (MS, PhD); computer science and engineering (MS, PhD); electrical engineering (MEE); lasers, microwaves, and solid-state electronics (MS, PhD); MBA/MEE. *Program availability:* Part-time. *Degree requirements:* For master's, thesis (for some programs); for doctorate, thesis/dissertation. *Entrance requirements:* For master's and doctorate, GRE General Test, GRE Subject Test, minimum GPA of 3.0. Additional exam requirements/recommendations for international students: Required—TOEFL (minimum score 600 paper-based; 90 iBT). Electronic applications accepted. *Faculty research:* Physical electronics, systems, computer engineering, bioengineering.

Santa Clara University, School of Engineering, Santa Clara, CA 95053. Offers applied mathematics (MS); bioengineering (MS); civil engineering (MS); computer science and engineering (MS, PhD); electrical engineering (MS, PhD); engineering (Engineer); engineering management and leadership (MS); mechanical engineering (MS, PhD); software engineering (MS); sustainable energy (MS). *Program availability:* Part-time, evening/weekend. *Faculty:* 66 full-time (22 women), 59 part-time/adjunct (12 women). *Students:* 449 full-time (188 women), 315 part-time (114 women); includes 197 minority (3 Black or African American, non-Hispanic/Latino; 144 Asian, non-Hispanic/Latino; 33 Hispanic/Latino; 1 Native Hawaiian or other Pacific Islander, non-Hispanic/Latino; 16

Two or more races, non-Hispanic/Latino), 418 international. Average age 28. 1,217 applicants, 45% accepted, 293 enrolled. In 2016, 466 master's awarded. *Entrance requirements:* For master's, GRE, transcript; for doctorate, GRE, master's degree or equivalent, 3 letters of recommendation, statement of purpose; for Engineer, master's degree. Additional exam requirements/recommendations for international students: Required—TOEFL (minimum score 79 iBT) or IELTS (6.5). *Application deadline:* For fall admission, 4/1 for domestic and international students; for winter admission, 9/9 for domestic students, 9/2 for international students; for spring admission, 2/17 for domestic students, 12/9 for international students. Application fee: $60. Electronic applications accepted. *Expenses:* $928 per unit. *Financial support:* Fellowships, research assistantships, teaching assistantships, career-related internships or fieldwork, Federal Work-Study, scholarships/grants, traineeships, health care benefits, tuition waivers, and unspecified assistantships available. Support available to part-time students. Financial award applicants required to submit FAFSA. *Unit head:* Dr. Alfonso Ortega, Dean. *Application contact:* Stacey Tinker, Director of Admissions and Marketing, 408-554-4313, Fax: 408-554-4323, E-mail: stinker@scu.edu.
Website: http://www.scu.edu/engineering/graduate/

South Dakota School of Mines and Technology, Graduate Division, Program in Chemical and Biological Engineering, Rapid City, SD 57701-3995. Offers PhD. *Program availability:* Part-time. *Degree requirements:* For doctorate, thesis/dissertation. *Entrance requirements:* Additional exam requirements/recommendations for international students: Required—TOEFL (minimum score 520 paper-based; 68 iBT). Electronic applications accepted.

Stanford University, School of Engineering, Department of Mechanical Engineering, Program in Biomechanical Engineering, Stanford, CA 94305-2004. Offers MS. *Entrance requirements:* For master's, GRE General Test, undergraduate degree in engineering, math or sciences. Additional exam requirements/recommendations for international students: Required—TOEFL. *Expenses: Tuition:* Full-time $47,331. *Required fees:* $609.

Stanford University, School of Medicine, Department of Bioengineering, Stanford, CA 94305-2004. Offers MS, PhD. *Degree requirements:* For master's, thesis optional; for doctorate, comprehensive exam, thesis/dissertation. *Entrance requirements:* For master's and doctorate, GRE General Test. Additional exam requirements/recommendations for international students: Required—TOEFL. Electronic applications accepted. *Expenses: Tuition:* Full-time $47,331. *Required fees:* $609. *Faculty research:* Biomedical computation, regenerative medicine/tissue engineering, molecular and cell bioengineering, biomedical imaging, biomedical devices.

Syracuse University, College of Engineering and Computer Science, Programs in Bioengineering, Syracuse, NY 13244. Offers MS, PhD. *Program availability:* Part-time. *Degree requirements:* For master's, thesis (for some programs); for doctorate, comprehensive exam, thesis/dissertation. *Entrance requirements:* For master's and doctorate, GRE General Test, three letters of recommendation, resume, personal statement, official transcripts. Additional exam requirements/recommendations for international students: Required—TOEFL (minimum score 100 iBT). *Application deadline:* For fall admission, 7/1 priority date for domestic students, 6/1 priority date for international students; for spring admission, 10/15 for domestic students, 11/15 priority date for international students. Applications are processed on a rolling basis. Application fee: $75. Electronic applications accepted. *Expenses: Tuition:* Full-time $25,974; part-time $1443 per credit hour. *Required fees:* $802; $50 per course. Tuition and fees vary according to course load and program. *Financial support:* Fellowships with full tuition reimbursements, research assistantships with tuition reimbursements, teaching assistantships with tuition reimbursements, and tuition waivers (partial) available. Financial award application deadline: 1/1; financial award applicants required to submit FAFSA. *Faculty research:* Biomaterials/tissue engineering, complex fluids, soft condensed matter, rheology. *Unit head:* Dr. James Henderson, Associate Professor/Bioengineering Graduate Program Director, 315-443-9739, E-mail: jhhender@syr.edu. *Application contact:* Kathleen Joyce, Assistant Dean, 315-443-2219, E-mail: topgrads@syr.edu.
Website: http://eng-cs.syr.edu/

Temple University, College of Engineering, Department of Bioengineering, Philadelphia, PA 19122-6096. Offers MS, PhD. *Program availability:* Part-time, evening/weekend. *Faculty:* 11 full-time (5 women), 1 part-time/adjunct (0 women). *Students:* 23 full-time (9 women), 2 part-time (0 women); includes 5 minority (2 Black or African American, non-Hispanic/Latino; 1 Asian, non-Hispanic/Latino; 2 Hispanic/Latino), 10 international. 50 applicants, 48% accepted, 8 enrolled. In 2016, 10 master's, 2 doctorates awarded. Terminal master's awarded for partial completion of doctoral program. *Degree requirements:* For master's, thesis optional; for doctorate, thesis/dissertation, preliminary exam, dissertation proposal and defense. *Entrance requirements:* For master's, GRE General Test, minimum undergraduate GPA of 3.0; BS in engineering from ABET-accredited or equivalent institution; resume; goals statement; three letters of reference; official transcripts; for doctorate, GRE General Test, minimum undergraduate GPA of 3.0; MS in engineering from ABET-accredited or equivalent institution (preferred); resume; goals statement; three letters of reference; official transcripts. Additional exam requirements/recommendations for international students: Required—TOEFL (minimum score 550 paper-based; 79 iBT), IELTS (minimum score 6.5), PTE (minimum score 53). *Application deadline:* For fall admission, 3/1 priority date for domestic and international students; for spring admission, 11/1 priority date for domestic students, 8/1 priority date for international students. Applications are processed on a rolling basis. Application fee: $60. Electronic applications accepted. *Expenses:* $995 per credit hour in-state tuition; $1,319 per credit hour out-of-state tuition. *Financial support:* In 2016–17, 2 fellowships with full tuition reimbursements, 7 research assistantships with full tuition reimbursements, 11 teaching assistantships with full tuition reimbursements were awarded; Federal Work-Study, scholarships/grants, health care benefits, and unspecified assistantships also available. Financial award application deadline: 3/1; financial award applicants required to submit FAFSA. *Faculty research:* Soft tissue mechanics, injury biomechanics, targeted drug delivery, brain-computer interface, regenerative medicine, smart nanotechnology-based biomaterials, tissue spectroscopy. *Unit head:* Dr. Peter Lelkes, Chair, Department of Bioengineering, 215-204-3307, Fax: 215-204-6936, E-mail: pilelkes@temple.edu. *Application contact:* Leslie Levin, Director, Admissions and Graduate Student Services, 215-204-7800, Fax: 215-204-6936, E-mail: gradengr@temple.edu.
Website: http://engineering.temple.edu/bioengineering

Temple University, College of Engineering, PhD in Engineering Program, Philadelphia, PA 19122-6096. Offers bioengineering (PhD); civil engineering (PhD); electrical engineering (PhD); environmental engineering (PhD); mechanical engineering (PhD). *Program availability:* Part-time, evening/weekend. *Faculty:* 67 full-time (13 women), 11 part-time/adjunct (1 woman). *Students:* 32 full-time (11 women), 7 part-time (2 women); includes 10 minority (3 Black or African American, non-Hispanic/Latino; 5 Asian, non-Hispanic/Latino; 1 Hispanic/Latino; 1 Two or more races, non-Hispanic/Latino), 19 international. 11 applicants, 64% accepted, 3 enrolled. In 2016, 6 doctorates awarded. *Degree requirements:* For doctorate, thesis/dissertation, preliminary exam, dissertation proposal and defense. *Entrance requirements:* For doctorate, GRE, minimum undergraduate GPA of 3.0; MS in engineering from ABET-accredited or equivalent

institution (preferred); resume; goals statement; three letters of reference; official transcripts. Additional exam requirements/recommendations for international students: Required—TOEFL (minimum score 550 paper-based; 79 iBT), IELTS (minimum score 6.5), PTE (minimum score 53). *Application deadline:* For fall admission, 1/15 priority date for domestic and international students; for spring admission, 11/1 priority date for domestic students, 8/1 priority date for international students. Applications are processed on a rolling basis. Application fee: $60. Electronic applications accepted. *Expenses:* $995 per credit hour in-state tuition; $1,319 per credit hour out-of-state. *Financial support:* Fellowships with tuition reimbursements, research assistantships with tuition reimbursements, teaching assistantships with tuition reimbursements, Federal Work-Study, scholarships/grants, health care benefits, and unspecified assistantships available. Financial award application deadline: 3/1; financial award applicants required to submit FAFSA. *Faculty research:* Advanced/computer-aided manufacturing and advanced materials processing; bioengineering; computer engineering; construction engineering and management; dynamics, controls, and systems; energy and environmental science; engineering physics and engineering mathematics; green engineering; signal processing and communication; transportation engineering; water resources, hydrology, and environmental engineering. *Unit head:* Dr. Saroj Biswas, Associate Dean, College of Engineering, 215-204-8403, E-mail: sbiswas@temple.edu. *Application contact:* Leslie Levin, Director, Admissions and Graduate Student Services, 215-204-7800, Fax: 215-204-6936, E-mail: gradengr@temple.edu.
Website: http://engineering.temple.edu/additional-programs/phd-engineering

See Display on page 63 and Close-Up on page 83.

Texas A&M University, College of Agriculture and Life Sciences and College of Engineering, Department of Biological and Agricultural Engineering, College Station, TX 77843. Offers agricultural systems management (M Agr, MS); biological and agricultural engineering (M Engr, MS, PhD). *Program availability:* Part-time. *Faculty:* 19. *Students:* 66 full-time (24 women), 24 part-time (9 women); includes 14 minority (3 Black or African American, non-Hispanic/Latino; 1 Asian, non-Hispanic/Latino; 8 Hispanic/Latino; 2 Two or more races, non-Hispanic/Latino), 54 international. Average age 28. 23 applicants, 96% accepted, 17 enrolled. In 2016, 15 master's, 5 doctorates awarded. *Degree requirements:* For master's, thesis (MS), preliminary and final exams; for doctorate, thesis/dissertation, preliminary and final exams. *Entrance requirements:* For master's and doctorate, GRE General Test. Additional exam requirements/recommendations for international students: Required—TOEFL (minimum score 550 paper-based; 80 iBT), IELTS (minimum score 6), PTE (minimum score 53). *Application deadline:* For fall admission, 12/15 priority date for domestic students. Applications are processed on a rolling basis. Application fee: $50 ($90 for international students). Electronic applications accepted. *Expenses:* Contact institution. *Financial support:* In 2016–17, 63 students received support, including 4 fellowships with tuition reimbursements available (averaging $8,642 per year), 37 research assistantships with tuition reimbursements available (averaging $5,471 per year), 11 teaching assistantships with tuition reimbursements available (averaging $9,384 per year); career-related internships or fieldwork, institutionally sponsored loans, scholarships/grants, traineeships, health care benefits, tuition waivers (full and partial), and unspecified assistantships also available. Support available to part-time students. Financial award application deadline: 3/15; financial award applicants required to submit FAFSA. *Faculty research:* Water quality and quantity; air quality; biological, food, ecological engineering; off-road equipment; mechatronics. *Unit head:* Dr. Steve Searcy, Professor and Head, 979-845-3940, Fax: 979-862-3442, E-mail: s-searcy@tamu.edu. *Application contact:* Dr. Sandun Fernando, Director of Graduate Programs, 979-845-9793, E-mail: sfernando@tamu.edu.
Website: http://baen.tamu.edu

Texas Tech University, Graduate School, Edward E. Whitacre Jr. College of Engineering, Interdisciplinary Program in Bioengineering, Lubbock, TX 79409-3103. Offers MS. *Students:* 5 full-time (3 women); includes 2 minority (1 Asian, non-Hispanic/Latino; 1 Hispanic/Latino), 1 international. Average age 24. 28 applicants, 32% accepted, 3 enrolled. In 2016, 3 master's awarded. *Degree requirements:* For master's, comprehensive exam, thesis (for some programs). *Entrance requirements:* For master's, GRE (Verbal and Quantitative). Additional exam requirements/recommendations for international students: Required—TOEFL (minimum score 550 paper-based; 79 iBT). *Application deadline:* For fall admission, 6/1 priority date for domestic students, 1/15 priority date for international students; for spring admission, 9/1 priority date for domestic students, 6/15 priority date for international students. Applications are processed on a rolling basis. Application fee: $75. Electronic applications accepted. *Expenses:* $325 per credit hour full-time resident tuition, $733 per credit hour full-time non-resident tuition; $53.75 per credit hour fee plus $608 per term fee. *Financial support:* In 2016–17, 2 students received support. Fellowships, research assistantships, teaching assistantships, scholarships/grants, tuition waivers (partial), and unspecified assistantships available. Financial award application deadline: 4/15; financial award applicants required to submit FAFSA. *Faculty research:* Bioengineering, biomaterials, environmental science, biomedical imaging. *Unit head:* Dr. Mary Baker, Director, 806-834-0065, Fax: 806-742-1245, E-mail: mary.baker@ttu.edu. *Application contact:* Judy Bailey, Administrative Assistant, 806-834-2573, Fax: 806-742-1245, E-mail: judy.bailey@ttu.edu.
Website: http://www.depts.ttu.edu/coe/bioengineering/

Tufts University, Graduate School of Arts and Sciences, Graduate Certificate Programs, Program in Bioengineering, Medford, MA 02155. Offers Certificate. *Program availability:* Part-time, evening/weekend. Electronic applications accepted. *Expenses: Tuition:* Full-time $49,892; part-time $1248 per credit hour. *Required fees:* $844. Full-time tuition and fees vary according to degree level, program and student level. Part-time tuition and fees vary according to course load.

Tufts University, School of Engineering, Department of Biomedical Engineering, Medford, MA 02155. Offers bioengineering (ME, MS), including biomaterials; biomedical engineering (PhD). *Program availability:* Part-time. Terminal master's awarded for partial completion of doctoral program. *Degree requirements:* For master's, thesis (for some programs); for doctorate, thesis/dissertation. *Entrance requirements:* For master's and doctorate, GRE General Test. Additional exam requirements/recommendations for international students: Required—TOEFL (minimum score 550 paper-based; 80 iBT), IELTS (minimum score 6.5). Electronic applications accepted. *Expenses: Tuition:* Full-time $49,892; part-time $1248 per credit hour. *Required fees:* $844. Full-time tuition and fees vary according to degree level, program and student level. Part-time tuition and fees vary according to course load. *Faculty research:* Regenerative medicine with biomaterials and tissue engineering, diffuse optical imaging and spectroscopy, optics in the development of biomedical devices, ultrafast nonlinear optics and biophotonics, optical diagnostics for diseased and engineered tissues.

Tufts University, School of Engineering, Department of Chemical and Biological Engineering, Medford, MA 02155. Offers bioengineering (ME, MS), including cell and bioprocess engineering; biotechnology engineering (PhD); chemical and biological engineering (ME, MS, PhD). *Program availability:* Part-time. Terminal master's awarded for partial completion of doctoral program. *Degree requirements:* For master's, thesis (for some programs); for doctorate, thesis/dissertation. *Entrance requirements:* For master's and doctorate, GRE General Test. Additional exam requirements/recommendations for international students: Required—TOEFL (minimum score 550 paper-based; 80 iBT), IELTS (minimum score 6.5). Electronic applications accepted. *Expenses: Tuition:* Full-time $49,892; part-time $1248 per credit hour. *Required fees:* $844. Full-time tuition and fees vary according to degree level, program and student level. Part-time tuition and fees vary according to course load. *Faculty research:* Clean energy with materials, biomaterials, colloids; metabolic engineering, biotechnology; process control; reaction kinetics, catalysis; transport phenomena.

Tufts University, School of Engineering, Department of Civil and Environmental Engineering, Medford, MA 02155. Offers bioengineering (ME, MS), including environmental technology; civil engineering (ME, MS, PhD), including geotechnical engineering, structural engineering, water diplomacy (PhD); environmental engineering (ME, MS, PhD), including environmental engineering and environmental sciences, environmental geotechnology, environmental health, environmental science and management, hazardous materials management, water diplomacy (PhD), water resources engineering. *Program availability:* Part-time. Terminal master's awarded for partial completion of doctoral program. *Degree requirements:* For master's, thesis or alternative; for doctorate, thesis/dissertation. *Entrance requirements:* For master's and doctorate, GRE General Test. Additional exam requirements/recommendations for international students: Required—TOEFL (minimum score 550 paper-based; 80 iBT), IELTS (minimum score 6.5). Electronic applications accepted. *Expenses: Tuition:* Full-time $49,892; part-time $1248 per credit hour. *Required fees:* $844. Full-time tuition and fees vary according to degree level, program and student level. Part-time tuition and fees vary according to course load. *Faculty research:* Environmental and water resources engineering, environmental health, geotechnical and geoenvironmental engineering, structural engineering and mechanics, water diplomacy.

Tufts University, School of Engineering, Department of Computer Science, Medford, MA 02155. Offers bioengineering (ME, MS), including bioinformatics; cognitive science (PhD); computer science (MS, PhD). *Program availability:* Part-time. Terminal master's awarded for partial completion of doctoral program. *Degree requirements:* For master's, thesis (for some programs); for doctorate, thesis/dissertation. *Entrance requirements:* For master's and doctorate, GRE General Test. Additional exam requirements/recommendations for international students: Required—TOEFL (minimum score 550 paper-based; 80 iBT), IELTS (minimum score 6.5). Electronic applications accepted. *Expenses: Tuition:* Full-time $49,892; part-time $1248 per credit hour. *Required fees:* $844. Full-time tuition and fees vary according to degree level, program and student level. Part-time tuition and fees vary according to course load. *Faculty research:* Computational biology, computational geometry, and computational systems biology; cognitive sciences, human-computer interaction, and human-robotic interaction; visualization and graphics, educational technologies; machine learning and data mining; programming languages and systems.

Tufts University, School of Engineering, Department of Electrical and Computer Engineering, Medford, MA 02155. Offers bioengineering (ME, MS), including signals and systems; electrical engineering (MS, PhD). *Program availability:* Part-time. Terminal master's awarded for partial completion of doctoral program. *Degree requirements:* For master's, thesis or alternative; for doctorate, thesis/dissertation. *Entrance requirements:* For master's and doctorate, GRE General Test. Additional exam requirements/recommendations for international students: Required—TOEFL (minimum score 550 paper-based; 80 iBT), IELTS (minimum score 6.5). Electronic applications accepted. *Expenses: Tuition:* Full-time $49,892; part-time $1248 per credit hour. *Required fees:* $844. Full-time tuition and fees vary according to degree level, program and student level. Part-time tuition and fees vary according to course load. *Faculty research:* Communication theory, networks, protocol, and transmission technology; simulation and modeling; digital processing technology; image and signal processing for security and medical applications; integrated circuits and VLSI.

Tufts University, School of Engineering, Department of Mechanical Engineering, Medford, MA 02155. Offers bioengineering (ME, MS), including bioinformatics, biomechanical systems and devices, signals and systems; bioinformatics (MS); human factors (MS); mechanical engineering (ME, MS, PhD). *Program availability:* Part-time. Terminal master's awarded for partial completion of doctoral program. *Degree requirements:* For master's, thesis; for doctorate, thesis/dissertation. *Entrance requirements:* For master's and doctorate, GRE General Test. Additional exam requirements/recommendations for international students: Required—TOEFL (minimum score 550 paper-based; 80 iBT), IELTS (minimum score 6.5). Electronic applications accepted. *Expenses: Tuition:* Full-time $49,892; part-time $1248 per credit hour. *Required fees:* $844. Full-time tuition and fees vary according to degree level, program and student level. Part-time tuition and fees vary according to course load. *Faculty research:* Applied mechanics, biomaterials, controls/robotics, design/systems, human factors.

University at Buffalo, the State University of New York, Graduate School, School of Engineering and Applied Sciences, Department of Chemical and Biological Engineering, Buffalo, NY 14260. Offers ME, MS, PhD. *Program availability:* Part-time. *Degree requirements:* For master's, thesis (for some programs); for doctorate, comprehensive exam, thesis/dissertation. *Entrance requirements:* For master's and doctorate, GRE General Test. Additional exam requirements/recommendations for international students: Required—TOEFL (minimum score 550 paper-based; 79 iBT). Electronic applications accepted. *Faculty research:* Transport, polymers, nanomaterials, biochemical engineering, catalysis.

University of Arkansas, Graduate School, College of Engineering, Department of Biological and Agricultural Engineering, Program in Biological Engineering, Fayetteville, AR 72701. Offers MSBE. In 2016, 5 master's awarded. *Application deadline:* For fall admission, 4/1 for international students; for spring admission, 10/1 for international students. Applications are processed on a rolling basis. Application fee: $40 ($50 for international students). Electronic applications accepted. *Financial support:* In 2016–17, 17 research assistantships, 1 teaching assistantship were awarded; fellowships also available. *Unit head:* Dr. Lalit Verma, Department Head, 479-575-2351, Fax: 479-575-2846, E-mail: lverma@uark.edu. *Application contact:* Dr. Jin-Woo Kim, Program Coordinator, 479-575-2351, Fax: 479-575-2846, E-mail: jwkim@uark.edu.
Website: http://www.baeg.uark.edu/

The University of British Columbia, Faculty of Applied Science, Department of Chemical and Biological Engineering, Vancouver, BC V6T 1Z3, Canada. Offers M Eng, M Sc, MA Sc, PhD. *Program availability:* Part-time, evening/weekend. *Degree requirements:* For master's, thesis (for some programs); for doctorate, thesis/dissertation. *Entrance requirements:* Additional exam requirements/recommendations for international students: Required—TOEFL, IELTS. Application fee: $100 Canadian dollars ($162 Canadian dollars for international students). Electronic applications accepted. *Expenses:* $4,802 per year tuition and fees, $8,436 per year international. *Financial support:* Fellowships, research assistantships, teaching assistantships, career-related internships or fieldwork, institutionally sponsored loans, scholarships/grants, and tuition waivers (full and partial) available. *Faculty research:* Biotechnology, catalysis, polymers, fluidization, pulp and paper. *Application contact:* Gina Abernethy, Graduate Program Staff, 604-827-4758, E-mail: chbe.gradsec@ubc.ca.
Website: http://www.chbe.ubc.ca/academics/graduate/

University of California, Berkeley, Graduate Division, Bioengineering Graduate Program Berkeley/UCSF, Berkeley, CA 94720-1762. Offers PhD. Program offered jointly with University of California, San Francisco. *Degree requirements:* For doctorate, comprehensive exam, thesis/dissertation. *Entrance requirements:* For doctorate, GRE General Test, minimum GPA of 3.0. Additional exam requirements/recommendations for international students: Required—TOEFL (minimum score 570 paper-based; 68 iBT). Electronic applications accepted. *Faculty research:* Biomaterials, biomechanics, biomedical imaging and instrumentation, computational biology, drug delivery systems and pharmacogenomics, neural systems engineering and vision science, systems and synthetic biology, tissue engineering and regenerative medicine.

University of California, Berkeley, Graduate Division, College of Engineering, Department of Bioengineering, Berkeley, CA 94720-1500. Offers M Eng, MTM. *Students:* 63 full-time (24 women); includes 24 minority (2 Black or African American, non-Hispanic/Latino; 18 Asian, non-Hispanic/Latino; 4 Hispanic/Latino), 18 international. 199 applicants, 62 enrolled. In 2016, 31 master's awarded. *Degree requirements:* For master's, comprehensive exam. *Entrance requirements:* Additional exam requirements/recommendations for international students: Required—TOEFL (minimum score 570 paper-based; 90 iBT). *Application deadline:* For fall admission, 1/6 for domestic students. Application fee: $105 ($125 for international students). Electronic applications accepted. *Financial support:* Fellowships, research assistantships, teaching assistantships, career-related internships or fieldwork, health care benefits, and unspecified assistantships available. *Unit head:* John Dueber, Chair, 510-642-9931, Fax: 510-642-5835, E-mail: bioe-grad@berkeley.edu. *Application contact:* 510-642-9931, E-mail: bioe-grad@berkeley.edu.
Website: http://bioegrad.berkeley.edu

University of California, Davis, College of Engineering, Program in Biological Systems Engineering, Davis, CA 95616. Offers M Engr, MS, D Engr, PhD, M Engr/MBA. Terminal master's awarded for partial completion of doctoral program. *Degree requirements:* For master's, thesis; for doctorate, thesis/dissertation. *Entrance requirements:* For master's, minimum GPA of 3.0; for doctorate, GRE, minimum graduate GPA of 3.25. Additional exam requirements/recommendations for international students: Required—TOEFL (minimum score 550 paper-based). Electronic applications accepted. *Faculty research:* Forestry, irrigation and drainage, power and machinery, structures and environment, information and energy technologies.

University of California, Los Angeles, Graduate Division, Henry Samueli School of Engineering and Applied Science, Department of Chemical and Biomolecular Engineering, Los Angeles, CA 90095-1592. Offers MS, PhD. *Faculty:* 14 full-time (3 women), 2 part-time/adjunct (0 women). *Students:* 105 full-time (24 women); includes 28 minority (1 Black or African American, non-Hispanic/Latino; 1 American Indian or Alaska Native, non-Hispanic/Latino; 19 Asian, non-Hispanic/Latino; 5 Hispanic/Latino; 2 Two or more races, non-Hispanic/Latino), 55 international. 420 applicants, 12% accepted, 27 enrolled. In 2016, 9 master's, 16 doctorates awarded. *Degree requirements:* For master's, comprehensive exam (for some programs), thesis (for some programs); for doctorate, thesis/dissertation, qualifying exams. *Entrance requirements:* For master's, GRE General Test, minimum GPA of 3.0; for doctorate, GRE General Test, minimum GPA of 3.25. Additional exam requirements/recommendations for international students: Required—TOEFL (minimum score 560 paper-based; 87 iBT), IELTS (minimum score 7). *Application deadline:* 12/31 for domestic and international students. Application fee: $105 ($125 for international students). Electronic applications accepted. *Financial support:* In 2016–17, 51 fellowships, 159 research assistantships, 57 teaching assistantships were awarded; Federal Work-Study, institutionally sponsored loans, and tuition waivers (full and partial) also available. Financial award application deadline: 12/31; financial award applicants required to submit FAFSA. *Faculty research:* Biomolecular engineering, renewable energy, water technology, advanced materials processing, process systems engineering. *Total annual research expenditures:* $9.4 million. *Unit head:* Dr. Panagiotis D. Christofides, Chair, 310-794-1015, E-mail: pdc@seas.ucla.edu. *Application contact:* Miguel Perez, Student Affairs Officer, 310-825-1203, E-mail: miguel@seas.ucla.edu.
Website: http://www.chemeng.ucla.edu/

University of California, Merced, Graduate Division, School of Engineering, Merced, CA 95343. Offers biological engineering and small scale technologies (MS, PhD); electrical engineering and computer science (MS, PhD); environmental systems (MS, PhD); mechanical engineering (MS); mechanical engineering and applied mechanics (PhD). *Faculty:* 44 full-time (7 women). *Students:* 170 full-time (52 women), 2 part-time (0 women); includes 34 minority (2 Black or African American, non-Hispanic/Latino; 11 Asian, non-Hispanic/Latino; 14 Hispanic/Latino; 2 Native Hawaiian or other Pacific Islander, non-Hispanic/Latino; 5 Two or more races, non-Hispanic/Latino), 99 international. Average age 28. 307 applicants, 35% accepted, 46 enrolled. In 2016, 15 master's, 12 doctorates awarded. Terminal master's awarded for partial completion of doctoral program. *Degree requirements:* For master's, variable foreign language requirement, comprehensive exam, thesis or alternative; for doctorate, variable foreign language requirement, comprehensive exam, thesis/dissertation. *Entrance requirements:* For master's and doctorate, GRE. Additional exam requirements/recommendations for international students: Required—TOEFL (minimum score 550 paper-based; 80 iBT); Recommended—IELTS (minimum score 7). *Application deadline:* For fall admission, 1/15 priority date for domestic and international students. Applications are processed on a rolling basis. Application fee: $90 ($110 for international students). Electronic applications accepted. *Expenses:* Contact institution. *Financial support:* In 2016–17, 150 students received support, including 16 fellowships with full tuition reimbursements available (averaging $19,088 per year), 45 research assistantships with full tuition reimbursements available (averaging $18,389 per year), 89 teaching assistantships with full tuition reimbursements available (averaging $19,249 per year); scholarships/grants, traineeships, and health care benefits also available. Financial award application deadline: 1/15. *Faculty research:* Water resources, biotechnology, renewable energy, big data, cyber-physical systems. *Total annual research expenditures:* $3.3 million. *Unit head:* Dr. Mark Matsumoto, Dean, Fax: 209-228-4047, E-mail: mmatsumoto@ucmerced.edu. *Application contact:* Tsu Ya, Director of Admissions and Academic Services, 209-228-4521, Fax: 209-228-6906, E-mail: tya@ucmerced.edu.

University of California, Riverside, Graduate Division, Department of Bioengineering, Riverside, CA 92521-0102. Offers MS, PhD. *Program availability:* Part-time. *Degree requirements:* For doctorate, thesis/dissertation, qualifying exams. *Entrance requirements:* Additional exam requirements/recommendations for international students: Required—TOEFL (minimum score 550 paper-based; 80 iBT). *Expenses:* Tuition, state resident: full-time $16,666. Tuition, nonresident: full-time $31,768. *Required fees:* $11,055.54 per quarter. $3685.18 per quarter. Tuition and fees vary according to campus/location and program.

University of California, San Diego, Graduate Division, Department of Bioengineering, La Jolla, CA 92093. Offers M Eng, MS, PhD. *Students:* 177 full-time (55 women), 2 part-time (both women). 812 applicants, 20% accepted, 52 enrolled. In 2016, 42 master's, 25 doctorates awarded. *Degree requirements:* For doctorate, comprehensive exam, thesis/dissertation, 2 quarters teaching 20 hours a week or 4 quarters teaching 10 hours a week. *Entrance requirements:* For master's, GRE General Test, minimum GPA of 3.0 (for M Eng), 3.4 (for MS); for doctorate, GRE General Test, minimum GPA of 3.4. Additional exam requirements/recommendations for international students: Required—TOEFL (minimum score 550 paper-based; 80 iBT), IELTS (minimum score 7). *Application deadline:* For fall admission, 11/30 for domestic students. Application fee: $105 ($125 for international students). Electronic applications accepted. *Expenses:* Tuition, state resident: full-time $11,220. Tuition, nonresident: full-time $26,322. *Required fees:* $1864. *Financial support:* Fellowships, research assistantships, teaching assistantships, scholarships/grants, traineeships, and unspecified assistantships available. Financial award applicants required to submit FAFSA. *Faculty research:* Bioinformatics and systems biology, multi-scale biology, quantitative biology, biomaterials, biosensors, neural engineering, integrative genomics, bio photonics. *Unit head:* Geert W. Schmid-Schoenbein, Chair, 858-534-3852, E-mail: chair@bioeng.ucsd.edu. *Application contact:* Jan Lenington, Graduate Coordinator, 858-822-1604, E-mail: jlenington@ucsd.edu.
Website: http://www.be.ucsd.edu/prospective-graduate-students

See Close-Up on page 119.

University of California, San Francisco, Graduate Division, Program in Bioengineering, Berkeley, CA 94720-1762. Offers PhD. Program offered jointly with University of California, Berkeley. *Degree requirements:* For doctorate, thesis/dissertation, qualifying exam. *Entrance requirements:* For doctorate, GRE General Test, minimum GPA of 3.0. Additional exam requirements/recommendations for international students: Required—TOEFL (minimum score 570 paper-based). Electronic applications accepted. *Faculty research:* Bioengineering, biomaterials, biomedical imaging and instrumentation, biomechanics, microfluidics, computational biology, systems biology, drug delivery systems and pharmacogenomics, neural systems engineering and vision science, synthetic biology, tissue engineering, regenerative medicine.

University of California, Santa Barbara, Graduate Division, College of Engineering, Department of Mechanical Engineering, Santa Barbara, CA 93106-5070. Offers bioengineering (PhD); mechanical engineering (MS); MS/PhD. Terminal master's awarded for partial completion of doctoral program. *Degree requirements:* For master's, thesis optional; for doctorate, comprehensive exam, thesis/dissertation. *Entrance requirements:* For master's and doctorate, GRE. Additional exam requirements/recommendations for international students: Required—TOEFL (minimum score 550 paper-based; 80 iBT), IELTS (minimum score 7). Electronic applications accepted. *Faculty research:* Micro/nanoscale technology; bioengineering and systems biology; computational science and engineering; dynamics systems, controls and robotics; thermofluid sciences; solid mechanics, materials, and structures.

University of California, Santa Barbara, Graduate Division, College of Letters and Sciences, Division of Mathematics, Life, and Physical Sciences, Department of Statistics and Applied Probability, Santa Barbara, CA 93106-3110. Offers bioengineering (PhD); financial mathematics and statistics (PhD); quantitative methods in the social sciences (PhD); statistics (MA), including applied statistics, mathematical statistics; statistics and applied probability (PhD); MA/PhD. Terminal master's awarded for partial completion of doctoral program. *Degree requirements:* For master's, comprehensive exam, thesis optional; for doctorate, comprehensive exam, thesis/dissertation. *Entrance requirements:* For master's and doctorate, GRE General Test. Additional exam requirements/recommendations for international students: Required—TOEFL (minimum score 550 paper-based; 80 iBT), IELTS (minimum score 7). Electronic applications accepted. *Faculty research:* Bayesian inference, financial mathematics, stochastic processes, environmental statistics, biostatistical modeling.

University of California, Santa Barbara, Graduate Division, College of Letters and Sciences, Division of Mathematics, Life, and Physical Sciences, Interdepartmental Graduate Program in Biomolecular Science and Engineering, Santa Barbara, CA 93106-2014. Offers biochemistry and molecular biology (PhD), including biochemistry and molecular biology, biophysics and bioengineering. Terminal master's awarded for partial completion of doctoral program. *Degree requirements:* For doctorate, thesis/dissertation. *Entrance requirements:* For doctorate, GRE General Test. Additional exam requirements/recommendations for international students: Required—TOEFL (minimum score 630 paper-based; 109 iBT), IELTS (minimum score 7). Electronic applications accepted. *Faculty research:* Biochemistry and molecular biology, biophysics, biomaterials, bioengineering, systems biology.

University of Chicago, Institute for Molecular Engineering, Chicago, IL 60637. Offers MA, PhD. *Faculty:* 21 full-time (4 women). *Students:* 73 full-time (22 women); includes 11 minority (5 Asian, non-Hispanic/Latino; 2 Hispanic/Latino; 4 Two or more races, non-Hispanic/Latino), 32 international. 242 applicants, 29% accepted, 25 enrolled. In 2016, 1 master's, 7 doctorates awarded. *Degree requirements:* For doctorate, thesis/dissertation, qualifying research presentation, teaching requirement. *Entrance requirements:* For doctorate, GRE General Test. Additional exam requirements/recommendations for international students: Required—TOEFL (minimum score 90 iBT), IELTS (minimum score 7). *Application deadline:* For fall admission, 1/5 for domestic and international students. Application fee: $0. Electronic applications accepted. *Financial support:* In 2016–17, 36 students received support, including 7 fellowships (averaging $4,000 per year), 45 research assistantships with full tuition reimbursements available (averaging $31,362 per year); career-related internships or fieldwork, scholarships/grants, traineeships, health care benefits, and unspecified assistantships also available. *Faculty research:* Bimolecular engineering, spintronics, nanotechnology, quantum computing, protein folding and aggregation, liquid crystals, theoretical and computational modeling of materials, immunology, nanolithography, directed self-assembly, cancer research. *Total annual research expenditures:* $2.9 million. *Unit head:* Dr. Sharon Feng, Senior Associate Dean. *Application contact:* Dr. Novia Pagone, Associate Dean of Students, 773-834-1437, E-mail: ime@uchicago.edu.
Website: http://ime.uchicago.edu/

University of Colorado Denver, College of Engineering and Applied Science, Department of Bioengineering, Aurora, CO 80045-2560. Offers basic research (MS, PhD); biomedical device design (MS); entrepreneurship (MS, PhD); translational bioengineering (PhD). *Program availability:* Part-time. *Faculty:* 26 full-time (11 women), 7 part-time/adjunct (2 women). *Students:* 48 full-time (20 women), 11 part-time (4 women); includes 17 minority (3 Black or African American, non-Hispanic/Latino; 9 Asian, non-Hispanic/Latino; 2 Hispanic/Latino; 3 Two or more races, non-Hispanic/Latino), 3 international. Average age 26. 84 applicants, 71% accepted, 15 enrolled. In 2016, 15 master's, 1 doctorate awarded. Terminal master's awarded for partial completion of doctoral program. *Degree requirements:* For master's, thesis or alternative, 30 credit hours; for doctorate, comprehensive exam, 36 credit hours of classwork (18 core, 18 elective), additional 30 hours of thesis work, three formal examinations, approval of dissertations. *Entrance requirements:* For master's and doctorate, GRE, transcripts, three letters of recommendation, resume, statement of purpose. Additional exam requirements/recommendations for international students: Required—TOEFL (minimum score 550 paper-based; 79 iBT), TOEFL (minimum score 600 paper-based; 100 iBT) for PhD. *Application deadline:* For fall admission, 1/15 priority date for domestic students, 1/1 priority date for international students. Application fee: $50 ($75 for international students). Electronic applications accepted. *Expenses:* Contact institution. *Financial support:* In 2016–17, 34 students received support.

Fellowships, research assistantships, teaching assistantships, Federal Work-Study, institutionally sponsored loans, scholarships/grants, and traineeships available. Financial award application deadline: 4/1; financial award applicants required to submit FAFSA. *Faculty research:* Imaging and bio photonics, cardiovascular biomechanics and hemodynamics, orthopedic biomechanics, ophthalmology, neuroscience engineering, diabetes, surgery and urological sciences. *Unit head:* Dr. Robin Shandas, Professor/ Founding Chair, 303-724-4196, E-mail: robin.shandas@ucdenver.edu. *Application contact:* Angela VanDijk, Director of Bioengineering Student Services, 303-724-9972, E-mail: angela.vandijk@ucdenver.edu.
Website: http://www.ucdenver.edu/academics/colleges/Engineering/Programs/bioengineering/Pages/Home.aspx

University of Dayton, Department of Chemical Engineering, Dayton, OH 45469. Offers bioengineering (MS); chemical engineering (MS Ch E). *Program availability:* Part-time, evening/weekend. *Faculty:* 9 full-time (2 women), 2 part-time/adjunct (0 women). *Students:* 26 full-time (8 women), 6 part-time (1 woman); includes 1 minority (Black or African American, non-Hispanic/Latino), 24 international. Average age 26. 92 applicants, 22% accepted. In 2016, 33 master's awarded. *Degree requirements:* For master's, thesis. *Entrance requirements:* For master's, GRE (preferred), minimum GPA of 3.0 as undergraduate, transcript, 3 letters of recommendation, bachelor's degree in chemical engineering (preferred). Additional exam requirements/recommendations for international students: Required—TOEFL (minimum score 550 paper-based; 80 iBT); Recommended—IELTS. *Application deadline:* Applications are processed on a rolling basis. Application fee: $0 ($50 for international students). Electronic applications accepted. *Expenses:* $890 per credit hour, $25 registration fee. *Financial support:* In 2016–17, 2 research assistantships with full tuition reimbursements (averaging $15,000 per year) were awarded; teaching assistantships, institutionally sponsored loans, and health care benefits also available. Financial award application deadline: 3/1; financial award applicants required to submit FAFSA. *Faculty research:* Nonmaterial cellular interactions; mixing, chemical reaction; oxidative and pyrolytic reaction chemistry; hydrocarbon fuel chemistry; kinetics and reaction engineering; electrochemistry and electrochemical engineering; fuel cells; modeling, control and automation of polymer processing. *Unit head:* Dr. Charles Browning, Chair, 937-229-2627, E-mail: cbrowning1@udayton.edu. *Application contact:* Dr. Kevin Myers, Graduate Program Director, 937-229-2627, E-mail: kmyers1@udayton.edu.
Website: https://www.udayton.edu/engineering/departments/chemical_and_materials/index.php

University of Denver, Daniel Felix Ritchie School of Engineering and Computer Science, Department of Mechanical and Materials Engineering, Denver, CO 80208. Offers bioengineering (MS); engineering (MS, PhD), including management (MS); materials science (MS, PhD); mechanical engineering (MS, PhD). *Program availability:* Part-time. *Faculty:* 11 full-time (1 woman), 2 part-time/adjunct (both women). *Students:* 2 full-time (0 women), 27 part-time (7 women); includes 6 minority (1 Asian, non-Hispanic/Latino; 5 Hispanic/Latino), 13 international. Average age 28. 57 applicants, 79% accepted, 13 enrolled. In 2016, 11 master's, 5 doctorates awarded. Terminal master's awarded for partial completion of doctoral program. *Degree requirements:* For master's, thesis optional; for doctorate, comprehensive exam, thesis/dissertation. *Entrance requirements:* For master's, GRE General Test, bachelor's degree, transcripts, personal statement, resume or curriculum vitae, two letters of recommendation; for doctorate, GRE General Test, master's degree, transcripts, personal statement, resume or curriculum vitae, two letters of recommendation. Additional exam requirements/ recommendations for international students: Required—TOEFL (minimum score 550 paper-based; 80 iBT). *Application deadline:* For fall admission, 2/1 priority date for domestic and international students. Applications are processed on a rolling basis. Application fee: $65. Electronic applications accepted. *Expenses:* $29,022 per year full-time. *Financial support:* In 2016–17, 15 students received support, including 4 research assistantships with tuition reimbursements available (averaging $11,667 per year), 5 teaching assistantships with tuition reimbursements available (averaging $12,084 per year); Federal Work-Study, institutionally sponsored loans, scholarships/grants, health care benefits, and unspecified assistantships also available. Financial award application deadline: 2/15; financial award applicants required to submit FAFSA. *Faculty research:* Cardiac biomechanics, novel high voltage/temperature materials and structures, high speed stereo radiography, musculoskeletal modeling, composites. *Total annual research expenditures:* $996,915. *Unit head:* Dr. Matt Gordon, Professor and Chair, 303-871-3580, Fax: 303-871-4450, E-mail: matthew.gordon@du.edu. *Application contact:* Yvonne Petitt, Assistant to the Chair, 303-871-2107, Fax: 303-871-4450, E-mail: yvonne.petitt@du.edu.
Website: http://ritchieschool.du.edu/departments/mme/

University of Florida, Graduate School, Herbert Wertheim College of Engineering and College of Agricultural and Life Sciences, Department of Agricultural and Biological Engineering, Gainesville, FL 32611. Offers agricultural and biological engineering (ME, MS, PhD), including geographic information systems, hydrologic sciences, wetland sciences; biological systems modeling (Certificate). *Program availability:* Part-time. Terminal master's awarded for partial completion of doctoral program. *Degree requirements:* For master's, comprehensive exam, thesis (for some programs); for doctorate, comprehensive exam, thesis/dissertation. *Entrance requirements:* For master's and doctorate, minimum GPA of 3.0, 3 letters of recommendation, statement of purpose. Additional exam requirements/recommendations for international students: Required—TOEFL (minimum score 550 paper-based; 80 iBT), IELTS (minimum score 6). Electronic applications accepted. *Faculty research:* Bioenergy and bioprocessing; hydrological, biological and agricultural modeling; biosensors; precision agriculture and robotics; food packaging and food security.

University of Guelph, Graduate Studies, College of Physical and Engineering Science, School of Engineering, Guelph, ON N1G 2W1, Canada. Offers biological engineering (M Eng, M Sc, MA Sc, PhD); engineering systems and computing (M Eng, M Sc, MA Sc, PhD); environmental engineering (M Eng, M Sc, MA Sc, PhD); water resources engineering (M Eng, M Sc, MA Sc, PhD). *Program availability:* Part-time. *Degree requirements:* For master's, thesis (for some programs); for doctorate, comprehensive exam, thesis/dissertation. *Entrance requirements:* For master's, minimum B- average during previous 2 years of course work; for doctorate, minimum B average. Additional exam requirements/recommendations for international students: Required—TOEFL (minimum score 550 paper-based; 89 iBT), IELTS (minimum score 6.5). Electronic applications accepted. *Faculty research:* Water and food safety, environmental contaminant fates and mechanisms, computer systems, robotics and mechatronics, waste treatment.

University of Hawaii at Manoa, Graduate Division, College of Tropical Agriculture and Human Resources, Department of Molecular Biosciences and Bioengineering, Program in Bioengineering, Honolulu, HI 96822. Offers MS. *Program availability:* Part-time. *Degree requirements:* For master's, thesis optional. *Entrance requirements:* For master's, GRE General Test. Additional exam requirements/recommendations for international students: Required—TOEFL (minimum score 500 paper-based; 61 iBT), IELTS (minimum score 5).

University of Idaho, College of Graduate Studies, College of Engineering, Department of Biological Engineering, Moscow, ID 83844-2282. Offers M Engr, MS, PhD. *Degree requirements:* For doctorate, variable foreign language requirement. *Entrance requirements:* For master's, minimum GPA of 3.0. Additional exam requirements/ recommendations for international students: Required—TOEFL. Electronic applications accepted. *Expenses:* Tuition, state resident: full-time $6460; part-time $414 per credit hour. Tuition, nonresident: full-time $21,268; part-time $1237 per credit hour. *Required fees:* $2070; $60 per credit hour. Full-time tuition and fees vary according to course load and reciprocity agreements.

University of Idaho, College of Graduate Studies, College of Engineering, Department of Engineering, Moscow, ID 83844. Offers biological engineering (M Engr, MS, PhD); technology management (MS). *Faculty:* 8 full-time. *Students:* 1 full-time, 25 part-time. Average age 42. In 2016, 6 master's, 1 doctorate awarded. *Entrance requirements:* For master's, minimum GPA of 3.0. Additional exam requirements/recommendations for international students: Required—TOEFL. *Application deadline:* Applications are processed on a rolling basis. Application fee: $60. Electronic applications accepted. *Expenses:* Tuition, state resident: full-time $6460; part-time $414 per credit hour. Tuition, nonresident: full-time $21,268; part-time $1237 per credit hour. *Required fees:* $2070; $60 per credit hour. Full-time tuition and fees vary according to course load and reciprocity agreements. *Financial support:* Applicants required to submit FAFSA. *Unit head:* Dr. Larry Stauffer, Dean, 208-885-6479. *Application contact:* Stephanie Thomas, Graduate Recruitment Coordinator, 208-885-4001, Fax: 208-885-4406, E-mail: gadms@uidaho.edu.
Website: http://www.uidaho.edu/engr/

University of Illinois at Chicago, College of Engineering, Department of Bioengineering, Chicago, IL 60607-7128. Offers MS, PhD. Terminal master's awarded for partial completion of doctoral program. *Degree requirements:* For master's, thesis; for doctorate, thesis/dissertation. *Entrance requirements:* For master's and doctorate, GRE Subject Test, minimum GPA of 3.0. Additional exam requirements/ recommendations for international students: Required—TOEFL. Electronic applications accepted. *Expenses:* Contact institution. *Faculty research:* Imaging systems, bioinstrumentation, electrophysiology, biological control, laser scattering.

University of Illinois at Urbana–Champaign, Graduate College, College of Agricultural, Consumer and Environmental Sciences, Department of Agricultural and Biological Engineering, Champaign, IL 61820. Offers agricultural and biological engineering (MS, PhD); technical systems management (MS, PSM).

University of Illinois at Urbana–Champaign, Graduate College, College of Engineering, Department of Bioengineering, Champaign, IL 61820. Offers MS, PhD.

University of Illinois at Urbana–Champaign, Graduate College, College of Liberal Arts and Sciences, School of Chemical Sciences, Department of Chemical and Biomolecular Engineering, Champaign, IL 61820. Offers bioinformatics: chemical and biomolecular engineering (MS); chemical engineering (MS, PhD). *Entrance requirements:* For master's, minimum GPA of 3.0.

The University of Kansas, Graduate Studies, School of Engineering, Program in Bioengineering, Lawrence, KS 66045. Offers MS, PhD. *Program availability:* Part-time. *Students:* 44 full-time (18 women), 2 part-time (both women); includes 9 minority (2 Black or African American, non-Hispanic/Latino; 1 American Indian or Alaska Native, non-Hispanic/Latino; 2 Asian, non-Hispanic/Latino; 1 Hispanic/Latino; 3 Two or more races, non-Hispanic/Latino), 5 international. Average age 26. 47 applicants, 45% accepted, 11 enrolled. In 2016, 10 master's, 5 doctorates awarded. Terminal master's awarded for partial completion of doctoral program. *Entrance requirements:* For master's and doctorate, GRE, statement of academic objectives, curriculum vitae or resume, official transcripts, 3 letters of recommendation. Additional exam requirements/ recommendations for international students: Required—TOEFL or IELTS. *Application deadline:* For fall admission, 12/12 for domestic and international students; for spring admission, 9/30 for domestic and international students. Application fee: $65 ($85 for international students). Electronic applications accepted. *Financial support:* Fellowships, research assistantships, teaching assistantships, and scholarships/grants available. Financial award application deadline: 12/12. *Faculty research:* Biomaterials and tissue engineering, biomechanics and neural engineering, biomedical product design and development, biomolecular engineering, bio imaging and bioinformatics. *Unit head:* Dr. Sara Wilson, Academic Director, Bioengineering Graduate Program, 785-864-2103, E-mail: sewilson@ku.edu. *Application contact:* Denise Bridwell, Program Assistant, 785-864-5258, E-mail: dbridwell@ku.edu.
Website: http://bio.engr.ku.edu/

University of Louisville, J. B. Speed School of Engineering, Department of Bioengineering, Louisville, KY 40292-0001. Offers M Eng. *Accreditation:* ABET. *Program availability:* Part-time, online learning. *Students:* 17 full-time (5 women), 11 part-time (3 women); includes 6 minority (2 Black or African American, non-Hispanic/ Latino; 2 Asian, non-Hispanic/Latino; 1 Hispanic/Latino; 1 Two or more races, non-Hispanic/Latino). Average age 24. 1 applicant, 1 enrolled. In 2016, 10 master's awarded. *Degree requirements:* For master's, thesis optional, minimum GPA of 2.75. *Entrance requirements:* For master's, GRE, letters of recommendation, final official transcripts. Additional exam requirements/recommendations for international students: Required—PTE (minimum score 550), TOEFL (minimum score 80 iBT) or IELTS. *Application deadline:* Applications are processed on a rolling basis. Electronic applications accepted. *Expenses:* Tuition, state resident: full-time $12,246; part-time $681 per credit hour. Tuition, nonresident: full-time $25,486; part-time $1417 per credit hour. *Required fees:* $196. Tuition and fees vary according to program and reciprocity agreements. *Financial support:* Fellowships with full tuition reimbursements, research assistantships with full tuition reimbursements, and teaching assistantships with full tuition reimbursements available. Financial award application deadline: 2/3. *Total annual research expenditures:* $5.2 million. *Unit head:* Dr. Ayman El-Baz, Chair, 502-852-5092, E-mail: aselba01@louisville.edu. *Application contact:* Dr. Michael Harris, Director of Graduate Student Affairs, 502-852-6278, Fax: 502-852-7294, E-mail: mharris@louisville.edu.
Website: https://louisville.edu/speed/bioengineering/

University of Maryland, College Park, Academic Affairs, A. James Clark School of Engineering, Department of Chemical and Biomolecular Engineering, College Park, MD 20742. Offers bioengineering (MS, PhD); chemical engineering (M Eng, MS, PhD). *Program availability:* Part-time, evening/weekend. *Degree requirements:* For master's, thesis optional; for doctorate, variable foreign language requirement, thesis/dissertation, exam, oral presentation. *Entrance requirements:* For master's and doctorate, GRE General Test, 3 letters of recommendation. Additional exam requirements/ recommendations for international students: Required—TOEFL. Electronic applications accepted. *Faculty research:* Applied polymer science, biochemical engineering, thermal properties, bioprocess monitoring.

University of Maryland, College Park, Academic Affairs, A. James Clark School of Engineering, Fischell Department of Bioengineering, College Park, MD 20742. Offers MS, PhD. *Degree requirements:* For master's, thesis optional; for doctorate, thesis/ dissertation. *Entrance requirements:* For master's, GRE General Test, minimum GPA of 3.0, 3 letters of recommendation. Electronic applications accepted. *Faculty research:* Bioengineering, bioenvironmental and water resources engineering, natural resources management.

University of Michigan–Dearborn, College of Engineering and Computer Science, MSE Program in Bioengineering, Dearborn, MI 48128. Offers MSE. *Program availability:* Part-time, evening/weekend. *Faculty:* 24 full-time (4 women), 12 part-time/adjunct (2 women). *Students:* 1 (woman) full-time, 1 part-time (0 women), 1 international. Average age 23. 2 applicants, 100% accepted, 2 enrolled. *Entrance requirements:* Additional exam requirements/recommendations for international students: Required—TOEFL (minimum score 560 paper-based; 84 iBT), IELTS (minimum score 6.5). *Application deadline:* For fall admission, 8/1 for domestic students, 5/1 for international students; for winter admission, 12/1 for domestic students, 9/1 for international students; for spring admission, 4/1 for domestic students, 1/1 for international students. Applications are processed on a rolling basis. Application fee: $60. Electronic applications accepted. *Expenses:* Tuition, state resident: full-time $13,118; part-time $2280 per term. Tuition, nonresident: full-time $21,816; part-time $3771 per term. *Required fees:* $866; $658 per unit. $329 per term. Tuition and fees vary according to program. *Financial support:* Research assistantships, scholarships/grants, and non-resident tuition scholarships available. Financial award application deadline: 3/1; financial award applicants required to submit FAFSA. *Faculty research:* Biomaterials and tissue engineering, cell preservation and biomimetics, microfluidics, drug delivery, biomechanics. *Unit head:* Dr. Alan Argento, Program Director, 313-593-5029, E-mail: aargento@umich.edu. *Application contact:* Office of Graduate Studies Staff, 313-583-6321, E-mail: umd-graduatestudies@umich.edu.
Website: https://umdearborn.edu/cecs/departments/mechanical-engineering/graduate-programs/mse-bioengineering

University of Missouri, Office of Research and Graduate Studies, College of Engineering, Department of Biological Engineering, Columbia, MO 65211. Offers agricultural engineering (MS); biological engineering (MS, PhD). *Faculty:* 9 full-time (3 women), 1 (woman) part-time/adjunct. *Students:* 26 full-time (7 women), 25 part-time (7 women). *Degree requirements:* For master's, thesis; for doctorate, thesis/dissertation. *Entrance requirements:* For master's and doctorate, GRE General Test, minimum GPA of 3.0. Additional exam requirements/recommendations for international students: Required—TOEFL (minimum score 550 paper-based; 80 iBT). *Application deadline:* For fall admission, 4/1 for domestic students. Applications are processed on a rolling basis. Application fee: $75 ($90 for international students). Electronic applications accepted. *Expenses:* Tuition, state resident: full-time $6347; part-time $352.60 per credit hour. Tuition, nonresident: full-time $17,379; part-time $965.50 per credit hour. *Required fees:* $1035. Tuition and fees vary according to course load, campus/location and program. *Financial support:* Fellowships, research assistantships, teaching assistantships, institutionally sponsored loans, scholarships/grants, traineeships, health care benefits, and unspecified assistantships available. Support available to part-time students.
Website: http://bioengineering.missouri.edu/graduate/

University of Nebraska–Lincoln, Graduate College, College of Engineering, Department of Biological Systems Engineering, Interdepartmental Area of Agricultural and Biological Systems Engineering, Lincoln, NE 68588. Offers MS, PhD. *Degree requirements:* For master's, thesis optional. *Entrance requirements:* Additional exam requirements/recommendations for international students: Required—TOEFL (minimum score 550 paper-based). Electronic applications accepted. *Faculty research:* Hydrological engineering, tractive performance, biomedical engineering, irrigation systems.

University of Nebraska–Lincoln, Graduate College, College of Engineering, Department of Chemical and Biomolecular Engineering, Lincoln, NE 68588. Offers MS, PhD. *Degree requirements:* For master's, thesis; for doctorate, comprehensive exam, thesis/dissertation. *Entrance requirements:* For master's and doctorate, GRE. Additional exam requirements/recommendations for international students: Required—TOEFL (minimum score 550 paper-based). Electronic applications accepted. *Faculty research:* Fermentation, radioactive waste remediation, chemical fuels from renewable feedstocks.

University of Notre Dame, Graduate School, College of Engineering, Department of Civil Engineering and Geological Sciences, Notre Dame, IN 46556. Offers bioengineering (MS Bio E); civil engineering (MSCE); civil engineering and geological sciences (PhD); environmental engineering (MS Env E); geological sciences (MS). Terminal master's awarded for partial completion of doctoral program. *Degree requirements:* For master's, comprehensive exam; for doctorate, thesis/dissertation, candidacy exam. *Entrance requirements:* For master's and doctorate, GRE General Test. Additional exam requirements/recommendations for international students: Required—TOEFL (minimum score 600 paper-based; 80 iBT). Electronic applications accepted. *Faculty research:* Environmental modeling, biological-waste treatment, petrology, environmental geology, geochemistry.

University of Ottawa, Faculty of Graduate and Postdoctoral Studies, Faculty of Engineering, Department of Chemical and Biological Engineering, Ottawa, ON K1N 6N5, Canada. Offers M Eng, MA Sc, PhD. *Degree requirements:* For master's, thesis or alternative; for doctorate, comprehensive exam, thesis/dissertation. *Entrance requirements:* For master's, honors degree or equivalent, minimum B average; for doctorate, master's degree, minimum B+ average. Electronic applications accepted. *Faculty research:* Material development, process engineering, clean technologies.

University of Pennsylvania, School of Engineering and Applied Science, Department of Bioengineering, Philadelphia, PA 19104. Offers MSE, PhD, PhD/MD, VMD/PhD. *Program availability:* Part-time. *Faculty:* 36 full-time (6 women), 15 part-time/adjunct (0 women). *Students:* 142 full-time (64 women), 25 part-time (10 women); includes 59 minority (3 Black or African American, non-Hispanic/Latino; 42 Asian, non-Hispanic/Latino; 11 Hispanic/Latino; 3 Two or more races, non-Hispanic/Latino), 41 international. Average age 25. 545 applicants, 21% accepted, 66 enrolled. In 2016, 44 master's, 21 doctorates awarded. *Degree requirements:* For master's, comprehensive exam, thesis optional; for doctorate, comprehensive exam, thesis/dissertation. *Entrance requirements:* For master's and doctorate, GRE. Additional exam requirements/recommendations for international students: Required—TOEFL (minimum score 100 iBT), IELTS (minimum score 7). *Application deadline:* For fall admission, 3/15 priority date for domestic and international students. Application fee: $80. Electronic applications accepted. *Expenses: Tuition:* Full-time $31,068; part-time $5762 per course. *Required fees:* $3200; $336 per course. Full-time tuition and fees vary according to degree level, program and student level. Part-time tuition and fees vary according to course load, degree level and program. *Faculty research:* Biomaterials, cell mechanics, molecular engineering, neuroengineering, theoretical computational bioengineering. *Application contact:* William Fenton, Assistant Director of Graduate Admissions, 215-898-4542, Fax: 215-573-5577, E-mail: gradstudies@seas.upenn.edu.
Website: http://www.be.seas.upenn.edu/prospective-students/masters/index.php

University of Pennsylvania, School of Engineering and Applied Science, Department of Chemical and Biomolecular Engineering, Philadelphia, PA 19104. Offers MSE, PhD. *Program availability:* Part-time. *Faculty:* 18 full-time (3 women), 5 part-time/adjunct (0 women). *Students:* 102 full-time (33 women), 5 part-time (0 women); includes 10 minority (1 Black or African American, non-Hispanic/Latino; 8 Asian, non-Hispanic/Latino; 1 Hispanic/Latino), 72 international. Average age 25. 482 applicants, 27% accepted, 59 enrolled. In 2016, 29 master's, 13 doctorates awarded. *Degree requirements:* For master's, comprehensive exam, thesis optional; for doctorate, comprehensive exam, thesis/dissertation. *Entrance requirements:* For master's and doctorate, GRE. Additional exam requirements/recommendations for international students: Required—TOEFL (minimum score 100 iBT), IELTS (minimum score 7). *Application deadline:* For fall admission, 3/15 priority date for domestic and international students. Application fee: $80. Electronic applications accepted. *Expenses: Tuition:* Full-time $31,068; part-time $5762 per course. *Required fees:* $3200; $336 per course. Full-time tuition and fees vary according to degree level, program and student level. Part-time tuition and fees vary according to course load, degree level and program. *Faculty research:* Advanced materials and nanotechnology, catalysis and reaction engineering, cellular and biomolecular engineering, energy and environmental engineering, molecular simulation and thermodynamics. *Application contact:* William Fenton, Assistant Director of Graduate Admissions, 215-898-4542, Fax: 215-573-5577, E-mail: gradstudies@seas.upenn.edu.
Website: http://www.cbe.seas.upenn.edu/prospective-students/masters/index.php

University of Pittsburgh, Swanson School of Engineering, Department of Bioengineering, Pittsburgh, PA 15260. Offers MSBENG, PhD, MD/PhD. *Program availability:* Part-time, 100% online. *Faculty:* 27 full-time (3 women), 22 part-time/adjunct (3 women). *Students:* 173 full-time (62 women), 18 part-time (7 women); includes 51 minority (10 Black or African American, non-Hispanic/Latino; 1 American Indian or Alaska Native, non-Hispanic/Latino; 22 Asian, non-Hispanic/Latino; 8 Hispanic/Latino; 10 Two or more races, non-Hispanic/Latino), 52 international. 309 applicants, 32% accepted, 45 enrolled. In 2016, 22 master's, 24 doctorates awarded. Terminal master's awarded for partial completion of doctoral program. *Degree requirements:* For doctorate, comprehensive exam, thesis/dissertation, final oral exams. *Entrance requirements:* For master's and doctorate, GRE General Test, minimum GPA of 3.0. Additional exam requirements/recommendations for international students: Required—TOEFL (minimum score 550 paper-based; 80 iBT). *Application deadline:* For fall admission, 3/1 priority date for domestic and international students; for spring admission, 7/1 priority date for domestic and international students. Applications are processed on a rolling basis. Application fee: $50. Electronic applications accepted. *Expenses:* $24,962 full-time per academic year in-state tuition, $41,222 full-time per academic year out-of-state tuition; $830 mandatory fees per academic year. *Financial support:* In 2016–17, 39 fellowships with full tuition reimbursements (averaging $30,720 per year), 55 research assistantships with full tuition reimbursements (averaging $27,396 per year), 18 teaching assistantships with full tuition reimbursements (averaging $26,328 per year) were awarded; scholarships/grants and traineeships also available. Financial award application deadline: 3/1. *Faculty research:* Artificial organs, biomechanics, biomaterials, signal processing, biotechnology. *Total annual research expenditures:* $52.7 million. *Unit head:* Dr. Sanjeev G. Shroff, Chairman, 412-624-4705, Fax: 412-383-8788, E-mail: sshroff@pitt.edu. *Application contact:* Rama Bazaz, Director, 412-624-9800, Fax: 412-624-9808, E-mail: ssoeadm@pitt.edu.
Website: http://www.engineering.pitt.edu/bioengineering/

University of Puerto Rico, Mayagüez Campus, Graduate Studies, College of Engineering, Department of Mechanical Engineering, Mayagüez, PR 00681-9000. Offers mechanical engineering (ME, MS, PhD), including aerospace and unmanned vehivles (ME), automation/mechatronics, bioengineering, cae and design, fluid mechanics, heat transfer/energy systems, manufacturing, mechanics of materials, micro and nano engineering. *Program availability:* Part-time. *Faculty:* 22 full-time (4 women), 1 part-time/adjunct (0 women). *Students:* 34 full-time (4 women), 8 part-time (2 women); includes 38 minority (all Hispanic/Latino), 3 international. Average age 25. 22 applicants, 100% accepted, 7 enrolled. In 2016, 17 master's awarded. Terminal master's awarded for partial completion of doctoral program. *Degree requirements:* For master's, one foreign language, comprehensive exam, thesis; for doctorate, one foreign language, comprehensive exam, thesis/dissertation. *Entrance requirements:* For master's, BS in mechanical engineering or its equivalent; for doctorate, GRE, BS or MS in mechanical engineering or its equivalent; minimum GPA of 3.0. Additional exam requirements/recommendations for international students: Required—TOEFL (minimum score 80 paper-based; 80 iBT). *Application deadline:* For fall admission, 2/15 for domestic and international students; for spring admission, 9/15 for domestic and international students. Applications are processed on a rolling basis. Application fee: $25. Electronic applications accepted. *Expenses: Tuition, area resident:* Full-time $2466. *International tuition:* $7166 full-time. *Required fees:* $210. One-time fee: $5 full-time. Tuition and fees vary according to course level, campus/location, program and student level. *Financial support:* In 2016–17, 39 students received support, including 26 research assistantships with full and partial tuition reimbursements available (averaging $3,801 per year), 30 teaching assistantships with full and partial tuition reimbursements available (averaging $3,293 per year); unspecified assistantships also available. *Faculty research:* Computational fluid dynamics, thermal sciences, mechanical design, material health, microfluidics. *Unit head:* Paul Sundaram, Ph.D., Chairperson, 787-832-4040 Ext. 3659, Fax: 787-265-3817, E-mail: paul.sundaram@upr.edu. *Application contact:* Yolanda Perez, Academic Orientation Officer, 787-832-4040 Ext. 2362, Fax: 787-265-3817, E-mail: yolanda.perez4@upr.edu.
Website: https://wordpress.uprm.edu/inme/

University of Saskatchewan, College of Graduate Studies and Research, College of Engineering, Biological Engineering Program, Saskatoon, SK S7N 5A9, Canada. Offers M Eng, M Sc, PhD. *Program availability:* Part-time. *Degree requirements:* For master's, thesis (for some programs), 30 credits (for M Eng); thesis and 12 credits (for MS); for doctorate, comprehensive exam, thesis/dissertation, qualifying exam, 18 credits. *Entrance requirements:* For master's and doctorate, GRE. Additional exam requirements/recommendations for international students: Required—TOEFL, TOEFL (minimum iBT score of 80), IELTS (6.5), CanTEST (4.5), or PTE (59). Electronic applications accepted. *Faculty research:* Agricultural machinery systems, animal welfare, biomechanical engineering, feed processing, food and bioprocess engineering, irrigation, livestock odor control, post-harvest technologies, soil and water conservation.

The University of Texas at Arlington, Graduate School, College of Engineering, Bioengineering Department, Arlington, TX 76019. Offers MS, PhD. Programs offered jointly with The University of Texas Southwestern Medical Center at Dallas. *Program availability:* Part-time. Terminal master's awarded for partial completion of doctoral program. *Degree requirements:* For master's, comprehensive exam (for some programs), thesis (for some programs); for doctorate, comprehensive exam, thesis/dissertation, qualifying exam. *Entrance requirements:* For master's, GRE General Test (minimum total of 1100 with minimum verbal score of 400), minimum GPA of 3.0 in last 60 hours of course work, 3 letters of recommendation; for doctorate, GRE General Test (minimum total of 1175 with minimum verbal score of 400), minimum GPA of 3.4 in last 60 hours of course work, 3 letters of recommendation. Additional exam requirements/recommendations for international students: Required—TOEFL. *Application deadline:* For fall admission, 6/6 for domestic students, 4/4 for international students; for spring admission, 10/15 for domestic students, 9/5 for international students. Applications are processed on a rolling basis. Application fee: $35 ($50 for international students). *Financial support:* Fellowships, research assistantships, teaching assistantships, career-related internships or fieldwork, Federal Work-Study, institutionally sponsored loans, scholarships/grants, and tuition waivers (partial) available. Financial award application deadline: 6/1; financial award applicants required to submit FAFSA. *Faculty research:* Instrumentation, mechanics, materials. *Unit head:* Dr. Khosrow Behbehani,

Bioengineering

Chair, 817-272-2249, Fax: 817-272-2251, E-mail: kb@uta.edu. *Application contact:* Amanda Kerby, Academic Advisor, 817-272-0783, Fax: 817-272-5388, E-mail: akerby@uta.edu.

The University of Toledo, College of Graduate Studies, College of Engineering, Department of Bioengineering, Toledo, OH 43606-3390. Offers MS, PhD. Terminal master's awarded for partial completion of doctoral program. *Degree requirements:* For master's, thesis optional; for doctorate, thesis/dissertation, qualifying exam. *Entrance requirements:* For master's, GRE General Test, minimum GPA of 3.0; for doctorate, GRE General Test, minimum GPA of 3.3. Additional exam requirements/recommendations for international students: Required—TOEFL (minimum score 550 paper-based; 80 iBT). Electronic applications accepted. *Faculty research:* Artificial organs, biochemical engineering, bioelectrical systems, biomechanics, cellular engineering.

★ **University of Utah,** Graduate School, College of Engineering, Department of Bioengineering, Salt Lake City, UT 84112-9202. Offers MS, PhD, MS/MBA. MS/MBA offered with David Eccles School of Business. *Faculty:* 25 full-time (4 women), 73 part-time/adjunct (14 women). *Students:* 143 full-time (43 women), 9 part-time (2 women); includes 18 minority (10 Asian, non-Hispanic/Latino; 3 Hispanic/Latino; 1 Native Hawaiian or other Pacific Islander, non-Hispanic/Latino; 4 Two or more races, non-Hispanic/Latino), 8 international. Average age 28. 310 applicants, 42% accepted, 64 enrolled. In 2016, 24 master's, 20 doctorates awarded. Terminal master's awarded for partial completion of doctoral program. *Degree requirements:* For master's, comprehensive exam (for some programs), thesis (for some programs), project presentation, oral exam; for doctorate, comprehensive exam, thesis/dissertation, seminar presentation, TA mentorship. *Entrance requirements:* For master's and doctorate, GRE General Test or MCAT, bachelor's degree from accredited institution, college, or university; minimum undergraduate GPA of 3.0. Additional exam requirements/recommendations for international students: Required—TOEFL (minimum score 575 paper-based; 90 iBT); Recommended—IELTS (minimum score 7.5). *Application deadline:* For fall admission, 4/1 for domestic and international students. Application fee: $10 ($25 for international students). Electronic applications accepted. *Expenses:* $27,295 per year (non-resident, 11 credit hours per semester). *Financial support:* In 2016–17, 162 students received support, including 16 fellowships with full and partial tuition reimbursements available (averaging $26,000 per year), 137 research assistantships with full and partial tuition reimbursements available (averaging $24,250 per year), 9 teaching assistantships with full and partial tuition reimbursements available (averaging $24,250 per year); traineeships, health care benefits, and unspecified assistantships also available. Financial award application deadline: 4/1; financial award applicants required to submit FAFSA. *Faculty research:* Neural engineering and prosthesis; cardiovascular engineering and computer modeling; biomedical imaging and ultrasonic bioinstrumentation; biomedical device innovation and design; cellular, molecular and tissue therapeutics. *Total annual research expenditures:* $7.9 million. *Unit head:* Dr. David W. Grainger, Professor and Chair, Bioengineering/Professor of Pharmaceutics and Pharmaceutical Chemistry, 801-587-9263, Fax: 801-585-5361, E-mail: david.grainger@utah.edu. *Application contact:* Laura L. Olsen, Academic Advisor, Graduate Program, 801-581-8559, Fax: 801-585-5361, E-mail: laura.l.olsen@utah.edu. Website: http://www.bioen.utah.edu/

See Display below and Close-Up on page 121.

University of Washington, Graduate School, College of Engineering and School of Medicine, Department of Bioengineering, Seattle, WA 98195-5061. Offers applied bioengineering (MAB); bioengineering (MS, PhD); bioengineering and nanotechnology (PhD); pharmaceutical bioengineering (MS). *Faculty:* 41 full-time (15 women), 15 part-time/adjunct (0 women). *Students:* 137 full-time (51 women), 34 part-time (14 women); includes 53 minority (1 Black or African American, non-Hispanic/Latino; 41 Asian, non-Hispanic/Latino; 5 Hispanic/Latino; 1 Native Hawaiian or other Pacific Islander, non-Hispanic/Latino; 5 Two or more races, non-Hispanic/Latino), 50 international. 640 applicants, 24% accepted, 62 enrolled. In 2016, 17 master's, 8 doctorates awarded. *Degree requirements:* For master's, comprehensive exam, thesis; for doctorate, comprehensive exam, thesis/dissertation, qualifying exam, general exam, thesis defense. *Entrance requirements:* For master's and doctorate, GRE General Test, minimum GPA of 3.0, transcripts, statement of purpose, letters of recommendation, resume/curriculum vitae. Additional exam requirements/recommendations for international students: Required—TOEFL (minimum score 500 paper-based; 80 iBT), IELTS (minimum score 6.5). *Application deadline:* For fall admission, 12/15 for domestic and international students. Application fee: $85. Electronic applications accepted. *Expenses:* Contact institution. *Financial support:* In 2016–17, 119 students received support, including 34 fellowships with full tuition reimbursements available (averaging $2,799 per year), 78 research assistantships with full tuition reimbursements available (averaging $2,616 per year), 7 teaching assistantships with full tuition reimbursements available (averaging $2,616 per year); Federal Work-Study, institutionally sponsored loans, traineeships, health care benefits, and tuition waivers (full) also available. Support available to part-time students. Financial award application deadline: 12/1; financial award applicants required to submit FAFSA. *Faculty research:* Imaging and image guided therapy, molecular and cellular engineering, biomaterials and regenerative medicine, technology for expanding access to healthcare, synthetic and quantitative biology. *Total annual research expenditures:* $24.1 million. *Unit head:* Dr. Cecilia Giachelli, Professor/Chair, 206-685-2000, Fax: 206-685-3300, E-mail: ceci@uw.edu. *Application contact:* Peggy Sharp, Graduate Academic Counselor, 206-685-3494, Fax: 206-685-3300, E-mail: peggys55@uw.edu. Website: http://depts.washington.edu/bioe/

Virginia Polytechnic Institute and State University, Graduate School, College of Engineering, Blacksburg, VA 24061. Offers aerospace engineering (ME, MS, PhD); biological systems engineering (ME, MS, PhD); biomedical engineering (MS, PhD); chemical engineering (ME, MS, PhD); civil engineering (ME, MS, PhD); computer engineering (ME, MS, PhD); computer science (MS, PhD); electrical engineering (ME, PhD); engineering education (PhD); engineering mechanics (ME, MS, PhD); environmental engineering (MS); environmental science and engineering (MS); industrial and systems engineering (ME, MS, PhD); materials science and engineering (ME, MS, PhD); mechanical engineering (ME, MS, PhD); mining and minerals engineering (PhD); mining engineering (ME, MS); nuclear engineering (MS, PhD); ocean engineering (MS); systems engineering (ME, MS). *Faculty:* 400 full-time (73 women), 3 part-time/adjunct (2 women). *Students:* 1,949 full-time (487 women), 393 part-time (69 women); includes 251 minority (56 Black or African American, non-Hispanic/Latino; 3 American Indian or Alaska Native, non-Hispanic/Latino; 87 Asian, non-Hispanic/Latino; 70 Hispanic/Latino; 35 Two or more races, non-Hispanic/Latino), 1,354 international. Average age 27. 4,903 applicants, 19% accepted, 569 enrolled. In 2016, 364 master's, 200 doctorates awarded. *Degree requirements:* For master's, comprehensive exam (for some programs), thesis (for some programs); for doctorate, comprehensive exam (for some programs), thesis/dissertation (for some programs). *Entrance requirements:* For master's and doctorate, GRE/GMAT. Additional exam requirements/recommendations for international students: Required—TOEFL (minimum score 80 iBT). *Application deadline:* For fall admission, 8/1 for domestic students, 4/1 for international students; for spring admission, 1/1 for domestic students, 9/1 for international students. Applications are processed on a rolling basis. Application fee: $75. Electronic applications accepted. *Expenses:* Tuition, state resident: full-time $12,467; part-time $692.50 per credit hour. Tuition, nonresident: full-time $25,095; part-time $1394.25 per credit hour. *Required fees:* $2669; $491.50 per semester. Tuition and

Department of Bioengineering
UNIVERSITY OF UTAH

The Department of Bioengineering at the University of Utah, established in 1974, is an internationally renowned center of interdisciplinary basic and applied medically related research. It has a rich history in artificial organs, including the heart-lung machine, the intra-aortic balloon pump heart assist device, the artificial eye, the artificial heart and the dialysis machine—the first of which was engineered out of sausage casing and part of a Ford automobile water pump during WWII by Willem Kolff. In addition, the Department has a history of developments in biomaterials, drug delivery, and entrepreneurial activity.

Current research activities of the Department include biobased engineering, biosensors, medical imaging, biomaterials, biomechanics, computation/modeling, drug/gene delivery, neural interfaces, computational bioengineering, tissue engineering, and other specialty areas. Among these strong areas of research, five current initiatives are particularly noteworthy: Neural Engineering; Cell, Molecular, and Tissue Therapeutics; Cardiovascular Engineering; Biomedical Imaging; BioDesign.

For more information, contact:
Laura L. Olsen, Graduate Academic Advisor
Department of Bioengineering
University of Utah
Salt Lake City, Utah 84112

Laura.l.olsen@utah.edu   http://www.bioen.utah.edu/

fees vary according to course load, campus/location and program. *Financial support:* In 2016–17, 160 fellowships with full tuition reimbursements (averaging $7,387 per year), 872 research assistantships with full tuition reimbursements (averaging $22,329 per year), 313 teaching assistantships with full tuition reimbursements (averaging $18,714 per year) were awarded. Financial award application deadline: 3/1; financial award applicants required to submit FAFSA. *Total annual research expenditures:* $91.8 million. *Unit head:* Dr. Julia Ross, Dean, 540-231-9752, Fax: 540-231-3031, E-mail: deaneng@vt.edu. *Application contact:* Linda Perkins, Executive Assistant, 540-231-9752, Fax: 540-231-3031, E-mail: lperkins@vt.edu.
Website: http://www.eng.vt.edu/

Washington State University, College of Agricultural, Human, and Natural Resource Sciences, Department of Biological Systems Engineering, Pullman, WA 99164-6120. Offers biological and agricultural engineering (MS, PhD). Program applications must be made through the Pullman campus. *Degree requirements:* For master's, comprehensive exam, thesis (for some programs), written and oral exam; for doctorate, comprehensive exam, thesis/dissertation, written and oral exam. *Entrance requirements:* For master's and doctorate, minimum GPA of 3.0, bachelor's degree in engineering or closely-related subject. Additional exam requirements/recommendations for international students: Required—TOEFL. Electronic applications accepted. *Faculty research:* Agricultural

automation engineering; bioenergy and bioproducts engineering; food engineering; land, air, and water resources and environmental engineering.

Wilkes University, College of Graduate and Professional Studies, College of Science and Engineering, Department of Electrical Engineering and Physics, Wilkes-Barre, PA 18766-0002. Offers bioengineering (MS); electrical engineering (MSEE). *Program availability:* Part-time. *Students:* 13 full-time (5 women), 13 part-time (4 women); includes 3 minority (1 Black or African American, non-Hispanic/Latino; 1 Asian, non-Hispanic/Latino; 1 Hispanic/Latino), 9 international. Average age 26. In 2016, 5 master's awarded. *Entrance requirements:* For master's, GRE General Test. Additional exam requirements/recommendations for international students: Required—TOEFL (minimum score 550 paper-based; 79 iBT). *Application deadline:* Applications are processed on a rolling basis. Application fee: $45 ($65 for international students). Electronic applications accepted. Tuition and fees vary according to degree level and program. *Financial support:* Unspecified assistantships available. Financial award application deadline: 3/1; financial award applicants required to submit FAFSA. *Unit head:* Dr. William Hudson, Dean, 570-408-4600, Fax: 570-408-7846, E-mail: william.hudson@wilkes.edu. *Application contact:* Director of Graduate Enrollment, 570-408-4234, Fax: 570-408-7846.
Website: http://www.wilkes.edu/academics/colleges/science-and-engineering/engineering-physics/electrical-engineering-physics/index.aspx

Biosystems Engineering

Auburn University, Graduate School, Ginn College of Engineering, Department of Biosystems Engineering, Auburn University, AL 36849. *Faculty:* 11 full-time (1 woman). *Students:* 21 full-time (8 women), 9 part-time (2 women); includes 1 minority (American Indian or Alaska Native, non-Hispanic/Latino), 17 international. Average age 26. 24 applicants, 58% accepted, 6 enrolled. In 2016, 7 master's, 4 doctorates awarded. *Expenses:* Tuition, state resident: full-time $9072; part-time $504 per credit hour. Tuition, nonresident: full-time $27,216; part-time $1512 per credit hour. *Required fees:* $812 per semester. Tuition and fees vary according to degree level and program. *Unit head:* Oladiran Fasina, Head, 334-844-4180. *Application contact:* Dr. George Flowers, Dean of the Graduate School, 334-844-2125.
Website: http://www.eng.auburn.edu/programs/bsen/programs/graduate/index.html

Clemson University, Graduate School, College of Engineering, Computing and Applied Sciences, Department of Environmental Engineering and Earth Sciences and College of Engineering, Computing and Applied Sciences, Program in Biosystems Engineering, Anderson, SC 29625. Offers MS, PhD. *Program availability:* Part-time. *Faculty:* 5 full-time (1 woman), 3 part-time/adjunct (1 woman). *Students:* 9 full-time (4 women), 1 (woman) part-time; includes 2 minority (1 Black or African American, non-Hispanic/Latino; 1 Two or more races, non-Hispanic/Latino), 5 international. Average age 26. 10 applicants, 40% accepted, 3 enrolled. In 2016, 1 master's awarded. *Degree requirements:* For master's, comprehensive exam, thesis; for doctorate, comprehensive exam, thesis/dissertation. *Entrance requirements:* For master's and doctorate, GRE General Test (minimum scores: 150 Verbal, 155 Quantitative, 3.5 Analytical Writing), unofficial transcripts, letters of recommendation. Additional exam requirements/recommendations for international students: Required—TOEFL, IELTS (minimum score 6.5). *Application deadline:* For fall admission, 2/15 for domestic and international students. Applications are processed on a rolling basis. Application fee: $80 ($90 for international students). Electronic applications accepted. *Expenses:* $4,841 per semester full-time resident, $9,640 per semester full-time non-resident, $612 per credit hour full-time resident, $1,223 per credit hour part-time non-resident. *Financial support:* In 2016–17, 10 students received support, including 2 fellowships with partial tuition reimbursements available (averaging $3,500 per year), 5 research assistantships with partial tuition reimbursements available (averaging $22,226 per year), 2 teaching assistantships with partial tuition reimbursements available (averaging $14,283 per year); career-related internships or fieldwork and unspecified assistantships also available. Financial award application deadline: 2/15. *Faculty research:* Ecological engineering, sustainable bioprocessing, biofuels and biomass co-products, biopharmaceuticals and nutraceuticals, non-point source pollution engineering. *Unit head:* Dr. David Freedman, Department Chair, 864-656-5566, E-mail: dfreedm@clemson.edu. *Application contact:* Dr. Terry Walker, Graduate Program Coordinator, 864-656-0351, E-mail: walker4@clemson.edu.
Website: http://www.clemson.edu/cecas/departments/eees/academics/gradprog/biosys/index.html

Michigan State University, The Graduate School, College of Agriculture and Natural Resources and College of Engineering, Department of Biosystems and Agricultural Engineering, East Lansing, MI 48824. Offers biosystems engineering (MS, PhD). *Entrance requirements:* Additional exam requirements/recommendations for international students: Required—TOEFL. Electronic applications accepted.

South Dakota State University, Graduate School, College of Agriculture and Biological Sciences, Department of Agricultural and Biosystems Engineering, Brookings, SD 57007. Offers MS, PhD. *Program availability:* Part-time. *Degree requirements:* For master's, thesis; for doctorate, comprehensive exam, thesis/dissertation, preliminary oral and written exams. *Entrance requirements:* Additional exam requirements/

recommendations for international students: Required—TOEFL (minimum score 525 paper-based; 71 iBT).

South Dakota State University, Graduate School, College of Engineering, Department of Agricultural and Biosystems Engineering, Brookings, SD 57007. Offers biological sciences (MS, PhD); engineering (MS). PhD offered jointly with Iowa State University of Science and Technology. *Program availability:* Part-time. *Degree requirements:* For master's, thesis (for some programs), oral exam; for doctorate, thesis/dissertation, preliminary oral and written exams. *Entrance requirements:* For master's and doctorate, engineering degree. Additional exam requirements/recommendations for international students: Required—TOEFL (minimum score 550 paper-based; 79 iBT). *Faculty research:* Water resources, food engineering, natural resources engineering, machine design, bioprocess engineering.

The University of Arizona, College of Agriculture and Life Sciences, Department of Agricultural and Biosystems Engineering, Tucson, AZ 85721. Offers MS, PhD. Terminal master's awarded for partial completion of doctoral program. *Degree requirements:* For master's, thesis; for doctorate, thesis/dissertation. *Entrance requirements:* For master's, minimum GPA of 3.0 in last 2 years of undergraduate study, 3 letters of recommendation; for doctorate, minimum GPA of 3.0 in last 2 years of undergraduate study, 3 letters of recommendation, statement of purpose. Additional exam requirements/recommendations for international students: Required—TOEFL (minimum score 550 paper-based; 79 iBT). Electronic applications accepted. *Faculty research:* Irrigation system design, energy-use management, equipment for alternative crops, food properties enhancement.

University of Manitoba, Faculty of Graduate Studies, Faculty of Engineering, Department of Biosystems Engineering, Winnipeg, MB R3T 2N2, Canada. Offers M Eng, M Sc, PhD.

University of Minnesota, Twin Cities Campus, Graduate School, College of Food, Agricultural and Natural Resource Sciences, Bioproducts and Biosystems Science, Engineering and Management Graduate Program, Saint Paul, MN 55108. Offers MS, PhD. *Program availability:* Part-time. Terminal master's awarded for partial completion of doctoral program. *Degree requirements:* For master's, comprehensive exam, thesis, written and oral preliminary exams; for doctorate, comprehensive exam, thesis/dissertation, written and oral preliminary exams. *Entrance requirements:* For master's and doctorate, GRE, BS in engineering, mathematics, physical or biological sciences, or related field. Additional exam requirements/recommendations for international students: Required—TOEFL (minimum score 550 paper-based; 79 iBT), IELTS (minimum score 6.5). Electronic applications accepted. *Faculty research:* Water quality, bioprocessing, food engineering, terramechanics, process and machine control.

The University of Tennessee, Graduate School, College of Agricultural Sciences and Natural Resources, Department of Biosystems Engineering and Environmental Science, Program in Biosystems Engineering, Knoxville, TN 37996. Offers MS, PhD. *Degree requirements:* For master's, thesis; for doctorate, thesis/dissertation. *Entrance requirements:* For master's and doctorate, GRE General Test, minimum GPA of 2.7. Additional exam requirements/recommendations for international students: Required—TOEFL. Electronic applications accepted.

The University of Tennessee, Graduate School, College of Agricultural Sciences and Natural Resources, Department of Biosystems Engineering and Environmental Science, Program in Biosystems Engineering Technology, Knoxville, TN 37996. Offers MS. *Degree requirements:* For master's, thesis or alternative. *Entrance requirements:* For master's, GRE General Test, minimum GPA of 2.7. Additional exam requirements/recommendations for international students: Required—TOEFL. Electronic applications accepted.

UNIVERSITY OF CALIFORNIA, SAN DIEGO

Department of Bioengineering

 For more information, visit http://petersons.to/uc-sandiego-bioeng

Programs of Study

The Department of Bioengineering at the University of California, San Diego (UCSD), offers graduate instruction leading to the Master of Engineering (M.Eng.), Master of Science (M.S.), and Doctor of Philosophy (Ph.D.) degrees. The bioengineering graduate program began in 1966, and the Department was established in the Jacobs School of Engineering in 1994. The graduate programs provide an excellent education, integrating the fields of engineering and biomedical sciences. Students with an undergraduate education in engineering learn how to use engineering concepts and methodology to analyze and solve biological problems associated with genes, molecules, cells, tissues, organs, and systems, with applications to clinical medicine and biology.

The M.S. program is intended to equip the student with fundamental knowledge in bioengineering. There are two options for the M.S. degree: Plan I requires 48 units combining coursework and research, culminating in a thesis. Plan II is 48 units of coursework with no research requirement. The degree may be terminal or obtained on the way to earning the Ph.D. degree. In addition to the M.S. degree, the Department offers the M.Eng. degree. This degree is intended to prepare design and project engineers for careers in the biomedical and biotechnology industries within the framework of the graduate program of the bioengineering department. It is a terminal professional degree in engineering.

The Ph.D. program is designed to prepare students for a career in research and/or teaching in bioengineering. Each student takes courses in engineering physics and the life sciences to prepare him or her for the Departmental Ph.D. qualifying examination, which tests students' capabilities and ascertains their potential for independent study and research. The degree requires the completion of a dissertation and defense of that research.

The Department of Bioengineering also participates in a number of training programs: interdisciplinary graduate training program at the interfaces between the biological, medical, physical, and engineering sciences; Integrative Bioengineering of Heart, Vessels, and Blood; Translational Muskoskeletal Research; Computational Neuroscience; and Quantitative Biology.

There is also an M.D./Ph.D. degree offered in conjunction with the UCSD Medical School, pending independent admission to the Medical School.

Research Facilities

The Department is housed in a modern research building constructed in 2003 with funds from the Whitaker and Powell Foundations. This building houses a majority of the bioengineering research laboratories in addition to premier core and instructional facilities. The research laboratories in the Department are fully equipped for modern bioengineering research. The Department houses several state-of-the-art core facilities, including biotechnology, microfabrication, cell engineering, and microscopy, and a vivarium. The state-of-the-art instrumentation includes access to high-throughput (Solexa) sequencers, mass spectrometry for proteomics and metabolomics, live-cell imaging, and new-generation cell-sorting/selection equipment. The Department maintains excellent computing and network facilities, including a multimedia laboratory and two 105-node Linux clusters.

Financial Aid

The Department supports full-time graduate students at the Ph.D. level in the first year if the student does not have external funding. There are a limited number of TAships within the Department for master level students. Students are also eligible to apply for TAships outside of the Department. TAships provide most of resident tuition and fees in addition to a modest stipend. Awarding of financial support is competitive, and Ph.D. stipends average $33,000 a year, plus tuition, fees, and health insurance. The adviser provides financial support to students in good standing from year two through graduation. Sources of funding include University fellowship, traineeships from an NIH training grant, and research grants.

Cost of Study

In 2017–18, full-time students who are California residents are expected to pay $5,668.06 per quarter in registration and incidental fees. Nonresidents paid a total of $10,702.06 per quarter in registration and incidental fees. Fees are subject to change.

Living and Housing Costs

UCSD provides 1,625 apartments for graduate students. Current monthly rates range from $483 for a single student to $1,430 for a family. There is also a variety of off-campus housing in the surrounding communities. Prevailing rents range from $613 per month for a room in a private home to $1,500 or more per month for a two-bedroom apartment. Information may be obtained from the UCSD Affiliated Housing Office.

Student Group

The current campus enrollment is 35,821 students, of whom 26,590 are undergraduates and 5,784 are graduate students. The Department of Bioengineering has an undergraduate enrollment of 680 and a graduate enrollment of 186.

Location

The 2,040-acre campus spreads from the coastline, where the Scripps Institution of Oceanography is located, across a large wooded portion of the Torrey Pines Mesa overlooking the Pacific Ocean. To the east and north lie mountains, and to the south are Mexico and the almost uninhabited seacoast of Baja California.

The University

One of ten campuses in the University of California System, UCSD comprises the general campus, the School of Medicine, and the Scripps Institution of Oceanography. Established in La Jolla in 1960, UCSD is one of the newer campuses, but in this short time, it has become one of the major universities in the country.

Applying

A minimum GPA of 3.4 (on a 4.0 scale) is required for Ph.D. and M.S. admission. For the M.Eng. degree, a minimum GPA of 3.0 (on a 4.0 scale) is required for admission. The average GPA for Ph.D students offered support in 2017–18 was 3.80. All applicants are required to take the GRE General Test. International applicants whose native language is not English are required to take the TOEFL and obtain a minimum score of 23 in speaking on the Internet-based version. In addition to test scores, applicants must submit a completed Graduate Admission Application, all official transcripts (English translation must accompany official transcripts written in other languages), a statement of purpose, and three letters of recommendation. The deadline for filing applications for both international students and U.S. residents is December 1, 2017. Applicants are considered for admission for the fall quarter only.

Correspondence and Information

Department of Bioengineering 0419
University of California, San Diego
La Jolla, California 92093-0419
United States
E-mail: jlenington@eng.ucsd.edu
Website: http://be.uscd.edu

THE FACULTY AND THEIR RESEARCH

Shu Chien, M.D., Ph.D., University Professor of Bioengineering and Medicine. Effects of mechanical forces on endothelial gene expression and signal transduction, molecular bioengineering, DNA microarrays, nanotechnology, circulatory regulation in health and disease, energy balance and molecular basis of leukocyte-endothelial interactions, vascular tissue engineering.

Pedro Cabrales, Ph.D., Associate Professor. Transport of biological gases and their ability to regulate or affect cardiovascular function and cellular metabolism in order to design novel therapeutic interventions to treat, manage, and ultimately prevent disease using an integrative analysis of physical and chemical phenomena, based on engineering sciences principles and methods.

Gert Cauwenberghs, Ph.D., Professor. Cross-cutting advances at the interface between in vivo and in silico neural information processing; silicon adaptive microsystems and emerging nanotechnologies as tools for basic neuroscience research and clinical biomedical applications, and the insights they provide regarding the inner workings of nervous systems; facilitating the development of sensory and neural prostheses and brain-machine interfaces.

Karen Christman, Ph.D., Professor. Regeneration of injured and diseased cardiovascular tissues in vivo, using polymer chemistry and nanotechnology methods to develop novel biomaterials for tissue implantation and cell delivery.

Todd P. Coleman, Ph.D., Professor. Information theory, neuroscience, machine learning, bioelectronics.

Francisco Contijoch, Ph.D., Assistant Professor. Imaging for advanced assessment of cardiovascular structure, function, and disease.

Adam Engler, Ph.D., Associate Professor. Interactions between cells and their extracellular matrix (ECM), especially the role of mechanical properties of the matrix in regulating stem cell differentiation, applying basic studies of cell-matrix interactions and mechanobiology to design new models for studying cancer progress, new strategies for engineering nerve and muscle tissues.

Stephanie Fraley, Ph.D., Assistant Professor. 3-D matrix systems biology, digital PCR, machine learning, Raman spectroscopy, infectious disease, cancer.

David A. Gough, Ph.D., Professor. Implantable glucose sensor for diabetes; glucose and oxygen transport through tissues, sensor biocompatibility; dynamic models of the natural pancreas on based glucose input and insulin output; machine learning for prediction of protein-protein interactions.

Jeff M. Hasty, Ph.D., Professor. Computational genomics and the dynamics of gene regulatory networks; dissection and analysis of the complex dynamical interactions involved in gene regulation using techniques from nonlinear dynamics, statistical physics, and molecular biology to model, design, and construct synthetic gene networks.

Xiaohua Huang, Ph.D., Associate Professor. Genomics, molecular biotechnology, and bioinformatics, including chemistry and biophysics of protein and DNA molecules and technologies to uncover greater information regarding the human genome and genetics.

Marcos Intaglietta, Ph.D., Professor. Development of plasma expanders and artificial blood, theory of tissue oxygenation at the microvascular level, optical methods for the study of microcirculation.

Kevin King, M.D., Ph.D., Assistant Professor. Cardiovascular bioengineering.

Ratnesh Lal, Ph.D., Professor. Nano-bio-interface science and technology; atomic force microscopy-based multimodality imaging and functional mapping to study protein misfolding, cell-cell, and cell-surround interactions; design and application of biosensors and devices to study normal and pathophysiology, preventive strategies, and therapeutics.

Prashant Mali, Ph.D., Assistant Professor. Synthetic biology, regenerative medicine, genome engineering, stem cell engineering.

Christian Metallo, Ph.D., Associate Professor. Metabolism, system biology, mass spectrometry, flux analysis, cancer, stem cell biology.

Andrew D. McCulloch, Ph.D., Professor. In vivo, in vitro, and in silico studies of the normal and diseased heart in model organisms and humans; cardiac phenotyping in gene-targeted animal models; cardiac muscle tissue engineering; myocyte mechanotransduction and mechanoelectric feedback; computational modeling of cardiac electromechanics; excitation-contraction coupling; metabolism and cell signaling; systems biology of cardiac function in *Drosophila.*

Elliot R. McVeigh, Ph.D., Professor. Cardiovascular imaging, MRI CT image guided therapy, novel MRI and CT methods.

Bernhard Palsson, Ph.D., Professor. Hematopoietic tissue engineering, stem cell technology, bioreactor design, metabolic dynamics and regulation, whole cell simulators, metabolic engineering, genetic circuits.

Robert L. Sah, M.D., Sc.D., Professor of Bioengineering and HHMI Professor. Bioengineering of cartilage tissue and synovial fluid at the molecular, cellular, tissue, and joint scales; cartilage growth, aging, degeneration, and repair; cartilage biophysics, biomechanics, and transport; chondrocyte and cartilage mechanoregulation.

Geert W. Schmid-Schönbein, Ph.D., Professor and Chair. Microcirculation, biomechanics, molecular, and cellular mechanisms for transport in living tissues; mechanisms for cell activation in cardiovascular disease with applications to shock, ischemia, inflammation, and hypertension.

Gabriel A. Silva, Ph.D., Adjunct Professor. Retinal and central nervous system neural engineering; use of microtechnology and nanotechnology applied to molecular neurobiology and cell biology for regeneration of the neural retina and central nervous system; theoretical and computational neuroscience applied to understanding the retinal neural code; focus on retinal neurophysiology and pathophysiology of degenerative retinal disorders, tissue engineering, and cellular replacement theories; adult stem cell biology for neuroscience applications.

Shankar Subramaniam, Ph.D., Professor. Bioinformatics and systems biology and bioengineering; measurement and integration of cellular data to reconstruct context-specific metabolic, signaling, and regulatory pathways; development of quantitative systems models for deciphering phenotypes in mammalian cells.

Amy Sung, Ph.D., Professor Emeritus. Geneticist who studies the molecular basis of cell and membrane mechanics.

Yingxiao Wang, Ph.D., Professor, Molecular engineering, fluorescence resonance energy transfer (FRET), live cell imaging, and bionanotechnology to visualize and elucidate the molecular mechanisms by which live cells perceive the environment and to engineer machinery molecules for the reprogramming of cellular functions.

John T. Watson, Ph.D., Professor. Heart failure and mechanical circulatory support; biomaterials; medical implant design; bioimaging; creativity, innovation, and technology transfer.

Kun Zhang, Ph.D., Professor. Development and scientific application of new genomic technologies, with an emphasis on high-throughput genomic analyses of single DNA molecules.

Sheng Zhong, Ph.D., Professor. Computational genomics, epigenomics, stem cells and developmental biology, single-cell nanotechnology.

Bioengineering Adjunct Faculty

Michael Berns, Professor. Application of lasers and associated optical technologies in biology, medicine, and biomedical engineering; laser-tissue interactions; laser microbeam studies on cell structure and function; development of photonics-based biomedical instrumentation; clinical research in oncology, fertility, and ophthalmology.

Trey Ideker, Ph.D., Professor of Medicine. Bioinformatics and systems biology, computational modeling of cellular regulatory networks, yeast genetic

Bruce C. Wheeler, Ph.D., Adjunct Professor. Brain-on-a-chip, micropatterning neurons and microelectrode arrays, neural signal processing, bioengineering education.

Bioengineering Affiliate Faculty

Adah Almutairi, Ph.D., Associate Professor. On-demand drug delivery in precise locations, safe image-based diagnosis, regenerative medicine.

Vineet Bafna, Ph.D., Professor. Computational molecular biology, bioinformatics, proteomics, approximational algorithms, human genome, human proteome, protein identification, Expressed Sequence Tags (EST) analysis.

Charles Cantor, Ph.D., Professor. Genomics, biochemical assays, protein immobilization and pharmacology, biophysical chemistry, bioassays.

Shaochen Chen, Ph.D., Professor of Nanoengineering. Biomaterials and tissue engineering; stem cell and regenerative medicine; nanomanufacturing and biomanufacturing; nanophotonics and biophotonics.

Eva-Maria Collins, Ph.D., Assistant Professor of Physics. Physical principles of living systems.

Neal Devaraj, Ph.D., Assistant Professor of Chemistry and Biochemistry. Chemical biology with an emphasis on developing bioorthogonal reactions for addressing questions in synthetic biology and molecular imaging.

David Hall, Ph.D., Assistant Adjunct Professor of Radiology. Using optical imaging approaches to interrogate tissue in vivo.

Erik Kistler, M.D., Ph.D., Associate Clinical Professor. Multiple organ failure, shock, expectorants, small intestine, pancreas.

Juan Lasheras, Ph.D., Distinguished Professor of Mechanical and Aerospace Engineering. Turbulent flows; two-phase flows; biomedical fluid mechanics; biomechanics.

Nathan Lewis, Ph.D., Assistant Professor.

Klaus F. Ley, M.D., La Jolla Allergy Institute. Inflammation and the defense reaction caused by tissue damage or injury, characterized by redness, heat, swelling, and pain. The primary objective of inflammation is to localize and eradicate the irritant and repair the surrounding tissue. For the survival of the host, inflammation is a necessary and beneficial process. The inflammatory response involves three major stages: first, dilation of capillaries to increase blood flow; second, microvascular structural changes and escape of plasma proteins from the bloodstream; and third, leukocyte transmigration through endothelium and accumulation at the site of injury.

Thomas Liu, Ph.D., Associate Professor of Radiology. Design and analysis of experiments for functional MRI (fMRI), with emphasis on statistical optimization, nonlinear signal processing, and physiological noise reduction; characterization and modeling of hemodynamic response to neural activity, including effects of drugs such as caffeine; development of novel imaging methods to measure cerebral blood flow and volume; characterization of cerebral blood flow in Alzheimer's disease and glaucoma.

Jeffrey H. Omens, Ph.D., Professor of Medicine. Regional mechanics of the normal and diseased heart; miniaturization of functional measurement techniques for rat and mouse hearts; role of mechanical factors in cardiac hypertrophy, remodeling, and growth; residual stress in the heart; computer-assisted analysis of cardiac mechanics.

James C. Perry, M.D., Associate Clinical Professor. Congenital heart disease.

Padmini Rangamani, Ph.D., Assistant Professor. Biological systems design, transport phenomena in biological membranes, influence of cell shape on biological activation of signaling networks, morphological and topological changes to lipid membranes mediated by proteins and cytoskeletal forces, computational biology and biophysics.

Erkki Ruoslahti, M.D., Ph.D. The Ruoslahti laboratory studies peptides that home to specific targets in the body, such as tumors, atherosclerotic plaques, and injured tissues. These peptides, which usually bind to receptors in the vessels of the target tissue, can be used to selectively deliver diagnostic probes and drugs to the target.

Julian Schroeder, Ph.D., Professor. Identifying the basic molecular mechanisms by which plants respond to and mount resistance to environmental stresses is fundamental to understanding stress resistance mechanisms to these "abiotic" in plants and is an important goal for developing future strategies for engineering stress resistance in plants.

Sameer Shah, Ph.D., Associate Professor. Alzheimer's disease, imaging, peripheral nerve injury/disease.

Scott Thomson, M.D., Ph.D., Professor-in-Residence of Orthopedics. Kidney physiology, using animal models; studies of regulation of kidney function by the juxtaglomerular apparatus, using a variety of adaptations on the technique of renal micropuncture.

Peter D. Wagner, M.D., Professor of Medicine. Theoretical and experimental basis of oxygen transport in the lungs and skeletal muscles; muscle capillary growth regulation using molecular biological approaches in integrated systems—the role of oxygen, microvascular hemodynamics, physical factors, and inflammatory mediators; mechanisms of exercise limitation in health and disease, especially the role of muscle dysfunction in heart failure, emphysema, and renal failure.

Sam Ward, Ph.D., Associate Professor in Residence of Radiology. Muscle Physiology Laboratory.

Robert N. Weinreb, M.D., Professor. Glaucoma surgery, optic neuropathy, and aging of the eye; cell and molecular biology of uveoscleral outflow; imaging of the optic disc and retinal nerve fiber layer; mechanisms of optic nerve damage in glaucoma; neuroprotection in glaucoma; measurement of intraocular pressure; drug delivery to eye; cataract surgery.

John B. West, M.D., Ph.D., D.Sc., Professor Emeritus of Medicine. Bioengineering aspects of the lung; stress failure and physiology of pulmonary capillaries when exposed to high transmural pressures; distribution of ventilation and blood flow in the lung; effect of gravity on the lung; measurements of pulmonary function during sustained weightlessness; distortion of the lung resulting from its weight; regulation of the structure of capillary walls, including changes of gene expression as the result of stress; high-altitude physiology, especially extreme altitude.

Thomas Yellen-Nelson, Ph.D., Professor of Radiology. Early detection of breast cancer, visualization, computer modeling, 3-D ultrasound, breast imaging, medical imaging.

Jin Zhang, Ph.D., Professor. Spatiotemporal regulation of signal transduction.

Liangfang Zhang, Professor. Drug and vaccine delivery using nanoparticles, including immune evasion and reversible liposome stabilization; prevention and treatment of infectious disease and cancer.

Faculty and students at the Department's 50th anniversary celebration with Father of Modern Biomechanics, Y.C. Fung.

UNIVERSITY OF UTAH
Department of Bioengineering

 For more information, visit http://petersons.to/utahbioengineering

Programs of Study

The Department of Bioengineering at the University of Utah prepares graduates to be leaders in the integration of engineering, biology, and medicine to detect and treat human disease and disability. The Department's programs are consistently ranked among the highest in the United States. The students are among the highest achieving students entering any interdepartmental program on campus. Graduate instruction leads to the Master of Science (M.S.) and Doctor of Philosophy (Ph.D.) degrees. Research programs include biomechanics, biomaterials, biosensors, computation and modeling, drug and gene delivery, medical imaging, neural interfaces, tissue engineering, and other specialty areas. The graduate program draws more than 150 faculty members from over thirty departments across four colleges.

Students in the M.S. program must complete the master's-level core curriculum and elective courses in one of the following areas: bioInnovate, biomaterials and therapeutics, biomechanics, cardiac electrophysiology and biophysics, computational systems and synthetic bioengineering, imaging, or neural interfaces. In addition, all M.S. thesis-option students are required to defend their thesis in a public forum. The Department also offers M.S. non-thesis option programs (project-based or course only).

Students may be admitted directly to the Ph.D. program at the time of admission, depending upon the decision of the Graduate Admissions Committee. Ph.D. students must successfully complete the bioengineering graduate core curriculum or its equivalent and take additional advanced graduate courses. Ph.D. students must also pass a written comprehensive qualifying exam, write and present a research proposal on their dissertation topic, publicly defend their dissertation, and publish their final dissertation manuscript.

The Ph.D. degree program typically takes five years to complete. It is strongly recommended that all graduate students select a research direction and begin thesis research as soon as they begin their studies. In addition, the program is individually tailored to meet the specific objectives of each candidate and may involve collaboration with faculty members in other departments.

Research Facilities and Initiatives

The Department of Bioengineering at the University of Utah is an internationally renowned center of interdisciplinary basic and applied medically related research. It has a rich history in artificial organs, biomaterials, and drug delivery. Research laboratories and Department offices are located in the state-of-the-art Sorenson Molecular Biotechnology Building (a USTAR innovation center). Additional labs are sited across campus in locations including: Merrill Engineering Building, Warnock Engineering Building, Biomedical Polymers Research Building, University Hospital, Huntsman Cancer Institute, Primary Children's Hospital, University Orthopaedic Center, the School of Medicine, and the College of Pharmacy. Centers and institutes include: Scientific Computing and Imaging Institute (SCI), Cardiovascular Research and Training Institute (CVRTI), Huntsman Cancer Institute (HCI), Utah Center for Advanced Imaging Research (UCAIR), Center for Controlled Chemical Delivery (CCCD), Keck Center for Tissue Engineering (KCTE), Center for Neural Interfaces, and Nano Institute. The University as a whole boasts cutting-edge research facilities, exceptional libraries, and computer centers, as well as superior entrepreneurial services.

Financial Aid

Ph.D. students making satisfactory progress in the Department typically receive financial support from their research advisor throughout their graduate studies. A limited number of University and Department fellowships are offered on a competitive basis to exceptionally well-qualified applicants.

Cost of Study

Bioengineering graduate students may receive full-time traineeships, fellowships, or assistantships. In addition, graduate students receiving financial support through the University of Utah may qualify for Graduate School tuition waivers. Tuition and fees for 2017–18 for 11 credit hours are $5,016 for Utah residents and $14,164 for nonresidents per semester.

Living and Housing Costs

Housing for unmarried graduate students ranges from approximately $400 (double room) per month to $1,000 (single pod) per month. Unfurnished apartments for married students range from $600 to $2,200 per month in the University Village, Medical Plaza, and historic Fort Douglas. Off-campus housing near the University is also available. For more specific rates and information, students should visit the following websites: for married student housing, http://www.apartments.utah.edu; for single student housing, http://www.housing.utah.edu.

Students

The University of Utah has a student population of more than 31,000, representing all fifty states and fifty other countries. The Department of Bioengineering welcomes approximately 40 to 60 new students each year and maintains an average total graduate enrollment of 150 students. Graduates are successful in industry, academics, medicine, government, and entrepreneurial pursuits.

Location

Salt Lake City is the center of a metropolitan area of nearly a million people. It lies in a valley with an elevation varying between 4,200 and 5,500 feet and is surrounded by mountain peaks reaching nearly 12,000 feet in elevation. The city is the cultural center of the intermountain area, with world-class ballet and modern dance companies, theater and opera companies, and a symphony orchestra. It also supports professional basketball, hockey, soccer, arena football, and baseball. Salt Lake City was the proud host of the 2002 Winter Olympics and is within 30 minutes of several world-class ski resorts. Several major recreation and wilderness areas are within a 2-hour drive from campus, and ten national parks are within a day's drive of the city.

The University

As Utah's flagship research university and PAC-12 school, the University of Utah is a leader in scholarship, innovation, athletics, and the arts. The 1,500-acre campus is nestled in the foothills of the Wasatch Mountains and is characterized by an eclectic mix of historic and modern buildings with attractive landscaping. Within a few minutes' walk of the University is Red Butte Gardens, an ecological center with 21 acres of developed gardens and more than 5 miles of hiking trails. The University also encompasses cutting-edge recreational facilities, museums, and performing arts. An international faculty of 3,600 members provides comprehensive instruction and research in disciplines ranging from medicine and law to fine arts and business.

Applying

Instructions for applying to the program can be found on the Department's Graduate Studies website at http://www.bioen.utah.edu/education/graduate. In addition to the application form and fee, students must submit three letters of recommendation, General Test of the Graduate Record Examinations (GRE) scores, university transcripts, and a written statement of interests and goals

Detailed information on the various aspects of the Department of Bioengineering at the University of Utah can be accessed from the Department's home page: http://www.bioen.utah.edu.

Correspondence and Information

Chair, Graduate Admissions Committee
Department of Bioengineering
University of Utah
Sorenson Molecular Biotechnology Building
36 S. Wasatch Drive, Room 3223
Salt Lake City, Utah 84112
United States
Website: http://www.bioen.utah.edu

THE FACULTY AND THEIR RESEARCH

[**Bold** *indicates primary faculty (tenure and career line);* *Adjunct faculty; **Emeritus faculty*]

Orly Alter, Ph.D., Stanford. *Genomic signal processing and systems biology.*
*M. Aman, Ph.D., Utah. Cardiovascular physiology, neurosciences.
*B. Ambati, Ph.D., Nanomedicine and imaging.
**J. D. Andrade, Ph.D., Denver. Interfacial biochemistry, biochemical sensors, proteins engineering, integrated science education, bioluminescence.
*A. E. Anderson, Ph.D., Utah. Computational modeling, tissue experimental biomechanics.
*J. Anderson, M.D., Ph.D., Northwestern. Clinical radiology, imaging sciences.
*A. Angelucci, M.D., Rome (Italy); Ph.D., MIT. Mammalian visual system.
*K. N. Bachus, Ph.D., Utah. Bone biomechanics, fracture analysis, implant failure mechanisms.
*Y. H. Bae, Ph.D., Korea. Pharmaceutical chemistry.
*K. Balagurunathan, Ph.D., Iowa. Biomaterials, chemical biology.
*S. Bamberg, Ph.D., Harvard-MIT. Bioinstrumentation, gait analysis, aging.
*H. Barkan, Ph.D. Neurology.
*A. Bild, Ph.D., Colorado. Pharmacology.
*S. M. Blair, Ph.D., Colorado. Integrated-optics resonance biosensors.
*R. D. Bloebaum, Ph.D., Western Australia. Orthopedic implants.
*D. Bloswick, Ph.D., Michigan. Biomechanics, ergonomics.
Susan C. Bock, Ph.D., California, Irvine. Conformational activation of antithrombin III anticoagulant activity, antithrombin III targeting to HSPG and heparin surfaces.

University of Utah

Robert D. Bowles, Ph.D., Cornell. Tissue engineering, regenerative medicine, gene therapy, CRISPR, immunoengineering, back pain.
*L. Brewer, Ph.D. Anesthesiology.
*D.W. Britt, Ph.D., Utah. High-resolution microscopy, thin films, protein-surface interactions.
Kelly W. Broadhead, Ph.D., Utah. Tissue engineering.*M. B. Bromberg, Ph.D., Vermont; M.D., Michigan. Bioelectric signals from nerve/muscle, neurophysiology.
*R. B. Brown, Ph.D., Utah. Medical applications for sensors, bioinstrumentation, implantable electronics.
*J. B. Bunnell, Sc.D., MIT. Medical device development.
Christopher R. Buston, Ph.D., Utah. Neuromodulation therapy.
**K. D. Caldwell, Ph.D., Uppsala (Sweden). Separation and characterization of biopolymers, subcellular particles, and cells.
*T. E. Cheatham III, Ph.D., California, San Francisco. Computer simulation of biological macromolecules.
*E. Cherkaev, Ph.D., St. Petersburg (Russia). Mathematics.
Douglas A. Christensen, Ph.D., Utah. Waves used for biomedical applications, including therapeutic ultrasound, utrasonic imaging, and optical biosensors.
*E. B. Clark, M.D., Albany Medical. Pediatrics.
Gregory A. Clark, Ph.D., California, Irvine. Electrophysiological, cellular, and computational analyses of neuronal plasticity in simple systems; neural information processing; bio-based neuroprostheses.
*B. Coats, Ph.D., Pennsylvania. Head and eye injury biomechanics.
Tara L. Deans, Ph.D., Boston. Synthetic biology, tissue engineering, materials science, regenerative medicine.
*E. V. R. DiBella, Ph.D., Georgia Tech. Medical imaging, dynamic cardiac SPECT.
Alan D. "Chuck" Dorval, Ph.D. Boston. Neuropathophysiology, translational neuroscience, neuromodulation, neuronal semiotics.
*D. J. Dosdall, Ph.D., Arizona State. Cardiac mapping and electrophyusiology.
*A. Douglass, Ph.D., UC San Francisco. Neurobiology and anatomy.
**C. Durney, Ph.D., Piezoelectric and magnetic resonance.
*T. D. Egan, M.D., Utah. Anesthesiology.
Benjamin J. Ellis, Ph.D., Utah. Musculoskeletal research.
*C. Farmer, Ph.D. Brown, Pulmonary fluid dynamics.
*P. Fitzgerald, Ph.D. Tissue remodeling.
*A. L. Fogelson, Ph.D., NYU. Physiological systems modeling.
*B. K. Gale, Ph.D., Utah. MEMS devices and their applications to biology and medicine.
*G. Gerig, Ph.D., ETH Zurich. Medical imaging analysis.
*J. Gertz, Ph.D., Washington (St. Louis). Computational biology, oncological sciences.
Hamid Ghandehari, Ph.D., Utah. Pharmaceutics, drug/gene delivery, nanomedicine.
*K. Golden, Ph.D., NYU. Applied mathematics, modeling and simulating multiscale systems in geophysics and materials science.
David W. Grainger, Ph.D., Utah. Drug delivery and medical device innovation; bioanalytical sensing, diagnostics and microarrays, foreign body response, device infection and bacterial-surface interactions, drug delivery, antibody drugs, novel vaccines.
*J. M. Harris, Ph.D., Purdue. Laser-based bioinstrumentation, interfacial spectroscopy.
*T. C. Henderson, Ph.D., Texas at Austin. Artificial intelligence, computer vision, robotics.
*H. B. Henninger, Ph.D., Utah, Orthopaedics.
*J. N. Herron, Ph.D., Illinois. Protein engineering, molecular graphics, biosensors.
Robert W. Hitchcock, Ph.D., Utah. Medical device design and development, infusion systems, biosensors, drug delivery, tissue engineering.
Vladimir Hlady, Ph.D., Zagreb (Croatia). Research in the proteins–polymers–interfaces group (PPIG) focuses on proteins and other macromolecules at biomaterial-host tissue interfaces.
**K. W. Horch, D.Sc., Yale. Neuroprostheses, biomedical instrumentation, information processing in the somatosensory system, tactile aids.
*H. Hopf, Ph.D., Dartmouth. Genetics of health-care associated infection.
*E. Hunter, Ph.D., Iowa. Vibration, exposure, acoustics.
Edward W. Hsu, Ph.D., Johns Hopkins. Magnetic resonance imaging and microscopy, tissue functional anatomy.
*D. T. Hutchinson, M.D., Jefferson Medical. Orthopedics implants for the hand.
*M. M. Janát Amsbury, Ph.D., Koeln (Germany). Animal cancer models; gynecologic malignancies: ovarian, endometrial, cervical cancer; gene and drug delivery, women's health.**J. Janatova, Ph.D., Utah. Biomaterials and biosensors.
*C. R. Johnson, Ph.D., Utah. Theoretical/computational electrophysiology, inverse electrocardiography, dynamical systems theory.
*K. Johnson, M.D., Tulane. Anesthesiology.
*E. M. Jorgensen, Ph.D., Washington (Seattle). Molecular biology, genetics, cellular neurophysiology.
Sarang C. Joshi, D.Sc., Washington (St. Louis). Computational anatomy, statistical shape analysis in medical imaging.
*D. J. Kadrmas, Ph.D., North Carolina. Molecular imaging, positron emission tomography (PET) of cancerous tissues.
*J. P. Keener, Ph.D., Caltech. Applied mathematics, nonlinear differential equations, chemical/biological dynamics.
*P. S. Khanwilkar, Ph.D., Utah. Artificial heart/assist devices, design, control, surgical implantation/physiologic interfaces.
*H. Kim, Ph.D., Michigan. Bionano-micro systems in moving fluids.
Sung Wan Kim, Ph.D., Utah. Blood compatibility; medical polymers; and drug-delivery systems such as hydrogels, biodegradable drug conjugates, self-regulating drug delivery, and stimuli sensitive polymers.
*R. D. King, Ph.D., Harvard. Alzheimer's image analysis.
*M. Kirby, Ph.D., Brown. Large-scale scientific computation and visualization.
**Willem Kolff, Ph.D., Leiden (The Netherlands). Late Distinguished Professor of bioengineering, surgery, and medicine. Widely considered the "father" of the field of artificial organs.
Jindrich Kopecek, Ph.D., Czechoslovak Academy of Sciences. Biomaterials; chemistry/biochemistry of macromolecules; drug-delivery systems; design, synthesis, and characterization of biorecognizable biomedical polymers.
Jessica R. Kramer, Ph.D., UCLA. Biomaterials, cancer diagnostics and therapeutics, glycobiology, regenerative medicine, drug delivery to the CNS.
*D. Krizaj, Ph.D., NYU, Physiology and ophthalmology.
*E. Kubiak, M.D., Washington (Seattle). Scientific computing and visualization, modeling, stimulation of ECG drug diffusion.
*K. Kuck, Ph.D. Anesthesiology.
*T. E. Lane, Ph.D., UCLA. Neuroinflammation, demyelinating diseases, neural stem cells.
*J. T. Langell, M.D., Ph.D., Drexel. Surgery.
*P. LaStayo, Ph.D. Northern Arizona. Physical therapy
*G. Lazzi, Ph.D., Utah. Computation, electromagnetics.
*V. Lee, M.D., Ph.D., M.B.A. Radiology and ocological sciences.
*D. Li, Ph.D. Molecular medicine.
Yang Li, Ph.D., Johns Hopkins. Extracellular matrix, biomaterials, molecular imaging, drug delivery, tissue engineering, regenerative medicine.
**D. Lyman, Ph.D. Oncology.
Robert S. MacLeod, Ph.D., Dalhousie. Cardiac electrophysiology, computational electrophysiology, cardiac arrhythmias, electrocardiographic mapping, scientific visualization, bioelectric signal and image processing.
*B. A. MacWilliams, Ph.D., Worcester Polytechnic. Vascular fluid dynamics, kinematic/kinetic biomechanics.
*B. Mann, Ph.D., Iowa State. Tissue engineering.
*C. Mastrangelo, Ph.D., Berekley. Microfabricated systems, bioMEMS.
*J. P. McAllister, Ph.D., Purdue. Pathophysiology of hydrocephalus and brain injury, neural prostheses and implantable intracranial devices, biocompatibility.
*D. McDonnall, Ph.D., Utah. Medical devices, neural interfaces.
*J. C. McRea, Ph.D., Utah. Medical device development.
*S. G. Meek, Ph.D., Utah. Prosthetic design and control, EMG signal processing, biomechanics.
*R. Menon, Ph.D. Electrical and computer engineering.
*B. Mickey, M.D., Ph.D., Michigan. Neuroscience and psychiatry.
*K. L. Monson, Ph.D., Berkeley, Traumatic brain injury, biomechanics.
*A. P. Moreno, Ph.D., IPN (Mexico). Molecular and biophysical properties of gap junctions, intercellular heterologous communication.
*C. J. Myers, Ph.D., Stanford. Modeling/analysis of biological networks.
*J. R. Nelson, Ph.D., Utah. Microbiology, immunology.
*F. Noo, Ph.D., Liege (Belgium). 3-D tomographic reconstruction.
**R. A. Normann, Ph.D., Berkeley. Cell physiology, bioinstrumentation, neuroprosthetics.
**D. B. Olsen, D.V.M., Colorado State. Artificial heart/assist devices, design, control, surgical implantation/physiologic interfaces.
*J. A. Orr, Ph.D., Utah. Anesthesia, physiologic monitoring, medical device development.
*A. E. Ostafin, Ph.D., Minnesota. Nanobiotechnology.
*S. Owen, Ph.D., Utah. Pharmaceutics and pharmaceutical chemistry.
*D. L. Parker, Ph.D., Utah. Medical imaging, applications of physics in medicine.
*A. Patel, Ph.D. Cardiovascular regenerative medicine.
*N. Patwari, Ph.D., Michigan. Electrical and computer engineering.
*A. Payne, Ph.D. Radiology.
Tomasz J. Petelenz, Ph.D., Utah. Medical instrumentation.
*C. Peters, M.D., Ph.D. Orthopedic surgery.
*J. Phillips, Ph.D. Hematology.
*W. G. Pitt, Ph.D., Wisconsin–Madison. Polymers and composite materials for biomedical applications, surface chemistry.
*M. Porter, Ph.D., Ohio State. Discovery, rapid screening therapeutic compounds.
*G. D. Prestwich, Ph.D., Stanford. Bioorganic chemistry.
*A. Pungor, Ph.D., Technical University (Hungary). Scanning-force microscopy, near-field optical microscopy, bioinstrumentation.
*B. B. Punske, Ph.D., North Carolina (Chapel Hill). Optical and electrical imaging of genetically altered hearts.
Richard D. Rabbitt, Ph.D., Rensselaer. Biophysics, biosensors, neural engineering, biomechanics, hearing/vestibular mechanisms, computational mechanics, computational neuroscience.
*R. Ranjan, Ph.D., John's Hopkins. Cardiac electrophysiology.
**N. Rapoport, Ph.D., Moscow State; D.Sc., Academy of Sciences (USSR). Polymeric materials, biological magnetic resonance.
*R. B. Roemer, Ph.D., Stanford. Heat transfer, thermodynamics, design, optimization to biomedical problems.
*J. Rosenblatt, Ph.D. Cell and tissue engineering.
Frank B. Sachse, Dr.-Ing., Karlsruhe (Germany). Cardiac biophysics, cardiac remodeling in disease, clinical translation of microscopic imaging technology.
*D. Sakata, M.D., Loma Linda. Ophthalmology.
*C. Saltzman, Ph.D., North Carolina. Orthopaedics.
*O. Shcheglovitov, Ph.D., Bogomoletz Institute (Ukraine). Neurobiology and anatomy.
*J. Shea, Ph.D., Utah. Radiobiology, oncological sciences.
*C. Shelton, M.D., Texas Southwestern Medical Center at Dallas. Hearing systems physiology.
*M. E. Smith, M.D., Illinois. Otolaryngology, neural interfaces.
*F. Solzbacher, Ph.D., Technical University (Germany). MEMS, micromachining.
*K. W. Spitzer, Ph.D., Buffalo, SUNY. Cardiac cellular electrophysiology, intracellular pH regulation.
Russell J. Stewart, Ph.D., California, Santa Barbara. Biomimetic underwater adhesives, natural bioadhesives.
*A. Stuart, Ph.D. Orthopedics.
*M. Tabib-Azar, Ph.D., Rensselaer. Advanced metrology and nano-device applications.
*C. M. Terry, Ph.D. Pharmaceutical chemistry.
*N. Tian, M.D., Ph.D. Ophthalmology and visual science.
Lucas H. Timmins, Ph.D., Texas A&M. Vascular biomechanics, computational and experimental biomechanics, medical device design.
*I. Titze, Ph.D., Otolaryngology.
Patrick A. Tresco, Ph.D., Brown. Biomaterials and tissue engineering, as applied to neural interfaces, neuroscience and connective tissue.
*P. Triolo, Ph.D., Utah. Development/regulatory approval of biomaterials/diagnostic devices, tissue-engineered products.
David J. Warren, Ph.D., Utah. Applied peripheral nervous system neuroscience.
Mark Warren, Ph.D., Universitat Autonoma De Barcelona (Spain).
Jeffrey A. Weiss, Ph.D., Utah. Experimental and computational biomechanics, orthopedic biomechanics, mechanics of angiogenesis.
**D. R. Westenskow, Ph.D., Utah. Bioinstrumentation, microprocessor applications in medicine.
*R. Whitaker, Ph.D., North Carolina. Image processing, computer vision, visualization.
*J. White, Ph.D., Johns Hopkins. Neural engineering and interfaces.
*B. Wirostko, M.D., Columbia. Developing a biodegradable hyaluronic acid polymer for use as an ocular therapy as well as an ophthalmic drug delivery device.
*C. T. Wittwer, Ph.D., Michigan. Real-time PCR and DNA analysis.
*M. Yoshigi, M.D., Kyoto (Japan); Ph.D., Tokyo Women's Medical College. Cardiovascular physiology and embryology.
*D. Young, Ph.D., Berkeley. Wireless micro-nano-system.
S. Michael Yu, Ph.D., Massachusetts (Amherst). Polymer science and engineering, collagen hybridization, tissue engineering, designing new peptide/protein architectures.
Alexey V. Zaitsev, Ph.D., Moscow State (Russia). Mechanisms of cardiac arrhythmias, myocardial ischemia, real-time physiological imaging of single cardiac myocytes and whole hearts.
*L. J. Zhang, Ph.D., Nanyang Tech (Singapore). Radiology, functional MRI.

Section 4
Architectural Engineering

This section contains a directory of institutions offering graduate work in architectural engineering. Additional information about programs listed in the directory may be obtained by writing directly to the dean of a graduate school or chair of a department at the address given in the directory.

For programs offering related work, see also in this book *Engineering and Applied Sciences* and *Management of Engineering and Technology.* In the other guides in this series:

Graduate Programs in the Humanities, Arts & Social Sciences
See *Applied Arts and Design (Industrial Design and Interior Design), Architecture (Environmental Design), Political Science and International Affairs,* and *Public, Regional, and Industrial Affairs (Urban and Regional Planning and Urban Studies)*

Graduate Programs in the Physical Sciences, Mathematics, Agricultural Sciences, the Environment & Natural Resources
See *Environmental Sciences and Management*

CONTENTS

Program Directory

Featured School: Display and Close-Up

Architectural Engineering

California Polytechnic State University, San Luis Obispo, College of Architecture and Environmental Design, Department of Architectural Engineering, San Luis Obispo, CA 93407. Offers MS. *Program availability:* Online learning. In 2016, 15 degrees awarded. *Application deadline:* For fall admission, 4/1 for domestic students. *Expenses:* Tuition, state resident: full-time $6738; part-time $3906 per year. Tuition, nonresident: full-time $15,666; part-time $8370 per year. *Required fees:* $3603; $3141 per unit. $1047 per term. *Financial support:* Fellowships, teaching assistantships, scholarships/grants, tuition waivers, and unspecified assistantships available. Financial award application deadline: 4/1; financial award applicants required to submit FAFSA. *Unit head:* Dr. Allen C. Estes, Head, 805-756-1314, Fax: 805-756-6054, E-mail: acestes@calpoly.edu. Website: http://www.arce.calpoly.edu

See Display on next page and Close-Up on page 127.

California State University, Fullerton, Graduate Studies, College of Engineering and Computer Science, Department of Civil and Environmental Engineering, Fullerton, CA 92834-9480. Offers civil engineering (MS), including architectural engineering, environmental engineering. *Program availability:* Part-time. *Degree requirements:* For master's, comprehensive exam, project or thesis. *Entrance requirements:* For master's, minimum undergraduate GPA of 2.5. Application fee: $55. *Expenses:* Tuition, state resident: full-time $3369; part-time $1953 per unit. Tuition, nonresident: full-time $3915; part-time $2499 per unit. Tuition and fees vary according to course load, degree level and program. *Financial support:* Career-related internships or fieldwork, Federal Work-Study, institutionally sponsored loans, and scholarships/grants available. Support available to part-time students. Financial award application deadline: 3/1; financial award applicants required to submit FAFSA. *Faculty research:* Soil-structure interaction, finite-element analysis, computer-aided analysis and design. *Unit head:* Dr. Prasada Rao, Chair, 657-278-3012. *Application contact:* Admissions/Applications, 657-278-2371. Website: http://www.fullerton.edu/ecs/cee/

Carnegie Mellon University, College of Fine Arts, School of Architecture, Pittsburgh, PA 15213-3891. Offers architecture (MSA); architecture, engineering, and construction management (PhD); building performance and diagnostics (MS, PhD); computational design (MS, PhD); engineering construction management (MSA); tangible interaction design (MTID); urban design (MUD). Terminal master's awarded for partial completion of doctoral program. *Degree requirements:* For doctorate, thesis/dissertation. *Entrance requirements:* For master's and doctorate, GRE General Test. Additional exam requirements/recommendations for international students: Required—TOEFL.

Drexel University, College of Engineering, Department of Civil, Architectural, and Environmental Engineering, Philadelphia, PA 19104-2875. Offers architectural/building systems engineering (MS, PhD); civil engineering (MS, PhD); environmental engineering (MS, PhD); geotechnical, geoenvironmental and geosynthetics engineering (MS, PhD); hydraulics, hydrology and water resources engineering (MS, PhD); structures (MS). *Program availability:* Part-time, evening/weekend. *Faculty:* 27 full-time (8 women). *Students:* 63 full-time (24 women), 27 part-time (6 women); includes 11 minority (2 Black or African American, non-Hispanic/Latino; 5 Asian, non-Hispanic/Latino; 2 Hispanic/Latino; 2 Two or more races, non-Hispanic/Latino), 39 international. Average age 30. In 2016, 48 master's, 10 doctorates awarded. *Degree requirements:* For master's, thesis optional; for doctorate, thesis/dissertation. *Entrance requirements:* For master's, minimum GPA of 3.0; for doctorate, minimum GPA of 3.5, MS in civil engineering. Additional exam requirements/recommendations for international students: Required—TOEFL. *Application deadline:* For fall admission, 8/21 for domestic students. Applications are processed on a rolling basis. Application fee: $50. Electronic applications accepted. *Expenses: Tuition:* Full-time $32,184; part-time $1192 per credit hour. *Required fees:* $280. Tuition and fees vary according to campus/location and program. *Financial support:* Research assistantships, teaching assistantships, career-related internships or fieldwork, Federal Work-Study, institutionally sponsored loans, tuition waivers (partial), and unspecified assistantships available. Financial award application deadline: 2/1. *Faculty research:* Structural dynamics, hazardous wastes, water resources, pavement materials, groundwater. *Unit head:* Dr. Richard Weggel, Interim Department Head, 215-895-2355. *Application contact:* Director of Graduate Admissions, 215-895-6700, Fax: 215-895-5939, E-mail: enroll@drexel.edu.

Illinois Institute of Technology, Graduate College, Armour College of Engineering, Department of Civil, Architectural and Environmental Engineering, Chicago, IL 60616. Offers architectural engineering (M Arch E); civil engineering (MS, PhD), including architectural engineering (MS), construction engineering and management (MS), geoenvironmental engineering (MS), geotechnical engineering (MS), structural engineering (MS), transportation engineering (MS); construction engineering and management (MCEM); environmental engineering (M Env E, MS, PhD); geoenvironmental engineering (M Geoenv E); geotechnical engineering (MGE); infrastructure engineering and management (MPW); structural engineering (MSE); transportation engineering (M Trans E). *Program availability:* Part-time, evening/weekend, online learning. Terminal master's

awarded for partial completion of doctoral program. *Degree requirements:* For master's, thesis (for some programs); for doctorate, comprehensive exam, thesis/dissertation. *Entrance requirements:* For master's, GRE General Test (minimum score 900 Quantitative and Verbal, 2.5 Analytical Writing), minimum undergraduate GPA of 3.0; for doctorate, GRE General Test (minimum score 1000 Quantitative and Verbal, 3.0 Analytical Writing), minimum undergraduate GPA of 3.0. Additional exam requirements/recommendations for international students: Required—TOEFL (minimum score 550 paper-based; 80 iBT). Electronic applications accepted. *Faculty research:* Structural, architectural, geotechnical and geoenvironmental engineering; construction engineering and management; transportation engineering; environmental engineering and public works.

Kansas State University, Graduate School, College of Engineering, Department of Architectural Engineering and Construction Science, Manhattan, KS 66506. Offers MS. *Faculty:* 15 full-time (2 women), 3 part-time/adjunct (0 women). *Students:* 11 full-time (5 women), 5 part-time (2 women); includes 5 minority (3 Asian, non-Hispanic/Latino; 1 Hispanic/Latino; 1 Two or more races, non-Hispanic/Latino), 2 international. Average age 25. 8 applicants, 75% accepted, 2 enrolled. In 2016, 5 master's awarded. *Degree requirements:* For master's, thesis or alternative. *Entrance requirements:* For master's, GRE, minimum GPA of 3.0, undergraduate degree (BS) from ABET-accredited engineering program. Additional exam requirements/recommendations for international students: Required—TOEFL. *Application deadline:* For fall admission, 2/1 priority date for domestic students, 1/1 priority date for international students; for spring admission, 8/1 priority date for domestic and international students. Applications are processed on a rolling basis. Application fee: $50 ($75 for international students). Electronic applications accepted. *Expenses:* Tuition, state resident: full-time $9670. Tuition, nonresident: full-time $21,828. *Required fees:* $862. *Financial support:* Fellowships, research assistantships, teaching assistantships, career-related internships or fieldwork, institutionally sponsored loans, and scholarships/grants available. Support available to part-time students. Financial award application deadline: 3/1; financial award applicants required to submit FAFSA. *Faculty research:* Structural systems design and analysis, building electrical and lighting systems, building HVAC and plumbing systems, sustainable engineering. *Unit head:* Raphael Yunk, Head, 785-532-5964, Fax: 785-532-3556, E-mail: yunk@k-state.edu. *Application contact:* Dr. Kimberly Kramer, Director of Graduate Studies, 785-532-5964, Fax: 785-532-3556, E-mail: arecns@k-state.edu. Website: http://www.k-state.edu/are-cns/

Lawrence Technological University, College of Engineering, Southfield, MI 48075-1058. Offers architectural engineering (MS); automotive engineering (MS); biomedical engineering (MS); civil engineering (MA, MS, PhD), including environmental engineering (MS), geotechnical engineering (MS), structural engineering (MS), transportation engineering (MS), water resource engineering (MS); construction engineering management (MA); electrical and computer engineering (MS); engineering management (MA); engineering technology (MS); fire engineering (MS); industrial engineering (MS), including healthcare; manufacturing systems (ME); mechanical engineering (MS, DE, PhD), including manufacturing (DE), solid mechanics (MS), thermal-fluids (MS); mechatronic systems engineering (MS). *Program availability:* Part-time, evening/weekend. *Faculty:* 24 full-time (5 women), 26 part-time/adjunct (2 women). *Students:* 22 full-time (7 women), 588 part-time (81 women); includes 23 minority (11 Black or African American, non-Hispanic/Latino; 4 Asian, non-Hispanic/Latino; 7 Hispanic/Latino; 1 Two or more races, non-Hispanic/Latino), 469 international. Average age 27. 1,186 applicants, 39% accepted, 99 enrolled. In 2016, 293 master's, 3 doctorates awarded. Terminal master's awarded for partial completion of doctoral program. *Degree requirements:* For master's, thesis optional; for doctorate, comprehensive exam, thesis/dissertation optional. *Entrance requirements:* Additional exam requirements/recommendations for international students: Required—TOEFL (minimum score 550 paper-based; 79 iBT), IELTS (minimum score 6.5). *Application deadline:* For fall admission, 5/22 for international students; for spring admission, 10/11 for international students; for summer admission, 2/16 for international students. Applications are processed on a rolling basis. Application fee: $50. Electronic applications accepted. *Expenses: Tuition:* Full-time $14,868; part-time $1062 per credit. *Required fees:* $75 per semester. Tuition and fees vary according to campus/location. *Financial support:* In 2016–17, 25 students received support, including 5 research assistantships with full tuition reimbursements available; unspecified assistantships also available. Financial award application deadline: 4/1; financial award applicants required to submit FAFSA. *Faculty research:* Carbon fiber reinforced polymer reinforced concrete structures; low impact storm water management solutions; vehicle battery energy management; wireless communication; entrepreneurial mindset and engineering. *Total annual research expenditures:* $1.7 million. *Unit head:* Dr. Nabil Grace, Dean, 248-204-2500, Fax: 248-204-2509, E-mail: engrdean@ltu.edu. *Application contact:* Jane Rohrback, Director of Admissions, 248-204-3160, Fax: 248-204-2228, E-mail: admissions@ltu.edu. Website: http://www.ltu.edu/engineering/index.asp

Milwaukee School of Engineering, Civil and Architectural Engineering and Construction Management Department, Program in Architectural Engineering, Milwaukee, WI 53202-3109. Offers MSAE. *Program availability:* Part-time, evening/weekend. *Faculty:* 1 full-time (0 women), 2 part-time/adjunct (0 women). *Students:* 2 full-time (0 women), 6 part-time (2 women), 1 international. Average age 26. 16 applicants, 56% accepted, 7 enrolled. In 2016, 14 master's awarded. *Degree requirements:* For master's, thesis, design project. *Entrance requirements:* For master's, GRE General Test or GMAT if undergraduate GPA less than 3.0, 2 letters of recommendation; BS in architectural, structural, or civil engineering or a related field. Additional exam requirements/recommendations for international students: Required—TOEFL (minimum score 90 iBT), IELTS (minimum score 6.5). *Application deadline:* Applications are processed on a rolling basis. Application fee: $0. Electronic applications accepted. *Expenses:* Tuition: Full-time $31,440; part-time $655 per credit. *Financial support:* Research assistantships, career-related internships or fieldwork, institutionally sponsored loans, and scholarships/grants available. Financial award application deadline: 3/15; financial award applicants required to submit FAFSA. *Faculty research:* Steel, materials. *Unit head:* Dr. Richard DeVries, Director, 414-277-7596, E-mail: devries@msoe.edu. *Application contact:* Ian Dahlinghaus, Graduate Program Associate, 414-277-7208, E-mail: dahlinghaus@msoe.edu. Website: http://www.msoe.edu/community/academics/engineering/page/1290/structural-engineering-overview

Penn State University Park, Graduate School, College of Engineering, Department of Architectural Engineering, University Park, PA 16802. Offers architectural engineering (M Eng, MAE, MS, PhD); facilities engineering and management (M Eng). *Unit head:* Dr. Amr S. Elnashai, Dean, 814-865-7537, Fax: 814-863-4749. *Application contact:* Lori Hawn, Director, Graduate Student Services, 814-865-1795, Fax: 814-863-4627, E-mail: l-gswww@lists.psu.edu. Website: http://www.ae.psu.edu/

University of California, San Diego, Graduate Division, Program in Architecture-based Enterprise Systems Engineering, La Jolla, CA 92093. Offers MAS. *Program availability:* Part-time. *Students:* 34 full-time (8 women). 36 applicants, 94% accepted, 32 enrolled. In 2016, 24 master's awarded. *Degree requirements:* For master's, capstone project. *Entrance requirements:* For master's, 3 letters of recommendation, statement of purpose, resume or curriculum vitae. Additional exam requirements/recommendations for international students: Required—TOEFL (minimum score 550 paper-based; 80 iBT), IELTS (minimum score 7). *Application deadline:* For fall admission, 5/1 for domestic students. Application fee: $105 ($125 for international students). Electronic applications accepted. *Expenses:* Contact institution. *Financial support:* Applicants required to submit FAFSA. *Faculty research:* Emerging enterprise solution approaches, globally distributed operations challenges. *Unit head:* Harold Sorenson, Chair, 858-534-4406, E-mail: hsorenson@ucsd.edu. *Application contact:* Stacey Williams, Coordinator, 858-534-1069, E-mail: staceyw@eng.ucsd.edu. Website: http://maseng.ucsd.edu/aese/

University of Colorado Boulder, Graduate School, College of Engineering and Applied Science, Department of Civil, Environmental, and Architectural Engineering, Boulder, CO 80309. Offers MS, PhD. *Faculty:* 43 full-time (10 women). *Students:* 275 full-time (102 women), 19 part-time (11 women); includes 31 minority (3 Black or African American, non-Hispanic/Latino; 1 American Indian or Alaska Native, non-Hispanic/Latino; 8 Asian, non-Hispanic/Latino; 9 Hispanic/Latino; 1 Native Hawaiian or other Pacific Islander, non-Hispanic/Latino; 9 Two or more races, non-Hispanic/Latino), 75 international. Average age 28. 482 applicants, 55% accepted, 79 enrolled. In 2016, 69 master's, 34 doctorates awarded. Terminal master's awarded for partial completion of doctoral program. *Degree requirements:* For master's, comprehensive exam, thesis or alternative; for doctorate, thesis/dissertation. *Entrance requirements:* For master's, GRE General Test, minimum undergraduate GPA of 3.0. *Application deadline:* For fall admission, 1/31 for domestic and international students; for spring admission, 10/1 for domestic and international students. Application fee: $60 ($80 for international students). Electronic applications accepted. Application fee is waived when completed online. *Financial support:* In 2016–17, 498 students received support, including 168 fellowships (averaging $10,048 per year), 81 research assistantships with full and partial tuition reimbursements available (averaging $36,827 per year), 32 teaching assistantships with full and partial tuition reimbursements available (averaging $38,824 per year); institutionally sponsored loans, scholarships/grants, health care benefits, and unspecified assistantships also available. Financial award application deadline: 1/15; financial award applicants required to submit FAFSA. *Faculty research:* Civil engineering, environmental engineering, architectural engineering, hydrology, water resources engineering. *Total annual research expenditures:* $12.5 million. *Application contact:* E-mail: cvengrad@colorado.edu. Website: http://civil.colorado.edu/

University of Detroit Mercy, School of Architecture, Detroit, MI 48221. Offers architecture (M Arch); community development (MA). *Entrance requirements:* For master's, BS in architecture, minimum GPA of 3.0, portfolio.

The University of Kansas, Graduate Studies, School of Engineering, Program in Architectural Engineering, Lawrence, KS 66045. Offers MS. *Program availability:* Part-time. *Students:* 8 full-time (1 woman), 1 (woman) part-time, 5 international. Average age 26. 11 applicants, 73% accepted, 6 enrolled. In 2016, 4 master's awarded. *Entrance requirements:* For master's, GRE, two letters of

Architectural Engineering

recommendation, statement of purpose. Additional exam requirements/recommendations for international students: Required—TOEFL or IELTS. *Application deadline:* For fall admission, 12/31 priority date for domestic students, 9/15 priority date for international students; for spring admission, 12/30 for domestic students, 10/15 for international students; for summer admission, 5/15 for domestic students. Application fee: $65 ($85 for international students). Electronic applications accepted. *Financial support:* Fellowships, research assistantships, teaching assistantships, career-related internships or fieldwork, and scholarships/grants available. Financial award application deadline: 12/15. *Faculty research:* Building mechanical systems, energy management, lighting and electrical systems, construction engineering. *Unit head:* David Darwin, Chair, 785-864-3827, E-mail: daved@ku.edu. *Application contact:* Graduate Secretary, 785-864-3826, Fax: 785-864-5631, E-mail: s523s307@ku.edu. Website: http://www.ceae.ku.edu/

University of Louisiana at Lafayette, College of the Arts, School of Architecture, Lafayette, LA 70504. Offers M Arch. *Degree requirements:* For master's, thesis. *Entrance requirements:* For master's, GRE General Test. Additional exam requirements/recommendations for international students: Required—TOEFL (minimum score 550 paper-based). Electronic applications accepted.

University of Massachusetts Amherst, Graduate School, College of Natural Sciences, Department of Environmental Conservation, Amherst, MA 01003. Offers building systems (MS, PhD); environmental policy and human dimensions (MS, PhD); forest resources (MS, PhD); sustainability science (MS); water, wetlands and watersheds (MS, PhD); wildlife and fisheries conservation (MS, PhD). *Program availability:* Part-time. Terminal master's awarded for partial completion of doctoral program. *Degree requirements:* For master's, thesis or alternative; for doctorate, comprehensive exam, thesis/dissertation. *Entrance requirements:* For master's and doctorate, GRE General Test. Additional exam requirements/recommendations for international students: Required—TOEFL (minimum score 550 paper-based; 80 iBT), IELTS (minimum score 6.5). Electronic applications accepted.

University of Miami, Graduate School, College of Engineering, Department of Civil, Architectural, and Environmental Engineering, Coral Gables, FL 33124. Offers architectural engineering (MSAE); civil engineering (MSCE, PhD). *Program availability:* Part-time. Terminal master's awarded for partial completion of doctoral program. *Degree requirements:* For master's, thesis (for some programs); for doctorate, comprehensive exam, thesis/dissertation. *Entrance requirements:* For master's, GRE General Test (minimum score 1000 verbal and quantitative), minimum GPA of 3.0; for doctorate, GRE General Test, minimum GPA of 3.5 in preceding degree. Additional exam requirements/recommendations for international students: Required—TOEFL (minimum score 550 paper-based). Electronic applications accepted. *Faculty research:* Structural assessment and wind engineering, sustainable construction and materials, moisture transport and management, wastewater and waste engineering, water management and risk analysis.

University of Nebraska–Lincoln, Graduate College, College of Engineering, Program in Architectural Engineering, Lincoln, NE 68588. Offers M Eng, MAE, MS, PhD. *Accreditation:* ABET. *Entrance requirements:* Additional exam requirements/recommendations for international students: Required—TOEFL (minimum score 550 paper-based).

The University of Texas at Austin, Graduate School, Cockrell School of Engineering, Department of Civil, Architectural and Environmental Engineering, Program in Architectural Engineering, Austin, TX 78712-1111. Offers MSE. *Program availability:* Part-time. *Degree requirements:* For master's, thesis. *Entrance requirements:* For master's, GRE General Test. Additional exam requirements/recommendations for international students: Required—TOEFL. Electronic applications accepted. *Faculty research:* Materials engineering, structural engineering, construction engineering, project management.

CALIFORNIA POLYTECHNIC STATE UNIVERSITY
Department of Architectural Engineering

Programs of Study

The Architectural Engineering Department at California Polytechnic State University offers a Master of Science in Architectural Engineering (M.S.A.E.)program that integrates theory and practice to thoroughly prepare students for careers in the building industry.

The program is designed for individuals who want to strengthen their knowledge of structural behavior. It allows them to become more familiar with the relationship between architecture, construction, and structures. It also increases their understanding of analysis and design trends in the structural engineering field.

The program consists of 45 units of courses including 24 units of core required and 12 units of elective courses. It also includes 9 units for a Master's Design Project and a comprehensive exam.

Students take core courses in architectural design, structural mechanics, nonlinear structural behavior, and structural system behavior.

The Department of Architectural Engineering seeks to provide the best preparation for structural engineering practice in California. Its program, which has accreditation from ABET, focuses primarily on structural engineering that emphasizes seismic design. Curricula go beyond the traditional structures program to provide in-depth knowledge about architecture and construction management as they relate to total project design.

The department is part of the College of Architecture and Environmental Design (CAED). This highly-regarded college is the only one of its kind in the country to offer nine degree programs in five closely related departments: Architectural Engineering, Architecture, City and Regional Planning, Construction Management, and Landscape Architecture.

CAED provides a low student-to-teacher ratio, state-of-the-art facilities, and meaningful hands-on experience. This gives students the opportunity to develop innovative solutions to real-world problems, collaborate with industry partners, and work across disciplines.

Research Focus

The M.S.A.E. degree program is designed for students holding an accredited degree in architectural engineering or civil engineering who wish to pursue advanced studies in structural engineering. The mission of the program is to better prepare students for practice in the structural engineering profession. Core curriculum courses expose students to emerging topics in structures, advanced methodologies to predict and analyze structural behavior in response to earthquakes, and cutting-edge design procedures used in industry. In addition, related topics in architecture and construction management may be integrated into the curriculum to create a unique master's-level education. The project culminates with a written report and oral presentation.

Financial Aid

California Polytechnic State University offers graduate students in the Department of Architectural Engineering several financial aid options including Federal loans, emergency loans, alternative loans, state grants, and scholarships.

Cost of Study

For the 2017–18 academic year, tuition and fees for the M.S. in Architectural Engineering program are $10,866 for California residents and $17,202 for nonresidents. The most current information on tuition and fees can be found at https://afd.calpoly.edu/fees/.

Living and Housing Costs

Graduate students can live in campus apartments complete with a full kitchen, private bathrooms, and the option of private or shared bedrooms. Costs for a University apartment per academic year range from $5,770 for an apartment with a double suite bedroom to $9,014 for an apartment with a private bedroom. These costs are subject to change. There are also many opportunities for off-campus housing.

Location

California Polytechnic State University is located in San Luis Obispo, California. According to Colleges in California, its campus is one of the most beautiful in the state. The University is situated in an area known for its mild climate, natural beauty, and outdoor recreational options. Biking, hiking, and sailing are just some of the activities students can enjoy most of the year.

The University

California Polytechnic State University provides a balanced education in the arts, sciences, and technology. It offers approximately 21,300 students nearly 190 major, master's, minor, and credential programs through six colleges: Agriculture, Food and Environmental Sciences; Architecture and Environmental Design; Engineering; Liberal Arts; Science and Mathematics; and the Orfalea College of Business

Learning by Doing is the cornerstone of the university's academic programs. Classes emphasize active-learning techniques and include extensive field and laboratory work.

California Polytechnic State University

On- and off-campus activities allow students to apply theory to real-world situations.

The university's commitment to rigorous, comprehensive education ensures that students graduate prepared to obtain rewarding positions.

California Polytechnic State University's commitment to providing high quality education earns it top honors. In its 2017 guidebook, *U.S. News & World Report* named it the best public, master's-level university in the west. This is the 24th consecutive year that the university has received this honor. The publisher also ranked it ninth among the best universities in the western region. PayScale.com ranked California Polytechnic State University seventh on its list of public universities with the best return on investment.

Faculty

Faculty members in the Department of Architectural Engineering are excellent teachers, accomplished researchers, skillful practitioners, and lifelong learners.

Professor Craig V. Baltimore is one of the department's distinguished faculty members. His teaching interests at the graduate level include communication methods and engineering mechanics. His research focuses on producing alternative energy and assisting the residents of rural Tanzania with planning and building a polytechnic college. Before beginning his career in academia, Professor Baltimore was a structural engineer for ARUP and KPFF Consulting Engineering. He continues to be active in the masonry and structural engineering professions.

Applying

Applicants to the Master of Science in Architectural Engineering must submit the following information: application, $55 application fee, certified transcripts from all schools attended, GRE results, a statement of purpose, and three letters of recommendation.

The program accepts qualified applicants on a rolling admission basis. Applicants who have submitted complete files can be reviewed and accepted anytime during the filing periods. Applications are accepted through the online system Cal State Apply. The filing periods are listed at https://admissions.calpoly.edu/applicants/graduate/deadlines.html. All applicants are responsible for using the University's established applicant checklist for meeting admission deadlines.

More information is available at grad.calpoly.edu. Application information for international students can be found at http://admissions.calpoly.edu/applicants/international/.

California Polytechnic State University
Department of Admissions
1 Grand Avenue
San Luis Obispo, California 93407
Phone: 805-756-1314
E-mail: arce@calpoly.edu
Website: www.arce.calpoly.edu

Section 5
Biomedical Engineering and Biotechnology

This section contains a directory of institutions offering graduate work in biomedical engineering and biotechnology, followed by an in-depth entry submitted by an institution that chose to prepare a detailed program description. Additional information about programs listed in the directory but not augmented by an in-depth entry may be obtained by writing directly to the dean of a graduate school or chair of a department at the address given in the directory.

For programs offering related work, see also in this book *Aerospace/ Aeronautical Engineering, Engineering and Applied Sciences, Engineering Design, Engineering Physics, Management of Engineering and Technology,* and *Mechanical Engineering and Mechanics.* In the other guides in this series:

Graduate Programs in the Biological/Biomedical Sciences & Health-Related Medical Professions
See *Allied Health, Biological and Biomedical Sciences,* and *Physiology*
Graduate Programs in the Physical Sciences, Mathematics, Agricultural Sciences, the Environment & Natural Resources
See *Mathematical Sciences (Biometrics and Biostatistics)*

CONTENTS

Program Directories

Featured School: Display and Close-Up

Biomedical Engineering

American University of Beirut, Graduate Programs, Faculty of Medicine, Beirut, Lebanon. Offers biochemistry (MS); biomedical engineering (MS); biomedical sciences (PhD); human morphology (MS); medicine (MD); microbiology and immunology (MS); neuroscience (MS); orthodontics (MS); pharmacology and therapeutics (MS); physiology (MS). *Program availability:* Part-time. *Faculty:* 292 full-time (87 women), 58 part-time/adjunct (5 women). *Students:* 491 full-time (248 women). Average age 23. 431 applicants, 50% accepted, 127 enrolled. In 2016, 18 master's, 88 doctorates awarded. *Degree requirements:* For master's, one foreign language, comprehensive exam, thesis (for some programs); for doctorate, one foreign language, comprehensive exam, thesis/dissertation. *Entrance requirements:* For doctorate, MCAT (for MD); GRE (for PhD). Additional exam requirements/recommendations for international students: Required—TOEFL (minimum score 600 paper-based; 100 iBT), IELTS (minimum score 7.5). *Application deadline:* For fall admission, 4/3 for domestic and international students. Applications are processed on a rolling basis. Application fee: $75. Electronic applications accepted. *Expenses:* Contact institution. *Financial support:* In 2016–17, 281 students received support. Institutionally sponsored loans, scholarships/grants, and unspecified assistantships available. Total annual research expenditures: $1.4 million. *Unit head:* Dr. Mohamed Sayegh, Dean, 961-1350000 Ext. 4700, Fax: 961-1744489, E-mail: msayegh@aub.edu.lb. *Application contact:* Dr. Salim Kanaan, Director, Admissions Office, 961-1350000 Ext. 2594, Fax: 961-1750775, E-mail: sk00@aub.edu.lb. Website: http://www.aub.edu.lb/fm/fm_home/Pages/index.aspx

Arizona State University at the Tempe campus, Ira A. Fulton Schools of Engineering, School of Biological and Health Systems Engineering, Tempe, AZ 85287-9709. Offers biological design (PhD); biomedical engineering (MS, PhD). *Program availability:* Part-time, evening/weekend. Terminal master's awarded for partial completion of doctoral program. *Degree requirements:* For master's, thesis and oral defense or applied project; interactive Program of Study (iPOS) submitted before completing 50 percent of required credit hours; for doctorate, comprehensive exam, thesis/dissertation, interactive Program of Study (iPOS) submitted before completing 50 percent of required credit hours. *Entrance requirements:* For master's and doctorate, GRE General Test, minimum GPA of 3.0 or equivalent in last 2 years of work leading to bachelor's degree, 3 letters of recommendation, one-page personal statement. Additional exam requirements/recommendations for international students: Required—TOEFL (minimum score 580 paper-based; 92 iBT). Electronic applications accepted. *Expenses:* Contact institution. *Faculty research:* Cardiovascular engineering; synthetic/computational biology; medical devices and diagnostics; neuroengineering; rehabilitation; regenerative medicine; imaging; molecular, cellular and tissue engineering; virtual reality healthcare delivery systems.

Baylor College of Medicine, Graduate School of Biomedical Sciences, Program in Translational Biology and Molecular Medicine, Houston, TX 77030-3498. Offers PhD. *Degree requirements:* For doctorate, thesis/dissertation, public defense. *Entrance requirements:* For doctorate, GRE, minimum GPA of 3.0. Additional exam requirements/recommendations for international students: Required—TOEFL. Electronic applications accepted. *Faculty research:* Molecular medicine, translational biology, human disease biology and therapy.

Baylor University, Graduate School, School of Engineering and Computer Science, Department of Mechanical Engineering, Waco, TX 76798. Offers biomedical engineering (MSBME); engineering (ME); mechanical engineering (MS, PhD). *Program availability:* Part-time. *Faculty:* 13 full-time (2 women). *Students:* 30 full-time (3 women), 1 part-time (0 women); includes 4 minority (1 Black or African American, non-Hispanic/Latino; 1 Asian, non-Hispanic/Latino; 2 Hispanic/Latino), 10 international. 20 applicants, 35% accepted, 3 enrolled. In 2016, 8 master's awarded. *Degree requirements:* For master's, thesis (for some programs), 33 coursework credits or 6 project credits and 27 coursework credits (for ME); for doctorate, thesis/dissertation (for some programs). *Entrance requirements:* For master's, GRE. Additional exam requirements/recommendations for international students: Required—TOEFL (minimum score 550 paper-based; 80 iBT), IELTS (minimum score 6.5), PTE (minimum score 58). *Application deadline:* For fall admission, 2/15 priority date for domestic and international students; for winter admission, 12/1 priority date for domestic and international students; for summer admission, 5/1 priority date for domestic students. Application fee: $50. Electronic applications accepted. *Expenses: Tuition:* Full-time $28,494; part-time $1583 per credit hour. *Required fees:* $167 per credit hour. Tuition and fees vary according to course load and program. *Financial support:* In 2016–17, 15 students received support, including 8 research assistantships with full tuition reimbursements available (averaging $15,000 per year), 7 teaching assistantships with full tuition reimbursements available (averaging $15,000 per year). Financial award application deadline: 2/15. *Unit head:* Dr. Dennis L. O'Neal, Dean, 254-710-3871, Fax: 254-710-3839, E-mail: dennis_oneal@baylor.edu. *Application contact:* Dr. Carolyn Skurla, Associate Professor and Graduate Program Director, 254-710-7371, Fax: 254-710-3360, E-mail: carolyn_skurla@baylor.edu. Website: http://www.ecs.baylor.edu/mechanicalengineering/

Binghamton University, State University of New York, Graduate School, Thomas J. Watson School of Engineering and Applied Science, Department of Biomedical Engineering, Binghamton, NY 13902-6000. Offers MS, PhD. *Program availability:* Part-time, online learning. *Faculty:* 9 full-time (4 women), 2 part-time/adjunct (0 women). *Students:* 43 full-time (16 women), 34 part-time (14 women); includes 16 minority (6 Black or African American, non-Hispanic/Latino; 6 Asian, non-Hispanic/Latino; 4 Hispanic/Latino), 43 international. Average age 26. 105 applicants, 86% accepted, 25 enrolled. In 2016, 15 master's awarded. *Degree requirements:* For master's, thesis; for doctorate, comprehensive exam, thesis/dissertation. *Entrance requirements:* For master's and doctorate, GRE General Test. Additional exam requirements/recommendations for international students: Required—TOEFL (minimum score 550 paper-based; 80 iBT). *Application deadline:* Applications are processed on a rolling basis. Application fee: $75. Electronic applications accepted. *Expenses:* Contact institution. *Financial support:* In 2016–17, 21 students received support, including 7 research assistantships (averaging $16,500 per year), 8 teaching assistantships with full tuition reimbursements available (averaging $16,500 per year); career-related internships or fieldwork, Federal Work-Study, institutionally sponsored loans, scholarships/grants, health care benefits, tuition waivers (full and partial), and unspecified assistantships also available. Financial award application deadline: 1/15; financial award applicants required to submit FAFSA. *Unit head:* Gretchen Mahler, Graduate Program Director, 607-777-5238, E-mail: gmahler@binghamton.edu. *Application contact:* Ben Balkaya, Assistant Dean and Director, 607-777-2151, Fax: 607-777-2501, E-mail: balkaya@binghamton.edu. Website: http://www.binghamton.edu/biomedical-engineering/grad/

Boston University, College of Engineering, Department of Biomedical Engineering, Boston, MA 02215. Offers biomedical engineering (M Eng, MS, PhD); MD/PhD. *Program availability:* Part-time. *Students:* 188 full-time (85 women), 11 part-time (4 women); includes 48 minority (2 Black or African American, non-Hispanic/Latino; 33 Asian, non-Hispanic/Latino; 6 Hispanic/Latino; 7 Two or more races, non-Hispanic/Latino), 59 international. Average age 25. 802 applicants, 27% accepted, 54 enrolled. In 2016, 41 master's, 20 doctorates awarded. Terminal master's awarded for partial completion of doctoral program. *Degree requirements:* For master's, thesis (for some programs); for doctorate, comprehensive exam, thesis/dissertation. *Entrance requirements:* For master's and doctorate, GRE General Test. Additional exam requirements/recommendations for international students: Required—TOEFL (minimum score 90 iBT), IELTS (minimum score 7). *Financial support:* Applicants required to submit FAFSA. *Faculty research:* Biomaterials, tissue engineering and drug delivery; modeling of biological systems; molecular bioengineering and biophysics; neuroscience and neural disease; synthetic biology and systems biology. *Unit head:* Dr. John White, Chairman, 617-353-2805, Fax: 617-353-6766. Website: http://www.bu.edu/bme/

Brown University, Graduate School, Division of Biology and Medicine, Department of Molecular Pharmacology, Physiology and Biotechnology, Providence, RI 02912. Offers biomedical engineering (Sc M, PhD); biotechnology (PhD); molecular pharmacology and physiology (PhD); MD/PhD. *Degree requirements:* For doctorate, thesis/dissertation, preliminary exam. *Entrance requirements:* For master's and doctorate, GRE General Test, GRE Subject Test. Additional exam requirements/recommendations for international students: Required—TOEFL. Electronic applications accepted. *Faculty research:* Structural biology, antiplatelet drugs, nicotinic receptor structure/function.

Brown University, Graduate School, Division of Biology and Medicine and School of Engineering, Program in Biomedical Engineering, Providence, RI 02912. Offers Sc M, PhD. *Entrance requirements:* For master's and doctorate, GRE General Test, interview. Additional exam requirements/recommendations for international students: Required—TOEFL.

Brown University, Graduate School, School of Engineering and Division of Biology and Medicine, Center for Biomedical Engineering, Providence, RI 02912. Offers Sc M, PhD. *Degree requirements:* For master's, thesis.

Carleton University, Faculty of Graduate Studies, Faculty of Engineering and Design, Ottawa-Carleton Institute for Biomedical Engineering, Ottawa, ON K1S 5B6, Canada. Offers MA Sc. *Degree requirements:* For master's, thesis optional. *Entrance requirements:* For master's, honours degree. Additional exam requirements/recommendations for international students: Required—TOEFL.

Carnegie Mellon University, Carnegie Institute of Technology, Biomedical and Health Engineering Program, Pittsburgh, PA 15213-3891. Offers bioengineering (MS, PhD); MD/PhD. *Degree requirements:* For master's, thesis; for doctorate, thesis/dissertation, qualifying exam. *Entrance requirements:* For master's and doctorate, GRE General Test. Additional exam requirements/recommendations for international students: Required—TOEFL. Electronic applications accepted. *Faculty research:* Cellular and molecular systematics, signal and image processing, materials and mechanics.

Case Western Reserve University, School of Graduate Studies, Case School of Engineering, Department of Biomedical Engineering, Cleveland, OH 44106. Offers MS, PhD, MD/MS, MD/PhD. *Faculty:* 21 full-time (2 women). *Students:* 117 full-time (41 women), 13 part-time (3 women); includes 29 minority (1 Black or African American, non-Hispanic/Latino; 22 Asian, non-Hispanic/Latino; 4 Hispanic/Latino; 2 Two or more races, non-Hispanic/Latino), 53 international. In 2016, 20 master's, 11 doctorates awarded. Terminal master's awarded for partial completion of doctoral program. *Degree requirements:* For master's, thesis (for some programs); for doctorate, thesis/dissertation, qualifying exam, teaching experience. *Entrance requirements:* For master's and doctorate, GRE General Test. Additional exam requirements/recommendations for international students: Required—TOEFL. *Application deadline:* For fall admission, 4/1 priority date for domestic students; for spring admission, 10/1 priority date for domestic students. Applications are processed on a rolling basis. Application fee: $50. *Expenses: Tuition:* Full-time $42,576; part-time $1774 per credit hour. *Required fees:* $34. Tuition and fees vary according to course load and program. *Financial support:* In 2016–17, 24 fellowships with full tuition reimbursements, 65 research assistantships with tuition reimbursements were awarded; traineeships also available. Financial award application deadline: 2/15; financial award applicants required to submit FAFSA. *Faculty research:* Neuroengineering, biomaterials/tissue engineering, drug delivery, biomedical imaging, biomedical sensors/systems. Total annual research expenditures: $15.9 million. *Unit head:* Dr. Robert Kirsch, Department Chair, 216-368-3158, Fax: 216-368-4969, E-mail: robert.kirsch@case.edu. *Application contact:* Carol Adrine, Academic Operations Coordinator, 216-368-4094, Fax: 216-368-4969, E-mail: caa7@case.edu. Website: http://bme.case.edu

See Display below and Close-Up on page 155.

The Catholic University of America, School of Engineering, Department of Biomedical Engineering, Washington, DC 20064. Offers MBE, PhD. *Program availability:* Part-time. *Faculty:* 7 full-time (1 woman), 1 (woman) part-time/adjunct. *Students:* 7 full-time (4 women), 15 part-time (4 women); includes 4 minority (1 Asian, non-Hispanic/Latino; 2 Hispanic/Latino; 1 Two or more races, non-Hispanic/Latino), 9 international. Average age 30. 28 applicants, 64% accepted, 6 enrolled. In 2016, 11 master's, 1 doctorate awarded. *Degree requirements:* For master's, thesis or alternative; for doctorate, comprehensive exam, thesis/dissertation, oral exams. *Entrance requirements:* For master's, minimum GPA of 3.0, statement of purpose, official copies of academic transcripts, three letters of recommendation; for doctorate, minimum GPA of 3.4, statement of purpose, official copies of academic transcripts, three letters of recommendation. Additional exam requirements/recommendations for international students: Required—TOEFL (minimum score 550 paper-based; 80 iBT). *Application deadline:* For fall admission, 7/15 priority date for domestic students, 7/1 for international students; for spring admission, 11/15 priority date for domestic students, 11/1 for international students. Applications are processed on a rolling basis. Application fee: $55. Electronic applications accepted. *Expenses:* $43,380 per year; $1,170 per credit; $200 per semester part-time fees. *Financial support:* Fellowships, research assistantships, teaching assistantships, Federal Work-Study, scholarships/grants, tuition waivers (full and partial), and unspecified assistantships available. Financial award application deadline: 2/1; financial award applicants required to submit FAFSA. *Faculty research:* Biomedical optics, robotics and human motor control, cell and tissue engineering, biomechanics, rehabilitation engineering. Total annual research expenditures: $259,822. *Unit head:* Dr. Peter S. Lum, Chair, 202-319-5181, Fax: 202-319-4287, E-mail: tran@cua.edu. *Application contact:* Director of Graduate Admissions, 202-319-5057, Fax: 202-319-6533, E-mail: cua-admissions@cua.edu. Website: http://biomedical.cua.edu/

City College of the City University of New York, Graduate School, Grove School of Engineering, Department of Biomedical Engineering, New York, NY 10031-9198. Offers MS, PhD. *Entrance requirements:* For master's, GRE. Additional exam requirements/recommendations for international students: Required—TOEFL (minimum score 550 paper-based). Tuition and fees vary according to course load, degree level and program.

Clemson University, Graduate School, College of Engineering, Computing and Applied Sciences, Department of Bioengineering, Clemson, SC 29634-0905. Offers bioengineering (MS, PhD); biomedical engineering (M Engr); medical device recycling and reprocessing (Certificate). *Program availability:* Part-time. *Faculty:* 27 full-time (8 women), 1 (woman) part-time/adjunct. *Students:* 80 full-time (31 women), 12 part-time (5 women); includes 6 minority (1 Black or African American, non-Hispanic/Latino; 2 Asian, non-Hispanic/Latino; 2 Hispanic/Latino; 1 Two or more races, non-Hispanic/Latino), 31 international. Average age 25. 96 applicants, 33% accepted, 18 enrolled. In 2016, 31 master's, 12 doctorates awarded. *Degree requirements:* For master's, thesis optional; for doctorate, comprehensive exam, thesis/dissertation. *Entrance requirements:* For master's and doctorate, GRE General Test, unofficial transcripts, letters of recommendation. Additional exam requirements/recommendations for international students: Required—TOEFL (minimum score 100 iBT), IELTS (minimum score 7). *Application deadline:* For fall admission, 2/15 priority date for domestic students, 1/15 priority date for international students. Applications are processed on a rolling basis. Application fee: $80 ($90 for international students). Electronic applications accepted. *Expenses:* $4,841 per semester full-time resident, $9,640 per semester full-time non-resident, $612 per credit hour part-time resident, $1,223 per credit hour part-time non-resident. *Financial support:* In 2016–17, 69 students received support, including 1 fellowship with partial tuition reimbursement available (averaging $22,667 per year), 29 research assistantships with partial tuition reimbursements available (averaging $19,838 per year), 32 teaching assistantships with partial tuition reimbursements available (averaging $19,151 per year); career-related internships or fieldwork and unspecified assistantships also available. Financial award application deadline: 2/15; financial award applicants required to submit FAFSA. *Faculty research:* Biomaterials, biomechanics, bioinstrumentation, tissue engineering, vascular engineering. *Total annual research expenditures:* $5.1 million. *Unit head:* Dr. Martine LaBerge, Department Chair, 864-656-5557, E-mail: laberge@clemson.edu. *Application contact:* Dr. Agneta Simionescu, Graduate Coordinator, 864-650-2575, E-mail: agneta@clemson.edu. Website: https://www.clemson.edu/cecas/departments/bioe/

Cleveland State University, College of Graduate Studies, Fenn College of Engineering, Department of Chemical and Biomedical Engineering, Program in Applied Biomedical Engineering, Cleveland, OH 44115. Offers D Eng. *Program availability:* Part-time, evening/weekend. *Faculty:* 8 full-time (1 woman), 1 part-time/adjunct (0 women). *Students:* 14 full-time (6 women), 1 part-time (0 women); includes 2 minority (both Black or African American, non-Hispanic/Latino), 11 international. Average age 31. 38 applicants, 18% accepted, 1 enrolled. In 2016, 6 doctorates awarded. *Degree requirements:* For doctorate, thesis/dissertation. *Entrance requirements:* For doctorate, GRE, minimum undergraduate GPA of 2.75, MS or MD 3.25; degree in engineering. Additional exam requirements/recommendations for international students: Required—TOEFL (minimum score 550 paper-based; 78 iBT). *Application deadline:* For fall admission, 3/15 for domestic and international students. Applications are processed on a rolling basis. Application fee: $40. Electronic applications accepted. *Expenses:* Tuition, state resident: full-time $9565. Tuition, nonresident: full-time $17,980. Tuition and fees vary according to program. *Financial support:* In 2016–17, research assistantships with tuition reimbursements (averaging $5,696 per year) were awarded; career-related internships or fieldwork, scholarships/grants, and tuition waivers (full) also available. Financial award application deadline: 3/30. *Faculty research:* Biomechanics, drug delivery systems, medical imaging, tissue engineering, artificial heart valves. *Unit head:* Dr. Dhananjai B. Shah, Director, 216-687-3569, Fax: 216-687-9220, E-mail: d.shah@csuohio.edu. *Application contact:* Becky Laird, Administrative Coordinator, 216-687-2571, Fax: 216-687-9220, E-mail: b.laird@csuohio.edu. Website: http://www.csuohio.edu/engineering/chemical/ABE/index.html

Colorado State University, Walter Scott, Jr. College of Engineering, School of Biomedical Engineering, Fort Collins, CO 80523-1376. Offers bioengineering (MS, PhD); biomedical engineering (ME). *Program availability:* Part-time, evening/weekend, 100% online. *Faculty:* 1 (woman) part-time/adjunct. *Students:* 15 full-time (6 women), 20 part-time (11 women); includes 4 minority (2 Asian, non-Hispanic/Latino; 2 Hispanic/Latino), 6 international. Average age 27. 52 applicants, 17% accepted, 7 enrolled. In 2016, 2 master's, 3 doctorates awarded. Terminal master's awarded for partial completion of doctoral program. *Degree requirements:* For master's, thesis (for some programs); for doctorate, thesis/dissertation, qualifying process (minimum B average in core classes); preliminary exam. *Entrance requirements:* For master's and doctorate, GRE General Test, minimum GPA of 3.0, resume, statement of purpose, official transcripts, three letters of recommendation. Additional exam requirements/recommendations for international students: Required—TOEFL (minimum score 550 paper-based; 80 iBT). *Application deadline:* For fall admission, 1/15 priority date for domestic and international students; for spring admission, 9/1 priority date for domestic and international students. Application fee: $60 ($70 for international students). Electronic applications accepted. *Expenses:* Contact institution. *Financial support:* In 2016–17, 18 students received support, including 17 research assistantships with full tuition reimbursements available (averaging $23,940 per year), 2 teaching assistantships with full tuition reimbursements available (averaging $18,000 per year); unspecified assistantships also available. Financial award application deadline: 1/15; financial award applicants required to submit FAFSA. *Faculty research:* Regenerative and rehabilitative medicine, imaging and diagnostics, medical devices and therapeutics. *Unit head:* Dr. Stu Tobet, Director and Professor, 970-491-7157, Fax: 970-491-5569, E-mail: stuart.tobet@colostate.edu. *Application contact:* Sara Mattern, Graduate Academic Adviser, 970-491-7157, Fax: 970-491-5569, E-mail: sara.mattern@colostate.edu. Website: http://www.engr.colostate.edu/sbme/

Columbia University, Fu Foundation School of Engineering and Applied Science, Department of Biomedical Engineering, New York, NY 10027. Offers MS, Eng Sc D, PhD. *Program availability:* Part-time, online learning. *Degree requirements:* For doctorate, thesis/dissertation, qualifying exam. *Entrance requirements:* For master's and doctorate, GRE General Test. Additional exam requirements/recommendations for international students: Required—TOEFL, IELTS, PTE. Electronic applications accepted. *Faculty research:* Biomechanics, biosignal and biomedical imaging, cellular and tissue engineering.

Cornell University, Graduate School, Graduate Fields of Engineering, Field of Biomedical Engineering, Ithaca, NY 14853. Offers M Eng, MS, PhD. *Degree requirements:* For master's, thesis; for doctorate, comprehensive exam, thesis/dissertation. *Entrance requirements:* For master's and doctorate, GRE General Test, GRE Subject Test (engineering), 3 letters of recommendation. Additional exam requirements/recommendations for international students: Required—TOEFL (minimum score 77 iBT). Electronic applications accepted. *Faculty research:* Biomaterials; biomedical instrumentation and diagnostics; biomedical mechanics; drug delivery, design, and metabolism.

Dalhousie University, Faculty of Engineering and Faculty of Medicine, Department of Biomedical Engineering, Halifax, NS B3H3J5, Canada. Offers MA Sc, PhD. *Entrance requirements:* Additional exam requirements/recommendations for international students: Required—TOEFL, IELTS, CANTEST, CAEL, or Michigan English Language Assessment Battery. Electronic applications accepted.

Dartmouth College, Thayer School of Engineering, Program in Biomedical Engineering, Hanover, NH 03755. Offers M Eng, MS, PhD. *Faculty research:* Imaging,

Department of Biomedical Engineering

Case Western Reserve University offers distinctive education programs ranging from the B.S. through Ph.D., including two new innovations:

- Master of Engineering and Management in Biomedical Entrepreneurship
- Physician Engineering Training Program (MD/PhD)

Research foci are in Biomaterials and Tissue Engineering, Neural Engineering and Neuroprostheses, Cardiac Bioelectricity, Imaging and Sensing, and Metabolic Engineering.

For more information contact:

Admissions Coordinator

Department of Biomedical Engineering

Case School of Engineering and School of

Medicine Wickenden Building-Room 325

10900 Euclid Avenue

Cleveland, Ohio 44106-7207

E-mail: bmedept@case.edu

Web site: http://bme.case.edu

physiological modeling, cancer hyperthermia and radiation therapy, bioelectromagnetics, biomedical optics and lasers. *Total annual research expenditures:* $9.8 million. *Unit head:* Dr. Joseph J. Helbie, Dean, 603-646-2238, Fax: 603-646-2580, E-mail: joseph.j.helbie@dartmouth.edu. *Application contact:* Candace S. Potter, Graduate Admissions Administrator, 603-646-3844, Fax: 603-646-1620, E-mail: candace.s.potter@dartmouth.edu.

Drexel University, School of Biomedical Engineering, Science and Health Systems, Program in Biomedical Engineering, Philadelphia, PA 19104-2875. Offers MS, PhD. *Faculty:* 28 full-time (8 women), 4 part-time/adjunct (1 woman). *Students:* 111 full-time (49 women), 14 part-time (5 women); includes 22 minority (3 Black or African American, non-Hispanic/Latino; 16 Asian, non-Hispanic/Latino; 3 Hispanic/Latino), 47 international. Average age 26. In 2016, 83 master's, 13 doctorates awarded. *Degree requirements:* For master's, thesis (for some programs); for doctorate, thesis/dissertation. *Application deadline:* For fall admission, 8/21 for domestic students. Applications are processed on a rolling basis. Application fee: $50. Electronic applications accepted. *Expenses: Tuition:* Full-time $32,184; part-time $1192 per credit hour. *Required fees:* $280. Tuition and fees vary according to campus/location and program. *Financial support:* Research assistantships, teaching assistantships, career-related internships or fieldwork, Federal Work-Study, institutionally sponsored loans, tuition waivers (full and partial), and unspecified assistantships available. Financial award application deadline: 2/1. *Total annual research expenditures:* $4.9 million. *Unit head:* Dr. Banu Onaral, Director, 215-895-2215. *Application contact:* Director of Graduate Admissions, 215-895-6700, Fax: 215-895-5939, E-mail: enroll@drexel.edu.

Duke University, Graduate School, Pratt School of Engineering, Department of Biomedical Engineering, Durham, NC 27708. Offers MS, PhD. *Degree requirements:* For doctorate, thesis/dissertation. *Entrance requirements:* For master's and doctorate, GRE General Test. Additional exam requirements/recommendations for international students: Required—TOEFL (minimum score 90 iBT), IELTS (minimum score 7).

Duke University, Graduate School, Pratt School of Engineering, Master of Engineering Program, Durham, NC 27708-0271. Offers biomedical engineering (M Eng); civil engineering (M Eng); electrical and computer engineering (M Eng); environmental engineering (M Eng); materials science and engineering (M Eng); mechanical engineering (M Eng); photonics and optical sciences (M Eng). *Program availability:* Part-time. *Entrance requirements:* For master's, GRE General Test, resume, 3 letters of recommendation, statement of purpose, transcripts. Additional exam requirements/recommendations for international students: Required—TOEFL.

East Carolina University, Graduate School, College of Engineering and Technology, Department of Engineering, Greenville, NC 27858-4353. Offers biomedical engineering (MS). *Students:* 12 full-time (5 women), 4 part-time (1 woman); includes 6 minority (3 Black or African American, non-Hispanic/Latino; 2 Hispanic/Latino; 1 Two or more races, non-Hispanic/Latino), 1 international. Average age 25. 14 applicants, 86% accepted, 9 enrolled. *Unit head:* Dr. Hayden Griffen, Chair, 252-737-1026, E-mail: griffen@ecu.edu. *Application contact:* Dean of Graduate School, 252-328-6012, Fax: 252-328-6071, E-mail: gradschool@ecu.edu.

École Polytechnique de Montréal, Graduate Programs, Institute of Biomedical Engineering, Montréal, QC H3C 3A7, Canada. Offers M Sc A, PhD, DESS. M Sc A and PhD programs offered jointly with Université de Montréal. *Program availability:* Part-time. *Degree requirements:* For master's, one foreign language, thesis; for doctorate, one foreign language, thesis/dissertation. *Entrance requirements:* For master's, minimum GPA of 2.75; for doctorate, minimum GPA of 3.0. *Faculty research:* Cardiac electrophysiology, biomedical instrumentation, biomechanics, biomaterials, medical imagery.

Florida Agricultural and Mechanical University, Division of Graduate Studies, Research, and Continuing Education, FAMU-FSU College of Engineering, Department of Chemical and Biomedical Engineering, Tallahassee, FL 32307-3200. Offers biomedical engineering (MS, PhD); chemical engineering (MS, PhD). *Degree requirements:* For master's, thesis optional; for doctorate, thesis/dissertation, paper presentation at professional meeting. *Entrance requirements:* For master's, GRE General Test, minimum GPA of 3.3, letters of recommendation (3); for doctorate, minimum GPA of 3.3. Additional exam requirements/recommendations for international students: Required—TOEFL (minimum score 550 paper-based). *Faculty research:* Cellular signaling, cancer therapy, drug delivery, cellular and tissue engineering, brain physiology.

Florida Institute of Technology, College of Engineering, Program in Biomedical Engineering, Melbourne, FL 32901-6975. Offers MS, PhD. *Program availability:* Part-time. *Students:* 27 full-time (15 women), 11 part-time (4 women); includes 3 minority (2 Black or African American, non-Hispanic/Latino; 1 Hispanic/Latino), 21 international. Average age 26. 85 applicants, 47% accepted, 12 enrolled. In 2016, 9 master's awarded. Terminal master's awarded for partial completion of doctoral program. *Degree requirements:* For master's, thesis or supervised project with 6 credits of elective courses; for doctorate, comprehensive exam, thesis/dissertation, 42 credit hours beyond the master's degree, minimum of GPA of 3.2. *Entrance requirements:* For master's, GRE, 3 letters of recommendation, resume, statement of objectives; for doctorate, GRE, minimum GPA of 3.2, 3 letters of recommendation, resume, statement of objectives. Additional exam requirements/recommendations for international students: Required—TOEFL (minimum score 550 paper-based; 79 iBT). *Application deadline:* For fall admission, 4/1 priority date for international students; for spring admission, 9/30 for international students. Applications are processed on a rolling basis. Electronic applications accepted. *Expenses: Tuition:* Full-time $22,338; part-time $1241 per credit hour. *Required fees:* $250. Tuition and fees vary according to degree level, campus/location and program. *Financial support:* Research assistantships with tuition reimbursements, teaching assistantships with tuition reimbursements, career-related internships or fieldwork, institutionally sponsored loans, tuition waivers (partial), unspecified assistantships, and tuition remissions available. Support available to part-time students. Financial award application deadline: 3/1; financial award applicants required to submit FAFSA. *Faculty research:* Biosensors, biomechanics, short pulse lasers, bioactive materials, medical photonics. *Unit head:* Dr. Ted Conway, Department Head, 321-674-8491, Fax: 321-674-7270, E-mail: tconway@fit.edu. *Application contact:* Cheryl A. Brown, Associate Director of Graduate Admissions, 321-674-7581, Fax: 321-723-9468, E-mail: cbrown@fit.edu.
Website: http://coe.fit.edu/biomedical-engineering/

Florida International University, College of Engineering and Computing, Department of Biomedical Engineering, Miami, FL 33175. Offers MS, PhD. *Program availability:* Part-time, evening/weekend. *Faculty:* 12 full-time (2 women). *Students:* 46 full-time (19 women), 5 part-time (0 women); includes 23 minority (4 Black or African American, non-Hispanic/Latino; 2 Asian, non-Hispanic/Latino; 14 Hispanic/Latino; 3 Two or more races, non-Hispanic/Latino), 21 international. Average age 28. 85 applicants, 46% accepted, 16 enrolled. In 2016, 7 master's, 4 doctorates awarded. *Degree requirements:* For master's, thesis; for doctorate, comprehensive exam, thesis/dissertation. *Entrance requirements:* For master's, GRE General Test (minimum combined score 1000, verbal 350, quantitative 650), minimum GPA of 3.0; for doctorate, GRE General Test (minimum combined score 1150, verbal 450, quantitative 700), minimum GPA of 3.0, letter of intent, letters of recommendation. Additional exam requirements/recommendations for international students: Required—TOEFL (minimum score 550 paper-based; 80 iBT). *Application deadline:* For fall admission, 6/1 for domestic students, 4/1 for international students; for spring admission, 10/1 for domestic students, 9/1 for international students. Applications are processed on a rolling basis. Application fee: $30. Electronic applications accepted. *Expenses:* Tuition, state resident: full-time $8912; part-time $446 per credit hour. Tuition, nonresident: full-time $21,393; part-time $992 per credit hour. *Required fees:* $2185; $195 per semester. Tuition and fees vary according to program. *Financial support:* Institutionally sponsored loans, scholarships/grants, and unspecified assistantships available. Financial award application deadline: 3/1; financial award applicants required to submit FAFSA. *Faculty research:* Bioimaging and biosignal processing, bioinstrumentation, devices and sensors, biomaterials and bio-nanotechnology, cellular and tissue engineering. *Unit head:* Dr. Wei-Chiang Lin, Interim Chair, 305-348-6112, Fax: 305-348-6954, E-mail: wclin@fiu.edu. *Application contact:* Sara-Michelle Lemus, Engineering Admissions Officer, 305-348-1890, E-mail: grad_eng@fiu.edu. Website: http://cec.fiu.edu/

Florida State University, The Graduate School, FAMU-FSU College of Engineering, Department of Chemical and Biomedical Engineering, Tallahassee, FL 32310-6046. Offers biomedical engineering (MS, PhD); chemical engineering (MS, PhD). *Program availability:* Part-time. *Faculty:* 18 full-time (3 women). *Students:* 48 full-time (12 women); includes 4 minority (all Black or African American, non-Hispanic/Latino), 37 international. Average age 25. 84 applicants, 30% accepted, 8 enrolled. In 2016, 11 master's, 4 doctorates awarded. Terminal master's awarded for partial completion of doctoral program. *Degree requirements:* For master's, thesis (for some programs); for doctorate, comprehensive exam, thesis/dissertation, qualifying exam. *Entrance requirements:* For master's, GRE General Test (recommended minimum scores: verbal 151/8th percentile; quantitative: 158/75th percentile), BS in chemical engineering or other physical science/engineering, minimum GPA of 3.0; for doctorate, GRE General Test (recommended minimum scores: verbal 151/8th percentile; quantitative: 158/75th percentile), BS in chemical engineering or other physical science/engineering, minimum GPA of 3.0, or MS in chemical or biomedical engineering. Additional exam requirements/recommendations for international students: Required—TOEFL (minimum score 550 paper-based; 80 iBT), Michigan English Language Assessment Battery (minimum score 77); Recommended—IELTS (minimum score 6.5). *Application deadline:* For fall admission, 3/1 priority date for domestic students, 3/1 for international students; for spring admission, 10/1 for domestic and international students. Applications are processed on a rolling basis. Application fee: $30. Electronic applications accepted. *Expenses:* Contact institution. *Financial support:* In 2016–17, 33 students received support, including 4 fellowships with full tuition reimbursements available (averaging $21,500 per year), 14 research assistantships with full tuition reimbursements available (averaging $21,500 per year), 14 teaching assistantships with full tuition reimbursements available (averaging $21,500 per year); scholarships/grants and unspecified assistantships also available. Financial award application deadline: 3/1; financial award applicants required to submit FAFSA. *Faculty research:* Macromolecular transport and reaction; polymer characterization and processing; solid NMR-MRI for solid state spectroscopy and cell microscopy; protein, cell, and tissue engineering; electrochemical and fuel cell engineering. *Total annual research expenditures:* $1.2 million. *Unit head:* Dr. Teng Ma, Chair and Professor, 850-410-6149, Fax: 850-410-6150, E-mail: tma@fsu.edu. *Application contact:* Lisa Fowler, Office Administrator, 850-410-6151, Fax: 850-410-6150, E-mail: lfowler@fsu.edu.
Website: http://www.eng.famu.fsu.edu/cbe

The George Washington University, School of Engineering and Applied Science, Department of Biomedical Engineering, Washington, DC 20052. Offers biomedical engineering (MS, PhD); regulatory biomedical engineering (MS). MS in regulatory biomedical engineering offered in partnership with the School of Medicine and Health Sciences Regulatory Affairs Program. *Faculty:* 4 full-time (1 woman). *Students:* 30 full-time (19 women), 19 part-time (9 women); includes 14 minority (3 Black or African American, non-Hispanic/Latino; 7 Asian, non-Hispanic/Latino; 1 Hispanic/Latino; 3 Two or more races, non-Hispanic/Latino), 24 international. Average age 27. 128 applicants, 72% accepted, 20 enrolled. In 2016, 5 master's, 1 doctorate awarded. *Unit head:* Igor Efimov, Chair. *Application contact:* Adina Lav, Marketing, Recruiting and Admissions, 202-994-5827, Fax: 202-994-0909, E-mail: engineering@gwu.edu.

Georgia Institute of Technology, Graduate Studies, College of Engineering, Wallace H. Coulter Department of Biomedical Engineering, Atlanta, GA 30332-0001. Offers PhD, MD/PhD. PhD offered jointly with Emory University (Georgia) and Peking University (China). *Program availability:* Part-time. *Degree requirements:* For doctorate, thesis/dissertation. *Entrance requirements:* For doctorate, GRE. Additional exam requirements/recommendations for international students: Required—TOEFL (minimum score 600 paper-based; 100 iBT). Electronic applications accepted. *Expenses:* Contact institution. *Faculty research:* Biomechanics and tissue engineering, bioinstrumentation and medical imaging.

The Graduate Center, City University of New York, Graduate Studies, Program in Engineering, New York, NY 10016-4039. Offers biomedical engineering (PhD); chemical engineering (PhD); civil engineering (PhD); electrical engineering (PhD); mechanical engineering (PhD). *Degree requirements:* For doctorate, thesis/dissertation. *Entrance requirements:* For doctorate, GRE General Test. Additional exam requirements/recommendations for international students: Required—TOEFL. Electronic applications accepted.

Harvard University, Graduate School of Arts and Sciences, Department of Physics, Cambridge, MA 02138. Offers experimental physics (PhD); medical engineering/medical physics (PhD), including applied physics, engineering sciences, physics; theoretical physics (PhD). *Degree requirements:* For doctorate, thesis/dissertation, final exams, laboratory experience. *Entrance requirements:* For doctorate, GRE General Test, GRE Subject Test. Additional exam requirements/recommendations for international students: Required—TOEFL. *Faculty research:* Particle physics, condensed matter physics, atomic physics.

Illinois Institute of Technology, Graduate College, Armour College of Engineering, Department of Biomedical Engineering, Chicago, IL 60616. Offers MAS, MS, PhD. *Program availability:* Part-time. *Degree requirements:* For doctorate, comprehensive exam, thesis/dissertation. *Entrance requirements:* For master's and doctorate, GRE (minimum 1800 combined; 1200 quantitative and verbal; 3.0 analytical writing), minimum cumulative undergraduate GPA of 3.2. Electronic applications accepted. *Faculty research:* Cell and tissue engineering, medical imaging, neural engineering.

Indiana University–Purdue University Indianapolis, School of Engineering and Technology, Biomedical Engineering Program, Indianapolis, IN 46202. Offers MS, PhD. *Program availability:* Part-time, evening/weekend. *Degree requirements:* For master's, thesis optional. *Entrance requirements:* For master's, GRE, minimum B average; for doctorate, GRE General Test. Additional exam requirements/recommendations for international students: Required—TOEFL. *Expenses:* Contact institution.

Johns Hopkins University, Engineering Program for Professionals, Part-time Program in Applied Biomedical Engineering, Baltimore, MD 21218. Offers MS, Post-Master's Certificate. *Program availability:* Part-time, evening/weekend, 100% online, blended/

hybrid learning. *Faculty:* 1 full-time (0 women), 10 part-time/adjunct (3 women). *Students:* 2 full-time (0 women), 44 part-time (13 women); includes 15 minority (1 Black or African American, non-Hispanic/Latino; 7 Asian, non-Hispanic/Latino; 5 Hispanic/Latino; 2 Two or more races, non-Hispanic/Latino), 4 international. Average age 29. 55 applicants, 33% accepted, 13 enrolled. In 2016, 11 master's awarded. *Entrance requirements:* Additional exam requirements/recommendations for international students: Required—TOEFL (minimum score 600 paper-based; 100 iBT). *Application deadline:* Applications are processed on a rolling basis. Application fee: $75. Electronic applications accepted. *Unit head:* Dr. Eileen Haase, Program Chair, 443-778-6201, E-mail: ehaase1@jhu.edu. *Application contact:* Doug Schiller, Admissions Director, 410-516-2300, Fax: 410-579-8049, E-mail: schiller@jhu.edu.
Website: http://www.ep.jhu.edu

Johns Hopkins University, G. W. C. Whiting School of Engineering and School of Medicine, Department of Biomedical Engineering, Baltimore, MD 21205. Offers bioengineering innovation and design (MSE); biomedical engineering (MSE, PhD). *Faculty:* 21 full-time (4 women), 2 part-time/adjunct (0 women). *Students:* 246 full-time (92 women); includes 85 minority (5 Black or African American, non-Hispanic/Latino; 55 Asian, non-Hispanic/Latino; 14 Hispanic/Latino; 11 Two or more races, non-Hispanic/Latino), 73 international. Average age 25. 312 applicants, 29% accepted, 42 enrolled. In 2016, 33 master's, 29 doctorates awarded. Terminal master's awarded for partial completion of doctoral program. *Degree requirements:* For master's, thesis; for doctorate, comprehensive exam, thesis/dissertation. *Entrance requirements:* For master's and doctorate, GRE General Test, 3 letters of recommendation, statement of purpose, transcripts. Additional exam requirements/recommendations for international students: Required—TOEFL (minimum score 600 paper-based, 100 iBT) or IELTS (7). *Application deadline:* For fall admission, 1/6 for domestic and international students. Application fee: $75. Electronic applications accepted. *Financial support:* In 2016–17, 224 students received support, including 57 fellowships with partial tuition reimbursements available (averaging $30,396 per year), 134 research assistantships with partial tuition reimbursements available (averaging $30,396 per year), 33 teaching assistantships (averaging $8,937 per year); Federal Work-Study, institutionally sponsored loans, scholarships/grants, health care benefits, tuition waivers (full), and unspecified assistantships also available. Financial award application deadline: 1/15. *Faculty research:* Systems neuroscience and neuroengineering, molecular and cellular systems biology, biomedical imaging, cell and tissue engineering, cardiovascular systems engineering. *Total annual research expenditures:* $18.4 million. *Unit head:* Dr. Les Tung, Interim Director, 410-955-3132, Fax: 410-516-4771, E-mail: ltung@jhu.edu. *Application contact:* Samuel Bourne, Academic Program Administrator, 410-516-8482, Fax: 410-516-4771, E-mail: sbourne@jhu.edu.
Website: http://www.bme.jhu.edu/

Lawrence Technological University, College of Engineering, Southfield, MI 48075-1058. Offers architectural engineering (MS); automotive engineering (MS); biomedical engineering (MS); civil engineering (MA, MS, PhD), including environmental engineering (MS), geotechnical engineering (MS), structural engineering (MS), transportation engineering (MS), water resource engineering (MS); construction engineering management (MA); electrical and computer engineering (MS); engineering management (MA); engineering technology (MS); fire engineering (MS); industrial engineering (MS), including healthcare; manufacturing systems (ME); mechanical engineering (MS, DE, PhD), including manufacturing (DE), solid mechanics (MS), thermal-fluids (MS); mechatronic systems engineering (MS). *Program availability:* Part-time, evening/weekend. *Faculty:* 24 full-time (5 women), 26 part-time/adjunct (2 women). *Students:* 22 full-time (7 women), 588 part-time (81 women); includes 23 minority (11 Black or African American, non-Hispanic/Latino; 4 Asian, non-Hispanic/Latino; 7 Hispanic/Latino; 1 Two or more races, non-Hispanic/Latino), 469 international. Average age 27. 1,186 applicants, 39% accepted, 99 enrolled. In 2016, 293 master's, 3 doctorates awarded. Terminal master's awarded for partial completion of doctoral program. *Degree requirements:* For master's, thesis optional; for doctorate, comprehensive exam, thesis/dissertation optional. *Entrance requirements:* Additional exam requirements/recommendations for international students: Required—TOEFL (minimum score 550 paper-based; 79 iBT), IELTS (minimum score 6.5). *Application deadline:* For fall admission, 5/22 for international students; for spring admission, 10/11 for international students; for summer admission, 2/16 for international students. Applications are processed on a rolling basis. Application fee: $50. Electronic applications accepted. *Expenses: Tuition:* Full-time $14,868; part-time $1062 per credit. *Required fees:* $75 per semester. Tuition and fees vary according to campus/location. *Financial support:* In 2016–17, 25 students received support, including 5 research assistantships with full tuition reimbursements available; unspecified assistantships also available. Financial award application deadline: 4/1; financial award applicants required to submit FAFSA. *Faculty research:* Carbon fiber reinforced polymer reinforced concrete structures; low impact storm water management solutions; vehicle battery energy management; wireless communication; entrepreneurial mindset and engineering. *Total annual research expenditures:* $1.7 million. *Unit head:* Dr. Nabil Grace, Dean, 248-204-2500, Fax: 248-204-2509, E-mail: engrdean@ltu.edu. *Application contact:* Jane Rohrback, Director of Admissions, 248-204-3160, Fax: 248-204-2228, E-mail: admissions@ltu.edu.
Website: http://www.ltu.edu/engineering/index.asp

Louisiana Tech University, Graduate School, College of Engineering and Science, Department of Biomedical Engineering, Ruston, LA 71272. Offers PhD. *Program availability:* Part-time. Terminal master's awarded for partial completion of doctoral program. *Degree requirements:* For doctorate, thesis/dissertation. *Entrance requirements:* For doctorate, minimum graduate GPA of 3.25 (with MS) or GRE General Test. Additional exam requirements/recommendations for international students: Required—TOEFL. *Application deadline:* For fall admission, 8/1 for domestic students; for spring admission, 2/1 for domestic students. Applications are processed on a rolling basis. Application fee: $20 ($30 for international students). *Financial support:* Fellowships, research assistantships, teaching assistantships, Federal Work-Study, and unspecified assistantships available. Financial award application deadline: 4/1. *Faculty research:* Microbiosensors and microcirculatory transport, speech recognition, artificial intelligence, rehabilitation engineering, bioelectromagnetics. *Unit head:* Emily J. Born, Academic Director, 318-257-5206, Fax: 318-257-5000. *Application contact:* Marilyn J. Robinson, Assistant to the Dean, 318-257-2924, Fax: 318-257-4487.
Website: http://coes.latech.edu/biomedical-engineering/

Marquette University, Graduate School, College of Engineering, Department of Biomedical Engineering, Milwaukee, WI 53201-1881. Offers biocomputing (ME); bioimaging (ME); bioinstrumentation (ME); bioinstrumentation/computers (MS, PhD); biomechanics (ME); biomechanics/biomaterials (MS, PhD); biorehabilitation (ME); functional imaging (PhD); healthcare technologies management (MS); rehabilitation bioengineering (PhD); systems physiology (MS, PhD). *Program availability:* Part-time, evening/weekend. *Faculty:* 17 full-time (6 women), 8 part-time/adjunct (4 women). *Students:* 37 full-time (14 women), 16 part-time (6 women); includes 8 minority (1 Black or African American, non-Hispanic/Latino; 6 Asian, non-Hispanic/Latino; 1 Hispanic/Latino), 6 international. Average age 26. 83 applicants, 59% accepted, 14 enrolled. In 2016, 15 master's, 4 doctorates awarded. Terminal master's awarded for partial completion of doctoral program. *Degree requirements:* For master's, comprehensive exam, thesis; for doctorate, comprehensive exam, thesis/dissertation, dissertation defense, qualifying exam. *Entrance requirements:* For master's, GRE General Test, minimum GPA of 3.0, official transcripts from all current and previous colleges/universities except Marquette, three letters of recommendation, brief statement of purpose that includes proposed area of research specialization, interview with program director (for ME), one year of post-baccalaureate professional work experience; for doctorate, GRE General Test, minimum GPA of 3.0, official transcripts from all current and previous colleges/universities except Marquette, three letters of recommendation, brief statement of purpose that includes proposed area of research specialization. Additional exam requirements/recommendations for international students: Required—TOEFL (minimum score 530 paper-based). *Application deadline:* For fall admission, 2/15 priority date for domestic students; for spring admission, 11/15 priority date for domestic students. Applications are processed on a rolling basis. Application fee: $50. Electronic applications accepted. *Financial support:* Fellowships, research assistantships, teaching assistantships, scholarships/grants, health care benefits, tuition waivers (partial), and unspecified assistantships available. Support available to part-time students. Financial award application deadline: 2/15. *Faculty research:* Cell and organ physiology, signal processing, gait analysis, orthopedic rehabilitation engineering, telemedicine. *Total annual research expenditures:* $2.1 million. *Unit head:* Dr. Lars Olson, Interim Chair, 414-288-3539. *Application contact:* Dr. Robert Scheidt, 414-288-6125. Website: http://www.marquette.edu/engineering/biomedical/

Massachusetts Institute of Technology, School of Engineering, Department of Biological Engineering, Cambridge, MA 02139. Offers applied biosciences (PhD, Sc D); bioengineering (PhD, Sc D); biological engineering (PhD, Sc D); biomedical engineering (M Eng); toxicology (SM); SM/MBA. *Faculty:* 34 full-time (5 women). *Students:* 140 full-time (60 women); includes 54 minority (2 Black or African American, non-Hispanic/Latino; 36 Asian, non-Hispanic/Latino; 9 Hispanic/Latino; 7 Two or more races, non-Hispanic/Latino), 24 international. Average age 26. 513 applicants, 8% accepted, 23 enrolled. In 2016, 3 master's, 19 doctorates awarded. Terminal master's awarded for partial completion of doctoral program. *Degree requirements:* For master's, thesis; for doctorate, comprehensive exam, thesis/dissertation. *Entrance requirements:* For master's and doctorate, GRE General Test. Additional exam requirements/recommendations for international students: Required—IELTS. *Application deadline:* For fall admission, 12/15 for domestic and international students. Application fee: $75. Electronic applications accepted. *Expenses: Tuition:* Full-time $46,400; part-time $725 per credit. One-time fee: $312 full-time. Full-time tuition and fees vary according to course load and program. *Financial support:* In 2016–17, 131 students received support, including fellowships (averaging $41,900 per year), 80 research assistantships (averaging $40,900 per year), 1 teaching assistantship (averaging $40,600 per year); Federal Work-Study, institutionally sponsored loans, scholarships/grants, traineeships, health care benefits, unspecified assistantships, and resident tutors also available. Support available to part-time students. Financial award application deadline: 5/1; financial award applicants required to submit FAFSA. *Faculty research:* Biomaterials; biophysics; cell and tissue engineering; computational modeling of biological and physiological systems; discovery and delivery of molecular therapeutics; new tools for genomics; functional genomics; proteomics and glycomics; macromolecular biochemistry and biophysics; molecular, cell and tissue biomechanics; synthetic biology; systems biology. *Total annual research expenditures:* $55 million. *Unit head:* Prof. Douglas A. Lauffenburger, Department Head, 617-452-4086. *Application contact:* 617-253-1712, Fax: 617-253-5208, E-mail: be-acad@mit.edu.
Website: http://be.mit.edu

Massachusetts Institute of Technology, School of Engineering, Harvard-MIT Health Sciences and Technology Program, Cambridge, MA 02139. Offers health sciences and technology (SM, PhD, Sc D), including bioastronautics (PhD, Sc D), bioinformatics and integrative genomics (PhD, Sc D), medical engineering and medical physics (PhD, Sc D), speech and hearing bioscience and technology (PhD, Sc D). *Faculty:* 132 full-time (23 women). *Students:* 268 full-time (121 women), 7 part-time (2 women); includes 78 minority (1 Black or African American, non-Hispanic/Latino; 1 American Indian or Alaska Native, non-Hispanic/Latino; 58 Asian, non-Hispanic/Latino; 15 Hispanic/Latino; 3 Two or more races, non-Hispanic/Latino), 51 international. Average age 26. 223 applicants, 14% accepted, 21 enrolled. In 2016, 1 master's, 20 doctorates awarded. Terminal master's awarded for partial completion of doctoral program. *Degree requirements:* For doctorate, comprehensive exam, thesis/dissertation. *Entrance requirements:* For doctorate, GRE General Test. Additional exam requirements/recommendations for international students: Required—TOEFL, IELTS. *Application deadline:* For fall admission, 12/15 for domestic and international students. Application fee: $75. Electronic applications accepted. *Expenses: Tuition:* Full-time $46,400; part-time $725 per credit. One-time fee: $312 full-time. Full-time tuition and fees vary according to course load and program. *Financial support:* In 2016–17, 132 students received support, including fellowships (averaging $36,300 per year), 60 research assistantships (averaging $37,800 per year), 3 teaching assistantships (averaging $37,400 per year); Federal Work-Study, institutionally sponsored loans, scholarships/grants, traineeships, health care benefits, and unspecified assistantships also available. Support available to part-time students. Financial award application deadline: 5/1; financial award applicants required to submit FAFSA. *Faculty research:* Biomedical imaging, drug delivery, medical devices, medical diagnostics, regenerative biomedical technologies. *Unit head:* Prof. Emery N. Brown, Director, 617-452-4091. *Application contact:* 617-253-3609, E-mail: hst-phd-admissions@mit.edu.
Website: http://hst.mit.edu/

Mayo Clinic Graduate School of Biomedical Sciences, Graduate Programs in Biomedical Sciences, Program in Biomedical Engineering, Rochester, MN 55905. Offers PhD. *Degree requirements:* For doctorate, oral defense of dissertation, qualifying oral and written exam. *Entrance requirements:* For doctorate, GRE, 1 year of chemistry, biology, calculus, and physics. Additional exam requirements/recommendations for international students: Required—TOEFL. Electronic applications accepted.

McGill University, Faculty of Graduate and Postdoctoral Studies, Faculty of Medicine, Department of Biomedical Engineering, Montréal, QC H3A 2T5, Canada. Offers M Eng, PhD.

Mercer University, Graduate Studies, Macon Campus, School of Engineering, Macon, GA 31207. Offers biomedical engineering (MSE); computer engineering (MSE); electrical engineering (MSE); engineering management (MSE); environmental engineering (MSE); environmental systems (MS); mechanical engineering (MSE); software engineering (MSE); software systems (MS); technical communications management (MS); technical management (MS). *Program availability:* Part-time-only, evening/weekend, online learning. *Faculty:* 21 full-time (5 women), 1 part-time/adjunct (0 women). *Students:* 44 full-time (9 women), 60 part-time (12 women); includes 14 minority (3 Black or African American, non-Hispanic/Latino; 1 American Indian or Alaska Native, non-Hispanic/Latino; 4 Asian, non-Hispanic/Latino; 3 Hispanic/Latino; 3 Two or more races, non-Hispanic/Latino), 2 international. Average age 27. In 2016, 64 master's awarded. *Degree requirements:* For master's, thesis or alternative. *Entrance requirements:* For master's, GRE (minimum score 300), minimum undergraduate GPA of 3.0. Additional exam requirements/recommendations for international students: Required—TOEFL (minimum score 550 paper-based; 80 iBT). *Application deadline:* For fall admission, 4/1 priority date for domestic and international students; for spring

admission, 11/1 priority date for domestic and international students. Applications are processed on a rolling basis. Application fee: $75. *Expenses:* $865 per credit hour. *Financial support:* Applicants required to submit FAFSA. *Faculty research:* Designing prostheses and orthotics, oxygen transfer and limitations in biological systems, low-cost groundwater development, lung airway and transport, autonomous mobile robots. *Unit head:* Dr. Laura W. Lackey, Dean, 478-301-4106, Fax: 478-301-5593, E-mail: lackey_l@mercer.edu. *Application contact:* Dr. Richard O. Mines, Jr., Program Director, 478-301-2347, Fax: 478-301-5433, E-mail: mines_ro@mercer.edu.
Website: http://engineering.mercer.edu/

Michigan Technological University, Graduate School, College of Engineering, Department of Biomedical Engineering, Houghton, MI 49931. Offers MS, PhD. *Program availability:* Part-time. *Faculty:* 16 full-time (6 women), 5 part-time/adjunct. *Students:* 31 full-time (13 women), 5 part-time; includes 3 minority (2 Black or African American, non-Hispanic/Latino; 1 Two or more races, non-Hispanic/Latino), 25 international. Average age 25. 127 applicants, 24% accepted, 12 enrolled. In 2016, 11 master's, 5 doctorates awarded. *Degree requirements:* For master's, comprehensive exam (for some programs), thesis (for some programs); for doctorate, comprehensive exam, thesis/dissertation. *Entrance requirements:* For master's, GRE (recommended for students with a Michigan Tech degree), statement of purpose, personal statement, official transcripts, 3 letters of recommendation, resume/curriculum vitae; for doctorate, GRE, statement of purpose, personal statement, official transcripts, 3 letters of recommendation, resume/curriculum vitae. Additional exam requirements/recommendations for international students: Required—TOEFL (recommended minimum score 110 iBT) or IELTS. *Application deadline:* Applications are processed on a rolling basis. Electronic applications accepted. *Expenses:* Contact institution. *Financial support:* In 2016–17, 28 students received support, including 2 fellowships with tuition reimbursements available (averaging $15,242 per year), 8 research assistantships with tuition reimbursements available (averaging $15,242 per year), 6 teaching assistantships with tuition reimbursements available (averaging $15,242 per year); career-related internships or fieldwork, Federal Work-Study, scholarships/grants, health care benefits, unspecified assistantships, and cooperative program also available. Financial award applicants required to submit FAFSA. *Faculty research:* Biomaterials/tissue engineering, physiology measurement and biosensors, biomechanics, mechanotransduction, biomedical optics, micro devices. *Total annual research expenditures:* $988,516. *Unit head:* Dr. Sean J. Kirkpatrick, Chair, 906-487-2167, Fax: 906-487-1717, E-mail: sjkirkpa@mtu.edu. *Application contact:* Stacey L. Sedar, Department Coordinator, 906-487-2772, Fax: 906-487-1717, E-mail: slsedar@mtu.edu.
Website: http://www.mtu.edu/biomedical/

Mississippi State University, College of Agriculture and Life Sciences, Department of Agricultural and Biological Engineering, Mississippi State, MS 39762. Offers biological engineering (MS, PhD); biomedical engineering (MS, PhD). *Faculty:* 17 full-time (6 women). *Students:* 29 full-time (17 women), 6 part-time (0 women); includes 6 minority (3 Black or African American, non-Hispanic/Latino; 1 Asian, non-Hispanic/Latino; 2 Two or more races, non-Hispanic/Latino), 7 international. Average age 27. 27 applicants, 48% accepted, 9 enrolled. In 2016, 3 master's, 7 doctorates awarded. *Degree requirements:* For master's, thesis (for some programs); for doctorate, thesis/dissertation, preliminary exam. *Entrance requirements:* For master's, GRE General Test, minimum undergraduate GPA of 2.75 (3.0 for biomedical engineering); for doctorate, GRE General Test, minimum GPA of 3.0 (biomedical engineering). Additional exam requirements/recommendations for international students: Required—TOEFL (minimum score 550 paper-based; 79 iBT); Recommended—IELTS (minimum score 6.5). *Application deadline:* For fall admission, 7/1 for domestic students, 5/1 for international students; for spring admission, 11/1 for domestic students, 9/1 for international students. Applications are processed on a rolling basis. Application fee: $60. Electronic applications accepted. *Expenses:* Tuition, state resident: full-time $7670; part-time $852.50 per credit hour. Tuition, nonresident: full-time $20,790; part-time $2310.50 per credit hour. Part-time tuition and fees vary according to course load. *Financial support:* In 2016–17, 12 research assistantships with partial tuition reimbursements (averaging $15,733 per year) were awarded; Federal Work-Study, institutionally sponsored loans, and unspecified assistantships also available. Financial award application deadline: 4/1; financial award applicants required to submit FAFSA. *Faculty research:* Bioenvironmental engineering, bioinstrumentation, biomechanics/biomaterials, precision agriculture, tissue engineering, ergonomics human factors, biosimulation and modeling. *Total annual research expenditures:* $3.1 million. *Unit head:* Dr. Jonathan Pote, Department Head and Professor, 662-325-3570, Fax: 662-325-3853, E-mail: jpote@abe.msstate.edu. *Application contact:* Marina Hunt, Admissions Assistant, 662-325-5188, E-mail: mhunt@grad.msstate.edu.
Website: http://www.abe.msstate.edu/

New Jersey Institute of Technology, Newark College of Engineering, Newark, NJ 07102. Offers biomedical engineering (MS, PhD); chemical engineering (MS, PhD); computer engineering (MS, PhD); electrical engineering (MS, PhD); engineering management (MS); environmental engineering (PhD); healthcare systems management (MS); industrial engineering (MS, PhD); Internet engineering (MS); manufacturing engineering (MS); mechanical engineering (MS, PhD); occupational safety and health engineering (MS); pharmaceutical bioprocessing (MS); pharmaceutical engineering (MS); pharmaceutical systems management (MS); power and energy systems (MS); telecommunications (MS); transportation (MS, PhD). *Program availability:* Part-time, evening/weekend. *Faculty:* 146 full-time (21 women), 119 part-time/adjunct (10 women). *Students:* 804 full-time (191 women), 550 part-time (129 women); includes 357 minority (82 Black or African American, non-Hispanic/Latino; 1 American Indian or Alaska Native, non-Hispanic/Latino; 138 Asian, non-Hispanic/Latino; 114 Hispanic/Latino; 22 Two or more races, non-Hispanic/Latino), 675 international. Average age 27. 2,959 applicants, 51% accepted, 442 enrolled. In 2016, 595 master's, 29 doctorates awarded. Terminal master's awarded for partial completion of doctoral program. *Degree requirements:* For master's, thesis optional; for doctorate, thesis/dissertation. *Entrance requirements:* For master's, GRE General Test; for doctorate, GRE General Test, minimum graduate GPA of 3.5. Additional exam requirements/recommendations for international students: Required—TOEFL (minimum score 550 paper-based; 79 iBT). *Application deadline:* For fall admission, 6/1 priority date for domestic students, 5/1 priority date for international students; for spring admission, 11/15 priority date for domestic and international students. Applications are processed on a rolling basis. Application fee: $75. Electronic applications accepted. *Expenses:* Contact institution. *Financial support:* In 2016–17, 172 students received support, including 1 fellowship (averaging $1,528 per year), 79 research assistantships (averaging $13,336 per year), 92 teaching assistantships (averaging $20,619 per year); scholarships/grants also available. Financial award application deadline: 1/15. *Faculty research:* Nonlinear signal processing, intelligent medical image analysis, calibration issues in coherent localization, computer-aided design, neural network for tool wear measurement. *Total annual research expenditures:* $11.1 million. *Unit head:* Dr. Moshe Kam, Dean, 973-596-5534, E-mail: moshe.kam@njit.edu. *Application contact:* Stephen Eck, Director of Admissions, 973-596-3300, Fax: 973-596-3461, E-mail: admissions@njit.edu.
Website: http://engineering.njit.edu/

New York University, Polytechnic School of Engineering, Department of Chemical and Biomolecular Engineering, Major in Biomedical Engineering, New York, NY 10012-1019. Offers MS, PhD. *Degree requirements:* For master's, comprehensive exam (for some programs), thesis (for some programs); for doctorate, comprehensive exam, thesis/dissertation. *Entrance requirements:* Additional exam requirements/recommendations for international students: Required—TOEFL (minimum score 550 paper-based; 80 iBT); Recommended—IELTS (minimum score 6.5). Electronic applications accepted.

North Carolina State University, Graduate School, College of Engineering, Joint Department of Biomedical Engineering UNC-Chapel Hill and NC State, Raleigh, NC 27695. Offers MS, PhD. Programs offered jointly with the University of North Carolina at Chapel Hill. Terminal master's awarded for partial completion of doctoral program. *Degree requirements:* For master's, comprehensive exam, thesis, research laboratory experience; for doctorate, one foreign language, comprehensive exam, thesis/dissertation, written and oral examinations, dissertation defense, teaching experience, research laboratory experience. *Entrance requirements:* For master's and doctorate, GRE General Test. Additional exam requirements/recommendations for international students: Required—TOEFL. Electronic applications accepted.

Northwestern University, McCormick School of Engineering and Applied Science, Department of Biomedical Engineering, Evanston, IL 60208. Offers MS, PhD. Admissions and degrees offered through The Graduate School. *Program availability:* Part-time. Terminal master's awarded for partial completion of doctoral program. *Degree requirements:* For master's, comprehensive exam, thesis (for some programs); for doctorate, comprehensive exam, thesis/dissertation. *Entrance requirements:* For master's and doctorate, GRE General Test. Additional exam requirements/recommendations for international students: Required—TOEFL (minimum score 577 paper-based; 90 iBT), IELTS (minimum score 7). Electronic applications accepted. *Faculty research:* Imaging and biophotonics; biomaterials and regenerative medicine; neural engineering and rehabilitation.

The Ohio State University, Graduate School, College of Engineering, Department of Biomedical Engineering, Columbus, OH 43210. Offers MS, PhD. *Program availability:* Evening/weekend. *Faculty:* 25. *Students:* 73 full-time (27 women), 1 part-time. Average age 26. In 2016, 18 master's, 8 doctorates awarded. *Degree requirements:* For master's, thesis optional; for doctorate, thesis/dissertation. *Entrance requirements:* For master's and doctorate, GRE General Test. Additional exam requirements/recommendations for international students: Required—TOEFL (minimum score 550 paper-based; 79 iBT), Michigan English Language Assessment Battery (minimum score 82); Recommended—IELTS (minimum score 7). *Application deadline:* For fall admission, 12/13 priority date for domestic students, 11/29 priority date for international students; for spring admission, 11/1 for domestic and international students. Applications are processed on a rolling basis. Application fee: $60 ($70 for international students). Electronic applications accepted. *Financial support:* Fellowships with tuition reimbursements, research assistantships with tuition reimbursements, career-related internships or fieldwork, Federal Work-Study, and institutionally sponsored loans available. Support available to part-time students. *Unit head:* Dr. Richard T. Hart, Chair, 614-292-1285, E-mail: hart.322@osu.edu. *Application contact:* Graduate and Professional Admissions, 614-292-9444, Fax: 614-292-3895, E-mail: gpadmissions@osu.edu. Website: http://bme.osu.edu

Ohio University, Graduate College, Russ College of Engineering and Technology, Department of Chemical and Biomolecular Engineering, Program in Biomedical Engineering, Athens, OH 45701-2979. Offers MS. *Program availability:* Part-time. *Degree requirements:* For master's, thesis. *Entrance requirements:* For master's, GRE General Test. Additional exam requirements/recommendations for international students: Required—TOEFL (minimum score 590 paper-based; 96 iBT), IELTS (minimum score 7). *Application deadline:* For fall admission, 2/1 priority date for domestic and international students. Applications are processed on a rolling basis. Application fee: $50 ($55 for international students). Electronic applications accepted. *Financial support:* Fellowships with full tuition reimbursements, research assistantships with full tuition reimbursements, and institutionally sponsored loans available. Financial award application deadline: 2/1. *Faculty research:* Molecular mechanisms of human disease, molecular therapeutics, biomedical information analysis and management, image analysis, biomechanics. *Unit head:* Dr. Dennis Irwin, Dean, 740-593-1474, E-mail: irwind@ohio.edu. *Application contact:* Tom Riggs, Biomedical Engineering Assistant, 740-597-2797, Fax: 740-593-0873, E-mail: biomed@ohio.edu.
Website: http://www.ohio.edu/engineering/biomedical

Ohio University, Graduate College, Russ College of Engineering and Technology, Department of Mechanical Engineering, Athens, OH 45701-2979. Offers biomedical engineering (MS); mechanical engineering (MS), including CAD/CAM, design, energy, manufacturing, materials, robotics, thermofluids. *Program availability:* Part-time. In 2016, 8 master's awarded. *Degree requirements:* For master's, comprehensive exam (for some programs), thesis. *Entrance requirements:* For master's, GRE, BS in engineering or science, minimum GPA of 2.8. Additional exam requirements/recommendations for international students: Required—TOEFL (minimum score 550 paper-based; 80 iBT) or IELTS (minimum score 6.5). *Application deadline:* For fall admission, 2/15 priority date for domestic and international students. Applications are processed on a rolling basis. Application fee: $50 ($55 for international students). Electronic applications accepted. *Financial support:* Research assistantships with tuition reimbursements, teaching assistantships with tuition reimbursements, career-related internships or fieldwork, Federal Work-Study, institutionally sponsored loans, tuition waivers (full and partial), and unspecified assistantships available. Financial award application deadline: 2/15; financial award applicants required to submit FAFSA. *Faculty research:* Biomedical, energy and the environment, materials and manufacturing, bioengineering. *Unit head:* Dr. Greg Kremer, Chairman, 740-593-1561, Fax: 740-593-0476, E-mail: kremer@bobcat.ent.ohiou.edu. *Application contact:* Dr. Frank F. Kraft, Graduate Chairman, 740-597-1478, Fax: 740-593-0476, E-mail: kraft@ohio.edu. Website: http://www.ohio.edu/mechanical

Old Dominion University, Frank Batten College of Engineering and Technology, Program in Biomedical Engineering, Norfolk, VA 23529. Offers ME, MS, PhD. *Program availability:* Part-time, evening/weekend. *Faculty:* 3 full-time (0 women). *Students:* 13 full-time (6 women), 5 part-time (1 woman); includes 3 minority (1 Asian, non-Hispanic/Latino; 2 Two or more races, non-Hispanic/Latino), 3 international. Average age 27. 10 applicants, 90% accepted, 5 enrolled. In 2016, 1 doctorate awarded. Terminal master's awarded for partial completion of doctoral program. *Degree requirements:* For master's, thesis (for some programs); for doctorate, thesis/dissertation, candidacy exam. *Entrance requirements:* For master's, GRE, master's degree, minimum graduate GPA of 3.0, two letters of recommendation, statement of purpose; for doctorate, GRE, master's degree, minimum graduate GPA of 3.5, three letters of recommendation, statement of purpose. Additional exam requirements/recommendations for international students: Required—TOEFL (minimum score 550 paper-based). *Application deadline:* For fall admission, 6/1 for domestic students, 2/15 priority date for international students; for spring admission, 11/1 for domestic students, 10/1 for international students. Applications are processed on a rolling basis. Application fee: $50. Electronic applications accepted. *Expenses:* Tuition, state resident: full-time $8604; part-time $478 per credit hour. Tuition, nonresident: full-time $21,510; part-time $1195 per credit hour. *Required fees:* $66 per semester. Tuition and fees vary according to campus/location, program and reciprocity agreements. *Financial support:* In 2016–17, 9 students received support. Unspecified

assistantships available. Financial award applicants required to submit FAFSA. *Faculty research:* Cellular and molecular bioengineering, cardiovascular engineering, musculoskeletal biomechanics, neural engineering, systems biology and computational bioengineering. *Unit head:* Dr. Dean Krusienski, Graduate Program Director, 757-683-3752, Fax: 757-683-3220, E-mail: dkrusien@odu.edu.
Website: https://www.odu.edu/eng/programs/biomedical

Oregon Health & Science University, School of Medicine, Graduate Programs in Medicine, Department of Biomedical Engineering, Portland, OR 97239-3098. Offers PhD. *Program availability:* Part-time. *Faculty:* 28 full-time (13 women), 5 part-time/adjunct (0 women). *Students:* 25 full-time (14 women), 2 part-time (1 woman); includes 8 minority (5 Asian, non-Hispanic/Latino; 2 Hispanic/Latino; 1 Two or more races, non-Hispanic/Latino), 6 international. Average age 28. 26 applicants, 3 enrolled. In 2016, 4 doctorates awarded. *Degree requirements:* For doctorate, comprehensive exam, thesis/dissertation, qualifying exam. *Entrance requirements:* For doctorate, GRE General Test (minimum scores: 153 Verbal/148 Quantitative/4.5 Analytical). Additional exam requirements/recommendations for international students: Required—IELTS or TOEFL. *Application deadline:* For fall admission, 1/15 for domestic students, 1/15 priority date for international students; for winter admission, 10/15 for domestic students, 9/15 for international students; for spring admission, 1/15 for domestic students, 12/15 for international students. Applications are processed on a rolling basis. Application fee: $70. Electronic applications accepted. *Financial support:* Health care benefits, tuition waivers (full), and full-tuition and stipends (for PhD students) available. Financial award applicants required to submit FAFSA. *Faculty research:* Blood cells in cancer and cancer biology, smart homes and machine learning, computational mechanics and multiscale modeling, tissue optics and biophotonics, nanomedicine and Nano biotechnology. *Unit head:* Dr. Monica Hinds, Program Director, 503-418-9309, E-mail: hindsm@ohsu.edu. *Application contact:* Nermina Radaslic, Administrative Coordinator, 503-418-9462, E-mail: radaslic@ohsu.edu.

Purdue University, College of Engineering, Weldon School of Biomedical Engineering, West Lafayette, IN 47907-2032. Offers MSBME, PhD, MD/PhD. Degree programs offered jointly with School of Mechanical Engineering, School of Electrical and Computer Engineering, and School of Chemical Engineering. *Faculty:* 53. *Students:* 90. In 2016, 8 master's, 13 doctorates awarded. *Degree requirements:* For master's, thesis optional; for doctorate, thesis/dissertation. *Entrance requirements:* For master's and doctorate, GRE General Test, minimum GPA of 3.25. *Application deadline:* For fall admission, 12/15 priority date for domestic and international students; for spring admission, 10/31 priority date for domestic students, 10/1 priority date for international students. Applications are processed on a rolling basis. Application fee: $60 ($75 for international students). Electronic applications accepted. *Financial support:* Fellowships with full and partial tuition reimbursements, research assistantships with full and partial tuition reimbursements, teaching assistantships with full and partial tuition reimbursements, scholarships/grants, health care benefits, and unspecified assistantships available. Financial award applicants required to submit FAFSA. *Faculty research:* Engineered biomaterials and biomechanics, imaging, instrumentation, quantitative cellular and systems engineering. *Unit head:* Dr. George R. Wodicka, Head of Biomedical Engineering. *Application contact:* Vickie Maris, Graduate Programs Director, E-mail: weldonbmegrad@purdue.edu.
Website: https://engineering.purdue.edu/BME

Rensselaer Polytechnic Institute, Graduate School, School of Engineering, Program in Biomedical Engineering, Troy, NY 12180-3590. Offers MS, D Eng, PhD. *Faculty:* 18 full-time (4 women), 1 part-time/adjunct (0 women). *Students:* 47 full-time (16 women); includes 9 minority (2 Black or African American, non-Hispanic/Latino; 6 Asian, non-Hispanic/Latino; 1 Hispanic/Latino), 9 international. Average age 25. 130 applicants, 38% accepted, 7 enrolled. In 2016, 9 master's, 3 doctorates awarded. Terminal master's awarded for partial completion of doctoral program. *Degree requirements:* For master's, thesis optional; for doctorate, thesis/dissertation. *Entrance requirements:* For master's and doctorate, GRE. Additional exam requirements/recommendations for international students: Required—TOEFL (minimum score 570 paper-based; 88 iBT), IELTS (minimum score 6.5), PTE (minimum score 60). *Application deadline:* For fall admission, 1/1 priority date for domestic and international students; for spring admission, 8/15 priority date for domestic and international students. Applications are processed on a rolling basis. Application fee: $75. Electronic applications accepted. *Expenses: Tuition:* Full-time $49,520; part-time $2060 per credit hour. *Required fees:* $2617. *Financial support:* In 2016–17, research assistantships with full tuition reimbursements (averaging $22,000 per year), teaching assistantships with full tuition reimbursements (averaging $22,000 per year) were awarded; fellowships also available. Financial award application deadline: 1/1. *Faculty research:* Biomolecular science and engineering, biomedical imaging, musculoskeletal engineering, neural engineering, systems biology and bio computation, vascular engineering. *Unit head:* Dr. Deanna Thompson, Graduate Program Director, 518-276-6293, E-mail: thompd4@rpi.edu. *Application contact:* Office of Graduate Admissions, 518-276-6216, E-mail: gradadmissions@rpi.edu.
Website: http://www.bme.rpi.edu/

Rice University, Graduate Programs, George R. Brown School of Engineering, Department of Chemical and Biomolecular Engineering, Houston, TX 77251-1892. Offers chemical and biomolecular engineering (MS, PhD); chemical engineering (M Ch E). *Program availability:* Part-time. *Degree requirements:* For master's, thesis (for some programs); for doctorate, thesis/dissertation. *Entrance requirements:* For master's and doctorate, GRE General Test, minimum GPA of 3.0. Additional exam requirements/recommendations for international students: Required—TOEFL (minimum score 600 paper-based; 90 iBT). Electronic applications accepted. *Faculty research:* Thermodynamics, phase equilibria, rheology, fluid mechanics, polymers, biomedical engineering, interfacial phenomena, process control, petroleum engineering, reaction engineering and catalysis, biomaterials, metabolic engineering.

Rose-Hulman Institute of Technology, Faculty of Engineering and Applied Sciences, Department of Biology and Biomedical Engineering, Terre Haute, IN 47803-3999. Offers MS, MD/MS. *Program availability:* Part-time. *Faculty:* 11 full-time (6 women). *Students:* 1 (woman) full-time; minority (Hispanic/Latino). Average age 24. 7 applicants, 71% accepted. In 2016, 1 master's awarded. *Degree requirements:* For master's, thesis. *Entrance requirements:* For master's, GRE, minimum GPA of 3.0. Additional exam requirements/recommendations for international students: Required—TOEFL (minimum score 580 paper-based; 92 iBT). *Application deadline:* For fall admission, 2/1 priority date for domestic students. Applications are processed on a rolling basis. Application fee: $0. Electronic applications accepted. *Expenses: Tuition:* Full-time $43,122. *Financial support:* In 2016–17, 1 student received support. Fellowships with tuition reimbursements available, research assistantships with tuition reimbursements available, institutionally sponsored loans, scholarships/grants, and tuition waivers (full and partial) available. *Faculty research:* Biomedical instrumentation, biomechanics, biomedical fluid mechanics, biomedical materials, quantitative physiology, soft tissue biomechanics, tissue-biomaterial interaction, biomaterials, biomedical instrumentation, biomedical fluid mechanics. *Total annual research expenditures:* $18,766. *Unit head:* Dr. Kay C. Dee, Interim Chairman, 812-877-8502, Fax: 812-877-8545, E-mail: dee@rose-hulman.edu. *Application contact:* Dr. Azad Siahmakoun, Associate Dean of the Faculty, 812-877-8400, Fax: 812-877-8061, E-mail: siahmako@rose-hulman.edu.
Website: http://www.rose-hulman.edu/abbe/

Rutgers University–Newark, Graduate School of Biomedical Sciences, Department of Biomedical Engineering, Newark, NJ 07107. Offers Certificate. *Entrance requirements:* Additional exam requirements/recommendations for international students: Required—TOEFL. Electronic applications accepted.

Rutgers University–New Brunswick, Graduate School of Biomedical Sciences, Program in Biomedical Engineering, Piscataway, NJ 08854-5635. Offers MS, PhD, MD/PhD. MS, PhD offered jointly with Rutgers, The State University of New Jersey, New Brunswick. *Degree requirements:* For master's, thesis, qualifying exam; for doctorate, thesis/dissertation, qualifying exam. *Entrance requirements:* For master's and doctorate, GRE General Test. Additional exam requirements/recommendations for international students: Required—TOEFL. Electronic applications accepted.

St. Cloud State University, School of Graduate Studies, College of Science and Engineering, Program in Regulatory Affairs and Services, St. Cloud, MN 56301-4498. Offers MS. *Program availability:* Part-time. *Degree requirements:* For master's, final paper. *Entrance requirements:* For master's, GRE General Test, minimum GPA of 2.75. Additional exam requirements/recommendations for international students: Required—TOEFL (minimum score 550 paper-based; 79 iBT), IELTS (minimum score 6.5). *Expenses:* Contact institution.

Saint Louis University, Graduate Education, Parks College of Engineering, Aviation, and Technology and Graduate Education, Department of Biomedical Engineering, St. Louis, MO 63103. Offers MS, MS-R, PhD. *Degree requirements:* For master's, thesis optional; for doctorate, thesis/dissertation. *Entrance requirements:* For master's, GRE General Test, letters of recommendation, resume, interview; for doctorate, GRE General Test, letters of recommendation, resumé, interview, transcripts, goal statement. Additional exam requirements/recommendations for international students: Required—TOEFL (minimum score 525 paper-based). *Faculty research:* Tissue engineering and biomaterials;neural cardiovascular and orthopedic tissue engineering; tissue engineering; airway remodeling, vasculopathy, and elastic, biodegradable scaffolds; biomechanics; orthopedics, trauma biomechanics and biomechanical modeling; biosignals;electrophysiology, signal processing, and biomechanical instrumentation.

South Dakota School of Mines and Technology, Graduate Division, Program in Biomedical Engineering, Rapid City, SD 57701-3995. Offers MS, PhD. *Program availability:* Part-time. *Degree requirements:* For master's, thesis (for some programs); for doctorate, thesis/dissertation. *Entrance requirements:* For doctorate, GRE General Test, 3 letters of recommendation, minimum GPA of 3.0. Additional exam requirements/recommendations for international students: Required—TOEFL (minimum score 520 paper-based; 68 iBT). Electronic applications accepted.

Southern Illinois University Carbondale, Graduate School, College of Engineering, Program in Biomedical Engineering, Carbondale, IL 62901-4701. Offers ME, MS. *Degree requirements:* For master's, thesis. *Entrance requirements:* For master's, GRE. Additional exam requirements/recommendations for international students: Required—TOEFL.

Stanford University, School of Engineering, Department of Mechanical Engineering, Stanford, CA 94305-2004. Offers biomechanical engineering (MS); mechanical engineering (MS, PhD, Engr); product design (MS). *Degree requirements:* For doctorate, thesis/dissertation; for Engr, thesis. *Entrance requirements:* For master's, GRE General Test, undergraduate degree in engineering, math or sciences; for doctorate and Engr, GRE General Test, MS in engineering, math or sciences. Additional exam requirements/recommendations for international students: Required—TOEFL. *Expenses: Tuition:* Full-time $47,331. *Required fees:* $609.

State University of New York Downstate Medical Center, School of Graduate Studies, Program in Biomedical Engineering, Brooklyn, NY 11203-2098. Offers bioimaging and neuroengineering (PhD); biomedical engineering (MS); MD/PhD. *Degree requirements:* For doctorate, comprehensive exam, thesis/dissertation.

Stevens Institute of Technology, Graduate School, Charles V. Schaefer Jr. School of Engineering and Science, Department of Chemistry, Chemical Biology and Biomedical Engineering, Program in Biomedical Engineering, Hoboken, NJ 07030. Offers M Eng, PhD, Certificate. *Program availability:* Part-time, evening/weekend. *Students:* 40 full-time (14 women), 12 part-time (7 women); includes 9 minority (2 Black or African American, non-Hispanic/Latino; 5 Asian, non-Hispanic/Latino; 2 Hispanic/Latino), 23 international. Average age 27. 159 applicants, 30% accepted, 17 enrolled. In 2016, 11 master's, 4 doctorates awarded. *Degree requirements:* For master's, thesis optional, minimum B average in major field and overall; for doctorate, comprehensive exam (for some programs), thesis/dissertation; for Certificate, minimum B average. *Entrance requirements:* Additional exam requirements/recommendations for international students: Required—TOEFL (minimum score 74 iBT), IELTS (minimum score 6). *Application deadline:* For fall admission, 6/1 for domestic students, 4/15 for international students; for spring admission, 11/30 for domestic students, 11/1 for international students. Applications are processed on a rolling basis. Application fee: $65. Electronic applications accepted. *Expenses:* Contact institution. *Financial support:* Fellowships, research assistantships, teaching assistantships, career-related internships or fieldwork, Federal Work-Study, scholarships/grants, and unspecified assistantships available. Financial award application deadline: 2/15; financial award applicants required to submit FAFSA. *Unit head:* Vikki Hazelwood, Program Director, 201-216-5051, Fax: 201-216-8306, E-mail: vikki.hazelwood@stevens.edu. *Application contact:* Graduate Admissions, 888-783-8367, Fax: 888-511-1306, E-mail: graduate@stevens.edu.

Stony Brook University, State University of New York, Graduate School, College of Engineering and Applied Sciences, Department of Biomedical Engineering, Stony Brook, NY 11794. Offers biomedical engineering (MS, PhD, Certificate); medical physics (MS, PhD). *Faculty:* 11 full-time (2 women). *Students:* 80 full-time (30 women), 1 (woman) part-time; includes 20 minority (15 Asian, non-Hispanic/Latino; 4 Hispanic/Latino; 1 Two or more races, non-Hispanic/Latino), 30 international. Average age 26. 176 applicants, 32% accepted, 29 enrolled. In 2016, 27 master's, 14 doctorates awarded. *Degree requirements:* For doctorate, thesis/dissertation, qualifying exams. *Entrance requirements:* For master's and doctorate, GRE General Test. Additional exam requirements/recommendations for international students: Required—TOEFL (minimum score 90 iBT). *Application deadline:* For fall admission, 1/15 for domestic students; for spring admission, 10/1 for domestic students. Application fee: $100. *Expenses:* Contact institution. *Financial support:* In 2016–17, 3 fellowships, 22 research assistantships, 19 teaching assistantships were awarded. *Faculty research:* Bioimaging, tissue engineering, biomedical engineering, carbon nanotubes, chemistry. *Total annual research expenditures:* $6.1 million. *Unit head:* Dr. Clinton Rubin, Chair, 631-632-1188, E-mail: clinton.rubin@stonybrook.edu. *Application contact:* Jessica Anne Kuhn, Coordinator, 631-632-8371, Fax: 631-632-8577, E-mail: jessica.kuhn@stonybrook.edu.
Website: http://www.bme.sunysb.edu/

Tennessee State University, The School of Graduate Studies and Research, College of Engineering, Nashville, TN 37209-1561. Offers biomedical engineering (ME); civil engineering (ME); computer and information systems engineering (MS, PhD); electrical engineering (ME); environmental engineering (ME); manufacturing engineering (ME);

mathematical sciences (MS); mechanical engineering (ME). *Program availability:* Part-time, evening/weekend. *Degree requirements:* For master's, project; for doctorate, comprehensive exam, thesis/dissertation. *Entrance requirements:* For doctorate, minimum GPA of 3.3. *Faculty research:* Robotics, intelligent systems, human-computer interaction software systems, biomedical engineering, signal/image processing, probabilistic design, intelligent manufacturing, cooperative mobile robots, condition based maintenance, sensor fusion.

Texas A&M University, College of Engineering, Department of Biomedical Engineering, College Station, TX 77840. Offers M Eng, MS, PhD. *Program availability:* Part-time. *Faculty:* 27. *Students:* 114 full-time (42 women), 6 part-time (0 women); includes 28 minority (4 Black or African American, non-Hispanic/Latino; 7 Asian, non-Hispanic/Latino; 16 Hispanic/Latino; 1 Two or more races, non-Hispanic/Latino), 35 international. Average age 27. 254 applicants, 25% accepted, 25 enrolled. In 2016, 11 master's, 12 doctorates awarded. *Degree requirements:* For master's, thesis (for MS); for doctorate, dissertation (for PhD). *Entrance requirements:* For master's and doctorate, GRE General Test, leveling courses if non-engineering undergraduate major. Additional exam requirements/recommendations for international students: Required—TOEFL (minimum score 550 paper-based; 80 iBT), TWE, PTE (minimum score 53). *Application deadline:* For fall admission, 5/1 for domestic students, 3/1 for international students; for spring admission, 10/1 for domestic students, 7/1 for international students. Applications are processed on a rolling basis. Application fee: $50 ($90 for international students). Electronic applications accepted. *Expenses:* Contact institution. *Financial support:* In 2016–17, 116 students received support, including 33 fellowships with tuition reimbursements available (averaging $19,377 per year), 66 research assistantships with tuition reimbursements available (averaging $6,352 per year), 23 teaching assistantships with tuition reimbursements available (averaging $10,288 per year); career-related internships or fieldwork, institutionally sponsored loans, scholarships/grants, traineeships, health care benefits, tuition waivers (full and partial), and unspecified assistantships also available. Support available to part-time students. Financial award application deadline: 3/15; financial award applicants required to submit FAFSA. *Faculty research:* Medical devices, cardiovascular biomechanics, biomedical optics and sensing, imaging, tissue engineering, biomaterials. *Unit head:* Dr. Gerard L. Cote, Department Head, 979-845-4196, Fax: 979-845-4450, E-mail: gcote@tamu.edu. *Application contact:* Dr. John C. Criscione, Assistant Dean for Graduate Programs, 979-845-5428, Fax: 979-845-4450, E-mail: jccriscione@tamu.edu.
Website: http://engineering.tamu.edu/biomedical

Tufts University, School of Engineering, Department of Biomedical Engineering, Medford, MA 02155. Offers bioengineering (ME, MS), including biomaterials; biomedical engineering (PhD). *Program availability:* Part-time. Terminal master's awarded for partial completion of doctoral program. *Degree requirements:* For master's, thesis (for some programs); for doctorate, thesis/dissertation. *Entrance requirements:* For master's and doctorate, GRE General Test. Additional exam requirements/recommendations for international students: Required—TOEFL (minimum score 550 paper-based; 80 iBT), IELTS (minimum score 6.5). Electronic applications accepted. *Expenses: Tuition:* Full-time $49,892; part-time $1248 per credit hour. *Required fees:* $844. Full-time tuition and fees vary according to degree level, program and student level. Part-time tuition and fees vary according to course load. *Faculty research:* Regenerative medicine with biomaterials and tissue engineering, diffuse optical imaging and spectroscopy, optics in the development of biomedical devices, ultrafast nonlinear optics and biophotonics, optical diagnostics for diseased and engineered tissues.

Tulane University, School of Science and Engineering, Department of Biomedical Engineering, New Orleans, LA 70118-5669. Offers MS, PhD. MS and PhD offered through the Graduate School. *Program availability:* Part-time. Terminal master's awarded for partial completion of doctoral program. *Degree requirements:* For master's, thesis (for some programs); for doctorate, thesis/dissertation. *Entrance requirements:* For master's and doctorate, GRE General Test, minimum B average in undergraduate course work. Additional exam requirements/recommendations for international students: Required—TOEFL. Electronic applications accepted. *Expenses: Tuition:* Full-time $50,920; part-time $2829 per credit hour. *Required fees:* $2040; $44.50 per credit hour. $580 per term. Tuition and fees vary according to course load, degree level and program. *Faculty research:* Pulmonary and biofluid mechanics and biomechanics of bone, biomaterials science, finite element analysis, electric fields of the brain.

Université de Montréal, Faculty of Medicine, Institute of Biomedical Engineering, Montréal, QC H3C 3J7, Canada. Offers M Sc A, PhD, DESS. M Sc A and PhD programs offered jointly with École Polytechnique de Montréal. *Degree requirements:* For master's, thesis; for doctorate, thesis/dissertation, general exam. *Entrance requirements:* For master's and doctorate, proficiency in French, knowledge of English. Electronic applications accepted. *Faculty research:* Electrophysiology, biomechanics, instrumentation, imaging, simulation.

University at Buffalo, the State University of New York, Graduate School, School of Engineering and Applied Sciences, Department of Biomedical Engineering, Buffalo, NY 14260. Offers MS, PhD. *Program availability:* Part-time. *Degree requirements:* For master's, thesis (for some programs); for doctorate, comprehensive exam, thesis/dissertation. *Entrance requirements:* For master's and doctorate, GRE General Test. Additional exam requirements/recommendations for international students: Required—TOEFL (minimum score 550 paper-based; 79 iBT). Electronic applications accepted.

The University of Akron, Graduate School, College of Engineering, Department of Biomedical Engineering, Akron, OH 44325. Offers biomedical engineering (MS); engineering (PhD). *Program availability:* Part-time, evening/weekend. *Faculty:* 9 full-time (4 women), 3 part-time/adjunct (0 women). *Students:* 33 full-time (15 women), 1 part-time (0 women); includes 3 minority (1 Asian, non-Hispanic/Latino; 2 Hispanic/Latino), 20 international. Average age 28. 39 applicants, 62% accepted, 9 enrolled. In 2016, 3 master's, 3 doctorates awarded. *Degree requirements:* For master's, thesis; for doctorate, one foreign language, thesis/dissertation, candidacy exam, qualifying exam. *Entrance requirements:* For master's, GRE, minimum GPA of 2.75, three letters of recommendation, statement of purpose; for doctorate, GRE, minimum GPA of 3.0 with bachelor's degree, 3.5 with master's degree; three letters of recommendation; statement of purpose; resume. Additional exam requirements/recommendations for international students: Required—TOEFL (minimum score 590 paper-based; 96 iBT). *Application deadline:* For fall admission, 2/1 priority date for domestic and international students; for spring admission, 9/1 priority date for domestic and international students. Applications are processed on a rolling basis. Application fee: $45 ($70 for international students). Electronic applications accepted. *Expenses:* Tuition, state resident: full-time $8618; part-time $359 per credit hour. Tuition, nonresident: full-time $17,149; part-time $715 per credit hour. *Required fees:* $1652. *Financial support:* In 2016–17, 1 fellowship with full tuition reimbursement, 15 research assistantships with full tuition reimbursements, 11 teaching assistantships with full tuition reimbursements were awarded; instructional support assistantships also available. *Faculty research:* Signal and image processing, physiological controls and instrumentation, biomechanics - orthopedic and hemodynamic, biomaterials for gene and drug delivery systems, telemedicine. *Total annual research expenditures:* $1.5 million. *Unit head:* Dr. Brian Davis, Chair, 330-972-6977, E-mail: bdavis3@uakron.edu. *Application contact:* Dr. Rebecca Willits, Associate Graduate Chair for Biomedical Engineering, 330-972-6587, E-mail: willits@uakron.edu.
Website: http://www.uakron.edu/engineering/BME/

The University of Alabama at Birmingham, School of Engineering, Program in Biomedical Engineering, Birmingham, AL 35294. Offers MSBME, PhD. *Program availability:* Part-time. *Faculty:* 33 full-time (7 women). *Students:* 27 full-time (6 women), 6 part-time (4 women); includes 11 minority (3 Black or African American, non-Hispanic/Latino; 4 Asian, non-Hispanic/Latino; 1 Hispanic/Latino; 3 Two or more races, non-Hispanic/Latino), 2 international. Average age 25. In 2016, 9 master's, 6 doctorates awarded. *Degree requirements:* For master's, thesis or alternative; for doctorate, comprehensive exam, thesis/dissertation. *Entrance requirements:* For master's and doctorate, GRE General Test. Additional exam requirements/recommendations for international students: Required—TOEFL (minimum score 90 iBT), IELTS (minimum score 6.5). *Application deadline:* For fall admission, 1/15 for domestic students. Application fee: $50 ($60 for international students). *Expenses:* $396 per hour resident tuition; $935 per hour non-resident tuition; $150 per course online course fee. *Financial support:* In 2016–17, 21 students received support, including 10 fellowships with full tuition reimbursements available (averaging $23,952 per year), 11 research assistantships with full tuition reimbursements available (averaging $22,368 per year). *Faculty research:* Biomedical imaging, biomedical implants and devices, cardiac electrophysiology, multiscale computational modeling, tissue engineering and regenerative medicine. *Total annual research expenditures:* $2.4 million. *Unit head:* Dr. Jianyi Zhang, Chair, 205-934-8420, E-mail: jayzhang@uab.edu. *Application contact:* Holly Hebard, Director of Graduate School Operations, 205-934-8227 Ext. 205, E-mail: gradschool@uab.edu.
Website: https://www.uab.edu/engineering/home/departments-research/bme

University of Alberta, Faculty of Medicine and Dentistry and Faculty of Graduate Studies and Research, Graduate Programs in Medicine, Department of Biomedical Engineering, Edmonton, AB T6G 2E1, Canada. Offers biomedical engineering (M Sc); medical sciences (PhD). *Degree requirements:* For master's, thesis; for doctorate, thesis/dissertation. Electronic applications accepted. *Faculty research:* Medical imaging, rehabilitation engineering, biomaterials and tissue engineering, biomechanics, cryobiology.

The University of Arizona, Graduate Interdisciplinary Programs, Graduate Interdisciplinary Program in Biomedical Engineering, Tucson, AZ 85721. Offers MS, PhD. *Entrance requirements:* For master's, GRE, 3 letters of recommendation; for doctorate, GRE, 3 letters of recommendation, statement of purpose. Additional exam requirements/recommendations for international students: Required—TOEFL (minimum score 600 paper-based). Electronic applications accepted.

University of Arkansas, Graduate School, College of Engineering, Department of Biological and Agricultural Engineering, Program in Biomedical Engineering, Fayetteville, AR 72701. Offers MSBME. In 2016, 6 master's awarded. *Application deadline:* For fall admission, 4/1 for international students; for spring admission, 10/1 for international students. Applications are processed on a rolling basis. Application fee: $40 ($50 for international students). Electronic applications accepted. *Financial support:* In 2016–17, 4 research assistantships, 2 teaching assistantships were awarded; fellowships also available. *Unit head:* Dr. Raj Rao, Department Head, 479-575-2351, Fax: 479-575-2846, E-mail: rajrao@uark.edu. *Application contact:* Dr. Kartik Balachandran, Program Coordinator, 479-575-4667, Fax: 479-575-2846, E-mail: kbalacha@uark.edu. Website: http://www.bmeg.uark.edu/

University of Bridgeport, School of Engineering, Department of Biomedical Engineering, Bridgeport, CT 06604. Offers MS. *Program availability:* Part-time, evening/weekend. *Degree requirements:* For master's, thesis optional. *Entrance requirements:* Additional exam requirements/recommendations for international students: Recommended—TOEFL (minimum score 550 paper-based; 80 iBT), IELTS (minimum score 6.5). *Expenses:* Contact institution.

University of Calgary, Faculty of Graduate Studies, Schulich School of Engineering, Biomedical Engineering Graduate Program, Calgary, AB T2N 1N4, Canada. Offers M Sc, PhD. *Degree requirements:* For master's, comprehensive exam, thesis, defense exam; for doctorate, comprehensive exam, thesis/dissertation, defense exam. *Entrance requirements:* For master's, B Sc, minimum GPA of 3.2, confirmed faculty supervisor; for doctorate, M Sc, minimum GPA of 3.5, confirmed faculty supervisor. Additional exam requirements/recommendations for international students: Required—TOEFL, IELTS. *Faculty research:* Bioelectricity, biomechanics, cell and tissue engineering (or biomaterials), imaging, bioinstrumentation, clinical engineering, rehabilitation engineering.

University of California, Davis, College of Engineering, Graduate Group in Biomedical Engineering, Davis, CA 95616. Offers MS, PhD. *Degree requirements:* For master's, thesis; for doctorate, thesis/dissertation. *Entrance requirements:* For master's and doctorate, GRE General Test, minimum GPA of 3.25. Additional exam requirements/recommendations for international students: Required—TOEFL (minimum score 550 paper-based), IELTS (minimum score 7). Electronic applications accepted. *Faculty research:* Orthopedic biomechanics, cell/molecular biomechanics and transport, biosensors and instrumentation, human movement, biomedical image analysis, spectroscopy.

University of California, Irvine, Henry Samueli School of Engineering, Department of Biomedical Engineering, Irvine, CA 92697. Offers MS, PhD. *Program availability:* Part-time. *Students:* 125 full-time (47 women), 1 part-time (0 women); includes 41 minority (32 Asian, non-Hispanic/Latino; 7 Hispanic/Latino; 2 Two or more races, non-Hispanic/Latino), 39 international. Average age 26. 359 applicants, 36% accepted, 36 enrolled. In 2016, 24 master's, 15 doctorates awarded. Terminal master's awarded for partial completion of doctoral program. *Degree requirements:* For doctorate, thesis/dissertation. *Entrance requirements:* For master's and doctorate, GRE General Test, minimum GPA of 3.0, 3 letters of recommendation. Additional exam requirements/recommendations for international students: Required—TOEFL (minimum score 550 paper-based). *Application deadline:* For fall admission, 1/15 priority date for domestic students, 1/15 for international students. Applications are processed on a rolling basis. Application fee: $105 ($125 for international students). Electronic applications accepted. *Financial support:* Fellowships, research assistantships with full tuition reimbursements, teaching assistantships, institutionally sponsored loans, traineeships, health care benefits, and unspecified assistantships available. Financial award application deadline: 3/1; financial award applicants required to submit FAFSA. *Faculty research:* Biomedical photonics, biomedical imaging, biomedical Nano- and micro-scale systems, biomedical computation/modeling, neuroengineering, tissue engineering. *Unit head:* Prof. Abraham P. Lee, Chair, 949-824-8155, Fax: 949-824-1727, E-mail: aplee@uci.edu. *Application contact:* Connie Cheng, Assistant Director of Graduate Student Affairs, 949-824-3562, Fax: 949-824-9096, E-mail: connie.cheng@uci.edu.
Website: http://www.eng.uci.edu/dept/bme

University of California, Los Angeles, Graduate Division, Henry Samueli School of Engineering and Applied Science, Department of Bioengineering, Los Angeles, CA 90095-1600. Offers MS, PhD. *Faculty:* 11 full-time (2 women), 4 part-time/adjunct. *Students:* 149 full-time (52 women); includes 51 minority (1 Black or African American, non-Hispanic/Latino; 39 Asian, non-Hispanic/Latino; 6 Hispanic/Latino; 5 Two or more races, non-Hispanic/Latino), 66 international. 421 applicants, 33% accepted, 31 enrolled. In 2016, 41 master's, 19 doctorates awarded. *Degree requirements:* For master's, comprehensive exam or thesis; for doctorate, thesis/dissertation, qualifying exams. *Entrance requirements:* For master's, GRE General Test, minimum GPA of 3.0; for doctorate, GRE General Test, minimum GPA of 3.25. Additional exam requirements/recommendations for international students: Required—TOEFL (minimum score 560 paper-based; 87 iBT), IELTS (minimum score 7). *Application deadline:* For fall admission, 12/1 for domestic and international students. Application fee: $105 ($125 for international students). Electronic applications accepted. *Financial support:* In 2016–17, 67 fellowships, 121 research assistantships, 52 teaching assistantships were awarded; career-related internships or fieldwork, Federal Work-Study, institutionally sponsored loans, and tuition waivers (full and partial) also available. Financial award application deadline: 12/1; financial award applicants required to submit FAFSA. *Faculty research:* Biomedical instrumentation; biomedical signal and image processing; biosystems science and engineering; medical imaging informatics; molecular cellular tissue therapeutics; neuroengineering. *Total annual research expenditures:* $6.8 million. *Unit head:* Dr. Song Li, Chair, 310-794-5072, E-mail: songli@ucla.edu. *Application contact:* Anne-Marie Wright, Student Affairs Officer, 310-794-5945, E-mail: awright@seas.ucla.edu. Website: http://www.bioeng.ucla.edu/

University of Central Oklahoma, The Jackson College of Graduate Studies, College of Mathematics and Science, Department of Engineering and Physics, Edmond, OK 73034-5209. Offers biomedical engineering (MS); electrical engineering (MS); mechanical systems (MS); physics (MS). *Program availability:* Part-time. *Degree requirements:* For master's, thesis optional. *Entrance requirements:* For master's, GRE, 24 hours of course work in physics or equivalent, mathematics through differential equations, minimum GPA of 2.75 overall and 3.0 in last 60 hours attempted. Additional exam requirements/recommendations for international students: Required—TOEFL (minimum score 550 paper-based). Electronic applications accepted.

University of Cincinnati, Graduate School, College of Engineering and Applied Science, Department of Biomedical, Chemical and Environmental Engineering, Cincinnati, OH 45221. Offers biomechanics (PhD); chemical engineering (MS, PhD); environmental engineering (MS, PhD); environmental sciences (MS, PhD); medical imaging (PhD); tissue engineering (PhD). *Program availability:* Part-time. *Degree requirements:* For master's, thesis or alternative; for doctorate, one foreign language, thesis/dissertation. *Entrance requirements:* For master's and doctorate, GRE General Test. Additional exam requirements/recommendations for international students: Required—TOEFL (minimum score 600 paper-based). *Expenses:* Tuition, area resident: Full-time $12,790; part-time $389 per credit hour. Tuition, state resident: full-time $13,290; part-time $419 per credit hour. Tuition, nonresident: full-time $24,532; part-time $976 per credit hour. *International tuition:* $24,832 full-time. *Required fees:* $3958; $140 per credit hour. Tuition and fees vary according to course load, degree level, program and reciprocity agreements.

University of Connecticut, Graduate School, School of Engineering, Department of Electrical and Computer Engineering, Field of Biomedical Engineering, Storrs, CT 06269. Offers MS, PhD. Terminal master's awarded for partial completion of doctoral program. *Degree requirements:* For master's, comprehensive exam, thesis or alternative; for doctorate, thesis/dissertation. *Entrance requirements:* For master's and doctorate, GRE General Test. Additional exam requirements/recommendations for international students: Required—TOEFL (minimum score 550 paper-based). Electronic applications accepted.

University of Florida, Graduate School, Herbert Wertheim College of Engineering, J. Crayton Pruitt Family Department of Biomedical Engineering, Gainesville, FL 32611. Offers biomedical engineering (ME, MS, PhD, Certificate); clinical and translational science (PhD); medical physics (MS, PhD); MD/PhD. Terminal master's awarded for partial completion of doctoral program. *Degree requirements:* For master's, comprehensive exam (for some programs), thesis (for some programs); for doctorate, comprehensive exam (for some programs), thesis/dissertation (for some programs). *Entrance requirements:* Additional exam requirements/recommendations for international students: Required—TOEFL (minimum score 550 paper-based; 80 iBT), IELTS (minimum score 6). Electronic applications accepted. *Faculty research:* Neural engineering, imaging and medical physics, biomaterials and regenerative medicine, biomedical informatics and modeling.

University of Houston, Cullen College of Engineering, Department of Biomedical Engineering, Houston, TX 77204. Offers PhD. *Program availability:* Part-time. *Degree requirements:* For doctorate, seminar. *Entrance requirements:* For doctorate, GRE, BS or MS in biomedical engineering or related field, minimum GPA of 3.3 on last 60 hours. Additional exam requirements/recommendations for international students: Required—TOEFL (minimum score 580 paper-based; 92 iBT), IELTS (minimum score 6). Electronic applications accepted.

The University of Iowa, Graduate College, College of Engineering, Department of Biomedical Engineering, Iowa City, IA 52242-1316. Offers MS, PhD. *Program availability:* Part-time. *Faculty:* 14 full-time (2 women), 4 part-time/adjunct (2 women). *Students:* 57 full-time (15 women), 12 part-time (4 women); includes 9 minority (1 Black or African American, non-Hispanic/Latino; 3 Asian, non-Hispanic/Latino; 2 Hispanic/Latino; 3 Two or more races, non-Hispanic/Latino), 18 international. Average age 26. 102 applicants, 22% accepted, 12 enrolled. In 2016, 14 master's, 11 doctorates awarded. Terminal master's awarded for partial completion of doctoral program. *Degree requirements:* For master's, thesis (for some programs), written and oral exam; for doctorate, comprehensive exam, thesis/dissertation, written and oral exam. *Entrance requirements:* For master's, GRE (minimum combined score of 310 on verbal and quantitative), minimum undergraduate GPA of 3.0; for doctorate, GRE (minimum combined score of 310 on verbal and quantitative), minimum undergraduate GPA of 3.25. Additional exam requirements/recommendations for international students: Required—TOEFL (minimum score 553 paper-based; 85 iBT), IELTS (minimum score 7). *Application deadline:* For fall admission, 3/1 for domestic and international students; for spring admission, 8/1 for domestic and international students; for summer admission, 1/1 for domestic and international students. Applications are processed on a rolling basis. Application fee: $60 ($100 for international students). Electronic applications accepted. *Financial support:* In 2016–17, 62 students received support, including 6 fellowships with partial tuition reimbursements available (averaging $25,500 per year), 51 research assistantships with partial tuition reimbursements available (averaging $22,981 per year), 5 teaching assistantships with partial tuition reimbursements available (averaging $18,809 per year); scholarships/grants, traineeships, health care benefits, and unspecified assistantships also available. Support available to part-time students. Financial award application deadline: 3/1. *Faculty research:* Biomaterials, tissue engineering and cellular mechanics; cell motion analysis and modeling; spinal and joint biomechanics, digital human modeling, and biomedical imaging; bioinformatics and computational biology; fluid and cardiovascular biomechanics; wound healing; mechanobiology. *Total annual research expenditures:* $3.9 million. *Unit head:* Dr. Nicole M. Grosland, Departmental Executive Officer, 319-335-5632, Fax: 319-335-5631, E-mail: nicole-grosland@uiowa.edu. *Application contact:* Joshua Lobb, Academic Program Specialist, 319-335-5632, Fax: 319-335-5631,

E-mail: bme@engineering.uiowa.edu.
Website: https://bme.engineering.uiowa.edu

University of Kentucky, Graduate School, College of Engineering, Program in Biomedical Engineering, Lexington, KY 40506-0032. Offers MSBE, PBME, PhD. *Degree requirements:* For master's, comprehensive exam, thesis optional; for doctorate, comprehensive exam, thesis/dissertation. *Entrance requirements:* For master's, GRE General Test, minimum undergraduate GPA of 2.75; for doctorate, GRE General Test, minimum graduate GPA of 3.0. Additional exam requirements/recommendations for international students: Required—TOEFL (minimum score 550 paper-based). Electronic applications accepted. *Faculty research:* Signal processing and dynamical systems, cardiopulmonary mechanics and systems, bioelectromagnetics, neuromotor control and electrical stimulation, biomaterials and musculoskeletal biomechanics.

University of Maine, Graduate School, Graduate School of Biomedical Science and Engineering, Orono, ME 04469. Offers bioinformatics (PSM); biomedical engineering (PhD); biomedical science (PhD). *Faculty:* 149 full-time (47 women). *Students:* 28 full-time (17 women), 16 part-time (9 women); includes 1 minority (Two or more races, non-Hispanic/Latino), 13 international. Average age 30. 51 applicants, 20% accepted, 8 enrolled. In 2016, 8 doctorates awarded. *Degree requirements:* For doctorate, comprehensive exam, thesis/dissertation. *Entrance requirements:* For doctorate, GRE General Test, master's degree. Additional exam requirements/recommendations for international students: Required—TOEFL (minimum score 90 iBT), IELTS (minimum score 7). *Application deadline:* For fall admission, 1/1 priority date for domestic and international students. Application fee: $65. *Expenses:* Tuition, state resident: full-time $7524; part-time $2508 per credit. Tuition, nonresident: full-time $24,498; part-time $8166 per credit. *Required fees:* $1148; $571 per credit. *Financial support:* In 2016–17, 33 students received support, including 2 fellowships with full tuition reimbursements available (averaging $21,500 per year), 28 research assistantships with full tuition reimbursements available (averaging $22,500 per year), 3 teaching assistantships (averaging $9,300 per year). Financial award application deadline: 3/1. *Faculty research:* Molecular and cellular biology, neuroscience, biomedical engineering, toxicology, bioinformatics and computational biology. *Total annual research expenditures:* $1.4 million. *Unit head:* Dr. David Neivandt, Director, 207-581-2803. *Application contact:* Scott G. Delcourt, Assistant Vice President for Graduate Studies and Senior Associate Dean, 207-581-3291, Fax: 207-581-3232, E-mail: graduate@maine.edu.
Website: http://gsbse.umaine.edu/

University of Massachusetts Boston, College of Science and Mathematics, Program in Biomedical Engineering and Biotechnology, Boston, MA 02125-3393. Offers PhD. *Students:* 1 (woman) full-time, 3 part-time (1 woman), 3 international. Average age 32. 10 applicants, 10% accepted, 1 enrolled. In 2016, 1 doctorate awarded. *Expenses:* Tuition, state resident: full-time $16,863. Tuition, nonresident: full-time $32,913. *Required fees:* $177. *Unit head:* Dr. William Hagar, 617-287-5776. *Application contact:* Peggy Roldan Patel, Graduate Admissions Coordinator, 617-287-6400, Fax: 617-287-6236, E-mail: bos.gadm@dpc.umassp.edu.

University of Massachusetts Dartmouth, Graduate School, College of Engineering, Program in Biomedical Engineering and Biotechnology, North Dartmouth, MA 02747-2300. Offers bioengineering (PhD); biology (PhD); biomedical engineering/biotechnology (MS, PhD); chemistry (PhD); civil engineering (PhD); computer and information science (PhD); electrical and computer engineering (PhD); mathematics (PhD); mechanical engineering (PhD); medical laboratory science (MS); physics (PhD). *Program availability:* Part-time. *Students:* 12 full-time (6 women), 8 part-time (5 women); includes 2 minority (both Hispanic/Latino), 7 international. Average age 31. 18 applicants, 44% accepted, 2 enrolled. In 2016, 2 master's, 6 doctorates awarded. *Degree requirements:* For doctorate, comprehensive exam, thesis/dissertation. *Entrance requirements:* For master's, GRE (recommended), statement of purpose (minimum of 300 words), resume, 3 letters of recommendation, official transcripts; for doctorate, GRE, statement of purpose (minimum of 300 words), resume, 3 letters of recommendation, official transcripts. Additional exam requirements/recommendations for international students: Required—TOEFL (minimum score 550 paper-based). *Application deadline:* For fall admission, 2/15 priority date for domestic students, 1/15 priority date for international students; for spring admission, 11/15 priority date for domestic students, 10/15 priority date for international students. Application fee: $60. Electronic applications accepted. *Expenses:* Tuition, state resident: full-time $14,994; part-time $624.75 per credit. Tuition, nonresident: full-time $27,068; part-time $1127.83 per credit. *Required fees:* $405; $25.88 per credit. Tuition and fees vary according to course load and reciprocity agreements. *Financial support:* In 2016–17, 5 fellowships (averaging $6,000 per year), 4 research assistantships (averaging $5,429 per year), 5 teaching assistantships (averaging $7,125 per year) were awarded. Financial award application deadline: 3/1; financial award applicants required to submit FAFSA. *Faculty research:* Comparative immunology, vaccine design, biosensors, biomimetic materials, polymer science, soft electronics, hydrogels, regenerative biological materials. *Total annual research expenditures:* $984,000. *Unit head:* Alex Fowler, Graduate Program Director, 508-999-8449, E-mail: afowler@umassd.edu. *Application contact:* Steven Briggs, Director of Marketing and Recruitment for Graduate Studies, 508-999-8604, Fax: 508-999-8183, E-mail: graduate@umassd.edu.
Website: http://www.umassd.edu/engineering/graduate/doctoraldegreeprograms/biomedicalengineeringandbiotechnology/

University of Memphis, Graduate School, Herff College of Engineering, Program in Biomedical Engineering, Memphis, TN 38152. Offers MS, PhD. *Faculty:* 7 full-time (2 women), 1 part-time/adjunct (0 women). *Students:* 20 full-time (9 women), 4 part-time (1 woman); includes 6 minority (1 Black or African American, non-Hispanic/Latino; 1 American Indian or Alaska Native, non-Hispanic/Latino; 2 Asian, non-Hispanic/Latino; 2 Hispanic/Latino), 5 international. Average age 30. 25 applicants, 20% accepted, 4 enrolled. In 2016, 3 master's, 2 doctorates awarded. *Degree requirements:* For master's, thesis or alternative, oral exam; for doctorate, comprehensive exam, thesis/dissertation. *Entrance requirements:* For master's, GRE, minimum undergraduate GPA of 3.0, three letters of recommendation; for doctorate, GRE, minimum undergraduate GPA of 3.25 or master's degree in biomedical engineering, three letters of recommendation. Additional exam requirements/recommendations for international students: Required—TOEFL (minimum score 550 paper-based; 79 iBT). *Application deadline:* For fall admission, 8/1 priority date for domestic students; for spring admission, 12/1 for domestic students. Applications are processed on a rolling basis. Application fee: $35 ($60 for international students). Electronic applications accepted. *Expenses:* $5,231.50 per semester full-time in-state, $9,623.50 full-time out-of-state. *Financial support:* In 2016–17, 8 students received support, including 14 fellowships with full tuition reimbursements available (averaging $16,714 per year); research assistantships with full tuition reimbursements available, career-related internships or fieldwork, Federal Work-Study, scholarships/grants, and unspecified assistantships also available. Financial award application deadline: 2/1; financial award applicants required to submit FAFSA. *Faculty research:* Biomaterials and cell/tissue engineering, especially for orthopedic applications; biosensors; biomechanics (hemodynamics, soft tissue, lung, gait); electrophysiology; novel medical image-acquisition devices. *Unit head:* Dr. Eugene C. Eckstein, Chairman, 901-678-3733, Fax: 901-678-5281, E-mail: eckstein@memphis.edu. *Application*

contact: Dr. Joel Bumgardner, Coordinator of Graduate Studies, Fax: 901-678-5281, E-mail: jbmgrdnr@memphis.edu.
Website: http://www.memphis.edu/bme/index.php

University of Miami, Graduate School, College of Engineering, Department of Biomedical Engineering, Coral Gables, FL 33124. Offers MSBE, PhD. *Program availability:* Part-time. *Degree requirements:* For master's, thesis (for some programs); for doctorate, comprehensive exam, thesis/dissertation. *Entrance requirements:* For master's and doctorate, GRE General Test, minimum GPA of 3.0. Additional exam requirements/recommendations for international students: Required—TOEFL (minimum score 550 paper-based). Electronic applications accepted. *Faculty research:* Biomedical signal processing and instrumentation, cardiovascular engineering, optics and lasers, rehabilitation engineering, tissue mechanics.

University of Michigan, College of Engineering, Department of Biomedical Engineering, Ann Arbor, MI 48109. Offers MS, MSE, PhD. *Program availability:* Part-time. *Students:* 208 full-time (97 women), 3 part-time (1 woman). 673 applicants, 29% accepted, 87 enrolled. In 2016, 72 master's, 18 doctorates awarded. *Degree requirements:* For master's, thesis optional; for doctorate, comprehensive exam, oral defense of dissertation. *Entrance requirements:* For master's, GRE General Test; for doctorate, GRE General Test, master's degree. Additional exam requirements/recommendations for international students: Required—TOEFL. *Application deadline:* Applications are processed on a rolling basis. Electronic applications accepted. *Expenses:* Tuition, state resident: full-time $21,466; part-time $1152 per credit hour. Tuition, nonresident: full-time $43,346; part-time $2367 per credit hour. Part-time tuition and fees vary according to course load, degree level and program. *Financial support:* Fellowships, research assistantships, teaching assistantships, Federal Work-Study, scholarships/grants, traineeships, and tuition waivers (partial) available. Financial award applicants required to submit FAFSA. *Faculty research:* Cellular and tissue engineering, biotechnology, biomedical materials, biomechanics, biomedical imaging, rehabilitation engineering. *Total annual research expenditures:* $36.4 million. *Unit head:* Lonnie Shea, Department Chair, 734-647-6319, Fax: 734-936-1905, E-mail: ldshea@umich.edu. *Application contact:* Maria E. Steele, Graduate Student Program Coordinator, 734-647-1091, Fax: 734-936-1905, E-mail: msteele@umich.edu.
Website: http://www.bme.umich.edu/

University of Minnesota, Twin Cities Campus, College of Science and Engineering and Medical School, Department of Biomedical Engineering, Minneapolis, MN 55455-0213. Offers MS, PhD, MD/PhD. *Program availability:* Part-time. Terminal master's awarded for partial completion of doctoral program. *Degree requirements:* For master's, thesis optional; for doctorate, thesis/dissertation. *Entrance requirements:* For master's and doctorate, GRE General Test. Additional exam requirements/recommendations for international students: Required—TOEFL. Electronic applications accepted. *Faculty research:* Bioinstrumentation and medical devices; biomaterials; biomechanics; biomedical optics and imaging; biomolecular, cellular, and tissue engineering; cardiovascular engineering; neural engineering.

University of Nebraska–Lincoln, Graduate College, College of Engineering, Department of Mechanical and Materials Engineering, Lincoln, NE 68588-0526. Offers biomedical engineering (PhD); engineering mechanics (MS); materials engineering (PhD); mechanical engineering (MS), including materials science engineering, metallurgical engineering; mechanical engineering and applied mechanics (PhD); MS/MS. MS/MS offered with University of Rouen-France. *Degree requirements:* For master's, thesis optional; for doctorate, comprehensive exam, thesis/dissertation. *Entrance requirements:* For master's and doctorate, GRE General Test. Additional exam requirements/recommendations for international students: Required—TOEFL (minimum score 550 paper-based). Electronic applications accepted. *Faculty research:* Medical robotics, rehabilitation dynamics, and design; combustion, fluid mechanics, and heat transfer; nano-materials, manufacturing, and devices; fiber, tissue, bio-polymer, and adaptive composites; blast, impact, fracture, and failure; electro-active and magnetic materials and devices; functional materials, design, and added manufacturing; materials characterization, modeling, and computational simulation.

University of Nevada, Las Vegas, Graduate College, Howard R. Hughes College of Engineering, Department of Mechanical Engineering, Las Vegas, NV 89154-4027. Offers aerospace engineering (MS); biomedical engineering (MS); materials and nuclear engineering (MS); mechanical engineering (MS, PhD); nuclear criticality safety (Certificate); nuclear safeguards and security (Certificate). *Program availability:* Part-time. *Faculty:* 16 full-time (2 women), 3 part-time/adjunct (1 woman). *Students:* 47 full-time (13 women), 21 part-time (4 women); includes 15 minority (1 American Indian or Alaska Native, non-Hispanic/Latino; 6 Asian, non-Hispanic/Latino; 3 Hispanic/Latino; 5 Two or more races, non-Hispanic/Latino), 16 international. Average age 30. 68 applicants, 54% accepted, 15 enrolled. In 2016, 10 master's, 3 doctorates, 4 other advanced degrees awarded. *Degree requirements:* For master's, thesis optional, design project; for doctorate, comprehensive exam, thesis/dissertation. *Entrance requirements:* For master's, GRE General Test, statement of purpose; 2 letters of recommendation; for doctorate, GRE General Test, 3 letters of recommendation; statement of purpose; bachelor's degree with minimum GPA of 3.5/master's degree with minimum GPA of 3.3. Additional exam requirements/recommendations for international students: Required—TOEFL (minimum score 550 paper-based; 80 iBT), IELTS (minimum score 7). *Application deadline:* For fall admission, 8/1 for domestic students, 5/1 for international students; for spring admission, 12/1 for domestic students, 10/1 for international students. Application fee: $60 ($95 for international students). Electronic applications accepted. *Expenses:* $269.25 per credit, $792 per 3-credit course; $9,634 per year resident; $23,274 per year non-resident; $7,094 fees non-resident (7 credits or more); $1,307 annual health insurance fee. *Financial support:* In 2016–17, 1 fellowship with partial tuition reimbursement (averaging $15,000 per year), 13 research assistantships with partial tuition reimbursements (averaging $17,115 per year), 27 teaching assistantships with partial tuition reimbursements (averaging $16,172 per year) were awarded; institutionally sponsored loans, scholarships/grants, health care benefits, and unspecified assistantships also available. Financial award application deadline: 3/15. *Faculty research:* Dynamics and control systems; energy systems including renewable and nuclear; computational fluid and solid mechanics; structures, materials and manufacturing; vibrations and acoustics. *Total annual research expenditures:* $4.5 million. *Unit head:* Dr. Brendan O'Toole, Chair/Professor, 702-895-3885, Fax: 702-895-3936, E-mail: brendan.otoole@unlv.edu. *Application contact:* Dr. Hui Zhao, Graduate Coordinator, 702-895-1463, Fax: 702-895-3936, E-mail: hui.zhao@unlv.edu.
Website: http://me.unlv.edu/

University of Nevada, Reno, Graduate School, Interdisciplinary Program in Biomedical Engineering, Reno, NV 89557. Offers MS, PhD. Terminal master's awarded for partial completion of doctoral program. *Degree requirements:* For master's, thesis optional; for doctorate, thesis/dissertation. *Entrance requirements:* For master's, GRE General Test (recommended), minimum GPA of 2.75; for doctorate, GRE General Test (recommended), minimum GPA of 3.0. Additional exam requirements/recommendations for international students: Required—TOEFL (minimum score 500 paper-based; 61 iBT), IELTS (minimum score 6). Electronic applications accepted. *Faculty research:* Bioengineering, biophysics, biomedical instrumentation, biosensors.

University of New Haven, Graduate School, Tagliatela College of Engineering, Program in Biomedical Engineering, West Haven, CT 06516. Offers MS. *Students:* 5 full-time (2 women), 2 part-time (1 woman); includes 2 minority (1 Black or African American, non-Hispanic/Latino; 1 Asian, non-Hispanic/Latino), 2 international. Average age 27. 18 applicants, 100% accepted, 7 enrolled. *Application deadline:* Applications are processed on a rolling basis. Application fee: $50. *Expenses: Tuition:* Full-time $15,660; part-time $870 per credit hour. *Required fees:* $200; $85 per term. Tuition and fees vary according to program. *Unit head:* Dr. Ronald Harichandran, Dean, 203-932-7167, E-mail: rharichandran@newhaven.edu. *Application contact:* Michelle Mason, Director of Graduate Enrollment, 203-932-7440, E-mail: mmason@newhaven.edu.

University of New Mexico, Graduate Studies, School of Engineering, Program in Biomedical Engineering, Albuquerque, NM 87131-2039. Offers MS, PhD. *Program availability:* Part-time. *Faculty:* 2 full-time (1 woman). *Students:* 9 full-time (4 women), 1 (woman) part-time; includes 1 minority (Hispanic/Latino), 1 international. Average age 30. 22 applicants, 41% accepted, 8 enrolled. In 2016, 3 master's, 2 doctorates awarded. Terminal master's awarded for partial completion of doctoral program. *Degree requirements:* For master's, thesis (for some programs); for doctorate, comprehensive exam, thesis/dissertation. *Entrance requirements:* For master's and doctorate, GRE General Test, letters of recommendation, letter of intent. *Application deadline:* Applications are processed on a rolling basis. Application fee: $50. *Unit head:* Dr. Steven Graves, Program Director, 505-277-5521, E-mail: graves@unm.edu. *Application contact:* Jocelyn White, Program Coordinator for Advisement, 505-277-5606, Fax: 505-277-5433, E-mail: jowhite@unm.edu.
Website: http://bme.unm.edu/index.html

The University of North Carolina at Chapel Hill, School of Medicine and Graduate School, Graduate Programs in Medicine, Joint Department of Biomedical Engineering UNC-Chapel Hill and NC State, Chapel Hill, NC 27599. Offers MS, PhD. Terminal master's awarded for partial completion of doctoral program. *Degree requirements:* For master's, comprehensive exam, thesis, ethics seminar; for doctorate, comprehensive exam, thesis/dissertation, qualifying exam, teaching and ethics seminar. *Entrance requirements:* For master's, GRE General Test, minimum GPA of 3.0; for doctorate, GRE General Test, minimum GPA of 3.3. Additional exam requirements/recommendations for international students: Required—TOEFL. Electronic applications accepted. *Faculty research:* Biomedical imaging, rehabilitation engineering, microsystems engineering.

University of North Texas, Robert B. Toulouse School of Graduate Studies, Denton, TX 76203-5459. Offers accounting (MS); applied anthropology (MA, MS); applied behavior analysis (Certificate); applied geography (MA); applied technology and performance improvement (M Ed, MS); art education (MA); art history (MA); art museum education (Certificate); arts leadership (Certificate); audiology (Au D); behavior analysis (MS); behavioral science (PhD); biochemistry and molecular biology (MS); biology (MA, MS); biomedical engineering (MS); business analysis (MS); chemistry (MS); clinical health psychology (PhD); communication studies (MA, MS); computer engineering (MS); computer science (MS); counseling (M Ed, MS), including clinical mental health counseling (MS), college and university counseling, elementary school counseling, secondary school counseling; creative writing (MA); criminal justice (MS); curriculum and instruction (M Ed); decision sciences (MBA); design (MA, MFA), including fashion design (MFA), innovation studies, interior design (MFA); early childhood studies (MS); economics (MS); educational leadership (M Ed, Ed D); educational psychology (MS, PhD), including family studies (MS), gifted and talented (MS), human development (MS), learning and cognition (MS), research, measurement and evaluation (MS); electrical engineering (MS); emergency management (MPA); engineering technology (MS); English (MA); English as a second language (MA); environmental science (MS); finance (MBA, MS); financial management (MPA); French (MA); health services management (MBA); higher education (M Ed, Ed D); history (MA, MS); hospitality management (MS); human resources management (MPA); information science (MS); information systems (PhD); information technologies (MBA); interdisciplinary studies (MA, MS); international studies (MA); international sustainable tourism (MS); jazz studies (MM); journalism (MA, MJ, Graduate Certificate), including interactive and virtual digital communication (Graduate Certificate), narrative journalism (Graduate Certificate), public relations (Graduate Certificate); kinesiology (MS); linguistics (MA); local government management (MPA); logistics (PhD); logistics and supply chain management (MBA); long-term care, senior housing, and aging services (MA); management (PhD); marketing (MBA); mathematics (MA, MS); mechanical and energy engineering (MS, PhD); music (MA), including ethnomusicology, music theory, musicology, performance; music composition (PhD); music education (MM Ed, PhD); nonprofit management (MPA); operations and supply chain management (MBA); performance (MM, DMA); philosophy (MA); political science (MA); professional and technical communication (MA); radio, television and film (MA, MFA); rehabilitation counseling (Certificate); sociology (MA); Spanish (MA); special education (M Ed); speech-language pathology (MA); strategic management (MBA); studio art (MFA); teaching (M Ed); MBA/MS. *Program availability:* Part-time, evening/weekend, online learning. Terminal master's awarded for partial completion of doctoral program. *Degree requirements:* For master's, variable foreign language requirement, comprehensive exam (for some programs), thesis (for some programs); for doctorate, variable foreign language requirement, comprehensive exam (for some programs), thesis/dissertation; for other advanced degree, variable foreign language requirement, comprehensive exam (for some programs). *Entrance requirements:* For master's and doctorate, GRE, GMAT. Additional exam requirements/recommendations for international students: Required—TOEFL (minimum score 550 paper-based; 79 iBT). Electronic applications accepted.

University of Oklahoma, Gallogly College of Engineering, School of Biomedical Engineering, Norman, OK 73019. Offers MS, PhD. *Program availability:* Part-time. *Faculty:* 17 full-time (2 women). *Students:* 16 full-time (7 women), 2 part-time (1 woman); includes 4 minority (1 Black or African American, non-Hispanic/Latino; 1 Asian, non-Hispanic/Latino; 2 Two or more races, non-Hispanic/Latino), 7 international. Average age 27. 22 applicants, 27% accepted, 5 enrolled. In 2016, 1 master's awarded. *Degree requirements:* For master's, thesis; for doctorate, comprehensive exam, thesis/dissertation. *Entrance requirements:* For master's and doctorate, GRE. Additional exam requirements/recommendations for international students: Required—TOEFL (minimum score 100 iBT) or IELTS (minimum score 7). *Application deadline:* For fall admission, 1/15 priority date for domestic and international students; for spring admission, 9/15 priority date for domestic and international students. Application fee: $50 ($100 for international students). Electronic applications accepted. *Expenses:* Tuition, state resident: full-time $4886; part-time $203.60 per credit hour. Tuition, nonresident: full-time $18,989; part-time $791.20 per credit hour. *Required fees:* $3283; $126.25 per credit hour. $126.50 per semester. *Financial support:* In 2016–17, 18 students received support, including 13 research assistantships with tuition reimbursements available (averaging $14,586 per year), 3 teaching assistantships with partial tuition reimbursements available (averaging $12,975 per year); fellowships with full tuition reimbursements available, scholarships/grants, health care benefits, and unspecified assistantships also available. Financial award application deadline: 6/1; financial award applicants required to submit FAFSA. *Faculty research:* Cancer nanomedicine, neural engineering, regenerative medicine, medical imaging, musculoskeletal medicine. *Total annual research expenditures:* $191,854. *Unit head:* Dr. Michael Detamore, Director,

405-325-2144, E-mail: detamore@ou.edu. *Application contact:* Shayla Palmer, Student Programs Coordinator, 405-325-3947, E-mail: chrishaylapalmer@ou.edu.
Website: http://www.ou.edu/coe/sbme

University of Ottawa, Faculty of Graduate and Postdoctoral Studies, Ottawa—Carlton Joint Program in Biomedical Engineering, Ottawa, ON K1N 6N5, Canada. Offers MA Sc. *Degree requirements:* For master's, thesis or alternative. *Entrance requirements:* For master's, honors degree or equivalent, minimum B average.

University of Portland, School of Engineering, Portland, OR 97203-5798. Offers biomedical engineering (MBME); civil engineering (ME); computer science (ME); electrical engineering (ME); mechanical engineering (ME). *Program availability:* Part-time, evening/weekend. *Degree requirements:* For master's, thesis optional. *Entrance requirements:* For master's, GRE General Test, minimum GPA of 3.0, 3 letters of recommendation, resume, statement of goals, official transcripts. Additional exam requirements/recommendations for international students: Required—TOEFL (minimum score 550 paper-based; 80 iBT), IELTS (minimum score 7). *Expenses:* Contact institution.

University of Rhode Island, Graduate School, College of Engineering, Department of Electrical, Computer and Biomedical Engineering, Kingston, RI 02881. Offers acoustics and underwater acoustics (MS, PhD); biomedical engineering (MS, PhD); circuits and devices (MS); communication theory (MS, PhD); computer architectures and digital systems (MS, PhD); computer networks (MS, PhD); digital signal processing (MS); embedded systems and computer applications (MS, PhD); fault-tolerant computing (MS, PhD); materials and optics (MS, PhD); systems theory (MS, PhD). *Program availability:* Part-time. *Faculty:* 22 full-time (3 women). *Students:* 27 full-time (5 women), 17 part-time (3 women); includes 6 minority (1 American Indian or Alaska Native, non-Hispanic/Latino; 3 Asian, non-Hispanic/Latino; 1 Hispanic/Latino; 1 Two or more races, non-Hispanic/Latino), 21 international. In 2016, 8 master's, 7 doctorates awarded. *Degree requirements:* For master's, comprehensive exam (for some programs), thesis optional; for doctorate, comprehensive exam, thesis/dissertation. *Entrance requirements:* For master's and doctorate, GRE, 2 letters of recommendation (3 for international applicants). Additional exam requirements/recommendations for international students: Required—TOEFL. *Application deadline:* For fall admission, 7/15 for domestic students, 2/1 for international students; for spring admission, 11/15 for domestic students, 7/15 for international students; for summer admission, 4/15 for domestic students. Application fee: $65. Electronic applications accepted. *Expenses:* Tuition, state resident: full-time $11,796; part-time $655 per credit. Tuition, nonresident: full-time $24,206; part-time $1345 per credit. *Required fees:* $1546; $44 per credit. One-time fee: $155 full-time; $35 part-time. *Financial support:* In 2016–17, 11 research assistantships with tuition reimbursements (averaging $9,825 per year), 4 teaching assistantships with tuition reimbursements (averaging $8,681 per year) were awarded. Financial award application deadline: 7/15; financial award applicants required to submit FAFSA. *Unit head:* Dr. Godi Fischer, Chair, 401-874-5879, Fax: 401-782-6422, E-mail: fischer@ele.uri.edu. *Application contact:* Dr. Frederick J. Vetter, Graduate Director, 401-874-5141,
E-mail: vetter@ele.uri.edu. Website: http://www.ele.uri.edu/

University of Rochester, Hajim School of Engineering and Applied Sciences, Department of Biomedical Engineering, Rochester, NY 14627. Offers MS, PhD. *Program availability:* Part-time. *Faculty:* 12 full-time (6 women). *Students:* 64 full-time (30 women), 2 part-time (1 woman); includes 14 minority (5 Black or African American, non-Hispanic/Latino; 4 Asian, non-Hispanic/Latino; 3 Hispanic/Latino; 2 Two or more races, non-Hispanic/Latino), 17 international. Average age 25. 277 applicants, 42% accepted, 26 enrolled. In 2016, 24 master's, 8 doctorates awarded. Terminal master's awarded for partial completion of doctoral program. *Degree requirements:* For master's, comprehensive exam, thesis, final exam; for doctorate, thesis/dissertation, qualifying exam. *Entrance requirements:* For master's and doctorate, GRE General Test. Additional exam requirements/recommendations for international students: Required—TOEFL (minimum score 600 paper-based; 100 iBT). *Application deadline:* For fall admission, 4/15 priority date for domestic and international students. Application fee: $60. Electronic applications accepted. *Expenses:* $1,538 per credit hour. *Financial support:* In 2016–17, 40 students received support, including 9 fellowships with full tuition reimbursements available (averaging $29,155 per year), 31 research assistantships with full and partial tuition reimbursements available (averaging $26,181 per year); traineeships, health care benefits, tuition waivers (full and partial), and unspecified assistantships also available. Financial award application deadline: 4/15. *Faculty research:* Biomechanics, biomedical optics, cell and tissue engineering, medical imaging, neuroengineering. *Unit head:* Diane Dalecki, Chair, 585-275-7378,
E-mail: diane.dalecki@rochester.edu. *Application contact:* Donna Porcelli, Graduate Program Coordinator, 585-275-3891.
Website: http://www.urmc.rochester.edu/bme/graduate/

University of Rochester, Hajim School of Engineering and Applied Sciences, Master of Science in Technical Entrepreneurship and Management Program, Rochester, NY 14642. Offers biomedical engineering (MS); chemical engineering (MS); computer science (MS); electrical and computer engineering (MS); energy and the environment (MS); materials science (MS); mechanical engineering (MS); optics (MS). Program offered in collaboration with the Simon School of Business. *Program availability:* Part-time. *Students:* 42 full-time (13 women), 6 part-time (3 women); includes 7 minority (1 Black or African American, non-Hispanic/Latino; 1 Asian, non-Hispanic/Latino; 4 Hispanic/Latino; 1 Two or more races, non-Hispanic/Latino), 28 international. Average age 24. 245 applicants, 65% accepted, 29 enrolled. In 2016, 31 master's awarded. *Degree requirements:* For master's, comprehensive exam, final exam. *Entrance requirements:* For master's, GRE or GMAT, 3 letters of recommendation; personal statement; official transcript; bachelor's degree (or equivalent for international students) in engineering, science, or mathematics. Additional exam requirements/recommendations for international students: Required—TOEFL (minimum score 600 paper-based; 100 iBT). *Application deadline:* For fall admission, 2/1 for domestic and international students. Application fee: $60. Electronic applications accepted. *Expenses:* $1,800 per credit. *Financial support:* In 2016–17, 45 students received support. Career-related internships or fieldwork and scholarships/grants available. Support available to part-time students. Financial award application deadline: 2/1. *Faculty research:* High efficiency solar cells, macromolecular self-assembly, digital signal processing, memory hierarchy management, molecular and physical mechanisms in cell migration, optical imaging systems. *Unit head:* Duncan T. Moore, Vice Provost for Entrepreneurship, 585-275-5248, Fax: 585-473-6745, E-mail: duncan.moore@rochester.edu. *Application contact:* Andrea Barrett, Executive Director, 585-276-3407, Fax: 585-276-2357,
E-mail: andrea.barrett@rochester.edu.
Website: http://www.rochester.edu/team

University of Saskatchewan, College of Graduate Studies and Research, College of Engineering, Biomedical Engineering Program, Saskatoon, SK S7N 5A9, Canada. Offers M Eng, M Sc, PhD. *Program availability:* Part-time. *Degree requirements:* For master's, thesis (for some programs), 30 credits (for M Eng); thesis and 12 credits (for MS); for doctorate, comprehensive exam, thesis/dissertation, qualifying exam, 18 credits. *Entrance requirements:* For master's and doctorate, GRE. Additional exam requirements/recommendations for international students: Required—TOEFL, TOEFL (minimum iBT score of 80), IELTS (6.5), CanTEST (4.5), or PTE (59). Electronic applications accepted. *Faculty research:* Bioinformatics, biomechanics, biomedical signal and image processing, biosensor, medical instrumentation, medical imaging, nano-drug delivery system, systems biology, tissue engineering.

University of Southern California, Graduate School, Viterbi School of Engineering, Department of Biomedical Engineering, Los Angeles, CA 90089. Offers biomedical engineering (PhD); medical device and diagnostic engineering (MS); medical imaging and imaging informatics (MS). *Program availability:* Online learning. Terminal master's awarded for partial completion of doctoral program. *Degree requirements:* For master's, thesis optional; for doctorate, thesis/dissertation. *Entrance requirements:* For master's and doctorate, GRE General Test. Additional exam requirements/recommendations for international students: Recommended—TOEFL. Electronic applications accepted. *Faculty research:* Medical ultrasound, BioMEMS, neural prosthetics, computational bioengineering, bioengineering of vision, medical devices.

University of South Florida, College of Engineering, Department of Chemical and Biomedical Engineering, Tampa, FL 33620. Offers biomedical engineering (MSBE, PhD); chemical engineering (MSCH, PhD). *Program availability:* Part-time. *Faculty:* 15 full-time (2 women). *Students:* 91 full-time (42 women), 20 part-time (5 women); includes 16 minority (7 Black or African American, non-Hispanic/Latino; 4 Asian, non-Hispanic/Latino; 5 Hispanic/Latino), 57 international. Average age 27. 195 applicants, 46% accepted, 43 enrolled. In 2016, 42 master's, 9 doctorates awarded. Terminal master's awarded for partial completion of doctoral program. *Degree requirements:* For master's, comprehensive exam, thesis (for some programs); for doctorate, comprehensive exam, thesis/dissertation. *Entrance requirements:* For master's, GRE General Test, undergraduate degree in engineering, science, or chemical engineering with minimum GPA of 3.0; at least two letters of recommendation; current resume; statement of research interests (for students who wish to pursue thesis option); for doctorate, GRE General Test, undergraduate degree in engineering, science, or chemical engineering with minimum GPA of 3.0; three letters of recommendation; current resume; statement of research interests. Additional exam requirements/recommendations for international students: Required—TOEFL (minimum score 550 paper-based; 79 iBT) or IELTS (minimum score 6.5). *Application deadline:* For fall admission, 2/15 for domestic and international students; for spring admission, 10/15 for domestic students, 9/15 for international students; for summer admission, 2/15 for domestic students, 1/15 for international students. Application fee: $30. Electronic applications accepted. *Expenses:* Tuition, state resident: full-time $7766; part-time $431.43 per credit hour. Tuition, nonresident: full-time $15,789; part-time $877.17 per credit hour. *Required fees:* $37 per term. *Financial support:* In 2016–17, 28 students received support, including 29 research assistantships with tuition reimbursements available (averaging $13,171 per year), 12 teaching assistantships with tuition reimbursements available (averaging $14,017 per year); unspecified assistantships also available. Financial award applicants required to submit FAFSA. *Faculty research:* Neuroengineering, tissue engineering, biomedicine and biotechnology, engineering education, functional materials and nanotechnology, energy, environment/sustainability. *Total annual research expenditures:* $987,111. *Unit head:* Dr. Venkat R. Bhethanabotla, Professor and Department Chair, 813-974-3997, E-mail: bhethana@usf.edu. *Application contact:* Dr. Robert Frisina, Jr., Professor and Graduate Program Director, 813-974-4013, Fax: 813-974-3651, E-mail: rfrisina@usf.edu.
Website: http://che.eng.usf.edu/

University of South Florida, Innovative Education, Tampa, FL 33620-9951. Offers adult, career and higher education (Graduate Certificate), including college teaching, leadership in developing human resources, leadership in higher education; Africana studies (Graduate Certificate), including diasporas and health disparities, genocide and human rights; aging studies (Graduate Certificate), including gerontology; art research (Graduate Certificate), including museum studies; business foundations (Graduate Certificate); chemical and biomedical engineering (Graduate Certificate), including materials science and engineering, water, health and sustainability; child and family studies (Graduate Certificate), including positive behavior support; civil and industrial engineering (Graduate Certificate), including transportation systems analysis; community and family health (Graduate Certificate), including maternal and child health, social marketing and public health, violence and injury: prevention and intervention, women's health; criminology (Graduate Certificate), including criminal justice administration; educational measurement and research (Graduate Certificate), including evaluation; English (Graduate Certificate), including comparative literary studies, creative writing, professional and technical communication; entrepreneurship (Graduate Certificate); environmental health (Graduate Certificate), including safety management; epidemiology and biostatistics (Graduate Certificate), including applied biostatistics, biostatistics, concepts and tools of epidemiology, epidemiology, epidemiology of infectious diseases; geography, environment and planning (Graduate Certificate), including community development, environmental policy and management, geographical information systems; geology (Graduate Certificate), including hydrogeology; global health (Graduate Certificate), including disaster management, global health and Latin American and Caribbean studies, global health practice, humanitarian assistance, infection control; government and international affairs (Graduate Certificate), including Cuban studies, globalization studies; health policy and management (Graduate Certificate), including health management and leadership, public health policy and programs; hearing specialist: early intervention (Graduate Certificate); industrial and management systems engineering (Graduate Certificate), including systems engineering, technology management; information studies (Graduate Certificate), including school library media specialist; information systems/decision sciences (Graduate Certificate), including analytics and business intelligence; instructional technology (Graduate Certificate), including distance education, Florida digital/virtual educator, instructional design, multimedia design, Web design; internal medicine, bioethics and medical humanities (Graduate Certificate), including biomedical ethics; Latin American and Caribbean studies (Graduate Certificate); mass communications (Graduate Certificate), including multimedia journalism; mathematics and statistics (Graduate Certificate), including mathematics; medicine (Graduate Certificate), including aging and neuroscience, bioinformatics, biotechnology, brain fitness and memory management, clinical investigation, health informatics, health sciences, integrative weight management, intellectual property, medicine and gender, metabolic and nutritional medicine, metabolic cardiology, pharmacy sciences; national and competitive intelligence (Graduate Certificate); psychological and social foundations (Graduate Certificate), including career counseling, college teaching, diversity in education, mental health counseling, school counseling; public affairs (Graduate Certificate), including nonprofit management, public management, research administration; public health (Graduate Certificate), including environmental health, health equity, public health generalist, translational research in adolescent behavioral health; public health practices (Graduate Certificate), including planning for healthy communities; rehabilitation and mental health counseling (Graduate Certificate), including integrative mental health care, marriage and family therapy, rehabilitation technology; secondary education (Graduate Certificate), including ESOL, foreign language education: culture and content, foreign language education: professional; social work (Graduate Certificate), including geriatric social work/clinical gerontology; special education (Graduate Certificate), including autism spectrum disorder, disabilities education: severe/profound; world languages (Graduate Certificate), including teaching

English as a second language (TESL) or foreign language. *Expenses:* Tuition, state resident: full-time $7766; part-time $431.43 per credit hour. Tuition, nonresident: full-time $15,789; part-time $877.17 per credit hour. *Required fees:* $37 per term. *Unit head:* Kathy Barnes, Interdisciplinary Programs Coordinator, 813-974-8031, Fax: 813-974-7061, E-mail: barnesk@usf.edu. *Application contact:* Karen Tylinski, Metro Initiatives, 813-974-9943, Fax: 813-974-7061, E-mail: ktylinsk@usf.edu.
Website: http://www.usf.edu/innovative-education/

The University of Tennessee, Graduate School, Tickle College of Engineering, Department of Mechanical, Aerospace and Biomedical Engineering, Program in Biomedical Engineering, Knoxville, TN 37996. Offers MS, PhD, MS/PhD. *Program availability:* Part-time, online learning. *Faculty:* 11 full-time (3 women), 1 part-time/adjunct (0 women). *Students:* 8 full-time (2 women), 2 part-time (0 women); includes 3 minority (1 American Indian or Alaska Native, non-Hispanic/Latino; 2 Asian, non-Hispanic/Latino), 5 international. Average age 28. 56 applicants, 57% accepted, 11 enrolled. In 2016, 6 master's, 6 doctorates awarded. *Degree requirements:* For master's, thesis or alternative; for doctorate, comprehensive exam, thesis/dissertation. *Entrance requirements:* For master's, GRE General Test (for MS students pursuing research thesis), minimum GPA of 2.7 (for U.S. degree holders), 3.0 (for international degree holders); 3 references; statement of purpose; for doctorate, GRE General Test, minimum GPA of 3.0 on previous graduate course work; 3 references; statement of purpose. Additional exam requirements/recommendations for international students: Required—TOEFL (minimum score 550 paper-based). *Application deadline:* For fall admission, 2/1 priority date for domestic and international students; for spring admission, 6/15 for domestic and international students. Applications are processed on a rolling basis. Application fee: $35. Electronic applications accepted. *Financial support:* In 2016–17, 12 students received support, including 3 research assistantships with full tuition reimbursements available (averaging $21,833 per year), 6 teaching assistantships with full tuition reimbursements available (averaging $18,983 per year); fellowships with full tuition reimbursements available, career-related internships or fieldwork, Federal Work-Study, institutionally sponsored loans, health care benefits, and unspecified assistantships also available. Financial award application deadline: 2/1; financial award applicants required to submit FAFSA. *Faculty research:* Bioimaging, biomechanics, biorobotics, biosensors, biomaterials. *Unit head:* Dr. Matthew Mench, Head, 865-974-5115, Fax: 865-974-5274, E-mail: mmench@utk.edu. *Application contact:* Dr. Kivanc Ekici, Associate Professor, Graduate Program Director, 865-974-6016, Fax: 865-974-5274, E-mail: ekici@utk.edu.
Website: http://www.engr.utk.edu/mabe

The University of Tennessee, The University of Tennessee Space Institute, Tullahoma, TN 37388. Offers aerospace engineering (MS, PhD); biomedical engineering (MS, PhD); engineering science (MS, PhD); industrial and systems engineering/engineering management (MS, PhD); mechanical engineering (MS, PhD); physics (MS, PhD). *Program availability:* Part-time, blended/hybrid learning. Terminal master's awarded for partial completion of doctoral program. *Degree requirements:* For doctorate, one foreign language, thesis/dissertation. *Entrance requirements:* Additional exam requirements/recommendations for international students: Required—TOEFL (minimum score 550 paper-based; 80 iBT), IELTS (minimum score 6.5). Electronic applications accepted. *Expenses:* Contact institution. *Faculty research:* Fluid mechanics/aerodynamics, chemical and electric propulsion and laser diagnostics, computational mechanics and simulations, carbon fiber production and composite materials.

The University of Tennessee Health Science Center, College of Graduate Health Sciences, Memphis, TN 38163. Offers biomedical engineering (MS, PhD); biomedical sciences (PhD); dental sciences (MDS); epidemiology (MS); health outcomes and policy research (PhD); laboratory research and management (MS); nursing science (PhD); pharmaceutical sciences (PhD); pharmacology (MS); speech and hearing science (PhD); DDS/PhD; DNP/PhD; MD/PhD; Pharm D/PhD. Biomedical engineering offered jointly with University of Memphis. *Faculty:* 528 full-time (176 women). *Students:* 258 full-time (130 women); includes 87 minority (14 Black or African American, non-Hispanic/Latino; 68 Asian, non-Hispanic/Latino; 5 Hispanic/Latino). Average age 28. 673 applicants, 17% accepted, 102 enrolled. In 2016, 23 master's, 30 doctorates awarded. Terminal master's awarded for partial completion of doctoral program. *Degree requirements:* For master's, comprehensive exam, thesis; for doctorate, thesis/dissertation, oral and written preliminary and comprehensive exams. *Entrance requirements:* For master's and doctorate, GRE General Test, minimum GPA of 3.0. Additional exam requirements/recommendations for international students: Required—TOEFL (minimum score 79 iBT); Recommended—IELTS (minimum score 6.5). *Application deadline:* Applications are processed on a rolling basis. Application fee: $0. Electronic applications accepted. *Financial support:* In 2016–17, 150 students received support, including 150 research assistantships (averaging $25,000 per year); fellowships, Federal Work-Study, institutionally sponsored loans, scholarships/grants, health care benefits, and tuition waivers (full and partial) also available. Support available to part-time students. Financial award application deadline: 2/25. *Faculty research:* Cell biology, epidemiology, biomedical engineering, speech and hearing science, health policy. *Unit head:* Dr. Donald B. Thomason, Dean, 901-448-5538, E-mail: dthomaso@uthsc.edu. *Application contact:* Dr. Isaac O. Donkor, Associate Dean for Student Affairs, 901-448-5538, E-mail: idonkor@uthsc.edu.
Website: http://grad.uthsc.edu/

The University of Texas at Austin, Graduate School, Cockrell School of Engineering, Department of Biomedical Engineering, Austin, TX 78712-1111. Offers MS, PhD, MD/PhD. MD/PhD offered jointly with The University of Texas Medical Branch. *Program availability:* Part-time. *Degree requirements:* For master's, thesis optional; for doctorate, comprehensive exam, thesis/dissertation. *Entrance requirements:* For master's and doctorate, GRE General Test. Additional exam requirements/recommendations for international students: Required—TOEFL (minimum score 550 paper-based). Electronic applications accepted. *Faculty research:* Biomechanics, bioengineering, tissue engineering, tissue optics, biothermal studies.

The University of Texas at Dallas, Erik Jonson School of Engineering and Computer Science, Department of Bioengineering, Richardson, TX 75080. Offers biomedical engineering (MS, PhD). *Faculty:* 18 full-time (4 women), 2 part-time/adjunct (both women). *Students:* 87 full-time (42 women), 21 part-time (12 women); includes 23 minority (1 Black or African American, non-Hispanic/Latino; 1 American Indian or Alaska Native, non-Hispanic/Latino; 13 Asian, non-Hispanic/Latino; 6 Hispanic/Latino; 2 Two or more races, non-Hispanic/Latino), 50 international. Average age 27. 124 applicants, 48% accepted, 32 enrolled. In 2016, 15 master's, 10 doctorates awarded. *Degree requirements:* For master's, thesis (for some programs); for doctorate, comprehensive exam, thesis/dissertation. *Entrance requirements:* For master's, GRE (minimum scores of 500 in verbal, 700 in quantitative and 4 in analytical writing), minimum GPA of 3.0 in upper-division quantitative course work; for doctorate, GRE (minimum scores of 500 in verbal, 700 in quantitative and 4 in analytical writing), minimum GPA of 3.5 in upper-division quantitative course work. Additional exam requirements/recommendations for international students: Required—TOEFL (minimum score 550 paper-based). *Application deadline:* For fall admission, 7/15 for domestic students, 5/1 priority date for international students; for spring admission, 11/15 for domestic students, 9/1 priority date for international students. Applications are processed on a rolling basis. Application fee: $50 ($100 for international students). Electronic applications accepted. *Expenses:* Tuition, state resident: full-time $12,418; part-time $690 per semester hour. Tuition, nonresident: full-time $24,150; part-time $1342 per semester hour. Tuition and fees vary according to course load. *Financial support:* In 2016–17, 75 students received support, including 4 fellowships (averaging $4,369 per year), 31 research assistantships with partial tuition reimbursements available (averaging $24,910 per year), 27 teaching assistantships with partial tuition reimbursements available (averaging $17,000 per year); career-related internships or fieldwork, Federal Work-Study, institutionally sponsored loans, scholarships/grants, and unspecified assistantships also available. Support available to part-time students. Financial award application deadline: 4/30; financial award applicants required to submit FAFSA. *Faculty research:* Bio-nanotechnology, organic electronics, system-level design for medical devices, computational geometry and biomedical computing. *Unit head:* Dr. Robert L. Rennaker, Department Head, 972-883-3562, E-mail: renn@utdallas.edu. *Application contact:* Ben Porter, Associate Dean, 972-883-5155, E-mail: gradecs@utdallas.edu.
Website: http://be.utdallas.edu/

The University of Texas at El Paso, Graduate School, College of Engineering, El Paso, TX 79968-0001. Offers biomedical engineering (PhD); civil engineering (MEENE, MS, MSENE, PhD, Certificate), including civil engineering (MS), civil engineering (PhD), construction management (MS, Certificate), environmental engineering (MEENE, MSENE); computer science (MS, MSIT, PhD), including computer science (MS, PhD), information technology (MSIT); education engineering (M Eng); electrical and computer engineering (MS, PhD), including computer engineering (MS), electrical and computer engineering (PhD), electrical engineering (MS); industrial engineering (MS, Certificate), including industrial engineering (MS), manufacturing engineering (MS), systems engineering; mechanical engineering (MS, PhD), including environmental science and engineering (PhD), mechanical engineering (MS); metallurgical and materials engineering (MS, PhD), including materials science and engineering (PhD), metallurgical and materials engineering (MS); software engineering (M Eng). *Program availability:* Part-time, evening/weekend. *Degree requirements:* For master's, thesis optional; for doctorate, thesis/dissertation. *Entrance requirements:* For master's, GRE, minimum GPA of 3.0, letters of reference; for doctorate, GRE, statement of purpose, letters of reference. Additional exam requirements/recommendations for international students: Required—TOEFL; Recommended—IELTS. Electronic applications accepted. *Expenses:* Contact institution.

The University of Texas at San Antonio, College of Engineering, Department of Biomedical Engineering, San Antonio, TX 78207. Offers MS, PhD. *Program availability:* Part-time. *Faculty:* 4 full-time (0 women), 1 part-time/adjunct (0 women). *Students:* 22 full-time (14 women), 36 part-time (15 women); includes 23 minority (4 Black or African American, non-Hispanic/Latino; 3 Asian, non-Hispanic/Latino; 14 Hispanic/Latino; 2 Two or more races, non-Hispanic/Latino), 17 international. Average age 28. 75 applicants, 48% accepted, 13 enrolled. In 2016, 24 master's, 1 doctorate awarded. Terminal master's awarded for partial completion of doctoral program. *Degree requirements:* For master's, comprehensive exam, thesis; for doctorate, comprehensive exam, thesis/dissertation. *Entrance requirements:* For master's, GRE, three letters of recommendation, statement of purpose, BS in any of the science or engineering disciplines; for doctorate, GRE, resume, three letters of recommendation, statement of purpose, BS in any of the science or engineering disciplines. Additional exam requirements/recommendations for international students: Required—TOEFL (minimum score 550 paper-based; 79 iBT), IELTS (minimum score 6.5). *Application deadline:* For fall admission, 2/1 for domestic and international students; for spring admission, 10/1 for domestic and international students. Applications are processed on a rolling basis. Application fee: $45 ($80 for international students). Electronic applications accepted. *Expenses:* Contact institution. *Financial support:* In 2016–17, 11 students received support, including 11 fellowships with full tuition reimbursements available (averaging $21,000 per year); unspecified assistantships also available. Financial award application deadline: 2/1. *Faculty research:* Tissue engineering and biomaterials, ocular biomechanics and cardiovascular biomechanics, biophotonics, cellular bioengineering, nano-biomaterials and nano-biotechnology. *Total annual research expenditures:* $416,896. *Unit head:* Dr. Anson Ong, Interim Department Chair/Professor, 210-458-7084, E-mail: anson.ong@utsa.edu. *Application contact:* Monica Rodriguez, Director of the Graduate School, 210-458-4331, E-mail: graduateadmissions@utsa.edu.
Website: http://engineering.utsa.edu/bme/BME_program/index.html

The University of Texas Health Science Center at San Antonio, Graduate School of Biomedical Sciences, Biomedical Engineering Program, San Antonio, TX 78229-3900. Offers MS, PhD. Program offered jointly with The University of Texas at San Antonio. *Program availability:* Part-time. Terminal master's awarded for partial completion of doctoral program. *Degree requirements:* For master's, comprehensive exam, thesis; for doctorate, comprehensive exam, thesis/dissertation.

The University of Texas Southwestern Medical Center, Southwestern Graduate School of Biomedical Sciences, Division of Basic Science, Biomedical Engineering Program, Dallas, TX 75390. Offers MS, PhD. Programs offered jointly with The University of Texas at Arlington. *Degree requirements:* For master's, comprehensive exam or thesis; for doctorate, comprehensive exam, thesis/dissertation. *Entrance requirements:* For master's, GRE General Test, minimum GPA of 3.0; for doctorate, GRE General Test, minimum GPA of 3.4. Additional exam requirements/recommendations for international students: Required—TOEFL. Electronic applications accepted. *Faculty research:* Noninvasive image analysis, biomaterials development, rehabilitation engineering, biomechanics, bioinstrumentation.

The University of Toledo, College of Graduate Studies, College of Engineering and College of Medicine and Life Sciences, PhD Program in Biomedical Engineering, Toledo, OH 43606-3390. Offers PhD. *Degree requirements:* For doctorate, thesis/dissertation, qualifying exam. *Entrance requirements:* For doctorate, GRE General Test, minimum GPA of 3.3. Additional exam requirements/recommendations for international students: Required—TOEFL (minimum score 550 paper-based; 80 iBT). Electronic applications accepted. *Faculty research:* Biomechanics, biomaterials, tissue engineering, artificial organs, biosensors.

University of Toronto, School of Graduate Studies, Faculty of Applied Science and Engineering, Institute of Biomaterials and Biomedical Engineering, Toronto, ON M5S 1A1, Canada. Offers biomedical engineering (MA Sc, PhD); clinical engineering (MH Sc, PhD). *Program availability:* Part-time. *Degree requirements:* For master's, thesis (for some programs), research project (MH Sc), oral presentation (MA Sc); for doctorate, thesis/dissertation, qualifying exam. *Entrance requirements:* For master's, minimum A-average; bachelor's degree or equivalent in engineering, physical or biological science (for MA Sc), applied science or engineering (for MH Sc); for doctorate, master's degree in engineering, engineering science, medicine, dentistry, or a physical or biological science. Additional exam requirements/recommendations for international students: Required—TOEFL (minimum score 600 paper-based), TWE (minimum score 4), IELTS, Michigan English Language Assessment Battery, or COPE. Electronic applications accepted.

University of Vermont, Graduate College, College of Engineering and Mathematics, Program in Bioengineering, Burlington, VT 05405. Offers PhD. *Entrance requirements:*

For doctorate, GRE General Test. Additional exam requirements/recommendations for international students: Required—TOEFL (minimum score 550 paper-based; 80 iBT). Electronic applications accepted. *Expenses:* Tuition, state resident: full-time $5814. Tuition, nonresident: full-time $14,670.

University of Virginia, School of Engineering and Applied Science, Department of Biomedical Engineering, Charlottesville, VA 22903. Offers ME, MS, PhD. *Faculty:* 22 full-time (4 women), 1 part-time/adjunct (0 women). *Students:* 79 full-time (38 women), 3 part-time (1 woman); includes 19 minority (2 Black or African American, non-Hispanic/Latino; 9 Asian, non-Hispanic/Latino; 6 Hispanic/Latino; 2 Two or more races, non-Hispanic/Latino), 13 international. Average age 25. 193 applicants, 22% accepted, 18 enrolled. In 2016, 4 master's, 8 doctorates awarded. *Degree requirements:* For master's, project or thesis; for doctorate, thesis/dissertation. *Entrance requirements:* For master's, GRE General Test, 3 letters of recommendation; for doctorate, GRE General Test, 3 letters of recommendation, essay. Additional exam requirements/recommendations for international students: Required—TOEFL (minimum score 600 paper-based; 90 iBT), IELTS (minimum score 7). *Application deadline:* For fall admission, 8/1 for domestic students, 4/1 for international students; for winter admission, 12/1 for domestic students, 8/1 for international students; for spring admission, 5/1 for domestic students, 1/1 for international students. Applications are processed on a rolling basis. Application fee: $60. Electronic applications accepted. *Expenses:* Tuition, state resident: full-time $15,026; part-time $834 per credit hour. Tuition, nonresident: full-time $25,168; part-time $1378 per credit hour. *Required fees:* $2654. *Financial support:* Fellowships, research assistantships, and teaching assistantships available. Financial award application deadline: 1/15; financial award applicants required to submit FAFSA. *Faculty research:* Cardiopulmonary and neural engineering, cellular engineering, image processing, orthopedics and rehabilitation engineering. *Unit head:* Frederick Epstein, Chair, 434-924-5101, Fax: 434-982-3870, E-mail: bme-dept@virginia.edu. *Application contact:* Jason Papin, Director of Graduate Programs, 434-243-6906, Fax: 434-982-3870, E-mail: bmegrad@virginia.edu.
Website: http://bme.virginia.edu/grad/

University of Wisconsin–Madison, Graduate School, College of Engineering, Department of Biomedical Engineering, Madison, WI 53706. Offers MS, PhD. *Program availability:* Part-time. *Faculty:* 16 full-time (7 women). *Students:* 93 full-time (39 women), 4 part-time (1 woman); includes 20 minority (2 Black or African American, non-Hispanic/Latino; 1 American Indian or Alaska Native, non-Hispanic/Latino; 9 Asian, non-Hispanic/Latino; 6 Hispanic/Latino; 2 Two or more races, non-Hispanic/Latino), 15 international. Average age 26. 407 applicants, 16% accepted, 32 enrolled. In 2016, 21 master's, 19 doctorates awarded. Terminal master's awarded for partial completion of doctoral program. *Degree requirements:* For master's, thesis optional, at least 30 credits of coursework; for doctorate, comprehensive exam, thesis/dissertation, 30 additional credits of coursework beyond MS. *Entrance requirements:* For master's and doctorate, GRE, bachelor's degree in engineering (biomedical, chemical, electrical, industrial, mechanical, etc.) or science (biology, biochemistry, chemistry, genetics, immunology, physics, etc.). Additional exam requirements/recommendations for international students: Required—TOEFL (minimum score 625 paper-based) or IELTS. *Application deadline:* For fall admission, 12/1 for domestic and international students; for spring admission, 10/1 for domestic and international students; for summer admission, 2/1 for domestic and international students. Application fee: $75 ($81 for international students). Electronic applications accepted. *Expenses:* $13,157 per year in-state tuition and fees; $26,484 per year out-of-state tuition and fees. *Financial support:* In 2016–17, 60 students received support, including 5 fellowships with full tuition reimbursements available, 42 research assistantships with full tuition reimbursements available, 13 teaching assistantships with full tuition reimbursements available; career-related internships or fieldwork, Federal Work-Study, scholarships/grants, traineeships, and health care benefits also available. Financial award application deadline: 12/1; financial award applicants required to submit FAFSA. *Faculty research:* Cellular and molecular engineering; bioinstrumentation; biomedical imaging; cancer research; biomechanics; biomaterials and tissue engineering. *Total annual research expenditures:* $10.6 million. *Unit head:* Dr. Justin Williams, Professor and Chair, 608-263-4660, E-mail: info@bme.wisc.edu. *Application contact:* Pam Peterson, Student Services Coordinator, 608-263-4025, Fax: 608-262-8454, E-mail: prpeterson@wisc.edu.
Website: http://www.engr.wisc.edu/department/bme

University of Wisconsin–Milwaukee, Graduate School, College of Engineering and Applied Science, Program in Engineering, Milwaukee, WI 53201-0413. Offers biomedical engineering (MS); civil engineering (MS, PhD); computer science (PhD); electrical and computer engineering (MS); electrical engineering (PhD); engineering mechanics (MS); industrial and management engineering (MS); industrial engineering (PhD); manufacturing engineering (MS); materials (PhD); materials engineering (MS); mechanical engineering (MS). *Program availability:* Part-time. *Students:* 199 full-time (52 women), 156 part-time (32 women); includes 27 minority (2 Black or African American, non-Hispanic/Latino; 15 Asian, non-Hispanic/Latino; 3 Hispanic/Latino; 7 Two or more races, non-Hispanic/Latino), 244 international. Average age 30. 396 applicants, 61% accepted, 102 enrolled. In 2016, 72 master's, 26 doctorates awarded. *Degree requirements:* For master's, comprehensive exam (for some programs), thesis or alternative; for doctorate, comprehensive exam, thesis/dissertation, internship. *Entrance requirements:* For master's, GRE, minimum GPA of 2.75; for doctorate, GRE, minimum GPA of 3.5. Additional exam requirements/recommendations for international students: Required—TOEFL (minimum score 550 paper-based; 79 iBT), IELTS (minimum score 6.5). *Application deadline:* For fall admission, 1/1 priority date for domestic students; for spring admission, 9/1 for domestic students. Applications are processed on a rolling basis. Application fee: $56 ($96 for international students). *Financial support:* In 2016–17, 3 fellowships, 55 research assistantships, 77 teaching assistantships were awarded; career-related internships or fieldwork, Federal Work-Study, unspecified assistantships, and project assistantships also available. Support available to part-time students. Financial award application deadline: 4/15. *Unit head:* David Yu, Representative, 414-229-6169, E-mail: yu@uwm.edu. *Application contact:* Betty Warras, General Information Contact, 414-229-6169, Fax: 414-229-6967, E-mail: bwarras@uwm.edu.
Website: http://www4.uwm.edu/ceas/academics/graduate_programs/

Vanderbilt University, School of Engineering and Graduate School, Department of Biomedical Engineering, Nashville, TN 37240-1001. Offers M Eng, MS, PhD, MD/PhD. *Degree requirements:* For master's, thesis (for some programs); for doctorate, thesis/dissertation. *Entrance requirements:* For master's, GRE General Test (for all except M Eng); for doctorate, GRE General Test. Additional exam requirements/recommendations for international students: Required—TOEFL. Electronic applications accepted. *Expenses: Tuition:* Part-time $1854 per credit hour. *Faculty research:* Biomedical imaging, cell bioengineering, biomedical optics, technology-guided therapy, laser-tissue interaction and spectroscopy.

Virginia Commonwealth University, Graduate School, School of Engineering, Department of Biomedical Engineering, Richmond, VA 23284-9005. Offers MS, PhD. *Degree requirements:* For master's, thesis; for doctorate, thesis/dissertation, comprehensive oral and written exams. *Entrance requirements:* For master's and doctorate, GRE General Test. Additional exam requirements/recommendations for international students: Required—TOEFL (minimum score 600 paper-based; 100 iBT).

Application deadline: For fall admission, 2/1 priority date for domestic students; for spring admission, 11/15 for domestic students. Application fee: $50. Electronic applications accepted. *Financial support:* Applicants required to submit FAFSA. *Faculty research:* Clinical instrumentation, mathematical modeling, neurosciences, radiation physics and rehabilitation. *Unit head:* Dr. Rosalyn S. Hobson, Associate Dean for Graduate Affairs, 804-828-3925, E-mail: rhobson@vcu.edu. *Application contact:* Dr. Jennifer S. Wayne, Graduate Program Director, 804-828-7956, E-mail: jwayne@vcu.edu.
Website: http://www.egr.vcu.edu/Page.aspx?id-93

Virginia Polytechnic Institute and State University, Graduate School, College of Engineering, Blacksburg, VA 24061. Offers aerospace engineering (ME, MS, PhD); biological systems engineering (ME, MS, PhD); biomedical engineering (MS, PhD); chemical engineering (ME, MS, PhD); civil engineering (ME, MS, PhD); computer engineering (ME, MS, PhD); computer science (MS, PhD); electrical engineering (ME, PhD); engineering education (PhD); engineering mechanics (ME, MS, PhD); environmental engineering (MS); environmental science and engineering (MS); industrial and systems engineering (ME, MS, PhD); materials science and engineering (ME, MS, PhD); mechanical engineering (ME, MS, PhD); mining and minerals engineering (PhD); mining engineering (ME, MS); nuclear engineering (MS, PhD); ocean engineering (MS); systems engineering (ME, MS). *Faculty:* 400 full-time (73 women), 3 part-time/adjunct (2 women). *Students:* 1,949 full-time (487 women), 393 part-time (69 women); includes 251 minority (56 Black or African American, non-Hispanic/Latino; 3 American Indian or Alaska Native, non-Hispanic/Latino; 87 Asian, non-Hispanic/Latino; 70 Hispanic/Latino; 35 Two or more races, non-Hispanic/Latino), 1,354 international. Average age 27. 4,903 applicants, 19% accepted, 569 enrolled. In 2016, 364 master's, 200 doctorates awarded. *Degree requirements:* For master's, comprehensive exam (for some programs), thesis (for some programs); for doctorate, comprehensive exam (for some programs), thesis/dissertation (for some programs). *Entrance requirements:* For master's and doctorate, GRE/GMAT. Additional exam requirements/recommendations for international students: Required—TOEFL (minimum score 80 iBT). *Application deadline:* For fall admission, 8/1 for domestic students, 4/1 for international students; for spring admission, 1/1 for domestic students, 9/1 for international students. Applications are processed on a rolling basis. Application fee: $75. Electronic applications accepted. *Expenses:* Tuition, state resident: full-time $12,467; part-time $692.50 per credit hour. Tuition, nonresident: full-time $25,095; part-time $1394.25 per credit hour. *Required fees:* $2669; $491.50 per semester. Tuition and fees vary according to course load, campus/location and program. *Financial support:* In 2016–17, 160 fellowships with full tuition reimbursements (averaging $7,387 per year), 872 research assistantships with full tuition reimbursements (averaging $22,329 per year), 313 teaching assistantships with full tuition reimbursements (averaging $18,714 per year) were awarded. Financial award application deadline: 3/1; financial award applicants required to submit FAFSA. *Total annual research expenditures:* $91.8 million. *Unit head:* Dr. Julia Ross, Dean, 540-231-9752, Fax: 540-231-3031, E-mail: deaneng@vt.edu. *Application contact:* Linda Perkins, Executive Assistant, 540-231-9752, Fax: 540-231-3031, E-mail: lperkins@vt.edu.
Website: http://www.eng.vt.edu/

Wake Forest University, Virginia Tech-Wake Forest University School of Biomedical Engineering and Sciences, Winston-Salem, NC 27106. Offers biomedical engineering (MS, PhD); DVM/PhD; MD/PhD. Terminal master's awarded for partial completion of doctoral program. *Degree requirements:* For master's, comprehensive exam, thesis; for doctorate, comprehensive exam, thesis/dissertation. *Entrance requirements:* For master's and doctorate, GRE, 3 letters of recommendation. Additional exam requirements/recommendations for international students: Required—TOEFL (minimum score 603 paper-based). Electronic applications accepted. *Faculty research:* Biomechanics, cell and tissue engineering, medical imaging, medical physics.

Washington University in St. Louis, School of Engineering and Applied Science, Department of Biomedical Engineering, St. Louis, MO 63130-4899. Offers MS, D Sc, PhD. Terminal master's awarded for partial completion of doctoral program. *Degree requirements:* For master's, thesis optional; for doctorate, thesis/dissertation. *Entrance requirements:* For master's, GRE, minimum GPA of 3.0; for doctorate, GRE General Test, minimum GPA of 3.5. Additional exam requirements/recommendations for international students: Required—TOEFL. Electronic applications accepted. *Faculty research:* Cell and tissue engineering, molecular engineering, neural engineering.

Wayne State University, College of Engineering, Department of Biomedical Engineering, Detroit, MI 48202. Offers biomedical engineering (MS, PhD), including biomedical imaging (PhD); injury biomechanics (Graduate Certificate). *Faculty:* 18. *Students:* 84 full-time (42 women), 37 part-time (14 women); includes 13 minority (6 Black or African American, non-Hispanic/Latino; 5 Asian, non-Hispanic/Latino; 2 Two or more races, non-Hispanic/Latino), 55 international. Average age 28. 165 applicants, 52% accepted, 38 enrolled. In 2016, 18 master's, 4 doctorates awarded. Terminal master's awarded for partial completion of doctoral program. *Degree requirements:* For master's, thesis optional; for doctorate, thesis/dissertation. *Entrance requirements:* For master's, GRE (recommended), bachelor's degree, minimum undergraduate GPA of 3.0, one-page statement of purpose, completion of prerequisite coursework in calculus and engineering physics; for doctorate, GRE, bachelor's degree with minimum undergraduate GPA of 3.5, undergraduate major or substantial specialized work in proposed doctoral major field, personal statement, three letters of recommendation; for Graduate Certificate, minimum undergraduate GPA of 3.0, bachelor's degree in engineering. Additional exam requirements/recommendations for international students: Required—TOEFL (minimum score 550 paper-based; 79 iBT), TWE (minimum score 5.5), Michigan English Language Assessment Battery (minimum score 85); Recommended—IELTS (minimum score 6.5). *Application deadline:* For fall admission, 6/1 priority date for domestic students, 5/1 priority date for international students; for winter admission, 10/1 priority date for domestic students, 9/1 priority date for international students; for spring admission, 2/1 priority date for domestic students, 1/1 priority date for international students. Applications are processed on a rolling basis. Application fee: $50. Electronic applications accepted. *Expenses:* $18,871 per year resident tuition and fees, $36,065 per year non-resident tuition and fees. *Financial support:* In 2016–17, 38 students received support, including 3 fellowships with tuition reimbursements available (averaging $16,000 per year), 6 research assistantships with tuition reimbursements available (averaging $16,799 per year), 9 teaching assistantships with tuition reimbursements available (averaging $19,177 per year); Federal Work-Study, scholarships/grants, health care benefits, and unspecified assistantships also available. Support available to part-time students. Financial award applicants required to submit FAFSA. *Faculty research:* Injury and orthopedic biomechanics, neurophysiology of pain, smart sensors, biomaterials and imaging. *Total annual research expenditures:* $1.9 million. *Unit head:* Dr. John Cavanaugh, Interim Department Chair, 313-577-3916, E-mail: jmc@wayne.edu. *Application contact:* Ellen Cope, Graduate Program Coordinator, 313-577-0409, Fax: 313-577-8333, E-mail: escope@wayne.edu.
Website: http://engineering.wayne.edu/bme/

Wichita State University, Graduate School, College of Engineering, Department of Biomedical Engineering, Wichita, KS 67260. Offers MS. *Degree requirements:* For master's, thesis. *Entrance requirements:* For master's, GRE, bachelor's degree, transcript, minimum undergraduate GPA of 3.0, statement of purpose, three letters of recommendation. Additional exam requirements/recommendations for international students: Required—TOEFL.

Widener University, Graduate Programs in Engineering, Program in Biomedical Engineering, Chester, PA 19013. Offers M Eng. *Students:* 3 full-time (1 woman), 3 part-time (2 women); includes 1 minority (Hispanic/Latino), 3 international. *Entrance requirements:* For master's, BS in engineering. Application fee: $0. Electronic applications accepted. Tuition and fees vary according to degree level and program. *Unit head:* Rudolph Treichel, Assistant Dean/Director of Graduate Programs, 610-499-1294, Fax: 610-499-4059, E-mail: rjtreichel@widener.edu.
Website: http://www.widener.edu/academics/schools/engineering/graduate/masters/biomedical.aspx

Worcester Polytechnic Institute, Graduate Studies and Research, Department of Biomedical Engineering, Worcester, MA 01609-2280. Offers M Eng, MS, PhD, Graduate Certificate. *Program availability:* Part-time, evening/weekend. *Faculty:* 9 full-time (3 women), 3 part-time/adjunct (0 women). *Students:* 44 full-time (23 women), 7 part-time (2 women); includes 7 minority (4 Asian, non-Hispanic/Latino; 2 Hispanic/Latino; 1 Two or more races, non-Hispanic/Latino), 7 international. 118 applicants, 36% accepted, 24 enrolled. In 2016, 15 master's, 4 doctorates awarded. Terminal master's awarded for partial completion of doctoral program. *Degree requirements:* For master's, thesis optional; for doctorate, comprehensive exam, thesis/dissertation. *Entrance requirements:* For master's and doctorate, GRE General Test, 3 letters of recommendation, statement of purpose. Additional exam requirements/recommendations for international students: Required—TOEFL (minimum score 563 paper-based; 84 iBT), IELTS (minimum score 7). *Application deadline:* For fall admission, 1/1 priority date for domestic and international students. Application fee: $70. Electronic applications accepted. *Financial support:* Research assistantships, teaching assistantships, career-related internships or fieldwork, institutionally sponsored loans, scholarships/grants, and unspecified assistantships available. Financial award application deadline: 1/1; financial award applicants required to submit FAFSA. *Unit head:* Dr. Chris Billiar, Head, 508-831-5447, Fax: 508-831-5541, E-mail: kbilliar@wpi.edu. *Application contact:* Dr. Marsha Rolle, Graduate Coordinator, 508-831-5447, Fax: 508-831-5447, E-mail: mrolle@wpi.edu.
Website: http://www.wpi.edu/Academics/Depts/BME/

Wright State University, Graduate School, College of Engineering and Computer Science, Department of Biomedical, Industrial and Human Factors Engineering, Dayton, OH 45435. Offers biomedical engineering (MS); industrial and human factors engineering (MS). *Program availability:* Part-time. *Degree requirements:* For master's, thesis or course option alternative. *Entrance requirements:* Additional exam requirements/recommendations for international students: Required—TOEFL. *Application deadline:* For fall admission, 5/30 for domestic students. Application fee: $25. *Expenses:* Tuition, state resident: full-time $9952; part-time $622 per credit hour. Tuition, nonresident: full-time $16,960; part-time $1060 per credit hour. *Financial support:* Fellowships, research assistantships, teaching assistantships, Federal Work-Study, institutionally sponsored loans, and unspecified assistantships available. Support available to part-time students. Financial award application deadline: 3/15; financial award applicants required to submit FAFSA. *Faculty research:* Medical imaging, functional electrical stimulation, implantable aids, man-machine interfaces, expert systems. *Unit head:* Dr. S. Narayanan, Chair, 937-775-5044, Fax: 937-775-7364, E-mail: sundaram.narayanan@wright.edu. *Application contact:* John Kimble, Associate Director of Graduate Admissions and Records, 937-775-2957, Fax: 937-775-2453, E-mail: john.kimble@wright.edu.
Website: https://engineering-computer-science.wright.edu/biomedical-industrial-and-human-factors-engineering

Yale University, Graduate School of Arts and Sciences, School of Engineering and Applied Science, Department of Biomedical Engineering, New Haven, CT 06520. Offers MS, PhD. *Faculty research:* Biomedical imaging and biosignals; biomechanics; biomolecular engineering and biotechnology.

Biotechnology

Adelphi University, College of Arts and Sciences, Department of Biology, Garden City, NY 11530-0701. Offers biology (MS); biotechnology (MS). *Program availability:* Part-time, evening/weekend. *Students:* 25 full-time (17 women), 13 part-time (9 women); includes 50 minority (11 Black or African American, non-Hispanic/Latino; 18 Asian, non-Hispanic/Latino; 18 Hispanic/Latino; 3 Two or more races, non-Hispanic/Latino), 10 international. Average age 25. 65 applicants, 60% accepted, 18 enrolled. In 2016, 13 master's awarded. *Degree requirements:* For master's, thesis or alternative. *Entrance requirements:* For master's, bachelor's degree in biology or allied sciences, essay, 3 letters of recommendation, official transcripts. Additional exam requirements/recommendations for international students: Required—TOEFL (minimum score 550 paper-based; 80 iBT), IELTS (minimum score 6.5). *Application deadline:* For fall admission, 5/1 for international students; for spring admission, 12/1 for international students. Applications are processed on a rolling basis. Application fee: $50. Electronic applications accepted. *Expenses:* Contact institution. *Financial support:* Research assistantships with full and partial tuition reimbursements, teaching assistantships, career-related internships or fieldwork, institutionally sponsored loans, scholarships/grants, traineeships, and unspecified assistantships available. Support available to part-time students. Financial award application deadline: 2/15; financial award applicants required to submit FAFSA. *Faculty research:* Plant-animal interactions, physiology (plant, cornea), reproductive behavior, topics in evolution, fish biology. *Unit head:* Dr. Alan Schoenfeld, Chair, 516-877-4211, E-mail: schoenfeld@adelphi.edu. *Application contact:* Christine Murphy, Director of Admissions, 516-877-3050, Fax: 516-877-3039, E-mail: graduateadmissions@adelphi.edu.
Website: http://academics.adelphi.edu/artsci/bio/index.php

The American University in Cairo, School of Sciences and Engineering, Cairo, Egypt. Offers biotechnology (MS); chemistry (MS); computer science (MS); computing (M Comp); construction engineering (M Eng, MS); electronics and communications engineering (M Eng); environmental engineering (MS); environmental system design (M Eng); mechanical engineering (M Eng, MS); nanotechnology (MS); physics (MS); robotics, control and smart systems (MS); sciences and engineering (PhD); sustainable development (MS, Graduate Diploma). *Program availability:* Part-time, evening/weekend. *Faculty:* 43 full-time (4 women), 12 part-time/adjunct (1 woman). *Students:* 50 full-time (21 women), 262 part-time (128 women), 13 international. Average age 28. 193 applicants, 46% accepted, 55 enrolled. In 2016, 71 master's, 5 doctorates awarded. *Degree requirements:* For master's, comprehensive exam (for some programs), thesis (for some programs); for doctorate, comprehensive exam (for some programs), thesis/dissertation. *Entrance requirements:* Additional exam requirements/recommendations for international students: Required—TOEFL (minimum score 450 paper-based; 45 iBT), IELTS (minimum score 5). *Application deadline:* For fall admission, 2/1 priority date for domestic and international students; for spring admission, 10/15 priority date for domestic and international students. Applications are processed on a rolling basis. Application fee: $80. Electronic applications accepted. *Expenses:* Contact institution. *Financial support:* Fellowships with partial tuition reimbursements, scholarships/grants, and unspecified assistantships available. Financial award application deadline: 3/10. *Faculty research:* Construction, mechanical and electronics engineering, physics, computer science, biotechnology and nanotechnology. *Unit head:* Dr. Hassan El Fawal, Dean, 20-2-2615-2926, E-mail: hassan.elfawal@aucegypt.edu. *Application contact:* Maha Hegazi, Director for Graduate Admissions, 20-2-2615-1462, E-mail: mahahegazi@aucegypt.edu.
Website: http://www.aucegypt.edu/sse/Pages/default.aspx

Arizona State University at the Tempe campus, Sandra Day O'Connor College of Law, Phoenix, AZ 85004-4467. Offers biotechnology and genomics (LL M); law (JD); legal studies (MLS); patent practice (MLS); sports law and business (MSLB); tribal policy, law and government (LL M); JD/MBA; JD/MD; JD/MSW; JD/PhD. *Accreditation:* ABA. *Program availability:* 100% online. *Faculty:* 71 full-time (31 women), 67 part-time/adjunct (16 women). *Students:* 718 full-time (300 women); includes 195 minority (17 Black or African American, non-Hispanic/Latino; 14 American Indian or Alaska Native, non-Hispanic/Latino; 27 Asian, non-Hispanic/Latino; 98 Hispanic/Latino; 3 Native Hawaiian or other Pacific Islander, non-Hispanic/Latino; 36 Two or more races, non-Hispanic/Latino), 13 international. Average age 28. 1,860 applicants, 42% accepted, 228 enrolled. In 2016, 52 master's, 190 doctorates awarded. *Entrance requirements:* For master's, bachelor's degree and JD (for LL M); for doctorate, LSAT, bachelor's degree. Additional exam requirements/recommendations for international students: Required—TOEFL (minimum score 550 paper-based; 80 iBT). *Application deadline:* For fall admission, 3/1 priority date for domestic and international students. Applications are processed on a rolling basis. Application fee: $65. Electronic applications accepted. *Expenses:* Contact institution. *Financial support:* In 2016–17, 432 students received support. Institutionally sponsored loans and scholarships/grants available. Financial award application deadline: 3/15; financial award applicants required to submit FAFSA. *Faculty research:* Emerging technologies and the law, Indian law, international law, intellectual property, health law, sports law and business. *Total annual research expenditures:* $1.9 million. *Unit head:* Douglas Sylvester, Dean/Professor, 480-965-6188, Fax: 480-965-6521, E-mail: douglas.sylvester@asu.edu. *Application contact:* Chitra Damania, Director of Operations, 480-965-1474, Fax: 480-727-7930, E-mail: law.admissions@asu.edu.
Website: http://www.law.asu.edu/

Arkansas State University, Graduate School, College of Sciences and Mathematics, Department of Biological Sciences, State University, AR 72467. Offers biological sciences (MA); biology (MS); biology education (MSE, SCCT); biotechnology (PSM). *Program availability:* Part-time. *Degree requirements:* For master's, comprehensive exam, thesis (for some programs); for SCCT, comprehensive exam. *Entrance requirements:* For master's, GRE General Test, appropriate bachelor's degree, letters of reference, interview, official transcripts, immunization records, statement of educational objectives and career goals, teaching certificate (for MSE); for SCCT, GRE General Test or MAT, interview, master's degree, letters of reference, official transcript, personal statement, immunization records. Additional exam requirements/recommendations for international students: Required—TOEFL (minimum score 550 paper-based; 79 iBT), IELTS (minimum score 6), PTE (minimum score 56). Electronic applications accepted.

Brandeis University, Graduate School of Arts and Sciences, Program in Biotechnology, Waltham, MA 02454-9110. Offers MS, MS/MBA. *Faculty:* 7 full-time (4 women), 4 part-time/adjunct (1 woman). *Students:* 14 full-time (9 women); includes 2 minority (both Black or African American, non-Hispanic/Latino), 9 international. 76 applicants, 51% accepted, 9 enrolled. In 2016, 7 master's awarded. *Degree requirements:* For master's, poster presentation; summer internship. *Entrance requirements:* For master's, GRE or GMAT, official transcript(s), 2 recommendation letters, curriculum vitae or resume, statement of purpose. Additional exam requirements/recommendations for international students: Required—TOEFL (minimum score 600 paper-based; 100 iBT); Recommended—IELTS (minimum score 7), TSE (minimum score 68). *Application deadline:* For fall admission, 5/1 for domestic students. Application fee: $75. Electronic applications accepted. *Expenses:* Contact institution. *Financial support:* In 2016–17, 9 students received support. Federal Work-Study, scholarships/grants, and tuition waivers (partial) available. Financial award application deadline: 4/15; financial award applicants required to submit FAFSA. *Faculty research:* Biotechnology, biotechnology and business administration. *Unit head:* Dr. Neil Simister, Director of Graduate Studies, 781-736-4952, Fax: 781-736-3107, E-mail: simister@brandeis.edu. *Application contact:* Rachel Krebs, Academic Administrator, 781-736-3100, Fax: 781-736-3107, E-mail: scigradoffice@brandeis.edu.
Website: http://www.brandeis.edu/gsas

Brigham Young University, Graduate Studies, College of Life Sciences, Department of Plant and Wildlife Sciences, Provo, UT 84602. Offers environmental science (MS); genetics and biotechnology (MS); wildlife and wildlands conservation (MS, PhD). *Faculty:* 23 full-time (1 woman), 1 (woman) part-time/adjunct. *Students:* 17 full-time (6 women), 34 part-time (11 women); includes 2 minority (both Hispanic/Latino). Average age 29. 28 applicants, 57% accepted, 16 enrolled. In 2016, 12 master's, 2 doctorates awarded. *Degree requirements:* For master's, thesis, no C grades or below, 30 hours (24 coursework, 6 thesis); for doctorate, comprehensive exam, thesis/dissertation, no C grades or below, 54 hours (18 dissertation, 36 coursework). *Entrance requirements:* For master's, GRE General Test, minimum GPA of 3.2; for doctorate, GRE, minimum GPA of 3.2. Additional exam requirements/recommendations for international students: Required—TOEFL (minimum score 580 paper-based; 85 iBT). *Application deadline:* 2/1 for domestic and international students. Applications are processed on a rolling basis. Application fee: $49. Electronic applications accepted. *Expenses:* Contact institution. *Financial support:* In 2016–17, 37 students received support, including 55 research assistantships with partial tuition reimbursements available (averaging $5,462 per year), 35 teaching assistantships with partial tuition reimbursements available (averaging $5,483 per year); scholarships/grants and tuition waivers (partial) also available. Financial award application deadline: 3/1. *Faculty research:* Environmental science, plant genetics, plant ecology, plant nutrition and pathology, wildlife and wildlands conservation. *Total annual research expenditures:* $3 million. *Unit head:* Brock R. McMillan, Chair, 801-422-3527, Fax: 801-422-0008, E-mail: brock_mcmillan@byu.edu.

Application contact: Bradley D. Geary, Graduate Coordinator, 801-422-1228, Fax: 801-422-0008, E-mail: bradley_geary@byu.edu.
Website: http://pws.byu.edu/home/

Brock University, Faculty of Graduate Studies, Faculty of Mathematics and Science, Program in Biotechnology, St. Catharines, ON L2S 3A1, Canada. Offers M Sc, PhD. *Program availability:* Part-time. *Degree requirements:* For master's, thesis; for doctorate, thesis/dissertation. *Entrance requirements:* For master's, honors B Sc; for doctorate, M Sc. Additional exam requirements/recommendations for international students: Required—TOEFL (minimum score 550 paper-based; 80 iBT), IELTS (minimum score 6.5), TWE (minimum score 4). Electronic applications accepted. *Faculty research:* Bioorganic chemistry, structural chemistry, electrochemistry, cell and molecular biology, plant sciences, oenology, and viticulture.

Brown University, Graduate School, Division of Biology and Medicine, Department of Molecular Pharmacology, Physiology and Biotechnology, Providence, RI 02912. Offers biomedical engineering (Sc M, PhD); biotechnology (PhD); molecular pharmacology and physiology (PhD); MD/PhD. *Degree requirements:* For doctorate, thesis/dissertation, preliminary exam. *Entrance requirements:* For master's and doctorate, GRE General Test, GRE Subject Test. Additional exam requirements/recommendations for international students: Required—TOEFL. Electronic applications accepted. *Faculty research:* Structural biology, antiplatelet drugs, nicotinic receptor structure/function.

California State University Channel Islands, Extended University and International Programs, Programs in Biotechnology, Camarillo, CA 93012. Offers biotechnology and bioinformatics (MS); MS/MBA. *Entrance requirements:* Additional exam requirements/recommendations for international students: Required—TOEFL (minimum score 550 paper-based; 80 iBT), IELTS (minimum score 6).

California State University, Fullerton, Graduate Studies, College of Natural Science and Mathematics, Department of Biological Science, Fullerton, CA 92834-9480. Offers biology (MS); biotechnology (MBT). *Program availability:* Part-time. *Degree requirements:* For master's, thesis. *Entrance requirements:* For master's, GRE General and Subject Tests, MCAT, or DAT, minimum GPA of 3.0 in biology. Application fee: $55. *Expenses:* Tuition, state resident: full-time $3369; part-time $1953 per unit. Tuition, nonresident: full-time $3915; part-time $2499 per unit. Tuition and fees vary according to course load, degree level and program. *Financial support:* Research assistantships, teaching assistantships, career-related internships or fieldwork, Federal Work-Study, institutionally sponsored loans, and scholarships/grants available. Support available to part-time students. Financial award application deadline: 3/1; financial award applicants required to submit FAFSA. *Faculty research:* Glycosidase release and the block to polyspermy in ascidian eggs. *Unit head:* Karen Lau, Department Coordinator, 657-278-2461, E-mail: skarl@fullerton.edu. *Application contact:* Admissions/Applications, 657-278-2371.

Carnegie Mellon University, Heinz College, School of Public Policy and Management, Master of Science Program in Biotechnology and Management, Pittsburgh, PA 15213-3891. Offers MS. *Accreditation:* AACSB. *Entrance requirements:* For master's, GRE or GMAT, college-level course in advanced algebra/pre-calculus; college-level courses in economics and statistics (recommended). Additional exam requirements/recommendations for international students: Required—TOEFL or IELTS.

The Catholic University of America, School of Arts and Sciences, Department of Biology, Washington, DC 20064. Offers biotechnology (MS); cell and microbial biology (MS, PhD), including cell biology; clinical laboratory science (MS, PhD); MSLS/MS. MSLS/MS offered joitnly with Department of Library and Information Science. *Program availability:* Part-time. *Faculty:* 10 full-time (4 women), 5 part-time/adjunct (2 women). *Students:* 21 full-time (14 women), 33 part-time (19 women); includes 8 minority (4 Black or African American, non-Hispanic/Latino; 2 Asian, non-Hispanic/Latino; 1 Hispanic/Latino; 1 Two or more races, non-Hispanic/Latino), 36 international. Average age 31. 53 applicants, 57% accepted, 12 enrolled. In 2016, 19 master's, 5 doctorates awarded. Terminal master's awarded for partial completion of doctoral program. *Degree requirements:* For master's and doctorate, comprehensive exam. *Entrance requirements:* For master's and doctorate, GRE General Test, GRE Subject Test, statement of purpose, official copies of academic transcripts, three letters of recommendation. Additional exam requirements/recommendations for international students: Required—TOEFL (minimum score 550 paper-based; 80 iBT). *Application deadline:* For fall admission, 7/15 priority date for domestic students, 7/1 for international students; for spring admission, 11/15 priority date for domestic students, 11/1 for international students. Applications are processed on a rolling basis. Application fee: $55. Electronic applications accepted. *Expenses:* $42,850 per year; $1,170 per credit; $200 per semester part-time fees. *Financial support:* Fellowships, research assistantships, teaching assistantships, Federal Work-Study, scholarships/grants, tuition waivers (full and partial), and unspecified assistantships available. Financial award application deadline: 2/1; financial award applicants required to submit FAFSA. *Faculty research:* Virus structure and assembly, hepatic and epithelial cell biology, drug resistance and genome stabilization in yeast, biophysics of ion-conductive nanostructures, eukaryotic gene regulation, cancer and vaccine research. *Total annual research expenditures:* $2 million. *Unit head:* Dr. Venigalla Rao, Chair, 202-319-5271, Fax: 202-319-5721, E-mail: rao@cua.edu. *Application contact:* Director of Graduate Admissions, 202-319-5057, Fax: 202-319-6533, E-mail: cua-admissions@cua.edu.
Website: http://biology.cua.edu/

Claflin University, Graduate Programs, Orangeburg, SC 29115. Offers biotechnology (MS); business administration (MBA). *Program availability:* Part-time. *Degree requirements:* For master's, comprehensive exam, thesis. *Entrance requirements:* For master's, GRE, GMAT, baccalaureate degree, 3 letters of recommendation, resume, statement of purpose. Additional exam requirements/recommendations for international students: Recommended—TOEFL (minimum score 550 paper-based).

Clarkson University, School of Arts and Sciences, Program in Interdisciplinary Bioscience and Biotechnology, Potsdam, NY 13699. Offers PhD. *Students:* 10 full-time (3 women); includes 1 minority (Black or African American, non-Hispanic/Latino), 5 international. 25 applicants, 8% accepted, 1 enrolled. *Degree requirements:* For doctorate, comprehensive exam, thesis/dissertation. *Entrance requirements:* For doctorate, GRE. Additional exam requirements/recommendations for international students: Required—TOEFL (minimum score 550 paper-based, 80 iBT) or IELTS (6.5). *Application deadline:* Applications are processed on a rolling basis. Application fee: $50. Electronic applications accepted. *Expenses: Tuition:* Full-time $23,400; part-time $1300 per credit hour. Tuition and fees vary according to campus/location and program. *Financial support:* Scholarships/grants and unspecified assistantships available. *Unit head:* Dr. Tom Langen, Chair of Biology, 315-268-2342, E-mail: tlangen@clarkson.edu. *Application contact:* Dan Capogna, Graduate Admissions Contact, 518-631-9910, E-mail: graduate@clarkson.edu.
Website: http://graduate.clarkson.edu

Columbia University, Graduate School of Arts and Sciences, New York, NY 10027. Offers African-American studies (MA); American studies (MA); anthropology (MA, PhD); art history and archaeology (MA, PhD); astronomy (PhD); biological sciences (PhD); biotechnology (MA); chemical physics (PhD); chemistry (PhD); classical studies (MA, PhD); classics (MA, PhD); climate and society (MA); conservation biology (MA); earth and environmental sciences (PhD); East Asia: regional studies (MA); East Asian languages and cultures (MA, PhD); ecology, evolution and environmental biology (MA), including conservation biology; ecology, evolution, and environmental biology (PhD), including ecology and evolutionary biology, evolutionary primatology; economics (MA, PhD); English and comparative literature (MA, PhD); French and Romance philology (MA, PhD); Germanic languages (MA, PhD); global French studies (MA); global thought (MA); Hispanic cultural studies (MA); history (PhD); history and literature (MA); human rights studies (MA); Islamic studies (MA); Italian (MA, PhD); Japanese pedagogy (MA); Jewish studies (MA); Latin America and the Caribbean: regional studies (MA); Latin American and Iberian cultures (PhD); mathematics (MA, PhD), including finance (MA); medieval and Renaissance studies (MA); Middle Eastern, South Asian, and African studies (MA, PhD); modern art: critical and curatorial studies (MA); modern European studies (MA); museum anthropology (MA); music (DMA, PhD); oral history (MA); philosophical foundations of physics (MA); philosophy (MA, PhD); physics (PhD); political science (MA, PhD); psychology (PhD); quantitative methods in the social sciences (MA); religion (MA, PhD); Russia, Eurasia and East Europe: regional studies (MA); Russian translation (MA); Slavic cultures (MA); Slavic languages (MA, PhD); sociology (MA, PhD); South Asian studies (MA); statistics (MA, PhD); theatre (PhD). Dual-degree programs require admission to both Graduate School of Arts and Sciences and another Columbia school. *Program availability:* Part-time. Terminal master's awarded for partial completion of doctoral program. *Degree requirements:* For master's, variable foreign language requirement, comprehensive exam (for some programs), thesis (for some programs); for doctorate, variable foreign language requirement, comprehensive exam (for some programs), thesis/dissertation. *Entrance requirements:* For master's and doctorate, GRE General Test, GRE Subject Test (for some programs). Additional exam requirements/recommendations for international students: Required—TOEFL, IELTS. Electronic applications accepted.

Concordia University, School of Graduate Studies, Faculty of Arts and Science, Department of Biology, Montréal, QC H3G 1M8, Canada. Offers biology (M Sc, PhD); biotechnology and genomics (Diploma). *Degree requirements:* For master's, thesis; for doctorate, thesis/dissertation, pedagogical training. *Entrance requirements:* For master's, honors degree in biology; for doctorate, M Sc in life science. *Faculty research:* Cell biology, animal physiology, ecology, microbiology/molecular biology, plant physiology/biochemistry and biotechnology.

Cornell University, Graduate School, Graduate Fields of Agriculture and Life Sciences and Graduate Fields of Engineering, Field of Biological and Environmental Engineering, Ithaca, NY 14853. Offers bioenergy and integrated energy systems (M Eng, MPS, MS, PhD); biological engineering (M Eng, MPS, MS, PhD); bioprocess engineering (M Eng, MPS, MS, PhD); ecohydrology (M Eng, MPS, MS, PhD); environmental engineering (M Eng, MPS, MS, PhD); environmental management (MPS); food engineering (M Eng, MPS, MS, PhD); industrial biotechnology (M Eng, MPS, MS, PhD); nanobiotechnology (M Eng, MPS, MS, PhD); sustainable systems (M Eng, MPS, MS, PhD); synthetic biology (MS); syntheticbiology (M Eng, MPS, PhD). Terminal master's awarded for partial completion of doctoral program. *Degree requirements:* For master's, thesis (MS); for doctorate, comprehensive exam, thesis/dissertation. *Entrance requirements:* For master's, letters of recommendation (3 for MS, 2 for M Eng and MPS); for doctorate, GRE General Test, 3 letters of recommendation. Additional exam requirements/recommendations for international students: Required—TOEFL (minimum score 550 paper-based; 77 iBT). Electronic applications accepted. *Faculty research:* Biological and food engineering, environmental, soil and water engineering, international agricultural engineering, structures and controlled environments, machine systems and energy.

Dartmouth College, Thayer School of Engineering, Program in Biotechnology and Biochemical Engineering, Hanover, NH 03755. Offers MS, PhD. *Degree requirements:* For master's, thesis; for doctorate, thesis/dissertation, candidacy oral exam. *Entrance requirements:* For master's and doctorate, GRE General Test. *Application deadline:* For fall admission, 1/1 priority date for domestic students. Application fee: $45. *Financial support:* Fellowships, research assistantships, teaching assistantships, career-related internships or fieldwork, Federal Work-Study, institutionally sponsored loans, and tuition waivers (full and partial) available. Financial award application deadline: 1/15. *Faculty research:* Biomass processing, metabolic engineering, kinetics and reactor design, applied microbiology, resource and environmental analysis. *Total annual research expenditures:* $2.6 million. *Unit head:* Dr. Joseph J. Helbie, Dean, 603-646-2238, Fax: 603-646-2580, E-mail: joseph.j.helbie@dartmouth.edu. *Application contact:* Candace S. Potter, Graduate Admissions Administrator, 603-646-3844, Fax: 603-646-1620, E-mail: candace.s.potter@dartmouth.edu.
Website: http://engineering.dartmouth.edu/

Duquesne University, Bayer School of Natural and Environmental Sciences, Program in Biotechnology, Pittsburgh, PA 15282-0001. Offers MS. *Program availability:* Part-time, evening/weekend. *Faculty:* 1 full-time (0 women), 2 part-time/adjunct (0 women). *Students:* 12 full-time (5 women), 6 part-time (2 women); includes 3 minority (1 Asian, non-Hispanic/Latino; 2 Two or more races, non-Hispanic/Latino), 10 international. Average age 26. 24 applicants, 83% accepted, 5 enrolled. In 2016, 7 master's awarded. *Entrance requirements:* For master's, GRE General Test, statement of purpose, 3 letters of recommendation, official transcripts. Additional exam requirements/recommendations for international students: Required—TOEFL (minimum score 80 iBT) or IELTS. *Application deadline:* For fall admission, 5/1 priority date for domestic students, 5/1 for international students; for spring admission, 10/1 priority date for domestic students, 10/1 for international students. Applications are processed on a rolling basis. Application fee: $0. Electronic applications accepted. *Expenses:* $1,264 per credit. *Financial support:* In 2016–17, 20 students received support. Career-related internships or fieldwork and tuition waivers (partial) available. *Unit head:* Dr. Alan W. Seadler, Director, 412-396-1568, E-mail: seadlera@duq.edu. *Application contact:* Heather Costello, Senior Graduate Academic Advisor, 412-396-6339, E-mail: costelloh@duq.edu.
Website: http://www.duq.edu/academics/schools/natural-and-environmental-sciences/academic-programs/biotechnology

East Carolina University, Graduate School, Thomas Harriot College of Arts and Sciences, Department of Biology, Greenville, NC 27858-4353. Offers biology (MS); molecular biology and biotechnology (MS). *Program availability:* Part-time. *Students:* 48 full-time (23 women), 15 part-time (5 women); includes 6 minority (2 Black or African American, non-Hispanic/Latino; 2 Asian, non-Hispanic/Latino; 1 Hispanic/Latino; 1 Two or more races, non-Hispanic/Latino). Average age 26. 60 applicants, 42% accepted, 23 enrolled. In 2016, 14 master's awarded. *Degree requirements:* For master's, one foreign language, comprehensive exam, thesis. *Entrance requirements:* For master's, GRE General Test, GRE Subject Test. Additional exam requirements/recommendations for international students: Required—TOEFL. *Application deadline:* For fall admission, 6/1 priority date for domestic students; for spring admission, 10/15 for domestic students. Applications are processed on a rolling basis. Application fee: $50. *Financial support:* Fellowships with partial tuition reimbursements, research assistantships with partial tuition reimbursements, teaching assistantships with partial tuition reimbursements, career-related internships or fieldwork, Federal Work-Study, scholarships/grants, and unspecified assistantships available. Support available to part-time students. Financial award application deadline: 6/1. *Faculty research:* Biochemistry, microbiology, cell biology. *Unit head:* Dr. Jeff McKinnon, Chair, 252-328-6718, E-mail: mckinnonj@

ecu.edu. *Application contact:* Dean of Graduate School, 252-328-6012, Fax: 252-328-6071, E-mail: gradschool@ecu.edu.
Website: http://www.ecu.edu/cs-cas/biology/graduate.cfm

Eastern Virginia Medical School, Biotechnology Program, Norfolk, VA 23501-1980. Offers MS. *Entrance requirements:* For master's, GRE. Additional exam requirements/recommendations for international students: Required—TOEFL. Electronic applications accepted.

Florida Institute of Technology, College of Science, Program in Biological Sciences, Melbourne, FL 32901-6975. Offers biological science (PhD); biotechnology (MS); cell and molecular biology (MS); ecology (MS); marine biology (MS). *Program availability:* Part-time. *Students:* 56 full-time (38 women), 9 part-time (4 women); includes 2 minority (1 Asian, non-Hispanic/Latino; 1 Hispanic/Latino), 33 international. Average age 26. 230 applicants, 24% accepted, 21 enrolled. In 2016, 27 master's, 3 doctorates awarded. *Degree requirements:* For master's, thesis (for some programs), research, seminar, internship, or summer lab; for doctorate, comprehensive exam, thesis/dissertation, dissertations seminar, publications. *Entrance requirements:* For master's, GRE General Test, 3 letters of recommendation; statement of objectives; bachelor's degree in biology, chemistry, biochemistry or equivalent; for doctorate, GRE General Test, resume, 3 letters of recommendation, minimum GPA of 3.2, statement of objectives. Additional exam requirements/recommendations for international students: Required—TOEFL (minimum score 550 paper-based; 79 iBT). *Application deadline:* For fall admission, 3/1 for domestic students, 4/1 for international students; for spring admission, 9/1 for domestic and international students. Applications are processed on a rolling basis. Electronic applications accepted. *Expenses: Tuition:* Full-time $22,338; part-time $1241 per credit hour. *Required fees:* $250. Tuition and fees vary according to degree level, campus/location and program. *Financial support:* Career-related internships or fieldwork, institutionally sponsored loans, tuition waivers (partial), unspecified assistantships, and tuition remissions available. Support available to part-time students. Financial award application deadline: 3/1; financial award applicants required to submit FAFSA. *Faculty research:* Initiation of protein synthesis in eukaryotic cells, fixation of radioactive carbon, changes in DNA molecule, endangered or threatened avian and mammalian species, hydro acoustics and feeding preference of the West Indian manatee. *Unit head:* Dr. Richard B. Aronson, Department Head, 321-674-8034, Fax: 321-674-7238, E-mail: raronson@fit.edu. *Application contact:* Cheryl A. Brown, Associate Director of Graduate Admissions, 321-674-7581, Fax: 321-723-9468, E-mail: cbrown@fit.edu.
Website: http://cos.fit.edu/biology/

The George Washington University, School of Medicine and Health Sciences, Health Sciences Programs, Washington, DC 20052. Offers clinical practice management (MSHS); clinical research administration (MSHS); emergency services management (MSHS); end-of-life care (MSHS); immunohematology (MSHS); immunohematology and biotechnology (MSHS); physical therapy (DPT); physician assistant (MSHS). *Program availability:* Online learning. *Faculty:* 49 full-time (40 women). *Students:* 291 full-time (211 women), 316 part-time (244 women); includes 188 minority (68 Black or African American, non-Hispanic/Latino; 1 American Indian or Alaska Native, non-Hispanic/Latino; 49 Asian, non-Hispanic/Latino; 57 Hispanic/Latino; 2 Native Hawaiian or other Pacific Islander, non-Hispanic/Latino; 11 Two or more races, non-Hispanic/Latino), 13 international. Average age 33. 2,202 applicants, 18% accepted, 237 enrolled. In 2016, 162 master's, 40 doctorates, 1 other advanced degree awarded. *Entrance requirements:* Additional exam requirements/recommendations for international students: Required—TOEFL (minimum score 550 paper-based). *Application deadline:* Applications are processed on a rolling basis. Application fee: $75. *Expenses:* Contact institution. *Unit head:* Jean E. Johnson, Senior Associate Dean, 202-994-3725, E-mail: jejohns@gwu.edu. *Application contact:* Joke Ogundiran, Director of Admission, 202-994-1668, Fax: 202-994-0870, E-mail: jokeogun@gwu.edu.

Harvard University, Extension School, Cambridge, MA 02138-3722. Offers applied sciences (CAS); biotechnology (ALM); educational technologies (ALM); educational technology (CET); English for graduate and professional studies (DGP); environmental management (ALM, CEM); information technology (ALM); journalism (ALM); liberal arts (ALM); management (ALM, CM); mathematics for teaching (ALM); museum studies (ALM); premedical studies (Diploma); publication and communication (CPC). *Program availability:* Part-time, evening/weekend. *Degree requirements:* For master's, thesis. *Entrance requirements:* For master's, 3 completed graduate courses with grade of B or higher. Additional exam requirements/recommendations for international students: Required—TOEFL (minimum score 600 paper-based), TWE (minimum score 5). *Expenses:* Contact institution.

Hood College, Graduate School, Program in Biomedical Science, Frederick, MD 21701-8575. Offers biomedical science (MS), including biotechnology/molecular biology, microbiology/immunology/virology. *Program availability:* Part-time, evening/weekend. *Faculty:* 4 full-time, 13 part-time/adjunct. *Students:* 11 full-time (4 women), 73 part-time (42 women); includes 26 minority (13 Black or African American, non-Hispanic/Latino; 8 Asian, non-Hispanic/Latino; 3 Hispanic/Latino; 2 Two or more races, non-Hispanic/Latino), 8 international. Average age 31. 37 applicants, 78% accepted, 22 enrolled. In 2016, 15 master's awarded. *Degree requirements:* For master's, thesis or alternative. *Entrance requirements:* For master's, bachelor's degree in biology; minimum GPA of 3.0; undergraduate course work in cell biology, chemistry, organic chemistry, and genetics. Additional exam requirements/recommendations for international students: Required—TOEFL (minimum score 575 paper-based; 89 iBT), IELTS (minimum score 6). *Application deadline:* For fall admission, 8/15 priority date for domestic students, 8/5 for international students; for spring admission, 12/1 priority date for domestic students, 12/1 for international students; for summer admission, 5/1 priority date for domestic students, 4/15 for international students. Applications are processed on a rolling basis. Application fee: $35. Electronic applications accepted. *Expenses:* $475 per credit; $110 comprehensive fee per semester. *Financial support:* Research assistantships with full tuition reimbursements, tuition waivers (partial), and unspecified assistantships available. Financial award applicants required to submit FAFSA. *Faculty research:* Molecular signaling in cell tumor initiation, biomedical ethics, genetic and biochemical approaches to study regulation of gene expression. *Unit head:* April Boulton, Interim Dean of the Graduate School, 301-696-3600, E-mail: gofurther@hood.edu. *Application contact:* Larbi Bricha, Assistant Director of Graduate Admissions, 301-696-3600, E-mail: gofurther@hood.edu.
Website: http://www.hood.edu/graduate

Howard University, College of Medicine, Department of Biochemistry and Molecular Biology, Washington, DC 20059-0002. Offers biochemistry and molecular biology (PhD); biotechnology (MS); MD/PhD. *Program availability:* Part-time. *Degree requirements:* For master's, externship; for doctorate, comprehensive exam, thesis/dissertation. *Entrance requirements:* For master's and doctorate, GRE General Test, minimum GPA of 3.0. *Faculty research:* Cellular and molecular biology of olfaction, gene regulation and expression, enzymology, NMR spectroscopy of molecular structure, hormone regulation/metabolism.

Husson University, Master of Business Administration Program, Bangor, ME 04401-2999. Offers athletic administration (MBA); biotechnology and innovation (MBA); general business administration (MBA); healthcare management (MBA); hospitality and tourism management (MBA); organizational management (MBA); risk management (MBA). *Program availability:* Part-time, evening/weekend, 100% online, blended/hybrid learning. *Faculty:* 8 full-time (4 women), 20 part-time/adjunct (5 women). *Students:* 81 full-time (47 women), 249 part-time (142 women); includes 32 minority (9 Black or African American, non-Hispanic/Latino; 2 American Indian or Alaska Native, non-Hispanic/Latino; 17 Asian, non-Hispanic/Latino; 3 Hispanic/Latino; 1 Two or more races, non-Hispanic/Latino), 11 international. Average age 34. 199 applicants, 78% accepted, 119 enrolled. In 2016, 109 master's awarded. *Degree requirements:* For master's, comprehensive exam (for some programs), thesis optional. *Entrance requirements:* For master's, minimum GPA of 3.0, letter of recommendation. Additional exam requirements/recommendations for international students: Required—TOEFL (minimum score 550 paper-based; 80 iBT), IELTS (minimum score 6.5). *Application deadline:* Applications are processed on a rolling basis. Application fee: $50. Electronic applications accepted. *Expenses:* $450 per credit; $450 fees per full-time year or $220 part-time. *Financial support:* Career-related internships or fieldwork, Federal Work-Study, scholarships/grants, and unspecified assistantships available. Financial award application deadline: 4/15; financial award applicants required to submit FAFSA. *Unit head:* Prof. Stephanie Shayne, Director, Graduate and Online Programs, 207-404-5632, Fax: 207-992-4987, E-mail: shaynes@husson.edu. *Application contact:* Kristen Card, Director of Graduate Admissions, 207-404-5660, Fax: 207-941-7935, E-mail: cardk@husson.edu.
Website: http://www.husson.edu/college-of-business/school-of-business-and-management/master-of-business-administration-mba/

Illinois State University, Graduate School, College of Arts and Sciences, School of Biological Sciences, Program in Biotechnology, Normal, IL 61790-2200. Offers MS. *Degree requirements:* For master's, thesis or alternative. *Entrance requirements:* For master's, GRE General Test, minimum GPA of 2.6 in last 60 hours of course work.

Indiana University Bloomington, University Graduate School, College of Arts and Sciences, Department of Biology, Bloomington, IN 47405. Offers biology teaching (MAT); biotechnology (MA); evolution, ecology, and behavior (MA, PhD); genetics (PhD); microbiology (MA, PhD); molecular, cellular, and developmental biology (PhD); plant sciences (MA, PhD); zoology (MA, PhD). Terminal master's awarded for partial completion of doctoral program. *Degree requirements:* For master's, thesis, oral defense; for doctorate, thesis/dissertation, oral defense. *Entrance requirements:* For master's and doctorate, GRE General Test. Additional exam requirements/recommendations for international students: Required—TOEFL (minimum score 100 iBT). Electronic applications accepted. *Faculty research:* Evolution, ecology and behavior; microbiology; molecular biology and genetics; plant biology.

Instituto Tecnológico y de Estudios Superiores de Monterrey, Campus Monterrey, Graduate and Research Division, Program in Natural and Social Sciences, Monterrey, Mexico. Offers biotechnology (MS); chemistry (MS, PhD); communications (MS); education (MA). *Program availability:* Part-time. *Degree requirements:* For master's, one foreign language, thesis; for doctorate, one foreign language, thesis/dissertation. *Entrance requirements:* For master's, EXADEP; for doctorate, EXADEP, master's degree in related field. Additional exam requirements/recommendations for international students: Required—TOEFL. *Faculty research:* Cultural industries, mineral substances, bioremediation, food processing, CQ in industrial chemical processing.

Inter American University of Puerto Rico, Bayamón Campus, Graduate School, Bayamón, PR 00957. Offers biology (MS), including environmental sciences and ecology, molecular biotechnology; electrical engineering (ME), including control system, potence system; human resources (MBA); mechanical engineering (ME, MS), including aerospace, energy. *Program availability:* Part-time, evening/weekend. *Faculty:* 12 full-time (5 women), 4 part-time/adjunct (2 women). *Students:* 7 full-time (5 women), 115 part-time (69 women); includes 119 minority (1 Black or African American, non-Hispanic/Latino; 118 Hispanic/Latino). Average age 28. 94 applicants, 72% accepted, 56 enrolled. In 2016, 22 master's awarded. *Degree requirements:* For master's, comprehensive exam, research project. *Entrance requirements:* For master's, EXADEP, GRE General Test, letters of recommendation. *Application deadline:* For fall admission, 7/1 for domestic students, 5/1 priority date for international students; for winter admission, 11/15 priority date for domestic and international students; for spring admission, 2/15 priority date for domestic and international students. Application fee: $31. *Expenses: Tuition:* Part-time $207 per credit. *Required fees:* $328 per semester. *Unit head:* Prof. Juan F. Martinez, Chancellor, 787-279-1200 Ext. 2295, Fax: 787-279-2205, E-mail: jmartinez@bayamon.inter.edu. *Application contact:* Aurelis Baez, Director of Student Services, 787-279-1912 Ext. 2017, Fax: 787-279-2205, E-mail: abaez@bayamon.inter.edu.

Johns Hopkins University, G. W. C. Whiting School of Engineering, Master of Science in Engineering Management Program, Baltimore, MD 21218. Offers biomaterials (MSEM); civil engineering (MSEM); communications science (MSEM); computer science (MSEM); environmental systems analysis, economics and public policy (MSEM); fluid mechanics (MSEM); materials science and engineering (MSEM); mechanical engineering (MSEM); mechanics and materials (MSEM); nano-biotechnology (MSEM); nanomaterials and nanotechnology (MSEM); operations research (MSEM); probability and statistics (MSEM); smart product and device design (MSEM). *Faculty:* 7 full-time (4 women), 1 part-time/adjunct (0 women). *Students:* 35 full-time (14 women), 8 part-time (3 women); includes 7 minority (4 Asian, non-Hispanic/Latino; 3 Hispanic/Latino), 26 international. Average age 24. 228 applicants, 28% accepted, 25 enrolled. In 2016, 18 master's awarded. *Entrance requirements:* For master's, GRE, 3 letters of recommendation, statement of purpose, transcripts. Additional exam requirements/recommendations for international students: Required—TOEFL (minimum score 600 paper-based, 100 iBT) or IELTS (7). *Application deadline:* For fall admission, 2/1 for domestic and international students. Application fee: $75. Electronic applications accepted. *Financial support:* Fellowships and health care benefits available. *Unit head:* Dr. Pamela Sheff, Director, 410-516-7056, Fax: 410-516-4880, E-mail: pamsheff@gmail.com. *Application contact:* Richard Helman, Director of Graduate Admissions, 410-516-8174, Fax: 410-516-0780,
E-mail: graduateadmissions@jhu.edu.
Website: http://engineering.jhu.edu/msem/

Johns Hopkins University, Zanvyl Krieger School of Arts and Sciences, Advanced Academic Programs, Program in Biotechnology, Washington, DC 20036. Offers MS, MS/MBA. *Program availability:* Part-time, evening/weekend, online learning. *Degree requirements:* For master's, thesis (for some programs). *Entrance requirements:* For master's, minimum GPA of 3.0; coursework in biology and chemistry. Additional exam requirements/recommendations for international students: Required—TOEFL (minimum score 100 iBT). Electronic applications accepted.

Johns Hopkins University, Zanvyl Krieger School of Arts and Sciences, Advanced Academic Programs, Program in Biotechnology Enterprise and Entrepreneurship, Washington, DC 20036. Offers MBEE. *Program availability:* Part-time, evening/weekend, online learning. *Degree requirements:* For master's, practicum. *Entrance requirements:* For master's, minimum GPA of 3.0, coursework in biochemistry and cell biology. Additional exam requirements/recommendations for international students: Required—TOEFL (minimum score 100 iBT). Electronic applications accepted.

Kean University, New Jersey Center for Science, Technology and Mathematics, Program in Biotechnology Science, Union, NJ 07083. Offers MS. *Program availability:* Part-time. *Faculty:* 8 full-time (1 woman). *Students:* 18 full-time (13 women), 4 part-time (3 women); includes 15 minority (2 Black or African American, non-Hispanic/Latino; 10 Asian, non-Hispanic/Latino; 3 Hispanic/Latino), 4 international. Average age 29. In 2016, 6 master's awarded. *Degree requirements:* For master's, written research project paper, presentation of research. *Entrance requirements:* For master's, GRE General Test, minimum GPA of 3.0 cumulative and in all science and math courses; official transcripts from all institutions attended; three letters of recommendation; professional resume/curriculum vitae; personal statement. Additional exam requirements/recommendations for international students: Required—TOEFL (minimum score 550 paper-based; 79 iBT), IELTS. *Application deadline:* For fall admission, 6/1 for domestic and international students; for spring admission, 12/1 for domestic and international students. Applications are processed on a rolling basis. Application fee: $75. Electronic applications accepted. *Expenses:* Tuition, state resident: full-time $13,156; part-time $640 per credit. Tuition, nonresident: full-time $17,831; part-time $785 per credit. *Required fees:* $3316; $151 per credit. Tuition and fees vary according to course level, course load, degree level and program. *Financial support:* Scholarships/grants and unspecified assistantships available. Financial award applicants required to submit FAFSA. *Unit head:* Dr. Salvatore Coniglio, Program Coordinator, 908-737-7216, E-mail: coniglsa@kean.edu. *Application contact:* Helen Ramirez, Associate Director of Graduate Admissions, 908-737-7100, E-mail: grad-adm@kean.edu.
Website: http://grad.kean.edu/masters-programs/biotechnology

Long Island University–Hudson, Graduate School, Purchase, NY 10577. Offers autism (Advanced Certificate); childhood education (MS Ed); early childhood education (MS Ed); educational leadership (MS Ed); finance (MBA); health administration (MPA); healthcare sector management (MBA); literacy (MS Ed); management (MBA); marriage and family therapy (MS); mental health counseling (MS), including credentialed alcoholism and substance abuse counselor; middle childhood and adolescence education (MS Ed); pharmaceutics (MS), including cosmetic science, industrial pharmacy; public administration (MPA); school counseling (MS Ed, Advanced Certificate); school psychology (MS Ed); special education (MS Ed); TESOL (all grades) (Advanced Certificate); TESOL and bilingual education (MS Ed); the business of pharmaceutics and biotechnology (MBA). *Program availability:* Part-time, evening/weekend, online learning. *Faculty:* 7 full-time (5 women), 42 part-time/adjunct (25 women). *Students:* 55 full-time (41 women), 158 part-time (123 women); includes 40 minority (8 Black or African American, non-Hispanic/Latino; 1 Asian, non-Hispanic/Latino; 31 Hispanic/Latino). Average age 35. *Entrance requirements:* Additional exam requirements/recommendations for international students: Required—TOEFL (minimum score 550 paper-based; 79 iBT). *Application deadline:* Applications are processed on a rolling basis. Application fee: $50. Electronic applications accepted. *Expenses:* Contact institution. *Unit head:* Dr. Sylvia Blake, Dean and Chief Operating Officer, 914-831-2700, E-mail: westchester@liu.edu. *Application contact:* Cindy Pagnotta, Director of Marketing and Enrollment, 914-831-2701, Fax: 914-251-5959, E-mail: cindy.pagnotta@liu.edu.

Marywood University, Academic Affairs, Munley College of Liberal Arts and Sciences, Science Department, Scranton, PA 18509-1598. Offers biotechnology (MS). *Program availability:* Part-time. Electronic applications accepted.

McGill University, Faculty of Graduate and Postdoctoral Studies, Faculty of Agricultural and Environmental Sciences, Institute of Parasitology, Montréal, QC H3A 2T5, Canada. Offers biotechnology (M Sc A, Certificate); parasitology (M Sc, PhD).

Michigan Technological University, Graduate School, School of Forest Resources and Environmental Science, Houghton, MI 49931. Offers applied ecology (MS); forest molecular genetics and biotechnology (MS, PhD); forest resources and environmental science (MF, MGIS); forest science (PhD); forestry (MS); forestry ecology and management (MS). *Accreditation:* SAF. *Program availability:* Part-time. *Faculty:* 44 full-time (12 women), 55 part-time/adjunct (17 women). *Students:* 50 full-time (20 women), 18 part-time (5 women); includes 1 minority (Two or more races, non-Hispanic/Latino), 16 international. Average age 31. 95 applicants, 28% accepted, 15 enrolled. In 2016, 20 master's, 8 doctorates awarded. Terminal master's awarded for partial completion of doctoral program. *Degree requirements:* For master's, thesis (for some programs), comprehensive exam (for non-research degrees); for doctorate, comprehensive exam, thesis/dissertation. *Entrance requirements:* For master's and doctorate, GRE, statement of purpose, personal statement, official transcripts, 3 letters of recommendation, resume/curriculum vitae. Additional exam requirements/recommendations for international students: Required—TOEFL (recommended minimum score 79 iBT) or IELTS (recommended minimum score of 6.5). *Application deadline:* Applications are processed on a rolling basis. Electronic applications accepted. *Expenses:* Tuition, state resident: full-time $16,290; part-time $905 per credit. Tuition, nonresident: full-time $16,290; part-time $905 per credit. *Required fees:* $248; $124 per term. Tuition and fees vary according to course load and program. *Financial support:* In 2016–17, 51 students received support, including 4 fellowships with tuition reimbursements available (averaging $15,242 per year), 18 research assistantships with tuition reimbursements available (averaging $15,242 per year), 5 teaching assistantships with tuition reimbursements available (averaging $15,242 per year); career-related internships or fieldwork, Federal Work-Study, scholarships/grants, health care benefits, unspecified assistantships, and cooperative program also available. Financial award applicants required to submit FAFSA. *Faculty research:* Forestry, wildlife ecology and management; natural resources, applied ecology and environmental science; biotechnology and molecular genetics; forest biomaterials; geospatial science and technology. *Total annual research expenditures:* $3.2 million. *Unit head:* Dr. Terry Sharik, Dean, 906-487-2352, Fax: 906-487-2915, E-mail: tlsharik@mtu.edu. *Application contact:* Dr. Andrew J. Storer, Associate Dean, 906-487-3470, Fax: 906-487-2915, E-mail: storer@mtu.edu.
Website: http://www.mtu.edu/forest/

Middle Tennessee State University, College of Graduate Studies, College of Basic and Applied Sciences, Program in Professional Science, Murfreesboro, TN 37132. Offers actuarial sciences (MS); biostatistics (MS); biotechnology (MS); engineering management (MS); health care informatics (MS). *Program availability:* Part-time, evening/weekend, online learning. *Degree requirements:* For master's, comprehensive exam. *Entrance requirements:* For master's, GRE. Additional exam requirements/recommendations for international students: Required—TOEFL (minimum score 525 paper-based; 71 iBT) or IELTS (minimum score 6).

Mount St. Mary's University, Program in Biotechnology and Management, Emmitsburg, MD 21727-7799. Offers MS. *Program availability:* Part-time-only, evening/weekend. *Faculty:* 1 (woman) full-time, 1 part-time/adjunct (0 women). *Students:* 2 full-time (1 woman), 21 part-time (13 women); includes 11 minority (7 Black or African American, non-Hispanic/Latino; 1 Asian, non-Hispanic/Latino; 2 Hispanic/Latino; 1 Two or more races, non-Hispanic/Latino), 2 international. Average age 30. 24 applicants, 54% accepted, 6 enrolled. *Degree requirements:* For master's, capstone experience (written paper and formal oral presentation of the project outcomes). *Entrance requirements:* For master's, bachelor's degree in biology or related field, undergraduate transcripts from accredited four-year institution with minimum GPA of 2.75, two letters of recommendation. Additional exam requirements/recommendations for international students: Required—TOEFL (minimum score 550 paper-based; 83 iBT). *Application deadline:* Applications are processed on a rolling basis. Electronic applications accepted. *Expenses:* $610 per credit hour. *Financial support:* Unspecified assistantships available. Financial award applicants required to submit FAFSA. *Unit head:* Dr. Connie E. Dudley, Director of Graduate Programs in Science, 301-447-5090, E-mail: cdudley@msmary.edu.
Website: http://msmary.edu/School_of_natural_science_and_math/Graduate_Programs/index.html

New Mexico State University, College of Arts and Sciences, Department of Biology, Las Cruces, NM 88003. Offers biology (MS, PhD); biotechnology (MS). *Program availability:* Part-time. *Faculty:* 21 full-time (11 women). *Students:* 51 full-time (28 women), 7 part-time (4 women); includes 19 minority (1 American Indian or Alaska Native, non-Hispanic/Latino; 2 Asian, non-Hispanic/Latino; 13 Hispanic/Latino; 3 Two or more races, non-Hispanic/Latino), 16 international. Average age 31. 30 applicants, 50% accepted, 11 enrolled. In 2016, 10 master's, 4 doctorates awarded. *Degree requirements:* For master's, thesis (for some programs), defense or oral exam; for doctorate, comprehensive exam, thesis/dissertation, qualifying exam. *Entrance requirements:* For master's and doctorate, GRE. Additional exam requirements/recommendations for international students: Required—TOEFL (minimum score 550 paper-based; 79 iBT), IELTS (minimum score 6.5). *Application deadline:* For fall admission, 1/15 priority date for domestic students, 1/15 for international students; for spring admission, 10/4 priority date for domestic students, 10/4 for international students. Applications are processed on a rolling basis. Application fee: $40 ($50 for international students). Electronic applications accepted. *Expenses:* Tuition, state resident: full-time $4086. Tuition, nonresident: full-time $14,254. *Required fees:* $853. Tuition and fees vary according to course load. *Financial support:* In 2016–17, 46 students received support, including 2 fellowships (averaging $4,088 per year), 16 research assistantships (averaging $22,418 per year), 28 teaching assistantships (averaging $17,893 per year); career-related internships or fieldwork, Federal Work-Study, scholarships/grants, traineeships, health care benefits, and unspecified assistantships also available. Support available to part-time students. Financial award application deadline: 3/1. *Faculty research:* Microbiology, cell and organismal physiology, ecology and ethology, evolution, genetics, developmental biology. *Total annual research expenditures:* $2.5 million. *Unit head:* Dr. Michele K. Nishiguchi, Department Head, 575-646-3611, Fax: 575-646-5665, E-mail: nish@nmsu.edu. *Application contact:* Dr. Jennifer Curtiss, Associate Professor, 575-646-3611, Fax: 575-646-5665, E-mail: curtij01@nmsu.edu.
Website: http://bio.nmsu.edu

New York University, Polytechnic School of Engineering, Department of Chemical and Biomolecular Engineering, Major in Biotechnology, New York, NY 10012-1019. Offers MS. *Entrance requirements:* Additional exam requirements/recommendations for international students: Required—TOEFL (minimum score 550 paper-based; 80 iBT); Recommended—IELTS (minimum score 6.5). Electronic applications accepted.

New York University, Polytechnic School of Engineering, Department of Chemical and Biomolecular Engineering, Major in Biotechnology and Entrepreneurship, New York, NY 10012-1019. Offers MS. *Entrance requirements:* Additional exam requirements/recommendations for international students: Required—TOEFL (minimum score 550 paper-based; 80 iBT); Recommended—IELTS (minimum score 6.5). Electronic applications accepted.

North Carolina State University, Graduate School, College of Agriculture and Life Sciences, Department of Microbiology, Program in Microbial Biotechnology, Raleigh, NC 27695. Offers MMB. *Entrance requirements:* For master's, GRE. Electronic applications accepted.

Northeastern University, College of Science, Boston, MA 02115-5096. Offers applied mathematics (MS); bioinformatics (MS); biology (PhD); biotechnology (MS); chemistry (MS, PhD); ecology, evolution, and marine biology (PhD); marine biology (MS); mathematics (MS, PhD); network science (PhD); operations research (MSOR); physics (MS, PhD); psychology (PhD). *Program availability:* Part-time. *Faculty:* 217 full-time (76 women), 58 part-time/adjunct (20 women). *Students:* 578 full-time (268 women), 63 part-time (27 women). In 2016, 121 master's, 50 doctorates awarded. Terminal master's awarded for partial completion of doctoral program. *Degree requirements:* For master's, comprehensive exam (for some programs), thesis; for doctorate, comprehensive exam (for some programs), thesis/dissertation. *Entrance requirements:* For master's, GRE General Test. *Application deadline:* Applications are processed on a rolling basis. Application fee: $75. Electronic applications accepted. *Expenses:* Contact institution. *Financial support:* Fellowships with tuition reimbursements, research assistantships with tuition reimbursements, teaching assistantships with tuition reimbursements, career-related internships or fieldwork, scholarships/grants, health care benefits, tuition waivers (full and partial), and unspecified assistantships available. Support available to part-time students. Financial award applicants required to submit FAFSA. *Unit head:* Dr. Kenneth Henderson, Dean. *Application contact:* Graduate Student Services, 617-373-4275, E-mail: gradcos@northeastern.edu.
Website: http://www.northeastern.edu/cos/

Northwestern University, The Graduate School, Interdisciplinary Biological Sciences Program (IBiS), Evanston, IL 60208. Offers biochemistry (PhD); bioengineering and biotechnology (PhD); biotechnology (PhD); cell and molecular biology (PhD); developmental and systems biology (PhD); nanotechnology (PhD); neurobiology (PhD); structural biology and biophysics (PhD). *Degree requirements:* For doctorate, thesis/dissertation, qualifying exam. *Entrance requirements:* For doctorate, GRE General Test. Additional exam requirements/recommendations for international students: Required—TOEFL (minimum score 600 paper-based). Electronic applications accepted. *Faculty research:* Biophysics/structural biology, cell/molecular biology, synthetic biology, developmental systems biology, chemical biology/nanotechnology.

Northwestern University, McCormick School of Engineering and Applied Science, Department of Chemical and Biological Engineering, MS in Biotechnology Program, Evanston, IL 60208. Offers MS. *Entrance requirements:* For master's, GRE General Test. Additional exam requirements/recommendations for international students: Required—TOEFL, IELTS. Electronic applications accepted.

Oregon State University, College of Agricultural Sciences, Program in Food Science and Technology, Corvallis, OR 97331. Offers brewing (MS, PhD); enology (MS, PhD); flavor chemistry (MS, PhD); food and seafood processing (MS, PhD); food chemistry/biochemistry (MS, PhD); food engineering (MS, PhD); food microbiology/biotechnology (MS, PhD); sensory evaluation (MS, PhD). *Faculty:* 16 full-time (5 women). *Students:* 34 full-time (24 women), 4 part-time (2 women), 17 international. Average age 28. 118 applicants, 13% accepted, 13 enrolled. In 2016, 12 master's, 5 doctorates awarded. *Degree requirements:* For master's, thesis (for some programs); for doctorate, thesis/dissertation. *Entrance requirements:* For master's and doctorate, GRE (minimum Verbal and Quantitative scores of 300), minimum GPA of 3.0 in last 90 hours. Additional exam requirements/recommendations for international students: Required—TOEFL (minimum score 80 iBT), IELTS (minimum score 6.5). *Application deadline:* For fall admission, 4/1 for international students; for winter admission, 7/1 for international students; for spring admission, 10/1 for international students; for summer admission, 1/1 for international

students. Application fee: $75 ($85 for international students). *Expenses:* Tuition, state resident: full-time $12,150; part-time $450 per credit. Tuition, nonresident: full-time $21,789; part-time $807 per credit. *Required fees:* $1651; $1507 per credit. One-time fee: $350. Tuition and fees vary according to course load, campus/location and program. *Financial support:* Fellowships, research assistantships, teaching assistantships, career-related internships or fieldwork, Federal Work-Study, and institutionally sponsored loans available. Support available to part-time students. *Unit head:* Dr. Robert McGorrin, Department Head and Professor. *Application contact:* Holly Templeton, Food Science and Technology Advisor, 541-737-6486,
E-mail: holly.templeton@oregonstate.edu.
Website: http://oregonstate.edu/foodsci/graduate-program

Oregon State University, College of Agricultural Sciences, Program in Horticulture, Corvallis, OR 97331. Offers breeding, genetics and biotechnology (MS, PhD); community and landscape horticultural systems (MS, PhD); sustainable crop production (MS). *Faculty:* 14 full-time (4 women), 1 part-time/adjunct (0 women). *Students:* 35 full-time (13 women), 3 part-time (1 woman); includes 6 minority (1 Asian, non-Hispanic/Latino; 5 Hispanic/Latino), 11 international. Average age 32. 46 applicants, 24% accepted, 11 enrolled. In 2016, 6 master's awarded. *Degree requirements:* For master's, thesis (for some programs); for doctorate, thesis/dissertation. *Entrance requirements:* For master's and doctorate, GRE General Test, minimum GPA of 3.0 in last 90 hours. Additional exam requirements/recommendations for international students: Required—TOEFL (minimum score 80 iBT), IELTS (minimum score 6.5). *Application deadline:* For fall admission, 4/1 for international students; for winter admission, 7/1 for international students; for spring admission, 10/1 for international students; for summer admission, 1/1 for international students. Application fee: $75 ($85 for international students). *Expenses:* Tuition, state resident: full-time $12,150; part-time $450 per credit. Tuition, nonresident: full-time $21,789; part-time $807 per credit. *Required fees:* $1651; $1507 per credit. One-time fee: $350. Tuition and fees vary according to course load, campus/location and program. *Financial support:* Research assistantships, teaching assistantships, career-related internships or fieldwork, Federal Work-Study, and institutionally sponsored loans available. Support available to part-time students. *Unit head:* Dr. Bill Braunworth, Department Head, 541-737-1317, E-mail: bill.braunworth@oregonstate.edu. *Application contact:* John Lambrinos, Horticulture Advisor, 541-737-3484, E-mail: lambrinj@hort.oregonstate.edu.
Website: http://horticulture.oregonstate.edu/content/graduate-students

Oregon State University, Interdisciplinary/Institutional Programs, Program in Molecular and Cellular Biology, Corvallis, OR 97331. Offers bioinformatics (PhD); biotechnology (PhD); cell biology (PhD); developmental biology (PhD); genome biology (PhD); molecular biology (PhD); molecular pathogenesis (PhD); molecular virology (PhD); plant molecular biology (PhD); structural biology (PhD). *Students:* 30 full-time (16 women), 2 part-time (1 woman); includes 4 minority (2 Asian, non-Hispanic/Latino; 2 Hispanic/Latino), 12 international. Average age 29. 43 applicants, 7% accepted, 3 enrolled. In 2016, 2 doctorates awarded. *Degree requirements:* For doctorate, thesis/dissertation, oral and written qualifying exams. *Entrance requirements:* For doctorate, GRE. Additional exam requirements/recommendations for international students: Required—TOEFL (minimum score 80 iBT), IELTS (minimum score 6.5). *Application deadline:* For fall admission, 8/1 for domestic students, 4/1 for international students; for winter admission, 12/1 for domestic students, 7/1 for international students; for spring admission, 2/1 for domestic students, 10/1 for international students; for summer admission, 5/1 for domestic students, 1/1 for international students. Application fee: $75 ($85 for international students). *Expenses:* Tuition, state resident: full-time $12,150; part-time $450 per credit. Tuition, nonresident: full-time $21,789; part-time $807 per credit. *Required fees:* $1651; $1507 per credit. One-time fee: $350. Tuition and fees vary according to course load, campus/location and program. *Financial support:* Fellowships, career-related internships or fieldwork, Federal Work-Study, and institutionally sponsored loans available. Support available to part-time students. Financial award application deadline: 1/1. *Unit head:* Dr. Kristin Carroll, Assistant Director, Molecular and Cellular Biology Program,
E-mail: kirstin.carroll@oregonstate.edu.
Website: http://gradschool.oregonstate.edu/molecular-and-cellular-biology-graduate-program

Penn State University Park, Graduate School, Eberly College of Science, Department of Biochemistry and Molecular Biology, University Park, PA 16802. Offers biochemistry, microbiology, and molecular biology (MS, PhD); biotechnology (MBIOT). *Unit head:* Dr. Douglas R. Cavener, Dean, 814-865-9591, Fax: 814-865-3634. *Application contact:* Lori Hawn, Director, Graduate Student Services, 814-865-1795, Fax: 814-863-4627, E-mail: l-gswww@lists.psu.edu.
Website: http://bmb.psu.edu/

Pontifical John Paul II Institute for Studies on Marriage and Family, Graduate Programs, Washington, DC 20064. Offers biotechnology and ethics (MTS); marriage and family (MTS, STD, STL); theology (PhD).

Purdue University, Graduate School, PULSe - Purdue University Life Sciences Program, West Lafayette, IN 47907. Offers biomolecular structure and biophysics (PhD); biotechnology (PhD); chemical biology (PhD); chromatin and regulation of gene expression (PhD); integrative neuroscience (PhD); integrative plant sciences (PhD); membrane biology (PhD); microbiology (PhD); molecular evolutionary and cancer biology (PhD); molecular evolutionary genetics (PhD); molecular virology (PhD). *Students:* 60 full-time (29 women); includes 6 minority (4 Hispanic/Latino; 2 Two or more races, non-Hispanic/Latino), 36 international. Average age 25. 127 applicants, 39% accepted, 25 enrolled. *Entrance requirements:* For doctorate, GRE, minimum undergraduate GPA of 3.0. Additional exam requirements/recommendations for international students: Required—TOEFL (minimum score 550 paper-based; 77 iBT). *Application deadline:* For fall admission, 1/15 priority date for domestic and international students. Applications are processed on a rolling basis. Application fee: $60 ($75 for international students). Electronic applications accepted. *Financial support:* In 2016–17, research assistantships with tuition reimbursements (averaging $22,500 per year), teaching assistantships with tuition reimbursements (averaging $22,500 per year) were awarded. *Unit head:* Dr. Christine A. Hrycyna, Head, 765-494-7322, E-mail: hrycyna@purdue.edu. *Application contact:* Lindsey Springer, Graduate Contact, 765-496-9667, E-mail: lbcampbe@purdue.edu.
Website: http://www.gradschool.purdue.edu/pulse

Purdue University Northwest, Graduate Studies Office, School of Engineering, Mathematics, and Science, Department of Biological Sciences, Program in Biotechnology, Hammond, IN 46323-2094. Offers MS. *Degree requirements:* For master's, thesis (for some programs). *Entrance requirements:* For master's, GRE General Test, 3 letters of recommendation.

Regis College, Program in Regulatory and Clinical Research Management, Weston, MA 02493. Offers MS. *Program availability:* Part-time, evening/weekend, blended/hybrid learning. *Degree requirements:* For master's, thesis optional, internship/field experience. *Entrance requirements:* For master's, GRE or MAT. Additional exam requirements/recommendations for international students: Required—TOEFL; Recommended—IELTS. *Application deadline:* Applications are processed on a rolling basis. Application fee: $65. Electronic applications accepted. *Financial support:* Career-related internships or fieldwork, scholarships/grants, and unspecified assistantships available. Financial award applicants required to submit FAFSA. *Faculty research:* FDA regulatory affairs medical device. *Unit head:* Joni Beshansky, Director, 781-768-7008, E-mail: joni.beshansky@regiscollege.edu.

Roosevelt University, Graduate Division, College of Arts and Sciences, Department of Biological, Chemical, and Physical Sciences, Chicago, IL 60605. Offers biotechnology and chemical science (MS). *Program availability:* Part-time, evening/weekend. *Degree requirements:* For master's, thesis optional. *Entrance requirements:* For master's, minimum GPA of 2.7, undergraduate course work in science and mathematics. *Faculty research:* Phase-transfer catalysts, bioinorganic chemistry, long chain dicarboxylic acids, organosilicon compounds, spectroscopic studies.

St. John's University, Institute for Biotechnology, Queens, NY 11439. Offers biological/pharmaceutical biotechnology (MS). *Degree requirements:* For master's, comprehensive exam, thesis optional. *Entrance requirements:* For master's, GRE General Test, minimum GPA of 3.0, 2 letters of recommendation, bachelor's degree in life or physical sciences. Additional exam requirements/recommendations for international students: Required—TOEFL (minimum score 600 paper-based; 100 iBT), IELTS (minimum score 7). Electronic applications accepted. *Expenses:* Contact institution.

San Francisco State University, Division of Graduate Studies, College of Science and Engineering, Department of Biology, Professional Science Master's Program, San Francisco, CA 94132-1722. Offers biotechnology (PSM); stem cell science (PSM). *Expenses:* Tuition, state resident: full-time $6738. Tuition, nonresident: full-time $15,666. *Required fees:* $1012. Tuition and fees vary according to degree level and program. *Unit head:* Dr. Lily Chen, Director, 415-338-6763, Fax: 415-338-2295, E-mail: lilychen@sfsu.edu. *Application contact:* Dr. Linda H. Chen, Associate Director and Program Coordinator, 415-338-1696, Fax: 415-338-2295, E-mail: psm@sfsu.edu.
Website: http://psm.sfsu.edu/

San Jose State University, Graduate Studies and Research, College of Science, San Jose, CA 95192-0001. Offers biological sciences (MA, MS), including molecular biology and microbiology (MS), organismal biology, conservation and ecology (MS), physiology (MS); biotechnology (MBT); chemistry (MA, MS); computer science (MS); cybersecurity (Certificate); cybersecurity: core technologies (Certificate); geology (MS); marine science (MS); mathematics (MA, MS), including mathematics education (MA), science; meteorology (MS); physics (MS), including computational physics, modern optics, science (MA, MS); science education (MA); statistics (MS); Unix system administration (Certificate). *Program availability:* Part-time, evening/weekend. *Entrance requirements:* For master's, GRE. Electronic applications accepted. *Faculty research:* Radiochemistry/environmental analysis, health physics, radiation effects.

Simon Fraser University, Office of Graduate Studies and Postdoctoral Fellows, Faculty of Business Administration, Vancouver, BC V6B 5K3, Canada. Offers business administration (EMBA, PhD, Graduate Diploma); finance (M Sc); management of technology (MBA); management of technology/biotechnology (MBA). *Program availability:* Online learning. *Faculty:* 91 full-time (33 women). *Students:* 554 full-time (252 women), 161 part-time (58 women). 928 applicants, 45% accepted, 279 enrolled. In 2016, 178 master's, 3 doctorates, 78 other advanced degrees awarded. *Degree requirements:* For master's, thesis (for some programs); for doctorate, comprehensive exam, thesis/dissertation. *Entrance requirements:* For master's, GMAT, minimum GPA of 3.0 (on scale of 4.33) or 3.33 based on last 60 credits of undergraduate courses; for doctorate, minimum GPA of 3.5 (on scale of 4.33); for Graduate Diploma, minimum GPA of 2.5 (on scale of 4.33) or 2.67 based on last 60 credits of undergraduate courses. Additional exam requirements/recommendations for international students: Recommended—TOEFL (minimum score 580 paper-based; 93 iBT), IELTS (minimum score 7), TWE (minimum score 5). *Application deadline:* For fall admission, 4/2 for domestic students; for winter admission, 10/1 for domestic students; for spring admission, 2/2 for domestic students. Application fee: $90 ($125 for international students). *Expenses:* Contact institution. *Financial support:* In 2016–17, 71 students received support, including 9 fellowships (averaging $6,139 per year), teaching assistantships (averaging $5,608 per year); research assistantships, career-related internships or fieldwork, and scholarships/grants also available. *Faculty research:* Accounting, management and organizational studies, technology and operations management, finance, international business. *Unit head:* Dr. Ian McCarthy, Associate Dean, Graduate Programs, 778-782-9255, Fax: 778-782-4920, E-mail: grad-business@sfu.ca. *Application contact:* Graduate Secretary, 778-782-5013, Fax: 778-782-5122, E-mail: grad-business@sfu.ca.
Website: http://beedie.sfu.ca/graduate/index.php

Southeastern Oklahoma State University, School of Arts and Sciences, Durant, OK 74701-0609. Offers biology (MT); computer information systems (MT); occupational safety and health (MT). *Program availability:* Part-time, evening/weekend. *Degree requirements:* For master's, thesis optional. *Entrance requirements:* For master's, minimum GPA of 3.0 in last 60 hours or 2.75 overall. Additional exam requirements/recommendations for international students: Required—TOEFL (minimum score 550 paper-based; 79 iBT). Electronic applications accepted.

Stephen F. Austin State University, Graduate School, College of Sciences and Mathematics, Division of Biotechnology, Nacogdoches, TX 75962. Offers MS. *Degree requirements:* For master's, comprehensive exam, thesis. *Entrance requirements:* For master's, GRE General Test, minimum GPA of 2.8 in last 60 hours, 2.5 overall. Additional exam requirements/recommendations for international students: Required—TOEFL.

Temple University, College of Science and Technology, Department of Biology, Philadelphia, PA 19122. Offers biology (MS, PMS, PhD); biotechnology (MS). Terminal master's awarded for partial completion of doctoral program. *Degree requirements:* For master's, comprehensive exam (for some programs), thesis (for some programs); for doctorate, comprehensive exam (for some programs), thesis/dissertation. *Entrance requirements:* For master's and doctorate, GRE General Test, minimum GPA of 3.0. Additional exam requirements/recommendations for international students: Required—TOEFL (minimum score 550 paper-based; 79 iBT). *Faculty research:* Membrane proteins, genetics, molecular biology, neuroscience, aquatic biology.

Tennessee State University, The School of Graduate Studies and Research, College of Agriculture, Human and Natural Sciences, Nashville, TN 37209-1561. Offers agricultural sciences (MS), including agribusiness, agricultural and extension education, animal science, plant and soil science; biological sciences (MS, PhD); biotechnology (PhD); chemistry (MS). *Program availability:* Part-time, evening/weekend. *Degree requirements:* For master's, thesis. *Entrance requirements:* For master's, GRE General Test, GRE Subject Test, MAT. *Faculty research:* Small farm economics, ornamental horticulture, beef cattle production, rural elderly.

Texas Tech University, Graduate School, Interdisciplinary Programs, Lubbock, TX 79409. Offers arid land studies (MS); biotechnology (MS); interdisciplinary studies (MA, MS); museum science (MA); wind science and engineering (PhD); JD/MS. *Program availability:* Part-time. *Faculty:* 10 full-time (4 women). *Students:* 122 full-time (56 women), 83 part-time (46 women); includes 78 minority (25 Black or African American, non-Hispanic/Latino; 1 American Indian or Alaska Native, non-Hispanic/Latino; 2 Asian, non-Hispanic/Latino; 41 Hispanic/Latino; 1 Native Hawaiian or other Pacific Islander, non-Hispanic/Latino; 8 Two or more races, non-Hispanic/Latino), 32 international. Average age 29. 114 applicants, 71% accepted, 60 enrolled. In 2016, 55 master's, 1 doctorate awarded. Terminal master's awarded for partial completion of doctoral program. *Degree requirements:* For master's, comprehensive exam (for some programs), thesis (for some programs); for doctorate, comprehensive exam, thesis/dissertation (for some programs). *Entrance requirements:* Additional exam requirements/recommendations for international students: Required—TOEFL (minimum score 550 paper-based; 79 iBT), IELTS (minimum score 6.5), PTE (minimum score 60), Cambridge Advanced (B), Cambridge Proficiency (C), ELS English for Academic Purposes (Level 112). *Application deadline:* For fall admission, 6/1 priority date for domestic students, 1/15 priority date for international students; for spring admission, 9/1 priority date for domestic students, 6/15 priority date for international students. Applications are processed on a rolling basis. Application fee: $75. Electronic applications accepted. *Expenses:* Tuition, state resident: full-time $7200; part-time $300 per credit hour. Tuition, nonresident: full-time $16,992; part-time $708 per credit hour. *Required fees:* $2428; $50.50 per credit hour. $608 per semester. Tuition and fees vary according to program. *Financial support:* In 2016–17, 116 students received support, including 107 fellowships (averaging $4,360 per year), 10 research assistantships (averaging $10,619 per year), 7 teaching assistantships (averaging $9,152 per year); scholarships/grants and unspecified assistantships also available. Financial award application deadline: 4/15; financial award applicants required to submit FAFSA. *Total annual research expenditures:* $2 million. *Unit head:* Dr. Mark Sheridan, Vice Provost for Graduate and Postdoctoral Affairs/Dean of the Graduate School, 806-742-2787, Fax: 806-742-1746, E-mail: mark.sheridan@ttu.edu. *Application contact:* Amanda Wysinger, Academic Advisor, 806-834-0822, Fax: 806-742-4038, E-mail: amanda.wysinger@ttu.edu. Website: http://www.depts.ttu.edu/gradschool/about/INDS/index.php

Texas Tech University Health Sciences Center, Graduate School of Biomedical Sciences, Program in Biotechnology, Lubbock, TX 79430. Offers MS. *Entrance requirements:* For master's, GRE General Test, minimum GPA of 3.0. Additional exam requirements/recommendations for international students: Required—TOEFL (minimum score 550 paper-based). *Faculty research:* Reproductive endocrinology, immunology, molecular biology and developmental biochemistry, biology of developing systems.

Thomas Jefferson University, Jefferson College of Health Professions, Department of Medical Laboratory Sciences and Biotechnology, Philadelphia, PA 19107. Offers biotechnology (MS); cytotechnology (MS); medical laboratory science (MS). *Program availability:* Part-time. *Faculty:* 6 full-time (3 women), 4 part-time/adjunct (2 women). *Students:* 57 full-time (43 women), 1 (woman) part-time; includes 11 minority (2 Black or African American, non-Hispanic/Latino; 9 Asian, non-Hispanic/Latino), 12 international. Average age 25. 77 applicants, 71% accepted, 46 enrolled. *Degree requirements:* For master's, comprehensive exam. *Entrance requirements:* Additional exam requirements/recommendations for international students: Required—TOEFL (minimum score 87 iBT), IELTS (minimum score 6.5). *Application deadline:* For spring admission, 5/15 for international students; for summer admission, 7/15 for domestic students. Applications are processed on a rolling basis. Application fee: $50. Electronic applications accepted. *Expenses:* $1,475 (1 year program); $1,600 (2 year program). *Financial support:* In 2016–17, 9 students received support. Federal Work-Study, institutionally sponsored loans, scholarships/grants, and unspecified assistantships available. Financial award application deadline: 4/1; financial award applicants required to submit FAFSA. *Faculty research:* Women's health; transportation of islet cells to remedy diabetes/insulin deficiency; bone regeneration; the use of stem cells to remedy cardiac injuries. *Unit head:* Dr. Barbara Goldsmith, Chair, 215-955-1327, E-mail: barbara.goldsmith@jefferson.edu. *Application contact:* Sarah McNabb, Senior Associate Director of Admissions, 215-503-1045, Fax: 215-503-7241, E-mail: sarah.mcnabb@jefferson.edu. Website: http://www.jefferson.edu/health_professions/departments/bioscience_technologies

Tufts University, Graduate School of Arts and Sciences, Department of Chemistry, Medford, MA 02155. Offers chemical physics (PhD); chemistry (MS, PhD); chemistry/biotechnology (PhD). *Students:* 76 full-time (35 women); includes 11 minority (1 Black or African American, non-Hispanic/Latino; 5 Asian, non-Hispanic/Latino; 3 Hispanic/Latino; 2 Two or more races, non-Hispanic/Latino), 13 international. Average age 26. 96 applicants, 56% accepted, 18 enrolled. In 2016, 5 master's, 6 doctorates awarded. Terminal master's awarded for partial completion of doctoral program. *Degree requirements:* For master's, thesis optional; for doctorate, comprehensive exam, thesis/dissertation. *Entrance requirements:* For master's and doctorate, GRE General Test; GRE Subject Test (recommended). Additional exam requirements/recommendations for international students: Required—TOEFL (minimum score 550 paper-based; 80 iBT), IELTS (minimum score 6.5). *Application deadline:* For fall admission, 1/15 for domestic and international students; for spring admission, 10/15 for domestic and international students. Applications are processed on a rolling basis. Application fee: $85. Electronic applications accepted. *Expenses:* $49,982 full-time tuition (for MS); $29,936 full-time tuition (for PhD). *Financial support:* In 2016–17, 76 students received support. Fellowships, research assistantships, teaching assistantships, Federal Work-Study, scholarships/grants, tuition waivers (full and partial), and unspecified assistantships available. Financial award application deadline: 1/15. *Unit head:* Samuel Thomas, Graduate Program Director. *Application contact:* Office of Graduate Admissions, 617-627-3395.
Website: http://chem.tufts.edu/

Tufts University, Graduate School of Arts and Sciences, Graduate Certificate Programs, Biotechnology Engineering Program, Medford, MA 02155. Offers Certificate. *Program availability:* Part-time, evening/weekend. Electronic applications accepted. *Expenses:* Tuition: Full-time $49,892; part-time $1248 per credit hour. *Required fees:* $844. Full-time tuition and fees vary according to degree level, program and student level. Part-time tuition and fees vary according to course load.

Tufts University, Graduate School of Arts and Sciences, Graduate Certificate Programs, Biotechnology Program, Medford, MA 02155. Offers Certificate. *Program availability:* Part-time, evening/weekend. Electronic applications accepted. *Expenses:* Tuition: Full-time $49,892; part-time $1248 per credit hour. *Required fees:* $844. Full-time tuition and fees vary according to degree level, program and student level. Part-time tuition and fees vary according to course load.

Tufts University, School of Engineering, Department of Chemical and Biological Engineering, Medford, MA 02155. Offers bioengineering (ME, MS), including cell and bioprocess engineering; biotechnology engineering (PhD); chemical and biological engineering (ME, MS, PhD). *Program availability:* Part-time. Terminal master's awarded for partial completion of doctoral program. *Degree requirements:* For master's, thesis (for some programs); for doctorate, thesis/dissertation. *Entrance requirements:* For master's and doctorate, GRE General Test. Additional exam requirements/recommendations for international students: Required—TOEFL (minimum score 550 paper-based; 80 iBT), IELTS (minimum score 6.5). Electronic applications accepted. *Expenses: Tuition:* Full-time $49,892; part-time $1248 per credit hour. *Required fees:* $844. Full-time tuition and fees vary according to degree level, program and student level. Part-time tuition and fees vary according to course load. *Faculty research:* Clean

energy with materials, biomaterials, colloids; metabolic engineering, biotechnology; process control; reaction kinetics, catalysis; transport phenomena.

Universidad de las Américas Puebla, Division of Graduate Studies, School of Sciences, Program in Biotechnology, Puebla, Mexico. Offers MS. *Degree requirements:* For master's, one foreign language, thesis.

University at Buffalo, the State University of New York, Graduate School, Jacobs School of Medicine and Biomedical Sciences, Graduate Programs in Medicine and Biomedical Sciences, Department of Biotechnical and Clinical Laboratory Sciences, Buffalo, NY 14214. Offers biotechnology (MS). *Accreditation:* NAACLS. *Program availability:* Part-time. *Faculty:* 7 full-time (3 women). *Students:* 9 full-time (6 women), 1 (woman) part-time, 6 international. Average age 22. 44 applicants, 43% accepted, 5 enrolled. In 2016, 4 master's awarded. *Degree requirements:* For master's, thesis. *Entrance requirements:* For master's, GRE General Test, minimum GPA of 3.0 or equivalent. Additional exam requirements/recommendations for international students: Required—TOEFL (minimum score 79 iBT), IELTS. *Application deadline:* For fall admission, 3/1 priority date for domestic students, 2/1 priority date for international students. Applications are processed on a rolling basis. Application fee: $75. Electronic applications accepted. *Financial support:* In 2016–17, 6 students received support, including 1 research assistantship with tuition reimbursement available (averaging $15,000 per year), 5 teaching assistantships with full tuition reimbursements available (averaging $10,000 per year). Financial award application deadline: 3/1. *Faculty research:* Immunology, cancer biology, toxicology, analytical clinical chemistry, hematology, chemistry, microbial genomics. *Total annual research expenditures:* $1.2 million. *Unit head:* Dr. Paul J. Kostyniak, Chair, 716-829-5188, Fax: 716-829-3601, E-mail: pjkost@buffalo.edu. *Application contact:* Dr. Stephen T. Koury, Director of Graduate Studies, 716-829-5188, Fax: 716-829-3601, E-mail: stvkoury@buffalo.edu. Website: http://www.smbs.buffalo.edu/cls/biotech-ms.html

The University of Alabama at Birmingham, School of Health Professions, Program in Biotechnology, Birmingham, AL 35294. Offers MS. *Entrance requirements:* For master's, GRE (minimum score of 500 in each area), minimum GPA of 3.0 overall or on last 60 hours attempted, interview. Additional exam requirements/recommendations for international students: Required—TOEFL, TWE. Full-time tuition and fees vary according to course load and program.

The University of Alabama in Huntsville, School of Graduate Studies, College of Engineering, Department of Chemical and Materials Engineering, Huntsville, AL 35899. Offers biotechnology science and engineering (PhD); chemical and materials engineering (MSE); materials science (PhD); mechanical engineering (PhD), including chemical engineering. *Program availability:* Part-time, evening/weekend. *Degree requirements:* For master's, comprehensive exam, thesis or alternative, oral and written exams; for doctorate, comprehensive exam, thesis/dissertation. *Entrance requirements:* For master's, GRE General Test, appropriate bachelor's degree, minimum GPA of 3.0; for doctorate, GRE General Test, minimum GPA of 3.0. Additional exam requirements/recommendations for international students: Required—TOEFL (minimum score 500 paper-based; 80 iBT), IELTS (minimum score 6.5). Electronic applications accepted. *Expenses:* Tuition, state resident: full-time $9834; part-time $600 per credit hour. Tuition, nonresident: full-time $21,830; part-time $1325 per credit hour. *Faculty research:* Ultrathin films for optical, sensor and biological applications; materials processing including low gravity; hypergolic reactants; computational fluid dynamics; biofuels and renewable resources.

The University of Alabama in Huntsville, School of Graduate Studies, College of Science, Department of Biological Sciences, Huntsville, AL 35899. Offers biology (MS); biotechnology science and engineering (PhD); education (MS). *Program availability:* Part-time, evening/weekend. *Degree requirements:* For master's, comprehensive exam, thesis or alternative, oral and written exams. *Entrance requirements:* For master's, GRE General Test, previous course work in biochemistry and organic chemistry, minimum GPA of 3.0. Additional exam requirements/recommendations for international students: Required—TOEFL (minimum score 550 paper-based; 80 iBT), IELTS (minimum score 6.5). Electronic applications accepted. *Expenses:* Tuition, state resident: full-time $9834; part-time $600 per credit hour. Tuition, nonresident: full-time $21,830; part-time $1325 per credit hour. *Faculty research:* Physiology, microbiology, genomics and protemics, ecology and evolution, drug discovery.

The University of Alabama in Huntsville, School of Graduate Studies, College of Science, Department of Chemistry, Huntsville, AL 35899. Offers biotechnology science and engineering (PhD); chemistry (MS); education (MS); materials science (MS, PhD). *Program availability:* Part-time, evening/weekend. *Degree requirements:* For master's, comprehensive exam, thesis or alternative, oral and written exams. *Entrance requirements:* For master's, GRE General Test, minimum GPA of 3.0. Additional exam requirements/recommendations for international students: Required—TOEFL (minimum score 550 paper-based; 80 iBT), IELTS (minimum score 6.5). Electronic applications accepted. *Expenses:* Tuition, state resident: full-time $9834; part-time $600 per credit hour. Tuition, nonresident: full-time $21,830; part-time $1325 per credit hour. *Faculty research:* Natural products drug discovery, protein biochemistry, macromolecular biophysics, polymer synthesis, surface modification and analysis of materials.

University of Alberta, Faculty of Graduate Studies and Research, Department of Biological Sciences, Edmonton, AB T6G 2E1, Canada. Offers environmental biology and ecology (M Sc, PhD); microbiology and biotechnology (M Sc, PhD); molecular biology and genetics (M Sc, PhD); physiology and cell biology (M Sc, PhD); plant biology (M Sc, PhD); systematics and evolution (M Sc, PhD). Terminal master's awarded for partial completion of doctoral program. *Degree requirements:* For master's, thesis; for doctorate, thesis/dissertation. *Entrance requirements:* Additional exam requirements/recommendations for international students: Required—TOEFL.

University of Calgary, Cumming School of Medicine and Faculty of Graduate Studies, Program in Biomedical Technology, Calgary, AB T2N 1N4, Canada. Offers MBT. *Program availability:* Part-time. *Degree requirements:* For master's, comprehensive exam, practicum. *Entrance requirements:* For master's, minimum GPA of 3.2 in last 2 years, B Sc in biological science. Additional exam requirements/recommendations for international students: Required—TOEFL (minimum score 600 paper-based). Electronic applications accepted. *Expenses:* Contact institution. *Faculty research:* Patent law, intellectual proprietorship.

University of California, Irvine, Francisco J. Ayala School of Biological Sciences, Department of Molecular Biology and Biochemistry, Program in Biotechnology, Irvine, CA 92697. Offers MS. *Students:* 23 full-time (12 women); includes 11 minority (6 Asian, non-Hispanic/Latino; 4 Hispanic/Latino; 1 Two or more races, non-Hispanic/Latino), 4 international. Average age 25. 143 applicants, 12% accepted, 11 enrolled. In 2016, 17 master's awarded. *Entrance requirements:* For master's, GRE General Test, GRE Subject Test, minimum GPA of 3.0. *Application deadline:* For fall admission, 3/1 priority date for domestic and international students. Applications are processed on a rolling basis. Application fee: $105 ($125 for international students). Electronic applications accepted. *Financial support:* Application deadline: 3/1; applicants required to submit FAFSA. *Unit head:* Michael G. Cumsky, Director, 949-824-7766, Fax: 949-824-8551, E-mail: mgcumsky@uci.edu. *Application contact:* Morgan Oldham, Administrative Contact, 949-824-6034, Fax: 949-824-8551, E-mail: morgano@uci.edu.

Biotechnology

University of California, Irvine, Francisco J. Ayala School of Biological Sciences, Department of Molecular Biology and Biochemistry, Program in Biotechnology Management, Irvine, CA 92697. Offers MS. Program offered jointly with the Paul Merage School of Business and the Department of Biomedical Engineering. *Students:* 23 full-time (14 women); includes 5 minority (all Asian, non-Hispanic/Latino), 16 international. Average age 24. 39 applicants, 41% accepted, 9 enrolled. In 2016, 12 master's awarded. *Application deadline:* For fall admission, 3/15 for domestic students. Application fee: $105 ($125 for international students). *Unit head:* Michael G. Cumsky, Program Director, 949-824-7766, Fax: 949-824-8551, E-mail: mgcumsky@uci.edu. *Application contact:* Morgan Oldham, Student Affairs Assistant, 949-826-6034, Fax: 949-824-8551, E-mail: morgano@uci.edu.
Website: http://mbb.bio.uci.edu/graduates/masters-science-degree-biotechnology-management/

University of Central Florida, College of Medicine, Burnett School of Biomedical Sciences, Orlando, FL 32816. Offers biomedical sciences (MS, PhD); biotechnology (MS). *Faculty:* 67 full-time (28 women), 7 part-time/adjunct (3 women). *Students:* 86 full-time (49 women), 12 part-time (8 women); includes 32 minority (11 Black or African American, non-Hispanic/Latino; 5 Asian, non-Hispanic/Latino; 15 Hispanic/Latino; 1 Two or more races, non-Hispanic/Latino), 23 international. Average age 27. 123 applicants, 60% accepted, 46 enrolled. In 2016, 21 master's, 9 doctorates awarded. *Degree requirements:* For master's, comprehensive exam, thesis or alternative. *Entrance requirements:* For master's, GRE. Additional exam requirements/recommendations for international students: Required—TOEFL. *Application deadline:* For fall admission, 1/15 for domestic students. Application fee: $30. Electronic applications accepted. *Expenses:* Tuition, state resident: part-time $288.16 per credit hour. Tuition, nonresident: part-time $1071.31 per credit hour. *Financial support:* In 2016–17, 49 students received support, including 8 fellowships with partial tuition reimbursements available (averaging $5,411 per year), 41 research assistantships with partial tuition reimbursements available (averaging $6,925 per year), 36 teaching assistantships with partial tuition reimbursements available (averaging $8,129 per year). Financial award application deadline: 3/1; financial award applicants required to submit FAFSA. *Unit head:* Dr. Griffith Parks, Director, 407-226-1000, E-mail: griffith.parks@ucf.edu. *Application contact:* Assistant Director, Graduate Admissions, 407-823-2766, Fax: 407-823-6442, E-mail: gradadmissions@ucf.edu.
Website: http://www.biomed.ucf.edu/

University of Delaware, College of Arts and Sciences, Department of Biological Sciences, Newark, DE 19716. Offers biotechnology (MS); cancer biology (MS, PhD); cell and extracellular matrix biology (MS, PhD); cell and systems physiology (MS, PhD); developmental biology (MS, PhD); ecology and evolution (MS, PhD); microbiology (MS, PhD); molecular biology and genetics (MS, PhD). Terminal master's awarded for partial completion of doctoral program. *Degree requirements:* For master's, thesis, preliminary exam; for doctorate, comprehensive exam, thesis/dissertation, preliminary exam. *Entrance requirements:* For master's and doctorate, GRE General Test. Additional exam requirements/recommendations for international students: Required—TOEFL (minimum score 600 paper-based); Recommended—TWE. Electronic applications accepted. *Faculty research:* Microorganisms, bone, cancer metastasis, developmental biology, cell biology, DNA.

University of Guelph, Graduate Studies, Ontario Agricultural College, Department of Environmental Biology, Guelph, ON N1G 2W1, Canada. Offers entomology (M Sc, PhD); environmental microbiology and biotechnology (M Sc, PhD); environmental toxicology (M Sc, PhD); plant and forest systems (M Sc, PhD); plant pathology (M Sc, PhD). *Program availability:* Part-time. *Degree requirements:* For master's, thesis; for doctorate, comprehensive exam, thesis/dissertation. *Entrance requirements:* For master's, minimum 75% average during previous 2 years of course work; for doctorate, minimum 75% average. Additional exam requirements/recommendations for international students: Required—TOEFL or IELTS. Electronic applications accepted. *Faculty research:* Entomology, environmental microbiology and biotechnology, environmental toxicology, forest ecology, plant pathology.

University of Houston–Clear Lake, School of Science and Computer Engineering, Program in Biotechnology, Houston, TX 77058-1002. Offers MS.

University of Illinois at Chicago, College of Pharmacy, Department of Biopharmaceutical Sciences, Chicago, IL 60607-7173. Offers MS, PhD. *Faculty research:* Lipid and polymer-based drug delivery systems, targeted drug delivery, pharmacokinetic membrane transport and absorption, behavioral and cardiovascular pharmacology; neuropharmacology, environmental toxicology, cancer chemotherapy.

The University of Kansas, University of Kansas Medical Center, School of Health Professions, Program in Molecular Biotechnology, Kansas City, KS 66160. Offers MS. *Faculty:* 4. *Students:* 3 full-time (2 women); includes 1 minority (Asian, non-Hispanic/Latino), 2 international. Average age 25. 14 applicants, 21% accepted, 3 enrolled. In 2016, 1 master's awarded. *Degree requirements:* For master's, comprehensive exam. *Entrance requirements:* For master's, GRE General Test. Additional exam requirements/recommendations for international students: Required—TOEFL or IELTS. *Application deadline:* For fall admission, 2/1 priority date for domestic and international students. Application fee: $60. Electronic applications accepted. *Financial support:* Career-related internships or fieldwork available. Financial award application deadline: 3/1; financial award applicants required to submit FAFSA. *Faculty research:* Diabetes, obesity, polycystic kidney disease, protein structure and function, cell signaling pathways. *Unit head:* Dr. Eric Elsinghorst, Director of Graduate Studies, 913-588-1089, E-mail: eelsinghorst@kumc.edu. *Application contact:* Valerie Noack, Senior Coordinator, 913-945-7347, Fax: 913-588-4697, E-mail: vnoack@kumc.edu.
Website: http://www.mb.kumc.edu

The University of Manchester, Faculty of Life Sciences, Manchester, United Kingdom. Offers adaptive organismal biology (M Phil, PhD); animal biology (M Phil, PhD); biochemistry (M Phil, PhD); bioinformatics (M Phil, PhD); biomolecular sciences (M Phil, PhD); biotechnology (M Phil, PhD); cell biology (M Phil, PhD); cell matrix research (M Phil, PhD); channels and transporters (M Phil, PhD); developmental biology (M Phil, PhD); Egyptology (M Phil, PhD); environmental biology (M Phil, PhD); evolutionary biology (M Phil, PhD); gene expression (M Phil, PhD); genetics (M Phil, PhD); history of science, technology and medicine (M Phil, PhD); immunology (M Phil, PhD); integrative neurobiology and behavior (M Phil, PhD); membrane trafficking (M Phil, PhD); microbiology (M Phil, PhD); molecular and cellular neuroscience (M Phil, PhD); molecular biology (M Phil, PhD); molecular cancer studies (M Phil, PhD); neuroscience (M Phil, PhD); ophthalmology (M Phil, PhD); optometry (M Phil, PhD); organelle function (M Phil, PhD); pharmacology (M Phil, PhD); physiology (M Phil, PhD); plant sciences (M Phil, PhD); stem cell research (M Phil, PhD); structural biology (M Phil, PhD); systems neuroscience (M Phil, PhD); toxicology (M Phil, PhD).

University of Maryland, Baltimore County, The Graduate School, College of Natural and Mathematical Sciences, Department of Biological Sciences, Programs in Biotechnology, Baltimore, MD 21250. Offers biotechnology (MPS); biotechnology management (Graduate Certificate). *Program availability:* Part-time, evening/weekend. *Faculty:* 17 part-time/adjunct (6 women). *Students:* 3 full-time (2 women), 17 part-time (10 women); includes 11 minority (1 Black or African American, non-Hispanic/Latino; 8 Asian, non-Hispanic/Latino; 2 Hispanic/Latino). Average age 29. 25 applicants, 64% accepted, 9 enrolled. In 2016, 11 master's, 4 other advanced degrees awarded. *Entrance requirements:* Additional exam requirements/recommendations for international students: Required—TOEFL (minimum score 99 iBT). *Application deadline:* For fall admission, 8/1 for domestic students, 1/1 for international students; for spring admission, 12/1 for domestic students. Applications are processed on a rolling basis. Application fee: $50. Electronic applications accepted. *Expenses:* $603 per credit resident tuition; $126 per credit fees. *Financial support:* Unspecified assistantships available. Financial award applicants required to submit FAFSA. *Unit head:* Sonya Crosby, Director, Professional Studies, 410-455-3899, E-mail: scrosby@umbc.edu. *Application contact:* Nancy Clements, Program Specialist, 410-455-5536, E-mail: nancyc@umbc.edu. Website: http://www.umbc.edu/biotech/

University of Maryland University College, The Graduate School, Program in Biotechnology, Adelphi, MD 20783. Offers MS, Certificate. *Program availability:* Part-time, evening/weekend, online learning. *Students:* 6 full-time (3 women), 401 part-time (260 women); includes 203 minority (118 Black or African American, non-Hispanic/Latino; 2 American Indian or Alaska Native, non-Hispanic/Latino; 42 Asian, non-Hispanic/Latino; 32 Hispanic/Latino; 9 Two or more races, non-Hispanic/Latino), 9 international. Average age 31. 81 applicants, 100% accepted, 62 enrolled. In 2016, 82 master's, 20 other advanced degrees awarded. *Degree requirements:* For master's, thesis or alternative, capstone course. *Application deadline:* Applications are processed on a rolling basis. Application fee: $50. Electronic applications accepted. *Expenses:* Tuition, state resident: part-time $458 per credit. Tuition, nonresident: part-time $659 per credit. *Financial support:* Federal Work-Study and scholarships/grants available. Support available to part-time students. Financial award application deadline: 6/1; financial award applicants required to submit FAFSA. *Unit head:* Rana Khan, Director, 240-684-2400, Fax: 240-684-2401, E-mail: rana.khan@umuc.edu. *Application contact:* Coordinator, Graduate Admissions, 800-888-8682, Fax: 240-684-2151, E-mail: newgrad@umuc.edu.
Website: http://www.umuc.edu/academic-programs/masters-degrees/biotechnology.cfm

University of Massachusetts Amherst, Graduate School, College of Natural Sciences, Department of Animal Biotechnology and Biomedical Sciences, Amherst, MA 01003. Offers MS, PhD. *Program availability:* Part-time. Terminal master's awarded for partial completion of doctoral program. *Degree requirements:* For master's, thesis or alternative; for doctorate, comprehensive exam, thesis/dissertation. *Entrance requirements:* For doctorate, GRE General Test. Additional exam requirements/recommendations for international students: Required—TOEFL (minimum score 550 paper-based; 80 iBT), IELTS (minimum score 6.5). Electronic applications accepted.

University of Massachusetts Boston, College of Science and Mathematics, Program in Biomedical Engineering and Biotechnology, Boston, MA 02125-3393. Offers PhD. *Students:* 1 (woman) full-time, 3 part-time (1 woman), 3 international. Average age 32. 10 applicants, 10% accepted, 1 enrolled. In 2016, 1 doctorate awarded. *Expenses:* Tuition, state resident: full-time $16,863. Tuition, nonresident: full-time $32,913. *Required fees:* $177. *Unit head:* Dr. William Hagar, 617-287-5776. *Application contact:* Peggy Roldan Patel, Graduate Admissions Coordinator, 617-287-6400, Fax: 617-287-6236, E-mail: bos.gadm@dpc.umassp.edu.

University of Massachusetts Boston, College of Science and Mathematics, Program in Biotechnology and Biomedical Sciences, Boston, MA 02125-3393. Offers MS. *Program availability:* Part-time, evening/weekend. *Students:* 1 (woman) full-time, 2 part-time (1 woman). Average age 39. 38 applicants. In 2016, 2 master's awarded. *Degree requirements:* For master's, comprehensive exam, thesis optional, oral exams. *Entrance requirements:* For master's, GRE General Test, GRE Subject Test, minimum GPA of 2.75, 3.0 in science and math. *Application deadline:* For fall admission, 3/1 for domestic students; for spring admission, 11/1 for domestic students. *Expenses:* Tuition, state resident: full-time $16,863. Tuition, nonresident: full-time $32,913. *Required fees:* $177. *Financial support:* Research assistantships with full tuition reimbursements, teaching assistantships with full tuition reimbursements, career-related internships or fieldwork, Federal Work-Study, and unspecified assistantships available. Support available to part-time students. Financial award application deadline: 3/1; financial award applicants required to submit FAFSA. *Faculty research:* Evolutionary and molecular immunology, molecular genetics, tissue culture, computerized laboratory technology. *Unit head:* Dr. Greg Beck, Director, 617-287-6600. *Application contact:* Peggy Roldan Patel, Graduate Admissions Coordinator, 617-287-6400, Fax: 617-287-6236, E-mail: bos.gadm@dpc.umassp.edu.

University of Massachusetts Dartmouth, Graduate School, College of Engineering, Program in Biomedical Engineering and Biotechnology, North Dartmouth, MA 02747-2300. Offers bioengineering (PhD); biology (PhD); biomedical engineering/biotechnology (MS, PhD); chemistry (PhD); civil engineering (PhD); computer and information science (PhD); electrical and computer engineering (PhD); mathematics (PhD); mechanical engineering (PhD); medical laboratory science (MS); physics (PhD). *Program availability:* Part-time. *Students:* 12 full-time (6 women), 8 part-time (5 women); includes 2 minority (both Hispanic/Latino), 7 international. Average age 31. 18 applicants, 44% accepted, 2 enrolled. In 2016, 2 master's, 6 doctorates awarded. *Degree requirements:* For doctorate, comprehensive exam, thesis/dissertation. *Entrance requirements:* For master's, GRE (recommended), statement of purpose (minimum of 300 words), resume, 3 letters of recommendation, official transcripts; for doctorate, GRE, statement of purpose (minimum of 300 words), resume, 3 letters of recommendation, official transcripts. Additional exam requirements/recommendations for international students: Required—TOEFL (minimum score 550 paper-based). *Application deadline:* For fall admission, 2/15 priority date for domestic students, 1/15 priority date for international students; for spring admission, 11/15 priority date for domestic students, 10/15 priority date for international students. Application fee: $60. Electronic applications accepted. *Expenses:* Tuition, state resident: full-time $14,994; part-time $624.75 per credit. Tuition, nonresident: full-time $27,068; part-time $1127.83 per credit. *Required fees:* $405; $25.88 per credit. Tuition and fees vary according to course load and reciprocity agreements. *Financial support:* In 2016–17, 5 fellowships (averaging $6,000 per year), 4 research assistantships (averaging $5,429 per year), 5 teaching assistantships (averaging $7,125 per year) were awarded. Financial award application deadline: 3/1; financial award applicants required to submit FAFSA. *Faculty research:* Comparative immunology, vaccine design, biosensors, biomimetic materials, polymer science, soft electronics, hydrogels, regenerative biological materials. *Total annual research expenditures:* $984,000. *Unit head:* Alex Fowler, Graduate Program Director, 508-999-8449, E-mail: afowler@umassd.edu. *Application contact:* Steven Briggs, Director of Marketing and Recruitment for Graduate Studies, 508-999-8604, Fax: 508-999-8183, E-mail: graduate@umassd.edu.
Website: http://www.umassd.edu/engineering/graduate/doctoraldegreeprograms/biomedicalengineeringandbiotechnology/

University of Minnesota, Twin Cities Campus, Graduate School, Program in Microbial Engineering, Minneapolis, MN 55455-0213. Offers MS. *Program availability:* Part-time. *Degree requirements:* For master's, thesis. *Entrance requirements:* For master's, GRE General Test. Additional exam requirements/recommendations for international students: Required—TOEFL. *Faculty research:* Microbial genetics, oncogenesis, gene transfer, fermentation, bioreactors, genetics of antibiotic biosynthesis.

University of Missouri–St. Louis, College of Arts and Sciences, Department of Chemistry and Biochemistry, St. Louis, MO 63121. Offers biochemistry and biotechnology (MS); chemistry (MS, PhD). *Program availability:* Part-time, evening/weekend. *Faculty:* 22 full-time (3 women), 3 part-time/adjunct (1 woman). *Students:* 45 full-time (17 women), 15 part-time (5 women); includes 7 minority (1 Black or African American, non-Hispanic/Latino; 2 Asian, non-Hispanic/Latino; 2 Hispanic/Latino; 1 Native Hawaiian or other Pacific Islander, non-Hispanic/Latino; 1 Two or more races, non-Hispanic/Latino), 24 international. 43 applicants, 47% accepted, 12 enrolled. Terminal master's awarded for partial completion of doctoral program. *Degree requirements:* For master's, thesis optional; for doctorate, thesis/dissertation. *Entrance requirements:* For master's, 2 letters of recommendation; for doctorate, GRE General Test, 3 letters of recommendation. Additional exam requirements/recommendations for international students: Required—TOEFL (minimum score 550 paper-based; 79 iBT), IELTS (minimum score 6.5). *Application deadline:* For fall admission, 7/1 priority date for domestic and international students; for spring admission, 12/1 priority date for domestic and international students. Applications are processed on a rolling basis. Application fee: $50 ($40 for international students). Electronic applications accepted. *Financial support:* Fellowships with tuition reimbursements, research assistantships with tuition reimbursements, and teaching assistantships with tuition reimbursements available. *Faculty research:* Metallaborane chemistry, serum transferrin chemistry, natural products chemistry, organic synthesis. *Unit head:* Cynthia Dupureur, Chair, 314-516-4392, Fax: 314-516-5342, E-mail: cdup@umsl.edu. *Application contact:* Graduate Admissions, 314-516-5458, Fax: 314-516-6996, E-mail: gradadm@umsl.edu.
Website: http://www.umsl.edu/chemistry/

University of Nevada, Reno, Graduate School, College of Agriculture, Biotechnology and Natural Resources, Program in Biotechnology, Reno, NV 89557. Offers MS. 5 year degree; students are admitted to as undergraduates. *Degree requirements:* For master's, thesis. *Entrance requirements:* For master's, GRE, minimum GPA of 2.75. Additional exam requirements/recommendations for international students: Required—TOEFL (minimum score 500 paper-based; 61 iBT), IELTS (minimum score 6). Electronic applications accepted. *Faculty research:* Cancer biology, plant virology.

University of North Texas Health Science Center at Fort Worth, Graduate School of Biomedical Sciences, Fort Worth, TX 76107-2699. Offers anatomy and cell biology (MS, PhD); biochemistry and molecular biology (MS, PhD); biomedical sciences (MS, PhD); biotechnology (MS); forensic genetics (MS); integrative physiology (MS, PhD); medical science (MS); microbiology and immunology (MS, PhD); pharmacology (MS, PhD); science education (MS); DO/MS; DO/PhD. Terminal master's awarded for partial completion of doctoral program. *Degree requirements:* For master's, thesis; for doctorate, thesis/dissertation. *Entrance requirements:* For master's and doctorate, GRE General Test. Additional exam requirements/recommendations for international students: Required—TOEFL. *Expenses:* Contact institution. *Faculty research:* Alzheimer's disease, aging, eye diseases, cancer, cardiovascular disease.

University of Pennsylvania, School of Engineering and Applied Science, Program in Biotechnology, Philadelphia, PA 19104. Offers MBT. *Program availability:* Part-time. *Students:* 55 full-time (27 women), 17 part-time (12 women); includes 12 minority (1 Black or African American, non-Hispanic/Latino; 9 Asian, non-Hispanic/Latino; 2 Hispanic/Latino), 46 international. Average age 25. 156 applicants, 43% accepted, 47 enrolled. In 2016, 45 master's awarded. *Degree requirements:* For master's, comprehensive exam, thesis optional. *Entrance requirements:* For master's, GRE. Additional exam requirements/recommendations for international students: Required—TOEFL (minimum score 100 iBT), IELTS (minimum score 7). *Application deadline:* For fall admission, 3/15 priority date for domestic and international students. Application fee: $80. Electronic applications accepted. *Expenses: Tuition:* Full-time $31,068; part-time $5762 per course. *Required fees:* $3200; $336 per course. Full-time tuition and fees vary according to degree level, program and student level. Part-time tuition and fees vary according to course load, degree level and program. *Faculty research:* Biopharmaceuticals, biomedical technologies, engineering biotechnology, molecular biology. *Application contact:* William Fenton, Assistant Director of Graduate Admissions, 215-898-4542, Fax: 215-573-5577, E-mail: gradstudies@seas.upenn.edu.
Website: http://www.upenn.edu/biotech/

University of Rhode Island, Graduate School, College of the Environment and Life Sciences, Department of Cell and Molecular Biology, Kingston, RI 02881. Offers biochemistry (MS, PhD); clinical laboratory sciences (MS), including biotechnology, clinical laboratory science, cytopathology; microbiology (MS, PhD); molecular genetics (MS, PhD). *Program availability:* Part-time. *Faculty:* 22 full-time (10 women), 2 part-time/adjunct (1 woman). *Students:* 18 full-time (13 women), 26 part-time (20 women); includes 10 minority (2 Black or African American, non-Hispanic/Latino; 1 American Indian or Alaska Native, non-Hispanic/Latino; 5 Asian, non-Hispanic/Latino; 1 Hispanic/Latino; 1 Two or more races, non-Hispanic/Latino), 10 international. In 2016, 19 master's, 3 doctorates awarded. *Degree requirements:* For master's, comprehensive exam (for some programs), thesis optional; for doctorate, comprehensive exam, thesis/dissertation. *Entrance requirements:* For master's and doctorate, GRE, 2 letters of recommendation. Additional exam requirements/recommendations for international students: Required—TOEFL. *Application deadline:* For fall admission, 1/15 for domestic and international students. Application fee: $65. Electronic applications accepted. *Expenses:* Tuition, state resident: full-time $11,796; part-time $655 per credit. Tuition, nonresident: full-time $24,206; part-time $1345 per credit. *Required fees:* $1546; $44 per credit. One-time fee: $155 full-time; $35 part-time. *Financial support:* In 2016–17, 8 research assistantships with tuition reimbursements (averaging $11,986 per year), 4 teaching assistantships with tuition reimbursements (averaging $17,273 per year) were awarded; traineeships also available. Financial award application deadline: 1/15; financial award applicants required to submit FAFSA. *Unit head:* Dr. Gongqing Sun, Chair and Professor, 401-874-5937, Fax: 401-874-2202, E-mail: gsun@mail.uri.edu. *Application contact:* Graduate Admissions, 401-874-2872,
E-mail: gradadm@etal.uri.edu.
Website: http://cels.uri.edu/cmb/

University of San Francisco, College of Arts and Sciences, Biotechnology Program, San Francisco, CA 94117-1080. Offers PSM. *Program availability:* Part-time. *Faculty:* 2 full-time (0 women), 1 part-time/adjunct (0 women). *Students:* 41 full-time (26 women), 4 part-time (1 woman); includes 21 minority (1 Black or African American, non-Hispanic/Latino; 14 Asian, non-Hispanic/Latino; 3 Hispanic/Latino; 1 Native Hawaiian or other Pacific Islander, non-Hispanic/Latino; 2 Two or more races, non-Hispanic/Latino), 10 international. Average age 26. 65 applicants, 66% accepted, 21 enrolled. In 2016, 14 master's awarded. *Entrance requirements:* For master's, GRE. Additional exam requirements/recommendations for international students: Required—TOEFL, IELTS, PTE. *Application deadline:* For fall admission, 4/15 for domestic and international students; for spring admission, 10/15 for domestic and international students. Electronic applications accepted. *Expenses: Tuition:* Full-time $23,310; part-time $1295 per credit. Tuition and fees vary according to course load, degree level, campus/location and program. *Financial support:* In 2016–17, 14 students received support. Applicants required to submit FAFSA. *Unit head:* Dr. Jennifer Dever, Director, 415-422-6755, E-mail: jadever@usfca.edu. *Application contact:* Mark Landerghini, Information Contact, 415-422-5101, Fax: 415-422-2217, E-mail: asgraduate@usfca.edu.
Website: https://www.usfca.edu/arts-sciences/graduate-programs/biotechnology

University of Saskatchewan, College of Graduate Studies and Research, Edwards School of Business, Program in Business Administration, Saskatoon, SK S7N 5A2, Canada. Offers agribusiness management (MBA); biotechnology management (MBA); health services management (MBA); indigenous management (MBA); international business management (MBA).

University of Southern California, Keck School of Medicine and Graduate School, Graduate Programs in Medicine, Program in Global Biotechnology, Los Angeles, CA 90089. Offers biotechnology (MS). *Program availability:* Part-time. *Faculty:* 4 full-time (2 women). *Students:* 2 full-time (1 woman), 2 part-time (0 women); includes 1 minority (Asian, non-Hispanic/Latino), 2 international. Average age 22. *Degree requirements:* For master's, experiential projects. *Entrance requirements:* Additional exam requirements/recommendations for international students: Recommended—TOEFL (minimum score 90 iBT), IELTS (minimum score 6.5). *Application deadline:* For fall admission, 6/1 for domestic students, 5/1 for international students; for spring admission, 12/1 for domestic students, 11/1 for international students; for summer admission, 5/1 for domestic students, 4/1 for international students. Applications are processed on a rolling basis. Electronic applications accepted. *Expenses:* $51,442 tuition, $2,222 fees. *Faculty research:* Stem cells, cell biology, oncogenesis, drug discovery and development. *Unit head:* Dr. Carol S. Lin, Director, 323-442-3237, E-mail: carollin@usc.edu. *Application contact:* Marisela Zuniga, Administrative Coordinator, 323-442-1607, Fax: 323-442-1199, E-mail: mzuniga@usc.edu.
Website: http://keck.usc.edu/global-biotechnology-program/

University of South Florida, Innovative Education, Tampa, FL 33620-9951. Offers adult, career and higher education (Graduate Certificate), including college teaching, leadership in developing human resources, leadership in higher education; Africana studies (Graduate Certificate), including diasporas and health disparities, genocide and human rights; aging studies (Graduate Certificate), including gerontology; art research (Graduate Certificate), including museum studies; business foundations (Graduate Certificate); chemical and biomedical engineering (Graduate Certificate), including materials science and engineering, water, health and sustainability; child and family studies (Graduate Certificate), including positive behavior support; civil and industrial engineering (Graduate Certificate), including transportation systems analysis; community and family health (Graduate Certificate), including maternal and child health, social marketing and public health, violence and injury: prevention and intervention, women's health; criminology (Graduate Certificate), including criminal justice administration; educational measurement and research (Graduate Certificate), including evaluation; English (Graduate Certificate), including comparative literary studies, creative writing, professional and technical communication; entrepreneurship (Graduate Certificate); environmental health (Graduate Certificate), including safety management; epidemiology and biostatistics (Graduate Certificate), including applied biostatistics, biostatistics, concepts and tools of epidemiology, epidemiology, epidemiology of infectious diseases; geography, environment and planning (Graduate Certificate), including community development, environmental policy and management, geographical information systems; geology (Graduate Certificate), including hydrogeology; global health (Graduate Certificate), including disaster management, global health and Latin American and Caribbean studies, global health practice, humanitarian assistance, infection control; government and international affairs (Graduate Certificate), including Cuban studies, globalization studies; health policy and management (Graduate Certificate), including health management and leadership, public health policy and programs; hearing specialist: early intervention (Graduate Certificate); industrial and management systems engineering (Graduate Certificate), including systems engineering, technology management; information studies (Graduate Certificate), including school library media specialist; information systems/decision sciences (Graduate Certificate), including analytics and business intelligence; instructional technology (Graduate Certificate), including distance education, Florida digital/virtual educator, instructional design, multimedia design, Web design; internal medicine, bioethics and medical humanities (Graduate Certificate), including biomedical ethics; Latin American and Caribbean studies (Graduate Certificate); mass communications (Graduate Certificate), including multimedia journalism; mathematics and statistics (Graduate Certificate), including mathematics; medicine (Graduate Certificate), including aging and neuroscience, bioinformatics, biotechnology, brain fitness and memory management, clinical investigation, health informatics, health sciences, integrative weight management, intellectual property, medicine and gender, metabolic and nutritional medicine, metabolic cardiology, pharmacy sciences; national and competitive intelligence (Graduate Certificate); psychological and social foundations (Graduate Certificate), including career counseling, college teaching, diversity in education, mental health counseling, school counseling; public affairs (Graduate Certificate), including nonprofit management, public management, research administration; public health (Graduate Certificate), including environmental health, health equity, public health generalist, translational research in adolescent behavioral health; public health practices (Graduate Certificate), including planning for healthy communities; rehabilitation and mental health counseling (Graduate Certificate), including integrative mental health care, marriage and family therapy, rehabilitation technology; secondary education (Graduate Certificate), including ESOL, foreign language education: culture and content, foreign language education: professional; social work (Graduate Certificate), including geriatric social work/clinical gerontology; special education (Graduate Certificate), including autism spectrum disorder, disabilities education: severe/profound; world languages (Graduate Certificate), including teaching English as a second language (TESL) or foreign language. *Expenses:* Tuition, state resident: full-time $7766; part-time $431.43 per credit hour. Tuition, nonresident: full-time $15,789; part-time $877.17 per credit hour. *Required fees:* $37 per term. *Unit head:* Kathy Barnes, Interdisciplinary Programs Coordinator, 813-974-8031, Fax: 813-974-7061, E-mail: barnesk@usf.edu. *Application contact:* Karen Tylinski, Metro Initiatives, 813-974-9943, Fax: 813-974-7061, E-mail: ktylinsk@usf.edu.
Website: http://www.usf.edu/innovative-education/

University of South Florida, Morsani College of Medicine and College of Graduate Studies, Graduate Programs in Medical Sciences, Tampa, FL 33620-9951. Offers advanced athletic training (MS); athletic training (MS); bioinformatics and computational biology (MSBCB); biotechnology (MSB); health informatics (MSHI); medical sciences (MSMS, PhD), including aging and neuroscience (MSMS), allergy, immunology and infectious disease (PhD), anatomy, biochemistry and molecular biology, clinical and translational research, health science (MSMS), interdisciplinary medical sciences (MSMS), medical microbiology and immunology (MSMS), metabolic and nutritional medicine (MSMS), microbiology and immunology (PhD), molecular medicine, molecular pharmacology and physiology (PhD), neuroscience (PhD), pathology and cell biology (PhD), women's health (MSMS). *Students:* 454 full-time (239 women), 273 part-time (173 women); includes 347 minority (110 Black or African American, non-Hispanic/Latino; 1 American Indian or Alaska Native, non-Hispanic/Latino; 99 Asian, non-Hispanic/Latino; 113 Hispanic/Latino; 1 Native Hawaiian or other Pacific Islander, non-Hispanic/Latino; 23 Two or more races, non-Hispanic/Latino), 61 international. Average age 27. 7,242 applicants, 8% accepted, 395 enrolled. In 2016, 374 master's, 13 doctorates awarded. Terminal master's awarded for partial completion of doctoral program. *Degree requirements:* For master's, comprehensive exam, thesis; for doctorate, comprehensive exam, thesis/dissertation. *Entrance requirements:* For master's, GRE General Test or GMAT, bachelor's degree or equivalent from regionally-accredited university with minimum GPA of 3.0 in upper-division sciences coursework; prerequisites in general biology, general chemistry, general physics, organic chemistry, quantitative analysis, and integral and differential calculus; for doctorate, GRE General Test, bachelor's degree from regionally-accredited university with minimum GPA of 3.0 in upper-division sciences coursework; 3 letters of recommendation; personal interview; 1-2 page personal statement; prerequisites in biology, chemistry, physics, organic chemistry, quantitative analysis, and integral/differential calculus. Additional exam requirements/recommendations for international students: Required—TOEFL (minimum score 550 paper-based; 79 iBT) or IELTS (minimum score 6.5). *Application deadline:* For fall admission, 2/1 for domestic and international students. Application fee: $30. Electronic applications accepted. *Expenses:* Contact institution. *Financial support:* In 2016–17, 116 students received support. *Faculty research:* Anatomy, biochemistry, cancer biology, cardiovascular disease, cell biology, immunology, microbiology, molecular biology, neuroscience, pharmacology, physiology. *Total annual research expenditures:* $42.3 million. *Unit head:* Dr. Michael Barber, Professor/Associate Dean for Graduate and Postdoctoral Affairs, 813-974-9908, Fax: 813-974-4317, E-mail: mbarber@health.usf.edu. *Application contact:* Dr. Eric Bennett, Graduate Director, PhD Program in Medical Sciences, 813-974-1545, Fax: 813-974-4317, E-mail: esbennet@health.usf.edu. Website: http://health.usf.edu/nocms/medicine/graduatestudies/

The University of Texas at Dallas, School of Natural Sciences and Mathematics, Department of Biological Sciences, Richardson, TX 75080. Offers bioinformatics and computational biology (MS); biotechnology (MS); molecular and cell biology (MS, PhD). *Program availability:* Part-time, evening/weekend. *Faculty:* 22 full-time (4 women), 1 (woman) part-time/adjunct. *Students:* 118 full-time (72 women), 21 part-time (10 women); includes 27 minority (2 Black or African American, non-Hispanic/Latino; 15 Asian, non-Hispanic/Latino; 6 Hispanic/Latino; 4 Two or more races, non-Hispanic/Latino), 80 international. Average age 28. 355 applicants, 26% accepted, 34 enrolled. In 2016, 37 master's, 6 doctorates awarded. *Degree requirements:* For master's, thesis optional; for doctorate, thesis/dissertation, publishable paper. *Entrance requirements:* For master's and doctorate, GRE (minimum combined score of 1000 on verbal and quantitative). Additional exam requirements/recommendations for international students: Required—TOEFL (minimum score 550 paper-based; 80 iBT). *Application deadline:* For fall admission, 7/15 for domestic students, 5/1 priority date for international students; for spring admission, 11/15 for domestic students, 9/1 priority date for international students. Applications are processed on a rolling basis. Application fee: $50 ($100 for international students). Electronic applications accepted. *Expenses:* Tuition, state resident: full-time $12,418; part-time $690 per semester hour. Tuition, nonresident: full-time $24,150; part-time $1342 per semester hour. Tuition and fees vary according to course load. *Financial support:* In 2016–17, 77 students received support, including 2 fellowships with partial tuition reimbursements available (averaging $675 per year), 16 research assistantships with partial tuition reimbursements available (averaging $24,013 per year), 53 teaching assistantships with partial tuition reimbursements available (averaging $17,153 per year); career-related internships or fieldwork, Federal Work-Study, institutionally sponsored loans, scholarships/grants, and unspecified assistantships also available. Support available to part-time students. Financial award application deadline: 4/30; financial award applicants required to submit FAFSA. *Faculty research:* Role of mitochondria in neurodegenerative diseases, protein-DNA interactions in site-specific recombination, eukaryotic gene expression, bio-nanotechnology, sickle cell research. *Unit head:* Dr. Stephen Spiro, Department Head, 972-883-6032, Fax: 972-883-4551, E-mail: stephen.spiro@utdallas.edu. *Application contact:* Dr. Lawrence Reitzer, Graduate Advisor, 972-883-2502, Fax: 972-883-4551, E-mail: reitzer@utdallas.edu. Website: http://www.utdallas.edu/biology/

The University of Texas at San Antonio, College of Sciences, Department of Biology, San Antonio, TX 78249-0617. Offers biology (MS); biotechnology (MS); cell and molecular biology (PhD); neurobiology (PhD). *Faculty:* 36 full-time (10 women), 3 part-time/adjunct (1 woman). *Students:* 107 full-time (59 women), 52 part-time (31 women); includes 64 minority (5 Black or African American, non-Hispanic/Latino; 1 American Indian or Alaska Native, non-Hispanic/Latino; 8 Asian, non-Hispanic/Latino; 47 Hispanic/Latino; 3 Two or more races, non-Hispanic/Latino), 30 international. Average age 27. 178 applicants, 59% accepted, 61 enrolled. In 2016, 50 master's, 9 doctorates awarded. Terminal master's awarded for partial completion of doctoral program. *Degree requirements:* For master's, comprehensive exam, thesis or alternative; for doctorate, comprehensive exam, thesis/dissertation. *Entrance requirements:* For master's, GRE General Test, bachelor's degree with 18 credit hours in field of study or in another appropriate field of study; for doctorate, GRE General Test, 3 letters of recommendation, statement of purpose, resume. Additional exam requirements/recommendations for international students: Required—TOEFL (minimum score 500 paper-based; 100 iBT), IELTS (minimum score 5). *Application deadline:* For fall admission, 7/1 for domestic students, 4/1 for international students; for spring admission, 11/1 for domestic students, 9/1 for international students. Application fee: $45 ($80 for international students). Electronic applications accepted. *Faculty research:* Development of human and veterinary vaccines against a fungal disease, mammalian germ cells and stem cells, dopamine neuron physiology and addiction, plant biochemistry, dendritic computation and synaptic plasticity. *Total annual research expenditures:* $9.7 million. *Unit head:* Dr. Garry Sunter, Chair, 210-458-5657, E-mail: garry.sunter@utsa.edu.
Website: http://bio.utsa.edu/

University of the Sciences, Program in Cell Biology and Biotechnology, Philadelphia, PA 19104-4495. Offers MS. *Program availability:* Part-time, evening/weekend. *Degree requirements:* For master's, thesis optional. *Entrance requirements:* For master's, GRE General Test. Additional exam requirements/recommendations for international students: Required—TOEFL, TWE. *Expenses:* Contact institution.

University of Toronto, School of Graduate Studies, Program in Biotechnology, Toronto, ON M5S 1A1, Canada. Offers MBiotech. *Entrance requirements:* For master's, minimum B+ average in the last two years of study and/or GRE. Additional exam requirements/recommendations for international students: Required—TOEFL (minimum score 580 paper-based; 93 iBT), TWE (minimum score 5). Electronic applications accepted.

University of Utah, Graduate School, Professional Master of Science and Technology Program, Salt Lake City, UT 84112. Offers biotechnology (PSM); computational science (PSM); environmental science (PSM); science instrumentation (PSM). *Program availability:* Part-time. *Students:* 12 full-time (5 women), 41 part-time (14 women); includes 2 minority (1 Asian, non-Hispanic/Latino; 1 Two or more races, non-Hispanic/Latino), 3 international. Average age 33. 32 applicants, 50% accepted, 9 enrolled. In 2016, 14 master's awarded. *Degree requirements:* For master's, professional experience project (internship). *Entrance requirements:* For master's, GRE (recommended), minimum undergraduate GPA of 3.0, bachelor's degree from accredited university or college. Additional exam requirements/recommendations for international students: Required—TOEFL (minimum score 550 paper-based; 80 iBT), IELTS (minimum score 6.5). *Application deadline:* For fall admission, 2/1 for domestic and international students. Application fee: $55 ($65 for international students). Electronic applications accepted. *Expenses:* Contact institution. *Financial support:* Fellowships, research assistantships, teaching assistantships, and unspecified assistantships available. *Unit head:* Ray Hoobler, Program Director, 801-585-5630, E-mail: ray.hoobler@utah.edu. *Application contact:* Jay Derek Payne, Project Coordinator, 801-585-3650, E-mail: derek.payne@gradschool.utah.edu.
Website: http://pmst.utah.edu/

University of Washington, Graduate School, School of Medicine, Graduate Programs in Medicine, Department of Genome Sciences, Seattle, WA 98195. Offers PhD. *Degree requirements:* For doctorate, thesis/dissertation, general exam. *Entrance requirements:* For doctorate, GRE General Test, minimum GPA of 3.0. Additional exam requirements/recommendations for international students: Required—TOEFL. Electronic applications accepted. *Faculty research:* Model organism genetics, human and medical genetics, genomics and proteomics, computational biology.

University of West Florida, College of Science and Engineering, School of Allied Health and Life Sciences, Department of Biology, Pensacola, FL 32514-5750. Offers biological chemistry (MS); biology (MS); biology education (MST); biotechnology (MS); coastal zone studies (MS); environmental biology (MS). *Degree requirements:* For master's, thesis. *Entrance requirements:* For master's, GRE (minimum score: verbal 450, quantitative 550), official transcripts; BS in biology or related field; letter of interest; relevant past experience; three letters of recommendation from individuals who can evaluate applicant's academic ability. Additional exam requirements/recommendations for international students: Required—TOEFL (minimum score 550 paper-based). *Application deadline:* For fall admission, 6/1 for domestic and international students; for spring admission, 10/1 for domestic and international students. Applications are processed on a rolling basis. Application fee: $30. *Expenses:* Tuition, state resident: full-time $5316.12. Tuition, nonresident: full-time $11,308. *Required fees:* $583.92. Tuition and fees vary according to course load and program. *Financial support:* Fellowships with partial tuition reimbursements, research assistantships with partial tuition reimbursements, teaching assistantships with partial tuition reimbursements, and unspecified assistantships available. Financial award application deadline: 4/15; financial award applicants required to submit FAFSA. *Unit head:* Dr. Philip Darby, Graduate Coordinator; Associate Chair, 850-474-2647, E-mail: pdarby@uwf.edu. *Application contact:* Terry McCray, Assistant Director of Graduate Admissions, 850-473-7718, Fax: 850-473-7714, E-mail: gradadmissions@uwf.edu.

University of Wyoming, Graduate Program in Molecular and Cellular Life Sciences, Laramie, WY 82071. Offers PhD. *Degree requirements:* For doctorate, thesis/dissertation, four eight-week laboratory rotations, comprehensive basic practical exam, two-part qualifying exam, seminars, symposium.

Virginia Polytechnic Institute and State University, Graduate School, College of Science, Blacksburg, VA 24061. Offers biological sciences (MS, PhD); biomedical technology development and management (MS); chemistry (MS, PhD); data analysis and applied statistics (MA); economics (MA, PhD); geosciences (MS, PhD); mathematics (MS, PhD); physics (MS, PhD); psychology (MS, PhD); statistics (MS, PhD). *Faculty:* 299 full-time (92 women), 1 part-time/adjunct (0 women). *Students:* 567 full-time (222 women), 47 part-time (19 women); includes 66 minority (14 Black or African American, non-Hispanic/Latino; 12 Asian, non-Hispanic/Latino; 29 Hispanic/Latino; 11 Two or more races, non-Hispanic/Latino), 247 international. Average age 27. 956 applicants, 17% accepted, 118 enrolled. In 2016, 75 master's, 71 doctorates awarded. *Degree requirements:* For master's, comprehensive exam (for some programs), thesis (for some programs); for doctorate, comprehensive exam (for some programs), thesis/dissertation (for some programs). *Entrance requirements:* For master's and doctorate, GRE/GMAT. Additional exam requirements/recommendations for international students: Required—TOEFL (minimum score 80 iBT). *Application deadline:* For fall admission, 8/1 for domestic students, 4/1 for international students; for spring admission, 1/1 for domestic students, 9/1 for international students. Applications are processed on a rolling basis. Application fee: $75. Electronic applications accepted. *Expenses:* Tuition, state resident: full-time $12,467; part-time $692.50 per credit hour. Tuition, nonresident: full-time $25,095; part-time $1394.25 per credit hour. *Required fees:* $2669; $491.50 per semester. Tuition and fees vary according to course load, campus/location and program. *Financial support:* In 2016–17, 156 research assistantships with full tuition reimbursements (averaging $21,863 per year), 379 teaching assistantships with full tuition reimbursements (averaging $18,980 per year) were awarded. Financial award application deadline: 3/1; financial award applicants required to submit FAFSA. *Total annual research expenditures:* $22.3 million. *Unit head:* Dr. Sally C. Morton, Dean, 540-231-5422, Fax: 540-231-3380, E-mail: scmorton@vt.edu. *Application contact:* Teresa Price, Executive Assistant to the Dean and Grants Specialist, 540-231-6394, Fax: 540-231-3380, E-mail: tfprice@vt.edu.
Website: http://www.science.vt.edu/

Wayne State University, College of Liberal Arts and Sciences, Department of Biological Sciences, Detroit, MI 48202. Offers biological sciences (MA, MS); cell development and neurobiology (PhD); evolution and organismal biology (PhD); molecular biology and biotechnology (PhD); molecular biotechnology (MS). PhD and MS programs admit for fall only. *Faculty:* 27. *Students:* 55 full-time (28 women), 9 part-time (5 women); includes 5 minority (3 Black or African American, non-Hispanic/Latino; 1 Asian, non-Hispanic/Latino; 1 Two or more races, non-Hispanic/Latino), 30 international. Average age 29. 213 applicants, 14% accepted, 18 enrolled. In 2016, 7 master's, 3 doctorates awarded. *Degree requirements:* For master's, thesis (for some programs); for doctorate, thesis/dissertation. *Entrance requirements:* For master's, GRE (for MS applicants), minimum GPA of 3.0; adequate preparation in biological sciences and supporting courses in chemistry, physics and mathematics; curriculum vitae; personal statement; three letters of recommendation (two for MA); for doctorate, GRE, curriculum vitae, statement of goals and career objectives, three letters of reference, bachelor's or master's degree in biological or other science. Additional exam requirements/recommendations for international students: Required—TOEFL (minimum score 550 paper-based; 79 iBT), TWE (minimum score 5.5), Michigan English Language Assessment Battery (minimum score 85); Recommended—IELTS (minimum score 6.5). Application fee: $50. Electronic applications accepted. *Expenses:* $16,503 per year resident tuition and fees, $33,697 per year non-resident tuition and fees. *Financial support:* In 2016–17, 51 students received support, including 1 fellowship with tuition reimbursement available (averaging $19,944 per year), 6 research assistantships with tuition reimbursements available (averaging $19,816 per year), 44 teaching assistantships with tuition reimbursements available (averaging $19,743 per year); scholarships/grants and unspecified assistantships also available. Financial award applicants required to submit FAFSA. *Faculty research:* Transcription and chromatin remodeling, genomic and developmental evolution, community and landscape ecology and environmental degradation, microbiology and virology, cell and neurobiology. *Unit head:* Dr. David Njus, Professor and Chair, 313-577-3105, E-mail: dnjus@wayne.edu. *Application contact:* Rose Mary Priest, Graduate Secretary, 313-577-6818, E-mail: rpriest@wayne.edu.
Website: http://clas.wayne.edu/Biology/

West Virginia State University, Biotechnology Graduate Program, Institute, WV 25112-1000. Offers MA, MS. *Degree requirements:* For master's, comprehensive exam.

Entrance requirements: For master's, GRE (Verbal 140, Quantitative 150), International Students: Affidavit of Support, Proof of Immunization, TOEFL (80), evaluation of academic transcripts. Additional exam requirements/recommendations for international students: Required—TOEFL. Electronic applications accepted. *Faculty research:* Plant physiology, microbiology, molecular biology, social insect biology, insect population biology, ecology, fish biology, aquaculture, nutrigenomics, nutritional immunology, tumor biology, gene therapy, muscle physiology, environmental microbiology, microbial genomics, biofilms, anaeromic digestion, plant genomics, parasitic platyhelminths, environmental parasitology, horticulture, plant breeding and genetics, plant reproductive barriers, sustainable agriculture, DNA-assisted plant breeding.

William Paterson University of New Jersey, College of Science and Health, Wayne, NJ 07470-8420. Offers biology (MS); biotechnology (MS); communication disorders (MS); exercise and sport studies (MS); nursing (MSN); nursing practice (DNP). *Program availability:* Part-time, evening/weekend. *Faculty:* 30 full-time (19 women), 26 part-time/adjunct (24 women). *Students:* 63 full-time (53 women), 199 part-time (171 women); includes 110 minority (14 Black or African American, non-Hispanic/Latino; 45 Asian, non-Hispanic/Latino; 44 Hispanic/Latino; 7 Two or more races, non-Hispanic/Latino), 2 international. Average age 33. 118 applicants, 98% accepted, 83 enrolled. In 2016, 51 master's, 2 doctorates awarded. *Degree requirements:* For master's, comprehensive exam (for some programs), thesis (for some programs), non-thesis internship/practicum (for some programs). *Entrance requirements:* For master's, GRE/MAT, minimum GPA of 3.0; 2-3 letters of recommendation; personal statement; work experience (for some programs); for doctorate, GRE/MAT, minimum GPA of 3.3; work experience; 3 letters of recommendation; interview; master's degree in nursing. Additional exam requirements/recommendations for international students: Required—TOEFL (minimum score 550 paper-based; 79 iBT), IELTS (minimum score 6). *Application deadline:* For fall admission, 8/1 for domestic students, 4/1 for international students; for spring admission, 12/1 for domestic students, 11/1 for international students; for summer admission, 5/1 for domestic students, 2/1 for international students. Applications are processed on a rolling basis. Application fee: $50. Electronic applications accepted. *Expenses:* Tuition, state resident: full-time $12,480; part-time $611 per credit. Tuition, nonresident: full-time $20,263; part-time $992 per credit. *Required fees:* $1573; $77 per credit. Tuition and fees vary according to course load, degree level and program. *Financial support:* Career-related internships or fieldwork, Federal Work-Study, scholarships/grants, and unspecified assistantships available. Support available to part-time students. Financial award applicants required to submit FAFSA. *Faculty research:* Alcohol prevention in Passaic county, plant genome and gene expression, human and animal genomes, predicting molecular motion in certain situations, traumatic brain injury. *Total annual research expenditures:* $177,820. *Unit head:* Dr. Kenneth Wolf, Dean, 973-720-2194, Fax: 973-720-3414, E-mail: wolfk@wpunj.edu. *Application contact:* Christina Aiello, Assistant Director, Graduate Admissions, 973-720-2506, Fax: 973-720-2035, E-mail: aielloc@wpunj.edu. Website: http://www.wpunj.edu/cosh

Worcester Polytechnic Institute, Graduate Studies and Research, Department of Biology and Biotechnology, Worcester, MA 01609-2280. Offers biology and biotechnology (MS); biotechnology (PhD). *Faculty:* 12 full-time (7 women). *Students:* 18 full-time (8 women), 5 international. 71 applicants, 15% accepted, 4 enrolled. In 2016, 3 master's, 4 doctorates awarded. Terminal master's awarded for partial completion of doctoral program. *Degree requirements:* For master's, thesis; for doctorate, comprehensive exam, thesis/dissertation, qualifying exam. *Entrance requirements:* For master's and doctorate, GRE General Test, 3 letters of recommendation, statement of purpose. Additional exam requirements/recommendations for international students: Required—TOEFL (minimum score 563 paper-based; 84 iBT), IELTS (minimum score 7). *Application deadline:* For fall admission, 1/1 priority date for domestic and international students. Application fee: $70. Electronic applications accepted. *Financial support:* Research assistantships, teaching assistantships, career-related internships or fieldwork, institutionally sponsored loans, scholarships/grants, and unspecified assistantships available. Financial award application deadline: 1/1; financial award applicants required to submit FAFSA. *Unit head:* Dr. Joseph Duffy, Head, 508-831-4111, Fax: 508-831-5936, E-mail: jduffy@wpi.edu. *Application contact:* Dr. Reeta Rao, Graduate Coordinator, 508-831-5538, Fax: 508-831-5936, E-mail: rpr@wpi.edu. Website: http://www.wpi.edu/Academics/Depts/BBT/

Worcester State University, Graduate Studies, Program in Biotechnology, Worcester, MA 01602-2597. Offers MS. *Program availability:* Part-time, evening/weekend. *Faculty:* 7 full-time (3 women), 1 part-time/adjunct (0 women). *Students:* 5 full-time (3 women), 18 part-time (11 women); includes 4 minority (1 Black or African American, non-Hispanic/Latino; 1 American Indian or Alaska Native, non-Hispanic/Latino; 2 Asian, non-Hispanic/Latino), 2 international. Average age 30. 34 applicants, 59% accepted, 7 enrolled. In 2016, 9 master's awarded. *Degree requirements:* For master's, comprehensive exam, thesis. *Entrance requirements:* For master's, GRE General Test or MAT, baccalaureate degree in biology, biotechnology, chemistry or similar major; minimum GPA of 2.75 in all undergraduate work, 3.0 in all course work within major at the junior and senior level. Additional exam requirements/recommendations for international students: Required—TOEFL (minimum score 550 paper-based; 79 iBT). *Application deadline:* For fall admission, 6/15 for domestic and international students; for spring admission, 11/1 for domestic and international students; for summer admission, 4/1 for domestic and international students. Applications are processed on a rolling basis. Application fee: $50. Electronic applications accepted. *Expenses:* Tuition, state resident: part-time $150 per credit. Tuition, nonresident: part-time $150 per credit. *Financial support:* Career-related internships or fieldwork, scholarships/grants, and unspecified assistantships available. Financial award application deadline: 3/1; financial award applicants required to submit FAFSA. *Unit head:* Dr. Ellen Fynan, Program Coordinator, 508-929-8596, Fax: 508-929-8171, E-mail: efynan@worcester.edu. *Application contact:* Sara Grady, Associate Dean, Graduate and Professional Development, 508-929-8787, Fax: 508-929-8100, E-mail: sara.grady@worcester.edu.

Nanotechnology

The American University in Cairo, School of Sciences and Engineering, Cairo, Egypt. Offers biotechnology (MS); chemistry (MS); computer science (MS); computing (M Comp); construction engineering (M Eng, MS); electronics and communications engineering (M Eng); environmental engineering (MS); environmental system design (M Eng); mechanical engineering (M Eng, MS); nanotechnology (MS); physics (MS); robotics, control and smart systems (MS); sciences and engineering (PhD); sustainable development (MS, Graduate Diploma). *Program availability:* Part-time, evening/weekend. *Faculty:* 43 full-time (4 women), 12 part-time/adjunct (1 woman). *Students:* 50 full-time (21 women), 262 part-time (128 women), 13 international. Average age 28. 193 applicants, 46% accepted, 55 enrolled. In 2016, 71 master's, 5 doctorates awarded. *Degree requirements:* For master's, comprehensive exam (for some programs), thesis (for some programs); for doctorate, comprehensive exam (for some programs), thesis/dissertation. *Entrance requirements:* Additional exam requirements/recommendations for international students: Required—TOEFL (minimum score 450 paper-based; 45 iBT), IELTS (minimum score 5). *Application deadline:* For fall admission, 2/1 priority date for domestic and international students; for spring admission, 10/15 priority date for domestic and international students. Applications are processed on a rolling basis. Application fee: $80. Electronic applications accepted. *Expenses:* Contact institution. *Financial support:* Fellowships with partial tuition reimbursements, scholarships/grants, and unspecified assistantships available. Financial award application deadline: 3/10. *Faculty research:* Construction, mechanical and electronics engineering, physics, computer science, biotechnology and nanotechnology. *Unit head:* Dr. Hassan El Fawal, Dean, 20-2-2615-2926, E-mail: hassan.elfawal@aucegypt.edu. *Application contact:* Maha Hegazi, Director for Graduate Admissions, 20-2-2615-1462, E-mail: mahahegazi@aucegypt.edu. Website: http://www.aucegypt.edu/sse/Pages/default.aspx

Arizona State University at the Tempe campus, College of Liberal Arts and Sciences, Department of Chemistry and Biochemistry, Tempe, AZ 85287-1604. Offers biochemistry (MS, PhD); chemistry (MS, PhD); nanoscience (PSM). Terminal master's awarded for partial completion of doctoral program. *Degree requirements:* For master's, thesis, interactive Program of Study (iPOS) submitted before completing 50 percent of required credit hours; for doctorate, comprehensive exam, thesis/dissertation, interactive Program of Study (iPOS) submitted before completing 50 percent of required credit hours. *Entrance requirements:* For master's and doctorate, GRE, minimum GPA of 3.0 or equivalent in last 2 years of work leading to bachelor's degree. Additional exam requirements/recommendations for international students: Required—TOEFL, IELTS, or PTE. Electronic applications accepted.

Arizona State University at the Tempe campus, College of Liberal Arts and Sciences, Department of Physics, Tempe, AZ 85287-1504. Offers nanoscience (PSM); physics (MNS, PhD). *Program availability:* Part-time. Terminal master's awarded for partial completion of doctoral program. *Degree requirements:* For master's, comprehensive exam, thesis or alternative, interactive Program of Study (iPOS) submitted before completing 50 percent of required credit hours; for doctorate, comprehensive exam, thesis/dissertation, interactive Program of Study (iPOS) submitted before completing 50 percent of required credit hours. *Entrance requirements:* For master's and doctorate, GRE, minimum GPA of 3.0 or equivalent in last 2 years of work leading to bachelor's degree. Additional exam requirements/recommendations for international students: Required—TOEFL, IELTS, or PTE. Electronic applications accepted. *Expenses:* Contact institution.

Carnegie Mellon University, Mellon College of Science, Department of Chemistry, Pittsburgh, PA 15213-3891. Offers atmospheric chemistry (PhD); bioinorganic chemistry (PhD); bioorganic chemistry and chemical biology (PhD); biophysical chemistry (PhD); catalysis (PhD); green and environmental chemistry (PhD); materials and nanoscience (PhD); renewable energy (PhD); sensors, probes, and imaging (PhD); spectroscopy and

single molecule analysis (PhD); theoretical and computational chemistry (PhD). *Program availability:* Part-time. Terminal master's awarded for partial completion of doctoral program. *Degree requirements:* For doctorate, thesis/dissertation, departmental qualifying and oral exams, teaching experience. *Entrance requirements:* For doctorate, GRE General Test, GRE Subject Test. Additional exam requirements/recommendations for international students: Required—TOEFL. Electronic applications accepted. *Faculty research:* Physical and theoretical chemistry, chemical synthesis, biophysical/bioinorganic chemistry.

The College of William and Mary, Faculty of Arts and Sciences, Department of Applied Science, Williamsburg, VA 23185. Offers accelerator science (PhD); applied mathematics (PhD); applied mechanics (PhD); applied robotics (PhD); applied science (MS); atmospheric and environmental science (PhD); computational neuroscience (PhD); interface, thin film and surface science (PhD); lasers and optics (PhD); magnetic resonance (PhD); materials science and engineering (PhD); mathematical and computational biology (PhD); medical imaging (PhD); nanotechnology (PhD); neuroscience (PhD); non-destructive evaluation (PhD); polymer chemistry (PhD); remote sensing (PhD). *Program availability:* Part-time. *Faculty:* 8 full-time (2 women), 2 part-time/adjunct (0 women). *Students:* 30 full-time (11 women), 4 part-time (0 women); includes 16 minority (2 Black or African American, non-Hispanic/Latino; 12 Asian, non-Hispanic/Latino; 2 Hispanic/Latino), 12 international. Average age 28. 37 applicants, 27% accepted, 7 enrolled. In 2016, 6 doctorates awarded. Terminal master's awarded for partial completion of doctoral program. *Degree requirements:* For master's, comprehensive exam, thesis; for doctorate, comprehensive exam, thesis/dissertation, 4 core courses. *Entrance requirements:* For master's and doctorate, GRE General Test, GRE Subject Test. Additional exam requirements/recommendations for international students: Required—TOEFL, IELTS. *Application deadline:* For fall admission, 2/3 priority date for domestic students, 2/3 for international students; for spring admission, 10/15 priority date for domestic students, 10/14 for international students. Applications are processed on a rolling basis. Application fee: $45. Electronic applications accepted. *Expenses:* Contact institution. *Financial support:* In 2016–17, 7 students received support, including 27 research assistantships (averaging $25,000 per year), 1 teaching assistantship (averaging $9,500 per year); fellowships, scholarships/grants, health care benefits, tuition waivers (full), and unspecified assistantships also available. Financial award application deadline: 4/15; financial award applicants required to submit FAFSA. *Faculty research:* Computational biology, non-destructive evaluation, neurophysiology, laser spectroscopy, nanotechnology. *Total annual research expenditures:* $536,220. *Unit head:* Dr. Christopher Del Negro, Chair, 757-221-7808, Fax: 757-221-2050, E-mail: cadeln@wm.edu. *Application contact:* Lianne Rios Ashburne, Graduate Program Coordinator, 757-221-2563, Fax: 757-221-2050, E-mail: lrashburne@wm.edu. Website: http://www.wm.edu/as/appliedscience

Cornell University, Graduate School, Graduate Fields of Agriculture and Life Sciences and Graduate Fields of Engineering, Field of Biological and Environmental Engineering, Ithaca, NY 14853. Offers bioenergy and integrated energy systems (M Eng, MPS, MS, PhD); biological engineering (M Eng, MPS, MS, PhD); bioprocess engineering (M Eng, MPS, MS, PhD); ecohydrology (M Eng, MPS, MS, PhD); environmental engineering (M Eng, MPS, MS, PhD); environmental management (MPS); food engineering (M Eng, MPS, MS, PhD); industrial biotechnology (M Eng, MPS, MS, PhD); nanobiotechnology (M Eng, MPS, MS, PhD); sustainable systems (M Eng, MPS, MS, PhD); synthetic biology (MS); syntheticbiology (M Eng, MPS, PhD). Terminal master's awarded for partial completion of doctoral program. *Degree requirements:* For master's, thesis (MS); for doctorate, comprehensive exam, thesis/dissertation. *Entrance requirements:* For master's, letters of recommendation (3 for MS, 2 for M Eng and MPS); for doctorate, GRE General Test, 3 letters of recommendation. Additional exam requirements/recommendations for international students: Required—TOEFL (minimum score 550 paper-based; 77 iBT). Electronic applications accepted. *Faculty research:* Biological and food engineering, environmental, soil and water engineering, international agricultural engineering, structures and controlled environments, machine systems and energy.

Indiana University of Pennsylvania, School of Graduate Studies and Research, College of Natural Sciences and Mathematics, Department of Physics, Program in Nanoscience/Industrial Materials, Indiana, PA 15705. Offers PSM. *Program availability:* Part-time. *Faculty:* 4 full-time (0 women). *Students:* 2 full-time (1 woman), 2 part-time (0 women); includes 1 minority (Black or African American, non-Hispanic/Latino), 2 international. Average age 31. 12 applicants, 75% accepted, 2 enrolled. In 2016, 1 master's awarded. *Degree requirements:* For master's, comprehensive exam (for some programs), thesis (for some programs). *Entrance requirements:* Additional exam requirements/recommendations for international students: Required—TOEFL (minimum score 540 paper-based). *Application deadline:* Applications are processed on a rolling basis. Application fee: $50. Electronic applications accepted. *Expenses:* Tuition, state resident: full-time $8694; part-time $483 per credit. Tuition, nonresident: full-time $13,050; part-time $725 per credit. *Required fees:* $157 per credit. $50 per term. Tuition and fees vary according to course load and program. *Financial support:* Fellowships with full tuition reimbursements, research assistantships with tuition reimbursements, career-related internships or fieldwork, Federal Work-Study, and scholarships/grants available. Support available to part-time students. Financial award application deadline: 4/15; financial award applicants required to submit FAFSA. *Unit head:* Dr. John Bradshaw, Graduate Coordinator, 724-357-7731, E-mail: bradshaw@iup.edu.

Johns Hopkins University, Engineering Program for Professionals, Part-time Program in Materials Science and Engineering, Baltimore, MD 21218. Offers nanotechnology (M Mat SE). *Program availability:* Part-time, evening/weekend. *Faculty:* 2 part-time/adjunct (1 woman). *Students:* 3 full-time (2 women), 16 part-time (3 women); includes 4 minority (2 Black or African American, non-Hispanic/Latino; 1 Asian, non-Hispanic/Latino; 1 Hispanic/Latino). Average age 28. 6 applicants, 83% accepted, 5 enrolled. In 2016, 5 master's awarded. *Entrance requirements:* Additional exam requirements/recommendations for international students: Required—TOEFL (minimum score 600 paper-based; 100 iBT). *Application deadline:* Applications are processed on a rolling basis. Application fee: $0. Electronic applications accepted. *Unit head:* Dr. James Spicer, Program Chair, 410-516-8524, E-mail: spicer@jhu.edu. *Application contact:* Doug Schiller, Admissions Director, 410-516-2300, Fax: 410-579-8049, E-mail: schiller@jhu.edu.
Website: http://www.ep.jhu.edu

Johns Hopkins University, G. W. C. Whiting School of Engineering, Master of Science in Engineering Management Program, Baltimore, MD 21218. Offers biomaterials (MSEM); civil engineering (MSEM); communications science (MSEM); computer science (MSEM); environmental systems analysis, economics and public policy (MSEM); fluid mechanics (MSEM); materials science and engineering (MSEM); mechanical engineering (MSEM); mechanics and materials (MSEM); nanobiotechnology (MSEM); nanomaterials and nanotechnology (MSEM); operations research (MSEM); probability and statistics (MSEM); smart product and device design (MSEM). *Faculty:* 7 full-time (4 women), 1 part-time/adjunct (0 women). *Students:* 35 full-time (14 women), 8 part-time (3 women); includes 7 minority (4 Asian, non-Hispanic/Latino; 3 Hispanic/Latino), 26 international. Average age 24. 228 applicants, 28% accepted, 25 enrolled. In 2016, 18 master's awarded. *Entrance requirements:* For master's, GRE, 3 letters of recommendation, statement of purpose, transcripts. Additional exam requirements/recommendations for international students: Required—TOEFL (minimum score 600 paper-based, 100 iBT) or IELTS (7). *Application deadline:* For fall admission, 2/1 for domestic and international students. Application fee: $75. Electronic applications accepted. *Financial support:* Fellowships and health care benefits available. *Unit head:* Dr. Pamela Sheff, Director, 410-516-7056, Fax: 410-516-4880, E-mail: pamsheff@gmail.com. *Application contact:* Richard Helman, Director of Graduate Admissions, 410-516-8174, Fax: 410-516-0780, E-mail: graduateadmissions@jhu.edu.
Website: http://engineering.jhu.edu/msem/

Louisiana Tech University, Graduate School, College of Engineering and Science, Department of Chemistry, Ruston, LA 71272. Offers molecular sciences and nanotechnology (MS, PhD). *Program availability:* Part-time. *Degree requirements:* For master's, thesis. *Entrance requirements:* For master's, GRE General Test, minimum GPA of 3.0 in last 60 hours. Additional exam requirements/recommendations for international students: Required—TOEFL. *Application deadline:* For fall admission, 8/1 for domestic students; for spring admission, 2/1 for domestic students. Applications are processed on a rolling basis. Application fee: $20 ($30 for international students). *Financial support:* Teaching assistantships and Federal Work-Study available. Financial award application deadline: 4/1. *Faculty research:* Vibrational spectroscopy, quantum studies of chemical reactions, enzyme kinetics, synthesis of transition metal compounds, nuclear magnetic resonance (NMR) spectrometry. *Unit head:* Dr. Lee Sawyer, Academic Director, 318-257-4053, Fax: 318-257-3823. *Application contact:* Marilyn J. Robinson, Assistant to the Dean, 318-257-2924, Fax: 318-257-4487.
Website: http://coes.latech.edu/chemistry/

Michigan Technological University, Graduate School, Interdisciplinary Programs, Houghton, MI 49931. Offers atmospheric sciences (PhD); biochemistry and molecular biology (PhD); computational science and engineering (PhD); data science (MS, Graduate Certificate); engineering (M Eng); environmental engineering (PhD); international profile (Graduate Certificate); nanotechnology (Graduate Certificate); sustainability (Graduate Certificate); sustainable water resources systems (Graduate Certificate). *Program availability:* Part-time. *Faculty:* 122 full-time (26 women), 13 part-time/adjunct. *Students:* 58 full-time (18 women), 17 part-time (5 women); includes 1 minority (Black or African American, non-Hispanic/Latino), 56 international. Average age 28. 395 applicants, 20% accepted, 22 enrolled. In 2016, 3 master's, 7 doctorates, 8 other advanced degrees awarded. Terminal master's awarded for partial completion of doctoral program. *Degree requirements:* For master's, comprehensive exam (for some programs), thesis (for some programs); for doctorate, comprehensive exam, thesis/dissertation. *Entrance requirements:* For master's, doctorate, and Graduate Certificate, GRE, statement of purpose, personal statement, official transcripts, 2-3 letters of recommendation. Additional exam requirements/recommendations for international students: Required—TOEFL or IELTS. *Application deadline:* Applications are processed on a rolling basis. Electronic applications accepted. *Expenses:* Tuition, state resident: full-time $16,290; part-time $905 per credit. Tuition, nonresident: full-time $16,290; part-time $905 per credit. *Required fees:* $248; $124 per term. Tuition and fees vary according to course load and program. *Financial support:* In 2016–17, 54 students received support, including 7 fellowships with tuition reimbursements available (averaging $15,242 per year), 19 research assistantships with tuition reimbursements available (averaging $15,242 per year), 5 teaching assistantships with tuition reimbursements available (averaging $15,242 per year); career-related internships or fieldwork, Federal Work-Study, scholarships/grants, health care benefits, unspecified assistantships, and cooperative program also available. Financial award applicants required to submit FAFSA. *Faculty research:* Big data, atmospheric sciences, bioinformatics and systems biology, molecular dynamics, environmental studies. *Unit head:* Dr. Pushpalathata Murthy, Dean of the Graduate School/Associate Provost for Graduate Education, 906-487-3007, Fax: 906-487-2284, E-mail: ppmurthy@mtu.edu. *Application contact:* Carol T. Wingerson, Administrative Aide, 906-487-2328, Fax: 906-487-2284, E-mail: gradadms@mtu.edu.

North Dakota State University, College of Graduate and Interdisciplinary Studies, College of Engineering, Doctoral Program in Engineering, Fargo, ND 58102. Offers environmental and conservation science (PhD); materials and nanotechnology (PhD); natural resource management (PhD); science, technology, engineering, mathematics education (STEM) (PhD); transportation and logistics (PhD). *Degree requirements:* For doctorate, comprehensive exam, thesis/dissertation. *Entrance requirements:* For doctorate, bachelor's degree in engineering, minimum GPA of 3.0. Additional exam requirements/recommendations for international students: Required—TOEFL. Electronic applications accepted. *Expenses:* Contact institution.

North Dakota State University, College of Graduate and Interdisciplinary Studies, Interdisciplinary Program in Materials and Nanotechnology, Fargo, ND 58102. Offers MS, PhD. *Entrance requirements:* For doctorate, GRE General Test. Additional exam requirements/recommendations for international students: Required—TOEFL (minimum score 525 paper-based; 71 iBT).

South Dakota School of Mines and Technology, Graduate Division, Program in Nanoscience and Nanoengineering, Rapid City, SD 57701-3995. Offers PhD. *Program availability:* Part-time. *Degree requirements:* For doctorate, thesis/dissertation. *Entrance requirements:* Additional exam requirements/recommendations for international students: Required—TOEFL (minimum score 520 paper-based; 68 iBT). Electronic applications accepted.

State University of New York Polytechnic Institute, Colleges of Nanoscale Science and Engineering, Albany, NY 12203. Offers nanoscale engineering (MS, PhD); nanoscale science (MS, PhD); MD/PhD. *Entrance requirements:* Additional exam requirements/recommendations for international students: Required—TOEFL (minimum score 550 paper-based). *Faculty research:* Thin film material structures, optoelectronic materials, design and fabrication of nano-mechanical systems, materials characterization.

Stevens Institute of Technology, Graduate School, Charles V. Schaefer Jr. School of Engineering and Science, Interdisciplinary Program in Nanotechnology, Hoboken, NJ 07030. Offers PhD. *Expenses: Tuition:* Full-time $33,328; part-time $1501 per credit. *Required fees:* $1186; $566 per credit. $283 per semester. *Unit head:* Dr. Keith G. Sheppard, Interim Dean, 201-216-5263. *Application contact:* Graduate Admissions, 888-783-8367, Fax: 888-555-1306, E-mail: graduate@stevens.edu.

University of Alberta, Faculty of Graduate Studies and Research, Department of Electrical and Computer Engineering, Edmonton, AB T6G 2E1, Canada. Offers communications (M Eng, M Sc, PhD); computer engineering (M Eng, M Sc, PhD); electromagnetics (M Eng, M Sc, PhD); nanotechnology and microdevices (M Eng, M Sc, PhD); power/power electronics (M Eng, M Sc, PhD); systems (M Eng, M Sc, PhD). Terminal master's awarded for partial completion of doctoral program. *Degree requirements:* For master's, thesis; for doctorate, thesis/dissertation. *Entrance requirements:* Additional exam requirements/recommendations for international students: Required—TOEFL. Electronic applications accepted. *Faculty research:* Controls, communications, microelectronics, electromagnetics.

University of California, Riverside, Graduate Division, Materials Science and Engineering Program, Riverside, CA 92521. Offers MS. *Entrance requirements:* For master's, GRE. Additional exam requirements/recommendations for international students: Required—TOEFL (minimum score 550 paper-based; 80 iBT). Electronic applications accepted. *Expenses:* Tuition, state resident: full-time $16,666. Tuition, nonresident: full-time $31,768. *Required fees:* $11,055.54 per quarter. $3685.18 per quarter. Tuition and fees vary according to campus/location and program.

University of California, San Diego, Graduate Division, Department of Electrical and Computer Engineering, La Jolla, CA 92093. Offers applied ocean science (MS, PhD); applied physics (MS, PhD); communication theory and systems (MS, PhD); computer engineering (MS, PhD); electronic circuits and systems (MS, PhD); intelligent systems, robotics and control (MS, PhD); medical devices and systems (MS, PhD); nanoscale devices and systems (MS, PhD); photonics (MS, PhD); signal and image processing (MS, PhD). *Students:* 612 full-time (119 women), 39 part-time (8 women). 2,885 applicants, 25% accepted, 269 enrolled. In 2016, 147 master's, 43 doctorates awarded. Terminal master's awarded for partial completion of doctoral program. *Degree requirements:* For master's, comprehensive exam (for some programs), thesis (for some programs); for doctorate, comprehensive exam, thesis/dissertation. *Entrance requirements:* For master's and doctorate, GRE General Test, minimum GPA of 3.0, resume or curriculum vitae (recommended). Additional exam requirements/recommendations for international students: Required—TOEFL (minimum score 550 paper-based; 80 iBT), IELTS (minimum score 7), PTE (minimum score 65). *Application deadline:* For fall admission, 12/13 for domestic students. Application fee: $105 ($125 for international students). Electronic applications accepted. *Expenses:* Tuition, state resident: full-time $11,220. Tuition, nonresident: full-time $26,322. *Required fees:* $1864. *Financial support:* Fellowships, research assistantships, teaching assistantships, scholarships/grants, traineeships, and unspecified assistantships available. Financial award applicants required to submit FAFSA. *Faculty research:* Applied ocean science; applied physics; communication theory and systems; computer engineering; electronic circuits and systems; intelligent systems, robotics and control; medical devices and systems; nanoscale devices and systems; photonics; signal and image processing. *Unit head:* Truong Nguyen, Chair, 858-822-5554, E-mail: nguyent@ece.ucsd.edu. *Application contact:* Melanie Lynn, Graduate Admissions Coordinator, 858-822-3213, E-mail: ecegradapps@ece.ucsd.edu.
Website: http://ece.ucsd.edu/

University of California, San Diego, Graduate Division, Department of Nanoengineering, La Jolla, CA 92093. Offers MS, PhD. *Students:* 103 full-time (33 women), 5 part-time (2 women). 224 applicants, 33% accepted, 34 enrolled. In 2016, 34 master's, 5 doctorates awarded. *Degree requirements:* For master's, comprehensive exam (for some programs), thesis (for some programs); for doctorate, comprehensive exam, thesis/dissertation, 1-quarter teaching assistantship. *Entrance requirements:* For master's and doctorate, GRE General Test, 3 letters of recommendation, statement of purpose, resume. Additional exam requirements/recommendations for international students: Required—TOEFL (minimum score 550 paper-based; 80 iBT), IELTS (minimum score 7). *Application deadline:* For fall admission, 12/19 for domestic students. Application fee: $105 ($125 for international students). Electronic applications accepted. *Expenses:* Tuition, state resident: full-time $11,220. Tuition, nonresident: full-time $26,322. *Required fees:* $1864. *Financial support:* Fellowships, research assistantships, teaching assistantships, and scholarships/grants available. Financial award applicants required to submit FAFSA. *Faculty research:* Biomedical nanotechnology, molecular and nanomaterials, nanotechnologies for energy and the environment. *Unit head:* Joseph Wang, Chair, 858-822-7640, E-mail: josephwang@ucsd.edu. *Application contact:* Dana Jimenez, Graduate Coordinator, 858-822-7981, E-mail: dljimenez@ucsd.edu. Website: http://nanoengineering.ucsd.edu

University of Central Florida, College of Graduate Studies, Program in Nanotechnology, Orlando, FL 32816. Offers MS, PSM. *Students:* 16 full-time (3 women),

13 part-time (5 women); includes 16 minority (7 Black or African American, non-Hispanic/Latino; 5 Asian, non-Hispanic/Latino; 4 Hispanic/Latino), 3 international. Average age 27. 26 applicants, 65% accepted, 15 enrolled. In 2016, 4 master's awarded. *Degree requirements:* For master's, thesis (for MS); internship (for PSM). *Entrance requirements:* Additional exam requirements/recommendations for international students: Required—TOEFL. *Application deadline:* For fall admission, 7/15 for domestic students; for spring admission, 12/1 for domestic students. Application fee: $30. Electronic applications accepted. *Expenses:* Tuition, state resident: part-time $288.16 per credit hour. Tuition, nonresident: part-time $1071.31 per credit hour. *Financial support:* In 2016–17, 6 students received support, including 2 fellowships with partial tuition reimbursements available (averaging $4,500 per year), 5 research assistantships with partial tuition reimbursements available (averaging $7,876 per year), 1 teaching assistantship with partial tuition reimbursement available (averaging $11,574 per year). Financial award application deadline: 3/1; financial award applicants required to submit FAFSA. *Unit head:* Dr. Sudipta Seal, Director, 407-823-5277, E-mail: sudipta.seal@ucf.edu. *Application contact:* Assistant Director, Graduate Admissions, 407-823-2766, Fax: 407-823-6442, E-mail: gradadmissions@ucf.edu.
Website: http://nano.ucf.edu/

University of New Mexico, Graduate Studies, School of Engineering, Program in Nanoscience and Microsystems Engineering, Albuquerque, NM 87131. Offers MS, PhD. *Program availability:* Part-time. *Faculty:* 10 full-time (2 women), 1 (woman) part-time/adjunct. *Students:* 31 full-time (7 women), 20 part-time (7 women); includes 11 minority (3 Black or African American, non-Hispanic/Latino; 1 Asian, non-Hispanic/Latino; 4 Hispanic/Latino; 3 Two or more races, non-Hispanic/Latino), 7 international. Average age 33. 28 applicants, 50% accepted, 11 enrolled. In 2016, 6 master's, 5 doctorates awarded. *Degree requirements:* For master's, comprehensive exam, thesis; for doctorate, comprehensive exam, thesis/dissertation. *Entrance requirements:* For master's and doctorate, GRE. Additional exam requirements/recommendations for international students: Required—TOEFL. *Application deadline:* For fall admission, 7/30 for domestic students, 2/1 for international students; for spring admission, 11/30 for domestic students, 6/1 for international students. Applications are processed on a rolling basis. Application fee: $50. Electronic applications accepted. *Financial support:* Research assistantships with full tuition reimbursements and teaching assistantships with full tuition reimbursements available. *Unit head:* Dr. Abhaya Datye, Professor, 505-277-0477, Fax: 505-277-1024, E-mail: datye@unm.edu. *Application contact:* Heather Elizabeth Armstrong, Program Specialist, 505-277-6824, Fax: 505-277-1024, E-mail: heathera@unm.edu.
Website: http://nsms.unm.edu

University of Pennsylvania, School of Engineering and Applied Science, Program in Nanotechnology, Philadelphia, PA 19104. Offers MSE. *Program availability:* Part-time. *Students:* 18 full-time (6 women), 8 part-time (4 women); includes 3 minority (1 Black or African American, non-Hispanic/Latino; 1 Asian, non-Hispanic/Latino; 1 Hispanic/Latino), 17 international. Average age 25. 26 applicants, 81% accepted, 16 enrolled. In 2016, 8 master's awarded. *Degree requirements:* For master's, comprehensive exam, thesis optional. *Entrance requirements:* For master's, GRE. Additional exam requirements/recommendations for international students: Required—TOEFL (minimum score 100 iBT), IELTS (minimum score 7). *Application deadline:* For fall admission, 3/15 priority date for domestic and international students. Application fee: $80. Electronic applications accepted. *Expenses: Tuition:* Full-time $31,068; part-time $5762 per course. *Required fees:* $3200; $336 per course. Full-time tuition and fees vary according to degree level, program and student level. Part-time tuition and fees vary according to course load, degree level and program. *Faculty research:* Nanofabrication, devices and properties, biotechnology, commercialization, societal impacts of technology. *Application contact:* William Fenton, Assistant Director of Graduate Admissions, 215-898-4542, Fax: 215-573-5577, E-mail: gradstudies@seas.upenn.edu.
Website: http://www.masters.nano.upenn.edu/

University of South Florida, College of Pharmacy, Tampa, FL 33620-9951. Offers pharmaceutical nanotechnology (MS); pharmacy (Pharm D), including pharmacy and health education. *Accreditation:* ACPE. *Faculty:* 41 full-time (28 women), 2 part-time/adjunct (0 women). *Students:* 391 full-time (233 women), 1 (woman) part-time; includes 170 minority (29 Black or African American, non-Hispanic/Latino; 63 Asian, non-Hispanic/Latino; 62 Hispanic/Latino; 4 Native Hawaiian or other Pacific Islander, non-Hispanic/Latino; 12 Two or more races, non-Hispanic/Latino). Average age 26. 679 applicants, 29% accepted, 102 enrolled. In 2016, 53 doctorates awarded. *Degree requirements:* For master's, comprehensive exam, thesis optional. *Entrance requirements:* For master's, GRE, MCAT or DAT, minimum GPA of 3.0, letters of reference, resume; for doctorate, PCAT, minimum GPA of 2.75 overall (preferred); completion of 72 prerequisite credit hours; U.S. citizenship or permanent resident. Additional exam requirements/recommendations for international students: Required—TOEFL (minimum score 550 paper-based; 79 iBT), IELTS (minimum score 6.5). *Application deadline:* For fall admission, 2/15 for domestic and international students; for spring admission, 10/15 for domestic students, 9/15 for international students; for summer admission, 2/15 for domestic and international students. Electronic applications accepted. *Expenses:* Tuition, state resident: full-time $7766; part-time $431.43 per credit hour. Tuition, nonresident: full-time $15,789; part-time $877.17 per credit hour. *Required fees:* $37 per term. *Financial support:* In 2016–17, 131 students received support. *Total annual research expenditures:* $1.1 million. *Unit head:* Dr. Kevin Sneed, Dean, 813-974-5699, E-mail: ksneed@health.usf.edu. *Application contact:* Dr. Amy Schwartz, Associate Dean, 813-974-2251, E-mail: aschwar1@health.usf.edu.

University of Washington, Graduate School, College of Engineering and School of Medicine, Department of Bioengineering, Seattle, WA 98195-5061. Offers applied bioengineering (MAB); bioengineering (MS, PhD); bioengineering and nanotechnology (PhD); pharmaceutical bioengineering (MS). *Faculty:* 41 full-time (15 women), 15 part-time/adjunct (0 women). *Students:* 137 full-time (51 women), 34 part-time (14 women); includes 53 minority (1 Black or African American, non-Hispanic/Latino; 41 Asian, non-Hispanic/Latino; 5 Hispanic/Latino; 1 Native Hawaiian or other Pacific Islander, non-Hispanic/Latino; 5 Two or more races, non-Hispanic/Latino), 50 international. 640 applicants, 24% accepted, 62 enrolled. In 2016, 17 master's, 8 doctorates awarded. *Degree requirements:* For master's, comprehensive exam, thesis; for doctorate, comprehensive exam, thesis/dissertation, qualifying exam, general exam, thesis defense. *Entrance requirements:* For master's and doctorate, GRE General Test, minimum GPA of 3.0, transcripts, statement of purpose, letters of recommendation, resume/curriculum vitae. Additional exam requirements/recommendations for international students: Required—TOEFL (minimum score 500 paper-based; 80 iBT), IELTS (minimum score 6.5). *Application deadline:* For fall admission, 12/15 for domestic and international students. Application fee: $85. Electronic applications accepted. *Expenses:* Contact institution. *Financial support:* In 2016–17, 119 students received support, including 34 fellowships with full tuition reimbursements available (averaging $2,799 per year), 78 research assistantships with full tuition reimbursements available (averaging $2,616 per year), 7 teaching assistantships with full tuition reimbursements available (averaging $2,616 per year); Federal Work-Study, institutionally sponsored loans, traineeships, health care benefits, and tuition waivers (full) also available. Support available to part-time students. Financial award application deadline: 12/1; financial award applicants required to submit FAFSA. *Faculty research:* Imaging and image guided therapy, molecular and cellular engineering, biomaterials and regenerative medicine, technology for expanding access to healthcare, synthetic and quantitative biology. *Total annual research expenditures:* $24.1 million. *Unit head:* Dr. Cecilia Giachelli, Professor/Chair, 206-685-2000, Fax: 206-685-3300, E-mail: ceci@uw.edu. *Application contact:* Peggy Sharp, Graduate Academic Counselor, 206-685-3494, Fax: 206-685-3300, E-mail: peggys55@uw.edu. Website: http://depts.washington.edu/bioe/

University of Washington, Graduate School, College of Engineering, Department of Chemical Engineering, Seattle, WA 98195-1750. Offers chemical engineering (MS, PhD); chemical engineering and advanced data science (PhD); chemical engineering and nanotechnology (PhD). *Faculty:* 19 full-time (3 women). *Students:* 116 full-time (39 women), 3 part-time (0 women); includes 21 minority (11 Asian, non-Hispanic/Latino; 7 Hispanic/Latino; 3 Two or more races, non-Hispanic/Latino), 49 international. 392 applicants, 27% accepted, 39 enrolled. In 2016, 25 master's, 10 doctorates awarded. Terminal master's awarded for partial completion of doctoral program. *Degree requirements:* For master's, comprehensive exam, thesis optional, final exam, research project, degree completed in 6 years; for doctorate, comprehensive exam, thesis/dissertation, general and final exams, research project, completion of all work within 10 years. *Entrance requirements:* For master's and doctorate, GRE General Test (minimum Quantitative score of 159), minimum GPA of 3.0, official transcripts, personal statement, confidential evaluations by 3 professors or other technical professional, high rank (top 5%) in respected chemical engineering program. Additional exam requirements/recommendations for international students: Required—TOEFL (minimum score 580 paper-based; 92 iBT); Recommended—IELTS (minimum score 7). *Application deadline:* For fall admission, 1/1 priority date for domestic students, 12/15 priority date for international students. Applications are processed on a rolling basis. Application fee: $85. Electronic applications accepted. *Expenses:* Contact institution. *Financial support:* In 2016–17, 125 students received support, including 15 fellowships with full tuition reimbursements available (averaging $2,573 per year), 66 research assistantships with full tuition reimbursements available (averaging $2,573 per year), 44 teaching assistantships with full tuition reimbursements available (averaging $2,573 per year); career-related internships or fieldwork, Federal Work-Study, health care benefits, and unspecified assistantships also available. Financial award application deadline: 1/15; financial award applicants required to submit FAFSA. *Faculty research:* Materials processing and characterization, optical and electronic polymers, surface science, biochemical engineering and bioengineering, computational chemistry, environmental studies. *Total annual research expenditures:* $12.7 million. *Unit head:* Dr. Francois Baneyx, Professor/Chair, 206-543-2250, Fax: 206-543-3778, E-mail: baneyx@uw.edu. *Application contact:* Allison Sherrill, Graduate Program Advisor, 206-685-9785, E-mail: sherra@uw.edu. Website: http://www.cheme.washington.edu/

University of Washington, Graduate School, College of Engineering, Department of Electrical Engineering, Seattle, WA 98195-2500. Offers electrical engineering (MS, PhD); electrical engineering and nanotechnology (PhD). *Program availability:* Part-time, evening/weekend. *Faculty:* 45 full-time (9 women). *Students:* 242 full-time (67 women), 117 part-time (18 women); includes 70 minority (3 Black or African American, non-Hispanic/Latino; 50 Asian, non-Hispanic/Latino; 12 Hispanic/Latino; 5 Two or more races, non-Hispanic/Latino), 163 international. 1,327 applicants, 12% accepted, 91 enrolled. In 2016, 70 master's, 30 doctorates awarded. Terminal master's awarded for partial completion of doctoral program. *Degree requirements:* For master's, thesis optional; for doctorate, thesis/dissertation, qualifying, general, and final exams. *Entrance requirements:* For master's and doctorate, GRE General Test (recommended minimum Quantitative score of 160), minimum GPA of 3.5 (recommended); resume or curriculum vitae, statement of purpose, 3 letters of recommendation, undergraduate and graduate transcripts. Additional exam requirements/recommendations for international students: Required—TOEFL (minimum score 600 paper-based; 92 iBT). *Application deadline:* For fall admission, 12/15 for domestic and international students. Applications are processed on a rolling basis. Application fee: $85. Electronic applications accepted. *Expenses:* Contact institution. *Financial support:* In 2016–17, 168 students received support, including 13 fellowships with full tuition reimbursements available (averaging $2,556 per year), 98 research assistantships with full tuition reimbursements available (averaging $2,463 per year), 57 teaching assistantships with full tuition reimbursements available (averaging $2,463 per year); career-related internships or fieldwork, Federal Work-Study, institutionally sponsored loans, and health care benefits also available. Financial award application deadline: 12/15; financial award applicants required to submit FAFSA. *Faculty research:* Computing and networking, photonics and nano-devices, power and energy systems, robotics and controls, data sciences and biosystems. *Total annual research expenditures:* $19 million. *Unit head:* Dr. Radha Poovendran, Professor/Chair, 206-543-6515, Fax: 206-543-3842, E-mail: chair@ee.washington.edu. *Application contact:* Brenda Larson, Graduate Program Lead Academic Counselor, 206-616-1351, Fax: 206-543-3842, E-mail: brenda@ee.washington.edu. Website: http://www.ee.washington.edu/

Virginia Commonwealth University, Graduate School, College of Humanities and Sciences, Department of Physics, Richmond, VA 23284-9005. Offers medical physics (MS, PhD); nanoscience and nanotechnology (PhD); physics and applied physics (MS). *Program availability:* Part-time. *Degree requirements:* For master's, comprehensive exam, thesis optional. *Entrance requirements:* For master's, GRE. Additional exam requirements/recommendations for international students: Required—TOEFL (minimum score 600 paper-based; 100 iBT); Recommended—IELTS (minimum score 6.5). *Application deadline:* For fall admission, 3/15 for domestic students; for spring admission, 11/15 for domestic students. Applications are processed on a rolling basis. Application fee: $50. Electronic applications accepted. *Financial support:* Fellowships, teaching assistantships, Federal Work-Study, institutionally sponsored loans, and tuition waivers (full and partial) available. Support available to part-time students. *Faculty research:* Condensed-matter theory and experimentation, electronic instrumentation, relativity. *Unit head:* Dr. Alison A. Baski, Chair, 804-828-8295, Fax: 804-828-7073, E-mail: aabaski@vcu.edu. *Application contact:* Dr. Shiv Khanna, Graduate Program Director, 804-828-1820, Fax: 804-828-7073, E-mail: snkhanna@vcu.edu.
Website: http://www.has.vcu.edu/phy/physic.html

Virginia Commonwealth University, Graduate School, College of Humanities and Sciences, Program in Nanosciences, Richmond, VA 23284-9005. Offers PhD. *Entrance requirements:* For doctorate, GRE General Test. Additional exam requirements/recommendations for international students: Required—TOEFL (minimum score 600 paper-based; 100 iBT); Recommended—IELTS (minimum score 6.5). *Application deadline:* For fall admission, 3/15 for domestic students; for spring admission, 11/15 for domestic students. Application fee: $50. Electronic applications accepted. *Faculty research:* Nanotechnology, nanoscience. *Unit head:* Dr. Everett E. Carpenter, Program Director, 804-828-7508, E-mail: ecarpenter2@vcu.edu. *Application contact:* Dr. Sherry T. Sandkam, Associate Dean, 804-828-6916, Fax: 804-827-4546,
E-mail: ssandkam@vcu.edu.
Website: http://www.nano.vcu.edu/

CASE WESTERN RESERVE UNIVERSITY
Department of Biomedical Engineering

Programs of Study

The Department offers many exceptional and innovative educational programs leading to career opportunities in biomedical engineering (BME) research, development, and design in industry, medical centers, and academic institutions. Graduate degrees offered include the M.S. and Ph.D. in BME, a combined M.D./M.S. degree offered to students admitted to the School of Medicine, and combined M.D./Ph.D. degrees in BME offered through the Physician Engineer Training Program or the Medical Scientist Training Program. Individualized BME programs of study allow students to develop strength in an engineering specialty and apply this expertise to an important biomedical problem under the supervision of a Faculty Guidance Committee. Students can choose from more than forty-three courses regularly taught in BME, as well as many courses in other departments. Typically, an M.S. program consists of seven to nine courses, and a Ph.D. program consists of about thirteen courses beyond the B.S. Students can select research projects from among the many strengths of the Department, including neural engineering and neural prostheses, biomaterials, tissue engineering, drug and gene delivery, biomedical imaging, sensors, optical imaging and diagnostics, the cardiovascular system, biomechanics, mass and heat transport, and metabolic systems. Collaborative research and training in basic biomedical sciences, as well as clinical and translational research, are available through primary faculty members, associated faculty members, and researchers in the nearby major medical centers.

Research Facilities

The primary faculty members have laboratories focusing on cardiovascular and skeletal biomaterials; cardiovascular, orthopaedic, and neural tissue engineering; materials and nanoparticles for drug and gene delivery, biomedical image processing, biomedical imaging in several modalities, cellular and tissue cardiac bioelectricity, ion channel function, electrochemical and fiber-optic sensors, neural engineering and brain electrophysiology, and neural prostheses. BME faculty members and students also make extensive use of campus research centers for special purposes such as microelectronic fabrication, biomedical imaging, and material analyses. Associated faculty members have labs devoted to eye movement control, gait analysis, implantable sensors/actuators, biomedical imaging, metabolism, and tissue pathology. These are located at four major medical centers and teaching hospitals that (with one exception) are within walking distance.

Financial Aid

Graduate students pursuing the Ph.D. may receive financial support from faculty members as research assistants, from training grants (NIH, NSF, DoE GAANN), or from the School of Medicine (M.D./Ph.D. only). These positions are awarded on a competitive basis. There are also opportunities for research assistantships in order to pursue the M.S.

Cost of Study

Tuition at Case in 2017–18 for graduate students is $1,827 per credit hour. A full load for graduate students is a minimum of 9 credits per semester. Fees for health insurance and activities are estimated at $880 per semester.

Living and Housing Costs

Within a 2-mile radius of the campus, numerous apartments are available for married and single graduate students, with rent ranging from $450 to $900 per month.

Student Group

The Department of Biomedical Engineering has 153 graduate students, of whom about 60 percent are advancing toward the Ph.D. At Case Western Reserve University, approximately 5,121 students are enrolled as undergraduates, and 6,219 in graduate studies and the professional schools.

Location

Case is located on the eastern boundary of Cleveland in University Circle, which is the city's cultural center. The area includes Severance Hall (home of the Cleveland Orchestra), the Museum of Art, the Museum of Natural History, the Garden Center, the Institute of Art, the Institute of Music, the Western Reserve Historical Society, and the Crawford Auto-Aviation Museum. Metropolitan Cleveland has a population of almost 2 million. The Cleveland Hopkins International Airport is 30 minutes away by rail transit. A network of parks encircles the greater Cleveland area. Opportunities are available for sailing on Lake Erie and for hiking and skiing nearby in Ohio, Pennsylvania, and New York. Major-league sports, theater, and all types of music provide a full range of entertainment.

The University and The Department

The Department of Biomedical Engineering at Case Western Reserve University is part of both the Case School of Engineering and the School of Medicine, which are located on the same campus. Established in 1967, the Department is one of the pioneers in biomedical engineering education and is currently among the nation's largest and highest rated (according to *U.S. News & World Report*). Case Western Reserve University was formed in 1967 by a federation of Western Reserve College and Case Institute of Technology. Numerous interdisciplinary programs exist with the professional Schools of Medicine, Dentistry, Nursing, Law, Social Work, and Management.

Applying

Applications that request financial aid should be submitted before February 1. The completed application requires official transcripts, scores on the GRE General Test, and three letters of reference. Application forms can be downloaded from the Case website (https://app.applyyourself.com/AYApplicantLogin/ApplicantConnectLogin.asp?id=casegrad). Applicants for the M.D./M.S. and M.D./Ph.D. programs can apply through the School of Medicine.

Correspondence and Information

Admissions Coordinator
Department of Biomedical Engineering
Wickenden Building 325
Case Western Reserve University
10900 Euclid Avenue
Cleveland, Ohio 44106-7207
Phone: 216-368-4094
Fax: 216-368-4969
Website: http://bme.case.edu

THE FACULTY AND THEIR RESEARCH

Primary Faculty

A. Bolu Ajiboye, Ph.D., Assistant Professor. Development and control of brain-computer-interface (BCI) technologies for restoring function to individuals with nervous system injuries.

Eben Alsberg, Ph.D., Professor. Biomimetic tissue engineering, innovative biomaterials and drug delivery vehicles for functional tissue regeneration and cancer therapy, control of stem cell differentiation, mechanotransduction and the influence of mechanics on cell and tissue function, cell-cell interactions.

James M. Anderson, M.D., Professor of Pathology, Macromolecular Science, and Biomedical Engineering. Blood and tissue/material interactions as they relate to implantable devices and biomaterials.

James P. Basilion, Ph.D., Professor of BME and Radiology. Molecular imaging, biomarkers, diagnosis and treatment of cancer.

Jeffery Capadona, Ph.D., Associate Professor. Advanced materials for neural interfacing, biomimetic and bio-inspired materials, host-implant integration, anti-inflammatory materials, and novel biomaterials for surface modification of cortical neuroprostheses.

Patrick E. Crago, Ph.D., Professor Emeritus. Control of neuroprostheses for motor function, neuromuscular control systems.

Colin Drummond, Ph.D., Professor and Assistant Chair. Medical device design, microfabrication packaging, sensor systems, and cross-platform software systems integration.

Dominique M. Durand, Ph.D., Professor. Neural engineering, neuro-prostheses, neural dynamics, magnetic and electric stimulation of the nervous system, neural interfaces with electronic devices, analysis and control of epilepsy.

Steven J. Eppell, Ph.D., Associate Professor. Nanoscale instrumentation for biomaterials, bone and cartilage structure and function.

Miklos Gratzl, Ph.D., Associate Professor. Fine chemical manipulation of microdroplets and single cells, cancer research and neurochemistry at the single-cell level, cost-effective biochemical diagnostics in microliter body fluids.

Kenneth Gustafson, Ph.D., Associate Professor. Neural engineering, neural prostheses, neurophysiology and neural control of genitourinary function, devices to restore genitourinary function, functional neuromuscular stimulation.

Efstathios Karathanasis, Ph.D., Associate Professor. Fabricating multifunctional agents that facilitate diagnosing, treating, and monitoring of therapies in a patient-specific manner.

Robert Kirsch, Ph.D., Professor and Chair, Executive Director, FES Center. Functional neuromuscular stimulation, biomechanics and neural control of human movement, modeling and simulation of musculoskeletal systems, identification of physiological systems.

Zheng-Rong Lu, Ph.D., Professor. Molecular imaging and drug delivery using novel nanotechnology.

Anant Madabhushi, Ph.D., Professor. Quantitative image analysis; multi-modal, multi-scale correlation of massive data sets for disease diagnostics, prognostics, theragnostics; cancer applications.

Cameron McIntyre, Ph.D., Professor. Theoretical modeling of the interaction between electric fields and the nervous system, deep brain stimulation.

J. Thomas Mortimer, Ph.D., Professor Emeritus. Neural prostheses, electrical activation of the nervous system, bowel and bladder assist device, respiratory assist device, selective stimulation and electrode development, electrochemical aspects of electrical stimulation.

P. Hunter Peckham, Ph.D., Professor. Neural prostheses, implantable stimulation and control of movement, rehabilitation engineering.

Andrew M. Rollins, Ph.D., Professor. Biomedical diagnosis; novel optical methods for high-resolution, minimally invasive imaging; tissue characterization and analyte sensing; real-time microstructural and functional imaging using coherence tomography; endoscopy.

Gerald M. Saidel, Ph.D., Professor and Director of the Center for Modeling Integrated Metabolic Systems. Mass and heat transport and metabolic analysis in cells, tissues, and organs; mathematical modeling, simulation, and parameter estimation; optimal experimental design; metabolic dynamics; minimally invasive thermal tumor ablation; slow-release drug delivery.

Nicole Seiberlich, Ph.D., Associate Professor. Advanced signal processing and data acquisition techniques for rapid Magnetic Resonance Imaging (MRI).

Anirban Sen Gupta, Ph.D., Associate Professor. Targeted drug delivery, targeted molecular imaging, image-guided therapy, platelet substitutes, novel polymeric biomaterials for tissue engineering scaffolds.

Samuel E. Senyo, Ph.D., Assistant Professor. Cardiovascular regeneration, microenvironment, stable isotopes, biomaterials, microfabrication, drug delivery.

Nicole F. Steinmetz, Ph.D., Associate Professor. Engineering of viral nanoparticles as smart devices for applications in medicine: tissue-specific imaging, drug-delivery, and tissue engineering.

Pallavi Tiwari, Ph.D., Assistant Professor. Developing image analysis and machine learning tools for neuroimaging applications.

Ronald Triolo, Ph.D., Associate Professor (Orthopaedics, VA Medical Center). Rehabilitation engineering, neuroprostheses, orthopaedic biomechanics.

Dustin Tyler, Ph.D., Professor. Neuromimetic neuroprostheses, laryngeal neuroprostheses, clinical implementation of nerve electrodes, cortical neuroprostheses, minimally invasive implantation techniques, modeling of neural stimulation and neuroprostheses.

Horst von Recum, Ph.D., Professor. Tissue-engineered epithelia, prevascularized polymer scaffolds, directed stem cell differentiation, novel stimuli-responsive biomaterials for gene and drug delivery, systems biology approaches to the identification of angiogenic factors.

Satish Viswanath, Ph.D., Assistant Professor. Medical image analysis, image radiomics, and machine-learning schemes, focused on the use of post-processing, co-registration, and biological quantitation.

David L. Wilson, Ph.D., Professor. In vivo microscopic and molecular imaging; medical image processing; image segmentation, registration, and analysis; quantitative image quality of X-ray fluoroscopy and fast MRI; interventional MRI treatment of cancer.

Xin Yu, Sc.D., Professor. Cardiovascular physiology, magnetic resonance imaging and spectroscopy, characterization of the structure-function and energy-function relationships in normal and diseased hearts, small-animal imaging and spectroscopy.

Associated Faculty (partial list)

Rigoberto Advincula, Ph.D., Professor. Design, synthesis, and characterization of polymers and nanostructured materials capable of controlled-assembly, tethering, and self-organization in ultrathin films.

Jay Alberts, Ph.D., Assistant Professor (BME, Cleveland Clinic Foundation). Neural basis of upper-extremity motor function and deep-brain stimulation in Parkinson's disease.

Harihara Baskaran, Ph.D., Associate Professor of BME and Chemical Engineering. Tissue engineering; cell/cellular transport processes in inflammation, wound healing, and cancer metastasis.

Richard C. Burgess, M.D./Ph.D., Adjunct Professor (Staff Physician, Neurology, Cleveland Clinic Foundation). Electrophysiological monitoring, EEG processing.

Arnold Caplan, Ph.D., Professor of Biology. Tissue engineering.

M. Cenk Cavusoglu, Ph.D., Professor. Robotics, systems and control theory, and human-machine interfaces, with emphasis on medical robotics, haptics, virtual environments, surgical simulation, and biosystem modeling and simulation.

John Chae, M.D., Professor (MED–Physical Medicine and Rehabilitation). Application of neuroprostheses in hemiplegia.

Hillel J. Chiel, Ph.D., Professor. Biomechanical and neural basis of feeding behavior in *Aplysia californica*, neuromechanical system modeling.

Margot Damaser, Ph.D., Associate Professor of Molecular Medicine (BME, Cleveland Clinic Foundation). Biomechanics as it relates to function and dysfunction of the lower urinary tract.

Kathleen Derwin, Ph.D., Assistant Professor (BME, Cleveland Clinic Foundation). Tendon mechanobiology and tissue engineering.

Isabelle Deschenes, Ph.D., Associate Professor (Cardiology, MED–Medicine). Molecular imaging, ion channel structure and function, genetic regulation of ion channels, cellular and molecular mechanisms of cardiac arrhythmias.

Agata Exner, Ph.D., Associate Professor (Radiology, University Hospitals). Image-guided drug delivery, polymers for interventional radiology, models of cancer.

Christopher Flask, Ph.D., Assistant Professor, Radiology. Development of quantitative and molecular MRI imaging methods, MRI physics.

Vikas Gulani, M.D., Ph.D., Assistant Professor. Diffusion tensor imaging and diffusion anisotropy, MRI microscopy, body MRI, functional MRI.

Elizabeth Fisher, Ph.D., Associate Professor (BME, Cleveland Clinic Foundation). Quantitative image analysis for monitoring multiple sclerosis.

Mark Griswold, Ph.D., Professor (Radiology, University Hospitals). Rapid magnetic resonance imaging, image reconstruction and processing, MRI hardware/instrumentation.

Michael Jenkins, Ph.D., Assistant Professor. Biomedical imaging and instrumentation to determine congenital heart defects.

Michael W. Keith, M.D., Professor (Orthopaedics, MED–Medicine). Restoration of motor function in hands.

Kevin Kilgore, Ph.D., Adjunct Assistant Professor (MED–Medicine). Functional electrical stimulation, restoration of hand function.

Kandice Kottke-Marchant, M.D./Ph.D., Professor (Staff, Clinical Pathology, Cleveland Clinic Foundation). Interaction of blood and materials, endothelial cell function on biomaterials.

Kenneth R. Laurita, Ph.D., Associate Professor (Heart and Vascular Research Center, MED–Medicine). Cardiac electrophysiology, arrhythmia mechanisms, intracellular calcium homeostasis, fluorescence imaging, instrumentation and software for potential mapping.

Zhenghong Lee, Ph.D., Associate Professor (Radiology, University Hospitals). Quantitative PET and SPECT imaging, multimodal image registration, 3-D visualization, molecular imaging, small-animal imaging systems.

George Muschler, M.D., Professor (Staff, BME, Cleveland Clinic Foundation). Musculoskeletal oncology, adult reconstructive orthopaedic surgery, fracture nonunion, research in bone healing and bone-grafting materials.

Raymond Muzic, Ph.D., Associate Professor (Radiology, University Hospitals). Modeling and experiment design for PET, image reconstruction.

Clare Rimnac, Ph.D., Professor and Director of the Musculoskeletal Mechanics and Materials Laboratories, Mechanical and Aerospace Engineering. Orthopaedic implant performance and design, mechanical behavior of hand tissues.

Mark S. Rzeszotarski, Ph.D., Professor (Radiology, MED–Medicine). Computers in radiology: MRI/CT/nuclear medicine, ultrasound.

Dawn Taylor, Ph.D., Assistant Professor (BME, Cleveland Clinic Foundation). Brain-computer interfaces for control of computers, neural prostheses, and robotic devices; invasive and noninvasive brain signal acquisition; adaptive decoding algorithms for retraining the brain to control alternative devices after paralysis.

Albert L. Waldo, M.D., Professor (Medicine, University Hospitals). Cardiac electrophysiology, cardiac excitation mapping, mechanisms of cardiac arrhythmias and conduction.

Barry W. Wessels, Ph.D., Professor (Radiation Oncology, University Hospitals). Radio-labeled antibody therapy (dosimeter and clinical trials); image-guided radiotherapy; intensity-modulated radiation therapy; image fusion of CT, MR, SPECT, and PET for adaptive radiation therapy treatment planning.

Guang H. Yue, Ph.D., Adjunct Associate Professor (Assistant Staff, BME, Cleveland Clinic Foundation). Neural control of movement, electrophysiology, MRI.

Marcie Zborowski, Ph.D., Adjunct Associate Professor (Assistant Staff, BME, Cleveland Clinic Foundation). High-speed magnetic cell sorting.

Nicholas P. Ziats, Ph.D., Associate Professor (Pathology, University Hospitals). Vascular grafts, cell-material interactions, extracellular matrix, tissue engineering, blood compatibility.

Section 6
Chemical Engineering

This section contains a directory of institutions offering graduate work in chemical engineering, followed by an in-depth entry submitted by an institution that chose to prepare a detailed program description. Additional information about programs listed in the directory but not augmented by an in-depth entry may be obtained by writing directly to the dean of a graduate school or chair of a department at the address given in the directory.

For programs offering related work, see also in this book *Engineering and Applied Sciences; Geological, Mineral/Mining, and Petroleum Engineering; Management of Engineering and Technology;* and *Materials Sciences and Engineering.* In the other guides in this series:

Graduate Programs in the Humanities, Arts & Social Sciences
See *Family and Consumer Sciences (Clothing and Textiles)*
Graduate Programs in the Biological/Biomedical Sciences & Health-Related Medical Professions
See *Biochemistry*
Graduate Programs in the Physical Sciences, Mathematics, Agricultural Sciences, the Environment & Natural Resources
See *Chemistry* and *Geosciences (Geochemistry* and *Geology)*

CONTENTS

Biochemical Engineering

Brown University, Graduate School, School of Engineering, Providence, RI 02912. Offers biomedical engineering (Sc M, PhD); chemical and biochemical engineering (Sc M, PhD); electrical sciences and computer engineering (Sc M, PhD); fluid and thermal sciences (Sc M, PhD); materials science and engineering (Sc M, PhD); mechanics of solids and structures (Sc M, PhD). *Degree requirements:* For doctorate, thesis/dissertation, preliminary exam.

Cornell University, Graduate School, Graduate Fields of Engineering, Field of Chemical Engineering, Ithaca, NY 14853. Offers advanced materials processing (M Eng, MS, PhD); applied mathematics and computational methods (M Eng, MS, PhD); biochemical engineering (M Eng, MS, PhD); chemical reaction engineering (M Eng, MS, PhD); classical and statistical thermodynamics (M Eng, MS, PhD); fluid dynamics, rheology and biorheology (M Eng, MS, PhD); heat and mass transfer (M Eng, MS, PhD); kinetics and catalysis (M Eng, MS, PhD); polymers (M Eng, MS, PhD); surface science (M Eng, MS, PhD). *Degree requirements:* For master's, thesis (MS); for doctorate, comprehensive exam, thesis/dissertation. *Entrance requirements:* For master's and doctorate, GRE General Test, 2 letters of recommendation. Additional exam requirements/recommendations for international students: Required—TOEFL (minimum score 600 paper-based; 77 iBT). Electronic applications accepted. *Faculty research:* Biochemical, biomedical and metabolic engineering; fluid and polymer dynamics; surface science and chemical kinetics; electronics materials; microchemical systems and nanotechnology.

Dartmouth College, Thayer School of Engineering, Program in Biotechnology and Biochemical Engineering, Hanover, NH 03755. Offers MS, PhD. *Degree requirements:* For master's, thesis; for doctorate, thesis/dissertation, candidacy oral exam. *Entrance requirements:* For master's and doctorate, GRE General Test. *Application deadline:* For fall admission, 1/1 priority date for domestic students. Application fee: $45. *Financial support:* Fellowships, research assistantships, teaching assistantships, career-related internships or fieldwork, Federal Work-Study, institutionally sponsored loans, and tuition waivers (full and partial) available. Financial award application deadline: 1/15. *Faculty research:* Biomass processing, metabolic engineering, kinetics and reactor design, applied microbiology, resource and environmental analysis. *Total annual research expenditures:* $2.6 million. *Unit head:* Dr. Joseph J. Helbie, Dean, 603-646-2238, Fax: 603-646-2580, E-mail: joseph.j.helbie@dartmouth.edu. *Application contact:* Candace S. Potter, Graduate Admissions Administrator, 603-646-3844, Fax: 603-646-1620, E-mail: candace.s.potter@dartmouth.edu.
Website: http://engineering.dartmouth.edu/

Drexel University, College of Engineering, Department of Chemical and Biological Engineering, Program in Biochemical Engineering, Philadelphia, PA 19104-2875. Offers MS. *Program availability:* Part-time, evening/weekend. *Faculty:* 14 full-time (1 woman). *Students:* 1 part-time (0 women). Average age 35. In 2016, 3 master's awarded. *Degree requirements:* For master's, thesis. *Entrance requirements:* For master's, minimum GPA of 3.0 in chemical engineering or biological sciences. Additional exam requirements/recommendations for international students: Required—TOEFL. *Application deadline:* For fall admission, 8/21 for domestic students. Applications are processed on a rolling basis. Application fee: $50. Electronic applications accepted. *Expenses: Tuition:* Full-time $32,184; part-time $1192 per credit hour. *Required fees:* $280. Tuition and fees vary according to campus/location and program. *Financial support:* Research assistantships, teaching assistantships, career-related internships or fieldwork, Federal Work-Study, tuition waivers (full and partial), and unspecified assistantships available. Financial award application deadline: 2/1. *Faculty research:* Monitoring and control of bioreactors, sensors for bioreactors, large-scale production of monoclonal antibodies. *Unit head:* Dr. Rajakkannu Mutharasan, Director, 215-895-2236. *Application contact:* Director of Graduate Admissions, 215-895-6700, Fax: 215-895-5939, E-mail: enroll@drexel.edu.

Lehigh University, P.C. Rossin College of Engineering and Applied Science, Department of Chemical and Biomolecular Engineering, Bethlehem, PA 18015. Offers biological chemical engineering (M Eng); chemical energy engineering (M Eng); chemical engineering (M Eng, MS, PhD); MBA/E. *Program availability:* Part-time, 100% online. *Faculty:* 23 full-time (4 women), 1 part-time/adjunct (0 women). *Students:* 56 full-time (24 women), 24 part-time (9 women); includes 11 minority (2 Black or African American, non-Hispanic/Latino; 6 Asian, non-Hispanic/Latino; 3 Hispanic/Latino), 44 international. Average age 27. 218 applicants, 32% accepted, 27 enrolled. In 2016, 14 master's, 6 doctorates awarded. Terminal master's awarded for partial completion of doctoral program. *Degree requirements:* For master's, thesis (for some programs); for doctorate, comprehensive exam, thesis/dissertation. *Entrance requirements:* For master's and doctorate, GRE General Test. Additional exam requirements/recommendations for international students: Required—TOEFL (minimum score 79 iBT), IELTS (minimum score 6.5). *Application deadline:* For fall admission, 7/15 for domestic students, 7/15 priority date for international students; for spring admission, 12/1 for domestic and international students. Application fee: $75. Electronic applications accepted. *Expenses:* $1,420 per credit. *Financial support:* In 2016–17, 42 students received support, including 4 fellowships with full tuition reimbursements available (averaging $28,140 per year), 33 research assistantships with full tuition reimbursements available (averaging $28,140 per year), 5 teaching assistantships with full tuition reimbursements available (averaging $28,704 per year); career-related internships or fieldwork, institutionally sponsored loans, scholarships/grants, health care benefits, and unspecified assistantships also available. Financial award application deadline: 1/15. *Faculty research:* Process control, energy, biotechnology, catalysis, polymers. *Total annual research expenditures:* $2.8 million. *Unit head:* Dr. Mayuresh V. Kothare, Chairman, 610-758-6654, Fax: 610-758-5057, E-mail: mvk2@lehigh.edu. *Application contact:* Barbara A. Kessler, Graduate Coordinator, 610-758-4261, Fax: 610-758-5057, E-mail: inchegs@mail.lehigh.edu.
Website: http://www.che.lehigh.edu/

Rutgers University–New Brunswick, Graduate School-New Brunswick, Program in Chemical and Biochemical Engineering, Piscataway, NJ 08854-8097. Offers MS, PhD. *Program availability:* Part-time, evening/weekend. Terminal master's awarded for partial completion of doctoral program. *Degree requirements:* For master's, thesis or alternative; for doctorate, thesis/dissertation. *Entrance requirements:* For master's and doctorate, GRE General Test. Additional exam requirements/recommendations for international students: Required—TOEFL. *Faculty research:* Biotechnology, pharmaceutical engineering, nanotechnology, process system engineering, materials and polymer science, chemical engineering sciences.

University of California, Irvine, Henry Samueli School of Engineering, Department of Chemical Engineering and Materials Science, Irvine, CA 92697. Offers chemical and biochemical engineering (MS, PhD); materials science and engineering (MS, PhD). *Program availability:* Part-time. *Students:* 141 full-time (60 women), 14 part-time (5 women); includes 42 minority (4 Black or African American, non-Hispanic/Latino; 29 Asian, non-Hispanic/Latino; 7 Hispanic/Latino; 2 Two or more races, non-Hispanic/

Latino), 71 international. Average age 26. 595 applicants, 23% accepted, 41 enrolled. In 2016, 47 master's, 11 doctorates awarded. Terminal master's awarded for partial completion of doctoral program. *Degree requirements:* For doctorate, thesis/dissertation. *Entrance requirements:* For master's and doctorate, GRE General Test, minimum GPA of 3.0, 3 letters of recommendation. Additional exam requirements/recommendations for international students: Required—TOEFL (minimum score 550 paper-based). *Application deadline:* For fall admission, 1/15 priority date for domestic students, 1/15 for international students. Applications are processed on a rolling basis. Application fee: $105 ($125 for international students). Electronic applications accepted. *Financial support:* Fellowships with tuition reimbursements, research assistantships with full tuition reimbursements, teaching assistantships with tuition reimbursements, institutionally sponsored loans, traineeships, health care benefits, and unspecified assistantships available. Financial award application deadline: 3/1; financial award applicants required to submit FAFSA. *Faculty research:* Molecular biotechnology, nanobiomaterials, biophotonics, synthesis, super plasticity and mechanical behavior, characterization of advanced and nanostructural materials. *Unit head:* Prof. Vasan Venugopalan, Chair, 949-824-5802, Fax: 949-824-2541, E-mail: vvenugop@uci.edu. *Application contact:* Grace Chau, Academic Program and Graduate Admission Coordinator, 949-824-3887, Fax: 949-824-2541, E-mail: chaug@uci.edu.
Website: http://www.eng.uci.edu/dept/chems

University of Georgia, College of Engineering, Athens, GA 30602. Offers MS. *Unit head:* Dr. E. Dale Threadgill, Dean, 706-542-1653. *Application contact:* Lawrence Hornak, Graduate coordinator, 706-542-2462, E-mail: lahornak@uga.edu.
Website: http://www.engineering.uga.edu/

The University of Iowa, Graduate College, College of Engineering, Department of Chemical and Biochemical Engineering, Iowa City, IA 52242-1316. Offers MS, PhD. *Program availability:* Part-time. *Faculty:* 12 full-time (3 women), 3 part-time/adjunct (1 woman). *Students:* 23 full-time (6 women), 7 part-time (3 women); includes 3 minority (1 Black or African American, non-Hispanic/Latino; 1 Asian, non-Hispanic/Latino; 1 Hispanic/Latino), 12 international. Average age 27. 66 applicants, 24% accepted, 6 enrolled. In 2016, 11 master's, 4 doctorates awarded. *Degree requirements:* For master's, comprehensive exam (for some programs), thesis (for some programs); for doctorate, comprehensive exam, thesis/dissertation. *Entrance requirements:* For master's and doctorate, GRE (minimum combined score of 310 on verbal and quantitative), minimum undergraduate GPA of 3.0. Additional exam requirements/recommendations for international students: Required—TOEFL (minimum score 600 paper-based; 100 iBT), IELTS (minimum score 7). *Application deadline:* For fall admission, 2/1 priority date for domestic and international students; for spring admission, 10/1 for domestic and international students. Applications are processed on a rolling basis. Application fee: $60 ($100 for international students). Electronic applications accepted. *Financial support:* In 2016–17, 38 students received support, including 6 fellowships with full tuition reimbursements available (averaging $25,500 per year), 25 research assistantships with full tuition reimbursements available (averaging $22,981 per year), 7 teaching assistantships with full tuition reimbursements available (averaging $18,809 per year); health care benefits and unspecified assistantships also available. Financial award application deadline: 2/1; financial award applicants required to submit FAFSA. *Faculty research:* Polymeric materials, photo polymerization, atmospheric chemistry and air pollution, biochemical engineering, bioprocessing and biomedical engineering. *Total annual research expenditures:* $1.9 million. *Unit head:* Dr. C. Allan Guymon, Department Executive Officer, 319-335-5015, Fax: 319-335-1415, E-mail: allan-guymon@uiowa.edu. *Application contact:* Sarah Hartman, Academic Program Specialist, 319-335-1215, Fax: 319-335-1415, E-mail: chemical-engineering@uiowa.edu.
Website: https://cbe.engineering.uiowa.edu

The University of Manchester, School of Chemical Engineering and Analytical Science, Manchester, United Kingdom. Offers biocatalysis (M Phil, PhD); chemical engineering (M Phil, PhD); chemical engineering and analytical science (M Phil, D Eng, PhD); colloids, crystals, interfaces and materials (M Phil, PhD); environment and sustainable technology (M Phil, PhD); instrumentation (M Phil, PhD); multi-scale modeling (M Phil, PhD); process integration (M Phil, PhD); systems biology (M Phil, PhD).

University of Maryland, Baltimore County, The Graduate School, College of Engineering and Information Technology, Department of Chemical, Biochemical, and Environmental Engineering, Post Baccalaureate Certificate Program in Biochemical Regulatory Engineering, Baltimore, MD 21250. Offers Postbaccalaureate Certificate. *Program availability:* Part-time. *Students:* 5 part-time (2 women); includes 3 minority (1 Black or African American, non-Hispanic/Latino; 2 Asian, non-Hispanic/Latino), 2 international. Average age 39. 5 applicants, 80% accepted, 4 enrolled. In 2016, 2 Postbaccalaureate Certificates awarded. *Application deadline:* For fall admission, 7/1 for domestic and international students; for spring admission, 2/1 for domestic students, 12/1 for international students. Applications are processed on a rolling basis. Application fee: $70. Electronic applications accepted. *Expenses:* Contact institution. *Unit head:* Dr. Antonio Moreira, Vice Provost for Academic Affairs, 410-455-6576, E-mail: moreira@umbc.edu. *Application contact:* 410-455-3400, Fax: 410-455-1049.
Website: http://cbee.umbc.edu/academics/graduate-degree-programs/graduate-certificate-in-biochemical-regulatory-engineering/

University of Maryland, Baltimore County, The Graduate School, College of Engineering and Information Technology, Department of Chemical, Biochemical, and Environmental Engineering, Program in Chemical and Biochemical Engineering, Baltimore, MD 21250. Offers MS, PhD. *Program availability:* Part-time. *Students:* 20 full-time (9 women), 3 part-time (2 women); includes 6 minority (3 Black or African American, non-Hispanic/Latino; 3 Asian, non-Hispanic/Latino), 9 international. Average age 23. 41 applicants, 34% accepted, 7 enrolled. In 2016, 8 master's, 1 doctorate awarded. *Degree requirements:* For master's, comprehensive exam (for some programs), thesis (for some programs); for doctorate, comprehensive exam, thesis/dissertation. *Entrance requirements:* For master's, GRE General Test, minimum GPA of 3.0, strong mathematical background; for doctorate, GRE General Test (taken within last 5 years), minimum GPA of 3.0. Additional exam requirements/recommendations for international students: Required—TOEFL (minimum score 550 paper-based; 80 iBT). *Application deadline:* For fall admission, 6/1 for domestic students, 1/1 for international students; for spring admission, 11/1 for domestic students, 6/1 for international students. Applications are processed on a rolling basis. Application fee: $70. Electronic applications accepted. Application fee is waived when completed online. *Expenses:* Contact institution. *Financial support:* In 2016–17, 3 students received support, including 1 fellowship with full tuition reimbursement available (averaging $25,000 per year), 16 research assistantships with full tuition reimbursements available (averaging $23,000 per year); teaching assistantships, career-related internships or fieldwork, Federal Work-Study, scholarships/grants, health care benefits, tuition waivers (partial),

and unspecified assistantships also available. Support available to part-time students. Financial award application deadline: 6/30; financial award applicants required to submit FAFSA. *Faculty research:* Biomaterials engineering, bioprocess engineering, cellular engineering, education, education and outreach, sensors and monitoring, systems biology and functional genomics. *Unit head:* Dr. Mark Marten, Professor and Interim Chair, 410-455-3400, Fax: 410-455-1049, E-mail: marten@umbc.edu. *Application contact:* Dr. Erin Lavik, Professor/Graduate Program Director, 410-455-3428, Fax: 410-455-1049, E-mail: elavik@umbc.edu.
Website: http://cbee.umbc.edu/

The University of Western Ontario, Faculty of Graduate Studies, Physical Sciences Division, Faculty of Engineering, London, ON N6A 5B8, Canada. Offers chemical and biochemical engineering (ME Sc, PhD); civil and environmental engineering (M Eng, ME Sc, PhD); electrical and computer engineering (M Eng, ME Sc, PhD); mechanical and materials engineering (M Eng, ME Sc, PhD). *Program availability:* Part-time. Terminal master's awarded for partial completion of doctoral program. *Degree requirements:* For master's, thesis; for doctorate, thesis/dissertation. *Entrance requirements:* For master's, minimum B average; for doctorate, minimum B+ average. *Faculty research:* Wind, geotechnical, chemical reactor engineering, applied electrostatics, biochemical engineering.

Villanova University, College of Engineering, Department of Chemical Engineering, Villanova, PA 19085-1699. Offers biochemical engineering (Certificate); chemical engineering (MSChE); environmental protection in the chemical process industries (Certificate). *Program availability:* Part-time, evening/weekend. *Degree requirements:* For master's, comprehensive exam, thesis optional. *Entrance requirements:* For master's, GRE General Test (for applicants with degrees from foreign universities), B Ch E, minimum GPA of 3.0. Additional exam requirements/recommendations for international students: Required—TOEFL (minimum score 600 paper-based; 100 iBT). *Faculty research:* Heat transfer, advanced materials, chemical vapor deposition, pyrolysis and combustion chemistry, industrial waste treatment.

Chemical Engineering

American University of Sharjah, Graduate Programs, Sharjah, United Arab Emirates. Offers accounting (MS); business (EMBA, MBA); chemical engineering (MS Ch E); civil engineering (MSCE); computer engineering (MS); electrical engineering (MSEE); engineering systems management (MS); mathematics (MS); mechanical engineering (MSME); mechatronics engineering (MS); teaching English to speakers of other languages (MA); translation and interpreting (MA); urban planning (MUP). *Program availability:* Part-time, evening/weekend. *Degree requirements:* For master's, thesis (for some programs). *Entrance requirements:* For master's, GMAT (for MBA). Additional exam requirements/recommendations for international students: Required—TOEFL (minimum score 550 paper-based; 80 iBT), TWE (minimum score 5); Recommended—IELTS (minimum score 6.5). Electronic applications accepted. *Faculty research:* Water pollution, management and waste water treatment, energy and sustainability, air pollution, Islamic finance, family business and small and medium enterprises.

Arizona State University at the Tempe campus, Ira A. Fulton Schools of Engineering, School for Engineering of Matter, Transport and Energy, Tempe, AZ 85281. Offers aerospace engineering (MS, PhD); chemical engineering (MS, PhD); materials science and engineering (MS, PhD); mechanical engineering (MS, PhD); solar energy engineering and commercialization (PSM). *Program availability:* Part-time, evening/weekend, online learning. Terminal master's awarded for partial completion of doctoral program. *Degree requirements:* For master's, thesis and oral defense (MS); applied project or comprehensive exam (MSE); interactive Program of Study (iPOS) submitted before completing 50 percent of required credit hours; for doctorate, comprehensive exam, thesis/dissertation, interactive Program of Study (iPOS) submitted before completing 50 percent of required credit hours. *Entrance requirements:* For master's, GRE, minimum GPA of 3.0 or equivalent in last 2 years of work leading to bachelor's degree; for doctorate, GRE, minimum GPA of 3.0 in last 2 years of work leading to bachelor's degree. Additional exam requirements/recommendations for international students: Required—TOEFL, IELTS, or PTE. Electronic applications accepted. *Expenses:* Contact institution. *Faculty research:* Electronic materials and packaging, materials for energy (batteries), adaptive/intelligent materials and structures, multiscale fluid mechanics, membranes, therapeutics and bioseparations, flexible structures, nanostructured materials, and micro/nano transport.

Auburn University, Graduate School, Ginn College of Engineering, Department of Chemical Engineering, Auburn University, AL 36849. Offers M Ch E, MS, PhD. *Program availability:* Part-time. *Faculty:* 20 full-time (4 women), 4 part-time/adjunct (0 women). *Students:* 50 full-time (14 women), 41 part-time (11 women); includes 7 minority (1 Black or African American, non-Hispanic/Latino; 3 Asian, non-Hispanic/Latino; 3 Hispanic/Latino), 48 international. Average age 27. 136 applicants, 24% accepted, 25 enrolled. In 2016, 6 master's, 13 doctorates awarded. *Degree requirements:* For master's, thesis (for some programs); for doctorate, comprehensive exam, thesis/dissertation. *Entrance requirements:* For master's and doctorate, GRE General Test. *Application deadline:* Applications are processed on a rolling basis. Application fee: $50 ($60 for international students). Electronic applications accepted. *Expenses:* Tuition, state resident: full-time $9072; part-time $504 per credit hour. Tuition, nonresident: full-time $27,216; part-time $1512 per credit hour. *Required fees:* $812 per semester. Tuition and fees vary according to degree level and program. *Financial support:* Fellowships, research assistantships, teaching assistantships, and Federal Work-Study available. Support available to part-time students. Financial award application deadline: 3/15; financial award applicants required to submit FAFSA. *Faculty research:* Coal liquefaction, asphalt research, pulp and paper engineering, surface science, biochemical engineering. *Unit head:* Dr. Mario Richard Eden, Chair, 334-844-2064. *Application contact:* Dr. George Flowers, Dean of the Graduate School, 334-844-2125.
Website: http://www.eng.auburn.edu/chen/

Brigham Young University, Graduate Studies, Ira A. Fulton College of Engineering and Technology, Department of Chemical Engineering, Provo, UT 84602. Offers MS, PhD. *Faculty:* 16 full-time (1 woman). *Students:* 53 full-time (11 women); includes 1 minority (Native Hawaiian or other Pacific Islander, non-Hispanic/Latino), 22 international. Average age 28. 36 applicants, 42% accepted, 12 enrolled. In 2016, 3 master's, 3 doctorates awarded. *Degree requirements:* For master's, comprehensive exam, thesis; for doctorate, comprehensive exam, thesis/dissertation. *Entrance requirements:* For master's and doctorate, GRE, BS in chemical engineering or related engineering field, minimum GPA of 3.3. Additional exam requirements/recommendations for international students: Required—TOEFL (minimum score 580 paper-based; 85 iBT), IELTS (minimum score 7). *Application deadline:* For fall admission, 1/31 for domestic and international students; for winter admission, 6/15 for domestic and international students; for spring admission, 10/15 for domestic and international students; for summer admission, 10/15 for domestic and international students. Application fee: $50. Electronic applications accepted. *Expenses: Tuition:* Full-time $6680; part-time $393 per credit. Tuition and fees vary according to course load, program and student's religious affiliation. *Financial support:* In 2016–17, 50 students received support, including 4 fellowships (averaging $25,764 per year), 114 research assistantships with full and partial tuition reimbursements available (averaging $23,304 per year), 20 teaching assistantships with full and partial tuition reimbursements available (averaging $22,956 per year); scholarships/grants also available. Financial award application deadline: 6/30; financial award applicants required to submit FAFSA. *Faculty research:* Energy and combustion, thermodynamics and thermophysical properties, biochemical and biomedical engineering, nano- and micro-technology, molecular modeling. *Total annual research expenditures:* $1.7 million. *Unit head:* Dr. Thomas H. Fletcher, Chair, 801-422-6236, Fax: 801-422-0151, E-mail: cheme@byu.edu. *Application contact:* Dr. William G. Pitt, Graduate Coordinator, 801-422-2588, Fax: 801-422-0151, E-mail: pitt@byu.edu.
Website: http://www.chemicalengineering.byu.edu

Brown University, Graduate School, School of Engineering, Providence, RI 02912. Offers biomedical engineering (Sc M, PhD); chemical and biochemical engineering (Sc M, PhD); electrical sciences and computer engineering (Sc M, PhD); fluid and thermal sciences (Sc M, PhD); materials science and engineering (Sc M, PhD); mechanics of solids and structures (Sc M, PhD). *Degree requirements:* For doctorate, thesis/dissertation, preliminary exam.

Bucknell University, Graduate Studies, College of Engineering, Department of Chemical Engineering, Lewisburg, PA 17837. Offers MS Ch E. *Degree requirements:* For master's, thesis. *Entrance requirements:* For master's, GRE General Test, minimum GPA of 3.0. Additional exam requirements/recommendations for international students: Required—TOEFL (minimum score 600 paper-based). *Faculty research:* Computer-aided design, software engineering, applied mathematics and modeling, polymer science, digital process control.

California Institute of Technology, Division of Chemistry and Chemical Engineering, Program in Chemical Engineering, Pasadena, CA 91125. Offers MS, PhD. *Faculty:* 12 full-time (2 women). *Students:* 49 full-time (11 women); includes 17 minority (12 Asian, non-Hispanic/Latino; 3 Hispanic/Latino; 2 Two or more races, non-Hispanic/Latino), 10 international. Average age 25. 231 applicants, 17% accepted, 11 enrolled. In 2016, 12 master's, 8 doctorates awarded. Terminal master's awarded for partial completion of doctoral program. *Degree requirements:* For master's, thesis; for doctorate, thesis/dissertation. *Entrance requirements:* For doctorate, GRE, BS. Additional exam requirements/recommendations for international students: Required—TOEFL; Recommended—IELTS, TWE. *Application deadline:* For fall admission, 12/15 for domestic and international students. Application fee: $100. Electronic applications accepted. *Financial support:* Fellowships, research assistantships, teaching assistantships, institutionally sponsored loans, scholarships/grants, traineeships, health care benefits, and unspecified assistantships available. Financial award application deadline: 12/15. *Faculty research:* Fluids, biomolecular engineering, atmospheric chemistry, polymers/materials, catalysis. *Unit head:* Prof. Jacqueline K. Barton, Chair, Chemistry and Chemical Engineering, 626-395-3646, Fax: 626-568-8824, E-mail: jkbarton@caltech.edu. *Application contact:* Natalie Gilmore, Assistant Dean of Graduate Studies, 626-395-3812, Fax: 626-577-9246, E-mail: ngilmore@caltech.edu.
Website: https://www.cce.caltech.edu/content/cheme

Carnegie Mellon University, Carnegie Institute of Technology, Department of Chemical Engineering, Pittsburgh, PA 15213-3891. Offers chemical engineering (M Ch E, MS, PhD); colloids, polymers and surfaces (MS). *Program availability:* Part-time, evening/weekend. Terminal master's awarded for partial completion of doctoral program. *Degree requirements:* For doctorate, thesis/dissertation, qualifying exam. *Entrance requirements:* For master's and doctorate, GRE General Test, GRE Subject Test. Additional exam requirements/recommendations for international students: Required—TOEFL. *Faculty research:* Computer-aided design in process engineering, biomedical engineering, biotechnology, complex fluids.

Case Western Reserve University, School of Graduate Studies, Case School of Engineering, Department of Chemical and Biomolecular Engineering, Cleveland, OH 44106. Offers MS, PhD. *Program availability:* Part-time, evening/weekend, online learning. *Faculty:* 12 full-time (3 women). *Students:* 32 full-time (10 women), 9 part-time (4 women); includes 3 minority (all Asian, non-Hispanic/Latino), 24 international. In 2016, 2 master's, 2 doctorates awarded. Terminal master's awarded for partial completion of doctoral program. *Degree requirements:* For master's, thesis (for some programs); for doctorate, thesis/dissertation, qualifying exam, research proposal, teaching experience. *Entrance requirements:* For master's and doctorate, GRE General Test. Additional exam requirements/recommendations for international students: Required—TOEFL. *Application deadline:* For fall admission, 2/15 priority date for domestic students; for spring admission, 11/1 for domestic students. Applications are processed on a rolling basis. Application fee: $50. *Expenses: Tuition:* Full-time $42,576; part-time $1774 per credit hour. *Required fees:* $34. Tuition and fees vary according to course load and program. *Financial support:* In 2016–17, 22 research assistantships with tuition reimbursements were awarded; Federal Work-Study and institutionally sponsored loans also available. Financial award application deadline: 3/1; financial award applicants required to submit FAFSA. *Faculty research:* Advanced separation methods; design, synthesis, processing and characterization of advanced materials; bio transport and bioprocessing; electrochemical engineering, materials engineering; energy storage and fuel cells. *Total annual research expenditures:* $2.8 million. *Unit head:* Daniel Lacks, Department Chair, 216-368-4238, Fax: 216-368-3016, E-mail: daniel.lacks@case.edu. *Application contact:* Theresa Claytor, Student Affairs Coordinator, 216-368-8555, E-mail: theresa.claytor@case.edu.
Website: http://www.case.edu/cse/eche

City College of the City University of New York, Graduate School, Grove School of Engineering, Department of Chemical Engineering, New York, NY 10031-9198. Offers ME, PhD. PhD program offered jointly with Graduate School and University Center of the City University of New York. *Program availability:* Part-time. *Degree requirements:* For master's, thesis optional; for doctorate, one foreign language, comprehensive exam, thesis/dissertation. *Entrance requirements:* For master's and doctorate, GRE General Test. Additional exam requirements/recommendations for international students: Required—TOEFL (minimum score 500 paper-based; 61 iBT). Tuition and fees vary according to course load, degree level and program. *Faculty research:* Theoretical turbulences, bio-fluid dynamics, polymers, fluidization, transport phenomena.

Chemical Engineering

Clarkson University, Wallace H. Coulter School of Engineering, Department of Chemical and Biomolecular Engineering, Potsdam, NY 13699. Offers chemical engineering (ME, MS, PhD). *Faculty:* 14 full-time (3 women), 1 part-time/adjunct (0 women). *Students:* 24 full-time (3 women), 20 international. 48 applicants, 46% accepted, 7 enrolled. *Degree requirements:* For master's, thesis (for MS); project (for ME); for doctorate, comprehensive exam, thesis/dissertation. *Entrance requirements:* For master's and doctorate, GRE. Additional exam requirements/recommendations for international students: Required—TOEFL (minimum score 550 paper-based, 80 iBT) or IELTS (6.5). *Application deadline:* Applications are processed on a rolling basis. Application fee: $50. Electronic applications accepted. *Expenses: Tuition:* Full-time $23,400; part-time $1300 per credit hour. Tuition and fees vary according to campus/location and program. *Financial support:* Scholarships/grants and unspecified assistantships available. *Unit head:* Dr. John McLaughlin, Chair of Chemical and Biomolecular Engineering, 315-268-6650, E-mail: jmclaugh@clarkson.edu. *Application contact:* Dan Capogna, Graduate Admissions Contact, 518-631-9910, E-mail: graduate@clarkson.edu.
Website: http://graduate.clarkson.edu

Clemson University, Graduate School, College of Engineering, Computing and Applied Sciences, Department of Chemical and Biomolecular Engineering, Clemson, SC 29364. Offers chemical engineering (MS, PhD). *Faculty:* 13 full-time (2 women). *Students:* 47 full-time (17 women); includes 4 minority (1 Black or African American, non-Hispanic/Latino; 3 Asian, non-Hispanic/Latino), 24 international. Average age 26. 131 applicants, 10% accepted, 8 enrolled. In 2016, 5 doctorates awarded. *Degree requirements:* For master's, thesis; for doctorate, comprehensive exam, thesis/dissertation. *Entrance requirements:* For master's and doctorate, GRE General Test, unofficial transcripts, letters of recommendation. Additional exam requirements/recommendations for international students: Required—TOEFL (minimum score 80 iBT), IELTS (minimum score 6.5). *Application deadline:* For fall admission, 2/1 for domestic and international students. Applications are processed on a rolling basis. Application fee: $80 ($90 for international students). Electronic applications accepted. *Expenses:* $4,841 per semester full-time resident, $9,640 per semester full-time non-resident, $612 per credit hour part-time resident, $1,223 per credit hour part-time non-resident. *Financial support:* In 2016–17, 40 students received support, including 2 fellowships with partial tuition reimbursements available (averaging $23,334 per year), 35 research assistantships with partial tuition reimbursements available (averaging $24,914 per year), 17 teaching assistantships with partial tuition reimbursements available (averaging $23,500 per year); career-related internships or fieldwork also available. Financial award application deadline: 2/1. *Faculty research:* Advanced materials, biotechnology, energy, molecular simulation, chemical and biochemical processing. *Total annual research expenditures:* $1.7 million. *Unit head:* Dr. David Bruce, Interim Department Chair, 864-656-5425, E-mail: dbruce@clemson.edu. *Application contact:* Dr. Mark Roberts, Graduate Coordinator, 864-656-6307, E-mail: mrober9@clemson.edu.
Website: https://www.clemson.edu/cecas/departments/chbe/

Cleveland State University, College of Graduate Studies, Fenn College of Engineering, Department of Chemical and Biomedical Engineering, Cleveland, OH 44115. Offers MS, D Eng. *Program availability:* Part-time, evening/weekend. *Faculty:* 12 full-time (1 woman), 26 part-time/adjunct (3 women). *Students:* 48 full-time (15 women), 32 part-time (12 women); includes 8 minority (3 Black or African American, non-Hispanic/Latino; 3 Asian, non-Hispanic/Latino; 2 Hispanic/Latino), 31 international. Average age 26. 126 applicants, 60% accepted, 22 enrolled. In 2016, 20 master's awarded. *Degree requirements:* For master's, project or thesis; for doctorate, thesis/dissertation, candidacy and qualifying exams. *Entrance requirements:* For master's, GRE General Test, minimum GPA of 2.75; for doctorate, GRE General Test, minimum GPA of 3.25. Additional exam requirements/recommendations for international students: Required—TOEFL (minimum score 550 paper-based; 78 iBT). *Application deadline:* For fall admission, 3/15 for domestic and international students. Applications are processed on a rolling basis. Application fee: $40. Electronic applications accepted. *Expenses:* Tuition, state resident: full-time $9565. Tuition, nonresident: full-time $17,980. Tuition and fees vary according to program. *Financial support:* In 2016–17, 34 students received support, including 1 fellowship, 24 research assistantships with tuition reimbursements available (averaging $21,000 per year), 9 teaching assistantships with tuition reimbursements available (averaging $15,000 per year); career-related internships or fieldwork, Federal Work-Study, institutionally sponsored loans, scholarships/grants, tuition waivers (full and partial), and unspecified assistantships also available. Financial award application deadline: 3/30. *Faculty research:* Absorption equilibrium and dynamics, advanced materials processing, biomaterials surface characterization, bioprocessing, cardiovascular mechanics, magnetic resonance imaging, mechanics of biomolecules, metabolic modeling, molecular simulation, process systems engineering, statistical mechanics. *Unit head:* Dr. Joanne M. Belovich, Chairperson, 216-687-3502, Fax: 216-687-9220, E-mail: j.belovich@csuohio.edu. *Application contact:* Becky Laird, Administrative Coordinator, 216-687-2571, Fax: 216-687-9220, E-mail: b.laird@csuohio.edu.
Website: http://www.csuohio.edu/engineering/chemical/

Colorado School of Mines, Office of Graduate Studies, Department of Chemical and Biological Engineering, Golden, CO 80401. Offers MS, PhD. *Program availability:* Part-time. Terminal master's awarded for partial completion of doctoral program. *Degree requirements:* For master's, thesis (for some programs); for doctorate, comprehensive exam, thesis/dissertation. *Entrance requirements:* For master's and doctorate, GRE General Test. Additional exam requirements/recommendations for international students: Required—TOEFL (minimum score 550 paper-based; 80 iBT). Electronic applications accepted. *Expenses:* Tuition, state resident: full-time $15,690. Tuition, nonresident: full-time $34,020. *Required fees:* $2152. Tuition and fees vary according to course load. *Faculty research:* Liquid fuels for the future, responsible management of hazardous substances, surface and interfacial engineering, advanced computational methods and process control, gas hydrates.

Colorado State University, Walter Scott, Jr. College of Engineering, Department of Chemical and Biological Engineering, Fort Collins, CO 80523-1370. Offers chemical engineering (ME, MS, PhD). *Faculty:* 13 full-time (1 woman), 3 part-time/adjunct (1 woman). *Students:* 16 full-time (5 women), 11 part-time (4 women); includes 1 minority (Hispanic/Latino), 14 international. Average age 28. 60 applicants, 2% accepted. In 2016, 2 master's, 3 doctorates awarded. Terminal master's awarded for partial completion of doctoral program. *Degree requirements:* For master's, comprehensive exam (for some programs), thesis (for some programs); for doctorate, comprehensive exam, thesis/dissertation. *Entrance requirements:* For master's and doctorate, GRE General Test, minimum GPA of 3.0. Additional exam requirements/recommendations for international students: Required—PTE (minimum score 58), TOEFL (minimum score 550 paper-based, 80 iBT) or IELTS (6.5). *Application deadline:* For fall admission, 1/15 for domestic and international students; for spring admission, 9/15 for domestic and international students. Application fee: $60 ($70 for international students). Electronic applications accepted. *Expenses:* Contact institution. *Financial support:* In 2016–17, 14 students received support, including 1 fellowship (averaging $20,000 per year), 8 research assistantships (averaging $26,400 per year), 3 teaching assistantships (averaging $19,800 per year); scholarships/grants also available. *Faculty research:* Biological engineering, environmental engineering, mathematical modeling, polymer science, transport phenomena. *Total annual research expenditures:* $2.1 million. *Unit head:* Dr. David Dandy, Department Head and Professor, 970-491-7437, Fax: 970-491-7369, E-mail: david.dandy@colostate.edu. *Application contact:* Denise Morgan, Administrative Assistant, 970-491-5252, Fax: 970-491-7369, E-mail: denise.morgan@colostate.edu. Website: http://www.engr.colostate.edu/cheme/

Columbia University, Fu Foundation School of Engineering and Applied Science, Department of Chemical Engineering, New York, NY 10027. Offers MS, Eng Sc D, PhD. PhD offered through the Graduate School of Arts and Sciences. *Program availability:* Part-time, online learning. *Degree requirements:* For doctorate, thesis/dissertation, qualifying exam. *Entrance requirements:* For master's and doctorate, GRE General Test. Additional exam requirements/recommendations for international students: Required—TOEFL, IELTS, PTE. Electronic applications accepted. *Faculty research:* Molecular design and modification of material surfaces, biophysics and soft matter physics, genomics engineering, interfacial engineering and electrochemistry, protein and metabolic engineering.

Cooper Union for the Advancement of Science and Art, Albert Nerken School of Engineering, New York, NY 10003. Offers chemical engineering (ME); civil engineering (ME); electrical engineering (ME); mechanical engineering (ME). *Program availability:* Part-time. *Faculty:* 27 full-time (1 woman), 15 part-time/adjunct (2 women). *Students:* 36 full-time (5 women), 39 part-time (8 women); includes 34 minority (3 Black or African American, non-Hispanic/Latino; 16 Asian, non-Hispanic/Latino; 5 Hispanic/Latino; 10 Two or more races, non-Hispanic/Latino), 3 international. Average age 24. 59 applicants, 75% accepted, 34 enrolled. In 2016, 25 master's awarded. *Degree requirements:* For master's, thesis (for some programs). *Entrance requirements:* For master's, BE or BS in an engineering discipline; official copies of school transcripts including secondary (high school), college and university work; two letters of recommendation; resume. Additional exam requirements/recommendations for international students: Required—TOEFL (minimum score 600 paper-based; 100 iBT). *Application deadline:* For fall admission, 3/31 for domestic and international students. Application fee: $75. Electronic applications accepted. *Expenses: Tuition:* Full-time $16,055; part-time $1235 per credit. *Required fees:* $925 per semester. One-time fee: $250. Tuition and fees vary according to course load. *Financial support:* In 2016–17, 70 students received support, including 4 fellowships with tuition reimbursements available (averaging $11,000 per year); career-related internships or fieldwork, tuition waivers (full and partial), and tuition scholarships offered to exceptional students also available. Support available to part-time students. Financial award application deadline: 5/1; financial award applicants required to submit FAFSA. *Faculty research:* Civil infrastructure, imaging and sensing technology, biomedical engineering, encryption technology, process engineering. *Unit head:* Richard Stock, Acting Dean of Albert Nerken School of Engineering, 212-353-4285, E-mail: stock@cooper.edu. *Application contact:* Chabeli Lajara, Administrative Assistant, 212-353-4120, E-mail: admissions@cooper.edu.
Website: http://cooper.edu/engineering

Cornell University, Graduate School, Graduate Fields of Engineering, Field of Chemical Engineering, Ithaca, NY 14853. Offers advanced materials processing (M Eng, MS, PhD); applied mathematics and computational methods (M Eng, MS, PhD); biochemical engineering (M Eng, MS, PhD); chemical reaction engineering (M Eng, MS, PhD); classical and statistical thermodynamics (M Eng, MS, PhD); fluid dynamics, rheology and biorheology (M Eng, MS, PhD); heat and mass transfer (M Eng, MS, PhD); kinetics and catalysis (M Eng, MS, PhD); polymers (M Eng, MS, PhD); surface science (M Eng, MS, PhD). *Degree requirements:* For master's, thesis (MS); for doctorate, comprehensive exam, thesis/dissertation. *Entrance requirements:* For master's and doctorate, GRE General Test, 2 letters of recommendation. Additional exam requirements/recommendations for international students: Required—TOEFL (minimum score 600 paper-based; 77 iBT). Electronic applications accepted. *Faculty research:* Biochemical, biomedical and metabolic engineering; fluid and polymer dynamics; surface science and chemical kinetics; electronics materials; microchemical systems and nanotechnology.

Dalhousie University, Faculty of Engineering, Department of Chemical Engineering, Halifax, NS B3J 1Z1, Canada. Offers M Eng, MA Sc, PhD. *Degree requirements:* For master's, thesis; for doctorate, thesis/dissertation. *Entrance requirements:* Additional exam requirements/recommendations for international students: Required—TOEFL, IELTS, CANTEST, CAEL, or Michigan English Language Assessment Battery. Electronic applications accepted. *Faculty research:* Explosions, process optimization, combustion synthesis of materials, waste minimization, treatment of industrial wastewater.

Drexel University, College of Engineering, Department of Chemical and Biological Engineering, Program in Chemical Engineering, Philadelphia, PA 19104-2875. Offers MS, PhD. *Faculty:* 17 full-time (3 women). *Students:* 53 full-time (18 women), 1 (woman) part-time; includes 7 minority (4 Asian, non-Hispanic/Latino; 2 Hispanic/Latino; 1 Two or more races, non-Hispanic/Latino), 28 international. Average age 26. In 2016, 17 master's, 8 doctorates awarded. *Degree requirements:* For doctorate, thesis/dissertation. *Entrance requirements:* For master's, minimum GPA of 3.0; for doctorate, minimum GPA of 3.5, MS in chemical engineering. Additional exam requirements/recommendations for international students: Required—TOEFL. *Application deadline:* For fall admission, 8/21 for domestic students. Applications are processed on a rolling basis. Application fee: $50. Electronic applications accepted. *Expenses: Tuition:* Full-time $32,184; part-time $1192 per credit hour. *Required fees:* $280. Tuition and fees vary according to campus/location and program. *Financial support:* Research assistantships, teaching assistantships, and unspecified assistantships available. Financial award application deadline: 2/1. *Total annual research expenditures:* $3.6 million. *Unit head:* Dr. Charles B. Weinberger, Head, 215-895-2226. *Application contact:* Director of Graduate Admissions, 215-895-6700, Fax: 215-895-5939, E-mail: enroll@drexel.edu.

École Polytechnique de Montréal, Graduate Programs, Department of Chemical Engineering, Montréal, QC H3C 3A7, Canada. Offers M Eng, M Sc A, PhD, DESS. *Program availability:* Part-time, evening/weekend. Terminal master's awarded for partial completion of doctoral program. *Degree requirements:* For master's, one foreign language, thesis; for doctorate, one foreign language, thesis/dissertation. *Entrance requirements:* For master's, minimum GPA of 2.75; for doctorate, minimum GPA of 3.0. Electronic applications accepted. *Faculty research:* Polymer engineering, biochemical and food engineering, reactor engineering and industrial processes pollution control engineering, gas technology.

Fairleigh Dickinson University, College at Florham, Silberman College of Business, Program in Pharmaceutical Studies, Madison, NJ 07940-1099. Offers MBA, Certificate.

Florida Agricultural and Mechanical University, Division of Graduate Studies, Research, and Continuing Education, FAMU-FSU College of Engineering, Department of Chemical and Biomedical Engineering, Tallahassee, FL 32307-3200. Offers biomedical engineering (MS, PhD); chemical engineering (MS, PhD). *Degree requirements:* For master's, thesis optional; for doctorate, thesis/dissertation, paper presentation at professional meeting. *Entrance requirements:* For master's, GRE General Test, minimum GPA of 3.3, letters of recommendation (3); for doctorate, minimum GPA of 3.3. Additional exam requirements/recommendations for international students: Required—TOEFL (minimum score 550 paper-based). *Faculty research:* Cellular signaling, cancer therapy, drug delivery, cellular and tissue engineering, brain physiology.

Florida Institute of Technology, College of Engineering, Program in Chemical Engineering, Melbourne, FL 32901-6975. Offers MS, PhD. *Program availability:* Part-time. *Students:* 8 full-time (4 women), 2 part-time (both women); includes 4 minority (1 Asian, non-Hispanic/Latino; 3 Hispanic/Latino), 4 international. Average age 29. 76 applicants, 16% accepted, 2 enrolled. In 2016, 7 master's awarded. Terminal master's awarded for partial completion of doctoral program. *Degree requirements:* For master's, 30 credit hours, seminar, thesis or capstone project with final exam; for doctorate, comprehensive exam, thesis/dissertation, publication in refereed journals, oral and written exams, research project, minimum of 72 credit hours. *Entrance requirements:* For master's, GRE, resume, 3 letters of recommendation, statement of objectives, undergraduate transcripts; for doctorate, GRE, minimum GPA of 3.5, resume, 3 letters of recommendation, statement of objectives. Additional exam requirements/recommendations for international students: Required—TOEFL (minimum score 550 paper-based; 79 iBT). *Application deadline:* For fall admission, 4/1 for international students; for spring admission, 9/30 for international students. Applications are processed on a rolling basis. Electronic applications accepted. *Expenses: Tuition:* Full-time $22,338; part-time $1241 per credit hour. *Required fees:* $250. Tuition and fees vary according to degree level, campus/location and program. *Financial support:* Research assistantships with tuition reimbursements, teaching assistantships with tuition reimbursements, career-related internships or fieldwork, institutionally sponsored loans, tuition waivers (partial), unspecified assistantships, and tuition remissions available. Support available to part-time students. Financial award application deadline: 3/1; financial award applicants required to submit FAFSA. *Faculty research:* Space technology, biotechnology, materials synthesis and processing, supercritical fluids, water treatment, process control. *Unit head:* Dr. Manolis M. Tomadakis, Department Head, 321-674-7243, Fax: 321-674-7565, E-mail: tomadaki@fit.edu. *Application contact:* Cheryl A. Brown, Associate Director of Graduate Admissions, 321-674-7581, Fax: 321-723-9468, E-mail: cbrown@fit.edu.
Website: http://coe.fit.edu/chemical/

Florida State University, The Graduate School, FAMU-FSU College of Engineering, Department of Chemical and Biomedical Engineering, Tallahassee, FL 32310-6046. Offers biomedical engineering (MS, PhD); chemical engineering (MS, PhD). *Program availability:* Part-time. *Faculty:* 18 full-time (3 women). *Students:* 48 full-time (12 women); includes 4 minority (all Black or African American, non-Hispanic/Latino), 37 international. Average age 25. 84 applicants, 30% accepted, 8 enrolled. In 2016, 11 master's, 4 doctorates awarded. Terminal master's awarded for partial completion of doctoral program. *Degree requirements:* For master's, thesis (for some programs); for doctorate, comprehensive exam, thesis/dissertation, qualifying exam. *Entrance requirements:* For master's, GRE General Test (recommended minimum scores: verbal 151/8th percentile; quantitative: 158/75th percentile), BS in chemical engineering or other physical science/engineering, minimum GPA of 3.0; for doctorate, GRE General Test (recommended minimum scores: verbal 151/8th percentile; quantitative: 158/75th percentile), BS in chemical engineering or other physical science/engineering, minimum GPA of 3.0, or MS in chemical or biomedical engineering. Additional exam requirements/recommendations for international students: Required—TOEFL (minimum score 550 paper-based; 80 iBT), Michigan English Language Assessment Battery (minimum score 77); Recommended—IELTS (minimum score 6.5). *Application deadline:* For fall admission, 3/1 priority date for domestic students, 3/1 for international students; for spring admission, 10/1 for domestic and international students. Applications are processed on a rolling basis. Application fee: $30. Electronic applications accepted. *Expenses:* Contact institution. *Financial support:* In 2016–17, 33 students received support, including 4 fellowships with full tuition reimbursements available (averaging $21,500 per year), 14 research assistantships with full tuition reimbursements available (averaging $21,500 per year), 14 teaching assistantships with full tuition reimbursements available (averaging $21,500 per year); scholarships/grants and unspecified assistantships also available. Financial award application deadline: 3/1; financial award applicants required to submit FAFSA. *Faculty research:* Macromolecular transport and reaction; polymer characterization and processing; solid NMR-MRI for solid state spectroscopy and cell microscopy; protein, cell, and tissue engineering; electrochemical and fuel cell engineering. *Total annual research expenditures:* $1.2 million. *Unit head:* Dr. Teng Ma, Chair and Professor, 850-410-6149, Fax: 850-410-6150, E-mail: tma@fsu.edu. *Application contact:* Lisa Fowler, Office Administrator, 850-410-6151, Fax: 850-410-6150, E-mail: lfowler@fsu.edu.
Website: http://www.eng.famu.fsu.edu/cbe

Georgia Institute of Technology, Graduate Studies, College of Engineering, School of Chemical and Biomolecular Engineering, Atlanta, GA 30332-0001. Offers chemical engineering (MS, PhD). Terminal master's awarded for partial completion of doctoral program. *Degree requirements:* For master's, thesis; for doctorate, comprehensive exam, thesis/dissertation. *Entrance requirements:* For master's and doctorate, GRE. Additional exam requirements/recommendations for international students: Required—TOEFL (minimum score 550 paper-based; 85 iBT). Electronic applications accepted. *Faculty research:* Biochemical engineering; process modeling, synthesis, and control; polymer science and engineering; thermodynamics and separations; surface and particle science.

The Graduate Center, City University of New York, Graduate Studies, Program in Engineering, New York, NY 10016-4039. Offers biomedical engineering (PhD); chemical engineering (PhD); civil engineering (PhD); electrical engineering (PhD); mechanical engineering (PhD). *Degree requirements:* For doctorate, thesis/dissertation. *Entrance requirements:* For doctorate, GRE General Test. Additional exam requirements/recommendations for international students: Required—TOEFL. Electronic applications accepted.

Howard University, College of Engineering, Architecture, and Computer Sciences, School of Engineering and Computer Science, Department of Chemical Engineering, Washington, DC 20059-0002. Offers MS. Offered through the Graduate School of Arts and Sciences. *Program availability:* Part-time. *Degree requirements:* For master's, thesis. *Entrance requirements:* For master's, GRE General Test, minimum GPA of 2.75. Additional exam requirements/recommendations for international students: Required—TOEFL. *Faculty research:* Bioengineering, reactor modeling, environmental engineering, nanotechnology, fuel cells.

Illinois Institute of Technology, Graduate College, Armour College of Engineering, Department of Chemical and Biological Engineering, Chicago, IL 60616. Offers biological engineering (MAS); chemical engineering (MAS, MS, PhD); MS/MAS. *Program availability:* Part-time, evening/weekend, online learning. Terminal master's awarded for partial completion of doctoral program. *Degree requirements:* For master's, comprehensive exam (for some programs), thesis (for some programs); for doctorate, comprehensive exam, thesis/dissertation. *Entrance requirements:* For master's, GRE General Test with minimum score of 950 Quantitative and Verbal, 2.5 Analytical Writing (for MAS); GRE General Test with minimum score of 1100 Quantitative and Verbal, 3.0 Analytical Writing (for MS), minimum undergraduate GPA of 3.0; for doctorate, GRE General Test (minimum score 1100 Quantitative and Verbal, 3.0 Analytical Writing), minimum undergraduate GPA of 3.0. Additional exam requirements/recommendations for international students: Required—TOEFL (minimum score 550 paper-based; 80 iBT). Electronic applications accepted. *Faculty research:* Energy and sustainability, biological engineering, advanced materials, systems engineering.

Instituto Tecnológico y de Estudios Superiores de Monterrey, Campus Monterrey, Graduate and Research Division, Programs in Engineering, Monterrey, Mexico. Offers applied statistics (M Eng); artificial intelligence (PhD); automation engineering (M Eng); chemical engineering (M Eng); civil engineering (M Eng); electrical engineering (M Eng); electronic engineering (M Eng); environmental engineering (M Eng); industrial engineering (M Eng, PhD); manufacturing engineering (M Eng); mechanical engineering (M Eng); systems and quality engineering (M Eng). M Eng program offered jointly with University of Waterloo; PhD in industrial engineering with Texas A&M University. *Program availability:* Part-time, evening/weekend. Terminal master's awarded for partial completion of doctoral program. *Degree requirements:* For master's, one foreign language, thesis; for doctorate, one foreign language, thesis/dissertation. *Entrance requirements:* For master's, EXADEP; for doctorate, GRE, master's degree in related field. Additional exam requirements/recommendations for international students: Required—TOEFL. *Faculty research:* Flexible manufacturing cells, materials, statistical methods, environmental prevention, control and evaluation.

Iowa State University of Science and Technology, Department of Chemical and Biological Engineering, Ames, IA 50011-2230. Offers M Eng, MS, PhD. *Degree requirements:* For master's, thesis (for some programs); for doctorate, thesis/dissertation. *Entrance requirements:* For master's and doctorate, GRE General Test. Additional exam requirements/recommendations for international students: Recommended—TOEFL (minimum score 587 paper-based; 94 iBT), IELTS (minimum score 7). *Application deadline:* For fall admission, 1/15 priority date for domestic and international students; for spring admission, 10/1 for domestic and international students. Application fee: $60 ($100 for international students). Electronic applications accepted. *Unit head:* 515-294-1660, Fax: 515-294-2689, E-mail: chemengr@iastate.edu. *Application contact:* Bellinda Hegelheimer, Application Contact, 515-294-1660, Fax: 515-294-2689, E-mail: chemengr@iastate.edu.
Website: http://www.cbe.iastate.edu

Johns Hopkins University, Engineering Program for Professionals, Part-time Program in Chemical and Biomolecular Engineering, Baltimore, MD 21218. Offers M Ch E. *Program availability:* Part-time, evening/weekend. *Faculty:* 1 full-time (0 women), 3 part-time/adjunct (0 women). *Students:* 6 part-time (4 women); includes 2 minority (1 Black or African American, non-Hispanic/Latino; 1 Hispanic/Latino). Average age 26. 3 applicants, 33% accepted. In 2016, 2 master's awarded. *Entrance requirements:* Additional exam requirements/recommendations for international students: Required—TOEFL (minimum score 600 paper-based; 100 iBT). *Application deadline:* Applications are processed on a rolling basis. Application fee: $0. Electronic applications accepted. *Unit head:* Dr. Michael Betenbaugh, Program Chair, 410-516-5461, E-mail: beten@jhu.edu. *Application contact:* Doug Schiller, Admissions Director, 410-516-2300, Fax: 410-579-8049, E-mail: schiller@jhu.edu.
Website: http://www.ep.jhu.edu

Johns Hopkins University, G. W. C. Whiting School of Engineering, Department of Chemical and Biomolecular Engineering, Baltimore, MD 21218. Offers MSE, PhD. *Faculty:* 21 full-time (7 women), 2 part-time/adjunct (1 woman). *Students:* 141 full-time (47 women); includes 26 minority (5 Black or African American, non-Hispanic/Latino; 11 Asian, non-Hispanic/Latino; 6 Hispanic/Latino; 4 Two or more races, non-Hispanic/Latino), 70 international. Average age 24. 306 applicants, 56% accepted, 56 enrolled. In 2016, 23 master's, 14 doctorates awarded. Terminal master's awarded for partial completion of doctoral program. *Degree requirements:* For master's, essay presentation; for doctorate, thesis/dissertation, oral exam; thesis presentation. *Entrance requirements:* For master's and doctorate, GRE General Test, 3 letters of recommendation, statement of purpose, transcripts. Additional exam requirements/recommendations for international students: Required—TOEFL (minimum score 600 paper-based, 100 iBT) or IELTS (7). *Application deadline:* For fall admission, 1/5 for domestic and international students. Application fee: $25. Electronic applications accepted. *Financial support:* In 2016–17, 84 students received support, including 9 fellowships with full and partial tuition reimbursements available (averaging $34,008 per year), 75 research assistantships with full tuition reimbursements available (averaging $29,496 per year); teaching assistantships with full and partial tuition reimbursements available, career-related internships or fieldwork, Federal Work-Study, institutionally sponsored loans, scholarships/grants, health care benefits, tuition waivers (partial), and unspecified assistantships also available. Support available to part-time students. Financial award application deadline: 1/15. *Faculty research:* Engineering in health and disease, biomolecular design and engineering, materials by design, micro and nanotechnology, alternative energy and sustainability. *Total annual research expenditures:* $14.7 million. *Unit head:* Dr. Konstantinos Konstantopoulos, Chair and Professor, 410-516-7170, Fax: 410-516-5510, E-mail: kkonsta1@jhu.edu. *Application contact:* Kailey Dille, Academic Program Coordinator, 410-516-4166, Fax: 410-516-5510, E-mail: kdille@jhu.edu.
Website: http://engineering.jhu.edu/chembe/

Kansas State University, Graduate School, College of Engineering, Department of Chemical Engineering, Manhattan, KS 66506. Offers MS, PhD, Graduate Certificate. *Program availability:* Online learning. *Faculty:* 8 full-time (2 women), 4 part-time/adjunct (0 women). *Students:* 21 full-time (6 women), 17 part-time (4 women); includes 7 minority (4 Black or African American, non-Hispanic/Latino; 1 Asian, non-Hispanic/Latino; 1 Hispanic/Latino; 1 Two or more races, non-Hispanic/Latino), 19 international. Average age 30. 53 applicants, 34% accepted, 11 enrolled. In 2016, 1 master's, 2 doctorates, 1 other advanced degree awarded. Terminal master's awarded for partial completion of doctoral program. *Degree requirements:* For master's, thesis, 24 hours of coursework; 6 hours of thesis; for doctorate, thesis/dissertation, 90 hours of credit. *Entrance requirements:* For doctorate, GRE. Additional exam requirements/recommendations for international students: Required—TOEFL. *Application deadline:* For fall admission, 2/1 priority date for domestic students, 1/1 priority date for international students; for spring admission, 8/1 priority date for domestic and international students. Applications are processed on a rolling basis. Application fee: $50 ($75 for international students). Electronic applications accepted. *Expenses:* Tuition, state resident: full-time $9670. Tuition, nonresident: full-time $21,828. *Required fees:* $862. *Financial support:* In 2016–17, 12 research assistantships with full tuition reimbursements (averaging $22,205 per year), 3 teaching assistantships with partial tuition reimbursements (averaging $22,300 per year) were awarded; fellowships with partial tuition reimbursements, scholarships/grants, and tuition waivers (full) also available. Financial award application deadline: 3/1; financial award applicants required to submit FAFSA. *Faculty research:* Renewable sustainable energy, molecular engineering, advanced materials. *Unit head:* Dr. James Edgar, Head, 785-532-5584, Fax: 785-532-7372, E-mail: che@ksu.edu.
Website: http://www.che.ksu.edu/

Lamar University, College of Graduate Studies, College of Engineering, Dan F. Smith Department of Chemical Engineering, Beaumont, TX 77710. Offers ME, PhD. *Faculty:* 12 full-time (1 woman). *Students:* 80 full-time (18 women), 47 part-time (6 women);

includes 6 minority (3 Asian, non-Hispanic/Latino; 2 Hispanic/Latino; 1 Two or more races, non-Hispanic/Latino), 118 international. Average age 26. 53 applicants, 100% accepted, 20 enrolled. In 2016, 41 master's, 5 doctorates awarded. *Degree requirements:* For master's, comprehensive exam (for some programs), thesis (for some programs); for doctorate, comprehensive exam, thesis/dissertation. *Entrance requirements:* For master's and doctorate, GRE General Test. Additional exam requirements/recommendations for international students: Required—TOEFL (minimum score 550 paper-based; 79 iBT), IELTS (minimum score 6.5). *Application deadline:* For fall admission, 8/10 for domestic students, 7/1 for international students; for spring admission, 1/5 for domestic students, 12/1 for international students. Applications are processed on a rolling basis. Application fee: $25 ($50 for international students). Electronic applications accepted. *Expenses:* $8,134 in-state full-time, $5,574 in-state part-time; $15,604 out-of-state full-time, $10,554 out-of-state part-time per year. *Financial support:* Fellowships with partial tuition reimbursements, research assistantships with partial tuition reimbursements, teaching assistantships with partial tuition reimbursements, and tuition waivers (full and partial) available. Financial award application deadline: 4/1; financial award applicants required to submit FAFSA. *Faculty research:* Flare minimization, process optimization, process integration. *Unit head:* Dr. Thomas C. Ho, Chair, 409-880-8784, Fax: 409-880-2197, E-mail: che_dept@lamar.edu. *Application contact:* Deidre Mayer, Interim Director, Admissions and Academic Services, 409-880-8888, Fax: 409-880-7419, E-mail: gradmissions@lamar.edu.
Website: http://engineering.lamar.edu/chemical

Lehigh University, P.C. Rossin College of Engineering and Applied Science, Department of Chemical and Biomolecular Engineering, Bethlehem, PA 18015. Offers biological chemical engineering (M Eng); chemical energy engineering (M Eng); chemical engineering (M Eng, MS, PhD); MBA/E. *Program availability:* Part-time, 100% online. *Faculty:* 23 full-time (4 women), 1 part-time/adjunct (0 women). *Students:* 56 full-time (24 women), 24 part-time (9 women); includes 11 minority (2 Black or African American, non-Hispanic/Latino; 6 Asian, non-Hispanic/Latino; 3 Hispanic/Latino), 44 international. Average age 27. 218 applicants, 32% accepted, 27 enrolled. In 2016, 14 master's, 6 doctorates awarded. Terminal master's awarded for partial completion of doctoral program. *Degree requirements:* For master's, thesis (for some programs); for doctorate, comprehensive exam, thesis/dissertation. *Entrance requirements:* For master's and doctorate, GRE General Test. Additional exam requirements/recommendations for international students: Required—TOEFL (minimum score 79 iBT), IELTS (minimum score 6.5). *Application deadline:* For fall admission, 7/15 for domestic students, 7/15 priority date for international students; for spring admission, 12/1 for domestic and international students. Application fee: $75. Electronic applications accepted. *Expenses:* $1,420 per credit. *Financial support:* In 2016–17, 42 students received support, including 4 fellowships with full tuition reimbursements available (averaging $28,140 per year), 33 research assistantships with full tuition reimbursements available (averaging $28,140 per year), 5 teaching assistantships with full tuition reimbursements available (averaging $28,704 per year); career-related internships or fieldwork, institutionally sponsored loans, scholarships/grants, health care benefits, and unspecified assistantships also available. Financial award application deadline: 1/15. *Faculty research:* Process control, energy, biotechnology, catalysis, polymers. *Total annual research expenditures:* $2.8 million. *Unit head:* Dr. Mayuresh V. Kothare, Chairman, 610-758-6654, Fax: 610-758-5057, E-mail: mvk2@lehigh.edu. *Application contact:* Barbara A. Kessler, Graduate Coordinator, 610-758-4261, Fax: 610-758-5057, E-mail: inchegs@mail.lehigh.edu.
Website: http://www.che.lehigh.edu/

Louisiana State University and Agricultural & Mechanical College, Graduate School, College of Engineering, Cain Department of Chemical Engineering, Baton Rouge, LA 70803. Offers MS Ch E, PhD.

Louisiana Tech University, Graduate School, College of Engineering and Science, Department of Chemical Engineering, Ruston, LA 71272. Offers MS. *Program availability:* Part-time. Terminal master's awarded for partial completion of doctoral program. *Degree requirements:* For master's, thesis. *Entrance requirements:* For master's, GRE General Test, minimum GPA of 3.0 in last 60 hours. Additional exam requirements/recommendations for international students: Required—TOEFL (minimum score 550 paper-based; 80 iBT). *Application deadline:* For fall admission, 8/1 for domestic students; for spring admission, 2/1 for domestic students. Applications are processed on a rolling basis. Application fee: $20 ($30 for international students). *Financial support:* Fellowships, research assistantships, teaching assistantships, Federal Work-Study, and unspecified assistantships available. Financial award application deadline: 4/1. *Faculty research:* Artificial intelligence, biotechnology, hazardous waste process safety. *Unit head:* Dr. Eric Sherer, Program Chair, 318-257-3236, Fax: 318-257-2562, E-mail: esherer@latech.edu. *Application contact:* Marilyn J. Robinson, Assistant to the Dean, 318-257-2924, Fax: 318-257-4487.
Website: http://coes.latech.edu/chemical-engineering/

Manhattan College, Graduate Programs, School of Engineering, Program in Chemical Engineering, Riverdale, NY 10471. Offers chemical engineering (MS). *Program availability:* Part-time, evening/weekend. *Faculty:* 2 full-time (0 women), 4 part-time/adjunct (0 women). *Students:* 25 full-time (14 women), 4 part-time (2 women); includes 10 minority (1 Black or African American, non-Hispanic/Latino; 6 Asian, non-Hispanic/Latino; 3 Hispanic/Latino). Average age 22. 33 applicants, 94% accepted, 25 enrolled. In 2016, 21 master's awarded. *Degree requirements:* For master's, 30 credits with minimum GPA of 3.0. *Entrance requirements:* For master's, GRE (recommended), minimum GPA of 3.0. Additional exam requirements/recommendations for international students: Required—TOEFL (minimum score 550 paper-based; 80 iBT), IELTS (minimum score 6). *Application deadline:* For fall admission, 8/10 priority date for domestic students, 8/10 for international students; for spring admission, 1/7 for domestic and international students. Applications are processed on a rolling basis. Application fee: $60. Electronic applications accepted. *Expenses:* Contact institution. *Financial support:* In 2016–17, 11 students received support. Scholarships/grants and unspecified assistantships available. Financial award application deadline: 2/1. *Faculty research:* Department of energy, collagen. *Unit head:* Dr. Moujalli Hourani, Interim Chairperson, 718-862-7172, Fax: 718-862-7819, E-mail: chmldept@manhattan.edu. *Application contact:* Kathy Ciarletta, Administrative Assistant, 718-862-7185, Fax: 718-862-7819, E-mail: kathy.ciarletta@manhattan.edu.

Massachusetts Institute of Technology, School of Engineering, Department of Chemical Engineering, Cambridge, MA 02139. Offers chemical engineering (PhD, Sc D); chemical engineering practice (SM, PhD); SM/MBA. *Faculty:* 35 full-time (8 women). *Students:* 232 full-time (67 women); includes 52 minority (2 Black or African American, non-Hispanic/Latino; 36 Asian, non-Hispanic/Latino; 8 Hispanic/Latino; 6 Two or more races, non-Hispanic/Latino), 90 international. Average age 26. 525 applicants, 12% accepted, 43 enrolled. In 2016, 45 master's, 31 doctorates awarded. *Degree requirements:* For master's, thesis (for some programs), one-semester industrial internship; for doctorate, comprehensive exam, thesis/dissertation. *Entrance requirements:* For master's and doctorate, GRE General Test. Additional exam requirements/recommendations for international students: Required—TOEFL, IELTS. *Application deadline:* For fall admission, 12/1 for domestic and international students. Application fee: $75. Electronic applications accepted. *Expenses: Tuition:* Full-time $46,400; part-time $725 per credit. One-time fee: $312 full-time. Full-time tuition and fees vary according to course load and program. *Financial support:* In 2016–17, 212 students received support, including fellowships (averaging $43,000 per year), 127 research assistantships (averaging $40,600 per year), 18 teaching assistantships (averaging $44,400 per year); Federal Work-Study, institutionally sponsored loans, scholarships/grants, traineeships, health care benefits, unspecified assistantships, and resident tutors also available. Support available to part-time students. Financial award application deadline: 5/1; financial award applicants required to submit FAFSA. *Faculty research:* Catalysis and reaction engineering, biological engineering, materials and polymers, surfaces and nanostructures, thermodynamics and molecular computation. *Total annual research expenditures:* $54 million. *Unit head:* Prof. Paula Hammond, Department Head, 617-253-4561, Fax: 617-258-8992. *Application contact:* 617-253-4561, E-mail: chemegrad@mit.edu.
Website: http://web.mit.edu/cheme/

McGill University, Faculty of Graduate and Postdoctoral Studies, Faculty of Engineering, Department of Chemical Engineering, Montréal, QC H3A 2T5, Canada. Offers chemical engineering (M Eng, PhD); environmental engineering (M Eng).

McMaster University, School of Graduate Studies, Faculty of Engineering, Department of Chemical Engineering, Hamilton, ON L8S 4M2, Canada. Offers M Eng, MA Sc, PhD. *Degree requirements:* For master's, thesis; for doctorate, comprehensive exam, thesis/dissertation. *Entrance requirements:* For master's, minimum B average in the last two years. Additional exam requirements/recommendations for international students: Required—TOEFL (minimum score 550 paper-based). *Faculty research:* Biomaterials, computer process control, polymer processing, environmental biotechnology, reverse osmosis.

McNeese State University, Doré School of Graduate Studies, College of Engineering and Engineering Technology, Department of Engineering, Master of Engineering Program, Lake Charles, LA 70609. Offers chemical engineering (M Eng); civil engineering (M Eng); electrical engineering (M Eng); engineering management (M Eng); mechanical engineering (M Eng). *Program availability:* Part-time, evening/weekend. *Degree requirements:* For master's, thesis or alternative. *Entrance requirements:* For master's, GRE, baccalaureate degree, minimum overall GPA of 3.0. Additional exam requirements/recommendations for international students: Required—TOEFL (minimum score 560 paper-based; 83 iBT).

Miami University, College of Engineering and Computing, Department of Chemical, Paper and Biomedical Engineering, Oxford, OH 45056. Offers MS. *Students:* 14 full-time (4 women), 4 part-time (3 women); includes 2 minority (both Asian, non-Hispanic/Latino), 11 international. Average age 24. In 2016, 7 master's awarded. *Expenses:* Tuition, state resident: full-time $12,890; part-time $564 per credit hour. Tuition, nonresident: full-time $29,604; part-time $1260 per credit hour. *Required fees:* $638. Part-time tuition and fees vary according to course load and program. *Unit head:* Dr. Shashi Lalvani, Chair, 513-529-0763, E-mail: lalvansb@miamioh.edu. *Application contact:* Department of Chemical, Paper and Biomedical Engineering, 513-529-0760, E-mail: paper@miamioh.edu.
Website: http://miamioh.edu/cec/academics/departments/cpb/

Michigan State University, The Graduate School, College of Engineering, Department of Chemical Engineering and Materials Science, East Lansing, MI 48824. Offers chemical engineering (MS, PhD); materials science and engineering (MS, PhD). *Entrance requirements:* Additional exam requirements/recommendations for international students: Required—TOEFL. Electronic applications accepted.

Michigan Technological University, Graduate School, College of Engineering, Department of Chemical Engineering, Houghton, MI 49931. Offers MS, PhD. *Program availability:* Part-time. *Faculty:* 22 full-time (5 women), 2 part-time/adjunct. *Students:* 37 full-time (12 women), 3 part-time; includes 3 minority (1 Black or African American, non-Hispanic/Latino; 2 Two or more races, non-Hispanic/Latino), 26 international. Average age 27. 185 applicants, 28% accepted, 5 enrolled. In 2016, 8 master's, 4 doctorates awarded. Terminal master's awarded for partial completion of doctoral program. *Degree requirements:* For master's, comprehensive exam (for some programs), thesis (for some programs); for doctorate, comprehensive exam, thesis/dissertation. *Entrance requirements:* For master's and doctorate, GRE, statement of purpose, personal statement, official transcripts, 2 letters of recommendation. Additional exam requirements/recommendations for international students: Required—TOEFL (minimum score 94 iBT) or IELTS (recommended minimum score of 7.0). *Application deadline:* For fall admission, 1/15 priority date for domestic and international students. Applications are processed on a rolling basis. Electronic applications accepted. *Expenses:* Contact institution. *Financial support:* In 2016–17, 36 students received support, including 2 fellowships with tuition reimbursements available (averaging $15,242 per year), 8 research assistantships with tuition reimbursements available (averaging $15,242 per year), 9 teaching assistantships with tuition reimbursements available (averaging $15,242 per year); career-related internships or fieldwork, Federal Work-Study, scholarships/grants, health care benefits, unspecified assistantships, and cooperative program also available. Financial award applicants required to submit FAFSA. *Faculty research:* Polymer engineering, thermodynamics, chemical process safety, surface science/catalysis, environmental chemical engineering. *Total annual research expenditures:* $900,305. *Unit head:* Dr. Komar Kawatra, Chair, 906-487-3132, Fax: 906-487-3213, E-mail: skkawatr@mtu.edu. *Application contact:* Taana Kalliainen, Staff Assistant, 906-487-3211, Fax: 906-487-3213, E-mail: taana@mtu.edu.
Website: http://www.mtu.edu/chemical/

Mississippi State University, Bagley College of Engineering, Dave C. Swalm School of Chemical Engineering, Mississippi State, MS 39762. Offers MS, PhD. *Faculty:* 9 full-time (1 woman). *Students:* 14 full-time (4 women), 5 part-time (1 woman); includes 1 minority (Black or African American, non-Hispanic/Latino), 16 international. Average age 29. 26 applicants, 31% accepted, 5 enrolled. In 2016, 5 master's, 1 doctorate awarded. *Degree requirements:* For master's, comprehensive exam or thesis; for doctorate, comprehensive exam, thesis/dissertation. *Entrance requirements:* For master's, GRE, minimum GPA of 3.0 on last 64 undergraduate hours; for doctorate, GRE, minimum GPA of 3.2 on last 64 undergraduate hours. Additional exam requirements/recommendations for international students: Required—TOEFL (minimum score 550 paper-based; 79 iBT); Recommended—IELTS (minimum score 6.5). *Application deadline:* For fall admission, 4/1 priority date for domestic students, 5/1 for international students; for spring admission, 8/1 priority date for domestic students, 9/1 for international students. Applications are processed on a rolling basis. Application fee: $60. Electronic applications accepted. *Expenses:* Tuition, state resident: full-time $7670; part-time $852.50 per credit hour. Tuition, nonresident: full-time $20,790; part-time $2310.50 per credit hour. Part-time tuition and fees vary according to course load. *Financial support:* In 2016–17, 10 research assistantships with full tuition reimbursements (averaging $16,589 per year), 4 teaching assistantships with full tuition reimbursements (averaging $16,288 per year) were awarded; Federal Work-Study, institutionally sponsored loans, and unspecified assistantships also available. Financial award application deadline: 4/1; financial award applicants required to submit FAFSA. *Faculty research:* Thermodynamics, composite materials, catalysis, surface science, environmental engineering. *Total annual research expenditures:* $2.2 million. *Unit head:* Dr. Bill Elmore, Interim Director, 662-325-2480, Fax: 662-325-2482, E-mail: elmore@

che.msstate.edu. *Application contact:* Doretta Martin, Senior Admissions Assistant, 662-325-9514, E-mail: dmartin@grad.msstate.edu.
Website: http://www.che.msstate.edu/

Missouri University of Science and Technology, Graduate School, Department of Chemical and Biological Engineering, Rolla, MO 65409. Offers chemical engineering (MS, DE, PhD). *Degree requirements:* For master's, thesis optional; for doctorate, comprehensive exam. *Entrance requirements:* For master's, GRE (minimum score 1100 verbal and quantitative, 4 writing); for doctorate, GRE (minimum score: verbal and quantitative 1200, writing 4). *Additional exam requirements/recommendations for international students:* Required—TOEFL (minimum score 550 paper-based). Electronic applications accepted. *Faculty research:* Mixing, fluid mechanics, bioengineering, freeze-drying, extraction.

Montana State University, The Graduate School, College of Engineering, Department of Chemical and Biological Engineering, Bozeman, MT 59717. Offers chemical engineering (MS); engineering (PhD), including chemical engineering option, environmental engineering option; environmental engineering (MS). *Program availability:* Part-time. *Degree requirements:* For master's, comprehensive exam, thesis (for some programs); for doctorate, comprehensive exam, thesis/dissertation. *Entrance requirements:* For master's and doctorate, GRE General Test. *Additional exam requirements/recommendations for international students:* Required—TOEFL (minimum score 550 paper-based). Electronic applications accepted. *Faculty research:* Metabolic network analysis and engineering; magnetic resonance microscopy; modeling of biological systems; the development of protective coatings on planar solid oxide fuel cell (SOFC) metallic interconnects; characterizing corrosion mechanisms of materials in precisely-controlled exposures; testing materials in poly-crystalline silicon production environments; environmental biotechnology and bioremediation.

New Jersey Institute of Technology, Newark College of Engineering, Newark, NJ 07102. Offers biomedical engineering (MS, PhD); chemical engineering (MS, PhD); computer engineering (MS, PhD); electrical engineering (MS, PhD); engineering management (MS); environmental engineering (PhD); healthcare systems management (MS); industrial engineering (MS, PhD); Internet engineering (MS); manufacturing engineering (MS); mechanical engineering (MS, PhD); occupational safety and health engineering (MS); pharmaceutical bioprocessing (MS); pharmaceutical engineering (MS); pharmaceutical systems management (MS); power and energy systems (MS); telecommunications (MS); transportation (MS, PhD). *Program availability:* Part-time, evening/weekend. *Faculty:* 146 full-time (21 women), 119 part-time/adjunct (10 women). *Students:* 804 full-time (191 women), 550 part-time (129 women); includes 357 minority (82 Black or African American, non-Hispanic/Latino; 1 American Indian or Alaska Native, non-Hispanic/Latino; 138 Asian, non-Hispanic/Latino; 114 Hispanic/Latino; 22 Two or more races, non-Hispanic/Latino), 675 international. Average age 27. 2,959 applicants, 51% accepted, 442 enrolled. In 2016, 595 master's, 29 doctorates awarded. Terminal master's awarded for partial completion of doctoral program. *Degree requirements:* For master's, thesis optional; for doctorate, thesis/dissertation. *Entrance requirements:* For master's, GRE General Test; for doctorate, GRE General Test, minimum graduate GPA of 3.5. *Additional exam requirements/recommendations for international students:* Required—TOEFL (minimum score 550 paper-based; 79 iBT). *Application deadline:* For fall admission, 6/1 priority date for domestic students, 5/1 priority date for international students; for spring admission, 11/15 priority date for domestic and international students. Applications are processed on a rolling basis. Application fee: $75. Electronic applications accepted. *Expenses:* Contact institution. *Financial support:* In 2016–17, 172 students received support, including 1 fellowship (averaging $1,528 per year), 79 research assistantships (averaging $13,336 per year), 92 teaching assistantships (averaging $20,619 per year); scholarships/grants also available. Financial award application deadline: 1/15. *Faculty research:* Nonlinear signal processing, intelligent medical image analysis, calibration issues in coherent localization, computer-aided design, neural network for tool wear measurement. *Total annual research expenditures:* $11.1 million. *Unit head:* Dr. Moshe Kam, Dean, 973-596-5534, E-mail: moshe.kam@njit.edu. *Application contact:* Stephen Eck, Director of Admissions, 973-596-3300, Fax: 973-596-3461, E-mail: admissions@njit.edu.
Website: http://engineering.njit.edu/

New Mexico State University, College of Engineering, Department of Chemical and Materials Engineering, Las Cruces, NM 88003. Offers MS Ch E, PhD. *Program availability:* Part-time. *Faculty:* 9 full-time (4 women). *Students:* 31 full-time (9 women), 6 part-time (1 woman); includes 5 minority (1 Asian, non-Hispanic/Latino; 3 Hispanic/Latino; 1 Two or more races, non-Hispanic/Latino), 24 international. Average age 28. 36 applicants, 56% accepted, 8 enrolled. In 2016, 16 master's, 6 doctorates awarded. Terminal master's awarded for partial completion of doctoral program. *Degree requirements:* For master's, thesis (for some programs); for doctorate, comprehensive exam, thesis/dissertation, qualifying exam. *Entrance requirements:* For master's and doctorate, GRE General Test. *Additional exam requirements/recommendations for international students:* Required—TOEFL (minimum score 550 paper-based; 79 iBT), IELTS (minimum score 6.5). *Application deadline:* For fall admission, 3/1 priority date for domestic and international students; for spring admission, 11/1 priority date for domestic and international students. Applications are processed on a rolling basis. Application fee: $40 ($50 for international students). Electronic applications accepted. *Expenses:* Tuition, state resident: full-time $4086. Tuition, nonresident: full-time $14,254. *Required fees:* $853. Tuition and fees vary according to course load. *Financial support:* In 2016–17, 34 students received support, including 3 fellowships (averaging $4,088 per year), 14 research assistantships (averaging $17,521 per year), 9 teaching assistantships (averaging $15,703 per year); career-related internships or fieldwork, Federal Work-Study, scholarships/grants, traineeships, health care benefits, and unspecified assistantships also available. Support available to part-time students. Financial award application deadline: 3/1. *Faculty research:* Separations, advanced materials, computer modeling and simulation, energy, biomaterials, polymers/rheology, water. *Total annual research expenditures:* $961,218. *Unit head:* Dr. David A. Rockstraw, Department Head, 575-646-1214, Fax: 575-646-7706, E-mail: drockstr@nmsu.edu. *Application contact:* Dr. Hongmei A. Luo, Graduate Student Admissions Coordinator, 575-646-1214, Fax: 575-646-7706, E-mail: hluo@nmsu.edu.
Website: http://chme.nmsu.edu/

New York University, Polytechnic School of Engineering, Department of Chemical and Biomolecular Engineering, Major in Chemical Engineering, New York, NY 10012-1019. Offers MS, PhD. *Program availability:* Part-time, evening/weekend. *Degree requirements:* For master's, comprehensive exam (for some programs), thesis (for some programs); for doctorate, comprehensive exam, thesis/dissertation. *Entrance requirements:* For master's, GRE General Test, BS in chemical engineering; for doctorate, GRE General Test. *Additional exam requirements/recommendations for international students:* Required—TOEFL (minimum score 550 paper-based; 80 iBT); Recommended—IELTS (minimum score 6.5). Electronic applications accepted. *Faculty research:* Plasma polymerization, crystallization of organic compounds, dipolar relaxations in reactive polymers.

North Carolina Agricultural and Technical State University, School of Graduate Studies, College of Engineering, Department of Chemical and Bioengineering, Greensboro, NC 27411. Offers bioengineering (MS); biological engineering (MS); chemical engineering (MS).

North Carolina State University, Graduate School, College of Engineering, Department of Chemical and Biomolecular Engineering, Raleigh, NC 27695. Offers chemical engineering (M Ch E, MS, PhD). *Program availability:* Part-time. Terminal master's awarded for partial completion of doctoral program. *Degree requirements:* For master's, thesis optional; for doctorate, thesis/dissertation. *Entrance requirements:* For master's and doctorate, GRE General Test. *Additional exam requirements/recommendations for international students:* Required—TOEFL. Electronic applications accepted. *Faculty research:* Molecular thermodynamics and computer simulation, catalysis, kinetics, electrochemical reaction engineering, biochemical engineering.

Northeastern University, College of Engineering, Boston, MA 02115-5096. Offers bioengineering (MS, PhD); chemical engineering (MS, PhD); civil engineering (MS, PhD); computer engineering (PhD); computer systems engineering (MS); electrical and computer engineering (MS); electrical and computer engineering leadership (MS); electrical engineering (PhD); energy systems (MS); engineering and public policy (MS); engineering management (MS, Certificate); environmental engineering (MS); industrial engineering (MS, PhD); information assurance (PhD); information systems (MS); interdisciplinary engineering (PhD); mechanical engineering (PhD); operations research (MS); telecommunication systems management (MS). *Program availability:* Part-time, online learning. *Faculty:* 202 full-time (59 women), 53 part-time/adjunct (9 women). *Students:* 2,982 full-time (954 women), 192 part-time (38 women). In 2016, 851 master's, 74 doctorates awarded. Application fee: $75. Electronic applications accepted. *Expenses:* $1,471 per credit. *Financial support:* Fellowships, research assistantships, teaching assistantships, career-related internships or fieldwork, scholarships/grants, health care benefits, tuition waivers, and unspecified assistantships available. Support available to part-time students. Financial award applicants required to submit FAFSA. *Unit head:* Dr. Nadine Aubry, Dean, College of Engineering. *Application contact:* Jeffery Hengel, Director of Graduate Admissions, 617-373-2711, E-mail: j.hengel@northeastern.edu.
Website: http://www.coe.neu.edu/academics/graduate-school-engineering

Northwestern University, McCormick School of Engineering and Applied Science, Department of Chemical and Biological Engineering, Evanston, IL 60208. Offers biotechnology (MS); chemical engineering (MS, PhD). Admissions and degrees offered through The Graduate School. *Program availability:* Part-time. Terminal master's awarded for partial completion of doctoral program. *Degree requirements:* For master's, comprehensive exam (for some programs), thesis optional; for doctorate, comprehensive exam, thesis/dissertation. *Entrance requirements:* For master's and doctorate, GRE General Test. *Additional exam requirements/recommendations for international students:* Required—TOEFL (minimum score 577 paper-based; 90 iBT), IELTS (minimum score 7). Electronic applications accepted. *Faculty research:* Biotechnology, bioengineering, complexity, energy, sustainability, materials, nanoengineering, and synthetic biology.

The Ohio State University, Graduate School, College of Engineering, Department of Chemical and Biomolecular Engineering, Columbus, OH 43210. Offers chemical engineering (MS, PhD). *Faculty:* 26. *Students:* 98 full-time (29 women), 4 part-time (2 women). Average age 25. In 2016, 7 master's, 16 doctorates awarded. *Degree requirements:* For master's, thesis; for doctorate, thesis/dissertation. *Entrance requirements:* For master's, GRE; for doctorate, GRE (highly recommend minimum score of 75% in Verbal and Quantitative and 4.0 in Analytical Writing). *Additional exam requirements/recommendations for international students:* Required—TOEFL (minimum score 600 paper-based; 100 iBT), Michigan English Language Assessment Battery (minimum score 86); Recommended—IELTS (minimum score 8). *Application deadline:* For fall admission, 12/13 priority date for domestic students, 11/30 priority date for international students; for spring admission, 10/1 for domestic and international students. Applications are processed on a rolling basis. Application fee: $60 ($70 for international students). Electronic applications accepted. *Financial support:* Fellowships with tuition reimbursements, research assistantships with tuition reimbursements, teaching assistantships with tuition reimbursements, career-related internships or fieldwork, Federal Work-Study, institutionally sponsored loans, and unspecified assistantships available. Support available to part-time students. *Unit head:* Dr. Andre Palmer, Chair, 614-292-6033, E-mail: palmer.351@osu.edu. *Application contact:* Graduate and Professional Admissions, 614-292-9444, Fax: 614-292-3895, E-mail: gpadmissions@osu.edu.
Website: http://www.cbe.osu.edu

Ohio University, Graduate College, Russ College of Engineering and Technology, Department of Chemical and Biomolecular Engineering, Athens, OH 45701-2979. Offers biomedical engineering (MS); chemical engineering (MS, PhD). *Program availability:* Part-time. *Degree requirements:* For master's, comprehensive exam (for some programs), thesis; for doctorate, comprehensive exam, thesis/dissertation, qualifying exams. *Entrance requirements:* For master's and doctorate, GRE General Test. *Additional exam requirements/recommendations for international students:* Required—TOEFL (minimum score 590 paper-based; 96 iBT) or IELTS (minimum score 7). *Application deadline:* For fall admission, 3/1 priority date for domestic and international students. Applications are processed on a rolling basis. Application fee: $50 ($55 for international students). Electronic applications accepted. *Financial support:* Fellowships with full tuition reimbursements, research assistantships with full tuition reimbursements, teaching assistantships with full tuition reimbursements, Federal Work-Study, institutionally sponsored loans, and unspecified assistantships available. Financial award application deadline: 3/1; financial award applicants required to submit FAFSA. *Faculty research:* Corrosion and multiphase flow, biochemical engineering, thin film materials, air pollution modeling and control, biomedical engineering. *Unit head:* Dr. Valerie L. Young, Chair, 740-593-1496, Fax: 740-593-0873, E-mail: youngv@ohio.edu. *Application contact:* Dr. Daniel A. Gulino, Assistant Chair for Graduate Studies, 740-593-1495, Fax: 740-593-0873, E-mail: gulino@ohio.edu.
Website: http://www.ohio.edu/chemical/

Oklahoma State University, College of Engineering, Architecture and Technology, School of Chemical Engineering, Stillwater, OK 74078. Offers MS, PhD. *Faculty:* 17 full-time (3 women), 1 part-time/adjunct (0 women). *Students:* 22 full-time (4 women), 22 part-time (6 women); includes 4 minority (1 American Indian or Alaska Native, non-Hispanic/Latino; 2 Asian, non-Hispanic/Latino; 1 Two or more races, non-Hispanic/Latino), 26 international. Average age 29. 65 applicants, 17% accepted, 11 enrolled. In 2016, 7 master's, 6 doctorates awarded. *Degree requirements:* For master's, thesis or alternative; for doctorate, comprehensive exam, thesis/dissertation. *Entrance requirements:* For master's and doctorate, GRE or GMAT. *Additional exam requirements/recommendations for international students:* Required—TOEFL (minimum score 550 paper-based; 79 iBT). *Application deadline:* For fall admission, 3/1 priority date for international students; for spring admission, 8/1 priority date for international students. Applications are processed on a rolling basis. Application fee: $40 ($75 for international students). Electronic applications accepted. *Expenses:* Tuition, state resident: full-time $3775; part-time $209.70 per credit hour. Tuition, nonresident: full-time $14,851; part-time $825.05 per credit hour. *Required fees:* $2027; $112.60 per credit hour. Tuition and fees vary according to campus/location. *Financial support:* In

2016–17, 26 research assistantships (averaging $15,000 per year), 7 teaching assistantships (averaging $14,143 per year) were awarded; career-related internships or fieldwork, Federal Work-Study, scholarships/grants, health care benefits, tuition waivers (partial), and unspecified assistantships also available. Support available to part-time students. Financial award application deadline: 3/1; financial award applicants required to submit FAFSA. *Unit head:* Dr. Rob Whiteley, Head, 405-744-5280, Fax: 405-744-6338, E-mail: rob.whiteley@okstate.edu.
Website: http://che.okstate.edu/

Oregon State University, College of Engineering, Program in Chemical Engineering, Corvallis, OR 97331. Offers M Eng, MS, PhD. *Faculty:* 19 full-time (3 women). *Students:* 75 full-time (23 women), 7 part-time (1 woman); includes 13 minority (3 Black or African American, non-Hispanic/Latino; 5 Asian, non-Hispanic/Latino; 2 Hispanic/Latino; 3 Two or more races, non-Hispanic/Latino), 49 international. Average age 27. 105 applicants, 38% accepted, 23 enrolled. In 2016, 22 master's, 5 doctorates awarded. *Entrance requirements:* For master's, GRE. Additional exam requirements/recommendations for international students: Required—TOEFL (minimum score 92 iBT). *Application deadline:* For fall admission, 12/20 for domestic students. Application fee: $75 ($85 for international students). *Expenses:* $14,130 resident full-time tuition, $23,769 non-resident. *Financial support:* Application deadline: 12/20. *Unit head:* Dr. James Sweeney, School Head/Professor. *Application contact:* Anita Hughes, Graduate Program Coordinator for Chemical, Biological and Environmental Engineering, E-mail: anita.hughes@oregonstate.edu.
Website: http://cbee.oregonstate.edu/che-graduate-program

Penn State University Park, Graduate School, College of Engineering, Department of Chemical Engineering, University Park, PA 16802. Offers MS, PhD. *Unit head:* Dr. Amr S. Elnashai, Dean, 814-865-7537, Fax: 814-863-4749. *Application contact:* Lori Hawn, Director, Graduate Student Services, 814-865-1795, Fax: 814-863-4627, E-mail: l-gswww@lists.psu.edu.
Website: http://che.psu.edu/

Princeton University, Graduate School, School of Engineering and Applied Science, Department of Chemical Engineering, Princeton, NJ 08544-1019. Offers M Eng, MSE, PhD. Terminal master's awarded for partial completion of doctoral program. *Degree requirements:* For master's, thesis (MSE); for doctorate, thesis/dissertation, general exam. *Entrance requirements:* For master's, GRE General Test, 3 letters of recommendation; for doctorate, GRE General Test, official transcript(s), 3 letters of recommendation, personal statement. Additional exam requirements/recommendations for international students: Required—TOEFL. Electronic applications accepted. *Faculty research:* Applied and computational mathematics, bioengineering, environmental and energy science and technology, fluid mechanics and transport phenomena, materials science.

Purdue University, College of Engineering, Davidson School of Chemical Engineering, West Lafayette, IN 47907-2100. Offers MSChE, PhD. *Faculty:* 43. *Students:* 158. In 2016, 10 master's, 31 doctorates awarded. Terminal master's awarded for partial completion of doctoral program. *Degree requirements:* For master's, thesis optional; for doctorate, thesis/dissertation. *Entrance requirements:* For master's and doctorate, GRE, minimum GPA of 3.0. *Application deadline:* For fall admission, 12/15 for domestic and international students. Applications are processed on a rolling basis. Application fee: $60 ($75 for international students). Electronic applications accepted. *Financial support:* Fellowships with full and partial tuition reimbursements, research assistantships with full and partial tuition reimbursements, teaching assistantships with full and partial tuition reimbursements, career-related internships or fieldwork, scholarships/grants, health care benefits, and unspecified assistantships available. Financial award applicants required to submit FAFSA. *Faculty research:* Biomedical and biomolecular engineering, catalysis and reaction engineering, fluid mechanics and interfacial phenomena, mass transfer and separations, nanoscale science and engineering, polymers and materials, product and process systems engineering, thermodynamics, molecular and nanoscale modeling. *Unit head:* Dr. Sangtae Kim, Head of Chemical Engineering/Professor, E-mail: kim55@purdue.edu. *Application contact:* Beverly Johnson, Graduate Program Administrator, 765-494-4057, E-mail: bevjohnson@purdue.edu.
Website: https://engineering.purdue.edu/ChE/

Queen's University at Kingston, School of Graduate Studies, Faculty of Applied Science, Department of Chemical Engineering, Kingston, ON K7L 3N6, Canada. Offers M Sc, PhD. *Program availability:* Part-time. *Degree requirements:* For master's, thesis or alternative; for doctorate, comprehensive exam, thesis/dissertation. *Entrance requirements:* Additional exam requirements/recommendations for international students: Required—TOEFL (minimum score 580 paper-based). Electronic applications accepted. *Faculty research:* Polymers and reaction engineering, process control and applied statistics, combustion, fermentation and bioremediation, biomaterials.

Rensselaer Polytechnic Institute, Graduate School, School of Engineering, Program in Chemical Engineering, Troy, NY 12180-3590. Offers M Eng, MS, D Eng, PhD. *Faculty:* 15 full-time (2 women). *Students:* 65 full-time (25 women), 3 part-time. 176 applicants, 21% accepted, 14 enrolled. In 2016, 8 master's, 14 doctorates awarded. Terminal master's awarded for partial completion of doctoral program. *Entrance requirements:* For master's and doctorate, GRE. Additional exam requirements/recommendations for international students: Required—TOEFL (minimum score 570 paper-based; 88 iBT), IELTS (minimum score 6.5), PTE (minimum score 60). *Application deadline:* For fall admission, 1/1 priority date for domestic and international students; for spring admission, 8/15 priority date for domestic and international students. Applications are processed on a rolling basis. Application fee: $75. Electronic applications accepted. *Expenses: Tuition:* Full-time $49,520; part-time $2060 per credit hour. *Required fees:* $2617. *Financial support:* In 2016–17, research assistantships with full tuition reimbursements (averaging $22,000 per year), teaching assistantships with full tuition reimbursements (averaging $22,000 per year) were awarded; fellowships also available. Financial award application deadline: 1/1. *Faculty research:* Advanced materials, biochemical engineering; biomedical engineering; biotechnology; drug delivery; energy; fluid mechanics; interfacial phenomena; mass transport; molecular simulations; molecular thermodynamics; nanotechnology; polymers; process control, design, and optimization; separation and bio separation processes; systems biology; systems engineering; transport phenomena. *Total annual research expenditures:* $5.3 million. *Unit head:* Dr. Cynthia Collins, Graduate Program Director, 518-276-4178, E-mail: ccollins@rpi.edu. *Application contact:* Office of Graduate Admissions, 518-276-6216, E-mail: gradadmissions@rpi.edu.
Website: http://cbe.rpi.edu/graduate

Rice University, Graduate Programs, George R. Brown School of Engineering, Department of Chemical and Biomolecular Engineering, Houston, TX 77251-1892. Offers chemical and biomolecular engineering (MS, PhD); chemical engineering (M Ch E). *Program availability:* Part-time. *Degree requirements:* For master's, thesis (for some programs); for doctorate, thesis/dissertation. *Entrance requirements:* For master's and doctorate, GRE General Test, minimum GPA of 3.0. Additional exam requirements/recommendations for international students: Required—TOEFL (minimum score 600 paper-based; 90 iBT). Electronic applications accepted. *Faculty research:* Thermodynamics, phase equilibria, rheology, fluid mechanics, polymers, biomedical engineering, interfacial phenomena, process control, petroleum engineering, reaction engineering and catalysis, biomaterials, metabolic engineering.

Rose-Hulman Institute of Technology, Faculty of Engineering and Applied Sciences, Department of Chemical Engineering, Terre Haute, IN 47803-3999. Offers M Eng, MS. *Program availability:* Part-time. *Faculty:* 11 full-time (5 women), 2 part-time/adjunct (0 women). *Students:* 5 full-time (1 woman), 1 part-time (0 women); includes 1 minority (Two or more races, non-Hispanic/Latino), 1 international. Average age 22. 8 applicants, 75% accepted, 4 enrolled. In 2016, 4 master's awarded. *Degree requirements:* For master's, thesis. *Entrance requirements:* For master's, GRE, minimum GPA of 3.0. Additional exam requirements/recommendations for international students: Required—TOEFL (minimum score 580 paper-based; 92 iBT). *Application deadline:* For fall admission, 2/1 priority date for domestic students. Applications are processed on a rolling basis. Application fee: $0. Electronic applications accepted. *Expenses: Tuition:* Full-time $43,122. *Financial support:* In 2016–17, 5 students received support. Fellowships with tuition reimbursements available, research assistantships with tuition reimbursements available, institutionally sponsored loans, scholarships/grants, and tuition waivers (full and partial) available. *Faculty research:* Thermodynamics and interfacial phenomena, reaction kinetics and separations, particle technology and materials, process systems and control, petrochemical processes. *Total annual research expenditures:* $1,135. *Unit head:* Dr. Adam Nolte, Chairman, 812-877-8096, Fax: 812-877-8992, E-mail: nolte@rose-hulman.edu. *Application contact:* Dr. Azad Siahmakoun, Associate Dean of the Faculty, 812-877-8400, Fax: 812-877-8061, E-mail: siahmako@rose-hulman.edu.
Website: http://www.rose-hulman.edu/academics/academic-departments/chemical-engineering.aspx

Rowan University, Graduate School, College of Engineering, Department of Chemical Engineering, Glassboro, NJ 08028-1701. Offers MS. Electronic applications accepted.

Royal Military College of Canada, Division of Graduate Studies and Research, Science Division, Department of Chemistry and Chemical and Materials Engineering, Kingston, ON K7K 7B4, Canada. Offers chemical engineering (M Eng, MA Sc, PhD); chemistry (M Sc, PhD). *Degree requirements:* For master's, thesis; for doctorate, comprehensive exam, thesis/dissertation. *Entrance requirements:* For master's, honour's degree with second-class standing; for doctorate, master's degree. Electronic applications accepted.

Rutgers University–New Brunswick, Graduate School-New Brunswick, Program in Chemical and Biochemical Engineering, Piscataway, NJ 08854-8097. Offers MS, PhD. *Program availability:* Part-time, evening/weekend. Terminal master's awarded for partial completion of doctoral program. *Degree requirements:* For master's, thesis or alternative; for doctorate, thesis/dissertation. *Entrance requirements:* For master's and doctorate, GRE General Test. Additional exam requirements/recommendations for international students: Required—TOEFL. *Faculty research:* Biotechnology, pharmaceutical engineering, nanotechnology, process system engineering, materials and polymer science, chemical engineering sciences.

South Dakota School of Mines and Technology, Graduate Division, Program in Chemical and Biological Engineering, Rapid City, SD 57701-3995. Offers PhD. *Program availability:* Part-time. *Degree requirements:* For doctorate, thesis/dissertation. *Entrance requirements:* Additional exam requirements/recommendations for international students: Required—TOEFL (minimum score 520 paper-based; 68 iBT). Electronic applications accepted.

South Dakota School of Mines and Technology, Graduate Division, Program in Chemical Engineering, Rapid City, SD 57701-3995. Offers MS. *Program availability:* Part-time. *Degree requirements:* For master's, thesis. *Entrance requirements:* For master's, GRE General Test. Additional exam requirements/recommendations for international students: Required—TOEFL (minimum score 520 paper-based; 68 iBT), TWE. Electronic applications accepted. *Faculty research:* Incineration chemistry, environmental chemistry, polymer surface chemistry.

Stanford University, School of Engineering, Department of Chemical Engineering, Stanford, CA 94305-2004. Offers MS, PhD. Terminal master's awarded for partial completion of doctoral program. *Degree requirements:* For doctorate, thesis/dissertation. *Entrance requirements:* For master's and doctorate, GRE General Test. Additional exam requirements/recommendations for international students: Required—TOEFL. Electronic applications accepted. *Expenses: Tuition:* Full-time $47,331. *Required fees:* $609.

Stevens Institute of Technology, Graduate School, Charles V. Schaefer Jr. School of Engineering and Science, Department of Chemical Engineering and Materials Science, Program in Chemical Engineering, Hoboken, NJ 07030. Offers M Eng, PhD, Engr. *Program availability:* Part-time, evening/weekend. *Students:* 30 full-time (11 women), 6 part-time (1 woman); includes 2 minority (both Asian, non-Hispanic/Latino), 26 international. Average age 25. 188 applicants, 43% accepted, 12 enrolled. In 2016, 22 master's, 1 doctorate awarded. *Degree requirements:* For master's, thesis optional, minimum B average in major field and overall; for doctorate, comprehensive exam (for some programs), thesis/dissertation; for Engr, minimum B average. *Entrance requirements:* Additional exam requirements/recommendations for international students: Required—TOEFL (minimum score 74 iBT), IELTS (minimum score 6). *Application deadline:* For fall admission, 6/1 for domestic students, 4/15 for international students; for spring admission, 11/30 for domestic students, 11/1 for international students. Applications are processed on a rolling basis. Application fee: $65. Electronic applications accepted. *Expenses:* Contact institution. *Financial support:* Fellowships, research assistantships, teaching assistantships, career-related internships or fieldwork, Federal Work-Study, scholarships/grants, and unspecified assistantships available. Financial award application deadline: 2/15; financial award applicants required to submit FAFSA. *Unit head:* Dr. Henry Du, Director, 201-216-5262, Fax: 201-216-8306, E-mail: hdu@stevens.edu. *Application contact:* Graduate Admissions, 888-783-8367, Fax: 888-511-1306, E-mail: graduate@stevens.edu.

Syracuse University, College of Engineering and Computer Science, Programs in Chemical Engineering, Syracuse, NY 13244. Offers MS, PhD. *Program availability:* Part-time. *Students:* Average age 25. *Degree requirements:* For master's, comprehensive exam (for some programs), thesis (for some programs); for doctorate, comprehensive exam, thesis/dissertation. *Entrance requirements:* For master's, GRE General Test, official transcripts, three letters of recommendation, resume, personal statement; for doctorate, GRE General Test. Additional exam requirements/recommendations for international students: Required—TOEFL (minimum score 100 iBT). *Application deadline:* For fall admission, 7/1 priority date for domestic students, 6/1 priority date for international students; for spring admission, 11/15 for domestic students, 10/15 priority date for international students. Applications are processed on a rolling basis. Application fee: $75. Electronic applications accepted. *Expenses: Tuition:* Full-time $25,974; part-time $1443 per credit hour. *Required fees:* $802; $50 per course. Tuition and fees vary according to course load and program. *Financial support:* Fellowships with full tuition reimbursements, research assistantships with tuition reimbursements, teaching assistantships with tuition reimbursements, and tuition waivers (partial) available. Financial award application deadline: 1/1; financial award applicants required to submit FAFSA. *Faculty research:* Complex fluids, soft condensed matter, rheology, energy

sources, conversion, and conservation, multiple phase systems, nanotechnology, rehabilitative and regenerative engineering, smart materials for healthcare, sustainable energy production, and systems biology / metabolic engineering. *Unit head:* Dr. Dacheng Ren, Professor, Chemical Engineering/Graduate Program Director, 315-443-4409, E-mail: dren@syr.edu. *Application contact:* Kathleen Joyce, Assistant Dean, 315-443-2219, E-mail: topgrads@syr.edu.
Website: http://eng-cs.syr.edu/

Tennessee Technological University, College of Graduate Studies, College of Engineering, Department of Chemical Engineering, Cookeville, TN 38505. Offers MS. *Program availability:* Part-time. *Faculty:* 8 full-time (0 women). *Students:* 4 full-time (2 women), 11 part-time (4 women), 9 international. Average age 26. 44 applicants, 41% accepted, 4 enrolled. In 2016, 6 master's awarded. *Degree requirements:* For master's, thesis. *Entrance requirements:* For master's, GRE General Test. Additional exam requirements/recommendations for international students: Required—TOEFL (minimum score 550 paper-based; 79 iBT), IELTS (minimum score 5.5), PTE (minimum score 53), or TOEIC (Test of English as an International Communication). *Application deadline:* For fall admission, 8/1 for domestic students, 5/1 for international students; for spring admission, 12/1 for domestic students, 10/1 for international students; for summer admission, 5/1 for domestic students, 2/1 for international students. Applications are processed on a rolling basis. Application fee: $35 ($40 for international students). Electronic applications accepted. *Expenses:* Tuition, state resident: full-time $9375; part-time $534 per credit hour. Tuition, nonresident: full-time $22,443; part-time $1260 per credit hour. *Financial support:* In 2016–17, fellowships (averaging $8,000 per year), 10 research assistantships (averaging $7,000 per year), 5 teaching assistantships (averaging $5,433 per year) were awarded; career-related internships or fieldwork also available. Financial award application deadline: 4/1. *Faculty research:* Biochemical conversion, insulation, fuel reprocessing. *Unit head:* Dr. Pedro Arce, Chairperson, 931-372-3297, Fax: 931-372-6372, E-mail: parce@tntech.edu. *Application contact:* Shelia K. Kendrick, Coordinator of Graduate Studies, 931-372-3808, Fax: 931-372-3497, E-mail: skendrick@tntech.edu.

Texas A&M University, College of Engineering, Artie McFerrin Department of Chemical Engineering, College Station, TX 77843. Offers M Eng, MS, PhD. *Faculty:* 36. *Students:* 230 full-time (81 women), 22 part-time (11 women); includes 25 minority (5 Black or African American, non-Hispanic/Latino; 11 Asian, non-Hispanic/Latino; 2 Hispanic/Latino; 7 Two or more races, non-Hispanic/Latino), 188 international. Average age 26. 681 applicants, 22% accepted, 71 enrolled. In 2016, 29 master's, 20 doctorates awarded. Terminal master's awarded for partial completion of doctoral program. *Degree requirements:* For master's, thesis (MS); for doctorate, thesis/dissertation. *Entrance requirements:* For master's and doctorate, GRE General Test. Additional exam requirements/recommendations for international students: Required—TOEFL (minimum score 550 paper-based; 80 iBT), IELTS (minimum score 6), PTE (minimum score 53). *Application deadline:* For fall admission, 12/1 for domestic students, 12/1 priority date for international students; for spring admission, 10/1 for domestic and international students. Applications are processed on a rolling basis. Application fee: $50 ($90 for international students). Electronic applications accepted. *Expenses:* Contact institution. *Financial support:* In 2016–17, 209 students received support, including 23 fellowships with tuition reimbursements available (averaging $8,672 per year), 147 research assistantships with tuition reimbursements available (averaging $7,210 per year), 9 teaching assistantships with tuition reimbursements available (averaging $6,326 per year); career-related internships or fieldwork, institutionally sponsored loans, scholarships/grants, traineeships, health care benefits, tuition waivers (full and partial), and unspecified assistantships also available. Support available to part-time students. Financial award application deadline: 3/15; financial award applicants required to submit FAFSA. *Faculty research:* Reaction engineering, interface phenomena, environmental applications, biochemical engineering, polymers. *Unit head:* Dr. M. Nazmul Karim, Head, 979-845-9806, E-mail: nazkarim@che.tamu.edu. *Application contact:* Dr. Hae-Kwon Jeong, Graduate Recruitment and Admissions Coordinator, 979-862-4850, E-mail: jeong@chemail.tamu.edu.
Website: http://engineering.tamu.edu/chemical

Texas A&M University–Kingsville, College of Graduate Studies, Frank H. Dotterweich College of Engineering, Wayne H. King Department of Chemical and Natural Gas Engineering, Program in Chemical Engineering, Kingsville, TX 78363. Offers ME, MS. *Degree requirements:* For master's, variable foreign language requirement, comprehensive exam, thesis (for some programs). *Entrance requirements:* For master's, GRE (minimum quantitative score of 150, verbal 145), MAT, GMAT, minimum GPA of 2.75. Additional exam requirements/recommendations for international students: Required—TOEFL (minimum score 550 paper-based; 79 iBT). Electronic applications accepted.

Texas Tech University, Graduate School, Edward E. Whitacre Jr. College of Engineering, Department of Chemical Engineering, Lubbock, TX 79409-3121. Offers MS Ch E, PhD. *Faculty:* 23 full-time (6 women). *Students:* 92 full-time (32 women), 4 part-time (0 women); includes 6 minority (2 Asian, non-Hispanic/Latino; 4 Hispanic/Latino), 83 international. Average age 26. 216 applicants, 16% accepted, 21 enrolled. In 2016, 8 master's, 6 doctorates awarded. Terminal master's awarded for partial completion of doctoral program. *Degree requirements:* For master's, comprehensive exam, thesis (for some programs); for doctorate, comprehensive exam, thesis/dissertation. *Entrance requirements:* For master's and doctorate, GRE (Verbal and Quantitative). Additional exam requirements/recommendations for international students: Required—TOEFL (minimum score 550 paper-based; 79 iBT). *Application deadline:* For fall admission, 6/1 priority date for domestic students, 1/15 priority date for international students; for spring admission, 9/1 priority date for domestic students, 6/15 priority date for international students. Applications are processed on a rolling basis. Application fee: $75. Electronic applications accepted. *Expenses:* $325 per credit hour full-time resident tuition, $733 per credit hour full-time non-resident tuition; $53.75 per credit hour fee plus $608 per term fee. *Financial support:* In 2016–17, 106 students received support, including 98 fellowships (averaging $2,509 per year), 96 research assistantships (averaging $19,019 per year), 25 teaching assistantships (averaging $10,572 per year); scholarships/grants, tuition waivers (partial), and unspecified assistantships also available. Financial award application deadline: 4/15; financial award applicants required to submit FAFSA. *Faculty research:* Bioengineering; energy and sustainability; polymers and materials; simulation and modeling in chemical engineering. *Total annual research expenditures:* $3.5 million. *Unit head:* Dr. Sindee Simon, Department Chair, 806-742-3553, Fax: 806-742-3552, E-mail: sindee.simon@ttu.edu. *Application contact:* Dr. Rajesh Khare, Professor, 806-742-3553, Fax: 806-742-3552, E-mail: rajesh.khare@ttu.edu.
Website: http://www.depts.ttu.edu/che/

Tufts University, School of Engineering, Department of Chemical and Biological Engineering, Medford, MA 02155. Offers bioengineering (ME, MS), including cell and bioprocess engineering (PhD); biotechnology engineering (PhD); chemical and biological engineering (ME, MS, PhD). *Program availability:* Part-time. Terminal master's awarded for partial completion of doctoral program. *Degree requirements:* For master's, thesis (for some programs); for doctorate, thesis/dissertation. *Entrance requirements:* For master's and doctorate, GRE General Test. Additional exam requirements/recommendations for international students: Required—TOEFL (minimum score 550 paper-based; 80 iBT), IELTS (minimum score 6.5). Electronic applications accepted. *Expenses: Tuition:* Full-time $49,892; part-time $1248 per credit hour. *Required fees:* $844. Full-time tuition and fees vary according to degree level, program and student level. Part-time tuition and fees vary according to course load. *Faculty research:* Clean energy with materials, biomaterials, colloids; metabolic engineering, biotechnology; process control; reaction kinetics, catalysis; transport phenomena.

Tulane University, School of Science and Engineering, Department of Chemical and Biomolecular Engineering, New Orleans, LA 70118-5669. Offers MS, PhD. *Program availability:* Part-time. Terminal master's awarded for partial completion of doctoral program. *Degree requirements:* For master's, thesis (for some programs); for doctorate, thesis/dissertation. *Entrance requirements:* For master's and doctorate, GRE General Test, minimum B average in undergraduate course work. Additional exam requirements/recommendations for international students: Required—TOEFL. Electronic applications accepted. *Expenses: Tuition:* Full-time $50,920; part-time $2829 per credit hour. *Required fees:* $2040; $44.50 per credit hour. $580 per term. Tuition and fees vary according to course load, degree level and program. *Faculty research:* Interfacial phenomena catalysis, electrochemical engineering, environmental science.

Universidad de las Américas Puebla, Division of Graduate Studies, School of Engineering, Program in Chemical Engineering, Puebla, Mexico. Offers chemical engineering (MS); food technology (MS). *Program availability:* Part-time, evening/weekend. *Degree requirements:* For master's, one foreign language, thesis. *Faculty research:* Food science, reactors, oil industry, biotechnology.

Université de Sherbrooke, Faculty of Engineering, Department of Chemical Engineering, Sherbrooke, QC J1K 2R1, Canada. Offers M Sc A, PhD. *Degree requirements:* For master's, one foreign language, thesis; for doctorate, comprehensive exam, thesis/dissertation. *Entrance requirements:* For doctorate, master's degree in engineering or equivalent. Electronic applications accepted. *Faculty research:* Conversion processes, high-temperature plasma technologies, system engineering, environmental engineering, textile technologies.

Université Laval, Faculty of Sciences and Engineering, Department of Chemical Engineering, Programs in Chemical Engineering, Québec, QC G1K 7P4, Canada. Offers M Sc, PhD. Terminal master's awarded for partial completion of doctoral program. *Degree requirements:* For master's, thesis (for some programs); for doctorate, comprehensive exam, thesis/dissertation. *Entrance requirements:* Additional exam requirements/recommendations for international students: Required—TOEFL (minimum score 500 paper-based). Electronic applications accepted.

University at Buffalo, the State University of New York, Graduate School, School of Engineering and Applied Sciences, Department of Chemical and Biological Engineering, Buffalo, NY 14260. Offers ME, MS, PhD. *Program availability:* Part-time. *Degree requirements:* For master's, thesis (for some programs); for doctorate, comprehensive exam, thesis/dissertation. *Entrance requirements:* For master's and doctorate, GRE General Test. Additional exam requirements/recommendations for international students: Required—TOEFL (minimum score 550 paper-based; 79 iBT). Electronic applications accepted. *Faculty research:* Transport, polymers, nanomaterials, biochemical engineering, catalysis.

The University of Akron, Graduate School, College of Engineering, Department of Chemical and Biomolecular Engineering, Akron, OH 44325. Offers MS, PhD. *Program availability:* Part-time, evening/weekend. *Faculty:* 18 full-time (5 women), 2 part-time/adjunct (0 women). *Students:* 72 full-time (30 women), 10 part-time (5 women); includes 4 minority (2 Asian, non-Hispanic/Latino; 2 Hispanic/Latino), 71 international. Average age 28. 66 applicants, 71% accepted, 16 enrolled. In 2016, 10 master's, 11 doctorates awarded. *Degree requirements:* For master's, thesis optional; for doctorate, one foreign language, thesis/dissertation, candidacy exam, qualifying exam. *Entrance requirements:* For master's, GRE, minimum GPA of 2.75, letters of recommendation, statement of purpose; for doctorate, GRE, minimum GPA of 3.0 with bachelor's degree, 3.5 with master's degree; letters of recommendation; personal statement; resume. Additional exam requirements/recommendations for international students: Required—TOEFL (minimum score 550 paper-based; 79 iBT), IELTS (minimum score 6.5). *Application deadline:* For fall admission, 5/1 priority date for domestic and international students; for spring admission, 10/31 priority date for domestic and international students; for summer admission, 2/15 for domestic and international students. Application fee: $45 ($70 for international students). Electronic applications accepted. *Expenses:* Tuition, state resident: full-time $8618; part-time $359 per credit hour. Tuition, nonresident: full-time $17,149; part-time $715 per credit hour. *Required fees:* $1652. *Financial support:* In 2016–17, 34 research assistantships with full tuition reimbursements, 2 teaching assistantships with full tuition reimbursements were awarded; scholarships/grants and instructional support assistantships also available. *Faculty research:* Renewable energy, fuel cell and CO2 sequestration, nanofiber synthesis and applications, materials for biomedical applications, engineering, surface characterization and modification. *Total annual research expenditures:* $2.7 million. *Unit head:* Dr. H. Michael Cheung, Chair, 330-972-7282, E-mail: cheung@uakron.edu. *Application contact:* Dr. George Chase, Graduate Director, 330-972-7943, E-mail: gchase@uakron.edu.
Website: http://www.uakron.edu/engineering/CBE/

The University of Alabama, Graduate School, College of Engineering, Department of Chemical and Biological Engineering, Tuscaloosa, AL 35487. Offers MS Ch E, PhD. *Faculty:* 14 full-time (2 women). *Students:* 20 full-time (7 women), 2 part-time (0 women); includes 2 minority (both Black or African American, non-Hispanic/Latino), 11 international. Average age 27. 43 applicants, 42% accepted, 5 enrolled. In 2016, 10 master's, 4 doctorates awarded. Terminal master's awarded for partial completion of doctoral program. *Degree requirements:* For master's, comprehensive exam, thesis; for doctorate, comprehensive exam, thesis/dissertation. *Entrance requirements:* For master's, GRE, minimum GPA of 3.0 overall; for doctorate, GRE, minimum GPA of 3.0. Additional exam requirements/recommendations for international students: Required—TOEFL (minimum score 550 paper-based); Recommended—IELTS (minimum score 6.5). *Application deadline:* For fall admission, 1/31 priority date for domestic and international students; for winter admission, 9/15 priority date for domestic and international students. Applications are processed on a rolling basis. Application fee: $50 ($60 for international students). Electronic applications accepted. *Expenses:* Tuition, state resident: full-time $10,470. Tuition, nonresident: full-time $26,950. *Financial support:* In 2016–17, 2 fellowships with full tuition reimbursements (averaging $25,000 per year), 14 research assistantships with full tuition reimbursements (averaging $25,000 per year), 4 teaching assistantships with full tuition reimbursements (averaging $25,000 per year) were awarded; Federal Work-Study also available. Financial award application deadline: 3/15. *Faculty research:* Nanotechnology, materials, electrochemistry, alternative energy, biological. *Total annual research expenditures:* $1.5 million. *Unit head:* Dr. Christopher S. Brazel, Associate Professor, 205-348-6450, Fax: 205-348-6579, E-mail: cbrazel@eng.ua.edu. *Application contact:* Dr. Christoffer H. Turner, Professor, 205-348-1733, Fax: 205-348-6579, E-mail: hturner@eng.ua.edu.
Website: http://che.eng.ua.edu/

Chemical Engineering

The University of Alabama in Huntsville, School of Graduate Studies, College of Engineering, Department of Chemical and Materials Engineering, Huntsville, AL 35899. Offers biotechnology science and engineering (PhD); chemical and materials engineering (MSE); materials science (PhD); mechanical engineering (PhD), including chemical engineering. *Program availability:* Part-time, evening/weekend. *Degree requirements:* For master's, comprehensive exam, thesis or alternative, oral and written exams; for doctorate, comprehensive exam, thesis/dissertation. *Entrance requirements:* For master's, GRE General Test, appropriate bachelor's degree, minimum GPA of 3.0; for doctorate, GRE General Test, minimum GPA of 3.0. Additional exam requirements/recommendations for international students: Required—TOEFL (minimum score 500 paper-based; 80 iBT), IELTS (minimum score 6.5). Electronic applications accepted. *Expenses:* Tuition, state resident: full-time $9834; part-time $600 per credit hour. Tuition, nonresident: full-time $21,830; part-time $1325 per credit hour. *Faculty research:* Ultrathin films for optical, sensor and biological applications; materials processing including low gravity; hypergolic reactants; computational fluid dynamics; biofuels and renewable resources.

University of Alberta, Faculty of Graduate Studies and Research, Department of Chemical and Materials Engineering, Edmonton, AB T6G 2E1, Canada. Offers chemical engineering (M Eng, M Sc, PhD); materials engineering (M Eng, M Sc, PhD); process control (M Eng, M Sc, PhD); welding (M Eng). *Program availability:* Part-time online learning. Terminal master's awarded for partial completion of doctoral program. *Degree requirements:* For master's, thesis; for doctorate, thesis/dissertation. *Faculty research:* Advanced materials and polymers, catalytic and reaction engineering, mineral processing, physical metallurgy, fluid mechanics.

The University of Arizona, College of Engineering, Department of Chemical and Environmental Engineering, Tucson, AZ 85721-0011. Offers chemical engineering (MS, PhD); environmental engineering (MS, PhD). *Program availability:* Part-time. *Degree requirements:* For master's, thesis; for doctorate, comprehensive exam, thesis/ dissertation, departmental qualifying exams. *Entrance requirements:* For master's and doctorate, GRE General Test, 3 letters of recommendation, resume, statement of purpose. Additional exam requirements/recommendations for international students: Required—TOEFL (minimum score 550 paper-based; 79 iBT). Electronic applications accepted. *Faculty research:* Energy and environment-hazardous waste incineration, sustainability, kinetics, bioremediation, semiconductor processing.

University of Arkansas, Graduate School, College of Engineering, Department of Chemical Engineering, Fayetteville, AR 72701. Offers MS Ch E, MSE, PhD. *Program availability:* Part-time. In 2016, 6 master's, 5 doctorates awarded. *Degree requirements:* For master's, thesis optional; for doctorate, one foreign language, thesis/dissertation. *Entrance requirements:* For master's and doctorate, GRE General Test. *Application deadline:* For fall admission, 4/1 for international students; for spring admission, 10/1 for international students. Applications are processed on a rolling basis. Application fee: $40 ($50 for international students). Electronic applications accepted. *Financial support:* In 2016–17, 18 research assistantships were awarded; fellowships with tuition reimbursements, teaching assistantships, career-related internships or fieldwork, and Federal Work-Study also available. Support available to part-time students. Financial award application deadline: 4/1; financial award applicants required to submit FAFSA. *Unit head:* Dr. David Ford, Department Chair, 479-575-4951, E-mail: daveford@uark.edu. *Application contact:* Dr. Christa Hestekin, Graduate Coordinator, 479-575-3416, E-mail: chesteki@uark.edu.
Website: http://www.cheg.uark.edu

The University of British Columbia, Faculty of Applied Science, Department of Chemical and Biological Engineering, Vancouver, BC V6T 1Z3, Canada. Offers M Eng, M Sc, MA Sc, PhD. *Program availability:* Part-time, evening/weekend. *Degree requirements:* For master's, thesis (for some programs); for doctorate, thesis/ dissertation. *Entrance requirements:* Additional exam requirements/recommendations for international students: Required—TOEFL, IELTS. Application fee: $100 Canadian dollars ($162 Canadian dollars for international students). Electronic applications accepted. *Expenses:* $4,802 per year tuition and fees, $8,436 per year international. *Financial support:* Fellowships, research assistantships, teaching assistantships, career-related internships or fieldwork, institutionally sponsored loans, scholarships/ grants, and tuition waivers (full and partial) available. *Faculty research:* Biotechnology, catalysis, polymers, fluidization, pulp and paper. *Application contact:* Gina Abernethy, Graduate Program Staff, 604-827-4758, E-mail: chbe.gradsec@ubc.ca.
Website: http://www.chbe.ubc.ca/academics/graduate/

University of Calgary, Faculty of Graduate Studies, Schulich School of Engineering, Department of Chemical and Petroleum Engineering, Calgary, AB T2N 1N4, Canada. Offers chemical engineering (M Eng, M Sc, PhD); energy and environment engineering (M Eng, M Sc, PhD); energy and environmental systems (M Eng, M Sc, PhD); environmental engineering (M Eng, M Sc, PhD); petroleum engineering (M Eng, M Sc, PhD); reservoir characterization (M Eng, M Sc). *Program availability:* Part-time. *Degree requirements:* For master's, thesis (for some programs); for doctorate, comprehensive exam, thesis/dissertation, candidacy exam. *Entrance requirements:* For master's, minimum GPA of 3.0 or equivalent; for doctorate, minimum GPA of 3.5 or equivalent. Additional exam requirements/recommendations for international students: Required—TOEFL (minimum score 550 paper-based; 80 iBT), IELTS (minimum score 7). Electronic applications accepted. *Faculty research:* Environmental engineering, biomedical engineering modeling, simulation and control, petroleum recovery and reservoir engineering, phase equilibria and transport properties.

University of California, Berkeley, Graduate Division, College of Chemistry, Department of Chemical and Biomolecular Engineering, Berkeley, CA 94720-1500. Offers chemical engineering (PhD); product development (MS). *Faculty:* 17 full-time, 2 part-time/adjunct. *Students:* 141 full-time (60 women); includes 40 minority (4 Black or African American, non-Hispanic/Latino; 1 American Indian or Alaska Native, non-Hispanic/Latino; 30 Asian, non-Hispanic/Latino; 5 Hispanic/Latino), 37 international. Average age 26. 597 applicants, 53 enrolled. In 2016, 36 master's, 20 doctorates awarded. Terminal master's awarded for partial completion of doctoral program. *Degree requirements:* For master's, comprehensive exam (for some programs), thesis (for some programs); for doctorate, thesis/dissertation, qualifying exam. *Entrance requirements:* For master's and doctorate, GRE General Test, minimum GPA of 3.0, 3 letters of recommendation. Additional exam requirements/recommendations for international students: Required—TOEFL (minimum score 570 paper-based; 90 iBT). *Application deadline:* For fall admission, 12/12 for domestic students. Application fee: $105 ($125 for international students). Electronic applications accepted. *Financial support:* Applicants required to submit FAFSA. *Faculty research:* Biochemical engineering, electrochemical engineering, electronic materials, heterogeneous catalysis and reaction engineering, complex fluids. *Unit head:* Jeffery Reimer, Chair, 510-642-8011, E-mail: cbechair@berkeley.edu. *Application contact:* E-mail: chegrad@cchem.berkeley.edu.
Website: http://cheme.berkeley.edu/

University of California, Davis, College of Engineering, Program in Chemical Engineering, Davis, CA 95616. Offers MS, PhD. Terminal master's awarded for partial completion of doctoral program. *Degree requirements:* For master's, comprehensive exam (for some programs), thesis (for some programs); for doctorate, thesis/ dissertation. *Entrance requirements:* For master's and doctorate, GRE General Test,

minimum GPA of 3.0. Additional exam requirements/recommendations for international students: Required—TOEFL (minimum score 550 paper-based). Electronic applications accepted. *Faculty research:* Transport phenomena, colloid science, catalysis, biotechnology, materials.

University of California, Irvine, Henry Samueli School of Engineering, Department of Chemical Engineering and Materials Science, Irvine, CA 92697. Offers chemical and biochemical engineering (MS, PhD); materials science and engineering (MS, PhD). *Program availability:* Part-time. *Students:* 141 full-time (60 women), 14 part-time (5 women); includes 42 minority (4 Black or African American, non-Hispanic/Latino; 29 Asian, non-Hispanic/Latino; 7 Hispanic/Latino; 2 Two or more races, non-Hispanic/ Latino), 71 international. Average age 26. 595 applicants, 23% accepted, 41 enrolled. In 2016, 47 master's, 11 doctorates awarded. Terminal master's awarded for partial completion of doctoral program. *Degree requirements:* For doctorate, thesis/ dissertation. *Entrance requirements:* For master's and doctorate, GRE General Test, minimum GPA of 3.0, 3 letters of recommendation. Additional exam requirements/ recommendations for international students: Required—TOEFL (minimum score 550 paper-based). *Application deadline:* For fall admission, 1/15 priority date for domestic students, 1/15 for international students. Applications are processed on a rolling basis. Application fee: $105 ($125 for international students). Electronic applications accepted. *Financial support:* Fellowships with tuition reimbursements, research assistantships with full tuition reimbursements, teaching assistantships with tuition reimbursements, institutionally sponsored loans, traineeships, health care benefits, and unspecified assistantships available. Financial award application deadline: 3/1; financial award applicants required to submit FAFSA. *Faculty research:* Molecular biotechnology, nanobiomaterials, biophotonics, synthesis, super plasticity and mechanical behavior, characterization of advanced and nanostructural materials. *Unit head:* Prof. Vasan Venugopalan, Chair, 949-824-5802, Fax: 949-824-2541, E-mail: vvenugop@uci.edu. *Application contact:* Grace Chau, Academic Program and Graduate Admission Coordinator, 949-824-3887, Fax: 949-824-2541, E-mail: chaug@uci.edu.
Website: http://www.eng.uci.edu/dept/chems

University of California, Los Angeles, Graduate Division, Henry Samueli School of Engineering and Applied Science, Department of Chemical and Biomolecular Engineering, Los Angeles, CA 90095-1592. Offers MS, PhD. *Faculty:* 14 full-time (3 women), 2 part-time/adjunct (0 women). *Students:* 105 full-time (24 women); includes 28 minority (1 Black or African American, non-Hispanic/Latino; 1 American Indian or Alaska Native, non-Hispanic/Latino; 19 Asian, non-Hispanic/Latino; 5 Hispanic/Latino; 2 Two or more races, non-Hispanic/Latino), 55 international. 420 applicants, 12% accepted, 27 enrolled. In 2016, 9 master's, 16 doctorates awarded. *Degree requirements:* For master's, comprehensive exam (for some programs), thesis (for some programs); for doctorate, thesis/dissertation, qualifying exams. *Entrance requirements:* For master's, GRE General Test, minimum GPA of 3.0; for doctorate, GRE General Test, minimum GPA of 3.25. Additional exam requirements/recommendations for international students: Required—TOEFL (minimum score 560 paper-based; 87 iBT), IELTS (minimum score 7). *Application deadline:* 12/31 for domestic and international students. Application fee: $105 ($125 for international students). Electronic applications accepted. *Financial support:* In 2016–17, 51 fellowships, 159 research assistantships, 57 teaching assistantships were awarded; Federal Work-Study, institutionally sponsored loans, and tuition waivers (full and partial) also available. Financial award application deadline: 12/ 31; financial award applicants required to submit FAFSA. *Faculty research:* Biomolecular engineering, renewable energy, water technology, advanced materials processing, process systems engineering. *Total annual research expenditures:* $9.4 million. *Unit head:* Dr. Panagiotis D. Christofides, Chair, 310-794-1015, E-mail: pdc@ seas.ucla.edu. *Application contact:* Miguel Perez, Student Affairs Officer, 310-825-1203, E-mail: miguel@seas.ucla.edu.
Website: http://www.chemeng.ucla.edu/

University of California, Riverside, Graduate Division, Department of Chemical and Environmental Engineering, Riverside, CA 92521-0102. Offers MS, PhD. *Program availability:* Part-time. Terminal master's awarded for partial completion of doctoral program. *Degree requirements:* For master's, thesis (for some programs); for doctorate, comprehensive exam, thesis/dissertation. *Entrance requirements:* For master's and doctorate, GRE General Test, minimum GPA of 3.0. Additional exam requirements/ recommendations for international students: Required—TOEFL (minimum score 550 paper-based; 80 iBT). Electronic applications accepted. *Expenses:* Tuition, state resident: full-time $16,666. Tuition, nonresident: full-time $31,768. *Required fees:* $11,055.54 per quarter. $3685.18 per quarter. Tuition and fees vary according to campus/location and program. *Faculty research:* Air quality systems, water quality systems, advanced materials and nanotechnology, energy systems/alternative fuels, theory and molecular modeling.

University of California, San Diego, Graduate Division, Program in Chemical Engineering, La Jolla, CA 92093. Offers MS, PhD. *Students:* 61 full-time (27 women), 5 part-time (0 women). 201 applicants, 48% accepted, 36 enrolled. In 2016, 16 master's, 3 doctorates awarded. *Degree requirements:* For master's, comprehensive exam (for some programs), thesis (for some programs); for doctorate, comprehensive exam, thesis/dissertation, 1-quarter teaching assistantship. *Entrance requirements:* For master's and doctorate, GRE General Test. Additional exam requirements/ recommendations for international students: Required—TOEFL (minimum score 550 paper-based; 80 iBT), IELTS (minimum score 7). *Application deadline:* For fall admission, 12/19 for domestic students. Application fee: $105 ($125 for international students). Electronic applications accepted. *Expenses:* Tuition, state resident: full-time $11,220. Tuition, nonresident: full-time $26,322. *Required fees:* $1864. *Financial support:* Fellowships, research assistantships, teaching assistantships, scholarships/ grants, and readerships available. Financial award applicants required to submit FAFSA. *Faculty research:* Regenerative medicine, development of new microfluidic devices, biomedical modeling, solar thermochemical hydrogen production. *Unit head:* Joseph Wang, Chair, 858-882-7640, E-mail: josephwang@ucsd.edu. *Application contact:* Dana Jimenez, Graduate Coordinator, 858-822-7981, E-mail: dljimenez@ ucsd.edu.
Website: http://nanoengineering.ucsd.edu/graduate-programs/degree/chemical-engineering

University of California, Santa Barbara, Graduate Division, College of Engineering, Department of Chemical Engineering, Santa Barbara, CA 93106. Offers MS, PhD. *Degree requirements:* For master's, thesis or comprehensive exam; for doctorate, thesis/dissertation, research progress reports (prior to candidacy), candidacy exam, thesis defense, seminar. *Entrance requirements:* For doctorate, GRE. Additional exam requirements/recommendations for international students: Required—TOEFL (minimum score 560 paper-based; 83 iBT), IELTS (minimum score 7). Electronic applications accepted. *Faculty research:* Biomaterials and bioengineering; energy, catalysis and reaction engineering; complex fluids and polymers; electronic and optical materials; fluids and transport phenomena; molecular thermodynamics and simulation; process systems engineering; surfaces and interfacial phenomena.

University of Cincinnati, Graduate School, College of Engineering and Applied Science, Department of Biomedical, Chemical and Environmental Engineering, Program in Chemical Engineering, Cincinnati, OH 45221. Offers MS, PhD. *Program availability:*

Part-time, evening/weekend. Terminal master's awarded for partial completion of doctoral program. *Degree requirements:* For master's, thesis; for doctorate, thesis/dissertation. *Entrance requirements:* For master's and doctorate, GRE General Test. Additional exam requirements/recommendations for international students: Required—TOEFL (minimum score 600 paper-based). *Expenses: Tuition, area resident:* Full-time $12,790; part-time $389 per credit hour. Tuition, state resident: full-time $13,290; part-time $419 per credit hour. Tuition, nonresident: full-time $24,532; part-time $976 per credit hour. *International tuition:* $24,832 full-time. *Required fees:* $3958; $140 per credit hour. Tuition and fees vary according to course load, degree level, program and reciprocity agreements.

University of Colorado Boulder, Graduate School, College of Engineering and Applied Science, Department of Chemical and Biological Engineering, Boulder, CO 80309. Offers ME, MS, PhD. *Faculty:* 24 full-time (5 women). *Students:* 158 full-time (55 women), 4 part-time (1 woman); includes 20 minority (1 Black or African American, non-Hispanic/Latino; 9 Asian, non-Hispanic/Latino; 6 Hispanic/Latino; 4 Two or more races, non-Hispanic/Latino), 44 international. Average age 25. 570 applicants, 28% accepted, 44 enrolled. In 2016, 15 master's, 17 doctorates awarded. Terminal master's awarded for partial completion of doctoral program. *Degree requirements:* For master's, comprehensive exam, thesis; for doctorate, thesis/dissertation. *Entrance requirements:* For master's, minimum undergraduate GPA of 3.0. *Application deadline:* For fall admission, 1/5 for domestic and international students. Applications are processed on a rolling basis. Application fee: $60 ($80 for international students). Electronic applications accepted. Application fee is waived when completed online. *Financial support:* In 2016–17, 440 students received support, including 104 fellowships (averaging $14,418 per year), 108 research assistantships with full and partial tuition reimbursements available (averaging $35,316 per year), 36 teaching assistantships with full and partial tuition reimbursements available (averaging $31,851 per year); institutionally sponsored loans, scholarships/grants, health care benefits, and unspecified assistantships also available. Financial award applicants required to submit FAFSA. *Faculty research:* Chemical engineering, materials engineering, interfacial phenomena, catalysis/kinetics, bioengineering. *Total annual research expenditures:* $14.7 million. *Application contact:* E-mail: chbegrad@colorado.edu.
Website: http://www.colorado.edu/chbe

University of Connecticut, Graduate School, School of Engineering, Department of Chemical, Materials and Biomolecular Engineering, Field of Chemical Engineering, Storrs, CT 06269. Offers MS, PhD. Terminal master's awarded for partial completion of doctoral program. *Degree requirements:* For master's, comprehensive exam, thesis or alternative; for doctorate, thesis/dissertation. *Entrance requirements:* For master's and doctorate, GRE General Test. Additional exam requirements/recommendations for international students: Required—TOEFL (minimum score 550 paper-based). Electronic applications accepted.

University of Dayton, Department of Chemical Engineering, Dayton, OH 45469. Offers bioengineering (MS); chemical engineering (MS Ch E). *Program availability:* Part-time, evening/weekend. *Faculty:* 9 full-time (2 women), 2 part-time/adjunct (0 women). *Students:* 26 full-time (8 women), 6 part-time (1 woman); includes 1 minority (Black or African American, non-Hispanic/Latino), 24 international. Average age 26. 92 applicants, 22% accepted. In 2016, 33 master's awarded. *Degree requirements:* For master's, thesis. *Entrance requirements:* For master's, GRE (preferred), minimum GPA of 3.0 as undergraduate, transcript, 3 letters of recommendation, bachelor's degree in chemical engineering (preferred). Additional exam requirements/recommendations for international students: Required—TOEFL (minimum score 550 paper-based; 80 iBT); Recommended—IELTS. *Application deadline:* Applications are processed on a rolling basis. Application fee: $0 ($50 for international students). Electronic applications accepted. *Expenses:* $890 per credit hour, $25 registration fee. *Financial support:* In 2016–17, 2 research assistantships with full tuition reimbursements (averaging $15,000 per year) were awarded; teaching assistantships, institutionally sponsored loans, and health care benefits also available. Financial award application deadline: 3/1; financial award applicants required to submit FAFSA. *Faculty research:* Nonmaterial cellular interactions; mixing, chemical reaction; oxidative and pyrolytic reaction chemistry; hydrocarbon fuel chemistry; kinetics and reaction engineering; electrochemistry and electrochemical engineering; fuel cells; modeling, control and automation of polymer processing. *Unit head:* Dr. Charles Browning, Chair, 937-229-2627, E-mail: cbrowning1@udayton.edu. *Application contact:* Dr. Kevin Myers, Graduate Program Director, 937-229-2627, E-mail: kmyers1@udayton.edu.
Website: https://www.udayton.edu/engineering/departments/chemical_and_materials/index.php

University of Delaware, College of Engineering, Department of Chemical Engineering, Newark, DE 19716. Offers M Ch E, PhD. *Program availability:* Part-time, evening/weekend, online learning. Terminal master's awarded for partial completion of doctoral program. *Degree requirements:* For master's, thesis (for some programs); for doctorate, thesis/dissertation. *Entrance requirements:* For master's and doctorate, GRE General Test. Additional exam requirements/recommendations for international students: Required—TOEFL. Electronic applications accepted. *Faculty research:* Biochemical/biomedical engineer, thermodynamics, polymers/composites, materials, catalysis/reactions, colloid/interfaces, expert systems/process control.

University of Florida, Graduate School, Herbert Wertheim College of Engineering, Department of Chemical Engineering, Gainesville, FL 32611. Offers ME, MS, PhD, Engr. *Program availability:* Part-time. Terminal master's awarded for partial completion of doctoral program. *Degree requirements:* For master's, thesis optional; for doctorate, comprehensive exam, thesis/dissertation. *Entrance requirements:* For master's and doctorate, minimum GPA of 3.0. Additional exam requirements/recommendations for international students: Required—TOEFL (minimum score 550 paper-based; 80 iBT), IELTS (minimum score 6). Electronic applications accepted. *Faculty research:* Complex fluids and interfacial and colloidal phenomena; materials for biological, energy and microelectronic applications; catalysis and reaction kinetics; transport and electrochemistry; biomolecular research including biomechanics, signal transduction, and tissue engineering.

University of Houston, Cullen College of Engineering, Department of Chemical and Biomolecular Engineering, Houston, TX 77204. Offers chemical engineering (MCHE, PhD); petroleum engineering (M Pet E). *Program availability:* Part-time. Terminal master's awarded for partial completion of doctoral program. *Entrance requirements:* For master's and doctorate, GRE General Test. Additional exam requirements/recommendations for international students: Required—TOEFL (minimum score 550 paper-based; 79 iBT), IELTS (minimum score 6.5). *Faculty research:* Chemical engineering.

University of Idaho, College of Graduate Studies, College of Engineering, Department of Chemical and Materials Engineering, Moscow, ID 83844. Offers chemical engineering (M Engr, MS, PhD); materials science and engineering (MS, PhD); metallurgical engineering (MS). *Faculty:* 10 full-time, 2 part-time/adjunct. *Students:* 16 full-time, 7 part-time. Average age 31. In 2016, 7 master's, 1 doctorate awarded. *Entrance requirements:* For master's and doctorate, GRE, minimum GPA of 3.0. *Application deadline:* For fall admission, 8/1 for domestic students; for spring admission, 12/15 for domestic students. Applications are processed on a rolling basis. Application fee: $60.

Electronic applications accepted. *Expenses:* Tuition, state resident: full-time $6460; part-time $414 per credit hour. Tuition, nonresident: full-time $21,268; part-time $1237 per credit hour. *Required fees:* $2070; $60 per credit hour. Full-time tuition and fees vary according to course load and reciprocity agreements. *Financial support:* Fellowships, research assistantships, and teaching assistantships available. Financial award applicants required to submit FAFSA. *Faculty research:* Geothermal energy utilization, alcohol production from agriculture waste material, energy conservation in pulp and paper mills. *Unit head:* Dr. Eric Aston, Department Chair, 208-885-7572, E-mail: che@uidaho.edu. *Application contact:* Sean Scoggin, Graduate Recruitment Coordinator, 208-885-4001, Fax: 208-885-4406, E-mail: graduateadmissions@uidaho.edu.
Website: https://www.uidaho.edu/engr/departments/cme

University of Illinois at Chicago, College of Engineering, Department of Chemical Engineering, Chicago, IL 60607-7128. Offers MS, PhD. *Program availability:* Part-time. *Degree requirements:* For master's, thesis or project; for doctorate, thesis/dissertation, departmental qualifying exam. *Entrance requirements:* For master's and doctorate, GRE General Test, minimum GPA of 2.75. Additional exam requirements/recommendations for international students: Required—TOEFL. *Expenses:* Contact institution. *Faculty research:* Multiphase flows, interfacial transport, heterogeneous catalysis, coal technology, molecular and static thermodynamics.

University of Illinois at Urbana–Champaign, Graduate College, College of Liberal Arts and Sciences, School of Chemical Sciences, Department of Chemical and Biomolecular Engineering, Champaign, IL 61820. Offers bioinformatics: chemical and biomolecular engineering (MS); chemical engineering (MS, PhD). *Entrance requirements:* For master's, minimum GPA of 3.0.

The University of Iowa, Graduate College, College of Engineering, Department of Chemical and Biochemical Engineering, Iowa City, IA 52242-1316. Offers MS, PhD. *Program availability:* Part-time. *Faculty:* 12 full-time (3 women), 3 part-time/adjunct (1 woman). *Students:* 23 full-time (6 women), 7 part-time (3 women); includes 3 minority (1 Black or African American, non-Hispanic/Latino; 1 Asian, non-Hispanic/Latino; 1 Hispanic/Latino), 12 international. Average age 27. 66 applicants, 24% accepted, 6 enrolled. In 2016, 11 master's, 4 doctorates awarded. *Degree requirements:* For master's, comprehensive exam (for some programs), thesis (for some programs); for doctorate, comprehensive exam, thesis/dissertation. *Entrance requirements:* For master's and doctorate, GRE (minimum combined score of 310 on verbal and quantitative), minimum undergraduate GPA of 3.0. Additional exam requirements/recommendations for international students: Required—TOEFL (minimum score 600 paper-based; 100 iBT), IELTS (minimum score 7). *Application deadline:* For fall admission, 2/1 priority date for domestic and international students; for spring admission, 10/1 for domestic and international students. Applications are processed on a rolling basis. Application fee: $60 ($100 for international students). Electronic applications accepted. *Financial support:* In 2016–17, 38 students received support, including 6 fellowships with full tuition reimbursements available (averaging $25,500 per year), 25 research assistantships with full tuition reimbursements available (averaging $22,981 per year), 7 teaching assistantships with full tuition reimbursements available (averaging $18,809 per year); health care benefits and unspecified assistantships also available. Financial award application deadline: 2/1; financial award applicants required to submit FAFSA. *Faculty research:* Polymeric materials, photo polymerization, atmospheric chemistry and air pollution, biochemical engineering, bioprocessing and biomedical engineering. *Total annual research expenditures:* $1.9 million. *Unit head:* Dr. C. Allan Guymon, Department Executive Officer, 319-335-5015, Fax: 319-335-1415, E-mail: allan-guymon@uiowa.edu. *Application contact:* Sarah Hartman, Academic Program Specialist, 319-335-1215, Fax: 319-335-1415, E-mail: chemical-engineering@uiowa.edu.
Website: https://cbe.engineering.uiowa.edu

The University of Kansas, Graduate Studies, School of Engineering, Program in Chemical and Petroleum Engineering, Lawrence, KS 66045. Offers chemical and petroleum engineering (PhD); chemical engineering (MS); petroleum engineering (MS); petroleum management (Certificate). *Program availability:* Part-time. *Students:* 46 full-time (16 women), 3 part-time (0 women); includes 1 minority (Two or more races, non-Hispanic/Latino), 36 international. Average age 26. 135 applicants, 11% accepted, 5 enrolled. In 2016, 4 master's, 5 doctorates, 6 other advanced degrees awarded. *Entrance requirements:* For master's, GRE General Test, minimum GPA of 3.0, resume, personal statement, transcripts, three letters of recommendation; for doctorate, GRE General Test, minimum GPA of 3.5, resume, personal statement, transcripts, three letters of recommendation. Additional exam requirements/recommendations for international students: Required—TOEFL or IELTS. *Application deadline:* For fall admission, 12/15 priority date for domestic and international students; for spring admission, 8/31 priority date for domestic and international students. Application fee: $65 ($85 for international students). Electronic applications accepted. *Financial support:* Fellowships, research assistantships, teaching assistantships, career-related internships or fieldwork, Federal Work-Study, scholarships/grants, traineeships, and unspecified assistantships available. Financial award application deadline: 12/15; financial award applicants required to submit FAFSA. *Faculty research:* Enhanced oil recovery, catalysis and kinetics, electrochemical engineering, biomedical engineering, semiconductor materials processing. *Unit head:* Laurence Weatherley, Chair, 785-864-3553, E-mail: lweather@ku.edu. *Application contact:* Graduate Admission Contact, 785-864-2900, E-mail: cpegrad@ku.edu.
Website: http://www.cpe.engr.ku.edu

The University of Kansas, Graduate Studies, School of Engineering, Program in Chemical Engineering, Lawrence, KS 66045. Offers MS. *Program availability:* Part-time. *Students:* 8 full-time (2 women), 2 part-time (0 women); includes 1 minority (Two or more races, non-Hispanic/Latino), 5 international. Average age 25. 20 applicants, 20% accepted, 1 enrolled. In 2016, 1 master's awarded. *Entrance requirements:* For master's, GRE, resume, personal statement, transcripts, three letters of recommendation. Additional exam requirements/recommendations for international students: Required—TOEFL or IELTS. *Application deadline:* For fall admission, 12/15 priority date for domestic and international students. Application fee: $65 ($85 for international students). Electronic applications accepted. *Financial support:* Fellowships, research assistantships, teaching assistantships, Federal Work-Study, and scholarships/grants available. Financial award application deadline: 12/15. *Unit head:* Laurence Weatherley, Chair, 785-864-3553, E-mail: lweather@ku.edu. *Application contact:* Graduate Admissions Contact, 785-864-4965, E-mail: cpegrad@ku.edu.
Website: http://www.cpe.engr.ku.edu/

University of Kentucky, Graduate School, College of Engineering, Program in Chemical Engineering, Lexington, KY 40506-0032. Offers MS, PhD. *Degree requirements:* For master's, comprehensive exam, thesis optional; for doctorate, comprehensive exam, thesis/dissertation. *Entrance requirements:* For master's, GRE General Test, minimum undergraduate GPA of 2.75; for doctorate, GRE General Test, minimum undergraduate GPA of 3.0. Additional exam requirements/recommendations for international students: Required—TOEFL (minimum score 550 paper-based). Electronic applications accepted. *Faculty research:* Aerosol physics and chemistry, biocellular engineering fuel science, poly and membrane science.

Chemical Engineering

University of Louisiana at Lafayette, College of Engineering, Department of Chemical Engineering, Lafayette, LA 70504. Offers MSE. *Program availability:* Evening/weekend. *Degree requirements:* For master's, comprehensive exam, thesis or alternative. *Entrance requirements:* For master's, GRE General Test, BS in chemical engineering, minimum GPA of 2.85. Additional exam requirements/recommendations for international students: Required—TOEFL (minimum score 550 paper-based). Electronic applications accepted. *Faculty research:* Corrosion, transport phenomena and thermodynamics in the oil and gas industry.

University of Louisville, J. B. Speed School of Engineering, Department of Chemical Engineering, Louisville, KY 40292-0001. Offers M Eng, MS, PhD. *Accreditation:* ABET (one or more programs are accredited). *Faculty:* 9 full-time (1 woman). *Students:* 39 full-time (10 women), 3 part-time (0 women); includes 6 minority (1 Black or African American, non-Hispanic/Latino; 2 Asian, non-Hispanic/Latino; 2 Hispanic/Latino; 1 Two or more races, non-Hispanic/Latino), 15 international. Average age 26. 45 applicants, 18% accepted, 8 enrolled. In 2016, 9 master's, 3 doctorates awarded. Terminal master's awarded for partial completion of doctoral program. *Degree requirements:* For master's, thesis optional, minimum GPA of 3.0; for doctorate, comprehensive exam, thesis/dissertation, minimum GPA of 3.0. *Entrance requirements:* For master's and doctorate, GRE, letters of recommendation, final official transcripts. Additional exam requirements/recommendations for international students: Required—TOEFL (minimum score 550 paper-based; 80 iBT), IELTS (minimum score 6.5), GRE. *Application deadline:* For fall admission, 5/1 priority date for international students; for spring admission, 11/1 priority date for international students; for summer admission, 3/1 priority date for international students. Applications are processed on a rolling basis. Application fee: $60. Electronic applications accepted. *Expenses:* Tuition, state resident: full-time $12,246; part-time $681 per credit hour. Tuition, nonresident: full-time $25,486; part-time $1417 per credit hour. *Required fees:* $196. Tuition and fees vary according to program and reciprocity agreements. *Financial support:* In 2016–17, 2 fellowships with full tuition reimbursements (averaging $22,000 per year) were awarded; research assistantships with full tuition reimbursements, teaching assistantships with full tuition reimbursements, scholarships/grants, and health care benefits also available. Financial award application deadline: 1/1. *Faculty research:* Mixing in chemical and biochemical systems; nanomaterials processing; nanoparticles; surface science; materials including polymers, thin films, and rapid prototyping. *Total annual research expenditures:* $926,743. *Unit head:* Dr. Joel R. Fried, Chair, 502-852-6350, Fax: 502-852-6355, E-mail: joel.fried@louisville.edu. *Application contact:* R. Eric Berson, Director of Graduate Studies, 502-852-1567, E-mail: eric.berson@louisville.edu.
Website: http://louisville.edu/speed/chemical/

University of Maine, Graduate School, College of Engineering, Department of Chemical and Biological Engineering, Orono, ME 04469. Offers chemical engineering (MS, PhD). *Program availability:* Part-time. *Faculty:* 9 full-time (1 woman). *Students:* 21 full-time (7 women), 5 part-time (1 woman); includes 3 minority (2 Asian, non-Hispanic/Latino; 1 Two or more races, non-Hispanic/Latino), 13 international. Average age 29. 25 applicants, 44% accepted, 4 enrolled. In 2016, 3 master's, 3 doctorates awarded. Terminal master's awarded for partial completion of doctoral program. *Degree requirements:* For master's, thesis; for doctorate, comprehensive exam, thesis/dissertation. *Entrance requirements:* For master's and doctorate, GRE General Test. Additional exam requirements/recommendations for international students: Required—TOEFL. *Application deadline:* For fall admission, 6/1 priority date for domestic students, 3/1 priority date for international students; for spring admission, 11/1 priority date for domestic students, 9/1 priority date for international students. Applications are processed on a rolling basis. Application fee: $65. Electronic applications accepted. *Expenses:* Tuition, state resident: full-time $7524; part-time $2508 per credit. Tuition, nonresident: full-time $24,498; part-time $8166 per credit. *Required fees:* $1148; $571 per credit. *Financial support:* In 2016–17, 15 students received support, including 11 research assistantships with full tuition reimbursements available (averaging $18,700 per year), 3 teaching assistantships (averaging $19,300 per year); Federal Work-Study and tuition waivers (full and partial) also available. Financial award application deadline: 3/1. *Faculty research:* Biofuels, catalysts, paper, nanotechnology, bio-based chemicals. *Total annual research expenditures:* $1.4 million. *Unit head:* Dr. Hemant Pendse, Chair, 207-581-2290, Fax: 207-581-2323, E-mail: pendse@maine.edu. *Application contact:* Scott G. Delcourt, Assistant Vice President for Graduate Studies and Senior Associate Dean, 207-581-3291, Fax: 207-581-3232, E-mail: graduate@maine.edu.
Website: http://www.umche.maine.edu/chb/

The University of Manchester, School of Chemical Engineering and Analytical Science, Manchester, United Kingdom. Offers biocatalysis (M Phil, PhD); chemical engineering (M Phil, PhD); chemical engineering and analytical science (M Phil, D Eng, PhD); colloids, crystals, interfaces and materials (M Phil, PhD); environment and sustainable technology (M Phil, PhD); instrumentation (M Phil, PhD); multi-scale modeling (M Phil, PhD); process integration (M Phil, PhD); systems biology (M Phil, PhD).

University of Maryland, Baltimore County, The Graduate School, College of Engineering and Information Technology, Department of Chemical, Biochemical, and Environmental Engineering, Program in Chemical and Biochemical Engineering, Baltimore, MD 21250. Offers MS, PhD. *Program availability:* Part-time. *Students:* 20 full-time (9 women), 3 part-time (2 women); includes 6 minority (3 Black or African American, non-Hispanic/Latino; 3 Asian, non-Hispanic/Latino), 9 international. Average age 23. 41 applicants, 34% accepted, 7 enrolled. In 2016, 8 master's, 1 doctorate awarded. *Degree requirements:* For master's, comprehensive exam (for some programs), thesis (for some programs); for doctorate, comprehensive exam, thesis/dissertation. *Entrance requirements:* For master's, GRE General Test, minimum GPA of 3.0, strong mathematical background; for doctorate, GRE General Test (taken within last 5 years), minimum GPA of 3.0. Additional exam requirements/recommendations for international students: Required—TOEFL (minimum score 550 paper-based; 80 iBT). *Application deadline:* For fall admission, 6/1 for domestic students, 1/1 for international students; for spring admission, 11/1 for domestic students, 6/1 for international students. Applications are processed on a rolling basis. Application fee: $70. Electronic applications accepted. Application fee is waived when completed online. *Expenses:* Contact institution. *Financial support:* In 2016–17, 3 students received support, including 1 fellowship with full tuition reimbursement available (averaging $25,000 per year), 16 research assistantships with full tuition reimbursements available (averaging $23,000 per year); teaching assistantships, career-related internships or fieldwork, Federal Work-Study, scholarships/grants, health care benefits, tuition waivers (partial), and unspecified assistantships also available. Support available to part-time students. Financial award application deadline: 6/30; financial award applicants required to submit FAFSA. *Faculty research:* Biomaterials engineering, bioprocess engineering, cellular engineering, education, education and outreach, sensors and monitoring, systems biology and functional genomics. *Unit head:* Dr. Mark Marten, Professor and Interim Chair, 410-455-3400, Fax: 410-455-1049, E-mail: marten@umbc.edu. *Application contact:* Dr. Erin Lavik, Professor/Graduate Program Director, 410-455-3428, Fax: 410-455-1049, E-mail: elavik@umbc.edu.
Website: http://cbee.umbc.edu/

University of Maryland, College Park, Academic Affairs, A. James Clark School of Engineering, Department of Chemical and Biomolecular Engineering, College Park, MD 20742. Offers bioengineering (MS, PhD); chemical engineering (M Eng, MS, PhD). *Program availability:* Part-time, evening/weekend. *Degree requirements:* For master's, thesis optional; for doctorate, variable foreign language requirement, thesis/dissertation, exam, oral presentation. *Entrance requirements:* For master's and doctorate, GRE General Test, 3 letters of recommendation. Additional exam requirements/recommendations for international students: Required—TOEFL. Electronic applications accepted. *Faculty research:* Applied polymer science, biochemical engineering, thermal properties, bioprocess monitoring.

University of Massachusetts Amherst, Graduate School, College of Engineering, Department of Chemical Engineering, Amherst, MA 01003. Offers MSChE, PhD. *Program availability:* Part-time. Terminal master's awarded for partial completion of doctoral program. *Degree requirements:* For master's, thesis; for doctorate, comprehensive exam, thesis/dissertation. *Entrance requirements:* For master's and doctorate, GRE General Test. Additional exam requirements/recommendations for international students: Required—TOEFL (minimum score 550 paper-based; 80 iBT), IELTS (minimum score 6.5). Electronic applications accepted.

University of Massachusetts Lowell, Francis College of Engineering, Department of Chemical Engineering, Lowell, MA 01854. Offers MS Eng, PhD. *Program availability:* Part-time. *Degree requirements:* For master's, thesis; for doctorate, thesis/dissertation, seminar, qualifying examination. *Entrance requirements:* For master's, GRE General Test. Electronic applications accepted. *Faculty research:* Biotechnology/bioprocessing, nanomaterials, ceramic materials, materials characterization.

University of Michigan, College of Engineering, Department of Chemical Engineering, Ann Arbor, MI 48109. Offers MSE, PhD, Ch E. *Program availability:* Part-time, online learning. *Students:* 156 full-time (57 women), 3 part-time (2 women). 511 applicants, 25% accepted, 39 enrolled. In 2016, 39 master's, 10 doctorates awarded. Terminal master's awarded for partial completion of doctoral program. *Degree requirements:* For doctorate, thesis/dissertation, oral defense of dissertation, preliminary exams. *Entrance requirements:* For master's and doctorate, GRE General Test. Additional exam requirements/recommendations for international students: Required—TOEFL. *Application deadline:* Applications are processed on a rolling basis. Electronic applications accepted. *Expenses:* Tuition, state resident: full-time $21,466; part-time $1152 per credit hour. Tuition, nonresident: full-time $43,346; part-time $2367 per credit hour. Part-time tuition and fees vary according to course load, degree level and program. *Financial support:* Fellowships, research assistantships, teaching assistantships, scholarships/grants, traineeships, health care benefits, tuition waivers (partial), and unspecified assistantships available. Financial award applicants required to submit FAFSA. *Faculty research:* Life sciences and biotechnology, energy and environment, complex fluids and nanostructured materials. *Total annual research expenditures:* $14.6 million. *Unit head:* Mark Burns, Department Chair, 734-936-3314, E-mail: maburns@umich.edu. *Application contact:* Sue Hamlin, Graduate Program Coordinator, 734-763-1148, Fax: 734-764-7453, E-mail: hamlins@umich.edu.
Website: http://www.engin.umich.edu/che

University of Minnesota, Twin Cities Campus, College of Science and Engineering, Department of Chemical Engineering and Materials Science, Program in Chemical Engineering, Minneapolis, MN 55455-0132. Offers M Ch E, MS Ch E, PhD. *Program availability:* Part-time. Terminal master's awarded for partial completion of doctoral program. *Degree requirements:* For master's, thesis; for doctorate, thesis/dissertation. *Entrance requirements:* For master's and doctorate, GRE General Test. Additional exam requirements/recommendations for international students: Required—TOEFL. Electronic applications accepted. *Faculty research:* Biotechnology and bioengineering, chemical kinetics, reaction engineering and chemical process synthesis.

University of Missouri, Office of Research and Graduate Studies, College of Engineering, Department of Chemical Engineering, Columbia, MO 65211. Offers MS, PhD. *Faculty:* 11 full-time (3 women), 1 part-time/adjunct (0 women). *Students:* 22 full-time (8 women), 2 part-time. *Degree requirements:* For master's, thesis; for doctorate, thesis/dissertation. *Entrance requirements:* For master's and doctorate, GRE General Test, minimum GPA of 3.0. Additional exam requirements/recommendations for international students: Required—TOEFL (minimum score 550 paper-based; 80 iBT). *Application deadline:* For fall admission, 3/15 for domestic and international students; for winter admission, 10/15 for domestic and international students. Applications are processed on a rolling basis. Application fee: $75 ($90 for international students). Electronic applications accepted. *Expenses:* Tuition, state resident: full-time $6347; part-time $352.60 per credit hour. Tuition, nonresident: full-time $17,379; part-time $965.50 per credit hour. *Required fees:* $1035. Tuition and fees vary according to course load, campus/location and program. *Financial support:* Fellowships, research assistantships, teaching assistantships, institutionally sponsored loans, scholarships/grants, traineeships, health care benefits, and unspecified assistantships available. Support available to part-time students.
Website: http://engineering.missouri.edu/chemical/

University of Nebraska–Lincoln, Graduate College, College of Engineering, Department of Chemical and Biomolecular Engineering, Lincoln, NE 68588. Offers MS, PhD. *Degree requirements:* For master's, thesis; for doctorate, comprehensive exam, thesis/dissertation. *Entrance requirements:* For master's and doctorate, GRE. Additional exam requirements/recommendations for international students: Required—TOEFL (minimum score 550 paper-based). Electronic applications accepted. *Faculty research:* Fermentation, radioactive waste remediation, chemical fuels from renewable feedstocks.

University of Nevada, Reno, Graduate School, College of Engineering, Department of Chemical and Materials Engineering, Program in Chemical Engineering, Reno, NV 89557. Offers MS, PhD. Terminal master's awarded for partial completion of doctoral program. *Degree requirements:* For master's, comprehensive exam, thesis optional; for doctorate, thesis/dissertation. *Entrance requirements:* For master's, GRE General Test, minimum GPA of 2.75; for doctorate, GRE General Test, minimum GPA of 3.0. Additional exam requirements/recommendations for international students: Required—TOEFL (minimum score 500 paper-based; 61 iBT), IELTS (minimum score 6). Electronic applications accepted. *Faculty research:* Energy conservation, fuel efficiency, development and fabrication of new materials.

University of New Brunswick Fredericton, School of Graduate Studies, Faculty of Engineering, Department of Chemical Engineering, Fredericton, NB E3B 5A3, Canada. Offers chemical engineering (M Eng, M Sc E, PhD); environmental studies (M Eng). *Program availability:* Part-time. *Degree requirements:* For master's, thesis; for doctorate, comprehensive exam, thesis/dissertation, qualifying exam. *Entrance requirements:* For master's and doctorate, minimum GPA of 3.0. Additional exam requirements/recommendations for international students: Required—TOEFL (minimum score 580 paper-based), TWE (minimum score 5), Michigan English Language Assessment Battery (minimum score 85) or CanTest (minimum score 4.5). Electronic applications accepted. *Faculty research:* Processing and characterizing nanoengineered composite materials based on carbon nanotubes, enhanced oil recovery processes and oil sweep strategies for conventional and heavy oils, pulp and paper, waste-water treatment, chemistry and corrosion of high and lower temperature water systems, adsorption, aquaculture systems, bioprocessing and biomass refining, nanotechnologies, nuclear, oil and gas, polymer and recirculation.

University of New Hampshire, Graduate School, College of Engineering and Physical Sciences, Department of Chemical Engineering, Durham, NH 03824. Offers M Engr, MS, PhD. *Degree requirements:* For master's, thesis; for doctorate, thesis/dissertation. *Entrance requirements:* For master's and doctorate, GRE. Additional exam requirements/recommendations for international students: Required—TOEFL (minimum score 550 paper-based). Electronic applications accepted.

University of New Mexico, Graduate Studies, School of Engineering, Program in Chemical Engineering, Albuquerque, NM 87131-2039. Offers MS, PhD. *Program availability:* Part-time. *Faculty:* 1 (woman) full-time, 2 part-time/adjunct (0 women). *Students:* 23 full-time (7 women), 10 part-time (2 women); includes 7 minority (1 Asian, non-Hispanic/Latino; 5 Hispanic/Latino; 1 Two or more races, non-Hispanic/Latino), 12 international. Average age 27. 21 applicants, 52% accepted, 15 enrolled. In 2016, 6 master's, 7 doctorates awarded. Terminal master's awarded for partial completion of doctoral program. *Degree requirements:* For master's, thesis (for some programs); for doctorate, comprehensive exam, thesis/dissertation, qualifying exam. *Entrance requirements:* For master's, GRE General Test, minimum GPA of 3.0, 3 letters of reference, letter of intent; for doctorate, GRE General Test, 3 letters of reference, minimum GPA of 3.0, letter of intent. Additional exam requirements/recommendations for international students: Required—TOEFL. *Application deadline:* For fall admission, 1/15 priority date for domestic and international students; for spring admission, 7/15 priority date for domestic and international students. Application fee: $50. Electronic applications accepted. *Financial support:* Fellowships, research assistantships with full tuition reimbursements, scholarships/grants, traineeships, and health care benefits available. Financial award application deadline: 1/15; financial award applicants required to submit FAFSA. *Faculty research:* Bioanalytical systems, ceramics, catalysis, colloidal science, bioengineering, biomaterials, fuel cells, protein engineering, semiconductors, tissue engineering. *Unit head:* Dr. Timothy Ward, Chair, 505-277-5431, Fax: 505-277-5433, E-mail: tward@unm.edu. *Application contact:* Jocelyn White, Coordinator/Program Advisor, 505-277-5606, Fax: 505-277-5433, E-mail: jowhite@unm.edu.
Website: http://cbe.unm.edu/programs-and-degrees/graduate/index.html

University of North Dakota, Graduate School, School of Engineering and Mines, Department of Chemical Engineering, Grand Forks, ND 58202. Offers M Engr, MS, PhD. *Program availability:* Part-time. *Degree requirements:* For master's, comprehensive exam, thesis or alternative. *Entrance requirements:* For master's, GRE General Test, minimum GPA of 3.0 (MS), 2.5 (M Engr). Additional exam requirements/recommendations for international students: Required—TOEFL (minimum score 550 paper-based; 79 iBT), IELTS (minimum score 6.5). *Application deadline:* For fall admission, 8/1 priority date for domestic students, 5/1 priority date for international students; for spring admission, 12/1 priority date for domestic students, 9/1 priority date for international students. Applications are processed on a rolling basis. Application fee: $35. Electronic applications accepted. *Financial support:* Fellowships with full and partial tuition reimbursements, research assistantships with full and partial tuition reimbursements, teaching assistantships with full and partial tuition reimbursements, career-related internships or fieldwork, Federal Work-Study, institutionally sponsored loans, scholarships/grants, health care benefits, tuition waivers (full and partial), and unspecified assistantships available. Support available to part-time students. Financial award application deadline: 3/15; financial award applicants required to submit FAFSA. *Faculty research:* Catalysis, fluid flow and heat transfer, application of fractals, modeling and simulation, reaction engineering. *Unit head:* Dr. Frank Burman, Graduate Director, 701-777-2958, Fax: 701-777-4838, E-mail: frank.burman@mail.und.nodak.edu. *Application contact:* Staci Wells, Admissions Associate, 701-777-2945, Fax: 701-777-3619, E-mail: staci.wells@gradschool.und.edu.
Website: http://www.und.edu/dept/sem/che/

University of Notre Dame, Graduate School, College of Engineering, Department of Chemical and Biomolecular Engineering, Notre Dame, IN 46556. Offers MS Ch E, PhD. *Degree requirements:* For master's, comprehensive exam, thesis; for doctorate, comprehensive exam, thesis/dissertation, candidacy exam. *Entrance requirements:* For master's, GRE General Test; for doctorate, GRE General Test, GRE Subject Test (strongly recommended). Additional exam requirements/recommendations for international students: Required—TOEFL (minimum score 600 paper-based; 80 iBT). Electronic applications accepted. *Faculty research:* Biomolecular engineering, green chemistry and engineering for the environment, advanced materials, nanoengineering, catalysis and reaction engineering.

University of Oklahoma, Gallogly College of Engineering, School of Chemical, Biological and Materials Engineering, Norman, OK 73019. Offers chemical engineering (MS, PhD). *Program availability:* Part-time. *Faculty:* 12 full-time (1 woman). *Students:* 23 full-time (5 women), 8 part-time (5 women); includes 2 minority (1 Black or African American, non-Hispanic/Latino; 1 American Indian or Alaska Native, non-Hispanic/Latino), 20 international. Average age 26. 83 applicants, 11% accepted, 9 enrolled. In 2016, 6 master's, 9 doctorates awarded. *Degree requirements:* For master's, thesis, oral defense of thesis; for doctorate, comprehensive exam, thesis/dissertation, oral defense of dissertation. *Entrance requirements:* For master's and doctorate, GRE. Additional exam requirements/recommendations for international students: Required—TOEFL (minimum score 79 iBT) or IELTS (minimum score 6.5). *Application deadline:* Applications are processed on a rolling basis. Application fee: $50 ($100 for international students). Electronic applications accepted. *Expenses:* Tuition, state resident: full-time $4886; part-time $203.60 per credit hour. Tuition, nonresident: full-time $18,989; part-time $791.20 per credit hour. *Required fees:* $3283; $126.25 per credit hour. $126.50 per semester. *Financial support:* In 2016–17, 31 students received support, including 29 research assistantships with full tuition reimbursements available (averaging $17,305 per year), 2 teaching assistantships (averaging $1,870 per year). Financial award application deadline: 6/1; financial award applicants required to submit FAFSA. *Faculty research:* Applied surfactant technologies, biofuels and bio-refining, biomedical and biochemical engineering, catalysis and surface characterization, nanomaterials. *Total annual research expenditures:* $3 million. *Unit head:* Dr. Brian Grady, Director, 405-325-5814, Fax: 405-325-5813, E-mail: cbme@ou.edu. *Application contact:* Donna King, Graduate Program Staff Assistant, 405-325-5812, Fax: 405-325-5813, E-mail: donnaking@ou.edu.
Website: http://www.ou.edu/coe/cbme.html

University of Ottawa, Faculty of Graduate and Postdoctoral Studies, Faculty of Engineering, Department of Chemical and Biological Engineering, Ottawa, ON K1N 6N5, Canada. Offers M Eng, MA Sc, PhD. *Degree requirements:* For master's, thesis or alternative; for doctorate, comprehensive exam, thesis/dissertation. *Entrance requirements:* For master's, honors degree or equivalent, minimum B average; for doctorate, master's degree, minimum B+ average. Electronic applications accepted. *Faculty research:* Material development, process engineering, clean technologies.

University of Pennsylvania, School of Engineering and Applied Science, Department of Chemical and Biomolecular Engineering, Philadelphia, PA 19104. Offers MSE, PhD. *Program availability:* Part-time. *Faculty:* 18 full-time (3 women), 5 part-time/adjunct (0 women). *Students:* 102 full-time (33 women), 5 part-time (0 women); includes 10 minority (1 Black or African American, non-Hispanic/Latino; 8 Asian, non-Hispanic/Latino; 1 Hispanic/Latino), 72 international. Average age 25. 482 applicants, 27% accepted, 59 enrolled. In 2016, 29 master's, 13 doctorates awarded. *Degree requirements:* For master's, comprehensive exam, thesis optional; for doctorate, comprehensive exam, thesis/dissertation. *Entrance requirements:* For master's and doctorate, GRE. Additional exam requirements/recommendations for international students: Required—TOEFL (minimum score 100 iBT), IELTS (minimum score 7). *Application deadline:* For fall admission, 3/15 priority date for domestic and international students. Application fee: $80. Electronic applications accepted. *Expenses: Tuition:* Full-time $31,068; part-time $5762 per course. *Required fees:* $3200; $336 per course. Full-time tuition and fees vary according to degree level, program and student level. Part-time tuition and fees vary according to course load, degree level and program. *Faculty research:* Advanced materials and nanotechnology, catalysis and reaction engineering, cellular and biomolecular engineering, energy and environmental engineering, molecular simulation and thermodynamics. *Application contact:* William Fenton, Assistant Director of Graduate Admissions, 215-898-4542, Fax: 215-573-5577, E-mail: gradstudies@seas.upenn.edu.
Website: http://www.cbe.seas.upenn.edu/prospective-students/masters/index.php

University of Pittsburgh, Swanson School of Engineering, Department of Chemical and Petroleum Engineering, Pittsburgh, PA 15260. Offers chemical engineering (MS Ch E, PhD); petroleum engineering (MSPE); MS Ch E/MSPE. *Program availability:* Part-time, 100% online. *Faculty:* 22 full-time (4 women), 12 part-time/adjunct (1 woman). *Students:* 106 full-time (36 women), 11 part-time (3 women); includes 11 minority (4 Black or African American, non-Hispanic/Latino; 3 Asian, non-Hispanic/Latino; 1 Hispanic/Latino; 3 Two or more races, non-Hispanic/Latino), 73 international. 336 applicants, 45% accepted, 42 enrolled. In 2016, 25 master's, 10 doctorates awarded. Terminal master's awarded for partial completion of doctoral program. *Degree requirements:* For doctorate, comprehensive exam, thesis/dissertation, final oral exams. *Entrance requirements:* For master's and doctorate, GRE General Test, minimum GPA of 3.0. Additional exam requirements/recommendations for international students: Required—TOEFL (minimum score 550 paper-based; 80 iBT). *Application deadline:* For fall admission, 3/1 priority date for domestic and international students; for spring admission, 7/1 priority date for domestic and international students. Applications are processed on a rolling basis. Application fee: $50. Electronic applications accepted. *Expenses:* $24,962 full-time per academic year in-state tuition, $41,222 full-time per academic year out-of-state tuition; $830 mandatory fees per academic year. *Financial support:* In 2016–17, 10 fellowships with full tuition reimbursements (averaging $30,720 per year), 33 research assistantships with full tuition reimbursements (averaging $27,396 per year), 29 teaching assistantships with full tuition reimbursements (averaging $26,328 per year) were awarded; scholarships/grants, traineeships, and tuition waivers (full) also available. Financial award application deadline: 3/1. *Faculty research:* Biotechnology, polymers, catalysis, energy and environment, computational modeling. *Total annual research expenditures:* $10 million. *Unit head:* Dr. Steven R. Little, Chairman, 412-624-9614, Fax: 412-624-9639, E-mail: srlittle@pitt.edu. *Application contact:* Rama Bazaz, Director, 412-624-9800, Fax: 412-624-9808, E-mail: ssoeadm@pitt.edu.
Website: http://www.engineering.pitt.edu/Departments/Chemical-Petroleum

University of Puerto Rico, Mayagüez Campus, Graduate Studies, College of Engineering, Department of Chemical Engineering, Mayagüez, PR 00681-9000. Offers ME, MS, PhD. *Program availability:* Part-time. *Faculty:* 24 full-time (9 women), 1 part-time/adjunct (0 women). *Students:* 44 full-time (18 women); includes 36 minority (all Hispanic/Latino), 8 international. Average age 25. 13 applicants, 46% accepted, 5 enrolled. In 2016, 3 master's, 9 doctorates awarded. Terminal master's awarded for partial completion of doctoral program. *Degree requirements:* For master's, one foreign language, comprehensive exam, thesis; for doctorate, one foreign language, comprehensive exam, thesis/dissertation. *Entrance requirements:* For master's, BS in chemical engineering or its equivalent; minimum GPA of 3.0; for doctorate, MS in chemical engineering or its equivalent; minimum GPA of 3.0. *Application deadline:* For fall admission, 2/15 for domestic and international students; for spring admission, 9/15 for domestic and international students. Applications are processed on a rolling basis. Application fee: $25. Electronic applications accepted. *Expenses: Tuition, area resident:* Full-time $2466. *International tuition:* $7166 full-time. *Required fees:* $210. One-time fee: $5 full-time. Tuition and fees vary according to course level, campus/location, program and student level. *Financial support:* In 2016–17, 37 students received support, including 34 research assistantships (averaging $4,277 per year), 16 teaching assistantships (averaging $3,774 per year); unspecified assistantships also available. *Faculty research:* Process simulation and optimization, air and water pollution control, mass transport, biochemical engineering, colloids and interfaces. *Unit head:* Aldo Acevedo, Ph.D., Chair and Associate Professor, 787-832-4040 Ext. 2587, Fax: 787-265-3818, E-mail: aldo.acevedo@upr.edu. *Application contact:* Waleska Velazquez, 787-832-4040 Ext. 3748, Fax: 787-265-3818, E-mail: waleska.velazquez@upr.edu.
Website: http://inqu.uprm.edu/home/

University of Rhode Island, Graduate School, College of Engineering, Department of Chemical Engineering, Kingston, RI 02881. Offers chemical engineering (MS, PhD). *Program availability:* Part-time. *Faculty:* 9 full-time (2 women). *Students:* 21 full-time (8 women), 8 part-time (2 women); includes 3 minority (1 Black or African American, non-Hispanic/Latino; 2 Hispanic/Latino), 14 international. In 2016, 3 master's, 2 doctorates, 1 other advanced degree awarded. *Degree requirements:* For master's, comprehensive exam (for some programs), thesis optional; for doctorate, comprehensive exam, thesis/dissertation. *Entrance requirements:* For master's and doctorate, 3 letters of recommendation. Additional exam requirements/recommendations for international students: Required—TOEFL. *Application deadline:* For fall admission, 12/1 for domestic and international students; for spring admission, 7/15 for domestic and international students; for summer admission, 12/1 for domestic students. Application fee: $65. Electronic applications accepted. *Expenses:* Tuition, state resident: full-time $11,796; part-time $655 per credit. Tuition, nonresident: full-time $24,206; part-time $1345 per credit. *Required fees:* $1546; $44 per credit. One-time fee: $155 full-time; $35 part-time. *Financial support:* In 2016–17, 5 research assistantships with tuition reimbursements (averaging $8,795 per year), 3 teaching assistantships with tuition reimbursements (averaging $8,810 per year) were awarded. Financial award application deadline: 12/1; financial award applicants required to submit FAFSA. *Unit head:* Dr. Geoffrey Bothun, Chair, 401-874-9518, E-mail: gbothun@uri.edu. *Application contact:* Brenda Moyer, Graduate Coordinator, 401-874-2656, E-mail: moyer@uri.edu.
Website: http://egr.uri.edu/che/

University of Rochester, Hajim School of Engineering and Applied Sciences, Master of Science in Technical Entrepreneurship and Management Program, Rochester, NY 14642. Offers biomedical engineering (MS); chemical engineering (MS); computer science (MS); electrical and computer engineering (MS); energy and the environment (MS); materials science (MS); mechanical engineering (MS); optics (MS). Program offered in collaboration with the Simon School of Business. *Program availability:* Part-time. *Students:* 42 full-time (13 women), 6 part-time (3 women); includes 7 minority (1 Black or African American, non-Hispanic/Latino; 1 Asian, non-Hispanic/Latino; 4 Hispanic/Latino; 1 Two or more races, non-Hispanic/Latino), 28 international. Average age 24. 245 applicants, 65% accepted, 29 enrolled. In 2016, 31 master's awarded.

Chemical Engineering

Degree requirements: For master's, comprehensive exam, final exam. *Entrance requirements:* For master's, GRE or GMAT, 3 letters of recommendation; personal statement; official transcript; bachelor's degree (or equivalent for international students) in engineering, science, or mathematics. Additional exam requirements/recommendations for international students: Required—TOEFL (minimum score 600 paper-based; 100 iBT). *Application deadline:* For fall admission, 2/1 for domestic and international students. Application fee: $60. Electronic applications accepted. *Expenses:* $1,800 per credit. *Financial support:* In 2016–17, 45 students received support. Career-related internships or fieldwork and scholarships/grants available. Support available to part-time students. Financial award application deadline: 2/1. *Faculty research:* High efficiency solar cells, macromolecular self-assembly, digital signal processing, memory hierarchy management, molecular and physical mechanisms in cell migration, optical imaging systems. *Unit head:* Duncan T. Moore, Vice Provost for Entrepreneurship, 585-275-5248, Fax: 585-473-6745, E-mail: duncan.moore@rochester.edu. *Application contact:* Andrea Barrett, Executive Director, 585-276-3407, Fax: 585-276-2357, E-mail: andrea.barrett@rochester.edu.
Website: http://www.rochester.edu/team

University of Rochester, Hajim School of Engineering and Applied Sciences, Program in Chemical Engineering, Rochester, NY 14627. Offers MS, PhD. *Program availability:* Part-time. *Faculty:* 11 full-time (1 woman). *Students:* 39 full-time (12 women); includes 5 minority (3 Asian, non-Hispanic/Latino; 2 Hispanic/Latino), 27 international. Average age 25. 136 applicants, 45% accepted, 12 enrolled. In 2016, 17 master's, 6 doctorates awarded. Terminal master's awarded for partial completion of doctoral program. *Degree requirements:* For master's, comprehensive exam, thesis, final exam; for doctorate, thesis/dissertation, qualifying exam. *Entrance requirements:* For master's and doctorate, GRE. Additional exam requirements/recommendations for international students: Required—TOEFL (minimum score 600 paper-based; 100 iBT). *Application deadline:* For fall admission, 1/15 for domestic and international students. Application fee: $60. Electronic applications accepted. *Expenses:* $1,583 per credit hour. *Financial support:* In 2016–17, 43 students received support, including 11 fellowships (averaging $28,000 per year), 12 research assistantships (averaging $28,000 per year); tuition waivers (partial) also available. Financial award application deadline: 4/15. *Faculty research:* Advanced materials, alternative energy, biotechnology, electrochemistry, theory and simulation, functional interfaces. *Unit head:* Matthew Yates, Chairman, 585-273-2335, E-mail: myates@che.rochester.edu. *Application contact:* Vicki Heberling, Graduate Program Coordinator, 585-275-4913, E-mail: victoria.heberling@rochester.edu.
Website: http://www.che.rochester.edu/graduate/index.html
See Display below and Close-Up on page 175.

University of Saskatchewan, College of Graduate Studies and Research, College of Engineering, Chemical Engineering Program, Saskatoon, SK S7N 5A9, Canada. Offers M Eng, M Sc, PhD. *Program availability:* Part-time. *Degree requirements:* For master's, thesis (for some programs), 30 credits (for M Eng); thesis and 12 credits (for MS); for doctorate, comprehensive exam, thesis/dissertation, qualifying exam, 18 credits. *Entrance requirements:* For master's and doctorate, GRE. Additional exam requirements/recommendations for international students: Required—TOEFL, TOEFL (minimum iBT score of 80), IELTS (6.5), CanTEST (4.5), or PTE (59). Electronic applications accepted. *Faculty research:* Applied thermodynamics, biochemical engineering, biosorption, chemical reaction engineering and catalysis, corrosion, environmental remediation, fluidization, fuel cell and microbial fuel cell technology, mineral processing, petroleum processing, process engineering, renewable energy.

University of South Africa, College of Science, Engineering and Technology, Pretoria, South Africa. Offers chemical engineering (M Tech); information technology (M Tech).

University of South Alabama, College of Engineering, Department of Chemical Engineering, Mobile, AL 36688. Offers MS Ch E. *Faculty:* 5 full-time (1 woman). *Students:* 7 full-time (3 women), 6 part-time (2 women); includes 4 minority (1 Black or African American, non-Hispanic/Latino; 1 Asian, non-Hispanic/Latino; 1 Hispanic/Latino; 1 Two or more races, non-Hispanic/Latino), 2 international. Average age 25. 33 applicants, 27% accepted, 4 enrolled. In 2016, 10 master's awarded. *Degree requirements:* For master's, comprehensive exam, project or thesis. *Entrance requirements:* For master's, GRE General Test, BS in engineering, minimum GPA of 3.0. Additional exam requirements/recommendations for international students: Required—TOEFL (minimum score 550 paper-based; 79 iBT). *Application deadline:* For fall admission, 7/1 priority date for domestic students, 6/1 priority date for international students; for spring admission, 12/1 priority date for domestic students, 11/1 priority date for international students; for summer admission, 5/1 priority date for domestic students, 4/1 priority date for international students. Applications are processed on a rolling basis. Application fee: $35. Electronic applications accepted. *Expenses:* Contact institution. *Financial support:* Fellowships, research assistantships, teaching assistantships, career-related internships or fieldwork, Federal Work-Study, institutionally sponsored loans, scholarships/grants, and unspecified assistantships available. Support available to part-time students. Financial award application deadline: 5/31; financial award applicants required to submit FAFSA. *Faculty research:* Molecular imaging, novel catalyst synthesis, gas separation and storage, lipidic ionic liquids, microscopy. *Unit head:* Dr. Nicholas D. Sylvester, Interim Department Chair, 251-460-6160, Fax: 251-461-1485, E-mail: engineering@southalabama.edu. *Application contact:* Brenda Poole, Academic Records Specialist, 251-460-6140, Fax: 251-460-6343, E-mail: engineering@southalabama.edu.
Website: http://www.southalabama.edu/colleges/engineering/chbe/index.html

University of South Carolina, The Graduate School, College of Engineering and Computing, Department of Chemical Engineering, Columbia, SC 29208. Offers ME, MS, PhD. *Program availability:* Part-time, evening/weekend, online learning. *Degree requirements:* For master's, comprehensive exam, thesis (for some programs); for doctorate, comprehensive exam, thesis/dissertation. *Entrance requirements:* For master's and doctorate, GRE General Test. Additional exam requirements/recommendations for international students: Required—TOEFL. Electronic applications accepted. *Faculty research:* Rheology, liquid and supercritical extractions, electrochemistry, corrosion, heterogeneous and homogeneous catalysis.

University of Southern California, Graduate School, Viterbi School of Engineering, Mork Family Department of Chemical Engineering and Materials Science, Los Angeles, CA 90089. Offers chemical engineering (MS, PhD, Engr); geoscience technologies (MS); materials engineering (MS); materials science (MS, PhD, Engr); petroleum engineering (MS, PhD, Engr); smart oilfield technologies (MS, Graduate Certificate). Terminal master's awarded for partial completion of doctoral program. *Degree requirements:* For master's, thesis optional; for doctorate, thesis/dissertation. *Entrance requirements:* For master's and doctorate, GRE General Test. Additional exam requirements/recommendations for international students: Recommended—TOEFL. Electronic applications accepted. *Expenses:* Contact institution. *Faculty research:* Heterogeneous materials and porous media, statistical mechanics, molecular simulation, polymer science and engineering, advanced materials, reaction engineering and catalysis, membrane processes and separation, biochemical engineering, cell culture, bioreactor modeling, petroleum engineering.

University of South Florida, College of Engineering, Department of Chemical and Biomedical Engineering, Tampa, FL 33620. Offers biomedical engineering (MSBE, PhD); chemical engineering (MSCH, PhD). *Program availability:* Part-time. *Faculty:* 15 full-time (2 women). *Students:* 91 full-time (42 women), 20 part-time (5 women); includes 16 minority (7 Black or African American, non-Hispanic/Latino; 4 Asian, non-Hispanic/

Latino; 5 Hispanic/Latino), 57 international. Average age 27. 195 applicants, 46% accepted, 43 enrolled. In 2016, 42 master's, 9 doctorates awarded. Terminal master's awarded for partial completion of doctoral program. *Degree requirements:* For master's, comprehensive exam, thesis (for some programs); for doctorate, comprehensive exam, thesis/dissertation. *Entrance requirements:* For master's, GRE General Test, undergraduate degree in engineering, science, or chemical engineering with minimum GPA of 3.0; at least two letters of recommendation; current resume; statement of research interests (for students who wish to pursue thesis option); for doctorate, GRE General Test, undergraduate degree in engineering, science, or chemical engineering with minimum GPA of 3.0; three letters of recommendation; current resume; statement of research interests. Additional exam requirements/recommendations for international students: Required—TOEFL (minimum score 550 paper-based; 79 iBT) or IELTS (minimum score 6.5). *Application deadline:* For fall admission, 2/15 for domestic and international students; for spring admission, 10/15 for domestic students, 9/15 for international students; for summer admission, 2/15 for domestic students, 1/15 for international students. Application fee: $30. Electronic applications accepted. *Expenses:* Tuition, state resident: full-time $7766; part-time $431.43 per credit hour. Tuition, nonresident: full-time $15,789; part-time $877.17 per credit hour. *Required fees:* $37 per term. *Financial support:* In 2016–17, 28 students received support, including 29 research assistantships with tuition reimbursements available (averaging $13,171 per year), 12 teaching assistantships with tuition reimbursements available (averaging $14,017 per year); unspecified assistantships also available. Financial award applicants required to submit FAFSA. *Faculty research:* Neuroengineering, tissue engineering, biomedicine and biotechnology, engineering education, functional materials and nanotechnology, energy, environment/sustainability. *Total annual research expenditures:* $987,111. *Unit head:* Dr. Venkat R. Bhethanabotla, Professor and Department Chair, 813-974-3997, E-mail: bhethana@usf.edu. *Application contact:* Dr. Robert Frisina, Jr., Professor and Graduate Program Director, 813-974-4013, Fax: 813-974-3651, E-mail: rfrisina@usf.edu.
Website: http://che.eng.usf.edu/

University of South Florida, Innovative Education, Tampa, FL 33620-9951. Offers adult, career and higher education (Graduate Certificate), including college teaching, leadership in developing human resources, leadership in higher education; Africana studies (Graduate Certificate), including diasporas and health disparities, genocide and human rights; aging studies (Graduate Certificate), including gerontology; art research (Graduate Certificate), including museum studies; business foundations (Graduate Certificate); chemical and biomedical engineering (Graduate Certificate), including materials science and engineering, water, health and sustainability; child and family studies (Graduate Certificate), including positive behavior support; civil and industrial engineering (Graduate Certificate), including transportation systems analysis; community and family health (Graduate Certificate), including maternal and child health, social marketing and public health, violence and injury: prevention and intervention, women's health; criminology (Graduate Certificate), including criminal justice administration; educational measurement and research (Graduate Certificate), including evaluation; English (Graduate Certificate), including comparative literary studies, creative writing, professional and technical communication; entrepreneurship (Graduate Certificate); environmental health (Graduate Certificate), including safety management; epidemiology and biostatistics (Graduate Certificate), including applied biostatistics, biostatistics, concepts and tools of epidemiology, epidemiology, epidemiology of infectious diseases; geography, environment and planning (Graduate Certificate), including community development, environmental policy and management, geographical information systems; geology (Graduate Certificate), including hydrogeology; global health (Graduate Certificate), including disaster management, global health and Latin American and Caribbean studies, global health practice, humanitarian assistance, infection control; government and international affairs (Graduate Certificate), including Cuban studies, globalization studies; health policy and management (Graduate Certificate), including health management and leadership, public health policy and programs; hearing specialist: early intervention (Graduate Certificate); industrial and management systems engineering (Graduate Certificate), including systems engineering, technology management; information studies (Graduate Certificate), including school library media specialist; information systems/decision sciences (Graduate Certificate), including analytics and business intelligence; instructional technology (Graduate Certificate), including distance education, Florida digital/virtual educator, instructional design, multimedia design, Web design; internal medicine, bioethics and medical humanities (Graduate Certificate), including biomedical ethics; Latin American and Caribbean studies (Graduate Certificate); mass communications (Graduate Certificate), including multimedia journalism; mathematics and statistics (Graduate Certificate), including mathematics; medicine (Graduate Certificate), including aging and neuroscience, bioinformatics, biotechnology, brain fitness and memory management, clinical investigation, health informatics, health sciences, integrative weight management, intellectual property, medicine and gender, metabolic and nutritional medicine, metabolic cardiology, pharmacy sciences; national and competitive intelligence (Graduate Certificate); psychological and social foundations (Graduate Certificate), including career counseling, college teaching, diversity in education, mental health counseling, school counseling; public affairs (Graduate Certificate), including nonprofit management, public management, research administration; public health (Graduate Certificate), including environmental health, health equity, public health generalist, translational research in adolescent behavioral health; public health practices (Graduate Certificate), including planning for healthy communities; rehabilitation and mental health counseling (Graduate Certificate), including integrative mental health care, marriage and family therapy, rehabilitation technology; secondary education (Graduate Certificate), including ESOL, foreign language education: culture and content, foreign language education: professional; social work (Graduate Certificate), including geriatric social work/clinical gerontology; special education (Graduate Certificate), including autism spectrum disorder, disabilities education: severe/profound; world languages (Graduate Certificate), including teaching English as a second language (TESL) or foreign language. *Expenses:* Tuition, state resident: full-time $7766; part-time $431.43 per credit hour. Tuition, nonresident: full-time $15,789; part-time $877.17 per credit hour. *Required fees:* $37 per term. *Unit head:* Kathy Barnes, Interdisciplinary Programs Coordinator, 813-974-8031, Fax: 813-974-7061, E-mail: barnesk@usf.edu. *Application contact:* Karen Tylinski, Metro Initiatives, 813-974-9943, Fax: 813-974-7061, E-mail: ktylinsk@usf.edu.
Website: http://www.usf.edu/innovative-education/

The University of Tennessee, Graduate School, Tickle College of Engineering, Department of Chemical and Biomolecular Engineering, Knoxville, TN 37996. Offers chemical engineering (MS, PhD); reliability and maintainability engineering (MS); MS/MBA. *Program availability:* Part-time. *Faculty:* 32 full-time (5 women). *Students:* 53 full-time (16 women), 2 part-time (0 women); includes 7 minority (2 Black or African American, non-Hispanic/Latino; 3 Hispanic/Latino; 2 Two or more races, non-Hispanic/Latino), 24 international. Average age 26. 82 applicants, 30% accepted, 10 enrolled. In 2016, 4 master's, 7 doctorates awarded. *Degree requirements:* For master's, thesis or alternative; for doctorate, comprehensive exam, thesis/dissertation. *Entrance requirements:* For master's, GRE General Test (for MS students pursuing research thesis), minimum GPA of 2.7 (for U.S. degree holders), 3.0 (for international degree holders); for doctorate, GRE General Test, minimum GPA of 3.0 on previous graduate course work. Additional exam requirements/recommendations for international students: Required—TOEFL (minimum score 550 paper-based). *Application deadline:* For fall admission, 2/1 priority date for domestic and international students; for spring admission, 6/15 for domestic and international students. Applications are processed on a rolling basis. Application fee: $35. Electronic applications accepted. *Financial support:* In 2016–17, 51 students received support, including 3 fellowships (averaging $25,333 per year), 28 research assistantships with full tuition reimbursements available (averaging $25,846 per year), 15 teaching assistantships with full tuition reimbursements available (averaging $24,126 per year); career-related internships or fieldwork, Federal Work-Study, institutionally sponsored loans, health care benefits, and unspecified assistantships also available. Financial award application deadline: 2/1; financial award applicants required to submit FAFSA. *Faculty research:* Bio-fuels; engineering of soft, functional and structural materials; fuel cells and energy storage devices; molecular and cellular bioengineering; molecular modeling and simulations. *Total annual research expenditures:* $3.9 million. *Unit head:* Dr. Bamin Khomami, Head, 865-974-2421, Fax: 865-974-7076, E-mail: bkhomami@utk.edu. *Application contact:* Dr. Paul Frymier, Graduate Program Coordinator, 865-974-4961, Fax: 865-974-7076, E-mail: pdf@utk.edu.
Website: http://www.engr.utk.edu/cbe/

The University of Tennessee at Chattanooga, Program in Engineering, Chattanooga, TN 37403. Offers automotive systems (MS Engr); chemical engineering (MS Engr); civil engineering (MS Engr); computational engineering (MS Engr); electrical engineering (MS Engr); industrial engineering (MS Engr); mechanical engineering (MS Engr). *Program availability:* Part-time. *Faculty:* 21 full-time (2 women), 2 part-time/adjunct (1 woman). *Students:* 21 full-time (5 women), 26 part-time (7 women); includes 11 minority (4 Black or African American, non-Hispanic/Latino; 5 Asian, non-Hispanic/Latino; 1 Hispanic/Latino; 1 Two or more races, non-Hispanic/Latino), 18 international. Average age 28. 30 applicants, 83% accepted, 14 enrolled. In 2016, 25 master's awarded. *Degree requirements:* For master's, comprehensive exam, thesis or alternative, engineering project. *Entrance requirements:* For master's, GRE General Test, minimum undergraduate GPA of 2.7 or 3.0 in last two years of undergraduate coursework. Additional exam requirements/recommendations for international students: Required—TOEFL (minimum score 550 paper-based; 79 iBT), IELTS (minimum score 6). *Application deadline:* For fall admission, 6/15 priority date for domestic students, 7/1 for international students; for spring admission, 11/1 priority date for domestic students, 11/1 for international students. Applications are processed on a rolling basis. Application fee: $35 ($40 for international students). Electronic applications accepted. *Expenses:* $9,876 full-time in-state; $25,994 full-time out-of-state; $450 per credit part-time in-state; $1,345 per credit part-time out-of-state. *Financial support:* In 2016–17, 6 research assistantships, 5 teaching assistantships were awarded; career-related internships or fieldwork, scholarships/grants, health care benefits, and unspecified assistantships also available. Support available to part-time students. Financial award application deadline: 7/1. *Faculty research:* Quality control and reliability engineering, financial management, thermal science, energy conservation, structural analysis. *Total annual research expenditures:* $921,122. *Unit head:* Dr. Daniel Pack, Dean, 423-425-2256, Fax: 423-425-5311, E-mail: daniel-pack@utc.edu. *Application contact:* Dr. Joanne Romagni, Dean of the Graduate School, 423-425-4478, Fax: 423-425-5223, E-mail: joanne-romagni@utc.edu.
Website: http://www.utc.edu/college-engineering-computer-science/graduate-programs/msengr.php

The University of Texas at Austin, Graduate School, Cockrell School of Engineering, Department of Chemical Engineering, Austin, TX 78712-1111. Offers MSE, PhD. Terminal master's awarded for partial completion of doctoral program. *Degree requirements:* For master's, thesis (for some programs); for doctorate, comprehensive exam, thesis/dissertation. *Entrance requirements:* For master's and doctorate, GRE General Test. Electronic applications accepted.

The University of Toledo, College of Graduate Studies, College of Engineering, Department of Chemical and Environmental Engineering, Toledo, OH 43606-3390. Offers chemical engineering (MS, PhD). *Program availability:* Part-time, evening/weekend. *Degree requirements:* For master's, thesis optional; for doctorate, thesis/dissertation, qualifying exam. *Entrance requirements:* For master's, GRE General Test, minimum GPA of 3.0; for doctorate, GRE General Test, minimum GPA of 3.3. Additional exam requirements/recommendations for international students: Required—TOEFL (minimum score 550 paper-based; 80 iBT). Electronic applications accepted. *Faculty research:* Polymers, applied computing, membranes, alternative energy (fuel cells).

University of Toronto, School of Graduate Studies, Faculty of Applied Science and Engineering, Department of Chemical Engineering and Applied Chemistry, Toronto, ON M5S 1A1, Canada. Offers M Eng, MA Sc, PhD. *Program availability:* Part-time. *Degree requirements:* For master's, thesis (for some programs); for doctorate, thesis/dissertation. *Entrance requirements:* For master's, minimum B+ average in final 2 years, four-year degree in engineering (M Eng, MA Sc) or physical sciences (MA Sc), 2 letters of reference; for doctorate, research master's degree, minimum B+ average, 2 letters of reference. Additional exam requirements/recommendations for international students: Required—TOEFL (minimum score 580 paper-based; 93 iBT), TWE (minimum score 4). Electronic applications accepted.

The University of Tulsa, Graduate School, College of Engineering and Natural Sciences, Department of Chemical Engineering, Tulsa, OK 74104-3189. Offers ME, MSE, PhD. *Program availability:* Part-time. *Faculty:* 9 full-time (3 women). *Students:* 18 full-time (3 women), 7 part-time (2 women); includes 3 minority (1 American Indian or Alaska Native, non-Hispanic/Latino; 2 Asian, non-Hispanic/Latino), 21 international. Average age 27. 55 applicants, 36% accepted, 3 enrolled. In 2016, 3 master's, 3 doctorates awarded. Terminal master's awarded for partial completion of doctoral program. *Degree requirements:* For master's, thesis (for some programs); for doctorate, comprehensive exam, thesis/dissertation. *Entrance requirements:* For master's and doctorate, GRE General Test. Additional exam requirements/recommendations for international students: Required—TOEFL (minimum score 550 paper-based; 80 iBT), IELTS (minimum score 6). *Application deadline:* Applications are processed on a rolling basis. Application fee: $55. Electronic applications accepted. *Expenses: Tuition:* Full-time $22,230; part-time $1235 per credit hour. *Required fees:* $990 per semester. Tuition and fees vary according to course load. *Financial support:* In 2016–17, 17 students received support, including 4 fellowships with full tuition reimbursements available (averaging $2,500 per year), 15 research assistantships with full tuition reimbursements available (averaging $10,399 per year), 6 teaching assistantships with full tuition reimbursements available (averaging $14,007 per year); career-related internships or fieldwork, Federal Work-Study, scholarships/grants, health care benefits, tuition waivers (full and partial), and unspecified assistantships also available. Support available to part-time students. Financial award application deadline: 2/1; financial award applicants required to submit FAFSA. *Faculty research:* Environment, surface science, catalysis, transport phenomena, process systems engineering, bioengineering, alternative energy, petrochemical processes. *Total annual research expenditures:* $928,438. *Unit head:* Dr. Geoffrey Price, Chairperson, 918-631-2575, Fax: 918-631-3268, E-mail: chegradadvisor@utulsa.edu. *Application contact:* Dr. Ty Johannes,

Advisor, 918-631-2947, Fax: 918-631-3268, E-mail: ty-johannes@utulsa.edu. Website: http://engineering.utulsa.edu/academics/chemical-engineering/

University of Utah, Graduate School, College of Engineering, Department of Chemical Engineering, Salt Lake City, UT 84112. Offers chemical engineering (MS, PhD); petroleum engineering (MS); MS/MBA. *Program availability:* Part-time, evening/weekend, online learning. *Faculty:* 14 full-time (2 women), 10 part-time/adjunct (2 women). *Students:* 75 full-time (17 women), 35 part-time (6 women); includes 13 minority (3 Black or African American, non-Hispanic/Latino; 5 Asian, non-Hispanic/Latino; 4 Hispanic/Latino; 1 Two or more races, non-Hispanic/Latino), 54 international. Average age 28. 210 applicants, 17% accepted, 29 enrolled. In 2016, 20 master's, 15 doctorates awarded. *Degree requirements:* For master's, comprehensive exam, thesis (for some programs); for doctorate, comprehensive exam, thesis/dissertation. *Entrance requirements:* For master's, GRE General Test, minimum GPA of 3.0; for doctorate, GRE General Test, minimum GPA of 3.0, degree or course work in chemical engineering. Additional exam requirements/recommendations for international students: Required—TOEFL (minimum score 550 paper-based; 80 iBT), IELTS (minimum score 6.5). *Application deadline:* For fall admission, 1/15 priority date for domestic and international students; for spring admission, 10/1 priority date for domestic and international students; for summer admission, 2/1 priority date for domestic and international students. Applications are processed on a rolling basis. Application fee: $0 ($15 for international students). Electronic applications accepted. *Expenses:* Contact institution. *Financial support:* In 2016–17, 53 students received support, including 5 fellowships with full tuition reimbursements available (averaging $25,450 per year), 41 research assistantships with full tuition reimbursements available (averaging $24,444 per year), 6 teaching assistantships (averaging $6,848 per year); Federal Work-Study, institutionally sponsored loans, scholarships/grants, and unspecified assistantships also available. Financial award application deadline: 4/15; financial award applicants required to submit FAFSA. *Faculty research:* Drug delivery, fossil fuel and biomass combustion and gasification, oil and gas reservoir characteristics and management, multi-scale simulation, micro-scale synthesis. *Unit head:* Dr. Milind D. Deo, Chair, 801-581-6915, Fax: 801-585-9291, E-mail: milind.deo@utah.edu. *Application contact:* Cynthia Ruiz, Graduate Coordinator, 801-587-3610, Fax: 801-585-9291, E-mail: cynthia.ruiz@chemeng.utah.edu. Website: http://www.che.utah.edu/

University of Virginia, School of Engineering and Applied Science, Department of Chemical Engineering, Charlottesville, VA 22903. Offers ME, MS, PhD. *Program availability:* Online learning. *Faculty:* 12 full-time (1 woman). *Students:* 46 full-time (16 women); includes 6 minority (1 Black or African American, non-Hispanic/Latino; 5 Asian, non-Hispanic/Latino), 18 international. Average age 25. 143 applicants, 24% accepted, 14 enrolled. In 2016, 7 master's, 4 doctorates awarded. *Degree requirements:* For master's, thesis (for some programs); for doctorate, thesis/dissertation. *Entrance requirements:* For master's, GRE General Test, 3 recommendations; for doctorate, GRE General Test, 3 recommendations, essay. Additional exam requirements/recommendations for international students: Required—TOEFL (minimum score 600 paper-based; 90 iBT), IELTS (minimum score 7). *Application deadline:* For fall admission, 8/1 for domestic students, 4/1 for international students; for winter admission, 12/1 for domestic students, 8/1 for international students; for spring admission, 5/1 for domestic students, 1/1 for international students. Applications are processed on a rolling basis. Application fee: $60. Electronic applications accepted. *Expenses:* Tuition, state resident: full-time $15,026; part-time $834 per credit hour. Tuition, nonresident: full-time $25,168; part-time $1378 per credit hour. *Required fees:* $2654. *Financial support:* Fellowships, research assistantships, and teaching assistantships available. Financial award application deadline: 1/15; financial award applicants required to submit FAFSA. *Faculty research:* Fluid mechanics, heat and mass transfer, chemical reactor analysis and engineering, biochemical engineering and biotechnology. *Unit head:* William Epling, Chair, 434-924-7778, Fax: 434-982-2658, E-mail: wse2t@virginia.edu. *Application contact:* Kyle Lampe, Graduate Admissions Coordinator, 434-924-7778, Fax: 434-982-2658, E-mail: lampe@virginia.edu.
Website: http://www.che.virginia.edu/

University of Washington, Graduate School, College of Engineering, Department of Chemical Engineering, Seattle, WA 98195-1750. Offers chemical engineering (MS, PhD); chemical engineering and advanced data science (PhD); chemical engineering and nanotechnology (PhD). *Faculty:* 19 full-time (3 women). *Students:* 116 full-time (39 women), 3 part-time (0 women); includes 21 minority (11 Asian, non-Hispanic/Latino; 7 Hispanic/Latino; 3 Two or more races, non-Hispanic/Latino), 49 international. 392 applicants, 27% accepted, 39 enrolled. In 2016, 25 master's, 10 doctorates awarded. Terminal master's awarded for partial completion of doctoral program. *Degree requirements:* For master's, comprehensive exam, thesis optional, final exam, research project, degree completed in 6 years; for doctorate, comprehensive exam, thesis/dissertation, general and final exams, research project, completion of all work within 10 years. *Entrance requirements:* For master's and doctorate, GRE General Test (minimum Quantitative score of 159), minimum GPA of 3.0, official transcripts, personal statement, confidential evaluations by 3 professors or other technical professional, high rank (top 5%) in respected chemical engineering program. Additional exam requirements/recommendations for international students: Required—TOEFL (minimum score 580 paper-based; 92 iBT); Recommended—IELTS (minimum score 7). *Application deadline:* For fall admission, 1/1 priority date for domestic students, 12/15 priority date for international students. Applications are processed on a rolling basis. Application fee: $85. Electronic applications accepted. *Expenses:* Contact institution. *Financial support:* In 2016–17, 125 students received support, including 15 fellowships with full tuition reimbursements available (averaging $2,573 per year), 66 research assistantships with full tuition reimbursements available (averaging $2,573 per year), 44 teaching assistantships with full tuition reimbursements available (averaging $2,573 per year); career-related internships or fieldwork, Federal Work-Study, health care benefits, and unspecified assistantships also available. Financial award application deadline: 1/15; financial award applicants required to submit FAFSA. *Faculty research:* Materials processing and characterization, optical and electronic polymers, surface science, biochemical engineering and bioengineering, computational chemistry, environmental studies. *Total annual research expenditures:* $12.7 million. *Unit head:* Dr. Francois Baneyx, Professor/Chair, 206-543-2250, Fax: 206-543-3778, E-mail: baneyx@uw.edu. *Application contact:* Allison Sherrill, Graduate Program Advisor, 206-685-9785, E-mail: sherra@uw.edu.
Website: http://www.cheme.washington.edu/

University of Waterloo, Graduate Studies, Faculty of Engineering, Department of Chemical Engineering, Waterloo, ON N2L 3G1, Canada. Offers M Eng, MA Sc, PhD. *Program availability:* Part-time. *Degree requirements:* For master's, research project or thesis, seminar; for doctorate, comprehensive exam, thesis/dissertation. *Entrance requirements:* For master's, honors degree, minimum B average; for doctorate, master's degree, minimum A- average. Additional exam requirements/recommendations for international students: Required—TOEFL, IELTS, PTE. Electronic applications accepted. *Faculty research:* Biotechnical and environmental engineering, mathematical analysis, statistics and control, polymer science and engineering.

The University of Western Ontario, Faculty of Graduate Studies, Physical Sciences Division, Faculty of Engineering, London, ON N6A 5B8, Canada. Offers chemical and biochemical engineering (ME Sc, PhD); civil and environmental engineering (M Eng, ME Sc, PhD); electrical and computer engineering (M Eng, ME Sc, PhD); mechanical and materials engineering (M Eng, ME Sc, PhD). *Program availability:* Part-time. Terminal master's awarded for partial completion of doctoral program. *Degree requirements:* For master's, thesis; for doctorate, thesis/dissertation. *Entrance requirements:* For master's, minimum B average; for doctorate, minimum B+ average. *Faculty research:* Wind, geotechnical, chemical reactor engineering, applied electrostatics, biochemical engineering.

University of Wisconsin–Madison, Graduate School, College of Engineering, Department of Chemical and Biological Engineering, Madison, WI 53706-0607. Offers chemical engineering (PhD). *Faculty:* 20 full-time (2 women). *Students:* 114 full-time (26 women); includes 10 minority (5 Asian, non-Hispanic/Latino; 4 Hispanic/Latino; 1 Two or more races, non-Hispanic/Latino), 53 international. Average age 25. 332 applicants, 25% accepted, 24 enrolled. In 2016, 17 doctorates awarded. *Degree requirements:* For doctorate, comprehensive exam, thesis/dissertation, at least 18 credits of coursework, 2 semesters of teaching assistantship. *Entrance requirements:* For doctorate, GRE General Test, bachelor's degree in chemical engineering. Additional exam requirements/recommendations for international students: Required—TOEFL (minimum score 580 paper-based; 92 iBT). *Application deadline:* For fall admission, 12/15 for domestic and international students; for spring admission, 10/15 for domestic and international students. Application fee: $75 ($81 for international students). Electronic applications accepted. *Expenses:* $13,157 per year in-state tuition and fees; $26,484 per year out-of-state tuition and fees. *Financial support:* In 2016–17, 149 students received support, including 9 fellowships with full tuition reimbursements available, 114 research assistantships with full tuition reimbursements available, 26 teaching assistantships with full tuition reimbursements available; traineeships and health care benefits also available. Financial award application deadline: 12/1; financial award applicants required to submit FAFSA. *Faculty research:* Fluid mechanics, colloids, bioengineering, reaction and systems engineering, materials and nanotechnology, polymer science and engineering, process control, optimization and scheduling, catalysis. *Total annual research expenditures:* $13.3 million. *Unit head:* Prof. Manos Mavrikakis, Chair, 608-263-2922, Fax: 608-262-5434, E-mail: emavrikakis@wisc.edu. *Application contact:* Kathy M. Heinzen, Senior Student Services Coordinator, 608-263-3138, Fax: 608-262-5434, E-mail: gradrecruit2017@che.wisc.edu.
Website: https://www.engr.wisc.edu/department/cbe/

University of Wyoming, College of Engineering and Applied Sciences, Department of Chemical and Petroleum Engineering, Program in Chemical Engineering, Laramie, WY 82071. Offers MS, PhD. *Program availability:* Part-time. Terminal master's awarded for partial completion of doctoral program. *Degree requirements:* For master's, thesis; for doctorate, thesis/dissertation. *Entrance requirements:* For master's and doctorate, GRE General Test, minimum GPA of 3.0. Additional exam requirements/recommendations for international students: Required—TOEFL (minimum score 600 paper-based; 76 iBT). Electronic applications accepted. *Faculty research:* Microwave reactor systems, synthetic fuels, fluidization, coal combustion/gasification, flue-gas cleanup.

Vanderbilt University, School of Engineering, Department of Chemical and Biomolecular Engineering, Nashville, TN 37240-1001. Offers M Eng, MS, PhD. MS and PhD offered through the Graduate School. *Program availability:* Part-time. *Degree requirements:* For master's, thesis; for doctorate, thesis/dissertation. *Entrance requirements:* For master's and doctorate, GRE General Test. Additional exam requirements/recommendations for international students: Required—TOEFL. Electronic applications accepted. *Expenses: Tuition:* Part-time $1854 per credit hour. *Faculty research:* Adsorption and surface chemistry; biochemical engineering and biotechnology; chemical reaction engineering, environment, materials, process modeling and control; molecular modeling and thermodynamics.

Villanova University, College of Engineering, Department of Chemical Engineering, Villanova, PA 19085-1699. Offers biochemical engineering (Certificate); chemical engineering (MSChE); environmental protection in the chemical process industries (Certificate). *Program availability:* Part-time, evening/weekend. *Degree requirements:* For master's, comprehensive exam, thesis optional. *Entrance requirements:* For master's, GRE General Test (for applicants with degrees from foreign universities), B Ch E, minimum GPA of 3.0. Additional exam requirements/recommendations for international students: Required—TOEFL (minimum score 600 paper-based; 100 iBT). *Faculty research:* Heat transfer, advanced materials, chemical vapor deposition, pyrolysis and combustion chemistry, industrial waste treatment.

Virginia Polytechnic Institute and State University, Graduate School, College of Engineering, Blacksburg, VA 24061. Offers aerospace engineering (ME, MS, PhD); biological systems engineering (ME, MS, PhD); biomedical engineering (MS, PhD); chemical engineering (ME, MS, PhD); civil engineering (ME, MS, PhD); computer engineering (ME, MS, PhD); computer science (MS, PhD); electrical engineering (ME, PhD); engineering education (PhD); engineering mechanics (ME, MS, PhD); environmental engineering (MS); environmental science and engineering (MS); industrial and systems engineering (ME, MS, PhD); materials science and engineering (ME, MS, PhD); mechanical engineering (ME, MS, PhD); mining and minerals engineering (PhD); mining engineering (ME, MS); nuclear engineering (MS, PhD); ocean engineering (MS); systems engineering (ME, MS). *Faculty:* 400 full-time (73 women), 3 part-time/adjunct (2 women). *Students:* 1,949 full-time (487 women), 393 part-time (69 women); includes 251 minority (56 Black or African American, non-Hispanic/Latino; 3 American Indian or Alaska Native, non-Hispanic/Latino; 87 Asian, non-Hispanic/Latino; 70 Hispanic/Latino; 35 Two or more races, non-Hispanic/Latino), 1,354 international. Average age 27. 4,903 applicants, 19% accepted, 569 enrolled. In 2016, 364 master's, 200 doctorates awarded. *Degree requirements:* For master's, comprehensive exam (for some programs), thesis (for some programs); for doctorate, comprehensive exam (for some programs), thesis/dissertation (for some programs). *Entrance requirements:* For master's and doctorate, GRE/GMAT. Additional exam requirements/recommendations for international students: Required—TOEFL (minimum score 80 iBT). *Application deadline:* For fall admission, 8/1 for domestic students, 4/1 for international students; for spring admission, 1/1 for domestic students, 9/1 for international students. Applications are processed on a rolling basis. Application fee: $75. Electronic applications accepted. *Expenses:* Tuition, state resident: full-time $12,467; part-time $692.50 per credit hour. Tuition, nonresident: full-time $25,095; part-time $1394.25 per credit hour. *Required fees:* $2669; $491.50 per semester. Tuition and fees vary according to course load, campus/location and program. *Financial support:* In 2016–17, 160 fellowships with full tuition reimbursements (averaging $7,387 per year), 872 research assistantships with full tuition reimbursements (averaging $22,329 per year), 313 teaching assistantships with full tuition reimbursements (averaging $18,714 per year) were awarded. Financial award application deadline: 3/1; financial award applicants required to submit FAFSA. *Total annual research expenditures:* $91.8 million. *Unit head:* Dr. Julia Ross, Dean, 540-231-9752, Fax: 540-231-3031, E-mail: deaneng@vt.edu. *Application contact:* Linda Perkins, Executive Assistant, 540-231-9752, Fax: 540-231-3031, E-mail: lperkins@vt.edu.
Website: http://www.eng.vt.edu/

Washington State University, Voiland College of Engineering and Architecture, The Gene and Linda Voiland School of Chemical Engineering and Bioengineering, Pullman,

WA 99164-6515. Offers MS, PhD. Terminal master's awarded for partial completion of doctoral program. *Degree requirements:* For master's, comprehensive exam, thesis (for some programs), oral exam; for doctorate, one foreign language, comprehensive exam, thesis/dissertation, oral exam. *Entrance requirements:* For master's and doctorate, minimum GPA of 3.0, 3 letters of recommendation by faculty. Additional exam requirements/recommendations for international students: Required—TOEFL (minimum score 580 paper-based). *Faculty research:* Kinetics and catalysis, biofilm engineering, muscle systems, engineering education.

Washington University in St. Louis, School of Engineering and Applied Science, Department of Energy, Environmental and Chemical Engineering, St. Louis, MO 63130-4899. Offers chemical engineering (MS, D Sc); environmental engineering (MS, D Sc). *Program availability:* Part-time. Terminal master's awarded for partial completion of doctoral program. *Degree requirements:* For master's, thesis optional; for doctorate, thesis/dissertation, preliminary exam, qualifying exam. *Entrance requirements:* For master's and doctorate, GRE, minimum B average during final 2 years of course work. Additional exam requirements/recommendations for international students: Required—TOEFL, TWE. Electronic applications accepted. *Faculty research:* Reaction engineering, materials processing, catalysis, process control, air pollution control.

Wayne State University, College of Engineering, Department of Chemical Engineering and Materials Science, Detroit, MI 48202. Offers chemical engineering (MS, PhD); materials science and engineering (MS, PhD, Graduate Certificate), including materials science and engineering (MS, PhD), polymer engineering (Graduate Certificate). *Program availability:* Part-time. *Faculty:* 11. *Students:* 44 full-time (12 women), 23 part-time (6 women); includes 3 minority (1 Black or African American, non-Hispanic/Latino; 2 Asian, non-Hispanic/Latino), 40 international. Average age 26. 230 applicants, 31% accepted, 18 enrolled. In 2016, 12 master's, 5 doctorates awarded. *Degree requirements:* For master's, thesis optional; for doctorate, thesis/dissertation. *Entrance requirements:* For master's, three letters of recommendation (at least two from the applicant's academic institution); personal statement; resume; for doctorate, GRE, three letters of recommendation (at least two from the applicant's academic institution); personal statement; resume; for Graduate Certificate, bachelor's degree in engineering, chemistry, or physics. Additional exam requirements/recommendations for international students: Required—TOEFL (minimum score 550 paper-based; 79 iBT), TWE (minimum score 5.5), Michigan English Language Assessment Battery (minimum score 85); Recommended—IELTS (minimum score 6.5). *Application deadline:* For fall admission, 3/1 priority date for domestic and international students; for winter admission, 10/1 priority date for domestic students, 9/1 priority date for international students; for spring admission, 2/1 priority date for domestic and international students; for summer admission, 2/1 priority date for domestic and international students. Application fee: $50. Electronic applications accepted. *Expenses:* $18,871 per year resident tuition and fees, $36,065 per year non-resident tuition and fees. *Financial support:* In 2016–17, 26 students received support, including 7 fellowships with tuition reimbursements available (averaging $14,884 per year), 10 research assistantships with tuition reimbursements available (averaging $19,546 per year), 12 teaching assistantships with tuition reimbursements available (averaging $19,017 per year); scholarships/grants, health care benefits, and unspecified assistantships also available. Support available to part-time students. Financial award applicants required to submit FAFSA. *Faculty research:* Thermodynamics and transport properties of polymer solutions; processing, rheology, and separation of polymers; heterogeneous catalysts; surface science of catalyst and polymeric materials; laser-based imaging of chemical species and reactions; environmental transport and management of hazardous waste; process design and synthesis based on waste minimization, biocatalysis in multiphase systems, biomaterials and tissue engineering. *Total annual research expenditures:* $1.6 million. *Unit head:* Dr. Guangzhao Mao, Professor and Chair, 313-577-3804, E-mail: gzmao@eng.wayne.edu. *Application contact:* Ellen Cope, Graduate Program Coordinator, E-mail: escope@wayne.edu. Website: http://engineering.wayne.edu/che/

Western Michigan University, Graduate College, College of Engineering and Applied Sciences, Department of Chemical and Paper Engineering, Kalamazoo, MI 49008. Offers MS, MSE, PhD. *Degree requirements:* For master's, thesis optional; for doctorate, one foreign language, comprehensive exam, thesis/dissertation.

West Virginia University, Statler College of Engineering and Mineral Resources, Department of Chemical Engineering, Morgantown, WV 26506. Offers MS Ch E, PhD. *Program availability:* Part-time. Terminal master's awarded for partial completion of doctoral program. *Degree requirements:* For master's, thesis; for doctorate, comprehensive exam, thesis/dissertation, original research proposal, dissertation research proposal. *Entrance requirements:* For master's and doctorate, minimum GPA of 3.0. Additional exam requirements/recommendations for international students: Required—TOEFL (minimum score 80 iBT). Electronic applications accepted. *Faculty research:* Biocatalysis and catalysis, fluid-particle systems, high-value non-fuel uses of coal, opto-electronic materials processing, polymer and polymer-composite nanotechnology.

Widener University, Graduate Programs in Engineering, Program in Chemical Engineering, Chester, PA 19013. Offers M Eng. *Program availability:* Part-time, evening/weekend. *Students:* 1 (woman) full-time, all international. Average age 28. In 2016, 13 master's awarded. *Degree requirements:* For master's, thesis optional. *Application deadline:* For fall admission, 8/1 priority date for domestic students; for spring admission, 12/1 for domestic students. Applications are processed on a rolling basis. Application fee: $0. Electronic applications accepted. Tuition and fees vary according to degree level and program. *Financial support:* Teaching assistantships with tuition reimbursements and unspecified assistantships available. Financial award application deadline: 3/15. *Faculty research:* Biotechnology, environmental engineering, computational fluid mechanics, reaction kinetics, process design. *Unit head:* Rudolph Treichel, Assistant Dean/Director of Graduate Programs, 610-499-1294, Fax: 610-499-4059, E-mail: rjtreichel@widener.edu.

Worcester Polytechnic Institute, Graduate Studies and Research, Department of Chemical Engineering, Worcester, MA 01609-2280. Offers MS, PhD. *Program availability:* Part-time, evening/weekend. *Faculty:* 8 full-time (3 women), 1 (woman) part-time/adjunct. *Students:* 29 full-time (9 women), 1 part-time (0 women); includes 2 minority (both Asian, non-Hispanic/Latino), 13 international. 105 applicants, 25% accepted, 6 enrolled. In 2016, 11 master's, 1 doctorate awarded. Terminal master's awarded for partial completion of doctoral program. *Degree requirements:* For master's, thesis; for doctorate, comprehensive exam, thesis/dissertation. *Entrance requirements:* For master's and doctorate, GRE (recommended), 3 letters of recommendation, statement of purpose. Additional exam requirements/recommendations for international students: Required—TOEFL (minimum score 550 paper-based; 84 iBT), IELTS (minimum score 7), GRE. *Application deadline:* For fall admission, 1/1 priority date for domestic and international students; for spring admission, 10/1 priority date for domestic and international students. Applications are processed on a rolling basis. Application fee: $70. Electronic applications accepted. *Financial support:* Fellowships, research assistantships, career-related internships or fieldwork, institutionally sponsored loans, scholarships/grants, and unspecified assistantships available. Financial award application deadline: 1/1; financial award applicants required to submit FAFSA. *Unit head:* Dr. Susan Roberts, Head, 508-831-5250, Fax: 508-831-5853, E-mail: scroberts@wpi.edu. *Application contact:* Dr. Aaron Deskins, Graduate Coordinator, 508-831-5250, Fax: 508-831-5853, E-mail: nadeskins@wpi.edu.
Website: http://www.wpi.edu/academics/che

Yale University, Graduate School of Arts and Sciences, School of Engineering and Applied Science, Department of Chemical Engineering, New Haven, CT 06520. Offers MS, PhD. Terminal master's awarded for partial completion of doctoral program. *Degree requirements:* For doctorate, thesis/dissertation, exam. *Entrance requirements:* For master's and doctorate, GRE General Test. Additional exam requirements/recommendations for international students: Required—TOEFL. *Faculty research:* Biochemical engineering, heterogeneous catalysis, high-temperature chemical reaction engineering, separation science and technology, colloids and complex fluids.

UNIVERSITY OF ROCHESTER

Edmund A. Hajim School of Engineering and Applied Sciences
Department of Chemical Engineering

 For more information, visit http://petersons.to/rochesterchemengineering

Programs of Study

The interdisciplinary nature of the University of Rochester's chemical engineering program manifests itself in active collaborations with other departments at the school. The faculty enjoys generous research support from government agencies and private industries. The University's graduate programs are among the highest ranked in the nation according to the 2010 National Research Council survey report (www.nap.edu/rdp).

To earn a Ph.D., students must complete 90 credit hours. It typically takes five years to complete the program, which includes successful defense of a dissertation. The first two semesters are devoted to graduate courses in chemical engineering and other sciences. Students are expected to provide undergraduate teaching assistance. At the end of this period, students take a first-year examination as a transition from classroom to full-time research.

Students without prior backgrounds in chemical engineering are encouraged to apply. The Department has a graduate curriculum devised for students with a background in science, such as chemistry, physics, and biology. The curriculum combines courses at the undergraduate and graduate levels and is designed to foster interdisciplinary research in advanced materials, nanotechnology, alternative energy, and biotechnology.

The Master of Science degree may be obtained through either a full-time or a part-time program. Graduate students may complete a thesis (Plan A) or choose a non-thesis (Plan B) option. All students who pursue Plan A are expected to earn 30 hours of credit, of which a minimum of 18 and a maximum of 24 hours should be formal course work. The balance of credit hours required for the degree is earned through M.S. research and/or reading courses. Satisfactory completion of the master thesis is also required. All students who pursue Plan B must earn a minimum of 32 credits of course work. At least 18 credits should be taken from courses within the Department. Overall, no more than 6 credits toward a degree may be earned by research and/or reading courses. Plan B students are required to pass a comprehensive oral exam toward the end of their program.

The Department of Chemical Engineering also awards the Master of Science degree in Alternative Energy. Courses and research projects focus on the fundamentals and applications of the generation, storage, and utilization of various forms of alternative energy as well as their impact on sustainability and energy conservation. This program is designed for graduate students with a bachelor's degree in engineering or science who are interested in pursuing a technical career in alternative energy. As with the other M.S. programs, the M.S. degree in Alternative Energy is available as a full- or part-time program, with a thesis (Plan A) or non-thesis (Plan B) option. All students who pursue Plan A are expected to earn 30 hours of credit; at least 18 should be attributed to 400-level courses. The balance of the credit-hour requirement can be satisfied through independent reading (no more than 4 credit hours) and thesis research (at least 6 credit hours), culminating in a master thesis. All students who pursue Plan B must earn a minimum of 32 credits of course work, with at least 18 credits from 400-level courses and no more than 4 through independent reading. Students may opt for industrial internship (1 credit hour), for which a final essay must be submitted as a part of their degree requirements. In addition to course work and the essay, all Plan B students must pass a comprehensive oral exam toward the end of their program.

Research Facilities

The River Campus Libraries hold approximately 2.5 million volumes and provide access to an extensive collection of electronic, multimedia, and interlibrary loan resources. Miner Library includes more than 230,000 volumes of journals, books, theses, and government documents for health-care and medical research. Located at the Medical Center, the library also maintains access to online databases and electronic resources.

The Laboratory for Laser Energetics and the Center for Optoelectronics and Imaging are two state-of-the-art facilities in which specialized material science research is conducted. The Laboratory for Laser Energetics was established in 1970 for the investigation of the interaction of intense radiation with matter, to conduct experiments in support of the National Inertial Confinement Fusion (ICF) program; develop new laser and materials technologies; provide education in electro-optics, high-power lasers, high-energy-density physics, plasma physics, and nuclear fusion technology; operate the National Laser User's Facility; and conduct research in advanced technology related to high-energy-density phenomena.

The renowned Medical Center, which is a few minutes' walk from the River Campus, houses the Peptide Sequencing/Mass Spectrometry Facilities, Cell Sorting Facility, Nucleic Acid Laboratory, Real-Time and Static Confocal Imaging Facility, Functional Genomics Center, and a network of nearly 1,000 investigators providing research, clinical trial, and education services. In addition, a recently founded research institute, the Aab Institute of Biomedical Sciences, is the centerpiece of a ten-year, $400-million strategic plan to expand the Medical Center's research programs in the basic sciences. It is headquartered in a 240,000-square-foot research building on the Medical Center campus.

Financial Aid

The University offers fellowships, scholarships, and assistantships for full-time graduate students, and individual departments provide support through research assistantships. Applicants are encouraged to apply for outside funding such as NSF or New York State fellowships. Full-time Ph.D. students receive an annual stipend of $28,000 plus full graduate tuition.

Cost of Study

In the 2017–18 academic year, tuition is $1,596 per credit hour. Students must also pay additional yearly fees of $600 for health services and $2,292 for optional health insurance. All amounts are subject to change.

Living and Housing Costs

Students are eligible to lease a University apartment if enrolled as a full-time graduate student or postgraduate trainee. In the 2017–18 academic year, rent, utilities, food, and supplies are estimated at $17,000 per year; books at $1,500; and personal expenses at $2,800. All amounts are subject to change.

Student Group

The chemical engineering discipline appeals to students who are proficient at both analytical and descriptive sciences, and are intrigued by the prospect of investigating new phenomena, and devising new materials and devices for the technologies of the future. Students in the master's degree program should have acquired technical background in chemistry, mathematics, and physics. For students interested in biotechnology, a technical background in biology is desirable.

Student Outcomes

In addition to the traditional jobs in the chemical process and petrochemical industries, chemical engineers work in pharmaceuticals, health care, pulp and paper, food processing, polymers, biotechnology, and environmental health and safety industries. Their expertise is also applied in law, education, publishing, finance, and medicine. Chemical engineers also are well equipped to analyze environmental issues and develop solutions to environmental problems, such as pollution control and remediation.

Location

Located at a bend of the Genesee River, the 85-acre River Campus is about 2 miles south of downtown Rochester, New York. Rochester has been ranked as one of the Northeast's ten "Best Places to Live in America" by *Money* magazine; Rochester has also been listed as one of the "Most Livable Cities" in America by the Partners for Livable Communities. Rochester claims more sites on the National Register of Historic Places than any other city its size. With Lake Ontario on its northern border and the scenic Finger Lakes to the south, the Rochester area of about 1 million people offers a wide variety of cultural and recreational opportunities through its museums, parks, orchestras, planetarium, theater companies, and professional sports teams.

The University

Founded in 1850, the University of Rochester ranks among the most highly regarded universities in the country, offering degree programs at the bachelor's, master's, and doctoral levels, as well as in several professional disciplines. In the last eighteen years, 27 faculty members have been named Guggenheim Fellows. Present faculty members include a MacArthur Foundation fellowship recipient and 6 National Endowment for the Humanities Senior Fellows. Past alumni have included 7 Nobel Prize winners and 11 Pulitzer Prize winners. The University's Eastman School of Music is consistently ranked as one of the top music schools in the nation.

University of Rochester

Applying

The official graduate application can be found online at **https://apply.grad. rochester.edu**. The entire application must be received by January 15 for fall admission. Late applications are considered for exceptional applicants only if scholarship slots are available. Applicants are required to send college transcripts, letters of recommendation, personal/research statement, curriculum vitae, and standardized test results along with a $60 application fee to the Department of Chemical Engineering.

Correspondence and Information

Graduate Program Coordinator
Department of Chemical Engineering
University of Rochester
4510 Wegman Hall, Box 270166
Rochester, New York 14627-0166
United States
Phone: 585-275-4913
Fax: 585-273-1348
E-mail: chegradinfo@che.rochester.edu
Website: http://www.che.rochester.edu

THE FACULTY AND THEIR RESEARCH

Mitchell Anthamatten, Professor and Scientist, LLE; Ph.D., MIT, 2001. Macromolecular self-assembly, associative and functional polymers, nanostructured materials, liquid crystals, interfacial phenomena, optoelectronic materials, vapor deposition polymerization, fuel cell membranes.

Danielle S. W. Benoit, Associate Professor Biomedical Engineering and Chemical Engineering; Ph.D., Colorado, 2006. The rational design, synthesis, characterization, and employment of materials to treat diseases or control cell behavior for applications in drug therapy, regenerative medicine, and tissue engineering.

Shaw H. Chen, Professor and Senior Scientist, LLE; Ph.D., Minnesota, 1981. Organic semiconductors, green chemical engineering, glassy liquid crystals, photoalignment of conjugated molecules, bipolar hosts for phosphorescent OLEDs, geometric surfactancy for bulk heterojunction solar cells.

Eldred H. Chimowitz, Professor; Ph.D., Connecticut, 1982. Critical phenomena, statistical mechanics of fluids, computer-aided design, supercritical fluids.

David G. Foster, Associate Professor; Ph.D., Rochester, 1999. Principles of transport phenomena, classic chemical engineering as well as biomedical engineering research, creation of nanoparticle coatings for enhanced capture of flowing cells in microtubes, capture cancer cells in blood flow, creating state-of-the-art videos for curricular purposes of fundamental fluid mechanics principles.

David R. Harding, Professor of Chemical Engineering and Senior Scientist, LLE; Ph.D., Cambridge, 1986. Thin-film deposition, properties of films and composite structures, and developing cryogenic fuel capsules for nuclear fusion experiments.

Jacob Jorné, Professor; Ph.D., Berkeley, 1972. Electrochemical engineering, microelectronics processing, fuel cells, polymer electrolyte membrane fuel cell, lithium batteries, green energy, copper electrodeposition, and reaction-diffusion interactions.

F. Douglas Kelley, Associate Professor; Ph.D., Rochester, 1990. Ways to exploit the divergent transport properties of fluids near the critical point, energy storage technologies that can be useful in balancing energy demand with sustainable energy generation, polymer mixtures and composites.

Tanya Z. Kosc, Lecturer of Chemical Engineering and Scientist, LLE; Ph.D., Rochester, 2003. Polymer cholesteric liquid crystals, optical materials.

Hitomi Mukaibo, Assistant Professor, Ph.D., Waseda (Japan), 2006. Template synthesis, microstructured/nanostructured materials, electrochemistry, nanoporous thin film, cell/nanostructure interface, gene delivery, energy storage and production, biosensors and bioanalytical chemistry.

Marc D. Porosoff, Assistant Professor, Ph.D. Columbia University, 2015. CO_2 reduction, heterogeneous catalysis, catalyst structure-property relationships, C1 chemistry, upgrading light alkanes.

Lewis Rothberg, Professor of Chemistry and Chemical Engineering; Ph.D., Harvard, 1984. Polymer electronics, optoelectronic devices, light-emitting diodes, thin-film transistors, organic photovoltaics and solar cells, biomolecular sensors, plasmon-enhanced devices.

Yonathon Shapir, Professor of Physics and Chemical Engineering; Ph.D., Tel-Aviv, 1981. Critical phenomena in ordered and disordered systems, classical and quantum transport in dirty metals and the metal-insulator transition, statistical properties of different polymer configurations, fractal properties of percolation and other clusters, kinetic models of growth and aggregation.

Alexander A. Shestopalov, Associate Professor; Ph.D., Duke, 2009. Development of new unconventional fabrication and patterning techniques and their use in preparation of functional micro- and nanostructured devices, organic chemistry and colloidal self-assembly.

Ching W. Tang, Emeritus Professor of Chemical Engineering; Ph.D., Cornell, 1975. Applications of organic electronic devices—organic light-emitting diodes, solar cells, photoconductors, image sensors, photoreceptors; basic studies of organic thin-film devices: charge injection, transport, recombination and luminescence properties; metal-organic and organic-organic junction phenomena; development of flat-panel display technology based on organic light-emitting diodes.

Wyatt Tenhaeff, Assistant Professor; Ph.D., MIT, 2009. Electrochemical energy storage, solid-state lithium batteries, solid electrolytes, polymer thin films and interfaces, thin film synthesis and characterization, vacuum deposition techniques.

Andrew D. White, Assistant Professor; Ph.D., Washington (Seattle), 2013. Computer simulation and data informatics design of material design for self-assembly, machine learning.

J. H. David Wu, Professor of Chemical Engineering and Biomedical Engineering and Associate Professor of Microbiology and Immunology; Ph.D., MIT, 1987. Biofuels development, molecular enzymology, transcriptional network, genomics and systems biology of biomass degradation for bioenergy conversion, artificial bone marrow and lymphoid tissue engineering, molecular control of hematopoiesis and immune response, stem cell and lymphocyte culture, biochemical engineering, fermentation, molecular biology.

Matthew Z. Yates, Professor, Chair, and Scientist, LLE; Ph.D., Texas, 1999. Particle synthesis and assembly, crystallization, fuel cell membranes, microemulsions and microencapsulation, supercritical fluids, microencapsulation, colloids and interfaces.

Meliora—"Ever Better"

Rochester fall colors.

Section 7
Civil and Environmental Engineering

This section contains a directory of institutions offering graduate work in civil and environmental engineering. Additional information about programs listed in the directory may be obtained by writing directly to the dean of a graduate school or chair of a department at the address given in the directory.

For programs offering related work, see also in this book *Agricultural Engineering and Bioengineering, Biomedical Engineering and Biotechnology, Engineering and Applied Sciences, Management of Engineering and Technology,* and *Ocean Engineering.* In the other guides in this series:

Graduate Programs in the Humanities, Arts & Social Sciences
See *Public, Regional, and Industrial Affairs (Urban and Regional Planning and Urban Studies)*

Graduate Programs in the Biological/Biomedical Sciences & Health-Related Medical Professions
See *Ecology, Environmental Biology,* and *Evolutionary Biology*

Graduate Programs in the Physical Sciences, Mathematics, Agricultural Sciences, the Environment & Natural Resources
See *Agricultural and Food Sciences, Environmental Sciences and Management, Geosciences,* and *Marine Sciences and Oceanography*

CONTENTS

Program Directories

Featured School: Display and Close-Up

See:

Civil Engineering

American University of Beirut, Graduate Programs, Faculty of Engineering and Architecture, 11-0236, Lebanon. Offers applied energy (ME); civil engineering (PhD); electrical and computer engineering (PhD); energy studies (MS); engineering management (MEM); environmental and water resources (ME); environmental technology (MSES); mechanical engineering (ME, PhD); urban design (MUD); urban planning and policy (MUPP). *Program availability:* Part-time, evening/weekend, 100% online. *Faculty:* 99 full-time (22 women), 1 part-time/adjunct (0 women). *Students:* 308 full-time (143 women), 86 part-time (39 women). Average age 26. 430 applicants, 69% accepted, 125 enrolled. In 2016, 103 master's, 7 doctorates awarded. Terminal master's awarded for partial completion of doctoral program. *Degree requirements:* For master's, comprehensive exam, thesis optional; for doctorate, comprehensive exam, thesis/ dissertation. *Entrance requirements:* For doctorate, GRE. Additional exam requirements/recommendations for international students: Required—TOEFL (minimum score 573 paper-based; 88 iBT); Recommended—IELTS (minimum score 7). *Application deadline:* For fall admission, 2/10 priority date for domestic and international students; for spring admission, 11/2 priority date for domestic students, 11/2 for international students. Application fee: $50. Electronic applications accepted. *Expenses:* Contact institution. *Financial support:* In 2016–17, 22 students received support, including 94 fellowships with full tuition reimbursements available (averaging $18,200 per year), 44 research assistantships with full tuition reimbursements available (averaging $7,596 per year), 124 teaching assistantships with full tuition reimbursements available (averaging $1,056 per year); career-related internships or fieldwork, Federal Work-Study, institutionally sponsored loans, scholarships/grants, traineeships, health care benefits, tuition waivers, and unspecified assistantships also available. Support available to part-time students. Financial award application deadline: 12/20. *Total annual research expenditures:* $1.5 million. *Unit head:* Prof. Alan Shihadeh, Interim Dean, 961-1350000 Ext. 3400, Fax: 961-1744462, E-mail: as20@aub.edu.lb. *Application contact:* Dr. Salim Kanaan, Director, Admissions Office, 961-1350000 Ext. 2594, Fax: 961-1750775, E-mail: sk00@aub.edu.lb.
Website: http://www.aub.edu.lb/fea/fea_home/Pages/index.aspx

American University of Sharjah, Graduate Programs, Sharjah, United Arab Emirates. Offers accounting (MS); business (EMBA, MBA); chemical engineering (MS Ch E); civil engineering (MSCE); computer engineering (MS); electrical engineering (MSEE); engineering systems management (MS); mathematics (MS); mechanical engineering (MSME); mechatronics engineering (MS); teaching English to speakers of other languages (MA); translation and interpreting (MA); urban planning (MUP). *Program availability:* Part-time, evening/weekend. *Degree requirements:* For master's, thesis (for some programs). *Entrance requirements:* For master's, GMAT (for MBA). Additional exam requirements/recommendations for international students: Required—TOEFL (minimum score 550 paper-based; 80 iBT), TWE (minimum score 5); Recommended— IELTS (minimum score 6.5). Electronic applications accepted. *Faculty research:* Water pollution, management and waste water treatment, energy and sustainability, air pollution, Islamic finance, family business and small and medium enterprises.

Arizona State University at the Tempe campus, Ira A. Fulton Schools of Engineering, School of Sustainable Engineering and the Built Environment, Tempe, AZ 85287-5306. Offers civil, environmental and sustainable engineering (MS, MSE, PhD); construction engineering (MSE); construction management (MS, PhD). *Program availability:* Part-time, evening/weekend, online learning. Terminal master's awarded for partial completion of doctoral program. *Degree requirements:* For master's, thesis optional, comprehensive exams (MSE); interactive Program of Study (iPOS) submitted before completing 50 percent of required credit hours; for doctorate, comprehensive exam, thesis/dissertation, interactive Program of Study (iPOS) submitted before completing 50 percent of required credit hours. *Entrance requirements:* For master's, GRE, minimum GPA of 3.0 or equivalent in last 2 years of work leading to bachelor's degree; for doctorate, GRE, minimum GPA of 3.0 in last 2 years of work leading to bachelor's degree, 3.2 in all graduate-level coursework with master's degree; 3 letters of recommendation; resume/curriculum vitae; letter of intent; thesis (if applicable); statement of research interests. Additional exam requirements/recommendations for international students: Required—TOEFL, IELTS, or PTE. Electronic applications accepted. *Expenses:* Contact institution. *Faculty research:* Water purification, transportation (safety and materials), construction management, environmental biotechnology, environmental nanotechnology, earth systems engineering and management, SMART innovations, project performance metrics, and underground infrastructure.

Auburn University, Graduate School, Ginn College of Engineering, Department of Civil Engineering, Auburn University, AL 36849. Offers MCE, MS, PhD. *Program availability:* Part-time. *Faculty:* 24 full-time (3 women), 1 part-time/adjunct (0 women). *Students:* 78 full-time (25 women), 54 part-time (12 women); includes 10 minority (3 Black or African American, non-Hispanic/Latino; 1 Asian, non-Hispanic/Latino; 4 Hispanic/Latino; 2 Two or more races, non-Hispanic/Latino), 67 international. Average age 27. 153 applicants, 62% accepted, 37 enrolled. In 2016, 28 master's, 10 doctorates awarded. *Degree requirements:* For master's, project (MCE), thesis (MS); for doctorate, comprehensive exam, thesis/dissertation. *Entrance requirements:* For master's and doctorate, GRE General Test. *Application deadline:* Applications are processed on a rolling basis. Application fee: $50 ($60 for international students). Electronic applications accepted. *Expenses:* Tuition, state resident: full-time $9072; part-time $504 per credit hour. Tuition, nonresident: full-time $27,216; part-time $1512 per credit hour. *Required fees:* $812 per semester. Tuition and fees vary according to degree level and program. *Financial support:* Fellowships, research assistantships, teaching assistantships, and Federal Work-Study available. Support available to part-time students. Financial award application deadline: 3/15; financial award applicants required to submit FAFSA. *Unit head:* Dr. Andy Nowak, Head, 334-844-4320. *Application contact:* Dr. George Flowers, Dean of the Graduate School, 334-844-2125.

Boise State University, College of Engineering, Department of Civil Engineering, Boise, ID 83725-2075. Offers civil engineering (M Engr, MS). *Program availability:* Part-time. *Faculty:* 8. *Students:* 19 full-time (8 women), 8 part-time (3 women); includes 1 minority (Asian, non-Hispanic/Latino), 9 international. Average age 29. 47 applicants, 38% accepted, 6 enrolled. In 2016, 9 master's awarded. *Degree requirements:* For master's, comprehensive exam, thesis (for some programs). *Entrance requirements:* For master's, GRE General Test, minimum GPA of 3.0. Additional exam requirements/ recommendations for international students: Required—TOEFL (minimum score 550 paper-based; 80 iBT), IELTS (minimum score 6). Application fee: $65 ($95 for international students). Electronic applications accepted. *Expenses:* Tuition, state resident: full-time $6058; part-time $358 per credit hour. Tuition, nonresident: full-time $20,108; part-time $608 per credit hour. *Required fees:* $2108. Tuition and fees vary according to program. *Financial support:* In 2016–17, 7 students received support, including 10 research assistantships (averaging $10,342 per year), 6 teaching assistantships (averaging $10,581 per year); scholarships/grants and unspecified

assistantships also available. Financial award applicants required to submit FAFSA. *Unit head:* Dr. Mandar Khanal, Department Chair, 208-426-1430, E-mail: mkhanal@ boisestate.edu. *Application contact:* Dr. Hao Chen, Graduate Program Coordinator, 208-426-1020, E-mail: haochen@boisestate.edu.
Website: http://coen.boisestate.edu/ce/graduate-students/

Bradley University, The Graduate School, Caterpillar College of Engineering and Technology, Department of Civil Engineering and Construction, Peoria, IL 61625-0002. Offers MSCE. *Program availability:* Part-time, evening/weekend. *Degree requirements:* For master's, comprehensive exam. *Entrance requirements:* Additional exam requirements/recommendations for international students: Required—TOEFL (minimum score 550 paper-based; 79 iBT), IELTS (minimum score 6.5). *Application deadline:* For fall admission, 5/15 priority date for domestic and international students; for spring admission, 10/15 priority date for domestic and international students. Applications are processed on a rolling basis. Application fee: $40 ($50 for international students). Electronic applications accepted. *Expenses: Tuition:* Full-time $7650; part-time $850 per credit. *Required fees:* $50 per credit. One-time fee: $100 full-time. *Financial support:* Research assistantships with full and partial tuition reimbursements, teaching assistantships, scholarships/grants, tuition waivers (partial), and unspecified assistantships available. Support available to part-time students. Financial award application deadline: 4/1. *Unit head:* Souhail Elhouar, Chairman, 309-677-3830, E-mail: selhouar@bradley.edu. *Application contact:* Kayla Carroll, Director of International Admissions and Student Services, 309-677-2375, E-mail: klcarroll@fsmail.bradley.edu. Website: http://www.bradley.edu/academic/departments/cec/

Brigham Young University, Graduate Studies, Ira A. Fulton College of Engineering and Technology, Department of Civil and Environmental Engineering, Provo, UT 84602. Offers civil engineering (MS, PhD). *Faculty:* 17 full-time (0 women), 2 part-time/adjunct (1 woman). *Students:* 57 full-time (9 women); includes 3 minority (1 Hispanic/Latino; 2 Native Hawaiian or other Pacific Islander, non-Hispanic/Latino), 10 international. Average age 27. 23 applicants, 70% accepted, 15 enrolled. In 2016, 39 master's, 4 doctorates awarded. *Degree requirements:* For master's, thesis (for some programs), Fundamentals of Engineering (FE) Exam; for doctorate, comprehensive exam, thesis/ dissertation. *Entrance requirements:* For master's and doctorate, GRE General Test, minimum cumulative GPA of 3.0 in last 60 hours of upper-division course work. Additional exam requirements/recommendations for international students: Required— TOEFL (minimum score 580 paper-based; 85 iBT), IELTS (minimum score 7). *Application deadline:* For fall admission, 2/15 for domestic and international students; for winter admission, 9/5 for domestic students, 9/15 for international students; for spring admission, 2/5 for domestic and international students; for summer admission, 2/5 for domestic and international students. Application fee: $50. Electronic applications accepted. *Expenses: Tuition:* Full-time $6680; part-time $393 per credit. Tuition and fees vary according to course load, program and student's religious affiliation. *Financial support:* In 2016–17, 69 students received support, including 1 fellowship (averaging $30,000 per year), 110 research assistantships (averaging $8,544 per year), 46 teaching assistantships (averaging $4,416 per year); scholarships/grants also available. Financial award application deadline: 3/1; financial award applicants required to submit FAFSA. *Faculty research:* Structural optimization; finite element modeling and earthquake resistant analysis; groundwater, surface water, watershed and hydrologic modeling and visualization; subsurface environmental issues including transport, remediation, monitoring and characterization; capacity of deep foundations under static and dynamic loading and the behavior and mitigation of liquefiable soils. *Total annual research expenditures:* $1.5 million. *Unit head:* Dr. Rollin H. Hotchkiss, Department Chair, 801-422-2811, Fax: 801-422-0159, E-mail: rhh@byu.edu. *Application contact:* Dr. Fernando S. Fonseca, Graduate Coordinator, 801-422-2811, Fax: 801-422-0159, E-mail: ffonseca@byu.edu.
Website: http://ceen.et.byu.edu/

Bucknell University, Graduate Studies, College of Engineering, Department of Civil and Environmental Engineering, Lewisburg, PA 17837. Offers MSCE, MSEV. *Degree requirements:* For master's, thesis. *Entrance requirements:* For master's, GRE General Test, minimum GPA of 3.0. Additional exam requirements/recommendations for international students: Required—TOEFL (minimum score 600 paper-based). *Faculty research:* Pile foundations, rehabilitation of bridges, deep-shaft biological-waste treatment, pre-cast concrete structures.

California Baptist University, Program in Civil Engineering, Riverside, CA 92504-3206. Offers MS. *Program availability:* Part-time. *Faculty:* 6 full-time (1 woman), 1 part-time/adjunct (0 women). *Students:* 6 full-time (3 women), 2 part-time (1 woman); includes 1 minority (Hispanic/Latino), 5 international. Average age 24. 7 applicants, 71% accepted, 5 enrolled. *Entrance requirements:* For master's, minimum undergraduate GPA of 3.0, bachelor's transcripts, three letters of recommendation, essay, resume, interview. Additional exam requirements/recommendations for international students: Required—TOEFL (minimum score 80 iBT). *Application deadline:* For fall admission, 8/1 priority date for domestic students, 7/1 priority date for international students; for spring admission, 12/1 priority date for domestic students, 11/1 priority date for international students. Applications are processed on a rolling basis. Application fee: $45. Electronic applications accepted. *Expenses:* Contact institution. *Financial support:* Federal Work-Study and scholarships/grants available. Financial award applicants required to submit CSS PROFILE or FAFSA. *Faculty research:* Resilient infrastructure, probabilistic capacity/demand model, pavement performance behavior, environmental nanotechnology, nanofabrication. *Unit head:* Dr. Helen Jung, Associate Dean, College of Engineering, 951-343-4510. *Application contact:* Taylor Neece, Director of Graduate Admissions, 951-343-4871, Fax: 877-228-8877, E-mail: graduateadmissions@ calbaptist.edu.

California Institute of Technology, Division of Engineering and Applied Science, Option in Civil Engineering, Pasadena, CA 91125-0001. Offers MS, PhD, Engr. *Degree requirements:* For doctorate, thesis/dissertation. *Faculty research:* Earthquake engineering, soil mechanics, finite-element analysis, hydraulics, coastal engineering.

California Polytechnic State University, San Luis Obispo, College of Engineering, Department of Civil and Environmental Engineering, San Luis Obispo, CA 93407. Offers MS. *Program availability:* Part-time. *Faculty:* 9 full-time (2 women), 1 part-time/adjunct (0 women). *Students:* 39 full-time (10 women), 3 part-time (2 women); includes 18 minority (2 Black or African American, non-Hispanic/Latino; 8 Asian, non-Hispanic/Latino; 4 Hispanic/Latino; 1 Native Hawaiian or other Pacific Islander, non-Hispanic/Latino; 3 Two or more races, non-Hispanic/Latino), 1 international. Average age 24. 52 applicants, 52% accepted, 22 enrolled. In 2016, 33 master's awarded. *Degree requirements:* For master's, comprehensive exam (for some programs), thesis (for some programs). *Entrance requirements:* For master's, GRE. Additional exam requirements/ recommendations for international students: Required—TOEFL (minimum score 80 iBT). *Application deadline:* For fall admission, 1/1 for domestic students, 3/1 priority date for international students. Applications are processed on a rolling basis. Application fee:

$55. Electronic applications accepted. *Expenses:* Tuition, state resident: full-time $6738; part-time $3906 per year. Tuition, nonresident: full-time $15,666; part-time $8370 per year. *Required fees:* $3603; $3141 per unit. $1047 per term. *Financial support:* Fellowships, research assistantships, teaching assistantships, career-related internships or fieldwork, and scholarships/grants available. Financial award application deadline: 3/2; financial award applicants required to submit FAFSA. *Faculty research:* Transportation and traffic, environmental protection, geotechnology, water engineering. *Unit head:* Dr. Bing Qu, Graduate Coordinator, 805-756-5645, E-mail: bqu@calpoly.edu.
Website: http://ceenve.calpoly.edu

California State Polytechnic University, Pomona, Program in Civil Engineering, Pomona, CA 91768-2557. Offers MS. *Program availability:* Part-time, evening/weekend. *Students:* 29 full-time (9 women), 86 part-time (73 women); includes 56 minority (2 Black or African American, non-Hispanic/Latino; 29 Asian, non-Hispanic/Latino; 24 Hispanic/Latino; 1 Two or more races, non-Hispanic/Latino), 14 international. Average age 27. 49 applicants, 96% accepted, 36 enrolled. In 2016, 32 master's awarded. *Degree requirements:* For master's, project or thesis. *Entrance requirements:* Additional exam requirements/recommendations for international students: Required—TOEFL. *Application deadline:* Applications are processed on a rolling basis. Application fee: $55. Electronic applications accepted. *Expenses:* Contact institution. *Financial support:* Application deadline: 3/2; applicants required to submit FAFSA. *Unit head:* Dr. Ronald Yeung, Graduate Coordinator, 909-869-2640, Fax: 909-869-4342, E-mail: mryeung@cpp.edu. *Application contact:* Andrew M. Wright, Director of Admissions, 909-869-3130, Fax: 909-869-4529, E-mail: awright@cpp.edu.
Website: http://www.cpp.edu/~engineering/CE/msce.shtml

California State University, Fresno, Division of Research and Graduate Studies, Lyles College of Engineering, Department of Civil and Geomatics Engineering, Fresno, CA 93740-8027. Offers MS. *Program availability:* Part-time, evening/weekend. *Degree requirements:* For master's, thesis or alternative. *Entrance requirements:* For master's, GRE General Test, minimum GPA of 2.75. Additional exam requirements/recommendations for international students: Required—TOEFL. *Application deadline:* For fall admission, 5/1 for domestic and international students; for spring admission, 10/1 for domestic and international students. Applications are processed on a rolling basis. Application fee: $55. Electronic applications accepted. *Financial support:* Career-related internships or fieldwork, Federal Work-Study, and scholarships/grants available. Financial award application deadline: 3/1; financial award applicants required to submit FAFSA. *Faculty research:* Surveying, water damage, instrumentation equipment, agricultural drainage, aerial triangulation, dairy manure particles. *Application contact:* Dr. C. Choo, Program Coordinator, 559-278-8746, Fax: 559-278-7002.
Website: http://www.fresnostate.edu/engineering/civil-geomatics/

California State University, Fullerton, Graduate Studies, College of Engineering and Computer Science, Department of Civil and Environmental Engineering, Fullerton, CA 92834-9480. Offers civil engineering (MS), including architectural engineering, environmental engineering. *Program availability:* Part-time. *Degree requirements:* For master's, comprehensive exam, project or thesis. *Entrance requirements:* For master's, minimum undergraduate GPA of 2.5. Application fee: $55. *Expenses:* Tuition, state resident: full-time $3369; part-time $1953 per unit. Tuition, nonresident: full-time $3915; part-time $2499 per unit. Tuition and fees vary according to course load, degree level and program. *Financial support:* Career-related internships or fieldwork, Federal Work-Study, institutionally sponsored loans, and scholarships/grants available. Support available to part-time students. Financial award application deadline: 3/1; financial award applicants required to submit FAFSA. *Faculty research:* Soil-structure interaction, finite-element analysis, computer-aided analysis and design. *Unit head:* Dr. Prasada Rao, Chair, 657-278-3012. *Application contact:* Admissions/Applications, 657-278-2371.
Website: http://www.fullerton.edu/ecs/cee/

California State University, Long Beach, Graduate Studies, College of Engineering, Department of Civil Engineering and Construction Engineering Management, Long Beach, CA 90840. Offers civil engineering (MSCE). *Program availability:* Part-time. *Degree requirements:* For master's, comprehensive exam or thesis. *Entrance requirements:* Additional exam requirements/recommendations for international students: Required—TOEFL. *Application deadline:* For fall admission, 3/1 for domestic students. Application fee: $55. Electronic applications accepted. *Financial support:* Career-related internships or fieldwork, Federal Work-Study, institutionally sponsored loans, scholarships/grants, and unspecified assistantships available. Financial award application deadline: 3/2. *Faculty research:* Soils, hydraulics, seismic structures, composite metals, computer-aided manufacturing. *Unit head:* Tesfai Goitom, Chair, 562-985-5118.

California State University, Los Angeles, Graduate Studies, College of Engineering, Computer Science, and Technology, Department of Civil Engineering, Los Angeles, CA 90032-8530. Offers MS. *Program availability:* Part-time, evening/weekend. *Degree requirements:* For master's, comprehensive exam or thesis. *Entrance requirements:* For master's, GRE or minimum GPA of 2.4. Additional exam requirements/recommendations for international students: Required—TOEFL (minimum score 550 paper-based). *Faculty research:* Structure, hydraulics, hydrology, soil mechanics.

California State University, Northridge, Graduate Studies, College of Engineering and Computer Science, Department of Civil Engineering and Construction Management, Northridge, CA 91330. Offers engineering (MS), including structural engineering. *Program availability:* Part-time, evening/weekend. *Faculty:* 8 full-time (6 women), 14 part-time/adjunct (all women). *Students:* 20 full-time (6 women), 45 part-time (7 women); includes 29 minority (1 Black or African American, non-Hispanic/Latino; 9 Asian, non-Hispanic/Latino; 17 Hispanic/Latino; 2 Two or more races, non-Hispanic/Latino), 7 international. Average age 28. 71 applicants, 52% accepted, 23 enrolled. *Degree requirements:* For master's, thesis. *Entrance requirements:* Additional exam requirements/recommendations for international students: Required—TOEFL. *Application deadline:* For fall admission, 11/30 for domestic students. Application fee: $55. *Expenses:* Tuition, state resident: full-time $4152. *Financial support:* Teaching assistantships available. Financial award application deadline: 3/1. *Faculty research:* Composite study. *Unit head:* Dr. Nazaret Dermendjian, Chair, 818-677-2166.
Website: http://www.csun.edu/~ceam/

California State University, Sacramento, Office of Graduate Studies, College of Engineering and Computer Science, Department of Civil Engineering, Sacramento, CA 95819. Offers MS. *Program availability:* Part-time, evening/weekend. *Students:* 24 full-time (5 women), 50 part-time (12 women); includes 40 minority (5 Black or African American, non-Hispanic/Latino; 19 Asian, non-Hispanic/Latino; 15 Hispanic/Latino; 1 Native Hawaiian or other Pacific Islander, non-Hispanic/Latino). Average age 30. 65 applicants, 62% accepted, 20 enrolled. In 2016, 10 master's awarded. *Degree requirements:* For master's, thesis, project, direct study, or comprehensive exam; writing proficiency exam. *Entrance requirements:* Additional exam requirements/recommendations for international students: Required—TOEFL (minimum score 550 paper-based; 80 iBT). *Application deadline:* For fall admission, 3/1 for domestic and international students; for spring admission, 9/15 for domestic students, 9/30 for international students. Applications are processed on a rolling basis. Application fee: $55. Electronic applications accepted. *Expenses:* $4,302 full-time tuition and fees per semester, $2,796 part-time. *Financial support:* Research assistantships, teaching assistantships, career-related internships or fieldwork, and Federal Work-Study available. Support available to part-time students. Financial award application deadline: 3/1; financial award applicants required to submit FAFSA. *Unit head:* Dr. Benjamin Fell, Chair, 916-278-8139, Fax: 916-278-7957, E-mail: fellb@csus.edu. *Application contact:* Jose Martinez, Graduate Admissions Supervisor, 916-278-7871, E-mail: martinj@skymail.csus.edu.
Website: http://www.ecs.csus.edu/ce

Carleton University, Faculty of Graduate Studies, Faculty of Engineering and Design, Department of Civil and Environmental Engineering, Ottawa, ON K1S 5B6, Canada. Offers M Eng, MA Sc, PhD. *Degree requirements:* For master's, thesis optional; for doctorate, thesis/dissertation. *Entrance requirements:* For master's, honors degree; for doctorate, MA Sc or M Eng. Additional exam requirements/recommendations for international students: Required—TOEFL. *Faculty research:* Pollution and wastewater management, fire safety engineering, earthquake engineering, structural design, bridge engineering.

Carnegie Mellon University, Carnegie Institute of Technology, Department of Civil and Environmental Engineering, Pittsburgh, PA 15213. Offers advanced infrastructure systems (MS, PhD); advanced infrastructure systems technology development and application (MS); air quality engineering and science (MS); civil and environmental engineering (MS, PhD); civil and environmental engineering/engineering and public policy (PhD); civil engineering (MS, PhD); computational mechanics (MS, PhD); computational modeling and monitoring for resilient structural and material systems (MS); energy infrastructure systems (MS); environmental engineering (MS, PhD); environmental management and science (MS, PhD); IT-based sustainable global infrastructure and construction management (MS); sustainability and green design (MS); water quality engineering and science (MS). *Program availability:* Part-time. *Faculty:* 23 full-time (5 women), 12 part-time/adjunct (3 women). *Students:* 230 full-time (87 women), 4 part-time (0 women); includes 17 minority (4 Black or African American, non-Hispanic/Latino; 12 Asian, non-Hispanic/Latino; 1 Two or more races, non-Hispanic/Latino), 179 international. Average age 25. 653 applicants, 60% accepted, 107 enrolled. In 2016, 145 master's, 15 doctorates awarded. Terminal master's awarded for partial completion of doctoral program. *Degree requirements:* For master's, thesis optional; for doctorate, comprehensive exam, thesis/dissertation, two-part qualifying exam, public defense of dissertation. *Entrance requirements:* For master's, GRE General Test, BS in engineering, science or mathematics; for doctorate, GRE General Test, BS or MS in engineering, science or mathematics. Additional exam requirements/recommendations for international students: Required—TOEFL (minimum score 84 iBT) or IELTS (6.0). *Application deadline:* For fall admission, 1/5 priority date for domestic and international students; for spring admission, 9/15 priority date for domestic and international students. Applications are processed on a rolling basis. Application fee: $65. Electronic applications accepted. *Expenses:* Contact institution. *Financial support:* In 2016–17, 129 students received support. Fellowships with tuition reimbursements available, research assistantships with tuition reimbursements available, scholarships/grants, tuition waivers (full and partial), unspecified assistantships, and service assistantships available. Financial award application deadline: 1/5. *Faculty research:* Advanced infrastructure systems; environmental engineering, sustainability, and science; mechanics, materials, and computing. *Total annual research expenditures:* $7.4 million. *Unit head:* Dr. David A. Dzombak, Professor and Department Head, 412-268-2941, Fax: 412-268-7813, E-mail: dzombak@cmu.edu. *Application contact:* David A. Vey, Graduate Admissions Manager, 412-268-2292, Fax: 412-268-7813, E-mail: dvey@andrew.cmu.edu.
Website: http://www.cmu.edu/cee/

Case Western Reserve University, School of Graduate Studies, Case School of Engineering, Department of Civil Engineering, Cleveland, OH 44106. Offers civil engineering (MS, PhD). *Program availability:* Part-time, 100% online. *Faculty:* 8 full-time (1 woman). *Students:* 21 full-time (7 women), 15 international. In 2016, 4 master's, 3 doctorates awarded. *Degree requirements:* For master's, thesis (for some programs); for doctorate, thesis/dissertation, qualifying exam, teaching experience. *Entrance requirements:* For master's and doctorate, GRE General Test. Additional exam requirements/recommendations for international students: Required—TOEFL. *Application deadline:* For fall admission, 8/1 priority date for domestic students; for spring admission, 1/1 for domestic students. Application fee: $50. *Expenses: Tuition:* Full-time $42,576; part-time $1774 per credit hour. *Required fees:* $34. Tuition and fees vary according to course load and program. *Financial support:* In 2016–17, 1 fellowship, 6 research assistantships with tuition reimbursements, 4 teaching assistantships were awarded; institutionally sponsored loans also available. Financial award application deadline: 8/1; financial award applicants required to submit FAFSA. *Faculty research:* Infrastructure performance and reliability, environmental, geotechnical, infrastructure reliability, mechanics, structures. *Total annual research expenditures:* $843,000. *Unit head:* Dr. David Zeng, Chairman/Professor, 216-368-2923, Fax: 216-368-5229, E-mail: xxz16@case.edu. *Application contact:* Carla Wilson, Student Affairs Coordinator, 216-368-4580, Fax: 216-368-3007, E-mail: cxw75@case.edu.
Website: http://civil.case.edu

The Catholic University of America, School of Engineering, Department of Civil Engineering, Washington, DC 20064. Offers civil engineering (MS, PhD); transportation and infrastructure systems (Certificate). *Program availability:* Part-time. *Faculty:* 7 full-time (0 women), 7 part-time/adjunct (0 women). *Students:* 18 full-time (3 women), 24 part-time (6 women); includes 13 minority (9 Black or African American, non-Hispanic/Latino; 1 Asian, non-Hispanic/Latino; 3 Two or more races, non-Hispanic/Latino), 22 international. Average age 34. 28 applicants, 79% accepted, 7 enrolled. In 2016, 9 master's, 1 doctorate awarded. *Degree requirements:* For master's, thesis optional; for doctorate, comprehensive exam, thesis/dissertation. *Entrance requirements:* For master's and doctorate, GRE General Test, statement of purpose, official copies of academic transcripts, three letters of recommendation. Additional exam requirements/recommendations for international students: Required—TOEFL (minimum score 550 paper-based; 80 iBT). *Application deadline:* For fall admission, 7/15 priority date for domestic students, 7/1 for international students; for spring admission, 11/15 priority date for domestic students, 11/1 for international students. Applications are processed on a rolling basis. Application fee: $55. Electronic applications accepted. *Expenses:* $43,380 per year; $1,170 per credit; $200 per semester part-time fees. *Financial support:* Fellowships, research assistantships, teaching assistantships, Federal Work-Study, scholarships/grants, tuition waivers (full and partial), and unspecified assistantships available. Financial award application deadline: 2/1; financial award applicants required to submit FAFSA. *Faculty research:* Transportation engineering, solid mechanics, construction engineering and management, environmental engineering and water resources, structural engineering. *Total annual research expenditures:* $241,311. *Unit head:* Dr. Lu Sun, Chair, 202-319-6671, Fax: 202-319-6677, E-mail: sunl@cua.edu. *Application contact:* Director of Graduate Admissions, 202-319-5057, Fax: 202-319-6533, E-mail: cua-admissions@cua.edu.
Website: http://civil.cua.edu/

The Citadel, The Military College of South Carolina, Citadel Graduate College, School of Engineering, Department of Civil and Environmental Engineering, Charleston, SC 29409. Offers built environment and public health (Graduate Certificate); civil

engineering (MS); geotechnical engineering (Graduate Certificate); structural engineering (Graduate Certificate); transportation engineering (Graduate Certificate). *Program availability:* Part-time, evening/weekend. *Faculty:* 1 full-time. *Students:* 11 part-time (1 woman); includes 1 minority (Black or African American, non-Hispanic/Latino). 8 applicants, 88% accepted, 4 enrolled. *Degree requirements:* For master's, plan of study outlining intended areas of interest and top four corresponding courses of interest. *Entrance requirements:* For master's, official transcript of baccalaureate degree from ABET-accredited engineering program or approved alternative; 2 letters of recommendation; for Graduate Certificate, official transcript of baccalaureate degree directly from an accredited college or university. Additional exam requirements/recommendations for international students: Required—TOEFL (minimum score 550 paper-based; 79 iBT). *Application deadline:* Applications are processed on a rolling basis. Application fee: $40. Electronic applications accepted. *Expenses:* Tuition, state resident: full-time $5121; part-time $569 per credit hour. Tuition, nonresident: full-time $8613; part-time $957 per credit hour. *Required fees:* $90 per term. *Financial support:* Fellowships and unspecified assistantships available. Support available to part-time students. Financial award application deadline: 7/1; financial award applicants required to submit FAFSA. *Unit head:* Dr. Kevin C. Bower, Head, 843-953-7683, E-mail: kevin.bower@citadel.edu. *Application contact:* Dr. Tara Hornor, Associate Provost for Planning, Assessment and Evaluation/Dean of Enrollment Management, 843-953-5089, E-mail: cgc@citadel.edu.
Website: http://www.citadel.edu/root/cee

City College of the City University of New York, Graduate School, Grove School of Engineering, Department of Civil Engineering, New York, NY 10031-9198. Offers ME, MS, PhD. PhD program offered jointly with Graduate School and University Center of the City University of New York. *Program availability:* Part-time. *Degree requirements:* For master's, thesis optional; for doctorate, one foreign language, comprehensive exam, thesis/dissertation. *Entrance requirements:* For master's and doctorate, GRE General Test. Additional exam requirements/recommendations for international students: Required—TOEFL (minimum score 500 paper-based; 61 iBT). Tuition and fees vary according to course load, degree level and program. *Faculty research:* Earthquake engineering, transportation systems, groundwater, environmental systems, highway systems.

Clarkson University, Wallace H. Coulter School of Engineering, Department of Civil and Environmental Engineering, Potsdam, NY 13699. Offers ME, MS, PhD. *Faculty:* 25 full-time (4 women), 9 part-time/adjunct (2 women). *Students:* 33 full-time (11 women); includes 1 minority (Hispanic/Latino), 25 international. 48 applicants, 58% accepted, 3 enrolled. In 2016, 9 master's, 3 doctorates awarded. *Degree requirements:* For master's, thesis (for MS); project (for ME); for doctorate, comprehensive exam, thesis/dissertation. *Entrance requirements:* For master's and doctorate, GRE. Additional exam requirements/recommendations for international students: Required—TOEFL (minimum score 550 paper-based, 80 iBT) or IELTS (6.5). *Application deadline:* Applications are processed on a rolling basis. Application fee: $50. Electronic applications accepted. *Expenses: Tuition:* Full-time $23,400; part-time $1300 per credit hour. Tuition and fees vary according to campus/location and program. *Financial support:* Scholarships/grants and unspecified assistantships available. *Unit head:* Dr. James Edzwald, Chair of Civil and Environmental Engineering, 315-268-6529, E-mail: jedzwald@clarkson.edu. *Application contact:* Dan Capogna, Graduate Admissions Contact, 518-631-9910, E-mail: graduate@clarkson.edu.
Website: http://graduate.clarkson.edu

Clemson University, Graduate School, College of Engineering, Computing and Applied Sciences, Glenn Department of Civil Engineering, Clemson, SC 29634. Offers MS, PhD. *Program availability:* Part-time. *Faculty:* 29 full-time (4 women), 2 part-time/adjunct (0 women). *Students:* 107 full-time (27 women), 23 part-time (6 women); includes 8 minority (3 Black or African American, non-Hispanic/Latino; 1 Asian, non-Hispanic/Latino; 1 Hispanic/Latino; 1 Native Hawaiian or other Pacific Islander, non-Hispanic/Latino; 2 Two or more races, non-Hispanic/Latino), 90 international. Average age 27. 307 applicants, 26% accepted, 29 enrolled. In 2016, 43 master's, 17 doctorates awarded. *Degree requirements:* For master's, thesis or alternative, oral exam, seminar; for doctorate, comprehensive exam, thesis/dissertation, oral exam, seminar. *Entrance requirements:* For master's and doctorate, GRE General Test, unofficial transcripts, letters of recommendation, statement of purpose. Additional exam requirements/recommendations for international students: Required—TOEFL (minimum score 80 iBT), IELTS (minimum score 6.5). *Application deadline:* For fall admission, 4/15 for domestic and international students; for spring admission, 9/15 for domestic and international students. Applications are processed on a rolling basis. Application fee: $80 ($90 for international students). Electronic applications accepted. *Expenses:* $4,841 per semester full-time resident, $9,640 per semester full-time non-resident, $612 per credit hour part-time resident, $1,223 per credit hour part-time non-resident. *Financial support:* In 2016–17, 106 students received support, including 7 fellowships with partial tuition reimbursements available (averaging $10,204 per year), 69 research assistantships with partial tuition reimbursements available (averaging $15,728 per year), 8 teaching assistantships with partial tuition reimbursements available (averaging $18,766 per year); career-related internships or fieldwork and unspecified assistantships also available. Financial award application deadline: 4/15. *Faculty research:* Applied fluid mechanics, construction materials, project management, structural and geotechnical engineering, transportation. *Total annual research expenditures:* $3.4 million. *Unit head:* Dr. James Martin, Department Chair, 864-656-3002, E-mail: jrmart@clemson.edu. *Application contact:* Dr. Abdul Khan, Graduate Program Coordinator, 864-656-3327, E-mail: abdkhan@clemson.edu.
Website: https://www.clemson.edu/cecas/departments/ce/

Cleveland State University, College of Graduate Studies, Fenn College of Engineering, Department of Civil and Environmental Engineering, Cleveland, OH 44115. Offers MS, D Eng. *Program availability:* Part-time, evening/weekend. *Faculty:* 8 full-time (2 women). *Students:* 65 full-time (13 women), 19 part-time (3 women); includes 3 minority (2 Asian, non-Hispanic/Latino; 1 Hispanic/Latino), 69 international. Average age 24. 214 applicants, 61% accepted, 21 enrolled. In 2016, 22 master's awarded. *Degree requirements:* For master's, project or thesis; for doctorate, comprehensive exam, thesis/dissertation, candidacy and qualifying exams. *Entrance requirements:* For master's, GRE General Test, GRE Subject Test, minimum GPA of 2.75; for doctorate, GRE General Test, GRE Subject Test, minimum GPA of 3.25. Additional exam requirements/recommendations for international students: Required—TOEFL (minimum score 550 paper-based; 78 iBT). *Application deadline:* For fall admission, 7/1 priority date for domestic students, 5/15 for international students; for spring admission, 11/15 for domestic students, 11/1 for international students; for summer admission, 4/1 for domestic students, 3/15 for international students. Applications are processed on a rolling basis. Application fee: $40. Electronic applications accepted. *Expenses:* Tuition, state resident: full-time $9565. Tuition, nonresident: full-time $17,980. Tuition and fees vary according to program. *Financial support:* In 2016–17, 9 research assistantships with tuition reimbursements (averaging $3,920 per year) were awarded; teaching assistantships with tuition reimbursements, career-related internships or fieldwork, scholarships/grants, and unspecified assistantships also available. Financial award application deadline: 9/1. *Faculty research:* Solid-waste disposal, constitutive modeling, transportation, safety engineering, concrete materials. *Total annual research expenditures:* $800,000. *Unit head:* Dr. Norbert Joseph Delatte, Chairperson, 216-687-9259, Fax: 216-687-5395, E-mail: n.delatte@csuohio.edu. *Application contact:* Deborah L. Brown, Interim Assistant Director, Graduate Admissions, 216-523-7572, Fax: 216-687-9214, E-mail: d.l.brown@csuohio.edu.
Website: http://www.csuohio.edu/engineering/civil

Colorado School of Mines, Office of Graduate Studies, Department of Civil and Environmental Engineering, Golden, CO 80401. Offers civil and environmental engineering (MS, PhD); environmental engineering science (MS, PhD); underground construction and tunneling (MS, PhD). *Program availability:* Part-time. *Degree requirements:* For master's, thesis (for some programs); for doctorate, comprehensive exam, thesis/dissertation. *Entrance requirements:* For master's and doctorate, GRE General Test. Additional exam requirements/recommendations for international students: Required—TOEFL (minimum score 550 paper-based; 80 iBT). Electronic applications accepted. *Expenses:* Tuition, state resident: full-time $15,690. Tuition, nonresident: full-time $34,020. *Required fees:* $2152. Tuition and fees vary according to course load. *Faculty research:* Treatment of water and wastes, environmental law: policy and practice, natural environment systems, hazardous waste management, environmental data analysis.

Colorado State University, Walter Scott, Jr. College of Engineering, Department of Civil and Environmental Engineering, Fort Collins, CO 80523-1372. Offers civil and environmental engineering (MS, PhD); civil engineering (ME). *Program availability:* Part-time, 100% online, blended/hybrid learning. *Faculty:* 29 full-time (5 women), 10 part-time/adjunct (2 women). *Students:* 96 full-time (36 women), 153 part-time (41 women); includes 10 minority (1 Black or African American, non-Hispanic/Latino; 2 Asian, non-Hispanic/Latino; 4 Hispanic/Latino; 3 Two or more races, non-Hispanic/Latino), 122 international. Average age 29. 245 applicants, 69% accepted, 60 enrolled. In 2016, 52 master's, 6 doctorates awarded. Terminal master's awarded for partial completion of doctoral program. *Degree requirements:* For master's, thesis, publication; for doctorate, comprehensive exam, thesis/dissertation, publication. *Entrance requirements:* For master's and doctorate, GRE. Additional exam requirements/recommendations for international students: Required—TOEFL (minimum score 550 paper-based, 80 iBT), IELTS (6.5), or PTE (58). *Application deadline:* For fall admission, 2/1 priority date for domestic and international students; for spring admission, 9/1 priority date for domestic and international students. Applications are processed on a rolling basis. Application fee: $60 ($70 for international students). Electronic applications accepted. *Expenses:* Contact institution. *Financial support:* In 2016–17, 80 students received support, including 9 fellowships (averaging $36,590 per year), 68 research assistantships (averaging $21,259 per year), 16 teaching assistantships (averaging $16,629 per year); scholarships/grants, health care benefits, and unspecified assistantships also available. Financial award application deadline: 2/1; financial award applicants required to submit FAFSA. *Faculty research:* Water resources, groundwater engineering, geoengineering, environmental engineering, structural engineering and structural mechanics. *Total annual research expenditures:* $12.8 million. *Unit head:* Dr. Charles Shackelford, Department Head, 970-491-5049, E-mail: charles.shackelford@colostate.edu. *Application contact:* Susheela Mallipudi, Graduate Advisor, 970-491-1174, E-mail: susheela.mallipudi@colostate.edu.
Website: http://www.engr.colostate.edu/ce/

Columbia University, Fu Foundation School of Engineering and Applied Science, Department of Civil Engineering and Engineering Mechanics, New York, NY 10027. Offers civil engineering (MS, Eng Sc D, PhD); construction engineering and management (MS); engineering mechanics (MS, Eng Sc D, PhD). *Program availability:* Part-time, online learning. Terminal master's awarded for partial completion of doctoral program. *Degree requirements:* For doctorate, thesis/dissertation, qualifying exam. *Entrance requirements:* For master's and doctorate, GRE General Test. Additional exam requirements/recommendations for international students: Required—TOEFL, IELTS, PTE. Electronic applications accepted. *Faculty research:* Structural dynamics, structural health and monitoring, fatigue and fracture mechanics, geo-environmental engineering, multiscale science and engineering.

Concordia University, School of Graduate Studies, Faculty of Engineering and Computer Science, Department of Building, Civil and Environmental Engineering, Montréal, QC H3G 1M8, Canada. Offers building engineering (M Eng, MA Sc, PhD, Certificate); civil engineering (M Eng, MA Sc, PhD); environmental engineering (Certificate). *Degree requirements:* For master's, thesis or alternative; for doctorate, comprehensive exam, thesis/dissertation. *Faculty research:* Structural engineering, geotechnical engineering, water resources and fluid engineering, transportation engineering, systems engineering.

Cooper Union for the Advancement of Science and Art, Albert Nerken School of Engineering, New York, NY 10003. Offers chemical engineering (ME); civil engineering (ME); electrical engineering (ME); mechanical engineering (ME). *Program availability:* Part-time. *Faculty:* 27 full-time (1 woman), 15 part-time/adjunct (2 women). *Students:* 36 full-time (5 women), 39 part-time (8 women); includes 34 minority (3 Black or African American, non-Hispanic/Latino; 16 Asian, non-Hispanic/Latino; 5 Hispanic/Latino; 10 Two or more races, non-Hispanic/Latino), 3 international. Average age 24. 59 applicants, 75% accepted, 34 enrolled. In 2016, 25 master's awarded. *Degree requirements:* For master's, thesis (for some programs). *Entrance requirements:* For master's, BE or BS in an engineering discipline; official copies of school transcripts including secondary (high school), college and university work; two letters of recommendation; resume. Additional exam requirements/recommendations for international students: Required—TOEFL (minimum score 600 paper-based; 100 iBT). *Application deadline:* For fall admission, 3/31 for domestic and international students. Application fee: $75. Electronic applications accepted. *Expenses: Tuition:* Full-time $16,055; part-time $1235 per credit. *Required fees:* $925 per semester. One-time fee: $250. Tuition and fees vary according to course load. *Financial support:* In 2016–17, 70 students received support, including 4 fellowships with tuition reimbursements available (averaging $11,000 per year); career-related internships or fieldwork, tuition waivers (full and partial), and tuition scholarships offered to exceptional students also available. Support available to part-time students. Financial award application deadline: 5/1; financial award applicants required to submit FAFSA. *Faculty research:* Civil infrastructure, imaging and sensing technology, biomedical engineering, encryption technology, process engineering. *Unit head:* Richard Stock, Acting Dean of Albert Nerken School of Engineering, 212-353-4285, E-mail: stock@cooper.edu. *Application contact:* Chabeli Lajara, Administrative Assistant, 212-353-4120, E-mail: admissions@cooper.edu.
Website: http://cooper.edu/engineering

Cornell University, Graduate School, Graduate Fields of Engineering, Field of Civil and Environmental Engineering, Ithaca, NY 14853. Offers engineering management (M Eng, MS, PhD); environmental engineering (M Eng, MS, PhD); environmental fluid mechanics and hydrology (M Eng, MS, PhD); environmental systems engineering (M Eng, MS, PhD); geotechnical engineering (M Eng, MS, PhD); remote sensing (M Eng, MS, PhD); structural engineering (M Eng, MS, PhD); structural mechanics (M Eng, MS); transportation engineering (MS, PhD); transportation systems engineering (M Eng); water resource systems (M Eng, MS, PhD). Terminal master's awarded for partial completion of doctoral program. *Degree requirements:* For master's, thesis (MS); for doctorate, comprehensive exam, thesis/dissertation. *Entrance requirements:* For master's and doctorate, GRE General Test (recommended), 2 letters of recommendation. Additional exam requirements/recommendations for international students: Required—TOEFL (minimum score 600 paper-based; 77 iBT). Electronic applications accepted. *Faculty research:* Environmental engineering, geotechnical engineering, remote sensing, environmental fluid mechanics and hydrology, structural engineering.

Dalhousie University, Faculty of Engineering, Department of Civil and Resource Engineering, Halifax, NS B3J 2X4, Canada. Offers M Eng, MA Sc, PhD. *Degree requirements:* For master's, thesis; for doctorate, thesis/dissertation. *Entrance requirements:* Additional exam requirements/recommendations for international students: Required—TOEFL, IELTS, CANTEST, CAEL, or Michigan English Language Assessment Battery. Electronic applications accepted. *Faculty research:* Environmental/ water resources, bridge engineering, geotechnical engineering, pavement design and management/highway materials, composite materials.

Drexel University, College of Engineering, Department of Civil, Architectural, and Environmental Engineering, Program in Civil Engineering, Philadelphia, PA 19104-2875. Offers MS, PhD. *Program availability:* Part-time, evening/weekend. *Faculty:* 27 full-time (8 women). *Students:* 24 full-time (6 women), 17 part-time (3 women); includes 7 minority (3 Asian, non-Hispanic/Latino; 2 Hispanic/Latino; 2 Two or more races, non-Hispanic/Latino), 16 international. Average age 30. In 2016, 26 master's, 9 doctorates awarded. *Degree requirements:* For master's, thesis optional; for doctorate, thesis/ dissertation. *Entrance requirements:* For master's, minimum GPA of 3.0; for doctorate, minimum GPA of 3.5, MS in civil engineering. Additional exam requirements/ recommendations for international students: Required—TOEFL. *Application deadline:* For fall admission, 8/21 for domestic students. Applications are processed on a rolling basis. Application fee: $50. Electronic applications accepted. *Expenses: Tuition:* Full-time $32,184; part-time $1192 per credit hour. *Required fees:* $280. Tuition and fees vary according to campus/location and program. *Financial support:* Research assistantships, teaching assistantships, career-related internships or fieldwork, Federal Work-Study, institutionally sponsored loans, tuition waivers (partial), and unspecified assistantships available. Financial award application deadline: 2/1. *Unit head:* Dr. Richard Weggel, Interim Department Head, 215-895-2355. *Application contact:* Director of Graduate Admissions, 215-895-6700, Fax: 215-895-5939, E-mail: enroll@drexel.edu.

Duke University, Graduate School, Pratt School of Engineering, Department of Civil and Environmental Engineering, Durham, NC 27708. Offers civil and environmental engineering (MS, PhD); environmental engineering (MS, PhD). Terminal master's awarded for partial completion of doctoral program. *Degree requirements:* For doctorate, thesis/dissertation. *Entrance requirements:* For master's and doctorate, GRE General Test. Additional exam requirements/recommendations for international students: Required—TOEFL (minimum score 550 paper-based; 90 iBT), IELTS (minimum score 7). Electronic applications accepted. *Faculty research:* Environmental process engineering, hydrology and fluid dynamics, materials, structures and geo-systems.

Duke University, Graduate School, Pratt School of Engineering, Master of Engineering Program, Durham, NC 27708-0271. Offers biomedical engineering (M Eng); civil engineering (M Eng); electrical and computer engineering (M Eng); environmental engineering (M Eng); materials science and engineering (M Eng); mechanical engineering (M Eng); photonics and optical sciences (M Eng). *Program availability:* Part-time. *Entrance requirements:* For master's, GRE General Test, resume, 3 letters of recommendation, statement of purpose, transcripts. Additional exam requirements/ recommendations for international students: Required—TOEFL.

École Polytechnique de Montréal, Graduate Programs, Department of Civil, Geological and Mining Engineering, Montréal, QC H3C 3A7, Canada. Offers civil, geological and mining engineering (DESS); environmental engineering (M Eng, M Sc A, PhD); geotechnical engineering (M Eng, M Sc A, PhD); hydraulics engineering (M Eng, M Sc A, PhD); structural engineering (M Eng, M Sc A, PhD); transportation engineering (M Eng, M Sc A, PhD). *Program availability:* Part-time. *Degree requirements:* For master's, one foreign language, thesis; for doctorate, one foreign language, thesis/ dissertation. *Entrance requirements:* For master's, minimum GPA of 2.75; for doctorate, minimum GPA of 3.0. *Faculty research:* Water resources management, characteristics of building materials, aging of dams, pollution control.

Embry-Riddle Aeronautical University–Daytona, Department of Civil Engineering, Daytona Beach, FL 32114-3900. Offers MS. *Program availability:* Part-time. *Faculty:* 3 full-time (1 woman). *Students:* 5 full-time (1 woman); includes 3 minority (2 Asian, non-Hispanic/Latino; 1 Two or more races, non-Hispanic/Latino), 2 international. Average age 26. 9 applicants, 67% accepted, 5 enrolled. *Degree requirements:* For master's, thesis or alternative. *Entrance requirements:* For master's, GRE. Additional exam requirements/recommendations for international students: Required—TOEFL (minimum score 550 paper-based, 79 iBT) or IELTS (6). *Application deadline:* For fall admission, 3/ 1 priority date for domestic students; for spring admission, 11/1 priority date for domestic students; for summer admission, 4/1 priority date for domestic students. Applications are processed on a rolling basis. Application fee: $50. Electronic applications accepted. *Expenses: Tuition:* Full-time $16,296; part-time $1358 per credit hour. *Required fees:* $1294; $647 per semester. One-time fee: $100 full-time. Tuition and fees vary according to course load, degree level and program. *Financial support:* Research assistantships, career-related internships or fieldwork, scholarships/grants, unspecified assistantships, and on-campus employment available. Financial award application deadline: 3/15; financial award applicants required to submit FAFSA. *Unit head:* Dr. Ashok Gurjar, Professor and Chair, Department of Civil Engineering, 386-226-6757, E-mail: gurjara@erau.edu. *Application contact:* Graduate Admissions, 800-388-3728, Fax: 386-226-7070, E-mail: graduate.admissions@erau.edu.
Website: https://daytonabeach.erau.edu/college-engineering/civil/index.html

Florida Agricultural and Mechanical University, Division of Graduate Studies, Research, and Continuing Education, FAMU-FSU College of Engineering, Department of Civil and Environmental Engineering, Tallahassee, FL 32307-3200. Offers civil engineering (M Eng, MS, PhD). *Degree requirements:* For master's, comprehensive exam, thesis optional; for doctorate, comprehensive exam, thesis/dissertation. *Entrance requirements:* For master's, GRE General Test, minimum GPA of 3.0; for doctorate, GRE General Test, minimum GPA of 3.0, letters of recommendation (3). Additional exam requirements/recommendations for international students: Required—TOEFL (minimum score 550 paper-based). *Faculty research:* Geotechnical, environmental, hydraulic, construction materials, and structures.

Florida Atlantic University, College of Engineering and Computer Science, Department of Civil, Environmental and Geomatics Engineering, Boca Raton, FL 33431-0991. Offers civil engineering (MS); environmental engineering (MS). *Program availability:* Part-time, evening/weekend. *Faculty:* 13 full-time (0 women), 2 part-time/ adjunct (0 women). *Students:* 13 full-time (5 women), 23 part-time (4 women); includes 13 minority (4 Black or African American, non-Hispanic/Latino; 1 Asian, non-Hispanic/ Latino; 7 Hispanic/Latino; 1 Two or more races, non-Hispanic/Latino), 10 international. Average age 31. 30 applicants, 53% accepted, 12 enrolled. In 2016, 11 master's awarded. *Degree requirements:* For master's, thesis optional. *Entrance requirements:* For master's, GRE General Test, minimum GPA of 3.0 in last 60 hours of undergraduate course work. Additional exam requirements/recommendations for international students: Required—TOEFL (minimum score 550 paper-based; 61 iBT), IELTS (minimum score 6). *Application deadline:* For fall admission, 7/1 priority date for domestic students, 2/15 for international students; for spring admission, 11/1 for domestic students, 7/15 for international students. Applications are processed on a rolling basis. Application fee: $30. *Expenses:* Tuition, state resident: full-time $7392; part-time $369.82 per credit hour. Tuition, nonresident: full-time $19,432; part-time $1024.81 per credit hour. *Financial support:* Research assistantships with full tuition reimbursements, teaching assistantships with full tuition reimbursements, career-related internships or fieldwork, Federal Work-Study, scholarships/grants, and unspecified assistantships available. Financial award applicants required to submit FAFSA. *Faculty research:* Structures, geotechnical engineering, environmental and water resources engineering, transportation engineering, materials. *Unit head:* Dr. Pete D. Scarlatos, Chair, 561-297-0466, Fax: 561-297-0493, E-mail: scarlatos@fau.edu. *Application contact:* Dr. Frederick Bloetscher, Assistant Professor, 561-297-0744, E-mail: fbloetscher@civil.fau.edu.
Website: http://www.cege.fau.edu/

Florida Institute of Technology, College of Engineering, Program in Civil Engineering, Melbourne, FL 32901-6975. Offers MS, PhD. *Program availability:* Part-time. *Students:* 29 full-time (2 women), 7 part-time (1 woman); includes 2 minority (1 Black or African American, non-Hispanic/Latino; 1 Hispanic/Latino), 30 international. Average age 27. 211 applicants, 25% accepted, 10 enrolled. In 2016, 11 master's, 2 doctorates awarded. *Degree requirements:* For master's, comprehensive exam (for some programs), thesis optional, 30 credit hours; teaching/internship (for thesis) or final examinations (for non-thesis); for doctorate, comprehensive exam, thesis/dissertation, 24 credit hours of coursework, 12 credit hours of formal coursework, 18 credit hours of dissertation, research project, preliminary examination. *Entrance requirements:* For master's, GRE, 2 letters of recommendation, statement of objectives; for doctorate, GRE, 3 letters of recommendation, minimum GPA of 3.2, resume, statement of objectives, degree from accredited institution. Additional exam requirements/recommendations for international students: Required—TOEFL (minimum score 550 paper-based; 79 iBT). *Application deadline:* For fall admission, 4/1 for international students; for spring admission, 9/30 for international students. Applications are processed on a rolling basis. Electronic applications accepted. *Expenses: Tuition:* Full-time $22,338; part-time $1241 per credit hour. *Required fees:* $250. Tuition and fees vary according to degree level, campus/ location and program. *Financial support:* Research assistantships, teaching assistantships, career-related internships or fieldwork, institutionally sponsored loans, tuition waivers (partial), unspecified assistantships, and tuition remissions available. Support available to part-time students. Financial award application deadline: 3/1; financial award applicants required to submit FAFSA. *Faculty research:* Groundwater and surface water modeling, pavements, waste materials, in situ soil testing, fiber optic sensors. *Unit head:* Dr. Ashok Pandit, Department Head, 321-674-7151, Fax: 321-768-7565, E-mail: apandit@fit.edu. *Application contact:* Cheryl A. Brown, Associate Director of Graduate Admissions, 321-674-7581, Fax: 321-723-9468, E-mail: cbrown@fit.edu.
Website: http://coe.fit.edu/civil/

Florida International University, College of Engineering and Computing, Department of Civil and Environmental Engineering, Miami, FL 33175. Offers civil engineering (MS, PhD); environmental engineering (MS). *Program availability:* Part-time, evening/ weekend, online learning. *Faculty:* 21 full-time (6 women), 7 part-time/adjunct (1 woman). *Students:* 55 full-time (21 women), 42 part-time (11 women); includes 36 minority (7 Black or African American, non-Hispanic/Latino; 1 Asian, non-Hispanic/ Latino; 27 Hispanic/Latino; 1 Two or more races, non-Hispanic/Latino), 56 international. Average age 31. 126 applicants, 33% accepted, 17 enrolled. In 2016, 26 master's, 11 doctorates awarded. Terminal master's awarded for partial completion of doctoral program. *Degree requirements:* For master's, thesis or alternative; for doctorate, comprehensive exam, thesis/dissertation. *Entrance requirements:* For master's, bachelor's degree in related field, 3 letters of recommendation, minimum GPA of 3.0; for doctorate, GRE General Test, minimum graduate GPA of 3.3, 3 letters of recommendation, master's degree, resume, statement of purpose. Additional exam requirements/recommendations for international students: Required—TOEFL (minimum score 550 paper-based; 80 iBT). *Application deadline:* For fall admission, 6/1 for domestic students, 4/1 for international students; for spring admission, 10/1 for domestic students, 9/1 for international students. Applications are processed on a rolling basis. Application fee: $30. Electronic applications accepted. *Expenses:* Tuition, state resident: full-time $8912; part-time $446 per credit hour. Tuition, nonresident: full-time $21,393; part-time $992 per credit hour. *Required fees:* $2185; $195 per semester. Tuition and fees vary according to program. *Financial support:* Federal Work-Study, institutionally sponsored loans, scholarships/grants, health care benefits, and unspecified assistantships available. Financial award application deadline: 3/1; financial award applicants required to submit FAFSA. *Faculty research:* Structural engineering, wind engineering, water resources engineering, transportation engineering, environmental engineering. *Unit head:* Dr. Atorod Azizinamini, Chair, 305-348-3821, Fax: 305-348-2802, E-mail: aazizina@fiu.edu. *Application contact:* Sara-Michelle Lemus, Engineering Admissions Officer, 305-348-1890, Fax: 305-348-7441, E-mail: grad_eng@fiu.edu.
Website: http://cec.fiu.edu

Florida State University, The Graduate School, FAMU-FSU College of Engineering, Department of Civil and Environmental Engineering, Tallahassee, FL 32306. Offers M Eng, MS, PhD. *Program availability:* Part-time. *Faculty:* 17 full-time (2 women), 1 part-time/adjunct (0 women). *Students:* 60 full-time (17 women); includes 12 minority (8 Black or African American, non-Hispanic/Latino; 2 Asian, non-Hispanic/Latino; 2 Hispanic/Latino), 34 international. Average age 23. 62 applicants, 50% accepted, 22 enrolled. In 2016, 13 master's, 2 doctorates awarded. *Degree requirements:* For master's, comprehensive exam, thesis optional; for doctorate, thesis/dissertation. *Entrance requirements:* For master's, GRE General Test (minimum score 1000 in old version), BS in engineering or related field, minimum GPA of 3.0; for doctorate, GRE General Test, master's degree in engineering or related field, minimum GPA of 3.0. Additional exam requirements/recommendations for international students: Required—TOEFL (minimum score 550 paper-based; 80 iBT); Recommended—IELTS (minimum score 6.5). *Application deadline:* For fall admission, 7/1 for domestic and international students; for spring admission, 11/1 for domestic and international students; for summer admission, 3/1 for domestic and international students. Applications are processed on a rolling basis. Application fee: $30. Electronic applications accepted. *Expenses:* Tuition, state resident: full-time $7263; part-time $403.51 per credit hour. Tuition, nonresident: full-time $18,087; part-time $1004.85 per credit hour. *Required fees:* $1365; $75.81 per credit hour. $20 per semester. Tuition and fees vary according to campus/location. *Financial support:* In 2016–17, 37 students received support, including 7 fellowships with full tuition reimbursements available, 17 research assistantships with full tuition reimbursements available, 13 teaching assistantships with full tuition reimbursements available; Federal Work-Study, scholarships/grants, tuition waivers (full), and unspecified assistantships also available. Financial award application deadline: 3/1; financial award applicants required to submit FAFSA. *Faculty research:* Tidal hydraulics, temperature effects on bridge girders, codes for coastal construction, field performance of pine bridges, river basin management, transportation pavement design, soil dynamics, structural analysis. *Total annual research expenditures:* $2.9 million. *Unit*

head: Dr. Kamal S. Tawfiq, Chair and Professor, 850-410-6143, Fax: 850-410-6142, E-mail: tawfiq@eng.famu.fsu.edu. *Application contact:* Mable Johnson, Office Manager, 850-410-6139, Fax: 850-410-6292, E-mail: mjohnson5@fsu.edu.
Website: http://www.eng.famu.fsu.edu/cee/

George Mason University, Volgenau School of Engineering, Sid and Reva Dewberry Department of Civil, Environmental, and Infrastructure Engineering, Fairfax, VA 22030. Offers construction project management (MS); geotechnical, construction, and structural engineering (M Eng); transportation engineering (PhD). *Faculty:* 14 full-time (6 women), 20 part-time/adjunct (4 women). *Students:* 47 full-time (12 women), 62 part-time (22 women); includes 23 minority (6 Black or African American, non-Hispanic/Latino; 9 Asian, non-Hispanic/Latino; 7 Hispanic/Latino; 1 Native Hawaiian or other Pacific Islander, non-Hispanic/Latino), 38 international. Average age 29. 109 applicants, 77% accepted, 39 enrolled. In 2016, 31 master's, 1 doctorate awarded. *Degree requirements:* For master's, thesis (for some programs), 30 credits, departmental seminars; for doctorate, thesis/dissertation, qualifying exams. *Entrance requirements:* For master's, GRE, photocopy of passport; 2 official college transcripts; resume; official bank statement; proof of financial support; expanded goals statement; self-evaluation form; BS in engineering or other related science; 3 letters of recommendation; for doctorate, GRE (for those who received degree outside of the U.S.), photocopy of passport; 2 official college transcripts; resume; official bank statement; proof of financial support; expanded goals statement; self-evaluation form; baccalaureate degree in engineering or related science; master's degree (preferred); 3 letters of recommendation. Additional exam requirements/recommendations for international students: Required—TOEFL (minimum score 575 paper-based; 88 iBT), IELTS (minimum score 6.5), PTE (minimum score 59). *Application deadline:* For fall admission, 1/15 priority date for domestic students. Application fee: $75 ($80 for international students). Electronic applications accepted. *Expenses:* Contact institution. *Financial support:* In 2016–17, 27 students received support, including 1 fellowship (averaging $10,000 per year), 16 research assistantships with tuition reimbursements available (averaging $20,150 per year), 10 teaching assistantships with tuition reimbursements available (averaging $21,000 per year); career-related internships or fieldwork, Federal Work-Study, scholarships/grants, unspecified assistantships, and health care benefits (for full-time research or teaching assistantship recipients) also available. Support available to part-time students. Financial award application deadline: 3/1; financial award applicants required to submit FAFSA. *Faculty research:* Evolutionary design, infrastructure security, intelligent transportation systems, national transportation networks, water quality modeling. *Total annual research expenditures:* $568,705. *Unit head:* LIza Wilson Durant, Acting Chair, 703-993-1687, Fax: 703-993-9790, E-mail: ldurant2@gmu.edu. *Application contact:* Laura Kosoglu, Director, Graduate Program, 703-993-1675, Fax: 703-993-9790, E-mail: ceiegrad@gmu.edu.
Website: http://civil.gmu.edu/

The George Washington University, School of Engineering and Applied Science, Department of Civil and Environmental Engineering, Washington, DC 20052. Offers MS, PhD, App Sc, Engr, Graduate Certificate. *Program availability:* Part-time, evening/weekend. *Faculty:* 12 full-time (3 women). *Students:* 31 full-time (7 women), 18 part-time (6 women); includes 1 minority (Asian, non-Hispanic/Latino), 38 international. Average age 27. 186 applicants, 54% accepted, 17 enrolled. In 2016, 7 master's, 2 doctorates awarded. *Degree requirements:* For master's, thesis optional; for doctorate, thesis/dissertation, final and qualifying exams. *Entrance requirements:* For master's, appropriate bachelor's degree, minimum GPA of 3.0; for doctorate, GRE (if highest earned degree is BS), appropriate bachelor's or master's degree, minimum GPA of 3.4; for other advanced degree, appropriate master's degree, minimum GPA of 3.0. Additional exam requirements/recommendations for international students: Required—TOEFL or The George Washington University English as a Foreign Language Test. *Application deadline:* For fall admission, 3/1 priority date for domestic students; for spring admission, 10/1 for domestic students. Applications are processed on a rolling basis. Application fee: $75. *Financial support:* In 2016–17, 42 students received support. Fellowships with tuition reimbursements available, research assistantships, teaching assistantships with tuition reimbursements available, career-related internships or fieldwork, Federal Work-Study, institutionally sponsored loans, and tuition waivers available. Financial award application deadline: 3/1; financial award applicants required to submit FAFSA. *Faculty research:* Computer-integrated manufacturing, materials engineering, electronic materials, fatigue and fracture, reliability. *Unit head:* Dr. Majid T. Manzari, Chair, 202-994-4901, Fax: 202-994-0127, E-mail: manzari@gwu.edu. *Application contact:* Adina Lav, Marketing, Recruiting and Admissions, 202-994-5827, Fax: 202-994-0909, E-mail: engineering@gwu.edu.
Website: http://www.cee.seas.gwu.edu/

Georgia Institute of Technology, Graduate Studies, College of Engineering, School of Civil and Environmental Engineering, Program in Civil Engineering, Atlanta, GA 30332-0001. Offers MS, PhD. *Program availability:* Part-time. Terminal master's awarded for partial completion of doctoral program. *Degree requirements:* For master's, thesis optional; for doctorate, comprehensive exam, thesis/dissertation. *Entrance requirements:* For master's and doctorate, GRE. Additional exam requirements/recommendations for international students: Required—TOEFL (minimum score 550 paper-based; 79 iBT). Electronic applications accepted. *Faculty research:* Structural analysis, fluid mechanics, geotechnical engineering, construction management, transportation engineering.

Georgia Southern University, Jack N. Averitt College of Graduate Studies, Allen E. Paulson College of Engineering and Information Technology, Program in Civil Engineering and Construction Management, Statesboro, GA 30458. Offers MSAE. *Students:* 11 full-time (2 women), 4 part-time (1 woman); includes 4 minority (3 Black or African American, non-Hispanic/Latino; 1 Asian, non-Hispanic/Latino), 7 international. Average age 29. 9 applicants, 100% accepted, 7 enrolled. *Entrance requirements:* For master's, bachelor's degree in engineering, information technology, or a scientific discipline; minimum cumulative GPA of 2.75. Additional exam requirements/recommendations for international students: Required—TOEFL. Electronic applications accepted. *Expenses:* Tuition, state resident: full-time $7236; part-time $277 per semester hour. Tuition, nonresident: full-time $27,118; part-time $1105 per semester hour. *Required fees:* $2092. *Financial support:* Applicants required to submit FAFSA. *Unit head:* Dr. David Williams, Associate Dean, 912-478-4848, E-mail: dwilliams@georgiasouthern.edu.
Website: http://ceit.georgiasouthern.edu/cecm/

The Graduate Center, City University of New York, Graduate Studies, Program in Engineering, New York, NY 10016-4039. Offers biomedical engineering (PhD); chemical engineering (PhD); civil engineering (PhD); electrical engineering (PhD); mechanical engineering (PhD). *Degree requirements:* For doctorate, thesis/dissertation. *Entrance requirements:* For doctorate, GRE General Test. Additional exam requirements/recommendations for international students: Required—TOEFL. Electronic applications accepted.

Howard University, College of Engineering, Architecture, and Computer Sciences, School of Engineering and Computer Science, Department of Civil Engineering, Washington, DC 20059-0002. Offers M Eng. Offered through the Graduate School of Arts and Sciences. *Degree requirements:* For master's, comprehensive exam, thesis. *Entrance requirements:* For master's, GRE General Test, minimum GPA of 3.0, bachelor's degree in engineering or related field. Additional exam requirements/recommendations for international students: Required—TOEFL. Electronic applications accepted. *Faculty research:* Modeling of concrete, structures, transportation planning, structural analysis, environmental and water resources.

Idaho State University, Office of Graduate Studies, College of Science and Engineering, Civil and Environmental Engineering Department, Pocatello, ID 83209-8060. Offers civil engineering (MS); environmental engineering (MS); environmental science and management (MS). *Program availability:* Part-time. *Degree requirements:* For master's, comprehensive exam (for some programs), thesis optional, thesis project, 2 semesters of seminar. *Entrance requirements:* For master's, GRE. Additional exam requirements/recommendations for international students: Required—TOEFL (minimum score 550 paper-based; 80 iBT). Electronic applications accepted. *Faculty research:* Floor vibration investigations, earthquake engineering, base isolation systems and seismic risk assessment, infrastructure revitalization (building foundations and damage, bridge structures, highways, and dams), slope stability and soil erosion, pavement rehabilitation, computational fluid dynamics and flood control structures, microbial fuel cells, water treatment and water quality modeling, environmental risk assessment, biotechnology, nanotechnology.

Illinois Institute of Technology, Graduate College, Armour College of Engineering, Department of Civil, Architectural and Environmental Engineering, Chicago, IL 60616. Offers architectural engineering (M Arch E); civil engineering (MS, PhD), including architectural engineering (MS), construction engineering and management (MS), geoenvironmental engineering (MS), geotechnical engineering (MS), structural engineering (MS), transportation engineering (MS); construction engineering and management (MCEM); environmental engineering (M Env E, MS, PhD); geoenvironmental engineering (M Geoenv E); geotechnical engineering (MGE); infrastructure engineering and management (MPW); structural engineering (MSE); transportation engineering (M Trans E). *Program availability:* Part-time, evening/weekend, online learning. Terminal master's awarded for partial completion of doctoral program. *Degree requirements:* For master's, thesis (for some programs); for doctorate, comprehensive exam, thesis/dissertation. *Entrance requirements:* For master's, GRE General Test (minimum score 900 Quantitative and Verbal, 2.5 Analytical Writing), minimum undergraduate GPA of 3.0; for doctorate, GRE General Test (minimum score 1000 Quantitative and Verbal, 3.0 Analytical Writing), minimum undergraduate GPA of 3.0. Additional exam requirements/recommendations for international students: Required—TOEFL (minimum score 550 paper-based; 80 iBT). Electronic applications accepted. *Faculty research:* Structural, architectural, geotechnical and geoenvironmental engineering; construction engineering and management; transportation engineering; environmental engineering and public works.

Indiana University–Purdue University Fort Wayne, College of Engineering, Technology, and Computer Science, Department of Civil and Mechanical Engineering, Fort Wayne, IN 46805-1499. Offers civil engineering (MSE); mechanical engineering (MSE). *Program availability:* Part-time. *Entrance requirements:* For master's, minimum GPA of 3.0, bachelor's degree in engineering discipline. Additional exam requirements/recommendations for international students: Required—TOEFL (minimum score 550 paper-based; 79 iBT); Recommended—TWE. Electronic applications accepted. *Faculty research:* Continuous space language model, sensor networks, wireless cloud architecture.

Instituto Tecnológico y de Estudios Superiores de Monterrey, Campus Monterrey, Graduate and Research Division, Programs in Engineering, Monterrey, Mexico. Offers applied statistics (M Eng); artificial intelligence (PhD); automation engineering (M Eng); chemical engineering (M Eng); civil engineering (M Eng); electrical engineering (M Eng); electronic engineering (M Eng); environmental engineering (M Eng); industrial engineering (M Eng, PhD); manufacturing engineering (M Eng); mechanical engineering (M Eng); systems and quality engineering (M Eng). M Eng program offered jointly with University of Waterloo; PhD in industrial engineering with Texas A&M University. *Program availability:* Part-time, evening/weekend. Terminal master's awarded for partial completion of doctoral program. *Degree requirements:* For master's, one foreign language, thesis; for doctorate, one foreign language, thesis/dissertation. *Entrance requirements:* For master's, EXADEP; for doctorate, GRE, master's degree in related field. Additional exam requirements/recommendations for international students: Required—TOEFL. *Faculty research:* Flexible manufacturing cells, materials, statistical methods, environmental prevention, control and evaluation.

Iowa State University of Science and Technology, Department of Civil and Construction Engineering, Ames, IA 50011. Offers civil engineering (MS, PhD), including civil engineering materials, construction engineering and management, environmental engineering, geotechnical engineering, structural engineering, transportation engineering. *Degree requirements:* For master's, thesis or alternative; for doctorate, thesis/dissertation. *Entrance requirements:* For master's and doctorate, GRE General Test. Additional exam requirements/recommendations for international students: Required—TOEFL (minimum score 550 paper-based; 82 iBT), IELTS (minimum score 6.5). *Application deadline:* For fall admission, 2/1 priority date for domestic students, 2/1 for international students; for spring admission, 8/1 priority date for domestic students, 8/1 for international students. Application fee: $60 ($90 for international students). Electronic applications accepted. *Application contact:* Kathy Petersen, Application Contact, 515-294-4975, Fax: 515-294-8216, E-mail: ccee-grad-inquiry@iastate.edu.
Website: http://www.ccee.iastate.edu/

Jackson State University, Graduate School, College of Science, Engineering and Technology, Department of Civil and Environmental Engineering and Industrial Systems and Technology, Jackson, MS 39217. Offers civil engineering (MS, PhD); coastal engineering (MS, PhD); environmental engineering (MS, PhD); hazardous materials management (MS); technology education (MS Ed). *Program availability:* Part-time, evening/weekend. *Degree requirements:* For master's, comprehensive exam, thesis or alternative. *Entrance requirements:* For master's, GRE General Test. Additional exam requirements/recommendations for international students: Required—TOEFL (minimum score 520 paper-based; 67 iBT). *Application deadline:* For fall admission, 3/1 priority date for domestic students, 3/1 for international students; for spring admission, 10/1 for domestic and international students. Applications are processed on a rolling basis. Application fee: $25. *Expenses:* Tuition, state resident: full-time $7141. Tuition, nonresident: full-time $17,494. *Required fees:* $1080. Tuition and fees vary according to class time, course level, course load, degree level, campus/location, program and student level. *Financial support:* Career-related internships or fieldwork, Federal Work-Study, scholarships/grants, and unspecified assistantships available. Support available to part-time students. Financial award application deadline: 3/1; financial award applicants required to submit FAFSA. *Unit head:* Dr. Farshad Amini, Chair, 601-979-3913, Fax: 601-979-3238, E-mail: famini@jsums.edu. *Application contact:* Fatoumatta Sisay, Manager of Graduate Admissions, 601-979-0342, Fax: 601-979-4325, E-mail: fatoumatta.sisay@jsums.edu.
Website: http://www.jsums.edu/ceeist/

Johns Hopkins University, Engineering Program for Professionals, Part-time Program in Civil Engineering, Baltimore, MD 21218. Offers MCE, Graduate Certificate. *Program availability:* Part-time, evening/weekend, 100% online, blended/hybrid learning. *Faculty:*

9 part-time/adjunct (2 women). *Students:* 24 part-time (3 women); includes 2 minority (both Asian, non-Hispanic/Latino), 1 international. Average age 27. 11 applicants, 45% accepted, 4 enrolled. In 2016, 5 master's awarded. *Entrance requirements:* Additional exam requirements/recommendations for international students: Required—TOEFL (minimum score 600 paper-based; 100 iBT). *Application deadline:* Applications are processed on a rolling basis. Application fee: $0. Electronic applications accepted. *Unit head:* Dr. Rachel Sangree, Chair, 410-516-7138, E-mail: sangree@jhu.edu. *Application contact:* Doug Schiller, Admissions Director, 410-516-2300, Fax: 410-579-8049, E-mail: schiller@jhu.edu.
Website: http://www.ep.jhu.edu

Johns Hopkins University, G. W. C. Whiting School of Engineering, Department of Civil Engineering, Baltimore, MD 21218. Offers MSE, PhD. *Faculty:* 12 full-time (3 women), 7 part-time/adjunct (0 women). *Students:* 60 full-time (12 women); includes 4 minority (3 Asian, non-Hispanic/Latino; 1 Two or more races, non-Hispanic/Latino), 45 international. Average age 26. 118 applicants, 61% accepted, 14 enrolled. In 2016, 10 master's, 5 doctorates awarded. *Degree requirements:* For master's, thesis (for some programs); for doctorate, comprehensive exam, thesis/dissertation, qualifying and oral exams. *Entrance requirements:* For master's and doctorate, GRE General Test, 3 letters of recommendation, statement of purpose, transcripts. Additional exam requirements/recommendations for international students: Required—TOEFL (minimum score 600 paper-based, 100 iBT) or IELTS (7). *Application deadline:* For fall admission, 12/31 for domestic and international students. Application fee: $75. Electronic applications accepted. *Financial support:* In 2016–17, 42 students received support, including 7 fellowships with full tuition reimbursements available (averaging $14,100 per year), 35 research assistantships with full tuition reimbursements available (averaging $14,472 per year); teaching assistantships with full tuition reimbursements available and tuition waivers (full and partial) also available. Financial award application deadline: 2/1. *Faculty research:* Mechanics of materials, structural engineering, systems engineering, probabilistic modeling, computational mechanics. *Total annual research expenditures:* $7.2 million. *Unit head:* Dr. Lori Brady, Chair, 410-516-8167, E-mail: lori@jhu.edu. *Application contact:* Lisa Wetzelberger, Academic Program Coordinator, 410-516-0617, Fax: 410-516-7473, E-mail: lawetzel@jhu.edu.
Website: http://www.ce.jhu.edu/

Johns Hopkins University, G. W. C. Whiting School of Engineering, Master of Science in Engineering Management Program, Baltimore, MD 21218. Offers biomaterials (MSEM); civil engineering (MSEM); communications science (MSEM); computer science (MSEM); environmental systems analysis, economics and public policy (MSEM); fluid mechanics (MSEM); materials science and engineering (MSEM); mechanical engineering (MSEM); mechanics and materials (MSEM); nano-biotechnology (MSEM); nanomaterials and nanotechnology (MSEM); operations research (MSEM); probability and statistics (MSEM); smart product and device design (MSEM). *Faculty:* 7 full-time (4 women), 1 part-time/adjunct (0 women). *Students:* 35 full-time (14 women), 8 part-time (3 women); includes 7 minority (4 Asian, non-Hispanic/Latino; 3 Hispanic/Latino), 26 international. Average age 24. 228 applicants, 28% accepted, 25 enrolled. In 2016, 18 master's awarded. *Entrance requirements:* For master's, GRE, 3 letters of recommendation, statement of purpose, transcripts. Additional exam requirements/recommendations for international students: Required—TOEFL (minimum score 600 paper-based, 100 iBT) or IELTS (7). *Application deadline:* For fall admission, 2/1 for domestic and international students. Application fee: $75. Electronic applications accepted. *Financial support:* Fellowships and health care benefits available. *Unit head:* Dr. Pamela Sheff, Director, 410-516-7056, Fax: 410-516-4880, E-mail: pamsheff@gmail.com. *Application contact:* Richard Helman, Director of Graduate Admissions, 410-516-8174, Fax: 410-516-0780, E-mail: graduateadmissions@jhu.edu.
Website: http://engineering.jhu.edu/msem/

Kansas State University, Graduate School, College of Engineering, Department of Civil Engineering, Manhattan, KS 66506. Offers civil engineering (MS, PhD); environmental engineering (MS, PhD); geotechnical engineering (MS, PhD); structural engineering (MS, PhD); transportation engineering (MS, PhD); water resources engineering (MS, PhD). *Program availability:* Part-time, evening/weekend, online learning. *Faculty:* 14 full-time (4 women), 3 part-time/adjunct (1 woman). *Students:* 36 full-time (11 women), 34 part-time (7 women); includes 5 minority (2 Asian, non-Hispanic/Latino; 2 Hispanic/Latino; 1 Two or more races, non-Hispanic/Latino), 28 international. Average age 29. 70 applicants, 60% accepted, 11 enrolled. In 2016, 21 master's, 7 doctorates awarded. *Degree requirements:* For master's, thesis or alternative; for doctorate, thesis/dissertation. *Entrance requirements:* For master's, GRE General Test, bachelor's degree or course work in related engineering fields; for doctorate, GRE General Test. Additional exam requirements/recommendations for international students: Required—TOEFL (minimum score 550 paper-based; 79 iBT). *Application deadline:* For fall admission, 2/1 priority date for domestic students, 1/1 priority date for international students; for spring admission, 8/1 priority date for domestic and international students. Applications are processed on a rolling basis. Application fee: $50 ($75 for international students). Electronic applications accepted. *Expenses:* Tuition, state resident: full-time $9670. Tuition, nonresident: full-time $21,828. *Required fees:* $862. *Financial support:* In 2016–17, 19 research assistantships with partial tuition reimbursements (averaging $13,431 per year), 12 teaching assistantships with partial tuition reimbursements (averaging $15,058 per year) were awarded; institutionally sponsored loans and scholarships/grants also available. Support available to part-time students. Financial award application deadline: 3/1; financial award applicants required to submit FAFSA. *Faculty research:* Transportation and materials engineering, water resources engineering, environmental engineering, geotechnical engineering, structural engineering. *Total annual research expenditures:* $2.4 million. *Unit head:* Dr. Robert Stokes, Head, 785-532-1595, Fax: 785-532-7717, E-mail: drbobb@k-state.edu. *Application contact:* Dr. Dunja Peric, Graduate Coordinator, 785-532-2468, Fax: 785-532-7717, E-mail: peric@k-state.edu.
Website: http://www.ce.ksu.edu/

Lawrence Technological University, College of Engineering, Southfield, MI 48075-1058. Offers architectural engineering (MS); automotive engineering (MS); biomedical engineering (MS); civil engineering (MA, MS, PhD), including environmental engineering (MS), geotechnical engineering (MS), structural engineering (MS), transportation engineering (MS), water resource engineering (MS); construction engineering management (MA); electrical and computer engineering (MS); engineering management (MA); engineering technology (MS); fire engineering (MS); industrial engineering (MS), including healthcare; manufacturing systems (ME); mechanical engineering (MS, DE, PhD), including manufacturing (DE), solid mechanics (MS), thermal-fluids (MS); mechatronic systems engineering (MS). *Program availability:* Part-time, evening/weekend. *Faculty:* 24 full-time (5 women), 26 part-time/adjunct (2 women). *Students:* 22 full-time (7 women), 588 part-time (81 women); includes 23 minority (11 Black or African American, non-Hispanic/Latino; 4 Asian, non-Hispanic/Latino; 7 Hispanic/Latino; 1 Two or more races, non-Hispanic/Latino), 469 international. Average age 27. 1,186 applicants, 39% accepted, 99 enrolled. In 2016, 293 master's, 3 doctorates awarded. Terminal master's awarded for partial completion of doctoral program. *Degree requirements:* For master's, thesis optional; for doctorate, comprehensive exam, thesis/dissertation optional. *Entrance requirements:* Additional exam requirements/

recommendations for international students: Required—TOEFL (minimum score 550 paper-based; 79 iBT), IELTS (minimum score 6.5). *Application deadline:* For fall admission, 5/22 for international students; for spring admission, 10/11 for international students; for summer admission, 2/16 for international students. Applications are processed on a rolling basis. Application fee: $50. Electronic applications accepted. *Expenses:* Tuition: Full-time $14,868; part-time $1062 per credit. *Required fees:* $75 per semester. Tuition and fees vary according to campus/location. *Financial support:* In 2016–17, 25 students received support, including 5 research assistantships with full tuition reimbursements available; unspecified assistantships also available. Financial award application deadline: 4/1; financial award applicants required to submit FAFSA. *Faculty research:* Carbon fiber reinforced polymer reinforced concrete structures; low impact storm water management solutions; vehicle battery energy management; wireless communication; entrepreneurial mindset and engineering. *Total annual research expenditures:* $1.7 million. *Unit head:* Dr. Nabil Grace, Dean, 248-204-2500, Fax: 248-204-2509, E-mail: engrdean@ltu.edu. *Application contact:* Jane Rohrback, Director of Admissions, 248-204-3160, Fax: 248-204-2228, E-mail: admissions@ltu.edu.
Website: http://www.ltu.edu/engineering/index.asp

Lehigh University, P.C. Rossin College of Engineering and Applied Science, Department of Civil and Environmental Engineering, Bethlehem, PA 18015. Offers M Eng, MS, PhD. *Program availability:* Part-time. *Faculty:* 21 full-time (4 women). *Students:* 78 full-time (24 women), 7 part-time (0 women); includes 6 minority (1 Black or African American, non-Hispanic/Latino; 2 Asian, non-Hispanic/Latino; 3 Hispanic/Latino), 51 international. Average age 27. 184 applicants, 27% accepted, 13 enrolled. In 2016, 29 master's, 14 doctorates awarded. Terminal master's awarded for partial completion of doctoral program. *Degree requirements:* For master's, thesis (for some programs); for doctorate, comprehensive exam, thesis/dissertation. *Entrance requirements:* For master's and doctorate, GRE. Additional exam requirements/recommendations for international students: Required—TOEFL (minimum score 550 paper-based; 79 iBT), IELTS (minimum score 6.5). *Application deadline:* For fall admission, 7/15 for domestic and international students; for spring admission, 12/1 for domestic and international students; for summer admission, 5/30 for domestic and international students. Application fee: $75. Electronic applications accepted. *Expenses:* $1,420 per credit. *Financial support:* In 2016–17, 5 fellowships with full tuition reimbursements (averaging $21,530 per year), 27 research assistantships with full and partial tuition reimbursements (averaging $23,000 per year), 7 teaching assistantships with full tuition reimbursements (averaging $21,530 per year) were awarded; unspecified assistantships also available. Financial award application deadline: 1/15; financial award applicants required to submit FAFSA. *Faculty research:* Structural engineering, geotechnical engineering, water resources engineering, environmental engineering. *Total annual research expenditures:* $4.5 million. *Unit head:* Dr. Panayiotis Diplas, Chair, 610-758-3554, E-mail: pad313@lehigh.edu. *Application contact:* Prisca Vidanage, Graduate Coordinator, 610-758-3530, E-mail: pmv1@lehigh.edu.
Website: http://www.lehigh.edu/~incee

Louisiana State University and Agricultural & Mechanical College, Graduate School, College of Engineering, Department of Civil and Environmental Engineering, Baton Rouge, LA 70803. Offers environmental engineering (MSCE, PhD); geotechnical engineering (MSCE, PhD); structural engineering and mechanics (MSCE, PhD); transportation engineering (MSCE, PhD); water resources (MSCE, PhD).

Louisiana Tech University, Graduate School, College of Engineering and Science, Department of Civil Engineering, Ruston, LA 71272. Offers MS. *Program availability:* Part-time. Terminal master's awarded for partial completion of doctoral program. *Degree requirements:* For master's, thesis or practicum. *Entrance requirements:* For master's, GRE General Test, minimum GPA of 3.0 in last 60 hours. Additional exam requirements/recommendations for international students: Required—TOEFL. *Application deadline:* For fall admission, 8/1 for domestic students; for spring admission, 2/1 for domestic students. Applications are processed on a rolling basis. Application fee: $20 ($30 for international students). *Financial support:* Fellowships, research assistantships, teaching assistantships, career-related internships or fieldwork, Federal Work-Study, and unspecified assistantships available. Financial award application deadline: 4/1. *Faculty research:* Environmental engineering, trenchless excavation construction, structural mechanics, transportation materials and planning, water quality modeling. *Unit head:* Dr. David E. Hall, Academic Director, 318-257-4127. *Application contact:* Marilyn J. Robinson, Assistant to the Dean, 318-257-2924, Fax: 318-257-4487.
Website: http://coes.latech.edu/civil-engineering/

Loyola Marymount University, College of Science and Engineering, Department of Civil Engineering and Environmental Science, Program in Civil Engineering, Los Angeles, CA 90045-2659. Offers MSE. *Program availability:* Part-time. *Students:* 6 full-time (2 women), 2 part-time (both women); includes 4 minority (1 Black or African American, non-Hispanic/Latino; 2 Hispanic/Latino; 1 Two or more races, non-Hispanic/Latino), 3 international. Average age 28. 6 applicants, 83% accepted, 3 enrolled. In 2016, 5 master's awarded. *Degree requirements:* For master's, comprehensive exam. *Entrance requirements:* For master's, 2 letters of recommendation, personal statement. Additional exam requirements/recommendations for international students: Required—TOEFL (minimum score 550 paper-based; 80 iBT). *Application deadline:* Applications are processed on a rolling basis. Application fee: $50. Electronic applications accepted. *Financial support:* In 2016–17, 5 students received support. Scholarships/grants and laboratory assistantships available. Support available to part-time students. Financial award application deadline: 6/30; financial award applicants required to submit FAFSA. *Unit head:* Jeremy Pal, Graduate Program Director, 310-568-6241, E-mail: jpal@lmu.edu. *Application contact:* Chake H. Kouyoumjian, Associate Dean of Graduate Studies, 310-338-2721, E-mail: ckouyoum@lmu.edu.
Website: http://cse.lmu.edu/department/civilengineering/

Manhattan College, Graduate Programs, School of Engineering, Program in Civil Engineering, Riverdale, NY 10471. Offers MS. *Program availability:* Part-time, evening/weekend. *Degree requirements:* For master's, thesis or alternative. *Entrance requirements:* For master's, GRE (recommended), minimum GPA of 3.0. Additional exam requirements/recommendations for international students: Required—TOEFL (minimum score 550 paper-based; 80 iBT), IELTS (minimum score 6). *Application deadline:* For fall admission, 8/10 priority date for domestic students, 8/10 for international students; for spring admission, 1/7 for domestic and international students. Applications are processed on a rolling basis. Application fee: $60. *Financial support:* Fellowships, research assistantships, teaching assistantships, career-related internships or fieldwork, Federal Work-Study, scholarships/grants, unspecified assistantships, and laboratory assistantships available. Support available to part-time students. Financial award application deadline: 2/1. *Faculty research:* Compressible-inclusion function for geofoams used with rigid walls under static loading, validation of sediment criteria. *Unit head:* Anirban De, Chairperson, 718-862-7175, Fax: 718-862-8035, E-mail: anirban.de@manhattan.edu.
Website: https://manhattan.edu/academics/graduate-programs/civil-engineering.php

Marquette University, Graduate School, College of Engineering, Department of Civil and Environmental Engineering, Milwaukee, WI 53201-1881. Offers construction engineering and management (MS, PhD, Certificate); environmental engineering (MS, PhD); structural design (Certificate); structural engineering and structural mechanics

(MS, PhD); transportation (Certificate); transportation engineering and materials (MS, PhD); waste and wastewater treatment processes (Certificate); water resources engineering (Certificate). *Program availability:* Part-time, evening/weekend. *Faculty:* 17 full-time (2 women), 2 part-time/adjunct (0 women). *Students:* 27 full-time (8 women), 6 part-time (0 women); includes 5 minority (1 Asian, non-Hispanic/Latino; 2 Hispanic/Latino; 2 Two or more races, non-Hispanic/Latino), 13 international. Average age 28. 70 applicants, 56% accepted, 9 enrolled. In 2016, 8 master's, 5 doctorates awarded. Terminal master's awarded for partial completion of doctoral program. *Degree requirements:* For master's, comprehensive exam (for some programs), thesis or alternative; for doctorate, thesis/dissertation. *Entrance requirements:* For master's, GRE General Test (recommended), minimum GPA of 3.0, official transcripts from all current and previous colleges/universities except Marquette, three letters of recommendation; for doctorate, GRE General Test, minimum GPA of 3.0, official transcripts from all current and previous colleges/universities except Marquette, three letters of recommendation, brief statement of purpose, submission of any English language publications authored by applicant (strongly recommended). Additional exam requirements/recommendations for international students: Required—TOEFL (minimum score 530 paper-based). *Application deadline:* For fall admission, 6/1 priority date for domestic students. Applications are processed on a rolling basis. Application fee: $50. Electronic applications accepted. *Financial support:* Fellowships, research assistantships, teaching assistantships, scholarships/grants, health care benefits, tuition waivers (partial), and unspecified assistantships available. Support available to part-time students. Financial award application deadline: 2/15. *Faculty research:* Highway safety, highway performance, and intelligent transportation systems; surface mount technology; watershed management. *Total annual research expenditures:* $480,876. *Unit head:* Dr. Christopher Foley, Chair, 414-288-5741. *Application contact:* Dr. Stephen M. Heinrich, Director of Graduate Studies, 414-288-5466.
Website: http://www.marquette.edu/civil-environmental-engineering/

Massachusetts Institute of Technology, School of Engineering, Department of Civil and Environmental Engineering, Cambridge, MA 02139. Offers biological oceanography (PhD, Sc D); chemical oceanography (PhD, Sc D); civil and environmental engineering (M Eng, SM, PhD, Sc D); civil and environmental systems (PhD, Sc D); civil engineering (PhD, Sc D, CE); civil engineering and computation (PhD); coastal engineering (PhD, Sc D); construction engineering and management (PhD, Sc D); environmental biology (PhD, Sc D); environmental chemistry (PhD, Sc D); environmental engineering (PhD, Sc D); environmental engineering and computation (PhD); environmental fluid mechanics (PhD, Sc D); geotechnical and geoenvironmental engineering (PhD, Sc D); hydrology (PhD, Sc D); information technology (PhD, Sc D); oceanographic engineering (PhD, Sc D); structures and materials (PhD, Sc D); transportation (PhD, Sc D); SM/MBA. *Faculty:* 35 full-time (6 women). *Students:* 192 full-time (64 women); includes 25 minority (2 Black or African American, non-Hispanic/Latino; 11 Asian, non-Hispanic/Latino; 8 Hispanic/Latino; 4 Two or more races, non-Hispanic/Latino), 113 international. Average age 27. 530 applicants, 20% accepted, 77 enrolled. In 2016, 56 master's, 16 doctorates, 1 other advanced degree awarded. *Degree requirements:* For master's, thesis; for doctorate, comprehensive exam, thesis/dissertation; for CE, comprehensive exam, thesis. *Entrance requirements:* For master's, doctorate, and CE, GRE General Test. Additional exam requirements/recommendations for international students: Required—TOEFL, IELTS. *Application deadline:* For fall admission, 12/15 for domestic and international students. Application fee: $75. Electronic applications accepted. *Expenses: Tuition:* Full-time $46,400; part-time $725 per credit. One-time fee: $312 full-time. Full-time tuition and fees vary according to course load and program. *Financial support:* In 2016–17, 150 students received support, including fellowships (averaging $41,900 per year), 124 research assistantships (averaging $36,900 per year), 9 teaching assistantships (averaging $36,900 per year); Federal Work-Study, institutionally sponsored loans, scholarships/grants, traineeships, health care benefits, unspecified assistantships, and resident tutors also available. Support available to part-time students. Financial award application deadline: 5/1; financial award applicants required to submit FAFSA. *Faculty research:* Environmental chemistry, environmental fluid mechanics and coastal engineering, environmental microbiology, geotechnical engineering and geomechanics, hydrology and hydro climatology, infrastructure systems, mechanics of materials and structures, transportation systems. *Total annual research expenditures:* $25 million. *Unit head:* Prof. Markus Buehler, Department Head, 617-253-7101. *Application contact:* 617-253-7119, E-mail: cee-admissions@mit.edu.
Website: http://cee.mit.edu/

McGill University, Faculty of Graduate and Postdoctoral Studies, Faculty of Engineering, Department of Civil Engineering and Applied Mechanics, Montréal, QC H3A 2T5, Canada. Offers environmental engineering (M Eng, M Sc, PhD); fluid mechanics (M Sc); fluid mechanics and hydraulic engineering (M Eng, PhD); materials engineering (M Eng, PhD); rehabilitation of urban infrastructure (M Eng, PhD); soil behavior (M Eng, PhD); soil mechanics and foundations (M Eng, PhD); structures and structural mechanics (M Eng, PhD); water resources (M Sc); water resources engineering (M Eng, PhD).

McMaster University, School of Graduate Studies, Faculty of Engineering, Department of Civil Engineering, Hamilton, ON L8S 4M2, Canada. Offers M Eng, MA Sc, PhD. *Degree requirements:* For master's, thesis; for doctorate, comprehensive exam, thesis/dissertation. *Entrance requirements:* Additional exam requirements/recommendations for international students: Required—TOEFL (minimum score 550 paper-based). *Faculty research:* Building science, environmental hydrology, bolted steel connections, research on highway materials, earthquake engineering.

McNeese State University, Doré School of Graduate Studies, College of Engineering and Engineering Technology, Department of Engineering, Master of Engineering Program, Lake Charles, LA 70609. Offers chemical engineering (M Eng); civil engineering (M Eng); electrical engineering (M Eng); engineering management (M Eng); mechanical engineering (M Eng). *Program availability:* Part-time, evening/weekend. *Degree requirements:* For master's, thesis or alternative. *Entrance requirements:* For master's, GRE, baccalaureate degree, minimum overall GPA of 3.0. Additional exam requirements/recommendations for international students: Required—TOEFL (minimum score 560 paper-based; 83 iBT).

Memorial University of Newfoundland, School of Graduate Studies, Faculty of Engineering and Applied Science, St. John's, NL A1C 5S7, Canada. Offers civil engineering (M Eng, PhD); electrical and computer engineering (M Eng, PhD); mechanical engineering (M Eng, PhD); ocean and naval architecture engineering (M Eng, PhD). *Program availability:* Part-time. *Degree requirements:* For master's, thesis; for doctorate, comprehensive exam, thesis/dissertation, oral thesis defense. *Entrance requirements:* For master's, 2nd class degree; for doctorate, master's degree in engineering. Electronic applications accepted. *Faculty research:* Engineering analysis, environmental and hydrotechnical studies, manufacturing and robotics, mechanics, structures and materials.

Merrimack College, School of Science and Engineering, North Andover, MA 01845-5800. Offers athletic training (MS); civil engineering (MS); community health education (MS); computer science (MS); data science (MS); exercise and sport science (MS); health and wellness management (MS); mechanical engineering (MS), including engineering management. *Program availability:* Part-time, evening/weekend, 100% online. *Faculty:* 16 full-time, 2 part-time/adjunct. *Students:* 88 full-time (32 women), 13 part-time (6 women); includes 6 minority (4 Hispanic/Latino; 2 Two or more races, non-Hispanic/Latino), 39 international. Average age 25. 156 applicants, 67% accepted, 59 enrolled. In 2016, 46 master's awarded. *Degree requirements:* For master's, comprehensive exam, thesis optional, internship or capstone (for some programs). *Entrance requirements:* For master's, official college transcripts, resume, personal statement, 2 recommendations. Additional exam requirements/recommendations for international students: Required—TOEFL (minimum score 84 iBT), IELTS (minimum score 6.5), PTE (minimum score 56). *Application deadline:* For fall admission, 8/14 for domestic students, 7/14 for international students; for spring admission, 1/10 for domestic students, 12/10 for international students; for summer admission, 5/10 for domestic students, 4/10 for international students. Applications are processed on a rolling basis. Application fee: $0. Electronic applications accepted. *Expenses:* Contact institution. *Financial support:* Fellowships with full tuition reimbursements, career-related internships or fieldwork, scholarships/grants, and health care benefits available. Support available to part-time students. Financial award application deadline: 5/1; financial award applicants required to submit FAFSA. *Faculty research:* Viral genomics and evolution (biology), robotics (mechanical engineering), knot theory (mathematics), computer graphics and network security (computer science), water management (civil engineering). *Application contact:* Allison Pena, Graduate Admissions Counselor, 978-837-3563, E-mail: penaa@merrimack.edu.
Website: http://www.merrimack.edu/academics/graduate/

Michigan State University, The Graduate School, College of Engineering, Department of Civil and Environmental Engineering, East Lansing, MI 48824. Offers civil engineering (MS, PhD); environmental engineering (MS, PhD); environmental engineering-environmental toxicology (PhD). *Program availability:* Part-time. *Entrance requirements:* Additional exam requirements/recommendations for international students: Required—TOEFL. Electronic applications accepted.

Milwaukee School of Engineering, Civil and Architectural Engineering and Construction Management Department, Program in Civil Engineering, Milwaukee, WI 53202-3109. Offers MS. *Program availability:* Part-time, evening/weekend. *Faculty:* 1 full-time (0 women), 2 part-time/adjunct (0 women). *Students:* 1 (woman) part-time, all international. Average age 22. 16 applicants, 13% accepted, 1 enrolled. In 2016, 10 master's awarded. *Degree requirements:* For master's, thesis. *Entrance requirements:* For master's, GRE General Test or GMAT if undergraduate GPA less than 3.0, 2 letters of recommendation; BS in architectural, structural, or civil engineering. Additional exam requirements/recommendations for international students: Required—TOEFL (minimum score 90 iBT), IELTS (minimum score 6.5). *Application deadline:* Applications are processed on a rolling basis. Application fee: $0. Electronic applications accepted. *Expenses: Tuition:* Full-time $31,440; part-time $655 per credit. *Financial support:* Federal Work-Study and scholarships/grants available. Financial award application deadline: 3/15; financial award applicants required to submit FAFSA. *Unit head:* Dr. Francis Mahuta, Director, 414-277-7599, E-mail: mahuta@msoe.edu. *Application contact:* Ian Dahlinghaus, Graduate Program Associate, 414-277-7208, E-mail: dahlinghaus@msoe.edu.
Website: http://www.msoe.edu/community/academics/engineering/page/2495/mscve-overview

Mississippi State University, Bagley College of Engineering, Department of Civil and Environmental Engineering, Mississippi State, MS 39762. Offers MS, PhD. *Program availability:* Part-time, blended/hybrid learning. *Faculty:* 12 full-time (0 women), 2 part-time/adjunct (0 women). *Students:* 16 full-time (6 women), 86 part-time (18 women); includes 20 minority (7 Black or African American, non-Hispanic/Latino; 12 Hispanic/Latino; 1 Two or more races, non-Hispanic/Latino), 9 international. Average age 30. 47 applicants, 47% accepted, 12 enrolled. In 2016, 15 master's, 8 doctorates awarded. Terminal master's awarded for partial completion of doctoral program. *Degree requirements:* For master's, thesis optional; for doctorate, thesis/dissertation, research on an approved topic, minimum 20 hours of dissertation research. *Entrance requirements:* For master's and doctorate, GRE (for graduates from program not accredited by EAC/ABET), minimum GPA of 3.0. Additional exam requirements/recommendations for international students: Required—TOEFL (minimum score 550 paper-based; 79 iBT); Recommended—IELTS (minimum score 6.5). *Application deadline:* For fall admission, 7/1 for domestic students, 5/1 for international students; for spring admission, 11/1 for domestic students, 9/1 for international students. Applications are processed on a rolling basis. Application fee: $60. Electronic applications accepted. *Expenses:* Tuition, state resident: full-time $7670; part-time $852.50 per credit hour. Tuition, nonresident: full-time $20,790; part-time $2310.50 per credit hour. Part-time tuition and fees vary according to course load. *Financial support:* In 2016–17, 5 research assistantships with full tuition reimbursements (averaging $16,164 per year), 4 teaching assistantships with full tuition reimbursements (averaging $16,074 per year) were awarded; Federal Work-Study, institutionally sponsored loans, and unspecified assistantships also available. Financial award application deadline: 4/1; financial award applicants required to submit FAFSA. *Faculty research:* Transportation, water modeling, construction materials, structures. *Total annual research expenditures:* $2.7 million. *Unit head:* Dr. Dennis D. Truax, Department Head, 662-325-7187, Fax: 662-325-7189, E-mail: truax@cee.msstate.edu. *Application contact:* Doretta Martin, Senior Admissions Assistant, 662-325-9514, E-mail: dmartin@grad.msstate.edu.
Website: http://www.cee.msstate.edu/

Missouri University of Science and Technology, Graduate School, Department of Civil, Architectural, and Environmental Engineering, Rolla, MO 65409. Offers civil engineering (MS, DE, PhD); construction engineering (MS, DE, PhD); environmental engineering (MS); fluid mechanics (MS, DE, PhD); geotechnical engineering (MS, DE, PhD); hydrology and hydraulic engineering (MS, DE, PhD). *Program availability:* Part-time, evening/weekend. Terminal master's awarded for partial completion of doctoral program. *Degree requirements:* For master's, thesis optional; for doctorate, comprehensive exam, thesis/dissertation. *Entrance requirements:* For master's, GRE General Test (minimum combined score 1100), minimum GPA of 3.0; for doctorate, GRE General Test (minimum score: verbal and quantitative 400, writing 3.5), minimum GPA of 3.0. Additional exam requirements/recommendations for international students: Required—TOEFL (minimum score 550 paper-based). Electronic applications accepted. *Faculty research:* Earthquake engineering, structural optimization and control systems, structural health monitoring/damage detection, soil-structure interaction, soil mechanics and foundation engineering.

Montana State University, The Graduate School, College of Engineering, Department of Civil Engineering, Bozeman, MT 59717. Offers civil engineering (MS); construction engineering management (MCEM); engineering (PhD), including applied mechanics option, civil engineering option. *Program availability:* Part-time. *Degree requirements:* For master's, comprehensive exam, thesis (for some programs); for doctorate, comprehensive exam, thesis/dissertation. *Entrance requirements:* For master's and doctorate, GRE General Test. Additional exam requirements/recommendations for international students: Required—TOEFL (minimum score 550 paper-based). Electronic applications accepted. *Faculty research:* Snow and ice mechanics, biofilm engineering, transportation, structural and geo materials, water resources.

Morgan State University, School of Graduate Studies, Clarence M. Mitchell, Jr. School of Engineering, Baltimore, MD 21251. Offers civil engineering (M Eng, D Eng); electrical and computer engineering (M Eng, MS, D Eng); industrial and systems engineering (M Eng, D Eng); transportation (MS). *Program availability:* Part-time, evening/weekend. *Degree requirements:* For master's, thesis, comprehensive exam or equivalent; for doctorate, thesis/dissertation, comprehensive exam or equivalent. *Entrance requirements:* For master's, GRE, minimum undergraduate GPA of 2.5; for doctorate, GRE, minimum GPA of 3.0. Additional exam requirements/recommendations for international students: Required—TOEFL (minimum score 550 paper-based).

New Mexico State University, College of Engineering, Department of Civil and Geological Engineering, Las Cruces, NM 88003. Offers civil and geological engineering (MSCE, PhD); environmental engineering (MS Env E). *Program availability:* Part-time. *Faculty:* 13 full-time (3 women). *Students:* 54 full-time (16 women), 16 part-time (4 women); includes 18 minority (2 Black or African American, non-Hispanic/Latino; 3 American Indian or Alaska Native, non-Hispanic/Latino; 1 Asian, non-Hispanic/Latino; 11 Hispanic/Latino; 1 Two or more races, non-Hispanic/Latino), 35 international. Average age 30. 64 applicants, 48% accepted, 17 enrolled. In 2016, 19 master's, 3 doctorates awarded. *Degree requirements:* For master's, thesis (for some programs); for doctorate, comprehensive exam, thesis/dissertation, qualifying exam. *Entrance requirements:* For master's and doctorate, BS in engineering, minimum GPA of 3.0. Additional exam requirements/recommendations for international students: Required—TOEFL (minimum score 550 paper-based; 79 iBT), IELTS (minimum score 6.5). *Application deadline:* For fall admission, 4/1 priority date for domestic and international students; for spring admission, 9/1 priority date for domestic and international students. Applications are processed on a rolling basis. Application fee: $40 ($50 for international students). Electronic applications accepted. *Expenses:* Tuition, state resident: full-time $4086. Tuition, nonresident: full-time $14,254. *Required fees:* $853. Tuition and fees vary according to course load. *Financial support:* In 2016–17, 61 students received support, including 5 fellowships (averaging $2,853 per year), 27 research assistantships (averaging $13,824 per year), 23 teaching assistantships (averaging $8,051 per year); career-related internships or fieldwork, Federal Work-Study, scholarships/grants, traineeships, health care benefits, and unspecified assistantships also available. Support available to part-time students. Financial award application deadline: 3/1. *Faculty research:* Structural engineering, water resources engineering, environmental engineering, geotechnical engineering, transportation. *Total annual research expenditures:* $3.1 million. *Unit head:* Dr. David Jauregui, Department Head, 575-646-3801, Fax: 575-646-6049, E-mail: jauregui@nmsu.edu. *Application contact:* Elvia Cisneros, Administrative Assistant, 575-646-3801, Fax: 575-646-6049, E-mail: civil@nmsu.edu.
Website: http://ce.nmsu.edu

New York University, Polytechnic School of Engineering, Department of Civil and Urban Engineering, Major in Civil Engineering, New York, NY 10012-1019. Offers MS, PhD. *Program availability:* Part-time, evening/weekend. *Degree requirements:* For master's, comprehensive exam (for some programs), thesis (for some programs); for doctorate, comprehensive exam, thesis/dissertation, qualifying exam. *Entrance requirements:* For doctorate, MS in civil engineering. Additional exam requirements/recommendations for international students: Required—TOEFL (minimum score 550 paper-based; 80 iBT); Recommended—IELTS (minimum score 6.5). Electronic applications accepted.

North Carolina Agricultural and Technical State University, School of Graduate Studies, College of Engineering, Department of Civil, Architectural, Agricultural and Environmental Engineering, Greensboro, NC 27411. Offers civil engineering (MSCE). *Program availability:* Part-time. *Degree requirements:* For master's, thesis optional. *Entrance requirements:* For master's, GRE General Test, GRE Subject Test (recommended). Additional exam requirements/recommendations for international students: Required—TOEFL. *Faculty research:* Lightning, indoor air quality, material behavior HVAC controls, structural masonry systems.

North Carolina State University, Graduate School, College of Engineering, Department of Civil, Construction, and Environmental Engineering, Raleigh, NC 27695. Offers civil engineering (MCE, MS, PhD). *Program availability:* Part-time, online learning. *Degree requirements:* For master's, thesis optional, oral exams; for doctorate, thesis/dissertation, oral exams. *Entrance requirements:* For master's, GRE General Test, minimum B average in major; for doctorate, GRE General Test. Additional exam requirements/recommendations for international students: Required—TOEFL. Electronic applications accepted. *Faculty research:* Materials; systems, environmental, geotechnical, structural, transportation and water rescue engineering.

North Dakota State University, College of Graduate and Interdisciplinary Studies, College of Engineering, Department of Civil and Environmental Engineering, Fargo, ND 58102. Offers civil and environmental engineering (PhD); civil engineering (MS, PhD); environmental engineering (MS). PhD in transportation and logistics offered jointly with Upper Great Plains Transportation Institute. *Program availability:* Part-time, online learning. *Degree requirements:* For master's, thesis; for doctorate, comprehensive exam, thesis/dissertation. *Entrance requirements:* Additional exam requirements/recommendations for international students: Required—TOEFL (minimum score 525 paper-based; 71 iBT). Electronic applications accepted. *Faculty research:* Wastewater, solid waste, composites, nanotechnology.

Northeastern University, College of Engineering, Boston, MA 02115-5096. Offers bioengineering (MS, PhD); chemical engineering (MS, PhD); civil engineering (MS, PhD); computer engineering (PhD); computer systems engineering (MS); electrical and computer engineering (MS); electrical and computer engineering leadership (MS); electrical engineering (PhD); energy systems (MS); engineering and public policy (MS); engineering management (MS, Certificate); environmental engineering (MS); industrial engineering (MS, PhD); information assurance (PhD); information systems (MS); interdisciplinary engineering (PhD); mechanical engineering (PhD); operations research (MS); telecommunication systems management (MS). *Program availability:* Part-time, online learning. *Faculty:* 202 full-time (59 women), 53 part-time/adjunct (9 women). *Students:* 2,982 full-time (954 women), 192 part-time (38 women). In 2016, 851 master's, 74 doctorates awarded. Application fee: $75. Electronic applications accepted. *Expenses:* $1,471 per credit. *Financial support:* Fellowships, research assistantships, teaching assistantships, career-related internships or fieldwork, scholarships/grants, health care benefits, tuition waivers, and unspecified assistantships available. Support available to part-time students. Financial award applicants required to submit FAFSA. *Unit head:* Dr. Nadine Aubry, Dean, College of Engineering. *Application contact:* Jeffery Hengel, Director of Graduate Admissions, 617-373-2711, E-mail: j.hengel@northeastern.edu.
Website: http://www.coe.neu.edu/academics/graduate-school-engineering

Northern Arizona University, Graduate College, College of Engineering, Forestry, and Natural Sciences, Programs in Engineering, Flagstaff, AZ 86011. Offers civil engineering (M Eng, MSE); computer science (MSE); electrical and computer engineering (M Eng, MSE); engineering (M Eng, MSE); environmental engineering (M Eng, MSE); mechanical engineering (M Eng, MSE). *Program availability:* Part-time, online learning. *Degree requirements:* For master's, thesis. *Entrance requirements:* For master's, GRE General Test. Additional exam requirements/recommendations for international students: Required—TOEFL (minimum score 550 paper-based; 80 iBT), IELTS (minimum score 7). Electronic applications accepted. *Expenses:* Tuition, state resident: full-time $8971; part-time $444 per credit hour. Tuition, nonresident: full-time $20,958; part-time $1164 per credit hour. *Required fees:* $1018; $644 per credit hour. Tuition and fees vary according to course load, campus/location and program.

Northwestern University, McCormick School of Engineering and Applied Science, Department of Civil and Environmental Engineering, Evanston, IL 60208-3109. Offers environmental engineering and science (MS, PhD); geotechnical engineering (MS, PhD); mechanics of materials and solids (MS, PhD); project management (MS); structural engineering and materials (MS, PhD); transportation systems analysis and planning (MS, PhD). MS and PhD admissions and degrees offered through The Graduate School. *Program availability:* Part-time. Terminal master's awarded for partial completion of doctoral program. *Degree requirements:* For master's, comprehensive exam (for some programs), thesis (for some programs); for doctorate, comprehensive exam, thesis/dissertation. *Entrance requirements:* For master's and doctorate, GRE General Test, minimum 2 letters of recommendation, transcripts from all academic institutions attended. Additional exam requirements/recommendations for international students: Required—TOEFL (minimum score 577 paper-based; 90 iBT), IELTS (minimum score 7). Electronic applications accepted. *Faculty research:* Environmental engineering and science, geotechnics, mechanics, materials, structures, and transportation systems analysis and planning.

Norwich University, College of Graduate and Continuing Studies, Master of Civil Engineering Program, Northfield, VT 05663. Offers construction management (MCE); environmental (MCE); geotechnical (MCE); structural (MCE). *Program availability:* Evening/weekend, online only, mostly all online with a week-long residency requirement. *Faculty:* 1 full-time (0 women), 11 part-time/adjunct (1 woman). *Students:* 70 full-time (17 women); includes 28 minority (16 Black or African American, non-Hispanic/Latino; 4 Asian, non-Hispanic/Latino; 5 Hispanic/Latino; 1 Native Hawaiian or other Pacific Islander, non-Hispanic/Latino; 2 Two or more races, non-Hispanic/Latino), 1 international. Average age 36. 35 applicants, 97% accepted, 18 enrolled. In 2016, 63 master's awarded. *Degree requirements:* For master's, capstone. *Entrance requirements:* For master's, minimum undergraduate GPA of 2.75. Additional exam requirements/recommendations for international students: Required—TOEFL (minimum score 550 paper-based; 80 iBT), IELTS (minimum score 6.5). *Application deadline:* For fall admission, 8/14 for domestic and international students; for spring admission, 2/12 for domestic and international students. Electronic applications accepted. *Expenses:* Contact institution. *Financial support:* In 2016–17, 10 students received support. Scholarships/grants available. Financial award application deadline: 8/4; financial award applicants required to submit FAFSA. *Unit head:* Dr. Thomas Descoteaux, Program Director, 802-485-2730, Fax: 802-485-2533, E-mail: tdescote@norwich.edu. *Application contact:* Admissions Advisor, 800-460-5597 Ext. 3369, Fax: 802-485-2533, E-mail: mce@online.norwich.edu.
Website: https://online.norwich.edu/degree-programs/masters/master-civil-engineering/overview

The Ohio State University, Graduate School, College of Engineering, Department of Civil, Environmental and Geodetic Engineering, Columbus, OH 43210. Offers civil engineering (MS, PhD). *Faculty:* 29. *Students:* 88 full-time (31 women), 13 part-time (1 woman). Average age 27. In 2016, 21 master's, 4 doctorates awarded. *Degree requirements:* For doctorate, thesis/dissertation. *Entrance requirements:* For master's and doctorate, GRE General Test (for all applicants whose undergraduate GPA is below 3.0 or whose undergraduate degree is not from an accredited U.S.-ABET or Canadian-CEAB institution). Additional exam requirements/recommendations for international students: Required—TOEFL (minimum score 550 paper-based; 79 iBT), Michigan English Language Assessment Battery (minimum score 82); Recommended—IELTS (minimum score 7). *Application deadline:* For fall admission, 12/13 priority date for domestic students, 11/30 priority date for international students. Applications are processed on a rolling basis. Application fee: $60 ($70 for international students). Electronic applications accepted. *Financial support:* Fellowships with tuition reimbursements, research assistantships with tuition reimbursements, teaching assistantships with tuition reimbursements, institutionally sponsored loans, and unspecified assistantships available. *Unit head:* Dr. Dorota Grejner-Brzezinska, Chair, 614-292-3455, E-mail: grejner-brzezinska.1@osu.edu. *Application contact:* Graduate and Professional Admissions, 614-292-9444, Fax: 614-292-3895, E-mail: gpadmissions@osu.edu.
Website: http://ceg.osu.edu/

Ohio University, Graduate College, Russ College of Engineering and Technology, Department of Civil Engineering, Athens, OH 45701-2979. Offers civil engineering (PhD); construction engineering and management (MS); environmental (MS); geotechnical and geoenvironmental (MS); mechanics (MS); structures (MS); transportation (MS); water resources (MS). *Program availability:* Part-time. *Degree requirements:* For master's, comprehensive exam (for some programs), thesis or alternative; for doctorate, comprehensive exam, thesis/dissertation. *Entrance requirements:* For master's, GRE General Test, minimum GPA of 3.0, 3 letters of recommendation; for doctorate, GRE General Test. Additional exam requirements/recommendations for international students: Required—TOEFL (minimum score 550 paper-based; 80 iBT) or IELTS (minimum score 6.5). *Application deadline:* For fall admission, 5/1 priority date for domestic students, 2/1 priority date for international students; for winter admission, 8/1 priority date for domestic students, 4/1 priority date for international students; for spring admission, 2/1 priority date for domestic students, 7/1 priority date for international students. Applications are processed on a rolling basis. Application fee: $50 ($55 for international students). Electronic applications accepted. *Financial support:* Research assistantships with full tuition reimbursements, teaching assistantships with full tuition reimbursements, Federal Work-Study, institutionally sponsored loans, scholarships/grants, and unspecified assistantships available. Financial award application deadline: 3/15; financial award applicants required to submit FAFSA. *Faculty research:* Noise abatement, materials and environment, highway infrastructure, subsurface investigation (pavements, pipes, bridges). *Unit head:* Dr. Gayle F. Mitchell, Chair, 740-593-0430, Fax: 740-593-0625, E-mail: mitchelg@ohio.edu. *Application contact:* Dr. Shad M. Sargand, Graduate Chair, 740-593-1465, Fax: 740-593-0625, E-mail: sargand@ohio.edu.
Website: http://www.ohio.edu/civil/

Oklahoma State University, College of Engineering, Architecture and Technology, School of Civil and Environmental Engineering, Stillwater, OK 74078. Offers civil engineering (MS, PhD); environmental engineering (MS). *Faculty:* 20 full-time (1 woman), 1 part-time/adjunct (0 women). *Students:* 28 full-time (5 women), 49 part-time (12 women); includes 1 minority (Black or African American, non-Hispanic/Latino), 52 international. Average age 28. 112 applicants, 32% accepted, 22 enrolled. In 2016, 28 master's, 7 doctorates awarded. *Degree requirements:* For master's, thesis or alternative; for doctorate, comprehensive exam, thesis/dissertation. *Entrance requirements:* For master's and doctorate, GRE or GMAT. Additional exam requirements/recommendations for international students: Required—TOEFL (minimum score 550 paper-based; 79 iBT). *Application deadline:* For fall admission, 3/1 priority date for international students; for spring admission, 8/1 priority date for international

students. Applications are processed on a rolling basis. Application fee: $40 ($75 for international students). Electronic applications accepted. *Expenses:* Tuition, state resident: full-time $3775; part-time $209.70 per credit hour. Tuition, nonresident: full-time $14,851; part-time $825.05 per credit hour. *Required fees:* $2027; $112.60 per credit hour. Tuition and fees vary according to campus/location. *Financial support:* In 2016–17, 41 research assistantships (averaging $11,139 per year), 2 teaching assistantships (averaging $8,500 per year) were awarded; career-related internships or fieldwork, Federal Work-Study, scholarships/grants, health care benefits, tuition waivers (partial), and unspecified assistantships also available. Support available to part-time students. Financial award application deadline: 3/1; financial award applicants required to submit FAFSA. *Unit head:* Dr. Norb Delatte, Department Head, 405-744-5190, Fax: 405-744-7554, E-mail: norb.delatte@okstate.edu.
Website: http://cive.okstate.edu

Old Dominion University, Frank Batten College of Engineering and Technology, Program in Civil and Environmental Engineering, Norfolk, VA 23529. Offers D Eng, PhD. *Program availability:* Part-time, evening/weekend, blended/hybrid learning. *Faculty:* 16 full-time (1 woman), 5 part-time/adjunct (0 women). *Students:* 17 full-time (7 women), 23 part-time (4 women); includes 8 minority (3 Black or African American, non-Hispanic/Latino; 2 Asian, non-Hispanic/Latino; 2 Hispanic/Latino; 1 Two or more races, non-Hispanic/Latino), 20 international. Average age 35. 47 applicants, 100% accepted, 19 enrolled. In 2016, 2 doctorates awarded. *Degree requirements:* For doctorate, comprehensive exam, thesis/dissertation, candidacy exam. *Entrance requirements:* For doctorate, GRE, minimum GPA of 3.5. Additional exam requirements/recommendations for international students: Required—TOEFL (minimum score 550 paper-based, 80 iBT) or IELTS (6.5). *Application deadline:* For fall admission, 6/1 priority date for domestic students, 4/15 priority date for international students; for spring admission, 11/1 priority date for domestic students, 10/1 priority date for international students. Applications are processed on a rolling basis. Application fee: $50. Electronic applications accepted. *Expenses:* Contact institution. *Financial support:* In 2016–17, 26 students received support, including 1 fellowship with full tuition reimbursement available (averaging $18,000 per year), 17 research assistantships with full and partial tuition reimbursements available (averaging $16,800 per year), 9 teaching assistantships with full and partial tuition reimbursements available (averaging $15,215 per year); scholarships/grants, health care benefits, and unspecified assistantships also available. Support available to part-time students. Financial award application deadline: 4/1. *Faculty research:* Structural engineering, coastal engineering, environmental engineering, geotechnical engineering, water resources, transportation engineering. *Total annual research expenditures:* $937,914. *Unit head:* Dr. Isao Ishibashi, Graduate Program Director, 757-683-4641, E-mail: cegpd@odu.edu. *Application contact:* Dr. Shirshak Dhali, Associate Dean, 757-683-3744, Fax: 757-683-4898, E-mail: sdhali@odu.edu.
Website: http://eng.odu.edu/cee/

Old Dominion University, Frank Batten College of Engineering and Technology, Program in Civil Engineering, Norfolk, VA 23529. Offers civil engineering (ME, MS), including coastal engineering, geotechnical engineering, hydraulics and water resources, structural engineering, transportation engineering. *Program availability:* Part-time, evening/weekend, blended/hybrid learning. *Faculty:* 16 full-time (1 woman), 5 part-time/adjunct (0 women). *Students:* 12 full-time (4 women), 30 part-time (6 women); includes 7 minority (2 Black or African American, non-Hispanic/Latino; 4 Hispanic/Latino; 1 Two or more races, non-Hispanic/Latino), 8 international. Average age 28. 79 applicants, 84% accepted, 33 enrolled. In 2016, 15 master's awarded. *Degree requirements:* For master's, comprehensive exam, thesis optional. *Entrance requirements:* For master's, GRE, minimum GPA of 3.0. Additional exam requirements/recommendations for international students: Required—TOEFL (minimum score 550 paper-based, 80 iBT) or IELTS (6.5). *Application deadline:* For fall admission, 6/1 priority date for domestic students, 4/15 priority date for international students; for spring admission, 11/1 priority date for domestic students, 10/1 priority date for international students. Applications are processed on a rolling basis. Application fee: $50. Electronic applications accepted. *Expenses:* Contact institution. *Financial support:* In 2016–17, 26 students received support, including 1 fellowship with full tuition reimbursement available (averaging $18,000 per year), 17 research assistantships with full and partial tuition reimbursements available (averaging $16,800 per year), 9 teaching assistantships with full and partial tuition reimbursements available (averaging $15,215 per year); scholarships/grants and health care benefits also available. Support available to part-time students. Financial award application deadline: 4/1; financial award applicants required to submit FAFSA. *Faculty research:* Structural engineering, coastal engineering, geotechnical engineering, water resources, transportation engineering. *Total annual research expenditures:* $937,914. *Unit head:* Dr. Isao Ishibashi, Graduate Program Director, 757-683-4641, E-mail: cegpd@odu.edu. *Application contact:* Dr. Shirshak Dhali, Associate Dean, 757-683-3744, Fax: 757-683-4898, E-mail: sdhali@odu.edu.
Website: http://eng.odu.edu/cee/

Oregon State University, College of Engineering, Program in Civil Engineering, Corvallis, OR 97331. Offers civil engineering (M Eng, MS, PhD); coastal and ocean engineering (M Eng, MS, PhD); construction engineering management (M Eng, MS, PhD); engineering education (M Eng, MS, PhD); geomatics (M Eng, MS, PhD); geotechnical engineering (M Eng, MS, PhD); infrastructure materials (M Eng, MS, PhD); structural engineering (M Eng, MS, PhD); transportation engineering (M Eng). *Faculty:* 42 full-time (8 women), 2 part-time/adjunct (0 women). *Students:* 157 full-time (48 women), 10 part-time (3 women); includes 18 minority (7 Asian, non-Hispanic/Latino; 7 Hispanic/Latino; 1 Native Hawaiian or other Pacific Islander, non-Hispanic/Latino; 3 Two or more races, non-Hispanic/Latino), 92 international. Average age 28. 379 applicants, 31% accepted, 50 enrolled. In 2016, 55 master's, 5 doctorates awarded. *Entrance requirements:* For master's and doctorate, GRE. Additional exam requirements/recommendations for international students: Required—TOEFL (minimum score 80 iBT), IELTS (minimum score 6.5). *Application deadline:* For fall admission, 8/1 for domestic students, 4/1 for international students; for winter admission, 12/1 for domestic students, 7/1 for international students; for spring admission, 2/1 for domestic students, 10/1 for international students; for summer admission, 5/1 for domestic students, 1/1 for international students. Application fee: $75 ($85 for international students). *Expenses:* $14,130 resident full-time tuition, $23,769 non-resident. *Financial support:* Application deadline: 1/15. *Unit head:* Dr. Jason Weiss, School Head/Professor. *Application contact:* Shannon Reed, Graduate Program Coordinator, 541-737-4575, E-mail: shannon.reed@oregonstate.edu.
Website: http://cce.oregonstate.edu/graduate-academics

Penn State University Park, Graduate School, College of Engineering, Department of Civil and Environmental Engineering, University Park, PA 16802. Offers civil engineering (M Eng, MS, PhD); environmental engineering (M Eng, MS, PhD). *Unit head:* Dr. Amr S. Elnashai, Dean, 814-865-7537, Fax: 814-863-4749. *Application contact:* Lori Hawn, Director, Graduate Student Services, 814-865-1795, Fax: 814-863-4627, E-mail: l-gswww@lists.psu.edu.
Website: http://cee.psu.edu/

Polytechnic University of Puerto Rico, Graduate School, Hato Rey, PR 00918. Offers business administration (MBA), including computer information systems, general management, management of information systems, management of international enterprises; civil engineering (ME, MS); computer engineering (ME, MS); computer science (MCS, MS); electrical engineering (ME, MS); engineering management (MEM); environmental management (MEM); landscape architecture (M Land Arch); manufacturing competitiveness (MMC, MS); manufacturing engineering (ME, MS); mechanical engineering (M Mech E). *Program availability:* Part-time, evening/weekend. *Entrance requirements:* For master's, 3 letters of recommendation.

Portland State University, Graduate Studies, College of Liberal Arts and Sciences, Systems Science Program, Portland, OR 97207-0751. Offers computational intelligence (Certificate); computer modeling and simulation (Certificate); systems science (MS); systems science/anthropology (PhD); systems science/business administration (PhD); systems science/civil engineering (PhD); systems science/economics (PhD); systems science/engineering management (PhD); systems science/general (PhD); systems science/mathematical sciences (PhD); systems science/mechanical engineering (PhD); systems science/psychology (PhD); systems science/sociology (PhD). *Faculty:* 2 full-time (0 women), 3 part-time/adjunct (1 woman). *Students:* 12 full-time (3 women), 21 part-time (5 women); includes 5 minority (1 Black or African American, non-Hispanic/Latino; 2 Hispanic/Latino; 2 Two or more races, non-Hispanic/Latino). Average age 39. 16 applicants, 69% accepted, 9 enrolled. In 2016, 4 master's, 6 doctorates awarded. *Degree requirements:* For master's, comprehensive exam (for some programs), thesis optional; for doctorate, variable foreign language requirement, comprehensive exam (for some programs), thesis/dissertation. *Entrance requirements:* For master's, GRE/GMAT (recommended), minimum GPA of 3.0 undergraduate or graduate work, 2 letters of recommendation, statement of interest; for doctorate, GMAT, GRE General Test, minimum GPA of 3.0 undergraduate, 3.25 graduate; 2 letters of recommendation; statement of interest. Additional exam requirements/recommendations for international students: Required—TOEFL (minimum score 550 paper-based; 80 iBT). *Application deadline:* For fall admission, 1/15 for domestic and international students; for spring admission, 11/1 for domestic students. Application fee: $65. Electronic applications accepted. *Expenses:* Contact institution. *Financial support:* In 2016–17, 2 research assistantships with tuition reimbursements (averaging $7,830 per year) were awarded; teaching assistantships, career-related internships or fieldwork, Federal Work-Study, scholarships/grants, and unspecified assistantships also available. Support available to part-time students. Financial award application deadline: 3/1; financial award applicants required to submit FAFSA. *Faculty research:* Systems theory and methodology, artificial intelligence neural networks, information theory, nonlinear dynamics/chaos, modeling and simulation. *Unit head:* Dr. Wayne Wakeland, Chair, 503-725-4975, E-mail: wakeland@pdx.edu.
Website: http://www.pdx.edu/sysc/

Portland State University, Graduate Studies, Maseeh College of Engineering and Computer Science, Department of Civil and Environmental Engineering, Portland, OR 97207-0751. Offers civil and environmental engineering (M Eng, MS, PhD); civil and environmental engineering management (M Eng); environmental sciences and resources (PhD); systems science (PhD). *Program availability:* Part-time, evening/weekend. *Faculty:* 27 full-time (5 women), 4 part-time/adjunct (2 women). *Students:* 50 full-time (11 women), 51 part-time (14 women); includes 10 minority (1 Black or African American, non-Hispanic/Latino; 1 Asian, non-Hispanic/Latino; 3 Hispanic/Latino; 5 Two or more races, non-Hispanic/Latino), 43 international. Average age 31. 89 applicants, 61% accepted, 26 enrolled. In 2016, 28 master's, 1 doctorate awarded. *Degree requirements:* For master's, comprehensive exam (for some programs), thesis (for some programs); for doctorate, one foreign language, comprehensive exam, thesis/dissertation, oral and written exams. *Entrance requirements:* For master's, BS in an engineering field, science, or closely-related area with minimum GPA of 3.0; for doctorate, MS in an engineering field, science, or closely-related area. Additional exam requirements/recommendations for international students: Required—TOEFL (minimum score 550 paper-based). *Application deadline:* For fall admission, 1/4 priority date for domestic and international students; for winter admission, 9/1 for domestic and international students; for spring admission, 11/1 for domestic and international students. Applications are processed on a rolling basis. Application fee: $65. *Expenses:* Contact institution. *Financial support:* In 2016–17, 21 research assistantships with tuition reimbursements (averaging $5,959 per year), 16 teaching assistantships with tuition reimbursements (averaging $6,096 per year) were awarded; career-related internships or fieldwork, Federal Work-Study, scholarships/grants, and unspecified assistantships also available. Support available to part-time students. Financial award application deadline: 3/1; financial award applicants required to submit FAFSA. *Faculty research:* Structures, water resources, geotechnical engineering, environmental engineering, transportation. *Total annual research expenditures:* $2.6 million. *Unit head:* Dr. Chris Monsere, Chair, 503-725-9746, Fax: 503-725-4298, E-mail: monserec@cecs.pdx.edu. *Application contact:* Ariel Lewis, Department Manager, 503-725-4244, Fax: 503-725-4298, E-mail: ariel.lewis@pdx.edu.
Website: http://www.pdx.edu/cee/

Princeton University, Graduate School, School of Engineering and Applied Science, Department of Civil and Environmental Engineering, Princeton, NJ 08544-1019. Offers M Eng, MSE, PhD. Terminal master's awarded for partial completion of doctoral program. *Degree requirements:* For master's, thesis (MSE); for doctorate, thesis/dissertation, general exam. *Entrance requirements:* For master's, GRE General Test, 3 letters of recommendation; for doctorate, GRE General Test, official transcript(s), 3 letters of recommendation, personal statement. Additional exam requirements/recommendations for international students: Required—TOEFL. Electronic applications accepted. *Faculty research:* Carbon mitigation; civil engineering materials and structures; climate and atmospheric dynamics; computational mechanics and risk assessment; hydrology, remote sensing, and sustainability.

Purdue University, College of Engineering, Lyles School of Civil Engineering, West Lafayette, IN 47907-2166. Offers MS, MSCE, MSE, PhD. *Program availability:* Part-time. *Faculty:* 73. *Students:* 356. In 2016, 105 master's, 28 doctorates awarded. Terminal master's awarded for partial completion of doctoral program. *Degree requirements:* For master's, thesis optional; for doctorate, thesis/dissertation. *Entrance requirements:* For master's and doctorate, GRE General Test, minimum GPA of 3.0. *Application deadline:* For fall admission, 1/1 priority date for domestic and international students; for spring admission, 9/15 for domestic and international students. Applications are processed on a rolling basis. Application fee: $60 ($75 for international students). Electronic applications accepted. *Financial support:* Fellowships with full and partial tuition reimbursements, research assistantships with full and partial tuition reimbursements, teaching assistantships with full and partial tuition reimbursements, scholarships/grants, health care benefits, and unspecified assistantships available. Support available to part-time students. Financial award applicants required to submit FAFSA. *Faculty research:* Architectural engineering, construction engineering, environmental engineering, geomatics engineering, geotechnical engineering, hydraulic and hydrologic engineering, materials engineering, structural engineering, transportation and infrastructure systems engineering. *Unit head:* Dr. Rao Govindaraju, Head/Professor, E-mail: govind@purdue.edu. *Application contact:* Jenny Ricksy, Graduate

Program Coordinator, 765-494-2436, E-mail: jricksy@purdue.edu. Website: https://engineering.purdue.edu/CE

Queen's University at Kingston, School of Graduate Studies, Faculty of Applied Science, Department of Civil Engineering, Kingston, ON K7L 3N6, Canada. Offers M Eng, M Sc Eng, PhD. *Program availability:* Part-time. *Degree requirements:* For master's, thesis (for some programs); for doctorate, comprehensive exam, thesis/dissertation. *Entrance requirements:* Additional exam requirements/recommendations for international students: Required—TOEFL. *Faculty research:* Structural, geotechnical, transportation, hydrotechnical, and environmental engineering.

Rensselaer Polytechnic Institute, Graduate School, School of Engineering, Program in Civil Engineering, Troy, NY 12180-3590. Offers M Eng, MS, D Eng, PhD. *Program availability:* Part-time. *Faculty:* 17 full-time (3 women), 3 part-time/adjunct (0 women). *Students:* 16 full-time (5 women). 61 applicants, 13% accepted, 3 enrolled. In 2016, 2 master's, 4 doctorates awarded. Terminal master's awarded for partial completion of doctoral program. *Degree requirements:* For master's, thesis (for some programs); for doctorate, thesis/dissertation. *Entrance requirements:* For master's and doctorate, GRE. Additional exam requirements/recommendations for international students: Required—TOEFL (minimum score 570 paper-based; 88 iBT), IELTS (minimum score 6.5), PTE (minimum score 60). *Application deadline:* For fall admission, 1/1 priority date for domestic and international students; for spring admission, 8/15 priority date for domestic and international students. Applications are processed on a rolling basis. Application fee: $75. Electronic applications accepted. *Expenses: Tuition:* Full-time $49,520; part-time $2060 per credit hour. *Required fees:* $2617. *Financial support:* In 2016–17, 16 students received support, including research assistantships (averaging $22,000 per year), teaching assistantships (averaging $22,000 per year); fellowships also available. Financial award application deadline: 1/1. *Faculty research:* Geotechnical, structural, transportation. *Total annual research expenditures:* $1.7 million. *Unit head:* Dr. Michael O'Rourke, Graduate Program Director, 518-276-6933, E-mail: orourm@rpi.edu. *Application contact:* Office of Graduate Admissions, 518-276-6216, E-mail: gradadmissions@rpi.edu.
Website: http://cee.rpi.edu/graduate

Rice University, Graduate Programs, George R. Brown School of Engineering, Department of Civil and Environmental Engineering, Houston, TX 77251-1892. Offers civil engineering (MCE, MS, PhD); environmental engineering (MEE, MES, MS, PhD); environmental science (MEE, MES, MS, PhD). *Program availability:* Part-time. *Degree requirements:* For master's, thesis (for some programs); for doctorate, thesis/dissertation. *Entrance requirements:* For master's and doctorate, GRE General Test, GRE Subject Test, minimum GPA of 3.25. Additional exam requirements/recommendations for international students: Required—TOEFL (minimum score 600 paper-based; 90 iBT). Electronic applications accepted. *Faculty research:* Biology and chemistry of groundwater, pollutant fate in groundwater systems, water quality monitoring, urban storm water runoff, urban air quality.

Rose-Hulman Institute of Technology, Faculty of Engineering and Applied Sciences, Department of Civil and Environmental Engineering, Terre Haute, IN 47803-3999. Offers civil engineering (MS); environmental engineering (MS). *Program availability:* Part-time. *Faculty:* 9 full-time (2 women), 1 part-time/adjunct (0 women). *Students:* 2 full-time (0 women). Average age 22. 10 applicants, 80% accepted. In 2016, 1 master's awarded. *Degree requirements:* For master's, thesis (for some programs). *Entrance requirements:* For master's, GRE, minimum GPA of 3.0. Additional exam requirements/recommendations for international students: Required—TOEFL (minimum score 580 paper-based; 92 iBT). *Application deadline:* For fall admission, 2/1 priority date for domestic students. Applications are processed on a rolling basis. Application fee: $0. Electronic applications accepted. *Expenses: Tuition:* Full-time $43,122. *Financial support:* In 2016–17, 2 students received support. Fellowships with tuition reimbursements available, research assistantships with tuition reimbursements available, institutionally sponsored loans, scholarships/grants, and tuition waivers (full and partial) available. Financial award application deadline: 2/1. *Faculty research:* Transportation, hydraulics/hydrology, environmental, construction, geotechnical, structural. *Total annual research expenditures:* $24,760. *Unit head:* Dr. Kevin Sutterer, Chairman, 812-877-8959, Fax: 812-877-8440, E-mail: sutterer@rose-hulman.edu. *Application contact:* Dr. Azad Siahmakoun, Associate Dean of the Faculty, 812-877-8400, Fax: 812-877-8061, E-mail: siahmako@rose-hulman.edu.
Website: http://www.rose-hulman.edu/ce/

Rowan University, Graduate School, College of Engineering, Department of Civil Engineering, Glassboro, NJ 08028-1701. Offers MEM, MS. Electronic applications accepted.

Royal Military College of Canada, Division of Graduate Studies and Research, Engineering Division, Department of Civil Engineering, Kingston, ON K7K 7B4, Canada. Offers M Eng, MA Sc, PhD. *Degree requirements:* For master's, thesis; for doctorate, comprehensive exam, thesis/dissertation. *Entrance requirements:* For master's, honours degree with second-class standing; for doctorate, master's degree. Electronic applications accepted.

Rutgers University–New Brunswick, Graduate School-New Brunswick, Department of Civil and Environmental Engineering, Piscataway, NJ 08854-8097. Offers MS, PhD. *Program availability:* Part-time, evening/weekend. Terminal master's awarded for partial completion of doctoral program. *Degree requirements:* For master's, comprehensive exam, thesis or alternative; for doctorate, comprehensive exam, thesis/dissertation. *Entrance requirements:* For master's and doctorate, GRE General Test. Additional exam requirements/recommendations for international students: Required—TOEFL (minimum score 580 paper-based). Electronic applications accepted. *Faculty research:* Civil engineering materials research, non-destructive evaluation of transportation infrastructure, transportation planning, intelligent transportation systems.

Saint Martin's University, Office of Graduate Studies, Program in Civil Engineering, Lacey, WA 98503. Offers MCE. *Program availability:* Part-time. *Faculty:* 5 full-time (2 women), 2 part-time/adjunct (0 women). *Students:* 6 full-time (1 woman), 1 international. Average age 28. 11 applicants, 27% accepted, 2 enrolled. In 2016, 6 master's awarded. *Degree requirements:* For master's, thesis optional. *Entrance requirements:* For master's, minimum GPA of 2.8 in undergraduate work; BS in civil engineering or other engineering/science with completion of calculus, differential equations, physics, chemistry, statistics, mechanics of materials and dynamics. Additional exam requirements/recommendations for international students: Required—TOEFL (minimum score 550 paper-based; 79 iBT); Recommended—IELTS (minimum score 6.5). *Application deadline:* For fall admission, 4/1 priority date for domestic students, 4/1 for international students; for spring admission, 11/1 priority date for domestic students, 11/1 for international students. Applications are processed on a rolling basis. Application fee: $50. Electronic applications accepted. *Expenses: Tuition:* Full-time $13,800; part-time $1150 per credit hour. *Required fees:* $720; $60 per credit hour. Tuition and fees vary according to course level and program. *Financial support:* Scholarships/grants and tuition waivers (partial) available. Support available to part-time students. Financial award application deadline: 3/1; financial award applicants required to submit FAFSA. *Faculty research:* Transportation engineering, metal fatigue and fracture, environmental engineering. *Unit head:* Dr. Pius O. Igharo, Program Chair, 360-438-4322, Fax: 360-438-4548, E-mail: pigharo@stmartin.edu. *Application contact:* Casey Caronna, Administrative Assistant, 360-412-6128, E-mail: ccaronna@stmartin.edu.
Website: https://www.stmartin.edu/directory/office-graduate-studies

San Diego State University, Graduate and Research Affairs, College of Engineering, Department of Civil and Environmental Engineering, San Diego, CA 92182. Offers civil engineering (MS). *Program availability:* Part-time, evening/weekend. *Degree requirements:* For master's, thesis optional. *Entrance requirements:* For master's, GRE General Test. Additional exam requirements/recommendations for international students: Required—TOEFL. Electronic applications accepted. *Faculty research:* Hydraulics, hydrology, transportation, smart material, concrete material.

Santa Clara University, School of Engineering, Santa Clara, CA 95053. Offers applied mathematics (MS); bioengineering (MS); civil engineering (MS); computer science and engineering (MS, PhD); electrical engineering (MS, PhD); engineering (Engineer); engineering management and leadership (MS); mechanical engineering (MS, PhD); software engineering (MS); sustainable energy (MS). *Program availability:* Part-time, evening/weekend. *Faculty:* 66 full-time (22 women), 59 part-time/adjunct (12 women). *Students:* 449 full-time (188 women), 315 part-time (114 women); includes 197 minority (3 Black or African American, non-Hispanic/Latino; 144 Asian, non-Hispanic/Latino; 33 Hispanic/Latino; 1 Native Hawaiian or other Pacific Islander, non-Hispanic/Latino; 16 Two or more races, non-Hispanic/Latino), 418 international. Average age 28. 1,217 applicants, 45% accepted, 293 enrolled. In 2016, 466 master's awarded. *Entrance requirements:* For master's, GRE, transcript; for doctorate, GRE, master's degree or equivalent, 3 letters of recommendation, statement of purpose; for Engineer, master's degree. Additional exam requirements/recommendations for international students: Required—TOEFL (minimum score 79 iBT) or IELTS (6.5). *Application deadline:* For fall admission, 4/1 for domestic and international students; for winter admission, 9/9 for domestic students, 9/2 for international students; for spring admission, 2/17 for domestic students, 12/9 for international students. Application fee: $60. Electronic applications accepted. *Expenses:* $928 per unit. *Financial support:* Fellowships, research assistantships, teaching assistantships, career-related internships or fieldwork, Federal Work-Study, scholarships/grants, traineeships, health care benefits, tuition waivers, and unspecified assistantships available. Support available to part-time students. Financial award applicants required to submit FAFSA. *Unit head:* Dr. Alfonso Ortega, Dean. *Application contact:* Stacey Tinker, Director of Admissions and Marketing, 408-554-4313, Fax: 408-554-4323, E-mail: stinker@scu.edu.
Website: http://www.scu.edu/engineering/graduate/

South Carolina State University, College of Graduate and Professional Studies, Department of Civil and Mechanical Engineering Technology, Orangeburg, SC 29117-0001. Offers transportation (MS). *Program availability:* Part-time, evening/weekend. *Faculty:* 2 full-time (1 woman), 1 part-time/adjunct (0 women). *Students:* 3 full-time (1 woman), 1 (woman) part-time; all minorities (all Black or African American, non-Hispanic/Latino). Average age 41. 1 applicant, 100% accepted. In 2016, 10 master's awarded. *Degree requirements:* For master's, comprehensive exam, thesis, departmental qualifying exam. *Entrance requirements:* For master's, GRE. Additional exam requirements/recommendations for international students: Recommended—TOEFL. *Application deadline:* For fall admission, 6/15 for domestic and international students; for spring admission, 11/1 for domestic and international students. Application fee: $25. Electronic applications accepted. *Expenses:* Tuition, state resident: full-time $8938; part-time $579 per credit hour. Tuition, nonresident: full-time $19,018; part-time $1139 per credit hour. *Required fees:* $1482; $82 per credit hour. *Financial support:* Fellowships, research assistantships, career-related internships or fieldwork, Federal Work-Study, scholarships/grants, and unspecified assistantships available. Financial award application deadline: 6/1. *Unit head:* Dr. Stanley Ihekweazu, Chair, 803-536-7117, Fax: 803-516-4607, E-mail: sihekwea@scsu.edu. *Application contact:* Curtis Foskey, Coordinator of Graduate Admission, 803-536-8419, Fax: 803-536-8812, E-mail: cfoskey@scsu.edu.
Website: http://www.scsu.edu/schoolofgraduatestudies.aspx

South Dakota School of Mines and Technology, Graduate Division, Program in Civil and Environmental Engineering, Rapid City, SD 57701-3995. Offers MS, PhD. *Program availability:* Part-time, online learning. *Degree requirements:* For master's, thesis (for some programs). *Entrance requirements:* Additional exam requirements/recommendations for international students: Required—TOEFL (minimum score 520 paper-based; 68 iBT), TWE. Electronic applications accepted.

South Dakota State University, Graduate School, College of Engineering, Department of Civil and Environmental Engineering, Brookings, SD 57007. Offers engineering (MS). *Program availability:* Part-time, online learning. *Degree requirements:* For master's, thesis (for some programs), oral exam. *Entrance requirements:* Additional exam requirements/recommendations for international students: Required—TOEFL (minimum score 525 paper-based). *Faculty research:* Structural, environmental, geotechnical, transportation engineering and water resources.

Southern Illinois University Carbondale, Graduate School, College of Engineering, Department of Civil and Environmental Engineering, Carbondale, IL 62901-4701. Offers civil and environmental engineering (ME); civil engineering (MS). *Degree requirements:* For master's, comprehensive exam, thesis. *Entrance requirements:* For master's, GRE, minimum GPA of 2.7. Additional exam requirements/recommendations for international students: Required—TOEFL. *Faculty research:* Composite materials, wastewater treatment, solid waste disposal, slurry transport, geotechnical engineering.

Southern Illinois University Carbondale, Graduate School, College of Engineering, Program in Engineering Science, Carbondale, IL 62901-4701. Offers engineering science (PhD), including civil and environmental engineering, electrical and computer engineering, mechanical engineering and energy processes, mining and mineral resources engineering. *Degree requirements:* For doctorate, thesis/dissertation. *Entrance requirements:* For doctorate, GRE General Test, minimum GPA of 3.5. Additional exam requirements/recommendations for international students: Required—TOEFL.

Southern Illinois University Edwardsville, Graduate School, School of Engineering, Department of Civil Engineering, Edwardsville, IL 62026. Offers environmental engineering (MS); geotechnical engineering (MS); structural engineering (MS); transportation engineering (MS). *Program availability:* Part-time, evening/weekend. *Degree requirements:* For master's, thesis (for some programs), research paper. *Entrance requirements:* For master's, minimum undergraduate GPA of 2.75 in science, math, and engineering courses. Additional exam requirements/recommendations for international students: Required—TOEFL (minimum score 550 paper-based; 79 iBT), IELTS (minimum score 6.5). Electronic applications accepted.

Southern Methodist University, Bobby B. Lyle School of Engineering, Department of Environmental and Civil Engineering, Dallas, TX 75275-0340. Offers air pollution control and atmospheric sciences (PhD); civil engineering (MS); environmental engineering (MS); environmental science (MS); structural engineering (PhD); sustainability and development (MA); water and wastewater engineering (PhD). *Program availability:* Part-time, evening/weekend, online learning. Terminal master's awarded for partial completion of doctoral program. *Degree requirements:* For master's, thesis optional; for doctorate, thesis/dissertation, oral and written qualifying exams. *Entrance requirements:*

For master's, GRE General Test, minimum GPA of 3.0 in last 2 years; bachelor's degree in engineering, mathematics, or sciences; for doctorate, GRE, BS and MS in related field, minimum GPA of 3.3. Additional exam requirements/recommendations for international students: Required—TOEFL. Electronic applications accepted. *Faculty research:* Human and environmental health effects of endocrine disrupters, development of air pollution control systems for diesel engines, structural analysis and design, modeling and design of waste treatment systems.

Stanford University, School of Engineering, Department of Civil and Environmental Engineering, Stanford, CA 94305-2004. Offers atmosphere and energy (MS, PhD); construction (MS), including construction engineering and management, design-construction integration, sustainable design and construction; environmental engineering and science (MS, PhD, Eng); environmental fluid mechanics and hydrology (PhD); geomechanics (MS); structural engineering (MS). Terminal master's awarded for partial completion of doctoral program. *Degree requirements:* For doctorate, thesis/dissertation, qualifying exam; for Eng, thesis. *Entrance requirements:* For master's, doctorate, and Eng, GRE General Test. Additional exam requirements/recommendations for international students: Required—TOEFL. Electronic applications accepted. *Expenses: Tuition:* Full-time $47,331. *Required fees:* $609.

Stevens Institute of Technology, Graduate School, Charles V. Schaefer Jr. School of Engineering and Science, Department of Civil, Environmental, and Ocean Engineering, Program in Civil Engineering, Hoboken, NJ 07030. Offers civil engineering (PhD, Certificate), including geotechnical engineering (Certificate); geotechnical/geoenvironmental engineering (M Eng, Engr); hydrologic modeling (M Eng); stormwater management (M Eng); structural engineering (M Eng, Engr); transportation engineering (M Eng); water resources engineering (M Eng). *Program availability:* Part-time, evening/weekend. *Students:* 63 full-time (12 women), 27 part-time (10 women); includes 5 minority (2 Black or African American, non-Hispanic/Latino; 2 Asian, non-Hispanic/Latino; 1 Hispanic/Latino), 55 international. Average age 25. 167 applicants, 57% accepted, 24 enrolled. In 2016, 50 master's, 1 other advanced degree awarded. *Degree requirements:* For master's, thesis optional, minimum B average in major field and overall; for doctorate, comprehensive exam (for some programs), thesis/dissertation; for other advanced degree, minimum B average. *Entrance requirements:* Additional exam requirements/recommendations for international students: Required—TOEFL (minimum score 74 iBT), IELTS (minimum score 6). *Application deadline:* For fall admission, 6/1 for domestic students, 4/15 for international students; for spring admission, 11/30 for domestic students, 11/1 for international students. Applications are processed on a rolling basis. Application fee: $65. Electronic applications accepted. *Expenses:* Contact institution. *Financial support:* Fellowships, research assistantships, teaching assistantships, career-related internships or fieldwork, Federal Work-Study, scholarships/grants, and unspecified assistantships available. Financial award application deadline: 2/15; financial award applicants required to submit FAFSA. *Unit head:* Dr. David A. Vaccari, Director, 201-216-5570, Fax: 201-216-8739, E-mail: dvaccari@stevens.edu. *Application contact:* Graduate Admission, 888-783-8367, Fax: 888-511-1306, E-mail: graduate@stevens.edu.

Stony Brook University, State University of New York, Graduate School, College of Engineering and Applied Sciences, Department of Civil Engineering, Stony Brook, NY 11794. Offers MS, PhD, Graduate Certificate. *Program availability:* Part-time. *Faculty:* 8 full-time (2 women), 3 part-time/adjunct (0 women). *Students:* 5 full-time (2 women), 1 international. Average age 24. 33 applicants, 33% accepted, 4 enrolled. Terminal master's awarded for partial completion of doctoral program. *Degree requirements:* For doctorate, thesis/dissertation, preliminary examination, qualifying examination, teaching requirement. *Entrance requirements:* For doctorate, GRE General Test. Additional exam requirements/recommendations for international students: Required—TOEFL (minimum score 90 iBT). *Application deadline:* For fall admission, 1/15 for domestic students; for spring admission, 10/1 for domestic students. Application fee: $100. *Expenses:* Contact institution. *Financial support:* In 2016–17, 3 teaching assistantships were awarded; fellowships and research assistantships also available. *Faculty research:* Air transportation, civil engineering, public transportation, transportation, transportation energy use, transportation engineering. *Total annual research expenditures:* $320,827. *Unit head:* Dr. Harold Walker, Chair, 631-632-8315, Fax: 631-632-8110, E-mail: harold.walker@stonybrook.edu. *Application contact:* 631-632-8777, E-mail: civil_engineering@stonybrook.edu.
Website: http://www.stonybrook.edu/commcms/civileng/

Syracuse University, College of Engineering and Computer Science, Programs in Civil Engineering, Syracuse, NY 13244. Offers MS, PhD. *Program availability:* Part-time. *Students:* Average age 26. *Degree requirements:* For master's, comprehensive exam (for some programs), thesis (for some programs); for doctorate, comprehensive exam, thesis/dissertation. *Entrance requirements:* For master's and doctorate, GRE General Test, official transcripts, resume, three letters of recommendation, personal statement. Additional exam requirements/recommendations for international students: Required—TOEFL (minimum score 100 iBT). *Application deadline:* For fall admission, 7/1 priority date for domestic students, 6/1 priority date for international students; for spring admission, 11/15 priority date for domestic students, 10/15 priority date for international students. Applications are processed on a rolling basis. Application fee: $75. Electronic applications accepted. *Expenses: Tuition:* Full-time $25,974; part-time $1443 per credit hour. *Required fees:* $802; $50 per course. Tuition and fees vary according to course load and program. *Financial support:* Fellowships with full tuition reimbursements, research assistantships with tuition reimbursements, teaching assistantships with tuition reimbursements, and tuition waivers (partial) available. Financial award application deadline: 1/1. *Faculty research:* Fate and transport of pollutants, methods for characterization and remediation of hazardous wastes, response of eco-systems to disturbances, water quality and engineering. *Unit head:* Dr. Dawit Negussey, Professor/Graduate Program Director, E-mail: negussey@syr.edu. *Application contact:* Kathleen Joyce, Assistant Dean, 315-443-2219, E-mail: topgrads@syr.edu.
Website: http://eng-cs.syr.edu/

Temple University, College of Engineering, Department of Civil and Environmental Engineering, Philadelphia, PA 19122-6096. Offers civil engineering (MSCE); environmental engineering (MS Env E); storm water management (Graduate Certificate). *Program availability:* Part-time, evening/weekend. *Faculty:* 19 full-time (4 women), 4 part-time/adjunct (0 women). *Students:* 20 full-time (6 women), 16 part-time (3 women); includes 9 minority (3 Black or African American, non-Hispanic/Latino; 4 Asian, non-Hispanic/Latino; 2 Hispanic/Latino), 11 international. 57 applicants, 47% accepted, 13 enrolled. In 2016, 9 master's, 2 other advanced degrees awarded. Terminal master's awarded for partial completion of doctoral program. *Degree requirements:* For master's, thesis optional. *Entrance requirements:* For master's, GRE General Test, minimum GPA of 3.0; BS in engineering from ABET-accredited or equivalent institution; resume; goals statement; three letters of reference; official transcripts. Additional exam requirements/recommendations for international students: Required—TOEFL (minimum score 550 paper-based; 79 iBT), IELTS (minimum score 6.5), PTE (minimum score 53). *Application deadline:* For fall admission, 3/1 priority date for domestic and international students; for spring admission, 11/1 priority date for domestic students, 8/1 priority date for international students. Applications are processed on a rolling basis. Application fee: $60. Electronic applications accepted. *Expenses:* $995 per credit hour in-state tuition; $1,319 per credit hour out-of-state tuition. *Financial support:* In 2016–17, 15 students received support, including 1 fellowship with tuition reimbursement available, 4 research assistantships with tuition reimbursements available, 10 teaching assistantships with tuition reimbursements available; Federal Work-Study, scholarships/grants, health care benefits, and unspecified assistantships also available. Financial award application deadline: 3/1; financial award applicants required to submit FAFSA. *Faculty research:* Analysis of the effect of scour on bridge stability, design of sustainable buildings, development of new highway pavement material using plastic waste, characterization of by-products and waste materials for pavement and geotechnical engineering applications, development of effective traffic signals in urban and rural settings, development of techniques for effective construction management. *Unit head:* Dr. Rominder Suri, Chair, Department of Civil and Environmental Engineering, 215-204-2378, Fax: 215-204-6936, E-mail: rominder.suri@temple.edu. *Application contact:* Leslie Levin, Director, Admissions and Graduate Student Services, 215-204-7800, Fax: 215-204-6936, E-mail: gradengr@temple.edu.
Website: http://engineering.temple.edu/department/civil-environmental-engineering

Temple University, College of Engineering, PhD in Engineering Program, Philadelphia, PA 19122-6096. Offers bioengineering (PhD); civil engineering (PhD); electrical engineering (PhD); environmental engineering (PhD); mechanical engineering (PhD). *Program availability:* Part-time, evening/weekend. *Faculty:* 67 full-time (13 women), 11 part-time/adjunct (1 woman). *Students:* 32 full-time (11 women), 7 part-time (2 women); includes 10 minority (3 Black or African American, non-Hispanic/Latino; 5 Asian, non-Hispanic/Latino; 1 Hispanic/Latino; 1 Two or more races, non-Hispanic/Latino), 19 international. 11 applicants, 64% accepted, 3 enrolled. In 2016, 6 doctorates awarded. *Degree requirements:* For doctorate, thesis/dissertation, preliminary exam, dissertation proposal and defense. *Entrance requirements:* For doctorate, GRE, minimum undergraduate GPA of 3.0; MS in engineering from ABET-accredited or equivalent institution (preferred); resume; goals statement; three letters of reference; official transcripts. Additional exam requirements/recommendations for international students: Required—TOEFL (minimum score 550 paper-based; 79 iBT), IELTS (minimum score 6.5), PTE (minimum score 53). *Application deadline:* For fall admission, 1/15 priority date for domestic and international students; for spring admission, 11/1 priority date for domestic students, 8/1 priority date for international students. Applications are processed on a rolling basis. Application fee: $60. Electronic applications accepted. *Expenses:* $995 per credit hour in-state tuition; $1,319 per credit hour out-of-state. *Financial support:* Fellowships with tuition reimbursements, research assistantships with tuition reimbursements, teaching assistantships with tuition reimbursements, Federal Work-Study, scholarships/grants, health care benefits, and unspecified assistantships available. Financial award application deadline: 3/1; financial award applicants required to submit FAFSA. *Faculty research:* Advanced/computer-aided manufacturing and advanced materials processing; bioengineering; computer engineering; construction engineering and management; dynamics, controls, and systems; energy and environmental science; engineering physics and engineering mathematics; green engineering; signal processing and communication; transportation engineering; water resources, hydrology, and environmental engineering. *Unit head:* Dr. Saroj Biswas, Associate Dean, College of Engineering, 215-204-8403, E-mail: sbiswas@temple.edu. *Application contact:* Leslie Levin, Director, Admissions and Graduate Student Services, 215-204-7800, Fax: 215-204-6936,
E-mail: gradengr@temple.edu.
Website: http://engineering.temple.edu/additional-programs/phd-engineering

See Display on page 63 and Close-Up on page 83.

Tennessee State University, The School of Graduate Studies and Research, College of Engineering, Nashville, TN 37209-1561. Offers biomedical engineering (ME); civil engineering (ME); computer and information systems engineering (MS, PhD); electrical engineering (ME); environmental engineering (ME); manufacturing engineering (ME); mathematical sciences (MS); mechanical engineering (ME). *Program availability:* Part-time, evening/weekend. *Degree requirements:* For master's, project; for doctorate, comprehensive exam, thesis/dissertation. *Entrance requirements:* For doctorate, minimum GPA of 3.3. *Faculty research:* Robotics, intelligent systems, human-computer interaction software systems, biomedical engineering, signal/image processing, probabilistic design, intelligent manufacturing, cooperative mobile robots, condition based maintenance, sensor fusion.

Tennessee Technological University, College of Graduate Studies, College of Engineering, Department of Civil and Environmental Engineering, Cookeville, TN 38505. Offers MS. *Program availability:* Part-time. *Faculty:* 17 full-time (0 women). *Students:* 9 full-time (4 women), 9 part-time (4 women); includes 4 minority (2 Black or African American, non-Hispanic/Latino; 1 Native Hawaiian or other Pacific Islander, non-Hispanic/Latino; 1 Two or more races, non-Hispanic/Latino), 3 international. Average age 27. 52 applicants, 21% accepted, 7 enrolled. In 2016, 7 master's awarded. *Degree requirements:* For master's, thesis. *Entrance requirements:* For master's, GRE. Additional exam requirements/recommendations for international students: Required—TOEFL (minimum score 550 paper-based; 79 iBT), IELTS (minimum score 5.5), PTE (minimum score 53), or TOEIC (Test of English as an International Communication). *Application deadline:* For fall admission, 8/1 for domestic students, 5/1 for international students; for spring admission, 12/1 for domestic students, 10/1 for international students; for summer admission, 5/1 for domestic students, 2/1 for international students. Applications are processed on a rolling basis. Application fee: $35 ($40 for international students). Electronic applications accepted. *Expenses:* Tuition, state resident: full-time $9375; part-time $534 per credit hour. Tuition, nonresident: full-time $22,443; part-time $1260 per credit hour. *Financial support:* In 2016–17, 7 research assistantships (averaging $8,227 per year), 8 teaching assistantships (averaging $7,200 per year) were awarded; career-related internships or fieldwork also available. Financial award application deadline: 4/1. *Faculty research:* Environmental engineering, transportation, structural engineering, water resources. *Unit head:* Dr. Ben Mohr, Interim Chairperson, 931-372-3454, Fax: 931-372-6352, E-mail: bmohr@tntech.edu. *Application contact:* Shelia K. Kendrick, Coordinator of Graduate Studies, 931-372-3808, Fax: 931-372-3497, E-mail: skendrick@tntech.edu.

Texas A&M University, College of Engineering, Zachry Department of Civil Engineering, College Station, TX 77843. Offers civil engineering (M Eng, MS, PhD). *Program availability:* Part-time. *Faculty:* 60. *Students:* 334 full-time (105 women), 50 part-time (7 women); includes 45 minority (7 Black or African American, non-Hispanic/Latino; 1 American Indian or Alaska Native, non-Hispanic/Latino; 11 Asian, non-Hispanic/Latino; 23 Hispanic/Latino; 3 Two or more races, non-Hispanic/Latino), 246 international. Average age 27. 918 applicants, 36% accepted, 127 enrolled. In 2016, 149 master's, 34 doctorates awarded. *Degree requirements:* For master's, thesis (MS); for doctorate, dissertation (PhD), internship (D Eng). *Entrance requirements:* For master's and doctorate, GRE General Test. Additional exam requirements/recommendations for international students: Required—TOEFL (minimum score 550 paper-based; 80 iBT), IELTS (minimum score 6), PTE (minimum score 53). *Application deadline:* For fall admission, 7/15 for domestic students, 4/15 for international students; for spring admission, 10/15 for domestic students, 9/15 for international students. Applications are processed on a rolling basis. Application fee: $50 ($90 for international students).

Electronic applications accepted. *Expenses:* Contact institution. *Financial support:* In 2016–17, 310 students received support, including 76 fellowships with tuition reimbursements available (averaging $4,414 per year), 137 research assistantships with tuition reimbursements available (averaging $5,564 per year), 62 teaching assistantships with tuition reimbursements available (averaging $7,334 per year); career-related internships or fieldwork, institutionally sponsored loans, scholarships/grants, traineeships, health care benefits, tuition waivers (full and partial), and unspecified assistantships also available. Support available to part-time students. Financial award application deadline: 3/15; financial award applicants required to submit FAFSA. *Unit head:* Dr. Robin Autenrieth, Department Head, 979-845-2438, E-mail: rautenrieth@civil.tamu.edu. *Application contact:* Laura Byrd, Program Assistant, Graduate Student Services, 979-845-2498, E-mail: lbyrd@civil.tamu.edu. Website: http://engineering.tamu.edu/civil/

Texas A&M University–Kingsville, College of Graduate Studies, Frank H. Dotterweich College of Engineering, Department of Civil and Architectural Engineering, Kingsville, TX 78363. Offers civil engineering (ME, MS). *Degree requirements:* For master's, variable foreign language requirement, comprehensive exam, thesis (for some programs). *Entrance requirements:* For master's, GRE (minimum Quantitative and Verbal score of 950 on old scale), MAT, GMAT, minimum GPA of 2.6. Additional exam requirements/recommendations for international students: Required—TOEFL (minimum score 550 paper-based; 79 iBT). Electronic applications accepted. *Faculty research:* Dam restoration.

Texas Tech University, Graduate School, Edward E. Whitacre Jr. College of Engineering, Department of Civil, Environmental, and Construction Engineering, Lubbock, TX 79409-1023. Offers civil engineering (MSCE, PhD); environmental engineering (MENVEGR). *Accreditation:* ABET. *Program availability:* Part-time. *Faculty:* 34 full-time (6 women), 7 part-time/adjunct (0 women). *Students:* 106 full-time (36 women), 13 part-time (3 women); includes 24 minority (3 Asian, non-Hispanic/Latino; 20 Hispanic/Latino; 1 Two or more races, non-Hispanic/Latino), 63 international. Average age 27. 170 applicants, 52% accepted, 39 enrolled. In 2016, 28 master's, 8 doctorates awarded. Terminal master's awarded for partial completion of doctoral program. *Degree requirements:* For master's, comprehensive exam, thesis or alternative; for doctorate, comprehensive exam, thesis/dissertation, preliminary examination. *Entrance requirements:* For master's and doctorate, GRE (Verbal and Quantitative). Additional exam requirements/recommendations for international students: Required—TOEFL (minimum score 550 paper-based; 79 iBT), IELTS (minimum score 6.5). *Application deadline:* For fall admission, 6/1 priority date for domestic students, 1/15 priority date for international students; for spring admission, 9/1 priority date for domestic students, 6/15 priority date for international students. Applications are processed on a rolling basis. Application fee: $75. Electronic applications accepted. *Expenses:* $325 per credit hour full-time resident tuition, $733 per credit hour full-time non-resident tuition; $53.75 per credit hour fee plus $608 per term fee. *Financial support:* In 2016–17, 99 students received support, including 71 fellowships (averaging $4,370 per year), 56 research assistantships (averaging $12,343 per year), 33 teaching assistantships (averaging $15,807 per year); scholarships/grants, tuition waivers (partial), and unspecified assistantships also available. Financial award application deadline: 3/1; financial award applicants required to submit FAFSA. *Faculty research:* Geotechnical engineering, transportation engineering, water resources engineering, environmental engineering, wind engineering, construction engineering management. *Total annual research expenditures:* $3.5 million. *Unit head:* Dr. David Ernst, Interim Chair, 806-834-8657, Fax: 806-742-3488, E-mail: david.ernst@ttu.edu. *Application contact:* Dr. Priyantha Jayawickrama, Associate Professor, 806-742-3523 Ext. 245, Fax: 806-742-3488, E-mail: priyantha.jayawickrama@ttu.edu. Website: http://www.depts.ttu.edu/ceweb/

Tufts University, School of Engineering, Department of Civil and Environmental Engineering, Medford, MA 02155. Offers bioengineering (ME, MS), including environmental technology; civil engineering (ME, MS, PhD), including geotechnical engineering, structural engineering, water diplomacy (PhD); environmental engineering (ME, MS, PhD), including environmental engineering and environmental sciences, environmental geotechnology, environmental health, environmental science and management, hazardous materials management, water diplomacy (PhD), water resources engineering. *Program availability:* Part-time. Terminal master's awarded for partial completion of doctoral program. *Degree requirements:* For master's, thesis or alternative; for doctorate, thesis/dissertation. *Entrance requirements:* For master's and doctorate, GRE General Test. Additional exam requirements/recommendations for international students: Required—TOEFL (minimum score 550 paper-based; 80 iBT), IELTS (minimum score 6.5). Electronic applications accepted. *Expenses: Tuition:* Full-time $49,892; part-time $1248 per credit hour. *Required fees:* $844. Full-time tuition and fees vary according to degree level, program and student level. Part-time tuition and fees vary according to course load. *Faculty research:* Environmental and water resources engineering, environmental health, geotechnical and geoenvironmental engineering, structural engineering and mechanics, water diplomacy.

United States Merchant Marine Academy, Graduate Program, Kings Point, NY 11024-1699. Offers MS.

Université de Moncton, Faculty of Engineering, Program in Civil Engineering, Moncton, NB E1A 3E9, Canada. Offers M Sc A. *Degree requirements:* For master's, thesis, proficiency in French. *Faculty research:* Structures and materials, hydrology and water resources, soil mechanics and statistical analysis, environment, transportation.

Université de Sherbrooke, Faculty of Engineering, Department of Civil Engineering, Sherbrooke, QC J1K 2R1, Canada. Offers M Sc A, PhD. *Degree requirements:* For master's, one foreign language, thesis; for doctorate, comprehensive exam, thesis/dissertation. *Entrance requirements:* For master's, bachelor's degree in engineering or equivalent; for doctorate, master's degree in engineering or equivalent. Electronic applications accepted. *Faculty research:* High-strength concrete, dynamics of structures, solid mechanics, geotechnical engineering, wastewater treatment.

Université Laval, Faculty of Sciences and Engineering, Department of Civil Engineering, Program in Urban Infrastructure Engineering, Québec, QC G1K 7P4, Canada. Offers Diploma. *Program availability:* Part-time, evening/weekend. *Entrance requirements:* For degree, knowledge of French. Electronic applications accepted.

Université Laval, Faculty of Sciences and Engineering, Department of Civil Engineering, Programs in Civil Engineering, Québec, QC G1K 7P4, Canada. Offers civil engineering (M Sc, PhD); environmental technology (M Sc). Terminal master's awarded for partial completion of doctoral program. *Degree requirements:* For master's, thesis (for some programs); for doctorate, comprehensive exam, thesis/dissertation. *Entrance requirements:* For master's and doctorate, knowledge of French and English. Electronic applications accepted.

University at Buffalo, the State University of New York, Graduate School, School of Engineering and Applied Sciences, Department of Civil, Structural, and Environmental Engineering, Buffalo, NY 14260. Offers civil engineering (ME, MS, PhD); engineering science (MS). *Program availability:* Part-time, online learning. Terminal master's awarded for partial completion of doctoral program. *Degree requirements:* For master's, project, thesis, or comprehensive exam; for doctorate, thesis/dissertation. *Entrance*

requirements: For master's and doctorate, GRE General Test, letters of reference. Additional exam requirements/recommendations for international students: Required—TOEFL (minimum score 550 paper-based; 79 iBT). Electronic applications accepted. *Faculty research:* Environmental engineering and fluid mechanics, structural dynamics, geomechanics, earthquake engineering computational mechanics.

The University of Akron, Graduate School, College of Engineering, Department of Civil Engineering, Akron, OH 44325. Offers civil engineering (MS); engineering (PhD). *Program availability:* Evening/weekend. *Faculty:* 17 full-time (2 women), 6 part-time/adjunct (0 women). *Students:* 75 full-time (16 women), 18 part-time (4 women); includes 4 minority (2 Asian, non-Hispanic/Latino; 1 Hispanic/Latino; 1 Two or more races, non-Hispanic/Latino), 66 international. Average age 30. 62 applicants, 90% accepted, 21 enrolled. In 2016, 18 master's, 16 doctorates awarded. *Degree requirements:* For master's, thesis optional; for doctorate, thesis/dissertation, candidacy exam, qualifying exam. *Entrance requirements:* For master's, GRE, minimum GPA of 2.75, statement of purpose, three letters of recommendation; for doctorate, GRE, minimum GPA of 3.0 with bachelor's degree, 3.5 with master's degree; three letters of recommendation; statement of purpose; resume. Additional exam requirements/recommendations for international students: Required—TOEFL (minimum score 550 paper-based; 79 iBT), IELTS (minimum score 6.5). *Application deadline:* Applications are processed on a rolling basis. Application fee: $45 ($70 for international students). Electronic applications accepted. *Expenses:* Tuition, state resident: full-time $8618; part-time $359 per credit hour. Tuition, nonresident: full-time $17,149; part-time $715 per credit hour. *Required fees:* $1652. *Financial support:* In 2016–17, 15 research assistantships with full and partial tuition reimbursements, 1 teaching assistantship with full tuition reimbursement were awarded; instructional support assistantships also available. *Faculty research:* Development of constitutive laws for numerical analysis of nonlinear problems in structural mechanics, multiscale modeling and simulation of novel materials, water quality and distribution system analysis, safety-related traffic control, dynamic pile testing and analysis. *Total annual research expenditures:* $3.4 million. *Unit head:* Dr. Wieslaw K. Binienda, Chair, 330-972-6693, E-mail: wbinienda@uakron.edu. *Application contact:* Dr. Anil Patnaik, Graduate Director, 330-972-5226, E-mail: patnaik@uakron.edu. Website: http://www.uakron.edu/engineering/CE/

The University of Alabama, Graduate School, College of Engineering, Department of Civil, Construction and Environmental Engineering, Tuscaloosa, AL 35487-0205. Offers civil engineering (MSCE, PhD); environmental engineering (MS). *Program availability:* Part-time. *Faculty:* 20 full-time (2 women). *Students:* 55 full-time (14 women), 7 part-time (2 women); includes 2 minority (1 Black or African American, non-Hispanic/Latino; 1 Asian, non-Hispanic/Latino), 29 international. Average age 28. 69 applicants, 52% accepted, 15 enrolled. In 2016, 24 master's, 2 doctorates awarded. Terminal master's awarded for partial completion of doctoral program. *Degree requirements:* For master's, thesis or alternative; for doctorate, comprehensive exam, thesis/dissertation. *Entrance requirements:* For master's and doctorate, GRE General Test (minimum combined score of 300), minimum overall GPA of 3.0 in last hours of course work. Additional exam requirements/recommendations for international students: Required—TOEFL (minimum score 550 paper-based; 79 iBT), IELTS (minimum score 6.5), PTE (minimum score 59). *Application deadline:* Applications are processed on a rolling basis. Application fee: $50 ($60 for international students). Electronic applications accepted. *Expenses:* Tuition, state resident: full-time $10,470. Tuition, nonresident: full-time $26,950. *Financial support:* In 2016–17, 40 students received support, including 2 fellowships with full tuition reimbursements available (averaging $30,000 per year), 17 research assistantships with full tuition reimbursements available (averaging $13,275 per year), 20 teaching assistantships with full tuition reimbursements available (averaging $13,275 per year); scholarships/grants, tuition waivers (partial), and unspecified assistantships also available. Financial award application deadline: 1/5. *Faculty research:* Experimental structures, modeling of structures, bridge management systems, geotechnological engineering, environmental remediation. *Total annual research expenditures:* $5.7 million. *Unit head:* Dr. W. Edward Back, Head/Professor, 205-348-6550, Fax: 205-348-0783, E-mail: eback@eng.ua.edu. *Application contact:* Dr. Andrew Graettinger, Professor and Graduate Program Director, 205-348-1707, Fax: 205-348-0783, E-mail: andrewg@eng.ua.edu. Website: http://cce.eng.ua.edu/

The University of Alabama at Birmingham, School of Engineering, Program in Civil Engineering, Birmingham, AL 35294. Offers construction engineering management (M Eng); structural engineering (M Eng); sustainable smart cities (M Eng). Program offered jointly with The University of Alabama in Huntsville. *Program availability:* Part-time, evening/weekend, 100% online. *Faculty:* 15 full-time (4 women), 3 part-time/adjunct. *Students:* 16 full-time (6 women), 24 part-time (5 women); includes 22 minority (5 Black or African American, non-Hispanic/Latino; 12 Asian, non-Hispanic/Latino; 4 Hispanic/Latino; 1 Two or more races, non-Hispanic/Latino). Average age 30. 16 applicants, 56% accepted, 5 enrolled. In 2016, 15 master's, 3 doctorates awarded. *Degree requirements:* For master's, comprehensive exam, thesis optional; for doctorate, comprehensive exam, thesis/dissertation. *Entrance requirements:* For master's, GRE General Test preferred (minimum score of 500 on each component), minimum GPA of 3.0 in all undergraduate degree major courses attempted, letters of evaluation. Additional exam requirements/recommendations for international students: Required—TOEFL (minimum score 550 paper-based), TWE (minimum score 3.5). *Application deadline:* For fall admission, 7/1 for domestic and international students; for spring admission, 11/1 for domestic and international students; for summer admission, 4/1 for domestic and international students. Applications are processed on a rolling basis. Application fee: $50 ($60 for international students). Electronic applications accepted. *Expenses:* $396 per hour resident tuition; $935 per hour non-resident tuition; $150 per course online course fee. *Financial support:* In 2016–17, 15 students received support, including 1 fellowship with full tuition reimbursement available (averaging $24,000 per year), 14 research assistantships with full and partial tuition reimbursements available (averaging $17,472 per year). *Total annual research expenditures:* $1.1 million. *Unit head:* Dr. Fouad H. Fouad, Chair, 205-934-8430, Fax: 205-934-9855, E-mail: ffouad@uab.edu. *Application contact:* Holly Hebard, Director of Graduate School Operations, 205-834-8227, Fax: 205-934-8413, E-mail: gradschool@uab.edu. Website: https://www.uab.edu/engineering/home/graduate-civil

The University of Alabama in Huntsville, School of Graduate Studies, College of Engineering, Department of Civil and Environmental Engineering, Huntsville, AL 35899. Offers civil and environmental engineering (PhD); civil engineering (MSE), including civil engineering. PhD offered jointly with The University of Alabama at Birmingham. *Program availability:* Part-time, evening/weekend. *Degree requirements:* For master's, comprehensive exam, thesis or alternative, oral and written exams; for doctorate, comprehensive exam, thesis/dissertation, oral and written exams. *Entrance requirements:* For master's, GRE General Test, BSE, minimum GPA of 3.0; for doctorate, GRE General Test, minimum GPA of 3.0. Additional exam requirements/recommendations for international students: Required—TOEFL (minimum score 500 paper-based; 80 iBT), IELTS (minimum score 6.5). Electronic applications accepted. *Expenses:* Tuition, state resident: full-time $9834; part-time $600 per credit hour. Tuition, nonresident: full-time $21,830; part-time $1325 per credit hour. *Faculty research:* Smart materials and smart structures, fiber-reinforced cementitious composites, processing and mechanics of composites, geographic information systems, environmental engineering.

University of Alaska Anchorage, School of Engineering, Program in Civil Engineering, Anchorage, AK 99508. Offers civil engineering (MCE, MS); coastal, ocean, and port engineering (Certificate). *Program availability:* Part-time, evening/weekend. *Degree requirements:* For master's, thesis (for some programs). *Entrance requirements:* For master's, bachelor's degree in engineering. Additional exam requirements/ recommendations for international students: Required—TOEFL (minimum score 550 paper-based). *Faculty research:* Structural engineering, engineering education, astronomical observations related to engineering.

University of Alaska Fairbanks, College of Engineering and Mines, Department of Civil and Environmental Engineering, Fairbanks, AK 99775-5900. Offers civil engineering (MS); design and construction management (Graduate Certificate); environmental engineering (PhD). *Program availability:* Part-time. *Faculty:* 9 full-time (3 women), 1 part-time/adjunct (0 women). *Students:* 10 full-time (3 women), 8 part-time (3 women); includes 4 minority (1 Black or African American, non-Hispanic/Latino; 2 Asian, non-Hispanic/Latino; 1 Two or more races, non-Hispanic/Latino), 2 international. Average age 29. 14 applicants, 43% accepted, 3 enrolled. In 2016, 9 master's, 1 other advanced degree awarded. *Degree requirements:* For master's, comprehensive exam, thesis (for some programs), oral defense of project or thesis; for doctorate, comprehensive exam, thesis/dissertation. *Entrance requirements:* For master's, bachelor's degree from accredited institution with minimum cumulative undergraduate and major GPA of 3.0. Additional exam requirements/recommendations for international students: Required—TOEFL (minimum score 550 paper-based; 79 iBT), IELTS (minimum score 6.5). *Application deadline:* For fall admission, 6/1 for domestic students, 3/1 for international students; for spring admission, 10/15 for domestic students, 9/1 for international students. Applications are processed on a rolling basis. Application fee: $60. Electronic applications accepted. *Expenses:* $533 per credit resident tuition, $673 per semester resident fees; $1,088 per credit non-resident tuition, $835 per semester non-resident fees. *Financial support:* In 2016–17, 5 research assistantships with full tuition reimbursements (averaging $4,248 per year), 6 teaching assistantships with full tuition reimbursements (averaging $5,781 per year) were awarded; fellowships with full tuition reimbursements, career-related internships or fieldwork, Federal Work-Study, scholarships/grants, health care benefits, and unspecified assistantships also available. Support available to part-time students. Financial award application deadline: 7/1; financial award applicants required to submit FAFSA. *Faculty research:* Soils, structures, culvert thawing with solar power, pavement drainage, contaminant hydrogeology. *Unit head:* Dr. Leroy Hulsey, Department Chair, 907-474-7241, Fax: 907-474-6087, E-mail: fycee@uaf.edu. *Application contact:* Mary Kreta, Director of Admissions, 907-474-7500, Fax: 907-474-7097, E-mail: admissions@uaf.edu.
Website: http://cem.uaf.edu/cee

University of Alberta, Faculty of Graduate Studies and Research, Department of Civil and Environmental Engineering, Edmonton, AB T6G 2E1, Canada. Offers construction engineering and management (M Eng, M Sc, PhD); environmental engineering (M Eng, M Sc, PhD); environmental science (M Sc, PhD); geoenvironmental engineering (M Eng, M Sc, PhD); geotechnical engineering (M Eng, M Sc, PhD); mining engineering (M Eng, M Sc, PhD); petroleum engineering (M Eng, M Sc, PhD); structural engineering (M Eng, M Sc, PhD); water resources (M Eng, M Sc, PhD). *Program availability:* Part-time, online learning. *Degree requirements:* For master's, thesis (for some programs); for doctorate, thesis/dissertation. *Entrance requirements:* For master's, minimum GPA of 3.0 in last 2 years of undergraduate studies; for doctorate, minimum GPA of 3.0. Additional exam requirements/recommendations for international students: Required—TOEFL (minimum score 550 paper-based). Electronic applications accepted. *Faculty research:* Mining.

University of Arkansas, Graduate School, College of Engineering, Department of Civil Engineering, Program in Civil Engineering, Fayetteville, AR 72701. Offers MSCE, MSE, PhD. In 2016, 15 master's, 5 doctorates awarded. *Degree requirements:* For master's, thesis optional; for doctorate, one foreign language, thesis/dissertation. *Application deadline:* For fall admission, 4/1 for international students; for spring admission, 10/1 for international students. Applications are processed on a rolling basis. Application fee: $40 ($50 for international students). Electronic applications accepted. *Financial support:* In 2016–17, 33 research assistantships, 1 teaching assistantship were awarded; fellowships, career-related internships or fieldwork, and Federal Work-Study also available. Support available to part-time students. Financial award application deadline: 4/1; financial award applicants required to submit FAFSA. *Unit head:* Dr. Micah Hale, Department Chair, 479-575-6348, Fax: 479-575-7168, E-mail: micah@uark.edu. *Application contact:* Dr. Julian Fairey, Graduate Coordinator, 479-575-4023, E-mail: julianf@uark.edu.
Website: http://www.cveg.uark.edu/

The University of British Columbia, Faculty of Applied Science, Department of Civil Engineering, Vancouver, BC V6T 1Z4, Canada. Offers M Eng, MA Sc, PhD. *Program availability:* Part-time. *Degree requirements:* For master's, thesis; for doctorate, thesis/ dissertation. *Entrance requirements:* Additional exam requirements/recommendations for international students: Required—TOEFL (minimum score 100 iBT), IELTS. *Application deadline:* For fall admission, 1/31 priority date for domestic students, 1/31 for international students. Application fee: $100 Canadian dollars ($162 Canadian dollars for international students). Electronic applications accepted. *Expenses:* $4,802 per year tuition and fees, $8,436 per year international. *Financial support:* Research assistantships, teaching assistantships, institutionally sponsored loans, scholarships/ grants, tuition waivers (full and partial), and unspecified assistantships available. *Faculty research:* Geotechnology; structural, water, and environmental engineering; transportation; materials and construction engineering. *Application contact:* Glenda Levins, Graduate Student Support, 604-822-0667, Fax: 604-822-6901, E-mail: gradsec@civil.ubc.ca.
Website: http://www.civil.ubc.ca/

University of Calgary, Faculty of Graduate Studies, Schulich School of Engineering, Department of Civil Engineering, Calgary, AB T2N 1N4, Canada. Offers avalanche mechanics (M Sc, PhD); civil engineering (M Eng, M Sc, PhD); energy and environment engineering (M Eng, M Sc, PhD); environmental engineering (M Eng, M Sc, PhD); geotechnical engineering (M Eng, M Sc, PhD); materials science (M Eng, M Sc, PhD); project management (M Eng, M Sc, PhD); structures and solid mechanics (M Eng, M Sc, PhD); transportation engineering (M Eng, M Sc, PhD); water resources (M Eng, M Sc, PhD). *Program availability:* Part-time. *Degree requirements:* For master's, thesis; for doctorate, thesis/dissertation, written and oral candidacy exam. *Entrance requirements:* For master's, minimum GPA of 3.0; for doctorate, minimum GPA of 3.5. Additional exam requirements/recommendations for international students: Required—TOEFL (minimum score 580 paper-based; 93 iBT), IELTS (minimum score 7). Electronic applications accepted. *Faculty research:* Geotechnical engineering, energy and environment, transportation, project management, structures and solid mechanics.

University of California, Berkeley, Graduate Division, College of Engineering, Department of Civil and Environmental Engineering, Berkeley, CA 94720-1500. Offers engineering and project management (M Eng, MS, PhD); environmental engineering (M Eng, MS, PhD); geoengineering (M Eng, MS, PhD); structural engineering, mechanics and materials (M Eng, MS, PhD); transportation engineering (M Eng, MS, PhD); M Arch/MS; MCP/MS; MPP/MS. *Students:* 360 full-time (143 women); includes 71 minority (15 Black or African American, non-Hispanic/Latino; 39 Asian, non-Hispanic/ Latino; 17 Hispanic/Latino), 148 international. Average age 27. 1,086 applicants, 185 enrolled. In 2016, 188 master's, 26 doctorates awarded. Terminal master's awarded for partial completion of doctoral program. *Degree requirements:* For master's, comprehensive exam (for some programs), thesis (for some programs), comprehensive exam or thesis (MS); for doctorate, thesis/dissertation, qualifying exam. *Entrance requirements:* For master's, GRE General Test, minimum GPA of 3.0, 3 letters of recommendation; for doctorate, GRE General Test, minimum GPA of 3.5, 3 letters of recommendation. Additional exam requirements/recommendations for international students: Required—TOEFL (minimum score 570 paper-based; 90 iBT). *Application deadline:* For fall admission, 12/16 for domestic students. Application fee: $105 ($125 for international students). Electronic applications accepted. *Financial support:* Applicants required to submit FAFSA. *Unit head:* Prof. Robert Harley, Chair, 510-643-8739, Fax: 510-643-5264, E-mail: chair@ce.berkeley.edu. *Application contact:* Shelly Okimoto, Graduate Advisor, 510-642-6464, Fax: 510-643-5264, E-mail: aao@ ce.berkeley.edu.
Website: http://www.ce.berkeley.edu/

University of California, Davis, College of Engineering, Program in Civil and Environmental Engineering, Davis, CA 95616. Offers M Engr, MS, D Engr, PhD, Certificate, M Engr/MBA. *Degree requirements:* For master's, comprehensive exam (for some programs), thesis (for some programs); for doctorate, thesis/dissertation. *Entrance requirements:* For master's, GRE General Test, minimum GPA of 3.0; for doctorate, GRE, minimum graduate GPA of 3.5. Additional exam requirements/recommendations for international students: Required—TOEFL (minimum score 550 paper-based). Electronic applications accepted. *Faculty research:* Environmental water resources, transportation, structural mechanics, structural engineering, geotechnical engineering.

University of California, Irvine, Henry Samueli School of Engineering, Department of Civil and Environmental Engineering, Irvine, CA 92697. Offers MS, PhD. *Program availability:* Part-time. *Students:* 161 full-time (51 women), 10 part-time (4 women); includes 17 minority (11 Asian, non-Hispanic/Latino; 5 Hispanic/Latino; 1 Two or more races, non-Hispanic/Latino), 117 international. Average age 27. 489 applicants, 46% accepted, 63 enrolled. In 2016, 70 master's, 14 doctorates awarded. Terminal master's awarded for partial completion of doctoral program. *Degree requirements:* For doctorate, thesis/dissertation. *Entrance requirements:* For master's and doctorate, GRE General Test, minimum GPA of 3.0, 3 letters of recommendation. Additional exam requirements/ recommendations for international students: Required—TOEFL (minimum score 550 paper-based). *Application deadline:* For fall admission, 1/15 priority date for domestic students, 1/15 for international students. Applications are processed on a rolling basis. Application fee: $105 ($125 for international students). Electronic applications accepted. *Financial support:* Fellowships, research assistantships with full tuition reimbursements, teaching assistantships, institutionally sponsored loans, traineeships, health care benefits, and unspecified assistantships available. Financial award application deadline: 3/1; financial award applicants required to submit FAFSA. *Faculty research:* Intelligent transportation systems and transportation economics, risk and reliability, fluid mechanics, environmental hydrodynamics, hydrological and climate systems, water resources. *Unit head:* Prof. Brett F. Sanders, Chair and Professor, 949-824-4327, Fax: 949-824-3672, E-mail: bsanders@uci.edu. *Application contact:* Connie Cheng, Assistant Director, 949-824-3562, Fax: 949-824-8200, E-mail: connie.cheng@uci.edu.
Website: http://www.eng.uci.edu/dept/cee

University of California, Los Angeles, Graduate Division, Henry Samueli School of Engineering and Applied Science, Department of Civil and Environmental Engineering, Los Angeles, CA 90095-1593. Offers MS, PhD. *Faculty:* 18 full-time (3 women), 5 part-time/adjunct (0 women). *Students:* 178 full-time (62 women); includes 33 minority (1 Black or African American, non-Hispanic/Latino; 19 Asian, non-Hispanic/Latino; 8 Hispanic/Latino; 5 Two or more races, non-Hispanic/Latino), 110 international. 434 applicants, 68% accepted, 89 enrolled. In 2016, 76 master's, 16 doctorates awarded. *Degree requirements:* For master's, comprehensive exam or thesis; for doctorate, thesis/dissertation, qualifying exams. *Entrance requirements:* For master's, GRE General Test, minimum GPA of 3.0; for doctorate, GRE General Test, minimum GPA of 3.25. Additional exam requirements/recommendations for international students: Required—TOEFL (minimum score 560 paper-based; 87 iBT), IELTS (minimum score 7). *Application deadline:* For fall admission, 12/15 priority date for domestic and international students. Application fee: $105 ($125 for international students). Electronic applications accepted. *Financial support:* In 2016–17, 126 fellowships, 71 research assistantships, 92 teaching assistantships were awarded; Federal Work-Study, institutionally sponsored loans, and tuition waivers (full and partial) also available. Financial award application deadline: 12/15; financial award applicants required to submit FAFSA. *Faculty research:* Civil engineering materials, environmental engineering, geotechnical engineering, hydrology and water resources, structures. *Total annual research expenditures:* $3.3 million. *Unit head:* Dr. Jonathan P. Stewart, Chair, 310-206-2990, E-mail: jstewart@seas.ucla.edu. *Application contact:* Jesse Dieker, Student Affairs Officer, 310-825-1851, E-mail: jdieker@seas.ucla.edu.
Website: http://cee.ucla.edu/

University of Central Florida, College of Engineering and Computer Science, Department of Civil, Environmental, and Construction Engineering, Program in Civil Engineering, Orlando, FL 32816. Offers MS, MSCE, PhD, Certificate. *Program availability:* Part-time, evening/weekend. *Students:* 83 full-time (9 women), 75 part-time (22 women); includes 41 minority (8 Black or African American, non-Hispanic/Latino; 9 Asian, non-Hispanic/Latino; 23 Hispanic/Latino; 1 Two or more races, non-Hispanic/ Latino), 70 international. Average age 30. 139 applicants, 71% accepted, 36 enrolled. In 2016, 33 master's, 13 doctorates, 3 other advanced degrees awarded. *Degree requirements:* For master's, thesis or alternative; for doctorate, thesis/dissertation, departmental qualifying exam, candidacy exam. *Entrance requirements:* For master's, minimum GPA of 3.0 in last 60 hours; for doctorate, GRE General Test, minimum GPA of 3.5 in last 60 hours. Additional exam requirements/recommendations for international students: Required—TOEFL. *Application deadline:* For fall admission, 7/15 priority date for domestic students; for spring admission, 12/1 priority date for domestic students. Application fee: $30. Electronic applications accepted. *Expenses:* Tuition, state resident: part-time $288.16 per credit hour. Tuition, nonresident: part-time $1071.31 per credit hour. *Financial support:* In 2016–17, 53 students received support, including 18 fellowships with partial tuition reimbursements available (averaging $13,311 per year), 38 research assistantships with partial tuition reimbursements available (averaging $10,478 per year), 13 teaching assistantships with partial tuition reimbursements available (averaging $10,630 per year); career-related internships or fieldwork, Federal Work-Study, institutionally sponsored loans, tuition waivers (partial), and unspecified assistantships also available. Financial award application deadline: 3/1; financial award applicants required to submit FAFSA. *Unit head:* Dr. Mohamed Abdel-Aty, Chair, 407-823-5657, E-mail: m.aty@ucf.edu. *Application contact:* Assistant Director, Graduate Admissions, 407-823-2766, Fax: 407-823-6442, E-mail: gradadmissions@ucf.edu.
Website: http://cece.ucf.edu/

University of Cincinnati, Graduate School, College of Engineering and Applied Science, Department of Civil and Architectural Engineering and Construction Management, Program in Civil Engineering, Cincinnati, OH 45221. Offers MS, PhD. *Program availability:* Part-time. Terminal master's awarded for partial completion of doctoral program. *Degree requirements:* For master's, project or thesis; for doctorate, one foreign language, thesis/dissertation. *Entrance requirements:* For master's and doctorate, GRE General Test. Additional exam requirements/recommendations for international students: Required—TOEFL (minimum score 580 paper-based; 92 iBT). Electronic applications accepted. *Expenses: Tuition, area resident:* Full-time $12,790; part-time $389 per credit hour. Tuition, state resident: full-time $13,290; part-time $419 per credit hour. Tuition, nonresident: full-time $24,532; part-time $976 per credit hour. *International tuition:* $24,832 full-time. *Required fees:* $3958; $140 per credit hour. Tuition and fees vary according to course load, degree level, program and reciprocity agreements. *Faculty research:* Soil mechanics and foundations, structures, transportation, water resources systems and hydraulics.

University of Colorado Boulder, Graduate School, College of Engineering and Applied Science, Department of Civil, Environmental, and Architectural Engineering, Boulder, CO 80309. Offers MS, PhD. *Faculty:* 43 full-time (10 women). *Students:* 275 full-time (102 women), 19 part-time (11 women); includes 31 minority (3 Black or African American, non-Hispanic/Latino; 1 American Indian or Alaska Native, non-Hispanic/Latino; 8 Asian, non-Hispanic/Latino; 9 Hispanic/Latino; 1 Native Hawaiian or other Pacific Islander, non-Hispanic/Latino; 9 Two or more races, non-Hispanic/Latino), 75 international. Average age 28. 482 applicants, 55% accepted, 79 enrolled. In 2016, 69 master's, 34 doctorates awarded. Terminal master's awarded for partial completion of doctoral program. *Degree requirements:* For master's, comprehensive exam, thesis or alternative; for doctorate, thesis/dissertation. *Entrance requirements:* For master's, GRE General Test, minimum undergraduate GPA of 3.0. *Application deadline:* For fall admission, 1/31 for domestic and international students; for spring admission, 10/1 for domestic and international students. Application fee: $60 ($80 for international students). Electronic applications accepted. Application fee is waived when completed online. *Financial support:* In 2016–17, 498 students received support, including 168 fellowships (averaging $10,048 per year), 81 research assistantships with full and partial tuition reimbursements available (averaging $36,827 per year), 32 teaching assistantships with full and partial tuition reimbursements available (averaging $38,824 per year); institutionally sponsored loans, scholarships/grants, health care benefits, and unspecified assistantships also available. Financial award application deadline: 1/15; financial award applicants required to submit FAFSA. *Faculty research:* Civil engineering, environmental engineering, architectural engineering, hydrology, water resources engineering. *Total annual research expenditures:* $12.5 million. *Application contact:* E-mail: cvengrad@colorado.edu.
Website: http://civil.colorado.edu/

University of Colorado Denver, College of Engineering and Applied Science, Department of Civil Engineering, Denver, CO 80217. Offers civil engineering (EASPh D); civil engineering systems (PhD); environmental and sustainability engineering (MS, PhD); geographic information systems (MS); geotechnical engineering (MS, PhD); hydrology and hydraulics (MS, PhD); structural engineering (MS, PhD); transportation engineering (MS, PhD). *Program availability:* Part-time, evening/weekend. *Faculty:* 15 full-time (3 women), 9 part-time/adjunct (0 women). *Students:* 50 full-time (15 women), 33 part-time (7 women); includes 10 minority (1 Black or African American, non-Hispanic/Latino; 2 Asian, non-Hispanic/Latino; 6 Hispanic/Latino; 1 Two or more races, non-Hispanic/Latino), 31 international. Average age 30. 105 applicants, 51% accepted, 14 enrolled. In 2016, 29 master's, 2 doctorates awarded. *Degree requirements:* For master's, comprehensive exam, 30 credit hours, project or thesis; for doctorate, comprehensive exam, thesis/dissertation, 60 credit hours (30 of which are dissertation research). *Entrance requirements:* For master's, GRE, statement of purpose, transcripts, three references; for doctorate, GRE, statement of purpose, transcripts, references, letter of support from faculty stating willingness to serve as dissertation advisor and outlining plan for financial support. Additional exam requirements/recommendations for international students: Required—TOEFL (minimum score 537 paper-based; 75 iBT); Recommended—IELTS (minimum score 6.5). *Application deadline:* For fall admission, 5/1 for domestic students, 4/1 for international students; for spring admission, 10/1 for domestic students, 9/1 for international students; for summer admission, 2/15 for domestic students, 1/15 for international students. Application fee: $50 ($75 for international students). Electronic applications accepted. *Expenses:* Contact institution. *Financial support:* In 2016–17, 62 students received support. Fellowships, research assistantships, teaching assistantships, career-related internships or fieldwork, Federal Work-Study, institutionally sponsored loans, scholarships/grants, traineeships, and unspecified assistantships available. Financial award application deadline: 4/1; financial award applicants required to submit FAFSA. *Faculty research:* Earthquake source physics, environmental biotechnology, hydrologic and hydraulic engineering, sustainability assessments, transportation energy use and greenhouse gas emissions. *Unit head:* Dr. Kevin Rens, Chair, 303-556-8017, E-mail: kevin.rens@ucdenver.edu. *Application contact:* Roxanne Pizano, Program Coordinator, 303-556-6274, E-mail: roxanne.pizano@ucdenver.edu.
Website: http://www.ucdenver.edu/academics/colleges/Engineering/Programs/Civil-Engineering/Pages/CivilEngineering.aspx

University of Colorado Denver, College of Engineering and Applied Science, Master of Engineering Program, Denver, CO 80217-3364. Offers civil engineering (M Eng), including civil engineering, geographic information systems, transportation systems; electrical engineering (M Eng); mechanical engineering (M Eng). *Program availability:* Part-time. *Students:* 35 full-time (9 women), 23 part-time (7 women); includes 5 minority (1 American Indian or Alaska Native, non-Hispanic/Latino; 2 Hispanic/Latino; 2 Two or more races, non-Hispanic/Latino), 11 international. Average age 31. 75 applicants, 63% accepted, 13 enrolled. In 2016, 17 master's awarded. *Degree requirements:* For master's, comprehensive exam, 27 credit hours of course work, 3 credit hours of report or thesis work. *Entrance requirements:* For master's, GRE (for those with GPA below 2.75), transcripts, references, statement of purpose. Additional exam requirements/recommendations for international students: Required—TOEFL (minimum score 537 paper-based; 75 iBT); Recommended—IELTS (minimum score 6.5). *Application deadline:* For fall admission, 4/1 for domestic students, 3/1 for international students; for spring admission, 10/1 for domestic students, 9/15 for international students. Applications are processed on a rolling basis. Application fee: $50 ($75 for international students). Electronic applications accepted. *Expenses:* Contact institution. *Financial support:* In 2016–17, 120 students received support. Fellowships, research assistantships, teaching assistantships, Federal Work-Study, institutionally sponsored loans, scholarships/grants, traineeships, and unspecified assistantships available. Financial award application deadline: 4/1; financial award applicants required to submit FAFSA. *Faculty research:* Civil, electrical and mechanical engineering. *Application contact:* Graduate School Admissions, 303-315-2179, E-mail: ceasgaapplications@ucdenver.edu.
Website: http://www.ucdenver.edu/academics/colleges/Engineering/admissions/Masters/Pages/MastersAdmissions.aspx

University of Connecticut, Graduate School, School of Engineering, Department of Civil and Environmental Engineering, Field of Civil Engineering, Storrs, CT 06269. Offers MS, PhD. Terminal master's awarded for partial completion of doctoral program. *Degree requirements:* For master's, comprehensive exam, thesis or alternative; for doctorate, thesis/dissertation. *Entrance requirements:* Additional exam requirements/recommendations for international students: Required—TOEFL (minimum score 550 paper-based). Electronic applications accepted.

University of Dayton, Department of Civil and Environmental Engineering and Engineering Mechanics, Dayton, OH 45469. Offers engineering mechanics (MSEM); environmental engineering (MSCE); geotechnical engineering (MSCE); structural engineering (MSCE); transportation engineering (MSCE); water resources engineering (MSCE). *Program availability:* Part-time, evening/weekend. *Faculty:* 9 full-time (2 women), 3 part-time/adjunct (1 woman). *Students:* 40 full-time (8 women), 2 part-time (0 women); includes 1 minority (Asian, non-Hispanic/Latino), 30 international. Average age 26. 137 applicants, 17% accepted. In 2016, 14 master's awarded. *Degree requirements:* For master's, thesis optional. *Entrance requirements:* For master's, minimum GPA of 3.0 in undergraduate work. Additional exam requirements/recommendations for international students: Required—TOEFL (minimum score 550 paper-based; 80 iBT); Recommended—IELTS. *Application deadline:* For fall admission, 8/1 priority date for domestic students, 5/1 priority date for international students; for spring admission, 11/1 priority date for international students. Applications are processed on a rolling basis. Application fee: $0 ($50 for international students). Electronic applications accepted. *Expenses:* $890 per credit hour, $25 registration fee. *Financial support:* Research assistantships, institutionally sponsored loans, scholarships/grants, and department-funded awards (averaging $2448 per year) available. Financial award application deadline: 3/1; financial award applicants required to submit FAFSA. *Faculty research:* Vertically-aligned carbon nanotubes infiltrated with temperature-responsive polymers; smart nanocomposite films for self-cleaning and controlled release; bilayer and bulk heterojunction solar cells using liquid crystalline porphyrins as donors by solution processing; DNA damage induced by multiwalled carbon nanotubes in mouse embryonic stem cells. *Total annual research expenditures:* $250,000. *Unit head:* Dr. Donald V. Chase, Chair, 937-229-3847, Fax: 937-229-3491, E-mail: dchase1@udayton.edu. *Application contact:* 937-229-4462, E-mail: graduateadmission@udayton.edu.
Website: https://www.udayton.edu/engineering/departments/civil/index.php

University of Delaware, College of Engineering, Department of Civil and Environmental Engineering, Newark, DE 19716. Offers environmental engineering (MAS, MCE, PhD); geotechnical engineering (MAS, MCE, PhD); ocean engineering (MAS, MCE, PhD); structural engineering (MAS, MCE, PhD); transportation engineering (MAS, MCE, PhD); water resource engineering (MAS, MCE, PhD). *Program availability:* Part-time. Terminal master's awarded for partial completion of doctoral program. *Degree requirements:* For master's, thesis; for doctorate, thesis/dissertation. *Entrance requirements:* For master's and doctorate, GRE General Test. Additional exam requirements/recommendations for international students: Required—TOEFL. Electronic applications accepted. *Faculty research:* Structural engineering and mechanics; transportation engineering; ocean engineering; soil mechanics and foundation; water resources and environmental engineering.

University of Detroit Mercy, College of Engineering and Science, Detroit, MI 48221. Offers chemistry (MS); civil and environmental engineering (DE); electrical and computer engineering (ME); electrical engineering (DE); engineering management (M Eng Mgt); environmental engineering (MEE); mechanical engineering (MME, DE); product development (MS); software engineering (MSSE); teaching of mathematics (MATM). *Program availability:* Part-time, evening/weekend. *Degree requirements:* For doctorate, thesis/dissertation. Electronic applications accepted. Application fee is waived when completed online. *Expenses:* Contact institution.

University of Florida, Graduate School, Herbert Wertheim College of Engineering, Department of Civil and Coastal Engineering, Gainesville, FL 32611. Offers civil engineering (ME, MS, PhD); coastal and oceanographic engineering (ME, MS, PhD); geographic information systems (ME, MS, PhD); hydrologic sciences (ME, MS, PhD); structural engineering (ME, MS); wetland sciences (ME, MS, PhD). *Program availability:* Part-time, online learning. Terminal master's awarded for partial completion of doctoral program. *Degree requirements:* For master's, thesis (for some programs); for doctorate, comprehensive exam, thesis/dissertation. *Entrance requirements:* For master's and doctorate, minimum GPA of 3.0. Additional exam requirements/recommendations for international students: Required—TOEFL (minimum score 550 paper-based; 80 iBT), IELTS (minimum score 6). Electronic applications accepted. *Faculty research:* Traffic congestion mitigation, wind mitigation, sustainable infrastructure materials, improved sensors for in situ measurements, storm surge modeling.

University of Hawaii at Manoa, Graduate Division, College of Engineering, Department of Civil and Environmental Engineering, Honolulu, HI 96822. Offers MS, PhD. *Program availability:* Part-time. *Degree requirements:* For master's, comprehensive exam, thesis; for doctorate, comprehensive exam, thesis/dissertation. *Entrance requirements:* For master's and doctorate, GRE General Test or EIT Exam. Additional exam requirements/recommendations for international students: Required—TOEFL (minimum score 540 paper-based; 76 iBT), IELTS (minimum score 5). *Faculty research:* Structures, transportation, environmental engineering, geotechnical engineering, construction.

University of Houston, Cullen College of Engineering, Department of Civil and Environmental Engineering, Houston, TX 77204. Offers civil engineering (MCE, PhD). *Program availability:* Part-time. Terminal master's awarded for partial completion of doctoral program. *Entrance requirements:* For master's and doctorate, GRE General Test. Additional exam requirements/recommendations for international students: Required—TOEFL (minimum score 550 paper-based; 79 iBT), IELTS (minimum score 6.5). Electronic applications accepted. *Faculty research:* Civil engineering.

University of Idaho, College of Graduate Studies, College of Engineering, Department of Civil Engineering, Moscow, ID 83844. Offers civil engineering (M Engr, MS, PhD); engineering management (M Engr); geological engineering (MS). *Faculty:* 17 full-time, 3 part-time/adjunct. *Students:* 19 full-time, 64 part-time. Average age 34. In 2016, 31 master's, 2 doctorates awarded. *Entrance requirements:* For master's and doctorate, minimum GPA of 3.0. Additional exam requirements/recommendations for international students: Required—TOEFL. *Application deadline:* For fall admission, 8/1 for domestic students; for spring admission, 12/15 for domestic students. Applications are processed on a rolling basis. Application fee: $60. Electronic applications accepted. *Expenses:* Tuition, state resident: full-time $6460; part-time $414 per credit hour. Tuition, nonresident: full-time $21,268; part-time $1237 per credit hour. *Required fees:* $2070; $60 per credit hour. Full-time tuition and fees vary according to course load and reciprocity agreements. *Financial support:* Fellowships, research assistantships, teaching assistantships, and career-related internships or fieldwork available. Financial award applicants required to submit FAFSA. *Unit head:* Patricia Colberg, Department Chair, 208-885-6782, E-mail: civilengr@uidaho.edu. *Application contact:* Sean Scoggin, Graduate Recruitment Coordinator, 208-885-4001, Fax: 208-885-4406, E-mail: graduateadmissions@uidaho.edu.
Website: http://www.uidaho.edu/engr/ce/

University of Illinois at Chicago, College of Engineering, Department of Civil and Materials Engineering, Chicago, IL 60607-7128. Offers MS, PhD. *Program availability:*

Evening/weekend. *Degree requirements:* For master's, thesis (for some programs); for doctorate, thesis/dissertation, preliminary and qualifying exams. *Entrance requirements:* For master's and doctorate, GRE General Test, minimum GPA of 3.0. Additional exam requirements/recommendations for international students: Required—TOEFL. Electronic applications accepted. *Expenses:* Contact institution. *Faculty research:* Integrated fiber optic, acoustic emission and MEMS-based sensors development; monitoring the state of repaired and strengthened structures; development of weigh-in-motion (WIM) systems; image processing techniques for characterization of concrete entrained air bubble systems.

University of Illinois at Urbana–Champaign, Graduate College, College of Engineering, Department of Civil and Environmental Engineering, Champaign, IL 61820. Offers civil engineering (MS, PhD); environmental engineering in civil engineering (MS, PhD); M Arch/MS; MBA/MS. *Program availability:* Part-time, evening/weekend, online learning.

The University of Iowa, Graduate College, College of Engineering, Department of Civil and Environmental Engineering, Iowa City, IA 52242-1316. Offers MS, PhD. *Program availability:* Part-time. *Faculty:* 22 full-time (2 women), 5 part-time/adjunct (0 women). *Students:* 55 full-time (17 women), 12 part-time (5 women); includes 3 minority (1 Black or African American, non-Hispanic/Latino; 1 Asian, non-Hispanic/Latino; 1 Two or more races, non-Hispanic/Latino), 30 international. Average age 27. 191 applicants, 20% accepted, 22 enrolled. In 2016, 22 master's, 7 doctorates awarded. Terminal master's awarded for partial completion of doctoral program. *Degree requirements:* For master's, thesis optional, exam; for doctorate, comprehensive exam, thesis/dissertation, exam. *Entrance requirements:* For master's, GRE (minimum combined score of 301 on verbal and quantitative), minimum undergraduate GPA of 3.0; for doctorate, GRE (minimum combined score of 301 on verbal and quantitative), minimum graduate GPA of 3.0. Additional exam requirements/recommendations for international students: Required—TOEFL (minimum score 550 paper-based; 81 iBT), IELTS (minimum score 7). *Application deadline:* For fall admission, 1/15 priority date for domestic and international students; for spring admission, 12/1 for domestic students, 10/1 for international students; for summer admission, 4/15 for domestic students, 3/1 for international students. Applications are processed on a rolling basis. Application fee: $60 ($100 for international students). Electronic applications accepted. *Financial support:* In 2016–17, 64 students received support, including 8 fellowships with partial tuition reimbursements available (averaging $25,500 per year), 50 research assistantships with partial tuition reimbursements available (averaging $22,981 per year), 6 teaching assistantships with partial tuition reimbursements available (averaging $18,809 per year); career-related internships or fieldwork, Federal Work-Study, scholarships/grants, traineeships, and unspecified assistantships also available. Support available to part-time students. Financial award application deadline: 1/15; financial award applicants required to submit FAFSA. *Faculty research:* Water resources; environmental engineering and science; hydraulics and hydrology; structures, mechanics, and materials; transportation engineering. *Total annual research expenditures:* $16.8 million. *Unit head:* Dr. Michelle Scherer, Department Executive Officer, 319-335-5654, Fax: 319-335-5660, E-mail: michelle-scherer@uiowa.edu. *Application contact:* Kim Lebeck, Academic Program Specialist, 319-335-5647, Fax: 319-335-5660, E-mail: cee@engineering.uiowa.edu.
Website: https://cee.engineering.uiowa.edu

The University of Kansas, Graduate Studies, School of Engineering, Program in Civil Engineering, Lawrence, KS 66045. Offers MCE, MS, PhD. *Program availability:* Part-time, evening/weekend. *Students:* 81 full-time (20 women), 45 part-time (11 women); includes 3 minority (2 Asian, non-Hispanic/Latino; 1 Hispanic/Latino), 75 international. Average age 28. 107 applicants, 65% accepted, 24 enrolled. In 2016, 23 master's, 8 doctorates awarded. *Entrance requirements:* For master's and doctorate, GRE, BS in engineering, two letters of recommendation, statement of purpose. Additional exam requirements/recommendations for international students: Required—TOEFL or IELTS. *Application deadline:* For fall admission, 12/15 priority date for domestic and international students; for spring admission, 9/15 priority date for domestic and international students. Application fee: $65 ($85 for international students). Electronic applications accepted. *Financial support:* Fellowships, research assistantships, teaching assistantships, and career-related internships or fieldwork available. Financial award application deadline: 12/15. *Faculty research:* Structural engineering, geotechnical engineering, transportation engineering, water resources engineering, construction engineering. *Unit head:* David Darwin, Chair, 785-864-3827, E-mail: daved@ku.edu. *Application contact:* Graduate Secretary, 785-864-3826, E-mail: s523s307@ku.edu.
Website: http://www.ceae.ku.edu/

University of Kentucky, Graduate School, College of Engineering, Program in Civil Engineering, Lexington, KY 40506-0032. Offers MSCE, PhD. *Degree requirements:* For master's, comprehensive exam, thesis optional; for doctorate, comprehensive exam, thesis/dissertation. *Entrance requirements:* For master's, GRE General Test, minimum undergraduate GPA of 2.75; for doctorate, GRE General Test, minimum undergraduate GPA of 3.0. Additional exam requirements/recommendations for international students: Required—TOEFL (minimum score 550 paper-based). Electronic applications accepted. *Faculty research:* Geotechnical engineering, structures, construction engineering and management, environmental engineering and water resources, transportation and materials.

University of Louisiana at Lafayette, College of Engineering, Department of Civil Engineering, Lafayette, LA 70504. Offers MSE. *Program availability:* Evening/weekend. *Degree requirements:* For master's, comprehensive exam, thesis or alternative. *Entrance requirements:* For master's, GRE General Test, BS in civil engineering, minimum GPA of 2.85. *Faculty research:* Structural mechanics, computer-aided design, environmental engineering.

University of Louisville, J. B. Speed School of Engineering, Department of Civil and Environmental Engineering, Louisville, KY 40292-0001. Offers civil engineering (M Eng, MS, PhD). *Accreditation:* ABET (one or more programs are accredited). *Program availability:* Blended/hybrid learning. *Faculty:* 10 full-time (1 woman), 2 part-time/adjunct (1 woman). *Students:* 32 full-time (7 women), 14 part-time (0 women); includes 3 minority (1 Asian, non-Hispanic/Latino; 2 Two or more races, non-Hispanic/Latino), 16 international. Average age 27. 31 applicants, 35% accepted, 8 enrolled. In 2016, 15 master's, 1 other advanced degree awarded. *Degree requirements:* For master's, thesis optional, minimum GPA of 3.0; for doctorate, comprehensive exam, thesis/dissertation, minimum GPA of 3.0. *Entrance requirements:* For master's and doctorate, GRE, letters of recommendation, final official transcripts; for Graduate Certificate, pursuit of graduate degree (M Eng, MS, PhD) at J.B. Speed School of Engineering; undergraduate degree. Additional exam requirements/recommendations for international students: Required—TOEFL (minimum score 550 paper-based, 80 iBT) or IELTS (6.5). *Application deadline:* For fall admission, 5/1 priority date for international students; for spring admission, 11/1 priority date for international students; for summer admission, 3/1 priority date for international students. Applications are processed on a rolling basis. Application fee: $60. Electronic applications accepted. *Expenses:* Tuition, state resident: full-time $12,246; part-time $681 per credit hour. Tuition, nonresident: full-time $25,486; part-time $1417 per credit hour. *Required fees:* $196. Tuition and fees vary according to program and reciprocity agreements. *Financial support:* In 2016–17, 2 fellowships with full tuition reimbursements (averaging $22,000 per year) were awarded; research assistantships with full tuition reimbursements, teaching assistantships with full tuition reimbursements, scholarships/grants, and health care benefits also available. Financial award application deadline: 1/1. *Faculty research:* Structures, hydraulics, transportation, environmental engineering, geomechanics. *Total annual research expenditures:* $648,296. *Unit head:* Dr. J. P. Mohsen, Chair, 502-852-4596, Fax: 502-852-8851, E-mail: jpm@louisville.edu. *Application contact:* Dr. Zhihui Sun, Director of Graduate Studies, 502-852-4583, Fax: 502-852-7294, E-mail: z.sun@louisville.edu.
Website: http://louisville.edu/speed/civil/

University of Maine, Graduate School, College of Engineering, Department of Civil and Environmental Engineering, Orono, ME 04469. Offers MS, PSM, PhD. *Faculty:* 12 full-time (4 women), 5 part-time/adjunct (1 woman). *Students:* 31 full-time (9 women), 8 part-time (2 women); includes 4 minority (1 Black or African American, non-Hispanic/Latino; 1 American Indian or Alaska Native, non-Hispanic/Latino; 1 Asian, non-Hispanic/Latino; 1 Hispanic/Latino), 16 international. Average age 32. 29 applicants, 76% accepted, 6 enrolled. In 2016, 12 master's, 1 doctorate awarded. Terminal master's awarded for partial completion of doctoral program. *Degree requirements:* For master's, thesis (for some programs); for doctorate, comprehensive exam, thesis/dissertation. *Entrance requirements:* For master's and doctorate, GRE General Test. Additional exam requirements/recommendations for international students: Required—TOEFL (minimum score 80 iBT), IELTS (minimum score 6.5). *Application deadline:* For fall admission, 2/1 priority date for domestic and international students. Applications are processed on a rolling basis. Application fee: $65. Electronic applications accepted. *Expenses:* Tuition, state resident: full-time $7524; part-time $2508 per credit. Tuition, nonresident: full-time $24,498; part-time $8166 per credit. *Required fees:* $1148; $571 per credit. *Financial support:* In 2016–17, 19 students received support, including 2 fellowships (averaging $27,700 per year), 7 research assistantships with full tuition reimbursements available (averaging $19,100 per year), 7 teaching assistantships with full tuition reimbursements available (averaging $14,600 per year); Federal Work-Study, institutionally sponsored loans, scholarships/grants, and tuition waivers (full and partial) also available. Financial award application deadline: 3/1. *Faculty research:* Offshore geotechnics; structures and mechanics; water quality and treatment processes; water resources including effects of climate change; ocean energy generation and aquaculture. *Total annual research expenditures:* $4 million. *Unit head:* Dr. Bill Davids, Chair, 207-581-2170, E-mail: william.davids@umit.maine.edu. *Application contact:* Scott G. Delcourt, Assistant Vice President for Graduate Studies and Senior Associate Dean, 207-581-3291, Fax: 207-581-3232, E-mail: graduate@maine.edu.
Website: http://www.civil.umaine.edu/

The University of Manchester, School of Mechanical, Aerospace and Civil Engineering, Manchester, United Kingdom. Offers advanced manufacturing technology (M Ent); aerospace engineering (M Phil, M Sc, PhD); civil engineering (M Phil, M Sc, PhD); environmental engineering (M Phil, PhD); management of projects (M Phil, M Sc, PhD); mechanical engineering (M Phil, M Sc, PhD); mechanical engineering design (M Ent); nuclear engineering (M Phil, D Eng, PhD).

University of Manitoba, Faculty of Graduate Studies, Faculty of Engineering, Department of Civil Engineering, Winnipeg, MB R3T 2N2, Canada. Offers M Eng, M Sc, PhD. *Degree requirements:* For master's, thesis.

University of Maryland, College Park, Academic Affairs, A. James Clark School of Engineering, Department of Civil and Environmental Engineering, College Park, MD 20742. Offers M Eng, MS, PhD. *Program availability:* Part-time, evening/weekend, online learning. *Degree requirements:* For master's, thesis optional; for doctorate, thesis/dissertation, qualifying exam. *Entrance requirements:* For master's and doctorate, GRE General Test, 3 letters of recommendation. Electronic applications accepted. *Faculty research:* Transportation and urban systems, environmental engineering, geotechnical engineering, construction engineering and management, hydraulics.

University of Massachusetts Amherst, Graduate School, College of Engineering, Department of Civil and Environmental Engineering, Amherst, MA 01003. Offers civil engineering (MSCE, PhD); environmental and water resources engineering (MSCE); geotechnical engineering (MSCE); structural engineering and mechanics (MSCE); transportation engineering (MSCE). *Program availability:* Part-time. Terminal master's awarded for partial completion of doctoral program. *Degree requirements:* For master's, thesis or alternative; for doctorate, comprehensive exam, thesis/dissertation. *Entrance requirements:* For master's and doctorate, GRE General Test. Additional exam requirements/recommendations for international students: Required—TOEFL (minimum score 550 paper-based; 80 iBT), IELTS (minimum score 6.5). Electronic applications accepted.

University of Massachusetts Amherst, Graduate School, Interdisciplinary Programs, Dual Degree Programs in Management and Engineering, Amherst, MA 01003. Offers MBA/MIE, MBA/MSEWRE, MSCE/MBA, MSME/MBA. *Program availability:* Part-time. *Entrance requirements:* Additional exam requirements/recommendations for international students: Required—TOEFL (minimum score 600 paper-based; 100 iBT), IELTS (minimum score 7). Electronic applications accepted.

University of Massachusetts Dartmouth, Graduate School, College of Engineering, Department of Civil and Environmental Engineering, North Dartmouth, MA 02747-2300. Offers civil engineering (MS). *Program availability:* Part-time. *Faculty:* 9 full-time (2 women), 2 part-time/adjunct (0 women). *Students:* 5 full-time (1 woman), 4 part-time (1 woman), 5 international. Average age 26. 23 applicants, 83% accepted, 5 enrolled. In 2016, 5 master's awarded. *Degree requirements:* For master's, thesis or project. *Entrance requirements:* For master's, GRE (UMass Dartmouth civil engineering bachelor's degree recipients are exempt), statement of purpose (minimum of 300 words), resume, 3 letters of recommendation, official transcripts. Additional exam requirements/recommendations for international students: Required—TOEFL (minimum score 550 paper-based; 80 iBT). *Application deadline:* For fall admission, 2/15 priority date for domestic students, 1/15 priority date for international students. Application fee: $60. Electronic applications accepted. *Expenses:* Tuition, state resident: full-time $14,994; part-time $624.75 per credit. Tuition, nonresident: full-time $27,068; part-time $1127.83 per credit. *Required fees:* $405; $25.88 per credit. Tuition and fees vary according to course load and reciprocity agreements. *Financial support:* In 2016–17, 7 research assistantships (averaging $5,696 per year), 1 teaching assistantship (averaging $7,500 per year) were awarded; institutionally sponsored loans and scholarships/grants also available. Support available to part-time students. Financial award application deadline: 3/1; financial award applicants required to submit FAFSA. *Faculty research:* Water/wastewater treatment systems, highway sustainability, structural analysis, cold-region engineering, surface treatments and overlays, development of PMA Asphalt mixtures, intersection of computational mechanics and applied probability and statistics. *Total annual research expenditures:* $1.8 million. *Unit head:* Mazdak Tootkaboni, Graduate Program Director, Civil and Environmental Engineering, 508-999-8465, Fax: 508-999-8964, E-mail: mtootkaboni@umassd.edu. *Application contact:* Steven Briggs, Director of Marketing and Recruitment for Graduate Studies, 508-999-8604, Fax: 508-999-8183, E-mail: graduate@umassd.edu.
Website: http://www.umassd.edu/engineering/cen/graduate

University of Massachusetts Lowell, Francis College of Engineering, Department of Civil and Environmental Engineering, Lowell, MA 01854. Offers environmental studies (PhD). *Program availability:* Part-time. *Degree requirements:* For master's, thesis optional. *Entrance requirements:* For master's, GRE General Test. *Faculty research:* Bridge design, traffic control, groundwater remediation, pile capacity.

University of Memphis, Graduate School, Herff College of Engineering, Department of Civil Engineering, Memphis, TN 38152. Offers civil engineering (PhD); engineering seismology (MS); environmental engineering (MS); freight transportation (Graduate Certificate); geotechnical engineering (MS); structural engineering (MS); transportation engineering (MS); water resources engineering (MS). *Faculty:* 12 full-time (1 woman). *Students:* 10 full-time (3 women), 15 part-time (3 women); includes 3 minority (2 Black or African American, non-Hispanic/Latino; 1 Two or more races, non-Hispanic/Latino), 9 international. Average age 29. 29 applicants, 69% accepted, 8 enrolled. In 2016, 5 master's awarded. Terminal master's awarded for partial completion of doctoral program. *Degree requirements:* For master's, comprehensive exam, thesis optional; for doctorate, comprehensive exam, thesis/dissertation. *Entrance requirements:* For master's, GRE General Test, minimum undergraduate GPA of 2.5; bachelor's degree in engineering or a related science or mathematics program; three letters of reference; for doctorate, GRE General Test, bachelor's degree in engineering or engineering science; three letters of reference; for Graduate Certificate, minimum undergraduate GPA of 2.75; bachelor's degree in engineering or engineering science. Additional exam requirements/recommendations for international students: Required—TOEFL (minimum score 550 paper-based; 79 iBT). *Application deadline:* For fall admission, 8/1 for domestic students; for spring admission, 12/1 for domestic students. Application fee: $35 ($60 for international students). Electronic applications accepted. *Expenses:* $5,231.50 per semester full-time in-state, $9,623.50 full-time out-of-state. *Financial support:* In 2016–17, 6 students received support, including 31 fellowships with full tuition reimbursements available (averaging $12,012 per year); research assistantships with full tuition reimbursements available, career-related internships or fieldwork, Federal Work-Study, scholarships/grants, and unspecified assistantships also available. Financial award application deadline: 2/1; financial award applicants required to submit FAFSA. *Faculty research:* Structural response to earthquakes, pavement design, water quality, transportation safety, intermodal transportation. *Unit head:* Dr. Sharam Pezeshk, Chair, 901-678-2746, Fax: 901-678-3026. *Application contact:* Dr. Roger Meier, Coordinator of Graduate Studies, 901-678-3284, E-mail: rwmeier@memphis.edu.
Website: http://www.ce.memphis.edu

University of Miami, Graduate School, College of Engineering, Department of Civil, Architectural, and Environmental Engineering, Coral Gables, FL 33124. Offers architectural engineering (MSAE); civil engineering (MSCE, PhD). *Program availability:* Part-time. Terminal master's awarded for partial completion of doctoral program. *Degree requirements:* For master's, thesis (for some programs); for doctorate, comprehensive exam, thesis/dissertation. *Entrance requirements:* For master's, GRE General Test (minimum score 1000 verbal and quantitative), minimum GPA of 3.0; for doctorate, GRE General Test, minimum GPA of 3.5 in preceding degree. Additional exam requirements/recommendations for international students: Required—TOEFL (minimum score 550 paper-based). Electronic applications accepted. *Faculty research:* Structural assessment and wind engineering, sustainable construction and materials, moisture transport and management, wastewater and waste engineering, water management and risk analysis.

University of Michigan, College of Engineering, Department of Civil and Environmental Engineering, Ann Arbor, MI 48109. Offers civil engineering (MSE, PhD, CE); construction engineering and management (M Eng, MSE); environmental engineering (MSE, PhD); structural engineering (M Eng); MBA/MSE. *Program availability:* Part-time. *Students:* 177 full-time (77 women), 3 part-time. 775 applicants, 42% accepted, 62 enrolled. In 2016, 57 master's, 9 doctorates awarded. *Degree requirements:* For master's, thesis optional; for doctorate, comprehensive exam, thesis/dissertation, oral defense of dissertation, preliminary and written exams. *Entrance requirements:* For master's and doctorate, GRE General Test. Additional exam requirements/recommendations for international students: Required—TOEFL. *Application deadline:* Applications are processed on a rolling basis. Electronic applications accepted. *Expenses:* Tuition, state resident: full-time $21,466; part-time $1152 per credit hour. Tuition, nonresident: full-time $43,346; part-time $2367 per credit hour. Part-time tuition and fees vary according to course load, degree level and program. *Financial support:* Fellowships, research assistantships, teaching assistantships, institutionally sponsored loans, and tuition waivers (partial) available. *Faculty research:* Construction engineering and management, geotechnical engineering, earthquake-resistant design of structures, environmental chemistry and microbiology, cost engineering, environmental and water resources engineering. *Total annual research expenditures:* $15.7 million. *Unit head:* Kim Hayes, Department Chair, 734-764-8495, Fax: 734-764-4292, E-mail: ford@umich.edu. *Application contact:* Jessica Randolph, Graduate Coordinator, 734-764-8405, Fax: 734-764-4292, E-mail: jrand@umich.edu.
Website: http://cee.engin.umich.edu/

University of Michigan, College of Engineering, Department of Naval Architecture and Marine Engineering, Ann Arbor, MI 48109. Offers MS, MSE, PhD, Mar Eng, Nav Arch, MBA/MSE. *Program availability:* Part-time. *Students:* 85 full-time (19 women), 5 part-time (0 women). 122 applicants, 46% accepted, 33 enrolled. In 2016, 44 master's, 7 doctorates awarded. Terminal master's awarded for partial completion of doctoral program. *Degree requirements:* For master's, thesis (for some programs); for doctorate, comprehensive exam, thesis/dissertation, oral defense of dissertation, written and oral preliminary exams; for other advanced degree, comprehensive exam, thesis, oral defense of thesis. *Entrance requirements:* For doctorate, GRE General Test, master's degree; for other advanced degree, GRE General Test. Additional exam requirements/recommendations for international students: Required—TOEFL. *Application deadline:* Applications are processed on a rolling basis. Electronic applications accepted. *Expenses:* Tuition, state resident: full-time $21,466; part-time $1152 per credit hour. Tuition, nonresident: full-time $43,346; part-time $2367 per credit hour. Part-time tuition and fees vary according to course load, degree level and program. *Financial support:* Fellowships, research assistantships, teaching assistantships, career-related internships or fieldwork, Federal Work-Study, institutionally sponsored loans, scholarships/grants, and unspecified assistantships available. *Faculty research:* System and structural reliability, design and analysis of offshore structures and vehicles, marine systems design, remote sensing of ship wakes and sea surfaces, marine hydrodynamics, nonlinear seakeeping analysis. *Total annual research expenditures:* $11 million. *Unit head:* Jing Sun, Department Chair, 734-615-8061, E-mail: jingsun@umich.edu. *Application contact:* Nathalie Fiveland, Graduate Program Coordinator, 734-936-0566, Fax: 734-936-8820, E-mail: fiveland@umich.edu.
Website: http://www.engin.umich.edu/name

University of Minnesota, Twin Cities Campus, College of Science and Engineering, Department of Civil, Environmental, and Geo-Engineering, Minneapolis, MN 55455-0213. Offers civil engineering (MCE, MS, PhD); geological engineering (M Geo E, MS); stream restoration science and engineering (Certificate). *Program availability:* Part-time. *Degree requirements:* For master's, thesis optional; for doctorate, thesis/dissertation. *Entrance requirements:* For master's and doctorate, GRE General Test. Additional exam requirements/recommendations for international students: Required—TOEFL. Electronic applications accepted. *Faculty research:* Environmental engineering, geomechanics, structural engineering, transportation, water resources.

University of Missouri, Office of Research and Graduate Studies, College of Engineering, Department of Civil and Environmental Engineering, Columbia, MO 65211. Offers civil engineering (MS, PhD); environmental engineering (MS, PhD); geotechnical engineering (MS, PhD); structural engineering (MS, PhD); transportation and highway engineering (MS); water resources (MS, PhD). *Faculty:* 16 full-time (3 women), 2 part-time/adjunct (1 woman). *Students:* 41 full-time (8 women), 30 part-time (8 women). *Degree requirements:* For master's, report or thesis; for doctorate, thesis/dissertation. *Entrance requirements:* For master's and doctorate, GRE General Test. Additional exam requirements/recommendations for international students: Required—TOEFL (minimum score 550 paper-based; 80 iBT). *Application deadline:* For fall admission, 2/15 priority date for domestic students, 2/15 for international students; for winter admission, 9/15 priority date for domestic students, 9/15 for international students. Application fee: $75 ($90 for international students). *Expenses:* Tuition, state resident: full-time $6347; part-time $352.60 per credit hour. Tuition, nonresident: full-time $17,379; part-time $965.50 per credit hour. *Required fees:* $1035. Tuition and fees vary according to course load, campus/location and program. *Financial support:* Fellowships, research assistantships, teaching assistantships, and institutionally sponsored loans available.
Website: http://engineering.missouri.edu/civil/

University of Missouri–Kansas City, School of Computing and Engineering, Kansas City, MO 64110-2499. Offers civil engineering (MS); computer and electrical engineering (PhD); computer science (MS), including bioinformatics, software engineering, telecommunications networking; computer science and informatics (PhD); computing (PhD); electrical engineering (MS); engineering (PhD); engineering and construction management (Graduate Certificate); mechanical engineering (MS); telecommunications and computer networking (PhD). PhD (interdisciplinary) offered through the School of Graduate Studies. *Program availability:* Part-time. *Faculty:* 45 full-time (6 women), 26 part-time/adjunct (4 women). *Students:* 473 full-time (155 women), 207 part-time (42 women); includes 24 minority (10 Black or African American, non-Hispanic/Latino; 10 Asian, non-Hispanic/Latino; 4 Hispanic/Latino), 581 international. Average age 25. 1,143 applicants, 44% accepted, 227 enrolled. In 2016, 446 master's, 2 other advanced degrees awarded. *Degree requirements:* For doctorate, thesis/dissertation. *Entrance requirements:* For master's, GRE General Test, minimum GPA of 3.0, 3 letters of recommendation from professors; for doctorate, GRE General Test, minimum GPA of 3.5. Additional exam requirements/recommendations for international students: Required—TOEFL (minimum score 550 paper-based; 80 iBT). *Application deadline:* For fall admission, 1/15 priority date for domestic students, 1/15 for international students. Applications are processed on a rolling basis. Application fee: $45 ($50 for international students). *Financial support:* In 2016–17, 37 research assistantships with partial tuition reimbursements (averaging $15,679 per year), 47 teaching assistantships with partial tuition reimbursements (averaging $16,830 per year) were awarded; career-related internships or fieldwork, Federal Work-Study, scholarships/grants, tuition waivers (partial), and unspecified assistantships also available. Support available to part-time students. Financial award application deadline: 3/1; financial award applicants required to submit FAFSA. *Faculty research:* Algorithms, bioinformatics and medical informatics, biomechanics/biomaterials, civil engineering materials, networking and telecommunications, thermal science. *Unit head:* Dr. Kevin Z. Truman, Dean, 816-235-2399, Fax: 816-235-5159. *Application contact:* 816-235-2399, Fax: 816-235-5159.
Website: http://sce.umkc.edu/

University of Nebraska–Lincoln, Graduate College, College of Engineering, Department of Civil Engineering, Lincoln, NE 68588. Offers MS, PhD. *Degree requirements:* For master's, thesis optional; for doctorate, comprehensive exam, thesis/dissertation. *Entrance requirements:* For master's and doctorate, GRE General Test. Additional exam requirements/recommendations for international students: Required—TOEFL (minimum score 550 paper-based). Electronic applications accepted. *Faculty research:* Water resources engineering, sediment transport, steel bridge systems, highway safety.

University of Nevada, Las Vegas, Graduate College, Howard R. Hughes College of Engineering, Department of Civil and Environmental Engineering and Construction, Las Vegas, NV 89154-4015. Offers civil and environmental engineering (PhD); transportation (MS). *Program availability:* Part-time. *Faculty:* 10 full-time (1 woman). *Students:* 34 full-time (8 women), 29 part-time (10 women); includes 12 minority (1 Black or African American, non-Hispanic/Latino; 7 Asian, non-Hispanic/Latino; 2 Hispanic/Latino; 2 Two or more races, non-Hispanic/Latino), 34 international. Average age 31. 41 applicants, 68% accepted, 13 enrolled. In 2016, 12 master's, 7 doctorates awarded. *Degree requirements:* For master's, thesis (for some programs); for doctorate, comprehensive exam, thesis/dissertation, preliminary exam. *Entrance requirements:* For master's, GRE General Test, bachelor's degree with minimum GPA of 3.0; statement of purpose; letter of recommendation; for doctorate, GRE General Test, master's degree; statement of purpose; 3 letters of recommendation. Additional exam requirements/recommendations for international students: Required—TOEFL (minimum score 550 paper-based; 80 iBT), IELTS (minimum score 7). *Application deadline:* For fall admission, 6/15 for domestic students, 3/15 for international students; for spring admission, 11/15 for domestic students, 8/30 for international students. Application fee: $60 ($95 for international students). Electronic applications accepted. *Expenses:* $269.25 per credit, $792 per 3-credit course; $9,634 per year resident; $23,274 per year non-resident; $7,094 fees non-resident (7 credits or more); $1,307 annual health insurance fee. *Financial support:* In 2016–17, 1 fellowship with partial tuition reimbursement (averaging $20,000 per year), 14 research assistantships with partial tuition reimbursements (averaging $14,616 per year), 24 teaching assistantships with partial tuition reimbursements (averaging $14,956 per year) were awarded; institutionally sponsored loans, scholarships/grants, health care benefits, and unspecified assistantships also available. Financial award application deadline: 3/15. *Faculty research:* Sustainable construction, construction safety, infrastructure project performance, construction education, construction performance improvement. *Total annual research expenditures:* $1.2 million. *Unit head:* Dr. Donald Hayes, Chair/Professor, 702-895-4723, Fax: 702-895-3936, E-mail: donald.hayes@unlv.edu. *Application contact:* Dr. Nader Ghafoori, Graduate Coordinator, 702-895-2531, Fax: 702-895-3936, E-mail: nader.ghafoori@unlv.edu.
Website: http://www.unlv.edu/ceec

University of Nevada, Reno, Graduate School, College of Engineering, Department of Civil and Environmental Engineering, Reno, NV 89557. Offers MS, PhD. Terminal master's awarded for partial completion of doctoral program. *Degree requirements:* For master's, thesis optional; for doctorate, thesis/dissertation. *Entrance requirements:* For master's, GRE General Test, minimum GPA of 3.0; for doctorate, GRE General Test, minimum GPA of 3.25. Additional exam requirements/recommendations for international students: Required—TOEFL (minimum score 500 paper-based; 61 iBT), IELTS (minimum score 6). Electronic applications accepted. *Faculty research:* Structural and earthquake engineering, geotechnical engineering, environmental engineering, transportation, pavements/materials.

Civil Engineering

University of New Brunswick Fredericton, School of Graduate Studies, Faculty of Engineering, Department of Civil Engineering, Fredericton, NB E3B 5A3, Canada. Offers construction engineering and management (M Eng, M Sc E, PhD); environmental engineering (M Eng, M Sc E, PhD); environmental studies (M Eng); geotechnical engineering (M Eng, M Sc E, PhD); groundwater/hydrology (M Eng, M Sc E, PhD); materials (M Eng, M Sc E, PhD); pavements (M Eng, M Sc E, PhD); structures (M Eng, M Sc E, PhD); transportation (M Eng, M Sc E, PhD). *Program availability:* Part-time. *Degree requirements:* For master's, thesis; for doctorate, comprehensive exam, thesis/dissertation, qualifying exam; 27 credit hours of courses. *Entrance requirements:* For master's, minimum GPA of 3.0; B Sc E in civil engineering or related engineering degree; for doctorate, minimum GPA of 3.0; graduate degree in engineering or applied science. Additional exam requirements/recommendations for international students: Required—IELTS (minimum score 7.5), TWE (minimum score 4), Michigan English Language Assessment Battery (minimum score 85) or CanTest (minimum score 4.5); Recommended—TOEFL (minimum score 580 paper-based). Electronic applications accepted. *Faculty research:* Construction engineering and management; engineering materials and infrastructure renewal; highway and pavement research; structures and solid mechanics; geotechnical and geoenvironmental engineering; structure interaction; transportation and planning; environment, solid waste management; structural engineering; water and environmental engineering.

University of New Hampshire, Graduate School, College of Engineering and Physical Sciences, Department of Civil and Environmental Engineering, Durham, NH 03824. Offers M Engr, MS, PhD. *Program availability:* Part-time. *Degree requirements:* For master's, thesis or alternative; for doctorate, thesis/dissertation. *Entrance requirements:* For master's and doctorate, GRE. Additional exam requirements/recommendations for international students: Required—TOEFL (minimum score 550 paper-based; 80 iBT). Electronic applications accepted. *Faculty research:* Environmental, structural materials, geotechnical engineering, water resources, systems analysis.

University of New Mexico, Graduate Studies, School of Engineering, Program in Civil Engineering, Albuquerque, NM 87131-0001. Offers civil engineering (M Eng, MSCE); construction management (MCM); engineering (PhD). *Program availability:* Part-time. *Faculty:* 17 full-time (3 women), 2 part-time/adjunct (1 woman). *Students:* 23 full-time (5 women), 35 part-time (14 women); includes 18 minority (2 American Indian or Alaska Native, non-Hispanic/Latino; 1 Asian, non-Hispanic/Latino; 12 Hispanic/Latino; 3 Two or more races, non-Hispanic/Latino), 17 international. Average age 32. 55 applicants, 31% accepted, 16 enrolled. In 2016, 20 master's, 4 doctorates awarded. Terminal master's awarded for partial completion of doctoral program. *Degree requirements:* For master's, comprehensive exam, thesis (for some programs); for doctorate, comprehensive exam, thesis/dissertation. *Entrance requirements:* For master's, GRE General Test (for MSCE and M Eng); GRE or GMAT (for MCM), minimum GPA of 3.0; for doctorate, GRE General Test, minimum GPA of 3.0. Additional exam requirements/recommendations for international students: Required—TOEFL (minimum score 550 paper-based; 80 iBT), IELTS (minimum score 6.5). *Application deadline:* For fall admission, 7/15 for domestic students, 3/1 for international students; for spring admission, 11/10 for domestic students, 8/1 for international students. Applications are processed on a rolling basis. Application fee: $50. Electronic applications accepted. *Financial support:* Research assistantships with tuition reimbursements, teaching assistantships with tuition reimbursements, scholarships/grants, health care benefits, and unspecified assistantships available. Support available to part-time students. Financial award application deadline: 3/1; financial award applicants required to submit FAFSA. *Faculty research:* Integrating design and construction, project delivery methods, sustainable design and construction, leadership and management in construction, project management and project supervision, production management and improvement. *Total annual research expenditures:* $4.2 million. *Unit head:* Dr. John C. Stormont, Chair, 505-277-2722, Fax: 505-277-1988, E-mail: jcstorm@unm.edu. *Application contact:* Missy Garoza, Professional Academic Advisor, 505-277-2722, Fax: 505-277-1988, E-mail: civil@unm.edu.
Website: http://civil.unm.edu

The University of North Carolina at Charlotte, William States Lee College of Engineering, Department of Civil and Environmental Engineering, Charlotte, NC 28223-0001. Offers civil engineering (MSCE); infrastructure and environmental systems (PhD), including infrastructure and environmental systems design. *Program availability:* Part-time, evening/weekend. *Faculty:* 24 full-time (4 women). *Students:* 56 full-time (16 women), 37 part-time (14 women); includes 13 minority (4 Black or African American, non-Hispanic/Latino; 3 Asian, non-Hispanic/Latino; 6 Hispanic/Latino), 37 international. Average age 31. 110 applicants, 56% accepted, 18 enrolled. In 2016, 19 master's, 11 doctorates awarded. *Degree requirements:* For master's, comprehensive exam (for some programs), thesis, project, or comprehensive exam; for doctorate, comprehensive exam, thesis/dissertation. *Entrance requirements:* For master's, GRE, undergraduate degree in civil and environmental engineering or a closely-related field; minimum undergraduate GPA of 3.0; for doctorate, GRE General Test, equivalent to U.S. baccalaureate or master's degree from regionally-accredited college or university in engineering, earth science and geology, chemical and biological sciences or a related field with minimum undergraduate GPA of 3.2, graduate 3.5. Additional exam requirements/recommendations for international students: Required—TOEFL (minimum score 523 paper-based, 70 iBT) or IELTS (6.5). *Application deadline:* For fall admission, 3/1 priority date for domestic and international students; for spring admission, 10/1 priority date for domestic and international students; for summer admission, 4/1 priority date for domestic and international students. Applications are processed on a rolling basis. Application fee: $75. Electronic applications accepted. *Expenses:* Contact institution. *Financial support:* In 2016–17, 36 students received support, including 2 fellowships (averaging $30,183 per year), 22 research assistantships (averaging $12,465 per year), 12 teaching assistantships (averaging $4,856 per year); career-related internships or fieldwork, institutionally sponsored loans, scholarships/grants, and unspecified assistantships also available. Support available to part-time students. Financial award application deadline: 3/1; financial award applicants required to submit FAFSA. *Total annual research expenditures:* $2.9 million. *Unit head:* Dr. John L. Daniels, Chair, 704-687-1219, E-mail: jodaniel@uncc.edu. *Application contact:* Kathy B. Giddings, Director of Graduate Admissions, 704-687-5503, Fax: 704-687-1668, E-mail: gradadm@uncc.edu.
Website: http://cee.uncc.edu/

University of North Dakota, Graduate School, School of Engineering and Mines, Department of Civil Engineering, Grand Forks, ND 58202. Offers civil engineering (M Engr). *Program availability:* Part-time. *Degree requirements:* For master's, comprehensive exam, thesis or alternative. *Entrance requirements:* For master's, GRE General Test, minimum GPA of 2.5. Additional exam requirements/recommendations for international students: Required—TOEFL (minimum score 550 paper-based; 79 iBT), IELTS (minimum score 6.5). *Application deadline:* For fall admission, 8/1 priority date for domestic students, 5/1 for international students; for spring admission, 12/1 priority date for domestic students, 9/1 priority date for international students. Applications are processed on a rolling basis. Application fee: $35. Electronic applications accepted. *Financial support:* Fellowships with full and partial tuition reimbursements, research assistantships with full and partial tuition reimbursements, teaching assistantships with full and partial tuition reimbursements, career-related internships or fieldwork, Federal Work-Study, scholarships/grants, health care benefits, tuition waivers (full and partial), and unspecified assistantships available. Support available to part-time students. Financial award application deadline: 3/15; financial award applicants required to submit FAFSA. *Faculty research:* Soil-structures, environmental-water resources. *Unit head:* Dr. Sukhvarsh Jerath, Graduate Director, 701-777-3564, Fax: 701-777-4838, E-mail: sukhvarshjerath@mail.und.edu. *Application contact:* Staci Wells, Admissions Associate, 701-777-2945, Fax: 701-777-3619, E-mail: staci.wells@gradschool.und.edu.
Website: http://www.civilengineering.und.edu/

University of North Florida, College of Computing, Engineering, and Construction, School of Engineering, Jacksonville, FL 32224. Offers MSCE, MSEE, MSME. *Program availability:* Part-time. *Faculty:* 19 full-time (1 woman). *Students:* 15 full-time (4 women), 34 part-time (6 women); includes 10 minority (2 Asian, non-Hispanic/Latino; 5 Hispanic/Latino; 3 Two or more races, non-Hispanic/Latino), 13 international. Average age 28. 43 applicants, 63% accepted, 17 enrolled. In 2016, 14 master's awarded. *Application deadline:* For fall admission, 8/1 priority date for domestic students, 5/1 for international students; for spring admission, 12/1 priority date for domestic students, 10/1 for international students; for summer admission, 3/15 priority date for domestic students, 2/1 for international students. Application fee: $30. Tuition and fees vary according to course load, campus/location and program. *Financial support:* In 2016–17, 30 students received support, including 11 research assistantships (averaging $3,925 per year), 8 teaching assistantships (averaging $2,552 per year); Federal Work-Study, scholarships/grants, tuition waivers, and unspecified assistantships also available. Financial award application deadline: 4/1; financial award applicants required to submit FAFSA. *Total annual research expenditures:* $804,835. *Unit head:* Dr. Murat Tiryakioglu, Director, 904-620-1393, E-mail: m.tiryakioglu@unf.edu. *Application contact:* Dr. Amanda Pascale, Director, The Graduate School, 904-320-1360, Fax: 904-620-1362, E-mail: graduateschool@unf.edu.
Website: http://www.unf.edu/ccec/engineering/

University of Notre Dame, Graduate School, College of Engineering, Department of Civil Engineering and Geological Sciences, Notre Dame, IN 46556. Offers bioengineering (MS Bio E); civil engineering (MSCE); civil engineering and geological sciences (PhD); environmental engineering (MS Env E); geological sciences (MS). Terminal master's awarded for partial completion of doctoral program. *Degree requirements:* For master's, comprehensive exam; for doctorate, thesis/dissertation, candidacy exam. *Entrance requirements:* For master's and doctorate, GRE General Test. Additional exam requirements/recommendations for international students: Required—TOEFL (minimum score 600 paper-based; 80 iBT). Electronic applications accepted. *Faculty research:* Environmental modeling, biological-waste treatment, petrology, environmental geology, geochemistry.

University of Oklahoma, Gallogly College of Engineering, School of Civil Engineering and Environmental Science, Program in Civil Engineering, Norman, OK 73019. Offers MS, PhD. *Program availability:* Part-time. *Students:* 31 full-time (8 women), 8 part-time (1 woman); includes 6 minority (2 Hispanic/Latino; 4 Two or more races, non-Hispanic/Latino), 20 international. Average age 27. 48 applicants, 31% accepted, 11 enrolled. In 2016, 3 master's, 5 doctorates awarded. Terminal master's awarded for partial completion of doctoral program. *Degree requirements:* For master's, thesis; for doctorate, comprehensive exam, thesis/dissertation. *Entrance requirements:* For master's and doctorate, GRE. Additional exam requirements/recommendations for international students: Required—TOEFL (minimum score 79 iBT) or IELTS (minimum score 6.5). *Application deadline:* For fall admission, 1/15 for domestic and international students; for spring admission, 8/15 for domestic and international students. Application fee: $50 ($100 for international students). Electronic applications accepted. *Expenses:* Tuition, state resident: full-time $4886; part-time $203.60 per credit hour. Tuition, nonresident: full-time $18,989; part-time $791.20 per credit hour. *Required fees:* $3283; $126.25 per credit hour. $126.50 per semester. *Financial support:* In 2016–17, 38 students received support. Research assistantships, teaching assistantships, and scholarships/grants available. Financial award application deadline: 6/1; financial award applicants required to submit FAFSA. *Faculty research:* Intelligent structures, composites, earthquake engineering, intelligent compaction, bridge engineering. *Unit head:* Dr. Randall Kolar, Director, 405-325-4267, Fax: 405-325-4217, E-mail: kolar@ou.edu. *Application contact:* Susan Williams, Graduate Programs Assistant, 405-325-2344, Fax: 405-325-4217, E-mail: srwilliams@ou.edu.
Website: http://www.ou.edu/coe/cees.html

University of Ottawa, Faculty of Graduate and Postdoctoral Studies, Faculty of Engineering, Ottawa-Carleton Institute for Civil Engineering, Ottawa, ON K1N 6N5, Canada. Offers M Eng, MA Sc, PhD. PhD, M Eng, MA Sc offered jointly with Carleton University. *Degree requirements:* For master's, thesis or alternative; for doctorate, comprehensive exam, thesis/dissertation, seminar series. *Entrance requirements:* For master's, honors degree or equivalent, minimum B average; for doctorate, master's degree, minimum B+ average. Electronic applications accepted. *Faculty research:* Environmental engineering, geotechnical engineering, structural engineering, transportation engineering, water resources engineering.

University of Pittsburgh, Swanson School of Engineering, Department of Civil and Environmental Engineering, Pittsburgh, PA 15260. Offers MSCEE, PhD. *Program availability:* Part-time, 100% online. *Faculty:* 17 full-time (5 women), 23 part-time/adjunct (1 woman). *Students:* 103 full-time (36 women), 44 part-time (9 women); includes 11 minority (2 Black or African American, non-Hispanic/Latino; 5 Asian, non-Hispanic/Latino; 4 Hispanic/Latino), 85 international. 333 applicants, 63% accepted, 44 enrolled. In 2016, 37 master's, 7 doctorates awarded. Terminal master's awarded for partial completion of doctoral program. *Degree requirements:* For doctorate, comprehensive exam, thesis/dissertation, final oral exams. *Entrance requirements:* For master's and doctorate, minimum GPA of 3.0. Additional exam requirements/recommendations for international students: Required—TOEFL (minimum score 550 paper-based; 80 iBT). *Application deadline:* For fall admission, 3/1 priority date for domestic and international students; for spring admission, 7/1 priority date for domestic and international students. Applications are processed on a rolling basis. Application fee: $50. Electronic applications accepted. *Expenses:* $24,962 full-time per academic year in-state tuition; $41,222 full-time per academic year out-of-state tuition; $830 mandatory fees per academic year. *Financial support:* In 2016–17, 5 fellowships with full tuition reimbursements (averaging $30,720 per year), 28 research assistantships with full tuition reimbursements (averaging $27,396 per year), 19 teaching assistantships with full tuition reimbursements (averaging $26,328 per year) were awarded; scholarships/grants, traineeships, and tuition waivers (full) also available. Financial award application deadline: 3/1. *Faculty research:* Environmental and water resources, structures and infrastructures, construction management. *Total annual research expenditures:* $4.2 million. *Unit head:* Dr. Radisav D. Vidic, Chairman, 412-624-9870, Fax: 412-624-0135, E-mail: vidic@pitt.edu. *Application contact:* Rama Bazaz, Director, 412-624-9800, Fax: 412-624-9808, E-mail: ssoeadm@pitt.edu.
Website: http://www.engineering.pitt.edu/Departments/Civil-Environmental//

University of Portland, School of Engineering, Portland, OR 97203-5798. Offers biomedical engineering (MBME); civil engineering (ME); computer science (ME); electrical engineering (ME); mechanical engineering (ME). *Program availability:* Part-time, evening/weekend. *Degree requirements:* For master's, thesis optional. *Entrance requirements:* For master's, GRE General Test, minimum GPA of 3.0, 3 letters of recommendation, resume, statement of goals, official transcripts. Additional exam requirements/recommendations for international students: Required—TOEFL (minimum score 550 paper-based; 80 iBT), IELTS (minimum score 7). *Expenses:* Contact institution.

University of Puerto Rico, Mayagüez Campus, Graduate Studies, College of Engineering, Department of Civil Engineering and Surveying, Mayagüez, PR 00681-9000. Offers civil engineering (ME, MS, PhD), including construction engineering and management (ME, MS), environmental engineering, geotechnical engineering (ME, MS), structural engineering, transportation engineering. *Program availability:* Part-time. *Faculty:* 37 full-time (7 women), 2 part-time/adjunct (0 women). *Students:* 118 full-time (37 women), 9 part-time (2 women); includes 110 minority (all Hispanic/Latino), 17 international. Average age 25. 35 applicants, 94% accepted, 16 enrolled. In 2016, 26 master's, 2 doctorates awarded. Terminal master's awarded for partial completion of doctoral program. *Degree requirements:* For master's, one foreign language, thesis; for doctorate, one foreign language, comprehensive exam, thesis/dissertation, qualifying exams. *Entrance requirements:* For master's, proficiency in English and Spanish; BS in civil engineering or its equivalent; for doctorate, proficiency in English and Spanish. *Application deadline:* For fall admission, 2/15 for domestic and international students; for spring admission, 9/15 for domestic and international students. Applications are processed on a rolling basis. Application fee: $25. Electronic applications accepted. *Expenses: Tuition, area resident:* Full-time $2466. *International tuition:* $7166 full-time. *Required fees:* $210. One-time fee: $5 full-time. Tuition and fees vary according to course level, campus/location, program and student level. *Financial support:* In 2016–17, 89 students received support, including 74 research assistantships with full and partial tuition reimbursements available (averaging $3,171 per year), 38 teaching assistantships with full and partial tuition reimbursements available (averaging $3,107 per year); unspecified assistantships also available. *Faculty research:* Structural design, concrete structure, finite elements, dynamic analysis, transportation, soils. *Unit head:* Ismael Pagan, Prof., Director, 787-832-4040 Ext. 3815, Fax: 787-833-8260, E-mail: ismael.pagan@upr.edu. *Application contact:* Myriam Hernandez, Administrative Officer III, 787-832-4040 Ext. 3815, Fax: 787-833-8260, E-mail: myriam.hernandez1@upr.edu.
Website: http://engineering.uprm.edu/inci/

University of Rhode Island, Graduate School, College of Engineering, Department of Civil and Environmental Engineering, Kingston, RI 02881. Offers environmental engineering (MS, PhD); geotechnical engineering (MS, PhD); structural engineering (MS, PhD); transportation engineering (MS, PhD). *Program availability:* Part-time. *Faculty:* 11 full-time (3 women). *Students:* 24 full-time (6 women), 8 part-time (4 women); includes 2 minority (1 Hispanic/Latino; 1 Two or more races, non-Hispanic/Latino), 14 international. In 2016, 11 master's, 3 doctorates awarded. *Degree requirements:* For master's, comprehensive exam (for some programs), thesis optional; for doctorate, comprehensive exam, thesis/dissertation. *Entrance requirements:* For master's and doctorate, 2 letters of recommendation. Additional exam requirements/recommendations for international students: Required—TOEFL. *Application deadline:* For fall admission, 7/15 for domestic students, 2/1 for international students; for spring admission, 11/15 for domestic students, 7/15 for international students. Application fee: $65. Electronic applications accepted. *Expenses:* Tuition, state resident: full-time $11,796; part-time $655 per credit. Tuition, nonresident: full-time $24,206; part-time $1345 per credit. *Required fees:* $1546; $44 per credit. One-time fee: $155 full-time; $35 part-time. *Financial support:* In 2016–17, 3 research assistantships with tuition reimbursements (averaging $8,774 per year), 4 teaching assistantships with tuition reimbursements (averaging $12,171 per year) were awarded. Financial award application deadline: 2/1; financial award applicants required to submit FAFSA. *Unit head:* Dr. Mayrai Gindy, Chair, 401-874-5117, Fax: 401-874-5587, E-mail: gindy@egr.uri.edu. *Application contact:* Dr. George Tsiatas, Graduate Program Director, 401-874-5117, E-mail: gt@uri.edu.
Website: http://www.uri.edu/cve/

University of Saskatchewan, College of Graduate Studies and Research, College of Engineering, Civil and Geological Engineering Program, Saskatoon, SK S7N 5A9, Canada. Offers M Eng, M Sc, PhD. *Program availability:* Part-time. *Degree requirements:* For master's, thesis (for some programs), 30 credits (for M Eng); thesis and 12 credits (for MS); for doctorate, comprehensive exam, thesis/dissertation, qualifying exam, 18 credits. *Entrance requirements:* For master's, GRE, minimum GPA of 5.0 on an 8.0 scale; for doctorate, GRE. Additional exam requirements/recommendations for international students: Required—TOEFL, TOEFL (minimum iBT score of 80), IELTS (6.5), CanTEST (4.5), or PTE (59). Electronic applications accepted. *Faculty research:* Geotechnical/geo-environmental engineering, structural engineering, water resources engineering, civil engineering materials, environmental/sanitary engineering, hydrogeology, rock mechanics and mining, transportation engineering.

University of South Alabama, College of Engineering, Department of Civil, Coastal, and Environmental Engineering, Mobile, AL 36688. Offers MSCE. *Faculty:* 7 full-time (1 woman). *Students:* 13 full-time (3 women), 4 part-time (1 woman); includes 1 minority (Black or African American, non-Hispanic/Latino), 5 international. Average age 26. 31 applicants, 39% accepted, 5 enrolled. In 2016, 17 master's awarded. *Degree requirements:* For master's, comprehensive exam, thesis or project. *Entrance requirements:* For master's, GRE, minimum GPA of 3.0, three references, portfolio. Additional exam requirements/recommendations for international students: Required—TOEFL (minimum score 525 paper-based; 71 iBT). *Application deadline:* For fall admission, 7/1 priority date for domestic students, 6/1 priority date for international students; for spring admission, 12/1 priority date for domestic students, 11/1 priority date for international students; for summer admission, 5/1 priority date for domestic students, 4/1 priority date for international students. Applications are processed on a rolling basis. Application fee: $35. Electronic applications accepted. *Expenses:* Contact institution. *Financial support:* Fellowships, research assistantships, teaching assistantships, career-related internships or fieldwork, Federal Work-Study, institutionally sponsored loans, scholarships/grants, and unspecified assistantships available. Support available to part-time students. Financial award application deadline: 5/31; financial award applicants required to submit FAFSA. *Faculty research:* Calibration of simulation model, monitoring coastal processes, reducing crashes. *Unit head:* Dr. Kevin White, Department Chair, 251-460-6174, Fax: 251-461-1400, E-mail: kwhite@southalabama.edu. *Application contact:* Brenda Poole, Academic Records Specialist, 251-460-6140, Fax: 251-460-6343, E-mail: engineering@alabama.edu.
Website: http://www.southalabama.edu/colleges/engineering/ce/index.html

University of South Carolina, The Graduate School, College of Engineering and Computing, Department of Civil and Environmental Engineering, Columbia, SC 29208. Offers civil engineering (ME, MS, PhD). *Program availability:* Part-time, evening/weekend, online learning. *Degree requirements:* For master's, comprehensive exam, thesis (for some programs); for doctorate, thesis/dissertation. *Entrance requirements:* For master's and doctorate, GRE General Test, 2 letters of recommendation. Additional exam requirements/recommendations for international students: Required—TOEFL (minimum score 570 paper-based). Electronic applications accepted. *Faculty research:* Structures, water resources.

University of Southern California, Graduate School, Viterbi School of Engineering, Sonny Astani Department of Civil Engineering, Los Angeles, CA 90089. Offers applied mechanics (MS); civil engineering (MS, PhD); computer-aided engineering (ME, Graduate Certificate); construction management (MCM); engineering technology commercialization (Graduate Certificate); environmental engineering (MS, PhD); environmental quality management (ME); structural design (ME); sustainable cities (Graduate Certificate); transportation systems (MS, Graduate Certificate); water and waste management (MS). *Program availability:* Part-time, evening/weekend. Terminal master's awarded for partial completion of doctoral program. *Degree requirements:* For master's, thesis optional; for doctorate, thesis/dissertation. *Entrance requirements:* For master's and doctorate, GRE General Test. Additional exam requirements/recommendations for international students: Recommended—TOEFL. Electronic applications accepted. *Faculty research:* Geotechnical engineering, transportation engineering, structural engineering, construction management, environmental engineering, water resources.

University of South Florida, College of Engineering, Department of Civil and Environmental Engineering, Tampa, FL 33620-9951. Offers civil engineering (MCE, MSCE, PhD), including geotechnical engineering, materials science and engineering, structures engineering, transportation engineering, water resources; environmental engineering (MEVE, MSEV, PhD), including engineering for international development (MSEV). *Program availability:* Part-time. *Faculty:* 20 full-time (5 women). *Students:* 117 full-time (41 women), 63 part-time (18 women); includes 33 minority (7 Black or African American, non-Hispanic/Latino; 2 Asian, non-Hispanic/Latino; 20 Hispanic/Latino; 4 Two or more races, non-Hispanic/Latino), 84 international. Average age 28. 250 applicants, 52% accepted, 51 enrolled. In 2016, 55 master's, 13 doctorates awarded. Terminal master's awarded for partial completion of doctoral program. *Degree requirements:* For master's, comprehensive exam, thesis (for some programs); for doctorate, comprehensive exam, thesis/dissertation. *Entrance requirements:* For master's, GRE General Test, minimum GPA of 3.0 in major, letters of reference, statement of purpose; for doctorate, GRE General Test, letters of recommendation, statement of purpose, resume. Additional exam requirements/recommendations for international students: Required—TOEFL (minimum score 550 paper-based; 79 iBT) or IELTS (minimum score 6.5). *Application deadline:* For fall admission, 2/15 for domestic students, 2/15 priority date for international students; for spring admission, 10/15 for domestic students, 9/15 priority date for international students. Application fee: $30. Electronic applications accepted. *Expenses:* Tuition, state resident: full-time $7766; part-time $431.43 per credit hour. Tuition, nonresident: full-time $15,789; part-time $877.17 per credit hour. *Required fees:* $37 per term. *Financial support:* In 2016–17, 36 students received support, including 44 research assistantships (averaging $14,123 per year), 21 teaching assistantships with tuition reimbursements available (averaging $15,329 per year). *Faculty research:* Environmental and water resources engineering, geotechnics and geoenvironmental systems, structures and materials systems, transportation systems. *Total annual research expenditures:* $3.7 million. *Unit head:* Dr. Manjriker Gunaratne, Professor and Department Chair, 813-974-5818, Fax: 813-974-2957, E-mail: gunaratn@usf.edu. *Application contact:* Dr. Sarina J. Ergas, Professor and Graduate Program Coordinator, 813-974-1119, Fax: 813-974-2957, E-mail: sergas@usf.edu.
Website: http://www.usf.edu/engineering/cee/

University of South Florida, Innovative Education, Tampa, FL 33620-9951. Offers adult, career and higher education (Graduate Certificate), including college teaching, leadership in developing human resources, leadership in higher education; Africana studies (Graduate Certificate), including diasporas and health disparities, genocide and human rights; aging studies (Graduate Certificate), including gerontology; art research (Graduate Certificate), including museum studies; business foundations (Graduate Certificate); chemical and biomedical engineering (Graduate Certificate), including materials science and engineering, water, health and sustainability; child and family studies (Graduate Certificate), including positive behavior support; civil and industrial engineering (Graduate Certificate), including transportation systems analysis; community and family health (Graduate Certificate), including maternal and child health, social marketing and public health, violence and injury: prevention and intervention, women's health; criminology (Graduate Certificate), including criminal justice administration; educational measurement and research (Graduate Certificate), including evaluation; English (Graduate Certificate), including comparative literary studies, creative writing, professional and technical communication; entrepreneurship (Graduate Certificate); environmental health (Graduate Certificate), including safety management; epidemiology and biostatistics (Graduate Certificate), including applied biostatistics, biostatistics, concepts and tools of epidemiology, epidemiology, epidemiology of infectious diseases; geography, environment and planning (Graduate Certificate), including community development, environmental policy and management, geographical information systems; geology (Graduate Certificate), including hydrogeology; global health (Graduate Certificate), including disaster management, global health and Latin American and Caribbean studies, global health practice, humanitarian assistance, infection control; government and international affairs (Graduate Certificate), including Cuban studies, globalization studies; health policy and management (Graduate Certificate), including health management and leadership, public health policy and programs; hearing specialist: early intervention (Graduate Certificate); industrial and management systems engineering (Graduate Certificate), including systems engineering, technology management; information studies (Graduate Certificate), including school library media specialist; information systems/decision sciences (Graduate Certificate), including analytics and business intelligence; instructional technology (Graduate Certificate), including distance education, Florida digital/virtual educator, instructional design, multimedia design, Web design; internal medicine, bioethics and medical humanities (Graduate Certificate), including biomedical ethics; Latin American and Caribbean studies (Graduate Certificate); mass communications (Graduate Certificate), including multimedia journalism; mathematics and statistics (Graduate Certificate), including mathematics; medicine (Graduate Certificate), including aging and neuroscience, bioinformatics, biotechnology, brain fitness and memory management, clinical investigation, health informatics, health sciences, integrative weight management, intellectual property, medicine and gender, metabolic and nutritional medicine, metabolic cardiology, pharmacy sciences; national and competitive intelligence (Graduate Certificate); psychological and social foundations (Graduate Certificate), including career counseling, college teaching, diversity in education, mental health counseling, school counseling; public affairs (Graduate Certificate), including nonprofit management, public management, research administration; public health (Graduate Certificate), including environmental health, health equity, public health generalist, translational research in adolescent behavioral health; public health practices (Graduate Certificate), including planning for healthy communities; rehabilitation and mental health counseling (Graduate Certificate), including integrative mental health care, marriage and family therapy, rehabilitation technology; secondary education (Graduate Certificate), including ESOL, foreign language education: culture and content, foreign language education: professional; social work (Graduate Certificate), including geriatric social work/clinical gerontology; special education (Graduate Certificate), including autism spectrum disorder, disabilities education: severe/profound; world languages (Graduate Certificate), including teaching English as a second language (TESL) or foreign language. *Expenses:* Tuition, state

resident: full-time $7766; part-time $431.43 per credit hour. Tuition, nonresident: full-time $15,789; part-time $877.17 per credit hour. *Required fees:* $37 per term. *Unit head:* Kathy Barnes, Interdisciplinary Programs Coordinator, 813-974-8031, Fax: 813-974-7061, E-mail: barnesk@usf.edu. *Application contact:* Karen Tylinski, Metro Initiatives, 813-974-9943, Fax: 813-974-7061, E-mail: ktylinsk@usf.edu.
Website: http://www.usf.edu/innovative-education/

The University of Tennessee, Graduate School, Tickle College of Engineering, Department of Civil and Environmental Engineering, Program in Civil Engineering, Knoxville, TN 37996. Offers MS, PhD, MS/MBA. *Program availability:* Part-time, online learning. *Faculty:* 17 full-time (3 women), 9 part-time/adjunct (3 women). *Students:* 98 full-time (25 women), 51 part-time (12 women); includes 13 minority (6 Black or African American, non-Hispanic/Latino; 4 Asian, non-Hispanic/Latino; 2 Hispanic/Latino; 1 Two or more races, non-Hispanic/Latino), 59 international. Average age 29. 108 applicants, 53% accepted, 22 enrolled. In 2016, 27 master's, 2 doctorates awarded. *Degree requirements:* For master's, thesis or alternative; for doctorate, comprehensive exam, thesis/dissertation. *Entrance requirements:* For master's, GRE General Test (for MS students pursuing research thesis), minimum GPA of 2.7 (for U.S. degree holders), 3.0 (for international degree holders); 3 references; statement of purpose; resume; for doctorate, GRE General Test, minimum GPA of 3.0 on previous graduate course work; 3 references; statement of purpose; resume. Additional exam requirements/recommendations for international students: Required—TOEFL (minimum score 550 paper-based). *Application deadline:* For fall admission, 2/1 priority date for domestic and international students; for spring admission, 6/15 for domestic and international students. Applications are processed on a rolling basis. Application fee: $35. Electronic applications accepted. *Financial support:* In 2016–17, 81 students received support, including 8 fellowships (averaging $27,875 per year), 38 research assistantships with full tuition reimbursements available (averaging $21,068 per year), 31 teaching assistantships with full tuition reimbursements available (averaging $20,491 per year); career-related internships or fieldwork, Federal Work-Study, institutionally sponsored loans, health care benefits, and unspecified assistantships also available. Financial award application deadline: 2/1; financial award applicants required to submit FAFSA. *Faculty research:* Multi-functional composites and mechanics of materials, geohydrologic investigations and monitoring, structures and vibrations, geotechnical and earthquake engineering, transportation system planning and design. *Unit head:* Dr. Chris Cox, Head, 865-974-2503, Fax: 865-974-2669, E-mail: ccox9@utk.edu. *Application contact:* Dr. Khalid Alshibli, Associate Head, 865-974-7728, Fax: 865-974-2669, E-mail: alshibli@utk.edu.
Website: http://www.engr.utk.edu/civil

The University of Tennessee at Chattanooga, Program in Engineering, Chattanooga, TN 37403. Offers automotive systems (MS Engr); chemical engineering (MS Engr); civil engineering (MS Engr); computational engineering (MS Engr); electrical engineering (MS Engr); industrial engineering (MS Engr); mechanical engineering (MS Engr). *Program availability:* Part-time. *Faculty:* 21 full-time (2 women), 2 part-time/adjunct (1 woman). *Students:* 21 full-time (5 women), 26 part-time (7 women); includes 11 minority (4 Black or African American, non-Hispanic/Latino; 5 Asian, non-Hispanic/Latino; 1 Hispanic/Latino; 1 Two or more races, non-Hispanic/Latino), 18 international. Average age 28. 30 applicants, 83% accepted, 14 enrolled. In 2016, 25 master's awarded. *Degree requirements:* For master's, comprehensive exam, thesis or alternative, engineering project. *Entrance requirements:* For master's, GRE General Test, minimum undergraduate GPA of 2.7 or 3.0 in last two years of undergraduate coursework. Additional exam requirements/recommendations for international students: Required—TOEFL (minimum score 550 paper-based; 79 iBT), IELTS (minimum score 6). *Application deadline:* For fall admission, 6/15 priority date for domestic students, 7/1 for international students; for spring admission, 11/1 priority date for domestic students, 11/1 for international students. Applications are processed on a rolling basis. Application fee: $35 ($40 for international students). Electronic applications accepted. *Expenses:* $9,876 full-time in-state; $25,994 full-time out-of-state; $450 per credit part-time in-state; $1,345 per credit part-time out-of-state. *Financial support:* In 2016–17, 6 research assistantships, 5 teaching assistantships were awarded; career-related internships or fieldwork, scholarships/grants, health care benefits, and unspecified assistantships also available. Support available to part-time students. Financial award application deadline: 7/1. *Faculty research:* Quality control and reliability engineering, financial management, thermal science, energy conservation, structural analysis. *Total annual research expenditures:* $921,122. *Unit head:* Dr. Daniel Pack, Dean, 423-425-2256, Fax: 423-425-5311, E-mail: daniel-pack@utc.edu. *Application contact:* Dr. Joanne Romagni, Dean of the Graduate School, 423-425-4478, Fax: 423-425-5223, E-mail: joanne-romagni@utc.edu.
Website: http://www.utc.edu/college-engineering-computer-science/graduate-programs/msengr.php

The University of Texas at Arlington, Graduate School, College of Engineering, Department of Civil Engineering, Arlington, TX 76019. Offers civil engineering (M Engr, MS, PhD); construction management (MCM). *Program availability:* Part-time, evening/weekend, online learning. Terminal master's awarded for partial completion of doctoral program. *Degree requirements:* For master's, comprehensive exam, thesis (for some programs), oral and written exams; for doctorate, comprehensive exam, thesis/dissertation, oral and written defense of dissertation. *Entrance requirements:* For master's, GRE General Test, minimum GPA of 3.0 in last 60 hours of undergraduate course work; for doctorate, GRE General Test, minimum GPA of 3.5. Additional exam requirements/recommendations for international students: Required—TOEFL. *Application deadline:* For fall admission, 6/6 for domestic students, 4/4 for international students; for spring admission, 10/15 for domestic students, 9/5 for international students. Applications are processed on a rolling basis. Application fee: $35 ($50 for international students). Electronic applications accepted. *Financial support:* Fellowships with partial tuition reimbursements, research assistantships with partial tuition reimbursements, teaching assistantships with partial tuition reimbursements, career-related internships or fieldwork, Federal Work-Study, scholarships/grants, tuition waivers (partial), and unspecified assistantships available. Financial award application deadline: 6/1; financial award applicants required to submit FAFSA. *Faculty research:* Environmental and water resources structures, geotechnical, transportation. *Unit head:* Dr. Ali Abolmaali, Chair, 817-272-5055, Fax: 817-272-2630, E-mail: abolmaali@uta.edu. *Application contact:* Dr. Stephen Mattingly, Graduate Advisor, 817-272-2201, Fax: 817-272-2630, E-mail: mattingly@uta.edu.
Website: http://www.uta.edu/ce/

The University of Texas at Austin, Graduate School, Cockrell School of Engineering, Department of Civil, Architectural and Environmental Engineering, Austin, TX 78712-1111. Offers architectural engineering (MSE); civil engineering (MS, PhD); environmental and water resources engineering (MS, PhD). *Program availability:* Part-time. *Degree requirements:* For master's, thesis or alternative; for doctorate, comprehensive exam, thesis/dissertation. *Entrance requirements:* For master's and doctorate, GRE General Test. Additional exam requirements/recommendations for international students: Required—TOEFL. Electronic applications accepted. *Faculty research:* Geotechnical structural engineering, transportation engineering, construction engineering/project management.

The University of Texas at El Paso, Graduate School, College of Engineering, Department of Civil Engineering, El Paso, TX 79968-0001. Offers civil engineering (MS, PhD); construction management (MS, Certificate); environmental engineering (MEENE, MSENE). *Program availability:* Part-time, evening/weekend. *Degree requirements:* For master's, comprehensive exam, thesis optional; for doctorate, comprehensive exam, thesis/dissertation. *Entrance requirements:* For master's, GRE, minimum GPA of 3.0; for doctorate, GRE. Additional exam requirements/recommendations for international students: Required—TOEFL. Electronic applications accepted. *Faculty research:* Non-destructive testing for geotechnical and pavement applications, transportation systems, wastewater treatment systems, air quality, linear and non-linear modeling of structures, structural reliability.

The University of Texas at San Antonio, College of Engineering, Department of Civil and Environmental Engineering, San Antonio, TX 78249-0617. Offers civil engineering (MCE, MSCE); environmental science and engineering (PhD). *Program availability:* Part-time. *Faculty:* 14 full-time (1 woman), 1 part-time/adjunct (0 women). *Students:* 45 full-time (9 women), 40 part-time (8 women); includes 23 minority (5 Black or African American, non-Hispanic/Latino; 5 Asian, non-Hispanic/Latino; 12 Hispanic/Latino; 1 Two or more races, non-Hispanic/Latino), 34 international. Average age 30. 88 applicants, 58% accepted, 22 enrolled. In 2016, 11 master's, 4 doctorates awarded. *Degree requirements:* For master's, comprehensive exam, thesis (for some programs); for doctorate, comprehensive exam, thesis/dissertation, written qualifying exam, dissertation proposal. *Entrance requirements:* For master's, GRE General Test, BS in civil engineering or related field from accredited institution, statement of research/specialization interest, recommendation by the Civil Engineering Master's Program Admissions Committee; for doctorate, GRE, BS and MS from accredited institution, minimum GPA of 3.0 in upper-division and graduate courses, three letters of recommendation, letter of research interest, resume/curriculum vitae. Additional exam requirements/recommendations for international students: Required—TOEFL (minimum score 550 paper-based; 79 iBT), IELTS (minimum score 6.5). *Application deadline:* For fall admission, 7/1 for domestic students, 4/1 for international students; for spring admission, 11/1 for domestic students, 9/1 for international students. Application fee: $45 ($80 for international students). Electronic applications accepted. *Expenses:* Contact institution. *Financial support:* In 2016–17, 42 students received support, including 28 research assistantships with full tuition reimbursements available (averaging $20,000 per year), 14 teaching assistantships (averaging $4,680 per year); scholarships/grants also available. Financial award application deadline: 2/1. *Faculty research:* Structures, application of geographic information systems in water resources, geotechnical engineering, pavement traffic loading, hydrogeology. *Total annual research expenditures:* $2.6 million. *Unit head:* Dr. Heather Shipley, Department Chair, 210-458-7517, Fax: 210-458-6475, E-mail: heather.shipley@utsa.edu. *Application contact:* Jessica Perez, Administrative Associate, 210-458-4428, Fax: 210-458-7469, E-mail: jessica.perez@utsa.edu.
Website: http://engineering.utsa.edu/CE/

The University of Texas at Tyler, College of Engineering, Department of Civil Engineering, Tyler, TX 75799-0001. Offers environmental engineering (MS); industrial safety (MS); structural engineering (MS); transportation engineering (MS); water resources engineering (MS). *Program availability:* Part-time, evening/weekend. *Degree requirements:* For master's, thesis optional. *Entrance requirements:* For master's, GRE General Test, bachelor's degree in engineering, associated science degree. Additional exam requirements/recommendations for international students: Required—TOEFL. *Faculty research:* Non-destructive strength testing, indoor air quality, transportation routing and signaling, pavement replacement criteria, flood water routing, construction and long-term behavior of innovative geotechnical foundation and embankment construction used in highway construction, engineering education.

The University of Toledo, College of Graduate Studies, College of Engineering, Department of Civil Engineering, Toledo, OH 43606-3390. Offers MS, PhD. *Program availability:* Part-time. Terminal master's awarded for partial completion of doctoral program. *Degree requirements:* For master's, thesis or alternative; for doctorate, thesis/dissertation, qualifying exam. *Entrance requirements:* For master's, GRE General Test, minimum GPA of 3.0; for doctorate, GRE General Test, minimum GPA of 3.3. Additional exam requirements/recommendations for international students: Required—TOEFL (minimum score 550 paper-based; 80 iBT). Electronic applications accepted. *Faculty research:* Environmental modeling, soil/pavement interaction, structural mechanics, earthquakes, transportation engineering.

University of Toronto, School of Graduate Studies, Faculty of Applied Science and Engineering, Department of Civil Engineering, Toronto, ON M5S 1A1, Canada. Offers M Eng, MA Sc, PhD. *Program availability:* Part-time. *Degree requirements:* For master's, thesis and oral presentation (MA Sc); for doctorate, thesis/dissertation, oral presentation. *Entrance requirements:* For master's, bachelor's degree in civil engineering, proficiency in computer usage, minimum B average in final 2 years, 3 letters of reference; for doctorate, proficiency in computer usage, minimum B average in final 2 years, 3 letters of reference. Additional exam requirements/recommendations for international students: Required—TOEFL (minimum score 580 paper-based; 93 iBT). Electronic applications accepted.

University of Utah, Graduate School, College of Engineering, Department of Civil and Environmental Engineering, Salt Lake City, UT 84112. Offers civil and environmental engineering (MS, PhD); nuclear engineering (MS, PhD). *Program availability:* Part-time. *Faculty:* 18 full-time (6 women), 21 part-time/adjunct (2 women). *Students:* 72 full-time (20 women), 31 part-time (5 women); includes 9 minority (3 Asian, non-Hispanic/Latino; 3 Hispanic/Latino; 3 Two or more races, non-Hispanic/Latino), 51 international. Average age 29. 156 applicants, 46% accepted, 28 enrolled. In 2016, 26 master's, 7 doctorates awarded. Terminal master's awarded for partial completion of doctoral program. *Degree requirements:* For master's, comprehensive exam (for some programs), thesis (for some programs); for doctorate, comprehensive exam, thesis/dissertation, departmental qualifying exam, preliminary exam. *Entrance requirements:* For master's and doctorate, GRE General Test, minimum GPA of 3.0. Additional exam requirements/recommendations for international students: Required—TOEFL (minimum score 550 paper-based; 80 iBT). *Application deadline:* For fall admission, 1/1 priority date for domestic students, 12/1 priority date for international students; for spring admission, 10/1 for domestic students, 9/1 for international students. Applications are processed on a rolling basis. Application fee: $10 ($25 for international students). Electronic applications accepted. *Expenses:* Contact institution. *Financial support:* In 2016–17, 76 students received support, including 3 fellowships with full tuition reimbursements available (averaging $24,000 per year), 45 research assistantships with full tuition reimbursements available (averaging $22,247 per year), 14 teaching assistantships with full tuition reimbursements available (averaging $22,088 per year); traineeships, health care benefits, and unspecified assistantships also available. Financial award application deadline: 12/1. *Faculty research:* Structural engineering, geotechnical engineering, transportation engineering, environmental engineering, water resources. *Total annual research expenditures:* $12.1 million. *Unit head:* Dr. Michael Barber, Chair, 801-581-6931, Fax: 801-585-5477, E-mail: barber@civil.utah.edu. *Application contact:* Bonnie Ogden, Academic Advisor, 801-581-6678, Fax: 801-585-5477, E-mail: bonnie.ogden@

utah.edu.
Website: http://www.civil.utah.edu

University of Vermont, Graduate College, College of Engineering and Mathematics, Department of Civil and Environmental Engineering, Burlington, VT 05405. Offers MS, PhD. *Degree requirements:* For master's, thesis or alternative; for doctorate, thesis/dissertation. *Entrance requirements:* For master's and doctorate, GRE General Test. Additional exam requirements/recommendations for international students: Required—TOEFL (minimum score 550 paper-based; 80 iBT). Electronic applications accepted. *Expenses:* Tuition, state resident: full-time $5814. Tuition, nonresident: full-time $14,670.

University of Virginia, School of Engineering and Applied Science, Department of Civil and Environmental Engineering, Charlottesville, VA 22903. Offers ME, MS, PhD. *Program availability:* Part-time, online learning. *Faculty:* 15 full-time (3 women), 2 part-time/adjunct (1 woman). *Students:* 61 full-time (26 women), 2 part-time (0 women); includes 5 minority (2 Asian, non-Hispanic/Latino; 2 Hispanic/Latino; 1 Two or more races, non-Hispanic/Latino), 37 international. Average age 27. 135 applicants, 50% accepted, 25 enrolled. In 2016, 13 master's, 5 doctorates awarded. Terminal master's awarded for partial completion of doctoral program. *Degree requirements:* For master's, thesis (for some programs); for doctorate, comprehensive exam, thesis/dissertation. *Entrance requirements:* For master's and doctorate, GRE General Test, 3 letters of recommendation. Additional exam requirements/recommendations for international students: Required—TOEFL (minimum score 600 paper-based; 90 iBT), IELTS (minimum score 7). *Application deadline:* For fall admission, 8/1 for domestic students, 4/1 for international students; for winter admission, 12/1 for domestic students, 8/1 for international students; for spring admission, 5/1 for domestic students, 1/1 for international students. Applications are processed on a rolling basis. Application fee: $60. Electronic applications accepted. *Expenses:* Tuition, state resident: full-time $15,026; part-time $834 per credit hour. Tuition, nonresident: full-time $25,168; part-time $1378 per credit hour. *Required fees:* $2654. *Financial support:* Fellowships with full tuition reimbursements, research assistantships with full tuition reimbursements, and teaching assistantships with full tuition reimbursements available. Financial award application deadline: 1/15. *Faculty research:* Groundwater, surface water, traffic engineering, composite materials. *Unit head:* Brian L. Smith, Chair, 434-924-7464, Fax: 434-982-2951, E-mail: civil@virginia.edu. *Application contact:* Graduate Program Coordinator, 434-924-7464, Fax: 434-982-2951, E-mail: civil@virginia.edu.
Website: http://www.ce.virginia.edu/

University of Washington, Graduate School, College of Engineering, Department of Civil and Environmental Engineering, Seattle, WA 98195-2700. Offers construction engineering (MSCE, PhD); environmental engineering (MSCE, PhD); geotechnical engineering (MSCE, PhD); hydrology and hydrodynamics (MSCE, PhD); structural engineering and mechanics (MSCE, PhD); transportation engineering (MSCE, PhD). *Program availability:* Part-time, 100% online. *Faculty:* 37 full-time (10 women). *Students:* 239 full-time (97 women), 153 part-time (41 women); includes 71 minority (7 Black or African American, non-Hispanic/Latino; 32 Asian, non-Hispanic/Latino; 22 Hispanic/Latino; 2 Native Hawaiian or other Pacific Islander, non-Hispanic/Latino; 8 Two or more races, non-Hispanic/Latino), 134 international. 782 applicants, 58% accepted, 157 enrolled. In 2016, 132 master's, 13 doctorates awarded. Terminal master's awarded for partial completion of doctoral program. *Degree requirements:* For master's, thesis optional; for doctorate, comprehensive exam, thesis/dissertation, qualifying, general and final exams; completion of degree within 10 years. *Entrance requirements:* For master's, GRE General Test, minimum GPA of 3.0, statement of purpose, letters of recommendation, transcripts; for doctorate, GRE General Test, minimum GPA of 3.5, statement of purpose, letters of recommendation, transcripts, resume. Additional exam requirements/recommendations for international students: Required—TOEFL (minimum score 580 paper-based; 92 iBT); Recommended—IELTS (minimum score 7), TSE. *Application deadline:* For fall admission, 12/15 for domestic and international students. Applications are processed on a rolling basis. Application fee: $85. Electronic applications accepted. *Expenses:* Contact institution. *Financial support:* In 2016–17, 110 students received support, including 10 fellowships with tuition reimbursements available (averaging $2,228 per year), 72 research assistantships with full tuition reimbursements available (averaging $2,351 per year), 28 teaching assistantships with full tuition reimbursements available (averaging $2,387 per year); scholarships/grants also available. Financial award application deadline: 12/15; financial award applicants required to submit FAFSA. *Faculty research:* Structural and geotechnical engineering, transportation and construction engineering, water and environmental engineering. *Total annual research expenditures:* $13.5 million. *Unit head:* Dr. Timothy V. Larson, Professor/Chair, 206-543-6815, Fax: 206-543-1543, E-mail: tlarson@uw.edu. *Application contact:* Melissa Pritchard, Graduate Adviser, 206-543-2574, Fax: 206-543-1543, E-mail: ceginfo@u.washington.edu.
Website: http://www.ce.washington.edu/

University of Waterloo, Graduate Studies, Faculty of Engineering, Department of Civil and Environmental Engineering, Waterloo, ON N2L 3G1, Canada. Offers M Eng, MA Sc, PhD. *Program availability:* Part-time. *Degree requirements:* For master's, research paper or thesis; for doctorate, comprehensive exam, thesis/dissertation. *Entrance requirements:* For master's, honors degree, minimum B average; for doctorate, master's degree, minimum A- average. Additional exam requirements/recommendations for international students: Required—TOEFL, IELTS, PTE. Electronic applications accepted. *Faculty research:* Water resources, structures, construction management, transportation, geotechnical engineering.

The University of Western Ontario, Faculty of Graduate Studies, Physical Sciences Division, Faculty of Engineering, London, ON N6A 5B8, Canada. Offers chemical and biochemical engineering (ME Sc, PhD); civil and environmental engineering (M Eng, ME Sc, PhD); electrical and computer engineering (M Eng, ME Sc, PhD); mechanical and materials engineering (M Eng, ME Sc, PhD). *Program availability:* Part-time. Terminal master's awarded for partial completion of doctoral program. *Degree requirements:* For master's, thesis; for doctorate, thesis/dissertation. *Entrance requirements:* For master's, minimum B average; for doctorate, minimum B+ average. *Faculty research:* Wind, geotechnical, chemical reactor engineering, applied electrostatics, biochemical engineering.

University of Windsor, Faculty of Graduate Studies, Faculty of Engineering, Department of Civil and Environmental Engineering, Windsor, ON N9B 3P4, Canada. Offers civil engineering (M Eng, MA Sc, PhD); environmental engineering (M Eng, MA Sc, PhD). *Program availability:* Part-time. *Degree requirements:* For master's, thesis; for doctorate, comprehensive exam, thesis/dissertation. *Entrance requirements:* For master's, minimum B average; for doctorate, master's degree, minimum A average. Additional exam requirements/recommendations for international students: Required—TOEFL (minimum score 580 paper-based). Electronic applications accepted. *Faculty research:* Odors: sampling, measurement, control; drinking water disinfection, hydrocarbon contaminated soil remediation, structural dynamics, numerical simulation of piezoelectric materials.

University of Wisconsin–Madison, Graduate School, College of Engineering, Department of Civil and Environmental Engineering, Madison, WI 53706. Offers MS, PhD. *Program availability:* Part-time. *Faculty:* 28 full-time (6 women). *Students:* 109 full-time (38 women), 28 part-time (10 women); includes 11 minority (2 Black or African American, non-Hispanic/Latino; 2 Asian, non-Hispanic/Latino; 6 Hispanic/Latino; 1 Two or more races, non-Hispanic/Latino), 69 international. Average age 27. 349 applicants, 24% accepted, 28 enrolled. In 2016, 29 master's, 7 doctorates awarded. Terminal master's awarded for partial completion of doctoral program. *Degree requirements:* For master's, thesis or alternative, minimum of 30 credits; minimum overall GPA of 3.0; for doctorate, comprehensive exam, thesis/dissertation, preliminary exam; qualifying exams; minimum of 51 credits; minimum overall GPA of 3.0. *Entrance requirements:* For master's, GRE General Test, bachelor's degree; minimum GPA of 3.0 for last 60 credits of course work; for doctorate, GRE General Test, minimum GPA of 3.0 for last 60 credits of course work. Additional exam requirements/recommendations for international students: Required—TOEFL (minimum score 580 paper-based; 92 iBT). *Application deadline:* For fall admission, 12/15 priority date for domestic and international students; for spring admission, 9/1 for domestic and international students. Application fee: $75 ($81 for international students). Electronic applications accepted. *Expenses:* $13,157 per year in-state tuition and fees; $26,484 per year out-of-state tuition and fees. *Financial support:* In 2016–17, 95 students received support, including 7 fellowships with full tuition reimbursements available, 52 research assistantships with full tuition reimbursements available, 26 teaching assistantships with full tuition reimbursements available; Federal Work-Study, scholarships/grants, health care benefits, unspecified assistantships, and project assistantships also available. Support available to part-time students. Financial award application deadline: 12/1; financial award applicants required to submit FAFSA. *Faculty research:* Environmental engineering; transportation; building systems; water resources; conventional and renewable energy; mineral extraction and byproducts management; geoenvironmental engineering. *Total annual research expenditures:* $12.5 million. *Unit head:* Prof. David Noyce, Chair, 608-265-1882, Fax: 608-262-5199, E-mail: danoyce@wisc.edu. *Application contact:* Cheryl Loschko, Student Services Coordinator, 608-890-2420, E-mail: loschko@wisc.edu.
Website: https://www.engr.wisc.edu/department/civil-environmental-engineering/academics/ms-phd-civil-and-environmental-engineering/

University of Wisconsin–Milwaukee, Graduate School, College of Engineering and Applied Science, Program in Engineering, Milwaukee, WI 53201-0413. Offers biomedical engineering (MS); civil engineering (MS, PhD); computer science (PhD); electrical and computer engineering (MS); electrical engineering (PhD); engineering mechanics (MS); industrial and management engineering (MS); industrial engineering (PhD); manufacturing engineering (MS); materials (PhD); materials engineering (MS); mechanical engineering (MS). *Program availability:* Part-time. *Students:* 199 full-time (52 women), 156 part-time (32 women); includes 27 minority (2 Black or African American, non-Hispanic/Latino; 15 Asian, non-Hispanic/Latino; 3 Hispanic/Latino; 7 Two or more races, non-Hispanic/Latino), 244 international. Average age 30. 396 applicants, 61% accepted, 102 enrolled. In 2016, 72 master's, 26 doctorates awarded. *Degree requirements:* For master's, comprehensive exam (for some programs), thesis or alternative; for doctorate, comprehensive exam, thesis/dissertation, internship. *Entrance requirements:* For master's, GRE, minimum GPA of 2.75; for doctorate, GRE, minimum GPA of 3.5. Additional exam requirements/recommendations for international students: Required—TOEFL (minimum score 550 paper-based; 79 iBT), IELTS (minimum score 6.5). *Application deadline:* For fall admission, 1/1 priority date for domestic students; for spring admission, 9/1 for domestic students. Applications are processed on a rolling basis. Application fee: $56 ($96 for international students). *Financial support:* In 2016–17, 3 fellowships, 55 research assistantships, 77 teaching assistantships were awarded; career-related internships or fieldwork, Federal Work-Study, unspecified assistantships, and project assistantships also available. Support available to part-time students. Financial award application deadline: 4/15. *Unit head:* David Yu, Representative, 414-229-6169, E-mail: yu@uwm.edu. *Application contact:* Betty Warras, General Information Contact, 414-229-6169, Fax: 414-229-6967, E-mail: bwarras@uwm.edu.
Website: http://www4.uwm.edu/ceas/academics/graduate_programs/

University of Wyoming, College of Engineering and Applied Sciences, Department of Civil and Architectural Engineering, Program in Civil Engineering, Laramie, WY 82071. Offers MS, PhD. *Program availability:* Part-time. Terminal master's awarded for partial completion of doctoral program. *Degree requirements:* For master's, thesis (for some programs); for doctorate, variable foreign language requirement, comprehensive exam, thesis/dissertation. *Entrance requirements:* For master's, GRE General Test (minimum score 900), minimum GPA of 3.0; for doctorate, GRE General Test (minimum score: 1000), minimum GPA of 3.0. Additional exam requirements/recommendations for international students: Required—TOEFL. Electronic applications accepted. *Faculty research:* Structures, water, resources, geotechnical, transportation.

Utah State University, School of Graduate Studies, College of Engineering, Department of Civil and Environmental Engineering, Logan, UT 84322. Offers ME, MS, PhD, CE. *Degree requirements:* For master's, thesis (for some programs); for doctorate, thesis/dissertation. *Entrance requirements:* For master's and doctorate, GRE General Test, minimum GPA of 3.0. Additional exam requirements/recommendations for international students: Required—TOEFL. Electronic applications accepted. *Faculty research:* Hazardous waste treatment, large space structures, river basin management, earthquake engineering, environmental impact.

Vanderbilt University, School of Engineering, Department of Civil and Environmental Engineering, Program in Civil Engineering, Nashville, TN 37240-1001. Offers M Eng, MS, PhD. MS and PhD offered through the Graduate School. *Program availability:* Part-time. Terminal master's awarded for partial completion of doctoral program. *Degree requirements:* For master's, thesis; for doctorate, thesis/dissertation. *Entrance requirements:* For master's and doctorate, GRE General Test. Additional exam requirements/recommendations for international students: Required—TOEFL. Electronic applications accepted. *Expenses: Tuition:* Part-time $1854 per credit hour. *Faculty research:* Structural mechanics, finite element analysis, urban transportation, hazardous material transport.

Villanova University, College of Engineering, Department of Civil and Environmental Engineering, Program in Civil Engineering, Villanova, PA 19085-1699. Offers MSCE. *Program availability:* Part-time, evening/weekend. *Degree requirements:* For master's, thesis optional. *Entrance requirements:* For master's, GRE General Test (for applicants with degrees from foreign universities), minimum GPA of 3.0. Additional exam requirements/recommendations for international students: Required—TOEFL (minimum score 600 paper-based; 100 iBT). Electronic applications accepted. *Faculty research:* Bridge inspection, environment maintenance, economy and risk.

Virginia Polytechnic Institute and State University, Graduate School, College of Engineering, Blacksburg, VA 24061. Offers aerospace engineering (ME, MS, PhD); biological systems engineering (ME, MS, PhD); biomedical engineering (MS, PhD); chemical engineering (ME, MS, PhD); civil engineering (ME, MS, PhD); computer engineering (ME, MS, PhD); computer science (MS, PhD); electrical engineering (ME, PhD); engineering education (PhD); engineering mechanics (ME, MS, PhD); environmental engineering (MS); environmental science and engineering (MS); industrial and systems engineering (ME, MS, PhD); materials science and engineering (ME, MS, PhD); mechanical engineering (ME, MS, PhD); mining and minerals engineering (PhD); mining engineering (ME, MS); nuclear engineering (MS, PhD); ocean engineering (MS); systems engineering (ME, MS). *Faculty:* 400 full-time (73

women), 3 part-time/adjunct (2 women). *Students:* 1,949 full-time (487 women), 393 part-time (69 women); includes 251 minority (56 Black or African American, non-Hispanic/Latino; 3 American Indian or Alaska Native, non-Hispanic/Latino; 87 Asian, non-Hispanic/Latino; 70 Hispanic/Latino; 35 Two or more races, non-Hispanic/Latino), 1,354 international. Average age 27. 4,903 applicants, 19% accepted, 569 enrolled. In 2016, 364 master's, 200 doctorates awarded. *Degree requirements:* For master's, comprehensive exam (for some programs), thesis (for some programs); for doctorate, comprehensive exam (for some programs), thesis/dissertation (for some programs). *Entrance requirements:* For master's and doctorate, GRE/GMAT. Additional exam requirements/recommendations for international students: Required—TOEFL (minimum score 80 iBT). *Application deadline:* For fall admission, 8/1 for domestic students, 4/1 for international students; for spring admission, 1/1 for domestic students, 9/1 for international students. Applications are processed on a rolling basis. Application fee: $75. Electronic applications accepted. *Expenses:* Tuition, state resident: full-time $12,467; part-time $692.50 per credit hour. Tuition, nonresident: full-time $25,095; part-time $1394.25 per credit hour. *Required fees:* $2669; $491.50 per semester. Tuition and fees vary according to course load, campus/location and program. *Financial support:* In 2016–17, 160 fellowships with full tuition reimbursements (averaging $7,387 per year), 872 research assistantships with full tuition reimbursements (averaging $22,329 per year), 313 teaching assistantships with full tuition reimbursements (averaging $18,714 per year) were awarded. Financial award application deadline: 3/1; financial award applicants required to submit FAFSA. *Total annual research expenditures:* $91.8 million. *Unit head:* Dr. Julia Ross, Dean, 540-231-9752, Fax: 540-231-3031, E-mail: deaneng@vt.edu. *Application contact:* Linda Perkins, Executive Assistant, 540-231-9752, Fax: 540-231-3031, E-mail: lperkins@vt.edu.
Website: http://www.eng.vt.edu/

Virginia Polytechnic Institute and State University, VT Online, Blacksburg, VA 24061. Offers advanced transportation systems (Certificate); aerospace engineering (MS); agricultural and life sciences (MSLFS); business information systems (Graduate Certificate); career and technical education (MS); civil engineering (MS); computer engineering (M Eng, MS); decision support systems (Graduate Certificate); eLearning leadership (MA); electrical engineering (M Eng, MS); engineering administration (MEA); environmental engineering (Certificate); environmental politics and policy (Graduate Certificate); environmental sciences and engineering (MS); foundations of political analysis (Graduate Certificate); health product risk management (Graduate Certificate); industrial and systems engineering (MS); information policy and society (Graduate Certificate); information security (Graduate Certificate); information technology (MIT); instructional technology (MA); integrative STEM education (MA Ed); liberal arts (Graduate Certificate); life sciences: health product risk management (MS); natural resources (MNR, Graduate Certificate); networking (Graduate Certificate); nonprofit and nongovernmental organization management (Graduate Certificate); ocean engineering (MS); political science (MA); security studies (Graduate Certificate); software development (Graduate Certificate). *Expenses:* Tuition, state resident: full-time $12,467; part-time $692.50 per credit hour. Tuition, nonresident: full-time $25,095; part-time $1394.25 per credit hour. *Required fees:* $2669; $491.50 per semester. Tuition and fees vary according to course load, campus/location and program.

Washington State University, Voiland College of Engineering and Architecture, Department of Civil and Environmental Engineering, Pullman, WA 99164-2910. Offers civil engineering (MS, PhD); environmental engineering (MS). MS programs also offered at Tri-Cities campus. *Program availability:* Part-time. Terminal master's awarded for partial completion of doctoral program. *Degree requirements:* For master's, comprehensive exam (for some programs), thesis (for some programs), oral exam; for doctorate, comprehensive exam, thesis/dissertation, oral exam, written exam. *Entrance requirements:* For master's, minimum GPA of 3.0, 3 letters of recommendation, statement of purpose; for doctorate, minimum GPA of 3.4, 3 letters of recommendation, statement of purpose. Additional exam requirements/recommendations for international students: Required—TOEFL (minimum score 550 paper-based), IELTS. Electronic applications accepted. *Faculty research:* Environmental engineering, water resources, structural engineering, geotechnical, transportation.

Wayne State University, College of Engineering, Department of Civil and Environmental Engineering, Detroit, MI 48202. Offers civil engineering (MS). *Faculty:* 10. *Students:* 61 full-time (12 women), 35 part-time (5 women); includes 9 minority (2 Black or African American, non-Hispanic/Latino; 4 Asian, non-Hispanic/Latino; 3 Hispanic/Latino), 43 international. Average age 30. 260 applicants, 38% accepted, 26 enrolled. In 2016, 33 master's, 4 doctorates awarded. *Degree requirements:* For master's, thesis optional; for doctorate, thesis/dissertation. *Entrance requirements:* For master's, BS in civil engineering from ABET-accredited institution with minimum GPA of 3.0, statement of purpose; for doctorate, BS in civil engineering from ABET-accredited institution with minimum GPA of 3.3, 3.4 in last two years, or MS in civil engineering with minimum GPA of 3.5. Additional exam requirements/recommendations for international students: Required—TOEFL (minimum score 550 paper-based; 79 iBT), TWE (minimum score 5.5), Michigan English Language Assessment Battery (minimum score 85); Recommended—IELTS (minimum score 6.5). *Application deadline:* For fall admission, 3/1 priority date for domestic and international students; for winter admission, 10/1 priority date for domestic students, 9/1 priority date for international students; for spring admission, 2/1 priority date for domestic students, 1/1 priority date for international students. Applications are processed on a rolling basis. Application fee: $50. Electronic applications accepted. *Expenses:* $18,871 per year resident tuition and fees, $36,065 per year non-resident tuition and fees. *Financial support:* In 2016–17, 29 students received support, including 1 fellowship with tuition reimbursement available (averaging $16,000 per year), 7 research assistantships with tuition reimbursements available (averaging $17,493 per year), 7 teaching assistantships with tuition reimbursements available (averaging $19,295 per year); scholarships/grants, health care benefits, and unspecified assistantships also available. Support available to part-time students. Financial award applicants required to submit FAFSA. *Faculty research:* Traffic engineering and safety, infrastructure information systems using GIS, intelligent transportation systems, non-destructive evaluation of structures, infrastructure appraisal and upgrade, geosynthetics, water quality modeling, waste containment systems, liquefaction effects on piles and underground utilities, construction safety and quality management. *Total annual research expenditures:* $1.7 million. *Unit head:* Dr. Mumtaz Usman, Professor and Chair, 313-577-3608, E-mail: musmen@eng.wayne.edu. *Application contact:* Ellen Cope, Graduate Program Coordinator, 313-577-0409, E-mail: escope@wayne.edu.
Website: http://engineering.wayne.edu/cee/

Wentworth Institute of Technology, Master of Engineering in Civil Engineering Program, Boston, MA 02115-5998. Offers construction engineering (M Eng); infrastructure engineering (M Eng). *Program availability:* Part-time-only, evening/weekend. *Faculty:* 12 part-time/adjunct (4 women). *Students:* 17 part-time (4 women); includes 4 minority (2 Black or African American, non-Hispanic/Latino; 1 Hispanic/Latino; 1 Two or more races, non-Hispanic/Latino), 1 international. Average age 27. 10 applicants, 100% accepted, 10 enrolled. In 2016, 7 master's awarded. *Degree requirements:* For master's, thesis optional, capstone course. *Entrance requirements:* For master's, resume, statement of purpose, official transcripts, two professional recommendations, bachelor's degree, minimum GPA of 3.0, one year of professional experience in a technical role and/or technical organization. Additional exam requirements/recommendations for international students: Recommended—TOEFL (minimum score 525 paper-based). *Application deadline:* For fall admission, 8/1 for domestic and international students. Applications are processed on a rolling basis. Application fee: $50. Electronic applications accepted. *Expenses:* Contact institution. *Financial support:* Scholarships/grants available. Support available to part-time students. Financial award application deadline: 8/1; financial award applicants required to submit FAFSA. *Unit head:* Philip Hammond, Director of Graduate Programs, 617-989-4594, Fax: 617-989-4399, E-mail: hammondp1@wit.edu. *Application contact:* Martha Sheehan, Director of Admissions and Marketing, 617-989-4661, Fax: 617-989-4399, E-mail: sheehanm@wit.edu.
Website: http://wit.edu/continuinged/programs/civil-engineering-masters.html

Western Michigan University, Graduate College, College of Engineering and Applied Sciences, Department of Civil and Construction Engineering, Kalamazoo, MI 49008. Offers MSE.

Western New England University, College of Engineering, Department of Civil and Environmental Engineering, Springfield, MA 01119. Offers civil engineering (MS). *Program availability:* Part-time, evening/weekend. *Faculty:* 5 full-time. *Students:* 2 part-time, both international. Average age 27. 27 applicants, 19% accepted, 2 enrolled. *Degree requirements:* For master's, thesis optional. *Entrance requirements:* For master's, transcript, two letters of recommendations, resume, bachelor's degree in engineering or related field. Additional exam requirements/recommendations for international students: Required—TOEFL (minimum score 79 iBT). *Application deadline:* Applications are processed on a rolling basis. Application fee: $30. Electronic applications accepted. *Expenses:* Contact institution. *Financial support:* Application deadline: 4/15; applicants required to submit FAFSA. *Unit head:* Kenneth Lee, Chair, 413-782-1739, E-mail: kenneth.lee@wne.edu. *Application contact:* Matthew Fox, Director of Admissions for Graduate Students and Adult Learners, 413-782-1410, Fax: 413-782-1777, E-mail: study@wne.edu.
Website: http://www1.wne.edu/academics/graduate/civil-engineering-ms.cfm

West Virginia University, Statler College of Engineering and Mineral Resources, Department of Civil and Environmental Engineering, Morgantown, WV 26506. Offers civil engineering (MSCE, MSE, PhD). *Program availability:* Part-time. *Degree requirements:* For master's, thesis; for doctorate, comprehensive exam, thesis/dissertation. *Entrance requirements:* For master's and doctorate, minimum GPA of 3.0. Additional exam requirements/recommendations for international students: Required—TOEFL. *Faculty research:* Habitat restoration, advanced materials for civil infrastructure, pavement modeling, infrastructure condition assessment.

Widener University, Graduate Programs in Engineering, Program in Civil Engineering, Chester, PA 19013. Offers M Eng. *Program availability:* Part-time, evening/weekend. *Students:* 1 full-time (0 women), 3 part-time (0 women); includes 1 minority (Asian, non-Hispanic/Latino). Average age 30. In 2016, 1 master's awarded. *Degree requirements:* For master's, thesis optional. *Application deadline:* For fall admission, 8/1 priority date for domestic students; for spring admission, 12/1 for domestic students. Applications are processed on a rolling basis. Application fee: $0. Electronic applications accepted. Tuition and fees vary according to degree level and program. *Financial support:* Teaching assistantships with full tuition reimbursements and unspecified assistantships available. Financial award application deadline: 3/15. *Faculty research:* Environmental engineering, laws and water supply, structural analysis and design. *Unit head:* Rudolph Treichel, Assistant Dean/Director of Graduate Programs, 610-499-1294, E-mail: rjtreichel@widener.edu.

Worcester Polytechnic Institute, Graduate Studies and Research, Department of Civil and Environmental Engineering, Worcester, MA 01609-2280. Offers civil and environmental engineering (Advanced Certificate, Graduate Certificate); civil engineering (ME, MS, PhD); construction project management (MS); environmental engineering (M Eng, MS); master builder (M Eng). *Program availability:* Part-time, evening/weekend, blended/hybrid learning. *Faculty:* 10 full-time (0 women), 4 part-time/adjunct (0 women). *Students:* 31 full-time (15 women), 20 part-time (8 women); includes 5 minority (1 Black or African American, non-Hispanic/Latino; 1 American Indian or Alaska Native, non-Hispanic/Latino; 1 Hispanic/Latino; 2 Two or more races, non-Hispanic/Latino), 19 international. 111 applicants, 58% accepted, 13 enrolled. In 2016, 20 master's, 6 doctorates awarded. *Degree requirements:* For master's, thesis optional; for doctorate, comprehensive exam, thesis/dissertation. *Entrance requirements:* For master's, GRE (recommended), 3 letters of recommendation; for doctorate, GRE (recommended), 3 letters of recommendation, statement of purpose. Additional exam requirements/recommendations for international students: Required—TOEFL (minimum score 563 paper-based; 84 iBT), IELTS (minimum score 7), GRE. *Application deadline:* For fall admission, 1/1 priority date for domestic and international students; for spring admission, 10/1 priority date for domestic and international students. Applications are processed on a rolling basis. Application fee: $70. Electronic applications accepted. *Financial support:* Research assistantships, teaching assistantships, career-related internships or fieldwork, institutionally sponsored loans, scholarships/grants, and unspecified assistantships available. Financial award application deadline: 1/1; financial award applicants required to submit FAFSA. *Unit head:* Dr. Tahar El-Korchi, Interim Head, 508-831-5530, Fax: 508-831-5808, E-mail: tek@wpi.edu. *Application contact:* Dr. Rajib Mallick, Graduate Coordinator, 508-831-5530, Fax: 508-831-5808, E-mail: rajib@wpi.edu.
Website: http://www.wpi.edu/academics/cee

Youngstown State University, Graduate School, College of Science, Technology, Engineering and Mathematics, Department of Civil and Environmental Engineering, Youngstown, OH 44555-0001. Offers MSE. *Program availability:* Part-time, evening/weekend. *Degree requirements:* For master's, thesis optional. *Entrance requirements:* For master's, minimum GPA of 2.75 in field. Additional exam requirements/recommendations for international students: Required—TOEFL. *Faculty research:* Structural mechanics, water quality modeling, surface and ground water hydrology, physical and chemical processes in aquatic systems.

Construction Engineering

The American University in Cairo, School of Sciences and Engineering, Cairo, Egypt. Offers biotechnology (MS); chemistry (MS); computer science (MS); computing (M Comp); construction engineering (M Eng, MS); electronics and communications engineering (M Eng); environmental engineering (MS); environmental system design (M Eng); mechanical engineering (M Eng, MS); nanotechnology (MS); physics (MS); robotics, control and smart systems (MS); sciences and engineering (PhD); sustainable development (MS, Graduate Diploma). *Program availability:* Part-time, evening/weekend. *Faculty:* 43 full-time (4 women), 12 part-time/adjunct (1 woman). *Students:* 50 full-time (21 women), 262 part-time (128 women), 13 international. Average age 28. 193 applicants, 46% accepted, 55 enrolled. In 2016, 71 master's, 5 doctorates awarded. *Degree requirements:* For master's, comprehensive exam (for some programs), thesis (for some programs); for doctorate, comprehensive exam (for some programs), thesis/dissertation. *Entrance requirements:* Additional exam requirements/recommendations for international students: Required—TOEFL (minimum score 450 paper-based; 45 iBT), IELTS (minimum score 5). *Application deadline:* For fall admission, 2/1 priority date for domestic and international students; for spring admission, 10/15 priority date for domestic and international students. Applications are processed on a rolling basis. Application fee: $80. Electronic applications accepted. *Expenses:* Contact institution. *Financial support:* Fellowships with partial tuition reimbursements, scholarships/grants, and unspecified assistantships available. Financial award application deadline: 3/10. *Faculty research:* Construction, mechanical and electronics engineering, physics, computer science, biotechnology and nanotechnology. *Unit head:* Dr. Hassan El Fawal, Dean, 20-2-2615-2926, E-mail: hassan.elfawal@aucegypt.edu. *Application contact:* Maha Hegazi, Director for Graduate Admissions, 20-2-2615-1462, E-mail: mahahegazi@aucegypt.edu.
Website: http://www.aucegypt.edu/sse/Pages/default.aspx

Arizona State University at the Tempe campus, Ira A. Fulton Schools of Engineering, School of Sustainable Engineering and the Built Environment, Tempe, AZ 85287-5306. Offers civil, environmental and sustainable engineering (MS, MSE, PhD); construction engineering (MSE); construction management (MS, PhD). *Program availability:* Part-time, evening/weekend, online learning. Terminal master's awarded for partial completion of doctoral program. *Degree requirements:* For master's, thesis optional, comprehensive exams (MSE); interactive Program of Study (iPOS) submitted before completing 50 percent of required credit hours; for doctorate, comprehensive exam, thesis/dissertation, interactive Program of Study (iPOS) submitted before completing 50 percent of required credit hours. *Entrance requirements:* For master's, GRE, minimum GPA of 3.0 or equivalent in last 2 years of work leading to bachelor's degree; for doctorate, GRE, minimum GPA of 3.0 in last 2 years of work leading to bachelor's degree, 3.2 in all graduate-level coursework with master's degree; 3 letters of recommendation; resume/curriculum vitae; letter of intent; thesis (if applicable); statement of research interests. Additional exam requirements/recommendations for international students: Required—TOEFL, IELTS, or PTE. Electronic applications accepted. *Expenses:* Contact institution. *Faculty research:* Water purification, transportation (safety and materials), construction management, environmental biotechnology, environmental nanotechnology, earth systems engineering and management, SMART innovations, project performance metrics, and underground infrastructure.

Auburn University, Graduate School, College of Architecture, Design, and Construction, McWhorter School of Building Science, Auburn University, AL 36849. Offers MBC, MIDC. *Faculty:* 17 full-time (2 women), 2 part-time/adjunct (1 woman). *Students:* 23 full-time (5 women), 61 part-time (20 women); includes 19 minority (6 Black or African American, non-Hispanic/Latino; 3 Asian, non-Hispanic/Latino; 7 Hispanic/Latino; 1 Native Hawaiian or other Pacific Islander, non-Hispanic/Latino; 2 Two or more races, non-Hispanic/Latino), 3 international. Average age 36. 123 applicants, 82% accepted, 39 enrolled. In 2016, 40 master's awarded. *Entrance requirements:* For master's, GRE General Test. *Application deadline:* Applications are processed on a rolling basis. Application fee: $50 ($60 for international students). Electronic applications accepted. *Expenses:* Tuition, state resident: full-time $9072; part-time $504 per credit hour. Tuition, nonresident: full-time $27,216; part-time $1512 per credit hour. *Required fees:* $812 per semester. Tuition and fees vary according to degree level and program. *Financial support:* Application deadline: 3/15; applicants required to submit FAFSA. *Unit head:* Dr. Richard Burt, Head, 334-844-5260. *Application contact:* Dr. George Flowers, Dean of the Graduate School, 334-844-2125.
Website: http://cadc.auburn.edu/construction

Bradley University, The Graduate School, Caterpillar College of Engineering and Technology, Department of Civil Engineering and Construction, Peoria, IL 61625-0002. Offers MSCE. *Program availability:* Part-time, evening/weekend. *Degree requirements:* For master's, comprehensive exam. *Entrance requirements:* Additional exam requirements/recommendations for international students: Required—TOEFL (minimum score 550 paper-based; 79 iBT), IELTS (minimum score 6.5). *Application deadline:* For fall admission, 5/15 priority date for domestic and international students; for spring admission, 10/15 priority date for domestic and international students. Applications are processed on a rolling basis. Application fee: $40 ($50 for international students). Electronic applications accepted. *Expenses: Tuition:* Full-time $7650; part-time $850 per credit. *Required fees:* $50 per credit. One-time fee: $100 full-time. *Financial support:* Research assistantships with full and partial tuition reimbursements, teaching assistantships, scholarships/grants, tuition waivers (partial), and unspecified assistantships available. Support available to part-time students. Financial award application deadline: 4/1. *Unit head:* Souhail Elhouar, Chairman, 309-677-3830, E-mail: selhouar@bradley.edu. *Application contact:* Kayla Carroll, Director of International Admissions and Student Services, 309-677-2375, E-mail: klcarroll@fsmail.bradley.edu.
Website: http://www.bradley.edu/academic/departments/cec/

Colorado School of Mines, Office of Graduate Studies, Department of Civil and Environmental Engineering, Golden, CO 80401. Offers civil and environmental engineering (MS, PhD); environmental engineering science (MS, PhD); underground construction and tunneling (MS, PhD). *Program availability:* Part-time. *Degree requirements:* For master's, thesis (for some programs); for doctorate, comprehensive exam, thesis/dissertation. *Entrance requirements:* For master's and doctorate, GRE General Test. Additional exam requirements/recommendations for international students: Required—TOEFL (minimum score 550 paper-based; 80 iBT). Electronic applications accepted. *Expenses:* Tuition, state resident: full-time $15,690. Tuition, nonresident: full-time $34,020. *Required fees:* $2152. Tuition and fees vary according to course load. *Faculty research:* Treatment of water and wastes, environmental law: policy and practice, natural environment systems, hazardous waste management, environmental data analysis.

Colorado School of Mines, Office of Graduate Studies, Department of Mining Engineering, Golden, CO 80401. Offers mining and earth systems engineering (MS); mining engineering (PhD); underground construction and tunneling (MS, PhD). *Program availability:* Part-time. *Degree requirements:* For master's, thesis (for some programs); for doctorate, comprehensive exam, thesis/dissertation. *Entrance requirements:* For master's and doctorate, GRE General Test. Additional exam requirements/recommendations for international students: Required—TOEFL (minimum score 550 paper-based; 80 iBT). Electronic applications accepted. *Expenses:* Tuition, state resident: full-time $15,690. Tuition, nonresident: full-time $34,020. *Required fees:* $2152. Tuition and fees vary according to course load. *Faculty research:* Mine evaluation and planning, geostatistics, mining robotics, water jet cutting, rock mechanics.

Columbia University, Fu Foundation School of Engineering and Applied Science, Department of Civil Engineering and Engineering Mechanics, New York, NY 10027. Offers civil engineering (MS, Eng Sc D, PhD); construction engineering and management (MS); engineering mechanics (MS, Eng Sc D, PhD). *Program availability:* Part-time, online learning. Terminal master's awarded for partial completion of doctoral program. *Degree requirements:* For doctorate, thesis/dissertation, qualifying exam. *Entrance requirements:* For master's and doctorate, GRE General Test. Additional exam requirements/recommendations for international students: Required—TOEFL, IELTS, PTE. Electronic applications accepted. *Faculty research:* Structural dynamics, structural health and monitoring, fatigue and fracture mechanics, geo-environmental engineering, multiscale science and engineering.

Concordia University, School of Graduate Studies, Faculty of Engineering and Computer Science, Department of Building, Civil and Environmental Engineering, Montréal, QC H3G 1M8, Canada. Offers building engineering (M Eng, MA Sc, PhD, Certificate); civil engineering (M Eng, MA Sc, PhD); environmental engineering (Certificate). *Degree requirements:* For master's, thesis or alternative; for doctorate, comprehensive exam, thesis/dissertation. *Faculty research:* Structural engineering, geotechnical engineering, water resources and fluid engineering, transportation engineering, systems engineering.

George Mason University, Volgenau School of Engineering, Sid and Reva Dewberry Department of Civil, Environmental, and Infrastructure Engineering, Fairfax, VA 22030. Offers construction project management (MS); geotechnical, construction, and structural engineering (M Eng); transportation engineering (PhD). *Faculty:* 14 full-time (6 women), 20 part-time/adjunct (4 women). *Students:* 47 full-time (12 women), 62 part-time (22 women); includes 23 minority (6 Black or African American, non-Hispanic/Latino; 9 Asian, non-Hispanic/Latino; 7 Hispanic/Latino; 1 Native Hawaiian or other Pacific Islander, non-Hispanic/Latino), 38 international. Average age 29. 109 applicants, 77% accepted, 39 enrolled. In 2016, 31 master's, 1 doctorate awarded. *Degree requirements:* For master's, thesis (for some programs), 30 credits, departmental seminars; for doctorate, thesis/dissertation, qualifying exams. *Entrance requirements:* For master's, GRE, photocopy of passport; 2 official college transcripts; resume; official bank statement; proof of financial support; expanded goals statement; self-evaluation form; BS in engineering or other related science; 3 letters of recommendation; for doctorate, GRE (for those who received degree outside of the U.S.), photocopy of passport; 2 official college transcripts; resume; official bank statement; proof of financial support; expanded goals statement; self-evaluation form; baccalaureate degree in engineering or related science; master's degree (preferred); 3 letters of recommendation. Additional exam requirements/recommendations for international students: Required—TOEFL (minimum score 575 paper-based; 88 iBT), IELTS (minimum score 6.5), PTE (minimum score 59). *Application deadline:* For fall admission, 1/15 priority date for domestic students. Application fee: $75 ($80 for international students). Electronic applications accepted. *Expenses:* Contact institution. *Financial support:* In 2016–17, 27 students received support, including 1 fellowship (averaging $10,000 per year), 16 research assistantships with tuition reimbursements available (averaging $20,150 per year), 10 teaching assistantships with tuition reimbursements available (averaging $21,000 per year); career-related internships or fieldwork, Federal Work-Study, scholarships/grants, unspecified assistantships, and health care benefits (for full-time research or teaching assistantship recipients) also available. Support available to part-time students. Financial award application deadline: 3/1; financial award applicants required to submit FAFSA. *Faculty research:* Evolutionary design, infrastructure security, intelligent transportation systems, national transportation networks, water quality modeling. *Total annual research expenditures:* $568,705. *Unit head:* LIza Wilson Durant, Acting Chair, 703-993-1687, Fax: 703-993-9790, E-mail: ldurant2@gmu.edu. *Application contact:* Laura Kosoglu, Director, Graduate Program, 703-993-1675, Fax: 703-993-9790, E-mail: ceiegrad@gmu.edu.
Website: http://civil.gmu.edu/

Illinois Institute of Technology, Graduate College, Armour College of Engineering, Department of Civil, Architectural and Environmental Engineering, Chicago, IL 60616. Offers architectural engineering (M Arch E); civil engineering (MS, PhD), including architectural engineering (MS), construction engineering and management (MS), geoenvironmental engineering (MS), geotechnical engineering (MS), structural engineering (MS), transportation engineering (MS); construction engineering and management (MCEM); environmental engineering (M Env E, MS, PhD); geoenvironmental engineering (M Geoenv E); geotechnical engineering (MGE); infrastructure engineering and management (MPW); structural engineering (MSE); transportation engineering (M Trans E). *Program availability:* Part-time, evening/weekend, online learning. Terminal master's awarded for partial completion of doctoral program. *Degree requirements:* For master's, thesis (for some programs); for doctorate, comprehensive exam, thesis/dissertation. *Entrance requirements:* For master's, GRE General Test (minimum score 900 Quantitative and Verbal, 2.5 Analytical Writing), minimum undergraduate GPA of 3.0; for doctorate, GRE General Test (minimum score 1000 Quantitative and Verbal, 3.0 Analytical Writing), minimum undergraduate GPA of 3.0. Additional exam requirements/recommendations for international students: Required—TOEFL (minimum score 550 paper-based; 80 iBT). Electronic applications accepted. *Faculty research:* Structural, architectural, geotechnical and geoenvironmental engineering; construction engineering and management; transportation engineering; environmental engineering and public works.

Iowa State University of Science and Technology, Department of Civil and Construction Engineering, Ames, IA 50011. Offers civil engineering (MS, PhD), including civil engineering materials, construction engineering and management, environmental engineering, geotechnical engineering, structural engineering, transportation engineering. *Degree requirements:* For master's, thesis or alternative; for doctorate, thesis/dissertation. *Entrance requirements:* For master's and doctorate, GRE General Test. Additional exam requirements/recommendations for international students: Required—TOEFL (minimum score 550 paper-based; 82 iBT), IELTS (minimum score 6.5). *Application deadline:* For fall admission, 2/1 priority date for domestic students, 2/1 for international students; for spring admission, 8/1 priority date for domestic students, 8/1 for international students. Application fee: $60 ($90 for international students). Electronic applications accepted. *Application contact:* Kathy Petersen, Application

Construction Engineering

Contact, 515-294-4975, Fax: 515-294-8216, E-mail: ccee-grad-inquiry@iastate.edu. Website: http://www.ccee.iastate.edu/

Lawrence Technological University, College of Engineering, Southfield, MI 48075-1058. Offers architectural engineering (MS); automotive engineering (MS); biomedical engineering (MS); civil engineering (MA, MS, PhD), including environmental engineering (MS), geotechnical engineering (MS), structural engineering (MS), transportation engineering (MS), water resource engineering (MS); construction engineering management (MA); electrical and computer engineering (MS); engineering management (MA); engineering technology (MS); fire engineering (MS); industrial engineering (MS), including healthcare; manufacturing systems (ME); mechanical engineering (MS, DE, PhD), including manufacturing (DE), solid mechanics (MS), thermal-fluids (MS); mechatronic systems engineering (MS). *Program availability:* Part-time, evening/weekend. *Faculty:* 24 full-time (5 women), 26 part-time/adjunct (2 women). *Students:* 22 full-time (7 women), 588 part-time (81 women); includes 23 minority (11 Black or African American, non-Hispanic/Latino; 4 Asian, non-Hispanic/Latino; 7 Hispanic/Latino; 1 Two or more races, non-Hispanic/Latino), 469 international. Average age 27. 1,186 applicants, 39% accepted, 99 enrolled. In 2016, 293 master's, 3 doctorates awarded. Terminal master's awarded for partial completion of doctoral program. *Degree requirements:* For master's, thesis optional; for doctorate, comprehensive exam, thesis/dissertation optional. *Entrance requirements:* Additional exam requirements/recommendations for international students: Required—TOEFL (minimum score 550 paper-based; 79 iBT), IELTS (minimum score 6.5). *Application deadline:* For fall admission, 5/22 for international students; for spring admission, 10/11 for international students; for summer admission, 2/16 for international students. Applications are processed on a rolling basis. Application fee: $50. Electronic applications accepted. *Expenses: Tuition:* Full-time $14,868; part-time $1062 per credit. *Required fees:* $75 per semester. Tuition and fees vary according to campus/location. *Financial support:* In 2016–17, 25 students received support, including 5 research assistantships with full tuition reimbursements available; unspecified assistantships also available. Financial award application deadline: 4/1; financial award applicants required to submit FAFSA. *Faculty research:* Carbon fiber reinforced polymer reinforced concrete structures; low impact storm water management solutions; vehicle battery energy management; wireless communication; entrepreneurial mindset and engineering. *Total annual research expenditures:* $1.7 million. *Unit head:* Dr. Nabil Grace, Dean, 248-204-2500, Fax: 248-204-2509, E-mail: engrdean@ltu.edu. *Application contact:* Jane Rohrback, Director of Admissions, 248-204-3160, Fax: 248-204-2228, E-mail: admissions@ltu.edu. Website: http://www.ltu.edu/engineering/index.asp

Marquette University, Graduate School, College of Engineering, Department of Civil and Environmental Engineering, Milwaukee, WI 53201-1881. Offers construction engineering and management (MS, PhD, Certificate); environmental engineering (MS, PhD); structural design (Certificate); structural engineering and structural mechanics (MS, PhD); transportation (Certificate); transportation engineering and materials (MS, PhD); waste and wastewater treatment processes (Certificate); water resources engineering (Certificate). *Program availability:* Part-time, evening/weekend. *Faculty:* 17 full-time (2 women), 2 part-time/adjunct (0 women). *Students:* 27 full-time (8 women), 6 part-time (0 women); includes 5 minority (1 Asian, non-Hispanic/Latino; 2 Hispanic/Latino; 2 Two or more races, non-Hispanic/Latino), 13 international. Average age 28. 70 applicants, 56% accepted, 9 enrolled. In 2016, 8 master's, 5 doctorates awarded. Terminal master's awarded for partial completion of doctoral program. *Degree requirements:* For master's, comprehensive exam (for some programs), thesis or alternative; for doctorate, thesis/dissertation. *Entrance requirements:* For master's, GRE General Test (recommended), minimum GPA of 3.0, official transcripts from all current and previous colleges/universities except Marquette, three letters of recommendation; for doctorate, GRE General Test, minimum GPA of 3.0, official transcripts from all current and previous colleges/universities except Marquette, three letters of recommendation, brief statement of purpose, submission of any English language publications authored by applicant (strongly recommended). Additional exam requirements/recommendations for international students: Required—TOEFL (minimum score 530 paper-based). *Application deadline:* For fall admission, 6/1 priority date for domestic students. Applications are processed on a rolling basis. Application fee: $50. Electronic applications accepted. *Financial support:* Fellowships, research assistantships, teaching assistantships, scholarships/grants, health care benefits, tuition waivers (partial), and unspecified assistantships available. Support available to part-time students. Financial award application deadline: 2/15. *Faculty research:* Highway safety, highway performance, and intelligent transportation systems; surface mount technology; watershed management. *Total annual research expenditures:* $480,876. *Unit head:* Dr. Christopher Foley, Chair, 414-288-5741. *Application contact:* Dr. Stephen M. Heinrich, Director of Graduate Studies, 414-288-5466.
Website: http://www.marquette.edu/civil-environmental-engineering/

Massachusetts Institute of Technology, School of Engineering, Department of Civil and Environmental Engineering, Cambridge, MA 02139. Offers biological oceanography (PhD, Sc D); chemical oceanography (PhD, Sc D); civil and environmental engineering (M Eng, SM, PhD, Sc D); civil and environmental systems (PhD, Sc D); civil engineering (PhD, Sc D, CE); civil engineering and computation (PhD); coastal engineering (PhD, Sc D); construction engineering and management (PhD, Sc D); environmental biology (PhD, Sc D); environmental chemistry (PhD, Sc D); environmental engineering (PhD, Sc D); environmental engineering and computation (PhD); environmental fluid mechanics (PhD, Sc D); geotechnical and geoenvironmental engineering (PhD, Sc D); hydrology (PhD, Sc D); information technology (PhD, Sc D); oceanographic engineering (PhD, Sc D); structures and materials (PhD, Sc D); transportation (PhD, Sc D); SM/MBA. *Faculty:* 35 full-time (6 women). *Students:* 192 full-time (64 women); includes 25 minority (2 Black or African American, non-Hispanic/Latino; 11 Asian, non-Hispanic/Latino; 8 Hispanic/Latino; 4 Two or more races, non-Hispanic/Latino), 113 international. Average age 27. 530 applicants, 20% accepted, 77 enrolled. In 2016, 56 master's, 16 doctorates, 1 other advanced degree awarded. *Degree requirements:* For master's, thesis; for doctorate, comprehensive exam, thesis/dissertation; for CE, comprehensive exam, thesis. *Entrance requirements:* For master's, doctorate, and CE, GRE General Test. Additional exam requirements/recommendations for international students: Required—TOEFL, IELTS. *Application deadline:* For fall admission, 12/15 for domestic and international students. Application fee: $75. Electronic applications accepted. *Expenses: Tuition:* Full-time $46,400; part-time $725 per credit. One-time fee: $312 full-time. Full-time tuition and fees vary according to course load and program. *Financial support:* In 2016–17, 150 students received support, including fellowships (averaging $41,900 per year), 124 research assistantships (averaging $36,900 per year), 9 teaching assistantships (averaging $36,900 per year); Federal Work-Study, institutionally sponsored loans, scholarships/grants, traineeships, health care benefits, unspecified assistantships, and resident tutors also available. Support available to part-time students. Financial award application deadline: 5/1; financial award applicants required to submit FAFSA. *Faculty research:* Environmental chemistry, environmental fluid mechanics and coastal engineering, environmental microbiology, geotechnical engineering and geomechanics, hydrology and hydro climatology, infrastructure systems, mechanics of materials and structures, transportation systems. *Total annual research expenditures:* $25 million. *Unit head:* Prof. Markus Buehler, Department Head, 617-253-7101. *Application contact:* 617-253-7119, E-mail: cee-admissions@mit.edu. Website: http://cee.mit.edu/

Missouri University of Science and Technology, Graduate School, Department of Civil, Architectural, and Environmental Engineering, Rolla, MO 65409. Offers civil engineering (MS, DE, PhD); construction engineering (MS, DE, PhD); environmental engineering (MS); fluid mechanics (MS, DE, PhD); geotechnical engineering (MS, DE, PhD); hydrology and hydraulic engineering (MS, DE, PhD). *Program availability:* Part-time, evening/weekend. Terminal master's awarded for partial completion of doctoral program. *Degree requirements:* For master's, thesis optional; for doctorate, comprehensive exam, thesis/dissertation. *Entrance requirements:* For master's, GRE General Test (minimum combined score 1100), minimum GPA of 3.0; for doctorate, GRE General Test (minimum score: verbal and quantitative 400, writing 3.5), minimum GPA of 3.0. Additional exam requirements/recommendations for international students: Required—TOEFL (minimum score 550 paper-based). Electronic applications accepted. *Faculty research:* Earthquake engineering, structural optimization and control systems, structural health monitoring/damage detection, soil-structure interaction, soil mechanics and foundation engineering.

Montana State University, The Graduate School, College of Engineering, Department of Civil Engineering, Bozeman, MT 59717. Offers civil engineering (MS); construction engineering management (MCEM); engineering (PhD), including applied mechanics option, civil engineering option. *Program availability:* Part-time. *Degree requirements:* For master's, comprehensive exam, thesis (for some programs); for doctorate, comprehensive exam, thesis/dissertation. *Entrance requirements:* For master's and doctorate, GRE General Test. Additional exam requirements/recommendations for international students: Required—TOEFL (minimum score 550 paper-based). Electronic applications accepted. *Faculty research:* Snow and ice mechanics, biofilm engineering, transportation, structural and geo materials, water resources.

Ohio University, Graduate College, Russ College of Engineering and Technology, Department of Civil Engineering, Athens, OH 45701-2979. Offers civil engineering (PhD); construction engineering and management (MS); environmental (MS); geotechnical and geoenvironmental (MS); mechanics (MS); structures (MS); transportation (MS); water resources (MS). *Program availability:* Part-time. *Degree requirements:* For master's, comprehensive exam (for some programs), thesis or alternative; for doctorate, comprehensive exam, thesis/dissertation. *Entrance requirements:* For master's, GRE General Test, minimum GPA of 3.0, 3 letters of recommendation; for doctorate, GRE General Test. Additional exam requirements/recommendations for international students: Required—TOEFL (minimum score 550 paper-based; 80 iBT) or IELTS (minimum score 6.5). *Application deadline:* For fall admission, 5/1 priority date for domestic students, 2/1 priority date for international students; for winter admission, 8/1 priority date for domestic students, 4/1 priority date for international students; for spring admission, 2/1 priority date for domestic students, 7/1 priority date for international students. Applications are processed on a rolling basis. Application fee: $50 ($55 for international students). Electronic applications accepted. *Financial support:* Research assistantships with full tuition reimbursements, teaching assistantships with full tuition reimbursements, Federal Work-Study, institutionally sponsored loans, scholarships/grants, and unspecified assistantships available. Financial award application deadline: 3/15; financial award applicants required to submit FAFSA. *Faculty research:* Noise abatement, materials and environment, highway infrastructure, subsurface investigation (pavements, pipes, bridges). *Unit head:* Dr. Gayle F. Mitchell, Chair, 740-593-0430, Fax: 740-593-0625, E-mail: mitchelg@ohio.edu. *Application contact:* Dr. Shad M. Sargand, Graduate Chair, 740-593-1465, Fax: 740-593-0625, E-mail: sargand@ohio.edu.
Website: http://www.ohio.edu/civil/

Oregon State University, College of Engineering, Program in Civil Engineering, Corvallis, OR 97331. Offers civil engineering (M Eng, MS, PhD); coastal and ocean engineering (M Eng, MS, PhD); construction engineering management (M Eng, MS, PhD); engineering education (M Eng, MS, PhD); geomatics (M Eng, MS, PhD); geotechnical engineering (M Eng, MS, PhD); infrastructure materials (M Eng, MS, PhD); structural engineering (M Eng, MS, PhD); transportation engineering (M Eng). *Faculty:* 42 full-time (8 women), 2 part-time/adjunct (0 women). *Students:* 157 full-time (48 women), 10 part-time (3 women); includes 18 minority (7 Asian, non-Hispanic/Latino; 7 Hispanic/Latino; 1 Native Hawaiian or other Pacific Islander, non-Hispanic/Latino; 3 Two or more races, non-Hispanic/Latino), 92 international. Average age 28. 379 applicants, 31% accepted, 50 enrolled. In 2016, 55 master's, 5 doctorates awarded. *Entrance requirements:* For master's and doctorate, GRE. Additional exam requirements/recommendations for international students: Required—TOEFL (minimum score 80 iBT), IELTS (minimum score 6.5). *Application deadline:* For fall admission, 8/1 for domestic students, 4/1 for international students; for winter admission, 12/1 for domestic students, 7/1 for international students; for spring admission, 2/1 for domestic students, 10/1 for international students; for summer admission, 5/1 for domestic students, 1/1 for international students. Application fee: $75 ($85 for international students). *Expenses:* $14,130 resident full-time tuition, $23,769 non-resident. *Financial support:* Application deadline: 1/15. *Unit head:* Dr. Jason Weiss, School Head/Professor. *Application contact:* Shannon Reed, Graduate Program Coordinator, 541-737-4575, E-mail: shannon.reed@oregonstate.edu.
Website: http://cce.oregonstate.edu/graduate-academics

Pittsburg State University, Graduate School, College of Technology, School of Construction, Pittsburg, KS 66762. Offers construction engineering technology (MET). *Program availability:* Part-time, 100% online, blended/hybrid learning. *Students:* 59 (9 women); includes 4 minority (2 Black or African American, non-Hispanic/Latino; 1 Asian, non-Hispanic/Latino; 1 Two or more races, non-Hispanic/Latino), 35 international. In 2016, 42 master's awarded. *Degree requirements:* For master's, thesis or alternative. *Entrance requirements:* Additional exam requirements/recommendations for international students: Required—TOEFL (minimum score 550 paper-based; 79 iBT), IELTS (minimum score 6.5), PTE (minimum score 53). *Application deadline:* For fall admission, 7/15 for domestic students, 6/1 for international students; for spring admission, 12/15 for domestic students, 10/15 for international students; for summer admission, 5/15 for domestic students, 4/1 for international students. Applications are processed on a rolling basis. Application fee: $35 ($60 for international students). Electronic applications accepted. *Expenses:* Contact institution. *Financial support:* In 2016–17, 4 teaching assistantships with full tuition reimbursements (averaging $5,500 per year) were awarded. Financial award application deadline: 2/1; financial award applicants required to submit FAFSA. *Unit head:* Jim Otter, Director/Professor, 620-235-4349. *Application contact:* Lisa Allen, Assistant Director of Graduate and Continuing Studies, 620-235-4218, Fax: 620-235-4219, E-mail: lallen@pittstate.edu.
Website: http://www.pittstate.edu/department/construction/

Stanford University, School of Engineering, Department of Civil and Environmental Engineering, Stanford, CA 94305-2004. Offers atmosphere and energy (MS, PhD); construction (MS), including construction engineering and management, design-construction integration, sustainable design and construction; environmental engineering and science (MS, PhD, Eng); environmental fluid mechanics and hydrology (PhD); geomechanics (MS); structural engineering (MS). Terminal master's awarded for partial completion of doctoral program. *Degree requirements:* For doctorate, thesis/

dissertation, qualifying exam; for Eng, thesis. *Entrance requirements:* For master's, doctorate, and Eng, GRE General Test. Additional exam requirements/recommendations for international students: Required—TOEFL. Electronic applications accepted. *Expenses: Tuition:* Full-time $47,331. *Required fees:* $609.

Stevens Institute of Technology, Graduate School, Charles V. Schaefer Jr. School of Engineering and Science, Department of Civil, Environmental, and Ocean Engineering, Program in Construction Management, Hoboken, NJ 07030. Offers construction management (MS, Certificate), including construction accounting/estimating (Certificate), construction engineering (Certificate), construction law/disputes (Certificate), construction/quality management (Certificate). *Program availability:* Part-time, evening/weekend. *Students:* 50 full-time (21 women), 22 part-time (6 women); includes 3 minority (all Black or African American, non-Hispanic/Latino), 49 international. Average age 25. 157 applicants, 72% accepted, 28 enrolled. In 2016, 39 master's, 15 other advanced degrees awarded. *Degree requirements:* For master's, thesis optional, minimum B average in major field and overall; for Certificate, minimum B average. *Entrance requirements:* Additional exam requirements/recommendations for international students: Required—TOEFL (minimum score 74 iBT), IELTS (minimum score 6). *Application deadline:* For fall admission, 6/1 for domestic students, 4/15 for international students; for spring admission, 11/30 for domestic students, 11/1 for international students. Applications are processed on a rolling basis. Application fee: $65. Electronic applications accepted. *Expenses:* Contact institution. *Financial support:* Fellowships, research assistantships, teaching assistantships, career-related internships or fieldwork, Federal Work-Study, scholarships/grants, and unspecified assistantships available. Financial award application deadline: 2/15; financial award applicants required to submit FAFSA. *Unit head:* Dr. Linda Thomas, Director, 201-216-5681, E-mail: lthomas2@stevens.edu. *Application contact:* Graduate Admission, 888-783-8367, Fax: 888-511-1306, E-mail: graduate@stevens.edu.

Texas Tech University, Graduate School, Edward E. Whitacre Jr. College of Engineering, Department of Civil, Environmental, and Construction Engineering, Lubbock, TX 79409-1023. Offers civil engineering (MSCE, PhD); environmental engineering (MENVEGR). *Accreditation:* ABET. *Program availability:* Part-time. *Faculty:* 34 full-time (6 women), 7 part-time/adjunct (0 women). *Students:* 106 full-time (36 women), 13 part-time (3 women); includes 24 minority (3 Asian, non-Hispanic/Latino; 20 Hispanic/Latino; 1 Two or more races, non-Hispanic/Latino), 63 international. Average age 27. 170 applicants, 52% accepted, 39 enrolled. In 2016, 28 master's, 8 doctorates awarded. Terminal master's awarded for partial completion of doctoral program. *Degree requirements:* For master's, comprehensive exam, thesis or alternative; for doctorate, comprehensive exam, thesis/dissertation, preliminary examination. *Entrance requirements:* For master's and doctorate, GRE (Verbal and Quantitative). Additional exam requirements/recommendations for international students: Required—TOEFL (minimum score 550 paper-based; 79 iBT), IELTS (minimum score 6.5). *Application deadline:* For fall admission, 6/1 priority date for domestic students, 1/15 priority date for international students; for spring admission, 9/1 priority date for domestic students, 6/15 priority date for international students. Applications are processed on a rolling basis. Application fee: $75. Electronic applications accepted. *Expenses:* $325 per credit hour full-time resident tuition, $733 per credit hour full-time non-resident tuition; $53.75 per credit hour fee plus $608 per term fee. *Financial support:* In 2016–17, 99 students received support, including 71 fellowships (averaging $4,370 per year), 56 research assistantships (averaging $12,343 per year), 33 teaching assistantships (averaging $15,807 per year); scholarships/grants, tuition waivers (partial), and unspecified assistantships also available. Financial award application deadline: 3/1; financial award applicants required to submit FAFSA. *Faculty research:* Geotechnical engineering, transportation engineering, water resources engineering, environmental engineering, wind engineering, construction engineering management. *Total annual research expenditures:* $3.5 million. *Unit head:* Dr. David Ernst, Interim Chair, 806-834-8657, Fax: 806-742-3488, E-mail: david.ernst@ttu.edu. *Application contact:* Dr. Priyantha Jayawickrama, Associate Professor, 806-742-3523 Ext. 245, Fax: 806-742-3488, E-mail: priyantha.jayawickrama@ttu.edu.
Website: http://www.depts.ttu.edu/ceweb/

The University of Alabama, Graduate School, College of Engineering, Department of Civil, Construction and Environmental Engineering, Tuscaloosa, AL 35487-0205. Offers civil engineering (MSCE, PhD); environmental engineering (MS). *Program availability:* Part-time. *Faculty:* 20 full-time (2 women). *Students:* 55 full-time (14 women), 7 part-time (2 women); includes 2 minority (1 Black or African American, non-Hispanic/Latino; 1 Asian, non-Hispanic/Latino), 29 international. Average age 28. 69 applicants, 52% accepted, 15 enrolled. In 2016, 24 master's, 2 doctorates awarded. Terminal master's awarded for partial completion of doctoral program. *Degree requirements:* For master's, thesis or alternative; for doctorate, comprehensive exam, thesis/dissertation. *Entrance requirements:* For master's and doctorate, GRE General Test (minimum combined score of 300), minimum overall GPA of 3.0 in last hours of course work. Additional exam requirements/recommendations for international students: Required—TOEFL (minimum score 550 paper-based; 79 iBT), IELTS (minimum score 6.5), PTE (minimum score 59). *Application deadline:* Applications are processed on a rolling basis. Application fee: $50 ($60 for international students). Electronic applications accepted. *Expenses:* Tuition, state resident: full-time $10,470. Tuition, nonresident: full-time $26,950. *Financial support:* In 2016–17, 40 students received support, including 2 fellowships with full tuition reimbursements available (averaging $30,000 per year), 17 research assistantships with full tuition reimbursements available (averaging $13,275 per year), 20 teaching assistantships with full tuition reimbursements available (averaging $13,275 per year); scholarships/grants, tuition waivers (partial), and unspecified assistantships also available. Financial award application deadline: 1/5. *Faculty research:* Experimental structures, modeling of structures, bridge management systems, geotechnological engineering, environmental remediation. *Total annual research expenditures:* $5.7 million. *Unit head:* Dr. W. Edward Back, Head/Professor, 205-348-6550, Fax: 205-348-0783, E-mail: eback@eng.ua.edu. *Application contact:* Dr. Andrew Graettinger, Professor and Graduate Program Director, 205-348-1707, Fax: 205-348-0783, E-mail: andrewg@eng.ua.edu.
Website: http://cce.eng.ua.edu/

The University of Alabama at Birmingham, School of Engineering, Program in Civil Engineering, Birmingham, AL 35294. Offers construction engineering management (M Eng); structural engineering (M Eng); sustainable smart cities (M Eng). Program offered jointly with The University of Alabama in Huntsville. *Program availability:* Part-time, evening/weekend, 100% online. *Faculty:* 15 full-time (4 women), 3 part-time/adjunct. *Students:* 16 full-time (6 women), 24 part-time (5 women); includes 22 minority (5 Black or African American, non-Hispanic/Latino; 12 Asian, non-Hispanic/Latino; 4 Hispanic/Latino; 1 Two or more races, non-Hispanic/Latino). Average age 30. 16 applicants, 56% accepted, 5 enrolled. In 2016, 15 master's, 3 doctorates awarded. *Degree requirements:* For master's, comprehensive exam, thesis optional; for doctorate, comprehensive exam, thesis/dissertation. *Entrance requirements:* For master's, GRE General Test preferred (minimum score of 500 on each component), minimum GPA of 3.0 in all undergraduate degree major courses attempted, letters of evaluation. Additional exam requirements/recommendations for international students: Required—TOEFL (minimum score 550 paper-based), TWE (minimum score 3.5). *Application deadline:* For fall admission, 7/1 for domestic and international students; for spring

admission, 11/1 for domestic and international students; for summer admission, 4/1 for domestic and international students. Applications are processed on a rolling basis. Application fee: $50 ($60 for international students). Electronic applications accepted. *Expenses:* $396 per hour resident tuition; $935 per hour non-resident tuition; $150 per course online course fee. *Financial support:* In 2016–17, 15 students received support, including 1 fellowship with full tuition reimbursement available (averaging $24,000 per year), 14 research assistantships with full and partial tuition reimbursements available (averaging $17,472 per year). *Total annual research expenditures:* $1.1 million. *Unit head:* Dr. Fouad H. Fouad, Chair, 205-934-8430, Fax: 205-934-9855, E-mail: ffouad@uab.edu. *Application contact:* Holly Hebard, Director of Graduate School Operations, 205-834-8227, Fax: 205-934-8413, E-mail: gradschool@uab.edu.
Website: https://www.uab.edu/engineering/home/graduate-civil

University of Alberta, Faculty of Graduate Studies and Research, Department of Civil and Environmental Engineering, Edmonton, AB T6G 2E1, Canada. Offers construction engineering and management (M Eng, M Sc, PhD); environmental engineering (M Eng, M Sc, PhD); environmental science (M Sc, PhD); geoenvironmental engineering (M Eng, M Sc, PhD); geotechnical engineering (M Eng, M Sc, PhD); mining engineering (M Eng, M Sc, PhD); petroleum engineering (M Eng, M Sc, PhD); structural engineering (M Eng, M Sc, PhD); water resources (M Eng, M Sc, PhD). *Program availability:* Part-time, online learning. *Degree requirements:* For master's, thesis (for some programs); for doctorate, thesis/dissertation. *Entrance requirements:* For master's, minimum GPA of 3.0 in last 2 years of undergraduate studies; for doctorate, minimum GPA of 3.0. Additional exam requirements/recommendations for international students: Required—TOEFL (minimum score 550 paper-based). Electronic applications accepted. *Faculty research:* Mining.

University of Central Florida, College of Engineering and Computer Science, Department of Civil, Environmental, and Construction Engineering, Orlando, FL 32816. Offers civil engineering (MS, MSCE, PhD, Certificate), including civil engineering (MS, MSCE, PhD), construction engineering (Certificate), structural engineering (Certificate), transportation engineering (Certificate); environmental engineering (MS, MS Env E, PhD). *Program availability:* Part-time, evening/weekend. *Faculty:* 29 full-time (3 women), 19 part-time/adjunct (1 woman). *Students:* 105 full-time (15 women), 90 part-time (26 women); includes 52 minority (11 Black or African American, non-Hispanic/Latino; 9 Asian, non-Hispanic/Latino; 29 Hispanic/Latino; 3 Two or more races, non-Hispanic/Latino), 79 international. Average age 29. 190 applicants, 73% accepted, 48 enrolled. In 2016, 42 master's, 17 doctorates, 3 other advanced degrees awarded. *Degree requirements:* For master's, thesis or alternative; for doctorate, thesis/dissertation, departmental qualifying exam, candidacy exam. *Entrance requirements:* For master's, GRE General Test, minimum GPA of 3.0 in last 60 hours of course work; for doctorate, GRE General Test, minimum GPA of 3.5 in last 60 hours of course work. Additional exam requirements/recommendations for international students: Required—TOEFL. *Application deadline:* For fall admission, 7/15 priority date for domestic students; for spring admission, 12/1 priority date for domestic students. Application fee: $30. Electronic applications accepted. *Expenses:* Tuition, state resident: part-time $288.16 per credit hour. Tuition, nonresident: part-time $1071.31 per credit hour. *Financial support:* In 2016–17, 70 students received support, including 20 fellowships with partial tuition reimbursements available (averaging $13,530 per year), 53 research assistantships with partial tuition reimbursements available (averaging $10,634 per year), 16 teaching assistantships with partial tuition reimbursements available (averaging $11,057 per year); career-related internships or fieldwork, Federal Work-Study, institutionally sponsored loans, tuition waivers (partial), and unspecified assistantships also available. Financial award application deadline: 3/1; financial award applicants required to submit FAFSA. *Unit head:* Dr. Mohamed Abdel-Aty, Chair, 407-823-2841, E-mail: m.aty@ucf.edu. *Application contact:* Assistant Director, Graduate Admissions, 407-823-2766, Fax: 407-823-6442, E-mail: gradadmissions@ucf.edu.
Website: http://cece.ucf.edu/

University of Michigan, College of Engineering, Department of Civil and Environmental Engineering, Ann Arbor, MI 48109. Offers civil engineering (MSE, PhD, CE); construction engineering and management (M Eng, MSE); environmental engineering (MSE, PhD); structural engineering (M Eng); MBA/MSE. *Program availability:* Part-time. *Students:* 177 full-time (77 women), 3 part-time. 775 applicants, 42% accepted, 62 enrolled. In 2016, 57 master's, 9 doctorates awarded. *Degree requirements:* For master's, thesis optional; for doctorate, comprehensive exam, thesis/dissertation, oral defense of dissertation, preliminary and written exams. *Entrance requirements:* For master's and doctorate, GRE General Test. Additional exam requirements/recommendations for international students: Required—TOEFL. *Application deadline:* Applications are processed on a rolling basis. Electronic applications accepted. *Expenses:* Tuition, state resident: full-time $21,466; part-time $1152 per credit hour. Tuition, nonresident: full-time $43,346; part-time $2367 per credit hour. Part-time tuition and fees vary according to course load, degree level and program. *Financial support:* Fellowships, research assistantships, teaching assistantships, institutionally sponsored loans, and tuition waivers (partial) available. *Faculty research:* Construction engineering and management, geotechnical engineering, earthquake-resistant design of structures, environmental chemistry and microbiology, cost engineering, environmental and water resources engineering. *Total annual research expenditures:* $15.7 million. *Unit head:* Kim Hayes, Department Chair, 734-764-8495, Fax: 734-764-4292, E-mail: ford@umich.edu. *Application contact:* Jessica Randolph, Graduate Coordinator, 734-764-8405, Fax: 734-764-4292, E-mail: jrand@umich.edu.
Website: http://cee.engin.umich.edu/

University of Missouri–Kansas City, School of Computing and Engineering, Kansas City, MO 64110-2499. Offers civil engineering (MS); computer and electrical engineering (PhD); computer science (MS), including bioinformatics, software engineering, telecommunications networking; computer science and informatics (PhD); computing (PhD); electrical engineering (MS); engineering (PhD); engineering and construction management (Graduate Certificate); mechanical engineering (MS); telecommunications and computer networking (PhD). PhD (interdisciplinary) offered through the School of Graduate Studies. *Program availability:* Part-time. *Faculty:* 45 full-time (6 women), 26 part-time/adjunct (4 women). *Students:* 473 full-time (155 women), 207 part-time (42 women); includes 24 minority (10 Black or African American, non-Hispanic/Latino; 10 Asian, non-Hispanic/Latino; 4 Hispanic/Latino), 581 international. Average age 25. 1,143 applicants, 44% accepted, 227 enrolled. In 2016, 446 master's, 2 other advanced degrees awarded. *Degree requirements:* For doctorate, thesis/dissertation. *Entrance requirements:* For master's, GRE General Test, minimum GPA of 3.0, 3 letters of recommendation from professors; for doctorate, GRE General Test, minimum GPA of 3.5. Additional exam requirements/recommendations for international students: Required—TOEFL (minimum score 550 paper-based; 80 iBT). *Application deadline:* For fall admission, 1/15 priority date for domestic students, 1/15 for international students. Applications are processed on a rolling basis. Application fee: $45 ($50 for international students). *Financial support:* In 2016–17, 37 research assistantships with partial tuition reimbursements (averaging $15,679 per year), 47 teaching assistantships with partial tuition reimbursements (averaging $16,830 per year) were awarded; career-related internships or fieldwork, Federal Work-Study, scholarships/grants, tuition waivers (partial), and unspecified assistantships also available. Support available to part-time students. Financial award application deadline: 3/1; financial award applicants required

to submit FAFSA. *Faculty research:* Algorithms, bioinformatics and medical informatics, biomechanics/biomaterials, civil engineering materials, networking and telecommunications, thermal science. *Unit head:* Dr. Kevin Z. Truman, Dean, 816-235-2399, Fax: 816-235-5159. *Application contact:* 816-235-2399, Fax: 816-235-5159.
Website: http://sce.umkc.edu/

University of New Brunswick Fredericton, School of Graduate Studies, Faculty of Engineering, Department of Civil Engineering, Fredericton, NB E3B 5A3, Canada. Offers construction engineering and management (M Eng, M Sc E, PhD); environmental engineering (M Eng, M Sc E, PhD); environmental studies (M Eng); geotechnical engineering (M Eng, M Sc E, PhD); groundwater/hydrology (M Eng, M Sc E, PhD); materials (M Eng, M Sc E, PhD); pavements (M Eng, M Sc E, PhD); structures (M Eng, M Sc E, PhD); transportation (M Eng, M Sc E, PhD). *Program availability:* Part-time. *Degree requirements:* For master's, thesis; for doctorate, comprehensive exam, thesis/dissertation, qualifying exam; 27 credit hours of courses. *Entrance requirements:* For master's, minimum GPA of 3.0; B Sc E in civil engineering or related engineering degree; for doctorate, minimum GPA of 3.0; graduate degree in engineering or applied science. Additional exam requirements/recommendations for international students: Required—IELTS (minimum score 7.5), TWE (minimum score 4), Michigan English Language Assessment Battery (minimum score 85) or CanTest (minimum score 4.5); Recommended—TOEFL (minimum score 580 paper-based). Electronic applications accepted. *Faculty research:* Construction engineering and management; engineering materials and infrastructure renewal; highway and pavement research; structures and solid mechanics; geotechnical and geoenvironmental engineering; structure interaction; transportation and planning; environment, solid waste management; structural engineering; water and environmental engineering.

University of Puerto Rico, Mayagüez Campus, Graduate Studies, College of Engineering, Department of Civil Engineering and Surveying, Mayagüez, PR 00681-9000. Offers civil engineering (ME, MS, PhD), including construction engineering and management (ME, MS), environmental engineering, geotechnical engineering (ME, MS), structural engineering, transportation engineering. *Program availability:* Part-time. *Faculty:* 37 full-time (7 women), 2 part-time/adjunct (0 women). *Students:* 118 full-time (37 women), 9 part-time (2 women); includes 110 minority (all Hispanic/Latino), 17 international. Average age 25. 35 applicants, 94% accepted, 16 enrolled. In 2016, 26 master's, 2 doctorates awarded. Terminal master's awarded for partial completion of doctoral program. *Degree requirements:* For master's, one foreign language, thesis; for doctorate, one foreign language, comprehensive exam, thesis/dissertation, qualifying exams. *Entrance requirements:* For master's, proficiency in English and Spanish; BS in civil engineering or its equivalent; for doctorate, proficiency in English and Spanish. *Application deadline:* For fall admission, 2/15 for domestic and international students; for spring admission, 9/15 for domestic and international students. Applications are processed on a rolling basis. Application fee: $25. Electronic applications accepted. *Expenses: Tuition, area resident:* Full-time $2466. *International tuition:* $7166 full-time. *Required fees:* $210. One-time fee: $5 full-time. Tuition and fees vary according to course level, campus/location, program and student level. *Financial support:* In 2016–17, 89 students received support, including 74 research assistantships with full and partial tuition reimbursements available (averaging $3,171 per year), 38 teaching assistantships with full and partial tuition reimbursements available (averaging $3,107 per year); unspecified assistantships also available. *Faculty research:* Structural design, concrete structure, finite elements, dynamic analysis, transportation, soils. *Unit head:* Ismael Pagan, Prof., Director, 787-832-4040 Ext. 3815, Fax: 787-833-8260, E-mail: ismael.pagan@upr.edu. *Application contact:* Myriam Hernandez, Administrative Officer III, 787-832-4040 Ext. 3815, Fax: 787-833-8260, E-mail: myriam.hernandez1@upr.edu.
Website: http://engineering.uprm.edu/inci/

University of Southern Mississippi, Graduate School, College of Science and Technology, School of Construction, Hattiesburg, MS 39406. Offers logistics, trade and transportation (MS). *Program availability:* Part-time, online learning. *Degree requirements:* For master's, comprehensive exam, thesis optional. *Entrance requirements:* For master's, GMAT or GRE General Test, minimum GPA of 2.75 in last 60 hours. Additional exam requirements/recommendations for international students: Required—TOEFL, IELTS. *Application deadline:* For fall admission, 3/1 priority date for domestic students, 3/1 for international students. Applications are processed on a rolling basis. Application fee: $60. *Expenses: Tuition, area resident:* Full-time $15,708; part-time $437 per credit hour. *Financial support:* Research assistantships with full tuition reimbursements, teaching assistantships with full tuition reimbursements, career-related internships or fieldwork, Federal Work-Study, scholarships/grants, health care benefits, and unspecified assistantships available. Financial award application deadline: 3/15; financial award applicants required to submit FAFSA. *Faculty research:* Robotics; CAD/CAM; simulation; computer-integrated manufacturing processes; construction scheduling, estimating, and computer systems. *Unit head:* Dr. Erich Connell, Director, 601-266-4895.
Website: http://www.usm.edu/construction

University of Virginia, School of Architecture, Program in the Constructed Environment, Charlottesville, VA 22903. Offers PhD. *Students:* 12 full-time (8 women), 1 (woman) part-time, 6 international. Average age 29. 43 applicants, 16% accepted, 4 enrolled. *Degree requirements:* For doctorate, thesis/dissertation. *Entrance requirements:* For doctorate, GRE, master's degree or equivalent, official transcripts, sample of academic writing, three letters of recommendation, resume or curriculum vitae, graphic portfolio. Additional exam requirements/recommendations for international students: Required—TOEFL. *Expenses:* Tuition, state resident: full-time $15,026; part-time $834 per credit hour. Tuition, nonresident: full-time $25,168; part-time $1378 per credit hour. *Required fees:* $2654. *Unit head:* Nana Last, Director, 434-924-6446, E-mail: ndl5g@virginia.edu. *Application contact:* Kristine Nelson, Director of Graduate Admissions and Financial Aid, 434-924-6442, Fax: 434-982-2678, E-mail: arch-admissions@virginia.edu.
Website: http://www.arch.virginia.edu/academics/phd

University of Washington, Graduate School, College of Engineering, Department of Civil and Environmental Engineering, Seattle, WA 98195-2700. Offers construction engineering (MSCE, PhD); environmental engineering (MSCE, PhD); geotechnical engineering (MSCE, PhD); hydrology and hydrodynamics (MSCE, PhD); structural engineering and mechanics (MSCE, PhD); transportation engineering (MSCE, PhD). *Program availability:* Part-time, 100% online. *Faculty:* 37 full-time (10 women). *Students:* 239 full-time (97 women), 153 part-time (41 women); includes 71 minority (7 Black or African American, non-Hispanic/Latino; 32 Asian, non-Hispanic/Latino; 22 Hispanic/Latino; 2 Native Hawaiian or other Pacific Islander, non-Hispanic/Latino; 8 Two or more races, non-Hispanic/Latino), 134 international. 782 applicants, 58% accepted, 157 enrolled. In 2016, 132 master's, 13 doctorates awarded. Terminal master's awarded for partial completion of doctoral program. *Degree requirements:* For master's, thesis optional; for doctorate, comprehensive exam, thesis/dissertation, qualifying, general and final exams; completion of degree within 10 years. *Entrance requirements:* For master's, GRE General Test, minimum GPA of 3.0, statement of purpose, letters of recommendation, transcripts; for doctorate, GRE General Test, minimum GPA of 3.5, statement of purpose, letters of recommendation, transcripts, resume. Additional exam requirements/recommendations for international students: Required—TOEFL (minimum score 580 paper-based; 92 iBT); Recommended—IELTS (minimum score 7), TSE. *Application deadline:* For fall admission, 12/15 for domestic and international students. Applications are processed on a rolling basis. Application fee: $85. Electronic applications accepted. *Expenses:* Contact institution. *Financial support:* In 2016–17, 110 students received support, including 10 fellowships with tuition reimbursements available (averaging $2,228 per year), 72 research assistantships with full tuition reimbursements available (averaging $2,351 per year), 28 teaching assistantships with full tuition reimbursements available (averaging $2,387 per year); scholarships/grants also available. Financial award application deadline: 12/15; financial award applicants required to submit FAFSA. *Faculty research:* Structural and geotechnical engineering, transportation and construction engineering, water and environmental engineering. *Total annual research expenditures:* $13.5 million. *Unit head:* Dr. Timothy V. Larson, Professor/Chair, 206-543-6815, Fax: 206-543-1543, E-mail: tlarson@uw.edu. *Application contact:* Melissa Pritchard, Graduate Adviser, 206-543-2574, Fax: 206-543-1543, E-mail: ceginfo@u.washington.edu.
Website: http://www.ce.washington.edu/

Virginia Polytechnic Institute and State University, Graduate School, College of Architecture and Urban Studies, Blacksburg, VA 24061. Offers architecture (MS Arch); architecture and design research (PhD); building/construction science and management (MS); creative technologies (MFA); environmental design and planning (PhD); landscape architecture (MLA); planning, governance, and globalization (PhD); public administration (MPA); public administration/public affairs (PhD, Certificate); public and international affairs (MPIA); urban and regional planning (MURP). *Accreditation:* ASLA (one or more programs are accredited). *Faculty:* 136 full-time (53 women). *Students:* 371 full-time (185 women), 210 part-time (104 women); includes 118 minority (49 Black or African American, non-Hispanic/Latino; 1 American Indian or Alaska Native, non-Hispanic/Latino; 30 Asian, non-Hispanic/Latino; 32 Hispanic/Latino; 6 Two or more races, non-Hispanic/Latino), 137 international. Average age 31. 566 applicants, 55% accepted, 160 enrolled. In 2016, 137 master's, 24 doctorates awarded. *Degree requirements:* For master's, comprehensive exam (for some programs), thesis (for some programs); for doctorate, comprehensive exam (for some programs), thesis/dissertation (for some programs). *Entrance requirements:* For master's and doctorate, GRE/GMAT. Additional exam requirements/recommendations for international students: Required—TOEFL (minimum score 80 iBT). *Application deadline:* For fall admission, 8/1 for domestic students, 4/1 for international students; for spring admission, 1/1 for domestic students, 9/1 for international students. Applications are processed on a rolling basis. Application fee: $75. Electronic applications accepted. *Expenses:* Tuition, state resident: full-time $12,467; part-time $692.50 per credit hour. Tuition, nonresident: full-time $25,095; part-time $1394.25 per credit hour. *Required fees:* $2669; $491.50 per semester. Tuition and fees vary according to course load, campus/location and program. *Financial support:* In 2016–17, 11 research assistantships with full tuition reimbursements (averaging $19,474 per year), 45 teaching assistantships with full tuition reimbursements (averaging $16,014 per year) were awarded. Financial award application deadline: 3/1; financial award applicants required to submit FAFSA. *Total annual research expenditures:* $3.6 million. *Unit head:* Dr. A. J. Davis, Dean, 540-231-6416, Fax: 540-231-6332, E-mail: davisa@vt.edu. *Application contact:* Christine Mattsson-Coon, Executive Assistant, 540-231-6416, Fax: 540-231-6332, E-mail: cmattsso@vt.edu.
Website: http://www.caus.vt.edu/

Wentworth Institute of Technology, Master of Engineering in Civil Engineering Program, Boston, MA 02115-5998. Offers construction engineering (M Eng); infrastructure engineering (M Eng). *Program availability:* Part-time-only, evening/weekend. *Faculty:* 12 part-time/adjunct (4 women). *Students:* 17 part-time (4 women); includes 4 minority (2 Black or African American, non-Hispanic/Latino; 1 Hispanic/Latino; 1 Two or more races, non-Hispanic/Latino), 1 international. Average age 27. 10 applicants, 100% accepted, 10 enrolled. In 2016, 7 master's awarded. *Degree requirements:* For master's, thesis optional, capstone course. *Entrance requirements:* For master's, resume, statement of purpose, official transcripts, two professional recommendations, bachelor's degree, minimum GPA of 3.0, one year of professional experience in a technical role and/or technical organization. Additional exam requirements/recommendations for international students: Recommended—TOEFL (minimum score 525 paper-based). *Application deadline:* For fall admission, 8/1 for domestic and international students. Applications are processed on a rolling basis. Application fee: $50. Electronic applications accepted. *Expenses:* Contact institution. *Financial support:* Scholarships/grants available. Support available to part-time students. Financial award application deadline: 8/1; financial award applicants required to submit FAFSA. *Unit head:* Philip Hammond, Director of Graduate Programs, 617-989-4594, Fax: 617-989-4399, E-mail: hammondp1@wit.edu. *Application contact:* Martha Sheehan, Director of Admissions and Marketing, 617-989-4661, Fax: 617-989-4399, E-mail: sheehanm@wit.edu.
Website: http://wit.edu/continuinged/programs/civil-engineering-masters.html

Environmental Engineering

Air Force Institute of Technology, Graduate School of Engineering and Management, Department of Systems and Engineering Management, Dayton, OH 45433-7765. Offers cost analysis (MS); environmental and engineering management (MS); environmental engineering science (MS); information resource/systems management (MS). *Accreditation:* ABET. *Program availability:* Part-time. *Degree requirements:* For master's, thesis. *Entrance requirements:* For master's, GRE, GMAT, minimum GPA of 3.0.

The American University in Cairo, School of Sciences and Engineering, Cairo, Egypt. Offers biotechnology (MS); chemistry (MS); computer science (MS); computing (M Comp); construction engineering (M Eng, MS); electronics and communications engineering (M Eng); environmental engineering (MS); environmental system design (M Eng); mechanical engineering (M Eng, MS); nanotechnology (MS); physics (MS); robotics, control and smart systems (MS); sciences and engineering (PhD); sustainable development (MS, Graduate Diploma). *Program availability:* Part-time, evening/weekend. *Faculty:* 43 full-time (4 women), 12 part-time/adjunct (1 woman). *Students:* 50

full-time (21 women), 262 part-time (128 women), 13 international. Average age 28. 193 applicants, 46% accepted, 55 enrolled. In 2016, 71 master's, 5 doctorates awarded. *Degree requirements:* For master's, comprehensive exam (for some programs), thesis (for some programs); for doctorate, comprehensive exam (for some programs), thesis/dissertation. *Entrance requirements:* Additional exam requirements/recommendations for international students: Required—TOEFL (minimum score 450 paper-based; 45 iBT), IELTS (minimum score 5). *Application deadline:* For fall admission, 2/1 priority date for domestic and international students; for spring admission, 10/15 priority date for domestic and international students. Applications are processed on a rolling basis. Application fee: $80. Electronic applications accepted. *Expenses:* Contact institution. *Financial support:* Fellowships with partial tuition reimbursements, scholarships/grants, and unspecified assistantships available. Financial award application deadline: 3/10. *Faculty research:* Construction, mechanical and electronics engineering, physics, computer science, biotechnology and nanotechnology. *Unit head:* Dr. Hassan El Fawal, Dean, 20-2-2615-2926, E-mail: hassan.elfawal@aucegypt.edu. *Application contact:* Maha Hegazi, Director for Graduate Admissions, 20-2-2615-1462, E-mail: mahahegazi@aucegypt.edu.
Website: http://www.aucegypt.edu/sse/Pages/default.aspx

Arizona State University at the Tempe campus, Ira A. Fulton Schools of Engineering, School of Sustainable Engineering and the Built Environment, Tempe, AZ 85287-5306. Offers civil, environmental and sustainable engineering (MS, MSE, PhD); construction engineering (MSE); construction management (MS, PhD). *Program availability:* Part-time, evening/weekend, online learning. Terminal master's awarded for partial completion of doctoral program. *Degree requirements:* For master's, thesis optional, comprehensive exams (MSE); interactive Program of Study (iPOS) submitted before completing 50 percent of required credit hours; for doctorate, comprehensive exam, thesis/dissertation, interactive Program of Study (iPOS) submitted before completing 50 percent of required credit hours. *Entrance requirements:* For master's, GRE, minimum GPA of 3.0 or equivalent in last 2 years of work leading to bachelor's degree; for doctorate, GRE, minimum GPA of 3.0 in last 2 years of work leading to bachelor's degree, 3.2 in all graduate-level coursework with master's degree; 3 letters of recommendation; resume/curriculum vitae; letter of intent; thesis (if applicable); statement of research interests. Additional exam requirements/recommendations for international students: Required—TOEFL, IELTS, or PTE. Electronic applications accepted. *Expenses:* Contact institution. *Faculty research:* Water purification, transportation (safety and materials), construction management, environmental biotechnology, environmental nanotechnology, earth systems engineering and management, SMART innovations, project performance metrics, and underground infrastructure.

California Institute of Technology, Division of Engineering and Applied Science, Option in Environmental Science and Engineering, Pasadena, CA 91125-0001. Offers MS, PhD. *Degree requirements:* For doctorate, thesis/dissertation. Electronic applications accepted. *Faculty research:* Chemistry of natural waters, physics and chemistry of particulates, fluid mechanics of the natural environment, pollutant formation and control, environmental modeling systems.

California Institute of Technology, Division of Geological and Planetary Sciences, Pasadena, CA 91125-0001. Offers environmental science and engineering (MS, PhD); geobiology (MS, PhD); geochemistry (MS, PhD); geology (MS, PhD); geophysics (MS, PhD); planetary science (MS, PhD). *Degree requirements:* For doctorate, thesis/dissertation. *Entrance requirements:* For doctorate, GRE General Test. Additional exam requirements/recommendations for international students: Required—TOEFL; Recommended—IELTS, TWE. Electronic applications accepted. *Faculty research:* Planetary surfaces, evolution of anaerobic respiratory processes, structural geology and tectonics, theoretical and numerical seismology, global biogeochemical cycles.

California Polytechnic State University, San Luis Obispo, College of Engineering, Department of Civil and Environmental Engineering, San Luis Obispo, CA 93407. Offers MS. *Program availability:* Part-time. *Faculty:* 9 full-time (2 women), 1 part-time/adjunct (0 women). *Students:* 39 full-time (10 women), 3 part-time (2 women); includes 18 minority (2 Black or African American, non-Hispanic/Latino; 8 Asian, non-Hispanic/Latino; 4 Hispanic/Latino; 1 Native Hawaiian or other Pacific Islander, non-Hispanic/Latino; 3 Two or more races, non-Hispanic/Latino), 1 international. Average age 24. 52 applicants, 52% accepted, 22 enrolled. In 2016, 33 master's awarded. *Degree requirements:* For master's, comprehensive exam (for some programs), thesis (for some programs). *Entrance requirements:* For master's, GRE. Additional exam requirements/recommendations for international students: Required—TOEFL (minimum score 80 iBT). *Application deadline:* For fall admission, 1/1 for domestic students, 3/1 priority date for international students. Applications are processed on a rolling basis. Application fee: $55. Electronic applications accepted. *Expenses:* Tuition, state resident: full-time $6738; part-time $3906 per year. Tuition, nonresident: full-time $15,666; part-time $8370 per year. Required fees: $3603; $3141 per unit. $1047 per term. *Financial support:* Fellowships, research assistantships, teaching assistantships, career-related internships or fieldwork, and scholarships/grants available. Financial award application deadline: 3/2; financial award applicants required to submit FAFSA. *Faculty research:* Transportation and traffic, environmental protection, geotechnology, water engineering. *Unit head:* Dr. Bing Qu, Graduate Coordinator, 805-756-5645, E-mail: bqu@calpoly.edu. Website: http://ceenve.calpoly.edu/

California State University, Fullerton, Graduate Studies, College of Engineering and Computer Science, Department of Civil and Environmental Engineering, Fullerton, CA 92834-9480. Offers civil engineering (MS), including architectural engineering, environmental engineering. *Program availability:* Part-time. *Degree requirements:* For master's, comprehensive exam, project or thesis. *Entrance requirements:* For master's, minimum undergraduate GPA of 2.5. Application fee: $55. *Expenses:* Tuition, state resident: full-time $3369; part-time $1953 per unit. Tuition, nonresident: full-time $3915; part-time $2499 per unit. Tuition and fees vary according to course load, degree level and program. *Financial support:* Career-related internships or fieldwork, Federal Work-Study, institutionally sponsored loans, and scholarships/grants available. Support available to part-time students. Financial award application deadline: 3/1; financial award applicants required to submit FAFSA. *Faculty research:* Soil-structure interaction, finite-element analysis, computer-aided analysis and design. *Unit head:* Dr. Prasada Rao, Chair, 657-278-3012. *Application contact:* Admissions/Applications, 657-278-2371. Website: http://www.fullerton.edu/ecs/cee/

Carleton University, Faculty of Graduate Studies, Faculty of Engineering and Design, Department of Civil and Environmental Engineering, Ottawa, ON K1S 5B6, Canada. Offers M Eng, MA Sc, PhD. *Degree requirements:* For master's, thesis optional; for doctorate, thesis/dissertation. *Entrance requirements:* For master's, honors degree; for doctorate, MA Sc or M Eng. Additional exam requirements/recommendations for international students: Required—TOEFL. *Faculty research:* Pollution and wastewater management, fire safety engineering, earthquake engineering, structural design, bridge engineering.

Carnegie Mellon University, Carnegie Institute of Technology, Department of Civil and Environmental Engineering, Pittsburgh, PA 15213. Offers advanced infrastructure systems (MS, PhD); advanced infrastructure systems technology development and application (MS); air quality engineering and science (MS); civil and environmental

engineering (MS, PhD); civil and environmental engineering/engineering and public policy (PhD); civil engineering (MS, PhD); computational mechanics (MS, PhD); computational modeling and monitoring for resilient structural and material systems (MS); energy infrastructure systems (MS); environmental engineering (MS, PhD); environmental management and science (MS, PhD); IT-based sustainable global infrastructure and construction management (MS); sustainability and green design (MS); water quality engineering and science (MS). *Program availability:* Part-time. *Faculty:* 23 full-time (5 women), 12 part-time/adjunct (3 women). *Students:* 230 full-time (87 women), 4 part-time (0 women); includes 17 minority (4 Black or African American, non-Hispanic/Latino; 12 Asian, non-Hispanic/Latino; 1 Two or more races, non-Hispanic/Latino), 179 international. Average age 25. 653 applicants, 60% accepted, 107 enrolled. In 2016, 145 master's, 15 doctorates awarded. Terminal master's awarded for partial completion of doctoral program. *Degree requirements:* For master's, thesis optional; for doctorate, comprehensive exam, thesis/dissertation, two-part qualifying exam, public defense of dissertation. *Entrance requirements:* For master's, GRE General Test, BS in engineering, science or mathematics; for doctorate, GRE General Test, BS or MS in engineering, science or mathematics. Additional exam requirements/recommendations for international students: Required—TOEFL (minimum score 84 iBT) or IELTS (6.0). *Application deadline:* For fall admission, 1/5 priority date for domestic and international students; for spring admission, 9/15 priority date for domestic and international students. Applications are processed on a rolling basis. Application fee: $65. Electronic applications accepted. *Expenses:* Contact institution. *Financial support:* In 2016–17, 129 students received support. Fellowships with tuition reimbursements available, research assistantships with tuition reimbursements available, scholarships/grants, tuition waivers (full and partial), unspecified assistantships, and service assistantships available. Financial award application deadline: 1/5. *Faculty research:* Advanced infrastructure systems; environmental engineering, sustainability, and science; mechanics, materials, and computing. Total annual research expenditures: $7.4 million. *Unit head:* Dr. David A. Dzombak, Professor and Department Head, 412-268-2941, Fax: 412-268-7813, E-mail: dzombak@cmu.edu. *Application contact:* David A. Vey, Graduate Admissions Manager, 412-268-2292, Fax: 412-268-7813, E-mail: dvey@andrew.cmu.edu.
Website: http://www.cmu.edu/cee/

Carnegie Mellon University, Tepper School of Business, Pittsburgh, PA 15213-3891. Offers accounting (PhD); business management and software engineering (MBMSE); business technologies (PhD); civil engineering and industrial management (MS); computational finance (MSCF); economics (PhD); environmental engineering and management (MEEM); financial economics (PhD); industrial administration (MBA), including administration and public management; marketing (PhD); mathematical finance (PhD); operations management (PhD); operations research (PhD); organizational behavior and theory (PhD); production and operations management (PhD); public policy and management (MS, MSED); software engineering and business management (MS); JD/MS; JD/MSIA; M Div/MS; MOM/MSIA; MSCF/MSIA. JD/MSIA offered jointly with University of Pittsburgh. *Program availability:* Part-time. Terminal master's awarded for partial completion of doctoral program. *Degree requirements:* For doctorate, thesis/dissertation. *Entrance requirements:* For master's, GMAT. Additional exam requirements/recommendations for international students: Required—TOEFL. *Expenses:* Contact institution.

The Catholic University of America, School of Engineering, Department of Mechanical Engineering, Washington, DC 20064. Offers energy and environment (MME); general (MME); mechanical engineering (MSE, PhD). *Program availability:* Part-time. *Faculty:* 9 full-time (0 women), 7 part-time/adjunct (0 women). *Students:* 7 full-time (1 woman), 12 part-time (2 women); includes 4 minority (3 Black or African American, non-Hispanic/Latino; 1 Two or more races, non-Hispanic/Latino), 8 international. Average age 32. 26 applicants, 85% accepted, 9 enrolled. In 2016, 16 master's, 1 doctorate awarded. Terminal master's awarded for partial completion of doctoral program. *Degree requirements:* For master's, thesis (for some programs); for doctorate, comprehensive exam, thesis/dissertation. *Entrance requirements:* For master's and doctorate, statement of purpose, official copies of academic transcripts, three letters of recommendation. Additional exam requirements/recommendations for international students: Required—TOEFL (minimum score 550 paper-based; 80 iBT). *Application deadline:* For fall admission, 7/15 priority date for domestic students, 7/1 for international students; for spring admission, 11/15 priority date for domestic students, 11/1 for international students. Applications are processed on a rolling basis. Application fee: $55. Electronic applications accepted. *Expenses:* $43,380 per year; $1,170 per credit; $200 per semester part-time fees. *Financial support:* Fellowships, research assistantships, teaching assistantships, Federal Work-Study, scholarships/grants, tuition waivers (full and partial), and unspecified assistantships available. Financial award application deadline: 2/1; financial award applicants required to submit FAFSA. *Faculty research:* Energy and environment, acoustics and vibration, bio fabrication and lab-on-chip, experimental mechanics, smart materials. Total annual research expenditures: $243,170. *Unit head:* Dr. Sen Nieh, Chair, 202-319-5170, Fax: 202-319-5173, E-mail: nieh@cua.edu. *Application contact:* Director of Graduate Admissions, 202-319-5057, Fax: 202-319-6533, E-mail: cua-admissions@cua.edu.
Website: http://mechanical.cua.edu/

Clarkson University, Institute for a Sustainable Environment, Program in Environmental Science and Engineering, Potsdam, NY 13699. Offers MS, PhD. *Program availability:* Part-time. *Students:* 19 full-time (6 women), 12 international. 19 applicants, 74% accepted, 6 enrolled. In 2016, 8 master's, 1 doctorate awarded. *Degree requirements:* For master's, thesis; for doctorate, comprehensive exam, thesis/dissertation. *Entrance requirements:* For master's and doctorate, GRE. Additional exam requirements/recommendations for international students: Required—TOEFL (minimum score 550 paper-based, 80 iBT) or IELTS (6.5). *Application deadline:* Applications are processed on a rolling basis. Application fee: $50. Electronic applications accepted. *Expenses:* Tuition: Full-time $23,400; part-time $1300 per credit hour. Tuition and fees vary according to campus/location and program. *Financial support:* Scholarships/grants and unspecified assistantships available. *Unit head:* Dr. Susan Powers, Interim Director of the Institute for a Sustainable Environment/Associate Director of Sustainability, 315-268-6542, E-mail: spowers@clarkson.edu. *Application contact:* Dan Capogna, Graduate Admissions Contact, 518-631-9910, E-mail: graduate@clarkson.edu.
Website: http://graduate.clarkson.edu

Clarkson University, Wallace H. Coulter School of Engineering, Department of Civil and Environmental Engineering, Potsdam, NY 13699. Offers ME, MS, PhD. *Faculty:* 25 full-time (4 women), 9 part-time/adjunct (2 women). *Students:* 33 full-time (11 women); includes 1 minority (Hispanic/Latino), 25 international. 48 applicants, 58% accepted, 3 enrolled. In 2016, 9 master's, 3 doctorates awarded. *Degree requirements:* For master's, thesis (for MS); project (for ME); for doctorate, comprehensive exam, thesis/dissertation. *Entrance requirements:* For master's and doctorate, GRE. Additional exam requirements/recommendations for international students: Required—TOEFL (minimum score 550 paper-based, 80 iBT) or IELTS (6.5). *Application deadline:* Applications are processed on a rolling basis. Application fee: $50. Electronic applications accepted. *Expenses:* Tuition: Full-time $23,400; part-time $1300 per credit hour. Tuition and fees vary according to campus/location and program. *Financial support:* Scholarships/grants and unspecified assistantships available. *Unit head:* Dr. James Edzwald, Chair of Civil

and Environmental Engineering, 315-268-6529, E-mail: jedzwald@clarkson.edu. *Application contact:* Dan Capogna, Graduate Admissions Contact, 518-631-9910, E-mail: graduate@clarkson.edu.
Website: http://graduate.clarkson.edu

Clemson University, Graduate School, College of Engineering, Computing and Applied Sciences, Department of Environmental Engineering and Earth Sciences, Program in Environmental Engineering and Science, Anderson, SC 29625. Offers MS, PhD. *Accreditation:* ABET. *Faculty:* 21 full-time (5 women). *Students:* 64 full-time (34 women), 15 part-time (4 women); includes 8 minority (2 Black or African American, non-Hispanic/Latino; 2 Asian, non-Hispanic/Latino; 4 Two or more races, non-Hispanic/Latino), 29 international. Average age 27. 126 applicants, 29% accepted, 18 enrolled. In 2016, 24 master's, 7 doctorates awarded. *Degree requirements:* For master's, thesis; for doctorate, comprehensive exam, thesis/dissertation, qualifying exam. *Entrance requirements:* For master's and doctorate, GRE General Test, unofficial transcripts, letters of recommendation. Additional exam requirements/recommendations for international students: Required—TOEFL (minimum score 80 iBT), IELTS (minimum score 6.5). *Application deadline:* For fall admission, 2/15 priority date for domestic students, 2/15 for international students. Applications are processed on a rolling basis. Application fee: $80 ($90 for international students). Electronic applications accepted. *Expenses:* $4,841 per semester full-time resident, $9,640 per semester full-time non-resident, $612 per credit hour part-time resident, $1,223 per credit hour part-time non-resident. *Financial support:* In 2016–17, 56 students received support, including 9 fellowships with partial tuition reimbursements available (averaging $9,283 per year), 30 research assistantships with partial tuition reimbursements available (averaging $21,312 per year), 17 teaching assistantships with partial tuition reimbursements available (averaging $21,447 per year); career-related internships or fieldwork also available. Financial award application deadline: 2/15. *Faculty research:* Drinking water treatment, hazardous waste treatment, environmental chemistry and microbiology, containment transport modeling, life cycle assessment and sustainable systems. *Unit head:* Dr. David Freedman, Department Chair, 864-656-5566, E-mail: dfreedm@clemson.edu. *Application contact:* Dr. Kevin Finneran, Graduate Program Coordinator, 864-656-5019, E-mail: ktf@clemson.edu.
Website: https://www.clemson.edu/cecas/departments/eees/academics/gradprog/ee/index.html

Cleveland State University, College of Graduate Studies, Fenn College of Engineering, Department of Civil and Environmental Engineering, Cleveland, OH 44115. Offers MS, D Eng. *Program availability:* Part-time, evening/weekend. *Faculty:* 8 full-time (2 women). *Students:* 65 full-time (13 women), 19 part-time (3 women); includes 3 minority (2 Asian, non-Hispanic/Latino; 1 Hispanic/Latino), 69 international. Average age 24. 214 applicants, 61% accepted, 21 enrolled. In 2016, 22 master's awarded. *Degree requirements:* For master's, project or thesis; for doctorate, comprehensive exam, thesis/dissertation, candidacy and qualifying exams. *Entrance requirements:* For master's, GRE General Test, GRE Subject Test, minimum GPA of 2.75; for doctorate, GRE General Test, GRE Subject Test, minimum GPA of 3.25. Additional exam requirements/recommendations for international students: Required—TOEFL (minimum score 550 paper-based; 78 iBT). *Application deadline:* For fall admission, 7/1 priority date for domestic students, 5/15 for international students; for spring admission, 11/15 for domestic students, 11/1 for international students; for summer admission, 4/1 for domestic students, 3/15 for international students. Applications are processed on a rolling basis. Application fee: $40. Electronic applications accepted. *Expenses:* Tuition, state resident: full-time $9565. Tuition, nonresident: full-time $17,980. Tuition and fees vary according to program. *Financial support:* In 2016–17, 9 research assistantships with tuition reimbursements (averaging $3,920 per year) were awarded; teaching assistantships with tuition reimbursements, career-related internships or fieldwork, scholarships/grants, and unspecified assistantships also available. Financial award application deadline: 9/1. *Faculty research:* Solid-waste disposal, constitutive modeling, transportation, safety engineering, concrete materials. *Total annual research expenditures:* $800,000. *Unit head:* Dr. Norbert Joseph Delatte, Chairperson, 216-687-9259, Fax: 216-687-5395, E-mail: n.delatte@csuohio.edu. *Application contact:* Deborah L. Brown, Interim Assistant Director, Graduate Admissions, 216-523-7572, Fax: 216-687-9214, E-mail: d.l.brown@csuohio.edu.
Website: http://www.csuohio.edu/engineering/civil

Colorado School of Mines, Office of Graduate Studies, Department of Civil and Environmental Engineering, Golden, CO 80401. Offers civil and environmental engineering (MS, PhD); environmental engineering science (MS, PhD); underground construction and tunneling (MS, PhD). *Program availability:* Part-time. *Degree requirements:* For master's, thesis (for some programs); for doctorate, comprehensive exam, thesis/dissertation. *Entrance requirements:* For master's and doctorate, GRE General Test. Additional exam requirements/recommendations for international students: Required—TOEFL (minimum score 550 paper-based; 80 iBT). Electronic applications accepted. *Expenses:* Tuition, state resident: full-time $15,690. Tuition, nonresident: full-time $34,020. *Required fees:* $2152. Tuition and fees vary according to course load. *Faculty research:* Treatment of water and wastes, environmental law: policy and practice, natural environment systems, hazardous waste management, environmental data analysis.

Columbia University, Fu Foundation School of Engineering and Applied Science, Department of Earth and Environmental Engineering, New York, NY 10027. Offers earth and environmental engineering (MS, Eng Sc D, PhD); MS/MBA. *Program availability:* Part-time, online learning. Terminal master's awarded for partial completion of doctoral program. *Degree requirements:* For master's, thesis; for doctorate, thesis/dissertation, qualifying exam. *Entrance requirements:* For master's and doctorate, GRE General Test. Additional exam requirements/recommendations for international students: Required—TOEFL, IELTS, PTE. Electronic applications accepted. *Faculty research:* Sustainable energy and materials, waste to energy, water resources and climate risks, environmental health engineering, life cycle analysis.

Concordia University, School of Graduate Studies, Faculty of Engineering and Computer Science, Department of Building, Civil and Environmental Engineering, Montréal, QC H3G 1M8, Canada. Offers building engineering (M Eng, MA Sc, PhD, Certificate); civil engineering (M Eng, MA Sc, PhD); environmental engineering (Certificate). *Degree requirements:* For master's, thesis or alternative; for doctorate, comprehensive exam, thesis/dissertation. *Faculty research:* Structural engineering, geotechnical engineering, water resources and fluid engineering, transportation engineering, systems engineering.

Cornell University, Graduate School, Graduate Fields of Engineering, Field of Civil and Environmental Engineering, Ithaca, NY 14853. Offers engineering management (M Eng, MS, PhD); environmental engineering (M Eng, MS, PhD); environmental fluid mechanics and hydrology (M Eng, MS, PhD); environmental systems engineering (M Eng, MS, PhD); geotechnical engineering (M Eng, MS, PhD); remote sensing (M Eng, MS, PhD); structural engineering (M Eng, MS, PhD); structural mechanics (M Eng, MS); transportation engineering (MS, PhD); transportation systems engineering (M Eng); water resource systems (M Eng, MS, PhD). Terminal master's awarded for partial completion of doctoral program. *Degree requirements:* For master's, thesis (MS); for doctorate, comprehensive exam, thesis/dissertation. *Entrance requirements:* For master's and doctorate, GRE General Test (recommended), 2 letters of recommendation. Additional exam requirements/recommendations for international students: Required—TOEFL (minimum score 600 paper-based; 77 iBT). Electronic applications accepted. *Faculty research:* Environmental engineering, geotechnical engineering, remote sensing, environmental fluid mechanics and hydrology, structural engineering.

Dalhousie University, Faculty of Engineering, Department of Environmental Engineering, Halifax, NS B3J 2X4, Canada. Offers M Eng, MA Sc, PhD. *Entrance requirements:* Additional exam requirements/recommendations for international students: Required—TOEFL, IELTS, CANTEST, CAEL, or Michigan English Language Assessment Battery. Electronic applications accepted.

Dartmouth College, Thayer School of Engineering, Program in Environmental Engineering, Hanover, NH 03755. Offers MS, PhD. Application fee: $45. *Faculty research:* Resource and environmental analysis, decision theory, risk assessment and public policy, environmental fluid mechanics. *Total annual research expenditures:* $290,384. *Unit head:* Dr. Joseph J. Helbie, Dean, 603-646-2238, Fax: 603-646-2580, E-mail: joseph.j.helbie@dartmouth.edu. *Application contact:* Candace S. Potter, Graduate Admissions Administrator, 603-646-3844, Fax: 603-646-1620, E-mail: candace.s.potter@dartmouth.edu.

Drexel University, College of Engineering, Department of Civil, Architectural, and Environmental Engineering, Program in Environmental Engineering, Philadelphia, PA 19104-2875. Offers MS, PhD. *Program availability:* Part-time, evening/weekend. *Faculty:* 27 full-time (8 women). *Students:* 31 full-time (15 women), 6 part-time (3 women); includes 4 minority (2 Black or African American, non-Hispanic/Latino; 2 Asian, non-Hispanic/Latino), 15 international. Average age 30. In 2016, 17 master's, 1 doctorate awarded. Terminal master's awarded for partial completion of doctoral program. *Degree requirements:* For master's, thesis optional; for doctorate, thesis/dissertation. *Application deadline:* For fall admission, 8/21 for domestic students. Applications are processed on a rolling basis. Application fee: $50. Electronic applications accepted. *Expenses:* *Tuition:* Full-time $32,184; part-time $1192 per credit hour. *Required fees:* $280. Tuition and fees vary according to campus/location and program. *Financial support:* Research assistantships, teaching assistantships, career-related internships or fieldwork, and unspecified assistantships available. Financial award application deadline: 2/1. *Unit head:* Dr. Richard Weggel, Interim Department Head, 215-895-2355. *Application contact:* Director of Graduate Admissions, 215-895-6700, Fax: 215-895-5939, E-mail: enroll@drexel.edu.

Drexel University, College of Engineering, Department of Civil, Architectural, and Environmental Engineering, Program in Geotechnical, Geoenvironmental and Geosynthetics Engineering, Philadelphia, PA 19104-2875. Offers MS, PhD. *Expenses:* *Tuition:* Full-time $32,184; part-time $1192 per credit hour. *Required fees:* $280. Tuition and fees vary according to campus/location and program. *Unit head:* Dr. Richard Weggel, Interim Department Head, 215-895-2355. *Application contact:* Director of Graduate Admissions, 215-895-6700, Fax: 215-895-5939, E-mail: enroll@drexel.edu.

Duke University, Graduate School, Pratt School of Engineering, Department of Civil and Environmental Engineering, Durham, NC 27708. Offers civil and environmental engineering (MS, PhD); environmental engineering (MS, PhD). Terminal master's awarded for partial completion of doctoral program. *Degree requirements:* For doctorate, thesis/dissertation. *Entrance requirements:* For master's and doctorate, GRE General Test. Additional exam requirements/recommendations for international students: Required—TOEFL (minimum score 550 paper-based; 90 iBT), IELTS (minimum score 7). Electronic applications accepted. *Faculty research:* Environmental process engineering, hydrology and fluid dynamics, materials, structures and geo-systems.

Duke University, Graduate School, Pratt School of Engineering, Master of Engineering Program, Durham, NC 27708-0271. Offers biomedical engineering (M Eng); civil engineering (M Eng); electrical and computer engineering (M Eng); environmental engineering (M Eng); materials science and engineering (M Eng); mechanical engineering (M Eng); photonics and optical sciences (M Eng). *Program availability:* Part-time. *Entrance requirements:* For master's, GRE General Test, resume, 3 letters of recommendation, statement of purpose, transcripts. Additional exam requirements/recommendations for international students: Required—TOEFL.

École Polytechnique de Montréal, Graduate Programs, Department of Civil, Geological and Mining Engineering, Montréal, QC H3C 3A7, Canada. Offers civil, geological and mining engineering (DESS); environmental engineering (M Eng, M Sc A, PhD); geotechnical engineering (M Eng, M Sc A, PhD); hydraulics engineering (M Eng, M Sc A, PhD); structural engineering (M Eng, M Sc A, PhD); transportation engineering (M Eng, M Sc A, PhD). *Program availability:* Part-time. *Degree requirements:* For master's, one foreign language, thesis; for doctorate, one foreign language, thesis/dissertation. *Entrance requirements:* For master's, minimum GPA of 2.75; for doctorate, minimum GPA of 3.0. *Faculty research:* Water resources management, characteristics of building materials, aging of dams, pollution control.

Florida Atlantic University, College of Engineering and Computer Science, Department of Civil, Environmental and Geomatics Engineering, Boca Raton, FL 33431-0991. Offers civil engineering (MS); environmental engineering (MS). *Program availability:* Part-time, evening/weekend. *Faculty:* 13 full-time (0 women), 2 part-time/adjunct (0 women). *Students:* 13 full-time (5 women), 23 part-time (4 women); includes 13 minority (4 Black or African American, non-Hispanic/Latino; 1 Asian, non-Hispanic/Latino; 7 Hispanic/Latino; 1 Two or more races, non-Hispanic/Latino), 10 international. Average age 31. 30 applicants, 53% accepted, 12 enrolled. In 2016, 11 master's awarded. *Degree requirements:* For master's, thesis optional. *Entrance requirements:* For master's, GRE General Test, minimum GPA of 3.0 in last 60 hours of undergraduate course work. Additional exam requirements/recommendations for international students: Required—TOEFL (minimum score 550 paper-based; 61 iBT), IELTS (minimum score 6). *Application deadline:* For fall admission, 7/1 priority date for domestic students, 2/15 for international students; for spring admission, 11/1 for domestic students, 7/15 for international students. Applications are processed on a rolling basis. Application fee: $30. *Expenses:* Tuition, state resident: full-time $7392; part-time $369.82 per credit hour. Tuition, nonresident: full-time $19,432; part-time $1024.81 per credit hour. *Financial support:* Research assistantships with full tuition reimbursements, teaching assistantships with full tuition reimbursements, career-related internships or fieldwork, Federal Work-Study, scholarships/grants, and unspecified assistantships available. Financial award applicants required to submit FAFSA. *Faculty research:* Structures, geotechnical engineering, environmental and water resources engineering, transportation engineering, materials. *Unit head:* Dr. Pete D. Scarlatos, Chair, 561-297-0466, Fax: 561-297-0493, E-mail: scarlatos@fau.edu. *Application contact:* Dr. Frederick Bloetscher, Assistant Professor, 561-297-0744, E-mail: fbloetscher@civil.fau.edu.
Website: http://www.cege.fau.edu/

Florida International University, College of Engineering and Computing, Department of Civil and Environmental Engineering, Miami, FL 33175. Offers civil engineering (MS, PhD); environmental engineering (MS). *Program availability:* Part-time, evening/weekend, online learning. *Faculty:* 21 full-time (6 women), 7 part-time/adjunct (1 woman). *Students:* 55 full-time (21 women), 42 part-time (11 women); includes 36 minority (7 Black or African American, non-Hispanic/Latino; 1 Asian, non-Hispanic/

Latino; 27 Hispanic/Latino; 1 Two or more races, non-Hispanic/Latino), 56 international. Average age 31. 126 applicants, 33% accepted, 17 enrolled. In 2016, 26 master's, 11 doctorates awarded. Terminal master's awarded for partial completion of doctoral program. *Degree requirements:* For master's, thesis or alternative; for doctorate, comprehensive exam, thesis/dissertation. *Entrance requirements:* For master's, bachelor's degree in related field, 3 letters of recommendation, minimum GPA of 3.0; for doctorate, GRE General Test, minimum graduate GPA of 3.3, 3 letters of recommendation, master's degree, resume, statement of purpose. Additional exam requirements/recommendations for international students: Required—TOEFL (minimum score 550 paper-based; 80 iBT). *Application deadline:* For fall admission, 6/1 for domestic students, 4/1 for international students; for spring admission, 10/1 for domestic students, 9/1 for international students. Applications are processed on a rolling basis. Application fee: $30. Electronic applications accepted. *Expenses:* Tuition, state resident: full-time $8912; part-time $446 per credit hour. Tuition, nonresident: full-time $21,393; part-time $992 per credit hour. *Required fees:* $2185; $195 per semester. Tuition and fees vary according to program. *Financial support:* Federal Work-Study, institutionally sponsored loans, scholarships/grants, health care benefits, and unspecified assistantships available. Financial award application deadline: 3/1; financial award applicants required to submit FAFSA. *Faculty research:* Structural engineering, wind engineering, water resources engineering, transportation engineering, environmental engineering. *Unit head:* Dr. Atorod Azizinamini, Chair, 305-348-3821, Fax: 305-348-2802, E-mail: aazizina@fiu.edu. *Application contact:* Sara-Michelle Lemus, Engineering Admissions Officer, 305-348-1890, Fax: 305-348-7441, E-mail: grad_eng@fiu.edu.
Website: http://cec.fiu.edu

Florida State University, The Graduate School, FAMU-FSU College of Engineering, Department of Civil and Environmental Engineering, Tallahassee, FL 32306. Offers M Eng, MS, PhD. *Program availability:* Part-time. *Faculty:* 17 full-time (2 women), 1 part-time/adjunct (0 women). *Students:* 60 full-time (17 women); includes 12 minority (8 Black or African American, non-Hispanic/Latino; 2 Asian, non-Hispanic/Latino; 2 Hispanic/Latino), 34 international. Average age 23. 62 applicants, 50% accepted, 22 enrolled. In 2016, 13 master's, 2 doctorates awarded. *Degree requirements:* For master's, comprehensive exam, thesis optional; for doctorate, thesis/dissertation. *Entrance requirements:* For master's, GRE General Test (minimum score 1000 in old version), BS in engineering or related field, minimum GPA of 3.0; for doctorate, GRE General Test, master's degree in engineering or related field, minimum GPA of 3.0. Additional exam requirements/recommendations for international students: Required—TOEFL (minimum score 550 paper-based; 80 iBT); Recommended—IELTS (minimum score 6.5). *Application deadline:* For fall admission, 7/1 for domestic and international students; for spring admission, 11/1 for domestic and international students; for summer admission, 3/1 for domestic and international students. Applications are processed on a rolling basis. Application fee: $30. Electronic applications accepted. *Expenses:* Tuition, state resident: full-time $7263; part-time $403.51 per credit hour. Tuition, nonresident: full-time $18,087; part-time $1004.85 per credit hour. *Required fees:* $1365; $75.81 per credit hour. $20 per semester. Tuition and fees vary according to campus/location. *Financial support:* In 2016–17, 37 students received support, including 7 fellowships with full tuition reimbursements available, 17 research assistantships with full tuition reimbursements available, 13 teaching assistantships with full tuition reimbursements available; Federal Work-Study, scholarships/grants, tuition waivers (full), and unspecified assistantships also available. Financial award application deadline: 3/1; financial award applicants required to submit FAFSA. *Faculty research:* Tidal hydraulics, temperature effects on bridge girders, codes for coastal construction, field performance of pine bridges, river basin management, transportation pavement design, soil dynamics, structural analysis. *Total annual research expenditures:* $2.9 million. *Unit head:* Dr. Kamal S. Tawfiq, Chair and Professor, 850-410-6143, Fax: 850-410-6142, E-mail: tawfiq@eng.famu.fsu.edu. *Application contact:* Mable Johnson, Office Manager, 850-410-6139, Fax: 850-410-6292, E-mail: mjohnson5@fsu.edu.
Website: http://www.eng.famu.fsu.edu/cee/

Gannon University, School of Graduate Studies, College of Engineering and Business, School of Engineering and Computer Science, Program in Environmental Science and Engineering, Erie, PA 16541-0001. Offers environmental health (MSEH); environmental health and engineering (MS). *Program availability:* Part-time, evening/weekend. *Students:* 6 full-time (4 women), 3 international. Average age 28. 35 applicants, 43% accepted, 4 enrolled. In 2016, 3 master's awarded. *Degree requirements:* For master's, thesis (for some programs), research paper or project (for some programs). *Entrance requirements:* For master's, GRE, bachelor's degree in science or engineering from an accredited college or university. Additional exam requirements/recommendations for international students: Required—TOEFL (minimum score 79 iBT), GRE. *Application deadline:* Applications are processed on a rolling basis. Application fee: $25. Electronic applications accepted. Application fee is waived when completed online. *Expenses:* Tuition: Full-time $17,370. *Required fees:* $550. Tuition and fees vary according to course load and program. *Financial support:* Federal Work-Study and unspecified assistantships available. Financial award application deadline: 7/1; financial award applicants required to submit FAFSA. *Unit head:* Dr. Harry Diz, Chair, 814-871-7633, E-mail: diz001@gannon.edu. *Application contact:* Bridget Philip, Director of Graduate Admissions, 814-871-7412, E-mail: graduate@gannon.edu.

The George Washington University, School of Engineering and Applied Science, Department of Civil and Environmental Engineering, Washington, DC 20052. Offers MS, PhD, App Sc, Engr, Graduate Certificate. *Program availability:* Part-time, evening/weekend. *Faculty:* 12 full-time (3 women). *Students:* 31 full-time (7 women), 18 part-time (6 women); includes 1 minority (Asian, non-Hispanic/Latino), 38 international. Average age 27. 186 applicants, 54% accepted, 17 enrolled. In 2016, 7 master's, 2 doctorates awarded. *Degree requirements:* For master's, thesis optional; for doctorate, thesis/dissertation, final and qualifying exams. *Entrance requirements:* For master's, appropriate bachelor's degree, minimum GPA of 3.0; for doctorate, GRE (if highest earned degree is BS), appropriate bachelor's or master's degree, minimum GPA of 3.4; for other advanced degree, appropriate master's degree, minimum GPA of 3.0. Additional exam requirements/recommendations for international students: Required—TOEFL or The George Washington University English as a Foreign Language Test. *Application deadline:* For fall admission, 3/1 priority date for domestic students; for spring admission, 10/1 for domestic students. Applications are processed on a rolling basis. Application fee: $75. *Financial support:* In 2016–17, 42 students received support. Fellowships with tuition reimbursements available, research assistantships, teaching assistantships with tuition reimbursements available, career-related internships or fieldwork, Federal Work-Study, institutionally sponsored loans, and tuition waivers available. Financial award application deadline: 3/1; financial award applicants required to submit FAFSA. *Faculty research:* Computer-integrated manufacturing, materials engineering, electronic materials, fatigue and fracture, reliability. *Unit head:* Dr. Majid T. Manzari, Chair, 202-994-4901, Fax: 202-994-0127, E-mail: manzari@gwu.edu. *Application contact:* Adina Lav, Marketing, Recruiting and Admissions, 202-994-5827, Fax: 202-994-0909, E-mail: engineering@gwu.edu.
Website: http://www.cee.seas.gwu.edu/

Georgia Institute of Technology, Graduate Studies, College of Engineering, School of Civil and Environmental Engineering, Program in Environmental Engineering, Atlanta,

GA 30332-0001. Offers MS. *Program availability:* Part-time. Terminal master's awarded for partial completion of doctoral program. *Degree requirements:* For master's, thesis optional. *Entrance requirements:* For master's, GRE. Additional exam requirements/recommendations for international students: Required—TOEFL (minimum score 550 paper-based; 79 iBT). Electronic applications accepted. *Faculty research:* Advanced microbiology of water and wastes, industrial waste treatment and disposal, air pollution measurements and control.

Harvard University, Graduate School of Arts and Sciences, Harvard John A. Paulson School of Engineering and Applied Sciences, Cambridge, MA 02138. Offers applied mathematics (PhD); applied physics (PhD); computational science and engineering (ME, SM); computer science (PhD); design engineering (MDE); engineering science (ME), including electrical engineering (ME, SM, PhD); engineering sciences (SM, PhD), including bioengineering (PhD), electrical engineering (ME, SM, PhD), environmental science and engineering (PhD), materials science and mechanical engineering (PhD). MDE offered in collaboration with Graduate School of Design. *Program availability:* Part-time. *Faculty:* 80 full-time (13 women), 47 part-time/adjunct (10 women). *Students:* 459 full-time (135 women), 19 part-time (7 women); includes 79 minority (2 Black or African American, non-Hispanic/Latino; 49 Asian, non-Hispanic/Latino; 15 Hispanic/Latino; 1 Native Hawaiian or other Pacific Islander, non-Hispanic/Latino; 12 Two or more races, non-Hispanic/Latino), 233 international. Average age 27. 2,486 applicants, 11% accepted, 126 enrolled. In 2016, 37 master's, 48 doctorates awarded. Terminal master's awarded for partial completion of doctoral program. *Degree requirements:* For master's, thesis (for ME); for doctorate, comprehensive exam, thesis/dissertation. *Entrance requirements:* For master's and doctorate, GRE General Test, GRE Subject Test (recommended), 3 letters of recommendation. Additional exam requirements/recommendations for international students: Required—TOEFL (minimum score 80 iBT). *Application deadline:* For fall admission, 12/15 priority date for domestic and international students. Application fee: $105. Electronic applications accepted. *Expenses:* $43,296 full-time tuition, $3,718 fees. *Financial support:* In 2016–17, 394 students received support, including 86 fellowships with full tuition reimbursements available (averaging $26,424 per year), 258 research assistantships with tuition reimbursements available (averaging $35,232 per year), 106 teaching assistantships with tuition reimbursements available (averaging $6,313 per year); health care benefits also available. *Faculty research:* Applied mathematics, applied physics, computer science and electrical engineering, environmental engineering, mechanical and biomedical engineering. *Total annual research expenditures:* $50.1 million. *Unit head:* Francis J. Doyle, III, Dean, 617-495-5829, Fax: 617-495-5264, E-mail: dean@seas.harvard.edu. *Application contact:* Office of Admissions and Financial Aid, 617-495-5315, E-mail: admissions@seas.harvard.edu.
Website: http://www.seas.harvard.edu/

Idaho State University, Office of Graduate Studies, College of Science and Engineering, Civil and Environmental Engineering Department, Pocatello, ID 83209-8060. Offers civil engineering (MS); environmental engineering (MS); environmental science and management (MS). *Program availability:* Part-time. *Degree requirements:* For master's, comprehensive exam (for some programs), thesis optional, thesis project, 2 semesters of seminar. *Entrance requirements:* For master's, GRE. Additional exam requirements/recommendations for international students: Required—TOEFL (minimum score 550 paper-based; 80 iBT). Electronic applications accepted. *Faculty research:* Floor vibration investigations, earthquake engineering, base isolation systems and seismic risk assessment, infrastructure revitalization (building foundations and damage, bridge structures, highways, and dams), slope stability and soil erosion, pavement rehabilitation, computational fluid dynamics and flood control structures, microbial fuel cells, water treatment and water quality modeling, environmental risk assessment, biotechnology, nanotechnology.

Illinois Institute of Technology, Graduate College, Armour College of Engineering, Department of Civil, Architectural and Environmental Engineering, Chicago, IL 60616. Offers architectural engineering (M Arch E); civil engineering (MS, PhD), including architectural engineering (MS), construction engineering and management (MS), geoenvironmental engineering (MS), geotechnical engineering (MS), structural engineering (MS), transportation engineering (MS); construction engineering and management (MCEM); environmental engineering (M Env E, MS, PhD); geoenvironmental engineering (M Geoenv E); geotechnical engineering (MGE); infrastructure engineering and management (MPW); structural engineering (MSE); transportation engineering (M Trans E). *Program availability:* Part-time, evening/weekend, online learning. Terminal master's awarded for partial completion of doctoral program. *Degree requirements:* For master's, thesis (for some programs); for doctorate, comprehensive exam, thesis/dissertation. *Entrance requirements:* For master's, GRE General Test (minimum score 900 Quantitative and Verbal, 2.5 Analytical Writing), minimum undergraduate GPA of 3.0; for doctorate, GRE General Test (minimum score 1000 Quantitative and Verbal, 3.0 Analytical Writing), minimum undergraduate GPA of 3.0. Additional exam requirements/recommendations for international students: Required—TOEFL (minimum score 550 paper-based; 80 iBT). Electronic applications accepted. *Faculty research:* Structural, architectural, geotechnical and geoenvironmental engineering; construction engineering and management; transportation engineering; environmental engineering and public works.

Instituto Tecnologico de Santo Domingo, Graduate School, Area of Engineering, Santo Domingo, Dominican Republic. Offers construction administration (MS, Certificate); data telecommunications (M Eng, MS, Certificate); industrial engineering (M Eng, Certificate); industrial management (M Mgmt); information technology (Certificate); maintenance engineering (M Eng); occupational hazard prevention (M Mgmt); production management (Certificate); quantitative methods (Certificate); sanitary and environmental engineering (M Eng); structural engineering (M Eng); systems engineering and electronic data processing (Certificate); transportation (Certificate).

Instituto Tecnológico y de Estudios Superiores de Monterrey, Campus Ciudad de México, Virtual University Division, Ciudad de Mexico, Mexico. Offers administration of information technologies (MA); computer sciences (MA); education (MA, PhD); educational technology (MA); environmental engineering (MA); environmental systems (MA); humanistic studies (MA); industrial engineering (MA); international business for Latin America (MA); quality systems (MA); quality systems and productivity (MA). *Program availability:* Part-time, evening/weekend, online learning. *Entrance requirements:* For master's and doctorate, Instituto entrance exam. Additional exam requirements/recommendations for international students: Required—TOEFL.

Instituto Tecnológico y de Estudios Superiores de Monterrey, Campus Monterrey, Graduate and Research Division, Programs in Engineering, Monterrey, Mexico. Offers applied statistics (M Eng); artificial intelligence (PhD); automation engineering (M Eng); chemical engineering (M Eng); civil engineering (M Eng); electrical engineering (M Eng); electronic engineering (M Eng); environmental engineering (M Eng); industrial engineering (M Eng, PhD); manufacturing engineering (M Eng); mechanical engineering (M Eng); systems and quality engineering (M Eng). M Eng program offered jointly with University of Waterloo; PhD in industrial engineering with Texas A&M University. *Program availability:* Part-time, evening/weekend. Terminal master's awarded for partial completion of doctoral program. *Degree requirements:* For master's, one foreign language, thesis; for doctorate, one foreign language, thesis/dissertation. *Entrance requirements:* For master's, EXADEP; for doctorate, GRE, master's degree in related field. Additional exam requirements/recommendations for international students: Required—TOEFL. *Faculty research:* Flexible manufacturing cells, materials, statistical methods, environmental prevention, control and evaluation.

Iowa State University of Science and Technology, Department of Civil and Construction Engineering, Ames, IA 50011. Offers civil engineering (MS, PhD), including civil engineering materials, construction engineering and management, environmental engineering, geotechnical engineering, structural engineering, transportation engineering. *Degree requirements:* For master's, thesis or alternative; for doctorate, thesis/dissertation. *Entrance requirements:* For master's and doctorate, GRE General Test. Additional exam requirements/recommendations for international students: Required—TOEFL (minimum score 550 paper-based; 82 iBT), IELTS (minimum score 6.5). *Application deadline:* For fall admission, 2/1 priority date for domestic students, 2/1 for international students; for spring admission, 8/1 priority date for domestic students, 8/1 for international students. Application fee: $60 ($90 for international students). Electronic applications accepted. *Application contact:* Kathy Petersen, Application Contact, 515-294-4975, Fax: 515-294-8216, E-mail: ccee-grad-inquiry@iastate.edu.
Website: http://www.ccee.iastate.edu/

Jackson State University, Graduate School, College of Science, Engineering and Technology, Department of Civil and Environmental Engineering and Industrial Systems and Technology, Jackson, MS 39217. Offers civil engineering (MS, PhD); coastal engineering (MS, PhD); environmental engineering (MS, PhD); hazardous materials management (MS); technology education (MS Ed). *Program availability:* Part-time, evening/weekend. *Degree requirements:* For master's, comprehensive exam, thesis or alternative. *Entrance requirements:* For master's, GRE General Test. Additional exam requirements/recommendations for international students: Required—TOEFL (minimum score 520 paper-based; 67 iBT). *Application deadline:* For fall admission, 3/1 priority date for domestic students, 3/1 for international students; for spring admission, 10/1 for domestic and international students. Applications are processed on a rolling basis. Application fee: $25. *Expenses:* Tuition, state resident: full-time $7141. Tuition, nonresident: full-time $17,494. *Required fees:* $1080. Tuition and fees vary according to class time, course level, course load, degree level, campus/location, program and student level. *Financial support:* Career-related internships or fieldwork, Federal Work-Study, scholarships/grants, and unspecified assistantships available. Support available to part-time students. Financial award application deadline: 3/1; financial award applicants required to submit FAFSA. *Unit head:* Dr. Farshad Amini, Chair, 601-979-3913, Fax: 601-979-3238, E-mail: famini@jsums.edu. *Application contact:* Fatoumatta Sisay, Manager of Graduate Admissions, 601-979-0342, Fax: 601-979-4325, E-mail: fatoumatta.sisay@jsums.edu.
Website: http://www.jsums.edu/ceeist/

Johns Hopkins University, Bloomberg School of Public Health, Department of Environmental Health Sciences, Baltimore, MD 21218. Offers environmental health engineering (PhD); environmental health sciences (MHS, Dr PH); occupational and environmental health (PhD); physiology (PhD); toxicology (PhD). *Program availability:* Online learning. *Degree requirements:* For master's, essay, presentation; for doctorate, comprehensive exam, thesis/dissertation, 1-year full-time residency, oral and written exams. *Entrance requirements:* For master's, GRE General Test or MCAT, 3 letters of recommendation, transcripts; for doctorate, GRE General Test or MCAT, 3 letters of recommendation. Additional exam requirements/recommendations for international students: Required—TOEFL (minimum score 600 paper-based). Electronic applications accepted. *Faculty research:* Chemical carcinogenesis/toxicology, lung disease, occupational and environmental health, nuclear imaging, molecular epidemiology.

Johns Hopkins University, Engineering Program for Professionals, Part-time Program in Environmental Engineering, Baltimore, MD 21218. Offers MS, Graduate Certificate, Post-Master's Certificate. *Program availability:* Part-time, evening/weekend, online only, 100% online. *Faculty:* 1 full-time (0 women), 6 part-time/adjunct (1 woman). *Students:* 1 full-time (0 women), 35 part-time (15 women); includes 5 minority (1 Black or African American, non-Hispanic/Latino; 4 Asian, non-Hispanic/Latino), 1 international. Average age 29. 17 applicants, 71% accepted, 9 enrolled. In 2016, 4 master's awarded. *Entrance requirements:* Additional exam requirements/recommendations for international students: Required—TOEFL (minimum score 600 paper-based; 100 iBT). Application fee: $0. *Unit head:* Dr. Hedy Alavi, Program Chair, 410-516-7091, Fax: 410-516-8996, E-mail: hedy.alavi@jhu.edu. *Application contact:* Doug Schiller, Admissions Director, 410-516-2300, Fax: 410-579-8049, E-mail: schiller@jhu.edu.
Website: http://www.ep.jhu.edu

Johns Hopkins University, Engineering Program for Professionals, Part-time Program in Environmental Engineering and Science, Baltimore, MD 21218. Offers MEE, MS, Graduate Certificate, Post-Master's Certificate. *Program availability:* Part-time, evening/weekend, online only, 100% online. *Faculty:* 9 part-time/adjunct (2 women). *Students:* 2 full-time (1 woman), 42 part-time (25 women); includes 7 minority (1 Black or African American, non-Hispanic/Latino; 4 Asian, non-Hispanic/Latino; 2 Hispanic/Latino), 1 international. Average age 30. 35 applicants, 49% accepted, 13 enrolled. In 2016, 17 master's awarded. *Entrance requirements:* Additional exam requirements/recommendations for international students: Required—TOEFL (minimum score 600 paper-based; 100 iBT). *Application deadline:* Applications are processed on a rolling basis. Application fee: $0. Electronic applications accepted. *Unit head:* Dr. Hedy Alavi, Program Chair, 410-516-7091, Fax: 410-516-8996, E-mail: hedy.alavi@jhu.edu. *Application contact:* Doug Schiller, Admissions Director, 410-516-2300, Fax: 410-579-8049, E-mail: schiller@jhu.edu.
Website: http://www.ep.jhu.edu/

Kansas State University, Graduate School, College of Engineering, Department of Civil Engineering, Manhattan, KS 66506. Offers civil engineering (MS, PhD); environmental engineering (MS, PhD); geotechnical engineering (MS, PhD); structural engineering (MS, PhD); transportation engineering (MS, PhD); water resources engineering (MS, PhD). *Program availability:* Part-time, evening/weekend, online learning. *Faculty:* 14 full-time (4 women), 3 part-time/adjunct (1 woman). *Students:* 36 full-time (11 women), 34 part-time (7 women); includes 5 minority (2 Asian, non-Hispanic/Latino; 2 Hispanic/Latino; 1 Two or more races, non-Hispanic/Latino), 28 international. Average age 29. 70 applicants, 60% accepted, 11 enrolled. In 2016, 21 master's, 7 doctorates awarded. *Degree requirements:* For master's, thesis or alternative; for doctorate, thesis/dissertation. *Entrance requirements:* For master's, GRE General Test, bachelor's degree or course work in related engineering fields; for doctorate, GRE General Test. Additional exam requirements/recommendations for international students: Required—TOEFL (minimum score 550 paper-based; 79 iBT). *Application deadline:* For fall admission, 2/1 priority date for domestic students, 1/1 priority date for international students; for spring admission, 8/1 priority date for domestic and international students. Applications are processed on a rolling basis. Application fee: $50 ($75 for international students). Electronic applications accepted. *Expenses:* Tuition, state resident: full-time $9670. Tuition, nonresident: full-time $21,828. *Required fees:* $862. *Financial support:* In 2016–17, 19 research assistantships with partial tuition reimbursements (averaging $13,431 per year), 12 teaching assistantships with partial tuition reimbursements (averaging $15,058 per year) were awarded; institutionally sponsored loans and scholarships/grants also available. Support available to part-time students. Financial award application deadline: 3/1; financial award applicants required to submit FAFSA. *Faculty research:* Transportation and materials engineering, water resources engineering, environmental engineering, geotechnical engineering, structural engineering. *Total annual research expenditures:* $2.4 million. *Unit head:* Dr. Robert Stokes, Head, 785-532-1595, Fax: 785-532-7717, E-mail: drbobb@k-state.edu. *Application contact:* Dr. Dunja Peric, Graduate Coordinator, 785-532-2468, Fax: 785-532-7717, E-mail: peric@k-state.edu.
Website: http://www.ce.ksu.edu/

Lakehead University, Graduate Studies, Faculty of Engineering, Thunder Bay, ON P7B 5E1, Canada. Offers control engineering (M Sc Engr); electrical/computer engineering (M Sc Engr); environmental engineering (M Sc Engr). *Program availability:* Part-time. *Degree requirements:* For master's, thesis. *Entrance requirements:* For master's, bachelor's degree in chemical, electrical or mechanical engineering, minimum B average. Additional exam requirements/recommendations for international students: Required—TOEFL. *Faculty research:* Pulp and paper, adaptive/process control, robust/interactive learning control, vibration control.

Lamar University, College of Graduate Studies, College of Engineering, Department of Civil and Environmental Engineering, Beaumont, TX 77710. Offers civil engineering (ME, MES); environmental engineering (MS); environmental studies (MS, DE). *Program availability:* Part-time. *Faculty:* 7 full-time (1 woman). *Students:* 41 full-time (13 women), 18 part-time (5 women); includes 2 minority (1 Black or African American, non-Hispanic/Latino; 1 American Indian or Alaska Native, non-Hispanic/Latino), 49 international. Average age 26. 54 applicants, 83% accepted, 20 enrolled. In 2016, 32 master's, 1 doctorate awarded. *Degree requirements:* For master's, thesis optional; for doctorate, thesis/dissertation. *Entrance requirements:* For master's and doctorate, GRE General Test. Additional exam requirements/recommendations for international students: Required—TOEFL (minimum score 550 paper-based; 79 iBT), IELTS (minimum score 6.5). *Application deadline:* For fall admission, 8/1 for domestic students, 7/1 for international students; for spring admission, 1/5 for domestic students, 12/1 for international students. Applications are processed on a rolling basis. Application fee: $25 ($50 for international students). Electronic applications accepted. *Expenses:* $8,134 in-state full-time, $5,574 in-state part-time; $15,604 out-of-state full-time, $10,554 out-of-state part-time per year. *Financial support:* Fellowships with partial tuition reimbursements, research assistantships with partial tuition reimbursements, teaching assistantships with partial tuition reimbursements, scholarships/grants, and tuition waivers (partial) available. Financial award application deadline: 4/1; financial award applicants required to submit FAFSA. *Faculty research:* Environmental remediation's, construction productivity, geotechnical soil stabilization, lake/reservoir hydrodynamics, air pollution. *Unit head:* Dr. Liv Haselbach, Chair, 409-880-8759, Fax: 409-880-8121. *Application contact:* Deidre Mayer, Interim Director, Admissions and Academic Services, 409-880-8888, Fax: 409-880-7419, E-mail: gradmissions@lamar.edu.
Website: http://engineering.lamar.edu/civil

Lehigh University, P.C. Rossin College of Engineering and Applied Science, Department of Civil and Environmental Engineering, Bethlehem, PA 18015. Offers M Eng, MS, PhD. *Program availability:* Part-time. *Faculty:* 21 full-time (4 women). *Students:* 78 full-time (24 women), 7 part-time (0 women); includes 6 minority (1 Black or African American, non-Hispanic/Latino; 2 Asian, non-Hispanic/Latino; 3 Hispanic/Latino), 51 international. Average age 27. 184 applicants, 27% accepted, 13 enrolled. In 2016, 29 master's, 14 doctorates awarded. Terminal master's awarded for partial completion of doctoral program. *Degree requirements:* For master's, thesis (for some programs); for doctorate, comprehensive exam, thesis/dissertation. *Entrance requirements:* For master's and doctorate, GRE. Additional exam requirements/recommendations for international students: Required—TOEFL (minimum score 550 paper-based; 79 iBT), IELTS (minimum score 6.5). *Application deadline:* For fall admission, 7/15 for domestic and international students; for spring admission, 12/1 for domestic and international students; for summer admission, 5/30 for domestic and international students. Application fee: $75. Electronic applications accepted. *Expenses:* $1,420 per credit. *Financial support:* In 2016–17, 5 fellowships with full tuition reimbursements (averaging $21,530 per year), 27 research assistantships with full and partial tuition reimbursements (averaging $23,000 per year), 7 teaching assistantships with full tuition reimbursements (averaging $21,530 per year) were awarded; unspecified assistantships also available. Financial award application deadline: 1/15; financial award applicants required to submit FAFSA. *Faculty research:* Structural engineering, geotechnical engineering, water resources engineering, environmental engineering. *Total annual research expenditures:* $4.5 million. *Unit head:* Dr. Panayiotis Diplas, Chair, 610-758-3554, E-mail: pad313@lehigh.edu. *Application contact:* Prisca Vidanage, Graduate Coordinator, 610-758-3530, E-mail: pmv1@lehigh.edu.
Website: http://www.lehigh.edu/~incee/

Louisiana State University and Agricultural & Mechanical College, Graduate School, College of Engineering, Department of Civil and Environmental Engineering, Baton Rouge, LA 70803. Offers environmental engineering (MSCE, PhD); geotechnical engineering (MSCE, PhD); structural engineering and mechanics (MSCE, PhD); transportation engineering (MSCE, PhD); water resources (MSCE, PhD).

Manhattan College, Graduate Programs, School of Engineering, Program in Environmental Engineering, Riverdale, NY 10471. Offers ME, MS. *Accreditation:* ABET. *Program availability:* Part-time, evening/weekend. *Degree requirements:* For master's, thesis optional, 30 credits, minimum GPA of 3.0. *Entrance requirements:* For master's, GRE (recommended), minimum GPA of 3.0. Additional exam requirements/recommendations for international students: Required—TOEFL (minimum score 550 paper-based; 80 iBT), IELTS (minimum score 6). *Application deadline:* For fall admission, 8/10 priority date for domestic students, 8/10 for international students; for spring admission, 1/7 for domestic and international students. Applications are processed on a rolling basis. Application fee: $60. *Financial support:* Fellowships with full tuition reimbursements, research assistantships with full tuition reimbursements, teaching assistantships with partial tuition reimbursements, career-related internships or fieldwork, Federal Work-Study, scholarships/grants, unspecified assistantships, and laboratory assistantships available. Support available to part-time students. Financial award application deadline: 3/1. *Faculty research:* Water quality modeling, environmental chemistry, air modeling, biological treatment, environmental chemistry. *Unit head:* Dr. Robert Sharp, Graduate Program Director, 718-862-7169, Fax: 718-862-8035, E-mail: robert.sharp@manhattan.edu.
Website: https://manhattan.edu/academics/graduate-programs/environmental-engineering.php

Marquette University, Graduate School, College of Engineering, Department of Civil and Environmental Engineering, Milwaukee, WI 53201-1881. Offers construction engineering and management (MS, PhD, Certificate); environmental engineering (MS, PhD); structural design (Certificate); structural engineering and structural mechanics (MS, PhD); transportation (Certificate); transportation engineering and materials (MS, PhD); waste and wastewater treatment processes (Certificate); water resources engineering (Certificate). *Program availability:* Part-time, evening/weekend. *Faculty:* 17 full-time (2 women), 2 part-time/adjunct (0 women). *Students:* 27 full-time (8 women), 6 part-time (0 women); includes 5 minority (1 Asian, non-Hispanic/Latino; 2 Hispanic/

Latino; 2 Two or more races, non-Hispanic/Latino), 13 international. Average age 28. 70 applicants, 56% accepted, 9 enrolled. In 2016, 8 master's, 5 doctorates awarded. Terminal master's awarded for partial completion of doctoral program. *Degree requirements:* For master's, comprehensive exam (for some programs), thesis or alternative; for doctorate, thesis/dissertation. *Entrance requirements:* For master's, GRE General Test (recommended), minimum GPA of 3.0, official transcripts from all current and previous colleges/universities except Marquette, three letters of recommendation; for doctorate, GRE General Test, minimum GPA of 3.0, official transcripts from all current and previous colleges/universities except Marquette, three letters of recommendation, brief statement of purpose, submission of any English language publications authored by applicant (strongly recommended). Additional exam requirements/recommendations for international students: Required—TOEFL (minimum score 530 paper-based). *Application deadline:* For fall admission, 6/1 priority date for domestic students. Applications are processed on a rolling basis. Application fee: $50. Electronic applications accepted. *Financial support:* Fellowships, research assistantships, teaching assistantships, scholarships/grants, health care benefits, tuition waivers (partial), and unspecified assistantships available. Support available to part-time students. Financial award application deadline: 2/15. *Faculty research:* Highway safety, highway performance, and intelligent transportation systems; surface mount technology; watershed management. *Total annual research expenditures:* $480,876. *Unit head:* Dr. Christopher Foley, Chair, 414-288-5741. *Application contact:* Dr. Stephen M. Heinrich, Director of Graduate Studies, 414-288-5466.
Website: http://www.marquette.edu/civil-environmental-engineering/

Marshall University, Academic Affairs Division, College of Information Technology and Engineering, Program in Engineering, Huntington, WV 25755. Offers engineering (MSME); engineering management (MSE); environmental engineering (MSE); transportation and infrastructure engineering (MSE). *Program availability:* Part-time, evening/weekend. *Degree requirements:* For master's, final project, oral exam. *Entrance requirements:* For master's, GMAT or GRE General Test, minimum undergraduate GPA of 2.75.

Massachusetts Institute of Technology, School of Engineering, Department of Civil and Environmental Engineering, Cambridge, MA 02139. Offers biological oceanography (PhD, Sc D); chemical oceanography (PhD, Sc D); civil and environmental engineering (M Eng, SM, PhD, Sc D); civil and environmental systems (PhD, Sc D); civil engineering (PhD, Sc D, CE); civil engineering and computation (PhD); coastal engineering (PhD, Sc D); construction engineering and management (PhD, Sc D); environmental biology (PhD, Sc D); environmental chemistry (PhD, Sc D); environmental engineering (PhD, Sc D); environmental engineering and computation (PhD); environmental fluid mechanics (PhD, Sc D); geotechnical and geoenvironmental engineering (PhD, Sc D); hydrology (PhD, Sc D); information technology (PhD, Sc D); oceanographic engineering (PhD, Sc D); structures and materials (PhD, Sc D); transportation (PhD, Sc D); SM/MBA. *Faculty:* 35 full-time (6 women). *Students:* 192 full-time (64 women); includes 25 minority (2 Black or African American, non-Hispanic/Latino; 11 Asian, non-Hispanic/Latino; 8 Hispanic/Latino; 4 Two or more races, non-Hispanic/Latino), 113 international. Average age 27. 530 applicants, 20% accepted, 77 enrolled. In 2016, 56 master's, 16 doctorates, 1 other advanced degree awarded. *Degree requirements:* For master's, thesis; for doctorate, comprehensive exam, thesis/dissertation; for CE, comprehensive exam, thesis. *Entrance requirements:* For master's, doctorate, and CE, GRE General Test. Additional exam requirements/recommendations for international students: Required—TOEFL, IELTS. *Application deadline:* For fall admission, 12/15 for domestic and international students. Application fee: $75. Electronic applications accepted. *Expenses: Tuition:* Full-time $46,400; part-time $725 per credit. One-time fee: $312 full-time. Full-time tuition and fees vary according to course load and program. *Financial support:* In 2016–17, 150 students received support, including fellowships (averaging $41,900 per year), 124 research assistantships (averaging $36,900 per year), 9 teaching assistantships (averaging $36,900 per year); Federal Work-Study, institutionally sponsored loans, scholarships/grants, traineeships, health care benefits, unspecified assistantships, and resident tutors also available. Support available to part-time students. Financial award application deadline: 5/1; financial award applicants required to submit FAFSA. *Faculty research:* Environmental chemistry, environmental fluid mechanics and coastal engineering, environmental microbiology, geotechnical engineering and geomechanics, hydrology and hydro climatology, infrastructure systems, mechanics of materials and structures, transportation systems. *Total annual research expenditures:* $25 million. *Unit head:* Prof. Markus Buehler, Department Head, 617-253-7101. *Application contact:* 617-253-7119, E-mail: cee-admissions@mit.edu.
Website: http://cee.mit.edu/

McGill University, Faculty of Graduate and Postdoctoral Studies, Faculty of Engineering, Department of Chemical Engineering, Montréal, QC H3A 2T5, Canada. Offers chemical engineering (M Eng, PhD); environmental engineering (M Eng).

McGill University, Faculty of Graduate and Postdoctoral Studies, Faculty of Engineering, Department of Civil Engineering and Applied Mechanics, Montréal, QC H3A 2T5, Canada. Offers environmental engineering (M Eng, M Sc, PhD); fluid mechanics (M Sc); fluid mechanics and hydraulic engineering (M Eng, PhD); materials engineering (M Eng, PhD); rehabilitation of urban infrastructure (M Eng, PhD); soil behavior (M Eng, PhD); soil mechanics and foundations (M Eng, PhD); structures and structural mechanics (M Eng, PhD); water resources (M Sc); water resources engineering (M Eng, PhD).

Memorial University of Newfoundland, School of Graduate Studies, Interdisciplinary Program in Environmental Systems Engineering and Management, St. John's, NL A1C 5S7, Canada. Offers MA Sc. *Degree requirements:* For master's, project course. *Entrance requirements:* For master's, 2nd class engineering degree. *Expenses:* Contact institution.

Mercer University, Graduate Studies, Macon Campus, School of Engineering, Macon, GA 31207. Offers biomedical engineering (MSE); computer engineering (MSE); electrical engineering (MSE); engineering management (MSE); environmental engineering (MSE); environmental systems (MS); mechanical engineering (MSE); software engineering (MSE); software systems (MS); technical communications management (MS); technical management (MS). *Program availability:* Part-time-only, evening/weekend, online learning. *Faculty:* 21 full-time (5 women), 1 part-time/adjunct (0 women). *Students:* 44 full-time (9 women), 60 part-time (12 women); includes 14 minority (3 Black or African American, non-Hispanic/Latino; 1 American Indian or Alaska Native, non-Hispanic/Latino; 4 Asian, non-Hispanic/Latino; 3 Hispanic/Latino; 3 Two or more races, non-Hispanic/Latino), 2 international. Average age 27. In 2016, 64 master's awarded. *Degree requirements:* For master's, thesis or alternative. *Entrance requirements:* For master's, GRE (minimum score 300), minimum undergraduate GPA of 3.0. Additional exam requirements/recommendations for international students: Required—TOEFL (minimum score 550 paper-based; 80 iBT). *Application deadline:* For fall admission, 4/1 priority date for domestic and international students; for spring admission, 11/1 priority date for domestic and international students. Applications are processed on a rolling basis. Application fee: $75. *Expenses:* $865 per credit hour. *Financial support:* Applicants required to submit FAFSA. *Faculty research:* Designing prostheses and orthotics, oxygen transfer and limitations in biological systems, low-cost groundwater development, lung airway and transport, autonomous mobile robots. *Unit*

head: Dr. Laura W. Lackey, Dean, 478-301-4106, Fax: 478-301-5593, E-mail: lackey_l@mercer.edu. *Application contact:* Dr. Richard O. Mines, Jr., Program Director, 478-301-2347, Fax: 478-301-5433, E-mail: mines_ro@mercer.edu.
Website: http://engineering.mercer.edu/

Michigan State University, The Graduate School, College of Engineering, Department of Civil and Environmental Engineering, East Lansing, MI 48824. Offers civil engineering (MS, PhD); environmental engineering (MS, PhD); environmental engineering-environmental toxicology (PhD). *Program availability:* Part-time. *Entrance requirements:* Additional exam requirements/recommendations for international students: Required—TOEFL. Electronic applications accepted.

Michigan Technological University, Graduate School, Interdisciplinary Programs, Houghton, MI 49931. Offers atmospheric sciences (PhD); biochemistry and molecular biology (PhD); computational science and engineering (PhD); data science (MS, Graduate Certificate); engineering (M Eng); environmental engineering (PhD); international profile (Graduate Certificate); nanotechnology (Graduate Certificate); sustainability (Graduate Certificate); sustainable water resources systems (Graduate Certificate). *Program availability:* Part-time. *Faculty:* 122 full-time (26 women), 13 part-time/adjunct. *Students:* 58 full-time (18 women), 17 part-time (5 women); includes 1 minority (Black or African American, non-Hispanic/Latino), 56 international. Average age 28. 395 applicants, 20% accepted, 22 enrolled. In 2016, 3 master's, 7 doctorates, 8 other advanced degrees awarded. Terminal master's awarded for partial completion of doctoral program. *Degree requirements:* For master's, comprehensive exam (for some programs), thesis (for some programs); for doctorate, comprehensive exam, thesis/ dissertation. *Entrance requirements:* For master's, doctorate, and Graduate Certificate, GRE, statement of purpose, personal statement, official transcripts, 2-3 letters of recommendation. Additional exam requirements/recommendations for international students: Required—TOEFL or IELTS. *Application deadline:* Applications are processed on a rolling basis. Electronic applications accepted. *Expenses:* Tuition, state resident: full-time $16,290; part-time $905 per credit. Tuition, nonresident: full-time $16,290; part-time $905 per credit. *Required fees:* $248; $124 per term. Tuition and fees vary according to course load and program. *Financial support:* In 2016–17, 54 students received support, including 7 fellowships with tuition reimbursements available (averaging $15,242 per year), 19 research assistantships with tuition reimbursements available (averaging $15,242 per year), 5 teaching assistantships with tuition reimbursements available (averaging $15,242 per year); career-related internships or fieldwork, Federal Work-Study, scholarships/grants, health care benefits, unspecified assistantships, and cooperative program also available. Financial award applicants required to submit FAFSA. *Faculty research:* Big data, atmospheric sciences, bioinformatics and systems biology, molecular dynamics, environmental studies. *Unit head:* Dr. Pushpalatha Murthy, Dean of the Graduate School/Associate Provost for Graduate Education, 906-487-3007, Fax: 906-487-2284, E-mail: ppmurthy@mtu.edu. *Application contact:* Carol T. Wingerson, Administrative Aide, 906-487-2328, Fax: 906-487-2284, E-mail: gradadms@mtu.edu.

Missouri University of Science and Technology, Graduate School, Department of Civil, Architectural, and Environmental Engineering, Rolla, MO 65409. Offers civil engineering (MS, DE, PhD); construction engineering (MS, DE, PhD); environmental engineering (MS); fluid mechanics (MS, DE, PhD); geotechnical engineering (MS, DE, PhD); hydrology and hydraulic engineering (MS, DE, PhD). *Program availability:* Part-time, evening/weekend. Terminal master's awarded for partial completion of doctoral program. *Degree requirements:* For master's, thesis optional; for doctorate, comprehensive exam, thesis/dissertation. *Entrance requirements:* For master's, GRE General Test (minimum combined score 1100), minimum GPA of 3.0; for doctorate, GRE General Test (minimum score: verbal and quantitative 400, writing 3.5), minimum GPA of 3.0. Additional exam requirements/recommendations for international students: Required—TOEFL (minimum score 550 paper-based). Electronic applications accepted. *Faculty research:* Earthquake engineering, structural optimization and control systems, structural health monitoring/damage detection, soil-structure interaction, soil mechanics and foundation engineering.

Montana State University, The Graduate School, College of Engineering, Department of Chemical and Biological Engineering, Bozeman, MT 59717. Offers chemical engineering (MS); engineering (PhD), including chemical engineering option, environmental engineering option; environmental engineering (MS). *Program availability:* Part-time. *Degree requirements:* For master's, comprehensive exam, thesis (for some programs); for doctorate, comprehensive exam, thesis/dissertation. *Entrance requirements:* For master's and doctorate, GRE General Test. Additional exam requirements/recommendations for international students: Required—TOEFL (minimum score 550 paper-based). Electronic applications accepted. *Faculty research:* Metabolic network analysis and engineering; magnetic resonance microscopy; modeling of biological systems; the development of protective coatings on planar solid oxide fuel cell (SOFC) metallic interconnects; characterizing corrosion mechanisms of materials in precisely-controlled exposures; testing materials in poly-crystalline silicon production environments; environmental biotechnology and bioremediation.

Montana Tech of The University of Montana, Department of Environmental Engineering, Butte, MT 59701-8997. Offers MS. *Program availability:* Part-time. *Faculty:* 7 full-time (2 women). *Students:* 8 full-time (2 women), 3 part-time (0 women); includes 3 minority (2 Black or African American, non-Hispanic/Latino; 1 American Indian or Alaska Native, non-Hispanic/Latino), 1 international. Average age 26. 5 applicants, 100% accepted, 5 enrolled. In 2016, 3 master's awarded. *Degree requirements:* For master's, thesis. *Entrance requirements:* For master's, GRE General Test, minimum GPA of 3.0. Additional exam requirements/recommendations for international students: Required— TOEFL (minimum score 525 paper-based; 78 iBT), IELTS (minimum score 6.5). *Application deadline:* For fall admission, 4/1 priority date for domestic students, 3/1 priority date for international students; for spring admission, 10/1 priority date for domestic students, 6/1 priority date for international students. Applications are processed on a rolling basis. Application fee: $50. Electronic applications accepted. *Expenses:* Tuition, state resident: full-time $2901; part-time $1450.68 per degree program. Tuition, nonresident: full-time $8432; part-time $4215.84 per degree program. *Required fees:* $668; $354 per degree program. Tuition and fees vary according to course load and program. *Financial support:* In 2016–17, 3 students received support, including 4 teaching assistantships with partial tuition reimbursements available (averaging $4,000 per year); research assistantships with full tuition reimbursements available, career-related internships or fieldwork, tuition waivers (full and partial), and unspecified assistantships also available. Financial award application deadline: 4/1; financial award applicants required to submit FAFSA. *Faculty research:* Mine waste reclamation, modeling, air pollution control, wetlands, water pollution control. *Unit head:* Dr. Kumar Ganesan, Head, 406-496-4239, Fax: 406-496-4650, E-mail: kganesan@ mtech.edu. *Application contact:* Daniel Stirling, Administrator, Graduate School, 406-496-4304, Fax: 406-496-4710, E-mail: gradschool@mtech.edu.
Website: http://www.mtech.edu/academics/gradschool/degreeprograms/degrees-environmental-engineering.htm

New Jersey Institute of Technology, Newark College of Engineering, Newark, NJ 07102. Offers biomedical engineering (MS, PhD); chemical engineering (MS, PhD); computer engineering (MS, PhD); electrical engineering (MS, PhD); engineering

management (MS); environmental engineering (PhD); healthcare systems management (MS); industrial engineering (MS, PhD); Internet engineering (MS); manufacturing engineering (MS); mechanical engineering (MS, PhD); occupational safety and health engineering (MS); pharmaceutical bioprocessing (MS); pharmaceutical engineering (MS); pharmaceutical systems management (MS); power and energy systems (MS); telecommunications (MS); transportation (MS, PhD). *Program availability:* Part-time, evening/weekend. *Faculty:* 146 full-time (21 women), 119 part-time/adjunct (10 women). *Students:* 804 full-time (191 women), 550 part-time (129 women); includes 357 minority (82 Black or African American, non-Hispanic/Latino; 1 American Indian or Alaska Native, non-Hispanic/Latino; 138 Asian, non-Hispanic/Latino; 114 Hispanic/Latino; 22 Two or more races, non-Hispanic/Latino), 675 international. Average age 27. 2,959 applicants, 51% accepted, 442 enrolled. In 2016, 595 master's, 29 doctorates awarded. Terminal master's awarded for partial completion of doctoral program. *Degree requirements:* For master's, thesis optional; for doctorate, thesis/dissertation. *Entrance requirements:* For master's, GRE General Test; for doctorate, GRE General Test, minimum graduate GPA of 3.5. Additional exam requirements/recommendations for international students: Required—TOEFL (minimum score 550 paper-based; 79 iBT). *Application deadline:* For fall admission, 6/1 priority date for domestic students, 5/1 priority date for international students; for spring admission, 11/15 priority date for domestic and international students. Applications are processed on a rolling basis. Application fee: $75. Electronic applications accepted. *Expenses:* Contact institution. *Financial support:* In 2016–17, 172 students received support, including 1 fellowship (averaging $1,528 per year), 79 research assistantships (averaging $13,336 per year), 92 teaching assistantships (averaging $20,619 per year); scholarships/grants also available. Financial award application deadline: 1/15. *Faculty research:* Nonlinear signal processing, intelligent medical image analysis, calibration issues in coherent localization, computer-aided design, neural network for tool wear measurement. *Total annual research expenditures:* $11.1 million. *Unit head:* Dr. Moshe Kam, Dean, 973-596-5534, E-mail: moshe.kam@njit.edu. *Application contact:* Stephen Eck, Director of Admissions, 973-596-3300, Fax: 973-596-3461, E-mail: admissions@njit.edu.
Website: http://engineering.njit.edu/

New Mexico Institute of Mining and Technology, Center for Graduate Studies, Department of Civil and Environmental Engineering, Socorro, NM 87801. Offers environmental engineering (MS), including air quality engineering and science, hazardous waste engineering, water quality engineering and science. *Degree requirements:* For master's, thesis, thesis or independent study. *Entrance requirements:* Additional exam requirements/recommendations for international students: Required—TOEFL (minimum score 540 paper-based). *Faculty research:* Air quality, hazardous waste management, wastewater management and treatment, site remediation.

New Mexico State University, College of Engineering, Department of Civil and Geological Engineering, Las Cruces, NM 88003. Offers civil and geological engineering (MSCE, PhD); environmental engineering (MS Env E). *Program availability:* Part-time. *Faculty:* 13 full-time (3 women). *Students:* 54 full-time (16 women), 16 part-time (4 women); includes 18 minority (2 Black or African American, non-Hispanic/Latino; 3 American Indian or Alaska Native, non-Hispanic/Latino; 1 Asian, non-Hispanic/Latino; 11 Hispanic/Latino; 1 Two or more races, non-Hispanic/Latino), 35 international. Average age 30. 64 applicants, 48% accepted, 17 enrolled. In 2016, 19 master's, 3 doctorates awarded. *Degree requirements:* For master's, thesis (for some programs); for doctorate, comprehensive exam, thesis/dissertation, qualifying exam. *Entrance requirements:* For master's and doctorate, BS in engineering, minimum GPA of 3.0. Additional exam requirements/recommendations for international students: Required—TOEFL (minimum score 550 paper-based; 79 iBT), IELTS (minimum score 6.5). *Application deadline:* For fall admission, 4/1 priority date for domestic and international students; for spring admission, 9/1 priority date for domestic and international students. Applications are processed on a rolling basis. Application fee: $40 ($50 for international students). Electronic applications accepted. *Expenses:* Tuition, state resident: full-time $4086. Tuition, nonresident: full-time $14,254. *Required fees:* $853. Tuition and fees vary according to course load. *Financial support:* In 2016–17, 61 students received support, including 5 fellowships (averaging $2,853 per year), 27 research assistantships (averaging $13,824 per year), 23 teaching assistantships (averaging $8,051 per year); career-related internships or fieldwork, Federal Work-Study, scholarships/grants, traineeships, health care benefits, and unspecified assistantships also available. Support available to part-time students. Financial award application deadline: 3/1. *Faculty research:* Structural engineering, water resources engineering, environmental engineering, geotechnical engineering, transportation. *Total annual research expenditures:* $3.1 million. *Unit head:* Dr. David Jauregui, Department Head, 575-646-3801, Fax: 575-646-6049, E-mail: jauregui@nmsu.edu. *Application contact:* Elvia Cisneros, Administrative Assistant, 575-646-3801, Fax: 575-646-6049, E-mail: civil@nmsu.edu.
Website: http://ce.nmsu.edu

New York Institute of Technology, School of Engineering and Computing Sciences, Department of Environmental Technology and Sustainability, Old Westbury, NY 11568-8000. Offers MS. *Program availability:* Part-time, evening/weekend. *Faculty:* 3 full-time (1 woman), 3 part-time/adjunct (0 women). *Students:* 44 full-time (14 women), 32 part-time (9 women); includes 10 minority (5 Black or African American, non-Hispanic/Latino; 4 Asian, non-Hispanic/Latino; 1 Hispanic/Latino), 54 international. Average age 26. 129 applicants, 81% accepted, 21 enrolled. In 2016, 43 master's awarded. *Degree requirements:* For master's, capstone project. *Entrance requirements:* For master's, minimum undergraduate GPA of 2.85; BS in engineering, technology, sciences, or related area. Additional exam requirements/recommendations for international students: Required—TOEFL (minimum score 79 iBT), IELTS (minimum score 6). *Application deadline:* For fall admission, 7/1 for domestic students, 6/1 for international students; for spring admission, 12/1 for domestic and international students. Applications are processed on a rolling basis. Application fee: $50. Electronic applications accepted. *Expenses:* $1,215 per credit. *Financial support:* Fellowships with partial tuition reimbursements, teaching assistantships with partial tuition reimbursements, career-related internships or fieldwork, Federal Work-Study, scholarships/grants, tuition waivers (full and partial), and unspecified assistantships available. Support available to part-time students. Financial award application deadline: 3/1; financial award applicants required to submit FAFSA. *Faculty research:* Clean water, pathways to cleaner production, development and testing of methodology to assess health risks and environmental impacts from separate sanitary sewage, introduction of technology innovation (including geographical information systems). *Unit head:* Dr. Stanley Greenwald, Department Chair, 516-686-7717, Fax: 516-686-7919, E-mail: sgreenwa@nyit.edu. *Application contact:* Alice Dolitsky, Director, Graduate Admissions, 516-686-7520, Fax: 516-686-1116, E-mail: nyitgrad@nyit.edu.
Website: http://www.nyit.edu/engineering/environmental_technology

New York University, Polytechnic School of Engineering, Department of Civil and Urban Engineering, Major in Environmental Engineering, New York, NY 10012-1019. Offers MS. *Program availability:* Part-time, evening/weekend. *Degree requirements:* For master's, comprehensive exam (for some programs), thesis (for some programs). *Entrance requirements:* Additional exam requirements/recommendations for international students: Required—TOEFL (minimum score 550 paper-based; 80 iBT); Recommended—IELTS (minimum score 6.5). Electronic applications accepted.

North Dakota State University, College of Graduate and Interdisciplinary Studies, College of Engineering, Department of Civil and Environmental Engineering, Fargo, ND 58102. Offers civil and environmental engineering (PhD); civil engineering (MS, PhD); environmental engineering (MS). PhD in transportation and logistics offered jointly with Upper Great Plains Transportation Institute. *Program availability:* Part-time, online learning. *Degree requirements:* For master's, thesis; for doctorate, comprehensive exam, thesis/dissertation. *Entrance requirements:* Additional exam requirements/recommendations for international students: Required—TOEFL (minimum score 525 paper-based; 71 iBT). Electronic applications accepted. *Faculty research:* Wastewater, solid waste, composites, nanotechnology.

Northeastern University, College of Engineering, Boston, MA 02115-5096. Offers bioengineering (MS, PhD); chemical engineering (MS, PhD); civil engineering (MS, PhD); computer engineering (PhD); computer systems engineering (MS); electrical and computer engineering (MS); electrical and computer engineering leadership (MS); electrical engineering (PhD); energy systems (MS); engineering and public policy (MS); engineering management (MS, Certificate); environmental engineering (MS); industrial engineering (MS, PhD); information assurance (PhD); information systems (MS); interdisciplinary engineering (PhD); mechanical engineering (PhD); operations research (MS); telecommunication systems management (MS). *Program availability:* Part-time, online learning. *Faculty:* 202 full-time (59 women), 53 part-time/adjunct (9 women). *Students:* 2,982 full-time (954 women), 192 part-time (38 women). In 2016, 851 master's, 74 doctorates awarded. Application fee: $75. Electronic applications accepted. *Expenses:* $1,471 per credit. *Financial support:* Fellowships, research assistantships, teaching assistantships, career-related internships or fieldwork, scholarships/grants, health care benefits, tuition waivers, and unspecified assistantships available. Support available to part-time students. Financial award applicants required to submit FAFSA. *Unit head:* Dr. Nadine Aubry, Dean, College of Engineering. *Application contact:* Jeffery Hengel, Director of Graduate Admissions, 617-373-2711, E-mail: j.hengel@northeastern.edu.
Website: http://www.coe.neu.edu/academics/graduate-school-engineering

Northern Arizona University, Graduate College, College of Engineering, Forestry, and Natural Sciences, Programs in Engineering, Flagstaff, AZ 86011. Offers civil engineering (M Eng, MSE); computer science (MSE); electrical and computer engineering (M Eng, MSE); engineering (M Eng, MSE); environmental engineering (M Eng, MSE); mechanical engineering (M Eng, MSE). *Program availability:* Part-time, online learning. *Degree requirements:* For master's, thesis. *Entrance requirements:* For master's, GRE General Test. Additional exam requirements/recommendations for international students: Required—TOEFL (minimum score 550 paper-based; 80 iBT), IELTS (minimum score 7). Electronic applications accepted. *Expenses:* Tuition, state resident: full-time $8971; part-time $444 per credit hour. Tuition, nonresident: full-time $20,958; part-time $1164 per credit hour. *Required fees:* $1018; $644 per credit hour. Tuition and fees vary according to course load, campus/location and program.

Northwestern University, McCormick School of Engineering and Applied Science, Department of Civil and Environmental Engineering, Evanston, IL 60208-3109. Offers environmental engineering and science (MS, PhD); geotechnical engineering (MS, PhD); mechanics of materials and solids (MS, PhD); project management (MS); structural engineering and materials (MS, PhD); transportation systems analysis and planning (MS, PhD). MS and PhD admissions and degrees offered through The Graduate School. *Program availability:* Part-time. Terminal master's awarded for partial completion of doctoral program. *Degree requirements:* For master's, comprehensive exam (for some programs), thesis (for some programs); for doctorate, comprehensive exam, thesis/dissertation. *Entrance requirements:* For master's and doctorate, GRE General Test, minimum 2 letters of recommendation, transcripts from all academic institutions attended. Additional exam requirements/recommendations for international students: Required—TOEFL (minimum score 577 paper-based; 90 iBT), IELTS (minimum score 7). Electronic applications accepted. *Faculty research:* Environmental engineering and science, geotechnics, mechanics, materials, structures, and transportation systems analysis and planning.

Norwich University, College of Graduate and Continuing Studies, Master of Civil Engineering Program, Northfield, VT 05663. Offers construction management (MCE); environmental (MCE); geotechnical (MCE); structural (MCE). *Program availability:* Evening/weekend, online only, mostly all online with a week-long residency requirement. *Faculty:* 1 full-time (0 women), 11 part-time/adjunct (1 woman). *Students:* 70 full-time (17 women); includes 28 minority (16 Black or African American, non-Hispanic/Latino; 4 Asian, non-Hispanic/Latino; 5 Hispanic/Latino; 1 Native Hawaiian or other Pacific Islander, non-Hispanic/Latino; 2 Two or more races, non-Hispanic/Latino), 1 international. Average age 36. 35 applicants, 97% accepted, 18 enrolled. In 2016, 63 master's awarded. *Degree requirements:* For master's, capstone. *Entrance requirements:* For master's, minimum undergraduate GPA of 2.75. Additional exam requirements/recommendations for international students: Required—TOEFL (minimum score 550 paper-based; 80 iBT), IELTS (minimum score 6.5). *Application deadline:* For fall admission, 8/14 for domestic and international students; for spring admission, 2/12 for domestic and international students. Electronic applications accepted. *Expenses:* Contact institution. *Financial support:* In 2016–17, 10 students received support. Scholarships/grants available. Financial award application deadline: 8/4; financial award applicants required to submit FAFSA. *Unit head:* Dr. Thomas Descoteaux, Program Director, 802-485-2730, Fax: 802-485-2533, E-mail: tdescote@norwich.edu. *Application contact:* Admissions Advisor, 800-460-5597 Ext. 3369, Fax: 802-485-2533, E-mail: mce@online.norwich.edu.
Website: https://online.norwich.edu/degree-programs/masters/master-civil-engineering/overview

Ohio University, Graduate College, Russ College of Engineering and Technology, Department of Civil Engineering, Athens, OH 45701-2979. Offers civil engineering (PhD); construction engineering and management (MS); environmental (MS); geotechnical and geoenvironmental (MS); mechanics (MS); structures (MS); transportation (MS); water resources (MS). *Program availability:* Part-time. *Degree requirements:* For master's, comprehensive exam (for some programs), thesis or alternative; for doctorate, comprehensive exam, thesis/dissertation. *Entrance requirements:* For master's, GRE General Test, minimum GPA of 3.0, 3 letters of recommendation; for doctorate, GRE General Test. Additional exam requirements/recommendations for international students: Required—TOEFL (minimum score 550 paper-based; 80 iBT) or IELTS (minimum score 6.5). *Application deadline:* For fall admission, 5/1 priority date for domestic students, 2/1 priority date for international students; for winter admission, 8/1 priority date for domestic students, 4/1 priority date for international students; for spring admission, 2/1 priority date for domestic students, 7/1 priority date for international students. Applications are processed on a rolling basis. Application fee: $50 ($55 for international students). Electronic applications accepted. *Financial support:* Research assistantships with full tuition reimbursements, teaching assistantships with full tuition reimbursements, Federal Work-Study, institutionally sponsored loans, scholarships/grants, and unspecified assistantships available. Financial award application deadline: 3/15; financial award applicants required to submit FAFSA. *Faculty research:* Noise abatement, materials and environment, highway infrastructure, subsurface investigation (pavements, pipes, bridges). *Unit head:* Dr.

Gayle F. Mitchell, Chair, 740-593-0430, Fax: 740-593-0625, E-mail: mitchelg@ohio.edu. *Application contact:* Dr. Shad M. Sargand, Graduate Chair, 740-593-1465, Fax: 740-593-0625, E-mail: sargand@ohio.edu.
Website: http://www.ohio.edu/civil/

Oklahoma State University, College of Agricultural Science and Natural Resources, Department of Biosystems and Agricultural Engineering, Stillwater, OK 74078. Offers biosystems engineering (MS, PhD); environmental and natural resources (MS, PhD). *Faculty:* 26 full-time (6 women), 2 part-time/adjunct (0 women). *Students:* 20 full-time (7 women), 11 part-time (3 women); includes 3 minority (2 Hispanic/Latino; 1 Two or more races, non-Hispanic/Latino), 14 international. Average age 29. 21 applicants, 24% accepted, 4 enrolled. In 2016, 9 master's, 8 doctorates awarded. *Degree requirements:* For master's, thesis; for doctorate, comprehensive exam, thesis/dissertation. *Entrance requirements:* For master's and doctorate, GRE or GMAT. Additional exam requirements/recommendations for international students: Required—TOEFL (minimum score 550 paper-based; 79 iBT). *Application deadline:* For fall admission, 3/1 priority date for international students; for spring admission, 8/1 priority date for international students. Applications are processed on a rolling basis. Application fee: $40 ($75 for international students). Electronic applications accepted. *Expenses:* Tuition, state resident: full-time $3775; part-time $209.70 per credit hour. Tuition, nonresident: full-time $14,851; part-time $825.05 per credit hour. *Required fees:* $2027; $112.60 per credit hour. Tuition and fees vary according to campus/location. *Financial support:* In 2016–17, 24 research assistantships (averaging $19,202 per year) were awarded; teaching assistantships, career-related internships or fieldwork, Federal Work-Study, scholarships/grants, health care benefits, tuition waivers (partial), and unspecified assistantships also available. Support available to part-time students. Financial award application deadline: 3/1; financial award applicants required to submit FAFSA. *Unit head:* Dr. John Veenstra, Department Head, 405-744-5431, Fax: 405-744-6059, E-mail: jveenst@okstate.edu. *Application contact:* Dr. Ning Wang, Professor/Graduate Coordinator, 405-744-2877, E-mail: ning.wang@okstate.edu.
Website: http://bae.okstate.edu/

Oklahoma State University, College of Engineering, Architecture and Technology, School of Civil and Environmental Engineering, Stillwater, OK 74078. Offers civil engineering (MS, PhD); environmental engineering (MS). *Faculty:* 20 full-time (1 woman), 1 part-time/adjunct (0 women). *Students:* 28 full-time (5 women), 49 part-time (12 women); includes 1 minority (Black or African American, non-Hispanic/Latino), 52 international. Average age 28. 112 applicants, 32% accepted, 22 enrolled. In 2016, 28 master's, 7 doctorates awarded. *Degree requirements:* For master's, thesis or alternative; for doctorate, comprehensive exam, thesis/dissertation. *Entrance requirements:* For master's and doctorate, GRE or GMAT. Additional exam requirements/recommendations for international students: Required—TOEFL (minimum score 550 paper-based; 79 iBT). *Application deadline:* For fall admission, 3/1 priority date for international students; for spring admission, 8/1 priority date for international students. Applications are processed on a rolling basis. Application fee: $40 ($75 for international students). Electronic applications accepted. *Expenses:* Tuition, state resident: full-time $3775; part-time $209.70 per credit hour. Tuition, nonresident: full-time $14,851; part-time $825.05 per credit hour. *Required fees:* $2027; $112.60 per credit hour. Tuition and fees vary according to campus/location. *Financial support:* In 2016–17, 41 research assistantships (averaging $11,139 per year), 2 teaching assistantships (averaging $8,500 per year) were awarded; career-related internships or fieldwork, Federal Work-Study, scholarships/grants, health care benefits, tuition waivers (partial), and unspecified assistantships also available. Support available to part-time students. Financial award application deadline: 3/1; financial award applicants required to submit FAFSA. *Unit head:* Dr. Norb Delatte, Department Head, 405-744-5190, Fax: 405-744-7554, E-mail: norb.delatte@okstate.edu.
Website: http://cive.okstate.edu

Old Dominion University, Frank Batten College of Engineering and Technology, Program in Civil and Environmental Engineering, Norfolk, VA 23529. Offers D Eng, PhD. *Program availability:* Part-time, evening/weekend, blended/hybrid learning. *Faculty:* 16 full-time (1 woman), 5 part-time/adjunct (0 women). *Students:* 17 full-time (7 women), 23 part-time (4 women); includes 8 minority (3 Black or African American, non-Hispanic/Latino; 2 Asian, non-Hispanic/Latino; 2 Hispanic/Latino; 1 Two or more races, non-Hispanic/Latino), 20 international. Average age 35. 47 applicants, 100% accepted, 19 enrolled. In 2016, 2 doctorates awarded. *Degree requirements:* For doctorate, comprehensive exam, thesis/dissertation, candidacy exam. *Entrance requirements:* For doctorate, GRE, minimum GPA of 3.5. Additional exam requirements/recommendations for international students: Required—TOEFL (minimum score 550 paper-based, 80 iBT) or IELTS (6.5). *Application deadline:* For fall admission, 6/1 priority date for domestic students, 4/15 priority date for international students; for spring admission, 11/1 priority date for domestic students, 10/1 priority date for international students. Applications are processed on a rolling basis. Application fee: $50. Electronic applications accepted. *Expenses:* Contact institution. *Financial support:* In 2016–17, 26 students received support, including 1 fellowship with full tuition reimbursement available (averaging $18,000 per year), 17 research assistantships with full and partial tuition reimbursements available (averaging $16,800 per year), 9 teaching assistantships with full and partial tuition reimbursements available (averaging $15,215 per year); scholarships/grants, health care benefits, and unspecified assistantships also available. Support available to part-time students. Financial award application deadline: 4/1. *Faculty research:* Structural engineering, coastal engineering, environmental engineering, geotechnical engineering, water resources, transportation engineering. *Total annual research expenditures:* $937,914. *Unit head:* Dr. Isao Ishibashi, Graduate Program Director, 757-683-4641, E-mail: cegpd@odu.edu. *Application contact:* Dr. Shirshak Dhali, Associate Dean, 757-683-3744, Fax: 757-683-4898, E-mail: sdhali@odu.edu.
Website: http://eng.odu.edu/cee/

Old Dominion University, Frank Batten College of Engineering and Technology, Program in Environmental Engineering, Norfolk, VA 23529. Offers ME, MS. *Program availability:* Part-time, evening/weekend, blended/hybrid learning. *Faculty:* 16 full-time (1 woman), 5 part-time/adjunct (0 women). *Students:* 2 full-time (0 women), 22 part-time (10 women); includes 6 minority (3 Black or African American, non-Hispanic/Latino; 1 Asian, non-Hispanic/Latino; 2 Hispanic/Latino), 1 international. Average age 29. 37 applicants, 89% accepted, 15 enrolled. In 2016, 13 master's awarded. *Degree requirements:* For master's, comprehensive exam, thesis optional. *Entrance requirements:* For master's, GRE, minimum GPA of 3.0. Additional exam requirements/recommendations for international students: Required—TOEFL (minimum score 550 paper-based, 80 iBT) or IELTS (6.5). *Application deadline:* For fall admission, 6/1 priority date for domestic students, 4/15 priority date for international students; for spring admission, 11/1 priority date for domestic students, 10/1 priority date for international students. Applications are processed on a rolling basis. Application fee: $50. Electronic applications accepted. *Expenses:* Contact institution. *Financial support:* In 2016–17, 26 students received support, including 1 fellowship with full tuition reimbursement available (averaging $18,000 per year), 17 research assistantships with partial tuition reimbursements available (averaging $16,800 per year), 9 teaching assistantships with partial tuition reimbursements available (averaging $15,215 per year); scholarships/grants and unspecified assistantships also available. Support available to part-time students. Financial award application deadline: 4/1; financial award applicants required to submit FAFSA. *Faculty research:* Water quality, water and wastewater treatment, hydrologic processes, water resources, environmental engineering microbiology, air quality, hazardous and solid waste, biofuels, nutrient cycling, and pollution prevention. *Total annual research expenditures:* $937,914. *Unit head:* Dr. Isao Ishibashi, Graduate Program Director, 757-683-4641, E-mail: cegpd@odu.edu. *Application contact:* Dr. Shirshak Dhali, Associate Dean, 757-683-3744, Fax: 757-683-4898, E-mail: sdhali@odu.edu.
Website: http://eng.odu.edu/cee/

Oregon Health & Science University, School of Medicine, Graduate Programs in Medicine, Department of Environmental and Biomolecular Systems, Portland, OR 97239-3098. Offers biochemistry and molecular biology (MS, PhD); environmental science and engineering (MS, PhD). *Program availability:* Part-time. *Faculty:* 13 full-time (4 women). *Students:* 27 full-time (15 women), 5 part-time (3 women); includes 8 minority (1 Black or African American, non-Hispanic/Latino; 3 Asian, non-Hispanic/Latino; 3 Hispanic/Latino; 1 Two or more races, non-Hispanic/Latino), 2 international. Average age 31. 15 applicants, 6 enrolled. In 2016, 12 master's, 7 doctorates awarded. Terminal master's awarded for partial completion of doctoral program. *Degree requirements:* For master's, thesis (for some programs); for doctorate, comprehensive exam, thesis/dissertation, qualifying exam. *Entrance requirements:* For master's and doctorate, GRE General Test (minimum scores: 153 Verbal/148 Quantitative/4.5 Analytical) or MCAT (for some programs). Additional exam requirements/recommendations for international students: Required—TOEFL or IELTS. *Application deadline:* For fall admission, 7/15 for domestic students, 5/15 for international students; for winter admission, 10/15 for domestic students, 9/15 for international students; for spring admission, 1/15 for domestic students, 12/15 for international students. Applications are processed on a rolling basis. Application fee: $70. Electronic applications accepted. *Financial support:* Health care benefits and full-tuition and stipends (for PhD students) available. Financial award application deadline: 3/1; financial award applicants required to submit FAFSA. *Faculty research:* Metalloprotein biochemistry, molecular microbiology, environmental microbiology, environmental chemistry, biogeochemistry. *Unit head:* Dr. Michiko Nakano, Program Director, 503-346-3430, E-mail: tebob@ohsu.edu. *Application contact:* Vanessa Green, Program Coordinator, 503-346-3411, E-mail: greenva@ohsu.edu.

Oregon State University, College of Engineering, Program in Environmental Engineering, Corvallis, OR 97331. Offers bioremediation (M Eng, MS, PhD); environmental fluid mechanics (M Eng, MS, PhD); environmental microbiology (M Eng, MS, PhD); environmental modeling (M Eng, MS, PhD); multiphase phenomena (M Eng, MS, PhD); subsurface flow and transport (M Eng, MS, PhD); water and wastewater treatment (M Eng, MS, PhD). *Faculty:* 19 full-time (3 women). *Students:* 40 full-time (19 women), 1 (woman) part-time; includes 3 minority (1 Asian, non-Hispanic/Latino; 1 Hispanic/Latino; 1 Two or more races, non-Hispanic/Latino), 16 international. Average age 27. 78 applicants, 41% accepted, 15 enrolled. In 2016, 12 master's awarded. *Entrance requirements:* For master's and doctorate, GRE. Additional exam requirements/recommendations for international students: Required—TOEFL (minimum score 92 iBT). *Application deadline:* For fall admission, 12/20 for domestic students. Application fee: $75 ($85 for international students). Electronic applications accepted. *Expenses:* $14,130 resident full-time tuition, $23,769 non-resident. *Financial support:* Unspecified assistantships available. Financial award application deadline: 1/1. *Unit head:* Dr. James Sweeney, School Head/Professor. *Application contact:* Anita Hughes, Graduate Program Coordinator, E-mail: anita.hughes@oregonstate.edu.
Website: http://cbee.oregonstate.edu/enve-graduate-program

Penn State Harrisburg, Graduate School, School of Science, Engineering and Technology, Middletown, PA 17057. Offers computer science (MS); electrical engineering (M Eng, MS); engineering management (MPS); engineering science (M Eng); environmental engineering (M Eng); environmental pollution control (MEPC, MS); structural engineering (Certificate). *Program availability:* Part-time, evening/weekend. *Unit head:* Dr. Mukund S. Kulkarni, Chancellor, 717-948-6105, Fax: 717-948-6452. *Application contact:* Robert W. Coffman, Jr., Director of Enrollment Management, Admissions, 717-948-6250, Fax: 717-948-6325, E-mail: hbgadmit@psu.edu.
Website: https://harrisburg.psu.edu/science-engineering-technology

Penn State University Park, Graduate School, College of Engineering, Department of Civil and Environmental Engineering, University Park, PA 16802. Offers civil engineering (M Eng, MS, PhD); environmental engineering (M Eng, MS, PhD). *Unit head:* Dr. Amr S. Elnashai, Dean, 814-865-7537, Fax: 814-863-4749. *Application contact:* Lori Hawn, Director, Graduate Student Services, 814-865-1795, Fax: 814-863-4627, E-mail: l-gswww@lists.psu.edu.
Website: http://cee.psu.edu/

Polytechnic University of Puerto Rico, Miami Campus, Graduate School, Miami, FL 33166. Offers accounting (MBA); business administration (MBA); construction management (MEM); environmental management (MEM); finance (MBA); human resources management (MBA); logistics and supply chain management (MBA); management of international enterprises (MBA); manufacturing management (MEM); marketing management (MBA); project management (MBA). *Program availability:* Part-time, evening/weekend, online learning. *Entrance requirements:* For master's, minimum GPA of 3.0. Electronic applications accepted.

Polytechnic University of Puerto Rico, Orlando Campus, Graduate School, Orlando, FL 32825. Offers accounting (MBA); business administration (MBA); construction management (MEM); engineering management (MEM); environmental management (MEM); finance (MBA); human resources management (MBA); management of international enterprises (MBA); management of technology (MBA); manufacturing management (MEM). *Program availability:* Part-time, evening/weekend, online learning. *Entrance requirements:* For master's, minimum GPA of 3.0. Additional exam requirements/recommendations for international students: Recommended—TOEFL. Electronic applications accepted.

Portland State University, Graduate Studies, Maseeh College of Engineering and Computer Science, Department of Civil and Environmental Engineering, Portland, OR 97207-0751. Offers civil and environmental engineering (M Eng, MS, PhD); civil and environmental engineering management (M Eng); environmental sciences and resources (PhD); systems science (PhD). *Program availability:* Part-time, evening/weekend. *Faculty:* 27 full-time (5 women), 4 part-time/adjunct (2 women). *Students:* 50 full-time (11 women), 51 part-time (14 women); includes 10 minority (1 Black or African American, non-Hispanic/Latino; 1 Asian, non-Hispanic/Latino; 3 Hispanic/Latino; 5 Two or more races, non-Hispanic/Latino), 43 international. Average age 31. 89 applicants, 61% accepted, 26 enrolled. In 2016, 28 master's, 1 doctorate awarded. *Degree requirements:* For master's, comprehensive exam (for some programs), thesis (for some programs); for doctorate, one foreign language, comprehensive exam, thesis/dissertation, oral and written exams. *Entrance requirements:* For master's, BS in an engineering field, science, or closely-related area with minimum GPA of 3.0; for doctorate, MS in an engineering field, science, or closely-related area. Additional exam requirements/recommendations for international students: Required—TOEFL (minimum score 550 paper-based). *Application deadline:* For fall admission, 1/4 priority date for domestic and international students; for winter admission, 9/1 for domestic and

international students; for spring admission, 11/1 for domestic and international students. Applications are processed on a rolling basis. Application fee: $65. *Expenses:* Contact institution. *Financial support:* In 2016–17, 21 research assistantships with tuition reimbursements (averaging $5,959 per year), 16 teaching assistantships with tuition reimbursements (averaging $6,096 per year) were awarded; career-related internships or fieldwork, Federal Work-Study, scholarships/grants, and unspecified assistantships also available. Support available to part-time students. Financial award application deadline: 3/1; financial award applicants required to submit FAFSA. *Faculty research:* Structures, water resources, geotechnical engineering, environmental engineering, transportation. *Total annual research expenditures:* $2.6 million. *Unit head:* Dr. Chris Monsere, Chair, 503-725-9746, Fax: 503-725-4298, E-mail: monserec@cecs.pdx.edu. *Application contact:* Ariel Lewis, Department Manager, 503-725-4244, Fax: 503-725-4298, E-mail: ariel.lewis@pdx.edu.
Website: http://www.pdx.edu/cee/

Princeton University, Graduate School, School of Engineering and Applied Science, Department of Civil and Environmental Engineering, Princeton, NJ 08544-1019. Offers M Eng, MSE, PhD. Terminal master's awarded for partial completion of doctoral program. *Degree requirements:* For master's, thesis (MSE); for doctorate, thesis/dissertation, general exam. *Entrance requirements:* For master's, GRE General Test, 3 letters of recommendation; for doctorate, GRE General Test, official transcript(s), 3 letters of recommendation, personal statement. Additional exam requirements/recommendations for international students: Required—TOEFL. Electronic applications accepted. *Faculty research:* Carbon mitigation; civil engineering materials and structures; climate and atmospheric dynamics; computational mechanics and risk assessment; hydrology, remote sensing, and sustainability.

Purdue University, College of Engineering, Division of Environmental and Ecological Engineering, West Lafayette, IN 47907. Offers MS, PhD. *Faculty:* 59. *Students:* 18. *Degree requirements:* For master's, thesis optional; for doctorate, thesis/dissertation. *Entrance requirements:* For master's and doctorate, GRE, minimum GPA of 3.0. *Application deadline:* For fall admission, 1/1 for domestic and international students. Application fee: $60 ($75 for international students). *Financial support:* Fellowships with full and partial tuition reimbursements, research assistantships with full and partial tuition reimbursements, teaching assistantships with full and partial tuition reimbursements, career-related internships or fieldwork, scholarships/grants, health care benefits, and unspecified assistantships available. Financial award applicants required to submit FAFSA. *Faculty research:* Water quality engineering, sustainable energy systems and impacts, greening the built environment, air quality engineering, watershed engineering and management, environmental remediation, life cycle engineering, reducing impacts of chemicals and materials. *Unit head:* Dr. John W. Sutherland, Professor/Head of Environmental and Ecological Engineering, E-mail: jwsuther@purdue.edu. *Application contact:* Patricia Finney, Graduate Administrative Assistant, 765-496-0545, E-mail: eee@purdue.edu.
Website: https://engineering.purdue.edu/EEE

Rensselaer Polytechnic Institute, Graduate School, School of Engineering, Program in Environmental Engineering, Troy, NY 12180-3590. Offers M Eng, MS, D Eng, PhD. *Faculty:* 17 full-time (3 women), 3 part-time/adjunct (0 women). *Students:* 4 full-time (3 women). 35 applicants, 9% accepted. In 2016, 1 master's awarded. Terminal master's awarded for partial completion of doctoral program. *Degree requirements:* For master's, thesis (for some programs); for doctorate, thesis/dissertation. *Entrance requirements:* For master's and doctorate, GRE. Additional exam requirements/recommendations for international students: Required—TOEFL (minimum score 570 paper-based; 88 iBT), IELTS (minimum score 6.5), PTE (minimum score 60). *Application deadline:* For fall admission, 1/1 priority date for domestic students, 1/1 for international students; for spring admission, 8/15 for domestic and international students. Applications are processed on a rolling basis. Application fee: $75. Electronic applications accepted. *Expenses: Tuition:* Full-time $49,520; part-time $2060 per credit hour. *Required fees:* $2617. *Financial support:* In 2016–17, research assistantships (averaging $22,000 per year), teaching assistantships with full tuition reimbursements (averaging $22,000 per year) were awarded; fellowships also available. Financial award application deadline: 1/1. *Faculty research:* Environmental systems, pollutant fate and transport, site remediation and bioremediation, waste treatment, water treatment. *Unit head:* Dr. Marianne Nyman, Graduate Program Director, 518-276-2268, E-mail: nymanm@rpi.edu. *Application contact:* Office of Graduate Admissions, 518-276-6216, E-mail: gradadmissions@rpi.edu.
Website: http://cee.rpi.edu/graduate

Rice University, Graduate Programs, George R. Brown School of Engineering, Department of Civil and Environmental Engineering, Houston, TX 77251-1892. Offers civil engineering (MCE, MS, PhD); environmental engineering (MEE, MES, MS, PhD); environmental science (MEE, MES, MS, PhD). *Program availability:* Part-time. *Degree requirements:* For master's, thesis (for some programs); for doctorate, thesis/dissertation. *Entrance requirements:* For master's and doctorate, GRE General Test, GRE Subject Test, minimum GPA of 3.25. Additional exam requirements/recommendations for international students: Required—TOEFL (minimum score 600 paper-based; 90 iBT). Electronic applications accepted. *Faculty research:* Biology and chemistry of groundwater, pollutant fate in groundwater systems, water quality monitoring, urban storm water runoff, urban air quality.

Rose-Hulman Institute of Technology, Faculty of Engineering and Applied Sciences, Department of Civil and Environmental Engineering, Terre Haute, IN 47803-3999. Offers civil engineering (MS); environmental engineering (MS). *Program availability:* Part-time. *Faculty:* 9 full-time (2 women), 1 part-time/adjunct (0 women). *Students:* 2 full-time (0 women). Average age 22. 10 applicants, 80% accepted. In 2016, 1 master's awarded. *Degree requirements:* For master's, thesis (for some programs). *Entrance requirements:* For master's, GRE, minimum GPA of 3.0. Additional exam requirements/recommendations for international students: Required—TOEFL (minimum score 580 paper-based; 92 iBT). *Application deadline:* For fall admission, 2/1 priority date for domestic students. Applications are processed on a rolling basis. Application fee: $0. Electronic applications accepted. *Expenses: Tuition:* Full-time $43,122. *Financial support:* In 2016–17, 2 students received support. Fellowships with tuition reimbursements available, research assistantships with tuition reimbursements available, institutionally sponsored loans, scholarships/grants, and tuition waivers (full and partial) available. Financial award application deadline: 2/1. *Faculty research:* Transportation, hydraulics/hydrology, environmental, construction, geotechnical, structural. *Total annual research expenditures:* $24,760. *Unit head:* Dr. Kevin Sutterer, Chairman, 812-877-8959, Fax: 812-877-8440, E-mail: sutterer@rose-hulman.edu. *Application contact:* Dr. Azad Siahmakoun, Associate Dean of the Faculty, 812-877-8400, Fax: 812-877-8061, E-mail: siahmako@rose-hulman.edu.
Website: http://www.rose-hulman.edu/ce/

Royal Military College of Canada, Division of Graduate Studies and Research, Engineering Division, Department of Chemistry and Chemical Engineering, Program in Environmental Engineering, Kingston, ON K7K 7B4, Canada. Offers chemical and materials (M Eng); chemistry (M Eng); environmental (PhD); nuclear (PhD). *Degree requirements:* For master's, thesis; for doctorate, comprehensive exam, thesis/dissertation. *Entrance requirements:* For master's, honours degree with second-class standing; for doctorate, master's degree. Electronic applications accepted.

Rutgers University–New Brunswick, Graduate School-New Brunswick, Department of Civil and Environmental Engineering, Piscataway, NJ 08854-8097. Offers MS, PhD. *Program availability:* Part-time, evening/weekend. Terminal master's awarded for partial completion of doctoral program. *Degree requirements:* For master's, comprehensive exam, thesis or alternative; for doctorate, comprehensive exam, thesis/dissertation. *Entrance requirements:* For master's and doctorate, GRE General Test. Additional exam requirements/recommendations for international students: Required—TOEFL (minimum score 580 paper-based). Electronic applications accepted. *Faculty research:* Civil engineering materials research, non-destructive evaluation of transportation infrastructure, transportation planning, intelligent transportation systems.

Southern Illinois University Carbondale, Graduate School, College of Engineering, Program in Engineering Science, Carbondale, IL 62901-4701. Offers engineering science (PhD), including civil and environmental engineering, electrical and computer engineering, mechanical engineering and energy processes, mining and mineral resources engineering. *Degree requirements:* For doctorate, thesis/dissertation. *Entrance requirements:* For doctorate, GRE General Test, minimum GPA of 3.5. Additional exam requirements/recommendations for international students: Required—TOEFL.

Southern Illinois University Edwardsville, Graduate School, School of Engineering, Department of Civil Engineering, Program in Environmental Engineering, Edwardsville, IL 62026. Offers MS. *Program availability:* Part-time, evening/weekend. *Degree requirements:* For master's, thesis (for some programs), research paper. *Entrance requirements:* For master's, minimum undergraduate GPA of 2.75 in science, math, and engineering courses. Additional exam requirements/recommendations for international students: Required—TOEFL (minimum score 550 paper-based, 79 iBT), IELTS (minimum score 6.5), Michigan Test of English Language Proficiency or PTE. Electronic applications accepted.

Southern Methodist University, Bobby B. Lyle School of Engineering, Department of Environmental and Civil Engineering, Dallas, TX 75275-0340. Offers air pollution control and atmospheric sciences (PhD); civil engineering (MS); environmental engineering (MS); environmental science (MS); structural engineering (PhD); sustainability and development (MA); water and wastewater engineering (PhD). *Program availability:* Part-time, evening/weekend, online learning. Terminal master's awarded for partial completion of doctoral program. *Degree requirements:* For master's, thesis optional; for doctorate, thesis/dissertation, oral and written qualifying exams. *Entrance requirements:* For master's, GRE General Test, minimum GPA of 3.0 in last 2 years; bachelor's degree in engineering, mathematics, or sciences; for doctorate, GRE, BS and MS in related field, minimum GPA of 3.3. Additional exam requirements/recommendations for international students: Required—TOEFL. Electronic applications accepted. *Faculty research:* Human and environmental health effects of endocrine disrupters, development of air pollution control systems for diesel engines, structural analysis and design, modeling and design of waste treatment systems.

Stanford University, School of Engineering, Department of Civil and Environmental Engineering, Stanford, CA 94305-2004. Offers atmosphere and energy (MS, PhD); construction (MS), including construction engineering and management, design-construction integration, sustainable design and construction; environmental engineering and science (MS, PhD, Eng); environmental fluid mechanics and hydrology (PhD); geomechanics (MS); structural engineering (MS). Terminal master's awarded for partial completion of doctoral program. *Degree requirements:* For doctorate, thesis/dissertation, qualifying exam; for Eng, thesis. *Entrance requirements:* For master's, doctorate, and Eng, GRE General Test. Additional exam requirements/recommendations for international students: Required—TOEFL. Electronic applications accepted. *Expenses: Tuition:* Full-time $47,331. *Required fees:* $609.

State University of New York College of Environmental Science and Forestry, Department of Environmental Resources Engineering, Syracuse, NY 13210-2779. Offers ecological engineering (MPS, MS, PhD); environmental management (MPS); environmental resources engineering (MPS, MS, PhD); geospatial information science and engineering (MPS, MS, PhD); water resources engineering (MPS, MS, PhD). *Program availability:* Part-time. *Faculty:* 8 full-time (1 woman), 9 part-time/adjunct (3 women). *Students:* 34 full-time (13 women), 13 part-time (2 women); includes 3 minority (1 Black or African American, non-Hispanic/Latino; 1 Asian, non-Hispanic/Latino; 1 Hispanic/Latino), 21 international. Average age 28. 44 applicants, 48% accepted, 10 enrolled. In 2016, 8 master's, 1 doctorate awarded. *Degree requirements:* For master's, thesis (for some programs); for doctorate, comprehensive exam, thesis/dissertation. *Entrance requirements:* For master's and doctorate, GRE General Test, minimum GPA of 3.0. Additional exam requirements/recommendations for international students: Required—TOEFL (minimum score 550 paper-based; 80 iBT), IELTS (minimum score 6). *Application deadline:* For fall admission, 1/15 priority date for domestic and international students; for spring admission, 11/1 priority date for domestic and international students. Applications are processed on a rolling basis. Application fee: $60. *Expenses:* Tuition, state resident: full-time $10,870; part-time $453 per credit. Tuition, nonresident: full-time $22,210; part-time $925 per credit. *Required fees:* $1075; $89.22 per credit. *Financial support:* In 2016–17, 7 students received support. Application deadline: 6/30; applicants required to submit FAFSA. *Faculty research:* Ecological engineering, environmental resources engineering, geospatial information science and engineering, water resources engineering, environmental science. *Unit head:* Dr. Theodore Endreny, Chair, 315-470-6565, Fax: 315-470-6958, E-mail: te@esf.edu. *Application contact:* Scott Shannon, Associate Provost for Instruction/Dean of the Graduate School, 315-470-6599, Fax: 315-470-6978, E-mail: esfgrad@esf.edu.
Website: http://www.esf.edu/ere

Stevens Institute of Technology, Graduate School, Charles V. Schaefer Jr. School of Engineering and Science, Department of Civil, Environmental, and Ocean Engineering, Program in Environmental Engineering, Hoboken, NJ 07030. Offers environmental engineering (PhD, Certificate), including environmental compatibility in engineering (Certificate), environmental hydrology (Certificate), environmental processes (Certificate), soil and groundwater pollution control (Certificate), water quality control (Certificate); environmental processes (M Eng); inland and coastal environmental hydrodynamics (M Eng); modeling of environmental systems (M Eng); soil and groundwater pollution control (M Eng). *Program availability:* Part-time, evening/weekend. *Students:* 30 full-time (11 women), 10 part-time (3 women); includes 4 minority (2 Black or African American, non-Hispanic/Latino; 2 Asian, non-Hispanic/Latino), 27 international. Average age 25. 133 applicants, 61% accepted, 21 enrolled. In 2016, 13 master's, 1 doctorate, 9 other advanced degrees awarded. *Degree requirements:* For master's, thesis optional, minimum B average in major field and overall; for doctorate, comprehensive exam (for some programs), thesis/dissertation; for Certificate, minimum B average. *Entrance requirements:* Additional exam requirements/recommendations for international students: Required—TOEFL (minimum score 74 iBT), IELTS (minimum score 6). *Application deadline:* For fall admission, 6/1 for domestic students, 4/15 for international students; for spring admission, 11/30 for domestic students, 11/1 for international students. Applications are processed on a rolling basis. Application fee: $65. Electronic applications accepted. *Expenses:* Contact institution. *Financial support:* Fellowships, research assistantships, teaching assistantships, career-related internships or fieldwork, Federal Work-Study, scholarships/grants, and unspecified assistantships available. Financial award application deadline: 2/15; financial award applicants required to submit FAFSA. *Unit head:* Dr. David A. Vaccari, Director, 201-216-5570, Fax: 201-216-8739, E-mail: dvaccari@stevens.edu. *Application contact:* Graduate Admission, 888-783-8367, Fax: 888-511-1306, E-mail: graduate@stevens.edu.

Stevens Institute of Technology, Graduate School, Charles V. Schaefer Jr. School of Engineering and Science, Department of Physics and Engineering Physics, Hoboken, NJ 07030. Offers applied optics (Certificate); atmospheric and environmental science and engineering (Certificate); microdevices and microsystems (Certificate); microelectronics (Certificate); photonics (Certificate); physics (M Eng, MS, PhD). *Program availability:* Part-time, evening/weekend. *Faculty:* 12 full-time (1 woman), 3 part-time/adjunct (1 woman). *Students:* 35 full-time (11 women), 7 part-time (2 women); includes 4 minority (2 Black or African American, non-Hispanic/Latino; 2 Asian, non-Hispanic/Latino), 26 international. Average age 27. 79 applicants, 51% accepted, 11 enrolled. In 2016, 9 master's, 4 doctorates, 4 other advanced degrees awarded. Terminal master's awarded for partial completion of doctoral program. *Degree requirements:* For master's, thesis optional, minimum B average in major field and overall; for doctorate, comprehensive exam (for some programs), thesis/dissertation; for Certificate, minimum B average. *Entrance requirements:* Additional exam requirements/recommendations for international students: Required—TOEFL (minimum score 74 iBT), IELTS (minimum score 6). *Application deadline:* For fall admission, 6/1 for domestic students, 4/15 for international students; for spring admission, 11/30 for domestic students, 11/1 for international students. Applications are processed on a rolling basis. Application fee: $65. Electronic applications accepted. *Expenses:* Contact institution. *Financial support:* Fellowships, research assistantships, teaching assistantships, career-related internships or fieldwork, Federal Work-Study, scholarships/grants, and unspecified assistantships available. Financial award application deadline: 2/15; financial award applicants required to submit FAFSA. *Faculty research:* Quantum systems, nanophotonics, optics. *Unit head:* Rainer Martini, Director, 201-216-5634, Fax: 201-216-5638, E-mail: rmartini@stevens.edu. *Application contact:* Graduate Admission, 888-783-8367, Fax: 888-511-1306, E-mail: graduate@stevens.edu.
Website: http://www.stevens.edu/schaefer-school-engineering-science/departments/physics-engineering-physics

Syracuse University, College of Engineering and Computer Science, MS Program in Environmental Engineering, Syracuse, NY 13244. Offers MS. *Program availability:* Part-time. *Students:* Average age 24. In 2016, 6 master's awarded. *Degree requirements:* For master's, thesis optional. *Entrance requirements:* For master's, GRE General Test, three letters of recommendation, personal statement, resume, official transcripts. Additional exam requirements/recommendations for international students: Required—TOEFL (minimum score 100 iBT). *Application deadline:* For fall admission, 7/1 priority date for domestic students, 6/1 priority date for international students; for spring admission, 11/15 priority date for domestic students, 10/15 priority date for international students. Applications are processed on a rolling basis. Application fee: $75. Electronic applications accepted. *Expenses: Tuition:* Full-time $25,974; part-time $1443 per credit hour. *Required fees:* $802; $50 per course. Tuition and fees vary according to course load and program. *Financial support:* Fellowships with full tuition reimbursements, research assistantships with tuition reimbursements, teaching assistantships with tuition reimbursements, and tuition waivers available. Financial award application deadline: 1/1. *Faculty research:* Environmental transport and fate of pollutants, sources of airborne particles in urban and remote areas, measurement and modeling of atmospheric dry and wet deposition of pollutants, emission inventories for airborne lead, assessment of performance of green infrastructure for storm water management. *Unit head:* Dr. Cliff Davidson, Program Director, 315-443-2311, E-mail: davidson@syr.edu. *Application contact:* Kathleen Joyce, Assistant Dean, 315-443-2219, E-mail: topgrads@syr.edu.
Website: http://eng-cs.syr.edu/

Syracuse University, College of Engineering and Computer Science, MS Program in Environmental Engineering Science, Syracuse, NY 13244. Offers MS. *Program availability:* Part-time. *Students:* Average age 24. In 2016, 2 master's awarded. *Degree requirements:* For master's, thesis optional. *Entrance requirements:* For master's, GRE General Test, three letters of recommendation, personal statement, resume, official transcripts. Additional exam requirements/recommendations for international students: Required—TOEFL (minimum score 100 iBT). *Application deadline:* For fall admission, 7/1 for domestic students, 6/1 for international students; for spring admission, 11/15 for domestic students, 10/15 priority date for international students. Applications are processed on a rolling basis. Application fee: $75. Electronic applications accepted. *Expenses: Tuition:* Full-time $25,974; part-time $1443 per credit hour. *Required fees:* $802; $50 per course. Tuition and fees vary according to course load and program. *Financial support:* Fellowships with full tuition reimbursements, research assistantships with tuition reimbursements, teaching assistantships with tuition reimbursements, and tuition waivers available. Financial award application deadline: 1/1. *Faculty research:* Sustainable development in urban areas, human perceptions of energy use from day-to-day activities, emission inventories for airborne ammonia, assessment of performance of green infrastructure for storm water management. *Unit head:* Dr. Cliff Davidson, Program Director, 315-443-2311, E-mail: davidson@syr.edu. *Application contact:* Kathleen Joyce, Assistant Dean, 315-443-2219, E-mail: topgrads@syr.edu.
Website: http://eng-cs.syr.edu/

Temple University, College of Engineering, Department of Civil and Environmental Engineering, Philadelphia, PA 19122-6096. Offers civil engineering (MSCE); environmental engineering (MS Env E); storm water management (Graduate Certificate). *Program availability:* Part-time, evening/weekend. *Faculty:* 19 full-time (4 women), 4 part-time/adjunct (0 women). *Students:* 20 full-time (6 women), 16 part-time (3 women); includes 9 minority (3 Black or African American, non-Hispanic/Latino; 4 Asian, non-Hispanic/Latino; 2 Hispanic/Latino), 11 international. 57 applicants, 47% accepted, 13 enrolled. In 2016, 9 master's, 2 other advanced degrees awarded. Terminal master's awarded for partial completion of doctoral program. *Degree requirements:* For master's, thesis optional. *Entrance requirements:* For master's, GRE General Test, minimum GPA of 3.0; BS in engineering from ABET-accredited or equivalent institution; resume; goals statement; three letters of reference; official transcripts. Additional exam requirements/recommendations for international students: Required—TOEFL (minimum score 550 paper-based; 79 iBT), IELTS (minimum score 6.5), PTE (minimum score 53). *Application deadline:* For fall admission, 3/1 priority date for domestic and international students; for spring admission, 11/1 priority date for domestic students, 8/1 priority date for international students. Applications are processed on a rolling basis. Application fee: $60. Electronic applications accepted. *Expenses:* $995 per credit hour in-state tuition; $1,319 per credit hour out-of-state tuition. *Financial support:* In 2016–17, 15 students received support, including 1 fellowship with tuition reimbursement available, 4 research assistantships with tuition reimbursements available, 10 teaching assistantships with tuition reimbursements available; Federal Work-Study, scholarships/grants, health care benefits, and unspecified assistantships also available. Financial award application deadline: 3/1; financial award applicants required to submit FAFSA. *Faculty research:* Analysis of the

effect of scour on bridge stability, design of sustainable buildings, development of new highway pavement material using plastic waste, characterization of by-products and waste materials for pavement and geotechnical engineering applications, development of effective traffic signals in urban and rural settings, development of techniques for effective construction management. *Unit head:* Dr. Rominder Suri, Chair, Department of Civil and Environmental Engineering, 215-204-2378, Fax: 215-204-6936, E-mail: rominder.suri@temple.edu. *Application contact:* Leslie Levin, Director, Admissions and Graduate Student Services, 215-204-7800, Fax: 215-204-6936, E-mail: gradengr@temple.edu.
Website: http://engineering.temple.edu/department/civil-environmental-engineering

Temple University, College of Engineering, PhD in Engineering Program, Philadelphia, PA 19122-6096. Offers bioengineering (PhD); civil engineering (PhD); electrical engineering (PhD); environmental engineering (PhD); mechanical engineering (PhD). *Program availability:* Part-time, evening/weekend. *Faculty:* 67 full-time (13 women), 11 part-time/adjunct (1 woman). *Students:* 32 full-time (11 women), 7 part-time (2 women); includes 10 minority (3 Black or African American, non-Hispanic/Latino; 5 Asian, non-Hispanic/Latino; 1 Hispanic/Latino; 1 Two or more races, non-Hispanic/Latino), 19 international. 11 applicants, 64% accepted, 3 enrolled. In 2016, 6 doctorates awarded. *Degree requirements:* For doctorate, thesis/dissertation, preliminary exam, dissertation proposal and defense. *Entrance requirements:* For doctorate, GRE, minimum undergraduate GPA of 3.0; MS in engineering from ABET-accredited or equivalent institution (preferred); resume; goals statement; three letters of reference; official transcripts. Additional exam requirements/recommendations for international students: Required—TOEFL (minimum score 550 paper-based; 79 iBT), IELTS (minimum score 6.5), PTE (minimum score 53). *Application deadline:* For fall admission, 1/15 priority date for domestic and international students; for spring admission, 11/1 priority date for domestic students, 8/1 priority date for international students. Applications are processed on a rolling basis. Application fee: $60. Electronic applications accepted. *Expenses:* $995 per credit hour in-state tuition; $1,319 per credit hour out-of-state. *Financial support:* Fellowships with tuition reimbursements, research assistantships with tuition reimbursements, teaching assistantships with tuition reimbursements, Federal Work-Study, scholarships/grants, health care benefits, and unspecified assistantships available. Financial award application deadline: 3/1; financial award applicants required to submit FAFSA. *Faculty research:* Advanced/computer-aided manufacturing and advanced materials processing; bioengineering; computer engineering; construction engineering and management; dynamics, controls, and systems; energy and environmental science; engineering physics and engineering mathematics; green engineering; signal processing and communication; transportation engineering; water resources, hydrology, and environmental engineering. *Unit head:* Dr. Saroj Biswas, Associate Dean, College of Engineering, 215-204-8403, E-mail: sbiswas@temple.edu. *Application contact:* Leslie Levin, Director, Admissions and Graduate Student Services, 215-204-7800, Fax: 215-204-6936, E-mail: gradengr@temple.edu.
Website: http://engineering.temple.edu/additional-programs/phd-engineering
See Display on page 63 and Close-Up on page 83.

Tennessee State University, The School of Graduate Studies and Research, College of Engineering, Nashville, TN 37209-1561. Offers biomedical engineering (ME); civil engineering (ME); computer and information systems engineering (MS, PhD); electrical engineering (ME); environmental engineering (ME); manufacturing engineering (ME); mathematical sciences (MS); mechanical engineering (ME). *Program availability:* Part-time, evening/weekend. *Degree requirements:* For master's, project; for doctorate, comprehensive exam, thesis/dissertation. *Entrance requirements:* For doctorate, minimum GPA of 3.3. *Faculty research:* Robotics, intelligent systems, human-computer interaction software systems, biomedical engineering, signal/image processing, probabilistic design, intelligent manufacturing, cooperative mobile robots, condition based maintenance, sensor fusion.

Texas A&M University–Kingsville, College of Graduate Studies, Frank H. Dotterweich College of Engineering, Department of Environmental Engineering, Kingsville, TX 78363. Offers ME, MS, PhD. *Degree requirements:* For master's, variable foreign language requirement, comprehensive exam, thesis (for some programs); for doctorate, variable foreign language requirement, comprehensive exam, thesis/dissertation (for some programs). *Entrance requirements:* For master's, GRE (minimum quantitative and verbal score of 294), MAT, GMAT, minimum undergraduate GPA of 2.8; for doctorate, GRE, MAT, GMAT. Additional exam requirements/recommendations for international students: Required—TOEFL (minimum score 550 paper-based; 79 iBT). Electronic applications accepted. *Faculty research:* Water sampling in the Lower Rio Grande, urban stormwater management.

Texas Tech University, Graduate School, Edward E. Whitacre Jr. College of Engineering, Department of Civil, Environmental, and Construction Engineering, Lubbock, TX 79409-1023. Offers civil engineering (MSCE, PhD); environmental engineering (MENVEGR). *Accreditation:* ABET. *Program availability:* Part-time. *Faculty:* 34 full-time (6 women), 7 part-time/adjunct (0 women). *Students:* 106 full-time (36 women), 13 part-time (3 women); includes 24 minority (3 Asian, non-Hispanic/Latino; 20 Hispanic/Latino; 1 Two or more races, non-Hispanic/Latino), 63 international. Average age 27. 170 applicants, 52% accepted, 39 enrolled. In 2016, 28 master's, 8 doctorates awarded. Terminal master's awarded for partial completion of doctoral program. *Degree requirements:* For master's, comprehensive exam, thesis or alternative; for doctorate, comprehensive exam, thesis/dissertation, preliminary examination. *Entrance requirements:* For master's and doctorate, GRE (Verbal and Quantitative). Additional exam requirements/recommendations for international students: Required—TOEFL (minimum score 550 paper-based; 79 iBT), IELTS (minimum score 6.5). *Application deadline:* For fall admission, 6/1 priority date for domestic students, 1/15 priority date for international students; for spring admission, 9/1 priority date for domestic students, 6/15 priority date for international students. Applications are processed on a rolling basis. Application fee: $75. Electronic applications accepted. *Expenses:* $325 per credit hour full-time resident tuition, $733 per credit hour full-time non-resident tuition; $53.75 per credit hour fee plus $608 per term fee. *Financial support:* In 2016–17, 99 students received support, including 71 fellowships (averaging $4,370 per year), 56 research assistantships (averaging $12,343 per year), 33 teaching assistantships (averaging $15,807 per year); scholarships/grants, tuition waivers (partial), and unspecified assistantships also available. Financial award application deadline: 3/1; financial award applicants required to submit FAFSA. *Faculty research:* Geotechnical engineering, transportation engineering, water resources engineering, environmental engineering, wind engineering, construction engineering management. *Total annual research expenditures:* $3.5 million. *Unit head:* Dr. David Ernst, Interim Chair, 806-834-8657, Fax: 806-742-3488, E-mail: david.ernst@ttu.edu. *Application contact:* Dr. Priyantha Jayawickrama, Associate Professor, 806-742-3523 Ext. 245, Fax: 806-742-3488, E-mail: priyantha.jayawickrama@ttu.edu.
Website: http://www.depts.ttu.edu/ceweb/

Tufts University, School of Engineering, Department of Civil and Environmental Engineering, Medford, MA 02155. Offers bioengineering (ME, MS), including environmental technology; civil engineering (ME, MS, PhD), including geotechnical engineering, structural engineering, water diplomacy (PhD); environmental engineering

(ME, MS, PhD), including environmental engineering and environmental sciences, environmental geotechnology, environmental health, environmental science and management, hazardous materials management, water diplomacy (PhD), water resources engineering. *Program availability:* Part-time. Terminal master's awarded for partial completion of doctoral program. *Degree requirements:* For master's, thesis or alternative; for doctorate, thesis/dissertation. *Entrance requirements:* For master's and doctorate, GRE General Test. Additional exam requirements/recommendations for international students: Required—TOEFL (minimum score 550 paper-based; 80 iBT), IELTS (minimum score 6.5). Electronic applications accepted. *Expenses: Tuition:* Full-time $49,892; part-time $1248 per credit hour. *Required fees:* $844. Full-time tuition and fees vary according to degree level, program and student level. Part-time tuition and fees vary according to course load. *Faculty research:* Environmental and water resources engineering, environmental health, geotechnical and geoenvironmental engineering, structural engineering and mechanics, water diplomacy.

Universidad Central del Este, Graduate School, San Pedro de Macoris, Dominican Republic. Offers environmental engineering (ME); financial management (M Ad); higher education (M Ed), including higher education management, higher education pedagogy; human resources (M Ad). *Entrance requirements:* For master's, letters of recommendation.

Universidad Nacional Pedro Henriquez Urena, Graduate School, Santo Domingo, Dominican Republic. Offers agricultural diversity (MS), including horticultural/fruit production, tropical animal production; conservation of monuments and cultural assets (M Arch); ecology and environment (MS); environmental engineering (MEE); international relations (MA); natural resource management (MS); political science (MA); project optimization (MPM); project feasibility (MPM); project management (MPM); sanitation engineering (ME); science for teachers (MS); tropical Caribbean architecture (M Arch).

Université de Sherbrooke, Faculty of Engineering, Program in the Environment, Sherbrooke, QC J1K 2R1, Canada. Offers M Env. *Degree requirements:* For master's, thesis.

Université Laval, Faculty of Sciences and Engineering, Department of Civil Engineering, Programs in Civil Engineering, Québec, QC G1K 7P4, Canada. Offers civil engineering (M Sc, PhD); environmental technology (M Sc). Terminal master's awarded for partial completion of doctoral program. *Degree requirements:* For master's, thesis (for some programs); for doctorate, comprehensive exam, thesis/dissertation. *Entrance requirements:* For master's and doctorate, knowledge of French and English. Electronic applications accepted.

University at Buffalo, the State University of New York, Graduate School, School of Engineering and Applied Sciences, Department of Civil, Structural, and Environmental Engineering, Buffalo, NY 14260. Offers civil engineering (ME, MS, PhD); engineering science (MS). *Program availability:* Part-time, online learning. Terminal master's awarded for partial completion of doctoral program. *Degree requirements:* For master's, project, thesis, or comprehensive exam; for doctorate, thesis/dissertation. *Entrance requirements:* For master's and doctorate, GRE General Test, letters of reference. Additional exam requirements/recommendations for international students: Required—TOEFL (minimum score 550 paper-based; 79 iBT). Electronic applications accepted. *Faculty research:* Environmental engineering and fluid mechanics, structural dynamics, geomechanics, earthquake engineering computational mechanics.

The University of Alabama, Graduate School, College of Engineering, Department of Civil, Construction and Environmental Engineering, Tuscaloosa, AL 35487-0205. Offers civil engineering (MSCE, PhD); environmental engineering (MS). *Program availability:* Part-time. *Faculty:* 20 full-time (2 women). *Students:* 55 full-time (14 women), 7 part-time (2 women); includes 2 minority (1 Black or African American, non-Hispanic/Latino; 1 Asian, non-Hispanic/Latino), 29 international. Average age 28. 69 applicants, 52% accepted, 15 enrolled. In 2016, 24 master's, 2 doctorates awarded. Terminal master's awarded for partial completion of doctoral program. *Degree requirements:* For master's, thesis or alternative; for doctorate, comprehensive exam, thesis/dissertation. *Entrance requirements:* For master's and doctorate, GRE General Test (minimum combined score of 300), minimum overall GPA of 3.0 in last hours of course work. Additional exam requirements/recommendations for international students: Required—TOEFL (minimum score 550 paper-based; 79 iBT), IELTS (minimum score 6.5), PTE (minimum score 59). *Application deadline:* Applications are processed on a rolling basis. Application fee: $50 ($60 for international students). Electronic applications accepted. *Expenses:* Tuition, state resident: full-time $10,470. Tuition, nonresident: full-time $26,950. *Financial support:* In 2016–17, 40 students received support, including 2 fellowships with full tuition reimbursements available (averaging $30,000 per year), 17 research assistantships with full tuition reimbursements available (averaging $13,275 per year), 20 teaching assistantships with full tuition reimbursements available (averaging $13,275 per year); scholarships/grants, tuition waivers (partial), and unspecified assistantships also available. Financial award application deadline: 1/5. *Faculty research:* Experimental structures, modeling of structures, bridge management systems, geotechnological engineering, environmental remediation. *Total annual research expenditures:* $5.7 million. *Unit head:* Dr. W. Edward Back, Head/Professor, 205-348-6550, Fax: 205-348-0783, E-mail: eback@eng.ua.edu. *Application contact:* Dr. Andrew Graettinger, Professor and Graduate Program Director, 205-348-1707, Fax: 205-348-0783, E-mail: andrewg@eng.ua.edu.
Website: http://cce.eng.ua.edu/

The University of Alabama in Huntsville, School of Graduate Studies, College of Engineering, Department of Civil and Environmental Engineering, Huntsville, AL 35899. Offers civil and environmental engineering (PhD); civil engineering (MSE), including civil engineering. PhD offered jointly with The University of Alabama at Birmingham. *Program availability:* Part-time, evening/weekend. *Degree requirements:* For master's, comprehensive exam, thesis or alternative, oral and written exams; for doctorate, comprehensive exam, thesis/dissertation, oral and written exams. *Entrance requirements:* For master's, GRE General Test, BSE, minimum GPA of 3.0; for doctorate, GRE General Test, minimum GPA of 3.0. Additional exam requirements/recommendations for international students: Required—TOEFL (minimum score 500 paper-based; 80 iBT), IELTS (minimum score 6.5). Electronic applications accepted. *Expenses:* Tuition, state resident: full-time $9834; part-time $600 per credit hour. Tuition, nonresident: full-time $21,830; part-time $1325 per credit hour. *Faculty research:* Smart materials and smart structures, fiber-reinforced cementitious composites, processing and mechanics of composites, geographic information systems, environmental engineering.

University of Alaska Anchorage, School of Engineering, Program in Applied Environmental Science and Technology, Anchorage, AK 99508. Offers M AEST, MS. *Program availability:* Part-time, evening/weekend. *Degree requirements:* For master's, comprehensive exam, thesis (for some programs). *Entrance requirements:* For master's, GRE General Test. Additional exam requirements/recommendations for international students: Required—TOEFL (minimum score 550 paper-based). *Faculty research:* Wastewater treatment, environmental regulations, water resources management, justification of public facilities, rural sanitation, biological treatment process.

University of Alaska Fairbanks, College of Engineering and Mines, Department of Civil and Environmental Engineering, Fairbanks, AK 99775-5900. Offers civil engineering (MS); design and construction management (Graduate Certificate); environmental engineering (PhD). *Program availability:* Part-time. *Faculty:* 9 full-time (3 women), 1 part-time/adjunct (0 women). *Students:* 10 full-time (3 women), 8 part-time (3 women); includes 4 minority (1 Black or African American, non-Hispanic/Latino; 2 Asian, non-Hispanic/Latino; 1 Two or more races, non-Hispanic/Latino), 2 international. Average age 29. 14 applicants, 43% accepted, 3 enrolled. In 2016, 9 master's, 1 other advanced degree awarded. *Degree requirements:* For master's, comprehensive exam, thesis (for some programs), oral defense of project or thesis; for doctorate, comprehensive exam, thesis/dissertation. *Entrance requirements:* For master's, bachelor's degree from accredited institution with minimum cumulative undergraduate and major GPA of 3.0. Additional exam requirements/recommendations for international students: Required—TOEFL (minimum score 550 paper-based; 79 iBT), IELTS (minimum score 6.5). *Application deadline:* For fall admission, 6/1 for domestic students, 3/1 for international students; for spring admission, 10/15 for domestic students, 9/1 for international students. Applications are processed on a rolling basis. Application fee: $60. Electronic applications accepted. *Expenses:* $533 per credit resident tuition, $673 per semester resident fees; $1,088 per credit non-resident tuition, $835 per semester non-resident fees. *Financial support:* In 2016–17, 5 research assistantships with full tuition reimbursements (averaging $4,248 per year), 6 teaching assistantships with full tuition reimbursements (averaging $5,781 per year) were awarded; fellowships with full tuition reimbursements, career-related internships or fieldwork, Federal Work-Study, scholarships/grants, health care benefits, and unspecified assistantships also available. Support available to part-time students. Financial award application deadline: 7/1; financial award applicants required to submit FAFSA. *Faculty research:* Soils, structures, culvert thawing with solar power, pavement drainage, contaminant hydrogeology. *Unit head:* Dr. Leroy Hulsey, Department Chair, 907-474-7241, Fax: 907-474-6087, E-mail: fycee@uaf.edu. *Application contact:* Mary Kreta, Director of Admissions, 907-474-7500, Fax: 907-474-7097, E-mail: admissions@uaf.edu.
Website: http://cem.uaf.edu/cee

University of Alberta, Faculty of Graduate Studies and Research, Department of Civil and Environmental Engineering, Edmonton, AB T6G 2E1, Canada. Offers construction engineering and management (M Eng, M Sc, PhD); environmental engineering (M Eng, M Sc, PhD); environmental science (M Sc, PhD); geoenvironmental engineering (M Eng, M Sc, PhD); geotechnical engineering (M Eng, M Sc, PhD); mining engineering (M Eng, M Sc, PhD); petroleum engineering (M Eng, M Sc, PhD); structural engineering (M Eng, M Sc, PhD); water resources (M Eng, M Sc, PhD). *Program availability:* Part-time, online learning. *Degree requirements:* For master's, thesis (for some programs); for doctorate, thesis/dissertation. *Entrance requirements:* For master's, minimum GPA of 3.0 in last 2 years of undergraduate studies; for doctorate, minimum GPA of 3.0. Additional exam requirements/recommendations for international students: Required—TOEFL (minimum score 550 paper-based). Electronic applications accepted. *Faculty research:* Mining.

The University of Arizona, College of Engineering, Department of Chemical and Environmental Engineering, Tucson, AZ 85721-0011. Offers chemical engineering (MS, PhD); environmental engineering (MS, PhD). *Program availability:* Part-time. *Degree requirements:* For master's, thesis; for doctorate, comprehensive exam, thesis/dissertation, departmental qualifying exams. *Entrance requirements:* For master's and doctorate, GRE General Test, 3 letters of recommendation, resume, statement of purpose. Additional exam requirements/recommendations for international students: Required—TOEFL (minimum score 550 paper-based; 79 iBT). Electronic applications accepted. *Faculty research:* Energy and environment-hazardous waste incineration, sustainability, kinetics, bioremediation, semiconductor processing.

University of Arkansas, Graduate School, College of Engineering, Department of Civil Engineering, Program in Environmental Engineering, Fayetteville, AR 72701. Offers MS En E, MSE. *Degree requirements:* For master's, thesis optional. *Application deadline:* For fall admission, 4/1 for international students; for spring admission, 10/1 for international students. Applications are processed on a rolling basis. Application fee: $40 ($50 for international students). Electronic applications accepted. *Financial support:* In 2016–17, 4 research assistantships were awarded; fellowships, teaching assistantships, career-related internships or fieldwork, and Federal Work-Study also available. Support available to part-time students. Financial award application deadline: 4/1; financial award applicants required to submit FAFSA. *Unit head:* Dr. Micah Hale, Department Chair, 479-575-4954, Fax: 479-575-7168, E-mail: micah@uark.edu. *Application contact:* Dr. Julian Fairey, Graduate Coordinator, 479-575-5356, E-mail: julianf@uark.edu.
Website: http://www.cveg.uark.edu/

University of Calgary, Faculty of Graduate Studies, Schulich School of Engineering, Department of Chemical and Petroleum Engineering, Calgary, AB T2N 1N4, Canada. Offers chemical engineering (M Eng, M Sc, PhD); energy and environment engineering (M Eng, M Sc, PhD); energy and environmental systems (M Eng, M Sc, PhD); environmental engineering (M Eng, M Sc, PhD); petroleum engineering (M Eng, M Sc, PhD); reservoir characterization (M Eng, M Sc). *Program availability:* Part-time. *Degree requirements:* For master's, thesis (for some programs); for doctorate, comprehensive exam, thesis/dissertation, candidacy exam. *Entrance requirements:* For master's, minimum GPA of 3.0 or equivalent; for doctorate, minimum GPA of 3.5 or equivalent. Additional exam requirements/recommendations for international students: Required—TOEFL (minimum score 550 paper-based; 80 iBT), IELTS (minimum score 7). Electronic applications accepted. *Faculty research:* Environmental engineering, biomedical engineering modeling, simulation and control, petroleum recovery and reservoir engineering, phase equilibria and transport properties.

University of Calgary, Faculty of Graduate Studies, Schulich School of Engineering, Department of Civil Engineering, Calgary, AB T2N 1N4, Canada. Offers avalanche mechanics (M Sc, PhD); civil engineering (M Eng, M Sc, PhD); energy and environment engineering (M Eng, M Sc, PhD); environmental engineering (M Eng, M Sc, PhD); geotechnical engineering (M Eng, M Sc, PhD); materials science (M Eng, M Sc, PhD); project management (M Eng, M Sc, PhD); structures and solid mechanics (M Eng, M Sc, PhD); transportation engineering (M Eng, M Sc, PhD); water resources (M Eng, M Sc, PhD). *Program availability:* Part-time. *Degree requirements:* For master's, thesis; for doctorate, thesis/dissertation, written and oral candidacy exam. *Entrance requirements:* For master's, minimum GPA of 3.0; for doctorate, minimum GPA of 3.5. Additional exam requirements/recommendations for international students: Required—TOEFL (minimum score 580 paper-based; 93 iBT), IELTS (minimum score 7). Electronic applications accepted. *Faculty research:* Geotechnical engineering, energy and environment, transportation, project management, structures and solid mechanics.

University of California, Berkeley, Graduate Division, College of Engineering, Department of Civil and Environmental Engineering, Berkeley, CA 94720-1500. Offers engineering and project management (M Eng, MS, PhD); environmental engineering (M Eng, MS, PhD); geoengineering (M Eng, MS, PhD); structural engineering, mechanics and materials (M Eng, MS, PhD); transportation engineering (M Eng, MS, PhD); M Arch/MS; MCP/MS; MPP/MS. *Students:* 360 full-time (143 women); includes 71 minority (15 Black or African American, non-Hispanic/Latino; 39 Asian, non-Hispanic/

Latino; 17 Hispanic/Latino), 148 international. Average age 27. 1,086 applicants, 185 enrolled. In 2016, 188 master's, 26 doctorates awarded. Terminal master's awarded for partial completion of doctoral program. *Degree requirements:* For master's, comprehensive exam (for some programs), thesis (for some programs), comprehensive exam or thesis (MS); for doctorate, thesis/dissertation, qualifying exam. *Entrance requirements:* For master's, GRE General Test, minimum GPA of 3.0, 3 letters of recommendation; for doctorate, GRE General Test, minimum GPA of 3.5, 3 letters of recommendation. Additional exam requirements/recommendations for international students: Required—TOEFL (minimum score 570 paper-based; 90 iBT). *Application deadline:* For fall admission, 12/16 for domestic students. Application fee: $105 ($125 for international students). Electronic applications accepted. *Financial support:* Applicants required to submit FAFSA. *Unit head:* Prof. Robert Harley, Chair, 510-643-8739, Fax: 510-643-5264, E-mail: chair@ce.berkeley.edu. *Application contact:* Shelly Okimoto, Graduate Advisor, 510-642-6464, Fax: 510-643-5264, E-mail: aao@ce.berkeley.edu.
Website: http://www.ce.berkeley.edu/

University of California, Davis, College of Engineering, Program in Civil and Environmental Engineering, Davis, CA 95616. Offers M Engr, MS, D Engr, PhD, Certificate, M Engr/MBA. *Degree requirements:* For master's, comprehensive exam (for some programs), thesis (for some programs); for doctorate, thesis/dissertation. *Entrance requirements:* For master's, GRE General Test, minimum GPA of 3.0; for doctorate, GRE, minimum graduate GPA of 3.5. Additional exam requirements/recommendations for international students: Required—TOEFL (minimum score 550 paper-based). Electronic applications accepted. *Faculty research:* Environmental water resources, transportation, structural mechanics, structural engineering, geotechnical engineering.

University of California, Irvine, Henry Samueli School of Engineering, Department of Civil and Environmental Engineering, Irvine, CA 92697. Offers MS, PhD. *Program availability:* Part-time. *Students:* 161 full-time (51 women), 10 part-time (4 women); includes 17 minority (11 Asian, non-Hispanic/Latino; 5 Hispanic/Latino; 1 Two or more races, non-Hispanic/Latino), 117 international. Average age 27. 489 applicants, 46% accepted, 63 enrolled. In 2016, 70 master's, 14 doctorates awarded. Terminal master's awarded for partial completion of doctoral program. *Degree requirements:* For doctorate, thesis/dissertation. *Entrance requirements:* For master's and doctorate, GRE General Test, minimum GPA of 3.0, 3 letters of recommendation. Additional exam requirements/recommendations for international students: Required—TOEFL (minimum score 550 paper-based). *Application deadline:* For fall admission, 1/15 priority date for domestic students, 1/15 for international students. Applications are processed on a rolling basis. Application fee: $105 ($125 for international students). Electronic applications accepted. *Financial support:* Fellowships, research assistantships with full tuition reimbursements, teaching assistantships, institutionally sponsored loans, traineeships, health care benefits, and unspecified assistantships available. Financial award application deadline: 3/1; financial award applicants required to submit FAFSA. *Faculty research:* Intelligent transportation systems and transportation economics, risk and reliability, fluid mechanics, environmental hydrodynamics, hydrological and climate systems, water resources. *Unit head:* Prof. Brett F. Sanders, Chair and Professor, 949-824-4327, Fax: 949-824-3672, E-mail: bsanders@uci.edu. *Application contact:* Connie Cheng, Assistant Director, 949-824-3562, Fax: 949-824-8200, E-mail: connie.cheng@uci.edu.
Website: http://www.eng.uci.edu/dept/cee

University of California, Los Angeles, Graduate Division, Henry Samueli School of Engineering and Applied Science, Department of Civil and Environmental Engineering, Los Angeles, CA 90095-1593. Offers MS, PhD. *Faculty:* 18 full-time (3 women), 5 part-time/adjunct (0 women). *Students:* 178 full-time (62 women); includes 33 minority (1 Black or African American, non-Hispanic/Latino; 19 Asian, non-Hispanic/Latino; 8 Hispanic/Latino; 5 Two or more races, non-Hispanic/Latino), 110 international. 434 applicants, 68% accepted, 89 enrolled. In 2016, 76 master's, 16 doctorates awarded. *Degree requirements:* For master's, comprehensive exam or thesis; for doctorate, thesis/dissertation, qualifying exams. *Entrance requirements:* For master's, GRE General Test, minimum GPA of 3.0; for doctorate, GRE General Test, minimum GPA of 3.25. Additional exam requirements/recommendations for international students: Required—TOEFL (minimum score 560 paper-based; 87 iBT), IELTS (minimum score 7). *Application deadline:* For fall admission, 12/15 priority date for domestic and international students. Application fee: $105 ($125 for international students). Electronic applications accepted. *Financial support:* In 2016–17, 126 fellowships, 71 research assistantships, 92 teaching assistantships were awarded; Federal Work-Study, institutionally sponsored loans, and tuition waivers (full and partial) also available. Financial award application deadline: 12/15; financial award applicants required to submit FAFSA. *Faculty research:* Civil engineering materials, environmental engineering, geotechnical engineering, hydrology and water resources, structures. *Total annual research expenditures:* $3.3 million. *Unit head:* Dr. Jonathan P. Stewart, Chair, 310-206-2990, E-mail: jstewart@seas.ucla.edu. *Application contact:* Jesse Dieker, Student Affairs Officer, 310-825-1851, E-mail: jdieker@seas.ucla.edu.
Website: http://cee.ucla.edu/

University of California, Los Angeles, Graduate Division, Institute of the Environment and Sustainability, Los Angeles, CA 90095-1496. Offers environmental science and engineering (D Env). *Degree requirements:* For doctorate, thesis/dissertation, oral and written qualifying exams. *Entrance requirements:* For doctorate, GRE General Test, minimum undergraduate GPA of 3.0, master's degree or equivalent in a natural science, engineering, or public health. *Faculty research:* Toxic and hazardous substances, air and water pollution, risk assessment/management, water resources, marine science.

University of California, Los Angeles, Graduate Division, School of Public Health, Department of Environmental Health Sciences, Los Angeles, CA 90095. Offers environmental health sciences (MS, PhD); environmental science and engineering (D Env); molecular toxicology (PhD); JD/MPH. *Accreditation:* ABET (one or more programs are accredited); CEPH. *Degree requirements:* For master's, comprehensive exam or thesis; for doctorate, thesis/dissertation, oral and written qualifying exams. *Entrance requirements:* For master's, GRE General Test, minimum GPA of 3.0; for doctorate, GRE General Test, minimum undergraduate GPA of 3.0. Electronic applications accepted.

University of California, Merced, Graduate Division, School of Engineering, Merced, CA 95343. Offers biological engineering and small scale technologies (MS, PhD); electrical engineering and computer science (MS, PhD); environmental systems (MS, PhD); mechanical engineering (MS); mechanical engineering and applied mechanics (PhD). *Faculty:* 44 full-time (7 women). *Students:* 170 full-time (52 women), 2 part-time (0 women); includes 34 minority (2 Black or African American, non-Hispanic/Latino; 11 Asian, non-Hispanic/Latino; 14 Hispanic/Latino; 2 Native Hawaiian or other Pacific Islander, non-Hispanic/Latino; 5 Two or more races, non-Hispanic/Latino), 99 international. Average age 28. 307 applicants, 35% accepted, 46 enrolled. In 2016, 15 master's, 12 doctorates awarded. Terminal master's awarded for partial completion of doctoral program. *Degree requirements:* For master's, variable foreign language requirement, comprehensive exam, thesis or alternative; for doctorate, variable foreign language requirement, comprehensive exam, thesis/dissertation. *Entrance requirements:* For master's and doctorate, GRE. Additional exam requirements/recommendations for international students: Required—TOEFL (minimum score 550 paper-based; 80 iBT); Recommended—IELTS (minimum score 7). *Application deadline:* For fall admission, 1/15 priority date for domestic and international students. Applications are processed on a rolling basis. Application fee: $90 ($110 for international students). Electronic applications accepted. *Expenses:* Contact institution. *Financial support:* In 2016–17, 150 students received support, including 16 fellowships with full tuition reimbursements available (averaging $19,088 per year), 45 research assistantships with full tuition reimbursements available (averaging $18,389 per year), 89 teaching assistantships with full tuition reimbursements available (averaging $19,249 per year); scholarships/grants, traineeships, and health care benefits also available. Financial award application deadline: 1/15. *Faculty research:* Water resources, biotechnology, renewable energy, big data, cyber-physical systems. *Total annual research expenditures:* $3.3 million. *Unit head:* Dr. Mark Matsumoto, Dean, Fax: 209-228-4047, E-mail: mmatsumoto@ucmerced.edu. *Application contact:* Tsu Ya, Director of Admissions and Academic Services, 209-228-4521, Fax: 209-228-6906, E-mail: tya@ucmerced.edu.

University of California, Riverside, Graduate Division, Department of Chemical and Environmental Engineering, Riverside, CA 92521-0102. Offers MS, PhD. *Program availability:* Part-time. Terminal master's awarded for partial completion of doctoral program. *Degree requirements:* For master's, thesis (for some programs); for doctorate, comprehensive exam, thesis/dissertation. *Entrance requirements:* For master's and doctorate, GRE General Test, minimum GPA of 3.0. Additional exam requirements/recommendations for international students: Required—TOEFL (minimum score 550 paper-based; 80 iBT). Electronic applications accepted. *Expenses:* Tuition, state resident: full-time $16,666. Tuition, nonresident: full-time $31,768. *Required fees:* $11,055.54 per quarter. $3685.18 per quarter. Tuition and fees vary according to campus/location and program. *Faculty research:* Air quality systems, water quality systems, advanced materials and nanotechnology, energy systems/alternative fuels, theory and molecular modeling.

University of Central Florida, College of Engineering and Computer Science, Department of Civil, Environmental, and Construction Engineering, Program in Environmental Engineering, Orlando, FL 32816. Offers MS, MS Env E, PhD. *Program availability:* Part-time, evening/weekend. *Students:* 22 full-time (6 women), 15 part-time (4 women); includes 11 minority (3 Black or African American, non-Hispanic/Latino; 6 Hispanic/Latino; 2 Two or more races, non-Hispanic/Latino), 9 international. Average age 27. 51 applicants, 76% accepted, 12 enrolled. In 2016, 9 master's, 4 doctorates awarded. *Degree requirements:* For master's, thesis or alternative; for doctorate, thesis/dissertation, departmental qualifying exam, candidacy exam. *Entrance requirements:* For master's, minimum GPA of 3.0 in last 60 hours of course work; for doctorate, GRE General Test, minimum GPA of 3.5 in last 60 hours of course work, interview. Additional exam requirements/recommendations for international students: Required—TOEFL. *Application deadline:* For fall admission, 7/15 for domestic students; for spring admission, 12/1 for domestic students. Application fee: $30. Electronic applications accepted. *Expenses:* Tuition, state resident: part-time $288.16 per credit hour. Tuition, nonresident: part-time $1071.31 per credit hour. *Financial support:* In 2016–17, 17 students received support, including 2 fellowships with partial tuition reimbursements available (averaging $15,550 per year), 15 research assistantships with partial tuition reimbursements available (averaging $11,030 per year), 3 teaching assistantships with partial tuition reimbursements available (averaging $12,040 per year); career-related internships or fieldwork, Federal Work-Study, institutionally sponsored loans, tuition waivers (partial), and unspecified assistantships also available. Financial award application deadline: 3/1; financial award applicants required to submit FAFSA. *Unit head:* Dr. Mohamed Abdel-Aty, Chair, 407-823-5657, E-mail: m.aty@ucf.edu. *Application contact:* Assistant Director, Graduate Admissions, 407-823-2766, Fax: 407-823-6442, E-mail: gradadmissions@ucf.edu.
Website: http://cece.ucf.edu/

University of Cincinnati, Graduate School, College of Engineering and Applied Science, Department of Biomedical, Chemical and Environmental Engineering, Program in Environmental Engineering, Cincinnati, OH 45221. Offers MS, PhD. *Accreditation:* ABET (one or more programs are accredited). *Program availability:* Part-time. *Degree requirements:* For master's, project or thesis; for doctorate, one foreign language, thesis/dissertation. *Entrance requirements:* For master's and doctorate, GRE General Test. Additional exam requirements/recommendations for international students: Required—TOEFL (minimum score 580 paper-based; 92 iBT). Electronic applications accepted. *Expenses: Tuition, area resident:* Full-time $12,790; part-time $389 per credit hour. Tuition, state resident: full-time $13,290; part-time $419 per credit hour. Tuition, nonresident: full-time $24,532; part-time $976 per credit hour. *International tuition:* $24,832 full-time. *Required fees:* $3958; $140 per credit hour. Tuition and fees vary according to course load, degree level, program and reciprocity agreements. *Faculty research:* Environmental microbiology, solid-waste management, air pollution control, water pollution control, aerosols.

University of Colorado Boulder, Graduate School, College of Engineering and Applied Science, Department of Civil, Environmental, and Architectural Engineering, Boulder, CO 80309. Offers MS, PhD. *Faculty:* 43 full-time (10 women). *Students:* 275 full-time (102 women), 19 part-time (11 women); includes 31 minority (3 Black or African American, non-Hispanic/Latino; 1 American Indian or Alaska Native, non-Hispanic/Latino; 8 Asian, non-Hispanic/Latino; 9 Hispanic/Latino; 1 Native Hawaiian or other Pacific Islander, non-Hispanic/Latino; 9 Two or more races, non-Hispanic/Latino), 75 international. Average age 28. 482 applicants, 55% accepted, 79 enrolled. In 2016, 69 master's, 34 doctorates awarded. Terminal master's awarded for partial completion of doctoral program. *Degree requirements:* For master's, comprehensive exam, thesis or alternative; for doctorate, thesis/dissertation. *Entrance requirements:* For master's, GRE General Test, minimum undergraduate GPA of 3.0. *Application deadline:* For fall admission, 1/31 for domestic and international students; for spring admission, 10/1 for domestic and international students. Application fee: $60 ($80 for international students). Electronic applications accepted. Application fee is waived when completed online. *Financial support:* In 2016–17, 498 students received support, including 168 fellowships (averaging $10,048 per year), 81 research assistantships with full and partial tuition reimbursements available (averaging $36,827 per year), 32 teaching assistantships with full and partial tuition reimbursements available (averaging $38,824 per year); institutionally sponsored loans, scholarships/grants, health care benefits, and unspecified assistantships also available. Financial award application deadline: 1/15; financial award applicants required to submit FAFSA. *Faculty research:* Civil engineering, environmental engineering, architectural engineering, hydrology, water resources engineering. *Total annual research expenditures:* $12.5 million. *Application contact:* E-mail: cvengrad@colorado.edu.
Website: http://civil.colorado.edu/

University of Colorado Denver, College of Engineering and Applied Science, Department of Civil Engineering, Denver, CO 80217. Offers civil engineering (EASPh D); civil engineering systems (PhD); environmental and sustainability engineering (MS, PhD); geographic information systems (MS); geotechnical engineering (MS, PhD); hydrology and hydraulics (MS, PhD); structural engineering (MS, PhD); transportation engineering (MS, PhD). *Program availability:* Part-time, evening/weekend. *Faculty:* 15 full-time (3 women), 9 part-time/adjunct (0 women). *Students:* 50

full-time (15 women), 33 part-time (7 women); includes 10 minority (1 Black or African American, non-Hispanic/Latino; 2 Asian, non-Hispanic/Latino; 6 Hispanic/Latino; 1 Two or more races, non-Hispanic/Latino), 31 international. Average age 30. 105 applicants, 51% accepted, 14 enrolled. In 2016, 29 master's, 2 doctorates awarded. *Degree requirements:* For master's, comprehensive exam, 30 credit hours, project or thesis; for doctorate, comprehensive exam, thesis/dissertation, 60 credit hours (30 of which are dissertation research). *Entrance requirements:* For master's, GRE, statement of purpose, transcripts, three references; for doctorate, GRE, statement of purpose, transcripts, references, letter of support from faculty stating willingness to serve as dissertation advisor and outlining plan for financial support. Additional exam requirements/recommendations for international students: Required—TOEFL (minimum score 537 paper-based; 75 iBT); Recommended—IELTS (minimum score 6.5). *Application deadline:* For fall admission, 5/1 for domestic students, 4/1 for international students; for spring admission, 10/1 for domestic students, 9/1 for international students; for summer admission, 2/15 for domestic students, 1/15 for international students. Application fee: $50 ($75 for international students). Electronic applications accepted. *Expenses:* Contact institution. *Financial support:* In 2016–17, 62 students received support. Fellowships, research assistantships, teaching assistantships, career-related internships or fieldwork, Federal Work-Study, institutionally sponsored loans, scholarships/grants, traineeships, and unspecified assistantships available. Financial award application deadline: 4/1; financial award applicants required to submit FAFSA. *Faculty research:* Earthquake source physics, environmental biotechnology, hydrologic and hydraulic engineering, sustainability assessments, transportation energy use and greenhouse gas emissions. *Unit head:* Dr. Kevin Rens, Chair, 303-556-8017, E-mail: kevin.rens@ucdenver.edu. *Application contact:* Roxanne Pizano, Program Coordinator, 303-556-6274, E-mail: roxanne.pizano@ucdenver.edu.
Website: http://www.ucdenver.edu/academics/colleges/Engineering/Programs/Civil-Engineering/Pages/CivilEngineering.aspx

University of Connecticut, Graduate School, School of Engineering, Department of Civil and Environmental Engineering, Field of Environmental Engineering, Storrs, CT 06269. Offers MS, PhD. *Degree requirements:* For master's, comprehensive exam; for doctorate, thesis/dissertation. *Entrance requirements:* For master's and doctorate, GRE General Test. Additional exam requirements/recommendations for international students: Required—TOEFL (minimum score 550 paper-based). Electronic applications accepted.

University of Dayton, Department of Civil and Environmental Engineering and Engineering Mechanics, Dayton, OH 45469. Offers engineering mechanics (MSEM); environmental engineering (MSCE); geotechnical engineering (MSCE); structural engineering (MSCE); transportation engineering (MSCE); water resources engineering (MSCE). *Program availability:* Part-time, evening/weekend. *Faculty:* 9 full-time (2 women), 3 part-time/adjunct (1 woman). *Students:* 40 full-time (8 women), 2 part-time (0 women); includes 1 minority (Asian, non-Hispanic/Latino), 30 international. Average age 26. 137 applicants, 17% accepted. In 2016, 14 master's awarded. *Degree requirements:* For master's, thesis optional. *Entrance requirements:* For master's, minimum GPA of 3.0 in undergraduate work. Additional exam requirements/recommendations for international students: Required—TOEFL (minimum score 550 paper-based; 80 iBT); Recommended—IELTS. *Application deadline:* For fall admission, 8/1 priority date for domestic students, 5/1 priority date for international students; for spring admission, 11/1 priority date for international students. Applications are processed on a rolling basis. Application fee: $0 ($50 for international students). Electronic applications accepted. *Expenses:* $890 per credit hour, $25 registration fee. *Financial support:* Research assistantships, institutionally sponsored loans, scholarships/grants, and department-funded awards (averaging $2448 per year) available. Financial award application deadline: 3/1; financial award applicants required to submit FAFSA. *Faculty research:* Vertically-aligned carbon nanotubes infiltrated with temperature-responsive polymers; smart nanocomposite films for self-cleaning and controlled release; bilayer and bulk heterojunction solar cells using liquid crystalline porphyrins as donors by solution processing; DNA damage induced by multiwalled carbon nanotubes in mouse embryonic stem cells. *Total annual research expenditures:* $250,000. *Unit head:* Dr. Donald V. Chase, Chair, 937-229-3847, Fax: 937-229-3491, E-mail: dchase1@udayton.edu. *Application contact:* 937-229-4462, E-mail: graduateadmission@udayton.edu.
Website: https://www.udayton.edu/engineering/departments/civil/index.php

University of Delaware, College of Engineering, Department of Civil and Environmental Engineering, Newark, DE 19716. Offers environmental engineering (MAS, MCE, PhD); geotechnical engineering (MAS, MCE, PhD); ocean engineering (MAS, MCE, PhD); structural engineering (MAS, MCE, PhD); transportation engineering (MAS, MCE, PhD); water resource engineering (MAS, MCE, PhD). *Program availability:* Part-time. Terminal master's awarded for partial completion of doctoral program. *Degree requirements:* For master's, thesis; for doctorate, thesis/dissertation. *Entrance requirements:* For master's and doctorate, GRE General Test. Additional exam requirements/recommendations for international students: Required—TOEFL. Electronic applications accepted. *Faculty research:* Structural engineering and mechanics; transportation engineering; ocean engineering; soil mechanics and foundation; water resources and environmental engineering.

University of Detroit Mercy, College of Engineering and Science, Detroit, MI 48221. Offers chemistry (MS); civil and environmental engineering (DE); electrical and computer engineering (ME); electrical engineering (DE); engineering management (M Eng Mgt); environmental engineering (MEE); mechanical engineering (MME, DE); product development (MS); software engineering (MSSE); teaching of mathematics (MATM). *Program availability:* Part-time, evening/weekend. *Degree requirements:* For doctorate, thesis/dissertation. Electronic applications accepted. Application fee is waived when completed online. *Expenses:* Contact institution.

University of Florida, Graduate School, Herbert Wertheim College of Engineering, Department of Environmental Engineering Sciences, Gainesville, FL 32611. Offers environmental engineering sciences (ME, MS, PhD, Engr); geographic information systems (ME, MS, PhD); hydrologic sciences (ME, MS, PhD); wetland sciences (ME, MS, PhD); JD/MS. *Program availability:* Part-time, evening/weekend, online learning. Terminal master's awarded for partial completion of doctoral program. *Degree requirements:* For master's, comprehensive exam (for some programs), thesis (for some programs), project, thesis or coursework; for doctorate, comprehensive exam, thesis/dissertation; for Engr, project or thesis. *Entrance requirements:* For master's and doctorate, minimum GPA of 3.0; for Engr, GRE General Test. Additional exam requirements/recommendations for international students: Required—TOEFL (minimum score 550 paper-based; 80 iBT), IELTS (minimum score 6). Electronic applications accepted. *Faculty research:* Air resources; system ecology and ecological engineering; water systems; geosystems engineering; environmental nanotechnology.

University of Georgia, College of Engineering, Athens, GA 30602. Offers MS. *Unit head:* Dr. E. Dale Threadgill, Dean, 706-542-1653. *Application contact:* Lawrence Hornak, Graduate coordinator, 706-542-2462, E-mail: lahornak@uga.edu.
Website: http://www.engineering.uga.edu/

University of Guelph, Graduate Studies, College of Physical and Engineering Science, School of Engineering, Guelph, ON N1G 2W1, Canada. Offers biological engineering (M Eng, M Sc, MA Sc, PhD); engineering systems and computing (M Eng, M Sc, MA Sc, PhD); environmental engineering (M Eng, M Sc, MA Sc, PhD); water resources engineering (M Eng, M Sc, MA Sc, PhD). *Program availability:* Part-time. *Degree requirements:* For master's, thesis (for some programs); for doctorate, comprehensive exam, thesis/dissertation. *Entrance requirements:* For master's, minimum B- average during previous 2 years of course work; for doctorate, minimum B average. Additional exam requirements/recommendations for international students: Required—TOEFL (minimum score 550 paper-based; 89 iBT), IELTS (minimum score 6.5). Electronic applications accepted. *Faculty research:* Water and food safety, environmental contaminant fates and mechanisms, computer systems, robotics and mechatronics, waste treatment.

University of Hawaii at Manoa, Graduate Division, College of Engineering, Department of Civil and Environmental Engineering, Honolulu, HI 96822. Offers MS, PhD. *Program availability:* Part-time. *Degree requirements:* For master's, comprehensive exam, thesis; for doctorate, comprehensive exam, thesis/dissertation. *Entrance requirements:* For master's and doctorate, GRE General Test or EIT Exam. Additional exam requirements/recommendations for international students: Required—TOEFL (minimum score 540 paper-based; 76 iBT), IELTS (minimum score 5). *Faculty research:* Structures, transportation, environmental engineering, geotechnical engineering, construction.

University of Illinois at Urbana–Champaign, Graduate College, College of Engineering, Department of Civil and Environmental Engineering, Champaign, IL 61820. Offers civil engineering (MS, PhD); environmental engineering in civil engineering (MS, PhD); M Arch/MS; MBA/MS. *Program availability:* Part-time, evening/weekend, online learning.

The University of Iowa, Graduate College, College of Engineering, Department of Civil and Environmental Engineering, Iowa City, IA 52242-1316. Offers MS, PhD. *Program availability:* Part-time. *Faculty:* 22 full-time (2 women), 5 part-time/adjunct (0 women). *Students:* 55 full-time (17 women), 12 part-time (5 women); includes 3 minority (1 Black or African American, non-Hispanic/Latino; 1 Asian, non-Hispanic/Latino; 1 Two or more races, non-Hispanic/Latino), 30 international. Average age 27. 191 applicants, 20% accepted, 22 enrolled. In 2016, 22 master's, 7 doctorates awarded. Terminal master's awarded for partial completion of doctoral program. *Degree requirements:* For master's, thesis optional, exam; for doctorate, comprehensive exam, thesis/dissertation, exam. *Entrance requirements:* For master's, GRE (minimum combined score of 301 on verbal and quantitative), minimum undergraduate GPA of 3.0; for doctorate, GRE (minimum combined score of 301 on verbal and quantitative), minimum graduate GPA of 3.0. Additional exam requirements/recommendations for international students: Required—TOEFL (minimum score 550 paper-based; 81 iBT), IELTS (minimum score 7). *Application deadline:* For fall admission, 1/15 priority date for domestic and international students; for spring admission, 12/1 for domestic students, 10/1 for international students; for summer admission, 4/15 for domestic students, 3/1 for international students. Applications are processed on a rolling basis. Application fee: $60 ($100 for international students). Electronic applications accepted. *Financial support:* In 2016–17, 64 students received support, including 8 fellowships with partial tuition reimbursements available (averaging $25,500 per year), 50 research assistantships with partial tuition reimbursements available (averaging $22,981 per year), 6 teaching assistantships with partial tuition reimbursements available (averaging $18,809 per year); career-related internships or fieldwork, Federal Work-Study, scholarships/grants, traineeships, and unspecified assistantships also available. Support available to part-time students. Financial award application deadline: 1/15; financial award applicants required to submit FAFSA. *Faculty research:* Water resources; environmental engineering and science; hydraulics and hydrology; structures, mechanics, and materials; transportation engineering. *Total annual research expenditures:* $16.8 million. *Unit head:* Dr. Michelle Scherer, Department Executive Officer, 319-335-5654, Fax: 319-335-5660, E-mail: michelle-scherer@uiowa.edu. *Application contact:* Kim Lebeck, Academic Program Specialist, 319-335-5647, Fax: 319-335-5660, E-mail: cee@engineering.uiowa.edu.
Website: https://cee.engineering.uiowa.edu

The University of Kansas, Graduate Studies, School of Engineering, Program in Environmental Engineering, Lawrence, KS 66045. Offers MS, PhD. *Program availability:* Part-time. *Students:* 8 full-time (4 women), 3 part-time (1 woman); includes 5 minority (2 Black or African American, non-Hispanic/Latino; 1 American Indian or Alaska Native, non-Hispanic/Latino; 1 Native Hawaiian or other Pacific Islander, non-Hispanic/Latino; 1 Two or more races, non-Hispanic/Latino), 7 international. Average age 29. 32 applicants, 63% accepted, 2 enrolled. In 2016, 1 master's, 2 doctorates awarded. *Degree requirements:* For doctorate, thesis/dissertation or alternative. *Entrance requirements:* For master's and doctorate, GRE, BS in engineering, recommendations, resume, statement of purpose. Additional exam requirements/recommendations for international students: Required—TOEFL (minimum score 80 iBT) or IELTS (5.5). *Application deadline:* For fall admission, 12/15 priority date for domestic and international students; for spring admission, 9/15 priority date for domestic and international students. Application fee: $65 ($85 for international students). Electronic applications accepted. *Financial support:* Fellowships, research assistantships, teaching assistantships, career-related internships or fieldwork, and scholarships/grants available. Financial award application deadline: 12/15. *Faculty research:* Water quality, water treatment, wastewater treatment, air quality, air pollution control, solid waste, hazardous waste, water resources engineering. *Unit head:* David Darwin, Chair, 785-864-3827, E-mail: daved@ku.edu. *Application contact:* Susan Scott, Administrative Assistant, 785-864-3826, E-mail: sbscott@ku.edu.
Website: http://ceae.ku.edu/overview-3

University of Louisville, J. B. Speed School of Engineering, Department of Civil and Environmental Engineering, Louisville, KY 40292-0001. Offers civil engineering (M Eng, MS, PhD). *Accreditation:* ABET (one or more programs are accredited). *Program availability:* Blended/hybrid learning. *Faculty:* 10 full-time (1 woman), 2 part-time/adjunct (1 woman). *Students:* 32 full-time (7 women), 14 part-time (0 women); includes 3 minority (1 Asian, non-Hispanic/Latino; 2 Two or more races, non-Hispanic/Latino), 16 international. Average age 27. 31 applicants, 35% accepted, 8 enrolled. In 2016, 15 master's, 1 other advanced degree awarded. *Degree requirements:* For master's, thesis optional, minimum GPA of 3.0; for doctorate, comprehensive exam, thesis/dissertation, minimum GPA of 3.0. *Entrance requirements:* For master's and doctorate, GRE, letters of recommendation, final official transcripts; for Graduate Certificate, pursuit of graduate degree (M Eng, MS, PhD) at J.B. Speed School of Engineering; undergraduate degree. Additional exam requirements/recommendations for international students: Required—TOEFL (minimum score 550 paper-based, 80 iBT) or IELTS (6.5). *Application deadline:* For fall admission, 5/1 priority date for international students; for spring admission, 11/1 priority date for international students; for summer admission, 3/1 priority date for international students. Applications are processed on a rolling basis. Application fee: $60. Electronic applications accepted. *Expenses:* Tuition, state resident: full-time $12,246; part-time $681 per credit hour. Tuition, nonresident: full-time $25,486; part-time $1417 per credit hour. *Required fees:* $196. Tuition and fees vary according to program and reciprocity agreements. *Financial support:* In 2016–17, 2 fellowships with full tuition reimbursements (averaging $22,000 per year) were awarded; research assistantships with full tuition reimbursements, teaching assistantships with full tuition reimbursements, scholarships/grants, and health care benefits also available. Financial

award application deadline: 1/1. *Faculty research:* Structures, hydraulics, transportation, environmental engineering, geomechanics. *Total annual research expenditures:* $648,296. *Unit head:* Dr. J. P. Mohsen, Chair, 502-852-4596, Fax: 502-852-8851, E-mail: jpm@louisville.edu. *Application contact:* Dr. Zhihui Sun, Director of Graduate Studies, 502-852-4583, Fax: 502-852-7294, E-mail: z.sun@louisville.edu.
Website: http://louisville.edu/speed/civil/

The University of Manchester, School of Mechanical, Aerospace and Civil Engineering, Manchester, United Kingdom. Offers advanced manufacturing technology (M Ent); aerospace engineering (M Phil, M Sc, PhD); civil engineering (M Phil, M Sc, PhD); environmental engineering (M Phil, PhD); management of projects (M Phil, M Sc, PhD); mechanical engineering (M Phil, M Sc, PhD); mechanical engineering design (M Ent); nuclear engineering (M Phil, D Eng, PhD).

University of Maryland, Baltimore County, The Graduate School, College of Engineering and Information Technology, Department of Chemical, Biochemical, and Environmental Engineering, Program in Environmental Engineering, Baltimore, MD 21227. Offers MS, PhD. *Program availability:* Part-time. *Faculty:* 5 full-time (1 woman). *Students:* 11 full-time (4 women), 3 part-time (1 woman); includes 2 minority (1 Asian, non-Hispanic/Latino; 1 Hispanic/Latino), 8 international. Average age 29. 24 applicants, 33% accepted, 2 enrolled. In 2016, 1 master's, 2 doctorates awarded. *Degree requirements:* For master's, comprehensive exam (for some programs), thesis (for some programs); for doctorate, comprehensive exam, thesis/dissertation. *Entrance requirements:* For master's and doctorate, GRE General Test, BS in environmental engineering or related field of engineering. Additional exam requirements/recommendations for international students: Required—TOEFL (minimum score 550 paper-based; 80 iBT). *Application deadline:* For fall admission, 6/1 for domestic students, 1/1 for international students; for spring admission, 11/1 for domestic students, 6/1 for international students. Applications are processed on a rolling basis. Application fee: $70. Electronic applications accepted. *Expenses:* Contact institution. *Financial support:* In 2016–17, 10 research assistantships with full tuition reimbursements (averaging $23,000 per year) were awarded; teaching assistantships with full tuition reimbursements, career-related internships or fieldwork, Federal Work-Study, scholarships/grants, health care benefits, tuition waivers (partial), and unspecified assistantships also available. Support available to part-time students. Financial award application deadline: 6/30; financial award applicants required to submit FAFSA. *Faculty research:* Environmental fate and transport, water resources treatment/remediation. *Unit head:* Dr. Mark Marten, Professor and Interim Chair, 410-455-3400, Fax: 410-455-1049, E-mail: reedb@umbc.edu. *Application contact:* Dr. Erin Lavik, Professor and Graduate Program Director, 410-455-3428, Fax: 410-455-6500, E-mail: mariajose@umbc.edu.
Website: http://cbee.umbc.edu/

University of Maryland, College Park, Academic Affairs, A. James Clark School of Engineering, Department of Civil and Environmental Engineering, College Park, MD 20742. Offers M Eng, MS, PhD. *Program availability:* Part-time, evening/weekend, online learning. *Degree requirements:* For master's, thesis optional; for doctorate, thesis/dissertation, qualifying exam. *Entrance requirements:* For master's and doctorate, GRE General Test, 3 letters of recommendation. Electronic applications accepted. *Faculty research:* Transportation and urban systems, environmental engineering, geotechnical engineering, construction engineering and management, hydraulics.

University of Massachusetts Amherst, Graduate School, College of Engineering, Department of Civil and Environmental Engineering, Amherst, MA 01003. Offers civil engineering (MSCE, PhD); environmental and water resources engineering (MSCE); geotechnical engineering (MSCE); structural engineering and mechanics (MSCE); transportation engineering (MSCE). *Program availability:* Part-time. Terminal master's awarded for partial completion of doctoral program. *Degree requirements:* For master's, thesis or alternative; for doctorate, comprehensive exam, thesis/dissertation. *Entrance requirements:* For master's and doctorate, GRE General Test. Additional exam requirements/recommendations for international students: Required—TOEFL (minimum score 550 paper-based; 80 iBT), IELTS (minimum score 6.5). Electronic applications accepted.

University of Massachusetts Lowell, Francis College of Engineering, Department of Civil and Environmental Engineering and College of Sciences, Program in Environmental Studies, Lowell, MA 01854. Offers MS, PhD. *Program availability:* Part-time. *Degree requirements:* For master's, thesis optional. *Entrance requirements:* For master's, GRE General Test. *Faculty research:* Remote sensing of air pollutants, atmospheric deposition of toxic metals, contaminant transport in groundwater, soil remediation.

University of Memphis, Graduate School, Herff College of Engineering, Department of Civil Engineering, Memphis, TN 38152. Offers civil engineering (PhD); engineering seismology (MS); environmental engineering (MS); freight transportation (Graduate Certificate); geotechnical engineering (MS); structural engineering (MS); transportation engineering (MS); water resources engineering (MS). *Faculty:* 12 full-time (1 woman). *Students:* 10 full-time (3 women), 15 part-time (3 women); includes 3 minority (2 Black or African American, non-Hispanic/Latino; 1 Two or more races, non-Hispanic/Latino), 9 international. Average age 29. 29 applicants, 69% accepted, 8 enrolled. In 2016, 5 master's awarded. Terminal master's awarded for partial completion of doctoral program. *Degree requirements:* For master's, comprehensive exam, thesis optional; for doctorate, comprehensive exam, thesis/dissertation. *Entrance requirements:* For master's, GRE General Test, minimum undergraduate GPA of 2.5; bachelor's degree in engineering or a related science or mathematics program; three letters of reference; for doctorate, GRE General Test, bachelor's degree in engineering or engineering science; three letters of reference; for Graduate Certificate, minimum undergraduate GPA of 2.75; bachelor's degree in engineering or engineering science. Additional exam requirements/recommendations for international students: Required—TOEFL (minimum score 550 paper-based; 79 iBT). *Application deadline:* For fall admission, 8/1 for domestic students; for spring admission, 12/1 for domestic students. Application fee: $35 ($60 for international students). Electronic applications accepted. *Expenses:* $5,231.50 per semester full-time in-state, $9,623.50 full-time out-of-state. *Financial support:* In 2016–17, 6 students received support, including 31 fellowships with full tuition reimbursements available (averaging $12,012 per year); research assistantships with full tuition reimbursements available, career-related internships or fieldwork, Federal Work-Study, scholarships/grants, and unspecified assistantships also available. Financial award application deadline: 2/1; financial award applicants required to submit FAFSA. *Faculty research:* Structural response to earthquakes, pavement design, water quality, transportation safety, intermodal transportation. *Unit head:* Dr. Sharam Pezeshk, Chair, 901-678-2746, Fax: 901-678-3026. *Application contact:* Dr. Roger Meier, Coordinator of Graduate Studies, 901-678-3284, E-mail: rwmeier@memphis.edu.
Website: http://www.ce.memphis.edu

University of Michigan, College of Engineering, Department of Civil and Environmental Engineering, Ann Arbor, MI 48109. Offers civil engineering (MSE, PhD, CE); construction engineering and management (M Eng, MSE); environmental engineering (MSE, PhD); structural engineering (M Eng); MBA/MSE. *Program availability:* Part-time. *Students:* 177 full-time (77 women), 3 part-time. 775 applicants, 42% accepted, 62 enrolled. In 2016, 57 master's, 9 doctorates awarded. *Degree requirements:* For master's, thesis optional; for doctorate, comprehensive exam, thesis/dissertation, oral defense of dissertation, preliminary and written exams. *Entrance requirements:* For master's and doctorate, GRE General Test. Additional exam requirements/recommendations for international students: Required—TOEFL. *Application deadline:* Applications are processed on a rolling basis. Electronic applications accepted. *Expenses:* Tuition, state resident: full-time $21,466; part-time $1152 per credit hour. Tuition, nonresident: full-time $43,346; part-time $2367 per credit hour. Part-time tuition and fees vary according to course load, degree level and program. *Financial support:* Fellowships, research assistantships, teaching assistantships, institutionally sponsored loans, and tuition waivers (partial) available. *Faculty research:* Construction engineering and management, geotechnical engineering, earthquake-resistant design of structures, environmental chemistry and microbiology, cost engineering, environmental and water resources engineering. *Total annual research expenditures:* $15.7 million. *Unit head:* Kim Hayes, Department Chair, 734-764-8495, Fax: 734-764-4292, E-mail: ford@umich.edu. *Application contact:* Jessica Randolph, Graduate Coordinator, 734-764-8405, Fax: 734-764-4292, E-mail: jrand@umich.edu.
Website: http://cee.engin.umich.edu/

University of Missouri, Office of Research and Graduate Studies, College of Engineering, Department of Civil and Environmental Engineering, Columbia, MO 65211. Offers civil engineering (MS, PhD); environmental engineering (MS, PhD); geotechnical engineering (MS, PhD); structural engineering (MS, PhD); transportation and highway engineering (MS); water resources (MS, PhD). *Faculty:* 16 full-time (3 women), 2 part-time/adjunct (1 woman). *Students:* 41 full-time (8 women), 30 part-time (8 women). *Degree requirements:* For master's, report or thesis; for doctorate, thesis/dissertation. *Entrance requirements:* For master's and doctorate, GRE General Test. Additional exam requirements/recommendations for international students: Required—TOEFL (minimum score 550 paper-based; 80 iBT). *Application deadline:* For fall admission, 2/15 priority date for domestic students, 2/15 for international students; for winter admission, 9/15 priority date for domestic students, 9/15 for international students. Application fee: $75 ($90 for international students). *Expenses:* Tuition, state resident: full-time $6347; part-time $352.60 per credit hour. Tuition, nonresident: full-time $17,379; part-time $965.50 per credit hour. *Required fees:* $1035. Tuition and fees vary according to course load, campus/location and program. *Financial support:* Fellowships, research assistantships, teaching assistantships, and institutionally sponsored loans available.
Website: http://engineering.missouri.edu/civil/

University of Nebraska–Lincoln, Graduate College, College of Engineering, Interdepartmental Area of Environmental Engineering, Lincoln, NE 68588. Offers MS, PhD. *Degree requirements:* For master's, thesis optional; for doctorate, comprehensive exam, thesis/dissertation. *Entrance requirements:* For master's and doctorate, GRE General Test. Additional exam requirements/recommendations for international students: Required—TOEFL (minimum score 550 paper-based). Electronic applications accepted. *Faculty research:* Wastewater engineering, hazardous waste management, solid waste management, groundwater engineering.

University of Nevada, Las Vegas, Graduate College, Howard R. Hughes College of Engineering, Department of Civil and Environmental Engineering and Construction, Las Vegas, NV 89154-4015. Offers civil and environmental engineering (PhD); transportation (MS). *Program availability:* Part-time. *Faculty:* 10 full-time (1 woman). *Students:* 34 full-time (8 women), 29 part-time (10 women); includes 12 minority (1 Black or African American, non-Hispanic/Latino; 7 Asian, non-Hispanic/Latino; 2 Hispanic/Latino; 2 Two or more races, non-Hispanic/Latino), 34 international. Average age 31. 41 applicants, 68% accepted, 13 enrolled. In 2016, 12 master's, 7 doctorates awarded. *Degree requirements:* For master's, thesis (for some programs); for doctorate, comprehensive exam, thesis/dissertation, preliminary exam. *Entrance requirements:* For master's, GRE General Test, bachelor's degree with minimum GPA of 3.0; statement of purpose; letter of recommendation; for doctorate, GRE General Test, master's degree; statement of purpose; 3 letters of recommendation. Additional exam requirements/recommendations for international students: Required—TOEFL (minimum score 550 paper-based; 80 iBT), IELTS (minimum score 7). *Application deadline:* For fall admission, 6/15 for domestic students, 3/15 for international students; for spring admission, 11/15 for domestic students, 8/30 for international students. Application fee: $60 ($95 for international students). Electronic applications accepted. *Expenses:* $269.25 per credit, $792 per 3-credit course; $9,634 per year resident; $23,274 per year non-resident; $7,094 fees non-resident (7 credits or more); $1,307 annual health insurance fee. *Financial support:* In 2016–17, 1 fellowship with partial tuition reimbursement (averaging $20,000 per year), 14 research assistantships with partial tuition reimbursements (averaging $14,616 per year), 24 teaching assistantships with partial tuition reimbursements (averaging $14,956 per year) were awarded; institutionally sponsored loans, scholarships/grants, health care benefits, and unspecified assistantships also available. Financial award application deadline: 3/15. *Faculty research:* Sustainable construction, construction safety, infrastructure project performance, construction education, construction performance improvement. *Total annual research expenditures:* $1.2 million. *Unit head:* Dr. Donald Hayes, Chair/Professor, 702-895-4723, Fax: 702-895-3936, E-mail: donald.hayes@unlv.edu. *Application contact:* Dr. Nader Ghafoori, Graduate Coordinator, 702-895-2531, Fax: 702-895-3936, E-mail: nader.ghafoori@unlv.edu.
Website: http://www.unlv.edu/ceec

University of New Brunswick Fredericton, School of Graduate Studies, Faculty of Engineering, Department of Civil Engineering, Fredericton, NB E3B 5A3, Canada. Offers construction engineering and management (M Eng, M Sc E, PhD); environmental engineering (M Eng, M Sc E, PhD); environmental studies (M Eng); geotechnical engineering (M Eng, M Sc E, PhD); groundwater/hydrology (M Eng, M Sc E, PhD); materials (M Eng, M Sc E, PhD); pavements (M Eng, M Sc E, PhD); structures (M Eng, M Sc E, PhD); transportation (M Eng, M Sc E, PhD). *Program availability:* Part-time. *Degree requirements:* For master's, thesis; for doctorate, comprehensive exam, thesis/dissertation, qualifying exam; 27 credit hours of courses. *Entrance requirements:* For master's, minimum GPA of 3.0; B Sc E in civil engineering or related engineering degree; for doctorate, minimum GPA of 3.0; graduate degree in engineering or applied science. Additional exam requirements/recommendations for international students: Required—IELTS (minimum score 7.5), TWE (minimum score 4), Michigan English Language Assessment Battery (minimum score 85) or CanTest (minimum score 4.5); Recommended—TOEFL (minimum score 580 paper-based). Electronic applications accepted. *Faculty research:* Construction engineering and management; engineering materials and infrastructure renewal; highway and pavement research; structures and solid mechanics; geotechnical and geoenvironmental engineering; structure interaction; transportation and planning; environment, solid waste management; structural engineering; water and environmental engineering.

University of New Hampshire, Graduate School, College of Engineering and Physical Sciences, Department of Civil and Environmental Engineering, Durham, NH 03824. Offers M Engr, MS, PhD. *Program availability:* Part-time. *Degree requirements:* For master's, thesis or alternative; for doctorate, thesis/dissertation. *Entrance requirements:* For master's and doctorate, GRE. Additional exam requirements/recommendations for international students: Required—TOEFL (minimum score 550 paper-based; 80 iBT). Electronic applications accepted. *Faculty research:* Environmental, structural materials, geotechnical engineering, water resources, systems analysis.

Environmental Engineering

University of New Haven, Graduate School, Tagliatela College of Engineering, Program in Environmental Engineering, West Haven, CT 06516. Offers environmental engineering (MS); industrial and hazardous waste (MS); water and wastewater treatment (MS); water resources (MS). *Program availability:* Part-time, evening/weekend. *Students:* 47 full-time (13 women), 26 part-time (10 women); includes 3 minority (2 Black or African American, non-Hispanic/Latino; 1 American Indian or Alaska Native, non-Hispanic/Latino), 54 international. Average age 27. 80 applicants, 89% accepted, 19 enrolled. In 2016, 31 master's awarded. *Degree requirements:* For master's, thesis or alternative, research project. *Entrance requirements:* For master's, bachelor's degree in engineering. Additional exam requirements/recommendations for international students: Required—TOEFL (minimum score 75 iBT), IELTS, PTE (minimum score 50). *Application deadline:* Applications are processed on a rolling basis. Application fee: $50. Electronic applications accepted. Application fee is waived when completed online. *Expenses: Tuition:* Full-time $15,660; part-time $870 per credit hour. *Required fees:* $200; $85 per term. Tuition and fees vary according to program. *Financial support:* Research assistantships with partial tuition reimbursements, teaching assistantships with partial tuition reimbursements, career-related internships or fieldwork, Federal Work-Study, scholarships/grants, and unspecified assistantships available. Support available to part-time students. Financial award application deadline: 5/1; financial award applicants required to submit FAFSA. *Unit head:* Dr. Agamemnon Koutsospyros, Coordinator, 203-932-7398, E-mail: akoutsospyros@newhaven.edu. *Application contact:* Michelle Mason, Director of Graduate Enrollment, 203-932-7067, E-mail: mmason@newhaven.edu.
Website: http://www.newhaven.edu/10140/

The University of North Carolina at Chapel Hill, Graduate School, Gillings School of Global Public Health, Department of Environmental Sciences and Engineering, Chapel Hill, NC 27599-7431. Offers environmental engineering (MPH, MS, MSEE, MSPH); environmental health sciences (MPH, MS, MSPH, PhD); MPH/MCRP; MS/MCRP; MSPH/MCRP. *Faculty:* 40 full-time (11 women), 30 part-time/adjunct (5 women). *Students:* 87 full-time (53 women), 3 part-time (2 women); includes 14 minority (1 Black or African American, non-Hispanic/Latino; 7 Asian, non-Hispanic/Latino; 1 Hispanic/Latino; 5 Two or more races, non-Hispanic/Latino), 23 international. Average age 28. 159 applicants, 31% accepted, 9 enrolled. In 2016, 30 master's, 16 doctorates awarded. Terminal master's awarded for partial completion of doctoral program. *Degree requirements:* For master's, comprehensive exam, thesis (for some programs), research paper; for doctorate, comprehensive exam, thesis/dissertation. *Entrance requirements:* For master's and doctorate, GRE General Test, 3 letters of recommendation (academic and/or professional; at least one academic). Additional exam requirements/recommendations for international students: Required—TOEFL (minimum score 90 iBT), IELTS (minimum score 7). *Application deadline:* For fall admission, 4/11 for domestic and international students. Applications are processed on a rolling basis. Application fee: $85. Electronic applications accepted. *Financial support:* Fellowships with tuition reimbursements, research assistantships with tuition reimbursements, teaching assistantships with tuition reimbursements, career-related internships or fieldwork, Federal Work-Study, traineeships, health care benefits, and unspecified assistantships available. Support available to part-time students. Financial award application deadline: 12/10; financial award applicants required to submit FAFSA. *Faculty research:* Air, radiation and industrial hygiene, aquatic and atmospheric sciences, environmental health sciences, environmental management and policy, water resources engineering. *Unit head:* Dr. Barbara J. Turpin, Professor and Chair, 919-966-1024, Fax: 919-966-7911, E-mail: esechair@unc.edu. *Application contact:* Jack Whaley, Registrar, 919-966-3844, Fax: 919-966-7911, E-mail: jack_whaley@unc.edu.
Website: http://sph.unc.edu/envr/environmental-sciences-and-engineering-home/

The University of North Carolina at Charlotte, William States Lee College of Engineering, Department of Civil and Environmental Engineering, Charlotte, NC 28223-0001. Offers civil engineering (MSCE); infrastructure and environmental systems (PhD), including infrastructure and environmental systems design. *Program availability:* Part-time, evening/weekend. *Faculty:* 24 full-time (4 women). *Students:* 56 full-time (16 women), 37 part-time (14 women); includes 13 minority (4 Black or African American, non-Hispanic/Latino; 3 Asian, non-Hispanic/Latino; 6 Hispanic/Latino), 37 international. Average age 31. 110 applicants, 56% accepted, 18 enrolled. In 2016, 19 master's, 11 doctorates awarded. *Degree requirements:* For master's, comprehensive exam (for some programs), thesis, project, or comprehensive exam; for doctorate, comprehensive exam, thesis/dissertation. *Entrance requirements:* For master's, GRE, undergraduate degree in civil and environmental engineering or a closely-related field; minimum undergraduate GPA of 3.0; for doctorate, GRE General Test, equivalent to U.S. baccalaureate or master's degree from regionally-accredited college or university in engineering, earth science and geology, chemical and biological sciences or a related field with minimum undergraduate GPA of 3.2, graduate 3.5. Additional exam requirements/recommendations for international students: Required—TOEFL (minimum score 523 paper-based, 70 iBT) or IELTS (6.5). *Application deadline:* For fall admission, 3/1 priority date for domestic and international students; for spring admission, 10/1 priority date for domestic and international students; for summer admission, 4/1 priority date for domestic and international students. Applications are processed on a rolling basis. Application fee: $75. Electronic applications accepted. *Expenses:* Contact institution. *Financial support:* In 2016–17, 36 students received support, including 2 fellowships (averaging $30,183 per year), 22 research assistantships (averaging $12,465 per year), 12 teaching assistantships (averaging $4,856 per year); career-related internships or fieldwork, institutionally sponsored loans, scholarships/grants, and unspecified assistantships also available. Support available to part-time students. Financial award application deadline: 3/1; financial award applicants required to submit FAFSA. *Total annual research expenditures:* $2.9 million. *Unit head:* Dr. John L. Daniels, Chair, 704-687-1219, E-mail: jodaniel@uncc.edu. *Application contact:* Kathy B. Giddings, Director of Graduate Admissions, 704-687-5503, Fax: 704-687-1668, E-mail: gradadm@uncc.edu.
Website: http://cee.uncc.edu/

University of North Dakota, Graduate School, School of Engineering and Mines, Department of Environmental Engineering, Grand Forks, ND 58202. Offers M Engr, MS, PhD. *Degree requirements:* For master's, thesis. *Entrance requirements:* For master's, GRE General Test, minimum GPA of 3.0. Additional exam requirements/recommendations for international students: Required—TOEFL (minimum score 550 paper-based; 79 iBT), IELTS (minimum score 6.5). *Application deadline:* For fall admission, 2/28 for domestic and international students; for spring admission, 9/15 for domestic and international students. Application fee: $35. Electronic applications accepted. *Financial support:* Fellowships with full and partial tuition reimbursements, research assistantships with full and partial tuition reimbursements, teaching assistantships with full and partial tuition reimbursements, Federal Work-Study, scholarships/grants, health care benefits, tuition waivers (full and partial), and unspecified assistantships available. Support available to part-time students. Financial award applicants required to submit FAFSA. *Unit head:* Dr. Frank Bowman, Graduate Director, 701-777-4245, Fax: 701-777-4838, E-mail: frankbowman@mail.und.edu. *Application contact:* Staci Wells, Admissions Associate, 701-777-2945, Fax: 701-777-3619, E-mail: staci.wells@gradschool.und.edu.

University of Notre Dame, Graduate School, College of Engineering, Department of Civil Engineering and Geological Sciences, Notre Dame, IN 46556. Offers bioengineering (MS Bio E); civil engineering (MSCE); civil engineering and geological sciences (PhD); environmental engineering (MS Env E); geological sciences (MS). Terminal master's awarded for partial completion of doctoral program. *Degree requirements:* For master's, comprehensive exam; for doctorate, thesis/dissertation, candidacy exam. *Entrance requirements:* For master's and doctorate, GRE General Test. Additional exam requirements/recommendations for international students: Required—TOEFL (minimum score 600 paper-based; 80 iBT). Electronic applications accepted. *Faculty research:* Environmental modeling, biological-waste treatment, petrology, environmental geology, geochemistry.

University of Oklahoma, Gallogly College of Engineering, School of Civil Engineering and Environmental Science, Program in Environmental Engineering, Norman, OK 73019. Offers MS, PhD. *Program availability:* Part-time. *Students:* 7 full-time (all women), 4 part-time (3 women); includes 2 minority (both Black or African American, non-Hispanic/Latino), 4 international. Average age 28. 9 applicants, 33% accepted, 1 enrolled. In 2016, 1 master's, 1 doctorate awarded. Terminal master's awarded for partial completion of doctoral program. *Degree requirements:* For master's, thesis; for doctorate, comprehensive exam, thesis/dissertation, general exam. *Entrance requirements:* For master's and doctorate, GRE. Additional exam requirements/recommendations for international students: Required—TOEFL (minimum score 79 iBT) or IELTS (minimum score 6.5). *Application deadline:* For fall admission, 1/15 for domestic and international students; for spring admission, 8/15 for domestic and international students. Application fee: $50 ($100 for international students). Electronic applications accepted. *Expenses:* Tuition, state resident: full-time $4886; part-time $203.60 per credit hour. Tuition, nonresident: full-time $18,989; part-time $791.20 per credit hour. *Required fees:* $3283; $126.25 per credit hour. $126.50 per semester. *Financial support:* In 2016–17, 10 students received support. Research assistantships, teaching assistantships, and scholarships/grants available. Financial award application deadline: 6/1; financial award applicants required to submit FAFSA. *Faculty research:* Coastal zone flood prediction, inland runoff modeling, flooding and drought due to climate change, water treatment. *Unit head:* Dr. Randall Kolar, Director, 405-325-4267, Fax: 405-325-4217, E-mail: kolar@ou.edu. *Application contact:* Susan Williams, Graduate Programs Assistant, 405-325-2344, Fax: 405-325-4217, E-mail: srwilliams@ou.edu.
Website: http://www.ou.edu/content/coe/cees.html

University of Pittsburgh, Swanson School of Engineering, Department of Civil and Environmental Engineering, Pittsburgh, PA 15260. Offers MSCEE, PhD. *Program availability:* Part-time, 100% online. *Faculty:* 17 full-time (5 women), 23 part-time/adjunct (1 woman). *Students:* 103 full-time (36 women), 44 part-time (9 women); includes 11 minority (2 Black or African American, non-Hispanic/Latino; 5 Asian, non-Hispanic/Latino; 4 Hispanic/Latino), 85 international. 333 applicants, 63% accepted, 44 enrolled. In 2016, 37 master's, 7 doctorates awarded. Terminal master's awarded for partial completion of doctoral program. *Degree requirements:* For doctorate, comprehensive exam, thesis/dissertation, final oral exams. *Entrance requirements:* For master's and doctorate, minimum GPA of 3.0. Additional exam requirements/recommendations for international students: Required—TOEFL (minimum score 550 paper-based; 80 iBT). *Application deadline:* For fall admission, 3/1 priority date for domestic and international students; for spring admission, 7/1 priority date for domestic and international students. Applications are processed on a rolling basis. Application fee: $50. Electronic applications accepted. *Expenses:* $24,962 full-time per academic year in-state tuition, $41,222 full-time per academic year out-of-state tuition; $830 mandatory fees per academic year. *Financial support:* In 2016–17, 5 fellowships with full tuition reimbursements (averaging $30,720 per year), 28 research assistantships with full tuition reimbursements (averaging $27,396 per year), 19 teaching assistantships with full tuition reimbursements (averaging $26,328 per year) were awarded; scholarships/grants, traineeships, and tuition waivers (full) also available. Financial award application deadline: 3/1. *Faculty research:* Environmental and water resources, structures and infrastructures, construction management. *Total annual research expenditures:* $4.2 million. *Unit head:* Dr. Radisav D. Vidic, Chairman, 412-624-9870, Fax: 412-624-0135, E-mail: vidic@pitt.edu. *Application contact:* Rama Bazaz, Director, 412-624-9800, Fax: 412-624-9808, E-mail: ssoeadm@pitt.edu.
Website: http://www.engineering.pitt.edu/Departments/Civil-Environmental//

University of Puerto Rico, Mayagüez Campus, Graduate Studies, College of Engineering, Department of Civil Engineering and Surveying, Mayagüez, PR 00681-9000. Offers civil engineering (ME, MS, PhD), including construction engineering and management (ME, MS), environmental engineering, geotechnical engineering (ME, MS), structural engineering, transportation engineering. *Program availability:* Part-time. *Faculty:* 37 full-time (7 women), 2 part-time/adjunct (0 women). *Students:* 118 full-time (37 women), 9 part-time (2 women); includes 110 minority (all Hispanic/Latino), 17 international. Average age 25. 35 applicants, 94% accepted, 16 enrolled. In 2016, 26 master's, 2 doctorates awarded. Terminal master's awarded for partial completion of doctoral program. *Degree requirements:* For master's, one foreign language, thesis; for doctorate, one foreign language, comprehensive exam, thesis/dissertation, qualifying exams. *Entrance requirements:* For master's, proficiency in English and Spanish; BS in civil engineering or its equivalent; for doctorate, proficiency in English and Spanish. *Application deadline:* For fall admission, 2/15 for domestic and international students; for spring admission, 9/15 for domestic and international students. Applications are processed on a rolling basis. Application fee: $25. Electronic applications accepted. *Expenses: Tuition, area resident:* Full-time $2466. *International tuition:* $7166 full-time. *Required fees:* $210. One-time fee: $5 full-time. Tuition and fees vary according to course level, campus/location, program and student level. *Financial support:* In 2016–17, 89 students received support, including 74 research assistantships with full and partial tuition reimbursements available (averaging $3,171 per year), 38 teaching assistantships with full and partial tuition reimbursements available (averaging $3,107 per year); unspecified assistantships also available. *Faculty research:* Structural design, concrete structure, finite elements, dynamic analysis, transportation, soils. *Unit head:* Ismael Pagan, Prof., Director, 787-832-4040 Ext. 3815, Fax: 787-833-8260, E-mail: ismael.pagan@upr.edu. *Application contact:* Myriam Hernandez, Administrative Officer III, 787-832-4040 Ext. 3815, Fax: 787-833-8260, E-mail: myriam.hernandez1@upr.edu.
Website: http://engineering.uprm.edu/inci/

University of Regina, Faculty of Graduate Studies and Research, Faculty of Engineering and Applied Science, Program in Environmental Systems Engineering, Regina, SK S4S 0A2, Canada. Offers M Eng, MA Sc, PhD. *Program availability:* Part-time. *Faculty:* 11 full-time (2 women), 24 part-time/adjunct (0 women). *Students:* 42 full-time (20 women), 2 part-time (0 women). 59 applicants, 17% accepted. In 2016, 14 master's, 7 doctorates awarded. *Degree requirements:* For master's, thesis, project, report; for doctorate, thesis/dissertation. *Entrance requirements:* For doctorate, master's degree. Additional exam requirements/recommendations for international students: Required—TOEFL (minimum score 550 paper-based; 80 iBT), IELTS (minimum score 6.5), PTE (minimum score 59). *Application deadline:* For fall admission, 3/31 for domestic and international students; for winter admission, 7/31 for domestic and international students; for spring admission, 11/30 for domestic and international students. Application fee: $100. Electronic applications accepted. *Expenses:* Contact institution. *Financial support:* In 2016–17, 10 fellowships (averaging $6,300 per year), 10 teaching assistantships (averaging $2,550 per year) were awarded; career-related internships or fieldwork and scholarships/grants also available. Financial award application deadline: 6/15. *Faculty research:* Design of water and wastewater treatment systems, urban and regional transportation planning, environmental fluid mechanics, air quality management, environmental modeling and decision-making. *Unit head:* Dr. Amr Henni, Associate Dean, Research and Graduate Studies, 306-585-4960, Fax: 306-585-4855, E-mail: amr.henni@uregina.ca. *Application contact:* Dr. Kelvin Ng, Graduate Coordinator, 306-585-8487, Fax: 306-585-4855, E-mail: kelvin.ng@uregina.ca. Website: http://www.uregina.ca/engineering/

University of Rhode Island, Graduate School, College of Engineering, Department of Civil and Environmental Engineering, Kingston, RI 02881. Offers environmental engineering (MS, PhD); geotechnical engineering (MS, PhD); structural engineering (MS, PhD); transportation engineering (MS, PhD). *Program availability:* Part-time. *Faculty:* 11 full-time (3 women). *Students:* 24 full-time (6 women), 8 part-time (4 women); includes 2 minority (1 Hispanic/Latino; 1 Two or more races, non-Hispanic/Latino), 14 international. In 2016, 11 master's, 3 doctorates awarded. *Degree requirements:* For master's, comprehensive exam (for some programs), thesis optional; for doctorate, comprehensive exam, thesis/dissertation. *Entrance requirements:* For master's and doctorate, 2 letters of recommendation. Additional exam requirements/recommendations for international students: Required—TOEFL. *Application deadline:* For fall admission, 7/15 for domestic students, 2/1 for international students; for spring admission, 11/15 for domestic students, 7/15 for international students. Application fee: $65. Electronic applications accepted. *Expenses:* Tuition, state resident: full-time $11,796; part-time $655 per credit. Tuition, nonresident: full-time $24,206; part-time $1345 per credit. *Required fees:* $1546; $44 per credit. One-time fee: $155 full-time; $35 part-time. *Financial support:* In 2016–17, 3 research assistantships with tuition reimbursements (averaging $8,774 per year), 4 teaching assistantships with tuition reimbursements (averaging $12,171 per year) were awarded. Financial award application deadline: 2/1; financial award applicants required to submit FAFSA. *Unit head:* Dr. Mayrai Gindy, Chair, 401-874-5117, Fax: 401-874-5587, E-mail: gindy@egr.uri.edu. *Application contact:* Dr. George Tsiatas, Graduate Program Director, 401-874-5117, E-mail: gt@uri.edu. Website: http://www.uri.edu/cve/

University of South Alabama, College of Engineering, Department of Civil, Coastal, and Environmental Engineering, Mobile, AL 36688. Offers MSCE. *Faculty:* 7 full-time (1 woman). *Students:* 13 full-time (3 women), 4 part-time (1 woman); includes 1 minority (Black or African American, non-Hispanic/Latino), 5 international. Average age 26. 31 applicants, 39% accepted, 5 enrolled. In 2016, 17 master's awarded. *Degree requirements:* For master's, comprehensive exam, thesis or project. *Entrance requirements:* For master's, GRE, minimum GPA of 3.0, three references, portfolio. Additional exam requirements/recommendations for international students: Required—TOEFL (minimum score 525 paper-based; 71 iBT). *Application deadline:* For fall admission, 7/1 priority date for domestic students, 6/1 priority date for international students; for spring admission, 12/1 priority date for domestic students, 11/1 priority date for international students; for summer admission, 5/1 priority date for domestic students, 4/1 priority date for international students. Applications are processed on a rolling basis. Application fee: $35. Electronic applications accepted. *Expenses:* Contact institution. *Financial support:* Fellowships, research assistantships, teaching assistantships, career-related internships or fieldwork, Federal Work-Study, institutionally sponsored loans, scholarships/grants, and unspecified assistantships available. Support available to part-time students. Financial award application deadline: 5/31; financial award applicants required to submit FAFSA. *Faculty research:* Calibration of simulation model, monitoring coastal processes, reducing crashes. *Unit head:* Dr. Kevin White, Department Chair, 251-460-6174, Fax: 251-461-1400, E-mail: kwhite@southalabama.edu. *Application contact:* Brenda Poole, Academic Records Specialist, 251-460-6140, Fax: 251-460-6343, E-mail: engineering@alabama.edu. Website: http://www.southalabama.edu/colleges/engineering/ce/index.html

University of Southern California, Graduate School, Viterbi School of Engineering, Sonny Astani Department of Civil Engineering, Los Angeles, CA 90089. Offers applied mechanics (MS); civil engineering (MS, PhD); computer-aided engineering (ME, Graduate Certificate); construction management (MCM); engineering technology commercialization (Graduate Certificate); environmental engineering (MS, PhD); environmental quality management (ME); structural design (ME); sustainable cities (Graduate Certificate); transportation systems (MS, Graduate Certificate); water and waste management (MS). *Program availability:* Part-time, evening/weekend. Terminal master's awarded for partial completion of doctoral program. *Degree requirements:* For master's, thesis optional; for doctorate, thesis/dissertation. *Entrance requirements:* For master's and doctorate, GRE General Test. Additional exam requirements/recommendations for international students: Recommended—TOEFL. Electronic applications accepted. *Faculty research:* Geotechnical engineering, transportation engineering, structural engineering, construction management, environmental engineering, water resources.

University of South Florida, College of Engineering, Department of Civil and Environmental Engineering, Tampa, FL 33620-9951. Offers civil engineering (MCE, MSCE, PhD), including geotechnical engineering, materials science and engineering, structures engineering, transportation engineering, water resources; environmental engineering (MEVE, MSEV, PhD), including engineering for international development (MSEV). *Program availability:* Part-time. *Faculty:* 20 full-time (5 women). *Students:* 117 full-time (41 women), 63 part-time (18 women); includes 33 minority (7 Black or African American, non-Hispanic/Latino; 2 Asian, non-Hispanic/Latino; 20 Hispanic/Latino; 4 Two or more races, non-Hispanic/Latino), 84 international. Average age 28. 250 applicants, 52% accepted, 51 enrolled. In 2016, 55 master's, 13 doctorates awarded. Terminal master's awarded for partial completion of doctoral program. *Degree requirements:* For master's, comprehensive exam, thesis (for some programs); for doctorate, comprehensive exam, thesis/dissertation. *Entrance requirements:* For master's, GRE General Test, minimum GPA of 3.0 in major, letters of reference, statement of purpose; for doctorate, GRE General Test, letters of recommendation, statement of purpose, resume. Additional exam requirements/recommendations for international students: Required—TOEFL (minimum score 550 paper-based; 79 iBT) or IELTS (minimum score 6.5). *Application deadline:* For fall admission, 2/15 for domestic students, 2/15 priority date for international students; for spring admission, 10/15 for domestic students, 9/15 priority date for international students. Application fee: $30. Electronic applications accepted. *Expenses:* Tuition, state resident: full-time $7766; part-time $431.43 per credit hour. Tuition, nonresident: full-time $15,789; part-time $877.17 per credit hour. *Required fees:* $37 per term. *Financial support:* In 2016–17, 36 students received support, including 44 research assistantships (averaging $14,123 per year), 21 teaching assistantships with tuition reimbursements available (averaging $15,329 per year). *Faculty research:* Environmental and water resources engineering, geotechnics and geoenvironmental systems, structures and materials systems, transportation systems. *Total annual research expenditures:* $3.7 million. *Unit head:* Dr. Manjriker Gunaratne, Professor and Department Chair, 813-974-5818, Fax: 813-974-2957, E-mail: gunaratn@usf.edu. *Application contact:* Dr. Sarina J. Ergas, Professor and Graduate

Program Coordinator, 813-974-1119, Fax: 813-974-2957, E-mail: sergas@usf.edu. Website: http://www.usf.edu/engineering/cee/

The University of Tennessee, Graduate School, Tickle College of Engineering, Department of Civil and Environmental Engineering, Program in Environmental Engineering, Knoxville, TN 37996. Offers MS, MS/MBA. *Program availability:* Part-time, online learning. *Faculty:* 15 full-time (2 women), 6 part-time/adjunct (0 women). *Students:* 10 full-time (7 women), 7 part-time (1 woman); includes 3 minority (2 Hispanic/Latino; 1 Two or more races, non-Hispanic/Latino). Average age 25. 18 applicants, 33% accepted, 3 enrolled. In 2016, 4 master's awarded. *Degree requirements:* For master's, thesis or alternative. *Entrance requirements:* For master's, GRE General Test (for MS students pursuing research thesis), minimum GPA of 2.7 (for U.S. degree holders), 3.0 (for international degree holders); 3 references; statement of purpose; resume. Additional exam requirements/recommendations for international students: Required—TOEFL (minimum score 550 paper-based). *Application deadline:* For fall admission, 2/1 priority date for domestic and international students; for spring admission, 6/15 for domestic and international students. Applications are processed on a rolling basis. Application fee: $35. Electronic applications accepted. *Financial support:* In 2016–17, 8 students received support, including 5 research assistantships with full tuition reimbursements available (averaging $19,488 per year), 2 teaching assistantships with full tuition reimbursements available (averaging $15,800 per year); career-related internships or fieldwork, Federal Work-Study, institutionally sponsored loans, health care benefits, and unspecified assistantships also available. Financial award application deadline: 2/1; financial award applicants required to submit FAFSA. *Faculty research:* Air pollution control technologies; climate change and engineering impact on environment; environmental sampling, monitoring, and restoration; soil erosion prediction and control; waste management and utilization. *Unit head:* Dr. Chris Cox, Head, 865-974-2503, Fax: 865-974-2669, E-mail: gdreed@utk.edu. *Application contact:* Dr. Khalid Alshibli, Associate Head, 865-974-7728, Fax: 865-974-2669, E-mail: alshibli@utk.edu. Website: http://www.engr.utk.edu/civil/

The University of Texas at Austin, Graduate School, Cockrell School of Engineering, Department of Civil, Architectural and Environmental Engineering, Program in Environmental and Water Resources Engineering, Austin, TX 78712-1111. Offers MS, PhD. *Program availability:* Part-time. *Degree requirements:* For master's, thesis or alternative. *Entrance requirements:* For master's, GRE General Test. Additional exam requirements/recommendations for international students: Required—TOEFL. Electronic applications accepted.

The University of Texas at El Paso, Graduate School, College of Engineering, Department of Civil Engineering, El Paso, TX 79968-0001. Offers civil engineering (MS, PhD); construction management (MS, Certificate); environmental engineering (MEENE, MSENE). *Program availability:* Part-time, evening/weekend. *Degree requirements:* For master's, comprehensive exam, thesis optional; for doctorate, comprehensive exam, thesis/dissertation. *Entrance requirements:* For master's, GRE, minimum GPA of 3.0; for doctorate, GRE. Additional exam requirements/recommendations for international students: Required—TOEFL. Electronic applications accepted. *Faculty research:* Non-destructive testing for geotechnical and pavement applications, transportation systems, wastewater treatment systems, air quality, linear and non-linear modeling of structures, structural reliability.

The University of Texas at El Paso, Graduate School, College of Engineering, Department of Mechanical Engineering, El Paso, TX 79968-0001. Offers environmental science and engineering (PhD); mechanical engineering (MS). *Program availability:* Part-time. *Degree requirements:* For master's, thesis optional; for doctorate, thesis/dissertation. *Entrance requirements:* For master's, GRE, minimum GPA of 3.0, letter of reference; for doctorate, GRE, minimum GPA of 3.5, letters of reference, BS or equivalent. Additional exam requirements/recommendations for international students: Required—TOEFL; Recommended—IELTS. Electronic applications accepted. *Faculty research:* Aerospace, energy, combustion and propulsion, design engineering, high temperature materials.

The University of Texas at El Paso, Graduate School, Interdisciplinary Program in Environmental Science and Engineering, El Paso, TX 79968-0001. Offers PhD. *Program availability:* Part-time, evening/weekend. *Degree requirements:* For doctorate, thesis/dissertation. *Entrance requirements:* For doctorate, GRE, letters of recommendation. Additional exam requirements/recommendations for international students: Required—TOEFL; Recommended—IELTS. Electronic applications accepted.

The University of Texas at San Antonio, College of Engineering, Department of Civil and Environmental Engineering, San Antonio, TX 78249-0617. Offers civil engineering (MCE, MSCE); environmental science and engineering (PhD). *Program availability:* Part-time. *Faculty:* 14 full-time (1 woman), 1 part-time/adjunct (0 women). *Students:* 45 full-time (9 women), 40 part-time (8 women); includes 23 minority (5 Black or African American, non-Hispanic/Latino; 5 Asian, non-Hispanic/Latino; 12 Hispanic/Latino; 1 Two or more races, non-Hispanic/Latino), 34 international. Average age 30. 88 applicants, 58% accepted, 22 enrolled. In 2016, 11 master's, 4 doctorates awarded. *Degree requirements:* For master's, comprehensive exam, thesis (for some programs); for doctorate, comprehensive exam, thesis/dissertation, written qualifying exam, dissertation proposal. *Entrance requirements:* For master's, GRE General Test, BS in civil engineering or related field from accredited institution, statement of research/specialization interest, recommendation by the Civil Engineering Master's Program Admissions Committee; for doctorate, GRE, BS and MS from accredited institution, minimum GPA of 3.0 in upper-division and graduate courses, three letters of recommendation, letter of research interest, resume/curriculum vitae. Additional exam requirements/recommendations for international students: Required—TOEFL (minimum score 550 paper-based; 79 iBT), IELTS (minimum score 6.5). *Application deadline:* For fall admission, 7/1 for domestic students, 4/1 for international students; for spring admission, 11/1 for domestic students, 9/1 for international students. Application fee: $45 ($80 for international students). Electronic applications accepted. *Expenses:* Contact institution. *Financial support:* In 2016–17, 42 students received support, including 28 research assistantships with full tuition reimbursements available (averaging $20,000 per year), 14 teaching assistantships (averaging $4,680 per year); scholarships/grants also available. Financial award application deadline: 2/1. *Faculty research:* Structures, application of geographic information systems in water resources, geotechnical engineering, pavement traffic loading, hydrogeology. *Total annual research expenditures:* $2.6 million. *Unit head:* Dr. Heather Shipley, Department Chair, 210-458-7517, Fax: 210-458-6475, E-mail: heather.shipley@utsa.edu. *Application contact:* Jessica Perez, Administrative Associate, 210-458-4428, Fax: 210-458-7469, E-mail: jessica.perez@utsa.edu. Website: http://engineering.utsa.edu/CE/

The University of Texas at Tyler, College of Engineering, Department of Civil Engineering, Tyler, TX 75799-0001. Offers environmental engineering (MS); industrial safety (MS); structural engineering (MS); transportation engineering (MS); water resources engineering (MS). *Program availability:* Part-time, evening/weekend. *Degree requirements:* For master's, thesis optional. *Entrance requirements:* For master's, GRE General Test, bachelor's degree in engineering, associated science degree. Additional exam requirements/recommendations for international students: Required—TOEFL.

Environmental Engineering

Faculty research: Non-destructive strength testing, indoor air quality, transportation routing and signaling, pavement replacement criteria, flood water routing, construction and long-term behavior of innovative geotechnical foundation and embankment construction used in highway construction, engineering education.

University of Utah, Graduate School, College of Mines and Earth Sciences, Department of Geology and Geophysics, Salt Lake City, UT 84112. Offers environmental engineering (ME, MS, PhD); geological engineering (ME, MS, PhD); geology (MS, PhD); geophysics (MS, PhD). *Faculty:* 32 full-time (8 women), 4 part-time/adjunct (2 women). *Students:* 54 full-time (21 women), 26 part-time (11 women); includes 6 minority (1 American Indian or Alaska Native, non-Hispanic/Latino; 4 Hispanic/Latino; 1 Two or more races, non-Hispanic/Latino), 16 international. Average age 30. 228 applicants, 14% accepted, 22 enrolled. In 2016, 18 master's, 3 doctorates awarded. Terminal master's awarded for partial completion of doctoral program. *Degree requirements:* For master's, comprehensive exam, thesis; for doctorate, thesis/dissertation, qualifying exam (written and oral). *Entrance requirements:* For master's and doctorate, GRE General Test, minimum GPA of 3.25. Additional exam requirements/recommendations for international students: Required—TOEFL (minimum score 500 paper-based; 61 iBT). *Application deadline:* For fall admission, 1/15 priority date for domestic and international students. Application fee: $55 ($65 for international students). Electronic applications accepted. *Expenses:* Tuition, state resident: full-time $7011; part-time $3918.24 per credit hour. Tuition, nonresident: full-time $22,154; part-time $11,665.42 per credit hour. *Financial support:* In 2016–17, 62 students received support, including 14 fellowships with full tuition reimbursements available (averaging $17,500 per year), 32 research assistantships with full tuition reimbursements available (averaging $23,000 per year), 16 teaching assistantships with full tuition reimbursements available (averaging $17,500 per year); career-related internships or fieldwork, institutionally sponsored loans, scholarships/grants, health care benefits, unspecified assistantships, and stipends also available. Financial award application deadline: 1/15; financial award applicants required to submit FAFSA. *Faculty research:* Igneous, metamorphic, and sedimentary petrology; stratigraphy; paleoclimatology; hydrology; seismology. *Total annual research expenditures:* $4.1 million. *Unit head:* Dr. John Bartley, Chair, 801-585-1670, Fax: 801-581-7065, E-mail: john.bartley@utah.edu. *Application contact:* Dr. Gabriel J. Bowen, Director of Graduate Studies, 801-585-7925, Fax: 801-581-7065, E-mail: gabe.bowen@utah.edu.
Website: http://www.earth.utah.edu/

University of Vermont, Graduate College, College of Engineering and Mathematics, Department of Civil and Environmental Engineering, Burlington, VT 05405. Offers MS, PhD. *Degree requirements:* For master's, thesis or alternative; for doctorate, thesis/dissertation. *Entrance requirements:* For master's and doctorate, GRE General Test. Additional exam requirements/recommendations for international students: Required—TOEFL (minimum score 550 paper-based; 80 iBT). Electronic applications accepted. *Expenses:* Tuition, state resident: full-time $5814. Tuition, nonresident: full-time $14,670.

University of Washington, Graduate School, College of Engineering, Department of Civil and Environmental Engineering, Seattle, WA 98195-2700. Offers construction engineering (MSCE, PhD); environmental engineering (MSCE, PhD); geotechnical engineering (MSCE, PhD); hydrology and hydrodynamics (MSCE, PhD); structural engineering and mechanics (MSCE, PhD); transportation engineering (MSCE, PhD). *Program availability:* Part-time, 100% online. *Faculty:* 37 full-time (10 women). *Students:* 239 full-time (97 women), 153 part-time (41 women); includes 71 minority (7 Black or African American, non-Hispanic/Latino; 32 Asian, non-Hispanic/Latino; 22 Hispanic/Latino; 2 Native Hawaiian or other Pacific Islander, non-Hispanic/Latino; 8 Two or more races, non-Hispanic/Latino), 134 international. 782 applicants, 58% accepted, 157 enrolled. In 2016, 132 master's, 13 doctorates awarded. Terminal master's awarded for partial completion of doctoral program. *Degree requirements:* For master's, thesis optional; for doctorate, comprehensive exam, thesis/dissertation, qualifying, general and final exams; completion of degree within 10 years. *Entrance requirements:* For master's, GRE General Test, minimum GPA of 3.0, statement of purpose, letters of recommendation, transcripts; for doctorate, GRE General Test, minimum GPA of 3.5, statement of purpose, letters of recommendation, transcripts, resume. Additional exam requirements/recommendations for international students: Required—TOEFL (minimum score 580 paper-based; 92 iBT); Recommended—IELTS (minimum score 7), TSE. *Application deadline:* For fall admission, 12/15 for domestic and international students. Applications are processed on a rolling basis. Application fee: $85. Electronic applications accepted. *Expenses:* Contact institution. *Financial support:* In 2016–17, 110 students received support, including 10 fellowships with tuition reimbursements available (averaging $2,228 per year), 72 research assistantships with full tuition reimbursements available (averaging $2,351 per year), 28 teaching assistantships with full tuition reimbursements available (averaging $2,387 per year); scholarships/grants also available. Financial award application deadline: 12/15; financial award applicants required to submit FAFSA. *Faculty research:* Structural and geotechnical engineering, transportation and construction engineering, water and environmental engineering. *Total annual research expenditures:* $13.5 million. *Unit head:* Dr. Timothy V. Larson, Professor/Chair, 206-543-6815, Fax: 206-543-1543, E-mail: tlarson@uw.edu. *Application contact:* Melissa Pritchard, Graduate Adviser, 206-543-2574, Fax: 206-543-1543, E-mail: ceginfo@u.washington.edu.
Website: http://www.ce.washington.edu/

University of Waterloo, Graduate Studies, Faculty of Engineering, Department of Civil and Environmental Engineering, Waterloo, ON N2L 3G1, Canada. Offers M Eng, MA Sc, PhD. *Program availability:* Part-time. *Degree requirements:* For master's, research paper or thesis; for doctorate, comprehensive exam, thesis/dissertation. *Entrance requirements:* For master's, honors degree, minimum B average; for doctorate, master's degree, minimum A- average. Additional exam requirements/recommendations for international students: Required—TOEFL, IELTS, PTE. Electronic applications accepted. *Faculty research:* Water resources, structures, construction management, transportation, geotechnical engineering.

The University of Western Ontario, Faculty of Graduate Studies, Physical Sciences Division, Faculty of Engineering, London, ON N6A 5B8, Canada. Offers chemical and biochemical engineering (ME Sc, PhD); civil and environmental engineering (M Eng, ME Sc, PhD); electrical and computer engineering (M Eng, ME Sc, PhD); mechanical and materials engineering (M Eng, ME Sc, PhD). *Program availability:* Part-time. Terminal master's awarded for partial completion of doctoral program. *Degree requirements:* For master's, thesis; for doctorate, thesis/dissertation. *Entrance requirements:* For master's, minimum B average; for doctorate, minimum B+ average. *Faculty research:* Wind, geotechnical, chemical reactor engineering, applied electrostatics, biochemical engineering.

University of Windsor, Faculty of Graduate Studies, Faculty of Engineering, Department of Civil and Environmental Engineering, Windsor, ON N9B 3P4, Canada. Offers civil engineering (M Eng, MA Sc, PhD); environmental engineering (M Eng, MA Sc, PhD). *Program availability:* Part-time. *Degree requirements:* For master's, thesis; for doctorate, comprehensive exam, thesis/dissertation. *Entrance requirements:* For master's, minimum B average; for doctorate, master's degree, minimum A average. Additional exam requirements/recommendations for international students: Required—

TOEFL (minimum score 580 paper-based). Electronic applications accepted. *Faculty research:* Odors: sampling, measurement, control; drinking water disinfection, hydrocarbon contaminated soil remediation, structural dynamics, numerical simulation of piezoelectric materials.

University of Wisconsin–Madison, Graduate School, College of Engineering, Department of Civil and Environmental Engineering, Madison, WI 53706. Offers MS, PhD. *Program availability:* Part-time. *Faculty:* 28 full-time (6 women). *Students:* 109 full-time (38 women), 28 part-time (10 women); includes 11 minority (2 Black or African American, non-Hispanic/Latino; 2 Asian, non-Hispanic/Latino; 6 Hispanic/Latino; 1 Two or more races, non-Hispanic/Latino), 69 international. Average age 27. 349 applicants, 24% accepted, 28 enrolled. In 2016, 29 master's, 7 doctorates awarded. Terminal master's awarded for partial completion of doctoral program. *Degree requirements:* For master's, thesis or alternative, minimum of 30 credits; minimum overall GPA of 3.0; for doctorate, comprehensive exam, thesis/dissertation, preliminary exam; qualifying exams; minimum of 51 credits; minimum overall GPA of 3.0. *Entrance requirements:* For master's, GRE General Test, bachelor's degree; minimum GPA of 3.0 for last 60 credits of course work; for doctorate, GRE General Test, minimum GPA of 3.0 for last 60 credits of course work. Additional exam requirements/recommendations for international students: Required—TOEFL (minimum score 580 paper-based; 92 iBT). *Application deadline:* For fall admission, 12/15 priority date for domestic and international students; for spring admission, 9/1 for domestic and international students. Application fee: $75 ($81 for international students). Electronic applications accepted. *Expenses:* $13,157 per year in-state tuition and fees; $26,484 per year out-of-state tuition and fees. *Financial support:* In 2016–17, 95 students received support, including 7 fellowships with full tuition reimbursements available, 52 research assistantships with full tuition reimbursements available, 26 teaching assistantships with full tuition reimbursements available; Federal Work-Study, scholarships/grants, health care benefits, unspecified assistantships, and project assistantships also available. Support available to part-time students. Financial award application deadline: 12/1; financial award applicants required to submit FAFSA. *Faculty research:* Environmental engineering; transportation; building systems; water resources; conventional and renewable energy; mineral extraction and byproducts management; geoenvironmental engineering. *Total annual research expenditures:* $12.5 million. *Unit head:* Prof. David Noyce, Chair, 608-265-1882, Fax: 608-262-5199, E-mail: danoyce@wisc.edu. *Application contact:* Cheryl Loschko, Student Services Coordinator, 608-890-2420, E-mail: loschko@wisc.edu.
Website: https://www.engr.wisc.edu/department/civil-environmental-engineering/academics/ms-phd-civil-and-environmental-engineering/

University of Wyoming, College of Engineering and Applied Sciences, Department of Civil and Architectural Engineering and Department of Chemical and Petroleum Engineering, Program in Environmental Engineering, Laramie, WY 82071. Offers MS. *Program availability:* Part-time. *Degree requirements:* For master's, thesis optional. *Entrance requirements:* For master's, GRE General Test, minimum GPA of 3.0. Additional exam requirements/recommendations for international students: Required—TOEFL (minimum score 550 paper-based). Electronic applications accepted. *Faculty research:* Water and waste water, solid and hazardous waste management, air pollution control, flue-gas cleanup.

Utah State University, School of Graduate Studies, College of Engineering, Department of Civil and Environmental Engineering, Logan, UT 84322. Offers ME, MS, PhD, CE. *Degree requirements:* For master's, thesis (for some programs); for doctorate, thesis/dissertation. *Entrance requirements:* For master's and doctorate, GRE General Test, minimum GPA of 3.0. Additional exam requirements/recommendations for international students: Required—TOEFL. Electronic applications accepted. *Faculty research:* Hazardous waste treatment, large space structures, river basin management, earthquake engineering, environmental impact.

Vanderbilt University, School of Engineering, Department of Civil and Environmental Engineering, Program in Environmental Engineering, Nashville, TN 37240-1001. Offers environmental engineering (M Eng); environmental management (MS, PhD). MS and PhD offered through the Graduate School. *Program availability:* Part-time. Terminal master's awarded for partial completion of doctoral program. *Degree requirements:* For master's, thesis or alternative; for doctorate, thesis/dissertation. *Entrance requirements:* For master's and doctorate, GRE General Test. Additional exam requirements/recommendations for international students: Required—TOEFL. Electronic applications accepted. *Expenses:* Tuition: Part-time $1854 per credit hour. *Faculty research:* Waste treatment, hazardous waste management, chemical waste treatment, water quality.

Villanova University, College of Engineering, Department of Civil and Environmental Engineering, Program in Water Resources and Environmental Engineering, Villanova, PA 19085-1699. Offers urban water resources design (Certificate); water resources and environmental engineering (MSWREE). *Program availability:* Part-time, evening/weekend, online learning. *Degree requirements:* For master's, thesis optional. *Entrance requirements:* For master's, GRE General Test (for applicants with degrees from foreign universities), BCE or bachelor's degree in science or related engineering field, minimum GPA of 3.0. Additional exam requirements/recommendations for international students: Required—TOEFL (minimum score 600 paper-based; 100 iBT). Electronic applications accepted. *Faculty research:* Photocatalytic decontamination and disinfection of water, urban storm water wetlands, economy and risk, removal and destruction of organic acids in water, sludge treatment.

Virginia Polytechnic Institute and State University, Graduate School, College of Engineering, Blacksburg, VA 24061. Offers aerospace engineering (ME, MS, PhD); biological systems engineering (ME, MS, PhD); biomedical engineering (MS, PhD); chemical engineering (ME, MS, PhD); civil engineering (ME, MS, PhD); computer engineering (ME, MS, PhD); computer science (MS, PhD); electrical engineering (ME, PhD); engineering education (PhD); engineering mechanics (ME, MS, PhD); environmental engineering (MS); environmental science and engineering (MS); industrial and systems engineering (ME, MS, PhD); materials science and engineering (ME, MS, PhD); mechanical engineering (ME, MS, PhD); mining and minerals engineering (PhD); mining engineering (ME, MS); nuclear engineering (MS, PhD); ocean engineering (MS); systems engineering (ME, MS). *Faculty:* 400 full-time (73 women), 3 part-time/adjunct (2 women). *Students:* 1,949 full-time (487 women), 393 part-time (69 women); includes 251 minority (56 Black or African American, non-Hispanic/Latino; 3 American Indian or Alaska Native, non-Hispanic/Latino; 87 Asian, non-Hispanic/Latino; 70 Hispanic/Latino; 35 Two or more races, non-Hispanic/Latino), 1,354 international. Average age 27. 4,903 applicants, 19% accepted, 569 enrolled. In 2016, 364 master's, 200 doctorates awarded. *Degree requirements:* For master's, comprehensive exam (for some programs), thesis (for some programs); for doctorate, comprehensive exam (for some programs), thesis/dissertation (for some programs). *Entrance requirements:* For master's and doctorate, GRE/GMAT. Additional exam requirements/recommendations for international students: Required—TOEFL (minimum score 80 iBT). *Application deadline:* For fall admission, 8/1 for domestic students, 4/1 for international students; for spring admission, 1/1 for domestic students, 9/1 for international students. Applications are processed on a rolling basis. Application fee: $75. Electronic applications accepted. *Expenses:* Tuition, state resident: full-time $12,467; part-time $692.50 per credit hour. Tuition, nonresident: full-time $25,095; part-time $1394.25 per credit hour. *Required fees:* $2669; $491.50 per semester. Tuition and

fees vary according to course load, campus/location and program. *Financial support:* In 2016–17, 160 fellowships with full tuition reimbursements (averaging $7,387 per year), 872 research assistantships with full tuition reimbursements (averaging $22,329 per year), 313 teaching assistantships with full tuition reimbursements (averaging $18,714 per year) were awarded. Financial award application deadline: 3/1; financial award applicants required to submit FAFSA. *Total annual research expenditures:* $91.8 million. *Unit head:* Dr. Julia Ross, Dean, 540-231-9752, Fax: 540-231-3031, E-mail: deaneng@vt.edu. *Application contact:* Linda Perkins, Executive Assistant, 540-231-9752, Fax: 540-231-3031, E-mail: lperkins@vt.edu.
Website: http://www.eng.vt.edu/

Virginia Polytechnic Institute and State University, VT Online, Blacksburg, VA 24061. Offers advanced transportation systems (Certificate); aerospace engineering (MS); agricultural and life sciences (MSLFS); business information systems (Graduate Certificate); career and technical education (MS); civil engineering (MS); computer engineering (M Eng, MS); decision support systems (Graduate Certificate); eLearning leadership (MA); electrical engineering (M Eng, MS); engineering administration (MEA); environmental engineering (Certificate); environmental politics and policy (Graduate Certificate); environmental sciences and engineering (MS); foundations of political analysis (Graduate Certificate); health product risk management (Graduate Certificate); industrial and systems engineering (MS); information policy and society (Graduate Certificate); information security (Graduate Certificate); information technology (MIT); instructional technology (MA); integrative STEM education (MA Ed); liberal arts (Graduate Certificate); life sciences: health product risk management (MS); natural resources (MNR, Graduate Certificate); networking (Graduate Certificate); nonprofit and nongovernmental organization management (Graduate Certificate); ocean engineering (MS); political science (MA); security studies (Graduate Certificate); software development (Graduate Certificate). *Expenses:* Tuition, state resident: full-time $12,467; part-time $692.50 per credit hour. Tuition, nonresident: full-time $25,095; part-time $1394.25 per credit hour. *Required fees:* $2669; $491.50 per semester. Tuition and fees vary according to course load, campus/location and program.

Washington State University, Voiland College of Engineering and Architecture, Department of Civil and Environmental Engineering, Pullman, WA 99164-2910. Offers civil engineering (MS, PhD); environmental engineering (MS). MS programs also offered at Tri-Cities campus. *Program availability:* Part-time. Terminal master's awarded for partial completion of doctoral program. *Degree requirements:* For master's, comprehensive exam (for some programs), thesis (for some programs), oral exam; for doctorate, comprehensive exam, thesis/dissertation, oral exam, written exam. *Entrance requirements:* For master's, minimum GPA of 3.0, 3 letters of recommendation, statement of purpose; for doctorate, minimum GPA of 3.4, 3 letters of recommendation, statement of purpose. Additional exam requirements/recommendations for international students: Required—TOEFL (minimum score 550 paper-based), IELTS. Electronic applications accepted. *Faculty research:* Environmental engineering, water resources, structural engineering, geotechnical, transportation.

Washington University in St. Louis, School of Engineering and Applied Science, Department of Energy, Environmental and Chemical Engineering, St. Louis, MO 63130-4899. Offers chemical engineering (MS, D Sc); environmental engineering (MS, D Sc). *Program availability:* Part-time. Terminal master's awarded for partial completion of doctoral program. *Degree requirements:* For master's, thesis optional; for doctorate, thesis/dissertation, preliminary exam, qualifying exam. *Entrance requirements:* For master's and doctorate, GRE, minimum B average during final 2 years of course work. Additional exam requirements/recommendations for international students: Required—TOEFL, TWE. Electronic applications accepted. *Faculty research:* Reaction engineering, materials processing, catalysis, process control, air pollution control.

West Virginia University, Statler College of Engineering and Mineral Resources, Department of Civil and Environmental Engineering, Morgantown, WV 26506. Offers civil engineering (MSCE, MSE, PhD). *Program availability:* Part-time. *Degree requirements:* For master's, thesis; for doctorate, comprehensive exam, thesis/dissertation. *Entrance requirements:* For master's and doctorate, minimum GPA of 3.0. Additional exam requirements/recommendations for international students: Required—TOEFL. *Faculty research:* Habitat restoration, advanced materials for civil infrastructure, pavement modeling, infrastructure condition assessment.

Worcester Polytechnic Institute, Graduate Studies and Research, Department of Civil and Environmental Engineering, Worcester, MA 01609-2280. Offers civil and environmental engineering (Advanced Certificate, Graduate Certificate); civil engineering (ME, MS, PhD); construction project management (MS); environmental engineering (M Eng, MS); master builder (M Eng). *Program availability:* Part-time, evening/weekend, blended/hybrid learning. *Faculty:* 10 full-time (0 women), 4 part-time/adjunct (0 women). *Students:* 31 full-time (15 women), 20 part-time (8 women); includes 5 minority (1 Black or African American, non-Hispanic/Latino; 1 American Indian or Alaska Native, non-Hispanic/Latino; 1 Hispanic/Latino; 2 Two or more races, non-Hispanic/Latino), 19 international. 111 applicants, 58% accepted, 13 enrolled. In 2016, 20 master's, 6 doctorates awarded. *Degree requirements:* For master's, thesis optional; for doctorate, comprehensive exam, thesis/dissertation. *Entrance requirements:* For master's, GRE (recommended), 3 letters of recommendation; for doctorate, GRE (recommended), 3 letters of recommendation, statement of purpose. Additional exam requirements/recommendations for international students: Required—TOEFL (minimum score 563 paper-based; 84 iBT), IELTS (minimum score 7), GRE. *Application deadline:* For fall admission, 1/1 priority date for domestic and international students; for spring admission, 10/1 priority date for domestic and international students. Applications are processed on a rolling basis. Application fee: $70. Electronic applications accepted. *Financial support:* Research assistantships, teaching assistantships, career-related internships or fieldwork, institutionally sponsored loans, scholarships/grants, and unspecified assistantships available. Financial award application deadline: 1/1; financial award applicants required to submit FAFSA. *Unit head:* Dr. Tahar El-Korchi, Interim Head, 508-831-5530, Fax: 508-831-5808, E-mail: tek@wpi.edu. *Application contact:* Dr. Rajib Mallick, Graduate Coordinator, 508-831-5530, Fax: 508-831-5808, E-mail: rajib@wpi.edu.
Website: http://www.wpi.edu/academics/cee

Worcester Polytechnic Institute, Graduate Studies and Research, Programs in Interdisciplinary Studies, Worcester, MA 01609-2280. Offers bioscience administration (MS); impact engineering (MS); manufacturing engineering management (MS); power systems management (MS); social science (PhD); systems modeling (MS). *Program availability:* Part-time, evening/weekend. *Faculty:* 1 part-time/adjunct (0 women). *Students:* 5 full-time (2 women), 54 part-time (21 women); includes 14 minority (3 Black or African American, non-Hispanic/Latino; 5 Asian, non-Hispanic/Latino; 5 Hispanic/Latino; 1 Two or more races, non-Hispanic/Latino), 4 international. 18 applicants, 89% accepted, 8 enrolled. *Degree requirements:* For master's, thesis; for doctorate, comprehensive exam, thesis/dissertation. *Entrance requirements:* For master's and doctorate, 3 letters of recommendation. Additional exam requirements/recommendations for international students: Required—TOEFL (minimum score 563 paper-based; 84 iBT), IELTS (minimum score 7). *Application deadline:* For fall admission, 1/1 priority date for domestic students, 1/1 for international students; for spring admission, 10/1 priority date for domestic students, 10/1 for international students. Applications are processed on a rolling basis. Application fee: $70. Electronic applications accepted. *Financial support:* Institutionally sponsored loans, scholarships/grants, and unspecified assistantships available. Financial award application deadline: 1/1; financial award applicants required to submit FAFSA. *Unit head:* Dr. Fred J. Looft, Head, 508-831-5231, Fax: 508-831-5491, E-mail: fjlooft@wpi.edu. *Application contact:* Lynne Dougherty, Administrative Assistant, 508-831-5301, Fax: 508-831-5717, E-mail: grad@wpi.edu.

Yale University, Graduate School of Arts and Sciences, School of Engineering and Applied Science, Program in Environmental Engineering, New Haven, CT 06520. Offers MS, PhD.

Youngstown State University, Graduate School, College of Science, Technology, Engineering and Mathematics, Department of Civil and Environmental Engineering, Youngstown, OH 44555-0001. Offers MSE. *Program availability:* Part-time, evening/weekend. *Degree requirements:* For master's, thesis optional. *Entrance requirements:* For master's, minimum GPA of 2.75 in field. Additional exam requirements/recommendations for international students: Required—TOEFL. *Faculty research:* Structural mechanics, water quality modeling, surface and ground water hydrology, physical and chemical processes in aquatic systems.

Fire Protection Engineering

Oklahoma State University, College of Arts and Sciences, Department of Political Science, Stillwater, OK 74078. Offers fire and emergency management administration (MS, PhD); political science (MA). *Faculty:* 23 full-time (9 women), 3 part-time/adjunct (1 woman). *Students:* 24 full-time (2 women), 46 part-time (12 women); includes 10 minority (1 Black or African American, non-Hispanic/Latino; 1 Asian, non-Hispanic/Latino; 8 Hispanic/Latino), 11 international. Average age 36. 46 applicants, 65% accepted, 20 enrolled. In 2016, 17 master's, 3 doctorates awarded. *Degree requirements:* For master's, comprehensive exam, thesis or creative component; for doctorate, comprehensive exam, thesis/dissertation. *Entrance requirements:* For master's and doctorate, GRE. Additional exam requirements/recommendations for international students: Required—TOEFL (minimum score 550 paper-based; 79 iBT). *Application deadline:* For fall admission, 3/1 priority date for international students; for spring admission, 8/1 priority date for international students. Applications are processed on a rolling basis. Application fee: $40 ($75 for international students). Electronic applications accepted. *Expenses:* Tuition, state resident: full-time $3775; part-time $209.70 per credit hour. Tuition, nonresident: full-time $14,851; part-time $825.05 per credit hour. *Required fees:* $2027; $112.60 per credit hour. Tuition and fees vary according to campus/location. *Financial support:* In 2016–17, 7 teaching assistantships (averaging $14,035 per year) were awarded; research assistantships, career-related internships or fieldwork, Federal Work-Study, scholarships/grants, health care benefits, tuition waivers (partial), and unspecified assistantships also available. Support available to part-time students. Financial award application deadline: 3/1; financial award applicants required to submit FAFSA. *Faculty research:* Fire and emergency management, environmental dispute resolution, voting and elections, women and politics, urban politics. *Unit head:* Dr. Jeanette Mendez, Department Head, 405-744-5607, E-mail: jeanette.mendez@okstate.edu.
Website: http://polsci.okstate.edu

University of Maryland, College Park, Academic Affairs, A. James Clark School of Engineering, Department of Fire Protection Engineering, College Park, MD 20742. Offers M Eng, MS. *Program availability:* Part-time, evening/weekend. *Degree requirements:* For master's, thesis optional. *Entrance requirements:* For master's, GRE General Test, minimum GPA of 3.0, BS in any engineering or physical science area, 3 letters of recommendation. Electronic applications accepted. *Faculty research:* Fire and thermal degradation of materials, fire modeling, fire dynamics, smoke detection and management, fire resistance.

University of New Haven, Graduate School, Henry C. Lee College of Criminal Justice and Forensic Sciences, Program in Fire Science, West Haven, CT 06516. Offers fire administration (MS); fire science (MS); fire/arson investigation (MS, Graduate Certificate); public safety management (MS, Graduate Certificate). *Program availability:* Part-time, evening/weekend. *Students:* 15 full-time (4 women), 2 part-time (0 women); includes 2 minority (1 Asian, non-Hispanic/Latino; 1 Hispanic/Latino), 10 international. Average age 28. 13 applicants, 100% accepted, 7 enrolled. In 2016, 10 master's, 7 other advanced degrees awarded. *Degree requirements:* For master's, thesis or alternative, research project or internship. *Entrance requirements:* Additional exam requirements/recommendations for international students: Required—TOEFL (minimum score 80 iBT), IELTS, PTE (minimum score 53). *Application deadline:* Applications are processed on a rolling basis. Application fee: $50. Electronic applications accepted. Application fee is waived when completed online. *Expenses: Tuition:* Full-time $15,660; part-time $870 per credit hour. *Required fees:* $200; $85 per term. Tuition and fees vary according to program. *Financial support:* Research assistantships with partial tuition reimbursements, teaching assistantships with partial tuition reimbursements, career-related internships or fieldwork, Federal Work-Study, scholarships/grants, and unspecified assistantships available. Support available to part-time students. Financial award applicants required to submit FAFSA. *Unit head:* Dr. Sorin Iliescu, Director, 203-932-7239, E-mail: siliescu@newhaven.edu. *Application contact:* Michelle Mason, Director of Graduate Enrollment, 203-932-7067, E-mail: mmason@newhaven.edu.
Website: http://www.newhaven.edu/5922/

The University of North Carolina at Charlotte, William States Lee College of Engineering, Department of Engineering Technology and Construction Management, Charlotte, NC 28223-0001. Offers applied energy (Graduate Certificate); applied energy and electromechanical systems (MS); construction and facilities management (MS); fire protection and administration (MS). *Program availability:* Part-time. *Faculty:* 26 full-time (5 women). *Students:* 46 full-time (8 women), 19 part-time (1 woman); includes 9 minority (4 Black or African American, non-Hispanic/Latino; 2 Asian, non-Hispanic/Latino; 3 Hispanic/Latino), 31 international. Average age 27. 71 applicants, 83% accepted, 24 enrolled. In 2016, 34 master's awarded. *Degree requirements:* For master's, thesis, capstone, or comprehensive exam. *Entrance requirements:* For

master's, GRE, minimum undergraduate GPA of 3.0, recommendations, statistics; integral and differential calculus (for students pursuing fire protection concentration or applied energy and electromechanical systems program); for Graduate Certificate, bachelor's degree in engineering, engineering technology, construction management or a closely-related technical or scientific field; undergraduate coursework of at least 3 semesters in engineering analysis or calculus; minimum GPA of 3.0. Additional exam requirements/recommendations for international students: Required—TOEFL (minimum score 523 paper-based, 70 iBT) or IELTS (6.5). *Application deadline:* For fall admission, 3/1 priority date for domestic and international students; for spring admission, 10/1 priority date for domestic and international students. Applications are processed on a rolling basis. Application fee: $75. Electronic applications accepted. *Expenses:* Contact institution. *Financial support:* In 2016–17, 22 students received support, including 22 research assistantships (averaging $8,235 per year); career-related internships or fieldwork, institutionally sponsored loans, scholarships/grants, and unspecified assistantships also available. Support available to part-time students. Financial award application deadline: 3/1; financial award applicants required to submit FAFSA. *Total annual research expenditures:* $1.5 million. *Unit head:* Dr. Anthony Brizendine, Chair, 704-687-5050, E-mail: albrizen@uncc.edu. *Application contact:* Kathy B. Giddings, Director of Graduate Admissions, 704-687-5503, Fax: 704-687-1668, E-mail: gradadm@uncc.edu.
Website: http://et.uncc.edu/

Worcester Polytechnic Institute, Graduate Studies and Research, Department of Fire Protection Engineering, Worcester, MA 01609-2280. Offers MS, PhD, Advanced Certificate, Graduate Certificate. *Program availability:* Part-time, evening/weekend, 100% online, blended/hybrid learning. *Faculty:* 4 full-time (1 woman), 2 part-time/adjunct (0 women). *Students:* 64 full-time (18 women), 33 part-time (6 women); includes 10 minority (3 Black or African American, non-Hispanic/Latino; 1 American Indian or Alaska Native, non-Hispanic/Latino; 2 Asian, non-Hispanic/Latino; 4 Hispanic/Latino), 24 international. 77 applicants, 100% accepted, 49 enrolled. In 2016, 26 master's awarded. *Degree requirements:* For master's, thesis optional; for doctorate, comprehensive exam, thesis/dissertation. *Entrance requirements:* For master's, GRE (recommended), BS in engineering or physical sciences, 3 letters of recommendation, work experience or statement of purpose; for doctorate, GRE General Test, 3 letters of recommendation, statement of purpose. Additional exam requirements/recommendations for international students: Required—TOEFL (minimum score 563 paper-based; 84 iBT), IELTS (minimum score 7), GRE. *Application deadline:* For fall admission, 1/1 priority date for domestic students, 1/1 for international students; for spring admission, 10/1 priority date for domestic students, 10/1 for international students. Applications are processed on a rolling basis. Application fee: $70. Electronic applications accepted. *Financial support:* Research assistantships, teaching assistantships, career-related internships or fieldwork, institutionally sponsored loans, scholarships/grants, and unspecified assistantships available. Financial award application deadline: 1/1; financial award applicants required to submit FAFSA. *Unit head:* Dr. Tahar El-Korchi, Head, 508-831-5593, Fax: 508-831-5862, E-mail: tek@wpi.edu. *Application contact:* Dr. Ali Rangwala, Graduate Coordinator, 508-831-5593, Fax: 508-831-5862, E-mail: rangwala@wpi.edu.
Website: http://www.wpi.edu/academics/fpe

Geotechnical Engineering

The Citadel, The Military College of South Carolina, Citadel Graduate College, School of Engineering, Department of Civil and Environmental Engineering, Charleston, SC 29409. Offers built environment and public health (Graduate Certificate); civil engineering (MS); geotechnical engineering (Graduate Certificate); structural engineering (Graduate Certificate); transportation engineering (Graduate Certificate). *Program availability:* Part-time, evening/weekend. *Faculty:* 1 full-time. *Students:* 11 part-time (1 woman); includes 1 minority (Black or African American, non-Hispanic/Latino). 8 applicants, 88% accepted, 4 enrolled. *Degree requirements:* For master's, plan of study outlining intended areas of interest and top four corresponding courses of interest. *Entrance requirements:* For master's, official transcript of baccalaureate degree from ABET-accredited engineering program or approved alternative; 2 letters of recommendation; for Graduate Certificate, official transcript of baccalaureate degree directly from an accredited college or university. Additional exam requirements/recommendations for international students: Required—TOEFL (minimum score 550 paper-based; 79 iBT). *Application deadline:* Applications are processed on a rolling basis. Application fee: $40. Electronic applications accepted. *Expenses:* Tuition, state resident: full-time $5121; part-time $569 per credit hour. Tuition, nonresident: full-time $8613; part-time $957 per credit hour. *Required fees:* $90 per term. *Financial support:* Fellowships and unspecified assistantships available. Support available to part-time students. Financial award application deadline: 7/1; financial award applicants required to submit FAFSA. *Unit head:* Dr. Kevin C. Bower, Head, 843-953-7683, E-mail: kevin.bower@citadel.edu. *Application contact:* Dr. Tara Hornor, Associate Provost for Planning, Assessment and Evaluation/Dean of Enrollment Management, 843-953-5089, E-mail: cgc@citadel.edu.
Website: http://www.citadel.edu/root/cee

Cornell University, Graduate School, Graduate Fields of Engineering, Field of Civil and Environmental Engineering, Ithaca, NY 14853. Offers engineering management (M Eng, MS, PhD); environmental engineering (M Eng, MS, PhD); environmental fluid mechanics and hydrology (M Eng, MS, PhD); environmental systems engineering (M Eng, MS, PhD); geotechnical engineering (M Eng, MS, PhD); remote sensing (M Eng, MS, PhD); structural engineering (M Eng, MS, PhD); structural mechanics (M Eng, MS); transportation engineering (MS, PhD); transportation systems engineering (M Eng); water resource systems (M Eng, MS, PhD). Terminal master's awarded for partial completion of doctoral program. *Degree requirements:* For master's, thesis (MS); for doctorate, comprehensive exam, thesis/dissertation. *Entrance requirements:* For master's and doctorate, GRE General Test (recommended), 2 letters of recommendation. Additional exam requirements/recommendations for international students: Required—TOEFL (minimum score 600 paper-based; 77 iBT). Electronic applications accepted. *Faculty research:* Environmental engineering, geotechnical engineering, remote sensing, environmental fluid mechanics and hydrology, structural engineering.

Drexel University, College of Engineering, Department of Civil, Architectural, and Environmental Engineering, Program in Geotechnical, Geoenvironmental and Geosynthetics Engineering, Philadelphia, PA 19104-2875. Offers MS, PhD. *Expenses: Tuition:* Full-time $32,184; part-time $1192 per credit hour. *Required fees:* $280. Tuition and fees vary according to campus/location and program. *Unit head:* Dr. Richard Weggel, Interim Department Head, 215-895-2355. *Application contact:* Director of Graduate Admissions, 215-895-6700, Fax: 215-895-5939, E-mail: enroll@drexel.edu.

École Polytechnique de Montréal, Graduate Programs, Department of Civil, Geological and Mining Engineering, Montréal, QC H3C 3A7, Canada. Offers civil, geological and mining engineering (DESS); environmental engineering (M Eng, M Sc A, PhD); geotechnical engineering (M Eng, M Sc A, PhD); hydraulics engineering (M Eng, M Sc A, PhD); structural engineering (M Eng, M Sc A, PhD); transportation engineering (M Eng, M Sc A, PhD). *Program availability:* Part-time. *Degree requirements:* For master's, one foreign language, thesis; for doctorate, one foreign language, thesis/dissertation. *Entrance requirements:* For master's, minimum GPA of 2.75; for doctorate, minimum GPA of 3.0. *Faculty research:* Water resources management, characteristics of building materials, aging of dams, pollution control.

Illinois Institute of Technology, Graduate College, Armour College of Engineering, Department of Civil, Architectural and Environmental Engineering, Chicago, IL 60616. Offers architectural engineering (M Arch E); civil engineering (MS, PhD), including architectural engineering (MS), construction engineering and management (MS), geoenvironmental engineering (MS), geotechnical engineering (MS), structural engineering (MS), transportation engineering (MS); construction engineering and management (MCEM); environmental engineering (M Env E, MS, PhD); geoenvironmental engineering (M Geoenv E); geotechnical engineering (MGE); infrastructure engineering and management (MPW); structural engineering (MSE); transportation engineering (M Trans E). *Program availability:* Part-time, evening/weekend, online learning. Terminal master's awarded for partial completion of doctoral program. *Degree requirements:* For master's, thesis (for some programs); for doctorate, comprehensive exam, thesis/dissertation. *Entrance requirements:* For master's, GRE General Test (minimum score 900 Quantitative and Verbal, 2.5 Analytical Writing), minimum undergraduate GPA of 3.0; for doctorate, GRE General Test (minimum score 1000 Quantitative and Verbal, 3.0 Analytical Writing), minimum undergraduate GPA of 3.0. Additional exam requirements/recommendations for international students: Required—TOEFL (minimum score 550 paper-based; 80 iBT). Electronic applications accepted. *Faculty research:* Structural, architectural, geotechnical and geoenvironmental engineering; construction engineering and management; transportation engineering; environmental engineering and public works.

Iowa State University of Science and Technology, Department of Civil and Construction Engineering, Ames, IA 50011. Offers civil engineering (MS, PhD), including civil engineering materials, construction engineering and management, environmental engineering, geotechnical engineering, structural engineering, transportation engineering. *Degree requirements:* For master's, thesis or alternative; for doctorate, thesis/dissertation. *Entrance requirements:* For master's and doctorate, GRE General Test. Additional exam requirements/recommendations for international students: Required—TOEFL (minimum score 550 paper-based; 82 iBT), IELTS (minimum score 6.5). *Application deadline:* For fall admission, 2/1 priority date for domestic students, 2/1 for international students; for spring admission, 8/1 priority date for domestic students, 8/1 for international students. Application fee: $60 ($90 for international students). Electronic applications accepted. *Application contact:* Kathy Petersen, Application Contact, 515-294-4975, Fax: 515-294-8216, E-mail: ccee-grad-inquiry@iastate.edu.
Website: http://www.ccee.iastate.edu/

Kansas State University, Graduate School, College of Engineering, Department of Civil Engineering, Manhattan, KS 66506. Offers civil engineering (MS, PhD); environmental engineering (MS, PhD); geotechnical engineering (MS, PhD); structural engineering (MS, PhD); transportation engineering (MS, PhD); water resources engineering (MS, PhD). *Program availability:* Part-time, evening/weekend, online learning. *Faculty:* 14 full-time (4 women), 3 part-time/adjunct (1 woman). *Students:* 36 full-time (11 women), 34 part-time (7 women); includes 5 minority (2 Asian, non-Hispanic/Latino; 2 Hispanic/Latino; 1 Two or more races, non-Hispanic/Latino), 28 international. Average age 29. 70 applicants, 60% accepted, 11 enrolled. In 2016, 21 master's, 7 doctorates awarded. *Degree requirements:* For master's, thesis or alternative; for doctorate, thesis/dissertation. *Entrance requirements:* For master's, GRE General Test, bachelor's degree or course work in related engineering fields; for doctorate, GRE General Test. Additional exam requirements/recommendations for international students: Required—TOEFL (minimum score 550 paper-based; 79 iBT). *Application deadline:* For fall admission, 2/1 priority date for domestic students, 1/1 priority date for international students; for spring admission, 8/1 priority date for domestic and international students. Applications are processed on a rolling basis. Application fee: $50 ($75 for international students). Electronic applications accepted. *Expenses:* Tuition, state resident: full-time $9670. Tuition, nonresident: full-time $21,828. *Required fees:* $862. *Financial support:* In 2016–17, 19 research assistantships with partial tuition reimbursements (averaging $13,431 per year), 12 teaching assistantships with partial tuition reimbursements (averaging $15,058 per year) were awarded; institutionally sponsored loans and scholarships/grants also available. Support available to part-time students. Financial award application deadline: 3/1; financial award applicants required to submit FAFSA. *Faculty research:* Transportation and materials engineering, water resources engineering, environmental engineering, geotechnical engineering, structural engineering. *Total annual research expenditures:* $2.4 million. *Unit head:* Dr. Robert Stokes, Head, 785-532-1595, Fax: 785-532-7717, E-mail: drbobb@k-state.edu. *Application contact:* Dr. Dunja Peric, Graduate Coordinator, 785-532-2468, Fax: 785-532-7717, E-mail: peric@k-state.edu.
Website: http://www.ce.ksu.edu/

Louisiana State University and Agricultural & Mechanical College, Graduate School, College of Engineering, Department of Civil and Environmental Engineering, Baton Rouge, LA 70803. Offers environmental engineering (MSCE, PhD); geotechnical engineering (MSCE, PhD); structural engineering and mechanics (MSCE, PhD); transportation engineering (MSCE, PhD); water resources (MSCE, PhD).

Massachusetts Institute of Technology, School of Engineering, Department of Civil and Environmental Engineering, Cambridge, MA 02139. Offers biological oceanography (PhD, Sc D); chemical oceanography (PhD, Sc D); civil and environmental engineering (M Eng, SM, PhD, Sc D); civil and environmental systems (PhD, Sc D); civil engineering (PhD, Sc D, CE); civil engineering and computation (PhD); coastal engineering (PhD, Sc D); construction engineering and management (PhD, Sc D); environmental biology (PhD, Sc D); environmental chemistry (PhD, Sc D); environmental engineering (PhD, Sc D); environmental engineering and computation (PhD); environmental fluid mechanics (PhD, Sc D); geotechnical and geoenvironmental engineering (PhD, Sc D); hydrology (PhD, Sc D); information technology (PhD, Sc D); oceanographic engineering (PhD, Sc D); structures and materials (PhD, Sc D); transportation (PhD, Sc D); SM/MBA. *Faculty:* 35 full-time (6 women). *Students:* 192 full-time (64 women); includes 25 minority (2 Black or African American, non-Hispanic/Latino; 11 Asian, non-Hispanic/Latino; 8 Hispanic/Latino; 4 Two or more races, non-Hispanic/Latino), 113 international. Average age 27. 530 applicants, 20% accepted, 77 enrolled. In 2016, 56 master's, 16

doctorates, 1 other advanced degree awarded. *Degree requirements:* For master's, thesis; for doctorate, comprehensive exam, thesis/dissertation; for CE, comprehensive exam, thesis. *Entrance requirements:* For master's, doctorate, and CE, GRE General Test. Additional exam requirements/recommendations for international students: Required—TOEFL, IELTS. *Application deadline:* For fall admission, 12/15 for domestic and international students. Application fee: $75. Electronic applications accepted. *Expenses: Tuition:* Full-time $46,400; part-time $725 per credit. One-time fee: $312 full-time. Full-time tuition and fees vary according to course load and program. *Financial support:* In 2016–17, 150 students received support, including fellowships (averaging $41,900 per year), 124 research assistantships (averaging $36,900 per year), 9 teaching assistantships (averaging $36,900 per year); Federal Work-Study, institutionally sponsored loans, scholarships/grants, traineeships, health care benefits, unspecified assistantships, and resident tutors also available. Support available to part-time students. Financial award application deadline: 5/1; financial award applicants required to submit FAFSA. *Faculty research:* Environmental chemistry, environmental fluid mechanics and coastal engineering, environmental microbiology, geotechnical engineering and geomechanics, hydrology and hydro climatology, infrastructure systems, mechanics of materials and structures, transportation systems. *Total annual research expenditures:* $25 million. *Unit head:* Prof. Markus Buehler, Department Head, 617-253-7101. *Application contact:* 617-253-7119, E-mail: cee-admissions@mit.edu.
Website: http://cee.mit.edu/

McGill University, Faculty of Graduate and Postdoctoral Studies, Faculty of Engineering, Department of Civil Engineering and Applied Mechanics, Montréal, QC H3A 2T5, Canada. Offers environmental engineering (M Eng, M Sc, PhD); fluid mechanics (M Sc); fluid mechanics and hydraulic engineering (M Eng, PhD); materials engineering (M Eng, PhD); rehabilitation of urban infrastructure (M Eng, PhD); soil behavior (M Eng, PhD); soil mechanics and foundations (M Eng, PhD); structures and structural mechanics (M Eng, PhD); water resources (M Sc); water resources engineering (M Eng, PhD).

Missouri University of Science and Technology, Graduate School, Department of Civil, Architectural, and Environmental Engineering, Rolla, MO 65409. Offers civil engineering (MS, DE, PhD); construction engineering (MS, DE, PhD); environmental engineering (MS); fluid mechanics (MS, DE, PhD); geotechnical engineering (MS, DE, PhD); hydrology and hydraulic engineering (MS, DE, PhD). *Program availability:* Part-time, evening/weekend. Terminal master's awarded for partial completion of doctoral program. *Degree requirements:* For master's, thesis optional; for doctorate, comprehensive exam, thesis/dissertation. *Entrance requirements:* For master's, GRE General Test (minimum combined score 1100), minimum GPA of 3.0; for doctorate, GRE General Test (minimum score: verbal and quantitative 400, writing 3.5), minimum GPA of 3.0. Additional exam requirements/recommendations for international students: Required—TOEFL (minimum score 550 paper-based). Electronic applications accepted. *Faculty research:* Earthquake engineering, structural optimization and control systems, structural health monitoring/damage detection, soil-structure interaction, soil mechanics and foundation engineering.

Northwestern University, McCormick School of Engineering and Applied Science, Department of Civil and Environmental Engineering, Evanston, IL 60208-3109. Offers environmental engineering and science (MS, PhD); geotechnical engineering (MS, PhD); mechanics of materials and solids (MS, PhD); project management (MS); structural engineering and materials (MS, PhD); transportation systems analysis and planning (MS, PhD). MS and PhD admissions and degrees offered through The Graduate School. *Program availability:* Part-time. Terminal master's awarded for partial completion of doctoral program. *Degree requirements:* For master's, comprehensive exam (for some programs), thesis (for some programs); for doctorate, comprehensive exam, thesis/dissertation. *Entrance requirements:* For master's and doctorate, GRE General Test, minimum 2 letters of recommendation, transcripts from all academic institutions attended. Additional exam requirements/recommendations for international students: Required—TOEFL (minimum score 577 paper-based; 90 iBT), IELTS (minimum score 7). Electronic applications accepted. *Faculty research:* Environmental engineering and science, geotechnics, mechanics, materials, structures, and transportation systems analysis and planning.

Norwich University, College of Graduate and Continuing Studies, Master of Civil Engineering Program, Northfield, VT 05663. Offers construction management (MCE); environmental (MCE); geotechnical (MCE); structural (MCE). *Program availability:* Evening/weekend, online only, mostly all online with a week-long residency requirement. *Faculty:* 1 full-time (0 women), 11 part-time/adjunct (1 woman). *Students:* 70 full-time (17 women); includes 28 minority (16 Black or African American, non-Hispanic/Latino; 4 Asian, non-Hispanic/Latino; 5 Hispanic/Latino; 1 Native Hawaiian or other Pacific Islander, non-Hispanic/Latino; 2 Two or more races, non-Hispanic/Latino), 1 international. Average age 36. 35 applicants, 97% accepted, 18 enrolled. In 2016, 63 master's awarded. *Degree requirements:* For master's, capstone. *Entrance requirements:* For master's, minimum undergraduate GPA of 2.75. Additional exam requirements/recommendations for international students: Required—TOEFL (minimum score 550 paper-based; 80 iBT), IELTS (minimum score 6.5). *Application deadline:* For fall admission, 8/14 for domestic and international students; for spring admission, 2/12 for domestic and international students. Electronic applications accepted. *Expenses:* Contact institution. *Financial support:* In 2016–17, 10 students received support. Scholarships/grants available. Financial award application deadline: 8/4; financial award applicants required to submit FAFSA. *Unit head:* Dr. Thomas Descoteaux, Program Director, 802-485-2730, Fax: 802-485-2533, E-mail: tdescote@norwich.edu. *Application contact:* Admissions Advisor, 800-460-5597 Ext. 3369, Fax: 802-485-2533, E-mail: mce@online.norwich.edu.
Website: https://online.norwich.edu/degree-programs/masters/master-civil-engineering/overview

Ohio University, Graduate College, Russ College of Engineering and Technology, Department of Civil Engineering, Athens, OH 45701-2979. Offers civil engineering (PhD); construction engineering and management (MS); environmental (MS); geotechnical and geoenvironmental (MS); mechanics (MS); structures (MS); transportation (MS); water resources (MS). *Program availability:* Part-time. *Degree requirements:* For master's, comprehensive exam (for some programs), thesis or alternative; for doctorate, comprehensive exam, thesis/dissertation. *Entrance requirements:* For master's, GRE General Test, minimum GPA of 3.0, 3 letters of recommendation; for doctorate, GRE General Test. Additional exam requirements/recommendations for international students: Required—TOEFL (minimum score 550 paper-based; 80 iBT) or IELTS (minimum score 6.5). *Application deadline:* For fall admission, 5/1 priority date for domestic students, 2/1 priority date for international students; for winter admission, 8/1 priority date for domestic students, 4/1 priority date for international students; for spring admission, 2/1 priority date for domestic students, 7/1 priority date for international students. Applications are processed on a rolling basis. Application fee: $50 ($55 for international students). Electronic applications accepted. *Financial support:* Research assistantships with full tuition reimbursements, teaching assistantships with full tuition reimbursements, Federal Work-Study, institutionally sponsored loans, scholarships/grants, and unspecified assistantships available. Financial award application deadline: 3/15; financial award applicants required to submit FAFSA. *Faculty research:* Noise abatement, materials and environment, highway infrastructure, subsurface investigation (pavements, pipes, bridges). *Unit head:* Dr. Gayle F. Mitchell, Chair, 740-593-0430, Fax: 740-593-0625, E-mail: mitchelg@ohio.edu. *Application contact:* Dr. Shad M. Sargand, Graduate Chair, 740-593-1465, Fax: 740-593-0625, E-mail: sargand@ohio.edu.
Website: http://www.ohio.edu/civil/

Old Dominion University, Frank Batten College of Engineering and Technology, Program in Civil Engineering, Norfolk, VA 23529. Offers civil engineering (ME, MS), including coastal engineering, geotechnical engineering, hydraulics and water resources, structural engineering, transportation engineering. *Program availability:* Part-time, evening/weekend, blended/hybrid learning. *Faculty:* 16 full-time (1 woman), 5 part-time/adjunct (0 women). *Students:* 12 full-time (4 women), 30 part-time (6 women); includes 7 minority (2 Black or African American, non-Hispanic/Latino; 4 Hispanic/Latino; 1 Two or more races, non-Hispanic/Latino), 8 international. Average age 28. 79 applicants, 84% accepted, 33 enrolled. In 2016, 15 master's awarded. *Degree requirements:* For master's, comprehensive exam, thesis optional. *Entrance requirements:* For master's, GRE, minimum GPA of 3.0. Additional exam requirements/recommendations for international students: Required—TOEFL (minimum score 550 paper-based, 80 iBT) or IELTS (6.5). *Application deadline:* For fall admission, 6/1 priority date for domestic students, 4/15 priority date for international students; for spring admission, 11/1 priority date for domestic students, 10/1 priority date for international students. Applications are processed on a rolling basis. Application fee: $50. Electronic applications accepted. *Expenses:* Contact institution. *Financial support:* In 2016–17, 26 students received support, including 1 fellowship with full tuition reimbursement available (averaging $18,000 per year), 17 research assistantships with full and partial tuition reimbursements available (averaging $16,800 per year), 9 teaching assistantships with full and partial tuition reimbursements available (averaging $15,215 per year); scholarships/grants and health care benefits also available. Support available to part-time students. Financial award application deadline: 4/1; financial award applicants required to submit FAFSA. *Faculty research:* Structural engineering, coastal engineering, geotechnical engineering, water resources, transportation engineering. *Total annual research expenditures:* $937,914. *Unit head:* Dr. Isao Ishibashi, Graduate Program Director, 757-683-4641, E-mail: cegpd@odu.edu. *Application contact:* Dr. Shirshak Dhali, Associate Dean, 757-683-3744, Fax: 757-683-4898, E-mail: sdhali@odu.edu.
Website: http://eng.odu.edu/cee/

Oregon State University, College of Engineering, Program in Civil Engineering, Corvallis, OR 97331. Offers civil engineering (M Eng, MS, PhD); coastal and ocean engineering (M Eng, MS, PhD); construction engineering management (M Eng, MS, PhD); engineering education (M Eng, MS, PhD); geomatics (M Eng, MS, PhD); geotechnical engineering (M Eng, MS, PhD); infrastructure materials (M Eng, MS, PhD); structural engineering (M Eng, MS, PhD); transportation engineering (M Eng). *Faculty:* 42 full-time (8 women), 2 part-time/adjunct (0 women). *Students:* 157 full-time (48 women), 10 part-time (3 women); includes 18 minority (7 Asian, non-Hispanic/Latino; 7 Hispanic/Latino; 1 Native Hawaiian or other Pacific Islander, non-Hispanic/Latino; 3 Two or more races, non-Hispanic/Latino), 92 international. Average age 28. 379 applicants, 31% accepted, 50 enrolled. In 2016, 55 master's, 5 doctorates awarded. *Entrance requirements:* For master's and doctorate, GRE. Additional exam requirements/recommendations for international students: Required—TOEFL (minimum score 80 iBT), IELTS (minimum score 6.5). *Application deadline:* For fall admission, 8/1 for domestic students, 4/1 for international students; for winter admission, 12/1 for domestic students, 7/1 for international students; for spring admission, 2/1 for domestic students, 10/1 for international students; for summer admission, 5/1 for domestic students, 1/1 for international students. Application fee: $75 ($85 for international students). *Expenses:* $14,130 resident full-time tuition, $23,769 non-resident. *Financial support:* Application deadline: 1/15. *Unit head:* Dr. Jason Weiss, School Head/Professor. *Application contact:* Shannon Reed, Graduate Program Coordinator, 541-737-4575, E-mail: shannon.reed@oregonstate.edu.
Website: http://cce.oregonstate.edu/graduate-academics

Penn State University Park, Graduate School, College of Earth and Mineral Sciences, John and Willie Leone Family Department of Energy and Mineral Engineering, University Park, PA 16802. Offers MS, PhD. *Unit head:* Dr. William E. Easterling, III, Dean, 814-865-7482, Fax: 814-863-7708. *Application contact:* Lori Hawn, Director, Graduate Student Services, 814-865-1795, Fax: 814-863-4627, E-mail: l-gswww@lists.psu.edu.
Website: http://eme.psu.edu/

Southern Illinois University Edwardsville, Graduate School, School of Engineering, Department of Civil Engineering, Program in Geotechnical Engineering, Edwardsville, IL 62026. Offers MS. *Program availability:* Part-time, evening/weekend. *Degree requirements:* For master's, thesis (for some programs), research paper. *Entrance requirements:* For master's, minimum undergraduate GPA of 2.75 in science, math, and engineering courses. Additional exam requirements/recommendations for international students: Required—TOEFL (minimum score 550 paper-based, 79 iBT), IELTS (minimum score 6.5), Michigan Test of English Language Proficiency or PTE. Electronic applications accepted.

Stanford University, School of Engineering, Department of Civil and Environmental Engineering, Stanford, CA 94305-2004. Offers atmosphere and energy (MS, PhD); construction (MS), including construction engineering and management, design-construction integration, sustainable design and construction; environmental engineering and science (MS, PhD, Eng); environmental fluid mechanics and hydrology (PhD); geomechanics (MS); structural engineering (MS). Terminal master's awarded for partial completion of doctoral program. *Degree requirements:* For doctorate, thesis/dissertation, qualifying exam; for Eng, thesis. *Entrance requirements:* For master's, doctorate, and Eng, GRE General Test. Additional exam requirements/recommendations for international students: Required—TOEFL. Electronic applications accepted. *Expenses: Tuition:* Full-time $47,331. *Required fees:* $609.

Tufts University, School of Engineering, Department of Civil and Environmental Engineering, Medford, MA 02155. Offers bioengineering (ME, MS), including environmental technology; civil engineering (ME, MS, PhD), including geotechnical engineering, structural engineering, water diplomacy (PhD); environmental engineering (ME, MS, PhD), including environmental engineering and environmental sciences, environmental geotechnology, environmental health, environmental science and management, hazardous materials management, water diplomacy (PhD), water resources engineering. *Program availability:* Part-time. Terminal master's awarded for partial completion of doctoral program. *Degree requirements:* For master's, thesis or alternative; for doctorate, thesis/dissertation. *Entrance requirements:* For master's and doctorate, GRE General Test. Additional exam requirements/recommendations for international students: Required—TOEFL (minimum score 550 paper-based; 80 iBT), IELTS (minimum score 6.5). Electronic applications accepted. *Expenses: Tuition:* Full-time $49,892; part-time $1248 per credit hour. *Required fees:* $844. Full-time tuition and fees vary according to degree level, program and student level. Part-time tuition and fees vary according to course load. *Faculty research:* Environmental and water resources engineering, environmental health, geotechnical and geoenvironmental engineering, structural engineering and mechanics, water diplomacy.

University of Alberta, Faculty of Graduate Studies and Research, Department of Civil and Environmental Engineering, Edmonton, AB T6G 2E1, Canada. Offers construction engineering and management (M Eng, M Sc, PhD); environmental engineering (M Eng, M Sc, PhD); environmental science (M Sc, PhD); geoenvironmental engineering (M Eng, M Sc, PhD); geotechnical engineering (M Eng, M Sc, PhD); mining engineering (M Eng, M Sc, PhD); petroleum engineering (M Eng, M Sc, PhD); structural engineering (M Eng, M Sc, PhD); water resources (M Eng, M Sc, PhD). *Program availability:* Part-time, online learning. *Degree requirements:* For master's, thesis (for some programs); for doctorate, thesis/dissertation. *Entrance requirements:* For master's, minimum GPA of 3.0 in last 2 years of undergraduate studies; for doctorate, minimum GPA of 3.0. Additional exam requirements/recommendations for international students: Required—TOEFL (minimum score 550 paper-based). Electronic applications accepted. *Faculty research:* Mining.

University of Calgary, Faculty of Graduate Studies, Schulich School of Engineering, Department of Civil Engineering, Calgary, AB T2N 1N4, Canada. Offers avalanche mechanics (M Sc, PhD); civil engineering (M Eng, M Sc, PhD); energy and environment engineering (M Eng, M Sc, PhD); environmental engineering (M Eng, M Sc, PhD); geotechnical engineering (M Eng, M Sc, PhD); materials science (M Eng, M Sc, PhD); project management (M Eng, M Sc, PhD); structures and solid mechanics (M Eng, M Sc, PhD); transportation engineering (M Eng, M Sc, PhD); water resources (M Eng, M Sc, PhD). *Program availability:* Part-time. *Degree requirements:* For master's, thesis; for doctorate, thesis/dissertation, written and oral candidacy exam. *Entrance requirements:* For master's, minimum GPA of 3.0; for doctorate, minimum GPA of 3.5. Additional exam requirements/recommendations for international students: Required—TOEFL (minimum score 580 paper-based; 93 iBT), IELTS (minimum score 7). Electronic applications accepted. *Faculty research:* Geotechnical engineering, energy and environment, transportation, project management, structures and solid mechanics.

University of Calgary, Faculty of Graduate Studies, Schulich School of Engineering, Department of Geomatics Engineering, Calgary, AB T2N 1N4, Canada. Offers M Eng, M Sc, PhD. *Program availability:* Part-time. *Degree requirements:* For master's, thesis (for some programs), minimum of 4 half-courses, completion of seminar course; for doctorate, comprehensive exam, thesis/dissertation, minimum of 3 half-courses, completion of two seminar courses, candidacy exam. *Entrance requirements:* For master's, B Sc or equivalent with minimum GPA of 3.0; for doctorate, M Sc or transfer from M Sc program with minimum GPA of 3.5. Additional exam requirements/recommendations for international students: Required—TOEFL (minimum score 550 paper-based; 80 iBT) or IELTS (minimum score 7). Electronic applications accepted. *Faculty research:* Digital imaging systems, earth observation, geospatial information systems, and land tenure positioning, navigation and wireless location.

University of California, Berkeley, Graduate Division, College of Engineering, Department of Civil and Environmental Engineering, Berkeley, CA 94720-1500. Offers engineering and project management (M Eng, MS, PhD); environmental engineering (M Eng, MS, PhD); geoengineering (M Eng, MS, PhD); structural engineering, mechanics and materials (M Eng, MS, PhD); transportation engineering (M Eng, MS, PhD); M Arch/MS; MCP/MS; MPP/MS. *Students:* 360 full-time (143 women); includes 71 minority (15 Black or African American, non-Hispanic/Latino; 39 Asian, non-Hispanic/Latino; 17 Hispanic/Latino), 148 international. Average age 27. 1,086 applicants, 185 enrolled. In 2016, 188 master's, 26 doctorates awarded. Terminal master's awarded for partial completion of doctoral program. *Degree requirements:* For master's, comprehensive exam (for some programs), thesis (for some programs), comprehensive exam or thesis (MS); for doctorate, thesis/dissertation, qualifying exam. *Entrance requirements:* For master's, GRE General Test, minimum GPA of 3.0, 3 letters of recommendation; for doctorate, GRE General Test, minimum GPA of 3.5, 3 letters of recommendation. Additional exam requirements/recommendations for international students: Required—TOEFL (minimum score 570 paper-based; 90 iBT). *Application deadline:* For fall admission, 12/16 for domestic students. Application fee: $105 ($125 for international students). Electronic applications accepted. *Financial support:* Applicants required to submit FAFSA. *Unit head:* Prof. Robert Harley, Chair, 510-643-8739, Fax: 510-643-5264, E-mail: chair@ce.berkeley.edu. *Application contact:* Shelly Okimoto, Graduate Advisor, 510-642-6464, Fax: 510-643-5264, E-mail: aao@ce.berkeley.edu.
Website: http://www.ce.berkeley.edu/

University of Colorado Denver, College of Engineering and Applied Science, Department of Civil Engineering, Denver, CO 80217. Offers civil engineering (EASPh D); civil engineering systems (PhD); environmental and sustainability engineering (MS, PhD); geographic information systems (MS); geotechnical engineering (MS, PhD); hydrology and hydraulics (MS, PhD); structural engineering (MS, PhD); transportation engineering (MS, PhD). *Program availability:* Part-time, evening/weekend. *Faculty:* 15 full-time (3 women), 9 part-time/adjunct (0 women). *Students:* 50 full-time (15 women), 33 part-time (7 women); includes 10 minority (1 Black or African American, non-Hispanic/Latino; 2 Asian, non-Hispanic/Latino; 6 Hispanic/Latino; 1 Two or more races, non-Hispanic/Latino), 31 international. Average age 30. 105 applicants, 51% accepted, 14 enrolled. In 2016, 29 master's, 2 doctorates awarded. *Degree requirements:* For master's, comprehensive exam, 30 credit hours, project or thesis; for doctorate, comprehensive exam, thesis/dissertation, 60 credit hours (30 of which are dissertation research). *Entrance requirements:* For master's, GRE, statement of purpose, transcripts, three references; for doctorate, GRE, statement of purpose, transcripts, references, letter of support from faculty stating willingness to serve as dissertation advisor and outlining plan for financial support. Additional exam requirements/recommendations for international students: Required—TOEFL (minimum score 537 paper-based; 75 iBT); Recommended—IELTS (minimum score 6.5). *Application deadline:* For fall admission, 5/1 for domestic students, 4/1 for international students; for spring admission, 10/1 for domestic students, 9/1 for international students; for summer admission, 2/15 for domestic students, 1/15 for international students. Application fee: $50 ($75 for international students). Electronic applications accepted. *Expenses:* Contact institution. *Financial support:* In 2016–17, 62 students received support. Fellowships, research assistantships, teaching assistantships, career-related internships or fieldwork, Federal Work-Study, institutionally sponsored loans, scholarships/grants, traineeships, and unspecified assistantships available. Financial award application deadline: 4/1; financial award applicants required to submit FAFSA. *Faculty research:* Earthquake source physics, environmental biotechnology, hydrologic and hydraulic engineering, sustainability assessments, transportation energy use and greenhouse gas emissions. *Unit head:* Dr. Kevin Rens, Chair, 303-556-8017, E-mail: kevin.rens@ucdenver.edu. *Application contact:* Roxanne Pizano, Program Coordinator, 303-556-6274, E-mail: roxanne.pizano@ucdenver.edu.
Website: http://www.ucdenver.edu/academics/colleges/Engineering/Programs/Civil-Engineering/Pages/CivilEngineering.aspx

University of Dayton, Department of Civil and Environmental Engineering and Engineering Mechanics, Dayton, OH 45469. Offers engineering mechanics (MSEM); environmental engineering (MSCE); geotechnical engineering (MSCE); structural engineering (MSCE); transportation engineering (MSCE); water resources engineering (MSCE). *Program availability:* Part-time, evening/weekend. *Faculty:* 9 full-time (2 women), 3 part-time/adjunct (1 woman). *Students:* 40 full-time (8 women), 2 part-time (0 women); includes 1 minority (Asian, non-Hispanic/Latino), 30 international. Average age 26. 137 applicants, 17% accepted. In 2016, 14 master's awarded. *Degree requirements:* For master's, thesis optional. *Entrance requirements:* For master's, minimum GPA of 3.0 in undergraduate work. Additional exam requirements/recommendations for international students: Required—TOEFL (minimum score 550 paper-based; 80 iBT); Recommended—IELTS. *Application deadline:* For fall admission, 8/1 priority date for domestic students, 5/1 priority date for international students; for spring admission, 11/1 priority date for international students. Applications are processed on a rolling basis. Application fee: $0 ($50 for international students). Electronic applications accepted. *Expenses:* $890 per credit hour, $25 registration fee. *Financial support:* Research assistantships, institutionally sponsored loans, scholarships/grants, and department-funded awards (averaging $2448 per year) available. Financial award application deadline: 3/1; financial award applicants required to submit FAFSA. *Faculty research:* Vertically-aligned carbon nanotubes infiltrated with temperature-responsive polymers; smart nanocomposite films for self-cleaning and controlled release; bilayer and bulk heterojunction solar cells using liquid crystalline porphyrins as donors by solution processing; DNA damage induced by multiwalled carbon nanotubes in mouse embryonic stem cells. *Total annual research expenditures:* $250,000. *Unit head:* Dr. Donald V. Chase, Chair, 937-229-3847, Fax: 937-229-3491, E-mail: dchase1@udayton.edu. *Application contact:* 937-229-4462, E-mail: graduateadmission@udayton.edu.
Website: https://www.udayton.edu/engineering/departments/civil/index.php

University of Delaware, College of Engineering, Department of Civil and Environmental Engineering, Newark, DE 19716. Offers environmental engineering (MAS, MCE, PhD); geotechnical engineering (MAS, MCE, PhD); ocean engineering (MAS, MCE, PhD); structural engineering (MAS, MCE, PhD); transportation engineering (MAS, MCE, PhD); water resource engineering (MAS, MCE, PhD). *Program availability:* Part-time. Terminal master's awarded for partial completion of doctoral program. *Degree requirements:* For master's, thesis; for doctorate, thesis/dissertation. *Entrance requirements:* For master's and doctorate, GRE General Test. Additional exam requirements/recommendations for international students: Required—TOEFL. Electronic applications accepted. *Faculty research:* Structural engineering and mechanics; transportation engineering; ocean engineering; soil mechanics and foundation; water resources and environmental engineering.

University of Massachusetts Amherst, Graduate School, College of Engineering, Department of Civil and Environmental Engineering, Amherst, MA 01003. Offers civil engineering (MSCE, PhD); environmental and water resources engineering (MSCE); geotechnical engineering (MSCE); structural engineering and mechanics (MSCE); transportation engineering (MSCE). *Program availability:* Part-time. Terminal master's awarded for partial completion of doctoral program. *Degree requirements:* For master's, thesis or alternative; for doctorate, comprehensive exam, thesis/dissertation. *Entrance requirements:* For master's and doctorate, GRE General Test. Additional exam requirements/recommendations for international students: Required—TOEFL (minimum score 550 paper-based; 80 iBT), IELTS (minimum score 6.5). Electronic applications accepted.

University of Memphis, Graduate School, Herff College of Engineering, Department of Civil Engineering, Memphis, TN 38152. Offers civil engineering (PhD); engineering seismology (MS); environmental engineering (MS); freight transportation (Graduate Certificate); geotechnical engineering (MS); structural engineering (MS); transportation engineering (MS); water resources engineering (MS). *Faculty:* 12 full-time (1 woman). *Students:* 10 full-time (3 women), 15 part-time (3 women); includes 3 minority (2 Black or African American, non-Hispanic/Latino; 1 Two or more races, non-Hispanic/Latino), 9 international. Average age 29. 29 applicants, 69% accepted, 8 enrolled. In 2016, 5 master's awarded. Terminal master's awarded for partial completion of doctoral program. *Degree requirements:* For master's, comprehensive exam, thesis optional; for doctorate, comprehensive exam, thesis/dissertation. *Entrance requirements:* For master's, GRE General Test, minimum undergraduate GPA of 2.5; bachelor's degree in engineering or a related science or mathematics program; three letters of reference; for doctorate, GRE General Test, bachelor's degree in engineering or engineering science; three letters of reference; for Graduate Certificate, minimum undergraduate GPA of 2.75; bachelor's degree in engineering or engineering science. Additional exam requirements/recommendations for international students: Required—TOEFL (minimum score 550 paper-based; 79 iBT). *Application deadline:* For fall admission, 8/1 for domestic students; for spring admission, 12/1 for domestic students. Application fee: $35 ($60 for international students). Electronic applications accepted. *Expenses:* $5,231.50 per semester full-time in-state, $9,623.50 full-time out-of-state. *Financial support:* In 2016–17, 6 students received support, including 31 fellowships with full tuition reimbursements available (averaging $12,012 per year); research assistantships with full tuition reimbursements available, career-related internships or fieldwork, Federal Work-Study, scholarships/grants, and unspecified assistantships also available. Financial award application deadline: 2/1; financial award applicants required to submit FAFSA. *Faculty research:* Structural response to earthquakes, pavement design, water quality, transportation safety, intermodal transportation. *Unit head:* Dr. Sharam Pezeshk, Chair, 901-678-2746, Fax: 901-678-3026. *Application contact:* Dr. Roger Meier, Coordinator of Graduate Studies, 901-678-3284, E-mail: rwmeier@memphis.edu.
Website: http://www.ce.memphis.edu

University of Missouri, Office of Research and Graduate Studies, College of Engineering, Department of Civil and Environmental Engineering, Columbia, MO 65211. Offers civil engineering (MS, PhD); environmental engineering (MS, PhD); geotechnical engineering (MS, PhD); structural engineering (MS, PhD); transportation and highway engineering (MS); water resources (MS, PhD). *Faculty:* 16 full-time (3 women), 2 part-time/adjunct (1 woman). *Students:* 41 full-time (8 women), 30 part-time (8 women). *Degree requirements:* For master's, report or thesis; for doctorate, thesis/dissertation. *Entrance requirements:* For master's and doctorate, GRE General Test. Additional exam requirements/recommendations for international students: Required—TOEFL (minimum score 550 paper-based; 80 iBT). *Application deadline:* For fall admission, 2/15 priority date for domestic students, 2/15 for international students; for winter admission, 9/15 priority date for domestic students, 9/15 for international students. Application fee: $75 ($90 for international students). *Expenses:* Tuition, state resident: full-time $6347; part-time $352.60 per credit hour. Tuition, nonresident: full-time $17,379; part-time $965.50 per credit hour. *Required fees:* $1035. Tuition and fees vary according to course load, campus/location and program. *Financial support:* Fellowships, research assistantships, teaching assistantships, and institutionally sponsored loans available.
Website: http://engineering.missouri.edu/civil/

University of New Brunswick Fredericton, School of Graduate Studies, Faculty of Engineering, Department of Civil Engineering, Fredericton, NB E3B 5A3, Canada. Offers construction engineering and management (M Eng, M Sc E, PhD); environmental engineering (M Eng, M Sc E, PhD); environmental studies (M Eng); geotechnical engineering (M Eng, M Sc E, PhD); groundwater/hydrology (M Eng, M Sc E, PhD); materials (M Eng, M Sc E, PhD); pavements (M Eng, M Sc E, PhD); structures (M Eng, M Sc E, PhD); transportation (M Eng, M Sc E, PhD). *Program availability:* Part-time.

Degree requirements: For master's, thesis; for doctorate, comprehensive exam, thesis/dissertation, qualifying exam; 27 credit hours of courses. *Entrance requirements:* For master's, minimum GPA of 3.0; B Sc E in civil engineering or related engineering degree; for doctorate, minimum GPA of 3.0; graduate degree in engineering or applied science. Additional exam requirements/recommendations for international students: Required—IELTS (minimum score 7.5), TWE (minimum score 4), Michigan English Language Assessment Battery (minimum score 85) or CanTest (minimum score 4.5); Recommended—TOEFL (minimum score 580 paper-based). Electronic applications accepted. *Faculty research:* Construction engineering and management; engineering materials and infrastructure renewal; highway and pavement research; structures and solid mechanics; geotechnical and geoenvironmental engineering; structure interaction; transportation and planning; environment, solid waste management; structural engineering; water and environmental engineering.

University of Puerto Rico, Mayagüez Campus, Graduate Studies, College of Engineering, Department of Civil Engineering and Surveying, Mayagüez, PR 00681-9000. Offers civil engineering (ME, MS, PhD), including construction engineering and management (ME, MS), environmental engineering, geotechnical engineering (ME, MS), structural engineering, transportation engineering. *Program availability:* Part-time. *Faculty:* 37 full-time (7 women), 2 part-time/adjunct (0 women). *Students:* 118 full-time (37 women), 9 part-time (2 women); includes 110 minority (all Hispanic/Latino), 17 international. Average age 25. 35 applicants, 94% accepted, 16 enrolled. In 2016, 26 master's, 2 doctorates awarded. Terminal master's awarded for partial completion of doctoral program. *Degree requirements:* For master's, one foreign language, thesis; for doctorate, one foreign language, comprehensive exam, thesis/dissertation, qualifying exams. *Entrance requirements:* For master's, proficiency in English and Spanish; BS in civil engineering or its equivalent; for doctorate, proficiency in English and Spanish. *Application deadline:* For fall admission, 2/15 for domestic and international students; for spring admission, 9/15 for domestic and international students. Applications are processed on a rolling basis. Application fee: $25. Electronic applications accepted. *Expenses: Tuition, area resident:* Full-time $2466. *International tuition:* $7166 full-time. *Required fees:* $210. One-time fee: $5 full-time. Tuition and fees vary according to course level, campus/location, program and student level. *Financial support:* In 2016–17, 89 students received support, including 74 research assistantships with full and partial tuition reimbursements available (averaging $3,171 per year), 38 teaching assistantships with full and partial tuition reimbursements available (averaging $3,107 per year); unspecified assistantships also available. *Faculty research:* Structural design, concrete structure, finite elements, dynamic analysis, transportation, soils. *Unit head:* Ismael Pagan, Prof., Director, 787-832-4040 Ext. 3815, Fax: 787-833-8260, E-mail: ismael.pagan@upr.edu. *Application contact:* Myriam Hernandez, Administrative Officer III, 787-832-4040 Ext. 3815, Fax: 787-833-8260, E-mail: myriam.hernandez1@upr.edu.
Website: http://engineering.uprm.edu/inci/

University of Southern California, Graduate School, Viterbi School of Engineering, Mork Family Department of Chemical Engineering and Materials Science, Los Angeles, CA 90089. Offers chemical engineering (MS, PhD, Engr); geoscience technologies (MS); materials engineering (MS); materials science (MS, PhD, Engr); petroleum engineering (MS, PhD, Engr); smart oilfield technologies (MS, Graduate Certificate). Terminal master's awarded for partial completion of doctoral program. *Degree requirements:* For master's, thesis optional; for doctorate, thesis/dissertation. *Entrance requirements:* For master's and doctorate, GRE General Test. Additional exam requirements/recommendations for international students: Recommended—TOEFL. Electronic applications accepted. *Expenses:* Contact institution. *Faculty research:* Heterogeneous materials and porous media, statistical mechanics, molecular simulation, polymer science and engineering, advanced materials, reaction engineering and catalysis, membrane processes and separation, biochemical engineering, cell culture, bioreactor modeling, petroleum engineering.

University of South Florida, College of Engineering, Department of Civil and Environmental Engineering, Tampa, FL 33620-9951. Offers civil engineering (MCE, MSCE, PhD), including geotechnical engineering, materials science and engineering, structures engineering, transportation engineering, water resources; environmental engineering (MEVE, MSEV, PhD), including engineering for international development (MSEV). *Program availability:* Part-time. *Faculty:* 20 full-time (5 women). *Students:* 117 full-time (41 women), 63 part-time (18 women); includes 33 minority (7 Black or African American, non-Hispanic/Latino; 2 Asian, non-Hispanic/Latino; 20 Hispanic/Latino; 4 Two or more races, non-Hispanic/Latino), 84 international. Average age 28. 250 applicants, 52% accepted, 51 enrolled. In 2016, 55 master's, 13 doctorates awarded. Terminal master's awarded for partial completion of doctoral program. *Degree requirements:* For master's, comprehensive exam, thesis (for some programs); for doctorate, comprehensive exam, thesis/dissertation. *Entrance requirements:* For master's, GRE General Test, minimum GPA of 3.0 in major, letters of reference, statement of purpose; for doctorate, GRE General Test, letters of recommendation, statement of purpose, resume. Additional exam requirements/recommendations for international students: Required—TOEFL (minimum score 550 paper-based; 79 iBT) or IELTS (minimum score 6.5). *Application deadline:* For fall admission, 2/15 for domestic students, 2/15 priority date for international students; for spring admission, 10/15 for domestic students, 9/15 priority date for international students. Application fee: $30. Electronic applications accepted. *Expenses:* Tuition, state resident: full-time $7766; part-time $431.43 per credit hour. Tuition, nonresident: full-time $15,789; part-time $877.17 per credit hour. *Required fees:* $37 per term. *Financial support:* In 2016–17, 36 students received support, including 44 research assistantships (averaging $14,123 per year), 21 teaching assistantships with tuition reimbursements available (averaging $15,329 per year). *Faculty research:* Environmental and water resources engineering, geotechnics and geoenvironmental systems, structures and materials systems, transportation systems. *Total annual research expenditures:* $3.7 million. *Unit head:* Dr. Manjriker Gunaratne, Professor and Department Chair, 813-974-5818, Fax: 813-974-2957, E-mail: gunaratn@usf.edu. *Application contact:* Dr. Sarina J. Ergas, Professor and Graduate Program Coordinator, 813-974-1119, Fax: 813-974-2957, E-mail: sergas@usf.edu.
Website: http://www.usf.edu/engineering/cee/

The University of Texas at Austin, Graduate School, Cockrell School of Engineering, Department of Petroleum and Geosystems Engineering, Austin, TX 78712-1111. Offers energy and earth resources (MA); petroleum engineering (MS, PhD). *Program availability:* Evening/weekend, online learning. *Entrance requirements:* For master's and doctorate, GRE General Test. Electronic applications accepted.

University of Washington, Graduate School, College of Engineering, Department of Civil and Environmental Engineering, Seattle, WA 98195-2700. Offers construction engineering (MSCE, PhD); environmental engineering (MSCE, PhD); geotechnical engineering (MSCE, PhD); hydrology and hydrodynamics (MSCE, PhD); structural engineering and mechanics (MSCE, PhD); transportation engineering (MSCE, PhD). *Program availability:* Part-time, 100% online. *Faculty:* 37 full-time (10 women). *Students:* 239 full-time (97 women), 153 part-time (41 women); includes 71 minority (7 Black or African American, non-Hispanic/Latino; 32 Asian, non-Hispanic/Latino; 22 Hispanic/Latino; 2 Native Hawaiian or other Pacific Islander, non-Hispanic/Latino; 8 Two or more races, non-Hispanic/Latino), 134 international. 782 applicants, 58% accepted, 157 enrolled. In 2016, 132 master's, 13 doctorates awarded. Terminal master's awarded for partial completion of doctoral program. *Degree requirements:* For master's, thesis optional; for doctorate, comprehensive exam, thesis/dissertation, qualifying, general and final exams; completion of degree within 10 years. *Entrance requirements:* For master's, GRE General Test, minimum GPA of 3.0, statement of purpose, letters of recommendation, transcripts; for doctorate, GRE General Test, minimum GPA of 3.5, statement of purpose, letters of recommendation, transcripts, resume. Additional exam requirements/recommendations for international students: Required—TOEFL (minimum score 580 paper-based; 92 iBT); Recommended—IELTS (minimum score 7), TSE. *Application deadline:* For fall admission, 12/15 for domestic and international students. Applications are processed on a rolling basis. Application fee: $85. Electronic applications accepted. *Expenses:* Contact institution. *Financial support:* In 2016–17, 110 students received support, including 10 fellowships with tuition reimbursements available (averaging $2,228 per year), 72 research assistantships with full tuition reimbursements available (averaging $2,351 per year), 28 teaching assistantships with full tuition reimbursements available (averaging $2,387 per year); scholarships/grants also available. Financial award application deadline: 12/15; financial award applicants required to submit FAFSA. *Faculty research:* Structural and geotechnical engineering, transportation and construction engineering, water and environmental engineering. *Total annual research expenditures:* $13.5 million. *Unit head:* Dr. Timothy V. Larson, Professor/Chair, 206-543-6815, Fax: 206-543-1543, E-mail: tlarson@uw.edu. *Application contact:* Melissa Pritchard, Graduate Adviser, 206-543-2574, Fax: 206-543-1543, E-mail: ceginfo@u.washington.edu.
Website: http://www.ce.washington.edu/

Hazardous Materials Management

Humboldt State University, Academic Programs, College of Natural Resources and Sciences, Programs in Natural Resources, Arcata, CA 95521-8299. Offers natural resources (MS), including fisheries, forestry, natural resources planning and interpretation, rangeland resources and wildland soils, wastewater utilization, watershed management, wildlife. *Degree requirements:* For master's, thesis or alternative. *Entrance requirements:* For master's, GRE, appropriate bachelor's degree, minimum GPA of 2.5, 3 letters of recommendation, resume. Additional exam requirements/recommendations for international students: Required—TOEFL (minimum score 500 paper-based). *Expenses:* Tuition, state resident: full-time $6738; part-time $1953 per semester. Tuition, nonresident: full-time $13,434; part-time $3813 per semester. *Required fees:* $1738; $653 per semester. Tuition and fees vary according to program. *Faculty research:* Spotted owl habitat, pre-settlement vegetation, hardwood utilization, tree physiology, fisheries.

Idaho State University, Office of Graduate Studies, Department of Interdisciplinary Studies, Pocatello, ID 83209. Offers general interdisciplinary (M Ed, MA, MNS); waste management and environmental science (MS). *Program availability:* Part-time. *Degree requirements:* For master's, comprehensive exam, thesis optional. *Entrance requirements:* For master's, GRE General Test or MAT, minimum GPA of 3.0. Additional exam requirements/recommendations for international students: Required—TOEFL (minimum score 550 paper-based; 80 iBT).

Marquette University, Graduate School, College of Engineering, Department of Civil and Environmental Engineering, Milwaukee, WI 53201-1881. Offers construction engineering and management (MS, PhD, Certificate); environmental engineering (MS, PhD); structural design (Certificate); structural engineering and structural mechanics (MS, PhD); transportation (Certificate); transportation engineering and materials (MS, PhD); waste and wastewater treatment processes (Certificate); water resources engineering (Certificate). *Program availability:* Part-time, evening/weekend. *Faculty:* 17 full-time (2 women), 2 part-time/adjunct (0 women). *Students:* 27 full-time (8 women), 6 part-time (0 women); includes 5 minority (1 Asian, non-Hispanic/Latino; 2 Hispanic/Latino; 2 Two or more races, non-Hispanic/Latino), 13 international. Average age 28. 70 applicants, 56% accepted, 9 enrolled. In 2016, 8 master's, 5 doctorates awarded. Terminal master's awarded for partial completion of doctoral program. *Degree requirements:* For master's, comprehensive exam (for some programs), thesis or alternative; for doctorate, thesis/dissertation. *Entrance requirements:* For master's, GRE General Test (recommended), minimum GPA of 3.0, official transcripts from all current and previous colleges/universities except Marquette, three letters of recommendation; for doctorate, GRE General Test, minimum GPA of 3.0, official transcripts from all current and previous colleges/universities except Marquette, three letters of recommendation, brief statement of purpose, submission of any English language publications authored by applicant (strongly recommended). Additional exam requirements/recommendations for international students: Required—TOEFL (minimum score 530 paper-based). *Application deadline:* For fall admission, 6/1 priority date for domestic students. Applications are processed on a rolling basis. Application fee: $50. Electronic applications accepted. *Financial support:* Fellowships, research assistantships, teaching assistantships, scholarships/grants, health care benefits, tuition waivers (partial), and unspecified assistantships available. Support available to part-time students. Financial award application deadline: 2/15. *Faculty research:* Highway safety, highway performance, and intelligent transportation systems; surface mount technology; watershed management. *Total annual research expenditures:* $480,876. *Unit head:* Dr. Christopher Foley, Chair, 414-288-5741. *Application contact:* Dr. Stephen M. Heinrich, Director of Graduate Studies, 414-288-5466.
Website: http://www.marquette.edu/civil-environmental-engineering/

New Mexico Institute of Mining and Technology, Center for Graduate Studies, Department of Civil and Environmental Engineering, Socorro, NM 87801. Offers environmental engineering (MS), including air quality engineering and science, hazardous waste engineering, water quality engineering and science. *Degree requirements:* For master's, thesis, thesis or independent study. *Entrance requirements:* Additional exam requirements/recommendations for international students: Required—TOEFL (minimum score 540 paper-based). *Faculty research:* Air quality, hazardous waste management, wastewater management and treatment, site remediation.

Rutgers University–New Brunswick, Graduate School-New Brunswick, Department of Environmental Sciences, Piscataway, NJ 08854-8097. Offers air pollution and resources (MS, PhD); aquatic biology (MS, PhD); aquatic chemistry (MS, PhD); atmospheric science (MS, PhD); chemistry and physics of aerosol and hydrosol systems (MS, PhD);

environmental chemistry (MS, PhD); environmental microbiology (MS, PhD); environmental toxicology (PhD); exposure assessment (PhD); fate and effects of pollutants (MS, PhD); pollution prevention and control (MS, PhD); water and wastewater treatment (MS, PhD); water resources (MS, PhD). Terminal master's awarded for partial completion of doctoral program. *Degree requirements:* For master's, comprehensive exam, thesis or alternative, oral final exam; for doctorate, comprehensive exam, thesis/dissertation, thesis defense, qualifying exam. *Entrance requirements:* For master's and doctorate, GRE General Test. Additional exam requirements/recommendations for international students: Required—TOEFL. Electronic applications accepted. *Faculty research:* Biological waste treatment; contaminant fate and transport; air, soil and water quality.

Tufts University, School of Engineering, Department of Civil and Environmental Engineering, Medford, MA 02155. Offers bioengineering (ME, MS), including environmental technology; civil engineering (ME, MS, PhD), including geotechnical engineering, structural engineering, water diplomacy (PhD); environmental engineering (ME, MS, PhD), including environmental engineering and environmental sciences, environmental geotechnology, environmental health, environmental science and management, hazardous materials management, water diplomacy (PhD), water resources engineering. *Program availability:* Part-time. Terminal master's awarded for partial completion of doctoral program. *Degree requirements:* For master's, thesis or alternative; for doctorate, thesis/dissertation. *Entrance requirements:* For master's and doctorate, GRE General Test. Additional exam requirements/recommendations for international students: Required—TOEFL (minimum score 550 paper-based; 80 iBT), IELTS (minimum score 6.5). Electronic applications accepted. *Expenses: Tuition:* Full-time $49,892; part-time $1248 per credit hour. *Required fees:* $844. Full-time tuition and fees vary according to degree level, program and student level. Part-time tuition and fees vary according to course load. *Faculty research:* Environmental and water resources engineering, environmental health, geotechnical and geoenvironmental engineering, structural engineering and mechanics, water diplomacy.

The University of Manchester, School of Materials, Manchester, United Kingdom. Offers advanced aerospace materials engineering (M Sc); advanced metallic systems (PhD); biomedical materials (M Phil, M Sc, PhD); ceramics and glass (M Phil, M Sc, PhD); composite materials (M Sc, PhD); corrosion and protection (M Phil, M Sc, PhD); materials (M Phil, PhD); metallic materials (M Phil, M Sc, PhD); nanostructural materials (M Phil, M Sc, PhD); paper science (M Phil, M Sc, PhD); polymer science and engineering (M Phil, M Sc, PhD); technical textiles (M Sc); textile design, fashion and management (M Phil, M Sc, PhD); textile science and technology (M Phil, M Sc, PhD); textiles (M Phil, PhD); textiles and fashion (M Ent).

University of New Haven, Graduate School, Tagliatela College of Engineering, Program in Environmental Engineering, West Haven, CT 06516. Offers environmental engineering (MS); industrial and hazardous waste (MS); water and wastewater treatment (MS); water resources (MS). *Program availability:* Part-time, evening/weekend. *Students:* 47 full-time (13 women), 26 part-time (10 women); includes 3 minority (2 Black or African American, non-Hispanic/Latino; 1 American Indian or Alaska Native, non-Hispanic/Latino), 54 international. Average age 27. 80 applicants, 89% accepted, 19 enrolled. In 2016, 31 master's awarded. *Degree requirements:* For master's, thesis or alternative, research project. *Entrance requirements:* For master's, bachelor's degree in engineering. Additional exam requirements/recommendations for international students: Required—TOEFL (minimum score 75 iBT), IELTS, PTE (minimum score 50). *Application deadline:* Applications are processed on a rolling basis. Application fee: $50. Electronic applications accepted. Application fee is waived when completed online. *Expenses: Tuition:* Full-time $15,660; part-time $870 per credit hour. *Required fees:* $200; $85 per term. Tuition and fees vary according to program. *Financial support:* Research assistantships with partial tuition reimbursements, teaching assistantships with partial tuition reimbursements, career-related internships or fieldwork, Federal Work-Study, scholarships/grants, and unspecified assistantships available. Support available to part-time students. Financial award application deadline: 5/1; financial award applicants required to submit FAFSA. *Unit head:* Dr. Agamemnon Koutsospyros, Coordinator, 203-932-7398, E-mail: akoutsospyros@newhaven.edu. *Application contact:* Michelle Mason, Director of Graduate Enrollment, 203-932-7067, E-mail: mmason@newhaven.edu.
Website: http://www.newhaven.edu/10140/

University of South Carolina, The Graduate School, Arnold School of Public Health, Department of Environmental Health Sciences, Program in Hazardous Materials Management, Columbia, SC 29208. Offers MPH, MSPH, PhD. *Degree requirements:* For master's, comprehensive exam, thesis (for some programs), practicum (MPH); for doctorate, one foreign language, comprehensive exam, thesis/dissertation. *Entrance requirements:* Additional exam requirements/recommendations for international students: Required—TOEFL (minimum score 570 paper-based). Electronic applications accepted. *Faculty research:* Environmental/human health protection; use and disposal of hazardous materials; site safety; exposure assessment; migration, fate and transformation of materials.

University of Southern California, Graduate School, Viterbi School of Engineering, Sonny Astani Department of Civil Engineering, Los Angeles, CA 90089. Offers applied mechanics (MS); civil engineering (MS, PhD); computer-aided engineering (ME, Graduate Certificate); construction management (MCM); engineering technology commercialization (Graduate Certificate); environmental engineering (MS, PhD); environmental quality management (ME); structural design (ME); sustainable cities (Graduate Certificate); transportation systems (MS, Graduate Certificate); water and waste management (MS). *Program availability:* Part-time, evening/weekend. Terminal master's awarded for partial completion of doctoral program. *Degree requirements:* For master's, thesis optional; for doctorate, thesis/dissertation. *Entrance requirements:* For master's and doctorate, GRE General Test. Additional exam requirements/recommendations for international students: Recommended—TOEFL. Electronic applications accepted. *Faculty research:* Geotechnical engineering, transportation engineering, structural engineering, construction management, environmental engineering, water resources.

Hydraulics

Drexel University, College of Engineering, Department of Civil, Architectural, and Environmental Engineering, Philadelphia, PA 19104-2875. Offers architectural/building systems engineering (MS, PhD); civil engineering (MS, PhD); environmental engineering (MS, PhD); geotechnical, geoenvironmental and geosynthetics engineering (MS, PhD); hydraulics, hydrology and water resources engineering (MS, PhD); structures (MS). *Program availability:* Part-time, evening/weekend. *Faculty:* 27 full-time (8 women). *Students:* 63 full-time (24 women), 27 part-time (6 women); includes 11 minority (2 Black or African American, non-Hispanic/Latino; 5 Asian, non-Hispanic/Latino; 2 Hispanic/Latino; 2 Two or more races, non-Hispanic/Latino), 39 international. Average age 30. In 2016, 48 master's, 10 doctorates awarded. *Degree requirements:* For master's, thesis optional; for doctorate, thesis/dissertation. *Entrance requirements:* For master's, minimum GPA of 3.0; for doctorate, minimum GPA of 3.5, MS in civil engineering. Additional exam requirements/recommendations for international students: Required—TOEFL. *Application deadline:* For fall admission, 8/21 for domestic students. Applications are processed on a rolling basis. Application fee: $50. Electronic applications accepted. *Expenses: Tuition:* Full-time $32,184; part-time $1192 per credit hour. *Required fees:* $280. Tuition and fees vary according to campus/location and program. *Financial support:* Research assistantships, teaching assistantships, career-related internships or fieldwork, Federal Work-Study, institutionally sponsored loans, tuition waivers (partial), and unspecified assistantships available. Financial award application deadline: 2/1. *Faculty research:* Structural dynamics, hazardous wastes, water resources, pavement materials, groundwater. *Unit head:* Dr. Richard Weggel, Interim Department Head, 215-895-2355. *Application contact:* Director of Graduate Admissions, 215-895-6700, Fax: 215-895-5939, E-mail: enroll@drexel.edu.

École Polytechnique de Montréal, Graduate Programs, Department of Civil, Geological and Mining Engineering, Montréal, QC H3C 3A7, Canada. Offers civil, geological and mining engineering (DESS); environmental engineering (M Eng, M Sc A, PhD); geotechnical engineering (M Eng, M Sc A, PhD); hydraulics engineering (M Eng, M Sc A, PhD); structural engineering (M Eng, M Sc A, PhD); transportation engineering (M Eng, M Sc A, PhD). *Program availability:* Part-time. *Degree requirements:* For master's, one foreign language, thesis; for doctorate, one foreign language, thesis/dissertation. *Entrance requirements:* For master's, minimum GPA of 2.75; for doctorate, minimum GPA of 3.0. *Faculty research:* Water resources management, characteristics of building materials, aging of dams, pollution control.

McGill University, Faculty of Graduate and Postdoctoral Studies, Faculty of Engineering, Department of Civil Engineering and Applied Mechanics, Montréal, QC H3A 2T5, Canada. Offers environmental engineering (M Eng, M Sc, PhD); fluid mechanics (M Sc); fluid mechanics and hydraulic engineering (M Eng, PhD); materials engineering (M Eng, PhD); rehabilitation of urban infrastructure (M Eng, PhD); soil behavior (M Eng, PhD); soil mechanics and foundations (M Eng, PhD); structures and structural mechanics (M Eng, PhD); water resources (M Sc); water resources engineering (M Eng, PhD).

Missouri University of Science and Technology, Graduate School, Department of Civil, Architectural, and Environmental Engineering, Rolla, MO 65409. Offers civil engineering (MS, DE, PhD); construction engineering (MS, DE, PhD); environmental engineering (MS); fluid mechanics (MS, DE, PhD); geotechnical engineering (MS, DE, PhD); hydrology and hydraulic engineering (MS, DE, PhD). *Program availability:* Part-time, evening/weekend. Terminal master's awarded for partial completion of doctoral program. *Degree requirements:* For master's, thesis optional; for doctorate, comprehensive exam, thesis/dissertation. *Entrance requirements:* For master's, GRE General Test (minimum combined score 1100), minimum GPA of 3.0; for doctorate, GRE General Test (minimum score: verbal and quantitative 400, writing 3.5), minimum GPA of 3.0. Additional exam requirements/recommendations for international students: Required—TOEFL (minimum score 550 paper-based). Electronic applications accepted. *Faculty research:* Earthquake engineering, structural optimization and control systems, structural health monitoring/damage detection, soil-structure interaction, soil mechanics and foundation engineering.

Old Dominion University, Frank Batten College of Engineering and Technology, Program in Civil Engineering, Norfolk, VA 23529. Offers civil engineering (ME, MS), including coastal engineering, geotechnical engineering, hydraulics and water resources, structural engineering, transportation engineering. *Program availability:* Part-time, evening/weekend, blended/hybrid learning. *Faculty:* 16 full-time (1 woman), 5 part-time/adjunct (0 women). *Students:* 12 full-time (4 women), 30 part-time (6 women); includes 7 minority (2 Black or African American, non-Hispanic/Latino; 4 Hispanic/Latino; 1 Two or more races, non-Hispanic/Latino), 8 international. Average age 28. 79 applicants, 84% accepted, 33 enrolled. In 2016, 15 master's awarded. *Degree requirements:* For master's, comprehensive exam, thesis optional. *Entrance requirements:* For master's, GRE, minimum GPA of 3.0. Additional exam requirements/recommendations for international students: Required—TOEFL (minimum score 550 paper-based, 80 iBT) or IELTS (6.5). *Application deadline:* For fall admission, 6/1 priority date for domestic students, 4/15 priority date for international students; for spring admission, 11/1 priority date for domestic students, 10/1 priority date for international students. Applications are processed on a rolling basis. Application fee: $50. Electronic applications accepted. *Expenses:* Contact institution. *Financial support:* In 2016–17, 26 students received support, including 1 fellowship with full tuition reimbursement available (averaging $18,000 per year), 17 research assistantships with full and partial tuition reimbursements available (averaging $16,800 per year), 9 teaching assistantships with full and partial tuition reimbursements available (averaging $15,215 per year); scholarships/grants and health care benefits also available. Support available to part-time students. Financial award application deadline: 4/1; financial award applicants required to submit FAFSA. *Faculty research:* Structural engineering, coastal engineering, geotechnical engineering, water resources, transportation engineering. *Total annual research expenditures:* $937,914. *Unit head:* Dr. Isao Ishibashi, Graduate Program Director, 757-683-4641, E-mail: cegpd@odu.edu. *Application contact:* Dr. Shirshak Dhali, Associate Dean, 757-683-3744, Fax: 757-683-4898, E-mail: sdhali@odu.edu.
Website: http://eng.odu.edu/cee/

University of Colorado Denver, College of Engineering and Applied Science, Department of Civil Engineering, Denver, CO 80217. Offers civil engineering (EASPh D); civil engineering systems (PhD); environmental and sustainability engineering (MS, PhD); geographic information systems (MS); geotechnical engineering (MS, PhD); hydrology and hydraulics (MS, PhD); structural engineering (MS, PhD); transportation engineering (MS, PhD). *Program availability:* Part-time, evening/weekend. *Faculty:* 15 full-time (3 women), 9 part-time/adjunct (0 women). *Students:* 50 full-time (15 women), 33 part-time (7 women); includes 10 minority (1 Black or African American, non-Hispanic/Latino; 2 Asian, non-Hispanic/Latino; 6 Hispanic/Latino; 1 Two or more races, non-Hispanic/Latino), 31 international. Average age 30. 105 applicants, 51% accepted, 14 enrolled. In 2016, 29 master's, 2 doctorates awarded. *Degree requirements:* For master's, comprehensive exam, 30 credit hours, project or thesis; for doctorate, comprehensive exam, thesis/dissertation, 60 credit hours (30 of which are dissertation research). *Entrance requirements:* For master's, GRE, statement of purpose, transcripts, three references; for doctorate, GRE, statement of purpose,

transcripts, references, letter of support from faculty stating willingness to serve as dissertation advisor and outlining plan for financial support. Additional exam requirements/recommendations for international students: Required—TOEFL (minimum score 537 paper-based; 75 iBT); Recommended—IELTS (minimum score 6.5). *Application deadline:* For fall admission, 5/1 for domestic students, 4/1 for international students; for spring admission, 10/1 for domestic students, 9/1 for international students; for summer admission, 2/15 for domestic students, 1/15 for international students. Application fee: $50 ($75 for international students). Electronic applications accepted. *Expenses:* Contact institution. *Financial support:* In 2016–17, 62 students received support. Fellowships, research assistantships, teaching assistantships, career-related internships or fieldwork, Federal Work-Study, institutionally sponsored loans, scholarships/grants, traineeships, and unspecified assistantships available. Financial award application deadline: 4/1; financial award applicants required to submit FAFSA. *Faculty research:* Earthquake source physics, environmental biotechnology, hydrologic and hydraulic engineering, sustainability assessments, transportation energy use and greenhouse gas emissions. *Unit head:* Dr. Kevin Rens, Chair, 303-556-8017, E-mail: kevin.rens@ucdenver.edu. *Application contact:* Roxanne Pizano, Program Coordinator, 303-556-6274, E-mail: roxanne.pizano@ucdenver.edu.
Website: http://www.ucdenver.edu/academics/colleges/Engineering/Programs/Civil-Engineering/Pages/CivilEngineering.aspx

Structural Engineering

California State University, Northridge, Graduate Studies, College of Engineering and Computer Science, Department of Civil Engineering and Construction Management, Northridge, CA 91330. Offers engineering (MS), including structural engineering. *Program availability:* Part-time, evening/weekend. *Faculty:* 8 full-time (6 women), 14 part-time/adjunct (all women). *Students:* 20 full-time (6 women), 45 part-time (7 women); includes 29 minority (1 Black or African American, non-Hispanic/Latino; 9 Asian, non-Hispanic/Latino; 17 Hispanic/Latino; 2 Two or more races, non-Hispanic/Latino), 7 international. Average age 28. 71 applicants, 52% accepted, 23 enrolled. *Degree requirements:* For master's, thesis. *Entrance requirements:* Additional exam requirements/recommendations for international students: Required—TOEFL. *Application deadline:* For fall admission, 11/30 for domestic students. Application fee: $55. *Expenses:* Tuition, state resident: full-time $4152. *Financial support:* Teaching assistantships available. Financial award application deadline: 3/1. *Faculty research:* Composite study. *Unit head:* Dr. Nazaret Dermendjian, Chair, 818-677-2166.
Website: http://www.csun.edu/~ceam/

The Citadel, The Military College of South Carolina, Citadel Graduate College, School of Engineering, Department of Civil and Environmental Engineering, Charleston, SC 29409. Offers built environment and public health (Graduate Certificate); civil engineering (MS); geotechnical engineering (Graduate Certificate); structural engineering (Graduate Certificate); transportation engineering (Graduate Certificate). *Program availability:* Part-time, evening/weekend. *Faculty:* 1 full-time. *Students:* 11 part-time (1 woman); includes 1 minority (Black or African American, non-Hispanic/Latino). 8 applicants, 88% accepted, 4 enrolled. *Degree requirements:* For master's, plan of study outlining intended areas of interest and top four corresponding courses of interest. *Entrance requirements:* For master's, official transcript of baccalaureate degree from ABET-accredited engineering program or approved alternative; 2 letters of recommendation; for Graduate Certificate, official transcript of baccalaureate degree directly from an accredited college or university. Additional exam requirements/recommendations for international students: Required—TOEFL (minimum score 550 paper-based; 79 iBT). *Application deadline:* Applications are processed on a rolling basis. Application fee: $40. Electronic applications accepted. *Expenses:* Tuition, state resident: full-time $5121; part-time $569 per credit hour. Tuition, nonresident: full-time $8613; part-time $957 per credit hour. *Required fees:* $90 per term. *Financial support:* Fellowships and unspecified assistantships available. Support available to part-time students. Financial award application deadline: 7/1; financial award applicants required to submit FAFSA. *Unit head:* Dr. Kevin C. Bower, Head, 843-953-7683, E-mail: kevin.bower@citadel.edu. *Application contact:* Dr. Tara Hornor, Associate Provost for Planning, Assessment and Evaluation/Dean of Enrollment Management, 843-953-5089, E-mail: cgc@citadel.edu.
Website: http://www.citadel.edu/root/cee

Cornell University, Graduate School, Graduate Fields of Engineering, Field of Civil and Environmental Engineering, Ithaca, NY 14853. Offers engineering management (M Eng, MS, PhD); environmental engineering (M Eng, MS, PhD); environmental fluid mechanics and hydrology (M Eng, MS, PhD); environmental systems engineering (M Eng, MS, PhD); geotechnical engineering (M Eng, MS, PhD); remote sensing (M Eng, MS, PhD); structural engineering (M Eng, MS, PhD); structural mechanics (M Eng, MS); transportation engineering (MS, PhD); transportation systems engineering (M Eng); water resource systems (M Eng, MS, PhD). Terminal master's awarded for partial completion of doctoral program. *Degree requirements:* For master's, thesis (MS); for doctorate, comprehensive exam, thesis/dissertation. *Entrance requirements:* For master's and doctorate, GRE General Test (recommended), 2 letters of recommendation. Additional exam requirements/recommendations for international students: Required—TOEFL (minimum score 600 paper-based; 77 iBT). Electronic applications accepted. *Faculty research:* Environmental engineering, geotechnical engineering, remote sensing, environmental fluid mechanics and hydrology, structural engineering.

Drexel University, College of Engineering, Department of Civil, Architectural, and Environmental Engineering, Philadelphia, PA 19104-2875. Offers architectural/building systems engineering (MS, PhD); civil engineering (MS, PhD); environmental engineering (MS, PhD); geotechnical, geoenvironmental and geosynthetics engineering (MS, PhD); hydraulics, hydrology and water resources engineering (MS, PhD); structures (MS). *Program availability:* Part-time, evening/weekend. *Faculty:* 27 full-time (8 women). *Students:* 63 full-time (24 women), 27 part-time (6 women); includes 11 minority (2 Black or African American, non-Hispanic/Latino; 5 Asian, non-Hispanic/Latino; 2 Hispanic/Latino; 2 Two or more races, non-Hispanic/Latino), 39 international. Average age 30. In 2016, 48 master's, 10 doctorates awarded. *Degree requirements:* For master's, thesis optional; for doctorate, thesis/dissertation. *Entrance requirements:* For master's, minimum GPA of 3.0; for doctorate, minimum GPA of 3.5, MS in civil engineering. Additional exam requirements/recommendations for international students: Required—TOEFL. *Application deadline:* For fall admission, 8/21 for domestic students. Applications are processed on a rolling basis. Application fee: $50. Electronic applications accepted. *Expenses:* Tuition: Full-time $32,184; part-time $1192 per credit hour. *Required fees:* $280. Tuition and fees vary according to campus/location and program. *Financial support:* Research assistantships, teaching assistantships, career-related internships or fieldwork, Federal Work-Study, institutionally sponsored loans, tuition waivers (partial), and unspecified assistantships available. Financial award application deadline: 2/1. *Faculty research:* Structural dynamics, hazardous wastes, water resources, pavement materials, groundwater. *Unit head:* Dr. Richard Weggel, Interim Department Head, 215-895-2355. *Application contact:* Director of Graduate Admissions, 215-895-6700, Fax: 215-895-5939, E-mail: enroll@drexel.edu.

École Polytechnique de Montréal, Graduate Programs, Department of Civil, Geological and Mining Engineering, Montréal, QC H3C 3A7, Canada. Offers civil, geological and mining engineering (DESS); environmental engineering (M Eng, M Sc A, PhD); geotechnical engineering (M Eng, M Sc A, PhD); hydraulics engineering (M Eng, M Sc A, PhD); structural engineering (M Eng, M Sc A, PhD); transportation engineering (M Eng, M Sc A, PhD). *Program availability:* Part-time. *Degree requirements:* For master's, one foreign language, thesis; for doctorate, one foreign language, thesis/dissertation. *Entrance requirements:* For master's, minimum GPA of 2.75; for doctorate, minimum GPA of 3.0. *Faculty research:* Water resources management, characteristics of building materials, aging of dams, pollution control.

George Mason University, Volgenau School of Engineering, Sid and Reva Dewberry Department of Civil, Environmental, and Infrastructure Engineering, Fairfax, VA 22030. Offers construction project management (MS); geotechnical, construction, and structural engineering (M Eng); transportation engineering (PhD). *Faculty:* 14 full-time (6 women), 20 part-time/adjunct (4 women). *Students:* 47 full-time (12 women), 62 part-time (22 women); includes 23 minority (6 Black or African American, non-Hispanic/Latino; 9 Asian, non-Hispanic/Latino; 7 Hispanic/Latino; 1 Native Hawaiian or other Pacific Islander, non-Hispanic/Latino), 38 international. Average age 29. 109 applicants, 77% accepted, 39 enrolled. In 2016, 31 master's, 1 doctorate awarded. *Degree requirements:* For master's, thesis (for some programs), 30 credits, departmental seminars; for doctorate, thesis/dissertation, qualifying exams. *Entrance requirements:* For master's, GRE, photocopy of passport; 2 official college transcripts; resume; official bank statement; proof of financial support; expanded goals statement; self-evaluation form; BS in engineering or other related science; 3 letters of recommendation; for doctorate, GRE (for those who received degree outside of the U.S.), photocopy of passport; 2 official college transcripts; resume; official bank statement; proof of financial support; expanded goals statement; self-evaluation form; baccalaureate degree in engineering or related science; master's degree (preferred); 3 letters of recommendation. Additional exam requirements/recommendations for international students: Required—TOEFL (minimum score 575 paper-based; 88 iBT), IELTS (minimum score 6.5), PTE (minimum score 59). *Application deadline:* For fall admission, 1/15 priority date for domestic students. Application fee: $75 ($80 for international students). Electronic applications accepted. *Expenses:* Contact institution. *Financial support:* In 2016–17, 27 students received support, including 1 fellowship (averaging $10,000 per year), 16 research assistantships with tuition reimbursements available (averaging $20,150 per year), 10 teaching assistantships with tuition reimbursements available (averaging $21,000 per year); career-related internships or fieldwork, Federal Work-Study, scholarships/grants, unspecified assistantships, and health care benefits (for full-time research or teaching assistantship recipients) also available. Support available to part-time students. Financial award application deadline: 3/1; financial award applicants required to submit FAFSA. *Faculty research:* Evolutionary design, infrastructure security, intelligent transportation systems, national transportation networks, water quality modeling. *Total annual research expenditures:* $568,705. *Unit head:* Llza Wilson Durant, Acting Chair, 703-993-1687, Fax: 703-993-9790, E-mail: ldurant2@gmu.edu. *Application contact:* Laura Kosoglu, Director, Graduate Program, 703-993-1675, Fax: 703-993-9790, E-mail: ceiegrad@gmu.edu.
Website: http://civil.gmu.edu/

Illinois Institute of Technology, Graduate College, Armour College of Engineering, Department of Civil, Architectural and Environmental Engineering, Chicago, IL 60616. Offers architectural engineering (M Arch E); civil engineering (MS, PhD), including architectural engineering (MS), construction engineering and management (MS), geoenvironmental engineering (MS), geotechnical engineering (MS), structural engineering (MS), transportation engineering (MS); construction engineering and management (MCEM); environmental engineering (M Env E, MS, PhD); geoenvironmental engineering (M Geoenv E); geotechnical engineering (MGE); infrastructure engineering and management (MPW); structural engineering (MSE); transportation engineering (M Trans E). *Program availability:* Part-time, evening/weekend, online learning. Terminal master's awarded for partial completion of doctoral program. *Degree requirements:* For master's, thesis (for some programs); for doctorate, comprehensive exam, thesis/dissertation. *Entrance requirements:* For master's, GRE General Test (minimum score 900 Quantitative and Verbal, 2.5 Analytical Writing), minimum undergraduate GPA of 3.0; for doctorate, GRE General Test (minimum score 1000 Quantitative and Verbal, 3.0 Analytical Writing), minimum undergraduate GPA of 3.0. Additional exam requirements/recommendations for international students: Required—TOEFL (minimum score 550 paper-based; 80 iBT). Electronic applications accepted. *Faculty research:* Structural, architectural, geotechnical and geoenvironmental engineering; construction engineering and management; transportation engineering; environmental engineering and public works.

Instituto Tecnologico de Santo Domingo, Graduate School, Area of Engineering, Santo Domingo, Dominican Republic. Offers construction administration (MS, Certificate); data telecommunications (M Eng, MS, Certificate); industrial engineering (M Eng, Certificate); industrial management (M Mgmt); information technology (Certificate); maintenance engineering (M Eng); occupational hazard prevention (M Mgmt); production management (Certificate); quantitative methods (Certificate); sanitary and environmental engineering (M Eng); structural engineering (M Eng); systems engineering and electronic data processing (Certificate); transportation (Certificate).

Iowa State University of Science and Technology, Department of Civil and Construction Engineering, Ames, IA 50011. Offers civil engineering (MS, PhD), including civil engineering materials, construction engineering and management, environmental engineering, geotechnical engineering, structural engineering, transportation engineering. *Degree requirements:* For master's, thesis or alternative; for doctorate, thesis/dissertation. *Entrance requirements:* For master's and doctorate, GRE General Test. Additional exam requirements/recommendations for international students: Required—TOEFL (minimum score 550 paper-based; 82 iBT), IELTS (minimum score 6.5). *Application deadline:* For fall admission, 2/1 priority date for domestic students, 2/1 for international students; for spring admission, 8/1 priority date for domestic students, 8/1 for international students. Application fee: $60 ($90 for international students). Electronic applications accepted. *Application contact:* Kathy Petersen, Application

Contact, 515-294-4975, Fax: 515-294-8216, E-mail: ccee-grad-inquiry@iastate.edu.
Website: http://www.ccee.iastate.edu/

Kansas State University, Graduate School, College of Engineering, Department of Civil Engineering, Manhattan, KS 66506. Offers civil engineering (MS, PhD); environmental engineering (MS, PhD); geotechnical engineering (MS, PhD); structural engineering (MS, PhD); transportation engineering (MS, PhD); water resources engineering (MS, PhD). *Program availability:* Part-time, evening/weekend, online learning. *Faculty:* 14 full-time (4 women), 3 part-time/adjunct (1 woman). *Students:* 36 full-time (11 women), 34 part-time (7 women); includes 5 minority (2 Asian, non-Hispanic/Latino; 2 Hispanic/Latino; 1 Two or more races, non-Hispanic/Latino), 28 international. Average age 29. 70 applicants, 60% accepted, 11 enrolled. In 2016, 21 master's, 7 doctorates awarded. *Degree requirements:* For master's, thesis or alternative; for doctorate, thesis/dissertation. *Entrance requirements:* For master's, GRE General Test, bachelor's degree or course work in related engineering fields; for doctorate, GRE General Test. Additional exam requirements/recommendations for international students: Required—TOEFL (minimum score 550 paper-based; 79 iBT). *Application deadline:* For fall admission, 2/1 priority date for domestic students, 1/1 priority date for international students; for spring admission, 8/1 priority date for domestic and international students. Applications are processed on a rolling basis. Application fee: $50 ($75 for international students). Electronic applications accepted. *Expenses:* Tuition, state resident: full-time $9670. Tuition, nonresident: full-time $21,828. *Required fees:* $862. *Financial support:* In 2016–17, 19 research assistantships with partial tuition reimbursements (averaging $13,431 per year), 12 teaching assistantships with partial tuition reimbursements (averaging $15,058 per year) were awarded; institutionally sponsored loans and scholarships/grants also available. Support available to part-time students. Financial award application deadline: 3/1; financial award applicants required to submit FAFSA. *Faculty research:* Transportation and materials engineering, water resources engineering, environmental engineering, geotechnical engineering, structural engineering. *Total annual research expenditures:* $2.4 million. *Unit head:* Dr. Robert Stokes, Head, 785-532-1595, Fax: 785-532-7717, E-mail: drbobb@k-state.edu. *Application contact:* Dr. Dunja Peric, Graduate Coordinator, 785-532-2468, Fax: 785-532-7717, E-mail: peric@k-state.edu.
Website: http://www.ce.ksu.edu/

Louisiana State University and Agricultural & Mechanical College, Graduate School, College of Engineering, Department of Civil and Environmental Engineering, Baton Rouge, LA 70803. Offers environmental engineering (MSCE, PhD); geotechnical engineering (MSCE, PhD); structural engineering and mechanics (MSCE, PhD); transportation engineering (MSCE, PhD); water resources (MSCE, PhD).

Marquette University, Graduate School, College of Engineering, Department of Civil and Environmental Engineering, Milwaukee, WI 53201-1881. Offers construction engineering and management (MS, PhD, Certificate); environmental engineering (MS, PhD); structural design (Certificate); structural engineering and structural mechanics (MS, PhD); transportation (Certificate); transportation engineering and materials (MS, PhD); waste and wastewater treatment processes (Certificate); water resources engineering (Certificate). *Program availability:* Part-time, evening/weekend. *Faculty:* 17 full-time (2 women), 2 part-time/adjunct (0 women). *Students:* 27 full-time (8 women), 6 part-time (0 women); includes 5 minority (1 Asian, non-Hispanic/Latino; 2 Hispanic/Latino; 2 Two or more races, non-Hispanic/Latino), 13 international. Average age 28. 70 applicants, 56% accepted, 9 enrolled. In 2016, 8 master's, 5 doctorates awarded. Terminal master's awarded for partial completion of doctoral program. *Degree requirements:* For master's, comprehensive exam (for some programs), thesis or alternative; for doctorate, thesis/dissertation. *Entrance requirements:* For master's, GRE General Test (recommended), minimum GPA of 3.0, official transcripts from all current and previous colleges/universities except Marquette, three letters of recommendation; for doctorate, GRE General Test, minimum GPA of 3.0, official transcripts from all current and previous colleges/universities except Marquette, three letters of recommendation, brief statement of purpose, submission of any English language publications authored by applicant (strongly recommended). Additional exam requirements/recommendations for international students: Required—TOEFL (minimum score 530 paper-based). *Application deadline:* For fall admission, 6/1 priority date for domestic students. Applications are processed on a rolling basis. Application fee: $50. Electronic applications accepted. *Financial support:* Fellowships, research assistantships, teaching assistantships, scholarships/grants, health care benefits, tuition waivers (partial), and unspecified assistantships available. Support available to part-time students. Financial award application deadline: 2/15. *Faculty research:* Highway safety, highway performance, and intelligent transportation systems; surface mount technology; watershed management. *Total annual research expenditures:* $480,876. *Unit head:* Dr. Christopher Foley, Chair, 414-288-5741. *Application contact:* Dr. Stephen M. Heinrich, Director of Graduate Studies, 414-288-5466.
Website: http://www.marquette.edu/civil-environmental-engineering/

Massachusetts Institute of Technology, School of Engineering, Department of Civil and Environmental Engineering, Cambridge, MA 02139. Offers biological oceanography (PhD, Sc D); chemical oceanography (PhD, Sc D); civil and environmental engineering (M Eng, SM, PhD, Sc D); civil and environmental systems (PhD, Sc D); civil engineering (PhD, Sc D, CE); civil engineering and computation (PhD); coastal engineering (PhD, Sc D); construction engineering and management (PhD, Sc D); environmental biology (PhD, Sc D); environmental chemistry (PhD, Sc D); environmental engineering (PhD, Sc D); environmental engineering and computation (PhD); environmental fluid mechanics (PhD, Sc D); geotechnical and geoenvironmental engineering (PhD, Sc D); hydrology (PhD, Sc D); information technology (PhD, Sc D); oceanographic engineering (PhD, Sc D); structures and materials (PhD, Sc D); transportation (PhD, Sc D); SM/MBA. *Faculty:* 35 full-time (6 women). *Students:* 192 full-time (64 women); includes 25 minority (2 Black or African American, non-Hispanic/Latino; 11 Asian, non-Hispanic/Latino; 8 Hispanic/Latino; 4 Two or more races, non-Hispanic/Latino), 113 international. Average age 27. 530 applicants, 20% accepted, 77 enrolled. In 2016, 56 master's, 16 doctorates, 1 other advanced degree awarded. *Degree requirements:* For master's, thesis; for doctorate, comprehensive exam, thesis/dissertation; for CE, comprehensive exam, thesis. *Entrance requirements:* For master's, doctorate, and CE, GRE General Test. Additional exam requirements/recommendations for international students: Required—TOEFL, IELTS. *Application deadline:* For fall admission, 12/15 for domestic and international students. Application fee: $75. Electronic applications accepted. *Expenses: Tuition:* Full-time $46,400; part-time $725 per credit. One-time fee: $312 full-time. Full-time tuition and fees vary according to course load and program. *Financial support:* In 2016–17, 150 students received support, including fellowships (averaging $41,900 per year), 124 research assistantships (averaging $36,900 per year), 9 teaching assistantships (averaging $36,900 per year); Federal Work-Study, institutionally sponsored loans, scholarships/grants, traineeships, health care benefits, unspecified assistantships, and resident tutors also available. Support available to part-time students. Financial award application deadline: 5/1; financial award applicants required to submit FAFSA. *Faculty research:* Environmental chemistry, environmental fluid mechanics and coastal engineering, environmental microbiology, geotechnical engineering and geomechanics, hydrology and hydro climatology, infrastructure systems, mechanics of materials and structures, transportation systems. *Total annual research expenditures:* $25 million. *Unit head:* Prof. Markus Buehler, Department Head, 617-253-7101. *Application contact:* 617-253-7119, E-mail: cee-admissions@mit.edu.
Website: http://cee.mit.edu/

McGill University, Faculty of Graduate and Postdoctoral Studies, Faculty of Engineering, Department of Civil Engineering and Applied Mechanics, Montréal, QC H3A 2T5, Canada. Offers environmental engineering (M Eng, M Sc, PhD); fluid mechanics (M Sc); fluid mechanics and hydraulic engineering (M Eng, PhD); materials engineering (M Eng, PhD); rehabilitation of urban infrastructure (M Eng, PhD); soil behavior (M Eng, PhD); soil mechanics and foundations (M Eng, PhD); structures and structural mechanics (M Eng, PhD); water resources (M Sc); water resources engineering (M Eng, PhD).

Northwestern University, McCormick School of Engineering and Applied Science, Department of Civil and Environmental Engineering, Evanston, IL 60208-3109. Offers environmental engineering and science (MS, PhD); geotechnical engineering (MS, PhD); mechanics of materials and solids (MS, PhD); project management (MS); structural engineering and materials (MS, PhD); transportation systems analysis and planning (MS, PhD). MS and PhD admissions and degrees offered through The Graduate School. *Program availability:* Part-time. Terminal master's awarded for partial completion of doctoral program. *Degree requirements:* For master's, comprehensive exam (for some programs), thesis (for some programs); for doctorate, comprehensive exam, thesis/dissertation. *Entrance requirements:* For master's and doctorate, GRE General Test, minimum 2 letters of recommendation, transcripts from all academic institutions attended. Additional exam requirements/recommendations for international students: Required—TOEFL (minimum score 577 paper-based; 90 iBT), IELTS (minimum score 7). Electronic applications accepted. *Faculty research:* Environmental engineering and science, geotechnics, mechanics, materials, structures, and transportation systems analysis and planning.

Norwich University, College of Graduate and Continuing Studies, Master of Civil Engineering Program, Northfield, VT 05663. Offers construction management (MCE); environmental (MCE); geotechnical (MCE); structural (MCE). *Program availability:* Evening/weekend, online only, mostly all online with a week-long residency requirement. *Faculty:* 1 full-time (0 women), 11 part-time/adjunct (1 woman). *Students:* 70 full-time (17 women); includes 28 minority (16 Black or African American, non-Hispanic/Latino; 4 Asian, non-Hispanic/Latino; 5 Hispanic/Latino; 1 Native Hawaiian or other Pacific Islander, non-Hispanic/Latino; 2 Two or more races, non-Hispanic/Latino), 1 international. Average age 36. 35 applicants, 97% accepted, 18 enrolled. In 2016, 63 master's awarded. *Degree requirements:* For master's, capstone. *Entrance requirements:* For master's, minimum undergraduate GPA of 2.75. Additional exam requirements/recommendations for international students: Required—TOEFL (minimum score 550 paper-based; 80 iBT), IELTS (minimum score 6.5). *Application deadline:* For fall admission, 8/14 for domestic and international students; for spring admission, 2/12 for domestic and international students. Electronic applications accepted. *Expenses:* Contact institution. *Financial support:* In 2016–17, 10 students received support. Scholarships/grants available. Financial award application deadline: 8/4; financial award applicants required to submit FAFSA. *Unit head:* Dr. Thomas Descoteaux, Program Director, 802-485-2730, Fax: 802-485-2533, E-mail: tdescote@norwich.edu. *Application contact:* Admissions Advisor, 800-460-5597 Ext. 3369, Fax: 802-485-2533, E-mail: mce@online.norwich.edu.
Website: https://online.norwich.edu/degree-programs/masters/master-civil-engineering/overview

Ohio University, Graduate College, Russ College of Engineering and Technology, Department of Civil Engineering, Athens, OH 45701-2979. Offers civil engineering (PhD); construction engineering and management (MS); environmental (MS); geotechnical and geoenvironmental (MS); mechanics (MS); structures (MS); transportation (MS); water resources (MS). *Program availability:* Part-time. *Degree requirements:* For master's, comprehensive exam (for some programs), thesis or alternative; for doctorate, comprehensive exam, thesis/dissertation. *Entrance requirements:* For master's, GRE General Test, minimum GPA of 3.0, 3 letters of recommendation; for doctorate, GRE General Test. Additional exam requirements/recommendations for international students: Required—TOEFL (minimum score 550 paper-based; 80 iBT) or IELTS (minimum score 6.5). *Application deadline:* For fall admission, 5/1 priority date for domestic students, 2/1 priority date for international students; for winter admission, 8/1 priority date for domestic students, 4/1 priority date for international students; for spring admission, 2/1 priority date for domestic students, 7/1 priority date for international students. Applications are processed on a rolling basis. Application fee: $50 ($55 for international students). Electronic applications accepted. *Financial support:* Research assistantships with full tuition reimbursements, teaching assistantships with full tuition reimbursements, Federal Work-Study, institutionally sponsored loans, scholarships/grants, and unspecified assistantships available. Financial award application deadline: 3/15; financial award applicants required to submit FAFSA. *Faculty research:* Noise abatement, materials and environment, highway infrastructure, subsurface investigation (pavements, pipes, bridges). *Unit head:* Dr. Gayle F. Mitchell, Chair, 740-593-0430, Fax: 740-593-0625, E-mail: mitchelg@ohio.edu. *Application contact:* Dr. Shad M. Sargand, Graduate Chair, 740-593-1465, Fax: 740-593-0625, E-mail: sargand@ohio.edu.
Website: http://www.ohio.edu/civil/

Old Dominion University, Frank Batten College of Engineering and Technology, Program in Civil Engineering, Norfolk, VA 23529. Offers civil engineering (ME, MS), including coastal engineering, geotechnical engineering, hydraulics and water resources, structural engineering, transportation engineering. *Program availability:* Part-time, evening/weekend, blended/hybrid learning. *Faculty:* 16 full-time (1 woman), 5 part-time/adjunct (0 women). *Students:* 12 full-time (4 women), 30 part-time (6 women); includes 7 minority (2 Black or African American, non-Hispanic/Latino; 4 Hispanic/Latino; 1 Two or more races, non-Hispanic/Latino), 8 international. Average age 28. 79 applicants, 84% accepted, 33 enrolled. In 2016, 15 master's awarded. *Degree requirements:* For master's, comprehensive exam, thesis optional. *Entrance requirements:* For master's, GRE, minimum GPA of 3.0. Additional exam requirements/recommendations for international students: Required—TOEFL (minimum score 550 paper-based, 80 iBT) or IELTS (6.5). *Application deadline:* For fall admission, 6/1 priority date for domestic students, 4/15 priority date for international students; for spring admission, 11/1 priority date for domestic students, 10/1 priority date for international students. Applications are processed on a rolling basis. Application fee: $50. Electronic applications accepted. *Expenses:* Contact institution. *Financial support:* In 2016–17, 26 students received support, including 1 fellowship with full tuition reimbursement available (averaging $18,000 per year), 17 research assistantships with full and partial tuition reimbursements available (averaging $16,800 per year), 9 teaching assistantships with full and partial tuition reimbursements available (averaging $15,215 per year); scholarships/grants and health care benefits also available. Support available to part-time students. Financial award application deadline: 4/1; financial award applicants required to submit FAFSA. *Faculty research:* Structural engineering, coastal engineering, geotechnical engineering, water resources, transportation engineering. *Total annual research expenditures:* $937,914. *Unit head:* Dr. Isao Ishibashi, Graduate Program Director, 757-683-4641, E-mail: cegpd@odu.edu. *Application contact:* Dr. Shirshak Dhali, Associate Dean, 757-683-3744, Fax: 757-683-4898, E-mail: sdhali@

odu.edu.
Website: http://eng.odu.edu/cee/

Oregon State University, College of Engineering, Program in Civil Engineering, Corvallis, OR 97331. Offers civil engineering (M Eng, MS, PhD); coastal and ocean engineering (M Eng, MS, PhD); construction engineering management (M Eng, MS, PhD); engineering education (M Eng, MS, PhD); geomatics (M Eng, MS, PhD); geotechnical engineering (M Eng, MS, PhD); infrastructure materials (M Eng, MS, PhD); structural engineering (M Eng, MS, PhD); transportation engineering (M Eng). *Faculty:* 42 full-time (8 women), 2 part-time/adjunct (0 women). *Students:* 157 full-time (48 women), 10 part-time (3 women); includes 18 minority (7 Asian, non-Hispanic/Latino; 7 Hispanic/Latino; 1 Native Hawaiian or other Pacific Islander, non-Hispanic/Latino; 3 Two or more races, non-Hispanic/Latino), 92 international. Average age 28. 379 applicants, 31% accepted, 50 enrolled. In 2016, 55 master's, 5 doctorates awarded. *Entrance requirements:* For master's and doctorate, GRE. Additional exam requirements/recommendations for international students: Required—TOEFL (minimum score 80 iBT), IELTS (minimum score 6.5). *Application deadline:* For fall admission, 8/1 for domestic students, 4/1 for international students; for winter admission, 12/1 for domestic students, 7/1 for international students; for spring admission, 2/1 for domestic students, 10/1 for international students; for summer admission, 5/1 for domestic students, 1/1 for international students. Application fee: $75 ($85 for international students). *Expenses:* $14,130 resident full-time tuition, $23,769 non-resident. *Financial support:* Application deadline: 1/15. *Unit head:* Dr. Jason Weiss, School Head/Professor. *Application contact:* Shannon Reed, Graduate Program Coordinator, 541-737-4575, E-mail: shannon.reed@oregonstate.edu.
Website: http://cce.oregonstate.edu/graduate-academics

Penn State Harrisburg, Graduate School, School of Science, Engineering and Technology, Middletown, PA 17057. Offers computer science (MS); electrical engineering (M Eng, MS); engineering management (MPS); engineering science (M Eng); environmental engineering (M Eng); environmental pollution control (MEPC, MS); structural engineering (Certificate). *Program availability:* Part-time, evening/weekend. *Unit head:* Dr. Mukund S. Kulkarni, Chancellor, 717-948-6105, Fax: 717-948-6452. *Application contact:* Robert W. Coffman, Jr., Director of Enrollment Management, Admissions, 717-948-6250, Fax: 717-948-6325, E-mail: hbgadmit@psu.edu.
Website: https://harrisburg.psu.edu/science-engineering-technology

Pontificia Universidad Catolica Madre y Maestra, Graduate School, Faculty of Engineering Sciences, Santiago, Dominican Republic. Offers earthquake engineering (ME); logistics management (ME).

Southern Illinois University Edwardsville, Graduate School, School of Engineering, Department of Civil Engineering, Program in Structural Engineering, Edwardsville, IL 62026. Offers MS. *Program availability:* Part-time, evening/weekend. *Degree requirements:* For master's, thesis (for some programs), research paper. *Entrance requirements:* For master's, minimum undergraduate GPA of 2.75 in science, math, and engineering courses. Additional exam requirements/recommendations for international students: Required—TOEFL (minimum score 550 paper-based, 79 iBT), IELTS (minimum score 6.5), Michigan Test of English Language Proficiency or PTE. Electronic applications accepted.

Southern Methodist University, Bobby B. Lyle School of Engineering, Department of Environmental and Civil Engineering, Dallas, TX 75275-0340. Offers air pollution control and atmospheric sciences (PhD); civil engineering (MS); environmental engineering (MS); environmental science (MS); structural engineering (PhD); sustainability and development (MA); water and wastewater engineering (PhD). *Program availability:* Part-time, evening/weekend, online learning. Terminal master's awarded for partial completion of doctoral program. *Degree requirements:* For master's, thesis optional; for doctorate, thesis/dissertation, oral and written qualifying exams. *Entrance requirements:* For master's, GRE General Test, minimum GPA of 3.0 in last 2 years; bachelor's degree in engineering, mathematics, or sciences; for doctorate, GRE, BS and MS in related field, minimum GPA of 3.3. Additional exam requirements/recommendations for international students: Required—TOEFL. Electronic applications accepted. *Faculty research:* Human and environmental health effects of endocrine disrupters, development of air pollution control systems for diesel engines, structural analysis and design, modeling and design of waste treatment systems.

Stanford University, School of Engineering, Department of Civil and Environmental Engineering, Stanford, CA 94305-2004. Offers atmosphere and energy (MS, PhD); construction (MS), including construction engineering and management, design-construction integration, sustainable design and construction; environmental engineering and science (MS, PhD, Eng); environmental fluid mechanics and hydrology (PhD); geomechanics (MS); structural engineering (MS). Terminal master's awarded for partial completion of doctoral program. *Degree requirements:* For doctorate, thesis/dissertation, qualifying exam; for Eng, thesis. *Entrance requirements:* For master's, doctorate, and Eng, GRE General Test. Additional exam requirements/recommendations for international students: Required—TOEFL. Electronic applications accepted. *Expenses: Tuition:* Full-time $47,331. *Required fees:* $609.

Stevens Institute of Technology, Graduate School, Charles V. Schaefer Jr. School of Engineering and Science, Department of Civil, Environmental, and Ocean Engineering, Program in Civil Engineering, Hoboken, NJ 07030. Offers civil engineering (PhD, Certificate), including geotechnical engineering (Certificate); geotechnical/geoenvironmental engineering (M Eng, Engr); hydrologic modeling (M Eng); stormwater management (M Eng); structural engineering (M Eng, Engr); transportation engineering (M Eng); water resources engineering (M Eng). *Program availability:* Part-time, evening/weekend. *Students:* 63 full-time (12 women), 27 part-time (10 women); includes 5 minority (2 Black or African American, non-Hispanic/Latino; 2 Asian, non-Hispanic/Latino; 1 Hispanic/Latino), 55 international. Average age 25. 167 applicants, 57% accepted, 24 enrolled. In 2016, 50 master's, 1 other advanced degree awarded. *Degree requirements:* For master's, thesis optional, minimum B average in major field and overall; for doctorate, comprehensive exam (for some programs), thesis/dissertation; for other advanced degree, minimum B average. *Entrance requirements:* Additional exam requirements/recommendations for international students: Required—TOEFL (minimum score 74 iBT), IELTS (minimum score 6). *Application deadline:* For fall admission, 6/1 for domestic students, 4/15 for international students; for spring admission, 11/30 for domestic students, 11/1 for international students. Applications are processed on a rolling basis. Application fee: $65. Electronic applications accepted. *Expenses:* Contact institution. *Financial support:* Fellowships, research assistantships, teaching assistantships, career-related internships or fieldwork, Federal Work-Study, scholarships/grants, and unspecified assistantships available. Financial award application deadline: 2/15; financial award applicants required to submit FAFSA. *Unit head:* Dr. David A. Vaccari, Director, 201-216-5570, Fax: 201-216-8739, E-mail: dvaccari@stevens.edu. *Application contact:* Graduate Admission, 888-783-8367, Fax: 888-511-1306, E-mail: graduate@stevens.edu.

Tufts University, School of Engineering, Department of Civil and Environmental Engineering, Medford, MA 02155. Offers bioengineering (ME, MS), including environmental technology; civil engineering (ME, MS, PhD), including geotechnical engineering, structural engineering, water diplomacy (PhD); environmental engineering (ME, MS, PhD), including environmental engineering and environmental sciences, environmental geotechnology, environmental health, environmental science and management, hazardous materials management, water diplomacy (PhD), water resources engineering. *Program availability:* Part-time. Terminal master's awarded for partial completion of doctoral program. *Degree requirements:* For master's, thesis or alternative; for doctorate, thesis/dissertation. *Entrance requirements:* For master's and doctorate, GRE General Test. Additional exam requirements/recommendations for international students: Required—TOEFL (minimum score 550 paper-based; 80 iBT), IELTS (minimum score 6.5). Electronic applications accepted. *Expenses: Tuition:* Full-time $49,892; part-time $1248 per credit hour. *Required fees:* $844. Full-time tuition and fees vary according to degree level, program and student level. Part-time tuition and fees vary according to course load. *Faculty research:* Environmental and water resources engineering, environmental health, geotechnical and geoenvironmental engineering, structural engineering and mechanics, water diplomacy.

University at Buffalo, the State University of New York, Graduate School, School of Engineering and Applied Sciences, Department of Civil, Structural, and Environmental Engineering, Buffalo, NY 14260. Offers civil engineering (ME, MS, PhD); engineering science (MS). *Program availability:* Part-time, online learning. Terminal master's awarded for partial completion of doctoral program. *Degree requirements:* For master's, project, thesis, or comprehensive exam; for doctorate, thesis/dissertation. *Entrance requirements:* For master's and doctorate, GRE General Test, letters of reference. Additional exam requirements/recommendations for international students: Required—TOEFL (minimum score 550 paper-based; 79 iBT). Electronic applications accepted. *Faculty research:* Environmental engineering and fluid mechanics, structural dynamics, geomechanics, earthquake engineering computational mechanics.

The University of Alabama at Birmingham, School of Engineering, Program in Civil Engineering, Birmingham, AL 35294. Offers construction engineering management (M Eng); structural engineering (M Eng); sustainable smart cities (M Eng). Program offered jointly with The University of Alabama in Huntsville. *Program availability:* Part-time, evening/weekend, 100% online. *Faculty:* 15 full-time (4 women), 3 part-time/adjunct. *Students:* 16 full-time (6 women), 24 part-time (5 women); includes 22 minority (5 Black or African American, non-Hispanic/Latino; 12 Asian, non-Hispanic/Latino; 4 Hispanic/Latino; 1 Two or more races, non-Hispanic/Latino). Average age 30. 16 applicants, 56% accepted, 5 enrolled. In 2016, 15 master's, 3 doctorates awarded. *Degree requirements:* For master's, comprehensive exam, thesis optional; for doctorate, comprehensive exam, thesis/dissertation. *Entrance requirements:* For master's, GRE General Test preferred (minimum score of 500 on each component), minimum GPA of 3.0 in all undergraduate degree major courses attempted, letters of evaluation. Additional exam requirements/recommendations for international students: Required—TOEFL (minimum score 550 paper-based), TWE (minimum score 3.5). *Application deadline:* For fall admission, 7/1 for domestic and international students; for spring admission, 11/1 for domestic and international students; for summer admission, 4/1 for domestic and international students. Applications are processed on a rolling basis. Application fee: $50 ($60 for international students). Electronic applications accepted. *Expenses:* $396 per hour resident tuition; $935 per hour non-resident tuition; $150 per course online course fee. *Financial support:* In 2016–17, 15 students received support, including 1 fellowship with full tuition reimbursement available (averaging $24,000 per year), 14 research assistantships with full and partial tuition reimbursements available (averaging $17,472 per year). *Total annual research expenditures:* $1.1 million. *Unit head:* Dr. Fouad H. Fouad, Chair, 205-934-8430, Fax: 205-934-9855, E-mail: ffouad@uab.edu. *Application contact:* Holly Hebard, Director of Graduate School Operations, 205-834-8227, Fax: 205-934-8413, E-mail: gradschool@uab.edu.
Website: https://www.uab.edu/engineering/home/graduate-civil

University of Alberta, Faculty of Graduate Studies and Research, Department of Civil and Environmental Engineering, Edmonton, AB T6G 2E1, Canada. Offers construction engineering and management (M Eng, M Sc, PhD); environmental engineering (M Eng, M Sc, PhD); environmental science (M Sc, PhD); geoenvironmental engineering (M Eng, M Sc, PhD); geotechnical engineering (M Eng, M Sc, PhD); mining engineering (M Eng, M Sc, PhD); petroleum engineering (M Eng, M Sc, PhD); structural engineering (M Eng, M Sc, PhD); water resources (M Eng, M Sc, PhD). *Program availability:* Part-time, online learning. *Degree requirements:* For master's, thesis (for some programs); for doctorate, thesis/dissertation. *Entrance requirements:* For master's, minimum GPA of 3.0 in last 2 years of undergraduate studies; for doctorate, minimum GPA of 3.0. Additional exam requirements/recommendations for international students: Required—TOEFL (minimum score 550 paper-based). Electronic applications accepted. *Faculty research:* Mining.

University of Calgary, Faculty of Graduate Studies, Schulich School of Engineering, Department of Civil Engineering, Calgary, AB T2N 1N4, Canada. Offers avalanche mechanics (M Sc, PhD); civil engineering (M Eng, M Sc, PhD); energy and environment engineering (M Eng, M Sc, PhD); environmental engineering (M Eng, M Sc, PhD); geotechnical engineering (M Eng, M Sc, PhD); materials science (M Eng, M Sc, PhD); project management (M Eng, M Sc, PhD); structures and solid mechanics (M Eng, M Sc, PhD); transportation engineering (M Eng, M Sc, PhD); water resources (M Eng, M Sc, PhD). *Program availability:* Part-time. *Degree requirements:* For master's, thesis; for doctorate, thesis/dissertation, written and oral candidacy exam. *Entrance requirements:* For master's, minimum GPA of 3.0; for doctorate, minimum GPA of 3.5. Additional exam requirements/recommendations for international students: Required—TOEFL (minimum score 580 paper-based; 93 iBT), IELTS (minimum score 7). Electronic applications accepted. *Faculty research:* Geotechnical engineering, energy and environment, transportation, project management, structures and solid mechanics.

University of California, Berkeley, Graduate Division, College of Engineering, Department of Civil and Environmental Engineering, Berkeley, CA 94720-1500. Offers engineering and project management (M Eng, MS, PhD); environmental engineering (M Eng, MS, PhD); geoengineering (M Eng, MS, PhD); structural engineering, mechanics and materials (M Eng, MS, PhD); transportation engineering (M Eng, MS, PhD); M Arch/MS; MCP/MS; MPP/MS. *Students:* 360 full-time (143 women); includes 71 minority (15 Black or African American, non-Hispanic/Latino; 39 Asian, non-Hispanic/Latino; 17 Hispanic/Latino), 148 international. Average age 27. 1,086 applicants, 185 enrolled. In 2016, 188 master's, 26 doctorates awarded. Terminal master's awarded for partial completion of doctoral program. *Degree requirements:* For master's, comprehensive exam (for some programs), thesis (for some programs), comprehensive exam or thesis (MS); for doctorate, thesis/dissertation, qualifying exam. *Entrance requirements:* For master's, GRE General Test, minimum GPA of 3.0, 3 letters of recommendation; for doctorate, GRE General Test, minimum GPA of 3.5, 3 letters of recommendation. Additional exam requirements/recommendations for international students: Required—TOEFL (minimum score 570 paper-based; 90 iBT). *Application deadline:* For fall admission, 12/16 for domestic students. Application fee: $105 ($125 for international students). Electronic applications accepted. *Financial support:* Applicants required to submit FAFSA. *Unit head:* Prof. Robert Harley, Chair, 510-643-8739, Fax: 510-643-5264, E-mail: chair@ce.berkeley.edu. *Application contact:* Shelly Okimoto, Graduate Advisor, 510-642-6464, Fax: 510-643-5264, E-mail: aao@ce.berkeley.edu.
Website: http://www.ce.berkeley.edu/

Structural Engineering

University of California, San Diego, Graduate Division, Department of Structural Engineering, La Jolla, CA 92093. Offers structural engineering (MS, PhD); structural health monitoring, prognosis, and validated simulations (MS). PhD in engineering sciences offered jointly with San Diego State University. *Students:* 195 full-time (39 women), 3 part-time (1 woman). 424 applicants, 57% accepted, 82 enrolled. In 2016, 70 master's, 11 doctorates awarded. *Degree requirements:* For master's, comprehensive exam (for some programs), thesis (for some programs); for doctorate, comprehensive exam, thesis/dissertation, 1-quarter teaching assistantship. *Entrance requirements:* For master's and doctorate, GRE General Test. Additional exam requirements/recommendations for international students: Required—TOEFL (minimum score 550 paper-based; 80 iBT), IELTS (minimum score 7). *Application deadline:* For fall admission, 12/20 for domestic students. Application fee: $105 ($125 for international students). Electronic applications accepted. *Expenses:* Tuition, state resident: full-time $11,220. Tuition, nonresident: full-time $26,322. *Required fees:* $1864. *Financial support:* Fellowships, research assistantships, teaching assistantships, scholarships/grants, and readerships available. Financial award applicants required to submit FAFSA. *Faculty research:* Earthquake engineering, advanced composites and aerospace structural systems, geotechnical, marine/offshore engineering; renewal engineering, structural health monitoring, prognosis and validated simulations, structural materials; computational mechanics; solid mechanics. *Unit head:* P. Benson Shing, Chair, 858-534-4567, E-mail: pshing@ucsd.edu. *Application contact:* Yvonne C. Wollman, Graduate Coordinator, 858-822-1421, E-mail: se-info@ucsd.edu. Website: http://www.structures.ucsd.edu/

University of Central Florida, College of Engineering and Computer Science, Department of Civil, Environmental, and Construction Engineering, Orlando, FL 32816. Offers civil engineering (MS, MSCE, PhD, Certificate), including civil engineering (MS, MSCE, PhD), construction engineering (Certificate), structural engineering (Certificate), transportation engineering (Certificate); environmental engineering (MS, MS Env E, PhD). *Program availability:* Part-time, evening/weekend. *Faculty:* 29 full-time (3 women), 19 part-time/adjunct (1 woman). *Students:* 105 full-time (15 women), 90 part-time (26 women); includes 52 minority (11 Black or African American, non-Hispanic/Latino; 9 Asian, non-Hispanic/Latino; 29 Hispanic/Latino; 3 Two or more races, non-Hispanic/Latino), 79 international. Average age 29. 190 applicants, 73% accepted, 48 enrolled. In 2016, 42 master's, 17 doctorates, 3 other advanced degrees awarded. *Degree requirements:* For master's, thesis or alternative; for doctorate, thesis/dissertation, departmental qualifying exam, candidacy exam. *Entrance requirements:* For master's, GRE General Test, minimum GPA of 3.0 in last 60 hours of course work; for doctorate, GRE General Test, minimum GPA of 3.5 in last 60 hours of course work. Additional exam requirements/recommendations for international students: Required—TOEFL. *Application deadline:* For fall admission, 7/15 priority date for domestic students; for spring admission, 12/1 priority date for domestic students. Application fee: $30. Electronic applications accepted. *Expenses:* Tuition, state resident: part-time $288.16 per credit hour. Tuition, nonresident: part-time $1071.31 per credit hour. *Financial support:* In 2016–17, 70 students received support, including 20 fellowships with partial tuition reimbursements available (averaging $13,530 per year), 53 research assistantships with partial tuition reimbursements available (averaging $10,634 per year), 16 teaching assistantships with partial tuition reimbursements available (averaging $11,057 per year); career-related internships or fieldwork, Federal Work-Study, institutionally sponsored loans, tuition waivers (partial), and unspecified assistantships also available. Financial award application deadline: 3/1; financial award applicants required to submit FAFSA. *Unit head:* Dr. Mohamed Abdel-Aty, Chair, 407-823-2841, E-mail: m.aty@ucf.edu. *Application contact:* Assistant Director, Graduate Admissions, 407-823-2766, Fax: 407-823-6442, E-mail: gradadmissions@ucf.edu. Website: http://cece.ucf.edu/

University of Colorado Denver, College of Engineering and Applied Science, Department of Civil Engineering, Denver, CO 80217. Offers civil engineering (EASPh D); civil engineering systems (PhD); environmental and sustainability engineering (MS, PhD); geographic information systems (MS); geotechnical engineering (MS, PhD); hydrology and hydraulics (MS, PhD); structural engineering (MS, PhD); transportation engineering (MS, PhD). *Program availability:* Part-time, evening/weekend. *Faculty:* 15 full-time (3 women), 9 part-time/adjunct (0 women). *Students:* 50 full-time (15 women), 33 part-time (7 women); includes 10 minority (1 Black or African American, non-Hispanic/Latino; 2 Asian, non-Hispanic/Latino; 6 Hispanic/Latino; 1 Two or more races, non-Hispanic/Latino), 31 international. Average age 30. 105 applicants, 51% accepted, 14 enrolled. In 2016, 29 master's, 2 doctorates awarded. *Degree requirements:* For master's, comprehensive exam, 30 credit hours, project or thesis; for doctorate, comprehensive exam, thesis/dissertation, 60 credit hours (30 of which are dissertation research). *Entrance requirements:* For master's, GRE, statement of purpose, transcripts, three references; for doctorate, GRE, statement of purpose, transcripts, references, letter of support from faculty stating willingness to serve as dissertation advisor and outlining plan for financial support. Additional exam requirements/recommendations for international students: Required—TOEFL (minimum score 537 paper-based; 75 iBT); Recommended—IELTS (minimum score 6.5). *Application deadline:* For fall admission, 5/1 for domestic students, 4/1 for international students; for spring admission, 10/1 for domestic students, 9/1 for international students; for summer admission, 2/15 for domestic students, 1/15 for international students. Application fee: $50 ($75 for international students). Electronic applications accepted. *Expenses:* Contact institution. *Financial support:* In 2016–17, 62 students received support. Fellowships, research assistantships, teaching assistantships, career-related internships or fieldwork, Federal Work-Study, institutionally sponsored loans, scholarships/grants, traineeships, and unspecified assistantships available. Financial award application deadline: 4/1; financial award applicants required to submit FAFSA. *Faculty research:* Earthquake source physics, environmental biotechnology, hydrologic and hydraulic engineering, sustainability assessments, transportation energy use and greenhouse gas emissions. *Unit head:* Dr. Kevin Rens, Chair, 303-556-8017, E-mail: kevin.rens@ucdenver.edu. *Application contact:* Roxanne Pizano, Program Coordinator, 303-556-6274, E-mail: roxanne.pizano@ucdenver.edu. Website: http://www.ucdenver.edu/academics/colleges/Engineering/Programs/Civil-Engineering/Pages/CivilEngineering.aspx

University of Dayton, Department of Civil and Environmental Engineering and Engineering Mechanics, Dayton, OH 45469. Offers engineering mechanics (MSEM); environmental engineering (MSCE); geotechnical engineering (MSCE); structural engineering (MSCE); transportation engineering (MSCE); water resources engineering (MSCE). *Program availability:* Part-time, evening/weekend. *Faculty:* 9 full-time (2 women), 3 part-time/adjunct (1 woman). *Students:* 40 full-time (8 women), 2 part-time (0 women); includes 1 minority (Asian, non-Hispanic/Latino), 30 international. Average age 26. 137 applicants, 17% accepted. In 2016, 14 master's awarded. *Degree requirements:* For master's, thesis optional. *Entrance requirements:* For master's, minimum GPA of 3.0 in undergraduate work. Additional exam requirements/recommendations for international students: Required—TOEFL (minimum score 550 paper-based; 80 iBT); Recommended—IELTS. *Application deadline:* For fall admission, 8/1 priority date for domestic students, 5/1 priority date for international students; for spring admission, 11/1 priority date for international students. Applications are processed on a rolling basis. Application fee: $0 ($50 for international students). Electronic applications accepted.

Expenses: $890 per credit hour, $25 registration fee. *Financial support:* Research assistantships, institutionally sponsored loans, scholarships/grants, and department-funded awards (averaging $2448 per year) available. Financial award application deadline: 3/1; financial award applicants required to submit FAFSA. *Faculty research:* Vertically-aligned carbon nanotubes infiltrated with temperature-responsive polymers; smart nanocomposite films for self-cleaning and controlled release; bilayer and bulk heterojunction solar cells using liquid crystalline porphyrins as donors by solution processing; DNA damage induced by multiwalled carbon nanotubes in mouse embryonic stem cells. *Total annual research expenditures:* $250,000. *Unit head:* Dr. Donald V. Chase, Chair, 937-229-3847, Fax: 937-229-3491, E-mail: dchase1@udayton.edu. *Application contact:* 937-229-4462, E-mail: graduateadmission@udayton.edu.
Website: https://www.udayton.edu/engineering/departments/civil/index.php

University of Delaware, College of Engineering, Department of Civil and Environmental Engineering, Newark, DE 19716. Offers environmental engineering (MAS, MCE, PhD); geotechnical engineering (MAS, MCE, PhD); ocean engineering (MAS, MCE, PhD); structural engineering (MAS, MCE, PhD); transportation engineering (MAS, MCE, PhD); water resource engineering (MAS, MCE, PhD). *Program availability:* Part-time. Terminal master's awarded for partial completion of doctoral program. *Degree requirements:* For master's, thesis; for doctorate, thesis/dissertation. *Entrance requirements:* For master's and doctorate, GRE General Test. Additional exam requirements/recommendations for international students: Required—TOEFL. Electronic applications accepted. *Faculty research:* Structural engineering and mechanics; transportation engineering; ocean engineering; soil mechanics and foundation; water resources and environmental engineering.

The University of Manchester, School of Materials, Manchester, United Kingdom. Offers advanced aerospace materials engineering (M Sc); advanced metallic systems (PhD); biomedical materials (M Phil, M Sc, PhD); ceramics and glass (M Phil, M Sc, PhD); composite materials (M Sc, PhD); corrosion and protection (M Phil, M Sc, PhD); materials (M Phil, PhD); metallic materials (M Phil, M Sc, PhD); nanostructural materials (M Phil, M Sc, PhD); paper science (M Phil, M Sc, PhD); polymer science and engineering (M Phil, M Sc, PhD); technical textiles (M Sc); textile design, fashion and management (M Phil, M Sc, PhD); textile science and technology (M Phil, M Sc, PhD); textiles (M Phil, PhD); textiles and fashion (M Ent).

University of Massachusetts Amherst, Graduate School, College of Engineering, Department of Civil and Environmental Engineering, Amherst, MA 01003. Offers civil engineering (MSCE, PhD); environmental and water resources engineering (MSCE); geotechnical engineering (MSCE); structural engineering and mechanics (MSCE); transportation engineering (MSCE). *Program availability:* Part-time. Terminal master's awarded for partial completion of doctoral program. *Degree requirements:* For master's, thesis or alternative; for doctorate, comprehensive exam, thesis/dissertation. *Entrance requirements:* For master's and doctorate, GRE General Test. Additional exam requirements/recommendations for international students: Required—TOEFL (minimum score 550 paper-based; 80 iBT), IELTS (minimum score 6.5). Electronic applications accepted.

University of Memphis, Graduate School, Herff College of Engineering, Department of Civil Engineering, Memphis, TN 38152. Offers civil engineering (PhD); engineering seismology (MS); environmental engineering (MS); freight transportation (Graduate Certificate); geotechnical engineering (MS); structural engineering (MS); transportation engineering (MS); water resources engineering (MS). *Faculty:* 12 full-time (1 woman). *Students:* 10 full-time (3 women), 15 part-time (3 women); includes 3 minority (2 Black or African American, non-Hispanic/Latino; 1 Two or more races, non-Hispanic/Latino), 9 international. Average age 29. 29 applicants, 69% accepted, 8 enrolled. In 2016, 5 master's awarded. Terminal master's awarded for partial completion of doctoral program. *Degree requirements:* For master's, comprehensive exam, thesis optional; for doctorate, comprehensive exam, thesis/dissertation. *Entrance requirements:* For master's, GRE General Test, minimum undergraduate GPA of 2.5; bachelor's degree in engineering or a related science or mathematics program; three letters of reference; for doctorate, GRE General Test, bachelor's degree in engineering or engineering science; three letters of reference; for Graduate Certificate, minimum undergraduate GPA of 2.75; bachelor's degree in engineering or engineering science. Additional exam requirements/recommendations for international students: Required—TOEFL (minimum score 550 paper-based; 79 iBT). *Application deadline:* For fall admission, 8/1 for domestic students; for spring admission, 12/1 for domestic students. Application fee: $35 ($60 for international students). Electronic applications accepted. *Expenses:* $5,231.50 per semester full-time in-state, $9,623.50 full-time out-of-state. *Financial support:* In 2016–17, 6 students received support, including 31 fellowships with full tuition reimbursements available (averaging $12,012 per year); research assistantships with full tuition reimbursements available, career-related internships or fieldwork, Federal Work-Study, scholarships/grants, and unspecified assistantships also available. Financial award application deadline: 2/1; financial award applicants required to submit FAFSA. *Faculty research:* Structural response to earthquakes, pavement design, water quality, transportation safety, intermodal transportation. *Unit head:* Dr. Sharam Pezeshk, Chair, 901-678-2746, Fax: 901-678-3026. *Application contact:* Dr. Roger Meier, Coordinator of Graduate Studies, 901-678-3284, E-mail: rwmeier@memphis.edu. Website: http://www.ce.memphis.edu

University of Michigan, College of Engineering, Department of Civil and Environmental Engineering, Ann Arbor, MI 48109. Offers civil engineering (MSE, PhD, CE); construction engineering and management (M Eng, MSE); environmental engineering (MSE, PhD); structural engineering (M Eng); MBA/MSE. *Program availability:* Part-time. *Students:* 177 full-time (77 women), 3 part-time. 775 applicants, 42% accepted, 62 enrolled. In 2016, 57 master's, 9 doctorates awarded. *Degree requirements:* For master's, thesis optional; for doctorate, comprehensive exam, thesis/dissertation, oral defense of dissertation, preliminary and written exams. *Entrance requirements:* For master's and doctorate, GRE General Test. Additional exam requirements/recommendations for international students: Required—TOEFL. *Application deadline:* Applications are processed on a rolling basis. Electronic applications accepted. *Expenses:* Tuition, state resident: full-time $21,466; part-time $1152 per credit hour. Tuition, nonresident: full-time $43,346; part-time $2367 per credit hour. Part-time tuition and fees vary according to course load, degree level and program. *Financial support:* Fellowships, research assistantships, teaching assistantships, institutionally sponsored loans, and tuition waivers (partial) available. *Faculty research:* Construction engineering and management, geotechnical engineering, earthquake-resistant design of structures, environmental chemistry and microbiology, cost engineering, environmental and water resources engineering. *Total annual research expenditures:* $15.7 million. *Unit head:* Kim Hayes, Department Chair, 734-764-8495, Fax: 734-764-4292, E-mail: ford@umich.edu. *Application contact:* Jessica Randolph, Graduate Coordinator, 734-764-8405, Fax: 734-764-4292, E-mail: jrand@umich.edu.
Website: http://cee.engin.umich.edu/

University of Missouri, Office of Research and Graduate Studies, College of Engineering, Department of Civil and Environmental Engineering, Columbia, MO 65211. Offers civil engineering (MS, PhD); environmental engineering (MS, PhD); geotechnical engineering (MS, PhD); structural engineering (MS, PhD); transportation and highway engineering (MS); water resources (MS, PhD). *Faculty:* 16 full-time (3 women), 2 part-time/adjunct (1 woman). *Students:* 41 full-time (8 women), 30 part-time (8 women). *Degree requirements:* For master's, report or thesis; for doctorate, thesis/dissertation. *Entrance requirements:* For master's and doctorate, GRE General Test. Additional exam requirements/recommendations for international students: Required—TOEFL (minimum score 550 paper-based; 80 iBT). *Application deadline:* For fall admission, 2/15 priority date for domestic students, 2/15 for international students; for winter admission, 9/15 priority date for domestic students, 9/15 for international students. Application fee: $75 ($90 for international students). *Expenses:* Tuition, state resident: full-time $6347; part-time $352.60 per credit hour. Tuition, nonresident: full-time $17,379; part-time $965.50 per credit hour. *Required fees:* $1035. Tuition and fees vary according to course load, campus/location and program. *Financial support:* Fellowships, research assistantships, teaching assistantships, and institutionally sponsored loans available. Website: http://engineering.missouri.edu/civil/

University of New Brunswick Fredericton, School of Graduate Studies, Faculty of Engineering, Department of Civil Engineering, Fredericton, NB E3B 5A3, Canada. Offers construction engineering and management (M Eng, M Sc E, PhD); environmental engineering (M Eng, M Sc E, PhD); environmental studies (M Eng); geotechnical engineering (M Eng, M Sc E, PhD); groundwater/hydrology (M Eng, M Sc E, PhD); materials (M Eng, M Sc E, PhD); pavements (M Eng, M Sc E, PhD); structures (M Eng, M Sc E, PhD); transportation (M Eng, M Sc E, PhD). *Program availability:* Part-time. *Degree requirements:* For master's, thesis; for doctorate, comprehensive exam, thesis/dissertation, qualifying exam; 27 credit hours of courses. *Entrance requirements:* For master's, minimum GPA of 3.0; B Sc E in civil engineering or related engineering degree; for doctorate, minimum GPA of 3.0; graduate degree in engineering or applied science. Additional exam requirements/recommendations for international students: Required—IELTS (minimum score 7.5), TWE (minimum score 4), Michigan English Language Assessment Battery (minimum score 85) or CanTest (minimum score 4.5); Recommended—TOEFL (minimum score 580 paper-based). Electronic applications accepted. *Faculty research:* Construction engineering and management; engineering materials and infrastructure renewal; highway and pavement research; structures and solid mechanics; geotechnical and geoenvironmental engineering; structure interaction; transportation and planning; environment, solid waste management; structural engineering; water and environmental engineering.

University of Puerto Rico, Mayagüez Campus, Graduate Studies, College of Engineering, Department of Civil Engineering and Surveying, Mayagüez, PR 00681-9000. Offers civil engineering (ME, MS, PhD), including construction engineering and management (ME, MS); environmental engineering, geotechnical engineering (ME, MS), structural engineering, transportation engineering. *Program availability:* Part-time. *Faculty:* 37 full-time (7 women), 2 part-time/adjunct (0 women). *Students:* 118 full-time (37 women), 9 part-time (2 women); includes 110 minority (all Hispanic/Latino), 17 international. Average age 25. 35 applicants, 94% accepted, 16 enrolled. In 2016, 26 master's, 2 doctorates awarded. Terminal master's awarded for partial completion of doctoral program. *Degree requirements:* For master's, one foreign language, thesis; for doctorate, one foreign language, comprehensive exam, thesis/dissertation, qualifying exams. *Entrance requirements:* For master's, proficiency in English and Spanish; BS in civil engineering or its equivalent; for doctorate, proficiency in English and Spanish. *Application deadline:* For fall admission, 2/15 for domestic and international students; for spring admission, 9/15 for domestic and international students. Applications are processed on a rolling basis. Application fee: $25. Electronic applications accepted. *Expenses:* Tuition, area resident: Full-time $2466. *International tuition:* $7166 full-time. *Required fees:* $210. One-time fee: $5 full-time. Tuition and fees vary according to course level, campus/location, program and student level. *Financial support:* In 2016–17, 89 students received support, including 74 research assistantships with full and partial tuition reimbursements available (averaging $3,171 per year), 38 teaching assistantships with full and partial tuition reimbursements available (averaging $3,107 per year); unspecified assistantships also available. *Faculty research:* Structural design, concrete structure, finite elements, dynamic analysis, transportation, soils. *Unit head:* Ismael Pagan, Prof., Director, 787-832-4040 Ext. 3815, Fax: 787-833-8260, E-mail: ismael.pagan@upr.edu. *Application contact:* Myriam Hernandez, Administrative Officer III, 787-832-4040 Ext. 3815, Fax: 787-833-8260, E-mail: myriam.hernandez1@upr.edu. Website: http://engineering.uprm.edu/inci/

University of South Florida, College of Engineering, Department of Civil and Environmental Engineering, Tampa, FL 33620-9951. Offers civil engineering (MCE, MSCE, PhD), including geotechnical engineering, materials science and engineering, structures engineering, transportation engineering, water resources; environmental engineering (MEVE, MSEV, PhD), including engineering for international development (MSEV). *Program availability:* Part-time. *Faculty:* 20 full-time (5 women). *Students:* 117 full-time (41 women), 63 part-time (18 women); includes 33 minority (7 Black or African American, non-Hispanic/Latino; 2 Asian, non-Hispanic/Latino; 20 Hispanic/Latino; 4 Two

or more races, non-Hispanic/Latino), 84 international. Average age 28. 250 applicants, 52% accepted, 51 enrolled. In 2016, 55 master's, 13 doctorates awarded. Terminal master's awarded for partial completion of doctoral program. *Degree requirements:* For master's, comprehensive exam, thesis (for some programs); for doctorate, comprehensive exam, thesis/dissertation. *Entrance requirements:* For master's, GRE General Test, minimum GPA of 3.0 in major, letters of reference, statement of purpose; for doctorate, GRE General Test, letters of recommendation, statement of purpose, resume. Additional exam requirements/recommendations for international students: Required—TOEFL (minimum score 550 paper-based; 79 iBT) or IELTS (minimum score 6.5). *Application deadline:* For fall admission, 2/15 for domestic students, 2/15 priority date for international students; for spring admission, 10/15 for domestic students, 9/15 priority date for international students. Application fee: $30. Electronic applications accepted. *Expenses:* Tuition, state resident: full-time $7766; part-time $431.43 per credit hour. Tuition, nonresident: full-time $15,789; part-time $877.17 per credit hour. *Required fees:* $37 per term. *Financial support:* In 2016–17, 36 students received support, including 44 research assistantships (averaging $14,123 per year), 21 teaching assistantships with tuition reimbursements available (averaging $15,329 per year). *Faculty research:* Environmental and water resources engineering, geotechnics and geoenvironmental systems, structures and materials systems, transportation systems. *Total annual research expenditures:* $3.7 million. *Unit head:* Dr. Manjriker Gunaratne, Professor and Department Chair, 813-974-5818, Fax: 813-974-2957, E-mail: gunaratn@usf.edu. *Application contact:* Dr. Sarina J. Ergas, Professor and Graduate Program Coordinator, 813-974-1119, Fax: 813-974-2957, E-mail: sergas@usf.edu. Website: http://www.usf.edu/engineering/cee/

The University of Texas at Tyler, College of Engineering, Department of Civil Engineering, Tyler, TX 75799-0001. Offers environmental engineering (MS); industrial safety (MS); structural engineering (MS); transportation engineering (MS); water resources engineering (MS). *Program availability:* Part-time, evening/weekend. *Degree requirements:* For master's, thesis optional. *Entrance requirements:* For master's, GRE General Test, bachelor's degree in engineering, associated science degree. Additional exam requirements/recommendations for international students: Required—TOEFL. *Faculty research:* Non-destructive strength testing, indoor air quality, transportation routing and signaling, pavement replacement criteria, flood water routing, construction and long-term behavior of innovative geotechnical foundation and embankment construction used in highway construction, engineering education.

University of Washington, Graduate School, College of Engineering, Department of Civil and Environmental Engineering, Seattle, WA 98195-2700. Offers construction engineering (MSCE, PhD); environmental engineering (MSCE, PhD); geotechnical engineering (MSCE, PhD); hydrology and hydrodynamics (MSCE, PhD); structural engineering and mechanics (MSCE, PhD); transportation engineering (MSCE, PhD). *Program availability:* Part-time, 100% online. *Faculty:* 37 full-time (10 women). *Students:* 239 full-time (97 women), 153 part-time (41 women); includes 71 minority (7 Black or African American, non-Hispanic/Latino; 32 Asian, non-Hispanic/Latino; 22 Hispanic/Latino; 2 Native Hawaiian or other Pacific Islander, non-Hispanic/Latino; 8 Two or more races, non-Hispanic/Latino), 134 international. 782 applicants, 58% accepted, 157 enrolled. In 2016, 132 master's, 13 doctorates awarded. Terminal master's awarded for partial completion of doctoral program. *Degree requirements:* For master's, thesis optional; for doctorate, comprehensive exam, thesis/dissertation, qualifying, general and final exams; completion of degree within 10 years. *Entrance requirements:* For master's, GRE General Test, minimum GPA of 3.0, statement of purpose, letters of recommendation, transcripts; for doctorate, GRE General Test, minimum GPA of 3.5, statement of purpose, letters of recommendation, transcripts, resume. Additional exam requirements/recommendations for international students: Required—TOEFL (minimum score 580 paper-based; 92 iBT); Recommended—IELTS (minimum score 7), TSE. *Application deadline:* For fall admission, 12/15 for domestic and international students. Applications are processed on a rolling basis. Application fee: $85. Electronic applications accepted. *Expenses:* Contact institution. *Financial support:* In 2016–17, 110 students received support, including 10 fellowships with tuition reimbursements available (averaging $2,228 per year), 72 research assistantships with full tuition reimbursements available (averaging $2,351 per year), 28 teaching assistantships with full tuition reimbursements available (averaging $2,387 per year); scholarships/grants also available. Financial award application deadline: 12/15; financial award applicants required to submit FAFSA. *Faculty research:* Structural and geotechnical engineering, transportation and construction engineering, water and environmental engineering. *Total annual research expenditures:* $13.5 million. *Unit head:* Dr. Timothy V. Larson, Professor/Chair, 206-543-6815, Fax: 206-543-1543, E-mail: tlarson@uw.edu. *Application contact:* Melissa Pritchard, Graduate Adviser, 206-543-2574, Fax: 206-543-1543, E-mail: ceginfo@u.washington.edu. Website: http://www.ce.washington.edu/

Surveying Science and Engineering

University of New Brunswick Fredericton, School of Graduate Studies, Faculty of Engineering, Department of Geodesy and Geomatics Engineering, Fredericton, NB E3B 5A3, Canada. Offers M Eng, M Sc E, PhD. *Degree requirements:* For master's, thesis; for doctorate, comprehensive exam, thesis/dissertation, qualifying exam. *Entrance requirements:* For master's and doctorate, minimum GPA of 3.0. Additional exam requirements/recommendations for international students: Required—TOEFL (minimum

score 550 paper-based; 80 iBT), IELTS (minimum score 7), TWE (minimum score 4), Michigan English Language Assessment Battery (minimum score 85) or CanTest (minimum score 4.5). Electronic applications accepted. *Faculty research:* GIS, GPS, remote sensing, ocean mapping, land administration, hydrography, engineering surveys.

Transportation and Highway Engineering

Arizona State University at the Tempe campus, College of Liberal Arts and Sciences, School of Geographical Sciences and Urban Planning, Tempe, AZ 85287-5302. Offers geographic information systems (MAS); geographical information science (Graduate Certificate); geography (MA, PhD); transportation systems (Graduate Certificate); urban and environmental planning (MUEP); urban planning (PhD). *Accreditation:* ACSP. Terminal master's awarded for partial completion of doctoral program. *Degree requirements:* For master's, thesis, interactive Program of Study (iPOS) submitted before completing 50 percent of required credit hours; for doctorate, comprehensive exam, thesis/dissertation, interactive Program of Study (iPOS) submitted before completing 50 percent of required credit hours. *Entrance requirements:* For master's and doctorate, GRE, minimum GPA of 3.0 or equivalent in last 2 years of work leading to

bachelor's degree. Additional exam requirements/recommendations for international students: Required—TOEFL, IELTS, or PTE. Electronic applications accepted. *Expenses:* Contact institution.

ArtCenter College of Design, Graduate Transportation Design Program, Pasadena, CA 91103. Offers transportation systems (MS). *Degree requirements:* For master's, thesis. *Entrance requirements:* For master's, portfolio. Additional exam requirements/recommendations for international students: Required—TOEFL (minimum score 100 iBT), IELTS (minimum score 7). Electronic applications accepted.

The Catholic University of America, School of Engineering, Department of Civil Engineering, Washington, DC 20064. Offers civil engineering (MS, PhD); transportation and infrastructure systems (Certificate). *Program availability:* Part-time. *Faculty:* 7 full-

time (0 women), 7 part-time/adjunct (0 women). *Students:* 18 full-time (3 women), 24 part-time (6 women); includes 13 minority (9 Black or African American, non-Hispanic/Latino; 1 Asian, non-Hispanic/Latino; 3 Two or more races, non-Hispanic/Latino), 22 international. Average age 34. 28 applicants, 79% accepted, 7 enrolled. In 2016, 9 master's, 1 doctorate awarded. *Degree requirements:* For master's, thesis optional; for doctorate, comprehensive exam, thesis/dissertation. *Entrance requirements:* For master's and doctorate, GRE General Test, statement of purpose, official copies of academic transcripts, three letters of recommendation. Additional exam requirements/recommendations for international students: Required—TOEFL (minimum score 550 paper-based; 80 iBT). *Application deadline:* For fall admission, 7/15 priority date for domestic students, 7/1 for international students; for spring admission, 11/15 priority date for domestic students, 11/1 for international students. Applications are processed on a rolling basis. Application fee: $55. Electronic applications accepted. *Expenses:* $43,380 per year; $1,170 per credit; $200 per semester part-time fees. *Financial support:* Fellowships, research assistantships, teaching assistantships, Federal Work-Study, scholarships/grants, tuition waivers (full and partial), and unspecified assistantships available. Financial award application deadline: 2/1; financial award applicants required to submit FAFSA. *Faculty research:* Transportation engineering, solid mechanics, construction engineering and management, environmental engineering and water resources, structural engineering. *Total annual research expenditures:* $241,311. *Unit head:* Dr. Lu Sun, Chair, 202-319-6671, Fax: 202-319-6677, E-mail: sunl@cua.edu. *Application contact:* Director of Graduate Admissions, 202-319-5057, Fax: 202-319-6533, E-mail: cua-admissions@cua.edu.
Website: http://civil.cua.edu/

The Citadel, The Military College of South Carolina, Citadel Graduate College, School of Engineering, Department of Civil and Environmental Engineering, Charleston, SC 29409. Offers built environment and public health (Graduate Certificate); civil engineering (MS); geotechnical engineering (Graduate Certificate); structural engineering (Graduate Certificate); transportation engineering (Graduate Certificate). *Program availability:* Part-time, evening/weekend. *Faculty:* 1 full-time. *Students:* 11 part-time (1 woman); includes 1 minority (Black or African American, non-Hispanic/Latino). 8 applicants, 88% accepted, 4 enrolled. *Degree requirements:* For master's, plan of study outlining intended areas of interest and top four corresponding courses of interest. *Entrance requirements:* For master's, official transcript of baccalaureate degree from ABET-accredited engineering program or approved alternative; 2 letters of recommendation; for Graduate Certificate, official transcript of baccalaureate degree directly from an accredited college or university. Additional exam requirements/recommendations for international students: Required—TOEFL (minimum score 550 paper-based; 79 iBT). *Application deadline:* Applications are processed on a rolling basis. Application fee: $40. Electronic applications accepted. *Expenses:* Tuition, state resident: full-time $5121; part-time $569 per credit hour. Tuition, nonresident: full-time $8613; part-time $957 per credit hour. *Required fees:* $90 per term. *Financial support:* Fellowships and unspecified assistantships available. Support available to part-time students. Financial award application deadline: 7/1; financial award applicants required to submit FAFSA. *Unit head:* Dr. Kevin C. Bower, Head, 843-953-7683, E-mail: kevin.bower@citadel.edu. *Application contact:* Dr. Tara Hornor, Associate Provost for Planning, Assessment and Evaluation/Dean of Enrollment Management, 843-953-5089, E-mail: cgc@citadel.edu.
Website: http://www.citadel.edu/root/cee

College for Creative Studies, Graduate Programs, Detroit, MI 48202-4034. Offers color and materials design (MFA); integrated design (MFA); interaction design (MFA); transportation design (MFA). *Accreditation:* NASAD.

Cornell University, Graduate School, Graduate Fields of Engineering, Field of Civil and Environmental Engineering, Ithaca, NY 14853. Offers engineering management (M Eng, MS, PhD); environmental engineering (M Eng, MS, PhD); environmental fluid mechanics and hydrology (M Eng, MS, PhD); environmental systems engineering (M Eng, MS, PhD); geotechnical engineering (M Eng, MS, PhD); remote sensing (M Eng, MS, PhD); structural engineering (M Eng, MS, PhD); structural mechanics (M Eng, MS); transportation engineering (MS, PhD); transportation systems engineering (M Eng); water resource systems (M Eng, MS, PhD). Terminal master's awarded for partial completion of doctoral program. *Degree requirements:* For master's, thesis (MS); for doctorate, comprehensive exam, thesis/dissertation. *Entrance requirements:* For master's and doctorate, GRE General Test (recommended), 2 letters of recommendation. Additional exam requirements/recommendations for international students: Required—TOEFL (minimum score 600 paper-based; 77 iBT). Electronic applications accepted. *Faculty research:* Environmental engineering, geotechnical engineering, remote sensing, environmental fluid mechanics and hydrology, structural engineering.

École Polytechnique de Montréal, Graduate Programs, Department of Civil, Geological and Mining Engineering, Montréal, QC H3C 3A7, Canada. Offers civil, geological and mining engineering (DESS); environmental engineering (M Eng, M Sc A, PhD); geotechnical engineering (M Eng, M Sc A, PhD); hydraulics engineering (M Eng, M Sc A, PhD); structural engineering (M Eng, M Sc A, PhD); transportation engineering (M Eng, M Sc A, PhD). *Program availability:* Part-time. *Degree requirements:* For master's, one foreign language, thesis; for doctorate, one foreign language, thesis/dissertation. *Entrance requirements:* For master's, minimum GPA of 2.75; for doctorate, minimum GPA of 3.0. *Faculty research:* Water resources management, characteristics of building materials, aging of dams, pollution control.

George Mason University, Volgenau School of Engineering, Sid and Reva Dewberry Department of Civil, Environmental, and Infrastructure Engineering, Fairfax, VA 22030. Offers construction project management (MS); geotechnical, construction, and structural engineering (M Eng); transportation engineering (PhD). *Faculty:* 14 full-time (6 women), 20 part-time/adjunct (4 women). *Students:* 47 full-time (12 women), 62 part-time (22 women); includes 23 minority (6 Black or African American, non-Hispanic/Latino; 9 Asian, non-Hispanic/Latino; 7 Hispanic/Latino; 1 Native Hawaiian or other Pacific Islander, non-Hispanic/Latino), 38 international. Average age 29. 109 applicants, 77% accepted, 39 enrolled. In 2016, 31 master's, 1 doctorate awarded. *Degree requirements:* For master's, thesis (for some programs), 30 credits, departmental seminars; for doctorate, thesis/dissertation, qualifying exams. *Entrance requirements:* For master's, GRE, photocopy of passport; 2 official college transcripts; resume; official bank statement; proof of financial support; expanded goals statement; self-evaluation form; BS in engineering or other related science; 3 letters of recommendation; for doctorate, GRE (for those who received degree outside of the U.S.), photocopy of passport; 2 official college transcripts; resume; official bank statement; proof of financial support; expanded goals statement; self-evaluation form; baccalaureate degree in engineering or related science; master's degree (preferred); 3 letters of recommendation. Additional exam requirements/recommendations for international students: Required—TOEFL (minimum score 575 paper-based; 88 iBT), IELTS (minimum score 6.5), PTE (minimum score 59). *Application deadline:* For fall admission, 1/15 priority date for domestic students. Application fee: $75 ($80 for international students). Electronic applications accepted. *Expenses:* Contact institution. *Financial support:* In 2016–17, 27 students received support, including 1 fellowship (averaging $10,000 per year), 16 research assistantships with tuition reimbursements available (averaging $20,150 per year), 10 teaching assistantships with tuition reimbursements available (averaging $21,000 per year); career-related internships or fieldwork, Federal Work-Study, scholarships/grants, unspecified assistantships, and health care benefits (for full-time research or teaching assistantship recipients) also available. Support available to part-time students. Financial award application deadline: 3/1; financial award applicants required to submit FAFSA. *Faculty research:* Evolutionary design, infrastructure security, intelligent transportation systems, national transportation networks, water quality modeling. *Total annual research expenditures:* $568,705. *Unit head:* LIza Wilson Durant, Acting Chair, 703-993-1687, Fax: 703-993-9790, E-mail: ldurant2@gmu.edu. *Application contact:* Laura Kosoglu, Director, Graduate Program, 703-993-1675, Fax: 703-993-9790, E-mail: ceiegrad@gmu.edu.
Website: http://civil.gmu.edu/

Illinois Institute of Technology, Graduate College, Armour College of Engineering, Department of Civil, Architectural and Environmental Engineering, Chicago, IL 60616. Offers architectural engineering (M Arch E); civil engineering (MS, PhD), including architectural engineering (MS), construction engineering and management (MS), geoenvironmental engineering (MS), geotechnical engineering (MS), structural engineering (MS), transportation engineering (MS); construction engineering and management (MCEM); environmental engineering (M Env E, MS, PhD); geoenvironmental engineering (M Geoenv E); geotechnical engineering (MGE); infrastructure engineering and management (MPW); structural engineering (MSE); transportation engineering (M Trans E). *Program availability:* Part-time, evening/weekend, online learning. Terminal master's awarded for partial completion of doctoral program. *Degree requirements:* For master's, thesis (for some programs); for doctorate, comprehensive exam, thesis/dissertation. *Entrance requirements:* For master's, GRE General Test (minimum score 900 Quantitative and Verbal, 2.5 Analytical Writing), minimum undergraduate GPA of 3.0; for doctorate, GRE General Test (minimum score 1000 Quantitative and Verbal, 3.0 Analytical Writing), minimum undergraduate GPA of 3.0. Additional exam requirements/recommendations for international students: Required—TOEFL (minimum score 550 paper-based; 80 iBT). Electronic applications accepted. *Faculty research:* Structural, architectural, geotechnical and geoenvironmental engineering; construction engineering and management; transportation engineering; environmental engineering and public works.

Iowa State University of Science and Technology, Department of Civil and Construction Engineering, Ames, IA 50011. Offers civil engineering (MS, PhD), including civil engineering materials, construction engineering and management, environmental engineering, geotechnical engineering, structural engineering, transportation engineering. *Degree requirements:* For master's, thesis or alternative; for doctorate, thesis/dissertation. *Entrance requirements:* For master's and doctorate, GRE General Test. Additional exam requirements/recommendations for international students: Required—TOEFL (minimum score 550 paper-based; 82 iBT), IELTS (minimum score 6.5). *Application deadline:* For fall admission, 2/1 priority date for domestic students, 2/1 for international students; for spring admission, 8/1 priority date for domestic students, 8/1 for international students. Application fee: $60 ($90 for international students). Electronic applications accepted. *Application contact:* Kathy Petersen, Application Contact, 515-294-4975, Fax: 515-294-8216, E-mail: ccee-grad-inquiry@iastate.edu.
Website: http://www.ccee.iastate.edu/

Kansas State University, Graduate School, College of Engineering, Department of Civil Engineering, Manhattan, KS 66506. Offers civil engineering (MS, PhD); environmental engineering (MS, PhD); geotechnical engineering (MS, PhD); structural engineering (MS, PhD); transportation engineering (MS, PhD); water resources engineering (MS, PhD). *Program availability:* Part-time, evening/weekend, online learning. *Faculty:* 14 full-time (4 women), 3 part-time/adjunct (1 woman). *Students:* 36 full-time (11 women), 34 part-time (7 women); includes 5 minority (2 Asian, non-Hispanic/Latino; 2 Hispanic/Latino; 1 Two or more races, non-Hispanic/Latino), 28 international. Average age 29. 70 applicants, 60% accepted, 11 enrolled. In 2016, 21 master's, 7 doctorates awarded. *Degree requirements:* For master's, thesis or alternative; for doctorate, thesis/dissertation. *Entrance requirements:* For master's, GRE General Test, bachelor's degree or course work in related engineering fields; for doctorate, GRE General Test. Additional exam requirements/recommendations for international students: Required—TOEFL (minimum score 550 paper-based; 79 iBT). *Application deadline:* For fall admission, 2/1 priority date for domestic students, 1/1 priority date for international students; for spring admission, 8/1 priority date for domestic and international students. Applications are processed on a rolling basis. Application fee: $50 ($75 for international students). Electronic applications accepted. *Expenses:* Tuition, state resident: full-time $9670. Tuition, nonresident: full-time $21,828. *Required fees:* $862. *Financial support:* In 2016–17, 19 research assistantships with partial tuition reimbursements (averaging $13,431 per year), 12 teaching assistantships with partial tuition reimbursements (averaging $15,058 per year) were awarded; institutionally sponsored loans and scholarships/grants also available. Support available to part-time students. Financial award application deadline: 3/1; financial award applicants required to submit FAFSA. *Faculty research:* Transportation and materials engineering, water resources engineering, environmental engineering, geotechnical engineering, structural engineering. *Total annual research expenditures:* $2.4 million. *Unit head:* Dr. Robert Stokes, Head, 785-532-1595, Fax: 785-532-7717, E-mail: drbobb@k-state.edu. *Application contact:* Dr. Dunja Peric, Graduate Coordinator, 785-532-2468, Fax: 785-532-7717, E-mail: peric@k-state.edu.
Website: http://www.ce.ksu.edu/

Louisiana State University and Agricultural & Mechanical College, Graduate School, College of Engineering, Department of Civil and Environmental Engineering, Baton Rouge, LA 70803. Offers environmental engineering (MSCE, PhD); geotechnical engineering (MSCE, PhD); structural engineering and mechanics (MSCE, PhD); transportation engineering (MSCE, PhD); water resources (MSCE, PhD).

Marquette University, Graduate School, College of Engineering, Department of Civil and Environmental Engineering, Milwaukee, WI 53201-1881. Offers construction engineering and management (MS, PhD, Certificate); environmental engineering (MS, PhD); structural design (Certificate); structural engineering and structural mechanics (MS, PhD); transportation (Certificate); transportation engineering and materials (MS, PhD); waste and wastewater treatment processes (Certificate); water resources engineering (Certificate). *Program availability:* Part-time, evening/weekend. *Faculty:* 17 full-time (2 women), 2 part-time/adjunct (0 women). *Students:* 27 full-time (8 women), 6 part-time (0 women); includes 5 minority (1 Asian, non-Hispanic/Latino; 2 Hispanic/Latino; 2 Two or more races, non-Hispanic/Latino), 13 international. Average age 28. 70 applicants, 56% accepted, 9 enrolled. In 2016, 8 master's, 5 doctorates awarded. Terminal master's awarded for partial completion of doctoral program. *Degree requirements:* For master's, comprehensive exam (for some programs), thesis or alternative; for doctorate, thesis/dissertation. *Entrance requirements:* For master's, GRE General Test (recommended), minimum GPA of 3.0, official transcripts from all current and previous colleges/universities except Marquette, three letters of recommendation; for doctorate, GRE General Test, minimum GPA of 3.0, official transcripts from all current and previous colleges/universities except Marquette, three letters of recommendation, brief statement of purpose, submission of any English language publications authored by applicant (strongly recommended). Additional exam

requirements/recommendations for international students: Required—TOEFL (minimum score 530 paper-based). *Application deadline:* For fall admission, 6/1 priority date for domestic students. Applications are processed on a rolling basis. Application fee: $50. Electronic applications accepted. *Financial support:* Fellowships, research assistantships, teaching assistantships, scholarships/grants, health care benefits, tuition waivers (partial), and unspecified assistantships available. Support available to part-time students. Financial award application deadline: 2/15. *Faculty research:* Highway safety, highway performance, and intelligent transportation systems; surface mount technology; watershed management. *Total annual research expenditures:* $480,876. *Unit head:* Dr. Christopher Foley, Chair, 414-288-5741. *Application contact:* Dr. Stephen M. Heinrich, Director of Graduate Studies, 414-288-5466.
Website: http://www.marquette.edu/civil-environmental-engineering/

Marshall University, Academic Affairs Division, College of Information Technology and Engineering, Program in Engineering, Huntington, WV 25755. Offers engineering (MSME); engineering management (MSE); environmental engineering (MSE); transportation and infrastructure engineering (MSE). *Program availability:* Part-time, evening/weekend. *Degree requirements:* For master's, final project, oral exam. *Entrance requirements:* For master's, GMAT or GRE General Test, minimum undergraduate GPA of 2.75.

Massachusetts Institute of Technology, School of Engineering, Department of Civil and Environmental Engineering, Cambridge, MA 02139. Offers biological oceanography (PhD, Sc D); chemical oceanography (PhD, Sc D); civil and environmental engineering (M Eng, SM, PhD, Sc D); civil and environmental systems (PhD, Sc D); civil engineering (PhD, Sc D, CE); civil engineering and computation (PhD); coastal engineering (PhD, Sc D); construction engineering and management (PhD, Sc D); environmental biology (PhD, Sc D); environmental chemistry (PhD, Sc D); environmental engineering (PhD, Sc D); environmental engineering and computation (PhD); environmental fluid mechanics (PhD, Sc D); geotechnical and geoenvironmental engineering (PhD, Sc D); hydrology (PhD, Sc D); information technology (PhD, Sc D); oceanographic engineering (PhD, Sc D); structures and materials (PhD, Sc D); transportation (PhD, Sc D); SM/MBA. *Faculty:* 35 full-time (6 women). *Students:* 192 full-time (64 women); includes 25 minority (2 Black or African American, non-Hispanic/Latino; 11 Asian, non-Hispanic/Latino; 8 Hispanic/Latino; 4 Two or more races, non-Hispanic/Latino), 113 international. Average age 27. 530 applicants, 20% accepted, 77 enrolled. In 2016, 56 master's, 16 doctorates, 1 other advanced degree awarded. *Degree requirements:* For master's, thesis; for doctorate, comprehensive exam, thesis/dissertation; for CE, comprehensive exam, thesis. *Entrance requirements:* For master's, doctorate, and CE, GRE General Test. Additional exam requirements/recommendations for international students: Required—TOEFL, IELTS. *Application deadline:* For fall admission, 12/15 for domestic and international students. Application fee: $75. Electronic applications accepted. *Expenses:* Tuition: Full-time $46,400; part-time $725 per credit. One-time fee: $312 full-time. Full-time tuition and fees vary according to course load and program. *Financial support:* In 2016–17, 150 students received support, including fellowships (averaging $41,900 per year), 124 research assistantships (averaging $36,900 per year), 9 teaching assistantships (averaging $36,900 per year); Federal Work-Study, institutionally sponsored loans, scholarships/grants, traineeships, health care benefits, unspecified assistantships, and resident tutors also available. Support available to part-time students. Financial award application deadline: 5/1; financial award applicants required to submit FAFSA. *Faculty research:* Environmental chemistry, environmental fluid mechanics and coastal engineering, environmental microbiology, geotechnical engineering and geomechanics, hydrology and hydro climatology, infrastructure systems, mechanics of materials and structures, transportation systems. *Total annual research expenditures:* $25 million. *Unit head:* Prof. Markus Buehler, Department Head, 617-253-7101. *Application contact:* 617-253-7119, E-mail: cee-admissions@mit.edu.
Website: http://cee.mit.edu/

Morgan State University, School of Graduate Studies, Clarence M. Mitchell, Jr. School of Engineering, Department of Transportation, Baltimore, MD 21251. Offers MS. *Program availability:* Part-time, evening/weekend. *Degree requirements:* For master's, thesis optional, comprehensive exam or equivalent. *Entrance requirements:* For master's, minimum undergraduate GPA of 2.5. Additional exam requirements/ recommendations for international students: Required—TOEFL (minimum score 550 paper-based). *Faculty research:* Distributional impacts of congestion, pricing education and training for intelligent vehicle highway systems.

New Jersey Institute of Technology, Newark College of Engineering, Newark, NJ 07102. Offers biomedical engineering (MS, PhD); chemical engineering (MS, PhD); computer engineering (MS, PhD); electrical engineering (MS, PhD); engineering management (MS); environmental engineering (PhD); healthcare systems management (MS); industrial engineering (MS, PhD); Internet engineering (MS); manufacturing engineering (MS); mechanical engineering (MS, PhD); occupational safety and health engineering (MS); pharmaceutical bioprocessing (MS); pharmaceutical engineering (MS); pharmaceutical systems management (MS); power and energy systems (MS); telecommunications (MS); transportation (MS, PhD). *Program availability:* Part-time, evening/weekend. *Faculty:* 146 full-time (21 women), 119 part-time/adjunct (10 women). *Students:* 804 full-time (191 women), 550 part-time (129 women); includes 357 minority (82 Black or African American, non-Hispanic/Latino; 1 American Indian or Alaska Native, non-Hispanic/Latino; 138 Asian, non-Hispanic/Latino; 114 Hispanic/Latino; 22 Two or more races, non-Hispanic/Latino), 675 international. Average age 27. 2,959 applicants, 51% accepted, 442 enrolled. In 2016, 595 master's, 29 doctorates awarded. Terminal master's awarded for partial completion of doctoral program. *Degree requirements:* For master's, thesis optional; for doctorate, thesis/dissertation. *Entrance requirements:* For master's, GRE General Test; for doctorate, GRE General Test, minimum graduate GPA of 3.5. Additional exam requirements/recommendations for international students: Required—TOEFL (minimum score 550 paper-based; 79 iBT). *Application deadline:* For fall admission, 6/1 priority date for domestic students, 5/1 priority date for international students; for spring admission, 11/15 priority date for domestic and international students. Applications are processed on a rolling basis. Application fee: $75. Electronic applications accepted. *Expenses:* Contact institution. *Financial support:* In 2016–17, 172 students received support, including 1 fellowship (averaging $1,528 per year), 79 research assistantships (averaging $13,336 per year), 92 teaching assistantships (averaging $20,619 per year); scholarships/grants also available. Financial award application deadline: 1/15. *Faculty research:* Nonlinear signal processing, intelligent medical image analysis, calibration issues in coherent localization, computer-aided design, neural network for tool wear measurement. *Total annual research expenditures:* $11.1 million. *Unit head:* Dr. Moshe Kam, Dean, 973-596-5534, E-mail: moshe.kam@njit.edu. *Application contact:* Stephen Eck, Director of Admissions, 973-596-3300, Fax: 973-596-3461, E-mail: admissions@njit.edu.
Website: http://engineering.njit.edu/

New York University, Polytechnic School of Engineering, Department of Civil and Urban Engineering, Major in Transportation Planning and Engineering, New York, NY 10012-1019. Offers MS, PhD. *Program availability:* Part-time, evening/weekend. *Degree requirements:* For master's, comprehensive exam (for some programs), thesis (for some programs); for doctorate, comprehensive exam, thesis/dissertation. *Entrance requirements:* Additional exam requirements/recommendations for international

students: Required—TOEFL (minimum score 550 paper-based; 80 iBT); Recommended—IELTS (minimum score 6.5). Electronic applications accepted.

North Dakota State University, College of Graduate and Interdisciplinary Studies, College of Engineering, Doctoral Program in Engineering, Fargo, ND 58102. Offers environmental and conservation science (PhD); materials and nanotechnology (PhD); natural resource management (PhD); science, technology, engineering, mathematics education (STEM) (PhD); transportation and logistics (PhD). *Degree requirements:* For doctorate, comprehensive exam, thesis/dissertation. *Entrance requirements:* For doctorate, bachelor's degree in engineering, minimum GPA of 3.0. Additional exam requirements/recommendations for international students: Required—TOEFL. Electronic applications accepted. *Expenses:* Contact institution.

Northwestern University, McCormick School of Engineering and Applied Science, Department of Civil and Environmental Engineering, Evanston, IL 60208-3109. Offers environmental engineering and science (MS, PhD); geotechnical engineering (MS, PhD); mechanics of materials and solids (MS, PhD); project management (MS); structural engineering and materials (MS, PhD); transportation systems analysis and planning (MS, PhD). MS and PhD admissions and degrees offered through The Graduate School. *Program availability:* Part-time. Terminal master's awarded for partial completion of doctoral program. *Degree requirements:* For master's, comprehensive exam (for some programs), thesis (for some programs); for doctorate, comprehensive exam, thesis/dissertation. *Entrance requirements:* For master's and doctorate, GRE General Test, minimum 2 letters of recommendation, transcripts from all academic institutions attended. Additional exam requirements/recommendations for international students: Required—TOEFL (minimum score 577 paper-based; 90 iBT), IELTS (minimum score 7). Electronic applications accepted. *Faculty research:* Environmental engineering and science, geotechnics, mechanics, materials, structures, and transportation systems analysis and planning.

Ohio University, Graduate College, Russ College of Engineering and Technology, Department of Civil Engineering, Athens, OH 45701-2979. Offers civil engineering (PhD); construction engineering and management (MS); environmental (MS); geotechnical and geoenvironmental (MS); mechanics (MS); structures (MS); transportation (MS); water resources (MS). *Program availability:* Part-time. *Degree requirements:* For master's, comprehensive exam (for some programs), thesis or alternative; for doctorate, comprehensive exam, thesis/dissertation. *Entrance requirements:* For master's, GRE General Test, minimum GPA of 3.0, 3 letters of recommendation; for doctorate, GRE General Test. Additional exam requirements/recommendations for international students: Required—TOEFL (minimum score 550 paper-based; 80 iBT) or IELTS (minimum score 6.5). *Application deadline:* For fall admission, 5/1 priority date for domestic students, 2/1 priority date for international students; for winter admission, 8/1 priority date for domestic students, 4/1 priority date for international students; for spring admission, 2/1 priority date for domestic students, 7/1 priority date for international students. Applications are processed on a rolling basis. Application fee: $50 ($55 for international students). Electronic applications accepted. *Financial support:* Research assistantships with full tuition reimbursements, teaching assistantships with full tuition reimbursements, Federal Work-Study, institutionally sponsored loans, scholarships/grants, and unspecified assistantships available. Financial award application deadline: 3/15; financial award applicants required to submit FAFSA. *Faculty research:* Noise abatement, materials and environment, highway infrastructure, subsurface investigation (pavements, pipes, bridges). *Unit head:* Dr. Gayle F. Mitchell, Chair, 740-593-0430, Fax: 740-593-0625, E-mail: mitchelg@ohio.edu. *Application contact:* Dr. Shad M. Sargand, Graduate Chair, 740-593-1465, Fax: 740-593-0625, E-mail: sargand@ohio.edu.
Website: http://www.ohio.edu/civil/

Old Dominion University, Frank Batten College of Engineering and Technology, Program in Civil Engineering, Norfolk, VA 23529. Offers civil engineering (ME, MS), including coastal engineering, geotechnical engineering, hydraulics and water resources, structural engineering, transportation engineering. *Program availability:* Part-time, evening/weekend, blended/hybrid learning. *Faculty:* 16 full-time (1 woman), 5 part-time/adjunct (0 women). *Students:* 12 full-time (4 women), 30 part-time (6 women); includes 7 minority (2 Black or African American, non-Hispanic/Latino; 4 Hispanic/Latino; 1 Two or more races, non-Hispanic/Latino), 8 international. Average age 28. 79 applicants, 84% accepted, 33 enrolled. In 2016, 15 master's awarded. *Degree requirements:* For master's, comprehensive exam, thesis optional. *Entrance requirements:* For master's, GRE, minimum GPA of 3.0. Additional exam requirements/recommendations for international students: Required—TOEFL (minimum score 550 paper-based, 80 iBT) or IELTS (6.5). *Application deadline:* For fall admission, 6/1 priority date for domestic students, 4/15 priority date for international students; for spring admission, 11/1 priority date for domestic students, 10/1 priority date for international students. Applications are processed on a rolling basis. Application fee: $50. Electronic applications accepted. *Expenses:* Contact institution. *Financial support:* In 2016–17, 26 students received support, including 1 fellowship with full tuition reimbursement available (averaging $18,000 per year), 17 research assistantships with full and partial tuition reimbursements available (averaging $16,800 per year), 9 teaching assistantships with full and partial tuition reimbursements available (averaging $15,215 per year); scholarships/grants and health care benefits also available. Support available to part-time students. Financial award application deadline: 4/1; financial award applicants required to submit FAFSA. *Faculty research:* Structural engineering, coastal engineering, geotechnical engineering, water resources, transportation engineering. *Total annual research expenditures:* $937,914. *Unit head:* Dr. Isao Ishibashi, Graduate Program Director, 757-683-4641, E-mail: cegpd@odu.edu. *Application contact:* Dr. Shirshak Dhali, Associate Dean, 757-683-3744, Fax: 757-683-4898, E-mail: sdhali@odu.edu.
Website: http://eng.odu.edu/cee/

Oregon State University, College of Engineering, Program in Civil Engineering, Corvallis, OR 97331. Offers civil engineering (M Eng, MS, PhD); coastal and ocean engineering (M Eng, MS, PhD); construction engineering management (M Eng, MS, PhD); engineering education (M Eng, MS, PhD); geomatics (M Eng, MS, PhD); geotechnical engineering (M Eng, MS, PhD); infrastructure materials (M Eng, MS, PhD); structural engineering (M Eng, MS, PhD); transportation engineering (M Eng). *Faculty:* 42 full-time (8 women), 2 part-time/adjunct (0 women). *Students:* 157 full-time (48 women), 10 part-time (3 women); includes 18 minority (7 Asian, non-Hispanic/Latino; 7 Hispanic/Latino; 1 Native Hawaiian or other Pacific Islander, non-Hispanic/Latino; 3 Two or more races, non-Hispanic/Latino), 92 international. Average age 28. 379 applicants, 31% accepted, 50 enrolled. In 2016, 55 master's, 5 doctorates awarded. *Entrance requirements:* For master's and doctorate, GRE. Additional exam requirements/recommendations for international students: Required—TOEFL (minimum score 80 iBT), IELTS (minimum score 6.5). *Application deadline:* For fall admission, 8/1 for domestic students, 4/1 for international students; for winter admission, 12/1 for domestic students, 7/1 for international students; for spring admission, 2/1 for domestic students, 10/1 for international students; for summer admission, 5/1 for domestic students, 1/1 for international students. Application fee: $75 ($85 for international students). *Expenses:* $14,130 resident full-time tuition, $23,769 non-resident. *Financial support:* Application deadline: 1/15. *Unit head:* Dr. Jason Weiss, School Head/Professor. *Application contact:*

Transportation and Highway Engineering

Shannon Reed, Graduate Program Coordinator, 541-737-4575, E-mail: shannon.reed@oregonstate.edu.
Website: http://cce.oregonstate.edu/graduate-academics

Rensselaer Polytechnic Institute, Graduate School, School of Engineering, Program in Transportation Engineering, Troy, NY 12180-3590. Offers M Eng, MS, D Eng, PhD. *Faculty:* 17 full-time (3 women), 3 part-time/adjunct (0 women). *Students:* 5 full-time (4 women). 9 applicants. In 2016, 1 master's, 2 doctorates awarded. Terminal master's awarded for partial completion of doctoral program. *Degree requirements:* For master's, thesis (for some programs); for doctorate, thesis/dissertation. *Entrance requirements:* For master's and doctorate, GRE. Additional exam requirements/recommendations for international students: Required—TOEFL (minimum score 570 paper-based; 88 iBT), IELTS (minimum score 6.5), PTE (minimum score 60). *Application deadline:* For fall admission, 1/1 priority date for domestic and international students; for spring admission, 8/15 priority date for domestic and international students. Applications are processed on a rolling basis. Application fee: $75. Electronic applications accepted. *Expenses: Tuition:* Full-time $49,520; part-time $2060 per credit hour. *Required fees:* $2617. *Financial support:* In 2016–17, research assistantships (averaging $22,000 per year), teaching assistantships (averaging $22,000 per year) were awarded; fellowships also available. Financial award application deadline: 1/1. *Faculty research:* Advanced econometrics, freight transportation systems: operations and modeling, intelligent transportation systems, traffic simulation and network modeling, transportation economics, transportation planning. *Total annual research expenditures:* $1.2 million. *Unit head:* Dr. Michael O'Rourke, Graduate Program Director, 518-276-6933, E-mail: orourm@rpi.edu. *Application contact:* Office of Graduate Admissions, 518-276-6216, E-mail: gradadmissions@rpi.edu.
Website: http://cee.rpi.edu/graduate

South Carolina State University, College of Graduate and Professional Studies, Department of Civil and Mechanical Engineering Technology, Orangeburg, SC 29117-0001. Offers transportation (MS). *Program availability:* Part-time, evening/weekend. *Faculty:* 2 full-time (1 woman), 1 part-time/adjunct (0 women). *Students:* 3 full-time (1 woman), 1 (woman) part-time; all minorities (all Black or African American, non-Hispanic/Latino). Average age 41. 1 applicant, 100% accepted. In 2016, 10 master's awarded. *Degree requirements:* For master's, comprehensive exam, thesis, departmental qualifying exam. *Entrance requirements:* For master's, GRE. Additional exam requirements/recommendations for international students: Recommended—TOEFL. *Application deadline:* For fall admission, 6/15 for domestic and international students; for spring admission, 11/1 for domestic and international students. Application fee: $25. Electronic applications accepted. *Expenses:* Tuition, state resident: full-time $8938; part-time $579 per credit hour. Tuition, nonresident: full-time $19,018; part-time $1139 per credit hour. *Required fees:* $1482; $82 per credit hour. *Financial support:* Fellowships, research assistantships, career-related internships or fieldwork, Federal Work-Study, scholarships/grants, and unspecified assistantships available. Financial award application deadline: 6/1. *Unit head:* Dr. Stanley Ihekweazu, Chair, 803-536-7117, Fax: 803-516-4607, E-mail: sihekwea@scsu.edu. *Application contact:* Curtis Foskey, Coordinator of Graduate Admission, 803-536-8419, Fax: 803-536-8812, E-mail: cfoskey@scsu.edu.
Website: http://www.scsu.edu/schoolofgraduatestudies.aspx

Southern Illinois University Edwardsville, Graduate School, School of Engineering, Department of Civil Engineering, Program in Transportation Engineering, Edwardsville, IL 62026. Offers MS. *Program availability:* Part-time, evening/weekend. *Degree requirements:* For master's, thesis (for some programs), research paper. *Entrance requirements:* For master's, minimum undergraduate GPA of 2.75 in science, math, and engineering courses. Additional exam requirements/recommendations for international students: Required—TOEFL (minimum score 550 paper-based, 79 iBT), IELTS (minimum score 6.5), Michigan Test of English Language Proficiency or PTE. Electronic applications accepted.

Stevens Institute of Technology, Graduate School, Charles V. Schaefer Jr. School of Engineering and Science, Department of Civil, Environmental, and Ocean Engineering, Program in Civil Engineering, Hoboken, NJ 07030. Offers civil engineering (PhD, Certificate), including geotechnical engineering (Certificate); geotechnical/geoenvironmental engineering (M Eng, Engr); hydrologic modeling (M Eng); stormwater management (M Eng); structural engineering (M Eng, Engr); transportation engineering (M Eng); water resources engineering (M Eng). *Program availability:* Part-time, evening/weekend. *Students:* 63 full-time (12 women), 27 part-time (10 women); includes 5 minority (2 Black or African American, non-Hispanic/Latino; 2 Asian, non-Hispanic/Latino; 1 Hispanic/Latino), 55 international. Average age 25. 167 applicants, 57% accepted, 24 enrolled. In 2016, 50 master's, 1 other advanced degree awarded. *Degree requirements:* For master's, thesis optional, minimum B average in major field and overall; for doctorate, comprehensive exam (for some programs), thesis/dissertation; for other advanced degree, minimum B average. *Entrance requirements:* Additional exam requirements/recommendations for international students: Required—TOEFL (minimum score 74 iBT), IELTS (minimum score 6). *Application deadline:* For fall admission, 6/1 for domestic students, 4/15 for international students; for spring admission, 11/30 for domestic students, 11/1 for international students. Applications are processed on a rolling basis. Application fee: $65. Electronic applications accepted. *Expenses:* Contact institution. *Financial support:* Fellowships, research assistantships, teaching assistantships, career-related internships or fieldwork, Federal Work-Study, scholarships/grants, and unspecified assistantships available. Financial award application deadline: 2/15; financial award applicants required to submit FAFSA. *Unit head:* Dr. David A. Vaccari, Director, 201-216-5570, Fax: 201-216-8739, E-mail: dvaccari@stevens.edu. *Application contact:* Graduate Admission, 888-783-8367, Fax: 888-511-1306, E-mail: graduate@stevens.edu.

Texas Southern University, School of Science and Technology, Program in Transportation, Planning and Management, Houston, TX 77004-4584. Offers MS. *Program availability:* Part-time, evening/weekend. *Degree requirements:* For master's, comprehensive exam, thesis optional. *Entrance requirements:* For master's, GRE General Test, minimum GPA of 2.5. Additional exam requirements/recommendations for international students: Required—TOEFL. Electronic applications accepted. *Faculty research:* Highway traffic operations, transportation and policy planning, air quality in transportation, transportation modeling.

University of Arkansas, Graduate School, College of Engineering, Department of Civil Engineering, Fayetteville, AR 72701. Offers civil engineering (MSCE, MSE, PhD); environmental engineering (MS En E, MSE); transportation engineering (MSE, MSTE). In 2016, 15 master's, 5 doctorates awarded. *Degree requirements:* For master's, thesis optional; for doctorate, one foreign language, thesis/dissertation. *Application deadline:* For fall admission, 4/1 for international students; for spring admission, 10/1 for international students. Applications are processed on a rolling basis. Application fee: $40 ($50 for international students). Electronic applications accepted. *Financial support:* In 2016–17, 37 research assistantships, 1 teaching assistantship were awarded; fellowships with tuition reimbursements, career-related internships or fieldwork, and Federal Work-Study also available. Support available to part-time students. Financial award application deadline: 4/1; financial award applicants required to submit FAFSA. *Unit head:* Dr. Micah Hale, Departmental Chair, 479-575-4954, Fax: 479-575-7168, E-mail: micah@uark.edu. *Application contact:* Dr. Julian Fairey, Graduate Coordinator, 479-575-4023, E-mail: julianf@uark.edu.
Website: http://www.cveg.uark.edu

University of Calgary, Faculty of Graduate Studies, Schulich School of Engineering, Department of Civil Engineering, Calgary, AB T2N 1N4, Canada. Offers avalanche mechanics (M Sc, PhD); civil engineering (M Eng, M Sc, PhD); energy and environment engineering (M Eng, M Sc, PhD); environmental engineering (M Eng, M Sc, PhD); geotechnical engineering (M Eng, M Sc, PhD); materials science (M Eng, M Sc, PhD); project management (M Eng, M Sc, PhD); structures and solid mechanics (M Eng, M Sc, PhD); transportation engineering (M Eng, M Sc, PhD); water resources (M Eng, M Sc, PhD). *Program availability:* Part-time. *Degree requirements:* For master's, thesis; for doctorate, thesis/dissertation, written and oral candidacy exam. *Entrance requirements:* For master's, minimum GPA of 3.0; for doctorate, minimum GPA of 3.5. Additional exam requirements/recommendations for international students: Required—TOEFL (minimum score 580 paper-based; 93 iBT), IELTS (minimum score 7). Electronic applications accepted. *Faculty research:* Geotechnical engineering, energy and environment, transportation, project management, structures and solid mechanics.

University of California, Berkeley, Graduate Division, College of Engineering, Department of Civil and Environmental Engineering, Berkeley, CA 94720-1500. Offers engineering and project management (M Eng, MS, PhD); environmental engineering (M Eng, MS, PhD); geoengineering (M Eng, MS, PhD); structural engineering, mechanics and materials (M Eng, MS, PhD); transportation engineering (M Eng, MS, PhD); M Arch/MS; MCP/MS; MPP/MS. *Students:* 360 full-time (143 women); includes 71 minority (15 Black or African American, non-Hispanic/Latino; 39 Asian, non-Hispanic/Latino; 17 Hispanic/Latino), 148 international. Average age 27. 1,086 applicants, 185 enrolled. In 2016, 188 master's, 26 doctorates awarded. Terminal master's awarded for partial completion of doctoral program. *Degree requirements:* For master's, comprehensive exam (for some programs), thesis (for some programs), comprehensive exam or thesis (MS); for doctorate, thesis/dissertation, qualifying exam. *Entrance requirements:* For master's, GRE General Test, minimum GPA of 3.0, 3 letters of recommendation; for doctorate, GRE General Test, minimum GPA of 3.5, 3 letters of recommendation. Additional exam requirements/recommendations for international students: Required—TOEFL (minimum score 570 paper-based; 90 iBT). *Application deadline:* For fall admission, 12/16 for domestic students. Application fee: $105 ($125 for international students). Electronic applications accepted. *Financial support:* Applicants required to submit FAFSA. *Unit head:* Prof. Robert Harley, Chair, 510-643-8739, Fax: 510-643-5264, E-mail: chair@ce.berkeley.edu. *Application contact:* Shelly Okimoto, Graduate Advisor, 510-642-6464, Fax: 510-643-5264, E-mail: aao@ce.berkeley.edu.
Website: http://www.ce.berkeley.edu/

University of California, Davis, College of Engineering, Graduate Group in Transportation Technology and Policy, Davis, CA 95616. Offers MS, PhD. Terminal master's awarded for partial completion of doctoral program. *Degree requirements:* For master's, comprehensive exam (for some programs), thesis (for some programs); for doctorate, thesis/dissertation. *Entrance requirements:* For master's, GRE General Test, minimum GPA of 3.0; for doctorate, GRE General Test, minimum GPA of 3.5. Additional exam requirements/recommendations for international students: Required—TOEFL (minimum score 550 paper-based). Electronic applications accepted.

University of California, Irvine, Institute of Transportation Studies, Irvine, CA 92697. Offers MA, PhD. *Students:* 15 full-time (9 women); includes 4 minority (all Asian, non-Hispanic/Latino), 10 international. Average age 29. 29 applicants, 55% accepted, 4 enrolled. *Entrance requirements:* For master's and doctorate, GRE General Test, minimum GPA of 3.0. *Application deadline:* For fall admission, 1/15 for domestic and international students. Application fee: $105 ($125 for international students). *Financial support:* Fellowships, research assistantships with full tuition reimbursements, teaching assistantships, institutionally sponsored loans, traineeships, health care benefits, and unspecified assistantships available. Financial award application deadline: 3/1. *Unit head:* Stephen G. Ritchie, Director, 949-824-4214, E-mail: sritchie@uci.edu. *Application contact:* Anne Marie DeFeo, Administrative Manager, 949-824-6564, E-mail: amdefeo@uci.edu.
Website: http://www.its.uci.edu/

University of Central Florida, College of Engineering and Computer Science, Department of Civil, Environmental, and Construction Engineering, Orlando, FL 32816. Offers civil engineering (MS, MSCE, PhD, Certificate), including civil engineering (MS, MSCE, PhD), construction engineering (Certificate), structural engineering (Certificate), transportation engineering (Certificate); environmental engineering (MS, MS Env E, PhD). *Program availability:* Part-time, evening/weekend. *Faculty:* 29 full-time (3 women), 19 part-time/adjunct (1 woman). *Students:* 105 full-time (15 women), 90 part-time (26 women); includes 52 minority (11 Black or African American, non-Hispanic/Latino; 9 Asian, non-Hispanic/Latino; 29 Hispanic/Latino; 3 Two or more races, non-Hispanic/Latino), 79 international. Average age 29. 190 applicants, 73% accepted, 48 enrolled. In 2016, 42 master's, 17 doctorates, 3 other advanced degrees awarded. *Degree requirements:* For master's, thesis or alternative; for doctorate, thesis/dissertation, departmental qualifying exam, candidacy exam. *Entrance requirements:* For master's, GRE General Test, minimum GPA of 3.0 in last 60 hours of course work; for doctorate, GRE General Test, minimum GPA of 3.5 in last 60 hours of course work. Additional exam requirements/recommendations for international students: Required—TOEFL. *Application deadline:* For fall admission, 7/15 priority date for domestic students; for spring admission, 12/1 priority date for domestic students. Application fee: $30. Electronic applications accepted. *Expenses:* Tuition, state resident: part-time $288.16 per credit hour. Tuition, nonresident: part-time $1071.31 per credit hour. *Financial support:* In 2016–17, 70 students received support, including 20 fellowships with partial tuition reimbursements available (averaging $13,530 per year), 53 research assistantships with partial tuition reimbursements available (averaging $10,634 per year), 16 teaching assistantships with partial tuition reimbursements available (averaging $11,057 per year); career-related internships or fieldwork, Federal Work-Study, institutionally sponsored loans, tuition waivers (partial), and unspecified assistantships also available. Financial award application deadline: 3/1; financial award applicants required to submit FAFSA. *Unit head:* Dr. Mohamed Abdel-Aty, Chair, 407-823-2841, E-mail: m.aty@ucf.edu. *Application contact:* Assistant Director, Graduate Admissions, 407-823-2766, Fax: 407-823-6442, E-mail: gradadmissions@ucf.edu.
Website: http://cece.ucf.edu/

University of Colorado Denver, College of Engineering and Applied Science, Department of Civil Engineering, Denver, CO 80217. Offers civil engineering (EASPh D); civil engineering systems (PhD); environmental and sustainability engineering (MS, PhD); geographic information systems (MS); geotechnical engineering (MS, PhD); hydrology and hydraulics (MS, PhD); structural engineering (MS, PhD); transportation engineering (MS, PhD). *Program availability:* Part-time, evening/weekend. *Faculty:* 15 full-time (3 women), 9 part-time/adjunct (0 women). *Students:* 50 full-time (15 women), 33 part-time (7 women); includes 10 minority (1 Black or African American, non-Hispanic/Latino; 2 Asian, non-Hispanic/Latino; 6 Hispanic/Latino; 1 Two or more races, non-Hispanic/Latino), 31 international. Average age 30. 105 applicants, 51% accepted, 14 enrolled. In 2016, 29 master's, 2 doctorates awarded. *Degree*

requirements: For master's, comprehensive exam, 30 credit hours, project or thesis; for doctorate, comprehensive exam, thesis/dissertation, 60 credit hours (30 of which are dissertation research). *Entrance requirements:* For master's, GRE, statement of purpose, transcripts, three references; for doctorate, GRE, statement of purpose, transcripts, references, letter of support from faculty stating willingness to serve as dissertation advisor and outlining plan for financial support. Additional exam requirements/recommendations for international students: Required—TOEFL (minimum score 537 paper-based; 75 iBT); Recommended—IELTS (minimum score 6.5). *Application deadline:* For fall admission, 5/1 for domestic students, 4/1 for international students; for spring admission, 10/1 for domestic students, 9/1 for international students; for summer admission, 2/15 for domestic students, 1/15 for international students. Application fee: $50 ($75 for international students). Electronic applications accepted. *Expenses:* Contact institution. *Financial support:* In 2016–17, 62 students received support. Fellowships, research assistantships, teaching assistantships, career-related internships or fieldwork, Federal Work-Study, institutionally sponsored loans, scholarships/grants, traineeships, and unspecified assistantships available. Financial award application deadline: 4/1; financial award applicants required to submit FAFSA. *Faculty research:* Earthquake source physics, environmental biotechnology, hydrologic and hydraulic engineering, sustainability assessments, transportation energy use and greenhouse gas emissions. *Unit head:* Dr. Kevin Rens, Chair, 303-556-8017, E-mail: kevin.rens@ucdenver.edu. *Application contact:* Roxanne Pizano, Program Coordinator, 303-556-6274, E-mail: roxanne.pizano@ucdenver.edu.
Website: http://www.ucdenver.edu/academics/colleges/Engineering/Programs/Civil-Engineering/Pages/CivilEngineering.aspx

University of Colorado Denver, College of Engineering and Applied Science, Master of Engineering Program, Denver, CO 80217-3364. Offers civil engineering (M Eng), including civil engineering, geographic information systems, transportation systems; electrical engineering (M Eng); mechanical engineering (M Eng). *Program availability:* Part-time. *Students:* 35 full-time (9 women), 23 part-time (7 women); includes 5 minority (1 American Indian or Alaska Native, non-Hispanic/Latino; 2 Hispanic/Latino; 2 Two or more races, non-Hispanic/Latino), 11 international. Average age 31. 75 applicants, 63% accepted, 13 enrolled. In 2016, 17 master's awarded. *Degree requirements:* For master's, comprehensive exam, 27 credit hours of course work, 3 credit hours of report or thesis work. *Entrance requirements:* For master's, GRE (for those with GPA below 2.75), transcripts, references, statement of purpose. Additional exam requirements/recommendations for international students: Required—TOEFL (minimum score 537 paper-based; 75 iBT); Recommended—IELTS (minimum score 6.5). *Application deadline:* For fall admission, 4/1 for domestic students, 3/1 for international students; for spring admission, 10/1 for domestic students, 9/15 for international students. Applications are processed on a rolling basis. Application fee: $50 ($75 for international students). Electronic applications accepted. *Expenses:* Contact institution. *Financial support:* In 2016–17, 120 students received support. Fellowships, research assistantships, teaching assistantships, Federal Work-Study, institutionally sponsored loans, scholarships/grants, traineeships, and unspecified assistantships available. Financial award application deadline: 4/1; financial award applicants required to submit FAFSA. *Faculty research:* Civil, electrical and mechanical engineering. *Application contact:* Graduate School Admissions, 303-315-2179, E-mail: ceasgaapplications@ucdenver.edu.
Website: http://www.ucdenver.edu/academics/colleges/Engineering/admissions/Masters/Pages/MastersAdmissions.aspx

University of Dayton, Department of Civil and Environmental Engineering and Engineering Mechanics, Dayton, OH 45469. Offers engineering mechanics (MSEM); environmental engineering (MSCE); geotechnical engineering (MSCE); structural engineering (MSCE); transportation engineering (MSCE); water resources engineering (MSCE). *Program availability:* Part-time, evening/weekend. *Faculty:* 9 full-time (2 women), 3 part-time/adjunct (1 woman). *Students:* 40 full-time (8 women), 2 part-time (0 women); includes 1 minority (Asian, non-Hispanic/Latino), 30 international. Average age 26. 137 applicants, 17% accepted. In 2016, 14 master's awarded. *Degree requirements:* For master's, thesis optional. *Entrance requirements:* For master's, minimum GPA of 3.0 in undergraduate work. Additional exam requirements/recommendations for international students: Required—TOEFL (minimum score 550 paper-based; 80 iBT); Recommended—IELTS. *Application deadline:* For fall admission, 8/1 priority date for domestic students, 5/1 priority date for international students; for spring admission, 11/1 priority date for international students. Applications are processed on a rolling basis. Application fee: $0 ($50 for international students). Electronic applications accepted. *Expenses:* $890 per credit hour, $25 registration fee. *Financial support:* Research assistantships, institutionally sponsored loans, scholarships/grants, and department-funded awards (averaging $2448 per year) available. Financial award application deadline: 3/1; financial award applicants required to submit FAFSA. *Faculty research:* Vertically-aligned carbon nanotubes infiltrated with temperature-responsive polymers; smart nanocomposite films for self-cleaning and controlled release; bilayer and bulk heterojunction solar cells using liquid crystalline porphyrins as donors by solution processing; DNA damage induced by multiwalled carbon nanotubes in mouse embryonic stem cells. *Total annual research expenditures:* $250,000. *Unit head:* Dr. Donald V. Chase, Chair, 937-229-3847, Fax: 937-229-3491, E-mail: dchase1@udayton.edu. *Application contact:* 937-229-4462, E-mail: graduateadmission@udayton.edu.
Website: https://www.udayton.edu/engineering/departments/civil/index.php

University of Delaware, College of Engineering, Department of Civil and Environmental Engineering, Newark, DE 19716. Offers environmental engineering (MAS, MCE, PhD); geotechnical engineering (MAS, MCE, PhD); ocean engineering (MAS, MCE, PhD); structural engineering (MAS, MCE, PhD); transportation engineering (MAS, MCE, PhD); water resource engineering (MAS, MCE, PhD). *Program availability:* Part-time. Terminal master's awarded for partial completion of doctoral program. *Degree requirements:* For master's, thesis; for doctorate, thesis/dissertation. *Entrance requirements:* For master's and doctorate, GRE General Test. Additional exam requirements/recommendations for international students: Required—TOEFL. Electronic applications accepted. *Faculty research:* Structural engineering and mechanics; transportation engineering; ocean engineering; soil mechanics and foundation; water resources and environmental engineering.

University of Massachusetts Amherst, Graduate School, College of Engineering, Department of Civil and Environmental Engineering, Amherst, MA 01003. Offers civil engineering (MSCE, PhD); environmental and water resources engineering (MSCE); geotechnical engineering (MSCE); structural engineering and mechanics (MSCE); transportation engineering (MSCE). *Program availability:* Part-time. Terminal master's awarded for partial completion of doctoral program. *Degree requirements:* For master's, thesis or alternative; for doctorate, comprehensive exam, thesis/dissertation. *Entrance requirements:* For master's and doctorate, GRE General Test. Additional exam requirements/recommendations for international students: Required—TOEFL (minimum score 550 paper-based; 80 iBT), IELTS (minimum score 6.5). Electronic applications accepted.

University of Memphis, Graduate School, Herff College of Engineering, Department of Civil Engineering, Memphis, TN 38152. Offers civil engineering (PhD); engineering

seismology (MS); environmental engineering (MS); freight transportation (Graduate Certificate); geotechnical engineering (MS); structural engineering (MS); transportation engineering (MS); water resources engineering (MS). *Faculty:* 12 full-time (1 woman). *Students:* 10 full-time (3 women), 15 part-time (3 women); includes 3 minority (2 Black or African American, non-Hispanic/Latino; 1 Two or more races, non-Hispanic/Latino), 9 international. Average age 29. 29 applicants, 69% accepted, 8 enrolled. In 2016, 5 master's awarded. Terminal master's awarded for partial completion of doctoral program. *Degree requirements:* For master's, comprehensive exam, thesis optional; for doctorate, comprehensive exam, thesis/dissertation. *Entrance requirements:* For master's, GRE General Test, minimum undergraduate GPA of 2.5; bachelor's degree in engineering or a related science or mathematics program; three letters of reference; for doctorate, GRE General Test, bachelor's degree in engineering or engineering science; three letters of reference; for Graduate Certificate, minimum undergraduate GPA of 2.75; bachelor's degree in engineering or engineering science. Additional exam requirements/recommendations for international students: Required—TOEFL (minimum score 550 paper-based; 79 iBT). *Application deadline:* For fall admission, 8/1 for domestic students; for spring admission, 12/1 for domestic students. Application fee: $35 ($60 for international students). Electronic applications accepted. *Expenses:* $5,231.50 per semester full-time in-state, $9,623.50 full-time out-of-state. *Financial support:* In 2016–17, 6 students received support, including 31 fellowships with full tuition reimbursements available (averaging $12,012 per year); research assistantships with full tuition reimbursements available, career-related internships or fieldwork, Federal Work-Study, scholarships/grants, and unspecified assistantships also available. Financial award application deadline: 2/1; financial award applicants required to submit FAFSA. *Faculty research:* Structural response to earthquakes, pavement design, water quality, transportation safety, intermodal transportation. *Unit head:* Dr. Sharam Pezeshk, Chair, 901-678-2746, Fax: 901-678-3026. *Application contact:* Dr. Roger Meier, Coordinator of Graduate Studies, 901-678-3284, E-mail: rwmeier@memphis.edu.
Website: http://www.ce.memphis.edu

University of Missouri, Office of Research and Graduate Studies, College of Engineering, Department of Civil and Environmental Engineering, Columbia, MO 65211. Offers civil engineering (MS, PhD); environmental engineering (MS, PhD); geotechnical engineering (MS, PhD); structural engineering (MS, PhD); transportation and highway engineering (MS); water resources (MS, PhD). *Faculty:* 16 full-time (3 women), 2 part-time/adjunct (1 woman). *Students:* 41 full-time (8 women), 30 part-time (8 women). *Degree requirements:* For master's, report or thesis; for doctorate, thesis/dissertation. *Entrance requirements:* For master's and doctorate, GRE General Test. Additional exam requirements/recommendations for international students: Required—TOEFL (minimum score 550 paper-based; 80 iBT). *Application deadline:* For fall admission, 2/15 priority date for domestic students, 2/15 for international students; for winter admission, 9/15 priority date for domestic students, 9/15 for international students. Application fee: $75 ($90 for international students). *Expenses:* Tuition, state resident: full-time $6347; part-time $352.60 per credit hour. Tuition, nonresident: full-time $17,379; part-time $965.50 per credit hour. Required fees: $1035. Tuition and fees vary according to course load, campus/location and program. *Financial support:* Fellowships, research assistantships, teaching assistantships, and institutionally sponsored loans available.
Website: http://engineering.missouri.edu/civil/

University of Nevada, Las Vegas, Graduate College, Howard R. Hughes College of Engineering, Department of Civil and Environmental Engineering and Construction, Las Vegas, NV 89154-4015. Offers civil and environmental engineering (PhD); transportation (MS). *Program availability:* Part-time. *Faculty:* 10 full-time (1 woman). *Students:* 34 full-time (8 women), 29 part-time (10 women); includes 12 minority (1 Black or African American, non-Hispanic/Latino; 7 Asian, non-Hispanic/Latino; 2 Hispanic/Latino; 2 Two or more races, non-Hispanic/Latino), 34 international. Average age 31. 41 applicants, 68% accepted, 13 enrolled. In 2016, 12 master's, 7 doctorates awarded. *Degree requirements:* For master's, thesis (for some programs); for doctorate, comprehensive exam, thesis/dissertation, preliminary exam. *Entrance requirements:* For master's, GRE General Test, bachelor's degree with minimum GPA of 3.0; statement of purpose; letter of recommendation; for doctorate, GRE General Test, master's degree; statement of purpose; 3 letters of recommendation. Additional exam requirements/recommendations for international students: Required—TOEFL (minimum score 550 paper-based; 80 iBT), IELTS (minimum score 7). *Application deadline:* For fall admission, 6/15 for domestic students, 3/15 for international students; for spring admission, 11/15 for domestic students, 8/30 for international students. Application fee: $60 ($95 for international students). Electronic applications accepted. *Expenses:* $269.25 per credit, $792 per 3-credit course; $9,634 per year resident; $23,274 per year non-resident; $7,094 fees non-resident (7 credits or more); $1,307 annual health insurance fee. *Financial support:* In 2016–17, 1 fellowship with partial tuition reimbursement (averaging $20,000 per year), 14 research assistantships with partial tuition reimbursements (averaging $14,616 per year), 24 teaching assistantships with partial tuition reimbursements (averaging $14,956 per year) were awarded; institutionally sponsored loans, scholarships/grants, health care benefits, and unspecified assistantships also available. Financial award application deadline: 3/15. *Faculty research:* Sustainable construction, construction safety, infrastructure project performance, construction education, construction performance improvement. *Total annual research expenditures:* $1.2 million. *Unit head:* Dr. Donald Hayes, Chair/Professor, 702-895-4723, Fax: 702-895-3936, E-mail: donald.hayes@unlv.edu. *Application contact:* Dr. Nader Ghafoori, Graduate Coordinator, 702-895-2531, Fax: 702-895-3936, E-mail: nader.ghafoori@unlv.edu.
Website: http://www.unlv.edu/ceec

University of New Brunswick Fredericton, School of Graduate Studies, Faculty of Engineering, Department of Civil Engineering, Fredericton, NB E3B 5A3, Canada. Offers construction engineering and management (M Eng, M Sc E, PhD); environmental engineering (M Eng, M Sc E, PhD); environmental studies (M Eng); geotechnical engineering (M Eng, M Sc E, PhD); groundwater/hydrology (M Eng, M Sc E, PhD); materials (M Eng, M Sc E, PhD); pavements (M Eng, M Sc E, PhD); structures (M Eng, M Sc E, PhD); transportation (M Eng, M Sc E, PhD). *Program availability:* Part-time. *Degree requirements:* For master's, thesis; for doctorate, comprehensive exam, thesis/dissertation, qualifying exam; 27 credit hours of courses. *Entrance requirements:* For master's, minimum GPA of 3.0; B Sc E in civil engineering or related engineering degree; for doctorate, minimum GPA of 3.0; graduate degree in engineering or applied science. Additional exam requirements/recommendations for international students: Required—IELTS (minimum score 7.5), TWE (minimum score 4), Michigan English Language Assessment Battery (minimum score 85) or CanTest (minimum score 4.5); Recommended—TOEFL (minimum score 580 paper-based). Electronic applications accepted. *Faculty research:* Construction engineering and management; engineering materials and infrastructure renewal; highway and pavement research; structures and solid mechanics; geotechnical and geoenvironmental engineering; structure interaction; transportation and planning; environment, solid waste management; structural engineering; water and environmental engineering.

University of Puerto Rico, Mayagüez Campus, Graduate Studies, College of Engineering, Department of Civil Engineering and Surveying, Mayagüez, PR 00681-9000. Offers civil engineering (ME, MS, PhD), including construction engineering and management (ME, MS), environmental engineering, geotechnical engineering (ME,

MS), structural engineering, transportation engineering. *Program availability:* Part-time. *Faculty:* 37 full-time (7 women), 2 part-time/adjunct (0 women). *Students:* 118 full-time (37 women), 9 part-time (2 women); includes 110 minority (all Hispanic/Latino), 17 international. Average age 25. 35 applicants, 94% accepted, 16 enrolled. In 2016, 26 master's, 2 doctorates awarded. Terminal master's awarded for partial completion of doctoral program. *Degree requirements:* For master's, one foreign language, thesis; for doctorate, one foreign language, comprehensive exam, thesis/dissertation, qualifying exams. *Entrance requirements:* For master's, proficiency in English and Spanish; BS in civil engineering or its equivalent; for doctorate, proficiency in English and Spanish. *Application deadline:* For fall admission, 2/15 for domestic and international students; for spring admission, 9/15 for domestic and international students. Applications are processed on a rolling basis. Application fee: $25. Electronic applications accepted. *Expenses: Tuition, area resident:* Full-time $2466. *International tuition:* $7166 full-time. *Required fees:* $210. One-time fee: $5 full-time. Tuition and fees vary according to course level, campus/location, program and student level. *Financial support:* In 2016–17, 89 students received support, including 74 research assistantships with full and partial tuition reimbursements available (averaging $3,171 per year), 38 teaching assistantships with full and partial tuition reimbursements available (averaging $3,107 per year); unspecified assistantships also available. *Faculty research:* Structural design, concrete structure, finite elements, dynamic analysis, transportation, soils. *Unit head:* Ismael Pagan, Prof., Director, 787-832-4040 Ext. 3815, Fax: 787-833-8260, E-mail: ismael.pagan@upr.edu. *Application contact:* Myriam Hernandez, Administrative Officer III, 787-832-4040 Ext. 3815, Fax: 787-833-8260, E-mail: myriam.hernandez1@upr.edu. Website: http://engineering.uprm.edu/inci/

University of Southern California, Graduate School, School of Policy, Planning, and Development, Master of Planning Program, Los Angeles, CA 90089. Offers sustainable cities (Graduate Certificate); transportation systems (Graduate Certificate); urban planning (M Pl); M Arch/M Pl; M Pl/MA; M Pl/MPP; M Pl/MRED; M Pl/MS; M Pl/MSW; MBA/M Pl; ML Arch/M Pl; MPA/M Pl. *Accreditation:* ACSP. *Program availability:* Part-time. *Degree requirements:* For master's, comprehensive exam, internship. *Entrance requirements:* For master's, GRE, GMAT. Additional exam requirements/recommendations for international students: Required—TOEFL (minimum score 600 paper-based; 100 iBT). Electronic applications accepted. *Faculty research:* Transportation and infrastructure, comparative international development, healthy communities, social economic development, sustainable community planning.

University of Southern California, Graduate School, Viterbi School of Engineering, Daniel J. Epstein Department of Industrial and Systems Engineering, Los Angeles, CA 90089. Offers digital supply chain management (MS); engineering management (MS); engineering technology communication (Graduate Certificate); health systems operations (Graduate Certificate); industrial and systems engineering (MS, PhD, Engr); manufacturing engineering (MS); operations research engineering (MS); optimization and supply chain management (Graduate Certificate); product development engineering (MS); safety systems and security (MS); systems architecting and engineering (MS, Graduate Certificate); systems safety and security (Graduate Certificate); transportation systems (Graduate Certificate); MS/MBA. *Program availability:* Part-time, evening/weekend, online learning. Terminal master's awarded for partial completion of doctoral program. *Degree requirements:* For master's, thesis optional; for doctorate, thesis/dissertation. *Entrance requirements:* For master's and doctorate, GRE General Test. Additional exam requirements/recommendations for international students: Recommended—TOEFL. Electronic applications accepted. *Faculty research:* Health systems, music cognition and retrieval, transportation and logistics, manufacturing and automation, engineering systems design, risk and economic analysis.

University of Southern California, Graduate School, Viterbi School of Engineering, Sonny Astani Department of Civil Engineering, Los Angeles, CA 90089. Offers applied mechanics (MS); civil engineering (MS, PhD); computer-aided engineering (ME, Graduate Certificate); construction management (MCM); engineering technology commercialization (Graduate Certificate); environmental engineering (MS, PhD); environmental quality management (ME); structural design (ME); sustainable cities (Graduate Certificate); transportation systems (MS, Graduate Certificate); water and waste management (MS). *Program availability:* Part-time, evening/weekend. Terminal master's awarded for partial completion of doctoral program. *Degree requirements:* For master's, thesis optional; for doctorate, thesis/dissertation. *Entrance requirements:* For master's and doctorate, GRE General Test. Additional exam requirements/recommendations for international students: Recommended—TOEFL. Electronic applications accepted. *Faculty research:* Geotechnical engineering, transportation engineering, structural engineering, construction management, environmental engineering, water resources.

University of South Florida, College of Engineering, Department of Civil and Environmental Engineering, Tampa, FL 33620-9951. Offers civil engineering (MCE, MSCE, PhD), including geotechnical engineering, materials science and engineering, structures engineering, transportation engineering, water resources; environmental engineering (MEVE, MSEV, PhD), including engineering for international development (MSEV). *Program availability:* Part-time. *Faculty:* 20 full-time (5 women). *Students:* 117 full-time (41 women), 63 part-time (18 women); includes 33 minority (7 Black or African American, non-Hispanic/Latino; 2 Asian, non-Hispanic/Latino; 20 Hispanic/Latino; 4 Two or more races, non-Hispanic/Latino), 84 international. Average age 28. 250 applicants, 52% accepted, 51 enrolled. In 2016, 55 master's, 13 doctorates awarded. Terminal master's awarded for partial completion of doctoral program. *Degree requirements:* For master's, comprehensive exam, thesis (for some programs); for doctorate, comprehensive exam, thesis/dissertation. *Entrance requirements:* For master's, GRE General Test, minimum GPA of 3.0 in major, letters of reference, statement of purpose; for doctorate, GRE General Test, letters of recommendation, statement of purpose, resume. Additional exam requirements/recommendations for international students: Required—TOEFL (minimum score 550 paper-based; 79 iBT) or IELTS (minimum score 6.5). *Application deadline:* For fall admission, 2/15 for domestic students, 2/15 priority date for international students; for spring admission, 10/15 for domestic students, 9/15 priority date for international students. Application fee: $30. Electronic applications accepted. *Expenses:* Tuition, state resident: full-time $7766; part-time $431.43 per credit hour. Tuition, nonresident: full-time $15,789; part-time $877.17 per credit hour. *Required fees:* $37 per term. *Financial support:* In 2016–17, 36 students received support, including 44 research assistantships (averaging $14,123 per year), 21 teaching assistantships with tuition reimbursements available (averaging $15,329 per year). *Faculty research:* Environmental and water resources engineering, geotechnics and geoenvironmental systems, structures and materials systems, transportation systems. *Total annual research expenditures:* $3.7 million. *Unit head:* Dr. Manjriker Gunaratne, Professor and Department Chair, 813-974-5818, Fax: 813-974-2957, E-mail: gunaratn@usf.edu. *Application contact:* Dr. Sarina J. Ergas, Professor and Graduate Program Coordinator, 813-974-1119, Fax: 813-974-2957, E-mail: sergas@usf.edu. Website: http://www.usf.edu/engineering/cee/

University of South Florida, Innovative Education, Tampa, FL 33620-9951. Offers adult, career and higher education (Graduate Certificate), including college teaching, leadership in developing human resources, leadership in higher education; Africana studies (Graduate Certificate), including diasporas and health disparities, genocide and human rights; aging studies (Graduate Certificate), including gerontology; art research (Graduate Certificate), including museum studies; business foundations (Graduate Certificate); chemical and biomedical engineering (Graduate Certificate), including materials science and engineering, water, health and sustainability; child and family studies (Graduate Certificate), including positive behavior support; civil and industrial engineering (Graduate Certificate), including transportation systems analysis; community and family health (Graduate Certificate), including maternal and child health, social marketing and public health, violence and injury: prevention and intervention, women's health; criminology (Graduate Certificate), including criminal justice administration; educational measurement and research (Graduate Certificate), including evaluation; English (Graduate Certificate), including comparative literary studies, creative writing, professional and technical communication; entrepreneurship (Graduate Certificate); environmental health (Graduate Certificate), including safety management; epidemiology and biostatistics (Graduate Certificate), including applied biostatistics, biostatistics, concepts and tools of epidemiology, epidemiology, epidemiology of infectious diseases; geography, environment and planning (Graduate Certificate), including community development, environmental policy and management, geographical information systems; geology (Graduate Certificate), including hydrogeology; global health (Graduate Certificate), including disaster management, global health and Latin American and Caribbean studies, global health practice, humanitarian assistance, infection control; government and international affairs (Graduate Certificate), including Cuban studies, globalization studies; health policy and management (Graduate Certificate), including health management and leadership, public health policy and programs; hearing specialist: early intervention (Graduate Certificate); industrial and management systems engineering (Graduate Certificate), including systems engineering, technology management; information studies (Graduate Certificate), including school library media specialist; information systems/decision sciences (Graduate Certificate), including analytics and business intelligence; instructional technology (Graduate Certificate), including distance education, Florida digital/virtual educator, instructional design, multimedia design, Web design; internal medicine, bioethics and medical humanities (Graduate Certificate), including biomedical ethics; Latin American and Caribbean studies (Graduate Certificate); mass communications (Graduate Certificate), including multimedia journalism; mathematics and statistics (Graduate Certificate), including mathematics; medicine (Graduate Certificate), including aging and neuroscience, bioinformatics, biotechnology, brain fitness and memory management, clinical investigation, health informatics, health sciences, integrative weight management, intellectual property, medicine and gender, metabolic and nutritional medicine, metabolic cardiology, pharmacy sciences; national and competitive intelligence (Graduate Certificate); psychological and social foundations (Graduate Certificate), including career counseling, college teaching, diversity in education, mental health counseling, school counseling; public affairs (Graduate Certificate), including nonprofit management, public management, research administration; public health (Graduate Certificate), including environmental health, health equity, public health generalist, translational research in adolescent behavioral health; public health practices (Graduate Certificate), including planning for healthy communities; rehabilitation and mental health counseling (Graduate Certificate), including integrative mental health care, marriage and family therapy, rehabilitation technology; secondary education (Graduate Certificate), including ESOL, foreign language education: culture and content, foreign language education: professional; social work (Graduate Certificate), including geriatric social work/clinical gerontology; special education (Graduate Certificate), including autism spectrum disorder, disabilities education: severe/profound; world languages (Graduate Certificate), including teaching English as a second language (TESL) or foreign language. *Expenses:* Tuition, state resident: full-time $7766; part-time $431.43 per credit hour. Tuition, nonresident: full-time $15,789; part-time $877.17 per credit hour. *Required fees:* $37 per term. *Unit head:* Kathy Barnes, Interdisciplinary Programs Coordinator, 813-974-8031, Fax: 813-974-7061, E-mail: barnesk@usf.edu. *Application contact:* Karen Tylinski, Metro Initiatives, 813-974-9943, Fax: 813-974-7061, E-mail: ktylinsk@usf.edu. Website: http://www.usf.edu/innovative-education/

The University of Texas at Tyler, College of Engineering, Department of Civil Engineering, Tyler, TX 75799-0001. Offers environmental engineering (MS); industrial safety (MS); structural engineering (MS); transportation engineering (MS); water resources engineering (MS). *Program availability:* Part-time, evening/weekend. *Degree requirements:* For master's, thesis optional. *Entrance requirements:* For master's, GRE General Test, bachelor's degree in engineering, associated science degree. Additional exam requirements/recommendations for international students: Required—TOEFL. *Faculty research:* Non-destructive strength testing, indoor air quality, transportation routing and signaling, pavement replacement criteria, flood water routing, construction and long-term behavior of innovative geotechnical foundation and embankment construction used in highway construction, engineering education.

University of Washington, Graduate School, College of Engineering, Department of Civil and Environmental Engineering, Seattle, WA 98195-2700. Offers construction engineering (MSCE, PhD); environmental engineering (MSCE, PhD); geotechnical engineering (MSCE, PhD); hydrology and hydrodynamics (MSCE, PhD); structural engineering and mechanics (MSCE, PhD); transportation engineering (MSCE, PhD). *Program availability:* Part-time, 100% online. *Faculty:* 37 full-time (10 women). *Students:* 239 full-time (97 women), 153 part-time (41 women); includes 71 minority (7 Black or African American, non-Hispanic/Latino; 32 Asian, non-Hispanic/Latino; 22 Hispanic/Latino; 2 Native Hawaiian or other Pacific Islander, non-Hispanic/Latino; 8 Two or more races, non-Hispanic/Latino), 134 international. 782 applicants, 58% accepted, 157 enrolled. In 2016, 132 master's, 13 doctorates awarded. Terminal master's awarded for partial completion of doctoral program. *Degree requirements:* For master's, thesis optional; for doctorate, comprehensive exam, thesis/dissertation, qualifying, general and final exams; completion of degree within 10 years. *Entrance requirements:* For master's, GRE General Test, minimum GPA of 3.0, statement of purpose, letters of recommendation, transcripts; for doctorate, GRE General Test, minimum GPA of 3.5, statement of purpose, letters of recommendation, transcripts, resume. Additional exam requirements/recommendations for international students: Required—TOEFL (minimum score 580 paper-based; 92 iBT); Recommended—IELTS (minimum score 7), TSE. *Application deadline:* For fall admission, 12/15 for domestic and international students. Applications are processed on a rolling basis. Application fee: $85. Electronic applications accepted. *Expenses:* Contact institution. *Financial support:* In 2016–17, 110 students received support, including 10 fellowships with tuition reimbursements available (averaging $2,228 per year), 72 research assistantships with full tuition reimbursements available (averaging $2,351 per year), 28 teaching assistantships with full tuition reimbursements available (averaging $2,387 per year); scholarships/grants also available. Financial award application deadline: 12/15; financial award applicants required to submit FAFSA. *Faculty research:* Structural and geotechnical engineering, transportation and construction engineering, water and environmental engineering. *Total annual research expenditures:* $13.5 million. *Unit head:* Dr. Timothy V. Larson, Professor/Chair, 206-543-6815, Fax: 206-543-1543, E-mail: tlarson@uw.edu. *Application contact:* Melissa Pritchard, Graduate Adviser, 206-543-2574, Fax: 206-543-1543, E-mail: ceginfo@u.washington.edu. Website: http://www.ce.washington.edu/

Virginia Polytechnic Institute and State University, VT Online, Blacksburg, VA 24061. Offers advanced transportation systems (Certificate); aerospace engineering (MS); agricultural and life sciences (MSLFS); business information systems (Graduate Certificate); career and technical education (MS); civil engineering (MS); computer engineering (M Eng, MS); decision support systems (Graduate Certificate); eLearning leadership (MA); electrical engineering (M Eng, MS); engineering administration (MEA); environmental engineering (Certificate); environmental politics and policy (Graduate Certificate); environmental sciences and engineering (MS); foundations of political analysis (Graduate Certificate); health product risk management (Graduate Certificate); industrial and systems engineering (MS); information policy and society (Graduate Certificate); information security (Graduate Certificate); information technology (MIT); instructional technology (MA); integrative STEM education (MA Ed); liberal arts (Graduate Certificate); life sciences: health product risk management (MS); natural resources (MNR, Graduate Certificate); networking (Graduate Certificate); nonprofit and nongovernmental organization management (Graduate Certificate); ocean engineering (MS); political science (MA); security studies (Graduate Certificate); software development (Graduate Certificate). *Expenses:* Tuition, state resident: full-time $12,467; part-time $692.50 per credit hour. Tuition, nonresident: full-time $25,095; part-time $1394.25 per credit hour. *Required fees:* $2669; $491.50 per semester. Tuition and fees vary according to course load, campus/location and program.

Wentworth Institute of Technology, Master of Engineering in Civil Engineering Program, Boston, MA 02115-5998. Offers construction engineering (M Eng); infrastructure engineering (M Eng). *Program availability:* Part-time-only, evening/weekend. *Faculty:* 12 part-time/adjunct (4 women). *Students:* 17 part-time (4 women); includes 4 minority (2 Black or African American, non-Hispanic/Latino; 1 Hispanic/Latino; 1 Two or more races, non-Hispanic/Latino), 1 international. Average age 27. 10 applicants, 100% accepted, 10 enrolled. In 2016, 7 master's awarded. *Degree requirements:* For master's, thesis optional, capstone course. *Entrance requirements:* For master's, resume, statement of purpose, official transcripts, two professional recommendations, bachelor's degree, minimum GPA of 3.0, one year of professional experience in a technical role and/or technical organization. Additional exam requirements/recommendations for international students: Recommended—TOEFL (minimum score 525 paper-based). *Application deadline:* For fall admission, 8/1 for domestic and international students. Applications are processed on a rolling basis. Application fee: $50. Electronic applications accepted. *Expenses:* Contact institution. *Financial support:* Scholarships/grants available. Support available to part-time students. Financial award application deadline: 8/1; financial award applicants required to submit FAFSA. *Unit head:* Philip Hammond, Director of Graduate Programs, 617-989-4594, Fax: 617-989-4399, E-mail: hammondp1@wit.edu. *Application contact:* Martha Sheehan, Director of Admissions and Marketing, 617-989-4661, Fax: 617-989-4399, E-mail: sheehanm@wit.edu.
Website: http://wit.edu/continuinged/programs/civil-engineering-masters.html

Water Resources Engineering

American University of Beirut, Graduate Programs, Faculty of Engineering and Architecture, 11-0236, Lebanon. Offers applied energy (ME); civil engineering (PhD); electrical and computer engineering (PhD); energy studies (MS); engineering management (MEM); environmental and water resources (ME); environmental technology (MSES); mechanical engineering (ME, PhD); urban design (MUD); urban planning and policy (MUPP). *Program availability:* Part-time, evening/weekend, 100% online. *Faculty:* 99 full-time (22 women), 1 part-time/adjunct (0 women). *Students:* 308 full-time (143 women), 86 part-time (39 women). Average age 26. 430 applicants, 69% accepted, 125 enrolled. In 2016, 103 master's, 7 doctorates awarded. Terminal master's awarded for partial completion of doctoral program. *Degree requirements:* For master's, comprehensive exam, thesis optional; for doctorate, comprehensive exam, thesis/dissertation. *Entrance requirements:* For doctorate, GRE. Additional exam requirements/recommendations for international students: Required—TOEFL (minimum score 573 paper-based; 88 iBT); Recommended—IELTS (minimum score 7). *Application deadline:* For fall admission, 2/10 priority date for domestic and international students; for spring admission, 11/2 priority date for domestic students, 11/2 for international students. Application fee: $50. Electronic applications accepted. *Expenses:* Contact institution. *Financial support:* In 2016–17, 22 students received support, including 94 fellowships with full tuition reimbursements available (averaging $18,200 per year), 44 research assistantships with full tuition reimbursements available (averaging $7,596 per year), 124 teaching assistantships with full tuition reimbursements available (averaging $1,056 per year); career-related internships or fieldwork, Federal Work-Study, institutionally sponsored loans, scholarships/grants, traineeships, health care benefits, tuition waivers, and unspecified assistantships also available. Support available to part-time students. Financial award application deadline: 12/20. *Total annual research expenditures:* $1.5 million. *Unit head:* Prof. Alan Shihadeh, Interim Dean, 961-1350000 Ext. 3400, Fax: 961-1744462, E-mail: as20@aub.edu.lb. *Application contact:* Dr. Salim Kanaan, Director, Admissions Office, 961-1350000 Ext. 2594, Fax: 961-1750775, E-mail: sk00@aub.edu.lb.
Website: http://www.aub.edu.lb/fea/fea_home/Pages/index.aspx

Carnegie Mellon University, Carnegie Institute of Technology, Department of Civil and Environmental Engineering, Pittsburgh, PA 15213. Offers advanced infrastructure systems (MS, PhD); advanced infrastructure systems technology development and application (MS); air quality engineering and science (MS); civil and environmental engineering (MS, PhD); civil and environmental engineering/engineering and public policy (PhD); civil engineering (MS, PhD); computational mechanics (MS, PhD); computational modeling and monitoring for resilient structural and material systems (MS); energy infrastructure systems (MS); environmental engineering (MS, PhD); environmental management and science (MS, PhD); IT-based sustainable global infrastructure and construction management (MS); sustainability and green design (MS); water quality engineering and science (MS). *Program availability:* Part-time. *Faculty:* 23 full-time (5 women), 12 part-time/adjunct (3 women). *Students:* 230 full-time (87 women), 4 part-time (0 women); includes 17 minority (4 Black or African American, non-Hispanic/Latino; 12 Asian, non-Hispanic/Latino; 1 Two or more races, non-Hispanic/Latino), 179 international. Average age 25. 653 applicants, 60% accepted, 107 enrolled. In 2016, 145 master's, 15 doctorates awarded. Terminal master's awarded for partial completion of doctoral program. *Degree requirements:* For master's, thesis optional; for doctorate, comprehensive exam, thesis/dissertation, two-part qualifying exam, public defense of dissertation. *Entrance requirements:* For master's, GRE General Test, BS in engineering, science or mathematics; for doctorate, GRE General Test, BS or MS in engineering, science or mathematics. Additional exam requirements/recommendations for international students: Required—TOEFL (minimum score 84 iBT) or IELTS (6.0). *Application deadline:* For fall admission, 1/5 priority date for domestic and international students; for spring admission, 9/15 priority date for domestic and international students. Applications are processed on a rolling basis. Application fee: $65. Electronic applications accepted. *Expenses:* Contact institution. *Financial support:* In 2016–17, 129 students received support. Fellowships with tuition reimbursements available, research assistantships with tuition reimbursements available, scholarships/grants, tuition waivers (full and partial), unspecified assistantships, and service assistantships available. Financial award application deadline: 1/5. *Faculty research:* Advanced infrastructure systems; environmental engineering, sustainability, and science; mechanics, materials, and computing. *Total annual research expenditures:* $7.4 million. *Unit head:* Dr. David A. Dzombak, Professor and Department Head, 412-268-2941, Fax: 412-268-7813, E-mail: dzombak@cmu.edu. *Application contact:* David A. Vey, Graduate Admissions Manager, 412-268-2292, Fax: 412-268-7813, E-mail: dvey@andrew.cmu.edu.
Website: http://www.cmu.edu/cee/

Cornell University, Graduate School, Graduate Fields of Engineering, Field of Civil and Environmental Engineering, Ithaca, NY 14853. Offers engineering management (M Eng, MS, PhD); environmental engineering (M Eng, MS, PhD); environmental fluid mechanics and hydrology (M Eng, MS, PhD); environmental systems engineering (M Eng, MS, PhD); geotechnical engineering (M Eng, MS, PhD); remote sensing (M Eng, MS, PhD); structural engineering (M Eng, MS, PhD); structural mechanics (M Eng, MS); transportation engineering (MS, PhD); transportation systems engineering (M Eng);

water resource systems (M Eng, MS, PhD). Terminal master's awarded for partial completion of doctoral program. *Degree requirements:* For master's, thesis (MS); for doctorate, comprehensive exam, thesis/dissertation. *Entrance requirements:* For master's and doctorate, GRE General Test (recommended), 2 letters of recommendation. Additional exam requirements/recommendations for international students: Required—TOEFL (minimum score 600 paper-based; 77 iBT). Electronic applications accepted. *Faculty research:* Environmental engineering, geotechnical engineering, remote sensing, environmental fluid mechanics and hydrology, structural engineering.

Indiana University Bloomington, School of Public and Environmental Affairs, Environmental Science Programs, Bloomington, IN 47405. Offers applied ecology (MSES); energy (MSES); environmental chemistry, toxicology, and risk assessment (MSES); environmental science (PhD); hazardous materials management (Certificate); specialized environmental science (MSES); water resources (MSES); JD/MSES; MSES/MA; MSES/MPA; MSES/MS. *Program availability:* Part-time. Terminal master's awarded for partial completion of doctoral program. *Degree requirements:* For master's, capstone or thesis; internship; for doctorate, comprehensive exam, thesis/dissertation. *Entrance requirements:* For master's, GRE General Test or GMAT, official transcripts, 3 letters of recommendation, resume, personal statement; for doctorate, GRE General Test or LSAT, official transcripts, 3 letters of recommendation, resume or curriculum vitae, statement of purpose. Additional exam requirements/recommendations for international students: Required—TOEFL (minimum score 600 paper-based; 96 iBT); Recommended—IELTS (minimum score 7). Electronic applications accepted. *Faculty research:* Applied ecology, bio-geochemistry, toxicology, wetlands ecology, environmental microbiology, forest ecology, environmental chemistry.

Kansas State University, Graduate School, College of Engineering, Department of Civil Engineering, Manhattan, KS 66506. Offers civil engineering (MS, PhD); environmental engineering (MS, PhD); geotechnical engineering (MS, PhD); structural engineering (MS, PhD); transportation engineering (MS, PhD); water resources engineering (MS, PhD). *Program availability:* Part-time, evening/weekend, online learning. *Faculty:* 14 full-time (4 women), 3 part-time/adjunct (1 woman). *Students:* 36 full-time (11 women), 34 part-time (7 women); includes 5 minority (2 Asian, non-Hispanic/Latino; 2 Hispanic/Latino; 1 Two or more races, non-Hispanic/Latino), 28 international. Average age 29. 70 applicants, 60% accepted, 11 enrolled. In 2016, 21 master's, 7 doctorates awarded. *Degree requirements:* For master's, thesis or alternative; for doctorate, thesis/dissertation. *Entrance requirements:* For master's, GRE General Test, bachelor's degree or course work in related engineering fields; for doctorate, GRE General Test. Additional exam requirements/recommendations for international students: Required—TOEFL (minimum score 550 paper-based; 79 iBT). *Application deadline:* For fall admission, 2/1 priority date for domestic students, 1/1 priority date for international students; for spring admission, 8/1 priority date for domestic and international students. Applications are processed on a rolling basis. Application fee: $50 ($75 for international students). Electronic applications accepted. *Expenses:* Tuition, state resident: full-time $9670. Tuition, nonresident: full-time $21,828. *Required fees:* $862. *Financial support:* In 2016–17, 19 research assistantships with partial tuition reimbursements (averaging $13,431 per year), 12 teaching assistantships with partial tuition reimbursements (averaging $15,058 per year) were awarded; institutionally sponsored loans and scholarships/grants also available. Support available to part-time students. Financial award application deadline: 3/1; financial award applicants required to submit FAFSA. *Faculty research:* Transportation and materials engineering, water resources engineering, environmental engineering, geotechnical engineering, structural engineering. *Total annual research expenditures:* $2.4 million. *Unit head:* Dr. Robert Stokes, Head, 785-532-1595, Fax: 785-532-7717, E-mail: drbobb@k-state.edu. *Application contact:* Dr. Dunja Peric, Graduate Coordinator, 785-532-2468, Fax: 785-532-7717, E-mail: peric@k-state.edu.
Website: http://www.ce.ksu.edu/

Lawrence Technological University, College of Engineering, Southfield, MI 48075-1058. Offers architectural engineering (MS); automotive engineering (MS); biomedical engineering (MS); civil engineering (MA, MS, PhD), including environmental engineering (MS), geotechnical engineering (MS), structural engineering (MS), transportation engineering (MS), water resource engineering (MS); construction engineering management (MA); electrical and computer engineering (MS); engineering management (MA); engineering technology (MS); fire engineering (MS); industrial engineering (MS), including healthcare; manufacturing systems (ME); mechanical engineering (MS, DE, PhD), including manufacturing (DE), solid mechanics (MS), thermal-fluids (MS); mechatronic systems engineering (MS). *Program availability:* Part-time, evening/weekend. *Faculty:* 24 full-time (5 women), 26 part-time/adjunct (2 women). *Students:* 22 full-time (7 women), 588 part-time (81 women); includes 23 minority (11 Black or African American, non-Hispanic/Latino; 4 Asian, non-Hispanic/Latino; 7 Hispanic/Latino; 1 Two or more races, non-Hispanic/Latino), 469 international. Average age 27. 1,186 applicants, 39% accepted, 99 enrolled. In 2016, 293 master's, 3 doctorates awarded. Terminal master's awarded for partial completion of doctoral program. *Degree requirements:* For master's, thesis optional; for doctorate, comprehensive exam, thesis/dissertation optional. *Entrance requirements:* Additional exam requirements/

recommendations for international students: Required—TOEFL (minimum score 550 paper-based; 79 iBT), IELTS (minimum score 6.5). *Application deadline:* For fall admission, 5/22 for international students; for spring admission, 10/11 for international students; for summer admission, 2/16 for international students. Applications are processed on a rolling basis. Application fee: $50. Electronic applications accepted. *Expenses: Tuition:* Full-time $14,868; part-time $1062 per credit. *Required fees:* $75 per semester. Tuition and fees vary according to campus/location. *Financial support:* In 2016–17, 25 students received support, including 5 research assistantships with full tuition reimbursements available; unspecified assistantships also available. Financial award application deadline: 4/1; financial award applicants required to submit FAFSA. *Faculty research:* Carbon fiber reinforced polymer reinforced concrete structures; low impact storm water management solutions; vehicle battery energy management; wireless communication; entrepreneurial mindset and engineering. *Total annual research expenditures:* $1.7 million. *Unit head:* Dr. Nabil Grace, Dean, 248-204-2500, Fax: 248-204-2509, E-mail: engrdean@ltu.edu. *Application contact:* Jane Rohrback, Director of Admissions, 248-204-3160, Fax: 248-204-2228, E-mail: admissions@ltu.edu.
Website: http://www.ltu.edu/engineering/index.asp

Louisiana State University and Agricultural & Mechanical College, Graduate School, College of Engineering, Department of Civil and Environmental Engineering, Baton Rouge, LA 70803. Offers environmental engineering (MSCE, PhD); geotechnical engineering (MSCE, PhD); structural engineering and mechanics (MSCE, PhD); transportation engineering (MSCE, PhD); water resources (MSCE, PhD).

Marquette University, Graduate School, College of Engineering, Department of Civil and Environmental Engineering, Milwaukee, WI 53201-1881. Offers construction engineering and management (MS, PhD, Certificate); environmental engineering (MS, PhD); structural design (Certificate); structural engineering and structural mechanics (MS, PhD); transportation (Certificate); transportation engineering and materials (MS, PhD); waste and wastewater treatment processes (Certificate); water resources engineering (Certificate). *Program availability:* Part-time, evening/weekend. *Faculty:* 17 full-time (2 women), 2 part-time/adjunct (0 women). *Students:* 27 full-time (8 women), 6 part-time (0 women); includes 5 minority (1 Asian, non-Hispanic/Latino; 2 Hispanic/Latino; 2 Two or more races, non-Hispanic/Latino), 13 international. Average age 28. 70 applicants, 56% accepted, 9 enrolled. In 2016, 8 master's, 5 doctorates awarded. Terminal master's awarded for partial completion of doctoral program. *Degree requirements:* For master's, comprehensive exam (for some programs), thesis or alternative; for doctorate, thesis/dissertation. *Entrance requirements:* For master's, GRE General Test (recommended), minimum GPA of 3.0, official transcripts from all current and previous colleges/universities except Marquette, three letters of recommendation; for doctorate, GRE General Test, minimum GPA of 3.0, official transcripts from all current and previous colleges/universities except Marquette, three letters of recommendation, brief statement of purpose, submission of any English language publications authored by applicant (strongly recommended). Additional exam requirements/recommendations for international students: Required—TOEFL (minimum score 530 paper-based). *Application deadline:* For fall admission, 6/1 priority date for domestic students. Applications are processed on a rolling basis. Application fee: $50. Electronic applications accepted. *Financial support:* Fellowships, research assistantships, teaching assistantships, scholarships/grants, health care benefits, tuition waivers (partial), and unspecified assistantships available. Support available to part-time students. Financial award application deadline: 2/15. *Faculty research:* Highway safety, highway performance, and intelligent transportation systems; surface mount technology; watershed management. *Total annual research expenditures:* $480,876. *Unit head:* Dr. Christopher Foley, Chair, 414-288-5741. *Application contact:* Dr. Stephen M. Heinrich, Director of Graduate Studies, 414-288-5466.
Website: http://www.marquette.edu/civil-environmental-engineering/

McGill University, Faculty of Graduate and Postdoctoral Studies, Faculty of Engineering, Department of Civil Engineering and Applied Mechanics, Montréal, QC H3A 2T5, Canada. Offers environmental engineering (M Eng, M Sc, PhD); fluid mechanics (M Sc); fluid mechanics and hydraulic engineering (M Eng, PhD); materials engineering (M Eng, PhD); rehabilitation of urban infrastructure (M Eng, PhD); soil behavior (M Eng, PhD); soil mechanics and foundations (M Eng, PhD); structures and structural mechanics (M Eng, PhD); water resources (M Sc); water resources engineering (M Eng, PhD).

New Mexico Institute of Mining and Technology, Center for Graduate Studies, Department of Civil and Environmental Engineering, Socorro, NM 87801. Offers environmental engineering (MS), including air quality engineering and science, hazardous waste engineering, water quality engineering and science. *Degree requirements:* For master's, thesis, thesis or independent study. *Entrance requirements:* Additional exam requirements/recommendations for international students: Required—TOEFL (minimum score 540 paper-based). *Faculty research:* Air quality, hazardous waste management, wastewater management and treatment, site remediation.

Ohio University, Graduate College, Russ College of Engineering and Technology, Department of Civil Engineering, Athens, OH 45701-2979. Offers civil engineering (PhD); construction engineering and management (MS); environmental (MS); geotechnical and geoenvironmental (MS); mechanics (MS); structures (MS); transportation (MS); water resources (MS). *Program availability:* Part-time. *Degree requirements:* For master's, comprehensive exam (for some programs), thesis or alternative; for doctorate, comprehensive exam, thesis/dissertation. *Entrance requirements:* For master's, GRE General Test, minimum GPA of 3.0, 3 letters of recommendation; for doctorate, GRE General Test. Additional exam requirements/recommendations for international students: Required—TOEFL (minimum score 550 paper-based; 80 iBT) or IELTS (minimum score 6.5). *Application deadline:* For fall admission, 5/1 priority date for domestic students, 2/1 priority date for international students; for winter admission, 8/1 priority date for domestic students, 4/1 priority date for international students; for spring admission, 2/1 priority date for domestic students, 7/1 priority date for international students. Applications are processed on a rolling basis. Application fee: $50 ($55 for international students). Electronic applications accepted. *Financial support:* Research assistantships with full tuition reimbursements, teaching assistantships with full tuition reimbursements, Federal Work-Study, institutionally sponsored loans, scholarships/grants, and unspecified assistantships available. Financial award application deadline: 3/15; financial award applicants required to submit FAFSA. *Faculty research:* Noise abatement, materials and environment, highway infrastructure, subsurface investigation (pavements, pipes, bridges). *Unit head:* Dr. Gayle F. Mitchell, Chair, 740-593-0430, Fax: 740-593-0625, E-mail: mitchelg@ohio.edu. *Application contact:* Dr. Shad M. Sargand, Graduate Chair, 740-593-1465, Fax: 740-593-0625, E-mail: sargand@ohio.edu.
Website: http://www.ohio.edu/civil/

Oregon State University, College of Engineering, Program in Biological and Ecological Engineering, Corvallis, OR 97331. Offers bio-based products and fuels (M Eng, MS, PhD); biological systems analysis (M Eng, MS, PhD); bioprocessing (M Eng, MS, PhD); ecosystems analysis and modeling (M Eng, MS, PhD); water quality (M Eng, MS, PhD); water resources (M Eng, MS, PhD). *Faculty:* 8 full-time (1 woman), 2 part-time/adjunct (1 woman). *Students:* 9 full-time (1 woman), 1 part-time (0 women), 6 international. Average age 35. 18 applicants, 17% accepted, 2 enrolled. In 2016, 2 master's, 1 doctorate awarded. Terminal master's awarded for partial completion of doctoral program. *Degree requirements:* For master's, thesis or alternative; for doctorate, thesis/dissertation. *Entrance requirements:* For master's and doctorate, GRE, minimum GPA of 3.0 in last 90 hours. Additional exam requirements/recommendations for international students: Required—TOEFL (minimum score 80 iBT), IELTS (minimum score 6.5). *Application deadline:* For fall admission, 1/3 for domestic students. Application fee: $75 ($85 for international students). *Expenses:* $14,130 resident full-time tuition, $23,769 non-resident. *Financial support:* Fellowships with full tuition reimbursements, research assistantships with full tuition reimbursements, teaching assistantships, Federal Work-Study, and institutionally sponsored loans available. Support available to part-time students. *Faculty research:* Bioengineering, water resources engineering, food engineering, cell culture and fermentation, vadose zone transport. *Unit head:* Dr. John P. Bolte, Head, 541-737-2041, E-mail: info-bee@engr.orst.edu. *Application contact:* Ganti Murthy, Biological and Ecological Engineering Advisor, 541-737-6291, E-mail: info-bee@engr.orst.edu.
Website: http://bee.oregonstate.edu/programs/graduate

Oregon State University, Interdisciplinary/Institutional Programs, Program in Water Resources Engineering, Corvallis, OR 97331. Offers groundwater engineering (MS, PhD); surface water engineering (MS, PhD); watershed engineering (MS, PhD). *Students:* 23 full-time (11 women), 2 part-time (1 woman); includes 3 minority (1 Black or African American, non-Hispanic/Latino; 1 American Indian or Alaska Native, non-Hispanic/Latino; 1 Hispanic/Latino), 2 international. Average age 31. 54 applicants, 31% accepted, 10 enrolled. In 2016, 9 master's, 3 doctorates awarded. *Entrance requirements:* For master's and doctorate, GRE. Additional exam requirements/recommendations for international students: Required—TOEFL (minimum score 80 iBT), IELTS (minimum score 6.5). *Application deadline:* For fall admission, 1/5 for domestic students. Application fee: $75 ($85 for international students). *Expenses:* Tuition, state resident: full-time $12,150; part-time $450 per credit. Tuition, nonresident: full-time $21,789; part-time $807 per credit. *Required fees:* $1651; $1507 per credit. One-time fee: $350. Tuition and fees vary according to course load, campus/location and program. *Financial support:* Application deadline: 1/5. *Unit head:* Dr. Mary Santelmann, Director, Water Resources Graduate Program, 541-737-1215, E-mail: santelmm@oregonstate.edu.
Website: http://oregonstate.edu/gradwater/water-resources-engineering-wre

Southern Methodist University, Bobby B. Lyle School of Engineering, Department of Environmental and Civil Engineering, Dallas, TX 75275-0340. Offers air pollution control and atmospheric sciences (PhD); civil engineering (MS); environmental engineering (MS); environmental science (MS); structural engineering (PhD); sustainability and development (MA); water and wastewater engineering (PhD). *Program availability:* Part-time, evening/weekend, online learning. Terminal master's awarded for partial completion of doctoral program. *Degree requirements:* For master's, thesis optional; for doctorate, thesis/dissertation, oral and written qualifying exams. *Entrance requirements:* For master's, GRE General Test, minimum GPA of 3.0 in last 2 years; bachelor's degree in engineering, mathematics, or sciences; for doctorate, GRE, BS and MS in related field, minimum GPA of 3.3. Additional exam requirements/recommendations for international students: Required—TOEFL. Electronic applications accepted. *Faculty research:* Human and environmental health effects of endocrine disrupters, development of air pollution control systems for diesel engines, structural analysis and design, modeling and design of waste treatment systems.

State University of New York College of Environmental Science and Forestry, Department of Environmental Resources Engineering, Syracuse, NY 13210-2779. Offers ecological engineering (MPS, MS, PhD); environmental management (MPS); environmental resources engineering (MPS, MS, PhD); geospatial information science and engineering (MPS, MS, PhD); water resources engineering (MPS, MS, PhD). *Program availability:* Part-time. *Faculty:* 8 full-time (1 woman), 9 part-time/adjunct (3 women). *Students:* 34 full-time (13 women), 13 part-time (2 women); includes 3 minority (1 Black or African American, non-Hispanic/Latino; 1 Asian, non-Hispanic/Latino; 1 Hispanic/Latino), 21 international. Average age 28. 44 applicants, 48% accepted, 10 enrolled. In 2016, 8 master's, 1 doctorate awarded. *Degree requirements:* For master's, thesis (for some programs); for doctorate, comprehensive exam, thesis/dissertation. *Entrance requirements:* For master's and doctorate, GRE General Test, minimum GPA of 3.0. Additional exam requirements/recommendations for international students: Required—TOEFL (minimum score 550 paper-based; 80 iBT), IELTS (minimum score 6). *Application deadline:* For fall admission, 1/15 priority date for domestic and international students; for spring admission, 11/1 priority date for domestic and international students. Applications are processed on a rolling basis. Application fee: $60. *Expenses:* Tuition, state resident: full-time $10,870; part-time $453 per credit. Tuition, nonresident: full-time $22,210; part-time $925 per credit. *Required fees:* $1075; $89.22 per credit. *Financial support:* In 2016–17, 7 students received support. Application deadline: 6/30; applicants required to submit FAFSA. *Faculty research:* Ecological engineering, environmental resources engineering, geospatial information science and engineering, water resources engineering, environmental science. *Unit head:* Dr. Theodore Endreny, Chair, 315-470-6565, Fax: 315-470-6958, E-mail: te@esf.edu. *Application contact:* Scott Shannon, Associate Provost for Instruction/Dean of the Graduate School, 315-470-6599, Fax: 315-470-6978, E-mail: esfgrad@esf.edu.
Website: http://www.esf.edu/ere

Stevens Institute of Technology, Graduate School, Charles V. Schaefer Jr. School of Engineering and Science, Department of Civil, Environmental, and Ocean Engineering, Program in Civil Engineering, Hoboken, NJ 07030. Offers civil engineering (PhD, Certificate), including geotechnical engineering (Certificate); geotechnical/geoenvironmental engineering (M Eng, Engr); hydrologic modeling (M Eng); stormwater management (M Eng); structural engineering (M Eng, Engr); transportation engineering (M Eng); water resources engineering (M Eng). *Program availability:* Part-time, evening/weekend. *Students:* 63 full-time (12 women), 27 part-time (10 women); includes 5 minority (2 Black or African American, non-Hispanic/Latino; 2 Asian, non-Hispanic/Latino; 1 Hispanic/Latino), 55 international. Average age 25. 167 applicants, 57% accepted, 24 enrolled. In 2016, 50 master's, 1 other advanced degree awarded. *Degree requirements:* For master's, thesis optional, minimum B average in major field and overall; for doctorate, comprehensive exam (for some programs), thesis/dissertation; for other advanced degree, minimum B average. *Entrance requirements:* Additional exam requirements/recommendations for international students: Required—TOEFL (minimum score 74 iBT), IELTS (minimum score 6). *Application deadline:* For fall admission, 6/1 for domestic students, 4/15 for international students; for spring admission, 11/30 for domestic students, 11/1 for international students. Applications are processed on a rolling basis. Application fee: $65. Electronic applications accepted. *Expenses:* Contact institution. *Financial support:* Fellowships, research assistantships, teaching assistantships, career-related internships or fieldwork, Federal Work-Study, scholarships/grants, and unspecified assistantships available. Financial award application deadline: 2/15; financial award applicants required to submit FAFSA. *Unit head:* Dr. David A. Vaccari, Director, 201-216-5570, Fax: 201-216-8739, E-mail: dvaccari@stevens.edu. *Application contact:* Graduate Admission, 888-783-8367, Fax: 888-511-1306, E-mail: graduate@stevens.edu.

Tufts University, School of Engineering, Department of Civil and Environmental Engineering, Medford, MA 02155. Offers bioengineering (ME, MS), including environmental technology; civil engineering (ME, MS, PhD), including geotechnical engineering, structural engineering, water diplomacy (PhD); environmental engineering (ME, MS, PhD), including environmental engineering and environmental sciences, environmental geotechnology, environmental health, environmental science and management, hazardous materials management, water diplomacy (PhD), water resources engineering. *Program availability:* Part-time. Terminal master's awarded for partial completion of doctoral program. *Degree requirements:* For master's, thesis or alternative; for doctorate, thesis/dissertation. *Entrance requirements:* For master's and doctorate, GRE General Test. Additional exam requirements/recommendations for international students: Required—TOEFL (minimum score 550 paper-based; 80 iBT), IELTS (minimum score 6.5). Electronic applications accepted. *Expenses: Tuition:* Full-time $49,892; part-time $1248 per credit hour. *Required fees:* $844. Full-time tuition and fees vary according to degree level, program and student level. Part-time tuition and fees vary according to course load. *Faculty research:* Environmental and water resources engineering, environmental health, geotechnical and geoenvironmental engineering, structural engineering and mechanics, water diplomacy.

University of Alberta, Faculty of Graduate Studies and Research, Department of Civil and Environmental Engineering, Edmonton, AB T6G 2E1, Canada. Offers construction engineering and management (M Eng, M Sc, PhD); environmental engineering (M Eng, M Sc, PhD); environmental science (M Sc, PhD); geoenvironmental engineering (M Eng, M Sc, PhD); geotechnical engineering (M Eng, M Sc, PhD); mining engineering (M Eng, M Sc, PhD); petroleum engineering (M Eng, M Sc, PhD); structural engineering (M Eng, M Sc, PhD); water resources (M Eng, M Sc, PhD). *Program availability:* Part-time, online learning. *Degree requirements:* For master's, thesis (for some programs); for doctorate, thesis/dissertation. *Entrance requirements:* For master's, minimum GPA of 3.0 in last 2 years of undergraduate studies; for doctorate, minimum GPA of 3.0. Additional exam requirements/recommendations for international students: Required—TOEFL (minimum score 550 paper-based). Electronic applications accepted. *Faculty research:* Mining.

University of California, Berkeley, Graduate Division, College of Engineering, Department of Civil and Environmental Engineering, Berkeley, CA 94720-1500. Offers engineering and project management (M Eng, MS, PhD); environmental engineering (M Eng, MS, PhD); geoengineering (M Eng, MS, PhD); structural engineering, mechanics and materials (M Eng, MS, PhD); transportation engineering (M Eng, MS, PhD); M Arch/MS; MCP/MS; MPP/MS. *Students:* 360 full-time (143 women); includes 71 minority (15 Black or African American, non-Hispanic/Latino; 39 Asian, non-Hispanic/Latino; 17 Hispanic/Latino), 148 international. Average age 27. 1,086 applicants, 185 enrolled. In 2016, 188 master's, 26 doctorates awarded. Terminal master's awarded for partial completion of doctoral program. *Degree requirements:* For master's, comprehensive exam (for some programs), thesis (for some programs), comprehensive exam or thesis (MS); for doctorate, thesis/dissertation, qualifying exam. *Entrance requirements:* For master's, GRE General Test, minimum GPA of 3.0, 3 letters of recommendation; for doctorate, GRE General Test, minimum GPA of 3.5, 3 letters of recommendation. Additional exam requirements/recommendations for international students: Required—TOEFL (minimum score 570 paper-based; 90 iBT). *Application deadline:* For fall admission, 12/16 for domestic students. Application fee: $105 ($125 for international students). Electronic applications accepted. *Financial support:* Applicants required to submit FAFSA. *Unit head:* Prof. Robert Harley, Chair, 510-643-8739, Fax: 510-643-5264, E-mail: chair@ce.berkeley.edu. *Application contact:* Shelly Okimoto, Graduate Advisor, 510-642-6464, Fax: 510-643-5264, E-mail: aao@ce.berkeley.edu.
Website: http://www.ce.berkeley.edu/

University of Dayton, Department of Civil and Environmental Engineering and Engineering Mechanics, Dayton, OH 45469. Offers engineering mechanics (MSEM); environmental engineering (MSCE); geotechnical engineering (MSCE); structural engineering (MSCE); transportation engineering (MSCE); water resources engineering (MSCE). *Program availability:* Part-time, evening/weekend. *Faculty:* 9 full-time (2 women), 3 part-time/adjunct (1 woman). *Students:* 40 full-time (8 women), 2 part-time (0 women); includes 1 minority (Asian, non-Hispanic/Latino), 30 international. Average age 26. 137 applicants, 17% accepted. In 2016, 14 master's awarded. *Degree requirements:* For master's, thesis optional. *Entrance requirements:* For master's, minimum GPA of 3.0 in undergraduate work. Additional exam requirements/recommendations for international students: Required—TOEFL (minimum score 550 paper-based; 80 iBT); Recommended—IELTS. *Application deadline:* For fall admission, 8/1 priority date for domestic students, 5/1 priority date for international students; for spring admission, 11/1 priority date for international students. Applications are processed on a rolling basis. Application fee: $0 ($50 for international students). Electronic applications accepted. *Expenses:* $890 per credit hour, $25 registration fee. *Financial support:* Research assistantships, institutionally sponsored loans, scholarships/grants, and department-funded awards (averaging $2448 per year) available. Financial award application deadline: 3/1; financial award applicants required to submit FAFSA. *Faculty research:* Vertically-aligned carbon nanotubes infiltrated with temperature-responsive polymers; smart nanocomposite films for self-cleaning and controlled release; bilayer and bulk heterojunction solar cells using liquid crystalline porphyrins as donors by solution processing; DNA damage induced by multiwalled carbon nanotubes in mouse embryonic stem cells. *Total annual research expenditures:* $250,000. *Unit head:* Dr. Donald V. Chase, Chair, 937-229-3847, Fax: 937-229-3491, E-mail: dchase1@udayton.edu. *Application contact:* 937-229-4462, E-mail: graduateadmission@udayton.edu.
Website: https://www.udayton.edu/engineering/departments/civil/index.php

University of Delaware, College of Engineering, Department of Civil and Environmental Engineering, Newark, DE 19716. Offers environmental engineering (MAS, MCE, PhD); geotechnical engineering (MAS, MCE, PhD); ocean engineering (MAS, MCE, PhD); structural engineering (MAS, MCE, PhD); transportation engineering (MAS, MCE, PhD); water resource engineering (MAS, MCE, PhD). *Program availability:* Part-time. Terminal master's awarded for partial completion of doctoral program. *Degree requirements:* For master's, thesis; for doctorate, thesis/dissertation. *Entrance requirements:* For master's and doctorate, GRE General Test. Additional exam requirements/recommendations for international students: Required—TOEFL. Electronic applications accepted. *Faculty research:* Structural engineering and mechanics; transportation engineering; ocean engineering; soil mechanics and foundation; water resources and environmental engineering.

University of Guelph, Graduate Studies, College of Physical and Engineering Science, School of Engineering, Guelph, ON N1G 2W1, Canada. Offers biological engineering (M Eng, M Sc, MA Sc, PhD); engineering systems and computing (M Eng, M Sc, MA Sc, PhD); environmental engineering (M Eng, M Sc, MA Sc, PhD); water resources engineering (M Eng, M Sc, MA Sc, PhD). *Program availability:* Part-time. *Degree requirements:* For master's, thesis (for some programs); for doctorate, comprehensive exam, thesis/dissertation. *Entrance requirements:* For master's, minimum B- average during previous 2 years of course work; for doctorate, minimum B average. Additional exam requirements/recommendations for international students: Required—TOEFL (minimum score 550 paper-based; 89 iBT), IELTS (minimum score 6.5). Electronic applications accepted. *Faculty research:* Water and food safety, environmental contaminant fates and mechanisms, computer systems, robotics and mechatronics, waste treatment.

University of Idaho, College of Graduate Studies, College of Agricultural and Life Sciences, Water Resources Program, Moscow, ID 83844. Offers engineering and science (PhD); engineering and science (MS); law, management and policy (MS, PhD); science and management (MS, PhD). *Faculty:* 17 full-time (5 women). *Students:* 27 full-time, 7 part-time. Average age 34. In 2016, 3 master's, 4 doctorates awarded. *Entrance requirements:* Additional exam requirements/recommendations for international students: Required—TOEFL. *Application deadline:* Applications are processed on a rolling basis. Application fee: $60. Electronic applications accepted. *Expenses:* Tuition, state resident: full-time $6460; part-time $414 per credit hour. Tuition, nonresident: full-time $21,268; part-time $1237 per credit hour. *Required fees:* $2070; $60 per credit hour. Full-time tuition and fees vary according to course load and reciprocity agreements. *Financial support:* Applicants required to submit FAFSA. *Faculty research:* Water resource systems, biological wastewater treatment and water reclamation, invasive species, aquatics ecosystem restoration, watershed science and management. *Unit head:* Dr. Mark David Solomon, Associate Director, 208-885-6430, E-mail: iwrri@uidaho.edu. *Application contact:* Sean Scoggin, Graduate Recruitment Coordinator, 208-885-4723, Fax: 208-885-4406, E-mail: graduateadmissions@uidaho.edu.
Website: http://www.uidaho.edu/cals/departments/water-resources

University of Massachusetts Amherst, Graduate School, College of Engineering, Department of Civil and Environmental Engineering, Amherst, MA 01003. Offers civil engineering (MSCE, PhD); environmental and water resources engineering (MSCE); geotechnical engineering (MSCE); structural engineering and mechanics (MSCE); transportation engineering (MSCE). *Program availability:* Part-time. Terminal master's awarded for partial completion of doctoral program. *Degree requirements:* For master's, thesis or alternative; for doctorate, comprehensive exam, thesis/dissertation. *Entrance requirements:* For master's and doctorate, GRE General Test. Additional exam requirements/recommendations for international students: Required—TOEFL (minimum score 550 paper-based; 80 iBT), IELTS (minimum score 6.5). Electronic applications accepted.

University of Memphis, Graduate School, Herff College of Engineering, Department of Civil Engineering, Memphis, TN 38152. Offers civil engineering (PhD); engineering seismology (MS); environmental engineering (MS); freight transportation (Graduate Certificate); geotechnical engineering (MS); structural engineering (MS); transportation engineering (MS); water resources engineering (MS). *Faculty:* 12 full-time (1 woman). *Students:* 10 full-time (3 women), 15 part-time (3 women); includes 3 minority (2 Black or African American, non-Hispanic/Latino; 1 Two or more races, non-Hispanic/Latino), 9 international. Average age 29. 29 applicants, 69% accepted, 8 enrolled. In 2016, 5 master's awarded. Terminal master's awarded for partial completion of doctoral program. *Degree requirements:* For master's, comprehensive exam, thesis optional; for doctorate, comprehensive exam, thesis/dissertation. *Entrance requirements:* For master's, GRE General Test, minimum undergraduate GPA of 2.5; bachelor's degree in engineering or a related science or mathematics program; three letters of reference; for doctorate, GRE General Test, bachelor's degree in engineering or engineering science; three letters of reference; for Graduate Certificate, minimum undergraduate GPA of 2.75; bachelor's degree in engineering or engineering science. Additional exam requirements/recommendations for international students: Required—TOEFL (minimum score 550 paper-based; 79 iBT). *Application deadline:* For fall admission, 8/1 for domestic students; for spring admission, 12/1 for domestic students. Application fee: $35 ($60 for international students). Electronic applications accepted. *Expenses:* $5,231.50 per semester full-time in-state, $9,623.50 full-time out-of-state. *Financial support:* In 2016–17, 6 students received support, including 31 fellowships with full tuition reimbursements available (averaging $12,012 per year); research assistantships with full tuition reimbursements available, career-related internships or fieldwork, Federal Work-Study, scholarships/grants, and unspecified assistantships also available. Financial award application deadline: 2/1; financial award applicants required to submit FAFSA. *Faculty research:* Structural response to earthquakes, pavement design, water quality, transportation safety, intermodal transportation. *Unit head:* Dr. Sharam Pezeshk, Chair, 901-678-2746, Fax: 901-678-3026. *Application contact:* Dr. Roger Meier, Coordinator of Graduate Studies, 901-678-3284, E-mail: rwmeier@memphis.edu.
Website: http://www.ce.memphis.edu

University of Missouri, Office of Research and Graduate Studies, College of Engineering, Department of Civil and Environmental Engineering, Columbia, MO 65211. Offers civil engineering (MS, PhD); environmental engineering (MS, PhD); geotechnical engineering (MS, PhD); structural engineering (MS, PhD); transportation and highway engineering (MS); water resources (MS, PhD). *Faculty:* 16 full-time (3 women), 2 part-time/adjunct (1 woman). *Students:* 41 full-time (8 women), 30 part-time (8 women). *Degree requirements:* For master's, report or thesis; for doctorate, thesis/dissertation. *Entrance requirements:* For master's and doctorate, GRE General Test. Additional exam requirements/recommendations for international students: Required—TOEFL (minimum score 550 paper-based; 80 iBT). *Application deadline:* For fall admission, 2/15 priority date for domestic students, 2/15 for international students; for winter admission, 9/15 priority date for domestic students, 9/15 for international students. Application fee: $75 ($90 for international students). *Expenses:* Tuition, state resident: full-time $6347; part-time $352.60 per credit hour. Tuition, nonresident: full-time $17,379; part-time $965.50 per credit hour. *Required fees:* $1035. Tuition and fees vary according to course load, campus/location and program. *Financial support:* Fellowships, research assistantships, teaching assistantships, and institutionally sponsored loans available.
Website: http://engineering.missouri.edu/civil/

University of New Haven, Graduate School, Tagliatela College of Engineering, Program in Environmental Engineering, West Haven, CT 06516. Offers environmental engineering (MS); industrial and hazardous waste (MS); water and wastewater treatment (MS); water resources (MS). *Program availability:* Part-time, evening/weekend. *Students:* 47 full-time (13 women), 26 part-time (10 women); includes 3 minority (2 Black or African American, non-Hispanic/Latino; 1 American Indian or Alaska Native, non-Hispanic/Latino), 54 international. Average age 27. 80 applicants, 89% accepted, 19 enrolled. In 2016, 31 master's awarded. *Degree requirements:* For master's, thesis or alternative, research project. *Entrance requirements:* For master's, bachelor's degree in engineering. Additional exam requirements/recommendations for international students: Required—TOEFL (minimum score 75 iBT), IELTS, PTE (minimum score 50). *Application deadline:* Applications are processed on a rolling basis. Application fee: $50. Electronic applications accepted. Application fee is waived when completed online. *Expenses: Tuition:* Full-time $15,660; part-time $870 per credit hour. *Required fees:* $200; $85 per term. Tuition and fees vary according to program. *Financial support:* Research assistantships with partial tuition reimbursements, teaching assistantships with partial tuition reimbursements, career-related internships or fieldwork, Federal Work-Study, scholarships/grants, and unspecified assistantships available. Support available to part-time students. Financial award application deadline: 5/1; financial award applicants required to submit FAFSA. *Unit head:* Dr. Agamemnon Koutsospyros, Coordinator, 203-932-7398, E-mail: akoutsospyros@newhaven.edu.

Water Resources Engineering

Application contact: Michelle Mason, Director of Graduate Enrollment, 203-932-7067, E-mail: mmason@newhaven.edu. Website: http://www.newhaven.edu/10140/

University of South Florida, College of Engineering, Department of Civil and Environmental Engineering, Tampa, FL 33620-9951. Offers civil engineering (MCE, MSCE, PhD), including geotechnical engineering, materials science and engineering, structures engineering, transportation engineering, water resources; environmental engineering (MEVE, MSEV, PhD), including engineering for international development (MSEV). *Program availability:* Part-time. *Faculty:* 20 full-time (5 women). *Students:* 117 full-time (41 women), 63 part-time (18 women); includes 33 minority (7 Black or African American, non-Hispanic/Latino; 2 Asian, non-Hispanic/Latino; 20 Hispanic/Latino; 4 Two or more races, non-Hispanic/Latino), 84 international. Average age 28. 250 applicants, 52% accepted, 51 enrolled. In 2016, 55 master's, 13 doctorates awarded. Terminal master's awarded for partial completion of doctoral program. *Degree requirements:* For master's, comprehensive exam, thesis (for some programs); for doctorate, comprehensive exam, thesis/dissertation. *Entrance requirements:* For master's, GRE General Test, minimum GPA of 3.0 in major, letters of reference, statement of purpose; for doctorate, GRE General Test, letters of recommendation, statement of purpose, resume. Additional exam requirements/recommendations for international students: Required—TOEFL (minimum score 550 paper-based; 79 iBT) or IELTS (minimum score 6.5). *Application deadline:* For fall admission, 2/15 for domestic students, 2/15 priority date for international students; for spring admission, 10/15 for domestic students, 9/15 priority date for international students. Application fee: $30. Electronic applications accepted. *Expenses:* Tuition, state resident: full-time $7766; part-time $431.43 per credit hour. Tuition, nonresident: full-time $15,789; part-time $877.17 per credit hour. *Required fees:* $37 per term. *Financial support:* In 2016–17, 36 students received support, including 44 research assistantships (averaging $14,123 per year), 21 teaching assistantships with tuition reimbursements available (averaging $15,329 per year). *Faculty research:* Environmental and water resources engineering, geotechnics and geoenvironmental systems, structures and materials systems, transportation systems. *Total annual research expenditures:* $3.7 million. *Unit head:* Dr. Manjriker Gunaratne, Professor and Department Chair, 813-974-5818, Fax: 813-974-2957, E-mail: gunaratn@usf.edu. *Application contact:* Dr. Sarina J. Ergas, Professor and Graduate Program Coordinator, 813-974-1119, Fax: 813-974-2957, E-mail: sergas@usf.edu. Website: http://www.usf.edu/engineering/cee/

University of South Florida, College of Global Sustainability, Tampa, FL 33620-9951. Offers energy, global, water and sustainable tourism (Graduate Certificate); global sustainability (MA), including building sustainable enterprise, climate change and sustainability, coastal sustainability, entrepreneurship, food sustainability and security, sustainable energy, sustainable tourism, sustainable transportation, water. *Faculty:* 4 full-time (0 women). *Students:* 59 full-time (35 women), 51 part-time (29 women); includes 25 minority (3 Black or African American, non-Hispanic/Latino; 1 American Indian or Alaska Native, non-Hispanic/Latino; 2 Asian, non-Hispanic/Latino; 16 Hispanic/Latino; 3 Two or more races, non-Hispanic/Latino), 30 international. Average age 28. 134 applicants, 59% accepted, 55 enrolled. In 2016, 36 master's awarded. *Degree requirements:* For master's, comprehensive exam (for some programs), thesis or alternative, internship. *Entrance requirements:* For master's, minimum GPA of 3.0 in undergraduate coursework; at least two letters of recommendation (one must be academic); 200-250 word essay on student's background, professional goals, and reasons for seeking degree. Additional exam requirements/recommendations for international students: Required—TOEFL (minimum score 550 paper-based; 79 iBT). *Application deadline:* For fall admission, 6/1 for domestic students, 5/1 for international students; for spring admission, 10/15 for domestic students, 9/15 for international students. Electronic applications accepted. *Expenses:* Tuition, state resident: full-time $7766; part-time $431.43 per credit hour. Tuition, nonresident: full-time $15,789; part-time $877.17 per credit hour. *Required fees:* $37 per term. *Financial support:* In 2016–17, 20 students received support. *Faculty research:* Global sustainability, integrated resource management, systems thinking, green communities, entrepreneurship, ecotourism. *Total annual research expenditures:* $208,988. *Unit head:* Dr. Rafael Perez, Interim Dean, 813-974-9694, E-mail: perez@usf.edu. Website: http://psgs.usf.edu/

University of South Florida, Innovative Education, Tampa, FL 33620-9951. Offers adult, career and higher education (Graduate Certificate), including college teaching, leadership in developing human resources, leadership in higher education; Africana studies (Graduate Certificate), including diasporas and health disparities, genocide and human rights; aging studies (Graduate Certificate), including gerontology; art research (Graduate Certificate), including museum studies; business foundations (Graduate Certificate); chemical and biomedical engineering (Graduate Certificate), including materials science and engineering, water, health and sustainability; child and family studies (Graduate Certificate), including positive behavior support; civil and industrial engineering (Graduate Certificate), including transportation systems analysis; community and family health (Graduate Certificate), including maternal and child health, social marketing and public health, violence and injury: prevention and intervention, women's health; criminology (Graduate Certificate), including criminal justice administration; educational measurement and research (Graduate Certificate), including evaluation; English (Graduate Certificate), including comparative literary studies, creative writing, professional and technical communication; entrepreneurship (Graduate Certificate); environmental health (Graduate Certificate), including safety management; epidemiology and biostatistics (Graduate Certificate), including applied biostatistics, biostatistics, concepts and tools of epidemiology, epidemiology, epidemiology of infectious diseases; geography, environment and planning (Graduate Certificate), including community development, environmental policy and management, geographical information systems; geology (Graduate Certificate), including hydrogeology; global health (Graduate Certificate), including disaster management, global health and Latin American and Caribbean studies, global health practice, humanitarian assistance, infection control; government and international affairs (Graduate Certificate), including Cuban studies, globalization studies; health policy and management (Graduate Certificate), including health management and leadership, public health policy and programs; hearing specialist: early intervention (Graduate Certificate); industrial and management systems engineering (Graduate Certificate), including systems engineering, technology management; information studies (Graduate Certificate), including school library media specialist; information systems/decision sciences (Graduate Certificate), including analytics and business intelligence; instructional technology (Graduate Certificate), including distance education, Florida digital/virtual educator, instructional design, multimedia design, Web design; internal medicine, bioethics and medical humanities (Graduate Certificate), including biomedical ethics; Latin American and Caribbean studies (Graduate Certificate); mass communications (Graduate Certificate), including multimedia journalism; mathematics and statistics (Graduate Certificate), including mathematics; medicine (Graduate Certificate), including aging and neuroscience, bioinformatics, biotechnology, brain fitness and memory management, clinical investigation, health informatics, health sciences, integrative weight management, intellectual property, medicine and gender, metabolic and nutritional medicine, metabolic cardiology, pharmacy sciences; national and competitive intelligence (Graduate Certificate); psychological and social foundations (Graduate Certificate), including career counseling, college teaching, diversity in education, mental health counseling, school counseling; public affairs (Graduate Certificate), including nonprofit management, public management, research administration; public health (Graduate Certificate), including environmental health, health equity, public health generalist, translational research in adolescent behavioral health; public health practices (Graduate Certificate), including planning for healthy communities; rehabilitation and mental health counseling (Graduate Certificate), including integrative mental health care, marriage and family therapy, rehabilitation technology; secondary education (Graduate Certificate), including ESOL, foreign language education: culture and content, foreign language education: professional; social work (Graduate Certificate), including geriatric social work/clinical gerontology; special education (Graduate Certificate), including autism spectrum disorder, disabilities education: severe/profound; world languages (Graduate Certificate), including teaching English as a second language (TESL) or foreign language. *Expenses:* Tuition, state resident: full-time $7766; part-time $431.43 per credit hour. Tuition, nonresident: full-time $15,789; part-time $877.17 per credit hour. *Required fees:* $37 per term. *Unit head:* Kathy Barnes, Interdisciplinary Programs Coordinator, 813-974-8031, Fax: 813-974-7061, E-mail: barnesk@usf.edu. *Application contact:* Karen Tylinski, Metro Initiatives, 813-974-9943, Fax: 813-974-7061, E-mail: ktylinsk@usf.edu. Website: http://www.usf.edu/innovative-education/

The University of Texas at Austin, Graduate School, Cockrell School of Engineering, Department of Civil, Architectural and Environmental Engineering, Program in Environmental and Water Resources Engineering, Austin, TX 78712-1111. Offers MS, PhD. *Program availability:* Part-time. *Degree requirements:* For master's, thesis or alternative. *Entrance requirements:* For master's, GRE General Test. Additional exam requirements/recommendations for international students: Required—TOEFL. Electronic applications accepted.

The University of Texas at Tyler, College of Engineering, Department of Civil Engineering, Tyler, TX 75799-0001. Offers environmental engineering (MS); industrial safety (MS); structural engineering (MS); transportation engineering (MS); water resources engineering (MS). *Program availability:* Part-time, evening/weekend. *Degree requirements:* For master's, thesis optional. *Entrance requirements:* For master's, GRE General Test, bachelor's degree in engineering, associated science degree. Additional exam requirements/recommendations for international students: Required—TOEFL. *Faculty research:* Non-destructive strength testing, indoor air quality, transportation routing and signaling, pavement replacement criteria, flood water routing, construction and long-term behavior of innovative geotechnical foundation and embankment construction used in highway construction, engineering education.

Utah State University, School of Graduate Studies, College of Engineering, Department of Biological and Irrigation Engineering, Logan, UT 84322. Offers biological and agricultural engineering (MS, PhD); irrigation engineering (MS, PhD). *Program availability:* Part-time. Terminal master's awarded for partial completion of doctoral program. *Degree requirements:* For master's, thesis (for some programs); for doctorate, thesis/dissertation. *Entrance requirements:* For master's and doctorate, GRE General Test, minimum GPA of 3.0. Additional exam requirements/recommendations for international students: Required—TOEFL. *Faculty research:* On-farm water management, crop-water yield modeling, irrigation, biosensors, biological engineering.

Villanova University, College of Engineering, Department of Civil and Environmental Engineering, Program in Water Resources and Environmental Engineering, Villanova, PA 19085-1699. Offers urban water resources design (Certificate); water resources and environmental engineering (MSWREE). *Program availability:* Part-time, evening/weekend, online learning. *Degree requirements:* For master's, thesis optional. *Entrance requirements:* For master's, GRE General Test (for applicants with degrees from foreign universities), BCE or bachelor's degree in science or related engineering field, minimum GPA of 3.0. Additional exam requirements/recommendations for international students: Required—TOEFL (minimum score 600 paper-based; 100 iBT). Electronic applications accepted. *Faculty research:* Photocatalytic decontamination and disinfection of water, urban storm water wetlands, economy and risk, removal and destruction of organic acids in water, sludge treatment.

Section 8
Computer Science and Information Technology

This section contains a directory of institutions offering graduate work in computer science and information technology, followed by in-depth entries submitted by institutions that chose to prepare detailed program descriptions. Additional information about programs listed in the directory but not augmented by an in-depth entry may be obtained by writing directly to the dean of a graduate school or chair of a department at the address given in the directory.

For programs offering related work, see also in this book *Electrical and Computer Engineering, Engineering and Applied Sciences,* and *Industrial Engineering.* In the other guides in this series:

Graduate Programs in the Humanities, Arts & Social Sciences
See *Communication and Media*
Graduate Programs in the Biological/Biomedical Sciences & Health-Related Medical Professions
See *Allied Health*
Graduate Programs in the Physical Sciences, Mathematics, Agricultural Sciences, the Environment & Natural Resources
See *Mathematical Sciences*
Graduate Programs in Business, Education, Information Studies, Law & Social Work
See *Business Administration and Management* and *Library and Information Studies*

CONTENTS

Artificial Intelligence/Robotics

The American University in Cairo, School of Sciences and Engineering, Cairo, Egypt. Offers biotechnology (MS); chemistry (MS); computer science (MS); computing (M Comp); construction engineering (M Eng, MS); electronics and communications engineering (M Eng); environmental engineering (MS); environmental system design (M Eng); mechanical engineering (M Eng, MS); nanotechnology (MS); physics (MS); robotics, control and smart systems (MS); sciences and engineering (PhD); sustainable development (MS, Graduate Diploma). *Program availability:* Part-time, evening/weekend. *Faculty:* 43 full-time (4 women), 12 part-time/adjunct (1 woman). *Students:* 50 full-time (21 women), 262 part-time (128 women), 13 international. Average age 28. 193 applicants, 46% accepted, 55 enrolled. In 2016, 71 master's, 5 doctorates awarded. *Degree requirements:* For master's, comprehensive exam (for some programs), thesis (for some programs); for doctorate, comprehensive exam (for some programs), thesis/dissertation. *Entrance requirements:* Additional exam requirements/recommendations for international students: Required—TOEFL (minimum score 450 paper-based; 45 iBT), IELTS (minimum score 5). *Application deadline:* For fall admission, 2/1 priority date for domestic and international students; for spring admission, 10/15 priority date for domestic and international students. Applications are processed on a rolling basis. Application fee: $80. Electronic applications accepted. *Expenses:* Contact institution. *Financial support:* Fellowships with partial tuition reimbursements, scholarships/grants, and unspecified assistantships available. Financial award application deadline: 3/10. *Faculty research:* Construction, mechanical and electronics engineering, physics, computer science, biotechnology and nanotechnology. *Unit head:* Dr. Hassan El Fawal, Dean, 20-2-2615-2926, E-mail: hassan.elfawal@aucegypt.edu. *Application contact:* Maha Hegazi, Director for Graduate Admissions, 20-2-2615-1462, E-mail: mahahegazi@aucegypt.edu.
Website: http://www.aucegypt.edu/sse/Pages/default.aspx

California State University, Northridge, Graduate Studies, College of Engineering and Computer Science, Department of Manufacturing Systems Engineering and Management, Northridge, CA 91330. Offers engineering automation (MS); engineering management (MS); manufacturing systems engineering (MS); materials engineering (MS). *Program availability:* Online learning. *Faculty:* 8 full-time (7 women), 21 part-time/adjunct (16 women). *Students:* 124 full-time (29 women), 94 part-time (19 women); includes 27 minority (1 American Indian or Alaska Native, non-Hispanic/Latino; 11 Asian, non-Hispanic/Latino; 13 Hispanic/Latino; 2 Two or more races, non-Hispanic/Latino), 145 international. Average age 27. 302 applicants, 33% accepted, 45 enrolled. *Entrance requirements:* For master's, GRE (if cumulative undergraduate GPA less than 3.0). *Application deadline:* For fall admission, 3/30 for domestic students; for spring admission, 9/30 for domestic students. Application fee: $55. *Expenses:* Tuition, state resident: full-time $4152. *Unit head:* Ahmad Sarfaraz, Chair, 818-677-2167.
Website: http://www.csun.edu/~msem/

Carnegie Mellon University, Dietrich College of Humanities and Social Sciences, Department of Statistics, Pittsburgh, PA 15213-3891. Offers machine learning and statistics (PhD); mathematical finance (PhD); statistics (MS, PhD), including applied statistics (PhD), computational statistics (PhD), theoretical statistics (PhD); statistics and public policy (PhD). Terminal master's awarded for partial completion of doctoral program. *Degree requirements:* For doctorate, comprehensive exam, thesis/dissertation. *Entrance requirements:* For master's and doctorate, GRE General Test. Additional exam requirements/recommendations for international students: Required—TOEFL. *Faculty research:* Stochastic processes, Bayesian statistics, statistical computing, decision theory, psychiatric statistics.

Carnegie Mellon University, School of Computer Science, Department of Machine Learning, Pittsburgh, PA 15213-3891. Offers MS, PhD.

Carnegie Mellon University, School of Computer Science and Carnegie Institute of Technology, Robotics Institute, Pittsburgh, PA 15213-3891. Offers computer vision (MS); robotic systems development (MS); robotics (MS, PhD); robotics technology (MS). *Degree requirements:* For doctorate, thesis/dissertation. *Entrance requirements:* For doctorate, GRE General Test, GRE Subject Test. Additional exam requirements/recommendations for international students: Required—TOEFL. *Faculty research:* Perception, cognition, manipulation, robot systems, manufacturing.

The College of William and Mary, Faculty of Arts and Sciences, Department of Applied Science, Williamsburg, VA 23185. Offers accelerator science (PhD); applied mathematics (PhD); applied mechanics (PhD); applied robotics (PhD); applied science (MS); atmospheric and environmental science (PhD); computational neuroscience (PhD); interface, thin film and surface science (PhD); lasers and optics (PhD); magnetic resonance (PhD); materials science and engineering (PhD); mathematical and computational biology (PhD); medical imaging (PhD); nanotechnology (PhD); neuroscience (PhD); non-destructive evaluation (PhD); polymer chemistry (PhD); remote sensing (PhD). *Program availability:* Part-time. *Faculty:* 8 full-time (2 women), 2 part-time/adjunct (0 women). *Students:* 30 full-time (11 women), 4 part-time (0 women); includes 16 minority (2 Black or African American, non-Hispanic/Latino; 12 Asian, non-Hispanic/Latino; 2 Hispanic/Latino), 12 international. Average age 28. 37 applicants, 27% accepted, 7 enrolled. In 2016, 6 doctorates awarded. Terminal master's awarded for partial completion of doctoral program. *Degree requirements:* For master's, comprehensive exam, thesis; for doctorate, comprehensive exam, thesis/dissertation, 4 core courses. *Entrance requirements:* For master's and doctorate, GRE General Test, GRE Subject Test. Additional exam requirements/recommendations for international students: Required—TOEFL, IELTS. *Application deadline:* For fall admission, 2/3 priority date for domestic students, 2/3 for international students; for spring admission, 10/15 priority date for domestic students, 10/14 for international students. Applications are processed on a rolling basis. Application fee: $45. Electronic applications accepted. *Expenses:* Contact institution. *Financial support:* In 2016–17, 7 students received support, including 27 research assistantships (averaging $25,000 per year), 1 teaching assistantship (averaging $9,500 per year); fellowships, scholarships/grants, health care benefits, tuition waivers (full), and unspecified assistantships also available. Financial award application deadline: 4/15; financial award applicants required to submit FAFSA. *Faculty research:* Computational biology, non-destructive evaluation, neurophysiology, laser spectroscopy, nanotechnology. *Total annual research expenditures:* $536,220. *Unit head:* Dr. Christopher Del Negro, Chair, 757-221-7808, Fax: 757-221-2050, E-mail: cadeln@wm.edu. *Application contact:* Lianne Rios Ashburne, Graduate Program Coordinator, 757-221-2563, Fax: 757-221-2050, E-mail: lrashburne@wm.edu.
Website: http://www.wm.edu/as/appliedscience

Cornell University, Graduate School, Graduate Fields of Engineering, Field of Computer Science, Ithaca, NY 14853. Offers algorithms (M Eng, PhD); applied logic and automated reasoning (M Eng, PhD); artificial intelligence (M Eng, PhD); computer graphics (M Eng, PhD); computer science (M Eng, PhD); computer vision (M Eng, PhD); concurrency and distributed computing (M Eng, PhD); information organization and retrieval (M Eng, PhD); operating systems (M Eng, PhD); parallel computing (M Eng, PhD); programming environments (M Eng, PhD); programming languages and

methodology (M Eng, PhD); robotics (M Eng, PhD); scientific computing (M Eng, PhD); theory of computation (M Eng, PhD). *Degree requirements:* For doctorate, comprehensive exam, thesis/dissertation. *Entrance requirements:* For master's, GRE General Test, 2 letters of recommendation; for doctorate, GRE General Test, GRE Subject Test (computer science or mathematics), 3 letters of recommendation. Additional exam requirements/recommendations for international students: Required—TOEFL (minimum score 505 paper-based; 77 iBT). Electronic applications accepted. *Faculty research:* Artificial intelligence, operating systems and databases, programming languages and security, scientific computing, theory of computing, computational biology and graphics.

Georgia Institute of Technology, Graduate Studies, College of Computing, Multidisciplinary Program in Robotics, Atlanta, GA 30332-0001. Offers PhD. Program offered jointly with College of Computing, School of Aerospace Engineering, Wallace H. Coulter Department of Biomedical Engineering, George W. Woodruff School of Mechanical Engineering, and School of Electrical and Computer Engineering. *Program availability:* Part-time. *Degree requirements:* For doctorate, comprehensive exam, thesis/dissertation. *Entrance requirements:* For doctorate, GRE General Test. Additional exam requirements/recommendations for international students: Required—TOEFL (minimum score 600 paper-based; 100 iBT). Electronic applications accepted.

Illinois Institute of Technology, Graduate College, College of Science, Department of Computer Science, Chicago, IL 60616. Offers business (MCS); computational intelligence (MCS); computer science (MCS, MS, PhD); cyber-physical systems (MCS); data analytics (MCS); data science (MAS); database systems (MCS); distributed and cloud computing (MCS); education (MCS); finance (MCS); information security and assurance (MCS); networking and communications (MCS); software engineering (MCS); telecommunications and software engineering (MAS); MS/MAS. *Program availability:* Part-time, evening/weekend, online learning. Terminal master's awarded for partial completion of doctoral program. *Degree requirements:* For master's, thesis optional; for doctorate, comprehensive exam, thesis/dissertation. *Entrance requirements:* For master's, GRE General Test with minimum scores of 298 Quantitative and Verbal, 3.0 Analytical Writing (for MS); GRE General Test with minimum scores of 292 Quantitative and Verbal, 2.5 Analytical Writing (for MAS), minimum undergraduate GPA of 3.0; for doctorate, GRE General Test (minimum scores: 304 Quantitative and Verbal, 3.5 Analytical Writing), minimum undergraduate GPA of 3.0. Additional exam requirements/recommendations for international students: Required—TOEFL (minimum score 523 paper-based; 70 iBT). Electronic applications accepted. *Faculty research:* Parallel and distributed processing, high-performance computing, computational linguistics, information retrieval, data mining, grid computing.

Indiana University Bloomington, School of Informatics and Computing, Program in Intelligent Systems Engineering, Bloomington, IN 47405-7000. Offers PhD. *Program availability:* Part-time. *Faculty:* 13 full-time (3 women). *Students:* 19. Average age 30. 31 applicants, 19 enrolled. *Degree requirements:* For doctorate, thesis/dissertation, qualifying exam. *Entrance requirements:* For doctorate, GRE, statement of purpose, curriculum vitae, 3 letters of recommendation, transcripts. Additional exam requirements/recommendations for international students: Required—TOEFL. *Application deadline:* Applications are processed on a rolling basis. Application fee: $55 ($65 for international students). Electronic applications accepted. *Financial support:* Fellowships, research assistantships, scholarships/grants, health care benefits, and unspecified assistantships available. *Faculty research:* Data mining, data modeling, computer networks, biophysics, biocomplexity, high performance computing, large scale computing, parallel and distributed computing, bioengineering, systems biology, computational, toxicology, experimental imaging analysis, medical modeling and data analysis, cyberinfrastructure, neuroengineering, 3D pranging, nanoengineering, high performance hardware, computer engineering, intelligent systems multimedia. *Unit head:* Geoffrey Fox, Chair, 812-856-7977, E-mail: gcf@indiana.edu. *Application contact:* Rebecca Winkle, Director of Graduate Administration, 812-855-2917, E-mail: isegrad@indiana.edu.

Instituto Tecnológico y de Estudios Superiores de Monterrey, Campus Monterrey, Graduate and Research Division, Program in Computer Science, Monterrey, Mexico. Offers artificial intelligence (PhD); computer science (MS); information systems (MS); information technology (MS). *Program availability:* Part-time. *Degree requirements:* For master's, one foreign language, thesis; for doctorate, one foreign language, thesis/dissertation. *Entrance requirements:* For master's, EXADEP; for doctorate, master's degree in related field. Additional exam requirements/recommendations for international students: Required—TOEFL. *Faculty research:* Distributed systems, software engineering, decision support systems.

Instituto Tecnológico y de Estudios Superiores de Monterrey, Campus Monterrey, Graduate and Research Division, Programs in Engineering, Monterrey, Mexico. Offers applied statistics (M Eng); artificial intelligence (PhD); automation engineering (M Eng); chemical engineering (M Eng); civil engineering (M Eng); electrical engineering (M Eng); electronic engineering (M Eng); environmental engineering (M Eng); industrial engineering (M Eng, PhD); manufacturing engineering (M Eng); mechanical engineering (M Eng); systems and quality engineering (M Eng). M Eng program offered jointly with University of Waterloo; PhD in industrial engineering with Texas A&M University. *Program availability:* Part-time, evening/weekend. Terminal master's awarded for partial completion of doctoral program. *Degree requirements:* For master's, one foreign language, thesis; for doctorate, one foreign language, thesis/dissertation. *Entrance requirements:* For master's, EXADEP; for doctorate, GRE, master's degree in related field. Additional exam requirements/recommendations for international students: Required—TOEFL. *Faculty research:* Flexible manufacturing cells, materials, statistical methods, environmental prevention, control and evaluation.

Johns Hopkins University, G. W. C. Whiting School of Engineering, Master of Science in Engineering in Robotics Program, Baltimore, MD 21218. Offers robotics (MSE). *Faculty:* 19 full-time (3 women), 4 part-time/adjunct (0 women). *Students:* 26 full-time (4 women), 2 part-time (0 women); includes 4 minority (3 Asian, non-Hispanic/Latino; 1 Two or more races, non-Hispanic/Latino), 14 international. Average age 23. 106 applicants, 50% accepted, 17 enrolled. In 2016, 9 master's awarded. *Degree requirements:* For master's, thesis optional, 10 courses or 8 courses and an essay. *Entrance requirements:* For master's, GRE, proficiencies in multivariable integral and differential calculus, linear algebra, ordinary differential equations, physics, probability and statistics, basic numerical methods using existing programming environments, and standard programming languages (C++, Java, or MATLAB); 3 letters of recommendation; statement of purpose; transcripts. Additional exam requirements/recommendations for international students: Required—IELTS preferred (minimum score 7) or TOEFL (minimum score 600 paper-based, 100 iBT). *Application deadline:* For fall admission, 12/5 for domestic and international students. Application fee: $75. Electronic applications accepted. *Financial support:* Scholarships/grants available. *Faculty research:* Perception and cognitive systems; medical robotics; dynamical

systems and controls; bio robotics; aerospace and marine robotics systems. *Total annual research expenditures:* $4.5 million. *Unit head:* Dr. Russ Taylor, Director, 410-516-4639, E-mail: rht@jhu.edu. *Application contact:* Alison Morrow, Robotics Academic Manager, 410-516-4639, E-mail: alison.morrow@jhu.edu.
Website: https://www.lcsr.jhu.edu/

Northwestern University, McCormick School of Engineering and Applied Science, Department of Mechanical Engineering, MS in Robotics Program, Evanston, IL 60208. Offers MS. *Entrance requirements:* For master's, GRE General Test (recommended). Additional exam requirements/recommendations for international students: Required—TOEFL (minimum score 100 iBT), IELTS (minimum score 7). Electronic applications accepted.

Oregon State University, College of Engineering, Program in Electrical and Computer Engineering, Corvallis, OR 97331. Offers analog and mixed signal (M Eng, MS, PhD); artificial intelligence and machine learning (M Eng, MS, PhD); communications and signal processing (M Eng, MS, PhD); computer systems (M Eng, MS, PhD); energy systems (M Eng, MS, PhD); materials and devices (M Eng, MS, PhD); radio frequencies/microwaves/optoelectronics (M Eng, MS, PhD). *Faculty:* 58 full-time (9 women), 3 part-time/adjunct (1 woman). *Students:* 202 full-time (26 women), 31 part-time (9 women); includes 11 minority (9 Asian, non-Hispanic/Latino; 2 Two or more races, non-Hispanic/Latino), 182 international. Average age 28. 535 applicants, 11% accepted, 49 enrolled. In 2016, 52 master's, 8 doctorates awarded. *Entrance requirements:* For master's and doctorate, GRE. Additional exam requirements/recommendations for international students: Required—TOEFL (minimum score 600 paper-based; 80 iBT), IELTS (minimum score 7). *Application deadline:* For fall admission, 1/15 for domestic students. Application fee: $75 ($85 for international students). *Expenses:* $14,130 resident full-time tuition, $23,769 non-resident. *Financial support:* Application deadline: 1/15. *Unit head:* V. John Mathews, Professor and School Head. *Application contact:* Graduate Coordinator, 541-737-7234, E-mail: eecs.gradinfo@oregonstate.edu.
Website: http://eecs.oregonstate.edu/current-students/graduate/ece-program

Oregon State University, College of Engineering, Program in Robotics, Corvallis, OR 97331. Offers assistive robots (M Eng, MS, PhD); autonomous robots (M Eng, MS, PhD); human-robot interaction (M Eng, MS, PhD); legged locomotion (M Eng, MS, PhD); manipulation (M Eng, MS); mobile robots (M Eng, MS, PhD); multi-robot coordination (M Eng, MS, PhD). *Students:* 41 full-time (7 women), 2 part-time (0 women); includes 5 minority (1 Black or African American, non-Hispanic/Latino; 2 Asian, non-Hispanic/Latino; 2 Hispanic/Latino), 9 international. Average age 26. 278 applicants, 8% accepted, 14 enrolled. In 2016, 5 master's, 1 doctorate awarded. *Entrance requirements:* For master's and doctorate, GRE. *Application deadline:* For fall admission, 8/1 for domestic students, 4/1 for international students. Application fee: $75 ($85 for international students). *Expenses:* $14,130 resident full-time tuition, $23,769 non-resident. *Financial support:* Application deadline: 1/15. *Unit head:* Dr. Harriet Nembhard, School Head. *Application contact:* Jean Robinson, Mechanical Engineering Advisor, 541-737-9191, E-mail: jean.robinson@oregonstate.edu.
Website: http://robotics.oregonstate.edu/graduate-program-robotics

Portland State University, Graduate Studies, College of Liberal Arts and Sciences, Systems Science Program, Portland, OR 97207-0751. Offers computational intelligence (Certificate); computer modeling and simulation (Certificate); systems science (MS); systems science/anthropology (PhD); systems science/business administration (PhD); systems science/civil engineering (PhD); systems science/economics (PhD); systems science/engineering management (PhD); systems science/general (PhD); systems science/mathematical sciences (PhD); systems science/mechanical engineering (PhD); systems science/psychology (PhD); systems science/sociology (PhD). *Faculty:* 2 full-time (0 women), 3 part-time/adjunct (1 woman). *Students:* 12 full-time (3 women), 21 part-time (5 women); includes 5 minority (1 Black or African American, non-Hispanic/Latino; 2 Hispanic/Latino; 2 Two or more races, non-Hispanic/Latino). Average age 39. 16 applicants, 69% accepted, 9 enrolled. In 2016, 4 master's, 6 doctorates awarded. *Degree requirements:* For master's, comprehensive exam (for some programs), thesis optional; for doctorate, variable foreign language requirement, comprehensive exam (for some programs), thesis/dissertation. *Entrance requirements:* For master's, GRE/GMAT (recommended), minimum GPA of 3.0 undergraduate or graduate work, 2 letters of recommendation, statement of interest; for doctorate, GMAT, GRE General Test, minimum GPA of 3.0 undergraduate, 3.25 graduate; 2 letters of recommendation, statement of interest. Additional exam requirements/recommendations for international students: Required—TOEFL (minimum score 550 paper-based; 80 iBT). *Application deadline:* For fall admission, 1/15 for domestic and international students; for spring admission, 11/1 for domestic students. Application fee: $65. Electronic applications accepted. *Expenses:* Contact institution. *Financial support:* In 2016–17, 2 research assistantships with tuition reimbursements (averaging $7,830 per year) were awarded; teaching assistantships, career-related internships or fieldwork, Federal Work-Study, scholarships/grants, and unspecified assistantships also available. Support available to part-time students. Financial award application deadline: 3/1; financial award applicants required to submit FAFSA. *Faculty research:* Systems theory and methodology, artificial intelligence neural networks, information theory, nonlinear dynamics/chaos, modeling and simulation. *Unit head:* Dr. Wayne Wakeland, Chair, 503-725-4975, E-mail: wakeland@pdx.edu.
Website: http://www.pdx.edu/sysc/

South Dakota School of Mines and Technology, Graduate Division, Program in Computational Sciences and Robotics, Rapid City, SD 57701-3995. Offers MS. *Program availability:* Part-time. *Entrance requirements:* Additional exam requirements/recommendations for international students: Required—TOEFL (minimum score 520 paper-based; 68 iBT), TWE. Electronic applications accepted.

Stevens Institute of Technology, Graduate School, Charles V. Schaefer Jr. School of Engineering and Science, Department of Electrical and Computer Engineering, Program in Electrical Engineering, Hoboken, NJ 07030. Offers autonomous robotics (Certificate); electrical engineering (M Eng, PhD, Certificate), including computer architecture and digital systems (M Eng), microelectronics and photonics science and technology (M Eng), signal processing for communications (M Eng), telecommunications systems engineering (M Eng), wireless communications (M Eng, Certificate). *Program availability:* Part-time, evening/weekend. *Students:* 190 full-time (47 women), 31 part-time (5 women); includes 14 minority (6 Black or African American, non-Hispanic/Latino; 8 Asian, non-Hispanic/Latino), 181 international. Average age 25. 851 applicants, 59% accepted, 93 enrolled. In 2016, 152 master's, 6 doctorates awarded. *Degree requirements:* For master's, thesis optional, minimum B average in major field and overall; for doctorate, comprehensive exam (for some programs), thesis/dissertation; for Certificate, minimum B average. *Entrance requirements:* Additional exam requirements/recommendations for international students: Required—TOEFL (minimum score 74 iBT), IELTS (minimum score 6). *Application deadline:* For fall admission, 6/1 for domestic students, 4/15 for international students; for spring admission, 11/30 for domestic students, 11/1 for international students. Applications are processed on a rolling basis. Application fee: $65. Electronic applications accepted. *Expenses:* Contact institution. *Financial support:* Fellowships, research assistantships, teaching assistantships, career-related internships or fieldwork, Federal Work-Study,

scholarships/grants, and unspecified assistantships available. Financial award application deadline: 2/15; financial award applicants required to submit FAFSA. *Unit head:* Cristina Comaniciu, Program Director, 201-216-5606, Fax: 201-216-8246, E-mail: ccomanic@stevens.edu. *Application contact:* Graduate Admissions, 888-783-8367, Fax: 888-511-1306, E-mail: graduate@stevens.edu.

University of California, Riverside, Graduate Division, Department of Electrical Engineering, Riverside, CA 92521-0102. Offers electrical engineering (MS, PhD), including computer engineering (MS), control and robotics (PhD). Terminal master's awarded for partial completion of doctoral program. *Degree requirements:* For master's, thesis optional; for doctorate, thesis/dissertation, qualifying exams. *Entrance requirements:* For master's and doctorate, GRE General Test, minimum GPA of 3.25. Additional exam requirements/recommendations for international students: Required—TOEFL (minimum score 550 paper-based; 80 iBT). Electronic applications accepted. *Expenses:* Tuition, state resident: full-time $16,666. Tuition, nonresident: full-time $31,768. *Required fees:* $11,055.54 per quarter. $3685.18 per quarter. Tuition and fees vary according to campus/location and program. *Faculty research:* Solid state devices, integrated circuits, signal processing.

University of California, San Diego, Graduate Division, Department of Electrical and Computer Engineering, La Jolla, CA 92093. Offers applied ocean science (MS, PhD); applied physics (MS, PhD); communication theory and systems (MS, PhD); computer engineering (MS, PhD); electronic circuits and systems (MS, PhD); intelligent systems, robotics and control (MS, PhD); medical devices and systems (MS, PhD); nanoscale devices and systems (MS, PhD); photonics (MS, PhD); signal and image processing (MS, PhD). *Students:* 612 full-time (119 women), 39 part-time (8 women). 2,885 applicants, 25% accepted, 269 enrolled. In 2016, 147 master's, 43 doctorates awarded. Terminal master's awarded for partial completion of doctoral program. *Degree requirements:* For master's, comprehensive exam (for some programs), thesis (for some programs); for doctorate, comprehensive exam, thesis/dissertation. *Entrance requirements:* For master's and doctorate, GRE General Test, minimum GPA of 3.0, resume or curriculum vitae (recommended). Additional exam requirements/recommendations for international students: Required—TOEFL (minimum score 550 paper-based; 80 iBT), IELTS (minimum score 7), PTE (minimum score 65). *Application deadline:* For fall admission, 12/13 for domestic students. Application fee: $105 ($125 for international students). Electronic applications accepted. *Expenses:* Tuition, state resident: full-time $11,220. Tuition, nonresident: full-time $26,322. *Required fees:* $1864. *Financial support:* Fellowships, research assistantships, teaching assistantships, scholarships/grants, traineeships, and unspecified assistantships available. Financial award applicants required to submit FAFSA. *Faculty research:* Applied ocean science; applied physics; communication theory and systems; computer engineering; electronic circuits and systems; intelligent systems, robotics and control; medical devices and systems; nanoscale devices and systems; photonics; signal and image processing. *Unit head:* Truong Nguyen, Chair, 858-822-5554, E-mail: nguyent@ece.ucsd.edu. *Application contact:* Melanie Lynn, Graduate Admissions Coordinator, 858-822-3213, E-mail: ecegradapps@ece.ucsd.edu.
Website: http://ece.ucsd.edu/

University of Georgia, Franklin College of Arts and Sciences, Artificial Intelligence Center, Athens, GA 30602. Offers MS. *Degree requirements:* For master's, thesis. *Entrance requirements:* For master's, GRE General Test. *Application deadline:* For fall admission, 7/1 priority date for domestic students; for spring admission, 11/15 for domestic students. Application fee: $50. Electronic applications accepted. *Financial support:* Unspecified assistantships available. *Unit head:* Dr. Walter Don Potter, Director, 706-542-0361, E-mail: potter@uga.edu. *Application contact:* Adam Goodle, Graduate Coordinator, 706-542-3444, E-mail: goodie@uga.edu.
Website: http://ai.uga.edu

University of Michigan, College of Engineering, Department of Integrative Systems and Design, Ann Arbor, MI 48109. Offers automotive engineering (M Eng); design science (MS, PhD); energy systems engineering (M Eng, MS); global automotive and manufacturing engineering (M Eng); manufacturing engineering (M Eng, D Eng); pharmaceutical engineering (M Eng); robotics and autonomous vehicles (M Eng); systems engineering and design (M Eng); MBA/M Eng; MSE/MS. *Program availability:* Part-time, online learning. *Students:* 147 full-time (33 women), 234 part-time (39 women). 315 applicants, 8% accepted, 13 enrolled. In 2016, 158 master's, 2 doctorates awarded. Terminal master's awarded for partial completion of doctoral program. *Degree requirements:* For master's, capstone project; for doctorate, thesis/dissertation. *Entrance requirements:* For master's, GRE; for doctorate, GRE, 2 years of work experience. Additional exam requirements/recommendations for international students: Required—TOEFL (minimum score 560 paper-based). *Application deadline:* Applications are processed on a rolling basis. Electronic applications accepted. *Expenses:* Tuition, state resident: full-time $21,466; part-time $1152 per credit hour. Tuition, nonresident: full-time $43,346; part-time $2367 per credit hour. Part-time tuition and fees vary according to course load, degree level and program. *Financial support:* Fellowships, research assistantships with full tuition reimbursements, teaching assistantships with full tuition reimbursements, career-related internships or fieldwork, scholarships/grants, and unspecified assistantships available. Financial award applicants required to submit FAFSA. *Faculty research:* Automotive engineering, design science, energy systems engineering, engineering sustainable systems, financial engineering, global automotive and manufacturing engineering, integrated microsystems, manufacturing engineering, pharmaceutical engineering, robotics and autonomous vehicles. *Total annual research expenditures:* $292,225. *Unit head:* Prof. Panos Papalambros, Department Chair, 734-647-8401, E-mail: pyp@umich.edu. *Application contact:* Kathy Bishar, Senior Graduate Coordinator, 734-764-3312, E-mail: kbishar@umich.edu.
Website: http://www.isd.engin.umich.edu

University of Michigan, College of Engineering, Program in Robotics, Ann Arbor, MI 48109. Offers MS, PhD. *Students:* 73 full-time (9 women), 1 part-time (0 women). 393 applicants, 23% accepted, 52 enrolled. In 2016, 4 master's awarded. *Entrance requirements:* For master's and doctorate, GRE General Test. Additional exam requirements/recommendations for international students: Required—TOEFL. *Expenses:* Tuition, state resident: full-time $21,466; part-time $1152 per credit hour. Tuition, nonresident: full-time $43,346; part-time $2367 per credit hour. Part-time tuition and fees vary according to course load, degree level and program. *Faculty research:* Autonomous vehicles, human-robot interaction, legged locomotion, manipulation, manufacturing. *Unit head:* Jessy Grizzle, Director, 734-763-3598, E-mail: grizzle@umich.edu. *Application contact:* Sarah Sobek, Graduate Coordinator, E-mail: um-robotics@umich.edu.
Website: http://robotics.umich.edu/

University of Nebraska at Omaha, Graduate Studies, College of Information Science and Technology, Department of Computer Science, Omaha, NE 68182. Offers artificial intelligence (Certificate); communication networks (Certificate); computer science (MA, MS); computer science education (MS, Certificate); software engineering (Certificate); system and architecture (Certificate). *Program availability:* Part-time, evening/weekend. *Faculty:* 13 full-time (4 women). *Students:* 73 full-time (19 women), 44 part-time (15 women); includes 8 minority (3 Asian, non-Hispanic/Latino; 1 Hispanic/Latino; 4 Two or more races, non-Hispanic/Latino), 87 international. Average age 27. 132 applicants, 59% accepted, 33 enrolled. In 2016, 58 master's awarded. *Degree requirements:* For master's, comprehensive exam, thesis (for some programs). *Entrance requirements:* For master's, GRE General Test, minimum GPA of 3.0, prior course work in computer science, official transcripts, resume, 2 letters of recommendation; for Certificate, minimum GPA of 3.0, resume. Additional exam requirements/recommendations for international students: Required—TOEFL, IELTS, PTE. *Application deadline:* For fall admission, 7/1 priority date for domestic and international students; for spring admission, 11/1 priority date for domestic and international students; for summer admission, 3/1 for domestic and international students. Applications are processed on a rolling basis. Application fee: $45. Electronic applications accepted. *Financial support:* In 2016–17, 16 students received support, including 16 research assistantships with tuition reimbursements available; teaching assistantships with tuition reimbursements available, Federal Work-Study, institutionally sponsored loans, scholarships/grants, health care benefits, tuition waivers (full), and unspecified assistantships also available. Support available to part-time students. Financial award application deadline: 3/1; financial award applicants required to submit FAFSA. *Unit head:* Dr. Qiuming Zhu, Chairperson, 402-554-2341, E-mail: graduate@unomaha.edu. *Application contact:* Dr. Azad Azadmanesh, Graduate Program Chair, 402-554-2341, E-mail: graduate@unomaha.edu.

University of Pennsylvania, School of Engineering and Applied Science, Program in Robotics, Philadelphia, PA 19104. Offers MSE. *Program availability:* Part-time. *Students:* 40 full-time (5 women), 23 part-time (4 women); includes 9 minority (8 Asian, non-Hispanic/Latino; 1 Hispanic/Latino), 28 international. Average age 25. 347 applicants, 16% accepted, 33 enrolled. In 2016, 39 master's awarded. *Degree requirements:* For master's, comprehensive exam, thesis optional. *Entrance requirements:* For master's, GRE. Additional exam requirements/recommendations for international students: Required—TOEFL (minimum score 100 iBT), IELTS (minimum score 7). *Application deadline:* For fall admission, 3/15 priority date for domestic and international students. Application fee: $80. Electronic applications accepted. *Expenses: Tuition:* Full-time $31,068; part-time $5762 per course. *Required fees:* $3200; $336 per course. Full-time tuition and fees vary according to degree level, program and student level. Part-time tuition and fees vary according to course load, degree level and program. *Faculty research:* Robotics and automation, control systems design, hybrid systems, machine learning, mechanics. *Unit head:* Vijay Kumar, Dean, 215-898-7244, E-mail: seasdean@seas.upenn.edu. *Application contact:* School of Engineering and Applied Science Graduate Admissions, 215-898-4542, E-mail: gradstudies@seas.upenn.edu.
Website: http://www.grasp.upenn.edu

University of Pittsburgh, Dietrich School of Arts and Sciences, Intelligent Systems Program, Pittsburgh, PA 15260. Offers MS, PhD. *Faculty:* 27 full-time (9 women). *Students:* 22 full-time (9 women), 1 part-time (0 women), 19 international. Average age 28. 39 applicants, 8% accepted, 3 enrolled. In 2016, 4 master's, 3 doctorates awarded. Terminal master's awarded for partial completion of doctoral program. *Degree requirements:* For doctorate, comprehensive exam, thesis/dissertation. *Entrance requirements:* For master's and doctorate, GRE General Test. Additional exam requirements/recommendations for international students: Required—TOEFL (minimum score 90 iBT), IELTS (minimum score 7). *Application deadline:* For fall admission, 1/15 for domestic and international students. Application fee: $50. Electronic applications accepted. *Expenses:* Contact institution. *Financial support:* In 2016–17, 5 fellowships with full tuition reimbursements (averaging $23,000 per year) were awarded; research assistantships with full tuition reimbursements, career-related internships or fieldwork, institutionally sponsored loans, scholarships/grants, traineeships, health care benefits, tuition waivers, and unspecified assistantships also available. Financial award application deadline: 1/15. *Faculty research:* Medical artificial intelligence, clinical decision support, expert systems, special cognition, plan generation and recognition. *Unit head:* Dr. Diane Litman, Director, 412-624-8838, Fax: 412-624-8561, E-mail: litman@cs.pitt.edu. *Application contact:* Michele Thomas, Administrator, 412-624-5755, Fax: 412-624-8561.
Website: http://www.isp.pitt.edu/

University of Southern California, Graduate School, Viterbi School of Engineering, Department of Computer Science, Los Angeles, CA 90089. Offers computer networks (MS); computer science (MS, PhD); computer security (MS); game development (MS); high performance computing and simulations (MS); human language technology (MS); intelligent robotics (MS); multimedia and creative technologies (MS); software engineering (MS). *Program availability:* Part-time, evening/weekend, online learning. *Entrance requirements:* For master's and doctorate, GRE General Test. Additional exam requirements/recommendations for international students: Required—TOEFL. Electronic applications accepted. *Faculty research:* Databases, computer graphics and computer vision, software engineering, networks and security, robotics, multimedia and virtual reality.

Villanova University, College of Engineering, Department of Electrical and Computer Engineering, Program in Computer Engineering, Villanova, PA 19085-1699. Offers computer architectures (Certificate); computer engineering (MSCPE); intelligent control systems (Certificate). *Program availability:* Part-time, evening/weekend. *Degree requirements:* For master's, thesis optional. *Entrance requirements:* For master's, GRE General Test (for applicants with degrees from foreign universities), BEE, minimum GPA of 3.0. Additional exam requirements/recommendations for international students: Required—TOEFL (minimum score 600 paper-based; 100 iBT). Electronic applications accepted. *Faculty research:* Expert systems, computer vision, neural networks, image processing, computer architectures.

Villanova University, College of Engineering, Department of Electrical and Computer Engineering, Program in Electrical Engineering, Villanova, PA 19085-1699. Offers electric power systems (Certificate); electrical engineering (MSEE); electro mechanical systems (Certificate); high frequency systems (Certificate); intelligent control systems (Certificate); wireless and digital communications (Certificate). *Program availability:* Part-time, evening/weekend. *Degree requirements:* For master's, thesis optional. *Entrance requirements:* For master's, GRE General Test (for applicants with degrees from foreign universities), BEE, minimum GPA of 3.0. Additional exam requirements/recommendations for international students: Required—TOEFL (minimum score 600 paper-based; 100 iBT). *Faculty research:* Signal processing, communications, antennas, devices.

Worcester Polytechnic Institute, Graduate Studies and Research, Program in Robotics Engineering, Worcester, MA 01609-2280. Offers MS, PhD. *Program availability:* Part-time, evening/weekend, online only, 100% online, blended/hybrid learning. *Faculty:* 1 part-time/adjunct. *Students:* 130 full-time (19 women), 37 part-time (5 women); includes 17 minority (4 Black or African American, non-Hispanic/Latino; 7 Asian, non-Hispanic/Latino; 6 Hispanic/Latino), 96 international. 320 applicants, 49% accepted, 61 enrolled. In 2016, 14 master's awarded. *Degree requirements:* For master's, thesis or capstone design project; for doctorate, thesis/dissertation. *Entrance requirements:* For master's and doctorate, GRE, 3 letters of recommendation, statement of purpose. Additional exam requirements/recommendations for international students: Required—TOEFL (minimum score 563 paper-based; 84 iBT), IELTS (minimum score 7). *Application deadline:* For fall admission, 1/1 priority date for domestic and international students; for spring admission, 10/1 priority date for domestic and international students. Applications are processed on a rolling basis. Application fee: $70. Electronic applications accepted. *Financial support:* Research assistantships, teaching assistantships, career-related internships or fieldwork, institutionally sponsored loans, scholarships/grants, and unspecified assistantships available. Financial award application deadline: 1/1; financial award applicants required to submit FAFSA. *Unit head:* Dr. Michael Gennert, Director, 508-831-5357, Fax: 508-831-5776, E-mail: michaelg@wpi.edu. *Application contact:* Deborah Baron, Graduate Coordinator, 508-831-5357, Fax: 508-831-5776, E-mail: dabaron@wpi.edu.
Website: http://www.wpi.edu/academics/robotics/gradprograms.html

Bioinformatics

Arizona State University at the Tempe campus, College of Health Solutions, Department of Biomedical Informatics, Phoenix, AZ 85004. Offers MS, PhD. Terminal master's awarded for partial completion of doctoral program. *Degree requirements:* For master's, interactive Program of Study (iPOS) submitted before completing 50 percent of required credit hours; for doctorate, comprehensive exam, thesis/dissertation, interactive Program of Study (iPOS) submitted before completing 50 percent of required credit hours. *Entrance requirements:* For master's, GRE or MCAT, bachelor's degree with minimum GPA of 3.25 in computer science, biology, physiology, nursing, statistics, engineering, related fields, or unrelated fields with appropriate academic backgrounds; resume/curriculum vitae; statement of purpose; 3 letters of recommendation; all official transcripts; for doctorate, GRE or MCAT, bachelor's degree with minimum GPA of 3.5 in computer science, biology, physiology, nursing, statistics, engineering, related fields, or unrelated fields with appropriate academic backgrounds; resume/curriculum vitae; statement of purpose; 3 letters of recommendation; all official transcripts. Additional exam requirements/recommendations for international students: Required—TOEFL (minimum score 550 paper-based; 83 iBT), IELTS (minimum score 6.5). Electronic applications accepted.

Boston University, Graduate School of Arts and Sciences and College of Engineering, Intercollegiate Program in Bioinformatics, Boston, MA 02215. Offers MS, PhD. *Students:* 87 full-time (33 women), 14 part-time (6 women); includes 24 minority (2 Black or African American, non-Hispanic/Latino; 12 Asian, non-Hispanic/Latino; 9 Hispanic/Latino; 1 Two or more races, non-Hispanic/Latino), 32 international. Average age 27. 174 applicants, 43% accepted, 27 enrolled. In 2016, 10 master's, 12 doctorates awarded. Terminal master's awarded for partial completion of doctoral program. *Degree requirements:* For master's, thesis or alternative, internship; for doctorate, comprehensive exam, thesis/dissertation. *Entrance requirements:* For master's, 3 letters of recommendation, transcripts, personal statement, resume; for doctorate, GRE General Test, 3 letters of recommendation, transcripts, personal statement, resume. Additional exam requirements/recommendations for international students: Required—TOEFL (minimum score 550 paper-based; 84 iBT). *Application deadline:* For fall and spring admission, 12/1 for domestic and international students. Application fee: $95. Electronic applications accepted. *Financial support:* In 2016–17, 55 students received support, including 12 fellowships with full tuition reimbursements available (averaging $21,500 per year), 41 research assistantships with full tuition reimbursements available (averaging $21,500 per year); career-related internships or fieldwork, Federal Work-Study, scholarships/grants, traineeships, and health care benefits also available. Financial award application deadline: 12/1. *Unit head:* Tom Tullius, Director, 617-353-2482, E-mail: tullius@bu.edu. *Application contact:* David King, Administrator, 617-358-0751, Fax: 617-353-5929, E-mail: dking@bu.edu.
Website: http://www.bu.edu/bioinformatics

Brandeis University, Rabb School of Continuing Studies, Division of Graduate Professional Studies, Master of Science in Bioinformatics Program, Waltham, MA 02454-9110. Offers MS. *Program availability:* Part-time-only. *Faculty:* 45 part-time/adjunct (16 women). *Students:* 25 part-time (8 women); includes 8 minority (2 Black or African American, non-Hispanic/Latino; 5 Asian, non-Hispanic/Latino; 1 Two or more races, non-Hispanic/Latino), 1 international. Average age 37. 6 applicants, 83% accepted, 5 enrolled. In 2016, 5 master's awarded. *Entrance requirements:* For master's, undergraduate-level coursework in molecular biology, organic chemistry, and programming in Java, C++ or C; four-year bachelor's degree from regionally-accredited U.S. institution or equivalent; official transcript(s) from every college or university attended; resume or curriculum vitae; statement of goals; letter of recommendation. Additional exam requirements/recommendations for international students: Required—TWE (minimum score 4.5), TOEFL (minimum scores: 600 paper-based, 100 iBT), IELTS (7), or PTE (68). *Application deadline:* For fall admission, 6/21 priority date for domestic and international students; for winter admission, 9/13 priority date for domestic and international students; for spring admission, 12/20 priority date for domestic and international students; for summer admission, 3/14 priority date for domestic and international students. Applications are processed on a rolling basis. Application fee: $50. Electronic applications accepted. *Expenses:* $3,400 per course, $100 graduation fee. *Financial support:* Applicants required to submit FAFSA. *Unit head:* Dr. Alan Cheng, Program Chair, 781-736-8787, E-mail: acheng@brandeis.edu. *Application contact:* Frances Stearns, Director of Admissions and Recruitment, 781-736-8785, E-mail: fstearns@brandeis.edu.
Website: http://www.brandeis.edu/gps

California State University Channel Islands, Extended University and International Programs, Programs in Biotechnology, Camarillo, CA 93012. Offers biotechnology and bioinformatics (MS); MS/MBA. *Entrance requirements:* Additional exam requirements/recommendations for international students: Required—TOEFL (minimum score 550 paper-based; 80 iBT), IELTS (minimum score 6).

California State University, Dominguez Hills, College of Natural and Behavioral Sciences, Department of Biology, Carson, CA 90747-0001. Offers MS. *Program availability:* Part-time, evening/weekend. *Degree requirements:* For master's, thesis. *Entrance requirements:* For master's, minimum GPA of 2.75. Additional exam requirements/recommendations for international students: Required—TOEFL (minimum score 550 paper-based). Electronic applications accepted. *Faculty research:* Cancer biology, infectious diseases, ecology of native plants, remediation, community ecology.

Dalhousie University, Faculty of Computer Science, Halifax, NS B3H 1W5, Canada. Offers computational biology and bioinformatics (M Sc); computer science (MA Sc, MC Sc, PhD); electronic commerce (MEC); health informatics (MHI). *Degree requirements:* For master's, thesis (for some programs); for doctorate, thesis/dissertation. *Entrance requirements:* Additional exam requirements/recommendations for international students: Required—1 of 5 approved tests: TOEFL, IELTS, CANTEST, CAEL, Michigan English Language Assessment Battery. Electronic applications accepted.

Duke University, Graduate School, Department of Computational Biology and Bioinformatics, Durham, NC 27708. Offers PhD, Certificate. *Degree requirements:* For doctorate, thesis/dissertation. *Entrance requirements:* For doctorate, GRE General Test. Additional exam requirements/recommendations for international students: Required—TOEFL (minimum score 577 paper-based; 90 iBT) or IELTS (minimum score 7). Electronic applications accepted.

Emory University, Rollins School of Public Health, Department of Biostatistics and Bioinformatics, Atlanta, GA 30322-1100. Offers bioinformatics (PhD); biostatistics (MPH, MSPH); public health informatics (MSPH). PhD offered through the Graduate School of Arts and Sciences. *Program availability:* Part-time. *Degree requirements:* For master's, thesis, practicum. *Entrance requirements:* For master's, GRE General Test. Additional exam requirements/recommendations for international students: Required—TOEFL (minimum score 550 paper-based; 80 iBT). Electronic applications accepted.

George Mason University, College of Science, School of Systems Biology, Manassas, VA 20110. Offers bioinformatics and computational biology (MS, PhD, Certificate); bioinformatics management (MS); biology (MS); biosciences (PhD); personalized medicine (Certificate). *Faculty:* 10 full-time (3 women), 2 part-time/adjunct (0 women). *Students:* 102 full-time (53 women), 81 part-time (46 women); includes 52 minority (4 Black or African American, non-Hispanic/Latino; 29 Asian, non-Hispanic/Latino; 11 Hispanic/Latino; 1 Native Hawaiian or other Pacific Islander, non-Hispanic/Latino; 7 Two or more races, non-Hispanic/Latino), 41 international. Average age 31. 133 applicants, 78% accepted, 68 enrolled. In 2016, 27 master's, 15 doctorates, 1 other advanced degree awarded. *Degree requirements:* For master's, research project or thesis; for doctorate, comprehensive exam, thesis/dissertation. *Entrance requirements:* For master's, GRE, resume; 3 letters of recommendation; expanded goals statement; 2 copies of official transcripts; bachelor's degree in related field with minimum GPA of 3.0 in last 60 hours; for doctorate, GRE, self-assessment form; resume; 3 letters of recommendation; expanded goals statement; 2 copies of official transcripts; bachelor's degree in related field with minimum GPA of 3.0 in last 60 hours; for Certificate, resume; 2 copies of official transcripts. Additional exam requirements/recommendations for international students: Required—TOEFL (minimum score 575 paper-based; 88 iBT), IELTS (minimum score 6.5), PTE (minimum score 59). Application fee: $75 ($80 for international students). Electronic applications accepted. *Expenses:* Tuition, state resident: full-time $10,628; part-time $443 per credit. Tuition, nonresident: full-time $29,306; part-time $1221 per credit. *Required fees:* $3096; $129 per credit. Tuition and fees vary according to program. *Financial support:* In 2016–17, 53 students received support, including 11 fellowships (averaging $6,688 per year), 14 research assistantships with tuition reimbursements available (averaging $15,875 per year), 40 teaching assistantships with tuition reimbursements available (averaging $15,740 per year); career-related internships or fieldwork, Federal Work-Study, scholarships/grants, unspecified assistantships, and health care benefits (for full-time research or teaching assistantship recipients) also available. Support available to part-time students. Financial award application deadline: 3/1; financial award applicants required to submit FAFSA. *Faculty research:* Functional genomics of chronic human diseases, ecology of vector-borne infectious diseases, neurogenetics, molecular biology, computational modeling, proteomics, chronic metabolic diseases, nanotechnology. *Total annual research expenditures:* $1.4 million. *Unit head:* Dr. Iosif Vaisman, Director, 703-993-8431, Fax: 703-993-8976, E-mail: ivaisman@gmu.edu. *Application contact:* Diane St. Germain, Graduate Student Services Coordinator, 703-993-4263, Fax: 703-993-8976, E-mail: dstgerma@gmu.edu.
Website: http://ssb.gmu.edu/

Georgetown University, Graduate School of Arts and Sciences, Department of Biostatistics, Bioinformatics and Biomathematics, Washington, DC 20057-1484. Offers biostatistics (MS, Certificate), including bioinformatics (MS), epidemiology (MS); epidemiology (Certificate). *Entrance requirements:* For master's, GRE General Test. Additional exam requirements/recommendations for international students: Required—TOEFL. *Faculty research:* Occupation epidemiology, cancer.

Georgia Institute of Technology, Graduate Studies, Multidisciplinary Program in Bioinformatics, Atlanta, GA 30332-0001. Offers MS, PhD. Program offered jointly with School of Biology, Wallace H. Coulter Department of Biomedical Engineering, School of Chemistry and Biochemistry, School of Computational Science and Engineering, School of Mathematics, and School of Industrial and Systems Engineering. *Program availability:* Part-time. Terminal master's awarded for partial completion of doctoral program. *Degree requirements:* For master's, research with faculty, professional internships, co-op work experience; for doctorate, comprehensive exam, thesis/dissertation. *Entrance requirements:* For master's and doctorate, GRE General Test. Additional exam requirements/recommendations for international students: Required—TOEFL (minimum score 600 paper-based; 100 iBT). Electronic applications accepted. *Expenses:* Contact institution.

Georgia State University, College of Arts and Sciences, Department of Biology, Program in Applied and Environmental Microbiology, Atlanta, GA 30302-3083. Offers applied and environmental microbiology (MS, PhD); bioinformatics (MS). *Program availability:* Part-time. Terminal master's awarded for partial completion of doctoral program. *Degree requirements:* For master's, comprehensive exam (for some programs), thesis optional; for doctorate, comprehensive exam, thesis/dissertation. *Entrance requirements:* For master's and doctorate, GRE. Additional exam requirements/recommendations for international students: Required—TOEFL (minimum score 550 paper-based; 82 iBT) or IELTS (minimum score 7). *Application deadline:* For fall admission, 7/1 priority date for domestic students, 6/1 priority date for international students; for spring admission, 11/15 priority date for domestic students, 10/15 priority date for international students. Applications are processed on a rolling basis. Application fee: $50. Electronic applications accepted. *Expenses:* Tuition, state resident: full-time $6876; part-time $382 per credit hour. Tuition, nonresident: full-time $22,374; part-time $1243 per credit hour. *Required fees:* $2128; $1064 per term. Part-time tuition and fees vary according to course load and program. *Financial support:* In 2016–17, fellowships with full tuition reimbursements (averaging $22,000 per year), research assistantships with full tuition reimbursements (averaging $20,000 per year) were awarded. Financial award application deadline: 12/3. *Faculty research:* Bioremediation, biofilms, indoor air quality control, environmental toxicology, product biosynthesis. *Unit head:* Dr. Charles Derby, Director of Graduate Studies, 404-413-5393, Fax: 404-413-5446, E-mail: cderby@gsu.edu.
Website: http://biology.gsu.edu/

Georgia State University, College of Arts and Sciences, Department of Biology, Program in Cellular and Molecular Biology and Physiology, Atlanta, GA 30302-3083. Offers bioinformatics (MS); cellular and molecular biology and physiology (MS, PhD). *Program availability:* Part-time. Terminal master's awarded for partial completion of doctoral program. *Degree requirements:* For master's, comprehensive exam (for some programs), thesis optional; for doctorate, comprehensive exam, thesis/dissertation. *Entrance requirements:* For master's and doctorate, GRE. Additional exam requirements/recommendations for international students: Required—TOEFL (minimum score 550 paper-based; 82 iBT) or IELTS (minimum score 7). *Application deadline:* For fall admission, 7/1 priority date for domestic students, 6/1 priority date for international students; for spring admission, 11/15 priority date for domestic students, 10/15 priority date for international students. Applications are processed on a rolling basis. Application fee: $50. Electronic applications accepted. *Expenses:* Tuition, state resident: full-time $6876; part-time $382 per credit hour. Tuition, nonresident: full-time $22,374; part-time $1243 per credit hour. *Required fees:* $2128; $1064 per term. Part-time tuition and fees vary according to course load and program. *Financial support:* In 2016–17, fellowships with full tuition reimbursements (averaging $22,000 per year), research assistantships with full tuition reimbursements (averaging $20,000 per year) were awarded. Financial award application deadline: 12/3. *Faculty research:* Membrane transport, viral infection, molecular immunology, protein modeling, gene regulation. *Unit head:* Dr. Charles Derby, Director of Graduate Studies, 404-413-5393, Fax: 404-413-5446, E-mail: cderby@gsu.edu.
Website: http://biology.gsu.edu/

Georgia State University, College of Arts and Sciences, Department of Biology, Program in Molecular Genetics and Biochemistry, Atlanta, GA 30302-3083. Offers bioinformatics (MS); molecular genetics and biochemistry (MS, PhD). *Program availability:* Part-time. Terminal master's awarded for partial completion of doctoral program. *Degree requirements:* For master's, comprehensive exam (for some programs), thesis optional; for doctorate, comprehensive exam, thesis/dissertation. *Entrance requirements:* For master's and doctorate, GRE. Additional exam requirements/recommendations for international students: Required—TOEFL (minimum score 550 paper-based; 82 iBT) or IELTS (minimum score 7). *Application deadline:* For fall admission, 7/1 priority date for domestic students, 6/1 priority date for international students; for spring admission, 11/15 priority date for domestic students, 10/15 priority date for international students. Applications are processed on a rolling basis. Application fee: $50. Electronic applications accepted. *Expenses:* Tuition, state resident: full-time $6876; part-time $382 per credit hour. Tuition, nonresident: full-time $22,374; part-time $1243 per credit hour. *Required fees:* $2128; $1064 per term. Part-time tuition and fees vary according to course load and program. *Financial support:* In 2016–17, fellowships with full tuition reimbursements (averaging $22,000 per year), research assistantships with full tuition reimbursements (averaging $20,000 per year) were awarded. Financial award application deadline: 12/3. *Faculty research:* Gene regulation, microbial pathogenesis, molecular transport, protein modeling, viral pathogenesis. *Unit head:* Dr. Charles Derby, Director of Graduate Studies, 404-413-5393, Fax: 404-413-5446, E-mail: cderby@gsu.edu.
Website: http://biology.gsu.edu/

Georgia State University, College of Arts and Sciences, Department of Biology, Program in Neurobiology and Behavior, Atlanta, GA 30302-3083. Offers bioinformatics (MS); neurobiology and behavior (MS, PhD). *Program availability:* Part-time. Terminal master's awarded for partial completion of doctoral program. *Degree requirements:* For master's, comprehensive exam (for some programs), thesis optional; for doctorate, comprehensive exam, thesis/dissertation. *Entrance requirements:* For master's and doctorate, GRE. Additional exam requirements/recommendations for international students: Required—TOEFL (minimum score 550 paper-based; 82 iBT) or IELTS (minimum score 7). *Application deadline:* For fall admission, 7/1 priority date for domestic students, 6/1 priority date for international students; for spring admission, 11/15 priority date for domestic students, 10/15 priority date for international students. Applications are processed on a rolling basis. Application fee: $50. Electronic applications accepted. *Expenses:* Tuition, state resident: full-time $6876; part-time $382 per credit hour. Tuition, nonresident: full-time $22,374; part-time $1243 per credit hour. *Required fees:* $2128; $1064 per term. Part-time tuition and fees vary according to course load and program. *Financial support:* In 2016–17, fellowships with full tuition reimbursements (averaging $22,000 per year), research assistantships with full tuition reimbursements (averaging $20,000 per year) were awarded. Financial award application deadline: 12/3. *Faculty research:* Behavior, circadian and circa-annual rhythms, developmental genetics, neuroendocrinology, cytoskeletal dynamics. *Unit head:* Dr. Charles Derby, Director of Graduate Studies, 404-413-5393, Fax: 404-413-5446, E-mail: cderby@gsu.edu.
Website: http://biology.gsu.edu/

Georgia State University, College of Arts and Sciences, Department of Chemistry, Atlanta, GA 30302-3083. Offers analytical chemistry (MS, PhD); biochemistry (MS, PhD); bioinformatics (MS, PhD); biophysical chemistry (PhD); computational chemistry (MS, PhD); geochemistry (PhD); organic/medicinal chemistry (MS, PhD); physical chemistry (MS). PhD in geochemistry offered jointly with Department of Geosciences. *Program availability:* Part-time. *Faculty:* 41 full-time (17 women). *Students:* 160 full-time (64 women), 7 part-time (3 women); includes 44 minority (21 Black or African American, non-Hispanic/Latino; 1 American Indian or Alaska Native, non-Hispanic/Latino; 10 Asian, non-Hispanic/Latino; 6 Hispanic/Latino; 6 Two or more races, non-Hispanic/Latino), 79 international. Average age 29. 117 applicants, 33% accepted, 29 enrolled. In 2016, 38 master's, 13 doctorates awarded. Terminal master's awarded for partial completion of doctoral program. *Degree requirements:* For master's, one foreign language, comprehensive exam (for some programs), thesis (for some programs); for doctorate, one foreign language, comprehensive exam, thesis/dissertation. *Entrance requirements:* For master's and doctorate, GRE. Additional exam requirements/recommendations for international students: Required—TOEFL (minimum score 550 paper-based; 80 iBT) or IELTS (minimum score 6.5). *Application deadline:* For fall admission, 7/1 priority date for domestic and international students; for winter admission, 11/15 priority date for domestic and international students; for spring admission, 4/15 priority date for domestic and international students. Applications are processed on a rolling basis. Application fee: $50. Electronic applications accepted. *Expenses:* Tuition, state resident: full-time $6876; part-time $382 per credit hour. Tuition, nonresident: full-time $22,374; part-time $1243 per credit hour. *Required fees:* $2128; $1064 per term. Part-time tuition and fees vary according to course load and program. *Financial support:* Fellowships with full tuition reimbursements, research assistantships with full tuition reimbursements, and teaching assistantships with full tuition reimbursements available. Financial award applicants required to submit FAFSA. *Faculty research:* Analytical chemistry, biological/biochemistry, biophysical/computational chemistry, chemical education, organic/medicinal chemistry. *Unit head:* Dr. Peng George Wang, Department Chair, 404-413-3591, Fax: 404-413-5505, E-mail: pwang11@gsu.edu.
Website: http://chemistry.gsu.edu/

Georgia State University, College of Arts and Sciences, Department of Computer Science, Atlanta, GA 30302-3083. Offers bioinformatics (MS, PhD); computer science (MS, PhD). *Program availability:* Part-time. *Faculty:* 21 full-time (4 women). *Students:* 147 full-time (61 women), 30 part-time (11 women); includes 18 minority (7 Black or

African American, non-Hispanic/Latino; 5 Asian, non-Hispanic/Latino; 2 Hispanic/Latino; 4 Two or more races, non-Hispanic/Latino), 141 international. Average age 28. 303 applicants, 41% accepted, 52 enrolled. In 2016, 48 master's, 10 doctorates awarded. Terminal master's awarded for partial completion of doctoral program. *Degree requirements:* For master's, comprehensive exam, thesis (for some programs); for doctorate, comprehensive exam, thesis/dissertation, proposal defense. *Entrance requirements:* For master's and doctorate, GRE General Test. Additional exam requirements/recommendations for international students: Required—TOEFL (minimum score 550 paper-based; 80 iBT). *Application deadline:* For fall admission, 3/15 for domestic and international students; for spring admission, 10/15 for domestic and international students. Application fee: $50. Electronic applications accepted. *Expenses:* Tuition, state resident: full-time $6876; part-time $382 per credit hour. Tuition, nonresident: full-time $22,374; part-time $1243 per credit hour. *Required fees:* $2128; $1064 per term. Part-time tuition and fees vary according to course load and program. *Financial support:* In 2016–17, fellowships with full tuition reimbursements (averaging $22,000 per year), research assistantships with full tuition reimbursements (averaging $16,000 per year), teaching assistantships with full tuition reimbursements (averaging $16,000 per year) were awarded; institutionally sponsored loans, health care benefits, and unspecified assistantships also available. Financial award application deadline: 2/15; financial award applicants required to submit FAFSA. *Faculty research:* Artificial intelligence and computational intelligence, bioinformatics, computer software systems, databases, graphics and human computer interaction, networks and parallel and distributed computing. *Unit head:* Dr. Yi Pan, Acting Chair, 404-413-5342, Fax: 404-413-5717, E-mail: yipan@gsu.edu.
Website: http://www.cs.gsu.edu/

Georgia State University, College of Arts and Sciences, Department of Mathematics and Statistics, Atlanta, GA 30302-3083. Offers bioinformatics (MS, PhD); biostatistics (MS, PhD); discrete mathematics (MS); mathematics (MS, PhD); scientific computing (MS); statistics (MS). *Program availability:* Part-time. *Faculty:* 38 full-time (11 women). *Students:* 97 full-time (47 women), 24 part-time (7 women); includes 43 minority (11 Black or African American, non-Hispanic/Latino; 21 Asian, non-Hispanic/Latino; 3 Hispanic/Latino; 8 Two or more races, non-Hispanic/Latino), 57 international. Average age 32. 72 applicants, 69% accepted, 26 enrolled. In 2016, 39 master's, 6 doctorates awarded. Terminal master's awarded for partial completion of doctoral program. *Degree requirements:* For master's, comprehensive exam (for some programs), thesis optional; for doctorate, comprehensive exam, thesis/dissertation. *Entrance requirements:* For master's and doctorate, GRE. Additional exam requirements/recommendations for international students: Required—TOEFL (minimum score 550 paper-based; 80 iBT). *Application deadline:* For fall admission, 7/1 priority date for domestic and international students; for spring admission, 11/15 priority date for domestic and international students. Application fee: $50. Electronic applications accepted. *Expenses:* Tuition, state resident: full-time $6876; part-time $382 per credit hour. Tuition, nonresident: full-time $22,374; part-time $1243 per credit hour. *Required fees:* $2128; $1064 per term. Part-time tuition and fees vary according to course load and program. *Financial support:* In 2016–17, fellowships with full tuition reimbursements (averaging $22,000 per year), research assistantships with full tuition reimbursements (averaging $9,000 per year), teaching assistantships with full tuition reimbursements (averaging $9,000 per year) were awarded; institutionally sponsored loans, scholarships/grants, health care benefits, and unspecified assistantships also available. Financial award application deadline: 2/1. *Faculty research:* Algebra, matrix theory, graph theory and combinatorics; applied mathematics and analysis; collegiate mathematics education; statistics, biostatistics and applications; bioinformatics, dynamical systems. *Unit head:* Dr. Guantao Chen, Chair, 404-413-6436, Fax: 404-413-6403, E-mail: gchen@gsu.edu.
Website: http://www2.gsu.edu/~wwwmat/

Grand Valley State University, Padnos College of Engineering and Computing, Medical and Bioinformatics Program, Allendale, MI 49401-9403. Offers MS. *Program availability:* Part-time, evening/weekend. *Faculty:* 13 full-time (4 women), 3 part-time/adjunct (2 women). *Students:* 12 full-time (6 women), 6 part-time (3 women); includes 2 minority (1 Asian, non-Hispanic/Latino; 1 Hispanic/Latino), 14 international. Average age 26. 16 applicants, 94% accepted, 6 enrolled. In 2016, 5 master's awarded. *Degree requirements:* For master's, capstone course. *Entrance requirements:* For master's, GRE or GMAT, minimum GPA of 3.0, resume, personal statement, minimum of 2 letters of recommendation, previous academic study or work experience. Additional exam requirements/recommendations for international students: Required—TOEFL, Michigan English Language Assessment Battery or completion of ELS 112; Recommended—IELTS. *Application deadline:* For fall admission, 2/1 priority date for domestic students. Applications are processed on a rolling basis. Application fee: $30. Electronic applications accepted. *Expenses:* $633 per credit hour. *Financial support:* In 2016–17, 11 students received support, including 4 fellowships, 7 research assistantships with full and partial tuition reimbursements available (averaging $8,000 per year); career-related internships or fieldwork, tuition waivers (full and partial), and unspecified assistantships also available. *Faculty research:* Biomedical informatics, information visualization, data mining, high-performance computing, computational biology. *Unit head:* Dr. Paul Leidig, Director, 616-331-2308, Fax: 616-331-2106, E-mail: leidigp@gvsu.edu. *Application contact:* Dr. Guenter Tusch, Graduate Program Director, 616-331-2046, E-mail: tuschg@gvsu.edu.

Hood College, Graduate School, Program in Bioinformatics, Frederick, MD 21701-8575. Offers MS, Certificate. *Program availability:* Part-time, evening/weekend. *Faculty:* 1 full-time, 2 part-time/adjunct. *Students:* 2 full-time (0 women), 19 part-time (10 women); includes 3 minority (1 Black or African American, non-Hispanic/Latino; 2 Asian, non-Hispanic/Latino), 3 international. Average age 38. 14 applicants, 93% accepted, 9 enrolled. *Degree requirements:* For master's, capstone project. *Entrance requirements:* For master's, bachelor's degree in life science or computer science field, minimum GPA of 2.75, essay. Additional exam requirements/recommendations for international students: Required—TOEFL (minimum score 575 paper-based; 89 iBT), IELTS (minimum score 6.5). *Application deadline:* For fall admission, 8/15 priority date for domestic students, 8/5 for international students; for spring admission, 12/1 priority date for domestic students, 12/1 for international students; for summer admission, 5/1 priority date for domestic students, 4/15 for international students. Applications are processed on a rolling basis. Application fee: $35. Electronic applications accepted. *Expenses:* $475 per credit hour; $110 comprehensive fee per semester. *Financial support:* Research assistantships with full tuition reimbursements, tuition waivers (partial), and unspecified assistantships available. Financial award applicants required to submit FAFSA. *Unit head:* April Boulton, Interim Dean of the Graduate School, 301-696-3600, E-mail: gofurther@hood.edu. *Application contact:* Larbi Bricha, Assistant Director of Graduate Admissions, 301-696-3600, E-mail: gofurther@hood.edu.

Hunter College of the City University of New York, Graduate School, School of Arts and Sciences, Department of Mathematics and Statistics, New York, NY 10065-5085. Offers adolescent mathematics education (MA); applied mathematics (MA); bioinformatics (MA); pure mathematics (MA); statistics (MA). *Program availability:* Part-time, evening/weekend. *Students:* 1 full-time (0 women), 47 part-time (19 women); includes 14 minority (4 Black or African American, non-Hispanic/Latino; 8 Asian, non-Hispanic/Latino; 2 Hispanic/Latino), 8 international. Average age 32. 41 applicants, 73% accepted, 13 enrolled. In 2016, 8 master's awarded. *Degree requirements:* For master's, one foreign language, comprehensive exam, thesis (for some programs). *Entrance requirements:* For master's, GRE General Test, 24 credits in mathematics. Additional exam requirements/recommendations for international students: Required—TOEFL. *Application deadline:* For fall admission, 4/1 for domestic students, 2/1 for international students; for spring admission, 11/1 for domestic students, 9/1 for international students. *Financial support:* Federal Work-Study, institutionally sponsored loans, scholarships/grants, and tuition waivers (partial) available. Support available to part-time students. *Faculty research:* Data analysis, dynamical systems, computer graphics, topology, statistical decision theory. *Unit head:* Robert Thompson, Chair, 212-650-3831, Fax: 212-772-4858, E-mail: robert.thompson@hunter.cuny.edu. *Application contact:* Ada Peluso, Director for Graduate Admissions, 212-772-4632, Fax: 212-772-4858, E-mail: peluso@math.hunter.cuny.edu.
Website: http://math.hunter.cuny.edu/

Indiana University Bloomington, School of Informatics and Computing, Department of Computer Science, Bloomington, IN 47405. Offers bioinformatics (MS); computer science (MS, PhD); cybersecurity risk management (MS); secure computing (MS, Graduate Certificate). MS in cybersecurity risk management offered in partnership with Kelley School of Business and Maurer School of Law. *Faculty:* 75 full-time (15 women). *Students:* 438 full-time (96 women), 14 part-time (2 women); includes 9 minority (2 Black or African American, non-Hispanic/Latino; 2 Asian, non-Hispanic/Latino; 4 Hispanic/Latino; 1 Two or more races, non-Hispanic/Latino), 401 international. Average age 27. 523 applicants, 56% accepted, 133 enrolled. In 2016, 122 master's, 12 doctorates awarded. Terminal master's awarded for partial completion of doctoral program. *Degree requirements:* For master's, thesis optional; for doctorate, comprehensive exam, thesis/dissertation, oral and written exams. *Entrance requirements:* For master's and doctorate, GRE General Test, statement of purpose, bachelor's degree. Additional exam requirements/recommendations for international students: Required—TOEFL. *Application deadline:* For fall admission, 1/15 priority date for domestic students, 12/1 priority date for international students. Application fee: $55 ($65 for international students). Electronic applications accepted. *Financial support:* In 2016–17, 1 fellowship with full tuition reimbursement (averaging $25,000 per year), 66 research assistantships with full tuition reimbursements (averaging $19,150 per year), 38 teaching assistantships with full tuition reimbursements (averaging $19,150 per year) were awarded; scholarships/grants, health care benefits, and tuition waivers also available. Financial award application deadline: 12/1. *Faculty research:* Algorithms, applied logic and computational theory, artificial intelligence, bioinformatics, case-based reasoning, chemical informatics, citation analysis, cognitive science, community informatics, compilers, complex networks and systems, computer optimization, computer-supported cooperative work, computer vision, cyberinfrastructure and e-science, database theory and systems, data mining, digital design and preservation, design pedagogy, digital humanities, digital learning environments. *Total annual research expenditures:* $19.4 million. *Unit head:* Dr. Funda Ergun, Director of Graduate Studies, 812-855-6586, Fax: 812-855-4829, E-mail: fergun@indiana.edu. *Application contact:* Rachel Harris, Admissions and Records Coordinator, 812-855-6487, E-mail: soiccsgr@soic.indiana.edu.
Website: http://www.cs.indiana.edu

Indiana University Bloomington, School of Informatics and Computing, Program in Informatics, Bloomington, IN 47405. Offers informatics (MS, PhD), including bioinformatics (PhD), complex systems (PhD), computing, culture and society (PhD), health informatics (PhD), human-computer interaction (MS), human-computer interaction design (PhD), music informatics (PhD), security informatics (PhD); visual heritage (PhD). *Program availability:* Part-time. *Faculty:* 75 full-time (15 women). *Students:* 206 full-time (85 women), 10 part-time (3 women); includes 30 minority (11 Black or African American, non-Hispanic/Latino; 10 Asian, non-Hispanic/Latino; 5 Hispanic/Latino; 4 Two or more races, non-Hispanic/Latino), 95 international. Average age 28. 395 applicants, 36% accepted, 69 enrolled. In 2016, 50 master's, 11 doctorates awarded. Terminal master's awarded for partial completion of doctoral program. *Degree requirements:* For master's, thesis, capstone project; for doctorate, variable foreign language requirement, comprehensive exam, thesis/dissertation. *Entrance requirements:* For master's and doctorate, GRE, resume/curriculum vitae, transcripts, 3 letters of recommendation. Additional exam requirements/recommendations for international students: Required—TOEFL (minimum score 600 paper-based; 100 iBT). *Application deadline:* For fall admission, 12/1 priority date for domestic and international students. Application fee: $55 ($65 for international students). Electronic applications accepted. *Financial support:* Fellowships, research assistantships, scholarships/grants, health care benefits, and unspecified assistantships available. Financial award application deadline: 12/1. *Faculty research:* Algorithms, applied logic and computational theory, artificial intelligence, bioinformatics, case-based reasoning, chemical informatics, citation analysis, cognitive science, community informatics, compilers, complex networks and systems, computer optimization, computer-supported cooperative work, computer vision, cyberinfrastructure and e-science, database theory and systems, data mining, digital design and preservation, design pedagogy, digital humanities, digital learning environments. *Total annual research expenditures:* $19.4 million. *Unit head:* Dr. Martin Siegel, Director of Graduate Studies, 812-856-3960, E-mail: msiegel@indiana.edu. *Application contact:* Informatics Graduate Studies Office, 812-856-3960, E-mail: infograd@indiana.edu.
Website: http://www.informatics.indiana.edu/graduate/index.html

Indiana University–Purdue University Indianapolis, School of Informatics and Computing, Department of BioHealth Informatics, Indianapolis, IN 46202. Offers bioinformatics (MS, PhD); health informatics (MS, PhD). *Students:* 82 full-time (46 women), 44 part-time (21 women); includes 25 minority (14 Black or African American, non-Hispanic/Latino; 7 Asian, non-Hispanic/Latino; 2 Hispanic/Latino; 2 Two or more races, non-Hispanic/Latino), 69 international. Average age 40. 107 applicants, 63% accepted, 35 enrolled. In 2016, 31 master's awarded. *Financial support:* Fellowships, scholarships/grants, and unspecified assistantships available. *Unit head:* Dr. Huanmei Wu, Chair, 317-278-1692, E-mail: hw9@iupui.edu. *Application contact:* Elizabeth Bunge, Graduate Admissions Coordinator, 317-278-9200, E-mail: ebunge@iupui.edu.
Website: http://soic.iupui.edu/biohealth/

Iowa State University of Science and Technology, Bioinformatics and Computational Biology Program, Ames, IA 50011. Offers MS, PhD. *Degree requirements:* For doctorate, thesis/dissertation. *Entrance requirements:* For master's and doctorate, GRE General Test. Additional exam requirements/recommendations for international students: Recommended—TOEFL, IELTS. *Application deadline:* For fall admission, 1/15 priority date for domestic students, 1/15 for international students; for spring admission, 10/15 for domestic and international students. Application fee: $40 ($90 for international students). Electronic applications accepted. *Faculty research:* Functional and structural genomics, genome evolution, macromolecular structure and function, mathematical biology and biological statistics, metabolic and developmental networks. *Application contact:* Trish Stauble, Information Contact, 515-294-5122, Fax: 515-294-2592, E-mail: bcb@iastate.edu.
Website: http://www.bcb.iastate.edu/

Johns Hopkins University, Bloomberg School of Public Health, Department of Biostatistics, Baltimore, MD 21205-2179. Offers bioinformatics (MHS); biostatistics

(MHS, Sc M, PhD). *Program availability:* Part-time. *Degree requirements:* For master's, comprehensive exam (for some programs), thesis (for some programs), written exam, final project; for doctorate, comprehensive exam, thesis/dissertation, 1-year full-time residency, oral and written exams. *Entrance requirements:* For master's and doctorate, GRE General Test, course work in calculus and matrix algebra, 3 letters of recommendation, curriculum vitae. Additional exam requirements/recommendations for international students: Required—TOEFL (minimum score 600 paper-based). Electronic applications accepted. *Faculty research:* Statistical genetics, bioinformatics, statistical computing, statistical methods, environmental statistics.

Johns Hopkins University, Zanvyl Krieger School of Arts and Sciences, Advanced Academic Programs, Program in Bioinformatics, Washington, DC 20036. Offers MS. *Program availability:* Part-time, evening/weekend, online learning. *Degree requirements:* For master's, thesis (for some programs). *Entrance requirements:* For master's, minimum GPA of 3.0; coursework in programming and data structures, biology, and chemistry. Additional exam requirements/recommendations for international students: Required—TOEFL (minimum score 100 iBT). Electronic applications accepted.

Lawrence Technological University, College of Arts and Sciences, Southfield, MI 48075-1058. Offers bioinformatics (Graduate Certificate); computer science (MS), including data science, big data, and data mining, intelligent systems; instructional design, communication, and presentation (Graduate Certificate); instructional technology (Graduate Certificate); premedical studies (Graduate Certificate); technical and professional communication (MS, Graduate Certificate); writing for the digital age (Graduate Certificate). *Program availability:* Part-time, evening/weekend. *Faculty:* 6 full-time (2 women), 10 part-time/adjunct (5 women). *Students:* 37 part-time (18 women); includes 4 minority (1 Black or African American, non-Hispanic/Latino; 1 Asian, non-Hispanic/Latino; 2 Hispanic/Latino), 8 international. Average age 33. 301 applicants, 23% accepted, 9 enrolled. In 2016, 22 master's, 2 other advanced degrees awarded. *Degree requirements:* For master's, thesis (for some programs). *Entrance requirements:* Additional exam requirements/recommendations for international students: Required—TOEFL (minimum score 550 paper-based; 79 iBT), IELTS (minimum score 6.5). *Application deadline:* For fall admission, 5/22 for international students; for spring admission, 10/11 for international students; for summer admission, 2/16 for international students. Applications are processed on a rolling basis. Application fee: $50. Electronic applications accepted. *Expenses: Tuition:* Full-time $14,868; part-time $1062 per credit. *Required fees:* $75 per semester. Tuition and fees vary according to campus/location. *Financial support:* In 2016–17, 9 students received support. Scholarships/grants and tuition reduction available. Financial award application deadline: 4/1; financial award applicants required to submit FAFSA. *Faculty research:* Computer analysis of visual art, psychology of numbers games, neural basis of moral judgement, synthesis of glycosylated warfarin analogs for potential use as antiviral drugs, observation of chemotaxis behavior in c. elegans. *Total annual research expenditures:* $530,625. *Unit head:* Dr. Hsiao-Ping Moore, Dean, 248-204-3500, Fax: 248-204-3518, E-mail: scidean@itu.edu. *Application contact:* Jane Rohrback, Director of Admissions, 248-204-3160, Fax: 248-204-2228, E-mail: admissions@ltu.edu.

Marquette University, Graduate School, College of Arts and Sciences, Department of Mathematics, Statistics, and Computer Science, Milwaukee, WI 53201-1881. Offers bioinformatics (MS); computational sciences (MS, PhD); computing (MS); mathematics education (MS). *Program availability:* Part-time, evening/weekend, online learning. *Faculty:* 33 full-time (9 women), 8 part-time/adjunct (1 woman). *Students:* 21 full-time (5 women), 20 part-time (9 women); includes 6 minority (4 Asian, non-Hispanic/Latino; 2 Two or more races, non-Hispanic/Latino), 21 international. Average age 31. 40 applicants, 55% accepted, 10 enrolled. In 2016, 6 master's, 6 doctorates awarded. Terminal master's awarded for partial completion of doctoral program. *Degree requirements:* For master's, thesis (for some programs), essay with oral presentation; for doctorate, comprehensive exam, thesis/dissertation, qualifying examination. *Entrance requirements:* For master's, official transcripts from all current and previous colleges/universities except Marquette, three letters of recommendation; for doctorate, GRE General Test, official transcripts from all current and previous colleges/universities except Marquette, three letters of recommendation. Additional exam requirements/recommendations for international students: Required—TOEFL (minimum score 530 paper-based). *Application deadline:* For fall admission, 1/15 for domestic and international students. Applications are processed on a rolling basis. Application fee: $50. Electronic applications accepted. *Financial support:* Fellowships, research assistantships with full tuition reimbursements, teaching assistantships with full tuition reimbursements, scholarships/grants, health care benefits, tuition waivers (full and partial), and unspecified assistantships available. Support available to part-time students. Financial award application deadline: 2/15. *Faculty research:* Models of physiological systems, mathematical immunology, computational group theory, mathematical logic, computational science. *Total annual research expenditures:* $836,671. *Unit head:* Dr. Rebecca Sanders, Chair, 414-288-7573, Fax: 414-288-1578. *Application contact:* Dr. Gary Krenz.
Website: http://www.marquette.edu/mscs/grad.shtml

Marquette University, Graduate School, College of Arts and Sciences, Program in Bioinformatics, Milwaukee, WI 53201-1881. Offers MS. Program offered jointly with Medical College of Wisconsin. *Program availability:* Part-time, evening/weekend, online learning. *Students:* 3 full-time (1 woman), 4 part-time (0 women); includes 1 minority (Asian, non-Hispanic/Latino), 3 international. Average age 30. 4 applicants, 50% accepted, 3 enrolled. In 2016, 4 master's awarded. *Degree requirements:* For master's, research practicum or thesis. *Entrance requirements:* For master's, GRE (strongly recommended), official transcripts from all current and previous colleges/universities except Marquette; essay outlining relevant work experience or education, career goals, possible areas of interest, and reasons for seeking admission; three letters of reference. Additional exam requirements/recommendations for international students: Required—TOEFL (minimum score 530 paper-based). *Application deadline:* Applications are processed on a rolling basis. Application fee: $50. Electronic applications accepted. *Financial support:* Fellowships, research assistantships, and teaching assistantships available. Financial award application deadline: 2/15. *Unit head:* Dr. Rebecca Sanders, Chair, 414-288-6345. *Application contact:* Dr. Anne Clough.
Website: http://www.brc.mcw.edu/ap

Massachusetts Institute of Technology, School of Engineering, Harvard-MIT Health Sciences and Technology Program, Cambridge, MA 02139. Offers health sciences and technology (SM, PhD, Sc D), including bioastronautics (PhD, Sc D), bioinformatics and integrative genomics (PhD, Sc D), medical engineering and medical physics (PhD, Sc D), speech and hearing bioscience and technology (PhD, Sc D). *Faculty:* 132 full-time (23 women). *Students:* 268 full-time (121 women), 7 part-time (2 women); includes 78 minority (1 Black or African American, non-Hispanic/Latino; 1 American Indian or Alaska Native, non-Hispanic/Latino; 58 Asian, non-Hispanic/Latino; 15 Hispanic/Latino; 3 Two or more races, non-Hispanic/Latino), 51 international. Average age 26. 223 applicants, 14% accepted, 21 enrolled. In 2016, 1 master's, 20 doctorates awarded. Terminal master's awarded for partial completion of doctoral program. *Degree requirements:* For doctorate, comprehensive exam, thesis/dissertation. *Entrance requirements:* For doctorate, GRE General Test. Additional exam requirements/recommendations for international students: Required—TOEFL, IELTS. *Application deadline:* For fall admission, 12/15 for domestic and international students. Application fee: $75. Electronic applications accepted. *Expenses: Tuition:* Full-time $46,400; part-time $725 per credit. One-time fee: $312 full-time. Full-time tuition and fees vary according to course load and program. *Financial support:* In 2016–17, 132 students received support, including fellowships (averaging $36,300 per year), 60 research assistantships (averaging $37,800 per year), 3 teaching assistantships (averaging $37,400 per year); Federal Work-Study, institutionally sponsored loans, scholarships/grants, traineeships, health care benefits, and unspecified assistantships also available. Support available to part-time students. Financial award application deadline: 5/1; financial award applicants required to submit FAFSA. *Faculty research:* Biomedical imaging, drug delivery, medical devices, medical diagnostics, regenerative biomedical technologies. *Unit head:* Prof. Emery N. Brown, Director, 617-452-4091. *Application contact:* 617-253-3609, E-mail: hst-phd-admissions@mit.edu.
Website: http://hst.mit.edu/

McGill University, Faculty of Graduate and Postdoctoral Studies, Faculty of Science, Department of Biology, Montréal, QC H3A 2T5, Canada. Offers bioinformatics (M Sc, PhD); environment (M Sc, PhD); neo-tropical environment (M Sc, PhD).

Morgan State University, School of Graduate Studies, School of Computer, Mathematical, and Natural Sciences, Department of Computer Science, Baltimore, MD 21251. Offers bioinformatics (MS). *Entrance requirements:* Additional exam requirements/recommendations for international students: Required—TOEFL (minimum score 550 paper-based).

New Jersey Institute of Technology, Ying Wu College of Computing, Newark, NJ 07102. Offers big data management and mining (Certificate); business and information systems (Certificate); computer science (MS, PhD), including bioinformatics (MS), computer science, computing and business (MS), cyber security and privacy (MS), software engineering (MS); data mining (Certificate); information security (Certificate); information systems (MS, PhD), including business and information systems (MS), emergency management and business continuity (MS), information systems; information technology administration and security (MS); IT administration (Certificate); network security and information assurance (Certificate); software engineering analysis/design (Certificate); Web systems development (Certificate). *Program availability:* Part-time, evening/weekend. *Faculty:* 64 full-time (10 women), 38 part-time/adjunct (4 women). *Students:* 818 full-time (241 women), 225 part-time (53 women); includes 162 minority (35 Black or African American, non-Hispanic/Latino; 77 Asian, non-Hispanic/Latino; 41 Hispanic/Latino; 9 Two or more races, non-Hispanic/Latino), 772 international. Average age 27. 2,666 applicants, 51% accepted, 377 enrolled. In 2016, 398 master's, 10 doctorates, 9 other advanced degrees awarded. Terminal master's awarded for partial completion of doctoral program. *Degree requirements:* For master's, thesis optional; for doctorate, thesis/dissertation. *Entrance requirements:* For master's, GRE General Test; for doctorate, GRE General Test, minimum graduate GPA of 3.5. Additional exam requirements/recommendations for international students: Required—TOEFL (minimum score 550 paper-based; 79 iBT). *Application deadline:* For fall admission, 6/1 priority date for domestic students, 5/1 priority date for international students; for spring admission, 11/15 priority date for domestic and international students. Applications are processed on a rolling basis. Application fee: $75. Electronic applications accepted. *Expenses:* Contact institution. *Financial support:* In 2016–17, 57 students received support, including 18 research assistantships (averaging $16,073 per year), 39 teaching assistantships (averaging $20,194 per year); fellowships, career-related internships or fieldwork, Federal Work-Study, institutionally sponsored loans, and unspecified assistantships also available. Financial award application deadline: 1/15. *Faculty research:* Computer systems, communications and networking, artificial intelligence, database engineering, systems analysis, analytics and optimization in crowdsourcing. *Total annual research expenditures:* $3 million. *Unit head:* Dr. Craig Gotsman, Dean, 973-542-5488, Fax: 973-596-5777, E-mail: marek.rusinkiewicz@njit.edu. *Application contact:* Stephen Eck, Director of Admissions, 973-596-3300, Fax: 973-596-3461, E-mail: admissions@njit.edu.
Website: http://computing.njit.edu/

New Mexico State University, College of Arts and Sciences, Department of Computer Science, Las Cruces, NM 88003. Offers bioinformatics (MS); computer science (MS, PhD). *Program availability:* Part-time. *Faculty:* 11 full-time (2 women). *Students:* 72 full-time (17 women), 18 part-time (8 women); includes 10 minority (1 Black or African American, non-Hispanic/Latino; 1 Asian, non-Hispanic/Latino; 7 Hispanic/Latino; 1 Two or more races, non-Hispanic/Latino), 65 international. Average age 30. 155 applicants, 48% accepted, 8 enrolled. In 2016, 9 master's, 1 doctorate awarded. Terminal master's awarded for partial completion of doctoral program. *Degree requirements:* For master's, comprehensive exam, thesis or alternative; for doctorate, comprehensive exam, thesis/dissertation, qualifying exam, thesis proposal. *Entrance requirements:* For master's and doctorate, BS in computer science. Additional exam requirements/recommendations for international students: Required—TOEFL (minimum score 550 paper-based; 79 iBT), IELTS (minimum score 6.5). *Application deadline:* For fall admission, 3/1 priority date for domestic and international students; for spring admission, 11/1 priority date for domestic and international students. Applications are processed on a rolling basis. Application fee: $40 ($50 for international students). Electronic applications accepted. *Expenses:* Tuition, state resident: full-time $4086. Tuition, nonresident: full-time $14,254. *Required fees:* $853. Tuition and fees vary according to course load. *Financial support:* In 2016–17, 61 students received support, including 2 fellowships (averaging $4,088 per year), 16 research assistantships (averaging $15,325 per year), 30 teaching assistantships (averaging $8,611 per year); career-related internships or fieldwork, Federal Work-Study, scholarships/grants, traineeships, health care benefits, and unspecified assistantships also available. Support available to part-time students. Financial award application deadline: 3/1. *Faculty research:* Bioinformatics, database and data mining, networks and systems optimization, artificial intelligence, human factors and user interfaces. *Total annual research expenditures:* $1.7 million. *Unit head:* Dr. Jonathan Cook, Interim Department Head, 575-646-3723, Fax: 575-646-1002, E-mail: joncook@cs.nmsu.edu. *Application contact:* Dr. Joe Song, Associate Professor, 575-646-3723, Fax: 575-646-1002, E-mail: gradcs@cs.nmsu.edu.
Website: http://www.cs.nmsu.edu/

New York University, Polytechnic School of Engineering, Major in Bioinformatics, New York, NY 10012-1019. Offers MS. *Program availability:* Part-time, online learning. *Entrance requirements:* Additional exam requirements/recommendations for international students: Required—TOEFL (minimum score 550 paper-based; 80 iBT). Electronic applications accepted.

New York University, School of Medicine and Graduate School of Arts and Science, Sackler Institute of Graduate Biomedical Sciences, Program in Biomedical Informatics, New York, NY 10012-1019. Offers PhD. *Degree requirements:* For doctorate, comprehensive exam, thesis/dissertation, qualifying exam. *Faculty research:* Microbiomics, molecular signatures, sequencing informatics, evidence based medicine and scientometrics, computational proteomics.

North Carolina State University, Graduate School, College of Agriculture and Life Sciences and College of Engineering, Program in Bioinformatics, Raleigh, NC 27695. Offers MB, PhD. *Degree requirements:* For master's, thesis optional; for doctorate, thesis/dissertation. *Entrance requirements:* For master's and doctorate, GRE, minimum

B average. Additional exam requirements/recommendations for international students: Required—TOEFL. Electronic applications accepted. *Faculty research:* Statistical genetics, molecular evolution, pedigree analysis, quantitative genetics, protein structure.

North Dakota State University, College of Graduate and Interdisciplinary Studies, Interdisciplinary Program in Genomics and Bioinformatics, Fargo, ND 58102. Offers MS, PhD. *Program availability:* Part-time. *Degree requirements:* For master's, thesis; for doctorate, comprehensive exam, thesis/dissertation. *Entrance requirements:* For master's and doctorate, minimum GPA of 3.0. Additional exam requirements/recommendations for international students: Required—TOEFL (minimum score 525 paper-based; 71 iBT). Electronic applications accepted. *Faculty research:* Genome evolution, genome mapping, genome expression, bioinformatics, data mining.

Northeastern University, College of Science, Boston, MA 02115-5096. Offers applied mathematics (MS); bioinformatics (MS); biology (PhD); biotechnology (MS); chemistry (MS, PhD); ecology, evolution, and marine biology (PhD); marine biology (MS); mathematics (MS, PhD); network science (PhD); operations research (MSOR); physics (MS, PhD); psychology (PhD). *Program availability:* Part-time. *Faculty:* 217 full-time (76 women), 58 part-time/adjunct (20 women). *Students:* 578 full-time (268 women), 63 part-time (27 women). In 2016, 121 master's, 50 doctorates awarded. Terminal master's awarded for partial completion of doctoral program. *Degree requirements:* For master's, comprehensive exam (for some programs), thesis; for doctorate, comprehensive exam (for some programs), thesis/dissertation. *Entrance requirements:* For master's, GRE General Test. *Application deadline:* Applications are processed on a rolling basis. Application fee: $75. Electronic applications accepted. *Expenses:* Contact institution. *Financial support:* Fellowships with tuition reimbursements, research assistantships with tuition reimbursements, teaching assistantships with tuition reimbursements, career-related internships or fieldwork, scholarships/grants, health care benefits, tuition waivers (full and partial), and unspecified assistantships available. Support available to part-time students. Financial award applicants required to submit FAFSA. *Unit head:* Dr. Kenneth Henderson, Dean. *Application contact:* Graduate Student Services, 617-373-4275, E-mail: gradcos@northeastern.edu.
Website: http://www.northeastern.edu/cos/

Nova Southeastern University, College of Osteopathic Medicine, Fort Lauderdale, FL 33328. Offers biomedical informatics (MS, Graduate Certificate), including biomedical informatics (MS), clinical informatics (Graduate Certificate), public health informatics (Graduate Certificate); disaster and emergency management (MS); medical education (MS); nutrition (MS, Graduate Certificate), including functional nutrition and herbal therapy (Graduate Certificate); osteopathic medicine (DO); public health (MPH, Graduate Certificate), including health education (Graduate Certificate); social medicine (Graduate Certificate). *Accreditation:* AOsA. *Faculty:* 126 full-time (64 women), 1,411 part-time/adjunct (352 women). *Students:* 1,040 full-time (476 women), 196 part-time (135 women); includes 635 minority (95 Black or African American, non-Hispanic/Latino; 298 Asian, non-Hispanic/Latino; 208 Hispanic/Latino; 1 Native Hawaiian or other Pacific Islander, non-Hispanic/Latino; 33 Two or more races, non-Hispanic/Latino), 54 international. Average age 27. 5,383 applicants, 7% accepted, 248 enrolled. In 2016, 94 master's, 231 doctorates, 2 other advanced degrees awarded. *Degree requirements:* For master's, comprehensive exam (for MPH); field/special projects; for doctorate, comprehensive exam, COMLEX Boards; for Graduate Certificate, thesis or alternative. *Entrance requirements:* For master's, GRE; for doctorate, MCAT, biology, chemistry, organic chemistry, physics (all with labs), biochemistry, and English. *Application deadline:* For fall admission, 1/15 for domestic students. Applications are processed on a rolling basis. Application fee: $50. Electronic applications accepted. *Expenses:* $49,639 residents, $54,806 non-residentsfor out-of-state students; $100 microscope/laboratory fee (for first-year students); $145 per year Health Professions Division student access fee; $1,050 per year student service fee. *Financial support:* In 2016–17, 46 students received support, including 8 fellowships (averaging $30,690 per year); research assistantships, teaching assistantships, Federal Work-Study, and scholarships/grants also available. Financial award application deadline: 6/1; financial award applicants required to submit FAFSA. *Faculty research:* Teaching strategies, simulated patient use, HIV/AIDS education, minority health issues, managed care education. *Unit head:* Elaine M. Wallace, Dean, 954-262-1457, Fax: 954-262-2250, E-mail: ewallace@nova.edu. *Application contact:* HPD Admissions, 877-640-0218, E-mail: hpdinfo@nova.edu.
Website: http://www.osteopathic.nova.edu/

Oregon Health & Science University, School of Medicine, Graduate Programs in Medicine, Department of Medical Informatics and Clinical Epidemiology, Portland, OR 97239-3098. Offers bioinformatics (MS, PhD); clinical informatics (MBI, MS, PhD, Certificate); health information management (Certificate). *Program availability:* Part-time, online learning. *Faculty:* 12 full-time (6 women), 15 part-time/adjunct (7 women). *Students:* 31 full-time (7 women), 95 part-time (38 women); includes 34 minority (4 Black or African American, non-Hispanic/Latino; 22 Asian, non-Hispanic/Latino; 2 Hispanic/Latino; 6 Two or more races, non-Hispanic/Latino), 8 international. Average age 38. 42 applicants, 29 enrolled. In 2016, 21 master's, 2 doctorates, 20 other advanced degrees awarded. Terminal master's awarded for partial completion of doctoral program. *Degree requirements:* For master's, thesis or capstone project; for doctorate, comprehensive exam, thesis/dissertation, qualifying exam. *Entrance requirements:* For master's and doctorate, GRE General Test (minimum scores: 153 Verbal/148 Quantitative/4.5 Analytical), coursework in computer programming, human anatomy and physiology. Additional exam requirements/recommendations for international students: Required—IELTS or TOEFL. *Application deadline:* For fall admission, 12/1 for domestic students; for winter admission, 11/1 for domestic students; for spring admission, 2/1 for domestic students. Applications are processed on a rolling basis. Application fee: $70. Electronic applications accepted. *Expenses:* Contact institution. *Financial support:* Fellowships with full tuition reimbursements, research assistantships, Federal Work-Study, scholarships/grants, health care benefits, and full-tuition and stipends (for PhD students) available. Financial award application deadline: 3/1; financial award applicants required to submit FAFSA. *Faculty research:* Clinical informatics, computational biology, health information management, genomics, data analytics. *Unit head:* Dr. William Hersh, Program Director, 503-494-4563, E-mail: hersh@ohsu.edu. *Application contact:* Lauren Ludwig, Administrative Coordinator, 503-494-2252, E-mail: informat@ohsu.edu.
Website: http://www.ohsu.edu/dmice/

Oregon State University, Interdisciplinary/Institutional Programs, Program in Molecular and Cellular Biology, Corvallis, OR 97331. Offers bioinformatics (PhD); biotechnology (PhD); cell biology (PhD); developmental biology (PhD); genome biology (PhD); molecular biology (PhD); molecular pathogenesis (PhD); molecular virology (PhD); plant molecular biology (PhD); structural biology (PhD). *Students:* 30 full-time (16 women), 2 part-time (1 woman); includes 4 minority (2 Asian, non-Hispanic/Latino; 2 Hispanic/Latino), 12 international. Average age 29. 43 applicants, 7% accepted, 3 enrolled. In 2016, 2 doctorates awarded. *Degree requirements:* For doctorate, thesis/dissertation, oral and written qualifying exams. *Entrance requirements:* For doctorate, GRE. Additional exam requirements/recommendations for international students: Required—TOEFL (minimum score 80 iBT), IELTS (minimum score 6.5). *Application deadline:* For fall admission, 8/1 for domestic students, 4/1 for international students; for winter admission, 12/1 for domestic students, 7/1 for international students; for spring admission, 2/1 for domestic students, 10/1 for international students; for summer admission, 5/1 for domestic students, 1/1 for international students. Application fee: $75 ($85 for international students). *Expenses:* Tuition, state resident: full-time $12,150; part-time $450 per credit. Tuition, nonresident: full-time $21,789; part-time $807 per credit. *Required fees:* $1651; $1507 per credit. One-time fee: $350. Tuition and fees vary according to course load, campus/location and program. *Financial support:* Fellowships, career-related internships or fieldwork, Federal Work-Study, and institutionally sponsored loans available. Support available to part-time students. Financial award application deadline: 1/1. *Unit head:* Dr. Kristin Carroll, Assistant Director, Molecular and Cellular Biology Program, E-mail: kirstin.carroll@oregonstate.edu.
Website: http://gradschool.oregonstate.edu/molecular-and-cellular-biology-graduate-program

Rice University, Graduate Programs, George R. Brown School of Engineering, Department of Statistics, Houston, TX 77251-1892. Offers bioinformatics (PhD); biostatistics (PhD); computational finance (PhD); general statistics (PhD); statistics (M Stat, MA); MBA/M Stat. *Program availability:* Part-time. *Degree requirements:* For master's, comprehensive exam; for doctorate, comprehensive exam, thesis/dissertation. *Entrance requirements:* For master's and doctorate, GRE General Test, minimum GPA of 3.0. Additional exam requirements/recommendations for international students: Required—TOEFL (minimum score 630 paper-based; 90 iBT). Electronic applications accepted. *Faculty research:* Statistical genetics, non parametric function estimation, computational statistics and visualization, stochastic processes.

Rochester Institute of Technology, Graduate Enrollment Services, College of Science, School of Life Sciences, MS Program in Bioinformatics, Rochester, NY 14623. Offers MS. *Program availability:* Part-time. *Students:* 7 full-time (1 woman), 7 part-time (3 women); includes 2 minority (1 Asian, non-Hispanic/Latino; 1 Two or more races, non-Hispanic/Latino), 2 international. Average age 30. 30 applicants, 20% accepted, 2 enrolled. In 2016, 6 master's awarded. *Degree requirements:* For master's, thesis. *Entrance requirements:* For master's, GRE, minimum GPA of 3.2 (recommended). Additional exam requirements/recommendations for international students: Required—TOEFL (minimum score 570 paper-based; 79 iBT), IELTS (minimum score 6.5), PTE (minimum score 58). *Application deadline:* For fall admission, 2/15 priority date for domestic and international students; for spring admission, 12/15 priority date for domestic and international students. Applications are processed on a rolling basis. Application fee: $60. Electronic applications accepted. *Expenses:* $1,742 per credit hour. *Financial support:* In 2016–17, 11 students received support. Research assistantships with partial tuition reimbursements available, teaching assistantships with partial tuition reimbursements available, career-related internships or fieldwork, scholarships/grants, and unspecified assistantships available. Support available to part-time students. Financial award applicants required to submit FAFSA. *Faculty research:* Gene expression analysis, genomic sequence analysis, computational biology and evolution, machine learning of big data in biology, metabolomics. *Unit head:* Dr. Michael Osier, Graduate Program Director, 585-475-4392, Fax: 585-475-6970, E-mail: mvosd@rit.edu. *Application contact:* Diane Ellison, Associate Vice President, Graduate Enrollment Services, 585-475-2229, Fax: 585-475-7164, E-mail: gradinfo@rit.edu.
Website: https://www.rit.edu/science/programs/ms/bioinformatics

Rowan University, Graduate School, College of Science and Mathematics, Program in Bioinformatics, Glassboro, NJ 08028-1701. Offers MS. *Entrance requirements:* For master's, GRE, BS in biology, biochemistry, chemistry, computer science, or related field with minimum GPA of 2.5. Additional exam requirements/recommendations for international students: Required—TOEFL. Electronic applications accepted.

Rutgers University–Newark, School of Health Related Professions, Department of Health Informatics, Program in Biomedical Informatics, Newark, NJ 07102. Offers MS, PhD, DMD/MS, MD/MS. *Program availability:* Part-time, evening/weekend, online learning. *Degree requirements:* For master's, thesis; for doctorate, comprehensive exam, thesis/dissertation. *Entrance requirements:* For master's, BS, transcript of highest degree, statement of research interests, curriculum vitae, basic understanding of database concepts and calculus, 3 reference letters; for doctorate, master's degree, transcripts of highest degree, statement of research interests, curriculum vitae, basic understanding of database concepts and calculus, 3 reference letters. Additional exam requirements/recommendations for international students: Required—TOEFL. Electronic applications accepted.

Simon Fraser University, Office of Graduate Studies and Postdoctoral Fellows, Faculty of Science, Department of Biological Sciences, Burnaby, BC V5A 1S6, Canada. Offers bioinformatics (Graduate Diploma); biological sciences (M Sc, PhD); environmental toxicology (MET); pest management (MPM). *Faculty:* 43 full-time (16 women). *Students:* 126 full-time (71 women). 95 applicants, 29% accepted, 21 enrolled. In 2016, 16 master's, 10 doctorates awarded. *Degree requirements:* For master's, thesis; for doctorate, thesis/dissertation, candidacy exam; for Graduate Diploma, practicum. *Entrance requirements:* For master's, minimum GPA of 3.0 (on scale of 4.33) or 3.33 based on last 60 credits of undergraduate courses; for doctorate, minimum GPA of 3.5 (on scale of 4.33); for Graduate Diploma, minimum GPA of 2.5 (on scale of 4.33) or 2.67 based on last 60 credits of undergraduate courses. Additional exam requirements/recommendations for international students: Recommended—TOEFL (minimum score 580 paper-based; 93 iBT), IELTS (minimum score 7), TWE (minimum score 5). *Application deadline:* For fall admission, 6/1 for domestic and international students; for winter admission, 10/1 for domestic and international students; for spring admission, 2/1 for domestic and international students. Applications are processed on a rolling basis. Application fee: $90 ($125 for international students). Electronic applications accepted. *Financial support:* In 2016–17, 73 students received support, including 38 fellowships (averaging $6,329 per year), teaching assistantships (averaging $5,608 per year); research assistantships and scholarships/grants also available. *Faculty research:* Cell biology, wildlife ecology, environmental and evolutionary physiology, environmental toxicology, pest management. *Unit head:* Dr. Margo Moore, Graduate Chair, 778-782-3441, Fax: 778-782-3496, E-mail: bisc-grad-chair@sfu.ca. *Application contact:* Marlene Nguyen, Graduate Secretary, 778-782-3120, Fax: 778-782-3496, E-mail: biscgrad@sfu.ca.
Website: http://www.sfu.ca/biology

Simon Fraser University, Office of Graduate Studies and Postdoctoral Fellows, Faculty of Science, Department of Molecular Biology and Biochemistry, Burnaby, BC V5A 1S6, Canada. Offers bioinformatics (Graduate Diploma); molecular biology and biochemistry (M Sc, PhD). *Faculty:* 25 full-time (10 women). *Students:* 59 full-time (27 women). 19 applicants, 47% accepted, 7 enrolled. In 2016, 5 master's, 4 doctorates awarded. *Degree requirements:* For master's, thesis; for doctorate, thesis/dissertation; for Graduate Diploma, practicum. *Entrance requirements:* For master's, minimum GPA of 3.0 (on scale of 4.33) or 3.33 based on last 60 credits of undergraduate courses; for doctorate, minimum GPA of 3.5; for Graduate Diploma, minimum GPA of 2.5 (on scale of 4.33) or 2.67 based on last 60 credits of undergraduate courses. Additional exam requirements/recommendations for international students: Recommended—TOEFL (minimum score 580 paper-based; 100 iBT), IELTS (minimum score 7.5), TWE (minimum score 5). *Application deadline:* Applications are processed on a rolling basis. Application fee: $90 ($125 for international students). Electronic applications accepted.

Financial support: In 2016–17, 42 students received support, including 29 fellowships (averaging $6,500 per year), teaching assistantships (averaging $5,608 per year); research assistantships and scholarships/grants also available. *Faculty research:* Genomics and bioinformatics, cell and developmental biology, structural biology/biochemistry, immunology, nucleic acid function. *Unit head:* Dr. Mark Paetzel, Graduate Chair, 778-782-4230, Fax: 778-782-5583, E-mail: mbb-grad-chair@sfu.ca. *Application contact:* Mimi Fourie, Graduate Secretary, 778-782-5631, Fax: 778-782-5583, E-mail: mbb@sfu.ca.
Website: http://www.sfu.ca/mbb

Stevens Institute of Technology, Graduate School, Charles V. Schaefer Jr. School of Engineering and Science, Department of Chemistry, Chemical Biology and Biomedical Engineering, Hoboken, NJ 07030. Offers analytical chemistry (Certificate), including analytical chemistry; bioinformatics (Certificate), including bioinformatics; biomedical chemistry (Certificate), including biomedical chemistry; biomedical engineering (M Eng, PhD); chemical biology (MS, PhD, Certificate), including chemical physiology (Certificate); chemical physiology (Certificate), including polymer chemistry; chemistry (MS, PhD); polymer chemistry (Certificate). *Program availability:* Part-time, evening/weekend, online learning. *Faculty:* 27 full-time (11 women), 9 part-time/adjunct (2 women). *Students:* 86 full-time (36 women), 18 part-time (11 women); includes 14 minority (4 Black or African American, non-Hispanic/Latino; 7 Asian, non-Hispanic/Latino; 3 Hispanic/Latino), 58 international. Average age 27. 311 applicants, 37% accepted, 33 enrolled. In 2016, 28 master's, 6 doctorates, 6 other advanced degrees awarded. Terminal master's awarded for partial completion of doctoral program. *Degree requirements:* For master's, thesis optional, minimum B average in major field and overall; for doctorate, comprehensive exam (for some programs), thesis/dissertation; for Certificate, minimum B average. *Entrance requirements:* Additional exam requirements/recommendations for international students: Required—TOEFL (minimum score 74 iBT), IELTS (minimum score 6). *Application deadline:* Applications are processed on a rolling basis. Application fee: $65. Electronic applications accepted. *Expenses:* Contact institution. *Financial support:* Fellowships, research assistantships, teaching assistantships, career-related internships or fieldwork, Federal Work-Study, scholarships/grants, and unspecified assistantships available. Financial award application deadline: 2/15; financial award applicants required to submit FAFSA. *Faculty research:* Polymerization engineering, methods of instrumental analysis, medicinal chemistry, structural chemistry, protein trafficking, proteomics. *Unit head:* Dr. Peter Tolias, Interim Director, 201-216-8253, Fax: 201-216-8196, E-mail: ptolias@stevens.edu. *Application contact:* Graduate Admissions, 888-783-8367, Fax: 888-511-1306, E-mail: graduate@stevens.edu.

Stony Brook University, State University of New York, Graduate School, College of Engineering and Applied Sciences, Department of Biomedical Informatics, Stony Brook, NY 11794-8322. Offers MS, PhD, AGC. *Faculty:* 10 full-time (2 women). *Degree requirements:* For doctorate, thesis/dissertation, qualifying examination, teaching requirement. *Entrance requirements:* For master's, GRE, minimum B average or equivalent, two letters of recommendation; for doctorate, GRE; for AGC, minimum B average or equivalent, statement of purpose, three letters of recommendation. Additional exam requirements/recommendations for international students: Required—TOEFL. *Application deadline:* For fall admission, 1/15 for domestic students; for spring admission, 10/1 for domestic students. *Expenses:* Contact institution. *Financial support:* Research assistantships available. *Faculty research:* Ecological risk, health care, health care administration, medical informatics, public health. *Total annual research expenditures:* $1.1 million. *Unit head:* Dr. Joel H. Saltz, Professor/Founding Chair, 631-638-1420, Fax: 631-638-1323, E-mail: joel.saltz@stonybrook.edu. *Application contact:* Melissa Jordan, Assistant Dean, 631-632-9712, Fax: 631-632-7243, E-mail: melissa.jordan@stonybrook.edu.
Website: http://bmi.stonybrookmedicine.edu/

Tufts University, School of Engineering, Department of Computer Science, Medford, MA 02155. Offers bioengineering (ME, MS), including bioinformatics; cognitive science (PhD); computer science (MS, PhD). *Program availability:* Part-time. Terminal master's awarded for partial completion of doctoral program. *Degree requirements:* For master's, thesis (for some programs); for doctorate, thesis/dissertation. *Entrance requirements:* For master's and doctorate, GRE General Test. Additional exam requirements/recommendations for international students: Required—TOEFL (minimum score 550 paper-based; 80 iBT), IELTS (minimum score 6.5). Electronic applications accepted. *Expenses: Tuition:* Full-time $49,892; part-time $1248 per credit hour. *Required fees:* $844. Full-time tuition and fees vary according to degree level, program and student level. Part-time tuition and fees vary according to course load. *Faculty research:* Computational biology, computational geometry, and computational systems biology; cognitive sciences, human-computer interaction, and human-robotic interaction; visualization and graphics, educational technologies; machine learning and data mining; programming languages and systems.

Tufts University, School of Engineering, Department of Mechanical Engineering, Medford, MA 02155. Offers bioengineering (ME, MS), including bioinformatics, biomechanical systems and devices, signals and systems; bioinformatics (MS); human factors (MS); mechanical engineering (ME, MS, PhD). *Program availability:* Part-time. Terminal master's awarded for partial completion of doctoral program. *Degree requirements:* For master's, thesis; for doctorate, thesis/dissertation. *Entrance requirements:* For master's and doctorate, GRE General Test. Additional exam requirements/recommendations for international students: Required—TOEFL (minimum score 550 paper-based; 80 iBT), IELTS (minimum score 6.5). Electronic applications accepted. *Expenses: Tuition:* Full-time $49,892; part-time $1248 per credit hour. *Required fees:* $844. Full-time tuition and fees vary according to degree level, program and student level. Part-time tuition and fees vary according to course load. *Faculty research:* Applied mechanics, biomaterials, controls/robotics, design/systems, human factors.

Université de Montréal, Faculty of Medicine, Biochemistry Department, Montréal, QC H3C 3J7, Canada. Offers M Sc, PhD. Electronic applications accepted.

Université de Montréal, Faculty of Medicine, Program in Bioinformatics, Montréal, QC H3C 3J7, Canada. Offers M Sc, PhD.

University at Buffalo, the State University of New York, Graduate School, Jacobs School of Medicine and Biomedical Sciences, Graduate Programs in Medicine and Biomedical Sciences, Program in Genetics, Genomics and Bioinformatics, Buffalo, NY 14203. Offers MS, PhD. *Faculty:* 59 full-time (16 women). *Students:* 5 full-time (2 women); includes 1 minority (Asian, non-Hispanic/Latino). Average age 28. 14 applicants, 57% accepted, 6 enrolled. In 2016, 3 master's awarded. Terminal master's awarded for partial completion of doctoral program. *Degree requirements:* For master's, thesis or alternative; for doctorate, thesis/dissertation. *Entrance requirements:* For master's and doctorate, GRE. Additional exam requirements/recommendations for international students: Required—TOEFL (minimum score 100 iBT); Recommended—IELTS (minimum score 6.5). *Application deadline:* For fall admission, 3/1 for domestic and international students. Application fee: $85. Electronic applications accepted. *Expenses:* Contact institution. *Financial support:* Support by faculty mentor available. *Faculty research:* Human and medical genetics and genomics, developmental genomics and genetics, microbial genetics and pathogenesis, bioinformatics. *Unit head:* Dr. Richard Gronostajski, Director, 716-829-3471, Fax: 716-849-6655, E-mail: rgron@buffalo.edu. *Application contact:* Renad Aref, Program Administrator, 716-881-8209, Fax: 716-849-6655, E-mail: raaref@buffalo.edu.
Website: http://medicine.buffalo.edu/education/ggb.html

The University of Alabama at Birmingham, Graduate Programs in Joint Health Sciences, Genetics, Genomics and Bioinformatics Theme, Birmingham, AL 35294. Offers PhD. *Students:* 36 full-time (21 women); includes 6 minority (2 Black or African American, non-Hispanic/Latino; 1 Asian, non-Hispanic/Latino; 1 Hispanic/Latino; 2 Two or more races, non-Hispanic/Latino), 1 international. Average age 26. 52 applicants, 21% accepted, 6 enrolled. In 2016, 5 doctorates awarded. *Degree requirements:* For doctorate, comprehensive exam, thesis/dissertation. *Entrance requirements:* For doctorate, GRE General Test, interview, previous research experience. Additional exam requirements/recommendations for international students: Required—TOEFL. *Application deadline:* For fall admission, 12/1 priority date for domestic and international students. Applications are processed on a rolling basis. Application fee: $0 ($60 for international students). Electronic applications accepted. Application fee is waived when completed online. *Expenses:* Contact institution. *Financial support:* Fellowships and competitive annual stipends, health insurance, and fully-paid tuition and fees available. *Unit head:* Dr. Daniel C. Bullard, Program Director, 205-934-7768, E-mail: dcbullard@uab.edu. *Application contact:* Nan Travis, Graduate Program Manager, 205-934-1003, Fax: 205-996-6749, E-mail: ntravis@uab.edu.
Website: http://www.uab.edu/gbs/genomic/

University of Arkansas at Little Rock, Graduate School, George W. Donaghey College of Engineering and Information Technology, Program in Bioinformatics, Little Rock, AR 72204-1099. Offers MS, PhD. *Entrance requirements:* For doctorate, MS in bioinformatics. Additional exam requirements/recommendations for international students: Required—TOEFL.

University of Arkansas for Medical Sciences, Graduate School, Little Rock, AR 72205. Offers biochemistry and molecular biology (MS, PhD); bioinformatics (MS, PhD); cellular physiology and molecular biophysics (MS, PhD); clinical nutrition (MS); interdisciplinary biomedical sciences (MS, PhD, Certificate); interdisciplinary toxicology (MS); microbiology and immunology (PhD); neurobiology and developmental sciences (PhD); pharmacology (PhD); MD/PhD. Bioinformatics programs hosted jointly with the University of Arkansas at Little Rock. *Program availability:* Part-time. Terminal master's awarded for partial completion of doctoral program. *Degree requirements:* For master's, comprehensive exam (for some programs), thesis (for some programs); for doctorate, thesis/dissertation. *Entrance requirements:* For master's and doctorate, GRE. Additional exam requirements/recommendations for international students: Required—TOEFL. Electronic applications accepted. *Expenses:* Contact institution.

The University of British Columbia, Faculty of Medicine, Department of Cellular and Physiological Sciences, Vancouver, BC V6T 1Z3, Canada. Offers bioinformatics (M Sc, PhD); cell and developmental biology (M Sc, PhD); genome science and technology (M Sc, PhD); neuroscience (M Sc, PhD). *Degree requirements:* For master's, thesis, oral defense; for doctorate, comprehensive exam, thesis/dissertation, oral defense. *Entrance requirements:* For master's, minimum overall B+ average in third- and fourth-year courses; for doctorate, minimum overall B+ average in master's degree (or equivalent) from approved institution with clear evidence of research ability or potential. Additional exam requirements/recommendations for international students: Required—TOEFL, IELTS. Application fee: $100 ($162 for international students). *Expenses:* $4,802 per year tuition and fees, $8,436 per year international. *Financial support:* Fellowships, research assistantships, teaching assistantships, Federal Work-Study, institutionally sponsored loans, scholarships/grants, traineeships, tuition waivers (full), and unspecified assistantships available. *Application contact:* Peggy Faulkner, Graduate Program Staff, 604-822-2671, Fax: 604-822-5802, E-mail: cell.grad@ubc.ca.
Website: http://cps.med.ubc.ca/

University of California, Los Angeles, Graduate Division, College of Letters and Science, Interdepartmental Program in Bioinformatics, Los Angeles, CA 90095. Offers MS, PhD. Terminal master's awarded for partial completion of doctoral program. *Degree requirements:* For master's, comprehensive exam, thesis, one quarter of teaching experience; for doctorate, thesis/dissertation, oral and written qualifying exams; one quarter of teaching experience. *Entrance requirements:* For doctorate, GRE General Test, bachelor's degree; minimum undergraduate GPA of 3.0 (or its equivalent if letter grade system not used). Additional exam requirements/recommendations for international students: Required—TOEFL. Electronic applications accepted.

University of California, Riverside, Graduate Division, Graduate Program in Genetics, Genomics, and Bioinformatics, Riverside, CA 92521-0102. Offers PhD. *Degree requirements:* For doctorate, thesis/dissertation, qualifying exams, teaching experience. *Entrance requirements:* For doctorate, GRE General Test, minimum GPA of 3.2. Additional exam requirements/recommendations for international students: Required—TOEFL (minimum score 550 paper-based; 80 iBT). Electronic applications accepted. *Expenses:* Tuition, state resident: full-time $16,666. Tuition, nonresident: full-time $31,768. *Required fees:* $11,055.54 per quarter. $3685.18 per quarter. Tuition and fees vary according to campus/location and program. *Faculty research:* Molecular genetics, evolution and population genetics, genomics and bioinformatics.

University of California, San Diego, School of Medicine and Graduate Division, Graduate Studies in Biomedical Sciences, La Jolla, CA 92093. Offers anthropogeny (PhD); bioinformatics (PhD); biomedical science (PhD); multi-scale biology (PhD). *Students:* 178 full-time (95 women). 513 applicants, 18% accepted, 26 enrolled. In 2016, 26 doctorates awarded. *Degree requirements:* For doctorate, comprehensive exam, thesis/dissertation, 1-quarter teaching assistantship. *Entrance requirements:* For doctorate, GRE General Test; GRE Subject Test in either biology, biochemistry, cell and molecular biology or chemistry (recommended). Additional exam requirements/recommendations for international students: Required—TOEFL (minimum score 550 paper-based; 80 iBT), IELTS (minimum score 7). *Application deadline:* For fall admission, 12/21 for domestic students. Application fee: $105 ($125 for international students). Electronic applications accepted. *Expenses:* Tuition, state resident: full-time $11,220. Tuition, nonresident: full-time $26,322. *Required fees:* $1864. *Financial support:* Fellowships, research assistantships, teaching assistantships, scholarships/grants, traineeships, unspecified assistantships, and stipends available. Financial award applicants required to submit FAFSA. *Faculty research:* Genetics, microbiology and immunology, molecular cell biology, molecular pharmacology, molecular pathology. *Unit head:* Arshad Desai, Chair, 858-534-9698, E-mail: abdesai@ucsd.edu. *Application contact:* Leanne Nordeman, Graduate Coordinator, 858-534-3982, E-mail: biomedsci@ucsd.edu.
Website: http://biomedsci.ucsd.edu

University of California, San Francisco, School of Pharmacy and Graduate Division, Program in Bioinformatics, San Francisco, CA 94158-2517. Offers PhD. Terminal master's awarded for partial completion of doctoral program. *Degree requirements:* For doctorate, thesis/dissertation, cumulative qualifying exams, proposal defense. *Entrance requirements:* For doctorate, GRE General Test, minimum GPA of 3.0, bachelor's degree. Additional exam requirements/recommendations for international students:

Required—TOEFL (minimum score 550 paper-based; 80 iBT). *Faculty research:* Bioinformatics and computational biology, genetics and genomics, systems biology.

University of California, Santa Cruz, Jack Baskin School of Engineering, Program in Biomolecular Engineering and Bioinformatics, Santa Cruz, CA 95064. Offers MS, PhD. *Faculty:* 16 full-time (3 women), 4 part-time/adjunct (0 women). *Students:* 53 full-time (13 women), 1 part-time (0 women); includes 11 minority (1 Black or African American, non-Hispanic/Latino; 1 American Indian or Alaska Native, non-Hispanic/Latino; 8 Asian, non-Hispanic/Latino; 1 Hispanic/Latino), 5 international. Average age 27. 104 applicants, 35% accepted, 18 enrolled. In 2016, 6 master's, 4 doctorates awarded. Terminal master's awarded for partial completion of doctoral program. *Degree requirements:* For master's, thesis, research project with written report; for doctorate, thesis/dissertation. *Entrance requirements:* For master's and doctorate, GRE General Test. Additional exam requirements/recommendations for international students: Required—TOEFL (minimum score 570 paper-based; 89 iBT); Recommended—IELTS (minimum score 8). *Application deadline:* For fall admission, 12/1 for domestic and international students. Application fee: $105 ($125 for international students). Electronic applications accepted. *Financial support:* In 2016–17, 104 students received support, including 9 fellowships (averaging $22,995 per year), 60 research assistantships (averaging $22,995 per year), 29 teaching assistantships (averaging $20,052 per year); institutionally sponsored loans, scholarships/grants, and tuition waivers (full and partial) also available. Financial award application deadline: 12/1; financial award applicants required to submit FAFSA. *Faculty research:* Bioinformatics, genomics, stem cell. *Unit head:* Todd Lowe, Chair/Professor, E-mail: tmjlowe@ucsc.edu. *Application contact:* Tracie Tucker, Graduate Student Advisor, 831-459-5737, E-mail: bsoe-ga@rt.ucsc.edu.
Website: http://www.cse.ucsc.edu/

University of Cincinnati, Graduate School, College of Medicine, Graduate Programs in Biomedical Sciences, Department of Biomedical Informatics, Cincinnati, OH 45229. Offers PhD, Graduate Certificate. *Expenses: Tuition, area resident:* Full-time $12,790; part-time $389 per credit hour. Tuition, state resident: full-time $13,290; part-time $419 per credit hour. Tuition, nonresident: full-time $24,532; part-time $976 per credit hour. *International tuition:* $24,832 full-time. *Required fees:* $3958; $140 per credit hour. Tuition and fees vary according to course load, degree level, program and reciprocity agreements.

University of Colorado Denver, School of Medicine, Program in Pharmacology, Aurora, CO 80206. Offers bioinformatics (PhD); biomolecular structure (PhD); pharmacology (PhD). *Students:* 25 full-time (12 women); includes 7 minority (2 Asian, non-Hispanic/Latino; 4 Hispanic/Latino; 1 Two or more races, non-Hispanic/Latino), 2 international. Average age 27. 22 applicants, 18% accepted, 4 enrolled. In 2016, 4 doctorates awarded. *Degree requirements:* For doctorate, comprehensive exam, thesis/dissertation, major seminar, 3 research rotations in the first year, 30 hours each of course work and thesis. *Entrance requirements:* For doctorate, GRE General Test, three letters of recommendation, personal statement. Additional exam requirements/recommendations for international students: Required—TOEFL (minimum score 550 paper-based; 80 iBT). *Application deadline:* For fall admission, 12/15 for domestic students, 11/15 for international students. Application fee: $50 ($75 for international students). Electronic applications accepted. *Expenses:* Contact institution. *Financial support:* In 2016–17, 27 students received support. Fellowships, research assistantships, teaching assistantships, institutionally sponsored loans, scholarships/grants, traineeships, health care benefits, tuition waivers (full), and unspecified assistantships available. Financial award application deadline: 3/15; financial award applicants required to submit FAFSA. *Faculty research:* Cancer biology, drugs of abuse, neuroscience, signal transduction, structural biology. *Unit head:* Dr. Andrew Thorburn, Interim Chair, 303-724-3290, Fax: 303-724-3663, E-mail: andrew.thorburn@ucdenver.edu. *Application contact:* Elizabeth Bowen, Graduate Program Coordinator, 303-724-3565, E-mail: elizabeth.bowen@ucdenver.edu.
Website: http://www.ucdenver.edu/academics/colleges/medicalschool/departments/Pharmacology/Pages/Pharmacology.aspx

University of Georgia, Institute of Bioinformatics, Athens, GA 30602. Offers MS, PhD. *Unit head:* Dr. Jessica Kissinger, Director, 706-542-6562, E-mail: jkissing@uga.edu. *Application contact:* Jonathan Arnold, Graduate Coordinator, 706-542-7783, E-mail: arnold@uga.edu.
Website: http://www.bioinformatics.uga.edu/

University of Idaho, College of Graduate Studies, College of Science, Department of Bioinformatics and Computational Biology, Moscow, ID 83844. Offers MS, PhD. *Faculty:* 23 full-time (7 women). *Students:* 19 full-time, 1 part-time. Average age 29. In 2016, 3 doctorates awarded. *Degree requirements:* For master's, thesis; for doctorate, thesis/dissertation. *Entrance requirements:* For master's, GRE, minimum GPA of 3.0. Additional exam requirements/recommendations for international students: Required—TOEFL. *Application deadline:* For fall admission, 8/1 for domestic students; for spring admission, 12/15 for domestic students. Applications are processed on a rolling basis. Application fee: $60. Electronic applications accepted. *Expenses:* Tuition, state resident: full-time $6460; part-time $414 per credit hour. Tuition, nonresident: full-time $21,268; part-time $1237 per credit hour. *Required fees:* $2070; $60 per credit hour. Full-time tuition and fees vary according to course load and reciprocity agreements. *Financial support:* Applicants required to submit FAFSA. *Unit head:* Dr. Eva Top, Director, 208-885-6010, E-mail: bcb@uidaho.edu. *Application contact:* Sean Scoggin, Graduate Recruitment Coordinator, 208-885-4723, Fax: 208-885-4406, E-mail: graduateadmissions@uidaho.edu.
Website: http://www.uidaho.edu/cogs/bcb

University of Illinois at Chicago, College of Engineering, Department of Bioengineering, Chicago, IL 60607-7128. Offers MS, PhD. Terminal master's awarded for partial completion of doctoral program. *Degree requirements:* For master's, thesis; for doctorate, thesis/dissertation. *Entrance requirements:* For master's and doctorate, GRE Subject Test, minimum GPA of 3.0. Additional exam requirements/recommendations for international students: Required—TOEFL. Electronic applications accepted. *Expenses:* Contact institution. *Faculty research:* Imaging systems, bioinstrumentation, electrophysiology, biological control, laser scattering.

University of Illinois at Urbana–Champaign, Graduate College, College of Agricultural, Consumer and Environmental Sciences, Department of Crop Sciences, Champaign, IL 61820. Offers bioinformatics: crop sciences (MS); crop sciences (MS, PhD). *Program availability:* Online learning.

University of Illinois at Urbana–Champaign, Graduate College, College of Engineering, Department of Computer Science, Champaign, IL 61820. Offers bioinformatics (MS); computer science (MCS, MS, PhD); MCS/JD; MCS/M Arch; MCS/MBA. *Program availability:* Part-time, evening/weekend, online learning.

University of Illinois at Urbana–Champaign, Graduate College, School of Information Sciences, Champaign, IL 61820. Offers bioinformatics (MS); digital libraries (CAS); information management (MS); library and information science (MS, PhD, CAS). *Accreditation:* ALA (one or more programs are accredited). *Program availability:* Part-time, online learning. *Entrance requirements:* For degree, master's degree in library and information science or related field with minimum GPA of 3.0.

The University of Iowa, Graduate College, Program in Informatics, Iowa City, IA 52242-1316. Offers bioinformatics (MS, PhD); bioinformatics and computational biology (Certificate); geoinformatics (MS, PhD, Certificate); health informatics (MS, PhD, Certificate); information science (MS, PhD, Certificate). *Degree requirements:* For master's, thesis optional; for doctorate, comprehensive exam, thesis/dissertation. *Entrance requirements:* For master's and doctorate, GRE General Test, minimum GPA of 3.0. Additional exam requirements/recommendations for international students: Required—TOEFL (minimum score 550 paper-based; 81 iBT). Electronic applications accepted.

University of Louisville, School of Interdisciplinary and Graduate Studies, Louisville, KY 40292. Offers interdisciplinary (MA, MS, PhD), including bioethics and medical humanities (MA), bioinformatics (PhD), sustainability (MA, MS), translational bioengineering (PhD), translational neuroscience (PhD). *Program availability:* Part-time. *Students:* 24 full-time (16 women), 8 part-time (4 women); includes 4 minority (1 Asian, non-Hispanic/Latino; 1 Hispanic/Latino; 2 Two or more races, non-Hispanic/Latino), 7 international. Average age 31. 35 applicants, 51% accepted, 12 enrolled. *Degree requirements:* For master's, variable foreign language requirement, comprehensive exam (for some programs), thesis (for some programs); for doctorate, variable foreign language requirement, comprehensive exam, thesis/dissertation. *Entrance requirements:* For master's and doctorate, GRE General Test, 3 letters of recommendation, transcripts from previous post-secondary educational institutions. Additional exam requirements/recommendations for international students: Required—TOEFL (minimum score 550 paper-based; 79 iBT), IELTS (minimum score 6.5). *Application deadline:* For fall admission, 12/1 priority date for domestic and international students; for winter admission, 11/1 for domestic students, 6/1 for international students; for spring admission, 11/1 for domestic students, 6/1 for international students; for summer admission, 4/1 for domestic students, 1/1 for international students. Applications are processed on a rolling basis. Application fee: $65. Electronic applications accepted. *Expenses:* Tuition, state resident: full-time $12,246; part-time $681 per credit hour. Tuition, nonresident: full-time $25,486; part-time $1417 per credit hour. *Required fees:* $196. Tuition and fees vary according to program and reciprocity agreements. *Financial support:* In 2016–17, 120 fellowships with full tuition reimbursements (averaging $20,000 per year) were awarded. Financial award application deadline: 1/15. *Unit head:* Dr. Beth A. Boehm, Dean and Vice Provost for Graduate Affairs, 502-852-6495, E-mail: beth.boehm@louisville.edu. *Application contact:* Dr. Paul DeMarco, Associate Dean, 502-852-6490, E-mail: gradadm@louisville.edu.
Website: http://www.graduate.louisville.edu

University of Maine, Graduate School, Graduate School of Biomedical Science and Engineering, Orono, ME 04469. Offers bioinformatics (PSM); biomedical engineering (PhD); biomedical science (PhD). *Faculty:* 149 full-time (47 women). *Students:* 28 full-time (17 women), 16 part-time (9 women); includes 1 minority (Two or more races, non-Hispanic/Latino), 13 international. Average age 30. 51 applicants, 20% accepted, 8 enrolled. In 2016, 8 doctorates awarded. *Degree requirements:* For doctorate, comprehensive exam, thesis/dissertation. *Entrance requirements:* For doctorate, GRE General Test, master's degree. Additional exam requirements/recommendations for international students: Required—TOEFL (minimum score 90 iBT), IELTS (minimum score 7). *Application deadline:* For fall admission, 1/1 priority date for domestic and international students. Application fee: $65. *Expenses:* Tuition, state resident: full-time $7524; part-time $2508 per credit. Tuition, nonresident: full-time $24,498; part-time $8166 per credit. *Required fees:* $1148; $571 per credit. *Financial support:* In 2016–17, 33 students received support, including 2 fellowships with full tuition reimbursements available (averaging $21,500 per year), 28 research assistantships with full tuition reimbursements available (averaging $22,500 per year), 3 teaching assistantships (averaging $9,300 per year). Financial award application deadline: 3/1. *Faculty research:* Molecular and cellular biology, neuroscience, biomedical engineering, toxicology, bioinformatics and computational biology. *Total annual research expenditures:* $1.4 million. *Unit head:* Dr. David Neivandt, Director, 207-581-2803. *Application contact:* Scott G. Delcourt, Assistant Vice President for Graduate Studies and Senior Associate Dean, 207-581-3291, Fax: 207-581-3232, E-mail: graduate@maine.edu.
Website: http://gsbse.umaine.edu/

The University of Manchester, Faculty of Life Sciences, Manchester, United Kingdom. Offers adaptive organismal biology (M Phil, PhD); animal biology (M Phil, PhD); biochemistry (M Phil, PhD); bioinformatics (M Phil, PhD); biomolecular sciences (M Phil, PhD); biotechnology (M Phil, PhD); cell biology (M Phil, PhD); cell matrix research (M Phil, PhD); channels and transporters (M Phil, PhD); developmental biology (M Phil, PhD); Egyptology (M Phil, PhD); environmental biology (M Phil, PhD); evolutionary biology (M Phil, PhD); gene expression (M Phil, PhD); genetics (M Phil, PhD); history of science, technology and medicine (M Phil, PhD); immunology (M Phil, PhD); integrative neurobiology and behavior (M Phil, PhD); membrane trafficking (M Phil, PhD); microbiology (M Phil, PhD); molecular and cellular neuroscience (M Phil, PhD); molecular biology (M Phil, PhD); molecular cancer studies (M Phil, PhD); neuroscience (M Phil, PhD); ophthalmology (M Phil, PhD); optometry (M Phil, PhD); organelle function (M Phil, PhD); pharmacology (M Phil, PhD); physiology (M Phil, PhD); plant sciences (M Phil, PhD); stem cell research (M Phil, PhD); structural biology (M Phil, PhD); systems neuroscience (M Phil, PhD); toxicology (M Phil, PhD).

University of Maryland, College Park, Academic Affairs, College of Computer, Mathematical and Natural Sciences, Department of Biology, PhD Program in Biological Sciences, College Park, MD 20742. Offers behavior, ecology, evolution, and systematics (PhD); computational biology, bioinformatics, and genomics (PhD); molecular and cellular biology (PhD); physiological systems (PhD). *Degree requirements:* For doctorate, comprehensive exam, thesis/dissertation, thesis work presentation in seminar. *Entrance requirements:* For doctorate, GRE General Test; GRE Subject Test in biology (recommended), academic transcripts, statement of purpose/research interests, 3 letters of recommendation. Additional exam requirements/recommendations for international students: Required—TOEFL. Electronic applications accepted.

University of Massachusetts Medical School, Graduate School of Biomedical Sciences, Worcester, MA 01655-0115. Offers biomedical sciences (PhD), including biochemistry and molecular pharmacology, bioinformatics and computational biology, cancer biology, cell biology, immunology and microbiology, interdisciplinary, neuroscience, translational science; biomedical sciences (millennium program) (PhD); clinical and population health research (PhD); clinical investigation (MS). *Faculty:* 1,354 full-time (540 women), 311 part-time/adjunct (192 women). *Students:* 341 full-time (176 women); includes 57 minority (12 Black or African American, non-Hispanic/Latino; 1 American Indian or Alaska Native, non-Hispanic/Latino; 31 Asian, non-Hispanic/Latino; 13 Hispanic/Latino), 129 international. Average age 29. 617 applicants, 29% accepted, 51 enrolled. In 2016, 4 master's, 55 doctorates awarded. Terminal master's awarded for partial completion of doctoral program. *Degree requirements:* For master's, comprehensive exam, thesis; for doctorate, comprehensive exam, thesis/dissertation. *Entrance requirements:* For master's, MD, PhD, DVM, or PharmD; for doctorate, GRE General Test, bachelor's degree. Additional exam requirements/recommendations for

international students: Required—TOEFL (minimum score 90 iBT) or IELTS (minimum score 7.0). *Application deadline:* For fall admission, 12/15 for domestic and international students; for spring admission, 5/15 for domestic students. Application fee: $80. Electronic applications accepted. *Expenses:* $7,356 in-state tuition and fees per year, $14,572 out-of-state. *Financial support:* In 2016–17, 7 fellowships (averaging $34,000 per year), 391 research assistantships with full tuition reimbursements (averaging $31,000 per year) were awarded; scholarships/grants also available. Support available to part-time students. Financial award application deadline: 5/15. *Faculty research:* RNA biology, molecular/cell/developmental/metabolic biology, bioinformatics and computational biology, clinical/translational research, infectious disease and immunology. *Total annual research expenditures:* $253 million. *Unit head:* Dr. Anthony Carruthers, Dean, 508-856-4135, E-mail: anthony.carruthers@umassmed.edu. *Application contact:* Dr. Kendall Knight, Assistant Vice Provost for Admissions, 508-856-5628, Fax: 508-856-3659, E-mail: kendall.knight@umassmed.edu.
Website: http://www.umassmed.edu/gsbs/

University of Memphis, Graduate School, College of Arts and Sciences, Department of Computer Science, Memphis, TN 38152. Offers bioinformatics (MS); computer science (MS, PhD). *Faculty:* 11 full-time (1 woman), 2 part-time/adjunct (0 women). *Students:* 54 full-time (14 women), 22 part-time (5 women); includes 8 minority (4 Black or African American, non-Hispanic/Latino; 3 Asian, non-Hispanic/Latino; 1 Two or more races, non-Hispanic/Latino), 60 international. Average age 29. 74 applicants, 74% accepted, 16 enrolled. In 2016, 27 master's, 3 doctorates awarded. Terminal master's awarded for partial completion of doctoral program. *Degree requirements:* For master's, comprehensive exam, thesis; for doctorate, comprehensive exam, thesis/dissertation, qualifying exam, final exam. *Entrance requirements:* For master's and doctorate, GRE, letters of recommendation. Additional exam requirements/recommendations for international students: Required—TOEFL (minimum score 550 paper-based; 79 iBT). *Application deadline:* Applications are processed on a rolling basis. Application fee: $35 ($60 for international students). *Expenses:* $5,231.50 per semester full-time in-state, $9,623.50 full-time out-of-state. *Financial support:* In 2016–17, 9 students received support, including 15 research assistantships with full tuition reimbursements available (averaging $13,114 per year); fellowships, teaching assistantships with full tuition reimbursements available, Federal Work-Study, scholarships/grants, and unspecified assistantships also available. Financial award application deadline: 2/1; financial award applicants required to submit FAFSA. *Faculty research:* Network security, biomolecular and distributed computing, wireless sensor networks, artificial intelligence. *Unit head:* Dr. Lan Wang, Chair, 901-678-5465, Fax: 901-678-2480, E-mail: lanwang@memphis.edu. *Application contact:* Dr. Wasile Rus, Graduate Studies Coordinator, E-mail: info@cs.memphis.edu.
Website: http://www.cs.memphis.edu

University of Michigan, Rackham Graduate School, Program in Biomedical Sciences (PIBS) and Rackham Graduate School, Program in Bioinformatics, Ann Arbor, MI 48109-2218. Offers MS, PhD. *Program availability:* Part-time. Terminal master's awarded for partial completion of doctoral program. *Degree requirements:* For master's, thesis optional, summer internship or rotation; for doctorate, thesis/dissertation, oral defense of dissertation, preliminary exam, two rotations. *Entrance requirements:* For master's and doctorate, GRE or MCAT. Additional exam requirements/recommendations for international students: Required—TOEFL (minimum score 100 iBT). Electronic applications accepted. *Expenses:* Contact institution. *Faculty research:* Clinical and biomedical informatics, databases and computing, genomics, proteomics and metabolomics, medical and translational research.

University of Minnesota Rochester, Graduate Programs, Rochester, MN 55904. Offers bioinformatics and computational biology (MS, PhD); business administration (MBA); occupational therapy (MOT).

University of Missouri, Office of Research and Graduate Studies, Informatics Institute, Columbia, MO 65211. Offers PhD. *Students:* 25 full-time (10 women), 20 part-time (6 women). *Entrance requirements:* Additional exam requirements/recommendations for international students: Required—TOEFL (minimum score 577 paper-based; 90 iBT), IELTS (minimum score 6.5). *Application deadline:* For fall admission, 1/15 priority date for domestic and international students. Applications are processed on a rolling basis. Application fee: $75 ($90 for international students). Electronic applications accepted. *Expenses:* Tuition, state resident: full-time $6347; part-time $352.60 per credit hour. Tuition, nonresident: full-time $17,379; part-time $965.50 per credit hour. *Required fees:* $1035. Tuition and fees vary according to course load, campus/location and program. *Financial support:* Scholarships/grants, health care benefits, and unspecified assistantships available. Support available to part-time students. *Faculty research:* Human-computer interaction, human factors, information technology standards, IT sophistication in nursing homes, data mining and knowledge discovery in genomics and epigenomics, pathology decision support systems, digital image analysis, pathology text mining, computational biophysics, RNA folding and gene regulation, computer graphics and scientific visualization, biomedical imaging and computer vision, 3D shape modeling.
Website: http://muii.missouri.edu/

University of Missouri–Kansas City, School of Computing and Engineering, Kansas City, MO 64110-2499. Offers civil engineering (MS); computer and electrical engineering (PhD); computer science (MS), including bioinformatics, software engineering, telecommunications networking; computer science and informatics (PhD); computing (PhD); electrical engineering (MS); engineering (PhD); engineering and construction management (Graduate Certificate); mechanical engineering (MS); telecommunications and computer networking (PhD). PhD (interdisciplinary) offered through the School of Graduate Studies. *Program availability:* Part-time. *Faculty:* 45 full-time (6 women), 26 part-time/adjunct (4 women). *Students:* 473 full-time (155 women), 207 part-time (42 women); includes 24 minority (10 Black or African American, non-Hispanic/Latino; 10 Asian, non-Hispanic/Latino; 4 Hispanic/Latino), 581 international. Average age 25. 1,143 applicants, 44% accepted, 227 enrolled. In 2016, 446 master's, 2 other advanced degrees awarded. *Degree requirements:* For doctorate, thesis/dissertation. *Entrance requirements:* For master's, GRE General Test, minimum GPA of 3.0, 3 letters of recommendation from professors; for doctorate, GRE General Test, minimum GPA of 3.5. Additional exam requirements/recommendations for international students: Required—TOEFL (minimum score 550 paper-based; 80 iBT). *Application deadline:* For fall admission, 1/15 priority date for domestic students, 1/15 for international students. Applications are processed on a rolling basis. Application fee: $45 ($50 for international students). *Financial support:* In 2016–17, 37 research assistantships with partial tuition reimbursements (averaging $15,679 per year), 47 teaching assistantships with partial tuition reimbursements (averaging $16,830 per year) were awarded; career-related internships or fieldwork, Federal Work-Study, scholarships/grants, tuition waivers (partial), and unspecified assistantships also available. Support available to part-time students. Financial award application deadline: 3/1; financial award applicants required to submit FAFSA. *Faculty research:* Algorithms, bioinformatics and medical informatics, biomechanics/biomaterials, civil engineering materials, networking and telecommunications, thermal science. *Unit head:* Dr. Kevin Z. Truman, Dean, 816-235-2399, Fax: 816-235-5159. *Application contact:* 816-235-2399, Fax: 816-235-5159.
Website: http://sce.umkc.edu/

University of Nebraska at Omaha, Graduate Studies, College of Information Science and Technology, School of Interdisciplinary Informatics, Omaha, NE 68182. Offers biomedical informatics (MS, PhD); information assurance (MS). *Program availability:* Part-time, evening/weekend. *Faculty:* 10 full-time (3 women). *Students:* 26 full-time (9 women), 34 part-time (5 women); includes 9 minority (5 Black or African American, non-Hispanic/Latino; 2 Asian, non-Hispanic/Latino; 2 Hispanic/Latino), 13 international. Average age 31. 53 applicants, 58% accepted, 15 enrolled. In 2016, 14 master's awarded. *Degree requirements:* For master's, comprehensive exam, thesis (for some programs); for doctorate, comprehensive exam, thesis/dissertation. *Entrance requirements:* For master's and doctorate, GRE General Test, letters of recommendation, resume, transcripts. Additional exam requirements/recommendations for international students: Required—TOEFL, IELTS, PTE. *Financial support:* In 2016–17, 6 students received support, including 6 research assistantships with tuition reimbursements available; fellowships, teaching assistantships with tuition reimbursements available, career-related internships or fieldwork, Federal Work-Study, scholarships/grants, health care benefits, tuition waivers (partial), and unspecified assistantships also available. Financial award application deadline: 3/1; financial award applicants required to submit FAFSA. *Unit head:* Dr. Ann Fruhling, Director, 402-554-2341, E-mail: graduate@unomaha.edu. *Application contact:* Dr. Dhundy Bastola, Graduate Program Chair, 402-554-2341, E-mail: graduate@unomaha.edu.

University of Nebraska–Lincoln, Graduate College, College of Arts and Sciences and College of Engineering, Department of Computer Science and Engineering, Lincoln, NE 68588. Offers bioinformatics (MS, PhD); computer engineering (MS, PhD); computer science (MS, PhD); information technology (PhD). *Degree requirements:* For master's, thesis optional; for doctorate, comprehensive exam, thesis/dissertation. *Entrance requirements:* For master's and doctorate, GRE General Test. Additional exam requirements/recommendations for international students: Required—TOEFL (minimum score 600 paper-based). Electronic applications accepted. *Faculty research:* Software engineering, geo- and bio-informatics, scientific computation, secure communication.

University of Nebraska Medical Center, Program in Biomedical Informatics, Omaha, NE 68198. Offers MS, PhD. *Program availability:* Part-time. *Faculty:* 29 full-time (7 women). *Students:* 4 full-time (2 women), 6 part-time (2 women), 3 international. Average age 32. 3 applicants, 67% accepted, 2 enrolled. In 2016, 1 doctorate awarded. *Degree requirements:* For master's, comprehensive exam, thesis; for doctorate, comprehensive exam, thesis/dissertation. *Entrance requirements:* For master's and doctorate, GRE, clinical training and experience (medicine, nursing, dentistry, or allied health degree). Additional exam requirements/recommendations for international students: Required—TOEFL (minimum score 550 paper-based; 80 iBT). *Application deadline:* For fall admission, 6/1 for domestic students, 4/1 for international students; for spring admission, 10/1 for domestic students, 9/1 for international students; for summer admission, 3/1 for domestic students, 1/1 for international students. Applications are processed on a rolling basis. Application fee: $60. Electronic applications accepted. *Expenses:* $297.25 resident tuition per credit, $850.50 non-resident tuition per credit; $140 fees per semester. *Financial support:* In 2016–17, 8 students received support, including 1 fellowship with full tuition reimbursement available (averaging $23,400 per year), 4 research assistantships with full tuition reimbursements available (averaging $23,400 per year); scholarships/grants also available. Support available to part-time students. Financial award application deadline: 2/15; financial award applicants required to submit FAFSA. *Faculty research:* Genomics, bioinformatics, clinical research informatics, health informatics, pathology informatics. *Unit head:* Dr. Jim McClay, Director, 402-559-3587, E-mail: jmcclay@unmc.edu. *Application contact:* Rhonda Sheibal-Carver, Academic Program Coordinator, 402-559-5141, E-mail: rhonda.sheibalcarver@unmc.edu.
Website: http://www.unmc.edu/bmi/

The University of North Carolina at Chapel Hill, School of Medicine and Graduate School, Graduate Programs in Medicine, Curriculum in Bioinformatics and Computational Biology, Chapel Hill, NC 27599. Offers PhD. *Degree requirements:* For doctorate, comprehensive exam, thesis/dissertation. *Entrance requirements:* For doctorate, GRE, minimum GPA of 3.0. Additional exam requirements/recommendations for international students: Required—TOEFL. Electronic applications accepted. *Faculty research:* Protein folding, design and evolution and molecular biophysics of disease; mathematical modeling of signaling pathways and regulatory networks; bioinformatics, medical informatics, user interface design; statistical genetics and genetic epidemiology datamining, classification and clustering analysis of gene-expression data.

The University of North Carolina at Charlotte, College of Computing and Informatics, Department of Bioinformatics and Genomics, Charlotte, NC 28223-0001. Offers bioinformatics (PSM); bioinformatics and computational biology (PhD); bioinformatics applications (Graduate Certificate); bioinformatics technology (Graduate Certificate). *Program availability:* Part-time. *Faculty:* 11 full-time (6 women). *Students:* 37 full-time (13 women), 17 part-time (14 women); includes 17 minority (5 Black or African American, non-Hispanic/Latino; 5 Asian, non-Hispanic/Latino; 4 Hispanic/Latino; 1 Native Hawaiian or other Pacific Islander, non-Hispanic/Latino; 2 Two or more races, non-Hispanic/Latino), 10 international. Average age 30. 38 applicants, 63% accepted, 13 enrolled. In 2016, 17 master's, 3 doctorates, 5 other advanced degrees awarded. Terminal master's awarded for partial completion of doctoral program. *Degree requirements:* For master's, internship, research project, or thesis; for doctorate, comprehensive exam, thesis/dissertation. *Entrance requirements:* For master's, GRE, baccalaureate degree from accredited college or university in biology, biochemistry, chemistry, physics, mathematics, statistics, computer science, or another related field that provides sound background in life sciences, computing, or both; minimum undergraduate GPA of 3.0 overall and in major; recommendation letters; for doctorate, GRE, baccalaureate degree from recognized institution; adequate preparation in chemistry, biology, mathematics (preferably statistics), and computer science; evidence of scholarly and creative activity; minimum GPA of 3.0; essay; reference letters; for Graduate Certificate, bachelor's degree in related field; practical experience and confidence with computers, for instance use of common Web browsers, word processing, plotting, and spreadsheet applications. Additional exam requirements/recommendations for international students: Required—TOEFL (minimum score 523 paper-based, 70 iBT) or IELTS (6.5). *Application deadline:* For fall admission, 12/15 for domestic and international students; for spring admission, 9/1 for domestic and international students. Applications are processed on a rolling basis. Application fee: $75. Electronic applications accepted. *Expenses:* Contact institution. *Financial support:* In 2016–17, 29 students received support, including 7 fellowships (averaging $39,112 per year), 9 research assistantships (averaging $9,897 per year), 12 teaching assistantships (averaging $14,627 per year); career-related internships or fieldwork, institutionally sponsored loans, scholarships/grants, unspecified assistantships, and administrative assistantships also available. Support available to part-time students. Financial award application deadline: 3/1; financial award applicants required to submit FAFSA. *Total annual research expenditures:* $2.2 million. *Unit head:* Dr. Lawrence Mays, Chair, 704-687-8555, E-mail: lemays@uncc.edu. *Application contact:* Kathy B. Giddings, Director of Graduate Admissions, 704-687-5503, Fax: 704-687-1668, E-mail: gradadm@uncc.edu.
Website: http://bioinformatics.uncc.edu/

Bioinformatics

The University of North Carolina at Charlotte, College of Computing and Informatics, Program in Computing and Information Systems, Charlotte, NC 28223-0001. Offers computing and information systems (PhD), including bioinformatics, business information systems and operations management, computer science, interdisciplinary, software and information systems. *Faculty:* 3 full-time (0 women). *Students:* 91 full-time (30 women), 23 part-time (3 women); includes 8 minority (2 Black or African American, non-Hispanic/Latino; 4 Asian, non-Hispanic/Latino; 1 Hispanic/Latino; 1 Two or more races, non-Hispanic/Latino), 76 international. Average age 31. 90 applicants, 41% accepted, 18 enrolled. In 2016, 13 doctorates awarded. *Degree requirements:* For doctorate, comprehensive exam, thesis/dissertation. *Entrance requirements:* For doctorate, GRE or GMAT, baccalaureate degree, minimum GPA of 3.0 on courses related to the chosen field of PhD study, essay, reference letters. Additional exam requirements/recommendations for international students: Required—TOEFL (minimum score 523 paper-based, 70 iBT) or IELTS (6.5). *Application deadline:* For fall admission, 2/1 for domestic and international students; for spring admission, 9/1 for domestic and international students. Applications are processed on a rolling basis. Application fee: $75. Electronic applications accepted. *Expenses:* Tuition, state resident: full-time $4252. Tuition, nonresident: full-time $17,423. *Required fees:* $3026. Tuition and fees vary according to course load and program. *Financial support:* Career-related internships or fieldwork, institutionally sponsored loans, scholarships/grants, health care benefits, and unspecified assistantships available. Support available to part-time students. Financial award applicants required to submit FAFSA. *Unit head:* Manuel A. Perez Quinones, Director, 704-687-8553, E-mail: perez.quinones@uncc.edu. *Application contact:* Kathy B. Giddings, Director of Graduate Admissions, 704-687-5503, Fax: 704-687-1668, E-mail: gradadm@uncc.edu.

University of Pittsburgh, School of Medicine, Graduate Programs in Medicine, Biomedical Informatics Programs, Pittsburgh, PA 15206. Offers MS, PhD, Certificate. *Program availability:* Part-time. Terminal master's awarded for partial completion of doctoral program. *Degree requirements:* For master's, comprehensive exam, thesis; for doctorate, comprehensive exam, thesis/dissertation. *Entrance requirements:* For master's, GRE; for doctorate, GRE, MCAT. Additional exam requirements/recommendations for international students: Required—TOEFL (minimum score 600 paper-based; 100 iBT), IELTS (minimum score 7). *Application deadline:* For fall admission, 2/1 priority date for domestic and international students. Application fee: $50. Electronic applications accepted. Tuition and fees vary according to program. *Financial support:* Fellowships with full tuition reimbursements, research assistantships with full tuition reimbursements, teaching assistantships, scholarships/grants, traineeships, and health care benefits available. Financial award application deadline: 2/1. *Faculty research:* Biomedical informatics; bioinformatics; global health informatics; translational informatics; causal discovery from biomedical data. *Unit head:* Dr. Rebecca Jacobson, Director, 412-648-9203, Fax: 412-648-9118, E-mail: rebeccaj@pitt.edu. *Application contact:* Toni L. Porterfield, Training Program Manager, 412-648-9203, Fax: 412-648-9118, E-mail: tls18@pitt.edu.
Website: http://www.dbmi.pitt.edu

University of Southern California, Graduate School, Dana and David Dornsife College of Letters, Arts and Sciences, Department of Biological Sciences, Program in Molecular and Computational Biology, Los Angeles, CA 90089. Offers computational biology and bioinformatics (PhD); molecular biology (PhD). *Degree requirements:* For doctorate, comprehensive exam, thesis/dissertation, qualifying examination, dissertation defense. *Entrance requirements:* For doctorate, GRE, 3 letters of recommendation, personal statement, resume, minimum GPA of 3.0. Additional exam requirements/recommendations for international students: Required—TOEFL (minimum score 600 paper-based; 100 iBT). Electronic applications accepted. *Faculty research:* Biochemistry and molecular biology; genomics; computational biology and bioinformatics; cell and developmental biology, and genetics; DNA replication and repair, and cancer biology.

University of South Florida, Innovative Education, Tampa, FL 33620-9951. Offers adult, career and higher education (Graduate Certificate), including college teaching, leadership in developing human resources, leadership in higher education; Africana studies (Graduate Certificate), including diasporas and health disparities, genocide and human rights; aging studies (Graduate Certificate), including gerontology; art research (Graduate Certificate), including museum studies; business foundations (Graduate Certificate); chemical and biomedical engineering (Graduate Certificate), including materials science and engineering, water, health and sustainability; child and family studies (Graduate Certificate), including positive behavior support; civil and industrial engineering (Graduate Certificate), including transportation systems analysis; community and family health (Graduate Certificate), including maternal and child health, social marketing and public health, violence and injury: prevention and intervention, women's health; criminology (Graduate Certificate), including criminal justice administration; educational measurement and research (Graduate Certificate), including evaluation; English (Graduate Certificate), including comparative literary studies, creative writing, professional and technical communication; entrepreneurship (Graduate Certificate); environmental health (Graduate Certificate), including safety management; epidemiology and biostatistics (Graduate Certificate), including applied biostatistics, biostatistics, concepts and tools of epidemiology, epidemiology, epidemiology of infectious diseases; geography, environment and planning (Graduate Certificate), including community development, environmental policy and management, geographical information systems; geology (Graduate Certificate), including hydrogeology; global health (Graduate Certificate), including disaster management, global health and Latin American and Caribbean studies, global health practice, humanitarian assistance, infection control; government and international affairs (Graduate Certificate), including Cuban studies, globalization studies; health policy and management (Graduate Certificate), including health management and leadership, public health policy and programs; hearing specialist: early intervention (Graduate Certificate); industrial and management systems engineering (Graduate Certificate), including systems engineering, technology management; information studies (Graduate Certificate), including school library media specialist; information systems/decision sciences (Graduate Certificate), including analytics and business intelligence; instructional technology (Graduate Certificate), including distance education, Florida digital/virtual educator, instructional design, multimedia design, Web design; internal medicine, bioethics and medical humanities (Graduate Certificate), including biomedical ethics; Latin American and Caribbean studies (Graduate Certificate); mass communications (Graduate Certificate), including multimedia journalism; mathematics and statistics (Graduate Certificate), including mathematics; medicine (Graduate Certificate), including aging and neuroscience, bioinformatics, biotechnology, brain fitness and memory management, clinical investigation, health informatics, health sciences, integrative weight management, intellectual property, medicine and gender, metabolic and nutritional medicine, metabolic cardiology, pharmacy sciences; national and competitive intelligence (Graduate Certificate); psychological and social foundations (Graduate Certificate), including career counseling, college teaching, diversity in education, mental health counseling, school counseling; public affairs (Graduate Certificate), including nonprofit management, public management, research administration; public health (Graduate Certificate), including environmental health, health equity, public health generalist, translational research in adolescent behavioral health; public health practices (Graduate Certificate), including planning for healthy communities; rehabilitation and mental health counseling (Graduate Certificate), including integrative mental health care, marriage and family therapy, rehabilitation technology; secondary education (Graduate Certificate), including ESOL, foreign language education: culture and content, foreign language education: professional; social work (Graduate Certificate), including geriatric social work/clinical gerontology; special education (Graduate Certificate), including autism spectrum disorder, disabilities education: severe/profound; world languages (Graduate Certificate), including teaching English as a second language (TESL) or foreign language. *Expenses:* Tuition, state resident: full-time $7766; part-time $431.43 per credit hour. Tuition, nonresident: full-time $15,789; part-time $877.17 per credit hour. *Required fees:* $37 per term. *Unit head:* Kathy Barnes, Interdisciplinary Programs Coordinator, 813-974-8031, Fax: 813-974-7061, E-mail: barnesk@usf.edu. *Application contact:* Karen Tylinski, Metro Initiatives, 813-974-9943, Fax: 813-974-7061, E-mail: ktylinsk@usf.edu.
Website: http://www.usf.edu/innovative-education/

University of South Florida, Morsani College of Medicine and College of Graduate Studies, Graduate Programs in Medical Sciences, Tampa, FL 33620-9951. Offers advanced athletic training (MS); athletic training (MS); bioinformatics and computational biology (MSBCB); biotechnology (MSB); health informatics (MSHI); medical sciences (MSMS, PhD), including aging and neuroscience (MSMS), allergy, immunology and infectious disease (PhD), anatomy, biochemistry and molecular biology, clinical and translational research, health science (MSMS), interdisciplinary medical sciences (MSMS), medical microbiology and immunology (MSMS), metabolic and nutritional medicine (MSMS), microbiology and immunology (PhD), molecular medicine, molecular pharmacology and physiology (PhD), neuroscience (PhD), pathology and cell biology (PhD), women's health (MSMS). *Students:* 454 full-time (239 women), 273 part-time (173 women); includes 347 minority (110 Black or African American, non-Hispanic/Latino; 1 American Indian or Alaska Native, non-Hispanic/Latino; 99 Asian, non-Hispanic/Latino; 113 Hispanic/Latino; 1 Native Hawaiian or other Pacific Islander, non-Hispanic/Latino; 23 Two or more races, non-Hispanic/Latino), 61 international. Average age 27. 7,242 applicants, 8% accepted, 395 enrolled. In 2016, 374 master's, 13 doctorates awarded. Terminal master's awarded for partial completion of doctoral program. *Degree requirements:* For master's, comprehensive exam, thesis; for doctorate, comprehensive exam, thesis/dissertation. *Entrance requirements:* For master's, GRE General Test or GMAT, bachelor's degree or equivalent from regionally-accredited university with minimum GPA of 3.0 in upper-division sciences coursework; prerequisites in general biology, general chemistry, general physics, organic chemistry, quantitative analysis, and integral and differential calculus; for doctorate, GRE General Test, bachelor's degree from regionally-accredited university with minimum GPA of 3.0 in upper-division sciences coursework; 3 letters of recommendation; personal interview; 1-2 page personal statement; prerequisites in biology, chemistry, physics, organic chemistry, quantitative analysis, and integral/differential calculus. Additional exam requirements/recommendations for international students: Required—TOEFL (minimum score 550 paper-based; 79 iBT) or IELTS (minimum score 6.5). *Application deadline:* For fall admission, 2/1 for domestic and international students. Application fee: $30. Electronic applications accepted. *Expenses:* Contact institution. *Financial support:* In 2016–17, 116 students received support. *Faculty research:* Anatomy, biochemistry, cancer biology, cardiovascular disease, cell biology, immunology, microbiology, molecular biology, neuroscience, pharmacology, physiology. *Total annual research expenditures:* $42.3 million. *Unit head:* Dr. Michael Barber, Professor/Associate Dean for Graduate and Postdoctoral Affairs, 813-974-9908, Fax: 813-974-4317, E-mail: mbarber@health.usf.edu. *Application contact:* Dr. Eric Bennett, Graduate Director, PhD Program in Medical Sciences, 813-974-1545, Fax: 813-974-4317, E-mail: esbennet@health.usf.edu.
Website: http://health.usf.edu/nocms/medicine/graduatestudies/

The University of Texas at El Paso, Graduate School, College of Science, Department of Biological Sciences, El Paso, TX 79968-0001. Offers bioinformatics (MS); biological sciences (MS, PhD). *Program availability:* Part-time, evening/weekend. *Degree requirements:* For master's, thesis; for doctorate, thesis/dissertation. *Entrance requirements:* For master's, GRE, minimum GPA of 3.0, letters of recommendation; for doctorate, GRE, statement of purpose, letters of recommendation. Additional exam requirements/recommendations for international students: Required—TOEFL; Recommended—IELTS. Electronic applications accepted.

The University of Texas at El Paso, Graduate School, College of Science, Program in Bioinformatics, El Paso, TX 79968-0001. Offers MS. *Program availability:* Part-time. *Entrance requirements:* For master's, GRE, minimum GPA of 3.0. Additional exam requirements/recommendations for international students: Required—TOEFL. Electronic applications accepted.

The University of Texas Health Science Center at Houston, School of Biomedical Informatics, Houston, TX 77225-0036. Offers MS, PhD, Certificate, MPH/MS, MPH/PhD. *Program availability:* Part-time, online learning. *Degree requirements:* For master's, thesis; for doctorate, thesis/dissertation. *Entrance requirements:* For master's and doctorate, GRE or MAT. Additional exam requirements/recommendations for international students: Required—TOEFL (minimum score 550 paper-based; 87 iBT). Electronic applications accepted. *Faculty research:* Patient safety, human computer interface, artificial intelligence, decision support tools, 3-D visualization, biomedical engineering.

The University of Texas Medical Branch, Graduate School of Biomedical Sciences, Program in Biochemistry and Molecular Biology, Galveston, TX 77555. Offers biochemistry (PhD); bioinformatics (PhD); biophysics (PhD); cell biology (PhD); computational biology (PhD); structural biology (PhD). *Degree requirements:* For doctorate, thesis/dissertation. *Entrance requirements:* Additional exam requirements/recommendations for international students: Required—TOEFL (minimum score 550 paper-based). Electronic applications accepted.

University of the Sciences, Program in Bioinformatics, Philadelphia, PA 19104-4495. Offers MS. *Program availability:* Part-time, evening/weekend. *Entrance requirements:* Additional exam requirements/recommendations for international students: Required—TOEFL, TWE. *Expenses:* Contact institution. *Faculty research:* Genomics, microarray analysis, computer-aided drug design, molecular biophysics, cell structure, molecular dynamics, computational chemistry.

The University of Toledo, College of Graduate Studies, College of Medicine and Life Sciences, Interdepartmental Programs, Toledo, OH 43606-3390. Offers bioinformatics and proteomics/genomics (MSBS); biomarkers and bioinformatics (Certificate); biomarkers and diagnostics (PSM); human donation sciences (MSBS); medical sciences (MSBS); MD/MSBS. *Degree requirements:* For master's, thesis or alternative. *Entrance requirements:* For master's, GRE, minimum undergraduate GPA of 3.0, three letters of recommendation, statement of purpose, transcripts from all prior institutions attended, resume; for Certificate, minimum undergraduate GPA of 3.0, three letters of recommendation, statement of purpose, transcripts from all prior institutions attended, resume. Additional exam requirements/recommendations for international students: Required—TOEFL (minimum score 550 paper-based; 80 iBT). Electronic applications accepted.

University of Utah, School of Medicine and Graduate School, Graduate Programs in Medicine, Department of Biomedical Informatics, Salt Lake City, UT 84112-1107. Offers MS, PhD, Certificate. *Program availability:* Part-time, online learning. *Degree requirements:* For master's, comprehensive exam, thesis; for doctorate, comprehensive exam, thesis/dissertation, qualifying exam. *Entrance requirements:* For master's and doctorate, GRE General Test (minimum 60th percentile), minimum GPA of 3.3. Additional exam requirements/recommendations for international students: Required—TOEFL (minimum score 600 paper-based). Electronic applications accepted. *Expenses:* Tuition, state resident: full-time $7011; part-time $3918.24 per credit hour. Tuition, nonresident: full-time $22,154; part-time $11,665.42 per credit hour. *Faculty research:* Health information systems and expert systems, genetic epidemiology, medical imaging, bioinformatics, public health informatics.

University of Washington, Graduate School, School of Medicine, Graduate Programs in Medicine, Department of Medical Education and Biomedical Informatics, Division of Biomedical and Health Informatics, Seattle, WA 98195. Offers MS, PhD. *Entrance requirements:* For master's and doctorate, GRE General Test, minimum GPA of 3.0; previous undergraduate course work in biology, computer programming, and mathematics. Additional exam requirements/recommendations for international students: Required—TOEFL (minimum score 580 paper-based; 70 iBT). Electronic applications accepted. *Faculty research:* Bio-clinical informatics, information retrieval, human-computer interaction, knowledge-based systems, telehealth.

University of Wisconsin–Madison, School of Medicine and Public Health, Biomedical Data Science Graduate Program, Madison, WI 53706-1380. Offers MS.
Website: https://www.biostat.wisc.edu/content/ms_program_in_biomedical_data_science

Vanderbilt University, Department of Biomedical Informatics, Nashville, TN 37240-1001. Offers MS, PhD. *Program availability:* Part-time. *Faculty:* 26 full-time (7 women). *Students:* 20 full-time (11 women); includes 5 minority (2 Black or African American, non-Hispanic/Latino; 3 Asian, non-Hispanic/Latino), 1 international. Average age 30. 48 applicants, 4% accepted. In 2016, 5 master's, 5 doctorates awarded. Terminal master's awarded for partial completion of doctoral program. *Degree requirements:* For master's, thesis; for doctorate, thesis/dissertation, final and qualifying exams. *Entrance requirements:* For master's and doctorate, GRE General Test. Additional exam requirements/recommendations for international students: Required—TOEFL (minimum score 570 paper-based; 88 iBT). *Application deadline:* For fall admission, 1/15 for domestic and international students. Electronic applications accepted. *Expenses: Tuition:* Part-time $1854 per credit hour. *Financial support:* Fellowships with tuition reimbursements, research assistantships with tuition reimbursements, teaching assistantships with tuition reimbursements, Federal Work-Study, institutionally sponsored loans, scholarships/grants, traineeships, and health care benefits available. Financial award application deadline: 1/15; financial award applicants required to submit CSS PROFILE or FAFSA. *Faculty research:* Organizational informatics, the application of informatics to the role of information technology in organizational change, clinical research and translational informatics, applications of informatics to facilitating and quota; bench to bedside and quote; translational research. *Unit head:* Dr. Kevin Johnson, Chair, 615-936-1423, Fax: 615-936-1427, E-mail: kevin.johnson@vanderbilt.edu. *Application contact:* Gretchen Jackson, Director of Graduate Studies, 615-936-1050, Fax: 615-936-1427, E-mail: rischelle.jenkins@vanderbilt.edu.
Website: https://medschool.vanderbilt.edu/dbmi/

Virginia Polytechnic Institute and State University, Graduate School, Intercollege, Blacksburg, VA 24061. Offers genetics, bioinformatics and computational biology (PhD); information technology (MIT); macromolecular science and engineering (MS, PhD); translational biology, medicine, and health (PhD). *Students:* 175 full-time (82 women), 763 part-time (279 women); includes 217 minority (71 Black or African American, non-Hispanic/Latino; 1 American Indian or Alaska Native, non-Hispanic/Latino; 77 Asian, non-Hispanic/Latino; 43 Hispanic/Latino; 1 Native Hawaiian or other Pacific Islander, non-Hispanic/Latino; 24 Two or more races, non-Hispanic/Latino), 83 international. Average age 33. 626 applicants, 74% accepted, 373 enrolled. In 2016, 91 master's, 18 doctorates awarded. *Degree requirements:* For master's, comprehensive exam (for some programs), thesis (for some programs); for doctorate, comprehensive exam (for some programs), thesis/dissertation (for some programs). *Entrance requirements:* For master's and doctorate, GRE/GMAT. Additional exam requirements/recommendations for international students: Required—TOEFL (minimum score 80 iBT). *Application deadline:* For fall admission, 8/1 for domestic students, 4/1 for international students; for spring admission, 1/1 for domestic students, 9/1 for international students. Applications are processed on a rolling basis. Application fee: $75. Electronic applications accepted. *Expenses:* Tuition, state resident: full-time $12,467; part-time $692.50 per credit hour. Tuition, nonresident: full-time $25,095; part-time $1394.25 per credit hour. *Required fees:* $2669; $491.50 per semester. Tuition and fees vary according to course load, campus/location and program. *Financial support:* In 2016–17, 100 research assistantships with full tuition reimbursements (averaging $23,321 per year), 10 teaching assistantships with full tuition reimbursements (averaging $20,748 per year) were awarded. Financial award application deadline: 3/1; financial award applicants required to submit FAFSA. *Unit head:* Dr. Karen P. DePauw, Vice President and Dean for Graduate Education, 540-231-7581, Fax: 540-231-1670, E-mail: kpdepauw@vt.edu.
Website: http://www.graduateschool.vt.edu/graduate_catalog/colleges.htm

Wayne State University, College of Engineering, Department of Computer Science, Detroit, MI 48202. Offers computer science (MS, PhD), including bioinformatics (PhD), computational biology (PhD); data science and business analytics (MS). Application deadline for PhD is February 17. *Faculty:* 22. *Students:* 117 full-time (41 women), 37 part-time (11 women); includes 11 minority (1 Black or African American, non-Hispanic/Latino; 8 Asian, non-Hispanic/Latino; 2 Two or more races, non-Hispanic/Latino), 121 international. Average age 27. 596 applicants, 24% accepted, 29 enrolled. In 2016, 63 master's, 13 doctorates awarded. *Degree requirements:* For master's, thesis (for some programs); for doctorate, thesis/dissertation. *Entrance requirements:* For master's, GRE, minimum GPA of 3.0, three letters of recommendation, adequate preparation in computer science and mathematics courses, personal statement; for doctorate, GRE, bachelor's or master's degree in computer science or related field; minimum GPA of 3.3 in most recent degree; three letters of recommendation; personal statement; adequate preparation in computer science and mathematics courses. Additional exam requirements/recommendations for international students: Required—TOEFL (minimum score 550 paper-based; 79 iBT), TWE (minimum score 5.5), Michigan English Language Assessment Battery (minimum score 85); Recommended—IELTS (minimum score 6.5). *Application deadline:* For fall admission, 6/1 priority date for domestic students, 5/1 priority date for international students; for winter admission, 10/1 priority date for domestic students, 9/1 priority date for international students; for spring admission, 2/1 priority date for domestic students, 1/2 priority date for international students. Applications are processed on a rolling basis. Application fee: $50. Electronic applications accepted. *Expenses:* $18,871 per year resident tuition and fees, $36,065 per year non-resident tuition and fees. *Financial support:* In 2016–17, 67 students received support, including 4 fellowships with tuition reimbursements available (averaging $17,250 per year), 22 research assistantships with tuition reimbursements available (averaging $22,361 per year), 36 teaching assistantships with tuition reimbursements available (averaging $19,177 per year); scholarships/grants, health care benefits, and unspecified assistantships also available. Financial award applicants required to submit FAFSA. *Faculty research:* Software engineering, databases, bioinformatics, artificial intelligence, networking, distributed and parallel computing, security, graphics, visualizations. *Total annual research expenditures:* $1.5 million. *Unit head:* Dr. Loren Schwiebert, Interim Chair, 313-577-5474, E-mail: loren@wayne.edu. *Application contact:* Eric Scimeca, Graduate Program Director, 313-577-5421, E-mail: eric.scimeca@wayne.edu.
Website: http://engineering.wayne.edu/cs/

Wesleyan University, Graduate Studies, Department of Biology, Middletown, CT 06459. Offers cell and developmental biology (PhD); evolution and ecology (PhD); genetics and genomics (PhD), including bioinformatics; neurobiology and behavior (PhD). Terminal master's awarded for partial completion of doctoral program. *Degree requirements:* For doctorate, comprehensive exam, thesis/dissertation, public seminar. *Entrance requirements:* For doctorate, GRE, official transcripts, three recommendation letters, essay. Additional exam requirements/recommendations for international students: Required—TOEFL. *Application deadline:* For fall admission, 1/15 for domestic and international students. Application fee: $0. Electronic applications accepted. *Financial support:* Stipends available. *Faculty research:* Evolution and ecology, neurobiology and behavior, cell and developmental biology, genetics, genomics and bioinformatics. *Unit head:* Dr. John Kirn, Chair/Professor, 860-685-3494, E-mail: jrkirn@wesleyan.edu. *Application contact:* Diane Meredith, Administrative Assistant IV, 860-685-2157, E-mail: dmeredith@wesleyan.edu.
Website: http://www.wesleyan.edu/bio/

Worcester Polytechnic Institute, Graduate Studies and Research, Program in Bioinformatics and Computational Biology, Worcester, MA 01609-2280. Offers MS, PhD. *Program availability:* Evening/weekend. *Students:* 8 full-time (3 women), 5 international. 20 applicants, 95% accepted, 4 enrolled. In 2016, 2 master's awarded. *Entrance requirements:* For master's and doctorate, GRE, 3 letters of recommendation, statement of purpose. Additional exam requirements/recommendations for international students: Required—TOEFL (minimum score 563 paper-based; 84 iBT), IELTS (minimum score 7). *Application deadline:* For fall admission, 1/1 priority date for domestic and international students; for spring admission, 10/1 priority date for domestic and international students. Applications are processed on a rolling basis. Application fee: $70. Electronic applications accepted. *Financial support:* Research assistantships, teaching assistantships, and career-related internships or fieldwork available. Financial award application deadline: 1/1; financial award applicants required to submit FAFSA. *Unit head:* Elizabeth Ryder, Professor, 508-831-5543, Fax: 508-831-5936, E-mail: ryder@wpi.edu. *Application contact:* Barbara Milanese, Administrative Assistant, 508-831-5543, Fax: 508-831-5936, E-mail: milanese@wpi.edu.
Website: http://www.wpi.edu/academics/bcb

Yale University, Yale School of Medicine and Graduate School of Arts and Sciences, Combined Program in Biological and Biomedical Sciences (BBS), Computational Biology and Bioinformatics Track, New Haven, CT 06520. Offers PhD, MD/PhD. *Entrance requirements:* Additional exam requirements/recommendations for international students: Required—TOEFL.

Computer and Information Systems Security

American InterContinental University Online, Program in Information Technology, Schaumburg, IL 60173. Offers Internet security (MIT); IT project management (MIT). *Program availability:* Evening/weekend, online learning. *Entrance requirements:* Additional exam requirements/recommendations for international students: Required—TOEFL (minimum score 550 paper-based). Electronic applications accepted.

American Public University System, AMU/APU Graduate Programs, Charles Town, WV 25414. Offers accounting (MBA, MS); applied business analytics (MBA, MS); criminal justice (MA), including business administration, emergency and disaster management, general (MA, MS); educational leadership (M Ed); emergency and disaster management (MA); entrepreneurship (MBA); environmental policy and management (MS), including environmental planning, environmental sustainability, fish and wildlife management, general (MA, MS), global environmental management; finance (MBA); general (MBA); government contracting and acquisition (MBA); health care administration (MBA); health information management (MS); history (MA), including American history, ancient and classical history, European history, global history, public history; homeland security (MA), including business administration, counterterrorism studies, criminal justice, cyber, emergency management and public health, intelligence studies, transportation security; homeland security resource allocation (MBA); humanities (MA); information technology (MS), including digital forensics, enterprise software development, information assurance and security, IT project management; information technology management (MBA); intelligence studies (MA), including criminal intelligence, cyber, general (MA, MS), homeland security, intelligence analysis, intelligence collection, intelligence management, intelligence operations, terrorism studies; international relations and conflict resolution (MA), including comparative and security issues, conflict resolution, international and transnational security issues, peacekeeping; legal studies (MA); management (MA), including strategic consulting; marketing (MBA); military history (MA), including American military history, American Revolution, civil war, war since 1945, World War II; military studies (MA), including joint warfare, strategic leadership; national security studies (MA), including cyber, general (MA, MS), homeland security, regional security studies, security and intelligence analysis, terrorism studies; nonprofit management (MBA); political science (MA), including American politics and government, comparative government and development, general (MA, MS), international relations, public policy; psychology (MA); public administration (MPA), including disaster management, environmental policy, health policy, human resources, national security, organizational management, security management; public health (MPH); reverse logistics management (MA); security management (MA); space studies (MS), including aerospace science, general (MA, MS), planetary science; sports and health sciences (MS); sports management (MBA); teaching (M Ed), including autism spectrum disorder, curriculum and instruction for elementary teachers, elementary reading, English language learners, instructional

leadership, online learning, special education, STEAM (STEM plus the arts); transportation and logistics management (MA). *Program availability:* Part-time, evening/weekend, online only, 100% online. *Faculty:* 401 full-time (228 women), 1,678 part-time/adjunct (781 women). *Students:* 378 full-time (184 women), 8,455 part-time (3,484 women); includes 2,972 minority (1,552 Black or African American, non-Hispanic/Latino; 52 American Indian or Alaska Native, non-Hispanic/Latino; 211 Asian, non-Hispanic/Latino; 791 Hispanic/Latino; 70 Native Hawaiian or other Pacific Islander, non-Hispanic/Latino; 296 Two or more races, non-Hispanic/Latino), 109 international. Average age 37. In 2016, 3,185 master's awarded. *Degree requirements:* For master's, comprehensive exam or practicum. *Entrance requirements:* For master's, official transcript showing earned bachelor's degree from institution accredited by recognized accrediting body. Additional exam requirements/recommendations for international students: Required—TOEFL (minimum score 550 paper-based), IELTS (minimum score 6.5). *Application deadline:* Applications are processed on a rolling basis. Application fee: $0. Electronic applications accepted. *Expenses: Tuition:* Part-time $350 per credit hour. *Required fees:* $50 per course. *Financial support:* Scholarships/grants available. Financial award applicants required to submit FAFSA. *Unit head:* Dr. Karan Powell, President, 877-468-6268, Fax: 304-724-3780. *Application contact:* Terry Grant, Vice President of Enrollment Management, 877-468-6268, Fax: 304-724-3780, E-mail: info@apus.edu.
Website: http://www.apus.edu

Armstrong State University, School of Graduate Studies, Program in Criminal Justice, Savannah, GA 31419-1997. Offers criminal justice (MS); cyber crime (Certificate). *Program availability:* Part-time, online learning. *Faculty:* 6 full-time (4 women), 1 (woman) part-time/adjunct. *Students:* 4 full-time (3 women), 20 part-time (12 women); includes 9 minority (all Black or African American, non-Hispanic/Latino). Average age 29. 42 applicants, 31% accepted, 12 enrolled. In 2016, 5 master's, 11 other advanced degrees awarded. *Degree requirements:* For master's, comprehensive exam, field practicum or thesis. *Entrance requirements:* For master's, GRE General Test (minimum score 150 on verbal, 141 on quantitative, or 4 on analytical section) or MAT, minimum GPA of 2.5, 2 letters of recommendation, letter of intent (500-1000 words). Additional exam requirements/recommendations for international students: Required—TOEFL (minimum score 523 paper-based; 70 iBT). *Application deadline:* For fall admission, 6/1 priority date for domestic students, 5/1 priority date for international students; for spring admission, 11/15 priority date for domestic students, 9/15 priority date for international students; for summer admission, 4/15 priority date for domestic students, 9/15 for international students. Applications are processed on a rolling basis. Application fee: $30. Electronic applications accepted. *Expenses:* Tuition, state resident: full-time $1781; part-time $161.93 per credit hour. Tuition, nonresident: full-time $6482; part-time $589.27 per credit hour. *Required fees:* $1224 per unit. $612 per semester. Tuition and fees vary according to course load, campus/location and program. *Financial support:* In 2016–17, research assistantships with full tuition reimbursements (averaging $5,000 per year) were awarded; career-related internships or fieldwork, Federal Work-Study, scholarships/grants, and unspecified assistantships also available. Support available to part-time students. Financial award application deadline: 3/15; financial award applicants required to submit FAFSA. *Faculty research:* International crime/globalization, cyber-crime, influence of social science research on judicial decision-making. *Unit head:* Dr. Daniel Skidmore-Hess, Department Head, 912-344-2532, Fax: 912-344-3438, E-mail: daniel.skidmore-hess@armstrong.edu. *Application contact:* McKenzie Peterman, Assistant Director of Graduate Admissions, 912-344-2503, Fax: 912-344-3417, E-mail: graduate@armstrong.edu.
Website: https://www.armstrong.edu/academic-departments/cjsps-master-of-science-in-criminal-justice

Auburn University at Montgomery, College of Arts and Sciences, Department of Mathematics and Computer Science, Montgomery, AL 36124-4023. Offers cybersystems and information security (MS).

Bay Path University, Program in Cybersecurity Management, Longmeadow, MA 01106-2292. Offers MS. *Program availability:* Part-time, evening/weekend, online only, 100% online. *Students:* 10 full-time (6 women), 19 part-time (11 women); includes 13 minority (6 Black or African American, non-Hispanic/Latino; 6 Hispanic/Latino; 1 Two or more races, non-Hispanic/Latino). Average age 36. 19 applicants, 95% accepted, 14 enrolled. In 2016, 4 master's awarded. *Degree requirements:* For master's, 12 core courses. *Application deadline:* Applications are processed on a rolling basis. Application fee: $45. Electronic applications accepted. Application fee is waived when completed online. *Expenses:* $21,465. *Financial support:* Unspecified assistantships available. Financial award applicants required to submit FAFSA. *Unit head:* Dr. Larry Snyder, Director, 413-565-1294, E-mail: lsnyder@baypath.edu. *Application contact:* Diane Ranaldi, Dean of Graduate Admissions, 413-565-1332, Fax: 413-565-1250, E-mail: dranaldi@baypath.edu.
Website: http://graduate.baypath.edu/graduate-programs/programs-online/ms-programs/cybersecurity-management

Benedictine University, Graduate Programs, Program in Business Administration, Lisle, IL 60532. Offers accounting (MBA); entrepreneurship and managing innovation (MBA); financial management (MBA); health administration (MBA); human resource management (MBA); information systems security (MBA); international business (MBA); management consulting (MBA); management information systems (MBA); marketing management (MBA); operations management and logistics (MBA); organizational leadership (MBA). *Program availability:* Part-time, evening/weekend, online learning. *Faculty:* 4 full-time (2 women), 24 part-time/adjunct (3 women). *Students:* 90 full-time (51 women), 440 part-time (262 women); includes 147 minority (65 Black or African American, non-Hispanic/Latino; 1 American Indian or Alaska Native, non-Hispanic/Latino; 58 Asian, non-Hispanic/Latino; 20 Hispanic/Latino; 3 Native Hawaiian or other Pacific Islander, non-Hispanic/Latino), 2 international. Average age 34. 211 applicants, 89% accepted, 155 enrolled. In 2016, 350 master's awarded. *Entrance requirements:* For master's, GMAT. Additional exam requirements/recommendations for international students: Required—TOEFL (minimum score 550 paper-based). *Application deadline:* For fall admission, 9/1 for domestic students; for winter admission, 12/1 for domestic students; for spring admission, 2/15 for domestic students. Applications are processed on a rolling basis. Application fee: $40. Electronic applications accepted. *Expenses: Tuition:* Full-time $15,600; part-time $650 per hour. *Required fees:* $300. One-time fee: $125 part-time. Tuition and fees vary according to class time, course load, campus/location and program. *Financial support:* Career-related internships or fieldwork and health care benefits available. Support available to part-time students. *Faculty research:* Strategic leadership in professional organizations, sociology of professions, organizational change, social identity theory, applications to change management. *Unit head:* Dr. Sharon Borowicz, Director, 630-829-6219, E-mail: sborowicz@ben.edu. *Application contact:* Kari Gibbons, Director, Admissions, 630-829-6200, Fax: 630-829-6584, E-mail: kgibbons@ben.edu.

Boston University, Graduate School of Arts and Sciences, Department of Computer Science, Boston, MA 02215. Offers computer science (MS, PhD); cyber security (MS); data-centric computing (MS). *Students:* 137 full-time (37 women), 15 part-time (1 woman); includes 4 minority (3 Asian, non-Hispanic/Latino; 1 Hispanic/Latino), 120 international. Average age 26. 951 applicants, 22% accepted, 53 enrolled. In 2016, 20 master's, 8 doctorates awarded. Terminal master's awarded for partial completion of doctoral program. *Degree requirements:* For master's, thesis optional, project; for doctorate, comprehensive exam, thesis/dissertation. *Entrance requirements:* For master's and doctorate, GRE General Test, 3 letters of recommendation, transcripts, personal statement. Additional exam requirements/recommendations for international students: Required—TOEFL (minimum score 550 paper-based; 84 iBT). *Application deadline:* For fall admission, 12/15 for domestic and international students; for spring admission, 11/1 for domestic and international students. Application fee: $95. Electronic applications accepted. *Financial support:* In 2016–17, 56 students received support, including fellowships with full tuition reimbursements available (averaging $21,500 per year), 19 research assistantships with full tuition reimbursements available (averaging $21,500 per year), 23 teaching assistantships with full tuition reimbursements available (averaging $21,500 per year); Federal Work-Study, scholarships/grants, and health care benefits also available. Support available to part-time students. Financial award application deadline: 12/15. *Unit head:* Mark Crovella, Chair, 617-353-8919, Fax: 617-353-6457, E-mail: crovella@bu.edu. *Application contact:* Jennifer Streubel, Program Coordinator, 617-353-8919, Fax: 617-353-6457, E-mail: jenn4@bu.edu.
Website: http://cs-www.bu.edu/

Boston University, Metropolitan College, Department of Computer Science, Boston, MA 02215. Offers computer information systems (MS), including computer networks, data analytics, database management and business intelligence, health informatics, IT project management, security, Web application development; computer networks (Certificate); computer science (MS); data analytics (Certificate); digital forensics (Certificate); health informatics (Certificate); information technology project management (Certificate); software development (MS); software engineering in health care systems (Certificate); telecommunications (MS), including security. *Program availability:* Part-time, evening/weekend, online learning. *Faculty:* 13 full-time (3 women), 43 part-time/adjunct (3 women). *Students:* 108 full-time (36 women), 1,294 part-time (364 women); includes 428 minority (115 Black or African American, non-Hispanic/Latino; 2 American Indian or Alaska Native, non-Hispanic/Latino; 187 Asian, non-Hispanic/Latino; 98 Hispanic/Latino; 2 Native Hawaiian or other Pacific Islander, non-Hispanic/Latino; 24 Two or more races, non-Hispanic/Latino), 314 international. Average age 33. 463 applicants, 79% accepted, 248 enrolled. In 2016, 311 master's awarded. *Degree requirements:* For master's, thesis optional. *Entrance requirements:* For master's and Certificate, official transcripts from regionally-accredited bachelor's degree program, 3 letters of recommendation, professional resume, personal statement. Additional exam requirements/recommendations for international students: Required—TOEFL (minimum score 84 iBT), IELTS. *Application deadline:* For fall admission, 6/1 priority date for international students; for spring admission, 10/1 priority date for international students. Applications are processed on a rolling basis. Application fee: $85. Electronic applications accepted. *Expenses:* Contact institution. *Financial support:* In 2016–17, 11 research assistantships (averaging $8,400 per year) were awarded; unspecified assistantships also available. Support available to part-time students. Financial award applicants required to submit FAFSA. *Faculty research:* Medical informatics, Web technologies, telecom and networks, security and forensics, software engineering, programming languages, multimedia and artificial intelligence (AI), information systems and IT project management. *Unit head:* Dr. Anatoly Temkin, Chair, 617-353-2566, Fax: 617-353-2367, E-mail: csinfo@bu.edu. *Application contact:* Lesley Moreau, Academic Program Coordinator, 617-353-2566, Fax: 617-353-2367, E-mail: metcs@bu.edu.
Website: http://www.bu.edu/csmet/

Brandeis University, Rabb School of Continuing Studies, Division of Graduate Professional Studies, Master of Science in Information Security Program, Waltham, MA 02454-9110. Offers MS. *Program availability:* Part-time-only. *Faculty:* 45 part-time/adjunct (16 women). *Students:* 29 part-time (1 woman); includes 25 minority (22 Black or African American, non-Hispanic/Latino; 1 Asian, non-Hispanic/Latino; 1 Hispanic/Latino; 1 Two or more races, non-Hispanic/Latino). Average age 37. 9 applicants, 89% accepted, 8 enrolled. In 2016, 10 master's awarded. *Entrance requirements:* For master's, undergraduate degree with work experience and/or coursework in networking, computer science, and computer security; 4-year bachelor's degree from regionally-accredited U.S. institution or equivalent; official transcript(s) from every college/university attended; resume or curriculum vitae; statement of goals; letter of recommendation. Additional exam requirements/recommendations for international students: Required—TWE (minimum score 4.5), TOEFL (minimum scores: 600 paper-based, 100 iBT), IELTS (7), or PTE (68). *Application deadline:* For fall admission, 6/21 priority date for domestic and international students; for winter admission, 9/13 priority date for domestic and international students; for spring admission, 12/20 priority date for domestic and international students; for summer admission, 3/14 priority date for domestic and international students. Applications are processed on a rolling basis. Application fee: $50. Electronic applications accepted. *Expenses:* $3,400 per course, $100 graduation fee. *Financial support:* Applicants required to submit FAFSA. *Unit head:* Joseph Dalessandro, Program Chair, 781-736-8787, E-mail: jdalessa@brandeis.edu. *Application contact:* Frances Stearns, Director of Admissions and Recruitment, 781-736-8785, E-mail: fstearns@brandeis.edu.
Website: http://www.brandeis.edu/gps

California State University, San Bernardino, Graduate Studies, College of Business and Public Administration, Program in Business Administration, San Bernardino, CA 92407. Offers accounting (MBA); entrepreneurship (MBA); finance (MBA); global business (MBA); information management (MBA); information security (MBA); management (MBA); supply chain management (MBA). *Accreditation:* AACSB. *Program availability:* Part-time, evening/weekend, online learning. *Faculty:* 7 full-time (4 women), 3 part-time/adjunct (2 women). *Students:* 37 full-time (11 women), 141 part-time (51 women); includes 85 minority (16 Black or African American, non-Hispanic/Latino; 1 American Indian or Alaska Native, non-Hispanic/Latino; 20 Asian, non-Hispanic/Latino; 45 Hispanic/Latino; 3 Two or more races, non-Hispanic/Latino), 46 international. 260 applicants, 37% accepted, 34 enrolled. In 2016, 180 master's awarded. *Degree requirements:* For master's, comprehensive exam, thesis. *Entrance requirements:* Additional exam requirements/recommendations for international students: Required—TOEFL. *Application deadline:* For fall admission, 7/16 for domestic students, 7/20 for international students; for winter admission, 10/23 for domestic students, 10/20 for international students; for spring admission, 1/22 for domestic students, 1/20 for international students. Application fee: $55. *Expenses:* Contact institution. *Financial support:* Application deadline: 3/1. *Unit head:* Dr. Lawrence C. Rose, Dean, 909-537-3703, Fax: 909-537-7026, E-mail: lrose@csusb.edu. *Application contact:* Dr. Vipin Gupta, Associate Dean/MBA Director, 909-537-7380, Fax: 909-537-7026, E-mail: vgupta@csusb.edu.
Website: http://mba.csusb.edu/

California State University, San Bernardino, Graduate Studies, College of Social and Behavioral Sciences, Program in National Cyber Security Studies, San Bernardino, CA 92407. Offers MA. *Students:* 5 full-time (3 women), 3 part-time (2 women); includes 4 minority (all Hispanic/Latino). 7 applicants, 57% accepted, 4 enrolled. In 2016, 1 master's awarded. *Degree requirements:* For master's, thesis. *Entrance requirements:* Additional exam requirements/recommendations for international students: Required—TOEFL. *Application deadline:* For fall admission, 4/15 for domestic students; for winter admission, 10/16 for domestic students; for spring admission, 1/22 for domestic students. Application fee: $55. *Expenses:* Tuition, state resident: full-time $7843; part-time $5011.20 per year. Tuition and fees vary according to course load, degree level, program and reciprocity agreements. *Financial support:* Unspecified assistantships available. *Unit head:* Dr. Mark Clark, Director, 909-537-5491, E-mail: mtclark@csusb.edu. *Application contact:* Dr. Francisca Beer, Dean, 909-537-5058, E-mail: fbeer@csusb.edu.

Capella University, School of Business and Technology, Doctoral Programs in Technology, Minneapolis, MN 55402. Offers general information technology (PhD); global operations and supply chain management (DBA); information assurance and security (PhD); information technology education (PhD); information technology management (DBA, PhD).

Capella University, School of Business and Technology, Master's Programs in Technology, Minneapolis, MN 55402. Offers enterprise software architecture (MS); general information systems and technology management (MS); global operations and supply chain management (MBA); information assurance and security (MS); information technology management (MBA); network management (MS).

Capitol Technology University, Graduate Programs, Laurel, MD 20708-9759. Offers business administration (MBA); computer science (MS); electrical engineering (MS); information and telecommunications systems management (MS); information architecture (MS); network security (MS). *Program availability:* Part-time, evening/weekend, online learning. *Entrance requirements:* For master's, minimum GPA of 3.0. Electronic applications accepted.

Carlow University, College of Leadership and Social Change, Program in Fraud and Forensics, Pittsburgh, PA 15213-3165. Offers MS. *Program availability:* Online only, 100% online. *Students:* 29 full-time (24 women); includes 10 minority (7 Black or African American, non-Hispanic/Latino; 2 Asian, non-Hispanic/Latino; 1 Two or more races, non-Hispanic/Latino). Average age 32. 45 applicants, 87% accepted, 29 enrolled. In 2016, 29 master's awarded. *Entrance requirements:* For master's, bachelor's degree in any discipline with minimum GPA of 3.0; ability to work in online environment; competency in Microsoft Word, Excel, and PowerPoint; one year of experience in setting appropriate to degree (preferred); resume/curriculum vitae; two professional recommendations. Additional exam requirements/recommendations for international students: Required—TOEFL (minimum score 550 paper-based). *Application deadline:* Applications are processed on a rolling basis. Electronic applications accepted. *Expenses:* Contact institution. *Financial support:* Application deadline: 4/1; applicants required to submit FAFSA. *Unit head:* Dr. Diane Matthews, Director, Fraud and Forensics Program, 412-578-6384, Fax: 412-587-6367, E-mail: damatthews@carlow.edu. *Application contact:* E-mail: gradstudies@carlow.edu.
Website: http://www.carlow.edu/Fraud_and_Forensics_(MS).aspx

Carnegie Mellon University, Carnegie Institute of Technology, Information Networking Institute, Pittsburgh, PA 15213. Offers information networking (MS); information security (MS); information technology - information security (MS); information technology - mobility (MS); information technology - software management (MS). *Degree requirements:* For master's, thesis optional. *Entrance requirements:* For master's, GRE General Test, bachelor's degree in computer science, computer engineering, or electrical engineering, or related technology degree; programming skills (C/C++ fluency for some programs). Additional exam requirements/recommendations for international students: Required—TOEFL. *Faculty research:* Computer forensics and incident response; dependable systems, embedded systems, mobile systems, and sensor networks; computer and information networks, network and information security, human and socio-economic factors in secure system design; wireless sensor networks, survivable embedded systems, signal processing/compression; strategic management, international strategic management, group dynamics and decision-making structures, simulated competitive environments.

Carnegie Mellon University, Heinz College, School of Information Systems and Management, Master of Science in Information Security Policy and Management Program, Pittsburgh, PA 15213-3891. Offers MSISPM. *Entrance requirements:* For master's, GRE or GMAT, college-level course in advanced algebra/pre-calculus; college-level courses in economics and statistics (recommended). Additional exam requirements/recommendations for international students: Required—TOEFL or IELTS.

Central Michigan University, Central Michigan University Global Campus, Program in Cybersecurity, Mount Pleasant, MI 48859. Offers Certificate. *Program availability:* Part-time, evening/weekend. *Faculty:* 8 part-time/adjunct. *Students:* 36 (9 women); includes 19 minority (13 Black or African American, non-Hispanic/Latino; 6 Two or more races, non-Hispanic/Latino). Average age 42. Application fee: $50. Electronic applications accepted. *Financial support:* Scholarships/grants available. Support available to part-time students. *Unit head:* Karl Smart, Chairperson, Business Information Systems, 989-774-6447, E-mail: smart1kl@cmich.edu. *Application contact:* Global Campus Call Center, 877-268-4636, Fax: 989-774-2461, E-mail: cmuglobal@cmich.edu.

Champlain College, Graduate Studies, Burlington, VT 05402-0670. Offers business (MBA); digital forensic science (MS); early childhood education (M Ed); emergent media (MFA, MS); executive leadership (MS); health care administration (MS); information security operations (MS); law (MS); mediation and applied conflict studies (MS). MS in emergent media program held in Shanghai. *Program availability:* Part-time, online learning. *Degree requirements:* For master's, capstone project. *Entrance requirements:* Additional exam requirements/recommendations for international students: Required—TOEFL (minimum score 550 paper-based; 80 iBT). Electronic applications accepted.

City University of Seattle, Graduate Division, School of Management, Seattle, WA 98121. Offers accounting (Certificate); change leadership (MBA, Certificate); computer systems (MS); finance (Certificate); financial management (MBA); general management (MBA); general management-Europe (MBA); global marketing (MBA); human resources management (Certificate); individualized study (MBA); information security (MS); information systems (MBA); leadership (MA); marketing (MBA, Certificate); project management (MBA, MS, Certificate); sustainable business (Certificate); technology management (MBA, Certificate). *Program availability:* Part-time, evening/weekend, online learning. *Degree requirements:* For master's, comprehensive exam (for some programs), thesis (for some programs). *Entrance requirements:* For master's, baccalaureate degree or equivalent from an accredited or otherwise recognized institution. Additional exam requirements/recommendations for international students: Required—TOEFL (minimum score 567 paper-based; 87 iBT); Recommended—IELTS. Electronic applications accepted.

Claremont Graduate University, Graduate Programs, Center for Information Systems and Technology, Claremont, CA 91711-6160. Offers cybersecurity and networking (MS); data science and analytics (MS); electronic commerce (PhD); geographic information systems (MS); health informatics (MS); information systems (Certificate); IT strategy and innovation (MS); knowledge management (PhD); systems development (PhD); telecommunications and networking (PhD); MBA/MS. *Program availability:* Part-time. *Faculty:* 8 full-time (1 woman), 1 part-time/adjunct (0 women). *Students:* 60 full-time (18 women), 81 part-time (27 women); includes 34 minority (7 Black or African American, non-Hispanic/Latino; 18 Asian, non-Hispanic/Latino; 7 Hispanic/Latino; 1 Native Hawaiian or other Pacific Islander, non-Hispanic/Latino; 1 Two or more races, non-Hispanic/Latino), 80 international. Average age 35. In 2016, 21 master's, 10 doctorates awarded. *Degree requirements:* For doctorate, comprehensive exam, thesis/dissertation, portfolio. *Entrance requirements:* For master's and doctorate, GMAT, GRE General Test. Additional exam requirements/recommendations for international students: Required—TOEFL (minimum score 75 iBT). *Application deadline:* For fall admission, 2/1 priority date for domestic and international students. Applications are processed on a rolling basis. Application fee: $80. Electronic applications accepted. *Expenses: Tuition:* Full-time $44,328; part-time $1847 per unit. *Required fees:* $600; $300 per semester. Tuition and fees vary according to course load and program. *Financial support:* Fellowships, research assistantships, teaching assistantships, Federal Work-Study, institutionally sponsored loans, and scholarships/grants available. Support available to part-time students. Financial award application deadline: 2/15; financial award applicants required to submit FAFSA. *Faculty research:* Man-machine interaction, organizational aspects of computing, implementation of information systems, information systems practice. *Unit head:* Lorne Olfman, Acting Director, 909-607-3035, E-mail: lorne.olfman@cgu.edu. *Application contact:* Jake Campbell, Senior Assistant Director of Admissions, 909-607-3024, E-mail: jake.campbell@cgu.edu.
Website: https://www.cgu.edu/school/center-for-information-systems-and-technology/

Colorado Christian University, Program in Business Administration, Lakewood, CO 80226. Offers corporate training (MBA); information security (MA); leadership (MBA); project management (MBA). *Program availability:* Part-time, evening/weekend, online learning. *Degree requirements:* For master's, thesis optional. *Entrance requirements:* For master's, GMAT, 2 letters of recommendation, resume. Additional exam requirements/recommendations for international students: Required—TOEFL. Electronic applications accepted. *Expenses:* Contact institution.

Colorado Technical University Aurora, Program in Computer Science, Aurora, CO 80014. Offers computer systems security (MSCS); database systems (MSCS); software engineering (MSCS). *Program availability:* Part-time, evening/weekend. *Degree requirements:* For master's, thesis or alternative. *Entrance requirements:* For master's, minimum undergraduate GPA of 3.0, resume.

Colorado Technical University Aurora, Program in Information Science, Aurora, CO 80014. Offers information systems security (MSM).

Colorado Technical University Colorado Springs, Graduate Studies, Program in Computer Science, Colorado Springs, CO 80907. Offers computer science (DCS); computer systems security (MSCS); database systems (MSCS); software engineering (MSCS). *Program availability:* Part-time, evening/weekend, online learning. *Degree requirements:* For master's, thesis or alternative; for doctorate, thesis/dissertation. *Entrance requirements:* For doctorate, minimum graduate GPA of 3.0, 5 years of related work experience. *Faculty research:* Software engineering, systems engineering.

Colorado Technical University Colorado Springs, Graduate Studies, Program in Information Science, Colorado Springs, CO 80907. Offers information systems security (MSM). *Program availability:* Online learning.

Columbus State University, Graduate Studies, Turner College of Business, Columbus, GA 31907-5645. Offers applied computer science (MS), including informational assurance, modeling and simulation, software development; business administration (MBA); human resource management (Certificate); information systems security (Certificate); modeling and simulation (Certificate); organizational leadership (MS), including human resource management, leader development, servant leadership; servant leadership (Certificate). *Accreditation:* AACSB. *Program availability:* Part-time, evening/weekend, 100% online, blended/hybrid learning. *Faculty:* 10 full-time (3 women). *Students:* 93 full-time (21 women), 132 part-time (47 women); includes 69 minority (36 Black or African American, non-Hispanic/Latino; 1 American Indian or Alaska Native, non-Hispanic/Latino; 11 Asian, non-Hispanic/Latino; 14 Hispanic/Latino; 7 Two or more races, non-Hispanic/Latino), 35 international. Average age 31. 279 applicants, 44% accepted, 64 enrolled. In 2016, 106 master's awarded. *Entrance requirements:* For master's, GMAT, GRE, minimum undergraduate GPA of 2.75, letters of recommendation. Additional exam requirements/recommendations for international students: Required—TOEFL (minimum score 550 paper-based; 79 iBT). *Application deadline:* For fall admission, 6/30 for domestic students, 5/1 for international students; for spring admission, 11/1 for domestic and international students; for summer admission, 3/1 for domestic and international students. Applications are processed on a rolling basis. Application fee: $50. Electronic applications accepted. *Expenses:* Contact institution. *Financial support:* In 2016–17, 18 students received support, including 16 research assistantships (averaging $3,000 per year); Federal Work-Study also available. Financial award application deadline: 5/1; financial award applicants required to submit FAFSA. *Unit head:* Dr. Linda U. Hadley, Dean, 706-507-8153, Fax: 706-568-2184, E-mail: hadley_linda@columbusstate.edu. *Application contact:* Kristin Williams, Director of International and Graduate Recruitment, 706-507-8848, Fax: 706-568-5091, E-mail: thornton_katie@colstate.edu.
Website: http://turner.columbusstate.edu/

Concordia University, School of Graduate Studies, Faculty of Engineering and Computer Science, Concordia Institute for Information Systems Engineering (CIISE), Montréal, QC H3G 1M8, Canada. Offers 3D graphics and game development (Certificate); information and systems engineering (PhD); information systems security (M Eng, MA Sc); quality systems engineering (M Eng, MA Sc); service engineering and network management (Certificate).

Concordia University, Nebraska, Program in Computer Science, Seward, NE 68434-1556. Offers cyber operations (MS). *Program availability:* Online learning.

Concordia University of Edmonton, Program in Information Systems Security Management, Edmonton, AB T5B 4E4, Canada. Offers MA.

Concordia University, St. Paul, College of Business, St. Paul, MN 55104-5494. Offers business administration (MBA), including cyber-security leadership; business and organizational leadership (MBA); health care management (MBA); human resource management (MA); leadership and management (MA); strategic communication management (MA). *Accreditation:* ACBSP. *Program availability:* Part-time, evening/weekend, 100% online, blended/hybrid learning. *Faculty:* 12 full-time (4 women), 36 part-time/adjunct (15 women). *Students:* 462 full-time (288 women), 25 part-time (16 women); includes 123 minority (59 Black or African American, non-Hispanic/Latino; 1 American Indian or Alaska Native, non-Hispanic/Latino; 36 Asian, non-Hispanic/Latino; 10 Hispanic/Latino; 1 Native Hawaiian or other Pacific Islander, non-Hispanic/Latino; 16 Two or more races, non-Hispanic/Latino), 28 international. Average age 34. 269 applicants, 73% accepted, 137 enrolled. In 2016, 192 master's awarded. *Degree requirements:* For master's, thesis (for some programs). *Entrance requirements:* For master's, official transcripts from regionally-accredited institution stating the conferral of a bachelor's degree with minimum cumulative GPA of 3.0; personal statement; professional resume. Additional exam requirements/recommendations for international students: Recommended—TOEFL (minimum score 547 paper-based; 78 iBT), IELTS (minimum score 6). *Application deadline:* For fall admission, 8/1 for domestic and international students; for spring admission, 12/1 for domestic and international students; for summer admission, 5/1 for domestic and international students. Applications are processed on a rolling basis. Application fee: $50. Electronic applications accepted. *Expenses:* Contact institution. *Financial support:* In 2016–17, 259 students received support. Scholarships/grants and unspecified assistantships available. Financial award applicants required to submit FAFSA. *Faculty research:*

Computer and Information Systems Security

Alternative dispute resolution, franchising, entrepreneurship, applied business ethics, strategic leadership development. *Unit head:* Dr. Kevin Hall, Dean, 651-603-6165, Fax: 651-641-8807, E-mail: khall@csp.edu. *Application contact:* Kimberly Craig, Associate Vice President, Cohort Enrollment Management, 651-603-6223, Fax: 651-603-6320, E-mail: craig@csp.edu.

Dakota State University, College of Business and Information Systems, Madison, SD 57042-1799. Offers analytics (MSA); applied computer science (MSACS); banking security (Graduate Certificate); business analytics (Graduate Certificate); cyber security (D Sc); ethical hacking (Graduate Certificate); general management (MBA); health informatics (MSHI); information assurance and computer security (MSIA); information systems (MSIS, D Sc IS); information technology (Graduate Certificate). *Accreditation:* ACBSP. *Program availability:* Part-time, evening/weekend, 100% online, blended/hybrid learning. *Degree requirements:* For master's, comprehensive exam, thesis optional, examination, integrative project; for doctorate, comprehensive exam, thesis/dissertation, portfolio. *Entrance requirements:* For master's, GRE General Test, demonstration of information systems skills, minimum GPA of 2.7; for doctorate, GRE General Test, demonstration of information systems skills; for Graduate Certificate, GMAT. Additional exam requirements/recommendations for international students: Required—PTE (minimum score 53), TOEFL (minimum score 550 paper-based, 79 iBT) or IELTS (6.5). *Application deadline:* For fall admission, 6/15 for domestic students, 4/15 for international students; for spring admission, 11/15 for domestic students, 9/15 priority date for international students; for summer admission, 4/15 for domestic and international students. Applications are processed on a rolling basis. Application fee: $35. *Expenses:* Contact institution. *Financial support:* Fellowships with partial tuition reimbursements, research assistantships with partial tuition reimbursements, teaching assistantships with partial tuition reimbursements, career-related internships or fieldwork, Federal Work-Study, scholarships/grants, and unspecified assistantships available. Support available to part-time students. Financial award applicants required to submit FAFSA. *Faculty research:* Data mining and analytics, biometrics and information assurance, decision support systems, health informatics, STEM education for K-12 teachers/students and underrepresented populations. *Unit head:* Mark Hawkes, Dean for Graduate Studies and Research, 605-256-5274, E-mail: mark.hawkes@dsu.edu. *Application contact:* Erin Blankespoor, Senior Secretary, Office of Graduate Studies and Research, 605-256-5799, E-mail: erin.blankespoor@dsu.edu.
Website: http://dsu.edu/academics/colleges/college-of-business-and-information-systems

Davenport University, Sneden Graduate School, Grand Rapids, MI 49512. Offers accounting (MBA); business administration (EMBA); finance (MBA); health care management (MBA); human resources (MBA); information assurance (MS); public health (MPH); strategic management (MBA). *Program availability:* Evening/weekend. *Entrance requirements:* For master's, GMAT, minimum undergraduate GPA of 2.75. Additional exam requirements/recommendations for international students: Required—TOEFL. Electronic applications accepted. *Faculty research:* Leadership, management, marketing, organizational culture.

DePaul University, College of Computing and Digital Media, Chicago, IL 60604. Offers animation (MA, MFA); business information technology (MS); cinema (MFA); cinema production (MS); computational finance (MS); computer and information sciences (PhD); computer game development (MS); computer information and network security (MS); computer science (MS); e-commerce technology (MS); health informatics (MS); human-computer interaction (MS); information systems (MS); information technology project management (MS); network engineering and management (MS); predictive analytics (MS); screenwriting (MFA); software engineering (MS); JD/MS. *Program availability:* Part-time, evening/weekend, online learning. *Degree requirements:* For master's, thesis (for some programs); for doctorate, comprehensive exam, thesis/dissertation. *Entrance requirements:* For master's, GRE or GMAT (for MS in computational finance only), bachelor's degree, resume (MS in predictive analytics only), IT experience (MS in information technology project management only), portfolio review (all MFA programs and MA in animation); for doctorate, GRE, master's degree in computer science. Additional exam requirements/recommendations for international students: Required—TOEFL (minimum score 590 paper-based; 80 iBT), IELTS (minimum score 6.5), PTE (minimum score 53). Electronic applications accepted. *Expenses:* Contact institution. *Faculty research:* Data mining, computer science, human-computer interaction, security, animation and film.

DeSales University, Division of Science and Mathematics, Center Valley, PA 18034-9568. Offers cyber security (Postbaccalaureate Certificate); data analytics (Postbaccalaureate Certificate); information systems (MS), including cyber security, digital forensics, healthcare information management, project management. *Program availability:* Part-time, evening/weekend, 100% online, blended/hybrid learning. *Faculty:* 1 (woman) full-time, 3 part-time/adjunct (0 women). *Students:* 8 full-time (1 woman), 12 part-time (6 women); includes 1 minority (Asian, non-Hispanic/Latino). Average age 34. 20 applicants, 30% accepted, 6 enrolled. In 2016, 7 master's awarded. *Entrance requirements:* For master's, GRE or GMAT, bachelor's degree in computer-related discipline from accredited college or university, minimum undergraduate GPA of 3.0, personal statement, three letters of recommendation. Additional exam requirements/recommendations for international students: Required—TOEFL. *Application deadline:* Applications are processed on a rolling basis. Application fee: $50. Electronic applications accepted. *Expenses:* Contact institution. *Financial support:* Applicants required to submit FAFSA. *Unit head:* Dr. Patricia Riola, MSIS Director/Assistant Professor of Computer Science, 610-282-1100 Ext. 1647, E-mail: patricia.riola@desales.edu. *Application contact:* Julia Ferraro, Director of Graduate Admissions, 610-282-1100 Ext. 1768, E-mail: gradadmissions@desales.edu.
Website: http://www.desales.edu/home/academics/graduate-studies/programs-of-study/msis—-master-of-science-in-information-systems

Drury University, Cybersecurity Leadership Certificate Program, Springfield, MO 65802. Offers Certificate. *Program availability:* Part-time, evening/weekend. *Faculty:* 3 full-time (1 woman), 2 part-time/adjunct (0 women). *Entrance requirements:* For degree, bachelor's degree, minimum GPA of 3.0. Additional exam requirements/recommendations for international students: Recommended—TOEFL (minimum score 80 iBT), IELTS (minimum score 6.5). *Application deadline:* For fall admission, 8/4 for domestic and international students; for spring admission, 1/5 for domestic and international students; for summer admission, 5/26 for domestic and international students. Applications are processed on a rolling basis. Application fee: $25 ($50 for international students). Electronic applications accepted. *Expenses:* $530 per credit hour; $100 graduation fee; $27 per credit hour technology/enhancement fee. *Financial support:* Career-related internships or fieldwork, scholarships/grants, and unspecified assistantships available. Financial award application deadline: 6/30; financial award applicants required to submit FAFSA. *Faculty research:* Cybersecurity leadership, health care management, cross cultural management, corporate finance, social entrepreneurship. *Unit head:* Angie Adamick, Director, Cybersecurity Leadership Certificate, 417-873-7612, E-mail: aadamick@drury.edu.
Website: http://www.drury.edu/cybersecurity

East Carolina University, Graduate School, College of Engineering and Technology, Department of Technology Systems, Greenville, NC 27858-4353. Offers computer network professional (Certificate); information assurance (Certificate); Lean Six Sigma Black Belt (Certificate); network technology (MS), including computer networking management, digital communications technology, information security, Web technologies; occupational safety (MS); technology management (PhD); technology systems (MS), including industrial distribution and logistics, manufacturing systems, performance improvement, quality systems; Website developer (Certificate). *Students:* 23 full-time (1 woman), 199 part-time (55 women); includes 59 minority (39 Black or African American, non-Hispanic/Latino; 3 American Indian or Alaska Native, non-Hispanic/Latino; 4 Asian, non-Hispanic/Latino; 10 Hispanic/Latino; 3 Two or more races, non-Hispanic/Latino), 5 international. Average age 38. 85 applicants, 87% accepted, 61 enrolled. In 2016, 23 master's awarded. *Entrance requirements:* For master's and Certificate, GRE General Test or MAT, minimum GPA of 2.5; for doctorate, GRE General Test, related work experience. *Application deadline:* For fall admission, 6/1 priority date for domestic students. Applications are processed on a rolling basis. Application fee: $50. *Financial support:* Application deadline: 6/1. *Unit head:* Dr. Tijjani Mohammed, Chair, 252-328-9668, E-mail: mohammedt@ecu.edu. *Application contact:* Dean of Graduate School, 252-328-6012, Fax: 252-328-6071, E-mail: gradschool@ecu.edu.

Eastern Illinois University, Graduate School, Lumpkin College of Business and Applied Sciences, School of Technology, Charleston, IL 61920. Offers computer technology (Certificate); quality systems (Certificate); technology (MS); technology security (Certificate); work performance improvement (Certificate); MS/MBA; MS/MS. *Program availability:* Part-time, evening/weekend.

Eastern Michigan University, Graduate School, College of Technology, School of Information Security and Applied Computing, Programs in Information Assurance, Ypsilanti, MI 48197. Offers Graduate Certificate. *Students:* 2 applicants. Application fee: $45. *Application contact:* Xiangdong Sean Che, Program Coordinator, 734-487-3685, Fax: 734-483-8755, E-mail: xche@emich.edu.

EC-Council University, Program in Security Science, Albuquerque, NM 87109. Offers MSS. *Program availability:* Online learning. *Degree requirements:* For master's, capstone.

Embry-Riddle Aeronautical University–Daytona, Department of Electrical, Computer, Software and Systems Engineering, Daytona Beach, FL 32114-3900. Offers computer engineering (MS); cybersecurity engineering (MS); electrical engineering (MSECE); electrical engineering and computer science (PhD), including electrical, computer, software, and systems engineering; software engineering (MSSE); systems engineering (MS). *Program availability:* Part-time. *Faculty:* 13 full-time (1 woman), 1 part-time/adjunct (0 women). *Students:* 63 full-time (17 women), 8 part-time (3 women); includes 6 minority (1 Black or African American, non-Hispanic/Latino; 1 Asian, non-Hispanic/Latino; 1 Hispanic/Latino; 3 Two or more races, non-Hispanic/Latino), 41 international. Average age 25. 93 applicants, 45% accepted, 21 enrolled. In 2016, 30 master's awarded. *Degree requirements:* For master's, thesis or alternative; for doctorate, thesis/dissertation. *Entrance requirements:* For master's, GRE (for some programs); for doctorate, GRE. Additional exam requirements/recommendations for international students: Required—TOEFL (minimum score 550 paper-based, 79 iBT) or IELTS (6). *Application deadline:* For fall admission, 3/1 priority date for domestic students; for spring admission, 11/1 priority date for domestic students; for summer admission, 4/1 priority date for domestic students. Applications are processed on a rolling basis. Application fee: $50. Electronic applications accepted. *Expenses: Tuition:* Full-time $16,296; part-time $1358 per credit hour. *Required fees:* $1294; $647 per semester. One-time fee: $100 full-time. Tuition and fees vary according to course load, degree level and program. *Financial support:* Research assistantships, teaching assistantships, career-related internships or fieldwork, scholarships/grants, unspecified assistantships, and on-campus employment available. Financial award application deadline: 3/15; financial award applicants required to submit FAFSA. *Faculty research:* Cybersecurity and assured systems engineering, radar, unmanned and autonomous systems, modeling and simulation, cyber-physical systems. *Unit head:* Timothy Wilson, PhD, Professor of Electrical and Computer Engineering/Chair, Department of Electrical, Computer, Software and Systems Engineering, 386-226-6100, E-mail: timothy.wilson@erau.edu. *Application contact:* Graduate Admissions, 386-226-6176, Fax: 386-226-7070, E-mail: graduate.admissions@erau.edu.
Website: https://daytonabeach.erau.edu/college-engineering/electrical-computer-software-systems/index.html

Embry-Riddle Aeronautical University–Worldwide, Department of Security and Emergency Services, Daytona Beach, FL 32114-3900. Offers cybersecurity management and policy (MSCMP); human security and resilience (MSHSR). *Program availability:* Part-time, evening/weekend, 100% online, blended/hybrid learning, EagleVision Classroom (between classrooms), EagleVision Home (faculty and students at home), and a blend of Classroom or Home. *Faculty:* 4 full-time (3 women), 5 part-time/adjunct (1 woman). *Students:* 2 full-time (both women), 5 part-time (2 women); includes 27 minority (10 Black or African American, non-Hispanic/Latino; 3 Asian, non-Hispanic/Latino; 2 Hispanic/Latino; 12 Two or more races, non-Hispanic/Latino), 1 international. Average age 37. *Degree requirements:* For master's, capstone project. *Entrance requirements:* Additional exam requirements/recommendations for international students: Required—TOEFL (minimum score 550 paper-based, 79 iBT) or IELTS (6). *Application deadline:* Applications are processed on a rolling basis. Application fee: $50. Electronic applications accepted. *Expenses:* $620 per credit (for civilians), $530 per credit (for military). *Financial support:* Career-related internships or fieldwork and scholarships/grants available. Financial award applicants required to submit FAFSA. *Unit head:* Ronald Wakeham, Department Chair, E-mail: ronald.wakeham@erau.edu. *Application contact:* Worldwide Campus, 800-522-6787, E-mail: worldwide@erau.edu.
Website: http://worldwide.erau.edu/colleges/arts-sciences/department-emergency-services

Embry-Riddle Aeronautical University–Worldwide, Department of Technology Management, Daytona Beach, FL 32114-3900. Offers information security and assurance (MS), including information assurance in a global context, information systems security, protecting business intelligence; management information systems (MS), including business intelligence siness and analytics, information security and assurance, information systems project management. *Program availability:* Part-time, evening/weekend, 100% online, blended/hybrid learning, EagleVision is a virtual classroom that combines Web video conferencing and a learning management system. EagleVision Classroom (between classrooms), EagleVision Home (faculty and students at home), and a blend of Classroom or Home. *Entrance requirements:* Additional exam requirements/recommendations for international students: Required—TOEFL (minimum score 550 paper-based; 79 iBT), IELTS (minimum score 6), TOEFL or IELTS accepted. Electronic applications accepted. *Expenses:* Contact institution.

Fairfield University, School of Engineering, Fairfield, CT 06824. Offers database management (CAS); electrical and computer engineering (MS); information security (CAS); management of technology (MS); mechanical engineering (MS); network technology (CAS); software engineering (MS); Web application development (CAS). *Program availability:* Part-time, evening/weekend. *Faculty:* 7 full-time (1 woman), 15 part-time/adjunct (2 women). *Students:* 104 full-time (31 women), 56 part-time (15

women); includes 17 minority (8 Black or African American, non-Hispanic/Latino; 5 Asian, non-Hispanic/Latino; 4 Hispanic/Latino), 108 international. Average age 28. 193 applicants, 63% accepted, 20 enrolled. In 2016, 173 master's awarded. *Degree requirements:* For master's, capstone course. *Entrance requirements:* For master's, resume, 2 recommendations. Additional exam requirements/recommendations for international students: Required—TOEFL (minimum score 550 paper-based; 80 iBT) or IELTS (minimum score 6.5). *Application deadline:* For fall admission, 5/15 for international students; for spring admission, 10/15 for international students. Applications are processed on a rolling basis. Application fee: $60. Electronic applications accepted. *Expenses:* $800 per credit hour. *Financial support:* In 2016–17, 27 students received support. Scholarships/grants and unspecified assistantships available. Financial award applicants required to submit FAFSA. *Faculty research:* Artificial intelligence and information visualization, natural language processing, thermofluids, microwaves and electromagnetics, micro-/nano-manufacturing. *Unit head:* Dr. Bruce Berdanier, Dean, 203-254-4147, Fax: 203-254-4013, E-mail: bberdanier@fairfield.edu. *Application contact:* Marianne Gumpper, Director of Graduate and Continuing Studies Admission, 203-254-4184, Fax: 203-254-4073, E-mail: gradadmis@fairfield.edu.
Website: http://www.fairfield.edu/soe

Ferris State University, College of Business, Big Rapids, MI 49307. Offers business intelligence (MBA); design and innovation management (MBA); incident response (MBA); information security and intelligence (MS), including business intelligence, incident response, project management; lean systems and leadership (MBA); performance metrics (MBA); project management (MBA); supply chain management and lean logistics (MBA). *Accreditation:* ACBSP. *Program availability:* Part-time, evening/weekend, 100% online, blended/hybrid learning. *Faculty:* 18 full-time (7 women), 6 part-time/adjunct (3 women). *Students:* 25 full-time (11 women), 113 part-time (47 women); includes 12 minority (2 Black or African American, non-Hispanic/Latino; 1 American Indian or Alaska Native, non-Hispanic/Latino; 3 Asian, non-Hispanic/Latino; 3 Hispanic/Latino; 3 Two or more races, non-Hispanic/Latino), 50 international. Average age 31. 128 applicants, 59% accepted, 39 enrolled. In 2016, 94 master's awarded. *Degree requirements:* For master's, comprehensive exam, thesis. *Entrance requirements:* For master's, GRE or GMAT, minimum GPA of 3.0 in junior/senior-level classes and overall; statement of purpose; 3 letters of reference; resume; transcripts. Additional exam requirements/recommendations for international students: Required—TOEFL (minimum score 500 paper-based; 70 iBT), IELTS (minimum score 6.5). *Application deadline:* For fall admission, 7/1 priority date for domestic students, 6/15 for international students; for winter admission, 11/1 priority date for domestic students, 10/15 for international students; for spring admission, 3/1 priority date for domestic students, 2/15 for international students. Applications are processed on a rolling basis. Application fee: $0 ($30 for international students). Electronic applications accepted. *Expenses:* Contact institution. *Financial support:* Career-related internships or fieldwork, Federal Work-Study, scholarships/grants, and unspecified assistantships available. Support available to part-time students. Financial award application deadline: 3/15; financial award applicants required to submit FAFSA. *Faculty research:* Lifestyle medicine business models, lean systems value chain pptimization, digital forensics/incident response, location-based services, passive data capture and analysis. *Unit head:* Dr. David Nicol, College of Business Dean, 231-591-2168, Fax: 231-591-3521, E-mail: davidnicol@ferris.edu. *Application contact:* Dr. Greg Gogolin, Professor, 231-591-3159, Fax: 231-591-3521, E-mail: greggogolin@ferris.edu.
Website: http://cbgp.ferris.edu/

Florida Institute of Technology, College of Engineering, Program in Information Assurance and Cybersecurity, Melbourne, FL 32901-6975. Offers MS. *Program availability:* Part-time, evening/weekend, 100% online. *Students:* 10 full-time (4 women), 6 part-time (1 woman); includes 2 minority (both Hispanic/Latino), 11 international. Average age 25. 55 applicants, 38% accepted, 5 enrolled. In 2016, 16 master's awarded. *Degree requirements:* For master's, comprehensive exam (for some programs), thesis optional, minimum of 33 credit hours. *Entrance requirements:* For master's, GRE General Test, transcripts. Additional exam requirements/recommendations for international students: Required—TOEFL (minimum score 550 paper-based; 79 iBT). *Application deadline:* Applications are processed on a rolling basis. Electronic applications accepted. *Expenses: Tuition:* Full-time $22,338; part-time $1241 per credit hour. *Required fees:* $250. Tuition and fees vary according to degree level, campus/location and program. *Financial support:* Applicants required to submit FAFSA. *Unit head:* Dr. Richard Newman, Department Head, 321-674-7487, E-mail: jrnewman@fit.edu. *Application contact:* Cheryl A. Brown, Associate Director of Graduate Admissions, 321-674-7581, Fax: 321-723-9468, E-mail: cbrown@fit.edu.
Website: http://www.fit.edu/programs/

Florida International University, College of Engineering and Computing, School of Computing and Information Sciences, Miami, FL 33199. Offers computer science (MS, PhD); cybersecurity (MS); data science (MS); information technology (MS); telecommunications and networking (MS). *Program availability:* Part-time, evening/weekend. *Faculty:* 46 full-time (11 women), 28 part-time/adjunct (5 women). *Students:* 145 full-time (39 women), 109 part-time (16 women); includes 124 minority (14 Black or African American, non-Hispanic/Latino; 1 American Indian or Alaska Native, non-Hispanic/Latino; 10 Asian, non-Hispanic/Latino; 97 Hispanic/Latino; 2 Two or more races, non-Hispanic/Latino), 115 international. Average age 29. 407 applicants, 54% accepted, 78 enrolled. In 2016, 90 master's, 8 doctorates awarded. *Degree requirements:* For master's, thesis or alternative; for doctorate, comprehensive exam, thesis/dissertation. *Entrance requirements:* For master's and doctorate, GRE General Test, 3 letters of recommendation, minimum GPA of 3.0. Additional exam requirements/recommendations for international students: Required—TOEFL (minimum score 550 paper-based; 80 iBT). *Application deadline:* For fall admission, 6/1 for domestic students, 4/1 for international students; for spring admission, 10/1 for domestic students, 9/1 for international students. Applications are processed on a rolling basis. Application fee: $30. Electronic applications accepted. *Expenses: Tuition,* state resident: full-time $8912; part-time $446 per credit hour. Tuition, nonresident: full-time $21,393; part-time $992 per credit hour. *Required fees:* $2185; $195 per semester. Tuition and fees vary according to program. *Financial support:* Research assistantships, teaching assistantships, institutionally sponsored loans, scholarships/grants, and unspecified assistantships available. Financial award application deadline: 3/1; financial award applicants required to submit FAFSA. *Faculty research:* Database systems, software engineering, operating systems, networks. *Unit head:* Dr. S. S. Iyengar, Director, 305-348-3947, E-mail: iyengar@cis.fiu.edu. *Application contact:* Sara-Michelle Lemus, Engineering Admissions Officer, 305-348-1890, E-mail: grad_eng@fiu.edu.

Florida State University, The Graduate School, College of Arts and Sciences, Department of Computer Science, Tallahassee, FL 32306. Offers computer criminology (MS); computer network and system administration (MS); computer science (MS, PhD); cyber security (MS). *Program availability:* Part-time. *Faculty:* 26 full-time (3 women), 1 part-time/adjunct (0 women). *Students:* 153 full-time (38 women), 5 part-time (1 woman); includes 25 minority (4 Black or African American, non-Hispanic/Latino; 5 Asian, non-Hispanic/Latino; 2 Hispanic/Latino; 14 Two or more races, non-Hispanic/Latino), 90 international. Average age 28. 344 applicants, 45% accepted, 42 enrolled. In 2016, 49 master's, 6 doctorates awarded. Terminal master's awarded for partial completion of

doctoral program. *Degree requirements:* For master's, comprehensive exam (for some programs), thesis (for some programs); for doctorate, comprehensive exam, thesis/dissertation, qualifying exam, preliminary exam, prospectus defense. *Entrance requirements:* For master's, GRE General Test, minimum undergraduate GPA of 3.0; for doctorate, GRE General Test, minimum GPA of 3.0. Additional exam requirements/recommendations for international students: Required—TOEFL (minimum score 550 paper-based; 80 iBT), IELTS (minimum score 6.5). *Application deadline:* For fall admission, 6/1 for domestic students, 1/15 priority date for international students; for spring admission, 11/1 for domestic students, 9/1 priority date for international students. Applications are processed on a rolling basis. Application fee: $30. Electronic applications accepted. *Expenses:* Tuition, state resident: full-time $7263; part-time $403.51 per credit hour. Tuition, nonresident: full-time $18,087; part-time $1004.85 per credit hour. *Required fees:* $1365; $75.81 per credit hour. $20 per semester. Tuition and fees vary according to campus/location. *Financial support:* In 2016–17, 114 students received support, including 21 fellowships with full tuition reimbursements available (averaging $32,500 per year), 22 research assistantships with full tuition reimbursements available (averaging $24,387 per year), 62 teaching assistantships with full tuition reimbursements available (averaging $18,751 per year); scholarships/grants, health care benefits, tuition waivers (full), and unspecified assistantships also available. Financial award application deadline: 1/15; financial award applicants required to submit FAFSA. *Faculty research:* Embedded systems, high performance computing, networking, operating systems, security, databases, algorithms, big data, visualization. *Total annual research expenditures:* $1 million. *Unit head:* Dr. Xin Yuan, Chairman, 850-644-9133, Fax: 850-644-0058, E-mail: xyuan@cs.fsu.edu. *Application contact:* Daniel B. Clawson, Graduate Coordinator, 850-645-4975, Fax: 850-644-0058, E-mail: clawson@cs.fsu.edu.
Website: http://www.cs.fsu.edu/

Fordham University, Graduate School of Arts and Sciences, Department of Computer and Information Sciences, New York, NY 10458. Offers computer science (MS); cyber security (MS); data analytics (MS). *Program availability:* Part-time, evening/weekend. *Faculty:* 11 full-time (1 woman). *Students:* 62 full-time (12 women), 17 part-time (5 women); includes 26 minority (10 Black or African American, non-Hispanic/Latino; 10 Asian, non-Hispanic/Latino; 1 Hispanic/Latino; 5 Two or more races, non-Hispanic/Latino), 19 international. Average age 31. 104 applicants, 39% accepted, 12 enrolled. In 2016, 5 master's awarded. *Degree requirements:* For master's, thesis optional. *Entrance requirements:* For master's, GRE General Test. Additional exam requirements/recommendations for international students: Required—TOEFL (minimum score 550 paper-based). *Application deadline:* For fall admission, 1/4 priority date for domestic students; for spring admission, 11/1 for domestic students. Application fee: $70. Electronic applications accepted. *Financial support:* In 2016–17, 5 students received support, including 3 research assistantships with tuition reimbursements available (averaging $15,000 per year); career-related internships or fieldwork, institutionally sponsored loans, tuition waivers (full and partial), and unspecified assistantships also available. Financial award application deadline: 1/4; financial award applicants required to submit CSS PROFILE or FAFSA. *Faculty research:* Robotics and computer vision, data mining and informatics, information and networking, computation and algorithms, biomedical informatics. *Total annual research expenditures:* $213,000. *Unit head:* Dr. Damian Lyons, Chair, 718-817-4485, Fax: 718-817-4488, E-mail: dlyons@fordham.edu. *Application contact:* Bernadette Valentino-Morrison, Director of Graduate Admissions, 718-817-4420, Fax: 718-817-3566, E-mail: valentinomor@fordham.edu.

George Mason University, School of Business, Program in Management of Secure Information Systems, Fairfax, VA 22030. Offers MS. *Faculty:* 6 full-time (1 woman), 2 part-time/adjunct. *Students:* 21 full-time (2 women); includes 10 minority (3 Black or African American, non-Hispanic/Latino; 2 Asian, non-Hispanic/Latino; 4 Hispanic/Latino; 1 Native Hawaiian or other Pacific Islander, non-Hispanic/Latino), 1 international. Average age 36. In 2016, 29 master's awarded. *Entrance requirements:* For master's, current resume; official copies of transcripts from all colleges or universities attended; two professional letters of recommendation; goal statement; interview. Additional exam requirements/recommendations for international students: Required—TOEFL (minimum score 650 paper-based; 93 iBT), IELTS, PTE. Application fee: $75 ($80 for international students). Electronic applications accepted. *Expenses:* Tuition, state resident: full-time $10,628; part-time $443 per credit. Tuition, nonresident: full-time $29,306; part-time $1221 per credit. *Required fees:* $3096; $129 per credit. Tuition and fees vary according to program. *Financial support:* In 2016–17, 1 student received support, including 1 teaching assistantship (averaging $12,480 per year); career-related internships or fieldwork, Federal Work-Study, and scholarships/grants also available. Support available to part-time students. Financial award applicants required to submit FAFSA. *Unit head:* Kumar Mehta, Director, 703-993-9412, Fax: 703-993-1809, E-mail: kmehta1@gmu.edu. *Application contact:* Jacky Buchy, Assistant Dean of Graduate Enrollment, 703-993-1856, Fax: 703-993-1778, E-mail: jbuchy@gmu.edu.
Website: http://business.gmu.edu/cyber-security-degree/

The George Washington University, School of Engineering and Applied Science, Department of Computer Science, Washington, DC 20052. Offers computer science (MS, D Sc); cybersecurity (MS). *Program availability:* Part-time, evening/weekend. *Faculty:* 15 full-time (6 women). *Students:* 323 full-time (75 women), 171 part-time (50 women); includes 42 minority (17 Black or African American, non-Hispanic/Latino; 19 Asian, non-Hispanic/Latino; 5 Hispanic/Latino; 1 Two or more races, non-Hispanic/Latino), 372 international. Average age 28. 956 applicants, 73% accepted, 230 enrolled. In 2016, 150 master's, 8 doctorates, 19 other advanced degrees awarded. *Degree requirements:* For master's, thesis optional; for doctorate, thesis/dissertation, dissertation defense, qualifying exam. *Entrance requirements:* For master's, appropriate bachelor's degree, minimum GPA of 3.0; for doctorate, GRE (if highest earned degree is BS), appropriate bachelor's or master's degree, minimum GPA of 3.3; for other advanced degree, appropriate master's degree, minimum GPA of 3.4. Additional exam requirements/recommendations for international students: Required—TOEFL or The George Washington University English as a Foreign Language Test. *Application deadline:* For fall admission, 3/1 priority date for domestic students; for spring admission, 10/1 for domestic students. Applications are processed on a rolling basis. Application fee: $75. *Financial support:* In 2016–17, 49 students received support. Fellowships with tuition reimbursements available, research assistantships, teaching assistantships with tuition reimbursements available, career-related internships or fieldwork, institutionally sponsored loans, and tuition waivers available. Financial award application deadline: 3/1; financial award applicants required to submit FAFSA. *Faculty research:* Computer graphics, multimedia, VLSI, parallel processing. *Unit head:* Prof. Abdou Youssef, Chair, 202-994-4953, E-mail: ayoussef@gwu.edu. *Application contact:* Adina Lav, Marketing, Recruiting and Admissions, 202-994-5827, Fax: 202-994-0909, E-mail: engineering@gwu.edu.
Website: http://www.cs.gwu.edu/

Georgia Institute of Technology, Graduate Studies, College of Computing, Program in Information Security, Atlanta, GA 30332-0001. Offers MS. *Program availability:* Part-time. *Entrance requirements:* For master's, GRE General Test. Additional exam requirements/recommendations for international students: Required—TOEFL (minimum score 600 paper-based; 100 iBT). Electronic applications accepted.

Computer and Information Systems Security

Hampton University, School of Science, Program in Information Assurance, Hampton, VA 23668. Offers MS. *Faculty:* 5 full-time (2 women), 2 part-time/adjunct. *Students:* 3 full-time (2 women); includes 2 minority (both Black or African American, non-Hispanic/Latino). Average age 28. 4 applicants, 50% accepted, 2 enrolled. In 2016, 3 master's awarded. *Expenses: Tuition:* Full-time $10,776; part-time $548 per credit hour. *Required fees:* $35; $35 per credit hour. Tuition and fees vary according to course load and program. *Unit head:* Dr. Chutima Boonthum-Denecke, Director, 757-727-5082.

Harrisburg University of Science and Technology, Program in Information Systems Engineering and Management, Harrisburg, PA 17101. Offers analytics (MS); digital government (MS); digital health (MS); entrepreneurship (MS); information security (MS); software engineering and systems development (MS). *Program availability:* Part-time, evening/weekend. *Faculty:* 9 full-time (0 women), 1 (woman) part-time/adjunct. *Students:* 1,031 full-time (264 women), 35 part-time (10 women); includes 2 minority (1 Black or African American, non-Hispanic/Latino; 1 Asian, non-Hispanic/Latino), 1,060 international. In 2016, 83 master's awarded. *Degree requirements:* For master's, thesis optional. *Entrance requirements:* For master's, baccalaureate degree. Additional exam requirements/recommendations for international students: Required—TOEFL (minimum score 520 paper-based; 80 iBT); Recommended—IELTS (minimum score 6). *Application deadline:* Applications are processed on a rolling basis. Application fee: $0. Electronic applications accepted. *Expenses: Tuition:* Full-time $4800; part-time $800 per semester hour. *Financial support:* In 2016–17, 2 students received support. Teaching assistantships available. Financial award applicants required to submit FAFSA. *Faculty research:* Healthcare Informatics, material analysis, enterprise systems, circuit design, enterprise architectures. *Unit head:* Dr. Amjad Umar, Director and Professor, 717-901-5141, Fax: 717-901-3141, E-mail: aumar@harrisburgu.edu.

Hofstra University, School of Engineering and Applied Science, Hempstead, NY 11549. Offers computer science (MS), including cybersecurity, Web engineering. *Program availability:* Part-time, evening/weekend, blended/hybrid learning. *Faculty:* 10 full-time (3 women), 6 part-time/adjunct (1 woman). *Students:* 34 full-time (8 women), 20 part-time (5 women); includes 13 minority (1 American Indian or Alaska Native, non-Hispanic/Latino; 6 Asian, non-Hispanic/Latino; 4 Hispanic/Latino; 1 Native Hawaiian or other Pacific Islander, non-Hispanic/Latino; 1 Two or more races, non-Hispanic/Latino), 20 international. Average age 30. 48 applicants, 90% accepted, 15 enrolled. In 2016, 12 master's awarded. *Degree requirements:* For master's, thesis optional, 30 credits, minimum GPA of 3.0. *Entrance requirements:* For master's, GRE, minimum GPA of 3.0. Additional exam requirements/recommendations for international students: Required—TOEFL (minimum score 550 paper-based; 80 iBT). *Application deadline:* Applications are processed on a rolling basis. Application fee: $75. Electronic applications accepted. *Expenses: Tuition:* Full-time $1240. *Required fees:* $970. Tuition and fees vary according to program. *Financial support:* In 2016–17, 24 students received support, including 6 fellowships with full and partial tuition reimbursements available (averaging $2,647 per year); research assistantships with full and partial tuition reimbursements available, career-related internships or fieldwork, Federal Work-Study, institutionally sponsored loans, scholarships/grants, tuition waivers (full and partial), and unspecified assistantships also available. Support available to part-time students. Financial award applicants required to submit FAFSA. *Faculty research:* Data mining; system and network security; cell and tissue engineering; experimental fluid mechanics; stem education. *Total annual research expenditures:* $1.5 million. *Unit head:* Dr. Sina Rabbany, Dean, 516-463-6672, E-mail: sina.y.rabbany@hofstra.edu. *Application contact:* Sunil Samuel, Assistant Vice President of Admissions, 516-463-4723, Fax: 516-463-4664, E-mail: graduateadmission@hofstra.edu.
Website: http://www.hofstra.edu/academics/colleges/seas/

Hood College, Graduate School, Programs in Computer and Information Sciences, Frederick, MD 21701-8575. Offers computer science (MS); cyber security (Certificate); information technology (MS). *Program availability:* Part-time, evening/weekend. *Faculty:* 7 full-time, 8 part-time/adjunct. *Students:* 82 full-time (29 women), 51 part-time (13 women); includes 8 minority (2 Black or African American, non-Hispanic/Latino; 4 Asian, non-Hispanic/Latino; 1 Hispanic/Latino; 1 Two or more races, non-Hispanic/Latino), 89 international. Average age 30. 79 applicants, 84% accepted, 36 enrolled. In 2016, 75 master's, 35 other advanced degrees awarded. *Degree requirements:* For master's, thesis optional. *Entrance requirements:* For master's, minimum GPA of 2.75, essay, resume. Additional exam requirements/recommendations for international students: Required—TOEFL (minimum score 575 paper-based; 89 iBT), IELTS (minimum score 6.5). *Application deadline:* For fall admission, 8/15 priority date for domestic students, 8/5 for international students; for spring admission, 12/1 priority date for domestic students, 12/1 for international students; for summer admission, 5/1 for domestic students, 4/15 for international students. Applications are processed on a rolling basis. Application fee: $35. Electronic applications accepted. *Expenses:* $475 per credit hour; $110 comprehensive fee per semester. *Financial support:* Tuition waivers (partial) and unspecified assistantships available. Financial award applicants required to submit FAFSA. *Faculty research:* Systems engineering, natural language, processing, database design, artificial intelligence and parallel distributed computing. *Unit head:* April Boulton, Interim Dean of the Graduate School, 301-696-3600, E-mail: gofurther@hood.edu. *Application contact:* Spencer Berk, Assistant Director of Graduate Admissions, 301-696-3600, E-mail: gofurther@hood.edu.
Website: http://www.hood.edu/graduate

Illinois Institute of Technology, Graduate College, College of Science, Department of Computer Science, Chicago, IL 60616. Offers business (MCS); computational intelligence (MCS); computer science (MCS, MS, PhD); cyber-physical systems (MCS); data analytics (MCS); data science (MAS); database systems (MCS); distributed and cloud computing (MCS); education (MCS); finance (MCS); information security and assurance (MCS); networking and communications (MCS); software engineering (MCS); telecommunications and software engineering (MAS); MS/MAS. *Program availability:* Part-time, evening/weekend, online learning. Terminal master's awarded for partial completion of doctoral program. *Degree requirements:* For master's, thesis optional; for doctorate, comprehensive exam, thesis/dissertation. *Entrance requirements:* For master's, GRE General Test with minimum scores of 298 Quantitative and Verbal, 3.0 Analytical Writing (for MS); GRE General Test with minimum scores of 292 Quantitative and Verbal, 2.5 Analytical Writing (for MAS), minimum undergraduate GPA of 3.0; for doctorate, GRE General Test (minimum scores: 304 Quantitative and Verbal, 3.5 Analytical Writing), minimum undergraduate GPA of 3.0. Additional exam requirements/recommendations for international students: Required—TOEFL (minimum score 523 paper-based; 70 iBT). Electronic applications accepted. *Faculty research:* Parallel and distributed processing, high-performance computing, computational linguistics, information retrieval, data mining, grid computing.

Illinois Institute of Technology, Graduate College, School of Applied Technology, Department of Information Technology and Management, Wheaton, IL 60189. Offers cyber forensics and security (MAS); information technology and management (MAS). *Program availability:* Part-time, evening/weekend, online learning. *Entrance requirements:* For master's, GRE (minimum score 300 Quantitative and Verbal, 2.5 Analytical Writing), bachelor's degree with minimum cumulative undergraduate GPA of 3.0 (or its equivalent) from accredited institution. Additional exam requirements/recommendations for international students: Required—TOEFL (minimum score 523 paper-based; 70 iBT); Recommended—IELTS (minimum score 5.5). Electronic applications accepted. *Faculty research:* Database design, voice over IP, process engineering, object-oriented programming, computer networking, online design, system administration.

Indiana University Bloomington, School of Informatics and Computing, Program in Informatics, Bloomington, IN 47405. Offers informatics (MS, PhD), including bioinformatics (PhD), complex systems (PhD), computing, culture and society (PhD), health informatics (PhD), human-computer interaction (MS), human-computer interaction design (PhD), music informatics (PhD), security informatics (PhD); visual heritage (PhD). *Program availability:* Part-time. *Faculty:* 75 full-time (15 women). *Students:* 206 full-time (85 women), 10 part-time (3 women); includes 30 minority (11 Black or African American, non-Hispanic/Latino; 10 Asian, non-Hispanic/Latino; 5 Hispanic/Latino; 4 Two or more races, non-Hispanic/Latino), 95 international. Average age 28. 395 applicants, 36% accepted, 69 enrolled. In 2016, 50 master's, 11 doctorates awarded. Terminal master's awarded for partial completion of doctoral program. *Degree requirements:* For master's, thesis, capstone project; for doctorate, variable foreign language requirement, comprehensive exam, thesis/dissertation. *Entrance requirements:* For master's and doctorate, GRE, resume/curriculum vitae, transcripts, 3 letters of recommendation. Additional exam requirements/recommendations for international students: Required—TOEFL (minimum score 600 paper-based; 100 iBT). *Application deadline:* For fall admission, 12/1 priority date for domestic and international students. Application fee: $55 ($65 for international students). Electronic applications accepted. *Financial support:* Fellowships, research assistantships, scholarships/grants, health care benefits, and unspecified assistantships available. Financial award application deadline: 12/1. *Faculty research:* Algorithms, applied logic and computational theory, artificial intelligence, bioinformatics, case-based reasoning, chemical informatics, citation analysis, cognitive science, community informatics, compilers, complex networks and systems, computer optimization, computer-supported cooperative work, computer vision, cyberinfrastructure and e-science, database theory and systems, data mining, digital design and preservation, design pedagogy, digital humanities, digital learning environments. *Total annual research expenditures:* $19.4 million. *Unit head:* Dr. Martin Siegel, Director of Graduate Studies, 812-856-3960, E-mail: msiegel@indiana.edu. *Application contact:* Informatics Graduate Studies Office, 812-856-3960, E-mail: infograd@indiana.edu.
Website: http://www.informatics.indiana.edu/graduate/index.html

Indiana University–Purdue University Indianapolis, School of Engineering and Technology, MS in Technology Program, Indianapolis, IN 46202. Offers applied data management and analytics (MS); facilities management (MS); information security and assurance (MS); motorsports (MS); organizational leadership (MS); technical communication (MS). *Program availability:* Online learning.

Indiana University–Purdue University Indianapolis, School of Science, Department of Computer and Information Science, Indianapolis, IN 46202-5132. Offers biocomputing (Graduate Certificate); biometrics (Graduate Certificate); computer science (MS, PhD); computer security (Graduate Certificate); databases and data mining (Graduate Certificate); software engineering (Graduate Certificate). *Program availability:* Part-time. *Faculty:* 16 full-time (2 women), 10 part-time/adjunct (4 women). *Students:* 95 full-time (36 women), 44 part-time (15 women); includes 8 minority (3 Black or African American, non-Hispanic/Latino; 5 Asian, non-Hispanic/Latino), 119 international. Average age 27. 275 applicants, 30% accepted, 41 enrolled. In 2016, 52 master's, 3 doctorates, 3 other advanced degrees awarded. Terminal master's awarded for partial completion of doctoral program. *Degree requirements:* For master's and Graduate Certificate, thesis optional; for doctorate, thesis/dissertation. *Entrance requirements:* For master's and doctorate, GRE, BS in computer science or the equivalent with a minimum GPA of 3.0 (or equivalent); for Graduate Certificate, BS in computer science or the equivalent with a minimum GPA of 3.0 (or equivalent). Additional exam requirements/recommendations for international students: Required—PTE (minimum score 58), TOEFL (minimum score 550 paper-based; 79 iBT) or IELTS (6.5). *Application deadline:* For fall admission, 1/15 priority date for domestic and international students; for spring admission, 9/15 for domestic students. Application fee: $60 ($65 for international students). *Financial support:* In 2016–17, 45 students received support, including 2 fellowships with full tuition reimbursements available (averaging $20,000 per year), 15 research assistantships with full and partial tuition reimbursements available (averaging $18,000 per year), 20 teaching assistantships with full and partial tuition reimbursements available (averaging $18,000 per year); scholarships/grants, health care benefits, and tuition waivers (full and partial) also available. Financial award application deadline: 1/15. *Faculty research:* Imaging and visualization; networking and security; software engineering; distributed and parallel computing; database, data mining and machine learning. *Total annual research expenditures:* $550,196. *Unit head:* Dr. Shiaofen Fang, Chair, 317-274-9727, Fax: 317-274-9742, E-mail: sfang@cs.iupui.edu. *Application contact:* Nicole Wittlief, Graduate Admissions and Program Coordinator, 317-274-3883, Fax: 317-274-9742, E-mail: wittlief@cs.iupui.edu.
Website: http://www.cs.iupui.edu/

Inter American University of Puerto Rico, Guayama Campus, Department of Natural and Applied Sciences, Guayama, PR 00785. Offers computer security and networks (MS); networking and security (MCS).

Iona College, School of Arts and Science, Department of Computer Science, New Rochelle, NY 10801-1890. Offers computer science (MS); cyber security (MS); game development (MS). *Program availability:* Part-time, evening/weekend. *Faculty:* 6 full-time (3 women), 1 (woman) part-time/adjunct. *Students:* 13 full-time (2 women), 9 part-time (1 woman); includes 4 minority (2 Black or African American, non-Hispanic/Latino; 2 Hispanic/Latino), 8 international. Average age 27. 28 applicants, 79% accepted, 6 enrolled. In 2016, 7 master's awarded. *Degree requirements:* For master's, thesis optional. *Entrance requirements:* For master's, minimum GPA of 3.0. Additional exam requirements/recommendations for international students: Required—TOEFL (minimum score 550 paper-based; 80 iBT), IELTS (minimum score 6.5). *Application deadline:* For fall admission, 8/1 priority date for domestic students, 5/1 priority date for international students; for spring admission, 1/1 priority date for domestic students, 9/1 priority date for international students. Applications are processed on a rolling basis. Application fee: $50. Electronic applications accepted. *Expenses: Tuition:* Full-time $19,692; part-time $1094 per credit. *Required fees:* $245 per term. Tuition and fees vary according to program. *Financial support:* In 2016–17, 7 students received support, including 2 research assistantships with full tuition reimbursements available; tuition waivers (partial) and unspecified assistantships also available. Support available to part-time students. Financial award application deadline: 4/15; financial award applicants required to submit FAFSA. *Faculty research:* Parallel procession, data mining, machine learning, cyber security, medical imaging. *Unit head:* Robert Schiaffino, PhD, Chair, 914-633-2338, E-mail: rschiaffino@iona.edu. *Application contact:* Katelyn Brunck, Assistant Director, Graduate Admissions, 914-633-2451, Fax: 914-633-2277, E-mail: kbrunck@iona.edu.
Website: http://www.iona.edu/Academics/School-of-Arts-Science/Departments/Computer-Science/Graduate-Programs.aspx

Iona College, School of Arts and Science, Department of Criminal Justice, New Rochelle, NY 10801-1890. Offers criminal justice (MS); cybercrime and security (AC); forensic criminology and criminal justice systems (Certificate). *Program availability:* Part-time, evening/weekend. *Faculty:* 2 full-time (0 women), 4 part-time/adjunct (1 woman). *Students:* 8 full-time (6 women), 14 part-time (4 women); includes 9 minority (5 Black or African American, non-Hispanic/Latino; 4 Hispanic/Latino), 1 international. Average age 26. 11 applicants, 100% accepted, 7 enrolled. In 2016, 12 master's, 3 other advanced degrees awarded. *Degree requirements:* For master's, thesis (for some programs), thesis or literature review. *Entrance requirements:* For master's, minimum GPA of 3.0. Additional exam requirements/recommendations for international students: Required—TOEFL (minimum score 550 paper-based; 80 iBT), IELTS (minimum score 6.5). *Application deadline:* For fall admission, 8/1 priority date for domestic students, 5/1 priority date for international students; for spring admission, 1/1 priority date for domestic students, 9/1 priority date for international students. Applications are processed on a rolling basis. Application fee: $50. Electronic applications accepted. *Expenses: Tuition:* Full-time $19,692; part-time $1094 per credit. *Required fees:* $245 per term. Tuition and fees vary according to program. *Financial support:* In 2016–17, 13 students received support. Unspecified assistantships available. Financial award application deadline: 4/15; financial award applicants required to submit FAFSA. *Faculty research:* Juvenile justice, criminology, victimology, policing, social justice, security threat assessment. *Unit head:* Cathryn Lavery, PhD, Chair, 914-633-2597, E-mail: clavery@iona.edu. *Application contact:* Katelyn Brunck, Assistant Director of Graduate Admissions, 914-633-2451, Fax: 914-633-2277, E-mail: kbrunck@iona.edu.
Website: http://www.iona.edu/Academics/School-of-Arts-Science/Departments/Criminal-Justice/Graduate-Programs.aspx

James Madison University, The Graduate School, College of Integrated Science and Engineering, Program in Computer Science, Harrisonburg, VA 22802. Offers digital forensics (MS); information security (MS). *Program availability:* Online learning. *Faculty:* 15 full-time (1 woman), 1 part-time/adjunct (0 women). *Students:* 7 full-time (3 women), 21 part-time (4 women); includes 6 minority (3 Black or African American, non-Hispanic/Latino; 1 Asian, non-Hispanic/Latino; 1 Hispanic/Latino; 1 Two or more races, non-Hispanic/Latino), 3 international. Average age 30. 29 applicants, 97% accepted, 18 enrolled. In 2016, 15 master's awarded. Application fee: $55. Electronic applications accepted. *Financial support:* Fellowships, Federal Work-Study, and 3 assistantships (averaging $7911) available. Financial award application deadline: 3/1; financial award applicants required to submit FAFSA. *Unit head:* Dr. Sharon J. Simmons, Department Head, 540-568-4196, E-mail: simmonsj@jmu.edu. *Application contact:* Lynette D. Michael, Director of Graduate Admissions, 540-568-6131 Ext. 6395, Fax: 540-568-7860, E-mail: michaeld@jmu.edu.
Website: http://www.jmu.edu/cs/

Johns Hopkins University, Engineering Program for Professionals, Part-time Program in Cybersecurity, Baltimore, MD 21218. Offers MS, Post-Master's Certificate. *Program availability:* Part-time, evening/weekend, 100% online, blended/hybrid learning. *Faculty:* 17 part-time/adjunct (3 women). *Students:* 5 full-time (1 woman), 95 part-time (21 women); includes 20 minority (9 Black or African American, non-Hispanic/Latino; 5 Asian, non-Hispanic/Latino; 5 Hispanic/Latino; 1 Two or more races, non-Hispanic/Latino), 4 international. Average age 32. 98 applicants, 27% accepted, 15 enrolled. In 2016, 14 master's awarded. *Entrance requirements:* Additional exam requirements/recommendations for international students: Required—TOEFL (minimum score 600 paper-based; 100 iBT). Application fee: $0. Electronic applications accepted. *Unit head:* Dr. Thomas A. Longstaff, Program Chair, 443-778-9389, E-mail: thomas.longstaff@jhuapl.edu. *Application contact:* Doug Schiller, Admissions Director, 410-516-2300, Fax: 410-579-8049, E-mail: schiller@jhu.edu.
Website: http://ep.jhu.edu/graduate-programs/cybersecurity

Johns Hopkins University, G. W. C. Whiting School of Engineering, Master of Science in Security Informatics Program, Baltimore, MD 21218. Offers MSSI. *Faculty:* 6 full-time (1 woman), 11 part-time/adjunct (0 women). *Students:* 69 full-time (17 women), 29 part-time (5 women); includes 7 minority (1 Black or African American, non-Hispanic/Latino; 2 Asian, non-Hispanic/Latino; 3 Hispanic/Latino; 1 Two or more races, non-Hispanic/Latino), 84 international. Average age 24. 167 applicants, 72% accepted, 54 enrolled. In 2016, 31 master's awarded. *Degree requirements:* For master's, 10 courses, capstone project. *Entrance requirements:* For master's, GRE, minimum GPA of 3.0, 2 letters of recommendation, statement of purpose, transcripts. Additional exam requirements/recommendations for international students: Required—TOEFL (minimum score 600 paper-based, 100 iBT) or IELTS (7). *Application deadline:* For fall admission, 3/1 for domestic and international students; for spring admission, 11/15 for domestic students, 9/15 for international students. Applications are processed on a rolling basis. Application fee: $75. Electronic applications accepted. *Financial support:* In 2016–17, 5 students received support, including 2 fellowships with full tuition reimbursements available (averaging $34,000 per year); career-related internships or fieldwork, Federal Work-Study, institutionally sponsored loans, scholarships/grants, traineeships, health care benefits, tuition waivers (partial), and unspecified assistantships also available. Financial award application deadline: 1/31. *Faculty research:* Cryptography and encryption methodologies; security and privacy in applications such as electronic voting, consumer transactions and electronic medical records; security in healthcare it; bitcoin and electronic currencies; security policy and management. *Total annual research expenditures:* $1.3 million. *Unit head:* Dr. Anton Dahbura, Executive Director, 410-516-0211, Fax: 410-516-3301, E-mail: antondahbura@jhu.edu. *Application contact:* Zach Burwell, Academic Program Administrator, 410-516-7451, Fax: 410-516-3301, E-mail: zburwel1@jhu.edu.
Website: http://www.jhuisi.jhu.edu/

Johnson & Wales University, Graduate Studies, MS Program in Information Security/Assurance, Providence, RI 02903-3703. Offers MS. *Program availability:* Online learning.

Kaplan University, Davenport Campus, School of Information Technology, Davenport, IA 52807. Offers decision support systems (MS); information security and assurance (MS). *Program availability:* Part-time, evening/weekend, online learning. *Entrance requirements:* Additional exam requirements/recommendations for international students: Required—TOEFL (minimum score 550 paper-based; 80 iBT).

Keiser University, Master of Business Administration Program, Ft. Lauderdale, FL 33309. Offers accounting (MBA); health services management (MBA); information security management (MBA); international business (MBA); leadership for managers (MBA); marketing (MBA). All concentrations except information security management also offered in Mandarin; leadership for managers and international business also offered in Spanish. *Program availability:* Part-time, online learning.

Keiser University, MS in Information Security Program, Ft. Lauderdale, FL 33309. Offers MS.

Kennesaw State University, College of Computing and Software Engineering, Department of Information Technology, Kennesaw, GA 30144. Offers health information technology (Postbaccalaureate Certificate); information security and assurance (Graduate Certificate); information technology (MSIT, Graduate Certificate); information technology fundamentals (Postbaccalaureate Certificate). *Program availability:* Part-time, evening/weekend, online learning. *Degree requirements:* For master's, thesis optional. *Entrance requirements:* For master's, minimum GPA of 2.75; for other advanced degree, bachelor's degree. Additional exam requirements/recommendations for international students: Required—TOEFL (minimum score 550 paper-based; 79 iBT), IELTS (minimum score 6.5). Electronic applications accepted. *Faculty research:* IT ethics, user interface design, IT security, IT integration, IT management, health information technology, business intelligence, networks, business continuity.

Kent State University, School of Digital Sciences, Kent, OH 44242-0001. Offers digital sciences (MDS), including data sciences; digital sciences management (MDS); digital sciences software development (MDS); digital sciences telecommunication network (MDS); digital sciences training technology (MDS); enterprise architecture (MDS). *Program availability:* Part-time. *Students:* 409 full-time (153 women), 156 part-time (51 women); includes 1 minority (Asian, non-Hispanic/Latino), 539 international. Average age 24. 617 applicants, 67% accepted, 94 enrolled. In 2016, 231 master's awarded. *Degree requirements:* For master's, thesis optional, capstone. *Entrance requirements:* For master's, minimum GPA of 3.0, transcripts, goal statement, resume, 3 letters of recommendation. Additional exam requirements/recommendations for international students: Required—TOEFL (minimum score of 525 paper-based, 71 iBT), IELTS (minimum score of 6), Michigan English Language Assessment Battery (minimum score of 75), or PTE (minimum score of 48). *Application deadline:* For fall admission, 7/1 for domestic students, 5/15 for international students; for spring admission, 11/15 for domestic students, 10/15 for international students; for summer admission, 4/15 for domestic students, 3/15 for international students. Applications are processed on a rolling basis. Application fee: $45 ($70 for international students). Electronic applications accepted. *Expenses:* Tuition, state resident: full-time $10,864; part-time $495 per credit hour. Tuition, nonresident: full-time $18,380; part-time $837 per credit hour. *Financial support:* Career-related internships or fieldwork available. *Unit head:* Jeffery Fruit, Interim Director, 330-672-9105, E-mail: jfruit@kent.edu. *Application contact:* Amy Copus, Academic Advisor II for Graduate Students, 330-672-9105, E-mail: acopus@kent.edu.
Website: http://www.kent.edu/dsci

Lawrence Technological University, College of Management, Southfield, MI 48075-1058. Offers business administration (MBA), including business analytics (MBA, MS), finance, information technology, marketing, project management (MBA, MS); information technology (MS), including business analytics (MBA, MS), information assurance, project management (MBA, MS); project management (Graduate Certificate). *Accreditation:* ACBSP. *Program availability:* Part-time, evening/weekend, 100% online. *Faculty:* 14 full-time (6 women), 10 part-time/adjunct (2 women). *Students:* 7 full-time (3 women), 323 part-time (120 women); includes 60 minority (29 Black or African American, non-Hispanic/Latino; 2 American Indian or Alaska Native, non-Hispanic/Latino; 17 Asian, non-Hispanic/Latino; 8 Hispanic/Latino; 4 Two or more races, non-Hispanic/Latino), 118 international. Average age 33. 275 applicants, 56% accepted, 72 enrolled. In 2016, 167 master's, 12 other advanced degrees awarded. Terminal master's awarded for partial completion of doctoral program. *Degree requirements:* For master's, thesis (for some programs). *Entrance requirements:* Additional exam requirements/recommendations for international students: Required—TOEFL (minimum score 550 paper-based; 79 iBT), IELTS (minimum score 6.5). *Application deadline:* For fall admission, 5/22 for international students; for spring admission, 10/11 for international students; for summer admission, 2/16 for international students. Applications are processed on a rolling basis. Application fee: $50. Electronic applications accepted. *Expenses: Tuition:* Full-time $14,868; part-time $1062 per credit. *Required fees:* $75 per semester. Tuition and fees vary according to campus/location. *Financial support:* In 2016–17, 35 students received support, including 8 research assistantships with partial tuition reimbursements available (averaging $3,250 per year); career-related internships or fieldwork, unspecified assistantships, and corporate tuition incentives also available. Financial award application deadline: 4/1; financial award applicants required to submit FAFSA. *Faculty research:* Cybersecurity; risk management; IT governance; security controls and countermeasures; threat modeling cyber resilience; autonomous cars; natural language processing; text mining; machine learning; reflective leadership; emerging leadership theories and practice; motivational studies; teaching effectiveness strategies; teamwork; organization development; strategic planning; strengths-based and positive organizational scholarship; global leadership; globalization; corporate governance. *Unit head:* Dr. Bahman Mirshab, Dean, 248-204-3050, E-mail: mgtdean@ltu.edu. *Application contact:* Jane Rohrback, Director of Admissions, 248-204-3160, Fax: 248-204-2228, E-mail: admissions@ltu.edu.
Website: http://www.ltu.edu/management/index.asp

Lewis University, College of Arts and Sciences, Program in Information Security, Romeoville, IL 60446. Offers management (MS); technical (MS). Program offered jointly with College of Business. *Program availability:* Part-time, evening/weekend, 100% online, blended/hybrid learning. *Students:* 26 full-time (1 woman), 59 part-time (19 women); includes 23 minority (11 Black or African American, non-Hispanic/Latino; 2 Asian, non-Hispanic/Latino; 7 Hispanic/Latino; 1 Native Hawaiian or other Pacific Islander, non-Hispanic/Latino; 2 Two or more races, non-Hispanic/Latino), 18 international. Average age 32. *Entrance requirements:* For master's, bachelor's degree, minimum GPA of 3.0, resume, 2-page statement of purpose, 3 letters of recommendation. Additional exam requirements/recommendations for international students: Required—TOEFL (minimum score 550 paper-based; 80 iBT). *Application deadline:* For fall admission, 5/1 priority date for international students; for spring admission, 11/15 priority date for international students. Applications are processed on a rolling basis. Application fee: $40. Electronic applications accepted. *Expenses: Tuition:* Full-time $13,860; part-time $770 per credit hour. *Required fees:* $75 per semester. Tuition and fees vary according to degree level and program. *Financial support:* Federal Work-Study and unspecified assistantships available. Financial award application deadline: 5/1; financial award applicants required to submit FAFSA. *Total annual research expenditures:* $33. *Unit head:* Dr. Raymond Klump, Program Director, 815-836-5528, E-mail: klumpra@lewisu.edu. *Application contact:* Office of Graduate Admission, 800-897-9000 Ext. 5610, E-mail: grad@lewisu.edu.
Website: http://www.lewisu.edu/academics/msinfosec/index.htm

Lewis University, College of Business, Graduate School of Management, Romeoville, IL 60446. Offers business administration (MBA), including accounting, custom elective option, e-business, finance, healthcare management, human resources management, international business, management information systems, marketing, project management, technology and operations management; business analytics (MS), including financial analytics, healthcare analytics, marketing analytics, operations analytics; finance (MS); information security-managerial (MA); project management (MS). *Accreditation:* ACBSP. *Program availability:* Part-time, evening/weekend, 100% online, blended/hybrid learning. *Students:* 2 part-time (1 woman). Average age 32. *Entrance requirements:* Additional exam requirements/recommendations for international students: Required—TOEFL. *Application deadline:* Applications are processed on a rolling basis. Application fee: $40. Electronic applications accepted. *Expenses: Tuition:* Full-time $13,860; part-time $770 per credit hour. *Required fees:* $75 per semester. Tuition and fees vary according to degree level and program. *Financial support:* Career-related internships or fieldwork, Federal Work-Study, and unspecified assistantships available. Financial award application deadline: 5/1; financial award applicants required to submit FAFSA. *Unit head:* Dr. Rami Khasawneh, Dean, 800-838-0500 Ext. 5360, E-mail: khasawra@lewisu.edu. *Application contact:* Michele Ryan, Director of Admission, 815-836-5384, E-mail: gsm@lewisu.edu.

Liberty University, School of Business, Lynchburg, VA 24515. Offers accounting (MBA, MS); business administration (MBA); criminal justice (MBA); cyber security (MS); executive leadership (MA); information systems (MS), including information assurance, technology management; international business (MBA, DBA); leadership (DBA); marketing (MBA, MS, DBA), including digital marketing and advertising (MS), project management (MS), public relations (MS), sports marketing and media (MS); project management (MBA, DBA); public administration (MBA); public relations (MBA). *Program availability:* Part-time, online learning. *Students:* 1,458 full-time (807 women), 4,188 part-time (2,041 women); includes 1,372 minority (1,060 Black or African American, non-Hispanic/Latino; 19 American Indian or Alaska Native, non-Hispanic/Latino; 85 Asian, non-Hispanic/Latino; 75 Hispanic/Latino; 10 Native Hawaiian or other Pacific Islander, non-Hispanic/Latino; 123 Two or more races, non-Hispanic/Latino), 124 international. Average age 35. 5,424 applicants, 45% accepted, 1242 enrolled. In 2016, 1,859 master's, 87 other advanced degrees awarded. *Entrance requirements:* For master's, minimum undergraduate GPA of 3.0, 15 hours of upper-level business courses. Additional exam requirements/recommendations for international students: Required—TOEFL (minimum score 600 paper-based; 100 iBT). *Application deadline:* Applications are processed on a rolling basis. Application fee: $50. Electronic applications accepted. *Expenses:* Contact institution. *Financial support:* Applicants required to submit FAFSA. *Unit head:* Dr. Scott Hicks, Dean, 434-592-4808, Fax: 434-582-2366, E-mail: smhicks@liberty.edu. *Application contact:* Jay Bridge, Director of Graduate Admissions, 800-424-9595, Fax: 800-628-7977, E-mail: gradadmissions@liberty.edu.
Website: http://www.liberty.edu/academics/business/index.cfm?PID-149

Liberty University, School of Engineering and Computational Sciences, Lynchburg, VA 24515. Offers cyber security (MS). *Program availability:* Part-time, online learning. *Students:* 44 full-time (10 women), 145 part-time (18 women); includes 53 minority (38 Black or African American, non-Hispanic/Latino; 1 American Indian or Alaska Native, non-Hispanic/Latino; 6 Asian, non-Hispanic/Latino; 1 Hispanic/Latino; 1 Native Hawaiian or other Pacific Islander, non-Hispanic/Latino; 6 Two or more races, non-Hispanic/Latino), 3 international. Average age 37. 223 applicants, 24% accepted, 24 enrolled. In 2016, 27 master's awarded. *Entrance requirements:* For master's, baccalaureate degree or its equivalent in computer science, information technology, or other technical degree, or baccalaureate degree in any field along with significant technical work experience. *Application deadline:* Applications are processed on a rolling basis. Application fee: $50. Electronic applications accepted. *Financial support:* Applicants required to submit FAFSA. *Unit head:* David Donahoo, Dean, 434-592-7150. *Application contact:* Jay Bridge, Director of Admissions, 800-424-9595, Fax: 800-628-7977, E-mail: gradadmissions@liberty.edu.

Lindenwood University, Graduate Programs, School of Accelerated Degree Programs, St. Charles, MO 63301-1695. Offers administration (MSA), including management, marketing, project management; business administration (MBA); communications (MA), including digital and multimedia, media management, promotions, training and development; criminal justice and administration (MS); healthcare administration (MS); human resource management (MS); information technology (Certificate); managing information security (MS); managing information technology (MS); managing virtualization and cloud computing (MS); writing (MFA). *Program availability:* Part-time, evening/weekend, 100% online. *Faculty:* 16 full-time (7 women), 75 part-time/adjunct (27 women). *Students:* 609 full-time (386 women), 179 part-time (121 women); includes 257 minority (202 Black or African American, non-Hispanic/Latino; 4 American Indian or Alaska Native, non-Hispanic/Latino; 5 Asian, non-Hispanic/Latino; 28 Hispanic/Latino; 1 Native Hawaiian or other Pacific Islander, non-Hispanic/Latino; 17 Two or more races, non-Hispanic/Latino), 28 international. Average age 36. 332 applicants, 70% accepted, 205 enrolled. In 2016, 479 master's awarded. *Degree requirements:* For master's, thesis (for some programs), minimum cumulative GPA of 3.0; for Certificate, minimum cumulative GPA of 3.0. *Entrance requirements:* For master's, resume, personal statement, official undergraduate transcript, minimum undergraduate cumulative GPA of 3.0. Additional exam requirements/recommendations for international students: Required—TOEFL (minimum score 550 paper-based; 80 iBT); Recommended—IELTS (minimum score 6.5). *Application deadline:* For fall admission, 9/26 priority date for domestic and international students; for winter admission, 1/3 priority date for domestic and international students; for spring admission, 3/31 priority date for domestic and international students; for summer admission, 7/3 priority date for domestic and international students. Applications are processed on a rolling basis. Application fee: $30 ($100 for international students). Electronic applications accepted. *Expenses: Tuition:* Full-time $15,672; part-time $453 per credit hour. *Required fees:* $205 per semester. Tuition and fees vary according to course level, course load and degree level. *Financial support:* In 2016–17, 467 students received support. Career-related internships or fieldwork, institutionally sponsored loans, scholarships/grants, tuition waivers (partial), and unspecified assistantships available. Financial award application deadline: 6/30; financial award applicants required to submit FAFSA. *Unit head:* Dr. Gina Ganahl, Dean, Accelerated Degree Programs, 636-949-4501, Fax: 636-949-4505, E-mail: gganahl@lindenwood.edu. *Application contact:* Tyler Kostich, Director, Evening and Graduate Admissions, 636-949-4138, Fax: 636-949-4109, E-mail: adultadmissions@lindenwood.edu.
Website: http://www.lindenwood.edu/academics/academic-schools/school-of-accelerated-degree-programs/

Lipscomb University, College of Business, Nashville, TN 37204-3951. Offers accountancy (M Acc); accounting (MBA); business administration (MM); conflict management (MBA); financial services (MBA); health care informatics (MBA); healthcare management (MBA); information security (MBA); leadership (MBA); nonprofit management (MBA); professional accountancy (Certificate); sports management (MBA); strategic human resources (MBA); sustainability (MBA); MBA/MS; Pharm D/MM. *Accreditation:* ACBSP. *Program availability:* Part-time, evening/weekend. *Faculty:* 22 full-time (4 women), 12 part-time/adjunct (4 women). *Students:* 112 full-time (51 women), 69 part-time (34 women); includes 30 minority (17 Black or African American, non-Hispanic/Latino; 3 Asian, non-Hispanic/Latino; 8 Hispanic/Latino; 2 Two or more races, non-Hispanic/Latino), 5 international. Average age 32. 244 applicants, 55% accepted, 54 enrolled. In 2016, 164 master's awarded. *Entrance requirements:* For master's, GMAT, transcripts, interview, 2 references, resume. Additional exam requirements/recommendations for international students: Required—TOEFL (minimum score 570 paper-based). *Application deadline:* For fall admission, 6/15 for domestic students, 2/1 for international students; for winter admission, 6/1 for international students; for spring admission, 11/15 for domestic students. Applications are processed on a rolling basis. Application fee: $50 ($75 for international students). Electronic applications accepted. *Expenses:* $1,150-$1,290 per hour, depending on program. *Financial support:* Career-related internships or fieldwork, scholarships/grants, tuition waivers (partial), and unspecified assistantships available. Support available to part-time students. Financial award application deadline: 7/1; financial award applicants required to submit FAFSA. *Faculty research:* Impact of spirituality on organization commitment, women in corporate leadership, psychological empowerment, training. *Unit head:* Allison Duke, Associate Dean of Graduate Business Programs, 615-966-5732, Fax: 615-966-1818, E-mail: allison.duke@lipscomb.edu. *Application contact:* Karen Risley, Manager, Graduate Business Recruiting, 615-966-5145, E-mail: karen.risley@lipscomb.edu.
Website: http://www.lipscomb.edu/business/Graduate-Programs

Lipscomb University, College of Computing and Technology, Nashville, TN 37204-3951. Offers data science (MS); information technology (MS), including data science, information security, information technology management, software engineering; software engineering (MS). *Program availability:* Part-time, evening/weekend. *Faculty:* 7 full-time (0 women), 6 part-time/adjunct (1 woman). *Students:* 21 full-time (10 women), 10 part-time (3 women); includes 9 minority (5 Black or African American, non-Hispanic/Latino; 4 Asian, non-Hispanic/Latino), 1 international. Average age 34. 47 applicants, 49% accepted, 12 enrolled. In 2016, 26 degrees awarded. *Degree requirements:* For master's, capstone project. *Entrance requirements:* For master's, GRE, 2 references, transcripts, resume, personal statement. Additional exam requirements/recommendations for international students: Required—TOEFL (minimum score 570 paper-based; 80 iBT). *Application deadline:* Applications are processed on a rolling basis. Application fee: $50 ($75 for international students). Electronic applications accepted. *Expenses:* $1,226 per hour. *Financial support:* Scholarships/grants and employer agreements available. Financial award applicants required to submit FAFSA. *Unit head:* Dr. Fortune S. Mhlanga, Dean, 615-966-5073, E-mail: fortune.mhlanga@lipscomb.edu. *Application contact:* Brett Ramsey, Enrollment Management Specialist, 615-966-1193, E-mail: brett.ramsey@lipscomb.edu.
Website: http://www.lipscomb.edu/technology/

London Metropolitan University, Graduate Programs, London, United Kingdom. Offers applied psychology (M Sc); architecture (MA); biomedical science (M Sc); blood science (M Sc); cancer pharmacology (M Sc); computer networking and cyber security (M Sc); computing and information systems (M Sc); conference interpreting (MA); counter-terrorism studies (M Sc); creative, digital and professional writing (MA); crime, violence and prevention (M Sc); criminology (M Sc); curating contemporary art (MA); data analytics (M Sc); digital media (MA); early childhood studies (MA); education (MA, Ed D); financial services law, regulation and compliance (LL M); food science (M Sc); forensic psychology (M Sc); health and social care management and policy (M Sc); human nutrition (M Sc); human resource management (MA); human rights and international conflict (MA); information technology (M Sc); intelligence and security studies (M Sc); international oil, gas and energy law (LL M); international relations (MA); interpreting (MA); learning and teaching in higher education (MA); legal practice (LL M); media and entertainment law (LL M); organizational and consumer psychology (M Sc); psychological therapy (M Sc); psychology of mental health (M Sc); public health (M Sc); public policy and management (MPA); security studies (M Sc); social work (M Sc); spatial planning and urban design (MA); sports therapy (M Sc); supporting older children and young people with dyslexia (MA); teaching languages (MA), including Arabic, English; translation (MA); woman and child abuse (MA).

Marymount University, School of Business Administration, Program in Cybersecurity, Arlington, VA 22207-4299. Offers MS, Certificate, MS/MS. *Program availability:* Part-time, evening/weekend. *Faculty:* 2 full-time (both women), 6 part-time/adjunct (1 woman). *Students:* 25 full-time (10 women), 32 part-time (16 women); includes 29 minority (15 Black or African American, non-Hispanic/Latino; 5 Asian, non-Hispanic/Latino; 7 Hispanic/Latino; 2 Two or more races, non-Hispanic/Latino), 8 international. Average age 34. 41 applicants, 98% accepted, 27 enrolled. In 2016, 11 master's, 1 other advanced degree awarded. *Degree requirements:* For master's, thesis or alternative. *Entrance requirements:* For master's, resume, certification or demonstrated work experience in computer networking. Additional exam requirements/recommendations for international students: Required—TOEFL (minimum score 600 paper-based; 96 iBT), IELTS (minimum score 6.5). *Application deadline:* For fall admission, 7/16 priority date for domestic and international students; for spring admission, 11/16 priority date for domestic and international students; for summer admission, 4/16 for domestic and international students. Applications are processed on a rolling basis. Application fee: $40. Electronic applications accepted. *Expenses:* $960 per credit hour. *Financial support:* In 2016–17, 6 students received support, including 2 research assistantships with tuition reimbursements available; career-related internships or fieldwork, Federal Work-Study, scholarships/grants, and unspecified assistantships also available. Support available to part-time students. Financial award applicants required to submit FAFSA. *Unit head:* Dr. Diane Murphy, Chair/Director, Information Technology, Management Sciences and Cybersecurity, 703-284-5958, Fax: 703-527-3830, E-mail: diane.murphy@marymount.edu. *Application contact:* Francesca Reed, Director, Graduate Admissions, 703-284-5901, Fax: 703-527-3815, E-mail: grad.admissions@marymount.edu.
Website: http://www.marymount.edu/Academics/School-of-Business-Administration/Graduate-Programs/Cybersecurity-(M-S-)

Marymount University, School of Business Administration, Program in Information Technology, Arlington, VA 22207-4299. Offers health care informatics (Certificate); information technology (MS, Certificate), including computer security (MS), health care informatics (MS), project management and technology leadership (MS), software engineering (MS); information technology project management and technology leadership (Certificate); MS/MBA; MS/MS. *Program availability:* Part-time, evening/weekend. *Faculty:* 7 full-time (6 women), 7 part-time/adjunct (0 women). *Students:* 39 full-time (23 women), 31 part-time (13 women); includes 24 minority (12 Black or African American, non-Hispanic/Latino; 5 Asian, non-Hispanic/Latino; 6 Hispanic/Latino; 1 Two or more races, non-Hispanic/Latino), 31 international. Average age 30. 67 applicants, 97% accepted, 23 enrolled. In 2016, 29 master's, 12 other advanced degrees awarded. *Degree requirements:* For master's, thesis or alternative. *Entrance requirements:* For master's, resume, bachelor's degree in computer-related field or another subject with certificate in computer-related field or related work experience; bachelor's degree in computer science or work in software development (for software engineering track). Additional exam requirements/recommendations for international students: Required—TOEFL (minimum score 600 paper-based; 96 iBT), IELTS (minimum score 6.5). *Application deadline:* For fall admission, 7/16 priority date for domestic and international students; for spring admission, 11/16 priority date for domestic and international students; for summer admission, 4/16 for domestic and international students. Applications are processed on a rolling basis. Application fee: $40. Electronic applications accepted. *Expenses:* $960 per credit hour. *Financial support:* In 2016–17, 5 students received support, including 2 research assistantships with tuition reimbursements available; career-related internships or fieldwork, Federal Work-Study, scholarships/grants, and unspecified assistantships also available. Support available to part-time students. Financial award applicants required to submit FAFSA. *Unit head:* Dr. Diane Murphy, Chair/Director, Information Technology, Management Sciences and Cybersecurity, 703-284-5958, Fax: 703-527-3830, E-mail: diane.murphy@marymount.edu. *Application contact:* Francesca Reed, Director, Graduate Admissions, 703-284-5901, Fax: 703-527-3815, E-mail: grad.admissions@marymount.edu.
Website: http://www.marymount.edu/Academics/School-of-Business-Administration/Graduate-Programs/Information-Technology-(M-S-)

Maryville University of Saint Louis, The John E. Simon School of Business, St. Louis, MO 63141-7299. Offers accounting (MBA, Certificate); business studies (Certificate); cyber security (MBA); cybersecurity (Certificate); financial services (MBA, Certificate);

healthcare practice management (MBA, Certificate); human resource management (MBA); information technology (MBA, Certificate); management (MBA, Certificate); management and leadership (MA); marketing (MBA, Certificate); project management (MBA); sport business management (MBA); supply chain management/logistics (MBA). *Accreditation:* ACBSP. *Program availability:* Part-time, evening/weekend, 100% online, blended/hybrid learning. *Faculty:* 7 full-time (3 women), 34 part-time/adjunct (9 women). *Students:* 84 full-time (40 women), 223 part-time (118 women); includes 67 minority (40 Black or African American, non-Hispanic/Latino; 2 American Indian or Alaska Native, non-Hispanic/Latino; 8 Asian, non-Hispanic/Latino; 12 Hispanic/Latino; 1 Native Hawaiian or other Pacific Islander, non-Hispanic/Latino; 4 Two or more races, non-Hispanic/Latino), 15 international. Average age 32. In 2016, 67 master's awarded. *Entrance requirements:* Additional exam requirements/recommendations for international students: Required—TOEFL (minimum score 563 paper-based; 85 iBT). *Application deadline:* Applications are processed on a rolling basis. Electronic applications accepted. *Expenses:* $650 per credit hour. *Financial support:* Career-related internships or fieldwork, Federal Work-Study, tuition waivers (partial), and campus employment available. Financial award application deadline: 3/1; financial award applicants required to submit FAFSA. *Faculty research:* Global business, e-marketing, strategic planning, interpersonal management skills, financial analysis. *Unit head:* Pam Horwitz, Interim Dean, 314-529-9680, Fax: 314-529-9975. *Application contact:* Dustin Loeffler, Director for Graduate Studies in Business, 314-529-9571, Fax: 314-529-9975, E-mail: dloeffler@maryville.edu.
Website: http://www.maryville.edu/bu/business-administration-masters/

Marywood University, Academic Affairs, Munley College of Liberal Arts and Sciences, Department of Mathematics and Computer Science, Scranton, PA 18509-1598. Offers information security (MS).

Mercy College, School of Liberal Arts, Program in Cybersecurity, Dobbs Ferry, NY 10522-1189. Offers MS. *Program availability:* Part-time, evening/weekend, 100% online, blended/hybrid learning. *Students:* 27 full-time (7 women), 20 part-time (4 women); includes 19 minority (9 Black or African American, non-Hispanic/Latino; 1 Asian, non-Hispanic/Latino; 9 Hispanic/Latino), 8 international. Average age 35. 50 applicants, 60% accepted, 18 enrolled. In 2016, 21 master's awarded. *Entrance requirements:* For master's, essay, letter of recommendation, undergraduate transcripts. Additional exam requirements/recommendations for international students: Required—TOEFL (minimum score 600 paper-based; 100 iBT), IELTS (minimum score 8). *Application deadline:* For fall admission, 8/1 for international students. Applications are processed on a rolling basis. Application fee: $40. Electronic applications accepted. *Expenses:* Contact institution. *Financial support:* Career-related internships or fieldwork, Federal Work-Study, scholarships/grants, and unspecified assistantships available. Support available to part-time students. Financial award applicants required to submit FAFSA. *Unit head:* Dean, School of Liberal Arts, 914-674-7593. *Application contact:* Allison Gurdineer, Senior Director of Admissions, 877-637-2946, Fax: 914-674-7382, E-mail: admissions@mercy.edu.
Website: https://www.mercy.edu/degrees-programs/ms-cybersecurity

Mercyhurst University, Graduate Studies, Program in Data Science, Erie, PA 16546. Offers MS. Electronic applications accepted.

Metropolitan State University, College of Management, St. Paul, MN 55106-5000. Offers business administration (MBA, DBA); database administration (Graduate Certificate); healthcare information technology management (Graduate Certificate); information assurance security (Graduate Certificate); management information systems (MMIS); MIS generalist (Graduate Certificate); MIS systems analysis and design (Graduate Certificate); project management (Graduate Certificate); public and nonprofit administration (MPNA). *Program availability:* Part-time, evening/weekend. *Degree requirements:* For master's, thesis optional, computer language (MMIS). *Entrance requirements:* For master's, GMAT (for MBA), resume. Additional exam requirements/recommendations for international students: Required—TOEFL (minimum score 550 paper-based). Electronic applications accepted. *Faculty research:* Yugoslav economic system, workers' cooperatives, participative management and job enrichment, global business systems.

Michigan Technological University, Graduate School, College of Sciences and Arts, Department of Computer Science, Houghton, MI 49931. Offers computational science and engineering (PhD); computer science (MS, PhD); cybersecurity (MS). *Program availability:* Part-time. *Faculty:* 21 full-time, 9 part-time/adjunct. *Students:* 41 full-time (13 women), 6 part-time; includes 1 minority (Two or more races, non-Hispanic/Latino), 32 international. Average age 27. 466 applicants, 19% accepted, 15 enrolled. In 2016, 3 master's, 5 doctorates awarded. *Degree requirements:* For master's, comprehensive exam (for some programs), thesis (for some programs); for doctorate, comprehensive exam, thesis/dissertation. *Entrance requirements:* For master's and doctorate, GRE, statement of purpose, personal statement, official transcripts, 3 letters of recommendation. Additional exam requirements/recommendations for international students: Required—TOEFL (recommended minimum score 90 iBT) or IELTS. *Application deadline:* For fall admission, 5/1 priority date for domestic and international students; for spring admission, 9/1 priority date for domestic and international students. Applications are processed on a rolling basis. Electronic applications accepted. *Expenses:* Contact institution. *Financial support:* In 2016–17, 36 students received support, including 4 fellowships (averaging $15,242 per year), 12 research assistantships with tuition reimbursements available (averaging $15,242 per year), 13 teaching assistantships with tuition reimbursements available (averaging $15,242 per year); career-related internships or fieldwork, Federal Work-Study, scholarships/grants, health care benefits, unspecified assistantships, and cooperative program also available. Financial award applicants required to submit FAFSA. *Faculty research:* Artificial intelligence, graphics/visualization, software engineering, architecture and compiler optimization, human computing interaction. *Total annual research expenditures:* $856,922. *Unit head:* Dr. Min Song, Chair, 906-487-2602, Fax: 906-487-2283, E-mail: mins@mtu.edu. *Application contact:* Cheryl Simpkins, Office Assistant, 906-487-2209, Fax: 906-487-2283, E-mail: cisimpki@mtu.edu.
Website: http://www.mtu.edu/cs/

Middle Georgia State University, Office of Graduate Studies, Macon, GA 31206. Offers adult/gerontology acute care nurse practitioner (MSN); information technology (MS), including health informatics, information security and digital forensics, software development. *Entrance requirements:* For master's, GRE. Additional exam requirements/recommendations for international students: Required—TOEFL (minimum score 523 paper-based; 69 iBT). *Expenses:* Contact institution.

Missouri State University, Graduate College, College of Business Administration, Department of Computer Information Systems, Springfield, MO 65897. Offers cybersecurity (MS). *Program availability:* Part-time, evening/weekend, online learning. *Faculty:* 12 full-time (2 women), 7 part-time/adjunct (0 women). *Students:* 4 full-time (1 woman), 31 part-time (6 women); includes 6 minority (3 Black or African American, non-Hispanic/Latino; 2 Asian, non-Hispanic/Latino; 1 Two or more races, non-Hispanic/Latino), 3 international. Average age 36. 36 applicants, 50% accepted, 10 enrolled. In 2016, 8 master's awarded. *Degree requirements:* For master's, comprehensive exam (for some programs), thesis optional. *Entrance requirements:* For master's, GMAT, 3 years of work experience in computer information systems, minimum GPA of 2.75 (MS),

9-12 teaching certification (MS Ed). Additional exam requirements/recommendations for international students: Required—TOEFL (minimum score 550 paper-based; 79 iBT), IELTS (minimum score 6). *Application deadline:* For fall admission, 7/20 priority date for domestic students, 5/1 for international students; for spring admission, 12/20 priority date for domestic students, 9/1 for international students; for summer admission, 5/20 priority date for domestic students. Applications are processed on a rolling basis. Application fee: $35 ($50 for international students). Electronic applications accepted. *Expenses:* Contact institution. *Financial support:* Federal Work-Study, institutionally sponsored loans, scholarships/grants, and unspecified assistantships available. Support available to part-time students. Financial award application deadline: 3/31; financial award applicants required to submit FAFSA. *Faculty research:* Information systems development, computer applications, information security. *Unit head:* Josh Davis, Department Head, 417-836-4426, Fax: 417-836-6907, E-mail: joshdavis@missouristate.edu. *Application contact:* Michael Edwards, Coordinator of Graduate Admissions, 417-836-5330, Fax: 417-836-6200, E-mail: michaeledwards@missouristate.edu.
Website: http://cis.missouristate.edu/

Missouri Western State University, Program in Information Technology Assurance Administration, St. Joseph, MO 64507-2294. Offers MS. *Program availability:* Part-time. *Students:* 12 full-time (1 woman), 4 part-time (0 women), 13 international. Average age 26. 17 applicants, 47% accepted, 3 enrolled. In 2016, 9 master's awarded. *Entrance requirements:* For master's, minimum GPA of 3.0. Additional exam requirements/recommendations for international students: Recommended—TOEFL (minimum score 79 iBT), IELTS (minimum score 6). *Application deadline:* For fall admission, 7/15 for domestic and international students; for spring admission, 10/1 for domestic and international students; for summer admission, 3/15 for domestic students. Applications are processed on a rolling basis. Application fee: $50. Electronic applications accepted. *Expenses:* Tuition, state resident: full-time $6548; part-time $327.39 per credit hour. Tuition, nonresident: full-time $11,848; part-time $592.39 per credit hour. *Required fees:* $542; $99 per credit hour. $176 per semester. One-time fee: $50. Tuition and fees vary according to course load and program. *Financial support:* Scholarships/grants and unspecified assistantships available. Support available to part-time students. *Unit head:* Dr. Baoqiang Yan, Associate Professor, 816-271-4372, E-mail: byan@missouriwestern.edu. *Application contact:* Dr. Benjamin D. Caldwell, Dean of the Graduate School, 816-271-4394, Fax: 816-271-4525, E-mail: graduate@missouriwestern.edu.
Website: https://www.missouriwestern.edu/itaa/

Naval Postgraduate School, Departments and Academic Groups, Department of Computer Science, Monterey, CA 93943. Offers computer science (MS, PhD); identity management and cyber security (MA); modeling of virtual environments and simulations (MS, PhD); software engineering (MS, PhD). Program only open to commissioned officers of the United States and friendly nations and selected United States federal civilian employees. *Program availability:* Part-time, online learning. *Degree requirements:* For master's, thesis; for doctorate, thesis/dissertation.

New Jersey City University, College of Professional Studies, Program in National Security Studies, Jersey City, NJ 07305-1597. Offers civil security leadership (D Sc); national security studies (MS, Certificate). *Program availability:* Part-time. *Entrance requirements:* Additional exam requirements/recommendations for international students: Required—TOEFL (minimum score 79 iBT).

New Jersey Institute of Technology, Ying Wu College of Computing, Newark, NJ 07102. Offers big data management and mining (Certificate); business and information systems (Certificate); computer science (MS, PhD), including bioinformatics (MS), computer science, computing and business (MS), cyber security and privacy (MS), software engineering (MS); data mining (Certificate); information security (Certificate); information systems (MS, PhD), including business and information systems (MS), emergency management and business continuity (MS), information systems, information technology administration and security (MS); IT administration (Certificate); network security and information assurance (Certificate); software engineering analysis/design (Certificate); Web systems development (Certificate). *Program availability:* Part-time, evening/weekend. *Faculty:* 64 full-time (10 women), 38 part-time/adjunct (4 women). *Students:* 818 full-time (241 women), 225 part-time (53 women); includes 162 minority (35 Black or African American, non-Hispanic/Latino; 77 Asian, non-Hispanic/Latino; 41 Hispanic/Latino; 9 Two or more races, non-Hispanic/Latino), 772 international. Average age 27. 2,666 applicants, 51% accepted, 377 enrolled. In 2016, 398 master's, 10 doctorates, 9 other advanced degrees awarded. Terminal master's awarded for partial completion of doctoral program. *Degree requirements:* For master's, thesis optional; for doctorate, thesis/dissertation. *Entrance requirements:* For master's, GRE General Test; for doctorate, GRE General Test, minimum graduate GPA of 3.5. Additional exam requirements/recommendations for international students: Required—TOEFL (minimum score 550 paper-based; 79 iBT). *Application deadline:* For fall admission, 6/1 priority date for domestic students, 5/1 priority date for international students; for spring admission, 11/15 priority date for domestic and international students. Applications are processed on a rolling basis. Application fee: $75. Electronic applications accepted. *Expenses:* Contact institution. *Financial support:* In 2016–17, 57 students received support, including 18 research assistantships (averaging $16,073 per year), 39 teaching assistantships (averaging $20,194 per year); fellowships, career-related internships or fieldwork, Federal Work-Study, institutionally sponsored loans, and unspecified assistantships also available. Financial award application deadline: 1/15. *Faculty research:* Computer systems, communications and networking, artificial intelligence, database engineering, systems analysis, analytics and optimization in crowdsourcing. *Total annual research expenditures:* $3 million. *Unit head:* Dr. Craig Gotsman, Dean, 973-542-5488, Fax: 973-596-5777, E-mail: marek.rusinkiewicz@njit.edu. *Application contact:* Stephen Eck, Director of Admissions, 973-596-3300, Fax: 973-596-3461, E-mail: admissions@njit.edu.
Website: http://computing.njit.edu/

New York Institute of Technology, School of Engineering and Computing Sciences, Department of Computer Science, Old Westbury, NY 11568-8000. Offers computer science (MS); information, network, and computer security (MS). *Program availability:* Part-time, evening/weekend. *Faculty:* 12 full-time (3 women), 19 part-time/adjunct (3 women). *Students:* 508 full-time (195 women), 158 part-time (43 women); includes 41 minority (6 Black or African American, non-Hispanic/Latino; 25 Asian, non-Hispanic/Latino; 9 Hispanic/Latino; 1 Two or more races, non-Hispanic/Latino), 602 international. Average age 25. 1,654 applicants, 62% accepted, 172 enrolled. In 2016, 342 master's awarded. *Degree requirements:* For master's, thesis or alternative. *Entrance requirements:* For master's, BS or its equivalent from accredited college or university in computer science, engineering, management, mathematics, information technology, liberal arts, and related areas; minimum undergraduate GPA of 2.85. Additional exam requirements/recommendations for international students: Required—TOEFL (minimum score 79 iBT), IELTS (minimum score 6). *Application deadline:* For fall admission, 7/1 for domestic students, 6/1 for international students; for spring admission, 12/1 for domestic and international students. Applications are processed on a rolling basis. Application fee: $50. Electronic applications accepted. *Expenses:* $1,215 per credit. *Financial support:* Fellowships with partial tuition reimbursements, teaching assistantships with

partial tuition reimbursements, career-related internships or fieldwork, Federal Work-Study, scholarships/grants, tuition waivers (full and partial), and unspecified assistantships available. Support available to part-time students. Financial award application deadline: 3/1; financial award applicants required to submit FAFSA. *Faculty research:* Active authentication of mobile users; privacy-preserving authentication protocols; sensing cloud system for cybersecurity; cognitive rhythms as a new modality for continuous authentication; cloud-enabled and cloud source disaster detection. *Unit head:* Dr. Frank Lee, Department Chair, 516-686-7456, Fax: 516-686-7439, E-mail: fli@nyit.edu. *Application contact:* Alice Dolitsky, Director, Graduate Admissions, 516-686-7520, Fax: 516-686-1116, E-mail: nyitgrad@nyit.edu.
Website: http://www.nyit.edu/degrees/computer_science_ms

New York University, Polytechnic School of Engineering, Department of Computer Science and Engineering, Major in Cyber Security, New York, NY 10012-1019. Offers Graduate Certificate. *Program availability:* Online learning. Electronic applications accepted.

Northeastern University, College of Engineering, Boston, MA 02115-5096. Offers bioengineering (MS, PhD); chemical engineering (MS, PhD); civil engineering (MS, PhD); computer engineering (PhD); computer systems engineering (MS); electrical and computer engineering (MS); electrical and computer engineering leadership (MS); electrical engineering (PhD); energy systems (MS); engineering and public policy (MS); engineering management (MS, Certificate); environmental engineering (MS); industrial engineering (MS, PhD); information assurance (PhD); information systems (MS); interdisciplinary engineering (PhD); mechanical engineering (PhD); operations research (MS); telecommunication systems management (MS). *Program availability:* Part-time, online learning. *Faculty:* 202 full-time (59 women), 53 part-time/adjunct (9 women). *Students:* 2,982 full-time (954 women), 192 part-time (38 women). In 2016, 851 master's, 74 doctorates awarded. Application fee: $75. Electronic applications accepted. *Expenses:* $1,471 per credit. *Financial support:* Fellowships, research assistantships, teaching assistantships, career-related internships or fieldwork, scholarships/grants, health care benefits, tuition waivers, and unspecified assistantships available. Support available to part-time students. Financial award applicants required to submit FAFSA. *Unit head:* Dr. Nadine Aubry, Dean, College of Engineering. *Application contact:* Jeffery Hengel, Director of Graduate Admissions, 617-373-2711, E-mail: j.hengel@northeastern.edu.
Website: http://www.coe.neu.edu/academics/graduate-school-engineering

Northern Kentucky University, Office of Graduate Programs, College of Informatics, Department of Business Informatics, Highland Heights, KY 41099. Offers business informatics (MS, Certificate); corporate information security (Certificate); enterprise resource planning (Certificate). *Program availability:* Part-time, evening/weekend. *Entrance requirements:* For master's, GRE or GMAT. Additional exam requirements/recommendations for international students: Required—TOEFL (minimum score 79 iBT); Recommended—IELTS (minimum score 6.5). Electronic applications accepted. *Faculty research:* Data analytics, cloud computing, healthcare informatics, information systems security.

Northwestern University, School of Professional Studies, Program in Information Systems, Evanston, IL 60208. Offers analytics and business intelligence (MS); database and Internet technologies (MS); information systems (MS); information systems management (MS); information systems security (MS); medical informatics (MS); software project management and development (MS).

Norwich University, College of Graduate and Continuing Studies, Master of Science in Information Security and Assurance Program, Northfield, VT 05663. Offers information security and assurance (MS), including computer forensic investigation/incident response team management, critical infrastructure protection and cyber crime, cyber law and international perspectives on cyberspace, project management, vulnerability management. *Program availability:* Evening/weekend, online only, mostly all online with a week-long residency requirement. *Faculty:* 20 part-time/adjunct (3 women). *Students:* 110 full-time (23 women); includes 30 minority (10 Black or African American, non-Hispanic/Latino; 2 American Indian or Alaska Native, non-Hispanic/Latino; 9 Asian, non-Hispanic/Latino; 4 Hispanic/Latino; 5 Two or more races, non-Hispanic/Latino), 1 international. Average age 37. 38 applicants, 97% accepted, 26 enrolled. In 2016, 54 master's awarded. *Entrance requirements:* For master's, minimum undergraduate GPA of 2.75. Additional exam requirements/recommendations for international students: Required—TOEFL (minimum score 550 paper-based; 80 iBT), IELTS (minimum score 6.5). *Application deadline:* For fall admission, 8/14 for domestic and international students; for winter admission, 11/13 for domestic and international students; for spring admission, 2/12 for domestic and international students; for summer admission, 6/5 for domestic and international students. Electronic applications accepted. *Expenses:* Contact institution. *Financial support:* In 2016–17, 52 students received support. Scholarships/grants available. Financial award application deadline: 8/4; financial award applicants required to submit FAFSA. *Unit head:* Dr. Rosemarie Pelletier, Program Director, 802-485-2767, Fax: 802-485-2533, E-mail: rpellet2@norwich.edu. *Application contact:* Admissions Advisor, 800-460-5597 Ext. 3363, Fax: 802-485-2533, E-mail: msisa@online.norwich.edu.
Website: https://online.norwich.edu/degree-programs/masters/master-science-information-security-assurance/overview

Nova Southeastern University, College of Engineering and Computing, Fort Lauderdale, FL 33314-7796. Offers computer science (MS, PhD); information assurance (PhD); information assurance and cybersecurity (MS); information systems (PhD); information technology (MS); management information systems (MS). *Program availability:* Part-time, evening/weekend, blended/hybrid learning. *Faculty:* 18 full-time (4 women), 11 part-time/adjunct (2 women). *Students:* 309 full-time (87 women), 407 part-time (125 women); includes 321 minority (139 Black or African American, non-Hispanic/Latino; 2 American Indian or Alaska Native, non-Hispanic/Latino; 52 Asian, non-Hispanic/Latino; 117 Hispanic/Latino; 11 Two or more races, non-Hispanic/Latino), 160 international. Average age 40. 390 applicants, 74% accepted. In 2016, 188 master's, 53 doctorates awarded. Terminal master's awarded for partial completion of doctoral program. *Degree requirements:* For master's, thesis optional; for doctorate, thesis/dissertation. *Entrance requirements:* For master's, minimum undergraduate GPA of 2.5; 3.0 in major; for doctorate, master's degree, minimum graduate GPA of 3.25. Additional exam requirements/recommendations for international students: Required—TOEFL (minimum score 80 iBT), IELTS (minimum score 6), PTE (minimum score 54). *Application deadline:* Applications are processed on a rolling basis. Application fee: $50. Electronic applications accepted. *Expenses:* $745 per credit hour (for master's); $1,075 per credit hour (for doctoral). *Financial support:* In 2016–17, 43 students received support. Federal Work-Study, scholarships/grants, and traineeships available. Financial award application deadline: 4/15; financial award applicants required to submit FAFSA. *Faculty research:* Artificial intelligence, database management, human-computer interaction, distance education, information assurance and cybersecurity. *Unit head:* Dr. Yong X. Tao, Dean, 954-262-2063, Fax: 954-262-2752, E-mail: ytao@nova.edu. *Application contact:* Nancy Azoulay, Director, Admissions, 954-262-2026, Fax: 954-262-2752, E-mail: azoulayn@nova.edu.
Website: http://scis.nova.edu

Our Lady of the Lake University, School of Business and Leadership, Program in Information Systems and Security, San Antonio, TX 78207-4689. Offers MS. *Program availability:* Part-time, online only, 100% online. *Faculty:* 5 full-time (3 women), 2 part-time/adjunct (0 women). *Students:* 28 full-time (8 women), 15 part-time (5 women); includes 32 minority (2 Black or African American, non-Hispanic/Latino; 1 Asian, non-Hispanic/Latino; 28 Hispanic/Latino; 1 Two or more races, non-Hispanic/Latino). Average age 36. 17 applicants, 65% accepted, 9 enrolled. In 2016, 18 master's awarded. *Entrance requirements:* For master's, GRE or GMAT, official transcripts showing baccalaureate degree from regionally-accredited institution in technical discipline and minimum GPA of 3.0 for cumulative undergraduate work or 3.2 in the major field (technical discipline) of study. Additional exam requirements/recommendations for international students: Required—TOEFL. *Application deadline:* For fall admission, 6/15 for domestic and international students; for spring admission, 11/15 for domestic and international students; for summer admission, 4/15 for domestic and international students. Applications are processed on a rolling basis. Application fee: $40 ($50 for international students). Electronic applications accepted. Application fee is waived when completed online. *Expenses: Tuition:* Full-time $14,796. Tuition and fees vary according to course load, degree level, campus/location and program. *Financial support:* In 2016–17, 14 students received support. Federal Work-Study, scholarships/grants, unspecified assistantships, and tuition discounts available. Support available to part-time students. Financial award application deadline: 5/1; financial award applicants required to submit FAFSA. *Faculty research:* Computer information systems implementation and best practices, computer and network security, cyber security legal issues, information assurance, and information technology education. *Unit head:* Carol Jeffries-Horner, Chair, Computer Information Systems and Security Department, 210-528-6730, E-mail: cjeffries@ollusa.edu. *Application contact:* Office of Graduate Admissions, 210-431-3995, Fax: 210-431-3945, E-mail: gradadm@ollusa.edu.
Website: http://www.ollusa.edu/s/1190/hybrid/default-hybrid-ollu.aspx?sid-1190&gid-1&pgid-7901

Pace University, Seidenberg School of Computer Science and Information Systems, New York, NY 10038. Offers chief information security officer (APC); computer science (MS, PhD); enterprise analytics (MS); information and communication technology strategy and innovation (APC); information systems (MS, APC); Internet technology (MS); professional studies in computing (DPS); secure software and information engineering (APC); security and information assurance (Certificate); software development and engineering (MS, Certificate); telecommunications systems and networks (MS, Certificate). *Program availability:* Part-time, evening/weekend, online only, 100% online, blended/hybrid learning. *Faculty:* 26 full-time (7 women), 7 part-time/adjunct (2 women). *Students:* 537 full-time (175 women), 303 part-time (85 women); includes 192 minority (79 Black or African American, non-Hispanic/Latino; 3 American Indian or Alaska Native, non-Hispanic/Latino; 53 Asian, non-Hispanic/Latino; 49 Hispanic/Latino; 8 Two or more races, non-Hispanic/Latino), 486 international. Average age 32. 599 applicants, 89% accepted, 248 enrolled. In 2016, 180 master's, 19 doctorates, 1 other advanced degree awarded. *Degree requirements:* For master's, thesis or alternative, capstone course; for doctorate, comprehensive exam (for some programs), thesis/dissertation. *Entrance requirements:* For master's, GRE General Test. Additional exam requirements/recommendations for international students: Required—TOEFL (minimum score 78 iBT), IELTS (minimum score 6.5) or PTE (minimum score 52). *Application deadline:* For fall admission, 8/1 priority date for domestic students, 6/1 for international students; for spring admission, 12/1 for domestic students, 10/1 for international students. Applications are processed on a rolling basis. Application fee: $70. Electronic applications accepted. *Expenses:* Contact institution. *Financial support:* In 2016–17, 45 students received support. Research assistantships, career-related internships or fieldwork, scholarships/grants, and unspecified assistantships available. Support available to part-time students. Financial award application deadline: 2/15; financial award applicants required to submit FAFSA. *Faculty research:* Cyber security/digital forensics; mobile app development; big data/enterprise analytics; artificial intelligence; software development. *Total annual research expenditures:* $314,545. *Unit head:* Dr. Jonathan Hill, Dean, Seidenberg School of Computer Science and Information Systems, 212-346-1864, E-mail: jhill@pace.edu. *Application contact:* Susan Ford-Goldschein, Director of Graduate Admissions, 914-422-4283, Fax: 212-346-1585, E-mail: graduateadmission@pace.edu.
Website: http://www.pace.edu/seidenberg

Penn State Great Valley, Graduate Studies, Management Division, Malvern, PA 19355-1488. Offers business administration (MBA); cyber security (Certificate); data analytics (Certificate); distributed energy and grid modernization (Certificate); finance (M Fin, Certificate); health sector management (Certificate); human resource management (Certificate); information science (MSIS); leadership development (MLD); new ventures and entrepreneurship (Certificate); professional studies in data analytics (MPS); sustainable management practices (Certificate). *Accreditation:* AACSB. *Unit head:* Dr. James A. Nemes, Chancellor, 610-648-3202, Fax: 610-725-5296. *Application contact:* JoAnn Kelly, Director of Admissions, 610-648-3315, Fax: 610-725-5296, E-mail: jek2@psu.edu.
Website: http://greatvalley.psu.edu/academics/masters-degrees/engineering-management

Purdue University, Graduate School, Interdisciplinary Program in Information Security, West Lafayette, IN 47907. Offers MS. *Students:* 5 full-time (2 women), 2 part-time (0 women); includes 1 minority (Hispanic/Latino), 4 international. Average age 36. 25 applicants, 32% accepted, 3 enrolled. *Entrance requirements:* For master's, GRE, minimum undergraduate GPA of 3.0 or equivalent. Additional exam requirements/recommendations for international students: Required—TOEFL (minimum score 550 paper-based; 100 iBT); Recommended—TWE. *Application deadline:* For fall admission, 4/1 priority date for domestic and international students; for spring admission, 10/1 priority date for domestic and international students. Applications are processed on a rolling basis. Application fee: $60 ($75 for international students). Electronic applications accepted. *Unit head:* Dr. Eugene Spafford, Head, 765-454-7805. *Application contact:* Marlene G. Walls, Administrative Assistant, 765-494-7805, E-mail: walls@cerias.purdue.edu.
Website: http://www.cerias.purdue.edu/site/education/graduate_program/

Regis University, College of Computer and Information Sciences, Denver, CO 80221-1099. Offers agile technologies (Certificate); cybersecurity (Certificate); data science (M Sc); database administration with Oracle (Certificate); database development (Certificate); database technologies (M Sc); enterprise Java software development (Certificate); enterprise resource planning (Certificate); executive information technology (Certificate); health care informatics (Certificate); health care informatics and information management (M Sc); information assurance (M Sc); information assurance policy management (Certificate); information technology management (M Sc); mobile software development (Certificate); software engineering (M Sc, Certificate); software engineering and database technology (M Sc); storage area networks (Certificate); systems engineering (M Sc, Certificate). *Program availability:* Part-time, evening/weekend, 100% online, blended/hybrid learning. *Faculty:* 11 full-time (3 women), 30 part-time/adjunct (10 women). *Students:* 341 full-time (95 women), 318 part-time (98 women); includes 186 minority (56 Black or African American, non-Hispanic/Latino; 2

American Indian or Alaska Native, non-Hispanic/Latino; 48 Asian, non-Hispanic/Latino; 63 Hispanic/Latino; 17 Two or more races, non-Hispanic/Latino), 57 international. Average age 37. 342 applicants, 79% accepted, 174 enrolled. In 2016, 192 master's awarded. *Degree requirements:* For master's, thesis (for some programs), final research project. *Entrance requirements:* For master's, official transcript reflecting baccalaureate degree awarded from regionally-accredited college or university, 2 years of related experience, resume, interview. Additional exam requirements/recommendations for international students: Required—TOEFL (minimum score 550 paper-based; 82 iBT). *Application deadline:* For fall admission, 8/15 priority date for domestic students, 7/13 for international students; for winter admission, 10/10 priority date for domestic students, 9/8 for international students; for spring admission, 1/10 priority date for domestic students, 11/17 for international students; for summer admission, 5/1 priority date for domestic students. Applications are processed on a rolling basis. Application fee: $75. Electronic applications accepted. *Expenses:* $730 per credit hour. *Financial support:* Scholarships/grants available. Financial award application deadline: 4/15; financial award applicants required to submit FAFSA. *Faculty research:* Information policy, knowledge management, software architectures, data science. *Unit head:* Shari Plantz-Masters, Academic Dean. *Application contact:* Cate Clark, Director of Admissions, 303-458-4900, Fax: 303-964-5534, E-mail: ruadmissions@regis.edu.
Website: http://regis.edu/CCIS.aspx

Robert Morris University, School of Communications and Information Systems, Moon Township, PA 15108-1189. Offers communication and information systems (MS); cyber security (MS); data analytics (MS); information security and assurance (MS); information systems and communications (D Sc); information systems management (MS); information technology project management (MS); Internet information systems (MS); organizational leadership (MS). *Program availability:* Part-time, evening/weekend, online learning. *Faculty:* 28 full-time (11 women), 6 part-time/adjunct (0 women). *Students:* 269 part-time (110 women); includes 49 minority (29 Black or African American, non-Hispanic/Latino; 10 Asian, non-Hispanic/Latino; 5 Hispanic/Latino; 5 Two or more races, non-Hispanic/Latino), 49 international. Average age 34. 239 applicants, 46% accepted, 83 enrolled. In 2016, 110 master's, 15 doctorates awarded. *Degree requirements:* For doctorate, thesis/dissertation. *Entrance requirements:* For doctorate, employer letter of endorsement, interview. Additional exam requirements/recommendations for international students: Required—TOEFL (minimum score 550 paper-based; 79 iBT). *Application deadline:* For fall admission, 7/1 priority date for domestic and international students; for spring admission, 11/1 priority date for domestic and international students. Applications are processed on a rolling basis. Application fee: $35. Electronic applications accepted. Application fee is waived when completed online. *Expenses:* $870 per credit (for master's degree). *Financial support:* Institutionally sponsored loans available. Support available to part-time students. Financial award application deadline: 5/1. *Unit head:* Ann Marie M. Le Blanc, Dean, 412-397-6433, Fax: 412-397-6469, E-mail: leblanc@rmu.edu. *Application contact:* Kellie L. Laurenzi, Associate Vice President, 412-397-5200, Fax: 412-397-5915, E-mail: graduateadmissions@rmu.edu.
Website: http://www.rmu.edu/web/cms/schools/scis/Pages/default.aspx

Robert Morris University Illinois, Morris Graduate School of Management, Chicago, IL 60605. Offers accounting (MBA); accounting/finance (MBA); business analytics (MIS); design and media (MM); design management (MM); educational technology (MM); health care administration (MM); higher education administration (MM); human resource management (MBA); information security (MIS); information systems (MBA, MIS); law enforcement administration (MM); management (MBA); management/finance (MBA); management/human resource management (MBA); mobile computing (MIS); sports administration (MM). *Program availability:* Part-time, evening/weekend. *Faculty:* 4 full-time (1 woman), 25 part-time/adjunct (5 women). *Students:* 196 full-time (98 women), 151 part-time (85 women); includes 200 minority (114 Black or African American, non-Hispanic/Latino; 17 Asian, non-Hispanic/Latino; 67 Hispanic/Latino; 2 Two or more races, non-Hispanic/Latino), 23 international. Average age 33. 174 applicants, 61% accepted, 97 enrolled. In 2016, 190 master's awarded. *Entrance requirements:* For master's, official transcripts and letters of recommendation (for some programs); written personal statement. Additional exam requirements/recommendations for international students: Required—TOEFL (minimum score 550 paper-based). *Application deadline:* Applications are processed on a rolling basis. Application fee: $20 ($100 for international students). Electronic applications accepted. *Expenses: Tuition:* Full-time $16,500; part-time $2750 per course. *Financial support:* In 2016–17, 444 students received support. Federal Work-Study, scholarships/grants, and unspecified assistantships available. Support available to part-time students. Financial award applicants required to submit FAFSA. *Unit head:* Kayed Akkawi, Dean, 312-935-6050, Fax: 312-935-6020, E-mail: kakkawi@robertmorris.edu. *Application contact:* Danielle Naffziger, Vice President of Marketing and Enrollment, 312-935-4812, Fax: 312-935-6020, E-mail: dnaffziger@robertmorris.edu.

Rochester Institute of Technology, Graduate Enrollment Services, Golisano College of Computing and Information Sciences, Computing Security Department, Advanced Certificate Program in Information Assurance (Cybersecurity), Rochester, NY 14623. Offers Advanced Certificate. *Program availability:* Part-time, 100% online. *Students:* 2 applicants. *Entrance requirements:* For degree, minimum GPA of 3.0 (recommended). Additional exam requirements/recommendations for international students: Required—TOEFL (minimum score 570 paper-based; 88 iBT), IELTS (minimum score 6.5), PTE (minimum score 61). *Application deadline:* Applications are processed on a rolling basis. Application fee: $60. Electronic applications accepted. *Expenses:* $1,742 per credit hour (classroom), $993 per credit hour (online). *Financial support:* Available to part-time students. Applicants required to submit FAFSA. *Faculty research:* Enterprise level network security and computer system security, forensics. *Unit head:* Sumita Mishra, Graduate Program Director, 585-475-4475, Fax: 585-475-6584, E-mail: sumita.mishra@rit.edu. *Application contact:* Diane Ellison, Associate Vice President, Graduate Enrollment Services, 585-475-2229, Fax: 585-475-7164, E-mail: gradinfo@rit.edu.
Website: https://www.rit.edu/gccis/computingsecurity/academics/ms/certificates

Rochester Institute of Technology, Graduate Enrollment Services, Golisano College of Computing and Information Sciences, Computing Security Department, MS Program in Computing Security, Rochester, NY 14623. Offers MS. *Program availability:* Part-time, 100% online. *Students:* 38 full-time (5 women), 9 part-time (0 women); includes 2 minority (both Black or African American, non-Hispanic/Latino), 31 international. Average age 26. 118 applicants, 51% accepted, 22 enrolled. In 2016, 18 master's awarded. *Degree requirements:* For master's, thesis or alternative. *Entrance requirements:* For master's, GRE, minimum GPA of 3.0 (recommended). Additional exam requirements/recommendations for international students: Required—TOEFL (minimum score 570 paper-based; 88 iBT), IELTS (minimum score 6.5), PTE (minimum score 61). *Application deadline:* For fall admission, 2/15 priority date for domestic and international students; for spring admission, 12/15 priority date for domestic and international students. Applications are processed on a rolling basis. Application fee: $60. Electronic applications accepted. *Expenses:* $1,742 per credit hour (classroom), $993 per credit hour (online). *Financial support:* In 2016–17, 32 students received support. Research assistantships with partial tuition reimbursements available, teaching assistantships with partial tuition reimbursements available, career-related internships or fieldwork, scholarships/grants, and unspecified assistantships available. Support available to part-time students. Financial award applicants required to submit FAFSA. *Faculty research:* Game-based learning for digital forensics, anonymity and privacy, usable security, security of internet of things, risk management in information security. *Unit head:* Sumita Mishra, Graduate Program Director, 585-475-4475, Fax: 585-475-6584, E-mail: sumita.mishra@rit.edu. *Application contact:* Diane Ellison, Associate Vice President, Graduate Enrollment Services, 585-475-2229, Fax: 585-475-7164, E-mail: gradinfo@rit.edu.
Website: http://www.rit.edu/gccis/computingsecurity/academics/ms/overview

Roger Williams University, School of Justice Studies, Bristol, RI 02809. Offers criminal justice (MS); cybersecurity (MS); leadership (MS), including health care administration (MPA, MS), public management (MPA, MS); public administration (MPA), including health care administration (MPA, MS), public management (MPA, MS); MS/JD. *Program availability:* Part-time, evening/weekend, 100% online, blended/hybrid learning. *Faculty:* 10 full-time (5 women), 4 part-time/adjunct (0 women). *Students:* 63 full-time (37 women), 67 part-time (30 women); includes 30 minority (13 Black or African American, non-Hispanic/Latino; 1 American Indian or Alaska Native, non-Hispanic/Latino; 2 Asian, non-Hispanic/Latino; 13 Hispanic/Latino; 1 Native Hawaiian or other Pacific Islander, non-Hispanic/Latino), 3 international. Average age 36. 67 applicants, 96% accepted, 34 enrolled. In 2016, 27 master's awarded. *Degree requirements:* For master's, thesis optional. *Entrance requirements:* For master's, 2 letters of recommendation, college transcript, and resume (for MS in leadership and MPA programs); criminal background check (for MS in cybersecurity). Additional exam requirements/recommendations for international students: Required—TOEFL (minimum score 85 iBT), IELTS (minimum score 6.5). *Application deadline:* For fall admission, 8/1 for domestic students; for spring admission, 1/1 for domestic students. Applications are processed on a rolling basis. Application fee: $50. Electronic applications accepted. Application fee is waived when completed online. *Expenses:* $552 per credit hour tuition (for MS in leadership and MPA); $843 per credit hour tuition (for MS in criminal justice and MS in cybersecurity). *Financial support:* Research assistantships, scholarships/grants, and unspecified assistantships available. Financial award application deadline: 4/1; financial award applicants required to submit FAFSA. *Unit head:* Dr. Stephanie Manzi, Dean, 401-254-3021, Fax: 401-254-3431, E-mail: smanzi@rwu.edu. *Application contact:* Marcus Hanscom, Director of Graduate Admissions, 401-254-6200, Fax: 401-254-3557, E-mail: gradadmit@rwu.edu.
Website: http://www.rwu.edu/academics/departments/criminaljustice.htm#graduate

Rowan University, Graduate School, College of Science and Mathematics, Networks Certificate of Graduate Study Program, Glassboro, NJ 08028-1701. Offers CGS. Electronic applications accepted.

Sacred Heart University, Graduate Programs, College of Arts and Sciences, Department of Computer Science, Fairfield, CT 06825. Offers computer science (MS); computer science gaming (MS); cybersecurity (MS); information technology (MS). *Program availability:* Part-time, evening/weekend. *Faculty:* 7 full-time (2 women), 21 part-time/adjunct (4 women). *Students:* 256 full-time (93 women), 138 part-time (44 women); includes 28 minority (11 Black or African American, non-Hispanic/Latino; 3 Asian, non-Hispanic/Latino; 14 Hispanic/Latino), 319 international. Average age 25. 1,187 applicants, 65% accepted, 72 enrolled. In 2016, 275 master's awarded. *Degree requirements:* For master's, thesis or alternative. *Entrance requirements:* For master's, bachelor's degree, minimum GPA of 3.0. Additional exam requirements/recommendations for international students: Required—TOEFL (minimum score 570 paper-based, 80 iBT), TWE, or IELTS (6.5); Recommended—TSE. *Application deadline:* For fall admission, 5/15 for international students; for spring admission, 10/30 for international students. Applications are processed on a rolling basis. Application fee: $75. Electronic applications accepted. *Expenses:* $850 per credit part-time. *Financial support:* Unspecified assistantships available. Financial award applicants required to submit FAFSA. *Unit head:* Domenick Pinto, Director of the School of Computing, 203-371-7789, Fax: 203-371-0506, E-mail: pintod@sacredheart.edu. *Application contact:* William Sweeney, Director of Graduate Admissions Operations, 203-365-7619, Fax: 203-365-4732, E-mail: gradstudies@sacredheart.edu.
Website: http://www.sacredheart.edu/academics/collegeofartssciences/academicdepartments/computerscienceinformationtechnology/graduatedegreesandcertificates/

St. Cloud State University, School of Graduate Studies, College of Science and Engineering, Program in Information Assurance, St. Cloud, MN 56301-4498. Offers MS. *Program availability:* Part-time. *Degree requirements:* For master's, 30 to 33 credits of coursework. *Entrance requirements:* For master's, minimum overall GPA of 2.75 in previous undergraduate and graduate records or in last half of undergraduate work. Electronic applications accepted.

St. Cloud State University, School of Graduate Studies, Herberger Business School, Program in Business Administration, St. Cloud, MN 56301-4498. Offers business administration (MBA); information assurance (MS). *Accreditation:* AACSB. *Program availability:* Part-time, evening/weekend. *Degree requirements:* For master's, thesis or alternative. *Entrance requirements:* For master's, GMAT, minimum GPA of 2.75. Additional exam requirements/recommendations for international students: Required—Michigan English Language Assessment Battery; Recommended—TOEFL (minimum score 550 paper-based), IELTS (minimum score 6.5).

Saint Leo University, Graduate Business Studies, Saint Leo, FL 33574-6665. Offers accounting (M Acc, MBA, Certificate); cybersecurity (MS); health care management (MBA, Certificate); human resource management (MBA, Certificate); information security management (MBA, Certificate); management (MBA, DBA); marketing (MBA, Certificate); marketing research and social media analytics (MBA, Certificate); project management (MBA, Certificate); sport business (MBA); supply chain global integration management (MBA, Certificate). *Accreditation:* ACBSP. *Program availability:* Part-time, evening/weekend, 100% online, blended/hybrid learning. *Faculty:* 53 full-time (18 women), 53 part-time/adjunct (19 women). *Students:* 8 full-time (4 women), 2,001 part-time (1,160 women); includes 928 minority (650 Black or African American, non-Hispanic/Latino; 5 American Indian or Alaska Native, non-Hispanic/Latino; 43 Asian, non-Hispanic/Latino; 193 Hispanic/Latino; 2 Native Hawaiian or other Pacific Islander, non-Hispanic/Latino; 35 Two or more races, non-Hispanic/Latino), 51 international. Average age 37. 922 applicants, 85% accepted, 517 enrolled. In 2016, 874 master's, 17 other advanced degrees awarded. *Degree requirements:* For doctorate, comprehensive exam, thesis/dissertation. *Entrance requirements:* For master's, GMAT (minimum score 500), official transcripts, current resume, 2 professional recommendations, personal statement, bachelor's degree from regionally-accredited university; undergraduate degree in accounting and minimum undergraduate GPA of 3.0 (for M Acc); minimum undergraduate GPA of 3.0 in final 2 years of undergraduate study and 2 years' work experience (for MBA); for doctorate, GMAT (minimum score of 550) if master's GPA is under 3.25, official transcripts, current resume, 2 professional recommendations, personal statement, master's degree from regionally-accredited university with minimum GPA of 3.25, 3 years' work experience, interview. Additional exam requirements/recommendations for international students: Required—TOEFL (minimum score 550 paper-based; 80 iBT). *Application deadline:* For fall admission, 7/1 priority date for domestic and international students; for spring admission, 11/12 priority date for domestic students, 11/1 for international students. Applications are processed on a rolling basis. Application fee: $80. Electronic applications accepted. *Expenses:* Contact

institution. *Financial support:* In 2016–17, 118 students received support. Career-related internships or fieldwork, scholarships/grants, and health care benefits available. Financial award application deadline: 3/1; financial award applicants required to submit FAFSA. *Unit head:* Dr. Lorrie McGovern, Associate Dean, School of Business, 352-588-7869, Fax: 352-588-8912, E-mail: mbaslu@saintleo.edu. *Application contact:* Jennifer Shelley, Senior Associate Director of Graduate Admissions, 800-707-8846, Fax: 352-588-7873, E-mail: grad.admissions@saintleo.edu.
Website: http://www.saintleo.edu/academics/graduate.aspx

St. Mary's University, School of Science, Engineering and Technology, Program in Cybersecurity, San Antonio, TX 78228-8507. Offers MS. *Program availability:* Part-time, evening/weekend. *Students:* 12 applicants, 42% accepted, 3 enrolled. *Degree requirements:* For master's, project or thesis. *Entrance requirements:* For master's, GRE (minimum quantitative score 152), minimum GPA of 3.0, written statement of purpose indicating applicant's interests and objectives, two letters of recommendation concerning applicant's potential for succeeding in graduate program, official transcripts of all college-level work. Additional exam requirements/recommendations for international students: Required—TOEFL (minimum score 550 paper-based; 80 iBT), IELTS (minimum score 6). *Application deadline:* For fall admission, 7/1 for domestic students; for spring admission, 11/15 for domestic students; for summer admission, 4/1 for domestic students. Applications are processed on a rolling basis. Application fee: $0. Electronic applications accepted. *Expenses: Tuition:* Full-time $15,600; part-time $865 per credit hour. *Required fees:* $148 per semester. *Financial support:* Application deadline: 3/31; applicants required to submit FAFSA. *Faculty research:* Information and network security, replicating data over cloud servers, cryptographic protocols, data integrity in cloud computing systems, knowledge discovery and data mining. *Unit head:* Dr. Ayad Barsoum, Graduate Program Director, 210-436-3315, E-mail: abarsoum@stmarytx.edu.

Salem International University, School of Business, Salem, WV 26426-0500. Offers information security (MBA); international business (MBA). *Program availability:* Part-time, online learning. *Entrance requirements:* For master's, minimum undergraduate GPA of 2.5, course work in business, resume. Additional exam requirements/recommendations for international students: Recommended—TOEFL (minimum score 550 paper-based), IELTS (minimum score 6.5). Electronic applications accepted. *Expenses:* Contact institution. *Faculty research:* Organizational behavior strategy, marketing services.

Salve Regina University, Program in Administration of Justice and Homeland Security, Newport, RI 02840-4192. Offers administration of justice and homeland security (MS); cybersecurity and intelligence (CGS); digital forensics (CGS); leadership in justice (CGS). *Program availability:* Part-time, evening/weekend, online learning. *Entrance requirements:* For master's, GMAT, GRE General Test, or MAT. Additional exam requirements/recommendations for international students: Required—TOEFL (minimum score 600 paper-based; 100 iBT). Electronic applications accepted.

Salve Regina University, Program in Business Administration, Newport, RI 02840-4192. Offers cybersecurity issues in business (MBA); entrepreneurial enterprise (MBA); health care administration and management (MBA); social ventures (MBA). *Program availability:* Part-time, evening/weekend, online learning. *Entrance requirements:* For master's, GMAT, GRE General Test, or MAT, 6 undergraduate credits each in accounting, economics, quantitative analysis and calculus or statistics. Additional exam requirements/recommendations for international students: Required—TOEFL (minimum score 600 paper-based; 100 iBT) or IELTS. Electronic applications accepted.

Sam Houston State University, College of Sciences, Department of Computer Science, Huntsville, TX 77341. Offers computing and information science (MS); digital forensics (MS); information assurance and security (MS). *Program availability:* Part-time. *Degree requirements:* For master's, comprehensive exam, thesis optional, internship; for doctorate, comprehensive exam, thesis/dissertation. *Entrance requirements:* For master's, GRE General Test, letters of recommendation. Additional exam requirements/recommendations for international students: Required—TOEFL (minimum score 550 paper-based; 79 iBT), IELTS (minimum score 6.5). Electronic applications accepted.

San Jose State University, Graduate Studies and Research, College of Science, San Jose, CA 95192-0001. Offers biological sciences (MA, MS), including molecular biology and microbiology (MS), organismal biology, conservation and ecology (MS), physiology (MS); biotechnology (MBT); chemistry (MA, MS); computer science (MS); cybersecurity (Certificate); cybersecurity: core technologies (Certificate); geology (MS); marine science (MS); mathematics (MA, MS), including mathematics education (MA), science; meteorology (MS); physics (MS), including computational physics, modern optics, science (MA, MS); science education (MA); statistics (MS); Unix system administration (Certificate). *Program availability:* Part-time, evening/weekend. *Entrance requirements:* For master's, GRE. Electronic applications accepted. *Faculty research:* Radiochemistry/environmental analysis, health physics, radiation effects.

Shippensburg University of Pennsylvania, School of Graduate Studies, College of Arts and Sciences, Department of Computer Science and Engineering, Shippensburg, PA 17257-2299. Offers agile software engineering (Certificate); computer science (MS), including computer science, cybersecurity, IT leadership, management information systems, software engineering; IT leadership (Certificate). *Program availability:* Part-time, evening/weekend. *Faculty:* 7 full-time (3 women). *Students:* 16 full-time (8 women), 14 part-time (5 women); includes 3 minority (2 Black or African American, non-Hispanic/Latino; 1 Hispanic/Latino), 21 international. Average age 29. 89 applicants, 49% accepted, 9 enrolled. In 2016, 10 master's awarded. *Entrance requirements:* For master's, GRE (if GPA less than 2.75), professional resume. Additional exam requirements/recommendations for international students: Required—TOEFL (minimum score 70 iBT) or IELTS (minimum score 6). *Application deadline:* For fall admission, 4/30 for international students; for spring admission, 9/30 for international students. Applications are processed on a rolling basis. Application fee: $45. Electronic applications accepted. *Expenses:* Tuition, state resident: part-time $483 per credit. Tuition, nonresident: part-time $725 per credit. *Required fees:* $141 per credit. *Financial support:* In 2016–17, 7 students received support. Career-related internships or fieldwork, scholarships/grants, unspecified assistantships, and resident hall director and student payroll positions available. Support available to part-time students. Financial award application deadline: 3/1; financial award applicants required to submit FAFSA. *Unit head:* Dr. Jeonghwa Lee, Associate Professor and Program Coordinator, 717-477-1178, Fax: 717-477-4002, E-mail: jlee@ship.edu. *Application contact:* Megan N. Luft, Assistant Dean of Graduate Admissions, 717-477-1231, Fax: 717-477-4016, E-mail: mnluft@ship.edu.
Website: http://www.cs.ship.edu/

Southern Arkansas University–Magnolia, School of Graduate Studies, Magnolia, AR 71753. Offers agriculture (MS); business administration (MBA), including agri-business, social entrepreneurship, supply chain management; clinical and mental health counseling (MS); computer and information sciences (MS), including cyber security and privacy, data science, information technology; gifted and talented (M Ed), including curriculum and instruction, educational administration and supervision, gifted and talented P-8/7-12, instructional specialist P-4; higher, adult and lifelong education (M Ed); kinesiology (M Ed), including coaching; library media and information specialist (M Ed); public administration (MPA); school counseling K-12 (M Ed); student affairs and college counseling (M Ed); teaching (MAT). *Accreditation:* NCATE. *Program availability:* Part-time, 100% online, blended/hybrid learning. *Faculty:* 36 full-time (19 women), 33 part-time/adjunct (14 women). *Students:* 605 full-time (143 women), 879 part-time (352 women); includes 130 minority (113 Black or African American, non-Hispanic/Latino; 7 American Indian or Alaska Native, non-Hispanic/Latino; 2 Asian, non-Hispanic/Latino; 2 Hispanic/Latino; 6 Two or more races, non-Hispanic/Latino), 1,048 international. Average age 28. 904 applicants, 81% accepted, 262 enrolled. In 2016, 278 master's awarded. *Degree requirements:* For master's, comprehensive exam (for some programs), thesis optional. *Entrance requirements:* For master's, GRE, MAT or GMAT, minimum GPA of 2.5. Additional exam requirements/recommendations for international students: Required—TOEFL (minimum score 550 paper-based), IELTS (minimum score 6). *Application deadline:* For fall admission, 7/20 for domestic students, 7/10 for international students; for spring admission, 12/1 for domestic students, 11/15 for international students; for summer admission, 4/1 for domestic students, 5/1 for international students. Applications are processed on a rolling basis. Application fee: $25 ($50 for international students). Electronic applications accepted. *Expenses:* Tuition, state resident: full-time $2511; part-time $279 per credit hour. Tuition, nonresident: full-time $3726; part-time $414 per credit hour. *Required fees:* $307 per semester. Tuition and fees vary according to course load and program. *Financial support:* Career-related internships or fieldwork, Federal Work-Study, scholarships/grants, tuition waivers (full), and unspecified assistantships available. Financial award applicants required to submit FAFSA. *Faculty research:* Alternative certification for teachers, supervision of instruction, instructional leadership, counseling. *Unit head:* Dr. Kim Bloss, Dean, School of Graduate Studies, 870-235-4150, Fax: 870-235-5227, E-mail: kkbloss@saumag.edu. *Application contact:* Shrijana Malakar, Admissions Specialist, 870-235-4150, Fax: 870-235-5227, E-mail: smalakar@saumag.edu.
Website: http://www.saumag.edu/graduate

Southern Utah University, Program in Cyber Security and Information Assurance, Cedar City, UT 84720-2498. Offers MS. *Program availability:* Part-time, online only. *Faculty:* 2 full-time (1 woman), 1 part-time/adjunct (0 women). *Students:* 4 full-time (1 woman), 18 part-time (1 woman); includes 3 minority (1 Asian, non-Hispanic/Latino; 1 Hispanic/Latino; 1 Native Hawaiian or other Pacific Islander, non-Hispanic/Latino). Average age 36. 17 applicants, 71% accepted, 9 enrolled. *Degree requirements:* For master's, thesis. *Entrance requirements:* Additional exam requirements/recommendations for international students: Required—TOEFL (minimum score 550 paper-based; 79 iBT), IELTS (minimum score 6). Application fee: $60 ($65 for international students). Electronic applications accepted. *Expenses:* $11,398 per year (international online only). *Unit head:* Dr. Rob Robertson, Department Chair/Graduate Director, 435-865-8560, Fax: 435-865-8444, E-mail: robertson@suu.edu. *Application contact:* Mary Gillins, Administrative Assistant, 435-586-5405, Fax: 435-865-8444, E-mail: marygillins@suu.edu. Website: https://www.suu.edu/cose/csis/masters/

State University of New York Polytechnic Institute, Program in Network and Computer Security, Utica, NY 13502. Offers MS. *Program availability:* Part-time. *Degree requirements:* For master's, thesis or project. *Entrance requirements:* For master's, GRE General Test, minimum GPA of 3.0, letter of reference, resume, BS in network and computer security or related field. Additional exam requirements/recommendations for international students: Required—TOEFL (minimum score 550 paper-based; 79 iBT), IELTS (minimum score 6.5). Electronic applications accepted. *Faculty research:* Cloud security, virtualization, wireless networks, cyber physical system.

Stevens Institute of Technology, Graduate School, Charles V. Schaefer Jr. School of Engineering and Science, Department of Computer Science, Hoboken, NJ 07030. Offers computer graphics (Certificate), including computer graphics; computer science (MS, PhD); computer systems (Certificate), including computer systems; cybersecurity (MS); database management systems (Certificate), including databases; distributed systems (Certificate), including distributed systems; elements of computer science (Certificate), including cybersecurity; enterprise and cloud computing (MS); enterprise computing (Certificate), including enterprise and cloud computing; enterprise security and information assurance (Certificate), including enterprise security and information assurance; health informatics (Certificate), including health informatics; multimedia experience and management (Certificate), including multimedia experience and management; networks and systems administration (Certificate), including cloud computing; service oriented computing (Certificate), including service oriented computing. *Program availability:* Part-time, evening/weekend. *Faculty:* 21 full-time (4 women), 13 part-time/adjunct (2 women). *Students:* 436 full-time (124 women), 72 part-time (12 women); includes 27 minority (4 Black or African American, non-Hispanic/Latino; 21 Asian, non-Hispanic/Latino; 1 Hispanic/Latino; 1 Two or more races, non-Hispanic/Latino), 423 international. Average age 25. 1,183 applicants, 54% accepted, 184 enrolled. In 2016, 225 master's, 4 doctorates, 18 other advanced degrees awarded. Terminal master's awarded for partial completion of doctoral program. *Degree requirements:* For master's, thesis optional, minimum B average in major field and overall; for doctorate, comprehensive exam (for some programs), thesis/dissertation; for Certificate, minimum B average. *Entrance requirements:* Additional exam requirements/recommendations for international students: Required—TOEFL (minimum score 74 iBT), IELTS (minimum score 6). *Application deadline:* For fall admission, 6/1 for domestic students, 4/15 for international students; for spring admission, 11/30 for domestic students, 11/1 for international students. Applications are processed on a rolling basis. Application fee: $65. Electronic applications accepted. *Expenses:* Contact institution. *Financial support:* Fellowships, research assistantships, teaching assistantships, career-related internships or fieldwork, Federal Work-Study, scholarships/grants, and unspecified assistantships available. Financial award application deadline: 2/15; financial award applicants required to submit FAFSA. *Faculty research:* Computer security, computer vision, dynamic scene analysis, privacy-preserving data mining, visualization. *Unit head:* Giuseppe Ateniese, Director, 201-216-3741, E-mail: gatenies@stevens.edu. *Application contact:* Graduate Admissions, 888-783-8367, Fax: 888-511-1306, E-mail: graduate@stevens.edu.
Website: https://www.stevens.edu/schaefer-school-engineering-science/departments/computer-science

Stevens Institute of Technology, Graduate School, School of Business, Program in Information Systems, Hoboken, NJ 07030. Offers computer science (MS); e-commerce (MS); enterprise systems (MS); entrepreneurial information technology (MS); information architecture (MS); information management (MS, Certificate); information security (MS); information technology in financial services industry (MS); information technology in the pharmaceutical industry (MS); information technology outsourcing management (MS); project management (MS, Certificate); software engineering (MS); telecommunications (MS). *Program availability:* Part-time, evening/weekend. *Students:* 280 full-time (100 women), 84 part-time (21 women); includes 23 minority (9 Black or African American, non-Hispanic/Latino; 13 Asian, non-Hispanic/Latino; 1 Hispanic/Latino), 283 international. Average age 26. 925 applicants, 62% accepted, 114 enrolled. In 2016, 212 master's, 32 other advanced degrees awarded. *Degree requirements:* For master's, thesis optional, minimum B average in major field and overall; for Certificate, minimum B average. *Entrance requirements:* Additional exam requirements/recommendations for international students: Required—TOEFL (minimum score 74

iBT), IELTS (minimum score 6). *Application deadline:* For fall admission, 6/1 for domestic students, 4/15 for international students; for spring admission, 11/30 for domestic students, 11/1 for international students. Applications are processed on a rolling basis. Application fee: $65. Electronic applications accepted. *Expenses:* Contact institution. *Financial support:* Fellowships, research assistantships, teaching assistantships, career-related internships or fieldwork, Federal Work-Study, scholarships/grants, and unspecified assistantships available. Financial award application deadline: 2/15; financial award applicants required to submit FAFSA. *Unit head:* Dr. Gregory Prastacos, Dean, 201-216-8366, E-mail: gprastac@stevens.edu. *Application contact:* Graduate Admissions, 888-783-8367, Fax: 888-511-1306, E-mail: graduate@stevens.edu.
Website: https://www.stevens.edu/school-business/masters-programs/information-systems

Stevenson University, Program in Cyber Forensics, Owings Mills, MD 21117. Offers MS. *Program availability:* Part-time, 100% online. *Faculty:* 6 part-time/adjunct (0 women). *Students:* 4 full-time (1 woman), 30 part-time (14 women); includes 13 minority (11 Black or African American, non-Hispanic/Latino; 1 Asian, non-Hispanic/Latino; 1 Hispanic/Latino). Average age 38. 14 applicants, 50% accepted, 7 enrolled. In 2016, 13 master's awarded. *Degree requirements:* For master's, capstone. *Entrance requirements:* For master's, bachelor's degree in a related field and two years of related work experience or a bachelor's degree in an unrelated field with five years of experience in information technology, telecommunication systems, system administration, network management, or information assurance. Additional exam requirements/recommendations for international students: Required—TOEFL, IELTS. *Application deadline:* Applications are processed on a rolling basis. Electronic applications accepted. *Expenses:* $670 per credit hour. *Financial support:* Unspecified assistantships available. Financial award applicants required to submit FAFSA. *Unit head:* Thomas Byrd, Program Coordinator, E-mail: tbyrd6@stevenson.edu. *Application contact:* William Wellein, Enrollment Counselor, 443-352-5843, Fax: 443-394-0538, E-mail: wwellein@stevenson.edu.
Website: http://www.stevenson.edu

Stratford University, School of Graduate Studies, Falls Church, VA 22043. Offers accounting (MS); business administration (IMBA, MBA); cyber security (MS); cyber security leadership and policy (MS); digital forensics (MS); enterprise business management (MS); entrepreneurial management (MS); healthcare administration (MS); information systems (MS); international hospitality management (MS); networking and telecommunications (MS); software engineering (MS). *Program availability:* Part-time, evening/weekend, 100% online, blended/hybrid learning. *Students:* 505 full-time (186 women), 172 part-time (88 women); includes 532 minority (165 Black or African American, non-Hispanic/Latino; 18 American Indian or Alaska Native, non-Hispanic/Latino; 324 Asian, non-Hispanic/Latino; 13 Hispanic/Latino; 10 Native Hawaiian or other Pacific Islander, non-Hispanic/Latino; 2 Two or more races, non-Hispanic/Latino). Average age 27. In 2016, 520 master's awarded. *Degree requirements:* For master's, comprehensive exam, capstone project. *Entrance requirements:* For master's, GRE or GMAT, baccalaureate degree. Additional exam requirements/recommendations for international students: Required—TOEFL (minimum score 79 iBT), IELTS (minimum score 6.5), PTE (minimum score 5). *Application deadline:* Applications are processed on a rolling basis. Application fee: $50. Electronic applications accepted. *Expenses:* Tuition: Full-time $4455; part-time $2227.50 per course. One-time fee: $100. *Financial support:* Federal Work-Study and scholarships/grants available. Financial award applicants required to submit FAFSA. *Unit head:* Dr. Richard R. Shurtz, President, 703-539-6890, Fax: 703-539-6960. *Application contact:* Admissions, 800-444-0804, E-mail: fcadmissions@stratford.edu.

Strayer University, Graduate Studies, Washington, DC 20005-2603. Offers accounting (MS); acquisition (MBA); business administration (MBA); communications technology (MS); educational management (M Ed); finance (MBA); health services administration (MHSA); hospitality and tourism management (MBA); human resource management (MBA); information systems (MS), including computer security management, decision support system management, enterprise resource management, network management, software engineering management, systems development management; management (MBA); management information systems (MS); marketing (MBA); professional accounting (MS), including accounting information systems, controllership, taxation; public administration (MPA); supply chain management (MBA); technology in education (M Ed). Programs also offered at campus locations in Birmingham, AL; Chamblee, GA; Cobb County, GA; Morrow, GA; White Marsh, MD; Charleston, SC; Columbia, SC; Greensboro, NC; Greenville, SC; Lexington, KY; Louisville, KY; Nashville, TN; North Raleigh, NC; Washington, DC. *Accreditation:* ACBSP. *Program availability:* Part-time, evening/weekend, online learning. *Degree requirements:* For master's, thesis. *Entrance requirements:* For master's, GMAT, GRE General Test, bachelor's degree from an accredited college or university, minimum undergraduate GPA of 2.75. Electronic applications accepted.

Syracuse University, College of Engineering and Computer Science, Programs in Cybersecurity, Syracuse, NY 13244. Offers MS, CAS. *Program availability:* Part-time, evening/weekend. *Entrance requirements:* For master's, GRE, three letters of recommendation, personal statement, resume, official transcripts. Additional exam requirements/recommendations for international students: Required—TOEFL (minimum score 100 iBT). *Application deadline:* For fall admission, 7/1 priority date for domestic students, 6/1 priority date for international students; for spring admission, 11/15 for domestic students, 10/15 priority date for international students. Applications are processed on a rolling basis. Application fee: $75. Electronic applications accepted. *Expenses:* Tuition: Full-time $25,974; part-time $1443 per credit hour. *Required fees:* $802; $50 per course. Tuition and fees vary according to course load and program. *Financial support:* Fellowships, research assistantships, teaching assistantships, and tuition waivers available. Financial award application deadline: 1/1. *Faculty research:* Design of secure systems that exhibit confidentiality, integrity, and availability through authentication, reference monitoring, and sound design and implementation. *Unit head:* Dr. Kishan Mehrotra, Professor/Chair, 315-443-2811, E-mail: mehrotra@syr.edu. *Application contact:* Kathleen Joyce, Assistant Dean, 315-443-2219, E-mail: topgrads@syr.edu.
Website: http://eng-cs.syr.edu/

Syracuse University, School of Information Studies, CAS Program in Information Security Management, Syracuse, NY 13244. Offers CAS. *Program availability:* Part-time, evening/weekend, online learning. *Students:* Average age 26. *Entrance requirements:* For degree, resume, personal statement, official transcripts. Additional exam requirements/recommendations for international students: Required—TOEFL (minimum score 100 iBT). *Application deadline:* For fall admission, 1/1 priority date for domestic and international students; for spring admission, 10/15 priority date for domestic and international students; for summer admission, 2/1 priority date for domestic and international students. Applications are processed on a rolling basis. Application fee: $75. Electronic applications accepted. *Expenses:* Tuition: Full-time $25,974; part-time $1443 per credit hour. *Required fees:* $802; $50 per course. Tuition and fees vary according to course load and program. *Financial support:* Application deadline: 1/1. *Faculty research:* Information security, digital forensics, internet security,

risk management, security policy. *Unit head:* Carsten Oesterlund, Program Director, 315-443-2911, E-mail: igrad@syr.edu. *Application contact:* Susan Corieri, Director of Enrollment Management, 315-443-2575, E-mail: ischool@syr.edu.
Website: http://ischool.syr.edu/

Texas A&M University–San Antonio, School of Business, San Antonio, TX 78224. Offers business administration (MBA); enterprise resource planning systems (MBA); finance (MBA); healthcare management (MBA); human resources management (MBA); information assurance and security (MBA); international business (MBA); professional accounting (MPA); project management (MBA); supply chain management (MBA). *Program availability:* Part-time, evening/weekend. *Entrance requirements:* For master's, GMAT. Additional exam requirements/recommendations for international students: Required—TOEFL (minimum score 550 paper-based; 80 iBT), IELTS (minimum score 6). Electronic applications accepted.

Towson University, Program in Applied Information Technology, Towson, MD 21252-0001. Offers applied information technology (MS, D Sc); database management systems (Postbaccalaureate Certificate); information security and assurance (Postbaccalaureate Certificate); information systems management (Postbaccalaureate Certificate); Internet applications development (Postbaccalaureate Certificate); networking technologies (Postbaccalaureate Certificate); software engineering (Postbaccalaureate Certificate). *Students:* 135 full-time (50 women), 154 part-time (50 women); includes 119 minority (81 Black or African American, non-Hispanic/Latino; 26 Asian, non-Hispanic/Latino; 4 Hispanic/Latino; 8 Two or more races, non-Hispanic/Latino), 82 international. *Entrance requirements:* For master's and Postbaccalaureate Certificate, bachelor's degree, minimum GPA of 3.0; for doctorate, master's degree in computer science, information systems, information technology, or closely-related area; minimum GPA of 3.0; 2 letters of recommendation; resume. Additional exam requirements/recommendations for international students: Required—TOEFL. *Application deadline:* Applications are processed on a rolling basis. Application fee: $45. Electronic applications accepted. *Expenses:* Tuition, state resident: full-time $7580; part-time $379 per unit. Tuition, nonresident: full-time $15,700; part-time $785 per unit. *Required fees:* $2480. *Unit head:* Dr. Jinjuan Feng, Graduate Program Director, 410-704-3463, E-mail: ait@towson.edu. *Application contact:* Coverley Beidleman, Assistant Director of Graduate Admissions, 410-704-2113, Fax: 410-704-3030, E-mail: grads@towson.edu.
Website: https://www.towson.edu/fcsm/departments/emergingtech/

Trident University International, College of Business Administration, Program in Business Administration, Cypress, CA 90630. Offers business administration (PhD); conflict and negotiation management (MBA); criminal justice administration (MBA); entrepreneurship (MBA); finance (MBA); general management (MBA); government accounting (MBA); human resource management (MBA); information security and digital assurance management (MBA); information technology management (MBA); international business (MBA); logistics management (MBA); marketing (MBA); project management (MBA); public management (MBA); quality management (MBA); strategic leadership (MBA). *Program availability:* Part-time, evening/weekend, online learning. *Degree requirements:* For doctorate, comprehensive exam, thesis/dissertation, defense of dissertation. *Entrance requirements:* For master's, minimum GPA of 2.5 (students with GPA 3.0 or greater may transfer up to 30% of graduate level credits); for doctorate, minimum GPA of 3.4, curriculum vitae, course work in research methods or statistics. Additional exam requirements/recommendations for international students: Required—TOEFL. Electronic applications accepted.

Tuskegee University, Graduate Programs, Andrew F. Brimmer College of Business and Information Science, Tuskegee, AL 36088. Offers information systems and security management (MS). *Degree requirements:* For master's, thesis. *Entrance requirements:* For master's, GRE or GMAT, baccalaureate degree in computer science, management information systems, accounting, finance, management, information technology, or a closely-related field.

Universidad del Este, Graduate School, Carolina, PR 00984. Offers accounting (MBA); adult education (M Ed); agribusiness (MBA); criminal justice and criminology (MA); curriculum and instruction - early education (M Ed); curriculum and instruction - elementary (M Ed); curriculum and instruction - English (M Ed); curriculum and instruction - Spanish (M Ed); human resources (MBA); information security management (MBA); information technology and Web business development (MBA); management (MBA); public policy (MPA); social work (MA), including clinical social work; special education (M Ed); strategic leadership (MBA).

Université de Sherbrooke, Faculty of Administration, Program in Governance, Audit and Security of Information Technology, Longueuil, QC J4K0A8, Canada. Offers M Adm. *Program availability:* Part-time, evening/weekend, online learning. *Degree requirements:* For master's, thesis. *Entrance requirements:* For master's, bachelor's degree, related work experience. Electronic applications accepted.

University at Albany, State University of New York, College of Emergency Preparedness, Homeland Security and Cybersecurity, Albany, NY 12222-0001. Offers cybersecurity (Certificate); emergency preparedness (Certificate); homeland security (Certificate). *Faculty:* 3 part-time/adjunct (0 women). *Students:* 8 part-time (5 women). 13 applicants, 100% accepted, 5 enrolled. In 2016, 5 Certificates awarded. *Entrance requirements:* Additional exam requirements/recommendations for international students: Required—TOEFL. *Expenses:* Tuition, state resident: full-time $10,870; part-time $453 per credit hour. Tuition, nonresident: full-time $22,210; part-time $925 per credit hour. *International tuition:* $21,550 full-time. *Required fees:* $1864; $96 per credit hour. *Unit head:* Dr. Robert Griffin, Dean, 518-442-5258. *Application contact:* Michael DeRensis, Director, Graduate Admissions, 518-442-3980, Fax: 518-442-3922, E-mail: graduate@albany.edu.
Website: http://www.albany.edu/cehc/

University at Albany, State University of New York, School of Business, MBA Programs, Albany, NY 12222. Offers business administration (MBA); cyber security (MBA); entrepreneurship (MBA); finance (MBA); human resource information systems (MBA); information technology management (MBA); marketing (MBA); JD/MBA. JD/MBA offered with Albany Law School. *Program availability:* Part-time, evening/weekend. *Faculty:* 25 full-time (8 women), 4 part-time/adjunct (1 woman). *Students:* 92 full-time (39 women), 192 part-time (77 women); includes 63 minority (12 Black or African American, non-Hispanic/Latino; 1 American Indian or Alaska Native, non-Hispanic/Latino; 32 Asian, non-Hispanic/Latino; 13 Hispanic/Latino; 5 Two or more races, non-Hispanic/Latino), 27 international. Average age 25. 217 applicants, 73% accepted, 119 enrolled. In 2016, 122 master's awarded. *Degree requirements:* For master's, thesis (for some programs), field or research project. *Entrance requirements:* For master's, GMAT, minimum undergraduate GPA of 3.0; 3 letters of recommendation; resume; statement of goals. Additional exam requirements/recommendations for international students: Required—TOEFL (minimum score 100 iBT); Recommended—IELTS (minimum score 7). *Application deadline:* For fall admission, 4/1 priority date for domestic students, 3/1 for international students; for spring admission, 12/1 for domestic students; for summer admission, 5/1 for domestic students. Applications are processed on a rolling basis. Application fee: $75. Electronic applications accepted. *Expenses:* $16,274 Full-Time MBA per year; $696 Part-Time MBA per credit hour. *Financial support:* In 2016–17, 20

students received support, including 20 fellowships with partial tuition reimbursements available (averaging $6,500 per year); research assistantships, teaching assistantships, and unspecified assistantships also available. Financial award application deadline: 4/1; financial award applicants required to submit FAFSA. *Faculty research:* Cyber security, entrepreneurship, human resource information systems, information technology management, finance, marketing. *Total annual research expenditures:* $136,000. *Unit head:* Dr. Hany A. Shawky, Interim Dean, 518-956-8337, E-mail: hshawky@albany.edu. *Application contact:* Zina Mega Lawrence, Assistant Dean of Graduate Student Services, 518-956-8320, Fax: 518-442-4042, E-mail: zlawrence@albany.edu.
Website: http://graduatebusiness.albany.edu/

University of Advancing Technology, Master of Science Program in Technology, Tempe, AZ 85283-1042. Offers advancing computer science (MS); emerging technologies (MS); game production and management (MS); information assurance (MS); technology leadership (MS). *Degree requirements:* For master's, project or thesis. *Entrance requirements:* Additional exam requirements/recommendations for international students: Required—TOEFL (minimum score 550 paper-based). Electronic applications accepted. *Faculty research:* Artificial intelligence, fractals, organizational management.

The University of Alabama at Birmingham, Collat School of Business, Program in Management Information Systems, Birmingham, AL 35294. Offers management information systems (MS), including information security, information technology management, Web and mobile development. *Program availability:* Part-time, online learning. *Entrance requirements:* For master's, GMAT. Additional exam requirements/ recommendations for international students: Required—TOEFL. Full-time tuition and fees vary according to course load and program.

The University of Alabama at Birmingham, College of Arts and Sciences, Program in Computer Forensics and Security Management, Birmingham, AL 35294. Offers MS. Interdisciplinary program offered jointly with College of Arts and Sciences and School of Business. *Degree requirements:* For master's, field practicum (internship). *Entrance requirements:* For master's, GRE General Test (minimum combined score of 320) or GMAT (minimum total score of 550), minimum GPA of 3.0. Electronic applications accepted. Full-time tuition and fees vary according to course load and program.

The University of Alabama in Huntsville, School of Graduate Studies, College of Business Administration, Programs in Information Systems, Huntsville, AL 35899. Offers cybersecurity (MS, Certificate); enterprise resource planning (Certificate); information systems (MSIS); supply chain and logistics management (MS); supply chain management (Certificate). *Program availability:* Part-time, evening/weekend. *Degree requirements:* For master's, comprehensive exam, thesis or alternative. *Entrance requirements:* For master's, GMAT (minimum score 500), minimum AACSB index of 1080. Additional exam requirements/recommendations for international students: Required—TOEFL (minimum score 550 paper-based; 80 iBT), IELTS (minimum score 6.5). Electronic applications accepted. *Expenses:* Tuition, state resident: full-time $9834; part-time $600 per credit hour. Tuition, nonresident: full-time $21,830; part-time $1325 per credit hour. *Faculty research:* Supply chain information systems, information assurance and security, databases and conceptual schema, workflow management, inter-organizational information sharing.

The University of Alabama in Huntsville, School of Graduate Studies, College of Science, Department of Computer Science, Huntsville, AL 35899. Offers computer science (MS, PhD); cybersecurity (MS); modeling and simulation (MS, PhD, Certificate); software engineering (MSSE, Certificate). *Program availability:* Part-time, evening/ weekend, online learning. *Degree requirements:* For master's, comprehensive exam, thesis or alternative, oral and written exams; for doctorate, comprehensive exam, thesis/ dissertation, oral and written exams. *Entrance requirements:* For master's, doctorate, and Certificate, GRE General Test, minimum GPA of 3.0. Additional exam requirements/ recommendations for international students: Required—TOEFL (minimum score 550 paper-based; 80 iBT), IELTS (minimum score 6.5). Electronic applications accepted. *Expenses:* Tuition, state resident: full-time $9834; part-time $600 per credit hour. Tuition, nonresident: full-time $21,830; part-time $1325 per credit hour. *Faculty research:* Information assurance and cyber security, modeling and simulation, data science, computer graphics and visualization, multimedia systems.

University of Colorado Colorado Springs, College of Engineering and Applied Science, Program in General Engineering, Colorado Springs, CO 80918. Offers energy engineering (ME); engineering management (ME); information assurance (ME); software engineering (ME); space operations (ME); systems engineering (ME). *Program availability:* Part-time, evening/weekend, blended/hybrid learning. *Faculty:* 1 full-time (0 women), 15 part-time/adjunct (6 women). *Students:* 18 full-time (3 women), 166 part-time (34 women); includes 36 minority (6 Black or African American, non-Hispanic/ Latino; 8 Asian, non-Hispanic/Latino; 12 Hispanic/Latino; 10 Two or more races, non-Hispanic/Latino), 57 international. Average age 36. 89 applicants, 72% accepted, 41 enrolled. In 2016, 21 master's, 8 doctorates awarded. *Degree requirements:* For master's, thesis, portfolio, or project; for doctorate, comprehensive exam, thesis/ dissertation. *Entrance requirements:* For master's, GRE (minimum score of 148 new grading scale on quantitative portion if undergraduate GPA is less than 3.0); for doctorate, GRE (minimum score of 148 new grading scale on the quantitative portion if the applicant has not graduated from a program of recognized standing), minimum GPA of 3.3 in the bachelor's or master's degree program attempted. Additional exam requirements/recommendations for international students: Required—TOEFL (minimum score 80 iBT), IELTS (minimum score 6). *Application deadline:* For fall admission, 7/1 for domestic students, 6/1 for international students; for spring admission, 11/1 for domestic and international students; for summer admission, 4/15 for domestic and international students. Applications are processed on a rolling basis. Application fee: $60 ($100 for international students). Electronic applications accepted. *Expenses:* Contact institution. *Financial support:* In 2016–17, 28 students received support. Federal Work-Study, scholarships/grants, traineeships, and unspecified assistantships available. Support available to part-time students. Financial award application deadline: 3/1; financial award applicants required to submit FAFSA. *Unit head:* Dr. Ramaswami Dandapani, Dean, 719-255-3543, Fax: 719-255-3542, E-mail: rdan@cas.uccs.edu. *Application contact:* Dawn House, Coordinator, 719-255-3246, E-mail: dhouse@uccs.edu.

University of Dallas, Satish and Yasmin Gupta College of Business, Irving, TX 75062-4736. Offers accounting (MBA, MS); business administration (DBA); business analytics (MS); business management (MBA); corporate finance (MBA); cybersecurity (MS); finance (MS); financial services (MBA); global business (MBA, MS); health services management (MBA); human resource management (MBA); information and technology management (MS); information assurance (MBA); information technology (MBA); information technology service management (MBA); marketing management (MBA); organization development (MBA); project management (MBA); sports and entertainment management (MBA); strategic leadership (MBA); supply chain management (MBA). *Accreditation:* AACSB. *Program availability:* Part-time, evening/weekend, online learning. *Entrance requirements:* Additional exam requirements/recommendations for international students: Required—TOEFL. Electronic applications accepted. *Expenses:* Contact institution.

University of Dayton, School of Business Administration, Dayton, OH 45469. Offers accounting (MBA); cyber security (MBA); finance (MBA); marketing (MBA); JD/MBA. *Accreditation:* AACSB. *Program availability:* Part-time, evening/weekend, blended/ hybrid learning. *Faculty:* 23 full-time (5 women), 18 part-time/adjunct (9 women). *Students:* 94 full-time (35 women), 85 part-time (38 women); includes 14 minority (5 Black or African American, non-Hispanic/Latino; 4 Asian, non-Hispanic/Latino; 5 Hispanic/Latino), 26 international. Average age 30. 269 applicants, 31% accepted. In 2016, 93 master's awarded. *Entrance requirements:* For master's, GMAT (minimum score of 500 total, 19 verbal); GRE (minimum score of 149 verbal, 146 quantitative), minimum GPA of 3.0, current resume. Additional exam requirements/recommendations for international students: Required—TOEFL (minimum score 550 paper-based; 80 iBT); Recommended—IELTS (minimum score 6.5). *Application deadline:* Applications are processed on a rolling basis. Application fee: $0 ($50 for international students). Electronic applications accepted. *Expenses:* $970 per credit hour, $25 registration fee per term. *Financial support:* In 2016–17, 7 research assistantships with partial tuition reimbursements (averaging $8,535 per year), 2 teaching assistantships with partial tuition reimbursements (averaging $8,535 per year) were awarded; institutionally sponsored loans, health care benefits, and unspecified assistantships also available. Financial award application deadline: 3/1; financial award applicants required to submit FAFSA. *Faculty research:* Asset pricing, applied microeconomics, financial reporting and auditing, entrepreneurship. *Unit head:* Scott MacDonald, Director, MBA Program, 937-229-3733, Fax: 937-229-3882, E-mail: smacdonald1@udayton.edu. *Application contact:* Mandy Bingaman, MBA Program Manager, 937-229-3733, Fax: 937-229-3882, E-mail: mbingaman1@udayton.edu.
Website: https://www.udayton.edu/business/academics/ master_of_business_administration/index.php

University of Denver, Daniel Felix Ritchie School of Engineering and Computer Science, Department of Computer Science, Denver, CO 80208. Offers computer science (MS, PhD); cybersecurity (MS). *Program availability:* Part-time, evening/ weekend. *Faculty:* 14 full-time (2 women), 3 part-time/adjunct (1 woman). *Students:* 12 full-time (3 women), 21 part-time (9 women); includes 7 minority (5 Asian, non-Hispanic/ Latino; 1 Hispanic/Latino; 1 Two or more races, non-Hispanic/Latino), 14 international. Average age 27. 75 applicants, 51% accepted, 13 enrolled. In 2016, 14 master's, 2 doctorates awarded. *Degree requirements:* For doctorate, variable foreign language requirement, comprehensive exam, thesis/dissertation, reading competency in two languages, modern typesetting system, or additional coursework. *Entrance requirements:* For master's, GRE General Test, bachelor's degree, transcripts, personal statement, resume or curriculum vitae, three letters of recommendation; for doctorate, GRE General Test, bachelor's degree in computer science or a related discipline, transcripts, personal statement, resume or curriculum vitae, three letters of recommendation. Additional exam requirements/recommendations for international students: Required—TOEFL (minimum score 550 paper-based; 80 iBT). *Application deadline:* For fall admission, 2/15 priority date for domestic and international students. Applications are processed on a rolling basis. Application fee: $65. Electronic applications accepted. *Expenses:* $29,022 per year full-time. *Financial support:* In 2016–17, 23 students received support, including 1 research assistantship with tuition reimbursement available (averaging $20,000 per year), 8 teaching assistantships with tuition reimbursements available (averaging $15,626 per year); career-related internships or fieldwork, Federal Work-Study, institutionally sponsored loans, scholarships/grants, and unspecified assistantships also available. Financial award application deadline: 2/15; financial award applicants required to submit FAFSA. *Faculty research:* Algorithms, artificial intelligence, databases, game development, robotics. *Total annual research expenditures:* $383,540. *Unit head:* Dr. Scott Leutenegger, Professor and Chair, 303-871-3329, Fax: 303-871-2821, E-mail: leut@cs.du.edu. *Application contact:* Information Contact, 303-871-2458, E-mail: info@cs.du.edu.
Website: http://ritchieschool.du.edu/departments/computer-science/

University of Detroit Mercy, College of Liberal Arts and Education, Detroit, MI 48221. Offers addiction counseling (MA); addiction studies (Certificate); clinical mental health counseling (MA); clinical psychology (MA, PhD); computer and information systems (MS); criminal justice (MA); curriculum and instruction (MA); economics (MA); educational administration (MA); financial economics (MA); industrial/organizational psychology (MA); information assurance (MS); intelligence analysis (MA); liberal studies (MALS); religious studies (MA); school counseling (MA, Certificate); school psychology (Spec); security administration (MS); special education: emotionally impaired/ behaviorally disordered (MA); special education: learning disabilities (MA). *Program availability:* Part-time, evening/weekend. *Degree requirements:* For doctorate, departmental qualifying exam. *Faculty research:* Psychology of aging, history of technology, Renaissance humanism, U.S. and Japanese economic relations.

University of Houston, College of Technology, Department of Information and Logistics Technology, Houston, TX 77204. Offers information security (MS); supply chain and logistics technology (MS); technology project management (MS). *Program availability:* Part-time. *Degree requirements:* For master's, project or thesis (most programs). *Entrance requirements:* For master's, GMAT. Additional exam requirements/ recommendations for international students: Required—TOEFL (minimum score 550 paper-based; 79 iBT). Electronic applications accepted.

University of Louisville, J. B. Speed School of Engineering, Department of Computer Engineering and Computer Science, Louisville, KY 40292-0001. Offers computer engineering and computer science (M Eng, MS, PhD); data mining (Certificate); network and information security (Certificate). *Accreditation:* ABET (one or more programs are accredited). *Program availability:* Part-time, 100% online, blended/hybrid learning. *Students:* 76 full-time (24 women), 81 part-time (16 women); includes 17 minority (5 Black or African American, non-Hispanic/Latino; 7 Asian, non-Hispanic/Latino; 2 Hispanic/Latino; 3 Two or more races, non-Hispanic/Latino), 54 international. Average age 31. 80 applicants, 46% accepted, 29 enrolled. In 2016, 17 master's, 1 doctorate, 1 other advanced degree awarded. *Degree requirements:* For master's, thesis optional, minimum GPA of 3.0; for doctorate, comprehensive exam, thesis/dissertation, minimum GPA of 3.0. *Entrance requirements:* For master's, GRE, two letters of recommendation, personal statement; for doctorate, GRE, two letters of recommendation, official final transcripts; for Certificate, undergraduate degree. Additional exam requirements/ recommendations for international students: Required—TOEFL (minimum score 550 paper-based; 80 iBT), IELTS (minimum score 6.5). *Application deadline:* For fall admission, 5/1 priority date for international students; for spring admission, 11/1 priority date for international students; for summer admission, 3/1 priority date for international students. Applications are processed on a rolling basis. Application fee: $60. Electronic applications accepted. *Expenses:* Tuition, state resident: full-time $12,246; part-time $681 per credit hour. Tuition, nonresident: full-time $25,486; part-time $1417 per credit hour. *Required fees:* $196. Tuition and fees vary according to program and reciprocity agreements. *Financial support:* In 2016–17, 2 fellowships with full tuition reimbursements (averaging $22,000 per year) were awarded; research assistantships with full tuition reimbursements, teaching assistantships with full tuition reimbursements, scholarships/grants, health care benefits, and tuition waivers also available. Financial award application deadline: 1/1. *Faculty research:* Software systems engineering, information security and forensics, multimedia and vision, mobile and distributed computing, intelligent systems. *Total annual research expenditures:* $740,736. *Unit*

head: Dr. Adel S. Elmaghraby, Chair, 502-852-6304, Fax: 502-852-4713, E-mail: adel@louisville.edu. *Application contact:* Dr. Mehmed Kantardzic, Director of Graduate Studies, 502-852-3703, E-mail: mehmed.kantardzic@louisville.edu.
Website: http://louisville.edu/speed/computer

University of Maryland, Baltimore County, The Graduate School, College of Engineering and Information Technology, Department of Computer Science and Electrical Engineering, Program in Cybersecurity, Baltimore, MD 21250. Offers cybersecurity (MPS); cybersecurity strategy and policy (Postbaccalaureate Certificate). *Program availability:* Part-time. *Faculty:* 2 full-time (0 women). *Students:* 34 full-time (9 women), 148 part-time (36 women); includes 74 minority (35 Black or African American, non-Hispanic/Latino; 14 Asian, non-Hispanic/Latino; 19 Hispanic/Latino; 1 Native Hawaiian or other Pacific Islander, non-Hispanic/Latino; 5 Two or more races, non-Hispanic/Latino), 8 international. Average age 34. 118 applicants, 63% accepted, 50 enrolled. In 2016, 57 master's, 22 other advanced degrees awarded. *Degree requirements:* For master's, comprehensive exam (for some programs). *Entrance requirements:* For master's, bachelor's degree in computer science, computer engineering, engineering, math, or information systems, or in other field with relevant work experience; curriculum vitae and two letters of recommendation (for international students). *Application deadline:* For fall admission, 8/1 for domestic and international students; for spring admission, 11/1 for international students. Applications are processed on a rolling basis. Application fee: $70. Electronic applications accepted. *Expenses:* Contact institution. *Financial support:* In 2016–17, 1 research assistantship (averaging $18,000 per year) was awarded; teaching assistantships, career-related internships or fieldwork, Federal Work-Study, health care benefits, and unspecified assistantships also available. Support available to part-time students. Financial award application deadline: 6/30; financial award applicants required to submit FAFSA. *Faculty research:* Cybersecurity strategy and policy. *Unit head:* Dr. Anupam Joshi, Professor and Chair, 410-455-3500, E-mail: joshi@cs.umbc.edu. *Application contact:* Dr. Richard Forno, Lecturer and Graduate Program Director, 410-455-5536, Fax: 410-455-3969, E-mail: richard.forno@umbc.edu.
Website: http://www.umbc.edu/cyber/

University of Maryland University College, The Graduate School, Cybersecurity Management and Policy Program, Adelphi, MD 20783. Offers MS, Certificate. *Program availability:* Part-time, evening/weekend, online learning. *Students:* 151 full-time (59 women), 192 part-time (87 women); includes 170 minority (118 Black or African American, non-Hispanic/Latino; 1 American Indian or Alaska Native, non-Hispanic/Latino; 20 Asian, non-Hispanic/Latino; 20 Hispanic/Latino; 1 Native Hawaiian or other Pacific Islander, non-Hispanic/Latino; 10 Two or more races, non-Hispanic/Latino), 4 international. Average age 36. 214 applicants, 100% accepted, 126 enrolled. In 2016, 98 master's, 15 other advanced degrees awarded. *Degree requirements:* For master's, thesis or alternative, capstone course. *Application deadline:* Applications are processed on a rolling basis. Application fee: $50. Electronic applications accepted. *Expenses:* Tuition, state resident: part-time $458 per credit. Tuition, nonresident: part-time $659 per credit. *Financial support:* Federal Work-Study and scholarships/grants available. Support available to part-time students. Financial award application deadline: 6/1; financial award applicants required to submit FAFSA. *Unit head:* Dr. Bruce deGrazia, Program Chair, 240-684-2400, Fax: 240-684-2401, E-mail: bruce.degrazia@umuc.edu. *Application contact:* Coordinator, Graduate Admissions, 800-888-UMUC, Fax: 240-684-2151, E-mail: newgrad@umuc.edu.
Website: http://www.umuc.edu/academic-programs/masters-degrees/cybersecurity-policy.cfm

University of Maryland University College, The Graduate School, Cybersecurity Technology Program, Adelphi, MD 20783. Offers MS, Certificate. *Program availability:* Part-time, evening/weekend, online learning. *Students:* 465 full-time (127 women), 1,287 part-time (354 women); includes 983 minority (597 Black or African American, non-Hispanic/Latino; 6 American Indian or Alaska Native, non-Hispanic/Latino; 146 Asian, non-Hispanic/Latino; 157 Hispanic/Latino; 7 Native Hawaiian or other Pacific Islander, non-Hispanic/Latino; 70 Two or more races, non-Hispanic/Latino), 19 international. Average age 34. 599 applicants, 100% accepted, 408 enrolled. In 2016, 469 master's, 169 other advanced degrees awarded. *Degree requirements:* For master's, thesis or alternative, capstone course. *Application deadline:* Applications are processed on a rolling basis. Application fee: $50. Electronic applications accepted. *Expenses:* Tuition, state resident: part-time $458 per credit. Tuition, nonresident: part-time $659 per credit. *Financial support:* Federal Work-Study and scholarships/grants available. Support available to part-time students. Financial award application deadline: 6/1; financial award applicants required to submit FAFSA. *Unit head:* Dr. Emma Garrison-Alexander, Chair, 240-684-2400, Fax: 240-684-2401, E-mail: emma.garrison-alexander@umuc.edu. *Application contact:* Coordinator, Graduate Admissions, 800-888-8682, Fax: 240-684-2151, E-mail: newgrad@umuc.edu.
Website: http://www.umuc.edu/academic-programs/masters-degrees/cybersecurity.cfm

University of Maryland University College, The Graduate School, Program in Digital Forensics and Cyber Investigation, Adelphi, MD 20783. Offers MS. *Program availability:* Part-time, evening/weekend, online learning. *Students:* 123 full-time (73 women), 245 part-time (121 women); includes 208 minority (138 Black or African American, non-Hispanic/Latino; 2 American Indian or Alaska Native, non-Hispanic/Latino; 18 Asian, non-Hispanic/Latino; 37 Hispanic/Latino; 13 Two or more races, non-Hispanic/Latino). Average age 32. 154 applicants, 100% accepted, 102 enrolled. In 2016, 92 master's awarded. *Degree requirements:* For master's, thesis or alternative, capstone course. *Application deadline:* Applications are processed on a rolling basis. Application fee: $50. Electronic applications accepted. *Expenses:* Tuition, state resident: part-time $458 per credit. Tuition, nonresident: part-time $659 per credit. *Financial support:* Federal Work-Study and scholarships/grants available. Support available to part-time students. Financial award application deadline: 6/1; financial award applicants required to submit FAFSA. *Application contact:* Coordinator, Graduate Admissions, 800-888-8682, Fax: 240-684-2151, E-mail: newgrad@umuc.edu.
Website: http://www.umuc.edu/academic-programs/masters-degrees/digital-forensics-and-cyber-investigations.cfm

University of Michigan–Dearborn, College of Engineering and Computer Science, PhD Program in Computer and Information Science, Dearborn, MI 48128. Offers data management (PhD); data science (PhD); software engineering (PhD); systems and security (PhD). *Program availability:* Part-time, evening/weekend. *Degree requirements:* For doctorate, thesis/dissertation. *Entrance requirements:* For doctorate, GRE, bachelor's or master's degree in computer science or closely-related field. Additional exam requirements/recommendations for international students: Required—TOEFL (minimum score 84 iBT), IELTS (minimum score 6.5). *Application deadline:* For fall admission, 2/15 for domestic and international students. Application fee: $60. Electronic applications accepted. *Expenses:* Tuition, state resident: full-time $13,118; part-time $2280 per term. Tuition, nonresident: full-time $21,816; part-time $3771 per term. *Required fees:* $866; $658 per unit. $329 per term. Tuition and fees vary according to program. *Financial support:* Research assistantships, teaching assistantships, scholarships/grants, health care benefits, and unspecified assistantships available. Financial award application deadline: 2/15; financial award applicants required to submit FAFSA. *Unit head:* Dr. Brahim Medjahed, Director, 313-583-6449, E-mail: brahim@

umich.edu. *Application contact:* Office of Graduate Studies Staff, 313-583-6321, E-mail: umd-graduatestudies@umich.edu.
Website: https://umdearborn.edu/cecs/departments/computer-and-information-science/graduate-programs/phd-computer-and-information-science

University of Minnesota, Twin Cities Campus, College of Science and Engineering, Technological Leadership Institute, Program in Security Technologies, Minneapolis, MN 55455-0213. Offers MSST. *Program availability:* Part-time. *Degree requirements:* For master's, capstone project. *Entrance requirements:* Additional exam requirements/recommendations for international students: Required—TOEFL (minimum score 580 paper-based; 90 iBT). Electronic applications accepted.

University of Missouri–St. Louis, College of Business Administration, Program in Business Administration, St. Louis, MO 63121. Offers accounting (MBA); business administration (Certificate); business intelligence (Certificate); cybersecurity (Certificate); digital and social media marketing (Certificate); finance (MBA); human resources management (Certificate); information systems (MBA); international business (MBA); logistics and supply chain management (MBA, PhD, Certificate); management (MBA); marketing (MBA); marketing management (Certificate); operations management (MBA). *Accreditation:* AACSB. *Program availability:* Part-time, evening/weekend. *Faculty:* 32 full-time (10 women), 14 part-time/adjunct (3 women). *Students:* 181 full-time (88 women), 357 part-time (154 women); includes 83 minority (30 Black or African American, non-Hispanic/Latino; 36 Asian, non-Hispanic/Latino; 12 Hispanic/Latino; 2 Native Hawaiian or other Pacific Islander, non-Hispanic/Latino; 3 Two or more races, non-Hispanic/Latino), 100 international. Average age 31. 245 applicants, 83% accepted, 139 enrolled. *Degree requirements:* For doctorate, thesis/dissertation. *Entrance requirements:* For master's, GMAT, 2 letters of recommendation. Additional exam requirements/recommendations for international students: Recommended—TOEFL (minimum score 550 paper-based; 79 iBT), IELTS (minimum score 6.5). *Application deadline:* For fall admission, 7/1 for domestic and international students; for spring admission, 12/1 for domestic and international students. Applications are processed on a rolling basis. Application fee: $50 ($40 for international students). Electronic applications accepted. *Financial support:* Research assistantships with tuition reimbursements, teaching assistantships with tuition reimbursements, career-related internships or fieldwork, Federal Work-Study, and institutionally sponsored loans available. Support available to part-time students. Financial award application deadline: 4/1; financial award applicants required to submit FAFSA. *Faculty research:* Human resources, strategic management, marketing strategy, consumer behavior product development, advertising. *Unit head:* Dr. Thomas H. Eyssell, Associate Dean and Director of Graduate Studies, 314-516-5885, Fax: 314-516-6420, E-mail: mba@umsl.edu. *Application contact:* 314-516-5458, Fax: 314-516-6996, E-mail: gradadm@umsl.edu.

University of Nebraska at Omaha, Graduate Studies, College of Information Science and Technology, Department of Information Systems and Quantitative Analysis, Omaha, NE 68182. Offers data analytics (Certificate); information assurance (Certificate); information technology (MIT, PhD); management information systems (MS); project management (Certificate); systems analysis and design (Certificate). *Program availability:* Part-time, evening/weekend. *Faculty:* 6 full-time (1 woman). *Students:* 140 full-time (53 women), 102 part-time (29 women); includes 25 minority (9 Black or African American, non-Hispanic/Latino; 7 Asian, non-Hispanic/Latino; 6 Hispanic/Latino; 3 Two or more races, non-Hispanic/Latino), 161 international. Average age 29. 342 applicants, 50% accepted, 68 enrolled. In 2016, 84 master's, 8 doctorates, 54 other advanced degrees awarded. *Degree requirements:* For master's, comprehensive exam, thesis (for some programs); for doctorate, comprehensive exam, thesis/dissertation. *Entrance requirements:* For master's, GRE General Test, minimum GPA of 3.0, 3 letters of recommendation, writing sample, resume, official transcripts; for doctorate, GMAT or GRE General Test, minimum GPA of 3.0, 3 letters of recommendation, writing sample, resume, official transcripts; for Certificate, minimum GPA of 3.0, official transcripts. Additional exam requirements/recommendations for international students: Required—TOEFL, IELTS, PTE. *Application deadline:* For fall admission, 2/15 for domestic and international students; for spring admission, 9/15 for domestic and international students; for summer admission, 4/1 for domestic and international students. Applications are processed on a rolling basis. Application fee: $45. Electronic applications accepted. *Financial support:* In 2016–17, 30 students received support, including 24 research assistantships with tuition reimbursements available, 6 teaching assistantships with tuition reimbursements available; fellowships, career-related internships or fieldwork, Federal Work-Study, scholarships/grants, health care benefits, tuition waivers (partial), and unspecified assistantships also available. Financial award application deadline: 3/1; financial award applicants required to submit FAFSA. *Unit head:* Dr. Peter Wolcott, Chairperson, 402-554-2341, E-mail: graduate@unomaha.edu. *Application contact:* Dr. Martina Greiner, Graduate Program Chair, 402-554-2341, E-mail: graduate@unomaha.edu.

University of Nebraska at Omaha, Graduate Studies, College of Information Science and Technology, School of Interdisciplinary Informatics, Omaha, NE 68182. Offers biomedical informatics (MS, PhD); information assurance (MS). *Program availability:* Part-time, evening/weekend. *Faculty:* 10 full-time (3 women). *Students:* 26 full-time (9 women), 34 part-time (5 women); includes 9 minority (5 Black or African American, non-Hispanic/Latino; 2 Asian, non-Hispanic/Latino; 2 Hispanic/Latino), 13 international. Average age 31. 53 applicants, 58% accepted, 15 enrolled. In 2016, 14 master's awarded. *Degree requirements:* For master's, comprehensive exam, thesis (for some programs); for doctorate, comprehensive exam, thesis/dissertation. *Entrance requirements:* For master's and doctorate, GRE General Test, letters of recommendation, resume, transcripts. Additional exam requirements/recommendations for international students: Required—TOEFL, IELTS, PTE. *Financial support:* In 2016–17, 6 students received support, including 6 research assistantships with tuition reimbursements available; fellowships, teaching assistantships with tuition reimbursements available, career-related internships or fieldwork, Federal Work-Study, scholarships/grants, health care benefits, tuition waivers (partial), and unspecified assistantships also available. Financial award application deadline: 3/1; financial award applicants required to submit FAFSA. *Unit head:* Dr. Ann Fruhling, Director, 402-554-2341, E-mail: graduate@unomaha.edu. *Application contact:* Dr. Dhundy Bastola, Graduate Program Chair, 402-554-2341, E-mail: graduate@unomaha.edu.

University of New Haven, Graduate School, Henry C. Lee College of Criminal Justice and Forensic Sciences, Program in Criminal Justice, West Haven, CT 06516. Offers crime analysis (MS); criminal justice (MS, PhD); criminal justice management (MS, Graduate Certificate); forensic computer investigation (MS); forensic psychology (MS); information protection and security (Graduate Certificate); victim advocacy and services management (Graduate Certificate); victimology (MS). *Program availability:* Part-time, evening/weekend, online learning. *Students:* 120 full-time (83 women), 121 part-time (69 women); includes 84 minority (49 Black or African American, non-Hispanic/Latino; 10 Asian, non-Hispanic/Latino; 14 Hispanic/Latino; 1 Native Hawaiian or other Pacific Islander, non-Hispanic/Latino; 10 Two or more races, non-Hispanic/Latino), 10 international. Average age 29. 128 applicants, 90% accepted, 73 enrolled. In 2016, 52 master's, 2 doctorates, 8 other advanced degrees awarded. *Degree requirements:* For master's, thesis or alternative. *Entrance requirements:* Additional exam requirements/

recommendations for international students: Required—TOEFL (minimum score 80 iBT), IELTS, PTE (minimum score 53). *Application deadline:* Applications are processed on a rolling basis. Application fee: $50. Electronic applications accepted. Application fee is waived when completed online. *Expenses: Tuition:* Full-time $15,660; part-time $870 per credit hour. *Required fees:* $200; $85 per term. Tuition and fees vary according to program. *Financial support:* Research assistantships with partial tuition reimbursements, teaching assistantships with partial tuition reimbursements, career-related internships or fieldwork, Federal Work-Study, scholarships/grants, and unspecified assistantships available. Support available to part-time students. Financial award applicants required to submit FAFSA. *Application contact:* Michelle Mason, Director of Graduate Enrollment, 203-932-7067, E-mail: mmason@newhaven.edu.
Website: http://www.newhaven.edu/5921/

University of New Haven, Graduate School, Henry C. Lee College of Criminal Justice and Forensic Sciences, Program in National Security, West Haven, CT 06516. Offers information protection and security (MS); national security (MS, Graduate Certificate); national security administration (Graduate Certificate). *Program availability:* Part-time, evening/weekend. *Students:* 43 full-time (20 women), 34 part-time (13 women); includes 19 minority (6 Black or African American, non-Hispanic/Latino; 1 Asian, non-Hispanic/Latino; 9 Hispanic/Latino; 3 Two or more races, non-Hispanic/Latino), 6 international. Average age 31. 41 applicants, 98% accepted, 27 enrolled. In 2016, 27 master's, 2 other advanced degrees awarded. *Degree requirements:* For master's, thesis or alternative, research project or internship. *Entrance requirements:* Additional exam requirements/recommendations for international students: Required—TOEFL (minimum score 70 iBT), IELTS, or PTE (minimum score of 53). *Application deadline:* Applications are processed on a rolling basis. Application fee: $50. Electronic applications accepted. Application fee is waived when completed online. *Expenses: Tuition:* Full-time $15,660; part-time $870 per credit hour. *Required fees:* $200; $85 per term. Tuition and fees vary according to program. *Financial support:* Research assistantships with partial tuition reimbursements, teaching assistantships with partial tuition reimbursements, career-related internships or fieldwork, Federal Work-Study, scholarships/grants, and unspecified assistantships available. Support available to part-time students. Financial award applicants required to submit FAFSA. *Unit head:* Dr. Jibey Asthappan, Director, 203-479-4147, E-mail: jasthappan@newhaven.edu. *Application contact:* Michelle Mason, Director of Graduate Enrollment, 203-932-7067, E-mail: mmason@newhaven.edu.
Website: http://www.newhaven.edu/5924/

University of New Haven, Graduate School, Tagliatela College of Engineering, Program in Cyber Systems, West Haven, CT 06516. Offers MS. *Students:* 25 full-time (8 women), 3 part-time (1 woman); includes 2 minority (both Black or African American, non-Hispanic/Latino), 16 international. Average age 26. 76 applicants, 46% accepted, 8 enrolled. In 2016, 11 master's awarded. *Application deadline:* Applications are processed on a rolling basis. Application fee: $50. *Expenses: Tuition:* Full-time $15,660; part-time $870 per credit hour. *Required fees:* $200; $85 per term. Tuition and fees vary according to program. *Unit head:* Dr. David Eggert, Coordinator, 203-932-7097, E-mail: deggert@newhaven.edu. *Application contact:* Michelle Mason, Director of Graduate Enrollment, 203-932-7067, E-mail: mmason@newhaven.edu.
Website: http://www.newhaven.edu/engineering/academic-depts/graduate/cyber-systems/

University of New Mexico, Anderson School of Management, Department of Accounting, Albuquerque, NM 87131. Offers accounting (MBA); advanced accounting (M Acct); information assurance (M Acct); professional accounting (M Acct); tax accounting (M Acct); JD/M Acct. *Accreditation:* AACSB. *Program availability:* Part-time, evening/weekend. *Faculty:* 15 full-time (7 women), 3 part-time/adjunct (all women). *Students:* 81 applicants, 70% accepted, 51 enrolled. In 2016, 39 master's awarded. *Entrance requirements:* For master's, GMAT/GRE (minimum score of 500), minimum GPA of 3.25, 3.0 on last 60 hours of coursework (for M Acct in professional accounting). Additional exam requirements/recommendations for international students: Required—TOEFL (minimum score 550 paper-based; 79 iBT), IELTS (minimum score 6.5). *Application deadline:* For fall admission, 4/1 priority date for domestic and international students; for spring admission, 10/1 priority date for domestic and international students. Applications are processed on a rolling basis. Application fee: $50. Electronic applications accepted. *Expenses:* Contact institution. *Financial support:* In 2016–17, 2 fellowships (averaging $20,800 per year), 12 research assistantships with partial tuition reimbursements (averaging $15,488 per year) were awarded; career-related internships or fieldwork, Federal Work-Study, scholarships/grants, and unspecified assistantships also available. Support available to part-time students. Financial award application deadline: 6/1; financial award applicants required to submit FAFSA. *Faculty research:* Critical accounting, accounting pedagogy, theory, taxation, information fraud. *Unit head:* Dr. Leslie Oakes, Chair, 505-277-6471, E-mail: loakes@unm.edu. *Application contact:* Dr. Rich Brody, Professor, 505-277-6471, E-mail: tmarmijo@unm.edu.
Website: https://www.mgt.unm.edu/acct/default.asp?mm=faculty

University of New Mexico, Anderson School of Management, Department of Marketing, Information and Decision Sciences, Albuquerque, NM 87131. Offers information assurance (MBA); information systems and assurance (MS); management information systems (MBA); marketing management (MBA); operations management (MBA). *Program availability:* Part-time, evening/weekend. *Faculty:* 17 full-time (3 women), 7 part-time/adjunct (5 women). In 2016, 47 master's awarded. *Entrance requirements:* For master's, GMAT or GRE, minimum GPA of 3.0 on last 60 hours of coursework; bachelor's degree from regionally-accredited college or university in U.S. or its equivalent in another country. Additional exam requirements/recommendations for international students: Required—TOEFL (minimum score 550 paper-based; 79 iBT), IELTS (minimum score 6.5). *Application deadline:* For fall admission, 4/1 priority date for domestic and international students; for spring admission, 10/1 priority date for domestic and international students. Applications are processed on a rolling basis. Application fee: $50. Electronic applications accepted. *Expenses:* Contact institution. *Financial support:* In 2016–17, 8 fellowships (averaging $11,484 per year), 13 research assistantships with partial tuition reimbursements (averaging $9,382 per year) were awarded; career-related internships or fieldwork, Federal Work-Study, scholarships/grants, and unspecified assistantships also available. Support available to part-time students. Financial award application deadline: 6/1; financial award applicants required to submit FAFSA. *Faculty research:* Marketing, operations management, information systems, information assurance. *Unit head:* Dr. Steve Yourstone, Chair, 505-277-6471, E-mail: yourstone@unm.edu. *Application contact:* Lisa Beauchene, Student Recruitment Specialist, 505-277-6471, E-mail: andersonadvising@unm.edu.
Website: https://www.mgt.unm.edu/mids/default.asp?mm=faculty

The University of North Carolina at Charlotte, College of Computing and Informatics, Department of Software and Information Systems, Charlotte, NC 28223-0001. Offers information security and privacy (Graduate Certificate); information technology (MS); management of information technology (Graduate Certificate); network security (Graduate Certificate); secure software development (Graduate Certificate). *Program availability:* Part-time, evening/weekend. *Faculty:* 15 full-time (6 women), 7 part-time/adjunct (0 women). *Students:* 96 full-time (41 women), 92 part-time (33 women); includes 24 minority (16 Black or African American, non-Hispanic/Latino; 2 Asian, non-Hispanic/Latino; 2 Hispanic/Latino; 4 Two or more races, non-Hispanic/Latino), 144 international. Average age 27. 557 applicants, 38% accepted, 55 enrolled. In 2016, 139 master's, 5 other advanced degrees awarded. *Degree requirements:* For master's, project, internship, or thesis. *Entrance requirements:* For master's, GRE or GMAT, undergraduate or equivalent course work in data structures, object-oriented programming in C++, C#, or Java with minimum GPA of 3.0; for Graduate Certificate, bachelor's degree from accredited institution in computing, mathematical, engineering or business discipline with minimum overall GPA of 2.8, junior/senior 3.0; substantial knowledge of data structures and object-oriented programming in C++, C# or Java. Additional exam requirements/recommendations for international students: Required—TOEFL (minimum score 523 paper-based, 70 iBT) or IELTS (6.5). *Application deadline:* For fall admission, 3/1 for domestic and international students; for spring admission, 10/1 for domestic and international students. Applications are processed on a rolling basis. Application fee: $75. Electronic applications accepted. *Expenses:* Contact institution. *Financial support:* In 2016–17, 62 students received support, including 1 fellowship (averaging $70,000 per year), 28 research assistantships (averaging $9,899 per year), 33 teaching assistantships (averaging $9,193 per year); career-related internships or fieldwork, institutionally sponsored loans, scholarships/grants, and unspecified assistantships also available. Support available to part-time students. Financial award application deadline: 3/1; financial award applicants required to submit FAFSA. *Total annual research expenditures:* $2.8 million. *Unit head:* Dr. Mary Lou Maher, Chair, 704-687-1940, E-mail: mmaher9@uncc.edu. *Application contact:* Kathy B. Giddings, Director of Graduate Admissions, 704-687-5503, Fax: 704-687-1668, E-mail: gradadm@uncc.edu.
Website: http://sis.uncc.edu/

The University of North Carolina at Charlotte, College of Computing and Informatics, Program in Computing and Information Systems, Charlotte, NC 28223-0001. Offers computing and information systems (PhD), including bioinformatics, business information systems and operations management, computer science, interdisciplinary, software and information systems. *Faculty:* 3 full-time (0 women). *Students:* 91 full-time (30 women), 23 part-time (3 women); includes 8 minority (2 Black or African American, non-Hispanic/Latino; 4 Asian, non-Hispanic/Latino; 1 Hispanic/Latino; 1 Two or more races, non-Hispanic/Latino), 76 international. Average age 31. 90 applicants, 41% accepted, 18 enrolled. In 2016, 13 doctorates awarded. *Degree requirements:* For doctorate, comprehensive exam, thesis/dissertation. *Entrance requirements:* For doctorate, GRE or GMAT, baccalaureate degree, minimum GPA of 3.0 on courses related to the chosen field of PhD study, essay, reference letters. Additional exam requirements/recommendations for international students: Required—TOEFL (minimum score 523 paper-based, 70 iBT) or IELTS (6.5). *Application deadline:* For fall admission, 2/1 for domestic and international students; for spring admission, 9/1 for domestic and international students. Applications are processed on a rolling basis. Application fee: $75. Electronic applications accepted. *Expenses:* Tuition, state resident: full-time $4252. Tuition, nonresident: full-time $17,423. *Required fees:* $3026. Tuition and fees vary according to course load and program. *Financial support:* Career-related internships or fieldwork, institutionally sponsored loans, scholarships/grants, health care benefits, and unspecified assistantships available. Support available to part-time students. Financial award applicants required to submit FAFSA. *Unit head:* Manuel A. Perez Quinones, Director, 704-687-8553, E-mail: perez.quinones@uncc.edu. *Application contact:* Kathy B. Giddings, Director of Graduate Admissions, 704-687-5503, Fax: 704-687-1668, E-mail: gradadm@uncc.edu.

University of Pittsburgh, School of Information Sciences, Information Science and Technology Program, Pittsburgh, PA 15260. Offers big data (Post-Master's Certificate, Postbaccalaureate Certificate); information science (MSIS, PhD), including information science (PhD), telecommunications (PhD); information science and technology (Certificate); security assured information systems (Post-Master's Certificate, Postbaccalaureate Certificate). *Program availability:* Part-time, evening/weekend, 100% online. *Faculty:* 17 full-time (3 women), 14 part-time/adjunct (3 women). *Students:* 240 full-time (93 women), 58 part-time (24 women); includes 14 minority (2 Black or African American, non-Hispanic/Latino; 5 Asian, non-Hispanic/Latino; 4 Hispanic/Latino; 3 Two or more races, non-Hispanic/Latino), 248 international. Average age 28. 675 applicants, 71% accepted, 107 enrolled. In 2016, 133 master's, 6 doctorates awarded. *Degree requirements:* For master's, thesis optional; for doctorate, comprehensive exam, thesis/dissertation. *Entrance requirements:* For master's, GRE General Test, GMAT, bachelor's degree with minimum GPA of 3.0; course work in structured programming language, statistics, and mathematics; for doctorate, GRE General Test, GMAT, master's degree; minimum GPA of 3.3; course work in statistics or mathematics, programming, cognitive psychology, systems analysis and design, and data structures; for other advanced degree, master's degree in information science, telecommunications, or related field. Additional exam requirements/recommendations for international students: Required—TOEFL (minimum score 550 paper-based; 80 iBT). *Application deadline:* For fall admission, 7/15 priority date for domestic students, 1/15 priority date for international students; for winter admission, 11/1 priority date for domestic students, 6/15 priority date for international students; for spring admission, 11/1 priority date for domestic students, 6/15 priority date for international students; for summer admission, 3/15 priority date for domestic students, 12/15 priority date for international students. Applications are processed on a rolling basis. Application fee: $50. Electronic applications accepted. *Expenses:* $22,628 per year in-state, $37,754 per year out-of-state (fall and spring); $931 per credit in-state, $1,553 per credit out-of-state (summer). *Financial support:* Fellowships with full and partial tuition reimbursements, research assistantships with full and partial tuition reimbursements, teaching assistantships with full and partial tuition reimbursements, career-related internships or fieldwork, institutionally sponsored loans, scholarships/grants, traineeships, health care benefits, and unspecified assistantships available. Financial award application deadline: 1/15; financial award applicants required to submit FAFSA. *Faculty research:* Big data, systems analysis and design, geoinformatics, database and Web systems, information assurance and security, cloud computing, social computing. *Unit head:* Dr. Martin Weiss, Program Chair, 412-624-9430, Fax: 421-624-5231, E-mail: mbw@pitt.edu. *Application contact:* Shabana Reza, Enrollment Manager, 412-624-3988, Fax: 412-624-5231, E-mail: sreza@sis.pitt.edu.
Website: http://www.ischool.pitt.edu/ist/

University of San Diego, Division of Professional and Continuing Education, San Diego, CA 92110-2492. Offers cyber security operations and leadership (MS); law enforcement and public safety leadership, (MS). *Program availability:* Part-time-only, evening/weekend, 100% online. *Faculty:* 1 full-time (0 women). *Students:* 200 part-time (44 women); includes 88 minority (10 Black or African American, non-Hispanic/Latino; 22 Asian, non-Hispanic/Latino; 54 Hispanic/Latino; 2 Two or more races, non-Hispanic/Latino). Average age 37. 120 applicants, 88% accepted, 83 enrolled. *Entrance requirements:* For master's, GMAT, GRE, or LSAT if GPA is under 2.75. Additional exam requirements/recommendations for international students: Required—TOEFL (minimum score 90 iBT). *Application deadline:* For fall admission, 8/2 for domestic students; for spring admission, 11/7 for domestic students; for summer admission, 4/11 for domestic students. Applications are processed on a rolling basis. Application fee: $45. Electronic applications accepted. *Financial support:* Application deadline: 4/1; applicants required to submit FAFSA. *Unit head:* Dr. Jason Lemon, Dean, 619-260-

4585, E-mail: continuinged@sandiego.edu. *Application contact:* Monica Mahon, Associate Director of Graduate Admissions, 619-260-4524, Fax: 619-260-4158, E-mail: grads@sandiego.edu.
Website: http://pce.sandiego.edu/

University of San Diego, Shiley-Marcos School of Engineering, San Diego, CA 92110-2492. Offers cyber security engineering (MS). *Faculty:* 1 full-time (0 women). *Students:* 3 part-time (0 women); includes 1 minority (Asian, non-Hispanic/Latino). 17 applicants, 82% accepted, 3 enrolled. *Degree requirements:* For master's, capstone course. *Entrance requirements:* Additional exam requirements/recommendations for international students: Required—TOEFL (minimum score 120 iBT). *Application deadline:* For fall admission, 8/2 for domestic students; for spring admission, 11/7 for domestic students; for summer admission, 4/11 for domestic students. Application fee: $45. *Unit head:* Dr. Chell Roberts, Dean, 619-260-4627, E-mail: croberts@sandiego.edu. *Application contact:* Monica Mahon, Associate Director of Graduate Admissions, 619-260-4524, Fax: 619-260-4158, E-mail: grads@sandiego.edu.
Website: http://www.sandiego.edu/engineering/

University of Southern California, Graduate School, Viterbi School of Engineering, Department of Computer Science, Los Angeles, CA 90089. Offers computer networks (MS); computer science (MS, PhD); computer security (MS); game development (MS); high performance computing and simulations (MS); human language technology (MS); intelligent robotics (MS); multimedia and creative technologies (MS); software engineering (MS). *Program availability:* Part-time, evening/weekend, online learning. *Entrance requirements:* For master's and doctorate, GRE General Test. Additional exam requirements/recommendations for international students: Required—TOEFL. Electronic applications accepted. *Faculty research:* Databases, computer graphics and computer vision, software engineering, networks and security, robotics, multimedia and virtual reality.

University of South Florida, College of Arts and Sciences, School of Information, Tampa, FL 33620-9951. Offers intelligence studies (MS), including cyber intelligence, strategic intelligence; library and information science (MA). *Accreditation:* ALA (one or more programs are accredited). *Program availability:* Part-time, evening/weekend, online learning. *Faculty:* 17 full-time (8 women). *Students:* 112 full-time (73 women), 163 part-time (127 women); includes 80 minority (28 Black or African American, non-Hispanic/Latino; 11 Asian, non-Hispanic/Latino; 32 Hispanic/Latino; 1 Native Hawaiian or other Pacific Islander, non-Hispanic/Latino; 8 Two or more races, non-Hispanic/Latino), 1 international. Average age 33. 167 applicants, 84% accepted, 90 enrolled. In 2016, 61 master's awarded. *Degree requirements:* For master's, comprehensive exam, thesis (for some programs). *Entrance requirements:* For master's, GRE General Test (for some programs). Additional exam requirements/recommendations for international students: Required—TOEFL (minimum score 550 paper-based; 79 iBT) or IELTS (minimum score 6.5). *Application deadline:* For fall admission, 6/1 for domestic students, 2/15 for international students; for spring admission, 10/15 for domestic students, 9/15 for international students. Applications are processed on a rolling basis. Application fee: $30. Electronic applications accepted. *Expenses:* Tuition, state resident: full-time $7766; part-time $431.43 per credit hour. Tuition, nonresident: full-time $15,789; part-time $877.17 per credit hour. *Required fees:* $37 per term. *Financial support:* In 2016–17, 47 students received support. Unspecified assistantships available. Financial award application deadline: 6/30. *Faculty research:* Youth services in libraries, community engagement and libraries, information architecture, biomedical informatics, health informatics. *Total annual research expenditures:* $378,531. *Unit head:* Dr. Jim Andrews, Director and Associate Professor, 813-974-2108, Fax: 813-974-6840, E-mail: jimandrews@usf.edu. *Application contact:* Dr. Diane Austin, Assistant Director, 813-974-6364, Fax: 813-974-6840, E-mail: dianeaustin@usf.edu.
Website: http://si.usf.edu/

University of South Florida, College of Graduate Studies, Tampa, FL 33620-9951. Offers cybersecurity (MS), including computer security fundamentals, cyber intelligence, digital forensics, information assurance. *Program availability:* Part-time, evening/weekend, online learning. *Faculty:* 1 (woman) full-time. *Students:* 63 full-time (20 women), 199 part-time (55 women); includes 99 minority (33 Black or African American, non-Hispanic/Latino; 1 American Indian or Alaska Native, non-Hispanic/Latino; 9 Asian, non-Hispanic/Latino; 42 Hispanic/Latino; 3 Native Hawaiian or other Pacific Islander, non-Hispanic/Latino; 11 Two or more races, non-Hispanic/Latino), 1 international. Average age 35. 104 applicants, 68% accepted, 49 enrolled. In 2016, 24 master's awarded. Terminal master's awarded for partial completion of doctoral program. *Degree requirements:* For master's, variable foreign language requirement, comprehensive exam, thesis (for some programs), practicum. *Entrance requirements:* For master's, GRE General Test, minimum GPA of 3.0; official transcripts with confirmation that applicant has received bachelor's degree from regionally-accredited university; 250-500 word essay in which student describes academic and professional background, reasons for pursuing degree, and professional goals pertaining to cybersecurity; two letters of recommendation. Additional exam requirements/recommendations for international students: Required—TOEFL (minimum score 550 paper-based; 79 iBT) or IELTS (minimum score 6.5). *Application deadline:* For fall admission, 2/15 for domestic and international students; for spring admission, 10/15 for domestic students, 9/15 for international students; for summer admission, 2/15 for domestic and international students. Application fee: $30. Electronic applications accepted. *Expenses:* Tuition, state resident: full-time $7766; part-time $431.43 per credit hour. Tuition, nonresident: full-time $15,789; part-time $877.17 per credit hour. *Required fees:* $37 per term. *Financial support:* In 2016–17, 5 students received support. Teaching assistantships available. Financial award application deadline: 2/1; financial award applicants required to submit FAFSA. *Faculty research:* Integrated neuroscience, diabetes, sustainability of populations/environment, drug design and delivery, marine science. *Total annual research expenditures:* $625,111. *Unit head:* Dr. Dwayne Smith, Dean, 813-974-7359, Fax: 813-974-5762, E-mail: mdsmith8@usf.edu. *Application contact:* Paul Crawford, Associate Director for Graduate Admissions, 813-974-8800, E-mail: pjcrawford@usf.edu.
Website: http://www.grad.usf.edu/

The University of Texas at Austin, Graduate School, School of Information, Austin, TX 78712-1111. Offers identity management and security (MSIMS); information (PhD); information studies (MSIS); MSIS/MA. MSIMS program offered in conjunction with the Center for Identity. *Accreditation:* ALA (one or more programs are accredited). *Program availability:* Part-time. *Degree requirements:* For doctorate, 2 foreign languages, thesis/dissertation. *Entrance requirements:* For master's and doctorate, GRE General Test. Electronic applications accepted. *Faculty research:* Information retrieval and artificial intelligence, library history and administration, classification and cataloguing.

The University of Texas at San Antonio, College of Business, Department of Information Systems and Cyber Security, San Antonio, TX 78249-0617. Offers cyber security (MSIT); information technology (MS, PhD); management of technology (MBA); technology entrepreneurship and management (Certificate). *Program availability:* Part-time, evening/weekend. *Faculty:* 10 full-time (2 women), 4 part-time/adjunct (0 women). *Students:* 70 full-time (19 women), 73 part-time (21 women); includes 38 minority (6 Black or African American, non-Hispanic/Latino; 6 Asian, non-Hispanic/Latino; 24 Hispanic/Latino; 2 Two or more races, non-Hispanic/Latino), 38 international. Average age 30. 141 applicants, 59% accepted, 55 enrolled. In 2016, 45 master's, 1 doctorate, 6 other advanced degrees awarded. *Degree requirements:* For master's, comprehensive exam (for some programs), thesis optional; for doctorate, comprehensive exam, thesis/dissertation. *Entrance requirements:* For master's and doctorate, GMAT/GRE, official transcripts, statement of purpose, letters of recommendation. Additional exam requirements/recommendations for international students: Required—TOEFL (minimum score 550 paper-based; 79 iBT), IELTS (minimum score 6.5). *Application deadline:* For fall admission, 7/1 for domestic students, 4/1 for international students; for spring admission, 11/1 for domestic students, 9/1 for international students. Applications are processed on a rolling basis. Application fee: $45 ($80 for international students). Electronic applications accepted. *Expenses:* Contact institution. *Financial support:* In 2016–17, 15 students received support, including 1 fellowship with full tuition reimbursement available (averaging $25,000 per year), 10 research assistantships with tuition reimbursements available (averaging $9,000 per year), 12 teaching assistantships with tuition reimbursements available (averaging $9,000 per year); scholarships/grants, health care benefits, and unspecified assistantships also available. Support available to part-time students. Financial award application deadline: 2/15. *Faculty research:* Cyber security, digital forensics, economics of information systems, information systems privacy, information technology adoption. *Total annual research expenditures:* $650,902. *Unit head:* Dr. Yoris A. Au, Chair/Associate Professor, 210-458-6300, Fax: 210-458-6305, E-mail: yoris.au@utsa.edu.
Website: http://business.utsa.edu/directory/index.aspx?DepID-16

The University of Texas at Tyler, College of Business and Technology, Program in Business Administration, Tyler, TX 75799-0001. Offers cyber security (MBA); engineering management (MBA); general management (MBA); healthcare management (MBA); internal assurance and consulting (MBA); marketing (MBA); oil, gas and energy (MBA); organizational development (MBA); quality management (MBA). *Accreditation:* AACSB. *Program availability:* Part-time, online learning. *Entrance requirements:* Additional exam requirements/recommendations for international students: Required—TOEFL (minimum score 550 paper-based). *Faculty research:* General business, inventory control, institutional markets, service marketing, product distribution, accounting fraud, financial reporting and recognition.

The University of Tulsa, Graduate School, College of Engineering and Natural Sciences, Tandy School of Computer Science, Tulsa, OK 74104-3189. Offers computer science (MS, PhD); cyber security (MS); JD/MS; MBA/MS. *Program availability:* Part-time. *Faculty:* 12 full-time (1 woman). *Students:* 42 full-time (13 women), 14 part-time (2 women); includes 4 minority (1 American Indian or Alaska Native, non-Hispanic/Latino; 3 Asian, non-Hispanic/Latino), 18 international. Average age 28. 65 applicants, 58% accepted, 22 enrolled. In 2016, 18 master's, 3 doctorates awarded. Terminal master's awarded for partial completion of doctoral program. *Degree requirements:* For master's, thesis (for some programs); for doctorate, comprehensive exam, thesis/dissertation. *Entrance requirements:* For master's and doctorate, GRE General Test. Additional exam requirements/recommendations for international students: Required—TOEFL (minimum score 550 paper-based; 80 iBT), IELTS (minimum score 6). *Application deadline:* Applications are processed on a rolling basis. Application fee: $55. Electronic applications accepted. *Expenses: Tuition:* Full-time $22,230; part-time $1235 per credit hour. *Required fees:* $990 per semester. Tuition and fees vary according to course load. *Financial support:* In 2016–17, 41 students received support, including 8 fellowships with full tuition reimbursements available (averaging $1,618 per year), 33 research assistantships with full tuition reimbursements available (averaging $15,208 per year), 9 teaching assistantships with full tuition reimbursements available (averaging $12,318 per year); career-related internships or fieldwork, Federal Work-Study, scholarships/grants, health care benefits, tuition waivers (full and partial), and unspecified assistantships also available. Support available to part-time students. Financial award application deadline: 2/1; financial award applicants required to submit FAFSA. *Faculty research:* Robotics, human-computer interaction, systems security, information assurance, machine learning, intelligent systems, software engineering, distributed systems, evolutionary computation, computational biology, bioinformatics. *Total annual research expenditures:* $1.8 million. *Unit head:* Dr. Roger Wainwright, Chairperson, 918-631-3143, E-mail: rogerw@utulsa.edu. *Application contact:* Dr. Mauricio Papa, Advisor, 918-631-2987, Fax: 918-631-3077, E-mail: mauricio-papa@utulsa.edu.
Website: http://engineering.utulsa.edu/academics/computer-science/

University of Utah, Graduate School, David Eccles School of Business, Department of Operations and Information Systems, Salt Lake City, UT 84112. Offers information systems (MS, Graduate Certificate), including business intelligence and analytics, IT security, product and process management, software and systems architecture. *Program availability:* Part-time, evening/weekend, 100% online, blended/hybrid learning. *Faculty:* 12 full-time (5 women), 7 part-time/adjunct (0 women). *Students:* 143 full-time (43 women), 107 part-time (28 women); includes 127 minority (1 Black or African American, non-Hispanic/Latino; 120 Asian, non-Hispanic/Latino; 3 Hispanic/Latino; 3 Two or more races, non-Hispanic/Latino), 123 international. Average age 29. 334 applicants, 72% accepted, 127 enrolled. In 2016, 96 master's awarded. *Degree requirements:* For master's, capstone project. *Entrance requirements:* For master's, GMAT/GRE, minimum undergraduate GPA of 3.0, 2 letters of recommendation, personal statement, professional resume. Additional exam requirements/recommendations for international students: Required—TOEFL (minimum score 550 paper-based; 80 iBT), IELTS (minimum score 6.5). *Application deadline:* For fall admission, 7/28 for domestic students, 3/1 for international students; for spring admission, 12/7 for domestic students, 8/16 for international students. Applications are processed on a rolling basis. Application fee: $55 ($65 for international students). Electronic applications accepted. *Expenses:* Contact institution. *Financial support:* In 2016–17, 75 students received support, including 7 teaching assistantships (averaging $5,000 per year); fellowships with partial tuition reimbursements available, tuition waivers (partial), and unspecified assistantships also available. Financial award application deadline: 3/31; financial award applicants required to submit FAFSA. *Faculty research:* Business intelligence and analytics, software and system architecture, product and process management, IT security, Web and data mining, applications and management of IT in healthcare. *Unit head:* Dr. Bradden Blair, Director of the IS Programs, 801-587-9489, Fax: 801-581-3666, E-mail: b.blair@eccles.utah.edu. *Application contact:* Raven Clissold, Admissions Coordinator, 801-587-5838, Fax: 801-581-3666, E-mail: raven.clissold@eccles.utah.edu.
Website: http://msis.eccles.utah.edu

University of Washington, Graduate School, Information School, Seattle, WA 98195. Offers information management (MSIM), including business intelligence, data science, information architecture, information consulting, information security, user experience; information science (PhD); library and information science (MLIS). *Accreditation:* ALA (one or more programs are accredited). *Program availability:* Part-time, 100% online coursework with required attendance at on-campus orientation at start of program. *Faculty:* 35 full-time (19 women), 22 part-time/adjunct (12 women). *Students:* 367 full-time (233 women), 237 part-time (170 women); includes 132 minority (20 Black or African American, non-Hispanic/Latino; 9 American Indian or Alaska Native, non-Hispanic/Latino; 59 Asian, non-Hispanic/Latino; 41 Hispanic/Latino; 3 Native Hawaiian or other Pacific Islander, non-Hispanic/Latino), 151 international. Average age 32. 1,208 applicants, 39% accepted, 254 enrolled. In 2016, 237 master's, 2 doctorates awarded.

Computer and Information Systems Security

Terminal master's awarded for partial completion of doctoral program. *Degree requirements:* For master's, comprehensive exam (for some programs), thesis or alternative, capstone project; for doctorate, comprehensive exam, thesis/dissertation. *Entrance requirements:* For master's, GRE General Test, GMAT; for doctorate, GRE General Test. Additional exam requirements/recommendations for international students: Required—TOEFL (minimum score 590 paper-based; 100 iBT). *Application deadline:* For fall admission, 12/1 priority date for domestic and international students. Application fee: $85. Electronic applications accepted. *Expenses:* $785 per quarter credit hour, $23,550 per year full-time, $1,000 university fees per quarter. *Financial support:* In 2016–17, 69 students received support, including 1 fellowship with full tuition reimbursement available (averaging $6,651 per year), 27 research assistantships with full tuition reimbursements available (averaging $19,418 per year), 27 teaching assistantships with full tuition reimbursements available (averaging $19,521 per year); Federal Work-Study, institutionally sponsored loans, scholarships/grants, health care benefits, tuition waivers (full and partial), and unspecified assistantships also available. Support available to part-time students. Financial award application deadline: 10/1; financial award applicants required to submit FAFSA. *Faculty research:* Human/computer interaction, information policy and ethics, knowledge organization, information literacy and access, data science, information assurance and cyber security, digital youth, information architecture, project management, systems analyst, user experience design. *Total annual research expenditures:* $3.6 million. *Unit head:* Dr. Harry Bruce, Dean, 206-616-0985, E-mail: harryb@uw.edu. *Application contact:* Kari Brothers, Admissions Counselor, 206-616-5541, Fax: 206-616-3152, E-mail: kari683@uw.edu.
Website: http://ischool.uw.edu/

University of Wisconsin–Madison, Graduate School, Wisconsin School of Business, Wisconsin Full-Time MBA Program, Madison, WI 53706. Offers applied security analysis (MBA); arts administration (MBA); brand and product management (MBA); corporate finance and investment banking (MBA); marketing research (MBA); operations and technology management (MBA); real estate (MBA); risk management and insurance (MBA); strategic human resource management (MBA); supply chain management (MBA). *Faculty:* 125 full-time (32 women), 48 part-time/adjunct (11 women). *Students:* 197 full-time (73 women); includes 30 minority (11 Black or African American, non-Hispanic/Latino; 9 Asian, non-Hispanic/Latino; 10 Hispanic/Latino), 42 international. Average age 29. 728 applicants, 26% accepted, 99 enrolled. In 2016, 100 master's awarded. *Entrance requirements:* For master's, GMAT or GRE, bachelor's or equivalent degree, 2 years of work experience, essay, letter of recommendation, resume. Additional exam requirements/recommendations for international students: Required—TOEFL (minimum score 100 iBT), IELTS (minimum score 7.5). *Application deadline:* For fall admission, 9/28 for domestic students, 11/1 for international students; for winter admission, 11/2 for domestic students, 12/16 for international students; for spring admission, 1/11 for domestic students, 2/24 for international students; for summer admission, 3/1 for domestic students, 4/14 for international students. Applications are processed on a rolling basis. Application fee: $75 ($81 for international students). Electronic applications accepted. *Expenses:* $7,947 per semester resident tuition, $2,430 fees; $16,082 per semester resident tuition, $2,830 fees. *Financial support:* In 2016–17, 178 students received support, including 8 fellowships with full tuition reimbursements available (averaging $56,413 per year), 23 research assistantships with full tuition reimbursements available (averaging $42,151 per year), 51 teaching assistantships with full tuition reimbursements available (averaging $39,963 per year); scholarships/grants, health care benefits, and unspecified assistantships also available. Financial award application deadline: 4/11. *Faculty research:* Forms of competition and outcomes in dual distribution systems; explaining the accuracy of revised forecasts; supply chain planning for random demand surges; advanced demand information in a multi-product system; the effects of presentation salience and measurement subjectivity on nonprofessional investors' fair value judgments. *Unit head:* Prof. Ella Mae Matsumura, Associate Dean, Full-time MBA Program, 608-262-9731, E-mail: ematsumura@bus.wisc.edu. *Application contact:* Mary Lewitzke, Assistant Director of Admissions and Recruiting, Full-time MBA Program, 608-262-4000, E-mail: mlewitzke@bus.wisc.edu.
Website: http://www.bus.wisc.edu/mba

Utah Valley University, Program in Cybersecurity, Orem, UT 84058-5999. Offers Graduate Certificate. *Entrance requirements:* For degree, bachelor's degree; 2 years of IT or IT security industry experience; undergraduate courses in data communication, programming, and servers.

Utica College, Program in Cybersecurity, Utica, NY 13502-4892. Offers MS. *Program availability:* Part-time, evening/weekend, 100% online. *Faculty:* 5 full-time (0 women), 8 part-time/adjunct (0 women). *Students:* 3 full-time (2 women), 374 part-time (106 women); includes 108 minority (50 Black or African American, non-Hispanic/Latino; 2 American Indian or Alaska Native, non-Hispanic/Latino; 18 Asian, non-Hispanic/Latino; 28 Hispanic/Latino; 10 Two or more races, non-Hispanic/Latino). Average age 35. 163 applicants, 98% accepted, 155 enrolled. In 2016, 133 master's awarded. *Entrance requirements:* For master's, BS, minimum GPA of 3.0. Additional exam requirements/recommendations for international students: Recommended—TOEFL (minimum score 525 paper-based). *Application deadline:* Applications are processed on a rolling basis. Electronic applications accepted. *Expenses:* Contact institution. *Financial support:* Application deadline: 3/15; applicants required to submit FAFSA. *Faculty research:* Steganography and data hiding, cryptography. *Unit head:* Joseph Giordano, Chair, 315-792-2521. *Application contact:* John D. Rowe, Director of Graduate Admissions, 315-792-3824, Fax: 315-792-3003, E-mail: jrowe@utica.edu.
Website: http://programs.online.utica.edu/programs/masters-cybersecurity.asp

Valparaiso University, Graduate School and Continuing Education, Program in Cyber Security, Valparaiso, IN 46383. Offers MS. *Program availability:* Part-time, evening/weekend. *Degree requirements:* For master's, internship or research project. *Entrance requirements:* Additional exam requirements/recommendations for international students: Required—TOEFL (minimum score 550 paper-based; 80 iBT), IELTS (minimum score 6). Electronic applications accepted. *Expenses: Tuition:* Full-time $11,070; part-time $615 per credit hour. *Required fees:* $116 per semester. Tuition and fees vary according to course load, degree level and program.

Villanova University, Villanova School of Business, MBA - The Fast Track Program, Villanova, PA 19085. Offers analytics (MBA); cybersecurity (MBA); finance (MBA); healthcare (MBA); international business (MBA); management information systems (MBA); marketing (MBA); real estate (MBA); strategic management (MBA); sustainability (MBA). *Accreditation:* AACSB. *Program availability:* Part-time, evening/weekend. *Faculty:* 108 full-time (39 women), 32 part-time/adjunct (8 women). *Students:* 127 part-time (58 women); includes 18 minority (3 Black or African American, non-Hispanic/Latino; 7 Asian, non-Hispanic/Latino; 6 Hispanic/Latino; 2 Two or more races, non-Hispanic/Latino), 2 international. Average age 30. 88 applicants, 90% accepted, 66 enrolled. In 2016, 75 master's awarded. *Degree requirements:* For master's, minimum GPA of 3.0. *Entrance requirements:* For master's, GMAT or GRE, work experience, 2 letters of recommendation, 2 essays, resume, official transcripts, interview. Additional exam requirements/recommendations for international students: Required—TOEFL (minimum score 550 paper-based; 100 iBT). *Application deadline:* For fall admission, 6/30 for domestic and international students. Application fee: $65. Electronic applications

accepted. *Expenses:* Contact institution. *Financial support:* Scholarships/grants available. Financial award application deadline: 6/30; financial award applicants required to submit FAFSA. *Faculty research:* Business analytics; creativity, innovation and entrepreneurship; global leadership; real estate; church management; business ethics; marketing and consumer insights. *Unit head:* Michael L. Capella, Associate Dean of Graduate and Executive Business Programs, 610-519-4336, Fax: 610-519-6273, E-mail: michael.l.capella@villanova.edu. *Application contact:* Kimberly Kane, Manager of Admissions, 610-519-3701, Fax: 610-519-6273, E-mail: kimberly.kane@villanova.edu.
Website: http://www1.villanova.edu/villanova/business/graduate/mba.html

Virginia International University, School of Computer Information Systems, Fairfax, VA 22030. Offers business intelligence (Graduate Certificate); business intelligence and data analytics (MIS); computer science (MS), including computer animation and gaming, cybersecurity, data management networking, intelligent systems, software applications development, software engineering; cybersecurity (MIS); data management (MIS); enterprise project management (MIS); health informatics (MIS); information assurance (MIS); information systems (Graduate Certificate); information systems management (MS, Graduate Certificate); information technology (MS); information technology audit and compliance (Graduate Certificate); knowledge management (MIS); software engineering (MS). *Program availability:* Part-time, online learning. *Entrance requirements:* For master's, bachelor's degree. Additional exam requirements/recommendations for international students: Required—TOEFL (minimum score 550 paper-based; 80 iBT), IELTS. Electronic applications accepted.

Virginia Polytechnic Institute and State University, VT Online, Blacksburg, VA 24061. Offers advanced transportation systems (Certificate); aerospace engineering (MS); agricultural and life sciences (MSLFS); business information systems (Graduate Certificate); career and technical education (MS); civil engineering (MS); computer engineering (M Eng, MS); decision support systems (Graduate Certificate); eLearning leadership (MA); electrical engineering (M Eng, MS); engineering administration (MEA); environmental engineering (Certificate); environmental politics and policy (Graduate Certificate); environmental sciences and engineering (MS); foundations of political analysis (Graduate Certificate); health product risk management (Graduate Certificate); industrial and systems engineering (MS); information policy and society (Graduate Certificate); information security (Graduate Certificate); information technology (MIT); instructional technology (MA); integrative STEM education (MA Ed); liberal arts (Graduate Certificate); life sciences: health product risk management (MS); natural resources (MNR, Graduate Certificate); networking (Graduate Certificate); nonprofit and nongovernmental organization management (Graduate Certificate); ocean engineering (MS); political science (MA); security studies (Graduate Certificate); software development (Graduate Certificate). *Expenses:* Tuition, state resident: full-time $12,467; part-time $692.50 per credit hour. Tuition, nonresident: full-time $25,095; part-time $1394.25 per credit hour. *Required fees:* $2669; $491.50 per semester. Tuition and fees vary according to course load, campus/location and program.

Walden University, Graduate Programs, School of Information Systems and Technology, Minneapolis, MN 55401. Offers information systems (Graduate Certificate); information systems management (MISM); information technology (MS, DIT), including health informatics (MS), information assurance and cyber security (MS), information systems (MS), software engineering (MS). *Program availability:* Part-time, evening/weekend, online only, 100% online. *Degree requirements:* For doctorate, thesis/dissertation (for some programs), residency. *Entrance requirements:* For master's, bachelor's degree or higher; minimum GPA of 2.5; official transcripts; goal statement (for some programs); access to computer and Internet; for doctorate, master's degree or higher; three years of related professional or academic experience (preferred); minimum GPA of 3.0; goal statement and current resume (for select programs); official transcripts; access to computer and Internet; for Graduate Certificate, relevant work experience; access to computer and Internet. Additional exam requirements/recommendations for international students: Required—TOEFL (minimum score 550 paper-based, 79 iBT), IELTS (minimum score 6.5), Michigan English Language Assessment Battery (minimum score 82), or PTE (minimum score 53). Electronic applications accepted.

Walsh College of Accountancy and Business Administration, Graduate Programs, Program in Information Technology, Troy, MI 48083. Offers cybersecurity (MSIT). *Program availability:* Part-time, evening/weekend. *Faculty:* 1 (woman) full-time, 7 part-time/adjunct (4 women). *Students:* 56 (25 women); includes 14 minority (9 Black or African American, non-Hispanic/Latino; 2 Asian, non-Hispanic/Latino; 1 Hispanic/Latino; 2 Two or more races, non-Hispanic/Latino), 16 international. Average age 34. 34 applicants, 79% accepted, 20 enrolled. In 2016, 4 master's awarded. *Entrance requirements:* For master's, minimum overall cumulative GPA of 2.75 from all colleges previously attended. Additional exam requirements/recommendations for international students: Required—TOEFL (minimum score 550 paper-based, 79 iBT), IELTS (6.5), Michigan English Language Assessment Battery, or MTELP. *Application deadline:* Applications are processed on a rolling basis. Application fee: $35. Electronic applications accepted. *Expenses:* $740 per credit hour, $125 registration fee per semester. *Financial support:* In 2016–17, 6 students received support. Career-related internships or fieldwork and scholarships/grants available. Financial award application deadline: 6/30; financial award applicants required to submit FAFSA. *Faculty research:* Business intelligence, data and decision-making, cyber security, project management, mobile technologies. *Unit head:* Dr. Barbara Ciaramitaro, Chair, Information Technology and Decision Sciences, 248-823-1635, Fax: 248-689-0920, E-mail: bciara2@walshcollege.edu. *Application contact:* Heather Rigby, Director, Admissions and Academic Advising, 248-823-1610, Fax: 248-689-0938, E-mail: hrigby@walshcollege.edu.

Webster University, George Herbert Walker School of Business and Technology, Department of Mathematics and Computer Science, St. Louis, MO 63119-3194. Offers cybersecurity (MS). *Program availability:* Part-time, evening/weekend, online learning. *Entrance requirements:* For master's, 36 hours of graduate course work. Additional exam requirements/recommendations for international students: Required—TOEFL. *Application deadline:* Applications are processed on a rolling basis. Application fee: $25 ($50 for international students). *Expenses: Tuition:* Full-time $21,900; part-time $730 per credit hour. Tuition and fees vary according to campus/location and program. *Financial support:* Federal Work-Study available. Support available to part-time students. Financial award application deadline: 4/1; financial award applicants required to submit FAFSA. *Faculty research:* Databases, computer information systems networks, operating systems, computer architecture. *Unit head:* Al Cawns, Chair, 314-968-7127, Fax: 314-963-6050, E-mail: cawnsae@webster.edu. *Application contact:* Sarah Nandor, Director, Graduate and Transfer Admissions, 314-968-7109, E-mail: gadmit@webster.edu.

West Chester University of Pennsylvania, College of the Sciences and Mathematics, Department of Computer Science, West Chester, PA 19383. Offers computer science (MS); computer security (information assurance) (Certificate); information systems (Certificate); Web technology (Certificate). *Program availability:* Part-time, evening/weekend. *Faculty:* 10 full-time (3 women). *Students:* 7 full-time (2 women), 29 part-time (10 women); includes 11 minority (5 Black or African American, non-Hispanic/Latino; 5 Asian, non-Hispanic/Latino; 1 Hispanic/Latino), 8 international. Average age 31. 29

applicants, 69% accepted, 12 enrolled. In 2016, 16 master's, 3 other advanced degrees awarded. *Degree requirements:* For master's, thesis optional, 33 credits; for Certificate, 12 credits. *Entrance requirements:* For master's, GRE, two letters of recommendation; for Certificate, BS. Additional exam requirements/recommendations for international students: Required—TOEFL or IELTS. *Application deadline:* For fall admission, 5/15 for international students; for spring admission, 10/15 for international students. Applications are processed on a rolling basis. Application fee: $50. Electronic applications accepted. *Expenses:* Tuition, state resident: full-time $8694; part-time $483 per credit. Tuition, nonresident: full-time $13,050; part-time $725 per credit. *Required fees:* $2399; $119.05 per credit. Tuition and fees vary according to campus/location and program. *Financial support:* Scholarships/grants and unspecified assistantships available. Financial award application deadline: 2/15; financial award applicants required to submit FAFSA. *Faculty research:* Security in mobile ad-hoc networks, intrusion detection, security and trust in pervasive computing, cloud computing, wireless sensor networks, cloud computing and data mining. *Unit head:* Dr. James Fabrey, Chair, 610-436-2204, E-mail: jfabrey@wcupa.edu. *Application contact:* Dr. Afrand Agah, Graduate Coordinator, 610-430-4419, E-mail: aagah@wcupa.edu.
Website: http://www.cs.wcupa.edu/

Western Governors University, College of Information Technology, Salt Lake City, UT 84107. Offers cybersecurity and information assurance (MS); data analytics (MS);
information technology management (MS). *Program availability:* Online learning. *Degree requirements:* For master's, capstone project.

Wilmington University, College of Technology, New Castle, DE 19720-6491. Offers geographic information systems (MS); information assurance (MS); information systems technologies (MS); Internet/Web design (MS); management and management information systems (MS). *Program availability:* Part-time, evening/weekend. *Faculty:* 5 full-time (1 woman), 114 part-time/adjunct (31 women). *Students:* 1,316 full-time (321 women), 263 part-time (79 women); includes 71 minority (53 Black or African American, non-Hispanic/Latino; 5 American Indian or Alaska Native, non-Hispanic/Latino; 8 Asian, non-Hispanic/Latino; 4 Hispanic/Latino; 1 Two or more races, non-Hispanic/Latino), 1,437 international. Average age 26. 856 applicants, 100% accepted, 332 enrolled. In 2016, 756 master's awarded. *Entrance requirements:* Additional exam requirements/recommendations for international students: Required—TOEFL (minimum score 500 paper-based). *Application deadline:* Applications are processed on a rolling basis. Application fee: $35. Electronic applications accepted. *Expenses: Tuition:* Full-time $8388; part-time $466 per credit. *Required fees:* $25 per semester. Tuition and fees vary according to degree level. *Unit head:* Dr. Mary Ann K. Westerfield, Dean. *Application contact:* Laura Morris, Director of Admissions, 877-967-5464, E-mail: infocenter@wilmu.edu.
Website: http://www.wilmu.edu/technology/

Computer Science

Acadia University, Faculty of Pure and Applied Science, Jodrey School of Computer Science, Wolfville, NS B4P 2R6, Canada. Offers M Sc. *Degree requirements:* For master's, thesis. *Entrance requirements:* For master's, honors degree in computer science. Additional exam requirements/recommendations for international students: Required—TOEFL (minimum score 580 paper-based; 93 iBT), IELTS (minimum score 6.5). *Faculty research:* Visual and object-oriented programming, concurrency, artificial intelligence, hypertext and multimedia, algorithm analysis, xml.

Air Force Institute of Technology, Graduate School of Engineering and Management, Department of Electrical and Computer Engineering, Dayton, OH 45433-7765. Offers computer engineering (MS, PhD); computer systems/science (MS); electrical engineering (MS, PhD); electro-optics (MS, PhD). *Accreditation:* ABET (one or more programs are accredited). *Program availability:* Part-time. *Degree requirements:* For master's, thesis; for doctorate, thesis/dissertation. *Entrance requirements:* For master's and doctorate, GRE General Test, minimum GPA of 3.0, U.S. citizenship. *Faculty research:* Remote sensing, information survivability, microelectronics, computer networks, artificial intelligence.

Alabama Agricultural and Mechanical University, School of Graduate Studies, College of Engineering, Technology, and Physical Sciences, Department of Electrical Engineering and Computer Science, Huntsville, AL 35811. Offers computer science (MS); material engineering (M Eng), including electrical engineering. *Program availability:* Evening/weekend. *Degree requirements:* For master's, comprehensive exam, thesis optional. *Entrance requirements:* For master's, GRE General Test. Additional exam requirements/recommendations for international students: Required—TOEFL (minimum score 500 paper-based; 61 iBT). *Application deadline:* For fall admission, 5/1 for domestic students. Applications are processed on a rolling basis. Application fee: $25. Electronic applications accepted. *Expenses:* Tuition, nonresident: part-time $826 per credit hour. Full-time tuition and fees vary according to course load and program. *Financial support:* Research assistantships with tuition reimbursements and career-related internships or fieldwork available. Financial award application deadline: 4/1. *Faculty research:* Computer-assisted instruction, database management, software engineering, operating systems, neural networks. *Unit head:* Dr. Kaveh Heidary, Chair, 256-372-5587, E-mail: kaveh.heidary@aamu.edu.

Alcorn State University, School of Graduate Studies, School of Arts and Sciences, Department of Mathematical Sciences, Lorman, MS 39096-7500. Offers computer and information sciences (MS).

American Sentinel University, Graduate Programs, Aurora, CO 80014. Offers business administration (MBA); business intelligence (MS); computer science (MSCS); health information management (MS); healthcare (MBA); information systems (MSIS); nursing (MSN). *Program availability:* Part-time, evening/weekend, online learning. *Entrance requirements:* Additional exam requirements/recommendations for international students: Required—TOEFL (minimum score 600 paper-based). Electronic applications accepted.

The American University in Cairo, School of Sciences and Engineering, Cairo, Egypt. Offers biotechnology (MS); chemistry (MS); computer science (MS); computing (M Comp); construction engineering (M Eng, MS); electronics and communications engineering (M Eng); environmental engineering (MS); environmental system design (M Eng); mechanical engineering (M Eng, MS); nanotechnology (MS); physics (MS); robotics, control and smart systems (MS); sciences and engineering (PhD); sustainable development (MS, Graduate Diploma). *Program availability:* Part-time, evening/weekend. *Faculty:* 43 full-time (4 women), 12 part-time/adjunct (1 woman). *Students:* 50 full-time (21 women), 262 part-time (128 women), 13 international. Average age 28. 193 applicants, 46% accepted, 55 enrolled. In 2016, 71 master's, 5 doctorates awarded. *Degree requirements:* For master's, comprehensive exam (for some programs), thesis (for some programs); for doctorate, comprehensive exam (for some programs), thesis/dissertation. *Entrance requirements:* Additional exam requirements/recommendations for international students: Required—TOEFL (minimum score 450 paper-based; 45 iBT), IELTS (minimum score 5). *Application deadline:* For fall admission, 2/1 priority date for domestic and international students; for spring admission, 10/15 priority date for domestic and international students. Applications are processed on a rolling basis. Application fee: $80. Electronic applications accepted. *Expenses:* Contact institution. *Financial support:* Fellowships with partial tuition reimbursements, scholarships/grants, and unspecified assistantships available. Financial award application deadline: 3/10. *Faculty research:* Construction, mechanical and electronics engineering, physics, computer science, biotechnology and nanotechnology. *Unit head:* Dr. Hassan El Fawal, Dean, 20-2-2615-2926, E-mail: hassan.elfawal@aucegypt.edu. *Application contact:* Maha Hegazi, Director for Graduate Admissions, 20-2-2615-1462, E-mail: mahahegazi@aucegypt.edu.
Website: http://www.aucegypt.edu/sse/Pages/default.aspx

American University of Armenia, Graduate Programs, Yerevan, Armenia. Offers business administration (MBA); computer and information science (MS), including business management, design and manufacturing, energy (ME, MS), industrial engineering and systems management; economics (MS); industrial engineering and systems management (ME), including business, computer aided design/manufacturing, energy (ME, MS), information technology; law (LL M); political science and international

affairs (MPSIA); public health (MPH); teaching English as a foreign language (MA). *Program availability:* Part-time, evening/weekend. *Degree requirements:* For master's, thesis (for some programs), capstone/project. *Entrance requirements:* For master's, GRE, GMAT, or LSAT. Additional exam requirements/recommendations for international students: Recommended—TOEFL (minimum score 79 iBT), IELTS (minimum score 6.5). *Faculty research:* Microfinance, finance (rural/development, international, corporate), firm life cycle theory, TESOL, language proficiency testing, public policy, administrative law, economic development, cryptography, artificial intelligence, energy efficiency/renewable energy, computer-aided design/manufacturing, health financing, tuberculosis control, mother/child health, preventive ophthalmology, post-earthquake psychopathological investigations, tobacco control, environmental health risk assessments.

American University of Beirut, Graduate Programs, Faculty of Arts and Sciences, Beirut, Lebanon. Offers anthropology (MA); Arab and Middle Eastern history (PhD); Arabic language and literature (MA, PhD); archaeology (MA); art history and curating (MA); biology (MS); cell and molecular biology (PhD); chemistry (MS); clinical psychology (MA); computational sciences (MS); computer science (MS); economics (MA); education (MA); English language (MA); English literature (MA); environmental policy planning (MS); financial economics (MAFE); geology (MS); history (MA); Islamic studies (MA); mathematics (MS); media studies (MA); Middle Eastern studies (MA); physics (MS); political studies (MA); psychology (MA); public administration (MA); public policy and international affairs (MA); sociology (MA); statistics (MA, MS); theoretical physics (PhD); transnational American studies (MA). *Program availability:* Part-time. *Faculty:* 133 full-time (42 women), 6 part-time/adjunct (2 women). *Students:* 240 full-time (172 women), 227 part-time (166 women). Average age 27. 286 applicants, 67% accepted, 108 enrolled. In 2016, 60 master's, 3 doctorates awarded. Terminal master's awarded for partial completion of doctoral program. *Degree requirements:* For master's, one foreign language, comprehensive exam, thesis (for some programs); for doctorate, one foreign language, comprehensive exam, thesis/dissertation. *Entrance requirements:* For master's, GRE (for some MA, MS programs), letters of recommendation; for doctorate, GRE, letters of recommendation. Additional exam requirements/recommendations for international students: Required—TOEFL (minimum score 600 paper-based; 97 iBT), IELTS (minimum score 7). *Application deadline:* For fall admission, 4/3 for domestic students; for winter admission, 11/3 for domestic students. Application fee: $50. Electronic applications accepted. *Expenses:* Contact institution. *Financial support:* In 2016–17, 4 fellowships (averaging $11,200 per year), 18 research assistantships (averaging $5,400 per year) were awarded; teaching assistantships, career-related internships or fieldwork, Federal Work-Study, institutionally sponsored loans, scholarships/grants, traineeships, health care benefits, tuition waivers (full), and unspecified assistantships also available. Support available to part-time students. *Faculty research:* Development economics, spatial econometrics, health economics, labor economics, energy economics, hydrogeology, geophysics, petrophysics, structural geology, mineralogy, petrology, geochemistry, multilingualism, comparative/world literature, translation studies, book histories/ cultures, biocatalysis, molecular recognition, photocatalysis, photophysical and biophysical chemistry, probe chemistry, machine learning, data science. *Unit head:* Dr. Nadia Maria El Cheikh, Dean, Faculty of Arts and Sciences, 961-1374374 Ext. 3800, Fax: 961-1744461, E-mail: nmcheikh@aub.edu.lb. *Application contact:* Dr. Salim Kanaan, Director, Admissions Office, 961-1350000 Ext. 2590, Fax: 961-1750775, E-mail: sk00@aub.edu.lb.
Website: http://www.aub.edu.lb/fas/

Appalachian State University, Cratis D. Williams Graduate School, Department of Computer Science, Boone, NC 28608. Offers MS. *Program availability:* Part-time. *Degree requirements:* For master's, comprehensive exam, thesis. *Entrance requirements:* For master's, GRE General Test, 3 letters of recommendation. Additional exam requirements/recommendations for international students: Required—TOEFL (minimum score 570 paper-based; 79 iBT), IELTS (minimum score 6.5). *Application deadline:* For fall admission, 3/15 priority date for domestic students, 2/1 for international students; for spring admission, 11/1 for domestic students, 7/1 for international students. Applications are processed on a rolling basis. Application fee: $55. Electronic applications accepted. *Expenses:* Tuition, state resident: full-time $4744. Tuition, nonresident: full-time $17,913. Full-time tuition and fees vary according to program. *Financial support:* Fellowships, research assistantships, teaching assistantships, Federal Work-Study, scholarships/grants, and unspecified assistantships available. Financial award application deadline: 4/1; financial award applicants required to submit FAFSA. *Faculty research:* Graph theory, compilers, parallel architecture, image processing. *Unit head:* Dr. James Wilkes, Chairperson, 828-262-2612. *Application contact:* Dr. Jay Fenwick, Advisor, 828-262-2708, Fax: 828-265-8617, E-mail: fenwickjb@appstate.edu.
Website: http://www.cs.appstate.edu

Arizona State University at the Tempe campus, Ira A. Fulton Schools of Engineering, The Polytechnic School, Department of Engineering, Mesa, AZ 85212. Offers simulation, modeling, and applied cognitive science (PhD). *Program availability:* Part-time. *Degree requirements:* For doctorate, comprehensive exam, thesis/dissertation, interactive Program of Study (iPOS) submitted before completing 50 percent of required credit hours. *Entrance requirements:* For doctorate, GRE, master's degree in psychology, engineering, cognitive science, or computer science; 3 letters of recommendation; statement of research interests. Additional exam requirements/ recommendations for international students: Required—TOEFL, IELTS, or PTE. Electronic applications accepted. *Faculty research:* Software process and automated workflow, software architecture, dotal technologies, relational database systems, embedded systems.

Arizona State University at the Tempe campus, Ira A. Fulton Schools of Engineering, School of Computing, Informatics, and Decision Systems Engineering, Tempe, AZ 85287-8809. Offers computer engineering (MS, PhD); computer science (MCS, MS, PhD); industrial engineering (MS, PhD); software engineering (MS). *Program availability:* Part-time, evening/weekend, online learning. Terminal master's awarded for partial completion of doctoral program. *Degree requirements:* For master's, comprehensive exam (for some programs), portfolio (MCS); interactive Program of Study (iPOS) submitted before completing 50 percent of required credit hours; for doctorate, comprehensive exam, thesis/dissertation, interactive Program of Study (iPOS) submitted before completing 50 percent of required credit hours. *Entrance requirements:* For master's, GRE, minimum GPA of 3.0 or equivalent in last 2 years of work leading to bachelor's degree; for doctorate, GRE, minimum GPA of 3.0 in last 2 years of work leading to bachelor's degree. Additional exam requirements/ recommendations for international students: Required—TOEFL, IELTS, or PTE. Electronic applications accepted. *Expenses:* Contact institution. *Faculty research:* Artificial intelligence, cyberphysical and embedded systems, health informatics, information assurance and security, information management/multimedia/visualization, network science, personalized learning/educational games, production logistics, software and systems engineering, statistical modeling and data mining.

Arkansas State University, Graduate School, College of Sciences and Mathematics, Department of Computer Science, State University, AR 72467. Offers MS. *Program availability:* Part-time. *Degree requirements:* For master's, comprehensive exam, thesis or alternative. *Entrance requirements:* For master's, GRE General Test or MAT, appropriate bachelor's degree, official transcripts, immunization records. Additional exam requirements/recommendations for international students: Required—TOEFL (minimum score 550 paper-based; 79 iBT), IELTS (minimum score 6), PTE (minimum score 56). Electronic applications accepted.

Armstrong State University, School of Graduate Studies, Program in Computer and Information Science, Savannah, GA 31419-1997. Offers MSCIS. *Program availability:* Part-time. *Faculty:* 4 full-time (0 women). *Students:* 1 full-time (0 women), 4 part-time (2 women), 3 international. Average age 28. 15 applicants, 7% accepted, 1 enrolled. *Degree requirements:* For master's, project. *Entrance requirements:* For master's, GRE (minimum scores: verbal 156, quantitative 144, and writing 4), minimum GPA of 2.7, letters of recommendation, BS in computer science or related field. Additional exam requirements/recommendations for international students: Required—TOEFL (minimum score 523 paper-based; 70 iBT). *Application deadline:* For fall admission, 7/1 priority date for domestic students, 5/1 priority date for international students; for spring admission, 11/15 priority date for domestic students, 9/15 priority date for international students; for summer admission, 4/15 priority date for domestic students, 9/15 for international students. Applications are processed on a rolling basis. Application fee: $30. Electronic applications accepted. *Expenses:* Tuition, state resident: full-time $1781; part-time $161.93 per credit hour. Tuition, nonresident: full-time $6482; part-time $589.27 per credit hour. *Required fees:* $1224 per unit. $612 per semester. Tuition and fees vary according to course load, campus/location and program. *Financial support:* In 2016–17, research assistantships with full tuition reimbursements (averaging $5,000 per year) were awarded; career-related internships or fieldwork, Federal Work-Study, scholarships/grants, and unspecified assistantships also available. Support available to part-time students. Financial award application deadline: 3/15; financial award applicants required to submit FAFSA. *Faculty research:* Bioinformatics, data mining, graph theory, image processing, machine learning. *Unit head:* Dr. Hong Zhang, Department Head, 912-344-2542, Fax: 912-344-3415, E-mail: hong.zhang@armstrong.edu. *Application contact:* McKenzie Peterman, Assistant Director of Graduate Admissions, 912-344-2503, Fax: 912-344-3417, E-mail: graduate@armstrong.edu.
Website: https://www.armstrong.edu/degree-programs/computer-science-mscis

Auburn University, Graduate School, Ginn College of Engineering, Department of Computer Science and Software Engineering, Auburn University, AL 36849. Offers MS, MSWE, PhD. *Program availability:* Part-time. *Faculty:* 18 full-time (3 women), 1 (woman) part-time/adjunct. *Students:* 101 full-time (28 women), 41 part-time (14 women); includes 13 minority (8 Black or African American, non-Hispanic/Latino; 1 Asian, non-Hispanic/Latino; 3 Hispanic/Latino; 1 Two or more races, non-Hispanic/Latino), 96 international. Average age 28. 199 applicants, 51% accepted, 29 enrolled. In 2016, 27 master's, 8 doctorates awarded. *Degree requirements:* For master's, thesis (for some programs); for doctorate, thesis/dissertation. *Entrance requirements:* For master's and doctorate, GRE General Test, GRE Subject Test. *Application deadline:* Applications are processed on a rolling basis. Application fee: $50 ($60 for international students). Electronic applications accepted. *Expenses:* Tuition, state resident: full-time $9072; part-time $504 per credit hour. Tuition, nonresident: full-time $27,216; part-time $1512 per credit hour. *Required fees:* $812 per semester. Tuition and fees vary according to degree level and program. *Financial support:* Research assistantships, teaching assistantships, and Federal Work-Study available. Support available to part-time students. Financial award application deadline: 3/15; financial award applicants required to submit FAFSA. *Faculty research:* Parallelizable, scalable software translations; graphical representations of algorithms, structures, and processes; graph drawing. *Unit head:* Dr. Hari Narayanan, Chair, 334-844-6310. *Application contact:* Dr. George Flowers, Dean of the Graduate School, 334-844-2125.
Website: http://www.eng.auburn.edu/cse/

Ball State University, Graduate School, College of Sciences and Humanities, Department of Computer Science, Muncie, IN 47306. Offers computer science (MA, MS). *Program availability:* Part-time. *Entrance requirements:* For master's, GRE General Test, minimum baccalaureate GPA of 2.75 or 3.0 in latter half of baccalauareate, goals statement, three letters of recommendation. Additional exam requirements/ recommendations for international students: Required—TOEFL (minimum score 550 paper-based; 79 iBT), IELTS (minimum score 6.5). Electronic applications accepted. *Faculty research:* Numerical methods, programmer productivity, graphics.

Baylor University, Graduate School, School of Engineering and Computer Science, Department of Computer Science, Waco, TX 76798. Offers MS, PhD. *Program availability:* Part-time. *Faculty:* 11 full-time (1 woman). *Students:* 11 full-time (0 women), 2 part-time (0 women); includes 4 minority (1 Black or African American, non-Hispanic/ Latino; 2 Asian, non-Hispanic/Latino; 1 Hispanic/Latino), 8 international. 30 applicants, 27% accepted, 7 enrolled. In 2016, 10 master's awarded. Terminal master's awarded for partial completion of doctoral program. *Degree requirements:* For master's, thesis (for some programs); for doctorate, comprehensive exam, thesis/dissertation. *Entrance requirements:* For master's and doctorate, GRE, course training in computer science equivalent to BS in computer science from Baylor University. Additional exam requirements/recommendations for international students: Required—TOEFL (minimum score 550 paper-based; 90 iBT). *Application deadline:* For fall admission, 2/15 priority date for domestic and international students; for spring admission, 12/1 priority date for domestic students, 11/1 priority date for international students. Applications are processed on a rolling basis. Application fee: $40. Electronic applications accepted. *Expenses: Tuition:* Full-time $28,494; part-time $1583 per credit hour. *Required fees:* $167 per credit hour. Tuition and fees vary according to course load and program. *Financial support:* In 2016–17, 15 students received support, including 5 research assistantships with full tuition reimbursements available (averaging $15,600 per year), 10 teaching assistantships with full tuition reimbursements available (averaging $15,600 per year); tuition waivers (full) also available. Financial award application deadline: 2/15. *Faculty research:* Bioinformatics, databases, machine learning, software engineering, networking. *Unit head:* Dr. Eunjee Song, Associate Professor and Graduate Program Director, 254-710-1498, E-mail: eunjee_song@baylor.edu. *Application contact:* 254-710-3588, Fax: 254-710-3870.
Website: http://www.ecs.baylor.edu/computerscience

Binghamton University, State University of New York, Graduate School, Thomas J. Watson School of Engineering and Applied Science, Department of Computer Science, Binghamton, NY 13902-6000. Offers MS, PhD. *Program availability:* Part-time, online learning. *Faculty:* 27 full-time (4 women), 10 part-time/adjunct (3 women). *Students:* 355 full-time (82 women), 81 part-time (11 women); includes 13 minority (1 Black or African American, non-Hispanic/Latino; 7 Asian, non-Hispanic/Latino; 5 Hispanic/Latino), 383 international. Average age 26. 956 applicants, 64% accepted, 170 enrolled. In 2016, 142 master's, 7 doctorates awarded. *Degree requirements:* For master's, comprehensive exam (for some programs), thesis or alternative; for doctorate, comprehensive exam, thesis/dissertation. *Entrance requirements:* For master's and doctorate, GRE General Test. Additional exam requirements/recommendations for international students: Required—TOEFL (minimum score 550 paper-based; 80 iBT). *Application deadline:* Applications are processed on a rolling basis. Application fee: $75. Electronic applications accepted. *Expenses:* Contact institution. *Financial support:* In 2016–17, 76 students received support, including 1 fellowship (averaging $10,000 per year), 16 research assistantships with full tuition reimbursements available (averaging $16,500 per year), 27 teaching assistantships with full tuition reimbursements available (averaging $16,500 per year); career-related internships or fieldwork, Federal Work-Study, institutionally sponsored loans, scholarships/grants, health care benefits, and unspecified assistantships also available. Financial award application deadline: 2/28; financial award applicants required to submit FAFSA. *Unit head:* Ellen Tilden, Coordinator of Graduate Studies, 607-777-2873, E-mail: etilden@binghamton.edu. *Application contact:* Ben Balkaya, Assistant Dean and Director, 607-777-2151, Fax: 607-777-2501, E-mail: balkaya@binghamton.edu.

Boise State University, College of Engineering, Department of Computer Science, Boise, ID 83725. Offers computer science (MS); computer science teacher endorsement (Graduate Certificate); STEM education (MS), including computer science. *Program availability:* Part-time. *Faculty:* 14. *Students:* 31 full-time (6 women), 35 part-time (11 women); includes 8 minority (1 Black or African American, non-Hispanic/Latino; 1 Asian, non-Hispanic/Latino; 3 Hispanic/Latino; 3 Two or more races, non-Hispanic/Latino), 24 international. Average age 30. 57 applicants, 47% accepted, 16 enrolled. In 2016, 8 master's awarded. *Degree requirements:* For master's, comprehensive exam, thesis. *Entrance requirements:* For master's, GRE General Test, minimum GPA of 3.0. Additional exam requirements/recommendations for international students: Required—TOEFL (minimum score 550 paper-based; 80 iBT), IELTS (minimum score 6). Application fee: $65 ($95 for international students). Electronic applications accepted. *Expenses:* Tuition, state resident: full-time $6058; part-time $358 per credit hour. Tuition, nonresident: full-time $20,108; part-time $608 per credit hour. *Required fees:* $2108. Tuition and fees vary according to program. *Financial support:* In 2016–17, 20 students received support, including 2 research assistantships (averaging $10,060 per year); scholarships/grants and unspecified assistantships also available. Financial award applicants required to submit FAFSA. *Unit head:* Dr. Tim Andersen, Department Chair, 208-426-5768, E-mail: tim@cs.boisestate.edu. *Application contact:* Dr. Dianxiang Xu, Graduate Program Coordinator, 208-426-5734, E-mail: dianxiangxu@boisestate.edu.
Website: http://coen.boisestate.edu/cs/

Boston University, Graduate School of Arts and Sciences, Department of Computer Science, Boston, MA 02215. Offers computer science (MS, PhD); cyber security (MS); data-centric computing (MS). *Students:* 137 full-time (37 women), 15 part-time (1 woman); includes 4 minority (3 Asian, non-Hispanic/Latino; 1 Hispanic/Latino), 120 international. Average age 26. 951 applicants, 22% accepted, 53 enrolled. In 2016, 20 master's, 8 doctorates awarded. Terminal master's awarded for partial completion of doctoral program. *Degree requirements:* For master's, thesis optional, project; for doctorate, comprehensive exam, thesis/dissertation. *Entrance requirements:* For master's and doctorate, GRE General Test, 3 letters of recommendation, transcripts, personal statement. Additional exam requirements/recommendations for international students: Required—TOEFL (minimum score 550 paper-based; 84 iBT). *Application deadline:* For fall admission, 12/15 for domestic and international students; for spring admission, 11/1 for domestic and international students. Application fee: $95. Electronic applications accepted. *Financial support:* In 2016–17, 56 students received support, including fellowships with full tuition reimbursements available (averaging $21,500 per year), 19 research assistantships with full tuition reimbursements available (averaging $21,500 per year), 23 teaching assistantships with full tuition reimbursements available (averaging $21,500 per year); Federal Work-Study, scholarships/grants, and health care benefits also available. Support available to part-time students. Financial award application deadline: 12/15. *Unit head:* Mark Crovella, Chair, 617-353-8919, Fax: 617-353-6457, E-mail: crovella@bu.edu. *Application contact:* Jennifer Streubel, Program Coordinator, 617-353-8919, Fax: 617-353-6457, E-mail: jenn4@bu.edu.
Website: http://cs-www.bu.edu/

Boston University, Metropolitan College, Department of Computer Science, Boston, MA 02215. Offers computer information systems (MS), including computer networks, data analytics, database management and business intelligence, health informatics, IT project management, security, Web application development; computer networks (Certificate); computer science (MS); data analytics (Certificate); digital forensics (Certificate); health informatics (Certificate); information technology project management (Certificate); software development (MS); software engineering in health care systems (Certificate); telecommunications (MS), including security. *Program availability:* Part-time, evening/weekend, online learning. *Faculty:* 13 full-time (3 women), 43 part-time/ adjunct (3 women). *Students:* 108 full-time (36 women), 1,294 part-time (364 women); includes 428 minority (115 Black or African American, non-Hispanic/Latino; 2 American Indian or Alaska Native, non-Hispanic/Latino; 187 Asian, non-Hispanic/Latino; 98 Hispanic/Latino; 2 Native Hawaiian or other Pacific Islander, non-Hispanic/Latino; 24 Two or more races, non-Hispanic/Latino), 314 international. Average age 33. 463 applicants, 79% accepted, 248 enrolled. In 2016, 311 master's awarded. *Degree requirements:* For master's, thesis optional. *Entrance requirements:* For master's and Certificate, official transcripts from regionally-accredited bachelor's degree program, 3 letters of recommendation, professional resume, personal statement. Additional exam requirements/recommendations for international students: Required—TOEFL (minimum score 84 iBT), IELTS. *Application deadline:* For fall admission, 6/1 priority date for international students; for spring admission, 10/1 priority date for international students. Applications are processed on a rolling basis. Application fee: $85. Electronic applications accepted. *Expenses:* Contact institution. *Financial support:* In 2016–17, 11 research assistantships (averaging $8,400 per year) were awarded; unspecified assistantships also available. Support available to part-time students. Financial award applicants required to submit FAFSA. *Faculty research:* Medical informatics, Web technologies, telecom and networks, security and forensics, software engineering, programming languages, multimedia and artificial intelligence (AI), information systems and IT project management. *Unit head:* Dr. Anatoly Temkin, Chair, 617-353-2566, Fax: 617-353-2367, E-mail: csinfo@bu.edu. *Application contact:* Lesley Moreau, Academic Program Coordinator, 617-353-2566, Fax: 617-353-2367, E-mail: metcs@bu.edu. Website: http://www.bu.edu/csmet/

Bowie State University, Graduate Programs, Department of Computer Science, Bowie, MD 20715-9465. Offers MS. *Program availability:* Part-time, evening/weekend. *Degree requirements:* For master's, comprehensive exam, thesis optional, research paper. *Entrance requirements:* For master's, minimum undergraduate GPA of 2.5. Electronic applications accepted. *Faculty research:* Holographics, launch vehicle ground truth ephemera.

Bowie State University, Graduate Programs, Program in Computer Science, Bowie, MD 20715-9465. Offers App Sc D. *Program availability:* Part-time, evening/weekend. Electronic applications accepted.

Bowling Green State University, Graduate College, College of Arts and Sciences, Department of Computer Science, Bowling Green, OH 43403. Offers computer science (MS), including operations research, parallel and distributed computing, software engineering. *Program availability:* Part-time. *Degree requirements:* For master's, thesis or alternative. *Entrance requirements:* For master's, GRE General Test. Additional exam requirements/recommendations for international students: Required—TOEFL. *Application deadline:* For fall admission, 2/1 priority date for domestic students; for spring admission, 11/15 priority date for domestic students. Application fee: $30. Electronic applications accepted. *Financial support:* Research assistantships with full tuition reimbursements, teaching assistantships with full tuition reimbursements, career-related internships or fieldwork, tuition waivers (full and partial), and unspecified assistantships available. Financial award applicants required to submit FAFSA. *Faculty research:* Artificial intelligence, real time and concurrent programming languages, behavioral aspects of computing, network protocols. *Unit head:* Dr. Rob Green, Graduate Coordinator, 419-372-8782, E-mail: csgradstudies@bgsu.edu. *Application contact:* Dr. Ron Lancaster, Graduate Coordinator, 419-372-8697.

Bradley University, The Graduate School, College of Liberal Arts and Sciences, Department of Computer Science and Information Systems, Peoria, IL 61625-0002. Offers computer information systems (MS); computer science (MS). *Program availability:* Part-time, evening/weekend. *Degree requirements:* For master's, comprehensive exam, thesis or alternative, programming test. *Entrance requirements:* For master's, GRE. Additional exam requirements/recommendations for international students: Required—TOEFL (minimum score 550 paper-based; 79 iBT), IELTS (minimum score 6.5). *Application deadline:* For fall admission, 5/15 priority date for domestic and international students; for spring admission, 10/15 priority date for domestic and international students. Applications are processed on a rolling basis. Application fee: $40 ($50 for international students). Electronic applications accepted. *Expenses: Tuition:* Full-time $7650; part-time $850 per credit. *Required fees:* $50 per credit. One-time fee: $100 full-time. *Financial support:* Research assistantships with full and partial tuition reimbursements, teaching assistantships, scholarships/grants, tuition waivers (partial), and unspecified assistantships available. Support available to part-time students. Financial award application deadline: 4/1. *Unit head:* Dr. Steven Dolins, Chair, 309-677-3284, E-mail: sdolins@bradley.edu. *Application contact:* Kayla Carroll, Director of International Admissions and Student Services, 309-677-2375, E-mail: klcarroll@fsmail.bradley.edu.
Website: http://www.bradley.edu/academic/departments/csis/

Brandeis University, Graduate School of Arts and Sciences, Department of Computer Science, Waltham, MA 02454-9110. Offers MA, PhD. *Program availability:* Part-time. *Faculty:* 15 full-time (5 women), 2 part-time/adjunct (0 women). *Students:* 84 full-time (24 women), 2 part-time (0 women); includes 10 minority (6 Asian, non-Hispanic/Latino; 3 Hispanic/Latino; 1 Two or more races, non-Hispanic/Latino), 54 international. 441 applicants, 39% accepted, 37 enrolled. In 2016, 45 master's, 3 doctorates awarded. *Degree requirements:* For doctorate, thesis/dissertation, thesis proposal. *Entrance requirements:* For master's, GRE, official transcript(s), statement of purpose, resume, 2 letters of recommendation; for doctorate, GRE, official transcript(s), statement of purpose, resume, 3 letters of recommendation. Additional exam requirements/recommendations for international students: Required—TOEFL (minimum score 600 paper-based; 100 iBT); Recommended—IELTS (minimum score 7), TSE (minimum score 68). *Application deadline:* For fall admission, 1/15 for domestic students. Applications are processed on a rolling basis. Application fee: $75. Electronic applications accepted. *Financial support:* In 2016–17, 37 students received support, including 16 fellowships with full tuition reimbursements available (averaging $25,300 per year), 9 research assistantships with full tuition reimbursements available (averaging $23,300 per year); scholarships/grants, health care benefits, and tuition waivers (partial) also available. Support available to part-time students. Financial award application deadline: 4/15; financial award applicants required to submit FAFSA. *Faculty research:* Databases, programming languages, artificial intelligence, networks, distributed and parallel computing, data compression, human computer interaction and collaborative technology. *Unit head:* Dr. Jordan Pollack, Chair, 781-736-2700, Fax: 781-736-2741, E-mail: pollack@brandeis.edu. *Application contact:* Anne Gudaitis, Department Administrator, 781-736-2700, E-mail: gudaitis@brandeis.edu.
Website: http://www.brandeis.edu/gsas

Brandeis University, Graduate School of Arts and Sciences, Program in Computational Linguistics, Waltham, MA 02454-9110. Offers MA. *Faculty:* 15 full-time (5 women), 2 part-time/adjunct (0 women). *Students:* 31 full-time (15 women), 2 part-time (1 woman); includes 5 minority (1 Asian, non-Hispanic/Latino; 3 Hispanic/Latino; 1 Two or more races, non-Hispanic/Latino), 10 international. 50 applicants, 76% accepted, 12 enrolled. In 2016, 8 master's awarded. *Degree requirements:* For master's, internship in computational linguistics or thesis. *Entrance requirements:* For master's, GRE, statement of purpose, 2 letters of recommendation, transcript(s), resume or curriculum vitae. Additional exam requirements/recommendations for international students: Required—TOEFL (minimum score 650 paper-based; 100 iBT); Recommended—IELTS (minimum score 7), TSE (minimum score 68). *Application deadline:* For fall admission, 2/15 priority date for domestic and international students. Applications are processed on a rolling basis. Application fee: $75. Electronic applications accepted. *Financial support:* In 2016–17, 15 students received support. Federal Work-Study, scholarships/grants, and tuition waivers (partial) available. Financial award application deadline: 4/15; financial award applicants required to submit FAFSA. *Faculty research:* Computational linguistics, statistical natural language processing, machine learning, computer science, speech recognition, automated text analysis. *Unit head:* Dr. James Pustejovsky, Program Chair, 781-736-2701, Fax: 781-736-2741, E-mail: jamesp@brandeis.edu. *Application contact:* Anne Gudaitis, Department Administrator, 781-736-2723, E-mail: gudaitis@brandeis.edu.
Website: http://www.brandeis.edu/programs/comp-linguistics/

Bridgewater State University, College of Graduate Studies, Bartlett College of Science and Mathematics, Department of Computer Science, Bridgewater, MA 02325. Offers MS.

Brigham Young University, Graduate Studies, College of Physical and Mathematical Sciences, Department of Computer Science, Provo, UT 84602. Offers MS, PhD. *Faculty:* 31 full-time (0 women), 6 part-time/adjunct (0 women). *Students:* 89 full-time (13 women); includes 17 minority (15 Asian, non-Hispanic/Latino; 2 Hispanic/Latino). Average age 29. 36 applicants, 83% accepted, 25 enrolled. In 2016, 16 master's, 5 doctorates awarded. Terminal master's awarded for partial completion of doctoral program. *Degree requirements:* For master's, thesis; for doctorate, comprehensive exam, thesis/dissertation, residency. *Entrance requirements:* For master's, GRE General Test, minimum GPA of 3.25 in last 60 hours; for doctorate, GRE General Test, minimum GPA of 3.5 in last 60 hours, undergraduate degree in computer science. Additional exam requirements/recommendations for international students: Required—TOEFL (minimum score 600 paper-based; 105 iBT). *Application deadline:* For fall admission, 12/15 for domestic and international students; for winter admission, 7/15 for domestic and international students. Application fee: $50. Electronic applications accepted. *Expenses: Tuition:* Full-time $6680; part-time $393 per credit. Tuition and fees vary according to course load, program and student's religious affiliation. *Financial support:* In 2016–17, fellowships (averaging $32,000 per year), 124 research assistantships (averaging $15,000 per year), 41 teaching assistantships with full and partial tuition reimbursements (averaging $13,000 per year) were awarded; scholarships/grants and health care benefits also available. Financial award application deadline: 3/1. *Faculty research:* Graphics/animation and computer vision, artificial intelligence and machine learning, computer networks/systems and security, human-computer interaction and software development, data and text analytics. *Total annual research expenditures:* $505,780. *Unit head:* Dr. Michael A. Goodrich, Chair, 801-422-6468, Fax: 801-422-0169, E-mail: mike@cs.byu.edu. *Application contact:* Dr. Christophe Giraud-Carrier, Graduate Coordinator, 801-422-8602, Fax: 801-422-0169, E-mail: cgc@cs.byu.edu.
Website: https://cs.byu.edu/

Brock University, Faculty of Graduate Studies, Faculty of Mathematics and Science, Program in Computer Science, St. Catharines, ON L2S 3A1, Canada. Offers M Sc. *Program availability:* Part-time. *Degree requirements:* For master's, thesis. *Entrance requirements:* For master's, honors degree. Additional exam requirements/recommendations for international students: Required—TOEFL (minimum score 550 paper-based; 80 iBT), IELTS (minimum score 6.5), TWE (minimum score 4).

Brooklyn College of the City University of New York, School of Natural and Behavioral Sciences, Department of Computer and Information Science, Brooklyn, NY 11210-2889. Offers computer science (MA); health informatics (MS); information systems (MS); parallel and distributed computing (Advanced Certificate). *Program availability:* Part-time, evening/weekend. *Degree requirements:* For master's, comprehensive exam, thesis or alternative. *Entrance requirements:* For master's, previous course work in computer science, 2 letters of recommendation. Additional exam requirements/recommendations for international students: Required—TOEFL (minimum score 525 paper-based; 70 iBT). Electronic applications accepted. *Faculty research:* Networks and distributed systems, programming languages, modeling and computer applications, algorithms, artificial intelligence, theoretical computer science.

Brown University, Graduate School, Department of Computer Science, Providence, RI 02912. Offers Sc M, PhD. *Degree requirements:* For master's, thesis or alternative; for doctorate, one foreign language, comprehensive exam, thesis/dissertation. *Entrance requirements:* For master's and doctorate, GRE General Test, GRE Subject Test.

California Institute of Technology, Division of Engineering and Applied Science, Option in Computer Science, Pasadena, CA 91125-0001. Offers MS, PhD. *Degree requirements:* For master's, thesis; for doctorate, thesis/dissertation. Electronic applications accepted. *Faculty research:* VLSI systems, concurrent computation, high-level programming languages, signal and image processing, graphics.

California Polytechnic State University, San Luis Obispo, College of Engineering, Department of Computer Science, San Luis Obispo, CA 93407. Offers MS. *Program availability:* Part-time. *Faculty:* 12 full-time (2 women). *Students:* 33 full-time (6 women), 17 part-time (4 women); includes 14 minority (12 Asian, non-Hispanic/Latino; 2 Two or more races, non-Hispanic/Latino), 4 international. Average age 25. 147 applicants, 7% accepted, 10 enrolled. In 2016, 24 master's awarded. *Degree requirements:* For master's, thesis. *Entrance requirements:* For master's, GRE. Additional exam requirements/recommendations for international students: Required—TOEFL (minimum score 80 iBT). *Application deadline:* For fall admission, 3/1 for domestic and international students. Applications are processed on a rolling basis. Application fee: $55. Electronic applications accepted. *Expenses:* Tuition, state resident: full-time $6738; part-time $3906 per year. Tuition, nonresident: full-time $15,666; part-time $8370 per year. *Required fees:* $3603; $3141 per unit. $1047 per term. *Financial support:* Fellowships, research assistantships, teaching assistantships, career-related internships or fieldwork, institutionally sponsored loans, scholarships/grants, and unspecified assistantships available. Financial award application deadline: 3/2; financial award applicants required to submit FAFSA. *Faculty research:* Human-computer interaction, artificial intelligence, programming languages, computer graphics, database systems. *Unit head:* Dr. Alex Dekhtyar, Graduate Coordinator, 805-756-2387, Fax: 805-756-2956, E-mail: dekhtyar@calpoly.edu.
Website: http://www.csc.calpoly.edu/programs/ms-csc/

California State Polytechnic University, Pomona, Program in Computer Science, Pomona, CA 91768-2557. Offers MS. *Program availability:* Part-time, evening/weekend. *Students:* 13 full-time (5 women), 67 part-time (22 women); includes 31 minority (2 Black or African American, non-Hispanic/Latino; 20 Asian, non-Hispanic/Latino; 9 Hispanic/Latino), 32 international. Average age 28. 30 applicants, 100% accepted, 24 enrolled. In 2016, 22 master's awarded. *Degree requirements:* For master's, thesis. *Entrance requirements:* Additional exam requirements/recommendations for international students: Required—TOEFL. *Application deadline:* Applications are processed on a rolling basis. Application fee: $55. Electronic applications accepted. *Expenses:* Contact institution. *Financial support:* Application deadline: 3/2; applicants required to submit FAFSA. *Unit head:* Dr. Gilbert S. Young, Graduate Coordinator, 909-869-4413, Fax: 909-869-4733, E-mail: gsyoung@cpp.edu. *Application contact:* Andrew M. Wright, Director of Admissions, 909-869-3130, Fax: 909-869-4529, E-mail: awright@cpp.edu.
Website: http://www.cpp.edu/~sci/computer-science/prospective-graduate-students/

California State University Channel Islands, Extended University and International Programs, Program in Computer Science, Camarillo, CA 93012. Offers MS. *Program availability:* Part-time, evening/weekend. *Entrance requirements:* Additional exam requirements/recommendations for international students: Required—TOEFL (minimum score 550 paper-based; 80 iBT), IELTS (minimum score 6).

California State University, Chico, Office of Graduate Studies, College of Engineering, Computer Science, and Construction Management, Department of Computer Science, Chico, CA 95929-0722. Offers MS. *Program availability:* Online learning. *Faculty:* 11 full-time (5 women), 6 part-time/adjunct (1 woman). *Students:* 9 full-time (0 women), 31 part-time (5 women); includes 37 minority (36 Asian, non-Hispanic/Latino; 1 Hispanic/Latino).

Computer Science

1 applicant, 100% accepted, 1 enrolled. In 2016, 19 master's awarded. *Degree requirements:* For master's, thesis or project and oral defense. *Entrance requirements:* For master's, GRE General Test (waived if graduated from ABET-accredited institution), 2 letters of recommendation, statement of purpose. Additional exam requirements/recommendations for international students: Required—TOEFL (minimum score 550 paper-based; 80 iBT), IELTS (minimum score 6.5). *Application deadline:* For fall admission, 3/1 priority date for domestic students, 3/1 for international students; for spring admission, 9/15 priority date for domestic students, 9/15 for international students. Application fee: $55. Electronic applications accepted. *Financial support:* Fellowships, research assistantships, teaching assistantships, career-related internships or fieldwork, scholarships/grants, and traineeships available. Financial award application deadline: 3/1; financial award applicants required to submit FAFSA. *Unit head:* Dr. Melody J. Stapleton, Chair, 530-898-6442, Fax: 530-898-5995, E-mail: csci@csuchico.edu. *Application contact:* Judy L. Morris, Graduate Admissions Coordinator, 530-898-5416, Fax: 530-898-3342, E-mail: jlmorris@csuchico.edu.
Website: http://www.csuchico.edu/csci/

California State University, Dominguez Hills, College of Natural and Behavioral Sciences, Department of Computer Science, Carson, CA 90747-0001. Offers MSCS. *Degree requirements:* For master's, comprehensive exam (for some programs), thesis (for some programs). *Entrance requirements:* For master's, GRE (minimum score 900), minimum GPA of 2.75. Additional exam requirements/recommendations for international students: Required—TOEFL (minimum score 550 paper-based). Electronic applications accepted.

California State University, East Bay, Office of Graduate Studies, College of Science, Department of Computer Science, Hayward, CA 94542-3000. Offers computer networks (MS); computer science (MS). *Program availability:* Part-time. *Students:* 105 full-time (46 women), 135 part-time (67 women); includes 23 minority (1 Black or African American, non-Hispanic/Latino; 18 Asian, non-Hispanic/Latino; 1 Hispanic/Latino; 1 Native Hawaiian or other Pacific Islander, non-Hispanic/Latino; 2 Two or more races, non-Hispanic/Latino), 205 international. Average age 26. 887 applicants, 43% accepted, 105 enrolled. In 2016, 138 master's awarded. *Degree requirements:* For master's, thesis or capstone experience. *Entrance requirements:* For master's, GRE, minimum GPA of 3.0 in field, 2.75 overall; baccalaureate degree in computer science or related field. Additional exam requirements/recommendations for international students: Required—TOEFL (minimum score 550 paper-based). *Application deadline:* For fall admission, 6/30 for domestic and international students. Application fee: $55. Electronic applications accepted. *Financial support:* Fellowships, career-related internships or fieldwork, Federal Work-Study, institutionally sponsored loans, and scholarships/grants available. Support available to part-time students. Financial award application deadline: 3/2; financial award applicants required to submit FAFSA. *Unit head:* Matthew Johnson, Chair, 510-885-4136, E-mail: matt.johnson@csueastbay.edu. *Application contact:* Dr. Donna Wiley, Interim Associate Vice President for Academic Programs and Graduate Studies, 510-885-3716, Fax: 510-885-4777, E-mail: donna.wiley@csueastbay.edu.
Website: http://www.csueastbay.edu/csci/departments/cs/index.html

California State University, Fresno, Division of Research and Graduate Studies, College of Science and Mathematics, Department of Computer Science, Fresno, CA 93740-8027. Offers MS. *Program availability:* Part-time, evening/weekend. *Degree requirements:* For master's, thesis or alternative. *Entrance requirements:* For master's, GRE General Test, minimum GPA of 2.75. Additional exam requirements/recommendations for international students: Required—TOEFL. *Application deadline:* For fall admission, 5/1 for domestic and international students; for spring admission, 10/1 for domestic and international students. Applications are processed on a rolling basis. Application fee: $55. Electronic applications accepted. *Financial support:* Fellowships, research assistantships, teaching assistantships, career-related internships or fieldwork, Federal Work-Study, scholarships/grants, and unspecified assistantships available. Support available to part-time students. Financial award application deadline: 3/1; financial award applicants required to submit FAFSA. *Faculty research:* Software design, parallel processing, computer engineering, auto line research. *Unit head:* Dr. Ming Li, Chair, 559-278-4373, Fax: 559-278-6297, E-mail: mingli@csufresno.edu. *Application contact:* Dr. Alex Liu, Graduate Coordinator, 559-278-4373, Fax: 559-278-6297, E-mail: shliu@csufresno.edu.
Website: http://www.fresnostate.edu/csm/csci/

California State University, Fullerton, Graduate Studies, College of Engineering and Computer Science, Department of Computer Science, Fullerton, CA 92834-9480. Offers computer science (MS); software engineering (MS). *Program availability:* Part-time, online learning. *Degree requirements:* For master's, comprehensive exam, project or thesis. *Entrance requirements:* For master's, GRE General Test, minimum undergraduate GPA of 2.5. Application fee: $55. *Expenses:* Tuition, state resident: full-time $3369; part-time $1953 per unit. Tuition, nonresident: full-time $3915; part-time $2499 per unit. Tuition and fees vary according to course load, degree level and program. *Financial support:* Career-related internships or fieldwork, Federal Work-Study, institutionally sponsored loans, and scholarships/grants available. Support available to part-time students. Financial award application deadline: 3/1; financial award applicants required to submit FAFSA. *Faculty research:* Software engineering, development of computer networks. *Unit head:* Dr. Shawn Wang, Chair, 657-278-7258. *Application contact:* Admissions/Applications, 657-278-2371.

California State University, Long Beach, Graduate Studies, College of Engineering, Department of Computer Engineering and Computer Science, Long Beach, CA 90840. Offers computer engineering (MSCS); computer science (MSCS). *Program availability:* Part-time. *Degree requirements:* For master's, thesis or alternative. *Entrance requirements:* Additional exam requirements/recommendations for international students: Required—TOEFL. *Application deadline:* For fall admission, 3/1 for domestic students. Application fee: $55. Electronic applications accepted. *Financial support:* Teaching assistantships, Federal Work-Study, institutionally sponsored loans, scholarships/grants, and unspecified assistantships available. Financial award application deadline: 3/2. *Faculty research:* Artificial intelligence, software engineering, computer simulation and modeling, user-interface design, networking. *Unit head:* Burkhart Englert, Chair, 562-985-4285.

California State University, Los Angeles, Graduate Studies, College of Engineering, Computer Science, and Technology, Department of Computer Science, Los Angeles, CA 90032-8530. Offers MS. *Entrance requirements:* Additional exam requirements/recommendations for international students: Required—TOEFL (minimum score 550 paper-based). Electronic applications accepted.

California State University, Northridge, Graduate Studies, College of Engineering and Computer Science, Department of Computer Science, Northridge, CA 91330. Offers computer science (MS); software engineering (MS). *Program availability:* Part-time, evening/weekend. *Faculty:* 19 full-time (15 women), 32 part-time/adjunct (26 women). *Students:* 36 full-time (8 women), 40 part-time (6 women); includes 22 minority (1 Black or African American, non-Hispanic/Latino; 7 Asian, non-Hispanic/Latino; 11 Hispanic/Latino; 3 Two or more races, non-Hispanic/Latino), 23 international. Average age 29. 425 applicants, 12% accepted, 25 enrolled. *Degree requirements:* For master's, thesis. *Entrance requirements:* For master's, GRE General Test, minimum GPA of 2.5. Additional exam requirements/recommendations for international students: Required—

TOEFL. *Application deadline:* For fall admission, 11/30 for domestic students. Application fee: $55. *Expenses:* Tuition, state resident: full-time $4152. *Financial support:* Application deadline: 3/1. *Faculty research:* Radar data processing. *Unit head:* Rick Covington, Chair, 818-677-3398.
Website: http://www.csun.edu/computerscience/

California State University, Sacramento, Office of Graduate Studies, College of Engineering and Computer Science, Department of Computer Science, Sacramento, CA 95819. Offers computer science (MS); software engineering (MS). *Program availability:* Part-time, evening/weekend. *Students:* 67 full-time (26 women), 41 part-time (17 women); includes 96 minority (2 Black or African American, non-Hispanic/Latino; 1 American Indian or Alaska Native, non-Hispanic/Latino; 90 Asian, non-Hispanic/Latino; 3 Hispanic/Latino). Average age 26. 352 applicants, 70% accepted, 60 enrolled. In 2016, 23 master's awarded. *Degree requirements:* For master's, thesis or comprehensive exam; writing proficiency exam. *Entrance requirements:* For master's, GRE, minimum GPA of 3.0 in last 60 units attempted. Additional exam requirements/recommendations for international students: Required—TOEFL (minimum score 550 paper-based; 80 iBT). *Application deadline:* For fall admission, 3/1 for domestic and international students; for spring admission, 9/15 for domestic students, 9/30 for international students. Applications are processed on a rolling basis. Application fee: $55. Electronic applications accepted. *Expenses:* $4,302 full-time tuition and fees per semester, $2,796 part-time. *Financial support:* Research assistantships, teaching assistantships, career-related internships or fieldwork, and Federal Work-Study available. Support available to part-time students. Financial award application deadline: 3/1; financial award applicants required to submit FAFSA. *Unit head:* Dr. Cui Zhang, Chair, 916-278-6834, E-mail: cscchair@ecs.csus.edu. *Application contact:* Jose Martinez, Graduate Admissions Supervisor, 916-278-7871, E-mail: martinj@skymail.csus.edu.
Website: http://www.ecs.csus.edu/csc

California State University, San Bernardino, Graduate Studies, College of Natural Sciences, Program in Computer Science, San Bernardino, CA 92407. Offers MS. *Faculty:* 9 full-time (3 women). *Students:* 10 full-time (3 women), 31 part-time (5 women); includes 5 minority (1 Asian, non-Hispanic/Latino; 4 Hispanic/Latino), 33 international. 196 applicants, 12% accepted, 6 enrolled. In 2016, 25 master's awarded. *Entrance requirements:* Additional exam requirements/recommendations for international students: Required—TOEFL. *Application deadline:* For fall admission, 7/16 for domestic students; for winter admission, 10/16 for domestic students; for spring admission, 1/22 for domestic students. Application fee: $55. *Expenses:* Tuition, state resident: full-time $7843; part-time $5011.20 per year. Tuition and fees vary according to course load, degree level, program and reciprocity agreements. *Unit head:* Dr. Haiyan Qiao, Director, 909-537-5415, Fax: 909-537-7004, E-mail: hqiao@csusb.edu. *Application contact:* Dr. Francisca Beer, Dean of Graduate Studies, 909-537-5058, E-mail: fbeer@csusb.edu.

California State University, San Marcos, College of Science and Mathematics, Program in Computer Science, San Marcos, CA 92096-0001. Offers MS. *Program availability:* Part-time. *Entrance requirements:* For master's, GRE General Test, statement of purpose, letters of recommendation. Additional exam requirements/recommendations for international students: Required—TOEFL (minimum score 550 paper-based; 80 iBT). *Expenses:* Tuition, state resident: full-time $6738. Tuition, nonresident: full-time $13,434. *Required fees:* $1906. Tuition and fees vary according to campus/location and program. *Faculty research:* Networks, multimedia, parallel algorithms, software engineering, artificial intelligence.

Capitol Technology University, Graduate Programs, Laurel, MD 20708-9759. Offers business administration (MBA); computer science (MS); electrical engineering (MS); information and telecommunications systems management (MS); information architecture (MS); network security (MS). *Program availability:* Part-time, evening/weekend, online learning. *Entrance requirements:* For master's, minimum GPA of 3.0. Electronic applications accepted.

Carleton University, Faculty of Graduate Studies, Faculty of Science, School of Computer Science, Ottawa, ON K1S 5B6, Canada. Offers computer science (MCS, PhD); information and system science (M Sc). MCS and PhD programs offered jointly with University of Ottawa. *Program availability:* Part-time. *Degree requirements:* For master's, thesis optional, project; for doctorate, comprehensive exam, thesis/dissertation. *Entrance requirements:* For master's, honors degree. Additional exam requirements/recommendations for international students: Required—TOEFL. *Faculty research:* Programming systems, theory of computing, computer applications, computer systems.

Carnegie Mellon University, School of Computer Science, Department of Computer Science, Pittsburgh, PA 15213-3891. Offers algorithms, combinatorics, and optimization (PhD); computer science (MS, PhD); pure and applied logic (PhD). *Degree requirements:* For doctorate, thesis/dissertation. *Entrance requirements:* For doctorate, GRE General Test, GRE Subject Test, BS in computer science or equivalent. Additional exam requirements/recommendations for international students: Required—TOEFL. *Faculty research:* Software systems, theory of computations, artificial intelligence, computer systems, programming languages.

Carnegie Mellon University, School of Computer Science, Language Technologies Institute, Pittsburgh, PA 15213-3891. Offers MLT, MS, PhD. Terminal master's awarded for partial completion of doctoral program. *Degree requirements:* For doctorate, thesis/dissertation. *Entrance requirements:* For master's and doctorate, GRE General Test, GRE Subject Test. Additional exam requirements/recommendations for international students: Required—TOEFL. *Faculty research:* Machine translation, natural language processing, speech and information retrieval, literacy.

Case Western Reserve University, School of Graduate Studies, Case School of Engineering, Department of Electrical Engineering and Computer Science, Cleveland, OH 44106. Offers computer engineering (MS, PhD); computing and information sciences (MS, PhD); electrical engineering (MS, PhD); systems and control engineering (MS, PhD). *Program availability:* Part-time, evening/weekend, online only, 100% online. *Faculty:* 32 full-time (3 women). *Students:* 188 full-time (42 women), 14 part-time (3 women); includes 7 minority (1 Black or African American, non-Hispanic/Latino; 5 Asian, non-Hispanic/Latino; 1 Hispanic/Latino), 152 international. In 2016, 25 master's, 26 doctorates awarded. Terminal master's awarded for partial completion of doctoral program. *Degree requirements:* For master's, thesis; for doctorate, thesis/dissertation, qualifying exam, teaching experience. *Entrance requirements:* For master's and doctorate, GRE General Test. Additional exam requirements/recommendations for international students: Required—TOEFL. *Application deadline:* For fall admission, 2/1 for domestic students; for spring admission, 11/1 for domestic students. Applications are processed on a rolling basis. Application fee: $50. *Expenses:* Tuition: Full-time $42,576; part-time $1774 per credit hour. *Required fees:* $34. Tuition and fees vary according to course load and program. *Financial support:* In 2016–17, 1 fellowship with tuition reimbursement, 63 research assistantships with tuition reimbursements, 10 teaching assistantships were awarded; career-related internships or fieldwork, Federal Work-Study, and institutionally sponsored loans also available. Support available to part-time students. Financial award application deadline: 3/1; financial award applicants required

to submit FAFSA. *Faculty research:* Micro-/nano-systems; robotics and haptics; applied artificial intelligence; automation; computer-aided design and testing of digital systems. *Total annual research expenditures:* $4.9 million. *Unit head:* Dr. Kenneth Loparo, Department Chair, 216-368-4115, E-mail: kal4@case.edu. *Application contact:* Kimberly Yurchick, Student Affairs Specialist, 216-368-2920, Fax: 216-368-2801, E-mail: ksy4@case.edu.
Website: http://eecs.cwru.edu/

The Catholic University of America, School of Engineering, Department of Electrical Engineering and Computer Science, Washington, DC 20064. Offers computer science (MSCS, PhD); electrical engineering (MEE, PhD). *Program availability:* Part-time. *Faculty:* 10 full-time (2 women), 7 part-time/adjunct (1 woman). *Students:* 13 full-time (2 women), 40 part-time (11 women); includes 6 minority (1 Black or African American, non-Hispanic/Latino; 1 Asian, non-Hispanic/Latino; 4 Two or more races, non-Hispanic/Latino), 35 international. Average age 33. 40 applicants, 63% accepted, 12 enrolled. In 2016, 7 master's, 10 doctorates awarded. *Degree requirements:* For master's, thesis or alternative; for doctorate, comprehensive exam, thesis/dissertation, oral exams. *Entrance requirements:* For master's and doctorate, statement of purpose, official copies of academic transcripts, three letters of recommendation. Additional exam requirements/recommendations for international students: Required—TOEFL (minimum score 550 paper-based; 80 iBT). *Application deadline:* For fall admission, 7/15 priority date for domestic students, 7/1 for international students; for spring admission, 11/15 priority date for domestic students, 11/1 for international students. Applications are processed on a rolling basis. Application fee: $55. Electronic applications accepted. *Expenses:* $43,380 per year; $1,170 per credit; $200 per semester part-time fees. *Financial support:* Fellowships, research assistantships, teaching assistantships, Federal Work-Study, scholarships/grants, tuition waivers (full and partial), and unspecified assistantships available. Financial award application deadline: 2/1; financial award applicants required to submit FAFSA. *Faculty research:* Signal and image processing, computer communications, robotics, intelligent controls, bio-electromagnetics. *Total annual research expenditures:* $455,269. *Unit head:* Dr. Ozlem Kilic, Chair, 202-319-5879, Fax: 202-319-5195, E-mail: regalia@cua.edu. *Application contact:* Director of Graduate Admissions, 202-319-5057, Fax: 202-319-6533, E-mail: cua-admissions@cua.edu.
Website: http://eecs.cua.edu/

Central Connecticut State University, School of Graduate Studies, School of Engineering, Science and Technology, Department of Computer Science, New Britain, CT 06050-4010. Offers computer information technology (MS). *Program availability:* Part-time, evening/weekend. *Faculty:* 10 full-time (5 women), 1 part-time/adjunct (0 women). *Students:* 25 full-time (12 women), 45 part-time (16 women); includes 13 minority (4 Black or African American, non-Hispanic/Latino; 4 Asian, non-Hispanic/Latino; 4 Hispanic/Latino; 1 Two or more races, non-Hispanic/Latino), 37 international. Average age 30. 61 applicants, 59% accepted, 15 enrolled. In 2016, 23 master's awarded. *Degree requirements:* For master's, thesis or alternative, special project. *Entrance requirements:* For master's, minimum undergraduate GPA of 2.7, letters of recommendation, resume. Additional exam requirements/recommendations for international students: Required—TOEFL (minimum score 550 paper-based; 79 iBT). *Application deadline:* For fall admission, 6/1 for domestic students, 5/1 for international students; for spring admission, 11/1 for domestic and international students. Applications are processed on a rolling basis. Application fee: $50. Electronic applications accepted. *Expenses: Tuition, area resident:* Full-time $6497; part-time $606 per credit. Tuition, state resident: full-time $9748; part-time $622 per credit. Tuition, nonresident: full-time $18,102; part-time $622 per credit. *Required fees:* $4459; $246 per credit. *Financial support:* In 2016–17, 2 students received support. Career-related internships or fieldwork, Federal Work-Study, scholarships/grants, and unspecified assistantships available. Support available to part-time students. Financial award application deadline: 3/1; financial award applicants required to submit FAFSA. *Unit head:* Dr. Stanislav Kurkovsky, Chair, 860-832-2710, E-mail: kurkovsky@ccsu.edu. *Application contact:* Patricia Gardner, Associate Director of Graduate Studies, 860-832-2350, Fax: 860-832-2362.
Website: http://www.ccsu.edu/cs/

Central Connecticut State University, School of Graduate Studies, School of Engineering, Science and Technology, Department of Mathematical Sciences, New Britain, CT 06050-4010. Offers data mining (MS, Certificate); mathematics (MA, MS), including actuarial science (MA), computer science (MA), statistics (MA); mathematics education leadership (Sixth Year Certificate); mathematics for secondary education (Certificate). *Program availability:* Part-time, evening/weekend, 100% online. *Faculty:* 14 full-time (4 women). *Students:* 8 full-time (5 women), 73 part-time (37 women); includes 17 minority (4 Black or African American, non-Hispanic/Latino; 7 Asian, non-Hispanic/Latino; 4 Hispanic/Latino; 2 Two or more races, non-Hispanic/Latino), 4 international. Average age 37. 44 applicants, 68% accepted, 21 enrolled. In 2016, 23 master's, 1 other advanced degree awarded. *Degree requirements:* For master's, comprehensive exam, thesis or alternative, special project; for other advanced degree, qualifying exam. *Entrance requirements:* For master's, minimum undergraduate GPA of 2.7; for other advanced degree, minimum undergraduate GPA of 3.0, essay, letters of recommendation. Additional exam requirements/recommendations for international students: Required—TOEFL (minimum score 550 paper-based; 79 iBT). *Application deadline:* For fall admission, 5/1 for domestic and international students; for spring admission, 11/1 for domestic and international students. Applications are processed on a rolling basis. Application fee: $50. Electronic applications accepted. *Expenses: Tuition, area resident:* Full-time $6497; part-time $606 per credit. Tuition, state resident: full-time $9748; part-time $622 per credit. Tuition, nonresident: full-time $18,102; part-time $622 per credit. *Required fees:* $4459; $246 per credit. *Financial support:* In 2016–17, 18 students received support. Career-related internships or fieldwork, Federal Work-Study, and scholarships/grants available. Support available to part-time students. Financial award application deadline: 3/1; financial award applicants required to submit FAFSA. *Faculty research:* Statistics, actuarial mathematics, computer systems and engineering, computer programming techniques, operations research. *Unit head:* Dr. Philip Halloran, Chair, 860-832-2835, E-mail: halloranp@ccsu.edu. *Application contact:* Patricia Gardner, Associate Director of Graduate Studies, 860-832-2350, Fax: 860-832-2362.
Website: http://www.ccsu.edu/mathematics/

Central Michigan University, College of Graduate Studies, College of Science and Technology, Department of Computer Science, Mount Pleasant, MI 48859. Offers MS. *Program availability:* Part-time. *Degree requirements:* For master's, thesis or alternative. *Entrance requirements:* For master's, bachelor's degree from accredited institution with minimum GPA of 3.0 in last two years of study. Electronic applications accepted. *Faculty research:* Artificial intelligence, biocomputing, data mining, software engineering, operating systems, mobile applications.

Chicago State University, School of Graduate and Professional Studies, College of Arts and Sciences, Department of Mathematics and Computer Science, Chicago, IL 60628. Offers computer science (MS); mathematics (MS). *Degree requirements:* For master's, thesis optional, oral exam. *Entrance requirements:* For master's, minimum GPA of 2.75.

Christopher Newport University, Graduate Studies, Department of Physics, Computer Science, and Engineering, Newport News, VA 23606-3072. Offers applied physics and computer science (MS). *Program availability:* Part-time. *Faculty:* 6 full-time (0 women). *Students:* 8 full-time (0 women), 9 part-time (0 women); includes 1 minority (Two or more races, non-Hispanic/Latino), 2 international. Average age 23. 13 applicants, 85% accepted, 7 enrolled. In 2016, 5 master's awarded. *Degree requirements:* For master's, comprehensive exam (for some programs), thesis (for some programs). *Entrance requirements:* For master's, GRE General Test, minimum GPA of 3.0. Additional exam requirements/recommendations for international students: Required—TOEFL (minimum score 580 paper-based; 92 iBT), IELTS (minimum score 7). *Application deadline:* For fall admission, 7/15 priority date for domestic students, 3/1 for international students; for spring admission, 11/1 for domestic students, 10/1 for international students; for summer admission, 3/15 for domestic students, 3/1 for international students. Applications are processed on a rolling basis. Application fee: $65. Electronic applications accepted. *Expenses:* Tuition, state resident: full-time $6660; part-time $370 per credit hour. Tuition, nonresident: full-time $15,138; part-time $841 per credit hour. *Required fees:* $3906; $217 per credit hour. Tuition and fees vary according to course load. *Financial support:* In 2016–17, 5 students received support, including 2 research assistantships with full tuition reimbursements available (averaging $2,000 per year), 3 teaching assistantships (averaging $1,000 per year); unspecified assistantships also available. Financial award application deadline: 3/1; financial award applicants required to submit FAFSA. *Faculty research:* Advanced programming methodologies, experimental nuclear physics, computer architecture, semiconductor nanophysics, laser and optical fiber sensors. *Total annual research expenditures:* $844,000. *Unit head:* Dr. David Heddle, Coordinator, 757-594-8435, Fax: 757-594-7919, E-mail: heddle@cnu.edu. *Application contact:* Lyn Sawyer, Associate Director, Graduate Admissions and Records, 757-594-7544, Fax: 757-594-7649, E-mail: gradstdy@cnu.edu.

City College of the City University of New York, Graduate School, Grove School of Engineering, Department of Computer Science, New York, NY 10031-9198. Offers computer science (MS, PhD); information systems (MIS). PhD program offered jointly with Graduate School and University Center of the City University of New York. *Degree requirements:* For master's, thesis optional; for doctorate, one foreign language, comprehensive exam, thesis/dissertation. *Entrance requirements:* For master's and doctorate, GRE General Test. Additional exam requirements/recommendations for international students: Required—TOEFL (minimum score 500 paper-based; 61 iBT). Tuition and fees vary according to course load, degree level and program. *Faculty research:* Complexities of algebraic research, human issues in computer science, scientific computing, super compilers, parallel algorithms.

City University of Seattle, Graduate Division, School of Management, Seattle, WA 98121. Offers accounting (Certificate); change leadership (MBA, Certificate); computer systems (MS); finance (Certificate); financial management (MBA); general management (MBA); general management-Europe (MBA); global marketing (MBA); human resources management (Certificate); individualized study (MBA); information security (MS); information systems (MBA); leadership (MA); marketing (MBA, Certificate); project management (MBA, MS, Certificate); sustainable business (Certificate); technology management (MBA, Certificate). *Program availability:* Part-time, evening/weekend, online learning. *Degree requirements:* For master's, comprehensive exam (for some programs), thesis (for some programs). *Entrance requirements:* For master's, baccalaureate degree or equivalent from an accredited or otherwise recognized institution. Additional exam requirements/recommendations for international students: Required—TOEFL (minimum score 567 paper-based; 87 iBT); Recommended—IELTS. Electronic applications accepted.

Clark Atlanta University, School of Arts and Sciences, Department of Computer and Information Science, Atlanta, GA 30314. Offers MS. *Program availability:* Part-time. *Faculty:* 3 full-time (0 women). *Students:* 27 full-time (10 women), 11 part-time (2 women); includes 6 minority (3 Black or African American, non-Hispanic/Latino; 3 Asian, non-Hispanic/Latino), 21 international. Average age 29. 25 applicants, 96% accepted, 7 enrolled. In 2016, 15 master's awarded. *Degree requirements:* For master's, one foreign language, thesis. *Entrance requirements:* For master's, GRE General Test, minimum GPA of 2.5. Additional exam requirements/recommendations for international students: Required—TOEFL (minimum score 500 paper-based; 61 iBT). *Application deadline:* For fall admission, 4/1 for domestic and international students; for spring admission, 11/1 for domestic and international students. Applications are processed on a rolling basis. Application fee: $40 ($55 for international students). *Expenses: Tuition:* Full-time $15,498; part-time $861 per credit hour. *Required fees:* $1326; $1326 per credit hour. Tuition and fees vary according to course load. *Financial support:* Fellowships, career-related internships or fieldwork, Federal Work-Study, scholarships/grants, and unspecified assistantships available. Support available to part-time students. Financial award application deadline: 4/30; financial award applicants required to submit FAFSA. *Unit head:* Dr. Roy George, Chairperson, 404-880-6945, E-mail: rgeorge@cau.edu. *Application contact:* Graduate Program Admissions, 404-880-8483, E-mail: graduateadmissions@cau.edu.

Clarkson University, School of Arts and Sciences, Department of Computer Science, Potsdam, NY 13699. Offers MS, PhD. *Faculty:* 20 full-time (5 women), 1 part-time/adjunct (0 women). *Students:* 10 full-time (2 women), 1 part-time (0 women); includes 2 minority (1 Asian, non-Hispanic/Latino; 1 Two or more races, non-Hispanic/Latino), 3 international. 38 applicants, 61% accepted, 3 enrolled. In 2016, 3 master's awarded. *Degree requirements:* For master's, thesis; for doctorate, comprehensive exam, thesis/dissertation. *Entrance requirements:* For master's and doctorate, GRE. Additional exam requirements/recommendations for international students: Required—TOEFL (minimum score 550 paper-based, 80 iBT) or IELTS (6.5). *Application deadline:* Applications are processed on a rolling basis. Application fee: $50. Electronic applications accepted. *Expenses: Tuition:* Full-time $23,400; part-time $1300 per credit hour. Tuition and fees vary according to campus/location and program. *Financial support:* Scholarships/grants and unspecified assistantships available. *Unit head:* Dr. Christopher Lynch, Chair of Computer Science, 315-268-2334, E-mail: clynch@clarkson.edu. *Application contact:* Dan Capogna, Graduate Admissions Contact, 518-631-9910, E-mail: graduate@clarkson.edu.
Website: http://graduate.clarkson.edu

Clemson University, Graduate School, College of Engineering, Computing and Applied Sciences, School of Computing, Program in Computer Science, Clemson, SC 29634. Offers MS, PhD. *Program availability:* Part-time. *Faculty:* 16 full-time (3 women). *Students:* 166 full-time (46 women), 30 part-time (6 women); includes 10 minority (3 Black or African American, non-Hispanic/Latino; 2 Hispanic/Latino; 5 Two or more races, non-Hispanic/Latino), 153 international. Average age 26. 390 applicants, 40% accepted, 70 enrolled. In 2016, 57 master's, 4 doctorates awarded. Terminal master's awarded for partial completion of doctoral program. *Degree requirements:* For master's, thesis optional; for doctorate, comprehensive exam, thesis/dissertation. *Entrance requirements:* For master's and doctorate, GRE General Test, unofficial transcripts, letters of recommendation. Additional exam requirements/recommendations for international students: Required—TOEFL (minimum score 550 paper-based; 80 iBT), IELTS (minimum score 6.5). *Application deadline:* For fall admission, 5/15 priority date for domestic students, 4/15 priority date for international students; for spring admission,

10/15 priority date for domestic students, 9/15 priority date for international students. Applications are processed on a rolling basis. Application fee: $80 ($90 for international students). Electronic applications accepted. *Expenses:* $4,841 per semester full-time resident, $9,640 per semester full-time non-resident, $612 per credit hour part-time resident, $1,223 per credit hour part-time non-resident. *Financial support:* In 2016–17, 68 students received support, including 2 fellowships with partial tuition reimbursements available (averaging $19,513 per year), 30 research assistantships with partial tuition reimbursements available (averaging $18,632 per year), 28 teaching assistantships with partial tuition reimbursements available (averaging $17,737 per year); career-related internships or fieldwork, traineeships, and unspecified assistantships also available. Financial award application deadline: 1/1. *Faculty research:* Algorithms and data structures, computer graphics, parallel and distributed computing, security and privacy, software engineering. *Unit head:* Dr. Amy Apon, Computer Science Division Chair, 864-656-5769, E-mail: aapon@clemson.edu. *Application contact:* Dr. Brian Dean, PhD Program Coordinator, 864-656-5866, E-mail: bcdean@clemson.edu.
Website: http://www.clemson.edu/cecas/departments/computing/academics/graduates/programsofstudy/index.html

Coastal Carolina University, College of Science, Conway, SC 29528-6054. Offers applied computing and information systems (Certificate); coastal marine and wetland studies (MS); information systems technology (MS); marine science (PhD); sports management (MS). *Program availability:* Part-time, evening/weekend. *Faculty:* 23 full-time (5 women), 1 part-time/adjunct (0 women). *Students:* 41 full-time (14 women), 29 part-time (15 women); includes 7 minority (4 Black or African American, non-Hispanic/Latino; 1 American Indian or Alaska Native, non-Hispanic/Latino; 1 Hispanic/Latino; 1 Two or more races, non-Hispanic/Latino), 6 international. Average age 27. 72 applicants, 57% accepted, 35 enrolled. In 2016, 13 master's awarded. *Degree requirements:* For master's, thesis or internship; for doctorate, comprehensive exam, thesis/dissertation. *Entrance requirements:* For master's, GRE, 3 letters of recommendation, resume, official transcripts, written statement of educational and career goals, baccalaureate degree; for doctorate, GRE, official transcripts; baccalaureate or master's degree; minimum GPA of 3.0 for all collegiate coursework; successful completion of at least two semesters of college-level calculus, physics, and chemistry; 3 letters of recommendation; written statement of educational and career goals; resume; for Certificate, 2 letters of reference, official transcripts, minimum GPA of 3.0 in all computing and information systems courses, documentation of graduation from accredited four-year college or university. Additional exam requirements/recommendations for international students: Required—TOEFL (minimum score 550 paper-based; 79 iBT), IELTS (minimum score 6.5). *Application deadline:* For fall admission, 1/15 priority date for domestic and international students; for spring admission, 11/1 priority date for domestic and international students. Applications are processed on a rolling basis. Application fee: $45. Electronic applications accepted. *Expenses:* Tuition, state resident: full-time $9990; part-time $555 per credit hour. Tuition, nonresident: full-time $18,108; part-time $1006 per credit hour. *Required fees:* $90; $5 per credit hour. *Financial support:* Fellowships, research assistantships, and unspecified assistantships available. Support available to part-time students. Financial award application deadline: 3/1; financial award applicants required to submit FAFSA. *Unit head:* Dr. Michael H. Roberts, Dean, 843-349-2282, Fax: 843-349-2545, E-mail: mroberts@coastal.edu. *Application contact:* Dr. James O. Luken, Associate Provost/Vice-Dean of the Coastal Environment, 843-349-2235, Fax: 843-349-6444, E-mail: joluken@coastal.edu.
Website: http://www.coastal.edu/academics/colleges/science/

College of Charleston, Graduate School, School of Sciences and Mathematics, Program in Computer and Information Sciences, Charleston, SC 29424-0001. Offers MS. Program offered jointly with The Citadel, The Military College of South Carolina. *Program availability:* Part-time, evening/weekend. *Degree requirements:* For master's, thesis optional. *Entrance requirements:* For master's, GRE. Additional exam requirements/recommendations for international students: Required—TOEFL (minimum score 81 iBT). *Application deadline:* For fall admission, 6/1 for domestic students; for spring admission, 11/1 for domestic students. Application fee: $45. Electronic applications accepted. *Financial support:* Research assistantships, Federal Work-Study, scholarships/grants, and unspecified assistantships available. Support available to part-time students. Financial award application deadline: 4/1; financial award applicants required to submit FAFSA. *Unit head:* Aspen Olmsted, Director, 843-953-6600. *Application contact:* Aspen Olmsted, Director, 843-953-6600.

The College of Saint Rose, Graduate Studies, School of Mathematics and Sciences, Program in Computer Information Systems, Albany, NY 12203-1419. Offers MS, Advanced Certificate. *Program availability:* Part-time, evening/weekend. *Students:* 89 full-time (28 women), 16 part-time (6 women); includes 4 minority (2 Black or African American, non-Hispanic/Latino; 1 Asian, non-Hispanic/Latino; 1 Two or more races, non-Hispanic/Latino), 97 international. Average age 25. 220 applicants, 83% accepted, 13 enrolled. In 2016, 18 master's, 3 other advanced degrees awarded. *Degree requirements:* For master's, comprehensive exam, research component, project. *Entrance requirements:* For master's, minimum GPA of 3.0, 9 undergraduate credits in math. Additional exam requirements/recommendations for international students: Required—TOEFL (minimum score 550 paper-based; 80 iBT), IELTS (minimum score 6), PTE (minimum score 56). *Application deadline:* For fall admission, 4/1 priority date for domestic and international students; for spring admission, 10/15 priority date for domestic and international students; for summer admission, 3/15 priority date for domestic and international students. Applications are processed on a rolling basis. Application fee: $40. Electronic applications accepted. *Expenses: Tuition:* Full-time $14,382; part-time $799 per credit. *Required fees:* $814; $32 per credit. $88 per semester. Tuition and fees vary according to course load. *Financial support:* Career-related internships or fieldwork, scholarships/grants, tuition waivers (partial), and unspecified assistantships available. Support available to part-time students. Financial award application deadline: 4/15; financial award applicants required to submit FAFSA. *Unit head:* Dr. John Avitabile, Department Chair, 518-458-5317, E-mail: avitabij@strose.edu. *Application contact:* Cris Murray, Assistant Vice President for Graduate Recruitment and Enrollment, 518-485-3390.
Website: https://www.strose.edu/computer-information-systems/

College of Staten Island of the City University of New York, Graduate Programs, Division of Science and Technology, Program in Computer Science, Staten Island, NY 10314-6600. Offers MS. *Program availability:* Part-time, evening/weekend. *Faculty:* 4 full-time. *Students:* 3 full-time, 28 part-time. Average age 27. 72 applicants, 40% accepted, 13 enrolled. In 2016, 24 master's awarded. *Degree requirements:* For master's, thesis optional, 10 courses (30 credits) with minimum GPA of 3.0. *Entrance requirements:* For master's, GRE General Test, BS in computer science or related area with minimum B average overall and in major. Additional exam requirements/recommendations for international students: Required—TOEFL (minimum score 550 paper-based; 79 iBT), IELTS (minimum score 6.5). *Application deadline:* For fall admission, 7/20 priority date for domestic and international students; for spring admission, 11/2 priority date for domestic and international students. Applications are processed on a rolling basis. Application fee: $125. Electronic applications accepted. *Expenses:* Tuition, state resident: full-time $10,130; part-time $425 per credit. Tuition, nonresident: full-time $18,720; part-time $780 per credit. *Required fees:* $181.10 per semester. Tuition and fees vary according to program. *Faculty research:* Big data, pattern recognition, text mining, and frequent pattern mining; graph theory; parallel computing and stimulation; serious games; scheduling algorithms. *Unit head:* Dr. Shuqun Zhang, Graduate Program Coordinator, 718-982-3178, E-mail: shuqun.zhang@csi.cuny.edu. *Application contact:* Sasha Spence, Associate Director for Graduate Admissions, 718-982-2019, Fax: 718-982-2500, E-mail: sasha.spence@csi.cuny.edu.
Website: http://www.cs.csi.cuny.edu/content/grad.cs.csi.cuny.new.htm

The College of William and Mary, Faculty of Arts and Sciences, Department of Computer Science, Williamsburg, VA 23187-8795. Offers computational operations research (MS), including computer science; computer science (MS, PhD), including computational science (PhD). *Program availability:* Part-time. *Faculty:* 17 full-time (2 women), 1 part-time/adjunct (0 women). *Students:* 74 full-time (16 women), 7 part-time (4 women); includes 4 minority (2 Asian, non-Hispanic/Latino; 1 Hispanic/Latino; 1 Two or more races, non-Hispanic/Latino), 61 international. Average age 27. 116 applicants, 51% accepted, 22 enrolled. In 2016, 11 master's, 12 doctorates awarded. *Degree requirements:* For master's, comprehensive exam, thesis optional, research project; for doctorate, comprehensive exam, thesis/dissertation. *Entrance requirements:* For master's and doctorate, GRE General Test, minimum GPA of 3.0. Additional exam requirements/recommendations for international students: Required—TOEFL, TWE. *Application deadline:* For fall admission, 3/1 priority date for domestic students, 3/1 for international students; for spring admission, 10/15 for domestic and international students. Applications are processed on a rolling basis. Application fee: $45. Electronic applications accepted. *Expenses:* Tuition, state resident: full-time $9000; part-time $500 per credit hour. Tuition, nonresident: full-time $24,686; part-time $1200 per credit hour. *Required fees:* $5258. One-time fee: $400 full-time. *Financial support:* In 2016–17, 6 fellowships with full tuition reimbursements (averaging $9,000 per year), 35 research assistantships with full tuition reimbursements (averaging $24,000 per year), 24 teaching assistantships with full tuition reimbursements (averaging $24,000 per year) were awarded; scholarships/grants and unspecified assistantships also available. Financial award application deadline: 3/1; financial award applicants required to submit FAFSA. *Faculty research:* High-performance computing, wireless computing, algorithms, computer systems and network computing, modeling, simulation, and graphics. *Total annual research expenditures:* $1.7 million. *Unit head:* Dr. Robert Lewis, Chair, 757-221-3460, Fax: 757-221-1717, E-mail: rmlewi@wm.edu. *Application contact:* Vanessa Godwin, Administrative Director, 757-221-3455, Fax: 757-221-1717, E-mail: gradinfo@cs.wm.edu.
Website: http://www.wm.edu/computerscience

Colorado School of Mines, Office of Graduate Studies, Department of Electrical Engineering and Computer Science, Golden, CO 80401. Offers computer science (MS, PhD); electrical engineering (MS, PhD). *Program availability:* Part-time. *Degree requirements:* For master's, thesis (for some programs); for doctorate, comprehensive exam, thesis/dissertation. *Entrance requirements:* For master's and doctorate, GRE General Test. Additional exam requirements/recommendations for international students: Required—TOEFL (minimum score 550 paper-based; 80 iBT). Electronic applications accepted. *Expenses:* Tuition, state resident: full-time $15,690. Tuition, nonresident: full-time $34,020. *Required fees:* $2152. Tuition and fees vary according to course load.

Colorado State University, College of Natural Sciences, Department of Computer Science, Fort Collins, CO 80523-1873. Offers MCS, MS, PhD. *Program availability:* Part-time, 100% online. *Faculty:* 15 full-time (3 women). *Students:* 36 full-time (9 women), 106 part-time (15 women); includes 18 minority (1 Black or African American, non-Hispanic/Latino; 10 Asian, non-Hispanic/Latino; 5 Hispanic/Latino; 2 Two or more races, non-Hispanic/Latino), 76 international. Average age 32. 67 applicants, 88% accepted, 31 enrolled. In 2016, 50 master's, 5 doctorates awarded. Terminal master's awarded for partial completion of doctoral program. *Degree requirements:* For master's, thesis (for some programs); for doctorate, thesis/dissertation. *Entrance requirements:* For master's, minimum GPA of 3.2, BS in computer science; for doctorate, minimum GPA of 3.2, BS/MS in computer science, research experience. Additional exam requirements/recommendations for international students: Required—TOEFL (minimum score 580 paper-based; 92 iBT), IELTS (minimum score 6.5), PTE (minimum score 62), GRE. *Application deadline:* For fall admission, 2/1 for domestic and international students; for spring admission, 8/15 for domestic and international students. Application fee: $60 ($70 for international students). Electronic applications accepted. *Expenses:* $675-$793 per credit hour (online). *Financial support:* In 2016–17, 3 fellowships (averaging $70,000 per year), 30 research assistantships (averaging $19,853 per year), 22 teaching assistantships (averaging $16,669 per year) were awarded; health care benefits and unspecified assistantships also available. Financial award application deadline: 2/1. *Faculty research:* Artificial intelligence; software engineering; networks and security; big data/cloud computing; computer vision/graphics. *Total annual research expenditures:* $3.7 million. *Unit head:* Dr. L. Darrell Whitley, Professor and Chair, 970-491-5792, Fax: 970-491-2466, E-mail: whitley@cs.colostate.edu. *Application contact:* Graduate Processor, 970-491-5792, Fax: 970-491-2466, E-mail: gradinfo@cs.colostate.edu.
Website: http://www.cs.colostate.edu/cstop/index

Colorado Technical University Aurora, Program in Computer Science, Aurora, CO 80014. Offers computer systems security (MSCS); database systems (MSCS); software engineering (MSCS). *Program availability:* Part-time, evening/weekend. *Degree requirements:* For master's, thesis or alternative. *Entrance requirements:* For master's, minimum undergraduate GPA of 3.0, resume.

Colorado Technical University Colorado Springs, Graduate Studies, Program in Computer Science, Colorado Springs, CO 80907. Offers computer science (DCS); computer systems security (MSCS); database systems (MSCS); software engineering (MSCS). *Program availability:* Part-time, evening/weekend, online learning. *Degree requirements:* For master's, thesis or alternative; for doctorate, thesis/dissertation. *Entrance requirements:* For doctorate, minimum graduate GPA of 3.0, 5 years of related work experience. *Faculty research:* Software engineering, systems engineering.

Columbia University, Fu Foundation School of Engineering and Applied Science, Department of Computer Science, New York, NY 10027. Offers computer science (MS, Eng Sc D, PhD); computer science and journalism (MS). PhD offered through the Graduate School of Arts and Sciences. *Program availability:* Part-time, online learning. Terminal master's awarded for partial completion of doctoral program. *Degree requirements:* For master's, thesis optional; for doctorate, comprehensive exam, thesis/dissertation, candidacy exam. *Entrance requirements:* For master's and doctorate, GRE General Test. Additional exam requirements/recommendations for international students: Required—TOEFL, IELTS, PTE. Electronic applications accepted. *Faculty research:* Natural language processing, machine learning, software systems, network systems, computer security, computational biology, foundations of computer science, vision and graphics.

Columbus State University, Graduate Studies, Turner College of Business, Columbus, GA 31907-5645. Offers applied computer science (MS), including informational assurance, modeling and simulation, software development; business administration (MBA); human resource management (Certificate); information systems security (Certificate); modeling and simulation (Certificate); organizational leadership (MS),

including human resource management, leader development, servant leadership; servant leadership (Certificate). *Accreditation:* AACSB. *Program availability:* Part-time, evening/weekend, 100% online, blended/hybrid learning. *Faculty:* 10 full-time (3 women). *Students:* 93 full-time (21 women), 132 part-time (47 women); includes 69 minority (36 Black or African American, non-Hispanic/Latino; 1 American Indian or Alaska Native, non-Hispanic/Latino; 11 Asian, non-Hispanic/Latino; 14 Hispanic/Latino; 7 Two or more races, non-Hispanic/Latino), 35 international. Average age 31. 279 applicants, 44% accepted, 64 enrolled. In 2016, 106 master's awarded. *Entrance requirements:* For master's, GMAT, GRE, minimum undergraduate GPA of 2.75, letters of recommendation. Additional exam requirements/recommendations for international students: Required—TOEFL (minimum score 550 paper-based; 79 iBT). *Application deadline:* For fall admission, 6/30 for domestic students, 5/1 for international students; for spring admission, 11/1 for domestic and international students; for summer admission, 3/1 for domestic and international students. Applications are processed on a rolling basis. Application fee: $50. Electronic applications accepted. *Expenses:* Contact institution. *Financial support:* In 2016–17, 18 students received support, including 16 research assistantships (averaging $3,000 per year); Federal Work-Study also available. Financial award application deadline: 5/1; financial award applicants required to submit FAFSA. *Unit head:* Dr. Linda U. Hadley, Dean, 706-507-8153, Fax: 706-568-2184, E-mail: hadley_linda@columbusstate.edu. *Application contact:* Kristin Williams, Director of International and Graduate Recruitment, 706-507-8848, Fax: 706-568-5091, E-mail: thornton_katie@colstate.edu.
Website: http://turner.columbusstate.edu/

Concordia University, School of Graduate Studies, Faculty of Engineering and Computer Science, Department of Computer Science and Software Engineering, Montréal, QC H3G 1M8, Canada. Offers computer science (M App Comp Sc, M Comp Sc, PhD, Diploma); software engineering (M Eng, MA Sc). *Degree requirements:* For master's, one foreign language, thesis optional; for doctorate, one foreign language, comprehensive exam, thesis/dissertation. *Faculty research:* Computer systems and applications, mathematics of computation, pattern recognition, artificial intelligence and robotics.

Concordia University, Nebraska, Program in Computer Science, Seward, NE 68434-1556. Offers cyber operations (MS). *Program availability:* Online learning.

Cornell University, Graduate School, Graduate Fields of Engineering, Field of Computer Science, Ithaca, NY 14853. Offers algorithms (M Eng, PhD); applied logic and automated reasoning (M Eng, PhD); artificial intelligence (M Eng, PhD); computer graphics (M Eng, PhD); computer science (M Eng, PhD); computer vision (M Eng, PhD); concurrency and distributed computing (M Eng, PhD); information organization and retrieval (M Eng, PhD); operating systems (M Eng, PhD); parallel computing (M Eng, PhD); programming environments (M Eng, PhD); programming languages and methodology (M Eng, PhD); robotics (M Eng, PhD); scientific computing (M Eng, PhD); theory of computation (M Eng, PhD). *Degree requirements:* For doctorate, comprehensive exam, thesis/dissertation. *Entrance requirements:* For master's, GRE General Test, 2 letters of recommendation; for doctorate, GRE General Test, GRE Subject Test (computer science or mathematics), 3 letters of recommendation. Additional exam requirements/recommendations for international students: Required—TOEFL (minimum score 505 paper-based; 77 iBT). Electronic applications accepted. *Faculty research:* Artificial intelligence, operating systems and databases, programming languages and security, scientific computing, theory of computing, computational biology and graphics.

Dakota State University, College of Business and Information Systems, Madison, SD 57042-1799. Offers analytics (MSA); applied computer science (MSACS); banking security (Graduate Certificate); business analytics (Graduate Certificate); cyber security (D Sc); ethical hacking (Graduate Certificate); general management (MBA); health informatics (MSHI); information assurance and computer security (MSIA); information systems (MSIS, D Sc IS); information technology (Graduate Certificate). *Accreditation:* ACBSP. *Program availability:* Part-time, evening/weekend, 100% online, blended/hybrid learning. *Degree requirements:* For master's, comprehensive exam, thesis optional, examination, integrative project; for doctorate, comprehensive exam, thesis/dissertation, portfolio. *Entrance requirements:* For master's, GRE General Test, demonstration of information systems skills, minimum GPA of 2.7; for doctorate, GRE General Test, demonstration of information systems skills; for Graduate Certificate, GMAT. Additional exam requirements/recommendations for international students: Required—PTE (minimum score 53), TOEFL (minimum score 550 paper-based; 79 iBT) or IELTS (6.5). *Application deadline:* For fall admission, 6/15 for domestic students, 4/15 for international students; for spring admission, 11/15 for domestic students, 9/15 priority date for international students; for summer admission, 4/15 for domestic and international students. Applications are processed on a rolling basis. Application fee: $35. *Expenses:* Contact institution. *Financial support:* Fellowships with partial tuition reimbursements, research assistantships with partial tuition reimbursements, teaching assistantships with partial tuition reimbursements, career-related internships or fieldwork, Federal Work-Study, scholarships/grants, and unspecified assistantships available. Support available to part-time students. Financial award applicants required to submit FAFSA. *Faculty research:* Data mining and analytics, biometrics and information assurance, decision support systems, health informatics, STEM education for K-12 teachers/students and underrepresented populations. *Unit head:* Mark Hawkes, Dean for Graduate Studies and Research, 605-256-5274, E-mail: mark.hawkes@dsu.edu. *Application contact:* Erin Blankespoor, Senior Secretary, Office of Graduate Studies and Research, 605-256-5799, E-mail: erin.blankespoor@dsu.edu.
Website: http://dsu.edu/academics/colleges/college-of-business-and-information-systems

Dalhousie University, Faculty of Computer Science, Halifax, NS B3H 1W5, Canada. Offers computational biology and bioinformatics (M Sc); computer science (MA Sc, MC Sc, PhD); electronic commerce (MEC); health informatics (MHI). *Degree requirements:* For master's, thesis (for some programs); for doctorate, thesis/dissertation. *Entrance requirements:* Additional exam requirements/recommendations for international students: Required—1 of 5 approved tests: TOEFL, IELTS, CANTEST, CAEL, Michigan English Language Assessment Battery. Electronic applications accepted.

Dartmouth College, School of Graduate and Advanced Studies, Department of Computer Science, Hanover, NH 03755. Offers MS, PhD. *Faculty:* 20 full-time (3 women), 4 part-time/adjunct (2 women). *Students:* 100 full-time (30 women); includes 7 minority (3 Asian, non-Hispanic/Latino; 2 Hispanic/Latino; 2 Two or more races, non-Hispanic/Latino), 81 international. Average age 26. 442 applicants, 18% accepted, 26 enrolled. In 2016, 35 master's, 9 doctorates awarded. Terminal master's awarded for partial completion of doctoral program. *Degree requirements:* For master's, thesis; for doctorate, thesis/dissertation, oral presentation, research presentation exam. *Entrance requirements:* For master's and doctorate, GRE General Test, GRE Subject Test. Additional exam requirements/recommendations for international students: Required—TOEFL. *Application deadline:* For fall admission, 12/15 for domestic students. Application fee: $40. Electronic applications accepted. *Financial support:* Fellowships with full tuition reimbursements, research assistantships with full tuition reimbursements, teaching assistantships with full tuition reimbursements, career-related internships or

fieldwork, institutionally sponsored loans, scholarships/grants, and tuition waivers (full and partial) available. Support available to part-time students. Financial award application deadline: 4/1; financial award applicants required to submit CSS PROFILE or FAFSA. *Faculty research:* Algorithms, computational geometry and learning, computer vision, information retrieval, robotics. *Unit head:* Dr. Hany Farid, Chair, 603-646-2761. *Application contact:* Susan J. Perry, Department Administrator, 603-646-1358.
Website: http://www.cs.dartmouth.edu/

DePaul University, College of Computing and Digital Media, Chicago, IL 60604. Offers animation (MA, MFA); business information technology (MS); cinema (MFA); cinema production (MS); computational finance (MS); computer and information sciences (PhD); computer game development (MS); computer information and network security (MS); computer science (MS); e-commerce technology (MS); health informatics (MS); human-computer interaction (MS); information systems (MS); information technology project management (MS); network engineering and management (MS); predictive analytics (MS); screenwriting (MFA); software engineering (MS); JD/MS. *Program availability:* Part-time, evening/weekend, online learning. *Degree requirements:* For master's, thesis (for some programs); for doctorate, comprehensive exam, thesis/dissertation. *Entrance requirements:* For master's, GRE or GMAT (for MS in computational finance only), bachelor's degree, resume (MS in predictive analytics only), IT experience (MS in information technology project management only), portfolio review (all MFA programs and MA in animation); for doctorate, GRE, master's degree in computer science. Additional exam requirements/recommendations for international students: Required—TOEFL (minimum score 590 paper-based; 80 iBT), IELTS (minimum score 6.5), PTE (minimum score 53). Electronic applications accepted. *Expenses:* Contact institution. *Faculty research:* Data mining, computer science, human-computer interaction, security, animation and film.

DigiPen Institute of Technology, Graduate Programs, Redmond, WA 98052. Offers computer science (MS); digital art and animation (MFA). *Program availability:* Part-time. *Faculty:* 28 full-time (7 women), 14 part-time/adjunct (1 woman). *Students:* 51 full-time (8 women), 27 part-time (5 women); includes 8 minority (3 Asian, non-Hispanic/Latino; 4 Hispanic/Latino; 1 Two or more races, non-Hispanic/Latino), 41 international. Average age 28. 107 applicants, 47% accepted, 21 enrolled. In 2016, 23 master's awarded. *Degree requirements:* For master's, comprehensive exam (for some programs), thesis (for some programs). *Entrance requirements:* For master's, GRE General Test (for MS), art portfolio (for MFA); official transcripts from all post-secondary education including final transcript indicating degree earned, statement of purpose, and 2 letters of recommendation. Additional exam requirements/recommendations for international students: Required—TOEFL (minimum score 550 paper-based; 80 iBT). *Application deadline:* For fall admission, 2/1 priority date for domestic and international students; for spring admission, 7/1 for domestic and international students. Applications are processed on a rolling basis. Application fee: $35. Electronic applications accepted. *Expenses:* Contact institution. *Financial support:* In 2016–17, 4 students received support, including 1 fellowship (averaging $9,500 per year); career-related internships or fieldwork and scholarships/grants also available. Financial award application deadline: 5/1; financial award applicants required to submit FAFSA. *Faculty research:* Procedural modeling, computer graphics and visualization, human-computer interaction, fuzzy numbers and fuzzy analysis, modeling under spistemic uncertainty, nonlinear image processing, mathematical representation of surfaces, advanced computer graphic rendering techniques, mathematical physics, computer music and sound synthesis. *Unit head:* Angela Kugler, Senior Vice President, 425-895-4438, Fax: 425-558-0378, E-mail: akugler@digipen.edu. *Application contact:* Danial Powers, Director of Admissions, 425-629-5071, Fax: 425-558-0378, E-mail: dpowers@digipen.edu.

★ **Drexel University,** College of Computing and Informatics, Department of Computer Science, Philadelphia, PA 19104-2875. Offers computer science (MS, PhD, Postbaccalaureate Certificate); software engineering (MS). *Program availability:* Part-time, evening/weekend, 100% online. *Faculty:* 31 full-time (5 women). *Students:* 57 full-time (15 women), 63 part-time (6 women); includes 10 minority (1 Black or African American, non-Hispanic/Latino; 4 Asian, non-Hispanic/Latino; 5 Hispanic/Latino), 45 international. Average age 29. 396 applicants, 24% accepted, 35 enrolled. In 2016, 42 master's, 4 doctorates awarded. Terminal master's awarded for partial completion of doctoral program. *Degree requirements:* For doctorate, thesis/dissertation. *Entrance requirements:* For master's and doctorate, GRE General Test. Additional exam requirements/recommendations for international students: Required—TOEFL (minimum score 600 paper-based; 100 iBT), IELTS (minimum score 6.5). *Application deadline:* For fall admission, 8/15 for domestic students, 7/15 for international students; for spring admission, 3/1 for domestic students, 2/1 for international students. Applications are processed on a rolling basis. Application fee: $65. Electronic applications accepted. Application fee is waived when completed online. *Expenses:* Tuition: Full-time $32,184; part-time $1192 per credit hour. *Required fees:* $280. Tuition and fees vary according to campus/location and program. *Financial support:* In 2016–17, 15 students received support, including 1 fellowship with full tuition reimbursement available (averaging $35,000 per year), 19 research assistantships with full tuition reimbursements available (averaging $27,780 per year), 11 teaching assistantships with full tuition reimbursements available (averaging $26,250 per year); scholarships/grants and tuition waivers (partial) also available. Financial award application deadline: 3/1; financial award applicants required to submit FAFSA. *Total annual research expenditures:* $1.9 million. *Unit head:* Dr. Yi Deng, Dean/Professor, 215-895-2474, Fax: 215-895-2494, E-mail: yd362@drexel.edu. *Application contact:* Matthew Lechtenberg, Director, Recruitment, 215-895-2474, Fax: 215-895-2303, E-mail: cciinfo@drexel.edu.

See Display on next page and Close-Up on page 369.

Duke University, Graduate School, Department of Computer Science, Durham, NC 27708. Offers MS, PhD. Spring admission applies to MS program only. *Degree requirements:* For doctorate, thesis/dissertation. *Entrance requirements:* For master's, GRE General Test; for doctorate, GRE General Test, GRE Subject Test (recommended). Additional exam requirements/recommendations for international students: Required—TOEFL (minimum score 577 paper-based; 90 iBT) or IELTS (minimum score 7). Electronic applications accepted.

East Carolina University, Graduate School, College of Engineering and Technology, Department of Computer Science, Greenville, NC 27858-4353. Offers computer science (MS); software engineering (MS). *Program availability:* Part-time, evening/weekend. *Students:* 32 full-time (8 women), 54 part-time (14 women); includes 19 minority (7 Black or African American, non-Hispanic/Latino; 9 Asian, non-Hispanic/Latino; 3 Hispanic/Latino), 23 international. Average age 31. 66 applicants, 83% accepted, 28 enrolled. In 2016, 19 master's awarded. *Degree requirements:* For master's, comprehensive exam, thesis or alternative. *Entrance requirements:* For master's, GRE General Test. Additional exam requirements/recommendations for international students: Required—TOEFL. *Application deadline:* For fall admission, 11/1 priority date for domestic students, 10/1 priority date for international students; for spring admission, 3/1 priority date for domestic and international students. Applications are processed on a rolling basis. Application fee: $50. Electronic applications accepted. *Financial support:* Research assistantships, career-related internships or fieldwork, Federal Work-Study, tuition waivers (full), and unspecified assistantships available. Financial award

Computer Science

application deadline: 3/1. *Faculty research:* Software development, software engineering, artificial intelligence, bioinformatics, cryptography. *Unit head:* Dr. Karl Abrahamson, Interim Chair, 252-328-9689, E-mail: karl@cs.ecu.edu. *Application contact:* Dean of Graduate School, 252-328-6012, Fax: 252-328-6071, E-mail: gradschool@ecu.edu. Website: http://www.ecu.edu/cs-tecs/csci/index.cfm

East Carolina University, Graduate School, College of Engineering and Technology, Department of Technology Systems, Greenville, NC 27858-4353. Offers computer network professional (Certificate); information assurance (Certificate); Lean Six Sigma Black Belt (Certificate); network technology (MS), including computer networking management, digital communications technology, information security, Web technologies; occupational safety (MS); technology management (PhD); technology systems (MS), including industrial distribution and logistics, manufacturing systems, performance improvement, quality systems; Website developer (Certificate). *Students:* 23 full-time (1 woman), 199 part-time (55 women); includes 59 minority (39 Black or African American, non-Hispanic/Latino; 3 American Indian or Alaska Native, non-Hispanic/Latino; 4 Asian, non-Hispanic/Latino; 10 Hispanic/Latino; 3 Two or more races, non-Hispanic/Latino), 5 international. Average age 38. 85 applicants, 87% accepted, 61 enrolled. In 2016, 23 master's awarded. *Entrance requirements:* For master's and Certificate, GRE General Test or MAT, minimum GPA of 2.5; for doctorate, GRE General Test, related work experience. *Application deadline:* For fall admission, 6/1 priority date for domestic students. Applications are processed on a rolling basis. Application fee: $50. *Financial support:* Application deadline: 6/1. *Unit head:* Dr. Tijjani Mohammed, Chair, 252-328-9668, E-mail: mohammedt@ecu.edu. *Application contact:* Dean of Graduate School, 252-328-6012, Fax: 252-328-6071, E-mail: gradschool@ecu.edu.

Eastern Illinois University, Graduate School, Lumpkin College of Business and Applied Sciences, School of Technology, Program in Technology, Charleston, IL 61920. Offers MS. *Program availability:* Part-time, evening/weekend. *Degree requirements:* For master's, comprehensive exam (for some programs), thesis (for some programs). *Entrance requirements:* For master's, GMAT or GRE. Additional exam requirements/ recommendations for international students: Required—TOEFL (minimum score 500 paper-based; 61 iBT), IELTS (minimum score 6). Electronic applications accepted.

Eastern Michigan University, Graduate School, College of Arts and Sciences, Department of Computer Science, Ypsilanti, MI 48197. Offers MS, Graduate Certificate. *Program availability:* Part-time, evening/weekend, online learning. *Faculty:* 14 full-time (5 women). *Students:* 35 full-time (15 women), 17 part-time (5 women); includes 4 minority (3 Asian, non-Hispanic/Latino; 1 Hispanic/Latino), 35 international. Average age 27. 80 applicants, 61% accepted, 19 enrolled. In 2016, 24 master's awarded. *Degree requirements:* For master's, thesis or alternative. *Entrance requirements:* For master's, at least 18 credit hours of computer science courses including data structures, programming languages like java, C or C++, computer organization; courses in discrete mathematics, probability and statistics, linear algebra and calculus; minimum GPA of 2.75 in computer science. Additional exam requirements/recommendations for international students: Required—TOEFL. *Application deadline:* For fall admission, 8/1 for domestic students, 5/1 for international students; for winter admission, 12/1 for domestic students, 10/1 for international students; for spring admission, 4/1 for domestic students, 2/1 for international students. Application fee: $45. *Financial support:* Fellowships, research assistantships with full tuition reimbursements, teaching assistantships with full tuition reimbursements, career-related internships or fieldwork, Federal Work-Study, institutionally sponsored loans, scholarships/grants, tuition waivers (partial), and unspecified assistantships available. Support available to part-time students. Financial award applicants required to submit FAFSA. *Unit head:* Dr. Augustine C. Ikeji, Department Head, 734-487-0056, Fax: 734-487-6824, E-mail: aikeji@emich.edu. *Application contact:* Dr. Zenia Bahorski, Graduate Advisor, 734-487-0270, Fax: 734-487-6824, E-mail: zbahorski@emich.edu. Website: http://www.emich.edu/compsci

Eastern Washington University, Graduate Studies, College of Science, Technology, Engineering and Mathematics, Department of Computer Science, Cheney, WA 99004-2431. Offers computer science (MS). *Program availability:* Part-time. *Faculty:* 12 full-time (3 women). *Students:* 14 full-time (1 woman), 3 part-time (0 women); includes 3 minority (1 American Indian or Alaska Native, non-Hispanic/Latino; 1 Hispanic/Latino; 1 Native Hawaiian or other Pacific Islander, non-Hispanic/Latino). Average age 31. 27 applicants, 41% accepted, 5 enrolled. In 2016, 4 master's awarded. *Degree requirements:* For master's, comprehensive exam, thesis or alternative. *Entrance requirements:* For master's, minimum GPA of 3.0. Additional exam requirements/ recommendations for international students: Required—TOEFL (minimum score 580 paper-based; 92 iBT), IELTS (minimum score 7), PTE (minimum score 63). *Application deadline:* For fall admission, 4/1 priority date for domestic students; for spring admission, 1/15 for domestic students. Applications are processed on a rolling basis. Application fee: $75. Electronic applications accepted. *Expenses:* Tuition, state resident: full-time $11,000; part-time $5500 per credit. Tuition, nonresident: full-time $24,000; part-time $12,000 per credit. *Required fees:* $1300. One-time fee: $50 full-time. Part-time tuition and fees vary according to course load, campus/location and program. *Financial support:* In 2016–17, 16 teaching assistantships with partial tuition reimbursements (averaging $12,000 per year) were awarded; career-related internships or fieldwork, Federal Work-Study, institutionally sponsored loans, scholarships/grants, health care benefits, tuition waivers (partial), and unspecified assistantships also available. Support available to part-time students. Financial award application deadline: 2/1. *Unit head:* Dr. Carol Taylor, Chair, 509-359-6065, Fax: 509-359-2215, E-mail: ctaylor@ewu.edu. Website: http://www.ewu.edu/cshe/programs/computer-science.xml

East Stroudsburg University of Pennsylvania, Graduate and Extended Studies, College of Arts and Sciences, Department of Computer Science, East Stroudsburg, PA 18301-2999. Offers MS. *Program availability:* Part-time, evening/weekend. *Faculty:* 6 full-time (2 women). *Students:* 9 full-time (3 women), 7 part-time (0 women); includes 1 minority (Black or African American, non-Hispanic/Latino), 7 international. Average age 28. 25 applicants, 48% accepted, 6 enrolled. In 2016, 9 master's awarded. *Degree requirements:* For master's, comprehensive exam, thesis or alternative. *Entrance requirements:* For master's, bachelor's degree in computer science or related field. Additional exam requirements/recommendations for international students: Recommended—TOEFL (minimum score 560 paper-based; 83 iBT), IELTS. *Application deadline:* For fall admission, 7/31 priority date for domestic students, 6/30 priority date for international students; for spring admission, 11/30 for domestic students, 10/31 for international students. Applications are processed on a rolling basis. Application fee: $50. Electronic applications accepted. *Expenses:* Tuition, state resident: full-time $8694; part-time $5796 per year. Tuition, nonresident: full-time $13,050; part-time $8700 per year. *Required fees:* $2550; $1690 per unit. $845 per semester. Tuition and fees vary according to course load, campus/location and program. *Financial support:* Research assistantships with tuition reimbursements, career-related internships or fieldwork, Federal Work-Study, and unspecified assistantships available. Support available to part-time students. Financial award application deadline: 3/1; financial award applicants required to submit FAFSA. *Unit head:* Dr. Robert Marmelstein, Graduate Coordinator, 570-422-3666, Fax: 570-422-3490, E-mail: rmarmelstein@po-box.esu.edu. *Application contact:* Kevin Quintero, Associate Director, Graduate and Extended Studies, 570-422-3890, Fax: 570-422-3711, E-mail: kquintero@esu.edu. Website: http://www.esu.edu/cpsc/

East Tennessee State University, School of Graduate Studies, College of Business and Technology, Department of Computing, Johnson City, TN 37614. Offers MS, Postbaccalaureate Certificate. *Program availability:* Part-time, evening/weekend.

Degree requirements: For master's, comprehensive exam, thesis optional, capstone. *Entrance requirements:* For master's, GRE General Test, minimum GPA of 2.5, three letters of recommendation. Additional exam requirements/recommendations for international students: Required—TOEFL (minimum score 550 paper-based; 79 iBT). Electronic applications accepted. *Faculty research:* Data mining, security and forensics, numerical optimization, computer gaming, enterprise resource planning.

École Polytechnique de Montréal, Graduate Programs, Department of Electrical and Computer Engineering, Montréal, QC H3C 3A7, Canada. Offers automation (M Eng, M Sc A, PhD); computer science (M Eng, M Sc A, PhD); electrical engineering (DESS); electrotechnology (M Eng, M Sc A, PhD); microelectronics (M Eng, M Sc A, PhD); microwave technology (M Eng, M Sc A, PhD). *Program availability:* Part-time, evening/weekend. *Degree requirements:* For master's, one foreign language, thesis; for doctorate, one foreign language, thesis/dissertation. *Entrance requirements:* For master's, minimum GPA of 2.75; for doctorate, minimum GPA of 3.0. *Faculty research:* Microwaves, telecommunications, software engineering.

Embry-Riddle Aeronautical University–Daytona, Department of Electrical, Computer, Software and Systems Engineering, Daytona Beach, FL 32114-3900. Offers computer engineering (MS); cybersecurity engineering (MS); electrical engineering (MSECE); electrical engineering and computer science (PhD), including electrical, computer, software, and systems engineering; software engineering (MSSE); systems engineering (MS). *Program availability:* Part-time. *Faculty:* 13 full-time (1 woman), 1 part-time/adjunct (0 women). *Students:* 63 full-time (17 women), 8 part-time (3 women); includes 6 minority (1 Black or African American, non-Hispanic/Latino; 1 Asian, non-Hispanic/Latino; 1 Hispanic/Latino; 3 Two or more races, non-Hispanic/Latino), 41 international. Average age 25. 93 applicants, 45% accepted, 21 enrolled. In 2016, 30 master's awarded. *Degree requirements:* For master's, thesis or alternative; for doctorate, thesis/dissertation. *Entrance requirements:* For master's, GRE (for some programs); for doctorate, GRE. Additional exam requirements/recommendations for international students: Required—TOEFL (minimum score 550 paper-based, 79 iBT) or IELTS (6). *Application deadline:* For fall admission, 3/1 priority date for domestic students; for spring admission, 11/1 priority date for domestic students; for summer admission, 4/1 priority date for domestic students. Applications are processed on a rolling basis. Application fee: $50. Electronic applications accepted. *Expenses: Tuition:* Full-time $16,296; part-time $1358 per credit hour. *Required fees:* $1294; $647 per semester. One-time fee: $100 full-time. Tuition and fees vary according to course load, degree level and program. *Financial support:* Research assistantships, teaching assistantships, career-related internships or fieldwork, scholarships/grants, unspecified assistantships, and on-campus employment available. Financial award application deadline: 3/15; financial award applicants required to submit FAFSA. *Faculty research:* Cybersecurity and assured systems engineering, radar, unmanned and autonomous systems, modeling and simulation, cyber-physical systems. *Unit head:* Timothy Wilson, PhD, Professor of Electrical and Computer Engineering/Chair, Department of Electrical, Computer, Software and Systems Engineering, 386-226-6100, E-mail: timothy.wilson@erau.edu. *Application contact:* Graduate Admissions, 386-226-6176, Fax: 386-226-7070, E-mail: graduate.admissions@erau.edu.
Website: https://daytonabeach.erau.edu/college-engineering/electrical-computer-software-systems/index.html

Emory University, Laney Graduate School, Department of Mathematics and Computer Science, Atlanta, GA 30322-1100. Offers computer science (MS); computer science and informatics (PhD); mathematics (MS, PhD). Terminal master's awarded for partial completion of doctoral program. *Degree requirements:* For master's, thesis; for doctorate, one foreign language, comprehensive exam, thesis/dissertation. *Entrance requirements:* For master's and doctorate, GRE General Test. Additional exam requirements/recommendations for international students: Recommended—TOEFL. Electronic applications accepted.

Fairleigh Dickinson University, College at Florham, Maxwell Becton College of Arts and Sciences, Department of Computer Science, Madison, NJ 07940-1099. Offers MS.

Fairleigh Dickinson University, Metropolitan Campus, University College: Arts, Sciences, and Professional Studies, School of Computer Sciences and Engineering, Program in Computer Science, Teaneck, NJ 07666-1914. Offers MS.

Fitchburg State University, Division of Graduate and Continuing Education, Program in Computer Science, Fitchburg, MA 01420-2697. Offers MS. *Program availability:* Part-time, evening/weekend. *Entrance requirements:* Additional exam requirements/recommendations for international students: Required—TOEFL (minimum score 550 paper-based; 79 iBT). Electronic applications accepted. *Expenses:* Tuition, state resident: full-time $2871; part-time $1914 per year. Tuition, nonresident: full-time $2871; part-time $1914 per year. *Required fees:* $3828. Tuition and fees vary according to program.

Florida Atlantic University, College of Engineering and Computer Science, Department of Computer and Electrical Engineering and Computer Science, Boca Raton, FL 33431-0991. Offers bioengineering (MS); computer engineering (MS, PhD); computer science (MS, PhD); electrical engineering (MS, PhD). *Program availability:* Part-time, evening/weekend. *Faculty:* 23 full-time (5 women), 1 part-time/adjunct (0 women). *Students:* 103 full-time (30 women), 127 part-time (30 women); includes 77 minority (15 Black or African American, non-Hispanic/Latino; 10 Asian, non-Hispanic/Latino; 46 Hispanic/Latino; 6 Two or more races, non-Hispanic/Latino), 74 international. Average age 32. 215 applicants, 51% accepted, 85 enrolled. In 2016, 45 master's, 5 doctorates awarded. Terminal master's awarded for partial completion of doctoral program. *Degree requirements:* For master's, thesis optional; for doctorate, thesis/dissertation, qualifying exam. *Entrance requirements:* For master's, GRE General Test, minimum GPA of 3.0; for doctorate, GRE General Test, master's degree, minimum GPA of 3.5. Additional exam requirements/recommendations for international students: Required—TOEFL (minimum score 500 paper-based; 61 iBT), IELTS (minimum score 6). *Application deadline:* For fall admission, 7/1 priority date for domestic students, 2/15 for international students; for spring admission, 11/1 for domestic students, 7/15 for international students. Applications are processed on a rolling basis. Application fee: $30. *Expenses:* Tuition, state resident: full-time $7392; part-time $369.82 per credit hour. Tuition, nonresident: full-time $19,432; part-time $1024.81 per credit hour. *Financial support:* Fellowships, research assistantships with partial tuition reimbursements, teaching assistantships with full tuition reimbursements, career-related internships or fieldwork, and Federal Work-Study available. Support available to part-time students. Financial award application deadline: 4/1; financial award applicants required to submit FAFSA. *Faculty research:* VLSI and neural networks, communication networks, software engineering, computer architecture, multimedia and video processing. *Unit head:* Jean Mangiaracina, 561-297-3855, E-mail: jmangiar@fau.edu.
Website: http://www.ceecs.fau.edu/

Florida Institute of Technology, College of Engineering, Program in Computer Science, Melbourne, FL 32901-6975. Offers MS, PhD. *Program availability:* Part-time. *Students:* 80 full-time (17 women), 36 part-time (6 women); includes 2 minority (1 Black or African American, non-Hispanic/Latino; 1 Hispanic/Latino), 93 international. Average age 29. 626 applicants, 31% accepted, 24 enrolled. In 2016, 58 master's, 9 doctorates awarded. *Degree requirements:* For master's, comprehensive exam (for some programs), thesis optional, minimum of 30 credits; for doctorate, comprehensive exam, thesis/dissertation, minimum of 72 credits beyond bachelor's degree, publications. *Entrance requirements:* For master's, GRE General Test, 3 letters of recommendation, transcript, 12 credits of advanced coursework in computer science; for doctorate, GRE General Test, GRE Subject Test in computer science (recommended), 3 letters of recommendation, minimum GPA of 3.5 in both bachelor's and master's degree in computer science, resume, statement of objectives. Additional exam requirements/recommendations for international students: Required—TOEFL (minimum score 550 paper-based; 79 iBT). *Application deadline:* For fall admission, 4/1 for international students; for spring admission, 9/30 for international students. Applications are processed on a rolling basis. Electronic applications accepted. *Expenses: Tuition:* Full-time $22,338; part-time $1241 per credit hour. *Required fees:* $250. Tuition and fees vary according to degree level, campus/location and program. *Financial support:* Career-related internships or fieldwork, institutionally sponsored loans, tuition waivers (partial), unspecified assistantships, and tuition remissions available. Support available to part-time students. Financial award application deadline: 3/1; financial award applicants required to submit FAFSA. *Faculty research:* Artificial intelligence, software engineering, management and processes, programming languages, database systems. *Unit head:* Dr. Ronaldo Menezes, Department Head, 321-674-7623, E-mail: rmenezes@fit.edu. *Application contact:* Cheryl A. Brown, Associate Director of Graduate Admissions, 321-674-7581, Fax: 321-723-9468, E-mail: cbrown@fit.edu.
Website: http://coe.fit.edu/cs

Florida Institute of Technology, Extended Studies Division, Melbourne, FL 32901-6975. Offers acquisition and contract management (MS); aerospace engineering (MS); business administration (MBA, DBA); computer information systems (MS); computer science (MS); electrical engineering (MS); engineering management (MS); human resources management (MS); logistics management (MS), including humanitarian and disaster relief logistics; management (MS), including acquisition and contract management, e-business, human resources management, information systems, logistics management, management, transportation management; material acquisition management (MS); mechanical engineering (MS); operations research (MS); project management (MS), including information systems, operations research; public administration (MPA); quality management (MS); software engineering (MS); space systems (MS); space systems management (MS); supply chain management (MS); systems management (MS), including information systems, operations research; technology management (MS). *Program availability:* Part-time, evening/weekend, online learning. *Faculty:* 10 full-time (3 women), 122 part-time/adjunct (29 women). *Students:* 131 full-time (58 women), 997 part-time (348 women); includes 389 minority (231 Black or African American, non-Hispanic/Latino; 9 American Indian or Alaska Native, non-Hispanic/Latino; 26 Asian, non-Hispanic/Latino; 99 Hispanic/Latino; 3 Native Hawaiian or other Pacific Islander, non-Hispanic/Latino; 21 Two or more races, non-Hispanic/Latino), 53 international. Average age 36. 962 applicants, 48% accepted, 323 enrolled. In 2016, 403 master's awarded. *Degree requirements:* For master's, comprehensive exam (for some programs). *Entrance requirements:* For master's, GMAT or resume showing 8 years of supervised experience, minimum GPA of 3.0, 2 letters of recommendation, resume. Additional exam requirements/recommendations for international students: Required—TOEFL (minimum score 550 paper-based; 79 iBT). *Application deadline:* For fall admission, 4/1 for international students; for spring admission, 9/30 for international students. Applications are processed on a rolling basis. Electronic applications accepted. *Expenses:* Contact institution. *Financial support:* Application deadline: 3/1; applicants required to submit FAFSA. *Unit head:* Dr. Theodore R. Richardson, III, Dean, 321-674-8123, Fax: 321-674-7597, E-mail: trichardson@fit.edu. *Application contact:* Carolyn Farrior, Director of Graduate Admissions, Online Learning and Off-Campus Programs, 321-674-7118, Fax: 321-674-8216, E-mail: cfarrior@fit.edu.
Website: http://es.fit.edu

Florida International University, College of Engineering and Computing, School of Computing and Information Sciences, Miami, FL 33199. Offers computer science (MS, PhD); cybersecurity (MS); data science (MS); information technology (MS); telecommunications and networking (MS). *Program availability:* Part-time, evening/weekend. *Faculty:* 46 full-time (11 women), 28 part-time/adjunct (5 women). *Students:* 145 full-time (39 women), 109 part-time (16 women); includes 124 minority (14 Black or African American, non-Hispanic/Latino; 1 American Indian or Alaska Native, non-Hispanic/Latino; 10 Asian, non-Hispanic/Latino; 97 Hispanic/Latino; 2 Two or more races, non-Hispanic/Latino), 115 international. Average age 29. 407 applicants, 54% accepted, 78 enrolled. In 2016, 90 master's, 8 doctorates awarded. *Degree requirements:* For master's, thesis or alternative; for doctorate, comprehensive exam, thesis/dissertation. *Entrance requirements:* For master's and doctorate, GRE General Test, 3 letters of recommendation, minimum GPA of 3.0. Additional exam requirements/recommendations for international students: Required—TOEFL (minimum score 550 paper-based; 80 iBT). *Application deadline:* For fall admission, 6/1 for domestic students, 4/1 for international students; for spring admission, 10/1 for domestic students, 9/1 for international students. Applications are processed on a rolling basis. Application fee: $30. Electronic applications accepted. *Expenses:* Tuition, state resident: full-time $8912; part-time $446 per credit hour. Tuition, nonresident: full-time $21,393; part-time $992 per credit hour. *Required fees:* $2185; $195 per semester. Tuition and fees vary according to program. *Financial support:* Research assistantships, teaching assistantships, institutionally sponsored loans, scholarships/grants, and unspecified assistantships available. Financial award application deadline: 3/1; financial award applicants required to submit FAFSA. *Faculty research:* Database systems, software engineering, operating systems, networks. *Unit head:* Dr. S. S. Iyengar, Director, 305-348-3947, E-mail: iyengar@cis.fiu.edu. *Application contact:* Sara-Michelle Lemus, Engineering Admissions Officer, 305-348-1890, E-mail: grad_eng@fiu.edu.

Florida State University, The Graduate School, College of Arts and Sciences, Department of Computer Science, Tallahassee, FL 32306. Offers computer criminology (MS); computer network and system administration (MS); computer science (MS, PhD); cyber security (MS). *Program availability:* Part-time. *Faculty:* 26 full-time (3 women), 1 part-time/adjunct (0 women). *Students:* 153 full-time (38 women), 5 part-time (1 woman); includes 25 minority (4 Black or African American, non-Hispanic/Latino; 5 Asian, non-Hispanic/Latino; 2 Hispanic/Latino; 14 Two or more races, non-Hispanic/Latino), 90 international. Average age 28. 344 applicants, 45% accepted, 42 enrolled. In 2016, 49 master's, 6 doctorates awarded. Terminal master's awarded for partial completion of doctoral program. *Degree requirements:* For master's, comprehensive exam (for some programs), thesis (for some programs); for doctorate, comprehensive exam, thesis/dissertation, qualifying exam, preliminary exam, prospectus defense. *Entrance requirements:* For master's, GRE General Test, minimum undergraduate GPA of 3.0; for doctorate, GRE General Test, minimum GPA of 3.0. Additional exam requirements/recommendations for international students: Required—TOEFL (minimum score 550 paper-based; 80 iBT), IELTS (minimum score 6.5). *Application deadline:* For fall admission, 6/1 for domestic students, 1/15 priority date for international students; for spring admission, 11/1 for domestic students, 9/1 priority date for international students. Applications are processed on a rolling basis. Application fee: $30. Electronic applications accepted. *Expenses:* Tuition, state resident: full-time $7263; part-time $403.51 per credit hour. Tuition, nonresident: full-time $18,087; part-time $1004.85 per

credit hour. *Required fees:* $1365; $75.81 per credit hour. $20 per semester. Tuition and fees vary according to campus/location. *Financial support:* In 2016–17, 114 students received support, including 21 fellowships with full tuition reimbursements available (averaging $32,500 per year), 22 research assistantships with full tuition reimbursements available (averaging $24,387 per year), 62 teaching assistantships with full tuition reimbursements available (averaging $18,751 per year); scholarships/grants, health care benefits, tuition waivers (full), and unspecified assistantships also available. Financial award application deadline: 1/15; financial award applicants required to submit FAFSA. *Faculty research:* Embedded systems, high performance computing, networking, operating systems, security, databases, algorithms, big data, visualization. *Total annual research expenditures:* $1 million. *Unit head:* Dr. Xin Yuan, Chairman, 850-644-9133, Fax: 850-644-0058, E-mail: xyuan@cs.fsu.edu. *Application contact:* Daniel B. Clawson, Graduate Coordinator, 850-645-4975, Fax: 850-644-0058, E-mail: clawson@cs.fsu.edu.
Website: http://www.cs.fsu.edu/

Fontbonne University, Graduate Programs, St. Louis, MO 63105-3098. Offers accounting (MBA, MS); art (MA); art (K-12) (MAT); business (MBA); computer science (MS); deaf education (MA); early intervention in deaf education (MA); education (MA), including autism spectrum disorders, curriculum and instruction, diverse learners, early childhood education, reading, special education; elementary education (MAT); family and consumer sciences (MA), including multidisciplinary health communication studies; fine arts (MFA); instructional design and technology (MS); management and leadership (MM); middle school education (MAT); secondary education (MAT); special education (MAT); speech-language pathology (MS); supply chain management (MS); theatre (MA). *Program availability:* Part-time, evening/weekend, online learning. *Faculty:* 32 full-time (24 women), 43 part-time/adjunct (26 women). *Students:* 456 full-time (313 women), 102 part-time (77 women); includes 138 minority (118 Black or African American, non-Hispanic/Latino; 1 American Indian or Alaska Native, non-Hispanic/Latino; 7 Asian, non-Hispanic/Latino; 9 Hispanic/Latino; 3 Two or more races, non-Hispanic/Latino), 37 international. *Degree requirements:* For master's, comprehensive exam (for some programs), thesis (for some programs). *Entrance requirements:* Additional exam requirements/recommendations for international students: Required—TOEFL (minimum score 500 paper-based; 65 iBT). *Application deadline:* For fall admission, 8/1 for international students; for spring admission, 12/1 for international students. Applications are processed on a rolling basis. Application fee: $25 ($30 for international students). Electronic applications accepted. *Expenses: Tuition:* Full-time $8436; part-time $703 per credit hour. *Required fees:* $18 per credit hour. Tuition and fees vary according to course load. *Financial support:* Teaching assistantships with partial tuition reimbursements and scholarships/grants available. Support available to part-time students. Financial award application deadline: 4/1; financial award applicants required to submit FAFSA. *Unit head:* Dr. Carey Adams, Vice President for Academic Affairs, 314-719-3609, E-mail: cadams@fontbonne.edu. *Application contact:* Lauryn Filip, Coordinator, Graduate Admission and Professional Studies, 314-889-4650, E-mail: admissions@fontbonne.edu.
Website: https://www.fontbonne.edu/academics/graduate-programs/

Fordham University, Graduate School of Arts and Sciences, Department of Computer and Information Sciences, New York, NY 10458. Offers computer science (MS); cyber security (MS); data analytics (MS). *Program availability:* Part-time, evening/weekend. *Faculty:* 11 full-time (1 woman). *Students:* 62 full-time (12 women), 17 part-time (5 women); includes 26 minority (10 Black or African American, non-Hispanic/Latino; 10 Asian, non-Hispanic/Latino; 1 Hispanic/Latino; 5 Two or more races, non-Hispanic/Latino), 19 international. Average age 31. 104 applicants, 39% accepted, 12 enrolled. In 2016, 5 master's awarded. *Degree requirements:* For master's, thesis optional. *Entrance requirements:* For master's, GRE General Test. Additional exam requirements/recommendations for international students: Required—TOEFL (minimum score 550 paper-based). *Application deadline:* For fall admission, 1/4 priority date for domestic students; for spring admission, 11/1 for domestic students. Application fee: $70. Electronic applications accepted. *Financial support:* In 2016–17, 5 students received support, including 3 research assistantships with tuition reimbursements available (averaging $15,000 per year); career-related internships or fieldwork, institutionally sponsored loans, tuition waivers (full and partial), and unspecified assistantships also available. Financial award application deadline: 1/4; financial award applicants required to submit CSS PROFILE or FAFSA. *Faculty research:* Robotics and computer vision, data mining and informatics, information and networking, computation and algorithms, biomedical informatics. *Total annual research expenditures:* $213,000. *Unit head:* Dr. Damian Lyons, Chair, 718-817-4485, Fax: 718-817-4488, E-mail: dlyons@fordham.edu. *Application contact:* Bernadette Valentino-Morrison, Director of Graduate Admissions, 718-817-4420, Fax: 718-817-3566, E-mail: valentinomor@fordham.edu.

Franklin University, Computer Science Program, Columbus, OH 43215-5399. Offers MS. *Program availability:* Part-time, evening/weekend. *Entrance requirements:* For master's, minimum undergraduate GPA of 2.75. Additional exam requirements/recommendations for international students: Required—TOEFL (minimum score 550 paper-based). Electronic applications accepted. *Expenses:* Contact institution.

Frostburg State University, Graduate School, College of Liberal Arts and Sciences, Department of Computer Science, Program in Applied Computer Science, Frostburg, MD 21532-1099. Offers MS. *Entrance requirements:* Additional exam requirements/recommendations for international students: Required—TOEFL. Electronic applications accepted.

Gannon University, School of Graduate Studies, College of Engineering and Business, School of Engineering and Computer Science, Program in Computer and Information Science, Erie, PA 16541-0001. Offers information analytics (MSCIS); software engineering (MSCIS). *Program availability:* Part-time, evening/weekend. *Students:* 1 part-time (0 women); minority (Native Hawaiian or other Pacific Islander, non-Hispanic/Latino). Average age 42. In 2016, 27 master's awarded. *Degree requirements:* For master's, thesis (for some programs), directed research. *Entrance requirements:* For master's, 3 letters of recommendation; resume; transcripts; baccalaureate degree in computer science, information systems, information science, software engineering, or related field from regionally-accredited institution with minimum GPA of 2.5. Additional exam requirements/recommendations for international students: Required—TOEFL (minimum score 79 iBT). *Application deadline:* Applications are processed on a rolling basis. Application fee: $25. Electronic applications accepted. Application fee is waived when completed online. *Expenses: Tuition:* Full-time $17,370. *Required fees:* $550. Tuition and fees vary according to course load and program. *Financial support:* Federal Work-Study and unspecified assistantships available. Financial award application deadline: 7/1; financial award applicants required to submit FAFSA. *Unit head:* Dr. Mei-Huei Tang, Chair, 814-871-5393, E-mail: tang002@gannon.edu. *Application contact:* Bridget Philip, Director of Graduate Admissions, 814-871-7412, E-mail: graduate@gannon.edu.

George Mason University, Volgenau School of Engineering, Department of Computer Science, Fairfax, VA 22030. Offers MS, PhD, Certificate. MS programs offered jointly with Old Dominion University, University of Virginia, Virginia Commonwealth University, and Virginia Polytechnic Institute and State University. *Faculty:* 53 full-time (16 women), 21 part-time/adjunct (0 women). *Students:* 304 full-time (93 women), 204 part-time (42 women); includes 89 minority (17 Black or African American, non-Hispanic/Latino; 51 Asian, non-Hispanic/Latino; 11 Hispanic/Latino; 1 Native Hawaiian or other Pacific Islander, non-Hispanic/Latino; 9 Two or more races, non-Hispanic/Latino), 293 international. Average age 28. 681 applicants, 62% accepted, 154 enrolled. In 2016, 143 master's, 8 doctorates, 13 other advanced degrees awarded. *Degree requirements:* For master's, thesis optional; for doctorate, comprehensive exam, thesis/dissertation. *Entrance requirements:* For master's, GRE, proof of financial support; 2 official college transcripts; resume; self-evaluation form; official bank statement; photocopy of passport; 3 letters of recommendation; baccalaureate degree related to computer science; minimum GPA of 3.0 in last 2 years of undergraduate work; 1 year beyond 1st-year calculus; personal goals statement; for doctorate, GRE, personal goals statement; 2 official copies of transcripts; self-evaluation form; 3 letters of recommendation; photocopy of passport; proof of financial support; official bank statement; resume; 4-year baccalaureate degree with strong background in computer science. Additional exam requirements/recommendations for international students: Required—TOEFL (minimum score 575 paper-based; 88 iBT), IELTS (minimum score 6.5), PTE (minimum score 59). *Application deadline:* For fall admission, 1/15 priority date for domestic students. Application fee: $75 ($80 for international students). Electronic applications accepted. *Expenses:* Contact institution. *Financial support:* In 2016–17, 105 students received support, including 1 fellowship (averaging $10,000 per year), 32 research assistantships with tuition reimbursements available (averaging $18,129 per year), 74 teaching assistantships with tuition reimbursements available (averaging $14,760 per year); career-related internships or fieldwork, Federal Work-Study, scholarships/grants, unspecified assistantships, and health care benefits (for full-time research or teaching assistantship recipients) also available. Support available to part-time students. Financial award application deadline: 3/1; financial award applicants required to submit FAFSA. *Faculty research:* Artificial intelligence, image processing/graphics, parallel/distributed systems, software engineering systems. *Total annual research expenditures:* $2.8 million. *Unit head:* Sanjeev Setia, Chair, 703-993-4098, Fax: 703-993-1710, E-mail: setia@gmu.edu. *Application contact:* Michele Pieper, Office Manager, 703-993-9483, Fax: 703-993-1710, E-mail: mpieper@gmu.edu.
Website: http://cs.gmu.edu/

Georgetown University, Graduate School of Arts and Sciences, Department of Computer Science, Washington, DC 20057. Offers MS, PhD. *Program availability:* Part-time, evening/weekend. *Degree requirements:* For master's, thesis optional. *Entrance requirements:* For master's, GRE, basic course work in data structures, advanced math, and programming; 3 letters of recommendation. Additional exam requirements/recommendations for international students: Required—TOEFL. Electronic applications accepted. *Faculty research:* Data mining, artificial intelligence, software engineering, security.

The George Washington University, School of Engineering and Applied Science, Department of Computer Science, Washington, DC 20052. Offers computer science (MS, D Sc); cybersecurity (MS). *Program availability:* Part-time, evening/weekend. *Faculty:* 15 full-time (6 women). *Students:* 323 full-time (75 women), 171 part-time (50 women); includes 42 minority (17 Black or African American, non-Hispanic/Latino; 19 Asian, non-Hispanic/Latino; 5 Hispanic/Latino; 1 Two or more races, non-Hispanic/Latino), 372 international. Average age 28. 956 applicants, 73% accepted, 230 enrolled. In 2016, 150 master's, 8 doctorates, 19 other advanced degrees awarded. *Degree requirements:* For master's, thesis optional; for doctorate, thesis/dissertation, dissertation defense, qualifying exam. *Entrance requirements:* For master's, appropriate bachelor's degree, minimum GPA of 3.0; for doctorate, GRE (if highest earned degree is BS), appropriate bachelor's or master's degree, minimum GPA of 3.3; for other advanced degree, appropriate master's degree, minimum GPA of 3.4. Additional exam requirements/recommendations for international students: Required—TOEFL or The George Washington University English as a Foreign Language Test. *Application deadline:* For fall admission, 3/1 priority date for domestic students; for spring admission, 10/1 for domestic students. Applications are processed on a rolling basis. Application fee: $75. *Financial support:* In 2016–17, 49 students received support. Fellowships with tuition reimbursements available, research assistantships, teaching assistantships with tuition reimbursements available, career-related internships or fieldwork, institutionally sponsored loans, and tuition waivers available. Financial award application deadline: 3/1; financial award applicants required to submit FAFSA. *Faculty research:* Computer graphics, multimedia, VLSI, parallel processing. *Unit head:* Prof. Abdou Youssef, Chair, 202-994-4953, E-mail: ayoussef@gwu.edu. *Application contact:* Adina Lav, Marketing, Recruiting and Admissions, 202-994-5827, Fax: 202-994-0909, E-mail: engineering@gwu.edu.
Website: http://www.cs.gwu.edu/

Georgia Institute of Technology, Graduate Studies, College of Computing, Program in Computer Science, Atlanta, GA 30332-0001. Offers MS, PhD. *Program availability:* Part-time, online learning. Terminal master's awarded for partial completion of doctoral program. *Degree requirements:* For master's, thesis optional; for doctorate, comprehensive exam, thesis/dissertation. *Entrance requirements:* For master's, GRE General Test, GRE Subject Test (computer science); for doctorate, GRE General Test, GRE Subject Test (computer science, mathematics, or physics). Additional exam requirements/recommendations for international students: Required—TOEFL (minimum score 600 paper-based; 100 iBT). Electronic applications accepted. *Expenses:* Contact institution.

Georgia Southern University, Jack N. Averitt College of Graduate Studies, Allen E. Paulson College of Engineering and Information Technology, Program in Computer Science, Statesboro, GA 30458. Offers MS. *Program availability:* Part-time, blended/hybrid learning. *Students:* 1 full-time (0 women), 27 part-time (2 women); includes 13 minority (9 Black or African American, non-Hispanic/Latino; 2 Asian, non-Hispanic/Latino; 1 Hispanic/Latino; 1 Two or more races, non-Hispanic/Latino), 2 international. Average age 34. 27 applicants, 74% accepted, 9 enrolled. In 2016, 8 master's awarded. *Degree requirements:* For master's, thesis (for some programs). *Entrance requirements:* For master's, GRE. Additional exam requirements/recommendations for international students: Required—TOEFL (minimum score 550 paper-based; 80 iBT), IELTS (minimum score 6). *Application deadline:* For fall admission, 7/31 for domestic and international students. Application fee: $50. Electronic applications accepted. *Expenses:* Tuition, state resident: full-time $7236; part-time $277 per semester hour. Tuition, nonresident: full-time $27,118; part-time $1105 per semester hour. *Required fees:* $2092. *Financial support:* In 2016–17, 1 student received support. Unspecified assistantships available. Financial award application deadline: 4/20; financial award applicants required to submit FAFSA. *Faculty research:* Cyber physical systems, big data, data mining and analytics, cloud computing. *Total annual research expenditures:* $663. *Unit head:* Muralidhar Medidi, Program Coordinator, 912-478-5898, E-mail: lli@georgiasouthern.edu.
Website: http://ceit.georgiasouthern.edu/cs/

Georgia Southwestern State University, School of Computing and Mathematics, Americus, GA 31709-4693. Offers computer information systems (Graduate Certificate); computer science (MS). *Program availability:* Part-time, 100% online, blended/hybrid learning. *Faculty:* 3 full-time (0 women), 1 part-time/adjunct (0 women). *Students:* 7 full-time (0 women), 11 part-time (3 women); includes 5 minority (2 Black or African

American, non-Hispanic/Latino; 3 Asian, non-Hispanic/Latino), 8 international. Average age 34. 23 applicants, 57% accepted, 7 enrolled. In 2016, 5 master's, 1 other advanced degree awarded. *Degree requirements:* For master's, thesis optional, minimum cumulative GPA of 3.0; maximum of 6 credit hours with C grade; no courses with D grade; degree must be completed within 7 calendar years from date of initial enrollment in graduate course work; for Graduate Certificate, minimum cumulative GPA of 3.0; maximum of 6 credit hours with C grade; no courses with D grade; degree must be completed within 7 calendar years from date of initial enrollment in graduate course work. *Entrance requirements:* For master's and Graduate Certificate, GRE, bachelor's degree from regionally-accredited college; minimum undergraduate GPA of 2.5 as reported on official final transcripts from all institutions attended; letters of recommendation. Additional exam requirements/recommendations for international students: Required—TOEFL (minimum score 523 paper-based; 69 iBT), IELTS (minimum score 6.5). *Application deadline:* For fall admission, 5/31 for domestic students; for spring admission, 10/15 for domestic students; for summer admission, 3/15 for domestic students. Applications are processed on a rolling basis. Application fee: $25. Electronic applications accepted. *Expenses:* $257 per credit hour for online program courses, plus fees, which vary according to enrolled credit hours. *Financial support:* Application deadline: 6/1; applicants required to submit FAFSA. *Unit head:* Dr. Boris V. Peltsverger, Dean, 229-931-2100. *Application contact:* Whitney Ford, Admissions Specialist, Office of Graduate Admission, 800-338-0082,
Fax: 229-931-2983.
Website: https://gsw.edu/Academics/Schools-and-Departments/School-of-Computing-and-Mathematics/index

Georgia State University, College of Arts and Sciences, Department of Computer Science, Atlanta, GA 30302-3083. Offers bioinformatics (MS, PhD); computer science (MS, PhD). *Program availability:* Part-time. *Faculty:* 21 full-time (4 women). *Students:* 147 full-time (61 women), 30 part-time (11 women); includes 18 minority (7 Black or African American, non-Hispanic/Latino; 5 Asian, non-Hispanic/Latino; 2 Hispanic/Latino; 4 Two or more races, non-Hispanic/Latino), 141 international. Average age 28. 303 applicants, 41% accepted, 52 enrolled. In 2016, 48 master's, 10 doctorates awarded. Terminal master's awarded for partial completion of doctoral program. *Degree requirements:* For master's, comprehensive exam, thesis (for some programs); for doctorate, comprehensive exam, thesis/dissertation, proposal defense. *Entrance requirements:* For master's and doctorate, GRE General Test. Additional exam requirements/recommendations for international students: Required—TOEFL (minimum score 550 paper-based; 80 iBT). *Application deadline:* For fall admission, 3/15 for domestic and international students; for spring admission, 10/15 for domestic and international students. Application fee: $50. Electronic applications accepted. *Expenses:* Tuition, state resident: full-time $6876; part-time $382 per credit hour. Tuition, nonresident: full-time $22,374; part-time $1243 per credit hour. *Required fees:* $2128; $1064 per term. Part-time tuition and fees vary according to course load and program. *Financial support:* In 2016–17, fellowships with full tuition reimbursements (averaging $22,000 per year), research assistantships with full tuition reimbursements (averaging $16,000 per year), teaching assistantships with full tuition reimbursements (averaging $16,000 per year) were awarded; institutionally sponsored loans, health care benefits, and unspecified assistantships also available. Financial award application deadline: 2/15; financial award applicants required to submit FAFSA. *Faculty research:* Artificial intelligence and computational intelligence, bioinformatics, computer software systems, databases, graphics and human computer interaction, networks and parallel and distributed computing. *Unit head:* Dr. Yi Pan, Acting Chair, 404-413-5342, Fax: 404-413-5717, E-mail: yipan@gsu.edu.
Website: http://www.cs.gsu.edu/

Georgia State University, College of Arts and Sciences, Department of Mathematics and Statistics, Atlanta, GA 30302-3083. Offers bioinformatics (MS, PhD); biostatistics (MS, PhD); discrete mathematics (MS); mathematics (MS, PhD); scientific computing (MS); statistics (MS). *Program availability:* Part-time. *Faculty:* 38 full-time (11 women). *Students:* 97 full-time (47 women), 24 part-time (7 women); includes 43 minority (11 Black or African American, non-Hispanic/Latino; 21 Asian, non-Hispanic/Latino; 3 Hispanic/Latino; 8 Two or more races, non-Hispanic/Latino), 57 international. Average age 32. 72 applicants, 69% accepted, 26 enrolled. In 2016, 39 master's, 6 doctorates awarded. Terminal master's awarded for partial completion of doctoral program. *Degree requirements:* For master's, comprehensive exam (for some programs), thesis optional; for doctorate, comprehensive exam, thesis/dissertation. *Entrance requirements:* For master's and doctorate, GRE. Additional exam requirements/recommendations for international students: Required—TOEFL (minimum score 550 paper-based; 80 iBT). *Application deadline:* For fall admission, 7/1 priority date for domestic and international students; for spring admission, 11/15 priority date for domestic and international students. Application fee: $50. Electronic applications accepted. *Expenses:* Tuition, state resident: full-time $6876; part-time $382 per credit hour. Tuition, nonresident: full-time $22,374; part-time $1243 per credit hour. *Required fees:* $2128; $1064 per term. Part-time tuition and fees vary according to course load and program. *Financial support:* In 2016–17, fellowships with full tuition reimbursements (averaging $22,000 per year), research assistantships with full tuition reimbursements (averaging $9,000 per year), teaching assistantships with full tuition reimbursements (averaging $9,000 per year) were awarded; institutionally sponsored loans, scholarships/grants, health care benefits, and unspecified assistantships also available. Financial award application deadline: 2/1. *Faculty research:* Algebra, matrix theory, graph theory and combinatorics; applied mathematics and analysis; collegiate mathematics education; statistics, biostatistics and applications; bioinformatics, dynamical systems. *Unit head:* Dr. Guantao Chen, Chair, 404-413-6436, Fax: 404-413-6403, E-mail: gchen@gsu.edu.
Website: http://www2.gsu.edu/~wwwmat/

Governors State University, College of Arts and Sciences, Program in Computer Science, University Park, IL 60484. Offers MS. *Program availability:* Part-time. *Faculty:* 91 full-time (43 women), 125 part-time/adjunct (64 women). *Students:* 283 full-time (64 women), 75 part-time (19 women); includes 16 minority (14 Black or African American, non-Hispanic/Latino; 2 Asian, non-Hispanic/Latino), 332 international. Average age 25. 1,414 applicants, 52% accepted, 298 enrolled. In 2016, 203 master's awarded. *Entrance requirements:* Additional exam requirements/recommendations for international students: Required—TOEFL (minimum score 550 paper-based; 80 iBT), IELTS. *Application deadline:* For fall admission, 4/1 for domestic students. Application fee: $50. Electronic applications accepted. *Expenses:* $307 per credit hour; $38 per term or $76 per credit hour fees. *Financial support:* Application deadline: 5/1; applicants required to submit FAFSA. *Unit head:* Steve Shih, Chair, Division of Computing Mathematics and Technology, 708-534-4547, E-mail: sshih@govst.edu. *Application contact:* Yakeea Daniels, Assistant Vice President for Enrollment Services/Director of Admission, 708-534-4510, E-mail: ydaniels@govst.edu.

The Graduate Center, City University of New York, Graduate Studies, Program in Computer Science, New York, NY 10016-4039. Offers PhD. Program offered jointly with College of Staten Island of the City University of New York. *Degree requirements:* For doctorate, one foreign language, thesis/dissertation. *Entrance requirements:* For doctorate, GRE General Test. Additional exam requirements/recommendations for international students: Required—TOEFL. Electronic applications accepted.

Grand Valley State University, Padnos College of Engineering and Computing, School of Computing and Information Systems, Allendale, MI 49401-9403. Offers computer information systems (MS), including databases, distributed systems, management of information systems, object-oriented systems, software engineering. *Program availability:* Part-time, evening/weekend. *Faculty:* 10 full-time (3 women), 1 (woman) part-time/adjunct. *Students:* 28 full-time (3 women), 57 part-time (14 women); includes 11 minority (3 Black or African American, non-Hispanic/Latino; 4 Asian, non-Hispanic/Latino; 3 Hispanic/Latino; 1 Two or more races, non-Hispanic/Latino), 32 international. Average age 30. 97 applicants, 59% accepted, 17 enrolled. In 2016, 36 master's awarded. *Degree requirements:* For master's, capstone course, project, or thesis. *Entrance requirements:* For master's, GMAT or GRE General Test, minimum GPA of 3.0; knowledge of a programming language; coursework or experience in: computer architecture and/or organization, data structures and algorithms, databases, discrete math, networking, operating systems, and software engineering; minimum of 2 letters of recommendation; resume; personal statement. Additional exam requirements/recommendations for international students: Required—TOEFL, Michigan English Language Assessment Battery or completion of ELS 112; Recommended—IELTS. *Application deadline:* For fall admission, 6/1 for international students; for winter admission, 9/1 for international students. Applications are processed on a rolling basis. Application fee: $30. Electronic applications accepted. *Expenses:* $646 per credit hour. *Financial support:* In 2016–17, 11 students received support, including 3 fellowships, 10 research assistantships with full and partial tuition reimbursements available (averaging $8,000 per year). *Faculty research:* Object technology, distributed computing, information systems management database, software engineering. *Unit head:* Dr. Paul Leidig, Director, 616-331-2038, Fax: 616-331-2106, E-mail: leidigp@gvsu.edu. *Application contact:* Dr. D. Robert Adams, Graduate Program Director/Recruiting Contact, 616-331-3885, Fax: 616-331-2106, E-mail: adams@cis.gvsu.edu.
Website: http://www.cis.gvsu.edu/

Hampton University, School of Science, Department of Computer Science, Hampton, VA 23668. Offers MS. *Program availability:* Part-time, evening/weekend. *Faculty:* 5 full-time (2 women), 2 part-time/adjunct (0 women). *Students:* 2 full-time (1 woman), 5 part-time (2 women); all minorities (4 Black or African American, non-Hispanic/Latino; 3 Asian, non-Hispanic/Latino). Average age 30. 10 applicants, 30% accepted, 2 enrolled. *Degree requirements:* For master's, thesis or alternative. *Entrance requirements:* For master's, GRE General Test. Additional exam requirements/recommendations for international students: Required—TOEFL (minimum score 525 paper-based) or IELTS (6.5). *Application deadline:* For fall admission, 6/1 priority date for domestic students, 4/1 priority date for international students; for spring admission, 11/1 priority date for domestic students, 9/1 priority date for international students; for summer admission, 4/1 priority date for domestic students, 2/1 priority date for international students. Applications are processed on a rolling basis. Application fee: $35. Electronic applications accepted. *Expenses: Tuition:* Full-time $10,776; part-time $548 per credit hour. *Required fees:* $35; $35 per credit hour. Tuition and fees vary according to course load and program. *Financial support:* In 2016–17, 5 fellowships (averaging $38,900 per year), 1 research assistantship were awarded; career-related internships or fieldwork, Federal Work-Study, and scholarships/grants also available. Support available to part-time students. Financial award application deadline: 6/30; financial award applicants required to submit FAFSA. *Faculty research:* Software testing, neural networks, parallel processing, computer graphics, natural language processing. *Unit head:* Dr. Jean Muhammad, Chair, 757-727-5552.

Harvard University, Graduate School of Arts and Sciences, Harvard John A. Paulson School of Engineering and Applied Sciences, Cambridge, MA 02138. Offers applied mathematics (PhD); applied physics (PhD); computational science and engineering (ME, SM); computer science (PhD); design engineering (MDE); engineering science (ME), including electrical engineering (ME, SM, PhD); engineering sciences (SM, PhD), including bioengineering (PhD), electrical engineering (ME, SM, PhD), environmental science and engineering (PhD), materials science and mechanical engineering (PhD). MDE offered in collaboration with Graduate School of Design. *Program availability:* Part-time. *Faculty:* 80 full-time (13 women), 47 part-time/adjunct (10 women). *Students:* 459 full-time (135 women), 19 part-time (7 women); includes 79 minority (2 Black or African American, non-Hispanic/Latino; 49 Asian, non-Hispanic/Latino; 15 Hispanic/Latino; 1 Native Hawaiian or other Pacific Islander, non-Hispanic/Latino; 12 Two or more races, non-Hispanic/Latino), 233 international. Average age 27. 2,486 applicants, 11% accepted, 126 enrolled. In 2016, 37 master's, 48 doctorates awarded. Terminal master's awarded for partial completion of doctoral program. *Degree requirements:* For master's, thesis (for ME); for doctorate, comprehensive exam, thesis/dissertation. *Entrance requirements:* For master's and doctorate, GRE General Test, GRE Subject Test (recommended), 3 letters of recommendation. Additional exam requirements/recommendations for international students: Required—TOEFL (minimum score 80 iBT). *Application deadline:* For fall admission, 12/15 priority date for domestic and international students. Application fee: $105. Electronic applications accepted. *Expenses:* $43,296 full-time tuition, $3,718 fees. *Financial support:* In 2016–17, 394 students received support, including 86 fellowships with full tuition reimbursements available (averaging $26,424 per year), 258 research assistantships with tuition reimbursements available (averaging $35,232 per year), 106 teaching assistantships with tuition reimbursements available (averaging $6,313 per year); health care benefits also available. *Faculty research:* Applied mathematics, applied physics, computer science and electrical engineering, environmental engineering, mechanical and biomedical engineering. *Total annual research expenditures:* $50.1 million. *Unit head:* Francis J. Doyle, III, Dean, 617-495-5829, Fax: 617-495-5264, E-mail: dean@seas.harvard.edu. *Application contact:* Office of Admissions and Financial Aid, 617-495-5315, E-mail: admissions@seas.harvard.edu.
Website: http://www.seas.harvard.edu/

Hood College, Graduate School, Programs in Computer and Information Sciences, Frederick, MD 21701-8575. Offers computer science (MS); cyber security (Certificate); information technology (MS). *Program availability:* Part-time, evening/weekend. *Faculty:* 7 full-time, 8 part-time/adjunct. *Students:* 82 full-time (29 women), 51 part-time (13 women); includes 8 minority (2 Black or African American, non-Hispanic/Latino; 4 Asian, non-Hispanic/Latino; 1 Hispanic/Latino; 1 Two or more races, non-Hispanic/Latino), 89 international. Average age 30. 79 applicants, 84% accepted, 36 enrolled. In 2016, 75 master's, 35 other advanced degrees awarded. *Degree requirements:* For master's, thesis optional. *Entrance requirements:* For master's, minimum GPA of 2.75, essay, resume. Additional exam requirements/recommendations for international students: Required—TOEFL (minimum score 575 paper-based; 89 iBT), IELTS (minimum score 6.5). *Application deadline:* For fall admission, 8/15 priority date for domestic students, 8/5 for international students; for spring admission, 12/1 priority date for domestic students, 12/1 for international students; for summer admission, 5/1 for domestic students, 4/15 for international students. Applications are processed on a rolling basis. Application fee: $35. Electronic applications accepted. *Expenses:* $475 per credit hour; $110 comprehensive fee per semester. *Financial support:* Tuition waivers (partial) and unspecified assistantships available. Financial award applicants required to submit FAFSA. *Faculty research:* Systems engineering, natural language, processing, database design, artificial intelligence and parallel distributed computing. *Unit head:* April Boulton, Interim Dean of the Graduate School, 301-696-3600, E-mail: gofurther@

hood.edu. *Application contact:* Spencer Berk, Assistant Director of Graduate Admissions, 301-696-3600, E-mail: gofurther@hood.edu.
Website: http://www.hood.edu/graduate

Howard University, College of Engineering, Architecture, and Computer Sciences, School of Engineering and Computer Science, Department of Systems and Computer Science, Washington, DC 20059-0002. Offers MCS. Offered through the Graduate School of Arts and Sciences. *Program availability:* Part-time. *Degree requirements:* For master's, thesis. *Entrance requirements:* For master's, GRE General Test, minimum GPA of 3.0. Additional exam requirements/recommendations for international students: Required—TOEFL. Electronic applications accepted. *Faculty research:* Software engineering, software fault-tolerance, software reliability, artificial intelligence.

Illinois Institute of Technology, Graduate College, College of Science, Department of Computer Science, Chicago, IL 60616. Offers business (MCS); computational intelligence (MCS); computer science (MCS, MS, PhD); cyber-physical systems (MCS); data analytics (MCS); data science (MAS); database systems (MCS); distributed and cloud computing (MCS); education (MCS); finance (MCS); information security and assurance (MCS); networking and communications (MCS); software engineering (MCS); telecommunications and software engineering (MAS); MS/MAS. *Program availability:* Part-time, evening/weekend, online learning. Terminal master's awarded for partial completion of doctoral program. *Degree requirements:* For master's, thesis optional; for doctorate, comprehensive exam, thesis/dissertation. *Entrance requirements:* For master's, GRE General Test with minimum scores of 298 Quantitative and Verbal, 3.0 Analytical Writing (for MS); GRE General Test with minimum scores of 292 Quantitative and Verbal, 2.5 Analytical Writing (for MAS), minimum undergraduate GPA of 3.0; for doctorate, GRE General Test (minimum scores: 304 Quantitative and Verbal, 3.5 Analytical Writing), minimum undergraduate GPA of 3.0. Additional exam requirements/recommendations for international students: Required—TOEFL (minimum score 523 paper-based; 70 iBT). Electronic applications accepted. *Faculty research:* Parallel and distributed processing, high-performance computing, computational linguistics, information retrieval, data mining, grid computing.

Indiana State University, College of Graduate and Professional Studies, College of Arts and Sciences, Department of Mathematics and Computer Science, Terre Haute, IN 47809. Offers computer science (MS); mathematics (MA, MS). *Program availability:* Part-time. *Degree requirements:* For master's, thesis or alternative. *Entrance requirements:* For master's, 24 semester hours of course work in undergraduate mathematics. Electronic applications accepted.

Indiana University Bloomington, School of Informatics and Computing, Department of Computer Science, Bloomington, IN 47405. Offers bioinformatics (MS); computer science (MS, PhD); cybersecurity risk management (MS); secure computing (MS, Graduate Certificate). MS in cybersecurity risk management offered in partnership with Kelley School of Business and Maurer School of Law. *Faculty:* 75 full-time (15 women). *Students:* 438 full-time (96 women), 14 part-time (2 women); includes 9 minority (2 Black or African American, non-Hispanic/Latino; 2 Asian, non-Hispanic/Latino; 4 Hispanic/Latino; 1 Two or more races, non-Hispanic/Latino), 401 international. Average age 27. 523 applicants, 56% accepted, 133 enrolled. In 2016, 122 master's, 12 doctorates awarded. Terminal master's awarded for partial completion of doctoral program. *Degree requirements:* For master's, thesis optional; for doctorate, comprehensive exam, thesis/dissertation, oral and written exams. *Entrance requirements:* For master's and doctorate, GRE General Test, statement of purpose, bachelor's degree. Additional exam requirements/recommendations for international students: Required—TOEFL. *Application deadline:* For fall admission, 1/15 priority date for domestic students, 12/1 priority date for international students. Application fee: $55 ($65 for international students). Electronic applications accepted. *Financial support:* In 2016–17, 1 fellowship with full tuition reimbursement (averaging $25,000 per year), 66 research assistantships with full tuition reimbursements (averaging $19,150 per year), 38 teaching assistantships with full tuition reimbursements (averaging $19,150 per year) were awarded; scholarships/grants, health care benefits, and tuition waivers also available. Financial award application deadline: 12/1. *Faculty research:* Algorithms, applied logic and computational theory, artificial intelligence, bioinformatics, case-based reasoning, chemical informatics, citation analysis, cognitive science, community informatics, compilers, complex networks and systems, computer optimization, computer-supported cooperative work, computer vision, cyberinfrastructure and e-science, database theory and systems, data mining, digital design and preservation, design pedagogy, digital humanities, digital learning environments. *Total annual research expenditures:* $19.4 million. *Unit head:* Dr. Funda Ergun, Director of Graduate Studies, 812-855-6586, Fax: 812-855-4829, E-mail: fergun@indiana.edu. *Application contact:* Rachel Harris, Admissions and Records Coordinator, 812-855-6487,
E-mail: soiccsgr@soic.indiana.edu.
Website: http://www.cs.indiana.edu

Indiana University Bloomington, School of Informatics and Computing, Program in Informatics, Bloomington, IN 47405. Offers informatics (MS, PhD), including bioinformatics (PhD), complex systems (PhD), computing, culture and society (PhD), health informatics (PhD), human-computer interaction (MS), human-computer interaction design (PhD), music informatics (PhD), security informatics (PhD); visual heritage (PhD). *Program availability:* Part-time. *Faculty:* 75 full-time (15 women). *Students:* 206 full-time (85 women), 10 part-time (3 women); includes 30 minority (11 Black or African American, non-Hispanic/Latino; 10 Asian, non-Hispanic/Latino; 5 Hispanic/Latino; 4 Two or more races, non-Hispanic/Latino), 95 international. Average age 28. 395 applicants, 36% accepted, 69 enrolled. In 2016, 50 master's, 11 doctorates awarded. Terminal master's awarded for partial completion of doctoral program. *Degree requirements:* For master's, thesis, capstone project; for doctorate, variable foreign language requirement, comprehensive exam, thesis/dissertation. *Entrance requirements:* For master's and doctorate, GRE, resume/curriculum vitae, transcripts, 3 letters of recommendation. Additional exam requirements/recommendations for international students: Required—TOEFL (minimum score 600 paper-based; 100 iBT). *Application deadline:* For fall admission, 12/1 priority date for domestic and international students. Application fee: $55 ($65 for international students). Electronic applications accepted. *Financial support:* Fellowships, research assistantships, scholarships/grants, health care benefits, and unspecified assistantships available. Financial award application deadline: 12/1. *Faculty research:* Algorithms, applied logic and computational theory, artificial intelligence, bioinformatics, case-based reasoning, chemical informatics, citation analysis, cognitive science, community informatics, compilers, complex networks and systems, computer optimization, computer-supported cooperative work, computer vision, cyberinfrastructure and e-science, database theory and systems, data mining, digital design and preservation, design pedagogy, digital humanities, digital learning environments. *Total annual research expenditures:* $19.4 million. *Unit head:* Dr. Martin Siegel, Director of Graduate Studies, 812-856-3960, E-mail: msiegel@indiana.edu. *Application contact:* Informatics Graduate Studies Office, 812-856-3960, E-mail: infograd@indiana.edu.
Website: http://www.informatics.indiana.edu/graduate/index.html

Indiana University–Purdue University Fort Wayne, College of Engineering, Technology, and Computer Science, Department of Computer Science, Fort Wayne, IN 46805-1499. Offers applied computer science (MS). *Program availability:* Part-time. *Entrance requirements:* For master's, GRE General Test, minimum GPA of 3.0. Additional exam requirements/recommendations for international students: Required—TOEFL (minimum score 550 paper-based; 79 iBT); Recommended—TWE. Electronic applications accepted. *Faculty research:* Architecture, cloud computing and security.

Indiana University–Purdue University Indianapolis, School of Science, Department of Computer and Information Science, Indianapolis, IN 46202-5132. Offers biocomputing (Graduate Certificate); biometrics (Graduate Certificate); computer science (MS, PhD); computer security (Graduate Certificate); databases and data mining (Graduate Certificate); software engineering (Graduate Certificate). *Program availability:* Part-time. *Faculty:* 16 full-time (2 women), 10 part-time/adjunct (4 women). *Students:* 95 full-time (36 women), 44 part-time (15 women); includes 8 minority (3 Black or African American, non-Hispanic/Latino; 5 Asian, non-Hispanic/Latino), 119 international. Average age 27. 275 applicants, 30% accepted, 41 enrolled. In 2016, 52 master's, 3 doctorates, 3 other advanced degrees awarded. Terminal master's awarded for partial completion of doctoral program. *Degree requirements:* For master's and Graduate Certificate, thesis optional; for doctorate, thesis/dissertation. *Entrance requirements:* For master's and doctorate, GRE, BS in computer science or the equivalent with a minimum GPA of 3.0 (or equivalent); for Graduate Certificate, BS in computer science or the equivalent with a minimum GPA of 3.0 (or equivalent). Additional exam requirements/recommendations for international students: Required—PTE (minimum score 58), TOEFL (minimum score 550 paper-based, 79 iBT) or IELTS (6.5). *Application deadline:* For fall admission, 1/15 priority date for domestic and international students; for spring admission, 9/15 for domestic students. Application fee: $60 ($65 for international students). *Financial support:* In 2016–17, 45 students received support, including 2 fellowships with full tuition reimbursements available (averaging $20,000 per year), 15 research assistantships with full and partial tuition reimbursements available (averaging $18,000 per year), 20 teaching assistantships with full and partial tuition reimbursements available (averaging $18,000 per year); scholarships/grants, health care benefits, and tuition waivers (full and partial) also available. Financial award application deadline: 1/15. *Faculty research:* Imaging and visualization; networking and security; software engineering; distributed and parallel computing; database, data mining and machine learning. *Total annual research expenditures:* $550,196. *Unit head:* Dr. Shiaofen Fang, Chair, 317-274-9727, Fax: 317-274-9742, E-mail: sfang@cs.iupui.edu. *Application contact:* Nicole Wittlief, Graduate Admissions and Program Coordinator, 317-274-3883, Fax: 317-274-9742, E-mail: wittlief@cs.iupui.edu. Website: http://www.cs.iupui.edu/

Indiana University South Bend, College of Liberal Arts and Sciences, South Bend, IN 46634-7111. Offers advanced computer programming (Graduate Certificate); applied informatics (Graduate Certificate); applied mathematics and computer science (MS); behavior modification (Graduate Certificate); computer applications (Graduate Certificate); computer programming (Graduate Certificate); correctional management and supervision (Graduate Certificate); English (MA); health systems management (Graduate Certificate); international studies (Graduate Certificate); liberal studies (MLS); nonprofit management (Graduate Certificate); paralegal studies (Graduate Certificate); professional writing (Graduate Certificate); public affairs (MPA); public management (Graduate Certificate); social and cultural diversity (Graduate Certificate); strategic sustainability leadership (Graduate Certificate); technology for administration (Graduate Certificate). *Program availability:* Part-time, evening/weekend. *Faculty:* 79 full-time (33 women). *Students:* 31 full-time (11 women), 92 part-time (53 women); includes 28 minority (9 Black or African American, non-Hispanic/Latino; 8 Asian, non-Hispanic/Latino; 5 Hispanic/Latino; 6 Two or more races, non-Hispanic/Latino), 19 international. Average age 38. 51 applicants, 84% accepted, 31 enrolled. In 2016, 30 master's, 6 other advanced degrees awarded. *Degree requirements:* For master's, variable foreign language requirement, thesis (for some programs). *Entrance requirements:* For master's, minimum GPA of 3.0. Additional exam requirements/recommendations for international students: Required—TOEFL (minimum score 550 paper-based; 80 iBT). *Application deadline:* For fall admission, 7/31 priority date for domestic students, 7/1 priority date for international students; for spring admission, 3/31 priority date for domestic students, 11/1 priority date for international students. Applications are processed on a rolling basis. Application fee: $40 ($60 for international students). *Expenses:* $276.98 per credit hour in-state; $652.54 per credit hour out-of-state. *Financial support:* In 2016–17, 5 teaching assistantships were awarded; Federal Work-Study also available. Support available to part-time students. Financial award application deadline: 3/10. *Faculty research:* Artificial intelligence, bioinformatics, English language and literature, creative writing, computer networks. *Total annual research expenditures:* $127,000. *Unit head:* Dr. Elizabeth E. Dunn, Dean, 574-520-4290, E-mail: elizdunn@iusb.edu. *Application contact:* Admissions Counselor, 574-520-4839, Fax: 574-520-4834, E-mail: graduate@iusb.edu.
Website: https://www.iusb.edu/clas/

Instituto Tecnológico y de Estudios Superiores de Monterrey, Campus Central de Veracruz, Graduate Programs, Córdoba, Mexico. Offers administration (MA); administration of information technologies (MTI); computer sciences (MCC); education (MEE); educational institution administration (MAD); educational technology (MTE); electronic commerce (MCE); finance (MAF); humanistic studies (MEH); international business for Latin America (MNL); marketing (MMT); science (MCP). *Program availability:* Part-time, evening/weekend, online learning. *Degree requirements:* For master's, thesis (for some programs). *Entrance requirements:* For master's, PAEP College Board. Electronic applications accepted.

Instituto Tecnológico y de Estudios Superiores de Monterrey, Campus Ciudad de México, Virtual University Division, Ciudad de Mexico, Mexico. Offers administration of information technologies (MA); computer sciences (MA); education (MA, PhD); educational technology (MA); environmental engineering (MA); environmental systems (MA); humanistic studies (MA); industrial engineering (MA); international business for Latin America (MA); quality systems (MA); quality systems and productivity (MA). *Program availability:* Part-time, evening/weekend, online learning. *Entrance requirements:* For master's and doctorate, Instituto entrance exam. Additional exam requirements/recommendations for international students: Required—TOEFL.

Instituto Tecnológico y de Estudios Superiores de Monterrey, Campus Cuernavaca, Programs in Information Science, Temixco, Mexico. Offers administration of information technology (MATI); computer science (MCC, DCC); information technology (MTI).

Instituto Tecnológico y de Estudios Superiores de Monterrey, Campus Estado de México, Professional and Graduate Division, Estado de Mexico, Mexico. Offers administration of information technologies (MITA); architecture (M Arch); business administration (GMBA, MBA); computer sciences (MCS, PhD); education (M Ed); educational institution administration (MAD); educational technology and innovation (PhD); electronic commerce (MEC); environmental systems (MS); finance (MAF); humanistic studies (MHS); information sciences and knowledge management (MISKM); information systems (MS); manufacturing systems (MS); marketing (MEM); quality systems and productivity (MS); science and materials engineering (PhD); telecommunications management (MTM). *Program availability:* Part-time, online learning. *Degree requirements:* For master's, one foreign language, thesis (for some programs); for doctorate, one foreign language, thesis/dissertation. *Entrance* *requirements:* For master's, E-PAEP 500, interview; for doctorate, E-PAEP 500, research proposal. Additional exam requirements/recommendations for international students: Required—TOEFL (minimum score 550 paper-based). *Faculty research:* Surface treatments by plasmas, mechanical properties, robotics, graphical computing, mechatronics security protocols.

Instituto Tecnológico y de Estudios Superiores de Monterrey, Campus Irapuato, Graduate Programs, Irapuato, Mexico. Offers administration (MBA); administration of information technology (MAIT); administration of telecommunications (MAT); architecture (M Arch); computer science (MCS); education (M Ed); educational administration (MEA); educational innovation and technology (DEIT); educational technology (MET); electronic commerce (MBA); environmental administration and planning (MEAP); environmental systems (MES); finances (MBA); humanistic studies (MHS); international management for Latin American executives (MIMLAE); library and information science (MLIS); manufacturing quality management (MMQM); marketing research (MBA).

Instituto Tecnológico y de Estudios Superiores de Monterrey, Campus Monterrey, Graduate and Research Division, Program in Computer Science, Monterrey, Mexico. Offers artificial intelligence (PhD); computer science (MS); information systems (MS); information technology (MS). *Program availability:* Part-time. *Degree requirements:* For master's, one foreign language, thesis; for doctorate, one foreign language, thesis/dissertation. *Entrance requirements:* For master's, EXADEP; for doctorate, master's degree in related field. Additional exam requirements/recommendations for international students: Required—TOEFL. *Faculty research:* Distributed systems, software engineering, decision support systems.

Inter American University of Puerto Rico, Fajardo Campus, Graduate Programs, Fajardo, PR 00738-7003. Offers computer science (MS); educational management and leadership (MA Ed); elementary education (MA Ed); general business (MBA); management information systems (MBA); marketing (MBA); special education (MA Ed).

Inter American University of Puerto Rico, Guayama Campus, Department of Natural and Applied Sciences, Guayama, PR 00785. Offers computer security and networks (MS); networking and security (MCS).

Inter American University of Puerto Rico, Metropolitan Campus, Graduate Programs, Program in Open Information Systems, San Juan, PR 00919-1293. Offers MS. *Degree requirements:* For master's, 2 foreign languages.

Iona College, School of Arts and Science, Department of Computer Science, New Rochelle, NY 10801-1890. Offers computer science (MS); cyber security (MS); game development (MS). *Program availability:* Part-time, evening/weekend. *Faculty:* 6 full-time (3 women), 1 (woman) part-time/adjunct. *Students:* 13 full-time (2 women), 9 part-time (1 woman); includes 4 minority (2 Black or African American, non-Hispanic/Latino; 2 Hispanic/Latino), 8 international. Average age 27. 28 applicants, 79% accepted, 6 enrolled. In 2016, 7 master's awarded. *Degree requirements:* For master's, thesis optional. *Entrance requirements:* For master's, minimum GPA of 3.0. Additional exam requirements/recommendations for international students: Required—TOEFL (minimum score 550 paper-based; 80 iBT), IELTS (minimum score 6.5). *Application deadline:* For fall admission, 8/1 priority date for domestic students, 5/1 priority date for international students; for spring admission, 1/1 priority date for domestic students, 9/1 priority date for international students. Applications are processed on a rolling basis. Application fee: $50. Electronic applications accepted. *Expenses: Tuition:* Full-time $19,692; part-time $1094 per credit. *Required fees:* $245 per term. Tuition and fees vary according to program. *Financial support:* In 2016–17, 7 students received support, including 2 research assistantships with full tuition reimbursements available; tuition waivers (partial) and unspecified assistantships also available. Support available to part-time students. Financial award application deadline: 4/15; financial award applicants required to submit FAFSA. *Faculty research:* Parallel procession, data mining, machine learning, cyber security, medical imaging. *Unit head:* Robert Schiaffino, PhD, Chair, 914-633-2338, E-mail: rschiaffino@iona.edu. *Application contact:* Katelyn Brunck, Assistant Director, Graduate Admissions, 914-633-2451, Fax: 914-633-2277,
E-mail: kbrunck@iona.edu.
Website: http://www.iona.edu/Academics/School-of-Arts-Science/Departments/Computer-Science/Graduate-Programs.aspx

Iowa State University of Science and Technology, Department of Computer Science, Ames, IA 50011. Offers MS, PhD. *Degree requirements:* For master's, thesis; for doctorate, thesis/dissertation. *Entrance requirements:* For master's and doctorate, GRE General Test. Additional exam requirements/recommendations for international students: Recommended—TOEFL (minimum score 550 paper-based; 79 iBT), IELTS (minimum score 6.5). *Application deadline:* For fall admission, 1/1 priority date for domestic and international students; for spring admission, 9/1 priority date for domestic and international students. Application fee: $60 ($90 for international students). Electronic applications accepted. *Application contact:* Carla Harris, Application Contact, 515-294-1224, Fax: 515-294-0258, E-mail: csadmissions@iastate.edu.
Website: http://www.cs.iastate.edu/

Jackson State University, Graduate School, College of Science, Engineering and Technology, Department of Computer Science, Jackson, MS 39217. Offers MS. *Program availability:* Part-time, evening/weekend. *Degree requirements:* For master's, comprehensive exam, thesis. *Entrance requirements:* For master's, GRE General Test. Additional exam requirements/recommendations for international students: Required—TOEFL (minimum score 520 paper-based; 67 iBT). *Application deadline:* For fall admission, 3/1 priority date for domestic students, 3/1 for international students; for spring admission, 10/1 for domestic and international students. Applications are processed on a rolling basis. Application fee: $25. *Expenses:* Tuition, state resident: full-time $7141. Tuition, nonresident: full-time $17,494. *Required fees:* $1080. Tuition and fees vary according to class time, course level, course load, degree level, campus/location, program and student level. *Financial support:* Career-related internships or fieldwork, Federal Work-Study, scholarships/grants, and unspecified assistantships available. Support available to part-time students. Financial award application deadline: 3/1; financial award applicants required to submit FAFSA. *Unit head:* Jessie Walker, Chair, 601-979-2059, E-mail: jessie.j.walker@jsums.edu. *Application contact:* Fatoumatta Sisay, Manager of Graduate Admissions, 601-979-0342, Fax: 601-979-4325, E-mail: fatoumatta.sisay@jsums.edu.
Website: http://www.jsums.edu/compscience/

Jacksonville State University, College of Graduate Studies and Continuing Education, College of Arts and Sciences, Program in Computer Systems and Software Design, Jacksonville, AL 36265-1602. Offers MS. *Program availability:* Part-time, evening/weekend. *Faculty:* 11 full-time (4 women). *Students:* 6 full-time (3 women), 7 part-time (2 women); includes 1 minority (Hispanic/Latino), 6 international. Average age 29. 83 applicants, 25% accepted, 1 enrolled. In 2016, 5 master's awarded. *Degree requirements:* For master's, comprehensive exam, thesis (for some programs). *Entrance requirements:* Additional exam requirements/recommendations for international students: Required—TOEFL (minimum score 500 paper-based; 61 iBT). *Application deadline:* Applications are processed on a rolling basis. Application fee: $35. Electronic applications accepted. *Financial support:* In 2016–17, 7 students received support, including 3 teaching assistantships. Support available to part-time students. Financial award application deadline: 4/1; financial award applicants required to submit FAFSA. *Unit head:* Dr. David Thornton, Head, 256-782-5359, E-mail: thornton@jsu.edu. *Application contact:* Dr. Jean Pugliese, Associate Dean, 256-782-8278, Fax: 256-782-5321, E-mail: pugliese@jsu.edu.

James Madison University, The Graduate School, College of Integrated Science and Engineering, Program in Computer Science, Harrisonburg, VA 22802. Offers digital forensics (MS); information security (MS). *Program availability:* Online learning. *Faculty:* 15 full-time (1 woman), 1 part-time/adjunct (0 women). *Students:* 7 full-time (3 women), 21 part-time (4 women); includes 6 minority (3 Black or African American, non-Hispanic/Latino; 1 Asian, non-Hispanic/Latino; 1 Hispanic/Latino; 1 Two or more races, non-Hispanic/Latino), 3 international. Average age 30. 29 applicants, 97% accepted, 18 enrolled. In 2016, 15 master's awarded. Application fee: $55. Electronic applications accepted. *Financial support:* Fellowships, Federal Work-Study, and 3 assistantships (averaging $7911) available. Financial award application deadline: 3/1; financial award applicants required to submit FAFSA. *Unit head:* Dr. Sharon J. Simmons, Department Head, 540-568-4196, E-mail: simmonsj@jmu.edu. *Application contact:* Lynette D. Michael, Director of Graduate Admissions, 540-568-6131 Ext. 6395, Fax: 540-568-7860, E-mail: michaeld@jmu.edu. Website: http://www.jmu.edu/cs/

Johns Hopkins University, Engineering Program for Professionals, Part-time Program in Computer Science, Baltimore, MD 21218. Offers communications and networking (MS); computer science (Post-Master's Certificate). *Program availability:* Part-time, evening/weekend, 100% online, blended/hybrid learning. *Faculty:* 48 part-time/adjunct (7 women). *Students:* 15 full-time (3 women), 437 part-time (75 women); includes 79 minority (14 Black or African American, non-Hispanic/Latino; 31 Asian, non-Hispanic/Latino; 28 Hispanic/Latino; 1 Native Hawaiian or other Pacific Islander, non-Hispanic/Latino; 5 Two or more races, non-Hispanic/Latino), 17 international. Average age 29. 290 applicants, 34% accepted, 76 enrolled. In 2016, 131 master's awarded. *Entrance requirements:* Additional exam requirements/recommendations for international students: Required—TOEFL (minimum score 600 paper-based; 100 iBT). *Application deadline:* Applications are processed on a rolling basis. Application fee: $0. Electronic applications accepted. *Unit head:* Dr. Thomas A. Longstaff, Program Chair, 443-778-9389, E-mail: thomas.longstaff@jhuapl.edu. *Application contact:* Doug Schiller, Admissions Director, 410-516-2300, Fax: 410-579-8049, E-mail: schiller@jhu.edu.
Website: http://www.ep.jhu.edu/

Johns Hopkins University, Engineering Program for Professionals, Part-time Program in Electrical and Computer Engineering, Baltimore, MD 21218. Offers communications and networking (MS); electrical and computer engineering (Graduate Certificate, Post-Master's Certificate); photonics (MS). *Program availability:* Part-time, evening/weekend, 100% online, blended/hybrid learning. *Faculty:* 48 part-time/adjunct (2 women). *Students:* 5 full-time (0 women), 303 part-time (52 women); includes 63 minority (11 Black or African American, non-Hispanic/Latino; 24 Asian, non-Hispanic/Latino; 24 Hispanic/Latino; 4 Two or more races, non-Hispanic/Latino). Average age 28. 108 applicants, 68% accepted, 53 enrolled. In 2016, 78 master's, 2 other advanced degrees awarded. *Degree requirements:* For master's and other advanced degree, thesis optional. *Entrance requirements:* Additional exam requirements/recommendations for international students: Required—TOEFL (minimum score 600 paper-based; 100 iBT). *Application deadline:* Applications are processed on a rolling basis. Application fee: $0. Electronic applications accepted. *Unit head:* Dr. Brian Jennison, Program Chair, 443-778-6421, E-mail: brian.jennison@jhuapl.edu. *Application contact:* Doug Schiller, Admissions Director, 410-516-2300, Fax: 410-579-8049, E-mail: schiller@jhu.edu.
Website: http://www.ep.jhu.edu/

Johns Hopkins University, G. W. C. Whiting School of Engineering, Department of Computer Science, Baltimore, MD 21218. Offers MSE, MSSI, PhD. *Faculty:* 34 full-time (6 women), 9 part-time/adjunct (1 woman). *Students:* 194 full-time (37 women), 23 part-time (4 women); includes 20 minority (1 Black or African American, non-Hispanic/Latino; 13 Asian, non-Hispanic/Latino; 4 Hispanic/Latino; 2 Two or more races, non-Hispanic/Latino), 128 international. Average age 26. 866 applicants, 23% accepted, 84 enrolled. In 2016, 46 master's, 18 doctorates awarded. Terminal master's awarded for partial completion of doctoral program. *Degree requirements:* For master's, thesis optional; for doctorate, comprehensive exam, thesis/dissertation, oral exam. *Entrance requirements:* For master's, GRE General Test, 2 letters of recommendation, statement of purpose, transcripts; for doctorate, GRE General Test, 3 letters of recommendation, statement of purpose, transcripts. Additional exam requirements/recommendations for international students: Required—TOEFL (minimum score 600 paper-based, 100 iBT) or IELTS (7). *Application deadline:* For fall admission, 12/15 for domestic students, 2/15 for international students; for spring admission, 11/15 for domestic students, 9/15 for international students. Application fee: $75. Electronic applications accepted. *Financial support:* In 2016–17, 128 students received support, including 8 fellowships with full and partial tuition reimbursements available (averaging $31,800 per year), 99 research assistantships with full tuition reimbursements available (averaging $31,200 per year), 21 teaching assistantships with full tuition reimbursements available (averaging $23,400 per year); institutionally sponsored loans, scholarships/grants, health care benefits, tuition waivers (partial), and unspecified assistantships also available. Financial award application deadline: 12/15. *Faculty research:* Theory and programming languages, systems, information security, machine learning and data intensive computing, language and speech processing, computational biology and medicine, Robotics, Vision and Graphics. *Total annual research expenditures:* $15.1 million. *Unit head:* Dr. Yair Amir, Chair, 301-806-4803, Fax: 410-516-6134, E-mail: yairamir@cs.jhu.edu. *Application contact:* Zach Burwell, Academic Program Administrator, 410-516-7451, Fax: 410-516-6134, E-mail: zburwel1@jhu.edu.
Website: http://www.cs.jhu.edu/

Johns Hopkins University, G. W. C. Whiting School of Engineering, Master of Science in Engineering Management Program, Baltimore, MD 21218. Offers biomaterials (MSEM); civil engineering (MSEM); communications science (MSEM); computer science (MSEM); environmental systems analysis, economics and public policy (MSEM); fluid mechanics (MSEM); materials science and engineering (MSEM); mechanical engineering (MSEM); mechanics and materials (MSEM); nano-biotechnology (MSEM); nanomaterials and nanotechnology (MSEM); operations research (MSEM); probability and statistics (MSEM); smart product and device design (MSEM). *Faculty:* 7 full-time (4 women), 1 part-time/adjunct (0 women). *Students:* 35 full-time (14 women), 8 part-time (3 women); includes 7 minority (4 Asian, non-Hispanic/Latino; 3 Hispanic/Latino), 26 international. Average age 24. 228 applicants, 28% accepted, 25 enrolled. In 2016, 18 master's awarded. *Entrance requirements:* For master's, GRE, 3 letters of recommendation, statement of purpose, transcripts. Additional exam requirements/recommendations for international students: Required—TOEFL (minimum score 600 paper-based, 100 iBT) or IELTS (7). *Application deadline:* For fall admission, 2/1 for domestic and international students. Application fee: $75. Electronic applications accepted. *Financial support:* Fellowships and health care benefits available. *Unit head:* Dr. Pamela Sheff, Director, 410-516-7056, Fax: 410-516-4880, E-mail: pamsheff@gmail.com. *Application contact:* Richard Helman, Director of Graduate Admissions, 410-516-8174, Fax: 410-516-0780, E-mail: graduateadmissions@jhu.edu.
Website: http://engineering.jhu.edu/msem/

Computer Science

Kansas State University, Graduate School, College of Engineering, Department of Computer Science, Manhattan, KS 66506. Offers MS, MSE, PhD. *Program availability:* Part-time, online learning. *Faculty:* 17 full-time (1 woman), 5 part-time/adjunct (2 women). *Students:* 53 full-time (15 women), 13 part-time (2 women); includes 1 minority (Two or more races, non-Hispanic/Latino), 54 international. Average age 26. 131 applicants, 29% accepted, 16 enrolled. In 2016, 15 master's, 7 doctorates awarded. Terminal master's awarded for partial completion of doctoral program. *Degree requirements:* For master's, thesis or alternative; for doctorate, thesis/dissertation. *Entrance requirements:* For master's, GRE General Test, bachelor's degree in computer science, minimum GPA of 3.0; for doctorate, GRE General Test, master's degree in computer science or bachelor's degree and strong advanced computer knowledge. Additional exam requirements/recommendations for international students: Required—TOEFL (minimum score 575 paper-based; 90 iBT), IELTS, or PTE. *Application deadline:* For fall admission, 2/1 priority date for domestic students, 1/1 priority date for international students; for spring admission, 9/1 priority date for domestic students, 8/1 priority date for international students. Applications are processed on a rolling basis. Application fee: $50 ($75 for international students). Electronic applications accepted. *Expenses:* Tuition, state resident: full-time $9670. Tuition, nonresident: full-time $21,828. *Required fees:* $862. *Financial support:* In 2016–17, 23 research assistantships with tuition reimbursements (averaging $21,900 per year), 25 teaching assistantships with full tuition reimbursements (averaging $14,208 per year) were awarded; fellowships, career-related internships or fieldwork, institutionally sponsored loans, scholarships/grants, health care benefits, and unspecified assistantships also available. Support available to part-time students. Financial award application deadline: 3/15; financial award applicants required to submit FAFSA. *Faculty research:* High-assurance software and programming languages, data mining, parallel and distributed computing, computer security, embedded systems. *Total annual research expenditures:* $3.2 million. *Unit head:* Dr. Scott DeLoach, Interim Head, 785-532-6350, Fax: 785-532-7353, E-mail: sdeloach@ksu.edu. *Application contact:* Ami Ratzlaff, Program Coordinator, 785-532-6350, Fax: 785-532-7353, E-mail: cis-gradapps@ksu.edu.
Website: http://www.cis.k-state.edu/

Kennesaw State University, College of Computing and Software Engineering, Department of Computer Science, Kennesaw, GA 30144. Offers MS. *Program availability:* Part-time, online learning. *Degree requirements:* For master's, thesis optional. *Entrance requirements:* For master's, GMAT or GRE, minimum GPA of 2.75. Additional exam requirements/recommendations for international students: Required—TOEFL (minimum score 550 paper-based; 80 iBT), IELTS (minimum score 6.5). Electronic applications accepted. *Expenses:* Contact institution.

Kent State University, College of Arts and Sciences, Department of Computer Science, Kent, OH 44242-0001. Offers MA, MS, PhD. *Program availability:* Part-time. *Faculty:* 17 full-time (3 women). *Students:* 164 full-time (61 women), 31 part-time (12 women); includes 5 minority (1 Black or African American, non-Hispanic/Latino; 3 Asian, non-Hispanic/Latino; 1 Two or more races, non-Hispanic/Latino), 180 international. Average age 30. 623 applicants, 33% accepted, 38 enrolled. In 2016, 108 master's, 10 doctorates awarded. *Degree requirements:* For master's, thesis (for some programs); for doctorate, comprehensive exam, thesis/dissertation, preliminary examination, two public presentations of project/research work. *Entrance requirements:* For master's, GRE, minimum undergraduate GPA of 3.0, transcript, goal statement, 3 letters of recommendation; for doctorate, GRE, minimum undergraduate GPA of 3.0, transcript, goal statement, 3 letters of recommendation, master's degree in computer science or similar field. Additional exam requirements/recommendations for international students: Required—TOEFL (minimum score of 525 paper-based, 71 iBT), IELTS (minimum score of 6), Michigan English Language Assessment Battery (minimum score of 75), or PTE (minimum score of 48). *Application deadline:* For fall admission, 6/1 for domestic and international students; for spring admission, 10/10 for domestic and international students. Applications are processed on a rolling basis. Application fee: $45 ($70 for international students). Electronic applications accepted. *Expenses:* Tuition, state resident: full-time $10,864; part-time $495 per credit hour. Tuition, nonresident: full-time $18,380; part-time $837 per credit hour. *Financial support:* Fellowships with full tuition reimbursements, research assistantships with full tuition reimbursements, teaching assistantships with full tuition reimbursements, Federal Work-Study, and unspecified assistantships available. Financial award application deadline: 1/31. *Unit head:* Dr. Javed Khan, Professor and Chair, 330-672-9038, E-mail: javed@kent.edu. *Application contact:* Dr. Chen Chang Lu, Professor/Assistant Chair/Graduate Advisor, 330-672-9031, Fax: 330-672-0737, E-mail: clu@kent.edu.
Website: http://www.kent.edu/cs

Kentucky State University, College of Agriculture, Food Science and Sustainable Systems, Frankfort, KY 40601. Offers aquaculture (MS); environmental studies (MS). *Program availability:* Part-time, evening/weekend. *Faculty:* 9 full-time (0 women). *Students:* 31 full-time (13 women), 14 part-time (9 women); includes 10 minority (7 Black or African American, non-Hispanic/Latino; 1 Asian, non-Hispanic/Latino; 1 Hispanic/Latino; 1 Two or more races, non-Hispanic/Latino), 6 international. Average age 31. 21 applicants, 76% accepted, 14 enrolled. In 2016, 9 master's awarded. *Degree requirements:* For master's, comprehensive exam, thesis. *Entrance requirements:* For master's, GRE, GMAT, essay, resume, transcript, recommendation. Additional exam requirements/recommendations for international students: Required—TOEFL (minimum score 500 paper-based; 61 iBT). *Application deadline:* For fall admission, 7/1 for domestic students, 4/1 for international students; for spring admission, 11/15 for domestic students, 8/15 for international students; for summer admission, 5/1 for domestic students, 2/1 for international students. Applications are processed on a rolling basis. Application fee: $30 ($100 for international students). Electronic applications accepted. *Expenses:* Tuition, state resident: full-time $7524; part-time $418 per credit hour. Tuition, nonresident: full-time $11,322; part-time $629 per credit hour. Tuition and fees vary according to course load. *Financial support:* In 2016–17, 41 students received support, including 31 research assistantships (averaging $21,112 per year); scholarships/grants, tuition waivers (partial), and unspecified assistantships also available. Financial award application deadline: 4/15; financial award applicants required to submit FAFSA. *Faculty research:* Apiculture-honeybee, biotechnology and plant stress, insect management and ecology, fruit horticulture and plant genetics, sustainable and organic vegetable production. *Total annual research expenditures:* $9.6 million. *Unit head:* Dr. Kirk Pomper, Interim Director of Land Grant Programs, 502-597-5942, E-mail: kirk.pomper@kysu.edu. *Application contact:* Dr. James Obielodan, Director of Graduate Studies, 502-597-4723, E-mail: james.obielodan@kysu.edu.
Website: http://www.kysu.edu/academics/CAFSSS/

Kentucky State University, College of Business and Computer Science, Frankfort, KY 40601. Offers business administration (MBA); computer science technology (MS). *Accreditation:* ACBSP. *Program availability:* Part-time, evening/weekend. *Faculty:* 8 full-time (1 woman), 1 part-time/adjunct (0 women). *Students:* 29 full-time (8 women), 18 part-time (5 women); includes 18 minority (13 Black or African American, non-Hispanic/Latino; 5 Asian, non-Hispanic/Latino), 10 international. Average age 33. 39 applicants, 72% accepted, 20 enrolled. In 2016, 15 master's awarded. *Degree requirements:* For master's, comprehensive exam, thesis optional. *Entrance requirements:* For master's, GMAT, GRE, letters of recommendation, essay, transcript. Additional exam requirements/recommendations for international students: Required—TOEFL (minimum score 525 paper-based). *Application deadline:* For fall admission, 7/1 for domestic students, 4/1 for international students; for spring admission, 11/15 for domestic students, 8/15 for international students; for summer admission, 5/1 for domestic students, 2/1 for international students. Applications are processed on a rolling basis. Application fee: $30 ($100 for international students). Electronic applications accepted. *Expenses:* Tuition, state resident: full-time $7524; part-time $418 per credit hour. Tuition, nonresident: full-time $11,322; part-time $629 per credit hour. Tuition and fees vary according to course load. *Financial support:* In 2016–17, 43 students received support, including 5 research assistantships (averaging $9,200 per year); scholarships/grants, tuition waivers (partial), and unspecified assistantships also available. Financial award application deadline: 4/15; financial award applicants required to submit FAFSA. *Total annual research expenditures:* $303,741. *Unit head:* Dr. Candice L. Jackson, Vice President of Academic Affairs, 502-597-6442, E-mail: candice.jackson@kysu.edu. *Application contact:* Dr. James Obielodan, Director of Graduate Studies, 502-597-4723, E-mail: james.obielodan@kysu.edu.
Website: http://kysu.edu/academics/college-of-business-and-computer-science/

Knowledge Systems Institute, Program in Computer and Information Sciences, Skokie, IL 60076. Offers MS. *Program availability:* Part-time, evening/weekend, online learning. *Degree requirements:* For master's, comprehensive exam, thesis. *Entrance requirements:* Additional exam requirements/recommendations for international students: Required—TOEFL (minimum score 550 paper-based; 79 iBT). Electronic applications accepted. *Faculty research:* Data mining, web development, database programming and administration.

Kutztown University of Pennsylvania, College of Liberal Arts and Sciences, Program in Computer Science, Kutztown, PA 19530-0730. Offers MS. *Program availability:* Part-time, evening/weekend. *Faculty:* 4 full-time (0 women). *Students:* 10 full-time (3 women), 7 part-time (1 woman); includes 2 minority (1 Black or African American, non-Hispanic/Latino; 1 Asian, non-Hispanic/Latino), 2 international. Average age 26. 15 applicants, 100% accepted, 8 enrolled. In 2016, 10 master's awarded. *Degree requirements:* For master's, comprehensive exam or thesis. *Entrance requirements:* For master's, GRE General Test, 3 letters of recommendation. Additional exam requirements/recommendations for international students: Required—TOEFL (minimum score 550 paper-based, 79 iBT) or IELTS (minimum score 6.5). *Application deadline:* For fall admission, 8/1 for domestic and international students; for spring admission, 12/1 for domestic and international students. Application fee: $35. Electronic applications accepted. *Expenses:* Tuition, state resident: full-time $4347; part-time $483 per credit. Tuition, nonresident: full-time $6525; part-time $725 per credit. *Required fees:* $88 per credit. One-time fee: $50 full-time. *Financial support:* Career-related internships or fieldwork, Federal Work-Study, scholarships/grants, and unspecified assistantships available. Financial award application deadline: 3/1; financial award applicants required to submit FAFSA. *Faculty research:* Artificial intelligence, expert systems, neural networks. *Unit head:* Dr. Lisa Frye, Chairperson, 610-683-4422, Fax: 610-683-4129, E-mail: frye@kutztown.edu.
Website: https://www.kutztown.edu/academics/graduate-programs/computer-science.htm

Lakehead University, Graduate Studies, School of Mathematical Sciences, Thunder Bay, ON P7B 5E1, Canada. Offers computer science (M Sc); mathematical science (MA). *Program availability:* Part-time, evening/weekend. *Degree requirements:* For master's, thesis optional. *Entrance requirements:* For master's, minimum B average, honours degree in mathematics or computer science. Additional exam requirements/recommendations for international students: Required—TOEFL. *Faculty research:* Numerical analysis, classical analysis, theoretical computer science, abstract harmonic analysis, functional analysis.

Lamar University, College of Graduate Studies, College of Arts and Sciences, Department of Computer Science, Beaumont, TX 77710. Offers MS. *Program availability:* Part-time. *Faculty:* 8 full-time (2 women). *Students:* 164 full-time (23 women), 44 part-time (10 women); includes 1 minority (Asian, non-Hispanic/Latino), 205 international. Average age 25. 110 applicants, 82% accepted, 27 enrolled. In 2016, 95 master's awarded. *Degree requirements:* For master's, comprehensive exams and project or thesis. *Entrance requirements:* For master's, GRE General Test, minimum GPA of 3.3 in last 60 hours of undergraduate course work or 3.0 overall. Additional exam requirements/recommendations for international students: Required—TOEFL (minimum score 550 paper-based; 79 iBT), IELTS (minimum score 6.5). *Application deadline:* For fall admission, 8/10 for domestic students, 7/1 for international students; for spring admission, 1/5 for domestic students, 12/1 for international students. Applications are processed on a rolling basis. Application fee: $25 ($50 for international students). *Expenses:* $8,134 in-state full-time, $5,574 in-state part-time; $15,604 out-of-state full-time, $10,554 out-of-state part-time per year. *Financial support:* Research assistantships with partial tuition reimbursements, teaching assistantships with partial tuition reimbursements, institutionally sponsored loans, scholarships/grants, and tuition waivers (partial) available. Financial award application deadline: 4/1; financial award applicants required to submit FAFSA. *Faculty research:* Computer architecture, network security. *Unit head:* Dr. Stefan Andrei, Chair, 409-880-8775, Fax: 409-880-2364. *Application contact:* Deidre Mayer, Interim Director, Admissions and Academic Services, 409-880-8888, Fax: 409-880-7419, E-mail: gradmissions@lamar.edu.
Website: http://artssciences.lamar.edu/computer-science

La Salle University, School of Arts and Sciences, Program in Computer Information Science, Philadelphia, PA 19141-1199. Offers application development (Certificate); computer information science (MS). *Program availability:* Part-time, evening/weekend, online only, 100% online. *Faculty:* 1 (woman) full-time, 1 part-time/adjunct (0 women). *Students:* 15 part-time (4 women); includes 4 minority (2 Black or African American, non-Hispanic/Latino; 1 Hispanic/Latino; 1 Two or more races, non-Hispanic/Latino). Average age 30. 4 applicants, 100% accepted, 3 enrolled. In 2016, 2 other advanced degrees awarded. *Degree requirements:* For master's, capstone project. *Entrance requirements:* For master's, GRE, MAT, or GMAT, minimum undergraduate GPA of 3.0; two letters of recommendation; resume; telephone or in-person interview. Additional exam requirements/recommendations for international students: Required—TOEFL. *Application deadline:* For fall admission, 8/15 priority date for domestic students, 7/15 for international students; for spring admission, 12/15 priority date for domestic students, 11/15 for international students; for summer admission, 4/15 priority date for domestic students, 3/15 for international students. Applications are processed on a rolling basis. Application fee: $35. Electronic applications accepted. Application fee is waived when completed online. *Expenses:* Contact institution. *Financial support:* In 2016–17, 3 students received support. Scholarships/grants available. Support available to part-time students. Financial award application deadline: 8/31; financial award applicants required to submit FAFSA. *Faculty research:* Human-computer interaction, networks, technology trends, databases, groupware. *Unit head:* Margaret M. McCoey, Director, 215-951-1136, Fax: 215-951-1805, E-mail: itleader@lasalle.edu. *Application contact:* Elizabeth Heenan, Director, Graduate and Adult Enrollment, 215-951-1100, Fax: 215-951-1462, E-mail: heenan@lasalle.edu.
Website: http://www.lasalle.edu/computer-information-science/

Lawrence Technological University, College of Arts and Sciences, Southfield, MI 48075-1058. Offers bioinformatics (Graduate Certificate); computer science (MS), including data science, big data, and data mining, intelligent systems; instructional design, communication, and presentation (Graduate Certificate); instructional technology (Graduate Certificate); premedical studies (Graduate Certificate); technical and professional communication (MS, Graduate Certificate); writing for the digital age (Graduate Certificate). *Program availability:* Part-time, evening/weekend. *Faculty:* 6 full-time (2 women), 10 part-time/adjunct (5 women). *Students:* 37 part-time (18 women); includes 4 minority (1 Black or African American, non-Hispanic/Latino; 1 Asian, non-Hispanic/Latino; 2 Hispanic/Latino), 8 international. Average age 33. 301 applicants, 23% accepted, 9 enrolled. In 2016, 22 master's, 2 other advanced degrees awarded. *Degree requirements:* For master's, thesis (for some programs). *Entrance requirements:* Additional exam requirements/recommendations for international students: Required—TOEFL (minimum score 550 paper-based; 79 iBT), IELTS (minimum score 6.5). *Application deadline:* For fall admission, 5/22 for international students; for spring admission, 10/11 for international students; for summer admission, 2/16 for international students. Applications are processed on a rolling basis. Application fee: $50. Electronic applications accepted. *Expenses: Tuition:* Full-time $14,868; part-time $1062 per credit. *Required fees:* $75 per semester. Tuition and fees vary according to campus/location. *Financial support:* In 2016–17, 9 students received support. Scholarships/grants and tuition reduction available. Financial award application deadline: 4/1; financial award applicants required to submit FAFSA. *Faculty research:* Computer analysis of visual art, psychology of numbers games, neural basis of moral judgement, synthesis of glycosylated warfarin analogs for potential use as antiviral drugs, observation of chemotaxis behavior in c. elegans. *Total annual research expenditures:* $530,625. *Unit head:* Dr. Hsiao-Ping Moore, Dean, 248-204-3500, Fax: 248-204-3518, E-mail: scidean@ltu.edu. *Application contact:* Jane Rohrback, Director of Admissions, 248-204-3160, Fax: 248-204-2228, E-mail: admissions@ltu.edu.

Lebanese American University, School of Arts and Sciences, Beirut, Lebanon. Offers computer science (MS); international affairs (MA).

Lehigh University, P.C. Rossin College of Engineering and Applied Science, Department of Computer Science and Engineering, Bethlehem, PA 18015. Offers computer engineering (M Eng, MS, PhD); computer science (M Eng, MS, PhD); MBA/E. *Program availability:* Part-time. *Faculty:* 16 full-time (2 women), 2 part-time/adjunct (both women). *Students:* 44 full-time (6 women), 4 part-time (1 woman); includes 2 minority (1 Asian, non-Hispanic/Latino; 1 Hispanic/Latino), 35 international. Average age 25. 226 applicants, 31% accepted, 16 enrolled. In 2016, 24 master's, 3 doctorates awarded. Terminal master's awarded for partial completion of doctoral program. *Degree requirements:* For master's, thesis optional, oral presentation of thesis; for doctorate, thesis/dissertation, qualifying, general, and oral exams. *Entrance requirements:* For master's, GRE General Test, minimum GPA of 3.0; for doctorate, GRE General Test, minimum GPA of 3.5. Additional exam requirements/recommendations for international students: Required—TOEFL (minimum score 550 paper-based; 79 iBT), IELTS (minimum score 6.5). *Application deadline:* For fall admission, 4/1 for domestic and international students; for spring admission, 11/1 for domestic and international students. Application fee: $75. Electronic applications accepted. *Expenses:* $1,420 per credit hour. *Financial support:* In 2016–17, 24 students received support, including 1 fellowship with full tuition reimbursement available (averaging $21,105 per year), 5 research assistantships with full tuition reimbursements available (averaging $21,033 per year), 6 teaching assistantships with full tuition reimbursements available (averaging $21,530 per year). Financial award application deadline: 1/15. *Faculty research:* Artificial intelligence, networking-pattern recognition, multimedia e-learning/data mining/web search, mobile robotics, bioinformatics, computer vision, data science. *Total annual research expenditures:* $1.1 million. *Unit head:* Dr. Daniel P. Lopresti, Chair, 610-758-5782, Fax: 610-758-4096, E-mail: dal9@lehigh.edu. *Application contact:* Heidi Wegrzyn, Graduate Coordinator, 610-758-3065, Fax: 610-758-4096, E-mail: hew207@lehigh.edu.
Website: http://www.cse.lehigh.edu/

Lehman College of the City University of New York, School of Natural and Social Sciences, Department of Mathematics and Computer Science, Program in Computer Science, Bronx, NY 10468-1589. Offers MS. *Degree requirements:* For master's, one foreign language, thesis or alternative.

Long Island University–LIU Brooklyn, School of Business, Public Administration and Information Sciences, Brooklyn, NY 11201-8423. Offers accounting (MBA); accounting (MS); business administration (MBA); computer science (MS); gerontology (Advanced Certificate); health administration (MPA); human resources management (MS); not-for-profit management (Advanced Certificate); public administration (MPA); taxation (MS). *Program availability:* Part-time, evening/weekend, blended/hybrid learning. *Faculty:* 18 full-time (9 women), 32 part-time/adjunct (10 women). *Students:* 275 full-time (150 women), 238 part-time (161 women); includes 281 minority (200 Black or African American, non-Hispanic/Latino; 2 American Indian or Alaska Native, non-Hispanic/Latino; 38 Asian, non-Hispanic/Latino; 36 Hispanic/Latino; 1 Native Hawaiian or other Pacific Islander, non-Hispanic/Latino; 4 Two or more races, non-Hispanic/Latino), 140 international. 796 applicants, 66% accepted, 143 enrolled. In 2016, 185 master's, 17 other advanced degrees awarded. *Entrance requirements:* Additional exam requirements/recommendations for international students: Required—TOEFL (minimum score 527 paper-based; 75 iBT). *Application deadline:* Applications are processed on a rolling basis. Application fee: $50. Electronic applications accepted. *Expenses: Tuition:* Full-time $28,272; part-time $1178 per credit. *Required fees:* $451 per term. Tuition and fees vary according to degree level, program and student level. *Financial support:* In 2016–17, 94 students received support. Career-related internships or fieldwork, Federal Work-Study, institutionally sponsored loans, scholarships/grants, and unspecified assistantships available. Support available to part-time students. Financial award application deadline: 2/15; financial award applicants required to submit FAFSA. *Faculty research:* Corporate social responsibility; executive compensation and corporate governance; combinatorics; secure mobile coding; social equity and justice, particularly among the Latino population; public and healthcare finance. *Unit head:* Dr. Edward Rogoff, Dean, 718-488-1159, E-mail: edward.rogoff@liu.edu. *Application contact:* Gabrielle Gannon, Director of Graduate Admissions, 718-488-1011, Fax: 718-780-6110, E-mail: bkln-admissions@liu.edu.
Website: http://liu.edu/Brooklyn/Academics/School-of-Business-Public-Administration-and-Information-Sciences

Louisiana State University and Agricultural & Mechanical College, Graduate School, College of Engineering, Division of Computer Science, Baton Rouge, LA 70803. Offers computer science (MSSS, PhD); systems science (MSSS).

Louisiana State University in Shreveport, College of Arts and Sciences, Program in Computer Systems Technology, Shreveport, LA 71115-2399. Offers MS. *Program availability:* Part-time, evening/weekend. *Students:* 7 full-time (1 woman), 11 part-time (2 women); includes 5 minority (1 Black or African American, non-Hispanic/Latino; 2 Asian, non-Hispanic/Latino; 1 Hispanic/Latino; 1 Two or more races, non-Hispanic/Latino). Average age 31. 22 applicants, 95% accepted, 5 enrolled. In 2016, 5 master's awarded. *Degree requirements:* For master's, comprehensive exam (for some programs), thesis or alternative. *Entrance requirements:* For master's, GRE, programming course in high-level language, interview. Additional exam requirements/recommendations for international students: Required—TOEFL (minimum score 550 paper-based; 80 iBT). *Application deadline:* For fall admission, 6/30 for domestic and international students; for spring admission, 11/30 for domestic and international students; for summer admission, 4/30 for domestic and international students. Applications are processed on a rolling basis. Application fee: $20 ($30 for international students). Electronic applications accepted. *Expenses:* Tuition, state resident: full-time $5163; part-time $350 per credit hour. Tuition, nonresident: full-time $15,578; part-time $1038 per credit hour. *Required fees:* $63 per credit hour. Tuition and fees vary according to course load and program. *Financial support:* In 2016–17, 2 research assistantships (averaging $5,000 per year) were awarded. Financial award applicants required to submit FAFSA. *Unit head:* Dr. Alfred McKinney, Program Director, 318-797-5300, Fax: 318-795-2419, E-mail: alfred.mckinney@lsus.edu. *Application contact:* Mary Catherine Harvison, Director of Admissions, 318-797-2400, Fax: 318-797-5286, E-mail: mary.harvison@lsus.edu.

Louisiana Tech University, Graduate School, College of Engineering and Science, Department of Computer Science, Ruston, LA 71272. Offers computational analysis and modeling (PhD); computer science (MS). *Program availability:* Part-time. *Degree requirements:* For master's, thesis or alternative. *Entrance requirements:* For master's, GRE General Test, minimum GPA of 3.0 in last 60 hours. Additional exam requirements/recommendations for international students: Required—TOEFL. *Application deadline:* For fall admission, 8/1 for domestic students; for spring admission, 2/1 for domestic students. Applications are processed on a rolling basis. Application fee: $20 ($30 for international students). *Financial support:* Research assistantships, Federal Work-Study, and unspecified assistantships available. Financial award application deadline: 4/1. *Faculty research:* Computer systems organization, artificial intelligence, expert systems, graphics, program language. *Unit head:* Dr. Jean Gourd, Program Chair, 318-257-4301, Fax: 318-257-4922. *Application contact:* Marilyn J. Robinson, Assistant to the Dean, 318-257-2924, Fax: 318-257-4487.
Website: http://coes.latech.edu/cs/

Loyola University Chicago, Graduate School, Department of Computer Science, Chicago, IL 60611. Offers computer science (MS); information technology (MS); software engineering (MS). *Program availability:* Part-time, evening/weekend, 100% online, blended/hybrid learning. *Faculty:* 15 full-time (3 women), 10 part-time/adjunct (2 women). *Students:* 64 full-time (33 women), 50 part-time (14 women); includes 24 minority (7 Black or African American, non-Hispanic/Latino; 10 Asian, non-Hispanic/Latino; 5 Hispanic/Latino; 2 Two or more races, non-Hispanic/Latino), 56 international. Average age 28. 135 applicants, 43% accepted, 39 enrolled. In 2016, 49 master's awarded. *Degree requirements:* For master's, thesis optional, ten courses. *Entrance requirements:* For master's, 3 letters of recommendation, transcripts, statement of purpose. Additional exam requirements/recommendations for international students: Required—TOEFL (minimum score 550 paper-based; 79 iBT) or IELTS (minimum score 6.5). *Application deadline:* Applications are processed on a rolling basis. Application fee: $50. Electronic applications accepted. Application fee is waived when completed online. *Expenses:* $1,033 per credit hour. *Financial support:* In 2016–17, 17 students received support, including 2 fellowships with full tuition reimbursements available, 1 research assistantship with full tuition reimbursement available (averaging $17,000 per year), 11 teaching assistantships with partial tuition reimbursements available (averaging $9,575 per year); career-related internships or fieldwork, Federal Work-Study, health care benefits, and tuition waivers (full and partial) also available. Financial award application deadline: 3/15. *Faculty research:* Software engineering, machine learning, algorithms and complexity, parallel and distributed computing, databases and computer networks. *Total annual research expenditures:* $22,000. *Unit head:* Dr. Konstantin Laufer, Chair, 312-915-7983, Fax: 312-915-7998, E-mail: laufer@cs.luc.edu. *Application contact:* Cecilia Murphy, Graduate Program Secretary, 312-915-7990, Fax: 312-915-7998, E-mail: csinfo@cs.luc.edu.
Website: http://cs.luc.edu

Maharishi University of Management, Graduate Studies, Program in Computer Science, Fairfield, IA 52557. Offers MS. *Degree requirements:* For master's, thesis or alternative. *Entrance requirements:* For master's, GRE General Test, minimum GPA of 3.0. Additional exam requirements/recommendations for international students: Required—TOEFL. *Faculty research:* Parallel processing, computer systems in architecture.

Marist College, Graduate Programs, School of Computer Science and Mathematics, Poughkeepsie, NY 12601-1387. Offers computer science/software development (MS); information systems (MS, Adv C); technology management (MS). *Program availability:* Part-time, evening/weekend, online learning. *Entrance requirements:* For master's, resume. Additional exam requirements/recommendations for international students: Required—TOEFL (minimum score 550 paper-based; 80 iBT); Recommended—IELTS (minimum score 6.5). Electronic applications accepted. *Faculty research:* Data quality, artificial intelligence, imaging, analysis of algorithms, distributed systems and applications.

Marquette University, Graduate School, College of Arts and Sciences, Department of Mathematics, Statistics, and Computer Science, Milwaukee, WI 53201-1881. Offers bioinformatics (MS); computational sciences (MS, PhD); computing (MS); mathematics education (MS). *Program availability:* Part-time, evening/weekend, online learning. *Faculty:* 33 full-time (9 women), 8 part-time/adjunct (1 woman). *Students:* 21 full-time (5 women), 20 part-time (9 women); includes 6 minority (4 Asian, non-Hispanic/Latino; 2 Two or more races, non-Hispanic/Latino), 21 international. Average age 31. 40 applicants, 55% accepted, 10 enrolled. In 2016, 6 master's, 6 doctorates awarded. Terminal master's awarded for partial completion of doctoral program. *Degree requirements:* For master's, thesis (for some programs), essay with oral presentation; for doctorate, comprehensive exam, thesis/dissertation, qualifying examination. *Entrance requirements:* For master's, official transcripts from all current and previous colleges/universities except Marquette, three letters of recommendation; for doctorate, GRE General Test, official transcripts from all current and previous colleges/universities except Marquette, three letters of recommendation. Additional exam requirements/recommendations for international students: Required—TOEFL (minimum score 530 paper-based). *Application deadline:* For fall admission, 1/15 for domestic and international students. Applications are processed on a rolling basis. Application fee: $50. Electronic applications accepted. *Financial support:* Fellowships, research assistantships with full tuition reimbursements, teaching assistantships with full tuition reimbursements, scholarships/grants, health care benefits, tuition waivers (full and partial), and unspecified assistantships available. Support available to part-time students. Financial award application deadline: 2/15. *Faculty research:* Models of physiological systems, mathematical immunology, computational group theory, mathematical logic, computational science. *Total annual research expenditures:* $836,671. *Unit head:* Dr. Rebecca Sanders, Chair, 414-288-7573, Fax: 414-288-1578. *Application contact:* Dr. Gary Krenz.
Website: http://www.marquette.edu/mscs/grad.shtml

Marquette University, Graduate School, College of Arts and Sciences, Program in Computing, Milwaukee, WI 53201-1881. Offers MS. *Program availability:* Part-time, evening/weekend, online learning. *Students:* 16 full-time (4 women), 39 part-time (11 women); includes 8 minority (2 Black or African American, non-Hispanic/Latino; 4 Asian, non-Hispanic/Latino; 2 Hispanic/Latino), 25 international. Average age 28. 37 applicants, 89% accepted, 11 enrolled. In 2016, 24 master's awarded. *Degree requirements:* For master's, thesis optional, enrollment in the Professional Seminar in

Computing each term. *Entrance requirements:* For master's, official transcripts from all current and previous colleges/universities except Marquette, essay, three letters of reference. Additional exam requirements/recommendations for international students: Required—TOEFL (minimum score 530 paper-based). *Application deadline:* Applications are processed on a rolling basis. Application fee: $50. Electronic applications accepted. *Financial support:* Teaching assistantships available. Financial award application deadline: 2/15. *Unit head:* Dr. Rebecca Sanders, Chair, 414-288-6345. *Application contact:* Dr. Thomas Kaczmarek, Assistant Professor, 414-288-6734.
Website: http://www.comp.mu.edu/

Marshall University, Academic Affairs Division, College of Information Technology and Engineering, Program in Computer Science, Huntington, WV 25755. Offers MS. *Degree requirements:* For master's, thesis or project. *Entrance requirements:* Additional exam requirements/recommendations for international students: Required—IELTS (minimum score 5.5).

Massachusetts Institute of Technology, School of Engineering, Department of Electrical Engineering and Computer Science, Cambridge, MA 02139. Offers computer science (PhD, Sc D, ECS); computer science and engineering (PhD, Sc D); computer science and molecular biology (M Eng); electrical engineering (PhD, Sc D, EE); electrical engineering and computer science (M Eng, SM, PhD, Sc D); SM/MBA. *Faculty:* 116 full-time (18 women). *Students:* 864 full-time (210 women), 3 part-time (1 woman); includes 225 minority (11 Black or African American, non-Hispanic/Latino; 142 Asian, non-Hispanic/Latino; 50 Hispanic/Latino; 22 Two or more races, non-Hispanic/Latino), 406 international. Average age 26. 2,773 applicants, 8% accepted, 128 enrolled. In 2016, 236 master's, 87 doctorates awarded. *Degree requirements:* For master's and other advanced degree, thesis; for doctorate, comprehensive exam, thesis/dissertation. *Entrance requirements:* Additional exam requirements/recommendations for international students: Required—TOEFL, IELTS. *Application deadline:* For fall admission, 12/15 for domestic and international students. Application fee: $75. Electronic applications accepted. *Expenses: Tuition:* Full-time $46,400; part-time $725 per credit. One-time fee: $312 full-time. Full-time tuition and fees vary according to course load and program. *Financial support:* In 2016–17, 825 students received support, including fellowships (averaging $39,000 per year), 526 research assistantships (averaging $36,900 per year), 175 teaching assistantships (averaging $37,500 per year); Federal Work-Study, institutionally sponsored loans, scholarships/grants, traineeships, health care benefits, unspecified assistantships, and resident tutors also available. Support available to part-time students. Financial award application deadline: 5/1; financial award applicants required to submit FAFSA. *Faculty research:* Information systems, circuits, biomedical sciences and engineering, computer science: artificial intelligence, systems, theory. *Total annual research expenditures:* $108.1 million. *Unit head:* Prof. Anantha P. Chandrakasan, Department Head, 617-253-4600, Fax: 617-258-7254, E-mail: hq@eecs.mit.edu. *Application contact:* Graduate Admissions, 617-253-4603, E-mail: grad-ap@eecs.mit.edu.
Website: http://www.eecs.mit.edu/

McGill University, Faculty of Graduate and Postdoctoral Studies, Faculty of Science, School of Computer Science, Montréal, QC H3A 2T5, Canada. Offers M Sc, PhD.

McMaster University, School of Graduate Studies, Faculty of Engineering, Department of Computing and Software, Hamilton, ON L8S 4M2, Canada. Offers computer science (M Sc, PhD); software engineering (M Eng, MA Sc, PhD). *Program availability:* Part-time. *Degree requirements:* For master's, thesis. *Entrance requirements:* Additional exam requirements/recommendations for international students: Required—TOEFL (minimum score 550 paper-based). *Faculty research:* Software engineering; theory of non-sequential systems; parallel and distributed computing; artificial intelligence; complexity, design, and analysis of algorithms; combinatorial computing, especially applications to molecular biology.

McNeese State University, Doré School of Graduate Studies, College of Science, Department of Mathematics, Computer Science, and Statistics, Lake Charles, LA 70609. Offers computer science (MS); mathematics (MS); statistics (MS). *Program availability:* Evening/weekend. *Degree requirements:* For master's, comprehensive exam, thesis or alternative, written exam. *Entrance requirements:* For master's, GRE.

Memorial University of Newfoundland, School of Graduate Studies, Department of Computer Science, St. John's, NL A1C 5S7, Canada. Offers M Sc, PhD. *Program availability:* Part-time. *Degree requirements:* For master's, thesis; for doctorate, comprehensive exam, thesis/dissertation, oral thesis defense. *Entrance requirements:* For master's, GRE (strongly recommended), honors degree in computer science or related field; for doctorate, GRE (strongly recommended), master's degree in computer science. Electronic applications accepted. *Faculty research:* Theoretical computer science, parallel and distributed computing, scientific computing, software systems and artificial intelligence.

Merrimack College, School of Science and Engineering, North Andover, MA 01845-5800. Offers athletic training (MS); civil engineering (MS); community health education (MS); computer science (MS); data science (MS); exercise and sport science (MS); health and wellness management (MS); mechanical engineering (MS), including engineering management. *Program availability:* Part-time, evening/weekend, 100% online. *Faculty:* 16 full-time, 2 part-time/adjunct. *Students:* 88 full-time (32 women), 13 part-time (6 women); includes 6 minority (4 Hispanic/Latino; 2 Two or more races, non-Hispanic/Latino), 39 international. Average age 25. 156 applicants, 67% accepted, 59 enrolled. In 2016, 46 master's awarded. *Degree requirements:* For master's, comprehensive exam, thesis optional, internship or capstone (for some programs). *Entrance requirements:* For master's, official college transcripts, resume, personal statement, 2 recommendations. Additional exam requirements/recommendations for international students: Required—TOEFL (minimum score 84 iBT), IELTS (minimum score 6.5), PTE (minimum score 56). *Application deadline:* For fall admission, 8/14 for domestic students, 7/14 for international students; for spring admission, 1/10 for domestic students, 12/10 for international students; for summer admission, 5/10 for domestic students, 4/10 for international students. Applications are processed on a rolling basis. Application fee: $0. Electronic applications accepted. *Expenses:* Contact institution. *Financial support:* Fellowships with full tuition reimbursements, career-related internships or fieldwork, scholarships/grants, and health care benefits available. Support available to part-time students. Financial award application deadline: 5/1; financial award applicants required to submit FAFSA. *Faculty research:* Viral genomics and evolution (biology), robotics (mechanical engineering), knot theory (mathematics), computer graphics and network security (computer science), water management (civil engineering). *Application contact:* Allison Pena, Graduate Admissions Counselor, 978-837-3563, E-mail: penaa@merrimack.edu.
Website: http://www.merrimack.edu/academics/graduate/

Metropolitan State University, College of Arts and Sciences, St. Paul, MN 55106-5000. Offers computer science (MS); liberal studies (MA); technical communication (MS). *Program availability:* Part-time, evening/weekend. *Entrance requirements:* For master's, minimum GPA of 2.75, resume. Additional exam requirements/recommendations for international students: Required—TOEFL (minimum score 550 paper-based). Electronic applications accepted.

Michigan State University, The Graduate School, College of Engineering, Department of Computer Science and Engineering, East Lansing, MI 48824. Offers computer science (MS, PhD). *Entrance requirements:* Additional exam requirements/recommendations for international students: Required—TOEFL. Electronic applications accepted.

Michigan Technological University, Graduate School, College of Sciences and Arts, Department of Computer Science, Houghton, MI 49931. Offers computational science and engineering (PhD); computer science (MS, PhD); cybersecurity (MS). *Program availability:* Part-time. *Faculty:* 21 full-time, 9 part-time/adjunct. *Students:* 41 full-time (13 women), 6 part-time; includes 1 minority (Two or more races, non-Hispanic/Latino), 32 international. Average age 27. 466 applicants, 19% accepted, 15 enrolled. In 2016, 3 master's, 5 doctorates awarded. *Degree requirements:* For master's, comprehensive exam (for some programs), thesis (for some programs); for doctorate, comprehensive exam, thesis/dissertation. *Entrance requirements:* For master's and doctorate, GRE, statement of purpose, personal statement, official transcripts, 3 letters of recommendation. Additional exam requirements/recommendations for international students: Required—TOEFL (recommended minimum score 90 iBT) or IELTS. *Application deadline:* For fall admission, 5/1 priority date for domestic and international students; for spring admission, 9/1 priority date for domestic and international students. Applications are processed on a rolling basis. Electronic applications accepted. *Expenses:* Contact institution. *Financial support:* In 2016–17, 36 students received support, including 4 fellowships (averaging $15,242 per year), 12 research assistantships with tuition reimbursements available (averaging $15,242 per year), 13 teaching assistantships with tuition reimbursements available (averaging $15,242 per year); career-related internships or fieldwork, Federal Work-Study, scholarships/grants, health care benefits, unspecified assistantships, and cooperative program also available. Financial award applicants required to submit FAFSA. *Faculty research:* Artificial intelligence, graphics/visualization, software engineering, architecture and compiler optimization, human computing interaction. *Total annual research expenditures:* $856,922. *Unit head:* Dr. Min Song, Chair, 906-487-2602, Fax: 906-487-2283, E-mail: mins@mtu.edu. *Application contact:* Cheryl Simpkins, Office Assistant, 906-487-2209, Fax: 906-487-2283, E-mail: cisimpki@mtu.edu.
Website: http://www.mtu.edu/cs/

Middle Tennessee State University, College of Graduate Studies, College of Basic and Applied Sciences, Department of Computer Science, Murfreesboro, TN 37132. Offers MS. *Program availability:* Part-time, evening/weekend, online learning. *Degree requirements:* For master's, comprehensive exam, thesis. *Entrance requirements:* For master's, GRE. Additional exam requirements/recommendations for international students: Required—TOEFL (minimum score 525 paper-based; 71 iBT) or IELTS (minimum score 6). Electronic applications accepted. *Faculty research:* Computational science, parallel processing, artificial intelligence.

Midwestern State University, Billie Doris McAda Graduate School, College of Science and Mathematics, Department of Computer Science, Wichita Falls, TX 76308. Offers MS. *Program availability:* Part-time, evening/weekend. *Degree requirements:* For master's, comprehensive exam, thesis. *Entrance requirements:* For master's, GRE General Test. Additional exam requirements/recommendations for international students: Required—TOEFL (minimum score 573 paper-based). Electronic applications accepted. *Faculty research:* Software engineering, genetic algorithms and graphics, computational epidemiology, new ways of using GPS.

Mills College, Graduate Studies, Program in Computer Science, Oakland, CA 94613-1000. Offers computer science (Certificate); interdisciplinary computer science (MA). *Program availability:* Part-time. *Faculty:* 1 (woman) full-time, 1 part-time/adjunct (0 women). *Students:* 20 full-time (6 women), 2 part-time (1 woman); includes 10 minority (5 Asian, non-Hispanic/Latino; 3 Hispanic/Latino; 2 Two or more races, non-Hispanic/Latino). Average age 27. 21 applicants, 90% accepted, 14 enrolled. In 2016, 2 master's awarded. *Degree requirements:* For master's, thesis. *Entrance requirements:* For master's, three letters of recommendation. Additional exam requirements/recommendations for international students: Required—TOEFL (minimum score 600 paper-based; 100 iBT) or IELTS (minimum score 7). *Application deadline:* For fall admission, 2/1 priority date for domestic students, 12/15 for international students; for spring admission, 11/1 priority date for domestic students, 10/1 for international students. Applications are processed on a rolling basis. Application fee: $50. Electronic applications accepted. *Expenses: Tuition:* Full-time $31,620. *Required fees:* $1118. Tuition and fees vary according to course load, degree level and program. *Financial support:* In 2016–17, 30 students received support, including 15 fellowships with tuition reimbursements available (averaging $4,626 per year), 15 teaching assistantships with tuition reimbursements available (averaging $4,626 per year); career-related internships or fieldwork, institutionally sponsored loans, and scholarships/grants also available. Support available to part-time students. Financial award application deadline: 2/1; financial award applicants required to submit FAFSA. *Faculty research:* Dynamical systems, linear programming, theory of computer viruses, interface design, intelligent tutoring systems. *Total annual research expenditures:* $7,483. *Unit head:* Susan S. Wang, Department Head, 510-430-2138, E-mail: wang@mills.edu. *Application contact:* Robynne Lofton, Director of Admissions, 510-430-3295, Fax: 510-430-2159, E-mail: grad-admission@mills.edu.
Website: http://www.mills.edu/ics

Minnesota State University Mankato, College of Graduate Studies and Research, College of Science, Engineering and Technology, Department of Computer Information Science, Mankato, MN 56001. Offers information technology (MS). *Students:* 43 full-time (19 women), 24 part-time (7 women). *Degree requirements:* For master's, comprehensive exam, thesis or alternative. *Entrance requirements:* For master's, GRE General Test, minimum GPA of 3.0 during previous 2 years. Additional exam requirements/recommendations for international students: Required—TOEFL (minimum score 550 paper-based; 80 iBT). *Application deadline:* For fall admission, 7/1 priority date for domestic students; for spring admission, 11/1 for domestic students. Applications are processed on a rolling basis. Electronic applications accepted. *Financial support:* Research assistantships with full tuition reimbursements, teaching assistantships with full tuition reimbursements, and unspecified assistantships available. Financial award application deadline: 3/15; financial award applicants required to submit FAFSA. *Unit head:* Dr. Leon Tietz, Chair, 507-389-5319, E-mail: leon.tietz@mnsu.edu.
Website: http://cset.mnsu.edu/ist/

Mississippi College, Graduate School, College of Arts and Sciences, School of Science and Mathematics, Department of Computer Science, Clinton, MS 39058. Offers M Ed, MS. *Program availability:* Part-time. *Degree requirements:* For master's, comprehensive exam, thesis or alternative. *Entrance requirements:* For master's, GRE. Additional exam requirements/recommendations for international students: Recommended—TOEFL, IELTS.

Mississippi State University, Bagley College of Engineering, Department of Computer Science and Engineering, Mississippi State, MS 39762. Offers MS, PhD. *Program availability:* Part-time, blended/hybrid learning. *Faculty:* 20 full-time (5 women), 3 part-time/adjunct (0 women). *Students:* 64 full-time (18 women), 14 part-time (0 women); includes 12 minority (6 Black or African American, non-Hispanic/Latino; 3 Asian, non-Hispanic/Latino; 2 Hispanic/Latino; 1 Two or more races, non-Hispanic/Latino), 22

international. Average age 28. 125 applicants, 40% accepted, 26 enrolled. In 2016, 24 master's, 5 doctorates awarded. *Degree requirements:* For master's, thesis optional, comprehensive oral exam; for doctorate, thesis/dissertation, comprehensive oral or written exam. *Entrance requirements:* For master's, GRE, minimum GPA of 2.75; for doctorate, GRE. Additional exam requirements/recommendations for international students: Required—TOEFL (minimum score 550 paper-based; 79 iBT); Recommended—IELTS (minimum score 6.5). *Application deadline:* For fall admission, 7/1 for domestic students, 5/1 for international students; for spring admission, 11/1 for domestic students, 9/1 for international students. Applications are processed on a rolling basis. Application fee: $60. Electronic applications accepted. *Expenses:* Tuition, state resident: full-time $7670; part-time $852.50 per credit hour. Tuition, nonresident: full-time $20,790; part-time $2310.50 per credit hour. Part-time tuition and fees vary according to course load. *Financial support:* In 2016–17, 5 research assistantships with full tuition reimbursements (averaging $16,524 per year), 18 teaching assistantships with full tuition reimbursements (averaging $15,121 per year) were awarded; Federal Work-Study, institutionally sponsored loans, and unspecified assistantships also available. Financial award application deadline: 4/1; financial award applicants required to submit FAFSA. *Faculty research:* Artificial intelligence, software engineering, visualization, high performance computing. *Total annual research expenditures:* $10.5 million. *Unit head:* Dr. Donna Reese, Professor and Department Head, 662-325-2756, Fax: 662-325-8997, E-mail: office@cse.msstate.edu. *Application contact:* Doretta Martin, Senior Admissions Assistant, 662-325-9514, E-mail: dmartin@grad.msstate.edu.
Website: http://www.cse.msstate.edu/

Missouri State University, Graduate College, College of Natural and Applied Sciences, Department of Computer Science, Springfield, MO 65897. Offers natural and applied science (MNAS), including computer science. *Program availability:* Part-time. *Faculty:* 6 full-time (1 woman). *Students:* 3 part-time (1 woman), 2 international. Average age 26. 10 applicants, 10% accepted. In 2016, 2 master's awarded. *Degree requirements:* For master's, comprehensive exam, thesis or alternative. *Entrance requirements:* For master's, GRE, minimum GPA of 3.0. Additional exam requirements/recommendations for international students: Required—TOEFL (minimum score 550 paper-based; 79 iBT), IELTS (minimum score 6). *Application deadline:* For fall admission, 7/20 priority date for domestic students, 5/1 for international students; for spring admission, 12/20 priority date for domestic students, 9/1 for international students. Applications are processed on a rolling basis. Application fee: $35 ($50 for international students). Electronic applications accepted. *Expenses:* Tuition, state resident: full-time $5830. Tuition, nonresident: full-time $10,708. *Required fees:* $1130. Tuition and fees vary according to class time, course level, course load and program. *Financial support:* In 2016–17, 1 teaching assistantship with partial tuition reimbursement (averaging $2,150 per year) was awarded; Federal Work-Study, institutionally sponsored loans, scholarships/grants, and unspecified assistantships also available. Financial award application deadline: 3/31; financial award applicants required to submit FAFSA. *Faculty research:* Floating point numbers, data compression, graph theory. *Unit head:* Dr. Jorge Rebaza, Interim Department Head, 417-836-4157, Fax: 417-836-6659, E-mail: computerscience@missouristate.edu. *Application contact:* Michael Edwards, Coordinator of Graduate Admissions, 417-836-5330, Fax: 417-836-6200, E-mail: michaeledwards@missouristate.edu.
Website: http://computerscience.missouristate.edu/

Missouri University of Science and Technology, Graduate School, Department of Computer Science, Rolla, MO 65409. Offers MS, PhD. *Program availability:* Part-time. Terminal master's awarded for partial completion of doctoral program. *Degree requirements:* For doctorate, thesis/dissertation, departmental qualifying exam. *Entrance requirements:* For master's, GRE General Test (minimum score 700 quantitative, 4 writing); for doctorate, GRE Subject Test (minimum score: quantitative 600, writing 3.5). Additional exam requirements/recommendations for international students: Required—TOEFL (minimum score 550 paper-based). Electronic applications accepted. *Faculty research:* Intelligent systems, artificial intelligence software engineering, distributed systems, database systems, computer systems.

Monmouth University, Graduate Studies, Department of Computer Science, West Long Branch, NJ 07764-1898. Offers computer science (MS); computer science software design and development (Certificate); information systems (MS). *Program availability:* Part-time, evening/weekend. *Degree requirements:* For master's, thesis (for some programs), practicum. *Entrance requirements:* For master's, minimum GPA of 3.0 in major, 2.75 overall; two letters of recommendation; calculus I and II with minimum C grade; two semesters of computer programming within past five years with minimum B grade; undergraduate degree in major that requires substantial component of software development and/or business administration; for Certificate, minimum GPA of 3.0 in major, 2.75 overall; two letters of recommendation; calculus I and II with minimum C grade; two semesters of computer programming within past five years with minimum B grade. Additional exam requirements/recommendations for international students: Required—TOEFL (minimum score 550 paper-based, 79 iBT), IELTS (minimum score 6), Michigan English Language Assessment Battery (minimum score 77) or Certificate of Advanced English (minimum score B2). Electronic applications accepted. *Faculty research:* Databases, natural language processing, protocols, performance analysis, communications networks (systems), cybersecurity.

Monroe College, King Graduate School, Bronx, NY 10468. Offers accounting (MS); business administration (MBA), including entrepreneurship, finance, general business administration, healthcare management, human resources, information technology, marketing; computer science (MS); criminal justice (MS); hospitality management (MS); public health (MPH), including biostatistics and epidemiology, community health, health administration and leadership. *Program availability:* Online learning. Application fee: $50.
Website: https://www.monroecollege.edu/Degrees/King-Graduate-School/

Montana State University, The Graduate School, College of Engineering, Department of Computer Science, Bozeman, MT 59717. Offers computer science (MS, PhD). *Program availability:* Part-time. *Degree requirements:* For master's, comprehensive exam; for doctorate, comprehensive exam, thesis/dissertation. *Entrance requirements:* For master's and doctorate, GRE. Additional exam requirements/recommendations for international students: Required—TOEFL (minimum score 550 paper-based). Electronic applications accepted. *Faculty research:* Applied algorithms, artificial intelligence, data mining, software engineering, Web-based learning, wireless networking and robotics.

Montclair State University, The Graduate School, College of Science and Mathematics, CISCO Certificate Program, Montclair, NJ 07043-1624. Offers Certificate. *Expenses:* Tuition, state resident: part-time $553 per credit. Tuition, nonresident: part-time $854 per credit. *Required fees:* $91 per credit. Tuition and fees vary according to program.

Montclair State University, The Graduate School, College of Science and Mathematics, MS Program in Computer Science, Montclair, NJ 07043-1624. Offers computer science (MS); information technology (MS). *Program availability:* Part-time, evening/weekend. *Degree requirements:* For master's, comprehensive exam, thesis or alternative. *Entrance requirements:* For master's, GRE General Test, 2 letters of recommendation, essay. Additional exam requirements/recommendations for

international students: Required—TOEFL (minimum score 83 iBT) or IELTS (minimum score 6.5). Electronic applications accepted. *Expenses:* Tuition, state resident: part-time $553 per credit. Tuition, nonresident: part-time $854 per credit. *Required fees:* $91 per credit. Tuition and fees vary according to program. *Faculty research:* Software engineering, parallel and distributed systems, artificial intelligence, databases, human-computer interaction.

National University, Academic Affairs, School of Engineering and Computing, La Jolla, CA 92037-1011. Offers computer science (MS), including advanced computing. *Program availability:* Part-time, evening/weekend, 100% online, blended/hybrid learning. *Faculty:* 21 full-time (4 women), 24 part-time/adjunct (5 women). *Students:* 285 full-time (70 women), 107 part-time (33 women); includes 155 minority (49 Black or African American, non-Hispanic/Latino; 2 American Indian or Alaska Native, non-Hispanic/Latino; 44 Asian, non-Hispanic/Latino; 47 Hispanic/Latino; 2 Native Hawaiian or other Pacific Islander, non-Hispanic/Latino; 11 Two or more races, non-Hispanic/Latino), 90 international. Average age 33. In 2016, 273 master's awarded. *Degree requirements:* For master's, thesis (for some programs). *Entrance requirements:* For master's, interview, minimum GPA of 2.5. Additional exam requirements/recommendations for international students: Required—TOEFL (minimum score 550 paper-based; 79 iBT), IELTS (minimum score 6). *Application deadline:* Applications are processed on a rolling basis. Application fee: $60 ($65 for international students). Electronic applications accepted. *Financial support:* Career-related internships or fieldwork, institutionally sponsored loans, scholarships/grants, and tuition waivers (partial) available. Support available to part-time students. Financial award application deadline: 6/30; financial award applicants required to submit FAFSA. *Faculty research:* Educational technology, scholarships in science. *Unit head:* School of Engineering and Computing, 800-628-8648, E-mail: soec@nu.edu. *Application contact:* Brandon Jouganatos, Vice President for Enrollment Services, 800-628-8648, E-mail: advisor@nu.edu.
Website: http://www.nu.edu/OurPrograms/SchoolOfEngineeringAndTechnology.html

Naval Postgraduate School, Departments and Academic Groups, Department of Computer Science, Monterey, CA 93943. Offers computer science (MS, PhD); identity management and cyber security (MA); modeling of virtual environments and simulations (MS, PhD); software engineering (MS, PhD). Program only open to commissioned officers of the United States and friendly nations and selected United States federal civilian employees. *Program availability:* Part-time, online learning. *Degree requirements:* For master's, thesis; for doctorate, thesis/dissertation.

Naval Postgraduate School, Departments and Academic Groups, Space Systems Academic Group, Monterey, CA 93943. Offers applied physics (MS); astronautical engineering (MS); computer science (MS); electrical engineering (MS); mechanical engineering (MS); space systems (Engr); space systems operations (MS). Program only open to commissioned officers of the United States and friendly nations and selected United States federal civilian employees. *Program availability:* Part-time. *Degree requirements:* For master's and Engr, thesis; for doctorate, thesis/dissertation. *Faculty research:* Military applications for space; space reconnaissance and remote sensing; radiation-hardened electronics for space; design, construction and operations of small satellites; satellite communications systems.

New Jersey Institute of Technology, Ying Wu College of Computing, Newark, NJ 07102. Offers big data management and mining (Certificate); business and information systems (Certificate); computer science (MS, PhD), including bioinformatics (MS), computer science, computing and business (MS), cyber security and privacy (MS), software engineering (MS); data mining (Certificate); information security (Certificate); information systems (MS, PhD), including business and information systems (MS), emergency management and business continuity (MS), information systems; information technology administration and security (MS); IT administration (Certificate); network security and information assurance (Certificate); software engineering analysis/design (Certificate); Web systems development (Certificate). *Program availability:* Part-time, evening/weekend. *Faculty:* 64 full-time (10 women), 38 part-time/adjunct (4 women). *Students:* 818 full-time (241 women), 225 part-time (53 women); includes 162 minority (35 Black or African American, non-Hispanic/Latino; 77 Asian, non-Hispanic/Latino; 41 Hispanic/Latino; 9 Two or more races, non-Hispanic/Latino), 772 international. Average age 27. 2,666 applicants, 51% accepted, 377 enrolled. In 2016, 398 master's, 10 doctorates, 9 other advanced degrees awarded. Terminal master's awarded for partial completion of doctoral program. *Degree requirements:* For master's, thesis optional; for doctorate, thesis/dissertation. *Entrance requirements:* For master's, GRE General Test; for doctorate, GRE General Test, minimum graduate GPA of 3.5. Additional exam requirements/recommendations for international students: Required—TOEFL (minimum score 550 paper-based; 79 iBT). *Application deadline:* For fall admission, 6/1 priority date for domestic students, 5/1 priority date for international students; for spring admission, 11/15 priority date for domestic and international students. Applications are processed on a rolling basis. Application fee: $75. Electronic applications accepted. *Expenses:* Contact institution. *Financial support:* In 2016–17, 57 students received support, including 18 research assistantships (averaging $16,073 per year), 39 teaching assistantships (averaging $20,194 per year); fellowships, career-related internships or fieldwork, Federal Work-Study, institutionally sponsored loans, and unspecified assistantships also available. Financial award application deadline: 1/15. *Faculty research:* Computer systems, communications and networking, artificial intelligence, database engineering, systems analysis, analytics and optimization in crowdsourcing. *Total annual research expenditures:* $3 million. *Unit head:* Dr. Craig Gotsman, Dean, 973-542-5488, Fax: 973-596-5777, E-mail: marek.rusinkiewicz@njit.edu. *Application contact:* Stephen Eck, Director of Admissions, 973-596-3300, Fax: 973-596-3461, E-mail: admissions@njit.edu.
Website: http://computing.njit.edu/

New Mexico Highlands University, Graduate Studies, College of Arts and Sciences, Department of Computer Sciences, Las Vegas, NM 87701. Offers media arts and computer science (MS), including computer science. *Degree requirements:* For master's, comprehensive exam, thesis. *Entrance requirements:* For master's, minimum undergraduate GPA of 3.0. Additional exam requirements/recommendations for international students: Required—TOEFL (minimum score 540 paper-based). *Faculty research:* Advanced digital compositing, photographic installations and exhibition design, pattern recognition, parallel and distributed computing, computer security education.

New Mexico Institute of Mining and Technology, Center for Graduate Studies, Department of Computer Science and Engineering, Socorro, NM 87801. Offers computer science (MS, PhD). *Program availability:* Part-time. *Degree requirements:* For master's, thesis optional; for doctorate, thesis/dissertation. *Entrance requirements:* For master's, GRE General Test; for doctorate, GRE General Test, GRE Subject Test. Additional exam requirements/recommendations for international students: Required—TOEFL. Electronic applications accepted.

New Mexico State University, College of Arts and Sciences, Department of Computer Science, Las Cruces, NM 88003. Offers bioinformatics (MS); computer science (MS, PhD). *Program availability:* Part-time. *Faculty:* 11 full-time (2 women). *Students:* 72 full-time (17 women), 18 part-time (8 women); includes 10 minority (1 Black or African American, non-Hispanic/Latino; 1 Asian, non-Hispanic/Latino; 7 Hispanic/Latino; 1 Two or more races, non-Hispanic/Latino), 65 international. Average age 30. 155 applicants,

48% accepted, 8 enrolled. In 2016, 9 master's, 1 doctorate awarded. Terminal master's awarded for partial completion of doctoral program. *Degree requirements:* For master's, comprehensive exam, thesis or alternative; for doctorate, comprehensive exam, thesis/dissertation, qualifying exam, thesis proposal. *Entrance requirements:* For master's and doctorate, BS in computer science. Additional exam requirements/recommendations for international students: Required—TOEFL (minimum score 550 paper-based; 79 iBT), IELTS (minimum score 6.5). *Application deadline:* For fall admission, 3/1 priority date for domestic and international students; for spring admission, 11/1 priority date for domestic and international students. Applications are processed on a rolling basis. Application fee: $40 ($50 for international students). Electronic applications accepted. *Expenses:* Tuition, state resident: full-time $4086. Tuition, nonresident: full-time $14,254. *Required fees:* $853. Tuition and fees vary according to course load. *Financial support:* In 2016–17, 61 students received support, including 2 fellowships (averaging $4,088 per year), 16 research assistantships (averaging $15,325 per year), 30 teaching assistantships (averaging $8,611 per year); career-related internships or fieldwork, Federal Work-Study, scholarships/grants, traineeships, health care benefits, and unspecified assistantships also available. Support available to part-time students. Financial award application deadline: 3/1. *Faculty research:* Bioinformatics, database and data mining, networks and systems optimization, artificial intelligence, human factors and user interfaces. *Total annual research expenditures:* $1.7 million. *Unit head:* Dr. Jonathan Cook, Interim Department Head, 575-646-3723, Fax: 575-646-1002, E-mail: joncook@cs.nmsu.edu. *Application contact:* Dr. Joe Song, Associate Professor, 575-646-3723, Fax: 575-646-1002, E-mail: gradcs@cs.nmsu.edu.
Website: http://www.cs.nmsu.edu/

New York Institute of Technology, School of Engineering and Computing Sciences, Department of Computer Science, Old Westbury, NY 11568-8000. Offers computer science (MS); information, network, and computer security (MS). *Program availability:* Part-time, evening/weekend. *Faculty:* 12 full-time (3 women), 19 part-time/adjunct (3 women). *Students:* 508 full-time (195 women), 158 part-time (43 women); includes 41 minority (6 Black or African American, non-Hispanic/Latino; 25 Asian, non-Hispanic/Latino; 9 Hispanic/Latino; 1 Two or more races, non-Hispanic/Latino), 602 international. Average age 25. 1,654 applicants, 62% accepted, 172 enrolled. In 2016, 342 master's awarded. *Degree requirements:* For master's, thesis or alternative. *Entrance requirements:* For master's, BS or its equivalent from accredited college or university in computer science, engineering, management, mathematics, information technology, liberal arts, and related areas; minimum undergraduate GPA of 2.85. Additional exam requirements/recommendations for international students: Required—TOEFL (minimum score 79 iBT), IELTS (minimum score 6). *Application deadline:* For fall admission, 7/1 for domestic students, 6/1 for international students; for spring admission, 12/1 for domestic and international students. Applications are processed on a rolling basis. Application fee: $50. Electronic applications accepted. *Expenses:* $1,215 per credit. *Financial support:* Fellowships with partial tuition reimbursements, teaching assistantships with partial tuition reimbursements, career-related internships or fieldwork, Federal Work-Study, scholarships/grants, tuition waivers (full and partial), and unspecified assistantships available. Support available to part-time students. Financial award application deadline: 3/1; financial award applicants required to submit FAFSA. *Faculty research:* Active authentication of mobile users; privacy-preserving authentication protocols; sensing cloud system for cybersecurity; cognitive rhythms as a new modality for continuous authentication; cloud-enabled and cloud source disaster detection. *Unit head:* Dr. Frank Lee, Department Chair, 516-686-7456, Fax: 516-686-7439, E-mail: fli@nyit.edu. *Application contact:* Alice Dolitsky, Director, Graduate Admissions, 516-686-7520, Fax: 516-686-1116, E-mail: nyitgrad@nyit.edu.
Website: http://www.nyit.edu/degrees/computer_science_ms

New York University, Graduate School of Arts and Science, Courant Institute of Mathematical Sciences, Department of Computer Science, New York, NY 10012-1019. Offers computer science (MS, PhD); information systems (MS); scientific computing (MS). *Program availability:* Part-time, evening/weekend. *Degree requirements:* For doctorate, thesis/dissertation, oral and written exams. *Entrance requirements:* For master's and doctorate, GRE General Test. Additional exam requirements/recommendations for international students: Required—TOEFL. *Faculty research:* Distributed parallel and secure computing, computer graphics and vision, algorithmic and theory of computation, natural language processing, computational biology.

New York University, Polytechnic School of Engineering, Department of Computer Science and Engineering, Major in Computer Science, New York, NY 10012-1019. Offers MS, PhD. *Program availability:* Part-time, evening/weekend. *Degree requirements:* For master's, comprehensive exam (for some programs), thesis (for some programs); for doctorate, comprehensive exam, thesis/dissertation, qualifying exam. *Entrance requirements:* For master's, BA or BS in computer science, mathematics, science, or engineering; working knowledge of a high-level program; for doctorate, GRE General Test, GRE Subject Test, BA or BS in science, engineering, or management; MS or 1 year of graduate course work. Additional exam requirements/recommendations for international students: Required—TOEFL (minimum score 550 paper-based; 80 iBT); Recommended—IELTS (minimum score 6.5). Electronic applications accepted.

Norfolk State University, School of Graduate Studies, School of Science and Technology, Department of Computer Science, Norfolk, VA 23504. Offers MS.

North Carolina Agricultural and Technical State University, School of Graduate Studies, College of Engineering, Department of Computer Science, Greensboro, NC 27411. Offers MSCS. *Program availability:* Part-time. *Degree requirements:* For master's, thesis optional. *Faculty research:* Object-oriented analysis, artificial intelligence, distributed computing, societal implications of computing, testing.

North Carolina Agricultural and Technical State University, School of Graduate Studies, School of Technology, Department of Electronics, Computer, and Information Technology, Greensboro, NC 27411. Offers electronics and computer technology (MSIT, MSTM); information technology (MSIT, MSTM).

North Carolina State University, Graduate School, College of Engineering, Department of Computer Science, Raleigh, NC 27695. Offers MC Sc, MS, PhD. *Program availability:* Part-time, online learning. *Degree requirements:* For master's, thesis optional; for doctorate, thesis/dissertation. *Entrance requirements:* For master's, GRE General Test, GRE Subject Test, minimum GPA of 3.0; for doctorate, GRE General Test, GRE Subject Test (recommended), minimum GPA of 3.5. Additional exam requirements/recommendations for international students: Required—TOEFL. Electronic applications accepted. *Faculty research:* Networking and performance analysis, theory and algorithms of computation, data mining, graphics and human computer interaction, software engineering and information security.

North Carolina State University, Graduate School, College of Engineering, Department of Electrical and Computer Engineering and Department of Computer Science, Program in Computer Networking, Raleigh, NC 27695. Offers MS. *Degree requirements:* For master's, thesis optional. *Entrance requirements:* For master's, GRE General Test, GRE Subject Test (recommended). Electronic applications accepted. *Faculty research:* High-speed networks, performance modelling, security, wireless and mobile.

North Central College, School of Graduate and Professional Studies, Department of Computer Science, Naperville, IL 60566-7063. Offers MS. *Program availability:* Part-time, evening/weekend. *Faculty:* 2 full-time (0 women), 3 part-time/adjunct (0 women). *Students:* 2 full-time (1 woman), 7 part-time (3 women); includes 2 minority (1 Black or African American, non-Hispanic/Latino; 1 Asian, non-Hispanic/Latino). Average age 31. 27 applicants, 59% accepted, 10 enrolled. In 2016, 3 master's awarded. *Degree requirements:* For master's, thesis optional, project. *Entrance requirements:* For master's, interview. Additional exam requirements/recommendations for international students: Required—TOEFL (minimum score 550 paper-based; 80 iBT), IELTS (minimum score 6.5). *Application deadline:* For fall admission, 8/15 for domestic students, 7/15 for international students; for winter admission, 12/1 for domestic students, 11/1 for international students; for spring admission, 2/1 for domestic students, 12/1 for international students. Applications are processed on a rolling basis. Application fee: $25. Electronic applications accepted. Application fee is waived when completed online. *Expenses:* Contact institution. *Financial support:* Scholarships/grants available. Support available to part-time students. Financial award applicants required to submit FAFSA. *Unit head:* Dr. Stephen Renk, Program Coordinator, Computer Science, 630-637-5170, Fax: 630-637-5172, E-mail: screnk@noctrl.edu. *Application contact:* Wendy Kulpinski, Director of Graduate and Professional Studies Admission, 630-637-5808, Fax: 630-637-5819, E-mail: wekulpinski@noctrl.edu.

North Dakota State University, College of Graduate and Interdisciplinary Studies, College of Science and Mathematics, Department of Computer Science, Fargo, ND 58102. Offers computer science (MS, PhD); software engineering (MS, MSE, PhD, Certificate). *Program availability:* Part-time. *Degree requirements:* For master's, comprehensive exam, thesis optional; for doctorate, thesis/dissertation, qualifying exam. *Entrance requirements:* For master's, minimum GPA of 3.0, BS in computer science or related field; for doctorate, minimum GPA of 3.25, MS in computer science or related field. Additional exam requirements/recommendations for international students: Required—TOEFL (minimum score 550 paper-based; 79 iBT). Electronic applications accepted. *Faculty research:* Networking, software engineering, artificial intelligence, database, programming languages.

Northeastern Illinois University, College of Graduate Studies and Research, College of Arts and Sciences, Program in Computer Science, Chicago, IL 60625-4699. Offers MS. *Program availability:* Part-time, evening/weekend. *Degree requirements:* For master's, comprehensive exam, research project or thesis. *Entrance requirements:* For master's, minimum GPA of 2.75, proficiency in 2 higher-level computer languages, 1 course in discrete mathematics. Additional exam requirements/recommendations for international students: Required—TOEFL (minimum score 550 paper-based; 79 iBT). Electronic applications accepted. *Faculty research:* Telecommunications, database inference problems, decision-making under uncertainty, belief networks, analysis of algorithms.

Northeastern University, College of Computer and Information Science, Boston, MA 02115-5096. Offers computer science (MS, PhD); data science (MS); game science and design (MS); health informatics (MS); information assurance (MS); network science (PhD); personal health informatics (PhD). *Program availability:* Part-time, evening/weekend. *Faculty:* 79 full-time (21 women), 34 part-time/adjunct (7 women). *Students:* 1,064 full-time (306 women), 34 part-time (10 women). In 2016, 322 master's, 8 doctorates awarded. Terminal master's awarded for partial completion of doctoral program. *Degree requirements:* For master's, thesis optional; for doctorate, comprehensive exam, thesis/dissertation. Application fee: $75. Electronic applications accepted. *Expenses:* $1,495 per credit. *Financial support:* Research assistantships, teaching assistantships, scholarships/grants, health care benefits, and unspecified assistantships available. Financial award applicants required to submit FAFSA. *Unit head:* Dr. Carla Brodley, Professor and Dean. *Application contact:* Dr. Rajmohan Rajaraman, Professor/Associate Dean/Director of the Graduate School, 617-373-8493, E-mail: gradschool@ccs.neu.edu.
Website: http://www.ccs.neu.edu/

Northern Arizona University, Graduate College, College of Engineering, Forestry, and Natural Sciences, Programs in Engineering, Flagstaff, AZ 86011. Offers civil engineering (M Eng, MSE); computer science (MSE); electrical and computer engineering (M Eng, MSE); engineering (M Eng, MSE); environmental engineering (M Eng, MSE); mechanical engineering (M Eng, MSE). *Program availability:* Part-time, online learning. *Degree requirements:* For master's, thesis. *Entrance requirements:* For master's, GRE General Test. Additional exam requirements/recommendations for international students: Required—TOEFL (minimum score 550 paper-based; 80 iBT), IELTS (minimum score 7). Electronic applications accepted. *Expenses:* Tuition, state resident: full-time $8971; part-time $444 per credit hour. Tuition, nonresident: full-time $20,958; part-time $1164 per credit hour. *Required fees:* $1018; $644 per credit hour. Tuition and fees vary according to course load, campus/location and program.

Northern Illinois University, Graduate School, College of Liberal Arts and Sciences, Department of Computer Science, De Kalb, IL 60115-2854. Offers MS. *Program availability:* Part-time, evening/weekend. *Faculty:* 14 full-time (3 women). *Students:* 144 full-time (47 women), 48 part-time (16 women); includes 9 minority (2 Black or African American, non-Hispanic/Latino; 5 Asian, non-Hispanic/Latino; 1 Hispanic/Latino; 1 Two or more races, non-Hispanic/Latino), 255 international. Average age 25. 414 applicants, 63% accepted, 56 enrolled. In 2016, 144 master's awarded. *Degree requirements:* For master's, comprehensive exam. *Entrance requirements:* For master's, GRE General Test, minimum GPA of 2.75. Additional exam requirements/recommendations for international students: Required—TOEFL (minimum score 550 paper-based). *Application deadline:* For fall admission, 6/1 for domestic students, 5/1 for international students; for spring admission, 11/1 for domestic students, 10/1 for international students. Applications are processed on a rolling basis. Application fee: $40. Electronic applications accepted. *Financial support:* In 2016–17, 7 research assistantships with full tuition reimbursements, 29 teaching assistantships with full tuition reimbursements were awarded; fellowships with full tuition reimbursements, career-related internships or fieldwork, Federal Work-Study, scholarships/grants, tuition waivers (full), and unspecified assistantships also available. Support available to part-time students. Financial award applicants required to submit FAFSA. *Faculty research:* Databases, theorem proving, artificial intelligence, neural networks, computer ethics. *Unit head:* Dr. Nicholas Karonis, Chair, 815-753-0349, Fax: 815-753-0342, E-mail: karonis@niu.edu. *Application contact:* Graduate School Office, 815-753-0395, E-mail: gradsch@niu.edu.
Website: http://www.cs.niu.edu/

Northern Kentucky University, Office of Graduate Programs, College of Informatics, Department of Computer Science, Highland Heights, KY 41099. Offers computer science (MSCS); geographic information systems (Certificate); secure software engineering (Certificate). *Program availability:* Part-time, evening/weekend. *Degree requirements:* For master's, thesis optional. *Entrance requirements:* For master's, GRE, minimum GPA of 3.0, at least 4 semesters of undergraduate study in computer science including intermediate computer programming and data structures, one year of calculus, one course in discrete mathematics. Additional exam requirements/recommendations for international students: Required—TOEFL (minimum score 550 paper-based; 79 iBT); Recommended—IELTS (minimum score 6.5). Electronic applications accepted. *Faculty* *research:* Data privacy, data mining, wireless security, secure software engineering, secure networking.

Northwestern Polytechnic University, School of Engineering, Fremont, CA 94539-7482. Offers computer engineering (DCE); computer science (MS); computer systems engineering (MS); electrical engineering (MS). *Program availability:* Part-time, evening/weekend. *Degree requirements:* For master's, thesis optional; for doctorate, thesis/dissertation. *Entrance requirements:* For master's, minimum GPA of 3.0. Additional exam requirements/recommendations for international students: Required—TOEFL (minimum score 550 paper-based; 79 iBT). *Faculty research:* Computer networking, database design, Internet technology, software engineering, digital signal processing.

Northwestern University, McCormick School of Engineering and Applied Science, Department of Electrical Engineering and Computer Science, Evanston, IL 60208. Offers computer engineering (MS, PhD); computer science (MS, PhD); electrical engineering (MS, PhD); information technology (MS). MS and PhD admissions and degrees offered through The Graduate School. *Program availability:* Part-time. Terminal master's awarded for partial completion of doctoral program. *Degree requirements:* For master's, comprehensive exam (for some programs), thesis optional; for doctorate, comprehensive exam, thesis/dissertation. *Entrance requirements:* For master's and doctorate, GRE General Test. Additional exam requirements/recommendations for international students: Required—TOEFL (minimum score 577 paper-based; 90 iBT), IELTS (minimum score 7). Electronic applications accepted. *Faculty research:* Solid state and photonics; computing, algorithms, and applications; computer engineering and systems; cognitive systems; graphics and interactive media; signals and systems.

Northwest Missouri State University, Graduate School, School of Computer Science and Information Systems, Maryville, MO 64468-6001. Offers applied computer science (MS); information systems (MS); instructional technology (MS). *Program availability:* Part-time. *Degree requirements:* For master's, comprehensive exam. *Entrance requirements:* For master's, GRE General Test, minimum GPA of 3.0. Additional exam requirements/recommendations for international students: Required—TOEFL (minimum score 550 paper-based). *Expenses:* Tuition, state resident: full-time $3447; part-time $383 per credit hour. Tuition, nonresident: full-time $5724; part-time $636 per credit hour. *Required fees:* $130 per credit hour.

Notre Dame College, Graduate Programs, South Euclid, OH 44121-4293. Offers mild/moderate needs (M Ed); reading (M Ed); security policy studies (MA, Graduate Certificate); technology (M Ed). *Program availability:* Part-time, evening/weekend. *Degree requirements:* For master's, thesis. *Entrance requirements:* For master's, GRE General Test, MAT, minimum undergraduate GPA of 2.75, valid teaching certificate, bachelor's degree in an education-related field from accredited college or university, official transcripts of most recent college work. *Faculty research:* Cognitive psychology, teaching critical thinking in the classroom.

Nova Southeastern University, College of Engineering and Computing, Fort Lauderdale, FL 33314-7796. Offers computer science (MS, PhD); information assurance (PhD); information assurance and cybersecurity (MS); information systems (PhD); information technology (MS); management information systems (MS). *Program availability:* Part-time, evening/weekend, blended/hybrid learning. *Faculty:* 18 full-time (4 women), 11 part-time/adjunct (2 women). *Students:* 309 full-time (87 women), 407 part-time (125 women); includes 321 minority (139 Black or African American, non-Hispanic/Latino; 2 American Indian or Alaska Native, non-Hispanic/Latino; 52 Asian, non-Hispanic/Latino; 117 Hispanic/Latino; 11 Two or more races, non-Hispanic/Latino), 160 international. Average age 40. 390 applicants, 74% accepted. In 2016, 188 master's, 53 doctorates awarded. Terminal master's awarded for partial completion of doctoral program. *Degree requirements:* For master's, thesis optional; for doctorate, thesis/dissertation. *Entrance requirements:* For master's, minimum undergraduate GPA of 2.5; 3.0 in major; for doctorate, master's degree, minimum graduate GPA of 3.25. Additional exam requirements/recommendations for international students: Required—TOEFL (minimum score 80 iBT), IELTS (minimum score 6), PTE (minimum score 54). *Application deadline:* Applications are processed on a rolling basis. Application fee: $50. Electronic applications accepted. *Expenses:* $745 per credit hour (for master's); $1,075 per credit hour (for doctoral). *Financial support:* In 2016–17, 43 students received support. Federal Work-Study, scholarships/grants, and traineeships available. Financial award application deadline: 4/15; financial award applicants required to submit FAFSA. *Faculty research:* Artificial intelligence, database management, human-computer interaction, distance education, information assurance and cybersecurity. *Unit head:* Dr. Yong X. Tao, Dean, 954-262-2063, Fax: 954-262-2752, E-mail: ytao@nova.edu. *Application contact:* Nancy Azoulay, Director, Admissions, 954-262-2026, Fax: 954-262-2752, E-mail: azoulayn@nova.edu.
Website: http://scis.nova.edu

Oakland University, Graduate Study and Lifelong Learning, School of Engineering and Computer Science, Department of Computer Science and Engineering, Rochester, MI 48309-4401. Offers computer science (MS); computer science and informatics (PhD); software engineering and information technology (MS). *Program availability:* Part-time, evening/weekend. *Entrance requirements:* For master's, minimum GPA of 3.0. Electronic applications accepted. *Expenses:* Contact institution.

The Ohio State University, Graduate School, College of Engineering, Department of Computer Science and Engineering, Columbus, OH 43210. Offers MS, PhD. *Faculty:* 43. *Students:* 290 full-time (49 women), 8 part-time (0 women). Average age 26. In 2016, 94 master's, 32 doctorates awarded. *Degree requirements:* For master's, thesis optional; for doctorate, thesis/dissertation. *Entrance requirements:* For master's and doctorate, GRE (minimum score Quantitative 750 old, 159 new; Verbal 500 old, 155 new; Analytical Writing 3.0); GRE Subject Test in computer science (strongly recommended for those whose undergraduate degree is not in computer science). Additional exam requirements/recommendations for international students: Required—TOEFL (minimum score 550 paper-based; 79 iBT), Michigan English Language Assessment Battery (minimum score 82); Recommended—IELTS (minimum score 7). *Application deadline:* For fall admission, 12/13 priority date for domestic students, 11/30 priority date for international students. Applications are processed on a rolling basis. Application fee: $60 ($70 for international students). Electronic applications accepted. *Financial support:* Fellowships with tuition reimbursements, research assistantships with tuition reimbursements, teaching assistantships with tuition reimbursements, career-related internships or fieldwork, Federal Work-Study, institutionally sponsored loans, unspecified assistantships, and administrative assistantships available. Support available to part-time students. Financial award application deadline: 1/15. *Unit head:* Dr. Xiadong Zhang, Professor/Chair, 614-292-2770, E-mail: zhang.574@osu.edu. *Application contact:* Graduate and Professional Admissions, 614-292-9444, Fax: 614-292-3895, E-mail: gpadmissions@osu.edu.
Website: http://www.cse.osu.edu

Ohio University, Graduate College, Russ College of Engineering and Technology, School of Electrical Engineering and Computer Science, Athens, OH 45701-2979. Offers electrical engineering (MS); electrical engineering and computer science (PhD). *Degree requirements:* For master's, comprehensive exam (for some programs), thesis; for doctorate, comprehensive exam, thesis/dissertation, qualifying exams. *Entrance requirements:* For master's, GRE, BSEE or BSCS, minimum GPA of 3.0; for doctorate,

GRE, MSEE or MSCS, minimum GPA of 3.0. Additional exam requirements/recommendations for international students: Required—TOEFL (minimum score 550 paper-based; 80 iBT) or IELTS (minimum score 6.5). *Application deadline:* For fall admission, 2/1 priority date for domestic students, 1/1 priority date for international students; for winter admission, 6/1 priority date for domestic students, 5/1 priority date for international students; for spring admission, 8/15 priority date for domestic students, 7/15 priority date for international students. Applications are processed on a rolling basis. Application fee: $50 ($55 for international students). Electronic applications accepted. *Financial support:* Research assistantships with full tuition reimbursements, teaching assistantships with full tuition reimbursements, Federal Work-Study, institutionally sponsored loans, scholarships/grants, and unspecified assistantships available. Financial award applicants required to submit FAFSA. *Faculty research:* Avionics, networking/communications, intelligent distribution, real-time computing, control systems, optical properties of semiconductors. *Unit head:* Dr. David Juedes, Chair, 740-593-1566, Fax: 740-593-0007, E-mail: juedes@ohio.edu. *Application contact:* Dr. Douglas Lawrence, Graduate Chair, 740-593-1578, Fax: 740-593-0007, E-mail: lawrencd@ohio.edu.
Website: http://www.ohio.edu/eecs

Oklahoma Christian University, Graduate School of Engineering and Computer Science, Oklahoma City, OK 73136-1100. Offers electrical and computer engineering (MSE); engineering management (MSE); mechanical engineering (MSE); software engineering (MSCS, MSE). *Program availability:* Part-time. *Faculty:* 8 full-time (1 woman), 7 part-time/adjunct (0 women). *Students:* 187 full-time (27 women), 85 part-time (12 women). Average age 25. 255 applicants, 33% accepted, 69 enrolled. In 2016, 188 master's awarded. *Entrance requirements:* Additional exam requirements/recommendations for international students: Required—TOEFL (minimum score 550 paper-based). *Application deadline:* Applications are processed on a rolling basis. Application fee: $25. Electronic applications accepted. *Expenses:* Contact institution. *Unit head:* Mary Ann Brown, Director for Graduate School Engineering, 405-425-5579. *Application contact:* Angie Ricketts, Admissions Counselor, 405-425-5587, E-mail: angie.ricketts@oc.edu.
Website: http://www.oc.edu/academics/graduate/engineering/

Oklahoma City University, Meinders School of Business, Oklahoma City, OK 73106-1402. Offers business (MBA, MSA); computer science (MS); energy legal studies (MS); energy management (MS); JD/MBA. *Program availability:* Part-time, evening/weekend, 100% online. *Faculty:* 17 full-time (3 women), 5 part-time/adjunct (1 woman). *Students:* 170 full-time (68 women), 218 part-time (90 women); includes 82 minority (17 Black or African American, non-Hispanic/Latino; 10 American Indian or Alaska Native, non-Hispanic/Latino; 16 Asian, non-Hispanic/Latino; 24 Hispanic/Latino; 15 Two or more races, non-Hispanic/Latino), 103 international. Average age 30. 592 applicants, 50% accepted, 138 enrolled. In 2016, 171 master's awarded. *Degree requirements:* For master's, practicum/capstone. *Entrance requirements:* For master's, undergraduate degree from accredited institution, minimum GPA of 3.0, essay, letters of recommendation. Additional exam requirements/recommendations for international students: Required—TOEFL (minimum score 550 paper-based; 80 iBT). *Application deadline:* Applications are processed on a rolling basis. Application fee: $50. Electronic applications accepted. *Expenses:* Contact institution. *Financial support:* In 2016–17, 262 students received support. Career-related internships or fieldwork, Federal Work-Study, institutionally sponsored loans, scholarships/grants, and tuition waivers (full and partial) available. Support available to part-time students. Financial award application deadline: 6/1; financial award applicants required to submit FAFSA. *Faculty research:* Group support systems, leadership, decision models in accounting. *Unit head:* Dr. Steve Agee, Dean, 405-208-5275, Fax: 405-208-5008, E-mail: sagee@okcu.edu. *Application contact:* Michael Harrington, Director of Graduate Admission, 800-633-7242, Fax: 405-208-5916, E-mail: gadmissions@okcu.edu.
Website: http://msb.okcu.edu

Oklahoma State University, College of Arts and Sciences, Department of Computer Science, Stillwater, OK 74078. Offers MS, PhD. *Faculty:* 14 full-time (2 women), 1 part-time/adjunct (0 women). *Students:* 47 full-time (15 women), 34 part-time (8 women); includes 6 minority (1 Asian, non-Hispanic/Latino; 5 Two or more races, non-Hispanic/Latino), 70 international. Average age 27. 252 applicants, 23% accepted, 20 enrolled. In 2016, 24 master's, 5 doctorates awarded. *Degree requirements:* For master's, thesis optional; for doctorate, comprehensive exam, thesis/dissertation. *Entrance requirements:* For master's, GRE; for doctorate, GRE General Test, GRE Subject Test in computer science (recommended), 3 letters of recommendation. Additional exam requirements/recommendations for international students: Required—TOEFL (minimum score 550 paper-based; 79 iBT). *Application deadline:* For fall admission, 3/1 priority date for international students; for spring admission, 8/1 priority date for international students. Applications are processed on a rolling basis. Application fee: $40 ($75 for international students). Electronic applications accepted. *Expenses:* Tuition, state resident: full-time $3775; part-time $209.70 per credit hour. Tuition, nonresident: full-time $14,851; part-time $825.05 per credit hour. *Required fees:* $2027; $112.60 per credit hour. Tuition and fees vary according to campus/location. *Financial support:* In 2016–17, 8 research assistantships (averaging $6,121 per year), 24 teaching assistantships (averaging $7,258 per year) were awarded; career-related internships or fieldwork, Federal Work-Study, scholarships/grants, health care benefits, tuition waivers (partial), and unspecified assistantships also available. Support available to part-time students. Financial award application deadline: 3/1; financial award applicants required to submit FAFSA. *Unit head:* Dr. K. M. George, Department Head, 405-744-5668, Fax: 405-774-9097, E-mail: kmg@cs.okstate.edu.
Website: http://cs.okstate.edu/

Old Dominion University, College of Sciences, Program in Computer Science, Norfolk, VA 23529. Offers computer information systems (MS); computer science (MS, PhD). *Program availability:* Part-time, 100% online. *Faculty:* 16 full-time (3 women), 3 part-time/adjunct (0 women). *Students:* 69 full-time (26 women), 52 part-time (6 women); includes 12 minority (6 Black or African American, non-Hispanic/Latino; 2 Asian, non-Hispanic/Latino; 2 Hispanic/Latino; 2 Two or more races, non-Hispanic/Latino), 76 international. Average age 30. 155 applicants, 52% accepted, 30 enrolled. In 2016, 41 master's, 7 doctorates awarded. Terminal master's awarded for partial completion of doctoral program. *Degree requirements:* For master's, comprehensive exam, thesis optional, 34 credit hours; for doctorate, comprehensive exam, thesis/dissertation, 48 credit hours beyond the MS. *Entrance requirements:* For master's, GRE General Test, minimum GPA of 3.0; for doctorate, GRE General Test, MS in computer science. Additional exam requirements/recommendations for international students: Required—TOEFL (minimum score 550 paper-based; 79 iBT), IELTS (minimum score 6.5). *Application deadline:* For fall admission, 6/1 for domestic students, 4/15 for international students; for spring admission, 11/1 for domestic students, 10/1 for international students; for summer admission, 3/1 for domestic students, 2/1 for international students. Applications are processed on a rolling basis. Application fee: $50. Electronic applications accepted. *Expenses:* Tuition, state resident: full-time $8604; part-time $478 per credit hour. Tuition, nonresident: full-time $21,510; part-time $1195 per credit hour. *Required fees:* $66 per semester. Tuition and fees vary according to campus/location, program and reciprocity agreements. *Financial support:* In 2016–17, 98 students received support, including 5 fellowships with full tuition reimbursements available

(averaging $18,000 per year), 27 research assistantships with partial tuition reimbursements available (averaging $16,048 per year), 36 teaching assistantships with partial tuition reimbursements available (averaging $8,570 per year); career-related internships or fieldwork and scholarships/grants also available. Financial award application deadline: 2/15; financial award applicants required to submit FAFSA. *Faculty research:* Machine intelligence and data analytics, web science and digital libraries, networks and mobile computing, bioinformatics, scientific computing. *Total annual research expenditures:* $1.6 million. *Unit head:* Dr. Ravi Mukkamala, Interim Department Chair, 757-683-6001, Fax: 757-683-4900, E-mail: mukka@cs.odu.edu. *Application contact:* Dr. Yaohang Li, Graduate Program Director, 757-683-6001, E-mail: yaohang@cs.odu.edu.
Website: http://www.cs.odu.edu/

Oregon Health & Science University, School of Medicine, Graduate Programs in Medicine, Department of Computer Science and Engineering, Portland, OR 97239-3098. Offers computer science and engineering (MS, PhD); electrical engineering (MS, PhD). *Program availability:* Part-time. *Faculty:* 7 full-time (2 women), 1 part-time/adjunct (0 women). *Students:* 10 full-time (3 women), 14 part-time (5 women); includes 3 minority (all Asian, non-Hispanic/Latino), 10 international. Average age 33. 10 applicants, 3 enrolled. In 2016, 5 master's, 1 doctorate awarded. Terminal master's awarded for partial completion of doctoral program. *Degree requirements:* For master's, thesis (for some programs); for doctorate, comprehensive exam, thesis/dissertation, qualifying exam. *Entrance requirements:* For master's and doctorate, GRE General Test (minimum scores: 153 Verbal/148 Quantitative/4.5 Analytical). Additional exam requirements/recommendations for international students: Required—IELTS or TOEFL. *Application deadline:* For fall admission, 7/15 for domestic students, 5/15 for international students; for winter admission, 10/15 for domestic students, 9/15 for international students; for spring admission, 1/15 for domestic students, 12/15 for international students. Applications are processed on a rolling basis. Application fee: $70. Electronic applications accepted. *Financial support:* Health care benefits, tuition waivers (full), and full-tuition and stipends (for PhD students) available. Financial award applicants required to submit FAFSA. *Faculty research:* Natural language processing, speech signal processing, computational biology, autism spectrum disorders, hearing and speaking disorders. *Unit head:* Dr. Peter Heeman, Program Director, 503-748-1635, E-mail: heemanp@ohsu.edu. *Application contact:* Pat Dickerson, Administrative Coordinator, 503-748-1635, E-mail: dickersp@ohsu.edu.

Oregon State University, College of Engineering, Program in Computer Science, Corvallis, OR 97331. Offers algorithms and cryptography (M Eng, MS, PhD); artificial intelligence, machine learning and data science (M Eng, PhD); computer graphics, visualization, and vision (M Eng, MS, PhD); computer systems and networking (M Eng, MS, PhD); human-computer interaction (M Eng, MS, PhD); programming languages (M Eng, MS, PhD); software engineering (M Eng, MS, PhD). *Faculty:* 58 full-time (9 women), 3 part-time/adjunct (1 woman). *Students:* 221 full-time (53 women), 26 part-time (4 women); includes 10 minority (8 Asian, non-Hispanic/Latino; 1 Hispanic/Latino; 1 Two or more races, non-Hispanic/Latino), 190 international. Average age 29. 630 applicants, 14% accepted, 65 enrolled. In 2016, 41 master's, 5 doctorates awarded. *Entrance requirements:* For master's and doctorate, GRE. Additional exam requirements/recommendations for international students: Required—TOEFL (minimum score 600 paper-based; 80 iBT), IELTS (minimum score 6.5). *Application deadline:* For fall admission, 1/15 for domestic students. Application fee: $75 ($85 for international students). *Expenses:* $14,130 resident full-time tuition, $23,769 non-resident. *Financial support:* Application deadline: 1/15. *Unit head:* V. John Mathews, Professor and School Head. *Application contact:* Graduate Coordinator, 541-737-7234, E-mail: eecs.gradinfo@oregonstate.edu.
Website: http://eecs.oregonstate.edu/current-students/graduate/cs-program

Pace University, Seidenberg School of Computer Science and Information Systems, New York, NY 10038. Offers chief information security officer (APC); computer science (MS, PhD); enterprise analytics (MS); information and communication technology strategy and innovation (APC); information systems (MS, APC); Internet technology (MS); professional studies in computing (DPS); secure software and information engineering (APC); security and information assurance (Certificate); software development and engineering (MS, Certificate); telecommunications systems and networks (MS, Certificate). *Program availability:* Part-time, evening/weekend, online only, 100% online, blended/hybrid learning. *Faculty:* 26 full-time (7 women), 7 part-time/adjunct (2 women). *Students:* 537 full-time (175 women), 303 part-time (85 women); includes 192 minority (79 Black or African American, non-Hispanic/Latino; 3 American Indian or Alaska Native, non-Hispanic/Latino; 53 Asian, non-Hispanic/Latino; 49 Hispanic/Latino; 8 Two or more races, non-Hispanic/Latino), 486 international. Average age 32. 599 applicants, 89% accepted, 248 enrolled. In 2016, 180 master's, 19 doctorates, 1 other advanced degree awarded. *Degree requirements:* For master's, thesis or alternative, capstone course; for doctorate, comprehensive exam (for some programs), thesis/dissertation. *Entrance requirements:* For master's, GRE General Test. Additional exam requirements/recommendations for international students: Required—TOEFL (minimum score 78 iBT), IELTS (minimum score 6.5) or PTE (minimum score 52). *Application deadline:* For fall admission, 8/1 priority date for domestic students, 6/1 for international students; for spring admission, 12/1 for domestic students, 10/1 for international students. Applications are processed on a rolling basis. Application fee: $70. Electronic applications accepted. *Expenses:* Contact institution. *Financial support:* In 2016–17, 45 students received support. Research assistantships, career-related internships or fieldwork, scholarships/grants, and unspecified assistantships available. Support available to part-time students. Financial award application deadline: 2/15; financial award applicants required to submit FAFSA. *Faculty research:* Cyber security/digital forensics; mobile app development; big data/enterprise analytics; artificial intelligence; software development. *Total annual research expenditures:* $314,545. *Unit head:* Dr. Jonathan Hill, Dean, Seidenberg School of Computer Science and Information Systems, 212-346-1864, E-mail: jhill@pace.edu. *Application contact:* Susan Ford-Goldschein, Director of Graduate Admissions, 914-422-4283, Fax: 212-346-1585, E-mail: graduateadmission@pace.edu.
Website: http://www.pace.edu/seidenberg

Pacific States University, College of Computer Science and Information Systems, Los Angeles, CA 90010. Offers computer science (MS); information systems (MS). *Program availability:* Part-time, evening/weekend. *Entrance requirements:* For master's, bachelor's degree in physics, engineering, computer science, or applied mathematics; minimum undergraduate GPA of 2.5 during last 90 hours of course work. Additional exam requirements/recommendations for international students: Required—TOEFL (minimum score 500 paper-based; 61 iBT), IELTS (minimum score 5.5).

Penn State Harrisburg, Graduate School, School of Science, Engineering and Technology, Middletown, PA 17057. Offers computer science (MS); electrical engineering (M Eng, MS); engineering management (MPS); engineering science (M Eng); environmental engineering (M Eng); environmental pollution control (MEPC, MS); structural engineering (Certificate). *Program availability:* Part-time, evening/weekend. *Unit head:* Dr. Mukund S. Kulkarni, Chancellor, 717-948-6105, Fax: 717-948-6452. *Application contact:* Robert W. Coffman, Jr., Director of Enrollment Management, Admissions, 717-948-6250, Fax: 717-948-6325, E-mail: hbgadmit@psu.edu.
Website: https://harrisburg.psu.edu/science-engineering-technology

Penn State University Park, Graduate School, College of Engineering, Department of Electrical Engineering and Computer Science, University Park, PA 16802. Offers computer science and engineering (M Eng, MS, PhD). *Unit head:* Dr. Amr S. Elnashai, Dean, 814-865-7537, Fax: 814-863-4749. *Application contact:* Lori Hawn, Director, Graduate Student Services, 814-865-1795, Fax: 814-863-4627, E-mail: l-gswww@lists.psu.edu.
Website: http://eecs.psu.edu/

Polytechnic University of Puerto Rico, Graduate School, Hato Rey, PR 00918. Offers business administration (MBA), including computer information systems, general management, management of information systems, management of international enterprises; civil engineering (ME, MS); computer engineering (ME, MS); computer science (MCS, MS); electrical engineering (ME, MS); engineering management (MEM); environmental management (MEM); landscape architecture (M Land Arch); manufacturing competitiveness (MMC, MS); manufacturing engineering (ME, MS); mechanical engineering (M Mech E). *Program availability:* Part-time, evening/weekend. *Entrance requirements:* For master's, 3 letters of recommendation.

Portland State University, Graduate Studies, Maseeh College of Engineering and Computer Science, Department of Computer Science, Portland, OR 97207-0751. Offers computer science (MS, PhD); software engineering (MSE). *Program availability:* Part-time. *Faculty:* 27 full-time (6 women), 6 part-time/adjunct (0 women). *Students:* 86 full-time (31 women), 75 part-time (28 women); includes 24 minority (15 Asian, non-Hispanic/Latino; 4 Hispanic/Latino; 5 Two or more races, non-Hispanic/Latino), 74 international. Average age 30. 261 applicants, 28% accepted, 38 enrolled. In 2016, 40 master's, 4 doctorates awarded. *Degree requirements:* For master's, thesis or alternative; for doctorate, comprehensive exam, thesis/dissertation. *Entrance requirements:* For master's, GRE (minimum scores in 60th percentile in Quantitative and 25th percentile in Verbal for MS), minimum GPA of 3.0 or equivalent, 2 letters of recommendation, personal statement; for doctorate, GRE (minimum scores 60th percentile in Quantitative and 25th percentile in Verbal), MS in computer science or allied field. Additional exam requirements/recommendations for international students: Required—TOEFL (minimum score 550 paper-based). *Application deadline:* For fall admission, 3/1 for domestic and international students; for winter admission, 5/15 for domestic and international students; for spring admission, 11/1 for domestic students, 10/1 for international students. Applications are processed on a rolling basis. Application fee: $65. *Expenses:* Contact institution. *Financial support:* In 2016–17, 15 research assistantships with tuition reimbursements (averaging $10,283 per year), 16 teaching assistantships with tuition reimbursements (averaging $7,190 per year) were awarded; career-related internships or fieldwork, Federal Work-Study, scholarships/grants, tuition waivers (partial), and unspecified assistantships also available. Support available to part-time students. Financial award application deadline: 3/1; financial award applicants required to submit FAFSA. *Faculty research:* Formal methods, database systems, parallel programming environments, computer security, software tools. *Total annual research expenditures:* $1.7 million. *Unit head:* Dr. Wu-Chi Feng, Chair, 503-725-2408, Fax: 503-725-3211, E-mail: wuchang@cs.pdx.edu. *Application contact:* Krys Sarreal, Department Manager, 503-725-4255, Fax: 503-725-3211, E-mail: gc@cs.pdx.edu.
Website: http://www.pdx.edu/computer-science/

Prairie View A&M University, College of Engineering, Prairie View, TX 77446. Offers computer information systems (MSCIS); computer science (MSCS); electrical engineering (MSEE, PhDEE); general engineering (MS Engr). *Program availability:* Part-time, evening/weekend. *Faculty:* 27 full-time (7 women), 2 part-time/adjunct (both women). *Students:* 171 full-time (45 women), 50 part-time (17 women); includes 89 minority (70 Black or African American, non-Hispanic/Latino; 16 Asian, non-Hispanic/Latino; 3 Hispanic/Latino), 115 international. Average age 30. 155 applicants, 94% accepted, 85 enrolled. In 2016, 43 master's, 3 doctorates awarded. *Degree requirements:* For master's, thesis optional; for doctorate, comprehensive exam, thesis/dissertation. *Entrance requirements:* For master's, GRE General Test (minimum score of 900), bachelor's degree in engineering from ABET-accredited institution; for doctorate, minimum GPA of 3.0. Additional exam requirements/recommendations for international students: Required—TOEFL (minimum score 550 paper-based; 79 iBT). *Application deadline:* For fall admission, 5/1 priority date for domestic and international students; for spring admission, 10/1 priority date for domestic students, 9/1 priority date for international students; for summer admission, 3/1 priority date for domestic students, 2/1 priority date for international students. Applications are processed on a rolling basis. Application fee: $50. Electronic applications accepted. *Expenses:* Tuition, state resident: full-time $4362; part-time $273.48 per credit hour. Tuition, nonresident: full-time $12,390; part-time $534.10 per credit hour. *Required fees:* $2782; $178.26 per credit hour. *Financial support:* In 2016–17, 1 fellowship with full tuition reimbursement (averaging $14,000 per year), 33 research assistantships with full and partial tuition reimbursements (averaging $17,260 per year), 3 teaching assistantships with full and partial tuition reimbursements (averaging $15,000 per year) were awarded; career-related internships or fieldwork, institutionally sponsored loans, scholarships/grants, health care benefits, tuition waivers (full), and unspecified assistantships also available. Financial award application deadline: 4/1; financial award applicants required to submit FAFSA. *Faculty research:* Electrical and computer engineering: big data analysis, wireless communications, bioinformatics and computational biology, space radiation; computer science: cloud computing, cyber security; chemical engineering: thermochemical processing of biofuel, photochemical modeling; civil and environmental engineering: environmental sustainability, water resources, structure; mechanical engineering: thermal science, nanocomposites, computational fluid dynamics. *Unit head:* Dr. Kendall T. Harris, Dean, 936-261-9900, Fax: 936-261-9868, E-mail: tharris@pvamu.edu. *Application contact:* Pauline Walker, Administrative Assistant II, Research and Graduate Studies, 936-261-3521, Fax: 936-261-3529, E-mail: gradadmissions@pvamu.edu.

Princeton University, Graduate School, School of Engineering and Applied Science, Department of Computer Science, Princeton, NJ 08544-1019. Offers MSE, PhD. Terminal master's awarded for partial completion of doctoral program. *Degree requirements:* For master's, thesis; for doctorate, thesis/dissertation, general exam. *Entrance requirements:* For master's, GRE General Test, GRE Subject Test (recommended), 3 letters of recommendation; for doctorate, GRE General Test, GRE Subject Test (recommended), official transcript(s), 3 letters of recommendation, personal statement. Additional exam requirements/recommendations for international students: Required—TOEFL. Electronic applications accepted. *Faculty research:* Computational biology and bioinformatics; computer and network systems; graphics, vision, and sound; machine learning, programming languages and security; theory.

Purdue University, Graduate School, College of Science, Department of Computer Sciences, West Lafayette, IN 47907. Offers MS, PhD. *Program availability:* Part-time. *Faculty:* 51 full-time (45 women), 2 part-time/adjunct (1 woman). *Students:* 220 full-time (49 women), 103 part-time (18 women); includes 19 minority (3 Black or African American, non-Hispanic/Latino; 7 Asian, non-Hispanic/Latino; 7 Hispanic/Latino; 2 Two or more races, non-Hispanic/Latino), 264 international. Average age 27. 1,177 applicants, 17% accepted, 79 enrolled. In 2016, 55 master's, 21 doctorates awarded.

Terminal master's awarded for partial completion of doctoral program. *Degree requirements:* For master's, thesis optional; for doctorate, comprehensive exam, thesis/dissertation. *Entrance requirements:* For master's and doctorate, minimum GPA of 3.5. Additional exam requirements/recommendations for international students: Required—TOEFL (minimum score 600 paper-based; 95 iBT), TWE (minimum score 5). *Application deadline:* For fall admission, 12/15 for domestic and international students; for spring admission, 10/1 for domestic and international students. Application fee: $60 ($75 for international students). Electronic applications accepted. *Financial support:* Fellowships with partial tuition reimbursements, research assistantships with partial tuition reimbursements, teaching assistantships with partial tuition reimbursements, health care benefits, and unspecified assistantships available. Financial award application deadline: 12/15. *Faculty research:* Bioinformatics and computational biology, computational science and engineering, databases, data mining, distributed systems, graphics and visualization, information retrieval, information security and assurance, machine learning, networking and operation systems, programming languages and compilers, software engineering, theory of computing and algorithms. *Unit head:* Prof. Sunil K. Prabhakar, Head, 765-494-6003, E-mail: sunil@cs.purdue.edu. *Application contact:* Sandra K. Freeman, Graduate Contact, 765-494-6004, E-mail: skfreema@purdue.edu. Website: http://www.cs.purdue.edu/

Purdue University Northwest, Graduate Studies Office, School of Engineering, Mathematics, and Science, Department of Mathematics, Computer Science, and Statistics, Hammond, IN 46323-2094. Offers computer science (MS); mathematics (MAT, MS). *Program availability:* Part-time. *Entrance requirements:* Additional exam requirements/recommendations for international students: Required—TOEFL. *Faculty research:* Topology, analysis, algebra, mathematics education.

Queens College of the City University of New York, Mathematics and Natural Sciences Division, Department of Computer Science, Queens, NY 11367-1597. Offers MA. *Program availability:* Part-time, evening/weekend. *Faculty:* 20 full-time (5 women), 25 part-time/adjunct (8 women). *Students:* 8 full-time (4 women), 72 part-time (19 women); includes 30 minority (3 Black or African American, non-Hispanic/Latino; 16 Asian, non-Hispanic/Latino; 6 Hispanic/Latino; 5 Two or more races, non-Hispanic/Latino), 29 international. Average age 30. 72 applicants, 71% accepted, 26 enrolled. In 2016, 10 master's awarded. *Entrance requirements:* For master's, minimum GPA of 3.0. Additional exam requirements/recommendations for international students: Required—TOEFL (minimum score 61 iBT), IELTS (minimum score 5). *Application deadline:* For fall admission, 4/1 for domestic students; for spring admission, 11/1 for domestic students. Applications are processed on a rolling basis. Application fee: $125. Electronic applications accepted. *Expenses:* Tuition, state resident: full-time $5065; part-time $425 per credit. Tuition, nonresident: part-time $780 per credit. *Required fees:* $522; $397 per credit. Part-time tuition and fees vary according to course load and program. *Financial support:* Career-related internships or fieldwork and unspecified assistantships available. Financial award application deadline: 4/1; financial award applicants required to submit FAFSA. *Unit head:* Dr. Zhigang Xiang, Chairperson, 718-997-3500, E-mail: zhigang.xiang@qc.cuny.edu.

Queen's University at Kingston, School of Graduate Studies, Faculty of Arts and Sciences, School of Computing, Kingston, ON K7L 3N6, Canada. Offers M Sc, PhD. *Degree requirements:* For master's, thesis; for doctorate, comprehensive exam, thesis/dissertation. *Entrance requirements:* For master's, honours B Sc in computer science; for doctorate, M Sc in computer science. Additional exam requirements/recommendations for international students: Required—TOEFL, TWE. *Faculty research:* Software engineering, human computer interaction, data base, networks, computational geometry.

Regis University, College of Computer and Information Sciences, Denver, CO 80221-1099. Offers agile technologies (Certificate); cybersecurity (Certificate); data science (M Sc); database administration with Oracle (Certificate); database development (Certificate); database technologies (M Sc); enterprise Java software development (Certificate); enterprise resource planning (Certificate); executive information technology (Certificate); health care informatics (Certificate); health care informatics and information management (M Sc); information assurance (M Sc); information assurance policy management (Certificate); information technology management (M Sc); mobile software development (Certificate); software engineering (M Sc, Certificate); software engineering and database technology (M Sc); storage area networks (Certificate); systems engineering (M Sc, Certificate). *Program availability:* Part-time, evening/weekend, 100% online, blended/hybrid learning. *Faculty:* 11 full-time (3 women), 30 part-time/adjunct (10 women). *Students:* 341 full-time (95 women), 318 part-time (98 women); includes 186 minority (56 Black or African American, non-Hispanic/Latino; 2 American Indian or Alaska Native, non-Hispanic/Latino; 48 Asian, non-Hispanic/Latino; 63 Hispanic/Latino; 17 Two or more races, non-Hispanic/Latino), 57 international. Average age 37. 342 applicants, 79% accepted, 174 enrolled. In 2016, 192 master's awarded. *Degree requirements:* For master's, thesis (for some programs), final research project. *Entrance requirements:* For master's, official transcript reflecting baccalaureate degree awarded from regionally-accredited college or university, 2 years of related experience, resume, interview. Additional exam requirements/recommendations for international students: Required—TOEFL (minimum score 550 paper-based; 82 iBT). *Application deadline:* For fall admission, 8/15 priority date for domestic students, 7/13 for international students; for winter admission, 10/10 priority date for domestic students, 9/8 for international students; for spring admission, 1/10 priority date for domestic students, 11/17 for international students; for summer admission, 5/1 priority date for domestic students. Applications are processed on a rolling basis. Application fee: $75. Electronic applications accepted. *Expenses:* $730 per credit hour. *Financial support:* Scholarships/grants available. Financial award application deadline: 4/15; financial award applicants required to submit FAFSA. *Faculty research:* Information policy, knowledge management, software architectures, data science. *Unit head:* Shari Plantz-Masters, Academic Dean. *Application contact:* Cate Clark, Director of Admissions, 303-458-4900, Fax: 303-964-5534, E-mail: ruadmissions@regis.edu. Website: http://regis.edu/CCIS.aspx

Rensselaer at Hartford, Department of Computer and Information Science, Hartford, CT 06120-2991. Offers computer science (MS); information technology (MS). *Program availability:* Part-time, evening/weekend. *Degree requirements:* For master's, thesis optional. *Entrance requirements:* For master's, GRE. Additional exam requirements/recommendations for international students: Required—TOEFL (minimum score 600 paper-based; 100 iBT). Electronic applications accepted.

Rensselaer Polytechnic Institute, Graduate School, School of Science, Program in Computer Science, Troy, NY 12180-3590. Offers MS, PhD. *Program availability:* Part-time. *Faculty:* 30 full-time (8 women), 4 part-time/adjunct (2 women). *Students:* 87 full-time (12 women), 5 part-time (0 women). 240 applicants, 26% accepted, 19 enrolled. In 2016, 14 master's, 10 doctorates awarded. Terminal master's awarded for partial completion of doctoral program. *Degree requirements:* For master's, thesis; for doctorate, comprehensive exam, thesis/dissertation. *Entrance requirements:* For master's and doctorate, GRE. Additional exam requirements/recommendations for international students: Required—TOEFL (minimum score 570 paper-based; 88 iBT), IELTS (minimum score 6.5), PTE (minimum score 60). *Application deadline:* For fall admission, 1/1 priority date for domestic and international students; for spring

admission, 8/15 priority date for domestic and international students. Applications are processed on a rolling basis. Application fee: $75. Electronic applications accepted. *Expenses: Tuition:* Full-time $49,520; part-time $2060 per credit hour. *Required fees:* $2617. *Financial support:* In 2016–17, research assistantships (averaging $22,000 per year), teaching assistantships (averaging $22,000 per year) were awarded; fellowships also available. Financial award application deadline: 1/1. *Faculty research:* Algorithms and theory; artificial intelligence; bioinformatics; computational science and engineering; computer vision, graphics, and robotics; data mining and machine and computational learning; database systems; pervasive computing and networking; programming languages and software engineering; security; semantic web; social networking. *Total annual research expenditures:* $6.7 million. *Unit head:* Dr. Sibel Adali, Graduate Program Director, 518-276-8047, E-mail: sibel@cs.rpi.edu. *Application contact:* Office of Graduate Admissions, 518-276-6216, E-mail: gradadmissions@rpi.edu. Website: https://science.rpi.edu/computer-science

Rice University, Graduate Programs, George R. Brown School of Engineering, Department of Computer Science, Houston, TX 77251-1892. Offers MCS, MS, PhD. Terminal master's awarded for partial completion of doctoral program. *Degree requirements:* For master's, comprehensive exam; for doctorate, comprehensive exam, thesis/dissertation. *Entrance requirements:* For master's and doctorate, bachelor's degree. Additional exam requirements/recommendations for international students: Required—TOEFL. Electronic applications accepted. *Faculty research:* Programming languages and compiler construction; robotics, bioinformatics, algorithms - motion planning with emphasis on high-dimensional systems; network protocols, distributed systems, and operating systems - adaptive protocols for wireless; computer architecture, aperating systems - virtual machine monitors; computer graphics - application of computers to geometric problems and centered around general problem of representing geometric shapes.

Rivier University, School of Graduate Studies, Department of Computer Science and Mathematics, Nashua, NH 03060. Offers computer science (MS); mathematics (MAT). *Program availability:* Part-time, evening/weekend. *Entrance requirements:* For master's, GRE Subject Test. Electronic applications accepted.

Rochester Institute of Technology, Graduate Enrollment Services, Golisano College of Computing and Information Sciences, Computer Science Department, MS Program in Computer Science, Rochester, NY 14623. Offers MS. *Program availability:* Part-time. *Students:* 379 full-time (104 women), 52 part-time (11 women); includes 5 minority (1 American Indian or Alaska Native, non-Hispanic/Latino; 2 Asian, non-Hispanic/Latino; 2 Two or more races, non-Hispanic/Latino), 393 international. Average age 25. 1,152 applicants, 39% accepted, 121 enrolled. In 2016, 134 master's awarded. *Degree requirements:* For master's, thesis or alternative. *Entrance requirements:* For master's, GRE or GMAT, minimum GPA of 3.0. Additional exam requirements/recommendations for international students: Required—TOEFL (minimum score 570 paper-based; 88 iBT), IELTS (minimum score 6.5), PTE (minimum score 61). *Application deadline:* For fall admission, 2/15 priority date for domestic and international students; for spring admission, 12/15 priority date for domestic and international students. Applications are processed on a rolling basis. Application fee: $60. Electronic applications accepted. *Expenses:* $1,742 per credit hour. *Financial support:* In 2016–17, 286 students received support. Research assistantships with partial tuition reimbursements available, teaching assistantships with partial tuition reimbursements available, career-related internships or fieldwork, scholarships/grants, and unspecified assistantships available. Financial award applicants required to submit FAFSA. *Faculty research:* Mobile and pervasive computing, including Internet-of-Things (IoT) and cloud computing for big data analytics; privacy-preserving techniques for cloud computing, specifically homomorphic encryption; norms and normative behavior in AI, reversible computing and reversible logic; graph database; semantic queries with nodes, edges, and properties to represent and store data; machine learning with applications in document recognition and informational retrieval. *Unit head:* Dr. Hans-Peter Bischof, Graduate Program Coordinator, 585-475-2995, Fax: 585-475-4935, E-mail: csdept@cs.rit.edu. *Application contact:* Diane Ellison, Associate Vice President, Graduate Enrollment Services, 585-475-2229, Fax: 585-475-7164, E-mail: gradinfo@rit.edu. Website: https://www.cs.rit.edu/ms-computer-science-overview

Rochester Institute of Technology, Graduate Enrollment Services, Golisano College of Computing and Information Sciences, Computing and Information Sciences Department, PhD Program in Computing and Information Sciences, Rochester, NY 14623. Offers PhD. *Program availability:* Part-time. *Students:* 39 full-time (7 women), 5 part-time (0 women); includes 4 minority (1 Asian, non-Hispanic/Latino; 3 Hispanic/Latino), 34 international. Average age 30. 78 applicants, 33% accepted, 14 enrolled. In 2016, 3 doctorates awarded. *Degree requirements:* For doctorate, comprehensive exam, thesis/dissertation. *Entrance requirements:* For doctorate, GRE, minimum GPA of 3.0. Additional exam requirements/recommendations for international students: Required—TOEFL (minimum score 570 paper-based; 88 iBT), IELTS (minimum score 6.5), PTE (minimum score 61). *Application deadline:* For fall admission, 1/15 priority date for domestic and international students. Applications are processed on a rolling basis. Application fee: $0. Electronic applications accepted. *Expenses:* $1,742 per credit hour. *Financial support:* In 2016–17, 31 students received support. Research assistantships with full tuition reimbursements available, teaching assistantships with full tuition reimbursements available, career-related internships or fieldwork, scholarships/grants, health care benefits, and unspecified assistantships available. Financial award applicants required to submit FAFSA. *Faculty research:* Accessibility and HCI; algorithm and programming languages; bioinformatics and health IT; cybersecurity; machine learning and data science. *Unit head:* Dr. Pengcheng Shi, Director, 585-475-6193, E-mail: ljtdps@rit.edu. *Application contact:* Diane Ellison, Associate Vice President, Graduate Enrollment Services, 585-475-2229, Fax: 585-475-7164, E-mail: gradinfo@rit.edu. Website: http://www.rit.edu/gccis/academics/phd-program

Rochester Institute of Technology, Graduate Enrollment Services, Golisano College of Computing and Information Sciences, Information Science and Technologies Department, MS Program in Networking and Systems Administration, Rochester, NY 14623. Offers MS. *Program availability:* Part-time, 100% online. *Students:* 26 full-time (6 women), 16 part-time (3 women); includes 1 minority (Asian, non-Hispanic/Latino), 37 international. Average age 26. 135 applicants, 35% accepted, 15 enrolled. In 2016, 32 master's awarded. *Degree requirements:* For master's, thesis or alternative. *Entrance requirements:* For master's, GRE, minimum GPA of 3.0. Additional exam requirements/recommendations for international students: Required—TOEFL (minimum score 570 paper-based; 88 iBT), IELTS (minimum score 6.5), PTE (minimum score 61). *Application deadline:* For fall admission, 2/15 priority date for domestic and international students; for spring admission, 12/15 priority date for domestic and international students. Applications are processed on a rolling basis. Electronic applications accepted. *Expenses:* $1,742 per credit hour (classroom), $993 per credit hour (online). *Financial support:* In 2016–17, 33 students received support. Research assistantships with partial tuition reimbursements available, teaching assistantships with partial tuition reimbursements available, career-related internships or fieldwork, scholarships/grants, and unspecified assistantships available. Support available to part-time students. Financial award applicants required to submit FAFSA. *Faculty research:* Vehicle area

network, IoT networking and security, future internet, network protocols and algorithms, cloud computing. *Unit head:* Qi Yu, Graduate Program Director, 585-475-6929, Fax: 585-475-6584, E-mail: qyuvks@rit.edu. *Application contact:* Diane Ellison, Associate Vice President, Graduate Enrollment Services, 585-475-2229, Fax: 585-475-7164, E-mail: gradinfo@rit.edu.
Website: http://nsa.rit.edu/

Roosevelt University, Graduate Division, College of Arts and Sciences, Department of Computer Science and Telecommunications, Program in Computer Science, Chicago, IL 60605. Offers MSC. *Program availability:* Part-time, evening/weekend. *Faculty research:* Artificial intelligence, software engineering, distributed databases, parallel processing.

Rowan University, Graduate School, College of Science and Mathematics, Program in Computer Science, Glassboro, NJ 08028-1701. Offers MS. *Degree requirements:* For master's, thesis optional. *Entrance requirements:* For master's, bachelor's degree (or its equivalent) in related field from accredited institution; official transcripts from all colleges attended; current professional resume; two letters of recommendation; statement of professional objectives; minimum undergraduate cumulative GPA of 3.0. Electronic applications accepted.

Royal Military College of Canada, Division of Graduate Studies and Research, Science Division, Department of Mathematics and Computer Science, Kingston, ON K7K 7B4, Canada. Offers computer science (M Sc); mathematics (M Sc). *Degree requirements:* For master's, thesis. *Entrance requirements:* For master's, honours degree with second-class standing. Electronic applications accepted.

Rutgers University–Camden, Graduate School of Arts and Sciences, Program in Computer Science, Camden, NJ 08102. Offers MS. *Program availability:* Part-time, evening/weekend. *Degree requirements:* For master's, comprehensive exam, thesis (for some programs), 30 credits. *Entrance requirements:* For master's, GRE, 3 letters of recommendation; statement of personal, professional, and academic goals; computer science undergraduate degree (preferred). Additional exam requirements/recommendations for international students: Required—TOEFL, IELTS. Electronic applications accepted. *Faculty research:* Cryptography and computer security, approximation algorithms, optical networks and wireless communications, computational geometry, data compression and encoding.

Rutgers University–New Brunswick, Graduate School-New Brunswick, Program in Computer Science, Piscataway, NJ 08854-8097. Offers MS, PhD. *Program availability:* Part-time. Terminal master's awarded for partial completion of doctoral program. *Degree requirements:* For master's, comprehensive exam, thesis; for doctorate, comprehensive exam, thesis/dissertation. *Entrance requirements:* For master's and doctorate, GRE General Test, GRE Subject Test. Additional exam requirements/recommendations for international students: Required—TOEFL. *Faculty research:* Artificial intelligence and machine learning, bioinformatics, algorithms and complexity, networking and operating systems, computational graphics and vision.

Sacred Heart University, Graduate Programs, College of Arts and Sciences, Department of Computer Science, Fairfield, CT 06825. Offers computer science (MS); computer science gaming (MS); cybersecurity (MS); information technology (MS). *Program availability:* Part-time, evening/weekend. *Faculty:* 7 full-time (2 women), 21 part-time/adjunct (4 women). *Students:* 256 full-time (93 women), 138 part-time (44 women); includes 28 minority (11 Black or African American, non-Hispanic/Latino; 3 Asian, non-Hispanic/Latino; 14 Hispanic/Latino), 319 international. Average age 25. 1,187 applicants, 65% accepted, 72 enrolled. In 2016, 275 master's awarded. *Degree requirements:* For master's, thesis or alternative. *Entrance requirements:* For master's, bachelor's degree, minimum GPA of 3.0. Additional exam requirements/recommendations for international students: Required—TOEFL (minimum score 570 paper-based, 80 iBT), TWE, or IELTS (6.5); Recommended—TSE. *Application deadline:* For fall admission, 5/15 for international students; for spring admission, 10/30 for international students. Applications are processed on a rolling basis. Application fee: $75. Electronic applications accepted. *Expenses:* $850 per credit part-time. *Financial support:* Unspecified assistantships available. Financial award applicants required to submit FAFSA. *Unit head:* Domenick Pinto, Director of the School of Computing, 203-371-7789, Fax: 203-371-0506, E-mail: pintod@sacredheart.edu. *Application contact:* William Sweeney, Director of Graduate Admissions Operations, 203-365-7619, Fax: 203-365-4732, E-mail: gradstudies@sacredheart.edu.
Website: http://www.sacredheart.edu/academics/collegeofartssciences/academicdepartments/computerscienceinformationtechnology/graduatedegreesandcertificates/

St. Cloud State University, School of Graduate Studies, College of Science and Engineering, Department of Computer Science and Information Technology, St. Cloud, MN 56301-4498. Offers computer science (MS). *Degree requirements:* For master's, thesis or alternative. *Entrance requirements:* For master's, GRE General Test, minimum GPA of 2.75. Additional exam requirements/recommendations for international students: Required—Michigan English Language Assessment Battery; Recommended—TOEFL (minimum score 550 paper-based), IELTS (minimum score 6.5). Electronic applications accepted.

St. Francis Xavier University, Graduate Studies, Department of Mathematics, Statistics and Computer Science, Antigonish, NS B2G 2W5, Canada. Offers computer science (M Sc). *Degree requirements:* For master's, thesis. *Entrance requirements:* For master's, bachelor's degree or equivalent in computer science with minimum B average, 2 letters of recommendation. Additional exam requirements/recommendations for international students: Required—TOEFL (minimum score 580 paper-based). *Expenses: Tuition:* Full-time $9060 Canadian dollars; part-time $725 Canadian dollars per credit. *Required fees:* $789 Canadian dollars; $78.84 Canadian dollars per credit. Tuition and fees vary according to course load, degree level and program. *Financial support:* Research assistantships, scholarships/grants, and unspecified assistantships available. *Unit head:* Dr. Iker Gondra, Coordinator, 902-867-3857, Fax: 902-867-3302, E-mail: cs_masters@stfx.ca. *Application contact:* Dr. Iker Gondra, Coordinator, 902-867-3857, Fax: 902-867-3302, E-mail: cs_masters@stfx.ca.

Saint Joseph's University, College of Arts and Sciences, Department of Computer Science, Philadelphia, PA 19131-1395. Offers computer science (MS); mathematics and computer science (Post-Master's Certificate). *Program availability:* Part-time, evening/weekend. *Faculty:* 4 full-time (1 woman), 2 part-time/adjunct (1 woman). *Students:* 44 full-time (15 women), 7 part-time (5 women); includes 2 minority (1 Asian, non-Hispanic/Latino; 1 Hispanic/Latino), 47 international. Average age 28. 85 applicants, 56% accepted, 11 enrolled. In 2016, 12 master's awarded. *Entrance requirements:* For master's, 2 letters of recommendation, resume, personal statement, official transcripts. Additional exam requirements/recommendations for international students: Required—TOEFL (minimum score 550 paper-based; 80 iBT), IELTS (minimum score 6.5). *Application deadline:* For fall admission, 7/15 for domestic and international students; for spring admission, 11/15 for domestic and international students. Applications are processed on a rolling basis. Application fee: $35. Electronic applications accepted. *Expenses:* $934 per credit. *Financial support:* In 2016–17, 13 students received support. Scholarships/grants and unspecified assistantships available. Financial award application deadline: 5/1; financial award applicants required to submit FAFSA. *Faculty research:* Computer vision, artificial intelligence, computer graphics, database modelling, computer security. *Unit head:* Dr. Babak Forouraghi, Director, 610-660-3131, E-mail: gradcas@sju.edu. *Application contact:* Graduate Admissions, College of Arts and Sciences, 610-660-3131, E-mail: gradcas@sju.edu.
Website: http://sju.edu/majors-programs/graduate-arts-sciences/masters/computer-science-ms

St. Mary's University, School of Science, Engineering and Technology, Program in Computer Information Systems, San Antonio, TX 78228-8507. Offers MS. *Program availability:* Part-time, evening/weekend. *Faculty:* 4 full-time (2 women), 1 part-time/adjunct (0 women). *Students:* 11 full-time (4 women), 6 part-time (0 women); includes 3 minority (1 Asian, non-Hispanic/Latino; 2 Hispanic/Latino), 14 international. Average age 31. 26 applicants, 15% accepted, 1 enrolled. In 2016, 14 master's awarded. *Degree requirements:* For master's, comprehensive exam, thesis optional. *Entrance requirements:* For master's, GMAT (minimum score of 334) or GRE General Test (minimum quantitative score of 148, analytical writing 2.5), minimum GPA of 3.0 in a bachelor's degree, written statement of purpose indicating interest and objective, two letters of recommendation, official transcripts of all college-level work. Additional exam requirements/recommendations for international students: Required—TOEFL (minimum score 530 paper-based; 80 iBT), IELTS (minimum score 6). *Application deadline:* For fall admission, 7/1 for domestic students; for spring admission, 11/15 for domestic students; for summer admission, 4/1 for domestic students. Applications are processed on a rolling basis. Application fee: $0. Electronic applications accepted. *Expenses: Tuition:* Full-time $15,600; part-time $865 per credit hour. *Required fees:* $148 per semester. *Financial support:* Career-related internships or fieldwork, Federal Work-Study, institutionally sponsored loans, scholarships/grants, health care benefits, and unspecified assistantships available. Financial award application deadline: 3/31; financial award applicants required to submit FAFSA. *Faculty research:* Artificial intelligence, biological modeling, computer languages, computer security, educational computer gaming. *Unit head:* Dr. Carol Redfield, Graduate Program Director, 210-436-3298, E-mail: credfield@stmarytx.edu.
Website: https://www.stmarytx.edu/academics/set/graduate/cis/

St. Mary's University, School of Science, Engineering and Technology, Program in Computer Science, San Antonio, TX 78228-8507. Offers MS. *Program availability:* Part-time, evening/weekend. *Faculty:* 4 full-time (2 women), 1 part-time/adjunct (0 women). *Students:* 21 full-time (7 women), 11 part-time (1 woman); includes 2 minority (both Hispanic/Latino), 26 international. Average age 28. 65 applicants, 29% accepted, 3 enrolled. In 2016, 40 master's awarded. *Degree requirements:* For master's, thesis or project. *Entrance requirements:* For master's, GRE (minimum quantitative score 148, analytical writing 2.5), GMAT (minimum score 334), written statement of purpose indicating interest and objective, two letters of recommendation, official transcripts of all college-level work, minimum GPA of 3.0 in a bachelor's degree. Additional exam requirements/recommendations for international students: Required—TOEFL (minimum score 550 paper-based; 80 iBT), IELTS (minimum score 6). *Application deadline:* For fall admission, 7/1 for domestic students; for spring admission, 11/15 for domestic students; for summer admission, 4/1 for domestic students. Applications are processed on a rolling basis. Application fee: $0. Electronic applications accepted. *Expenses: Tuition:* Full-time $15,600; part-time $865 per credit hour. *Required fees:* $148 per semester. *Financial support:* Fellowships, research assistantships, career-related internships or fieldwork, Federal Work-Study, institutionally sponsored loans, scholarships/grants, and health care benefits available. Financial award application deadline: 3/31; financial award applicants required to submit FAFSA. *Faculty research:* Artificial intelligence, biological modeling, computer languages, computer security, educational computer gaming. *Unit head:* Dr. Carol Redfield, Graduate Program Director, 210-436-3298, E-mail: credfield@stmarytx.edu.
Website: https://www.stmarytx.edu/academics/set/graduate/computer-science/

Saint Xavier University, Graduate Studies, College of Arts and Sciences, Department of Computer Science, Chicago, IL 60655-3105. Offers MACS. *Degree requirements:* For master's, thesis optional.

Sam Houston State University, College of Sciences, Department of Computer Science, Huntsville, TX 77341. Offers computing and information science (MS); digital forensics (MS); information assurance and security (MS). *Program availability:* Part-time. *Degree requirements:* For master's, comprehensive exam, thesis optional, internship; for doctorate, comprehensive exam, thesis/dissertation. *Entrance requirements:* For master's, GRE General Test, letters of recommendation. Additional exam requirements/recommendations for international students: Required—TOEFL (minimum score 550 paper-based; 79 iBT), IELTS (minimum score 6.5). Electronic applications accepted.

San Diego State University, Graduate and Research Affairs, College of Sciences, Program in Computer Science, San Diego, CA 92182. Offers MS. *Program availability:* Part-time. *Degree requirements:* For master's, comprehensive exam or thesis. *Entrance requirements:* For master's, GRE General Test. Additional exam requirements/recommendations for international students: Required—TOEFL. Electronic applications accepted.

San Francisco State University, Division of Graduate Studies, College of Science and Engineering, Department of Computer Science, San Francisco, CA 94132-1722. Offers MS. *Program availability:* Part-time. *Application deadline:* Applications are processed on a rolling basis. *Expenses:* Tuition, state resident: full-time $6738. Tuition, nonresident: full-time $15,666. *Required fees:* $1012. Tuition and fees vary according to degree level and program. *Unit head:* Dr. William Hsu, Chair, 415-338-2156, Fax: 415-338-6826, E-mail: whsu@sfsu.edu. *Application contact:* Prof. Kazunori Okada, Graduate Coordinator, 415-338-7687, Fax: 415-338-6826, E-mail: kazokada@sfsu.edu.
Website: http://cs.sfsu.edu/grad/graduate.html

San Francisco State University, Division of Graduate Studies, College of Science and Engineering, School of Engineering, San Francisco, CA 94132-1722. Offers embedded electrical and computer systems (MS); energy systems (MS); structural/earthquake engineering (MS). *Program availability:* Part-time. *Application deadline:* Applications are processed on a rolling basis. Electronic applications accepted. *Expenses:* Tuition, state resident: full-time $6738. Tuition, nonresident: full-time $15,666. *Required fees:* $1012. Tuition and fees vary according to degree level and program. *Unit head:* Dr. Wenshen Pong, Director, 415-338-7738, Fax: 415-338-0525, E-mail: wspong@sfsu.edu. *Application contact:* Dr. Hamid Shahnasser, Graduate Coordinator, 415-338-2124, Fax: 415-338-0525, E-mail: hamid@sfsu.edu.
Website: http://engineering.sfsu.edu/

San Jose State University, Graduate Studies and Research, College of Science, San Jose, CA 95192-0001. Offers biological sciences (MA, MS), including molecular biology and microbiology (MS), organismal biology, conservation and ecology (MS), physiology (MS); biotechnology (MBT); chemistry (MA, MS); computer science (MS); cybersecurity (Certificate); cybersecurity: core technologies (Certificate); geology (MS); marine science (MS); mathematics (MA, MS), including mathematics education (MA), science; meteorology (MS); physics (MS), including computational physics, modern optics, science (MA, MS); science education (MA); statistics (MS); Unix system administration (Certificate). *Program availability:* Part-time, evening/weekend. *Entrance requirements:*

For master's, GRE. Electronic applications accepted. *Faculty research:* Radiochemistry/environmental analysis, health physics, radiation effects.

Santa Clara University, School of Engineering, Santa Clara, CA 95053. Offers applied mathematics (MS); bioengineering (MS); civil engineering (MS); computer science and engineering (MS, PhD); electrical engineering (MS, PhD); engineering (Engineer); engineering management and leadership (MS); mechanical engineering (MS, PhD); software engineering (MS); sustainable energy (MS). *Program availability:* Part-time, evening/weekend. *Faculty:* 66 full-time (22 women), 59 part-time/adjunct (12 women). *Students:* 449 full-time (188 women), 315 part-time (114 women); includes 197 minority (3 Black or African American, non-Hispanic/Latino; 144 Asian, non-Hispanic/Latino; 33 Hispanic/Latino; 1 Native Hawaiian or other Pacific Islander, non-Hispanic/Latino; 16 Two or more races, non-Hispanic/Latino), 418 international. Average age 28. 1,217 applicants, 45% accepted, 293 enrolled. In 2016, 466 master's awarded. *Entrance requirements:* For master's, GRE, transcript; for doctorate, GRE, master's degree or equivalent, 3 letters of recommendation, statement of purpose; for Engineer, master's degree. Additional exam requirements/recommendations for international students: Required—TOEFL (minimum score 79 iBT) or IELTS (6.5). *Application deadline:* For fall admission, 4/1 for domestic and international students; for winter admission, 9/9 for domestic students, 9/2 for international students; for spring admission, 2/17 for domestic students, 12/9 for international students. Application fee: $60. Electronic applications accepted. *Expenses:* $928 per unit. *Financial support:* Fellowships, research assistantships, teaching assistantships, career-related internships or fieldwork, Federal Work-Study, scholarships/grants, traineeships, health care benefits, tuition waivers, and unspecified assistantships available. Support available to part-time students. Financial award applicants required to submit FAFSA. *Unit head:* Dr. Alfonso Ortega, Dean. *Application contact:* Stacey Tinker, Director of Admissions and Marketing, 408-554-4313, Fax: 408-554-4323, E-mail: stinker@scu.edu.
Website: http://www.scu.edu/engineering/graduate/

Seattle University, College of Science and Engineering, Program in Computer Science, Seattle, WA 98122-1090. Offers MSCS. *Faculty:* 11 full-time (4 women), 5 part-time/adjunct (0 women). *Students:* 33 full-time (10 women), 47 part-time (12 women); includes 24 minority (1 Black or African American, non-Hispanic/Latino; 18 Asian, non-Hispanic/Latino; 3 Hispanic/Latino; 2 Two or more races, non-Hispanic/Latino), 18 international. Average age 27. 100 applicants, 48% accepted, 35 enrolled. In 2016, 10 master's awarded. *Entrance requirements:* For master's, GRE, bachelor's degree in computer science or related discipline from regionally-accredited institution; minimum GPA of 3.0; letter of intent; 2 academic or professional recommendations; official transcripts. Additional exam requirements/recommendations for international students: Required—TOEFL (minimum score 580 paper-based; 92 iBT). *Application deadline:* For fall admission, 7/20 for domestic students, 4/1 for international students; for winter admission, 11/20 for domestic students, 9/1 for international students; for spring admission, 2/20 for domestic students, 12/1 for international students. *Financial support:* In 2016–17, 5 students received support. *Unit head:* Dr. Richard LeBlanc, Chair, 206-296-5510, Fax: 206-296-2071, E-mail: leblanc@seattleu.edu. *Application contact:* Janet Shandley, Director of Graduate Admissions, 206-296-5900, Fax: 206-298-5656, E-mail: grad_admissions@seattleu.edu.
Website: https://www.seattleu.edu/scieng/computer-science/graduate-degrees/master-of-science-in-computer-science/

Shippensburg University of Pennsylvania, School of Graduate Studies, College of Arts and Sciences, Department of Computer Science and Engineering, Shippensburg, PA 17257-2299. Offers agile software engineering (Certificate); computer science (MS), including computer science, cybersecurity, IT leadership, management information systems, software engineering; IT leadership (Certificate). *Program availability:* Part-time, evening/weekend. *Faculty:* 7 full-time (3 women). *Students:* 16 full-time (8 women), 14 part-time (5 women); includes 3 minority (2 Black or African American, non-Hispanic/Latino; 1 Hispanic/Latino), 21 international. Average age 29. 89 applicants, 49% accepted, 9 enrolled. In 2016, 10 master's awarded. *Entrance requirements:* For master's, GRE (if GPA less than 2.75), professional resume. Additional exam requirements/recommendations for international students: Required—TOEFL (minimum score 70 iBT) or IELTS (minimum score 6). *Application deadline:* For fall admission, 4/30 for international students; for spring admission, 9/30 for international students. Applications are processed on a rolling basis. Application fee: $45. Electronic applications accepted. *Expenses:* Tuition, state resident: part-time $483 per credit. Tuition, nonresident: part-time $725 per credit. *Required fees:* $141 per credit. *Financial support:* In 2016–17, 7 students received support. Career-related internships or fieldwork, scholarships/grants, unspecified assistantships, and resident hall director and student payroll positions available. Support available to part-time students. Financial award application deadline: 3/1; financial award applicants required to submit FAFSA. *Unit head:* Dr. Jeonghwa Lee, Associate Professor and Program Coordinator, 717-477-1178, Fax: 717-477-4002, E-mail: jlee@ship.edu. *Application contact:* Megan N. Luft, Assistant Dean of Graduate Admissions, 717-477-1231, Fax: 717-477-4016, E-mail: mnluft@ship.edu.
Website: http://www.cs.ship.edu/

Silicon Valley University, Graduate Programs, San Jose, CA 95131. Offers business administration (MBA); computer engineering (MSCE); computer science (MSCS). *Degree requirements:* For master's, project (MSCS).

Simon Fraser University, Office of Graduate Studies and Postdoctoral Fellows, Faculty of Applied Sciences, School of Computing Science, Burnaby, BC V5A 1S6, Canada. Offers M Sc, PhD, M Sc/MSE. M Sc/MSE offered jointly with Zhejiang University. *Faculty:* 50 full-time (8 women). *Students:* 289 full-time (79 women), 2 part-time (0 women). 890 applicants, 20% accepted, 90 enrolled. In 2016, 68 master's, 19 doctorates awarded. *Degree requirements:* For master's, comprehensive exam, thesis or alternative; for doctorate, comprehensive exam, thesis/dissertation, qualifying exams. *Entrance requirements:* For master's, minimum GPA of 3.0 (on scale of 4.33) or 3.33 based on last 60 credits of undergraduate courses; for doctorate, minimum GPA of 3.5 (on scale of 4.33). Additional exam requirements/recommendations for international students: Recommended—TOEFL (minimum score 580 paper-based; 93 iBT), IELTS (minimum score 7), TWE (minimum score 5). *Application deadline:* For fall admission, 2/1 priority date for domestic and international students; for winter admission, 8/1 for domestic students; for spring admission, 8/1 priority date for domestic and international students. Application fee: $90 ($125 for international students). Electronic applications accepted. *Financial support:* In 2016–17, 137 students received support, including 58 fellowships (averaging $6,500 per year), teaching assistantships (averaging $5,608 per year); research assistantships and scholarships/grants also available. *Faculty research:* Artificial intelligence, computer hardware, computer systems, database systems, theory. *Unit head:* Dr. Ghassan Hamarneh, Graduate Program Director, 778-782-2214, Fax: 778-782-3045, E-mail: cmpt-grad-chair@sfu.ca. *Application contact:* Melissa Apostoli, Graduate Secretary, 778-782-4842, Fax: 778-782-3045, E-mail: csgrada@sfu.ca.
Website: http://www.sfu.ca/computing.html

Simon Fraser University, Office of Graduate Studies and Postdoctoral Fellows, Faculty of Communication, Art and Technology, School of Interactive Arts and Technology, Surrey, BC V3T 2W1, Canada. Offers M Sc, MA, PhD. *Faculty:* 29 full-time (10 women). *Students:* 96 full-time (54 women). 118 applicants, 26% accepted, 16 enrolled. In 2016, 8 master's, 7 doctorates awarded. *Degree requirements:* For master's, thesis, seminar presentation; for doctorate, comprehensive exam, thesis/dissertation, seminar presentations. *Entrance requirements:* For master's, minimum GPA of 3.0 (on scale of 4.33) or 3.33 based on last 60 credits of undergraduate courses; for doctorate, minimum GPA of 3.5 (on scale of 4.33). Additional exam requirements/recommendations for international students: Required—TOEFL (minimum score 580 paper-based; 93 iBT), IELTS (minimum score 7), TWE (minimum score 5). *Application deadline:* For fall admission, 3/15 for domestic and international students. Application fee: $90 Canadian dollars ($125 Canadian dollars for international students). Electronic applications accepted. *Financial support:* In 2016–17, 43 students received support, including 20 fellowships (averaging $6,500 per year), teaching assistantships (averaging $5,608 per year); research assistantships and scholarships/grants also available. Financial award application deadline: 2/28. *Faculty research:* Media and culture, scientific methods, social and human experience, knowledge computation, media art. *Unit head:* Dr. Lyn Bartram, Graduate Chair, 778-782-2439, Fax: 778-782-9422, E-mail: siatgrad-chair@sfu.ca. *Application contact:* Tiffany Taylor, Graduate Program Assistant, 778-782-7499, Fax: 778-782-9422, E-mail: siatgrad-admissions@sfu.ca.
Website: http://www.sfu.ca/siat.html

Sofia University, Residential Programs, Palo Alto, CA 94303. Offers clinical psychology (Psy D); computer science (MS); counseling psychology (MA); transpersonal psychology (MA, PhD). *Program availability:* Part-time, evening/weekend. Terminal master's awarded for partial completion of doctoral program. *Degree requirements:* For doctorate, thesis/dissertation. *Entrance requirements:* For master's, bachelor's degree; for doctorate, bachelor's degree; master's degree (for some programs). Electronic applications accepted.

Southern Arkansas University–Magnolia, School of Graduate Studies, Magnolia, AR 71753. Offers agriculture (MS); business administration (MBA), including agri-business, social entrepreneurship, supply chain management; clinical and mental health counseling (MS); computer and information sciences (MS), including cyber security and privacy, data science, information technology; gifted and talented (M Ed), including curriculum and instruction, educational administration and supervision, gifted and talented P-8/7-12, instructional specialist P-4; higher, adult and lifelong education (M Ed); kinesiology (M Ed), including coaching; library media and information specialist (M Ed); public administration (MPA); school counseling K-12 (M Ed); student affairs and college counseling (M Ed); teaching (MAT). *Accreditation:* NCATE. *Program availability:* Part-time, 100% online, blended/hybrid learning. *Faculty:* 36 full-time (19 women), 33 part-time/adjunct (14 women). *Students:* 605 full-time (143 women), 879 part-time (352 women); includes 130 minority (113 Black or African American, non-Hispanic/Latino; 7 American Indian or Alaska Native, non-Hispanic/Latino; 2 Asian, non-Hispanic/Latino; 2 Hispanic/Latino; 6 Two or more races, non-Hispanic/Latino), 1,048 international. Average age 28. 904 applicants, 81% accepted, 262 enrolled. In 2016, 278 master's awarded. *Degree requirements:* For master's, comprehensive exam (for some programs), thesis optional. *Entrance requirements:* For master's, GRE, MAT or GMAT, minimum GPA of 2.5. Additional exam requirements/recommendations for international students: Required—TOEFL (minimum score 550 paper-based), IELTS (minimum score 6). *Application deadline:* For fall admission, 7/20 for domestic students, 7/10 for international students; for spring admission, 12/1 for domestic students, 11/15 for international students; for summer admission, 4/1 for domestic students, 5/1 for international students. Applications are processed on a rolling basis. Application fee: $25 ($50 for international students). Electronic applications accepted. *Expenses:* Tuition, state resident: full-time $2511; part-time $279 per credit hour. Tuition, nonresident: full-time $3726; part-time $414 per credit hour. *Required fees:* $307 per semester. Tuition and fees vary according to course load and program. *Financial support:* Career-related internships or fieldwork, Federal Work-Study, scholarships/grants, tuition waivers (full), and unspecified assistantships available. Financial award applicants required to submit FAFSA. *Faculty research:* Alternative certification for teachers, supervision of instruction, instructional leadership, counseling. *Unit head:* Dr. Kim Bloss, Dean, School of Graduate Studies, 870-235-4150, Fax: 870-235-5227, E-mail: kkbloss@saumag.edu. *Application contact:* Shrijana Malakar, Admissions Specialist, 870-235-4150, Fax: 870-235-5227, E-mail: smalakar@saumag.edu.
Website: http://www.saumag.edu/graduate

Southern Connecticut State University, School of Graduate Studies, School of Arts and Sciences, Department of Computer Science, New Haven, CT 06515-1355. Offers MS. *Program availability:* Part-time, evening/weekend. *Faculty:* 6 full-time (1 woman), 1 part-time/adjunct (0 women). *Students:* 13 full-time (1 woman), 23 part-time (5 women); includes 9 minority (2 Black or African American, non-Hispanic/Latino; 4 Asian, non-Hispanic/Latino; 2 Hispanic/Latino; 1 Two or more races, non-Hispanic/Latino), 2 international. Average age 34. 46 applicants, 39% accepted, 14 enrolled. In 2016, 5 master's awarded. *Entrance requirements:* For master's, GRE. *Application deadline:* Applications are processed on a rolling basis. Application fee: $50. Electronic applications accepted. *Expenses:* Tuition, state resident: full-time $6497; part-time $519 per credit hour. Tuition, nonresident: full-time $18,102; part-time $535 per credit hour. *Required fees:* $4722; $55 per semester. Tuition and fees vary according to program. *Financial support:* Career-related internships or fieldwork, scholarships/grants, and unspecified assistantships available. *Unit head:* Dr. Lisa Lancor, Chairperson, 203-392-5890, Fax: 203-392-5898, E-mail: lancorl1@southernct.edu. *Application contact:* Lisa Galvin, Director of Graduate Admissions, 203-392-5240, Fax: 203-392-5235, E-mail: galvinl1@southernct.edu.

Southern Illinois University Carbondale, Graduate School, College of Science, Department of Computer Science, Carbondale, IL 62901-4701. Offers MS, PhD. *Degree requirements:* For master's, thesis; for doctorate, thesis/dissertation. *Entrance requirements:* For master's, previous undergraduate course work in computer science, minimum GPA of 2.7; for doctorate, GRE General Test, minimum GPA of 3.25. Additional exam requirements/recommendations for international students: Required—TOEFL. *Faculty research:* Analysis of algorithms, VLSI testing, database systems, artificial intelligence, computer architecture.

Southern Illinois University Edwardsville, Graduate School, School of Engineering, Department of Computer Science, Edwardsville, IL 62026. Offers MS. *Program availability:* Part-time, evening/weekend. *Degree requirements:* For master's, thesis (for some programs), final exam, final project. *Entrance requirements:* Additional exam requirements/recommendations for international students: Required—TOEFL (minimum score 550 paper-based; 79 iBT), IELTS (minimum score 6.5). Electronic applications accepted.

Southern Methodist University, Bobby B. Lyle School of Engineering, Department of Computer Science and Engineering, Dallas, TX 75275-0122. Offers computer engineering (MS, PhD); computer science (MS, PhD); security engineering (MS); software engineering (MS, DE). *Program availability:* Part-time, evening/weekend, online learning. Terminal master's awarded for partial completion of doctoral program. *Degree requirements:* For master's, thesis optional; for doctorate, thesis/dissertation, oral and written qualifying exams, oral final exam (PhD). *Entrance requirements:* For master's, GRE General Test, minimum GPA of 3.0 in last 2 years; bachelor's degree in engineering, mathematics, or sciences; for doctorate, preliminary counseling exam (PhD), minimum GPA of 3.0, bachelor's degree in related field, MA (for DE). Additional exam requirements/recommendations for international students: Required—TOEFL (minimum score 550 paper-based). *Faculty research:* Trusted and high performance network computing, software engineering and management, knowledge engineering and management, computer arithmetic, computer architecture and CAD.

Southern Oregon University, Graduate Studies, Department of Computer Science, Ashland, OR 97520. Offers applied computer science (PSM). *Program availability:* Part-time, online learning. *Faculty:* 3 full-time (1 woman), 2 part-time/adjunct (0 women). *Students:* 2 full-time (1 woman). Average age 39. 2 applicants. In 2016, 1 master's awarded. *Degree requirements:* For master's, thesis (for some programs). *Entrance requirements:* For master's, GRE General Test, minimum cumulative GPA of 3.0 in the last 90 quarter credits (60 semester credits) of undergraduate coursework. Additional exam requirements/recommendations for international students: Required—TOEFL (minimum score 540 paper-based; 76 iBT), IELTS (minimum score 6), ELPT (minimum score 964) or ELS (minimum score 112). *Application deadline:* For fall admission, 7/31 priority date for domestic students, 7/30 priority date for international students; for winter admission, 11/15 priority date for domestic and international students; for spring admission, 1/7 priority date for domestic and international students. Applications are processed on a rolling basis. Application fee: $60. Electronic applications accepted. *Expenses:* Tuition, state resident: full-time $10,719; part-time $397 per credit. Tuition, nonresident: full-time $13,419; part-time $497 per credit. *Required fees:* $548. *Financial support:* In 2016–17, 1 student received support, including 1 research assistantship with partial tuition reimbursement available; career-related internships or fieldwork, institutionally sponsored loans, scholarships/grants, and unspecified assistantships also available. *Unit head:* Dr. Kevin Sahr, Graduate Program Coordinator, 541-552-6978. *Application contact:* Kelly Moutsatson, Director of Admissions, 541-552-6411, Fax: 541-552-8403, E-mail: admissions@sou.edu.
Website: http://www.sou.edu/cs/

Southern University and Agricultural and Mechanical College, Graduate School, College of Sciences, Department of Computer Science, Baton Rouge, LA 70813. Offers information systems (MS); micro/minicomputer architecture (MS); operating systems (MS). *Program availability:* Part-time, online learning. *Degree requirements:* For master's, thesis. *Entrance requirements:* For master's, GRE General Test, minimum GPA of 3.0, bachelor's degree in computer science or related field. Additional exam requirements/recommendations for international students: Required—TOEFL (minimum score 525 paper-based). *Faculty research:* Network theory, computational complexity, high speed computing, neural networking, data warehousing/mining.

Stanford University, School of Engineering, Department of Computer Science, Stanford, CA 94305-2004. Offers MS, PhD. Terminal master's awarded for partial completion of doctoral program. *Degree requirements:* For doctorate, thesis/dissertation. *Entrance requirements:* For master's, GRE General Test; for doctorate, GRE General Test, GRE Subject Test (computer science). Additional exam requirements/recommendations for international students: Required—TOEFL. Electronic applications accepted. *Expenses: Tuition:* Full-time $47,331. *Required fees:* $609.

Stanford University, School of Engineering, Institute for Computational and Mathematical Engineering, Stanford, CA 94305-2004. Offers MS, PhD. Terminal master's awarded for partial completion of doctoral program. *Degree requirements:* For doctorate, thesis/dissertation, qualifying exam. *Entrance requirements:* For master's, GRE General Test; for doctorate, GRE General Test, GRE Subject Test. Additional exam requirements/recommendations for international students: Required—TOEFL. Electronic applications accepted. *Expenses: Tuition:* Full-time $47,331. *Required fees:* $609.

State University of New York at New Paltz, Graduate School, School of Science and Engineering, Department of Computer Science, New Paltz, NY 12561. Offers MS. *Program availability:* Part-time, evening/weekend. *Students:* 63 full-time (13 women), 22 part-time (4 women); includes 3 minority (all Black or African American, non-Hispanic/Latino), 66 international. 199 applicants, 50% accepted, 21 enrolled. In 2016, 26 master's awarded. *Degree requirements:* For master's, comprehensive exam, thesis. *Entrance requirements:* For master's, minimum GPA of 3.0, proficiency in program assembly. Additional exam requirements/recommendations for international students: Required—TOEFL (minimum score 550 paper-based; 80 iBT), IELTS (minimum score 6.5). *Application deadline:* For fall admission, 5/15 for domestic and international students; for spring admission, 11/15 for domestic and international students. Applications are processed on a rolling basis. Application fee: $50. Electronic applications accepted. *Financial support:* In 2016–17, 4 teaching assistantships with partial tuition reimbursements (averaging $5,000 per year) were awarded. Financial award application deadline: 8/1. *Unit head:* Dr. Paul Zuckerman, Chair, 845-257-3516, Fax: 845-257-3996, E-mail: zuckerpr@newpaltz.edu.
Website: http://www.newpaltz.edu/compsci/

State University of New York Polytechnic Institute, Program in Computer and Information Science, Utica, NY 13502. Offers MS. *Program availability:* Part-time, evening/weekend. *Degree requirements:* For master's, thesis or project. *Entrance requirements:* For master's, GRE General Test, minimum GPA of 3.0, one letter of reference, resume, BS in computer science or a related field. Additional exam requirements/recommendations for international students: Required—TOEFL (minimum score 550 paper-based; 79 iBT), IELTS (minimum score 6.5). Electronic applications accepted. *Faculty research:* Cryptography, distributed systems, computer-aided system theory, reasoning with uncertainty, grid computing.

Stephen F. Austin State University, Graduate School, College of Business, Department of Computer Science, Nacogdoches, TX 75962. Offers MS. *Program availability:* Part-time. *Degree requirements:* For master's, comprehensive exam, thesis optional. *Entrance requirements:* For master's, GRE General Test. Additional exam requirements/recommendations for international students: Required—TOEFL.

Stevens Institute of Technology, Graduate School, Charles V. Schaefer Jr. School of Engineering and Science, Department of Computer Science, Program in Computer Science, Hoboken, NJ 07030. Offers MS, PhD, Certificate. *Program availability:* Part-time, evening/weekend. *Students:* 417 full-time (117 women), 57 part-time (12 women); includes 22 minority (2 Black or African American, non-Hispanic/Latino; 19 Asian, non-Hispanic/Latino; 1 Two or more races, non-Hispanic/Latino), 409 international. Average age 25. 1,183 applicants, 54% accepted, 184 enrolled. In 2016, 214 master's, 4 doctorates, 1 other advanced degree awarded. *Degree requirements:* For master's, thesis optional, minimum B average in major field and overall; for doctorate, comprehensive exam (for some programs), thesis/dissertation; for Certificate, minimum B average. *Entrance requirements:* Additional exam requirements/recommendations for international students: Required—TOEFL (minimum score 74 iBT), IELTS (minimum score 6). *Application deadline:* For fall admission, 6/1 for domestic students, 4/15 for international students; for spring admission, 11/30 for domestic students, 11/1 for international students. Applications are processed on a rolling basis. Application fee: $65. Electronic applications accepted. *Expenses:* Contact institution. *Financial support:* Fellowships, research assistantships, teaching assistantships, career-related internships or fieldwork, Federal Work-Study, scholarships/grants, and unspecified assistantships available. Financial award application deadline: 2/15; financial award applicants required to submit FAFSA. *Unit head:* Giuseppe Ateniese, Director, 201-216-3741, E-mail: gatenies@stevens.edu. *Application contact:* Graduate Admissions, 888-783-8367, Fax: 888-511-1306, E-mail: graduate@stevens.edu.

Stevens Institute of Technology, Graduate School, School of Business, Program in Information Systems, Hoboken, NJ 07030. Offers computer science (MS); e-commerce (MS); enterprise systems (MS); entrepreneurial information technology (MS); information architecture (MS); information management (MS, Certificate); information security (MS); information technology in financial services industry (MS); information technology in the pharmaceutical industry (MS); information technology outsourcing management (MS); project management (MS, Certificate); software engineering (MS); telecommunications (MS). *Program availability:* Part-time, evening/weekend. *Students:* 280 full-time (100 women), 84 part-time (21 women); includes 23 minority (9 Black or African American, non-Hispanic/Latino; 13 Asian, non-Hispanic/Latino; 1 Hispanic/Latino), 283 international. Average age 26. 925 applicants, 62% accepted, 114 enrolled. In 2016, 212 master's, 32 other advanced degrees awarded. *Degree requirements:* For master's, thesis optional, minimum B average in major field and overall; for Certificate, minimum B average. *Entrance requirements:* Additional exam requirements/recommendations for international students: Required—TOEFL (minimum score 74 iBT); IELTS (minimum score 6). *Application deadline:* For fall admission, 6/1 for domestic students, 4/15 for international students; for spring admission, 11/30 for domestic students, 11/1 for international students. Applications are processed on a rolling basis. Application fee: $65. Electronic applications accepted. *Expenses:* Contact institution. *Financial support:* Fellowships, research assistantships, teaching assistantships, career-related internships or fieldwork, Federal Work-Study, scholarships/grants, and unspecified assistantships available. Financial award application deadline: 2/15; financial award applicants required to submit FAFSA. *Unit head:* Dr. Gregory Prastacos, Dean, 201-216-8366, E-mail: gprastac@stevens.edu. *Application contact:* Graduate Admissions, 888-783-8367, Fax: 888-511-1306, E-mail: graduate@stevens.edu.
Website: https://www.stevens.edu/school-business/masters-programs/information-systems

Stony Brook University, State University of New York, Graduate School, College of Engineering and Applied Sciences, Department of Computer Science, Stony Brook, NY 11794-2424. Offers computer science (MS, PhD); information systems (Certificate); information systems engineering (MS); software engineering (Certificate). *Faculty:* 49 full-time (7 women), 3 part-time/adjunct (1 woman). *Students:* 399 full-time (92 women), 113 part-time (27 women); includes 22 minority (17 Asian, non-Hispanic/Latino; 3 Hispanic/Latino; 2 Two or more races, non-Hispanic/Latino), 458 international. Average age 26. 2,225 applicants, 26% accepted, 192 enrolled. In 2016, 198 master's, 18 doctorates awarded. Terminal master's awarded for partial completion of doctoral program. *Degree requirements:* For master's, thesis or alternative; for doctorate, comprehensive exam, thesis/dissertation. *Entrance requirements:* For master's and doctorate, GRE General Test. Additional exam requirements/recommendations for international students: Required—TOEFL (minimum score 90 iBT). *Application deadline:* For fall admission, 1/15 for domestic students; for spring admission, 10/1 for domestic students. Application fee: $100. *Expenses:* Contact institution. *Financial support:* In 2016–17, 1 fellowship, 57 research assistantships, 62 teaching assistantships were awarded. *Faculty research:* Cyber security, computer security, computer software, computer operating systems, computer and information sciences. *Total annual research expenditures:* $7.3 million. *Unit head:* Prof. Arie Kaufman, Chair, 631-632-8441, E-mail: arie.kaufman@stonybrook.edu. *Application contact:* Cynthia Scalzo, Coordinator, 631-632-1521, E-mail: cscalzo@cs.stonybrook.edu.
Website: http://www.cs.sunysb.edu/

Stratford University, School of Graduate Studies, Falls Church, VA 22043. Offers accounting (MS); business administration (IMBA, MBA); cyber security (MS); cyber security leadership and policy (MS); digital forensics (MS); enterprise business management (MS); entrepreneurial management (MS); healthcare administration (MS); information systems (MS); international hospitality management (MS); networking and telecommunications (MS); software engineering (MS). *Program availability:* Part-time, evening/weekend, 100% online, blended/hybrid learning. *Students:* 505 full-time (186 women), 172 part-time (88 women); includes 532 minority (165 Black or African American, non-Hispanic/Latino; 18 American Indian or Alaska Native, non-Hispanic/Latino; 324 Asian, non-Hispanic/Latino; 13 Hispanic/Latino; 10 Native Hawaiian or other Pacific Islander, non-Hispanic/Latino; 2 Two or more races, non-Hispanic/Latino). Average age 27. In 2016, 520 master's awarded. *Degree requirements:* For master's, comprehensive exam, capstone project. *Entrance requirements:* For master's, GRE or GMAT, baccalaureate degree. Additional exam requirements/recommendations for international students: Required—TOEFL (minimum score 79 iBT), IELTS (minimum score 6.5), PTE (minimum score 5). *Application deadline:* Applications are processed on a rolling basis. Application fee: $50. Electronic applications accepted. *Expenses: Tuition:* Full-time $4455; part-time $2227.50 per course. One-time fee: $100. *Financial support:* Federal Work-Study and scholarships/grants available. Financial award applicants required to submit FAFSA. *Unit head:* Dr. Richard R. Shurtz, President, 703-539-6890, Fax: 703-539-6960. *Application contact:* Admissions, 800-444-0804, E-mail: fcadmissions@stratford.edu.

Syracuse University, College of Engineering and Computer Science, MS Program in Computer Science, Syracuse, NY 13244. Offers MS. *Program availability:* Part-time. *Students:* Average age 25. In 2016, 53 master's awarded. *Degree requirements:* For master's, comprehensive exam (for some programs), thesis (for some programs). *Entrance requirements:* For master's, GRE General Test, three letters of recommendation, resume, personal statement, official transcripts. Additional exam requirements/recommendations for international students: Required—TOEFL (minimum score 100 iBT). *Application deadline:* For fall admission, 7/1 priority date for domestic students, 6/1 priority date for international students; for spring admission, 11/15 priority date for domestic students, 10/15 priority date for international students. Applications are processed on a rolling basis. Application fee: $75. Electronic applications accepted. *Expenses: Tuition:* Full-time $25,974; part-time $1443 per credit hour. *Required fees:* $802; $50 per course. Tuition and fees vary according to course load and program. *Financial support:* Fellowships with full tuition reimbursements, research assistantships with tuition reimbursements, teaching assistantships with tuition reimbursements, and tuition waivers (partial) available. Financial award application deadline: 1/1; financial award applicants required to submit FAFSA. *Faculty research:* Structured programming and formal methods, computer architecture, operating systems, design and analysis of algorithms. *Unit head:* Dr. Susan Older, Program Director, 315-443-4679, Fax: 315-443-2583, E-mail: sueo@ecs.syr.edu. *Application contact:* Kathleen Joyce, Assistant Dean, 315-443-2219, E-mail: topgrads@syr.edu.
Website: http://eng-cs.syr.edu/

Télé-université, Graduate Programs, Québec, QC G1K 9H5, Canada. Offers computer science (PhD); corporate finance (MS); distance learning (MS). *Program availability:* Part-time.

Temple University, College of Science and Technology, Department of Computer and Information Sciences, Philadelphia, PA 19122. Offers computer and information science (PhD); computer science (MS); information science and technology (MS). *Program* *availability:* Part-time, evening/weekend. Terminal master's awarded for partial completion of doctoral program. *Degree requirements:* For doctorate, thesis/dissertation. *Entrance requirements:* For master's and doctorate, GRE General Test, minimum GPA of 3.0. Additional exam requirements/recommendations for international students: Required—TOEFL (minimum score 550 paper-based; 79 iBT). Electronic applications accepted. *Faculty research:* Artificial intelligence, information systems, software engineering, network-distributed systems.

Tennessee Technological University, College of Graduate Studies, College of Engineering, Department of Computer Science, Cookeville, TN 38505. Offers computer software and scientific applications (MS); Internet-based computing (MS). *Program availability:* Part-time. *Students:* 11 full-time (4 women), 9 part-time (0 women); includes 1 minority (Black or African American, non-Hispanic/Latino), 10 international. 99 applicants, 44% accepted, 8 enrolled. In 2016, 5 master's awarded. *Degree requirements:* For master's, thesis or alternative. *Entrance requirements:* For master's, GRE. Additional exam requirements/recommendations for international students: Required—TOEFL (minimum score 550 paper-based; 79 iBT), IELTS (minimum score 5.5), PTE (minimum score 53), or TOEIC (Test of English as an International Communication). *Application deadline:* For fall admission, 8/1 for domestic students, 5/1 for international students; for spring admission, 12/1 for domestic students, 10/1 for international students; for summer admission, 5/1 for domestic students, 2/1 for international students. Applications are processed on a rolling basis. Application fee: $35 ($40 for international students). Electronic applications accepted. *Expenses:* Tuition, state resident: full-time $9375; part-time $534 per credit hour. Tuition, nonresident: full-time $22,443; part-time $1260 per credit hour. *Financial support:* In 2016–17, 6 research assistantships (averaging $7,500 per year), 8 teaching assistantships (averaging $7,500 per year) were awarded. Financial award application deadline: 4/1. *Unit head:* Dr. Jerry Gannod, Chairperson, 931-372-3691, Fax: 931-372-3686, E-mail: jgannod@tntech.edu. *Application contact:* Shelia K. Kendrick, Coordinator of Graduate Studies, 931-372-3808, Fax: 931-372-3497, E-mail: skendrick@tntech.edu.

Texas A&M University, College of Engineering, Department of Computer Science and Engineering, College Station, TX 77843. Offers computer engineering (M Eng, MS, PhD); computer science (MCS, MS, PhD). *Program availability:* Part-time. *Faculty:* 45. *Students:* 273 full-time (46 women), 35 part-time (7 women); includes 38 minority (6 Black or African American, non-Hispanic/Latino; 12 Asian, non-Hispanic/Latino; 17 Hispanic/Latino; 1 Native Hawaiian or other Pacific Islander, non-Hispanic/Latino; 2 Two or more races, non-Hispanic/Latino), 228 international. Average age 27. 2,131 applicants, 10% accepted, 86 enrolled. In 2016, 80 master's, 28 doctorates awarded. *Degree requirements:* For master's, thesis (for some programs); for doctorate, thesis/dissertation. *Entrance requirements:* For master's and doctorate, GRE General Test. Additional exam requirements/recommendations for international students: Required—TOEFL (minimum score 550 paper-based; 80 iBT), IELTS (minimum score 6), PTE (minimum score 53). *Application deadline:* For fall admission, 1/1 priority date for domestic and international students; for spring admission, 8/1 priority date for domestic and international students. Applications are processed on a rolling basis. Application fee: $50 ($90 for international students). Electronic applications accepted. *Expenses:* Contact institution. *Financial support:* In 2016–17, 238 students received support, including 6 fellowships with tuition reimbursements available (averaging $19,491 per year), 110 research assistantships with tuition reimbursements available (averaging $6,088 per year), 68 teaching assistantships with tuition reimbursements available (averaging $10,385 per year); career-related internships or fieldwork, institutionally sponsored loans, scholarships/grants, traineeships, health care benefits, tuition waivers (full and partial), and unspecified assistantships also available. Support available to part-time students. Financial award application deadline: 3/15; financial award applicants required to submit FAFSA. *Faculty research:* Software, systems, informatics, human-centered systems, theory. *Unit head:* Dr. Dilma Da Silva, Department Head, 979-845-5820, E-mail: dilma@cse.tamu.edu. *Application contact:* Dr. Duncan M. Walker, Professor and Graduate Advisor, 979-458-4087, E-mail: grad-advisor@cse.tamu.edu. Website: http://engineering.tamu.edu/cse/

Texas A&M University–Corpus Christi, College of Graduate Studies, College of Science and Engineering, Program in Computer Science, Corpus Christi, TX 78412-5503. Offers MS. *Program availability:* Part-time, evening/weekend. *Students:* 51 full-time (15 women), 5 part-time (1 woman); includes 5 minority (1 Black or African American, non-Hispanic/Latino; 2 Asian, non-Hispanic/Latino; 2 Hispanic/Latino), 50 international. Average age 26. 154 applicants, 32% accepted, 14 enrolled. In 2016, 40 master's awarded. *Degree requirements:* For master's, thesis (for some programs), thesis or project. *Entrance requirements:* For master's, GRE (taken within 5 years), essay (500-1,000 words). Additional exam requirements/recommendations for international students: Required—TOEFL (minimum score 550 paper-based; 79 iBT), IELTS (minimum score 6.5). *Application deadline:* For fall admission, 2/1 priority date for domestic and international students; for spring admission, 11/15 priority date for domestic students, 10/1 priority date for international students; for summer admission, 4/15 priority date for domestic students, 2/1 priority date for international students. Applications are processed on a rolling basis. Application fee: $50 ($70 for international students). Electronic applications accepted. *Financial support:* Research assistantships, career-related internships or fieldwork, Federal Work-Study, institutionally sponsored loans, scholarships/grants, health care benefits, and unspecified assistantships available. Support available to part-time students. Financial award application deadline: 3/15; financial award applicants required to submit FAFSA. *Unit head:* Dr. Ajay Katangur, Program Coordinator, 361-825-2478, E-mail: scott.king@tamucc.edu. *Application contact:* Graduate Admissions Coordinator, 361-825-2177, Fax: 361-825-2755, E-mail: gradweb@tamucc.edu. Website: http://cs.tamucc.edu/masters.html

Texas A&M University–Kingsville, College of Graduate Studies, Frank H. Dotterweich College of Engineering, Department of Electrical Engineering and Computer Science, Program in Computer Science, Kingsville, TX 78363. Offers MS. *Degree requirements:* For master's, variable foreign language requirement, comprehensive exam, thesis (for some programs). *Entrance requirements:* For master's, GRE (minimum Quantitative and Verbal score of 288), MAT, GMAT, minimum undergraduate GPA of 3.0. Additional exam requirements/recommendations for international students: Required—TOEFL (minimum score 550 paper-based; 79 iBT). Electronic applications accepted.

Texas Southern University, School of Science and Technology, Department of Computer Science, Houston, TX 77004-4584. Offers MS. Electronic applications accepted.

Texas State University, The Graduate College, College of Science and Engineering, Program in Computer Science, San Marcos, TX 78666. Offers MA, MS. *Program availability:* Part-time. *Faculty:* 13 full-time (2 women). *Students:* 71 full-time (34 women), 42 part-time (20 women); includes 16 minority (3 Black or African American, non-Hispanic/Latino; 1 American Indian or Alaska Native, non-Hispanic/Latino; 6 Asian, non-Hispanic/Latino; 5 Hispanic/Latino; 1 Two or more races, non-Hispanic/Latino), 86 international. Average age 28. 274 applicants, 41% accepted, 32 enrolled. In 2016, 75 master's awarded. *Degree requirements:* For master's, comprehensive exam, thesis (for some programs). *Entrance requirements:* For master's, GRE General Test (minimum preferred score of 286 with no less than 140 on the verbal section and 148 on the

quantitative section), baccalaureate degree from regionally-accredited university with minimum GPA of 2.75 on last 60 undergraduate semester hours, 3 letters of recommendation, academic vitae (resume), statement of purpose. Additional exam requirements/recommendations for international students: Required—TOEFL (minimum score 550 paper-based; 78 iBT), IELTS (minimum score 6.5). *Application deadline:* For fall admission, 2/15 priority date for domestic and international students; for spring admission, 10/15 for domestic students, 10/1 for international students; for summer admission, 4/15 for domestic students, 3/15 for international students. Applications are processed on a rolling basis. Application fee: $40 ($90 for international students). Electronic applications accepted. *Expenses:* $4,851 per semester. *Financial support:* In 2016–17, 24 students received support, including 5 research assistantships (averaging $13,338 per year), 20 teaching assistantships (averaging $13,670 per year); Federal Work-Study, institutionally sponsored loans, scholarships/grants, health care benefits, and unspecified assistantships also available. Support available to part-time students. Financial award application deadline: 3/1; financial award applicants required to submit FAFSA. *Faculty research:* Power consumption based multicore task scheduling and load balancing; securing mobile cyber-physical systems (CPSs) against stealthy attacks; shared high performance data center;. *Total annual research expenditures:* $329,751. *Unit head:* Dr. Wuxu Peng, Graduate Advisor, 512-245-3874, Fax: 512-245-8750, E-mail: wp01@txstate.edu. *Application contact:* Dr. Andrea Golato, Dean of the Graduate College, 512-245-2581, E-mail: gradcollege@txstate.edu. Website: http://www.cs.txstate.edu/

Texas Tech University, Graduate School, Edward E. Whitacre Jr. College of Engineering, Department of Computer Science, Lubbock, TX 79409-3104. Offers computer science (MS, PhD); software engineering (MS). *Program availability:* Part-time, blended/hybrid learning. *Faculty:* 19 full-time (5 women). *Students:* 78 full-time (28 women), 33 part-time (10 women); includes 8 minority (1 Asian, non-Hispanic/Latino; 5 Hispanic/Latino; 2 Two or more races, non-Hispanic/Latino), 85 international. Average age 29. 257 applicants, 36% accepted, 34 enrolled. In 2016, 47 master's, 6 doctorates awarded. Terminal master's awarded for partial completion of doctoral program. *Degree requirements:* For master's, comprehensive exam (for some programs), thesis (for some programs); for doctorate, comprehensive exam, thesis/dissertation. *Entrance requirements:* For master's and doctorate, GRE (Verbal and Quantitative). Additional exam requirements/recommendations for international students: Required—TOEFL (minimum score 550 paper-based; 79 iBT). *Application deadline:* For fall admission, 6/1 priority date for domestic students, 1/15 priority date for international students; for spring admission, 9/1 priority date for domestic students, 6/15 priority date for international students. Applications are processed on a rolling basis. Application fee: $75. Electronic applications accepted. *Expenses:* $325 per credit hour full-time resident tuition, $733 per credit hour full-time non-resident tuition; $53.75 per credit hour fee plus $608 per term fee. *Financial support:* In 2016–17, 53 students received support, including 48 fellowships (averaging $4,116 per year), 26 research assistantships (averaging $8,503 per year), 15 teaching assistantships (averaging $15,336 per year); scholarships/grants, tuition waivers (partial), and unspecified assistantships also available. Financial award application deadline: 4/15; financial award applicants required to submit FAFSA. *Faculty research:* High performance and parallel computing; cyber security and data science; software engineering (quality assurance, testing, design specification); artificial intelligence (intelligent systems, knowledge representation); mobile and computer networks. *Total annual research expenditures:* $1 million. *Unit head:* Dr. Rattikorn Hewett, Professor and Chair, 806-742-3527, Fax: 806-742-3519, E-mail: rattikorn.hewett@ttu.edu. *Application contact:* Jeremy Herrera, Staff Graduate Advisor, 806-742-3527, Fax: 806-742-3519, E-mail: jeremy.herrera@ttu.edu. Website: http://www.cs.ttu.edu/

Towson University, Program in Computer Science, Towson, MD 21252-0001. Offers MS. *Program availability:* Part-time, evening/weekend. *Students:* 46 full-time (14 women), 91 part-time (25 women); includes 38 minority (12 Black or African American, non-Hispanic/Latino; 21 Asian, non-Hispanic/Latino; 2 Hispanic/Latino; 3 Two or more races, non-Hispanic/Latino), 29 international. *Degree requirements:* For master's, thesis optional. *Entrance requirements:* For master's, minimum GPA of 3.0, bachelor's degree in computer science or bachelor's degree in any other field and completion of 1-3 preparatory courses. *Application deadline:* Applications are processed on a rolling basis. Application fee: $45. Electronic applications accepted. *Expenses:* Tuition, state resident: full-time $7580; part-time $379 per unit. Tuition, nonresident: full-time $15,700; part-time $785 per unit. *Required fees:* $2480. *Financial support:* Application deadline: 4/1. *Unit head:* Dr. Yanggon Kim, Graduate Program Director, 410-704-3782, E-mail: ykim@towson.edu. *Application contact:* Coverley Beidleman, Assistant Director of Graduate Admissions, 410-704-2113, Fax: 410-704-3030, E-mail: grads@towson.edu. Website: http://www.towson.edu/fcsm/departments/computerinfosci/grad/computersci/

Toyota Technological Institute at Chicago, Program in Computer Science, Chicago, IL 60637. Offers PhD. *Degree requirements:* For doctorate, thesis/dissertation.

Trent University, Graduate Studies, Program in Applications of Modeling in the Natural and Social Sciences, Department of Computer Studies, Peterborough, ON K9J 7B8, Canada. Offers M Sc. *Degree requirements:* For master's, thesis. *Entrance requirements:* For master's, honours degree.

Troy University, Graduate School, College of Arts and Sciences, Program in Computer Science, Troy, AL 36082. Offers MS. *Program availability:* Part-time, evening/weekend. *Faculty:* 7 full-time (1 woman), 2 part-time/adjunct (1 woman). *Students:* 112 full-time (24 women), 47 part-time (10 women); includes 26 minority (10 Black or African American, non-Hispanic/Latino; 14 Asian, non-Hispanic/Latino; 1 Hispanic/Latino; 1 Two or more races, non-Hispanic/Latino). Average age 25. 495 applicants, 71% accepted, 10 enrolled. In 2016, 61 master's awarded. *Degree requirements:* For master's, thesis or research paper and comprehensive exam; minimum GPA of 3.0; admission to candidacy. *Entrance requirements:* For master's, GRE (minimum score of 850 on old exam or 286 on new exam), MAT (minimum score of 385) or GMAT (minimum score of 380), bachelor's degree; minimum undergraduate GPA of 2.5 or 3.0 on last 30 semester hours. Additional exam requirements/recommendations for international students: Required—TOEFL (minimum score 523 paper-based; 70 iBT), IELTS (minimum score 6). *Application deadline:* For fall admission, 6/1 for international students; for spring admission, 10/15 for international students. Applications are processed on a rolling basis. Application fee: $50. Electronic applications accepted. *Expenses:* Tuition, state resident: full-time $7146; part-time $397 per credit hour. Tuition, nonresident: full-time $14,292; part-time $794 per credit hour. *Required fees:* $802; $50 per semester. Tuition and fees vary according to campus/location and program. *Financial support:* Fellowships, career-related internships or fieldwork, and scholarships/grants available. Support available to part-time students. Financial award applicants required to submit FAFSA. *Unit head:* Dr. Bill Zhong, Department Chairman/Professor, 334-670-3388, Fax: 334-670-3796, E-mail: jzhong@troy.edu. *Application contact:* Jessica A. Kimbro, Director of Graduate Admissions, 334-670-3178, E-mail: jacord@troy.edu.

Tufts University, Graduate School of Arts and Sciences, Graduate Certificate Programs, Computer Science Program, Medford, MA 02155. Offers Certificate. *Program availability:* Part-time, evening/weekend. Electronic applications accepted. *Expenses:* Tuition: Full-time $49,892; part-time $1248 per credit hour. *Required fees:* $844. Full-time tuition and fees vary according to degree level, program and student level. Part-time tuition and fees vary according to course load.

Tufts University, Graduate School of Arts and Sciences, Graduate Certificate Programs, Post-Baccalaureate Minor Program in Computer Science, Medford, MA 02155. Offers Certificate. *Program availability:* Part-time, evening/weekend. Electronic applications accepted. *Expenses: Tuition:* Full-time $49,892; part-time $1248 per credit hour. *Required fees:* $844. Full-time tuition and fees vary according to degree level, program and student level. Part-time tuition and fees vary according to course load.

Tufts University, School of Engineering, Department of Computer Science, Medford, MA 02155. Offers bioengineering (ME, MS), including bioinformatics; cognitive science (PhD); computer science (MS, PhD). *Program availability:* Part-time. Terminal master's awarded for partial completion of doctoral program. *Degree requirements:* For master's, thesis (for some programs); for doctorate, thesis/dissertation. *Entrance requirements:* For master's and doctorate, GRE General Test. Additional exam requirements/recommendations for international students: Required—TOEFL (minimum score 550 paper-based; 80 iBT), IELTS (minimum score 6.5). Electronic applications accepted. *Expenses: Tuition:* Full-time $49,892; part-time $1248 per credit hour. *Required fees:* $844. Full-time tuition and fees vary according to degree level, program and student level. Part-time tuition and fees vary according to course load. *Faculty research:* Computational biology, computational geometry, and computational systems biology; cognitive sciences, human-computer interaction, and human-robotic interaction; visualization and graphics, educational technologies; machine learning and data mining; programming languages and systems.

Universidad Autonoma de Guadalajara, Graduate Programs, Guadalajara, Mexico. Offers administrative law and justice (LL M); advertising and corporate communications (MA); architecture (M Arch); business (MBA); computational science (MCC); education (Ed M, Ed D); English-Spanish translation (MA); entrepreneurship and management (MBA); integrated management of digital animation (MA); international business (MIB); international corporate law (LL M); internet technologies (MS); manufacturing systems (MMS); occupational health (MS); philosophy (MA, PhD); power electronics (MS); quality systems (MQS); renewable energy (MS); social evaluation of projects (MBA); strategic market research (MBA); tax law (MA); teaching mathematics (MA).

Universidad de las Américas Puebla, Division of Graduate Studies, School of Engineering, Program in Computer Engineering, Puebla, Mexico. Offers computer science (MS). *Program availability:* Part-time, evening/weekend. *Degree requirements:* For master's, one foreign language, thesis. *Faculty research:* Computers in education, robotics, artificial intelligence.

Universidad de las Américas Puebla, Division of Graduate Studies, School of Engineering, Program in Computer Science, Puebla, Mexico. Offers PhD.

Université de Moncton, Faculty of Sciences, Information Technology Programs, Moncton, NB E1A 3E9, Canada. Offers M Sc, Certificate, Diploma. *Program availability:* Part-time. *Degree requirements:* For master's, thesis. Electronic applications accepted. *Faculty research:* Programming, databases, networks.

Université de Montréal, Faculty of Arts and Sciences, Department of Computer Science and Operational Research, Montréal, QC H3C 3J7, Canada. Offers computer systems (M Sc, PhD); electronic commerce (M Sc). *Program availability:* Part-time. Terminal master's awarded for partial completion of doctoral program. *Degree requirements:* For master's, one foreign language, thesis; for doctorate, one foreign language, thesis/dissertation, general exam. *Entrance requirements:* For master's, B Sc in related field; for doctorate, MA or M Sc in related field. Electronic applications accepted. *Faculty research:* Optimization statistics, programming languages, telecommunications, theoretical computer science, artificial intelligence.

Université du Québec à Trois-Rivières, Graduate Programs, Program in Mathematics and Computer Science, Trois-Rivières, QC G9A 5H7, Canada. Offers M Sc. *Faculty research:* Probability, statistics.

Université du Québec en Outaouais, Graduate Programs, Program in Computer Network, Gatineau, QC J8X 3X7, Canada. Offers computer science (M Sc, PhD, DESS). *Program availability:* Part-time, evening/weekend. *Degree requirements:* For master's, thesis; for doctorate, thesis/dissertation.

Université Laval, Faculty of Sciences and Engineering, Department of Computer Science, Programs in Computer Science, Québec, QC G1K 7P4, Canada. Offers M Sc, PhD. Terminal master's awarded for partial completion of doctoral program. *Degree requirements:* For master's, thesis; for doctorate, thesis/dissertation. *Entrance requirements:* For master's and doctorate, knowledge of French and English. Electronic applications accepted.

University at Albany, State University of New York, College of Engineering and Applied Sciences, Programs in Computer Science, Albany, NY 12222-0001. Offers MS, PhD. *Faculty:* 29 full-time (10 women), 14 part-time/adjunct (3 women). *Students:* 116 full-time (31 women), 83 part-time (28 women); includes 11 minority (3 Black or African American, non-Hispanic/Latino; 6 Asian, non-Hispanic/Latino; 1 Hispanic/Latino; 1 Two or more races, non-Hispanic/Latino), 168 international. Average age 27. 455 applicants, 60% accepted, 83 enrolled. In 2016, 80 master's, 4 doctorates awarded. *Degree requirements:* For master's, comprehensive exam, project or thesis; for doctorate, comprehensive exam, thesis/dissertation, area exams. *Entrance requirements:* For master's and doctorate, GRE General Test. Additional exam requirements/recommendations for international students: Required—TOEFL (minimum score 550 paper-based). *Application deadline:* For fall admission, 8/1 for domestic students, 5/1 for international students; for spring admission, 11/1 for domestic and international students. Applications are processed on a rolling basis. Application fee: $75. Electronic applications accepted. *Expenses:* Tuition, state resident: full-time $10,870; part-time $453 per credit hour. Tuition, nonresident: full-time $22,210; part-time $925 per credit hour. *International tuition:* $21,550 full-time. *Required fees:* $1864; $96 per credit hour. *Financial support:* Fellowships, research assistantships, teaching assistantships, career-related internships or fieldwork, and Federal Work-Study available. Financial award application deadline: 3/1. *Faculty research:* Algorithm design and analysis, artificial intelligence, computational logic, databases, numerical analysis. *Total annual research expenditures:* $1.8 million. *Unit head:* Randy Moulic, Chair, 518-956-8242, Fax: 518-442-5638, E-mail: jmoulic@albany.edu.
Website: http://www.cs.albany.edu/

University at Buffalo, the State University of New York, Graduate School, School of Engineering and Applied Sciences, Department of Computer Science and Engineering, Buffalo, NY 14260. Offers computer science and engineering (MS, PhD); information assurance (Certificate). *Program availability:* Part-time. Terminal master's awarded for partial completion of doctoral program. *Degree requirements:* For master's, thesis or alternative; for doctorate, thesis/dissertation, comprehensive qualifying exam. *Entrance requirements:* For master's and doctorate, GRE General Test. Additional exam requirements/recommendations for international students: Required—TOEFL (minimum score 550 paper-based; 79 iBT). Electronic applications accepted. *Faculty research:* Bioinformatics, pattern recognition, computer networks and security, theory and algorithms, databases and data mining.

University of Advancing Technology, Master of Science Program in Technology, Tempe, AZ 85283-1042. Offers advancing computer science (MS); emerging technologies (MS); game production and management (MS); information assurance (MS); technology leadership (MS). *Degree requirements:* For master's, project or thesis. *Entrance requirements:* Additional exam requirements/recommendations for international students: Required—TOEFL (minimum score 550 paper-based). Electronic applications accepted. *Faculty research:* Artificial intelligence, fractals, organizational management.

The University of Akron, Graduate School, Buchtel College of Arts and Sciences, Department of Computer Science, Akron, OH 44325. Offers MS. *Faculty:* 7 full-time (2 women), 2 part-time/adjunct (0 women). *Students:* 40 full-time (15 women), 6 part-time (1 woman); includes 1 minority (Two or more races, non-Hispanic/Latino), 40 international. Average age 24. 123 applicants, 33% accepted, 10 enrolled. In 2016, 42 master's awarded. *Degree requirements:* For master's, thesis optional. *Entrance requirements:* For master's, baccalaureate degree in computer science or a related field; three letters of recommendation; statement of purpose; resume; knowledge of one high-level programming language; mathematical maturity; proficiency in data structures, computer organization, and operating systems. Additional exam requirements/recommendations for international students: Required—TOEFL (minimum score 550 paper-based; 79 iBT), IELTS (minimum score 6.5). *Application deadline:* For fall admission, 3/15 for domestic and international students; for spring admission, 10/15 for domestic and international students. Application fee: $45 ($70 for international students). Electronic applications accepted. *Expenses:* Tuition, state resident: full-time $8618; part-time $359 per credit hour. Tuition, nonresident: full-time $17,149; part-time $715 per credit hour. *Required fees:* $1652. *Financial support:* In 2016–17, 6 research assistantships with full tuition reimbursements, 6 teaching assistantships with full and partial tuition reimbursements were awarded; unspecified assistantships and instructional support assistantships also available. *Faculty research:* Bioinformatics, database/data mining, networking, parallel computing, visualization. *Total annual research expenditures:* $163,574. *Unit head:* Dr. David Steer, Interim Chair, 330-972-2099, E-mail: steer@uakron.edu. *Application contact:* Dr. Timothy O'Neil, Graduate Program Coordinator, 330-972-6492, E-mail: toneil@uakron.edu.
Website: http://www.uakron.edu/computer-science/

The University of Alabama, Graduate School, College of Engineering, Department of Computer Science, Tuscaloosa, AL 35487-0290. Offers MS, PhD. *Program availability:* Part-time. *Faculty:* 15 full-time (2 women). *Students:* 29 full-time (12 women), 8 part-time (0 women); includes 2 minority (1 Black or African American, non-Hispanic/Latino; 1 Hispanic/Latino), 23 international. Average age 28. 46 applicants, 30% accepted, 10 enrolled. In 2016, 11 master's, 2 doctorates awarded. Terminal master's awarded for partial completion of doctoral program. *Degree requirements:* For master's, comprehensive exam, thesis (for some programs); for doctorate, comprehensive exam, thesis/dissertation. *Entrance requirements:* For master's and doctorate, GRE. Additional exam requirements/recommendations for international students: Required—TOEFL (minimum score 550 paper-based; 79 iBT). *Application deadline:* For fall admission, 6/1 priority date for domestic students, 3/1 for international students; for winter admission, 8/1 for international students; for spring admission, 11/1 priority date for domestic students, 8/1 for international students; for summer admission, 1/1 for international students. Applications are processed on a rolling basis. Application fee: $50 ($60 for international students). Electronic applications accepted. *Expenses:* Tuition, state resident: full-time $10,470. Tuition, nonresident: full-time $26,950. *Financial support:* In 2016–17, 28 students received support, including 2 fellowships with full tuition reimbursements available (averaging $15,000 per year), 10 research assistantships with full tuition reimbursements available (averaging $15,750 per year), 15 teaching assistantships with full tuition reimbursements available (averaging $15,750 per year); health care benefits and unspecified assistantships also available. Financial award application deadline: 3/15. *Faculty research:* Software engineering, networking, database management, robotics, security, algorithms. *Total annual research expenditures:* $14.7 million. *Unit head:* Dr. David Cordes, Professor and Department Head, 205-348-6363, Fax: 205-348-0219, E-mail: david.cordes@ua.edu. *Application contact:* Dr. Susan Vrbsky, Associate Professor and Graduate Program Director, 205-348-6363, Fax: 205-348-0219, E-mail: vrbsky@cs.ua.edu.
Website: http://cs.ua.edu/

The University of Alabama at Birmingham, College of Arts and Sciences, Program in Computer and Information Sciences, Birmingham, AL 35294. Offers MS, PhD. Terminal master's awarded for partial completion of doctoral program. *Degree requirements:* For master's, thesis optional; for doctorate, thesis/dissertation. *Entrance requirements:* For master's, GRE General Test, minimum GPA of 3.0, letters of recommendation; for doctorate, GRE General Test, minimum GPA of 3.5 overall or on last 60 hours; letters of recommendation. Additional exam requirements/recommendations for international students: Required—TOEFL, IELTS. Electronic applications accepted. Full-time tuition and fees vary according to course load and program. *Faculty research:* Theory and software systems, intelligent systems, systems architecture, high performance computing, computer architecture, computer graphics, data mining, software engineering.

The University of Alabama in Huntsville, School of Graduate Studies, College of Science, Department of Computer Science, Huntsville, AL 35899. Offers computer science (MS, PhD); cybersecurity (MS); modeling and simulation (MS, PhD, Certificate); software engineering (MSSE, Certificate). *Program availability:* Part-time, evening/weekend, online learning. *Degree requirements:* For master's, comprehensive exam, thesis or alternative, oral and written exams; for doctorate, comprehensive exam, thesis/dissertation, oral and written exams. *Entrance requirements:* For master's, doctorate, and Certificate, GRE General Test, minimum GPA of 3.0. Additional exam requirements/recommendations for international students: Required—TOEFL (minimum score 550 paper-based; 80 iBT), IELTS (minimum score 6.5). Electronic applications accepted. *Expenses:* Tuition, state resident: full-time $9834; part-time $600 per credit hour. Tuition, nonresident: full-time $21,830; part-time $1325 per credit hour. *Faculty research:* Information assurance and cyber security, modeling and simulation, data science, computer graphics and visualization, multimedia systems.

University of Alaska Fairbanks, College of Engineering and Mines, Department of Computer Science, Fairbanks, AK 99775-6670. Offers MS. *Program availability:* Part-time. *Faculty:* 4 full-time (0 women). *Students:* 2 full-time (0 women). Average age 28. 6 applicants, 67% accepted. In 2016, 2 master's awarded. *Degree requirements:* For master's, comprehensive exam, oral defense of project or thesis. *Entrance requirements:* For master's, GRE General Test, GRE Subject Test (computer science), bachelor's degree from accredited institution with minimum cumulative undergraduate and major GPA of 3.0. Additional exam requirements/recommendations for international students: Required—TOEFL (minimum score 600 paper-based). *Application deadline:* For fall admission, 6/1 for domestic students, 3/1 for international students; for spring admission, 10/15 for domestic students, 9/1 for international students. Applications are processed on a rolling basis. Application fee: $60. Electronic applications accepted. *Expenses:* $533 per credit resident tuition, $673 per semester resident fees; $1,088 per credit non-resident tuition, $835 per semester non-resident fees. *Financial support:* In 2016–17, 1 research assistantship with full tuition reimbursement (averaging $7,088 per

year), 1 teaching assistantship with full tuition reimbursement (averaging $7,302 per year) were awarded; fellowships with full tuition reimbursements, career-related internships or fieldwork, Federal Work-Study, scholarships/grants, health care benefits, and unspecified assistantships also available. Support available to part-time students. Financial award application deadline: 7/1; financial award applicants required to submit FAFSA. *Faculty research:* Interaction with a virtual reality environment, synthetic aperture radar interferometry software. *Unit head:* Dr. Jon Genetti, Department Chair, 907-474-2777, Fax: 907-474-5030, E-mail: uaf-cs-dept@alaska.edu. *Application contact:* Mary Kreta, Director of Admissions, 907-474-7500, Fax: 907-474-7097, E-mail: admissions@uaf.edu.
Website: http://www.cs.uaf.edu

University of Alberta, Faculty of Graduate Studies and Research, Department of Computing Science, Edmonton, AB T6G 2E1, Canada. Offers M Sc, PhD. *Program availability:* Part-time. Terminal master's awarded for partial completion of doctoral program. *Degree requirements:* For master's, thesis (for some programs), oral exam, seminar; for doctorate, thesis/dissertation, oral exam, seminar. *Entrance requirements:* For master's and doctorate, GRE General Test. Additional exam requirements/recommendations for international students: Required—TOEFL. *Faculty research:* Artificial intelligence, multimedia, distributed computing, theory, software engineering.

The University of Arizona, College of Science, Department of Computer Science, Tucson, AZ 85721. Offers MS, PhD. *Program availability:* Part-time. *Faculty:* 18 full-time (2 women). *Students:* 60 full-time (16 women), 5 part-time (1 woman); includes 3 minority (1 Asian, non-Hispanic/Latino; 2 Two or more races, non-Hispanic/Latino), 18 international. Average age 29. 246 applicants, 19% accepted, 35 enrolled. In 2016, 17 master's, 9 doctorates awarded. Terminal master's awarded for partial completion of doctoral program. *Degree requirements:* For master's, thesis optional; for doctorate, comprehensive exam, thesis/dissertation. *Entrance requirements:* For master's, GRE General Test, minimum GPA of 3.2; for doctorate, GRE General Test, minimum undergraduate GPA of 3.5, graduate 3.7. Additional exam requirements/recommendations for international students: Required—TOEFL (minimum score 600 paper-based; 100 iBT). *Application deadline:* For fall admission, 1/15 for domestic and international students. Application fee: $85 ($95 for international students). Electronic applications accepted. *Expenses:* $11,400 per semester resident, $31,100 per semester non-resident. *Financial support:* In 2016–17, 55 students received support, including 3 fellowships with full tuition reimbursements available (averaging $10,000 per year), 33 research assistantships with full tuition reimbursements available (averaging $19,000 per year), 18 teaching assistantships with full tuition reimbursements available (averaging $18,000 per year); scholarships/grants, health care benefits, tuition waivers (full and partial), and unspecified assistantships also available. Financial award application deadline: 1/15. *Faculty research:* Operating systems, programming languages, algorithms, parallel and distributed computing, data visualization. *Total annual research expenditures:* $3.1 million. *Unit head:* Dr. Todd Proebsting, Department Head, 520-621-4324, Fax: 520-626-5997. *Application contact:* Bridget Radcliff, Manager, Academic Services and Student Support, 520-621-4632, Fax: 520-626-5997, E-mail: gradadvising@cs.arizona.edu.
Website: http://www.cs.arizona.edu/

University of Arkansas, Graduate School, College of Engineering, Department of Computer Science and Computer Engineering, Program in Computer Science, Fayetteville, AR 72701. Offers MS, PhD. *Degree requirements:* For doctorate, thesis/dissertation. *Application deadline:* For fall admission, 4/1 for international students; for spring admission, 10/1 for international students. Applications are processed on a rolling basis. Application fee: $40 ($50 for international students). Electronic applications accepted. *Financial support:* In 2016–17, 16 research assistantships, 6 teaching assistantships were awarded; fellowships with tuition reimbursements, career-related internships or fieldwork, and Federal Work-Study also available. Support available to part-time students. Financial award application deadline: 4/1; financial award applicants required to submit FAFSA. *Unit head:* Dr. Frank Liu, Departmental Chair, 479-575-6197, Fax: 479-575-5339, E-mail: frankliu@uark.edu. *Application contact:* Dr. Gordon Beavers, Graduate Coordinator, 479-575-6040, Fax: 479-575-5339, E-mail: gordonb@uark.edu.
Website: http://www.csce.uark.edu/

University of Arkansas at Little Rock, Graduate School, George W. Donaghey College of Engineering and Information Technology, Department of Computer Science, Little Rock, AR 72204-1099. Offers MS, PhD. *Program availability:* Part-time, evening/weekend. *Degree requirements:* For master's, thesis optional. *Entrance requirements:* For master's, GRE General Test, minimum GPA of 3.0; bachelor's degree in computer science, mathematics, or appropriate alternative.

University of Bridgeport, School of Engineering, Departments of Computer Science and Computer Engineering, Bridgeport, CT 06604. Offers computer engineering (MS); computer science (MS); computer science and engineering (PhD). *Degree requirements:* For master's, thesis optional; for doctorate, comprehensive exam, thesis/dissertation. *Entrance requirements:* Additional exam requirements/recommendations for international students: Recommended—TOEFL (minimum score 550 paper-based; 80 iBT), IELTS (minimum score 6.5). Electronic applications accepted. *Expenses:* Contact institution.

The University of British Columbia, Faculty of Science, Department of Computer Science, Vancouver, BC V6T 1Z4, Canada. Offers computer science (M Sc, PhD); data science (MDS). *Program availability:* Part-time. *Degree requirements:* For doctorate, comprehensive exam, thesis/dissertation. *Entrance requirements:* Additional exam requirements/recommendations for international students: Required—TOEFL. *Application deadline:* Applications are processed on a rolling basis. Application fee: $100 Canadian dollars ($162 Canadian dollars for international students). Electronic applications accepted. *Expenses:* $4,802 per year tuition and fees, $8,436 per year international. *Financial support:* Fellowships, research assistantships, teaching assistantships, career-related internships or fieldwork, institutionally sponsored loans, scholarships/grants, and tuition waivers (full and partial) available. *Faculty research:* Computational intelligence, data management and mining, theory, graphics, network security and systems. *Application contact:* Joyce Poon, Graduate Program Administrator, 604-822-2500, Fax: 604-822-5485, E-mail: grad_info@cs.ubc.ca.
Website: http://www.cs.ubc.ca/

University of Calgary, Faculty of Graduate Studies, Faculty of Science, Department of Computer Science, Calgary, AB T2N 1N4, Canada. Offers computer science (M Sc, PhD); software engineering (M Sc). *Program availability:* Part-time. *Degree requirements:* For master's, comprehensive exam (for some programs), thesis (for some programs); for doctorate, thesis/dissertation, oral and written departmental exam. *Entrance requirements:* For master's, bachelor's degree in computer science; for doctorate, M Sc in computer science. Additional exam requirements/recommendations for international students: Required—TOEFL (minimum score 600 paper-based); Recommended—TWE. Electronic applications accepted. *Faculty research:* Visual and interactive computing, quantum computing and cryptography, evolutionary software engineering, distributed systems and algorithms.

University of California, Berkeley, Graduate Division, College of Engineering, Department of Electrical Engineering and Computer Sciences, Berkeley, CA 94720-1500. Offers computer science (MS, PhD); electrical engineering (M Eng, MS, PhD). *Students:* 580 full-time (124 women); includes 146 minority (11 Black or African American, non-Hispanic/Latino; 110 Asian, non-Hispanic/Latino; 25 Hispanic/Latino), 329 international. Average age 27. 4,215 applicants, 142 enrolled. In 2016, 89 master's, 78 doctorates awarded. Terminal master's awarded for partial completion of doctoral program. *Degree requirements:* For master's, comprehensive exam (for some programs), thesis (for some programs), comprehensive exam or thesis; for doctorate, thesis/dissertation, qualifying exam. *Entrance requirements:* For master's and doctorate, GRE General Test, minimum GPA of 3.0, 3 letters of recommendation. Additional exam requirements/recommendations for international students: Required—TOEFL (minimum score 570 paper-based; 90 iBT). *Application deadline:* For fall admission, 12/15 for domestic students. Application fee: $105 ($125 for international students). Electronic applications accepted. *Financial support:* Fellowships, research assistantships, teaching assistantships, scholarships/grants, and unspecified assistantships available. Financial award applicants required to submit FAFSA. *Unit head:* Prof. Jitendra Malik, Chair, 510-642-3214, E-mail: eecs-chair@eecs.berkeley.edu. *Application contact:* Admission Assistant, 510-642-3068, Fax: 510-642-7644, E-mail: gradadmissions@eecs.berkeley.edu.
Website: http://eecs.berkeley.edu

University of California, Davis, College of Engineering, Graduate Group in Computer Science, Davis, CA 95616. Offers MS, PhD. Terminal master's awarded for partial completion of doctoral program. *Degree requirements:* For master's, comprehensive exam (for some programs), thesis optional; for doctorate, comprehensive exam, thesis/dissertation. *Entrance requirements:* For master's and doctorate, GRE General Test, GRE Subject Test, minimum GPA of 3.0. Additional exam requirements/recommendations for international students: Required—TOEFL (minimum score 550 paper-based). Electronic applications accepted. *Faculty research:* Intrusion detection, malicious code detection, next generation light wave computer networks, biological algorithms, parallel processing.

University of California, Irvine, Donald Bren School of Information and Computer Sciences, Department of Computer Science, Irvine, CA 92697. Offers MS, PhD. *Students:* 252 full-time (60 women), 19 part-time (3 women); includes 21 minority (2 Black or African American, non-Hispanic/Latino; 15 Asian, non-Hispanic/Latino; 2 Hispanic/Latino; 2 Two or more races, non-Hispanic/Latino), 217 international. Average age 27. 3,074 applicants, 8% accepted, 93 enrolled. In 2016, 74 master's, 20 doctorates awarded. Application fee: $105 ($125 for international students). *Unit head:* Alexandru Nicolau, Chair, 949-824-4079, E-mail: nicolau@ics.uci.edu. *Application contact:* Holly Byrnes, Department Manager, 949-824-6753, E-mail: hbyrnes@uci.edu.
Website: http://www.cs.uci.edu/

University of California, Irvine, Donald Bren School of Information and Computer Sciences, Program in Networked Systems, Irvine, CA 92697. Offers MS, PhD. *Students:* 39 full-time (9 women), 3 part-time (0 women); includes 2 minority (both Asian, non-Hispanic/Latino), 37 international. Average age 26. 263 applicants, 16% accepted, 22 enrolled. In 2016, 16 master's, 2 doctorates awarded. *Application deadline:* For fall admission, 1/15 for domestic students. Application fee: $105 ($125 for international students). *Financial support:* Fellowships, research assistantships, and teaching assistantships available. *Unit head:* Nalini Venkatasubramanian, Director, 949-824-5898, Fax: 949-824-4056, E-mail: nalini@uci.edu. *Application contact:* Athina Markopoulou, Co-Director, 949-824-0357, Fax: 949-824-3203, E-mail: athina@uci.edu.
Website: http://www.networkedsystems.uci.edu/

University of California, Irvine, Henry Samueli School of Engineering, Department of Electrical Engineering and Computer Science, Irvine, CA 92697. Offers electrical engineering and computer science (MS, PhD); networked systems (MS, PhD). *Program availability:* Part-time. *Students:* 305 full-time (77 women), 22 part-time (7 women); includes 21 minority (18 Asian, non-Hispanic/Latino; 1 Hispanic/Latino; 2 Two or more races, non-Hispanic/Latino), 280 international. Average age 26. 1,808 applicants, 21% accepted, 105 enrolled. In 2016, 109 master's, 15 doctorates awarded. Terminal master's awarded for partial completion of doctoral program. *Degree requirements:* For doctorate, thesis/dissertation. *Entrance requirements:* For master's and doctorate, GRE General Test, minimum GPA of 3.0, 3 letters of recommendation. Additional exam requirements/recommendations for international students: Required—TOEFL (minimum score 550 paper-based). *Application deadline:* For fall admission, 1/15 priority date for domestic students, 1/15 for international students. Applications are processed on a rolling basis. Application fee: $105 ($125 for international students). Electronic applications accepted. *Financial support:* Fellowships, research assistantships with full tuition reimbursements, teaching assistantships, institutionally sponsored loans, traineeships, health care benefits, and unspecified assistantships available. Financial award application deadline: 3/1; financial award applicants required to submit FAFSA. *Faculty research:* Optics and electronic devices and circuits, signal processing, communications, machine vision, power electronics. *Unit head:* Prof. H. Kumar Wickramasinghe, Chair, 949-824-2213, E-mail: hkwick@uci.edu. *Application contact:* Jean Bennett, Director of Graduate Student Affairs, 949-824-6475, Fax: 949-824-8200, E-mail: jean.bennett@uci.edu.
Website: http://www.eng.uci.edu/dept/eecs

University of California, Los Angeles, Graduate Division, Henry Samueli School of Engineering and Applied Science, Department of Computer Science, Los Angeles, CA 90095-1596. Offers MS, PhD, MBA/MS. *Faculty:* 33 full-time (3 women), 4 part-time/adjunct (0 women). *Students:* 344 full-time (93 women); includes 65 minority (3 Black or African American, non-Hispanic/Latino; 54 Asian, non-Hispanic/Latino; 6 Hispanic/Latino; 2 Two or more races, non-Hispanic/Latino), 233 international. 2,471 applicants, 11% accepted, 145 enrolled. In 2016, 162 master's, 26 doctorates awarded. *Degree requirements:* For master's, comprehensive exam or thesis; for doctorate, thesis/dissertation, qualifying exams. *Entrance requirements:* For master's, GRE General Test, GRE Subject Test, minimum GPA of 3.0; for doctorate, GRE General Test, GRE Subject Test, minimum GPA of 3.25. Additional exam requirements/recommendations for international students: Required—TOEFL (minimum score 560 paper-based; 87 iBT), IELTS (minimum score 7). *Application deadline:* For fall admission, 12/1 for domestic and international students. Application fee: $105 ($125 for international students). Electronic applications accepted. *Financial support:* In 2016–17, 48 fellowships, 161 research assistantships, 235 teaching assistantships were awarded; Federal Work-Study, institutionally sponsored loans, and tuition waivers (full and partial) also available. Financial award application deadline: 12/1; financial award applicants required to submit FAFSA. *Faculty research:* Artificial intelligence, computational systems biology, computer network systems, computer systems architecture, information and data management. *Total annual research expenditures:* $12.7 million. *Unit head:* Dr. Mario Gerla, Chair, 310-825-4367, E-mail: gerla@cs.ucla.edu. *Application contact:* Steve Arbuckle, Student Affairs Officer, 310-825-6830, E-mail: arbuckle@cs.ucla.edu.
Website: http://www.cs.ucla.edu/

University of California, Merced, Graduate Division, School of Engineering, Merced, CA 95343. Offers biological engineering and small scale technologies (MS, PhD); electrical engineering and computer science (MS, PhD); environmental systems (MS,

Computer Science

PhD); mechanical engineering (MS); mechanical engineering and applied mechanics (PhD). *Faculty:* 44 full-time (7 women). *Students:* 170 full-time (52 women), 2 part-time (0 women); includes 34 minority (2 Black or African American, non-Hispanic/Latino; 11 Asian, non-Hispanic/Latino; 14 Hispanic/Latino; 2 Native Hawaiian or other Pacific Islander, non-Hispanic/Latino; 5 Two or more races, non-Hispanic/Latino), 99 international. Average age 28. 307 applicants, 35% accepted, 46 enrolled. In 2016, 15 master's, 12 doctorates awarded. Terminal master's awarded for partial completion of doctoral program. *Degree requirements:* For master's, variable foreign language requirement, comprehensive exam, thesis or alternative; for doctorate, variable foreign language requirement, comprehensive exam, thesis/dissertation. *Entrance requirements:* For master's and doctorate, GRE. Additional exam requirements/ recommendations for international students: Required—TOEFL (minimum score 550 paper-based; 80 iBT); Recommended—IELTS (minimum score 7). *Application deadline:* For fall admission, 1/15 priority date for domestic and international students. Applications are processed on a rolling basis. Application fee: $90 ($110 for international students). Electronic applications accepted. *Expenses:* Contact institution. *Financial support:* In 2016–17, 150 students received support, including 16 fellowships with full tuition reimbursements available (averaging $19,088 per year), 45 research assistantships with full tuition reimbursements available (averaging $18,389 per year), 89 teaching assistantships with full tuition reimbursements available (averaging $19,249 per year); scholarships/grants, traineeships, and health care benefits also available. Financial award application deadline: 1/15. *Faculty research:* Water resources, biotechnology, renewable energy, big data, cyber-physical systems. *Total annual research expenditures:* $3.3 million. *Unit head:* Dr. Mark Matsumoto, Dean, Fax: 209-228-4047, E-mail: mmatsumoto@ucmerced.edu. *Application contact:* Tsu Ya, Director of Admissions and Academic Services, 209-228-4521, Fax: 209-228-6906, E-mail: tya@ucmerced.edu.

University of California, Riverside, Graduate Division, Department of Computer Science and Engineering, Riverside, CA 92521. Offers computer engineering (MS); computer science (MS, PhD). *Faculty:* 31 full-time (2 women), 3 part-time/adjunct (0 women). *Students:* 196 full-time (40 women); includes 26 minority (2 Black or African American, non-Hispanic/Latino; 13 Asian, non-Hispanic/Latino; 6 Hispanic/Latino; 5 Two or more races, non-Hispanic/Latino), 143 international. Average age 26. 1,019 applicants, 19% accepted, 80 enrolled. In 2016, 37 master's, 14 doctorates awarded. Terminal master's awarded for partial completion of doctoral program. *Degree requirements:* For master's, comprehensive exam, thesis or project; for doctorate, thesis/dissertation, written and oral qualifying exams, dissertation defense. *Entrance requirements:* For master's and doctorate, GRE General Test (minimum expected score: 1100 old scale or 300 new scale), minimum GPA of 3.2 in junior/senior years of undergraduate study (last two years). Additional exam requirements/recommendations for international students: Required—TOEFL (minimum score 550 paper-based; 80 iBT), IELTS (minimum score 7). *Application deadline:* For fall admission, 1/5 priority date for domestic and international students. Application fee: $0 ($100 for international students). Electronic applications accepted. *Expenses:* Tuition, state resident: full-time $16,666. Tuition, nonresident: full-time $31,768. *Required fees:* $11,055.54 per quarter. $3685.18 per quarter. Tuition and fees vary according to campus/location and program. *Financial support:* In 2016–17, 40 students received support, including 39 fellowships with full and partial tuition reimbursements available (averaging $18,800 per year), 187 research assistantships with full and partial tuition reimbursements available (averaging $14,000 per year), 123 teaching assistantships with full and partial tuition reimbursements available (averaging $15,300 per year); institutionally sponsored loans, scholarships/grants, health care benefits, and unspecified assistantships also available. Financial award application deadline: 1/5; financial award applicants required to submit FAFSA. *Faculty research:* Algorithms,

bioinformatics, logic; architecture, compilers, embedded systems, verification; databases, data mining, artificial intelligence, graphics; systems, networks. *Total annual research expenditures:* $4.8 million. *Unit head:* Prof. Marek Chrobak, Professor/Chair, 951-827-5639, Fax: 951-827-4643, E-mail: gradinfo@cs.ucr.edu. *Application contact:* Vanda Yamaguchi, Graduate Program Coordinator, 951-827-5639, Fax: 951-827-4643, E-mail: vanda.yamaguchi@ucr.edu.
Website: http://www1.cs.ucr.edu/index.php

See Display below and Close-Up on page 371.

University of California, San Diego, Graduate Division, Department of Computer Science and Engineering, La Jolla, CA 92093. Offers computer engineering (MS, PhD); computer science (MS, PhD). *Students:* 602 full-time (127 women), 76 part-time (13 women). 4,193 applicants, 18% accepted, 293 enrolled. In 2016, 102 master's, 15 doctorates awarded. Terminal master's awarded for partial completion of doctoral program. *Degree requirements:* For master's, comprehensive exam (for some programs), thesis (for some programs), comprehensive exam or thesis; for doctorate, comprehensive exam, thesis/dissertation, 1-quarter teaching assistantship. *Entrance requirements:* For master's and doctorate, GRE General Test, GRE Subject Test (recommended). Additional exam requirements/recommendations for international students: Required—TOEFL (minimum score 550 paper-based; 80 iBT), IELTS (minimum score 7). *Application deadline:* For fall admission, 12/14 for domestic students. Application fee: $105 ($125 for international students). Electronic applications accepted. *Expenses:* Tuition, state resident: full-time $11,220. Tuition, nonresident: full-time $26,322. *Required fees:* $1864. *Financial support:* Fellowships, research assistantships, teaching assistantships, career-related internships or fieldwork, and scholarships/grants available. Financial award applicants required to submit FAFSA. *Faculty research:* Artificial intelligence and machine learning, bioinformatics, computer architecture and compilers, visual computing, computer graphics, computer vision, databases and information management, embedded systems and software, high-performance computing, human-computer interaction, programming systems, security and cryptography, software engineering, systems and networking, ubiquitous computing and social dynamics, VLSI/CAD. *Unit head:* Dean Tullsen, Chair, 858-534-6181, E-mail: dtullsen@ucsd.edu. *Application contact:* Julie Connor, Graduate Coordinator, 858-534-8872, E-mail: gradinfo@cs.ucsd.edu.
Website: http://cse.ucsd.edu

University of California, Santa Barbara, Graduate Division, College of Engineering, Department of Computer Science, Santa Barbara, CA 93106-5110. Offers computer science (MS, PhD), including cognitive science (PhD), computational science and engineering (PhD), technology and society (PhD). Terminal master's awarded for partial completion of doctoral program. *Degree requirements:* For master's, comprehensive exam (for some programs), thesis (for some programs), project (for some programs); for doctorate, thesis/dissertation. *Entrance requirements:* For master's and doctorate, GRE. Additional exam requirements/recommendations for international students: Required—TOEFL (minimum score 600 paper-based; 100 iBT), IELTS (minimum score 7). Electronic applications accepted. *Faculty research:* Algorithms and theory, computational science and engineering, computer architecture, database and information systems, machine learning and data mining, networking, operating systems and distributed systems, programming languages and software engineering, security and cryptography, social computing, visual computing and interaction.

University of California, Santa Cruz, Jack Baskin School of Engineering, Department of Applied Mathematics and Statistics, Santa Cruz, CA 95064. Offers scientific computing and applied mathematics (MS); statistics and applied mathematics (MS, PhD), including applied mathematics, statistics. *Faculty:* 14 full-time (3 women), 1 part-time/adjunct (0 women). *Students:* 59 full-time (19 women), 4 part-time (2 women);

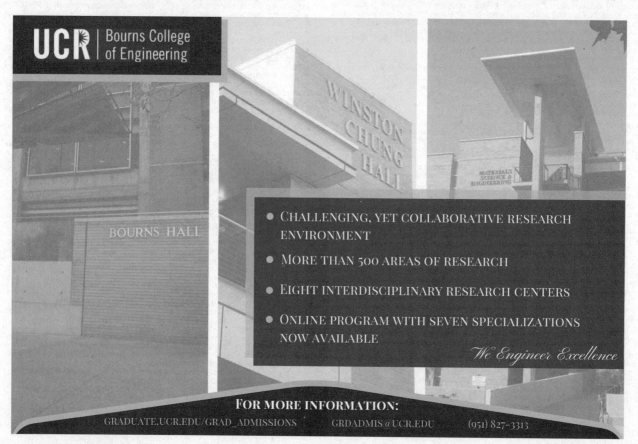

includes 14 minority (1 American Indian or Alaska Native, non-Hispanic/Latino; 6 Asian, non-Hispanic/Latino; 5 Hispanic/Latino; 2 Native Hawaiian or other Pacific Islander, non-Hispanic/Latino), 23 international. 122 applicants, 60% accepted, 25 enrolled. In 2016, 9 master's, 5 doctorates awarded. Terminal master's awarded for partial completion of doctoral program. *Degree requirements:* For master's, thesis, seminar, capstone project; for doctorate, thesis/dissertation, seminar, first-year exam, qualifying exam. *Entrance requirements:* For master's and doctorate, GRE General Test; GRE Subject Test in math (recommended). Additional exam requirements/recommendations for international students: Required—TOEFL (minimum score 570 paper-based; 89 iBT); Recommended—IELTS (minimum score 8). *Application deadline:* For fall admission, 1/3 for domestic and international students. Application fee: $105 ($125 for international students). Electronic applications accepted. *Financial support:* In 2016–17, 46 students received support, including 18 fellowships (averaging $16,497 per year), 33 research assistantships (averaging $20,043 per year), 86 teaching assistantships (averaging $20,052 per year); institutionally sponsored loans and tuition waivers (full and partial) also available. Financial award application deadline: 1/3; financial award applicants required to submit FAFSA. *Faculty research:* Bayesian nonparametric methods; computationally intensive Bayesian inference, prediction, and decision-making; envirometrics; fluid mechanics; mathematical biology. *Unit head:* Dr. Nicholas Brummell, Chair/Professor, E-mail: brummell@soe.ucsc.edu. *Application contact:* Lisa Slater, Graduate Student Advisor, 831-459-3609, E-mail: bsoe-ga@rt.ucsc.edu.
Website: https://www.soe.ucsc.edu/departments/applied-mathematics-statistics

University of California, Santa Cruz, Jack Baskin School of Engineering, Department of Computer Science, Santa Cruz, CA 95064. Offers MS, PhD. *Program availability:* Part-time. *Faculty:* 22 full-time (3 women), 6 part-time/adjunct (1 woman). *Students:* 168 full-time (52 women), 22 part-time (4 women); includes 21 minority (3 Black or African American, non-Hispanic/Latino; 12 Asian, non-Hispanic/Latino; 4 Hispanic/Latino; 2 Native Hawaiian or other Pacific Islander, non-Hispanic/Latino), 117 international. Average age 29. 900 applicants, 25% accepted, 86 enrolled. In 2016, 39 master's, 15 doctorates awarded. Terminal master's awarded for partial completion of doctoral program. *Degree requirements:* For master's, thesis, project; for doctorate, one foreign language, thesis/dissertation, qualifying exam. *Entrance requirements:* For master's and doctorate, GRE General Test. Additional exam requirements/recommendations for international students: Required—TOEFL (minimum score 570 paper-based; 89 iBT); Recommended—IELTS (minimum score 8). *Application deadline:* For fall admission, 1/3 for domestic and international students. Application fee: $105 ($125 for international students). Electronic applications accepted. *Financial support:* In 2016–17, 87 students received support, including 41 fellowships (averaging $19,494 per year), 90 research assistantships (averaging $20,511 per year), 131 teaching assistantships (averaging $20,052 per year); institutionally sponsored loans and tuition waivers (full and partial) also available. Financial award application deadline: 1/3; financial award applicants required to submit FAFSA. *Faculty research:* Algorithm analysis, data science, scientific visualization, machine learning, multimodal human-computer interaction. *Unit head:* Luca De Alvaro, Chair/Professor, E-mail: luca@soe.ucsc.edu. *Application contact:* Will Suh, Graduate Student Advisor, 831-459-2332, E-mail: bsoe-ga@rt.ucsc.edu.
Website: https://www.soe.ucsc.edu/departments/computer-science

University of Central Arkansas, Graduate School, College of Natural Sciences and Math, Department of Applied Computing, Conway, AR 72035-0001. Offers MS. *Entrance requirements:* For master's, GRE, minimum GPA of 2.7. Additional exam requirements/recommendations for international students: Required—TOEFL (minimum score 550 paper-based; 80 iBT). Electronic applications accepted.

University of Central Florida, College of Engineering and Computer Science, Department of Electrical Engineering and Computer Science, Program in Computer Science, Orlando, FL 32816. Offers computer science (MS, PhD); digital forensics (MS). *Program availability:* Part-time, evening/weekend. *Students:* 234 full-time (58 women), 126 part-time (24 women); includes 76 minority (15 Black or African American, non-Hispanic/Latino; 13 Asian, non-Hispanic/Latino; 42 Hispanic/Latino; 6 Two or more races, non-Hispanic/Latino), 173 international. Average age 30. 542 applicants, 71% accepted, 141 enrolled. In 2016, 97 master's, 9 doctorates awarded. *Degree requirements:* For master's, thesis or alternative; for doctorate, thesis/dissertation, candidacy exam, departmental qualifying exam. *Entrance requirements:* For master's, GRE General Test, GRE Subject Test, minimum GPA of 3.0 in last 60 hours; for doctorate, GRE Subject Test, minimum GPA of 3.0 in last 60 hours. Additional exam requirements/recommendations for international students: Required—TOEFL. *Application deadline:* For fall admission, 7/15 for domestic students; for spring admission, 12/1 for domestic students. Application fee: $30. Electronic applications accepted. *Expenses:* Tuition, state resident: part-time $288.16 per credit hour. Tuition, nonresident: part-time $1071.31 per credit hour. *Financial support:* In 2016–17, 138 students received support, including 29 fellowships with partial tuition reimbursements available (averaging $10,821 per year), 80 research assistantships with partial tuition reimbursements available (averaging $12,531 per year), 61 teaching assistantships with partial tuition reimbursements available (averaging $11,750 per year); career-related internships or fieldwork, Federal Work-Study, institutionally sponsored loans, tuition waivers (partial), and unspecified assistantships also available. Financial award application deadline: 3/1; financial award applicants required to submit FAFSA. *Faculty research:* Image and video processing, computer vision, AI and machine learning, virtual reality. *Unit head:* Dr. Gary Leavens, Chair, 407-882-0185, E-mail: leavens@ucf.edu. *Application contact:* Assistant Director, Graduate Admissions, 407-823-2766, Fax: 407-823-6442, E-mail: gradadmissions@ucf.edu.
Website: http://web.eecs.ucf.edu/

University of Central Missouri, The Graduate School, Warrensburg, MO 64093. Offers accountancy (MA); accounting (MBA); applied mathematics (MS); aviation safety (MA); biology (MS); business administration (MBA); career and technical education leadership (MS); college student personnel administration (MS); communication (MA); computer science (MS); counseling (MS); criminal justice (MS); educational leadership (Ed D); educational technology (MS); elementary and early childhood education (MSE); English (MA); environmental studies (MA); finance (MBA); history (MA); human services/educational technology (Ed S); human services/learning resources (Ed S); human services/professional counseling (Ed S); industrial hygiene (MS); industrial management (MS); information systems (MBA); information technology (MS); kinesiology (MS); library science and information services (MS); literacy education (MSE); marketing (MBA); mathematics (MS); music (MA); occupational safety management (MS); psychology (MS); rural family nursing (MS); school administration (MSE); social gerontology (MS); sociology (MA); special education (MSE); speech language pathology (MS); superintendency (Ed S); teaching (MAT); teaching English as a second language (MA); technology (MS); technology management (PhD); theatre (MA). *Program availability:* Part-time, 100% online, blended/hybrid learning. *Degree requirements:* For master's and Ed S, comprehensive exam (for some programs), thesis (for some programs). *Entrance requirements:* Additional exam requirements/recommendations for international students: Required—TOEFL (minimum score 550 paper-based; 79 iBT). Electronic applications accepted.

University of Central Oklahoma, The Jackson College of Graduate Studies, College of Mathematics and Science, Department of Mathematics and Statistics, Edmond, OK 73034-5209. Offers applied mathematical sciences (MS), including computer science, mathematics, statistics, teaching. *Program availability:* Part-time. *Degree requirements:* For master's, comprehensive exam (for some programs), thesis (for some programs). *Entrance requirements:* For master's, GRE. Additional exam requirements/recommendations for international students: Required—TOEFL (minimum score 550 paper-based; 79 iBT), IELTS (minimum score 6.5). Electronic applications accepted.

University of Chicago, Division of the Physical Sciences, Master's Program in Computer Science, Chicago, IL 60637-1513. Offers MS. *Program availability:* Part-time, evening/weekend. *Students:* 53 full-time (11 women), 80 part-time (12 women); includes 23 minority (2 Black or African American, non-Hispanic/Latino; 17 Asian, non-Hispanic/Latino; 3 Hispanic/Latino; 1 Two or more races, non-Hispanic/Latino), 45 international. 588 applicants, 30% accepted, 66 enrolled. *Entrance requirements:* For master's, GRE General Test. Additional exam requirements/recommendations for international students: Required—TOEFL (minimum score 600 paper-based; 90 iBT), IELTS (minimum score 7). *Application deadline:* For fall admission, 8/1 priority date for domestic students, 2/1 for international students; for winter admission, 12/1 priority date for domestic students, 10/1 for international students; for spring admission, 3/1 for domestic students, 12/31 for international students; for summer admission, 5/1 priority date for domestic students, 2/1 for international students. Applications are processed on a rolling basis. Application fee: $90. Electronic applications accepted. *Financial support:* Institutionally sponsored loans available. Financial award applicants required to submit FAFSA. *Unit head:* T. Andrew Binkowski, Assistant Clinical Professor, 773-702-8487, E-mail: masters-admin@cs.uchicago.edu. *Application contact:* Karin M. Czaplewski, Student Support Representative, 773-834-8587, Fax: 773-702-8487, E-mail: masters-admin@cs.uchicago.edu.
Website: https://csmasters.uchicago.edu/

University of Chicago, Division of the Physical Sciences, PhD Program in Computer Science, Chicago, IL 60637. Offers PhD. *Students:* 58 full-time (13 women); includes 7 minority (2 Black or African American, non-Hispanic/Latino; 2 Asian, non-Hispanic/Latino; 3 Hispanic/Latino), 37 international. 247 applicants, 21% accepted, 16 enrolled. *Entrance requirements:* For doctorate, GRE General Test. Additional exam requirements/recommendations for international students: Required—TOEFL (minimum score 90 iBT), IELTS (minimum score 7). *Application deadline:* For fall admission, 1/7 for domestic and international students. Application fee: $55. Electronic applications accepted. *Financial support:* In 2016–17, fellowships with full tuition reimbursements (averaging $22,950 per year), research assistantships with full tuition reimbursements (averaging $22,950 per year), teaching assistantships with full tuition reimbursements (averaging $22,950 per year) were awarded; institutionally sponsored loans, scholarships/grants, traineeships, health care benefits, and unspecified assistantships also available. Financial award applicants required to submit FAFSA. *Faculty research:* Systems, theoretical computer science, machine learning, programming languages, scientific computing and visualization. *Unit head:* Todd DuPont, Chair, 773-702-7950. *Application contact:* Margaret Jaffey, Student Support Representative, 773-702-6011, E-mail: admissions@cs.uchicago.edu.
Website: https://cs.uchicago.edu/page/phd-program

University of Cincinnati, Graduate School, College of Engineering and Applied Science, Department of Electrical Engineering and Computing Systems, Program in Computer Science, Cincinnati, OH 45221. Offers MS. *Degree requirements:* For master's, thesis. *Entrance requirements:* For master's, GRE General Test, GRE Subject Test or BS in computer science. Additional exam requirements/recommendations for international students: Required—TOEFL (minimum score 550 paper-based). *Expenses: Tuition, area resident:* Full-time $12,790; part-time $389 per credit hour. Tuition, state resident: full-time $13,290; part-time $419 per credit hour. Tuition, nonresident: full-time $24,532; part-time $976 per credit hour. *International tuition:* $24,832 full-time. *Required fees:* $3958; $140 per credit hour. Tuition and fees vary according to course load, degree level, program and reciprocity agreements.

University of Cincinnati, Graduate School, College of Engineering and Applied Science, Department of Electrical Engineering and Computing Systems, Program in Computer Science and Engineering, Cincinnati, OH 45221. Offers PhD. *Degree requirements:* For doctorate, thesis/dissertation. *Entrance requirements:* For doctorate, GRE General Test. Additional exam requirements/recommendations for international students: Required—TOEFL. *Expenses: Tuition, area resident:* Full-time $12,790; part-time $389 per credit hour. Tuition, state resident: full-time $13,290; part-time $419 per credit hour. Tuition, nonresident: full-time $24,532; part-time $976 per credit hour. *International tuition:* $24,832 full-time. *Required fees:* $3958; $140 per credit hour. Tuition and fees vary according to course load, degree level, program and reciprocity agreements.

University of Colorado Boulder, Graduate School, College of Engineering and Applied Science, Department of Computer Science, Boulder, CO 80309. Offers ME, MS, PhD. *Faculty:* 36 full-time (5 women). *Students:* 272 full-time (71 women), 19 part-time (6 women); includes 22 minority (1 Black or African American, non-Hispanic/Latino; 1 American Indian or Alaska Native, non-Hispanic/Latino; 9 Asian, non-Hispanic/Latino; 6 Hispanic/Latino; 5 Two or more races, non-Hispanic/Latino), 158 international. Average age 28. 909 applicants, 25% accepted, 69 enrolled. In 2016, 54 master's, 19 doctorates awarded. Terminal master's awarded for partial completion of doctoral program. *Degree requirements:* For master's, comprehensive exam, thesis or alternative; for doctorate, one foreign language, thesis/dissertation. *Entrance requirements:* For master's, minimum undergraduate GPA of 3.0. *Application deadline:* For fall admission, 12/15 for domestic and international students; for spring admission, 10/15 for domestic students, 9/1 for international students. Applications are processed on a rolling basis. Application fee: $60 ($80 for international students). Electronic applications accepted. Application fee is waived when completed online. *Financial support:* In 2016–17, 478 students received support, including 121 fellowships (averaging $5,362 per year), 72 research assistantships with full and partial tuition reimbursements available (averaging $39,653 per year), 43 teaching assistantships with full and partial tuition reimbursements available (averaging $41,279 per year); institutionally sponsored loans, scholarships/grants, health care benefits, and unspecified assistantships also available. Financial award applicants required to submit FAFSA. *Faculty research:* Computer science, distributed systems, computer interface, computer software, artificial intelligence/cybernetics. *Total annual research expenditures:* $6.5 million. *Application contact:* E-mail: gradadms@cs.colorado.edu.
Website: http://www.colorado.edu/cs

University of Colorado Colorado Springs, College of Engineering and Applied Science, Department of Computer Science, Colorado Springs, CO 80918. Offers MS. *Program availability:* Part-time. *Faculty:* 13 full-time (3 women), 2 part-time/adjunct (0 women). *Students:* 9 full-time (2 women), 44 part-time (9 women); includes 7 minority (3 Asian, non-Hispanic/Latino; 3 Hispanic/Latino; 1 Two or more races, non-Hispanic/Latino), 19 international. Average age 31. 34 applicants, 44% accepted, 7 enrolled. In 2016, 21 master's awarded. *Degree requirements:* For master's, thesis optional, oral final exam. *Entrance requirements:* For master's, GRE General Test, minimum undergraduate GPA of 3.0, 2 semesters of course work in calculus, 1 other math course, course work in computer science. Additional exam requirements/recommendations for international students: Required—TOEFL (minimum score 550 paper-based; 80 iBT).

Application deadline: For fall admission, 6/1 priority date for domestic students, 5/1 for international students; for spring admission, 11/1 priority date for domestic students, 10/1 for international students; for summer admission, 4/15 priority date for domestic students. Applications are processed on a rolling basis. Application fee: $60 ($100 for international students). Electronic applications accepted. *Expenses:* Contact institution. *Financial support:* In 2016–17, 4 students received support. Career-related internships or fieldwork, Federal Work-Study, and scholarships/grants available. Support available to part-time students. Financial award application deadline: 3/1; financial award applicants required to submit FAFSA. *Faculty research:* Neural networks, computer vision, pattern recognition, networking, medical imaging, computer game design and development, human motion tracking and reasoning, natural language processing, medical imaging, distributed systems, dynamic process, migration. *Total annual research expenditures:* $548,431. *Unit head:* Dr. Charles Zhou, Chair, 719-255-3493, Fax: 719-255-3369, E-mail: xzhou@uccs.edu. *Application contact:* Ali Langfels, Program Assistant, 719-255-3243, E-mail: alangfel@uccs.edu.
Website: http://eas.uccs.edu/cs/

University of Colorado Denver, Business School, Program in Computer Science and Information Systems, Denver, CO 80217. Offers PhD. *Students:* 6 full-time (2 women), 7 part-time (1 woman); includes 1 minority (Black or African American, non-Hispanic/Latino), 7 international. Average age 39. 15 applicants, 13% accepted, 2 enrolled. *Degree requirements:* For doctorate, comprehensive exam, thesis/dissertation. *Entrance requirements:* For doctorate, GMAT or GRE General Test, letters of recommendation, portfolio, essay describing applicant's motivation and initial plan for doctoral study, resume. Additional exam requirements/recommendations for international students: Required—TOEFL (minimum score 525 paper-based; 71 iBT); Recommended—IELTS (minimum score 6.5). *Application deadline:* For fall admission, 3/1 priority date for domestic and international students; for spring admission, 10/15 for domestic students, 10/1 for international students. Applications are processed on a rolling basis. Application fee: $50 ($75 for international students). Electronic applications accepted. *Expenses:* Contact institution. *Financial support:* In 2016–17, 16 students received support. Fellowships, research assistantships, teaching assistantships, Federal Work-Study, institutionally sponsored loans, scholarships/grants, and traineeships available. Financial award application deadline: 4/1; financial award applicants required to submit FAFSA. *Faculty research:* Design science of information systems, information system economics, organizational impacts of information technology, high performance parallel and distributed systems, performance measurement and prediction. *Unit head:* Dr. Michael Mannino, Associate Professor/Co-Director, 303-315-8427, E-mail: michael.mannino@ucdenver.edu. *Application contact:* 303-315-8200, E-mail: bschool.admissions@ucdenver.edu.
Website: http://www.ucdenver.edu/academics/colleges/business/degrees/phd/Pages/default.aspx

University of Colorado Denver, College of Engineering and Applied Science, Department of Computer Science and Engineering, Denver, CO 80217. Offers computer science (MS); computer science and engineering (EASPh D); computer science and information systems (PhD). *Program availability:* Part-time, evening/weekend. *Faculty:* 10 full-time (2 women), 2 part-time/adjunct (0 women). *Students:* 80 full-time (26 women), 21 part-time (6 women); includes 11 minority (2 Black or African American, non-Hispanic/Latino; 7 Asian, non-Hispanic/Latino; 2 Hispanic/Latino), 61 international. Average age 34. 217 applicants, 44% accepted, 28 enrolled. In 2016, 33 master's, 1 doctorate awarded. *Degree requirements:* For master's, thesis or alternative, at least 30 semester hours of computer science courses while maintaining minimum GPA of 3.0; for doctorate, comprehensive exam, thesis/dissertation, at least 60 hours beyond the master's degree level, 30 of which are dissertation research. *Entrance requirements:* For master's, GRE, minimum GPA of 3.0, 10 semester hours of university-level calculus, at least one math course beyond calculus, statement of purpose, letters of recommendation; for doctorate, GRE or GMAT. Additional exam requirements/recommendations for international students: Required—TOEFL (minimum score 537 paper-based; 75 iBT). *Application deadline:* For fall admission, 5/1 for domestic students, 4/1 for international students; for spring admission, 10/1 for domestic students, 9/1 for international students. Application fee: $50 ($75 for international students). Electronic applications accepted. *Expenses:* Tuition, state resident: full-time $11,006; part-time $474 per credit. Tuition, nonresident: full-time $28,212; part-time $1264 per credit hour. *Required fees:* $256 per semester. One-time fee: $94.32. Tuition and fees vary according to campus/location and program. *Financial support:* In 2016–17, 9 students received support. Research assistantships, teaching assistantships, Federal Work-Study, institutionally sponsored loans, scholarships/grants, traineeships, and unspecified assistantships available. Financial award application deadline: 4/1; financial award applicants required to submit FAFSA. *Faculty research:* Algorithms, automata theory, artificial intelligence, communication networks, combinatorial geometry, computational geometry, computer architectures, computer graphics, distributed computing, high performance computing, graph theory, Internet, operating systems, parallel processing, simulation and software engineering. *Unit head:* Dr. Gita Alaghband, Chair, 303-315-1400, E-mail: gita.alaghband@ucdenver.edu. *Application contact:* Sarah Mandos, Program Assistant, 303-315-1411, E-mail: sarah.mandos@ucdenver.edu.
Website: http://www.ucdenver.edu/academics/colleges/Engineering/Programs/Computer-Science-and-Engineering/Pages/ComputerScienceEngineering.aspx

University of Colorado Denver, College of Liberal Arts and Sciences, Program in Integrated Sciences, Denver, CO 80217. Offers applied science (MIS); computer science (MIS); mathematics (MIS). *Program availability:* Part-time, evening/weekend. *Students:* 6 full-time (2 women), 7 part-time (5 women); includes 2 minority (both Hispanic/Latino), 2 international. Average age 35. 8 applicants, 63% accepted, 5 enrolled. In 2016, 2 master's awarded. *Degree requirements:* For master's, 30 credit hours; thesis or project. *Entrance requirements:* For master's, GRE if undergraduate GPA is 3.0 or less, minimum of 40 semester hours in mathematics, computer science, physics, biology, chemistry and/or geology; essay; three letters of recommendation. Additional exam requirements/recommendations for international students: Required—TOEFL (minimum score 537 paper-based; 75 iBT); Recommended—IELTS (minimum score 6.5). *Application deadline:* For fall admission, 4/15 for domestic students, 4/15 priority date for international students; for spring admission, 10/15 for domestic students, 10/15 priority date for international students. Application fee: $50 ($75 for international students). Electronic applications accepted. *Expenses:* Tuition, state resident: full-time $11,006; part-time $474 per credit. Tuition, nonresident: full-time $28,212; part-time $1264 per credit hour. *Required fees:* $256 per semester. One-time fee: $94.32. Tuition and fees vary according to campus/location and program. *Financial support:* In 2016–17, 1 student received support. Fellowships, research assistantships, teaching assistantships, Federal Work-Study, institutionally sponsored loans, scholarships/grants, and traineeships available. Financial award application deadline: 4/1; financial award applicants required to submit FAFSA. *Faculty research:* Computer science, applied science, mathematics. *Unit head:* E-mail: integrated.sciences@ucdenver.edu. *Application contact:* Marissa Tornatore, Graduate School Application Specialist, 303-315-0049, E-mail: marissa.tornatore@ucdenver.edu.
Website: http://www.ucdenver.edu/academics/colleges/CLAS/Programs/MastersofIntegratedSciences/Pages/ProgramOverview.aspx

University of Connecticut, Graduate School, School of Engineering, Department of Computer Science and Engineering, Storrs, CT 06269. Offers computer science (MS, PhD), including artificial intelligence, computer architecture, computer science, operating systems, robotics, software engineering. Terminal master's awarded for partial completion of doctoral program. *Degree requirements:* For master's, comprehensive exam, thesis or alternative; for doctorate, thesis/dissertation. *Entrance requirements:* For master's and doctorate, GRE General Test. Additional exam requirements/recommendations for international students: Required—TOEFL (minimum score 550 paper-based). Electronic applications accepted.

University of Dayton, Department of Computer Science, Dayton, OH 45469. Offers MCS. *Program availability:* Part-time. *Faculty:* 9 full-time (1 woman). *Students:* 130 full-time (62 women), 19 part-time (5 women); includes 2 minority (1 Asian, non-Hispanic/Latino; 1 Hispanic/Latino), 139 international. Average age 24. 279 applicants, 36% accepted. In 2016, 16 master's awarded. *Degree requirements:* For master's, software project, additional coursework, or thesis. *Entrance requirements:* For master's, minimum GPA of 3.0 and undergraduate degree in computer science or related degree program. Additional exam requirements/recommendations for international students: Required—TOEFL (minimum score 550 paper-based; 80 iBT). *Application deadline:* Applications are processed on a rolling basis. Application fee: $0 ($50 for international students). Electronic applications accepted. *Expenses:* $899 per credit hour, $25 registration fee. *Financial support:* In 2016–17, 9 teaching assistantships with full tuition reimbursements (averaging $11,025 per year) were awarded; research assistantships, institutionally sponsored loans, health care benefits, and unspecified assistantships also available. Financial award application deadline: 5/1; financial award applicants required to submit FAFSA. *Faculty research:* Data mining, bib data, cyber security, virtual reality, multimedia. *Unit head:* Dr. Mehdi Zargham, Chair, 937-229-3831, E-mail: mzargham1@udayton.edu. *Application contact:* 937-229-4462, E-mail: graduateadmission@udayton.edu.
Website: https://www.udayton.edu/artssciences/academics/computerscience/welcome/index.php

University of Delaware, College of Engineering, Department of Computer and Information Sciences, Newark, DE 19716. Offers MS, PhD. *Program availability:* Part-time. Terminal master's awarded for partial completion of doctoral program. *Degree requirements:* For master's, thesis optional; for doctorate, comprehensive exam, thesis/dissertation. *Entrance requirements:* For master's and doctorate, GRE General Test. Additional exam requirements/recommendations for international students: Required—TOEFL (minimum score 550 paper-based). Electronic applications accepted. *Faculty research:* Artificial intelligence, computational theory, graphics and computer vision, networks, systems.

University of Denver, Daniel Felix Ritchie School of Engineering and Computer Science, Department of Computer Science, Denver, CO 80208. Offers computer science (MS, PhD); cybersecurity (MS). *Program availability:* Part-time, evening/weekend. *Faculty:* 14 full-time (2 women), 3 part-time/adjunct (1 woman). *Students:* 12 full-time (3 women), 21 part-time (9 women); includes 7 minority (5 Asian, non-Hispanic/Latino; 1 Hispanic/Latino; 1 Two or more races, non-Hispanic/Latino), 14 international. Average age 27. 75 applicants, 51% accepted, 13 enrolled. In 2016, 14 master's, 2 doctorates awarded. *Degree requirements:* For doctorate, variable foreign language requirement, comprehensive exam, thesis/dissertation, reading competency in two languages, modern typesetting system, or additional coursework. *Entrance requirements:* For master's, GRE General Test, bachelor's degree, transcripts, personal statement, resume or curriculum vitae, three letters of recommendation; for doctorate, GRE General Test, bachelor's degree in computer science or a related discipline, transcripts, personal statement, resume or curriculum vitae, three letters of recommendation. Additional exam requirements/recommendations for international students: Required—TOEFL (minimum score 550 paper-based; 80 iBT). *Application deadline:* For fall admission, 2/15 priority date for domestic and international students. Applications are processed on a rolling basis. Application fee: $65. Electronic applications accepted. *Expenses:* $29,022 per year full-time. *Financial support:* In 2016–17, 23 students received support, including 1 research assistantship with tuition reimbursement available (averaging $20,000 per year), 8 teaching assistantships with tuition reimbursements available (averaging $15,626 per year); career-related internships or fieldwork, Federal Work-Study, institutionally sponsored loans, scholarships/grants, and unspecified assistantships also available. Financial award application deadline: 2/15; financial award applicants required to submit FAFSA. *Faculty research:* Algorithms, artificial intelligence, databases, game development, robotics. *Total annual research expenditures:* $383,540. *Unit head:* Dr. Scott Leutenegger, Professor and Chair, 303-871-3329, Fax: 303-871-2821, E-mail: leut@cs.du.edu. *Application contact:* Information Contact, 303-871-2458, E-mail: info@cs.du.edu.
Website: http://ritchieschool.du.edu/departments/computer-science/

University of Detroit Mercy, College of Liberal Arts and Education, Detroit, MI 48221. Offers addiction counseling (MA); addiction studies (Certificate); clinical mental health counseling (MA); clinical psychology (MA, PhD); computer and information systems (MS); criminal justice (MA); curriculum and instruction (MA); economics (MA); educational administration (MA); financial economics (MA); industrial/organizational psychology (MA); information assurance (MS); intelligence analysis (MA); liberal studies (MALS); religious studies (MA); school counseling (MA, Certificate); school psychology (Spec); security administration (MS); special education: emotionally impaired/behaviorally disordered (MA); special education: learning disabilities (MA). *Program availability:* Part-time, evening/weekend. *Degree requirements:* For doctorate, departmental qualifying exam. *Faculty research:* Psychology of aging, history of technology, Renaissance humanism, U.S. and Japanese economic relations.

University of Florida, Graduate School, Herbert Wertheim College of Engineering and College of Liberal Arts and Sciences, Department of Computer and Information Science and Engineering, Gainesville, FL 32611. Offers computer engineering (ME, MS, PhD); computer science (MS); digital arts and sciences (MS). *Program availability:* Part-time, online learning. Terminal master's awarded for partial completion of doctoral program. *Degree requirements:* For master's, comprehensive exam, thesis optional; for doctorate, comprehensive exam, thesis/dissertation. *Entrance requirements:* For master's and doctorate, minimum GPA of 3.0. Additional exam requirements/recommendations for international students: Required—TOEFL (minimum score 550 paper-based; 80 iBT), IELTS (minimum score 6). Electronic applications accepted. *Faculty research:* Computer systems and computer networking; high-performance computing and algorithm; database and machine learning; computer graphics, vision, and intelligent systems; human center computing and digital art.

University of Georgia, Franklin College of Arts and Sciences, Department of Computer Science, Athens, GA 30602. Offers applied mathematical science (MAMS); computer science (MS, PhD). *Degree requirements:* For doctorate, thesis/dissertation. *Entrance requirements:* For master's and doctorate, GRE General Test. *Application deadline:* For fall admission, 7/1 priority date for domestic students, 4/15 for international students; for spring admission, 11/15 for domestic and international students. Applications are processed on a rolling basis. Application fee: $50. Electronic applications accepted. *Financial support:* Fellowships, research assistantships, teaching assistantships, tuition waivers (full), and unspecified assistantships available. *Unit head:* Dr. H. B. Schuttler,

Head, 706-542-3455, E-mail: hbs@cs.uga.edu. *Application contact:* Hamid Arabnia, Graduate Coordinator, 706-542-2911, E-mail: gradadvisor@cs.uga.edu.
Website: http://www.cs.uga.edu/

University of Guelph, Graduate Studies, College of Physical and Engineering Science, Department of Computing and Information Science, Guelph, ON N1G 2W1, Canada. Offers applied computer science (M Sc); computer science (PhD). *Degree requirements:* For master's, thesis; for doctorate, comprehensive exam, thesis/dissertation. *Entrance requirements:* For master's, major or minor in computer science, honors degree; for doctorate, M Sc in computer science or related discipline. Additional exam requirements/recommendations for international students: Required—TOEFL (minimum score 600 paper-based; 89 iBT), IELTS (minimum score 6.5). Electronic applications accepted. *Faculty research:* Modeling and theory, distributed computing, soft computing, software and information systems, data and knowledge management.

University of Hawaii at Manoa, Graduate Division, College of Natural Sciences, Department of Information and Computer Sciences, Honolulu, HI 96822. Offers computer science (MS, PhD); library and information science (MLI Sc, Graduate Certificate), including advanced library and information science (Graduate Certificate), library and information science (MLI Sc). *Program availability:* Part-time. *Degree requirements:* For master's, thesis optional; for doctorate, comprehensive exam, thesis/dissertation. *Entrance requirements:* For master's and doctorate, GRE. Additional exam requirements/recommendations for international students: Required—TOEFL (minimum score 580 paper-based; 92 iBT), IELTS (minimum score 5). *Faculty research:* Software engineering, telecommunications, artificial intelligence, multimedia.

University of Houston, College of Natural Sciences and Mathematics, Department of Computer Science, Houston, TX 77204. Offers MA, PhD. *Program availability:* Part-time. Terminal master's awarded for partial completion of doctoral program. *Degree requirements:* For master's, thesis or alternative; for doctorate, comprehensive exam, thesis/dissertation. *Entrance requirements:* For master's and doctorate, GRE. Additional exam requirements/recommendations for international students: Required—TOEFL (minimum score 550 paper-based; 79 iBT), IELTS (minimum score 6.5). Electronic applications accepted. *Faculty research:* Databases, networks, image analysis, security, animation.

University of Houston–Clear Lake, School of Science and Computer Engineering, Program in Computer Science, Houston, TX 77058-1002. Offers MS. *Program availability:* Part-time, evening/weekend. *Entrance requirements:* For master's, GRE General Test. Additional exam requirements/recommendations for international students: Required—TOEFL (minimum score 550 paper-based).

University of Houston–Victoria, School of Arts and Sciences, Department of Computer Science, Victoria, TX 77901-4450. Offers computer information systems (MS); computer science (MS). *Program availability:* Part-time, evening/weekend, online learning. *Degree requirements:* For master's, comprehensive exam (for some programs), thesis (for some programs). *Entrance requirements:* For master's, GRE. Additional exam requirements/recommendations for international students: Required—TOEFL (minimum score 550 paper-based).

University of Idaho, College of Graduate Studies, College of Engineering, Department of Computer Science, Moscow, ID 83844. Offers MS, PhD. *Faculty:* 10 full-time, 1 part-time/adjunct. *Students:* 29 full-time, 16 part-time. Average age 34. In 2016, 10 master's, 3 doctorates awarded. *Degree requirements:* For doctorate, thesis/dissertation. *Entrance requirements:* For master's, minimum GPA of 3.0; for doctorate, GRE, minimum GPA of 3.0. Additional exam requirements/recommendations for international students: Required—TOEFL. *Application deadline:* For fall admission, 8/1 for domestic students; for spring admission, 12/15 for domestic students. Applications are processed on a rolling basis. Application fee: $60. Electronic applications accepted. *Expenses:* Tuition, state resident: full-time $6460; part-time $414 per credit hour. Tuition, nonresident: full-time $21,268; part-time $1237 per credit hour. *Required fees:* $2070; $60 per credit hour. Full-time tuition and fees vary according to course load and reciprocity agreements. *Financial support:* Research assistantships, teaching assistantships, and career-related internships or fieldwork available. Financial award applicants required to submit FAFSA. *Faculty research:* Information assurance and security, collaborative virtual education, evolutionary computation, bioinformatics. *Unit head:* Dr. Frederick Sheldon, Chair, 208-885-6589, E-mail: csinfo@uidaho.edu. *Application contact:* Sean Scoggin, Graduate Recruitment Coordinator, 208-885-4001, Fax: 208-885-4406, E-mail: graduateadmissions@uidaho.edu.
Website: https://www.uidaho.edu/engr/departments/cs

University of Illinois at Chicago, College of Engineering, Department of Computer Science, Chicago, IL 60607-7128. Offers MS, PhD. *Program availability:* Part-time. *Degree requirements:* For master's, thesis or alternative; for doctorate, thesis/dissertation, departmental qualifying exam. *Entrance requirements:* For master's, BS in related field, minimum GPA of 2.75; for doctorate, GRE General Test, minimum GPA of 2.75, MS in related field. Additional exam requirements/recommendations for international students: Required—TOEFL. *Expenses:* Contact institution. *Faculty research:* Artificial intelligence; deployment of natural language discourse/dialogue coordinated with graphics tools; data management and mining, information retrieval; computational techniques for population biology; systems security research; scientific visualization.

University of Illinois at Chicago, College of Liberal Arts and Sciences, Department of Mathematics, Statistics, and Computer Science, Chicago, IL 60607-7128. Offers mathematics (DA); probability and statistics (PhD); secondary school mathematics (MST); statistics (MS). *Program availability:* Part-time. *Degree requirements:* For master's, comprehensive exam; for doctorate, one foreign language, thesis/dissertation. *Entrance requirements:* For master's and doctorate, GRE General Test, minimum GPA of 3.0. Additional exam requirements/recommendations for international students: Required—TOEFL (minimum score 100 iBT). Electronic applications accepted.

University of Illinois at Springfield, Graduate Programs, College of Liberal Arts and Sciences, Program in Computer Science, Springfield, IL 62703-5407. Offers MS. *Program availability:* Part-time, evening/weekend, 100% online, blended/hybrid learning. *Faculty:* 18 full-time (5 women), 7 part-time/adjunct (1 woman). *Students:* 483 full-time (141 women), 338 part-time (77 women); includes 77 minority (26 Black or African American, non-Hispanic/Latino; 1 American Indian or Alaska Native, non-Hispanic/Latino; 32 Asian, non-Hispanic/Latino; 15 Hispanic/Latino; 3 Two or more races, non-Hispanic/Latino), 569 international. Average age 27. 1,102 applicants, 51% accepted, 227 enrolled. In 2016, 442 master's awarded. *Degree requirements:* For master's, comprehensive closure exercise. *Entrance requirements:* For master's, minimum undergraduate GPA of 2.7; computer science undergraduate degree or stipulated prerequisite. Additional exam requirements/recommendations for international students: Required—TOEFL (minimum score 550 paper-based; 79 iBT). *Application deadline:* Applications are processed on a rolling basis. Application fee: $60 ($75 for international students). Electronic applications accepted. *Expenses:* $369.75 per hour in-state, $715.75 per hour out-of-state, $403 per hour online. *Financial support:* In 2016–17, fellowships with full tuition reimbursements (averaging $9,900 per year), research assistantships with full tuition reimbursements (averaging $9,991 per year), teaching assistantships with full tuition reimbursements (averaging $10,059 per year) were awarded; career-related internships or fieldwork, Federal Work-Study, scholarships/grants, health care benefits, and unspecified assistantships also available. Support available to part-time students. Financial award application deadline: 11/15; financial award applicants required to submit FAFSA. *Unit head:* Dr. Ted Mims, Program Administrator, 217-206-7326, Fax: 217-206-6217, E-mail: mims.ted@uis.edu. *Application contact:* Dr. Cecelia Cornell, Associate Vice Chancellor for Graduate Education, 217-206-7230, E-mail: ccorn1@uis.edu.

University of Illinois at Urbana–Champaign, Graduate College, College of Engineering, Department of Computer Science, Champaign, IL 61820. Offers bioinformatics (MS); computer science (MCS, MS, PhD); MCS/JD; MCS/M Arch; MCS/MBA. *Program availability:* Part-time, evening/weekend, online learning.

The University of Iowa, Graduate College, College of Liberal Arts and Sciences, Department of Computer Science, Iowa City, IA 52242-1316. Offers MCS, PhD. *Degree requirements:* For master's, thesis optional, exam; for doctorate, comprehensive exam, thesis/dissertation. *Entrance requirements:* For master's, minimum GPA of 3.0; for doctorate, GRE General Test, minimum GPA of 3.0. Additional exam requirements/recommendations for international students: Required—TOEFL (minimum score 550 paper-based; 81 iBT). Electronic applications accepted.

The University of Kansas, Graduate Studies, School of Engineering, Program in Computer Science, Lawrence, KS 66045. Offers MS, PhD. *Program availability:* Part-time, evening/weekend. *Students:* 56 full-time (15 women), 14 part-time (3 women); includes 6 minority (1 Black or African American, non-Hispanic/Latino; 1 Asian, non-Hispanic/Latino; 2 Hispanic/Latino; 2 Two or more races, non-Hispanic/Latino), 45 international. Average age 28. 126 applicants, 47% accepted, 13 enrolled. In 2016, 20 master's, 2 doctorates awarded. Terminal master's awarded for partial completion of doctoral program. *Entrance requirements:* For master's, GRE (minimum scores: 146 verbal and 155 quantitative), minimum GPA of 3.0, official transcript, three recommendations, statement of academic objectives, resume; for doctorate, GRE (minimum scores: 146 verbal and 155 quantitative), minimum GPA of 3.5, official transcript, three recommendations, statement of academic objectives, resume. Additional exam requirements/recommendations for international students: Required—TOEFL or IELTS. *Application deadline:* For fall admission, 12/15 priority date for domestic and international students; for spring admission, 10/1 for domestic and international students. Application fee: $65 ($85 for international students). Electronic applications accepted. *Financial support:* Fellowships, research assistantships, teaching assistantships, career-related internships or fieldwork, scholarships/grants, and unspecified assistantships available. Financial award application deadline: 12/15. *Faculty research:* Communication systems and networking, computer systems design, interactive intelligent systems, bioinformatics. *Unit head:* Victor Frost, Chair, 785-864-4833, E-mail: vsfrost@ku.edu. *Application contact:* Pam Shadoin, Graduate Admissions Contact, 785-864-4487, E-mail: pshadoin@ku.edu.
Website: http://www.eecs.ku.edu/prospective_students/graduate

University of Kentucky, Graduate School, College of Engineering, Program in Computer Science, Lexington, KY 40506-0032. Offers MS, PhD. *Degree requirements:* For master's, comprehensive exam, thesis optional; for doctorate, one foreign language, comprehensive exam, thesis/dissertation. *Entrance requirements:* For master's, GRE General Test, minimum undergraduate GPA of 2.75; for doctorate, GRE General Test, minimum undergraduate GPA of 3.0. Additional exam requirements/recommendations for international students: Required—TOEFL (minimum score 550 paper-based). Electronic applications accepted. *Faculty research:* Artificial intelligence and databases, communication networks and operating systems, graphics and vision, numerical analysis, theory.

University of Lethbridge, School of Graduate Studies, Lethbridge, AB T1K 3M4, Canada. Offers addictions counseling (M Sc); agricultural biotechnology (M Sc); agricultural studies (M Sc, MA); anthropology (MA); archaeology (M Sc, MA); art (MA, MFA); biochemistry (M Sc); biological sciences (M Sc); biomolecular science (PhD); biosystems and biodiversity (PhD); Canadian studies (MA); chemistry (M Sc); computer science (M Sc); computer science and geographical information science (M Sc); counseling (MC); counseling psychology (M Ed); dramatic arts (MA); earth, space, and physical science (PhD); economics (MA); education (MA, PhD); educational leadership (M Ed); English (MA); environmental science (M Sc); evolution and behavior (PhD); exercise science (M Sc); French (MA); French/German (MA); French/Spanish (MA); general education (M Ed); geography (M Sc, MA); German (MA); health sciences (M Sc); individualized multidisciplinary (M Sc, MA); kinesiology (M Sc, MA); management (M Sc), including accounting, finance, human resource management and labor relations, information systems, international management, marketing, policy and strategy; mathematics (M Sc); music (M Mus, MA); Native American studies (MA); neuroscience (M Sc, PhD); new media (MA, MFA); nursing (M Sc, MN); philosophy (MA); physics (M Sc); political science (MA); psychology (M Sc, MA); religious studies (MA); sociology (MA); theatre and dramatic arts (MFA); theoretical and computational science (PhD); urban and regional studies (MA); women and gender studies (MA). *Program availability:* Part-time, evening/weekend. *Degree requirements:* For master's, thesis (for some programs); for doctorate, comprehensive exam, thesis/dissertation. *Entrance requirements:* For master's, GMAT (for M Sc in management), bachelor's degree in related field, minimum GPA of 3.0 during previous 20 graded semester courses, 2 years' teaching or related experience (M Ed); for doctorate, master's degree, minimum graduate GPA of 3.5. Additional exam requirements/recommendations for international students: Required—TOEFL (minimum score 580 paper-based; 93 iBT). Electronic applications accepted. *Faculty research:* Movement and brain plasticity, gibberellin physiology, photosynthesis, carbon cycling, molecular properties of main-group ring components.

University of Louisiana at Lafayette, College of Engineering, Center for Advanced Computer Studies, Lafayette, LA 70504. Offers computer engineering (MS, PhD); computer science (MS, PhD). *Program availability:* Part-time. Terminal master's awarded for partial completion of doctoral program. *Degree requirements:* For master's, thesis or alternative; for doctorate, comprehensive exam, thesis/dissertation, final oral exam. *Entrance requirements:* For master's, GRE General Test, minimum GPA of 2.75; for doctorate, GRE General Test, minimum GPA of 3.0. Additional exam requirements/recommendations for international students: Required—TOEFL. Electronic applications accepted.

University of Louisville, J. B. Speed School of Engineering, Department of Computer Engineering and Computer Science, Louisville, KY 40292-0001. Offers computer engineering and computer science (M Eng, MS, PhD); data mining (Certificate); network and information security (Certificate). *Accreditation:* ABET (one or more programs are accredited). *Program availability:* Part-time, 100% online, blended/hybrid learning. *Students:* 76 full-time (24 women), 81 part-time (16 women); includes 17 minority (5 Black or African American, non-Hispanic/Latino; 7 Asian, non-Hispanic/Latino; 2 Hispanic/Latino; 3 Two or more races, non-Hispanic/Latino), 54 international. Average age 31. 80 applicants, 46% accepted, 29 enrolled. In 2016, 17 master's, 1 doctorate, 1 other advanced degree awarded. *Degree requirements:* For master's, thesis optional, minimum GPA of 3.0; for doctorate, comprehensive exam, thesis/dissertation, minimum GPA of 3.0. *Entrance requirements:* For master's, GRE, two letters of recommendation, personal statement; for doctorate, GRE, two letters of recommendation, official final

transcripts; for Certificate, undergraduate degree. Additional exam requirements/recommendations for international students: Required—TOEFL (minimum score 550 paper-based; 80 iBT), IELTS (minimum score 6.5). *Application deadline:* For fall admission, 5/1 priority date for international students; for spring admission, 11/1 priority date for international students; for summer admission, 3/1 priority date for international students. Applications are processed on a rolling basis. Application fee: $60. Electronic applications accepted. *Expenses:* Tuition, state resident: full-time $12,246; part-time $681 per credit hour. Tuition, nonresident: full-time $25,486; part-time $1417 per credit hour. *Required fees:* $196. Tuition and fees vary according to program and reciprocity agreements. *Financial support:* In 2016–17, 2 fellowships with full tuition reimbursements (averaging $22,000 per year) were awarded; research assistantships with full tuition reimbursements, teaching assistantships with full tuition reimbursements, scholarships/grants, health care benefits, and tuition waivers also available. Financial award application deadline: 1/1. *Faculty research:* Software systems engineering, information security and forensics, multimedia and vision, mobile and distributed computing, intelligent systems. *Total annual research expenditures:* $740,736. *Unit head:* Dr. Adel S. Elmaghraby, Chair, 502-852-6304, Fax: 502-852-4713, E-mail: adel@louisville.edu. *Application contact:* Dr. Mehmed Kantardzic, Director of Graduate Studies, 502-852-3703, E-mail: mehmed.kantardzic@louisville.edu.
Website: http://louisville.edu/speed/computer

University of Maine, Graduate School, College of Liberal Arts and Sciences, School of Computing and Information Science, Orono, ME 04469. Offers MS, PhD, CGS. *Program availability:* Part-time. *Faculty:* 13 full-time (2 women), 2 part-time/adjunct (1 woman). *Students:* 36 full-time (5 women), 12 part-time (4 women); includes 4 minority (1 American Indian or Alaska Native, non-Hispanic/Latino; 1 Asian, non-Hispanic/Latino; 1 Hispanic/Latino; 1 Two or more races, non-Hispanic/Latino), 10 international. Average age 31. 31 applicants, 77% accepted, 15 enrolled. In 2016, 6 master's, 5 doctorates, 2 other advanced degrees awarded. *Degree requirements:* For master's, thesis (for some programs); for doctorate, comprehensive exam, thesis/dissertation. *Entrance requirements:* For master's and doctorate, GRE General Test, GRE Subject Test. Additional exam requirements/recommendations for international students: Required—TOEFL (minimum score 550 paper-based; 80 iBT). *Application deadline:* Applications are processed on a rolling basis. Application fee: $65. Electronic applications accepted. *Expenses:* Tuition, state resident: full-time $7524; part-time $2508 per credit. Tuition, nonresident: full-time $24,498; part-time $8166 per credit. *Required fees:* $1148; $571 per credit. *Financial support:* In 2016–17, 21 students received support, including 2 fellowships (averaging $20,700 per year), 1 research assistantship with full tuition reimbursement available (averaging $14,600 per year), 10 teaching assistantships with full tuition reimbursements available (averaging $14,600 per year); career-related internships or fieldwork, Federal Work-Study, institutionally sponsored loans, and tuition waivers (full) also available. Financial award application deadline: 3/1. *Faculty research:* Geographic information science, spatial informatics, scientific computing. *Total annual research expenditures:* $1.3 million. *Unit head:* Dr. Max Egenhofer, Acting Director, 207-581-2114, Fax: 207-581-2206. *Application contact:* Scott G. Delcourt, Assistant Vice President for Graduate Studies and Senior Associate Dean, 207-581-3291, Fax: 207-581-3232, E-mail: graduate@maine.edu.
Website: http://umaine.edu/cis/

University of Management and Technology, Program in Computer Science, Arlington, VA 22209-1609. Offers computer science (MS); information technology (AC); project management (AC); software engineering (MS). *Program availability:* Part-time, evening/weekend, online learning. *Entrance requirements:* For master's, 3 recommendations, resume. Additional exam requirements/recommendations for international students: Required—TOEFL (minimum score 530 paper-based; 71 iBT). Electronic applications accepted.

The University of Manchester, School of Computer Science, Manchester, United Kingdom. Offers M Phil, PhD.

University of Manitoba, Faculty of Graduate Studies, Faculty of Science, Department of Computer Science, Winnipeg, MB R3T 2N2, Canada. Offers M Sc, PhD. *Degree requirements:* For master's, thesis or alternative; for doctorate, thesis/dissertation.

University of Maryland, Baltimore County, The Graduate School, College of Engineering and Information Technology, Department of Computer Science and Electrical Engineering, Program in Computer Science, Baltimore, MD 21250. Offers MS, PhD. *Program availability:* Part-time. *Faculty:* 27 full-time (7 women), 20 part-time/adjunct (3 women). *Students:* 132 full-time (38 women), 37 part-time (5 women); includes 23 minority (1 Black or African American, non-Hispanic/Latino; 1 American Indian or Alaska Native, non-Hispanic/Latino; 16 Asian, non-Hispanic/Latino; 4 Hispanic/Latino; 1 Two or more races, non-Hispanic/Latino), 103 international. Average age 28. 417 applicants, 35% accepted, 49 enrolled. In 2016, 42 master's, 5 doctorates awarded. *Degree requirements:* For master's, comprehensive exam (for some programs), thesis (for some programs); for doctorate, comprehensive exam, thesis/dissertation. *Entrance requirements:* For master's, GRE General Test, strong background in computer science and math courses; for doctorate, GRE General Test, MS in computer science (strongly recommended). Additional exam requirements/recommendations for international students: Required—TOEFL (minimum score 550 paper-based; 80 iBT). *Application deadline:* For fall admission, 6/1 for domestic students, 1/1 for international students; for spring admission, 11/1 for domestic students, 6/1 for international students. Applications are processed on a rolling basis. Application fee: $70. Electronic applications accepted. *Expenses:* Contact institution. *Financial support:* In 2016–17, 2 fellowships with full tuition reimbursements (averaging $18,000 per year), 24 research assistantships with full tuition reimbursements (averaging $18,000 per year), 50 teaching assistantships with full tuition reimbursements (averaging $16,000 per year) were awarded; career-related internships or fieldwork, Federal Work-Study, scholarships/grants, health care benefits, tuition waivers (partial), and unspecified assistantships also available. Support available to part-time students. Financial award application deadline: 6/30; financial award applicants required to submit FAFSA. *Faculty research:* Artificial intelligence, graphics and visualization, high performance computing, information and knowledge management, networking and systems, security, theory and algorithms. *Unit head:* Dr. Anupam Joshi, Professor and Chair, 410-455-3500, Fax: 410-455-3969, E-mail: joshi@cs.umbc.edu. *Application contact:* Dr. Charles Nicholas, Professor and Interim Graduate Program Director, 410-455-3000, Fax: 410-455-3969, E-mail: nicholas@umbc.edu.
Website: http://www.csee.umbc.edu/

University of Maryland, Baltimore County, The Graduate School, College of Engineering and Information Technology, Department of Information Systems, Program in Human-Centered Computing, Baltimore, MD 21227. Offers MS, PhD. *Program availability:* Part-time, evening/weekend. *Students:* 26 full-time (11 women), 23 part-time (11 women); includes 11 minority (6 Black or African American, non-Hispanic/Latino; 2 Asian, non-Hispanic/Latino; 2 Hispanic/Latino; 1 Two or more races, non-Hispanic/Latino), 14 international. Average age 32. 58 applicants, 66% accepted, 11 enrolled. In 2016, 16 master's, 3 doctorates awarded. Terminal master's awarded for partial completion of doctoral program. *Degree requirements:* For master's, comprehensive exam (for some programs), thesis optional; for doctorate, comprehensive exam, thesis/dissertation. *Entrance requirements:* For master's, minimum GPA of 3.0; for doctorate, GRE General Test or GMAT, competence in statistical analysis and experimental design. Additional exam requirements/recommendations for international students: Required—TOEFL (minimum score 550 paper-based; 80 iBT). *Application deadline:* For fall admission, 6/1 for domestic students, 1/1 for international students; for spring admission, 11/1 for domestic students, 6/1 for international students. Applications are processed on a rolling basis. Application fee: $70. Electronic applications accepted. *Expenses:* Contact institution. *Financial support:* In 2016–17, 1 fellowship with full tuition reimbursement (averaging $18,000 per year), 7 research assistantships with full tuition reimbursements (averaging $20,000 per year), 3 teaching assistantships with full tuition reimbursements (averaging $20,000 per year) were awarded; career-related internships or fieldwork, Federal Work-Study, scholarships/grants, health care benefits, tuition waivers (partial), and unspecified assistantships also available. Support available to part-time students. Financial award application deadline: 6/30; financial award applicants required to submit FAFSA. *Faculty research:* Human-centered computing. *Unit head:* Dr. Arrya Gangopadhyay, Professor and Chair, 410-455-2620, Fax: 410-455-1217, E-mail: gangopad@umbc.edu. *Application contact:* Dr. Amy Hurst, Associate Professor and Graduate Program Director, 410-455-8146, Fax: 410-455-1217, E-mail: amyhurst@umbc.edu.
Website: http://www.is.umbc.edu/

University of Maryland, College Park, Academic Affairs, College of Computer, Mathematical and Natural Sciences, Department of Computer Science, College Park, MD 20742. Offers MS, PhD. *Program availability:* Part-time, evening/weekend. Terminal master's awarded for partial completion of doctoral program. *Degree requirements:* For master's, thesis or scholarly paper and exam; for doctorate, thesis/dissertation. *Entrance requirements:* For master's and doctorate, GRE General Test, GRE Subject Test (recommended), minimum GPA of 3.0, 3 letters of recommendation. Additional exam requirements/recommendations for international students: Required—TOEFL; Recommended—TWE. Electronic applications accepted. *Faculty research:* Artificial intelligence, computer applications, information processing, bioinformatics and computational biology, human-computer interaction.

University of Maryland Eastern Shore, Graduate Programs, Department of Mathematics and Computer Science, Princess Anne, MD 21853-1299. Offers applied computer science (MS). *Program availability:* Part-time, evening/weekend. *Degree requirements:* For master's, thesis or alternative, research project. *Entrance requirements:* For master's, GRE General Test, minimum GPA of 3.0. Additional exam requirements/recommendations for international students: Required—TOEFL (minimum score 80 iBT). Electronic applications accepted.

University of Massachusetts Amherst, Graduate School, College of Natural Sciences, School of Computer Science, Amherst, MA 01003. Offers MS, PhD. *Program availability:* Part-time. Terminal master's awarded for partial completion of doctoral program. *Degree requirements:* For master's, thesis or alternative; for doctorate, comprehensive exam, thesis/dissertation. *Entrance requirements:* For master's and doctorate, GRE General Test. Additional exam requirements/recommendations for international students: Required—TOEFL (minimum score 550 paper-based; 80 iBT), IELTS (minimum score 6.5), TWE. Electronic applications accepted. *Faculty research:* Artificial intelligence, robotics, computer vision, and wearable computing; autonomous and multiagent systems; information retrieval, data mining and machine learning; networking, distributed systems and security.

University of Massachusetts Boston, College of Science and Mathematics, Program in Computer Science, Boston, MA 02125-3393. Offers MS, PhD. *Program availability:* Part-time, evening/weekend. *Faculty:* 22 full-time (4 women), 5 part-time/adjunct (0 women). *Students:* 136 full-time (39 women), 26 part-time (7 women); includes 13 minority (3 Black or African American, non-Hispanic/Latino; 8 Asian, non-Hispanic/Latino; 1 Hispanic/Latino; 1 Two or more races, non-Hispanic/Latino), 127 international. Average age 28. 196 applicants, 45% accepted, 43 enrolled. In 2016, 54 master's, 7 doctorates awarded. *Degree requirements:* For master's, comprehensive exam, thesis optional, capstone final project; for doctorate, comprehensive exam, thesis/dissertation, oral exams. *Entrance requirements:* For master's and doctorate, GRE General Test, minimum GPA of 2.75. Additional exam requirements/recommendations for international students: Required—TOEFL (minimum score 80 iBT). *Application deadline:* For fall admission, 3/1 for domestic students; for spring admission, 11/1 for domestic students. *Expenses:* Tuition, state resident: full-time $16,863. Tuition, nonresident: full-time $32,913. *Required fees:* $177. *Financial support:* Research assistantships with full tuition reimbursements, teaching assistantships with full tuition reimbursements, career-related internships or fieldwork, Federal Work-Study, and unspecified assistantships available. Support available to part-time students. Financial award application deadline: 3/1; financial award applicants required to submit FAFSA. *Faculty research:* Queuing theory, database design theory, computer networks, theory of database query languages, real-time systems. *Unit head:* Dr. Dan Simovici, Director, 617-287-6472. *Application contact:* Peggy Roldan Patel, Graduate Admissions Coordinator, 617-287-6400, Fax: 617-287-6236, E-mail: bos.gadm@dpc.umassp.edu.

University of Massachusetts Dartmouth, Graduate School, College of Engineering, Department of Computer Science, North Dartmouth, MA 02747-2300. Offers computer networks and distributed systems (Postbaccalaureate Certificate); computer science (MS, Postbaccalaureate Certificate); software development and design (Postbaccalaureate Certificate). *Program availability:* Part-time, 100% online, blended/hybrid learning. *Faculty:* 11 full-time (2 women), 1 part-time/adjunct (0 women). *Students:* 93 full-time (26 women), 31 part-time (7 women); includes 7 minority (1 Black or African American, non-Hispanic/Latino; 5 Asian, non-Hispanic/Latino; 1 Hispanic/Latino), 104 international. Average age 25. 138 applicants, 79% accepted, 42 enrolled. In 2016, 57 master's awarded. *Degree requirements:* For master's, thesis, project. *Entrance requirements:* For master's, GRE (UMass Dartmouth computer science bachelor's degree recipients are exempt), statement of purpose (minimum of 300 words), resume, 3 letters of recommendation, official transcripts; for Postbaccalaureate Certificate, statement of purpose (minimum of 300 words), resume, official transcripts. Additional exam requirements/recommendations for international students: Required—TOEFL (minimum score 533 paper-based; 72 iBT). *Application deadline:* For fall admission, 2/15 priority date for domestic students, 1/15 priority date for international students; for spring admission, 11/15 priority date for domestic students, 10/15 priority date for international students. Application fee: $60. Electronic applications accepted. *Expenses:* Tuition, state resident: full-time $14,994; part-time $624.75 per credit. Tuition, nonresident: full-time $27,068; part-time $1127.83 per credit. *Required fees:* $405; $25.88 per credit. Tuition and fees vary according to course load and reciprocity agreements. *Financial support:* In 2016–17, 3 fellowships (averaging $7,500 per year), 1 research assistantship (averaging $4,500 per year), 3 teaching assistantships (averaging $7,500 per year) were awarded; institutionally sponsored loans, scholarships/grants, and unspecified assistantships also available. Support available to part-time students. Financial award application deadline: 3/1; financial award applicants required to submit FAFSA. *Faculty research:* Human-computer interaction, visualization and imaging, software engineering, multi-agent systems, informatics and data processing, computer networks, self-organizing feature maps. *Total annual research expenditures:* $1 million. *Unit head:* Dr. Xiaoqin Zhang, Graduate Program Director, Computer Science, 508-999-8294, E-mail: x2zhang@umassd.edu. *Application contact:* Steven Briggs, Director of Marketing and Recruitment for Graduate Studies, 508-999-

8604, Fax: 508-999-8183, E-mail: graduate@umassd.edu. Website: http://www.umassd.edu/engineering/cis/graduate

University of Massachusetts Dartmouth, Graduate School, College of Engineering, Program in Engineering and Applied Science, North Dartmouth, MA 02747-2300. Offers applied mechanics and materials (PhD); computational science and engineering (PhD); computer science and information systems (PhD); engineering and applied science (PhD); industrial and systems engineering (PhD). *Program availability:* Part-time. *Students:* 23 full-time (7 women), 8 part-time (3 women); includes 2 minority (both Black or African American, non-Hispanic/Latino), 15 international. Average age 31. 14 applicants, 79% accepted, 7 enrolled. *Degree requirements:* For doctorate, comprehensive exam, thesis/dissertation. *Entrance requirements:* For doctorate, GRE, statement of purpose (minimum of 300 words), resume, 3 letters of recommendation, official transcripts. Additional exam requirements/recommendations for international students: Required—TOEFL (minimum score 550 paper-based; 79 iBT). *Application deadline:* For fall admission, 2/15 priority date for domestic students, 1/15 priority date for international students; for spring admission, 11/15 priority date for domestic students, 10/15 priority date for international students. Application fee: $60. Electronic applications accepted. *Expenses:* Tuition, state resident: full-time $14,994; part-time $624.75 per credit. Tuition, nonresident: full-time $27,068; part-time $1127.83 per credit. *Required fees:* $405; $25.88 per credit. Tuition and fees vary according to course load and reciprocity agreements. *Financial support:* In 2016–17, 11 fellowships (averaging $16,591 per year), 12 research assistantships (averaging $5,160 per year) were awarded; institutionally sponsored loans, scholarships/grants, and doctoral support also available. Support available to part-time students. Financial award application deadline: 3/1; financial award applicants required to submit FAFSA. *Faculty research:* Tissue/cell engineering, bio transport sensors/networks, marine systems biomimetic materials, composite/polymeric materials, resilient infrastructure robotics, renewable energy. *Total annual research expenditures:* $253,000. *Unit head:* Gaurav Khanna, Graduate Program Director, Engineering and Applied Science, 508-910-6605, Fax: 508-999-9115, E-mail: gkhanna@umassd.edu. *Application contact:* Steven Briggs, Director of Marketing and Recruitment for Graduate Studies, 508-999-8604, Fax: 508-999-8183, E-mail: graduate@umassd.edu. Website: http://www.umassd.edu/engineering/graduate/doctoraldegreeprograms/egrandappliedsciencephd/

University of Massachusetts Lowell, College of Sciences, Department of Computer Science, Lowell, MA 01854. Offers MS, PhD. *Program availability:* Part-time. *Degree requirements:* For master's, thesis optional; for doctorate, thesis/dissertation. *Entrance requirements:* For master's and doctorate, GRE General Test. *Faculty research:* Networks, multimedia systems, human-computer interaction, graphics and visualization databases.

University of Memphis, Graduate School, College of Arts and Sciences, Department of Computer Science, Memphis, TN 38152. Offers bioinformatics (MS); computer science (MS, PhD). *Faculty:* 11 full-time (1 woman), 2 part-time/adjunct (0 women). *Students:* 54 full-time (14 women), 22 part-time (5 women); includes 8 minority (4 Black or African American, non-Hispanic/Latino; 3 Asian, non-Hispanic/Latino; 1 Two or more races, non-Hispanic/Latino), 60 international. Average age 29. 74 applicants, 74% accepted, 16 enrolled. In 2016, 27 master's, 3 doctorates awarded. Terminal master's awarded for partial completion of doctoral program. *Degree requirements:* For master's, comprehensive exam, thesis; for doctorate, comprehensive exam, thesis/dissertation, qualifying exam, final exam. *Entrance requirements:* For master's and doctorate, GRE, letters of recommendation. Additional exam requirements/recommendations for international students: Required—TOEFL (minimum score 550 paper-based; 79 iBT). *Application deadline:* Applications are processed on a rolling basis. Application fee: $35 ($60 for international students). *Expenses:* $5,231.50 per semester full-time in-state, $9,623.50 full-time out-of-state. *Financial support:* In 2016–17, 9 students received support, including 15 research assistantships with full tuition reimbursements available (averaging $13,114 per year); fellowships, teaching assistantships with full tuition reimbursements available, Federal Work-Study, scholarships/grants, and unspecified assistantships also available. Financial award application deadline: 2/1; financial award applicants required to submit FAFSA. *Faculty research:* Network security, biomolecular and distributed computing, wireless sensor networks, artificial intelligence. *Unit head:* Dr. Lan Wang, Chair, 901-678-5465, Fax: 901-678-2480, E-mail: lanwang@memphis.edu. *Application contact:* Dr. Wasile Rus, Graduate Studies Coordinator, E-mail: info@cs.memphis.edu. Website: http://www.cs.memphis.edu

University of Miami, Graduate School, College of Arts and Sciences, Department of Computer Science, Coral Gables, FL 33124. Offers MS, PhD. *Program availability:* Part-time, online learning. *Degree requirements:* For master's, comprehensive exam (for some programs), thesis. *Entrance requirements:* For master's, GRE. Additional exam requirements/recommendations for international students: Required—TOEFL. Electronic applications accepted. *Faculty research:* Algorithm engineering, automated reasoning, computer graphics, cryptography, security network.

University of Michigan, College of Engineering, Department of Computer Science and Engineering, Ann Arbor, MI 48109. Offers MS, MSE, PhD. *Students:* 328 full-time (51 women), 5 part-time (3 women). 1,801 applicants, 15% accepted, 85 enrolled. In 2016, 86 master's, 30 doctorates awarded. *Expenses:* Tuition, state resident: full-time $21,466; part-time $1152 per credit hour. Tuition, nonresident: full-time $43,346; part-time $2367 per credit hour. Part-time tuition and fees vary according to course load, degree level and program. *Faculty research:* Solid state electronics and optics; communications, control, signal process; sensors and integrated circuitry; software systems; artificial intelligence; hardware systems. *Total annual research expenditures:* $27.3 million. *Unit head:* Prof. Peter Chen, Interim Chair, 734-763-4472, E-mail: pmchen@umich.edu. *Application contact:* Ashley Andreae, Graduate Programs Coordinator, 734-647-1807, E-mail: smash@umich.edu. Website: http://eecs.umich.edu/cse/

University of Michigan–Dearborn, College of Engineering and Computer Science, PhD Program in Computer and Information Science, Dearborn, MI 48128. Offers data management (PhD); data science (PhD); software engineering (PhD); systems and security (PhD). *Program availability:* Part-time, evening/weekend. *Degree requirements:* For doctorate, thesis/dissertation. *Entrance requirements:* For doctorate, GRE, bachelor's or master's degree in computer science or closely-related field. Additional exam requirements/recommendations for international students: Required—TOEFL (minimum score 84 iBT), IELTS (minimum score 6.5). *Application deadline:* For fall admission, 2/15 for domestic and international students. Application fee: $60. Electronic applications accepted. *Expenses:* Tuition, state resident: full-time $13,118; part-time $2280 per term. Tuition, nonresident: full-time $21,816; part-time $3771 per term. *Required fees:* $866; $658 per unit. $329 per term. Tuition and fees vary according to program. *Financial support:* Research assistantships, teaching assistantships, scholarships/grants, health care benefits, and unspecified assistantships available. Financial award application deadline: 2/15; financial award applicants required to submit FAFSA. *Unit head:* Dr. Brahim Medjahed, Director, 313-583-6449, E-mail: brahim@umich.edu. *Application contact:* Office of Graduate Studies Staff, 313-583-6321, E-mail: umd-graduatestudies@umich.edu.

Website: https://umdearborn.edu/cecs/departments/computer-and-information-science/graduate-programs/phd-computer-and-information-science

University of Michigan–Flint, College of Arts and Sciences, Program in Computer Science and Information Systems, Flint, MI 48502-1950. Offers computer science (MS); information systems (MS), including business information systems, health information systems. *Program availability:* Part-time, evening/weekend, 100% online. *Faculty:* 29 full-time (7 women), 12 part-time/adjunct (7 women). *Students:* 35 full-time (17 women), 91 part-time (24 women); includes 11 minority (3 Black or African American, non-Hispanic/Latino; 2 Asian, non-Hispanic/Latino; 4 Hispanic/Latino; 1 Native Hawaiian or other Pacific Islander, non-Hispanic/Latino; 1 Two or more races, non-Hispanic/Latino), 82 international. Average age 28. 712 applicants, 29% accepted, 29 enrolled. In 2016, 171 master's awarded. *Degree requirements:* For master's, thesis optional. *Entrance requirements:* For master's, BS from regionally-accredited institution in computer science, computer information systems, or computer engineering (preferred); minimum overall undergraduate GPA of 3.0. Additional exam requirements/recommendations for international students: Required—TOEFL (minimum score 84 iBT), IELTS (minimum score 6.5). *Application deadline:* For fall admission, 5/1 for domestic students, 2/1 for international students; for winter admission, 10/1 for domestic students, 8/1 for international students; for spring admission, 3/15 for domestic students, 1/1 for international students; for summer admission, 5/15 for domestic students, 3/1 for international students. Applications are processed on a rolling basis. Application fee: $55. Electronic applications accepted. *Expenses:* Contact institution. *Financial support:* Federal Work-Study, scholarships/grants, and unspecified assistantships available. Support available to part-time students. Financial award application deadline: 3/1; financial award applicants required to submit FAFSA. *Faculty research:* Computer network systems, database management systems, artificial intelligence and controlled systems. *Unit head:* Dr. Jeffrey Livermore, Director, 810-762-3131, Fax: 810-766-6780, E-mail: jefflive@umflint.edu. *Application contact:* Bradley T. Maki, Director of Graduate Admissions, 810-762-3171, Fax: 810-766-6789, E-mail: bmaki@umflint.edu. Website: http://www.umflint.edu/graduateprograms/computer-science-information-systems-ms

University of Minnesota, Duluth, Graduate School, Swenson College of Science and Engineering, Department of Computer Science, Duluth, MN 55812-2496. Offers MS. *Program availability:* Part-time. *Entrance requirements:* For master's, GRE General Test, minimum GPA of 3.0. Additional exam requirements/recommendations for international students: Required—TOEFL (minimum score 550 paper-based). Electronic applications accepted. *Faculty research:* Information retrieval, artificial intelligence, machine learning, parallel/distributed computing, graphics.

University of Minnesota, Twin Cities Campus, College of Science and Engineering, Department of Computer Science and Engineering, Minneapolis, MN 55455-0213. Offers computer science (MCS, MS, PhD); data science (MS); software engineering (MSSE). *Program availability:* Part-time. Terminal master's awarded for partial completion of doctoral program. *Degree requirements:* For doctorate, thesis/dissertation. *Entrance requirements:* For master's and doctorate, GRE General Test. Additional exam requirements/recommendations for international students: Required—TOEFL. Electronic applications accepted. *Faculty research:* Computer architecture, bioinformatics and computational biology, data mining, graphics and visualization, high performance computing, human-computer interaction, networks, software systems, theory, artificial intelligence.

University of Minnesota, Twin Cities Campus, College of Science and Engineering, Scientific Computation Program, Minneapolis, MN 55455-0213. Offers MS, PhD. *Program availability:* Part-time. *Degree requirements:* For master's, thesis; for doctorate, thesis/dissertation. *Entrance requirements:* For master's and doctorate, GRE General Test. Additional exam requirements/recommendations for international students: Required—TOEFL (minimum score 550 paper-based; 79 iBT), IELTS (minimum score 6.5). Electronic applications accepted. *Faculty research:* Parallel computations, quantum mechanical dynamics, computational materials science, computational fluid dynamics, computational neuroscience.

University of Missouri, Office of Research and Graduate Studies, College of Engineering, Department of Computer Science, Columbia, MO 65211. Offers MS, PhD. *Program availability:* Part-time. *Faculty:* 20 full-time (4 women). *Students:* 53 full-time (15 women), 68 part-time (17 women). *Degree requirements:* For doctorate, thesis/dissertation. *Entrance requirements:* For master's, GRE General Test, minimum GPA of 3.0; for doctorate, GRE General Test. Additional exam requirements/recommendations for international students: Required—TOEFL (minimum score 577 paper-based; 90 iBT). *Application deadline:* For fall admission, 1/15 priority date for domestic students, 1/15 for international students; for winter admission, 10/1 priority date for domestic students, 10/1 for international students. Applications are processed on a rolling basis. Application fee: $75 ($90 for international students). Electronic applications accepted. *Expenses:* Tuition, state resident: full-time $6347; part-time $352.60 per credit hour. Tuition, nonresident: full-time $17,379; part-time $965.50 per credit hour. *Required fees:* $1035. Tuition and fees vary according to course load, campus/location and program. *Financial support:* Fellowships, research assistantships, teaching assistantships, institutionally sponsored loans, scholarships/grants, traineeships, health care benefits, and unspecified assistantships available. Support available to part-time students. Website: http://engineering.missouri.edu/cs/degree-programs/

University of Missouri–Kansas City, School of Computing and Engineering, Kansas City, MO 64110-2499. Offers civil engineering (MS); computer and electrical engineering (PhD); computer science (MS), including bioinformatics, software engineering, telecommunications networking; computer science and informatics (PhD); computing (PhD); electrical engineering (MS); engineering (PhD); engineering and construction management (Graduate Certificate); mechanical engineering (MS); telecommunications and computer networking (PhD). PhD (interdisciplinary) offered through the School of Graduate Studies. *Program availability:* Part-time. *Faculty:* 45 full-time (6 women), 26 part-time/adjunct (4 women). *Students:* 473 full-time (155 women), 207 part-time (42 women); includes 24 minority (10 Black or African American, non-Hispanic/Latino; 10 Asian, non-Hispanic/Latino; 4 Hispanic/Latino), 581 international. Average age 25. 1,143 applicants, 44% accepted, 227 enrolled. In 2016, 446 master's, 2 other advanced degrees awarded. *Degree requirements:* For doctorate, thesis/dissertation. *Entrance requirements:* For master's, GRE General Test, minimum GPA of 3.0, 3 letters of recommendation from professors; for doctorate, GRE General Test, minimum GPA of 3.5. Additional exam requirements/recommendations for international students: Required—TOEFL (minimum score 550 paper-based; 80 iBT). *Application deadline:* For fall admission, 1/15 priority date for domestic students, 1/15 for international students. Applications are processed on a rolling basis. Application fee: $45 ($50 for international students). *Financial support:* In 2016–17, 37 research assistantships with partial tuition reimbursements (averaging $15,679 per year), 47 teaching assistantships with partial tuition reimbursements (averaging $16,830 per year) were awarded; career-related internships or fieldwork, Federal Work-Study, scholarships/grants, tuition waivers (partial), and unspecified assistantships also available. Support available to part-time students. Financial award application deadline: 3/1; financial award applicants required to submit FAFSA. *Faculty research:* Algorithms, bioinformatics and medical informatics, biomechanics/biomaterials, civil engineering materials, networking and

telecommunications, thermal science. *Unit head:* Dr. Kevin Z. Truman, Dean, 816-235-2399, Fax: 816-235-5159. *Application contact:* 816-235-2399, Fax: 816-235-5159.
Website: http://sce.umkc.edu/

University of Missouri–St. Louis, College of Arts and Sciences, Department of Mathematics and Computer Science, St. Louis, MO 63121. Offers computer science (MS); mathematical and computational sciences (PhD); mathematics (MA). *Program availability:* Part-time, evening/weekend. *Faculty:* 15 full-time (2 women), 1 part-time/adjunct (0 women). *Students:* 58 full-time (24 women), 39 part-time (10 women); includes 9 minority (1 Black or African American, non-Hispanic/Latino; 6 Asian, non-Hispanic/Latino; 1 Hispanic/Latino; 1 Two or more races, non-Hispanic/Latino), 52 international. Average age 31. 140 applicants, 61% accepted, 20 enrolled. *Degree requirements:* For master's, thesis optional; for doctorate, thesis/dissertation. *Entrance requirements:* For master's, GRE (for teaching assistantships), 2 letters of recommendation; C programming, C++ or Java (for computer science); for doctorate, GRE General Test, 3 letters of recommendation. Additional exam requirements/recommendations for international students: Required—TOEFL (minimum score 550 paper-based; 79 iBT), IELTS (minimum score 6.5). *Application deadline:* For fall admission, 7/1 priority date for domestic and international students; for spring admission, 12/1 priority date for domestic and international students. Applications are processed on a rolling basis. Application fee: $50 ($40 for international students). Electronic applications accepted. *Financial support:* Research assistantships with tuition reimbursements, teaching assistantships with tuition reimbursements, and scholarships/grants available. Financial award applicants required to submit FAFSA. *Faculty research:* Probability and statistics; algebra, geometry, and topology; evolutionary computation; computer graphics and image manipulations; networking and communications; computational mathematics; biological data. *Unit head:* Dr. Qingtang Jiang, Director of Graduate Studies, 314-516-6358, Fax: 314-516-5400, E-mail: jiangq@umsl.edu. *Application contact:* 314-516-5458, Fax: 314-516-6996, E-mail: gradadm@umsl.edu.
Website: http://umsl.edu/divisions/artscience/math_cs/

University of Montana, Graduate School, College of Humanities and Sciences, Department of Computer Science, Missoula, MT 59812-0002. Offers MS. *Program availability:* Part-time. *Degree requirements:* For master's, project or thesis. *Entrance requirements:* For master's, GRE General Test. Additional exam requirements/recommendations for international students: Required—TOEFL (minimum score 525 paper-based). *Faculty research:* Parallel and distributed systems, neural networks, genetic algorithms, machine learning, data visualization, artificial intelligence.

University of Nebraska at Omaha, Graduate Studies, College of Information Science and Technology, Department of Computer Science, Omaha, NE 68182. Offers artificial intelligence (Certificate); communication networks (Certificate); computer science (MA, MS); computer science education (MS, Certificate); software engineering (Certificate); system and architecture (Certificate). *Program availability:* Part-time, evening/weekend. *Faculty:* 13 full-time (4 women). *Students:* 73 full-time (19 women), 44 part-time (15 women); includes 8 minority (3 Asian, non-Hispanic/Latino; 1 Hispanic/Latino; 4 Two or more races, non-Hispanic/Latino), 87 international. Average age 27. 132 applicants, 59% accepted, 33 enrolled. In 2016, 58 master's awarded. *Degree requirements:* For master's, comprehensive exam, thesis (for some programs). *Entrance requirements:* For master's, GRE General Test, minimum GPA of 3.0, prior course work in computer science, official transcripts, resume, 2 letters of recommendation; for Certificate, minimum GPA of 3.0, resume. Additional exam requirements/recommendations for international students: Required—TOEFL, IELTS, PTE. *Application deadline:* For fall admission, 7/1 priority date for domestic and international students; for spring admission, 11/1 priority date for domestic and international students; for summer admission, 3/1 for domestic and international students. Applications are processed on a rolling basis. Application fee: $45. Electronic applications accepted. *Financial support:* In 2016–17, 16 students received support, including 16 research assistantships with tuition reimbursements available; teaching assistantships with tuition reimbursements available, Federal Work-Study, institutionally sponsored loans, scholarships/grants, health care benefits, tuition waivers (full), and unspecified assistantships also available. Support available to part-time students. Financial award application deadline: 3/1; financial award applicants required to submit FAFSA. *Unit head:* Dr. Qiuming Zhu, Chairperson, 402-554-2341, E-mail: graduate@unomaha.edu. *Application contact:* Dr. Azad Azadmanesh, Graduate Program Chair, 402-554-2341, E-mail: graduate@unomaha.edu.

University of Nebraska–Lincoln, Graduate College, College of Arts and Sciences and College of Engineering, Department of Computer Science and Engineering, Lincoln, NE 68588. Offers bioinformatics (MS, PhD); computer engineering (MS, PhD); computer science (MS, PhD); information technology (PhD). *Degree requirements:* For master's, thesis optional; for doctorate, comprehensive exam, thesis/dissertation. *Entrance requirements:* For master's and doctorate, GRE General Test. Additional exam requirements/recommendations for international students: Required—TOEFL (minimum score 600 paper-based). Electronic applications accepted. *Faculty research:* Software engineering, geo- and bio-informatics, scientific computation, secure communication.

University of Nevada, Las Vegas, Graduate College, Howard R. Hughes College of Engineering, School of Computer Science, Las Vegas, NV 89154-4019. Offers MS, PhD. *Program availability:* Part-time. *Faculty:* 13 full-time (2 women), 1 part-time/adjunct (0 women). *Students:* 36 full-time (11 women), 22 part-time (3 women); includes 9 minority (1 Asian, non-Hispanic/Latino; 4 Hispanic/Latino; 4 Two or more races, non-Hispanic/Latino), 32 international. Average age 29. 67 applicants, 60% accepted, 13 enrolled. In 2016, 17 master's awarded. *Degree requirements:* For master's, thesis optional, project; for doctorate, comprehensive exam, thesis/dissertation. *Entrance requirements:* For master's, GRE General Test, bachelor's degree with minimum GPA 2.75; 2 letters of recommendation; for doctorate, GRE General Test, bachelor's degree with minimum GPA of 3.5; 3 letters of recommendation; statement of purpose. Additional exam requirements/recommendations for international students: Required—TOEFL (minimum score 550 paper-based; 80 iBT), IELTS (minimum score 7). *Application deadline:* For fall admission, 6/1 for domestic students, 2/1 for international students; for spring admission, 11/1 for domestic students, 10/1 for international students. Application fee: $60 ($95 for international students). Electronic applications accepted. *Expenses:* $269.25 per credit, $792 per 3-credit course; $9,634 per year resident; $23,274 per year non-resident; $7,094 fees non-resident (7 credits or more); $1,307 annual health insurance fee. *Financial support:* In 2016–17, 13 research assistantships with partial tuition reimbursements (averaging $15,545 per year), 26 teaching assistantships with partial tuition reimbursements (averaging $10,923 per year) were awarded; institutionally sponsored loans, scholarships/grants, health care benefits, and unspecified assistantships also available. Financial award application deadline: 3/15. *Faculty research:* Algorithms, computer graphics, databases and data mining, distributed systems and networks, big data analytics. *Total annual research expenditures:* $141,922. *Unit head:* Dr. Laxmi Gewali, Chair/Professor, 702-895-4028, Fax: 702-895-2639, E-mail: laxmi.gewali@unlv.edu. *Application contact:* Dr. Ajoy Datta, Graduate Coordinator, 702-895-0870, Fax: 702-895-2639, E-mail: ajoy.datta@unlv.edu.
Website: http://cs.unlv.edu/

University of Nevada, Reno, Graduate School, College of Engineering, Department of Computer Science and Engineering, Reno, NV 89557. Offers MS, PhD. Terminal master's awarded for partial completion of doctoral program. *Degree requirements:* For master's, thesis optional; for doctorate, thesis/dissertation. *Entrance requirements:* For master's, GRE General Test, minimum GPA of 2.75; for doctorate, GRE General Test, minimum GPA of 3.0. Additional exam requirements/recommendations for international students: Required—TOEFL (minimum score 500 paper-based; 61 iBT), IELTS (minimum score 6). Electronic applications accepted. *Faculty research:* Evolutionary computing systems, computer vision/virtual reality, software engineering.

University of New Brunswick Fredericton, School of Graduate Studies, Faculty of Computer Science, Fredericton, NB E3B 5A3, Canada. Offers M Sc CS, PhD. *Program availability:* Part-time. *Degree requirements:* For master's, thesis; for doctorate, comprehensive exam, thesis/dissertation, qualifying exam. *Entrance requirements:* For master's, minimum GPA of 3.0; undergraduate degree with sufficient computer science background; for doctorate, research-based master's degree in computer science or related area. Additional exam requirements/recommendations for international students: Required—TOEFL (minimum score 550 paper-based; 80 iBT), IELTS (minimum score 7), TWE (minimum score 4.5), Michigan English Language Assessment Battery (minimum score 85) or CanTest (minimum score 4.5). Electronic applications accepted. *Faculty research:* Computer hardware, software engineering, embedded systems, e-business, e-learning, security, artificial intelligence, bioinformatics, computer-assisted drug design, high performance computing, Web services.

University of New Hampshire, Graduate School, College of Engineering and Physical Sciences, Department of Computer Science, Durham, NH 03824. Offers MS, PhD, Postbaccalaureate Certificate. *Program availability:* Part-time, evening/weekend. *Degree requirements:* For master's, thesis or alternative; for doctorate, thesis/dissertation. *Entrance requirements:* For master's and doctorate, GRE General Test. Additional exam requirements/recommendations for international students: Required—TOEFL (minimum score 550 paper-based; 80 iBT). Electronic applications accepted. *Faculty research:* Programming languages, compiler design, parallel algorithms, computer graphics, artificial intelligence.

University of New Haven, Graduate School, Henry C. Lee College of Criminal Justice and Forensic Sciences, Program in Criminal Justice, West Haven, CT 06516. Offers crime analysis (MS); criminal justice (MS, PhD); criminal justice management (MS, Graduate Certificate); forensic computer investigation (MS); forensic psychology (MS); information protection and security (Graduate Certificate); victim advocacy and services management (Graduate Certificate); victimology (MS). *Program availability:* Part-time, evening/weekend, online learning. *Students:* 120 full-time (83 women), 121 part-time (69 women); includes 84 minority (49 Black or African American, non-Hispanic/Latino; 10 Asian, non-Hispanic/Latino; 14 Hispanic/Latino; 1 Native Hawaiian or other Pacific Islander, non-Hispanic/Latino; 10 Two or more races, non-Hispanic/Latino), 10 international. Average age 29. 128 applicants, 90% accepted, 73 enrolled. In 2016, 52 master's, 2 doctorates, 8 other advanced degrees awarded. *Degree requirements:* For master's, thesis or alternative. *Entrance requirements:* Additional exam requirements/recommendations for international students: Required—TOEFL (minimum score 80 iBT), IELTS, PTE (minimum score 53). *Application deadline:* Applications are processed on a rolling basis. Application fee: $50. Electronic applications accepted. Application fee is waived when completed online. *Expenses: Tuition:* Full-time $15,660; part-time $870 per credit hour. *Required fees:* $200; $85 per term. Tuition and fees vary according to program. *Financial support:* Research assistantships with partial tuition reimbursements, teaching assistantships with partial tuition reimbursements, career-related internships or fieldwork, Federal Work-Study, scholarships/grants, and unspecified assistantships available. Support available to part-time students. Financial award applicants required to submit FAFSA. *Application contact:* Michelle Mason, Director of Graduate Enrollment, 203-932-7067, E-mail: mmason@newhaven.edu.
Website: http://www.newhaven.edu/5921/

University of New Haven, Graduate School, Tagliatela College of Engineering, Program in Computer Science, West Haven, CT 06516. Offers computer programming (Graduate Certificate); computer science (MS); network systems (MS); software development (MS). *Program availability:* Part-time, evening/weekend. *Students:* 96 full-time (46 women), 25 part-time (5 women); includes 9 minority (1 American Indian or Alaska Native, non-Hispanic/Latino; 7 Asian, non-Hispanic/Latino; 1 Two or more races, non-Hispanic/Latino), 86 international. Average age 27. 791 applicants, 43% accepted, 23 enrolled. In 2016, 80 master's, 1 other advanced degree awarded. *Degree requirements:* For master's, thesis or alternative. *Entrance requirements:* Additional exam requirements/recommendations for international students: Required—TOEFL (minimum score 75 iBT), IELTS, PTE (minimum score 50). *Application deadline:* Applications are processed on a rolling basis. Application fee: $50. Electronic applications accepted. Application fee is waived when completed online. *Expenses: Tuition:* Full-time $15,660; part-time $870 per credit hour. *Required fees:* $200; $85 per term. Tuition and fees vary according to program. *Financial support:* Research assistantships with partial tuition reimbursements, teaching assistantships with partial tuition reimbursements, career-related internships or fieldwork, Federal Work-Study, scholarships/grants, and unspecified assistantships available. Support available to part-time students. Financial award applicants required to submit FAFSA. *Unit head:* Dr. David Eggert, Coordinator, 203-932-7097, E-mail: deggert@newhaven.edu. *Application contact:* Michelle Mason, Director of Graduate Enrollment, 203-932-7067, E-mail: mmason@newhaven.edu.
Website: http://www.newhaven.edu/9591/

University of New Mexico, Graduate Studies, School of Engineering, Program in Computer Science, Albuquerque, NM 87131-2039. Offers MS, PhD. *Program availability:* Part-time. *Faculty:* 20 full-time (5 women), 1 part-time/adjunct (0 women). *Students:* 81 full-time (15 women), 61 part-time (8 women); includes 26 minority (1 Black or African American, non-Hispanic/Latino; 7 Asian, non-Hispanic/Latino; 14 Hispanic/Latino; 4 Two or more races, non-Hispanic/Latino), 58 international. Average age 30. 200 applicants, 17% accepted, 28 enrolled. In 2016, 33 master's, 11 doctorates awarded. Terminal master's awarded for partial completion of doctoral program. *Degree requirements:* For master's, thesis or alternative; for doctorate, thesis/dissertation. *Entrance requirements:* For master's and doctorate, GRE General Test, minimum GPA of 3.0. Additional exam requirements/recommendations for international students: Required—TOEFL (minimum score 550 paper-based; 79 iBT), IELTS (minimum score 6.5). *Application deadline:* For fall admission, 1/15 for domestic students, 3/1 for international students; for spring admission, 8/1 for domestic and international students. Applications are processed on a rolling basis. Application fee: $50. Electronic applications accepted. *Financial support:* Fellowships with full tuition reimbursements, research assistantships with full tuition reimbursements, teaching assistantships with full tuition reimbursements, career-related internships or fieldwork, scholarships/grants, and health care benefits available. Financial award application deadline: 1/15; financial award applicants required to submit FAFSA. *Faculty research:* Artificial life, genetic algorithms, computer security, complexity theory, interactive computer graphics, operating systems and networking, biology and computation, machine learning, automated reasoning, quantum computation. *Total annual research expenditures:* $2.7 million. *Unit head:* Dr. Michalis Faloutsos, Chairperson, 505-277-3112, Fax: 505-277-

6927, E-mail: michalis@cs.unm.edu. *Application contact:* Lynne Jacobsen, Coordinator, Program Advisement, 505-277-3112, Fax: 505-277-6927, E-mail: ljake@cs.unm.edu. Website: http://www.cs.unm.edu/

University of New Orleans, Graduate School, College of Sciences, Department of Computer Science, New Orleans, LA 70148. Offers MS. *Entrance requirements:* For master's, GRE General Test. Additional exam requirements/recommendations for international students: Required—TOEFL (minimum score 550 paper-based; 79 iBT), IELTS (minimum score 6.5). Electronic applications accepted.

The University of North Carolina at Chapel Hill, Graduate School, College of Arts and Sciences, Department of Computer Science, Chapel Hill, NC 27599. Offers MS, PhD. *Program availability:* Part-time, online learning. Terminal master's awarded for partial completion of doctoral program. *Degree requirements:* For master's, comprehensive exam, thesis or alternative, programming product; for doctorate, comprehensive exam, thesis/dissertation, programming product, teaching requirement. *Entrance requirements:* For master's and doctorate, GRE General Test, minimum GPA of 3.0. Additional exam requirements/recommendations for international students: Required—TOEFL (minimum score 575 paper-based). Electronic applications accepted. *Faculty research:* Bioinformatics, graphics, hardware, systems, theory.

The University of North Carolina at Charlotte, College of Computing and Informatics, Department of Computer Science, Charlotte, NC 28223-0001. Offers advanced databases and knowledge discovery (Graduate Certificate); computer science (MS); game design and development (Graduate Certificate). *Program availability:* Part-time, evening/weekend. *Faculty:* 27 full-time (7 women), 2 part-time/adjunct (1 woman). *Students:* 275 full-time (86 women), 87 part-time (35 women); includes 9 minority (5 Asian, non-Hispanic/Latino; 4 Hispanic/Latino), 335 international. Average age 24. 1,569 applicants, 37% accepted, 182 enrolled. In 2016, 224 master's, 9 other advanced degrees awarded. *Degree requirements:* For master's, thesis optional. *Entrance requirements:* For master's, GRE General Test, knowledge of two higher languages, data structures, algorithm analysis, operating systems or computer architecture, and two additional upper-division computer science courses; knowledge of calculus, discrete mathematics, and linear algebra; minimum undergraduate GPA of 3.0; for Graduate Certificate, BS in any scientific, engineering or business discipline; enrolled and in good standing in a graduate degree program at UNC Charlotte or have minimum GPA of 2.8 overall and 3.0 junior/senior year. Additional exam requirements/recommendations for international students: Required—TOEFL (minimum score 523 paper-based, 70 iBT) or IELTS (6.5). *Application deadline:* For fall admission, 3/1 priority date for domestic and international students; for spring admission, 10/1 priority date for domestic and international students; for summer admission, 4/1 priority date for domestic and international students. Applications are processed on a rolling basis. Application fee: $75. Electronic applications accepted. *Expenses:* Contact institution. *Financial support:* In 2016–17, 88 students received support, including 2 fellowships (averaging $36,833 per year), 23 research assistantships (averaging $10,463 per year), 62 teaching assistantships (averaging $7,000 per year); career-related internships or fieldwork, Federal Work-Study, institutionally sponsored loans, scholarships/grants, unspecified assistantships, and administrative assistantships also available. Support available to part-time students. Financial award application deadline: 3/1; financial award applicants required to submit FAFSA. *Total annual research expenditures:* $2.3 million. *Unit head:* Dr. Bojan Cukic, Chair, 704-687-6155, E-mail: bcukic@uncc.edu. *Application contact:* Kathy B. Giddings, Director of Graduate Admissions, 704-687-3366, Fax: 704-687-3279, E-mail: gradadm@uncc.edu. Website: http://cs.uncc.edu/

The University of North Carolina at Charlotte, College of Computing and Informatics, Program in Computing and Information Systems, Charlotte, NC 28223-0001. Offers computing and information systems (PhD), including bioinformatics, business information systems and operations management, computer science, interdisciplinary, software and information systems. *Faculty:* 3 full-time (0 women). *Students:* 91 full-time (30 women), 23 part-time (3 women); includes 8 minority (2 Black or African American, non-Hispanic/Latino; 4 Asian, non-Hispanic/Latino; 1 Hispanic/Latino; 1 Two or more races, non-Hispanic/Latino), 76 international. Average age 31. 90 applicants, 41% accepted, 18 enrolled. In 2016, 13 doctorates awarded. *Degree requirements:* For doctorate, comprehensive exam, thesis/dissertation. *Entrance requirements:* For doctorate, GRE or GMAT, baccalaureate degree, minimum GPA of 3.0 on courses related to the chosen field of PhD study, essay, reference letters. Additional exam requirements/recommendations for international students: Required—TOEFL (minimum score 523 paper-based, 70 iBT) or IELTS (6.5). *Application deadline:* For fall admission, 2/1 for domestic and international students; for spring admission, 9/1 for domestic and international students. Applications are processed on a rolling basis. Application fee: $75. Electronic applications accepted. *Expenses:* Tuition, state resident: full-time $4252. Tuition, nonresident: full-time $17,423. *Required fees:* $3026. Tuition and fees vary according to course load and program. *Financial support:* Career-related internships or fieldwork, institutionally sponsored loans, scholarships/grants, health care benefits, and unspecified assistantships available. Support available to part-time students. Financial award applicants required to submit FAFSA. *Unit head:* Manuel A. Perez Quinones, Director, 704-687-8553, E-mail: perez.quinones@uncc.edu. *Application contact:* Kathy B. Giddings, Director of Graduate Admissions, 704-687-5503, Fax: 704-687-1668, E-mail: gradadm@uncc.edu.

The University of North Carolina at Greensboro, Graduate School, College of Arts and Sciences, Department of Computer Science, Greensboro, NC 27412-5001. Offers MS.

The University of North Carolina Wilmington, Interdisciplinary Program in Computer Science and Information Systems, Wilmington, NC 28403-3297. Offers MS. *Program availability:* Part-time. *Faculty:* 11 full-time (3 women). *Students:* 13 full-time (3 women), 10 part-time (2 women); includes 3 minority (1 Black or African American, non-Hispanic/Latino; 1 Asian, non-Hispanic/Latino; 1 Hispanic/Latino), 6 international. Average age 28. 22 applicants, 73% accepted, 10 enrolled. In 2016, 10 master's awarded. *Degree requirements:* For master's, thesis or alternative, research project. *Entrance requirements:* For master's, GMAT or GRE, 3 letters of recommendation, resume, statement of interest. Additional exam requirements/recommendations for international students: Required—TOEFL (minimum score 79 iBT), IELTS (minimum score 6.5). *Application deadline:* For fall admission, 6/1 for domestic students; for spring admission, 11/1 for domestic students. Applications are processed on a rolling basis. Application fee: $60. Electronic applications accepted. *Expenses:* Contact institution. *Financial support:* Scholarships/grants and unspecified assistantships available. Financial award application deadline: 3/15; financial award applicants required to submit FAFSA. *Unit head:* Dr. Clayton Ferner, Program Coordinator, 910-962-7552, E-mail: cferner@uncw.edu. *Application contact:* Candace Wilhelm, Graduate Coordinator, 910-962-3903, Fax: 910-962-7457, E-mail: wilhelmc@uncw.edu. Website: http://csb.uncw.edu/mscsis/

University of North Dakota, Graduate School, John D. Odegard School of Aerospace Sciences, Department of Computer Science, Grand Forks, ND 58202. Offers MS. *Program availability:* Part-time. *Degree requirements:* For master's, comprehensive exam, thesis or alternative. *Entrance requirements:* For master's, GRE General Test, minimum GPA of 3.0. Additional exam requirements/recommendations for international

students: Required—TOEFL (minimum score 550 paper-based; 79 iBT), IELTS (minimum score 6.5). *Application deadline:* For fall admission, 8/1 priority date for domestic and international students; for spring admission, 12/1 priority date for domestic students, 9/1 priority date for international students. Applications are processed on a rolling basis. Application fee: $35. Electronic applications accepted. *Financial support:* Fellowships with full and partial tuition reimbursements, research assistantships with full and partial tuition reimbursements, teaching assistantships with full and partial tuition reimbursements, Federal Work-Study, institutionally sponsored loans, scholarships/grants, health care benefits, tuition waivers (full and partial), and unspecified assistantships available. Support available to part-time students. Financial award application deadline: 3/15; financial award applicants required to submit FAFSA. *Faculty research:* Operating systems, simulation, parallel computation, hypermedia, graph theory. *Unit head:* Dr. Emanuel Grant, Graduate Director, 701-777-4133, Fax: 701-777-3330, E-mail: grante@cs.und.edu. *Application contact:* Staci Wells, Admissions Specialist, 701-777-0748, Fax: 701-777-3619, E-mail: staci.wells@gradschool.und.edu. Website: http://www.cs.und.edu

University of Northern British Columbia, Office of Graduate Studies, Prince George, BC V2N 4Z9, Canada. Offers business administration (Diploma); community health science (M Sc); disability management (MA); education (M Ed); first nations studies (MA); gender studies (MA); history (MA); interdisciplinary studies (MA); international studies (MA); mathematical, computer and physical sciences (M Sc); natural resources and environmental studies (M Sc, MA, MNRES, PhD); political science (MA); psychology (M Sc, PhD); social work (MSW). *Program availability:* Part-time, evening/weekend, online learning. *Degree requirements:* For master's, thesis; for doctorate, thesis/dissertation. *Entrance requirements:* For master's, GRE, minimum B average in undergraduate course work; for doctorate, candidacy exam, minimum A average in graduate course work.

University of North Florida, College of Computing, Engineering, and Construction, School of Computing, Jacksonville, FL 32224. Offers computer science (MS); information systems (MS); software engineering (MS). *Program availability:* Part-time. *Faculty:* 12 full-time (2 women), 1 part-time/adjunct (0 women). *Students:* 13 full-time (5 women), 47 part-time (14 women); includes 14 minority (2 Black or African American, non-Hispanic/Latino; 9 Asian, non-Hispanic/Latino; 1 Hispanic/Latino; 2 Two or more races, non-Hispanic/Latino), 20 international. Average age 30. 62 applicants, 31% accepted, 7 enrolled. In 2016, 3 master's awarded. *Degree requirements:* For master's, thesis. *Entrance requirements:* For master's, GRE General Test, minimum GPA of 3.0 in last 60 hours of course work. Additional exam requirements/recommendations for international students: Required—TOEFL (minimum score 500 paper-based; 61 iBT). *Application deadline:* For fall admission, 8/1 priority date for domestic students, 5/1 for international students; for spring admission, 12/1 priority date for domestic students, 10/1 for international students; for summer admission, 3/15 priority date for domestic students, 2/1 for international students. Application fee: $30. Electronic applications accepted. Tuition and fees vary according to course load, campus/location and program. *Financial support:* In 2016–17, 4 research assistantships (averaging $2,332 per year) were awarded; teaching assistantships, Federal Work-Study, scholarships/grants, and unspecified assistantships also available. Financial award application deadline: 4/1; financial award applicants required to submit FAFSA. *Total annual research expenditures:* $196,076. *Unit head:* Dr. Sherif Elfayoumy, Director/Professor, 904-620-2985, E-mail: selfayou@unf.edu. *Application contact:* Dr. Amanda Pascale, Director, The Graduate School, 904-620-1360, Fax: 904-620-1362, E-mail: graduateschool@unf.edu. Website: http://www.unf.edu/ccec/computing/

University of North Texas, Robert B. Toulouse School of Graduate Studies, Denton, TX 76203-5459. Offers accounting (MS); applied anthropology (MA, MS); applied behavior analysis (Certificate); applied geography (MA); applied technology and performance improvement (M Ed, MS); art education (MA); art history (MA); art museum education (Certificate); arts leadership (Certificate); audiology (Au D); behavior analysis (MS); behavioral science (PhD); biochemistry and molecular biology (MS); biology (MA, MS); biomedical engineering (MS); business analysis (MS); chemistry (MS); clinical health psychology (PhD); communication studies (MA, MS); computer engineering (MS); computer science (MS); counseling (M Ed, MS), including clinical mental health counseling (MS), college and university counseling, elementary school counseling, secondary school counseling; creative writing (MA); criminal justice (MS); curriculum and instruction (M Ed); decision sciences (MBA); design (MA, MFA), including fashion design (MFA), innovation studies, interior design (MFA); early childhood studies (MS); economics (MS); educational leadership (M Ed, Ed D); educational psychology (MS, PhD), including family studies (MS), gifted and talented (MS), human development (MS), learning and cognition (MS), research, measurement and evaluation (MS); electrical engineering (MS); emergency management (MPA); engineering technology (MS); English (MA); English as a second language (MA); environmental science (MS); finance (MBA, MS); financial management (MPA); French (MA); health services management (MBA); higher education (M Ed, Ed D); history (MA, MS); hospitality management (MS); human resources management (MPA); information science (MS); information systems (PhD); information technologies (MBA); interdisciplinary studies (MA, MS); international studies (MA); international sustainable tourism (MS); jazz studies (MM); journalism (MA, MJ, Graduate Certificate), including interactive and virtual digital communication (Graduate Certificate), narrative journalism (Graduate Certificate), public relations (Graduate Certificate); kinesiology (MS); linguistics (MA); local government management (MPA); logistics (PhD); logistics and supply chain management (MBA); long-term care, senior housing, and aging services (MA); management (PhD); marketing (MBA); mathematics (MA, MS); mechanical and energy engineering (MS, PhD); music (MA), including ethnomusicology, music theory, musicology, performance; music composition (PhD); music education (MM Ed, PhD); nonprofit management (MPA); operations and supply chain management (MBA); performance (MM, DMA); philosophy (MA); political science (MA); professional and technical communication (MA); radio, television and film (MA, MFA); rehabilitation counseling (Certificate); sociology (MA); Spanish (MA); special education (M Ed); speech-language pathology (MA); strategic management (MBA); studio art (MFA); teaching (M Ed); MBA/MS. *Program availability:* Part-time, evening/weekend, online learning. Terminal master's awarded for partial completion of doctoral program. *Degree requirements:* For master's, variable foreign language requirement, comprehensive exam (for some programs), thesis (for some programs); for doctorate, variable foreign language requirement, comprehensive exam (for some programs), thesis/dissertation; for other advanced degree, variable foreign language requirement, comprehensive exam (for some programs). *Entrance requirements:* For master's and doctorate, GRE, GMAT. Additional exam requirements/recommendations for international students: Required—TOEFL (minimum score 550 paper-based; 79 iBT). Electronic applications accepted.

University of Notre Dame, Graduate School, College of Engineering, Department of Computer Science and Engineering, Notre Dame, IN 46556. Offers MSCSE, PhD. Terminal master's awarded for partial completion of doctoral program. *Degree requirements:* For master's, comprehensive exam; for doctorate, thesis/dissertation, candidacy exam. *Entrance requirements:* For master's and doctorate, GRE General Test. Additional exam requirements/recommendations for international students: Required—TOEFL (minimum score 600 paper-based; 80 iBT). Electronic applications accepted. *Faculty research:* Algorithms and theory of computer science, artificial intelligence, behavior-based robotics, biometrics, computer vision.

University of Oklahoma, Gallogly College of Engineering, School of Computer Science, Norman, OK 73019. Offers MS, PhD. *Program availability:* Part-time. *Faculty:* 17 full-time (3 women). *Students:* 56 full-time (14 women), 12 part-time (3 women); includes 1 minority (Black or African American, non-Hispanic/Latino), 61 international. Average age 26. 123 applicants, 32% accepted, 22 enrolled. In 2016, 33 master's, 4 doctorates awarded. *Degree requirements:* For master's, comprehensive exam (for some programs), thesis (for some programs), 5 seminars; for doctorate, comprehensive exam, thesis/dissertation, 5 seminars. *Entrance requirements:* For master's and doctorate, GRE, bachelor's degree, resume, 3 letters of recommendation, statement of purpose. Additional exam requirements/recommendations for international students: Required—TOEFL (minimum score 79 iBT) or IELTS (minimum score 6.5). *Application deadline:* For fall admission, 4/1 for domestic students, 3/1 for international students; for spring admission, 10/1 for domestic students, 9/1 for international students. Applications are processed on a rolling basis. Application fee: $50 ($100 for international students). Electronic applications accepted. *Expenses:* Tuition, state resident: full-time $4886; part-time $203.60 per credit hour. Tuition, nonresident: full-time $18,989; part-time $791.20 per credit hour. *Required fees:* $3283; $126.25 per credit hour. $126.50 per semester. *Financial support:* In 2016–17, 52 students received support, including 18 research assistantships with full tuition reimbursements available (averaging $15,167 per year), 23 teaching assistantships with full tuition reimbursements available (averaging $12,679 per year); fellowships with full tuition reimbursements available, career-related internships or fieldwork, scholarships/grants, and unspecified assistantships also available. Financial award application deadline: 6/1; financial award applicants required to submit FAFSA. *Faculty research:* Cybersecurity, data mining, algorithms and theory, mobile wireless and computer networks, parallel programming. *Total annual research expenditures:* $1.9 million. *Unit head:* Dr. Sridhar Radhakrishnan, Director, 405-325-4042, Fax: 405-325-4044, E-mail: sridhar@ou.edu. *Application contact:* Virginie Perez Woods, Academic Programs Coordinator, 405-325-0145, Fax: 405-325-4044, E-mail: vpw@cs.ou.edu.
Website: http://cs.ou.edu

University of Oregon, Graduate School, College of Arts and Sciences, Department of Computer and Information Science, Eugene, OR 97403. Offers MA, MS, PhD. *Program availability:* Part-time. Terminal master's awarded for partial completion of doctoral program. *Degree requirements:* For doctorate, thesis/dissertation. *Entrance requirements:* For master's and doctorate, GRE General Test, minimum GPA of 3.0. Additional exam requirements/recommendations for international students: Required—TOEFL. *Faculty research:* Artificial intelligence, graphics, natural-language processing, expert systems, operating systems.

University of Ottawa, Faculty of Graduate and Postdoctoral Studies, Faculty of Engineering, Ottawa-Carleton Institute for Computer Science, Ottawa, ON K1N 6N5, Canada. Offers MCS, PhD. MCS, PhD offered jointly with Carleton University. *Degree requirements:* For master's, thesis or alternative; for doctorate, comprehensive exam, thesis/dissertation, two seminars. *Entrance requirements:* For master's, honors degree or equivalent, minimum B average; for doctorate, minimum B+ average. Electronic applications accepted. *Faculty research:* Knowledge-based and intelligent systems, algorithms, parallel and distributed systems.

University of Pennsylvania, School of Engineering and Applied Science, Department of Computer and Information Science, Philadelphia, PA 19104. Offers computer and information science (MSE, PhD); computer and information technology (MCIT); computer graphics and game technology (MSE). *Program availability:* Part-time. *Faculty:* 53 full-time (6 women), 8 part-time/adjunct (2 women). *Students:* 304 full-time (84 women), 96 part-time (36 women); includes 38 minority (4 Black or African American, non-Hispanic/Latino; 26 Asian, non-Hispanic/Latino; 6 Hispanic/Latino; 2 Two or more races, non-Hispanic/Latino), 233 international. Average age 26. 2,114 applicants, 17% accepted, 209 enrolled. In 2016, 142 master's, 14 doctorates awarded. *Degree requirements:* For master's, comprehensive exam, thesis optional; for doctorate, comprehensive exam, thesis/dissertation. *Entrance requirements:* For master's and doctorate, GRE. Additional exam requirements/recommendations for international students: Required—TOEFL (minimum score 100 iBT), IELTS (minimum score 7). *Application deadline:* For fall admission, 3/15 priority date for domestic and international students. Application fee: $80. Electronic applications accepted. *Expenses: Tuition:* Full-time $31,068; part-time $5762 per course. *Required fees:* $3200; $336 per course. Full-time tuition and fees vary according to degree level, program and student level. Part-time tuition and fees vary according to course load, degree level and program. *Faculty research:* Artificial intelligence, robotics, software engineering, computational linguistics, machine learning. *Application contact:* William Fenton, Assistant Director of Graduate Admissions, 215-898-4542, Fax: 215-573-5577, E-mail: gradstudies@seas.upenn.edu.
Website: http://www.cis.upenn.edu/prospective-students/graduate/

University of Pittsburgh, Dietrich School of Arts and Sciences, Department of Computer Science, Pittsburgh, PA 15260. Offers MS, PhD. *Program availability:* Part-time. *Faculty:* 18 full-time (4 women). *Students:* 79 full-time (17 women), 6 part-time (0 women); includes 3 minority (all Asian, non-Hispanic/Latino), 64 international. Average age 26. 613 applicants, 5% accepted, 14 enrolled. In 2016, 24 master's, 6 doctorates awarded. Terminal master's awarded for partial completion of doctoral program. *Degree requirements:* For master's, thesis or alternative; for doctorate, comprehensive exam, thesis/dissertation, preliminary exam. *Entrance requirements:* For master's and doctorate, GRE General Test. Additional exam requirements/recommendations for international students: Required—TOEFL (minimum score 90 iBT), GRE. *Application deadline:* For fall admission, 1/15 for domestic and international students; for spring admission, 9/15 for domestic and international students. Application fee: $50. Electronic applications accepted. Tuition and fees vary according to program. *Financial support:* In 2016–17, 62 students received support, including 6 fellowships with full tuition reimbursements available (averaging $21,992 per year), 26 research assistantships with full tuition reimbursements available (averaging $18,950 per year), 29 teaching assistantships with full tuition reimbursements available (averaging $17,910 per year); career-related internships or fieldwork, Federal Work-Study, health care benefits, and tuition waivers (partial) also available. Financial award application deadline: 1/15. *Faculty research:* Algorithms and theory, artificial intelligence, parallel and distributed systems, software systems and interfaces. *Total annual research expenditures:* $2.9 million. *Unit head:* Dr. Taieb Znati, Chairman, 412-624-8493, Fax: 412-624-8854, E-mail: znati@cs.pitt.edu. *Application contact:* Keena M. Walker, Graduate Administrator, 412-624-8495, Fax: 412-624-8854, E-mail: keena@cs.pitt.edu.
Website: http://www.cs.pitt.edu/

University of Pittsburgh, Dietrich School of Arts and Sciences, Program in Computational Modeling and Simulation, Pittsburgh, PA 15260. Offers biological science (PhD); chemistry (PhD); computer science (PhD); economics (PhD); geology and environmental sciences (PhD); mathematics (PhD); physics and astronomy (PhD); psychology (PhD); statistics (PhD). *Program availability:* Part-time. *Faculty:* 4 full-time (1 woman). *Students:* 3 full-time (1 woman), 1 part-time (0 women); includes 1 minority (Asian, non-Hispanic/Latino). Average age 23. 7 applicants, 43% accepted, 2 enrolled. *Degree requirements:* For doctorate, comprehensive exam, thesis/dissertation, preliminary exam. *Entrance requirements:* For doctorate, GRE, statement of purpose, transcripts for all college-level institutions attended, three letters of reference. Additional exam requirements/recommendations for international students: Required—TOEFL (minimum score 90 iBT), IELTS (minimum score 7). *Application deadline:* For fall admission, 1/15 for domestic and international students. Applications are processed on a rolling basis. Application fee: $0 ($50 for international students). Electronic applications accepted. *Expenses:* Contact institution. *Financial support:* In 2016–17, 3 students received support, including 2 fellowships with full tuition reimbursements available (averaging $28,500 per year), 2 research assistantships with full tuition reimbursements available (averaging $23,000 per year); tuition waivers (full) also available. Financial award application deadline: 4/15. *Faculty research:* Econometric modeling, developing reduced-scaling first principles approaches for expedited predictions of molecular and materials properties, developing computational models to quantitatively describe origins of reactivity and selectivity in organ catalytic reactions, image retrieval, human-machine communication. *Unit head:* Dr. Holger Hoock, Associate Dean, 412-624-3939, Fax: 412-624-6855. *Application contact:* Wendy G. Janocha, Graduate Administrator, 412-648-7251, E-mail: wgj1@pitt.edu.
Website: http://cmsp.pitt.edu/

University of Portland, School of Engineering, Portland, OR 97203-5798. Offers biomedical engineering (MBME); civil engineering (ME); computer science (ME); electrical engineering (ME); mechanical engineering (ME). *Program availability:* Part-time, evening/weekend. *Degree requirements:* For master's, thesis optional. *Entrance requirements:* For master's, GRE General Test, minimum GPA of 3.0, 3 letters of recommendation, resume, statement of goals, official transcripts. Additional exam requirements/recommendations for international students: Required—TOEFL (minimum score 550 paper-based; 80 iBT), IELTS (minimum score 7). *Expenses:* Contact institution.

University of Puerto Rico, Mayagüez Campus, Graduate Studies, College of Engineering, Computer Science and Engineering Program, Mayagüez, PR 00681-9000. Offers PhD. *Program availability:* Part-time. *Faculty:* 10 full-time (1 woman). *Students:* 36 full-time (4 women), 9 part-time (1 woman); includes 37 minority (all Hispanic/Latino), 6 international. Average age 25. 13 applicants, 85% accepted, 5 enrolled. *Degree requirements:* For doctorate, one foreign language, comprehensive exam, thesis/dissertation. *Entrance requirements:* For doctorate, GRE General Test, BS in engineering or science; undergraduate courses in data structures, programming language, calculus III and linear algebra, or the equivalent. *Application deadline:* For fall admission, 2/15 for domestic and international students; for spring admission, 9/15 for domestic and international students. Applications are processed on a rolling basis. Application fee: $25. Electronic applications accepted. *Expenses: Tuition, area resident:* Full-time $2466. *International tuition:* $7166 full-time. *Required fees:* $210. One-time fee: $5 full-time. Tuition and fees vary according to course level, campus/location, program and student level. *Financial support:* In 2016–17, 12 students received support, including 7 research assistantships with full and partial tuition reimbursements available (averaging $1,919 per year), 11 teaching assistantships with full and partial tuition reimbursements available (averaging $5,252 per year); unspecified assistantships also available. *Faculty research:* Big data analysis, parallel and distributor processing, mobile computing and networking, remote sensing, channel capacity. *Unit head:* Bienvenido Velez, Ph.D., Acting Director, 787-832-4040 Ext. 5827, Fax: 787-833-3331, E-mail: bienvenido.velez@upr.edu. *Application contact:* Alida Minguela, Administrative Assistant, 787-832-4040 Ext. 5217, Fax: 787-833-3331, E-mail: alida@ece.uprm.edu.
Website: http://cse.uprm.edu/

University of Puerto Rico, Mayagüez Campus, Graduate Studies, College of Engineering, Department of Electrical and Computer Engineering, Mayagüez, PR 00681-9000. Offers computer engineering (ME, MS); computing and information sciences and engineering (PhD); electrical engineering (ME, MS). *Program availability:* Part-time. *Faculty:* 48 full-time (6 women). *Students:* 45 full-time (6 women), 8 part-time (3 women); includes 45 minority (all Hispanic/Latino), 5 international. Average age 25. 30 applicants, 83% accepted, 18 enrolled. In 2016, 12 master's awarded. Terminal master's awarded for partial completion of doctoral program. *Degree requirements:* For master's, one foreign language, comprehensive exam, thesis; for doctorate, one foreign language, comprehensive exam, thesis/dissertation. *Entrance requirements:* For master's and doctorate, proficiency in English and Spanish; BS in electrical or computer engineering, or equivalent; minimum GPA of 3.0. *Application deadline:* For fall admission, 2/15 for domestic and international students; for spring admission, 9/15 for domestic and international students. Applications are processed on a rolling basis. Application fee: $25. Electronic applications accepted. *Expenses: Tuition, area resident:* Full-time $2466. *International tuition:* $7166 full-time. *Required fees:* $210. One-time fee: $5 full-time. Tuition and fees vary according to course level, campus/location, program and student level. *Financial support:* In 2016–17, 50 students received support, including 41 research assistantships with full and partial tuition reimbursements available (averaging $3,442 per year), 26 teaching assistantships with full and partial tuition reimbursements available (averaging $4,149 per year); unspecified assistantships also available. *Faculty research:* Digital signal processing, power electronics, microwave ocean emissivity, parallel and distributed computing, microwave remote sensing. *Unit head:* Jose Colom-Ustaris, Ph.D., Department Head, 787-832-4040 Ext. 3086, Fax: 787-831-7564, E-mail: jose.colom1@upr.edu. *Application contact:* Claribel Lorenzo, Administrative Secretary V, 787-832-4040 Ext. 3821, E-mail: claribel.lorenzo@upr.edu.
Website: https://ece.uprm.edu/

University of Regina, Faculty of Graduate Studies and Research, Faculty of Science, Department of Computer Science, Regina, SK S4S 0A2, Canada. Offers M Sc, PhD. *Program availability:* Part-time. *Faculty:* 14 full-time (3 women), 10 part-time/adjunct (0 women). *Students:* 75 full-time (20 women), 5 part-time (3 women). 176 applicants, 13% accepted. In 2016, 26 master's, 2 doctorates awarded. *Degree requirements:* For master's, thesis (for some programs), project, report; for doctorate, thesis/dissertation. *Entrance requirements:* Additional exam requirements/recommendations for international students: Required—TOEFL (minimum score 580 paper-based; 80 iBT), IELTS (minimum score 6.5), PTE (minimum score 59). *Application deadline:* For fall admission, 3/31 for domestic and international students; for winter admission, 7/31 for domestic and international students; for spring admission, 11/30 for domestic and international students. Application fee: $100. Electronic applications accepted. *Financial support:* In 2016–17, 13 fellowships (averaging $6,308 per year), 13 teaching assistantships (averaging $2,586 per year) were awarded; career-related internships or fieldwork and scholarships/grants also available. Financial award application deadline: 6/15. *Faculty research:* Information retrieval, machine learning, computer visualization, theory and application of rough sets, human-computer interaction. *Unit head:* Dr. Howard Hamilton, Head, 306-585-4079, Fax: 306-585-4745, E-mail: hamilton@cs.uregina.ca. *Application contact:* Dr. JingTao Yao, Graduate Program Coordinator, 306-585-4071, Fax: 306-585-4745, E-mail: jintao.yao@uregina.ca.
Website: http://www.cs.uregina.ca

University of Rhode Island, Graduate School, College of Arts and Sciences, Department of Computer Science and Statistics, Kingston, RI 02881. Offers computer

science (MS, PhD); digital forensics (Graduate Certificate); statistics (MS). *Program availability:* Part-time. *Faculty:* 16 full-time (6 women). *Students:* 32 full-time (13 women), 111 part-time (25 women); includes 26 minority (12 Black or African American, non-Hispanic/Latino; 8 Asian, non-Hispanic/Latino; 5 Hispanic/Latino; 1 Two or more races, non-Hispanic/Latino), 20 international. In 2016, 10 master's, 10 other advanced degrees awarded. *Degree requirements:* For master's, comprehensive exam (for some programs), thesis optional; for doctorate, comprehensive exam, thesis/dissertation. *Entrance requirements:* For master's and doctorate, GRE, 2 letters of recommendation. Additional exam requirements/recommendations for international students: Required—TOEFL. *Application deadline:* For fall admission, 7/15 for domestic students, 2/1 for international students; for spring admission, 11/15 for domestic students, 7/15 for international students; for summer admission, 4/15 for domestic students. Application fee: $65. Electronic applications accepted. *Expenses:* Tuition, state resident: full-time $11,796; part-time $655 per credit. Tuition, nonresident: full-time $24,206; part-time $1345 per credit. *Required fees:* $1546; $44 per credit. One-time fee: $155 full-time; $35 part-time. *Financial support:* In 2016–17, 3 research assistantships with tuition reimbursements (averaging $14,320 per year), 11 teaching assistantships with tuition reimbursements (averaging $17,249 per year) were awarded. Financial award application deadline: 2/1; financial award applicants required to submit FAFSA. *Unit head:* Dr. Joan Peckham, Chair, 401-874-2701, Fax: 401-874-4617, E-mail: joan@cs.uri.edu. *Application contact:* E-mail: grad-inquiries@cs.uri.edu.
Website: http://www.cs.uri.edu/

University of Rochester, Hajim School of Engineering and Applied Sciences, Department of Computer Science, Rochester, NY 14627. Offers MS, PhD. *Program availability:* Part-time. *Faculty:* 17 full-time (1 woman). *Students:* 90 full-time (10 women), 4 part-time (0 women); includes 3 minority (2 Asian, non-Hispanic/Latino; 1 Two or more races, non-Hispanic/Latino), 74 international. Average age 25. 718 applicants, 18% accepted, 42 enrolled. In 2016, 19 master's, 5 doctorates awarded. *Degree requirements:* For doctorate, thesis/dissertation. *Entrance requirements:* For master's and doctorate, GRE General Test, personal statement, transcripts, three letters of recommendation. Additional exam requirements/recommendations for international students: Required—TOEFL (minimum score 600 paper-based; 100 iBT). *Application deadline:* For fall admission, 1/15 for domestic and international students. Application fee: $60. Electronic applications accepted. *Expenses:* $1,538 per credit. *Financial support:* In 2016–17, 111 students received support, including 1 fellowship with full tuition reimbursement available (averaging $25,000 per year), 58 research assistantships with full tuition reimbursements available (averaging $20,700 per year), 2 teaching assistantships (averaging $2,500 per year); tuition waivers (full and partial) also available. Financial award application deadline: 1/15. *Faculty research:* Artificial intelligence, human-computer interaction, systems research, theory research. *Unit head:* Sandhya Dwarkadas, Chair, 585-275-5647, E-mail: sandhya@cs.rochester.edu. *Application contact:* Michelle Kiso, Graduate Coordinator, 585-275-7737, E-mail: mkiso@cs.rochester.edu.
Website: http://www.cs.rochester.edu/

University of Rochester, Hajim School of Engineering and Applied Sciences, Master of Science in Technical Entrepreneurship and Management Program, Rochester, NY 14642. Offers biomedical engineering (MS); chemical engineering (MS); computer science (MS); electrical and computer engineering (MS); energy and the environment (MS); materials science (MS); mechanical engineering (MS); optics (MS). Program offered in collaboration with the Simon School of Business. *Program availability:* Part-time. *Students:* 42 full-time (13 women), 6 part-time (3 women); includes 7 minority (1 Black or African American, non-Hispanic/Latino; 1 Asian, non-Hispanic/Latino; 4 Hispanic/Latino; 1 Two or more races, non-Hispanic/Latino), 28 international. Average age 24. 245 applicants, 65% accepted, 29 enrolled. In 2016, 31 master's awarded. *Degree requirements:* For master's, comprehensive exam, final exam. *Entrance requirements:* For master's, GRE or GMAT, 3 letters of recommendation; personal statement; official transcript; bachelor's degree (or equivalent for international students) in engineering, science, or mathematics. Additional exam requirements/recommendations for international students: Required—TOEFL (minimum score 600 paper-based; 100 iBT). *Application deadline:* For fall admission, 2/1 for domestic and international students. Application fee: $60. Electronic applications accepted. *Expenses:* $1,800 per credit. *Financial support:* In 2016–17, 45 students received support. Career-related internships or fieldwork and scholarships/grants available. Support available to part-time students. Financial award application deadline: 2/1. *Faculty research:* High efficiency solar cells, macromolecular self-assembly, digital signal processing, memory hierarchy management, molecular and physical mechanisms in cell migration, optical imaging systems. *Unit head:* Duncan T. Moore, Vice Provost for Entrepreneurship, 585-275-5248, Fax: 585-473-6745, E-mail: duncan.moore@rochester.edu. *Application contact:* Andrea Barrett, Executive Director, 585-276-3407, Fax: 585-276-2357, E-mail: andrea.barrett@rochester.edu.
Website: http://www.rochester.edu/team

University of San Francisco, College of Arts and Sciences, Computer Science Program, San Francisco, CA 94117-1080. Offers MS. *Program availability:* Part-time. *Faculty:* 5 full-time (3 women), 1 (woman) part-time/adjunct. *Students:* 55 full-time (18 women), 3 part-time (1 woman); includes 5 minority (4 Asian, non-Hispanic/Latino; 1 Hispanic/Latino), 47 international. Average age 26. 285 applicants, 56% accepted, 40 enrolled. In 2016, 20 master's awarded. *Degree requirements:* For master's, thesis optional. *Entrance requirements:* For master's, GRE General Test, GRE Subject Test, BS in computer science or related field. Additional exam requirements/recommendations for international students: Required—TOEFL, IELTS, PTE. *Application deadline:* For fall admission, 3/15 for domestic and international students. Applications are processed on a rolling basis. Application fee: $55 ($65 for international students). *Expenses: Tuition:* Full-time $23,310; part-time $1295 per credit. Tuition and fees vary according to course load, degree level, campus/location and program. *Financial support:* In 2016–17, 16 students received support. Fellowships, teaching assistantships, career-related internships or fieldwork, and Federal Work-Study available. Financial award application deadline: 3/2; financial award applicants required to submit FAFSA. *Faculty research:* Software engineering, computer graphics, computer networks. *Unit head:* Gian Bruno, Program Manager, 415-422-5247. *Application contact:* Mark Landerghini, Graduate Adviser, 415-422-5101, E-mail: asgraduate@usfca.edu.
Website: https://www.usfca.edu/arts-sciences/graduate-programs/computer-science

University of Saskatchewan, College of Graduate Studies and Research, College of Arts and Science, Department of Computer Science, Saskatoon, SK S7N 5A2, Canada. Offers M Sc, PhD. *Degree requirements:* For master's, thesis; for doctorate, comprehensive exam (for some programs), thesis/dissertation. *Entrance requirements:* For master's and doctorate, GRE. Additional exam requirements/recommendations for international students: Required—TOEFL (minimum score 80 iBT); Recommended—IELTS (minimum score 6.5). Electronic applications accepted.

University of South Alabama, School of Computing, Mobile, AL 36688. Offers computer science (MS); information systems (MS). *Program availability:* Part-time, evening/weekend. *Faculty:* 18 full-time (2 women). *Students:* 121 full-time (35 women), 21 part-time (6 women); includes 10 minority (2 Black or African American, non-Hispanic/Latino; 4 Asian, non-Hispanic/Latino; 1 Hispanic/Latino; 1 Native Hawaiian or other Pacific Islander, non-Hispanic/Latino; 2 Two or more races, non-Hispanic/Latino), 87 international. Average age 27. 204 applicants, 53% accepted, 29 enrolled. In 2016, 67 master's awarded. *Degree requirements:* For master's, comprehensive exam, project, thesis, or coursework only with additional credit hours earned; for doctorate, comprehensive exam, thesis/dissertation, minimum GPA of 3.0. *Entrance requirements:* For master's, GRE General Test, undergraduate degree, official transcripts, three letters of recommendation, statement of purpose; for doctorate, GRE, master's degree in related discipline, minimum graduate GPA of 3.5, statement of purpose, three letters of recommendation, curriculum vitae, official transcripts. Additional exam requirements/recommendations for international students: Required—TOEFL (minimum score 525 paper-based; 71 iBT). *Application deadline:* For fall admission, 7/15 priority date for domestic students, 6/15 priority date for international students; for spring admission, 12/1 priority date for domestic students, 11/1 priority date for international students; for summer admission, 5/1 priority date for domestic students, 4/1 priority date for international students. Applications are processed on a rolling basis. Application fee: $35. Electronic applications accepted. *Expenses:* Tuition, state resident: full-time $9768; part-time $407 per credit hour. Tuition, nonresident: full-time $19,536; part-time $814 per credit hour. *Financial support:* Fellowships, research assistantships, teaching assistantships, Federal Work-Study, institutionally sponsored loans, scholarships/grants, and unspecified assistantships available. Support available to part-time students. Financial award application deadline: 5/31; financial award applicants required to submit FAFSA. *Faculty research:* Artificial intelligence, big data/data mining, STEM education, visual analytics. *Unit head:* Dr. Alec Yasinsac, Dean, School of Computing, 251-460-6390, Fax: 251-460-7274, E-mail: yasinsac@southalabama.edu. *Application contact:* Dr. Harold Pardue, Director of School of Computing Graduate Studies, 251-460-1600, Fax: 251-460-7274, E-mail: hpardue@southalabama.edu.
Website: http://www.cis.usouthal.edu

University of South Carolina, The Graduate School, College of Engineering and Computing, Department of Computer Science and Engineering, Columbia, SC 29208. Offers computer science and engineering (ME, MS, PhD); software engineering (MS). *Program availability:* Part-time, evening/weekend, online learning. *Degree requirements:* For master's, comprehensive exam, thesis (for some programs); for doctorate, comprehensive exam, thesis/dissertation. *Entrance requirements:* For master's and doctorate, GRE General Test. Additional exam requirements/recommendations for international students: Required—TOEFL (minimum score 570 paper-based). Electronic applications accepted. *Faculty research:* Computer security, computer vision, artificial intelligence, multiagent systems, bioinformatics.

The University of South Dakota, Graduate School, College of Arts and Sciences, Department of Computer Science, Vermillion, SD 57069. Offers MS. *Program availability:* Part-time. *Degree requirements:* For master's, thesis optional. *Entrance requirements:* For master's, GRE General Test, GRE Subject Test (recommended), minimum GPA of 2.7. Additional exam requirements/recommendations for international students: Required—TOEFL (minimum score 550 paper-based; 79 iBT). Electronic applications accepted.

University of Southern California, Graduate School, Viterbi School of Engineering, Department of Computer Science, Los Angeles, CA 90089. Offers computer networks (MS); computer science (MS, PhD); computer security (MS); game development (MS); high performance computing and simulations (MS); human language technology (MS); intelligent robotics (MS); multimedia and creative technologies (MS); software engineering (MS). *Program availability:* Part-time, evening/weekend, online learning. *Entrance requirements:* For master's and doctorate, GRE General Test. Additional exam requirements/recommendations for international students: Required—TOEFL. Electronic applications accepted. *Faculty research:* Databases, computer graphics and computer vision, software engineering, networks and security, robotics, multimedia and virtual reality.

University of Southern Maine, College of Science, Technology, and Health, Department of Computer Science, Portland, ME 04103. Offers computer science (MS); software systems (CGS). *Program availability:* Part-time. *Degree requirements:* For master's, thesis. *Entrance requirements:* For master's, GRE General Test, minimum GPA of 3.0. Additional exam requirements/recommendations for international students: Required—TOEFL. Electronic applications accepted. *Faculty research:* Software engineering, database systems, formal methods, object-oriented technology, artificial intelligence, bioinformatics, data analysis and data mining, health information systems.

University of Southern Mississippi, Graduate School, College of Science and Technology, School of Computing, Hattiesburg, MS 39406. Offers computational science (MS, PhD); computer science (MS). *Degree requirements:* For master's, comprehensive exam, thesis; for doctorate, comprehensive exam, thesis/dissertation. *Entrance requirements:* For master's, GRE General Test, minimum GPA of 2.75 in last 60 hours; for doctorate, GRE General Test, minimum GPA of 3.5. Additional exam requirements/recommendations for international students: Required—TOEFL, IELTS. *Application deadline:* For fall admission, 3/15 priority date for domestic students, 3/15 for international students; for spring admission, 1/10 priority date for domestic and international students. Applications are processed on a rolling basis. Application fee: $60. Electronic applications accepted. *Expenses: Tuition, area resident:* Full-time $15,708; part-time $437 per credit hour. *Financial support:* Research assistantships with full tuition reimbursements, teaching assistantships with full tuition reimbursements, Federal Work-Study, institutionally sponsored loans, scholarships/grants, health care benefits, and unspecified assistantships available. Financial award application deadline: 3/15; financial award applicants required to submit FAFSA. *Faculty research:* Satellite telecommunications, advanced life-support systems, artificial intelligence. *Unit head:* Andrew H. Sung, Director, 601-266-4949, Fax: 601-266-5829. *Application contact:* Dr. Chaoyang Zhang, Manager of Graduate Admissions, 601-266-4949, Fax: 601-266-6452.
Website: https://www.usm.edu/computing

University of South Florida, College of Engineering, Department of Computer Science and Engineering, Tampa, FL 33620-9951. Offers computer engineering (MSCP); computer science (MSCS); computer science and engineering (PhD). *Program availability:* Part-time. *Faculty:* 21 full-time (3 women). *Students:* 182 full-time (41 women), 43 part-time (11 women); includes 20 minority (4 Black or African American, non-Hispanic/Latino; 7 Asian, non-Hispanic/Latino; 8 Hispanic/Latino; 1 Two or more races, non-Hispanic/Latino), 171 international. Average age 27. 566 applicants, 43% accepted, 67 enrolled. In 2016, 41 master's, 10 doctorates awarded. Terminal master's awarded for partial completion of doctoral program. *Degree requirements:* For master's, comprehensive exam, thesis or alternative; for doctorate, comprehensive exam, thesis/dissertation, teaching of at least one undergraduate computer science and engineering course. *Entrance requirements:* For master's, GRE General Test, minimum GPA of 3.0 in last 60 hours of coursework, three letters of recommendation, statement of purpose; for doctorate, GRE General Test, minimum GPA of 3.0 in last 60 hours of coursework, three letters of recommendation, statement of purpose that includes three areas of research interest. Additional exam requirements/recommendations for international students: Required—TOEFL (minimum score 550 paper-based; 79 iBT) or IELTS (minimum score 6.5). *Application deadline:* For fall admission, 2/15 for domestic and international students; for spring admission, 10/15 for domestic students, 9/15 for

international students. Application fee: $30. Electronic applications accepted. *Expenses:* Tuition, state resident: full-time $7766; part-time $431.43 per credit hour. Tuition, nonresident: full-time $15,789; part-time $877.17 per credit hour. *Required fees:* $37 per term. *Financial support:* In 2016–17, 26 students received support, including 30 research assistantships with tuition reimbursements available (averaging $14,942 per year), 35 teaching assistantships with tuition reimbursements available (averaging $14,003 per year); unspecified assistantships also available. Financial award application deadline: 1/1; financial award applicants required to submit FAFSA. *Faculty research:* Artificial intelligence/intelligence systems; computational biology and bioinformatics; computer vision and pattern recognition; databases; distributed systems; graphics; information systems (networks) and location-aware information systems; robotics (biomorphic robotics and robot perception and action); software security; VLSI, computer architecture, and parallel processing. *Total annual research expenditures:* $1.2 million. *Unit head:* Dr. Lawrence Hall, Professor and Department Chair, 813-974-4195, Fax: 813-974-5094, E-mail: hall@cse.usf.edu. *Application contact:* Dr. Srivinas Katkoori, Associate Professor and Graduate Program Director, 813-974-5737, Fax: 813-974-5094, E-mail: katkoori@cse.usf.edu.
Website: http://www.cse.usf.edu/

The University of Tennessee, Graduate School, College of Arts and Sciences, Department of Computer Science, Knoxville, TN 37996. Offers MS, PhD. *Program availability:* Part-time. *Degree requirements:* For master's, thesis or alternative; for doctorate, thesis/dissertation. *Entrance requirements:* For master's and doctorate, GRE General Test, minimum GPA of 2.7. Additional exam requirements/recommendations for international students: Required—TOEFL. Electronic applications accepted.

The University of Tennessee, Graduate School, Tickle College of Engineering, Department of Electrical Engineering and Computer Science, Program in Computer Science, Knoxville, TN 37996. Offers MS, PhD. *Program availability:* Part-time. *Faculty:* 28 full-time (3 women), 3 part-time/adjunct (2 women). *Students:* 62 full-time (14 women), 15 part-time (2 women); includes 7 minority (1 Black or African American, non-Hispanic/Latino; 4 Asian, non-Hispanic/Latino; 1 Hispanic/Latino; 1 Two or more races, non-Hispanic/Latino), 27 international. Average age 29. 147 applicants, 18% accepted, 22 enrolled. In 2016, 8 master's, 6 doctorates awarded. *Degree requirements:* For master's, thesis or alternative; for doctorate, comprehensive exam, thesis/dissertation. *Entrance requirements:* For master's, GRE General Test (for MS students pursuing research thesis), minimum GPA of 2.7 (for U.S. degree holders), 3.0 (for international degree holders); 3 references; personal statement; for doctorate, GRE General Test, minimum GPA of 3.0 on previous graduate coursework; 3 references; personal statement. Additional exam requirements/recommendations for international students: Required—TOEFL (minimum score 550 paper-based). *Application deadline:* For fall admission, 2/1 priority date for domestic and international students; for spring admission, 6/15 for domestic and international students. Applications are processed on a rolling basis. Application fee: $35. Electronic applications accepted. *Financial support:* In 2016–17, 56 students received support, including 3 fellowships with full tuition reimbursements available (averaging $25,000 per year), 28 research assistantships with full tuition reimbursements available (averaging $24,078 per year), 20 teaching assistantships with full tuition reimbursements available (averaging $18,162 per year); career-related internships or fieldwork, Federal Work-Study, institutionally sponsored loans, health care benefits, and unspecified assistantships also available. Financial award application deadline: 2/1; financial award applicants required to submit FAFSA. *Unit head:* Dr. Leon Tolbert, Head, 865-974-3461, Fax: 865-974-5483, E-mail: tolbert@utk.edu. *Application contact:* Dr. Jens Gregor, Associate Head, 865-974-4399, Fax: 865-974-5483, E-mail: jgregor@utk.edu.
Website: http://www.eecs.utk.edu

The University of Tennessee at Chattanooga, Program in Computer Science, Chattanooga, TN 37403. Offers MS. *Program availability:* Part-time. *Faculty:* 10 full-time (4 women). *Students:* 21 full-time (8 women), 28 part-time (9 women); includes 15 minority (4 Black or African American, non-Hispanic/Latino; 1 American Indian or Alaska Native, non-Hispanic/Latino; 4 Asian, non-Hispanic/Latino; 2 Hispanic/Latino; 4 Two or more races, non-Hispanic/Latino), 10 international. Average age 30. 41 applicants, 83% accepted, 15 enrolled. In 2016, 12 master's awarded. *Degree requirements:* For master's, comprehensive exam, thesis. *Entrance requirements:* For master's, GRE General Test, minimum cumulative undergraduate GPA of 2.7 or 3.0 in senior year. Additional exam requirements/recommendations for international students: Required—TOEFL (minimum score 550 paper-based; 79 iBT), IELTS (minimum score 6). *Application deadline:* For fall admission, 6/15 priority date for domestic students, 7/1 for international students; for spring admission, 11/1 priority date for domestic students, 11/1 for international students. Applications are processed on a rolling basis. Application fee: $35 ($40 for international students). Electronic applications accepted. *Expenses:* $9,876 full-time in-state; $25,994 full-time out-of-state; $450 per credit part-time in-state; $1,345 per credit part-time out-of-state. *Financial support:* In 2016–17, 6 research assistantships, 1 teaching assistantship were awarded; career-related internships or fieldwork, scholarships/grants, health care benefits, and unspecified assistantships also available. Support available to part-time students. Financial award application deadline: 7/1; financial award applicants required to submit FAFSA. *Faculty research:* Power systems, computer architecture, pattern recognition, artificial intelligence, statistical data analysis. *Unit head:* Dr. Joseph Kizza, Department Head, 423-425-4043, Fax: 423-425-5442, E-mail: joseph-kizza@utc.edu. *Application contact:* Dr. Joanne Romagni, Dean of the Graduate School, 423-425-4478, Fax: 423-425-5223, E-mail: joanne-romagni@utc.edu.
Website: http://www.utc.edu/college-engineering-computer-science/programs/computer-science-engineering/graduateprogram.php

The University of Texas at Arlington, Graduate School, College of Engineering, Department of Computer Science and Engineering, Arlington, TX 76019. Offers computer engineering (MS, PhD); computer science (MS, PhD); mathematical sciences, computer science (PhD); software engineering (MS). *Program availability:* Part-time, online learning. Terminal master's awarded for partial completion of doctoral program. *Degree requirements:* For master's, comprehensive exam (for some programs), thesis; for doctorate, comprehensive exam, thesis/dissertation. *Entrance requirements:* For master's, GRE General Test, minimum GPA of 3.0 (3.2 in computer science-related classes); for doctorate, GRE General Test, minimum GPA of 3.5. Additional exam requirements/recommendations for international students: Required—TOEFL (minimum score 550 paper-based; 92 iBT), IELTS (minimum score 6.5). *Application deadline:* For fall admission, 6/1 for domestic students, 5/1 for international students; for spring admission, 12/1 for domestic students, 10/1 for international students. Applications are processed on a rolling basis. Application fee: $35 ($50 for international students). *Financial support:* Fellowships with full tuition reimbursements, research assistantships with partial tuition reimbursements, teaching assistantships with partial tuition reimbursements, career-related internships or fieldwork, and scholarships/grants available. Financial award application deadline: 6/1; financial award applicants required to submit FAFSA. *Faculty research:* Algorithms, homeland security, mobile pervasive computing, high performance computing bio information. *Unit head:* Dr. Fillia Makedon, Chairman, 817-272-3605, E-mail: makedon@uta.edu. *Application contact:* Dr. Bahram Khalili, Graduate Advisor, 817-272-5407, Fax: 817-272-3784, E-mail: khalili@uta.edu.
Website: http://www.cse.uta.edu/

The University of Texas at Austin, Graduate School, College of Natural Sciences, Department of Computer Sciences, Austin, TX 78712-1111. Offers MSCS, PhD. *Degree requirements:* For master's, thesis optional; for doctorate, thesis/dissertation, oral proposal, final defense. *Entrance requirements:* For master's and doctorate, GRE General Test, GRE Subject Test, bachelor's degree in computer sciences (preferred). Additional exam requirements/recommendations for international students: Required—TOEFL. Electronic applications accepted. *Faculty research:* Artificial intelligence, distributed computing, networks, algorithms, experimental systems.

The University of Texas at Dallas, Erik Jonson School of Engineering and Computer Science, Department of Computer Science, Richardson, TX 75080. Offers computer science (MS, PhD); software engineering (MS, PhD). *Program availability:* Part-time, evening/weekend. *Faculty:* 48 full-time (6 women), 9 part-time/adjunct (2 women). *Students:* 880 full-time (284 women), 256 part-time (66 women); includes 51 minority (2 Black or African American, non-Hispanic/Latino; 1 American Indian or Alaska Native, non-Hispanic/Latino; 32 Asian, non-Hispanic/Latino; 10 Hispanic/Latino; 6 Two or more races, non-Hispanic/Latino), 1,006 international. Average age 27. 3,675 applicants, 34% accepted, 412 enrolled. In 2016, 585 master's, 12 doctorates awarded. *Degree requirements:* For master's, thesis optional; for doctorate, comprehensive exam, thesis/dissertation. *Entrance requirements:* For master's, GRE General Test, minimum GPA of 3.0 in undergraduate course work, 3.3 in quantitative course work; for doctorate, GRE General Test, minimum GPA of 3.5. Additional exam requirements/recommendations for international students: Required—TOEFL (minimum score 550 paper-based). *Application deadline:* For fall admission, 7/15 for domestic students, 5/1 priority date for international students; for spring admission, 11/15 for domestic students, 9/1 priority date for international students. Applications are processed on a rolling basis. Application fee: $50 ($100 for international students). Electronic applications accepted. *Expenses:* Tuition, state resident: full-time $12,418; part-time $690 per semester hour. Tuition, nonresident: full-time $24,150; part-time $1342 per semester hour. Tuition and fees vary according to course load. *Financial support:* In 2016–17, 259 students received support, including 10 fellowships (averaging $1,650 per year), 77 research assistantships with partial tuition reimbursements available (averaging $23,115 per year), 79 teaching assistantships with partial tuition reimbursements available (averaging $17,231 per year); career-related internships or fieldwork, Federal Work-Study, institutionally sponsored loans, and scholarships/grants also available. Support available to part-time students. Financial award application deadline: 4/30; financial award applicants required to submit FAFSA. *Faculty research:* AI-based automated software synthesis and testing, quality of service in computer networks, wireless networks, cloud computing and IT security, speech recognition. *Unit head:* Dr. Gopal Gupta, Department Head, 972-883-4107, Fax: 972-883-2399, E-mail: gupta@utdallas.edu. *Application contact:* 972-883-2185, Fax: 972-883-2399, E-mail: gradecs@utdallas.edu.
Website: http://cs.utdallas.edu/

The University of Texas at El Paso, Graduate School, College of Engineering, Department of Computer Science, El Paso, TX 79968-0001. Offers computer science (MS, PhD); information technology (MSIT). *Program availability:* Part-time, evening/weekend. *Degree requirements:* For master's, thesis optional; for doctorate, thesis/dissertation. *Entrance requirements:* For master's, GRE, minimum GPA of 3.0; for doctorate, GRE, statement of purpose, letters of reference. Additional exam requirements/recommendations for international students: Required—TOEFL; Recommended—IELTS. Electronic applications accepted.

The University of Texas at San Antonio, College of Sciences, Department of Computer Science, San Antonio, TX 78249-0617. Offers MS, PhD. *Program availability:* Part-time. *Faculty:* 20 full-time (1 woman). *Students:* 88 full-time (30 women), 46 part-time (9 women); includes 32 minority (4 Black or African American, non-Hispanic/Latino; 7 Asian, non-Hispanic/Latino; 20 Hispanic/Latino; 1 Two or more races, non-Hispanic/Latino), 74 international. Average age 29. 269 applicants, 48% accepted, 41 enrolled. In 2016, 44 master's, 10 doctorates awarded. Terminal master's awarded for partial completion of doctoral program. *Degree requirements:* For master's, 36 credits of coursework; thesis or comprehensive exam within 6 years; minimum GPA of 3.0; for doctorate, comprehensive exam, thesis/dissertation, continuous enrollment until time of graduation; admission to candidacy; oral examination; 90 credits of coursework and research; minimum GPA of 3.0 on all coursework. *Entrance requirements:* For master's and doctorate, GRE General Test, bachelor's degree in computer science offered by UTSA or an equivalent academic preparation from an accredited college or university in the United States or a comparable foreign institution; minimum GPA of 3.0; at least 24 semester credit hours (12 of which must be at the upper-division level) in the area. Additional exam requirements/recommendations for international students: Required—TOEFL (minimum score 550 paper-based; 79 iBT), IELTS (minimum score 6.5). *Application deadline:* For fall admission, 7/1 for domestic students, 4/1 for international students; for spring admission, 11/1 for domestic students, 9/1 for international students. Application fee: $45 ($80 for international students). Electronic applications accepted. *Expenses:* Contact institution. *Financial support:* In 2016–17, 82 students received support, including 19 fellowships (averaging $1,000 per year), 3 research assistantships with full tuition reimbursements available (averaging $28,465 per year), 37 teaching assistantships with full tuition reimbursements available (averaging $28,465 per year); career-related internships or fieldwork, scholarships/grants, and unspecified assistantships also available. Financial award application deadline: 10/1; financial award applicants required to submit FAFSA. *Faculty research:* Cyber security, cloud computing, software engineering, data science, bioinformatics and computational biology, high performance computing and storage systems, programming languages, operating systems, real-time systems, embedded computing, human-computer Interaction, augmented reality, computer vision and multimedia, wireless networks, AI and machine learning. *Total annual research expenditures:* $5.7 million. *Unit head:* Dr. Rajendra V. Boppana, Department Chair, 210-458-4434, Fax: 210-458-4437, E-mail: rajendra.boppana@utsa.edu. *Application contact:* Dr. Weining Zhang, Graduate Advisor of Record, 210-458-5557, E-mail: wzhang@cs.utsa.edu.
Website: http://www.cs.utsa.edu/

The University of Texas at Tyler, College of Business and Technology, Department of Computer Science, Tyler, TX 75799-0001. Offers MS. *Degree requirements:* For master's, comprehensive exam, thesis optional. *Entrance requirements:* For master's, GRE General Test, previous course work in data structures and computer organization, 6 hours of course work in calculus and statistics. Additional exam requirements/recommendations for international students: Required—TOEFL. Electronic applications accepted. *Faculty research:* Database design, software engineering, client-server architecture, visual programming, data mining, computer security, digital image processing, simulation and modeling, computer science education.

The University of Texas of the Permian Basin, Office of Graduate Studies, College of Arts and Sciences, Department of Math and Computer Science, Odessa, TX 79762-0001. Offers computer science (MS). *Program availability:* Part-time, evening/weekend. *Degree requirements:* For master's, comprehensive exam, thesis or alternative. *Entrance requirements:* For master's, GRE General Test. Additional exam requirements/recommendations for international students: Required—TOEFL (minimum score 550 paper-based).

The University of Texas Rio Grande Valley, College of Engineering and Computer Science, Department of Computer Science, Edinburg, TX 78539. Offers computer science (MS); information technology (MS). *Program availability:* Part-time, evening/weekend, online learning. *Degree requirements:* For master's, final written exam, project. *Entrance requirements:* For master's, GRE General Test, minimum GPA of 3.0 in last 60 hours. Additional exam requirements/recommendations for international students: Required—TOEFL. Tuition and fees vary according to course load and program. *Faculty research:* Artificial intelligence, distributed systems, Internet computing, theoretical computer sciences, information visualization.

University of the District of Columbia, School of Engineering and Applied Sciences, Program in Computer Science, Washington, DC 20008-1175. Offers MS, MSCS. *Degree requirements:* For master's, thesis optional.

The University of Toledo, College of Graduate Studies, College of Engineering, Department of Electrical Engineering and Computer Science, Toledo, OH 43606-3390. Offers computer science (MS, PhD); electrical engineering (MS, PhD). *Program availability:* Part-time, evening/weekend. *Degree requirements:* For master's, thesis or alternative; for doctorate, thesis/dissertation, qualifying exam. *Entrance requirements:* For master's, GRE General Test, minimum GPA of 3.0; for doctorate, GRE General Test, minimum GPA of 3.3. Additional exam requirements/recommendations for international students: Required—TOEFL (minimum score 550 paper-based; 80 iBT). Electronic applications accepted. *Faculty research:* Communication and signal processing, high performance computing systems, intelligent systems, power electronics and energy systems, RF and microwave systems, sensors and medical devices, solid state devices.

University of Toronto, School of Graduate Studies, Faculty of Arts and Science, Department of Computer Science, Toronto, ON M5S 1A1, Canada. Offers applied computing (M Sc AC); computer science (M Sc, PhD). *Program availability:* Part-time. *Degree requirements:* For master's, thesis; for doctorate, thesis/dissertation, thesis defense/oral exam. *Entrance requirements:* For master's, GRE (recommended), minimum B+ average overall and in final year; resume; 3 letters of reference; background in computer science and mathematics (preferred); for doctorate, minimum B+ average overall and in final year; resume; 3 letters of reference; background in computer science and mathematics (preferred). Additional exam requirements/recommendations for international students: Required—TOEFL (minimum score 580 paper-based), TWE (minimum score 5). Electronic applications accepted.

The University of Tulsa, Graduate School, College of Engineering and Natural Sciences, Tandy School of Computer Science, Tulsa, OK 74104-3189. Offers computer science (MS, PhD); cyber security (MS); JD/MS; MBA/MS. *Program availability:* Part-time. *Faculty:* 12 full-time (1 woman). *Students:* 42 full-time (13 women), 14 part-time (2 women); includes 4 minority (1 American Indian or Alaska Native, non-Hispanic/Latino; 3 Asian, non-Hispanic/Latino), 18 international. Average age 28. 65 applicants, 58% accepted, 22 enrolled. In 2016, 18 master's, 3 doctorates awarded. Terminal master's awarded for partial completion of doctoral program. *Degree requirements:* For master's, thesis (for some programs); for doctorate, comprehensive exam, thesis/dissertation. *Entrance requirements:* For master's and doctorate, GRE General Test. Additional exam requirements/recommendations for international students: Required—TOEFL (minimum score 550 paper-based; 80 iBT), IELTS (minimum score 6). *Application deadline:* Applications are processed on a rolling basis. Application fee: $55. Electronic applications accepted. *Expenses: Tuition:* Full-time $22,230; part-time $1235 per credit hour. *Required fees:* $990 per semester. Tuition and fees vary according to course load. *Financial support:* In 2016–17, 41 students received support, including 8 fellowships with full tuition reimbursements available (averaging $1,618 per year), 33 research assistantships with full tuition reimbursements available (averaging $15,208 per year), 9 teaching assistantships with full tuition reimbursements available (averaging $12,318 per year); career-related internships or fieldwork, Federal Work-Study, scholarships/grants, health care benefits, tuition waivers (full and partial), and unspecified assistantships also available. Support available to part-time students. Financial award application deadline: 2/1; financial award applicants required to submit FAFSA. *Faculty research:* Robotics, human-computer interaction, systems security, information assurance, machine learning, intelligent systems, software engineering, distributed systems, evolutionary computation, computational biology, bioinformatics. *Total annual research expenditures:* $1.8 million. *Unit head:* Dr. Roger Wainwright, Chairperson, 918-631-3143, E-mail: rogerw@utulsa.edu. *Application contact:* Dr. Mauricio Papa, Advisor, 918-631-2987, Fax: 918-631-3077, E-mail: mauricio-papa@utulsa.edu.
Website: http://engineering.utulsa.edu/academics/computer-science/

The University of Tulsa, Graduate School, Collins College of Business, Business Administration/Computer Science Program, Tulsa, OK 74104-3189. Offers MBA/MS. *Program availability:* Part-time. *Entrance requirements:* Additional exam requirements/recommendations for international students: Required—TOEFL (minimum score 577 paper-based; 91 iBT), IELTS (minimum score 6.5). *Application deadline:* Applications are processed on a rolling basis. Application fee: $55. Electronic applications accepted. *Expenses: Tuition:* Full-time $22,230; part-time $1235 per credit hour. *Required fees:* $990 per semester. Tuition and fees vary according to course load. *Financial support:* Fellowships, research assistantships with full tuition reimbursements, teaching assistantships, career-related internships or fieldwork, Federal Work-Study, institutionally sponsored loans, scholarships/grants, health care benefits, tuition waivers (full and partial), and unspecified assistantships available. Support available to part-time students. Financial award application deadline: 2/1; financial award applicants required to submit FAFSA. *Unit head:* Dr. Ralph Jackson, Associate Dean, 918-631-2242, Fax: 918-631-2142, E-mail: ralph-jackson@utulsa.edu. *Application contact:* Information Contact, 918-631-2242, E-mail: graduate-business@utulsa.edu.

University of Utah, Graduate School, College of Engineering, School of Computing, Salt Lake City, UT 84112-9205. Offers computational engineering and science (MS); computer science (MS, PhD); computing (MS, PhD); MS/MBA. *Faculty:* 34 full-time (5 women), 12 part-time/adjunct (1 woman). *Students:* 204 full-time (53 women), 60 part-time (12 women); includes 16 minority (10 Asian, non-Hispanic/Latino; 2 Hispanic/Latino; 4 Two or more races, non-Hispanic/Latino), 169 international. Average age 28. 616 applicants, 36% accepted, 95 enrolled. In 2016, 75 master's, 13 doctorates awarded. Terminal master's awarded for partial completion of doctoral program. *Degree requirements:* For master's, comprehensive exam (for some programs), thesis (for some programs); for doctorate, comprehensive exam, thesis/dissertation. *Entrance requirements:* For master's and doctorate, GRE General Test, minimum GPA of 3.0. Additional exam requirements/recommendations for international students: Required—TOEFL (minimum score 500 paper-based; 61 iBT), IELTS (minimum score 6.5). *Application deadline:* For fall admission, 12/15 for domestic and international students. Application fee: $55 ($65 for international students). Electronic applications accepted. *Expenses:* Contact institution. *Financial support:* In 2016–17, 3 students received support, including 3 fellowships with full tuition reimbursements available (averaging $25,000 per year), 125 research assistantships with full tuition reimbursements available (averaging $33,375 per year), 55 teaching assistantships with full tuition reimbursements available (averaging $16,800 per year); Federal Work-Study, scholarships/grants, health care benefits, and unspecified assistantships also available. Financial award application deadline: 12/15; financial award applicants required to submit FAFSA. *Faculty research:* Operating systems, programming languages, formal methods, natural language processing, architecture, networks, image analysis, data analysis, visualization, graphics, scientific computing, robotics. *Total annual research expenditures:* $7.9 million. *Unit head:* Dr. Ross Whitaker, Director, 801-587-9549, Fax: 801-581-5843, E-mail: whitaker@cs.utah.edu. *Application contact:* Robert Barber, Graduate Advisor, 801-581-3479, Fax: 801-581-5843, E-mail: annc@cs.utah.edu.
Website: http://www.cs.utah.edu

University of Vermont, Graduate College, College of Engineering and Mathematics, Program in Computer Science, Burlington, VT 05405. Offers MS, PhD. *Degree requirements:* For master's, thesis or alternative. *Entrance requirements:* For master's and doctorate, GRE General Test. Additional exam requirements/recommendations for international students: Required—TOEFL (minimum score 550 paper-based; 80 iBT). Electronic applications accepted. *Expenses:* Tuition, state resident: full-time $5814. Tuition, nonresident: full-time $14,670.

University of Victoria, Faculty of Graduate Studies, Faculty of Engineering, Department of Computer Science, Victoria, BC V8W 2Y2, Canada. Offers M Sc, PhD. *Program availability:* Part-time. Terminal master's awarded for partial completion of doctoral program. *Degree requirements:* For master's, thesis or alternative; for doctorate, thesis/dissertation, candidacy exam. *Entrance requirements:* For master's, GRE (recommended), B Sc in computer science/software engineering or the equivalent or bachelor's degree in mathematics with emphasis on computer science (recommended); for doctorate, GRE (recommended), MS in computer science or equivalent (recommended). Additional exam requirements/recommendations for international students: Required—TOEFL (minimum score 575 paper-based), IELTS (minimum score 7). Electronic applications accepted. *Faculty research:* Functional and logic programming, numerical analysis, parallel and distributed computing, software systems, theoretical computer science, VLSI design and testing.

University of Virginia, School of Engineering and Applied Science, Department of Computer Science, Charlottesville, VA 22903. Offers MCS, MS, PhD. *Faculty:* 36 full-time (8 women), 1 part-time/adjunct (0 women). *Students:* 103 full-time (26 women), 18 part-time (6 women); includes 9 minority (6 Asian, non-Hispanic/Latino; 2 Hispanic/Latino; 1 Two or more races, non-Hispanic/Latino), 93 international. Average age 25. 433 applicants, 27% accepted, 55 enrolled. In 2016, 20 master's, 5 doctorates awarded. *Degree requirements:* For master's, thesis (for some programs); for doctorate, comprehensive exam, thesis/dissertation. *Entrance requirements:* For master's, GRE General Test, 3 letters of recommendation; for doctorate, GRE General Test, 3 letters of recommendation; essay. Additional exam requirements/recommendations for international students: Required—TOEFL (minimum score 650 paper-based; 90 iBT), IELTS (minimum score 7). *Application deadline:* For fall admission, 8/1 for domestic students, 4/1 for international students; for winter admission, 12/1 for domestic students, 8/1 for international students; for spring admission, 5/1 for domestic students, 1/1 for international students. Applications are processed on a rolling basis. Application fee: $60. Electronic applications accepted. *Expenses:* Tuition, state resident: full-time $15,026; part-time $834 per credit hour. Tuition, nonresident: full-time $25,168; part-time $1378 per credit hour. *Required fees:* $2654. *Financial support:* Fellowships available. Financial award application deadline: 10/15; financial award applicants required to submit FAFSA. *Faculty research:* Systems programming, operating systems, analysis of programs and computation theory, programming languages, software engineering. *Unit head:* Kevin Skadron, Chair, 434-982-2200, Fax: 434-982-2214, E-mail: deptchair@cs.virginia.edu. *Application contact:* Pamela M. Norris, Associate Dean for Research and Graduate Programs, 434-243-7863, E-mail: pmn3d@virginia.edu.
Website: http://www.cs.virginia.edu/

University of Waterloo, Graduate Studies, Faculty of Mathematics, David R. Cheriton School of Computer Science, Waterloo, ON N2L 3G1, Canada. Offers computer science (M Math, PhD); software engineering (M Math); statistics and computing (M Math). *Program availability:* Part-time. *Degree requirements:* For master's, research paper or thesis; for doctorate, comprehensive exam, thesis/dissertation. *Entrance requirements:* For master's, honors degree in field, minimum B+ average; for doctorate, master's degree, minimum B+ average. Additional exam requirements/recommendations for international students: Required—TOEFL, IELTS, PTE. Electronic applications accepted. *Faculty research:* Computer graphics, artificial intelligence, algorithms and complexity, distributed computing and networks, software engineering.

The University of Western Ontario, Faculty of Graduate Studies, Physical Sciences Division, Department of Computer Science, London, ON N6A 5B8, Canada. Offers M Sc, PhD. *Program availability:* Part-time. *Degree requirements:* For master's, thesis, project, or course work; for doctorate, thesis/dissertation. *Entrance requirements:* For master's, B Sc in computer science or comparable academic qualifications; for doctorate, M Sc in computer science or comparable academic qualifications. Additional exam requirements/recommendations for international students: Required—TOEFL. *Faculty research:* Artificial intelligence and logic programming, graphics and image processing, software and systems, theory of computing, symbolic mathematical computation.

University of West Florida, College of Science and Engineering, Department of Computer Science, Pensacola, FL 32514-5750. Offers computer science (MS); database systems (MS); software engineering (MS). *Program availability:* Part-time, evening/weekend. *Degree requirements:* For master's, thesis optional. *Entrance requirements:* For master's, GRE, MAT, or GMAT, official transcripts; minimum undergraduate GPA of 3.0; letter of intent; three letters of recommendation. Additional exam requirements/recommendations for international students: Required—TOEFL (minimum score 550 paper-based). *Application deadline:* For fall admission, 6/1 for domestic and international students; for spring admission, 10/1 for domestic and international students. Applications are processed on a rolling basis. Application fee: $30. *Expenses:* Tuition, state resident: full-time $5316.12. Tuition, nonresident: full-time $11,308. *Required fees:* $583.92. Tuition and fees vary according to course load and program. *Financial support:* Fellowships with partial tuition reimbursements, research assistantships with partial tuition reimbursements, teaching assistantships with partial tuition reimbursements, and unspecified assistantships available. Financial award application deadline: 4/15; financial award applicants required to submit FAFSA. *Unit head:* Dr. Sikha Bagui, Chairperson, 850-474-3022. *Application contact:* Terry McCray, Assistant Director of Graduate Admissions, 850-473-7718, Fax: 850-473-7714, E-mail: gradadmissions@uwf.edu.
Website: http://catalog.uwf.edu/graduate/computerscience/

University of West Georgia, College of Science and Mathematics, Carrollton, GA 30118. Offers biology (MS); computer science (MS); geographic information systems (Postbaccalaureate Certificate); mathematics (MS). *Program availability:* Part-time, evening/weekend, 100% online, blended/hybrid learning. *Faculty:* 49 full-time (17 women). *Students:* 15 full-time (7 women), 61 part-time (26 women); includes 19 minority (14 Black or African American, non-Hispanic/Latino; 1 American Indian or Alaska Native, non-Hispanic/Latino; 3 Asian, non-Hispanic/Latino; 1 Two or more races, non-Hispanic/Latino), 6 international. Average age 33. 64 applicants, 86% accepted, 43 enrolled. In 2016, 21 master's, 4 other advanced degrees awarded. *Entrance requirements:* Additional exam requirements/recommendations for international

students: Required—TOEFL (minimum score 523 paper-based; 69 iBT); Recommended—IELTS (minimum score 6.5). *Application deadline:* For fall admission, 6/1 for domestic and international students; for spring admission, 11/15 for domestic students, 10/15 for international students; for summer admission, 4/1 for domestic students, 3/30 for international students. Applications are processed on a rolling basis. Application fee: $40. Electronic applications accepted. *Expenses:* Tuition, state resident: full-time $5316; part-time $222 per semester hour. Tuition, nonresident: full-time $20,658; part-time $861 per semester hour. *Required fees:* $1962. Tuition and fees vary according to course load, degree level and program. *Financial support:* Fellowships, research assistantships, teaching assistantships, career-related internships or fieldwork, Federal Work-Study, institutionally sponsored loans, scholarships/grants, and unspecified assistantships available. Support available to part-time students. Financial award application deadline: 4/1; financial award applicants required to submit FAFSA. *Unit head:* Dr. Lok C. Lew Yan Voon, Dean of Science and Mathematics, 678-839-5190, Fax: 678-839-5191, E-mail: lokl@westga.edu. *Application contact:* Dr. Toby Ziglar, Assistant Dean of the Graduate School, 678-839-1394, Fax: 678-839-1395, E-mail: graduate@westga.edu.
Website: http://www.westga.edu/cosm

University of Windsor, Faculty of Graduate Studies, Faculty of Science, School of Computer Science, Windsor, ON N9B 3P4, Canada. Offers M Sc, PhD. *Program availability:* Part-time. *Degree requirements:* For master's, thesis; for doctorate, comprehensive exam, thesis/dissertation. *Entrance requirements:* For master's, GRE, minimum B average; for doctorate, master's degree in computer science, minimum B+ average. Additional exam requirements/recommendations for international students: Required—TOEFL (minimum score 580 paper-based). Electronic applications accepted. *Faculty research:* Data mining, distributed query optimization, distributed object based systems, grid computing, querying multimedia database systems.

University of Wisconsin–Madison, Graduate School, College of Letters and Science, Department of Computer Sciences, Madison, WI 53706-1380. Offers MS, PhD. *Program availability:* Part-time. Terminal master's awarded for partial completion of doctoral program. *Degree requirements:* For doctorate, thesis/dissertation. *Entrance requirements:* For master's and doctorate, GRE General Test, GRE Subject Test. Electronic applications accepted.

University of Wisconsin–Milwaukee, Graduate School, College of Engineering and Applied Science, Computer Science Program, Milwaukee, WI 53201-0413. Offers MS. *Program availability:* Part-time. *Students:* 32 full-time (15 women), 20 part-time (7 women); includes 7 minority (1 Black or African American, non-Hispanic/Latino; 6 Asian, non-Hispanic/Latino), 32 international. Average age 28. 121 applicants, 31% accepted, 13 enrolled. In 2016, 25 master's awarded. *Degree requirements:* For master's, comprehensive exam (for some programs), thesis or alternative. *Entrance requirements:* For master's, GRE, minimum GPA of 2.75. Additional exam requirements/recommendations for international students: Required—TOEFL (minimum score 550 paper-based; 79 iBT), IELTS (minimum score 6.5). *Application deadline:* For fall admission, 1/1 priority date for domestic students; for spring admission, 9/1 for domestic students. Applications are processed on a rolling basis. Application fee: $56 ($96 for international students). Electronic applications accepted. *Financial support:* Fellowships, research assistantships, teaching assistantships, career-related internships or fieldwork, unspecified assistantships, and project assistantships available. Support available to part-time students. Financial award application deadline: 4/15. *Unit head:* John Boyland, PhD, Department Chair, 414-229-6986, E-mail: boyland@uwm.edu. *Application contact:* Engineering and Computer Science Graduate Programs, 414-229-6169, E-mail: ceas-graduate@uwm.edu.
Website: http://uwm.edu/engineering/academics-2/departments/computer-science/

University of Wisconsin–Milwaukee, Graduate School, College of Engineering and Applied Science, Program in Engineering, Milwaukee, WI 53201-0413. Offers biomedical engineering (MS); civil engineering (MS, PhD); computer science (PhD); electrical and computer engineering (MS); electrical engineering (PhD); engineering mechanics (MS); industrial and management engineering (MS); industrial engineering (PhD); manufacturing engineering (MS); materials (PhD); materials engineering (MS); mechanical engineering (MS). *Program availability:* Part-time. *Students:* 199 full-time (52 women), 156 part-time (32 women); includes 27 minority (2 Black or African American, non-Hispanic/Latino; 15 Asian, non-Hispanic/Latino; 3 Hispanic/Latino; 7 Two or more races, non-Hispanic/Latino), 244 international. Average age 30. 396 applicants, 61% accepted, 102 enrolled. In 2016, 72 master's, 26 doctorates awarded. *Degree requirements:* For master's, comprehensive exam (for some programs), thesis or alternative; for doctorate, comprehensive exam, thesis/dissertation, internship. *Entrance requirements:* For master's, GRE, minimum GPA of 2.75; for doctorate, GRE, minimum GPA of 3.5. Additional exam requirements/recommendations for international students: Required—TOEFL (minimum score 550 paper-based; 79 iBT), IELTS (minimum score 6.5). *Application deadline:* For fall admission, 1/1 priority date for domestic students; for spring admission, 9/1 for domestic students. Applications are processed on a rolling basis. Application fee: $56 ($96 for international students). *Financial support:* In 2016–17, 3 fellowships, 55 research assistantships, 77 teaching assistantships were awarded; career-related internships or fieldwork, Federal Work-Study, unspecified assistantships, and project assistantships also available. Support available to part-time students. Financial award application deadline: 4/15. *Unit head:* David Yu, Representative, 414-229-6169, E-mail: yu@uwm.edu. *Application contact:* Betty Warras, General Information Contact, 414-229-6169, Fax: 414-229-6967, E-mail: bwarras@uwm.edu.
Website: http://www4.uwm.edu/ceas/academics/graduate_programs/

University of Wisconsin–Parkside, School of Business and Technology, Program in Computer and Information Systems, Kenosha, WI 53141-2000. Offers MSCIS. *Entrance requirements:* For master's, GRE General Test or GMAT, 3 letters of recommendation, minimum GPA of 3.0. *Faculty research:* Distributed systems, data bases, natural language processing, event-driven systems.

University of Wisconsin–Platteville, School of Graduate Studies, College of Engineering, Mathematics and Science, Program in Computer Science, Platteville, WI 53818-3099. Offers MS. *Program availability:* Part-time. *Students:* 2 full-time (both women), 1 part-time (0 women); includes 1 minority (Asian, non-Hispanic/Latino). 10 applicants, 20% accepted. In 2016, 1 master's awarded. *Degree requirements:* For master's, comprehensive exam, thesis or alternative. *Entrance requirements:* Additional exam requirements/recommendations for international students: Required—TOEFL (minimum score 550 paper-based; 79 iBT), IELTS (minimum score 6.5). *Application deadline:* For fall admission, 9/1 for domestic students, 7/1 for international students; for spring admission, 1/1 for domestic students, 11/15 for international students. Applications are processed on a rolling basis. Application fee: $56. Electronic applications accepted. *Financial support:* Research assistantships with partial tuition reimbursements available. *Unit head:* Dr. Qi Yang, Coordinator, 608-342-1418, Fax: 608-342-1965, E-mail: csse@uwplatt.edu. *Application contact:* Dee Dunbar, School of Graduate Studies, 608-342-1322, Fax: 608-342-1389, E-mail: gradstudies@uwplatt.edu.

University of Wyoming, College of Engineering and Applied Sciences, Department of Computer Science, Laramie, WY 82071. Offers MS, PhD. *Program availability:* Part-time. Terminal master's awarded for partial completion of doctoral program. *Degree requirements:* For master's, thesis; for doctorate, thesis/dissertation. *Entrance requirements:* For master's and doctorate, GRE General Test, minimum GPA of 3.0. Additional exam requirements/recommendations for international students: Required—TOEFL (minimum score 550 paper-based), IELTS (minimum score 6). Electronic applications accepted. *Faculty research:* Fault-tolerant computing, distributed systems, knowledge representation, automated reasoning, parallel database access, formal methods.

Utah State University, School of Graduate Studies, College of Science, Department of Computer Science, Logan, UT 84322. Offers MCS, MS, PhD. *Program availability:* Part-time, evening/weekend, online learning. *Degree requirements:* For master's, thesis (for some programs), research project; for doctorate, thesis/dissertation. *Entrance requirements:* For master's, GRE General Test, GRE Subject Test, minimum GPA of 3.25, prerequisite coursework in math, 3 recommendation letters; for doctorate, GRE General Test, minimum GPA of 3.25, BS or MS. Additional exam requirements/recommendations for international students: Required—TOEFL. Electronic applications accepted. *Faculty research:* Artificial intelligence, software engineering, parallelism.

Vanderbilt University, School of Engineering, Department of Electrical Engineering and Computer Science, Program in Computer Science, Nashville, TN 37240-1001. Offers M Eng, MS, PhD. MS and PhD offered through the Graduate School. *Program availability:* Part-time. Terminal master's awarded for partial completion of doctoral program. *Degree requirements:* For master's, thesis (for some programs); for doctorate, comprehensive exam, thesis/dissertation. *Entrance requirements:* For master's and doctorate, GRE General Test, 3 letters of recommendation. Additional exam requirements/recommendations for international students: Required—TOEFL. Electronic applications accepted. *Expenses: Tuition:* Part-time $1854 per credit hour. *Faculty research:* Artificial intelligence, performance evaluation, databases, software engineering, computational science.

Villanova University, College of Engineering, Department of Electrical and Computer Engineering, Program in Computer Engineering, Villanova, PA 19085-1699. Offers computer architectures (Certificate); computer engineering (MSCPE); intelligent control systems (Certificate). *Program availability:* Part-time, evening/weekend. *Degree requirements:* For master's, thesis optional. *Entrance requirements:* For master's, GRE General Test (for applicants with degrees from foreign universities), BEE, minimum GPA of 3.0. Additional exam requirements/recommendations for international students: Required—TOEFL (minimum score 600 paper-based; 100 iBT). Electronic applications accepted. *Faculty research:* Expert systems, computer vision, neural networks, image processing, computer architectures.

Villanova University, Graduate School of Liberal Arts and Sciences, Department of Computing Sciences, Villanova, PA 19085-1699. Offers computer science (MS); software engineering (MS). *Program availability:* Part-time, evening/weekend. *Faculty:* 19. *Students:* 92 full-time (47 women), 23 part-time (10 women); includes 7 minority (2 Black or African American, non-Hispanic/Latino; 3 Hispanic/Latino; 2 Two or more races, non-Hispanic/Latino), 86 international. Average age 26. 32 applicants, 59% accepted, 23 enrolled. In 2016, 48 master's awarded. *Degree requirements:* For master's, thesis optional, independent study project. *Entrance requirements:* For master's, GRE, minimum GPA of 3.0, 3 recommendation letters. Additional exam requirements/recommendations for international students: Required—TOEFL. *Application deadline:* For fall admission, 5/1 priority date for international students; for spring admission, 11/15 priority date for international students. Applications are processed on a rolling basis. Application fee: $50. Electronic applications accepted. *Financial support:* Research assistantships, scholarships/grants, and unspecified assistantships available. Financial award applicants required to submit FAFSA. *Unit head:* Dr. Vijay Gehlot, Chair, 610-519-5843.
Website: http://www1.villanova.edu/villanova/artsci/computerscience/graduate.html

Virginia Commonwealth University, Graduate School, School of Engineering, Department of Computer Science, Richmond, VA 23284-9005. Offers computer science (MS). *Degree requirements:* For master's, thesis optional. *Entrance requirements:* For master's, GRE General Test; for doctorate, GRE. Additional exam requirements/recommendations for international students: Required—TOEFL (minimum score 600 paper-based; 100 iBT). *Application deadline:* For fall admission, 2/1 priority date for domestic students; for spring admission, 11/15 for domestic students. Application fee: $50. Electronic applications accepted. *Financial support:* Applicants required to submit FAFSA. *Unit head:* Dr. Rosalyn S. Hobson, Associate Dean for Graduate Studies, 804-828-8308, E-mail: rhobson@vcu.edu. *Application contact:* Dr. Tom Arodz, Director, Graduate Studies, 804-827-3989, E-mail: tarodz@vcu.edu.
Website: http://www.egr.vcu.edu/cs/index.html

Virginia International University, School of Computer Information Systems, Fairfax, VA 22030. Offers business intelligence (Graduate Certificate); business intelligence and data analytics (MIS); computer science (MS), including computer animation and gaming, cybersecurity, data management networking, intelligent systems, software applications development, software engineering; cybersecurity (MIS); data management (MIS); enterprise project management (MIS); health informatics (MIS); information assurance (MIS); information systems (Graduate Certificate); information systems management (MS, Graduate Certificate); information technology (MS); information technology audit and compliance (Graduate Certificate); knowledge management (MIS); software engineering (MS). *Program availability:* Part-time, online learning. *Entrance requirements:* For master's, bachelor's degree. Additional exam requirements/recommendations for international students: Required—TOEFL (minimum score 550 paper-based; 80 iBT), IELTS. Electronic applications accepted.

Virginia Polytechnic Institute and State University, Graduate School, College of Engineering, Blacksburg, VA 24061. Offers aerospace engineering (ME, MS, PhD); biological systems engineering (ME, MS, PhD); biomedical engineering (MS, PhD); chemical engineering (ME, MS, PhD); civil engineering (ME, MS, PhD); computer engineering (ME, MS, PhD); computer science (MS, PhD); electrical engineering (ME, PhD); engineering education (PhD); engineering mechanics (ME, MS, PhD); environmental engineering (MS); environmental science and engineering (MS); industrial and systems engineering (ME, MS, PhD); materials science and engineering (ME, MS, PhD); mechanical engineering (ME, MS, PhD); mining and minerals engineering (PhD); mining engineering (ME, MS); nuclear engineering (MS, PhD); ocean engineering (MS); systems engineering (ME, MS). *Faculty:* 400 full-time (73 women), 3 part-time/adjunct (2 women). *Students:* 1,949 full-time (487 women), 393 part-time (69 women); includes 251 minority (56 Black or African American, non-Hispanic/Latino; 3 American Indian or Alaska Native, non-Hispanic/Latino; 87 Asian, non-Hispanic/Latino; 70 Hispanic/Latino; 35 Two or more races, non-Hispanic/Latino), 1,354 international. Average age 27. 4,903 applicants, 19% accepted, 569 enrolled. In 2016, 364 master's, 200 doctorates awarded. *Degree requirements:* For master's, comprehensive exam (for some programs), thesis (for some programs); for doctorate, comprehensive exam (for some programs), thesis/dissertation (for some programs). *Entrance requirements:* For master's and doctorate, GRE/GMAT. Additional exam requirements/recommendations for international students: Required—TOEFL (minimum score 80 iBT). *Application deadline:* For fall admission, 8/1 for domestic students, 4/1 for international students; for spring admission, 1/1 for domestic students, 9/1 for international students. Applications are processed on a rolling basis. Application fee:

$75. Electronic applications accepted. *Expenses:* Tuition, state resident: full-time $12,467; part-time $692.50 per credit hour. Tuition, nonresident: full-time $25,095; part-time $1394.25 per credit hour. *Required fees:* $2669; $491.50 per semester. Tuition and fees vary according to course load, campus/location and program. *Financial support:* In 2016–17, 160 fellowships with full tuition reimbursements (averaging $7,387 per year), 872 research assistantships with full tuition reimbursements (averaging $22,329 per year), 313 teaching assistantships with full tuition reimbursements (averaging $18,714 per year) were awarded. Financial award application deadline: 3/1; financial award applicants required to submit FAFSA. *Total annual research expenditures:* $91.8 million. *Unit head:* Dr. Julia Ross, Dean, 540-231-9752, Fax: 540-231-3031, E-mail: deaneng@vt.edu. *Application contact:* Linda Perkins, Executive Assistant, 540-231-9752, Fax: 540-231-3031, E-mail: lperkins@vt.edu.
Website: http://www.eng.vt.edu/

Virginia Polytechnic Institute and State University, VT Online, Blacksburg, VA 24061. Offers advanced transportation systems (Certificate); aerospace engineering (MS); agricultural and life sciences (MSLFS); business information systems (Graduate Certificate); career and technical education (MS); civil engineering (MS); computer engineering (M Eng, MS); decision support systems (Graduate Certificate); eLearning leadership (MA); electrical engineering (M Eng, MS); engineering administration (MEA); environmental engineering (Certificate); environmental politics and policy (Graduate Certificate); environmental sciences and engineering (MS); foundations of political analysis (Graduate Certificate); health product risk management (Graduate Certificate); industrial and systems engineering (MS); information policy and society (Graduate Certificate); information security (Graduate Certificate); information technology (MIT); instructional technology (MA); integrative STEM education (MA Ed); liberal arts (Graduate Certificate); life sciences: health product risk management (MS); natural resources (MNR, Graduate Certificate); networking (Graduate Certificate); nonprofit and nongovernmental organization management (Graduate Certificate); ocean engineering (MS); political science (MA); security studies (Graduate Certificate); software development (Graduate Certificate). *Expenses:* Tuition, state resident: full-time $12,467; part-time $692.50 per credit hour. Tuition, nonresident: full-time $25,095; part-time $1394.25 per credit hour. *Required fees:* $2669; $491.50 per semester. Tuition and fees vary according to course load, campus/location and program.

Virginia State University, College of Graduate Studies, College of Engineering and Technology, Department of Mathematics and Computer Science, Petersburg, VA 23806-0001. Offers computer science (MS); mathematics (MS); mathematics education (MS). *Degree requirements:* For master's, thesis (for some programs).

Wake Forest University, Graduate School of Arts and Sciences, Department of Computer Science, Winston-Salem, NC 27106. Offers MS. *Program availability:* Part-time. *Degree requirements:* For master's, one foreign language, thesis optional. *Entrance requirements:* For master's, GRE General Test. Additional exam requirements/recommendations for international students: Required—TOEFL (minimum score 79 iBT). Electronic applications accepted.

Washington State University, Voiland College of Engineering and Architecture, Engineering and Computer Science Programs, Vancouver Campus, Pullman, WA 99164. Offers MS. *Degree requirements:* For master's, comprehensive exam, thesis optional. *Entrance requirements:* For master's, official transcripts from all colleges and universities attended; one-page statement of purpose; three letters of recommendation. Additional exam requirements/recommendations for international students: Required—TOEFL; Recommended—IELTS. Electronic applications accepted. *Faculty research:* High yield production of bioenergy biofuels and bioproducts, nanomaterials, power systems, microfluidics, atmospheric research.

Washington State University, Voiland College of Engineering and Architecture, School of Electrical Engineering and Computer Science, Pullman, WA 99164-2752. Offers computer engineering (MS); computer science (MS); electrical engineering (MS); electrical engineering and computer science (PhD); electrical power engineering (MS). MS programs in computer engineering, computer science and electrical engineering also offered at Tri-Cities campus; MS in electrical power engineering offered at the Global (online) campus. *Program availability:* Part-time. *Degree requirements:* For master's, comprehensive exam (for some programs), thesis or alternative; for doctorate, comprehensive exam, thesis/dissertation. *Entrance requirements:* For master's and doctorate, GRE General Test, minimum GPA of 3.0, 3 letters of recommendation, statement of purpose, transcripts. Additional exam requirements/recommendations for international students: Required—TOEFL (minimum score 580 paper-based). *Faculty research:* Software engineering, networks, distributed computing, computer engineering, electrophysics, artificial intelligence, bioinformatics and computational biology, computer graphics, communications, control systems, signal processing, power systems, microelectronics, algorithms.

Washington University in St. Louis, School of Engineering and Applied Science, Department of Computer Science and Engineering, St. Louis, MO 63130-4899. Offers computer engineering (MS, PhD); computer science (MS, PhD); computer science and engineering (M Eng). *Program availability:* Part-time. Terminal master's awarded for partial completion of doctoral program. *Degree requirements:* For master's, thesis optional; for doctorate, thesis/dissertation. *Entrance requirements:* For doctorate, GRE General Test. Additional exam requirements/recommendations for international students: Required—TOEFL. Electronic applications accepted. *Faculty research:* Artificial intelligence, computational genomics, computer and systems architecture, media and machines, networking and communication, software systems.

Wayne State University, College of Engineering, Department of Computer Science, Detroit, MI 48202. Offers computer science (MS, PhD), including bioinformatics (PhD), computational biology (PhD); data science and business analytics (MS). Application deadline for PhD is February 17. *Faculty:* 22. *Students:* 117 full-time (41 women), 37 part-time (11 women); includes 11 minority (1 Black or African American, non-Hispanic/Latino; 8 Asian, non-Hispanic/Latino; 2 Two or more races, non-Hispanic/Latino), 121 international. Average age 27. 596 applicants, 24% accepted, 29 enrolled. In 2016, 63 master's, 13 doctorates awarded. *Degree requirements:* For master's, thesis (for some programs); for doctorate, thesis/dissertation. *Entrance requirements:* For master's, GRE, minimum GPA of 3.0, three letters of recommendation, adequate preparation in computer science and mathematics courses, personal statement; for doctorate, GRE, bachelor's or master's degree in computer science or related field; minimum GPA of 3.3 in most recent degree; three letters of recommendation; personal statement; adequate preparation in computer science and mathematics courses. Additional exam requirements/recommendations for international students: Required—TOEFL (minimum score 550 paper-based; 79 iBT), TWE (minimum score 5.5), Michigan English Language Assessment Battery (minimum score 85); Recommended—IELTS (minimum score 6.5). *Application deadline:* For fall admission, 6/1 priority date for domestic students, 5/1 priority date for international students; for winter admission, 10/1 priority date for domestic students, 9/1 priority date for international students; for spring admission, 2/1 priority date for domestic students, 1/2 priority date for international students. Applications are processed on a rolling basis. Application fee: $50. Electronic applications accepted. *Expenses:* $18,871 per year resident tuition and fees, $36,065 per year non-resident tuition and fees. *Financial support:* In 2016–17, 67 students received support, including 4 fellowships with tuition reimbursements available

(averaging $17,250 per year), 22 research assistantships with tuition reimbursements available (averaging $22,361 per year), 36 teaching assistantships with tuition reimbursements available (averaging $19,177 per year); scholarships/grants, health care benefits, and unspecified assistantships also available. Financial award applicants required to submit FAFSA. *Faculty research:* Software engineering, databases, bioinformatics, artificial intelligence, networking, distributed and parallel computing, security, graphics, visualizations. *Total annual research expenditures:* $1.5 million. *Unit head:* Dr. Loren Schwiebert, Interim Chair, 313-577-5474, E-mail: loren@wayne.edu. *Application contact:* Eric Scimeca, Graduate Program Director, 313-577-5421, E-mail: eric.scimeca@wayne.edu.
Website: http://engineering.wayne.edu/cs/

Webster University, George Herbert Walker School of Business and Technology, Department of Mathematics and Computer Science, St. Louis, MO 63119-3194. Offers cybersecurity (MS). *Program availability:* Part-time, evening/weekend, online learning. *Entrance requirements:* For master's, 36 hours of graduate course work. Additional exam requirements/recommendations for international students: Required—TOEFL. *Application deadline:* Applications are processed on a rolling basis. Application fee: $25 ($50 for international students). *Expenses: Tuition:* Full-time $21,900; part-time $730 per credit hour. Tuition and fees vary according to campus/location and program. *Financial support:* Federal Work-Study available. Support available to part-time students. Financial award application deadline: 4/1; financial award applicants required to submit FAFSA. *Faculty research:* Databases, computer information systems networks, operating systems, computer architecture. *Unit head:* Al Cawns, Chair, 314-968-7127, Fax: 314-963-6050, E-mail: cawnsae@webster.edu. *Application contact:* Sarah Nandor, Director, Graduate and Transfer Admissions, 314-968-7109, E-mail: gadmit@webster.edu.

Wesleyan University, Graduate Studies, Department of Mathematics and Computer Science, Middletown, CT 06459. Offers computer science (MA); mathematics (MA, PhD). *Faculty:* 23 full-time (5 women). *Students:* 19 full-time (10 women); includes 2 minority (1 Asian, non-Hispanic/Latino; 1 Hispanic/Latino), 4 international. Average age 25. 79 applicants, 14% accepted, 6 enrolled. In 2016, 4 master's, 2 doctorates awarded. Terminal master's awarded for partial completion of doctoral program. *Degree requirements:* For master's, one foreign language, thesis; for doctorate, one foreign language, comprehensive exam, thesis/dissertation. *Entrance requirements:* For master's, GRE General Test, GRE Subject Test; for doctorate, GRE Subject Test. Additional exam requirements/recommendations for international students: Recommended—TOEFL. *Application deadline:* For fall admission, 2/15 for domestic and international students. Applications are processed on a rolling basis. Application fee: $0. Electronic applications accepted. *Financial support:* In 2016–17, 19 teaching assistantships with full tuition reimbursements (averaging $23,000 per year) were awarded; tuition waivers (full) also available. Financial award application deadline: 4/15. *Faculty research:* Topology, analysis, algebra, geometry, number theory. *Unit head:* Dr. Adam Fieldsteel, Chair, 860-685-2196, E-mail: afieldsteel@wesleyan.edu. *Application contact:* Caryn Canalia, Administrative Assistant, 860-685-2182, Fax: 860-685-2571, E-mail: ccanalia@wesleyan.edu.
Website: http://www.wesleyan.edu/mathcs/index.html

West Chester University of Pennsylvania, College of the Sciences and Mathematics, Department of Computer Science, West Chester, PA 19383. Offers computer science (MS); computer security (information assurance) (Certificate); information systems (Certificate); Web technology (Certificate). *Program availability:* Part-time, evening/weekend. *Faculty:* 10 full-time (3 women). *Students:* 7 full-time (2 women), 29 part-time (10 women); includes 11 minority (5 Black or African American, non-Hispanic/Latino; 5 Asian, non-Hispanic/Latino; 1 Hispanic/Latino), 8 international. Average age 31. 29 applicants, 69% accepted, 12 enrolled. In 2016, 16 master's, 3 other advanced degrees awarded. *Degree requirements:* For master's, thesis optional, 33 credits; for Certificate, 12 credits. *Entrance requirements:* For master's, GRE, two letters of recommendation; for Certificate, BS. Additional exam requirements/recommendations for international students: Required—TOEFL or IELTS. *Application deadline:* For fall admission, 5/15 for international students; for spring admission, 10/15 for international students. Applications are processed on a rolling basis. Application fee: $50. Electronic applications accepted. *Expenses:* Tuition, state resident: full-time $8694; part-time $483 per credit. Tuition, nonresident: full-time $13,050; part-time $725 per credit. *Required fees:* $2399; $119.05 per credit. Tuition and fees vary according to campus/location and program. *Financial support:* Scholarships/grants and unspecified assistantships available. Financial award application deadline: 2/15; financial award applicants required to submit FAFSA. *Faculty research:* Security in mobile ad-hoc networks, intrusion detection, security and trust in pervasive computing, cloud computing, wireless sensor networks, cloud computing and data mining. *Unit head:* Dr. James Fabrey, Chair, 610-436-2204, E-mail: jfabrey@wcupa.edu. *Application contact:* Dr. Afrand Agah, Graduate Coordinator, 610-430-4419, E-mail: aagah@wcupa.edu.
Website: http://www.cs.wcupa.edu/

Western Illinois University, School of Graduate Studies, College of Business and Technology, School of Computer Science, Macomb, IL 61455-1390. Offers MS. *Program availability:* Part-time. *Students:* 143 full-time (44 women), 17 part-time (6 women); includes 5 minority (3 Black or African American, non-Hispanic/Latino; 2 Hispanic/Latino), 145 international. Average age 24. 267 applicants, 80% accepted, 67 enrolled. In 2016, 70 master's awarded. *Degree requirements:* For master's, thesis or alternative. *Entrance requirements:* For master's, proficiency in Java. Additional exam requirements/recommendations for international students: Required—TOEFL (minimum score 550 paper-based; 80 iBT). *Application deadline:* Applications are processed on a rolling basis. Application fee: $30. Electronic applications accepted. *Financial support:* In 2016–17, 25 students received support, including 6 teaching assistantships with full tuition reimbursements available (averaging $8,688 per year); unspecified assistantships also available. Financial award applicants required to submit FAFSA. *Unit head:* Dr. Dennis DeVolder, Program Director, 309-298-1452. *Application contact:* Dr. Nancy Parsons, Associate Provost and Director of Graduate Studies, 309-298-1806, Fax: 309-298-2345, E-mail: grad-office@wiu.edu.
Website: http://wiu.edu/computerscience

Western Kentucky University, Graduate Studies, Ogden College of Science and Engineering, Department of Mathematics and Computer Science, Bowling Green, KY 42101. Offers computational mathematics (MS); computer science (MS); mathematics (MA, MS). *Degree requirements:* For master's, comprehensive exam, thesis optional, written exam. *Entrance requirements:* For master's, GRE General Test, minimum GPA of 2.75. Additional exam requirements/recommendations for international students: Required—TOEFL (minimum score 555 paper-based; 79 iBT). *Faculty research:* Differential equations numerical analysis, probability statistics, algebra, typology, knot theory.

Western Michigan University, Graduate College, College of Engineering and Applied Sciences, Department of Computer Science, Kalamazoo, MI 49008. Offers MS, PhD. *Degree requirements:* For master's, thesis optional; for doctorate, 2 foreign languages, thesis/dissertation.

Western Washington University, Graduate School, College of Sciences and Technology, Department of Computer Science, Bellingham, WA 98225-5996. Offers

MS. *Program availability:* Part-time. *Degree requirements:* For master's, thesis optional, project. *Entrance requirements:* For master's, GRE General Test, minimum GPA of 3.0 in last 60 semester hours or last 90 quarter hours. Additional exam requirements/recommendations for international students: Required—TOEFL (minimum score 567 paper-based). Electronic applications accepted. *Faculty research:* Distributed operating systems, data mining, machine learning, robotics, information retrieval, graphics and visualization, parallel and distributed computing.

West Virginia University, Statler College of Engineering and Mineral Resources, Lane Department of Computer Science and Electrical Engineering, Program in Computer Science, Morgantown, WV 26506. Offers MSCS, PhD. *Program availability:* Part-time. *Degree requirements:* For master's, thesis; for doctorate, comprehensive exam, thesis/dissertation. *Entrance requirements:* For master's, GRE General Test, letters of recommendation; for doctorate, GRE General Test, GRE Subject Test, MS in computer science, letters of recommendation. Additional exam requirements/recommendations for international students: Required—TOEFL. *Faculty research:* Artificial intelligence, knowledge-based simulation, data communications, mathematical computations, software engineering.

Wichita State University, Graduate School, College of Engineering, Department of Electrical Engineering and Computer Science, Wichita, KS 67260. Offers computer networking (MS); computer science (MS); electrical engineering (MS); electrical engineering and computer science (PhD). *Program availability:* Part-time, evening/weekend. *Unit head:* Dr. John Watkins, Chair, 316-978-3156, Fax: 316-978-5408, E-mail: john.watkins@wichita.edu. *Application contact:* Jordan Oleson, Admissions Coordinator, 316-978-3095, Fax: 316-978-3253, E-mail: jordan.oleson@wichita.edu.
Website: http://www.wichita.edu/eecs

Winston-Salem State University, Program in Computer Science and Information Technology, Winston-Salem, NC 27110-0003. Offers MS. *Program availability:* Part-time. *Degree requirements:* For master's, thesis optional. *Entrance requirements:* For master's, GRE, resume. Electronic applications accepted. *Faculty research:* Artificial intelligence, network protocols, software engineering.

Worcester Polytechnic Institute, Graduate Studies and Research, Department of Computer Science, Worcester, MA 01609-2280. Offers computer and communications networks (MS); computer science (MS, PhD, Advanced Certificate, Graduate Certificate). *Program availability:* Part-time, evening/weekend. *Faculty:* 23 full-time (3 women), 15 part-time/adjunct (2 women). *Students:* 122 full-time (36 women), 17 part-time (3 women); includes 10 minority (2 Black or African American, non-Hispanic/Latino; 5 Asian, non-Hispanic/Latino; 2 Hispanic/Latino; 1 Two or more races, non-Hispanic/Latino), 105 international. 419 applicants, 44% accepted, 53 enrolled. In 2016, 61 master's, 4 doctorates awarded. Terminal master's awarded for partial completion of doctoral program. *Degree requirements:* For master's, thesis optional; for doctorate, comprehensive exam, thesis/dissertation. *Entrance requirements:* For master's and doctorate, GRE General Test, 3 letters of recommendation, statement of purpose. Additional exam requirements/recommendations for international students: Required—TOEFL (minimum score 563 paper-based; 84 iBT), IELTS (minimum score 7). *Application deadline:* For fall admission, 1/1 priority date for domestic and international students; for spring admission, 10/1 priority date for domestic and international students. Applications are processed on a rolling basis. Application fee: $70. Electronic applications accepted. *Financial support:* Research assistantships, teaching assistantships, career-related internships or fieldwork, institutionally sponsored loans, scholarships/grants, and unspecified assistantships available. Financial award application deadline: 1/1; financial award applicants required to submit FAFSA. *Unit head:* Dr. Craig Wills, Department Head, 508-831-5357, Fax: 508-831-5776, E-mail: cew@wpi.edu. *Application contact:* Dr. George Heineman, Graduate Coordinator, 508-831-5357, Fax: 508-831-5776, E-mail: rundenst@wpi.edu.
Website: http://www.wpi.edu/academics/cs

Wright State University, Graduate School, College of Engineering and Computer Science, Department of Computer Science and Engineering, Computer Science Program, Dayton, OH 45435. Offers MS. *Degree requirements:* For master's, thesis optional. *Entrance requirements:* For master's, GRE General Test, minimum GPA of 3.0 in major, 2.7 overall. Additional exam requirements/recommendations for international students: Required—TOEFL. Application fee: $25. *Expenses:* Tuition, state resident: full-time $9952; part-time $622 per credit hour. Tuition, nonresident: full-time $16,960; part-time $1060 per credit hour. *Financial support:* Fellowships, research assistantships, teaching assistantships, and unspecified assistantships available. Support available to part-time students. Financial award application deadline: 3/31; financial award applicants required to submit FAFSA. *Unit head:* Dr. Forouzan Golshani, Chair, 937-775-5131, Fax: 937-775-5133, E-mail: cse-dept@wright.edu. *Application contact:* Dr. Jay E. Dejongh, Graduate Program Director, 937-775-5136, Fax: 937-775-5133, E-mail: jay.dejongh@wright.edu.

Wright State University, Graduate School, College of Engineering and Computer Science, Department of Computer Science and Engineering, Program in Computer Science and Engineering, Dayton, OH 45435. Offers MSCE, PhD. *Degree requirements:* For doctorate, thesis/dissertation, candidacy and general exams. *Entrance requirements:* For doctorate, GRE General Test, minimum GPA of 3.3. Additional exam requirements/recommendations for international students: Required—TOEFL. Application fee: $25. *Expenses:* Tuition, state resident: full-time $9952; part-time $622 per credit hour. Tuition, nonresident: full-time $16,960; part-time $1060 per credit hour. *Financial support:* Application deadline: 3/31. *Unit head:* Dr. Thomas Sudkamp, Director, 937-775-5118, Fax: 937-775-5133, E-mail: thomas.sudkamp@wright.edu. *Application contact:* John Kimble, Associate Director of Graduate Admissions and Records, 937-775-2957, Fax: 937-775-2453, E-mail: john.kimble@wright.edu.

Yale University, Graduate School of Arts and Sciences, Department of Computer Science, New Haven, CT 06520. Offers MS, PhD. *Degree requirements:* For doctorate, thesis/dissertation. *Entrance requirements:* For doctorate, GRE General Test, GRE Subject Test.

York University, Faculty of Graduate Studies, Lassonde School of Engineering, Program in Computer Science, Toronto, ON M3J 1P3, Canada. Offers M Sc, PhD. *Degree requirements:* For master's, thesis or alternative; for doctorate, comprehensive exam, thesis/dissertation, internship or practicum. Electronic applications accepted.

Youngstown State University, Graduate School, College of Science, Technology, Engineering and Mathematics, Department of Computer Science and Information Systems, Youngstown, OH 44555-0001. Offers computing and information systems (MCIS). *Program availability:* Part-time. *Degree requirements:* For master's, thesis or capstone project. *Entrance requirements:* For master's, GRE or GMAT. Additional exam requirements/recommendations for international students: Required—TOEFL (minimum score 550 paper-based). *Faculty research:* Networking, computational science, graphics and visualization, database and data mining, biometrics, artificial intelligence, online learning environments.

Youngstown State University, Graduate School, College of Science, Technology, Engineering and Mathematics, Department of Mathematics and Statistics, Youngstown, OH 44555-0001. Offers applied mathematics (MS); computer science (MS); secondary mathematics (MS); statistics (MS). *Program availability:* Part-time. *Degree requirements:* For master's, comprehensive exam, thesis optional. *Entrance requirements:* For master's, minimum GPA of 2.7 in computer science and mathematics. Additional exam requirements/recommendations for international students: Required—TOEFL. *Faculty research:* Regression analysis, numerical analysis, statistics, Markov chain, topology and fuzzy sets.

Database Systems

Austin Peay State University, College of Graduate Studies, College of Science and Mathematics, Professional Science Master's Program, Clarksville, TN 37044. Offers data management and analysis (PSM); predictive analytics (PSM). *Program availability:* Part-time, online learning. *Faculty:* 9 full-time (5 women). *Students:* 6 full-time (2 women), 20 part-time (11 women); includes 3 minority (1 Black or African American, non-Hispanic/Latino; 2 Two or more races, non-Hispanic/Latino). Average age 26. 14 applicants, 43% accepted, 3 enrolled. In 2016, 6 master's awarded. *Entrance requirements:* For master's, GRE, minimum undergraduate GPA of 2.5. Additional exam requirements/recommendations for international students: Required—TOEFL (minimum score 500 paper-based). *Application deadline:* For fall admission, 8/9 priority date for domestic students. Applications are processed on a rolling basis. Application fee: $45 ($50 for international students). Electronic applications accepted. *Expenses:* Tuition, state resident: full-time $8300; part-time $415 per credit hour. Tuition, nonresident: full-time $22,280; part-time $1114 per credit hour. *Required fees:* $1473; $73.65 per credit hour. *Financial support:* Research assistantships with full tuition reimbursements, career-related internships or fieldwork, Federal Work-Study, institutionally sponsored loans, scholarships/grants, and unspecified assistantships available. Support available to part-time students. Financial award application deadline: 4/1; financial award applicants required to submit FAFSA. *Unit head:* Dr. Bruce Myers, Dean, 931-221-7833, Fax: 931-221-7984, E-mail: gradpsm@apsu.edu. *Application contact:* Brad Averitt, Coordinator of Graduate Admissions, 800-859-4723, Fax: 931-221-7641, E-mail: gradadmissions@apsu.edu.
Website: http://www.apsu.edu/csci/psm-information

Boston University, Metropolitan College, Department of Computer Science, Boston, MA 02215. Offers computer information systems (MS), including computer networks, data analytics, database management and business intelligence, health informatics, IT project management, security, Web application development; computer networks (Certificate); computer science (MS); data analytics (Certificate); digital forensics (Certificate); health informatics (Certificate); information technology project management (Certificate); software development (MS); software engineering in health care systems (Certificate); telecommunications (MS), including security. *Program availability:* Part-time, evening/weekend, online learning. *Faculty:* 13 full-time (3 women), 43 part-time/adjunct (3 women). *Students:* 108 full-time (36 women), 1,294 part-time (364 women); includes 428 minority (115 Black or African American, non-Hispanic/Latino; 2 American Indian or Alaska Native, non-Hispanic/Latino; 187 Asian, non-Hispanic/Latino; 98 Hispanic/Latino; 2 Native Hawaiian or other Pacific Islander, non-Hispanic/Latino; 24 Two or more races, non-Hispanic/Latino), 314 international. Average age 33. 463 applicants, 79% accepted, 248 enrolled. In 2016, 311 master's awarded. *Degree requirements:* For master's, thesis optional. *Entrance requirements:* For master's and Certificate, official transcripts from regionally-accredited bachelor's degree program, 3 letters of recommendation, professional resume, personal statement. Additional exam requirements/recommendations for international students: Required—TOEFL (minimum score 84 iBT), IELTS. *Application deadline:* For fall admission, 6/1 priority date for international students; for spring admission, 10/1 priority date for international students. Applications are processed on a rolling basis. Application fee: $85. Electronic applications accepted. *Expenses:* Contact institution. *Financial support:* In 2016–17, 11 research assistantships (averaging $8,400 per year) were awarded; unspecified assistantships also available. Support available to part-time students. Financial award applicants required to submit FAFSA. *Faculty research:* Medical informatics, Web technologies, telecom and networks, security and forensics, software engineering, programming languages, multimedia and artificial intelligence (AI), information systems and IT project management. *Unit head:* Dr. Anatoly Temkin, Chair, 617-353-2566, Fax: 617-353-2367, E-mail: csinfo@bu.edu. *Application contact:* Lesley Moreau, Academic Program Coordinator, 617-353-2566, Fax: 617-353-2367, E-mail: metcs@bu.edu.
Website: http://www.bu.edu/csmet/

California Polytechnic State University, San Luis Obispo, Orfalea College of Business, Program in Business Analytics, San Luis Obispo, CA 93407. Offers MS. *Students:* 26 full-time (7 women); includes 5 minority (3 Asian, non-Hispanic/Latino; 2 Hispanic/Latino), 7 international. Average age 25. *Degree requirements:* For master's, comprehensive exam (for some programs), thesis (for some programs). *Entrance requirements:* For master's, GMAT. Additional exam requirements/recommendations for international students: Required—TOEFL (minimum score 80 iBT). *Application deadline:* For fall admission, 4/1 for domestic students, 3/1 for international students. Applications are processed on a rolling basis. Application fee: $55. Electronic applications accepted. *Expenses:* Tuition, state resident: full-time $6738; part-time $3906 per year. Tuition, nonresident: full-time $15,666; part-time $8370 per year. *Required fees:* $3603; $3141 per unit. $1047 per term. *Financial support:* Fellowships, career-related internships or fieldwork, Federal Work-Study, institutionally sponsored loans, scholarships/grants, and unspecified assistantships available. Support available to part-time students. Financial award application deadline: 3/2; financial award applicants required to submit FAFSA. *Faculty research:* Management of high-tech firms, Pacific Rim, capital market structures, economics of environmental policy, marketing of services. *Unit head:* Dr. Scott Dawson, Dean, 805-756-2705, E-mail: scdawson@calpoly.edu. *Application contact:* Dr. Sanjiv Jaggia, Associate Dean, Graduate Programs, 805-756-7519, E-mail: sjaggia@calpoly.edu.
Website: http://www.cob.calpoly.edu/gradbusiness/degree-programs/ms-business-analytics/

California State University, East Bay, Office of Graduate Studies, College of Business and Economics, Program in Business Analytics, Hayward, CA 94542-3000. Offers MS. *Entrance requirements:* For master's, baccalaureate degree, minimum undergraduate

GPA of 2.5. Additional exam requirements/recommendations for international students: Required—TOEFL (minimum score 550 paper-based; 79 iBT), IELTS (minimum score 6.5).

Case Western Reserve University, Weatherhead School of Management, Program in Business Analytics, Cleveland, OH 44106. Offers MSM. *Expenses: Tuition:* Full-time $42,576; part-time $1774 per credit hour. *Required fees:* $34. Tuition and fees vary according to course load and program.

Central European University, Center for Network Science, Budapest, Hungary. Offers PhD. *Faculty:* 2 full-time (1 woman), 1 part-time/adjunct (0 women). *Students:* 10 full-time (4 women). Average age 33. 33 applicants, 27% accepted, 7 enrolled. *Degree requirements:* For doctorate, comprehensive exam, thesis/dissertation. *Entrance requirements:* For doctorate, master's degree in physics, mathematics, computer science, sociology, political science, economics, or equivalent; two references. Additional exam requirements/recommendations for international students: Required—TOEFL. *Application deadline:* For fall admission, 2/4 for domestic and international students. Application fee: $30. Electronic applications accepted. *Expenses: Tuition:* Full-time 13,500 euros. Tuition and fees vary according to degree level, program and student level. *Financial support:* In 2016–17, 10 students received support. Fellowships, research assistantships, teaching assistantships, scholarships/grants, health care benefits, and tuition waivers (full) available. Financial award applicants required to submit FAFSA. *Faculty research:* Social network analysis, complex systems in physics and biology, computational methods. *Unit head:* Balazs Vedres, Director, 36-1-327-3000. *Application contact:* Janos Kertesz, Program Director, 36-1-327-3000 Ext. 2655, E-mail: cns@ceu.edu.
Website: http://cns.ceu.edu

Central European University, CEU Business School, Budapest, Hungary. Offers business administration (PhD); business analytics (M Sc); executive business administration (EMBA); finance (M Sc); general management (MBA); information technology management (M Sc); international executive (MBA). *Program availability:* Part-time. *Faculty:* 16 full-time (4 women), 15 part-time/adjunct (5 women). *Students:* 73 full-time (29 women), 108 part-time (28 women). Average age 33. 218 applicants, 57% accepted, 69 enrolled. In 2016, 108 master's awarded. *Degree requirements:* For master's, one foreign language; for doctorate, thesis/dissertation or alternative. *Entrance requirements:* For master's, GMAT. Additional exam requirements/recommendations for international students: Required—TOEFL (minimum score 570 paper-based); Recommended—IELTS (minimum score 6.5). *Application deadline:* For fall admission, 2/4 for domestic and international students. Application fee: $30. Electronic applications accepted. *Expenses:* Contact institution. *Financial support:* Scholarships/grants, health care benefits, and tuition waivers (full and partial) available. *Faculty research:* Social and ethical business, marketing, international business, international trade and investment, management development in Central and East Europe, non-market strategies of emerging-market multinationals, macro and micro analysis of the business environment, international competitive analysis, the transition process from emerging economies to established market economies and its social impact, the regulation of natural monopolies. *Unit head:* Dr. Mel Horwitch, Dean/Managing Director, 36 1 887-5050, E-mail: mhorwitch@ceubusiness.com. *Application contact:* Agnes Schram, Admissions Coordinator, 361-887-5111, E-mail: schrama@business.ceu.edu.
Website: http://business.ceu.hu/

Central European University, Department of Economics, Budapest, Hungary. Offers business analytics (M Sc); economic policy in global markets (MA); economics (MA, PhD); global economic relations (MA). *Faculty:* 14 full-time (1 woman), 9 part-time/adjunct (1 woman). *Students:* 122 full-time (44 women). Average age 26. 300 applicants, 24% accepted, 51 enrolled. In 2016, 34 master's, 5 doctorates awarded. *Degree requirements:* For master's, one foreign language, thesis; for doctorate, one foreign language, comprehensive exam, thesis/dissertation. *Entrance requirements:* For master's and doctorate, interview. Additional exam requirements/recommendations for international students: Required—TOEFL (minimum score 570 paper-based); Recommended—IELTS (minimum score 6.5). *Application deadline:* For fall admission, 2/4 for domestic and international students. Application fee: $30. Electronic applications accepted. *Expenses: Tuition:* Full-time 13,500 euros. Tuition and fees vary according to degree level, program and student level. *Financial support:* Fellowships, teaching assistantships, career-related internships or fieldwork, institutionally sponsored loans, scholarships/grants, health care benefits, and tuition waivers (full and partial) available. *Faculty research:* Economic theory (microeconomics and macroeconomics) and econometrics, as well as study of many applied fields, including labor economics, health economics and economics of education, industrial organization, monetary economics, international economics, law and economics, comparative institutional economics, corporate governance, and economics of transition. *Unit head:* Miklos Koren, Head of Department, 36 1 327-3000 Ext. 2212, E-mail: econdept@ceu.edu. *Application contact:* Zsuzsanna Jaszberenyi, Admissions Officer, 361-324-3009, Fax: 367-327-3211, E-mail: admissions@ceu.edu.
Website: http://economics.ceu.edu/

Claremont Graduate University, Graduate Programs, Center for Information Systems and Technology, Claremont, CA 91711-6160. Offers cybersecurity and networking (MS); data science and analytics (MS); electronic commerce (PhD); geographic information systems (MS); health informatics (MS); information systems (Certificate); IT strategy and innovation (MS); knowledge management (PhD); systems development (PhD); telecommunications and networking (PhD); MBA/MS. *Program availability:* Part-time. *Faculty:* 8 full-time (1 woman), 1 part-time/adjunct (0 women). *Students:* 60 full-time (18 women), 81 part-time (27 women); includes 34 minority (7 Black or African American, non-Hispanic/Latino; 18 Asian, non-Hispanic/Latino; 7 Hispanic/Latino; 1 Native Hawaiian or other Pacific Islander, non-Hispanic/Latino; 1 Two or more races, non-Hispanic/Latino), 80 international. Average age 35. In 2016, 21 master's, 10 doctorates awarded. *Degree requirements:* For doctorate, comprehensive exam, thesis/dissertation, portfolio. *Entrance requirements:* For master's and doctorate, GMAT, GRE General Test. Additional exam requirements/recommendations for international students: Required—TOEFL (minimum score 75 iBT). *Application deadline:* For fall admission, 2/1 priority date for domestic and international students. Applications are processed on a rolling basis. Application fee: $80. Electronic applications accepted. *Expenses: Tuition:* Full-time $44,328; part-time $1847 per unit. *Required fees:* $600; $300 per semester. Tuition and fees vary according to course load and program. *Financial support:* Fellowships, research assistantships, teaching assistantships, Federal Work-Study, institutionally sponsored loans, and scholarships/grants available. Support available to part-time students. Financial award application deadline: 2/15; financial award applicants required to submit FAFSA. *Faculty research:* Man-machine interaction, organizational aspects of computing, implementation of information systems, information systems practice. *Unit head:* Lorne Olfman, Acting Director, 909-607-3035, E-mail: lorne.olfman@cgu.edu. *Application contact:* Jake Campbell, Senior Assistant Director of Admissions, 909-607-3024, E-mail: jake.campbell@cgu.edu.
Website: https://www.cgu.edu/school/center-for-information-systems-and-technology/

Clark University, Graduate School, Graduate School of Management, Program in Business Analytics, Worcester, MA 01610-1477. Offers MSBA. *Expenses: Tuition:* Full-time $44,050. *Required fees:* $80. Tuition and fees vary according to course load and program. *Unit head:* Dr. Catherine Usoff, Dean, 508-793-7670, Fax: 508-793-8822, E-mail: cusoff@clarku.edu. *Application contact:* Ethan Bernstein, Director of Admissions, 508-793-7543, E-mail: graduateadmissions@clarku.edu.
Website: http://www.clarku.edu/programs/ms-business-analytics

College of Staten Island of the City University of New York, Graduate Programs, School of Business, Program in Business Analytics of Large-Scale Data, Staten Island, NY 10314-6600. Offers Advanced Certificate. *Program availability:* Part-time, evening/weekend. *Students:* 2 applicants, 50% accepted. *Degree requirements:* For Advanced Certificate, minimum GPA of 3.0. *Entrance requirements:* For degree, assessment test in statistical methods, bachelor's degree in business, economics, or related field, or be in a graduate student program with minimum GPA of 3.0; 2 letters of recommendation; resume. Additional exam requirements/recommendations for international students: Required—TOEFL (minimum score 600 paper-based; 100 iBT), IELTS (minimum score 7). *Application deadline:* For fall admission, 4/25 priority date for domestic and international students; for spring admission, 11/25 priority date for domestic and international students. Applications are processed on a rolling basis. Application fee: $125. Electronic applications accepted. *Expenses:* Tuition, state resident: full-time $10,130; part-time $425 per credit. Tuition, nonresident: full-time $18,720; part-time $780 per credit. *Required fees:* $181.10 per semester. Tuition and fees vary according to program. *Faculty research:* Transportation policy, econometrics. *Unit head:* Prof. Jonathan Peters, Graduate Program Coordinator, 718-982-2963, E-mail: jonathan.peters@csi.cuny.edu. *Application contact:* Sasha Spence, Associate Director for Graduate Admissions, 718-982-2019, Fax: 718-982-2500, E-mail: sasha.spence@csi.cuny.edu.
Website: http://www.csi.cuny.edu/schoolofbusiness/programs_graduate.php

Colorado Technical University Aurora, Program in Computer Science, Aurora, CO 80014. Offers computer systems security (MSCS); database systems (MSCS); software engineering (MSCS). *Program availability:* Part-time, evening/weekend. *Degree requirements:* For master's, thesis or alternative. *Entrance requirements:* For master's, minimum undergraduate GPA of 3.0, resume.

Colorado Technical University Colorado Springs, Graduate Studies, Program in Computer Science, Colorado Springs, CO 80907. Offers computer science (DCS); computer systems security (MSCS); database systems (MSCS); software engineering (MSCS). *Program availability:* Part-time, evening/weekend, online learning. *Degree requirements:* For master's, thesis or alternative; for doctorate, thesis/dissertation. *Entrance requirements:* For doctorate, minimum graduate GPA of 3.0, 5 years of related work experience. *Faculty research:* Software engineering, systems engineering.

Columbia University, Fu Foundation School of Engineering and Applied Science, Data Science Institute, New York, NY 10027. Offers MS. *Program availability:* Part-time. *Entrance requirements:* For master's, GRE General Test. Additional exam requirements/recommendations for international students: Required—TOEFL, IELTS, PTE. *Faculty research:* Cybersecurity, financial and business analytics, foundations of data science, health analytics, new media, smart cities.

DeSales University, Division of Science and Mathematics, Center Valley, PA 18034-9568. Offers cyber security (Postbaccalaureate Certificate); data analytics (Postbaccalaureate Certificate); information systems (MS), including cyber security, digital forensics, healthcare information management, project management. *Program availability:* Part-time, evening/weekend, 100% online, blended/hybrid learning. *Faculty:* 1 (woman) full-time, 3 part-time/adjunct (0 women). *Students:* 8 full-time (1 woman), 12 part-time (6 women); includes 1 minority (Asian, non-Hispanic/Latino). Average age 34. 20 applicants, 30% accepted, 6 enrolled. In 2016, 7 master's awarded. *Entrance requirements:* For master's, GRE or GMAT, bachelor's degree in computer-related discipline from accredited college or university, minimum undergraduate GPA of 3.0, personal statement, three letters of recommendation. Additional exam requirements/recommendations for international students: Required—TOEFL. *Application deadline:* Applications are processed on a rolling basis. Application fee: $50. Electronic applications accepted. *Expenses:* Contact institution. *Financial support:* Applicants required to submit FAFSA. *Unit head:* Dr. Patricia Riola, MSIS Director/Assistant Professor of Computer Science, 610-282-1100 Ext. 1647, E-mail: patricia.riola@desales.edu. *Application contact:* Julia Ferraro, Director of Graduate Admissions, 610-282-1100 Ext. 1768, E-mail: gradadmissions@desales.edu.
Website: http://www.desales.edu/home/academics/graduate-studies/programs-of-study/msis—master-of-science-in-information-systems

Elmhurst College, Graduate Programs, Program in Data Science, Elmhurst, IL 60126-3296. Offers MS. *Program availability:* Part-time, evening/weekend, online learning. *Faculty:* 2 full-time (0 women), 1 part-time/adjunct (0 women). *Students:* 37 part-time (11 women); includes 6 minority (2 Asian, non-Hispanic/Latino; 4 Hispanic/Latino), 2 international. Average age 35. 28 applicants, 57% accepted, 14 enrolled. In 2016, 2 master's awarded. *Entrance requirements:* For master's, 3 recommendations, resume, statement of purpose, interview. Additional exam requirements/recommendations for international students: Required—TOEFL (minimum score 550 paper-based; 79 iBT). *Application deadline:* Applications are processed on a rolling basis. Application fee: $0. Electronic applications accepted. *Expenses:* $845 per semester hour. *Financial support:* In 2016–17, 7 students received support. Scholarships/grants available. Support available to part-time students. Financial award application deadline: 3/1; financial award applicants required to submit FAFSA. *Unit head:* Jim Kulich. *Application contact:* Timothy J. Panfil, Director of Enrollment Management, School for Professional Studies, 630-617-3300 Ext. 3256, Fax: 630-617-6471, E-mail: panfilt@elmhurst.edu.
Website: http://www.elmhurst.edu/data_science

Fairfield University, School of Engineering, Fairfield, CT 06824. Offers database management (CAS); electrical and computer engineering (MS); information security (CAS); management of technology (MS); mechanical engineering (MS); network technology (CAS); software engineering (MS); Web application development (CAS). *Program availability:* Part-time, evening/weekend. *Faculty:* 7 full-time (1 woman), 15 part-time/adjunct (2 women). *Students:* 104 full-time (31 women), 56 part-time (15 women); includes 17 minority (8 Black or African American, non-Hispanic/Latino; 5 Asian, non-Hispanic/Latino; 4 Hispanic/Latino), 108 international. Average age 28. 193 applicants, 63% accepted, 20 enrolled. In 2016, 173 master's awarded. *Degree requirements:* For master's, capstone course. *Entrance requirements:* For master's, resume, 2 recommendations. Additional exam requirements/recommendations for international students: Required—TOEFL (minimum score 550 paper-based; 80 iBT) or IELTS (minimum score 6.5). *Application deadline:* For fall admission, 5/15 for international students; for spring admission, 10/15 for international students. Applications are processed on a rolling basis. Application fee: $60. Electronic applications accepted. *Expenses:* $800 per credit hour. *Financial support:* In 2016–17, 27 students received support. Scholarships/grants and unspecified assistantships available. Financial award applicants required to submit FAFSA. *Faculty research:* Artificial intelligence and information visualization, natural language processing, thermofluids, microwaves and electromagnetics, micro-/nano-manufacturing. *Unit head:* Dr. Bruce Berdanier, Dean, 203-254-4147, Fax: 203-254-4013, E-mail: bberdanier@fairfield.edu. *Application contact:* Marianne Gumpper, Director of Graduate and Continuing Studies Admission, 203-254-4184, Fax: 203-254-4073, E-mail: gradadmis@

fairfield.edu.
Website: http://www.fairfield.edu/soe

Ferris State University, College of Business, Big Rapids, MI 49307. Offers business intelligence (MBA); design and innovation management (MBA); incident response (MBA); information security and intelligence (MS), including business intelligence, incident response, project management; lean systems and leadership (MBA); performance metrics (MBA); project management (MBA); supply chain management and lean logistics (MBA). *Accreditation:* ACBSP. *Program availability:* Part-time, evening/weekend, 100% online, blended/hybrid learning. *Faculty:* 18 full-time (7 women), 6 part-time/adjunct (3 women). *Students:* 25 full-time (11 women), 113 part-time (47 women); includes 12 minority (2 Black or African American, non-Hispanic/Latino; 1 American Indian or Alaska Native, non-Hispanic/Latino; 3 Asian, non-Hispanic/Latino; 3 Hispanic/Latino; 3 Two or more races, non-Hispanic/Latino), 50 international. Average age 31. 128 applicants, 59% accepted, 39 enrolled. In 2016, 94 master's awarded. *Degree requirements:* For master's, comprehensive exam, thesis. *Entrance requirements:* For master's, GRE or GMAT, minimum GPA of 3.0 in junior-/senior-level classes and overall; statement of purpose; 3 letters of reference; resume; transcripts. Additional exam requirements/recommendations for international students: Required—TOEFL (minimum score 500 paper-based; 70 iBT), IELTS (minimum score 6.5). *Application deadline:* For fall admission, 7/1 priority date for domestic students, 6/15 for international students; for winter admission, 11/1 priority date for domestic students, 10/15 for international students; for spring admission, 3/1 priority date for domestic students, 2/15 for international students. Applications are processed on a rolling basis. Application fee: $0 ($30 for international students). Electronic applications accepted. *Expenses:* Contact institution. *Financial support:* Career-related internships or fieldwork, Federal Work-Study, scholarships/grants, and unspecified assistantships available. Support available to part-time students. Financial award application deadline: 3/15; financial award applicants required to submit FAFSA. *Faculty research:* Lifestyle medicine business models, lean systems value chain pptimization, digital forensics/incident response, location-based services, passive data capture and analysis. *Unit head:* Dr. David Nicol, College of Business Dean, 231-591-2168, Fax: 231-591-3521, E-mail: davidnicol@ferris.edu. *Application contact:* Dr. Greg Gogolin, Professor, 231-591-3159, Fax: 231-591-3521, E-mail: greggogolin@ferris.edu.
Website: http://cbgp.ferris.edu/

Florida International University, College of Engineering and Computing, School of Computing and Information Sciences, Miami, FL 33199. Offers computer science (MS, PhD); cybersecurity (MS); data science (MS); information technology (MS); telecommunications and networking (MS). *Program availability:* Part-time, evening/weekend. *Faculty:* 46 full-time (11 women), 28 part-time/adjunct (5 women). *Students:* 145 full-time (39 women), 109 part-time (16 women); includes 124 minority (14 Black or African American, non-Hispanic/Latino; 1 American Indian or Alaska Native, non-Hispanic/Latino; 10 Asian, non-Hispanic/Latino; 97 Hispanic/Latino; 2 Two or more races, non-Hispanic/Latino), 115 international. Average age 29. 407 applicants, 54% accepted, 78 enrolled. In 2016, 90 master's, 8 doctorates awarded. *Degree requirements:* For master's, thesis or alternative; for doctorate, comprehensive exam, thesis/dissertation. *Entrance requirements:* For master's and doctorate, GRE General Test, 3 letters of recommendation, minimum GPA of 3.0. Additional exam requirements/recommendations for international students: Required—TOEFL (minimum score 550 paper-based; 80 iBT). *Application deadline:* For fall admission, 6/1 for domestic students, 4/1 for international students; for spring admission, 10/1 for domestic students, 9/1 for international students. Applications are processed on a rolling basis. Application fee: $30. Electronic applications accepted. *Expenses:* Tuition, state resident: full-time $8912; part-time $446 per credit hour. Tuition, nonresident: full-time $21,393; part-time $992 per credit hour. *Required fees:* $2185; $195 per semester. Tuition and fees vary according to program. *Financial support:* Research assistantships, teaching assistantships, institutionally sponsored loans, scholarships/grants, and unspecified assistantships available. Financial award application deadline: 3/1; financial award applicants required to submit FAFSA. *Faculty research:* Database systems, software engineering, operating systems, networks. *Unit head:* Dr. S. S. Iyengar, Director, 305-348-3947, E-mail: iyengar@cis.fiu.edu. *Application contact:* Sara-Michelle Lemus, Engineering Admissions Officer, 305-348-1890, E-mail: grad_eng@fiu.edu.

Fordham University, Graduate School of Arts and Sciences, Department of Computer and Information Sciences, New York, NY 10458. Offers computer science (MS); cyber security (MS); data analytics (MS). *Program availability:* Part-time, evening/weekend. *Faculty:* 11 full-time (1 woman). *Students:* 62 full-time (12 women), 17 part-time (5 women); includes 26 minority (10 Black or African American, non-Hispanic/Latino; 10 Asian, non-Hispanic/Latino; 1 Hispanic/Latino; 5 Two or more races, non-Hispanic/Latino), 19 international. Average age 31. 104 applicants, 39% accepted, 12 enrolled. In 2016, 5 master's awarded. *Degree requirements:* For master's, thesis optional. *Entrance requirements:* For master's, GRE General Test. Additional exam requirements/recommendations for international students: Required—TOEFL (minimum score 550 paper-based). *Application deadline:* For fall admission, 1/4 priority date for domestic students; for spring admission, 11/1 for domestic students. Application fee: $70. Electronic applications accepted. *Financial support:* In 2016–17, 5 students received support, including 3 research assistantships with tuition reimbursements available (averaging $15,000 per year); career-related internships or fieldwork, institutionally sponsored loans, tuition waivers (full and partial), and unspecified assistantships also available. Financial award application deadline: 1/4; financial award applicants required to submit CSS PROFILE or FAFSA. *Faculty research:* Robotics and computer vision, data mining and informatics, information and networking, computation and algorithms, biomedical informatics. *Total annual research expenditures:* $213,000. *Unit head:* Dr. Damian Lyons, Chair, 718-817-4485, Fax: 718-817-4488, E-mail: dlyons@fordham.edu. *Application contact:* Bernadette Valentino-Morrison, Director of Graduate Admissions, 718-817-4420, Fax: 718-817-3566, E-mail: valentinomor@fordham.edu.

Grand Canyon University, College of Doctoral Studies, Phoenix, AZ 85017-1097. Offers data analytics (DBA); general psychology (PhD), including cognition and instruction, industrial and organizational psychology, integrating technology, learning, and psychology, performance psychology; management (DBA); marketing (DBA); organizational leadership (Ed D), including behavioral health, Christian ministry, health care administration, organizational development. *Degree requirements:* For doctorate, comprehensive exam, thesis/dissertation. *Entrance requirements:* For doctorate, minimum GPA of 3.4 on earned advanced degree from regionally-accredited institution; transcripts; goals statement. Application fee: $0. *Unit head:* Michael Berger, Dean, 602-639-7255. *Application contact:* Michael Berger, Dean, 602-639-7255.
Website: https://www.gcu.edu/college-of-doctoral-studies.php

IGlobal University, Graduate Programs, Vienna, VA 22182. Offers accounting (MBA); data management and analytics (MSIT); entrepreneurship (MBA); finance (MBA); global business management (MBA); health care management (MBA); hospitality and tourism management (MBA); human resources management (MBA); information technology (MBA); information technology systems and management (MSIT); leadership and management (MBA); project management (MBA); public service and administration (MBA); software design and management (MSIT).

Illinois Institute of Technology, Graduate College, College of Science, Department of Applied Mathematics, Chicago, IL 60616. Offers applied mathematics (MS, PhD); data science (MAS); mathematical finance (MAS). MAS in mathematical finance program held jointly with Stuart School of Business. Terminal master's awarded for partial completion of doctoral program. *Degree requirements:* For master's, comprehensive exam, thesis; for doctorate, comprehensive exam, thesis/dissertation. *Entrance requirements:* For master's, GRE General Test (minimum scores: 304 Quantitative and Verbal, 2.5 Analytical Writing), minimum undergraduate GPA of 3.0; three letters of recommendation; for doctorate, GRE General Test (minimum scores: 304 Quantitative and Verbal, 3.0 Analytical Writing), minimum undergraduate GPA of 3.5; three letters of recommendation. Additional exam requirements/recommendations for international students: Required—TOEFL (minimum score 550 paper-based; 80 iBT). Electronic applications accepted. *Faculty research:* Applied analysis, computational mathematics, discrete applied mathematics, stochastics (including financial mathematics).

Illinois Institute of Technology, Graduate College, College of Science, Department of Computer Science, Chicago, IL 60616. Offers business (MCS); computational intelligence (MCS); computer science (MCS, MS, PhD); cyber-physical systems (MCS); data analytics (MCS); data science (MAS); database systems (MCS); distributed and cloud computing (MCS); education (MCS); finance (MCS); information security and assurance (MCS); networking and communications (MCS); software engineering (MCS); telecommunications and software engineering (MAS); MS/MAS. *Program availability:* Part-time, evening/weekend, online learning. Terminal master's awarded for partial completion of doctoral program. *Degree requirements:* For master's, thesis optional; for doctorate, comprehensive exam, thesis/dissertation. *Entrance requirements:* For master's, GRE General Test with minimum scores of 298 Quantitative and Verbal, 3.0 Analytical Writing (for MS); GRE General Test with minimum scores of 292 Quantitative and Verbal, 2.5 Analytical Writing (for MAS), minimum undergraduate GPA of 3.0; for doctorate, GRE General Test (minimum scores: 304 Quantitative and Verbal, 3.5 Analytical Writing), minimum undergraduate GPA of 3.0. Additional exam requirements/recommendations for international students: Required—TOEFL (minimum score 523 paper-based; 70 iBT). Electronic applications accepted. *Faculty research:* Parallel and distributed processing, high-performance computing, computational linguistics, information retrieval, data mining, grid computing.

Indiana University Bloomington, School of Informatics and Computing, Program in Data Science, Bloomington, IN 47408. Offers MS, Graduate Certificate. *Program availability:* Part-time, evening/weekend, 100% online, blended/hybrid learning. *Faculty:* 44. *Students:* 207 full-time (49 women), 240 part-time (51 women); includes 79 minority (20 Black or African American, non-Hispanic/Latino; 52 Asian, non-Hispanic/Latino; 7 Hispanic/Latino), 272 international. Average age 33. 719 applicants, 57% accepted, 247 enrolled. In 2016, 30 master's, 17 other advanced degrees awarded. *Entrance requirements:* For master's, GRE, statement of purpose, 3 recommendation letters, transcripts. Additional exam requirements/recommendations for international students: Required—TOEFL (minimum score 100 iBT). *Application deadline:* For fall admission, 1/1 for domestic and international students. Applications are processed on a rolling basis. Application fee: $55 ($65 for international students). Electronic applications accepted. *Expenses:* $50,000 non-resident/international; $17,000 resident. *Financial support:* In 2016–17, 265 students received support, including 262 fellowships (averaging $9,795 per year), 1 research assistantship with full tuition reimbursement available (averaging $24,000 per year); unspecified assistantships also available. Financial award application deadline: 1/1. *Faculty research:* 3D collaborative virtual environments, algorithms for big data, artificial intelligence, astronomy, Bayesian analysis, bioinformatics, case-based reasoning, causal inference, cheminformatics, citation analysis, classical multidimensional scaling, cognitive aspects of data management, cognitive science, complex networks and systems, computational linguistics, computational social science, computer networks, computer vision. *Unit head:* Dr. David Wild, 812-856-1848, E-mail: djwild@indiana.edu. *Application contact:* Kayla Scroggins, Data Science Graduate Manager, 812-856-9536, E-mail: datasci@indiana.edu.

Indiana University–Purdue University Indianapolis, School of Informatics and Computing, Department of Human-Centered Computing, Indianapolis, IN 46202. Offers human-computer interaction (MS, PhD); informatics (MS), including data analytics; media arts and science (MS). *Students:* 72 full-time (36 women), 40 part-time (11 women); includes 15 minority (4 Black or African American, non-Hispanic/Latino; 4 Asian, non-Hispanic/Latino; 5 Hispanic/Latino; 2 Two or more races, non-Hispanic/Latino), 52 international. Average age 35. 141 applicants, 42% accepted, 36 enrolled. In 2016, 40 master's awarded. *Unit head:* Dr. Davide Bolchini, Chair, 317-278-5144, E-mail: dbolchin@iupui.edu. *Application contact:* Elizabeth Bunge, Graduate Admissions Coordinator, 317-278-9200, E-mail: ebunge@iupui.edu.
Website: http://soic.iupui.edu/hcc/

Indiana University–Purdue University Indianapolis, School of Science, Department of Computer and Information Science, Indianapolis, IN 46202-5132. Offers biocomputing (Graduate Certificate); biometrics (Graduate Certificate); computer science (MS, PhD); computer security (Graduate Certificate); databases and data mining (Graduate Certificate); software engineering (Graduate Certificate). *Program availability:* Part-time. *Faculty:* 16 full-time (2 women), 10 part-time/adjunct (4 women). *Students:* 95 full-time (36 women), 44 part-time (15 women); includes 8 minority (3 Black or African American, non-Hispanic/Latino; 5 Asian, non-Hispanic/Latino), 119 international. Average age 27. 275 applicants, 30% accepted, 41 enrolled. In 2016, 52 master's, 3 doctorates, 3 other advanced degrees awarded. Terminal master's awarded for partial completion of doctoral program. *Degree requirements:* For master's and Graduate Certificate, thesis optional; for doctorate, thesis/dissertation. *Entrance requirements:* For master's and doctorate, GRE, BS in computer science or the equivalent with a minimum GPA of 3.0 (or equivalent); for Graduate Certificate, BS in computer science or the equivalent with a minimum GPA of 3.0 (or equivalent). Additional exam requirements/recommendations for international students: Required—PTE (minimum score 58), TOEFL (minimum score 550 paper-based, 79 iBT) or IELTS (6.5). *Application deadline:* For fall admission, 1/15 priority date for domestic and international students; for spring admission, 9/15 for domestic students. Application fee: $60 ($65 for international students). *Financial support:* In 2016–17, 45 students received support, including 2 fellowships with full tuition reimbursements available (averaging $20,000 per year), 15 research assistantships with full and partial tuition reimbursements available (averaging $18,000 per year), 20 teaching assistantships with full and partial tuition reimbursements available (averaging $18,000 per year); scholarships/grants, health care benefits, and tuition waivers (full and partial) also available. Financial award application deadline: 1/15. *Faculty research:* Imaging and visualization; networking and security; software engineering; distributed and parallel computing; database, data mining and machine learning. *Total annual research expenditures:* $550,196. *Unit head:* Dr. Shiaofen Fang, Chair, 317-274-9727, Fax: 317-274-9742, E-mail: sfang@cs.iupui.edu. *Application contact:* Nicole Wittlief, Graduate Admissions and Program Coordinator, 317-274-3883, Fax: 317-274-9742, E-mail: wittlief@cs.iupui.edu.
Website: http://www.cs.iupui.edu/

Iowa State University of Science and Technology, Program in Business Analytics, Ames, IA 50011. Offers MS. *Program availability:* Online learning.

Kansas State University, Graduate School, College of Business, Program in Business Administration, Manhattan, KS 66506. Offers data analytics (MBA); finance (MBA); management (MBA); marketing (MBA); technology entrepreneurship (MBA). *Accreditation:* AACSB. *Program availability:* Part-time, 100% online. *Faculty:* 35 full-time (8 women). *Students:* 50 full-time (19 women), 89 part-time (36 women); includes 25 minority (8 Black or African American, non-Hispanic/Latino; 6 Asian, non-Hispanic/Latino; 4 Hispanic/Latino; 7 Two or more races, non-Hispanic/Latino), 17 international. Average age 32. 78 applicants, 90% accepted, 31 enrolled. In 2016, 26 master's, 3 other advanced degrees awarded. *Entrance requirements:* For master's, GMAT (minimum score of 500), minimum undergraduate GPA of 3.0. Additional exam requirements/recommendations for international students: Required—TOEFL (minimum score 550 paper-based; 79 iBT); Recommended—IELTS (minimum score 7). *Application deadline:* For fall admission, 2/1 priority date for domestic and international students; for spring admission, 10/1 priority date for domestic students, 8/1 priority date for international students. Applications are processed on a rolling basis. Application fee: $70 ($80 for international students). Electronic applications accepted. *Expenses:* Contact institution. *Financial support:* In 2016–17, 6 students received support, including 5 research assistantships (averaging $6,400 per year), 6 teaching assistantships with partial tuition reimbursements available (averaging $6,400 per year); institutionally sponsored loans and scholarships/grants also available. Financial award application deadline: 3/1; financial award applicants required to submit FAFSA. *Faculty research:* Organizational citizenship behavior, service marketing, impression management, human resources management, lean manufacturing and supply chain management, financial market behavior and investment management, data analytics, corporate responsibility, technology entrepreneurship. *Unit head:* Dr. Kevin Gwinner, Dean, 785-532-7227, Fax: 785-532-7216, E-mail: kgwinner@ksu.edu. *Application contact:* Dr. Chwen Sheu, Associate Dean for Academic Programs, 785-532-4363, Fax: 785-532-1339, E-mail: gradbusiness@ksu.edu.
Website: http://www.cba.k-state.edu/

Lawrence Technological University, College of Arts and Sciences, Southfield, MI 48075-1058. Offers bioinformatics (Graduate Certificate); computer science (MS), including data science, big data, and data mining, intelligent systems; instructional design, communication, and presentation (Graduate Certificate); instructional technology (Graduate Certificate); premedical studies (Graduate Certificate); technical and professional communication (MS, Graduate Certificate); writing for the digital age (Graduate Certificate). *Program availability:* Part-time, evening/weekend. *Faculty:* 6 full-time (2 women), 10 part-time/adjunct (5 women). *Students:* 37 part-time (18 women); includes 4 minority (1 Black or African American, non-Hispanic/Latino; 1 Asian, non-Hispanic/Latino; 2 Hispanic/Latino), 8 international. Average age 33. 301 applicants, 23% accepted, 9 enrolled. In 2016, 22 master's, 2 other advanced degrees awarded. *Degree requirements:* For master's, thesis (for some programs). *Entrance requirements:* Additional exam requirements/recommendations for international students: Required—TOEFL (minimum score 550 paper-based; 79 iBT), IELTS (minimum score 6.5). *Application deadline:* For fall admission, 5/22 for international students; for spring admission, 10/11 for international students; for summer admission, 2/16 for international students. Applications are processed on a rolling basis. Application fee: $50. Electronic applications accepted. *Expenses: Tuition:* Full-time $14,868; part-time $1062 per credit. *Required fees:* $75 per semester. Tuition and fees vary according to campus/location. *Financial support:* In 2016–17, 9 students received support. Scholarships/grants and tuition reduction available. Financial award application deadline: 4/1; financial award applicants required to submit FAFSA. *Faculty research:* Computer analysis of visual art, psychology of numbers games, neural basis of moral judgement, synthesis of glycosylated warfarin analogs for potential use as antiviral drugs, observation of chemotaxis behavior in c. elegans. *Total annual research expenditures:* $530,625. *Unit head:* Dr. Hsiao-Ping Moore, Dean, 248-204-3500, Fax: 248-204-3518, E-mail: scidean@itu.edu. *Application contact:* Jane Rohrback, Director of Admissions, 248-204-3160, Fax: 248-204-2228, E-mail: admissions@ltu.edu.

Lewis University, College of Business, Graduate School of Management, Program in Business Analytics, Romeoville, IL 60446. Offers financial analytics (MS); healthcare analytics (MS); marketing analytics (MS); operations analytics (MS). *Program availability:* Part-time, evening/weekend, 100% online, blended/hybrid learning. *Students:* 12 full-time (5 women), 28 part-time (16 women); includes 8 minority (4 Black or African American, non-Hispanic/Latino; 3 Hispanic/Latino; 1 Two or more races, non-Hispanic/Latino), 4 international. Average age 32. *Degree requirements:* For master's, comprehensive exam. *Entrance requirements:* Additional exam requirements/recommendations for international students: Required—TOEFL. *Application deadline:* Applications are processed on a rolling basis. Electronic applications accepted. *Expenses: Tuition:* Full-time $13,860; part-time $770 per credit hour. *Required fees:* $75 per semester. Tuition and fees vary according to degree level and program. *Financial support:* Career-related internships or fieldwork, Federal Work-Study, and unspecified assistantships available. Financial award applicants required to submit FAFSA. *Unit head:* Dr. Rami Khasawneh, Dean, 800-838-0500 Ext. 5360, E-mail: khasawra@lewisu.edu. *Application contact:* Michele Ryan, Director of Admission, 815-836-5384, E-mail: gsm@lewisu.edu.
Website: http://www.lewisu.edu/academics/business-analytics/

Lipscomb University, College of Computing and Technology, Nashville, TN 37204-3951. Offers data science (MS); information technology (MS), including data science, information security, information technology management, software engineering; software engineering (MS). *Program availability:* Part-time, evening/weekend. *Faculty:* 7 full-time (0 women), 6 part-time/adjunct (1 woman). *Students:* 21 full-time (10 women), 10 part-time (3 women); includes 9 minority (5 Black or African American, non-Hispanic/Latino; 4 Asian, non-Hispanic/Latino), 1 international. Average age 34. 47 applicants, 49% accepted, 12 enrolled. In 2016, 26 degrees awarded. *Degree requirements:* For master's, capstone project. *Entrance requirements:* For master's, GRE, 2 references, transcripts, resume, personal statement. Additional exam requirements/recommendations for international students: Required—TOEFL (minimum score 570 paper-based; 80 iBT). *Application deadline:* Applications are processed on a rolling basis. Application fee: $50 ($75 for international students). Electronic applications accepted. *Expenses:* $1,226 per hour. *Financial support:* Scholarships/grants and employer agreements available. Financial award applicants required to submit FAFSA. *Unit head:* Dr. Fortune S. Mhlanga, Dean, 615-966-5073, E-mail: fortune.mhlanga@lipscomb.edu. *Application contact:* Brett Ramsey, Enrollment Management Specialist, 615-966-1193, E-mail: brett.ramsey@lipscomb.edu.
Website: http://www.lipscomb.edu/technology/

London Metropolitan University, Graduate Programs, London, United Kingdom. Offers applied psychology (M Sc); architecture (MA); biomedical science (M Sc); blood science (M Sc); cancer pharmacology (M Sc); computer networking and cyber security (M Sc); computing and information systems (M Sc); conference interpreting (MA); counter-terrorism studies (M Sc); creative, digital and professional writing (MA); crime, violence and prevention (M Sc); criminology (M Sc); curating contemporary art (MA); data analytics (M Sc); digital media (MA); early childhood studies (MA); education (MA, Ed D); financial services law, regulation and compliance (LL M); food science (M Sc); forensic psychology (M Sc); health and social care management and policy (M Sc); human nutrition (M Sc); human resource management (MA); human rights and international conflict (MA); information technology (M Sc); intelligence and security studies (M Sc); international oil, gas and energy law (LL M); international relations (MA); interpreting (MA); learning and teaching in higher education (MA); legal practice (LL M); media and entertainment law (LL M); organizational and consumer psychology (M Sc); psychological therapy (M Sc); psychology of mental health (M Sc); public health (M Sc); public policy and management (MPA); security studies (M Sc); social work (M Sc); spatial planning and urban design (MA); sports therapy (M Sc); supporting older children and young people with dyslexia (MA); teaching languages (MA), including Arabic, English; translation (MA); woman and child abuse (MA).

Manhattan College, Graduate Programs, School of Science, Program in Applied Mathematics - Data Analytics, Riverdale, NY 10471. Offers MS. *Program availability:* Part-time. *Faculty:* 9 full-time (4 women). *Students:* 7 full-time (2 women); includes 1 minority (Hispanic/Latino), 2 international. Average age 24. 7 applicants, 71% accepted, 5 enrolled. *Degree requirements:* For master's, comprehensive exam. *Entrance requirements:* Additional exam requirements/recommendations for international students: Required—TOEFL. *Application deadline:* Applications are processed on a rolling basis. Electronic applications accepted. *Financial support:* In 2016–17, 4 students received support. Unspecified assistantships available. *Faculty research:* Machine learning, statistical learning, search algorithms for textual data mining, probabilistic modeling, operations research, network theory, Monte Carlo methods. *Unit head:* Dr. Constantine Theodosiou, Dean of Science, 718-862-7368, E-mail: constantine.theodosiou@manhattan.edu. *Application contact:* William Bisset, Vice President for Enrollment, 718-862-7199, Fax: 718-862-8019, E-mail: william.bisset@manhattan.edu.
Website: https://manhattan.edu/academics/5-year-programs/applied-mathematics-data-analytics.php

Merrimack College, School of Science and Engineering, North Andover, MA 01845-5800. Offers athletic training (MS); civil engineering (MS); community health education (MS); computer science (MS); data science (MS); exercise and sport science (MS); health and wellness management (MS); mechanical engineering (MS), including engineering management. *Program availability:* Part-time, evening/weekend, 100% online. *Faculty:* 16 full-time, 2 part-time/adjunct. *Students:* 88 full-time (32 women), 13 part-time (6 women); includes 6 minority (4 Hispanic/Latino; 2 Two or more races, non-Hispanic/Latino), 39 international. Average age 25. 156 applicants, 67% accepted, 59 enrolled. In 2016, 46 master's awarded. *Degree requirements:* For master's, comprehensive exam, thesis optional, internship or capstone (for some programs). *Entrance requirements:* For master's, official college transcripts, resume, personal statement, 2 recommendations. Additional exam requirements/recommendations for international students: Required—TOEFL (minimum score 84 iBT), IELTS (minimum score 6.5), PTE (minimum score 56). *Application deadline:* For fall admission, 8/14 for domestic students, 7/14 for international students; for spring admission, 1/10 for domestic students, 12/10 for international students; for summer admission, 5/10 for domestic students, 4/10 for international students. Applications are processed on a rolling basis. Application fee: $0. Electronic applications accepted. *Expenses:* Contact institution. *Financial support:* Fellowships with full tuition reimbursements, career-related internships or fieldwork, scholarships/grants, and health care benefits available. Support available to part-time students. Financial award application deadline: 5/1; financial award applicants required to submit FAFSA. *Faculty research:* Viral genomics and evolution (biology), robotics (mechanical engineering), knot theory (mathematics), computer graphics and network security (computer science), water management (civil engineering). *Application contact:* Allison Pena, Graduate Admissions Counselor, 978-837-3563, E-mail: penaa@merrimack.edu.
Website: http://www.merrimack.edu/academics/graduate/

Metropolitan State University, College of Management, St. Paul, MN 55106-5000. Offers business administration (MBA, DBA); database administration (Graduate Certificate); healthcare information technology management (Graduate Certificate); information assurance security (Graduate Certificate); management information systems (MMIS); MIS generalist (Graduate Certificate); MIS systems analysis and design (Graduate Certificate); project management (Graduate Certificate); public and nonprofit administration (MPNA). *Program availability:* Part-time, evening/weekend. *Degree requirements:* For master's, thesis optional, computer language (MMIS). *Entrance requirements:* For master's, GMAT (for MBA), resume. Additional exam requirements/recommendations for international students: Required—TOEFL (minimum score 550 paper-based). Electronic applications accepted. *Faculty research:* Yugoslav economic system, workers' cooperatives, participative management and job enrichment, global business systems.

Michigan Technological University, Graduate School, Interdisciplinary Programs, Houghton, MI 49931. Offers atmospheric sciences (PhD); biochemistry and molecular biology (PhD); computational science and engineering (PhD); data science (MS, Graduate Certificate); engineering (M Eng); environmental engineering (PhD); international profile (Graduate Certificate); nanotechnology (Graduate Certificate); sustainability (Graduate Certificate); sustainable water resources systems (Graduate Certificate). *Program availability:* Part-time. *Faculty:* 122 full-time (26 women), 13 part-time/adjunct. *Students:* 58 full-time (18 women), 17 part-time (5 women); includes 1 minority (Black or African American, non-Hispanic/Latino), 56 international. Average age 28. 395 applicants, 20% accepted, 22 enrolled. In 2016, 3 master's, 7 doctorates, 8 other advanced degrees awarded. Terminal master's awarded for partial completion of doctoral program. *Degree requirements:* For master's, comprehensive exam (for some programs), thesis (for some programs); for doctorate, comprehensive exam, thesis/dissertation. *Entrance requirements:* For master's, doctorate, and Graduate Certificate, GRE, statement of purpose, personal statement, official transcripts, 2-3 letters of recommendation. Additional exam requirements/recommendations for international students: Required—TOEFL or IELTS. *Application deadline:* Applications are processed on a rolling basis. Electronic applications accepted. *Expenses:* Tuition, state resident: full-time $16,290; part-time $905 per credit. Tuition, nonresident: full-time $16,290; part-time $905 per credit. *Required fees:* $248; $124 per term. Tuition and fees vary according to course load and program. *Financial support:* In 2016–17, 54 students received support, including 7 fellowships with tuition reimbursements available (averaging $15,242 per year), 19 research assistantships with tuition reimbursements available (averaging $15,242 per year), 5 teaching assistantships with tuition reimbursements available (averaging $15,242 per year); career-related internships or fieldwork, Federal Work-Study, scholarships/grants, health care benefits, unspecified assistantships, and cooperative program also available. Financial award applicants required to submit FAFSA. *Faculty research:* Big data, atmospheric sciences, bioinformatics and systems biology, molecular dynamics, environmental studies. *Unit head:* Dr. Pushpalathata Murthy, Dean of the Graduate School/Associate Provost for Graduate Education, 906-487-3007, Fax: 906-487-2284, E-mail: ppmurthy@mtu.edu. *Application contact:* Carol T. Wingerson, Administrative Aide, 906-487-2328, Fax: 906-487-2284, E-mail: gradadms@mtu.edu.

Montclair State University, The Graduate School, College of Humanities and Social Sciences, Data Collection and Management Certificate Program, Montclair, NJ 07043-1624. Offers Certificate. *Expenses:* Tuition, state resident: part-time $553 per credit.

Database Systems

Tuition, nonresident: part-time $854 per credit. *Required fees:* $91 per credit. Tuition and fees vary according to program.

New College of Florida, Program in Data Science, Sarasota, FL 34243. Offers MDS. *Entrance requirements:* For master's, bachelor's degree, course in linear algebra, programming proficiency. Additional exam requirements/recommendations for international students: Required—TOEFL (minimum score 560 paper-based; 83 iBT), IELTS (minimum score 6.5).

New Jersey Institute of Technology, Martin Tuchman School of Management, Newark, NJ 07102. Offers business administration (MBA); business data science (PhD); finance for managers (Certificate); international business (MS); management (MS); management essentials (Certificate); management of technology (Certificate). *Accreditation:* AACSB. *Program availability:* Part-time, evening/weekend. *Faculty:* 29 full-time (9 women), 21 part-time/adjunct (3 women). *Students:* 90 full-time (35 women), 147 part-time (53 women); includes 104 minority (30 Black or African American, non-Hispanic/Latino; 30 Asian, non-Hispanic/Latino; 38 Hispanic/Latino; 6 Two or more races, non-Hispanic/Latino), 57 international. Average age 31. 385 applicants, 52% accepted, 80 enrolled. In 2016, 81 master's, 11 other advanced degrees awarded. Terminal master's awarded for partial completion of doctoral program. *Degree requirements:* For master's, thesis optional. *Entrance requirements:* For doctorate, GRE General Test, minimum graduate GPA of 3.5. Additional exam requirements/recommendations for international students: Required—TOEFL (minimum score 550 paper-based; 79 iBT). *Application deadline:* For fall admission, 6/1 priority date for domestic students, 5/1 priority date for international students; for spring admission, 11/15 priority date for domestic and international students. Applications are processed on a rolling basis. Application fee: $75. Electronic applications accepted. *Expenses:* Contact institution. *Financial support:* In 2016–17, 7 students received support, including 3 research assistantships (averaging $9,088 per year), 4 teaching assistantships (averaging $19,250 per year); fellowships, career-related internships or fieldwork, Federal Work-Study, institutionally sponsored loans, and unspecified assistantships also available. Financial award application deadline: 1/15. *Faculty research:* Manufacturing systems analysis, earnings management, knowledge-based view of the firm, data envelopment analysis, human factors in human/machine systems. *Unit head:* Dr. Reggie Caudill, Interim Dean, 973-596-5856, Fax: 973-596-3074, E-mail: reggie.j.caudill@njit.edu. *Application contact:* Stephen Eck, Director of Admissions, 973-596-3300, Fax: 973-596-3461, E-mail: admissions@njit.edu.
Website: http://management.njit.edu

The New School, Parsons School of Design, Program in Data Visualization, New York, NY 10011. Offers MS. *Program availability:* Part-time. *Faculty:* 23 full-time (16 women), 3 part-time/adjunct (1 woman). *Students:* 7 full-time (1 woman), 13 part-time (6 women); includes 3 minority (1 Asian, non-Hispanic/Latino; 1 Native Hawaiian or other Pacific Islander, non-Hispanic/Latino; 1 Two or more races, non-Hispanic/Latino), 8 international. Average age 32. 55 applicants, 49% accepted, 15 enrolled. In 2016, 7 master's awarded. *Degree requirements:* For master's, thesis or alternative. *Entrance requirements:* For master's, transcripts, resume, statement of purpose, recommendation letters, portfolio, programming sample and/or writing sample, interview. Additional exam requirements/recommendations for international students: Required—TOEFL (minimum score 92 iBT), IELTS (minimum score 7), PTE (minimum score 63). *Application deadline:* For fall admission, 1/1 priority date for domestic and international students. Applications are processed on a rolling basis. Application fee: $50. Electronic applications accepted. *Expenses: Tuition:* Full-time $42,610; part-time $1685 per credit. *Required fees:* $276; $138 per semester. Full-time tuition and fees vary according to degree level and program. Part-time tuition and fees vary according to course load and program. *Financial support:* Research assistantships, teaching assistantships, Federal Work-Study, scholarships/grants, and unspecified assistantships available. Support available to part-time students. Financial award application deadline: 2/1; financial award applicants required to submit FAFSA. *Unit head:* Aaron Hill, Director, 212-229-5600 Ext. 1284, E-mail: aaron.hill@newschool.edu. *Application contact:* Courtney Malenius, Director of Graduate Admission, 212-229-5150 Ext. 4011, E-mail: maleniuc@newschool.edu.
Website: http://www.newschool.edu/parsons/ms-data-visualization/

New York University, Graduate School of Arts and Science, Department of Data Science, New York, NY 10012-1019. Offers MS. *Entrance requirements:* For master's, GRE or GMAT. Additional exam requirements/recommendations for international students: Required—TOEFL. Electronic applications accepted.

New York University, School of Continuing and Professional Studies, Division of Programs in Business, Graduate Programs in Management and Systems, New York, NY 10012-1019. Offers core business competencies (Advanced Certificate); database technologies (MS); enterprise risk management (MS, Advanced Certificate); information technologies (Advanced Certificate); strategy and leadership (MS, Advanced Certificate); systems management (MS). *Program availability:* Part-time, evening/weekend, online learning. *Degree requirements:* For master's, thesis, capstone project. *Entrance requirements:* For master's, GRE or GMAT (only upon request), bachelor's degree, resume with relevant professional work, internship or volunteer experience, two letters of recommendation, statement of purpose. Additional exam requirements/recommendations for international students: Required—TOEFL (minimum score 600 paper-based; 100 iBT), IELTS (minimum score 7). Electronic applications accepted.

Northeastern University, College of Computer and Information Science, Boston, MA 02115-5096. Offers computer science (MS, PhD); data science (MS); game science and design (MS); health informatics (MS); information assurance (MS); network science (PhD); personal health informatics (PhD). *Program availability:* Part-time, evening/weekend. *Faculty:* 79 full-time (21 women), 34 part-time/adjunct (7 women). *Students:* 1,064 full-time (306 women), 34 part-time (10 women). In 2016, 322 master's, 8 doctorates awarded. Terminal master's awarded for partial completion of doctoral program. *Degree requirements:* For master's, thesis optional; for doctorate, comprehensive exam, thesis/dissertation. Application fee: $75. Electronic applications accepted. *Expenses:* $1,495 per credit. *Financial support:* Research assistantships, teaching assistantships, scholarships/grants, health care benefits, and unspecified assistantships available. Financial award applicants required to submit FAFSA. *Unit head:* Dr. Carla Brodley, Professor and Dean. *Application contact:* Dr. Rajmohan Rajaraman, Professor/Associate Dean/Director of the Graduate School, 617-373-8493, E-mail: gradschool@ccs.neu.edu.
Website: http://www.ccs.neu.edu/

Northwestern University, School of Professional Studies, Program in Information Systems, Evanston, IL 60208. Offers analytics and business intelligence (MS); database and Internet technologies (MS); information systems (MS); information systems management (MS); information systems security (MS); medical informatics (MS); software project management and development (MS).

Ohio Dominican University, Division of Business, Program in Business Administration, Columbus, OH 43219-2099. Offers accounting (MBA); data analytics (MBA); finance (MBA); leadership (MBA); risk management (MBA); sport management (MBA). *Program availability:* Part-time, evening/weekend, 100% online, blended/hybrid learning. *Faculty:* 8 full-time (4 women), 17 part-time/adjunct (3 women). *Students:* 63 full-time (26 women), 112 part-time (59 women); includes 50 minority (29 Black or African American, non-Hispanic/Latino; 2 American Indian or Alaska Native, non-Hispanic/Latino; 6 Asian, non-Hispanic/Latino; 6 Hispanic/Latino; 1 Native Hawaiian or other Pacific Islander, non-Hispanic/Latino; 6 Two or more races, non-Hispanic/Latino), 7 international. Average age 31. 65 applicants, 51% accepted, 26 enrolled. In 2016, 120 master's awarded. *Entrance requirements:* For master's, minimum overall GPA of 3.0 in undergraduate degree from regionally-accredited institution or 2.75 in last 60 semester hours of bachelor's degree. Additional exam requirements/recommendations for international students: Required—TOEFL (minimum score 550 paper-based), IELTS (minimum score 6.5). *Application deadline:* For fall admission, 8/15 for domestic students, 6/10 for international students; for spring admission, 1/4 for domestic students, 11/2 for international students; for summer admission, 5/30 for domestic students. Applications are processed on a rolling basis. Application fee: $25. Electronic applications accepted. *Expenses:* $590 per credit hour; $225 fees per semester. *Financial support:* Applicants required to submit FAFSA. *Unit head:* Dr. Steve Vickner, Director of Master of Business Administration Program, 614-251-4569, E-mail: vickners@ohiodominican.edu. *Application contact:* John W. Naughton, Director for Graduate Admissions, 614-251-4721, Fax: 614-251-6654, E-mail: grad@ohiodominican.edu.
Website: http://www.ohiodominican.edu/academics/graduate/mba

Penn State Great Valley, Graduate Studies, Management Division, Malvern, PA 19355-1488. Offers business administration (MBA); cyber security (Certificate); data analytics (Certificate); distributed energy and grid modernization (Certificate); finance (M Fin, Certificate); health sector management (Certificate); human resource management (Certificate); information science (MSIS); leadership development (MLD); new ventures and entrepreneurship (Certificate); professional studies in data analytics (MPS); sustainable management practices (Certificate). *Accreditation:* AACSB. *Unit head:* Dr. James A. Nemes, Chancellor, 610-648-3202, Fax: 610-725-5296. *Application contact:* JoAnn Kelly, Director of Admissions, 610-648-3315, Fax: 610-725-5296, E-mail: jek2@psu.edu.
Website: http://greatvalley.psu.edu/academics/masters-degrees/engineering-management

Queens College of the City University of New York, Division of Social Sciences, Department of Sociology, Queens, NY 11367-1597. Offers data analytics and applied social research (MA); sociology (MA). *Program availability:* Part-time, evening/weekend. *Faculty:* 30 full-time (15 women), 40 part-time/adjunct (22 women). *Students:* 7 full-time (4 women), 27 part-time (15 women); includes 17 minority (1 Black or African American, non-Hispanic/Latino; 6 Asian, non-Hispanic/Latino; 10 Hispanic/Latino), 4 international. Average age 27. 40 applicants, 75% accepted, 16 enrolled. In 2016, 11 master's awarded. *Degree requirements:* For master's, thesis optional. *Entrance requirements:* For master's, minimum GPA of 3.0. Additional exam requirements/recommendations for international students: Required—TOEFL (minimum score 100 iBT), IELTS (minimum score 7). *Application deadline:* For fall admission, 5/15 for domestic students; for spring admission, 12/1 for domestic students. Applications are processed on a rolling basis. Application fee: $125. Electronic applications accepted. *Expenses:* Tuition, state resident: full-time $5065; part-time $425 per credit. Tuition, nonresident: part-time $780 per credit. *Required fees:* $522; $397 per credit. Part-time tuition and fees vary according to course load and program. *Financial support:* Career-related internships or fieldwork and unspecified assistantships available. Financial award application deadline: 4/1; financial award applicants required to submit FAFSA. *Unit head:* Dr. Andrew Beveridge, Chairperson, 718-997-2800, E-mail: andrew.beveridge@qc.cuny.edu.

Radford University, College of Graduate Studies and Research, Program in Data and Information Management, Radford, VA 24142. Offers MS. *Program availability:* Part-time, evening/weekend. *Faculty:* 2 full-time (0 women). *Students:* 3 full-time (1 woman); includes 2 minority (both Asian, non-Hispanic/Latino), 1 international. Average age 27. 5 applicants, 80% accepted, 3 enrolled. *Entrance requirements:* For master's, GRE (minimum scores of 152 on quantitative portion and 148 on verbal portion, or 650 and 420, respectively, under old scoring system), minimum GPA of 3.0 overall from accredited educational institution, three letters of reference from faculty members familiar with academic performance in major coursework or from colleagues or supervisors familiar with work. Additional exam requirements/recommendations for international students: Required—TOEFL (minimum score 567 paper-based). *Application deadline:* Applications are processed on a rolling basis. Application fee: $50. Electronic applications accepted. *Expenses:* Tuition, state resident: full-time $7868; part-time $328 per credit hour. Tuition, nonresident: full-time $16,394; part-time $683 per credit hour. *Required fees:* $3090; $130 per credit hour. Tuition and fees vary according to course load and program. *Financial support:* In 2016–17, 2 students received support, including 1 research assistantship (averaging $11,000 per year); teaching assistantships, scholarships/grants, and unspecified assistantships also available. Support available to part-time students. *Unit head:* Dr. Jeff Pittges, Chair, Department of Information Technology, 540-831-5381, E-mail: jpittges@radford.edu.

Regis University, College of Computer and Information Sciences, Denver, CO 80221-1099. Offers agile technologies (Certificate); cybersecurity (Certificate); data science (M Sc); database administration with Oracle (Certificate); database development (Certificate); database technologies (M Sc); enterprise Java software development (Certificate); enterprise resource planning (Certificate); executive information technology (Certificate); health care informatics (Certificate); health care informatics and information management (M Sc); information assurance (M Sc); information assurance policy management (Certificate); information technology management (M Sc); mobile software development (Certificate); software engineering (M Sc, Certificate); software engineering and database technology (M Sc); storage area networks (Certificate); systems engineering (M Sc, Certificate). *Program availability:* Part-time, evening/weekend, 100% online, blended/hybrid learning. *Faculty:* 11 full-time (3 women), 30 part-time/adjunct (10 women). *Students:* 341 full-time (95 women), 318 part-time (98 women); includes 186 minority (56 Black or African American, non-Hispanic/Latino; 2 American Indian or Alaska Native, non-Hispanic/Latino; 48 Asian, non-Hispanic/Latino; 63 Hispanic/Latino; 17 Two or more races, non-Hispanic/Latino), 57 international. Average age 37. 342 applicants, 79% accepted, 174 enrolled. In 2016, 192 master's awarded. *Degree requirements:* For master's, thesis (for some programs), final research project. *Entrance requirements:* For master's, official transcript reflecting baccalaureate degree awarded from regionally-accredited college or university, 2 years of related experience, resume, interview. Additional exam requirements/recommendations for international students: Required—TOEFL (minimum score 550 paper-based; 82 iBT). *Application deadline:* For fall admission, 8/15 priority date for domestic students, 7/13 for international students; for winter admission, 10/10 priority date for domestic students, 9/8 for international students; for spring admission, 1/10 priority date for domestic students, 11/17 for international students; for summer admission, 5/1 priority date for domestic students. Applications are processed on a rolling basis. Application fee: $75. Electronic applications accepted. *Expenses:* $730 per credit hour. *Financial support:* Scholarships/grants available. Financial award application deadline: 4/15; financial award applicants required to submit FAFSA. *Faculty research:* Information policy, knowledge management, software architectures, data science. *Unit head:* Shari Plantz-Masters, Academic Dean. *Application contact:* Cate Clark, Director of Admissions, 303-458-4900, Fax: 303-964-5534, E-mail: ruadmissions@regis.edu.
Website: http://regis.edu/CCIS.aspx

Robert Morris University, School of Communications and Information Systems, Moon Township, PA 15108-1189. Offers communication and information systems (MS); cyber security (MS); data analytics (MS); information security and assurance (MS); information systems and communications (D Sc); information systems management (MS); information technology project management (MS); Internet information systems (MS); organizational leadership (MS). *Program availability:* Part-time, evening/weekend, online learning. *Faculty:* 28 full-time (11 women), 6 part-time/adjunct (0 women). *Students:* 269 part-time (110 women); includes 49 minority (29 Black or African American, non-Hispanic/Latino; 10 Asian, non-Hispanic/Latino; 5 Hispanic/Latino; 5 Two or more races, non-Hispanic/Latino), 49 international. Average age 34. 239 applicants, 46% accepted, 83 enrolled. In 2016, 110 master's, 15 doctorates awarded. *Degree requirements:* For doctorate, thesis/dissertation. *Entrance requirements:* For doctorate, employer letter of endorsement, interview. Additional exam requirements/recommendations for international students: Required—TOEFL (minimum score 550 paper-based; 79 iBT). *Application deadline:* For fall admission, 7/1 priority date for domestic and international students; for spring admission, 11/1 priority date for domestic and international students. Applications are processed on a rolling basis. Application fee: $35. Electronic applications accepted. Application fee is waived when completed online. *Expenses:* $870 per credit (for master's degree). *Financial support:* Institutionally sponsored loans available. Support available to part-time students. Financial award application deadline: 5/1. *Unit head:* Ann Marie M. Le Blanc, Dean, 412-397-6433, Fax: 412-397-6469, E-mail: leblanc@rmu.edu. *Application contact:* Kellie L. Laurenzi, Associate Vice President, 412-397-5200, Fax: 412-397-5915, E-mail: graduateadmissions@rmu.edu. Website: http://www.rmu.edu/web/cms/schools/scis/Pages/default.aspx

Rochester Institute of Technology, Graduate Enrollment Services, Golisano College of Computing and Information Sciences, Computer Science Department, Advanced Certificate Program in Big Data Analytics, Rochester, NY 14623. Offers Advanced Certificate. *Program availability:* Part-time, 100% online. *Students:* 4 part-time (2 women). 11 applicants, 45% accepted, 4 enrolled. In 2016, 50 Advanced Certificates awarded. *Entrance requirements:* For degree, minimum GPA of 3.0 (recommended). Additional exam requirements/recommendations for international students: Required—TOEFL (minimum score 550 paper-based; 79 iBT), IELTS (minimum score 6.5), PTE (minimum score 58). *Application deadline:* Applications are processed on a rolling basis. Application fee: $60. Electronic applications accepted. *Expenses:* $1,742 per credit hour (classroom), $993 per credit hour (online). *Financial support:* In 2016–17, 31 students received support. Available to part-time students. Applicants required to submit FAFSA. *Faculty research:* Data management, data analytics, data security, data warehousing. *Unit head:* Dr. Hans-Peter Bischof, Graduate Program Director, 585-475-5568, Fax: 585-475-4935, E-mail: hpb@cs.rit.edu. *Application contact:* Diane Ellison, Associate Vice President, Graduate Enrollment Services, 585-475-2229, Fax: 585-475-7164, E-mail: gradinfo@rit.edu. Website: https://www.rit.edu/gccis/advanced-certificate-big-data-analytics

Rockhurst University, Helzberg School of Management, Kansas City, MO 64110-2561. Offers accounting (MBA); business intelligence (MBA, Certificate); data science (MBA, Certificate); entrepreneurship (MBA); finance (MBA); fundraising leadership (MBA, Certificate); healthcare management (MBA, Certificate); human capital (Certificate); international business (Certificate); management (MBA, Certificate); nonprofit administration (Certificate); organizational development (Certificate); science leadership (Certificate). *Accreditation:* AACSB. *Program availability:* Part-time, evening/weekend. *Entrance requirements:* For master's, GMAT or GRE. Additional exam requirements/recommendations for international students: Required—TOEFL (minimum score 550 paper-based; 79 iBT). Electronic applications accepted. Application fee is waived when completed online. *Faculty research:* Offshoring/outsourcing, systems analysis/synthesis, work teams, multilateral trade, path dependencies/creation.

St. John's University, College of Professional Studies, Department of Computer Science, Mathematics and Science, Queens, NY 11439. Offers MS. *Program availability:* Part-time, evening/weekend. *Entrance requirements:* For master's, baccalaureate degree, two letters of recommendation. Additional exam requirements/recommendations for international students: Required—TOEFL (minimum score 600 paper-based; 100 iBT), IELTS (minimum score 7). Electronic applications accepted.

Saint Mary's College, Graduate Programs, Program in Data Science, Notre Dame, IN 46556. Offers MS. *Program availability:* Part-time-only, blended/hybrid learning. *Faculty:* 5 full-time (2 women). *Students:* 5 full-time (1 woman), 8 part-time (3 women); includes 7 minority (2 Black or African American, non-Hispanic/Latino; 3 Asian, non-Hispanic/Latino; 2 Hispanic/Latino). Average age 37. 24 applicants, 83% accepted, 8 enrolled. *Degree requirements:* For master's, thesis optional, practicum presentation. *Entrance requirements:* For master's, GRE, GMAT, or LSAT, bachelor's degree, official transcripts, current resume or curriculum vitae, letter of recommendation, personal statement. Additional exam requirements/recommendations for international students: Required—TOEFL or IELTS. *Application deadline:* For fall admission, 6/15 priority date for domestic students. Applications are processed on a rolling basis. Application fee: $50. Electronic applications accepted. *Expenses:* Contact institution. *Financial support:* Application deadline: 3/1; applicants required to submit FAFSA. *Faculty research:* Real analysis and number theory, algorithm design and analysis, probability theory and Brownian motion, topological data analysis, data science education. *Unit head:* Kristin Kuter, Program Director, Master of Science in Data Science, 574-284-4458, E-mail: kjehring@saintmarys.edu. *Application contact:* Melissa Fruscione, Graduate Admission, 574-284-5098, E-mail: graduateadmission@saintmarys.edu. Website: http://grad.saintmarys.edu/academic-programs/ms-data-science

Saint Mary's College of California, School of Economics and Business Administration, MS in Business Analytics Program, Moraga, CA 94575. Offers MS.

Saint Peter's University, Graduate Business Programs, Program in Data Science, Jersey City, NJ 07306-5997. Offers business analytics (MS). *Program availability:* Part-time. *Entrance requirements:* Additional exam requirements/recommendations for international students: Required—TOEFL (minimum score 550 paper-based; 79 iBT), IELTS (minimum score 6.5).

Seattle University, Albers School of Business and Economics, Master of Science in Business Analytics Program, Seattle, WA 98122-1090. Offers MSBA, Certificate. *Program availability:* Part-time. *Students:* 42 full-time (22 women), 29 part-time (10 women); includes 20 minority (1 Black or African American, non-Hispanic/Latino; 15 Asian, non-Hispanic/Latino; 4 Hispanic/Latino), 29 international. Average age 28. 113 applicants, 41% accepted, 30 enrolled. In 2016, 19 Certificates awarded. *Entrance requirements:* For master's, GMAT. Additional exam requirements/recommendations for international students: Required—TOEFL or IELTS. *Application deadline:* For fall admission, 7/20 for domestic students, 9/1 for international students; for winter admission, 12/1 for international students; for spring admission, 1/1 for international students; for summer admission, 4/20 for domestic students, 4/1 for international students. Applications are processed on a rolling basis. Application fee: $55. Electronic applications accepted. *Expenses:* Contact institution. *Financial support:* In 2016–17, 17 students received support. Application deadline: 6/1. *Unit head:* Dr. Carlos De Mello e Souza, Program Director, 206-296-5700, Fax: 206-296-5795, E-mail: albersgrad@seattleu.edu. *Application contact:* Jeff Millard, Assistant Dean of Graduate Programs, 206-296-5700, E-mail: albersgrad@seattleu.edu. Website: http://www.seattleu.edu/albers/msba/

Slippery Rock University of Pennsylvania, Graduate Studies (Recruitment), College of Health, Environment, and Science, Department of Mathematics and Statistics, Slippery Rock, PA 16057-1383. Offers data analytics (MS). *Program availability:* Part-time, blended/hybrid learning. *Faculty:* 2 full-time (both women). *Students:* 3 full-time (1 woman), 17 part-time (3 women); includes 2 minority (both Black or African American, non-Hispanic/Latino). Average age 36. 36 applicants, 72% accepted, 17 enrolled. *Entrance requirements:* For master's, official transcripts; minimum GPA of 3.0; completion of following prerequisite courses with minimum C grade: differential calculus, integral calculus, probability/inferential statistics, and a programming language (C, C++, C#, Java, Python); familiarity with multivariable calculus, linear algebra, and math statistics. Additional exam requirements/recommendations for international students: Required—TOEFL (minimum score 550 paper-based; 80 iBT). *Application deadline:* For fall admission, 5/1 priority date for domestic students, 3/1 priority date for international students; for spring admission, 10/1 priority date for domestic students, 9/1 priority date for international students. Applications are processed on a rolling basis. Application fee: $25 ($30 for international students). Electronic applications accepted. *Expenses:* $646.50 per credit in-state, $936.80 per credit out-of-state; $581.45 per online credit in-state, $648.65 per online credit out-of-state. *Financial support:* In 2016–17, 2 students received support. Career-related internships or fieldwork, Federal Work-Study, institutionally sponsored loans, scholarships/grants, tuition waivers (partial), and unspecified assistantships available. Support available to part-time students. Financial award application deadline: 5/1; financial award applicants required to submit FAFSA. *Unit head:* Dr. Christy Crute, Graduate Coordinator, 724-738-4286, Fax: 724-738-4807, E-mail: christy.crute@sru.edu. *Application contact:* Brandi Weber-Mortimer, Director of Graduate Admissions, 724-738-4340, E-mail: graduate.admissions@sru.edu. Website: http://www.sru.edu/academics/colleges-and-departments/ches/departments/mathematics-and-statistics

Southern Arkansas University–Magnolia, School of Graduate Studies, Magnolia, AR 71753. Offers agriculture (MS); business administration (MBA), including agri-business, social entrepreneurship, supply chain management; clinical and mental health counseling (MS); computer and information sciences (MS), including cyber security and privacy, data science, information technology; gifted and talented (M Ed), including curriculum and instruction, educational administration and supervision, gifted and talented P-8/7-12, instructional specialist P-4; higher, adult and lifelong education (M Ed); kinesiology (M Ed), including coaching; library media and information specialist (M Ed); public administration (MPA); school counseling K-12 (M Ed); student affairs and college counseling (M Ed); teaching (MAT). *Accreditation:* NCATE. *Program availability:* Part-time, 100% online, blended/hybrid learning. *Faculty:* 36 full-time (19 women), 33 part-time/adjunct (14 women). *Students:* 605 full-time (143 women), 879 part-time (352 women); includes 130 minority (113 Black or African American, non-Hispanic/Latino; 7 American Indian or Alaska Native, non-Hispanic/Latino; 2 Asian, non-Hispanic/Latino; 2 Hispanic/Latino; 6 Two or more races, non-Hispanic/Latino), 1,048 international. Average age 28. 904 applicants, 81% accepted, 262 enrolled. In 2016, 278 master's awarded. *Degree requirements:* For master's, comprehensive exam (for some programs), thesis optional. *Entrance requirements:* For master's, GRE, MAT or GMAT, minimum GPA of 2.5. Additional exam requirements/recommendations for international students: Required—TOEFL (minimum score 550 paper-based), IELTS (minimum score 6). *Application deadline:* For fall admission, 7/20 for domestic students, 7/10 for international students; for spring admission, 12/1 for domestic students, 11/15 for international students; for summer admission, 4/1 for domestic students, 5/1 for international students. Applications are processed on a rolling basis. Application fee: $25 ($50 for international students). Electronic applications accepted. *Expenses:* Tuition, state resident: full-time $2511; part-time $279 per credit hour. Tuition, nonresident: full-time $3726; part-time $414 per credit hour. Required fees: $307 per semester. Tuition and fees vary according to course load and program. *Financial support:* Career-related internships or fieldwork, Federal Work-Study, scholarships/grants, tuition waivers (full), and unspecified assistantships available. Financial award applicants required to submit FAFSA. *Faculty research:* Alternative certification for teachers, supervision of instruction, instructional leadership, counseling. *Unit head:* Dr. Kim Bloss, Dean, School of Graduate Studies, 870-235-4150, Fax: 870-235-5227, E-mail: kkbloss@saumag.edu. *Application contact:* Shrijana Malakar, Admissions Specialist, 870-235-4150, Fax: 870-235-5227, E-mail: smalakar@saumag.edu. Website: http://www.saumag.edu/graduate

Southern Methodist University, Bobby B. Lyle School of Engineering, Program in Datacenter Systems Engineering, Dallas, TX 75275. Offers MS. *Program availability:* Part-time, online learning. *Entrance requirements:* For master's, BS in one of the engineering disciplines, computer science, one of the quantitative sciences or mathematics; minimum of two years of college-level mathematics including one year of college-level calculus.

Stevens Institute of Technology, Graduate School, Charles V. Schaefer Jr. School of Engineering and Science, Department of Computer Science, Hoboken, NJ 07030. Offers computer graphics (Certificate), including computer graphics; computer science (MS, PhD); computer systems (Certificate), including computer systems; cybersecurity (MS); database management systems (Certificate), including databases; distributed systems (Certificate), including distributed systems; elements of computer science (Certificate), including cybersecurity; enterprise and cloud computing (MS); enterprise computing (Certificate), including enterprise and cloud computing; enterprise security and information assurance (Certificate), including enterprise security and information assurance; health informatics (Certificate), including health informatics; multimedia experience and management (Certificate), including multimedia experience and management; networks and systems administration (Certificate), including cloud computing; service oriented computing (Certificate), including service oriented computing. *Program availability:* Part-time, evening/weekend. *Faculty:* 21 full-time (4 women), 13 part-time/adjunct (2 women). *Students:* 436 full-time (124 women), 72 part-time (12 women); includes 27 minority (4 Black or African American, non-Hispanic/Latino; 21 Asian, non-Hispanic/Latino; 1 Hispanic/Latino; 1 Two or more races, non-Hispanic/Latino), 423 international. Average age 25. 1,183 applicants, 54% accepted, 184 enrolled. In 2016, 225 master's, 4 doctorates, 18 other advanced degrees awarded. Terminal master's awarded for partial completion of doctoral program. *Degree requirements:* For master's, thesis optional, minimum B average in major field and overall; for doctorate, comprehensive exam (for some programs), thesis/dissertation; for Certificate, minimum B average. *Entrance requirements:* Additional exam requirements/recommendations for international students: Required—TOEFL (minimum score 74 iBT), IELTS (minimum score 6). *Application deadline:* For fall admission, 6/1 for domestic students, 4/15 for international students; for spring admission, 11/30 for domestic students, 11/1 for international students. Applications are processed on a rolling basis. Application fee: $65. Electronic applications accepted. *Expenses:* Contact institution. *Financial support:* Fellowships, research assistantships, teaching assistantships, career-related internships or fieldwork, Federal Work-Study, scholarships/grants, and unspecified assistantships available. Financial award application deadline: 2/15; financial award applicants required to submit FAFSA. *Faculty research:* Computer security, computer vision, dynamic scene analysis, privacy-

preserving data mining, visualization. *Unit head:* Giuseppe Ateniese, Director, 201-216-3741, E-mail: gatenies@stevens.edu. *Application contact:* Graduate Admissions, 888-783-8367, Fax: 888-511-1306, E-mail: graduate@stevens.edu.
Website: https://www.stevens.edu/schaefer-school-engineering-science/departments/computer-science

Stevens Institute of Technology, Graduate School, School of Business, Program in Business Intelligence and Analytics, Hoboken, NJ 07030. Offers MS, Certificate. *Program availability:* Part-time, evening/weekend. *Students:* 147 full-time (54 women), 32 part-time (6 women); includes 16 minority (1 Black or African American, non-Hispanic/Latino; 15 Asian, non-Hispanic/Latino), 139 international. Average age 26. 576 applicants, 50% accepted, 95 enrolled. In 2016, 69 master's, 32 other advanced degrees awarded. *Degree requirements:* For master's, thesis optional, minimum B average in major field and overall; for Certificate, minimum B average. *Entrance requirements:* Additional exam requirements/recommendations for international students: Required—TOEFL (minimum score 74 iBT), IELTS (minimum score 6). *Application deadline:* For fall admission, 6/1 for domestic students, 4/15 for international students; for spring admission, 11/30 for domestic students, 11/1 for international students. Applications are processed on a rolling basis. Application fee: $65. Electronic applications accepted. *Expenses:* Contact institution. *Financial support:* Fellowships, research assistantships, teaching assistantships, career-related internships or fieldwork, Federal Work-Study, scholarships/grants, and unspecified assistantships available. Financial award application deadline: 2/15; financial award applicants required to submit FAFSA. *Unit head:* Dr. Christopher Asakiewicz, Director, 201-216-8012, E-mail: christopher.asakiewicz@stevens.edu. *Application contact:* Graduate Admissions, 888-783-8367, Fax: 888-511-1306, E-mail: graduate@stevens.edu.
Website: https://www.stevens.edu/school-business/masters-programs/business-intelligence-analytics

Syracuse University, Martin J. Whitman School of Management, MS in Business Analytics Program, Syracuse, NY 13244. Offers MS. *Program availability:* Part-time, evening/weekend, 100% online. *Students:* 27 part-time (10 women); includes 11 minority (4 Black or African American, non-Hispanic/Latino; 4 Asian, non-Hispanic/Latino; 2 Hispanic/Latino; 1 Native Hawaiian or other Pacific Islander, non-Hispanic/Latino). Average age 38. 45 applicants, 82% accepted, 27 enrolled. *Degree requirements:* For master's, comprehensive exam (for full-time and online degrees). *Entrance requirements:* For master's, GMAT or GRE, resume, essay, 5-minute video interview, two letters of recommendation, transcripts (unofficial). Additional exam requirements/recommendations for international students: Required—TOEFL (minimum score 100 iBT), IELTS (minimum score 7), PTE (minimum score 68). *Application deadline:* For fall admission, 11/30 for domestic and international students; for winter admission, 1/1 for domestic and international students; for spring admission, 2/15 for domestic and international students; for summer admission, 4/19 for domestic students. Application fee: $75. Electronic applications accepted. *Expenses:* Contact institution. *Financial support:* Merit-based scholarships available. Financial award application deadline: 2/15. *Faculty research:* Data analysis and decision making, business analytics, accounting analytics, financial Services analytics, marketing analytics. *Unit head:* Don Harter, Associate Dean for Master's Programs, 315-443-3502, Fax: 315-443-9517, E-mail: dharter@syr.edu. *Application contact:* Shri Ramakrishnan, Assistant Director, Graduate Recruitment, 315-443-3497, Fax: 315-443-9517, E-mail: sramak01@syr.edu.

Texas Tech University, Rawls College of Business Administration, Lubbock, TX 79409-2101. Offers accounting (MSA, PhD), including audit/financial reporting (MSA), taxation (MSA); business statistics (MS, PhD); data science (MS); finance (PhD); general business (MBA); healthcare management (MS); information systems and operations management (PhD); management (PhD); marketing (PhD); STEM (MBA); JD/MBA; JD/MSA; MBA/M Arch; MBA/MD; MBA/MS; MBA/Pharm D. *Accreditation:* AACSB; CAHME (one or more programs are accredited). *Program availability:* Evening/weekend. *Faculty:* 74 full-time (13 women). *Students:* 741 full-time (275 women); includes 198 minority (38 Black or African American, non-Hispanic/Latino; 1 American Indian or Alaska Native, non-Hispanic/Latino; 24 Asian, non-Hispanic/Latino; 116 Hispanic/Latino; 1 Native Hawaiian or other Pacific Islander, non-Hispanic/Latino; 18 Two or more races, non-Hispanic/Latino), 95 international. Average age 28. 905 applicants, 48% accepted, 251 enrolled. In 2016, 545 master's, 13 doctorates awarded. *Degree requirements:* For master's, capstone course; for doctorate, comprehensive exam, thesis/dissertation, qualifying exams. *Entrance requirements:* For master's, GMAT, GRE, MCAT, PCAT, LSAT, or DAT, holistic review of academic credentials, resume, essay, letters of recommendation; for doctorate, GMAT, GRE, holistic review of academic credentials, resume, statement of purpose, letters of recommendation. Additional exam requirements/recommendations for international students: Required—TOEFL (minimum score 95 iBT), IELTS. *Application deadline:* For fall admission, 7/1 priority date for domestic students, 1/15 for international students; for spring admission, 12/1 priority date for domestic students, 6/15 for international students; for summer admission, 5/1 for domestic students. Applications are processed on a rolling basis. Application fee: $60. Electronic applications accepted. *Expenses:* $48,000 (MBA for Working Professionals); $20,000 (STEM MBA). *Financial support:* In 2016–17, 157 students received support, including 25 research assistantships (averaging $22,725 per year), 27 teaching assistantships (averaging $22,725 per year); fellowships, career-related internships or fieldwork, Federal Work-Study, scholarships/grants, health care benefits, and unspecified assistantships also available. Financial award application deadline: 3/1; financial award applicants required to submit FAFSA. *Faculty research:* Governmental and nonprofit accounting, securities and options futures, statistical analysis and design, leadership, consumer behavior. *Unit head:* Dr. Margaret Williams, Dean, 806-742-3188, Fax: 806-742-1092, E-mail: margaret.l.williams@ttu.edu. *Application contact:* Chathry Keaton, Applications Manager, Graduate and Professional Programs, 806-742-3184, Fax: 806-742-3958, E-mail: rawlsgrad@ttu.edu.
Website: http://www.depts.ttu.edu/rawlsbusiness/graduate/

Towson University, Program in Applied Information Technology, Towson, MD 21252-0001. Offers applied information technology (MS, D Sc); database management systems (Postbaccalaureate Certificate); information security and assurance (Postbaccalaureate Certificate); information systems management (Postbaccalaureate Certificate); Internet applications development (Postbaccalaureate Certificate); networking technologies (Postbaccalaureate Certificate); software engineering (Postbaccalaureate Certificate). *Students:* 135 full-time (50 women), 154 part-time (50 women); includes 119 minority (81 Black or African American, non-Hispanic/Latino; 26 Asian, non-Hispanic/Latino; 4 Hispanic/Latino; 8 Two or more races, non-Hispanic/Latino), 82 international. *Entrance requirements:* For master's and Postbaccalaureate Certificate, bachelor's degree, minimum GPA of 3.0; for doctorate, master's degree in computer science, information systems, information technology, or closely-related area; minimum GPA of 3.0; 2 letters of recommendation; resume. Additional exam requirements/recommendations for international students: Required—TOEFL. *Application deadline:* Applications are processed on a rolling basis. Application fee: $45. Electronic applications accepted. *Expenses:* Tuition, state resident: full-time $7580; part-time $379 per unit. Tuition, nonresident: full-time $15,700; part-time $785 per unit. *Required fees:* $2480. *Unit head:* Dr. Jinjuan Feng, Graduate Program Director, 410-704-3463, E-mail: ait@towson.edu. *Application contact:* Coverley Beidleman, Assistant Director of Graduate Admissions, 410-704-2113, Fax: 410-704-3030, E-mail: grads@towson.edu.
Website: https://www.towson.edu/fcsm/departments/emergingtech/

University of California, Berkeley, Graduate Division, School of Information, Program in Information and Data Science, Berkeley, CA 94720-1500. Offers MIDS. *Program availability:* Online only, 100% online. *Students:* 334 full-time (88 women); includes 102 minority (2 Black or African American, non-Hispanic/Latino; 1 American Indian or Alaska Native, non-Hispanic/Latino; 86 Asian, non-Hispanic/Latino; 13 Hispanic/Latino), 74 international. 1,023 applicants, 172 enrolled. *Degree requirements:* For master's, capstone project. *Application deadline:* For fall admission, 5/29 for domestic students; for spring admission, 10/10 for domestic students. Application fee: $105 ($125 for international students). Electronic applications accepted. *Financial support:* Institutionally sponsored loans available. *Unit head:* Prof. AnnaLee Saxenian, Dean, 510-642-1464, E-mail: admissions@datascience.berkeley.edu. *Application contact:* 855-678-6437, E-mail: admissions@datascience.berkeley.edu.
Website: https://datascience.berkeley.edu

University of California, San Diego, Graduate Division, Program in Data Science and Engineering, La Jolla, CA 92093. Offers MAS. *Program availability:* Part-time. *Students:* 1 full-time (0 women), 56 part-time (16 women). 98 applicants, 40% accepted, 33 enrolled. In 2016, 16 master's awarded. *Degree requirements:* For master's, capstone team project. *Entrance requirements:* For master's, 2 letters of recommendation, statement of purpose, resume/curriculum vitae. Additional exam requirements/recommendations for international students: Required—TOEFL (minimum score 550 paper-based; 80 iBT), IELTS (minimum score 7). *Application deadline:* For fall admission, 5/1 for domestic students. Application fee: $105 ($125 for international students). Electronic applications accepted. *Expenses:* Contact institution. *Financial support:* Applicants required to submit FAFSA. *Unit head:* Dr. Yoav Freund, Co-Director, 858-534-0404, E-mail: datasciencemas@eng.ucsd.edu. *Application contact:* Stacey Williams, Program Coordinator, 858-534-1069, E-mail: staceyw@eng.ucsd.edu.
Website: http://jacobsschool.ucsd.edu/mas/dse/

University of Houston–Downtown, College of Sciences and Technology, Houston, TX 77002. Offers data analytics (MS). *Program availability:* Part-time, evening/weekend. *Faculty:* 5 full-time (2 women), 1 part-time/adjunct (0 women). *Students:* 35 full-time (19 women), 31 part-time (11 women); includes 36 minority (9 Black or African American, non-Hispanic/Latino; 13 Asian, non-Hispanic/Latino; 14 Hispanic/Latino), 15 international. Average age 33. 62 applicants, 81% accepted, 38 enrolled. *Degree requirements:* For master's, capstone course, internship course or approved directed study. *Entrance requirements:* For master's, GRE. Additional exam requirements/recommendations for international students: Required—TOEFL (minimum score 553 paper-based; 81 iBT), IELTS (minimum score 6.5). *Application deadline:* For fall admission, 7/15 for domestic and international students. Application fee: $35 ($60 for international students). Electronic applications accepted. *Expenses:* $305.50 in-state, per credit; $663.50 out-of-state, per credit. *Financial support:* Federal Work-Study and scholarships/grants available. Financial award application deadline: 4/1; financial award applicants required to submit FAFSA. *Unit head:* Dr. J. Akif Uzman, Dean, 713-221-8019, E-mail: st_dean@uhd.edu. *Application contact:* Ceshia Love, Director of Graduate and International Admissions, 713-221-8093, Fax: 713-221-8658, E-mail: gradadmissions@uhd.edu.
Website: https://www.uhd.edu/academics/sciences/pages/master-in-data-analytics.aspx

University of Illinois at Springfield, Graduate Programs, College of Liberal Arts and Sciences, Program in Data Analytics, Springfield, IL 62703-5407. Offers MS. Program administered jointly by the Departments of Computer Science and Mathematical Sciences. *Program availability:* Part-time, evening/weekend, 100% online, blended/hybrid learning. *Degree requirements:* For master's, thesis or alternative, Capstone Course. *Entrance requirements:* For master's, Baccalaureate in computer science or mathematics with a minimum undergraduate GPA of 3.0 on a 4.0 scale. Written evidence of ability to perform at a high academic level by submitting a personal and academic statement. Additional exam requirements/recommendations for international students: Required—TOEFL (minimum score 500 paper-based; 61 iBT). Electronic applications accepted. *Expenses:* Tuition, state resident: part-time $329 per credit hour. Tuition, nonresident: part-time $675 per credit hour.

The University of Iowa, Henry B. Tippie College of Business, MS Program in Business Analytics, Iowa City, IA 52242-1316. Offers MS. Program also offered at the Cedar Rapids and Des Moines locations. *Program availability:* Part-time-only, evening/weekend. *Faculty:* 24 full-time (4 women), 4 part-time/adjunct (0 women). *Students:* 86 part-time (21 women). Average age 37. 105 applicants, 48% accepted, 49 enrolled. In 2016, 3 master's awarded. *Degree requirements:* For master's, 30 hours. *Entrance requirements:* Additional exam requirements/recommendations for international students: Required—TOEFL (minimum score 100 iBT). *Application deadline:* For fall admission, 7/30 priority date for domestic and international students; for spring admission, 12/30 priority date for domestic and international students; for summer admission, 4/30 priority date for domestic and international students. Application fee: $60 ($100 for international students). Electronic applications accepted. *Unit head:* Prof. Nick Street, Department Executive Officer, 319-335-0858, Fax: 319-335-1956, E-mail: nick-street@uiowa.edu. *Application contact:* Renea L. Jay, Associate Director, Non-MBA Graduate Programs, 319-335-0830, Fax: 319-335-0860, E-mail: renea-jay@uiowa.edu.
Website: https://tippie.uiowa/management-sciences

University of Maryland University College, The Graduate School, Program in Data Analytics, Adelphi, MD 20783. Offers MS, Certificate. *Program availability:* Part-time, evening/weekend, online learning. *Students:* 380 part-time (168 women); includes 178 minority (105 Black or African American, non-Hispanic/Latino; 1 American Indian or Alaska Native, non-Hispanic/Latino; 37 Asian, non-Hispanic/Latino; 25 Hispanic/Latino; 1 Native Hawaiian or other Pacific Islander, non-Hispanic/Latino; 9 Two or more races, non-Hispanic/Latino), 11 international. Average age 35. 146 applicants, 100% accepted, 75 enrolled. In 2016, 23 master's, 35 other advanced degrees awarded. *Degree requirements:* For master's, practicum. *Application deadline:* Applications are processed on a rolling basis. Application fee: $50. Electronic applications accepted. *Expenses:* Tuition, state resident: part-time $458 per credit. Tuition, nonresident: part-time $659 per credit. *Financial support:* Federal Work-Study available. Support available to part-time students. Financial award application deadline: 6/1; financial award applicants required to submit FAFSA. *Unit head:* Elena Gortcheva, Program Director, 240-684-2400, Fax: 240-684-2401, E-mail: elena.gortcheva@umuc.edu. *Application contact:* Coordinator, Graduate Admissions, 800-888-8682, Fax: 240-684-2151, E-mail: newgrad@umuc.edu.
Website: http://www.umuc.edu/academic-programs/masters-degrees/data-analytics.cfm

University of Massachusetts Dartmouth, Graduate School, Program in Data Science, North Dartmouth, MA 02747-2300. Offers MS. Program offered jointly by the Department of Computer Science and the Department of Mathematics. *Program availability:* Part-time. *Students:* 9 full-time (1 woman), 2 part-time (1 woman); includes 1 minority (Hispanic/Latino), 8 international. Average age 27. 19 applicants, 74% accepted, 5 enrolled. *Degree requirements:* For master's, thesis or alternative, practicum. *Entrance requirements:* For master's, GRE, statement of purpose (minimum

300 words), resume, official transcripts, 2 letters of recommendation. Additional exam requirements/recommendations for international students: Required—TOEFL (minimum score 533 paper-based). *Application deadline:* For fall admission, 3/1 priority date for domestic students, 2/1 priority date for international students; for spring admission, 12/15 priority date for domestic students, 12/1 priority date for international students. Application fee: $60. Electronic applications accepted. *Expenses:* Tuition, state resident: full-time $14,994; part-time $624.75 per credit. Tuition, nonresident: full-time $27,068; part-time $1127.83 per credit. *Required fees:* $405; $25.88 per credit. Tuition and fees vary according to course load and reciprocity agreements. *Financial support:* Institutionally sponsored loans and scholarships/grants available. Support available to part-time students. Financial award application deadline: 3/1; financial award applicants required to submit FAFSA. *Faculty research:* Computer programming, statistics, data mining, machine learning, data analysis involving large, diverse data sets from different application domains. *Unit head:* Ramprasad Balasubramanian, Associate Dean, College of Engineering, 508-910-6919, E-mail: r.bala@umassd.edu. *Application contact:* Steven Briggs, Director of Marketing and Recruitment for Graduate Studies, 508-999-8604, Fax: 508-999-8183, E-mail: graduate@umassd.edu.
Website: http://www.umassd.edu/datascience/masterofscience/

University of Michigan, Rackham Graduate School, Program in Survey Methodology, Ann Arbor, MI 48106. Offers data science (MS, PhD); social and psychological (MS, PhD); statistical (MS, PhD); survey methodology (Certificate). *Program availability:* Part-time. Terminal master's awarded for partial completion of doctoral program. *Degree requirements:* For master's, internships; for doctorate, comprehensive exam, thesis/dissertation. *Entrance requirements:* For master's and doctorate, GRE, 3 letters of recommendation, academic statement of purpose, personal statement, resume or curriculum vitae, academic transcripts; for Certificate, 3 letters of recommendation, academic statement of purpose, personal statement, resume or curriculum vitae, academic transcripts. Additional exam requirements/recommendations for international students: Required—TOEFL (minimum score 560 paper-based; 84 iBT). Electronic applications accepted. *Expenses:* Contact institution. *Faculty research:* Survey methodology, web surveys, survey non-response, sample design methods, adaptive survey design.

University of Michigan–Dearborn, College of Business, MS Program in Business Analytics, Dearborn, MI 48126. Offers MS. *Program availability:* Part-time, evening/weekend. *Faculty:* 33 full-time (14 women), 10 part-time/adjunct (5 women). *Students:* 45 full-time (21 women), 44 part-time (16 women); includes 9 minority (2 Black or African American, non-Hispanic/Latino; 6 Asian, non-Hispanic/Latino; 1 Two or more races, non-Hispanic/Latino), 52 international. Average age 29. 175 applicants, 59% accepted, 46 enrolled. In 2016, 38 master's awarded. *Entrance requirements:* For master's, GMAT or GRE, equivalent of four-year U.S. bachelor's degree from regionally-accredited institution, undergraduate course in finite math, pre-calculus, or calculus. Additional exam requirements/recommendations for international students: Required—TOEFL (minimum score 560 paper-based; 84 iBT), IELTS (minimum score 6.5). *Application deadline:* For fall admission, 8/1 for domestic students, 5/1 for international students; for winter admission, 12/1 for domestic students, 9/1 for international students; for spring admission, 4/1 for domestic students, 1/1 for international students. Applications are processed on a rolling basis. Application fee: $60. Electronic applications accepted. *Expenses:* Contact institution. *Financial support:* In 2016–17, 46 students received support. Scholarships/grants and non-resident tuition scholarships available. Financial award application deadline: 3/1; financial award applicants required to submit FAFSA. *Faculty research:* Business intelligence, information technology, brand management and new media, management education, operations strategy. *Unit head:* Dr. Michael Kamen, Director, Graduate Programs, 313-593-5460, E-mail: mkamen@umich.edu. *Application contact:* Joan Doherty, Academic Advisor/Counselor, 313-593-5460, Fax: 313-271-9838, E-mail: umd-gradbusiness@umich.edu.
Website: http://umdearborn.edu/cob/ms-business-analytics/

University of Michigan–Dearborn, College of Engineering and Computer Science, PhD Program in Computer and Information Science, Dearborn, MI 48128. Offers data management (PhD); data science (PhD); software engineering (PhD); systems and security (PhD). *Program availability:* Part-time, evening/weekend. *Degree requirements:* For doctorate, thesis/dissertation. *Entrance requirements:* For doctorate, GRE, bachelor's or master's degree in computer science or closely-related field. Additional exam requirements/recommendations for international students: Required—TOEFL (minimum score 84 iBT), IELTS (minimum score 6.5). *Application deadline:* For fall admission, 2/15 for domestic and international students. Application fee: $60. Electronic applications accepted. *Expenses:* Tuition, state resident: full-time $13,118; part-time $2280 per term. Tuition, nonresident: full-time $21,816; part-time $3771 per term. *Required fees:* $866; $658 per unit. $329 per term. Tuition and fees vary according to program. *Financial support:* Research assistantships, teaching assistantships, scholarships/grants, health care benefits, and unspecified assistantships available. Financial award application deadline: 2/15; financial award applicants required to submit FAFSA. *Unit head:* Dr. Brahim Medjahed, Director, 313-583-6449, E-mail: brahim@umich.edu. *Application contact:* Office of Graduate Studies Staff, 313-583-6321, E-mail: umd-graduatestudies@umich.edu.
Website: https://umdearborn.edu/cecs/departments/computer-and-information-science/graduate-programs/phd-computer-and-information-science

University of Minnesota, Twin Cities Campus, Carlson School of Management, Master of Science in Business Analytics Program, Minneapolis, MN 55455-0213. Offers MS. *Program availability:* Part-time, evening/weekend. *Faculty:* 15 full-time (2 women), 1 part-time/adjunct. *Students:* 81 full-time (38 women), 15 part-time (6 women); includes 3 minority (all Asian, non-Hispanic/Latino), 73 international. Average age 26. 355 applicants, 50% accepted, 83 enrolled. In 2016, 40 master's awarded. *Entrance requirements:* For master's, semester of college-level calculus with minimum C grade; demonstrated proficiency in computer programming (Python, R, C, C++, C#, VB, Java, Pascal, and Fortran). Additional exam requirements/recommendations for international students: Required—TOEFL (minimum score 79 iBT), IELTS (minimum score 6.5). *Application deadline:* For fall admission, 6/1 for domestic students; for summer admission, 2/1 for domestic and international students. Application fee: $75 ($95 for international students). Electronic applications accepted. *Expenses:* $42,300 resident tuition (one-year full-time program); $58,500 non-resident tuition (one-year full-time program); $1,287 per semester fees (full-time program); $1,230 per credit tuition (part-time MSBA program); $842 per semester fees (part-time program). *Financial support:* In 2016–17, 17 students received support. Scholarships/grants available. Financial award application deadline: 2/1; financial award applicants required to submit FAFSA. *Unit head:* Prof. Alok Gupta, Dean, 612-626-1402, Fax: 612-624-6374, E-mail: gupta037@umn.edu. *Application contact:* 612-625-5555, E-mail: msba@umn.edu.
Website: http://www.carlsonschool.umn.edu/degrees/master-science-in-business-analytics

University of Minnesota, Twin Cities Campus, College of Science and Engineering, Department of Computer Science and Engineering, Program in Data Science, Minneapolis, MN 55455-0213. Offers MS. *Entrance requirements:* For master's, GRE. Additional exam requirements/recommendations for international students: Required—TOEFL. Electronic applications accepted. *Faculty research:* Data collection and management, data analytics, scalable data-driven pattern discovery, and the fundamental algorithmic and statistical concepts behind these methods.

University of Nebraska at Omaha, Graduate Studies, College of Information Science and Technology, Department of Information Systems and Quantitative Analysis, Omaha, NE 68182. Offers data analytics (Certificate); information assurance (Certificate); information technology (MIT, PhD); management information systems (MS); project management (Certificate); systems analysis and design (Certificate). *Program availability:* Part-time, evening/weekend. *Faculty:* 6 full-time (1 woman). *Students:* 140 full-time (53 women), 102 part-time (29 women); includes 25 minority (9 Black or African American, non-Hispanic/Latino; 7 Asian, non-Hispanic/Latino; 6 Hispanic/Latino; 3 Two or more races, non-Hispanic/Latino), 161 international. Average age 29. 342 applicants, 50% accepted, 68 enrolled. In 2016, 84 master's, 8 doctorates, 54 other advanced degrees awarded. *Degree requirements:* For master's, comprehensive exam, thesis (for some programs); for doctorate, comprehensive exam, thesis/dissertation. *Entrance requirements:* For master's, GRE General Test, minimum GPA of 3.0, 3 letters of recommendation, writing sample, resume, official transcripts; for doctorate, GMAT or GRE General Test, minimum GPA of 3.0, 3 letters of recommendation, writing sample, resume, official transcripts; for Certificate, minimum GPA of 3.0, official transcripts. Additional exam requirements/recommendations for international students: Required—TOEFL, IELTS, PTE. *Application deadline:* For fall admission, 2/15 for domestic and international students; for spring admission, 9/15 for domestic and international students; for summer admission, 4/1 for domestic and international students. Applications are processed on a rolling basis. Application fee: $45. Electronic applications accepted. *Financial support:* In 2016–17, 30 students received support, including 24 research assistantships with tuition reimbursements available, 6 teaching assistantships with tuition reimbursements available; fellowships, career-related internships or fieldwork, Federal Work-Study, scholarships/grants, health care benefits, tuition waivers (partial), and unspecified assistantships also available. Financial award application deadline: 3/1; financial award applicants required to submit FAFSA. *Unit head:* Dr. Peter Wolcott, Chairperson, 402-554-2341, E-mail: graduate@unomaha.edu. *Application contact:* Dr. Martina Greiner, Graduate Program Chair, 402-554-2341, E-mail: graduate@unomaha.edu.

University of Nevada, Las Vegas, Graduate College, Lee Business School, Department of Management, Entrepreneurship and Technology, Las Vegas, NV 89154-6034. Offers data analytics (Certificate); data analytics and applied economics (MS); management information systems (MS, Certificate); new venture management (Certificate); MS/MS. *Program availability:* Part-time, evening/weekend. *Faculty:* 11 full-time (1 woman). *Students:* 28 full-time (12 women), 45 part-time (19 women); includes 31 minority (6 Black or African American, non-Hispanic/Latino; 9 Asian, non-Hispanic/Latino; 11 Hispanic/Latino; 5 Two or more races, non-Hispanic/Latino), 21 international. Average age 33. 64 applicants, 81% accepted, 30 enrolled. In 2016, 19 master's, 2 other advanced degrees awarded. *Degree requirements:* For master's, thesis optional. *Entrance requirements:* For master's, GMAT or GRE, bachelor's degree with minimum GPA 3.0; 2 letters of recommendation; for Certificate, GMAT or GRE. Additional exam requirements/recommendations for international students: Required—TOEFL (minimum score 550 paper-based; 80 iBT), IELTS (minimum score 7). *Application deadline:* For fall admission, 8/1 for domestic students, 5/1 for international students; for spring admission, 11/15 for domestic students, 10/1 for international students. Application fee: $60 ($95 for international students). Electronic applications accepted. *Expenses:* $269.25 per credit, $792 per 3-credit course; $9,634 per year resident; $23,274 per year non-resident; $7,094 fees non-resident (7 credits or more); $1,307 annual health insurance fee. *Financial support:* In 2016–17, 5 research assistantships with partial tuition reimbursements (averaging $10,000 per year), 5 teaching assistantships with partial tuition reimbursements (averaging $13,000 per year) were awarded; institutionally sponsored loans, scholarships/grants, health care benefits, and unspecified assistantships also available. Financial award application deadline: 3/15. *Faculty research:* Decision-making, publish or perish, ethical issues in information systems, IT-enabled decision making, business ethics. *Unit head:* Dr. Stoney Alder, Chair/Associate Professor, 702-895-2052, Fax: 702-895-4370, E-mail: stoney.alder@unlv.edu. *Application contact:* Dr. Greg Moody, Graduate Coordinator, 702-895-1365, Fax: 702-895-4370, E-mail: gregory.moody@unlv.edu.
Website: https://www.unlv.edu/met

University of New Haven, Graduate School, Tagliatela College of Engineering, Program in Data Science, West Haven, CT 06516. Offers MS. Program offered in partnership with Galvanize, exclusively in San Francisco. *Program availability:* Part-time. *Students:* 9 full-time (2 women), 28 part-time (7 women); includes 5 minority (1 Black or African American, non-Hispanic/Latino; 4 Asian, non-Hispanic/Latino), 9 international. Average age 30. 63 applicants, 67% accepted, 26 enrolled. In 2016, 5 master's awarded. Application fee: $50. *Expenses:* Contact institution. *Unit head:* Dr. Ronald Harichandran, Dean, 203-932-7167, E-mail: rharichandran@newhaven.edu. *Application contact:* Michelle Mason, Director of Graduate Enrollment, 203-932-7067, E-mail: mmason@newhaven.edu.
Website: http://galvanizeu.newhaven.edu/

The University of North Carolina at Charlotte, College of Computing and Informatics, Department of Computer Science, Charlotte, NC 28223-0001. Offers advanced databases and knowledge discovery (Graduate Certificate); computer science (MS); game design and development (Graduate Certificate). *Program availability:* Part-time, evening/weekend. *Faculty:* 27 full-time (7 women), 2 part-time/adjunct (1 woman). *Students:* 275 full-time (86 women), 87 part-time (35 women); includes 9 minority (5 Asian, non-Hispanic/Latino; 4 Hispanic/Latino), 335 international. Average age 24. 1,569 applicants, 37% accepted, 182 enrolled. In 2016, 224 master's, 9 other advanced degrees awarded. *Degree requirements:* For master's, thesis optional. *Entrance requirements:* For master's, GRE General Test, knowledge of two higher languages, data structures, algorithm analysis, operating systems or computer architecture, and two additional upper-division computer science courses; knowledge of calculus, discrete mathematics, and linear algebra; minimum undergraduate GPA of 3.0; for Graduate Certificate, BS in any scientific, engineering or business discipline; enrolled and in good standing in a graduate degree program at UNC Charlotte or have minimum GPA of 2.8 overall and 3.0 junior/senior year. Additional exam requirements/recommendations for international students: Required—TOEFL (minimum score 523 paper-based, 70 iBT) or IELTS (6.5). *Application deadline:* For fall admission, 3/1 priority date for domestic and international students; for spring admission, 10/1 priority date for domestic and international students; for summer admission, 4/1 priority date for domestic and international students. Applications are processed on a rolling basis. Application fee: $75. Electronic applications accepted. *Expenses:* Contact institution. *Financial support:* In 2016–17, 88 students received support, including 2 fellowships (averaging $36,833 per year), 23 research assistantships (averaging $10,463 per year), 62 teaching assistantships (averaging $7,000 per year); career-related internships or fieldwork, Federal Work-Study, institutionally sponsored loans, scholarships/grants, unspecified assistantships, and administrative assistantships also available. Support available to part-time students. Financial award application deadline: 3/1; financial award applicants required to submit FAFSA. *Total annual research expenditures:* $2.3 million. *Unit head:* Dr. Bojan Cukic, Chair, 704-687-6155, E-mail: bcukic@uncc.edu. *Application contact:* Kathy B. Giddings, Director of Graduate Admissions, 704-687-3366, Fax: 704-687-3279,

Database Systems

E-mail: gradadm@uncc.edu.
Website: http://cs.uncc.edu/

University of Notre Dame, Mendoza College of Business, Master of Science in Business Analytics Program, Notre Dame, IN 46556. Offers MSBA. *Program availability:* Part-time. *Faculty:* 4 full-time, 6 part-time/adjunct. *Students:* 53 part-time (10 women); includes 16 minority (4 Black or African American, non-Hispanic/Latino; 3 Asian, non-Hispanic/Latino; 8 Hispanic/Latino; 1 Native Hawaiian or other Pacific Islander, non-Hispanic/Latino). Average age 34. In 2016, 32 master's awarded. *Entrance requirements:* For master's, minimum of two years of work experience, evidence of quantitative capabilities to complete a rigorous analytical curriculum. *Application deadline:* For fall admission, 9/15 for domestic students; for summer admission, 7/15 for domestic and international students. Applications are processed on a rolling basis. Application fee: $50. Electronic applications accepted. *Expenses:* Contact institution. *Financial support:* In 2016–17, 5 students received support, including 5 fellowships (averaging $8,000 per year). Financial award application deadline: 9/15; financial award applicants required to submit FAFSA. *Faculty research:* Methods and approaches for improving decision making, applied work on decision-making models and processes for accounting; financial management; resource allocation; risk management; the development, improvement and evaluation of statistical methods and measurement issues; supply chain management and integration; design of lean service processes; and adoption of lean manufacturing systems. *Unit head:* Don Kleinmutz, Academic Director, Master of Science in Business Analytics, 312-763-3608, E-mail: dkleinmu@nd.edu. *Application contact:* Stacey Dickson, Admissions Coordinator, 574-631-1593, Fax: 574-631-6783, E-mail: sdickso1@nd.edu.
Website: http://mendoza.nd.edu/programs/specialized-masters/ms-in-business-analytics/

University of Oklahoma, Gallogly College of Engineering, Program in Data Science and Analytics, Norman, OK 73019. Offers MS. *Program availability:* Part-time, evening/weekend, 100% online. *Students:* 32 full-time (9 women), 51 part-time (9 women); includes 26 minority (6 Black or African American, non-Hispanic/Latino; 11 Asian, non-Hispanic/Latino; 8 Hispanic/Latino; 1 Two or more races, non-Hispanic/Latino), 19 international. Average age 33. 55 applicants, 65% accepted, 30 enrolled. In 2016, 1 master's awarded. *Degree requirements:* For master's, comprehensive exam, thesis. *Entrance requirements:* For master's, GRE, calculus I, calculus II, linear algebra, one year of high-level language programming. Additional exam requirements/recommendations for international students: Required—TOEFL (minimum score 79 iBT) or IELTS (minimum score 6.5). *Application deadline:* For fall admission, 4/1 for international students; for spring admission, 9/1 for international students; for summer admission, 2/1 for international students. Applications are processed on a rolling basis. Application fee: $50 ($100 for international students). *Expenses:* Tuition, state resident: full-time $4886; part-time $203.60 per credit hour. Tuition, nonresident: full-time $18,989; part-time $791.20 per credit hour. *Required fees:* $3283; $126.25 per credit hour. $126.50 per semester. *Financial support:* In 2016–17, 29 students received support. Unspecified assistantships available. Financial award application deadline: 6/1; financial award applicants required to submit FAFSA. *Faculty research:* Metaheuristic and evolutionary search, applications on data mining, dynamic data assimilation, game theory. *Unit head:* Dr. Randa L. Shehab, Co-Director, 405-325-2307, E-mail: rishehab@ou.edu. *Application contact:* Nicola Manos, Academic Program Coordinator, 405-325-6417, E-mail: datascience@ou.edu.
Website: http://ou.edu/datascience

University of Oklahoma, Gallogly College of Engineering, School of Industrial and Systems Engineering, Norman, OK 73019. Offers data science and analytics (MS); industrial and systems engineering (MS, PhD). *Faculty:* 16 full-time (3 women). *Students:* 49 full-time (13 women), 21 part-time (8 women); includes 9 minority (3 Black or African American, non-Hispanic/Latino; 2 Asian, non-Hispanic/Latino; 1 Hispanic/Latino; 3 Two or more races, non-Hispanic/Latino), 51 international. Average age 27. 131 applicants, 24% accepted, 15 enrolled. In 2016, 19 master's, 4 doctorates awarded. *Degree requirements:* For master's, comprehensive exam, thesis or alternative, 30 units with thesis, 33 without thesis; for doctorate, comprehensive exam, thesis/dissertation, 90 units. *Entrance requirements:* For master's and doctorate, GRE, BS in engineering, mathematics or equivalent. Additional exam requirements/recommendations for international students: Required—TOEFL (minimum score 79 iBT) or IELTS (minimum score 6.5). *Application deadline:* For fall admission, 6/1 priority date for domestic students, 4/1 for international students; for spring admission, 10/15 priority date for domestic students, 9/1 for international students. Applications are processed on a rolling basis. Application fee: $50 ($100 for international students). Electronic applications accepted. *Expenses:* Tuition, state resident: full-time $4886; part-time $203.60 per credit hour. Tuition, nonresident: full-time $18,989; part-time $791.20 per credit hour. *Required fees:* $3283; $126.25 per credit hour. $126.50 per semester. *Financial support:* In 2016–17, 30 students received support, including 11 research assistantships with full tuition reimbursements available (averaging $12,961 per year), 11 teaching assistantships with full tuition reimbursements available (averaging $11,160 per year); Federal Work-Study, institutionally sponsored loans, scholarships/grants, and health care benefits also available. Financial award application deadline: 6/1; financial award applicants required to submit FAFSA. *Faculty research:* Manufacturing metrology, cyber-physical-social systems, engineering design, ergonomics, data science and analytics. *Total annual research expenditures:* $527,601. *Unit head:* Dr. Shivakumar Raman, Professor/Interim Director, 405-819-3710, Fax: 405-325-7555, E-mail: raman@ou.edu. *Application contact:* Dr. Janet Allen, Chair/Graduate Liaison, 405-550-3969, Fax: 405-325-7555, E-mail: janet.allen@ou.edu.
Website: http://www.ou.edu/coe/ise.html

University of Rochester, School of Arts and Sciences, Goergen Institute for Data Science, Rochester, NY 14627. Offers MS. *Students:* 28 full-time (7 women), 1 part-time (0 women); includes 2 minority (1 Black or African American, non-Hispanic/Latino; 1 Hispanic/Latino), 20 international. Average age 24. 144 applicants, 50% accepted, 29 enrolled. In 2016, 20 master's awarded. Terminal master's awarded for partial completion of doctoral program. *Degree requirements:* For master's, comprehensive exam, thesis optional, practicum, final exam. *Entrance requirements:* For master's, GRE, bachelor's degree in a STEM field (preferred). Additional exam requirements/recommendations for international students: Required—TOEFL (minimum score 600 paper-based; 100 iBT). *Application deadline:* For fall admission, 1/1 for domestic and international students. Application fee: $60. Electronic applications accepted. *Expenses:* $1,538 per credit hour. *Financial support:* In 2016–17, 33 students received support. Tuition waivers (partial) available. Financial award application deadline: 1/15. *Unit head:* Henry Kautz, Director, 585-520-1200, E-mail: kautz@cs.rochester.edu. *Application contact:* Michele Foster, Graduate Coordinator, 585-275-4054, E-mail: michele.foster@rochester.edu.
Website: http://www.rochester.edu/data-science/

University of St. Thomas, Graduate Studies, School of Engineering, St. Paul, MN 55105-1096. Offers data science (MS); electrical engineering (MS); information technology (MS); manufacturing engineering (MS); manufacturing systems (Certificate); mechanical engineering (MS); medical device development (Certificate); regulatory science (MS); software engineering (MS); software management (MS); systems engineering (MS); technology leadership (Certificate); technology management (MS). *Accreditation:* ABET (one or more programs are accredited). *Entrance requirements:* For master's, resume, official transcripts. Additional exam requirements/recommendations for international students: Required—TOEFL (minimum score 550 paper-based). *Application deadline:* For fall admission, 8/1 priority date for domestic students; for spring admission, 1/1 priority date for domestic students. Applications are processed on a rolling basis. Application fee: $50. Electronic applications accepted. *Expenses:* Contact institution. *Financial support:* Fellowships, research assistantships, institutionally sponsored loans, and scholarships/grants available. Support available to part-time students. Financial award application deadline: 4/1; financial award applicants required to submit FAFSA. *Unit head:* Don Weinkauf, Dean, 651-962-5760, Fax: 651-962-6419, E-mail: dhweinkauf@stthomas.edu. *Application contact:* Tina M. Hansen, Graduate Program Manager, 651-962-5755, Fax: 651-962-6419, E-mail: tina.hansen@stthomas.edu.
Website: http://www.stthomas.edu/engineering/

University of San Francisco, College of Arts and Sciences, Analytics Program, San Francisco, CA 94117-1080. Offers MS. Program offered jointly with School of Management. *Faculty:* 6 full-time (1 woman), 1 (woman) part-time/adjunct. *Students:* 62 full-time (30 women); includes 12 minority (1 Black or African American, non-Hispanic/Latino; 7 Asian, non-Hispanic/Latino; 4 Hispanic/Latino, 26 international. Average age 26. 559 applicants, 18% accepted, 61 enrolled. In 2016, 32 master's awarded. *Entrance requirements:* For master's, GRE or GMAT, prerequisite courses in inferential statistics, linear algebra, computer programming (Java, Mathematica, Matlab, Python or C++), and a social science course. Additional exam requirements/recommendations for international students: Required—TOEFL, IELTS, PTE. *Application deadline:* For summer admission, 3/1 for domestic and international students. *Expenses: Tuition:* Full-time $23,310; part-time $1295 per credit. Tuition and fees vary according to course load, degree level, campus/location and program. *Financial support:* In 2016–17, 49 students received support. Applicants required to submit FAFSA. *Unit head:* Kirsten Keihl, Program Manager, 415-422-2966. *Application contact:* Mark Landerghini, Information Contact, 415-422-5101, Fax: 415-422-2217, E-mail: asgraduate@usfca.edu.
Website: https://www.usfca.edu/arts-sciences/graduate-programs/analytics

The University of South Dakota, Graduate School, Beacom School of Business, Department of Business Administration, Vermillion, SD 57069. Offers business administration (MBA); business analytics (MBA); health services administration (MBA); JD/MBA. *Accreditation:* AACSB. *Program availability:* Part-time, evening/weekend, online learning. *Degree requirements:* For master's, thesis or alternative. *Entrance requirements:* For master's, GMAT, minimum GPA of 2.7, resume. Additional exam requirements/recommendations for international students: Required—TOEFL (minimum score 550 paper-based; 79 iBT). Electronic applications accepted. *Expenses:* Contact institution.

University of Southern Indiana, Graduate Studies, Romain College of Business, Program in Business Administration, Evansville, IN 47712-3590. Offers accounting (MBA); business administration (MBA); data analytics (MBA); engineering management (MBA); health administration (MBA); human resources (MBA). *Accreditation:* AACSB. *Program availability:* Part-time, evening/weekend, 100% online, blended/hybrid learning. *Faculty:* 22 full-time (4 women), 2 part-time/adjunct (0 women). *Students:* 149 full-time (70 women), 64 part-time (29 women); includes 25 minority (17 Black or African American, non-Hispanic/Latino; 1 Asian, non-Hispanic/Latino; 5 Hispanic/Latino; 2 Two or more races, non-Hispanic/Latino), 5 international. Average age 32. In 2016, 36 master's awarded. *Entrance requirements:* For master's, GMAT or GRE, minimum GPA of 2.5, resume, 3 professional references. Additional exam requirements/recommendations for international students: Required—TOEFL (minimum score 550 paper-based; 79 iBT), IELTS (minimum score 6). *Application deadline:* For fall admission, 8/1 for domestic students, 3/1 priority date for international students. Applications are processed on a rolling basis. Application fee: $40. Electronic applications accepted. *Expenses:* Tuition, state resident: full-time $8497. Tuition, nonresident: full-time $16,691. *Required fees:* $500. *Financial support:* In 2016–17, 8 students received support. Federal Work-Study, scholarships/grants, tuition waivers (full and partial), and unspecified assistantships available. Financial award application deadline: 3/1; financial award applicants required to submit FAFSA. *Unit head:* Dr. Jack E. Smothers, Program Director, 812-461-5248, E-mail: jesmothers@usi.edu. *Application contact:* Michelle Simmons, MBA Program Assistant, 812-464-1926, Fax: 812-465-1044, E-mail: masimmons3@usi.edu.
Website: http://www.usi.edu/business/mba

University of South Florida, Muma College of Business, Department of Information Systems and Decision Sciences, Tampa, FL 33620-9951. Offers business administration (PhD), including information systems; business analytics and information systems (MS), including analytics and business intelligence, information assurance. *Program availability:* Part-time. *Faculty:* 21 full-time (5 women), 1 part-time/adjunct (0 women). *Students:* 149 full-time (54 women), 73 part-time (22 women); includes 13 minority (1 Black or African American, non-Hispanic/Latino; 6 Asian, non-Hispanic/Latino; 5 Hispanic/Latino; 1 Two or more races, non-Hispanic/Latino), 186 international. Average age 27. 1,198 applicants, 44% accepted, 117 enrolled. In 2016, 163 master's awarded. Terminal master's awarded for partial completion of doctoral program. *Degree requirements:* For master's, comprehensive exam, thesis (for some programs), thesis or practicum project; for doctorate, comprehensive exam, thesis/dissertation. *Entrance requirements:* For master's, GMAT or GRE, letters of recommendation, statement of purpose, relevant work experience; for doctorate, GMAT or GRE, letters of recommendation, personal statement, interview. Additional exam requirements/recommendations for international students: Required—TOEFL (minimum score 550 paper-based; 79 iBT) or IELTS (minimum score 6.5). *Application deadline:* For fall admission, 6/1 for domestic students, 2/1 for international students; for spring admission, 10/15 for domestic students, 9/15 for international students. Applications are processed on a rolling basis. Application fee: $30. Electronic applications accepted. *Expenses:* Tuition, state resident: full-time $7766; part-time $431.43 per credit hour. Tuition, nonresident: full-time $15,789; part-time $877.17 per credit hour. *Required fees:* $37 per term. *Financial support:* In 2016¬17, 30 students received support, including 8 research assistantships with tuition reimbursements available (averaging $11,972 per year), 22 teaching assistantships with tuition reimbursements available (averaging $9,002 per year); scholarships/grants, health care benefits, and unspecified assistantships also available. Financial award applicants required to submit FAFSA. *Faculty research:* Data mining, business intelligence, bioterrorism surveillance, health informatics/informatics, software engineering, agent-based modeling, distributed systems, statistics, electronic markets, e-commerce, business process improvement, operations management, supply chain, LEAN management, global information systems, organizational impacts of IT, enterprise resource planning, business intelligence, Web and mobile technologies, social networks, information security. *Total annual research expenditures:* $496,876. *Unit head:* Dr. Kaushal Chari, Chair and Professor, 813-974-6768, Fax: 813-974-6749, E-mail: kchari@usf.edu. *Application contact:* Judy Oates, Office Assistant, 813-974-5524, Fax: 813-974-6749, E-mail: joates@usf.edu.
Website: http://business.usf.edu/departments/isds/

The University of Texas at Dallas, School of Natural Sciences and Mathematics, Department of Mathematical Sciences, Richardson, TX 75080. Offers actuarial science (MS); mathematics (MS, PhD), including applied mathematics, data science (MS), engineering mathematics (MS), mathematics (MS); statistics (MS, PhD). *Program availability:* Part-time, evening/weekend. *Faculty:* 29 full-time (6 women), 2 part-time/adjunct (0 women). *Students:* 150 full-time (51 women), 31 part-time (12 women); includes 37 minority (8 Black or African American, non-Hispanic/Latino; 19 Asian, non-Hispanic/Latino; 8 Hispanic/Latino; 2 Two or more races, non-Hispanic/Latino), 112 international. Average age 31. 240 applicants, 43% accepted, 56 enrolled. In 2016, 36 master's, 7 doctorates awarded. *Degree requirements:* For master's, thesis optional; for doctorate, thesis/dissertation. *Entrance requirements:* For master's, GRE General Test, minimum GPA of 3.0 in upper-level course work in field; for doctorate, GRE General Test, minimum GPA of 3.5 in upper-level course work in field. Additional exam requirements/recommendations for international students: Required—TOEFL (minimum score 550 paper-based). *Application deadline:* For fall admission, 7/15 for domestic students, 5/1 priority date for international students; for spring admission, 11/15 for domestic students, 9/1 priority date for international students. Applications are processed on a rolling basis. Application fee: $50 ($100 for international students). Electronic applications accepted. *Expenses:* Tuition, state resident: full-time $12,418; part-time $690 per semester hour. Tuition, nonresident: full-time $24,150; part-time $1342 per semester hour. Tuition and fees vary according to course load. *Financial support:* In 2016–17, 114 students received support, including 1 fellowship (averaging $1,000 per year), 12 research assistantships (averaging $23,300 per year), 73 teaching assistantships with partial tuition reimbursements available (averaging $17,100 per year); career-related internships or fieldwork, Federal Work-Study, institutionally sponsored loans, scholarships/grants, and unspecified assistantships also available. Support available to part-time students. Financial award application deadline: 4/30; financial award applicants required to submit FAFSA. *Faculty research:* Sequential analysis, applications in semiconductor manufacturing, medical image analysis, computational anatomy, information theory, probability theory. *Unit head:* Dr. Vladimir Dragovic, Department Head, 972-883-6402, Fax: 972-883-6622, E-mail: mathdepthead@utdallas.edu. *Application contact:* Evangelina Bustamante, Graduate Student Coordinator, 972-883-2161, Fax: 972-883-6622, E-mail: utdmath@utdallas.edu.
Website: http://www.utdallas.edu/math

University of Virginia, Data Science Institute, Charlottesville, VA 22903. Offers MS. *Students:* 49 full-time (16 women); includes 11 minority (2 Black or African American, non-Hispanic/Latino; 5 Asian, non-Hispanic/Latino; 2 Hispanic/Latino; 2 Two or more races, non-Hispanic/Latino), 10 international. Average age 25. 437 applicants, 23% accepted, 48 enrolled. In 2016, 49 master's awarded. *Entrance requirements:* For master's, GRE or GMAT, undergraduate degree, personal statement, official transcripts, two letters of recommendation. Additional exam requirements/recommendations for international students: Required—TOEFL or IELTS. *Application deadline:* Applications are processed on a rolling basis. Application fee: $85. *Expenses:* $22,550 tuition, $2,654 fees in-state; $36,900 tuition, $3,336 fees out-of-state. *Unit head:* Donald E. Brown, Director, 434-982-2074, E-mail: deb@virginia.edu. *Application contact:* Steven Boker, Program Director, 434-243-7275, E-mail: boker@virginia.edu.
Website: http://dsi.virginia.edu/

University of Washington, Graduate School, Information School, Seattle, WA 98195. Offers information management (MSIM), including business intelligence, data science, information architecture, information consulting, information security, user experience; information science (PhD); library and information science (MLIS). *Accreditation:* ALA (one or more programs are accredited). *Program availability:* Part-time, 100% online coursework with required attendance at on-campus orientation at start of program. *Faculty:* 35 full-time (19 women), 22 part-time/adjunct (12 women). *Students:* 367 full-time (233 women), 237 part-time (170 women); includes 132 minority (20 Black or African American, non-Hispanic/Latino; 9 American Indian or Alaska Native, non-Hispanic/Latino; 59 Asian, non-Hispanic/Latino; 41 Hispanic/Latino; 3 Native Hawaiian or other Pacific Islander, non-Hispanic/Latino), 151 international. Average age 32. 1,208 applicants, 39% accepted, 254 enrolled. In 2016, 237 master's, 2 doctorates awarded. Terminal master's awarded for partial completion of doctoral program. *Degree requirements:* For master's, comprehensive exam (for some programs), thesis or alternative, capstone project; for doctorate, comprehensive exam, thesis/dissertation. *Entrance requirements:* For master's, GRE General Test, GMAT; for doctorate, GRE General Test. Additional exam requirements/recommendations for international students: Required—TOEFL (minimum score 590 paper-based; 100 iBT). *Application deadline:* For fall admission, 12/1 priority date for domestic and international students. Application fee: $85. Electronic applications accepted. *Expenses:* $785 per quarter credit hour, $23,550 per year full-time, $1,000 university fees per quarter. *Financial support:* In 2016–17, 69 students received support, including 1 fellowship with full tuition reimbursement available (averaging $6,651 per year), 27 research assistantships with full tuition reimbursements available (averaging $19,418 per year), 27 teaching assistantships with full tuition reimbursements available (averaging $19,521 per year); Federal Work-Study, institutionally sponsored loans, scholarships/grants, health care benefits, tuition waivers (full and partial), and unspecified assistantships also available. Support available to part-time students. Financial award application deadline: 10/1; financial award applicants required to submit FAFSA. *Faculty research:* Human/computer interaction, information policy and ethics, knowledge organization, information literacy and access, data science, information assurance and cyber security, digital youth, information architecture, project management, systems analyst, user experience design. *Total annual research expenditures:* $3.6 million. *Unit head:* Dr. Harry Bruce, Dean, 206-616-0985, E-mail: harryb@uw.edu. *Application contact:* Kari Brothers, Admissions Counselor, 206-616-5541, Fax: 206-616-3152, E-mail: kari683@uw.edu.
Website: http://ischool.uw.edu/

University of West Florida, College of Science and Engineering, Department of Computer Science, Pensacola, FL 32514-5750. Offers computer science (MS); database systems (MS); software engineering (MS). *Program availability:* Part-time, evening/weekend. *Degree requirements:* For master's, thesis optional. *Entrance requirements:* For master's, GRE, MAT, or GMAT, official transcripts; minimum undergraduate GPA of 3.0; letter of intent; three letters of recommendation. Additional exam requirements/recommendations for international students: Required—TOEFL (minimum score 550 paper-based). *Application deadline:* For fall admission, 6/1 for domestic and international students; for spring admission, 10/1 for domestic and international students. Applications are processed on a rolling basis. Application fee: $30. *Expenses:* Tuition, state resident: full-time $5316.12. Tuition, nonresident: full-time $11,308. *Required fees:* $583.92. Tuition and fees vary according to course load and program. *Financial support:* Fellowships with partial tuition reimbursements, research assistantships with partial tuition reimbursements, teaching assistantships with partial tuition reimbursements, and unspecified assistantships available. Financial award application deadline: 4/15; financial award applicants required to submit FAFSA. *Unit head:* Dr. Sikha Bagui, Chairperson, 850-474-3022. *Application contact:* Terry McCray, Assistant Director of Graduate Admissions, 850-473-7718, Fax: 850-473-7714, E-mail: gradadmissions@uwf.edu.
Website: http://catalog.uwf.edu/graduate/computerscience/

University of Wisconsin–La Crosse, College of Science and Health, Department of Mathematics and Statistics, La Crosse, WI 54601-3742. Offers data science (MS). *Program availability:* Part-time, online learning. *Faculty:* 4 full-time (1 woman). *Students:* 3 full-time (0 women), 42 part-time (13 women); includes 3 minority (1 American Indian or Alaska Native, non-Hispanic/Latino; 1 Asian, non-Hispanic/Latino; 1 Hispanic/Latino), 2 international. Average age 41. 42 applicants, 100% accepted, 24 enrolled. Application fee: $56. Electronic applications accepted. *Faculty research:* Scientific computing, inverse problems and uncertainty analysis for environmental computer models, Bayesian optimization. *Unit head:* Rebecca LeDocq, Chair, 608-785-6615, E-mail: rledocq@uwlax.edu. *Application contact:* Jeffrey Baggett, Director, 608-785-8393, E-mail: jbaggett@uwlax.edu.
Website: http://www.uwlax.edu/mathematics/

Villanova University, Villanova School of Business, Master of Science in Analytics Program, Villanova, PA 19085-1699. Offers MSA. *Program availability:* Part-time-only, evening/weekend, online only, 100% online. *Faculty:* 108 full-time (39 women), 32 part-time/adjunct (8 women). *Students:* 134 part-time (50 women); includes 20 minority (9 Black or African American, non-Hispanic/Latino; 8 Asian, non-Hispanic/Latino; 3 Hispanic/Latino), 2 international. Average age 34. 112 applicants, 71% accepted, 58 enrolled. In 2016, 15 master's awarded. *Degree requirements:* For master's, minimum GPA of 3.0. *Entrance requirements:* For master's, two essays, professional resume, two letters of recommendation, official transcripts, completion of undergraduate statistics course. Additional exam requirements/recommendations for international students: Required—TOEFL (minimum score 550 paper-based; 100 iBT). *Application deadline:* For fall admission, 6/30 for domestic students; for spring admission, 11/15 for domestic students. Applications are processed on a rolling basis. Application fee: $65. Electronic applications accepted. *Expenses:* Contact institution. *Financial support:* Scholarships/grants available. Financial award application deadline: 6/30; financial award applicants required to submit FAFSA. *Faculty research:* Analytics, innovation, creativity and entrepreneurship, church management, ethics, global leadership, real estate, marketing and consumer insights. *Unit head:* Michael L. Capella, Associate Dean of Graduate and Executive Business Programs, 610-519-4336, Fax: 610-519-6273, E-mail: michael.l.capella@villanova.edu. *Application contact:* Claire Bruno, Director of Recruitment and Enrollment Management, 610-519-4336, Fax: 610-519-6745, E-mail: claire.bruno@villanova.edu.
Website: http://www1.villanova.edu/villanova/business/graduate/specializedprograms/msa.html

Virginia International University, School of Computer Information Systems, Fairfax, VA 22030. Offers business intelligence (Graduate Certificate); business intelligence and data analytics (MIS); computer science (MS), including computer animation and gaming, cybersecurity, data management networking, intelligent systems, software applications development, software engineering; cybersecurity (MIS); data management (MIS); enterprise project management (MIS); health informatics (MIS); information assurance (MIS); information systems (Graduate Certificate); information systems management (MS, Graduate Certificate); information technology (MS); information technology audit and compliance (Graduate Certificate); knowledge management (MIS); software engineering (MS). *Program availability:* Part-time, online learning. *Entrance requirements:* For master's, bachelor's degree. Additional exam requirements/recommendations for international students: Required—TOEFL (minimum score 550 paper-based; 80 iBT), IELTS. Electronic applications accepted.

Wake Forest University, School of Business, MS in Business Analytics Program, Winston-Salem, NC 27106. Offers MS. *Faculty:* 10 full-time (2 women), 3 part-time/adjunct (2 women). *Students:* 39 full-time (21 women); includes 2 minority (1 Asian, non-Hispanic/Latino; 1 Hispanic/Latino), 19 international. Average age 24. 119 applicants, 45% accepted, 39 enrolled. *Degree requirements:* For master's, 37 credit hours. *Entrance requirements:* For master's, GMAT, bachelors degree in business, engineering, mathematics, economics, computer science or liberal arts; coursework in calculus and statistics. Additional exam requirements/recommendations for international students: Required—TOEFL (minimum score 600 paper-based). *Application deadline:* For fall admission, 5/1 for domestic students, 2/2 for international students. Applications are processed on a rolling basis. Application fee: $100. Electronic applications accepted. *Expenses:* Contact institution. *Financial support:* Scholarships/grants available. Financial award application deadline: 4/15; financial award applicants required to submit FAFSA. *Unit head:* Jeffrey Camm, Associate Dean, Business Analytics, 336-758-5422, Fax: 336-758-5830, E-mail: busadmissions@wfu.edu. *Application contact:* Tamara Paquee, Administrative Assistant, 336-758-5422, Fax: 336-758-5830, E-mail: busadmissions@wfu.edu.
Website: http://business.wfu.edu/ms-analytics/

Washington University in St. Louis, Olin Business School, Program in Customer Analytics, St. Louis, MO 63130-4899. Offers MS. *Program availability:* Part-time. *Faculty:* 97 full-time (22 women), 44 part-time/adjunct (13 women). *Students:* 32 full-time (19 women), 4 part-time (1 woman); includes 4 minority (all Asian, non-Hispanic/Latino), 28 international. Average age 25. 299 applicants, 24% accepted, 32 enrolled. In 2016, 29 master's awarded. *Entrance requirements:* For master's, GMAT or GRE. Additional exam requirements/recommendations for international students: Required—TOEFL, IELTS. *Application deadline:* For fall admission, 10/3 for domestic students, 2/1 priority date for international students; for winter admission, 12/1 for domestic students; for spring admission, 4/3 for domestic students. Applications are processed on a rolling basis. Application fee: $100. Electronic applications accepted. *Financial support:* Institutionally sponsored loans and scholarships/grants available. Financial award applicants required to submit FAFSA. *Unit head:* Joe Fox, Associate Dean/Director of Specialized Master's Programs, 314-935-6322, Fax: 314-935-4464, E-mail: fox@wustl.edu. *Application contact:* 314-935-7301, E-mail: olingradadmissions@wustl.edu.

Wayne State University, College of Engineering, Department of Computer Science, Detroit, MI 48202. Offers computer science (MS, PhD), including bioinformatics (PhD), computational biology (PhD); data science and business analytics (MS). Application deadline for PhD is February 17. *Faculty:* 22. *Students:* 117 full-time (41 women), 37 part-time (11 women); includes 11 minority (1 Black or African American, non-Hispanic/Latino; 8 Asian, non-Hispanic/Latino; 2 Two or more races, non-Hispanic/Latino), 121 international. Average age 27. 596 applicants, 24% accepted, 29 enrolled. In 2016, 63 master's, 13 doctorates awarded. *Degree requirements:* For master's, thesis (for some programs); for doctorate, thesis/dissertation. *Entrance requirements:* For master's, GRE, minimum GPA of 3.0, three letters of recommendation, adequate preparation in computer science and mathematics courses, personal statement; for doctorate, GRE, bachelor's or master's degree in computer science or related field; minimum GPA of 3.3 in most recent degree; three letters of recommendation; personal statement; adequate preparation in computer science and mathematics courses. Additional exam requirements/recommendations for international students: Required—TOEFL (minimum score 550 paper-based; 79 iBT), TWE (minimum score 5.5), Michigan English Language Assessment Battery (minimum score 85); Recommended—IELTS (minimum score 6.5). *Application deadline:* For fall admission, 6/1 priority date for domestic students, 5/1 priority date for international students; for winter admission, 10/1 priority date for domestic students, 9/1 priority date for international students; for spring admission, 2/1 priority date for domestic students, 1/2 priority date for international students.

Applications are processed on a rolling basis. Application fee: $50. Electronic applications accepted. *Expenses:* $18,871 per year resident tuition and fees, $36,065 per year non-resident tuition and fees. *Financial support:* In 2016–17, 67 students received support, including 4 fellowships with tuition reimbursements available (averaging $17,250 per year), 22 research assistantships with tuition reimbursements available (averaging $22,361 per year), 36 teaching assistantships with tuition reimbursements available (averaging $19,177 per year); scholarships/grants, health care benefits, and unspecified assistantships also available. Financial award applicants required to submit FAFSA. *Faculty research:* Software engineering, databases, bioinformatics, artificial intelligence, networking, distributed and parallel computing, security, graphics, visualizations. *Total annual research expenditures:* $1.5 million. *Unit head:* Dr. Loren Schwiebert, Interim Chair, 313-577-5474, E-mail: loren@wayne.edu. *Application contact:* Eric Scimeca, Graduate Program Director, 313-577-5421, E-mail: eric.scimeca@wayne.edu.
Website: http://engineering.wayne.edu/cs/

Wayne State University, College of Engineering, Department of Industrial and Systems Engineering, Detroit, MI 48202. Offers data science and business analytics (MS); engineering management (MS); industrial engineering (MS, PhD); manufacturing engineering (MS); systems engineering (Certificate). *Faculty:* 10. *Students:* 313 full-time (37 women), 140 part-time (26 women); includes 37 minority (16 Black or African American, non-Hispanic/Latino; 15 Asian, non-Hispanic/Latino; 3 Hispanic/Latino; 3 Two or more races, non-Hispanic/Latino), 340 international. Average age 28. 1,171 applicants, 42% accepted, 105 enrolled. In 2016, 117 master's, 5 doctorates awarded. *Degree requirements:* For master's, thesis (for some programs); for doctorate, thesis/dissertation. *Entrance requirements:* For master's, BS from ABET-accredited institution; for doctorate, MS in industrial engineering or operations research with minimum graduate GPA of 3.5; for Certificate, BS in engineering or other technical field from ABET-accredited institution, full-time work experience as practicing engineer or technical leader. Additional exam requirements/recommendations for international students: Required—TOEFL (minimum score 550 paper-based; 79 iBT), TWE (minimum score 5.5), Michigan English Language Assessment Battery (minimum score 85); Recommended—IELTS (minimum score 6.5). *Application deadline:* For fall admission, 6/1 priority date for domestic students, 5/1 priority date for international students; for winter admission, 10/1 priority date for domestic students, 9/1 priority date for international students; for spring admission, 2/1 priority date for domestic students, 1/1 priority date for international students. Applications are processed on a rolling basis. Application fee: $50. Electronic applications accepted. *Expenses:* $18,871 per year resident tuition and fees, $36,065 per year non-resident tuition and fees. *Financial support:* In 2016–17, 118 students received support, including 2 fellowships with tuition reimbursements available (averaging $16,000 per year), 4 research assistantships with tuition reimbursements available (averaging $18,883 per year), 12 teaching assistantships with tuition reimbursements available (averaging $19,177 per year); scholarships/grants, tuition waivers (full), and unspecified assistantships also available. Financial award applicants required to submit FAFSA. *Faculty research:* Healthcare systems engineering, product design and development, quality and reliability engineering, supply chain management and logistics. *Total annual research expenditures:* $3.2 million. *Unit head:* Dr. Leslie Monplaisir, Associate Professor/Chair, 313-577-3821, Fax: 313-577-8833, E-mail: leslie.monplaisir@wayne.edu. *Application contact:* Eric Scimeca, Graduate Program Coordinator, 313-577-0412, E-mail: eric.scimeca@wayne.edu.
Website: http://engineering.wayne.edu/ise/

Wayne State University, Mike Ilitch School of Business, Detroit, MI 48202. Offers accounting (MS, Postbaccalaureate Certificate); business (Graduate Certificate); business administration (MBA, PhD); data science (MS), including business analytics; entrepreneurship and innovation (Postbaccalaureate Certificate); finance (MS); information systems management (Postbaccalaureate Certificate); taxation (MST); JD/MBA. Application deadline for PhD is February 15. *Accreditation:* AACSB. *Program availability:* Part-time, evening/weekend. *Faculty:* 32. *Students:* 219 full-time (105 women), 941 part-time (406 women); includes 314 minority (186 Black or African American, non-Hispanic/Latino; 3 American Indian or Alaska Native, non-Hispanic/Latino; 68 Asian, non-Hispanic/Latino; 33 Hispanic/Latino; 24 Two or more races, non-Hispanic/Latino), 88 international. Average age 30. 1,119 applicants, 49% accepted, 329 enrolled. In 2016, 203 master's, 1 doctorate, 3 other advanced degrees awarded. *Degree requirements:* For doctorate, thesis/dissertation. *Entrance requirements:* For master's, GMAT, GRE, LSAT, MCAT, at least three years of relevant work experience that shows increased responsibility, or minimum GPA of 3.0 from AACSB-accredited program or 3.2 from regionally-accredited program, undergraduate degree from accredited institution; undergraduate degree in accounting, business administration, or area of business administration (for MS and MST); for doctorate, GMAT (minimum score of 600), minimum undergraduate GPA of 3.0, 3.5 upper-division or graduate; three letters of recommendation; brief essay; undergraduate degree from accredited institution; personal statement; for other advanced degree, bachelor's degree from accredited institution. Additional exam requirements/recommendations for international students: Required—TOEFL (minimum score 550 paper-based; 79 iBT), Michigan English Language Assessment Battery (minimum score 85); Recommended—IELTS (minimum score 6.5), TWE (minimum score 5.5). *Application deadline:* For fall admission, 7/1 for domestic students, 5/1 priority date for international students; for winter admission, 11/1 for domestic students, 9/1 priority date for international students; for spring admission, 3/1 for domestic students, 1/1 priority date for international students. Applications are processed on a rolling basis. Application fee: $50. Electronic applications accepted. *Expenses:* $18,871 per year resident tuition and fees, $36,065 per year non-resident tuition and fees. *Financial support:* In 2016–17, 174 students received support, including 1 fellowship with tuition reimbursement available (averaging $18,000 per year), 2 research assistantships with tuition reimbursements available (averaging $18,000 per year), 5 teaching assistantships with tuition reimbursements available (averaging $18,000 per year); scholarships/grants, health care benefits, and unspecified assistantships also available. Support available to part-time students. Financial award applicants required to submit FAFSA. *Faculty research:* Executive compensation and stock performance, consumer reactions to pricing strategies, communication across the automotive supply chain, performance of firms in sub-Saharan Africa, implementation issues with ERP software. *Unit head:* Dr. Robert Forsythe, Dean, School of Business Administration, 313-577-4501, E-mail: robert.forsythe@wayne.edu. *Application contact:* Kiantee N. Rupert-Jones, Director, 313-577-4511, Fax: 313-577-9442, E-mail: gradbusiness@wayne.edu.
Website: http://ilitchbusiness.wayne.edu/

Western Governors University, College of Information Technology, Salt Lake City, UT 84107. Offers cybersecurity and information assurance (MS); data analytics (MS); information technology management (MS). *Program availability:* Online learning. *Degree requirements:* For master's, capstone project.

Worcester Polytechnic Institute, Graduate Studies and Research, Program in Data Science, Worcester, MA 01609-2280. Offers MS, PhD, Graduate Certificate. *Program availability:* Part-time, evening/weekend. *Students:* 104 full-time (45 women), 14 part-time (4 women); includes 13 minority (2 Black or African American, non-Hispanic/Latino; 8 Asian, non-Hispanic/Latino; 3 Hispanic/Latino), 93 international. 308 applicants, 57% accepted, 62 enrolled. *Entrance requirements:* For master's, GRE or GMAT (recommended), statement of purpose; 3 letters of recommendation; for doctorate, GRE or GMAT (recommended). Additional exam requirements/recommendations for international students: Required—TOEFL (minimum score 563 paper-based; 84 iBT), IELTS, GRE or GMAT. *Application deadline:* For fall admission, 1/1 for domestic and international students; for spring admission, 10/1 for domestic and international students. Applications are processed on a rolling basis. Application fee: $70. Electronic applications accepted. *Financial support:* Research assistantships, teaching assistantships, career-related internships or fieldwork, health care benefits, and unspecified assistantships available. Financial award application deadline: 1/1; financial award applicants required to submit FAFSA. *Unit head:* Dr. Elke Rundensteiner, Director, 508-831-5815, Fax: 508-831-5776, E-mail: rundenst@wpi.edu. *Application contact:* Mary Racicot, Administrative Assistant, 508-831-4883, E-mail: mracicot@wpi.edu.
Website: http://www.wpi.edu/academics/datascience/graduate-program.html

Financial Engineering

Baruch College of the City University of New York, Weissman School of Arts and Sciences, Program in Financial Engineering, New York, NY 10010-5585. Offers MS. *Program availability:* Part-time, evening/weekend. *Faculty:* 13 full-time (3 women), 6 part-time/adjunct (0 women). *Students:* 41 full-time (10 women), 13 part-time (2 women); includes 5 minority (all Asian, non-Hispanic/Latino), 44 international. 564 applicants, 10% accepted, 43 enrolled. In 2016, 27 master's awarded. *Entrance requirements:* For master's, 3 recommendations. *Application deadline:* For fall admission, 11/15 for domestic and international students. Application fee: $125. Electronic applications accepted. *Financial support:* Career-related internships or fieldwork, Federal Work-Study, traineeships, and tuition waivers (partial) available. Financial award applicants required to submit FAFSA. *Faculty research:* Two-dimensional random walks; Brownian motion; financial applications of probability; volatility modeling; modeling equity market micro-structure for algorithmic trading; mathematical physics; properties of spatially disordered systems; stochastic processes; interacting particle systems; algebra and number theory; discrete and computational geometry; Ramsey theory; additive number theory; numerical methods for financial applications; option pricing; dynamical systems. *Unit head:* Prof. Dan Stefanica, Director, 646-312-1000. *Application contact:* Cathy Levkulic, Assistant Director, Graduate Studies, 646-312-4493, Fax: 646-312-4491, E-mail: cathy.levkulic@baruch.cuny.edu.
Website: http://mfe.baruch.cuny.edu/

Claremont Graduate University, Graduate Programs, Financial Engineering Program, Claremont, CA 91711-6160. Offers MSFE, MS/EMBA, MS/MBA, MS/PhD. *Students:* 23 full-time (3 women), 15 part-time (4 women); includes 5 minority (1 Black or African American, non-Hispanic/Latino; 2 Asian, non-Hispanic/Latino; 2 Hispanic/Latino), 29 international. Average age 26. In 2016, 19 master's awarded. *Entrance requirements:* For master's, GRE General Test or GMAT. Additional exam requirements/recommendations for international students: Required—TOEFL (minimum score 75 iBT). *Application deadline:* For fall admission, 2/1 priority date for domestic and international students. Applications are processed on a rolling basis. Application fee: $80. Electronic applications accepted. *Expenses: Tuition:* Full-time $44,328; part-time $1847 per unit. *Required fees:* $600; $300 per semester. Tuition and fees vary according to course load and program. *Financial support:* Fellowships, Federal Work-Study, institutionally sponsored loans, and scholarships/grants available. Support available to part-time students. Financial award application deadline: 2/15; financial award applicants required to submit FAFSA. *Unit head:* Henry Schellhorn, Academic Director, 909-607-4168, E-mail: henry.schellhorn@cgu.edu. *Application contact:* Julianna Gomez-Anton, Assistant Director of Admissions, 909-607-4999, E-mail: julianna.gomez-anton@cgu.edu.
Website: https://www.cgu.edu/academics/program/financial-engineering/

Columbia University, Fu Foundation School of Engineering and Applied Science, Department of Industrial Engineering and Operations Research, New York, NY 10027. Offers financial engineering (MS); industrial engineering and operations research (MS, Eng Sc D, PhD); management science and engineering (MS); MS/MBA. *Program availability:* Part-time, evening/weekend, online learning. *Degree requirements:* For doctorate, thesis/dissertation, oral and written qualifying exams. *Entrance requirements:* For master's and doctorate, GRE General Test. Additional exam requirements/recommendations for international students: Required—TOEFL, IELTS, PTE. Electronic applications accepted. *Faculty research:* Applied probability and optimization; financial engineering, modeling risk including credit risk and systemic risk, asset allocation, portfolio execution, behavioral finance, agent-based model in finance; revenue management; management and optimization of service systems, call centers, capacity allocation in healthcare systems, inventory control for vaccines; energy, smart grids, demand shaping, managing renewable energy sources, energy-aware scheduling.

HEC Montreal, School of Business Administration, Master of Science Programs in Administration, Program in Financial Engineering, Montréal, QC H3T 2A7, Canada. Offers M Sc. All courses are given in English. *Students:* 56 full-time (10 women), 8 part-time (0 women). 38 applicants, 61% accepted, 11 enrolled. In 2016, 21 master's awarded. *Degree requirements:* For master's, one foreign language, thesis. *Entrance requirements:* For master's, Test de francais international (TFI) with minimum score of 850 (for those who have never studied in French), BBA, undergraduate degree in another field, degree deemed equivalent by program director and minimum GPA of 3.0 on 4.3 scale. *Application deadline:* For fall admission, 3/15 for domestic and international students; for winter admission, 9/15 for domestic and international students. Application fee: $86 Canadian dollars. Electronic applications accepted. *Expenses: Tuition, area resident:* Part-time $77.80 Canadian dollars per credit. Tuition, state resident: full-time $2797 Canadian dollars; part-time $240.92 Canadian dollars per credit. Tuition, nonresident: full-time $8673 Canadian dollars; part-time $531.43 Canadian dollars per credit. *International tuition:* $19,131 Canadian dollars full-time. *Required fees:* $1699 Canadian dollars; $40.58 Canadian dollars per credit. $67.32 Canadian dollars per term. Tuition and fees vary according to degree level and program. *Financial support:* Research assistantships, teaching assistantships, and scholarships/

grants available. Financial award application deadline: 9/2. *Unit head:* Dr. Marie-Helene Jobin, Director, 514-340-6283, E-mail: marie-helene.jobin@hec.ca. *Application contact:* Marianne de Moura, Administrative Director, 514-340-7106, Fax: 514-340-6411, E-mail: marianne.de-moura@hec.ca.
Website: http://www.hec.ca/programmes/maitrises/maitrise-ingenierie-financiere/index.html

The International University of Monaco, Graduate Programs, Monte Carlo, Monaco. Offers entrepreneurship (EMBA, MBA); financial engineering (M Sc); hedge fund and private equity (M Sc); international marketing (EMBA, MBA); international wealth management (M Sc); luxury goods and services (EMBA, M Sc, MBA); wealth and asset management (EMBA, MBA). *Program availability:* Part-time. *Degree requirements:* For master's, comprehensive exam (for some programs), applied research project. *Entrance requirements:* Additional exam requirements/recommendations for international students: Required—TOEFL (minimum score 550 paper-based), IELTS. Electronic applications accepted. *Faculty research:* Gaming, leadership, disintermediation.

New York University, Polytechnic School of Engineering, Department of Finance and Risk Engineering, New York, NY 10012-1019. Offers financial engineering (MS, Advanced Certificate), including capital markets (MS); computational finance (MS); financial technology (MS); financial technology management (Advanced Certificate); organizational behavior (Advanced Certificate); risk management (Advanced Certificate); technology management (Advanced Certificate). MS program also offered in Manhattan. *Program availability:* Part-time, evening/weekend. *Degree requirements:* For master's, comprehensive exam (for some programs), thesis (for some programs). *Entrance requirements:* For master's, GMAT, minimum B average in undergraduate course work. Additional exam requirements/recommendations for international students: Required—TOEFL (minimum score 550 paper-based; 80 iBT); Recommended—IELTS (minimum score 6.5). Electronic applications accepted. *Faculty research:* Optimal control theory, general modeling and analysis, risk parity optimality, a new algorithmic approach to entangled political economy.

North Carolina State University, Graduate School, College of Agriculture and Life Sciences and College of Engineering and College of Physical and Mathematical Sciences, Program in Financial Mathematics, Raleigh, NC 27695. Offers MFM. *Program availability:* Part-time. *Degree requirements:* For master's, thesis optional, project/internship. *Entrance requirements:* For master's, GRE General Test. Additional exam requirements/recommendations for international students: Required—TOEFL (minimum score 550 paper-based). Electronic applications accepted. *Faculty research:* Financial mathematics modeling and computation, futures, options and commodities markets, real options, credit risk, portfolio optimization.

Princeton University, Graduate School, School of Engineering and Applied Science, Department of Operations Research and Financial Engineering, Princeton, NJ 08544-1019. Offers M Eng, MSE, PhD. Terminal master's awarded for partial completion of doctoral program. *Degree requirements:* For master's, thesis (MSE); for doctorate, thesis/dissertation, general exam. *Entrance requirements:* For master's and doctorate, GRE General Test, official transcript(s), 3 letters of recommendation, personal statement. Additional exam requirements/recommendations for international students: Required—TOEFL. Electronic applications accepted. *Faculty research:* Applied and computational mathematics; financial mathematics; optimization, queuing theory, and machine learning; statistics and stochastic analysis; transportation and logistics.

Rensselaer Polytechnic Institute, Graduate School, Lally School of Management, Program in Quantitative Finance and Risk Analytics, Troy, NY 12180-3590. Offers MS, MS/MBA. *Program availability:* Part-time. *Faculty:* 35 full-time (10 women), 7 part-time/adjunct (0 women). *Students:* 56 full-time (26 women), 14 part-time (7 women). 405 applicants, 47% accepted, 47 enrolled. In 2016, 32 master's awarded. *Entrance requirements:* For master's, GMAT or GRE. Additional exam requirements/recommendations for international students: Required—TOEFL (minimum score 570 paper-based; 88 iBT), IELTS (minimum score 6.5), PTE (minimum score 60). *Application deadline:* For fall admission, 1/1 for domestic and international students. Applications are processed on a rolling basis. Application fee: $75. Electronic applications accepted. *Expenses:* Tuition: Full-time $49,520; part-time $2060 per credit hour. *Required fees:* $2617. *Financial support:* Scholarships/grants available. Financial award application deadline: 1/1. *Unit head:* Dr. Gina O'Connor, Associate Dean, 518-276-6842, E-mail: oconng@rpi.edu. *Application contact:* Office of Graduate Admissions, 518-276-6216, E-mail: gradadmissions@rpi.edu.
Website: https://lallyschool.rpi.edu/graduate-programs/ms-qfra

Stevens Institute of Technology, Graduate School, School of Systems and Enterprises, Program in Financial Engineering, Hoboken, NJ 07030. Offers MS, PhD, Certificate. *Program availability:* Part-time, evening/weekend. *Students:* 223 full-time (65 women), 55 part-time (10 women); includes 22 minority (4 Black or African American, non-Hispanic/Latino; 16 Asian, non-Hispanic/Latino; 2 Hispanic/Latino), 207 international. Average age 26. 535 applicants, 67% accepted, 132 enrolled. In 2016, 98 master's, 1 doctorate, 29 other advanced degrees awarded. *Degree requirements:* For master's, thesis optional, minimum B average in major field and overall; for doctorate, comprehensive exam (for some programs), thesis/dissertation; for Certificate, minimum B average. *Entrance requirements:* Additional exam requirements/recommendations for international students: Required—TOEFL (minimum score 74 iBT), IELTS (minimum score 6). *Application deadline:* For fall admission, 6/1 for domestic students, 4/15 for international students; for spring admission, 11/30 for domestic students, 11/1 for international students. Applications are processed on a rolling basis. Application fee: $65. Electronic applications accepted. *Expenses:* Contact institution. *Financial support:* Fellowships, research assistantships, teaching assistantships, career-related internships or fieldwork, Federal Work-Study, scholarships/grants, and unspecified assistantships available. Financial award application deadline: 2/15; financial award applicants required to submit FAFSA. *Faculty research:* Quantitative finance, financial services analytics, financial risk and regulation, financial systems. *Unit head:* Dr. Khaldoun Khashanah, Director, 201-216-5446, Fax: 201-216-5541, E-mail: kkhashan@stevens.edu. *Application contact:* Graduate Admissions, 888-783-8367, Fax: 888-511-1306, E-mail: graduate@stevens.edu.
Website: https://www.stevens.edu/school-systems-enterprises/masters-degree-programs/financial-engineering

Temple University, Fox School of Business, Specialized Master's Programs, Philadelphia, PA 19122-6096. Offers accountancy (MS); actuarial science (MS); finance (MS); financial engineering (MS); human resource management (MS); innovation management and entrepreneurship (MS); marketing (MS); statistics (MS). MS in innovation management and entrepreneurship delivered jointly with College of Engineering. *Accreditation:* AACSB. *Program availability:* Part-time. *Entrance*

requirements: For master's, GRE General Test or GMAT, minimum undergraduate GPA of 3.0. Additional exam requirements/recommendations for international students: Required—TOEFL (minimum score 600 paper-based; 100 iBT), IELTS (minimum score 7.5).

University of California, Berkeley, Graduate Division, Haas School of Business, Master of Financial Engineering Program, Berkeley, CA 94720-1500. Offers MFE. *Faculty:* 13 full-time (2 women), 7 part-time/adjunct. *Students:* 69 full-time (11 women); includes 3 minority (all Asian, non-Hispanic/Latino), 60 international. Average age 26. 543 applicants, 17% accepted, 69 enrolled. In 2016, 68 master's awarded. *Degree requirements:* For master's, comprehensive exam, internship/applied finance project. *Entrance requirements:* For master's, GMAT or GRE (waived if candidate holds PhD), bachelor's degree with minimum GPA of 3.0 or equivalent; two recommendation letters; proficiency in math, statistics, computer science, and economics/finance. Additional exam requirements/recommendations for international students: Required—TOEFL (minimum score 570 paper-based, 90 iBT) or IELTS (minimum score 7). *Application deadline:* For spring admission, 10/3 for domestic and international students. Applications are processed on a rolling basis. Application fee: $275. Electronic applications accepted. *Expenses:* Contact institution. *Financial support:* Non-resident tuition waivers for some students, such as veterans available. *Faculty research:* Financial economics, modern portfolio theory, valuation of exotic options, mortgage markets. *Unit head:* Linda Kreitzman, Assistant Dean and Executive Director, 510-643-4329, Fax: 510-643-4345, E-mail: lindak@haas.berkeley.edu. *Application contact:* Diane Nguyen, Admissions Specialist and Assistant Director, 510-642-4417, Fax: 510-643-4345, E-mail: mfe@haas.berkeley.edu.
Website: http://mfe.berkeley.edu

University of California, Los Angeles, Graduate Division, UCLA Anderson School of Management, Los Angeles, CA 90095-1481. Offers accounting (PhD); behavioral decision making (PhD); business administration (EMBA, MBA); decisions, operations, and technology management (PhD); finance (PhD); financial engineering (MFE); global economics and management (PhD); management and organizations (PhD); marketing (PhD); strategy and policy (PhD); DDS/MBA; MBA/JD; MBA/MD; MBA/MLAS; MBA/MLIS; MBA/MN; MBA/MPH; MBA/MPP; MBA/MSCS; MBA/MURP. *Accreditation:* AACSB. *Program availability:* Part-time, evening/weekend. *Faculty:* 90 full-time (20 women), 98 part-time/adjunct (19 women). *Students:* 865 full-time (263 women), 1,201 part-time (337 women); includes 710 minority (48 Black or African American, non-Hispanic/Latino; 1 American Indian or Alaska Native, non-Hispanic/Latino; 505 Asian, non-Hispanic/Latino; 88 Hispanic/Latino; 4 Native Hawaiian or other Pacific Islander, non-Hispanic/Latino; 64 Two or more races, non-Hispanic/Latino), 451 international. Average age 31. 5,643 applicants, 26% accepted, 881 enrolled. In 2016, 807 master's, 7 doctorates awarded. *Degree requirements:* For master's, comprehensive exam, field consulting project; internship (for MBA); thesis/dissertation (for MFE); for doctorate, comprehensive exam, thesis/dissertation, oral and written qualifying exams. *Entrance requirements:* For master's, GMAT or GRE, 4-year bachelor's degree or equivalent; 2 letters of recommendation; essays (1 for MBA, 2 for FEMBA and MFE); 4-8 years of full-time work experience (for FEMBA); minimum eight years of work experience with at least three years at management level (for EMBA); for doctorate, GMAT or GRE, bachelor's degree from college or university of fully-recognized standing, minimum B average during junior and senior years of undergraduate years, 3 letters of recommendation, statement of purpose. Additional exam requirements/recommendations for international students: Required—TOEFL (minimum score 560 paper-based; 87 iBT), IELTS (minimum score 7). *Application deadline:* For fall admission, 10/6 priority date for domestic and international students; for winter admission, 1/5 for domestic and international students; for spring admission, 4/12 for domestic and international students. Applications are processed on a rolling basis. Application fee: $200. Electronic applications accepted. *Expenses:* Contact institution. *Financial support:* In 2016–17, 633 students received support, including 455 fellowships (averaging $30,253 per year); research assistantships with partial tuition reimbursements available, teaching assistantships with partial tuition reimbursements available, career-related internships or fieldwork, institutionally sponsored loans, and scholarships/grants also available. Support available to part-time students. *Faculty research:* Finance/global economics, entrepreneurship, accounting, human resources/organizational behavior, marketing, behavioral decision making. *Total annual research expenditures:* $1.1 million. *Unit head:* Dr. Judy D. Olian, Dean/Chair in Management, 310-825-7982, Fax: 310-206-2073, E-mail: judy.olian@anderson.ucla.edu. *Application contact:* Alex Lawrence, Assistant Dean and Director of MBA Admissions, 310-825-6944, Fax: 310-825-8582, E-mail: mba.admissions@anderson.ucla.edu.
Website: http://www.anderson.ucla.edu/

University of Illinois at Urbana–Champaign, Graduate College, College of Engineering, Joint Program in Financial Engineering, Champaign, IL 61820. Offers MS. Program offered jointly with College of Business. *Degree requirements:* For master's, thesis or alternative.

The University of Tulsa, Graduate School, Collins College of Business, Program in Finance, Tulsa, OK 74104-3189. Offers corporate finance (MS); investments and portfolio management (MS); risk management (MS); JD/MSF; MBA/MSF; MSF/MSAM. *Program availability:* Part-time, evening/weekend. *Faculty:* 9 full-time (1 woman). *Students:* 7 full-time (2 women), 4 part-time (0 women); includes 2 minority (both Hispanic/Latino), 3 international. Average age 26. 72 applicants, 39% accepted, 3 enrolled. In 2016, 5 master's awarded. *Degree requirements:* For master's, thesis optional. *Entrance requirements:* For master's, GMAT. Additional exam requirements/recommendations for international students: Required—TOEFL (minimum score 577 paper-based; 91 iBT), IELTS (minimum score 6.5). *Application deadline:* Applications are processed on a rolling basis. Application fee: $55. Electronic applications accepted. *Expenses:* Tuition: Full-time $22,230; part-time $1235 per credit hour. *Required fees:* $990 per semester. Tuition and fees vary according to course load. *Financial support:* In 2016–17, 3 students received support, including 1 fellowship with full tuition reimbursement available (averaging $10,500 per year), 3 teaching assistantships with full tuition reimbursements available (averaging $10,347 per year); research assistantships with tuition reimbursements available, career-related internships or fieldwork, Federal Work-Study, institutionally sponsored loans, scholarships/grants, health care benefits, tuition waivers (full and partial), and unspecified assistantships also available. Support available to part-time students. Financial award application deadline: 2/1; financial award applicants required to submit FAFSA. *Unit head:* Dr. Ralph Jackson, Associate Dean, 918-631-2242, Fax: 918-631-2142, E-mail: ralph-jackson@utulsa.edu. *Application contact:* Information Contact, 918-631-2242, E-mail: graduate-business@utulsa.edu.

Game Design and Development

Academy of Art University, Graduate Programs, School of Game Development, San Francisco, CA 94105-3410. Offers MA, MFA. *Program availability:* Part-time, 100% online. *Faculty:* 11 full-time (0 women), 22 part-time/adjunct (1 woman). *Students:* 91 full-time (26 women), 35 part-time (8 women); includes 25 minority (5 Black or African American, non-Hispanic/Latino; 5 Asian, non-Hispanic/Latino; 11 Hispanic/Latino; 4 Two or more races, non-Hispanic/Latino), 63 international. Average age 29. 39 applicants, 100% accepted, 33 enrolled. In 2016, 28 master's awarded. *Degree requirements:* For master's, final review. *Entrance requirements:* For master's, statement of intent; resume; portfolio/reel; official college transcripts. *Application deadline:* Applications are processed on a rolling basis. Application fee: $50. Electronic applications accepted. *Expenses: Tuition:* Part-time $982 per unit. *Financial support:* Career-related internships or fieldwork, Federal Work-Study, and scholarships/grants available. Financial award application deadline: 8/10; financial award applicants required to submit FAFSA. *Unit head:* 800-544-ARTS, E-mail: info@academyart.edu. *Application contact:* 800-544-ARTS, E-mail: info@academyart.edu.
Website: http://www.academyart.edu/academics/game-development

Concordia University, School of Graduate Studies, Faculty of Engineering and Computer Science, Concordia Institute for Information Systems Engineering (CIISE), Montréal, QC H3G 1M8, Canada. Offers 3D graphics and game development (Certificate); information and systems engineering (PhD); information systems security (M Eng, MA Sc); quality systems engineering (M Eng, MA Sc); service engineering and network management (Certificate).

DePaul University, College of Computing and Digital Media, Chicago, IL 60604. Offers animation (MA, MFA); business information technology (MS); cinema (MFA); cinema production (MS); computational finance (MS); computer and information sciences (PhD); computer game development (MS); computer information and network security (MS); computer science (MS); e-commerce technology (MS); health informatics (MS); human-computer interaction (MS); information systems (MS); information technology project management (MS); network engineering and management (MS); predictive analytics (MS); screenwriting (MFA); software engineering (MS); JD/MS. *Program availability:* Part-time, evening/weekend, online learning. *Degree requirements:* For master's, thesis (for some programs); for doctorate, comprehensive exam, thesis/dissertation. *Entrance requirements:* For master's, GRE or GMAT (for MS in computational finance only), bachelor's degree, resume (MS in predictive analytics only), IT experience (MS in information technology project management only), portfolio review (all MFA programs and MA in animation); for doctorate, GRE, master's degree in computer science. Additional exam requirements/recommendations for international students: Required—TOEFL (minimum score 590 paper-based; 80 iBT), IELTS (minimum score 6.5), PTE (minimum score 53). Electronic applications accepted. *Expenses:* Contact institution. *Faculty research:* Data mining, computer science, human-computer interaction, security, animation and film.

Full Sail University, Game Design Master of Science Program - Campus, Winter Park, FL 32792-7437. Offers MS.

Iona College, School of Arts and Science, Department of Computer Science, New Rochelle, NY 10801-1890. Offers computer science (MS); cyber security (MS); game development (MS). *Program availability:* Part-time, evening/weekend. *Faculty:* 6 full-time (3 women), 1 (woman) part-time/adjunct. *Students:* 13 full-time (2 women), 9 part-time (1 woman); includes 4 minority (2 Black or African American, non-Hispanic/Latino; 2 Hispanic/Latino), 8 international. Average age 27. 28 applicants, 79% accepted, 6 enrolled. In 2016, 7 master's awarded. *Degree requirements:* For master's, thesis optional. *Entrance requirements:* For master's, minimum GPA of 3.0. Additional exam requirements/recommendations for international students: Required—TOEFL (minimum score 550 paper-based; 80 iBT), IELTS (minimum score 6.5). *Application deadline:* For fall admission, 8/1 priority date for domestic students, 5/1 priority date for international students; for spring admission, 1/1 priority date for domestic students, 9/1 priority date for international students. Applications are processed on a rolling basis. Application fee: $50. Electronic applications accepted. *Expenses: Tuition:* Full-time $19,692; part-time $1094 per credit. *Required fees:* $245 per term. Tuition and fees vary according to program. *Financial support:* In 2016–17, 7 students received support, including 2 research assistantships with full tuition reimbursements available; tuition waivers (partial) and unspecified assistantships also available. Support available to part-time students. Financial award application deadline: 4/15; financial award applicants required to submit FAFSA. *Faculty research:* Parallel procession, data mining, machine learning, cyber security, medical imaging. *Unit head:* Robert Schiaffino, PhD, Chair, 914-633-2338, E-mail: rschiaffino@iona.edu. *Application contact:* Katelyn Brunck, Assistant Director, Graduate Admissions, 914-633-2451, Fax: 914-633-2277, E-mail: kbrunck@iona.edu.
Website: http://www.iona.edu/Academics/School-of-Arts-Science/Departments/Computer-Science/Graduate-Programs.aspx

Long Island University–LIU Post, College of Arts, Communications and Design, Brookville, NY 11548-1300. Offers art (MA); clinical art therapy (MA); clinical art therapy and counseling (MA); digital game design and development (MA); fine arts and design (MFA); interactive multimedia arts (MA); music (MA); theater (MA); theatre (MFA). *Faculty:* 36 full-time (19 women), 144 part-time/adjunct (74 women). *Students:* 123 full-time (91 women), 21 part-time (18 women); includes 25 minority (6 Black or African American, non-Hispanic/Latino; 1 American Indian or Alaska Native, non-Hispanic/Latino; 6 Asian, non-Hispanic/Latino; 11 Hispanic/Latino; 1 Two or more races, non-Hispanic/Latino), 32 international. 175 applicants, 73% accepted, 46 enrolled. In 2016, 68 master's awarded. *Degree requirements:* For master's, variable foreign language requirement, comprehensive exam (for some programs), thesis (for some programs). *Entrance requirements:* For master's, performance audition or portfolio. Additional exam requirements/recommendations for international students: Required—TOEFL (minimum score 550 paper-based; 79 iBT). *Application deadline:* Applications are processed on a rolling basis. Application fee: $50. Electronic applications accepted. *Expenses: Tuition:* Full-time $28,272; part-time $1178 per credit. *Required fees:* $451 per term. Tuition and fees vary according to degree level and program. *Financial support:* In 2016–17, 6 research assistantships with partial tuition reimbursements (averaging $1,020 per year), 14 teaching assistantships with partial tuition reimbursements (averaging $670 per year) were awarded; career-related internships or fieldwork, Federal Work-Study, institutionally sponsored loans, scholarships/grants, tuition waivers (full and partial), and unspecified assistantships also available. Support available to part-time students. Financial award application deadline: 2/15; financial award applicants required to submit FAFSA. *Faculty research:* Game design, new plays, musical theatre, compositions for wind symphony, jazz ensemble, jazz combo and vocal jazz. *Unit head:* Dr. Christine Kerr, Acting Dean, 516-299-2309, E-mail: christine.kerr@liu.edu. *Application contact:* Carol Zerah, Director of Graduate Admissions, 516-299-2900, Fax: 516-299-2137, E-mail: post-enroll@liu.edu.

Website: http://www.liu.edu/CWPost/Academics/School-of-Visual-Arts-Communications-and-Digital-Technologies

Michigan State University, The Graduate School, College of Communication Arts and Sciences, Department of Telecommunication, Information Studies, and Media, East Lansing, MI 48824. Offers digital media arts and technology (MA); information and telecommunication management (MA); information, policy and society (MA); serious game design (MA). *Entrance requirements:* Additional exam requirements/recommendations for international students: Required—TOEFL. Electronic applications accepted.

New York University, Tisch School of the Arts, Game Center, Brooklyn, NY 11201. Offers MFA.

Rochester Institute of Technology, Graduate Enrollment Services, Golisano College of Computing and Information Sciences, Interactive Games and Media School, MS Program in Game Design and Development, Rochester, NY 14623. Offers MS. *Students:* 30 full-time (3 women), 1 part-time (0 women); includes 2 minority (1 Black or African American, non-Hispanic/Latino; 1 Hispanic/Latino), 24 international. Average age 23. 127 applicants, 43% accepted, 19 enrolled. In 2016, 7 master's awarded. *Degree requirements:* For master's, thesis or alternative, capstone experience. *Entrance requirements:* For master's, portfolio, minimum GPA of 3.0 (recommended). Additional exam requirements/recommendations for international students: Required—TOEFL (minimum score 570 paper-based; 88 iBT), IELTS (minimum score 6.5), PTE (minimum score 61). *Application deadline:* For fall admission, 2/15 priority date for domestic and international students. Applications are processed on a rolling basis. Application fee: $60. Electronic applications accepted. *Expenses:* $1,742 per credit hour. *Financial support:* In 2016–17, 28 students received support. Research assistantships with partial tuition reimbursements available, teaching assistantships with partial tuition reimbursements available, career-related internships or fieldwork, scholarships/grants, and unspecified assistantships available. Support available to part-time students. Financial award applicants required to submit FAFSA. *Faculty research:* Game balance, game engines, games for health, graphics, e-sports. *Unit head:* Dr. Jessica Bayliss, Graduate Program Director, 585-475-2507, E-mail: jdbics@rit.edu. *Application contact:* Diane Ellison, Associate Vice President, Graduate Enrollment Services, 585-475-2229, Fax: 585-475-7164, E-mail: gradinfo@rit.edu.
Website: https://www.rit.edu/gccis/igm/ms-game-design-development-overview

Sacred Heart University, Graduate Programs, College of Arts and Sciences, Department of Computer Science, Fairfield, CT 06825. Offers computer science (MS); computer science gaming (MS); cybersecurity (MS); information technology (MS). *Program availability:* Part-time, evening/weekend. *Faculty:* 7 full-time (2 women), 21 part-time/adjunct (4 women). *Students:* 256 full-time (93 women), 138 part-time (44 women); includes 28 minority (11 Black or African American, non-Hispanic/Latino; 3 Asian, non-Hispanic/Latino; 14 Hispanic/Latino), 319 international. Average age 25. 1,187 applicants, 65% accepted, 72 enrolled. In 2016, 275 master's awarded. *Degree requirements:* For master's, thesis or alternative. *Entrance requirements:* For master's, bachelor's degree, minimum GPA of 3.0. Additional exam requirements/recommendations for international students: Required—TOEFL (minimum score 570 paper-based, 80 iBT), TWE, or IELTS (6.5); Recommended—TSE. *Application deadline:* For fall admission, 5/15 for international students; for spring admission, 10/30 for international students. Applications are processed on a rolling basis. Application fee: $75. Electronic applications accepted. *Expenses:* $850 per credit part-time. *Financial support:* Unspecified assistantships available. Financial award applicants required to submit FAFSA. *Unit head:* Domenick Pinto, Director of the School of Computing, 203-371-7789, Fax: 203-371-0506, E-mail: pintod@sacredheart.edu. *Application contact:* William Sweeney, Director of Graduate Admissions Operations, 203-365-7619, Fax: 203-365-4732, E-mail: gradstudies@sacredheart.edu.
Website: http://www.sacredheart.edu/academics/collegeofartssciences/academicdepartments/computerscienceinformationtechnology/graduatedegreesandcertificates/

Savannah College of Art and Design, Graduate School, Program in Interactive Design and Game Development, Savannah, GA 31402-3146. Offers MA, MFA. *Program availability:* Part-time, 100% online. *Faculty:* 14 full-time (4 women), 5 part-time/adjunct (0 women). *Students:* 66 full-time (29 women), 34 part-time (8 women); includes 10 minority (2 Black or African American, non-Hispanic/Latino; 6 Asian, non-Hispanic/Latino; 2 Hispanic/Latino), 56 international. Average age 28. 124 applicants, 40% accepted, 22 enrolled. In 2016, 27 master's awarded. *Degree requirements:* For master's, final project (for MA); thesis (for MFA). *Entrance requirements:* For master's, GRE (recommended), portfolio (submitted in digital format), audition or writing submission, resume, statement of purpose, two letters of recommendation. Additional exam requirements/recommendations for international students: Required—TOEFL (minimum score 550 paper-based, 85 iBT), IELTS (minimum score 6.5), or ACTFL. *Application deadline:* For fall admission, 4/1 for domestic and international students. Applications are processed on a rolling basis. Application fee: $40. Electronic applications accepted. *Expenses: Tuition:* Full-time $36,045. Tuition and fees vary according to course load. *Financial support:* Career-related internships or fieldwork, Federal Work-Study, and scholarships/grants available. Financial award application deadline: 4/1; financial award applicants required to submit FAFSA. *Unit head:* SuAnne Fu, Chair, Interactive Design and Game Development. *Application contact:* Jenny Jaquillard, Executive Director of Admissions, Recruitment and Events, 912-525-5100, Fax: 912-525-5985, E-mail: admission@scad.edu.
Website: http://www.scad.edu/academics/programs/interactive-design-and-game-development

Shepherd University, Hollywood CG School of Digital Arts, Los Angeles, CA 90065. Offers game art and design (MSIT); visual effects and animation (MSIT). *Degree requirements:* For master's, exam, thesis, or portfolio.

University of Advancing Technology, Master of Science Program in Technology, Tempe, AZ 85283-1042. Offers advancing computer science (MS); emerging technologies (MS); game production and management (MS); information assurance (MS); technology leadership (MS). *Degree requirements:* For master's, project or thesis. *Entrance requirements:* Additional exam requirements/recommendations for international students: Required—TOEFL (minimum score 550 paper-based). Electronic applications accepted. *Faculty research:* Artificial intelligence, fractals, organizational management.

University of Central Florida, College of Arts and Humanities, Florida Interactive Entertainment Academy, Orlando, FL 32816. Offers MS. *Faculty:* 9 full-time (0 women), 3 part-time/adjunct (1 woman). *Students:* 70 full-time (17 women), 53 part-time (15 women); includes 36 minority (8 Black or African American, non-Hispanic/Latino; 5 Asian, non-Hispanic/Latino; 17 Hispanic/Latino; 6 Two or more races, non-Hispanic/Latino), 17 international. Average age 26. 138 applicants, 64% accepted, 70 enrolled. In

2016, 63 master's awarded. *Degree requirements:* For master's, thesis or alternative. *Entrance requirements:* For master's, GRE. Additional exam requirements/recommendations for international students: Required—TOEFL. *Application deadline:* For fall admission, 7/15 for domestic students. Application fee: $30. Electronic applications accepted. *Expenses:* Contact institution. *Financial support:* Application deadline: 3/1; applicants required to submit FAFSA. *Unit head:* Ben Noel, Executive Director, 407-235-3580, Fax: 407-317-7094, E-mail: bnoel@fiea.ucf.edu. *Application contact:* Assistant Director, Graduate Admissions, 407-823-2766, Fax: 407-823-6442, E-mail: gradadmissions@ucf.edu.
Website: http://www.fiea.ucf.edu/

The University of North Carolina at Charlotte, College of Computing and Informatics, Department of Computer Science, Charlotte, NC 28223-0001. Offers advanced databases and knowledge discovery (Graduate Certificate); computer science (MS); game design and development (Graduate Certificate). *Program availability:* Part-time, evening/weekend. *Faculty:* 27 full-time (7 women), 2 part-time/adjunct (1 woman). *Students:* 275 full-time (86 women), 87 part-time (35 women); includes 9 minority (5 Asian, non-Hispanic/Latino; 4 Hispanic/Latino), 335 international. Average age 24. 1,569 applicants, 37% accepted, 182 enrolled. In 2016, 224 master's, 9 other advanced degrees awarded. *Degree requirements:* For master's, thesis optional. *Entrance requirements:* For master's, GRE General Test, knowledge of two higher languages, data structures, algorithm analysis, operating systems or computer architecture, and two additional upper-division computer science courses; knowledge of calculus, discrete mathematics, and linear algebra; minimum undergraduate GPA of 3.0; for Graduate Certificate, BS in any scientific, engineering or business discipline; enrolled and in good standing in a graduate degree program at UNC Charlotte or have minimum GPA of 2.8 overall and 3.0 junior/senior year. Additional exam requirements/recommendations for international students: Required—TOEFL (minimum score 523 paper-based, 70 iBT) or IELTS (6.5). *Application deadline:* For fall admission, 3/1 priority date for domestic and international students; for spring admission, 10/1 priority date for domestic and international students; for summer admission, 4/1 priority date for domestic and international students. Applications are processed on a rolling basis. Application fee: $75. Electronic applications accepted. *Expenses:* Contact institution. *Financial support:* In 2016–17, 88 students received support, including 2 fellowships (averaging $36,833 per year), 23 research assistantships (averaging $10,463 per year), 62 teaching assistantships (averaging $7,000 per year); career-related internships or fieldwork, Federal Work-Study, institutionally sponsored loans, scholarships/grants, unspecified assistantships, and administrative assistantships also available. Support available to part-time students. Financial award application deadline: 3/1; financial award applicants required to submit FAFSA. *Total annual research expenditures:* $2.3 million. *Unit head:* Dr. Bojan Cukic, Chair, 704-687-6155, E-mail: bcukic@uncc.edu. *Application contact:* Kathy B. Giddings, Director of Graduate Admissions, 704-687-3366, Fax: 704-687-3279, E-mail: gradadm@uncc.edu.
Website: http://cs.uncc.edu/

University of Southern California, Graduate School, Viterbi School of Engineering, Department of Computer Science, Los Angeles, CA 90089. Offers computer networks (MS); computer science (MS, PhD); computer security (MS); game development (MS); high performance computing and simulations (MS); human language technology (MS); intelligent robotics (MS); multimedia and creative technologies (MS); software engineering (MS). *Program availability:* Part-time, evening/weekend, online learning. *Entrance requirements:* For master's and doctorate, GRE General Test. Additional exam requirements/recommendations for international students: Required—TOEFL. Electronic applications accepted. *Faculty research:* Databases, computer graphics and computer vision, software engineering, networks and security, robotics, multimedia and virtual reality.

University of Utah, Graduate School, College of Engineering, Program in Entertainment Arts and Engineering, Salt Lake City, UT 84112. Offers game art (MEAE); game engineering (MEAE); game production (MEAE); technical art (MEAE). *Program*

availability: Part-time. *Faculty:* 7 full-time (0 women). *Students:* 120 full-time (21 women), 1 part-time (0 women); includes 19 minority (1 Black or African American, non-Hispanic/Latino; 9 Asian, non-Hispanic/Latino; 5 Hispanic/Latino; 1 Native Hawaiian or other Pacific Islander, non-Hispanic/Latino; 3 Two or more races, non-Hispanic/Latino), 55 international. Average age 25. 160 applicants, 50% accepted, 60 enrolled. In 2016, 53 master's awarded. *Entrance requirements:* For master's, GRE (recommended for game engineering and game production track applicants). Additional exam requirements/recommendations for international students: Required—TOEFL (minimum score 550 paper-based; 80 iBT), IELTS (minimum score 6.5). *Application deadline:* For fall admission, 2/28 for domestic and international students. Application fee: $65. Electronic applications accepted. *Expenses:* Contact institution. *Financial support:* In 2016–17, 50 research assistantships with partial tuition reimbursements (averaging $7,000 per year), 53 teaching assistantships with partial tuition reimbursements (averaging $7,000 per year) were awarded; career-related internships or fieldwork, scholarships/grants, health care benefits, and unspecified assistantships also available. Financial award application deadline: 2/28; financial award applicants required to submit FAFSA. *Faculty research:* Games for health, simulation. *Unit head:* Corrinne Lewis, Academic Program Manager, 801-585-6491, E-mail: corrinne.lewis@utah.edu. *Application contact:* Hallie Huber, Program Coordinator/Academic Advisor, 801-581-5460, E-mail: hallie.huber@utah.edu.
Website: http://eae.utah.edu/

Virginia International University, School of Computer Information Systems, Fairfax, VA 22030. Offers business intelligence (Graduate Certificate); business intelligence and data analytics (MIS); computer science (MS), including computer animation and gaming, cybersecurity, data management networking, intelligent systems, software applications development, software engineering; cybersecurity (MIS); data management (MIS); enterprise project management (MIS); health informatics (MIS); information assurance (MIS); information systems (Graduate Certificate); information systems management (MS, Graduate Certificate); information technology (MS); information technology audit and compliance (Graduate Certificate); knowledge management (MIS); software engineering (MS). *Program availability:* Part-time, online learning. *Entrance requirements:* For master's, bachelor's degree. Additional exam requirements/recommendations for international students: Required—TOEFL (minimum score 550 paper-based; 80 iBT), IELTS. Electronic applications accepted.

West Virginia University, Statler College of Engineering and Mineral Resources, Lane Department of Computer Science and Electrical Engineering, Program in Interactive Technologies and Serious Gaming, Morgantown, WV 26506. Offers Graduate Certificate. *Entrance requirements:* Additional exam requirements/recommendations for international students: Required—TOEFL or IELTS. Electronic applications accepted.

Worcester Polytechnic Institute, Graduate Studies and Research, Program in Interactive Media and Game Development, Worcester, MA 01609-2280. Offers MS. *Program availability:* Part-time, evening/weekend. *Students:* 15 full-time (2 women), 9 international. 57 applicants, 67% accepted, 11 enrolled. In 2016, 7 master's awarded. *Entrance requirements:* For master's, GRE (recommended), 3 letters of recommendation, statement of purpose, portfolio (recommended). Additional exam requirements/recommendations for international students: Required—TOEFL (minimum score 563 paper-based; 84 iBT), IELTS (minimum score 7). *Application deadline:* For fall admission, 1/1 for domestic and international students; for spring admission, 10/1 for domestic and international students. Applications are processed on a rolling basis. Application fee: $70. Electronic applications accepted. *Financial support:* Research assistantships, teaching assistantships, and health care benefits available. Financial award application deadline: 1/1; financial award applicants required to submit FAFSA. *Unit head:* Jennifer DeWinter, Graduate Coordinator, 508-831-4977, Fax: 508-831-5776, E-mail: jdewinter@wpi.edu. *Application contact:* Alison Darling, Administrative Assistant, 508-831-4977, E-mail: ajdarling@wpi.edu.
Website: http://www.wpi.edu/academics/imgd

Health Informatics

Adelphi University, College of Nursing and Public Health, Program in Health Information Technology, Garden City, NY 11530-0701. Offers MS, Advanced Certificate. *Students:* 12 full-time (9 women), 104 part-time (79 women); includes 76 minority (33 Black or African American, non-Hispanic/Latino; 1 American Indian or Alaska Native, non-Hispanic/Latino; 29 Asian, non-Hispanic/Latino; 9 Hispanic/Latino; 4 Two or more races, non-Hispanic/Latino). Average age 35. 88 applicants, 61% accepted, 32 enrolled. In 2016, 2 master's awarded. *Entrance requirements:* Additional exam requirements/recommendations for international students: Required—TOEFL (minimum score 550 paper-based; 80 iBT), IELTS (minimum score 6.5). Application fee: $50. *Expenses:* Contact institution. *Financial support:* Research assistantships, teaching assistantships, career-related internships or fieldwork, institutionally sponsored loans, scholarships/grants, traineeships, and unspecified assistantships available. Support available to part-time students. *Unit head:* Dr. Thomas Virgona, Director, 516-877-4516, E-mail: tvirgona@adelphi.edu. *Application contact:* Christine Murphy, Director of Admissions, 516-877-3050, Fax: 516-877-3039, E-mail: graduateadmissions@adelphi.edu.

American Public University System, AMU/APU Graduate Programs, Charles Town, WV 25414. Offers accounting (MBA, MS); applied business analytics (MBA, MS); criminal justice (MA), including business administration, emergency and disaster management, general (MA, MS); educational leadership (M Ed); emergency and disaster management (MA); entrepreneurship (MBA); environmental policy and management (MS), including environmental planning, environmental sustainability, fish and wildlife management, general (MA, MS), global environmental management; finance (MBA); general (MBA); government contracting and acquisition (MBA); health care administration (MBA); health information management (MS); history (MA), including American history, ancient and classical history, European history, global history, public history; homeland security (MA), including business administration, counterterrorism studies, criminal justice, cyber, emergency management and public health, intelligence studies, transportation security; homeland security resource allocation (MBA); humanities (MA); information technology (MS), including digital forensics, enterprise software development, information assurance and security, IT project management; information technology management (MBA); intelligence studies (MA), including criminal intelligence, cyber, general (MA, MS), homeland security, intelligence analysis, intelligence collection, intelligence management, intelligence operations, terrorism studies; international relations and conflict resolution (MA), including comparative and security issues, conflict resolution, international and transnational security issues, peacekeeping; legal studies (MA); management (MA), including strategic consulting; marketing (MBA); military history (MA), including American military history, American Revolution, civil war, war since 1945, World War II; military studies (MA), including joint

warfare, strategic leadership; national security studies (MA), including cyber, general (MA, MS), homeland security, regional security studies, security and intelligence analysis, terrorism studies; nonprofit management (MBA); political science (MA), including American politics and government, comparative government and development, general (MA, MS), international relations, public policy; psychology (MA); public administration (MPA), including disaster management, environmental policy, health policy, human resources, national security, organizational management, security management; public health (MPH); reverse logistics management (MA); security management (MA); space studies (MS), including aerospace science, general (MA, MS), planetary science; sports and health sciences (MS); sports management (MBA); teaching (M Ed), including autism spectrum disorder, curriculum and instruction for elementary teachers, elementary reading, English language learners, instructional leadership, online learning, special education, STEAM (STEM plus the arts); transportation and logistics management (MA). *Program availability:* Part-time, evening/weekend, online only, 100% online. *Faculty:* 401 full-time (228 women), 1,678 part-time/adjunct (781 women). *Students:* 378 full-time (184 women), 8,455 part-time (3,484 women); includes 2,972 minority (1,552 Black or African American, non-Hispanic/Latino; 52 American Indian or Alaska Native, non-Hispanic/Latino; 211 Asian, non-Hispanic/Latino; 791 Hispanic/Latino; 70 Native Hawaiian or other Pacific Islander, non-Hispanic/Latino; 296 Two or more races, non-Hispanic/Latino), 109 international. Average age 37. In 2016, 3,185 master's awarded. *Degree requirements:* For master's, comprehensive exam or practicum. *Entrance requirements:* For master's, official transcript showing earned bachelor's degree from institution accredited by recognized accrediting body. Additional exam requirements/recommendations for international students: Required—TOEFL (minimum score 550 paper-based), IELTS (minimum score 6.5). *Application deadline:* Applications are processed on a rolling basis. Application fee: $0. Electronic applications accepted. *Expenses: Tuition:* Part-time $350 per credit hour. *Required fees:* $50 per course. *Financial support:* Scholarships/grants available. Financial award applicants required to submit FAFSA. *Unit head:* Dr. Karan Powell, President, 877-468-6268, Fax: 304-724-3780. *Application contact:* Terry Grant, Vice President of Enrollment Management, 877-468-6268, Fax: 304-724-3780, E-mail: info@apus.edu.
Website: http://www.apus.edu

American Sentinel University, Graduate Programs, Aurora, CO 80014. Offers business administration (MBA); business intelligence (MS); computer science (MSCS); health information management (MS); healthcare (MBA); information systems (MSIS); nursing (MSN). *Program availability:* Part-time, evening/weekend, online learning. *Entrance requirements:* Additional exam requirements/recommendations for international students: Required—TOEFL (minimum score 600 paper-based). Electronic applications accepted.

Arkansas Tech University, College of Natural and Health Sciences, Russellville, AR 72801. Offers fisheries and wildlife biology (MS); health informatics (MS); nursing (MSN). *Program availability:* Part-time. *Students:* 15 full-time (8 women), 43 part-time (27 women); includes 13 minority (8 Black or African American, non-Hispanic/Latino; 1 Asian, non-Hispanic/Latino; 3 Hispanic/Latino; 1 Two or more races, non-Hispanic/Latino). Average age 37. In 2016, 16 master's awarded. *Degree requirements:* For master's, thesis (for some programs), project. *Entrance requirements:* For master's, GRE General Test. Additional exam requirements/recommendations for international students: Required—TOEFL (minimum score 550 paper-based; 79 iBT), IELTS (minimum score 6). *Application deadline:* For fall admission, 3/1 priority date for domestic students, 5/1 priority date for international students; for spring admission, 10/1 priority date for domestic and international students. Applications are processed on a rolling basis. Application fee: $25 ($75 for international students). Electronic applications accepted. *Expenses:* Tuition, state resident: full-time $4932; part-time $274 per credit hour. Tuition, nonresident: full-time $9864; part-time $548 per credit hour. *Required fees:* $513 per semester. Tuition and fees vary according to course load. *Financial support:* In 2016–17, research assistantships with full tuition reimbursements (averaging $4,800 per year), teaching assistantships with full tuition reimbursements (averaging $4,800 per year) were awarded; career-related internships or fieldwork, Federal Work-Study, scholarships/grants, health care benefits, and unspecified assistantships also available. Support available to part-time students. Financial award application deadline: 4/15; financial award applicants required to submit FAFSA. *Unit head:* Dr. Jeff Robertson, Dean, 479-968-0498, E-mail: jrobertson@atu.edu. *Application contact:* Dr. Mary B. Gunter, Dean of Graduate College, 479-968-0398, Fax: 479-964-0542, E-mail: gradcollege@atu.edu.
Website: http://www.atu.edu/nhs/

Augusta University, College of Allied Health Sciences, Program in Public Health, Augusta, GA 30912. Offers environmental health (MPH); health informatics (MPH); health management (MPH); social and behavioral sciences (MPH). *Accreditation:* CEPH. *Program availability:* Part-time. *Degree requirements:* For master's, thesis (for some programs). *Entrance requirements:* For master's, GRE General Test, three letters of recommendation. Additional exam requirements/recommendations for international students: Required—TOEFL. Electronic applications accepted.

Barry University, College of Health Sciences, Graduate Certificate Programs, Miami Shores, FL 33161-6695. Offers health care leadership (Certificate); health care planning and informatics (Certificate); histotechnology (Certificate); long term care management (Certificate); medical group practice management (Certificate); quality improvement and outcomes management (Certificate).

Benedictine University, Graduate Programs, Program in Public Health, Lisle, IL 60532. Offers administration of health care institutions (MPH); dietetics (MPH); disaster management (MPH); health education (MPH); health information systems (MPH); MBA/MPH; MPH/MS. *Accreditation:* CEPH. *Program availability:* Part-time, evening/weekend, online learning. *Students:* 89 full-time (72 women), 462 part-time (358 women); includes 129 minority (61 Black or African American, non-Hispanic/Latino; 5 American Indian or Alaska Native, non-Hispanic/Latino; 51 Asian, non-Hispanic/Latino; 11 Hispanic/Latino; 1 Native Hawaiian or other Pacific Islander, non-Hispanic/Latino), 12 international. 195 applicants, 86% accepted, 143 enrolled. In 2016, 190 master's awarded. *Entrance requirements:* For master's, MAT, GRE, or GMAT. Additional exam requirements/recommendations for international students: Required—TOEFL (minimum score 550 paper-based). *Application deadline:* For fall admission, 9/1 for domestic students; for winter admission, 12/1 for domestic students; for spring admission, 2/15 for domestic students. Application fee: $40. *Expenses: Tuition:* Full-time $15,600; part-time $650 per hour. *Required fees:* $300. One-time fee: $125 part-time. Tuition and fees vary according to class time, course load, campus/location and program. *Financial support:* Career-related internships or fieldwork and health care benefits available. Support available to part-time students. *Unit head:* Dr. Georgeen Polyak, Director, 630-829-6217, E-mail: gpolyak@ben.edu. *Application contact:* Kari Gibbons, Associate Vice President, Enrollment Center, 630-829-6200, Fax: 630-829-6584, E-mail: kgibbons@ben.edu.

Boston University, Metropolitan College, Department of Computer Science, Boston, MA 02215. Offers computer information systems (MS), including computer networks, data analytics, database management and business intelligence, health informatics, IT project management, security, Web application development; computer networks (Certificate); computer science (MS); data analytics (Certificate); digital forensics (Certificate); health informatics (Certificate); information technology project management (Certificate); software development (MS); software engineering in health care systems (Certificate); telecommunications (MS), including security. *Program availability:* Part-time, evening/weekend, online learning. *Faculty:* 13 full-time (3 women), 43 part-time/adjunct (3 women). *Students:* 108 full-time (36 women), 1,294 part-time (364 women); includes 428 minority (115 Black or African American, non-Hispanic/Latino; 2 American Indian or Alaska Native, non-Hispanic/Latino; 187 Asian, non-Hispanic/Latino; 98 Hispanic/Latino; 2 Native Hawaiian or other Pacific Islander, non-Hispanic/Latino; 24 Two or more races, non-Hispanic/Latino), 314 international. Average age 33. 463 applicants, 79% accepted, 248 enrolled. In 2016, 311 master's awarded. *Degree requirements:* For master's, thesis optional. *Entrance requirements:* For master's and Certificate, official transcripts from regionally-accredited bachelor's degree program, 3 letters of recommendation, professional resume, personal statement. Additional exam requirements/recommendations for international students: Required—TOEFL (minimum score 84 iBT), IELTS. *Application deadline:* For fall admission, 6/1 priority date for international students; for spring admission, 10/1 priority date for international students. Applications are processed on a rolling basis. Application fee: $85. Electronic applications accepted. *Expenses:* Contact institution. *Financial support:* In 2016–17, 11 research assistantships (averaging $8,400 per year) were awarded; unspecified assistantships also available. Support available to part-time students. Financial award applicants required to submit FAFSA. *Faculty research:* Medical informatics, Web technologies, telecom and networks, security and forensics, software engineering, programming languages, multimedia and artificial intelligence (AI), information systems and IT project management. *Unit head:* Dr. Anatoly Temkin, Chair, 617-353-2566, Fax: 617-353-2367, E-mail: csinfo@bu.edu. *Application contact:* Lesley Moreau, Academic Program Coordinator, 617-353-2566, Fax: 617-353-2367, E-mail: metcs@bu.edu.
Website: http://www.bu.edu/csmet/

Brandeis University, Rabb School of Continuing Studies, Division of Graduate Professional Studies, Master of Science in Health and Medical Informatics Program, Waltham, MA 02454-9110. Offers MS. *Program availability:* Part-time-only. *Faculty:* 45 part-time/adjunct (16 women). *Students:* 43 part-time (24 women); includes 18 minority (8 Black or African American, non-Hispanic/Latino; 9 Asian, non-Hispanic/Latino; 1 Two or more races, non-Hispanic/Latino). Average age 37. 15 applicants, 100% accepted, 14 enrolled. In 2016, 12 master's awarded. *Entrance requirements:* For master's, four-year bachelor's degree from regionally-accredited U.S. institution or equivalent; official transcript(s) from every college or university attended; resume or curriculum vitae; statement of goals; letter of recommendation. Additional exam requirements/recommendations for international students: Required—TWE (minimum score 4.5), TOEFL (minimum scores: 600 paper-based, 100 iBT), IELTS (7), or PTE (68). *Application deadline:* For fall admission, 6/21 priority date for domestic and international students; for winter admission, 9/13 priority date for domestic and international students; for spring admission, 12/20 priority date for domestic and international students; for summer admission, 3/14 priority date for domestic and international students. Applications are processed on a rolling basis. Application fee: $50. Electronic applications accepted. *Expenses:* $3,400 per course, $100 graduation fee. *Financial support:* Applicants required to submit FAFSA. *Unit head:* Arthur Harvey, Chair, 781-736-8787, E-mail: aharv0001@brandeis.edu. *Application contact:* Frances Stearns, Director of Admissions and Recruitment, 781-736-8785, E-mail: fstearns@brandeis.edu.
Website: http://www.brandeis.edu/gps

Brooklyn College of the City University of New York, School of Natural and Behavioral Sciences, Department of Computer and Information Science, Brooklyn, NY 11210-2889. Offers computer science (MA); health informatics (MS); information systems (MS); parallel and distributed computing (Advanced Certificate). *Program availability:* Part-time, evening/weekend. *Degree requirements:* For master's, comprehensive exam, thesis or alternative. *Entrance requirements:* For master's, previous course work in computer science, 2 letters of recommendation. Additional exam requirements/recommendations for international students: Required—TOEFL (minimum score 525 paper-based; 70 iBT). Electronic applications accepted. *Faculty research:* Networks and distributed systems, programming languages, modeling and computer applications, algorithms, artificial intelligence, theoretical computer science.

Canisius College, Graduate Division, School of Education and Human Services, Office of Professional Studies, Buffalo, NY 14208-1098. Offers applied nutrition (MS, Certificate); community and school health (MS); health and human performance (MS); health information technology (MS); respiratory care (MS). *Program availability:* Part-time, evening/weekend, 100% online, blended/hybrid learning. *Faculty:* 2 full-time (0 women), 6 part-time/adjunct (3 women). *Students:* 18 full-time (13 women), 59 part-time (43 women); includes 11 minority (5 Black or African American, non-Hispanic/Latino; 2 Asian, non-Hispanic/Latino; 3 Hispanic/Latino; 1 Two or more races, non-Hispanic/Latino), 2 international. Average age 36. 48 applicants, 85% accepted, 25 enrolled. In 2016, 42 master's awarded. *Entrance requirements:* For master's, GRE (recommended), bachelor's degree transcript, two letters of recommendation, current licensure (for applied nutrition), minimum GPA of 2.7, current resume. Additional exam requirements/recommendations for international students: Required—TOEFL (minimum score 550 paper-based, 79 iBT), IELTS (minimum score 6.5), or CAEL (minimum score 70). *Application deadline:* Applications are processed on a rolling basis. Application fee: $25. Electronic applications accepted. Application fee is waived when completed online. *Expenses: Tuition:* Full-time $14,742. *Required fees:* $724. *Financial support:* Career-related internships or fieldwork, Federal Work-Study, scholarships/grants, tuition waivers (partial), and unspecified assistantships available. Support available to part-time students. Financial award application deadline: 4/30; financial award applicants required to submit FAFSA. *Faculty research:* Nutrition, community and school health; community and health; health and human performance applied; nutrition and respiratory care. *Unit head:* Sandy McKenna, Director, Professional Studies, 716-888-8296, E-mail: mckekkas@canisius.edu. *Application contact:* Kathleen B. Davis, Vice President of Enrollment Management, 716-888-2500, Fax: 716-888-3195, E-mail: daviskb@canisius.edu.
Website: http://www.canisius.edu/graduate/

Capella University, School of Public Service Leadership, Master's Programs in Nursing, Minneapolis, MN 55402. Offers diabetes nursing (MSN); general nursing (MSN); gerontology nursing (MSN); health information management (MS); nurse educator (MSN); nursing leadership and administration (MSN). *Accreditation:* AACN.

Chatham University, Program in Healthcare Informatics, Pittsburgh, PA 15232-2826. Offers MHI. *Program availability:* Online learning. *Expenses: Tuition:* Full-time $16,254; part-time $903 per credit hour. *Required fees:* $468; $26 per credit hour.

Claremont Graduate University, Graduate Programs, Center for Information Systems and Technology, Claremont, CA 91711-6160. Offers cybersecurity and networking (MS); data science and analytics (MS); electronic commerce (PhD); geographic information systems (MS); health informatics (MS); information systems (Certificate); IT strategy and innovation (MS); knowledge management (PhD); systems development (PhD); telecommunications and networking (PhD); MBA/MS. *Program availability:* Part-time. *Faculty:* 8 full-time (1 woman), 1 part-time/adjunct (0 women). *Students:* 60 full-time (18 women), 81 part-time (27 women); includes 34 minority (7 Black or African American, non-Hispanic/Latino; 18 Asian, non-Hispanic/Latino; 7 Hispanic/Latino; 1 Native Hawaiian or other Pacific Islander, non-Hispanic/Latino; 1 Two or more races, non-Hispanic/Latino), 80 international. Average age 35. In 2016, 21 master's, 10 doctorates awarded. *Degree requirements:* For doctorate, comprehensive exam, thesis/dissertation, portfolio. *Entrance requirements:* For master's and doctorate, GMAT, GRE General Test. Additional exam requirements/recommendations for international students: Required—TOEFL (minimum score 75 iBT). *Application deadline:* For fall admission, 2/1 priority date for domestic and international students. Applications are processed on a rolling basis. Application fee: $80. Electronic applications accepted. *Expenses: Tuition:* Full-time $44,328; part-time $1847 per unit. *Required fees:* $600; $300 per semester. Tuition and fees vary according to course load and program. *Financial support:* Fellowships, research assistantships, teaching assistantships, Federal Work-Study, institutionally sponsored loans, and scholarships/grants available. Support available to part-time students. Financial award application deadline: 2/15; financial award applicants required to submit FAFSA. *Faculty research:* Man-machine interaction, organizational aspects of computing, implementation of information systems, information systems practice. *Unit head:* Lorne Olfman, Acting Director, 909-607-3035, E-mail: lorne.olfman@cgu.edu. *Application contact:* Jake Campbell, Senior Assistant Director of Admissions, 909-607-3024, E-mail: jake.campbell@cgu.edu.
Website: https://www.cgu.edu/school/center-for-information-systems-and-technology/

Clarkson University, Program in Data Analytics, Potsdam, NY 13699. Offers MS. *Program availability:* Part-time, evening/weekend, 100% online. *Faculty:* 8 full-time (0 women). *Students:* 12 full-time (2 women), 2 part-time (1 woman); includes 1 minority (Black or African American, non-Hispanic/Latino), 9 international. 36 applicants, 92% accepted, 19 enrolled. In 2016, 11 master's awarded. *Degree requirements:* For master's, capstone project. *Entrance requirements:* For master's, GMAT or GRE. Additional exam requirements/recommendations for international students: Required—TOEFL (minimum score 550 paper-based, 80 iBT) or IELTS (6.5). *Application deadline:* Applications are processed on a rolling basis. Application fee: $50. Electronic applications accepted. *Expenses:* $1,504 per credit. *Financial support:* Scholarships/grants and unspecified assistantships available. *Unit head:* Dr. Boris Jukic, Director of Business Analytics, 315-268-3884, E-mail: bjukic@clarkson.edu. *Application contact:* Dan Capogna, Graduate Admissions Contact, 518-631-9910, E-mail: graduate@clarkson.edu.
Website: http://graduate.clarkson.edu

Clarkson University, School of Business, Potsdam, NY 13699. Offers health data analytics (MS); health systems administration (MBA); healthcare management and leadership (MBA, MS, Advanced Certificate), including clinical leadership in healthcare

management (MS), healthcare data analytics (MS), healthcare management (MBA, Advanced Certificate). *Faculty:* 46 full-time (11 women), 22 part-time/adjunct (6 women). *Students:* 176 full-time (78 women), 113 part-time (52 women); includes 64 minority (12 Black or African American, non-Hispanic/Latino; 1 American Indian or Alaska Native, non-Hispanic/Latino; 38 Asian, non-Hispanic/Latino; 6 Hispanic/Latino; 1 Native Hawaiian or other Pacific Islander, non-Hispanic/Latino; 6 Two or more races, non-Hispanic/Latino), 23 international. *Expenses: Tuition:* Full-time $23,400; part-time $1300 per credit hour. Tuition and fees vary according to campus/location and program. *Unit head:* Dr. Dayle Smith, Dean of Business, 315-268-2300, E-mail: dsmith@clarkson.edu. *Application contact:* Erin Wheeler, 518-631-9910, E-mail: ewheeler@clarkson.edu.
Website: http://graduate.clarkson.edu

The College of St. Scholastica, Graduate Studies, Department of Health Information Management, Duluth, MN 55811-4199. Offers MA, Certificate. *Program availability:* Part-time. *Degree requirements:* For master's, thesis. *Entrance requirements:* Additional exam requirements/recommendations for international students: Required—TOEFL (minimum score 550 paper-based; 79 iBT). Electronic applications accepted. *Expenses:* Contact institution. *Faculty research:* Electronic health record implementation, personal health records, Athens Project.

Colorado Mesa University, Department of Health Sciences, Grand Junction, CO 81501-3122. Offers advanced nursing practice (MSN); family nurse practitioner (DNP); health information technology systems (Graduate Certificate); nursing education (MSN). *Accreditation:* AACN. *Program availability:* Part-time, evening/weekend, 100% online, blended/hybrid learning. *Faculty:* 6 full-time (all women), 2 part-time/adjunct (0 women). *Students:* 3 full-time (all women), 39 part-time (35 women); includes 6 minority (1 American Indian or Alaska Native, non-Hispanic/Latino; 3 Asian, non-Hispanic/Latino; 1 Hispanic/Latino; 1 Two or more races, non-Hispanic/Latino), 1 international. Average age 38. 35 applicants, 34% accepted, 6 enrolled. In 2016, 3 master's, 6 doctorates, 1 other advanced degree awarded. *Degree requirements:* For master's and doctorate, capstone. *Entrance requirements:* For master's and doctorate, minimum GPA of 3.0 in BSN program. Additional exam requirements/recommendations for international students: Required—TOEFL (minimum score 550 paper-based). *Application deadline:* For fall admission, 4/1 for domestic and international students; for spring admission, 11/1 for domestic and international students. Applications are processed on a rolling basis. Application fee: $50. Electronic applications accepted. *Expenses:* Tuition, state resident: full-time $3582; part-time $398 per credit hour. Tuition, nonresident: full-time $10,080; part-time $1120 per credit hour. *Required fees:* $27.43 per credit hour. Tuition and fees vary according to course load and program. *Financial support:* In 2016–17, 1 student received support. Scholarships/grants available. Financial award applicants required to submit FAFSA. *Unit head:* Dr. Debra Bailey, Director, 970-248-1772, E-mail: dbailey@coloradomesa.edu. *Application contact:* Renae Phillips, Professional Staff Assistant, 970-248-1235, E-mail: rdphilli@coloradomesa.edu.
Website: http://www.coloradomesa.edu/healthsciences/index.html

Dakota State University, College of Business and Information Systems, Madison, SD 57042-1799. Offers analytics (MSA); applied computer science (MSACS); banking security (Graduate Certificate); business analytics (Graduate Certificate); cyber security (D Sc); ethical hacking (Graduate Certificate); general management (MBA); health informatics (MSHI); information assurance and computer security (MSIA); information systems (MSIS, D Sc IS); information technology (Graduate Certificate). *Accreditation:* ACBSP. *Program availability:* Part-time, evening/weekend, 100% online, blended/hybrid learning. *Degree requirements:* For master's, comprehensive exam, thesis optional, examination, integrative project; for doctorate, comprehensive exam, thesis/dissertation, portfolio. *Entrance requirements:* For master's, GRE General Test, demonstration of information systems skills, minimum GPA of 2.7; for doctorate, GRE General Test, demonstration of information systems skills; for Graduate Certificate, GMAT. Additional exam requirements/recommendations for international students: Required—PTE (minimum score 53), TOEFL (minimum score 550 paper-based, 79 iBT) or IELTS (6.5). *Application deadline:* For fall admission, 6/15 for domestic students, 4/15 for international students; for spring admission, 11/15 for domestic students, 9/15 priority date for international students; for summer admission, 4/15 for domestic and international students. Applications are processed on a rolling basis. Application fee: $35. *Expenses:* Contact institution. *Financial support:* Fellowships with partial tuition reimbursements, research assistantships with partial tuition reimbursements, teaching assistantships with partial tuition reimbursements, career-related internships or fieldwork, Federal Work-Study, scholarships/grants, and unspecified assistantships available. Support available to part-time students. Financial award applicants required to submit FAFSA. *Faculty research:* Data mining and analytics, biometrics and information assurance, decision support systems, health informatics, STEM education for K-12 teachers/students and underrepresented populations. *Unit head:* Mark Hawkes, Dean for Graduate Studies and Research, 605-256-5274, E-mail: mark.hawkes@dsu.edu. *Application contact:* Erin Blankespoor, Senior Secretary, Office of Graduate Studies and Research, 605-256-5799, E-mail: erin.blankespoor@dsu.edu.
Website: http://dsu.edu/academics/colleges/college-of-business-and-information-systems

DePaul University, College of Computing and Digital Media, Chicago, IL 60604. Offers animation (MA, MFA); business information technology (MS); cinema (MFA); cinema production (MS); computational finance (MS); computer and information sciences (PhD); computer game development (MS); computer information and network security (MS); computer science (MS); e-commerce technology (MS); health informatics (MS); human-computer interaction (MS); information systems (MS); information technology project management (MS); network engineering and management (MS); predictive analytics (MS); screenwriting (MFA); software engineering (MS); JD/MS. *Program availability:* Part-time, evening/weekend, online learning. *Degree requirements:* For master's, thesis (for some programs); for doctorate, comprehensive exam, thesis/dissertation. *Entrance requirements:* For master's, GRE or GMAT (for MS in computational finance only), bachelor's degree, resume (MS in predictive analytics only), IT experience (MS in information technology project management only), portfolio review (all MFA programs and MA in animation); for doctorate, GRE, master's degree in computer science. Additional exam requirements/recommendations for international students: Required—TOEFL (minimum score 590 paper-based; 80 iBT), IELTS (minimum score 6.5), PTE (minimum score 53). Electronic applications accepted. *Expenses:* Contact institution. *Faculty research:* Data mining, computer science, human-computer interaction, security, animation and film.

DeSales University, Division of Science and Mathematics, Center Valley, PA 18034-9568. Offers cyber security (Postbaccalaureate Certificate); data analytics (Postbaccalaureate Certificate); information systems (MS), including cyber security, digital forensics, healthcare information management, project management. *Program availability:* Part-time, evening/weekend, 100% online, blended/hybrid learning. *Faculty:* 1 (woman) full-time, 3 part-time/adjunct (0 women). *Students:* 8 full-time (1 woman), 12 part-time (6 women); includes 1 minority (Asian, non-Hispanic/Latino). Average age 34. 20 applicants, 30% accepted, 6 enrolled. In 2016, 7 master's awarded. *Entrance requirements:* For master's, GRE or GMAT, bachelor's degree in computer-related discipline from accredited college or university, minimum undergraduate GPA of 3.0, personal statement, three letters of recommendation. Additional exam requirements/recommendations for international students: Required—TOEFL. *Application deadline:* Applications are processed on a rolling basis. Application fee: $50. Electronic applications accepted. *Expenses:* Contact institution. *Financial support:* Applicants required to submit FAFSA. *Unit head:* Dr. Patricia Riola, MSIS Director/Assistant Professor of Computer Science, 610-282-1100 Ext. 1647, E-mail: patricia.riola@desales.edu. *Application contact:* Julia Ferraro, Director of Graduate Admissions, 610-282-1100 Ext. 1768, E-mail: gradadmissions@desales.edu.
Website: http://www.desales.edu/home/academics/graduate-studies/programs-of-study/msis---master-of-science-in-information-systems

Duke University, School of Medicine, Program in Clinical Informatics, Durham, NC 27710. Offers MS. *Program availability:* Part-time. *Faculty:* 7 full-time (3 women), 5 part-time/adjunct (2 women). *Students:* 37 full-time (15 women); includes 9 minority (1 Black or African American, non-Hispanic/Latino; 1 American Indian or Alaska Native, non-Hispanic/Latino; 5 Asian, non-Hispanic/Latino; 2 Hispanic/Latino), 3 international. 46 applicants, 80% accepted, 25 enrolled. In 2016, 23 master's awarded. *Entrance requirements:* For master's, essay; two letters of recommendation (one addressing work or educational experience and conveying ability to work at the level of a master's program and one addressing interpersonal skills, values, or character); interview with the program director. Additional exam requirements/recommendations for international students: Required—TOEFL. *Application deadline:* For fall admission, 6/30 for domestic students. Applications are processed on a rolling basis. Electronic applications accepted. *Financial support:* Scholarships/grants available. Financial award application deadline: 5/1; financial award applicants required to submit FAFSA. *Unit head:* Randy Sears, Operations Director, 919-681-8817, Fax: 919-681-4569, E-mail: r.sears@dm.duke.edu. *Application contact:* Cindy Seymour, Senior Program Coordinator, 919-613-0310, Fax: 919-681-4569, E-mail: cynthia.seymour@dm.duke.edu.
Website: http://www.dukemmci.org

East Carolina University, Graduate School, College of Allied Health Sciences, Department of Health Services and Information Management, Greenville, NC 27858-4353. Offers health informatics and information management (MS). *Students:* 32 full-time (22 women), 101 part-time (78 women); includes 51 minority (42 Black or African American, non-Hispanic/Latino; 1 American Indian or Alaska Native, non-Hispanic/Latino; 4 Asian, non-Hispanic/Latino; 3 Hispanic/Latino; 1 Two or more races, non-Hispanic/Latino), 1 international. Average age 35. 71 applicants, 94% accepted, 54 enrolled. In 2016, 7 master's awarded. *Unit head:* Dr. Xiaoming Zeng, Chair, 252-744-6176, E-mail: zengx@ecu.edu. *Application contact:* Dean of Graduate School, 252-328-6012, Fax: 252-328-6071, E-mail: gradschool@ecu.edu.
Website: http://www.ecu.edu/cs-dhs/hsim/

Emory University, Rollins School of Public Health, Department of Biostatistics and Bioinformatics, Atlanta, GA 30322-1100. Offers bioinformatics (PhD); biostatistics (MPH, MSPH); public health informatics (MSPH). PhD offered through the Graduate School of Arts and Sciences. *Program availability:* Part-time. *Degree requirements:* For master's, thesis, practicum. *Entrance requirements:* For master's, GRE General Test. Additional exam requirements/recommendations for international students: Required—TOEFL (minimum score 550 paper-based; 80 iBT). Electronic applications accepted.

Emory University, Rollins School of Public Health, Online Program in Public Health, Atlanta, GA 30322-1100. Offers applied epidemiology (MPH); applied public health informatics (MPH); prevention science (MPH). *Program availability:* Part-time, evening/weekend, online learning. *Degree requirements:* For master's, thesis, practicum. *Entrance requirements:* For master's, GRE. Additional exam requirements/recommendations for international students: Required—TOEFL (minimum score 550 paper-based; 80 iBT). Electronic applications accepted.

Excelsior College, School of Health Sciences, Albany, NY 12203-5159. Offers health administration (MS); health care informatics (Certificate); health professions education (MSHS); healthcare informatics (MS); organizational development (MS); public health (MSHS). *Program availability:* Part-time, evening/weekend, online learning. *Faculty:* 5 part-time/adjunct (4 women). *Students:* 307 part-time (240 women); includes 176 minority (101 Black or African American, non-Hispanic/Latino; 2 American Indian or Alaska Native, non-Hispanic/Latino; 17 Asian, non-Hispanic/Latino; 39 Hispanic/Latino; 3 Native Hawaiian or other Pacific Islander, non-Hispanic/Latino; 14 Two or more races, non-Hispanic/Latino), 1 international. Average age 39. In 2016, 21 master's awarded. *Entrance requirements:* For degree, bachelor's degree in applicable field. *Application deadline:* Applications are processed on a rolling basis. Application fee: $50. Electronic applications accepted. *Expenses: Tuition:* Part-time $645 per credit. *Required fees:* $265 per credit. *Financial support:* Scholarships/grants available. *Unit head:* Dr. Laurie Carbo-Porter, Dean, 518-464-8500, Fax: 518-464-8777. *Application contact:* Admissions Counselor, 518-464-8500, Fax: 518-464-8777, E-mail: admissions@excelsior.edu.

Georgia Southwestern State University, School of Nursing, Americus, GA 31709-4693. Offers family nurse practitioner (MSN); health informatics (Postbaccalaureate Certificate); nurse educator (Post Master's Certificate); nursing educator (MSN); nursing informatics (MSN); nursing leadership/management (MSN). MSN program offered by the Georgia Intercollegiate Consortium for Graduate Nursing Education, a partnership with Columbus State University. *Program availability:* Part-time, online only, all theory courses are offered online; clinical requirements (preceptorship, practicum internship) are not online. *Faculty:* 10 full-time, 3 part-time/adjunct. *Students:* 12 full-time (all women), 82 part-time (72 women); includes 32 minority (29 Black or African American, non-Hispanic/Latino; 1 Asian, non-Hispanic/Latino; 1 Hispanic/Latino; 1 Two or more races, non-Hispanic/Latino). Average age 34. 126 applicants, 59% accepted, 44 enrolled. In 2016, 6 master's awarded. *Entrance requirements:* For master's and other advanced degree, baccalaureate degree in nursing from regionally-accredited institution and nationally-accredited nursing program with minimum GPA of 3.0; three professional letters of recommendation; current unencumbered RN license in state where clinical course requirements will be met; background check/drug test; proof of immunizations. *Application deadline:* For fall admission, 2/15 for domestic students; for spring admission, 10/15 for domestic students; for summer admission, 2/15 for domestic students. Application fee: $25. Electronic applications accepted. *Expenses:* $385 per credit hour, plus fees, which vary according to enrolled credit hours. *Financial support:* Application deadline: 6/1; applicants required to submit FAFSA. *Unit head:* Dr. Sandra Daniel, Dean, 229-931-2275, E-mail: sandra.daniel@gsw.edu. *Application contact:* Whitney Ford, Admissions Specialist, Office of Graduate Admissions, 800-338-0082, Fax: 229-931-2983, E-mail: graduateadmissions@gsw.edu.
Website: https://gsw.edu/Academics/Schools-and-Departments/School-of-Nursing/index

Georgia State University, J. Mack Robinson College of Business, Department of Computer Information Systems, Atlanta, GA 30302-3083. Offers computer information systems (PhD); health informatics (MBA, MS); information systems (MSIS, Certificate); information systems development and project management (MBA); information systems management (MBA); managing information technology (Exec MS); the wireless organization (MBA). *Program availability:* Part-time, evening/weekend. *Faculty:* 24 full-time (2 women). *Students:* 209 full-time (84 women), 7 part-time (3 women); includes 41 minority (20 Black or African American, non-Hispanic/Latino; 16 Asian, non-Hispanic/Latino; 4 Hispanic/Latino; 1 Two or more races, non-Hispanic/Latino), 158 international.

Average age 28. 587 applicants, 56% accepted, 138 enrolled. In 2016, 126 master's, 4 doctorates awarded. *Degree requirements:* For master's, thesis optional; for doctorate, comprehensive exam, thesis/dissertation. *Entrance requirements:* For master's, GRE or GMAT, transcripts from all institutions attended, resume, essays; for doctorate, GRE or GMAT, three letters of recommendation, personal statement, transcripts from all institutions attended, resume. Additional exam requirements/recommendations for international students: Required—TOEFL (minimum score 610 paper-based; 101 iBT), IELTS (minimum score 7). *Application deadline:* For fall admission, 5/1 priority date for domestic students, 2/1 priority date for international students; for spring admission, 9/15 priority date for domestic students, 4/1 priority date for international students. Applications are processed on a rolling basis. Application fee: $50. Electronic applications accepted. *Expenses:* Tuition, state resident: full-time $6876; part-time $382 per credit hour. Tuition, nonresident: full-time $22,374; part-time $1243 per credit hour. *Required fees:* $2128; $1064 per term. Part-time tuition and fees vary according to course load and program. *Financial support:* Research assistantships, teaching assistantships, scholarships/grants, tuition waivers, and unspecified assistantships available. Financial award applicants required to submit FAFSA. *Faculty research:* Process and technological innovation, strategic IT management, intelligent systems, information systems security, software project risk. *Unit head:* Dr. Ephraim R. McLean, Professor/Chair, 404-413-7360, Fax: 404-413-7394. *Application contact:* Toby McChesney, Assistant Dean for Graduate Recruiting and Student Services, 404-413-7167, Fax: 404-413-7167, E-mail: rcbgradadmissions@gsu.edu.
Website: http://cis.robinson.gsu.edu/

Georgia State University, J. Mack Robinson College of Business, Institute of Health Administration, Atlanta, GA 30302-3083. Offers health administration (MBA, MSHA); health informatics (MBA, MSCIS); MBA/MHA; PMBA/MHA. *Accreditation:* CAHME. *Program availability:* Part-time, evening/weekend. *Faculty:* 8 full-time (2 women). *Students:* 58 full-time (33 women), 14 part-time (6 women); includes 33 minority (11 Black or African American, non-Hispanic/Latino; 14 Asian, non-Hispanic/Latino; 3 Hispanic/Latino; 5 Two or more races, non-Hispanic/Latino), 8 international. Average age 30. 55 applicants, 42% accepted, 15 enrolled. In 2016, 73 master's awarded. *Entrance requirements:* For master's, GRE or GMAT, transcripts from all institutions attended, resume, essays. Additional exam requirements/recommendations for international students: Required—TOEFL (minimum score 610 paper-based; 101 iBT), IELTS (minimum score 7). *Application deadline:* For fall admission, 5/1 priority date for domestic students, 2/1 priority date for international students; for spring admission, 9/15 priority date for domestic students, 4/1 priority date for international students. Applications are processed on a rolling basis. Application fee: $50. Electronic applications accepted. *Expenses:* Tuition, state resident: full-time $6876; part-time $382 per credit hour. Tuition, nonresident: full-time $22,374; part-time $1243 per credit hour. *Required fees:* $2128; $1064 per term. Part-time tuition and fees vary according to course load and program. *Financial support:* Research assistantships, teaching assistantships, scholarships/grants, tuition waivers, and unspecified assistantships available. *Faculty research:* Health information technology, health insurance exchanges, health policy and economic impact, healthcare quality, healthcare transformation. *Unit head:* Dr. Andrew T. Sumner, Chair in Health Administration/Director of the Institute of Health, 404-413-7630, Fax: 404-413-7631. *Application contact:* Toby McChesney, Assistant Dean for Graduate Recruiting and Student Services, 404-413-7167, Fax: 404-413-7162, E-mail: rcbgradadmissions@gsu.edu.
Website: http://www.hagsu.org/

Golden Gate University, Ageno School of Business, San Francisco, CA 94105-2968. Offers accounting (MBA); business administration (EMBA, MBA, PMBA, DBA); business analytics (MS); finance (MBA, MS, Certificate); financial planning (MS, Certificate); healthcare information systems (Certificate); human resource management (MBA, MS); human resources management (Certificate); information systems (MS); information technology (MBA); information technology management (Certificate); integrated marketing and communications (MS, Certificate); international business (MBA); management (MBA); marketing (MBA, MS, Certificate); operations supply chain management (Certificate); psychology (MA, Certificate); public administration (EMPA); public relations (MS, Certificate); technical market analysis (Certificate); JD/MBA. *Program availability:* Part-time, evening/weekend. *Faculty:* 18 full-time (3 women), 117 part-time/adjunct (44 women). *Students:* 458 full-time (254 women), 664 part-time (331 women); includes 346 minority (75 Black or African American, non-Hispanic/Latino; 2 American Indian or Alaska Native, non-Hispanic/Latino; 132 Asian, non-Hispanic/Latino; 105 Hispanic/Latino; 9 Native Hawaiian or other Pacific Islander, non-Hispanic/Latino; 23 Two or more races, non-Hispanic/Latino), 354 international. Average age 34. 905 applicants, 83% accepted, 165 enrolled. In 2016, 350 master's, 2 doctorates awarded. *Degree requirements:* For doctorate, thesis/dissertation, qualifying examination. *Entrance requirements:* For master's, GMAT (for MBA), minimum GPA of 2.5 (MS). Additional exam requirements/recommendations for international students: Required—TOEFL (minimum score 550 paper-based; 79 iBT). *Application deadline:* For fall admission, 5/15 for domestic and international students; for winter admission, 1/15 for domestic and international students; for spring admission, 9/15 for domestic and international students. Applications are processed on a rolling basis. Application fee: $70 ($110 for international students). Electronic applications accepted. *Expenses:* Contact institution. *Financial support:* In 2016–17, 372 students received support. Career-related internships or fieldwork, Federal Work-Study, institutionally sponsored loans, and scholarships/grants available. Support available to part-time students. Financial award applicants required to submit FAFSA. *Unit head:* Dr. Gordon Swartz, Dean, 415-442-7027, Fax: 415-442-6579, E-mail: gswartz@ggu.edu. *Application contact:* Angela Melero, Enrollment Services, 415-442-7800, Fax: 415-442-7807, E-mail: info@ggu.edu.
Website: http://www.ggu.edu/programs/business-and-management

Grand Canyon University, College of Nursing and Health Care Professions, Phoenix, AZ 85017-1097. Offers acute care nurse practitioner (MSN, PMC); family nurse practitioner (MSN, PMC); health care administration (MS); health care informatics (MS, MSN); leadership in health care systems (MSN); nursing (DNP); nursing education (MSN, PMC); public health (MPH, MSN); MBA/MSN. *Accreditation:* AACN. *Program availability:* Part-time, evening/weekend, online learning. *Degree requirements:* For master's and PMC, comprehensive exam (for some programs). *Entrance requirements:* For master's, minimum cumulative and science course undergraduate GPA of 3.0. Additional exam requirements/recommendations for international students: Required—TOEFL (minimum score 575 paper-based; 90 iBT), IELTS (minimum score 7). Application fee: $0. *Financial support:* Federal Work-Study available. Support available to part-time students. Financial award applicants required to submit FAFSA. *Unit head:* Lisa Smith, Dean, 602-639-6165, Fax: 602-589-2810. *Application contact:* Lisa Smith, Dean, 602-639-6165, Fax: 602-589-2810.
Website: https://www.gcu.edu/college-of-nursing-and-health-care-professions.php

Hofstra University, School of Health Professions and Human Services, Programs in Health, Hempstead, NY 11549. Offers health administration (MHA); health informatics (MS); occupational therapy (MS); public health (MPH); sport science (MS), including strength and conditioning. *Program availability:* Part-time, evening/weekend. *Students:* 213 full-time (133 women), 96 part-time (65 women); includes 155 minority (54 Black or African American, non-Hispanic/Latino; 1 American Indian or Alaska Native, non-Hispanic/Latino; 63 Asian, non-Hispanic/Latino; 32 Hispanic/Latino; 4 Native Hawaiian or other Pacific Islander, non-Hispanic/Latino; 1 Two or more races, non-Hispanic/Latino), 25 international. Average age 27. 582 applicants, 47% accepted, 140 enrolled. In 2016, 116 master's awarded. *Degree requirements:* For master's, internship, minimum GPA of 3.0. *Entrance requirements:* For master's, interview, 2 letters of recommendation, essay, resume. Additional exam requirements/recommendations for international students: Required—TOEFL (minimum score 550 paper-based; 80 iBT). *Application deadline:* Applications are processed on a rolling basis. Application fee: $75. Electronic applications accepted. *Expenses: Tuition:* Full-time $1240. *Required fees:* $970. Tuition and fees vary according to program. *Financial support:* In 2016–17, 127 students received support, including 74 fellowships with full and partial tuition reimbursements available (averaging $3,271 per year), 5 research assistantships with full and partial tuition reimbursements available (averaging $7,505 per year); career-related internships or fieldwork, Federal Work-Study, institutionally sponsored loans, scholarships/grants, traineeships, tuition waivers (full and partial), and unspecified assistantships also available. Support available to part-time students. Financial award applicants required to submit FAFSA. *Faculty research:* HIV/AIDS, LGBTQ health, correctional health, dental public health, fitness assessment and injury risk in collegiate athletes, fitness assessment and screening in wild land firefighters. *Unit head:* Dr. Jayne Ellinger, Chairperson, 516-463-6952, Fax: 516-463-6275, E-mail: jayne.ellinger@hofstra.edu. *Application contact:* Sunil Samuel, Assistant Vice President of Admissions, 516-463-4723, Fax: 516-463-4664, E-mail: graduateadmission@hofstra.edu.
Website: http://www.hofstra.edu/academics/colleges/healthscienceshumanservices/

Indiana University Bloomington, School of Informatics and Computing, Program in Informatics, Bloomington, IN 47405. Offers informatics (MS, PhD), including bioinformatics (PhD), complex systems (PhD), computing, culture and society (PhD), health informatics (PhD), human-computer interaction (MS), human-computer interaction design (PhD), music informatics (PhD), security informatics (PhD); visual heritage (PhD). *Program availability:* Part-time. *Faculty:* 75 full-time (15 women). *Students:* 206 full-time (85 women), 10 part-time (3 women); includes 30 minority (11 Black or African American, non-Hispanic/Latino; 10 Asian, non-Hispanic/Latino; 5 Hispanic/Latino; 4 Two or more races, non-Hispanic/Latino), 95 international. Average age 28. 395 applicants, 36% accepted, 69 enrolled. In 2016, 50 master's, 11 doctorates awarded. Terminal master's awarded for partial completion of doctoral program. *Degree requirements:* For master's, thesis, capstone project; for doctorate, variable foreign language requirement, comprehensive exam, thesis/dissertation. *Entrance requirements:* For master's and doctorate, GRE, resume/curriculum vitae, transcripts, 3 letters of recommendation. Additional exam requirements/recommendations for international students: Required—TOEFL (minimum score 600 paper-based; 100 iBT). *Application deadline:* For fall admission, 12/1 priority date for domestic and international students. Application fee: $55 ($65 for international students). Electronic applications accepted. *Financial support:* Fellowships, research assistantships, scholarships/grants, health care benefits, and unspecified assistantships available. Financial award application deadline: 12/1. *Faculty research:* Algorithms, applied logic and computational theory, artificial intelligence, bioinformatics, case-based reasoning, chemical informatics, citation analysis, cognitive science, community informatics, compilers, complex networks and systems, computer optimization, computer-supported cooperative work, computer vision, cyberinfrastructure and e-science, database theory and systems, data mining, digital design and preservation, design pedagogy, digital humanities, digital learning environments. *Total annual research expenditures:* $19.4 million. *Unit head:* Dr. Martin Siegel, Director of Graduate Studies, 812-856-3960, E-mail: msiegel@indiana.edu. *Application contact:* Informatics Graduate Studies Office, 812-856-3960, E-mail: infograd@indiana.edu.
Website: http://www.informatics.indiana.edu/graduate/index.html

Indiana University–Purdue University Indianapolis, School of Informatics and Computing, Department of BioHealth Informatics, Indianapolis, IN 46202. Offers bioinformatics (MS, PhD); health informatics (MS, PhD). *Students:* 82 full-time (46 women), 44 part-time (21 women); includes 25 minority (14 Black or African American, non-Hispanic/Latino; 7 Asian, non-Hispanic/Latino; 2 Hispanic/Latino; 2 Two or more races, non-Hispanic/Latino), 69 international. Average age 40. 107 applicants, 63% accepted, 35 enrolled. In 2016, 31 master's awarded. *Financial support:* Fellowships, scholarships/grants, and unspecified assistantships available. *Unit head:* Dr. Huanmei Wu, Chair, 317-278-1692, E-mail: hw9@iupui.edu. *Application contact:* Elizabeth Bunge, Graduate Admissions Coordinator, 317-278-9200, E-mail: ebunge@iupui.edu.
Website: http://soic.iupui.edu/biohealth/

Jacksonville University, Brooks Rehabilitation College of Healthcare Sciences, School of Applied Health Sciences, Program in Health Informatics, Jacksonville, FL 32211. Offers MS. *Program availability:* Online learning. Electronic applications accepted. *Expenses: Tuition:* Full-time $13,320. One-time fee: $50 part-time. Tuition and fees vary according to course load, degree level, campus/location and program.

Johns Hopkins University, School of Medicine, Division of Health Sciences Informatics, Baltimore, MD 21287. Offers applied health sciences informatics (MS); clinical informatics (Certificate); health sciences informatics (PhD); health sciences informatics research (MS). *Faculty:* 40 part-time/adjunct (10 women). *Students:* 7 full-time (2 women), 7 part-time (4 women); includes 4 minority (all Black or African American, non-Hispanic/Latino), 7 international. Average age 28. 64 applicants, 23% accepted, 8 enrolled. In 2016, 2 master's awarded. *Degree requirements:* For master's, thesis, publications, practica. *Entrance requirements:* Additional exam requirements/recommendations for international students: Recommended—TOEFL. *Application deadline:* For spring admission, 2/15 priority date for domestic students, 2/15 for international students. Application fee: $110. Electronic applications accepted. *Financial support:* Fellowships, career-related internships or fieldwork, and health care benefits available. *Faculty research:* Decision modeling, consumer health informatics, digital libraries, data standards, patient safety. *Total annual research expenditures:* $963,103. *Unit head:* Dr. Harold P. Lehmann, Director, Training Program, 410-502-2569, Fax: 410-614-2064, E-mail: lehmann@jhmi.edu. *Application contact:* Kersti Winny, Academic Program Administrator, 410-502-3768, Fax: 410-614-2064, E-mail: kwinny@jhmi.edu.
Website: http://dhsi.med.jhmi.edu

Kennesaw State University, College of Computing and Software Engineering, Department of Information Technology, Kennesaw, GA 30144. Offers health information technology (Postbaccalaureate Certificate); information security and assurance (Graduate Certificate); information technology (MSIT, Graduate Certificate); information technology fundamentals (Postbaccalaureate Certificate). *Program availability:* Part-time, evening/weekend, online learning. *Degree requirements:* For master's, thesis optional. *Entrance requirements:* For master's, minimum GPA of 2.75; for other advanced degree, bachelor's degree. Additional exam requirements/recommendations for international students: Required—TOEFL (minimum score 550 paper-based; 79 iBT), IELTS (minimum score 6.5). Electronic applications accepted. *Faculty research:* IT ethics, user interface design, IT security, IT integration, IT management, health information technology, business intelligence, networks, business continuity.

Kent State University, College of Communication and Information, School of Library and Information Science, Kent, OH 44242-0001. Offers information architecture and knowledge management (MS), including health informatics, knowledge management,

user experience design; library and information science (MLIS), including school library media; M Ed/MLIS; MBA/MLIS. *Accreditation:* ALA (one or more programs are accredited). *Program availability:* Part-time, online learning. *Faculty:* 19 full-time (16 women). *Students:* 208 full-time (163 women), 633 part-time (459 women); includes 112 minority (41 Black or African American, non-Hispanic/Latino; 2 American Indian or Alaska Native, non-Hispanic/Latino; 12 Asian, non-Hispanic/Latino; 36 Hispanic/Latino; 1 Native Hawaiian or other Pacific Islander, non-Hispanic/Latino; 20 Two or more races, non-Hispanic/Latino), 10 international. Average age 33. 269 applicants, 80% accepted, 175 enrolled. In 2016, 294 master's awarded. *Degree requirements:* For master's, thesis optional. *Entrance requirements:* For master's, GRE, minimum GPA of 3.0, statement of purpose, 3 letters of recommendation, curriculum vitae/resume, transcripts, writing sample, personal interview. Additional exam requirements/recommendations for international students: Required—TOEFL (minimum score of 600 paper-based, 100 iBT), IELTS (minimum score of 7.0), Michigan English Language Assessment Battery (minimum score of 85), or PTE (minimum score of 68). *Application deadline:* For fall admission, 3/15 for domestic and international students; for spring admission, 9/15 for domestic and international students; for summer admission, 1/15 for domestic and international students. Applications are processed on a rolling basis. Application fee: $45 ($70 for international students). Electronic applications accepted. *Expenses:* Tuition, state resident: full-time $10,864; part-time $495 per credit hour. Tuition, nonresident: full-time $18,380; part-time $837 per credit hour. *Financial support:* Fellowships with full tuition reimbursements, research assistantships with full tuition reimbursements, teaching assistantships with full tuition reimbursements, scholarships/grants, and unspecified assistantships available. Financial award application deadline: 3/1. *Unit head:* Dr. Kendra Albright, Director and Professor, 330-672-8535, E-mail: kalbrig7@kent.edu. *Application contact:* Dr. Karen Gracy, Graduate Co-Coordinator/Associate Professor, 330-672-2782, E-mail: kgracy@kent.edu.
Website: http://www.kent.edu/slis/

Lipscomb University, College of Business, Nashville, TN 37204-3951. Offers accountancy (M Acc); accounting (MBA); business administration (MM); conflict management (MBA); financial services (MBA); health care informatics (MBA); healthcare management (MBA); information security (MBA); leadership (MBA); nonprofit management (MBA); professional accountancy (Certificate); sports management (MBA); strategic human resources (MBA); sustainability (MBA); MBA/MS; Pharm D/MM. *Accreditation:* ACBSP. *Program availability:* Part-time, evening/weekend. *Faculty:* 22 full-time (4 women), 12 part-time/adjunct (4 women). *Students:* 112 full-time (51 women), 69 part-time (34 women); includes 30 minority (17 Black or African American, non-Hispanic/Latino; 3 Asian, non-Hispanic/Latino; 8 Hispanic/Latino; 2 Two or more races, non-Hispanic/Latino), 5 international. Average age 32. 244 applicants, 55% accepted, 54 enrolled. In 2016, 164 master's awarded. *Entrance requirements:* For master's, GMAT, transcripts, interview, 2 references, resume. Additional exam requirements/recommendations for international students: Required—TOEFL (minimum score 570 paper-based). *Application deadline:* For fall admission, 6/15 for domestic students, 2/1 for international students; for winter admission, 6/1 for international students; for spring admission, 11/15 for domestic students. Applications are processed on a rolling basis. Application fee: $50 ($75 for international students). Electronic applications accepted. *Expenses:* $1,150-$1,290 per hour, depending on program. *Financial support:* Career-related internships or fieldwork, scholarships/grants, tuition waivers (partial), and unspecified assistantships available. Support available to part-time students. Financial award application deadline: 7/1; financial award applicants required to submit FAFSA. *Faculty research:* Impact of spirituality on organization commitment, women in corporate leadership, psychological empowerment, training. *Unit head:* Allison Duke, Associate Dean of Graduate Business Programs, 615-966-5732, Fax: 615-966-1818, E-mail: allison.duke@lipscomb.edu. *Application contact:* Karen Risley, Manager, Graduate Business Recruiting, 615-966-5145, E-mail: karen.risley@lipscomb.edu.
Website: http://www.lipscomb.edu/business/Graduate-Programs

Lipscomb University, College of Pharmacy, Nashville, TN 37204-3951. Offers healthcare informatics (MS); pharmacy (Pharm D); Pharm D/MM; Pharm D/MS. *Accreditation:* ACPE. *Faculty:* 32 full-time (14 women), 6 part-time/adjunct (4 women). *Students:* 297 full-time (172 women); includes 74 minority (26 Black or African American, non-Hispanic/Latino; 4 American Indian or Alaska Native, non-Hispanic/Latino; 30 Asian, non-Hispanic/Latino; 7 Hispanic/Latino; 1 Native Hawaiian or other Pacific Islander, non-Hispanic/Latino; 6 Two or more races, non-Hispanic/Latino). Average age 26. In 2016, 3 master's, 69 doctorates awarded. *Degree requirements:* For master's, capstone project; for doctorate, comprehensive exam. *Entrance requirements:* For master's, GRE, 2 references, transcripts, resume, personal statement, eligibility documentation (degree and/or experience in related area); for doctorate, PCAT (minimum 45th percentile), 66 pre-professional semester hours, minimum GPA of 2.5, interview, PharmCAS application (for international students). Additional exam requirements/recommendations for international students: Required—TOEFL (minimum score 550 paper-based; 80 iBT). *Application deadline:* For fall admission, 2/7 for domestic students. Applications are processed on a rolling basis. Application fee: $50 ($75 for international students). Electronic applications accepted. *Expenses:* $37,938 per year (for Pharm D); $1,000 per hour (for MS); $1,150 per hour (for MM). *Financial support:* Application deadline: 2/15; applicants required to submit FAFSA. *Total annual research expenditures:* $1.3 million. *Unit head:* Dr. Roger Davis, Dean/Professor of Pharmacy Practice, 615-966-7161. *Application contact:* Laura Ward, Director of Admissions and Student Affairs, 615-966-7173, E-mail: laura.ward@lipscomb.edu.
Website: http://lipscomb.edu/pharmacy

Logan University, College of Health Sciences, Chesterfield, MO 63017. Offers health informatics (MS); health professionals education (DHPE); nutrition and human performance (MS); sports science and rehabilitation (MS). *Program availability:* Part-time, online only, 100% online. *Faculty:* 2 full-time (1 woman), 14 part-time/adjunct (6 women). *Students:* 54 full-time (40 women), 255 part-time (182 women); includes 38 minority (16 Black or African American, non-Hispanic/Latino; 4 Asian, non-Hispanic/Latino; 10 Hispanic/Latino; 8 Two or more races, non-Hispanic/Latino), 14 international. Average age 35. 229 applicants, 88% accepted, 164 enrolled. In 2016, 89 master's awarded. *Entrance requirements:* For master's, minimum GPA of 2.5; 6 hours of biology and physical science; bachelor's degree and 9 hours of business health administration (for health informatics). Additional exam requirements/recommendations for international students: Required—TOEFL (minimum score 500 paper-based; 79 iBT); Recommended—IELTS (minimum score 6.5). *Application deadline:* Applications are processed on a rolling basis. Application fee: $50. Electronic applications accepted. *Expenses:* $650 tuition per credit hour (for DHPE), $450 tuition per credit hour (for MS); $80 fees per trimester. *Financial support:* In 2016–17, 4 students received support. Federal Work-Study and scholarships/grants available. Support available to part-time students. Financial award applicants required to submit FAFSA. *Faculty research:* Ankle injury prevention in high school athletes, low back pain in college football players, short arc banding and low back pain, the effects of enzymes on inflammatory blood markers, gait analysis in high school and college athletes. *Unit head:* Dr. Sherri Cole, Dean, College of Health Sciences, 636-227-2100 Ext. 2702, Fax: 636-207-2418, E-mail: sherri.cole@logan.edu. *Application contact:* Jordan LaMarca, Assistant Director of Admissions, 636-227-2100 Ext. 1973, Fax: 636-207-2425, E-mail: admissions@logan.edu.

Louisiana Tech University, Graduate School, College of Applied and Natural Sciences, Department of Health Informatics and Information Management, Ruston, LA 71272. Offers health informatics (MHI). *Program availability:* Online learning. *Entrance requirements:* For master's, essay or GRE; three letters of recommendation; official transcripts; bachelor's degree from regionally-accredited institution; at least two years of work experience; resume; personal statement; interview. *Unit head:* Dr. Angela Kennedy, Head, 318-257-2854, E-mail: angelak@latech.edu.
Website: http://him.latech.edu/

Marshall University, Academic Affairs Division, College of Health Professions, Department of Health Informatics, Huntington, WV 25755. Offers MS. Offered jointly with College of Business and College of Information Technology and Engineering.

Marymount University, School of Business Administration, Program in Information Technology, Arlington, VA 22207-4299. Offers health care informatics (Certificate); information technology (MS, Certificate), including computer security (MS), health care informatics (MS), project management and technology leadership (MS), software engineering (MS); information technology project management and technology leadership (Certificate); MS/MBA; MS/MS. *Program availability:* Part-time, evening/weekend. *Faculty:* 7 full-time (6 women), 7 part-time/adjunct (0 women). *Students:* 39 full-time (23 women), 31 part-time (13 women); includes 24 minority (12 Black or African American, non-Hispanic/Latino; 5 Asian, non-Hispanic/Latino; 6 Hispanic/Latino; 1 Two or more races, non-Hispanic/Latino), 31 international. Average age 30. 67 applicants, 97% accepted, 23 enrolled. In 2016, 29 master's, 12 other advanced degrees awarded. *Degree requirements:* For master's, thesis or alternative. *Entrance requirements:* For master's, resume, bachelor's degree in computer-related field or another subject with certificate in computer-related field or related work experience; bachelor's degree in computer science or work in software development (for software engineering track). Additional exam requirements/recommendations for international students: Required—TOEFL (minimum score 600 paper-based; 96 iBT), IELTS (minimum score 6.5). *Application deadline:* For fall admission, 7/16 priority date for domestic and international students; for spring admission, 11/16 priority date for domestic and international students; for summer admission, 4/16 for domestic and international students. Applications are processed on a rolling basis. Application fee: $40. Electronic applications accepted. *Expenses:* $960 per credit hour. *Financial support:* In 2016–17, 5 students received support, including 2 research assistantships with tuition reimbursements available; career-related internships or fieldwork, Federal Work-Study, scholarships/grants, and unspecified assistantships also available. Support available to part-time students. Financial award applicants required to submit FAFSA. *Unit head:* Dr. Diane Murphy, Chair/Director, Information Technology, Management Sciences and Cybersecurity, 703-284-5958, Fax: 703-527-3830, E-mail: diane.murphy@marymount.edu. *Application contact:* Francesca Reed, Director, Graduate Admissions, 703-284-5901, Fax: 703-527-3815, E-mail: grad.admissions@marymount.edu.
Website: http://www.marymount.edu/Academics/School-of-Business-Administration/Graduate-Programs/Information-Technology-(M-S-)

Mercer University, Graduate Studies, Cecil B. Day Campus, Penfield College, Atlanta, GA 30341. Offers certified rehabilitation counseling (MS); clinical mental health (MS); counselor education and supervision (PhD); criminal justice and public safety leadership (MS); health informatics (MS); human services (MS), including child and adolescent services, gerontology services; organizational leadership (MS); school counseling (MS). *Program availability:* Part-time, evening/weekend, 100% online, blended/hybrid learning. *Faculty:* 15 full-time (8 women), 22 part-time/adjunct (18 women). *Students:* 168 full-time (136 women), 242 part-time (201 women); includes 231 minority (192 Black or African American, non-Hispanic/Latino; 1 American Indian or Alaska Native, non-Hispanic/Latino; 15 Asian, non-Hispanic/Latino; 19 Hispanic/Latino; 1 Native Hawaiian or other Pacific Islander, non-Hispanic/Latino; 3 Two or more races, non-Hispanic/Latino), 2 international. Average age 32. 300 applicants, 45% accepted, 114 enrolled. In 2016, 92 master's, 8 doctorates awarded. *Degree requirements:* For master's, comprehensive exam (for some programs), thesis (for some programs); for doctorate, thesis/dissertation. *Entrance requirements:* For master's, GRE or MAT, Georgia Professional Standards Commission (GPSC) Certification at the SC-5 level; for doctorate, GRE or MAT. Additional exam requirements/recommendations for international students: Recommended—TOEFL (minimum score 550 paper-based; 80 iBT), IELTS (minimum score 6.5). *Application deadline:* For fall admission, 7/1 priority date for domestic and international students; for spring admission, 11/1 priority date for domestic and international students; for summer admission, 4/1 priority date for domestic and international students. Application fee: $35. Electronic applications accepted. Application fee is waived when completed online. *Expenses:* $588 per credit hour. *Financial support:* In 2016–17, 32 students received support. Federal Work-Study, scholarships/grants, and unspecified assistantships available. Financial award applicants required to submit FAFSA. *Faculty research:* Marriage and families issues, leadership and ethics, cyber-bullying, trauma, narrative counseling and theory. *Total annual research expenditures:* $85,000. *Unit head:* Dr. Priscilla R. Danheiser, Dean, 678-547-6028, Fax: 678-547-6008, E-mail: danheiser_p@mercer.edu.
Website: http://penfield.mercer.edu/programs/graduate-professional/

Metropolitan State University, College of Management, St. Paul, MN 55106-5000. Offers business administration (MBA, DBA); database administration (Graduate Certificate); healthcare information technology management (Graduate Certificate); information assurance security (Graduate Certificate); management information systems (MMIS); MIS generalist (Graduate Certificate); MIS systems analysis and design (Graduate Certificate); project management (Graduate Certificate); public and nonprofit administration (MPNA). *Program availability:* Part-time, evening/weekend. *Degree requirements:* For master's, thesis optional, computer language (MMIS). *Entrance requirements:* For master's, GMAT (for MBA), resume. Additional exam requirements/recommendations for international students: Required—TOEFL (minimum score 550 paper-based). Electronic applications accepted. *Faculty research:* Yugoslav economic system, workers' cooperatives, participative management and job enrichment, global business systems.

Middle Georgia State University, Office of Graduate Studies, Macon, GA 31206. Offers adult/gerontology acute care nurse practitioner (MSN); information technology (MS), including health informatics, information security and digital forensics, software development. *Entrance requirements:* For master's, GRE. Additional exam requirements/recommendations for international students: Required—TOEFL (minimum score 523 paper-based; 69 iBT). *Expenses:* Contact institution.

Midwestern State University, Billie Doris McAda Graduate School, Robert D. and Carol Gunn College of Health Sciences and Human Services, Department of Criminal Justice and Health Services Administration, Wichita Falls, TX 76308. Offers criminal justice (MA); health information management (MHA); health services administration (Graduate Certificate); medical practice management (MHA); public and community sector health care management (MHA); rural and urban hospital management (MHA). *Program availability:* Part-time, evening/weekend. *Degree requirements:* For master's, comprehensive exam, thesis. *Entrance requirements:* For master's, GRE. Additional exam requirements/recommendations for international students: Required—TOEFL (minimum score 550 paper-based). Electronic applications accepted. *Faculty research:*

Universal service policy, telehealth, bullying, healthcare financial management, public health ethics.

Millennia Atlantic University, Graduate Programs, Doral, FL 33178. Offers accounting (MBA); business administration (MBA); health information management (MS); human resource management (MA). *Program availability:* Online learning.

Montana Tech of The University of Montana, Health Care Informatics Program, Butte, MT 59701-8997. Offers Certificate. *Program availability:* Part-time, evening/weekend, online learning. *Faculty:* 4 full-time (2 women). *Students:* 7 part-time (5 women). 1 applicant. In 2016, 4 Certificates awarded. *Entrance requirements:* Additional exam requirements/recommendations for international students: Required—TOEFL (minimum score 545 paper-based; 78 iBT), IELTS (minimum score 6.5). *Application deadline:* For fall admission, 4/1 priority date for domestic students, 3/1 priority date for international students; for spring admission, 10/1 priority date for domestic students, 6/1 priority date for international students. Applications are processed on a rolling basis. Application fee: $50. Electronic applications accepted. *Expenses:* Tuition, state resident: full-time $2901; part-time $1450.68 per degree program. Tuition, nonresident: full-time $8432; part-time $4215.84 per degree program. *Required fees:* $668; $354 per degree program. Tuition and fees vary according to course load and program. *Financial support:* Scholarships/grants available. Financial award application deadline: 4/1; financial award applicants required to submit FAFSA. *Faculty research:* Informatics, healthcare, computer science. *Unit head:* Dr. Charie Faught, Department Head, 406-496-4884, Fax: 406-496-4435, E-mail: cfaught@mtech.edu. *Application contact:* Daniel Stirling, Administrator, Graduate School, 406-496-4304, Fax: 406-496-4710, E-mail: gradschool@mtech.edu.
Website: http://www.mtech.edu/academics/gradschool/distancelearning/distancelearning-hci.htm

Northeastern University, College of Computer and Information Science, Boston, MA 02115-5096. Offers computer science (MS, PhD); data science (MS); game science and design (MS); health informatics (MS); information assurance (MS); network science (PhD); personal health informatics (PhD). *Program availability:* Part-time, evening/weekend. *Faculty:* 79 full-time (21 women), 34 part-time/adjunct (7 women). *Students:* 1,064 full-time (306 women), 34 part-time (10 women). In 2016, 322 master's, 8 doctorates awarded. Terminal master's awarded for partial completion of doctoral program. *Degree requirements:* For master's, thesis optional; for doctorate, comprehensive exam, thesis/dissertation. Application fee: $75. Electronic applications accepted. *Expenses:* $1,495 per credit. *Financial support:* Research assistantships, teaching assistantships, scholarships/grants, health care benefits, and unspecified assistantships available. Financial award applicants required to submit FAFSA. *Unit head:* Dr. Carla Brodley, Professor and Dean. *Application contact:* Dr. Rajmohan Rajaraman, Professor/Associate Dean/Director of the Graduate School, 617-373-8493, E-mail: gradschool@ccs.neu.edu.
Website: http://www.ccs.neu.edu/

Northern Kentucky University, Office of Graduate Programs, College of Informatics, Program in Health Informatics, Highland Heights, KY 41099. Offers MS, Certificate. *Program availability:* Part-time, evening/weekend, online learning. *Degree requirements:* For master's, capstone, electronic portfolio. *Entrance requirements:* For master's, MAT, GRE, or GMAT, official transcripts from accredited college or university, minimum GPA of 3.0, letter of career goals and background, statement addressing computer proficiencies; references (recommended). Additional exam requirements/recommendations for international students: Required—TOEFL (minimum score 79 iBT); Recommended—IELTS (minimum score 6.5). Electronic applications accepted. *Faculty research:* Health informatics course development, healthcare analytics, technology acceptance in healthcare, consumer engagement, population health outcome, systems implementation, healthcare operations.

Northwestern University, Feinberg School of Medicine and Interdepartmental Programs, Driskill Graduate Program in Life Sciences, Chicago, IL 60611. Offers biostatistics (PhD); epidemiology (PhD); health and biomedical informatics (PhD); health services and outcomes research (PhD); healthcare quality and patient safety (PhD); translational outcomes in science (PhD). *Degree requirements:* For doctorate, comprehensive exam, thesis/dissertation, written and oral qualifying exams. *Entrance requirements:* For doctorate, GRE General Test. Additional exam requirements/recommendations for international students: Required—TOEFL (minimum score 600 paper-based). Electronic applications accepted.

Nova Southeastern University, College of Osteopathic Medicine, Fort Lauderdale, FL 33328. Offers biomedical informatics (MS, Graduate Certificate), including biomedical informatics (MS), clinical informatics (Graduate Certificate), public health informatics (Graduate Certificate); disaster and emergency management (MS); medical education (MS); nutrition (MS, Graduate Certificate), including functional nutrition and herbal therapy (Graduate Certificate); osteopathic medicine (DO); public health (MPH, Graduate Certificate), including health education (Graduate Certificate); social medicine (Graduate Certificate). *Accreditation:* AOsA. *Faculty:* 126 full-time (64 women), 1,411 part-time/adjunct (352 women). *Students:* 1,040 full-time (476 women), 196 part-time (135 women); includes 635 minority (95 Black or African American, non-Hispanic/Latino; 298 Asian, non-Hispanic/Latino; 208 Hispanic/Latino; 1 Native Hawaiian or other Pacific Islander, non-Hispanic/Latino; 33 Two or more races, non-Hispanic/Latino), 54 international. Average age 27. 5,383 applicants, 7% accepted, 248 enrolled. In 2016, 94 master's, 231 doctorates, 2 other advanced degrees awarded. *Degree requirements:* For master's, comprehensive exam (for MPH); field/special projects; for doctorate, comprehensive exam, COMLEX Boards; for Graduate Certificate, thesis or alternative. *Entrance requirements:* For master's, GRE; for doctorate, MCAT, biology, chemistry, organic chemistry, physics (all with labs), biochemistry, and English. *Application deadline:* For fall admission, 1/15 for domestic students. Applications are processed on a rolling basis. Application fee: $50. Electronic applications accepted. *Expenses:* $49,639 residents, $54,806 non-residentsfor out-of-state students; $100 microscope/laboratory fee (for first-year students); $145 per year Health Professions Division student access fee; $1,050 per year student service fee. *Financial support:* In 2016–17, 46 students received support, including 8 fellowships (averaging $30,690 per year); research assistantships, teaching assistantships, Federal Work-Study, and scholarships/grants also available. Financial award application deadline: 6/1; financial award applicants required to submit FAFSA. *Faculty research:* Teaching strategies, simulated patient use, HIV/AIDS education, minority health issues, managed care education. *Unit head:* Elaine M. Wallace, Dean, 954-262-1457, Fax: 954-262-2250, E-mail: ewallace@nova.edu. *Application contact:* HPD Admissions, 877-640-0218, E-mail: hpdinfo@nova.edu.
Website: http://www.osteopathic.nova.edu/

Oregon Health & Science University, School of Medicine, Graduate Programs in Medicine, Department of Medical Informatics and Clinical Epidemiology, Portland, OR 97239-3098. Offers bioinformatics (MS, PhD); clinical informatics (MBI, MS, PhD, Certificate); health information management (Certificate). *Program availability:* Part-time, online learning. *Faculty:* 12 full-time (6 women), 15 part-time/adjunct (7 women). *Students:* 31 full-time (7 women), 95 part-time (38 women); includes 34 minority (4 Black or African American, non-Hispanic/Latino; 22 Asian, non-Hispanic/Latino; 2 Hispanic/Latino; 6 Two or more races, non-Hispanic/Latino), 8 international. Average age 38. 42 applicants, 29 enrolled. In 2016, 21 master's, 2 doctorates, 20 other advanced degrees awarded. Terminal master's awarded for partial completion of doctoral program. *Degree requirements:* For master's, thesis or capstone project; for doctorate, comprehensive exam, thesis/dissertation, qualifying exam. *Entrance requirements:* For master's and doctorate, GRE General Test (minimum scores: 153 Verbal/148 Quantitative/4.5 Analytical), coursework in computer programming, human anatomy and physiology. Additional exam requirements/recommendations for international students: Required—IELTS or TOEFL. *Application deadline:* For fall admission, 12/1 for domestic students; for winter admission, 11/1 for domestic students; for spring admission, 2/1 for domestic students. Applications are processed on a rolling basis. Application fee: $70. Electronic applications accepted. *Expenses:* Contact institution. *Financial support:* Fellowships with full tuition reimbursements, research assistantships, Federal Work-Study, scholarships/grants, health care benefits, and full-tuition and stipends (for PhD students) available. Financial award application deadline: 3/1; financial award applicants required to submit FAFSA. *Faculty research:* Clinical informatics, computational biology, health information management, genomics, data analytics. *Unit head:* Dr. William Hersh, Program Director, 503-494-4563, E-mail: hersh@ohsu.edu. *Application contact:* Lauren Ludwig, Administrative Coordinator, 503-494-2252, E-mail: informat@ohsu.edu.
Website: http://www.ohsu.edu/dmice/

Regis University, College of Computer and Information Sciences, Denver, CO 80221-1099. Offers agile technologies (Certificate); cybersecurity (Certificate); data science (M Sc); database administration with Oracle (Certificate); database development (Certificate); database technologies (M Sc); enterprise Java software development (Certificate); enterprise resource planning (Certificate); executive information technology (Certificate); health care informatics (Certificate); health care informatics and information management (M Sc); information assurance (M Sc); information assurance policy management (Certificate); information technology management (M Sc); mobile software development (Certificate); software engineering (M Sc, Certificate); software engineering and database technology (M Sc); storage area networks (Certificate); systems engineering (M Sc, Certificate). *Program availability:* Part-time, evening/weekend, 100% online, blended/hybrid learning. *Faculty:* 11 full-time (3 women), 30 part-time/adjunct (10 women). *Students:* 341 full-time (95 women), 318 part-time (98 women); includes 186 minority (56 Black or African American, non-Hispanic/Latino; 2 American Indian or Alaska Native, non-Hispanic/Latino; 48 Asian, non-Hispanic/Latino; 63 Hispanic/Latino; 17 Two or more races, non-Hispanic/Latino), 57 international. Average age 37. 342 applicants, 79% accepted, 174 enrolled. In 2016, 192 master's awarded. *Degree requirements:* For master's, thesis (for some programs), final research project. *Entrance requirements:* For master's, official transcript reflecting baccalaureate degree awarded from regionally-accredited college or university, 2 years of related experience, resume, interview. Additional exam requirements/recommendations for international students: Required—TOEFL (minimum score 550 paper-based; 82 iBT). *Application deadline:* For fall admission, 8/15 priority date for domestic students, 7/13 for international students; for winter admission, 10/10 priority date for domestic students, 9/8 for international students; for spring admission, 1/10 priority date for domestic students, 11/17 for international students; for summer admission, 5/1 priority date for domestic students. Applications are processed on a rolling basis. Application fee: $75. Electronic applications accepted. *Expenses:* $730 per credit hour. *Financial support:* Scholarships/grants available. Financial award application deadline: 4/15; financial award applicants required to submit FAFSA. *Faculty research:* Information policy, knowledge management, software architectures, data science. *Unit head:* Shari Plantz-Masters, Academic Dean. *Application contact:* Cate Clark, Director of Admissions, 303-458-4900, Fax: 303-964-5534, E-mail: ruadmissions@regis.edu.
Website: http://regis.edu/CCIS.aspx

Roberts Wesleyan College, Health Administration Programs, Rochester, NY 14624-1997. Offers health administration (MS); healthcare informatics administration (MS). *Program availability:* Evening/weekend, online learning. *Degree requirements:* For master's, thesis or alternative. *Entrance requirements:* For master's, minimum GPA of 3.0, verifiable work experience or recommendation.

Sacred Heart University, Graduate Programs, College of Health Professions, Program in Health Science and Leadership, Fairfield, CT 06825. Offers MS. *Program availability:* Part-time, evening/weekend. *Faculty:* 2 full-time (0 women), 10 part-time/adjunct (7 women). *Students:* 41 full-time (21 women), 30 part-time (24 women); includes 14 minority (6 Black or African American, non-Hispanic/Latino; 4 Asian, non-Hispanic/Latino; 3 Hispanic/Latino; 1 Native Hawaiian or other Pacific Islander, non-Hispanic/Latino), 39 international. Average age 30. 122 applicants, 93% accepted, 18 enrolled. In 2016, 5 master's awarded. *Degree requirements:* For master's, comprehensive exam (for some programs). *Entrance requirements:* For master's, bachelor's degree, minimum cumulative undergraduate GPA of 3.0, personal essay, two letters of recommendation, resume. Additional exam requirements/recommendations for international students: Required—TOEFL (minimum score 570 paper-based, 80 iBT), TWE, or IELTS (6.5); Recommended—TSE. *Application deadline:* Applications are processed on a rolling basis. Application fee: $75. Electronic applications accepted. *Expenses:* $775 per credit part-time. *Financial support:* Unspecified assistantships available. Financial award applicants required to submit FAFSA. *Unit head:* Dr. Stephen C. Burrows, Chair, Health Science and Leadership/Program Director, Healthcare Informatics, 203-416-3948, Fax: 203-416-3951, E-mail: burrowss@sacredheart.edu. *Application contact:* William Sweeney, Director of Graduate Admissions Operations, 203-365-4827, E-mail: sweeneyw@sacredheart.edu.
Website: http://www.sacredheart.edu/academics/collegeofhealthprofessions/academicprograms/healthcareinformatics/

St. Joseph's College, Long Island Campus, Programs in Health Care Administration, Field in Health Care Management - Health Information Systems, Patchogue, NY 11772-2399. Offers MBA. *Expenses: Tuition:* Full-time $16,182; part-time $899 per credit. *Required fees:* $440.

St. Joseph's College, New York, Programs in Health Care Administration, Field in Health Care Management - Health Information Systems, Brooklyn, NY 11205-3688. Offers MBA. *Program availability:* Part-time, evening/weekend, 100% online, blended/hybrid learning. *Faculty:* 2 full-time (both women), 6 part-time/adjunct (3 women). *Students:* 4 full-time (3 women), 12 part-time (7 women); includes 13 minority (10 Black or African American, non-Hispanic/Latino; 2 Asian, non-Hispanic/Latino; 1 Hispanic/Latino). Average age 37. 5 applicants, 60% accepted, 3 enrolled. In 2016, 4 master's awarded. *Entrance requirements:* For master's, official transcripts, resume, two letters of reference, verification of employment. Additional exam requirements/recommendations for international students: Required—TOEFL (minimum score 80 iBT). Application fee: $25. *Expenses:* Contact institution. *Financial support:* In 2016–17, 3 students received support. *Unit head:* Lauren Pete, Chair, 718-940-5890, E-mail: lpete@sjcny.edu. *Application contact:* John Fitzgerald, Associate Director, Admissions, 718-940-5810, Fax: 718-636-8303, E-mail: jfitzgerald3@sjcny.edu.
Website: https://www.sjcny.edu

Saint Joseph's University, College of Arts and Sciences, Department of Health Services, Philadelphia, PA 19131-1395. Offers health administration (MS); health education (MS); informatics (MS); organizations development and leadership (MS). *Program availability:* Part-time, evening/weekend. *Faculty:* 12 full-time (6 women), 32

part-time/adjunct (12 women). *Students:* 52 full-time (35 women), 469 part-time (346 women); includes 188 minority (117 Black or African American, non-Hispanic/Latino; 1 American Indian or Alaska Native, non-Hispanic/Latino; 38 Asian, non-Hispanic/Latino; 23 Hispanic/Latino; 1 Native Hawaiian or other Pacific Islander, non-Hispanic/Latino; 8 Two or more races, non-Hispanic/Latino), 34 international. Average age 32. 156 applicants, 72% accepted, 59 enrolled. In 2016, 204 master's awarded. *Entrance requirements:* For master's, GRE (if GPA less than 2.75), 2 letters of recommendation, resume, personal statement, official transcripts. Additional exam requirements/recommendations for international students: Required—TOEFL (minimum score 550 paper-based; 80 iBT), IELTS (minimum score 6.5). *Application deadline:* For fall admission, 7/15 for international students; for spring admission, 11/1 for international students. Applications are processed on a rolling basis. Application fee: $35. Electronic applications accepted. *Expenses:* $853 per credit. *Financial support:* In 2016–17, 12 students received support. Career-related internships or fieldwork and unspecified assistantships available. Financial award application deadline: 5/1; financial award applicants required to submit FAFSA. *Unit head:* Louis D. Horvath, Director, 610-660-3131, E-mail: gradcas@sju.edu. *Application contact:* Graduate Admissions, College of Arts and Sciences, 610-660-3131, E-mail: gradcas@sju.edu.
Website: http://sju.edu/majors-programs/graduate-arts-sciences/masters/health-administration-ms

Slippery Rock University of Pennsylvania, Graduate Studies (Recruitment), College of Health, Environment, and Science, Department of Computer Science, Slippery Rock, PA 16057-1383. Offers health informatics (MS). *Program availability:* Part-time, evening/weekend, online only, 100% online. *Faculty:* 2 full-time (0 women). *Students:* 4 full-time (2 women), 5 part-time (3 women). Average age 38. 15 applicants, 87% accepted, 9 enrolled. *Entrance requirements:* For master's, minimum GPA of 3.0. Additional exam requirements/recommendations for international students: Required—TOEFL (minimum score 550 paper-based; 80 iBT). *Application deadline:* For fall admission, 5/1 priority date for domestic students, 3/1 priority date for international students; for spring admission, 10/1 priority date for domestic students, 9/1 priority date for international students. Applications are processed on a rolling basis. Application fee: $25 ($30 for international students). Electronic applications accepted. *Expenses:* $581.45 per online credit in-state; $648.65 per online credit out-of-state. *Financial support:* In 2016–17, 1 student received support. Career-related internships or fieldwork, Federal Work-Study, institutionally sponsored loans, scholarships/grants, tuition waivers (partial), and unspecified assistantships available. Support available to part-time students. Financial award application deadline: 5/1; financial award applicants required to submit FAFSA. *Unit head:* Dr. Sam Thangiah, Department Chair, 724-738-2141, Fax: 724-738-4513, E-mail: sam.thangiah@sru.edu. *Application contact:* Brandi Weber-Mortimer, Director of Graduate Admissions, 724-738-2051, Fax: 724-738-2146, E-mail: graduate.admissions@sru.edu.
Website: http://www.sru.edu/academics/colleges-and-departments/ches/departments/computer-science

Southern Illinois University Edwardsville, Graduate School, Program in Healthcare Informatics, Edwardsville, IL 62026. Offers MS. *Program availability:* Part-time, evening/weekend. *Degree requirements:* For master's, comprehensive exam. *Entrance requirements:* For master's, baccalaureate degree with minimum GPA of 2.75. Additional exam requirements/recommendations for international students: Required—TOEFL (minimum score 550 paper-based; 79 iBT), IELTS (minimum score 6.5). Electronic applications accepted.

Southern New Hampshire University, School of Business, Manchester, NH 03106-1045. Offers accounting (MBA, MS, Graduate Certificate); accounting finance (MS); accounting/auditing (MS); accounting/forensic accounting (MS); accounting/taxation (MS); athletic administration (MBA, Graduate Certificate); business administration (IMBA, MBA, Certificate, Graduate Certificate), including accounting (Certificate), business administration (MBA), business information systems (Graduate Certificate), human resource management (Certificate); corporate social responsibility (MBA); entrepreneurship (MBA); finance (MBA, MS, Graduate Certificate); finance/corporate finance (MS); finance/investments and securities (MS); forensic accounting (MBA); healthcare informatics (MBA); healthcare management (MBA); human resource management (Graduate Certificate); information technology (MS, Graduate Certificate); information technology management (MBA); international business (Graduate Certificate); international business and information technology (Graduate Certificate); international finance (Graduate Certificate); international sport management (Graduate Certificate); justice studies (MBA); leadership of nonprofit organizations (Graduate Certificate); management (MS); marketing (MBA, MS, Graduate Certificate); operations and project management (MS); operations and supply chain management (MBA, Graduate Certificate); organizational leadership (MS); project management (MBA, Graduate Certificate); Six Sigma (MBA); Six Sigma quality (Graduate Certificate); social media marketing (MBA); sport management (MBA, MS, Graduate Certificate); sustainability and environmental compliance (MBA); workplace conflict management (MBA); MBA/Certificate. *Accreditation:* ACBSP. *Program availability:* Part-time, evening/weekend, online learning. Terminal master's awarded for partial completion of doctoral program. *Degree requirements:* For master's, one foreign language, comprehensive exam (for some programs), thesis or alternative. *Entrance requirements:* For master's, minimum GPA of 2.5. Additional exam requirements/recommendations for international students: Required—TOEFL (minimum score 500 paper-based). Electronic applications accepted.

Stephens College, Division of Graduate and Continuing Studies, Columbia, MO 65215-0002. Offers counseling (M Ed), including addictions counseling, clinical mental health counseling, school counseling; health information administration (Postbaccalaureate Certificate); physician assistant studies (MPAS); TV and screenwriting (MFA). *Program availability:* Part-time, evening/weekend, online learning. *Faculty:* 14 full-time (9 women), 30 part-time/adjunct (19 women). *Students:* 117 full-time (101 women), 107 part-time (96 women); includes 25 minority (2 Black or African American, non-Hispanic/Latino; 2 American Indian or Alaska Native, non-Hispanic/Latino; 1 Asian, non-Hispanic/Latino; 2 Hispanic/Latino; 1 Native Hawaiian or other Pacific Islander, non-Hispanic/Latino; 17 Two or more races, non-Hispanic/Latino), 1 international. Average age 35. 226 applicants, 43% accepted, 87 enrolled. In 2016, 44 master's awarded. *Entrance requirements:* For master's, minimum GPA of 3.0 in last 60 hours. Additional exam requirements/recommendations for international students: Required—TOEFL (minimum score 79 iBT). *Application deadline:* For fall admission, 8/15 priority date for domestic and international students; for winter admission, 1/9 priority date for domestic and international students; for spring admission, 6/5 priority date for domestic and international students. Applications are processed on a rolling basis. Application fee: $50. Electronic applications accepted. *Expenses: Tuition:* Full-time $3564; part-time $396 per credit hour. *Required fees:* $45 per credit hour. *Financial support:* In 2016–17, 5 fellowships with full tuition reimbursements (averaging $7,673 per year) were awarded; unspecified assistantships also available. Financial award applicants required to submit FAFSA. *Faculty research:* Educational psychology, outcomes assessment. *Unit head:* Dr. Brian Sajko, Vice President of Strategic Enrollment Management, 800-388-7579, Fax: 573-876-7237, E-mail: online@stephens.edu. *Application contact:* Lindsey Boudinot, Director of Graduate and Online Admissions, 800-388-7579, E-mail: online@stephens.edu.

Stevens Institute of Technology, Graduate School, Charles V. Schaefer Jr. School of Engineering and Science, Department of Computer Science, Hoboken, NJ 07030. Offers computer graphics (Certificate), including computer graphics; computer science (MS, PhD); computer systems (Certificate), including computer systems; cybersecurity (MS); database management systems (Certificate), including databases; distributed systems (Certificate), including distributed systems; elements of computer science (Certificate), including cybersecurity; enterprise and cloud computing (MS); enterprise computing (Certificate), including enterprise and cloud computing; enterprise security and information assurance (Certificate), including enterprise security and information assurance; health informatics (Certificate), including health informatics; multimedia experience and management (Certificate), including multimedia experience and management; networks and systems administration (Certificate), including cloud computing; service oriented computing (Certificate), including service oriented computing. *Program availability:* Part-time, evening/weekend. *Faculty:* 21 full-time (4 women), 13 part-time/adjunct (2 women). *Students:* 436 full-time (124 women), 72 part-time (12 women); includes 27 minority (4 Black or African American, non-Hispanic/Latino; 21 Asian, non-Hispanic/Latino; 1 Hispanic/Latino; 1 Two or more races, non-Hispanic/Latino), 423 international. Average age 25. 1,183 applicants, 54% accepted, 184 enrolled. In 2016, 225 master's, 4 doctorates, 18 other advanced degrees awarded. Terminal master's awarded for partial completion of doctoral program. *Degree requirements:* For master's, thesis optional, minimum B average in major field and overall; for doctorate, comprehensive exam (for some programs), thesis/dissertation; for Certificate, minimum B average. *Entrance requirements:* Additional exam requirements/recommendations for international students: Required—TOEFL (minimum score 74 iBT), IELTS (minimum score 6). *Application deadline:* For fall admission, 6/1 for domestic students, 4/15 for international students; for spring admission, 11/30 for domestic students, 11/1 for international students. Applications are processed on a rolling basis. Application fee: $65. Electronic applications accepted. *Expenses:* Contact institution. *Financial support:* Fellowships, research assistantships, teaching assistantships, career-related internships or fieldwork, Federal Work-Study, scholarships/grants, and unspecified assistantships available. Financial award application deadline: 2/15; financial award applicants required to submit FAFSA. *Faculty research:* Computer security, computer vision, dynamic scene analysis, privacy-preserving data mining, visualization. *Unit head:* Giuseppe Ateniese, Director, 201-216-3741, E-mail: gatenies@stevens.edu. *Application contact:* Graduate Admissions, 888-783-8367, Fax: 888-511-1306, E-mail: graduate@stevens.edu.
Website: https://www.stevens.edu/schaefer-school-engineering-science/departments/computer-science

Stony Brook University, State University of New York, Stony Brook Medicine, School of Health Technology and Management, Stony Brook, NY 11794. Offers applied health informatics (MS); disability studies (Certificate); health administration (MHA); health and rehabilitation sciences (PhD); health care management (Advanced Certificate); health care policy and management (MS); occupational therapy (MS); physical therapy (DPT); physician assistant (MS). *Accreditation:* APTA. *Faculty:* 62 full-time (41 women), 64 part-time/adjunct (44 women). *Students:* 573 full-time (381 women), 68 part-time (52 women); includes 186 minority (32 Black or African American, non-Hispanic/Latino; 1 American Indian or Alaska Native, non-Hispanic/Latino; 94 Asian, non-Hispanic/Latino; 50 Hispanic/Latino; 2 Native Hawaiian or other Pacific Islander, non-Hispanic/Latino; 7 Two or more races, non-Hispanic/Latino), 12 international. Average age 28. 2,672 applicants, 15% accepted, 258 enrolled. In 2016, 133 master's, 91 doctorates, 28 other advanced degrees awarded. *Degree requirements:* For master's, thesis; for doctorate, thesis/dissertation. *Entrance requirements:* For master's, GRE General Test, minimum GPA of 3.0, work experience in field, references; for doctorate, GRE, three references, essay. Additional exam requirements/recommendations for international students: Required—TOEFL (minimum score 550 paper-based). *Application deadline:* For fall admission, 1/15 for domestic students; for spring admission, 10/1 for domestic students. Application fee: $100. *Expenses:* Contact institution. *Financial support:* In 2016–17, 1 research assistantship was awarded; fellowships, teaching assistantships, career-related internships or fieldwork, Federal Work-Study, and institutionally sponsored loans also available. Financial award application deadline: 3/15. *Faculty research:* Developmental disabilities, disability studies, health promotion, multiple sclerosis, quality of life program, internal medicine, lung disease, palliative care, respiratory diseases, neuromuscular disorders, orthopedics, physical medicine and rehabilitation, physical therapy, prostheses or implants, advance directives, advocacy alienation, allied health education, allied health occupations, adolescents, adoption, child or adolescent mental health, multiple sclerosis, youth policy. *Total annual research expenditures:* $1.2 million. *Unit head:* Dr. Craig A. Lehmann, Dean, 631-444-2253, Fax: 631-444-7621, E-mail: craig.lehmann@stonybrook.edu. *Application contact:* Dr. Richard W. Johnson, Associate Dean for Graduate Studies, 631-444-3251, Fax: 631-444-7621, E-mail: richard.johnson@stonybrook.edu.
Website: http://healthtechnology.stonybrookmedicine.edu/

Temple University, College of Public Health, Department of Health Services Administration and Policy, Philadelphia, PA 19122. Offers health informatics (MS). *Program availability:* Part-time, evening/weekend, online learning. *Entrance requirements:* For master's, two letters of reference, statement of goals. Additional exam requirements/recommendations for international students: Required—TOEFL (minimum score 550 paper-based; 79 iBT). Electronic applications accepted.

Texas State University, The Graduate College, College of Health Professions, Program in Health Information Management, San Marcos, TX 78666. Offers MHIIM. *Program availability:* Part-time, evening/weekend. *Faculty:* 6 full-time (3 women), 1 (woman) part-time/adjunct. *Students:* 19 full-time (15 women), 13 part-time (all women); includes 22 minority (11 Black or African American, non-Hispanic/Latino; 10 Hispanic/Latino; 1 Two or more races, non-Hispanic/Latino). Average age 38. 41 applicants, 61% accepted, 20 enrolled. *Degree requirements:* For master's, comprehensive exam, thesis optional, committee review. *Entrance requirements:* For master's, baccalaureate degree from regionally-accredited institution with minimum GPA of 2.75 on last 60 hours of undergraduate work, 3 letters of reference, written statement of purpose, current resume. Additional exam requirements/recommendations for international students: Required—TOEFL (minimum score 550 paper-based; 78 iBT), IELTS (minimum score 6.5). *Application deadline:* For fall admission, 6/1 for domestic and international students. Applications are processed on a rolling basis. Application fee: $40 ($90 for international students). Electronic applications accepted. *Expenses:* $4,851 per semester. *Financial support:* In 2016–17, 18 students received support, including 2 teaching assistantships (averaging $13,502 per year); research assistantships, career-related internships or fieldwork, Federal Work-Study, and institutionally sponsored loans also available. Support available to part-time students. Financial award application deadline: 3/1; financial award applicants required to submit FAFSA. *Unit head:* Jackie Moczygemba, Graduate Advisor, 512-245-8242, E-mail: jm38@txstate.edu. *Application contact:* Dr. Andrea Golato, Dean of Graduate School, 512-245-2581, Fax: 512-245-8365, E-mail: gradcollege@txstate.edu.
Website: http://www.health.txstate.edu/hsr

Trident University International, College of Health Sciences, Program in Health Sciences, Cypress, CA 90630. Offers clinical research administration (MS, Certificate); emergency and disaster management (MS, Certificate); environmental health science

(Certificate); health care administration (PhD); health care management (MS), including health informatics; health education (MS, Certificate); health informatics (Certificate); health sciences (PhD); international health (MS); international health: educator or researcher option (PhD); international health: practitioner option (PhD); law and expert witness studies (MS, Certificate); public health (MS); quality assurance (Certificate). *Program availability:* Part-time, evening/weekend, online learning. *Degree requirements:* For doctorate, comprehensive exam, thesis/dissertation, defense of dissertation. *Entrance requirements:* For master's, minimum GPA of 2.5 (students with GPA 3.0 or greater may transfer up to 30% of graduate level credits); for doctorate, minimum GPA of 3.4, curriculum vitae, course work in research methods or statistics. Additional exam requirements/recommendations for international students: Required—TOEFL. Electronic applications accepted.

The University of Alabama at Birmingham, School of Health Professions, Program in Health Informatics, Birmingham, AL 35294. Offers MSHI. *Program availability:* Online learning. *Degree requirements:* For master's, thesis, administrative internship, or project. *Entrance requirements:* For master's, GRE General Test, MAT, minimum undergraduate GPA of 3.0, course work in computing fundamentals and programming, letters of recommendation, interview. Additional exam requirements/recommendations for international students: Recommended—TOEFL, IELTS. Electronic applications accepted. Full-time tuition and fees vary according to course load and program. *Faculty research:* Healthcare/medical informatics, natural language processing, application of expert systems, graphical user interface design.

University of Central Florida, College of Health and Public Affairs, Department of Health Management and Informatics, Orlando, FL 32816. Offers health care informatics (MS); health information administration (Certificate); health services administration (MS). *Accreditation:* CAHME. *Program availability:* Part-time, evening/weekend. *Faculty:* 27 full-time (15 women), 21 part-time/adjunct (11 women). *Students:* 159 full-time (122 women), 161 part-time (118 women); includes 188 minority (87 Black or African American, non-Hispanic/Latino; 1 American Indian or Alaska Native, non-Hispanic/ Latino; 41 Asian, non-Hispanic/Latino; 51 Hispanic/Latino; 8 Two or more races, non-Hispanic/Latino), 5 international. Average age 28. 203 applicants, 76% accepted, 107 enrolled. In 2016, 126 master's awarded. *Degree requirements:* For master's, comprehensive exam, thesis or alternative, research report. *Entrance requirements:* For master's, GRE General Test. Additional exam requirements/recommendations for international students: Required—TOEFL. *Application deadline:* For fall admission, 7/15 for domestic students; for spring admission, 12/1 for domestic students. Application fee: $30. Electronic applications accepted. *Expenses:* Tuition, state resident: part-time $288.16 per credit hour. Tuition, nonresident: part-time $1071.31 per credit hour. *Financial support:* In 2016–17, 7 students received support, including 7 research assistantships with partial tuition reimbursements available (averaging $8,425 per year), 1 teaching assistantship (averaging $9,998 per year); career-related internships or fieldwork, Federal Work-Study, institutionally sponsored loans, and unspecified assistantships also available. Financial award application deadline: 3/1; financial award applicants required to submit FAFSA. *Unit head:* Dr. Reid Oetjen, Interim Chair, 407-823-5668, E-mail: reid.oetjen@ucf.edu. *Application contact:* Assistant Director, Graduate Admissions, 407-823-2766, Fax: 407-823-6442, E-mail: gradadmissions@ucf.edu.
Website: http://www.cohpa.ucf.edu/hmi/

University of Cincinnati, Graduate School, College of Allied Health Sciences, Department of Clinical and Health Information Sciences, Cincinnati, OH 45221. Offers health informatics (MHI). *Program availability:* Part-time, online learning. *Expenses: Tuition, area resident:* Full-time $12,790; part-time $389 per credit hour. Tuition, state resident: full-time $13,290; part-time $419 per credit hour. Tuition, nonresident: full-time $24,532; part-time $976 per credit hour. *International tuition:* $24,832 full-time. *Required fees:* $3958; $140 per credit hour. Tuition and fees vary according to course load, degree level, program and reciprocity agreements.

The University of Findlay, Office of Graduate Admissions, Findlay, OH 45840-3653. Offers applied security and analytics (MSAS); athletic training (MAT); business (MBA), including certified management accountant, certified public accountant, health care management, hospitality management; education (MA Ed, Ed D), including children's literature (MA Ed), curriculum and teaching (MA Ed), education (MA Ed), educational administration (MA Ed), human resource development (MA Ed), reading (MA Ed), science education (MA Ed), superintendent (Ed D), teaching (Ed D), technology (MA Ed); environmental, safety and health management (MSEM); health informatics (MS); occupational therapy (MOT); pharmacy (Pharm D); physical therapy (DPT); physician assistant (MPA); rhetoric and writing (MA); teaching English to speakers of other languages (TESOL) and bilingual education (MA). *Program availability:* Part-time, evening/weekend, 100% online, blended/hybrid learning. *Faculty:* 114 full-time (63 women), 44 part-time/adjunct (18 women). *Students:* 751 full-time (452 women), 573 part-time (323 women); includes 164 minority (82 Black or African American, non-Hispanic/Latino; 1 American Indian or Alaska Native, non-Hispanic/Latino; 27 Asian, non-Hispanic/Latino; 37 Hispanic/Latino; 17 Two or more races, non-Hispanic/Latino), 280 international. Average age 28. 661 applicants, 52% accepted, 288 enrolled. In 2016, 366 master's, 137 doctorates awarded. *Degree requirements:* For master's, comprehensive exam (for some programs), thesis, cumulative project, capstone project; for doctorate, thesis/dissertation. *Entrance requirements:* For master's, GRE (for some programs), bachelor's degree from accredited institution, minimum undergraduate GPA of 3.0 in last 64 hours of course work; for doctorate, MAT, minimum cumulative GPA of 3.0, master's degree. Additional exam requirements/recommendations for international students: Recommended—TOEFL (minimum score 79 iBT), IELTS (minimum score 7). *Application deadline:* For fall admission, 6/15 for international students; for spring admission, 12/1 for international students; for summer admission, 4/1 for international students. Applications are processed on a rolling basis. Electronic applications accepted. *Expenses:* Contact institution. *Financial support:* In 2016–17, 139 students received support, including 15 research assistantships with partial tuition reimbursements available (averaging $7,200 per year), 25 teaching assistantships with partial tuition reimbursements available (averaging $7,200 per year); Federal Work-Study, institutionally sponsored loans, and unspecified assistantships also available. Financial award application deadline: 4/1; financial award applicants required to submit FAFSA. *Unit head:* Christopher M. Harris, Director of Admissions, 419-434-4347, E-mail: harrisc1@findlay.edu. *Application contact:* Madeline Fauser Brennan, Graduate Admissions Counselor, 419-434-4636, Fax: 419-434-4898, E-mail: fauserbrennan@findlay.edu.
Website: http://www.findlay.edu/admissions/graduate/Pages/default.aspx

University of Illinois at Chicago, College of Applied Health Sciences, Program in Health Informatics, Chicago, IL 60607-7128. Offers health informatics (MS, CAS); health information management (Certificate). *Program availability:* Part-time, online learning. *Expenses:* Contact institution. *Faculty research:* Information science, computer science, health informatics, health information management.

University of Illinois at Urbana–Champaign, Graduate College, School of Information Sciences, Champaign, IL 61820. Offers bioinformatics (MS); digital libraries (CAS); information management (MS); library and information science (MS, PhD, CAS). *Accreditation:* ALA (one or more programs are accredited). *Program availability:* Part-time, online learning. *Entrance requirements:* For degree, master's degree in library and information science or related field with minimum GPA of 3.0.

The University of Iowa, Graduate College, Program in Informatics, Iowa City, IA 52242-1316. Offers bioinformatics (MS, PhD); bioinformatics and computational biology (Certificate); geoinformatics (MS, PhD, Certificate); health informatics (MS, PhD, Certificate); information science (MS, PhD, Certificate). *Degree requirements:* For master's, thesis optional; for doctorate, comprehensive exam, thesis/dissertation. *Entrance requirements:* For master's and doctorate, GRE General Test, minimum GPA of 3.0. Additional exam requirements/recommendations for international students: Required—TOEFL (minimum score 550 paper-based; 81 iBT). Electronic applications accepted.

The University of Kansas, University of Kansas Medical Center, Interprofessional Program in Health Informatics, Kansas City, KS 66160. Offers MS, Post Master's Certificate. *Program availability:* Part-time, evening/weekend, 100% online, blended/hybrid learning. *Faculty:* 6. *Students:* 7 part-time (5 women); includes 2 minority (both Two or more races, non-Hispanic/Latino). Average age 30. 7 applicants, 43% accepted, 1 enrolled. In 2016, 3 master's awarded. *Degree requirements:* For master's, comprehensive exam, thesis or alternative, minimum GPA of 3.0; for Post Master's Certificate, minimum GPA of 3.0. *Entrance requirements:* For master's, minimum GPA of 3.0, official copies of transcripts, 3 references, resume, personal statement; for Post Master's Certificate, minimum cumulative GPA of 3.0, official copies of transcripts, 3 references, resume, personal statement. Additional exam requirements/recommendations for international students: Required—TOEFL or IELTS. *Application deadline:* For fall admission, 4/1 for domestic and international students; for spring admission, 9/1 for domestic and international students. Application fee: $60. Electronic applications accepted. *Financial support:* Application deadline: 3/1; applicants required to submit FAFSA. *Faculty research:* GIS in public health, symbolic representation of health data, inter-professional education and practice, usability of health systems, electronic health record systems quality and safety. *Unit head:* Dr. E. LaVerne Manos, Director, 913-588-1671, Fax: 913-588-1660, E-mail: lmanos@kumc.edu. *Application contact:* Teresa Stenner, Program Manager, 913-588-3362, Fax: 913-588-1660, E-mail: healthinformatics@kumc.edu.
Website: http://www.kumc.edu/health-informatics.html

University of Maryland, Baltimore County, The Graduate School, College of Engineering and Information Technology, Department of Information Systems, Program in Health Information Technology, Baltimore, MD 21227. Offers MPS. *Program availability:* Part-time. *Faculty:* 1 (woman) full-time, 1 part-time/adjunct (0 women). *Students:* 13 full-time (8 women), 36 part-time (21 women); includes 30 minority (18 Black or African American, non-Hispanic/Latino; 9 Asian, non-Hispanic/Latino; 3 Hispanic/Latino), 5 international. Average age 32. 28 applicants, 75% accepted, 16 enrolled. *Entrance requirements:* For master's, minimum undergraduate GPA of 3.0. Additional exam requirements/recommendations for international students: Required—TOEFL (minimum score 550 paper-based; 80 iBT), GRE. Application fee: $70. *Expenses:* Contact institution. *Financial support:* In 2016–17, 2 research assistantships (averaging $18,000 per year) were awarded; fellowships, teaching assistantships, health care benefits, and unspecified assistantships also available. *Faculty research:* Health information technology. *Unit head:* Dr. Aryya Gangopadhyay, Professor and Chair, 410-455-2620, Fax: 410-455-1217, E-mail: gangopad@umbc.edu. *Application contact:* Dr. George Karabatis, Associate Professor/Associate Chair for Academic Affairs, 410-455-2650, Fax: 410-455-1217, E-mail: georgek@umbc.edu.
Website: http://www.umbc.edu/hit/

University of Maryland University College, The Graduate School, Health Informatics Administration Program, Adelphi, MD 20783. Offers MS. *Program availability:* Part-time, evening/weekend, online learning. *Students:* 1 full-time (0 women), 350 part-time (254 women); includes 247 minority (177 Black or African American, non-Hispanic/Latino; 1 American Indian or Alaska Native, non-Hispanic/Latino; 47 Asian, non-Hispanic/Latino; 11 Hispanic/Latino; 11 Two or more races, non-Hispanic/Latino), 8 international. Average age 33. 141 applicants, 100% accepted, 112 enrolled. In 2016, 45 master's awarded. *Degree requirements:* For master's, thesis or alternative, capstone course. *Application deadline:* Applications are processed on a rolling basis. Application fee: $50. Electronic applications accepted. *Expenses:* Tuition, state resident: part-time $458 per credit. Tuition, nonresident: part-time $659 per credit. *Financial support:* Federal Work-Study and scholarships/grants available. Support available to part-time students. Financial award application deadline: 6/1; financial award applicants required to submit FAFSA. *Unit head:* Zakevia Green-Lawson, Program Chair, 240-684-2471, Fax: 240-684-2401, E-mail: zakevia.green-lawson@umuc.edu. *Application contact:* Coordinator, Graduate Admissions, 800-888-8682, Fax: 240-684-2151, E-mail: newgrad@umuc.edu.
Website: http://www.umuc.edu/academic-programs/masters-degrees/health-informatics-administration.cfm

★ **University of Michigan,** Rackham Graduate School, School of Information, Ann Arbor, MI 48109-1285. Offers health informatics (MHI); information (MSI, PhD). *Accreditation:* ALA (one or more programs are accredited). *Program availability:* Part-time. *Students:* 453 full-time (270 women), 32 part-time (20 women); includes 99 minority (16 Black or African American, non-Hispanic/Latino; 49 Asian, non-Hispanic/Latino; 21 Hispanic/Latino; 13 Two or more races, non-Hispanic/Latino), 212 international. Average age 27. 829 applicants, 53% accepted, 199 enrolled. In 2016, 179 master's, 7 doctorates awarded. Terminal master's awarded for partial completion of doctoral program. *Degree requirements:* For master's, thesis optional, internship; for doctorate, thesis/dissertation. *Entrance requirements:* For master's and doctorate, GRE General Test. Additional exam requirements/recommendations for international students: Required—TOEFL (minimum score 100 iBT). *Application deadline:* Applications are processed on a rolling basis. Application fee: $75 ($90 for international students). Electronic applications accepted. *Expenses:* Contact institution. *Financial support:* In 2016–17, 122 students received support, including 2 fellowships (averaging $28,200 per year), 33 research assistantships (averaging $28,200 per year), 41 teaching assistantships (averaging $28,200 per year); scholarships/grants and tuition waivers (full and partial) also available. *Unit head:* Dr. Thomas A. Finholt, Dean, School of Information, 734-647-3576. *Application contact:* School of Information Admissions, 734-763-2285, Fax: 734-615-3587, E-mail: umsi.admissions@umich.edu.
Website: http://www.si.umich.edu/

See Display on page 346 and Close-Up on page 375.

University of Michigan–Dearborn, College of Education, Health, and Human Services, Master of Science Program in Health Information Technology, Dearborn, MI 48126. Offers MS. *Program availability:* Part-time, evening/weekend. *Faculty:* 5 full-time (3 women), 2 part-time/adjunct (both women). *Students:* 10 full-time (8 women), 14 part-time (all women); includes 7 minority (2 Black or African American, non-Hispanic/Latino; 4 Asian, non-Hispanic/Latino; 1 Two or more races, non-Hispanic/Latino), 2 international. Average age 30. 26 applicants, 88% accepted, 14 enrolled. In 2016, 2 master's awarded. *Entrance requirements:* Additional exam requirements/recommendations for international students: Required—TOEFL (minimum score 560

paper-based; 84 iBT), IELTS (minimum score 6.5). *Application deadline:* For fall admission, 8/1 for domestic students, 5/1 for international students; for winter admission, 12/1 for domestic students, 9/1 for international students; for spring admission, 4/1 for domestic students, 1/1 for international students. Applications are processed on a rolling basis. Application fee: $60. Electronic applications accepted. *Expenses:* Contact institution. *Financial support:* In 2016–17, 8 students received support. Career-related internships or fieldwork and scholarships/grants available. Financial award application deadline: 3/1; financial award applicants required to submit FAFSA. *Faculty research:* Behavior and new technology, information quality, technology acceptance, healthcare systems, economics of recovery. *Unit head:* Dr. Stein Brunvand, Director, 313-583-6415, E-mail: sbrunvan@umich.edu. *Application contact:* Elizabeth Morden, Program Assistant, 313-593-5090, E-mail: emorden@umich.edu.
Website: http://umdearborn.edu/cehhs/cehhs_m_hit/

University of Michigan–Flint, College of Arts and Sciences, Program in Computer Science and Information Systems, Flint, MI 48502-1950. Offers computer science (MS); information systems (MS), including business information systems, health information systems. *Program availability:* Part-time, evening/weekend, 100% online. *Faculty:* 29 full-time (7 women), 12 part-time/adjunct (7 women). *Students:* 35 full-time (17 women), 91 part-time (24 women); includes 11 minority (3 Black or African American, non-Hispanic/Latino; 2 Asian, non-Hispanic/Latino; 4 Hispanic/Latino; 1 Native Hawaiian or other Pacific Islander, non-Hispanic/Latino; 1 Two or more races, non-Hispanic/Latino), 82 international. Average age 28. 712 applicants, 29% accepted, 29 enrolled. In 2016, 171 master's awarded. *Degree requirements:* For master's, thesis optional. *Entrance requirements:* For master's, BS from regionally-accredited institution in computer science, computer information systems, or computer engineering (preferred); minimum overall undergraduate GPA of 3.0. Additional exam requirements/recommendations for international students: Required—TOEFL (minimum score 84 iBT), IELTS (minimum score 6.5). *Application deadline:* For fall admission, 5/1 for domestic students, 2/1 for international students; for winter admission, 10/1 for domestic students, 8/1 for international students; for spring admission, 3/15 for domestic students, 1/1 for international students; for summer admission, 5/15 for domestic students, 3/1 for international students. Applications are processed on a rolling basis. Application fee: $55. Electronic applications accepted. *Expenses:* Contact institution. *Financial support:* Federal Work-Study, scholarships/grants, and unspecified assistantships available. Support available to part-time students. Financial award application deadline: 3/1; financial award applicants required to submit FAFSA. *Faculty research:* Computer network systems, database management systems, artificial intelligence and controlled systems. *Unit head:* Dr. Jeffrey Livermore, Director, 810-762-3131, Fax: 810-766-6780, E-mail: jefflive@umflint.edu. *Application contact:* Bradley T. Maki, Director of Graduate Admissions, 810-762-3171, Fax: 810-766-6789, E-mail: bmaki@umflint.edu.
Website: http://www.umflint.edu/graduateprograms/computer-science-information-systems-ms

University of Minnesota, Twin Cities Campus, Graduate School, Program in Health Informatics, Minneapolis, MN 55455-0213. Offers MHI, MS, PhD, MD/MHI. *Program availability:* Part-time. *Degree requirements:* For master's, thesis or alternative; for doctorate, thesis/dissertation. *Entrance requirements:* For master's and doctorate, GRE General Test, previous course work in life sciences, programming, calculus. Additional exam requirements/recommendations for international students: Required—TOEFL (minimum score 550 paper-based). Electronic applications accepted. *Faculty research:* Medical decision making, physiological control systems, population studies, clinical information systems, telemedicine.

University of Missouri, Office of Research and Graduate Studies, Department of Health Management and Informatics, Columbia, MO 65211. Offers health administration (MHA); health informatics (MS, Certificate). *Accreditation:* CAHME. *Program availability:* Part-time. *Faculty:* 19 full-time (8 women), 2 part-time/adjunct (0 women). *Students:* 76 full-time (40 women), 35 part-time (24 women); includes 21 minority (10 Black or African American, non-Hispanic/Latino; 6 Asian, non-Hispanic/Latino; 4 Hispanic/Latino; 1 Two or more races, non-Hispanic/Latino), 14 international. Average age 30. *Entrance requirements:* For master's, GRE General Test or GMAT, minimum GPA of 3.0. Additional exam requirements/recommendations for international students: Required—TOEFL (minimum score 550 paper-based; 80 iBT), IELTS (minimum score 6.5). *Application deadline:* Applications are processed on a rolling basis. Application fee: $75 ($90 for international students). Electronic applications accepted. *Expenses:* Tuition, state resident: full-time $6347; part-time $352.60 per credit hour. Tuition, nonresident: full-time $17,379; part-time $965.50 per credit hour. *Required fees:* $1035. Tuition and fees vary according to course load, campus/location and program. *Financial support:* Fellowships, research assistantships, teaching assistantships, institutionally sponsored loans, scholarships/grants, traineeships, health care benefits, and unspecified assistantships available. Support available to part-time students.
Website: http://www.hmi.missouri.edu/

University of New England, College of Graduate and Professional Studies, Portland, ME 04103. Offers applied nutrition (MS); career and technical education (MS Ed); curriculum and instruction (MS Ed); education (CAGS, Post-Master's Certificate); education leadership (Ed D); educational leadership (MS Ed); generalist (MS Ed); health informatics (MS, Graduate Certificate); inclusion education (MS Ed); literacy K-12 (MS Ed); medical education leadership (MMEL); public health (Graduate Certificate); reading specialist (MS Ed); social work (MSW). *Program availability:* Part-time, evening/weekend, online only, 100% online. *Faculty:* 67 part-time/adjunct (46 women). *Students:* 891 full-time (667 women), 359 part-time (261 women); includes 309 minority (215 Black or African American, non-Hispanic/Latino; 2 American Indian or Alaska Native, non-Hispanic/Latino; 63 Asian, non-Hispanic/Latino; 18 Hispanic/Latino; 2 Native Hawaiian or other Pacific Islander, non-Hispanic/Latino; 9 Two or more races, non-Hispanic/Latino). Average age 36. 777 applicants, 50% accepted, 316 enrolled. In 2016, 292 master's, 34 doctorates, 130 other advanced degrees awarded. *Application deadline:* Applications are processed on a rolling basis. Electronic applications accepted. Tuition and fees vary according to degree level, program and student level. *Financial support:* Application deadline: 5/1; applicants required to submit FAFSA. *Unit head:* Dr. Martha Wilson, Associate Provost for Online Worldwide Learning/Dean of the College of Graduate and Professional Studies, 207-221-4985, E-mail: mwilson13@une.edu.
Website: http://online.une.edu

The University of North Carolina at Charlotte, The Graduate School, Program in Health Informatics, Charlotte, NC 28223-0001. Offers PSM, Graduate Certificate. *Program availability:* Part-time, evening/weekend. *Students:* 23 full-time (18 women), 31 part-time (20 women); includes 22 minority (15 Black or African American, non-Hispanic/Latino; 5 Asian, non-Hispanic/Latino; 1 Native Hawaiian or other Pacific Islander, non-Hispanic/Latino; 1 Two or more races, non-Hispanic/Latino), 11 international. Average age 31. 54 applicants, 80% accepted, 29 enrolled. In 2016, 22 master's, 9 Graduate Certificates awarded. *Degree requirements:* For master's, thesis or alternative, internship/practicum. *Entrance requirements:* For master's, GRE, undergraduate degree in health, the life sciences, an informatics discipline or closely-related field; minimum undergraduate GPA of 3.0; three letters of recommendation; statement of purpose outlining goals for pursuing graduate education; for Graduate Certificate, bachelor's degree from regionally-accredited university in related field, including, but not limited to a life science, health science, health administration, business administration, or computing discipline; minimum undergraduate GPA of 2.75; statement of purpose outlining the goals for pursuing a graduate education in health informatics. Additional exam requirements/recommendations for international students: Required—TOEFL (minimum score 523 paper-based, 70 iBT) or IELTS (6.5). *Application deadline:* For fall admission, 3/1 priority date for domestic and international students; for spring admission, 10/1 priority date for domestic and international students. Applications are processed on a rolling basis. Application fee: $75. Electronic applications accepted. *Expenses:* Contact institution. *Financial support:* Career-related internships or fieldwork, institutionally sponsored loans, scholarships/grants, and unspecified assistantships available. Support available to part-time students. Financial award application deadline: 3/1; financial award applicants required to submit FAFSA. *Unit head:* Carly Mahedy, Director of Student Services, 704-687-0068, E-mail: healthinformatics@uncc.edu. *Application contact:* Kathy B. Giddings, Director of Graduate Admissions, 704-687-5503, Fax: 704-687-1668, E-mail: gradadm@uncc.edu.
Website: http://www.hi.uncc.edu/

University of Phoenix–Charlotte Campus, College of Nursing, Charlotte, NC 28273-3409. Offers education (MHA); gerontology (MHA); health administration (MHA); informatics (MHA, MSN); nursing (MSN); nursing/health care education (MSN). *Program availability:* Evening/weekend. *Degree requirements:* For master's, thesis (for some programs). *Entrance requirements:* For master's, minimum undergraduate GPA of 2.5, 3 years work experience. Additional exam requirements/recommendations for international students: Required—TOEFL (minimum score 550 paper-based; 79 iBT). Electronic applications accepted.

University of Phoenix–Online Campus, College of Health Sciences and Nursing, Phoenix, AZ 85034-7209. Offers family nurse practitioner (Certificate); health care (Certificate); health care education (Certificate); health care informatics (Certificate); informatics (MSN); nursing (MSN); nursing and health care education (MSN); MSN/MBA; MSN/MHA. *Accreditation:* AACN. *Program availability:* Evening/weekend, online learning. *Entrance requirements:* Additional exam requirements/recommendations for international students: Required—TOEFL, TOEIC (Test of English as an International Communication), Berlitz Online English Proficiency Exam, PTE, or IELTS. Electronic applications accepted. *Expenses:* Contact institution.

University of Phoenix–Washington D.C. Campus, College of Nursing, Washington, DC 20001. Offers education (MHA); gerontology (MHA); health administration (MHA, DHA); informatics (MHA, MSN); nursing (MSN, PhD); nursing/health care education (MSN); MSN/MBA; MSN/MHA.

University of Pittsburgh, School of Health and Rehabilitation Sciences, Master's Programs in Health and Rehabilitation Sciences, Pittsburgh, PA 15260. Offers health and rehabilitation sciences (MS), including health information systems, healthcare supervision and management, occupational therapy, physical therapy, rehabilitation counseling, rehabilitation science and technology, sports medicine, wellness and human performance. *Accreditation:* APTA. *Program availability:* Part-time, evening/weekend. *Faculty:* 30 full-time (19 women). *Students:* 93 full-time (65 women), 32 part-time (26 women); includes 15 minority (3 Black or African American, non-Hispanic/Latino; 1 American Indian or Alaska Native, non-Hispanic/Latino; 4 Asian, non-Hispanic/Latino; 4 Hispanic/Latino; 3 Two or more races, non-Hispanic/Latino), 58 international. Average age 29. 247 applicants, 64% accepted, 70 enrolled. In 2016, 37 master's awarded. *Degree requirements:* For master's, comprehensive exam (for some programs), thesis optional. *Entrance requirements:* For master's, minimum GPA of 3.0. Additional exam requirements/recommendations for international students: Required—TOEFL (minimum score 550 paper-based; 80 iBT), IELTS (minimum score 6.5). *Application deadline:* For fall admission, 3/1 for international students; for spring admission, 9/1 for international students; for summer admission, 2/1 for international students. Applications are processed on a rolling basis. Application fee: $50. Electronic applications accepted. Tuition and fees vary according to program. *Financial support:* In 2016–17, 6 fellowships with full tuition reimbursements (averaging $17,550 per year), 4 research assistantships with full tuition reimbursements (averaging $21,900 per year) were awarded; traineeships also available. *Faculty research:* Assistive technology, seating and wheelchair mobility, cellular neurophysiology, low back syndrome, augmentative communication. *Total annual research expenditures:* $2.7 million. *Unit head:* Dr. Anthony Delitto, Dean, 412-383-6560, Fax: 412-383-6535, E-mail: delitto@pitt.edu. *Application contact:* Jessica Maguire, Director of Admissions, 412-383-6557, Fax: 412-383-6535, E-mail: maguire@pitt.edu.

University of Puerto Rico, Medical Sciences Campus, School of Health Professions, Program in Health Information Administration, San Juan, PR 00936-5067. Offers MS. *Program availability:* Part-time. *Degree requirements:* For master's, one foreign language, thesis or alternative, internship. *Entrance requirements:* For master's, EXADEP or GRE General Test, minimum GPA of 2.5, interview, fluency in Spanish. *Faculty research:* Quality of medical records, health information data.

University of St. Augustine for Health Sciences, Graduate Programs, Master of Health Science Program, San Marcos, CA 92069. Offers athletic training (MHS); executive leadership (MHS); informatics (MHS); teaching and learning (MHS). *Program availability:* Online learning. *Degree requirements:* For master's, comprehensive project.

University of San Diego, Hahn School of Nursing and Health Science, San Diego, CA 92110-2492. Offers adult-gerontology clinical nurse specialist (MSN); adult-gerontology nurse practitioner/family nurse practitioner (MSN); executive nurse leader (MSN); family nurse practitioner (MSN); family/lifespan psychiatric-mental health nurse practitioner (MSN); healthcare informatics (MS, MSN); nursing (PhD); nursing practice (DNP). *Accreditation:* AACN. *Program availability:* Part-time, evening/weekend. *Faculty:* 24 full-time (19 women), 50 part-time/adjunct (44 women). *Students:* 193 full-time (159 women), 178 part-time (149 women); includes 169 minority (25 Black or African American, non-Hispanic/Latino; 1 American Indian or Alaska Native, non-Hispanic/Latino; 72 Asian, non-Hispanic/Latino; 58 Hispanic/Latino; 3 Native Hawaiian or other Pacific Islander, non-Hispanic/Latino; 10 Two or more races, non-Hispanic/Latino), 13 international. Average age 35. In 2016, 84 master's, 34 doctorates awarded. *Degree requirements:* For doctorate, thesis/dissertation (for some programs), residency (DNP). *Entrance requirements:* For master's, GRE General Test (for entry-level nursing), BSN, current California RN licensure (except for entry-level nursing), minimum GPA of 3.0; for doctorate, minimum GPA of 3.5, MSN, current California RN licensure. Additional exam requirements/recommendations for international students: Required—TOEFL (minimum score 580 paper-based; 83 iBT), TWE. *Application deadline:* Applications are processed on a rolling basis. Application fee: $45. Electronic applications accepted. *Financial support:* In 2016–17, 227 students received support. Scholarships/grants and traineeships available. Support available to part-time students. Financial award application deadline: 4/1; financial award applicants required to submit FAFSA. *Faculty research:* Maternal/neonatal health, palliative and end of life care, adolescent obesity, health disparities, cognitive dysfunction. *Unit head:* Dr. Sally Hardin, Dean, 619-260-4550, Fax: 619-260-6814, E-mail: nursing@sandiego.edu. *Application contact:* Monica Mahon, Associate Director of Graduate Admissions, 619-260-4524, Fax: 619-260-4158, E-mail: grads@sandiego.edu.
Website: http://www.sandiego.edu/nursing/

Health Informatics

University of San Francisco, School of Nursing and Health Professions, Program in Health Informatics, San Francisco, CA 94117-1080. Offers MS. *Faculty:* 4 full-time (2 women), 6 part-time/adjunct (2 women). *Students:* 39 full-time (21 women), 10 part-time (7 women); includes 19 minority (3 Black or African American, non-Hispanic/Latino; 15 Asian, non-Hispanic/Latino; 1 Two or more races, non-Hispanic/Latino), 16 international. Average age 33. 49 applicants, 84% accepted, 17 enrolled. In 2016, 29 master's awarded. Electronic applications accepted. *Expenses: Tuition:* Full-time $23,310; part-time $1295 per credit. Tuition and fees vary according to course load, degree level, campus/location and program. *Financial support:* In 2016–17, 5 students received support. *Unit head:* Dr. Margaret Baker, Dean, 415-422-6681, Fax: 415-422-6877, E-mail: nursing@usfca.edu. *Application contact:* Ingrid McVanner, Information Contact, 415-422-2746, Fax: 415-422-2217.
Website: https://www.usfca.edu/nursing/programs/masters/health-informatics

University of South Carolina Upstate, Graduate Programs, Spartanburg, SC 29303-4999. Offers early childhood education (M Ed); elementary education (M Ed); informatics (MS); special education: visual impairment (M Ed). *Accreditation:* NCATE. *Program availability:* Part-time, evening/weekend. *Degree requirements:* For master's, professional portfolio. *Entrance requirements:* For master's, GRE General Test or MAT, interview, minimum undergraduate GPA of 2.5, teaching certificate, 2 letters of recommendation. *Faculty research:* Promoting university diversity awareness, rough and tumble play, social justice education, American Indian literatures and cultures, diversity and multicultural education, science teaching strategy.

University of Southern Indiana, Graduate Studies, College of Nursing and Health Professions, Program in Health Administration, Evansville, IN 47712-3590. Offers health administration (MHA); health informatics (MHA). *Program availability:* Part-time, 3 required intensives in August (2.5 days), January (2.5 days) and May (2 days). *Faculty:* 3 full-time (1 woman). *Students:* 59 full-time (44 women); includes 6 minority (2 Black or African American, non-Hispanic/Latino; 1 Asian, non-Hispanic/Latino; 3 Hispanic/Latino). Average age 33. In 2016, 22 master's awarded. *Entrance requirements:* For master's, GRE, minimum GPA of 3.0, curriculum vitae, letter of intent, three professional references, focused essay(s). Additional exam requirements/recommendations for international students: Required—TOEFL (minimum score 550 paper-based; 79 iBT), IELTS (minimum score 6). *Application deadline:* For fall admission, 6/1 for domestic students, 1/1 priority date for international students. Applications are processed on a rolling basis. Application fee: $40. Electronic applications accepted. *Expenses:* Tuition, state resident: full-time $8497. Tuition, nonresident: full-time $16,691. *Required fees:* $500. *Financial support:* In 2016–17, 11 students received support. Federal Work-Study, scholarships/grants, tuition waivers (full and partial), and unspecified assistantships available. Financial award application deadline: 3/1; financial award applicants required to submit FAFSA. *Unit head:* Dr. Kevin J. Valadares, Program Chair, 812-461-5277, E-mail: kvaladar@usi.edu. *Application contact:* Dr. Mayola Rowser, Director, Graduate Studies, 812-465-7015, Fax: 812-464-1956, E-mail: mrowser@usi.edu.
Website: http://www.usi.edu/health/master-of-health-administration

University of South Florida, Innovative Education, Tampa, FL 33620-9951. Offers adult, career and higher education (Graduate Certificate), including college teaching, leadership in developing human resources, leadership in higher education; Africana studies (Graduate Certificate), including diasporas and health disparities, genocide and human rights; aging studies (Graduate Certificate), including gerontology; art research (Graduate Certificate), including museum studies; business foundations (Graduate Certificate); chemical and biomedical engineering (Graduate Certificate), including materials science and engineering, water, health and sustainability; child and family studies (Graduate Certificate), including positive behavior support; civil and industrial engineering (Graduate Certificate), including transportation systems analysis; community and family health (Graduate Certificate), including maternal and child health, social marketing and public health, violence and injury: prevention and intervention, women's health; criminology (Graduate Certificate), including criminal justice administration; educational measurement and research (Graduate Certificate), including evaluation; English (Graduate Certificate), including comparative literary studies, creative writing, professional and technical communication; entrepreneurship (Graduate Certificate); environmental health (Graduate Certificate), including safety management; epidemiology and biostatistics (Graduate Certificate), including applied biostatistics, biostatistics, concepts and tools of epidemiology, epidemiology, epidemiology of infectious diseases; geography, environment and planning (Graduate Certificate), including community development, environmental policy and management, geographical information systems; geology (Graduate Certificate), including hydrogeology; global health (Graduate Certificate), including disaster management, global health and Latin American and Caribbean studies, global health practice, humanitarian assistance, infection control; government and international affairs (Graduate Certificate), including Cuban studies, globalization studies; health policy and management (Graduate Certificate), including health management and leadership, public health policy and programs; hearing specialist: early intervention (Graduate Certificate); industrial and management systems engineering (Graduate Certificate), including systems engineering, technology management; information studies (Graduate Certificate), including school library media specialist; information systems/decision sciences (Graduate Certificate), including analytics and business intelligence; instructional technology (Graduate Certificate), including distance education, Florida digital/virtual educator, instructional design, multimedia design, Web design; internal medicine, bioethics and medical humanities (Graduate Certificate), including biomedical ethics; Latin American and Caribbean studies (Graduate Certificate); mass communications (Graduate Certificate), including multimedia journalism; mathematics and statistics (Graduate Certificate), including mathematics; medicine (Graduate Certificate), including aging and neuroscience, bioinformatics, biotechnology, brain fitness and memory management, clinical investigation, health informatics, health sciences, integrative weight management, intellectual property, medicine and gender, metabolic and nutritional medicine, metabolic cardiology, pharmacy sciences; national and competitive intelligence (Graduate Certificate); psychological and social foundations (Graduate Certificate), including career counseling, college teaching, diversity in education, mental health counseling, school counseling; public affairs (Graduate Certificate), including nonprofit management, public management, research administration; public health (Graduate Certificate), including environmental health, health equity, public health generalist, translational research in adolescent behavioral health; public health practices (Graduate Certificate), including planning for healthy communities; rehabilitation and mental health counseling (Graduate Certificate), including integrative mental health care, marriage and family therapy, rehabilitation technology; secondary education (Graduate Certificate), including ESOL, foreign language education: culture and content, foreign language education: professional; social work (Graduate Certificate), including geriatric social work/clinical gerontology; special education (Graduate Certificate), including autism spectrum disorder, disabilities education: severe/profound; world languages (Graduate Certificate), including teaching English as a second language (TESL) or foreign language. *Expenses:* Tuition, state resident: full-time $7766; part-time $431.43 per credit hour. Tuition, nonresident: full-time $15,789; part-time $877.17 per credit hour. *Required fees:* $37 per term. *Unit head:* Kathy Barnes, Interdisciplinary Programs Coordinator, 813-974-8031, Fax: 813-974-

7061, E-mail: barnesk@usf.edu. *Application contact:* Karen Tylinski, Metro Initiatives, 813-974-9943, Fax: 813-974-7061, E-mail: ktylinsk@usf.edu.
Website: http://www.usf.edu/innovative-education/

University of South Florida, Morsani College of Medicine and College of Graduate Studies, Graduate Programs in Medical Sciences, Tampa, FL 33620-9951. Offers advanced athletic training (MS); athletic training (MS); bioinformatics and computational biology (MSBCB); biotechnology (MSB); health informatics (MSHI); medical sciences (MSMS, PhD), including aging and neuroscience (MSMS), allergy, immunology and infectious disease (PhD), anatomy, biochemistry and molecular biology, clinical and translational research, health science (MSMS), interdisciplinary medical sciences (MSMS), medical microbiology and immunology (MSMS), metabolic and nutritional medicine (MSMS), microbiology and immunology (PhD), molecular medicine, molecular pharmacology and physiology (PhD), neuroscience (PhD), pathology and cell biology (PhD), women's health (MSMS). *Students:* 454 full-time (239 women), 273 part-time (173 women); includes 347 minority (110 Black or African American, non-Hispanic/Latino; 1 American Indian or Alaska Native, non-Hispanic/Latino; 99 Asian, non-Hispanic/Latino; 113 Hispanic/Latino; 1 Native Hawaiian or other Pacific Islander, non-Hispanic/Latino; 23 Two or more races, non-Hispanic/Latino), 61 international. Average age 27. 7,242 applicants, 8% accepted, 395 enrolled. In 2016, 374 master's, 13 doctorates awarded. Terminal master's awarded for partial completion of doctoral program. *Degree requirements:* For master's, comprehensive exam, thesis; for doctorate, comprehensive exam, thesis/dissertation. *Entrance requirements:* For master's, GRE General Test or GMAT, bachelor's degree or equivalent from regionally-accredited university with minimum GPA of 3.0 in upper-division sciences coursework; prerequisites in general biology, general chemistry, general physics, organic chemistry, quantitative analysis, and integral and differential calculus; for doctorate, GRE General Test, bachelor's degree from regionally-accredited university with minimum GPA of 3.0 in upper-division sciences coursework; 3 letters of recommendation; personal interview; 1-2 page personal statement; prerequisites in biology, chemistry, physics, organic chemistry, quantitative analysis, and integral/differential calculus. Additional exam requirements/recommendations for international students: Required—TOEFL (minimum score 550 paper-based; 79 iBT) or IELTS (minimum score 6.5). *Application deadline:* For fall admission, 2/1 for domestic and international students. Application fee: $30. Electronic applications accepted. *Expenses:* Contact institution. *Financial support:* In 2016–17, 116 students received support. *Faculty research:* Anatomy, biochemistry, cancer biology, cardiovascular disease, cell biology, immunology, microbiology, molecular biology, neuroscience, pharmacology, physiology. *Total annual research expenditures:* $42.3 million. *Unit head:* Dr. Michael Barber, Professor/Associate Dean for Graduate and Postdoctoral Affairs, 813-974-9908, Fax: 813-974-4317, E-mail: mbarber@health.usf.edu. *Application contact:* Dr. Eric Bennett, Graduate Director, PhD Program in Medical Sciences, 813-974-1545, Fax: 813-974-4317, E-mail: esbennet@health.usf.edu.
Website: http://health.usf.edu/nocms/medicine/graduatestudies/

The University of Tennessee Health Science Center, College of Health Professions, Memphis, TN 38163-0002. Offers audiology (MS, Au D); clinical laboratory science (MSCLS); cytopathology practice (MCP); health informatics and information management (MHIIM); occupational therapy (MOT); physical therapy (DPT, ScDPT); physician assistant (MMS); speech-language pathology (MS). *Accreditation:* AOTA; APTA. *Program availability:* Part-time, evening/weekend, online learning. Terminal master's awarded for partial completion of doctoral program. *Degree requirements:* For master's, comprehensive exam, thesis; for doctorate, comprehensive exam, residency. *Entrance requirements:* For master's, GRE (MOT, MSCLS), minimum GPA of 3.0, 3 letters of reference, national accreditation (MSCLS), GRE if GPA is less than 3.0 (MCP); for doctorate, GRE. Additional exam requirements/recommendations for international students: Required—TOEFL (minimum score 550 paper-based; 80 iBT). Electronic applications accepted. *Expenses:* Contact institution. *Faculty research:* Gait deviation, muscular dystrophy and strength, hemophilia and exercise, pediatric neurology, self-efficacy.

University of Toronto, Faculty of Medicine, Institute of Health Policy, Management and Evaluation, Program in Health Informatics, Toronto, ON M5S 1A1, Canada. Offers MHI. *Entrance requirements:* For master's, minimum B average in last academic year. Additional exam requirements/recommendations for international students: Required—TOEFL (minimum score 580 paper-based; 93 iBT), TWE (minimum score 5). Electronic applications accepted.

University of Victoria, Faculty of Graduate Studies, Faculty of Human and Social Development, School of Health Information Science, Victoria, BC V8W 2Y2, Canada. Offers M Sc. *Degree requirements:* For master's, thesis or research project. *Entrance requirements:* Additional exam requirements/recommendations for international students: Required—TOEFL (minimum score 575 paper-based).

University of Virginia, School of Medicine, Department of Public Health Sciences, Program in Clinical Research, Charlottesville, VA 22903. Offers clinical investigation and patient-oriented research (MS); informatics in medicine (MS). *Program availability:* Part-time. *Students:* 3 full-time (1 woman), 6 part-time (2 women); includes 2 minority (both Two or more races, non-Hispanic/Latino). Average age 34. 11 applicants, 55% accepted, 6 enrolled. In 2016, 7 master's awarded. *Degree requirements:* For master's, thesis (for some programs). *Entrance requirements:* For master's, 2 letters of recommendation. Additional exam requirements/recommendations for international students: Required—TOEFL (minimum score 600 paper-based; 90 iBT). *Application deadline:* For fall admission, 3/1 priority date for domestic and international students. Application fee: $60. Electronic applications accepted. *Expenses:* Tuition, state resident: full-time $15,026; part-time $834 per credit hour. Tuition, nonresident: full-time $25,168; part-time $1378 per credit hour. *Required fees:* $2654. *Financial support:* Career-related internships or fieldwork available. Financial award applicants required to submit FAFSA. *Unit head:* Dr. Jean Eby, Program Director, 434-924-8430, Fax: 434-924-8437, E-mail: jmg5b@virginia.edu. *Application contact:* Tracey L. Brookman, Academic Programs Administrator, 434-924-8430, Fax: 434-924-8437, E-mail: phsdegrees@virginia.edu.
Website: http://research.med.virginia.edu/clinicalresearch/

University of Washington, Graduate School, School of Medicine, Graduate Programs in Medicine, Department of Medical Education and Biomedical Informatics, Division of Biomedical and Health Informatics, Seattle, WA 98195. Offers MS, PhD. *Entrance requirements:* For master's and doctorate, GRE General Test, minimum GPA of 3.0; previous undergraduate course work in biology, computer programming, and mathematics. Additional exam requirements/recommendations for international students: Required—TOEFL (minimum score 580 paper-based; 70 iBT). Electronic applications accepted. *Faculty research:* Bio-clinical informatics, information retrieval, human-computer interaction, knowledge-based systems, telehealth.

University of Washington, Graduate School, School of Public Health, Department of Health Services, Program in Health Informatics and Health Information Management, Seattle, WA 98195. Offers MHIHIM. *Program availability:* Evening/weekend, online learning. *Degree requirements:* For master's, capstone project. *Entrance requirements:* For master's, resume or curriculum vitae, three recommendations, minimum GPA of 3.0. Additional exam requirements/recommendations for international students: Required—

TOEFL (minimum score 580 paper-based; 92 iBT), IELTS. Electronic applications accepted. *Expenses:* Contact institution.

University of Waterloo, Graduate Studies, Faculty of Applied Health Sciences, School of Public Health and Health Systems, Waterloo, ON N2L 3G1, Canada. Offers health evaluation (MHE); health informatics (MHI); health studies and gerontology (M Sc, PhD); public health (MPH). *Program availability:* Part-time. *Degree requirements:* For master's, thesis; for doctorate, comprehensive exam, thesis/dissertation. *Entrance requirements:* For master's, honors degree, minimum B average, resume, writing sample; for doctorate, GRE (recommended), master's degree, minimum B average, resume, writing sample. Additional exam requirements/recommendations for international students: Required—TOEFL, IELTS, PTE. Electronic applications accepted. *Faculty research:* Population health, health promotion and disease prevention, healthy aging, health policy, planning and evaluation, health information management and health informatics, aging, health and well-being, work and health.

University of Wisconsin–Milwaukee, Graduate School, College of Engineering and Applied Science, Biomedical and Health Informatics Program, Milwaukee, WI 53201-0413. Offers health information systems (PhD); health services management and policy (PhD); knowledge based systems (PhD); medical imaging and instrumentation (PhD); public health informatics (PhD). *Students:* 6 full-time (4 women), 12 part-time (3 women); includes 3 minority (2 Black or African American, non-Hispanic/Latino; 1 Asian, non-Hispanic/Latino), 7 international. Average age 37. 11 applicants, 55% accepted, 4 enrolled. In 2016, 3 doctorates awarded. *Degree requirements:* For doctorate, comprehensive exam, thesis/dissertation. *Entrance requirements:* For doctorate, GRE, GMAT or MCAT. Additional exam requirements/recommendations for international students: Required—TOEFL (minimum score 600 paper-based; 79 iBT), IELTS (minimum score 6.5). Application fee: $56 ($96 for international students). *Financial support:* Fellowships, research assistantships, teaching assistantships, and project assistantships available. *Unit head:* Devendra Misra, PhD, Chair, 414-229-3327, E-mail: misra@uwm.edu. *Application contact:* Betty Warras, Engineering and Computer Science Graduate Programs, 414-229-6169, E-mail: ceas-graduate@uwm.edu. Website: http://uwm.edu/engineering/academics-2/departments/biomedical-engineering/

University of Wisconsin–Milwaukee, Graduate School, College of Health Sciences, Department of Health Informatics and Administration, Milwaukee, WI 53201-0413. Offers health care informatics (MS); healthcare administration (MHA). *Students:* 31 full-time (19 women), 11 part-time (10 women); includes 9 minority (2 Black or African American, non-Hispanic/Latino; 5 Asian, non-Hispanic/Latino; 2 Two or more races, non-Hispanic/Latino), 5 international. Average age 32. 34 applicants, 76% accepted, 20 enrolled. In 2016, 8 master's awarded. *Degree requirements:* For master's, comprehensive exam, thesis optional. *Entrance requirements:* For master's, GRE General Test. Additional exam requirements/recommendations for international students: Required—TOEFL (minimum score 550 paper-based; 79 iBT), IELTS (minimum score 6.5). Application fee: $56 ($96 for international students). *Financial support:* Fellowships, research assistantships, and teaching assistantships available. *Unit head:* Priya Nambisan, Department Chair, 414-229-7136, Fax: 414-229-3373, E-mail: nambisap@uwm.edu. *Application contact:* Kathleen M. Olewinski, Educational Coordinator, 414-229-7110, Fax: 414-229-3373, E-mail: kmo@uwm.edu. Website: http://uwm.edu/healthsciences/academics/health-informatics-administration/

Virginia International University, School of Computer Information Systems, Fairfax, VA 22030. Offers business intelligence (Graduate Certificate); business intelligence and data analytics (MIS); computer science (MS), including computer animation and gaming, cybersecurity, data management networking, intelligent systems, software applications development, software engineering; cybersecurity (MIS); data management (MIS);

enterprise project management (MIS); health informatics (MIS); information assurance (MIS); information systems (Graduate Certificate); information systems management (MS, Graduate Certificate); information technology (MS); information technology audit and compliance (Graduate Certificate); knowledge management (MIS); software engineering (MS). *Program availability:* Part-time, online learning. *Entrance requirements:* For master's, bachelor's degree. Additional exam requirements/recommendations for international students: Required—TOEFL (minimum score 550 paper-based; 80 iBT), IELTS. Electronic applications accepted.

Walden University, Graduate Programs, School of Health Sciences, Minneapolis, MN 55401. Offers clinical research administration (MS, Graduate Certificate); health education and promotion (MS, PhD), including behavioral health (PhD), disease surveillance (PhD), emergency preparedness (MS), general (MHA, MS), global health (PhD), health policy (PhD), health policy and advocacy (MS), population health (PhD); health informatics (MS); health services (PhD), including community health, healthcare administration, leadership, public health policy, self-designed; healthcare administration (MHA, DHA), including general (MHA, MS); leadership and organizational development (MHA); public health (MPH, Dr PH, PhD, Graduate Certificate), including community health education (PhD), epidemiology (PhD); systems policy (MHA). *Program availability:* Part-time, evening/weekend, online only, 100% online. *Degree requirements:* For doctorate, thesis/dissertation, residency. *Entrance requirements:* For master's, bachelor's degree or higher; minimum GPA of 2.5; official transcripts; goal statement (for some programs); access to computer and Internet; for doctorate, master's degree or higher; three years of related professional or academic experience (preferred); minimum GPA of 3.0; goal statement and current resume (for select programs); official transcripts; access to computer and Internet; for Graduate Certificate, relevant work experience; access to computer and Internet. Additional exam requirements/recommendations for international students: Required—TOEFL (minimum score 550 paper-based, 79 iBT), IELTS (minimum score 6.5), Michigan English Language Assessment Battery (minimum score 82), or PTE (minimum score 53). Electronic applications accepted.

Walden University, Graduate Programs, School of Information Systems and Technology, Minneapolis, MN 55401. Offers information systems (Graduate Certificate); information systems management (MISM); information technology (MS, DIT), including health informatics (MS), information assurance and cyber security (MS), information systems (MS), software engineering (MS). *Program availability:* Part-time, evening/weekend, online only, 100% online. *Degree requirements:* For doctorate, thesis/dissertation (for some programs), residency. *Entrance requirements:* For master's, bachelor's degree or higher; minimum GPA of 2.5; official transcripts; goal statement (for some programs); access to computer and Internet; for doctorate, master's degree or higher; three years of related professional or academic experience (preferred); minimum GPA of 3.0; goal statement and current resume (for select programs); official transcripts; access to computer and Internet; for Graduate Certificate, relevant work experience; access to computer and Internet. Additional exam requirements/recommendations for international students: Required—TOEFL (minimum score 550 paper-based, 79 iBT), IELTS (minimum score 6.5), Michigan English Language Assessment Battery (minimum score 82), or PTE (minimum score 53). Electronic applications accepted.

Weill Cornell Medicine, Weill Cornell Graduate School of Medical Sciences, Program in Health Informatics, New York, NY 10065. Offers MS. *Program availability:* Part-time. *Degree requirements:* For master's, thesis. *Entrance requirements:* For master's, GRE, MCAT, or GMAT, official transcripts, resume, personal statement, 3 letters of reference. Additional exam requirements/recommendations for international students: Required—TOEFL. *Expenses:* Contact institution.

Human-Computer Interaction

Brandeis University, Rabb School of Continuing Studies, Division of Graduate Professional Studies, Master of Science in User-Centered Design Program, Waltham, MA 02454-9110. Offers MS. *Program availability:* Part-time-only. *Faculty:* 45 part-time/adjunct (16 women). *Students:* 9 part-time (5 women); includes 2 minority (both Asian, non-Hispanic/Latino). Average age 37. 4 applicants, 100% accepted, 4 enrolled. *Degree requirements:* For master's, capstone. *Entrance requirements:* For master's, four-year bachelor's degree from regionally-accredited U.S. institution or equivalent; official transcript(s) from every college or university attended; resume or curriculum vitae; statement of goals; letter of recommendation. Additional exam requirements/recommendations for international students: Required—TWE (minimum score 4.5), TOEFL (minimum scores: 600 paper-based, 100 iBT), IELTS (7), or PTE (68). *Application deadline:* For fall admission, 6/21 priority date for domestic and international students; for winter admission, 9/13 priority date for domestic and international students; for spring admission, 12/20 priority date for domestic and international students; for summer admission, 3/14 priority date for domestic and international students. Applications are processed on a rolling basis. Application fee: $50. Electronic applications accepted. *Expenses:* $3,400 per course, $100 graduation fee. *Financial support:* Applicants required to submit FAFSA. *Unit head:* Lou Susi, Program Chair, 781-736-8787, E-mail: loususi@brandeis.edu. *Application contact:* Frances Stearns, Director of Admissions and Recruitment, 781-736-8785, E-mail: fstearns@brandeis.edu.

Carnegie Mellon University, School of Computer Science, Department of Human-Computer Interaction, Pittsburgh, PA 15213-3891. Offers MHCI, PhD. *Entrance requirements:* For master's, GRE General Test, GRE Subject Test.

Clemson University, Graduate School, College of Engineering, Computing and Applied Sciences, School of Computing, Program in Human-Centered Computing, Clemson, SC 29634. Offers PhD. *Program availability:* Part-time. *Faculty:* 9 full-time (2 women). *Students:* 18 full-time (9 women), 1 part-time (0 women); includes 9 minority (8 Black or African American, non-Hispanic/Latino; 1 Asian, non-Hispanic/Latino), 7 international. Average age 29. 13 applicants, 15% accepted, 1 enrolled. In 2016, 2 doctorates awarded. *Degree requirements:* For doctorate, comprehensive exam, thesis/dissertation, qualifying exam. *Entrance requirements:* For doctorate, GRE General Test, unofficial transcripts, letters of recommendation. Additional exam requirements/recommendations for international students: Required—TOEFL (minimum score 550 paper-based; 80 iBT), IELTS (minimum score 6.5). *Application deadline:* For fall admission, 5/15 priority date for domestic students, 4/15 priority date for international students; for spring admission, 10/15 priority date for domestic students, 9/15 priority date for international students. Applications are processed on a rolling basis. Application fee: $80 ($90 for international students). Electronic applications accepted. *Expenses:* $4,841 per semester full-time resident, $9,640 per semester full-time non-resident, $612 per credit hour part-time resident, $1,223 per credit hour part-time non-resident. *Financial support:* In 2016–17, 22 students received support, including 2 fellowships with partial tuition reimbursements available (averaging $4,625 per year), 8 research

assistantships with partial tuition reimbursements available (averaging $21,393 per year), 9 teaching assistantships with partial tuition reimbursements available (averaging $19,726 per year); career-related internships or fieldwork, traineeships, and unspecified assistantships also available. Financial award application deadline: 1/1. *Faculty research:* Virtual worlds and virtual humans, user interfaces and user experience, identity science and biometrics, affective computing, advanced learning technologies. *Unit head:* Dr. Brygg Ullmer, Chair, Human-Centered Computing Division, 864-656-4846, E-mail: bullmer@clemson.edu. *Application contact:* Dr. Larry Hodges, Director, PhD Program, 864-656-7552, E-mail: lfh@clemson.edu. Website: http://www.clemson.edu/cecas/departments/computing/academics/graduates/programsofstudy/phdinhcc.html

Cornell University, Graduate School, Graduate Fields of Agriculture and Life Sciences, Field of Communication, Ithaca, NY 14853. Offers communication (MS, PhD); human-computer interaction (MS, PhD); language and communication (MS, PhD); media communication and society (MS, PhD); organizational communication (MS, PhD); science, environment and health communication (MS, PhD); social psychology of communication (MS, PhD). *Degree requirements:* For master's, thesis (MS); for doctorate, comprehensive exam, thesis/dissertation. *Entrance requirements:* For master's and doctorate, GRE General Test, 3 letters of recommendation. Additional exam requirements/recommendations for international students: Required—TOEFL (minimum score 600 paper-based; 100 iBT). Electronic applications accepted. *Faculty research:* Mass communication, communication technologies, science and environmental communication.

Cornell University, Graduate School, Graduate Fields of Arts and Sciences, Field of Information Science, Ithaca, NY 14853. Offers cognition (PhD); human computer interaction (PhD); information science (PhD); information systems (PhD); social aspects of information (PhD). *Degree requirements:* For doctorate, comprehensive exam, thesis/dissertation. *Entrance requirements:* For doctorate, GRE General Test, 3 letters of recommendation. Additional exam requirements/recommendations for international students: Required—TOEFL (minimum score 550 paper-based; 77 iBT). Electronic applications accepted. *Faculty research:* Digital libraries, game theory, data mining, human-computer interaction, computational linguistics.

Dalhousie University, Faculty of Engineering, Department of Internetworking, Halifax, NS B3J 1Z1, Canada. Offers M Eng. *Entrance requirements:* Additional exam requirements/recommendations for international students: Required—TOEFL, IELTS, CANTEST, CAEL, or Michigan English Language Assessment Battery. Electronic applications accepted.

DePaul University, College of Computing and Digital Media, Chicago, IL 60604. Offers animation (MA, MFA); business information technology (MS); cinema (MFA); cinema production (MS); computational finance (MS); computer and information sciences (PhD); computer game development (MS); computer information and network security (MS);

computer science (MS); e-commerce technology (MS); health informatics (MS); human-computer interaction (MS); information systems (MS); information technology project management (MS); network engineering and management (MS); predictive analytics (MS); screenwriting (MFA); software engineering (MS); JD/MS. *Program availability:* Part-time, evening/weekend, online learning. *Degree requirements:* For master's, thesis (for some programs); for doctorate, comprehensive exam, thesis/dissertation. *Entrance requirements:* For master's, GRE or GMAT (for MS in computational finance only), bachelor's degree, resume (MS in predictive analytics only), IT experience (MS in information technology project management only), portfolio review (all MFA programs and MA in animation); for doctorate, GRE, master's degree in computer science. Additional exam requirements/recommendations for international students: Required—TOEFL (minimum score 590 paper-based; 80 iBT), IELTS (minimum score 6.5), PTE (minimum score 53). Electronic applications accepted. *Expenses:* Contact institution. *Faculty research:* Data mining, computer science, human-computer interaction, security, animation and film.

Florida Institute of Technology, College of Aeronautics, Program in Aviation Human Factors, Melbourne, FL 32901-6975. Offers MS. *Program availability:* Part-time. *Students:* 7 full-time (2 women), 1 part-time, 2 international. Average age 25. 13 applicants, 69% accepted, 4 enrolled. In 2016, 2 master's awarded. *Degree requirements:* For master's, thesis optional, minimum of 36 credit hours. *Entrance requirements:* For master's, GRE General Test, 3 letters of recommendation, statement of objectives, resume. Additional exam requirements/recommendations for international students: Required—TOEFL (minimum score 550 paper-based; 79 iBT). *Application deadline:* Applications are processed on a rolling basis. Electronic applications accepted. *Expenses: Tuition:* Full-time $22,338; part-time $1241 per credit hour. *Required fees:* $250. Tuition and fees vary according to degree level, campus/location and program. *Financial support:* Applicants required to submit FAFSA. *Unit head:* Dr. Korhan Oyman, Dean, 321-674-8971, Fax: 321-674-8059, E-mail: koyman@fit.edu. *Application contact:* Cheryl A. Brown, Associate Director of Graduate Admissions, 321-674-7581, Fax: 321-723-9468, E-mail: cbrown@fit.edu.
Website: http://www.fit.edu/programs/8229/ms-aviation-human-factors#.VT_URE10ypo

Florida Institute of Technology, College of Aeronautics, Program in Human Factors in Aeronautics, Melbourne, FL 32901-6975. Offers MS. *Program availability:* Part-time, evening/weekend, online only, 100% online. *Students:* 3 full-time (0 women), 16 part-time (4 women); includes 2 minority (1 Asian, non-Hispanic/Latino; 1 Hispanic/Latino), 1 international. Average age 36. 15 applicants, 20% accepted, 3 enrolled. In 2016, 10 master's awarded. *Degree requirements:* For master's, thesis, 36 credit hours. *Entrance requirements:* For master's, GRE, 3 letters of recommendation, resume, statement of objectives. Additional exam requirements/recommendations for international students: Required—TOEFL (minimum score 550 paper-based; 79 iBT). *Application deadline:* Applications are processed on a rolling basis. Electronic applications accepted. *Expenses: Tuition:* Full-time $22,338; part-time $1241 per credit hour. *Required fees:* $250. Tuition and fees vary according to degree level, campus/location and program. *Unit head:* Dr. Korhan Oyman, Dean, 321-674-8971, Fax: 321-674-8059, E-mail: koyman@fit.edu. *Application contact:* Cheryl A. Brown, Associate Director of Graduate Admissions, 321-674-7581, Fax: 321-723-9468, E-mail: cbrown@fit.edu.
Website: http://coa.fit.edu

Georgia Institute of Technology, Graduate Studies, Multidisciplinary Program in Human Computer Interaction, Atlanta, GA 30332-0001. Offers MS. Program offered jointly with School of Industrial Design, School of Interactive Computing, School of Psychology, and School of Literature, Media, and Communication. *Program availability:* Part-time. *Degree requirements:* For master's, seminar, project. *Entrance requirements:* For master's, GRE General Test. Additional exam requirements/recommendations for international students: Required—TOEFL (minimum score 600 paper-based; 100 iBT). Electronic applications accepted. *Expenses:* Contact institution.

Indiana University Bloomington, School of Informatics and Computing, Program in Informatics, Bloomington, IN 47405. Offers informatics (MS, PhD), including bioinformatics (PhD), complex systems (PhD), computing, culture and society (PhD), health informatics (PhD), human-computer interaction (MS), human-computer interaction design (PhD), music informatics (PhD), security informatics (PhD); visual heritage (PhD). *Program availability:* Part-time. *Faculty:* 75 full-time (15 women). *Students:* 206 full-time (85 women), 10 part-time (3 women); includes 30 minority (11 Black or African American, non-Hispanic/Latino; 10 Asian, non-Hispanic/Latino; 5 Hispanic/Latino; 4 Two or more races, non-Hispanic/Latino), 95 international. Average age 28. 395 applicants, 36% accepted, 69 enrolled. In 2016, 50 master's, 11 doctorates awarded. Terminal master's awarded for partial completion of doctoral program. *Degree requirements:* For master's, thesis, capstone project; for doctorate, variable foreign language requirement, comprehensive exam, thesis/dissertation. *Entrance requirements:* For master's and doctorate, GRE, resume/curriculum vitae, transcripts, 3 letters of recommendation. Additional exam requirements/recommendations for international students: Required—TOEFL (minimum score 600 paper-based; 100 iBT). *Application deadline:* For fall admission, 12/1 priority date for domestic and international students. Application fee: $55 ($65 for international students). Electronic applications accepted. *Financial support:* Fellowships, research assistantships, scholarships/grants, health care benefits, and unspecified assistantships available. Financial award application deadline: 12/1. *Faculty research:* Algorithms, applied logic and computational theory, artificial intelligence, bioinformatics, case-based reasoning, chemical informatics, citation analysis, cognitive science, community informatics, compilers, complex networks and systems, computer optimization, computer-supported cooperative work, computer vision, cyberinfrastructure and e-science, database theory and systems, data mining, digital design and preservation, design pedagogy, digital humanities, digital learning environments. *Total annual research expenditures:* $19.4 million. *Unit head:* Dr. Martin Siegel, Director of Graduate Studies, 812-856-3960, E-mail: msiegel@indiana.edu. *Application contact:* Informatics Graduate Studies Office, 812-856-3960, E-mail: infograd@indiana.edu.
Website: http://www.informatics.indiana.edu/graduate/index.html

Indiana University–Purdue University Indianapolis, School of Informatics and Computing, Department of Human-Centered Computing, Indianapolis, IN 46202. Offers human-computer interaction (MS, PhD); informatics (MS), including data analytics; media arts and science (MS). *Students:* 72 full-time (36 women), 40 part-time (11 women); includes 15 minority (4 Black or African American, non-Hispanic/Latino; 4 Asian, non-Hispanic/Latino; 5 Hispanic/Latino; 2 Two or more races, non-Hispanic/Latino), 52 international. Average age 35. 141 applicants, 42% accepted, 36 enrolled. In 2016, 40 master's awarded. *Unit head:* Dr. Davide Bolchini, Chair, 317-278-5144, E-mail: dbolchin@iupui.edu. *Application contact:* Elizabeth Bunge, Graduate Admissions Coordinator, 317-278-9200, E-mail: ebunge@iupui.edu.
Website: http://soic.iupui.edu/hcc/

Iowa State University of Science and Technology, Program in Human-Computer Interaction, Ames, IA 50011. Offers MS, PhD. *Degree requirements:* For master's, thesis; for doctorate, thesis/dissertation. *Entrance requirements:* For master's, GRE General Test; for doctorate, GRE General Test, e-portfolio of research. Additional exam requirements/recommendations for international students: Required—TOEFL (minimum score 580 paper-based; 95 iBT), IELTS (minimum score 7). *Application deadline:* For fall admission, 1/15 priority date for domestic and international students. Application fee: $40 ($90 for international students). Electronic applications accepted. *Application contact:* Amy Carver, Application Contact, 515-294-2089, Fax: 515-294-5530, E-mail: info@hci.iastate.edu.
Website: http://www.hci.iastate.edu/

Rochester Institute of Technology, Graduate Enrollment Services, Golisano College of Computing and Information Sciences, Information Science and Technologies Department, MS Program in Human Computer Interaction, Rochester, NY 14623. Offers MS. *Program availability:* Part-time, evening/weekend, 100% online. *Students:* 31 full-time (13 women), 16 part-time (9 women); includes 5 minority (4 Asian, non-Hispanic/Latino; 1 Hispanic/Latino), 31 international. Average age 26. 171 applicants, 49% accepted, 15 enrolled. In 2016, 12 master's awarded. *Degree requirements:* For master's, thesis or alternative. *Entrance requirements:* For master's, GRE, minimum GPA of 3.0. Additional exam requirements/recommendations for international students: Required—TOEFL (minimum score 570 paper-based; 88 iBT), IELTS (minimum score 6.5), PTE (minimum score 61). *Application deadline:* For fall admission, 2/15 priority date for domestic and international students; for spring admission, 12/15 priority date for domestic and international students. Applications are processed on a rolling basis. Electronic applications accepted. *Expenses:* $1,742 per credit hour (classroom), $993 per credit hour (online). *Financial support:* In 2016–17, 38 students received support. Research assistantships with partial tuition reimbursements available, teaching assistantships with partial tuition reimbursements available, career-related internships or fieldwork, scholarships/grants, and unspecified assistantships available. Support available to part-time students. Financial award applicants required to submit FAFSA. *Faculty research:* Ubiquitous and wearable computing, computing accessibility for people with disabilities, social factors influencing technology use, empirical evaluation of human language technologies, personal fabrication technologies. *Unit head:* Qi Yu, Graduate Program Director, 585-475-2700, Fax: 585-475-6584, E-mail: informaticsgrad@rit.edu. *Application contact:* Diane Ellison, Associate Vice President, Graduate Enrollment Services, 585-475-2229, Fax: 585-475-7164, E-mail: gradinfo@rit.edu.
Website: http://hci.rit.edu/

State University of New York at Oswego, Graduate Studies, College of Liberal Arts and Sciences, Interdisciplinary Program in Human Computer Interaction, Oswego, NY 13126. Offers MA. *Program availability:* Part-time. *Entrance requirements:* For master's, GRE, minimum GPA of 3.0. Additional exam requirements/recommendations for international students: Required—TOEFL (minimum score 560 paper-based).

Tufts University, Graduate School of Arts and Sciences, Graduate Certificate Programs, Human-Computer Interaction Program, Medford, MA 02155. Offers Certificate. *Program availability:* Part-time, evening/weekend. Electronic applications accepted. *Expenses: Tuition:* Full-time $49,892; part-time $1248 per credit hour. *Required fees:* $844. Full-time tuition and fees vary according to degree level, program and student level. Part-time tuition and fees vary according to course load.

University of Baltimore, Graduate School, Yale Gordon College of Arts and Sciences, Program in Interaction Design and Information Architecture, Baltimore, MD 21201-5779. Offers MS. *Program availability:* Part-time, evening/weekend. *Degree requirements:* For master's, project or thesis. *Entrance requirements:* For master's, GRE General Test or Miller Analogy Test, undergraduate GPA of 3.0.

University of Illinois at Urbana–Champaign, Graduate College, School of Information Sciences, Champaign, IL 61820. Offers bioinformatics (MS); digital libraries (CAS); information management (MS); library and information science (MS, PhD, CAS). *Accreditation:* ALA (one or more programs are accredited). *Program availability:* Part-time, online learning. *Entrance requirements:* For degree, master's degree in library and information science or related field with minimum GPA of 3.0.

Information Science

Alcorn State University, School of Graduate Studies, School of Arts and Sciences, Department of Mathematical Sciences, Lorman, MS 39096-7500. Offers computer and information sciences (MS).

American InterContinental University Atlanta, Program in Information Technology, Atlanta, GA 30328. Offers MIT. *Program availability:* Part-time, evening/weekend. *Degree requirements:* For master's, technical proficiency demonstration. *Entrance requirements:* For master's, Computer Programmer Aptitude Battery Exam, interview. Electronic applications accepted. *Faculty research:* Operating systems, security issues, networks and routing, computer hardware.

American InterContinental University Online, Program in Information Technology, Schaumburg, IL 60173. Offers Internet security (MIT); IT project management (MIT). *Program availability:* Evening/weekend, online learning. *Entrance requirements:* Additional exam requirements/recommendations for international students: Required—TOEFL (minimum score 550 paper-based). Electronic applications accepted.

American University of Armenia, Graduate Programs, Yerevan, Armenia. Offers business administration (MBA); computer and information science (MS), including business management, design and manufacturing, energy (ME, MS), industrial engineering and systems management; economics (MS); industrial engineering and systems management (ME), including business, computer aided design/manufacturing, energy (ME, MS), information technology; law (LL M); political science and international affairs (MPSIA); public health (MPH); teaching English as a foreign language (MA). *Program availability:* Part-time, evening/weekend. *Degree requirements:* For master's, thesis (for some programs), capstone/project. *Entrance requirements:* For master's, GRE, GMAT, or LSAT. Additional exam requirements/recommendations for international students: Recommended—TOEFL (minimum score 79 iBT), IELTS (minimum score 6.5). *Faculty research:* Microfinance, finance (rural/development, international, corporate), firm life cycle theory, TESOL, language proficiency testing, public policy, administrative law, economic development, cryptography, artificial intelligence, energy efficiency/renewable energy, computer-aided design/manufacturing, health financing, tuberculosis control, mother/child health, preventive ophthalmology, post-earthquake psychopathological investigations, tobacco control, environmental health risk assessments.

Arizona State University at the Tempe campus, Ira A. Fulton Schools of Engineering, The Polytechnic School, Programs in Technology Management, Mesa, AZ 85212. Offers aviation management and human factors (MS); environmental technology management (MS); global technology and development (MS); graphic information technology (MS); management of technology (MS). *Program availability:* Part-time, evening/weekend, online learning. *Degree requirements:* For master's, thesis or applied project and oral defense; interactive Program of Study (iPOS) submitted before completing 50 percent of required credit hours. *Entrance requirements:* For master's, GRE, minimum GPA of 3.0 or equivalent in last 2 years of work leading to bachelor's degree. Additional exam requirements/recommendations for international students: Required—TOEFL, IELTS, or PTE. Electronic applications accepted. *Faculty research:* Digital imaging, digital publishing, Internet development/e-commerce, information aviation human factors, pilot selection, databases, multimedia, commercial digital photography, digital workflow, computer graphics modeling and animation, information design, sociotechnology, visual and technical literacy, environmental management, quality management, project management, industrial ethics, hazardous materials, environmental chemistry.

Arkansas Tech University, College of Engineering and Applied Sciences, Russellville, AR 72801. Offers emergency management (MS); engineering (M Engr); information technology (MS). *Program availability:* Part-time, online learning. *Students:* 59 full-time (15 women), 63 part-time (21 women); includes 22 minority (8 Black or African American, non-Hispanic/Latino; 2 American Indian or Alaska Native, non-Hispanic/Latino; 4 Asian, non-Hispanic/Latino; 4 Hispanic/Latino; 4 Two or more races, non-Hispanic/Latino), 41 international. Average age 31. In 2016, 43 master's awarded. *Degree requirements:* For master's, comprehensive exam (for some programs), thesis (for some programs), internship. *Entrance requirements:* For master's, GRE General Test. Additional exam requirements/recommendations for international students: Required—TOEFL (minimum score 550 paper-based; 79 iBT), IELTS (minimum score 6). *Application deadline:* For fall admission, 3/1 priority date for domestic students, 5/1 priority date for international students; for spring admission, 10/1 priority date for domestic and international students. Applications are processed on a rolling basis. Application fee: $25 ($75 for international students). Electronic applications accepted. *Expenses:* Tuition, state resident: full-time $4932; part-time $274 per credit hour. Tuition, nonresident: full-time $9864; part-time $548 per credit hour. *Required fees:* $513 per semester. Tuition and fees vary according to course load. *Financial support:* In 2016–17, research assistantships with full tuition reimbursements (averaging $4,800 per year), teaching assistantships with full tuition reimbursements (averaging $4,800 per year) were awarded; career-related internships or fieldwork, Federal Work-Study, scholarships/grants, health care benefits, and unspecified assistantships also available. Support available to part-time students. Financial award application deadline: 4/15; financial award applicants required to submit FAFSA. *Unit head:* Dr. Douglas Barlow, Dean, 479-968-0353, E-mail: dbarlow@atu.edu. *Application contact:* Dr. Mary B. Gunter, Dean of Graduate College, 479-968-0398, Fax: 479-964-0542, E-mail: gradcollege@atu.edu.
Website: http://www.atu.edu/appliedsci/

Armstrong State University, School of Graduate Studies, Program in Computer and Information Science, Savannah, GA 31419-1997. Offers MSCIS. *Program availability:* Part-time. *Faculty:* 4 full-time (0 women). *Students:* 1 full-time (0 women), 4 part-time (2 women), 3 international. Average age 28. 15 applicants, 7% accepted, 1 enrolled. *Degree requirements:* For master's, project. *Entrance requirements:* For master's, GRE (minimum scores: verbal 156, quantitative 144, and writing 4), minimum GPA of 2.7, letters of recommendation, BS in computer science or related field. Additional exam requirements/recommendations for international students: Required—TOEFL (minimum score 523 paper-based; 70 iBT). *Application deadline:* For fall admission, 7/1 priority date for domestic students, 5/1 priority date for international students; for spring admission, 11/15 priority date for domestic students, 9/15 priority date for international students; for summer admission, 4/15 priority date for domestic students, 9/15 for international students. Applications are processed on a rolling basis. Application fee: $30. Electronic applications accepted. *Expenses:* Tuition, state resident: full-time $1781; part-time $161.93 per credit hour. Tuition, nonresident: full-time $6482; part-time $589.27 per credit hour. *Required fees:* $1224 per unit. $612 per semester. Tuition and fees vary according to course load, campus/location and program. *Financial support:* In 2016–17, research assistantships with full tuition reimbursements (averaging $5,000 per year) were awarded; career-related internships or fieldwork, Federal Work-Study, scholarships/grants, and unspecified assistantships also available. Support available to part-time students. Financial award application deadline: 3/15; financial award applicants required to submit FAFSA. *Faculty research:* Bioinformatics, data mining, graph theory, image processing, machine learning. *Unit head:* Dr. Hong Zhang, Department Head, 912-344-2542, Fax: 912-344-3415, E-mail: hong.zhang@armstrong.edu. *Application contact:* McKenzie Peterman, Assistant Director of Graduate Admissions, 912-344-2503, Fax: 912-344-3417, E-mail: graduate@armstrong.edu.
Website: https://www.armstrong.edu/degree-programs/computer-science-mscis

Aspen University, Program in Information Technology, Denver, CO 80246-1930. Offers MS, Certificate. *Program availability:* Part-time, evening/weekend, online learning. Electronic applications accepted.

Auburn University at Montgomery, College of Arts and Sciences, Department of Mathematics and Computer Science, Montgomery, AL 36124-4023. Offers cybersystems and information security (MS).

Ball State University, Graduate School, College of Communication, Information, and Media, Center for Information and Communication Sciences, Muncie, IN 47306. Offers information and communication sciences (MS); information and communication technologies (Certificate). *Program availability:* Part-time, 100% online. *Entrance requirements:* For master's, minimum baccalaureate GPA of 2.75 or 3.0 in latter half of baccalaureate, statement of goals. Additional exam requirements/recommendations for international students: Required—TOEFL (minimum score 550 paper-based; 79 iBT), IELTS (minimum score 6.5). Electronic applications accepted.

Barry University, School of Adult and Continuing Education, Program in Information Technology, Miami Shores, FL 33161-6695. Offers MS. *Program availability:* Part-time, evening/weekend. *Entrance requirements:* For master's, GMAT, GRE or MAT, bachelor's degree in information technology, related area or professional experience. Electronic applications accepted.

Bellevue University, Graduate School, College of Information Technology, Bellevue, NE 68005-3098. Offers computer information systems (MS); cybersecurity (MS); management of information systems (MS); project management (MPM).

Bentley University, Graduate School of Business, Program in Information Technology, Waltham, MA 02452-4705. Offers MSIT. *Program availability:* Part-time, evening/weekend. *Faculty:* 71 full-time (25 women), 33 part-time/adjunct (15 women). *Students:* 42 full-time (29 women), 19 part-time (5 women); includes 3 minority (2 Asian, non-Hispanic/Latino; 1 Hispanic/Latino), 37 international. Average age 27. 91 applicants, 66% accepted, 26 enrolled. In 2016, 42 master's awarded. *Entrance requirements:* For master's, GMAT or GRE General Test, current resume; two letters of recommendation; official copies of all university level transcripts. Additional exam requirements/recommendations for international students: Required—TOEFL (minimum score 600 paper-based; 100 iBT), IELTS (minimum score 7), or PTE. *Application deadline:* Applications are processed on a rolling basis. Application fee: $50. Electronic applications accepted. *Expenses:* $4,225 per course, $480 fee per year. *Financial support:* In 2016–17, 16 students received support. Scholarships/grants and unspecified assistantships available. Financial award application deadline: 6/1; financial award applicants required to submit FAFSA. *Faculty research:* Business intelligence; enterprise networks and services; telemedicine; enterprise resource planning usability; information visualization, system design quality. *Unit head:* Dr. Wendy Lucas, Professor, 781-891-2554, E-mail: wlucas@bentley.edu. *Application contact:* Sharon Hill, Assistant Dean/Director of Graduate Admissions, 781-891-2108, Fax: 781-891-2464, E-mail: bentleygraduateadmissions@bentley.edu.
Website: http://www.bentley.edu/graduate/ms-programs/masters-in-information-technology

Bradley University, The Graduate School, College of Liberal Arts and Sciences, Department of Computer Science and Information Systems, Peoria, IL 61625-0002. Offers computer information systems (MS); computer science (MS). *Program availability:* Part-time, evening/weekend. *Degree requirements:* For master's, comprehensive exam, thesis or alternative, programming test. *Entrance requirements:* For master's, GRE. Additional exam requirements/recommendations for international students: Required—TOEFL (minimum score 550 paper-based; 79 iBT), IELTS (minimum score 6.5). *Application deadline:* For fall admission, 5/15 priority date for domestic and international students; for spring admission, 10/15 priority date for domestic and international students. Applications are processed on a rolling basis. Application fee: $40 ($50 for international students). Electronic applications accepted. *Expenses: Tuition:* Full-time $7650; part-time $850 per credit. *Required fees:* $50 per credit. One-time fee: $100 full-time. *Financial support:* Research assistantships with full and partial tuition reimbursements, teaching assistantships, scholarships/grants, tuition waivers (partial), and unspecified assistantships available. Support available to part-time students. Financial award application deadline: 4/1. *Unit head:* Dr. Steven Dolins, Chair, 309-677-3284, E-mail: sdolins@bradley.edu. *Application contact:* Kayla Carroll, Director of International Admissions and Student Services, 309-677-2375, E-mail: klcarroll@fsmail.bradley.edu.
Website: http://www.bradley.edu/academic/departments/csis/

Brigham Young University, Graduate Studies, Ira A. Fulton College of Engineering and Technology, School of Technology, Provo, UT 84602. Offers construction management (MS); information technology (MS); manufacturing engineering technology (MS); technology and engineering education (MS). *Faculty:* 25 full-time (0 women), 3 part-time/adjunct (0 women). *Students:* 36 full-time (4 women); includes 5 minority (2 American Indian or Alaska Native, non-Hispanic/Latino; 2 Asian, non-Hispanic/Latino; 1 Hispanic/Latino). Average age 29. 14 applicants, 100% accepted, 13 enrolled. In 2016, 11 master's awarded. *Degree requirements:* For master's, thesis. *Entrance requirements:* For master's, GRE General Test; GMAT or GRE (for construction management emphasis), minimum GPA of 3.0 in last 60 hours of course work. Additional exam requirements/recommendations for international students: Required—TOEFL (minimum score 580 paper-based; 85 iBT). *Application deadline:* For fall admission, 2/15 for domestic and international students; for winter admission, 9/10 for domestic students, 9/15 for international students; for spring admission, 2/15 for domestic and international students; for summer admission, 2/15 for domestic and international students. Application fee: $50. Electronic applications accepted. *Expenses: Tuition:* Full-time $6680; part-time $393 per credit. Tuition and fees vary according to course load, program and student's religious affiliation. *Financial support:* In 2016–17, 28 students received support, including 3 research assistantships (averaging $18,288 per year), 11 teaching assistantships (averaging $7,500 per year); scholarships/grants also available. *Faculty research:* Information assurance and security, HEI and databases, manufacturing materials, processes and systems, innovation in construction management scheduling and delivery methods. *Total annual research expenditures:* $844,333. *Unit head:* Dr. Barry M. Lunt, Director, 801-422-6300, Fax: 801-422-0490, E-mail: blunt@byu.edu. *Application contact:* Clifton Farnsworth, Graduate Coordinator, 801-422-6494, Fax: 801-422-0490, E-mail: clifton_farnsworth@byu.edu.
Website: http://www.et.byu.edu/sot/

Brooklyn College of the City University of New York, School of Natural and Behavioral Sciences, Department of Computer and Information Science, Brooklyn, NY 11210-2889. Offers computer science (MA); health informatics (MS); information systems (MS); parallel and distributed computing (Advanced Certificate). *Program availability:* Part-time, evening/weekend. *Degree requirements:* For master's, comprehensive exam, thesis or alternative. *Entrance requirements:* For master's, previous course work in computer science, 2 letters of recommendation. Additional exam requirements/recommendations for international students: Required—TOEFL (minimum score 525 paper-based; 70 iBT). Electronic applications accepted. *Faculty research:* Networks and distributed systems, programming languages, modeling and computer applications, algorithms, artificial intelligence, theoretical computer science.

California State University, Fullerton, Graduate Studies, College of Business and Economics, Department of Information Systems and Decision Sciences, Fullerton, CA 92834-9480. Offers decision science (MBA); information systems (MBA, MS); information systems and decision sciences (MS); information systems and e-commerce (MS); information technology (MS). *Program availability:* Part-time. *Degree requirements:* For master's, project or thesis. *Entrance requirements:* For master's, GMAT, minimum AACSB index of 950. Application fee: $55. *Expenses:* Tuition, state resident: full-time $3369; part-time $1953 per unit. Tuition, nonresident: full-time $3915; part-time $2499 per unit. Tuition and fees vary according to course load, degree level and program. *Financial support:* Career-related internships or fieldwork, Federal Work-Study, institutionally sponsored loans, and scholarships/grants available. Support available to part-time students. Financial award application deadline: 3/1; financial award applicants required to submit FAFSA. *Unit head:* Dr. Bhushan Kapoor, Chair, 657-278-2221. *Application contact:* Admissions/Applications, 657-278-2371.
Website: http://business.fullerton.edu/isds/

Capitol Technology University, Graduate Programs, Laurel, MD 20708-9759. Offers business administration (MBA); computer science (MS); electrical engineering (MS); information and telecommunications systems management (MS); information architecture (MS); network security (MS). *Program availability:* Part-time, evening/weekend, online learning. *Entrance requirements:* For master's, minimum GPA of 3.0. Electronic applications accepted.

Carleton University, Faculty of Graduate Studies, Faculty of Engineering and Design, Ottawa-Carleton Institute for Electrical Engineering, Department of Systems and Computer Engineering, Program in Information and Systems Science, Ottawa, ON K1S 5B6, Canada. Offers M Sc.

Carleton University, Faculty of Graduate Studies, Faculty of Science, Information and Systems Science Program, Ottawa, ON K1S 5B6, Canada. Offers M Sc. *Degree requirements:* For master's, thesis optional. *Entrance requirements:* For master's, honors degree. Additional exam requirements/recommendations for international students: Required—TOEFL. *Faculty research:* Software engineering, real-time and microprocessor programming, computer communications.

Carleton University, Faculty of Graduate Studies, Faculty of Science, School of Computer Science, Ottawa, ON K1S 5B6, Canada. Offers computer science (MCS, PhD); information and system science (M Sc). MCS and PhD programs offered jointly with University of Ottawa. *Program availability:* Part-time. *Degree requirements:* For master's, thesis optional, project; for doctorate, comprehensive exam, thesis/dissertation. *Entrance requirements:* For master's, honors degree. Additional exam requirements/recommendations for international students: Required—TOEFL. *Faculty research:* Programming systems, theory of computing, computer applications, computer systems.

Carnegie Mellon University, Heinz College Australia, Master of Science in Information Technology Program (Adelaide, South Australia), Adelaide SA 5000, Australia. Offers MSIT. *Entrance requirements:* For master's, GRE or GMAT, college-level course in advanced algebra/pre-calculus; college-level courses in economics and statistics (recommended). Additional exam requirements/recommendations for international students: Required—TOEFL or IELTS.

Carnegie Mellon University, Heinz College, School of Information Systems and Management, Master of Information Systems Management Program, Pittsburgh, PA 15213-3891. Offers MISM. *Entrance requirements:* For master's, GRE or GMAT, college-level course in advanced algebra/pre-calculus; college-level courses in economics and statistics (recommended). Additional exam requirements/recommendations for international students: Required—TOEFL or IELTS.

Carnegie Mellon University, School of Computer Science, Language Technologies Institute, Pittsburgh, PA 15213-3891. Offers MLT, MS, PhD. Terminal master's awarded for partial completion of doctoral program. *Degree requirements:* For doctorate, thesis/dissertation. *Entrance requirements:* For master's and doctorate, GRE General Test, GRE Subject Test. Additional exam requirements/recommendations for international students: Required—TOEFL. *Faculty research:* Machine translation, natural language processing, speech and information retrieval, literacy.

Case Western Reserve University, School of Graduate Studies, Case School of Engineering, Department of Electrical Engineering and Computer Science, Cleveland, OH 44106. Offers computer engineering (MS, PhD); computing and information sciences (MS, PhD); electrical engineering (MS, PhD); systems and control engineering (MS, PhD). *Program availability:* Part-time, evening/weekend, online only, 100% online. *Faculty:* 32 full-time (3 women). *Students:* 188 full-time (42 women), 14 part-time (3 women); includes 7 minority (1 Black or African American, non-Hispanic/Latino; 5 Asian, non-Hispanic/Latino; 1 Hispanic/Latino), 152 international. In 2016, 25 master's, 26 doctorates awarded. Terminal master's awarded for partial completion of doctoral program. *Degree requirements:* For master's, thesis; for doctorate, thesis/dissertation, qualifying exam, teaching experience. *Entrance requirements:* For master's and doctorate, GRE General Test. Additional exam requirements/recommendations for international students: Required—TOEFL. *Application deadline:* For fall admission, 2/1 for domestic students; for spring admission, 11/1 for domestic students. Applications are processed on a rolling basis. Application fee: $50. *Expenses: Tuition:* Full-time $42,576; part-time $1774 per credit hour. *Required fees:* $34. Tuition and fees vary according to course load and program. *Financial support:* In 2016–17, 1 fellowship with tuition reimbursement, 63 research assistantships with tuition reimbursements, 10 teaching assistantships were awarded; career-related internships or fieldwork, Federal Work-Study, and institutionally sponsored loans also available. Support available to part-time students. Financial award application deadline: 3/1; financial award applicants required to submit FAFSA. *Faculty research:* Micro-/nano-systems; robotics and haptics; applied artificial intelligence; automation; computer-aided design and testing of digital systems. *Total annual research expenditures:* $4.9 million. *Unit head:* Dr. Kenneth Loparo, Department Chair, 216-368-4115, E-mail: kal4@case.edu. *Application contact:* Kimberly Yurchick, Student Affairs Specialist, 216-368-2920, Fax: 216-368-2801, E-mail: ksy4@case.edu.
Website: http://eecs.cwru.edu/

The Citadel, The Military College of South Carolina, Citadel Graduate College, School of Science and Mathematics, Department of Mathematics and Computer Science, Charleston, SC 29409. Offers computer and information sciences (MS). MS computer and information sciences and cybersecurity graduate certificate offered jointly with the Graduate College of the College of Charleston. *Accreditation:* NCATE (one or more programs are accredited). *Program availability:* Part-time, evening/weekend. *Faculty:* 1 full-time (0 women). *Students:* 1 (woman) full-time, 7 part-time (3 women); includes 2 minority (both Black or African American, non-Hispanic/Latino). 17 applicants, 94% accepted, 2 enrolled. In 2016, 5 master's awarded. *Degree requirements:* For master's, comprehensive exam (for some programs), thesis (for some programs). *Entrance requirements:* For master's, GRE General Test (minimum combined score of 300 on the verbal and quantitative sections, 1000 under the old grading system, 4.0 on the writing assessment for MS); MAT with minimum raw score of 396 (for MA Ed), minimum undergraduate GPA of 3.0 and competency demonstrated through coursework, approved work experience, or a program-administrated competency exam, in the areas of basic computer architecture, object-oriented programming, discrete mathematics, and data structures (for MS). Additional exam requirements/recommendations for international students: Required—TOEFL (minimum score 550 paper-based; 79 iBT). *Application deadline:* Applications are processed on a rolling basis. Application fee: $40. Electronic applications accepted. *Expenses:* Tuition, state resident: full-time $5121; part-time $569 per credit hour. Tuition, nonresident: full-time $8613; part-time $957 per credit hour. *Required fees:* $90 per term. *Financial support:* Fellowships and unspecified assistantships available. Support available to part-time students. Financial award application deadline: 7/1; financial award applicants required to submit FAFSA. *Unit head:* Dr. Mei-Qin Chen, Department Head, 843-953-5048, E-mail: chenm@citadel.edu. *Application contact:* Dr. Shankar M. Banik, Program Director, 843-953-5039, E-mail: shankar.banik@citadel.edu.
Website: http://www.citadel.edu/root/mathcs

Claremont Graduate University, Graduate Programs, Center for Information Systems and Technology, Claremont, CA 91711-6160. Offers cybersecurity and networking (MS); data science and analytics (MS); electronic commerce (PhD); geographic information systems (MS); health informatics (MS); information systems (Certificate); IT strategy and innovation (MS); knowledge management (PhD); systems development (PhD); telecommunications and networking (PhD); MBA/MS. *Program availability:* Part-time. *Faculty:* 8 full-time (1 woman), 1 part-time/adjunct (0 women). *Students:* 60 full-time (18 women), 81 part-time (27 women); includes 34 minority (7 Black or African American, non-Hispanic/Latino; 18 Asian, non-Hispanic/Latino; 7 Hispanic/Latino; 1 Native Hawaiian or other Pacific Islander, non-Hispanic/Latino; 1 Two or more races, non-Hispanic/Latino), 80 international. Average age 35. In 2016, 21 master's, 10 doctorates awarded. *Degree requirements:* For doctorate, comprehensive exam, thesis/dissertation, portfolio. *Entrance requirements:* For master's and doctorate, GMAT, GRE General Test. Additional exam requirements/recommendations for international students: Required—TOEFL (minimum score 75 iBT). *Application deadline:* For fall admission, 2/1 priority date for domestic and international students. Applications are processed on a rolling basis. Application fee: $80. Electronic applications accepted. *Expenses: Tuition:* Full-time $44,328; part-time $1847 per unit. *Required fees:* $600; $300 per semester. Tuition and fees vary according to course load and program. *Financial support:* Fellowships, research assistantships, teaching assistantships, Federal Work-Study, institutionally sponsored loans, and scholarships/grants available. Support available to part-time students. Financial award application deadline: 2/15; financial award applicants required to submit FAFSA. *Faculty research:* Man-machine interaction, organizational aspects of computing, implementation of information systems, information systems practice. *Unit head:* Lorne Olfman, Acting Director, 909-607-3035, E-mail: lorne.olfman@cgu.edu. *Application contact:* Jake Campbell, Senior Assistant Director of Admissions, 909-607-3024, E-mail: jake.campbell@cgu.edu.
Website: https://www.cgu.edu/school/center-for-information-systems-and-technology/

Clark Atlanta University, School of Arts and Sciences, Department of Computer and Information Science, Atlanta, GA 30314. Offers MS. *Program availability:* Part-time. *Faculty:* 3 full-time (0 women). *Students:* 27 full-time (10 women), 11 part-time (2 women); includes 6 minority (3 Black or African American, non-Hispanic/Latino; 3 Asian, non-Hispanic/Latino), 21 international. Average age 29. 25 applicants, 96% accepted, 7 enrolled. In 2016, 15 master's awarded. *Degree requirements:* For master's, one foreign language, thesis. *Entrance requirements:* For master's, GRE General Test, minimum GPA of 2.5. Additional exam requirements/recommendations for international students: Required—TOEFL (minimum score 500 paper-based; 61 iBT). *Application deadline:* For fall admission, 4/1 for domestic and international students; for spring admission, 11/1 for domestic and international students. Applications are processed on a rolling basis. Application fee: $40 ($55 for international students). *Expenses: Tuition:* Full-time $15,498; part-time $861 per credit hour. *Required fees:* $1326; $1326 per credit hour. Tuition and fees vary according to course load. *Financial support:* Fellowships, career-related internships or fieldwork, Federal Work-Study, scholarships/grants, and unspecified assistantships available. Support available to part-time students. Financial award application deadline: 4/30; financial award applicants required to submit FAFSA. *Unit head:* Dr. Roy George, Chairperson, 404-880-6945, E-mail: rgeorge@cau.edu. *Application contact:* Graduate Program Admissions, 404-880-8483, E-mail: graduateadmissions@cau.edu.

Clarkson University, School of Arts and Sciences, Program in Information Technology, Potsdam, NY 13699. Offers MS. *Students:* 3 applicants. In 2016, 1 master's awarded. *Entrance requirements:* For master's, GRE. Additional exam requirements/recommendations for international students: Required—TOEFL (minimum score 550 paper-based, 80 iBT) or IELTS (6.5). *Application deadline:* Applications are processed on a rolling basis. Application fee: $50. Electronic applications accepted. *Expenses: Tuition:* Full-time $23,400; part-time $1300 per credit hour. Tuition and fees vary according to campus/location and program. *Financial support:* Scholarships/grants and unspecified assistantships available. *Unit head:* Dr. William Dennis Horn, Director of the IT Master's Program, 315-268-6420, E-mail: whorn@clarkson.edu. *Application contact:* Dan Capogna, Graduate Admissions Contact, 518-631-9910, E-mail: graduate@clarkson.edu.
Website: http://graduate.clarkson.edu

Clark University, Graduate School, School of Professional Studies, Program in Information Technology, Worcester, MA 01610-1477. Offers MSIT. *Students:* 33 full-time (19 women), 24 part-time (8 women); includes 6 minority (3 Black or African American, non-Hispanic/Latino; 2 Hispanic/Latino; 1 Two or more races, non-Hispanic/Latino), 39 international. Average age 31. 66 applicants, 79% accepted, 20 enrolled. In 2016, 22 master's awarded. *Degree requirements:* For master's, thesis or alternative. *Entrance requirements:* Additional exam requirements/recommendations for international students: Required—TOEFL. *Application deadline:* Applications are processed on a rolling basis. Application fee: $75. Electronic applications accepted. *Expenses: Tuition:* Full-time $44,050. *Required fees:* $80. Tuition and fees vary according to course load and program. *Financial support:* Tuition waivers (partial) available. *Application contact:* Dr. John Chetro-Szivos, Associate Dean of Professional Studies and Online Education, 508-793-7623, E-mail: jchetroszivos@clarku.edu.
Website: http://www.clarku.edu/programs/masters-information-technology

Coleman University, Program in Information Technology, San Diego, CA 92123. Offers MSIT. *Program availability:* Evening/weekend. *Entrance requirements:* For master's, bachelor's degree in computer field, minimum GPA of 3.0. Additional exam requirements/recommendations for international students: Required—TOEFL (minimum score 500 paper-based).

The College of Saint Rose, Graduate Studies, School of Mathematics and Sciences, Program in Computer Information Systems, Albany, NY 12203-1419. Offers MS, Advanced Certificate. *Program availability:* Part-time, evening/weekend. *Students:* 89 full-time (28 women), 16 part-time (6 women); includes 4 minority (2 Black or African American, non-Hispanic/Latino; 1 Asian, non-Hispanic/Latino; 1 Two or more races, non-Hispanic/Latino), 97 international. Average age 25. 220 applicants, 83% accepted, 13 enrolled. In 2016, 18 master's, 3 other advanced degrees awarded. *Degree requirements:* For master's, comprehensive exam, research component, project. *Entrance requirements:* For master's, minimum GPA of 3.0, 9 undergraduate credits in math. Additional exam requirements/recommendations for international students: Required—TOEFL (minimum score 550 paper-based; 80 iBT), IELTS (minimum score 6), PTE (minimum score 56). *Application deadline:* For fall admission, 4/1 priority date for domestic and international students; for spring admission, 10/15 priority date for domestic and international students; for summer admission, 3/15 priority date for domestic and international students. Applications are processed on a rolling basis. Application fee: $40. Electronic applications accepted. *Expenses: Tuition:* Full-time $14,382; part-time $799 per credit. *Required fees:* $814; $32 per credit. $88 per semester. Tuition and fees vary according to course load. *Financial support:* Career-related internships or fieldwork, scholarships/grants, tuition waivers (partial), and unspecified assistantships available. Support available to part-time students. Financial award application deadline: 4/15; financial award applicants required to submit FAFSA. *Unit head:* Dr. John Avitabile, Department Chair, 518-458-5317, E-mail: avitabij@strose.edu. *Application contact:* Cris Murray, Assistant Vice President for Graduate Recruitment and Enrollment, 518-485-3390.
Website: https://www.strose.edu/computer-information-systems/

Cornell University, Graduate School, Graduate Fields of Arts and Sciences, Field of Information Science, Ithaca, NY 14853. Offers cognition (PhD); human computer interaction (PhD); information science (PhD); information systems (PhD); social aspects of information (PhD). *Degree requirements:* For doctorate, comprehensive exam, thesis/dissertation. *Entrance requirements:* For doctorate, GRE General Test, 3 letters of recommendation. Additional exam requirements/recommendations for international students: Required—TOEFL (minimum score 550 paper-based; 77 iBT). Electronic applications accepted. *Faculty research:* Digital libraries, game theory, data mining, human-computer interaction, computational linguistics.

Dakota State University, College of Business and Information Systems, Madison, SD 57042-1799. Offers analytics (MSA); applied computer science (MSACS); banking security (Graduate Certificate); business analytics (Graduate Certificate); cyber security (D Sc); ethical hacking (Graduate Certificate); general management (MBA); health informatics (MSHI); information assurance and computer security (MSIA); information systems (MSIS, D Sc IS); information technology (Graduate Certificate). *Accreditation:*

ACBSP. *Program availability:* Part-time, evening/weekend, 100% online, blended/hybrid learning. *Degree requirements:* For master's, comprehensive exam, thesis optional, examination, integrative project; for doctorate, comprehensive exam, thesis/dissertation, portfolio. *Entrance requirements:* For master's, GRE General Test, demonstration of information systems skills, minimum GPA of 2.7; for doctorate, GRE General Test, demonstration of information systems skills; for Graduate Certificate, GMAT. Additional exam requirements/recommendations for international students: Required—PTE (minimum score 53), TOEFL (minimum score 550 paper-based, 79 iBT) or IELTS (6.5). *Application deadline:* For fall admission, 6/15 for domestic students, 4/15 for international students; for spring admission, 11/15 for domestic students, 9/15 priority date for international students; for summer admission, 4/15 for domestic and international students. Applications are processed on a rolling basis. Application fee: $35. *Expenses:* Contact institution. *Financial support:* Fellowships with partial tuition reimbursements, research assistantships with partial tuition reimbursements, teaching assistantships with partial tuition reimbursements, career-related internships or fieldwork, Federal Work-Study, scholarships/grants, and unspecified assistantships available. Support available to part-time students. Financial award applicants required to submit FAFSA. *Faculty research:* Data mining and analytics, biometrics and information assurance, decision support systems, health informatics, STEM education for K-12 teachers/students and underrepresented populations. *Unit head:* Mark Hawkes, Dean for Graduate Studies and Research, 605-256-5274, E-mail: mark.hawkes@dsu.edu. *Application contact:* Erin Blankespoor, Senior Secretary, Office of Graduate Studies and Research, 605-256-5799, E-mail: erin.blankespoor@dsu.edu.
Website: http://dsu.edu/academics/colleges/college-of-business-and-information-systems

DePaul University, College of Computing and Digital Media, Chicago, IL 60604. Offers animation (MA, MFA); business information technology (MS); cinema (MFA); cinema production (MS); computational finance (MS); computer and information sciences (PhD); computer game development (MS); computer information and network security (MS); computer science (MS); e-commerce technology (MS); health informatics (MS); human-computer interaction (MS); information systems (MS); information technology project management (MS); network engineering and management (MS); predictive analytics (MS); screenwriting (MFA); software engineering (MS); JD/MS. *Program availability:* Part-time, evening/weekend, online learning. *Degree requirements:* For master's, thesis (for some programs); for doctorate, comprehensive exam, thesis/dissertation. *Entrance requirements:* For master's, GRE or GMAT (for MS in computational finance only), bachelor's degree, resume (MS in predictive analytics only), IT experience (MS in information technology project management only), portfolio review (all MFA programs and MA in animation); for doctorate, GRE, master's degree in computer science. Additional exam requirements/recommendations for international students: Required—TOEFL (minimum score 590 paper-based; 80 iBT), IELTS (minimum score 6.5), PTE (minimum score 53). Electronic applications accepted. *Expenses:* Contact institution. *Faculty research:* Data mining, computer science, human-computer interaction, security, animation and film.

⭐ **Drexel University,** College of Computing and Informatics, Department of Information Science, Philadelphia, PA 19104-2875. Offers health informatics (MS); information science (PhD, Post-Master's Certificate, Postbaccalaureate Certificate); information systems (MS); library and information science (MS). *Program availability:* Part-time, evening/weekend, 100% online. *Faculty:* 33 full-time (18 women), 9 part-time/adjunct (3 women). *Students:* 115 full-time (61 women), 281 part-time (184 women); includes 78 minority (29 Black or African American, non-Hispanic/Latino; 16 Asian, non-Hispanic/Latino; 24 Hispanic/Latino; 9 Two or more races, non-Hispanic/Latino), 60 international. Average age 34. 475 applicants, 43% accepted, 102 enrolled. In 2016, 181 master's, 8 doctorates, 20 other advanced degrees awarded. *Degree requirements:* For doctorate, thesis/dissertation. *Entrance requirements:* For master's and doctorate, GRE General Test. Additional exam requirements/recommendations for international students: Required—TOEFL (minimum score 600 paper-based; 100 iBT), IELTS (minimum score 6.5). *Application deadline:* For fall admission, 8/15 for domestic students, 7/15 for international students; for spring admission, 3/1 for domestic students, 2/1 for international students. Applications are processed on a rolling basis. Application fee: $65. Electronic applications accepted. Application fee is waived when completed online. *Expenses: Tuition:* Full-time $32,184; part-time $1192 per credit hour. *Required fees:* $280. Tuition and fees vary according to campus/location and program. *Financial support:* In 2016–17, 82 students received support, including 15 research assistantships with full tuition reimbursements available (averaging $26,670 per year), 9 teaching assistantships with full tuition reimbursements available (averaging $26,750 per year); career-related internships or fieldwork, scholarships/grants, and tuition waivers (partial) also available. Support available to part-time students. Financial award application deadline: 3/1; financial award applicants required to submit FAFSA. *Total annual research expenditures:* $2 million. *Unit head:* Dr. Yi Deng, Dean/Professor, 215-895-2474, Fax: 215-895-2494, E-mail: yd362@drexel.edu. *Application contact:* Matthew Lechtenberg, Director, Recruitment, 215-895-2474, Fax: 215-895-2303, E-mail: cciinfo@drexel.edu.
Website: http://cci.drexel.edu/academics/graduate-programs/ms-in-health-informatics
See Display on page 275 and Close-Up on page 369.

East Tennessee State University, School of Graduate Studies, College of Business and Technology, Department of Computing, Johnson City, TN 37614. Offers MS, Postbaccalaureate Certificate. *Program availability:* Part-time, evening/weekend. *Degree requirements:* For master's, comprehensive exam, thesis optional, capstone. *Entrance requirements:* For master's, GRE General Test, minimum GPA of 2.5, three letters of recommendation. Additional exam requirements/recommendations for international students: Required—TOEFL (minimum score 550 paper-based; 79 iBT). Electronic applications accepted. *Faculty research:* Data mining, security and forensics, numerical optimization, computer gaming, enterprise resource planning.

Florida Institute of Technology, College of Engineering, Program in Computer Information Systems, Melbourne, FL 32901-6975. Offers MS. *Program availability:* Part-time, evening/weekend, 100% online. *Students:* 71 full-time (29 women), 58 part-time (15 women); includes 15 minority (6 Black or African American, non-Hispanic/Latino; 5 Asian, non-Hispanic/Latino; 4 Hispanic/Latino), 90 international. Average age 28. 295 applicants, 62% accepted, 34 enrolled. In 2016, 102 master's awarded. *Degree requirements:* For master's, comprehensive exam (for some programs), thesis optional, minimum of 30 credits. *Entrance requirements:* For master's, 3 letters of recommendation, resume, mathematical proficiency. *Application deadline:* Applications are processed on a rolling basis. Application fee: $50. Electronic applications accepted. *Expenses: Tuition:* Full-time $22,338; part-time $1241 per credit hour. *Required fees:* $250. Tuition and fees vary according to degree level, campus/location and program. *Financial support:* Tuition remissions available. Financial award application deadline: 3/1; financial award applicants required to submit FAFSA. *Faculty research:* Artificial intelligence, software engineering, computer graphics, programming languages, database systems. *Unit head:* Dr. Rhoda Baggs, Program Chair of Computer Information Systems, 321-674-8807, E-mail: rbaggs@fit.edu. *Application contact:* Cheryl A. Brown, Associate Director of Graduate Admissions, 321-674-7581, Fax: 321-723-9468, E-mail: cbrown@fit.edu.
Website: http://coe.fit.edu/computing/cis/

Florida International University, College of Engineering and Computing, School of Computing and Information Sciences, Miami, FL 33199. Offers computer science (MS, PhD); cybersecurity (MS); data science (MS); information technology (MS); telecommunications and networking (MS). *Program availability:* Part-time, evening/weekend. *Faculty:* 46 full-time (11 women), 28 part-time/adjunct (5 women). *Students:* 145 full-time (39 women), 109 part-time (16 women); includes 124 minority (14 Black or African American, non-Hispanic/Latino; 1 American Indian or Alaska Native, non-Hispanic/Latino; 10 Asian, non-Hispanic/Latino; 97 Hispanic/Latino; 2 Two or more races, non-Hispanic/Latino), 115 international. Average age 29. 407 applicants, 54% accepted, 78 enrolled. In 2016, 90 master's, 8 doctorates awarded. *Degree requirements:* For master's, thesis or alternative; for doctorate, comprehensive exam, thesis/dissertation. *Entrance requirements:* For master's and doctorate, GRE General Test, 3 letters of recommendation, minimum GPA of 3.0. Additional exam requirements/recommendations for international students: Required—TOEFL (minimum score 550 paper-based; 80 iBT). *Application deadline:* For fall admission, 6/1 for domestic students, 4/1 for international students; for spring admission, 10/1 for domestic students, 9/1 for international students. Applications are processed on a rolling basis. Application fee: $30. Electronic applications accepted. *Expenses:* Tuition, state resident: full-time $8912; part-time $446 per credit hour. Tuition, nonresident: full-time $21,393; part-time $992 per credit hour. *Required fees:* $2185; $195 per semester. Tuition and fees vary according to program. *Financial support:* Research assistantships, teaching assistantships, institutionally sponsored loans, scholarships/grants, and unspecified assistantships available. Financial award application deadline: 3/1; financial award applicants required to submit FAFSA. *Faculty research:* Database systems, software engineering, operating systems, networks. *Unit head:* Dr. S. S. Iyengar, Director, 305-348-3947, E-mail: iyengar@cis.fiu.edu. *Application contact:* Sara-Michelle Lemus, Engineering Admissions Officer, 305-348-1890, E-mail: grad_eng@fiu.edu.

Gannon University, School of Graduate Studies, College of Engineering and Business, School of Engineering and Computer Science, Program in Computer and Information Science, Erie, PA 16541-0001. Offers information analytics (MSCIS); software engineering (MSCIS). *Program availability:* Part-time, evening/weekend. *Students:* 1 part-time (0 women); minority (Native Hawaiian or other Pacific Islander, non-Hispanic/Latino). Average age 42. In 2016, 27 master's awarded. *Degree requirements:* For master's, thesis (for some programs), directed research. *Entrance requirements:* For master's, 3 letters of recommendation; resume; transcripts; baccalaureate degree in computer science, information systems, information science, software engineering, or related field from regionally-accredited institution with minimum GPA of 2.5. Additional exam requirements/recommendations for international students: Required—TOEFL (minimum score 79 iBT). *Application deadline:* Applications are processed on a rolling basis. Application fee: $25. Electronic applications accepted. Application fee is waived when completed online. *Expenses: Tuition:* Full-time $17,370. *Required fees:* $550. Tuition and fees vary according to course load and program. *Financial support:* Federal Work-Study and unspecified assistantships available. Financial award application deadline: 7/1; financial award applicants required to submit FAFSA. *Unit head:* Dr. Mei-Huei Tang, Chair, 814-871-5393, E-mail: tang002@gannon.edu. *Application contact:* Bridget Philip, Director of Graduate Admissions, 814-871-7412, E-mail: graduate@gannon.edu.

Gannon University, School of Graduate Studies, College of Engineering and Business, School of Engineering and Computer Science, Program in Information Analytics, Erie, PA 16541-0001. Offers MSCIS. *Program availability:* Part-time, evening/weekend. *Students:* 53 full-time (12 women), 13 part-time (5 women); includes 1 minority (Asian, non-Hispanic/Latino), 61 international. Average age 27. 143 applicants, 59% accepted, 6 enrolled. In 2016, 4 master's awarded. *Entrance requirements:* For master's, baccalaureate degree in computer science, information systems, information science, software engineering, or a related field from regionally-accredited institution with minimum GPA of 2.5; resume; transcripts; 3 letters of recommendation. Additional exam requirements/recommendations for international students: Required—TOEFL (minimum score 79 iBT). *Application deadline:* Applications are processed on a rolling basis. Application fee: $25. Electronic applications accepted. Application fee is waived when completed online. *Expenses: Tuition:* Full-time $17,370. *Required fees:* $550. Tuition and fees vary according to course load and program. *Financial support:* Federal Work-Study available. Financial award application deadline: 7/1; financial award applicants required to submit FAFSA. *Unit head:* Dr. Mei-Huei Tang, Chair, 814-871-5393, E-mail: tang002@gannon.edu. *Application contact:* Bridget Philip, Director of Graduate Admissions, 814-871-7412, E-mail: graduate@gannon.edu.

George Mason University, Volgenau School of Engineering, Department of Information Sciences and Technology, Fairfax, VA 22030. Offers applied information technology (MS); information sciences and technology (Certificate). *Faculty:* 21 full-time (6 women), 58 part-time/adjunct (10 women). *Students:* 142 full-time (48 women), 302 part-time (90 women); includes 152 minority (27 Black or African American, non-Hispanic/Latino; 95 Asian, non-Hispanic/Latino; 22 Hispanic/Latino; 1 Native Hawaiian or other Pacific Islander, non-Hispanic/Latino; 7 Two or more races, non-Hispanic/Latino), 101 international. Average age 31. 336 applicants, 84% accepted, 147 enrolled. In 2016, 86 master's, 25 other advanced degrees awarded. *Degree requirements:* For master's, capstone course. *Entrance requirements:* For master's, GRE/GMAT, personal goals statement; 2 copies of official transcripts; 3 letters of recommendation; resume; official bank statement; proof of financial support; photocopy of passport; baccalaureate degree from an accredited program with minimum B average in last 60 credit hours. Additional exam requirements/recommendations for international students: Required—TOEFL (minimum score 575 paper-based; 88 iBT), IELTS (minimum score 6.5), PTE (minimum score 59). *Application deadline:* For fall admission, 1/15 priority date for domestic students. Application fee: $75 ($80 for international students). Electronic applications accepted. *Expenses:* Contact institution. *Financial support:* In 2016–17, 11 students received support, including 4 research assistantships (averaging $7,975 per year), 8 teaching assistantships with tuition reimbursements available (averaging $10,156 per year); career-related internships or fieldwork, Federal Work-Study, scholarships/grants, unspecified assistantships, and health care benefits (for full-time research or teaching assistantship recipients) also available. Support available to part-time students. Financial award application deadline: 3/1; financial award applicants required to submit FAFSA. *Faculty research:* Secure information systems, document forensics, IT entrepreneurship, learning agents. *Unit head:* Ioulia Rytikova, Associate Chair for Graduate Studies, 703-993-6889, E-mail: irytikov@gmu.edu. *Application contact:* Academic Advisor, 703-993-3565, E-mail: msait@gmu.edu.
Website: http://ist.gmu.edu

George Mason University, Volgenau School of Engineering, Program in Data Analytics Engineering, Fairfax, VA 22030. Offers MS. *Faculty:* 1 full-time (0 women). *Students:* 98 full-time (30 women), 138 part-time (40 women); includes 64 minority (17 Black or African American, non-Hispanic/Latino; 34 Asian, non-Hispanic/Latino; 10 Hispanic/Latino; 3 Two or more races, non-Hispanic/Latino), 74 international. Average age 30. 206 applicants, 81% accepted, 80 enrolled. In 2016, 27 master's awarded. *Entrance*

requirements: For master's, three letters of recommendation; detailed statement of career goals and professional aspiration; self-evaluation form. Additional exam requirements/recommendations for international students: Required—TOEFL (minimum score 575 paper-based; 88 iBT), IELTS (minimum score 6.5), PTE (minimum score 59). *Application deadline:* For fall admission, 1/15 priority date for domestic students. Application fee: $75 ($80 for international students). Electronic applications accepted. *Expenses:* Tuition, state resident: full-time $10,628; part-time $443 per credit. Tuition, nonresident: full-time $29,306; part-time $1221 per credit. *Required fees:* $3096; $129 per credit. Tuition and fees vary according to program. *Financial support:* In 2016–17, 9 students received support, including 4 research assistantships (averaging $7,975 per year), 6 teaching assistantships (averaging $9,946 per year); career-related internships or fieldwork, Federal Work-Study, and scholarships/grants also available. Support available to part-time students. Financial award applicants required to submit FAFSA. *Unit head:* Robert Osgood, Director, 703-993-5443, Fax: 703-993-6137, E-mail: rosgood@gmu.edu. *Application contact:* Suddaf Ismail, Director, Graduate Admissions and Recruitment, 703-993-9115, Fax: 703-993-1242, E-mail: sismail@gmu.edu.
Website: http://volgenau.gmu.edu/data-analytics-engineering

George Mason University, Volgenau School of Engineering, Program in Information Technology, Fairfax, VA 22030. Offers PhD. *Faculty:* 21 full-time (6 women), 58 part-time/adjunct (10 women). *Students:* 33 full-time (14 women), 43 part-time (8 women); includes 21 minority (2 Black or African American, non-Hispanic/Latino; 13 Asian, non-Hispanic/Latino; 5 Hispanic/Latino; 1 Two or more races, non-Hispanic/Latino), 29 international. Average age 37. 25 applicants, 64% accepted, 7 enrolled. In 2016, 11 doctorates awarded. *Degree requirements:* For doctorate, comprehensive exam, thesis/dissertation, internship. *Entrance requirements:* For doctorate, GRE, MS and BS in a related field; 2 official copies of transcripts; 3 letters of recommendation; resume; expanded goals statement. Additional exam requirements/recommendations for international students: Required—TOEFL (minimum score 575 paper-based; 88 iBT), IELTS (minimum score 6.5), PTE (minimum score 59). *Application deadline:* For fall admission, 1/15 priority date for domestic students. Application fee: $75 ($80 for international students). Electronic applications accepted. *Expenses:* Contact institution. *Financial support:* In 2016–17, 23 students received support, including 1 fellowship (averaging $10,000 per year), 12 research assistantships with tuition reimbursements available (averaging $20,840 per year), 12 teaching assistantships with tuition reimbursements available (averaging $16,489 per year); career-related internships or fieldwork, Federal Work-Study, scholarships/grants, unspecified assistantships, and health care benefits (for full-time research or teaching assistantship recipients) also available. Support available to part-time students. Financial award application deadline: 3/1; financial award applicants required to submit FAFSA. *Faculty research:* Rapid pace of technological innovation, need for efficient and effective technology development, unwavering interoperability challenges, the scope and complexity of major system design requirements. *Unit head:* Stephen Nash, Senior Associate Dean, 703-993-1505, Fax: 703-993-1633, E-mail: snash@gmu.edu. *Application contact:* Jennifer Skorzawski-Ross, Director, Graduate Academic Affairs, 703-993-1505, Fax: 703-993-1633, E-mail: jskorzaw@gmu.edu.
Website: http://volgenau.gmu.edu/students/graduates/phd-in-information-technology

Georgia State University, J. Mack Robinson College of Business, Department of Computer Information Systems, Atlanta, GA 30302-3083. Offers computer information systems (PhD); health informatics (MBA, MS); information systems (MSIS, Certificate); information systems development and project management (MBA); information systems management (MBA); managing information technology (Exec MS); the wireless organization (MBA). *Program availability:* Part-time, evening/weekend. *Faculty:* 24 full-time (2 women). *Students:* 209 full-time (84 women), 7 part-time (3 women); includes 41 minority (20 Black or African American, non-Hispanic/Latino; 16 Asian, non-Hispanic/Latino; 4 Hispanic/Latino; 1 Two or more races, non-Hispanic/Latino), 158 international. Average age 28. 587 applicants, 56% accepted, 138 enrolled. In 2016, 126 master's, 4 doctorates awarded. *Degree requirements:* For master's, thesis optional; for doctorate, comprehensive exam, thesis/dissertation. *Entrance requirements:* For master's, GRE or GMAT, transcripts from all institutions attended, resume, essays; for doctorate, GRE or GMAT, three letters of recommendation, personal statement, transcripts from all institutions attended, resume. Additional exam requirements/recommendations for international students: Required—TOEFL (minimum score 610 paper-based; 101 iBT), IELTS (minimum score 7). *Application deadline:* For fall admission, 5/1 priority date for domestic students, 2/1 priority date for international students; for spring admission, 9/15 priority date for domestic students, 4/1 priority date for international students. Applications are processed on a rolling basis. Application fee: $50. Electronic applications accepted. *Expenses:* Tuition, state resident: full-time $6876; part-time $382 per credit hour. Tuition, nonresident: full-time $22,374; part-time $1243 per credit hour. *Required fees:* $2128; $1064 per term. Part-time tuition and fees vary according to course load and program. *Financial support:* Research assistantships, teaching assistantships, scholarships/grants, tuition waivers, and unspecified assistantships available. Financial award applicants required to submit FAFSA. *Faculty research:* Process and technological innovation, strategic IT management, intelligent systems, information systems security, software project risk. *Unit head:* Dr. Ephraim R. McLean, Professor/Chair, 404-413-7360, Fax: 404-413-7394. *Application contact:* Toby McChesney, Assistant Dean for Graduate Recruiting and Student Services, 404-413-7167, Fax: 404-413-7167, E-mail: rcbgradadmissions@gsu.edu.
Website: http://cis.robinson.gsu.edu/

Grand Valley State University, Padnos College of Engineering and Computing, School of Computing and Information Systems, Allendale, MI 49401-9403. Offers computer information systems (MS), including databases, distributed systems, management of information systems, object-oriented systems, software engineering. *Program availability:* Part-time, evening/weekend. *Faculty:* 10 full-time (3 women), 1 (woman) part-time/adjunct. *Students:* 28 full-time (3 women), 57 part-time (14 women); includes 11 minority (3 Black or African American, non-Hispanic/Latino; 4 Asian, non-Hispanic/Latino; 3 Hispanic/Latino; 1 Two or more races, non-Hispanic/Latino), 32 international. Average age 30. 97 applicants, 59% accepted, 17 enrolled. In 2016, 36 master's awarded. *Degree requirements:* For master's, capstone course, project, or thesis. *Entrance requirements:* For master's, GMAT or GRE General Test, minimum GPA of 3.0; knowledge of a programming language; coursework or experience in: computer architecture and/or organization, data structures and algorithms, databases, discrete math, networking, operating systems, and software engineering; minimum of 2 letters of recommendation; resume; personal statement. Additional exam requirements/recommendations for international students: Required—TOEFL, Michigan English Language Assessment Battery or completion of ELS 112; Recommended—IELTS. *Application deadline:* For fall admission, 6/1 for international students; for winter admission, 9/1 for international students. Applications are processed on a rolling basis. Application fee: $30. Electronic applications accepted. *Expenses:* $646 per credit hour. *Financial support:* In 2016–17, 11 students received support, including 3 fellowships, 10 research assistantships with full and partial tuition reimbursements available (averaging $8,000 per year). *Faculty research:* Object technology, distributed computing, information systems management database, software engineering. *Unit head:* Dr. Paul Leidig, Director, 616-331-2038, Fax: 616-331-2106, E-mail: leidigp@gvsu.edu. *Application contact:* Dr. D. Robert Adams, Graduate Program Director/Recruiting Contact, 616-331-3885, Fax: 616-331-2106, E-mail: adams@cis.gvsu.edu.
Website: http://www.cis.gvsu.edu/

Harvard University, Extension School, Cambridge, MA 02138-3722. Offers applied sciences (CAS); biotechnology (ALM); educational technologies (ALM); educational technology (CET); English for graduate and professional studies (DGP); environmental management (ALM, CEM); information technology (ALM); journalism (ALM); liberal arts (ALM); management (ALM, CM); mathematics for teaching (ALM); museum studies (ALM); premedical studies (Diploma); publication and communication (CPC). *Program availability:* Part-time, evening/weekend. *Degree requirements:* For master's, thesis. *Entrance requirements:* For master's, 3 completed graduate courses with grade of B or higher. Additional exam requirements/recommendations for international students: Required—TOEFL (minimum score 600 paper-based), TWE (minimum score 5). *Expenses:* Contact institution.

Harvard University, Graduate School of Arts and Sciences, Program in Information, Technology and Management, Cambridge, MA 02138. Offers PhD.

Hood College, Graduate School, Program in Management of Information Technology, Frederick, MD 21701-8575. Offers MS. *Program availability:* Part-time, evening/weekend. *Students:* 14 full-time (5 women), 3 part-time (1 woman); includes 1 minority (Asian, non-Hispanic/Latino), 14 international. Average age 33. 21 applicants, 71% accepted, 6 enrolled. In 2016, 12 master's awarded. *Entrance requirements:* For master's, minimum GPA of 2.75, essay, resume. Additional exam requirements/recommendations for international students: Required—TOEFL (minimum score 575 paper-based; 89 iBT), IELTS (minimum score 6.5). *Application deadline:* For fall admission, 8/15 priority date for domestic students, 8/5 for international students; for spring admission, 12/1 priority date for domestic students, 12/1 for international students; for summer admission, 5/1 priority date for domestic students, 4/15 for international students. Applications are processed on a rolling basis. Application fee: $35. Electronic applications accepted. *Expenses:* $475 per credit; $110 comprehensive fee per semester. *Financial support:* Tuition waivers (partial) and unspecified assistantships available. Financial award applicants required to submit FAFSA. *Faculty research:* Systems engineering, parallel distributed computing, strategy, business ethics, entrepreneurship. *Unit head:* April Boulton, Interim Dean of the Graduate School, 301-696-3600, E-mail: gofurther@hood.edu. *Application contact:* Larbi Bricha, Assistant Director of Graduate Admissions, 301-696-3600, E-mail: gofurther@hood.edu.
Website: http://www.hood.edu/graduate

Hood College, Graduate School, Programs in Computer and Information Sciences, Frederick, MD 21701-8575. Offers computer science (MS); cyber security (Certificate); information technology (MS). *Program availability:* Part-time, evening/weekend. *Faculty:* 7 full-time, 8 part-time/adjunct. *Students:* 82 full-time (29 women), 51 part-time (13 women); includes 8 minority (2 Black or African American, non-Hispanic/Latino; 4 Asian, non-Hispanic/Latino; 1 Hispanic/Latino; 1 Two or more races, non-Hispanic/Latino), 89 international. Average age 30. 79 applicants, 84% accepted, 36 enrolled. In 2016, 75 master's, 35 other advanced degrees awarded. *Degree requirements:* For master's, thesis optional. *Entrance requirements:* For master's, minimum GPA of 2.75, essay, resume. Additional exam requirements/recommendations for international students: Required—TOEFL (minimum score 575 paper-based; 89 iBT), IELTS (minimum score 6.5). *Application deadline:* For fall admission, 8/15 priority date for domestic students, 8/5 for international students; for spring admission, 12/1 priority date for domestic students, 12/1 for international students; for summer admission, 5/1 for domestic students, 4/15 for international students. Applications are processed on a rolling basis. Application fee: $35. Electronic applications accepted. *Expenses:* $475 per credit hour; $110 comprehensive fee per semester. *Financial support:* Tuition waivers (partial) and unspecified assistantships available. Financial award applicants required to submit FAFSA. *Faculty research:* Systems engineering, natural language, processing, database design, artificial intelligence and parallel distributed computing. *Unit head:* April Boulton, Interim Dean of the Graduate School, 301-696-3600, E-mail: gofurther@hood.edu. *Application contact:* Spencer Berk, Assistant Director of Graduate Admissions, 301-696-3600, E-mail: gofurther@hood.edu.
Website: http://www.hood.edu/graduate

Indiana University Bloomington, School of Informatics and Computing, Department of Information and Library Science, Bloomington, IN 47405-3907. Offers information architecture (Graduate Certificate); information science (MIS, PhD); library and information science (Sp LIS); library science (MLS); JD/MLS; MIS/MA; MLS/MA; MPA/MIS; MPA/MLS. *Accreditation:* ALA (one or more programs are accredited). *Program availability:* Part-time. *Faculty:* 12 full-time (6 women), 19 part-time/adjunct (11 women). *Students:* 151 full-time (109 women), 52 part-time (36 women); includes 23 minority (2 Black or African American, non-Hispanic/Latino; 5 Asian, non-Hispanic/Latino; 8 Hispanic/Latino; 8 Two or more races, non-Hispanic/Latino), 42 international. Average age 28. 943 applicants, 62% accepted, 73 enrolled. In 2016, 87 master's, 4 doctorates, 9 other advanced degrees awarded. Terminal master's awarded for partial completion of doctoral program. *Degree requirements:* For master's, internship; for doctorate, comprehensive exam, thesis/dissertation. *Entrance requirements:* For master's, GRE General Test (for applicants whose previous undergraduate degree GPA was below 3.0 or previous graduate degree GPA was below 3.2), 3 letters of reference, resume, personal statement (500 words minimum), transcripts; for doctorate, GRE General Test, resume, personal statement (800-1000 words), writing sample, transcripts, 3 letters of reference. Additional exam requirements/recommendations for international students: Required—TOEFL (minimum score 600 paper-based; 100 iBT), IELTS. *Application deadline:* For fall admission, 5/15 priority date for domestic students, 12/1 priority date for international students; for spring admission, 11/1 priority date for domestic students, 9/1 priority date for international students. Applications are processed on a rolling basis. Application fee: $55 ($65 for international students). Electronic applications accepted. *Expenses:* Contact institution. *Financial support:* In 2016–17, 55 students received support, including 20 fellowships; research assistantships with full and partial tuition reimbursements available, teaching assistantships, career-related internships or fieldwork, scholarships/grants, health care benefits, tuition waivers (partial), and unspecified assistantships also available. Financial award application deadline: 1/15. *Faculty research:* Scholarly communication, interface design, library and management policy, computer-mediated communication, information retrieval, documentation, web analysis, e-business, information architecture, social informatics, virtual groups and online communities, online deviant behaviors, knowledge sharing, indexing, philosophy of information, information policy, resource management, research methods digital humanities, digital libraries, semantic web, digital preservation, natural language processing. *Unit head:* Dr. John Walsh, Interim Director of Graduate Programs, 812-856-0707, E-mail: jawalsh@indiana.edu. *Application contact:* Corbet Tarbell, Director of Graduate Student Services, 812-856-7214, Fax: 812-855-6166, E-mail: ilsmain@indiana.edu.
Website: http://ils.indiana.edu/

Indiana University Bloomington, School of Informatics and Computing, Program in Informatics, Bloomington, IN 47405. Offers informatics (MS, PhD), including bioinformatics (PhD), complex systems (PhD), computing, culture and society (PhD), health informatics (PhD), human-computer interaction (MS), human-computer interaction design (PhD), music informatics (PhD), security informatics (PhD); visual

heritage (PhD). *Program availability:* Part-time. *Faculty:* 75 full-time (15 women). *Students:* 206 full-time (85 women), 10 part-time (3 women); includes 30 minority (11 Black or African American, non-Hispanic/Latino; 10 Asian, non-Hispanic/Latino; 5 Hispanic/Latino; 4 Two or more races, non-Hispanic/Latino), 95 international. Average age 28. 395 applicants, 36% accepted, 69 enrolled. In 2016, 50 master's, 11 doctorates awarded. Terminal master's awarded for partial completion of doctoral program. *Degree requirements:* For master's, thesis, capstone project; for doctorate, variable foreign language requirement, comprehensive exam, thesis/dissertation. *Entrance requirements:* For master's and doctorate, GRE, resume/curriculum vitae, transcripts, 3 letters of recommendation. Additional exam requirements/recommendations for international students: Required—TOEFL (minimum score 600 paper-based; 100 iBT). *Application deadline:* For fall admission, 12/1 priority date for domestic and international students. Application fee: $55 ($65 for international students). Electronic applications accepted. *Financial support:* Fellowships, research assistantships, scholarships/grants, health care benefits, and unspecified assistantships available. Financial award application deadline: 12/1. *Faculty research:* Algorithms, applied logic and computational theory, artificial intelligence, bioinformatics, case-based reasoning, chemical informatics, citation analysis, cognitive science, community informatics, compilers, complex networks and systems, computer optimization, computer-supported cooperative work, computer vision, cyberinfrastructure and e-science, database theory and systems, data mining, digital design and preservation, design pedagogy, digital humanities, digital learning environments. *Total annual research expenditures:* $19.4 million. *Unit head:* Dr. Martin Siegel, Director of Graduate Studies, 812-856-3960, E-mail: msiegel@indiana.edu. *Application contact:* Informatics Graduate Studies Office, 812-856-3960, E-mail: infograd@indiana.edu.
Website: http://www.informatics.indiana.edu/graduate/index.html

Indiana University–Purdue University Fort Wayne, College of Engineering, Technology, and Computer Science, Program in Technology, Fort Wayne, IN 46805-1499. Offers facilities/construction management (MS); industrial technology/manufacturing (MS); information technology/advanced computer applications (MS). *Program availability:* Part-time. *Entrance requirements:* For master's, minimum GPA of 3.0. Additional exam requirements/recommendations for international students: Required—TOEFL (minimum score 550 paper-based; 79 iBT), TWE. Electronic applications accepted.

Indiana University–Purdue University Indianapolis, School of Informatics and Computing, Department of Information and Library Science, Indianapolis, IN 46202. Offers MLS. *Program availability:* Part-time, evening/weekend. *Entrance requirements:* For master's, GRE General Test. Additional exam requirements/recommendations for international students: Required—TOEFL (minimum score 600 paper-based).

Instituto Tecnologico de Santo Domingo, Graduate School, Area of Engineering, Santo Domingo, Dominican Republic. Offers construction administration (MS, Certificate); data telecommunications (M Eng, MS, Certificate); industrial engineering (M Eng, Certificate); industrial management (M Mgmt); information technology (Certificate); maintenance engineering (M Eng); occupational hazard prevention (M Mgmt); production management (Certificate); quantitative methods (Certificate); sanitary and environmental engineering (M Eng); structural engineering (M Eng); systems engineering and electronic data processing (Certificate); transportation (Certificate).

Instituto Tecnológico y de Estudios Superiores de Monterrey, Campus Cuernavaca, Programs in Information Science, Temixco, Mexico. Offers administration of information technology (MATI); computer science (MCC, DCC); information technology (MTI).

Instituto Tecnológico y de Estudios Superiores de Monterrey, Campus Estado de México, Professional and Graduate Division, Estado de Mexico, Mexico. Offers administration of information technologies (MITA); architecture (M Arch); business administration (GMBA, MBA); computer sciences (MCS, PhD); education (M Ed); educational institution administration (MAD); educational technology and innovation (PhD); electronic commerce (MEC); environmental systems (MS); finance (MAF); humanistic studies (MHS); information sciences and knowledge management (MISKM); information systems (MS); manufacturing systems (MS); marketing (MEM); quality systems and productivity (MS); science and materials engineering (PhD); telecommunications management (MTM). *Program availability:* Part-time, online learning. *Degree requirements:* For master's, one foreign language, thesis (for some programs); for doctorate, one foreign language, thesis/dissertation. *Entrance requirements:* For master's, E-PAEP 500, interview; for doctorate, E-PAEP 500, research proposal. Additional exam requirements/recommendations for international students: Required—TOEFL (minimum score 550 paper-based). *Faculty research:* Surface treatments by plasmas, mechanical properties, robotics, graphical computing, mechatronics security protocols.

Instituto Tecnológico y de Estudios Superiores de Monterrey, Campus Irapuato, Graduate Programs, Irapuato, Mexico. Offers administration (MBA); administration of information technology (MAIT); administration of telecommunications (MAT); architecture (M Arch); computer science (MCS); education (M Ed); educational administration (MEA); educational innovation and technology (DEIT); educational technology (MET); electronic commerce (MBA); environmental administration and planning (MEAP); environmental systems (MES); finances (MBA); humanistic studies (MHS); international management for Latin American executives (MIMLAE); library and information science (MLIS); manufacturing quality management (MMQM); marketing research (MBA).

Instituto Tecnológico y de Estudios Superiores de Monterrey, Campus Monterrey, Graduate and Research Division, Program in Computer Science, Monterrey, Mexico. Offers artificial intelligence (PhD); computer science (MS); information systems (MS); information technology (MS). *Program availability:* Part-time. *Degree requirements:* For master's, one foreign language, thesis; for doctorate, one foreign language, thesis/dissertation. *Entrance requirements:* For master's, EXADEP; for doctorate, master's degree in related field. Additional exam requirements/recommendations for international students: Required—TOEFL. *Faculty research:* Distributed systems, software engineering, decision support systems.

Instituto Tecnológico y de Estudios Superiores de Monterrey, Campus Monterrey, Graduate and Research Division, Program in Informatics, Monterrey, Mexico. Offers PhD. *Program availability:* Part-time. *Degree requirements:* For doctorate, one foreign language, thesis/dissertation, technological project, arbitrated publication of articles. *Entrance requirements:* For doctorate, GRE General Test, GRE Subject Test, master's degree in related field. Additional exam requirements/recommendations for international students: Required—TOEFL. *Faculty research:* Artificial intelligence, distributed systems, software engineering, decision support systems.

Instituto Tecnológico y de Estudios Superiores de Monterrey, Campus Sonora Norte, Program in Technological Information Management, Hermosillo, Mexico. Offers MA.

Iowa State University of Science and Technology, Program in Information Assurance, Ames, IA 50011. Offers M Eng, MS. *Degree requirements:* For master's, thesis or alternative. *Entrance requirements:* For master's, GRE General Test.

Additional exam requirements/recommendations for international students: Required—TOEFL (minimum score 570 paper-based; 79 iBT), IELTS (minimum score 6.5). *Application deadline:* For fall admission, 5/1 priority date for domestic and international students; for spring admission, 11/1 priority date for domestic and international students. Application fee: $60 ($90 for international students). Electronic applications accepted. *Application contact:* Virginia Anderson, Application Contact, 515-294-0659, Fax: 515-294-7582, E-mail: infas@iastate.edu.
Website: http://www.iac.iastate.edu

Kennesaw State University, College of Computing and Software Engineering, Department of Information Technology, Kennesaw, GA 30144. Offers health information technology (Postbaccalaureate Certificate); information security and assurance (Graduate Certificate); information technology (MSIT, Graduate Certificate); information technology fundamentals (Postbaccalaureate Certificate). *Program availability:* Part-time, evening/weekend, online learning. *Degree requirements:* For master's, thesis optional. *Entrance requirements:* For master's, minimum GPA of 2.75; for other advanced degree, bachelor's degree. Additional exam requirements/recommendations for international students: Required—TOEFL (minimum score 550 paper-based; 79 iBT), IELTS (minimum score 6.5). Electronic applications accepted. *Faculty research:* IT ethics, user interface design, IT security, IT integration, IT management, health information technology, business intelligence, networks, business continuity.

Kennesaw State University, Michael J. Coles College of Business, Program in Information Systems, Kennesaw, GA 30144. Offers MSIS. *Program availability:* Part-time. *Entrance requirements:* For master's, GMAT or GRE General Test, minimum GPA of 2.75. Additional exam requirements/recommendations for international students: Required—TOEFL (minimum score 550 paper-based; 80 iBT), IELTS (minimum score 6.5). Electronic applications accepted.

Kent State University, College of Communication and Information, School of Library and Information Science, Kent, OH 44242-0001. Offers information architecture and knowledge management (MS), including health informatics, knowledge management, user experience design; library and information science (MLIS), including school library media; M Ed/MLIS; MBA/MLIS. *Accreditation:* ALA (one or more programs are accredited). *Program availability:* Part-time, online learning. *Faculty:* 19 full-time (16 women). *Students:* 208 full-time (163 women), 633 part-time (459 women); includes 112 minority (41 Black or African American, non-Hispanic/Latino; 2 American Indian or Alaska Native, non-Hispanic/Latino; 12 Asian, non-Hispanic/Latino; 36 Hispanic/Latino; 1 Native Hawaiian or other Pacific Islander, non-Hispanic/Latino; 20 Two or more races, non-Hispanic/Latino), 10 international. Average age 33. 269 applicants, 80% accepted, 175 enrolled. In 2016, 294 master's awarded. *Degree requirements:* For master's, thesis optional. *Entrance requirements:* For master's, GRE, minimum GPA of 3.0, statement of purpose, 3 letters of recommendation, curriculum vitae/resume, transcripts, writing sample, personal interview. Additional exam requirements/recommendations for international students: Required—TOEFL (minimum score of 600 paper-based, 100 iBT), IELTS (minimum score of 7.0), Michigan English Language Assessment Battery (minimum score of 85), or PTE (minimum score of 68). *Application deadline:* For fall admission, 3/15 for domestic and international students; for spring admission, 9/15 for domestic and international students; for summer admission, 1/15 for domestic and international students. Applications are processed on a rolling basis. Application fee: $45 ($70 for international students). Electronic applications accepted. *Expenses:* Tuition, state resident: full-time $10,864; part-time $495 per credit hour. Tuition, nonresident: full-time $18,380; part-time $837 per credit hour. *Financial support:* Fellowships with full tuition reimbursements, research assistantships with full tuition reimbursements, teaching assistantships with full tuition reimbursements, scholarships/grants, and unspecified assistantships available. Financial award application deadline: 3/1. *Unit head:* Dr. Kendra Albright, Director and Professor, 330-672-8535, E-mail: kalbrig7@kent.edu. *Application contact:* Dr. Karen Gracy, Graduate Co-Coordinator/Associate Professor, 330-672-2782, E-mail: kgracy@kent.edu.
Website: http://www.kent.edu/slis/

Knowledge Systems Institute, Program in Computer and Information Sciences, Skokie, IL 60076. Offers MS. *Program availability:* Part-time, evening/weekend, online learning. *Degree requirements:* For master's, comprehensive exam, thesis. *Entrance requirements:* Additional exam requirements/recommendations for international students: Required—TOEFL (minimum score 550 paper-based; 79 iBT). Electronic applications accepted. *Faculty research:* Data mining, web development, database programming and administration.

Lawrence Technological University, College of Management, Southfield, MI 48075-1058. Offers business administration (MBA), including business analytics (MBA, MS); finance, information technology, marketing, project management (MBA, MS); information technology (MS), including business analytics (MBA, MS), information assurance, project management (MBA, MS); project management (Graduate Certificate). *Accreditation:* ACBSP. *Program availability:* Part-time, evening/weekend, 100% online. *Faculty:* 14 full-time (6 women), 10 part-time/adjunct (2 women). *Students:* 7 full-time (3 women), 323 part-time (120 women); includes 60 minority (29 Black or African American, non-Hispanic/Latino; 2 American Indian or Alaska Native, non-Hispanic/Latino; 17 Asian, non-Hispanic/Latino; 8 Hispanic/Latino; 4 Two or more races, non-Hispanic/Latino), 118 international. Average age 33. 275 applicants, 56% accepted, 72 enrolled. In 2016, 167 master's, 12 other advanced degrees awarded. Terminal master's awarded for partial completion of doctoral program. *Degree requirements:* For master's, thesis (for some programs). *Entrance requirements:* Additional exam requirements/recommendations for international students: Required—TOEFL (minimum score 550 paper-based; 79 iBT), IELTS (minimum score 6.5). *Application deadline:* For fall admission, 5/22 for international students; for spring admission, 10/11 for international students; for summer admission, 2/16 for international students. Applications are processed on a rolling basis. Application fee: $50. Electronic applications accepted. *Expenses:* Tuition: Full-time $14,868; part-time $1062 per credit. *Required fees:* $75 per semester. Tuition and fees vary according to campus/location. *Financial support:* In 2016–17, 35 students received support, including 8 research assistantships with partial tuition reimbursements available (averaging $3,250 per year); career-related internships or fieldwork, unspecified assistantships, and corporate tuition incentives also available. Financial award application deadline: 4/1; financial award applicants required to submit FAFSA. *Faculty research:* Cybersecurity; risk management; IT governance; security controls and countermeasures; threat modeling cyber resilience; autonomous cars; natural language processing; text mining; machine learning; reflective leadership; emerging leadership theories and practice; motivational studies; teaching effectiveness strategies; teamwork; organization development; strategic planning; strengths-based and positive organizational scholarship; global leadership; globalization; corporate governance. *Unit head:* Dr. Bahman Mirshab, Dean, 248-204-3050, E-mail: mgtdean@ltu.edu. *Application contact:* Jane Rohrback, Director of Admissions, 248-204-3160, Fax: 248-204-2228, E-mail: admissions@ltu.edu.
Website: http://www.ltu.edu/management/index.asp

Lehigh University, College of Business and Economics, Department of Accounting, Bethlehem, PA 18015. Offers accounting and information analysis (MS). *Accreditation:* AACSB. *Faculty:* 6 full-time (0 women), 1 part-time/adjunct (0 women). *Students:* 31 full-time (16 women), 3 part-time (2 women); includes 4 minority (1 Black or African

American, non-Hispanic/Latino; 1 Asian, non-Hispanic/Latino; 2 Hispanic/Latino), 20 international. Average age 23. 118 applicants, 42% accepted, 10 enrolled. In 2016, 76 master's awarded. *Entrance requirements:* For master's, GMAT. Additional exam requirements/recommendations for international students: Required—TOEFL (minimum score 105 iBT). *Application deadline:* For fall admission, 2/28 for domestic and international students. Applications are processed on a rolling basis. Application fee: $75. Electronic applications accepted. *Expenses:* $1,200 per credit hour. *Financial support:* In 2016–17, 19 students received support. Research assistantships, scholarships/grants, tuition waivers, and unspecified assistantships available. Financial award application deadline: 1/15. *Faculty research:* Behavioral accounting, internal control, information systems, supply chain management, financial accounting. *Unit head:* Dr. C. Bryan Cloyd, Chairman, 610-758-2816, Fax: 610-758-6429, E-mail: cbc215@lehigh.edu. *Application contact:* Michael Tarantino, Director of Recruitment and Admissions, 610-758-3418, Fax: 610-758-5283, E-mail: mgt215@lehigh.edu.
Website: http://www4.lehigh.edu/business/academics/depts/accounting

Loyola University Chicago, Graduate School, Department of Computer Science, Chicago, IL 60611. Offers computer science (MS); information technology (MS); software engineering (MS). *Program availability:* Part-time, evening/weekend, 100% online, blended/hybrid learning. *Faculty:* 15 full-time (3 women), 10 part-time/adjunct (2 women). *Students:* 64 full-time (33 women), 50 part-time (14 women); includes 24 minority (7 Black or African American, non-Hispanic/Latino; 10 Asian, non-Hispanic/Latino; 5 Hispanic/Latino; 2 Two or more races, non-Hispanic/Latino), 56 international. Average age 28. 135 applicants, 43% accepted, 39 enrolled. In 2016, 49 master's awarded. *Degree requirements:* For master's, thesis optional, ten courses. *Entrance requirements:* For master's, 3 letters of recommendation, transcripts, statement of purpose. Additional exam requirements/recommendations for international students: Required—TOEFL (minimum score 550 paper-based; 79 iBT) or IELTS (minimum score 6.5). *Application deadline:* Applications are processed on a rolling basis. Application fee: $50. Electronic applications accepted. Application fee is waived when completed online. *Expenses:* $1,033 per credit hour. *Financial support:* In 2016–17, 17 students received support, including 2 fellowships with full tuition reimbursements available, 1 research assistantship with full tuition reimbursement available (averaging $17,000 per year), 11 teaching assistantships with partial tuition reimbursements available (averaging $9,575 per year); career-related internships or fieldwork, Federal Work-Study, health care benefits, and tuition waivers (full and partial) also available. Financial award application deadline: 3/15. *Faculty research:* Software engineering, machine learning, algorithms and complexity, parallel and distributed computing, databases and computer networks. *Total annual research expenditures:* $22,000. *Unit head:* Dr. Konstantin Laufer, Chair, 312-915-7983, Fax: 312-915-7998, E-mail: laufer@cs.luc.edu. *Application contact:* Cecilia Murphy, Graduate Program Secretary, 312-915-7990, Fax: 312-915-7998, E-mail: csinfo@cs.luc.edu.
Website: http://cs.luc.edu

Marshall University, Academic Affairs Division, College of Information Technology and Engineering, Program in Information Systems, Huntington, WV 25755. Offers MS. *Program availability:* Part-time, evening/weekend. *Degree requirements:* For master's, final project, oral exam. *Entrance requirements:* For master's, GRE General Test or MAT, minimum undergraduate GPA of 2.5.

Maryville University of Saint Louis, The John E. Simon School of Business, St. Louis, MO 63141-7299. Offers accounting (MBA, Certificate); business studies (Certificate); cyber security (MBA); cybersecurity (Certificate); financial services (MBA, Certificate); healthcare practice management (MBA, Certificate); human resource management (MBA); information technology (MBA, Certificate); management (MBA, Certificate); management and leadership (MA); marketing (MBA, Certificate); project management (MBA); sport business management (MBA); supply chain management/logistics (MBA). *Accreditation:* ACBSP. *Program availability:* Part-time, evening/weekend, 100% online, blended/hybrid learning. *Faculty:* 7 full-time (3 women), 34 part-time/adjunct (9 women). *Students:* 84 full-time (40 women), 223 part-time (118 women); includes 67 minority (40 Black or African American, non-Hispanic/Latino; 2 American Indian or Alaska Native, non-Hispanic/Latino; 8 Asian, non-Hispanic/Latino; 12 Hispanic/Latino; 1 Native Hawaiian or other Pacific Islander, non-Hispanic/Latino; 4 Two or more races, non-Hispanic/Latino), 15 international. Average age 32. In 2016, 67 master's awarded. *Entrance requirements:* Additional exam requirements/recommendations for international students: Required—TOEFL (minimum score 563 paper-based; 85 iBT). *Application deadline:* Applications are processed on a rolling basis. Electronic applications accepted. *Expenses:* $650 per credit hour. *Financial support:* Career-related internships or fieldwork, Federal Work-Study, tuition waivers (partial), and campus employment available. Financial award application deadline: 3/1; financial award applicants required to submit FAFSA. *Faculty research:* Global business, e-marketing, strategic planning, interpersonal management skills, financial analysis. *Unit head:* Pam Horwitz, Interim Dean, 314-529-9680, Fax: 314-529-9975. *Application contact:* Dustin Loeffler, Director for Graduate Studies in Business, 314-529-9571, Fax: 314-529-9975, E-mail: dloeffler@maryville.edu.
Website: http://www.maryville.edu/bu/business-administration-masters/

Massachusetts Institute of Technology, School of Engineering, Department of Civil and Environmental Engineering, Cambridge, MA 02139. Offers biological oceanography (PhD, Sc D); chemical oceanography (PhD, Sc D); civil and environmental engineering (M Eng, SM, PhD, Sc D); civil and environmental systems (PhD, Sc D); civil engineering (PhD, Sc D, CE); civil engineering and computation (PhD); coastal engineering (PhD, Sc D); construction engineering and management (PhD, Sc D); environmental biology (PhD, Sc D); environmental chemistry (PhD, Sc D); environmental engineering (PhD, Sc D); environmental engineering and computation (PhD); environmental fluid mechanics (PhD, Sc D); geotechnical and geoenvironmental engineering (PhD, Sc D); hydrology (PhD, Sc D); information technology (PhD, Sc D); oceanographic engineering (PhD, Sc D); structures and materials (PhD, Sc D); transportation (PhD, Sc D); SM/MBA. *Faculty:* 35 full-time (6 women). *Students:* 192 full-time (64 women); includes 25 minority (2 Black or African American, non-Hispanic/Latino; 11 Asian, non-Hispanic/Latino; 8 Hispanic/Latino; 4 Two or more races, non-Hispanic/Latino), 113 international. Average age 27. 530 applicants, 20% accepted, 77 enrolled. In 2016, 56 master's, 16 doctorates, 1 other advanced degree awarded. *Degree requirements:* For master's, thesis; for doctorate, comprehensive exam, thesis/dissertation; for CE, comprehensive exam, thesis. *Entrance requirements:* For master's, doctorate, and CE, GRE General Test. Additional exam requirements/recommendations for international students: Required—TOEFL, IELTS. *Application deadline:* For fall admission, 12/15 for domestic and international students. Application fee: $75. Electronic applications accepted. *Expenses: Tuition:* Full-time $46,400; part-time $725 per credit. One-time fee: $312 full-time. Full-time tuition and fees vary according to course load and program. *Financial support:* In 2016–17, 150 students received support, including fellowships (averaging $41,900 per year), 124 research assistantships (averaging $36,900 per year), 9 teaching assistantships (averaging $36,900 per year); Federal Work-Study, institutionally sponsored loans, scholarships/grants, traineeships, health care benefits, unspecified assistantships, and resident tutors also available. Support available to part-time students. Financial award application deadline: 5/1; financial award applicants required to submit FAFSA. *Faculty research:* Environmental chemistry, environmental fluid mechanics and coastal engineering, environmental microbiology, geotechnical engineering and geomechanics, hydrology and hydro climatology, infrastructure systems, mechanics of materials and structures, transportation systems. *Total annual research expenditures:* $25 million. *Unit head:* Prof. Markus Buehler, Department Head, 617-253-7101. *Application contact:* 617-253-7119, E-mail: cee-admissions@mit.edu.
Website: http://cee.mit.edu/

Minnesota State University Mankato, College of Graduate Studies and Research, College of Science, Engineering and Technology, Department of Computer Information Science, Mankato, MN 56001. Offers information technology (MS). *Students:* 43 full-time (19 women), 24 part-time (7 women). *Degree requirements:* For master's, comprehensive exam, thesis or alternative. *Entrance requirements:* For master's, GRE General Test, minimum GPA of 3.0 during previous 2 years. Additional exam requirements/recommendations for international students: Required—TOEFL (minimum score 550 paper-based; 80 iBT). *Application deadline:* For fall admission, 7/1 priority date for domestic students; for spring admission, 11/1 for domestic students. Applications are processed on a rolling basis. Electronic applications accepted. *Financial support:* Research assistantships with full tuition reimbursements, teaching assistantships with full tuition reimbursements, and unspecified assistantships available. Financial award application deadline: 3/15; financial award applicants required to submit FAFSA. *Unit head:* Dr. Leon Tietz, Chair, 507-389-5319, E-mail: leon.tietz@mnsu.edu.
Website: http://cset.mnsu.edu/ist/

Missouri University of Science and Technology, Graduate School, Department of Business and Information Technology, Rolla, MO 65409. Offers business and management systems (MBA); information science and technology (MS). *Degree requirements:* For master's, thesis or alternative. *Entrance requirements:* Additional exam requirements/recommendations for international students: Required—TOEFL (minimum score 600 paper-based); Recommended—IELTS. Electronic applications accepted.

Monroe College, King Graduate School, Bronx, NY 10468. Offers accounting (MS); business administration (MBA), including entrepreneurship, finance, general business administration, healthcare management, human resources, information technology, marketing; computer science (MS); criminal justice (MS); hospitality management (MS); public health (MPH), including biostatistics and epidemiology, community health, health administration and leadership. *Program availability:* Online learning. Application fee: $50.
Website: https://www.monroecollege.edu/Degrees/King-Graduate-School/

Naval Postgraduate School, Departments and Academic Groups, Department of Information Sciences, Monterey, CA 93943. Offers electronic warfare systems engineering (MS); information sciences (PhD); information systems and operations (MS); information technology management (MS); information warfare systems engineering (MS); knowledge superiority (Certificate); remote sensing intelligence (MS); system technology (command, control and communications) (MS). Program open only to commissioned officers of the United States and friendly nations and selected United States federal civilian employees. *Program availability:* Part-time. *Degree requirements:* For master's, thesis (for some programs); for doctorate, thesis/dissertation. *Faculty research:* Designing inter-organisational collectivities for dynamic fit: stability, manoeuvrability and application in disaster relief endeavours; system self-awareness and related methods for Improving the use and understanding of data within DoD; evaluating a macrocognition model of team collaboration using real-world data from the Haiti relief effort; cyber distortion in command and control; performance and QoS in service-based systems.

New Jersey Institute of Technology, Ying Wu College of Computing, Newark, NJ 07102. Offers big data management and mining (Certificate); business and information systems (Certificate); computer science (MS, PhD), including bioinformatics (MS), computer science, computing and business (MS), cyber security and privacy (MS), software engineering (MS); data mining (Certificate); information security (Certificate); information systems (MS, PhD), including business and information systems (MS), emergency management and business continuity (MS), information systems; information technology administration and security (MS); IT administration (Certificate); network security and information assurance (Certificate); software engineering analysis/design (Certificate); Web systems development (Certificate). *Program availability:* Part-time, evening/weekend. *Faculty:* 64 full-time (10 women), 38 part-time/adjunct (4 women). *Students:* 818 full-time (241 women), 225 part-time (53 women); includes 162 minority (35 Black or African American, non-Hispanic/Latino; 77 Asian, non-Hispanic/Latino; 41 Hispanic/Latino; 9 Two or more races, non-Hispanic/Latino), 772 international. Average age 27. 2,666 applicants, 51% accepted, 377 enrolled. In 2016, 398 master's, 10 doctorates, 9 other advanced degrees awarded. Terminal master's awarded for partial completion of doctoral program. *Degree requirements:* For master's, thesis optional; for doctorate, thesis/dissertation. *Entrance requirements:* For master's, GRE General Test; for doctorate, GRE General Test, minimum graduate GPA of 3.5. Additional exam requirements/recommendations for international students: Required—TOEFL (minimum score 550 paper-based; 79 iBT). *Application deadline:* For fall admission, 6/1 priority date for domestic students, 5/1 priority date for international students; for spring admission, 11/15 priority date for domestic and international students. Applications are processed on a rolling basis. Application fee: $75. Electronic applications accepted. *Expenses:* Contact institution. *Financial support:* In 2016–17, 57 students received support, including 18 research assistantships (averaging $16,073 per year), 39 teaching assistantships (averaging $20,194 per year); fellowships, career-related internships or fieldwork, Federal Work-Study, institutionally sponsored loans, and unspecified assistantships also available. Financial award application deadline: 1/15. *Faculty research:* Computer systems, communications and networking, artificial intelligence, database engineering, systems analysis, analytics and optimization in crowdsourcing. *Total annual research expenditures:* $3 million. *Unit head:* Dr. Craig Gotsman, Dean, 973-542-5488, Fax: 973-596-5777, E-mail: marek.rusinkiewicz@njit.edu. *Application contact:* Stephen Eck, Director of Admissions, 973-596-3300, Fax: 973-596-3461, E-mail: admissions@njit.edu.
Website: http://computing.njit.edu/

Northern Kentucky University, Office of Graduate Programs, College of Informatics, Department of Business Informatics, Highland Heights, KY 41099. Offers business informatics (MS, Certificate); corporate information security (Certificate); enterprise resource planning (Certificate). *Program availability:* Part-time, evening/weekend. *Entrance requirements:* For master's, GRE or GMAT. Additional exam requirements/recommendations for international students: Required—TOEFL (minimum score 79 iBT); Recommended—IELTS (minimum score 6.5). Electronic applications accepted. *Faculty research:* Data analytics, cloud computing, healthcare informatics, information systems security.

Northwestern University, McCormick School of Engineering and Applied Science, Department of Electrical Engineering and Computer Science, MS in Information Technology Program, Evanston, IL 60208. Offers MS. *Program availability:* Part-time, evening/weekend. *Entrance requirements:* For master's, GRE (recommended), work experience in an IT-related position. Additional exam requirements/recommendations for international students: Required—TOEFL (minimum score 80 iBT), IELTS (minimum score 7). Electronic applications accepted.

Nova Southeastern University, College of Engineering and Computing, Fort Lauderdale, FL 33314-7796. Offers computer science (MS, PhD); information assurance (PhD); information assurance and cybersecurity (MS); information systems (PhD); information technology (MS); management information systems (MS). *Program availability:* Part-time, evening/weekend, blended/hybrid learning. *Faculty:* 18 full-time (4 women), 11 part-time/adjunct (2 women). *Students:* 309 full-time (87 women), 407 part-time (125 women); includes 321 minority (139 Black or African American, non-Hispanic/Latino; 2 American Indian or Alaska Native, non-Hispanic/Latino; 52 Asian, non-Hispanic/Latino; 117 Hispanic/Latino; 11 Two or more races, non-Hispanic/Latino), 160 international. Average age 40. 390 applicants, 74% accepted. In 2016, 188 master's, 53 doctorates awarded. Terminal master's awarded for partial completion of doctoral program. *Degree requirements:* For master's, thesis optional; for doctorate, thesis/dissertation. *Entrance requirements:* For master's, minimum undergraduate GPA of 2.5; 3.0 in major; for doctorate, master's degree, minimum graduate GPA of 3.25. Additional exam requirements/recommendations for international students: Required—TOEFL (minimum score 80 iBT), IELTS (minimum score 6), PTE (minimum score 54). *Application deadline:* Applications are processed on a rolling basis. Application fee: $50. Electronic applications accepted. *Expenses:* $745 per credit hour (for master's); $1,075 per credit hour (for doctoral). *Financial support:* In 2016–17, 43 students received support. Federal Work-Study, scholarships/grants, and traineeships available. Financial award application deadline: 4/15; financial award applicants required to submit FAFSA. *Faculty research:* Artificial intelligence, database management, human-computer interaction, distance education, information assurance and cybersecurity. *Unit head:* Dr. Yong X. Tao, Dean, 954-262-2063, Fax: 954-262-2752, E-mail: ytao@nova.edu. *Application contact:* Nancy Azoulay, Director, Admissions, 954-262-2026, Fax: 954-262-2752, E-mail: azoulayn@nova.edu.
Website: http://scis.nova.edu

Oklahoma State University, Spears School of Business, Department of Management Science and Information Systems, Stillwater, OK 74078. Offers management information systems (MS); management science and information systems (PhD); telecommunications management (MS). *Program availability:* Part-time, online learning. *Faculty:* 21 full-time (1 woman), 5 part-time/adjunct (2 women). *Students:* 95 full-time (20 women), 67 part-time (19 women); includes 14 minority (1 Black or African American, non-Hispanic/Latino; 2 American Indian or Alaska Native, non-Hispanic/Latino; 3 Asian, non-Hispanic/Latino; 4 Hispanic/Latino; 1 Native Hawaiian or other Pacific Islander, non-Hispanic/Latino; 3 Two or more races, non-Hispanic/Latino), 112 international. Average age 28. 779 applicants, 12% accepted, 56 enrolled. In 2016, 89 master's, 1 doctorate awarded. *Degree requirements:* For master's, thesis or alternative; for doctorate, comprehensive exam, thesis/dissertation. *Entrance requirements:* For master's and doctorate, GRE or GMAT. Additional exam requirements/recommendations for international students: Required—TOEFL (minimum score 550 paper-based; 79 iBT). *Application deadline:* For fall admission, 3/1 priority date for international students; for spring admission, 8/1 priority date for international students. Applications are processed on a rolling basis. Application fee: $40 ($75 for international students). Electronic applications accepted. *Expenses:* Tuition, state resident: full-time $3775; part-time $209.70 per credit hour. Tuition, nonresident: full-time $14,851; part-time $825.05 per credit hour. *Required fees:* $2027; $112.60 per credit hour. Tuition and fees vary according to campus/location. *Financial support:* In 2016–17, 2 research assistantships (averaging $5,500 per year), 18 teaching assistantships (averaging $8,542 per year) were awarded; career-related internships or fieldwork, Federal Work-Study, scholarships/grants, health care benefits, tuition waivers (partial), and unspecified assistantships also available. Support available to part-time students. Financial award application deadline: 3/1; financial award applicants required to submit FAFSA. *Unit head:* Dr. Rick Wilson, Department Head, 405-744-3551, Fax: 405-744-5180, E-mail: rick.wilson@okstate.edu. *Application contact:* Dr. Rathin Sarathy, Graduate Coordinator, 405-744-8646, Fax: 405-744-5180, E-mail: rathin.sarathy@okstate.edu.
Website: http://spears.okstate.edu/msis

Old Dominion University, Strome College of Business, Doctoral Program in Business Administration, Norfolk, VA 23529. Offers finance (PhD); information technology (PhD); marketing (PhD); strategic management (PhD). *Accreditation:* AACSB. *Faculty:* 29 full-time (6 women). *Students:* 25 full-time (8 women), 23 part-time (5 women); includes 2 minority (both Asian, non-Hispanic/Latino), 38 international. Average age 34. 71 applicants, 17% accepted, 12 enrolled. In 2016, 15 doctorates awarded. *Degree requirements:* For doctorate, comprehensive exam, thesis/dissertation. *Entrance requirements:* For doctorate, GMAT. Additional exam requirements/recommendations for international students: Required—TOEFL (minimum score 550 paper-based; 79 iBT). *Application deadline:* For fall admission, 1/1 priority date for domestic and international students. Application fee: $50. Electronic applications accepted. *Expenses:* Tuition, state resident: full-time $8604; part-time $478 per credit hour. Tuition, nonresident: full-time $21,510; part-time $1195 per credit hour. *Required fees:* $66 per semester. Tuition and fees vary according to campus/location, program and reciprocity agreements. *Financial support:* In 2016–17, 36 students received support, including 15 research assistantships with full tuition reimbursements available (averaging $7,500 per year), 12 teaching assistantships with full tuition reimbursements available (averaging $7,500 per year); scholarships/grants and unspecified assistantships also available. Financial award application deadline: 3/1; financial award applicants required to submit FAFSA. *Faculty research:* International business, buyer behavior, financial markets, strategy, operations research. *Unit head:* Dr. John B. Ford, Graduate Program Director, 757-683-3587, Fax: 757-683-4076, E-mail: jbford@odu.edu. *Application contact:* Katrina Davenport, Program Coordinator, 757-683-5138, Fax: 757-683-4076, E-mail: kdavenpo@odu.edu.
Website: http://www.odu.edu/business/academics/graduate/scb-phd

Pace University, Seidenberg School of Computer Science and Information Systems, New York, NY 10038. Offers chief information security officer (APC); computer science (MS, PhD); enterprise analytics (MS); information and communication technology strategy and innovation (APC); information systems (MS, APC); Internet technology (MS); professional studies in computing (DPS); secure software and information engineering (APC); security and information assurance (Certificate); software development and engineering (MS, Certificate); telecommunications systems and networks (MS, Certificate). *Program availability:* Part-time, evening/weekend, online only, 100% online, blended/hybrid learning. *Faculty:* 26 full-time (7 women), 7 part-time/adjunct (2 women). *Students:* 537 full-time (175 women), 303 part-time (85 women); includes 192 minority (79 Black or African American, non-Hispanic/Latino; 3 American Indian or Alaska Native, non-Hispanic/Latino; 53 Asian, non-Hispanic/Latino; 49 Hispanic/Latino; 8 Two or more races, non-Hispanic/Latino), 486 international. Average age 32. 599 applicants, 89% accepted, 248 enrolled. In 2016, 180 master's, 19 doctorates, 1 other advanced degree awarded. *Degree requirements:* For master's, thesis or alternative, capstone course; for doctorate, comprehensive exam (for some programs), thesis/dissertation. *Entrance requirements:* For master's, GRE General Test. Additional exam requirements/recommendations for international students: Required—TOEFL (minimum score 78 iBT), IELTS (minimum score 6.5) or PTE (minimum score 52). *Application deadline:* For fall admission, 8/1 priority date for domestic students, 6/1 for international students; for spring admission, 12/1 for domestic students, 10/1 for

international students. Applications are processed on a rolling basis. Application fee: $70. Electronic applications accepted. *Expenses:* Contact institution. *Financial support:* In 2016–17, 45 students received support. Research assistantships, career-related internships or fieldwork, scholarships/grants, and unspecified assistantships available. Support available to part-time students. Financial award application deadline: 2/15; financial award applicants required to submit FAFSA. *Faculty research:* Cyber security/digital forensics; mobile app development; big data/enterprise analytics; artificial intelligence; software development. *Total annual research expenditures:* $314,545. *Unit head:* Dr. Jonathan Hill, Dean, Seidenberg School of Computer Science and Information Systems, 212-346-1864, E-mail: jhill@pace.edu. *Application contact:* Susan Ford-Goldschein, Director of Graduate Admissions, 914-422-4283, Fax: 212-346-1585, E-mail: graduateadmission@pace.edu.
Website: http://www.pace.edu/seidenberg

Penn State Great Valley, Graduate Studies, Management Division, Malvern, PA 19355-1488. Offers business administration (MBA); cyber security (Certificate); data analytics (Certificate); distributed energy and grid modernization (Certificate); finance (M Fin, Certificate); health sector management (Certificate); human resource management (Certificate); information science (MSIS); leadership development (MLD); new ventures and entrepreneurship (Certificate); professional studies in data analytics (MPS); sustainable management practices (Certificate). *Accreditation:* AACSB. *Unit head:* Dr. James A. Nemes, Chancellor, 610-648-3202, Fax: 610-725-5296. *Application contact:* JoAnn Kelly, Director of Admissions, 610-648-3315, Fax: 610-725-5296, E-mail: jek2@psu.edu.
Website: http://greatvalley.psu.edu/academics/masters-degrees/engineering-management

Penn State University Park, Graduate School, College of Information Sciences and Technology, University Park, PA 16802. Offers enterprise architecture (MPS); information sciences (MPS); information sciences and technology (MS, PhD). *Students:* 108 full-time (41 women), 9 part-time (0 women). Average age 28. 262 applicants, 28% accepted, 38 enrolled. In 2016, 19 master's, 12 doctorates awarded. *Entrance requirements:* Additional exam requirements/recommendations for international students: Required—TOEFL (minimum score 550 paper-based; 80 iBT), IELTS. *Application deadline:* For fall admission, 12/15 for domestic and international students. Applications are processed on a rolling basis. Application fee: $65. Electronic applications accepted. *Financial support:* Fellowships, research assistantships, teaching assistantships, career-related internships or fieldwork, Federal Work-Study, scholarships/grants, traineeships, health care benefits, and unspecified assistantships available. Support available to part-time students. Financial award application deadline: 3/1; financial award applicants required to submit FAFSA. *Unit head:* Dr. Andrew L. Sears, Dean, 814-865-3528, Fax: 814-865-7485. *Application contact:* Lori Hawn, Director, Graduate Student Services, 814-865-1795, Fax: 814-863-4627, E-mail: l-gswww@lists.psu.edu.
Website: http://ist.psu.edu/

Regis University, College of Computer and Information Sciences, Denver, CO 80221-1099. Offers agile technologies (Certificate); cybersecurity (Certificate); data science (M Sc); database administration with Oracle (Certificate); database development (Certificate); database technologies (M Sc); enterprise Java software development (Certificate); enterprise resource planning (Certificate); executive information technology (Certificate); health care informatics (Certificate); health care informatics and information management (M Sc); information assurance (M Sc); information assurance policy management (Certificate); information technology management (M Sc); mobile software development (Certificate); software engineering (M Sc, Certificate); software engineering and database technology (M Sc); storage area networks (Certificate); systems engineering (M Sc, Certificate). *Program availability:* Part-time, evening/weekend, 100% online, blended/hybrid learning. *Faculty:* 11 full-time (3 women), 30 part-time/adjunct (10 women). *Students:* 341 full-time (95 women), 318 part-time (98 women); includes 186 minority (56 Black or African American, non-Hispanic/Latino; 2 American Indian or Alaska Native, non-Hispanic/Latino; 48 Asian, non-Hispanic/Latino; 63 Hispanic/Latino; 17 Two or more races, non-Hispanic/Latino), 57 international. Average age 37. 342 applicants, 79% accepted, 174 enrolled. In 2016, 192 master's awarded. *Degree requirements:* For master's, thesis (for some programs), final research project. *Entrance requirements:* For master's, official transcript reflecting baccalaureate degree awarded from regionally-accredited college or university, 2 years of related experience, resume, interview. Additional exam requirements/recommendations for international students: Required—TOEFL (minimum score 550 paper-based; 82 iBT). *Application deadline:* For fall admission, 8/15 priority date for domestic students, 7/13 for international students; for winter admission, 10/10 priority date for domestic students, 9/8 for international students; for spring admission, 1/10 priority date for domestic students, 11/17 for international students; for summer admission, 5/1 priority date for domestic students. Applications are processed on a rolling basis. Application fee: $75. Electronic applications accepted. *Expenses:* $730 per credit hour. *Financial support:* Scholarships/grants available. Financial award application deadline: 4/15; financial award applicants required to submit FAFSA. *Faculty research:* Information policy, knowledge management, software architectures, data science. *Unit head:* Shari Plantz-Masters, Academic Dean. *Application contact:* Cate Clark, Director of Admissions, 303-458-4900, Fax: 303-964-5534, E-mail: ruadmissions@regis.edu.
Website: http://regis.edu/CCIS.aspx

Rensselaer at Hartford, Department of Computer and Information Science, Program in Information Technology, Hartford, CT 06120-2991. Offers MS. *Program availability:* Part-time, evening/weekend. *Entrance requirements:* For master's, GRE. Additional exam requirements/recommendations for international students: Required—TOEFL (minimum score 600 paper-based; 100 iBT). Electronic applications accepted.

Rensselaer Polytechnic Institute, Graduate School, School of Science, Program in Information Technology and Web Science, Troy, NY 12180-3590. Offers MS. *Program availability:* Part-time. *Students:* 36 full-time (12 women), 4 part-time (1 woman). 138 applicants, 37% accepted, 17 enrolled. In 2016, 29 master's awarded. *Entrance requirements:* For master's, GRE, IT Background Evaluation Form. Additional exam requirements/recommendations for international students: Required—TOEFL (minimum score 570 paper-based; 88 iBT), IELTS (minimum score 6.5), PTE (minimum score 60). *Application deadline:* For fall admission, 1/1 priority date for domestic and international students; for spring admission, 8/15 priority date for domestic and international students. Applications are processed on a rolling basis. Application fee: $75. Electronic applications accepted. *Expenses: Tuition:* Full-time $49,520; part-time $2060 per credit hour. *Required fees:* $2617. *Financial support:* In 2016–17, teaching assistantships with full tuition reimbursements (averaging $22,000 per year) were awarded. Financial award application deadline: 1/1. *Faculty research:* Database and intelligent systems, data science and analytics, financial engineering, human computer interaction, information dominance, information security, information systems engineering, management information systems, networking, software design and engineering, Web science. *Unit head:* Dr. Peter Fox, Graduate Program Director, 518-276-4862, E-mail: pfox@cs.rpi.edu. *Application contact:* Office of Graduate Admissions, 518-276-6216, E-mail: gradadmissions@rpi.edu.
Website: https://science.rpi.edu/itws

Information Science

Robert Morris University, School of Communications and Information Systems, Moon Township, PA 15108-1189. Offers communication and information systems (MS); cyber security (MS); data analytics (MS); information security and assurance (MS); information systems and communications (D Sc); information systems management (MS); information technology project management (MS); Internet information systems (MS); organizational leadership (MS). *Program availability:* Part-time, evening/weekend, online learning. *Faculty:* 28 full-time (11 women), 6 part-time/adjunct (0 women). *Students:* 269 part-time (110 women); includes 49 minority (29 Black or African American, non-Hispanic/Latino; 10 Asian, non-Hispanic/Latino; 5 Hispanic/Latino; 5 Two or more races, non-Hispanic/Latino), 49 international. Average age 34. 239 applicants, 46% accepted, 83 enrolled. In 2016, 110 master's, 15 doctorates awarded. *Degree requirements:* For doctorate, thesis/dissertation. *Entrance requirements:* For doctorate, employer letter of endorsement, interview. Additional exam requirements/recommendations for international students: Required—TOEFL (minimum score 550 paper-based; 79 iBT). *Application deadline:* For fall admission, 7/1 priority date for domestic and international students; for spring admission, 11/1 priority date for domestic and international students. Applications are processed on a rolling basis. Application fee: $35. Electronic applications accepted. Application fee is waived when completed online. *Expenses:* $870 per credit (for master's degree). *Financial support:* Institutionally sponsored loans available. Support available to part-time students. Financial award application deadline: 5/1. *Unit head:* Ann Marie M. Le Blanc, Dean, 412-397-6433, Fax: 412-397-6469, E-mail: leblanc@rmu.edu. *Application contact:* Kellie L. Laurenzi, Associate Vice President, 412-397-5200, Fax: 412-397-5915, E-mail: graduateadmissions@rmu.edu.
Website: http://www.rmu.edu/web/cms/schools/scis/Pages/default.aspx

Rochester Institute of Technology, Graduate Enrollment Services, Golisano College of Computing and Information Sciences, Computing and Information Sciences Department, PhD Program in Computing and Information Sciences, Rochester, NY 14623. Offers PhD. *Program availability:* Part-time. *Students:* 39 full-time (7 women), 5 part-time (0 women); includes 4 minority (1 Asian, non-Hispanic/Latino; 3 Hispanic/Latino), 34 international. Average age 30. 78 applicants, 33% accepted, 14 enrolled. In 2016, 3 doctorates awarded. *Degree requirements:* For doctorate, comprehensive exam, thesis/dissertation. *Entrance requirements:* For doctorate, GRE, minimum GPA of 3.0. Additional exam requirements/recommendations for international students: Required—TOEFL (minimum score 570 paper-based; 88 iBT), IELTS (minimum score 6.5), PTE (minimum score 61). *Application deadline:* For fall admission, 1/15 priority date for domestic and international students. Applications are processed on a rolling basis. Application fee: $0. Electronic applications accepted. *Expenses:* $1,742 per credit hour. *Financial support:* In 2016–17, 31 students received support. Research assistantships with full tuition reimbursements available, teaching assistantships with full tuition reimbursements available, career-related internships or fieldwork, scholarships/grants, health care benefits, and unspecified assistantships available. Financial award applicants required to submit FAFSA. *Faculty research:* Accessibility and HCI; algorithm and programming languages; bioinformatics and health IT; cybersecurity; machine learning and data science. *Unit head:* Dr. Pengcheng Shi, Director, 585-475-6193, E-mail: ljtdps@rit.edu. *Application contact:* Diane Ellison, Associate Vice President, Graduate Enrollment Services, 585-475-2229, Fax: 585-475-7164, E-mail: gradinfo@rit.edu.
Website: http://www.rit.edu/gccis/academics/phd-program

Rochester Institute of Technology, Graduate Enrollment Services, Golisano College of Computing and Information Sciences, Information Science and Technologies Department, MS Program in Information Sciences and Technologies, Rochester, NY 14623. Offers MS. *Program availability:* Part-time. *Students:* 102 full-time (47 women), 24 part-time (8 women); includes 5 minority (1 Black or African American, non-Hispanic/Latino; 1 American Indian or Alaska Native, non-Hispanic/Latino; 2 Asian, non-Hispanic/Latino; 1 Two or more races, non-Hispanic/Latino), 116 international. Average age 27. 441 applicants, 41% accepted, 29 enrolled. In 2016, 30 master's awarded. *Degree requirements:* For master's, thesis or alternative. *Entrance requirements:* For master's, GRE, minimum GPA of 3.0. Additional exam requirements/recommendations for international students: Required—TOEFL (minimum score 570 paper-based; 88 iBT), IELTS (minimum score 6.5), PTE (minimum score 61). *Application deadline:* For fall admission, 2/15 priority date for domestic and international students; for spring admission, 12/15 priority date for domestic and international students. Applications are processed on a rolling basis. Application fee: $60. Electronic applications accepted. *Expenses:* $1,742 per credit hour. *Financial support:* In 2016–17, 134 students received support. Research assistantships with partial tuition reimbursements available, teaching assistantships with partial tuition reimbursements available, career-related internships or fieldwork, scholarships/grants, and unspecified assistantships available. Support available to part-time students. Financial award applicants required to submit FAFSA. *Faculty research:* Machine learning, data analytics/management, service computing, web and mobile computing, geographic information science and technology. *Unit head:* Qi Yu, Graduate Program Director, 585-475-6929, E-mail: qyuvks@rit.edu. *Application contact:* Diane Ellison, Associate Vice President, Graduate Enrollment Services, 585-475-2229, Fax: 585-475-7164, E-mail: gradinfo@rit.edu.
Website: http://it.rit.edu/

Rutgers University–New Brunswick, School of Communication and Information, Program in Information, New Brunswick, NJ 08901. Offers MI. *Accreditation:* ALA. *Program availability:* Part-time, online learning. *Entrance requirements:* For master's, GRE General Test. Additional exam requirements/recommendations for international students: Required—TOEFL. Electronic applications accepted. *Faculty research:* Information science, library services, management of information services.

Sacred Heart University, Graduate Programs, College of Arts and Sciences, Department of Computer Science, Fairfield, CT 06825. Offers computer science (MS); computer science gaming (MS); cybersecurity (MS); information technology (MS). *Program availability:* Part-time, evening/weekend. *Faculty:* 7 full-time (2 women), 21 part-time/adjunct (4 women). *Students:* 256 full-time (93 women), 138 part-time (44 women); includes 28 minority (11 Black or African American, non-Hispanic/Latino; 3 Asian, non-Hispanic/Latino; 14 Hispanic/Latino), 319 international. Average age 25. 1,187 applicants, 65% accepted, 72 enrolled. In 2016, 275 master's awarded. *Degree requirements:* For master's, thesis or alternative. *Entrance requirements:* For master's, bachelor's degree, minimum GPA of 3.0. Additional exam requirements/recommendations for international students: Required—TOEFL (minimum score 570 paper-based, 80 iBT), TWE, or IELTS (6.5); Recommended—TSE. *Application deadline:* For fall admission, 5/15 for international students; for spring admission, 10/30 for international students. Applications are processed on a rolling basis. Application fee: $75. Electronic applications accepted. *Expenses:* $850 per credit part-time. *Financial support:* Unspecified assistantships available. Financial award applicants required to submit FAFSA. *Unit head:* Domenick Pinto, Director of the School of Computing, 203-371-7789, Fax: 203-371-0506, E-mail: pintod@sacredheart.edu. *Application contact:* William Sweeney, Director of Graduate Admissions Operations, 203-365-7619, Fax: 203-365-4732, E-mail: gradstudies@sacredheart.edu.
Website: http://www.sacredheart.edu/academics/collegeofartssciences/academicdepartments/computerscienceinformationtechnology/graduatedegreesandcertificates/

St. John's University, St. John's College of Liberal Arts and Sciences, Department of Government and Politics and Division of Library and Information Science, Program in Government and Library and Information Science, Queens, NY 11439. Offers MA/MS. *Program availability:* Part-time, evening/weekend. *Entrance requirements:* Additional exam requirements/recommendations for international students: Required—TOEFL (minimum score 600 paper-based; 100 iBT), IELTS (minimum score 7). Electronic applications accepted.

St. Mary's University, School of Science, Engineering and Technology, Program in Computer Information Systems, San Antonio, TX 78228-8507. Offers MS. *Program availability:* Part-time, evening/weekend. *Faculty:* 4 full-time (2 women), 1 part-time/adjunct (0 women). *Students:* 11 full-time (4 women), 6 part-time (0 women); includes 3 minority (1 Asian, non-Hispanic/Latino; 2 Hispanic/Latino), 14 international. Average age 31. 26 applicants, 15% accepted, 1 enrolled. In 2016, 14 master's awarded. *Degree requirements:* For master's, comprehensive exam, thesis optional. *Entrance requirements:* For master's, GMAT (minimum score of 334) or GRE General Test (minimum quantitative score of 148, analytical writing 2.5), minimum GPA of 3.0 in a bachelor's degree, written statement of purpose indicating interest and objective, two letters of recommendation, official transcripts of all college-level work. Additional exam requirements/recommendations for international students: Required—TOEFL (minimum score 530 paper-based; 80 iBT), IELTS (minimum score 6). *Application deadline:* For fall admission, 7/1 for domestic students; for spring admission, 11/15 for domestic students; for summer admission, 4/1 for domestic students. Applications are processed on a rolling basis. Application fee: $0. Electronic applications accepted. *Expenses: Tuition:* Full-time $15,600; part-time $865 per credit hour. *Required fees:* $148 per semester. *Financial support:* Career-related internships or fieldwork, Federal Work-Study, institutionally sponsored loans, scholarships/grants, health care benefits, and unspecified assistantships available. Financial award application deadline: 3/31; financial award applicants required to submit FAFSA. *Faculty research:* Artificial intelligence, biological modeling, computer languages, computer security, educational computer gaming. *Unit head:* Dr. Carol Redfield, Graduate Program Director, 210-436-3298, E-mail: credfield@stmarytx.edu.
Website: https://www.stmarytx.edu/academics/set/graduate/cis/

Sam Houston State University, College of Sciences, Department of Computer Science, Huntsville, TX 77341. Offers computing and information science (MS); digital forensics (MS); information assurance and security (MS). *Program availability:* Part-time. *Degree requirements:* For master's, comprehensive exam, thesis optional, internship; for doctorate, comprehensive exam, thesis/dissertation. *Entrance requirements:* For master's, GRE General Test, letters of recommendation. Additional exam requirements/recommendations for international students: Required—TOEFL (minimum score 550 paper-based; 79 iBT), IELTS (minimum score 6.5). Electronic applications accepted.

Shippensburg University of Pennsylvania, School of Graduate Studies, College of Arts and Sciences, Department of Computer Science and Engineering, Shippensburg, PA 17257-2299. Offers agile software engineering (Certificate); computer science (MS), including computer science, cybersecurity, IT leadership, management information systems, software engineering; IT leadership (Certificate). *Program availability:* Part-time, evening/weekend. *Faculty:* 7 full-time (3 women). *Students:* 16 full-time (8 women), 14 part-time (5 women); includes 3 minority (2 Black or African American, non-Hispanic/Latino; 1 Hispanic/Latino), 21 international. Average age 29. 89 applicants, 49% accepted, 9 enrolled. In 2016, 10 master's awarded. *Entrance requirements:* For master's, GRE (if GPA less than 2.75), professional resume. Additional exam requirements/recommendations for international students: Required—TOEFL (minimum score 70 iBT) or IELTS (minimum score 6). *Application deadline:* For fall admission, 4/30 for international students; for spring admission, 9/30 for international students. Applications are processed on a rolling basis. Application fee: $45. Electronic applications accepted. *Expenses:* Tuition, state resident: part-time $483 per credit. Tuition, nonresident: part-time $725 per credit. *Required fees:* $141 per credit. *Financial support:* In 2016–17, 7 students received support. Career-related internships or fieldwork, scholarships/grants, unspecified assistantships, and resident hall director and student payroll positions available. Support available to part-time students. Financial award application deadline: 3/1; financial award applicants required to submit FAFSA. *Unit head:* Dr. Jeonghwa Lee, Associate Professor and Program Coordinator, 717-477-1178, Fax: 717-477-4002, E-mail: jlee@ship.edu. *Application contact:* Megan N. Luft, Assistant Dean of Graduate Admissions, 717-477-1231, Fax: 717-477-4016, E-mail: mnluft@ship.edu.
Website: http://www.cs.ship.edu/

Simmons College, School of Library and Information Science, Boston, MA 02115. Offers children's literature (MA); library and information science (MS, PhD, Certificate), including archives management (MS), cultural heritage (MS), information science and technology (MS), school library teacher (MS); writing for children (MFA); MA/MA; MA/MAT; MA/MFA; MS/MA. *Accreditation:* ALA (one or more programs are accredited). *Program availability:* Part-time, evening/weekend, 100% online, blended/hybrid learning. *Faculty:* 23 full-time (17 women), 23 part-time/adjunct (16 women). *Students:* 313 full-time (262 women), 511 part-time (420 women); includes 88 minority (13 Black or African American, non-Hispanic/Latino; 10 Asian, non-Hispanic/Latino; 41 Hispanic/Latino; 24 Two or more races, non-Hispanic/Latino), 19 international. Average age 30. 568 applicants, 98% accepted, 319 enrolled. In 2016, 245 master's, 3 doctorates, 4 other advanced degrees awarded. *Degree requirements:* For master's, thesis optional, capstone project experience; for doctorate, comprehensive exam, thesis/dissertation, 36 credit hours. *Entrance requirements:* For doctorate, GRE, transcripts, personal statement, resume, recommendations, master's degree. Additional exam requirements/recommendations for international students: Required—TOEFL (minimum score 550 paper-based; 79 iBT), IELTS (minimum score 7). *Application deadline:* For fall admission, 3/1 for domestic and international students; for spring admission, 9/1 for domestic and international students; for summer admission, 2/1 for domestic and international students. Applications are processed on a rolling basis. Application fee: $65. Electronic applications accepted. *Expenses:* $1,210 per credit, $3,630 per course, $52 activity fee per semester. *Financial support:* In 2016–17, 10 fellowships with partial tuition reimbursements were awarded; scholarships/grants, tuition waivers, and unspecified assistantships also available. Support available to part-time students. Financial award application deadline: 2/1; financial award applicants required to submit FAFSA. *Faculty research:* Archives and social justice, information-seeking behavior, information retrieval, organization of information, cultural heritage informatics. *Unit head:* Dr. Eileen G. Abels, Dean, 617-521-2869. *Application contact:* Sarah Petrakos, Assistant Dean for Admission and Recruitment, 617-521-2868, Fax: 617-521-3192, E-mail: gslisadm@simmons.edu.
Website: http://www.simmons.edu/slis/

Southern Arkansas University–Magnolia, School of Graduate Studies, Magnolia, AR 71753. Offers agriculture (MS); business administration (MBA), including agri-business, social entrepreneurship, supply chain management; clinical and mental health counseling (MS); computer and information sciences (MS), including cyber security and privacy, data science, information technology; gifted and talented (M Ed), including curriculum and instruction, educational administration and supervision, gifted and

talented P-8/7-12, instructional specialist P-4; higher, adult and lifelong education (M Ed); kinesiology (M Ed), including coaching; library media and information specialist (M Ed); public administration (MPA); school counseling K-12 (M Ed); student affairs and college counseling (M Ed); teaching (MAT). *Accreditation:* NCATE. *Program availability:* Part-time, 100% online, blended/hybrid learning. *Faculty:* 36 full-time (19 women), 33 part-time/adjunct (14 women). *Students:* 605 full-time (143 women), 879 part-time (352 women); includes 130 minority (113 Black or African American, non-Hispanic/Latino; 7 American Indian or Alaska Native, non-Hispanic/Latino; 2 Asian, non-Hispanic/Latino; 2 Hispanic/Latino; 6 Two or more races, non-Hispanic/Latino), 1,048 international. Average age 28. 904 applicants, 81% accepted, 262 enrolled. In 2016, 278 master's awarded. *Degree requirements:* For master's, comprehensive exam (for some programs), thesis optional. *Entrance requirements:* For master's, GRE, MAT or GMAT, minimum GPA of 2.5. Additional exam requirements/recommendations for international students: Required—TOEFL (minimum score 550 paper-based), IELTS (minimum score 6). *Application deadline:* For fall admission, 7/20 for domestic students, 7/10 for international students; for spring admission, 12/1 for domestic students, 11/15 for international students; for summer admission, 4/1 for domestic students, 5/1 for international students. Applications are processed on a rolling basis. Application fee: $25 ($50 for international students). Electronic applications accepted. *Expenses:* Tuition, state resident: full-time $2511; part-time $279 per credit hour. Tuition, nonresident: full-time $3726; part-time $414 per credit hour. *Required fees:* $307 per semester. Tuition and fees vary according to course load and program. *Financial support:* Career-related internships or fieldwork, Federal Work-Study, scholarships/grants, tuition waivers (full), and unspecified assistantships available. Financial award applicants required to submit FAFSA. *Faculty research:* Alternative certification for teachers, supervision of instruction, instructional leadership, counseling. *Unit head:* Dr. Kim Bloss, Dean, School of Graduate Studies, 870-235-4150, Fax: 870-235-5227, E-mail: kkbloss@saumag.edu. *Application contact:* Shrijana Malakar, Admissions Specialist, 870-235-4150, Fax: 870-235-5227, E-mail: smalakar@saumag.edu.
Website: http://www.saumag.edu/graduate

Southern Methodist University, Bobby B. Lyle School of Engineering, Department of Engineering Management, Information, and Systems, Dallas, TX 75275. Offers engineering management (MSEM, DE); information engineering and management (MSIEM); operations research (MS, PhD); systems engineering (MS, PhD). *Program availability:* Part-time, evening/weekend, online learning. Terminal master's awarded for partial completion of doctoral program. *Degree requirements:* For master's, thesis optional; for doctorate, thesis/dissertation, oral and written qualifying exams. *Entrance requirements:* For master's, minimum GPA of 3.0 in last 2 years; bachelor's degree in engineering, mathematics, sciences, or technical area; for doctorate, GRE General Test (operations research, engineering management), bachelor's degree in related field. Additional exam requirements/recommendations for international students: Required—TOEFL. *Faculty research:* Telecommunications, decision systems, information engineering, operations research, software.

State University of New York Polytechnic Institute, Program in Computer and Information Science, Utica, NY 13502. Offers MS. *Program availability:* Part-time, evening/weekend. *Degree requirements:* For master's, thesis or project. *Entrance requirements:* For master's, GRE General Test, minimum GPA of 3.0, one letter of reference, resume, BS in computer science or a related field. Additional exam requirements/recommendations for international students: Required—TOEFL (minimum score 550 paper-based; 79 iBT), IELTS (minimum score 6.5). Electronic applications accepted. *Faculty research:* Cryptography, distributed systems, computer-aided system theory, reasoning with uncertainty, grid computing.

State University of New York Polytechnic Institute, Program in Information Design and Technology, Utica, NY 13502. Offers MS. *Program availability:* Part-time, online learning. *Degree requirements:* For master's, thesis or project. *Entrance requirements:* For master's, minimum GPA of 3.0; 2 letters of reference; writing samples or portfolio; resume, educational objective. Additional exam requirements/recommendations for international students: Required—TOEFL (minimum score 550 paper-based; 79 iBT), IELTS (minimum score 6.5). Electronic applications accepted. *Faculty research:* Textual-visualization, ethics and technology, behavioral information security.

Stevens Institute of Technology, Graduate School, School of Business, Program in Information Systems, Hoboken, NJ 07030. Offers computer science (MS); e-commerce (MS); enterprise systems (MS); entrepreneurial information technology (MS); information architecture (MS); information management (MS, Certificate); information security (MS); information technology in financial services industry (MS); information technology in the pharmaceutical industry (MS); information technology outsourcing management (MS); project management (MS, Certificate); software engineering (MS); telecommunications (MS). *Program availability:* Part-time, evening/weekend. *Students:* 280 full-time (100 women), 84 part-time (21 women); includes 23 minority (9 Black or African American, non-Hispanic/Latino; 13 Asian, non-Hispanic/Latino; 1 Hispanic/Latino), 283 international. Average age 26. 925 applicants, 62% accepted, 114 enrolled. In 2016, 212 master's, 32 other advanced degrees awarded. *Degree requirements:* For master's, thesis optional, minimum B average in major field and overall; for Certificate, minimum B average. *Entrance requirements:* Additional exam requirements/recommendations for international students: Required—TOEFL (minimum score 74 iBT), IELTS (minimum score 6). *Application deadline:* For fall admission, 6/1 for domestic students, 4/15 for international students; for spring admission, 11/30 for domestic students, 11/1 for international students. Applications are processed on a rolling basis. Application fee: $65. Electronic applications accepted. *Expenses:* Contact institution. *Financial support:* Fellowships, research assistantships, teaching assistantships, career-related internships or fieldwork, Federal Work-Study, scholarships/grants, and unspecified assistantships available. Financial award application deadline: 2/15; financial award applicants required to submit FAFSA. *Unit head:* Dr. Gregory Prastacos, Dean, 201-216-8366, E-mail: gprastac@stevens.edu. *Application contact:* Graduate Admissions, 888-783-8367, Fax: 888-511-1306, E-mail: graduate@stevens.edu.
Website: https://www.stevens.edu/school-business/masters-programs/information-systems

Strayer University, Graduate Studies, Washington, DC 20005-2603. Offers accounting (MS); acquisition (MBA); business administration (MBA); communications technology (MS); educational management (M Ed); finance (MBA); health services administration (MHSA); hospitality and tourism management (MBA); human resource management (MBA); information systems (MS), including computer security management, decision support system management, enterprise resource management, network management, software engineering management, systems development management; management (MBA); management information systems (MS); marketing (MBA); professional accounting (MS), including accounting information systems, controllership, taxation; public administration (MPA); supply chain management (MBA); technology in education (M Ed). Programs also offered at campus locations in Birmingham, AL; Chamblee, GA; Cobb County, GA; Morrow, GA; White Marsh, MD; Charleston, SC; Columbia, SC; Greensboro, NC; Greenville, SC; Lexington, KY; Louisville, KY; Nashville, TN; North Raleigh, NC; Washington, DC. *Accreditation:* ACBSP. *Program availability:* Part-time, evening/weekend, online learning. *Degree requirements:* For master's, thesis. *Entrance requirements:* For master's, GMAT, GRE General Test, bachelor's degree from an accredited college or university, minimum undergraduate GPA of 2.75. Electronic applications accepted.

Syracuse University, College of Engineering and Computer Science, PhD Program in Computer and Information Science and Engineering, Syracuse, NY 13244. Offers PhD. *Program availability:* Part-time. *Students:* Average age 29. In 2016, 3 doctorates awarded. *Degree requirements:* For doctorate, comprehensive exam, thesis/dissertation. *Entrance requirements:* For doctorate, GRE General Test, GRE Subject Test (computer science), three letters of recommendation, personal statement, official transcripts, resume. Additional exam requirements/recommendations for international students: Required—TOEFL (minimum score 100 iBT). *Application deadline:* For fall admission, 7/1 priority date for domestic students, 6/1 priority date for international students; for spring admission, 11/15 priority date for domestic students, 10/15 priority date for international students. Applications are processed on a rolling basis. Application fee: $75. Electronic applications accepted. *Expenses: Tuition:* Full-time $25,974; part-time $1443 per credit hour. *Required fees:* $802; $50 per course. Tuition and fees vary according to course load and program. *Financial support:* Fellowships with full tuition reimbursements, research assistantships with tuition reimbursements, teaching assistantships with tuition reimbursements, and tuition waivers (partial) available. Financial award application deadline: 1/1; financial award applicants required to submit FAFSA. *Faculty research:* Computer and information science, software aspects of the computer-engineering field. *Unit head:* Dr. Kishan Mehrotra, Professor and Chair, Department of Electrical Engineering and Computer Science, 315-443-2811, E-mail: mehrotra@syr.edu. *Application contact:* Kathleen Joyce, Assistant Dean, 315-443-2219, E-mail: topgrads@syr.edu.
Website: http://eng-cs.syr.edu/

Syracuse University, School of Information Studies, MS Program in Library and Information Science, Syracuse, NY 13244. Offers MS. *Accreditation:* ALA. *Program availability:* Part-time, evening/weekend, online learning. *Students:* Average age 30. *Degree requirements:* For master's, fieldwork or research paper. *Entrance requirements:* For master's, GRE General Test, two letters of recommendation, personal statement, resume. Additional exam requirements/recommendations for international students: Required—TOEFL (minimum score 100 iBT). *Application deadline:* For fall admission, 2/1 priority date for domestic and international students; for spring admission, 10/15 priority date for domestic and international students. Applications are processed on a rolling basis. Application fee: $75. Electronic applications accepted. *Expenses: Tuition:* Full-time $25,974; part-time $1443 per credit hour. *Required fees:* $802; $50 per course. Tuition and fees vary according to course load and program. *Financial support:* Fellowships with full tuition reimbursements and teaching assistantships available. Financial award application deadline: 1/1; financial award applicants required to submit FAFSA. *Faculty research:* Information environments, library planning and marketing, management principles, information policy. *Unit head:* Prof. Jill Hurst-Wahl, Program Director, 315-443-2911, E-mail: igrad@syr.edu. *Application contact:* Susan Corieri, Director of Enrollment Management, 315-443-1070, E-mail: ischool@syr.edu.
Website: http://ischool.syr.edu/

Syracuse University, School of Information Studies, PhD Program in Information Science and Technology, Syracuse, NY 13244. Offers PhD. *Students:* Average age 35. In 2016, 4 doctorates awarded. *Degree requirements:* For doctorate, comprehensive exam, thesis/dissertation. *Entrance requirements:* For doctorate, GRE General Test, writing sample, personal statement, three letters of recommendation, official transcripts. Additional exam requirements/recommendations for international students: Required—TOEFL (minimum score 100 iBT). *Application deadline:* For fall admission, 1/3 priority date for domestic and international students. Application fee: $75. Electronic applications accepted. *Expenses: Tuition:* Full-time $25,974; part-time $1443 per credit hour. *Required fees:* $802; $50 per course. Tuition and fees vary according to course load and program. *Financial support:* Fellowships with full tuition reimbursements, research assistantships with partial tuition reimbursements, and teaching assistantships with partial tuition reimbursements available. Financial award application deadline: 1/1. *Faculty research:* Information and public policy, human-computer interaction, emerging technologies, digital literacy. *Unit head:* Dr. Steve Sawyer, Director, 315-443-6147, Fax: 315-443-6886, E-mail: istphd@syr.edu. *Application contact:* Susan Corieri, Director of Enrollment Management, 315-443-2575, E-mail: ischool@syr.edu.
Website: http://ischool.syr.edu/

Temple University, College of Science and Technology, Department of Computer and Information Sciences, Philadelphia, PA 19122. Offers computer and information science (PhD); computer science (MS); information science and technology (MS). *Program availability:* Part-time, evening/weekend. Terminal master's awarded for partial completion of doctoral program. *Degree requirements:* For doctorate, thesis/dissertation. *Entrance requirements:* For master's and doctorate, GRE General Test, minimum GPA of 3.0. Additional exam requirements/recommendations for international students: Required—TOEFL (minimum score 550 paper-based; 79 iBT). Electronic applications accepted. *Faculty research:* Artificial intelligence, information systems, software engineering, network-distributed systems.

Texas Woman's University, Graduate School, College of Arts and Sciences, Department of Mathematics and Computer Science, Denton, TX 76201. Offers informatics (MS); mathematics (MS); mathematics teaching (MS). *Program availability:* Part-time, evening/weekend. *Students:* Average age 38. In 2016, 10 master's awarded. *Degree requirements:* For master's, comprehensive exam, thesis. *Entrance requirements:* For master's, 2 letters of reference. Additional exam requirements/recommendations for international students: Required—TOEFL (minimum score 550 paper-based; 79 iBT). *Application deadline:* For fall admission, 7/1 priority date for domestic students, 3/1 for international students; for spring admission, 12/1 priority date for domestic students, 7/1 for international students. Applications are processed on a rolling basis. Application fee: $50 ($75 for international students). Electronic applications accepted. *Expenses:* Tuition, state resident: full-time $9046; part-time $251 per credit hour. Tuition, nonresident: full-time $22,922; part-time $614 per credit hour. *International tuition:* $23,046 full-time. *Required fees:* $2690; $1285 per credit hour. One-time fee: $50. Tuition and fees vary according to course level, course load, program and reciprocity agreements. *Financial support:* Research assistantships, teaching assistantships, career-related internships or fieldwork, Federal Work-Study, institutionally sponsored loans, scholarships/grants, traineeships, health care benefits, and unspecified assistantships available. Support available to part-time students. Financial award application deadline: 3/1; financial award applicants required to submit FAFSA. *Faculty research:* Biopharmaceutical statistics, dynamic systems and control theory, Bayesian inference, math and computer science curriculum innovation, computer modeling of physical phenomenon. *Unit head:* Dr. Don E. Edwards, Chair, 940-898-3275, Fax: 940-898-2179, E-mail: mathcs@twu.edu. *Application contact:* Dr. Samuel Wheeler, Assistant Director of Admissions, 940-898-3188, Fax: 940-898-3081, E-mail: wheelersr@twu.edu.
Website: http://www.twu.edu/math-computer-science/

Towson University, Program in Applied Information Technology, Towson, MD 21252-0001. Offers applied information technology (MS, D Sc); database management

Information Science

systems (Postbaccalaureate Certificate); information security and assurance (Postbaccalaureate Certificate); information systems management (Postbaccalaureate Certificate); Internet applications development (Postbaccalaureate Certificate); networking technologies (Postbaccalaureate Certificate); software engineering (Postbaccalaureate Certificate). *Students:* 135 full-time (50 women), 154 part-time (50 women); includes 119 minority (81 Black or African American, non-Hispanic/Latino; 26 Asian, non-Hispanic/Latino; 4 Hispanic/Latino; 8 Two or more races, non-Hispanic/Latino), 82 international. *Entrance requirements:* For master's and Postbaccalaureate Certificate, bachelor's degree, minimum GPA of 3.0; for doctorate, master's degree in computer science, information systems, information technology, or closely-related area; minimum GPA of 3.0; 2 letters of recommendation; resume. Additional exam requirements/recommendations for international students: Required—TOEFL. *Application deadline:* Applications are processed on a rolling basis. Application fee: $45. Electronic applications accepted. *Expenses:* Tuition, state resident: full-time $7580; part-time $379 per unit. Tuition, nonresident: full-time $15,700; part-time $785 per unit. *Required fees:* $2480. *Unit head:* Dr. Jinjuan Feng, Graduate Program Director, 410-704-3463, E-mail: ait@towson.edu. *Application contact:* Coverley Beidleman, Assistant Director of Graduate Admissions, 410-704-2113, Fax: 410-704-3030, E-mail: grads@towson.edu.
Website: https://www.towson.edu/fcsm/departments/emergingtech/

Trevecca Nazarene University, Graduate Education Program, Nashville, TN 37210-2877. Offers accountability and instructional leadership (Ed S); curriculum and instruction for Christian school educators (M Ed); curriculum and instruction K-12 (M Ed); educational leadership (M Ed); English second language (M Ed); library and information science (MLI Sc); special education: visual impairments (M Ed); teaching (MAT), including teaching 6-12, teaching K-5. *Accreditation:* NCATE. *Program availability:* Part-time, evening/weekend, online learning. *Faculty:* 5 full-time (3 women), 18 part-time/adjunct (12 women). *Students:* 80 full-time (64 women), 16 part-time (13 women); includes 19 minority (17 Black or African American, non-Hispanic/Latino; 2 Hispanic/Latino). Average age 35. In 2016, 68 master's, 7 other advanced degrees awarded. *Degree requirements:* For master's, comprehensive exam, exit assessment/e-portfolio. *Entrance requirements:* For master's, GRE (minimum score of 290) or MAT (minimum score of 378); PRAXIS (for MAT), minimum GPA of 3.0, official transcript from regionally-accredited institution, at least 3 years' successful teaching experience (for M Ed in educational leadership major). Additional exam requirements/recommendations for international students: Required—TOEFL (minimum score 550 paper-based). *Application deadline:* Applications are processed on a rolling basis. Electronic applications accepted. *Expenses:* Contact institution. *Financial support:* Applicants required to submit FAFSA. *Unit head:* Dr. Suzie Harris, Dean, School of Education/Director of Graduate Education Programs, 615-248-1201, Fax: 615-248-1597, E-mail: admissions_ged@trevecca.edu. *Application contact:* 844-TNU-GRAD, E-mail: sgcsadmissions@trevecca.edu.
Website: http://www.trevecca.edu/soe

Université de Sherbrooke, Faculty of Sciences, Department of Informatics, Sherbrooke, QC J1K 2R1, Canada. Offers M Sc, PhD. *Degree requirements:* For master's, thesis. Electronic applications accepted.

University at Albany, State University of New York, College of Engineering and Applied Sciences, PhD Program in Informatics, Albany, NY 12222-0001. Offers PhD. *Faculty:* 8 full-time (2 women), 16 part-time/adjunct (3 women). *Students:* 11 full-time (3 women), 23 part-time (9 women); includes 7 minority (3 Asian, non-Hispanic/Latino; 4 Hispanic/Latino), 13 international. Average age 28. 18 applicants, 61% accepted, 5 enrolled. In 2016, 4 doctorates awarded. *Degree requirements:* For doctorate, comprehensive exam. *Entrance requirements:* Additional exam requirements/recommendations for international students: Required—TOEFL. *Expenses:* Tuition, state resident: full-time $10,870; part-time $453 per credit hour. Tuition, nonresident: full-time $22,210; part-time $925 per credit hour. *International tuition:* $21,550 full-time. *Required fees:* $1864; $96 per credit hour. *Total annual research expenditures:* $226,725. *Unit head:* George Berg, Chair, 518-437-4937, Fax: 518-442-5367, E-mail: gberg@albany.edu.

The University of Alabama at Birmingham, College of Arts and Sciences, Program in Computer and Information Sciences, Birmingham, AL 35294. Offers MS, PhD. Terminal master's awarded for partial completion of doctoral program. *Degree requirements:* For master's, thesis optional; for doctorate, thesis/dissertation. *Entrance requirements:* For master's, GRE General Test, minimum GPA of 3.0, letters of recommendation; for doctorate, GRE General Test, minimum GPA of 3.5 overall or on last 60 hours; letters of recommendation. Additional exam requirements/recommendations for international students: Required—TOEFL, IELTS. Electronic applications accepted. Full-time tuition and fees vary according to course load and program. *Faculty research:* Theory and software systems, intelligent systems, systems architecture, high performance computing, computer architecture, computer graphics, data mining, software engineering.

University of Arkansas at Little Rock, Graduate School, George W. Donaghey College of Engineering and Information Technology, Program in Information Quality, Little Rock, AR 72204-1099. Offers MS, PhD, Graduate Certificate.

University of California, Irvine, Donald Bren School of Information and Computer Sciences, Department of Informatics, Irvine, CA 92697. Offers information and computer science (MS, PhD). *Students:* 112 full-time (56 women), 4 part-time (1 woman); includes 22 minority (1 Black or African American, non-Hispanic/Latino; 15 Asian, non-Hispanic/Latino; 3 Hispanic/Latino; 3 Two or more races, non-Hispanic/Latino), 57 international. Average age 29. 495 applicants, 21% accepted, 55 enrolled. In 2016, 28 master's, 14 doctorates awarded. Application fee: $105 ($125 for international students). *Unit head:* Andre van der Hoek, Chair, 949-824-6326, Fax: 949-824-4056, E-mail: andre@uci.edu. *Application contact:* Gillian Hayes, Vice Chair for Graduate Affairs, 949-824-1483, E-mail: gillianrh@ics.uci.edu.
Website: http://www.informatics.uci.edu/

University of California, Merced, Graduate Division, School of Social Sciences, Humanities and Arts, Merced, CA 95343. Offers cognitive and information sciences (PhD); interdisciplinary humanities (MA, PhD); psychological sciences (MA, PhD); social sciences (MA, PhD); sociology (MA, PhD). *Faculty:* 93 full-time (41 women), 3 part-time/adjunct (all women). *Students:* 172 full-time (112 women), 3 part-time (2 women); includes 69 minority (4 Black or African American, non-Hispanic/Latino; 15 Asian, non-Hispanic/Latino; 43 Hispanic/Latino; 7 Two or more races, non-Hispanic/Latino), 25 international. Average age 31. 195 applicants, 50% accepted, 52 enrolled. In 2016, 13 master's, 11 doctorates awarded. Terminal master's awarded for partial completion of doctoral program. *Degree requirements:* For master's, variable foreign language requirement, comprehensive exam, thesis or alternative; for doctorate, variable foreign language requirement, comprehensive exam, thesis/dissertation. *Entrance requirements:* For master's and doctorate, GRE. Additional exam requirements/recommendations for international students: Required—TOEFL (minimum score 550 paper-based; 80 iBT); Recommended—IELTS (minimum score 7). *Application deadline:* For fall admission, 1/15 for domestic and international students. Application fee: $90 ($110 for international students). Electronic applications accepted. *Expenses:* Contact institution. *Financial support:* In 2016–17, 167 students received support, including 12 fellowships with full tuition reimbursements available (averaging $20,237 per year), 12 research assistantships with full tuition reimbursements available (averaging $18,842 per year), 121 teaching assistantships with full tuition reimbursements available (averaging $19,655 per year); scholarships/grants, traineeships, and health care benefits also available. Financial award application deadline: 1/15. *Faculty research:* Social inequality, critical race and ethnic studies, public health and health sciences, cognitive science and language acquisition, political institutions. *Total annual research expenditures:* $1.2 million. *Unit head:* Dr. Jill Robbins, Dean, E-mail: jillrobbins@ucmerced.edu. *Application contact:* Tsu Ya, Director of Admissions and Academic Services, 209-228-4521, Fax: 209-228-6906, E-mail: tya@ucmerced.edu.

University of Central Missouri, The Graduate School, Warrensburg, MO 64093. Offers accountancy (MA); accounting (MBA); applied mathematics (MS); aviation safety (MA); biology (MS); business administration (MBA); career and technical education leadership (MS); college student personnel administration (MS); communication (MA); computer science (MS); counseling (MS); criminal justice (MS); educational leadership (Ed D); educational technology (MS); elementary and early childhood education (MSE); English (MA); environmental studies (MA); finance (MBA); history (MA); human services/educational technology (Ed S); human services/learning resources (Ed S); human services/professional counseling (Ed S); industrial hygiene (MS); industrial management (MS); information systems (MBA); information technology (MS); kinesiology (MS); library science and information services (MS); literacy education (MSE); marketing (MBA); mathematics (MS); music (MA); occupational safety management (MS); psychology (MS); rural family nursing (MS); school administration (MSE); social gerontology (MS); sociology (MA); special education (MSE); speech language pathology (MS); superintendency (Ed S); teaching (MAT); teaching English as a second language (MA); technology (MS); technology management (PhD); theatre (MA). *Program availability:* Part-time, 100% online, blended/hybrid learning. *Degree requirements:* For master's and Ed S, comprehensive exam (for some programs), thesis (for some programs). *Entrance requirements:* Additional exam requirements/recommendations for international students: Required—TOEFL (minimum score 550 paper-based; 79 iBT). Electronic applications accepted.

University of Colorado Boulder, Graduate School, College of Media, Communication and Information, Program in Information Science, Boulder, CO 80309. Offers PhD. *Faculty:* 9 full-time (4 women). *Students:* 5 full-time (2 women), 3 international. Average age 24. 26 applicants, 38% accepted, 5 enrolled. Application fee: $60 ($80 for international students). Electronic applications accepted. *Financial support:* In 2016–17, 22 students received support, including 13 fellowships (averaging $10,602 per year), 3 research assistantships with full and partial tuition reimbursements available (averaging $43,659 per year); institutionally sponsored loans, scholarships/grants, health care benefits, and unspecified assistantships also available. Financial award application deadline: 2/1; financial award applicants required to submit FAFSA. *Faculty research:* Computer science; information science/systems; data analysis; collective behavior; computer interface. *Total annual research expenditures:* $61,683. *Application contact:* E-mail: cmci.info@colorado.edu.
Website: http://www.colorado.edu/cmci/academics/information-science

University of Colorado Denver, College of Engineering and Applied Science, Department of Computer Science and Engineering, Denver, CO 80217. Offers computer science (MS); computer science and engineering (EASPh D); computer science and information systems (PhD). *Program availability:* Part-time, evening/weekend. *Faculty:* 10 full-time (2 women), 2 part-time/adjunct (0 women). *Students:* 80 full-time (26 women), 21 part-time (6 women); includes 11 minority (2 Black or African American, non-Hispanic/Latino; 7 Asian, non-Hispanic/Latino; 2 Hispanic/Latino), 61 international. Average age 34. 217 applicants, 44% accepted, 28 enrolled. In 2016, 33 master's, 1 doctorate awarded. *Degree requirements:* For master's, thesis or alternative, at least 30 semester hours of computer science courses while maintaining minimum GPA of 3.0; for doctorate, comprehensive exam, thesis/dissertation, at least 60 hours beyond the master's degree level, 30 of which are dissertation research. *Entrance requirements:* For master's, GRE, minimum GPA of 3.0, 10 semester hours of university-level calculus, at least one math course beyond calculus, statement of purpose, letters of recommendation; for doctorate, GRE or GMAT. Additional exam requirements/recommendations for international students: Required—TOEFL (minimum score 537 paper-based; 75 iBT). *Application deadline:* For fall admission, 5/1 for domestic students, 4/1 for international students; for spring admission, 10/1 for domestic students, 9/1 for international students. Application fee: $50 ($75 for international students). Electronic applications accepted. *Expenses:* Tuition, state resident: full-time $11,006; part-time $474 per credit. Tuition, nonresident: full-time $28,212; part-time $1264 per credit hour. *Required fees:* $256 per semester. One-time fee: $94.32. Tuition and fees vary according to campus/location and program. *Financial support:* In 2016–17, 9 students received support. Research assistantships, teaching assistantships, Federal Work-Study, institutionally sponsored loans, scholarships/grants, traineeships, and unspecified assistantships available. Financial award application deadline: 4/1; financial award applicants required to submit FAFSA. *Faculty research:* Algorithms, automata theory, artificial intelligence, communication networks, combinatorial geometry, computational geometry, computer architectures, computer graphics, distributed computing, high performance computing, graph theory, Internet, operating systems, parallel processing, simulation and software engineering. *Unit head:* Dr. Gita Alaghband, Chair, 303-315-1400, E-mail: gita.alaghband@ucdenver.edu. *Application contact:* Sarah Mandos, Program Assistant, 303-315-1411, E-mail: sarah.mandos@ucdenver.edu.
Website: http://www.ucdenver.edu/academics/colleges/Engineering/Programs/Computer-Science-and-Engineering/Pages/ComputerScienceEngineering.aspx

University of Delaware, College of Engineering, Department of Computer and Information Sciences, Newark, DE 19716. Offers MS, PhD. *Program availability:* Part-time. Terminal master's awarded for partial completion of doctoral program. *Degree requirements:* For master's, thesis optional; for doctorate, comprehensive exam, thesis/dissertation. *Entrance requirements:* For master's and doctorate, GRE General Test. Additional exam requirements/recommendations for international students: Required—TOEFL (minimum score 550 paper-based). Electronic applications accepted. *Faculty research:* Artificial intelligence, computational theory, graphics and computer vision, networks, systems.

University of Denver, University College, Denver, CO 80208. Offers arts and culture (MA, Certificate); communication management (MS, Certificate), including translation studies (Certificate), world history and culture (Certificate); environmental policy and management (MS); geographic information systems (MS); global affairs (MA, Certificate), including human capital in organizations (Certificate), philanthropic leadership (Certificate), project management (Certificate), strategic innovation and change (Certificate); healthcare leadership (MS); information communications and technology (MS); leadership and organizations (MS); professional creative writing (MA, Certificate), including emergency planning and response (Certificate), organizational security (Certificate); security management (MS, Certificate); strategic human resources (Certificate). *Program availability:* Part-time, evening/weekend, online learning. *Faculty:* 118 part-time/adjunct (62 women). *Students:* 59 full-time (22 women), 1,285 part-time (750 women); includes 316 minority (111 Black or African American, non-Hispanic/Latino; 8 American Indian or Alaska Native, non-Hispanic/Latino; 39 Asian, non-

Hispanic/Latino; 123 Hispanic/Latino; 3 Native Hawaiian or other Pacific Islander, non-Hispanic/Latino; 32 Two or more races, non-Hispanic/Latino), 85 international. Average age 35. 703 applicants, 89% accepted, 390 enrolled. In 2016, 428 master's, 138 other advanced degrees awarded. *Degree requirements:* For master's, capstone project. *Entrance requirements:* For master's, transcripts, two letters of recommendation, personal statement, resume. Additional exam requirements/recommendations for international students: Required—TOEFL (minimum score 550 paper-based; 80 iBT). *Application deadline:* For fall admission, 6/21 priority date for domestic students, 5/1 priority date for international students; for winter admission, 9/14 priority date for domestic students, 9/19 priority date for international students; for spring admission, 1/11 priority date for domestic students, 12/12 priority date for international students; for summer admission, 3/29 priority date for domestic students, 3/6 priority date for international students. Applications are processed on a rolling basis. Application fee: $75. Electronic applications accepted. *Expenses:* $7,236 per year full-time. *Financial support:* In 2016–17, 27 students received support, including 1 teaching assistantship (averaging $1,489 per year). Financial award applicants required to submit FAFSA. *Unit head:* Dr. Michael McGuire, Dean, 303-871-3518, Fax: 303-871-3303, E-mail: mmcguire@du.edu. *Application contact:* Information Contact, 303-871-2291, E-mail: ucoladm@du.edu.
Website: http://universitycollege.du.edu/

University of Florida, Graduate School, Herbert Wertheim College of Engineering and College of Liberal Arts and Sciences, Department of Computer and Information Science and Engineering, Gainesville, FL 32611. Offers computer engineering (ME, MS, PhD); computer science (MS); digital arts and sciences (MS). *Program availability:* Part-time, online learning. Terminal master's awarded for partial completion of doctoral program. *Degree requirements:* For master's, comprehensive exam, thesis optional; for doctorate, comprehensive exam, thesis/dissertation. *Entrance requirements:* For master's and doctorate, minimum GPA of 3.0. Additional exam requirements/recommendations for international students: Required—TOEFL (minimum score 550 paper-based; 80 iBT), IELTS (minimum score 6). Electronic applications accepted. *Faculty research:* Computer systems and computer networking; high-performance computing and algorithm; database and machine learning; computer graphics, vision, and intelligent systems; human center computing and digital art.

University of Hawaii at Manoa, Graduate Division, Interdisciplinary Program in Communication and Information Sciences, Honolulu, HI 96822. Offers PhD. *Program availability:* Part-time. *Degree requirements:* For doctorate, comprehensive exam, thesis/dissertation. *Entrance requirements:* For doctorate, GRE or GMAT. Additional exam requirements/recommendations for international students: Required—TOEFL (minimum score 600 paper-based; 100 iBT), IELTS (minimum score 7).

University of Hawaii at Manoa, Graduate Division, Shidler College of Business, Program in Business Administration, Honolulu, HI 96822. Offers Asian business studies (MBA); Chinese business studies (MBA); decision sciences (MBA); entrepreneurship (MBA); finance (MBA); finance and banking (MBA); human resources management (MBA); information management (MBA); information technology (MBA); international business (MBA); Japanese business studies (MBA); marketing (MBA); organizational behavior (MBA); organizational management (MBA); real estate (MBA); student-designed track (MBA). *Accreditation:* AACSB. *Program availability:* Part-time, evening/weekend. *Degree requirements:* For master's, thesis optional. *Entrance requirements:* For master's, GMAT, minimum GPA of 3.0. Additional exam requirements/recommendations for international students: Required—TOEFL (minimum score 600 paper-based; 100 iBT), IELTS (minimum score 7). *Expenses:* Contact institution.

University of Houston, Bauer College of Business, Decision and Information Sciences Program, Houston, TX 77204. Offers PhD. *Program availability:* Evening/weekend.

University of Houston, College of Technology, Department of Information and Logistics Technology, Houston, TX 77204. Offers information security (MS); supply chain and logistics technology (MS); technology project management (MS). *Program availability:* Part-time. *Degree requirements:* For master's, project or thesis (most programs). *Entrance requirements:* For master's, GMAT. Additional exam requirements/recommendations for international students: Required—TOEFL (minimum score 550 paper-based; 79 iBT). Electronic applications accepted.

University of Houston–Clear Lake, School of Science and Computer Engineering, Program in Computer Information Systems, Houston, TX 77058-1002. Offers MS. *Program availability:* Part-time, evening/weekend. *Entrance requirements:* For master's, GRE General Test. Additional exam requirements/recommendations for international students: Required—TOEFL (minimum score 550 paper-based).

University of Illinois at Urbana–Champaign, Graduate College, School of Information Sciences, Champaign, IL 61820. Offers bioinformatics (MS); digital libraries (CAS); information management (MS); library and information science (MS, PhD, CAS). *Accreditation:* ALA (one or more programs are accredited). *Program availability:* Part-time, online learning. *Entrance requirements:* For degree, master's degree in library and information science or related field with minimum GPA of 3.0.

University of Illinois at Urbana–Champaign, Illinois Informatics Institute, Champaign, IL 61820. Offers PhD. *Degree requirements:* For doctorate, thesis/dissertation.

The University of Iowa, Graduate College, Program in Informatics, Iowa City, IA 52242-1316. Offers bioinformatics (MS, PhD); bioinformatics and computational biology (Certificate); geoinformatics (MS, PhD, Certificate); health informatics (MS, PhD, Certificate); information science (MS, PhD, Certificate). *Degree requirements:* For master's, thesis optional; for doctorate, comprehensive exam, thesis/dissertation. *Entrance requirements:* For master's and doctorate, GRE General Test, minimum GPA of 3.0. Additional exam requirements/recommendations for international students: Required—TOEFL (minimum score 550 paper-based; 81 iBT). Electronic applications accepted.

University of Kentucky, Graduate School, College of Communication and Information, Program in Library and Information Science, Lexington, KY 40506-0032. Offers MA, MSLS. *Accreditation:* ALA (one or more programs are accredited). *Program availability:* Part-time. *Degree requirements:* For master's, variable foreign language requirement, comprehensive exam. *Entrance requirements:* For master's, GRE General Test, minimum undergraduate GPA of 2.75. Additional exam requirements/recommendations for international students: Required—TOEFL (minimum score 550 paper-based). *Faculty research:* Information retrieval systems, information-seeking behavior, organizational behavior, computer cataloging, library resource sharing.

University of Maine, Graduate School, College of Liberal Arts and Sciences, School of Computing and Information Science, Orono, ME 04469. Offers MS, PhD, CGS. *Program availability:* Part-time. *Faculty:* 13 full-time (2 women), 2 part-time/adjunct (1 woman). *Students:* 36 full-time (5 women), 12 part-time (4 women); includes 4 minority (1 American Indian or Alaska Native, non-Hispanic/Latino; 1 Asian, non-Hispanic/Latino; 1 Hispanic/Latino; 1 Two or more races, non-Hispanic/Latino), 10 international. Average age 31. 31 applicants, 77% accepted, 15 enrolled. In 2016, 6 master's, 5 doctorates, 2 other advanced degrees awarded. *Degree requirements:* For master's, thesis (for some programs); for doctorate, comprehensive exam, thesis/dissertation. *Entrance requirements:* For master's and doctorate, GRE General Test, GRE Subject Test. Additional exam requirements/recommendations for international students: Required—TOEFL (minimum score 550 paper-based; 80 iBT). *Application deadline:* Applications are processed on a rolling basis. Application fee: $65. Electronic applications accepted. *Expenses:* Tuition, state resident: full-time $7524; part-time $2508 per credit. Tuition, nonresident: full-time $24,498; part-time $8166 per credit. *Required fees:* $1148; $571 per credit. *Financial support:* In 2016–17, 21 students received support, including 2 fellowships (averaging $20,700 per year), 1 research assistantship with full tuition reimbursement available (averaging $14,600 per year), 10 teaching assistantships with full tuition reimbursements available (averaging $14,600 per year); career-related internships or fieldwork, Federal Work-Study, institutionally sponsored loans, and tuition waivers (full) also available. Financial award application deadline: 3/1. *Faculty research:* Geographic information science, spatial informatics, scientific computing. *Total annual research expenditures:* $1.3 million. *Unit head:* Dr. Max Egenhofer, Acting Director, 207-581-2114, Fax: 207-581-2206. *Application contact:* Scott G. Delcourt, Assistant Vice President for Graduate Studies and Senior Associate Dean, 207-581-3291, Fax: 207-581-3232, E-mail: graduate@maine.edu.
Website: http://umaine.edu/cis/

University of Maryland, Baltimore County, The Graduate School, College of Engineering and Information Technology, Department of Information Systems, Program in Information Systems, Baltimore, MD 21227. Offers MS, PhD. *Program availability:* Part-time, 100% online. *Students:* 194 full-time (84 women), 235 part-time (89 women); includes 93 minority (37 Black or African American, non-Hispanic/Latino; 2 American Indian or Alaska Native, non-Hispanic/Latino; 41 Asian, non-Hispanic/Latino; 5 Hispanic/Latino; 8 Two or more races, non-Hispanic/Latino), 202 international. Average age 31. 426 applicants, 59% accepted, 102 enrolled. In 2016, 138 master's, 7 doctorates awarded. *Degree requirements:* For master's, comprehensive exam (for some programs), thesis optional; for doctorate, comprehensive exam, thesis/dissertation. *Entrance requirements:* For master's, minimum GPA of 3.0; for doctorate, GRE General Test or GMAT, competence in statistical analysis, experimental design, programming, databases, and computer networks. Additional exam requirements/recommendations for international students: Required—TOEFL (minimum score 550 paper-based; 80 iBT). *Application deadline:* For fall admission, 6/1 for domestic students, 1/1 for international students; for spring admission, 11/1 for domestic students, 6/1 for international students. Applications are processed on a rolling basis. Application fee: $70. Electronic applications accepted. *Expenses:* Contact institution. *Financial support:* In 2016–17, 21 research assistantships with full tuition reimbursements (averaging $20,000 per year), 14 teaching assistantships with full tuition reimbursements (averaging $17,000 per year) were awarded; fellowships with full tuition reimbursements, career-related internships or fieldwork, Federal Work-Study, scholarships/grants, health care benefits, tuition waivers (partial), and unspecified assistantships also available. Support available to part-time students. Financial award application deadline: 6/30; financial award applicants required to submit FAFSA. *Faculty research:* Artificial intelligence/knowledge management, database/data mining, software engineering. *Unit head:* Dr. Arrya Gangopadhyay, Professor and Chair, 410-455-2620, Fax: 410-455-1217, E-mail: gangopad@umbc.edu. *Application contact:* Dr. Zhiyuan Chen, Associate Professor and Graduate Program Director, 410-455-8833, Fax: 410-455-1217, E-mail: zhchen@umbc.edu.
Website: http://www.is.umbc.edu/

University of Maryland University College, The Graduate School, Program in Information Technology, Adelphi, MD 20783. Offers MS. *Program availability:* Part-time, evening/weekend, online learning. *Students:* 16 full-time (8 women), 1,082 part-time (389 women); includes 573 minority (367 Black or African American, non-Hispanic/Latino; 2 American Indian or Alaska Native, non-Hispanic/Latino; 84 Asian, non-Hispanic/Latino; 75 Hispanic/Latino; 4 Native Hawaiian or other Pacific Islander, non-Hispanic/Latino; 41 Two or more races, non-Hispanic/Latino), 40 international. Average age 34. 331 applicants, 100% accepted, 229 enrolled. In 2016, 229 master's awarded. *Degree requirements:* For master's, thesis or alternative, capstone course. *Application deadline:* Applications are processed on a rolling basis. Application fee: $50. Electronic applications accepted. *Expenses:* Tuition, state resident: part-time $458 per credit. Tuition, nonresident: part-time $659 per credit. *Financial support:* Federal Work-Study and scholarships/grants available. Support available to part-time students. Financial award application deadline: 6/1; financial award applicants required to submit FAFSA. *Unit head:* Les Pang, Program Director, 240-684-2400, Fax: 240-684-2401, E-mail: les.pang@umuc.edu. *Application contact:* Coordinator, Graduate Admissions, 800-888-8682, Fax: 240-684-2151, E-mail: newgrad@umuc.edu.
Website: http://www.umuc.edu/academic-programs/masters-degrees/information-technology.cfm

University of Massachusetts Dartmouth, Graduate School, College of Engineering, Program in Engineering and Applied Science, North Dartmouth, MA 02747-2300. Offers applied mechanics and materials (PhD); computational science and engineering (PhD); computer science and information systems (PhD); engineering and applied science (PhD); industrial and systems engineering (PhD). *Program availability:* Part-time. *Students:* 23 full-time (7 women), 8 part-time (3 women); includes 2 minority (both Black or African American, non-Hispanic/Latino), 15 international. Average age 31. 14 applicants, 79% accepted, 7 enrolled. *Degree requirements:* For doctorate, comprehensive exam, thesis/dissertation. *Entrance requirements:* For doctorate, GRE, statement of purpose (minimum of 300 words), resume, 3 letters of recommendation, official transcripts. Additional exam requirements/recommendations for international students: Required—TOEFL (minimum score 550 paper-based; 79 iBT). *Application deadline:* For fall admission, 2/15 priority date for domestic students, 1/15 priority date for international students; for spring admission, 11/15 priority date for domestic students, 10/15 priority date for international students. Application fee: $60. Electronic applications accepted. *Expenses:* Tuition, state resident: full-time $14,994; part-time $624.75 per credit. Tuition, nonresident: full-time $27,068; part-time $1127.83 per credit. *Required fees:* $405; $25.88 per credit. Tuition and fees vary according to course load and reciprocity agreements. *Financial support:* In 2016–17, 11 fellowships (averaging $16,591 per year), 12 research assistantships (averaging $5,160 per year) were awarded; institutionally sponsored loans, scholarships/grants, and doctoral support also available. Support available to part-time students. Financial award application deadline: 3/1; financial award applicants required to submit FAFSA. *Faculty research:* Tissue/cell engineering, bio transport sensors/networks, marine systems biomimetic materials, composite/polymeric materials, resilient infrastructure robotics, renewable energy. *Total annual research expenditures:* $253,000. *Unit head:* Gaurav Khanna, Graduate Program Director, Engineering and Applied Science, 508-910-6605, Fax: 508-999-9115, E-mail: gkhanna@umassd.edu. *Application contact:* Steven Briggs, Director of Marketing and Recruitment for Graduate Studies, 508-999-8604, Fax: 508-999-8183, E-mail: graduate@umassd.edu.
Website: http://www.umassd.edu/engineering/graduate/doctoraldegreeprograms/egrandappliedsciencephd/

University of Michigan, Rackham Graduate School, School of Information, Ann Arbor, MI 48109-1285. Offers health informatics (MHI); information (MSI, PhD). *Accreditation:* ALA (one or more programs are accredited). *Program availability:* Part-

time. *Students:* 453 full-time (270 women), 32 part-time (20 women); includes 99 minority (16 Black or African American, non-Hispanic/Latino; 49 Asian, non-Hispanic/Latino; 21 Hispanic/Latino; 13 Two or more races, non-Hispanic/Latino), 212 international. Average age 27. 829 applicants, 53% accepted, 199 enrolled. In 2016, 179 master's, 7 doctorates awarded. Terminal master's awarded for partial completion of doctoral program. *Degree requirements:* For master's, thesis optional, internship; for doctorate, thesis/dissertation. *Entrance requirements:* For master's and doctorate, GRE General Test. Additional exam requirements/recommendations for international students: Required—TOEFL (minimum score 100 iBT). *Application deadline:* Applications are processed on a rolling basis. Application fee: $75 ($90 for international students). Electronic applications accepted. *Expenses:* Contact institution. *Financial support:* In 2016–17, 122 students received support, including 2 fellowships (averaging $28,200 per year), 33 research assistantships (averaging $28,200 per year), 41 teaching assistantships (averaging $28,200 per year); scholarships/grants and tuition waivers (full and partial) also available. *Unit head:* Dr. Thomas A. Finholt, Dean, School of Information, 734-647-3576. *Application contact:* School of Information Admissions, 734-763-2285, Fax: 734-615-3587, E-mail: umsi.admissions@umich.edu.
Website: http://www.si.umich.edu/

See Display below and Close-Up on page 375.

University of Michigan–Dearborn, College of Engineering and Computer Science, Master of Science Program in Computer and Information Science, Dearborn, MI 48128. Offers MS. *Program availability:* Part-time, evening/weekend, 100% online. *Faculty:* 16 full-time (1 woman), 2 part-time/adjunct (0 women). *Students:* 39 full-time (17 women), 49 part-time (17 women); includes 14 minority (7 Black or African American, non-Hispanic/Latino; 4 Asian, non-Hispanic/Latino; 1 Hispanic/Latino; 2 Two or more races, non-Hispanic/Latino), 55 international. Average age 26. 113 applicants, 65% accepted, 34 enrolled. In 2016, 31 master's awarded. *Degree requirements:* For master's, thesis optional. *Entrance requirements:* For master's, bachelor's degree with minimum GPA of 3.0. Additional exam requirements/recommendations for international students: Required—TOEFL (minimum score 560 paper-based; 84 iBT), IELTS (minimum score 6.5). *Application deadline:* For fall admission, 8/1 priority date for domestic students, 5/1 for international students; for winter admission, 12/1 priority date for domestic students, 9/1 for international students; for spring admission, 4/1 priority date for domestic students, 1/1 for international students. Applications are processed on a rolling basis. Application fee: $60. Electronic applications accepted. *Expenses:* Tuition, state resident: full-time $13,118; part-time $2280 per term. Tuition, nonresident: full-time $21,816; part-time $3771 per term. *Required fees:* $866; $658 per unit. $329 per term. Tuition and fees vary according to program. *Financial support:* Research assistantships, teaching assistantships, career-related internships or fieldwork, scholarships/grants, unspecified assistantships, and non-resident tuition scholarships available. Support available to part-time students. Financial award application deadline: 3/1; financial award applicants required to submit FAFSA. *Faculty research:* Data science, security, networks, databases and information systems, natural language processing. *Unit head:* Dr. William I. Grosky, Chair, 313-583-6424, E-mail: wgrosky@umich.edu. *Application contact:* Office of Graduate Studies, 313-583-6321, Fax: 313-593-4256, E-mail: umd-graduatestudies@umich.edu.
Website: https://umdearborn.edu/cecs/departments/computer-and-information-science/graduate-programs/masters-computer-and-information-science

University of Michigan–Dearborn, College of Engineering and Computer Science, PhD Program in Computer and Information Science, Dearborn, MI 48128. Offers data management (PhD); data science (PhD); software engineering (PhD); systems and security (PhD). *Program availability:* Part-time, evening/weekend. *Degree requirements:* For doctorate, thesis/dissertation. *Entrance requirements:* For doctorate, GRE, bachelor's or master's degree in computer science or closely-related field. Additional exam requirements/recommendations for international students: Required—TOEFL (minimum score 84 iBT), IELTS (minimum score 6.5). *Application deadline:* For fall admission, 2/15 for domestic and international students. Application fee: $60. Electronic applications accepted. *Expenses:* Tuition, state resident: full-time $13,118; part-time $2280 per term. Tuition, nonresident: full-time $21,816; part-time $3771 per term. *Required fees:* $866; $658 per unit. $329 per term. Tuition and fees vary according to program. *Financial support:* Research assistantships, teaching assistantships, scholarships/grants, health care benefits, and unspecified assistantships available. Financial award application deadline: 2/15; financial award applicants required to submit FAFSA. *Unit head:* Dr. Brahim Medjahed, Director, 313-583-6449, E-mail: brahim@umich.edu. *Application contact:* Office of Graduate Studies Staff, 313-583-6321, E-mail: umd-graduatestudies@umich.edu.
Website: https://umdearborn.edu/cecs/departments/computer-and-information-science/graduate-programs/phd-computer-and-information-science

University of Michigan–Flint, College of Arts and Sciences, Program in Computer Science and Information Systems, Flint, MI 48502-1950. Offers computer science (MS); information systems (MS), including business information systems, health information systems. *Program availability:* Part-time, evening/weekend, 100% online. *Faculty:* 29 full-time (7 women), 12 part-time/adjunct (7 women). *Students:* 35 full-time (17 women), 91 part-time (24 women); includes 11 minority (3 Black or African American, non-Hispanic/Latino; 2 Asian, non-Hispanic/Latino; 4 Hispanic/Latino; 1 Native Hawaiian or other Pacific Islander, non-Hispanic/Latino; 1 Two or more races, non-Hispanic/Latino), 82 international. Average age 28. 712 applicants, 29% accepted, 29 enrolled. In 2016, 171 master's awarded. *Degree requirements:* For master's, thesis optional. *Entrance requirements:* For master's, BS from regionally-accredited institution in computer science, computer information systems, or computer engineering (preferred); minimum overall undergraduate GPA of 3.0. Additional exam requirements/recommendations for international students: Required—TOEFL (minimum score 84 iBT), IELTS (minimum score 6.5). *Application deadline:* For fall admission, 5/1 for domestic students, 2/1 for international students; for winter admission, 10/1 for domestic students, 8/1 for international students; for spring admission, 3/15 for domestic students, 1/1 for international students; for summer admission, 5/15 for domestic students, 3/1 for international students. Applications are processed on a rolling basis. Application fee: $55. Electronic applications accepted. *Expenses:* Contact institution. *Financial support:* Federal Work-Study, scholarships/grants, and unspecified assistantships available. Support available to part-time students. Financial award application deadline: 3/1; financial award applicants required to submit FAFSA. *Faculty research:* Computer network systems, database management systems, artificial intelligence and controlled systems. *Unit head:* Dr. Jeffrey Livermore, Director, 810-762-3131, Fax: 810-766-6780, E-mail: jefflive@umflint.edu. *Application contact:* Bradley T. Maki, Director of Graduate Admissions, 810-762-3171, Fax: 810-766-6789, E-mail: bmaki@umflint.edu.
Website: http://www.umflint.edu/graduateprograms/computer-science-information-systems-ms

University of Nebraska at Omaha, Graduate Studies, College of Information Science and Technology, Department of Information Systems and Quantitative Analysis, Omaha, NE 68182. Offers data analytics (Certificate); information assurance (Certificate); information technology (MIT, PhD); management information systems (MS); project management (Certificate); systems analysis and design (Certificate). *Program availability:* Part-time, evening/weekend. *Faculty:* 6 full-time (1 woman). *Students:* 140 full-time (53 women), 102 part-time (29 women); includes 25 minority (9 Black or African American, non-Hispanic/Latino; 7 Asian, non-Hispanic/Latino; 6 Hispanic/Latino; 3 Two or more races, non-Hispanic/Latino), 161 international. Average age 29. 342 applicants, 50% accepted, 68 enrolled. In 2016, 84 master's, 8 doctorates, 54 other advanced

degrees awarded. *Degree requirements:* For master's, comprehensive exam, thesis (for some programs); for doctorate, comprehensive exam, thesis/dissertation. *Entrance requirements:* For master's, GRE General Test, minimum GPA of 3.0, 3 letters of recommendation, writing sample, resume, official transcripts; for doctorate, GMAT or GRE General Test, minimum GPA of 3.0, 3 letters of recommendation, writing sample, resume, official transcripts; for Certificate, minimum GPA of 3.0, official transcripts. Additional exam requirements/recommendations for international students: Required—TOEFL, IELTS, PTE. *Application deadline:* For fall admission, 2/15 for domestic and international students; for spring admission, 9/15 for domestic and international students; for summer admission, 4/1 for domestic and international students. Applications are processed on a rolling basis. Application fee: $45. Electronic applications accepted. *Financial support:* In 2016–17, 30 students received support, including 24 research assistantships with tuition reimbursements available, 6 teaching assistantships with tuition reimbursements available; fellowships, career-related internships or fieldwork, Federal Work-Study, scholarships/grants, health care benefits, tuition waivers (partial), and unspecified assistantships also available. Financial award application deadline: 3/1; financial award applicants required to submit FAFSA. *Unit head:* Dr. Peter Wolcott, Chairperson, 402-554-2341, E-mail: graduate@unomaha.edu. *Application contact:* Dr. Martina Greiner, Graduate Program Chair, 402-554-2341, E-mail: graduate@unomaha.edu.

University of Nebraska–Lincoln, Graduate College, College of Arts and Sciences and College of Engineering, Department of Computer Science and Engineering, Lincoln, NE 68588. Offers bioinformatics (MS, PhD); computer engineering (MS, PhD); computer science (MS, PhD); information technology (PhD). *Degree requirements:* For master's, thesis optional; for doctorate, comprehensive exam, thesis/dissertation. *Entrance requirements:* For master's and doctorate, GRE General Test. Additional exam requirements/recommendations for international students: Required—TOEFL (minimum score 600 paper-based). Electronic applications accepted. *Faculty research:* Software engineering, geo- and bio-informatics, scientific computation, secure communication.

University of North Alabama, College of Arts and Sciences, Department of Interdisciplinary and Professional Studies, Florence, AL 35632-0001. Offers professional studies (MPS), including community development, information technology, security and safety leadership. *Program availability:* Part-time. *Faculty:* 1 full-time (0 women), 1 part-time/adjunct (0 women). *Students:* 12 full-time (8 women), 40 part-time (29 women); includes 6 minority (5 Black or African American, non-Hispanic/Latino; 1 Asian, non-Hispanic/Latino), 8 international. Average age 35. 25 applicants, 76% accepted, 15 enrolled. In 2016, 11 master's awarded. *Degree requirements:* For master's, thesis optional. *Entrance requirements:* For master's, ETS PPI, baccalaureate degree from accredited institution; minimum cumulative GPA of 2.75 or 3.0 in last 60 hours of undergraduate study; personal statement. Additional exam requirements/recommendations for international students: Required—TOEFL (minimum score 79 iBT), IELTS (minimum score 6), PTE (minimum score 54). *Application deadline:* Applications are processed on a rolling basis. Application fee: $50 ($100 for international students). Electronic applications accepted. *Expenses:* Tuition, state resident: full-time $2799; part-time $1866 per semester. Tuition, nonresident: full-time $5598; part-time $3732 per semester. *Required fees:* $915; $642 per semester. Tuition and fees vary according to course load. *Financial support:* In 2016–17, 9 students received support. Scholarships/grants and unspecified assistantships available. Financial award application deadline: 12/1; financial award applicants required to submit FAFSA. *Unit head:* Dr. Craig T. Robertson, Director, 256-765-5003, E-mail: ctrobertson@una.edu. *Application contact:* Hillary N. Coats, Graduate Admissions Coordinator, 256-765-4447, E-mail: graduate@una.edu.
Website: https://www.una.edu/interdisciplinary-studies/

The University of North Carolina at Charlotte, College of Computing and Informatics, Department of Software and Information Systems, Charlotte, NC 28223-0001. Offers information security and privacy (Graduate Certificate); information technology (MS); management of information technology (Graduate Certificate); network security (Graduate Certificate); secure software development (Graduate Certificate). *Program availability:* Part-time, evening/weekend. *Faculty:* 15 full-time (6 women), 7 part-time/adjunct (0 women). *Students:* 96 full-time (41 women), 92 part-time (33 women); includes 24 minority (16 Black or African American, non-Hispanic/Latino; 2 Asian, non-Hispanic/Latino; 2 Hispanic/Latino; 4 Two or more races, non-Hispanic/Latino), 144 international. Average age 27. 557 applicants, 38% accepted, 55 enrolled. In 2016, 139 master's, 5 other advanced degrees awarded. *Degree requirements:* For master's, project, internship, or thesis. *Entrance requirements:* For master's, GRE or GMAT, undergraduate or equivalent course work in data structures, object-oriented programming in C++, C#, or Java with minimum GPA of 3.0; for Graduate Certificate, bachelor's degree from accredited institution in computing, mathematical, engineering or business discipline with minimum overall GPA of 2.8, junior/senior 3.0; substantial knowledge of data structures and object-oriented programming in C++, C# or Java. Additional exam requirements/recommendations for international students: Required—TOEFL (minimum score 523 paper-based, 70 iBT) or IELTS (6.5). *Application deadline:* For fall admission, 3/1 for domestic and international students; for spring admission, 10/1 for domestic and international students. Applications are processed on a rolling basis. Application fee: $75. Electronic applications accepted. *Expenses:* Contact institution. *Financial support:* In 2016–17, 62 students received support, including 1 fellowship (averaging $70,000 per year), 28 research assistantships (averaging $9,899 per year), 33 teaching assistantships (averaging $9,193 per year); career-related internships or fieldwork, institutionally sponsored loans, scholarships/grants, and unspecified assistantships also available. Support available to part-time students. Financial award application deadline: 3/1; financial award applicants required to submit FAFSA. *Total annual research expenditures:* $2.8 million. *Unit head:* Dr. Mary Lou Maher, Chair, 704-687-1940, E-mail: mmaher9@uncc.edu. *Application contact:* Kathy B. Giddings, Director of Graduate Admissions, 704-687-5503, Fax: 704-687-1668, E-mail: gradadm@uncc.edu.
Website: http://sis.uncc.edu/

University of North Texas, Robert B. Toulouse School of Graduate Studies, Denton, TX 76203-5459. Offers accounting (MS); applied anthropology (MA, MS); applied behavior analysis (Certificate); applied geography (MA); applied technology and performance improvement (M Ed, MS); art education (MA); art history (MA); art museum education (Certificate); arts leadership (Certificate); audiology (Au D); behavior analysis (MS); behavioral science (PhD); biochemistry and molecular biology (MS); biology (MA, MS); biomedical engineering (MS); business analysis (MS); chemistry (MS); clinical health psychology (PhD); communication studies (MA, MS); computer engineering (MS); computer science (MS); counseling (M Ed, MS), including clinical mental health counseling (MS), college and university counseling, elementary school counseling, secondary school counseling; creative writing (MA); criminal justice (MS); curriculum and instruction (M Ed); decision sciences (MBA); design (MA, MFA), including fashion design (MFA), innovation studies, interior design (MFA); early childhood studies (MS); economics (MS); educational leadership (M Ed, Ed D); educational psychology (MS, PhD), including family studies (MS), gifted and talented (MS), human development (MS), learning and cognition (MS), research, measurement and evaluation (MS); electrical engineering (MS); emergency management (MPA); engineering technology (MS); English (MA); English as a second language (MA); environmental science (MS); finance (MBA, MS); financial management (MPA); French (MA); health services management (MBA); higher education (M Ed, Ed D); history (MA, MS); hospitality management (MS); human resources management (MPA); information science (MS); information systems (PhD); information technologies (MBA); interdisciplinary studies (MA, MS); international studies (MA); international sustainable tourism (MS); jazz studies (MM); journalism (MA, MJ, Graduate Certificate), including interactive and virtual digital communication (Graduate Certificate), narrative journalism (Graduate Certificate), public relations (Graduate Certificate); kinesiology (MS); linguistics (MA); local government management (MPA); logistics (PhD); logistics and supply chain management (MBA); long-term care, senior housing, and aging services (MA); management (PhD); marketing (MBA); mathematics (MA, MS); mechanical and energy engineering (MS, PhD); music (MA), including ethnomusicology, music theory, musicology, performance; music composition (PhD); music education (MM Ed, PhD); nonprofit management (MPA); operations and supply chain management (MBA); performance (MM, DMA); philosophy (MA); political science (MA); professional and technical communication (MA); radio, television and film (MA, MFA); rehabilitation counseling (Certificate); sociology (MA); Spanish (MA); special education (M Ed); speech-language pathology (MA); strategic management (MBA); studio art (MFA); teaching (M Ed); MBA/MS. *Program availability:* Part-time, evening/weekend, online learning. Terminal master's awarded for partial completion of doctoral program. *Degree requirements:* For master's, variable foreign language requirement, comprehensive exam (for some programs), thesis (for some programs); for doctorate, variable foreign language requirement, comprehensive exam (for some programs), thesis/dissertation; for other advanced degree, variable foreign language requirement, comprehensive exam (for some programs). *Entrance requirements:* For master's and doctorate, GRE, GMAT. Additional exam requirements/recommendations for international students: Required—TOEFL (minimum score 550 paper-based; 79 iBT). Electronic applications accepted.

University of Oregon, Graduate School, College of Arts and Sciences, Department of Computer and Information Science, Eugene, OR 97403. Offers MA, MS, PhD. *Program availability:* Part-time. Terminal master's awarded for partial completion of doctoral program. *Degree requirements:* For doctorate, thesis/dissertation. *Entrance requirements:* For master's and doctorate, GRE General Test, minimum GPA of 3.0. Additional exam requirements/recommendations for international students: Required—TOEFL. *Faculty research:* Artificial intelligence, graphics, natural-language processing, expert systems, operating systems.

University of Ottawa, Faculty of Graduate and Postdoctoral Studies, Faculty of Engineering, Engineering Management Program, Ottawa, ON K1N 6N5, Canada. Offers engineering management (M Eng); information technology (Certificate); project management (Certificate). *Degree requirements:* For master's, thesis or alternative. *Entrance requirements:* For master's and Certificate, honors degree or equivalent, minimum B average. Electronic applications accepted.

University of Pennsylvania, School of Engineering and Applied Science, Department of Computer and Information Science, Philadelphia, PA 19104. Offers computer and information science (MSE, PhD); computer and information technology (MCIT); computer graphics and game technology (MSE). *Program availability:* Part-time. *Faculty:* 53 full-time (6 women), 8 part-time/adjunct (2 women). *Students:* 304 full-time (84 women), 96 part-time (36 women); includes 38 minority (4 Black or African American, non-Hispanic/Latino; 26 Asian, non-Hispanic/Latino; 6 Hispanic/Latino; 2 Two or more races, non-Hispanic/Latino), 233 international. Average age 26. 2,114 applicants, 17% accepted, 209 enrolled. In 2016, 142 master's, 14 doctorates awarded. *Degree requirements:* For master's, comprehensive exam, thesis optional; for doctorate, comprehensive exam, thesis/dissertation. *Entrance requirements:* For master's and doctorate, GRE. Additional exam requirements/recommendations for international students: Required—TOEFL (minimum score 100 iBT), IELTS (minimum score 7). *Application deadline:* For fall admission, 3/15 priority date for domestic and international students. Application fee: $80. Electronic applications accepted. *Expenses: Tuition:* Full-time $31,068; part-time $5762 per course. *Required fees:* $3200; $336 per course. Full-time tuition and fees vary according to degree level, program and student level. Part-time tuition and fees vary according to course load, degree level and program. *Faculty research:* Artificial intelligence, robotics, software engineering, computational linguistics, machine learning. *Application contact:* William Fenton, Assistant Director of Graduate Admissions, 215-898-4542, Fax: 215-573-5577, E-mail: gradstudies@seas.upenn.edu.
Website: http://www.cis.upenn.edu/prospective-students/graduate/

University of Pittsburgh, School of Information Sciences, Information Science and Technology Program, Pittsburgh, PA 15260. Offers big data (Post-Master's Certificate, Postbaccalaureate Certificate); information science (MSIS, PhD), including information science (PhD), telecommunications (PhD); information science and technology (Certificate); security assured information systems (Post-Master's Certificate, Postbaccalaureate Certificate). *Program availability:* Part-time, evening/weekend, 100% online. *Faculty:* 17 full-time (3 women), 14 part-time/adjunct (3 women). *Students:* 240 full-time (93 women), 58 part-time (24 women); includes 14 minority (2 Black or African American, non-Hispanic/Latino; 5 Asian, non-Hispanic/Latino; 4 Hispanic/Latino; 3 Two or more races, non-Hispanic/Latino), 248 international. Average age 28. 675 applicants, 71% accepted, 107 enrolled. In 2016, 133 master's, 6 doctorates awarded. *Degree requirements:* For master's, thesis optional; for doctorate, comprehensive exam, thesis/dissertation. *Entrance requirements:* For master's, GRE General Test, GMAT, bachelor's degree with minimum GPA of 3.0; course work in structured programming language, statistics, and mathematics; for doctorate, GRE General Test, GMAT, master's degree; minimum GPA of 3.3; course work in statistics or mathematics, programming, cognitive psychology, systems analysis and design, and data structures; for other advanced degree, master's degree in information science, telecommunications, or related field. Additional exam requirements/recommendations for international students: Required—TOEFL (minimum score 550 paper-based; 80 iBT). *Application deadline:* For fall admission, 7/15 priority date for domestic students, 1/15 priority date for international students; for winter admission, 11/1 priority date for domestic students, 6/15 priority date for international students; for spring admission, 11/1 priority date for domestic students, 6/15 priority date for international students; for summer admission, 3/15 priority date for domestic students, 12/15 priority date for international students. Applications are processed on a rolling basis. Application fee: $50. Electronic applications accepted. *Expenses:* $22,628 per year in-state, $37,754 per year out-of-state (fall and spring); $931 per credit in-state, $1,553 per credit out-of-state (summer). *Financial support:* Fellowships with full and partial tuition reimbursements, research assistantships with full and partial tuition reimbursements, teaching assistantships with full and partial tuition reimbursements, career-related internships or fieldwork, institutionally sponsored loans, scholarships/grants, traineeships, health care benefits, and unspecified assistantships available. Financial award application deadline: 1/15; financial award applicants required to submit FAFSA. *Faculty research:* Big data, systems analysis and design, geoinformatics, database and Web systems, information assurance and security, cloud computing, social computing. *Unit head:* Dr. Martin Weiss, Program Chair, 412-624-9430, Fax: 421-624-5231, E-mail: mbw@pitt.edu. *Application contact:* Shabana Reza, Enrollment Manager, 412-624-3988, Fax: 412-624-5231, E-mail: sreza@sis.pitt.edu.
Website: http://www.ischool.pitt.edu/ist/

Information Science

University of Pittsburgh, School of Information Sciences, Telecommunications and Networking Program, Pittsburgh, PA 15260. Offers information science (PhD), including telecommunications; telecommunications and networking (MST, Certificate). *Program availability:* Part-time, evening/weekend, 100% online. *Faculty:* 4 full-time (0 women), 1 part-time/adjunct (0 women). *Students:* 41 full-time (9 women), 3 part-time (1 woman), 43 international. Average age 26. 131 applicants, 71% accepted, 20 enrolled. In 2016, 28 master's, 3 doctorates awarded. *Degree requirements:* For master's, thesis optional; for doctorate, comprehensive exam, thesis/dissertation. *Entrance requirements:* For master's, GRE, GMAT, bachelor's degree with minimum GPA of 3.0; previous course work in computer programming, calculus, and probability; for doctorate, GRE, GMAT, master's degree; minimum GPA of 3.3; course work in computer programming, differential and integral calculus, probability, and statistics; for Certificate, MSIS, MST from accredited university. Additional exam requirements/recommendations for international students: Required—TOEFL (minimum score 550 paper-based; 80 iBT). *Application deadline:* For fall admission, 1/15 priority date for domestic and international students; for winter admission, 9/15 priority date for domestic students, 6/15 priority date for international students; for spring admission, 9/15 priority date for domestic students, 6/15 priority date for international students; for summer admission, 1/15 priority date for domestic students, 12/15 priority date for international students. Applications are processed on a rolling basis. Application fee: $50. Electronic applications accepted. *Expenses:* $22,628 per year in-state, $37,754 per year out-of-state (fall and spring); $931 per credit in-state, $1,553 per credit out-of-state (summer). *Financial support:* Fellowships with full and partial tuition reimbursements, research assistantships with full and partial tuition reimbursements, teaching assistantships with full and partial tuition reimbursements, career-related internships or fieldwork, institutionally sponsored loans, scholarships/grants, traineeships, health care benefits, and unspecified assistantships available. Financial award application deadline: 1/15; financial award applicants required to submit FAFSA. *Faculty research:* Telecommunication systems, telecommunications policy, network design and management, wireless information systems, network security, cloud computing, big data. *Unit head:* Dr. Martin Weiss, Program Chair, 412-624-9430, Fax: 412-624-5231, E-mail: mbw@pitt.edu. *Application contact:* Shabana Reza, Enrollment Manager, 412-624-3988, Fax: 412-624-5231, E-mail: sreza@sis.pitt.edu.
Website: http://www.ischool.pitt.edu/tele/

University of Puerto Rico, Mayagüez Campus, Graduate Studies, College of Engineering, Department of Electrical and Computer Engineering, Mayagüez, PR 00681-9000. Offers computer engineering (ME, MS); computing and information sciences and engineering (PhD); electrical engineering (ME, MS). *Program availability:* Part-time. *Faculty:* 48 full-time (6 women). *Students:* 45 full-time (6 women), 8 part-time (3 women); includes 45 minority (all Hispanic/Latino), 5 international. Average age 25. 30 applicants, 83% accepted, 18 enrolled. In 2016, 12 master's awarded. Terminal master's awarded for partial completion of doctoral program. *Degree requirements:* For master's, one foreign language, comprehensive exam, thesis; for doctorate, one foreign language, comprehensive exam, thesis/dissertation. *Entrance requirements:* For master's and doctorate, proficiency in English and Spanish; BS in electrical or computer engineering, or equivalent; minimum GPA of 3.0. *Application deadline:* For fall admission, 2/15 for domestic and international students; for spring admission, 9/15 for domestic and international students. Applications are processed on a rolling basis. Application fee: $25. Electronic applications accepted. *Expenses: Tuition, area resident:* Full-time $2466. *International tuition:* $7166 full-time. *Required fees:* $210. One-time fee: $5 full-time. Tuition and fees vary according to course level, campus/location, program and student level. *Financial support:* In 2016–17, 50 students received support, including 41 research assistantships with full and partial tuition reimbursements available (averaging $3,442 per year), 26 teaching assistantships with full and partial tuition reimbursements available (averaging $4,149 per year); unspecified assistantships also available. *Faculty research:* Digital signal processing, power electronics, microwave ocean emissivity, parallel and distributed computing, microwave remote sensing. *Unit head:* Jose Colom-Ustaris, Ph.D., Department Head, 787-832-4040 Ext. 3086, Fax: 787-831-7564, E-mail: jose.colom1@upr.edu. *Application contact:* Claribel Lorenzo, Administrative Secretary V, 787-832-4040 Ext. 3821, E-mail: claribel.lorenzo@upr.edu.
Website: https://ece.uprm.edu/

University of Puerto Rico, Río Piedras Campus, Graduate School of Information Sciences and Technologies, San Juan, PR 00931-3300. Offers administration of academic libraries (PMC); administration of public libraries (PMC); administration of special libraries (PMC); consultant in information services (PMC); documents and files administration (Post-Graduate Certificate); electronic information resources analyst (Post-Graduate Certificate); information science (MIS); librarianship and information services (MLS); school librarian (Post-Graduate Certificate); school librarian distance education mode (Post-Graduate Certificate); specialist in legal information (PMC). *Accreditation:* ALA. *Program availability:* Part-time. *Degree requirements:* For master's, comprehensive exam, thesis, portfolio. *Entrance requirements:* For master's, PAEG, GRE, interview, minimum GPA of 3.0, 3 letters of recommendation; for other advanced degree, PAEG, GRE, minimum GPA of 3.0, IST master's degree. *Faculty research:* Investigating the users needs and preferences for a specialized environmental library.

University of St. Thomas, Graduate Studies, School of Engineering, St. Paul, MN 55105-1096. Offers data science (MS); electrical engineering (MS); information technology (MS); manufacturing engineering (MS); manufacturing systems (Certificate); mechanical engineering (MS); medical device development (Certificate); regulatory science (MS); software engineering (MS); software management (MS); systems engineering (MS); technology leadership (Certificate); technology management (MS). *Accreditation:* ABET (one or more programs are accredited). *Entrance requirements:* For master's, resume, official transcripts. Additional exam requirements/recommendations for international students: Required—TOEFL (minimum score 550 paper-based). *Application deadline:* For fall admission, 8/1 priority date for domestic students; for spring admission, 1/1 priority date for domestic students. Applications are processed on a rolling basis. Application fee: $50. Electronic applications accepted. *Expenses:* Contact institution. *Financial support:* Fellowships, research assistantships, institutionally sponsored loans, and scholarships/grants available. Support available to part-time students. Financial award application deadline: 4/1; financial award applicants required to submit FAFSA. *Unit head:* Don Weinkauf, Dean, 651-962-5760, Fax: 651-962-6419, E-mail: dhweinkauf@stthomas.edu. *Application contact:* Tina M. Hansen, Graduate Program Manager, 651-962-5755, Fax: 651-962-6419, E-mail: tina.hansen@stthomas.edu.
Website: http://www.stthomas.edu/engineering/

University of South Africa, College of Human Sciences, Pretoria, South Africa. Offers adult education (M Ed); African languages (MA, PhD); African politics (MA, PhD); Afrikaans (MA, PhD); ancient history (MA, PhD); ancient Near Eastern studies (MA, PhD); anthropology (MA, PhD); applied linguistics (MA); Arabic (MA, PhD); archaeology (MA); art history (MA); Biblical archaeology (MA); Biblical studies (M Th, D Th, PhD); Christian spirituality (M Th, D Th); church history (M Th, D Th); classical studies (MA, PhD); clinical psychology (MA); communication (MA, PhD); comparative education (M Ed, Ed D); consulting psychology (D Admin, D Com, PhD); curriculum studies (M Ed, Ed D); development studies (M Admin, MA, D Admin, PhD); didactics (M Ed, Ed D); education (M Tech); education management (M Ed, Ed D); educational psychology (M Ed); English (MA); environmental education (M Ed); French (MA, PhD); German (MA, PhD); Greek (MA); guidance and counseling (M Ed); health studies (MA, PhD), including health sciences education (MA), health services management (MA), medical and surgical nursing science (critical care general) (MA), midwifery and neonatal nursing science (MA), trauma and emergency care (MA); history (MA, PhD); history of education (Ed D); inclusive education (M Ed, Ed D); information and communications technology policy and regulation (MA); information science (MA, MIS, PhD); international politics (MA, PhD); Islamic studies (MA, PhD); Italian (MA, PhD); Judaica (MA, PhD); linguistics (MA, PhD); mathematical education (M Ed); mathematics education (MA); missiology (M Th, D Th); modern Hebrew (MA, PhD); musicology (MA, MMus, D Mus, PhD); natural science education (M Ed); New Testament (M Th, D Th); Old Testament (D Th); pastoral therapy (M Th, D Th); philosophy (MA); philosophy of education (M Ed, Ed D); politics (MA, PhD); Portuguese (MA, PhD); practical theology (M Th, D Th); psychology (MA, MS, PhD); psychology of education (M Ed, Ed D); public health (MA); religious studies (MA, D Th, PhD); Romance languages (MA); Russian (MA, PhD); Semitic languages (MA, PhD); social behavior studies in HIV/AIDS (MA); social science (mental health) (MA); social science in development studies (MA); social science in psychology (MA); social science in social work (MA); social science in sociology (MA); social work (MSW, DSW, PhD); socio-education (M Ed, Ed D); sociolinguistics (MA); sociology (MA, PhD); Spanish (MA, PhD); systematic theology (M Th, D Th); TESOL (teaching English to speakers of other languages) (MA); theological ethics (M Th, D Th); theory of literature (MA, PhD); urban ministries (D Th); urban ministry (M Th).

University of South Carolina Upstate, Graduate Programs, Spartanburg, SC 29303-4999. Offers early childhood education (M Ed); elementary education (M Ed); informatics (MS); special education: visual impairment (M Ed). *Accreditation:* NCATE. *Program availability:* Part-time, evening/weekend. *Degree requirements:* For master's, professional portfolio. *Entrance requirements:* For master's, GRE General Test or MAT, interview, minimum undergraduate GPA of 2.5, teaching certificate, 2 letters of recommendation. *Faculty research:* Promoting university diversity awareness, rough and tumble play, social justice education, American Indian literatures and cultures, diversity and multicultural education, science teaching strategy.

University of Southern Mississippi, Graduate School, College of Education and Psychology, School of Library and Information Science, Hattiesburg, MS 39406. Offers archives and special collections (Graduate Certificate); library and information science (MLIS); youth services and literature (Graduate Certificate). *Accreditation:* ALA (one or more programs are accredited). *Program availability:* Part-time, evening/weekend, online learning. *Degree requirements:* For master's, comprehensive exam, thesis. *Entrance requirements:* For master's, GRE General Test, minimum GPA of 3.0. Additional exam requirements/recommendations for international students: Required—TOEFL, IELTS. *Application deadline:* For fall admission, 3/15 priority date for domestic students, 3/15 for international students; for spring admission, 1/10 priority date for domestic and international students. Applications are processed on a rolling basis. Application fee: $60. Electronic applications accepted. *Expenses: Tuition, area resident:* Full-time $15,708; part-time $437 per credit hour. *Financial support:* Fellowships with tuition reimbursements, research assistantships with full tuition reimbursements, teaching assistantships with full tuition reimbursements, career-related internships or fieldwork, Federal Work-Study, institutionally sponsored loans, scholarships/grants, health care benefits, and unspecified assistantships available. Financial award application deadline: 3/15; financial award applicants required to submit FAFSA. *Faculty research:* Printing, library history, children's literature, telecommunications, management. *Unit head:* Dr. Melanie J. Norton, Director, 601-266-4236, Fax: 601-266-5774. *Application contact:* Shonna Breland, Manager of Graduate Admissions, 601-266-6563, Fax: 601-266-5138.
Website: https://www.usm.edu/library-information-science

University of South Florida, College of Arts and Sciences, School of Information, Tampa, FL 33620-9951. Offers intelligence studies (MS), including cyber intelligence, strategic intelligence; library and information science (MA). *Accreditation:* ALA (one or more programs are accredited). *Program availability:* Part-time, evening/weekend, online learning. *Faculty:* 17 full-time (8 women). *Students:* 112 full-time (73 women), 163 part-time (127 women); includes 80 minority (28 Black or African American, non-Hispanic/Latino; 11 Asian, non-Hispanic/Latino; 32 Hispanic/Latino; 1 Native Hawaiian or other Pacific Islander, non-Hispanic/Latino; 8 Two or more races, non-Hispanic/Latino), 1 international. Average age 33. 167 applicants, 84% accepted, 90 enrolled. In 2016, 61 master's awarded. *Degree requirements:* For master's, comprehensive exam, thesis (for some programs). *Entrance requirements:* For master's, GRE General Test (for some programs). Additional exam requirements/recommendations for international students: Required—TOEFL (minimum score 550 paper-based; 79 iBT) or IELTS (minimum score 6.5). *Application deadline:* For fall admission, 6/1 for domestic students, 2/15 for international students; for spring admission, 10/15 for domestic students, 9/15 for international students. Applications are processed on a rolling basis. Application fee: $30. Electronic applications accepted. *Expenses:* Tuition, state resident: full-time $7766; part-time $431.43 per credit hour. Tuition, nonresident: full-time $15,789; part-time $877.17 per credit hour. *Required fees:* $37 per term. *Financial support:* In 2016–17, 47 students received support. Unspecified assistantships available. Financial award application deadline: 6/30. *Faculty research:* Youth services in libraries, community engagement and libraries, information architecture, biomedical informatics, health informatics. *Total annual research expenditures:* $378,531. *Unit head:* Dr. Jim Andrews, Director and Associate Professor, 813-974-2108, Fax: 813-974-6840, E-mail: jimandrews@usf.edu. *Application contact:* Dr. Diane Austin, Assistant Director, 813-974-6364, Fax: 813-974-6840, E-mail: dianeaustin@usf.edu.
Website: http://si.usf.edu/

The University of Tennessee, Graduate School, College of Communication and Information, School of Information Sciences, Knoxville, TN 37996. Offers MS, PhD. *Accreditation:* ALA (one or more programs are accredited). *Program availability:* Part-time, evening/weekend, online learning. *Degree requirements:* For master's, 42 semester hours; written comprehensive exam, online e-portfolio, or thesis; for doctorate, thesis/dissertation or alternative. *Entrance requirements:* For master's, GRE General Test, minimum GPA of 2.7; for doctorate, GRE General Test (minimum scores at or above the 50th percentile on the 3 components, taken within the past five years), master's degree; minimum undergraduate GPA of 3.0, graduate 3.5; recommendation letters from at least three former instructors or professional supervisors; personal statement; interview. Additional exam requirements/recommendations for international students: Required—TOEFL. Electronic applications accepted.

The University of Texas at El Paso, Graduate School, College of Engineering, Department of Computer Science, El Paso, TX 79968-0001. Offers computer science (MS, PhD); information technology (MSIT). *Program availability:* Part-time, evening/weekend. *Degree requirements:* For master's, thesis optional; for doctorate, thesis/dissertation. *Entrance requirements:* For master's, GRE, minimum GPA of 3.0; for doctorate, GRE, statement of purpose, letters of reference. Additional exam requirements/recommendations for international students: Required—TOEFL; Recommended—IELTS. Electronic applications accepted.

The University of Texas at San Antonio, College of Business, Department of Information Systems and Cyber Security, San Antonio, TX 78249-0617. Offers cyber security (MSIT); information technology (MS, PhD); management of technology (MBA); technology entrepreneurship and management (Certificate). *Program availability:* Part-time, evening/weekend. *Faculty:* 10 full-time (2 women), 4 part-time/adjunct (0 women). *Students:* 70 full-time (19 women), 73 part-time (21 women); includes 38 minority (6 Black or African American, non-Hispanic/Latino; 6 Asian, non-Hispanic/Latino; 24 Hispanic/Latino; 2 Two or more races, non-Hispanic/Latino), 38 international. Average age 30. 141 applicants, 59% accepted, 55 enrolled. In 2016, 45 master's, 1 doctorate, 6 other advanced degrees awarded. *Degree requirements:* For master's, comprehensive exam (for some programs), thesis optional; for doctorate, comprehensive exam, thesis/dissertation. *Entrance requirements:* For master's and doctorate, GMAT/GRE, official transcripts, statement of purpose, letters of recommendation. Additional exam requirements/recommendations for international students: Required—TOEFL (minimum score 550 paper-based; 79 iBT), IELTS (minimum score 6.5). *Application deadline:* For fall admission, 7/1 for domestic students, 4/1 for international students; for spring admission, 11/1 for domestic students, 9/1 for international students. Applications are processed on a rolling basis. Application fee: $45 ($80 for international students). Electronic applications accepted. *Expenses:* Contact institution. *Financial support:* In 2016–17, 15 students received support, including 1 fellowship with full tuition reimbursement available (averaging $25,000 per year), 10 research assistantships with tuition reimbursements available (averaging $9,000 per year), 12 teaching assistantships with tuition reimbursements available (averaging $9,000 per year); scholarships/grants, health care benefits, and unspecified assistantships also available. Support available to part-time students. Financial award application deadline: 2/15. *Faculty research:* Cyber security, digital forensics, economics of information systems, information systems privacy, information technology adoption. *Total annual research expenditures:* $650,902. *Unit head:* Dr. Yoris A. Au, Chair/Associate Professor, 210-458-6300, Fax: 210-458-6305, E-mail: yoris.au@utsa.edu.
Website: http://business.utsa.edu/directory/index.aspx?DepID-16

University of the Sacred Heart, Graduate Programs, Department of Business Administration, Program in Information Technology, San Juan, PR 00914-0383. Offers Certificate.

University of Washington, Graduate School, Information School, Seattle, WA 98195. Offers information management (MSIM), including business intelligence, data science, information architecture, information consulting, information security, user experience; information science (PhD); library and information science (MLIS). *Accreditation:* ALA (one or more programs are accredited). *Program availability:* Part-time, 100% online coursework with required attendance at on-campus orientation at start of program. *Faculty:* 35 full-time (19 women), 22 part-time/adjunct (12 women). *Students:* 367 full-time (233 women), 237 part-time (170 women); includes 132 minority (20 Black or African American, non-Hispanic/Latino; 9 American Indian or Alaska Native, non-Hispanic/Latino; 59 Asian, non-Hispanic/Latino; 41 Hispanic/Latino; 3 Native Hawaiian or other Pacific Islander, non-Hispanic/Latino), 151 international. Average age 32. 1,208 applicants, 39% accepted, 254 enrolled. In 2016, 237 master's, 2 doctorates awarded. Terminal master's awarded for partial completion of doctoral program. *Degree requirements:* For master's, comprehensive exam (for some programs), thesis or alternative, capstone project; for doctorate, comprehensive exam, thesis/dissertation. *Entrance requirements:* For master's, GRE General Test, GMAT; for doctorate, GRE General Test. Additional exam requirements/recommendations for international students: Required—TOEFL (minimum score 590 paper-based; 100 iBT). *Application deadline:* For fall admission, 12/1 priority date for domestic and international students. Application fee: $85. Electronic applications accepted. *Expenses:* $785 per quarter credit hour, $23,550 per year full-time, $1,000 university fees per quarter. *Financial support:* In 2016–17, 69 students received support, including 1 fellowship with full tuition reimbursement available (averaging $6,651 per year), 27 research assistantships with full tuition reimbursements available (averaging $19,418 per year), 27 teaching assistantships with full tuition reimbursements available (averaging $19,521 per year); Federal Work-Study, institutionally sponsored loans, scholarships/grants, health care benefits, tuition waivers (full and partial), and unspecified assistantships also available. Support available to part-time students. Financial award application deadline: 10/1; financial award applicants required to submit FAFSA. *Faculty research:* Human/computer interaction, information policy and ethics, knowledge organization, information literacy and access, data science, information assurance and cyber security, digital youth, information architecture, project management, systems analyst, user experience design. *Total annual research expenditures:* $3.6 million. *Unit head:* Dr. Harry Bruce, Dean, 206-616-0985, E-mail: harryb@uw.edu. *Application contact:* Kari Brothers, Admissions Counselor, 206-616-5541, Fax: 206-616-3152, E-mail: kari683@uw.edu.
Website: http://ischool.uw.edu/

University of Waterloo, Graduate Studies, Faculty of Engineering, Department of Management Sciences, Waterloo, ON N2L 3G1, Canada. Offers applied operations research (MA Sc, MMS, PhD); information systems (MA Sc, MMS, PhD); management of technology (MA Sc, MMS, PhD). *Program availability:* Part-time, online learning. *Degree requirements:* For master's, research paper or thesis; for doctorate, comprehensive exam, thesis/dissertation. *Entrance requirements:* For master's, GMAT or GRE, honors degree, minimum B average, resume; for doctorate, GMAT or GRE, master's degree, minimum A- average, resume. Additional exam requirements/recommendations for international students: Required—TOEFL, IELTS, PTE. Electronic applications accepted. *Faculty research:* Operations research, manufacturing systems, scheduling, information systems.

University of Wisconsin–Parkside, School of Business and Technology, Program in Computer and Information Systems, Kenosha, WI 53141-2000. Offers MSCIS. *Entrance requirements:* For master's, GRE General Test or GMAT, 3 letters of recommendation, minimum GPA of 3.0. *Faculty research:* Distributed systems, data bases, natural language processing, event-driven systems.

University of Wisconsin–Stout, Graduate School, College of Science, Technology, Engineering and Mathematics, Program in Information and Communication Technologies, Menomonie, WI 54751. Offers MS. *Program availability:* Part-time, online learning. *Degree requirements:* For master's, thesis. *Entrance requirements:* For master's, minimum GPA of 2.75. Additional exam requirements/recommendations for international students: Required—TOEFL (minimum score 500 paper-based; 61 iBT). Electronic applications accepted.

Western Governors University, College of Information Technology, Salt Lake City, UT 84107. Offers cybersecurity and information assurance (MS); data analytics (MS); information technology management (MS). *Program availability:* Online learning. *Degree requirements:* For master's, capstone project.

Youngstown State University, Graduate School, College of Science, Technology, Engineering and Mathematics, Department of Computer Science and Information Systems, Youngstown, OH 44555-0001. Offers computing and information systems (MCIS). *Program availability:* Part-time. *Degree requirements:* For master's, thesis or capstone project. *Entrance requirements:* For master's, GRE or GMAT. Additional exam requirements/recommendations for international students: Required—TOEFL (minimum score 550 paper-based). *Faculty research:* Networking, computational science, graphics and visualization, database and data mining, biometrics, artificial intelligence, online learning environments.

Internet Engineering

Hofstra University, School of Engineering and Applied Science, Hempstead, NY 11549. Offers computer science (MS), including cybersecurity, Web engineering. *Program availability:* Part-time, evening/weekend, blended/hybrid learning. *Faculty:* 10 full-time (3 women), 6 part-time/adjunct (1 woman). *Students:* 34 full-time (8 women), 20 part-time (5 women); includes 13 minority (1 American Indian or Alaska Native, non-Hispanic/Latino; 6 Asian, non-Hispanic/Latino; 4 Hispanic/Latino; 1 Native Hawaiian or other Pacific Islander, non-Hispanic/Latino; 1 Two or more races, non-Hispanic/Latino), 20 international. Average age 30. 48 applicants, 90% accepted, 15 enrolled. In 2016, 12 master's awarded. *Degree requirements:* For master's, thesis optional, 30 credits, minimum GPA of 3.0. *Entrance requirements:* For master's, GRE, minimum GPA of 3.0. Additional exam requirements/recommendations for international students: Required—TOEFL (minimum score 550 paper-based; 80 iBT). *Application deadline:* Applications are processed on a rolling basis. Application fee: $75. Electronic applications accepted. *Expenses: Tuition:* Full-time $1240. *Required fees:* $970. Tuition and fees vary according to program. *Financial support:* In 2016–17, 24 students received support, including 6 fellowships with full and partial tuition reimbursements available (averaging $2,647 per year); research assistantships with full and partial tuition reimbursements available, career-related internships or fieldwork, Federal Work-Study, institutionally sponsored loans, scholarships/grants, tuition waivers (full and partial), and unspecified assistantships also available. Support available to part-time students. Financial award applicants required to submit FAFSA. *Faculty research:* Data mining; system and network security; cell and tissue engineering; experimental fluid mechanics; stem education. *Total annual research expenditures:* $1.5 million. *Unit head:* Dr. Sina Rabbany, Dean, 516-463-6672, E-mail: sina.y.rabbany@hofstra.edu. *Application contact:* Sunil Samuel, Assistant Vice President of Admissions, 516-463-4723, Fax: 516-463-4664, E-mail: graduateadmission@hofstra.edu.
Website: http://www.hofstra.edu/academics/colleges/seas/

New Jersey Institute of Technology, Newark College of Engineering, Newark, NJ 07102. Offers biomedical engineering (MS, PhD); chemical engineering (MS, PhD); computer engineering (MS, PhD); electrical engineering (MS, PhD); engineering management (MS); environmental engineering (PhD); healthcare systems management (MS); industrial engineering (MS, PhD); Internet engineering (MS); manufacturing engineering (MS); mechanical engineering (MS, PhD); occupational safety and health engineering (MS); pharmaceutical bioprocessing (MS); pharmaceutical engineering (MS); pharmaceutical systems management (MS); power and energy systems (MS); telecommunications (MS); transportation (MS, PhD). *Program availability:* Part-time, evening/weekend. *Faculty:* 146 full-time (21 women), 119 part-time/adjunct (10 women). *Students:* 804 full-time (191 women), 550 part-time (129 women); includes 357 minority (82 Black or African American, non-Hispanic/Latino; 1 American Indian or Alaska Native, non-Hispanic/Latino; 138 Asian, non-Hispanic/Latino; 114 Hispanic/Latino; 22 Two or more races, non-Hispanic/Latino), 675 international. Average age 27. 2,959 applicants, 51% accepted, 442 enrolled. In 2016, 595 master's, 29 doctorates awarded. Terminal master's awarded for partial completion of doctoral program. *Degree requirements:* For master's, thesis optional; for doctorate, thesis/dissertation. *Entrance requirements:* For master's, GRE General Test; for doctorate, GRE General Test, minimum graduate GPA of 3.5. Additional exam requirements/recommendations for international students: Required—TOEFL (minimum score 550 paper-based; 79 iBT). *Application deadline:* For fall admission, 6/1 priority date for domestic students, 5/1 priority date for international students; for spring admission, 11/15 priority date for domestic and international students. Applications are processed on a rolling basis. Application fee: $75. Electronic applications accepted. *Expenses:* Contact institution. *Financial support:* In 2016–17, 172 students received support, including 1 fellowship (averaging $1,528 per year), 79 research assistantships (averaging $13,336 per year), 92 teaching assistantships (averaging $20,619 per year); scholarships/grants also available. Financial award application deadline: 1/15. *Faculty research:* Nonlinear signal processing, intelligent medical image analysis, calibration issues in coherent localization, computer-aided design, neural network for tool wear measurement. *Total annual research expenditures:* $11.1 million. *Unit head:* Dr. Moshe Kam, Dean, 973-596-5534, E-mail: moshe.kam@njit.edu. *Application contact:* Stephen Eck, Director of Admissions, 973-596-3300, Fax: 973-596-3461, E-mail: admissions@njit.edu.
Website: http://engineering.njit.edu/

Wilmington University, College of Technology, New Castle, DE 19720-6491. Offers geographic information systems (MS); information assurance (MS); information systems technologies (MS); Internet/Web design (MS); management and management information systems (MS). *Program availability:* Part-time, evening/weekend. *Faculty:* 5 full-time (1 woman), 114 part-time/adjunct (31 women). *Students:* 1,316 full-time (321 women), 263 part-time (79 women); includes 71 minority (53 Black or African American, non-Hispanic/Latino; 5 American Indian or Alaska Native, non-Hispanic/Latino; 8 Asian, non-Hispanic/Latino; 4 Hispanic/Latino; 1 Two or more races, non-Hispanic/Latino), 1,437 international. Average age 26. 856 applicants, 100% accepted, 332 enrolled. In 2016, 756 master's awarded. *Entrance requirements:* Additional exam requirements/recommendations for international students: Required—TOEFL (minimum score 500 paper-based). *Application deadline:* Applications are processed on a rolling basis. Application fee: $35. Electronic applications accepted. *Expenses: Tuition:* Full-time $8388; part-time $466 per credit. *Required fees:* $25 per semester. Tuition and fees vary according to degree level. *Unit head:* Dr. Mary Ann K. Westerfield, Dean. *Application contact:* Laura Morris, Director of Admissions, 877-967-5464, E-mail: infocenter@wilmu.edu.
Website: http://www.wilmu.edu/technology/

Medical Informatics

Arizona State University at the Tempe campus, College of Health Solutions, Department of Biomedical Informatics, Phoenix, AZ 85004. Offers MS, PhD. Terminal master's awarded for partial completion of doctoral program. *Degree requirements:* For master's, interactive Program of Study (iPOS) submitted before completing 50 percent of required credit hours; for doctorate, comprehensive exam, thesis/dissertation, interactive Program of Study (iPOS) submitted before completing 50 percent of required credit hours. *Entrance requirements:* For master's, GRE or MCAT, bachelor's degree with minimum GPA of 3.25 in computer science, biology, physiology, nursing, statistics, engineering, related fields, or unrelated fields with appropriate academic backgrounds; resume/curriculum vitae; statement of purpose; 3 letters of recommendation; all official transcripts; for doctorate, GRE or MCAT, bachelor's degree with minimum GPA of 3.5 in computer science, biology, physiology, nursing, statistics, engineering, related fields, or unrelated fields with appropriate academic backgrounds; resume/curriculum vitae; statement of purpose; 3 letters of recommendation; all official transcripts. Additional exam requirements/recommendations for international students: Required—TOEFL (minimum score 550 paper-based; 83 iBT), IELTS (minimum score 6.5). Electronic applications accepted.

Brandeis University, Rabb School of Continuing Studies, Division of Graduate Professional Studies, Master of Science in Health and Medical Informatics Program, Waltham, MA 02454-9110. Offers MS. *Program availability:* Part-time-only. *Faculty:* 45 part-time/adjunct (16 women). *Students:* 43 part-time (24 women); includes 18 minority (8 Black or African American, non-Hispanic/Latino; 9 Asian, non-Hispanic/Latino; 1 Two or more races, non-Hispanic/Latino). Average age 37. 15 applicants, 100% accepted, 14 enrolled. In 2016, 12 master's awarded. *Entrance requirements:* For master's, four-year bachelor's degree from regionally-accredited U.S. institution or equivalent; official transcript(s) from every college or university attended; resume or curriculum vitae; statement of goals; letter of recommendation. Additional exam requirements/recommendations for international students: Required—TWE (minimum score 4.5), TOEFL (minimum scores: 600 paper-based, 100 iBT), IELTS (7), or PTE (68). *Application deadline:* For fall admission, 6/21 priority date for domestic and international students; for winter admission, 9/13 priority date for domestic and international students; for spring admission, 12/20 priority date for domestic and international students; for summer admission, 3/14 priority date for domestic and international students. Applications are processed on a rolling basis. Application fee: $50. Electronic applications accepted. *Expenses:* $3,400 per course, $100 graduation fee. *Financial support:* Applicants required to submit FAFSA. *Unit head:* Arthur Harvey, Chair, 781-736-8787, E-mail: aharv0001@brandeis.edu. *Application contact:* Frances Stearns, Director of Admissions and Recruitment, 781-736-8785, E-mail: fstearns@brandeis.edu. Website: http://www.brandeis.edu/gps

Cambridge College, School of Management, Cambridge, MA 02138-5304. Offers business negotiation and conflict resolution (M Mgt); general business (M Mgt); health care informatics (M Mgt); health care management (M Mgt); leadership in human and organizational dynamics (M Mgt); non-profit and public organization management (M Mgt); small business development (M Mgt); technology management (M Mgt). *Program availability:* Part-time, evening/weekend. *Degree requirements:* For master's, thesis, seminars. *Entrance requirements:* For master's, resume, 2 professional references. Additional exam requirements/recommendations for international students: Required—TOEFL (minimum score 550 paper-based; 79 iBT), Michigan English Language Assessment Battery (minimum score 85); Recommended—IELTS (minimum score 6). Electronic applications accepted. *Expenses:* Contact institution. *Faculty research:* Negotiation, mediation and conflict resolution; leadership; management of diverse organizations; case studies and simulation methodologies for management education, digital as a second language: social networking for digital immigrants, non-profit and public management.

Columbia University, College of Dental Medicine and Graduate School of Arts and Sciences, Programs in Dental Specialties, New York, NY 10027. Offers advanced education in general dentistry (Certificate); biomedical informatics (MA, PhD); endodontics (Certificate); orthodontics (MS, Certificate); periodontics (MS, Certificate); prosthodontics (MS, Certificate); science education (MA). *Degree requirements:* For master's, thesis, presentation of seminar. *Entrance requirements:* For master's, GRE General Test, DDS or equivalent. *Expenses:* Contact institution. *Faculty research:* Analysis of growth/form, pulpal microcirculation, implants, microbiology of oral environment, calcified tissues.

Columbia University, College of Physicians and Surgeons, Department of Biomedical Informatics, New York, NY 10032. Offers M Phil, MA, PhD, MD/PhD. *Degree requirements:* For doctorate, thesis/dissertation. *Entrance requirements:* For master's and doctorate, GRE General Test, knowledge of computational techniques. Additional exam requirements/recommendations for international students: Required—TOEFL. Electronic applications accepted. *Faculty research:* Bioinformatics, bioimaging, clinical informatics, public health informatics.

Dalhousie University, Faculty of Computer Science, Halifax, NS B3H 1W5, Canada. Offers computational biology and bioinformatics (M Sc); computer science (MA Sc, MC Sc, PhD); electronic commerce (MEC); health informatics (MHI). *Degree requirements:* For master's, thesis (for some programs); for doctorate, thesis/dissertation. *Entrance requirements:* Additional exam requirements/recommendations for international students: Required—1 of 5 approved tests: TOEFL, IELTS, CANTEST, CAEL, Michigan English Language Assessment Battery. Electronic applications accepted.

Excelsior College, School of Health Sciences, Albany, NY 12203-5159. Offers health administration (MS); health care informatics (Certificate); health professions education (MSHS); healthcare informatics (MS); organizational development (MS); public health (MSHS). *Program availability:* Part-time, evening/weekend, online learning. *Faculty:* 5 part-time/adjunct (4 women). *Students:* 307 part-time (240 women); includes 176 minority (101 Black or African American, non-Hispanic/Latino; 2 American Indian or Alaska Native, non-Hispanic/Latino; 17 Asian, non-Hispanic/Latino; 39 Hispanic/Latino; 3 Native Hawaiian or other Pacific Islander, non-Hispanic/Latino; 14 Two or more races, non-Hispanic/Latino), 1 international. Average age 39. In 2016, 21 master's awarded. *Entrance requirements:* For degree, bachelor's degree in applicable field. *Application deadline:* Applications are processed on a rolling basis. Application fee: $50. Electronic applications accepted. *Expenses: Tuition:* Part-time $645 per credit. *Required fees:* $265 per credit. *Financial support:* Scholarships/grants available. *Unit head:* Dr. Laurie Carbo-Porter, Dean, 518-464-8500, Fax: 518-464-8777. *Application contact:* Admissions Counselor, 518-464-8500, Fax: 518-464-8777, E-mail: admissions@excelsior.edu.

Grand Valley State University, Padnos College of Engineering and Computing, Medical and Bioinformatics Program, Allendale, MI 49401-9403. Offers MS. *Program availability:* Part-time, evening/weekend. *Faculty:* 13 full-time (4 women), 3 part-time/adjunct (2 women). *Students:* 12 full-time (6 women), 6 part-time (3 women); includes 2 minority (1 Asian, non-Hispanic/Latino; 1 Hispanic/Latino), 14 international. Average age 26. 16 applicants, 94% accepted, 6 enrolled. In 2016, 5 master's awarded. *Degree requirements:* For master's, capstone course. *Entrance requirements:* For master's, GRE or GMAT, minimum GPA of 3.0, resume, personal statement, minimum of 2 letters of recommendation, previous academic study or work experience. Additional exam requirements/recommendations for international students: Required—TOEFL, Michigan English Language Assessment Battery or completion of ELS 112; Recommended—IELTS. *Application deadline:* For fall admission, 2/1 priority date for domestic students. Applications are processed on a rolling basis. Application fee: $30. Electronic applications accepted. *Expenses:* $633 per credit hour. *Financial support:* In 2016–17, 11 students received support, including 4 fellowships, 7 research assistantships with full and partial tuition reimbursements available (averaging $8,000 per year); career-related internships or fieldwork, tuition waivers (full and partial), and unspecified assistantships also available. *Faculty research:* Biomedical informatics, information visualization, data mining, high-performance computing, computational biology. *Unit head:* Dr. Paul Leidig, Director, 616-331-2308, Fax: 616-331-2106, E-mail: leidigp@gvsu.edu. *Application contact:* Dr. Guenter Tusch, Graduate Program Director, 616-331-2046, E-mail: tuschg@gvsu.edu.

Johns Hopkins University, School of Medicine, Division of Health Sciences Informatics, Baltimore, MD 21287. Offers applied health sciences informatics (MS); clinical informatics (Certificate); health sciences informatics (PhD); health sciences informatics research (MS). *Faculty:* 40 part-time/adjunct (10 women). *Students:* 7 full-time (2 women), 7 part-time (4 women); includes 4 minority (all Black or African American, non-Hispanic/Latino), 7 international. Average age 28. 64 applicants, 23% accepted, 8 enrolled. In 2016, 2 master's awarded. *Degree requirements:* For master's, thesis, publications, practica. *Entrance requirements:* Additional exam requirements/recommendations for international students: Recommended—TOEFL. *Application deadline:* For spring admission, 2/15 priority date for domestic students, 2/15 for international students. Application fee: $110. Electronic applications accepted. *Financial support:* Fellowships, career-related internships or fieldwork, and health care benefits available. *Faculty research:* Decision modeling, consumer health informatics, digital libraries, data standards, patient safety. *Total annual research expenditures:* $963,103. *Unit head:* Dr. Harold P. Lehmann, Director, Training Program, 410-502-2569, Fax: 410-614-2064, E-mail: lehmann@jhmi.edu. *Application contact:* Kersti Winny, Academic Program Administrator, 410-502-3768, Fax: 410-614-2064, E-mail: kwinny@jhmi.edu. Website: http://dhsi.med.jhmi.edu

Michigan Technological University, Graduate School, School of Technology, Houghton, MI 49931. Offers integrated geospatial technology (MS); medical informatics (MS). *Program availability:* Part-time, 100% online, blended/hybrid learning. *Faculty:* 26 full-time, 4 part-time/adjunct. *Students:* 11 full-time (6 women), 9 part-time (4 women); includes 2 minority (1 Black or African American, non-Hispanic/Latino; 1 American Indian or Alaska Native, non-Hispanic/Latino), 8 international. Average age 36. 53 applicants, 43% accepted, 7 enrolled. In 2016, 6 master's awarded. *Degree requirements:* For master's, comprehensive exam (for some programs), thesis (for some programs), thesis or comprehensive exam. *Entrance requirements:* For master's, GRE (for some programs), statement of purpose, personal statement, official transcripts, 2-3 letters of recommendation, resume/curriculum vitae. Additional exam requirements/recommendations for international students: Required—TOEFL (recommended minimum score 79 iBT) or IELTS. *Application deadline:* Applications are processed on a rolling basis. Electronic applications accepted. *Expenses:* Tuition, state resident: full-time $16,290; part-time $905 per credit. Tuition, nonresident: full-time $16,290; part-time $905 per credit. *Required fees:* $248; $124 per term. Tuition and fees vary according to course load and program. *Financial support:* In 2016–17, 6 students received support, including 1 research assistantship (averaging $15,242 per year); career-related internships or fieldwork, Federal Work-Study, scholarships/grants, and health care benefits also available. Financial award applicants required to submit FAFSA. *Faculty research:* Cybersecurity, medical image processing, sensory data fusion, architectural and archaeological laser scanning, high resolution remote sensing. *Total annual research expenditures:* $437,518. *Unit head:* Dr. James O. Frendewey, Dean, 906-487-2260, Fax: 906-487-2583, E-mail: jimf@mtu.edu. *Application contact:* Peggy A. Gorton, Executive Assistant, 906-487-2260, Fax: 906-487-2583, E-mail: pagorton@mtu.edu.
Website: http://www.mtu.edu/technology/

Middle Tennessee State University, College of Graduate Studies, College of Basic and Applied Sciences, Program in Professional Science, Murfreesboro, TN 37132. Offers actuarial sciences (MS); biostatistics (MS); biotechnology (MS); engineering management (MS); health care informatics (MS). *Program availability:* Part-time, evening/weekend, online learning. *Degree requirements:* For master's, comprehensive exam. *Entrance requirements:* For master's, GRE. Additional exam requirements/recommendations for international students: Required—TOEFL (minimum score 525 paper-based; 71 iBT) or IELTS (minimum score 6).

Milwaukee School of Engineering, Rader School of Business, Program in Medical Informatics, Milwaukee, WI 53202-3109. Offers MS. *Program availability:* Part-time, evening/weekend. *Faculty:* 1 (woman) full-time, 2 part-time/adjunct (1 woman). *Students:* 3 part-time (2 women); includes 1 minority (Hispanic/Latino). Average age 27. 2 applicants. In 2016, 4 master's awarded. *Degree requirements:* For master's, thesis, capstone course, research project. *Entrance requirements:* For master's, GRE General Test or GMAT (with percentiles that average 60% or better), 3 letters of recommendation, minimum GPA of 3.0, personal essay, transcripts. Additional exam requirements/recommendations for international students: Required—TOEFL (minimum score 79 iBT), IELTS (minimum score 6.5). *Application deadline:* Applications are processed on a rolling basis. Application fee: $0. Electronic applications accepted. *Expenses: Tuition:* Full-time $31,440; part-time $655 per credit. *Financial support:* Career-related internships or fieldwork, institutionally sponsored loans, scholarships/grants, and tuition waivers (full) available. Financial award application deadline: 3/15; financial award applicants required to submit FAFSA. *Faculty research:* Information technology, databases. *Unit head:* Katie McCarthy, Program Director, 414-277-7279, Fax: 414-277-7279, E-mail: mccarthk@msoe.edu. *Application contact:* Ian Dahlinghaus, Graduate Admissions Counselor, 414-277-7208, E-mail: dahlinghaus@msoe.edu.
Website: http://www.msoe.edu/community/academics/business/page/1323/medical-informatics-overview

Northwestern University, Feinberg School of Medicine and Interdepartmental Programs, Driskill Graduate Program in Life Sciences, Chicago, IL 60611. Offers biostatistics (PhD); epidemiology (PhD); health and biomedical informatics (PhD); health services and outcomes research (PhD); healthcare quality and patient safety (PhD); translational outcomes in science (PhD). *Degree requirements:* For doctorate, comprehensive exam, thesis/dissertation, written and oral qualifying exams. *Entrance* *requirements:* For doctorate, GRE General Test. Additional exam requirements/recommendations for international students: Required—TOEFL (minimum score 600 paper-based). Electronic applications accepted.

Northwestern University, School of Professional Studies, Program in Information Systems, Evanston, IL 60208. Offers analytics and business intelligence (MS); database and Internet technologies (MS); information systems (MS); information systems management (MS); information systems security (MS); medical informatics (MS); software project management and development (MS).

Northwestern University, School of Professional Studies, Program in Medical Informatics, Evanston, IL 60208. Offers MS. *Program availability:* Online learning.

Nova Southeastern University, College of Osteopathic Medicine, Fort Lauderdale, FL 33328. Offers biomedical informatics (MS, Graduate Certificate), including biomedical informatics (MS), clinical informatics (Graduate Certificate), public health informatics (Graduate Certificate); disaster and emergency management (MS); medical education (MS); nutrition (MS, Graduate Certificate), including functional nutrition and herbal therapy (Graduate Certificate); osteopathic medicine (DO); public health (MPH, Graduate Certificate), including health education (Graduate Certificate); social medicine (Graduate Certificate). *Accreditation:* AOsA. *Faculty:* 126 full-time (64 women), 1,411 part-time/adjunct (352 women). *Students:* 1,040 full-time (476 women), 196 part-time (135 women); includes 635 minority (95 Black or African American, non-Hispanic/Latino; 298 Asian, non-Hispanic/Latino; 208 Hispanic/Latino; 1 Native Hawaiian or other Pacific Islander, non-Hispanic/Latino; 33 Two or more races, non-Hispanic/Latino), 54 international. Average age 27. 5,383 applicants, 7% accepted, 248 enrolled. In 2016, 94 master's, 231 doctorates, 2 other advanced degrees awarded. *Degree requirements:* For master's, comprehensive exam (for MPH); field/special projects; for doctorate, comprehensive exam, COMLEX Boards; for Graduate Certificate, thesis or alternative. *Entrance requirements:* For master's, GRE; for doctorate, MCAT, biology, chemistry, organic chemistry, physics (all with labs), biochemistry, and English. *Application deadline:* For fall admission, 1/15 for domestic students. Applications are processed on a rolling basis. Application fee: $50. Electronic applications accepted. *Expenses:* $49,639 residents, $54,806 non-residentsfor out-of-state students; $100 microscope/laboratory fee (for first-year students); $145 per year Health Professions Division student access fee; $1,050 per year student service fee. *Financial support:* In 2016–17, 46 students received support, including 8 fellowships (averaging $30,690 per year); research assistantships, teaching assistantships, Federal Work-Study, and scholarships/grants also available. Financial award application deadline: 6/1; financial award applicants required to submit FAFSA. *Faculty research:* Teaching strategies, simulated patient use, HIV/AIDS education, minority health issues, managed care education. *Unit head:* Elaine M. Wallace, Dean, 954-262-1457, Fax: 954-262-2250, E-mail: ewallace@nova.edu. *Application contact:* HPD Admissions, 877-640-0218, E-mail: hpdinfo@nova.edu.
Website: http://www.osteopathic.nova.edu/

Oregon Health & Science University, School of Medicine, Graduate Programs in Medicine, Department of Medical Informatics and Clinical Epidemiology, Portland, OR 97239-3098. Offers bioinformatics (MS, PhD); clinical informatics (MBI, MS, PhD, Certificate); health information management (Certificate). *Program availability:* Part-time, online learning. *Faculty:* 12 full-time (6 women), 15 part-time/adjunct (7 women). *Students:* 31 full-time (7 women), 95 part-time (38 women); includes 34 minority (4 Black or African American, non-Hispanic/Latino; 22 Asian, non-Hispanic/Latino; 2 Hispanic/Latino; 6 Two or more races, non-Hispanic/Latino), 8 international. Average age 38. 42 applicants, 29 enrolled. In 2016, 21 master's, 2 doctorates, 20 other advanced degrees awarded. Terminal master's awarded for partial completion of doctoral program. *Degree requirements:* For master's, thesis or capstone project; for doctorate, comprehensive exam, thesis/dissertation, qualifying exam. *Entrance requirements:* For master's and doctorate, GRE General Test (minimum scores: 153 Verbal/148 Quantitative/4.5 Analytical), coursework in computer programming, human anatomy and physiology. Additional exam requirements/recommendations for international students: Required—IELTS or TOEFL. *Application deadline:* For fall admission, 12/1 for domestic students; for winter admission, 11/1 for domestic students; for spring admission, 2/1 for domestic students. Applications are processed on a rolling basis. Application fee: $70. Electronic applications accepted. *Expenses:* Contact institution. *Financial support:* Fellowships with full tuition reimbursements, research assistantships, Federal Work-Study, scholarships/grants, health care benefits, and full-tuition and stipends (for PhD students) available. Financial award application deadline: 3/1; financial award applicants required to submit FAFSA. *Faculty research:* Clinical informatics, computational biology, health information management, genomics, data analytics. *Unit head:* Dr. William Hersh, Program Director, 503-494-4563, E-mail: hersh@ohsu.edu. *Application contact:* Lauren Ludwig, Administrative Coordinator, 503-494-2252, E-mail: informat@ohsu.edu.
Website: http://www.ohsu.edu/dmice/

Regis University, College of Computer and Information Sciences, Denver, CO 80221-1099. Offers agile technologies (Certificate); cybersecurity (Certificate); data science (M Sc); database administration with Oracle (Certificate); database development (Certificate); database technologies (M Sc); enterprise Java software development (Certificate); enterprise resource planning (Certificate); executive information technology (Certificate); health care informatics (Certificate); health care informatics and information management (M Sc); information assurance (M Sc); information assurance policy management (Certificate); information technology management (M Sc); mobile software development (Certificate); software engineering (M Sc, Certificate); software engineering and database technology (M Sc); storage area networks (Certificate); systems engineering (M Sc, Certificate). *Program availability:* Part-time, evening/weekend, 100% online, blended/hybrid learning. *Faculty:* 11 full-time (3 women), 30 part-time/adjunct (10 women). *Students:* 341 full-time (95 women), 318 part-time (98 women); includes 186 minority (56 Black or African American, non-Hispanic/Latino; 2 American Indian or Alaska Native, non-Hispanic/Latino; 48 Asian, non-Hispanic/Latino; 63 Hispanic/Latino; 17 Two or more races, non-Hispanic/Latino), 57 international. Average age 37. 342 applicants, 79% accepted, 174 enrolled. In 2016, 192 master's awarded. *Degree requirements:* For master's, thesis (for some programs), final research project. *Entrance requirements:* For master's, official transcript reflecting baccalaureate degree awarded from regionally-accredited college or university, 2 years of related experience, resume, interview. Additional exam requirements/recommendations for international students: Required—TOEFL (minimum score 550 paper-based; 82 iBT). *Application deadline:* For fall admission, 8/15 priority date for domestic students, 7/13 for international students; for winter admission, 10/10 priority date for domestic students, 9/8 for international students; for spring admission, 1/10 priority date for domestic students, 11/17 for international students; for summer admission, 5/1 priority date for domestic students. Applications are processed on a rolling basis. Application fee: $75. Electronic applications accepted. *Expenses:* $730 per credit hour. *Financial support:* Scholarships/grants available. Financial award application deadline: 4/15; financial award applicants required to submit FAFSA. *Faculty research:* Information policy, knowledge management, software architectures, data science. *Unit head:* Shari Plantz-Masters, Academic Dean. *Application contact:* Cate Clark, Director of Admissions, 303-458-4900, Fax: 303-964-5534, E-mail: ruadmissions@regis.edu.
Website: http://regis.edu/CCIS.aspx

Rutgers University–Newark, School of Health Related Professions, Department of Health Informatics, Program in Biomedical Informatics, Newark, NJ 07102. Offers MS, PhD, DMD/MS, MD/MS. *Program availability:* Part-time, evening/weekend, online learning. *Degree requirements:* For master's, thesis; for doctorate, comprehensive exam, thesis/dissertation. *Entrance requirements:* For master's, BS, transcript of highest degree, statement of research interests, curriculum vitae, basic understanding of database concepts and calculus, 3 reference letters; for doctorate, master's degree, transcripts of highest degree, statement of research interests, curriculum vitae, basic understanding of database concepts and calculus, 3 reference letters. Additional exam requirements/recommendations for international students: Required—TOEFL. Electronic applications accepted.

Rutgers University–Newark, School of Health Related Professions, Department of Health Informatics, Program in Health Care Informatics, Newark, NJ 07102. Offers Certificate. *Program availability:* Part-time, evening/weekend, online learning. *Entrance requirements:* For degree, all transcripts, basic proficiency in programming language, BS, 3 reference letters. Additional exam requirements/recommendations for international students: Required—TOEFL (minimum score 500 paper-based; 79 iBT). Electronic applications accepted.

Stanford University, School of Medicine, Stanford Center for Biomedical Informatics Research, Stanford, CA 94305-2004. Offers MS, PhD. Terminal master's awarded for partial completion of doctoral program. *Degree requirements:* For master's, thesis; for doctorate, thesis/dissertation. *Entrance requirements:* For doctorate, GRE or MCAT. Additional exam requirements/recommendations for international students: Required—TOEFL. Electronic applications accepted. *Expenses: Tuition:* Full-time $47,331. *Required fees:* $609.

University at Buffalo, the State University of New York, Graduate School, Jacobs School of Medicine and Biomedical Sciences, Graduate Programs in Medicine and Biomedical Sciences, Department of Biomedical Informatics, Buffalo, NY 14203. Offers bio-informatics (PhD); biomedical informatics (MS); biomedical ontology (PhD); clinical informatics (PhD). *Program availability:* Part-time. *Degree requirements:* For master's, thesis; for doctorate, variable foreign language requirement, comprehensive exam (for some programs), thesis/dissertation. *Entrance requirements:* For master's and doctorate, GRE, MCAT, 3 letters of recommendation. Additional exam requirements/recommendations for international students: Required—TOEFL (minimum score 600 paper-based; 100 iBT), IELTS (minimum score 7.5). Electronic applications accepted. *Expenses:* Contact institution. *Faculty research:* Integrated information systems planning and evaluation, management of knowledge-based information resources, scholarly communication in the health sciences, the economic value of health information, electronic health records, natural language understanding, ontologies, telemedicine/telehealth systems of healthcare, quality management information systems, implementation and evaluation of electronic health record systems, ethical and social issues in informatics.

The University of Arizona, College of Nursing, Tucson, AZ 85721. Offers health care informatics (Certificate); nurse practitioner (MS); nursing (DNP, PhD). *Accreditation:* AACN; AANA/CANAEP. *Program availability:* Part-time, online learning. Terminal master's awarded for partial completion of doctoral program. *Degree requirements:* For master's, thesis optional; for doctorate, comprehensive exam, thesis/dissertation. *Entrance requirements:* For master's, BSN, eligibility for RN license; for doctorate, BSN; for Certificate, GRE General Test, Arizona RN license, BSN, minimum GPA of 3.0. Additional exam requirements/recommendations for international students: Required—TOEFL (minimum score 550 paper-based; 79 iBT). Electronic applications accepted. *Expenses:* Contact institution. *Faculty research:* Vulnerable populations, injury mechanisms and biobehavioral responses, health care systems, informatics, rural health.

University of California, Davis, Graduate Studies, Graduate Group in Health Informatics, Davis, CA 95616. Offers MS. *Entrance requirements:* Additional exam requirements/recommendations for international students: Required—TOEFL (minimum score 550 paper-based).

University of Colorado Denver, College of Nursing, Aurora, CO 80045. Offers adult clinical nurse specialist (MS); adult nurse practitioner (MS); family nurse practitioner (MS); family psychiatric mental health nurse practitioner (MS); health care informatics (MS); nurse-midwifery (MS); nursing (DNP, PhD); nursing leadership and health care systems (MS); pediatric nurse practitioner (MS); women's health (MS); MS/PhD. *Accreditation:* AACN; ACNM/ACME (one or more programs are accredited). *Program availability:* Part-time, evening/weekend, online learning. *Faculty:* 118 full-time (110 women), 91 part-time/adjunct (83 women). *Students:* 408 full-time (376 women), 118 part-time (98 women); includes 91 minority (20 Black or African American, non-Hispanic/Latino; 2 American Indian or Alaska Native, non-Hispanic/Latino; 19 Asian, non-Hispanic/Latino; 36 Hispanic/Latino; 14 Two or more races, non-Hispanic/Latino), 3 international. Average age 39. 340 applicants, 42% accepted, 112 enrolled. In 2016, 138 master's, 23 doctorates awarded. Terminal master's awarded for partial completion of doctoral program. *Degree requirements:* For master's, thesis optional; for doctorate, comprehensive exam, thesis/dissertation, 42 credits of coursework. *Entrance requirements:* For master's, GRE if cumulative undergraduate GPA is less than 3.0, undergraduate nursing degree from NLNAC- or CCNE-accredited school or university; completion of research and statistics courses with minimum grade of C; copy of current and unencumbered nursing license; for doctorate, GRE, bachelor's and/or master's degrees in nursing from NLN- or CCNE-accredited institution; portfolio; minimum undergraduate GPA of 3.0, graduate 3.5; graduate-level intermediate statistics and master's-level nursing theory courses with minimum B grade; interview. Additional exam requirements/recommendations for international students: Required—TOEFL (minimum score 560 paper-based; 83 iBT). *Application deadline:* For fall admission, 2/15 for domestic students, 1/15 for international students; for spring admission, 7/1 for domestic students, 6/1 for international students. Application fee: $50 ($75 for international students). Electronic applications accepted. *Expenses:* Contact institution. *Financial support:* In 2016–17, 244 students received support. Fellowships, research assistantships, teaching assistantships, Federal Work-Study, institutionally sponsored loans, scholarships/grants, traineeships, and unspecified assistantships available. Support available to part-time students. Financial award application deadline: 4/1; financial award applicants required to submit FAFSA. *Faculty research:* Biological and behavioral phenomena in pregnancy and postpartum; patterns of glycaemia during the insulin resistance of pregnancy; obesity, gestational diabetes, and relationship to neonatal adiposity; men's awareness and knowledge of male breast cancer; cognitive-behavioral therapy for chronic insomnia after breast cancer treatment; massage therapy for the treatment of tension-type headaches. *Total annual research expenditures:* $6.8 million. *Unit head:* Dr. Sarah Thompson, Dean, 303-724-1679, E-mail: sarah.a.thompson@ucdenver.edu. *Application contact:* Judy Campbell, Graduate Programs Coordinator, 303-724-8503, E-mail: judy.campbell@ucdenver.edu.
Website: http://www.ucdenver.edu/academics/colleges/nursing/Pages/default.aspx

University of Illinois at Urbana–Champaign, Graduate College, School of Information Sciences, Champaign, IL 61820. Offers bioinformatics (MS); digital libraries (CAS); information management (MS); library and information science (MS, PhD, CAS). *Accreditation:* ALA (one or more programs are accredited). *Program availability:* Part-time, online learning. *Entrance requirements:* For degree, master's degree in library and information science or related field with minimum GPA of 3.0.

The University of Kansas, University of Kansas Medical Center, School of Nursing, Kansas City, KS 66160. Offers adult/gerontological clinical nurse specialist (PMC); adult/gerontological nurse practitioner (PMC); health care informatics (PMC); health professions educator (PMC); nurse midwife (PMC); nursing (MS, DNP, PhD); organizational leadership (PMC); psychiatric/mental health nurse practitioner (PMC); public health nursing (PMC). *Accreditation:* AACN; ACNM/ACME. *Program availability:* Part-time, 100% online, blended/hybrid learning. *Faculty:* 53. *Students:* 41 full-time (40 women), 270 part-time (244 women); includes 47 minority (15 Black or African American, non-Hispanic/Latino; 2 American Indian or Alaska Native, non-Hispanic/Latino; 9 Asian, non-Hispanic/Latino; 10 Hispanic/Latino; 11 Two or more races, non-Hispanic/Latino), 1 international. Average age 37. 95 applicants, 97% accepted, 67 enrolled. In 2016, 87 master's, 25 doctorates, 9 other advanced degrees awarded. Terminal master's awarded for partial completion of doctoral program. *Degree requirements:* For master's, comprehensive exam, thesis (for some programs), general oral exam; for doctorate, thesis/dissertation or alternative, comprehensive oral exam (for DNP); comprehensive written and oral exam, or three publications (for PhD). *Entrance requirements:* For master's, bachelor's degree in nursing, minimum GPA of 3.0, 1 year of clinical experience, RN license in KS and MO; for doctorate, GRE General Test (for PhD only), bachelor's degree in nursing, minimum GPA of 3.5, RN license in KS and MO. Additional exam requirements/recommendations for international students: Required—TOEFL. *Application deadline:* For fall admission, 4/1 for domestic and international students; for spring admission, 9/1 for domestic and international students. Application fee: $60. Electronic applications accepted. *Financial support:* In 2016–17, 50 students received support, including 5 research assistantships with tuition reimbursements available (averaging $20,000 per year), 30 teaching assistantships with tuition reimbursements available (averaging $20,000 per year); scholarships/grants and traineeships also available. Financial award application deadline: 3/1; financial award applicants required to submit FAFSA. *Faculty research:* Breastfeeding practices of teen mothers, national database of nursing quality indicators, caregiving of families of patients using technology in the home, simulation in nursing education, diaphragm fatigue. *Total annual research expenditures:* $1.2 million. *Unit head:* Dr. Sally Maliski, Dean, 913-588-1601, Fax: 913-588-1660, E-mail: smaliski@kumc.edu. *Application contact:* Dr. Pamela K. Barnes, Associate Dean, Student Affairs, 913-588-1619, Fax: 913-588-1615, E-mail: pbarnes2@kumc.edu.
Website: http://nursing.kumc.edu

University of Phoenix–Phoenix Campus, College of Health Sciences and Nursing, Tempe, AZ 85282-2371. Offers family nurse practitioner (MSN, Certificate); gerontology health care (Certificate); health care education (MSN, Certificate); health care informatics (Certificate); informatics (MSN); nursing (MSN); MSN/MHA. *Program availability:* Evening/weekend, online learning. *Entrance requirements:* Additional exam requirements/recommendations for international students: Required—TOEFL, TOEIC (Test of English as an International Communication), Berlitz Online English Proficiency Exam, PTE, or IELTS. Electronic applications accepted. *Expenses:* Contact institution.

The University of Tennessee at Chattanooga, School of Nursing, Chattanooga, TN 37403. Offers administration (MSN); certified nurse anesthetist (Post-Master's Certificate); education (MSN); family nurse practitioner (MSN, Post-Master's Certificate); health care informatics (Post-Master's Certificate); nurse anesthesia (MSN); nurse education (Post-Master's Certificate); nursing (DNP). *Accreditation:* AACN; AANA/CANAEP (one or more programs are accredited). *Faculty:* 12 full-time (9 women), 3 part-time/adjunct (2 women). *Students:* 61 full-time (32 women), 49 part-time (42 women); includes 15 minority (6 Black or African American, non-Hispanic/Latino; 2 Asian, non-Hispanic/Latino; 3 Hispanic/Latino; 4 Two or more races, non-Hispanic/Latino). Average age 35. 48 applicants, 98% accepted, 38 enrolled. In 2016, 36 master's, 5 doctorates, 1 other advanced degree awarded. *Degree requirements:* For master's, thesis optional, qualifying exams, professional project; for doctorate, professional project; for Post-Master's Certificate, thesis or alternative, practicum, seminar. *Entrance requirements:* For master's, GRE General Test, MAT, BSN, minimum GPA of 3.0, eligibility for Tennessee RN license, 1 year of direct patient care experience; for doctorate, GRE General Test or MAT (if applicant does not have MSN), minimum GPA of 3.0 for highest degree earned; for Post-Master's Certificate, GRE General Test, MAT, MSN, minimum GPA of 3.0, eligibility for Tennessee RN license, one year of direct patient care experience. Additional exam requirements/recommendations for international students: Required—TOEFL (minimum score 550 paper-based; 79 iBT), IELTS (minimum score 6). *Application deadline:* For fall admission, 6/15 priority date for domestic students, 7/1 for international students; for spring admission, 11/1 priority date for domestic students, 11/1 for international students. Applications are processed on a rolling basis. Application fee: $35 ($40 for international students). Electronic applications accepted. *Expenses:* $9,876 full-time in-state; $25,994 full-time out-of-state; $450 per credit part-time in-state; $1,345 per credit part-time out-of-state. *Financial support:* In 2016–17, 1 teaching assistantship was awarded; career-related internships or fieldwork and scholarships/grants also available. Support available to part-time students. Financial award application deadline: 7/1; financial award applicants required to submit FAFSA. *Faculty research:* Diabetes in women, health care for elderly, alternative medicine, hypertension, nurse anesthesia. *Total annual research expenditures:* $1.9 million. *Unit head:* Dr. Chris Smith, Director, 423-425-1741, Fax: 423-425-4668, E-mail: chris-smith@utc.edu. *Application contact:* Dr. Joanne Romagni, Dean of the Graduate School, 423-425-4478, Fax: 423-425-5223, E-mail: joanne-romagni@utc.edu.
Website: http://www.utc.edu/nursing/

University of Washington, Graduate School, School of Medicine, Graduate Programs in Medicine, Department of Medical Education and Biomedical Informatics, Division of Biomedical and Health Informatics, Seattle, WA 98195. Offers MS, PhD. *Entrance requirements:* For master's and doctorate, GRE General Test, minimum GPA of 3.0; previous undergraduate course work in biology, computer programming, and mathematics. Additional exam requirements/recommendations for international students: Required—TOEFL (minimum score 580 paper-based; 70 iBT). Electronic applications accepted. *Faculty research:* Bio-clinical informatics, information retrieval, human-computer interaction, knowledge-based systems, telehealth.

University of Wisconsin–Milwaukee, Graduate School, College of Health Sciences, Department of Health Informatics and Administration, Milwaukee, WI 53201-0413. Offers health care informatics (MS); healthcare administration (MHA). *Students:* 31 full-time (19 women), 11 part-time (10 women); includes 9 minority (2 Black or African American, non-Hispanic/Latino; 5 Asian, non-Hispanic/Latino; 2 Two or more races, non-Hispanic/Latino), 5 international. Average age 32. 34 applicants, 76% accepted, 20 enrolled. In 2016, 8 master's awarded. *Degree requirements:* For master's, comprehensive exam, thesis optional. *Entrance requirements:* For master's, GRE General Test. Additional exam requirements/recommendations for international students: Required—TOEFL (minimum score 550 paper-based; 79 iBT), IELTS (minimum score 6.5). Application fee: $56 ($96 for international students). *Financial support:* Fellowships, research assistantships, and teaching assistantships available. *Unit head:* Priya Nambisan, Department Chair, 414-229-7136, Fax: 414-229-3373, E-mail: nambisap@uwm.edu. *Application contact:* Kathleen M. Olewinski, Educational Coordinator, 414-229-7110, Fax: 414-229-3373, E-mail: kmo@uwm.edu.
Website: http://uwm.edu/healthsciences/academics/health-informatics-administration/

Modeling and Simulation

Arizona State University at the Tempe campus, Ira A. Fulton Schools of Engineering, ASU Engineering Online Programs, Tempe, AZ 85287. Offers construction (MS); embedded systems (M Eng); enterprise systems innovation and management (MSE); modeling and simulation (M Eng); quality and reliability engineering (M Eng); software engineering (MSE); systems engineering (M Eng).

Arizona State University at the Tempe campus, Ira A. Fulton Schools of Engineering, The Polytechnic School, Department of Engineering, Mesa, AZ 85212. Offers simulation, modeling, and applied cognitive science (PhD). *Program availability:* Part-time. *Degree requirements:* For doctorate, comprehensive exam, thesis/dissertation, interactive Program of Study (iPOS) submitted before completing 50 percent of required credit hours. *Entrance requirements:* For doctorate, GRE, master's degree in psychology, engineering, cognitive science, or computer science; 3 letters of recommendation; statement of research interests. Additional exam requirements/recommendations for international students: Required—TOEFL, IELTS, or PTE. Electronic applications accepted. *Faculty research:* Software process and automated workflow, software architecture, dotal technologies, relational database systems, embedded systems.

Carnegie Mellon University, Carnegie Institute of Technology, Department of Civil and Environmental Engineering, Pittsburgh, PA 15213. Offers advanced infrastructure systems (MS, PhD); advanced infrastructure systems technology development and application (MS); air quality engineering and science (MS); civil and environmental engineering (MS, PhD); civil and environmental engineering/engineering and public policy (PhD); civil engineering (MS, PhD); computational mechanics (MS, PhD); computational modeling and monitoring for resilient structural and material systems (MS); energy infrastructure systems (MS); environmental engineering (MS, PhD); environmental management and science (MS, PhD); IT-based sustainable global infrastructure and construction management (MS); sustainability and green design (MS); water quality engineering and science (MS). *Program availability:* Part-time. *Faculty:* 23 full-time (5 women), 12 part-time/adjunct (3 women). *Students:* 230 full-time (87 women), 4 part-time (0 women); includes 17 minority (4 Black or African American, non-Hispanic/Latino; 12 Asian, non-Hispanic/Latino; 1 Two or more races, non-Hispanic/Latino), 179 international. Average age 25. 653 applicants, 60% accepted, 107 enrolled. In 2016, 145 master's, 15 doctorates awarded. Terminal master's awarded for partial completion of doctoral program. *Degree requirements:* For master's, thesis optional; for doctorate, comprehensive exam, thesis/dissertation, two-part qualifying exam, public defense of dissertation. *Entrance requirements:* For master's, GRE General Test, BS in engineering, science or mathematics; for doctorate, GRE General Test, BS or MS in engineering, science or mathematics. Additional exam requirements/recommendations for international students: Required—TOEFL (minimum score 84 iBT) or IELTS (6.0). *Application deadline:* For fall admission, 1/5 priority date for domestic and international students; for spring admission, 9/15 priority date for domestic and international students. Applications are processed on a rolling basis. Application fee: $65. Electronic applications accepted. *Expenses:* Contact institution. *Financial support:* In 2016–17, 129 students received support. Fellowships with tuition reimbursements available, research assistantships with tuition reimbursements available, scholarships/grants, tuition waivers (full and partial), unspecified assistantships, and service assistantships available. Financial award application deadline: 1/5. *Faculty research:* Advanced infrastructure systems; environmental engineering, sustainability, and science; mechanics, materials, and computing. *Total annual research expenditures:* $7.4 million. *Unit head:* Dr. David A. Dzombak, Professor and Department Head, 412-268-2941, Fax: 412-268-7813, E-mail: dzombak@cmu.edu. *Application contact:* David A. Vey, Graduate Admissions Manager, 412-268-2292, Fax: 412-268-7813, E-mail: dvey@andrew.cmu.edu.
Website: http://www.cmu.edu/cee/

Columbus State University, Graduate Studies, Turner College of Business, Columbus, GA 31907-5645. Offers applied computer science (MS), including informational assurance, modeling and simulation, software development; business administration (MBA); human resource management (Certificate); information systems security (Certificate); modeling and simulation (Certificate); organizational leadership (MS), including human resource management, leader development, servant leadership; servant leadership (Certificate). *Accreditation:* AACSB. *Program availability:* Part-time, evening/weekend, 100% online, blended/hybrid learning. *Faculty:* 10 full-time (3 women). *Students:* 93 full-time (21 women), 132 part-time (47 women); includes 69 minority (36 Black or African American, non-Hispanic/Latino; 1 American Indian or Alaska Native, non-Hispanic/Latino; 11 Asian, non-Hispanic/Latino; 14 Hispanic/Latino; 7 Two or more races, non-Hispanic/Latino), 35 international. Average age 31. 279 applicants, 44% accepted, 64 enrolled. In 2016, 106 master's awarded. *Entrance requirements:* For master's, GMAT, GRE, minimum undergraduate GPA of 2.75, letters of recommendation. Additional exam requirements/recommendations for international students: Required—TOEFL (minimum score 550 paper-based; 79 iBT). *Application deadline:* For fall admission, 6/30 for domestic students, 5/1 for international students; for spring admission, 11/1 for domestic and international students; for summer admission, 3/1 for domestic and international students. Applications are processed on a rolling basis. Application fee: $50. Electronic applications accepted. *Expenses:* Contact institution. *Financial support:* In 2016–17, 18 students received support, including 16 research assistantships (averaging $3,000 per year); Federal Work-Study also available. Financial award application deadline: 5/1; financial award applicants required to submit FAFSA. *Unit head:* Dr. Linda U. Hadley, Dean, 706-507-8153, Fax: 706-568-2184, E-mail: hadley_linda@columbusstate.edu. *Application contact:* Kristin Williams, Director of International and Graduate Recruitment, 706-507-8848, Fax: 706-568-5091, E-mail: thornton_katie@colstate.edu.
Website: http://turner.columbusstate.edu/

Naval Postgraduate School, Departments and Academic Groups, Department of Computer Science, Monterey, CA 93943. Offers computer science (MS, PhD); identity management and cyber security (MA); modeling of virtual environments and simulations (MS, PhD); software engineering (MS, PhD). Program only open to commissioned officers of the United States and friendly nations and selected United States federal civilian employees. *Program availability:* Part-time, online learning. *Degree requirements:* For master's, thesis; for doctorate, thesis/dissertation.

Old Dominion University, College of Arts and Letters, Graduate Program in International Studies, Norfolk, VA 23529. Offers conflict and cooperation (MA, PhD); interdependence and transnationalism (MA, PhD); international cultural studies (MA, PhD); international political economy and development (MA, PhD); modeling and simulation (MA, PhD); U.S. foreign policy and international relations (MA, PhD). *Program availability:* Part-time. *Faculty:* 18 full-time (4 women). *Students:* 35 full-time (13 women), 38 part-time (20 women); includes 14 minority (9 Black or African American, non-Hispanic/Latino; 2 Asian, non-Hispanic/Latino; 1 Hispanic/Latino; 2 Two or more races, non-Hispanic/Latino), 19 international. Average age 37. 99 applicants, 54% accepted, 34 enrolled. In 2016, 24 master's, 11 doctorates awarded. Terminal master's awarded for partial completion of doctoral program. *Degree requirements:* For master's, one foreign language, comprehensive exam, thesis optional; for doctorate, one foreign language, comprehensive exam, thesis/dissertation. *Entrance requirements:* For master's, GRE General Test, sample of written work, 2 letters of recommendation; for doctorate, GRE General Test, sample of written work, 3 letters of recommendation. Additional exam requirements/recommendations for international students: Required—TOEFL (minimum score 570 paper-based). *Application deadline:* For fall admission, 1/15 for domestic and international students; for spring admission, 10/15 for domestic and international students. Application fee: $50. Electronic applications accepted. *Expenses:* Contact institution. *Financial support:* In 2016–17, 12 students received support, including 1 fellowship (averaging $15,000 per year), 5 research assistantships with tuition reimbursements available (averaging $15,000 per year), 4 teaching assistantships with tuition reimbursements available (averaging $15,000 per year); career-related internships or fieldwork, institutionally sponsored loans, and unspecified assistantships also available. Financial award application deadline: 1/15; financial award applicants required to submit FAFSA. *Faculty research:* U.S. foreign policy, international security, Transatlantic and Transpacific relations, transnational issues, international political economy and development. *Total annual research expenditures:* $330,391. *Unit head:* Dr. Regina Karp, Graduate Program Director, 757-683-5700, Fax: 757-683-5701, E-mail: rkarp@odu.edu. *Application contact:* Dr. David C. Earnest, Associate Dean, 757-683-6077, Fax: 757-683-5746, E-mail: dearnest@odu.edu.
Website: http://www.odu.edu/gpis

Old Dominion University, Frank Batten College of Engineering and Technology, Program in Modeling and Simulation, Norfolk, VA 23529. Offers ME, MS, D Eng, PhD. *Program availability:* Part-time, evening/weekend, 100% online, blended/hybrid learning. *Faculty:* 10 full-time (1 woman). *Students:* 19 full-time (2 women), 70 part-time (19 women); includes 23 minority (9 Black or African American, non-Hispanic/Latino; 7 Asian, non-Hispanic/Latino; 5 Hispanic/Latino; 2 Two or more races, non-Hispanic/Latino), 23 international. Average age 34. 38 applicants, 100% accepted, 21 enrolled. In 2016, 12 master's, 2 doctorates awarded. Terminal master's awarded for partial completion of doctoral program. *Degree requirements:* For master's, comprehensive exam, thesis optional; for doctorate, comprehensive exam, thesis/dissertation, candidacy exam. *Entrance requirements:* For master's, GRE, proficiency in calculus, calculus-based statistics, and computer science; for doctorate, GRE, graduate-level proficiency in calculus, calculus-based statistics, and computer science. Additional exam requirements/recommendations for international students: Required—TOEFL (minimum score 550 paper-based; 79 iBT). *Application deadline:* For fall admission, 6/1 for domestic students, 4/15 priority date for international students; for spring admission, 11/1 for domestic students, 10/1 for international students. Applications are processed on a rolling basis. Application fee: $50. Electronic applications accepted. *Expenses:* $478 per credit, in-state full-time tuition. *Financial support:* In 2016–17, 18 students received support, including 2 fellowships with full tuition reimbursements available (averaging $16,000 per year), 16 research assistantships with full tuition reimbursements available (averaging $18,000 per year); career-related internships or fieldwork, scholarships/grants, and unspecified assistantships also available. Financial award application deadline: 4/15; financial award applicants required to submit FAFSA. *Faculty research:* Distributed simulation and interoperability, medical modeling and simulation, transportation modeling and simulation, human factors, discrete event systems. *Total annual research expenditures:* $3.6 million. *Unit head:* Dr. Rick McKenzie, Department Chair, 757-683-5590, Fax: 757-683-3200, E-mail: rdmckenz@odu.edu. *Application contact:* Dr. Tammy Hanna, Academic Advisor/Program Manager, 757-683-5946, E-mail: tlhanna@odu.edu.
Website: http://eng.odu.edu/msve

Oregon State University, College of Engineering, Program in Environmental Engineering, Corvallis, OR 97331. Offers bioremediation (M Eng, MS, PhD); environmental fluid mechanics (M Eng, MS, PhD); environmental microbiology (M Eng, MS, PhD); environmental modeling (M Eng, MS, PhD); multiphase phenomena (M Eng, MS, PhD); subsurface flow and transport (M Eng, MS, PhD); water and wastewater treatment (M Eng, MS, PhD). *Faculty:* 19 full-time (3 women). *Students:* 40 full-time (19 women), 1 (woman) part-time; includes 3 minority (1 Asian, non-Hispanic/Latino; 1 Hispanic/Latino; 1 Two or more races, non-Hispanic/Latino), 16 international. Average age 27. 78 applicants, 41% accepted, 15 enrolled. In 2016, 12 master's awarded. *Entrance requirements:* For master's and doctorate, GRE. Additional exam requirements/recommendations for international students: Required—TOEFL (minimum score 92 iBT). *Application deadline:* For fall admission, 12/20 for domestic students. Application fee: $75 ($85 for international students). Electronic applications accepted. *Expenses:* $14,130 resident full-time tuition, $23,769 non-resident. *Financial support:* Unspecified assistantships available. Financial award application deadline: 1/1. *Unit head:* Dr. James Sweeney, School Head/Professor. *Application contact:* Anita Hughes, Graduate Program Coordinator, E-mail: anita.hughes@oregonstate.edu.
Website: http://cbee.oregonstate.edu/enve-graduate-program

Philadelphia University, School of Design and Engineering, Program in Modeling, Simulation and Data Analytics, Philadelphia, PA 19144. Offers MS. *Program availability:* Online learning.

Portland State University, Graduate Studies, College of Liberal Arts and Sciences, Systems Science Program, Portland, OR 97207-0751. Offers computational intelligence (Certificate); computer modeling and simulation (Certificate); systems science (MS); systems science/anthropology (PhD); systems science/business administration (PhD); systems science/civil engineering (PhD); systems science/economics (PhD); systems science/engineering management (PhD); systems science/general (PhD); systems science/mathematical sciences (PhD); systems science/mechanical engineering (PhD); systems science/psychology (PhD); systems science/sociology (PhD). *Faculty:* 2 full-time (0 women), 3 part-time/adjunct (1 woman). *Students:* 12 full-time (3 women), 21 part-time (5 women); includes 5 minority (1 Black or African American, non-Hispanic/Latino; 2 Hispanic/Latino; 2 Two or more races, non-Hispanic/Latino). Average age 39. 16 applicants, 69% accepted, 9 enrolled. In 2016, 4 master's, 6 doctorates awarded. *Degree requirements:* For master's, comprehensive exam (for some programs), thesis optional; for doctorate, variable foreign language requirement, comprehensive exam (for

some programs), thesis/dissertation. *Entrance requirements:* For master's, GRE/GMAT (recommended), minimum GPA of 3.0 undergraduate or graduate work, 2 letters of recommendation, statement of interest; for doctorate, GMAT, GRE General Test, minimum GPA of 3.0 undergraduate, 3.25 graduate; 2 letters of recommendation; statement of interest. Additional exam requirements/recommendations for international students: Required—TOEFL (minimum score 550 paper-based; 80 iBT). *Application deadline:* For fall admission, 1/15 for domestic and international students; for spring admission, 11/1 for domestic students. Application fee: $65. Electronic applications accepted. *Expenses:* Contact institution. *Financial support:* In 2016–17, 2 research assistantships with tuition reimbursements (averaging $7,830 per year) were awarded; teaching assistantships, career-related internships or fieldwork, Federal Work-Study, scholarships/grants, and unspecified assistantships also available. Support available to part-time students. Financial award application deadline: 3/1; financial award applicants required to submit FAFSA. *Faculty research:* Systems theory and methodology, artificial intelligence neural networks, information theory, nonlinear dynamics/chaos, modeling and simulation. *Unit head:* Dr. Wayne Wakeland, Chair, 503-725-4975, E-mail: wakeland@pdx.edu.
Website: http://www.pdx.edu/sysc/

Rochester Institute of Technology, Graduate Enrollment Services, College of Science, School of Mathematical Sciences, PhD Program in Mathematical Modeling, Rochester, NY 14623-5603. Offers PhD. *Degree requirements:* For doctorate, thesis/dissertation. *Entrance requirements:* For doctorate, GRE, official transcripts, minimum GPA of 3.0 in primary field of study, previous mathematical coursework beyond calculus, two letters of recommendation, personal statement. Additional exam requirements/recommendations for international students: Required—TOEFL (minimum score 100 iBT), IELTS (minimum score 7), PTE (minimum score 68). *Application deadline:* For fall admission, 1/15 priority date for domestic and international students. Applications are processed on a rolling basis. Application fee: $60. Electronic applications accepted. *Expenses:* $1,742 per credit hour. *Financial support:* Research assistantships with full tuition reimbursements, teaching assistantships with full tuition reimbursements, career-related internships or fieldwork, scholarships/grants, health care benefits, and unspecified assistantships available. Support available to part-time students. Financial award applicants required to submit FAFSA. *Faculty research:* Mathematical biology; dynamical systems and fluid dynamics; discrete mathematics; applied inverse problems; geometry, relativity and gravitation. *Unit head:* Dr. Elizabeth Cherry, Director, 585-475-4497, E-mail: excsma@rit.edu. *Application contact:* Diane Ellison, Associate Vice President, Graduate Enrollment Services, 585-475-2229, Fax: 585-475-7164, E-mail: gradinfo@rit.edu.
Website: https://www.rit.edu/science/programs/phd/mathematical-modeling

Stevens Institute of Technology, Graduate School, Charles V. Schaefer Jr. School of Engineering and Science, Department of Civil, Environmental, and Ocean Engineering, Program in Civil Engineering, Hoboken, NJ 07030. Offers civil engineering (PhD, Certificate), including geotechnical engineering (Certificate); geotechnical/geoenvironmental engineering (M Eng, Engr); hydrologic modeling (M Eng); stormwater management (M Eng); structural engineering (M Eng, Engr); transportation engineering (M Eng); water resources engineering (M Eng). *Program availability:* Part-time, evening/weekend. *Students:* 63 full-time (12 women), 27 part-time (10 women); includes 5 minority (2 Black or African American, non-Hispanic/Latino; 2 Asian, non-Hispanic/Latino; 1 Hispanic/Latino), 55 international. Average age 25. 167 applicants, 57% accepted, 24 enrolled. In 2016, 50 master's, 1 other advanced degree awarded. *Degree requirements:* For master's, thesis optional, minimum B average in major field and overall; for doctorate, comprehensive exam (for some programs), thesis/dissertation; for other advanced degree, minimum B average. *Entrance requirements:* Additional exam requirements/recommendations for international students: Required—TOEFL (minimum score 74 iBT), IELTS (minimum score 6). *Application deadline:* For fall admission, 6/1 for domestic students, 4/15 for international students; for spring admission, 11/30 for domestic students, 11/1 for international students. Applications are processed on a rolling basis. Application fee: $65. Electronic applications accepted. *Expenses:* Contact institution. *Financial support:* Fellowships, research assistantships, teaching assistantships, career-related internships or fieldwork, Federal Work-Study, scholarships/grants, and unspecified assistantships available. Financial award application deadline: 2/15; financial award applicants required to submit FAFSA. *Unit head:* Dr. David A. Vaccari, Director, 201-216-5570, Fax: 201-216-8739, E-mail: dvaccari@stevens.edu. *Application contact:* Graduate Admission, 888-783-8367, Fax: 888-511-1306, E-mail: graduate@stevens.edu.

Trent University, Graduate Studies, Program in Applications of Modeling in the Natural and Social Sciences, Peterborough, ON K9J 7B8, Canada. Offers applications of modeling in the natural and social sciences (MA); biology (M Sc, PhD); chemistry (M Sc); computer studies (M Sc); geography (M Sc, PhD); physics (M Sc). *Program availability:* Part-time. *Degree requirements:* For master's, thesis. *Entrance requirements:* For master's, honours degree. *Faculty research:* Computation of heat transfer, atmospheric physics, statistical mechanics, stress and coping, evolutionary ecology.

Université Laval, Faculty of Administrative Sciences, Programs in Business Administration, Québec, QC G1K 7P4, Canada. Offers accounting (MBA); agri-food management (MBA); electronic business (MBA, Diploma); factory management and logistics (MBA); finance (MBA); firm management (MBA); geomatic management (MBA); information technology management (MBA); international management (MBA); management (MBA); management accounting (MBA, Diploma); marketing (MBA); modeling and organizational decision (MBA); occupational health and safety management (MBA); pharmacy management (MBA); social and environmental responsibility (MBA); technological entrepreneurship (Diploma). *Accreditation:* AACSB. *Program availability:* Part-time, evening/weekend, online learning. *Entrance requirements:* For master's and Diploma, knowledge of French and English. Electronic applications accepted.

University at Buffalo, the State University of New York, Graduate School, College of Arts and Sciences, Department of Geography, Buffalo, NY 14214. Offers earth systems science (MA, MS); economic geography and business geographics (MS); environmental modeling and analysis (MA); geographic information science (MA, MS); geography (MA, PhD); health geography (MS); international trade (MA); urban and regional analysis (MA). *Program availability:* Part-time. *Faculty:* 18 full-time (8 women), 1 part-time/adjunct (0 women). *Students:* 45 full-time (29 women), 51 part-time (15 women); includes 64 minority (1 Black or African American, non-Hispanic/Latino; 61 Asian, non-Hispanic/Latino; 2 Hispanic/Latino), 41 international. Average age 28. 167 applicants, 34% accepted, 28 enrolled. In 2016, 23 master's, 7 doctorates awarded. Terminal master's awarded for partial completion of doctoral program. *Degree requirements:* For master's, thesis (for some programs), project or portfolio; for doctorate, thesis/dissertation. *Entrance requirements:* For master's, GRE General Test, minimum GPA of 2.9; for doctorate, GRE General Test, minimum GPA of 3.0. Additional exam requirements/recommendations for international students: Required—TOEFL (minimum score 550 paper-based; 79 iBT). *Application deadline:* For fall admission, 5/1 priority date for domestic students, 3/10 priority date for international students; for spring admission, 11/1 priority date for domestic students, 9/1 priority date for international students. Applications are processed on a rolling basis. Application fee: $75. Electronic applications accepted. *Expenses:* Contact institution. *Financial support:* In 2016–17, 15 students received support, including 7 fellowships with full tuition reimbursements available (averaging $3,070 per year), 7 research assistantships with full tuition reimbursements available (averaging $14,000 per year), 15 teaching assistantships with full tuition reimbursements available (averaging $14,080 per year); career-related internships or fieldwork, Federal Work-Study, institutionally sponsored loans, traineeships, health care benefits, and unspecified assistantships also available. Financial award application deadline: 1/10. *Faculty research:* International business and world trade, geographic information systems and cartography, transportation, urban and regional analysis, physical and environmental geography. *Total annual research expenditures:* $2.6 million. *Unit head:* Dr. Sean Bennett, Chairman, 716-645-0490, Fax: 716-645-2329, E-mail: seanb@buffalo.edu. *Application contact:* Wendy Zitzka, Graduate Secretary, 716-645-0471, Fax: 716-645-2329, E-mail: wzitzka@buffalo.edu. Website: http://www.geog.buffalo.edu/

The University of Alabama in Huntsville, School of Graduate Studies, College of Science, Department of Computer Science, Huntsville, AL 35899. Offers computer science (MS, PhD); cybersecurity (MS); modeling and simulation (MS, PhD, Certificate); software engineering (MSSE, Certificate). *Program availability:* Part-time, evening/weekend, online learning. *Degree requirements:* For master's, comprehensive exam, thesis or alternative, oral and written exams; for doctorate, comprehensive exam, thesis/dissertation, oral and written exams. *Entrance requirements:* For master's, doctorate, and Certificate, GRE General Test, minimum GPA of 3.0. Additional exam requirements/recommendations for international students: Required—TOEFL (minimum score 550 paper-based; 80 iBT), IELTS (minimum score 6.5). Electronic applications accepted. *Expenses:* Tuition, state resident: full-time $9834; part-time $600 per credit hour. Tuition, nonresident: full-time $21,830; part-time $1325 per credit hour. *Faculty research:* Information assurance and cyber security, modeling and simulation, data science, computer graphics and visualization, multimedia systems.

University of California, San Diego, Graduate Division, Department of Structural Engineering, La Jolla, CA 92093. Offers structural engineering (MS, PhD); structural health monitoring, prognosis, and validated simulations (MS). PhD in engineering sciences offered jointly with San Diego State University. *Students:* 195 full-time (39 women), 3 part-time (1 woman). 424 applicants, 57% accepted, 82 enrolled. In 2016, 70 master's, 11 doctorates awarded. *Degree requirements:* For master's, comprehensive exam (for some programs), thesis (for some programs); for doctorate, comprehensive exam, thesis/dissertation, 1-quarter teaching assistantship. *Entrance requirements:* For master's and doctorate, GRE General Test. Additional exam requirements/recommendations for international students: Required—TOEFL (minimum score 550 paper-based; 80 iBT), IELTS (minimum score 7). *Application deadline:* For fall admission, 12/20 for domestic students. Application fee: $105 ($125 for international students). Electronic applications accepted. *Expenses:* Tuition, state resident: full-time $11,220. Tuition, nonresident: full-time $26,322. *Required fees:* $1864. *Financial support:* Fellowships, research assistantships, teaching assistantships, scholarships/grants, and readerships available. Financial award applicants required to submit FAFSA. *Faculty research:* Earthquake engineering, advanced composites and aerospace structural systems, geotechnical, marine/offshore engineering; renewal engineering, structural health monitoring, prognosis and validated simulations, structural materials; computational mechanics; solid mechanics. *Unit head:* P. Benson Shing, Chair, 858-534-4567, E-mail: pshing@ucsd.edu. *Application contact:* Yvonne C. Wollman, Graduate Coordinator, 858-822-1421, E-mail: se-info@ucsd.edu. Website: http://www.structures.ucsd.edu/

University of Central Florida, College of Education and Human Performance, Department of Educational and Human Sciences, Program in Instructional Design and Technology, Orlando, FL 32816. Offers e-learning professional development (Certificate); instructional design and technology (MA); instructional design for simulations (Certificate); instructional/educational technology (Certificate). *Program availability:* Part-time. *Students:* 7 full-time (6 women), 46 part-time (36 women); includes 18 minority (6 Black or African American, non-Hispanic/Latino; 12 Hispanic/Latino), 1 international. Average age 38. 21 applicants, 76% accepted, 15 enrolled. In 2016, 9 master's, 9 other advanced degrees awarded. *Degree requirements:* For master's, thesis or alternative. *Entrance requirements:* Additional exam requirements/recommendations for international students: Required—TOEFL. *Application deadline:* For fall admission, 7/15 for domestic students; for spring admission, 12/1 for domestic students. Application fee: $30. Electronic applications accepted. *Expenses:* Tuition, state resident: part-time $288.16 per credit hour. Tuition, nonresident: part-time $1071.31 per credit hour. *Financial support:* In 2016–17, 1 student received support, including 1 teaching assistantship with partial tuition reimbursement available (averaging $9,088 per year). Financial award application deadline: 3/1; financial award applicants required to submit FAFSA. *Unit head:* Dr. Richard Hartshorne, Program Coordinator, 407-823-1861, E-mail: richard.hartshorne@ucf.edu. *Application contact:* Assistant Director, Graduate Admissions, 407-823-2766, Fax: 407-823-6442, E-mail: gradadmissions@ucf.edu. Website: http://education.ucf.edu/insttech/

University of Central Florida, College of Graduate Studies, Program in Modeling and Simulation, Orlando, FL 32816. Offers MS, PhD, Certificate. *Students:* 23 full-time (11 women), 22 part-time (3 women); includes 16 minority (5 Black or African American, non-Hispanic/Latino; 1 Asian, non-Hispanic/Latino; 9 Hispanic/Latino; 1 Two or more races, non-Hispanic/Latino), 3 international. Average age 35. 46 applicants, 57% accepted, 17 enrolled. In 2016, 1 other advanced degree awarded. *Degree*

requirements: For master's, thesis or alternative. *Entrance requirements:* Additional exam requirements/recommendations for international students: Required—TOEFL. *Application deadline:* For fall admission, 7/15 for domestic students; for spring admission, 12/1 for domestic students. Application fee: $30. Electronic applications accepted. *Expenses:* Tuition, state resident: part-time $288.16 per credit hour. Tuition, nonresident: part-time $1071.31 per credit hour. *Financial support:* In 2016–17, 15 students received support, including 8 fellowships with partial tuition reimbursements available (averaging $15,675 per year), 17 research assistantships with partial tuition reimbursements available (averaging $8,621 per year); teaching assistantships also available. Financial award application deadline: 3/1; financial award applicants required to submit FAFSA. *Unit head:* Dr. Joseph LaViola, Jr., Program Director, 407-882-2285, E-mail: jjl@eecs.ucf.edu. *Application contact:* Assistant Director, Graduate Admissions, 407-823-2766, Fax: 407-823-6442, E-mail: gradadmissions@ucf.edu. Website: http://www.ist.ucf.edu/

The University of Manchester, School of Chemical Engineering and Analytical Science, Manchester, United Kingdom. Offers biocatalysis (M Phil, PhD); chemical engineering (M Phil, PhD); chemical engineering and analytical science (M Phil, D Eng, PhD); colloids, crystals, interfaces and materials (M Phil, PhD); environment and sustainable technology (M Phil, PhD); instrumentation (M Phil, PhD); multi-scale modeling (M Phil, PhD); process integration (M Phil, PhD); systems biology (M Phil, PhD).

University of Pittsburgh, Dietrich School of Arts and Sciences, Program in Computational Modeling and Simulation, Pittsburgh, PA 15260. Offers biological science (PhD); chemistry (PhD); computer science (PhD); economics (PhD); geology and environmental sciences (PhD); mathematics (PhD); physics and astronomy (PhD); psychology (PhD); statistics (PhD). *Program availability:* Part-time. *Faculty:* 4 full-time (1 woman). *Students:* 3 full-time (1 woman), 1 part-time (0 women); includes 1 minority (Asian, non-Hispanic/Latino). Average age 23. 7 applicants, 43% accepted, 2 enrolled. *Degree requirements:* For doctorate, comprehensive exam, thesis/dissertation, preliminary exam. *Entrance requirements:* For doctorate, GRE, statement of purpose, transcripts for all college-level institutions attended, three letters of reference. Additional exam requirements/recommendations for international students: Required—TOEFL (minimum score 90 iBT), IELTS (minimum score 7). *Application deadline:* For fall admission, 1/15 for domestic and international students. Applications are processed on a rolling basis. Application fee: $0 ($50 for international students). Electronic applications accepted. *Expenses:* Contact institution. *Financial support:* In 2016–17, 3 students received support, including 2 fellowships with full tuition reimbursements available (averaging $28,500 per year), 2 research assistantships with full tuition reimbursements available (averaging $23,000 per year); tuition waivers (full) also available. Financial award application deadline: 4/15. *Faculty research:* Econometric modeling, developing reduced-scaling first principles approaches for expedited predictions of molecular and materials properties, developing computational models to quantitatively describe origins of reactivity and selectivity in organ catalytic reactions, image retrieval, human-machine communication. *Unit head:* Dr. Holger Hoock, Associate Dean, 412-624-3939, Fax: 412-624-6855. *Application contact:* Wendy G. Janocha, Graduate Administrator, 412-648-7251, E-mail: wgj1@pitt.edu. Website: http://cmsp.pitt.edu/

University of Southern California, Graduate School, Viterbi School of Engineering, Department of Computer Science, Los Angeles, CA 90089. Offers computer networks (MS); computer science (MS, PhD); computer security (MS); game development (MS); high performance computing and simulations (MS); human language technology (MS); intelligent robotics (MS); multimedia and creative technologies (MS); software engineering (MS). *Program availability:* Part-time, evening/weekend, online learning. *Entrance requirements:* For master's and doctorate, GRE General Test. Additional exam requirements/recommendations for international students: Required—TOEFL. Electronic applications accepted. *Faculty research:* Databases, computer graphics and computer vision, software engineering, networks and security, robotics, multimedia and virtual reality.

Worcester Polytechnic Institute, Graduate Studies and Research, Programs in Interdisciplinary Studies, Worcester, MA 01609-2280. Offers bioscience administration (MS); impact engineering (MS); manufacturing engineering management (MS); power systems management (MS); social science (PhD); systems modeling (MS). *Program availability:* Part-time, evening/weekend. *Faculty:* 1 part-time/adjunct (0 women). *Students:* 5 full-time (2 women), 54 part-time (21 women); includes 14 minority (3 Black or African American, non-Hispanic/Latino; 5 Asian, non-Hispanic/Latino; 5 Hispanic/Latino; 1 Two or more races, non-Hispanic/Latino), 4 international. 18 applicants, 89% accepted, 8 enrolled. *Degree requirements:* For master's, thesis; for doctorate, comprehensive exam, thesis/dissertation. *Entrance requirements:* For master's and doctorate, 3 letters of recommendation. Additional exam requirements/recommendations for international students: Required—TOEFL (minimum score 563 paper-based; 84 iBT), IELTS (minimum score 7). *Application deadline:* For fall admission, 1/1 priority date for domestic students, 1/1 for international students; for spring admission, 10/1 priority date for domestic students, 10/1 for international students. Applications are processed on a rolling basis. Application fee: $70. Electronic applications accepted. *Financial support:* Institutionally sponsored loans, scholarships/grants, and unspecified assistantships available. Financial award application deadline: 1/1; financial award applicants required to submit FAFSA. *Unit head:* Dr. Fred J. Looft, Head, 508-831-5231, Fax: 508-831-5491, E-mail: fjlooft@wpi.edu. *Application contact:* Lynne Dougherty, Administrative Assistant, 508-831-5301, Fax: 508-831-5717, E-mail: grad@wpi.edu.

Software Engineering

American Public University System, AMU/APU Graduate Programs, Charles Town, WV 25414. Offers accounting (MBA, MS); applied business analytics (MBA, MS); criminal justice (MA), including business administration, emergency and disaster management, general (MA, MS); educational leadership (M Ed); emergency and disaster management (MA); entrepreneurship (MBA); environmental policy and management (MS), including environmental planning, environmental sustainability, fish and wildlife management, general (MA, MS), global environmental management; finance (MBA); general (MBA); government contracting and acquisition (MBA); health care administration (MBA); health information management (MS); history (MA), including American history, ancient and classical history, European history, global history, public history; homeland security (MA), including business administration, counterterrorism studies, criminal justice, cyber, emergency management and public health, intelligence studies, transportation security; homeland security resource allocation (MBA); humanities (MA); information technology (MS), including digital forensics, enterprise software development, information assurance and security, IT project management;

information technology management (MBA); intelligence studies (MA), including criminal intelligence, cyber, general (MA, MS), homeland security, intelligence analysis, intelligence collection, intelligence management, intelligence operations, terrorism studies; international relations and conflict resolution (MA), including comparative and security issues, conflict resolution, international and transnational security issues, peacekeeping; legal studies (MA); management (MA), including strategic consulting; marketing (MBA); military history (MA), including American military history, American Revolution, civil war, war since 1945, World War II; military studies (MA), including joint warfare, strategic leadership; national security studies (MA), including cyber, general (MA, MS), homeland security, regional security studies, security and intelligence analysis, terrorism studies; nonprofit management (MBA); political science (MA), including American politics and government, comparative government and development, general (MA, MS), international relations, public policy; psychology (MA); public administration (MPA), including disaster management, environmental policy, health policy, human resources, national security, organizational management, security

management; public health (MPH); reverse logistics management (MA); security management (MA); space studies (MS), including aerospace science, general (MA, MS), planetary science; sports and health sciences (MS); sports management (MBA); teaching (M Ed), including autism spectrum disorder, curriculum and instruction for elementary teachers, elementary reading, English language learners, instructional leadership, online learning, special education, STEAM (STEM plus the arts); transportation and logistics management (MA). *Program availability:* Part-time, evening/weekend, online only, 100% online. *Faculty:* 401 full-time (228 women), 1,678 part-time/adjunct (781 women). *Students:* 378 full-time (184 women), 8,455 part-time (3,484 women); includes 2,972 minority (1,552 Black or African American, non-Hispanic/Latino; 52 American Indian or Alaska Native, non-Hispanic/Latino; 211 Asian, non-Hispanic/Latino; 791 Hispanic/Latino; 70 Native Hawaiian or other Pacific Islander, non-Hispanic/Latino; 296 Two or more races, non-Hispanic/Latino), 109 international. Average age 37. In 2016, 3,185 master's awarded. *Degree requirements:* For master's, comprehensive exam or practicum. *Entrance requirements:* For master's, official transcript showing earned bachelor's degree from institution accredited by recognized accrediting body. Additional exam requirements/recommendations for international students: Required—TOEFL (minimum score 550 paper-based), IELTS (minimum score 6.5). *Application deadline:* Applications are processed on a rolling basis. Application fee: $0. Electronic applications accepted. *Expenses: Tuition:* Part-time $350 per credit hour. *Required fees:* $50 per course. *Financial support:* Scholarships/grants available. Financial award applicants required to submit FAFSA. *Unit head:* Dr. Karan Powell, President, 877-468-6268, Fax: 304-724-3780. *Application contact:* Terry Grant, Vice President of Enrollment Management, 877-468-6268, Fax: 304-724-3780, E-mail: info@apus.edu.
Website: http://www.apus.edu

Arizona State University at the Tempe campus, Ira A. Fulton Schools of Engineering, ASU Engineering Online Programs, Tempe, AZ 85287. Offers construction (MS); embedded systems (M Eng); enterprise systems innovation and management (MSE); modeling and simulation (M Eng); quality and reliability engineering (M Eng); software engineering (MSE); systems engineering (M Eng).

Arizona State University at the Tempe campus, Ira A. Fulton Schools of Engineering, School of Computing, Informatics, and Decision Systems Engineering, Tempe, AZ 85287-8809. Offers computer engineering (MS, PhD); computer science (MCS, MS, PhD); industrial engineering (MS, PhD); software engineering (MS). *Program availability:* Part-time, evening/weekend, online learning. Terminal master's awarded for partial completion of doctoral program. *Degree requirements:* For master's, comprehensive exam (for some programs), portfolio (MCS); interactive Program of Study (iPOS) submitted before completing 50 percent of required credit hours; for doctorate, comprehensive exam, thesis/dissertation, interactive Program of Study (iPOS) submitted before completing 50 percent of required credit hours. *Entrance requirements:* For master's, GRE, minimum GPA of 3.0 or equivalent in last 2 years of work leading to bachelor's degree; for doctorate, GRE, minimum GPA of 3.0 in last 2 years of work leading to bachelor's degree. Additional exam requirements/recommendations for international students: Required—TOEFL, IELTS, or PTE. Electronic applications accepted. *Expenses:* Contact institution. *Faculty research:* Artificial intelligence, cyberphysical and embedded systems, health informatics, information assurance and security, information management/multimedia/visualization, network science, personalized learning/educational games, production logistics, software and systems engineering, statistical modeling and data mining.

Auburn University, Graduate School, Ginn College of Engineering, Department of Computer Science and Software Engineering, Auburn University, AL 36849. Offers MS, MSWE, PhD. *Program availability:* Part-time. *Faculty:* 18 full-time (3 women), 1 (woman) part-time/adjunct. *Students:* 101 full-time (28 women), 41 part-time (14 women); includes 13 minority (8 Black or African American, non-Hispanic/Latino; 1 Asian, non-Hispanic/Latino; 3 Hispanic/Latino; 1 Two or more races, non-Hispanic/Latino), 96 international. Average age 28. 199 applicants, 51% accepted, 29 enrolled. In 2016, 27 master's, 8 doctorates awarded. *Degree requirements:* For master's, thesis (for some programs); for doctorate, thesis/dissertation. *Entrance requirements:* For master's and doctorate, GRE General Test, GRE Subject Test. *Application deadline:* Applications are processed on a rolling basis. Application fee: $50 ($60 for international students). Electronic applications accepted. *Expenses:* Tuition, state resident: full-time $9072; part-time $504 per credit hour. Tuition, nonresident: full-time $27,216; part-time $1512 per credit hour. *Required fees:* $812 per semester. Tuition and fees vary according to degree level and program. *Financial support:* Research assistantships, teaching assistantships, and Federal Work-Study available. Support available to part-time students. Financial award application deadline: 3/15; financial award applicants required to submit FAFSA. *Faculty research:* Parallelizable, scalable software translations; graphical representations of algorithms, structures, and processes; graph drawing. *Unit head:* Dr. Hari Narayanan, Chair, 334-844-6310. *Application contact:* Dr. George Flowers, Dean of the Graduate School, 334-844-2125.
Website: http://www.eng.auburn.edu/cse/

Boston University, Metropolitan College, Department of Computer Science, Boston, MA 02215. Offers computer information systems (MS), including computer networks, data analytics, database management and business intelligence, health informatics, IT project management, security, Web application development; computer networks (Certificate); computer science (MS); data analytics (Certificate); digital forensics (Certificate); health informatics (Certificate); information technology project management (Certificate); software development (MS); software engineering in health care systems (Certificate); telecommunications (MS), including security. *Program availability:* Part-time, evening/weekend, online learning. *Faculty:* 13 full-time (3 women), 43 part-time/adjunct (3 women). *Students:* 108 full-time (36 women), 1,294 part-time (364 women); includes 428 minority (115 Black or African American, non-Hispanic/Latino; 2 American Indian or Alaska Native, non-Hispanic/Latino; 187 Asian, non-Hispanic/Latino; 98 Hispanic/Latino; 2 Native Hawaiian or other Pacific Islander, non-Hispanic/Latino; 24 Two or more races, non-Hispanic/Latino), 314 international. Average age 33. 463 applicants, 79% accepted, 248 enrolled. In 2016, 311 master's awarded. *Degree requirements:* For master's, thesis optional. *Entrance requirements:* For master's and Certificate, official transcripts from regionally-accredited bachelor's degree program, 3 letters of recommendation, professional resume, personal statement. Additional exam requirements/recommendations for international students: Required—TOEFL (minimum score 84 iBT), IELTS. *Application deadline:* For fall admission, 6/1 priority date for international students; for spring admission, 10/1 priority date for international students. Applications are processed on a rolling basis. Application fee: $85. Electronic applications accepted. *Expenses:* Contact institution. *Financial support:* In 2016–17, 11 research assistantships (averaging $8,400 per year) were awarded; unspecified assistantships also available. Support available to part-time students. Financial award applicants required to submit FAFSA. *Faculty research:* Medical informatics, Web technologies, telecom and networks, security and forensics, software engineering, programming languages, multimedia and artificial intelligence (AI), information systems and IT project management. *Unit head:* Dr. Anatoly Temkin, Chair, 617-353-2566, Fax: 617-353-2367, E-mail: csinfo@bu.edu. *Application contact:* Lesley Moreau, Academic Program Coordinator, 617-353-2566, Fax: 617-353-2367, E-mail: metcs@bu.edu.
Website: http://www.bu.edu/csmet/

Bowling Green State University, Graduate College, College of Arts and Sciences, Department of Computer Science, Bowling Green, OH 43403. Offers computer science (MS), including operations research, parallel and distributed computing, software engineering. *Program availability:* Part-time. *Degree requirements:* For master's, thesis or alternative. *Entrance requirements:* For master's, GRE General Test. Additional exam requirements/recommendations for international students: Required—TOEFL. *Application deadline:* For fall admission, 2/1 priority date for domestic students; for spring admission, 11/15 priority date for domestic students. Application fee: $30. Electronic applications accepted. *Financial support:* Research assistantships with full tuition reimbursements, teaching assistantships with full tuition reimbursements, career-related internships or fieldwork, tuition waivers (full and partial), and unspecified assistantships available. Financial award applicants required to submit FAFSA. *Faculty research:* Artificial intelligence, real time and concurrent programming languages, behavioral aspects of computing, network protocols. *Unit head:* Dr. Rob Green, Graduate Coordinator, 419-372-8782, E-mail: csgradstudies@bgsu.edu. *Application contact:* Dr. Ron Lancaster, Graduate Coordinator, 419-372-8697.

Brandeis University, Rabb School of Continuing Studies, Division of Graduate Professional Studies, Master of Software Engineering Program, Waltham, MA 02454-9110. Offers MSE. *Program availability:* Part-time-only. *Faculty:* 45 part-time/adjunct (16 women). *Students:* 37 part-time (9 women); includes 6 minority (2 Black or African American, non-Hispanic/Latino; 3 Asian, non-Hispanic/Latino; 1 Hispanic/Latino). Average age 37. 3 applicants, 100% accepted, 3 enrolled. In 2016, 16 master's awarded. *Entrance requirements:* For master's, programming language (Java, C++, C), software engineering, and data structures, or equivalent work experience; 4-year bachelor's degree from regionally-accredited U.S. institution or equivalent; official transcript(s) from every college/university attended; resume or curriculum vitae; statement of goals; letter of recommendation. Additional exam requirements/recommendations for international students: Required—TWE (minimum score 4.5), TOEFL (minimum scores: 600 paper-based, 100 iBT), IELTS (7), or PTE (68). *Application deadline:* For fall admission, 6/21 priority date for domestic and international students; for winter admission, 9/13 priority date for domestic and international students; for spring admission, 12/20 priority date for domestic and international students; for summer admission, 3/14 priority date for domestic and international students. Applications are processed on a rolling basis. Application fee: $50. Electronic applications accepted. *Expenses:* $3,400 per course, $100 graduation fee. *Financial support:* Applicants required to submit FAFSA. *Unit head:* Dr. Aline Yurik, Program Chair, 781-736-8787, E-mail: ayurik@brandeis.edu. *Application contact:* Frances Stearns, Director of Admissions and Recruitment, 781-736-8785, E-mail: fstearns@brandeis.edu.
Website: http://www.brandeis.edu/gps

California Baptist University, Program in Software Engineering, Riverside, CA 92504-3206. Offers MS. *Program availability:* Part-time. *Faculty:* 4 full-time (2 women). *Students:* 17 full-time (3 women), 2 part-time (0 women); includes 1 minority (Asian, non-Hispanic/Latino), 16 international. Average age 24. 57 applicants, 39% accepted, 11 enrolled. *Entrance requirements:* For master's, minimum undergraduate GPA of 3.0, bachelor's transcripts, three letters of recommendation, essay, resume, interview. Additional exam requirements/recommendations for international students: Required—TOEFL (minimum score 80 iBT). *Application deadline:* For fall admission, 8/1 priority date for domestic students, 7/1 priority date for international students; for spring admission, 12/1 priority date for domestic students, 11/1 priority date for international students. Applications are processed on a rolling basis. Application fee: $45. Electronic applications accepted. *Expenses:* Contact institution. *Financial support:* Federal Work-Study and scholarships/grants available. Financial award applicants required to submit CSS PROFILE or FAFSA. *Faculty research:* Mathematical modeling, computational statistics and programming, agile software development, database management systems. *Unit head:* Dr. Arlene Perkins, Chair, Computer Science and Software Engineering, 951-552-8630, E-mail: aperkins@calbaptist.edu. *Application contact:* Taylor Neece, Director of Graduate Admissions, 951-343-4871, Fax: 877-228-8877, E-mail: graduateadmissions@calbaptist.edu.

California State University, Fullerton, Graduate Studies, College of Engineering and Computer Science, Department of Computer Science, Fullerton, CA 92834-9480. Offers computer science (MS); software engineering (MS). *Program availability:* Part-time, online learning. *Degree requirements:* For master's, comprehensive exam, project or thesis. *Entrance requirements:* For master's, GRE General Test, minimum undergraduate GPA of 2.5. Application fee: $55. *Expenses:* Tuition, state resident: full-time $3369; part-time $1953 per unit. Tuition, nonresident: full-time $3915; part-time $2499 per unit. Tuition and fees vary according to course load, degree level and program. *Financial support:* Career-related internships or fieldwork, Federal Work-Study, institutionally sponsored loans, and scholarships/grants available. Support available to part-time students. Financial award application deadline: 3/1; financial award applicants required to submit FAFSA. *Faculty research:* Software engineering, development of computer networks. *Unit head:* Dr. Shawn Wang, Chair, 657-278-7258. *Application contact:* Admissions/Applications, 657-278-2371.

California State University, Northridge, Graduate Studies, College of Engineering and Computer Science, Department of Computer Science, Northridge, CA 91330. Offers computer science (MS); software engineering (MS). *Program availability:* Part-time, evening/weekend. *Faculty:* 19 full-time (15 women), 32 part-time/adjunct (26 women). *Students:* 36 full-time (8 women), 40 part-time (6 women); includes 22 minority (1 Black or African American, non-Hispanic/Latino; 7 Asian, non-Hispanic/Latino; 11 Hispanic/Latino; 3 Two or more races, non-Hispanic/Latino), 23 international. Average age 29. 425 applicants, 12% accepted, 25 enrolled. *Degree requirements:* For master's, thesis. *Entrance requirements:* For master's, GRE General Test, minimum GPA of 2.5. Additional exam requirements/recommendations for international students: Required—TOEFL. *Application deadline:* For fall admission, 11/30 for domestic students. Application fee: $55. *Expenses:* Tuition, state resident: full-time $4152. *Financial support:* Application deadline: 3/1. *Faculty research:* Radar data processing. *Unit head:* Rick Covington, Chair, 818-677-3398.
Website: http://www.csun.edu/computerscience/

California State University, Sacramento, Office of Graduate Studies, College of Engineering and Computer Science, Department of Computer Science, Sacramento, CA 95819. Offers computer science (MS); software engineering (MS). *Program availability:* Part-time, evening/weekend. *Students:* 67 full-time (26 women), 41 part-time (17 women); includes 96 minority (2 Black or African American, non-Hispanic/Latino; 1 American Indian or Alaska Native, non-Hispanic/Latino; 90 Asian, non-Hispanic/Latino; 3 Hispanic/Latino). Average age 26. 352 applicants, 70% accepted, 60 enrolled. In 2016, 23 master's awarded. *Degree requirements:* For master's, thesis or comprehensive exam; writing proficiency exam. *Entrance requirements:* For master's, GRE, minimum GPA of 3.0 in last 60 units attempted. Additional exam requirements/recommendations for international students: Required—TOEFL (minimum score 550 paper-based; 80 iBT). *Application deadline:* For fall admission, 3/1 for domestic and international students; for spring admission, 9/15 for domestic students, 9/30 for international students. Applications are processed on a rolling basis. Application fee: $55. Electronic applications accepted. *Expenses:* $4,302 full-time tuition and fees per

Software Engineering

semester, $2,796 part-time. *Financial support:* Research assistantships, teaching assistantships, career-related internships or fieldwork, and Federal Work-Study available. Support available to part-time students. Financial award application deadline: 3/1; financial award applicants required to submit FAFSA. *Unit head:* Dr. Cui Zhang, Chair, 916-278-6834, E-mail: cscchair@ecs.csus.edu. *Application contact:* Jose Martinez, Graduate Admissions Supervisor, 916-278-7871, E-mail: martinj@skymail.csus.edu.
Website: http://www.ecs.csus.edu/csc

Carnegie Mellon University, Carnegie Institute of Technology, Information Networking Institute, Pittsburgh, PA 15213. Offers information networking (MS); information security (MS); information technology - information security (MS); information technology - mobility (MS); information technology - software management (MS). *Degree requirements:* For master's, thesis optional. *Entrance requirements:* For master's, GRE General Test, bachelor's degree in computer science, computer engineering, or electrical engineering, or related technology degree; programming skills (C/C++ fluency for some programs). Additional exam requirements/recommendations for international students: Required—TOEFL. *Faculty research:* Computer forensics and incident response; dependable systems, embedded systems, mobile systems, and sensor networks; computer and information networks, network and information security, human and socio-economic factors in secure system design; wireless sensor networks, survivable embedded systems, signal processing/compression; strategic management, international strategic management, group dynamics and decision-making structures, simulated competitive environments.

Carnegie Mellon University, School of Computer Science, Software Engineering Program, Pittsburgh, PA 15213-3891. Offers MSE, PhD. *Entrance requirements:* For master's, GRE General Test, GRE Subject Test (computer science), 2 years of experience in large-scale software development project.

Carnegie Mellon University, Tepper School of Business, Pittsburgh, PA 15213-3891. Offers accounting (PhD); business management and software engineering (MBMSE); business technologies (PhD); civil engineering and industrial management (MS); computational finance (MSCF); economics (PhD); environmental engineering and management (MEEM); financial economics (PhD); industrial administration (MBA), including administration and public management; marketing (PhD); mathematical finance (PhD); operations management (PhD); operations research (PhD); organizational behavior and theory (PhD); production and operations management (PhD); public policy and management (MS, MSED); software engineering and business management (MS); JD/MS; JD/MSIA; M Div/MS; MOM/MSIA; MSCF/MSIA. JD/MSIA offered jointly with University of Pittsburgh. *Program availability:* Part-time. Terminal master's awarded for partial completion of doctoral program. *Degree requirements:* For doctorate, thesis/dissertation. *Entrance requirements:* For master's, GMAT. Additional exam requirements/recommendations for international students: Required—TOEFL. *Expenses:* Contact institution.

Carroll University, Program in Software Engineering, Waukesha, WI 53186-5593. Offers MSE. *Program availability:* Part-time, evening/weekend. *Degree requirements:* For master's, professional experience, capstone project. *Entrance requirements:* For master's, BA or BS, 2 years of professional experience. Additional exam requirements/recommendations for international students: Required—TOEFL. Electronic applications accepted. *Faculty research:* Networking, artificial intelligence, virtual reality, effective teaching of software design, computer science pedagogy.

Cleveland State University, College of Graduate Studies, Fenn College of Engineering, Department of Electrical and Computer Engineering, Cleveland, OH 44115. Offers electrical engineering (MS, D Eng); software engineering (MS). *Program availability:* Part-time, evening/weekend. *Faculty:* 15 full-time (2 women), 1 part-time/adjunct (0 women). *Students:* 209 full-time (36 women), 163 part-time (33 women); includes 17 minority (4 Black or African American, non-Hispanic/Latino; 13 Asian, non-Hispanic/Latino), 297 international. Average age 25. 1,083 applicants, 44% accepted, 89 enrolled. In 2016, 171 master's, 2 doctorates awarded. Terminal master's awarded for partial completion of doctoral program. *Degree requirements:* For master's, thesis optional; for doctorate, comprehensive exam, thesis/dissertation, qualifying and candidacy exams. *Entrance requirements:* For master's, GRE General Test (minimum score 650 quantitative), minimum GPA of 2.75; for doctorate, GRE General Test (minimum quantitative score in 80th percentile), minimum GPA of 3.25. Additional exam requirements/recommendations for international students: Required—TOEFL (minimum score 550 paper-based; 78 iBT) or IELTS (minimum score 6.0). *Application deadline:* For fall admission, 7/1 priority date for domestic students, 5/15 for international students; for spring admission, 11/15 for domestic students, 11/1 for international students; for summer admission, 4/1 for domestic students, 3/15 for international students. Applications are processed on a rolling basis. Application fee: $40. Electronic applications accepted. *Expenses:* Contact institution. *Financial support:* In 2016–17, 31 students received support, including 23 research assistantships with tuition reimbursements available (averaging $4,242 per year), 8 teaching assistantships with tuition reimbursements available (averaging $4,242 per year); career-related internships or fieldwork, scholarships/grants, and unspecified assistantships also available. Financial award applicants required to submit FAFSA. *Faculty research:* Computer networks, computer security and privacy, mobile computing, distributed computing, software engineering, knowledge-based control systems, artificial intelligence, digital communications, MEMS, sensors, power systems, power electronics. *Total annual research expenditures:* $484,362. *Unit head:* Dr. Chansu Yu, Chairperson, 216-687-2584, Fax: 216-687-5405, E-mail: f.xiong@csuohio.edu. *Application contact:* Deborah L. Brown, Interim Assistant Director, Graduate Admissions, 216-523-7572, Fax: 216-687-9214, E-mail: d.l.brown@csuohio.edu.
Website: http://www.csuohio.edu/ece

Colorado Technical University Aurora, Program in Computer Science, Aurora, CO 80014. Offers computer systems security (MSCS); database systems (MSCS); software engineering (MSCS). *Program availability:* Part-time, evening/weekend. *Degree requirements:* For master's, thesis or alternative. *Entrance requirements:* For master's, minimum undergraduate GPA of 3.0, resume.

Colorado Technical University Colorado Springs, Graduate Studies, Program in Computer Science, Colorado Springs, CO 80907. Offers computer science (DCS); computer systems security (MSCS); database systems (MSCS); software engineering (MSCS). *Program availability:* Part-time, evening/weekend, online learning. *Degree requirements:* For master's, thesis or alternative; for doctorate, thesis/dissertation. *Entrance requirements:* For doctorate, minimum graduate GPA of 3.0, 5 years of related work experience. *Faculty research:* Software engineering, systems engineering.

Concordia University, School of Graduate Studies, Faculty of Engineering and Computer Science, Department of Computer Science and Software Engineering, Montréal, QC H3G 1M8, Canada. Offers computer science (M App Comp Sc, M Comp Sc, PhD, Diploma); software engineering (M Eng, MA Sc). *Degree requirements:* For master's, one foreign language, thesis optional; for doctorate, one foreign language, comprehensive exam, thesis/dissertation. *Faculty research:* Computer systems and applications, mathematics of computation, pattern recognition, artificial intelligence and robotics.

DePaul University, College of Computing and Digital Media, Chicago, IL 60604. Offers animation (MA, MFA); business information technology (MS); cinema (MFA); cinema production (MS); computational finance (MS); computer and information sciences (PhD); computer game development (MS); computer information and network security (MS); computer science (MS); e-commerce technology (MS); health informatics (MS); human-computer interaction (MS); information systems (MS); information technology project management (MS); network engineering and management (MS); predictive analytics (MS); screenwriting (MFA); software engineering (MS); JD/MS. *Program availability:* Part-time, evening/weekend, online learning. *Degree requirements:* For master's, thesis (for some programs); for doctorate, comprehensive exam, thesis/dissertation. *Entrance requirements:* For master's, GRE or GMAT (for MS in computational finance only), bachelor's degree, resume (MS in predictive analytics only), IT experience (MS in information technology project management only), portfolio review (all MFA programs and MA in animation); for doctorate, GRE, master's degree in computer science. Additional exam requirements/recommendations for international students: Required—TOEFL (minimum score 590 paper-based; 80 iBT), IELTS (minimum score 6.5), PTE (minimum score 53). Electronic applications accepted. *Expenses:* Contact institution. *Faculty research:* Data mining, computer science, human-computer interaction, security, animation and film.

★ **Drexel University,** College of Computing and Informatics, Department of Computer Science, Philadelphia, PA 19104-2875. Offers computer science (MS, PhD, Postbaccalaureate Certificate); software engineering (MS). *Program availability:* Part-time, evening/weekend, 100% online. *Faculty:* 31 full-time (5 women). *Students:* 57 full-time (15 women), 63 part-time (6 women); includes 10 minority (1 Black or African American, non-Hispanic/Latino; 4 Asian, non-Hispanic/Latino; 5 Hispanic/Latino), 45 international. Average age 29. 396 applicants, 24% accepted, 35 enrolled. In 2016, 42 master's, 4 doctorates awarded. Terminal master's awarded for partial completion of doctoral program. *Degree requirements:* For doctorate, thesis/dissertation. *Entrance requirements:* For master's and doctorate, GRE General Test. Additional exam requirements/recommendations for international students: Required—TOEFL (minimum score 600 paper-based; 100 iBT), IELTS (minimum score 6.5). *Application deadline:* For fall admission, 8/15 for domestic students, 7/15 for international students; for spring admission, 3/1 for domestic students, 2/1 for international students. Applications are processed on a rolling basis. Application fee: $65. Electronic applications accepted. Application fee is waived when completed online. *Expenses:* Tuition: Full-time $32,184; part-time $1192 per credit hour. *Required fees:* $280. Tuition and fees vary according to campus/location and program. *Financial support:* In 2016–17, 15 students received support, including 1 fellowship with full tuition reimbursement available (averaging $35,000 per year), 19 research assistantships with full tuition reimbursements available (averaging $27,780 per year), 11 teaching assistantships with full tuition reimbursements available (averaging $26,250 per year); scholarships/grants and tuition waivers (partial) also available. Financial award application deadline: 3/1; financial award applicants required to submit FAFSA. *Total annual research expenditures:* $1.9 million. *Unit head:* Dr. Yi Deng, Dean/Professor, 215-895-2474, Fax: 215-895-2494, E-mail: yd362@drexel.edu. *Application contact:* Matthew Lechtenberg, Director, Recruitment, 215-895-2474, Fax: 215-895-2303, E-mail: cciinfo@drexel.edu.

See Display on page 275 and Close-Up on page 369.

Drexel University, College of Engineering, Department of Electrical and Computer Engineering, Program in Software Engineering, Philadelphia, PA 19104-2875. Offers MSSE. *Students:* 1 full-time (0 women), 17 part-time (0 women); includes 2 minority (1 Asian, non-Hispanic/Latino; 1 Hispanic/Latino), 1 international. Average age 31. In 2016, 15 master's awarded. *Entrance requirements:* For master's, GRE. Additional exam requirements/recommendations for international students: Required—TOEFL. *Application deadline:* For fall admission, 8/21 for domestic students. Applications are processed on a rolling basis. Application fee: $50. Electronic applications accepted. *Expenses:* Tuition: Full-time $32,184; part-time $1192 per credit hour. *Required fees:* $280. Tuition and fees vary according to campus/location and program. *Financial support:* Application deadline: 2/1. *Unit head:* Dr. Nihat M. Bilgutay, Head, 215-895-6806, Fax: 215-895-1695, E-mail: bilgutay@ece.drexel.edu. *Application contact:* Director of Graduate Admissions, 215-895-6700, Fax: 215-895-5939, E-mail: enroll@drexel.edu.

East Carolina University, Graduate School, College of Engineering and Technology, Department of Computer Science, Greenville, NC 27858-4353. Offers computer science (MS); software engineering (MS). *Program availability:* Part-time, evening/weekend. *Students:* 32 full-time (8 women), 54 part-time (14 women); includes 19 minority (7 Black or African American, non-Hispanic/Latino; 9 Asian, non-Hispanic/Latino; 3 Hispanic/Latino), 23 international. Average age 31. 66 applicants, 83% accepted, 28 enrolled. In 2016, 19 master's awarded. *Degree requirements:* For master's, comprehensive exam, thesis or alternative. *Entrance requirements:* For master's, GRE General Test. Additional exam requirements/recommendations for international students: Required—TOEFL. *Application deadline:* For fall admission, 11/1 priority date for domestic students, 10/1 priority date for international students; for spring admission, 3/1 priority date for domestic and international students. Applications are processed on a rolling basis. Application fee: $50. Electronic applications accepted. *Financial support:* Research assistantships, career-related internships or fieldwork, Federal Work-Study, tuition waivers (full), and unspecified assistantships available. Financial award application deadline: 3/1. *Faculty research:* Software development, software engineering, artificial intelligence, bioinformatics, cryptography. *Unit head:* Dr. Karl Abrahamson, Interim Chair, 252-328-9689, E-mail: karl@cs.ecu.edu. *Application contact:* Dean of Graduate School, 252-328-6012, Fax: 252-328-6071, E-mail: gradschool@ecu.edu.
Website: http://www.ecu.edu/cs-tecs/csci/index.cfm

Embry-Riddle Aeronautical University–Daytona, Department of Electrical, Computer, Software and Systems Engineering, Daytona Beach, FL 32114-3900. Offers computer engineering (MS); cybersecurity engineering (MS); electrical engineering (MSECE); electrical engineering and computer science (PhD), including electrical, computer, software, and systems engineering; software engineering (MSSE); systems engineering (MS). *Program availability:* Part-time. *Faculty:* 13 full-time (1 woman), 1 part-time/adjunct (0 women). *Students:* 63 full-time (17 women), 8 part-time (3 women); includes 6 minority (1 Black or African American, non-Hispanic/Latino; 1 Asian, non-Hispanic/Latino; 1 Hispanic/Latino; 3 Two or more races, non-Hispanic/Latino), 41 international. Average age 25. 93 applicants, 45% accepted, 21 enrolled. In 2016, 30 master's awarded. *Degree requirements:* For master's, thesis or alternative; for doctorate, thesis/dissertation. *Entrance requirements:* For master's, GRE (for some programs); for doctorate, GRE. Additional exam requirements/recommendations for international students: Required—TOEFL (minimum score 550 paper-based, 79 iBT) or IELTS (6.). *Application deadline:* For fall admission, 3/1 priority date for domestic students; for spring admission, 11/1 priority date for domestic students; for summer admission, 4/1 priority date for domestic students. Applications are processed on a rolling basis. Application fee: $50. Electronic applications accepted. *Expenses:* Tuition: Full-time $16,296; part-time $1358 per credit hour. *Required fees:* $1294; $647 per semester.

One-time fee: $100 full-time. Tuition and fees vary according to course load, degree level and program. *Financial support:* Research assistantships, teaching assistantships, career-related internships or fieldwork, scholarships/grants, unspecified assistantships, and on-campus employment available. Financial award application deadline: 3/15; financial award applicants required to submit FAFSA. *Faculty research:* Cybersecurity and assured systems engineering, radar, unmanned and autonomous systems, modeling and simulation, cyber-physical systems. *Unit head:* Timothy Wilson, PhD, Professor of Electrical and Computer Engineering/Chair, Department of Electrical, Computer, Software and Systems Engineering, 386-226-6100, E-mail: timothy.wilson@erau.edu. *Application contact:* Graduate Admissions, 386-226-6176, Fax: 386-226-7070, E-mail: graduate.admissions@erau.edu.
Website: https://daytonabeach.erau.edu/college-engineering/electrical-computer-software-systems/index.html

Fairfield University, School of Engineering, Fairfield, CT 06824. Offers database management (CAS); electrical and computer engineering (MS); information security (CAS); management of technology (MS); mechanical engineering (MS); network technology (CAS); software engineering (MS); Web application development (CAS). *Program availability:* Part-time, evening/weekend. *Faculty:* 7 full-time (1 woman), 15 part-time/adjunct (2 women). *Students:* 104 full-time (31 women), 56 part-time (15 women); includes 17 minority (8 Black or African American, non-Hispanic/Latino; 5 Asian, non-Hispanic/Latino; 4 Hispanic/Latino), 108 international. Average age 28. 193 applicants, 63% accepted, 20 enrolled. In 2016, 173 master's awarded. *Degree requirements:* For master's, capstone course. *Entrance requirements:* For master's, resume, 2 recommendations. Additional exam requirements/recommendations for international students: Required—TOEFL (minimum score 550 paper-based; 80 iBT) or IELTS (minimum score 6.5). *Application deadline:* For fall admission, 5/15 for international students; for spring admission, 10/15 for international students. Applications are processed on a rolling basis. Application fee: $60. Electronic applications accepted. *Expenses:* $800 per credit hour. *Financial support:* In 2016–17, 27 students received support. Scholarships/grants and unspecified assistantships available. Financial award applicants required to submit FAFSA. *Faculty research:* Artificial intelligence and information visualization, natural language processing, thermofluids, microwaves and electromagnetics, micro-/nano-manufacturing. *Unit head:* Dr. Bruce Berdanier, Dean, 203-254-4147, Fax: 203-254-4013, E-mail: bberdanier@fairfield.edu. *Application contact:* Marianne Gumpper, Director of Graduate and Continuing Studies Admission, 203-254-4184, Fax: 203-254-4073, E-mail: gradadmis@fairfield.edu.
Website: http://www.fairfield.edu/soe

Florida Agricultural and Mechanical University, Division of Graduate Studies, Research, and Continuing Education, College of Science and Technology, Department of Computer Information Sciences, Tallahassee, FL 32307-3200. Offers software engineering (MS). *Entrance requirements:* Additional exam requirements/recommendations for international students: Required—TOEFL.

Florida Institute of Technology, College of Engineering, Program in Software Engineering, Melbourne, FL 32901-6975. Offers MS. *Program availability:* Part-time. *Students:* 8 full-time (2 women), 2 part-time (1 woman); includes 2 minority (1 Black or African American, non-Hispanic/Latino; 1 Two or more races, non-Hispanic/Latino), 5 international. Average age 27. 43 applicants, 28% accepted, 2 enrolled. In 2016, 6 master's awarded. *Degree requirements:* For master's, comprehensive exam (for some programs), thesis optional, minimum of 30 credit hours. *Entrance requirements:* For master's, GRE General Test, 3 letters of recommendation, specific courses in mathematical studies. Additional exam requirements/recommendations for international students: Required—TOEFL (minimum score 550 paper-based; 79 iBT). *Application deadline:* Applications are processed on a rolling basis. Application fee: $50. Electronic applications accepted. *Expenses: Tuition:* Full-time $22,338; part-time $1241 per credit hour. *Required fees:* $250. Tuition and fees vary according to degree level, campus/location and program. *Financial support:* Career-related internships or fieldwork available. *Unit head:* Dr. Richard Newman, Interim Department Head, 321-674-7487, E-mail: jrnewman@fit.edu. *Application contact:* Cheryl A. Brown, Associate Director of Graduate Admissions, 321-674-7581, Fax: 321-723-9468, E-mail: cbrown@fit.edu.
Website: http://coe.fit.edu/

Florida Institute of Technology, Extended Studies Division, Melbourne, FL 32901-6975. Offers acquisition and contract management (MS); aerospace engineering (MS); business administration (MBA, DBA); computer information systems (MS); computer science (MS); electrical engineering (MS); engineering management (MS); human resources management (MS); logistics management (MS), including humanitarian and disaster relief logistics; management (MS), including acquisition and contract management, e-business, human resources management, information systems, logistics management, management, transportation management; material acquisition management (MS); mechanical engineering (MS); operations research (MS); project management (MS), including information systems, operations research; public administration (MPA); quality management (MS); software engineering (MS); space systems (MS); space systems management (MS); supply chain management (MS); systems management (MS), including information systems, operations research; technology management (MS). *Program availability:* Part-time, evening/weekend, online learning. *Faculty:* 10 full-time (3 women), 122 part-time/adjunct (29 women). *Students:* 131 full-time (58 women), 997 part-time (348 women); includes 389 minority (231 Black or African American, non-Hispanic/Latino; 9 American Indian or Alaska Native, non-Hispanic/Latino; 26 Asian, non-Hispanic/Latino; 99 Hispanic/Latino; 3 Native Hawaiian or other Pacific Islander, non-Hispanic/Latino; 21 Two or more races, non-Hispanic/Latino), 53 international. Average age 36. 962 applicants, 48% accepted, 323 enrolled. In 2016, 403 master's awarded. *Degree requirements:* For master's, comprehensive exam (for some programs). *Entrance requirements:* For master's, GMAT or resume showing 8 years of supervised experience, minimum GPA of 3.0, 2 letters of recommendation, resume. Additional exam requirements/recommendations for international students: Required—TOEFL (minimum score 550 paper-based; 79 iBT). *Application deadline:* For fall admission, 4/1 for international students; for spring admission, 9/30 for international students. Applications are processed on a rolling basis. Electronic applications accepted. *Expenses:* Contact institution. *Financial support:* Application deadline: 3/1; applicants required to submit FAFSA. *Unit head:* Dr. Theodore R. Richardson, III, Dean, 321-674-8123, Fax: 321-674-7597, E-mail: trichardson@fit.edu. *Application contact:* Carolyn Farrior, Director of Graduate Admissions, Online Learning and Off-Campus Programs, 321-674-7118, Fax: 321-674-8216, E-mail: cfarrior@fit.edu.
Website: http://es.fit.edu

Gannon University, School of Graduate Studies, College of Engineering and Business, School of Engineering and Computer Science, Program in Computer and Information Science, Erie, PA 16541-0001. Offers information analytics (MSCIS); software engineering (MSCIS). *Program availability:* Part-time, evening/weekend. *Students:* 1 part-time (0 women); minority (Native Hawaiian or other Pacific Islander, non-Hispanic/Latino). Average age 42. In 2016, 27 master's awarded. *Degree requirements:* For master's, thesis (for some programs), directed research. *Entrance requirements:* For master's, 3 letters of recommendation; resume; transcripts; baccalaureate degree in

computer science, information systems, information science, software engineering, or related field from regionally-accredited institution with minimum GPA of 2.5. Additional exam requirements/recommendations for international students: Required—TOEFL (minimum score 79 iBT). *Application deadline:* Applications are processed on a rolling basis. Application fee: $25. Electronic applications accepted. Application fee is waived when completed online. *Expenses: Tuition:* Full-time $17,370. *Required fees:* $550. Tuition and fees vary according to course load and program. *Financial support:* Federal Work-Study and unspecified assistantships available. Financial award application deadline: 7/1; financial award applicants required to submit FAFSA. *Unit head:* Dr. Mei-Huei Tang, Chair, 814-871-5393, E-mail: tang002@gannon.edu. *Application contact:* Bridget Philip, Director of Graduate Admissions, 814-871-7412, E-mail: graduate@gannon.edu.

Gannon University, School of Graduate Studies, College of Engineering and Business, School of Engineering and Computer Science, Program in Electrical and Computer Engineering, Erie, PA 16541-0001. Offers MSEE, MSES. *Program availability:* Part-time, evening/weekend. *Students:* 76 full-time (16 women), 29 part-time (4 women); includes 1 minority (Asian, non-Hispanic/Latino), 101 international. Average age 25. 267 applicants, 58% accepted, 17 enrolled. In 2016, 94 master's awarded. *Degree requirements:* For master's, thesis (for some programs), oral exam (for some programs), design project (for some programs). *Entrance requirements:* For master's, bachelor's degree in electrical or computer engineering from an ABET-accredited program or its equivalent with minimum GPA of 2.5, transcripts, 3 letters of recommendation. Additional exam requirements/recommendations for international students: Required—TOEFL (minimum score 79 iBT). *Application deadline:* Applications are processed on a rolling basis. Application fee: $25. Electronic applications accepted. Application fee is waived when completed online. *Expenses: Tuition:* Full-time $17,370. *Required fees:* $550. Tuition and fees vary according to course load and program. *Financial support:* Federal Work-Study available. Financial award application deadline: 7/1; financial award applicants required to submit FAFSA. *Unit head:* Dr. Wookwon Lee, Chair, 814-871-7630, E-mail: lee023@gannon.edu. *Application contact:* Bridget Philip, Director of Graduate Admissions, 814-871-7412, E-mail: graduate@gannon.edu.

Gannon University, School of Graduate Studies, College of Engineering and Business, School of Engineering and Computer Science, Program in Software Engineering, Erie, PA 16541-0001. Offers MSCIS. *Program availability:* Part-time, evening/weekend. *Students:* 20 full-time (8 women), 2 part-time (0 women), 20 international. Average age 27. 256 applicants, 61% accepted, 3 enrolled. In 2016, 10 master's awarded. *Entrance requirements:* For master's, baccalaureate degree in computer science, information systems, information science, software engineering, or a related field from regionally-accredited institution with minimum GPA of 2.5; resume; transcripts; 3 letters of recommendation. Additional exam requirements/recommendations for international students: Required—TOEFL (minimum score 79 iBT). *Application deadline:* Applications are processed on a rolling basis. Application fee: $25. Electronic applications accepted. Application fee is waived when completed online. *Expenses: Tuition:* Full-time $17,370. *Required fees:* $550. Tuition and fees vary according to course load and program. *Financial support:* Federal Work-Study available. Financial award application deadline: 7/1; financial award applicants required to submit FAFSA. *Unit head:* Dr. William L. Scheller, II, Dean, 814-871-7582, E-mail: scheller002@gannon.edu. *Application contact:* Bridget Philip, Director of Graduate Admissions, 814-871-7412, E-mail: graduate@gannon.edu.

Grand Valley State University, Padnos College of Engineering and Computing, School of Computing and Information Systems, Allendale, MI 49401-9403. Offers computer information systems (MS), including databases, distributed systems, management of information systems, object-oriented systems, software engineering. *Program availability:* Part-time, evening/weekend. *Faculty:* 10 full-time (3 women), 1 (woman) part-time/adjunct. *Students:* 28 full-time (3 women), 57 part-time (14 women); includes 11 minority (3 Black or African American, non-Hispanic/Latino; 4 Asian, non-Hispanic/Latino; 3 Hispanic/Latino; 1 Two or more races, non-Hispanic/Latino), 32 international. Average age 30. 97 applicants, 59% accepted, 17 enrolled. In 2016, 36 master's awarded. *Degree requirements:* For master's, capstone course, project, or thesis. *Entrance requirements:* For master's, GMAT or GRE General Test, minimum GPA of 3.0; knowledge of a programming language; coursework or experience in: computer architecture and/or organization, data structures and algorithms, databases, discrete math, networking, operating systems, and software engineering; minimum of 2 letters of recommendation; resume; personal statement. Additional exam requirements/recommendations for international students: Required—TOEFL, Michigan English Language Assessment Battery or completion of ELS 112; Recommended—IELTS. *Application deadline:* For fall admission, 6/1 for international students; for winter admission, 9/1 for international students. Applications are processed on a rolling basis. Application fee: $30. Electronic applications accepted. *Expenses:* $646 per credit hour. *Financial support:* In 2016–17, 11 students received support, including 3 fellowships, 10 research assistantships with full and partial tuition reimbursements available (averaging $8,000 per year). *Faculty research:* Object technology, distributed computing, information systems management database, software engineering. *Unit head:* Dr. Paul Leidig, Director, 616-331-2038, Fax: 616-331-2106, E-mail: leidigp@gvsu.edu. *Application contact:* Dr. D. Robert Adams, Graduate Program Director/Recruiting Contact, 616-331-3885, Fax: 616-331-2106, E-mail: adams@cis.gvsu.edu.
Website: http://www.cis.gvsu.edu/

Harrisburg University of Science and Technology, Program in Information Systems Engineering and Management, Harrisburg, PA 17101. Offers analytics (MS); digital government (MS); digital health (MS); entrepreneurship (MS); information security (MS); software engineering and systems development (MS). *Program availability:* Part-time, evening/weekend. *Faculty:* 9 full-time (0 women), 1 (woman) part-time/adjunct. *Students:* 1,031 full-time (264 women), 35 part-time (10 women); includes 2 minority (1 Black or African American, non-Hispanic/Latino; 1 Asian, non-Hispanic/Latino), 1,060 international. In 2016, 83 master's awarded. *Degree requirements:* For master's, thesis optional. *Entrance requirements:* For master's, baccalaureate degree. Additional exam requirements/recommendations for international students: Required—TOEFL (minimum score 520 paper-based; 80 iBT); Recommended—IELTS (minimum score 6). *Application deadline:* Applications are processed on a rolling basis. Application fee: $0. Electronic applications accepted. *Expenses: Tuition:* Full-time $4800; part-time $800 per semester hour. *Financial support:* In 2016–17, 2 students received support. Teaching assistantships available. Financial award applicants required to submit FAFSA. *Faculty research:* Healthcare Informatics, material analysis, enterprise systems, circuit design, enterprise architectures. *Unit head:* Dr. Amjad Umar, Director and Professor, 717-901-5141, Fax: 717-901-3141, E-mail: aumar@harrisburgu.edu.

Illinois Institute of Technology, Graduate College, Armour College of Engineering, Department of Electrical and Computer Engineering, Chicago, IL 60616. Offers biomedical imaging and signals (MAS); computer engineering (MS, PhD); electrical engineering (MS, PhD); electricity markets (MAS); network engineering (MAS); power engineering (MAS); telecommunications and software engineering (MAS); VLSI and microelectronics (MAS); MS/MS. *Program availability:* Part-time, evening/weekend, online learning. Terminal master's awarded for partial completion of doctoral program. *Degree requirements:* For master's, comprehensive exam (for some programs), thesis (for some programs); for doctorate, comprehensive exam, thesis/dissertation. *Entrance requirements:* For master's and doctorate, GRE General Test (minimum score 1100 Quantitative and Verbal, 3.5 Analytical Writing), minimum undergraduate GPA of 3.0. Additional exam requirements/recommendations for international students: Required—TOEFL (minimum score 550 paper-based; 80 iBT); Recommended—IELTS (minimum score 5.5). Electronic applications accepted. *Faculty research:* Communication systems, wireless networks, computer systems, computer networks, wireless security, cloud computing and micro-electronics; electromagnetics and electronics; power and control systems; signal and image processing.

Illinois Institute of Technology, Graduate College, College of Science, Department of Computer Science, Chicago, IL 60616. Offers business (MCS); computational intelligence (MCS); computer science (MCS, MS, PhD); cyber-physical systems (MCS); data analytics (MCS); data science (MAS); database systems (MCS); distributed and cloud computing (MCS); education (MCS); finance (MCS); information security and assurance (MCS); networking and communications (MCS); software engineering (MCS); telecommunications and software engineering (MAS); MS/MAS. *Program availability:* Part-time, evening/weekend, online learning. Terminal master's awarded for partial completion of doctoral program. *Degree requirements:* For master's, thesis optional; for doctorate, comprehensive exam, thesis/dissertation. *Entrance requirements:* For master's, GRE General Test with minimum scores of 298 Quantitative and Verbal, 3.0 Analytical Writing (for MS); GRE General Test with minimum scores of 292 Quantitative and Verbal, 2.5 Analytical Writing (for MAS), minimum undergraduate GPA of 3.0; for doctorate, GRE General Test (minimum scores: 304 Quantitative and Verbal, 3.5 Analytical Writing), minimum undergraduate GPA of 3.0. Additional exam requirements/recommendations for international students: Required—TOEFL (minimum score 523 paper-based; 70 iBT). Electronic applications accepted. *Faculty research:* Parallel and distributed processing, high-performance computing, computational linguistics, information retrieval, data mining, grid computing.

Indiana University–Purdue University Indianapolis, School of Science, Department of Computer and Information Science, Indianapolis, IN 46202-5132. Offers biocomputing (Graduate Certificate); biometrics (Graduate Certificate); computer science (MS, PhD); computer security (Graduate Certificate); databases and data mining (Graduate Certificate); software engineering (Graduate Certificate). *Program availability:* Part-time. *Faculty:* 16 full-time (2 women), 10 part-time/adjunct (4 women). *Students:* 95 full-time (36 women), 44 part-time (15 women); includes 8 minority (3 Black or African American, non-Hispanic/Latino; 5 Asian, non-Hispanic/Latino), 119 international. Average age 27. 275 applicants, 30% accepted, 41 enrolled. In 2016, 52 master's, 3 doctorates, 3 other advanced degrees awarded. Terminal master's awarded for partial completion of doctoral program. *Degree requirements:* For master's and Graduate Certificate, thesis optional; for doctorate, thesis/dissertation. *Entrance requirements:* For master's and doctorate, GRE, BS in computer science or the equivalent with a minimum GPA of 3.0 (or equivalent); for Graduate Certificate, BS in computer science or the equivalent with a minimum GPA of 3.0 (or equivalent). Additional exam requirements/recommendations for international students: Required—PTE (minimum score 58), TOEFL (minimum score 550 paper-based, 79 iBT) or IELTS (6.5). *Application deadline:* For fall admission, 1/15 priority date for domestic and international students; for spring admission, 9/15 for domestic students. Application fee: $60 ($65 for international students). *Financial support:* In 2016–17, 45 students received support, including 2 fellowships with full tuition reimbursements available (averaging $20,000 per year), 15 research assistantships with full and partial tuition reimbursements available (averaging $18,000 per year), 20 teaching assistantships with full and partial tuition reimbursements available (averaging $18,000 per year); scholarships/grants, health care benefits, and tuition waivers (full and partial) also available. Financial award application deadline: 1/15. *Faculty research:* Imaging and visualization; networking and security; software engineering; distributed and parallel computing; database, data mining and machine learning. *Total annual research expenditures:* $550,196. *Unit head:* Dr. Shiaofen Fang, Chair, 317-274-9727, Fax: 317-274-9742, E-mail: sfang@cs.iupui.edu. *Application contact:* Nicole Wittlief, Graduate Admissions and Program Coordinator, 317-274-3883, Fax: 317-274-9742, E-mail: wittlief@cs.iupui.edu.
Website: http://www.cs.iupui.edu/

Instituto Tecnologico de Santo Domingo, Graduate School, Area of Engineering, Santo Domingo, Dominican Republic. Offers construction administration (MS, Certificate); data telecommunications (M Eng, MS, Certificate); industrial engineering (M Eng, Certificate); industrial management (M Mgmt); information technology (Certificate); maintenance engineering (M Eng); occupational hazard prevention (M Mgmt); production management (Certificate); quantitative methods (Certificate); sanitary and environmental engineering (M Eng); structural engineering (M Eng); systems engineering and electronic data processing (Certificate); transportation (Certificate).

International Technological University, Program in Software Engineering, San Jose, CA 95134. Offers MSSE. *Program availability:* Part-time, evening/weekend. *Degree requirements:* For master's, thesis or alternative, capstone project. *Entrance requirements:* Additional exam requirements/recommendations for international students: Required—TOEFL, IELTS. Electronic applications accepted.

Jacksonville State University, College of Graduate Studies and Continuing Education, College of Arts and Sciences, Program in Computer Systems and Software Design, Jacksonville, AL 36265-1602. Offers MS. *Program availability:* Part-time, evening/weekend. *Faculty:* 11 full-time (4 women). *Students:* 6 full-time (3 women), 7 part-time (2 women); includes 1 minority (Hispanic/Latino), 6 international. Average age 29. 83 applicants, 25% accepted, 1 enrolled. In 2016, 5 master's awarded. *Degree requirements:* For master's, comprehensive exam, thesis (for some programs). *Entrance requirements:* Additional exam requirements/recommendations for international students: Required—TOEFL (minimum score 500 paper-based; 61 iBT). *Application deadline:* Applications are processed on a rolling basis. Application fee: $35. Electronic applications accepted. *Financial support:* In 2016–17, 7 students received support, including 3 teaching assistantships. Support available to part-time students. Financial award application deadline: 4/1; financial award applicants required to submit FAFSA. *Unit head:* Dr. David Thornton, Head, 256-782-5359, E-mail: thornton@jsu.edu. *Application contact:* Dr. Jean Pugliese, Associate Dean, 256-782-8278, Fax: 256-782-5321, E-mail: pugliese@jsu.edu.

Kennesaw State University, College of Computing and Software Engineering, Department of Software Engineering and Game Development, Kennesaw, GA 30144. Offers software engineering (MSSWE, Graduate Certificate); software engineering foundations (Graduate Certificate). *Program availability:* Part-time, evening/weekend, online learning. *Degree requirements:* For master's, thesis optional, capstone (software engineering). *Entrance requirements:* For master's, GRE (recommended). Additional exam requirements/recommendations for international students: Required—TOEFL (minimum score 550 paper-based; 79 iBT), IELTS (minimum score 6.5). Electronic applications accepted. *Faculty research:* Image processing and artificial intelligence, distributed computing, telemedicine applications, enterprise architectures, databases, software requirements engineering, software quality and metrics, usability, parallel and distributed computing, information security.

Lipscomb University, College of Computing and Technology, Nashville, TN 37204-3951. Offers data science (MS); information technology (MS), including data science, information security, information technology management, software engineering; software engineering (MS). *Program availability:* Part-time, evening/weekend. *Faculty:* 7 full-time (0 women), 6 part-time/adjunct (1 woman). *Students:* 21 full-time (10 women), 10 part-time (3 women); includes 9 minority (5 Black or African American, non-Hispanic/Latino; 4 Asian, non-Hispanic/Latino), 1 international. Average age 34. 47 applicants, 49% accepted, 12 enrolled. In 2016, 26 degrees awarded. *Degree requirements:* For master's, capstone project. *Entrance requirements:* For master's, GRE, 2 references, transcripts, resume, personal statement. Additional exam requirements/recommendations for international students: Required—TOEFL (minimum score 570 paper-based; 80 iBT). *Application deadline:* Applications are processed on a rolling basis. Application fee: $50 ($75 for international students). Electronic applications accepted. *Expenses:* $1,226 per hour. *Financial support:* Scholarships/grants and employer agreements available. Financial award applicants required to submit FAFSA. *Unit head:* Dr. Fortune S. Mhlanga, Dean, 615-966-5073, E-mail: fortune.mhlanga@lipscomb.edu. *Application contact:* Brett Ramsey, Enrollment Management Specialist, 615-966-1193, E-mail: brett.ramsey@lipscomb.edu.
Website: http://www.lipscomb.edu/technology/

Loyola University Chicago, Graduate School, Department of Computer Science, Chicago, IL 60611. Offers computer science (MS); information technology (MS); software engineering (MS). *Program availability:* Part-time, evening/weekend, 100% online, blended/hybrid learning. *Faculty:* 15 full-time (3 women), 10 part-time/adjunct (2 women). *Students:* 64 full-time (33 women), 50 part-time (14 women); includes 24 minority (7 Black or African American, non-Hispanic/Latino; 10 Asian, non-Hispanic/Latino; 5 Hispanic/Latino; 2 Two or more races, non-Hispanic/Latino), 56 international. Average age 28. 135 applicants, 43% accepted, 39 enrolled. In 2016, 49 master's awarded. *Degree requirements:* For master's, thesis optional, ten courses. *Entrance requirements:* For master's, 3 letters of recommendation, transcripts, statement of purpose. Additional exam requirements/recommendations for international students: Required—TOEFL (minimum score 550 paper-based; 79 iBT) or IELTS (minimum score 6.5). *Application deadline:* Applications are processed on a rolling basis. Application fee: $50. Electronic applications accepted. Application fee is waived when completed online. *Expenses:* $1,033 per credit hour. *Financial support:* In 2016–17, 17 students received support, including 2 fellowships with full tuition reimbursements available, 1 research assistantship with full tuition reimbursement available (averaging $17,000 per year), 11 teaching assistantships with partial tuition reimbursements available (averaging $9,575 per year); career-related internships or fieldwork, Federal Work-Study, health care benefits, and tuition waivers (full and partial) also available. Financial award application deadline: 3/15. *Faculty research:* Software engineering, machine learning, algorithms and complexity, parallel and distributed computing, databases and computer networks. *Total annual research expenditures:* $22,000. *Unit head:* Dr. Konstantin Laufer, Chair, 312-915-7983, Fax: 312-915-7998, E-mail: laufer@cs.luc.edu. *Application contact:* Cecilia Murphy, Graduate Program Secretary, 312-915-7990, Fax: 312-915-7998, E-mail: csinfo@cs.luc.edu.
Website: http://cs.luc.edu

Marist College, Graduate Programs, School of Computer Science and Mathematics, Poughkeepsie, NY 12601-1387. Offers computer science/software development (MS); information systems (MS, Adv C); technology management (MS). *Program availability:* Part-time, evening/weekend, online learning. *Entrance requirements:* For master's, resume. Additional exam requirements/recommendations for international students: Required—TOEFL (minimum score 550 paper-based; 80 iBT); Recommended—IELTS (minimum score 6.5). Electronic applications accepted. *Faculty research:* Data quality, artificial intelligence, imaging, analysis of algorithms, distributed systems and applications.

Marymount University, School of Business Administration, Program in Information Technology, Arlington, VA 22207-4299. Offers health care informatics (Certificate); information technology (MS, Certificate), including computer security (MS), health care informatics (MS), project management and technology leadership (MS), software engineering (MS); information technology project management and technology leadership (Certificate); MS/MBA; MS/MS. *Program availability:* Part-time, evening/weekend. *Faculty:* 7 full-time (6 women), 7 part-time/adjunct (0 women). *Students:* 39 full-time (23 women), 31 part-time (13 women); includes 24 minority (12 Black or African American, non-Hispanic/Latino; 5 Asian, non-Hispanic/Latino; 6 Hispanic/Latino; 1 Two or more races, non-Hispanic/Latino), 31 international. Average age 30. 67 applicants, 97% accepted, 23 enrolled. In 2016, 29 master's, 12 other advanced degrees awarded. *Degree requirements:* For master's, thesis or alternative. *Entrance requirements:* For master's, resume, bachelor's degree in computer-related field or another subject with certificate in computer-related field or related work experience; bachelor's degree in computer science or work in software development (for software engineering track). Additional exam requirements/recommendations for international students: Required—TOEFL (minimum score 600 paper-based; 96 iBT), IELTS (minimum score 6.5). *Application deadline:* For fall admission, 7/16 priority date for domestic and international students; for spring admission, 11/16 priority date for domestic and international students; for summer admission, 4/16 for domestic and international students. Applications are processed on a rolling basis. Application fee: $40. Electronic applications accepted. *Expenses:* $960 per credit hour. *Financial support:* In 2016–17, 5 students received support, including 2 research assistantships with tuition reimbursements available; career-related internships or fieldwork, Federal Work-Study, scholarships/grants, and unspecified assistantships also available. Support available to part-time students. Financial award applicants required to submit FAFSA. *Unit head:* Dr. Diane Murphy, Chair/Director, Information Technology, Management Sciences and Cybersecurity, 703-284-5958, Fax: 703-527-3830, E-mail: diane.murphy@marymount.edu. *Application contact:* Francesca Reed, Director, Graduate Admissions, 703-284-5901, Fax: 703-527-3815, E-mail: grad.admissions@marymount.edu.
Website: http://www.marymount.edu/Academics/School-of-Business-Administration/Graduate-Programs/Information-Technology-(M-S-)

McMaster University, School of Graduate Studies, Faculty of Engineering, Department of Computing and Software, Hamilton, ON L8S 4M2, Canada. Offers computer science (M Sc, PhD); software engineering (M Eng, MA Sc, PhD). *Program availability:* Part-time. *Degree requirements:* For master's, thesis. *Entrance requirements:* Additional exam requirements/recommendations for international students: Required—TOEFL (minimum score 550 paper-based). *Faculty research:* Software engineering; theory of non-sequential systems; parallel and distributed computing; artificial intelligence; complexity, design, and analysis of algorithms; combinatorial computing, especially applications to molecular biology.

Mercer University, Graduate Studies, Macon Campus, School of Engineering, Macon, GA 31207. Offers biomedical engineering (MSE); computer engineering (MSE); electrical engineering (MSE); engineering management (MSE); environmental engineering (MSE); environmental systems (MS); mechanical engineering (MSE); software engineering (MSE); software systems (MS); technical communications management (MS); technical management (MS). *Program availability:* Part-time-only, evening/weekend, online learning. *Faculty:* 21 full-time (5 women), 1 part-time/adjunct (0

women). *Students:* 44 full-time (9 women), 60 part-time (12 women); includes 14 minority (3 Black or African American, non-Hispanic/Latino; 1 American Indian or Alaska Native, non-Hispanic/Latino; 4 Asian, non-Hispanic/Latino; 3 Hispanic/Latino; 3 Two or more races, non-Hispanic/Latino), 2 international. Average age 27. In 2016, 64 master's awarded. *Degree requirements:* For master's, thesis or alternative. *Entrance requirements:* For master's, GRE (minimum score 300), minimum undergraduate GPA of 3.0. Additional exam requirements/recommendations for international students: Required—TOEFL (minimum score 550 paper-based; 80 iBT). *Application deadline:* For fall admission, 4/1 priority date for domestic and international students; for spring admission, 11/1 priority date for domestic and international students. Applications are processed on a rolling basis. Application fee: $75. *Expenses:* $865 per credit hour. *Financial support:* Applicants required to submit FAFSA. *Faculty research:* Designing prostheses and orthotics, oxygen transfer and limitations in biological systems, low-cost groundwater development, lung airway and transport, autonomous mobile robots. *Unit head:* Dr. Laura W. Lackey, Dean, 478-301-4106, Fax: 478-301-5593, E-mail: lackey_l@mercer.edu. *Application contact:* Dr. Richard O. Mines, Jr., Program Director, 478-301-2347, Fax: 478-301-5433, E-mail: mines_ro@mercer.edu.
Website: http://engineering.mercer.edu/

Monmouth University, Graduate Studies, Department of Computer Science, West Long Branch, NJ 07764-1898. Offers computer science (MS); computer science software design and development (Certificate); information systems (MS). *Program availability:* Part-time, evening/weekend. *Degree requirements:* For master's, thesis (for some programs), practicum. *Entrance requirements:* For master's, minimum GPA of 3.0 in major, 2.75 overall; two letters of recommendation; calculus I and II with minimum C grade; two semesters of computer programming within past five years with minimum B grade; undergraduate degree in major that requires substantial component of software development and/or business administration; for Certificate, minimum GPA of 3.0 in major, 2.75 overall; two letters of recommendation; calculus I and II with minimum C grade; two semesters of computer programming within past five years with minimum B grade. Additional exam requirements/recommendations for international students: Required—TOEFL (minimum score 550 paper-based, 79 iBT), IELTS (minimum score 6), Michigan English Language Assessment Battery (minimum score 77) or Certificate of Advanced English (minimum score B2). Electronic applications accepted. *Faculty research:* Databases, natural language processing, protocols, performance analysis, communications networks (systems), cybersecurity.

Monmouth University, Graduate Studies, Department of Computer Science and Software Engineering, West Long Branch, NJ 07764-1898. Offers software development (Certificate); software engineering (MS, Certificate). *Program availability:* Part-time, evening/weekend. *Degree requirements:* For master's, thesis optional, practicum. *Entrance requirements:* For master's and Certificate, bachelor's degree in software engineering, computer science, computer engineering or other engineering-related discipline; minimum GPA of 3.0 in major, 2.5 overall; completed course work in computer programming, data structures and algorithms, and software engineering. Additional exam requirements/recommendations for international students: Required—TOEFL (minimum score 550 paper-based, 79 iBT), IELTS (minimum score 6), Michigan English Language Assessment Battery (minimum score 77) or Certificate of Advanced English (minimum score B2). Electronic applications accepted. *Expenses:* Contact institution. *Faculty research:* Conceptual structures, real time software, business rules, project management, software related to homeland security.

Naval Postgraduate School, Departments and Academic Groups, Department of Computer Science, Monterey, CA 93943. Offers computer science (MS, PhD); identity management and cyber security (MA); modeling of virtual environments and simulations (MS, PhD); software engineering (MS, PhD). Program only open to commissioned officers of the United States and friendly nations and selected United States federal civilian employees. *Program availability:* Part-time, online learning. *Degree requirements:* For master's, thesis; for doctorate, thesis/dissertation.

New Jersey Institute of Technology, Ying Wu College of Computing, Newark, NJ 07102. Offers big data management and mining (Certificate); business and information systems (Certificate); computer science (MS, PhD), including bioinformatics (MS), computer science, computing and business (MS), cyber security and privacy (MS), software engineering (MS); data mining (Certificate); information security (Certificate); information systems (MS, PhD), including business and information systems (MS), emergency management and business continuity (MS), information systems; information technology administration and security (MS); IT administration (Certificate); network security and information assurance (Certificate); software engineering analysis/design (Certificate); Web systems development (Certificate). *Program availability:* Part-time, evening/weekend. *Faculty:* 64 full-time (10 women), 38 part-time/adjunct (4 women). *Students:* 818 full-time (241 women), 225 part-time (53 women); includes 162 minority (35 Black or African American, non-Hispanic/Latino; 77 Asian, non-Hispanic/Latino; 41 Hispanic/Latino; 9 Two or more races, non-Hispanic/Latino), 772 international. Average age 27. 2,666 applicants, 51% accepted, 377 enrolled. In 2016, 398 master's, 10 doctorates, 9 other advanced degrees awarded. Terminal master's awarded for partial completion of doctoral program. *Degree requirements:* For master's, thesis optional; for doctorate, thesis/dissertation. *Entrance requirements:* For master's, GRE General Test; for doctorate, GRE General Test, minimum graduate GPA of 3.5. Additional exam requirements/recommendations for international students: Required—TOEFL (minimum score 550 paper-based; 79 iBT). *Application deadline:* For fall admission, 6/1 priority date for domestic students, 5/1 priority date for international students; for spring admission, 11/15 priority date for domestic and international students. Applications are processed on a rolling basis. Application fee: $75. Electronic applications accepted. *Expenses:* Contact institution. *Financial support:* In 2016–17, 57 students received support, including 18 research assistantships (averaging $16,073 per year), 39 teaching assistantships (averaging $20,194 per year); fellowships, career-related internships or fieldwork, Federal Work-Study, institutionally sponsored loans, and unspecified assistantships also available. Financial award application deadline: 1/15. *Faculty research:* Computer systems, communications and networking, artificial intelligence, database engineering, systems analysis, analytics and optimization in crowdsourcing. *Total annual research expenditures:* $3 million. *Unit head:* Dr. Craig Gotsman, Dean, 973-542-5488, Fax: 973-596-5777, E-mail: marek.rusinkiewicz@njit.edu. *Application contact:* Stephen Eck, Director of Admissions, 973-596-3300, Fax: 973-596-3461, E-mail: admissions@njit.edu.
Website: http://computing.njit.edu/

New York University, Polytechnic School of Engineering, Department of Computer Science and Engineering, Major in Software Engineering, New York, NY 10012-1019. Offers Graduate Certificate. Electronic applications accepted.

North Dakota State University, College of Graduate and Interdisciplinary Studies, College of Science and Mathematics, Department of Computer Science, Program in Software Engineering, Fargo, ND 58102. Offers MS, MSE, PhD, Certificate. *Program availability:* Part-time, online learning. Terminal master's awarded for partial completion of doctoral program. *Degree requirements:* For master's, comprehensive exam, thesis optional; for doctorate, thesis/dissertation, qualifying exam. *Entrance requirements:* For master's and doctorate, minimum GPA of 3.0 in software engineering or related field. Additional exam requirements/recommendations for international students: Required—TOEFL (minimum score 550 paper-based; 79 iBT). Electronic applications accepted. *Faculty research:* Data knowledge and engineering requirements, formal methods for software, software measurement and mobile agents, software development process.

Northern Kentucky University, Office of Graduate Programs, College of Informatics, Department of Computer Science, Highland Heights, KY 41099. Offers computer science (MSCS); geographic information systems (Certificate); secure software engineering (Certificate). *Program availability:* Part-time, evening/weekend. *Degree requirements:* For master's, thesis optional. *Entrance requirements:* For master's, GRE, minimum GPA of 3.0, at least 4 semesters of undergraduate study in computer science including intermediate computer programming and data structures, one year of calculus, one course in discrete mathematics. Additional exam requirements/recommendations for international students: Required—TOEFL (minimum score 550 paper-based; 79 iBT); Recommended—IELTS (minimum score 6.5). Electronic applications accepted. *Faculty research:* Data privacy, data mining, wireless security, secure software engineering, secure networking.

Northwestern University, School of Professional Studies, Program in Information Systems, Evanston, IL 60208. Offers analytics and business intelligence (MS); database and Internet technologies (MS); information systems (MS); information systems management (MS); information systems security (MS); medical informatics (MS); software project management and development (MS).

Oakland University, Graduate Study and Lifelong Learning, School of Engineering and Computer Science, Department of Computer Science and Engineering, Rochester, MI 48309-4401. Offers computer science (MS); computer science and informatics (PhD); software engineering and information technology (MS). *Program availability:* Part-time, evening/weekend. *Entrance requirements:* For master's, minimum GPA of 3.0. Electronic applications accepted. *Expenses:* Contact institution.

Oklahoma Christian University, Graduate School of Engineering and Computer Science, Oklahoma City, OK 73136-1100. Offers electrical and computer engineering (MSE); engineering management (MSE); mechanical engineering (MSE); software engineering (MSCS, MSE). *Program availability:* Part-time. *Faculty:* 8 full-time (1 woman), 7 part-time/adjunct (0 women). *Students:* 187 full-time (27 women), 85 part-time (12 women). Average age 25. 255 applicants, 33% accepted, 69 enrolled. In 2016, 188 master's awarded. *Entrance requirements:* Additional exam requirements/recommendations for international students: Required—TOEFL (minimum score 550 paper-based). *Application deadline:* Applications are processed on a rolling basis. Application fee: $25. Electronic applications accepted. *Expenses:* Contact institution. *Unit head:* Mary Ann Brown, Director for Graduate School Engineering, 405-425-5579. *Application contact:* Angie Ricketts, Admissions Counselor, 405-425-5587, E-mail: angie.ricketts@oc.edu.
Website: http://www.oc.edu/academics/graduate/engineering/

Oregon State University, College of Engineering, Program in Computer Science, Corvallis, OR 97331. Offers algorithms and cryptography (M Eng, MS, PhD); artificial intelligence, machine learning and data science (M Eng, PhD); computer graphics, visualization, and vision (M Eng, MS, PhD); computer systems and networking (M Eng, MS, PhD); human-computer interaction (M Eng, MS, PhD); programming languages (M Eng, MS, PhD); software engineering (M Eng, MS, PhD). *Faculty:* 58 full-time (9 women), 3 part-time/adjunct (1 woman). *Students:* 221 full-time (53 women), 26 part-time (4 women); includes 10 minority (8 Asian, non-Hispanic/Latino; 1 Hispanic/Latino; 1 Two or more races, non-Hispanic/Latino), 190 international. Average age 29. 630 applicants, 14% accepted, 65 enrolled. In 2016, 41 master's, 5 doctorates awarded. *Entrance requirements:* For master's and doctorate, GRE. Additional exam requirements/recommendations for international students: Required—TOEFL (minimum score 600 paper-based; 80 iBT), IELTS (minimum score 6.5). *Application deadline:* For fall admission, 1/15 for domestic students. Application fee: $75 ($85 for international students). *Expenses:* $14,130 resident full-time tuition, $23,769 non-resident. *Financial support:* Application deadline: 1/15. *Unit head:* V. John Mathews, Professor and School Head. *Application contact:* Graduate Coordinator, 541-737-7234, E-mail: eecs.gradinfo@oregonstate.edu.
Website: http://eecs.oregonstate.edu/current-students/graduate/cs-program

Pace University, Seidenberg School of Computer Science and Information Systems, New York, NY 10038. Offers chief information security officer (APC); computer science (MS, PhD); enterprise analytics (MS); information and communication technology strategy and innovation (APC); information systems (MS, APC); Internet technology (MS); professional studies in computing (DPS); secure software and information engineering (APC); security and information assurance (Certificate); software development and engineering (MS, Certificate); telecommunications systems and networks (MS, Certificate). *Program availability:* Part-time, evening/weekend, online only, 100% online, blended/hybrid learning. *Faculty:* 26 full-time (7 women), 7 part-time/adjunct (2 women). *Students:* 537 full-time (175 women), 303 part-time (85 women); includes 192 minority (79 Black or African American, non-Hispanic/Latino; 3 American Indian or Alaska Native, non-Hispanic/Latino; 53 Asian, non-Hispanic/Latino; 49 Hispanic/Latino; 8 Two or more races, non-Hispanic/Latino), 486 international. Average age 32. 599 applicants, 89% accepted, 248 enrolled. In 2016, 180 master's, 19 doctorates, 1 other advanced degree awarded. *Degree requirements:* For master's, thesis or alternative, capstone course; for doctorate, comprehensive exam (for some programs), thesis/dissertation. *Entrance requirements:* For master's, GRE General Test. Additional exam requirements/recommendations for international students: Required—TOEFL (minimum score 78 iBT), IELTS (minimum score 6.5) or PTE (minimum score 52). *Application deadline:* For fall admission, 8/1 priority date for domestic students, 6/1 for international students; for spring admission, 12/1 for domestic students, 10/1 for international students. Applications are processed on a rolling basis. Application fee: $70. Electronic applications accepted. *Expenses:* Contact institution. *Financial support:* In 2016–17, 45 students received support. Research assistantships, career-related internships or fieldwork, scholarships/grants, and unspecified assistantships available. Support available to part-time students. Financial award application deadline: 2/15; financial award applicants required to submit FAFSA. *Faculty research:* Cyber security/digital forensics; mobile app development; big data/enterprise analytics; artificial intelligence; software development. *Total annual research expenditures:* $314,545. *Unit head:* Dr. Jonathan Hill, Dean, Seidenberg School of Computer Science and Information Systems, 212-346-1864, E-mail: jhill@pace.edu. *Application contact:* Susan Ford-Goldschein, Director of Graduate Admissions, 914-422-4283, Fax: 212-346-1585, E-mail: graduateadmission@pace.edu.
Website: http://www.pace.edu/seidenberg

Penn State Great Valley, Graduate Studies, Engineering Division, Malvern, PA 19355-1488. Offers engineering management (MEM); software engineering (MSE); systems engineering (M Eng, Certificate). *Unit head:* Dr. James A. Nemes, Chancellor, 610-648-3202 Ext. 610, Fax: 610-725-5296, E-mail: cse1@psu.edu. *Application contact:* JoAnn Kelly, Director of Admissions, 610-648-3315, Fax: 610-725-5296, E-mail: jek2@psu.edu.
Website: http://greatvalley.psu.edu/academics/masters-degrees/systems-engineering

Portland State University, Graduate Studies, Maseeh College of Engineering and Computer Science, Department of Computer Science, Portland, OR 97207-0751. Offers

computer science (MS, PhD); software engineering (MSE). *Program availability:* Part-time. *Faculty:* 27 full-time (6 women), 6 part-time/adjunct (0 women). *Students:* 86 full-time (31 women), 75 part-time (28 women); includes 24 minority (15 Asian, non-Hispanic/Latino; 4 Hispanic/Latino; 5 Two or more races, non-Hispanic/Latino), 74 international. Average age 30. 261 applicants, 28% accepted, 38 enrolled. In 2016, 40 master's, 4 doctorates awarded. *Degree requirements:* For master's, thesis or alternative; for doctorate, comprehensive exam, thesis/dissertation. *Entrance requirements:* For master's, GRE (minimum scores in 60th percentile in Quantitative and 25th percentile in Verbal for MS), minimum GPA of 3.0 or equivalent, 2 letters of recommendation, personal statement; for doctorate, GRE (minimum scores 60th percentile in Quantitative and 25th percentile in Verbal), MS in computer science or allied field. Additional exam requirements/recommendations for international students: Required—TOEFL (minimum score 550 paper-based). *Application deadline:* For fall admission, 3/1 for domestic and international students; for winter admission, 5/15 for domestic and international students; for spring admission, 11/1 for domestic students, 10/1 for international students. Applications are processed on a rolling basis. Application fee: $65. *Expenses:* Contact institution. *Financial support:* In 2016–17, 15 research assistantships with tuition reimbursements (averaging $10,283 per year), 16 teaching assistantships with tuition reimbursements (averaging $7,190 per year) were awarded; career-related internships or fieldwork, Federal Work-Study, scholarships/grants, tuition waivers (partial), and unspecified assistantships also available. Support available to part-time students. Financial award application deadline: 3/1; financial award applicants required to submit FAFSA. *Faculty research:* Formal methods, database systems, parallel programming environments, computer security, software tools. *Total annual research expenditures:* $1.7 million. *Unit head:* Dr. Wu-Chi Feng, Chair, 503-725-2408, Fax: 503-725-3211, E-mail: wuchang@cs.pdx.edu. *Application contact:* Krys Sarreal, Department Manager, 503-725-4255, Fax: 503-725-3211, E-mail: gc@cs.pdx.edu.
Website: http://www.pdx.edu/computer-science/

Regis University, College of Computer and Information Sciences, Denver, CO 80221-1099. Offers agile technologies (Certificate); cybersecurity (Certificate); data science (M Sc); database administration with Oracle (Certificate); database development (Certificate); database technologies (M Sc); enterprise Java software development (Certificate); enterprise resource planning (Certificate); executive information technology (Certificate); health care informatics (Certificate); health care informatics and information management (M Sc); information assurance (M Sc); information assurance policy management (Certificate); information technology management (M Sc); mobile software development (Certificate); software engineering (M Sc, Certificate); software engineering and database technology (M Sc); storage area networks (Certificate); systems engineering (M Sc, Certificate). *Program availability:* Part-time, evening/weekend, 100% online, blended/hybrid learning. *Faculty:* 11 full-time (3 women), 30 part-time/adjunct (10 women). *Students:* 341 full-time (95 women), 318 part-time (98 women); includes 186 minority (56 Black or African American, non-Hispanic/Latino; 2 American Indian or Alaska Native, non-Hispanic/Latino; 48 Asian, non-Hispanic/Latino; 63 Hispanic/Latino; 17 Two or more races, non-Hispanic/Latino), 57 international. Average age 37. 342 applicants, 79% accepted, 174 enrolled. In 2016, 192 master's awarded. *Degree requirements:* For master's, thesis (for some programs), final research project. *Entrance requirements:* For master's, official transcript reflecting baccalaureate degree awarded from regionally-accredited college or university, 2 years of related experience, resume, interview. Additional exam requirements/recommendations for international students: Required—TOEFL (minimum score 550 paper-based; 82 iBT). *Application deadline:* For fall admission, 8/15 priority date for domestic students, 7/13 for international students; for winter admission, 10/10 priority date for domestic students, 9/8 for international students; for spring admission, 1/10 priority date for domestic students, 11/17 for international students; for summer admission, 5/1 priority date for domestic students. Applications are processed on a rolling basis. Application fee: $75. Electronic applications accepted. *Expenses:* $730 per credit hour. *Financial support:* Scholarships/grants available. Financial award application deadline: 4/15; financial award applicants required to submit FAFSA. *Faculty research:* Information policy, knowledge management, software architectures, data science. *Unit head:* Shari Plantz-Masters, Academic Dean. *Application contact:* Cate Clark, Director of Admissions, 303-458-4900, Fax: 303-964-5534, E-mail: ruadmissions@regis.edu.
Website: http://regis.edu/CCIS.aspx

Rochester Institute of Technology, Graduate Enrollment Services, Golisano College of Computing and Information Sciences, Software Engineering Department, MS Program in Software Engineering, Rochester, NY 14623. Offers MS. *Program availability:* Part-time. *Students:* 46 full-time (14 women), 19 part-time (5 women); includes 2 minority (1 Black or African American, non-Hispanic/Latino; 1 Two or more races, non-Hispanic/Latino), 54 international. Average age 26. 127 applicants, 67% accepted, 23 enrolled. In 2016, 15 master's awarded. *Degree requirements:* For master's, thesis or alternative. *Entrance requirements:* For master's, GRE, minimum GPA of 3.0 (recommended). Additional exam requirements/recommendations for international students: Required—TOEFL (minimum score 570 paper-based; 88 iBT), IELTS (minimum score 6.5), PTE (minimum score 61). *Application deadline:* For fall admission, 2/15 priority date for domestic and international students; for spring admission, 12/15 priority date for domestic and international students. Applications are processed on a rolling basis. Application fee: $60. Electronic applications accepted. *Expenses:* $1,742 per credit hour. *Financial support:* In 2016–17, 42 students received support. Research assistantships with partial tuition reimbursements available, teaching assistantships with partial tuition reimbursements available, career-related internships or fieldwork, scholarships/grants, and unspecified assistantships available. Support available to part-time students. Financial award applicants required to submit FAFSA. *Faculty research:* Software engineering education, software architecture and design, architectural styles and design patterns, mathematical foundations of software engineering, object-oriented software development, augmented and virtual reality systems, engineering of real-time and embedded software systems, concurrent systems, distributed systems, data communications and networking, programming environments and tools, computer graphics, computer vision. *Unit head:* Dr. J. Scott Hawker, Graduate Program Director, 585-475-2705, E-mail: hawker@se.rit.edu. *Application contact:* Diane Ellison, Associate Vice President, Graduate Enrollment Services, 585-475-2229, Fax: 585-475-7164, E-mail: gradinfo@rit.edu.
Website: http://www.se.rit.edu/graduate/curriculum-overview

Rose-Hulman Institute of Technology, Faculty of Engineering and Applied Sciences, Department of Computer Science and Software Engineering, Terre Haute, IN 47803-3999. Offers software engineering (MS). *Program availability:* Part-time. *Faculty:* 20 full-time (2 women). *Students:* 2 part-time (0 women). Average age 42. 3 applicants, 67% accepted, 1 enrolled. In 2016, 2 master's awarded. *Degree requirements:* For master's, thesis. *Entrance requirements:* For master's, GRE, minimum GPA of 3.0. Additional exam requirements/recommendations for international students: Required—TOEFL (minimum score 580 paper-based; 92 iBT). *Application deadline:* For fall admission, 2/1 priority date for domestic students. Applications are processed on a rolling basis. Application fee: $0. Electronic applications accepted. *Expenses: Tuition:* Full-time $43,122. *Financial support:* Fellowships with tuition reimbursements, research assistantships with tuition reimbursements, and tuition waivers (full and partial) available. *Faculty research:* Software architecture, software project management, programming languages, database systems, computer graphics. *Unit head:* Dr. J.P. Mellor, Chairman, 812-877-8085, Fax: 812-872-6060, E-mail: mellor@rose-hulman.edu. *Application contact:* Dr. Azad Siahmakoun, Associate Dean of the Faculty, 812-877-8400, Fax: 812-877-8061, E-mail: siahmako@rose-hulman.edu.
Website: http://www.rose-hulman.edu/academics/academic-departments/computer-science-software-engineering.aspx

Royal Military College of Canada, Division of Graduate Studies and Research, Engineering Division, Department of Electrical and Computer Engineering, Kingston, ON K7K 7B4, Canada. Offers computer engineering (M Eng, PhD); electrical engineering (M Eng, PhD); software engineering (M Eng, PhD). *Degree requirements:* For master's, thesis; for doctorate, comprehensive exam, thesis/dissertation. *Entrance requirements:* For master's, honours degree with second-class standing in the appropriate field; for doctorate, master's degree. Electronic applications accepted.

St. Mary's University, School of Science, Engineering and Technology, Program in Software Engineering, San Antonio, TX 78228-8507. Offers MS, Certificate. *Program availability:* Part-time. *Faculty:* 4 full-time (0 women), 4 part-time/adjunct (0 women). *Students:* 5 full-time (0 women), 7 part-time (1 woman); includes 5 minority (all Hispanic/Latino), 3 international. Average age 32. 3 applicants, 33% accepted. In 2016, 1 master's awarded. *Degree requirements:* For master's, thesis (for some programs), thesis or project. *Entrance requirements:* For master's, GRE (minimum quantitative score of 148), bachelor's degree in software engineering, computer science, computer engineering or closely-related discipline; minimum GPA of 3.0. Additional exam requirements/recommendations for international students: Required—TOEFL (minimum score 550 paper-based; 80 iBT), IELTS (minimum score 6.5). *Application deadline:* For fall admission, 7/1 for domestic students; for spring admission, 11/15 for domestic students; for summer admission, 4/1 for domestic students. Applications are processed on a rolling basis. Application fee: $0. Electronic applications accepted. *Expenses: Tuition:* Full-time $15,600; part-time $865 per credit hour. *Required fees:* $148 per semester. *Financial support:* Career-related internships or fieldwork, Federal Work-Study, institutionally sponsored loans, scholarships/grants, and health care benefits available. Financial award application deadline: 3/31; financial award applicants required to submit FAFSA. *Faculty research:* Software analysis, software metrics, usability of web applications, component-based software development. *Unit head:* Dr. Djaffer Ibaroudene, Director, 210-431-2050, E-mail: dibaroudene@stmarytx.edu.
Website: https://www.stmarytx.edu/academics/set/graduate/software-engineering/

Santa Clara University, School of Engineering, Santa Clara, CA 95053. Offers applied mathematics (MS); bioengineering (MS); civil engineering (MS); computer science and engineering (MS, PhD); electrical engineering (MS, PhD); engineering (Engineer); engineering management and leadership (MS); mechanical engineering (MS, PhD); software engineering (MS); sustainable energy (MS). *Program availability:* Part-time, evening/weekend. *Faculty:* 66 full-time (22 women), 59 part-time/adjunct (12 women). *Students:* 449 full-time (188 women), 315 part-time (114 women); includes 197 minority (3 Black or African American, non-Hispanic/Latino; 144 Asian, non-Hispanic/Latino; 33 Hispanic/Latino; 1 Native Hawaiian or other Pacific Islander, non-Hispanic/Latino; 16 Two or more races, non-Hispanic/Latino), 418 international. Average age 28. 1,217 applicants, 45% accepted, 293 enrolled. In 2016, 466 master's awarded. *Entrance requirements:* For master's, GRE, transcript; for doctorate, GRE, master's degree or equivalent, 3 letters of recommendation, statement of purpose; for Engineer, master's degree. Additional exam requirements/recommendations for international students: Required—TOEFL (minimum score 79 iBT) or IELTS (6.5). *Application deadline:* For fall admission, 4/1 for domestic and international students; for winter admission, 9/9 for domestic students, 9/2 for international students; for spring admission, 2/17 for domestic students, 12/9 for international students. Application fee: $60. Electronic applications accepted. *Expenses:* $928 per unit. *Financial support:* Fellowships, research assistantships, teaching assistantships, career-related internships or fieldwork, Federal Work-Study, scholarships/grants, traineeships, health care benefits, tuition waivers, and unspecified assistantships available. Support available to part-time students. Financial award applicants required to submit FAFSA. *Unit head:* Dr. Alfonso Ortega, Dean. *Application contact:* Stacey Tinker, Director of Admissions and Marketing, 408-554-4313, Fax: 408-554-4323, E-mail: stinker@scu.edu.
Website: http://www.scu.edu/engineering/graduate/

Seattle University, College of Science and Engineering, Program in Software Engineering, Seattle, WA 98122-1090. Offers MSE. *Program availability:* Part-time, evening/weekend. *Faculty:* 11 full-time (4 women), 5 part-time/adjunct (0 women). *Students:* 11 full-time (4 women), 5 part-time (0 women); includes 4 minority (all Asian, non-Hispanic/Latino), 13 international. Average age 31. 15 applicants, 60% accepted, 5 enrolled. In 2016, 13 master's awarded. *Degree requirements:* For master's, thesis. *Entrance requirements:* For master's, GRE General Test, minimum GPA of 3.0; 2 years of related work experience; letter noting working knowledge of at least one programming language, such as C++, Java or C#; professional autobiography; 2 recommendations. Additional exam requirements/recommendations for international students: Required—TOEFL (minimum score 580 paper-based). *Application deadline:* For fall admission, 7/20 for domestic students, 4/1 for international students; for winter admission, 11/20 for domestic students, 9/1 for international students; for spring admission, 2/20 for domestic students, 12/1 for international students. Application fee: $55. Electronic applications accepted. *Financial support:* In 2016–17, 2 students received support. Career-related internships or fieldwork and Federal Work-Study available. Support available to part-time students. Financial award applicants required to submit FAFSA. *Unit head:* Dr. Richard LeBlanc, Chair, 206-296-5510, Fax: 206-296-5518, E-mail: leblanc@seattleu.edu. *Application contact:* Janet Shandley, Associate Dean of Graduate Admissions, 206-296-5900, Fax: 206-298-5656, E-mail: grad_admissions@seattleu.edu.
Website: https://www.seattleu.edu/scieng/computer-science/graduate-degrees/master-of-software-engineering/

Shippensburg University of Pennsylvania, School of Graduate Studies, College of Arts and Sciences, Department of Computer Science and Engineering, Shippensburg, PA 17257-2299. Offers agile software engineering (Certificate); computer science (MS), including computer science, cybersecurity, IT leadership, management information systems, software engineering; IT leadership (Certificate). *Program availability:* Part-time, evening/weekend. *Faculty:* 7 full-time (3 women). *Students:* 16 full-time (8 women), 14 part-time (5 women); includes 3 minority (2 Black or African American, non-Hispanic/Latino; 1 Hispanic/Latino), 21 international. Average age 29. 89 applicants, 49% accepted, 9 enrolled. In 2016, 10 master's awarded. *Entrance requirements:* For master's, GRE (if GPA less than 2.75), professional resume. Additional exam requirements/recommendations for international students: Required—TOEFL (minimum score 70 iBT) or IELTS (minimum score 6). *Application deadline:* For fall admission, 4/30 for international students; for spring admission, 9/30 for international students. Applications are processed on a rolling basis. Application fee: $45. Electronic applications accepted. *Expenses:* Tuition, state resident: part-time $483 per credit. Tuition, nonresident: part-time $725 per credit. *Required fees:* $141 per credit. *Financial support:* In 2016–17, 7 students received support. Career-related internships or fieldwork, scholarships/grants, unspecified assistantships, and resident hall director and student payroll positions available. Support available to part-time students. Financial

award application deadline: 3/1; financial award applicants required to submit FAFSA. *Unit head:* Dr. Jeonghwa Lee, Associate Professor and Program Coordinator, 717-477-1178, Fax: 717-477-4002, E-mail: jlee@ship.edu. *Application contact:* Megan N. Luft, Assistant Dean of Graduate Admissions, 717-477-1231, Fax: 717-477-4016, E-mail: mnluft@ship.edu.
Website: http://www.cs.ship.edu/

Southern Methodist University, Bobby B. Lyle School of Engineering, Department of Computer Science and Engineering, Dallas, TX 75275-0122. Offers computer engineering (MS, PhD); computer science (MS, PhD); security engineering (MS); software engineering (MS, DE). *Program availability:* Part-time, evening/weekend, online learning. Terminal master's awarded for partial completion of doctoral program. *Degree requirements:* For master's, thesis optional; for doctorate, thesis/dissertation, oral and written qualifying exams, oral final exam (PhD). *Entrance requirements:* For master's, GRE General Test, minimum GPA of 3.0 in last 2 years; bachelor's degree in engineering, mathematics, or sciences; for doctorate, preliminary counseling exam (PhD), minimum GPA of 3.0, bachelor's degree in related field, MA (for DE). Additional exam requirements/recommendations for international students: Required—TOEFL (minimum score 550 paper-based). *Faculty research:* Trusted and high performance network computing, software engineering and management, knowledge engineering and management, computer arithmetic, computer architecture and CAD.

Stevens Institute of Technology, Graduate School, School of Systems and Enterprises, Program in Software Engineering, Hoboken, NJ 07030. Offers MS, Certificate. *Program availability:* Part-time, evening/weekend. *Students:* 30 full-time (9 women), 33 part-time (5 women); includes 5 minority (1 Black or African American, non-Hispanic/Latino; 4 Asian, non-Hispanic/Latino), 25 international. Average age 30. 59 applicants, 69% accepted, 22 enrolled. In 2016, 23 master's, 48 other advanced degrees awarded. *Degree requirements:* For master's, thesis optional, minimum B average in major field and overall; for Certificate, minimum B average. *Entrance requirements:* Additional exam requirements/recommendations for international students: Required—TOEFL (minimum score 74 iBT), IELTS (minimum score 6). *Application deadline:* For fall admission, 6/1 for domestic students, 4/15 for international students; for spring admission, 11/30 for domestic students, 11/1 for international students. Applications are processed on a rolling basis. Application fee: $65. Electronic applications accepted. *Expenses:* Contact institution. *Financial support:* Fellowships, research assistantships, teaching assistantships, career-related internships or fieldwork, Federal Work-Study, scholarships/grants, and unspecified assistantships available. Financial award application deadline: 2/15; financial award applicants required to submit FAFSA. *Unit head:* Dr. Gregg Vesonder, Director, 201-216-8107, Fax: 201-216-5541, E-mail: gvesonde@stevens.edu. *Application contact:* Graduate Admissions, 888-783-8367, Fax: 888-511-1306, E-mail: graduate@stevens.edu.

Stony Brook University, State University of New York, Graduate School, College of Engineering and Applied Sciences, Department of Computer Science, Stony Brook, NY 11794-2424. Offers computer science (MS, PhD); information systems (Certificate); information systems engineering (MS); software engineering (Certificate). *Faculty:* 49 full-time (7 women), 3 part-time/adjunct (1 woman). *Students:* 399 full-time (92 women), 113 part-time (27 women); includes 22 minority (17 Asian, non-Hispanic/Latino; 3 Hispanic/Latino; 2 Two or more races, non-Hispanic/Latino), 458 international. Average age 26. 2,225 applicants, 26% accepted, 192 enrolled. In 2016, 198 master's, 18 doctorates awarded. Terminal master's awarded for partial completion of doctoral program. *Degree requirements:* For master's, thesis or alternative; for doctorate, comprehensive exam, thesis/dissertation. *Entrance requirements:* For master's and doctorate, GRE General Test. Additional exam requirements/recommendations for international students: Required—TOEFL (minimum score 90 iBT). *Application deadline:* For fall admission, 1/15 for domestic students; for spring admission, 10/1 for domestic students. Application fee: $100. *Expenses:* Contact institution. *Financial support:* In 2016–17, 1 fellowship, 57 research assistantships, 62 teaching assistantships were awarded. *Faculty research:* Cyber security, computer security, computer software, computer operating systems, computer and information sciences. *Total annual research expenditures:* $7.3 million. *Unit head:* Prof. Arie Kaufman, Chair, 631-632-8441, E-mail: arie.kaufman@stonybrook.edu. *Application contact:* Cynthia Scalzo, Coordinator, 631-632-1521, E-mail: cscalzo@cs.stonybrook.edu.
Website: http://www.cs.sunysb.edu/

Stratford University, School of Graduate Studies, Falls Church, VA 22043. Offers accounting (MS); business administration (IMBA, MBA); cyber security (MS); cyber security leadership and policy (MS); digital forensics (MS); enterprise business management (MS); entrepreneurial management (MS); healthcare administration (MS); information systems (MS); international hospitality management (MS); networking and telecommunications (MS); software engineering (MS). *Program availability:* Part-time, evening/weekend, 100% online, blended/hybrid learning. *Students:* 505 full-time (186 women), 172 part-time (88 women); includes 532 minority (165 Black or African American, non-Hispanic/Latino; 18 American Indian or Alaska Native, non-Hispanic/Latino; 324 Asian, non-Hispanic/Latino; 13 Hispanic/Latino; 10 Native Hawaiian or other Pacific Islander, non-Hispanic/Latino; 2 Two or more races, non-Hispanic/Latino). Average age 27. In 2016, 520 master's awarded. *Degree requirements:* For master's, comprehensive exam, capstone project. *Entrance requirements:* For master's, GRE or GMAT, baccalaureate degree. Additional exam requirements/recommendations for international students: Required—TOEFL (minimum score 79 iBT), IELTS (minimum score 6.5), PTE (minimum score 5). *Application deadline:* Applications are processed on a rolling basis. Application fee: $50. Electronic applications accepted. *Expenses: Tuition:* Full-time $4455; part-time $2227.50 per course. One-time fee: $100. *Financial support:* Federal Work-Study and scholarships/grants available. Financial award applicants required to submit FAFSA. *Unit head:* Dr. Richard R. Shurtz, President, 703-539-6890, Fax: 703-539-6960. *Application contact:* Admissions, 800-444-0804, E-mail: fcadmissions@stratford.edu.

Strayer University, Graduate Studies, Washington, DC 20005-2603. Offers accounting (MS); acquisition (MBA); business administration (MBA); communications technology (MS); educational management (M Ed); finance (MBA); health services administration (MHSA); hospitality and tourism management (MBA); human resource management (MBA); information systems (MS), including computer security management, decision support system management, enterprise resource management, network management, software engineering management, systems development management; management (MBA); management information systems (MS); marketing (MBA); professional accounting (MS), including accounting information systems, controllership, taxation; public administration (MPA); supply chain management (MBA); technology in education (M Ed). Programs also offered at campus locations in Birmingham, AL; Chamblee, GA; Cobb County, GA; Morrow, GA; White Marsh, MD; Charleston, SC; Columbia, SC; Greensboro, NC; Greenville, SC; Lexington, KY; Louisville, KY; Nashville, TN; North Raleigh, NC; Washington, DC. *Accreditation:* ACBSP. *Program availability:* Part-time, evening/weekend, online learning. *Degree requirements:* For master's, thesis. *Entrance requirements:* For master's, GMAT, GRE General Test, bachelor's degree from an accredited college or university, minimum undergraduate GPA of 2.75. Electronic applications accepted.

Tennessee Technological University, College of Graduate Studies, College of Engineering, Department of Computer Science, Cookeville, TN 38505. Offers computer software and scientific applications (MS); Internet-based computing (MS). *Program availability:* Part-time. *Students:* 11 full-time (4 women), 9 part-time (0 women); includes 1 minority (Black or African American, non-Hispanic/Latino), 10 international. 99 applicants, 44% accepted, 8 enrolled. In 2016, 5 master's awarded. *Degree requirements:* For master's, thesis or alternative. *Entrance requirements:* For master's, GRE. Additional exam requirements/recommendations for international students: Required—TOEFL (minimum score 550 paper-based; 79 iBT), IELTS (minimum score 5.5), PTE (minimum score 53), or TOEIC (Test of English as an International Communication). *Application deadline:* For fall admission, 8/1 for domestic students, 5/1 for international students; for spring admission, 12/1 for domestic students, 10/1 for international students; for summer admission, 5/1 for domestic students, 2/1 for international students. Applications are processed on a rolling basis. Application fee: $35 ($40 for international students). Electronic applications accepted. *Expenses:* Tuition, state resident: full-time $9375; part-time $534 per credit hour. Tuition, nonresident: full-time $22,443; part-time $1260 per credit hour. *Financial support:* In 2016–17, 6 research assistantships (averaging $7,500 per year), 8 teaching assistantships (averaging $7,500 per year) were awarded. Financial award application deadline: 4/1. *Unit head:* Dr. Jerry Gannod, Chairperson, 931-372-3691, Fax: 931-372-3686, E-mail: jgannod@tntech.edu. *Application contact:* Shelia K. Kendrick, Coordinator of Graduate Studies, 931-372-3808, Fax: 931-372-3497, E-mail: skendrick@tntech.edu.

Texas State University, The Graduate College, College of Science and Engineering, Program in Software Engineering, San Marcos, TX 78666. Offers MS. *Program availability:* Part-time. *Faculty:* 4 full-time (1 woman). *Students:* 7 full-time (3 women), 4 part-time (2 women); includes 1 minority (Asian, non-Hispanic/Latino), 6 international. Average age 29. 21 applicants, 24% accepted, 2 enrolled. In 2016, 4 master's awarded. *Degree requirements:* For master's, comprehensive exam, thesis optional. *Entrance requirements:* For master's, GRE General Test (preferred minimum score of 286 with no less than 140 on the verbal section and 148 on the quantitative section), baccalaureate degree from regionally-accredited university with minimum GPA of 2.75 on last 60 undergraduate semester hours, 3 letters of reference, academic vitae (resume), statement of purpose. Additional exam requirements/recommendations for international students: Required—TOEFL (minimum score 550 paper-based; 78 iBT), IELTS (minimum score 6.5). *Application deadline:* For fall admission, 2/15 priority date for domestic and international students; for spring admission, 10/15 for domestic students, 10/1 for international students; for summer admission, 4/15 for domestic students, 3/15 for international students. Applications are processed on a rolling basis. Application fee: $40 ($90 for international students). Electronic applications accepted. *Expenses:* $4,851 per semester. *Financial support:* In 2016–17, 1 student received support, including 1 research assistantship (averaging $13,509 per year); teaching assistantships, Federal Work-Study, institutionally sponsored loans, scholarships/grants, health care benefits, and unspecified assistantships also available. Support available to part-time students. Financial award application deadline: 3/1; financial award applicants required to submit FAFSA. *Faculty research:* Enabling and improving data-driven research, analysis and combination of eye movement traits for biometric ID and spoof protection, user experience for McCoy's building supply, eye movement-driven biometrics and interaction on google glass. *Total annual research expenditures:* $329,751. *Unit head:* Dr. Wuxu Peng, Graduate Advisor, 512-245-3874, Fax: 512-245-8750, E-mail: wp01@txstate.edu. *Application contact:* Dr. Andrea Golato, Dean of the Graduate College, 512-245-2581, E-mail: gradcollege@txstate.edu.
Website: http://www.gradcollege.txstate.edu/soen.html

Texas Tech University, Graduate School, Edward E. Whitacre Jr. College of Engineering, Department of Computer Science, Lubbock, TX 79409-3104. Offers computer science (MS, PhD); software engineering (MS). *Program availability:* Part-time, blended/hybrid learning. *Faculty:* 19 full-time (5 women). *Students:* 78 full-time (28 women), 33 part-time (10 women); includes 8 minority (1 Asian, non-Hispanic/Latino; 5 Hispanic/Latino; 2 Two or more races, non-Hispanic/Latino), 85 international. Average age 29. 257 applicants, 36% accepted, 34 enrolled. In 2016, 47 master's, 6 doctorates awarded. Terminal master's awarded for partial completion of doctoral program. *Degree requirements:* For master's, comprehensive exam (for some programs), thesis (for some programs); for doctorate, comprehensive exam, thesis/dissertation. *Entrance requirements:* For master's and doctorate, GRE (Verbal and Quantitative). Additional exam requirements/recommendations for international students: Required—TOEFL (minimum score 550 paper-based; 79 iBT). *Application deadline:* For fall admission, 6/1 priority date for domestic students, 1/15 priority date for international students; for spring admission, 9/1 priority date for domestic students, 6/15 priority date for international students. Applications are processed on a rolling basis. Application fee: $75. Electronic applications accepted. *Expenses:* $325 per credit hour full-time resident tuition, $733 per credit hour full-time non-resident tuition; $53.75 per credit hour fee plus $608 per term fee. *Financial support:* In 2016–17, 53 students received support, including 48 fellowships (averaging $4,116 per year), 26 research assistantships (averaging $8,503 per year), 15 teaching assistantships (averaging $15,336 per year); scholarships/grants, tuition waivers (partial), and unspecified assistantships also available. Financial award application deadline: 4/15; financial award applicants required to submit FAFSA. *Faculty research:* High performance and parallel computing; cyber security and data science; software engineering (quality assurance, testing, design specification); artificial intelligence (intelligent systems, knowledge representation); mobile and computer networks. *Total annual research expenditures:* $1 million. *Unit head:* Dr. Rattikorn Hewett, Professor and Chair, 806-742-3527, Fax: 806-742-3519, E-mail: rattikorn.hewett@ttu.edu. *Application contact:* Jeremy Herrera, Staff Graduate Advisor, 806-742-3527, Fax: 806-742-3519, E-mail: jeremy.herrera@ttu.edu.
Website: http://www.cs.ttu.edu/

Towson University, Program in Applied Information Technology, Towson, MD 21252-0001. Offers applied information technology (MS, D Sc); database management systems (Postbaccalaureate Certificate); information security and assurance (Postbaccalaureate Certificate); information systems management (Postbaccalaureate Certificate); Internet applications development (Postbaccalaureate Certificate); networking technologies (Postbaccalaureate Certificate); software engineering (Postbaccalaureate Certificate). *Students:* 135 full-time (50 women), 154 part-time (50 women); includes 119 minority (81 Black or African American, non-Hispanic/Latino; 26 Asian, non-Hispanic/Latino; 4 Hispanic/Latino; 8 Two or more races, non-Hispanic/Latino), 82 international. *Entrance requirements:* For master's and Postbaccalaureate Certificate, bachelor's degree, minimum GPA of 3.0; for doctorate, master's degree in computer science, information systems, information technology, or closely-related area; minimum GPA of 3.0; 2 letters of recommendation; resume. Additional exam requirements/recommendations for international students: Required—TOEFL. *Application deadline:* Applications are processed on a rolling basis. Application fee: $45. Electronic applications accepted. *Expenses:* Tuition, state resident: full-time $7580; part-time $379 per unit. Tuition, nonresident: full-time $15,700; part-time $785 per unit. *Required fees:* $2480. *Unit head:* Dr. Jinjuan Feng, Graduate Program Director, 410-704-3463, E-mail: ait@towson.edu. *Application contact:* Coverley Beidleman, Assistant Director of Graduate Admissions, 410-704-2113, Fax: 410-704-3030, E-mail: grads@

towson.edu.
Website: https://www.towson.edu/fcsm/departments/emergingtech/

Université Laval, Faculty of Sciences and Engineering, Program in Software Engineering, Québec, QC G1K 7P4, Canada. Offers Diploma. *Program availability:* Part-time. *Entrance requirements:* For degree, knowledge of French. Electronic applications accepted.

The University of Alabama in Huntsville, School of Graduate Studies, College of Engineering, Department of Electrical and Computer Engineering, Huntsville, AL 35899. Offers computer engineering (MSE, PhD); electrical engineering (MSE, PhD), including optics and photonics technology (MSE); optical science and engineering (PhD); software engineering (MSSE). *Program availability:* Part-time, evening/weekend. *Degree requirements:* For master's, comprehensive exam, thesis or alternative, oral and written exams; for doctorate, comprehensive exam, thesis/dissertation, oral and written exams. *Entrance requirements:* For master's, GRE General Test, appropriate bachelor's degree, minimum GPA of 3.0; for doctorate, GRE General Test, minimum GPA of 3.0. Additional exam requirements/recommendations for international students: Required—TOEFL (minimum score 500 paper-based; 80 iBT), IELTS (minimum score 6.5). Electronic applications accepted. *Expenses:* Tuition, state resident: full-time $9834; part-time $600 per credit hour. Tuition, nonresident: full-time $21,830; part-time $1325 per credit hour. *Faculty research:* Advanced computer architecture and systems, fault tolerant computing and verification, computational electro-magnetics, nano-photonics and plasmonics, micro electro-mechanical (MEMS) systems.

The University of Alabama in Huntsville, School of Graduate Studies, College of Science, Department of Computer Science, Huntsville, AL 35899. Offers computer science (MS, PhD); cybersecurity (MS); modeling and simulation (MS, PhD, Certificate); software engineering (MSSE, Certificate). *Program availability:* Part-time, evening/weekend, online learning. *Degree requirements:* For master's, comprehensive exam, thesis or alternative, oral and written exams; for doctorate, comprehensive exam, thesis/dissertation, oral and written exams. *Entrance requirements:* For master's, doctorate, and Certificate, GRE General Test, minimum GPA of 3.0. Additional exam requirements/recommendations for international students: Required—TOEFL (minimum score 550 paper-based; 80 iBT), IELTS (minimum score 6.5). Electronic applications accepted. *Expenses:* Tuition, state resident: full-time $9834; part-time $600 per credit hour. Tuition, nonresident: full-time $21,830; part-time $1325 per credit hour. *Faculty research:* Information assurance and cyber security, modeling and simulation, data science, computer graphics and visualization, multimedia systems.

University of Calgary, Faculty of Graduate Studies, Faculty of Science, Department of Computer Science, Calgary, AB T2N 1N4, Canada. Offers computer science (M Sc, PhD); software engineering (M Sc). *Program availability:* Part-time. *Degree requirements:* For master's, comprehensive exam (for some programs), thesis (for some programs); for doctorate, thesis/dissertation, oral and written departmental exam. *Entrance requirements:* For master's, bachelor's degree in computer science; for doctorate, M Sc in computer science. Additional exam requirements/recommendations for international students: Required—TOEFL (minimum score 600 paper-based); Recommended—TWE. Electronic applications accepted. *Faculty research:* Visual and interactive computing, quantum computing and cryptography, evolutionary software engineering, distributed systems and algorithms.

University of Colorado Colorado Springs, College of Engineering and Applied Science, Program in General Engineering, Colorado Springs, CO 80918. Offers energy engineering (ME); engineering management (ME); information assurance (ME); software engineering (ME); space operations (ME); systems engineering (ME). *Program availability:* Part-time, evening/weekend, blended/hybrid learning. *Faculty:* 1 full-time (0 women), 15 part-time/adjunct (6 women). *Students:* 18 full-time (3 women), 166 part-time (34 women); includes 36 minority (6 Black or African American, non-Hispanic/Latino; 8 Asian, non-Hispanic/Latino; 12 Hispanic/Latino; 10 Two or more races, non-Hispanic/Latino), 57 international. Average age 36. 89 applicants, 72% accepted, 41 enrolled. In 2016, 21 master's, 8 doctorates awarded. *Degree requirements:* For master's, thesis, portfolio, or project; for doctorate, comprehensive exam, thesis/dissertation. *Entrance requirements:* For master's, GRE (minimum score of 148 new grading scale on quantitative portion if undergraduate GPA is less than 3.0); for doctorate, GRE (minimum score of 148 new grading scale on the quantitative portion if the applicant has not graduated from a program of recognized standing), minimum GPA of 3.3 in the bachelor's or master's degree program attempted. Additional exam requirements/recommendations for international students: Required—TOEFL (minimum score 80 iBT), IELTS (minimum score 6). *Application deadline:* For fall admission, 7/1 for domestic students, 6/1 for international students; for spring admission, 11/1 for domestic and international students; for summer admission, 4/15 for domestic and international students. Applications are processed on a rolling basis. Application fee: $60 ($100 for international students). Electronic applications accepted. *Expenses:* Contact institution. *Financial support:* In 2016–17, 28 students received support. Federal Work-Study, scholarships/grants, traineeships, and unspecified assistantships available. Support available to part-time students. Financial award application deadline: 3/1; financial award applicants required to submit FAFSA. *Unit head:* Dr. Ramaswami Dandapani, Dean, 719-255-3543, Fax: 719-255-3542, E-mail: rdan@cas.uccs.edu. *Application contact:* Dawn House, Coordinator, 719-255-3246, E-mail: dhouse@uccs.edu.

University of Connecticut, Graduate School, School of Engineering, Department of Computer Science and Engineering, Storrs, CT 06269. Offers computer science (MS, PhD), including artificial intelligence, computer architecture, computer science, operating systems, robotics, software engineering. Terminal master's awarded for partial completion of doctoral program. *Degree requirements:* For master's, comprehensive exam, thesis or alternative; for doctorate, thesis/dissertation. *Entrance requirements:* For master's and doctorate, GRE General Test. Additional exam requirements/recommendations for international students: Required—TOEFL (minimum score 550 paper-based). Electronic applications accepted.

University of Detroit Mercy, College of Engineering and Science, Detroit, MI 48221. Offers chemistry (MS); civil and environmental engineering (DE); electrical and computer engineering (ME); electrical engineering (DE); engineering management (M Eng Mgt); environmental engineering (MEE); mechanical engineering (MME, DE); product development (MS); software engineering (MSSE); teaching of mathematics (MATM). *Program availability:* Part-time, evening/weekend. *Degree requirements:* For doctorate, thesis/dissertation. Electronic applications accepted. Application fee is waived when completed online. *Expenses:* Contact institution.

University of Houston–Clear Lake, School of Science and Computer Engineering, Program in Software Engineering, Houston, TX 77058-1002. Offers MS. *Program availability:* Part-time, evening/weekend. *Entrance requirements:* For master's, GRE General Test. Additional exam requirements/recommendations for international students: Required—TOEFL (minimum score 550 paper-based).

University of Management and Technology, Program in Computer Science, Arlington, VA 22209-1609. Offers computer science (MS); information technology (AC); project management (AC); software engineering (MS). *Program availability:* Part-time, evening/weekend, online learning. *Entrance requirements:* For master's, 3 recommendations, resume. Additional exam requirements/recommendations for international students: Required—TOEFL (minimum score 530 paper-based; 71 iBT). Electronic applications accepted.

University of Massachusetts Dartmouth, Graduate School, College of Engineering, Department of Computer Science, North Dartmouth, MA 02747-2300. Offers computer networks and distributed systems (Postbaccalaureate Certificate); computer science (MS, Postbaccalaureate Certificate); software development and design (Postbaccalaureate Certificate). *Program availability:* Part-time, 100% online, blended/hybrid learning. *Faculty:* 11 full-time (2 women), 1 part-time/adjunct (0 women). *Students:* 93 full-time (26 women), 31 part-time (7 women); includes 7 minority (1 Black or African American, non-Hispanic/Latino; 5 Asian, non-Hispanic/Latino; 1 Hispanic/Latino), 104 international. Average age 25. 138 applicants, 79% accepted, 42 enrolled. In 2016, 57 master's awarded. *Degree requirements:* For master's, thesis, project. *Entrance requirements:* For master's, GRE (UMass Dartmouth computer science bachelor's degree recipients are exempt), statement of purpose (minimum of 300 words), resume, 3 letters of recommendation, official transcripts; for Postbaccalaureate Certificate, statement of purpose (minimum of 300 words), resume, official transcripts. Additional exam requirements/recommendations for international students: Required—TOEFL (minimum score 533 paper-based; 72 iBT). *Application deadline:* For fall admission, 2/15 priority date for domestic students, 1/15 priority date for international students; for spring admission, 11/15 priority date for domestic students, 10/15 priority date for international students. Application fee: $60. Electronic applications accepted. *Expenses:* Tuition, state resident: full-time $14,994; part-time $624.75 per credit. Tuition, nonresident: full-time $27,068; part-time $1127.83 per credit. *Required fees:* $405; $25.88 per credit. Tuition and fees vary according to course load and reciprocity agreements. *Financial support:* In 2016–17, 3 fellowships (averaging $7,500 per year), 1 research assistantship (averaging $4,500 per year), 3 teaching assistantships (averaging $7,500 per year) were awarded; institutionally sponsored loans, scholarships/grants, and unspecified assistantships also available. Support available to part-time students. Financial award application deadline: 3/1; financial award applicants required to submit FAFSA. *Faculty research:* Human-computer interaction, visualization and imaging, software engineering, multi-agent systems, informatics and data processing, computer networks, self-organizing feature maps. *Total annual research expenditures:* $1 million. *Unit head:* Dr. Xiaoqin Zhang, Graduate Program Director, Computer Science, 508-999-8294, E-mail: x2zhang@umassd.edu. *Application contact:* Steven Briggs, Director of Marketing and Recruitment for Graduate Studies, 508-999-8604, Fax: 508-999-8183, E-mail: graduate@umassd.edu.
Website: http://www.umassd.edu/engineering/cis/graduate

University of Michigan–Dearborn, College of Engineering and Computer Science, Master of Science in Software Engineering Program, Dearborn, MI 48128. Offers MS. *Program availability:* Part-time, evening/weekend, 100% online. *Faculty:* 16 full-time (1 woman), 3 part-time/adjunct (1 woman). *Students:* 11 full-time (6 women), 26 part-time (4 women); includes 8 minority (2 Black or African American, non-Hispanic/Latino; 5 Asian, non-Hispanic/Latino; 1 Two or more races, non-Hispanic/Latino), 14 international. Average age 30. 38 applicants, 63% accepted, 15 enrolled. In 2016, 9 master's awarded. *Degree requirements:* For master's, thesis optional. *Entrance requirements:* For master's, bachelor's degree in mathematics, computer science or engineering; minimum GPA of 3.0. Additional exam requirements/recommendations for international students: Required—TOEFL (minimum score 560 paper-based; 84 iBT), IELTS (minimum score 6.5). *Application deadline:* For fall admission, 8/1 priority date for domestic students, 5/1 priority date for international students; for winter admission, 12/1 priority date for domestic students, 9/1 priority date for international students; for spring admission, 4/1 priority date for domestic students, 1/1 priority date for international students. Applications are processed on a rolling basis. Application fee: $60. Electronic applications accepted. *Expenses:* Tuition, state resident: full-time $13,118; part-time $2280 per term. Tuition, nonresident: full-time $21,816; part-time $3771 per term. *Required fees:* $866; $658 per unit. $329 per term. Tuition and fees vary according to program. *Financial support:* Research assistantships, teaching assistantships, scholarships/grants, health care benefits, and non-resident tuition scholarships available. Support available to part-time students. Financial award application deadline: 3/1; financial award applicants required to submit FAFSA. *Faculty research:* Analytics, security, computational intelligence, optimization. *Unit head:* Dr. William I. Grosky, Chair, 313-583-6424, E-mail: wgrosky@umich.edu. *Application contact:* Office of Graduate Studies, 313-583-6321, E-mail: umd-graduatestudies@umich.edu.
Website: https://umdearborn.edu/cecs/departments/computer-and-information-science/graduate-programs/masters-software-engineering

University of Michigan–Dearborn, College of Engineering and Computer Science, PhD Program in Computer and Information Science, Dearborn, MI 48128. Offers data management (PhD); data science (PhD); software engineering (PhD); systems and security (PhD). *Program availability:* Part-time, evening/weekend. *Degree requirements:* For doctorate, thesis/dissertation. *Entrance requirements:* For doctorate, GRE, bachelor's or master's degree in computer science or closely-related field. Additional exam requirements/recommendations for international students: Required—TOEFL (minimum score 84 iBT), IELTS (minimum score 6.5). *Application deadline:* For fall admission, 2/15 for domestic and international students. Application fee: $60. Electronic applications accepted. *Expenses:* Tuition, state resident: full-time $13,118; part-time $2280 per term. Tuition, nonresident: full-time $21,816; part-time $3771 per term. *Required fees:* $866; $658 per unit. $329 per term. Tuition and fees vary according to program. *Financial support:* Research assistantships, teaching assistantships, scholarships/grants, health care benefits, and unspecified assistantships available. Financial award application deadline: 2/15; financial award applicants required to submit FAFSA. *Unit head:* Dr. Brahim Medjahed, Director, 313-583-6449, E-mail: brahim@umich.edu. *Application contact:* Office of Graduate Studies Staff, 313-583-6321, E-mail: umd-graduatestudies@umich.edu.
Website: https://umdearborn.edu/cecs/departments/computer-and-information-science/graduate-programs/phd-computer-and-information-science

University of Minnesota, Twin Cities Campus, College of Science and Engineering, Department of Computer Science and Engineering, Program in Software Engineering, Minneapolis, MN 55455-0213. Offers MSSE. *Program availability:* Part-time, evening/weekend. *Degree requirements:* For master's, thesis optional, capstone project. *Entrance requirements:* For master's, 1 year of work experience in software field; minimum undergraduate GPA of 3.0. Additional exam requirements/recommendations for international students: Required—TOEFL. Electronic applications accepted. *Faculty research:* Database systems, human-computer interaction, software development, high performance neural systems, data mining.

University of Missouri–Kansas City, School of Computing and Engineering, Kansas City, MO 64110-2499. Offers civil engineering (MS); computer and electrical engineering (PhD); computer science (MS), including bioinformatics, software engineering, telecommunications networking; computer science and informatics (PhD); computing (PhD); electrical engineering (MS); engineering (PhD); engineering and construction management (Graduate Certificate); mechanical engineering (MS); telecommunications and computer networking (PhD). PhD (interdisciplinary) offered through the School of Graduate Studies. *Program availability:* Part-time. *Faculty:* 45 full-time (6 women), 26 part-time/adjunct (4 women). *Students:* 473 full-time (155 women), 207 part-time (42

women); includes 24 minority (10 Black or African American, non-Hispanic/Latino; 10 Asian, non-Hispanic/Latino; 4 Hispanic/Latino), 581 international. Average age 25. 1,143 applicants, 44% accepted, 227 enrolled. In 2016, 446 master's, 2 other advanced degrees awarded. *Degree requirements:* For doctorate, thesis/dissertation. *Entrance requirements:* For master's, GRE General Test, minimum GPA of 3.0, 3 letters of recommendation from professors; for doctorate, GRE General Test, minimum GPA of 3.5. Additional exam requirements/recommendations for international students: Required—TOEFL (minimum score 550 paper-based; 80 iBT). *Application deadline:* For fall admission, 1/15 priority date for domestic students, 1/15 for international students. Applications are processed on a rolling basis. Application fee: $45 ($50 for international students). *Financial support:* In 2016–17, 37 research assistantships with partial tuition reimbursements (averaging $15,679 per year), 47 teaching assistantships with partial tuition reimbursements (averaging $16,830 per year) were awarded; career-related internships or fieldwork, Federal Work-Study, scholarships/grants, tuition waivers (partial), and unspecified assistantships also available. Support available to part-time students. Financial award application deadline: 3/1; financial award applicants required to submit FAFSA. *Faculty research:* Algorithms, bioinformatics and medical informatics, biomechanics/biomaterials, civil engineering materials, networking and telecommunications, thermal science. *Unit head:* Dr. Kevin Z. Truman, Dean, 816-235-2399, Fax: 816-235-5159. *Application contact:* 816-235-2399, Fax: 816-235-5159.
Website: http://sce.umkc.edu/

University of Nebraska at Omaha, Graduate Studies, College of Information Science and Technology, Department of Computer Science, Omaha, NE 68182. Offers artificial intelligence (Certificate); communication networks (Certificate); computer science (MA, MS); computer science education (MS, Certificate); software engineering (Certificate); system and architecture (Certificate). *Program availability:* Part-time, evening/weekend. *Faculty:* 13 full-time (4 women). *Students:* 73 full-time (19 women), 44 part-time (15 women); includes 8 minority (3 Asian, non-Hispanic/Latino; 1 Hispanic/Latino; 4 Two or more races, non-Hispanic/Latino), 87 international. Average age 27. 132 applicants, 59% accepted, 33 enrolled. In 2016, 58 master's awarded. *Degree requirements:* For master's, comprehensive exam, thesis (for some programs). *Entrance requirements:* For master's, GRE General Test, minimum GPA of 3.0, prior course work in computer science, official transcripts, resume, 2 letters of recommendation; for Certificate, minimum GPA of 3.0, resume. Additional exam requirements/recommendations for international students: Required—TOEFL, IELTS, PTE. *Application deadline:* For fall admission, 7/1 priority date for domestic and international students; for spring admission, 11/1 priority date for domestic and international students; for summer admission, 3/1 for domestic and international students. Applications are processed on a rolling basis. Application fee: $45. Electronic applications accepted. *Financial support:* In 2016–17, 16 students received support, including 16 research assistantships with tuition reimbursements available; teaching assistantships with tuition reimbursements available, Federal Work-Study, institutionally sponsored loans, scholarships/grants, health care benefits, tuition waivers (full), and unspecified assistantships also available. Support available to part-time students. Financial award application deadline: 3/1; financial award applicants required to submit FAFSA. *Unit head:* Dr. Qiuming Zhu, Chairperson, 402-554-2341, E-mail: graduate@unomaha.edu. *Application contact:* Dr. Azad Azadmanesh, Graduate Program Chair, 402-554-2341, E-mail: graduate@unomaha.edu.

University of New Haven, Graduate School, Tagliatela College of Engineering, Program in Computer Science, West Haven, CT 06516. Offers computer programming (Graduate Certificate); computer science (MS); network systems (MS); software development (MS). *Program availability:* Part-time, evening/weekend. *Students:* 96 full-time (46 women), 25 part-time (5 women); includes 9 minority (1 American Indian or Alaska Native, non-Hispanic/Latino; 7 Asian, non-Hispanic/Latino; 1 Two or more races, non-Hispanic/Latino), 86 international. Average age 27. 791 applicants, 43% accepted, 23 enrolled. In 2016, 80 master's, 1 other advanced degree awarded. *Degree requirements:* For master's, thesis or alternative. *Entrance requirements:* Additional exam requirements/recommendations for international students: Required—TOEFL (minimum score 75 iBT), IELTS, PTE (minimum score 50). *Application deadline:* Applications are processed on a rolling basis. Application fee: $50. Electronic applications accepted. Application fee is waived when completed online. *Expenses: Tuition:* Full-time $15,660; part-time $870 per credit hour. *Required fees:* $200; $85 per term. Tuition and fees vary according to program. *Financial support:* Research assistantships with partial tuition reimbursements, teaching assistantships with partial tuition reimbursements, career-related internships or fieldwork, Federal Work-Study, scholarships/grants, and unspecified assistantships available. Support available to part-time students. Financial award applicants required to submit FAFSA. *Unit head:* Dr. David Eggert, Coordinator, 203-932-7097, E-mail: deggert@newhaven.edu. *Application contact:* Michelle Mason, Director of Graduate Enrollment, 203-932-7067, E-mail: mmason@newhaven.edu.
Website: http://www.newhaven.edu/9591/

University of North Florida, College of Computing, Engineering, and Construction, School of Computing, Jacksonville, FL 32224. Offers computer science (MS); information systems (MS); software engineering (MS). *Program availability:* Part-time. *Faculty:* 12 full-time (2 women), 1 part-time/adjunct (0 women). *Students:* 13 full-time (5 women), 47 part-time (14 women); includes 14 minority (2 Black or African American, non-Hispanic/Latino; 9 Asian, non-Hispanic/Latino; 1 Hispanic/Latino; 2 Two or more races, non-Hispanic/Latino), 20 international. Average age 30. 62 applicants, 31% accepted, 7 enrolled. In 2016, 3 master's awarded. *Degree requirements:* For master's, thesis. *Entrance requirements:* For master's, GRE General Test, minimum GPA of 3.0 in last 60 hours of course work. Additional exam requirements/recommendations for international students: Required—TOEFL (minimum score 500 paper-based; 61 iBT). *Application deadline:* For fall admission, 8/1 priority date for domestic students, 5/1 for international students; for spring admission, 12/1 priority date for domestic students, 10/1 for international students; for summer admission, 3/15 priority date for domestic students, 2/1 for international students. Application fee: $30. Electronic applications accepted. Tuition and fees vary according to course load, campus/location and program. *Financial support:* In 2016–17, 4 research assistantships (averaging $2,332 per year) were awarded; teaching assistantships, Federal Work-Study, scholarships/grants, and unspecified assistantships also available. Financial award application deadline: 4/1; financial award applicants required to submit FAFSA. *Total annual research expenditures:* $196,076. *Unit head:* Dr. Sherif Elfayoumy, Director/Professor, 904-620-2985, E-mail: selfayou@unf.edu. *Application contact:* Dr. Amanda Pascale, Director, The Graduate School, 904-620-1360, Fax: 904-620-1362, E-mail: graduateschool@unf.edu.
Website: http://www.unf.edu/ccec/computing/

University of Regina, Faculty of Graduate Studies and Research, Faculty of Engineering and Applied Science, Program in Software Systems Engineering, Regina, SK S4S 0A2, Canada. Offers M Eng, MA Sc. *Program availability:* Part-time. *Faculty:* 6 full-time (1 woman), 24 part-time/adjunct (0 women). *Students:* 13 full-time (1 woman), 2 part-time (0 women). 30 applicants, 20% accepted. In 2016, 6 master's awarded. *Degree requirements:* For master's, comprehensive exam, thesis, project, report. *Entrance requirements:* Additional exam requirements/recommendations for international students: Required—TOEFL (minimum score 550 paper-based; 80 iBT), IELTS (minimum score 6.5), PTE (minimum score 59). *Application deadline:* For fall admission, 3/31 for domestic and international students; for winter admission, 7/31 for domestic and international students; for spring admission, 11/30 for domestic and international students. Application fee: $100. Electronic applications accepted. *Expenses:* Contact institution. *Financial support:* In 2016–17, 3 fellowships (averaging $6,333 per year), 5 teaching assistantships (averaging $2,574 per year) were awarded; career-related internships or fieldwork and scholarships/grants also available. Financial award application deadline: 6/15. *Faculty research:* Software design and development, network computing, multimedia communication, computational theories to real-life programming techniques, embedded systems construction. *Unit head:* Dr. Amr Henni, Associate Dean, Research and Graduate Studies, 306-585-4960, Fax: 306-585-4855, E-mail: amr.henni@uregina.ca. *Application contact:* Dr. Christine Chan, Graduate Coordinator, 306-585-5225, Fax: 306-585-4855, E-mail: christine.chan@uregina.ca.
Website: http://www.uregina.ca/engineering/

University of St. Thomas, Graduate Studies, School of Engineering, St. Paul, MN 55105-1096. Offers data science (MS); electrical engineering (MS); information technology (MS); manufacturing engineering (MS); manufacturing systems (Certificate); mechanical engineering (MS); medical device development (Certificate); regulatory science (MS); software engineering (MS); software management (MS); systems engineering (MS); technology leadership (Certificate); technology management (MS). *Accreditation:* ABET (one or more programs are accredited). *Entrance requirements:* For master's, resume, official transcripts. Additional exam requirements/recommendations for international students: Required—TOEFL (minimum score 550 paper-based). *Application deadline:* For fall admission, 8/1 priority date for domestic students; for spring admission, 1/1 priority date for domestic students. Applications are processed on a rolling basis. Application fee: $50. Electronic applications accepted. *Expenses:* Contact institution. *Financial support:* Fellowships, research assistantships, institutionally sponsored loans, and scholarships/grants available. Support available to part-time students. Financial award application deadline: 4/1; financial award applicants required to submit FAFSA. *Unit head:* Don Weinkauf, Dean, 651-962-5760, Fax: 651-962-6419, E-mail: dhweinkauf@stthomas.edu. *Application contact:* Tina M. Hansen, Graduate Program Manager, 651-962-5755, Fax: 651-962-6419, E-mail: tina.hansen@stthomas.edu.
Website: http://www.stthomas.edu/engineering/

The University of Scranton, Kania School of Management, Program in Software Engineering, Scranton, PA 18510. Offers MS. *Program availability:* Part-time, evening/weekend. *Degree requirements:* For master's, comprehensive exam (for some programs), thesis (for some programs), capstone experience. *Entrance requirements:* For master's, minimum GPA of 3.0, three letters of reference. Additional exam requirements/recommendations for international students: Required—TOEFL (minimum score 500 paper-based; 80 iBT), IELTS (minimum score 6.5). Electronic applications accepted. *Faculty research:* Database, parallel and distributed systems, computer network, real time systems.

University of South Carolina, The Graduate School, College of Engineering and Computing, Department of Computer Science and Engineering, Columbia, SC 29208. Offers computer science and engineering (ME, MS, PhD); software engineering (MS). *Program availability:* Part-time, evening/weekend, online learning. *Degree requirements:* For master's, comprehensive exam, thesis (for some programs); for doctorate, comprehensive exam, thesis/dissertation. *Entrance requirements:* For master's and doctorate, GRE General Test. Additional exam requirements/recommendations for international students: Required—TOEFL (minimum score 570 paper-based). Electronic applications accepted. *Faculty research:* Computer security, computer vision, artificial intelligence, multiagent systems, bioinformatics.

University of Southern California, Graduate School, Viterbi School of Engineering, Department of Computer Science, Los Angeles, CA 90089. Offers computer networks (MS); computer science (MS, PhD); computer security (MS); game development (MS); high performance computing and simulations (MS); human language technology (MS); intelligent robotics (MS); multimedia and creative technologies (MS); software engineering (MS). *Program availability:* Part-time, evening/weekend, online learning. *Entrance requirements:* For master's and doctorate, GRE General Test. Additional exam requirements/recommendations for international students: Required—TOEFL. Electronic applications accepted. *Faculty research:* Databases, computer graphics and computer vision, software engineering, networks and security, robotics, multimedia and virtual reality.

University of Southern Maine, College of Science, Technology, and Health, Department of Computer Science, Portland, ME 04103. Offers computer science (MS); software systems (CGS). *Program availability:* Part-time. *Degree requirements:* For master's, thesis. *Entrance requirements:* For master's, GRE General Test, minimum GPA of 3.0. Additional exam requirements/recommendations for international students: Required—TOEFL. Electronic applications accepted. *Faculty research:* Software engineering, database systems, formal methods, object-oriented technology, artificial intelligence, bioinformatics, data analysis and data mining, health information systems.

The University of Texas at Arlington, Graduate School, College of Engineering, Department of Computer Science and Engineering, Arlington, TX 76019. Offers computer engineering (MS, PhD); computer science (MS, PhD); mathematical sciences, computer science (PhD); software engineering (MS). *Program availability:* Part-time, online learning. Terminal master's awarded for partial completion of doctoral program. *Degree requirements:* For master's, comprehensive exam (for some programs), thesis; for doctorate, comprehensive exam, thesis/dissertation. *Entrance requirements:* For master's, GRE General Test, minimum GPA of 3.0 (3.2 in computer science-related classes); for doctorate, GRE General Test, minimum GPA of 3.5. Additional exam requirements/recommendations for international students: Required—TOEFL (minimum score 550 paper-based; 92 iBT), IELTS (minimum score 6.5). *Application deadline:* For fall admission, 6/1 for domestic students, 5/1 for international students; for spring admission, 12/1 for domestic students, 10/1 for international students. Applications are processed on a rolling basis. Application fee: $35 ($50 for international students). *Financial support:* Fellowships with full tuition reimbursements, research assistantships with partial tuition reimbursements, teaching assistantships with partial tuition reimbursements, career-related internships or fieldwork, and scholarships/grants available. Financial award application deadline: 6/1; financial award applicants required to submit FAFSA. *Faculty research:* Algorithms, homeland security, mobile pervasive computing, high performance computing bio information. *Unit head:* Dr. Fillia Makedon, Chairman, 817-272-3605, E-mail: makedon@uta.edu. *Application contact:* Dr. Bahram Khalili, Graduate Advisor, 817-272-5407, Fax: 817-272-3784, E-mail: khalili@uta.edu.
Website: http://www.cse.uta.edu/

The University of Texas at Dallas, Erik Jonson School of Engineering and Computer Science, Department of Computer Science, Richardson, TX 75080. Offers computer science (MS, PhD); software engineering (MS, PhD). *Program availability:* Part-time, evening/weekend. *Faculty:* 48 full-time (6 women), 9 part-time/adjunct (2 women). *Students:* 880 full-time (284 women), 256 part-time (66 women); includes 51 minority (2 Black or African American, non-Hispanic/Latino; 1 American Indian or Alaska Native, non-Hispanic/Latino; 32 Asian, non-Hispanic/Latino; 10 Hispanic/Latino; 6 Two or more races, non-Hispanic/Latino), 1,006 international. Average age 27. 3,675 applicants, 34%

accepted, 412 enrolled. In 2016, 585 master's, 12 doctorates awarded. *Degree requirements:* For master's, thesis optional; for doctorate, comprehensive exam, thesis/dissertation. *Entrance requirements:* For master's, GRE General Test, minimum GPA of 3.0 in undergraduate course work, 3.3 in quantitative course work; for doctorate, GRE General Test, minimum GPA of 3.5. Additional exam requirements/recommendations for international students: Required—TOEFL (minimum score 550 paper-based). *Application deadline:* For fall admission, 7/15 for domestic students, 5/1 priority date for international students; for spring admission, 11/15 for domestic students, 9/1 priority date for international students. Applications are processed on a rolling basis. Application fee: $50 ($100 for international students). Electronic applications accepted. *Expenses:* Tuition, state resident: full-time $12,418; part-time $690 per semester hour. Tuition, nonresident: full-time $24,150; part-time $1342 per semester hour. Tuition and fees vary according to course load. *Financial support:* In 2016–17, 259 students received support, including 10 fellowships (averaging $1,650 per year), 77 research assistantships with partial tuition reimbursements available (averaging $23,115 per year), 79 teaching assistantships with partial tuition reimbursements available (averaging $17,231 per year); career-related internships or fieldwork, Federal Work-Study, institutionally sponsored loans, and scholarships/grants also available. Support available to part-time students. Financial award application deadline: 4/30; financial award applicants required to submit FAFSA. *Faculty research:* AI-based automated software synthesis and testing, quality of service in computer networks, wireless networks, cloud computing and IT security, speech recognition. *Unit head:* Dr. Gopal Gupta, Department Head, 972-883-4107, Fax: 972-883-2399, E-mail: gupta@utdallas.edu. *Application contact:* 972-883-2185, Fax: 972-883-2399, E-mail: gradecs@utdallas.edu.
Website: http://cs.utdallas.edu/

The University of Texas at El Paso, Graduate School, College of Engineering, El Paso, TX 79968-0001. Offers biomedical engineering (PhD); civil engineering (MEENE, MS, MSENE, PhD, Certificate), including civil engineering (MS), civil engineering (PhD), construction management (MS, Certificate), environmental engineering (MEENE, MSENE); computer science (MS, MSIT, PhD), including computer science (MS, PhD), information technology (MSIT); education engineering (M Eng); electrical and computer engineering (MS, PhD), including computer engineering (MS), electrical and computer engineering (PhD), electrical engineering (MS); industrial engineering (MS, Certificate), including industrial engineering (MS), manufacturing engineering (MS), systems engineering; mechanical engineering (MS, PhD), including environmental science and engineering (PhD), mechanical engineering (MS); metallurgical and materials engineering (MS, PhD), including materials science and engineering (PhD), metallurgical and materials engineering (MS); software engineering (M Eng). *Program availability:* Part-time, evening/weekend. *Degree requirements:* For master's, thesis optional; for doctorate, thesis/dissertation. *Entrance requirements:* For master's, GRE, minimum GPA of 3.0, letters of reference; for doctorate, GRE, statement of purpose, letters of reference. Additional exam requirements/recommendations for international students: Required—TOEFL; Recommended—IELTS. Electronic applications accepted. *Expenses:* Contact institution.

University of Utah, Graduate School, David Eccles School of Business, Department of Operations and Information Systems, Salt Lake City, UT 84112. Offers information systems (MS, Graduate Certificate), including business intelligence and analytics, IT security, product and process management, software and systems architecture. *Program availability:* Part-time, evening/weekend, 100% online, blended/hybrid learning. *Faculty:* 12 full-time (5 women), 7 part-time/adjunct (0 women). *Students:* 143 full-time (43 women), 107 part-time (28 women); includes 127 minority (1 Black or African American, non-Hispanic/Latino; 120 Asian, non-Hispanic/Latino; 3 Hispanic/Latino; 3 Two or more races, non-Hispanic/Latino), 123 international. Average age 29. 334 applicants, 72% accepted, 127 enrolled. In 2016, 96 master's awarded. *Degree requirements:* For master's, capstone project. *Entrance requirements:* For master's, GMAT/GRE, minimum undergraduate GPA of 3.0, 2 letters of recommendation, personal statement, professional resume. Additional exam requirements/recommendations for international students: Required—TOEFL (minimum score 550 paper-based; 80 iBT), IELTS (minimum score 6.5). *Application deadline:* For fall admission, 7/28 for domestic students, 3/1 for international students; for spring admission, 12/7 for domestic students, 8/16 for international students. Applications are processed on a rolling basis. Application fee: $55 ($65 for international students). Electronic applications accepted. *Expenses:* Contact institution. *Financial support:* In 2016–17, 75 students received support, including 7 teaching assistantships (averaging $5,000 per year); fellowships with partial tuition reimbursements available, tuition waivers (partial), and unspecified assistantships also available. Financial award application deadline: 3/31; financial award applicants required to submit FAFSA. *Faculty research:* Business intelligence and analytics, software and system architecture, product and process management, IT security, Web and data mining, applications and management of IT in healthcare. *Unit head:* Dr. Bradden Blair, Director of the IS Programs, 801-587-9489, Fax: 801-581-3666, E-mail: b.blair@eccles.utah.edu. *Application contact:* Raven Clissold, Admissions Coordinator, 801-587-5838, Fax: 801-581-3666, E-mail: raven.clissold@eccles.utah.edu.
Website: http://msis.eccles.utah.edu

University of Washington, Bothell, Program in Computing and Software Systems, Bothell, WA 98011. Offers MS. *Program availability:* Part-time, evening/weekend. *Degree requirements:* For master's, comprehensive exam (for some programs), thesis optional. *Entrance requirements:* For master's, GRE. Additional exam requirements/recommendations for international students: Required—TOEFL (minimum score 580 paper-based; 92 iBT) or IELTS (minimum score 7). Electronic applications accepted. *Expenses:* Contact institution. *Faculty research:* Computer science, software engineering, computer graphics, parallel and distributed systems, computer vision.

University of Washington, Tacoma, Graduate Programs, Program in Computing and Software Systems, Tacoma, WA 98402-3100. Offers MS. *Program availability:* Part-time. *Degree requirements:* For master's, capstone project/thesis or 15 credits elective coursework. *Entrance requirements:* For master's, GRE, personal statement, resume, transcripts, 3 recommendations. Additional exam requirements/recommendations for international students: Required—TOEFL (minimum score 580 paper-based; 92 iBT), IELTS (minimum score 7). Electronic applications accepted. *Faculty research:* Data stream analysis, formal methods, data mining, robotic systems, software development processes.

University of Waterloo, Graduate Studies, Faculty of Mathematics, David R. Cheriton School of Computer Science, Waterloo, ON N2L 3G1, Canada. Offers computer science (M Math, PhD); software engineering (M Math); statistics and computing (M Math). *Program availability:* Part-time. *Degree requirements:* For master's, research paper or thesis; for doctorate, comprehensive exam, thesis/dissertation. *Entrance requirements:* For master's, honors degree in field, minimum B+ average; for doctorate, master's degree, minimum B+ average. Additional exam requirements/recommendations for international students: Required—TOEFL, IELTS, PTE. Electronic applications accepted. *Faculty research:* Computer graphics, artificial intelligence, algorithms and complexity, distributed computing and networks, software engineering.

University of West Florida, College of Science and Engineering, Department of Computer Science, Pensacola, FL 32514-5750. Offers computer science (MS); database systems (MS); software engineering (MS). *Program availability:* Part-time, evening/weekend. *Degree requirements:* For master's, thesis optional. *Entrance requirements:* For master's, GRE, MAT, or GMAT, official transcripts; minimum undergraduate GPA of 3.0; letter of intent; three letters of recommendation. Additional exam requirements/recommendations for international students: Required—TOEFL (minimum score 550 paper-based). *Application deadline:* For fall admission, 6/1 for domestic and international students; for spring admission, 10/1 for domestic and international students. Applications are processed on a rolling basis. Application fee: $30. *Expenses:* Tuition, state resident: full-time $5316.12. Tuition, nonresident: full-time $11,308. *Required fees:* $583.92. Tuition and fees vary according to course load and program. *Financial support:* Fellowships with partial tuition reimbursements, research assistantships with partial tuition reimbursements, teaching assistantships with partial tuition reimbursements, and unspecified assistantships available. Financial award application deadline: 4/15; financial award applicants required to submit FAFSA. *Unit head:* Dr. Sikha Bagui, Chairperson, 850-474-3022. *Application contact:* Terry McCray, Assistant Director of Graduate Admissions, 850-473-7718, Fax: 850-473-7714, E-mail: gradadmissions@uwf.edu.
Website: http://catalog.uwf.edu/graduate/computerscience/

University of Wisconsin–La Crosse, College of Science and Health, Department of Computer Science, La Crosse, WI 54601-3742. Offers software engineering (MSE). *Program availability:* Part-time. *Faculty:* 10 full-time (2 women). *Students:* 23 full-time (6 women), 5 part-time (0 women), 19 international. Average age 23. 18 applicants, 83% accepted, 12 enrolled. In 2016, 20 master's awarded. *Degree requirements:* For master's, thesis. *Entrance requirements:* Additional exam requirements/recommendations for international students: Recommended—TOEFL (minimum score 550 paper-based; 79 iBT), IELTS (minimum score 6). *Application deadline:* For fall admission, 5/1 priority date for domestic and international students; for spring admission, 11/1 priority date for domestic and international students. Applications are processed on a rolling basis. Electronic applications accepted. *Financial support:* Research assistantships with partial tuition reimbursements, Federal Work-Study, scholarships/grants, health care benefits, and tuition waivers (partial) available. Support available to part-time students. *Unit head:* Dr. Kasi Periyasamy, Software Engineering Program Director, 608-785-6823, E-mail: periyasa.kas2@uwlax.edu. *Application contact:* Brandon Schaller, Senior Graduate Student Status Examiner, 608-785-8941, E-mail: admissions@uwlax.edu.
Website: http://www.cs.uwlax.edu/

Villanova University, Graduate School of Liberal Arts and Sciences, Department of Computing Sciences, Villanova, PA 19085-1699. Offers computer science (MS); software engineering (MS). *Program availability:* Part-time, evening/weekend. *Faculty:* 19. *Students:* 92 full-time (47 women), 23 part-time (10 women); includes 7 minority (2 Black or African American, non-Hispanic/Latino; 3 Hispanic/Latino; 2 Two or more races, non-Hispanic/Latino), 86 international. Average age 26. 32 applicants, 59% accepted, 23 enrolled. In 2016, 48 master's awarded. *Degree requirements:* For master's, thesis optional, independent study project. *Entrance requirements:* For master's, GRE, minimum GPA of 3.0, 3 recommendation letters. Additional exam requirements/recommendations for international students: Required—TOEFL. *Application deadline:* For fall admission, 5/1 priority date for international students; for spring admission, 11/15 priority date for international students. Applications are processed on a rolling basis. Application fee: $50. Electronic applications accepted. *Financial support:* Research assistantships, scholarships/grants, and unspecified assistantships available. Financial award applicants required to submit FAFSA. *Unit head:* Dr. Vijay Geholt, Chair, 610-519-5843.
Website: http://www1.villanova.edu/villanova/artsci/computerscience/graduate.html

Virginia International University, School of Computer Information Systems, Fairfax, VA 22030. Offers business intelligence (Graduate Certificate); business intelligence and data analytics (MIS); computer science (MS), including computer animation and gaming, cybersecurity, data management networking, intelligent systems, software applications development, software engineering; cybersecurity (MIS); data management (MIS); enterprise project management (MIS); health informatics (MIS); information assurance (MIS); information systems (Graduate Certificate); information systems management (MS, Graduate Certificate); information technology (MS); information technology audit and compliance (Graduate Certificate); knowledge management (MIS); software engineering (MS). *Program availability:* Part-time, online learning. *Entrance requirements:* For master's, bachelor's degree. Additional exam requirements/recommendations for international students: Required—TOEFL (minimum score 550 paper-based; 80 iBT), IELTS. Electronic applications accepted.

Virginia Polytechnic Institute and State University, VT Online, Blacksburg, VA 24061. Offers advanced transportation systems (Certificate); aerospace engineering (MS); agricultural and life sciences (MSLFS); business information systems (Graduate Certificate); career and technical education (MS); civil engineering (MS); computer engineering (M Eng, MS); decision support systems (Graduate Certificate); eLearning leadership (MA); electrical engineering (M Eng, MS); engineering administration (MEA); environmental engineering (Certificate); environmental politics and policy (Graduate Certificate); environmental sciences and engineering (MS); foundations of political analysis (Graduate Certificate); health product risk management (Graduate Certificate); industrial and systems engineering (MS); information policy and society (Graduate Certificate); information security (Graduate Certificate); information technology (MIT); instructional technology (MA); integrative STEM education (MA Ed); liberal arts (Graduate Certificate); life sciences: health product risk management (MS); natural resources (MNR, Graduate Certificate); networking (Graduate Certificate); nonprofit and nongovernmental organization management (Graduate Certificate); ocean engineering (MS); political science (MA); security studies (Graduate Certificate); software development (Graduate Certificate). *Expenses:* Tuition, state resident: full-time $12,467; part-time $692.50 per credit hour. Tuition, nonresident: full-time $25,095; part-time $1394.25 per credit hour. *Required fees:* $2669; $491.50 per semester. Tuition and fees vary according to course load, campus/location and program.

West Virginia University, Statler College of Engineering and Mineral Resources, Lane Department of Computer Science and Electrical Engineering, Program in Software Engineering, Morgantown, WV 26506. Offers MSSE. *Entrance requirements:* For master's, GRE or work experience.

Systems Science

Arizona State University at the Tempe campus, College of Liberal Arts and Sciences, School of Life Sciences, Tempe, AZ 85287-4601. Offers animal behavior (PhD); applied ethics (biomedical and health ethics) (MA); biology (MS, PhD), including biology, biology and society, complex adaptive systems science (PhD), plant biology and conservation (MS); environmental life sciences (PhD); evolutionary biology (PhD); history and philosophy of science (PhD); human and social dimensions of science and technology (PhD); microbiology (PhD); molecular and cellular biology (PhD); neuroscience (PhD). Terminal master's awarded for partial completion of doctoral program. *Degree requirements:* For master's, thesis (for some programs), interactive Program of Study (iPOS) submitted before completing 50 percent of required credit hours; for doctorate, variable foreign language requirement, comprehensive exam, thesis/dissertation, interactive Program of Study (iPOS) submitted before completing 50 percent of required credit hours. *Entrance requirements:* For master's and doctorate, GRE, minimum GPA of 3.0 or equivalent in last 2 years of work leading to bachelor's degree. Additional exam requirements/recommendations for international students: Required—TOEFL (minimum score 600 paper-based; 100 iBT). Electronic applications accepted.

Arizona State University at the Tempe campus, Ira A. Fulton Schools of Engineering, ASU Engineering Online Programs, Tempe, AZ 85287. Offers construction (MS); embedded systems (M Eng); enterprise systems innovation and management (MSE); modeling and simulation (M Eng); quality and reliability engineering (M Eng); software engineering (MSE); systems engineering (M Eng).

Binghamton University, State University of New York, Graduate School, Thomas J. Watson School of Engineering and Applied Science, Department of Systems Science and Industrial Engineering, Binghamton, NY 13902-6000. Offers executive health systems (MS); industrial and systems engineering (M Eng); systems science and industrial engineering (MS, PhD). MS in executive health systems also offered in Manhattan. *Program availability:* Part-time, evening/weekend, online learning. *Faculty:* 21 full-time (4 women), 4 part-time/adjunct (0 women). *Students:* 221 full-time (65 women), 125 part-time (40 women); includes 54 minority (18 Black or African American, non-Hispanic/Latino; 20 Asian, non-Hispanic/Latino; 16 Hispanic/Latino), 238 international. Average age 28. 468 applicants, 88% accepted, 117 enrolled. In 2016, 109 master's, 11 doctorates awarded. *Degree requirements:* For master's, thesis; for doctorate, thesis/dissertation. *Entrance requirements:* For master's and doctorate, GRE General Test. Additional exam requirements/recommendations for international students: Required—TOEFL (minimum score 550 paper-based; 80 iBT). *Application deadline:* For fall admission, 4/1 priority date for domestic and international students; for spring admission, 11/15 priority date for domestic and international students. Applications are processed on a rolling basis. Application fee: $75. Electronic applications accepted. *Expenses:* Contact institution. *Financial support:* In 2016–17, 97 students received support, including 1 fellowship with full tuition reimbursement available (averaging $10,000 per year), 45 research assistantships with full tuition reimbursements available (averaging $16,500 per year), 13 teaching assistantships with full tuition reimbursements available (averaging $16,500 per year); career-related internships or fieldwork, Federal Work-Study, institutionally sponsored loans, scholarships/grants, health care benefits, tuition waivers (full and partial), and unspecified assistantships also available. Financial award application deadline: 2/1; financial award applicants required to submit FAFSA. *Faculty research:* Problem restructuring, protein modeling. *Unit head:* Ellen Tilden, Coordinator of Graduate Studies, 607-777-2873, E-mail: etilden@binghamton.edu. *Application contact:* Ben Balkaya, Assistant Dean and Director, 607-777-2151, Fax: 607-777-2501, E-mail: balkaya@binghamton.edu.
Website: http://www.ssie.binghamton.edu

Carleton University, Faculty of Graduate Studies, Faculty of Engineering and Design, Ottawa-Carleton Institute for Electrical Engineering, Department of Systems and Computer Engineering, Program in Information and Systems Science, Ottawa, ON K1S 5B6, Canada. Offers M Sc.

Carleton University, Faculty of Graduate Studies, Faculty of Science, Information and Systems Science Program, Ottawa, ON K1S 5B6, Canada. Offers M Sc. *Degree requirements:* For master's, thesis optional. *Entrance requirements:* For master's, honors degree. Additional exam requirements/recommendations for international students: Required—TOEFL. *Faculty research:* Software engineering, real-time and microprocessor programming, computer communications.

Carleton University, Faculty of Graduate Studies, Faculty of Science, School of Computer Science, Ottawa, ON K1S 5B6, Canada. Offers computer science (MCS, PhD); information and system science (M Sc). MCS and PhD programs offered jointly with University of Ottawa. *Program availability:* Part-time. *Degree requirements:* For master's, thesis optional, project; for doctorate, comprehensive exam, thesis/ dissertation. *Entrance requirements:* For master's, honors degree. Additional exam requirements/recommendations for international students: Required—TOEFL. *Faculty research:* Programming systems, theory of computing, computer applications, computer systems.

Claremont Graduate University, Graduate Programs, Center for Information Systems and Technology, Claremont, CA 91711-6160. Offers cybersecurity and networking (MS); data science and analytics (MS); electronic commerce (PhD); geographic information systems (MS); health informatics (MS); information systems (Certificate); IT strategy and innovation (MS); knowledge management (PhD); systems development (PhD); telecommunications and networking (PhD); MBA/MS. *Program availability:* Part-time. *Faculty:* 8 full-time (1 woman), 1 part-time/adjunct (0 women). *Students:* 60 full-time (18 women), 81 part-time (27 women); includes 34 minority (7 Black or African American, non-Hispanic/Latino; 18 Asian, non-Hispanic/Latino; 7 Hispanic/Latino; 1 Native Hawaiian or other Pacific Islander, non-Hispanic/Latino; 1 Two or more races, non-Hispanic/Latino), 80 international. Average age 35. In 2016, 21 master's, 10 doctorates awarded. *Degree requirements:* For doctorate, comprehensive exam, thesis/ dissertation, portfolio. *Entrance requirements:* For master's and doctorate, GMAT, GRE General Test. Additional exam requirements/recommendations for international students: Required—TOEFL (minimum score 75 iBT). *Application deadline:* For fall admission, 2/1 priority date for domestic and international students. Applications are processed on a rolling basis. Application fee: $80. Electronic applications accepted. *Expenses:* Tuition: Full-time $44,328; part-time $1847 per unit. *Required fees:* $600; $300 per semester. Tuition and fees vary according to course load and program. *Financial support:* Fellowships, research assistantships, teaching assistantships, Federal Work-Study, institutionally sponsored loans, and scholarships/grants available. Support available to part-time students. Financial award application deadline: 2/15; financial award applicants required to submit FAFSA. *Faculty research:* Man-machine interaction, organizational aspects of computing, implementation of information systems, information systems practice. *Unit head:* Lorne Olfman, Acting Director, 909-607-3035, E-mail: lorne.olfman@cgu.edu. *Application contact:* Jake Campbell, Senior Assistant Director of Admissions, 909-607-3024, E-mail: jake.campbell@cgu.edu.
Website: https://www.cgu.edu/school/center-for-information-systems-and-technology/

Eastern Illinois University, Graduate School, Lumpkin College of Business and Applied Sciences, School of Technology, Charleston, IL 61920. Offers computer technology (Certificate); quality systems (Certificate); technology (MS); technology security (Certificate); work performance improvement (Certificate); MS/MBA; MS/MS. *Program availability:* Part-time, evening/weekend.

Fairleigh Dickinson University, Metropolitan Campus, University College: Arts, Sciences, and Professional Studies, Program in Systems Science, Teaneck, NJ 07666-1914. Offers MS. *Entrance requirements:* For master's, GRE General Test.

Harrisburg University of Science and Technology, Program in Information Systems Engineering and Management, Harrisburg, PA 17101. Offers analytics (MS); digital government (MS); digital health (MS); entrepreneurship (MS); information security (MS); software engineering and systems development (MS). *Program availability:* Part-time, evening/weekend. *Faculty:* 9 full-time (0 women), 1 (woman) part-time/adjunct. *Students:* 1,031 full-time (264 women), 35 part-time (10 women); includes 2 minority (1 Black or African American, non-Hispanic/Latino; 1 Asian, non-Hispanic/Latino), 1,060 international. In 2016, 83 master's awarded. *Degree requirements:* For master's, thesis optional. *Entrance requirements:* For master's, baccalaureate degree. Additional exam requirements/recommendations for international students: Required—TOEFL (minimum score 520 paper-based; 80 iBT); Recommended—IELTS (minimum score 6). *Application deadline:* Applications are processed on a rolling basis. Application fee: $0. Electronic applications accepted. *Expenses: Tuition:* Full-time $4800; part-time $800 per semester hour. *Financial support:* In 2016–17, 2 students received support. Teaching assistantships available. Financial award applicants required to submit FAFSA. *Faculty research:* Healthcare Informatics, material analysis, enterprise systems, circuit design, enterprise architectures. *Unit head:* Dr. Amjad Umar, Director and Professor, 717-901-5141, Fax: 717-901-3141, E-mail: aumar@harrisburgu.edu.

Hood College, Graduate School, Program in Management of Information Technology, Frederick, MD 21701-8575. Offers MS. *Program availability:* Part-time, evening/ weekend. *Students:* 14 full-time (5 women), 3 part-time (1 woman); includes 1 minority (Asian, non-Hispanic/Latino), 14 international. Average age 33. 21 applicants, 71% accepted, 6 enrolled. In 2016, 12 master's awarded. *Entrance requirements:* For master's, minimum GPA of 2.75, essay, resume. Additional exam requirements/ recommendations for international students: Required—TOEFL (minimum score 575 paper-based; 89 iBT), IELTS (minimum score 6.5). *Application deadline:* For fall admission, 8/15 priority date for domestic students, 8/5 for international students; for spring admission, 12/1 priority date for domestic students, 12/1 for international students; for summer admission, 5/1 priority date for domestic students, 4/15 for international students. Applications are processed on a rolling basis. Application fee: $35. Electronic applications accepted. *Expenses:* $475 per credit; $110 comprehensive fee per semester. *Financial support:* Tuition waivers (partial) and unspecified assistantships available. Financial award applicants required to submit FAFSA. *Faculty research:* Systems engineering, parallel distributed computing, strategy, business ethics, entrepreneurship. *Unit head:* April Boulton, Interim Dean of the Graduate School, 301-696-3600, E-mail: gofurther@hood.edu. *Application contact:* Larbi Bricha, Assistant Director of Graduate Admissions, 301-696-3600, E-mail: gofurther@hood.edu.
Website: http://www.hood.edu/graduate

Louisiana State University and Agricultural & Mechanical College, Graduate School, College of Engineering, Division of Computer Science, Baton Rouge, LA 70803. Offers computer science (MSSS, PhD); systems science (MSSS).

Louisiana State University in Shreveport, College of Arts and Sciences, Program in Computer Systems Technology, Shreveport, LA 71115-2399. Offers MS. *Program availability:* Part-time, evening/weekend. *Students:* 7 full-time (1 woman), 11 part-time (2 women); includes 5 minority (1 Black or African American, non-Hispanic/Latino; 2 Asian, non-Hispanic/Latino; 1 Hispanic/Latino; 1 Two or more races, non-Hispanic/Latino). Average age 31. 22 applicants, 95% accepted, 5 enrolled. In 2016, 5 master's awarded. *Degree requirements:* For master's, comprehensive exam (for some programs), thesis or alternative. *Entrance requirements:* For master's, GRE, programming course in high-level language, interview. Additional exam requirements/recommendations for international students: Required—TOEFL (minimum score 550 paper-based; 80 iBT). *Application deadline:* For fall admission, 6/30 for domestic and international students; for spring admission, 11/30 for domestic and international students; for summer admission, 4/30 for domestic and international students. Applications are processed on a rolling basis. Application fee: $20 ($30 for international students). Electronic applications accepted. *Expenses:* Tuition, state resident: full-time $5163; part-time $350 per credit hour. Tuition, nonresident: full-time $15,578; part-time $1038 per credit hour. *Required fees:* $63 per credit hour. Tuition and fees vary according to course load and program. *Financial support:* In 2016–17, 2 research assistantships (averaging $5,000 per year) were awarded. Financial award applicants required to submit FAFSA. *Unit head:* Dr. Alfred McKinney, Program Director, 318-797-5300, Fax: 318-795-2419, E-mail: alfred.mckinney@lsus.edu. *Application contact:* Mary Catherine Harvison, Director of Admissions, 318-797-2400, Fax: 318-797-5286, E-mail: mary.harvison@lsus.edu.

Miami University, College of Engineering and Computing, Department of Computer Science and Software Engineering, Oxford, OH 45056. Offers computer science (MCS). *Students:* 14 full-time (5 women), 1 (woman) part-time; includes 2 minority (1 Black or African American, non-Hispanic/Latino; 1 Two or more races, non-Hispanic/Latino), 8 international. Average age 25. In 2016, 10 master's awarded. *Expenses:* Tuition, state resident: full-time $12,890; part-time $564 per credit hour. Tuition, nonresident: full-time $29,604; part-time $1260 per credit hour. *Required fees:* $638. Part-time tuition and fees vary according to course load and program. *Unit head:* Dr. James Kiper, Chair, 513-529-0340, E-mail: kiperjd@miamioh.edu. *Application contact:* Graduate Director, 513-529-0340, E-mail: cecgrad@miamioh.edu.
Website: http://miamioh.edu/cec/academics/departments/cse/

New Jersey Institute of Technology, Ying Wu College of Computing, Newark, NJ 07102. Offers big data management and mining (Certificate); business and information systems (Certificate); computer science (MS, PhD), including bioinformatics (MS), computer science, computing and business (MS), cyber security and privacy (MS), software engineering (MS), data mining (Certificate); information security (Certificate); information systems (MS, PhD), including business and information systems (MS), emergency management and business continuity (MS), information systems; information technology administration and security (MS); IT administration (Certificate); network security and information assurance (Certificate); software engineering analysis/ design (Certificate); Web systems development (Certificate). *Program availability:* Part-time, evening/weekend. *Faculty:* 64 full-time (10 women), 38 part-time/adjunct (4 women). *Students:* 818 full-time (241 women), 225 part-time (53 women); includes 162 minority (35 Black or African American, non-Hispanic/Latino; 77 Asian, non-Hispanic/

Latino; 41 Hispanic/Latino; 9 Two or more races, non-Hispanic/Latino), 772 international. Average age 27. 2,666 applicants, 51% accepted, 377 enrolled. In 2016, 398 master's, 10 doctorates, 9 other advanced degrees awarded. Terminal master's awarded for partial completion of doctoral program. *Degree requirements:* For master's, thesis optional; for doctorate, thesis/dissertation. *Entrance requirements:* For master's, GRE General Test; for doctorate, GRE General Test, minimum graduate GPA of 3.5. Additional exam requirements/recommendations for international students: Required—TOEFL (minimum score 550 paper-based; 79 iBT). *Application deadline:* For fall admission, 6/1 priority date for domestic students, 5/1 priority date for international students; for spring admission, 11/15 priority date for domestic and international students. Applications are processed on a rolling basis. Application fee: $75. Electronic applications accepted. *Expenses:* Contact institution. *Financial support:* In 2016–17, 57 students received support, including 18 research assistantships (averaging $16,073 per year), 39 teaching assistantships (averaging $20,194 per year); fellowships, career-related internships or fieldwork, Federal Work-Study, institutionally sponsored loans, and unspecified assistantships also available. Financial award application deadline: 1/15. *Faculty research:* Computer systems, communications and networking, artificial intelligence, database engineering, systems analysis, analytics and optimization in crowdsourcing. *Total annual research expenditures:* $3 million. *Unit head:* Dr. Craig Gotsman, Dean, 973-542-5488, Fax: 973-596-5777, E-mail: marek.rusinkiewicz@njit.edu. *Application contact:* Stephen Eck, Director of Admissions, 973-596-3300, Fax: 973-596-3461, E-mail: admissions@njit.edu.
Website: http://computing.njit.edu/

Oakland University, Graduate Study and Lifelong Learning, School of Engineering and Computer Science, Department of Electrical and Computer Engineering, Rochester, MI 48309-4401. Offers electrical and computer engineering (MS, PhD); embedded systems (MS); mechatronics (MS). *Program availability:* Part-time, evening/weekend. *Entrance requirements:* For master's, minimum GPA of 3.0. Additional exam requirements/recommendations for international students: Required—TOEFL (minimum score 550 paper-based). Electronic applications accepted. *Expenses:* Contact institution.

Portland State University, Graduate Studies, College of Liberal Arts and Sciences, Systems Science Program, Portland, OR 97207-0751. Offers computational intelligence (Certificate); computer modeling and simulation (Certificate); systems science (MS); systems science/anthropology (PhD); systems science/business administration (PhD); systems science/civil engineering (PhD); systems science/economics (PhD); systems science/engineering management (PhD); systems science/general (PhD); systems science/mathematical sciences (PhD); systems science/mechanical engineering (PhD); systems science/psychology (PhD); systems science/sociology (PhD). *Faculty:* 2 full-time (0 women), 3 part-time/adjunct (1 woman). *Students:* 12 full-time (3 women), 21 part-time (5 women); includes 5 minority (1 Black or African American, non-Hispanic/Latino; 2 Hispanic/Latino; 2 Two or more races, non-Hispanic/Latino). Average age 39. 16 applicants, 69% accepted, 9 enrolled. In 2016, 4 master's, 6 doctorates awarded. *Degree requirements:* For master's, comprehensive exam (for some programs), thesis optional; for doctorate, variable foreign language requirement, comprehensive exam (for some programs), thesis/dissertation. *Entrance requirements:* For master's, GRE/GMAT (recommended), minimum GPA of 3.0 undergraduate or graduate work, 2 letters of recommendation, statement of interest; for doctorate, GMAT, GRE General Test, minimum GPA of 3.0 undergraduate, 3.25 graduate; 2 letters of recommendation; statement of interest. Additional exam requirements/recommendations for international students: Required—TOEFL (minimum score 550 paper-based; 80 iBT). *Application deadline:* For fall admission, 1/15 for domestic and international students; for spring admission, 11/1 for domestic students. Application fee: $65. Electronic applications accepted. *Expenses:* Contact institution. *Financial support:* In 2016–17, 2 research assistantships with tuition reimbursements (averaging $7,830 per year) were awarded; teaching assistantships, career-related internships or fieldwork, Federal Work-Study, scholarships/grants, and unspecified assistantships also available. Support available to part-time students. Financial award application deadline: 3/1; financial award applicants required to submit FAFSA. *Faculty research:* Systems theory and methodology, artificial intelligence neural networks, information theory, nonlinear dynamics/chaos, modeling and simulation. *Unit head:* Dr. Wayne Wakeland, Chair, 503-725-4975, E-mail: wakeland@pdx.edu.
Website: http://www.pdx.edu/sysc/

Portland State University, Graduate Studies, Maseeh College of Engineering and Computer Science, Department of Engineering and Technology Management, Portland, OR 97207-0751. Offers engineering and technology management (M Eng); engineering management (MS); manufacturing engineering (ME); manufacturing management (M Eng); systems science/engineering management (PhD); MS/MBA; MS/MS. *Program availability:* Part-time, evening/weekend. *Faculty:* 6 full-time (1 woman), 5 part-time/adjunct (0 women). *Students:* 53 full-time (19 women), 75 part-time (34 women); includes 18 minority (3 Black or African American, non-Hispanic/Latino; 11 Asian, non-Hispanic/Latino; 3 Hispanic/Latino; 1 Two or more races, non-Hispanic/Latino), 73 international. Average age 36. 76 applicants, 50% accepted, 20 enrolled. In 2016, 34 master's, 4 doctorates awarded. *Degree requirements:* For master's, thesis optional; for doctorate, one foreign language, comprehensive exam, thesis/dissertation, oral and written exams. *Entrance requirements:* For master's, minimum GPA of 2.75 undergraduate or 3.0 graduate (at least 12 credits); minimum 4 years of experience in engineering or related discipline; 3 letters of recommendation; background in probability/statistics, differential equations, computer programming and linear algebra; for doctorate, GRE General Test (minimum combined score of 1100 for verbal and quantitative), minimum GPA of 3.0 undergraduate, 3.25 graduate. Additional exam requirements/recommendations for international students: Required—TOEFL (minimum score 550 paper-based; 80 iBT). *Application deadline:* For fall admission, 4/1 for domestic students, 3/1 for international students; for winter admission, 9/1 for domestic students, 7/1 for international students; for spring admission, 11/1 for domestic students, 9/1 for international students; for summer admission, 2/1 for domestic students, 12/1 for international students. Application fee: $65. Electronic applications accepted. *Expenses:* Contact institution. *Financial support:* In 2016–17, 7 research assistantships with tuition reimbursements (averaging $2,885 per year), 3 teaching assistantships with tuition reimbursements (averaging $1,176 per year) were awarded; career-related internships or fieldwork, Federal Work-Study, scholarships/grants, and unspecified assistantships also available. Support available to part-time students. Financial award application deadline: 3/1; financial award applicants required to submit FAFSA. *Faculty research:* Scheduling, hierarchical decision modeling, operations research, knowledge-based information systems. *Total annual research expenditures:* $323,951. *Unit head:* Dr. Timothy Anderson, Chair, 503-725-4668, Fax: 503-725-4667, E-mail: tim.anderson@pdx.edu. *Application contact:* Shawn Wall, Department Manager, 503-725-4661, E-mail: shawnw@pdx.edu.
Website: http://www.pdx.edu/engineering-technology-management/

Rensselaer at Hartford, Department of Engineering, Program in Computer and Systems Engineering, Hartford, CT 06120-2991. Offers ME. *Entrance requirements:* For master's, GRE.

Southern Methodist University, Bobby B. Lyle School of Engineering, Department of Engineering Management, Information, and Systems, Dallas, TX 75275. Offers engineering management (MSEM, DE); information engineering and management (MSIEM); operations research (MS, PhD); systems engineering (MS, PhD). *Program availability:* Part-time, evening/weekend, online learning. Terminal master's awarded for partial completion of doctoral program. *Degree requirements:* For master's, thesis optional; for doctorate, thesis/dissertation, oral and written qualifying exams. *Entrance requirements:* For master's, minimum GPA of 3.0 in last 2 years; bachelor's degree in engineering, mathematics, sciences, or technical area; for doctorate, GRE General Test (operations research, engineering management), bachelor's degree in related field. Additional exam requirements/recommendations for international students: Required—TOEFL. *Faculty research:* Telecommunications, decision systems, information engineering, operations research, software.

Stevens Institute of Technology, Graduate School, Charles V. Schaefer Jr. School of Engineering and Science, Department of Mechanical Engineering, Program in Integrated Product Development, Hoboken, NJ 07030. Offers armament engineering (M Eng); computer and electrical engineering (M Eng); manufacturing technologies (M Eng); systems reliability and design (M Eng). *Program availability:* Part-time, evening/weekend. *Students:* 15 applicants. In 2016, 2 master's awarded. *Degree requirements:* For master's, thesis optional, minimum B average in major field and overall. *Entrance requirements:* Additional exam requirements/recommendations for international students: Required—TOEFL (minimum score 74 iBT), IELTS (minimum score 6). *Application deadline:* For fall admission, 6/1 for domestic students, 4/15 for international students; for spring admission, 11/30 for domestic students, 11/1 for international students. Applications are processed on a rolling basis. Application fee: $65. Electronic applications accepted. *Expenses:* Contact institution. *Financial support:* Fellowships, research assistantships, teaching assistantships, career-related internships or fieldwork, Federal Work-Study, scholarships/grants, and unspecified assistantships available. Financial award application deadline: 2/15; financial award applicants required to submit FAFSA. *Unit head:* Dr. Frank Fisher, Interim Department Director, 201-216-8913, Fax: 201-216-8315, E-mail: ffisher@stevens.edu. *Application contact:* Graduate Admissions, 888-783-8367, Fax: 888-511-1306, E-mail: graduate@stevens.edu.

Stevens Institute of Technology, Graduate School, School of Systems and Enterprises, Program in Enterprise Systems, Hoboken, NJ 07030. Offers Certificate. *Program availability:* Part-time, evening/weekend. *Students:* 65 applicants, 71% accepted, 22 enrolled. *Degree requirements:* For Certificate, minimum B average. *Entrance requirements:* Additional exam requirements/recommendations for international students: Required—TOEFL (minimum score 74 iBT), IELTS (minimum score 6). *Application deadline:* For fall admission, 6/1 for domestic students, 4/15 for international students; for spring admission, 11/30 for domestic students, 11/1 for international students. Applications are processed on a rolling basis. Application fee: $65. Electronic applications accepted. *Expenses:* Contact institution. *Financial support:* Fellowships, research assistantships, teaching assistantships, career-related internships or fieldwork, Federal Work-Study, scholarships/grants, and unspecified assistantships available. Financial award application deadline: 2/15; financial award applicants required to submit FAFSA. *Unit head:* Dr. Dinesh Verma, Dean, 201-216-8645, Fax: 201-216-5541, E-mail: dinesh.verma@stevens.edu. *Application contact:* Graduate Admissions, 888-783-8367, Fax: 888-511-1306, E-mail: graduate@stevens.edu.

Stevens Institute of Technology, Graduate School, School of Systems and Enterprises, Program in Socio-Technical Systems, Hoboken, NJ 07030. Offers MS, PhD. *Program availability:* Part-time, evening/weekend. *Students:* 2 full-time (0 women), 2 part-time (0 women), 1 international. Average age 37. 5 applicants, 60% accepted, 2 enrolled. *Degree requirements:* For master's, thesis optional, minimum B average in major field and overall; for doctorate, comprehensive exam (for some programs), thesis/dissertation. *Entrance requirements:* Additional exam requirements/recommendations for international students: Required—TOEFL (minimum score 74 iBT), IELTS (minimum score 6). *Application deadline:* For fall admission, 6/1 for domestic students, 4/15 for international students; for spring admission, 11/30 for domestic students, 11/1 for international students. Applications are processed on a rolling basis. Application fee: $65. Electronic applications accepted. *Expenses:* Contact institution. *Financial support:* Fellowships, research assistantships, teaching assistantships, career-related internships or fieldwork, Federal Work-Study, scholarships/grants, and unspecified assistantships available. Financial award application deadline: 2/15; financial award applicants required to submit FAFSA. *Unit head:* Dr. Dinesh Verma, Dean, 201-216-8645, Fax: 201-216-5541, E-mail: dinesh.verma@stevens.edu. *Application contact:* Graduate Admissions, 888-783-8367, Fax: 888-511-1306, E-mail: graduate@stevens.edu.

Strayer University, Graduate Studies, Washington, DC 20005-2603. Offers accounting (MS); acquisition (MBA); business administration (MBA); communications technology (MS); educational management (M Ed); finance (MBA); health services administration (MHSA); hospitality and tourism management (MBA); human resource management (MBA); information systems (MS), including computer security management, decision support system management, enterprise resource management, network management, software engineering management, systems development management; management (MBA); management information systems (MS); marketing (MBA); professional accounting (MS), including accounting information systems, controllership, taxation; public administration (MPA); supply chain management (MBA); technology in education (M Ed). Programs also offered at campus locations in Birmingham, AL; Chamblee, GA; Cobb County, GA; Morrow, GA; White Marsh, MD; Charleston, SC; Columbia, SC; Greensboro, NC; Greenville, SC; Lexington, KY; Louisville, KY; Nashville, TN; North Raleigh, NC; Washington, DC. *Accreditation:* ACBSP. *Program availability:* Part-time, evening/weekend, online learning. *Degree requirements:* For master's, thesis. *Entrance requirements:* For master's, GMAT, GRE General Test, bachelor's degree from an accredited college or university, minimum undergraduate GPA of 2.75. Electronic applications accepted.

Universidad Autonoma de Guadalajara, Graduate Programs, Guadalajara, Mexico. Offers administrative law and justice (LL M); advertising and corporate communications (MA); architecture (M Arch); business (MBA); computational science (MCC); education (Ed M, Ed D); English-Spanish translation (MA); entrepreneurship and management (MBA); integrated management of digital animation (MA); international business (MIB); international corporate law (LL M); internet technologies (MS); manufacturing systems (MMS); occupational health (MS); philosophy (MA, PhD); power electronics (MS); quality systems (MQS); renewable energy (MS); social evaluation of projects (MBA); strategic market research (MBA); tax law (MA); teaching mathematics (MA).

University of Michigan, College of Engineering, Department of Integrative Systems and Design, Ann Arbor, MI 48109. Offers automotive engineering (M Eng); design science (MS, PhD); energy systems engineering (M Eng, MS); global automotive and manufacturing engineering (M Eng); manufacturing engineering (M Eng, D Eng); pharmaceutical engineering (M Eng); robotics and autonomous vehicles (M Eng); systems engineering and design (M Eng); MBA/M Eng; MSE/MS. *Program availability:* Part-time, online learning. *Students:* 147 full-time (33 women), 234 part-time (39 women). 315 applicants, 8% accepted, 13 enrolled. In 2016, 158 master's, 2 doctorates awarded. Terminal master's awarded for partial completion of doctoral program. *Degree*

requirements: For master's, capstone project; for doctorate, thesis/dissertation. *Entrance requirements:* For master's, GRE; for doctorate, GRE, 2 years of work experience. Additional exam requirements/recommendations for international students: Required—TOEFL (minimum score 560 paper-based). *Application deadline:* Applications are processed on a rolling basis. Electronic applications accepted. *Expenses:* Tuition, state resident: full-time $21,466; part-time $1152 per credit hour. Tuition, nonresident: full-time $43,346; part-time $2367 per credit hour. Part-time tuition and fees vary according to course load, degree level and program. *Financial support:* Fellowships, research assistantships with full tuition reimbursements, teaching assistantships with full tuition reimbursements, career-related internships or fieldwork, scholarships/grants, and unspecified assistantships available. Financial award applicants required to submit FAFSA. *Faculty research:* Automotive engineering, design science, energy systems engineering, engineering sustainable systems, financial engineering, global automotive and manufacturing engineering, integrated microsystems, manufacturing engineering, pharmaceutical engineering, robotics and autonomous vehicles. *Total annual research expenditures:* $292,225. *Unit head:* Prof. Panos Papalambros, Department Chair, 734-647-8401, E-mail: pyp@umich.edu. *Application contact:* Kathy Bishar, Senior Graduate Coordinator, 734-764-3312, E-mail: kbishar@umich.edu.
Website: http://www.isd.engin.umich.edu

University of Ottawa, Faculty of Graduate and Postdoctoral Studies, Interdisciplinary Programs, Ottawa, ON K1N 6N5, Canada. Offers e-business (Certificate); e-commerce (Certificate); finance (Certificate); health services and policies research (Diploma); population health (PhD); population health risk assessment and management (Certificate); public management and governance (Certificate); systems science (Certificate).

University of Ottawa, Faculty of Graduate and Postdoctoral Studies, Systems Science Program, Ottawa, ON K1N 6N5, Canada. Offers M Sc, M Sys Sc, Certificate. *Program*

availability: Part-time, evening/weekend. *Degree requirements:* For master's and Certificate, thesis optional. *Entrance requirements:* For master's, bachelor's degree or equivalent, minimum B average; for Certificate, honors degree or equivalent, minimum B average. Additional exam requirements/recommendations for international students: Recommended—TOEFL. Electronic applications accepted. *Faculty research:* Software engineering, communication systems, information systems, production management, corporate managerial modeling.

Worcester Polytechnic Institute, Graduate Studies and Research, Department of Social Science and Policy Studies, Worcester, MA 01609-2280. Offers interdisciplinary social science (PhD); system dynamics (MS, Graduate Certificate). *Program availability:* Part-time, evening/weekend, 100% online. *Faculty:* 3 full-time (1 woman), 4 part-time/adjunct (1 woman). *Students:* 2 full-time (1 woman), 7 part-time (0 women), 2 international. 5 applicants, 100% accepted, 2 enrolled. In 2016, 2 master's awarded. *Entrance requirements:* For master's and doctorate, GRE General Test, 3 letters of recommendation, statement of purpose. Additional exam requirements/recommendations for international students: Required—TOEFL (minimum score 563 paper-based; 84 iBT), IELTS (minimum score 7). *Application deadline:* For fall admission, 1/1 priority date for domestic students, 1/1 for international students; for spring admission, 10/1 priority date for domestic students, 10/1 for international students. Applications are processed on a rolling basis. Application fee: $70. Electronic applications accepted. *Financial support:* Research assistantships, teaching assistantships, career-related internships or fieldwork, institutionally sponsored loans, scholarships/grants, and unspecified assistantships available. Financial award application deadline: 1/1; financial award applicants required to submit FAFSA. *Unit head:* Dr. James K. Doyle, Head, 508-831-5296, Fax: 508-831-5896, E-mail: doyle@wpi.edu. *Application contact:* Dr. Khalid Saeed, Graduate Coordinator, 508-831-5296, Fax: 508-831-5896, E-mail: saeed@wpi.edu.
Website: http://www.wpi.edu/academics/ssps

DREXEL UNIVERSITY
College of Computing & Informatics

For more information, visit http://petersons.to/drexel-cci

Programs of Study

The College of Computing & Informatics (CCI) is located at Drexel University, a private university in the heart of Philadelphia, Pennsylvania. CCI offers graduate degree programs including the online and on-campus Library and Information Science program; the online and on-campus Computer Science program; the online Health Informatics program; the online and on-campus Information Systems program; the online and on-campus Software Engineering program; and the online and on-campus Cybersecurity program (a joint program with the Electrical & Computer Engineering Department of Drexel's College of Engineering).

Founded in 2013, CCI instills the knowledge and skills necessary for students to lead and innovate across industries in a rapidly evolving technological landscape. Building on Drexel University's exceptional foundation of entrepreneurship and cooperative education, CCI provides unparalleled professional experiences and the on-the-job training that is vital to preparing today's students for tomorrow's world. CCI's unique structure brings computing and informatics together under one roof in a dynamic, collaborative college that allows faculty and students to spot trends before they emerge, to solve problems before they occur, and to build a better tomorrow, starting today.

The graduate programs offered by the College of Computing & Informatics include:

The Master of Science in Library & Informatics Science (M.S.L.I.S.) program, newly revised in 2017, addresses the contexts in which librarians and other information professionals work, the systems and services they provide, and the uses of new and emerging technologies in the field. The M.S.L.I.S. is one of the country's oldest and longest continually accredited library and information science master's degree programs, established in 1892. In 2010, the program was fully reaccredited with continuous accreditation status until 2017. The program presentation for reaccreditation is scheduled to occur in October 2017.

The **Master of Science in Computer Science (M.S.C.S.)** offers a multidisciplinary and in-depth understanding of the core and advanced topics in the rapidly growing field of computer science, while placing equal emphasis on theory and practice to prepare students for top professional positions.

The **Master of Science in Health Informatics (M.S.H.I.)** teaches students from diverse academic and professional backgrounds how to use information technology efficiently and responsibly to improve health outcomes. Drexel's M.S.H.I. degree program is in candidacy status, pending accreditation review by the Commission on Accreditation for Health Informatics and Information Management Education (CAHIIM). Drexel University's educational programs are accredited by MSCHE (Middle States Commission on Higher Education).

The **Master of Science in Information Systems (M.S.I.S.)** equips students with both the domain knowledge and practical competencies to compete in the ever-changing technical landscape of information system business requirements, software design and management, data-oriented informatics, and user experience design.

The **Master of Science in Software Engineering (M.S.S.E.)** prepares students to become professional software engineers across a wide variety of industries, and offers students a blend of theory and practice to provide a solid understanding of the fundamentals of software systems as well as a working knowledge of the many languages, methods, and systems used in the field.

The **Master of Science in Cybersecurity (M.S.C.)** is an interdisciplinary program that prepares students with both the academic and practical training to be competitive in the ever-changing technical landscape of cybersecurity. This is a joint program with the Electrical & Computer Engineering Department of Drexel's College of Engineering.

CCI also offers graduate students the opportunity to pursue a dual master's degree among any of their graduate programs. The Master of Science in Library and Information Science (M.S.L.I.S.) and the Master of Science in Information Systems (M.S.I.S.) dual program combines the focus of the M.S.L.I.S. program's concern with selecting, organizing, managing, and accessing information resources to meet user's information needs with the M.S.I.S. graduate's skills in creating and managing the databases, interfaces, and information systems. To be eligible for a dual master's degree program, graduate students must be currently working on their first degree when requesting admission to the second.

CCI has graduate minors in computer science and heathcare informatics. The computer science minor allows Drexel students from all backgrounds to obtain fundamental computer science knowledge as well as an introduction to advanced topics in computer science that will be suitable for their own graduate studies. The program is offered to current Drexel graduate students outside of the College's Computer Science Department. The minor in healthcare informatics provides a basic acquaintance with health informatics principles and practices for students pursuing careers in a wide variety of health-related professions. The program is offered to current Drexel graduate students in good standing (students in the M.S. in Health Informatics program are not eligible).

Graduate Co-op is available for the M.S. in Computer Science and M.S. in Information Systems programs. Graduate Co-op allows graduate students to alternate class terms with a six-month period of hands-on experience, gaining access to employers in their chosen industries.

CCI's interdisciplinary doctoral programs in information studies and computer science prepare students for leadership careers in research and education in the information and computer science fields. The College's **Ph.D. in Computer Science** program is designed to ensure core knowledge of the fundamental computer science areas and to conduct leading-edge research at the forefront of a selected area. Students are prepared for leadership careers in research and education in computer science and interdisciplinary work using computer science. The **Ph.D. in Information Studies** prepares students to become creative, interdisciplinary researchers with foundations in information science, data science, and human-centered computing. The main focus of the program is research with applications that benefit all sectors of society.

The College's professional development programs, such as the Post-Baccalaureate Certificate in Computer Science; Certificate in Healthcare Informatics; and the Advanced Certificate in Information Studies and Technology (ACIST), allow students holding a bachelor's or master's degree in any field to update their education and develop new expertise.

Research Facilities

Research at CCI spans a wide range of areas and topics all related in some way to the exciting world of computing and informatics. This research can be categorized in terms of six major research areas: computer science, computer security, human-centered computing, informatics and data science, library and information science, and systems and software engineering.

CCI is associated with a number of research centers and institutes that house a number of the University's leading-edge research initiatives. Collaboratively led by CCI faculty and members from partner colleges and institutions, these centers and institutes encompass a broad range of research topics and solutions in the computing and informatics fields. Some of those include the Center for the Study of Libraries, Information, & Society; Center for Visual and Decision Informatics (CVDI); the Drexel University Isaac L. Auerbach Cybersecurity Institute; and the Metadata Research Center.

Financial Aid

There are several options which can help CCI graduate students offset the cost of their studies, including CCI incentives, partner organization discounts, scholarships, student loans, the G.I. Bill for veterans, the Yellow Ribbon program, private scholarships, and employment with the University.

Cost of Study

The tuition rate for the 2017–18 academic year is $1,228 per credit hour plus general student fees.

Living and Housing Costs

On-campus housing is available. One-, two- and three- bedroom suites are available. Ample off-campus housing is also available.

Student Life

Both online and on-campus graduate students have the opportunity to participate in a variety of activities. CCI holds events, workshops, and hosts guest speakers throughout the year.

CCI graduate students have the opportunity to participate in student groups and professional organizations, many of which have local chapters that hold regular events. Student groups include the Drexel University Libraries & Archives Student Association, Upsilon Pi Epsilon, MCS Society, Women in Computing Society (WiCS), Drexel Game Developers Group (DGDG), and CCI Doctoral Student Association.

Drexel University

From graduate co-op programs and career workshops, to career counseling, career fairs, and national and international hands-on experience, the Steinbright Career Development Center at Drexel University helps give students the edge they need to succeed. Steinbright is also home to Dragon Jobs, Drexel's online job board of full-time and paid internship positions for graduating students and recent alums.

Location

Drexel University's lively urban campus is located in one of America's most exciting cities—Philadelphia. In a world-class city for business, art, and education, Philadelphia's skyscrapers are blended with distinct and culturally diverse neighborhoods, creating a unique metropolitan yet intimate urban experience. Surrounded by tree-lined residential blocks just minutes away from Philadelphia's downtown Center City district, Drexel makes its home in the neighborhood of University City. Philadelphia, a city steeped in history and tradition, is one of the nation's up-and-coming hubs for innovation, technology, and economic growth. Home to powerhouse companies such as Comcast and Urban Outfitters, as well as a quickly growing number of energetic start-ups, Philadelphia is a natural fit for Drexel's dynamic community. Philadelphia boasts some of the nation's best historical and cultural attractions and offers the vibrant nightlife, choice restaurants, dynamic arts, and major-league athletics of a first-class city. Drexel's location offers easy access to public transportation and the Drexel shuttle provides convenient, free transportation between campuses for Drexel students. Adjacent to Drexel's University City Campus, Amtrak's 30th Street Station is a hub for trains and buses to the Philadelphia suburbs, New York City, Washington, D.C., and the Philadelphia International Airport.

The University

Drexel is a comprehensive global research university ranked among the top 100 in the nation. With approximately 26,000 students, Drexel is one of America's 15 largest private universities. For nearly a decade, Drexel has been ranked in the category of Best National Universities in "America's Best Colleges" by *U.S. News & World Report*. The University placed 96th overall in the 2017 rankings. Drexel also ranked 14th (tied with Cornell, Harvard, George Mason University, and the University of Texas-Austin) in the Most Innovative Schools category. Drexel, the University of Pennsylvania, and Villanova are the only Philadelphia universities ranked in the *U.S. News* top 100. Drexel University is ranked in the top 8 percent of U.S. colleges and universities in a list compiled by the *Wall Street Journal* and *Times Higher Education*. In a 2017 report (Concept to Commercialization: The Best Universities for Technology Transfer) released by the Milken Institute, Drexel was ranked 46th out of 225 universities across the country based on its technology transfer, or ability to translate its academic innovators' research into actual technologies, products, and research-driven startups.

Drexel is known for its leadership in experiential learning and career-minded approach to education. Drexel has built its global reputation on core achievements that include leadership in experiential learning through Drexel Co-op; a history of academic technology firsts; and recognition as a model of best practices in translational, use-inspired research.

The Faculty and Their Research

With an emphasis on experiential learning, CCI's 68 full-time faculty members come from elite universities around the world, including Harvard University, Massachusetts Institute of Technology (MIT), University of Pennsylvania, New York University, Columbia University, and Brown University. Research is conducted in multidisciplinary clusters that are structured to address vital issues at the forefront of today's leading industries, including key areas such as computer science, computer security, human-centered computing, informatics and data science, library and information science, and systems and software engineering.

CCI faculty are engaged in collaborative, interdisciplinary initiatives in teaching and research among two departments: Computer Science and Information Science. The Department of Computer Science offers undergraduate and graduate degrees in computer science and software engineering, and includes world-class instructors and researchers in the field, integrating foundational computing theory with practical applications. The Department of Information Science leverages faculty research and teaching expertise in areas such as informatics and data science, library and information science, computer security, and human-centered computing to offer core undergraduate and graduate programs in information science. The department seeks to educate the next generation of informatics, computer, data, and library scientists to solve complex problems in an increasingly information-driven world.

Additional information on faculty members is available at http://drexel.edu/cci/contact/Faculty/.

Applying

Specific information about applying to any of the CCI graduate programs can be found at http://drexel.edu/cci/admissions/graduate-professional-development/.

Correspondence and Information

College of Computing & Informatics
306 Rush Building
Drexel University
3141 Chestnut Street
Philadelphia, Pennsylvania 19104
United States
Phone: 215-895-2474
E-mail: cciinfo@drexel.edu
Website: http://drexel.edu/cci/

UNIVERSITY OF CALIFORNIA, RIVERSIDE

Bourns College of Engineering

★ For more information, visit http://petersons.to/uc-riverside_compsci-eng

UCR
Bourns College
of Engineering

Programs of Study

The research and graduate programs at the Bourns College of Engineering (BCOE) provide students pursuing graduate degrees with a broad range of research opportunities in cutting-edge technology areas within a challenging, yet collaborative academic environment. Engineering students at the University of California, Riverside (UCR) enjoy the benefits of a smaller campus, which include a more personal research and educational approach with specialized attention and guidance. Students can become engaged with the world-class faculty at Bourns in any of a wide range of research projects, succeed in research, and benefit from their professional connections both within and outside the prestigious UC System.

The National Research Council's (NRC) data-based assessment of U.S. research doctorate programs shows the excellence of the Bourns College of Engineering's faculty and the rapid rise in the quality of its programs. All of the graduate programs in the Bourns College of Engineering were strongly rated in these rankings.

The graduate degree programs offered through the Bourns College of Engineering are designed to deepen student understanding of both fundamental principles and applications in their chosen field of study. The Ph.D. programs are heavily integrated with the College's research activities and are ideal for well-qualified individuals who wish to pursue careers in academia or industrial research. The College offers Master of Science (M.S.) and Doctor of Philosophy (Ph.D.) degrees in Bioengineering, Chemical and Environmental Engineering, Computer Science, Electrical and Computer Engineering, Materials Science and Engineering, and Mechanical Engineering as well as an online M.S. in Engineering.

Bioengineering (www.bioeng.ucr.edu): The Bioengineering program has a strong focus on state-of-the-art research, student training, and excellence in education. With bioengineering being a highly interdisciplinary field, its internationally recognized core faculty members are drawn from an eclectic mix of bioengineering-related disciplines including physics, biological sciences, chemistry, materials science, and engineering. Together they provide enriched, in-depth training for the students as well as forge the foundation for outstanding, collaborative, state-of-the-art research in specific focus areas. Efforts are concentrated in five critically important areas in bioengineering/biomedical engineering: biomaterials and regenerative medicine, biomedical imaging, computational bioengineering, medical devices, and molecular and cellular engineering.

Chemical and Environmental Engineering (www.cee.ucr.edu): The Department of Chemical and Environmental Engineering at UC Riverside offers leading-edge research and education in fields that will transform the future of health, energy, public safety, and the quality of our air, water, and land. Main research areas include: biotechnology, advanced materials and nanotechnology, air quality systems engineering, water quality systems engineering, sustainable energy, and molecular theory and modeling.

The department and two closely affiliated research centers (the College of Engineering–Center for Environmental Research and Technology and the Center for Nanoscale Science and Engineering) are leading the way in overcoming some of the most challenging scientific and technological problems of our time. For example, CEE faculty and students are leaders in the development of innovative methods to control air pollution and emissions from transportation and industrial sources. They are developing technologies to assure abundant supplies of safe drinking water, and applying nanoscience principles to the creation of new sensors that can detect toxic substances in air or water rapidly, accurately, and inexpensively. They are making other advancements toward the development of clean and renewable fuels and energy that can provide for society's needs sustainably and economically.

Computer Science and Engineering (www.cs.ucr.edu): The department offers B.S. degrees in Computer Science, Business Informatics, and Computer Engineering (jointly with the ECE department). It also offers the M.S. and Ph.D. degrees in Computer Science, as well as five-year joint B.S.+M.S. degrees in Computer Science and Computer Engineering. The Department has strong research programs, spanning the areas of architecture, compilers, embedded systems, algorithms, bioinformatics, databases, data mining, computer networks, distributed processing, artificial intelligence, machine learning, security, high-performance computing, software engineering, and graphics. CSE offers excellent career opportunities for alumni; new, state-of-the-art facilities; superior student recognition; a strong sense of community and pride; worldwide networking through UC connections,

graduate research, conferences, and more; and enthusiastic CSE staff and advisers that are able to assist students through their academic careers.

Materials Science and Engineering (www.mse.ucr.edu): The Materials Science and Engineering (MSE) graduate program at UCR offers M.S. and Ph.D. degrees (ABET accredited). The program comprises a large and diverse faculty from various disciplines in both the Bourns College of Engineering (BCOE) and the College of Natural and Agricultural Sciences (CNAS). Both BCOE and CNAS host a number of faculty members who carry out experimental, theoretical, and computational research in materials science and engineering. The program structure emphasizes the interdisciplinary nature of the field and encourages interdepartmental collaboration resulting in dynamic and original research. In addition to receiving a world-class education in the classroom, students enrolled in the MSE program benefit from unique research facilities, both existing and currently under development, at UCR. These facilities support research in the fields of materials synthesis, processing, characterization, and property measurement and are available in the departments of Bioengineering, Chemical and Environmental Engineering, Chemistry, Electrical and Computer Engineering, Mechanical Engineering, and Physics as well as those in the MSE program itself, which is housed in the Materials Science and Engineering Building. The Center for Nanoscale Science and Engineering (CNSE) and the Central Facility for Advanced Microscopy and Microanalysis (CFAMM) offer additional instrumentation, which is available for use by all students. Modern materials science and engineering allows those with both engineering and non-engineering backgrounds to join together in bringing technological innovations to fruition by applying the principles of engineering and the chemical and physical sciences.

Mechanical Engineering (www.me.ucr.edu): The Department of Mechanical Engineering (ME) at UCR offers opportunities for graduate study in a number of specialty areas of mechanical engineering, spanning seven broad areas: energy processing; bio-applications; nano- and micro-scale engineering; computation and design; materials properties and processing; multiphase flow, heat transfer, and combustion; and air quality and fire engineering. Disciplinary research by many faculty members and their groups is also carried out across interdepartmental programs and centers, such as Materials and Science and Engineering (MS&E), Center for Environmental Research and Technology (CE-CERT), and the Winston Chung Energy Center. Faculty-directed research is sponsored by federal agencies (NSF, NIH, DOE, ARO, AFOSR, USDAFS, ONR, etc.), state agencies (Cal Trans, CIEE, UCTC, etc.), and industrial sponsors (Raytheon, Aeptec, Lockheed, Bourns Inc., 3M, etc.). Highlights of the ME graduate program include active, modern, and inter/multidisciplinary research programs that are rapidly growing in size and prestige, combined with the diversity, personal advising, and close contact with all faculty.

Online M.S. in Engineering (MSOL): This program is the first of its kind at UCR and is designed for working professional engineers who wish to advance their knowledge in a field and enhance their value in the workplace. Students in the program receive course materials including lectures, notes, assignments, and announcements over the Internet. Exams are given by proctors at regional locations.

The BCOE online master's program is unique in that it combines engineering and professional development classes. Another key component is a significant design experience, incorporating additional readings and knowledge of the courses taken. This design experience is addressed in the online course 296A.

The MSOL concentrations include Bioengineering, Data Science, Electrical Engineering—Power Systems, Environmental Engineering Systems (Water), Materials at the Nanoscale, and Mechanical Engineering.

Research

BCOE is home to cutting-edge, high-risk, profoundly creative research. The colleg has invested in internationally recognized engineering research in hundreds of emerging areas focused on solving the world's greatest challenges. Faculty and their research teams collaborate in multidisciplinary research with colleagues at other colleges, campuses and industry leaders. Annual research expenditures total more than $30 million, with $313,000 in average research expenditures per faculty members and more than 590 different areas of research.

BCOE boasts nearly 300,000 square feet of laboratories and classrooms that feature state-of-the-art equipment to advance research efforts. From a $10 million nanofabrication clean room (with clean areas of Class 1,000 and Class 100 specifications) to the world's largest known indoor atmospheric chamber,

University of California, Riverside

BCOE's facilities help provide engineers the tools to conduct groundbreaking research.

BCOE's affiliated research centers each have a unique focus and specialize in areas of futuristic studies that are relevant to our core research areas. They enhance the college's capabilities by addressing some of today's most important engineering problems and creating valuable opportunities for students to prepare for their own careers of discovery. Centers include the Center for Bioengineering Research; College of Engineering–Center for Environmental Research and Technology; Southern California Initiative for Solar Energy; Winston Chung Global Energy Center; Center for Nanoscale Science and Engineering; Center for Research in Intelligent Systems; Center for Ubiquitous Communication by Light; Phonon Optimized Engineered Materials; and Center for Advanced Neuroimaging.

Financial Aid

Ph.D. students are usually fully funded, and application fees for domestic students are covered.

Costs

For the 2017–18 academic year, tuition and fees total $17,000.

Location

The University of California, Riverside, is set on a beautiful parklike campus of 1,200 acres at the foot of the Box Springs Mountains. One of ten campuses in the renowned University of California system, UCR offers the unique advantages of a large research institution along with opportunity for personal faculty attention. Located in Southern California's rapidly growing Inland Empire, the historic city of Riverside is noted for its palm-lined avenues, mild climate, and relatively low cost of living. Riverside is centrally located, offering easy access to the best geographical features of Southern California, including mountain resorts, ocean beaches, and desert playgrounds. The metropolitan areas of Los Angeles, Orange County, and San Diego are all within a short distance.

The University

The University of California, Riverside is one of 10 universities within the prestigious University of California system, and the only UC located in Inland Southern California.

Widely recognized as one of the most ethnically diverse research universities in the nation, UCR currently hosts about 22,000 students, with 900 instructional faculty. The campus is in the midst of a tremendous growth spurt with new and remodeled facilities coming on-line on a regular basis.

The Faculty

Faculty members are the Bourns College's greatest asset. Chosen for their dedication to research, teaching, and student success, they bring to the college more than $400,000 in research funding per person. In recent years, BCOE received more than $38 million in research support.

The distinguished faculty are well-recognized, and together include 90 Fellows of professional associations in their respective fields; 54 were awarded NSF CAREER and Young Investigator awards. Two are members of the National Academy of Engineering. Several of them have also won awards for mentoring of both graduates and undergraduates, as well as for teaching.

Details about the faculty members can be found at www.engr.ucr.edu/faculty.

Applying

Students should apply online at https://gradsis.ucr.edu/gradsis/GSIS_LOGIN. Login_student.

Correspondence and Information

Adrienne Thomas
Graduate Student Affairs Officer
Bourns College of Engineering
University of California, Riverside
900 University Avenue Bourns Hall A222
Riverside, California 92521
United States
Phone: 951-827-2859
E-mail: excellence@engr.ucr.edu
Website: www.engr.ucr.edu

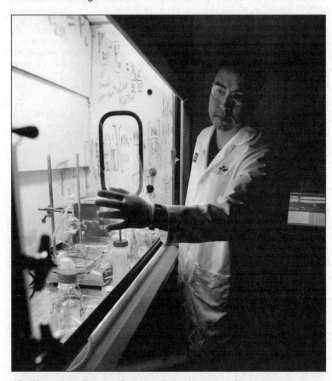

UC Riverside's Bourns College of Engineering offers degrees in five departments and two interdisciplinary programs.

UC Riverside's Bourns College of Engineering has a challenging, yet collaborative, research program that promotes interdisciplinary engagement with other colleges on campus, universities throughout the world, and business leaders in various fields of industry.

UNIVERSITY OF MICHIGAN
School of Information

Programs of Study

The University of Michigan School of Information (UMSI) is dedicated to studying information and all of its functions, from how it is created and collected to how it is preserved and accessed. The school offers three graduate degrees: A Master of Science in Information, a Ph.D. in Information, and a Master of Health Informatics. The programs accept those just embarking on careers in information science as well as seasoned scholars looking to enhance their research skills. There is a strong interdisciplinary emphasis at the school, and students come from as many as 100 different majors.

All the programs emphasize an academic knowledge base and research methods that train students to use information to effect positive changes. *U.S. News & World Report* consistently ranks the University of Michigan School of Information among the top 10 in archival and preservation programs, digital librarianship, and information systems.

Students work side by side with faculty members, researching and creating new ways of improving access to information and developing new uses for it in society, education, and the marketplace. Active research faculty grants include the study of relevant technological advances and their relationship to information. Major initiatives include in-depth studies into virtual collaboration, the impact of deploying large-scale electronic health records systems, usability challenges in smart homes, and social media sentiment analysis, among others.

The University of Michigan School of Information prepares students for careers in the field of information at Web/software design firms, universities, large IT organizations, healthcare systems, consulting firms, archives and records repositories, library systems, government, and museums.

Master of Science in Information (M.S.I.): The M.S.I. is a 48- credit professional degree which prepares students for emerging careers that meet the rapidly growing information-management needs of an increasingly interconnected world. Specific requirements vary, dependent on the selected Area of Interest (see below).

M.S.I. Areas of Interest: Students will focus their studies in one of three areas: Data Science/Data Analytics/Computational Social Science; Digital Archives and Library Science/Preservation; or User Experience (UX) Research and Design/Human-Computer Interaction/Social Computing.

Master of Health Informatics (M.H.I.): Conducted in partnership with the School of Public Health and the University of Michigan's Learning Health Services Initiatives, the School of Information offers a Master of Health Informatics degree program. One of the fastest-growing fields in the nation, health informatics develops innovative ways to put information and knowledge to use in promoting health and improving health care. Because clinical, consumer and public health fields are converging, students are required to acquire knowledge relevant to each of these areas. Defining features of the program include strengths in consumer informatics, population health applications, and system-related human and organizational issues.

The M.H.I. degree is 52 credits and takes 2 years (4 semesters) of full-time work on campus to complete. Students can attend part time and typically complete the program in three to four years. Requirements include 37–38 credits of core course work, 14–15 credits of elective course work, and 360 hours of internship.

Ph.D. in Information: Doctoral students in the School of Information are trained for research careers in academia or industry, focused on innovative information processes and technologies that affect classrooms, business, and society as a whole. Academic milestones for the doctoral degree in information include a pre-candidacy research project, a field preliminary exam, teaching requirements, and a successful defense of the student's final dissertation.

Doctoral program students complete a minimum of 24 hours of study in residence at the University of Michigan's Ann Arbor campus. Students must maintain full-time status and must complete their course work within seven years, although most students graduate in four or five years.

Dual-Degree Programs: The University of Michigan has developed six different programs that grant dual degrees in conjunction with the Master of Science in Information. The M.S.I. can be paired with an M.B.A. from the Ross School of Business, an M.P.P. from the Ford School of Public Policy, a J.D. from the Law School, an M.S.W. from the School of Social Work, an M.D. from the Medical School, or an M.S.N. from the School of Nursing. Degree requirements and length of study vary according to each dual-degree program's requirements. When students pursue degrees combined with Master of Science in Information degrees, the total number of credits required is less than the requirements for each degree if earned separately.

Research Facilities

The School of Information has a beautiful home in North Quad, along with the Department of Screen Arts and Cultures, the Department of Communication Studies, the Language Resource Center, and the Sweetland Writing Center. Features of this facility include the high-tech Media Gateway and Space 2435, which support students, faculty, and staff working with multimedia, network, and communication technologies. The complex also provides classrooms, academic studios, research labs, and offices. Within North Quad, UMSI has four dedicated classrooms, all with state-of-the-art audiovisual technology. North Quad also offers many spaces to facilitate meetings or to exchange ideas. There are several

UMSI project meeting rooms and a number of collaborative work spaces, such as the Media Gateway and Space 2435, which include video-teleconferences and electronic media sharing and editing.

An array of resources that support the School of Information and other users is available within the Graduate Library collection. The library maintains more than 65,000 volumes and 450 current journal titles covering all aspects of the School of Information academic programs. In addition, the University Library also provides access to a vast number of electronic and print resources such as OCLC FirstSearch, ProQuest, ISI Web of Science, JSTOR, Wilson Indexes, and dozens more, many including full-text content. In particular, library and information science resources such as Library Literature, LISA, ERIC, INSPEC, and many full-text journals may also be accessed across campus or from home. The library in the Duderstadt Center on North Campus specializes in engineering and computer science materials.

Financial Aid

There are many resources available to assist master's students with funding, including UMSI scholarships, UMSI diversity scholarships, and GSI/GSRA opportunities.

UMSI master's students (new and continuing) have also been successful when applying for external funding. In recent years, awards received by UMSI students have included American Library Association Spectrum Scholarships, ARMA International Educational Foundation Scholarships, Association for Women in Computing Scholarships, Society of American Archivist Scholarships, and more. All external tuition scholarship awards are eligible for matching funds from UMSI, up to a maximum of $10,000 and subject to availability of funds.

The U-M Office of Financial Aid has information on federal programs for aid for U.S. citizens. The University also provides funding information for international students.

Most students also choose to work part-time while in the program, for both a source of funding and an opportunity for professional experience.

Cost of Study

Graduate tuition and fees in the School of Information for the 2017–18 academic year are $11,184 (for Michigan residents) and $22,578 (non-Michigan residents) per term for the M.S.I. program and $13,918 (Michigan residents) and $22,996 (non-Michigan residents) per term for the M.H.I. program. Ph.D. students are guaranteed funding, including tuition and a stipend, contingent on their academic progress.

Living and Housing Costs

There are many options for housing both on and off campus that range from co-ops to rooms in houses to freestanding apartments. A new University graduate student residence opened in 2015. Housing information is provided to admitted students in the summer before they begin the program. Housing costs for the academic year are estimated at $15,000.

Student Outcomes

There are more than 8,400 alumni of the University of Michigan School of Information; many are leaders and experts in the field and in their communities. Recent graduates of the School of Information work for top organizations including Google, Facebook, the Federal Trade Commission, the Library of Congress, and Microsoft Corporation. Between 97 and 100 percent of new alumni have found employment or are pursuing additional education within one year of graduation.

Location

Ann Arbor is a vibrant college town with many restaurants, musical venues, museums, bars, and theaters to explore. There is a multitude of recreational activities for its students and residents, with over 1,900 acres of parks in the city, as well as golfing, ice skating, and canoeing facilities. Residents of Ann Arbor also enjoy the city's diverse cultural scene, evident in the many museums, galleries, theaters, and music venues. Ann Arbor is frequently ranked as one of the top cities in America by many media organizations, including CNNMoney, The Huffington Post, *Kiplinger*, and *USA Today*.

The University and The School

The University of Michigan celebrates its bicentennial in 2017. It was founded in 1817 as the Catholepistemiad, or University of Michigania. In 1821, it was officially renamed the University of Michigan. Originally located in Detroit, the institution's home moved to Ann Arbor in 1837. One of the original buildings on the Ann Arbor campus still stands and is used today as the President's house.

The University has grown to include nineteen schools and colleges, covering the liberal arts and sciences as well as most professions. The fall 2016 enrollment of undergraduate, graduate, and professional students was 44,718. According to the latest national data, the U-M spends more on research—$1.39 billion in FY2016—than any other U.S. public university.

University Of Michigan

The School of Information was chartered in 1996, but the school has had several other incarnations since its origin as the University of Michigan Department of Library Science in 1926. The department evolved to meet the needs of each new generation. In 1948, the department ended its undergraduate program, replaced the bachelor's degree in library science with a master's degree, and introduced a Ph.D. program. In 1969, the Department of Library Science became the School of Library Science. In 1986, the name was changed again, to the School of Information and Library Science.

Toward the end of the twentieth century, as the pace of change quickened in the information field, the School of Information was founded, taking on a new identity and mission: to prepare socially engaged information professionals, and to create people-centered knowledge, systems and institutions for the Information Age.

Correspondence and Information

School of Information
University of Michigan
MSI Admissions
3360 North Quad
105 South State Street
Ann Arbor, Michigan 48109-1285
Phone: 734-763-2285
Fax: 734-615-3587
E-mail: umsi.admissions@umich.edu
Website: umsi.info/pgpedu

THE FACULTY AND AREAS OF RESEARCH

Mark S. Ackerman, George Herbert Mead Collegiate Professor; Ph.D., MIT. Computer-supported cooperative work, expertise networks, organizational memory.

Eytan Adar, Associate Professor; Ph.D., Washington. Network science, Web re-visitation, network visualization.

Christopher Brooks, Research Assistant Professor; Ph.D., Saskatchewan. Educational discourse, lecture capture impact, predicting academic success, massive online open courses.

Ceren Budak, Assistant Professor; Ph.D., California, Santa Barbara. Information analysis and retrieval, computational social science.

Yan Chen, Daniel Kahneman Collegiate Professor; Ph.D., Caltech. Economics, incentive-centered design, contributions to public goods.

Kevyn Collins-Thompson, Associate Professor; Ph.D., Carnegie Mellon. Information retrieval, text mining, natural language processing, machine learning.

Paul Conway, Associate Professor; Ph.D., Michigan. Archives and records management, digitization and representation of visual and textual archives, modeling the use of digital archives in the visual studies and the humanities.

Tawanna Dillahunt, Assistant Professor; Ph.D., Carnegie Mellon. Human-computer interaction, ubiquitous computing, social computing.

Nicole Ellison, Professor; Ph.D., USC. Computer-supported cooperative work and communications; social computing, relationship formation and maintenance via social network sites.

Thomas Finholt, Dean, Professor; Ph.D., Carnegie Mellon. Computer-supported cooperative work, cyberinfrastructure, scientific collaboration via virtual organizations.

Barry Fishman, Arthur F Thurnau Professor; Ph.D., Northwestern. Learning science, teacher learning, learning technologies.

Kristin Fontichiaro, Clinical Associate Professor; M.I.L.S., Wayne State. Inquiry, digital literacy, makerspaces.

Patricia Garcia, Assistant Professor, Ph.D., UCLA. Culturally responsive computing, learning in libraries, community archives, participatory archives.

Margaret Hedstrom, Robert M Warner Collegiate Professor; Ph.D., Wisconsin. Archives and records management, sustainable digital data preservation, science and big data.

Matthew Kay, Assistant Professor; Ph.D., Washington. Designing/building/evaluating user interfaces and information visualizations.

John L. King, William Warner Bishop Collegiate Professor; Ph.D., UC Irvine. Public policy and computer science, requirement development for information systems design and implementation, organizational and institutional influences on information technology development.

Predrag "Pedja" Klasnja, Assistant Professor; Ph.D., Washington. Human-computer interaction, ubiquitous computing for chronic disease management, health informatics.

Erin L. Krupka, Assistant Professor; Ph.D., Carnegie Mellon. Economics and social psychology, effect of social and environmental factors on behavior, how social norms modify self-interest.

Carl Lagoze, Associate Professor; Ph.D., Cornell. Library and information science; digital libraries, metadata, and sociotechnical infrastructure for scholarly communication; scientific collaboration.

Cliff Lampe, Associate Professor; Ph.D., Michigan. Computer-supported cooperative work and communication studies, social computing, outcomes of participating in social network sites.

Walter Lasecki, Assistant Professor; Ph.D., Rochester. Crowdsourcing, human computation, HCI, collective intelligence, artificial intelligence.

Silvia Lindtner, Assistant Professor; Ph.D., UC Irvine. DIY "maker" and open source culture, IT development in urban China, global processes of work and labor.

Karen Markey, Professor; Ph.D., Syracuse. Library and information science, subject searching, visual persuasion, gaming for teaching information literacy.

Qiaozhu Mei, Associate Professor; Ph.D., Illinois. Computer science; information retrieval; text, Web, and social data mining.

Markus Mobius, Associate Professor; Ph.D., MIT. Economics of social networks, belief formations in labor market outcomes.

Michael Nebeling, Assistant Professor; Ph.D., ETH Zurich. HCI, interface engineering, ubiquitous computing, crowdsourcing.

Mark W. Newman, Associate Professor; Ph.D., UC Berkeley. Human-computer interaction, ubiquitous computing, end-user programming.

Sile O'Modhrain, Associate Professor; Ph.D., Stanford. Human-computer interaction, haptic output interfaces, movement as interaction design.

Stephen Oney, Assistant Professor; Ph.D., Carnegie-Mellon. Human-computer interaction, software engineering, programming environments.

Joyojeet Pal, Assistant Professor; Ph.D., UC Berkeley. Information and communication technology for development, assistive technology, computer-aided learning.

Sun Young Park, Assistant Professor; Ph.D., UC Irvine. HCI, computer supported cooperative work, health informatics, design.

Casey Pierce, Assistant Professor; Ph.D., Northwestern. Organizational communication and technology, knowledge management in organizations.

Dragomir Radev, Professor; Ph.D., Columbia. Computer science, natural language processing, information retrieval.

Paul Resnick, Associate Dean for Research and Faculty Affairs, Michael D. Cohen Collegiate Professor; Ph.D., MIT. Computer science, economics, and social psychology; social computing; reputation and recommender systems.

Soo Young Rieh, Associate Professor; Ph.D., Rutgers. Library and information science, credibility and cognitive authority judgment, human information behavior.

Lionel Robert, Assistant Professor; Ph.D., Indiana. Management information systems, diversity and team performance, collaboration technology.

Daniel Romero, Assistant Professor; Ph.D., Cornell. Social and information networks, network evolution, information diffusion, user interactions on Web.

Tanya Rosenblat, Associate Professor; Ph.D., MIT. Experimental economics, trust and altruism in social networks.

Christian Sandvig, Associate Professor; Ph.D., Stanford. Infrastructure studies, socio-technical systems, social computing, information policy.

Florian Schaub, Assistant Professor; Ph.D., Ulm. Privacy, HCI, usable privacy and security, ubiquitous computing, Internet of things.

Sarita Schoenebeck, Assistant Professor; Ph.D., Georgia Tech. Computer-supported cooperative work, social computing, youth and digital media.

Charles Severance, Clinical Associate Professor; Ph.D., Michigan State. Computer science and education; open educational resources; online learning, teaching, and collaboration systems.

Stephanie Teasley, Research Professor; Ph.D., Pittsburgh. Computer-supported cooperative work and learning science, collaboration and learning technologies, learning analytics.

Kentaro Toyama, W.K. Kellogg Professor of Community Information, Associate Professor; Ph.D., Yale. Information and communication technologies, international development (ICTD).

Douglas E. Van Houweling, Professor; Ph.D., Indiana. Public policy and management, information systems management and planning, large-scale network management.

Tiffany C.E. Veinot, Associate Professor; Ph.D., Western Ontario. Health informatics and library and information science; health information behavior within marginalized communities; social studies of health information technologies, policy, and practice.

Elizabeth Yakel, Senior Associate Dean for Academic Affairs, Professor; Ph.D., Michigan. Archives and records management, access to digital archives, Web 2.0 and cultural heritage institutions, archival metrics and evaluation.

North Quad, home of the School of Information, on the central campus of the University of Michigan.

Section 9
Electrical and Computer Engineering

This section contains a directory of institutions offering graduate work in electrical and computer engineering, followed by in-depth entries submitted by institutions that chose to prepare detailed program descriptions. Additional information about programs listed in the directory but not augmented by an in-depth entry may be obtained by writing directly to the dean of a graduate school or chair of a department at the address given in the directory.

For programs offering related work, see also in this book *Computer Science and Information Technology, Energy and Power Engineering, Engineering and Applied Sciences, Industrial Engineering,* and *Mechanical Engineering and Mechanics.* In another guide in this series:

Graduate Programs in the Physical Sciences, Mathematics, Agricultural Sciences, the Environment & Natural Resources
See *Mathematical Sciences* and *Physics*

CONTENTS

Program Directories

Featured Schools: Displays and Close-Ups

See also:

Computer Engineering

Air Force Institute of Technology, Graduate School of Engineering and Management, Department of Electrical and Computer Engineering, Dayton, OH 45433-7765. Offers computer engineering (MS, PhD); computer systems/science (MS); electrical engineering (MS, PhD); electro-optics (MS, PhD). *Accreditation:* ABET (one or more programs are accredited). *Program availability:* Part-time. *Degree requirements:* For master's, thesis; for doctorate, thesis/dissertation. *Entrance requirements:* For master's and doctorate, GRE General Test, minimum GPA of 3.0, U.S. citizenship. *Faculty research:* Remote sensing, information survivability, microelectronics, computer networks, artificial intelligence.

American University of Beirut, Graduate Programs, Faculty of Engineering and Architecture, 11-0236, Lebanon. Offers applied energy (ME); civil engineering (PhD); electrical and computer engineering (PhD); energy studies (MS); engineering management (MEM); environmental and water resources (ME); environmental technology (MSES); mechanical engineering (ME, PhD); urban design (MUD); urban planning and policy (MUPP). *Program availability:* Part-time, evening/weekend, 100% online. *Faculty:* 99 full-time (22 women), 1 part-time/adjunct (0 women). *Students:* 308 full-time (143 women), 86 part-time (39 women). Average age 26. 430 applicants, 69% accepted, 125 enrolled. In 2016, 103 master's, 7 doctorates awarded. Terminal master's awarded for partial completion of doctoral program. *Degree requirements:* For master's, comprehensive exam, thesis optional; for doctorate, comprehensive exam, thesis/dissertation. *Entrance requirements:* For doctorate, GRE. Additional exam requirements/recommendations for international students: Required—TOEFL (minimum score 573 paper-based; 88 iBT); Recommended—IELTS (minimum score 7). *Application deadline:* For fall admission, 2/10 priority date for domestic and international students; for spring admission, 11/2 priority date for domestic students, 11/2 for international students. Application fee: $50. Electronic applications accepted. *Expenses:* Contact institution. *Financial support:* In 2016–17, 22 students received support, including 94 fellowships with full tuition reimbursements available (averaging $18,200 per year), 44 research assistantships with full tuition reimbursements available (averaging $7,596 per year), 124 teaching assistantships with full tuition reimbursements available (averaging $1,056 per year); career-related internships or fieldwork, Federal Work-Study, institutionally sponsored loans, scholarships/grants, traineeships, health care benefits, tuition waivers, and unspecified assistantships also available. Support available to part-time students. Financial award application deadline: 12/20. *Total annual research expenditures:* $1.5 million. *Unit head:* Prof. Alan Shihadeh, Interim Dean, 961-1350000 Ext. 3400, Fax: 961-1744462, E-mail: as20@aub.edu.lb. *Application contact:* Dr. Salim Kanaan, Director, Admissions Office, 961-1350000 Ext. 2594, Fax: 961-1750775, E-mail: sk00@aub.edu.lb.
Website: http://www.aub.edu.lb/fea/fea_home/Pages/index.aspx

American University of Sharjah, Graduate Programs, Sharjah, United Arab Emirates. Offers accounting (MS); business (EMBA, MBA); chemical engineering (MS Ch E); civil engineering (MSCE); computer engineering (MS); electrical engineering (MSEE); engineering systems management (MS); mathematics (MS); mechanical engineering (MSME); mechatronics engineering (MS); teaching English to speakers of other languages (MA); translation and interpreting (MA); urban planning (MUP). *Program availability:* Part-time, evening/weekend. *Degree requirements:* For master's, thesis (for some programs). *Entrance requirements:* For master's, GMAT (for MBA). Additional exam requirements/recommendations for international students: Required—TOEFL (minimum score 550 paper-based; 80 iBT), TWE (minimum score 5); Recommended—IELTS (minimum score 6.5). Electronic applications accepted. *Faculty research:* Water pollution, management and waste water treatment, energy and sustainability, air pollution, Islamic finance, family business and small and medium enterprises.

Arizona State University at the Tempe campus, Ira A. Fulton Schools of Engineering, School of Computing, Informatics, and Decision Systems Engineering, Tempe, AZ 85287-8809. Offers computer engineering (MS, PhD); computer science (MCS, MS, PhD); industrial engineering (MS, PhD); software engineering (MS). *Program availability:* Part-time, evening/weekend, online learning. Terminal master's awarded for partial completion of doctoral program. *Degree requirements:* For master's, comprehensive exam (for some programs), portfolio (MCS); interactive Program of Study (iPOS) submitted before completing 50 percent of required credit hours; for doctorate, comprehensive exam, thesis/dissertation, interactive Program of Study (iPOS) submitted before completing 50 percent of required credit hours. *Entrance requirements:* For master's, GRE, minimum GPA of 3.0 or equivalent in last 2 years of work leading to bachelor's degree; for doctorate, GRE, minimum GPA of 3.0 in last 2 years of work leading to bachelor's degree. Additional exam requirements/recommendations for international students: Required—TOEFL, IELTS, or PTE. Electronic applications accepted. *Expenses:* Contact institution. *Faculty research:* Artificial intelligence, cyberphysical and embedded systems, health informatics, information assurance and security, information management/multimedia/visualization, network science, personalized learning/educational games, production logistics, software and systems engineering, statistical modeling and data mining.

Auburn University, Graduate School, Ginn College of Engineering, Department of Electrical and Computer Engineering, Auburn University, AL 36849. Offers MEE, MS, PhD. *Program availability:* Part-time. *Faculty:* 22 full-time (0 women), 4 part-time/adjunct (0 women). *Students:* 93 full-time (18 women), 42 part-time (3 women); includes 3 minority (1 Black or African American, non-Hispanic/Latino; 1 Asian, non-Hispanic/Latino; 1 Hispanic/Latino), 105 international. Average age 26. 240 applicants, 53% accepted, 27 enrolled. In 2016, 49 master's, 18 doctorates awarded. *Degree requirements:* For master's, comprehensive exam, thesis (for some programs); for doctorate, thesis/dissertation. *Entrance requirements:* For master's and doctorate, GRE General Test, GRE Subject Test. *Application deadline:* Applications are processed on a rolling basis. Application fee: $50 ($60 for international students). Electronic applications accepted. *Expenses:* Tuition, state resident: full-time $9072; part-time $504 per credit hour. Tuition, nonresident: full-time $27,216; part-time $1512 per credit hour. *Required fees:* $812 per semester. Tuition and fees vary according to degree level and program. *Financial support:* Fellowships, research assistantships, teaching assistantships, and Federal Work-Study available. Support available to part-time students. Financial award application deadline: 3/15; financial award applicants required to submit FAFSA. *Faculty research:* Power systems, energy conversion, electronics, electromagnetics, digital systems. *Unit head:* Dr. Mark Nelms, Head, 334-844-1830. *Application contact:* Dr. George Flowers, Dean of the Graduate School, 334-844-2125.
Website: http://www.eng.auburn.edu/ee/

Baylor University, Graduate School, School of Engineering and Computer Science, Department of Electrical and Computer Engineering, Waco, TX 76798. Offers MS, PhD. *Faculty:* 15 full-time (1 woman). *Students:* 38 full-time (7 women), 4 part-time (0 women); includes 3 minority (1 Black or African American, non-Hispanic/Latino; 1 Asian, non-Hispanic/Latino; 1 Two or more races, non-Hispanic/Latino), 19 international. Average age 25. 34 applicants, 38% accepted, 13 enrolled. In 2016, 6 master's, 2 doctorates awarded. Terminal master's awarded for partial completion of doctoral program. *Degree requirements:* For master's, thesis (for some programs); for doctorate, comprehensive exam, thesis/dissertation. *Entrance requirements:* For master's and doctorate, GRE. Additional exam requirements/recommendations for international students: Required—TOEFL (minimum score 550 paper-based; 100 iBT). *Application deadline:* For fall admission, 2/15 for domestic and international students; for spring admission, 12/1 for domestic and international students. Applications are processed on a rolling basis. Application fee: $50. Electronic applications accepted. *Expenses:* $1,583 per hour tuition, $174 per semester fees. *Financial support:* In 2016–17, 18 students received support, including 28 research assistantships with full tuition reimbursements available (averaging $21,500 per year), 16 teaching assistantships with full tuition reimbursements available (averaging $16,000 per year); fellowships, scholarships/grants, health care benefits, and unspecified assistantships also available. Financial award application deadline: 4/15. *Faculty research:* Biosensors, microwave frequency signals, wearable sensors, optoelectronic devices, energy efficient power electronics. *Unit head:* Dr. Kwang Y. Lee, Chair, 254-710-4817, Fax: 254-710-3010, E-mail: kwang_y_lee@baylor.edu. *Application contact:* Dr. B. Randall Jean, Graduate Director, 254-710-4194, Fax: 254-710-3010.
Website: http://www.ecs.baylor.edu/ece/

Boise State University, College of Engineering, Department of Electrical and Computer Engineering, Boise, ID 83725. Offers M Engr, MS, PhD. *Program availability:* Part-time. *Faculty:* 14. *Students:* 28 full-time (7 women), 23 part-time (0 women); includes 4 minority (3 Asian, non-Hispanic/Latino; 1 Hispanic/Latino), 23 international. Average age 30. 60 applicants, 45% accepted, 9 enrolled. In 2016, 9 master's awarded. Terminal master's awarded for partial completion of doctoral program. *Degree requirements:* For master's, comprehensive exam, thesis (for some programs); for doctorate, thesis/dissertation. *Entrance requirements:* For master's, GRE General Test, minimum GPA of 3.0. Additional exam requirements/recommendations for international students: Required—TOEFL (minimum score 550 paper-based; 80 iBT), IELTS (minimum score 6). *Application deadline:* For fall admission, 2/1 priority date for domestic and international students. Application fee: $65 ($95 for international students). Electronic applications accepted. *Expenses:* Tuition, state resident: full-time $6058; part-time $358 per credit hour. Tuition, nonresident: full-time $20,108; part-time $608 per credit hour. *Required fees:* $2108. Tuition and fees vary according to program. *Financial support:* In 2016–17, 11 students received support, including 17 research assistantships (averaging $10,214 per year); scholarships/grants and unspecified assistantships also available. Financial award application deadline: 2/1; financial award applicants required to submit FAFSA. *Unit head:* Dr. Nader Rafia, Department Chair, 208-426-3711, E-mail: nrafia@boisestate.edu. *Application contact:* Hao Chen, Graduate Program Coordinator, 208-426-1020, E-mail: haochen@boisestate.edu.
Website: http://coen.boisestate.edu/ece/

Boston University, College of Engineering, Department of Electrical and Computer Engineering, Boston, MA 02215. Offers computer engineering (M Eng, MS, PhD). *Program availability:* Part-time. *Students:* 305 full-time (77 women), 98 part-time (22 women); includes 31 minority (3 Black or African American, non-Hispanic/Latino; 19 Asian, non-Hispanic/Latino; 9 Hispanic/Latino), 296 international. Average age 25. 1,219 applicants, 25% accepted, 142 enrolled. In 2016, 133 master's, 17 doctorates awarded. Terminal master's awarded for partial completion of doctoral program. *Degree requirements:* For master's, thesis (for some programs); for doctorate, comprehensive exam, thesis/dissertation. *Entrance requirements:* For master's and doctorate, GRE General Test. Additional exam requirements/recommendations for international students: Required—TOEFL (minimum score 90 iBT), IELTS (minimum score 7). *Financial support:* Application deadline: 1/1. *Faculty research:* Communications and computer networks; signal, image, video, and multimedia processing; solid-state materials, devices, and photonics; systems, control, and reliable computing; VLSI, computer engineering and high-performance computing. *Unit head:* Dr. William C. Karl, Interim Chairman, 617-353-9880, Fax: 617-353-6440, E-mail: wckarl@bu.edu.
Website: http://www.bu.edu/ece/

Boston University, Metropolitan College, Department of Computer Science, Boston, MA 02215. Offers computer information systems (MS), including computer networks, data analytics, database management and business intelligence, health informatics, IT project management, security, Web application development; computer networks (Certificate); computer science (MS); data analytics (Certificate); digital forensics (Certificate); health informatics (Certificate); information technology project management (Certificate); software development (MS); software engineering in health care systems (Certificate); telecommunications (MS), including security. *Program availability:* Part-time, evening/weekend, online learning. *Faculty:* 13 full-time (3 women), 43 part-time/adjunct (3 women). *Students:* 108 full-time (36 women), 1,294 part-time (364 women); includes 428 minority (115 Black or African American, non-Hispanic/Latino; 2 American Indian or Alaska Native, non-Hispanic/Latino; 187 Asian, non-Hispanic/Latino; 98 Hispanic/Latino; 2 Native Hawaiian or other Pacific Islander, non-Hispanic/Latino; 24 Two or more races, non-Hispanic/Latino), 314 international. Average age 33. 463 applicants, 79% accepted, 248 enrolled. In 2016, 311 master's awarded. *Degree requirements:* For master's, thesis optional. *Entrance requirements:* For master's and Certificate, official transcripts from regionally-accredited bachelor's degree program, 3 letters of recommendation, professional resume, personal statement. Additional exam requirements/recommendations for international students: Required—TOEFL (minimum score 84 iBT), IELTS. *Application deadline:* For fall admission, 6/1 priority date for international students; for spring admission, 10/1 priority date for international students. Applications are processed on a rolling basis. Application fee: $85. Electronic applications accepted. *Expenses:* Contact institution. *Financial support:* In 2016–17, 11 research assistantships (averaging $8,400 per year) were awarded; unspecified assistantships also available. Support available to part-time students. Financial award applicants required to submit FAFSA. *Faculty research:* Medical informatics, Web technologies, telecom and networks, security and forensics, software engineering, programming languages, multimedia and artificial intelligence (AI), information systems and IT project management. *Unit head:* Dr. Anatoly Temkin, Chair, 617-353-2566, Fax: 617-353-2367, E-mail: csinfo@bu.edu. *Application contact:* Lesley Moreau, Academic Program Coordinator, 617-353-2566, Fax: 617-353-2367, E-mail: metcs@bu.edu.
Website: http://www.bu.edu/csmet/

Brigham Young University, Graduate Studies, Ira A. Fulton College of Engineering and Technology, Department of Electrical and Computer Engineering, Provo, UT 84602. Offers MS, PhD. *Faculty:* 23 full-time (1 woman). *Students:* 100 full-time (9 women); includes 2 minority (1 Asian, non-Hispanic/Latino; 1 Hispanic/Latino), 19 international. Average age 27. 59 applicants, 63% accepted, 27 enrolled. In 2016, 10 master's, 6 doctorates awarded. *Degree requirements:* For master's, thesis; for doctorate, comprehensive exam, thesis/dissertation. *Entrance requirements:* For master's and doctorate, GRE General Test, minimum GPA of 3.2 in last 60 hours of course work.

Additional exam requirements/recommendations for international students: Required—TOEFL (minimum score 580 paper-based; 85 iBT). *Application deadline:* For fall admission, 1/15 for domestic and international students; for winter admission, 8/15 for domestic and international students. Application fee: $50. Electronic applications accepted. *Expenses: Tuition:* Full-time $6680; part-time $393 per credit. Tuition and fees vary according to course load, program and student's religious affiliation. *Financial support:* In 2016–17, 168 students received support, including 5 fellowships with full tuition reimbursements available (averaging $20,250 per year), 140 research assistantships with full tuition reimbursements available (averaging $5,415 per year), 47 teaching assistantships with full tuition reimbursements available (averaging $5,340 per year); scholarships/grants also available. Financial award application deadline: 5/15; financial award applicants required to submit FAFSA. *Faculty research:* Microwave earth remote sensing, configurable computing and embedded systems, MEMS semiconductors, integrated electro-optics, multiple-agent intelligent coordinated control systems for unmanned air vehicles. *Total annual research expenditures:* $3.5 million. *Unit head:* Dr. Brent E. Nelson, Chair, 801-422-4012, Fax: 801-422-0201, E-mail: nelson@ee.byu.edu. *Application contact:* Janalyn L. Mergist, Graduate Secretary, 801-422-4013, Fax: 801-422-0201, E-mail: janalyn@ee.byu.edu.
Website: http://www.ee.byu.edu/

Brown University, Graduate School, School of Engineering, Program in Electrical Sciences and Computer Engineering, Providence, RI 02912. Offers Sc M, PhD. *Degree requirements:* For doctorate, thesis/dissertation, preliminary exam.

California State University, Chico, Office of Graduate Studies, College of Engineering, Computer Science, and Construction Management, Electrical and Computer Engineering Department, Option in Computer Engineering, Chico, CA 95929-0722. Offers MS. *Students:* 9 full-time (2 women), 5 part-time (2 women); includes 5 minority (all Asian, non-Hispanic/Latino). 25 applicants, 72% accepted, 3 enrolled. *Degree requirements:* For master's, comprehensive exam, thesis or project plan. *Entrance requirements:* For master's, GRE General Test, 2 letters of recommendation, statement of purpose, resume. Additional exam requirements/recommendations for international students: Required—TOEFL (minimum score 550 paper-based; 80 iBT), IELTS (minimum score 6.8), PTE (minimum score 59). *Application deadline:* For fall admission, 3/1 priority date for domestic students, 3/1 for international students; for spring admission, 9/15 priority date for domestic students, 9/15 for international students. Applications are processed on a rolling basis. Application fee: $55. Electronic applications accepted. *Financial support:* Career-related internships or fieldwork, scholarships/grants, and traineeships available. Financial award application deadline: 3/1; financial award applicants required to submit FAFSA. *Application contact:* Judy L. Morris, Graduate Admissions Coordinator, 530-898-5416, Fax: 530-898-3342, E-mail: jlmorris@csuchico.edu.

California State University, Fresno, Division of Research and Graduate Studies, Lyles College of Engineering, Department of Electrical and Computer Engineering, Fresno, CA 93740-8027. Offers computer engineering (MSE); electrical engineering (MSE). *Program availability:* Part-time, evening/weekend. *Degree requirements:* For master's, thesis or alternative. *Entrance requirements:* For master's, GRE General Test, minimum GPA of 2.7. Additional exam requirements/recommendations for international students: Required—TOEFL. *Application deadline:* For fall admission, 5/1 for domestic and international students; for spring admission, 10/1 for domestic and international students. Applications are processed on a rolling basis. Application fee: $55. Electronic applications accepted. *Financial support:* Career-related internships or fieldwork, Federal Work-Study, and scholarships/grants available. Support available to part-time students. Financial award application deadline: 3/1; financial award applicants required to submit FAFSA. *Faculty research:* Research in electromagnetic devices. *Unit head:* Dr. Reza Raeisi, Chair, 559-278-6038, Fax: 559-278-6297, E-mail: rraeisi@csufresno.edu. *Application contact:* Dr. Nagy Bengiamin, Graduate Program Coordinator, 559-278-8339.
Website: http://www.fresnostate.edu/engineering/elec-computer/

California State University, Fullerton, Graduate Studies, College of Engineering and Computer Science, Program in Computer Engineering, Fullerton, CA 92834-9480. Offers MS. *Application deadline:* For fall admission, 4/1 for domestic and international students. *Expenses:* Tuition, state resident: full-time $3369; part-time $1953 per unit. Tuition, nonresident: full-time $3915; part-time $2499 per unit. Tuition and fees vary according to course load, degree level and program. *Unit head:* Dr. Kiran George, Coordinator, 657-278-2640, E-mail: kgeorge@fullerton.edu. *Application contact:* Admissions/Applications, 657-278-2371.
Website: http://www.fullerton.edu/ecs/cpe/

California State University, Long Beach, Graduate Studies, College of Engineering, Department of Computer Engineering and Computer Science, Long Beach, CA 90840. Offers computer engineering (MSCS); computer science (MSCS). *Program availability:* Part-time. *Degree requirements:* For master's, thesis or alternative. *Entrance requirements:* Additional exam requirements/recommendations for international students: Required—TOEFL. *Application deadline:* For fall admission, 3/1 for domestic students. Application fee: $55. Electronic applications accepted. *Financial support:* Teaching assistantships, Federal Work-Study, institutionally sponsored loans, scholarships/grants, and unspecified assistantships available. Financial award application deadline: 3/2. *Faculty research:* Artificial intelligence, software engineering, computer simulation and modeling, user-interface design, networking. *Unit head:* Burkhart Englert, Chair, 562-985-4285.

Carnegie Mellon University, Carnegie Institute of Technology, Department of Electrical and Computer Engineering, Pittsburgh, PA 15213-3891. Offers MS, PhD. *Program availability:* Part-time. *Degree requirements:* For master's, thesis; for doctorate, thesis/dissertation, qualifying exam, teaching experience. *Entrance requirements:* For master's and doctorate, GRE General Test. Additional exam requirements/recommendations for international students: Required—TOEFL. *Faculty research:* Computer-aided design, solid-state devices, VLSI, processing, robotics and controls, signal processing, data systems storage.

Case Western Reserve University, School of Graduate Studies, Case School of Engineering, Department of Electrical Engineering and Computer Science, Cleveland, OH 44106. Offers computer engineering (MS, PhD); computing and information sciences (MS, PhD); electrical engineering (MS, PhD); systems and control engineering (MS, PhD). *Program availability:* Part-time, evening/weekend, online only, 100% online. *Faculty:* 32 full-time (3 women). *Students:* 188 full-time (42 women), 14 part-time (3 women); includes 7 minority (1 Black or African American, non-Hispanic/Latino; 5 Asian, non-Hispanic/Latino; 1 Hispanic/Latino), 152 international. In 2016, 25 master's, 26 doctorates awarded. Terminal master's awarded for partial completion of doctoral program. *Degree requirements:* For master's, thesis; for doctorate, thesis/dissertation, qualifying exam, teaching experience. *Entrance requirements:* For master's and doctorate, GRE General Test. Additional exam requirements/recommendations for international students: Required—TOEFL. *Application deadline:* For fall admission, 2/1 for domestic students; for spring admission, 11/1 for domestic students. Applications are processed on a rolling basis. Application fee: $50. *Expenses: Tuition:* Full-time $42,576; part-time $1774 per credit hour. *Required fees:* $34. Tuition and fees vary according to course load and program. *Financial support:* In 2016–17, 1 fellowship with tuition reimbursement, 63 research assistantships with tuition reimbursements, 10 teaching assistantships were awarded; career-related internships or fieldwork, Federal Work-Study, and institutionally sponsored loans also available. Support available to part-time students. Financial award application deadline: 3/1; financial award applicants required to submit FAFSA. *Faculty research:* Micro-/nano-systems; robotics and haptics; applied artificial intelligence; automation; computer-aided design and testing of digital systems. *Total annual research expenditures:* $4.9 million. *Unit head:* Dr. Kenneth Loparo, Department Chair, 216-368-4115, E-mail: kal4@case.edu. *Application contact:* Kimberly Yurchick, Student Affairs Specialist, 216-368-2920, Fax: 216-368-2801, E-mail: ksy4@case.edu.
Website: http://eecs.cwru.edu/

The Citadel, The Military College of South Carolina, Citadel Graduate College, School of Engineering, Department of Electrical and Computer Engineering, Charleston, SC 29409. Offers computer engineering (Graduate Certificate); electrical engineering (MS). *Program availability:* Part-time, evening/weekend. *Students:* 1 part-time. 2 applicants, 50% accepted. *Degree requirements:* For master's, 30 hours of coursework with minimum GPA of 3.0 on hours earned at The Citadel. *Entrance requirements:* For master's, GRE, 2 letters of recommendation; official transcript of baccalaureate degree from an ABET accredited engineering program or approved alternative. Additional exam requirements/recommendations for international students: Required—TOEFL (minimum score 550 paper-based; 79 iBT). *Application deadline:* Applications are processed on a rolling basis. Application fee: $40. Electronic applications accepted. *Expenses:* Tuition, state resident: full-time $5121; part-time $569 per credit hour. Tuition, nonresident: full-time $8613; part-time $957 per credit hour. *Required fees:* $90 per term. *Financial support:* Fellowships and unspecified assistantships available. Support available to part-time students. Financial award application deadline: 7/1; financial award applicants required to submit FAFSA. *Unit head:* Dr. Robert J. Barsanti, Jr., Department Head, 843-953-7593, E-mail: robert.barsanti@citadel.edu. *Application contact:* Dr. Tara Hornor, Associate Provost for Planning, Assessment and Evaluation/Dean of Enrollment Management, 843-953-5089, E-mail: cgc@citadel.edu.
Website: http://www.citadel.edu/root/ece

Clarkson University, Wallace H. Coulter School of Engineering, Department of Electrical and Computer Engineering, Potsdam, NY 13699. Offers electrical and computer engineering (PhD); electrical engineering (ME, MS). *Program availability:* Part-time, evening/weekend. *Faculty:* 33 full-time (8 women), 7 part-time/adjunct (1 woman). *Students:* 45 full-time (6 women), 24 part-time (2 women); includes 8 minority (1 Black or African American, non-Hispanic/Latino; 5 Asian, non-Hispanic/Latino; 2 Hispanic/Latino), 25 international. 60 applicants, 47% accepted, 14 enrolled. In 2016, 14 master's, 3 doctorates awarded. *Degree requirements:* For master's, thesis (for some programs), thesis or project (for MS); project (for ME); for doctorate, comprehensive exam, thesis/dissertation. *Entrance requirements:* For master's and doctorate, GRE. Additional exam requirements/recommendations for international students: Required—TOEFL (minimum score 550 paper-based, 80 iBT) or IELTS (6.5). *Application deadline:* Applications are processed on a rolling basis. Application fee: $50. Electronic applications accepted. *Expenses: Tuition:* Full-time $23,400; part-time $1300 per credit hour. Tuition and fees vary according to campus/location and program. *Financial support:* Scholarships/grants and unspecified assistantships available. *Unit head:* Dr. David Crouse, Chair of Electrical and Computer Engineering, 315-268-6529, E-mail: dcrouse@clarkson.edu. *Application contact:* Dan Capogna, Graduate Admissions Contact, 518-631-9910, E-mail: graduate@clarkson.edu.
Website: http://graduate.clarkson.edu

Clemson University, Graduate School, College of Engineering, Computing and Applied Sciences, Holcombe Department of Electrical and Computer Engineering, Program in Computer Engineering, Clemson, SC 29634. Offers MS, PhD. *Program availability:* Part-time. *Faculty:* 24 full-time (2 women), 3 part-time/adjunct (0 women). *Students:* 49 full-time (6 women), 6 part-time (2 women), 37 international. Average age 26. 91 applicants, 19% accepted, 11 enrolled. In 2016, 11 master's, 5 doctorates awarded. *Degree requirements:* For master's, comprehensive exam (for some programs), thesis or alternative; for doctorate, comprehensive exam, thesis/dissertation, departmental qualifying exam. *Entrance requirements:* For master's and doctorate, GRE General Test, unofficial transcripts, letters of recommendation. Additional exam requirements/recommendations for international students: Required—TOEFL (minimum score 95 iBT), IELTS (minimum score 7). *Application deadline:* For fall admission, 1/15 priority date for domestic students, 4/15 for international students; for spring admission, 9/15 priority date for domestic students, 9/15 for international students. Applications are processed on a rolling basis. Application fee: $80 ($90 for international students). Electronic applications accepted. *Expenses:* $4,841 per semester full-time resident, $9,640 per semester full-time non-resident, $612 per credit hour part-time resident, $1,223 per credit hour part-time non-resident. *Financial support:* In 2016–17, 56 students received support, including 6 fellowships with partial tuition reimbursements available (averaging $10,949 per year), 26 research assistantships with partial tuition reimbursements available (averaging $21,796 per year), 15 teaching assistantships with partial tuition reimbursements available (averaging $13,919 per year); unspecified assistantships also available. Financial award application deadline: 1/15. *Faculty research:* Applied use of emerging heterogeneous computing architectures; communications theory, coding theory, detection and estimation theory. *Unit head:* Dr. Daniel Noneaker, Department Chair, 864-656-0100, E-mail: dnoneak@clemson.edu. *Application contact:* Dr. Harlan Russell, Graduate Program Coordinator, 864-656-7214, E-mail: harlanr@clemson.edu.
Website: https://www.clemson.edu/cecas/departments/ece/

Colorado Technical University Aurora, Program in Computer Engineering, Aurora, CO 80014. Offers MS.

Colorado Technical University Colorado Springs, Graduate Studies, Program in Computer Engineering, Colorado Springs, CO 80907. Offers MSCE. *Program availability:* Part-time, evening/weekend, online learning. *Degree requirements:* For master's, thesis or alternative.

Columbia University, Fu Foundation School of Engineering and Applied Science, Department of Electrical Engineering, New York, NY 10027. Offers computer engineering (MS); electrical engineering (MS, Eng Sc D, PhD). PhD offered through the Graduate School of Arts and Sciences. *Program availability:* Part-time, online learning. *Degree requirements:* For doctorate, thesis/dissertation, qualifying exam. *Entrance requirements:* For master's and doctorate, GRE General Test. Additional exam requirements/recommendations for international students: Required—TOEFL, IELTS, PTE. Electronic applications accepted. *Faculty research:* Media informatics and signal processing, integrated circuits and cyberphysical systems, communications systems and networking, nanoscale electronics and photonics, systems biology and neuroengineering.

Concordia University, School of Graduate Studies, Faculty of Engineering and Computer Science, Department of Electrical and Computer Engineering, Montréal, QC H3G 1M8, Canada. Offers M Eng, MA Sc, PhD. *Degree requirements:* For master's, thesis optional; for doctorate, comprehensive exam, thesis/dissertation. *Faculty research:* Computer communications and protocols, circuits and systems, graph theory, VLSI systems, microelectronics.

Computer Engineering

Cornell University, Graduate School, Graduate Fields of Engineering, Field of Electrical and Computer Engineering, Ithaca, NY 14853. Offers computer engineering (M Eng, PhD); electrical engineering (M Eng, PhD); electrical systems (M Eng, PhD); electrophysics (M Eng, PhD). *Degree requirements:* For doctorate, comprehensive exam, thesis/dissertation. *Entrance requirements:* For master's, GRE General Test, 2 letters of recommendation; for doctorate, GRE General Test, 3 letters of recommendation. Additional exam requirements/recommendations for international students: Required—TOEFL (minimum score 600 paper-based; 77 iBT). Electronic applications accepted. *Faculty research:* Communications, information theory, signal processing and power control, computer engineering, microelectromechanical systems and nanotechnology.

Dalhousie University, Faculty of Engineering, Department of Electrical and Computer Engineering, Halifax, NS B3J 1Z1, Canada. Offers M Eng, MA Sc, PhD. *Degree requirements:* For master's, thesis; for doctorate, thesis/dissertation. *Entrance requirements:* Additional exam requirements/recommendations for international students: Required—TOEFL, IELTS, CANTEST, CAEL, or Michigan English Language Assessment Battery. Electronic applications accepted. *Faculty research:* Communications, computer engineering, power engineering, electronics, systems engineering.

Dartmouth College, Thayer School of Engineering, Program in Computer Engineering, Hanover, NH 03755. Offers MS, PhD. *Degree requirements:* For master's, thesis; for doctorate, thesis/dissertation, candidacy oral exam. *Entrance requirements:* For master's and doctorate, GRE General Test. *Application deadline:* For fall admission, 1/1 priority date for domestic students. Application fee: $45. *Financial support:* Fellowships, research assistantships, teaching assistantships, career-related internships or fieldwork, Federal Work-Study, institutionally sponsored loans, and tuition waivers (full and partial) available. Financial award application deadline: 1/15. *Faculty research:* Analog VLSI, electromagnetic fields and waves, electronic instrumentation, microelectromechanical systems, optics, lasers and non-linear optics, power electronics and integrated power converters, networking, parallel and distributed computing, simulation, VLSI design and testing, wireless networking. *Total annual research expenditures:* $2.8 million. *Unit head:* Dr. Joseph J. Helbie, Dean, 603-646-2238, Fax: 603-646-2580, E-mail: joseph.j.helbie@dartmouth.edu. *Application contact:* Candace S. Potter, Graduate Admissions Administrator, 603-646-3844, Fax: 603-646-1620, E-mail: candace.s.potter@dartmouth.edu.
Website: http://engineering.dartmouth.edu/

Drexel University, College of Engineering, Department of Electrical and Computer Engineering, Program in Computer Engineering, Philadelphia, PA 19104-2875. Offers MS. *Program availability:* Part-time, evening/weekend. *Faculty:* 34 full-time (4 women), 4 part-time/adjunct (0 women). *Students:* 18 full-time (2 women), 3 part-time (0 women); includes 3 minority (2 Asian, non-Hispanic/Latino; 1 Hispanic/Latino), 17 international. Average age 25. In 2016, 24 master's awarded. *Degree requirements:* For master's, thesis (for some programs). *Application deadline:* For fall admission, 8/21 for domestic students. Applications are processed on a rolling basis. Application fee: $50. Electronic applications accepted. *Expenses: Tuition:* Full-time $32,184; part-time $1192 per credit hour. *Required fees:* $280. Tuition and fees vary according to campus/location and program. *Financial support:* Career-related internships or fieldwork and unspecified assistantships available. Financial award application deadline: 2/1. *Unit head:* Dr. Nihat M. Bilgutay, Head, 215-895-6806, Fax: 215-895-1695, E-mail: bilgutay@ece.drexel.edu. *Application contact:* Director of Graduate Admissions, 215-895-6700, Fax: 215-895-5939, E-mail: enroll@drexel.edu.

Duke University, Graduate School, Pratt School of Engineering, Department of Electrical and Computer Engineering, Durham, NC 27708. Offers MS, PhD, JD/MS. Terminal master's awarded for partial completion of doctoral program. *Degree requirements:* For doctorate, thesis/dissertation. *Entrance requirements:* For master's and doctorate, GRE General Test. Additional exam requirements/recommendations for international students: Required—TOEFL (minimum score 90 iBT), IELTS (minimum score 7). Electronic applications accepted. *Faculty research:* Architecture and networking; biological applications circuits and systems; nanosystems, devices and materials; quantum computing and photonics; sensing and signals visualization; waves and metamaterials.

See Display on page 399 and Close-Up on page 425.

Duke University, Graduate School, Pratt School of Engineering, Master of Engineering Program, Durham, NC 27708-0271. Offers biomedical engineering (M Eng); civil engineering (M Eng); electrical and computer engineering (M Eng); environmental engineering (M Eng); materials science and engineering (M Eng); mechanical engineering (M Eng); photonics and optical sciences (M Eng). *Program availability:* Part-time. *Entrance requirements:* For master's, GRE General Test, resume, 3 letters of recommendation, statement of purpose, transcripts. Additional exam requirements/recommendations for international students: Required—TOEFL.

East Carolina University, Graduate School, College of Engineering and Technology, Greenville, NC 27858-4353. Offers MCM, MS, PhD, Certificate. *Accreditation:* ABET. *Program availability:* Part-time. *Students:* 74 full-time (15 women), 280 part-time (73 women); includes 89 minority (52 Black or African American, non-Hispanic/Latino; 3 American Indian or Alaska Native, non-Hispanic/Latino; 13 Asian, non-Hispanic/Latino; 16 Hispanic/Latino; 5 Two or more races, non-Hispanic/Latino), 31 international. Average age 35. 186 applicants, 86% accepted, 109 enrolled. In 2016, 50 master's awarded. *Degree requirements:* For master's, comprehensive exam. *Application deadline:* For fall admission, 6/1 priority date for domestic students. Applications are processed on a rolling basis. Application fee: $50. *Financial support:* Fellowships, research assistantships, teaching assistantships, and Federal Work-Study available. Support available to part-time students. Financial award application deadline: 6/1. *Unit head:* Dr. David White, Dean, 252-328-9604. *Application contact:* Dean of Graduate School, 252-328-6012, Fax: 252-328-6071, E-mail: gradschool@ecu.edu.
Website: http://www.ecu.edu/tecs/

École Polytechnique de Montréal, Graduate Programs, Department of Electrical and Computer Engineering, Montréal, QC H3C 3A7, Canada. Offers automation (M Eng, M Sc A, PhD); computer science (M Eng, M Sc A, PhD); electrical engineering (DESS); electrotechnology (M Eng, M Sc A, PhD); microelectronics (M Eng, M Sc A, PhD); microwave technology (M Eng, M Sc A, PhD). *Program availability:* Part-time, evening/weekend. *Degree requirements:* For master's, one foreign language, thesis; for doctorate, one foreign language, thesis/dissertation. *Entrance requirements:* For master's, minimum GPA of 2.75; for doctorate, minimum GPA of 3.0. *Faculty research:* Microwaves, telecommunications, software engineering.

Fairfield University, School of Engineering, Fairfield, CT 06824. Offers database management (CAS); electrical and computer engineering (MS); information security (CAS); management of technology (MS); mechanical engineering (MS); network technology (CAS); software engineering (MS); Web application development (CAS). *Program availability:* Part-time, evening/weekend. *Faculty:* 7 full-time (1 woman), 15 part-time/adjunct (2 women). *Students:* 104 full-time (31 women), 56 part-time (15 women); includes 17 minority (8 Black or African American, non-Hispanic/Latino; 5 Asian, non-Hispanic/Latino; 4 Hispanic/Latino), 108 international. Average age 28. 193 applicants, 63% accepted, 20 enrolled. In 2016, 173 master's awarded. *Degree requirements:* For master's, capstone course. *Entrance requirements:* For master's, resume, 2 recommendations. Additional exam requirements/recommendations for international students: Required—TOEFL (minimum score 550 paper-based; 80 iBT) or IELTS (minimum score 6.5). *Application deadline:* For fall admission, 5/15 for international students; for spring admission, 10/15 for international students. Applications are processed on a rolling basis. Application fee: $60. Electronic applications accepted. *Expenses:* $800 per credit hour. *Financial support:* In 2016–17, 27 students received support. Scholarships/grants and unspecified assistantships available. Financial award applicants required to submit FAFSA. *Faculty research:* Artificial intelligence and information visualization, natural language processing, thermofluids, microwaves and electromagnetics, micro-/nano-manufacturing. *Unit head:* Dr. Bruce Berdanier, Dean, 203-254-4147, Fax: 203-254-4013, E-mail: bberdanier@fairfield.edu. *Application contact:* Marianne Gumpper, Director of Graduate and Continuing Studies Admission, 203-254-4184, Fax: 203-254-4073, E-mail: gradadmis@fairfield.edu.
Website: http://www.fairfield.edu/soe

Fairleigh Dickinson University, Metropolitan Campus, University College: Arts, Sciences, and Professional Studies, School of Computer Sciences and Engineering, Program in Computer Engineering, Teaneck, NJ 07666-1914. Offers MS.

Florida Atlantic University, College of Engineering and Computer Science, Department of Computer and Electrical Engineering and Computer Science, Boca Raton, FL 33431-0991. Offers bioengineering (MS); computer engineering (MS, PhD); computer science (MS, PhD); electrical engineering (MS, PhD). *Program availability:* Part-time, evening/weekend. *Faculty:* 23 full-time (5 women), 1 part-time/adjunct (0 women). *Students:* 103 full-time (30 women), 127 part-time (30 women); includes 77 minority (15 Black or African American, non-Hispanic/Latino; 10 Asian, non-Hispanic/Latino; 46 Hispanic/Latino; 6 Two or more races, non-Hispanic/Latino), 74 international. Average age 32. 215 applicants, 51% accepted, 85 enrolled. In 2016, 45 master's, 5 doctorates awarded. Terminal master's awarded for partial completion of doctoral program. *Degree requirements:* For master's, thesis optional; for doctorate, thesis/dissertation, qualifying exam. *Entrance requirements:* For master's, GRE General Test, minimum GPA of 3.0; for doctorate, GRE General Test, master's degree, minimum GPA of 3.5. Additional exam requirements/recommendations for international students: Required—TOEFL (minimum score 500 paper-based; 61 iBT), IELTS (minimum score 6). *Application deadline:* For fall admission, 7/1 priority date for domestic students, 2/15 for international students; for spring admission, 11/1 for domestic students, 7/15 for international students. Applications are processed on a rolling basis. Application fee: $30. *Expenses:* Tuition, state resident: full-time $7392; part-time $369.82 per credit hour. Tuition, nonresident: full-time $19,432; part-time $1024.81 per credit hour. *Financial support:* Fellowships, research assistantships with partial tuition reimbursements, teaching assistantships with full tuition reimbursements, career-related internships or fieldwork, and Federal Work-Study available. Support available to part-time students. Financial award application deadline: 4/1; financial award applicants required to submit FAFSA. *Faculty research:* VLSI and neural networks, communication networks, software engineering, computer architecture, multimedia and video processing. *Unit head:* Jean Mangiaracina, 561-297-3855, E-mail: jmangiar@fau.edu.
Website: http://www.ceecs.fau.edu/

Florida Institute of Technology, College of Engineering, Program in Computer Engineering, Melbourne, FL 32901-6975. Offers MS, PhD. *Program availability:* Part-time. *Students:* 54 full-time (9 women), 17 part-time (3 women); includes 2 minority (1 Black or African American, non-Hispanic/Latino; 1 Hispanic/Latino), 64 international. Average age 30. 106 applicants, 58% accepted, 15 enrolled. In 2016, 34 master's, 4 doctorates awarded. *Degree requirements:* For master's, thesis or final examination, 30 credit hours; for doctorate, thesis/dissertation, 24 credit hours of coursework, 24 credit hours of dissertation, yearly seminar demonstrating progress. *Entrance requirements:* For master's, GRE; for doctorate, GRE, 3 letters of recommendation, resume, statement of objectives. Additional exam requirements/recommendations for international students: Required—TOEFL (minimum score 550 paper-based; 79 iBT). *Application deadline:* Applications are processed on a rolling basis. Application fee: $50. Electronic applications accepted. *Expenses: Tuition:* Full-time $22,338; part-time $1241 per credit hour. *Required fees:* $250. Tuition and fees vary according to degree level, campus/location and program. *Financial support:* Research assistantships, teaching assistantships, career-related internships or fieldwork, and tuition remissions available. Financial award application deadline: 3/1; financial award applicants required to submit FAFSA. *Faculty research:* Neural networks, parallel processing, reliability testing, image processing. *Unit head:* Dr. Samuel P. Kozaitis, Chair, 321-674-8060, Fax: 321-674-8192. *Application contact:* Cheryl A. Brown, Associate Director of Graduate Admissions, 321-674-7581, Fax: 321-723-9468, E-mail: cbrown@fit.edu.
Website: http://coe.fit.edu/cs/

Florida International University, College of Engineering and Computing, Department of Electrical and Computer Engineering, Miami, FL 33175. Offers computer engineering (MS); electrical engineering (MS, PhD). *Program availability:* Part-time, evening/weekend. *Faculty:* 27 full-time (3 women), 10 part-time/adjunct (0 women). *Students:* 139 full-time (25 women), 55 part-time (9 women); includes 65 minority (11 Black or African American, non-Hispanic/Latino; 7 Asian, non-Hispanic/Latino; 46 Hispanic/Latino; 1 Native Hawaiian or other Pacific Islander, non-Hispanic/Latino), 114 international. Average age 29. 271 applicants, 43% accepted, 47 enrolled. In 2016, 57 master's, 15 doctorates awarded. Terminal master's awarded for partial completion of doctoral program. *Degree requirements:* For master's, thesis optional; for doctorate, comprehensive exam, thesis/dissertation. *Entrance requirements:* For master's, minimum undergraduate GPA of 3.0 in upper-level coursework, resume, letters of recommendation, letter of intent; for doctorate, GRE General Test, minimum graduate GPA of 3.3, resume, letters of recommendation, letter of intent. Additional exam requirements/recommendations for international students: Required—TOEFL (minimum score 550 paper-based; 80 iBT). *Application deadline:* For fall admission, 6/1 for domestic students, 4/1 for international students; for spring admission, 10/1 for domestic students, 9/1 for international students. Applications are processed on a rolling basis. Application fee: $30. Electronic applications accepted. *Expenses:* Tuition, state resident: full-time $8912; part-time $446 per credit hour. Tuition, nonresident: full-time $21,393; part-time $992 per credit hour. *Required fees:* $2185; $195 per semester. Tuition and fees vary according to program. *Financial support:* Institutionally sponsored loans, scholarships/grants, and unspecified assistantships available. Financial award application deadline: 3/1; financial award applicants required to submit FAFSA. *Unit head:* Dr. Shekhar Bhansali, Chair, 305-348-4439, Fax: 305-348-3707, E-mail: sbhansa@fiu.edu. *Application contact:* Sara-Michelle Lemus, Engineering Admissions Officer, 305-348-1890, Fax: 305-348-7441, E-mail: grad_eng@fiu.edu.
Website: http://cec.fiu.edu

George Mason University, Volgenau School of Engineering, Department of Electrical and Computer Engineering, Fairfax, VA 22030. Offers computer engineering (MS); electrical and computer engineering (PhD, Certificate). MS programs offered jointly with Old Dominion University, University of Virginia, Virginia Commonwealth University, and Virginia Polytechnic Institute and State University. *Faculty:* 34 full-time (5 women), 42

part-time/adjunct (3 women). *Students:* 208 full-time (58 women), 196 part-time (38 women); includes 82 minority (24 Black or African American, non-Hispanic/Latino; 28 Asian, non-Hispanic/Latino; 22 Hispanic/Latino; 1 Native Hawaiian or other Pacific Islander, non-Hispanic/Latino; 7 Two or more races, non-Hispanic/Latino), 193 international. Average age 29. 353 applicants, 82% accepted, 107 enrolled. In 2016, 168 master's, 11 doctorates, 54 other advanced degrees awarded. *Degree requirements:* For master's, thesis optional; for doctorate, comprehensive exam, thesis or scholarly paper. *Entrance requirements:* For master's, GRE, personal goals statement; 2 official copies of transcripts; self-evaluation form; 3 letters of recommendation; resume; official bank statement; photocopy of passport; proof of financial support; for doctorate, GRE (waived for GMU electrical and computer engineering master's graduates with minimum GPA of 3.0), personal goals statement; 2 official copies of transcripts; self-evaluation form; 3 letters of recommendation; resume; official bank statement; photocopy of passport; proof of financial support. Additional exam requirements/recommendations for international students: Required—TOEFL (minimum score 575 paper-based; 88 iBT), IELTS (minimum score 6.5), PTE (minimum score 59). *Application deadline:* For fall admission, 1/15 priority date for domestic students. Application fee: $75 ($80 for international students). Electronic applications accepted. *Expenses:* Contact institution. *Financial support:* In 2016–17, 71 students received support, including 2 fellowships (averaging $10,814 per year), 29 research assistantships with tuition reimbursements available (averaging $17,506 per year), 42 teaching assistantships with tuition reimbursements available (averaging $11,959 per year); career-related internships or fieldwork, Federal Work-Study, scholarships/grants, unspecified assistantships, and health care benefits (for full-time research or teaching assistantship recipients) also available. Support available to part-time students. Financial award application deadline: 3/1; financial award applicants required to submit FAFSA. *Faculty research:* Communication networks, signal processing, system failure diagnosis, multiprocessors, material processing using microwave energy. *Total annual research expenditures:* $2.3 million. *Unit head:* Monson Hayes, Chair, 703-993-1570, Fax: 703-993-1601, E-mail: hayes@gmu.edu. *Application contact:* Jammie Chang, Academic Program Coordinator, 703-993-1570, Fax: 703-993-1601, E-mail: jchangn@gmu.edu.
Website: http://ece.gmu.edu/

The George Washington University, School of Engineering and Applied Science, Department of Electrical and Computer Engineering, Washington, DC 20052. Offers electrical engineering (MS, PhD); telecommunication and computers (MS). *Program availability:* Part-time, evening/weekend. *Faculty:* 26 full-time (2 women). *Students:* 191 full-time (43 women), 67 part-time (56 women); includes 19 minority (9 Black or African American, non-Hispanic/Latino; 7 Asian, non-Hispanic/Latino; 3 Hispanic/Latino), 218 international. Average age 27. 545 applicants, 88% accepted, 103 enrolled. In 2016, 48 master's, 7 doctorates, 1 other advanced degree awarded. *Degree requirements:* For master's, thesis optional; for doctorate, comprehensive exam, thesis/dissertation, dissertation defense, qualifying exam. *Entrance requirements:* For master's, appropriate bachelor's degree, minimum GPA of 3.0; for doctorate, GRE (if highest earned degree is BS), appropriate bachelor's or master's degree, minimum GPA of 3.3; for other advanced degree, appropriate master's degree, minimum GPA of 3.0. Additional exam requirements/recommendations for international students: Required—TOEFL or The George Washington University English as a Foreign Language Test. *Application deadline:* For fall admission, 3/1 priority date for domestic students; for spring admission, 10/1 for domestic students. Applications are processed on a rolling basis. Application fee: $75. *Financial support:* In 2016–17, 39 students received support. Fellowships with tuition reimbursements available, research assistantships, teaching assistantships with tuition reimbursements available, career-related internships or fieldwork, and institutionally sponsored loans available. Financial award application deadline: 3/1; financial award applicants required to submit FAFSA. *Faculty research:* Computer graphics, multimedia systems. *Unit head:* Prof. Ahmed Louri, Chair, 202-994-5905, E-mail: louri@gwu.edu. *Application contact:* Adina Lav, Marketing, Recruiting and Admissions, 202-994-5827, Fax: 202-994-0909, E-mail: engineering@gwu.edu.
Website: http://www.ece.gwu.edu/

Georgia Institute of Technology, Graduate Studies, College of Engineering, School of Electrical and Computer Engineering, Atlanta, GA 30332-0001. Offers MS, PhD. *Program availability:* Part-time, online learning. Terminal master's awarded for partial completion of doctoral program. *Degree requirements:* For master's, thesis optional; for doctorate, comprehensive exam, thesis/dissertation. *Entrance requirements:* For master's and doctorate, GRE General Test. Additional exam requirements/recommendations for international students: Required—TOEFL (minimum score 550 paper-based; 79 iBT). Electronic applications accepted. *Expenses:* Contact institution. *Faculty research:* Telecommunications, computer systems, microelectronics, optical engineering, digital signal processing.

Grand Valley State University, Padnos College of Engineering and Computing, School of Engineering, Allendale, MI 49401-9403. Offers electrical and computer engineering (MSE); manufacturing operations (MSE); mechanical engineering (MSE); product design and manufacturing engineering (MSE). *Program availability:* Part-time, evening/weekend. *Faculty:* 16 full-time (3 women). *Students:* 29 full-time (8 women), 38 part-time (5 women); includes 5 minority (2 Black or African American, non-Hispanic/Latino; 1 Asian, non-Hispanic/Latino; 2 Hispanic/Latino), 37 international. Average age 26. 129 applicants, 58% accepted, 23 enrolled. In 2016, 24 master's awarded. *Degree requirements:* For master's, project or thesis. *Entrance requirements:* For master's, engineering degree, minimum GPA of 3.0, resume, 3 confidential letters of recommendation, 1-2 page essay, base of underlying relevant knowledge/evidence from academic records or relevant wok experience. Additional exam requirements/recommendations for international students: Required—TOEFL (minimum score 80 iBT) or IELTS (6.5). *Application deadline:* Applications are processed on a rolling basis. Application fee: $30. Electronic applications accepted. *Expenses:* $661 per credit hour. *Financial support:* In 2016–17, 32 students received support, including 8 fellowships; career-related internships or fieldwork, Federal Work-Study, institutionally sponsored loans, scholarships/grants, and unspecified assistantships also available. *Faculty research:* Digital signal processing, computer aided design, computer aided manufacturing, manufacturing simulation, biomechanics, product design. *Total annual research expenditures:* $300,000. *Unit head:* Dr. Wael Mokhtar, Director, 616-331-6015, Fax: 616-331-7215, E-mail: mokhtarw@gvsu.edu. *Application contact:* Dr. Shabbir Choudhuri, Graduate Program Director, 616-331-6845, Fax: 616-331-7215, E-mail: choudhus@gvsu.edu.
Website: http://www.engineer.gvsu.edu/

Illinois Institute of Technology, Graduate College, Armour College of Engineering, Department of Electrical and Computer Engineering, Chicago, IL 60616. Offers biomedical imaging and signals (MAS); computer engineering (MS, PhD); electrical engineering (MS, PhD); electricity markets (MAS); network engineering (MAS); power engineering (MAS); telecommunications and software engineering (MAS); VLSI and microelectronics (MAS); MS/MS. *Program availability:* Part-time, evening/weekend, online learning. Terminal master's awarded for partial completion of doctoral program. *Degree requirements:* For master's, comprehensive exam (for some programs), thesis (for some programs); for doctorate, comprehensive exam, thesis/dissertation. *Entrance requirements:* For master's and doctorate, GRE General Test (minimum score 1100 Quantitative and Verbal, 3.5 Analytical Writing), minimum undergraduate GPA of 3.0. Additional exam requirements/recommendations for international students: Required—TOEFL (minimum score 550 paper-based; 80 iBT); Recommended—IELTS (minimum score 5.5). Electronic applications accepted. *Faculty research:* Communication systems, wireless networks, computer systems, computer networks, wireless security, cloud computing and micro-electronics; electromagnetics and electronics; power and control systems; signal and image processing.

Indiana State University, College of Graduate and Professional Studies, College of Technology, Department of Electronics and Computer Engineering Technology, Terre Haute, IN 47809. Offers electronics and computer technology (MS). *Degree requirements:* For master's, thesis or alternative. *Entrance requirements:* For master's, bachelor's degree in industrial technology or related field. Additional exam requirements/recommendations for international students: Required—TOEFL. Electronic applications accepted.

Indiana University–Purdue University Fort Wayne, College of Engineering, Technology, and Computer Science, Department of Electrical and Computer Engineering, Fort Wayne, IN 46805-1499. Offers computer engineering (MSE); electrical engineering (MSE); systems engineering (MSE). *Program availability:* Part-time. *Entrance requirements:* For master's, minimum GPA of 3.0, bachelor's degree in engineering discipline. Additional exam requirements/recommendations for international students: Required—TOEFL (minimum score 550 paper-based; 79 iBT); Recommended—TWE. Electronic applications accepted.

Indiana University–Purdue University Indianapolis, School of Engineering and Technology, Department of Electrical and Computer Engineering, Indianapolis, IN 46202. Offers electrical and computer engineering (MS, PhD); engineering (MSE). *Faculty:* 17 full-time (4 women), 5 part-time/adjunct. *Students:* 89 full-time (18 women), 66 part-time (15 women); includes 9 minority (4 Black or African American, non-Hispanic/Latino; 4 Asian, non-Hispanic/Latino; 1 Hispanic/Latino), 123 international. Average age 26. 173 applicants, 58% accepted, 49 enrolled. In 2016, 58 master's awarded. *Degree requirements:* For master's, thesis optional; for doctorate, thesis/dissertation. *Entrance requirements:* For master's, GRE, minimum GPA of 3.0, three recommendation letters, statement of purpose/intent; for doctorate, GRE, minimum GPA of 3.0, three recommendation letters, statement of purpose/intent, curriculum vitae. Additional exam requirements/recommendations for international students: Required—TOEFL; Recommended—IELTS, TSE. Application fee: $55 ($65 for international students). Electronic applications accepted. *Expenses:* $382 resident tuition per credit hour; $1,100 non-resident tuition per credit hour; $215-370 per term mandatory fees. *Financial support:* In 2016–17, 31 students received support. Fellowships, research assistantships, teaching assistantships, scholarships/grants, tuition waivers, and unspecified assistantships available. Financial award application deadline: 1/2. *Faculty research:* Modeling and control of advanced vehicle systems; data analytics and parallel processing; robotics and automation; 3-D imaging algorithms and image processing; signal/video processing and analysis; power electronics an renewable energy. *Total annual research expenditures:* $1 million. *Unit head:* Dr. Brian King, Chair, Department of Electrical and Computer Engineering, 317-274-9723, E-mail: briking@iupui.edu. *Application contact:* Sherrie Tucker, ECE Graduate Program Coordinator, 317-278-9726, E-mail: ecegrad@iupui.edu.
Website: http://www.engr.iupui.edu/departments/ece/

Instituto Tecnológico y de Estudios Superiores de Monterrey, Campus Chihuahua, Graduate Programs, Chihuahua, Mexico. Offers computer systems engineering (Ingeniero); electrical engineering (Ingeniero); electromechanical engineering (Ingeniero); electronic engineering (Ingeniero); engineering administration (MEA); industrial engineering (MIE, Ingeniero); international trade (MIT); mechanical engineering (Ingeniero).

International Technological University, Program in Computer Engineering, San Jose, CA 95134. Offers MSCE. *Program availability:* Part-time, evening/weekend. *Degree requirements:* For master's, thesis or alternative, capstone project. *Entrance requirements:* Additional exam requirements/recommendations for international students: Required—TOEFL, IELTS. Electronic applications accepted.

Iowa State University of Science and Technology, Department of Electrical and Computer Engineering, Ames, IA 50011. Offers computer engineering (M Eng, MS, PhD); electrical engineering (M Eng, MS, PhD). *Degree requirements:* For master's, thesis or alternative; for doctorate, thesis/dissertation. *Entrance requirements:* For master's and doctorate, GRE General Test. Additional exam requirements/recommendations for international students: Required—TOEFL (minimum score 570 paper-based; 79 iBT), IELTS (minimum score 6.5). *Application deadline:* For fall admission, 1/15 priority date for domestic and international students; for spring admission, 9/15 for domestic and international students. Application fee: $40 ($90 for international students). Electronic applications accepted. *Application contact:* Vicky Thorland-Oster, Application Contact, 515-294-8403, E-mail: ecegrad@iastate.edu.
Website: http://www.ece.iastate.edu/

Iowa State University of Science and Technology, Program in Computer Engineering, Ames, IA 50011. Offers M Eng, MS, PhD. *Entrance requirements:* For master's and doctorate, GRE. Additional exam requirements/recommendations for international students: Required—TOEFL (minimum score 570 paper-based; 79 iBT), IELTS (minimum score 6.5). *Application deadline:* For fall admission, 1/15 for domestic students; for spring admission, 9/15 for domestic students. Application fee: $60 ($90 for international students). Electronic applications accepted. *Application contact:* Stacey Ross, Application Contact, 515-294-9162, E-mail: ecpe_grad_questions@iastate.edu.
Website: http://www.ece.iastate.edu/

Johns Hopkins University, Engineering Program for Professionals, Part-time Program in Electrical and Computer Engineering, Baltimore, MD 21218. Offers communications and networking (MS); electrical and computer engineering (Graduate Certificate, Post-Master's Certificate); photonics (MS). *Program availability:* Part-time, evening/weekend, 100% online, blended/hybrid learning. *Faculty:* 48 part-time/adjunct (2 women). *Students:* 5 full-time (0 women), 303 part-time (52 women); includes 63 minority (11 Black or African American, non-Hispanic/Latino; 24 Asian, non-Hispanic/Latino; 24 Hispanic/Latino; 4 Two or more races, non-Hispanic/Latino). Average age 28. 108 applicants, 68% accepted, 53 enrolled. In 2016, 78 master's, 2 other advanced degrees awarded. *Degree requirements:* For master's and other advanced degree, thesis optional. *Entrance requirements:* Additional exam requirements/recommendations for international students: Required—TOEFL (minimum score 600 paper-based; 100 iBT). *Application deadline:* Applications are processed on a rolling basis. Application fee: $0. Electronic applications accepted. *Unit head:* Dr. Brian Jennison, Program Chair, 443-778-6421, E-mail: brian.jennison@jhuapl.edu. *Application contact:* Doug Schiller, Admissions Director, 410-516-2300, Fax: 410-579-8049, E-mail: schiller@jhu.edu.
Website: http://www.ep.jhu.edu/

Johns Hopkins University, G. W. C. Whiting School of Engineering, Department of Electrical and Computer Engineering, Baltimore, MD 21218. Offers MSE, PhD. *Faculty:* 23 full-time (4 women), 4 part-time/adjunct (1 woman). *Students:* 146 full-time (29 women), 3 part-time (0 women); includes 12 minority (6 Black or African American, non-Hispanic/Latino; 4 Asian, non-Hispanic/Latino; 2 Two or more races, non-Hispanic/Latino), 106 international. Average age 26. 394 applicants, 37% accepted, 51 enrolled.

Computer Engineering

In 2016, 20 master's, 13 doctorates awarded. Terminal master's awarded for partial completion of doctoral program. *Degree requirements:* For master's, thesis optional; for doctorate, thesis/dissertation, qualifying and oral exams, seminar. *Entrance requirements:* For master's and doctorate, GRE General Test, transcripts, 3 letters of recommendation, statement of purpose. Additional exam requirements/recommendations for international students: Required—TOEFL (minimum score 600 paper-based, 100 iBT) or IELTS (7). *Application deadline:* For fall admission, 12/18 for domestic and international students. Application fee: $75. Electronic applications accepted. *Financial support:* In 2016–17, 88 students received support, including 20 fellowships with full tuition reimbursements available (averaging $27,996 per year), 68 research assistantships with full tuition reimbursements available (averaging $27,996 per year); teaching assistantships with full tuition reimbursements available, career-related internships or fieldwork, Federal Work-Study, institutionally sponsored loans, scholarships/grants, health care benefits, tuition waivers (partial), and unspecified assistantships also available. Financial award application deadline: 12/15. *Faculty research:* Microsystems, neuromorphics and brain-machines interface; acoustics, speech and language processing; photonics, bio photonics and optoelectronics; signal processing and imaging science and technology; networks, controls and systems. *Total annual research expenditures:* $16.1 million. *Unit head:* Dr. Ralph Etienne-Cummings, Chair, 410-516-7031, Fax: 410-516-5566, E-mail: retienne@jhu.edu. *Application contact:* Debbie Race, Academic Program Administrator, 410-516-4808, Fax: 410-516-5566, E-mail: drace@jhu.edu.
Website: http://www.ece.jhu.edu/

Kansas State University, Graduate School, College of Engineering, Department of Electrical and Computer Engineering, Manhattan, KS 66506. Offers electrical engineering (MS), including bioengineering, communication systems, design of computer systems, electrical engineering, energy and power systems, integrated circuits and devices, real time embedded systems, renewable energy, signal processing. *Program availability:* Part-time, evening/weekend, online learning. *Faculty:* 21 full-time (4 women), 1 (woman) part-time/adjunct. *Students:* 47 full-time (11 women), 51 part-time (5 women); includes 13 minority (6 Black or African American, non-Hispanic/Latino; 6 Asian, non-Hispanic/Latino; 1 Two or more races, non-Hispanic/Latino), 40 international. Average age 31. 146 applicants, 29% accepted, 17 enrolled. In 2016, 16 master's, 5 doctorates awarded. *Degree requirements:* For master's, thesis or alternative, final exam; for doctorate, thesis/dissertation, final exam, preliminary exams. *Entrance requirements:* For master's, GRE General Test, bachelor's degree in electrical engineering or computer science, minimum GPA of 3.0; for doctorate, GRE General Test. Additional exam requirements/recommendations for international students: Required—TOEFL (minimum score 600 paper-based; 85 iBT). *Application deadline:* For fall admission, 1/1 priority date for domestic and international students; for spring admission, 8/1 priority date for domestic and international students. Applications are processed on a rolling basis. Application fee: $50 ($75 for international students). Electronic applications accepted. *Expenses:* Tuition, state resident: full-time $9670. Tuition, nonresident: full-time $21,828. *Required fees:* $862. *Financial support:* In 2016–17, 40 students received support, including 22 research assistantships with tuition reimbursements available (averaging $12,100 per year), 18 teaching assistantships with full tuition reimbursements available (averaging $12,220 per year); career-related internships or fieldwork, institutionally sponsored loans, and scholarships/grants also available. Support available to part-time students. Financial award application deadline: 3/1; financial award applicants required to submit FAFSA. *Faculty research:* Energy systems and renewable energy, computer systems and real time embedded systems, communication systems and signal processing, integrated circuits and devices, bioengineering. *Total annual research expenditures:* $1.3 million. *Unit head:* Dr. Don Gruenbacher, Head, 785-532-5600, Fax: 785-532-1188, E-mail: grue@k-state.edu. *Application contact:* Dr. Andrew Rys, Graduate Program Director, 785-532-4665, Fax: 785-532-1188, E-mail: andrys@k-state.edu.
Website: http://www.ece.k-state.edu/

Kennesaw State University, Southern Polytechnic College of Engineering and Engineering Technology, Department of Electrical and Computer Engineering Technology, Kennesaw, GA 30144. Offers electrical engineering technology (MS). *Program availability:* Part-time, evening/weekend. *Degree requirements:* For master's, thesis. *Entrance requirements:* For master's, GRE (minimum scores: 147 Verbal, 147 Quantitative, 3.5 Analytical), minimum GPA of 2.7. Additional exam requirements/recommendations for international students: Required—TOEFL (minimum score 550 paper-based; 79 iBT), IELTS (minimum score 6.5). Electronic applications accepted. *Faculty research:* Analog and digital communications, computer networking, analog and low power electronics design, control systems and digital signal processing, instrumentation (medical and industrial), biomedical signal analysis, biomedical imaging, renewable energy systems, electronics, power distribution, power electronics.

Lakehead University, Graduate Studies, Faculty of Engineering, Thunder Bay, ON P7B 5E1, Canada. Offers control engineering (M Sc Engr); electrical/computer engineering (M Sc Engr); environmental engineering (M Sc Engr). *Program availability:* Part-time. *Degree requirements:* For master's, thesis. *Entrance requirements:* For master's, bachelor's degree in chemical, electrical or mechanical engineering, minimum B average. Additional exam requirements/recommendations for international students: Required—TOEFL. *Faculty research:* Pulp and paper, adaptive/process control, robust/interactive learning control, vibration control.

Lawrence Technological University, College of Engineering, Southfield, MI 48075-1058. Offers architectural engineering (MS); automotive engineering (MS); biomedical engineering (MS); civil engineering (MA, MS, PhD), including environmental engineering (MS), geotechnical engineering (MS), structural engineering (MS), transportation engineering (MS), water resource engineering (MS); construction engineering management (MA); electrical and computer engineering (MS); engineering management (MA); engineering technology (MS); fire engineering (MS); industrial engineering (MS), including healthcare; manufacturing systems (ME); mechanical engineering (MS, DE, PhD), including manufacturing (DE), solid mechanics (MS), thermal-fluids (MS); mechatronic systems engineering (MS). *Program availability:* Part-time, evening/weekend. *Faculty:* 24 full-time (5 women), 26 part-time/adjunct (2 women). *Students:* 22 full-time (7 women), 588 part-time (81 women); includes 23 minority (11 Black or African American, non-Hispanic/Latino; 4 Asian, non-Hispanic/Latino; 7 Hispanic/Latino; 1 Two or more races, non-Hispanic/Latino), 469 international. Average age 27. 1,186 applicants, 39% accepted, 99 enrolled. In 2016, 293 master's, 3 doctorates awarded. Terminal master's awarded for partial completion of doctoral program. *Degree requirements:* For master's, thesis optional; for doctorate, comprehensive exam, thesis/dissertation optional. *Entrance requirements:* Additional exam requirements/recommendations for international students: Required—TOEFL (minimum score 550 paper-based; 79 iBT), IELTS (minimum score 6.5). *Application deadline:* For fall admission, 5/22 for international students; for spring admission, 10/11 for international students; for summer admission, 2/16 for international students. Applications are processed on a rolling basis. Application fee: $50. Electronic applications accepted. *Expenses: Tuition:* Full-time $14,868; part-time $1062 per credit. *Required fees:* $75 per semester. Tuition and fees vary according to campus/location. *Financial support:* In 2016–17, 25 students received support, including 5 research assistantships with full tuition reimbursements available; unspecified assistantships also available. Financial

award application deadline: 4/1; financial award applicants required to submit FAFSA. *Faculty research:* Carbon fiber reinforced polymer reinforced concrete structures; low impact storm water management solutions; vehicle battery energy management; wireless communication; entrepreneurial mindset and engineering. *Total annual research expenditures:* $1.7 million. *Unit head:* Dr. Nabil Grace, Dean, 248-204-2500, Fax: 248-204-2509, E-mail: engrdean@ltu.edu. *Application contact:* Jane Rohrback, Director of Admissions, 248-204-3160, Fax: 248-204-2228, E-mail: admissions@ltu.edu. Website: http://www.ltu.edu/engineering/index.asp

Lehigh University, P.C. Rossin College of Engineering and Applied Science, Department of Computer Science and Engineering, Bethlehem, PA 18015. Offers computer engineering (M Eng, MS, PhD); computer science (M Eng, MS, PhD); MBA/E. *Program availability:* Part-time. *Faculty:* 16 full-time (2 women), 2 part-time/adjunct (both women). *Students:* 44 full-time (6 women), 4 part-time (1 woman); includes 2 minority (1 Asian, non-Hispanic/Latino; 1 Hispanic/Latino), 35 international. Average age 25. 226 applicants, 31% accepted, 16 enrolled. In 2016, 24 master's, 3 doctorates awarded. Terminal master's awarded for partial completion of doctoral program. *Degree requirements:* For master's, thesis optional, oral presentation of thesis; for doctorate, thesis/dissertation, qualifying, general, and oral exams. *Entrance requirements:* For master's, GRE General Test, minimum GPA of 3.0; for doctorate, GRE General Test, minimum GPA of 3.5. Additional exam requirements/recommendations for international students: Required—TOEFL (minimum score 550 paper-based; 79 iBT), IELTS (minimum score 6.5). *Application deadline:* For fall admission, 4/1 for domestic and international students; for spring admission, 11/1 for domestic and international students. Application fee: $75. Electronic applications accepted. *Expenses:* $1,420 per credit hour. *Financial support:* In 2016–17, 24 students received support, including 1 fellowship with full tuition reimbursement available (averaging $21,105 per year), 5 research assistantships with full tuition reimbursements available (averaging $21,033 per year), 6 teaching assistantships with full tuition reimbursements available (averaging $21,530 per year). Financial award application deadline: 1/15. *Faculty research:* Artificial intelligence, networking-pattern recognition, multimedia e-learning/data mining/web search, mobile robotics, bioinformatics, computer vision, data science. *Total annual research expenditures:* $1.1 million. *Unit head:* Dr. Daniel P. Lopresti, Chair, 610-758-5782, Fax: 610-758-4096, E-mail: dal9@lehigh.edu. *Application contact:* Heidi Wegrzyn, Graduate Coordinator, 610-758-3065, Fax: 610-758-4096, E-mail: hew207@lehigh.edu. Website: http://www.cse.lehigh.edu/

Lehigh University, P.C. Rossin College of Engineering and Applied Science, Department of Electrical and Computer Engineering, Bethlehem, PA 18015. Offers electrical engineering (MS, PhD); wireless network engineering (MS). *Program availability:* Part-time. *Faculty:* 21 full-time (4 women). *Students:* 82 full-time (14 women), 8 part-time (1 woman); includes 1 minority (Hispanic/Latino), 74 international. Average age 25. 324 applicants, 33% accepted, 29 enrolled. In 2016, 12 master's, 8 doctorates awarded. Terminal master's awarded for partial completion of doctoral program. *Degree requirements:* For master's, thesis optional; for doctorate, thesis/dissertation, qualifying or comprehensive exam for all 1st year PhD's; general exam 7 months or more prior to completion/dissertation defense. *Entrance requirements:* For master's and doctorate, GRE General Test, BS in field or related field. Additional exam requirements/recommendations for international students: Required—TOEFL (minimum score 79 iBT), IELTS (minimum score 6.5). *Application deadline:* For fall admission, 4/1 for domestic and international students; for spring admission, 11/1 for domestic and international students. Application fee: $75. Electronic applications accepted. Application fee is waived when completed online. *Expenses:* $1,420 per credit hour. *Financial support:* In 2016–17, 50 students received support, including 6 fellowships with full tuition reimbursements available (averaging $28,140 per year), 35 research assistantships with full tuition reimbursements available (averaging $28,140 per year), 7 teaching assistantships with full tuition reimbursements available (averaging $21,530 per year). Financial award application deadline: 1/15. *Faculty research:* Nanostructures/nanodevices, terahertz generation, analog devices, mixed mode design and signal circuits, optoelectronic sensors, micro-fabrication technology and design, packaging/reliability of microsensors, coding and networking information theory, radio frequency, wireless and optical wireless communication, wireless networks. *Total annual research expenditures:* $2.8 million. *Unit head:* Dr. Svetlana Tatic-Lucic, Interim Chair, 610-758-4069, Fax: 610-758-6279, E-mail: svt2@lehigh.edu. *Application contact:* Diane Hubinsky, Graduate Coordinator, 610-758-4072, Fax: 610-758-6279, E-mail: dih2@lehigh.edu.
Website: http://www.ece.lehigh.edu/

Louisiana State University and Agricultural & Mechanical College, Graduate School, College of Engineering, Division of Electrical and Computer Engineering, Baton Rouge, LA 70803. Offers MSEE, PhD.

Manhattan College, Graduate Programs, School of Engineering, Program in Computer Engineering, Riverdale, NY 10471. Offers MS. *Program availability:* Part-time, evening/weekend. *Degree requirements:* For master's, thesis or alternative. *Entrance requirements:* For master's, GRE (recommended), minimum GPA of 3.0. Additional exam requirements/recommendations for international students: Required—TOEFL (minimum score 550 paper-based; 80 iBT), IELTS (minimum score 6). *Application deadline:* For fall admission, 8/10 priority date for domestic students, 8/10 for international students; for spring admission, 1/7 for domestic and international students. Applications are processed on a rolling basis. Application fee: $60. *Financial support:* Fellowships, research assistantships, teaching assistantships with partial tuition reimbursements, career-related internships or fieldwork, Federal Work-Study, scholarships/grants, and unspecified assistantships available. Support available to part-time students. Financial award application deadline: 2/1. *Unit head:* Dr. George Giakos, Chairperson, 718-862-7154, Fax: 718-862-7162, E-mail: george.giakos@manhattan.edu.
Website: https://manhattan.edu/academics/graduate-programs/computer-engineering.php

Marquette University, Graduate School, College of Engineering, Department of Electrical and Computer Engineering, Milwaukee, WI 53201-1881. Offers digital signal processing (Certificate); electric machines, drives, and controls (Certificate); electrical and computer engineering (MS, PhD); microwaves and antennas (Certificate); sensors and smart systems (Certificate). *Program availability:* Part-time, evening/weekend. *Faculty:* 15 full-time (2 women), 4 part-time/adjunct (0 women). *Students:* 24 full-time (3 women), 25 part-time (7 women); includes 4 minority (2 Black or African American, non-Hispanic/Latino; 2 Hispanic/Latino), 25 international. Average age 27. 108 applicants, 63% accepted, 14 enrolled. In 2016, 14 master's, 6 doctorates awarded. Terminal master's awarded for partial completion of doctoral program. *Degree requirements:* For master's, comprehensive exam (for some programs), thesis optional; for doctorate, thesis/dissertation, dissertation defense, qualifying exam. *Entrance requirements:* For master's, GRE General Test (recommended), official transcripts from all current and previous colleges/universities except Marquette, three letters of recommendation; for doctorate, GRE General Test, minimum GPA of 3.0, official transcripts from all current and previous colleges/universities except Marquette, three letters of recommendation, statement of purpose, submission of any English language publications authored by applicant (strongly recommended). Additional exam requirements/recommendations for

international students: Required—TOEFL (minimum score 530 paper-based). *Application deadline:* For fall admission, 7/15 priority date for domestic students; for spring admission, 11/15 for domestic students. Applications are processed on a rolling basis. Application fee: $50. Electronic applications accepted. *Financial support:* Fellowships, research assistantships, teaching assistantships, scholarships/grants, health care benefits, tuition waivers (partial), and unspecified assistantships available. Support available to part-time students. Financial award application deadline: 2/15. *Faculty research:* Electric machines, drives, and controls; applied solid-state electronics; computers and signal processing; microwaves and antennas; solid state devices and acoustic wave sensors. *Total annual research expenditures:* $947,209. *Unit head:* Dr. Edwin E. Yaz, Chair, 414-288-6820, Fax: 414-288-5579. *Application contact:* Dr. Fabien Josse, 414-288-6789.
Website: http://www.marquette.edu/engineering/electrical_computer/grad.shtml

Massachusetts Institute of Technology, School of Engineering, Department of Electrical Engineering and Computer Science, Cambridge, MA 02139. Offers computer science (PhD, Sc D, ECS); computer science and engineering (PhD, Sc D); computer science and molecular biology (M Eng); electrical engineering (PhD, Sc D, EE); electrical engineering and computer science (M Eng, SM, PhD, Sc D); SM/MBA. *Faculty:* 116 full-time (18 women). *Students:* 864 full-time (210 women), 3 part-time (1 woman); includes 225 minority (11 Black or African American, non-Hispanic/Latino; 142 Asian, non-Hispanic/Latino; 50 Hispanic/Latino; 22 Two or more races, non-Hispanic/Latino), 406 international. Average age 26. 2,773 applicants, 8% accepted, 128 enrolled. In 2016, 236 master's, 87 doctorates awarded. *Degree requirements:* For master's and other advanced degree, thesis; for doctorate, comprehensive exam, thesis/dissertation. *Entrance requirements:* Additional exam requirements/recommendations for international students: Required—TOEFL, IELTS. *Application deadline:* For fall admission, 12/15 for domestic and international students. Application fee: $75. Electronic applications accepted. *Expenses: Tuition:* Full-time $46,400; part-time $725 per credit. One-time fee: $312 full-time. Full-time tuition and fees vary according to course load and program. *Financial support:* In 2016–17, 825 students received support, including fellowships (averaging $39,000 per year), 526 research assistantships (averaging $36,900 per year), 175 teaching assistantships (averaging $37,500 per year); Federal Work-Study, institutionally sponsored loans, scholarships/grants, traineeships, health care benefits, unspecified assistantships, and resident tutors also available. Support available to part-time students. Financial award application deadline: 5/1; financial award applicants required to submit FAFSA. *Faculty research:* Information systems, circuits, biomedical sciences and engineering, computer science: artificial intelligence, systems, theory. *Total annual research expenditures:* $108.1 million. *Unit head:* Prof. Anantha P. Chandrakasan, Department Head, 617-253-4600, Fax: 617-258-7254, E-mail: hq@eecs.mit.edu. *Application contact:* Graduate Admissions, 617-253-4603, E-mail: grad-ap@eecs.mit.edu.
Website: http://www.eecs.mit.edu/

McGill University, Faculty of Graduate and Postdoctoral Studies, Faculty of Engineering, Department of Electrical and Computer Engineering, Montréal, QC H3A 2T5, Canada. Offers M Eng, PhD.

Memorial University of Newfoundland, School of Graduate Studies, Faculty of Engineering and Applied Science, St. John's, NL A1C 5S7, Canada. Offers civil engineering (M Eng, PhD); electrical and computer engineering (M Eng, PhD); mechanical engineering (M Eng, PhD); ocean and naval architecture engineering (M Eng, PhD). *Program availability:* Part-time. *Degree requirements:* For master's, thesis; for doctorate, comprehensive exam, thesis/dissertation, oral thesis defense. *Entrance requirements:* For master's, 2nd class degree; for doctorate, master's degree in engineering. Electronic applications accepted. *Faculty research:* Engineering analysis, environmental and hydrotechnical studies, manufacturing and robotics, mechanics, structures and materials.

Memorial University of Newfoundland, School of Graduate Studies, Interdisciplinary Program in Computer Engineering, St. John's, NL A1C 5S7, Canada. Offers MA Sc. *Degree requirements:* For master's, project course. *Entrance requirements:* For master's, 2nd class engineering degree. Electronic applications accepted. *Expenses:* Contact institution.

Mercer University, Graduate Studies, Macon Campus, School of Engineering, Macon, GA 31207. Offers biomedical engineering (MSE); computer engineering (MSE); electrical engineering (MSE); engineering management (MSE); environmental engineering (MSE); environmental systems (MS); mechanical engineering (MSE); software engineering (MSE); software systems (MS); technical communications management (MS); technical management (MS). *Program availability:* Part-time-only, evening/weekend, online learning. *Faculty:* 21 full-time (5 women), 1 part-time/adjunct (0 women). *Students:* 44 full-time (9 women), 60 part-time (12 women); includes 14 minority (3 Black or African American, non-Hispanic/Latino; 1 American Indian or Alaska Native, non-Hispanic/Latino; 4 Asian, non-Hispanic/Latino; 3 Hispanic/Latino; 3 Two or more races, non-Hispanic/Latino), 2 international. Average age 27. In 2016, 64 master's awarded. *Degree requirements:* For master's, thesis or alternative. *Entrance requirements:* For master's, GRE (minimum score 300), minimum undergraduate GPA of 3.0. Additional exam requirements/recommendations for international students: Required—TOEFL (minimum score 550 paper-based; 80 iBT). *Application deadline:* For fall admission, 4/1 priority date for domestic and international students; for spring admission, 11/1 priority date for domestic and international students. Applications are processed on a rolling basis. Application fee: $75. *Expenses:* $865 per credit hour. *Financial support:* Applicants required to submit FAFSA. *Faculty research:* Designing prostheses and orthotics, oxygen transfer and limitations in biological systems, low-cost groundwater development, lung airway and transport, autonomous mobile robots. *Unit head:* Dr. Laura W. Lackey, Dean, 478-301-4106, Fax: 478-301-5593, E-mail: lackey_l@mercer.edu. *Application contact:* Dr. Richard O. Mines, Jr., Program Director, 478-301-2347, Fax: 478-301-5433, E-mail: mines_ro@mercer.edu.
Website: http://engineering.mercer.edu/

Miami University, College of Engineering and Computing, Department of Electrical and Computer Engineering, Oxford, OH 45056. Offers MS. *Students:* 16 full-time (3 women), 1 part-time (0 women), 11 international. Average age 25. *Expenses:* Tuition, state resident: full-time $12,890; part-time $564 per credit hour. Tuition, nonresident: full-time $29,604; part-time $1260 per credit hour. *Required fees:* $638. Part-time tuition and fees vary according to course load and program. *Unit head:* Dr. Q. Herb Zhou, Chair, 513-523-0740, E-mail: zhouq@miamioh.edu. *Application contact:* 513-529-0340, E-mail: cecgrad@miamioh.edu.
Website: http://miamioh.edu/cec/academics/departments/ece/

Michigan Technological University, Graduate School, College of Engineering, Department of Electrical and Computer Engineering, Houghton, MI 49931. Offers advanced electric power engineering (Graduate Certificate); automotive systems and controls (Graduate Certificate); computer engineering (MS, PhD); electrical engineering (MS, PhD). *Program availability:* Part-time, online learning. *Faculty:* 44 full-time, 9 part-time/adjunct. *Students:* 197 full-time (28 women), 51 part-time; includes 11 minority (3 Black or African American, non-Hispanic/Latino; 2 Asian, non-Hispanic/Latino; 6 Hispanic/Latino), 205 international. Average age 27. 804 applicants, 36% accepted, 70 enrolled. In 2016, 100 master's, 4 doctorates, 56 other advanced degrees awarded. Terminal master's awarded for partial completion of doctoral program. *Degree requirements:* For master's, comprehensive exam (for some programs), thesis (for some programs); for doctorate, comprehensive exam, thesis/dissertation. *Entrance requirements:* For master's and doctorate, GRE, statement of purpose, personal statement, official transcripts, 2 letters of recommendation; for Graduate Certificate, statement of purpose, personal statement, official transcripts. Additional exam requirements/recommendations for international students: Required—TOEFL (recommended minimum score 100 iBT) or IELTS (recommended minimum score of 7.0). *Application deadline:* For fall admission, 2/15 priority date for domestic and international students; for spring admission, 8/15 priority date for domestic and international students. Applications are processed on a rolling basis. Electronic applications accepted. *Expenses:* Contact institution. *Financial support:* In 2016–17, 155 students received support, including 8 fellowships with tuition reimbursements available (averaging $15,242 per year), 26 research assistantships with tuition reimbursements available (averaging $15,242 per year), 20 teaching assistantships with tuition reimbursements available (averaging $15,242 per year); career-related internships or fieldwork, Federal Work-Study, scholarships/grants, health care benefits, unspecified assistantships, and cooperative program also available. Financial award applicants required to submit FAFSA. *Faculty research:* Electrical power systems, optics and photonics, embedded computing systems, computer networks, communication and information theory. *Total annual research expenditures:* $2.4 million. *Unit head:* Dr. Daniel R. Fuhrmann, Department Chair, 906-487-2550, Fax: 906-487-2949, E-mail: fuhrmann@mtu.edu. *Application contact:* Dr. John Pakkala, Graduate Academic Advisor, 906-487-2550, Fax: 906-487-2949, E-mail: jepakkal@mtu.edu.
Website: http://www.mtu.edu/ece/

Michigan Technological University, Graduate School, Interdisciplinary Programs, Houghton, MI 49931. Offers atmospheric sciences (PhD); biochemistry and molecular biology (PhD); computational science and engineering (PhD); data science (MS, Graduate Certificate); engineering (M Eng); environmental engineering (PhD); international profile (Graduate Certificate); nanotechnology (Graduate Certificate); sustainability (Graduate Certificate); sustainable water resources systems (Graduate Certificate). *Program availability:* Part-time. *Faculty:* 122 full-time (26 women), 13 part-time/adjunct. *Students:* 58 full-time (18 women), 17 part-time (5 women); includes 1 minority (Black or African American, non-Hispanic/Latino), 56 international. Average age 28. 395 applicants, 20% accepted, 22 enrolled. In 2016, 3 master's, 7 doctorates, 8 other advanced degrees awarded. Terminal master's awarded for partial completion of doctoral program. *Degree requirements:* For master's, comprehensive exam (for some programs), thesis (for some programs); for doctorate, comprehensive exam, thesis/dissertation. *Entrance requirements:* For master's, doctorate, and Graduate Certificate, GRE, statement of purpose, personal statement, official transcripts, 2-3 letters of recommendation. Additional exam requirements/recommendations for international students: Required—TOEFL or IELTS. *Application deadline:* Applications are processed on a rolling basis. Electronic applications accepted. *Expenses:* Tuition, state resident: full-time $16,290; part-time $905 per credit. Tuition, nonresident: full-time $16,290; part-time $905 per credit. *Required fees:* $248; $124 per term. Tuition and fees vary according to course load and program. *Financial support:* In 2016–17, 54 students received support, including 7 fellowships with tuition reimbursements available (averaging $15,242 per year), 19 research assistantships with tuition reimbursements available (averaging $15,242 per year), 5 teaching assistantships with tuition reimbursements available (averaging $15,242 per year); career-related internships or fieldwork, Federal Work-Study, scholarships/grants, health care benefits, unspecified assistantships, and cooperative program also available. Financial award applicants required to submit FAFSA. *Faculty research:* Big data, atmospheric sciences, bioinformatics and systems biology, molecular dynamics, environmental studies. *Unit head:* Dr. Pushpalathatha Murthy, Dean of the Graduate School/Associate Provost for Graduate Education, 906-487-3007, Fax: 906-487-2284, E-mail: ppmurthy@mtu.edu. *Application contact:* Carol T. Wingerson, Administrative Aide, 906-487-2328, Fax: 906-487-2284, E-mail: gradadms@mtu.edu.

Mississippi State University, Bagley College of Engineering, Department of Electrical and Computer Engineering, Mississippi State, MS 39762. Offers MS, PhD. *Program availability:* Part-time, blended/hybrid learning. *Faculty:* 19 full-time (2 women). *Students:* 53 full-time (10 women), 39 part-time (1 woman); includes 10 minority (6 Black or African American, non-Hispanic/Latino; 2 Asian, non-Hispanic/Latino; 2 Hispanic/Latino), 39 international. Average age 32. 142 applicants, 43% accepted, 25 enrolled. In 2016, 13 master's, 6 doctorates awarded. Terminal master's awarded for partial completion of doctoral program. *Degree requirements:* For master's, comprehensive exam, thesis optional; for doctorate, comprehensive exam, thesis/dissertation, written exam, oral preliminary exam. *Entrance requirements:* For master's, GRE (for graduates from program not accredited by EAC/ABET), minimum GPA of 3.0 on BS; for doctorate, GRE (for graduates from program not accredited by EAC/ABET), minimum GPA of 3.5 on BS or MS. Additional exam requirements/recommendations for international students: Required—TOEFL (minimum score 550 paper-based; 79 iBT); Recommended—IELTS (minimum score 6.5). *Application deadline:* For fall admission, 7/1 for domestic students, 5/1 for international students; for spring admission, 11/1 for domestic students, 9/1 for international students. Applications are processed on a rolling basis. Application fee: $60. Electronic applications accepted. *Expenses:* Tuition, state resident: full-time $7670; part-time $852.50 per credit hour. Tuition, nonresident: full-time $20,790; part-time $2310.50 per credit hour. Part-time tuition and fees vary according to course load. *Financial support:* In 2016–17, 17 research assistantships with full tuition reimbursements (averaging $18,824 per year), 19 teaching assistantships with full tuition reimbursements (averaging $16,011 per year) were awarded; Federal Work-Study, institutionally sponsored loans, scholarships/grants, and unspecified assistantships also available. Financial award application deadline: 4/1; financial award applicants required to submit FAFSA. *Faculty research:* Digital computing, power, controls, communication systems, microelectronics. *Total annual research expenditures:* $12.7 million. *Unit head:* Dr. Nicholas H. Younan, Jr., Professor and Department Head, 662-325-3912, Fax: 662-325-2298, E-mail: ece-head@ece.msstate.edu. *Application contact:* Doretta Martin, Senior Admissions Assistant, 662-325-9514, E-mail: dmartin@grad.msstate.edu.
Website: http://www.ece.msstate.edu/

Missouri University of Science and Technology, Graduate School, Department of Electrical and Computer Engineering, Rolla, MO 65409. Offers computer engineering (MS, DE, PhD); electrical engineering (MS, DE, PhD). *Program availability:* Part-time, evening/weekend. Terminal master's awarded for partial completion of doctoral program. *Degree requirements:* For master's, thesis optional; for doctorate, comprehensive exam, thesis/dissertation, departmental qualifying exam. *Entrance requirements:* For master's, GRE General Test (minimum score 1100 verbal and quantitative, writing 4.5); for doctorate, GRE General Test (minimum score: verbal and quantitative 1100, writing 3.5). Additional exam requirements/recommendations for international students: Required—TOEFL (minimum score 550 paper-based). Electronic applications accepted. *Faculty research:* Power systems, computer/communication networks, intelligent control/robotics, robust control, nanotechnologies.

Montana State University, The Graduate School, College of Engineering, Department of Electrical and Computer Engineering, Bozeman, MT 59717. Offers electrical engineering (MS); engineering (PhD), including electrical and computer engineering option. *Program availability:* Part-time. *Degree requirements:* For master's, comprehensive exam, thesis (for some programs); for doctorate, comprehensive exam, thesis/dissertation. *Entrance requirements:* For master's, GRE, BS in electrical or computer engineering or related field; for doctorate, GRE, MS in electrical or computer engineering or related field. Additional exam requirements/recommendations for international students: Required—TOEFL (minimum score 550 paper-based). Electronic applications accepted. *Faculty research:* Optics and optoelectonics, communications and signal processing, microfabrication, complex systems and control, energy systems.

Naval Postgraduate School, Departments and Academic Groups, Department of Electrical and Computer Engineering, Monterey, CA 93943-5216. Offers computer engineering (MS); electrical engineer (EE); electrical engineering (PhD); engineering acoustics (MS); engineering science (MS). Program only open to commissioned officers of the United States and friendly nations and selected United States federal civilian employees. *Accreditation:* ABET (one or more programs are accredited). *Program availability:* Part-time, online learning. *Degree requirements:* For master's and EE, thesis (for some programs), capstone project or research/dissertation paper (for some programs); for doctorate, thesis/dissertation. *Faculty research:* Theory and design of digital communication systems; behavior modeling for detection, identification, prediction and reaction in artificial intelligence (AI) systems solutions; waveform design for target class discrimination with closed-loop radar; iterative technique for system identification with adaptive signal design.

New Jersey Institute of Technology, Newark College of Engineering, Newark, NJ 07102. Offers biomedical engineering (MS, PhD); chemical engineering (MS, PhD); computer engineering (MS, PhD); electrical engineering (MS, PhD); engineering management (MS); environmental engineering (PhD); healthcare systems management (MS); industrial engineering (MS, PhD); Internet engineering (MS); manufacturing engineering (MS); mechanical engineering (MS, PhD); occupational safety and health engineering (MS); pharmaceutical bioprocessing (MS); pharmaceutical engineering (MS); pharmaceutical systems management (MS); power and energy systems (MS); telecommunications (MS); transportation (MS, PhD). *Program availability:* Part-time, evening/weekend. *Faculty:* 146 full-time (21 women), 119 part-time/adjunct (10 women). *Students:* 804 full-time (191 women), 550 part-time (129 women); includes 357 minority (82 Black or African American, non-Hispanic/Latino; 1 American Indian or Alaska Native, non-Hispanic/Latino; 138 Asian, non-Hispanic/Latino; 114 Hispanic/Latino; 22 Two or more races, non-Hispanic/Latino), 675 international. Average age 27. 2,959 applicants, 51% accepted, 442 enrolled. In 2016, 595 master's, 29 doctorates awarded. Terminal master's awarded for partial completion of doctoral program. *Degree requirements:* For master's, thesis optional; for doctorate, thesis/dissertation. *Entrance requirements:* For master's, GRE General Test; for doctorate, GRE General Test, minimum graduate GPA of 3.5. Additional exam requirements/recommendations for international students: Required—TOEFL (minimum score 550 paper-based; 79 iBT). *Application deadline:* For fall admission, 6/1 priority date for domestic students, 5/1 priority date for international students; for spring admission, 11/15 priority date for domestic and international students. Applications are processed on a rolling basis. Application fee: $75. Electronic applications accepted. *Expenses:* Contact institution. *Financial support:* In 2016–17, 172 students received support, including 1 fellowship (averaging $1,528 per year), 79 research assistantships (averaging $13,336 per year), 92 teaching assistantships (averaging $20,619 per year); scholarships/grants also available. Financial award application deadline: 1/15. *Faculty research:* Nonlinear signal processing, intelligent medical image analysis, calibration issues in coherent localization, computer-aided design, neural network for tool wear measurement. *Total annual research expenditures:* $11.1 million. *Unit head:* Dr. Moshe Kam, Dean, 973-596-5534, E-mail: moshe.kam@njit.edu. *Application contact:* Stephen Eck, Director of Admissions, 973-596-3300, Fax: 973-596-3461, E-mail: admissions@njit.edu.
Website: http://engineering.njit.edu/

New Mexico State University, College of Engineering, Klipsch School of Electrical and Computer Engineering, Las Cruces, NM 88003. Offers MSEE, PhD, Graduate Certificate. *Program availability:* Part-time, evening/weekend, 100% online. *Faculty:* 18 full-time (1 woman), 1 part-time/adjunct (0 women). *Students:* 73 full-time (11 women), 44 part-time (10 women); includes 30 minority (4 Black or African American, non-Hispanic/Latino; 1 American Indian or Alaska Native, non-Hispanic/Latino; 1 Asian, non-Hispanic/Latino; 22 Hispanic/Latino; 2 Two or more races, non-Hispanic/Latino), 55 international. Average age 30. 125 applicants, 48% accepted, 26 enrolled. In 2016, 37 master's, 6 doctorates awarded. Terminal master's awarded for partial completion of doctoral program. *Degree requirements:* For master's, thesis (for some programs), final oral or written exam; for doctorate, comprehensive exam, thesis/dissertation, qualifying exam. *Entrance requirements:* For master's, GRE, minimum GPA of 3.0; for doctorate, minimum GPA of 3.0. Additional exam requirements/recommendations for international students: Required—TOEFL (minimum score 550 paper-based; 79 iBT), IELTS (minimum score 6.5). *Application deadline:* For fall admission, 3/1 priority date for domestic and international students; for spring admission, 8/1 priority date for domestic and international students. Applications are processed on a rolling basis. Application fee: $40 ($50 for international students). Electronic applications accepted. *Expenses:* Tuition, state resident: full-time $4086. Tuition, nonresident: full-time $14,254. *Required fees:* $853. Tuition and fees vary according to course load. *Financial support:* In 2016–17, 66 students received support, including 1 fellowship (averaging $4,088 per year), 23 research assistantships (averaging $13,395 per year), 20 teaching assistantships (averaging $11,971 per year); career-related internships or fieldwork, Federal Work-Study, scholarships/grants, traineeships, health care benefits, and unspecified assistantships also available. Support available to part-time students. Financial award application deadline: 3/1. *Faculty research:* Image and digital signal processing, energy systems, wireless communications, analog and mixed-signal VLSI design, electro-optics. *Total annual research expenditures:* $1.5 million. *Unit head:* Dr. Satishkuma Ranade, Department Head, 575-646-3115, Fax: 575-646-1435, E-mail: sranade@nmsu.edu. *Application contact:* 575-646-3115, Fax: 575-646-1435, E-mail: eceoffice@nmsu.edu.
Website: http://ece.nmsu.edu

New York Institute of Technology, School of Engineering and Computing Sciences, Department of Electrical and Computer Engineering, Old Westbury, NY 11568-8000. Offers MS. *Program availability:* Part-time, evening/weekend. *Faculty:* 10 full-time (2 women), 8 part-time/adjunct (all women). *Students:* 193 full-time (38 women), 74 part-time (17 women); includes 22 minority (9 Black or African American, non-Hispanic/Latino; 7 Asian, non-Hispanic/Latino; 6 Hispanic/Latino), 233 international. Average age 24. 627 applicants, 65% accepted, 57 enrolled. In 2016, 175 master's awarded. *Degree requirements:* For master's, thesis or alternative. *Entrance requirements:* For master's, BS in electrical or computer engineering or closely-related field; minimum undergraduate GPA of 2.85. Additional exam requirements/recommendations for international students: Required—TOEFL (minimum score 79 iBT), IELTS (minimum score 6). *Application deadline:* For fall admission, 7/1 for domestic students, 6/1 for international students; for spring admission, 12/1 for domestic and international students. Applications are processed on a rolling basis. Application fee: $50. Electronic applications accepted. *Expenses:* $1,215 per credit. *Financial support:* Fellowships with partial tuition reimbursements, teaching assistantships with partial tuition reimbursements, career-related internships or fieldwork, Federal Work-Study, scholarships/grants, tuition waivers (full and partial), and unspecified assistantships available. Support available to part-time students. Financial award application deadline: 3/1; financial award applicants required to submit FAFSA. *Faculty research:* Securing inter-vehicular networks with time and driver identity considerations; security of mobile devices and wireless networks; implantable wireless system to study gastric neurophysiology; model-based software for configuring single switch scanning systems; family-based framework of quality assurance for biomedical ontologies. *Unit head:* Dr. Yoshikazu Saito, Department Chairperson, 212-261-1650, Fax: 516-686-7439, E-mail: ysaito@nyit.edu. *Application contact:* Alice Dolitsky, Director, Graduate Admissions, 516-686-7520, Fax: 516-686-1116, E-mail: nyitgrad@nyit.edu.
Website: http://www.nyit.edu/engineering/electrical_and_computer_engineering

New York University, Polytechnic School of Engineering, Department of Electrical and Computer Engineering, Major in Computer Engineering, New York, NY 10012-1019. Offers MS, Certificate. *Program availability:* Online learning. *Degree requirements:* For master's, comprehensive exam (for some programs), thesis (for some programs). *Entrance requirements:* For master's, BS in electrical engineering. Additional exam requirements/recommendations for international students: Required—TOEFL (minimum score 550 paper-based; 80 iBT); Recommended—IELTS (minimum score 6.5). Electronic applications accepted.

Norfolk State University, School of Graduate Studies, School of Science and Technology, Program in Electronics Engineering, Norfolk, VA 23504. Offers MS.

North Carolina Agricultural and Technical State University, School of Graduate Studies, College of Engineering, Department of Electrical and Computer Engineering, Greensboro, NC 27411. Offers electrical engineering (MSEE, PhD), including communications and signal processing, computer engineering, electronic and optical materials and devices, power systems and control. *Program availability:* Part-time. *Degree requirements:* For master's, project, thesis defense; for doctorate, thesis/dissertation. *Entrance requirements:* For master's, GRE General Test, GRE Subject Test, minimum GPA of 2.8; for doctorate, GRE General Test, minimum GPA of 3.0. *Faculty research:* Semiconductor compounds, VLSI design, image processing, optical systems and devices, fault-tolerant computing.

North Carolina State University, Graduate School, College of Engineering, Department of Electrical and Computer Engineering, Program in Computer Engineering, Raleigh, NC 27695. Offers MS, PhD. *Degree requirements:* For master's, thesis (for some programs); for doctorate, thesis/dissertation. *Entrance requirements:* For master's and doctorate, GRE. Additional exam requirements/recommendations for international students: Required—TOEFL (minimum score 575 paper-based). Electronic applications accepted. *Faculty research:* Computer architecture, parallel processing, embedded computer systems, VLSI design, computer networking performance and control.

North Dakota State University, College of Graduate and Interdisciplinary Studies, College of Engineering, Department of Electrical and Computer Engineering, Fargo, ND 58102. Offers ME, MS, PhD. *Program availability:* Part-time. Terminal master's awarded for partial completion of doctoral program. *Degree requirements:* For master's, comprehensive exam, thesis; for doctorate, comprehensive exam, thesis/dissertation. *Entrance requirements:* Additional exam requirements/recommendations for international students: Required—TOEFL (minimum score 525 paper-based; 71 iBT). Electronic applications accepted. *Faculty research:* Computers, power and control systems, microwaves, communications and signal processing, bioengineering.

Northeastern University, College of Engineering, Boston, MA 02115-5096. Offers bioengineering (MS, PhD); chemical engineering (MS, PhD); civil engineering (MS, PhD); computer engineering (PhD); computer systems engineering (MS); electrical and computer engineering (MS); electrical and computer engineering leadership (MS); electrical engineering (PhD); energy systems (MS); engineering and public policy (MS); engineering management (MS, Certificate); environmental engineering (MS); industrial engineering (MS, PhD); information assurance (PhD); information systems (MS); interdisciplinary engineering (PhD); mechanical engineering (PhD); operations research (MS); telecommunication systems management (MS). *Program availability:* Part-time, online learning. *Faculty:* 202 full-time (59 women), 53 part-time/adjunct (9 women). *Students:* 2,982 full-time (954 women), 192 part-time (38 women). In 2016, 851 master's, 74 doctorates awarded. Application fee: $75. Electronic applications accepted. *Expenses:* $1,471 per credit. *Financial support:* Fellowships, research assistantships, teaching assistantships, career-related internships or fieldwork, scholarships/grants, health care benefits, tuition waivers, and unspecified assistantships available. Support available to part-time students. Financial award applicants required to submit FAFSA. *Unit head:* Dr. Nadine Aubry, Dean, College of Engineering. *Application contact:* Jeffery Hengel, Director of Graduate Admissions, 617-373-2711, E-mail: j.hengel@northeastern.edu.
Website: http://www.coe.neu.edu/academics/graduate-school-engineering

Northern Arizona University, Graduate College, College of Engineering, Forestry, and Natural Sciences, Programs in Engineering, Flagstaff, AZ 86011. Offers civil engineering (M Eng, MSE); computer science (MSE); electrical and computer engineering (M Eng, MSE); engineering (M Eng, MSE); environmental engineering (M Eng, MSE); mechanical engineering (M Eng, MSE). *Program availability:* Part-time, online learning. *Degree requirements:* For master's, thesis. *Entrance requirements:* For master's, GRE General Test. Additional exam requirements/recommendations for international students: Required—TOEFL (minimum score 550 paper-based; 80 iBT), IELTS (minimum score 7). Electronic applications accepted. *Expenses:* Tuition, state resident: full-time $8971; part-time $444 per credit hour. Tuition, nonresident: full-time $20,958; part-time $1164 per credit hour. *Required fees:* $1018; $644 per credit hour. Tuition and fees vary according to course load, campus/location and program.

Northwestern Polytechnic University, School of Engineering, Fremont, CA 94539-7482. Offers computer engineering (DCE); computer science (MS); computer systems engineering (MS); electrical engineering (MS). *Program availability:* Part-time, evening/weekend. *Degree requirements:* For master's, thesis optional; for doctorate, thesis/dissertation. *Entrance requirements:* For master's, minimum GPA of 3.0. Additional exam requirements/recommendations for international students: Required—TOEFL (minimum score 550 paper-based; 79 iBT). *Faculty research:* Computer networking, database design, Internet technology, software engineering, digital signal processing.

Northwestern University, McCormick School of Engineering and Applied Science, Department of Electrical Engineering and Computer Science, Evanston, IL 60208. Offers computer engineering (MS, PhD); computer science (MS, PhD); electrical engineering (MS, PhD); information technology (MS). MS and PhD admissions and degrees offered through The Graduate School. *Program availability:* Part-time. Terminal master's awarded for partial completion of doctoral program. *Degree requirements:* For master's, comprehensive exam (for some programs), thesis optional; for doctorate, comprehensive exam, thesis/dissertation. *Entrance requirements:* For master's and doctorate, GRE General Test. Additional exam requirements/recommendations for international students: Required—TOEFL (minimum score 577 paper-based; 90 iBT), IELTS (minimum score 7). Electronic applications accepted. *Faculty research:* Solid state and photonics; computing, algorithms, and applications; computer engineering and systems; cognitive systems; graphics and interactive media; signals and systems.

Oakland University, Graduate Study and Lifelong Learning, School of Engineering and Computer Science, Department of Computer Science and Engineering, Rochester, MI 48309-4401. Offers computer science (MS); computer science and informatics (PhD); software engineering and information technology (MS). *Program availability:* Part-time, evening/weekend. *Entrance requirements:* For master's, minimum GPA of 3.0. Electronic applications accepted. *Expenses:* Contact institution.

Oakland University, Graduate Study and Lifelong Learning, School of Engineering and Computer Science, Department of Electrical and Computer Engineering, Rochester, MI 48309-4401. Offers electrical and computer engineering (MS, PhD); embedded systems (MS); mechatronics (MS). *Program availability:* Part-time, evening/weekend. *Entrance requirements:* For master's, minimum GPA of 3.0. Additional exam requirements/ recommendations for international students: Required—TOEFL (minimum score 550 paper-based). Electronic applications accepted. *Expenses:* Contact institution.

The Ohio State University, Graduate School, College of Engineering, Department of Computer Science and Engineering, Columbus, OH 43210. Offers MS, PhD. *Faculty:* 43. *Students:* 290 full-time (49 women), 8 part-time (0 women). Average age 26. In 2016, 94 master's, 32 doctorates awarded. *Degree requirements:* For master's, thesis optional; for doctorate, thesis/dissertation. *Entrance requirements:* For master's and doctorate, GRE (minimum score Quantitative 750 old, 159 new; Verbal 500 old, 155 new; Analytical Writing 3.0); GRE Subject Test in computer science (strongly recommended for those whose undergraduate degree is not in computer science). Additional exam requirements/recommendations for international students: Required—TOEFL (minimum score 550 paper-based; 79 iBT), Michigan English Language Assessment Battery (minimum score 82); Recommended—IELTS (minimum score 7). *Application deadline:* For fall admission, 12/13 priority date for domestic students, 11/30 priority date for international students. Applications are processed on a rolling basis. Application fee: $60 ($70 for international students). Electronic applications accepted. *Financial support:* Fellowships with tuition reimbursements, research assistantships with tuition reimbursements, teaching assistantships with tuition reimbursements, career-related internships or fieldwork, Federal Work-Study, institutionally sponsored loans, unspecified assistantships, and administrative assistantships available. Support available to part-time students. Financial award application deadline: 1/15. *Unit head:* Dr. Xiadong Zhang, Professor/Chair, 614-292-2770, E-mail: zhang.574@osu.edu. *Application contact:* Graduate and Professional Admissions, 614-292-9444, Fax: 614-292-3895, E-mail: gpadmissions@osu.edu.
Website: http://www.cse.osu.edu

The Ohio State University, Graduate School, College of Engineering, Department of Electrical and Computer Engineering, Columbus, OH 43210. Offers electrical and computer engineering (MS, PhD); electrical engineering (MS, PhD). *Program availability:* Part-time. *Faculty:* 62. *Students:* 421 full-time (78 women), 33 part-time (11 women); includes 6 minority (all Two or more races, non-Hispanic/Latino), 344 international. Average age 25. In 2016, 151 master's, 42 doctorates awarded. Terminal master's awarded for partial completion of doctoral program. *Degree requirements:* For master's, thesis optional; for doctorate, thesis/dissertation. *Entrance requirements:* For master's, GRE General Test (for all graduates of foreign universities and for applicants if undergraduate GPA below 3.2); for doctorate, GRE General Test (for all graduates of foreign universities and for applicants if graduate work GPA is below 3.5). Additional exam requirements/recommendations for international students: Required—TOEFL (minimum score 580 paper-based; 92 iBT); Recommended—IELTS (minimum score 7.5). *Application deadline:* For fall admission, 11/30 priority date for domestic and international students. Applications are processed on a rolling basis. Application fee: $60 ($70 for international students). Electronic applications accepted. *Financial support:* Fellowships with full tuition reimbursements, research assistantships with full tuition reimbursements, teaching assistantships with full tuition reimbursements, career-related internships or fieldwork, Federal Work-Study, institutionally sponsored loans, scholarships/grants, traineeships, health care benefits, and unspecified assistantships available. Support available to part-time students. *Unit head:* Dr. Joel T. Johnson, Chair, 614-292-1563, E-mail: johnson.1374@osu.edu. *Application contact:* Electrical and Computer Engineering Graduate Program, 614-292-2572, Fax: 614-292-7596, E-mail: ecegrad@ece.osu.edu.
Website: http://ece.osu.edu/

Oklahoma Christian University, Graduate School of Engineering and Computer Science, Oklahoma City, OK 73136-1100. Offers electrical and computer engineering (MSE); engineering management (MSE); mechanical engineering (MSE); software engineering (MSCS, MSE). *Program availability:* Part-time. *Faculty:* 8 full-time (1 woman), 7 part-time/adjunct (0 women). *Students:* 187 full-time (27 women), 85 part-time (12 women). Average age 25. 255 applicants, 33% accepted, 69 enrolled. In 2016, 188 master's awarded. *Entrance requirements:* Additional exam requirements/ recommendations for international students: Required—TOEFL (minimum score 550 paper-based). *Application deadline:* Applications are processed on a rolling basis. Application fee: $25. Electronic applications accepted. *Expenses:* Contact institution. *Unit head:* Mary Ann Brown, Director for Graduate School Engineering, 405-425-5579. *Application contact:* Angie Ricketts, Admissions Counselor, 405-425-5587, E-mail: angie.ricketts@oc.edu.
Website: http://www.oc.edu/academics/graduate/engineering/

Oklahoma State University, College of Engineering, Architecture and Technology, School of Electrical and Computer Engineering, Stillwater, OK 74078. Offers MS, PhD. *Program availability:* Online learning. *Faculty:* 22 full-time (2 women). *Students:* 53 full-time (12 women), 48 part-time (11 women); includes 8 minority (1 Black or African American, non-Hispanic/Latino; 2 Asian, non-Hispanic/Latino; 4 Hispanic/Latino; 1 Two or more races, non-Hispanic/Latino), 69 international. Average age 28. 285 applicants, 18% accepted, 24 enrolled. In 2016, 88 master's, 11 doctorates awarded. *Degree requirements:* For master's, thesis or alternative; for doctorate, comprehensive exam, thesis/dissertation. *Entrance requirements:* For master's and doctorate, GRE or GMAT. Additional exam requirements/recommendations for international students: Required—TOEFL (minimum score 550 paper-based; 79 iBT). *Application deadline:* For fall admission, 3/1 priority date for international students; for spring admission, 8/1 priority date for international students. Applications are processed on a rolling basis. Application fee: $40 ($75 for international students). Electronic applications accepted. *Expenses:* Tuition, state resident: full-time $3775; part-time $209.70 per credit hour. Tuition, nonresident: full-time $14,851; part-time $825.05 per credit hour. *Required fees:* $2027; $112.60 per credit hour. Tuition and fees vary according to campus/location. *Financial support:* In 2016–17, 18 research assistantships (averaging $10,061 per year), 21 teaching assistantships (averaging $6,318 per year) were awarded; career-related internships or fieldwork, Federal Work-Study, scholarships/grants, health care benefits, tuition waivers (partial), and unspecified assistantships also available. Support available to part-time students. Financial award application deadline: 3/1; financial award applicants required to submit FAFSA. *Unit head:* Dr. Jeffrey Young, Department Head, 405-744-5151, Fax: 405-744-9198, E-mail: jl.young@okstate.edu. *Application contact:* Dr. R. G. Ramakumar, Graduate Coordinator, 405-744-5157, Fax: 405-744-9198, E-mail: ramakum@okstate.edu.
Website: http://www.ece.okstate.edu

Old Dominion University, Frank Batten College of Engineering and Technology, Graduate Program in Electrical and Computer Engineering, Norfolk, VA 23529. Offers ME, MS, D Eng, PhD. *Program availability:* Part-time, online learning. *Faculty:* 23 full-time (2 women), 1 part-time/adjunct (0 women). *Students:* 24 full-time (6 women), 62 part-time (12 women); includes 14 minority (7 Black or African American, non-Hispanic/Latino; 4 Asian, non-Hispanic/Latino; 2 Hispanic/Latino; 1 Two or more races, non-Hispanic/Latino), 40 international. Average age 30. 63 applicants, 63% accepted, 9 enrolled. In 2016, 16 master's, 5 doctorates awarded. *Degree requirements:* For master's, comprehensive exam (for some programs), thesis (for some programs); for doctorate, thesis/dissertation, candidacy exam, diagnostic exam. *Entrance requirements:* For master's, GRE, two letters of recommendation, resume, personal statement of objectives; for doctorate, GRE, three letters of recommendation, resume, personal statement of objectives. Additional exam requirements/recommendations for international students: Required—TOEFL (minimum score 550 paper-based; 79 iBT), IELTS. *Application deadline:* For fall admission, 6/1 for domestic students, 4/15 for international students; for spring admission, 11/1 for domestic students, 10/1 for international students. Applications are processed on a rolling basis. Application fee: $50. Electronic applications accepted. *Expenses:* Tuition, state resident: full-time $8604; part-time $478 per credit hour. Tuition, nonresident: full-time $21,510; part-time $1195 per credit hour. *Required fees:* $66 per semester. Tuition and fees vary according to campus/location, program and reciprocity agreements. *Financial support:* In 2016–17, 26 research assistantships with full and partial tuition reimbursements (averaging $15,000 per year), 27 teaching assistantships with full and partial tuition reimbursements (averaging $15,000 per year) were awarded; scholarships/grants and unspecified assistantships also available. Financial award application deadline: 2/15. *Faculty research:* Cyber-physical systems, communications and networking, computer vision, computational modeling, controls, security and hardware, medical/biological systems, methods, and devices, bioelectrics, medical image processing, plasma medicine, signal processing for medical and biological systems, solid state and physical electronics, photovoltaics, plasma processing, thin films and nanotechnology. *Total annual research expenditures:* $2.3 million. *Unit head:* Dr. Chunsheng Xin, Graduate Program Director, 757-683-5294, Fax: 757-683-3220, E-mail: cxin@odu.edu.
Website: http://www.odu.edu/ece/

Oregon Health & Science University, School of Medicine, Graduate Programs in Medicine, Department of Computer Science and Engineering, Portland, OR 97239-3098. Offers computer science and engineering (MS, PhD); electrical engineering (MS, PhD). *Program availability:* Part-time. *Faculty:* 7 full-time (2 women), 1 part-time/adjunct (0 women). *Students:* 10 full-time (3 women), 14 part-time (5 women); includes 3 minority (all Asian, non-Hispanic/Latino), 10 international. Average age 33. 10 applicants, 3 enrolled. In 2016, 5 master's, 1 doctorate awarded. Terminal master's awarded for partial completion of doctoral program. *Degree requirements:* For master's, thesis (for some programs); for doctorate, comprehensive exam, thesis/dissertation, qualifying exam. *Entrance requirements:* For master's and doctorate, GRE General Test (minimum scores: 153 Verbal/148 Quantitative/4.5 Analytical). Additional exam requirements/recommendations for international students: Required—IELTS or TOEFL. *Application deadline:* For fall admission, 7/15 for domestic students, 5/15 for international students; for winter admission, 10/15 for domestic students, 9/15 for international students; for spring admission, 1/15 for domestic students, 12/15 for international students. Applications are processed on a rolling basis. Application fee: $70. Electronic applications accepted. *Financial support:* Health care benefits, tuition waivers (full), and full-tuition and stipends (for PhD students) available. Financial award applicants required to submit FAFSA. *Faculty research:* Natural language processing, speech signal processing, computational biology, autism spectrum disorders, hearing and speaking disorders. *Unit head:* Dr. Peter Heeman, Program Director, 503-748-1635, E-mail: heemanp@ohsu.edu. *Application contact:* Pat Dickerson, Administrative Coordinator, 503-748-1635, E-mail: dickersp@ohsu.edu.

Oregon State University, College of Engineering, Program in Electrical and Computer Engineering, Corvallis, OR 97331. Offers analog and mixed signal (M Eng, MS, PhD); artificial intelligence and machine learning (M Eng, MS, PhD); communications and signal processing (M Eng, MS, PhD); computer systems (M Eng, MS, PhD); energy systems (M Eng, MS, PhD); materials and devices (M Eng, MS, PhD); radio frequencies/microwaves/optoelectronics (M Eng, MS, PhD). *Faculty:* 58 full-time (9 women), 3 part-time/adjunct (1 woman). *Students:* 202 full-time (26 women), 31 part-time (9 women); includes 11 minority (9 Asian, non-Hispanic/Latino; 2 Two or more races, non-Hispanic/Latino), 182 international. Average age 28. 535 applicants, 11% accepted, 49 enrolled. In 2016, 52 master's, 8 doctorates awarded. *Entrance requirements:* For master's and doctorate, GRE. Additional exam requirements/ recommendations for international students: Required—TOEFL (minimum score 600 paper-based; 80 iBT), IELTS (minimum score 7). *Application deadline:* For fall admission, 1/15 for domestic students. Application fee: $75 ($85 for international students). *Expenses:* $14,130 resident full-time tuition, $23,769 non-resident. *Financial support:* Application deadline: 1/15. *Unit head:* V. John Mathews, Professor and School Head. *Application contact:* Graduate Coordinator, 541-737-7234, E-mail: eecs.gradinfo@oregonstate.edu.
Website: http://eecs.oregonstate.edu/current-students/graduate/ece-program

Oregon State University, College of Engineering, Program in Materials Science, Corvallis, OR 97331. Offers chemical engineering (MS, PhD); chemistry (MS, PhD); civil engineering (MS, PhD); electrical and computer engineering (MS, PhD); forest products (MS, PhD); mathematics (MS, PhD); mechanical engineering (MS, PhD); nuclear engineering (MS); physics (MS, PhD). *Faculty:* 52 full-time (12 women), 3 part-time/ adjunct (0 women). *Students:* 34 full-time (8 women), 10 part-time (3 women); includes 7 minority (4 Hispanic/Latino; 3 Two or more races, non-Hispanic/Latino), 15 international. Average age 30. 78 applicants, 24% accepted, 10 enrolled. In 2016, 7 master's, 6 doctorates awarded. *Degree requirements:* For master's, thesis or alternative. *Entrance requirements:* For master's and doctorate, GRE. Additional exam requirements/ recommendations for international students: Required—TOEFL (minimum score 80 iBT), IELTS (minimum score 6.5). *Application deadline:* For fall admission, 8/1 for domestic students, 4/1 for international students; for winter admission, 12/1 for domestic students, 7/1 for international students; for spring admission, 2/1 for domestic students, 10/1 for international students; for summer admission, 5/1 for domestic students, 1/1 for international students. Application fee: $75 ($85 for international students). *Expenses:* $14,130 resident full-time tuition, $23,769 non-resident. *Financial support:* Fellowships, research assistantships, teaching assistantships, Federal Work-Study, and institutionally sponsored loans available. Support available to part-time students. Financial award application deadline: 1/15. *Unit head:* Dr. Harriet Nembhard, School Head. *Application contact:* Jean Robinson, Advisor, E-mail: jean.robinson@oregonstate.edu.
Website: http://matsci.oregonstate.edu

Polytechnic University of Puerto Rico, Graduate School, Hato Rey, PR 00918. Offers business administration (MBA), including computer information systems, general management, management of information systems, management of international enterprises; civil engineering (ME, MS); computer engineering (ME, MS); computer science (MCS, MS); electrical engineering (ME, MS); engineering management (MEM); environmental management (MEM); landscape architecture (M Land Arch); manufacturing competitiveness (MMC, MS); manufacturing engineering (ME, MS);

mechanical engineering (M Mech E). *Program availability:* Part-time, evening/weekend. *Entrance requirements:* For master's, 3 letters of recommendation.

Portland State University, Graduate Studies, Maseeh College of Engineering and Computer Science, Department of Electrical and Computer Engineering, Portland, OR 97207-0751. Offers M Eng, MS, PhD. *Program availability:* Part-time, evening/weekend. *Faculty:* 22 full-time (2 women), 10 part-time/adjunct (1 woman). *Students:* 186 full-time (47 women), 134 part-time (25 women); includes 34 minority (2 Black or African American, non-Hispanic/Latino; 18 Asian, non-Hispanic/Latino; 8 Hispanic/Latino; 6 Two or more races, non-Hispanic/Latino), 203 international. Average age 29. 465 applicants, 38% accepted, 113 enrolled. In 2016, 127 master's, 7 doctorates awarded. *Degree requirements:* For master's, variable foreign language requirement, oral exam; for doctorate, one foreign language, comprehensive exam, thesis/dissertation, oral and written exams. *Entrance requirements:* For master's, GRE, minimum GPA of 2.75; for doctorate, GRE General Test, GRE Subject Test, master's degree in electrical engineering or related field, 3 reference letters, statement of purpose, writing sample. Additional exam requirements/recommendations for international students: Required—TOEFL (minimum score 550 paper-based; 80 iBT). *Application deadline:* For fall admission, 2/1 for domestic and international students; for winter admission, 8/15 for domestic and international students; for spring admission, 11/1 for domestic and international students. Application fee: $65. *Expenses:* Contact institution. *Financial support:* In 2016–17, 12 research assistantships with tuition reimbursements (averaging $9,339 per year), 25 teaching assistantships with tuition reimbursements (averaging $3,226 per year) were awarded; career-related internships or fieldwork, Federal Work-Study, scholarships/grants, and unspecified assistantships also available. Support available to part-time students. Financial award application deadline: 3/1; financial award applicants required to submit FAFSA. *Faculty research:* Optics and laser systems, design automation, VLSI design, computer systems, power electronics. *Total annual research expenditures:* $1.5 million. *Unit head:* Dr. James McNames, Chair, 503-725-5390, Fax: 503-725-3807, E-mail: mcnames@ece.pdx.edu. *Application contact:* Melisa Cehajic, Graduate Coordinator, 503-725-3002, Fax: 503-725-3807, E-mail: melisa@pdx.edu.
Website: http://www.pdx.edu/ece/

Purdue University, College of Engineering, School of Electrical and Computer Engineering, West Lafayette, IN 47907-2035. Offers MSECE, PhD. MS and PhD degree programs in biomedical engineering offered jointly with School of Mechanical Engineering and School of Chemical Engineering. *Program availability:* Part-time, online learning. *Faculty:* 129. *Students:* 675. In 2016, 127 master's, 80 doctorates awarded. Terminal master's awarded for partial completion of doctoral program. *Degree requirements:* For master's, thesis optional; for doctorate, thesis/dissertation. *Entrance requirements:* For master's and doctorate, GRE General Test, minimum GPA of 3.25. *Application deadline:* For fall admission, 12/15 priority date for domestic and international students; for spring admission, 9/15 for domestic and international students. Application fee: $60 ($75 for international students). Electronic applications accepted. *Financial support:* Fellowships with full and partial tuition reimbursements, research assistantships with full and partial tuition reimbursements, teaching assistantships with full and partial tuition reimbursements, scholarships/grants, health care benefits, and unspecified assistantships available. Financial award application deadline: 12/15. *Faculty research:* Automatic control, biomedical imaging and sensing, communications, networking, signal and image processing, computer engineering, education, fields and optics, microelectronics and nanotechnology, power and energy systems, VLSI and circuit design. *Unit head:* Ragu Balakrishnan, Head/Professor, E-mail: ragu@ecn.purdue.edu. *Application contact:* Debra Bowman, Graduate Admissions, E-mail: ecegrad@purdue.edu.
Website: https://engineering.purdue.edu/ECE

Purdue University Northwest, Graduate Studies Office, School of Engineering, Mathematics, and Science, Department of Engineering, Hammond, IN 46323-2094. Offers computer engineering (MSE); electrical engineering (MSE); engineering (MS); mechanical engineering (MSE). *Program availability:* Evening/weekend. *Entrance requirements:* Additional exam requirements/recommendations for international students: Required—TOEFL.

Queen's University at Kingston, School of Graduate Studies, Faculty of Applied Science, Department of Electrical and Computer Engineering, Kingston, ON K7L 3N6, Canada. Offers M Eng, M Sc, M Sc Eng, PhD. *Program availability:* Part-time. *Degree requirements:* For master's, thesis optional; for doctorate, comprehensive exam, thesis/dissertation. *Entrance requirements:* Additional exam requirements/recommendations for international students: Required—TOEFL (minimum score 580 paper-based). *Faculty research:* Communications and signal processing systems, computer engineering systems.

Rensselaer at Hartford, Department of Engineering, Program in Computer and Systems Engineering, Hartford, CT 06120-2991. Offers ME. *Entrance requirements:* For master's, GRE.

Rensselaer Polytechnic Institute, Graduate School, School of Engineering, Program in Computer and Systems Engineering, Troy, NY 12180-3590. Offers M Eng, MS, D Eng, PhD. *Faculty:* 39 full-time (7 women), 1 part-time/adjunct (0 women). *Students:* 13 full-time (4 women), 2 part-time (0 women), 10 international. Average age 27. 49 applicants, 24% accepted, 5 enrolled. In 2016, 2 master's, 1 doctorate awarded. Terminal master's awarded for partial completion of doctoral program. *Degree requirements:* For master's, thesis (for some programs); for doctorate, thesis/dissertation. *Entrance requirements:* For master's and doctorate, GRE. Additional exam requirements/recommendations for international students: Required—TOEFL (minimum score 570 paper-based; 88 iBT), IELTS (minimum score 6.5), PTE (minimum score 60). *Application deadline:* For fall admission, 1/1 priority date for domestic and international students; for spring admission, 8/15 priority date for domestic and international students. Applications are processed on a rolling basis. Application fee: $75. Electronic applications accepted. *Expenses: Tuition:* Full-time $49,520; part-time $2060 per credit hour. *Required fees:* $2617. *Financial support:* In 2016–17, research assistantships (averaging $22,000 per year), teaching assistantships (averaging $22,000 per year) were awarded; fellowships also available. Financial award application deadline: 1/1. *Faculty research:* Communications, information, and signals and systems; computer engineering, hardware, and architecture; computer networking; control, robotics, and automation; energy sources and systems; image science: computer vision, image processing, and geographic information science; microelectronics, photonics, VLSI, and mixed-signal design; plasma science and electromagnetics. *Unit head:* Dr. Ken Vastola, Graduate Program Director, 518-576-6074, E-mail: gpd@ecse.rpi.edu. *Application contact:* Office of Graduate Admissions, 518-276-6216, E-mail: gradadmissions@rpi.edu.
Website: http://www.ecse.rpi.edu/

Rice University, Graduate Programs, George R. Brown School of Engineering, Department of Electrical and Computer Engineering, Houston, TX 77251-1892. Offers bioengineering (MS, PhD); circuits, controls, and communication systems (MS, PhD); computer science and engineering (MS, PhD); electrical engineering (MEE); lasers, microwaves, and solid-state electronics (MS, PhD); MBA/MEE. *Program availability:* Part-time. *Degree requirements:* For master's, thesis (for some programs); for doctorate, thesis/dissertation. *Entrance requirements:* For master's and doctorate, GRE General Test, GRE Subject Test, minimum GPA of 3.0. Additional exam requirements/recommendations for international students: Required—TOEFL (minimum score 600 paper-based; 90 iBT). Electronic applications accepted. *Faculty research:* Physical electronics, systems, computer engineering, bioengineering.

Rice University, Graduate Programs, George R. Brown School of Engineering, Program in Computational Science and Engineering, Houston, TX 77251-1892. Offers MCSE.

Rochester Institute of Technology, Graduate Enrollment Services, Kate Gleason College of Engineering, Computer Engineering Department, MS Program in Computer Engineering, Rochester, NY 14623. Offers MS. *Program availability:* Part-time. *Students:* 44 full-time (9 women), 13 part-time (1 woman); includes 5 minority (1 Black or African American, non-Hispanic/Latino; 4 Asian, non-Hispanic/Latino), 36 international. Average age 24. 205 applicants, 16% accepted, 15 enrolled. In 2016, 18 master's awarded. *Degree requirements:* For master's, thesis. *Entrance requirements:* For master's, GRE, minimum GPA of 3.0 (recommended). Additional exam requirements/recommendations for international students: Required—TOEFL (minimum score 550 paper-based; 79 iBT), IELTS (minimum score 6.5), PTE (minimum score 58). *Application deadline:* For fall admission, 2/15 priority date for domestic and international students; for spring admission, 12/15 priority date for domestic and international students. Applications are processed on a rolling basis. Application fee: $60. Electronic applications accepted. *Expenses:* $1,742 per credit hour. *Financial support:* In 2016–17, 31 students received support. Fellowships, research assistantships with partial tuition reimbursements available, teaching assistantships with partial tuition reimbursements available, career-related internships or fieldwork, scholarships/grants, and unspecified assistantships available. Support available to part-time students. Financial award applicants required to submit FAFSA. *Faculty research:* Computer architecture; integrated circuits and systems; networks and security; computer vision and machine intelligence; signal processing, controls, and embedded systems. *Unit head:* Dr. Dhireesha Kudithipudi, Graduate Program Director, 585-475-5085, E-mail: dxkeec@rit.edu. *Application contact:* Diane Ellison, Associate Vice President, Graduate Enrollment Services, 585-475-2229, Fax: 585-475-7164, E-mail: gradinfo@rit.edu.
Website: https://www.rit.edu/kgcoe/computerengineering/

Rose-Hulman Institute of Technology, Faculty of Engineering and Applied Sciences, Department of Electrical and Computer Engineering, Terre Haute, IN 47803-3999. Offers electrical and computer engineering (M Eng); electrical engineering (MS); systems engineering and management (MS). *Program availability:* Part-time. *Faculty:* 18 full-time (2 women), 1 (woman) part-time/adjunct. *Students:* 7 full-time (3 women), 7 part-time (0 women), 12 international. Average age 25. 17 applicants, 65% accepted, 3 enrolled. In 2016, 7 master's awarded. *Degree requirements:* For master's, thesis (for some programs). *Entrance requirements:* For master's, GRE, minimum GPA of 3.0. Additional exam requirements/recommendations for international students: Required—TOEFL (minimum score 580 paper-based; 92 iBT). *Application deadline:* For fall admission, 2/1 priority date for domestic students. Applications are processed on a rolling basis. Application fee: $0. Electronic applications accepted. *Expenses: Tuition:* Full-time $43,122. *Financial support:* In 2016–17, 14 students received support. Fellowships with tuition reimbursements available, research assistantships with tuition reimbursements available, institutionally sponsored loans, scholarships/grants, and tuition waivers (full and partial) available. *Faculty research:* VLSI, power systems, analog electronics, communications, electromagnetics. *Total annual research expenditures:* $84,698. *Unit head:* Dr. Mario Simoni, Chairman, 812-877-8341, Fax: 812-877-8895, E-mail: simoni@rose-hulman.edu. *Application contact:* Dr. Azad Siahmakoun, Associate Dean of the Faculty, 812-877-8400, Fax: 812-877-8061, E-mail: siahmako@rose-hulman.edu.
Website: http://www.rose-hulman.edu/academics/academic-departments/electrical-computer-engineering.aspx

Royal Military College of Canada, Division of Graduate Studies and Research, Engineering Division, Department of Electrical and Computer Engineering, Kingston, ON K7K 7B4, Canada. Offers computer engineering (M Eng, PhD); electrical engineering (M Eng, PhD); software engineering (M Eng, PhD). *Degree requirements:* For master's, thesis; for doctorate, comprehensive exam, thesis/dissertation. *Entrance requirements:* For master's, honours degree with second-class standing in the appropriate field; for doctorate, master's degree. Electronic applications accepted.

Rutgers University–New Brunswick, Graduate School-New Brunswick, Department of Electrical and Computer Engineering, Piscataway, NJ 08854-8097. Offers communications and solid-state electronics (MS, PhD); computer engineering (MS, PhD); control systems (MS, PhD); digital signal processing (MS, PhD). *Program availability:* Part-time. Terminal master's awarded for partial completion of doctoral program. *Degree requirements:* For master's, thesis or alternative; for doctorate, thesis/dissertation. *Entrance requirements:* For master's and doctorate, GRE General Test. Additional exam requirements/recommendations for international students: Required—TOEFL. Electronic applications accepted. *Faculty research:* Communication and information processing, wireless information networks, micro-vacuum devices, machine vision, VLSI design.

St. Mary's University, School of Science, Engineering and Technology, Program in Computer Engineering, San Antonio, TX 78228-8507. Offers MS. *Program availability:* Part-time. *Faculty:* 2 full-time (0 women). *Students:* 2 full-time (1 woman), 4 part-time (1 woman); includes 5 minority (1 Black or African American, non-Hispanic/Latino; 4 Hispanic/Latino), 1 international. Average age 30. 11 applicants, 18% accepted, 1 enrolled. In 2016, 1 master's awarded. *Degree requirements:* For master's, thesis or project. *Entrance requirements:* For master's, GRE (minimum quantitative score of 148), bachelor's degree in computer engineering, electrical engineering or a closely-related discipline; minimum GPA of 3.0; written statement of purpose; two letters of recommendation; official transcripts. Additional exam requirements/recommendations for international students: Required—TOEFL (minimum score 550 paper-based; 80 iBT), IELTS (minimum score 6.5). *Application deadline:* For fall admission, 7/1 for domestic students; for spring admission, 11/15 for domestic students; for summer admission, 4/1 for domestic students. Applications are processed on a rolling basis. Electronic applications accepted. *Expenses: Tuition:* Full-time $15,600; part-time $865 per credit hour. *Required fees:* $148 per semester. *Financial support:* Research assistantships available. Financial award application deadline: 3/31; financial award applicants required to submit FAFSA. *Faculty research:* Computer security, parallel algorithms for 3-D image representation, computer architecture, computer networking. *Unit head:* Dr. Djaffer Ibaroudene, Graduate Program Director, 210-431-2050, E-mail: dibaroudene@stmarytx.edu.

Santa Clara University, School of Engineering, Santa Clara, CA 95053. Offers applied mathematics (MS); bioengineering (MS); civil engineering (MS); computer science and engineering (MS, PhD); electrical engineering (MS, PhD); engineering (Engineer); engineering management and leadership (MS); mechanical engineering (MS, PhD); software engineering (MS); sustainable energy (MS). *Program availability:* Part-time, evening/weekend. *Faculty:* 66 full-time (22 women), 59 part-time/adjunct (12 women). *Students:* 449 full-time (188 women), 315 part-time (114 women); includes 197 minority (3 Black or African American, non-Hispanic/Latino; 144 Asian, non-Hispanic/Latino; 33

Hispanic/Latino; 1 Native Hawaiian or other Pacific Islander, non-Hispanic/Latino; 16 Two or more races, non-Hispanic/Latino), 418 international. Average age 28. 1,217 applicants, 45% accepted, 293 enrolled. In 2016, 466 master's awarded. *Entrance requirements:* For master's, GRE, transcript; for doctorate, GRE, master's degree or equivalent, 3 letters of recommendation, statement of purpose; for Engineer, master's degree. Additional exam requirements/recommendations for international students: Required—TOEFL (minimum score 79 iBT) or IELTS (6.5). *Application deadline:* For fall admission, 4/1 for domestic and international students; for winter admission, 9/9 for domestic students, 9/2 for international students; for spring admission, 2/17 for domestic students, 12/9 for international students. Application fee: $60. Electronic applications accepted. *Expenses:* $928 per unit. *Financial support:* Fellowships, research assistantships, teaching assistantships, career-related internships or fieldwork, Federal Work-Study, scholarships/grants, traineeships, health care benefits, tuition waivers, and unspecified assistantships available. Support available to part-time students. Financial award applicants required to submit FAFSA. *Unit head:* Dr. Alfonso Ortega, Dean. *Application contact:* Stacey Tinker, Director of Admissions and Marketing, 408-554-4313, Fax: 408-554-4323, E-mail: stinker@scu.edu. Website: http://www.scu.edu/engineering/graduate/

Silicon Valley University, Graduate Programs, San Jose, CA 95131. Offers business administration (MBA); computer engineering (MSCE); computer science (MSCS). *Degree requirements:* For master's, project (MSCS).

Southern Illinois University Carbondale, Graduate School, College of Engineering, Department of Electrical and Computer Engineering, Carbondale, IL 62901-4701. Offers MS, PhD, JD/MS. *Degree requirements:* For master's, comprehensive exam, thesis. *Entrance requirements:* For master's, GRE, minimum GPA of 2.7; for doctorate, GRE, minimum GPA of 3.25. Additional exam requirements/recommendations for international students: Required—TOEFL. *Faculty research:* Circuits and power systems, communications and signal processing, controls and systems, electromagnetics and optics, electronics instrumentation and bioengineering.

Southern Illinois University Carbondale, Graduate School, College of Engineering, Program in Engineering Science, Carbondale, IL 62901-4701. Offers engineering science (PhD), including civil and environmental engineering, electrical and computer engineering, mechanical engineering and energy processes, mining and mineral resources engineering. *Degree requirements:* For doctorate, thesis/dissertation. *Entrance requirements:* For doctorate, GRE General Test, minimum GPA of 3.5. Additional exam requirements/recommendations for international students: Required—TOEFL.

Southern Methodist University, Bobby B. Lyle School of Engineering, Department of Computer Science and Engineering, Dallas, TX 75275-0122. Offers computer engineering (MS, PhD); computer science (MS, PhD); security engineering (MS); software engineering (MS, DE). *Program availability:* Part-time, evening/weekend, online learning. Terminal master's awarded for partial completion of doctoral program. *Degree requirements:* For master's, thesis optional; for doctorate, thesis/dissertation, oral and written qualifying exams, oral final exam (PhD). *Entrance requirements:* For master's, GRE General Test, minimum GPA of 3.0 in last 2 years; bachelor's degree in engineering, mathematics, or sciences; for doctorate, preliminary counseling exam (PhD), minimum GPA of 3.0, bachelor's degree in related field, MA (for DE) Additional exam requirements/recommendations for international students: Required—TOEFL (minimum score 550 paper-based). *Faculty research:* Trusted and high performance network computing, software engineering and management, knowledge engineering and management, computer arithmetic, computer architecture and CAD.

Stevens Institute of Technology, Graduate School, Charles V. Schaefer Jr. School of Engineering and Science, Department of Electrical and Computer Engineering, Program in Computer Engineering, Hoboken, NJ 07030. Offers computer engineering (PhD, Certificate), including digital signal processing (Certificate), digital systems and VLSI design (Certificate), multimedia technology (Certificate), networked information systems (Certificate), real-time and embedded systems (Certificate), secure network systems design (Certificate); computer systems (M Eng); data communications and networks (M Eng); digital systems design (M Eng); engineered software systems (M Eng); image processing and multimedia (M Eng); information system security (M Eng); information systems (M Eng). *Program availability:* Part-time, evening/weekend. *Students:* 102 full-time (26 women), 19 part-time (2 women); includes 5 minority (all Asian, non-Hispanic/Latino), 99 international. Average age 25. 183 applicants, 60% accepted, 37 enrolled. In 2016, 51 master's, 3 doctorates, 1 other advanced degree awarded. Terminal master's awarded for partial completion of doctoral program. *Degree requirements:* For master's, thesis optional, minimum B average in major field and overall; for doctorate, comprehensive exam (for some programs), thesis/dissertation; for Certificate, minimum B average. *Entrance requirements:* Additional exam requirements/recommendations for international students: Required—TOEFL (minimum score 74 iBT), IELTS (minimum score 6). *Application deadline:* For fall admission, 6/1 for domestic students, 4/15 for international students; for spring admission, 11/30 for domestic students, 11/1 for international students. Applications are processed on a rolling basis. Application fee: $65. Electronic applications accepted. *Expenses:* Contact institution. *Financial support:* Fellowships, research assistantships, teaching assistantships, career-related internships or fieldwork, Federal Work-Study, scholarships/grants, and unspecified assistantships available. Financial award application deadline: 2/15; financial award applicants required to submit FAFSA. *Unit head:* Bruce McNair, Program Director, 201-216-5549, Fax: 201-216-8246, E-mail: bmcnair@stevens.edu. *Application contact:* Graduate Admissions, 888-783-8367, Fax: 888-511-1306, E-mail: graduate@stevens.edu.

Stevens Institute of Technology, Graduate School, Charles V. Schaefer Jr. School of Engineering and Science, Department of Mechanical Engineering, Program in Integrated Product Development, Hoboken, NJ 07030. Offers armament engineering (M Eng); computer and electrical engineering (M Eng); manufacturing technologies (M Eng); systems reliability and design (M Eng). *Program availability:* Part-time, evening/weekend. *Students:* 15 applicants. In 2016, 2 master's awarded. *Degree requirements:* For master's, thesis optional, minimum B average in major field and overall. *Entrance requirements:* Additional exam requirements/recommendations for international students: Required—TOEFL (minimum score 74 iBT), IELTS (minimum score 6). *Application deadline:* For fall admission, 6/1 for domestic students, 4/15 for international students; for spring admission, 11/30 for domestic students, 11/1 for international students. Applications are processed on a rolling basis. Application fee: $65. Electronic applications accepted. *Expenses:* Contact institution. *Financial support:* Fellowships, research assistantships, teaching assistantships, career-related internships or fieldwork, Federal Work-Study, scholarships/grants, and unspecified assistantships available. Financial award application deadline: 2/15; financial award applicants required to submit FAFSA. *Unit head:* Dr. Frank Fisher, Interim Department Director, 201-216-8913, Fax: 201-216-8315, E-mail: ffisher@stevens.edu. *Application contact:* Graduate Admissions, 888-783-8367, Fax: 888-511-1306, E-mail: graduate@stevens.edu.

Stony Brook University, State University of New York, Graduate School, College of Engineering and Applied Sciences, Department of Electrical and Computer Engineering, Program in Computer Engineering, Stony Brook, NY 11794. Offers MS, PhD. *Students:*

41 full-time (7 women), 34 part-time (10 women); includes 3 minority (2 Asian, non-Hispanic/Latino; 1 Hispanic/Latino), 67 international. Average age 26. 313 applicants, 51% accepted, 26 enrolled. In 2016, 23 master's, 3 doctorates awarded. *Degree requirements:* For doctorate, thesis/dissertation. *Entrance requirements:* For master's, GRE; for doctorate, GRE, statement of purpose, resume, three recommendation letters. Additional exam requirements/recommendations for international students: Required—TOEFL (minimum score 90 iBT). *Application deadline:* For fall admission, 1/15 for domestic students; for spring admission, 10/1 for domestic students. Application fee: $100. *Expenses:* Contact institution. *Financial support:* Research assistantships and teaching assistantships available. *Unit head:* Prof. Petar M. Djuric, Chair, 631-632-8420, Fax: 631-632-8494, E-mail: petar.djuric@stonybrook.edu. *Application contact:* Susan Hayden, Coordinator, 631-632-8400, Fax: 631-632-8494, E-mail: susan.hayden@stonybrook.edu.

Syracuse University, College of Engineering and Computer Science, MS Program in Computer Engineering, Syracuse, NY 13244. Offers MS. *Program availability:* Part-time. *Students:* Average age 24. *Degree requirements:* For master's, comprehensive exam (for some programs), thesis (for some programs). *Entrance requirements:* For master's, GRE General Test, three letters of recommendation, personal statement, resume, official transcripts. Additional exam requirements/recommendations for international students: Required—TOEFL (minimum score 100 iBT). *Application deadline:* For fall admission, 6/1 priority date for domestic and international students; for spring admission, 11/15 priority date for domestic students, 10/15 priority date for international students. Applications are processed on a rolling basis. Application fee: $75. Electronic applications accepted. *Expenses: Tuition:* Full-time $25,974; part-time $1443 per credit hour. *Required fees:* $802; $50 per course. Tuition and fees vary according to course load and program. *Financial support:* Fellowships with full tuition reimbursements, research assistantships with tuition reimbursements, teaching assistantships with tuition reimbursements, and tuition waivers (partial) available. Financial award application deadline: 1/1; financial award applicants required to submit FAFSA. *Faculty research:* Software systems, hardware systems, security and assurance systems, computer engineering, digital machine design. *Unit head:* Dr. Qinru Qiu, Director, 315-443-1836, Fax: 315-443-2583, E-mail: qiqiu@syr.edu. *Application contact:* Kathleen Joyce, Assistant Dean, 315-443-2219, E-mail: topgrads@syr.edu. Website: http://eng-cs.syr.edu/

Syracuse University, College of Engineering and Computer Science, PhD Program in Electrical and Computer Engineering, Syracuse, NY 13244. Offers PhD. *Program availability:* Part-time. *Students:* Average age 29. In 2016, 12 doctorates awarded. *Degree requirements:* For doctorate, comprehensive exam, thesis/dissertation. *Entrance requirements:* For doctorate, GRE General Test, three letters of recommendation, personal statement, resume, official transcripts. Additional exam requirements/recommendations for international students: Required—TOEFL (minimum score 100 iBT). *Application deadline:* For fall admission, 7/1 priority date for domestic students, 6/1 priority date for international students; for spring admission, 11/1 priority date for domestic students, 10/1 priority date for international students. Applications are processed on a rolling basis. Application fee: $75. Electronic applications accepted. *Expenses: Tuition:* Full-time $25,974; part-time $1443 per credit hour. *Required fees:* $802; $50 per course. Tuition and fees vary according to course load and program. *Financial support:* Fellowships with full tuition reimbursements, research assistantships with tuition reimbursements, and teaching assistantships with tuition reimbursements available. Financial award application deadline: 1/1. *Faculty research:* Electrical engineering, computer engineering hardware. *Unit head:* Dr. Qinru Qiu, Professor, Computer Engineering/Program Director, Electrical Engineering and Computer Science, 315-443-1836, E-mail: qiqiu@syr.edu. *Application contact:* Kathleen Joyce, Assistant Dean, 315-443-2219, E-mail: bflowers@syr.edu. Website: http://eng-cs.syr.edu/

Tennessee State University, The School of Graduate Studies and Research, College of Engineering, Nashville, TN 37209-1561. Offers biomedical engineering (ME); civil engineering (ME); computer and information systems engineering (MS, PhD); electrical engineering (ME); environmental engineering (ME); manufacturing engineering (ME); mathematical sciences (MS); mechanical engineering (ME). *Program availability:* Part-time, evening/weekend. *Degree requirements:* For master's, project; for doctorate, comprehensive exam, thesis/dissertation. *Entrance requirements:* For doctorate, minimum GPA of 3.3. *Faculty research:* Robotics, intelligent systems, human-computer interaction software systems, biomedical engineering, signal/image processing, probabilistic design, intelligent manufacturing, cooperative mobile robots, condition based maintenance, sensor fusion.

Texas A&M University, College of Engineering, Department of Electrical and Computer Engineering, College Station, TX 77843. Offers computer engineering (M Eng, MS, PhD); electrical engineering (M Eng, MS, PhD). *Faculty:* 72. *Students:* 590 full-time (109 women), 112 part-time (20 women); includes 29 minority (3 Black or African American, non-Hispanic/Latino; 14 Asian, non-Hispanic/Latino; 9 Hispanic/Latino; 1 Native Hawaiian or other Pacific Islander, non-Hispanic/Latino; 2 Two or more races, non-Hispanic/Latino), 625 international. Average age 27. 1,958 applicants, 27% accepted, 217 enrolled. In 2016, 207 master's, 42 doctorates awarded. *Degree requirements:* For master's, thesis (MS); for doctorate, thesis/dissertation. *Entrance requirements:* For master's and doctorate, GRE General Test. Additional exam requirements/recommendations for international students: Required—TOEFL (minimum score 550 paper-based; 80 iBT), IELTS (minimum score 6), PTE (minimum score 53). *Application deadline:* For fall admission, 1/1 for domestic students, 2/1 for international students; for spring admission, 10/1 for domestic students, 8/1 for international students. Application fee: $50 ($90 for international students). *Expenses:* Contact institution. *Financial support:* In 2016–17, 448 students received support, including 24 fellowships with tuition reimbursements available (averaging $11,557 per year), 182 research assistantships with tuition reimbursements available (averaging $5,334 per year), 124 teaching assistantships with tuition reimbursements available (averaging $6,551 per year); career-related internships or fieldwork, institutionally sponsored loans, scholarships/grants, traineeships, health care benefits, tuition waivers (full and partial), and unspecified assistantships also available. Support available to part-time students. Financial award application deadline: 3/15; financial award applicants required to submit FAFSA. *Faculty research:* Solid-state, electric power systems, and communications engineering. *Unit head:* Dr. Miroslav M. Begovic, Department Head, 979-862-1553, E-mail: begovic@ece.tamu.edu. *Application contact:* Tammy Carda, Senior Academic Advisor II, 979-845-7467, E-mail: t-carda@tamu.edu. Website: http://engineering.tamu.edu/electrical/

Universidad del Turabo, Graduate Programs, School of Engineering, Gurabo, PR 00778-3030. Offers computer engineering (M Eng); electrical engineering (M Eng); mechanical engineering (M Eng); telecommunications and network systems administration (M Eng). *Students:* 14 full-time (0 women), 46 part-time (7 women); all minorities (all Hispanic/Latino). Average age 34. 74 applicants, 41% accepted, 20 enrolled. In 2016, 13 master's awarded. *Entrance requirements:* For master's, GRE, EXADEP or GMAT, interview, essay, official transcript, recommendation letters. *Application deadline:* Applications are processed on a rolling basis. Application fee: $25. Electronic applications accepted. *Financial support:* Institutionally sponsored loans

available. Financial award applicants required to submit FAFSA. *Unit head:* Hector Rodriguez, Dean, 787-743-7979 Ext. 4144. *Application contact:* Diriee Rodriguez, Admissions Director, 787-743-7979 Ext. 4453, E-mail: admisiones-ut@suagm.edu.
Website: http://ut.suagm.edu/es/engineering

The University of Akron, Graduate School, College of Engineering, Department of Electrical and Computer Engineering, Akron, OH 44325. Offers engineering (PhD). *Program availability:* Evening/weekend. *Faculty:* 17 full-time (2 women), 4 part-time/adjunct (1 woman). *Students:* 82 full-time (13 women), 4 part-time (1 woman); includes 1 minority (Two or more races, non-Hispanic/Latino), 80 international. Average age 27. 106 applicants, 52% accepted, 25 enrolled. In 2016, 17 master's, 3 doctorates awarded. *Degree requirements:* For master's, oral comprehensive exam or thesis; for doctorate, one foreign language, thesis/dissertation, candidacy exam, qualifying exam. *Entrance requirements:* For master's, GRE, minimum GPA of 2.75, three letters of recommendation, statement of purpose; for doctorate, GRE, minimum GPA of 3.0 with bachelor's degree, 3.5 with master's degree; three letters of recommendation; statement of purpose; resume. Additional exam requirements/recommendations for international students: Required—TOEFL (minimum score 550 paper-based; 79 iBT), IELTS (minimum score 6.5). *Application deadline:* Applications are processed on a rolling basis. Application fee: $45 ($70 for international students). Electronic applications accepted. *Expenses:* Tuition, state resident: full-time $8618; part-time $359 per credit hour. Tuition, nonresident: full-time $17,149; part-time $715 per credit hour. *Required fees:* $1652. *Financial support:* In 2016–17, 49 research assistantships with full and partial tuition reimbursements, 18 teaching assistantships with full tuition reimbursements were awarded. *Faculty research:* Computational electromagnetics and nondestructive testing, control systems, sensors and actuators applications and networks, alternative energy systems and hybrid vehicles, analog integrated circuit (IC) design, embedded systems. *Total annual research expenditures:* $1.5 million. *Unit head:* Dr. Joan Carletta, Interim Chair, 330-972-5993, E-mail: carlett@uakron.edu. *Application contact:* Dr. Hamid Bahrami, Graduate Director, 330-972-7940, E-mail: hrb@uakron.edu.
Website: http://www.uakron.edu/engineering/ECE/

The University of Alabama, Graduate School, College of Engineering, Department of Electrical and Computer Engineering, Tuscaloosa, AL 35487-0286. Offers electrical engineering (MS, PhD). *Program availability:* Part-time, online learning. *Faculty:* 23 full-time (4 women). *Students:* 54 full-time (8 women), 10 part-time (1 woman); includes 1 minority (Hispanic/Latino), 47 international. Average age 27. 82 applicants, 39% accepted, 17 enrolled. In 2016, 8 master's, 8 doctorates awarded. *Degree requirements:* For master's, thesis or alternative; for doctorate, one foreign language, comprehensive exam, thesis/dissertation. *Entrance requirements:* For master's, GRE (for students from non ABET-accredited schools), minimum GPA of 3.0 in last 60 hours of course work or overall; for doctorate, GRE (for students from non ABET-accredited schools), minimum GPA of 3.0 overall. Additional exam requirements/recommendations for international students: Required—TOEFL (minimum score 550 paper-based). *Application deadline:* For fall admission, 7/1 priority date for domestic students, 1/15 priority date for international students; for spring admission, 11/1 priority date for domestic students, 6/1 priority date for international students. Applications are processed on a rolling basis. Application fee: $50 ($60 for international students). Electronic applications accepted. *Expenses:* Tuition, state resident: full-time $10,470. Tuition, nonresident: full-time $26,950. *Financial support:* In 2016–17, 1 fellowship with full tuition reimbursement (averaging $15,000 per year), 14 research assistantships with full tuition reimbursements (averaging $14,000 per year), 6 teaching assistantships with full tuition reimbursements (averaging $11,025 per year) were awarded; health care benefits and unspecified assistantships also available. *Faculty research:* Devices and materials, electromechanical systems, embedded systems. *Total annual research expenditures:* $1.9 million. *Unit head:* Dr. Tim Haskew, Department Head, 205-348-1766, Fax: 205-348-6959, E-mail: thaskew@eng.ua.edu. *Application contact:* Steve Shepard, Graduate Program Coordinator/Professor, 205-348-1650, Fax: 205-348-6419, E-mail: sshepard@eng.ua.edu.
Website: http://ece.eng.ua.edu

The University of Alabama at Birmingham, School of Engineering, Program in Electrical Engineering, Birmingham, AL 35294. Offers computer engineering (PhD); electrical engineering (MSEE). *Program availability:* Part-time. *Faculty:* 10 full-time, 5 part-time/adjunct. *Students:* 10 full-time (2 women), 12 part-time (2 women); includes 18 minority (1 Black or African American, non-Hispanic/Latino; 15 Asian, non-Hispanic/Latino; 1 Hispanic/Latino; 1 Two or more races, non-Hispanic/Latino). Average age 29. 36 applicants, 83% accepted, 15 enrolled. In 2016, 9 master's awarded. *Degree requirements:* For master's, comprehensive exam, thesis (for some programs); for doctorate, comprehensive exam, thesis/dissertation. *Entrance requirements:* For master's, GRE, minimum GPA of 3.0 in all junior and senior electrical and computer engineering and mathematics courses attempted, letters of evaluation. Additional exam requirements/recommendations for international students: Required—TOEFL (minimum score 80 iBT), IELTS (minimum score 6.5). *Application deadline:* For fall admission, 7/1 for domestic and international students; for spring admission, 11/1 for domestic and international students; for summer admission, 4/1 for domestic and international students. Applications are processed on a rolling basis. Application fee: $50 ($60 for international students). Electronic applications accepted. *Expenses:* $396 per hour resident tuition; $935 per hour non-resident tuition; $150 per course online course fee. *Financial support:* In 2016–17, 18 students received support, including 3 research assistantships with full and partial tuition reimbursements available (averaging $15,960 per year), 14 teaching assistantships (averaging $5,520 per year); unspecified assistantships also available. *Total annual research expenditures:* $1,370. *Unit head:* Dr. Murat Tanik, Chair, 205-934-8440, Fax: 205-975-3337, E-mail: mtanik@uab.edu. *Application contact:* Holly Hebard, Director of Graduate School Operations, 205-934-8227, Fax: 205-934-8413, E-mail: gradschool@uab.edu.
Website: https://www.uab.edu/engineering/home/graduate#msee

The University of Alabama in Huntsville, School of Graduate Studies, College of Engineering, Department of Electrical and Computer Engineering, Huntsville, AL 35899. Offers computer engineering (MSE, PhD); electrical engineering (MSE, PhD), including optics and photonics technology (MSE); optical science and engineering (PhD); software engineering (MSSE). *Program availability:* Part-time, evening/weekend. *Degree requirements:* For master's, comprehensive exam, thesis or alternative, oral and written exams; for doctorate, comprehensive exam, thesis/dissertation, oral and written exams. *Entrance requirements:* For master's, GRE General Test, appropriate bachelor's degree, minimum GPA of 3.0; for doctorate, GRE General Test, minimum GPA of 3.0. Additional exam requirements/recommendations for international students: Required—TOEFL (minimum score 500 paper-based; 80 iBT), IELTS (minimum score 6.5). Electronic applications accepted. *Expenses:* Tuition, state resident: full-time $9834; part-time $600 per credit hour. Tuition, nonresident: full-time $21,830; part-time $1325 per credit hour. *Faculty research:* Advanced computer architecture and systems, fault tolerant computing and verification, computational electro-magnetics, nano-photonics and plasmonics, micro electro-mechanical (MEMS) systems.

University of Alberta, Faculty of Graduate Studies and Research, Department of Electrical and Computer Engineering, Edmonton, AB T6G 2E1, Canada. Offers communications (M Eng, M Sc, PhD); computer engineering (M Eng, M Sc, PhD); electromagnetics (M Eng, M Sc, PhD); nanotechnology and microdevices (M Eng, M Sc, PhD); power/power electronics (M Eng, M Sc, PhD); systems (M Eng, M Sc, PhD). Terminal master's awarded for partial completion of doctoral program. *Degree requirements:* For master's, thesis; for doctorate, thesis/dissertation. *Entrance requirements:* Additional exam requirements/recommendations for international students: Required—TOEFL. Electronic applications accepted. *Faculty research:* Controls, communications, microelectronics, electromagnetics.

The University of Arizona, College of Engineering, Department of Electrical and Computer Engineering, Tucson, AZ 85721. Offers MS, PhD. *Program availability:* Part-time. *Degree requirements:* For master's, thesis (for some programs); for doctorate, thesis/dissertation. *Entrance requirements:* For master's, GRE General Test, 3 letters of recommendation, statement of purpose; for doctorate, GRE General Test, master's degree in related field, 3 letters of recommendation, statement of purpose. Additional exam requirements/recommendations for international students: Required—TOEFL (minimum score 550 paper-based; 79 iBT). Electronic applications accepted. *Faculty research:* Communication systems, control systems, signal processing, computer-aided logic.

University of Arkansas, Graduate School, College of Engineering, Department of Computer Science and Computer Engineering, Program in Computer Engineering, Fayetteville, AR 72701. Offers MS Cmp E, MSE, PhD. In 2016, 8 master's, 1 doctorate awarded. *Degree requirements:* For master's, thesis optional; for doctorate, one foreign language, thesis/dissertation. *Application deadline:* For fall admission, 4/1 for international students; for spring admission, 10/1 for international students. Applications are processed on a rolling basis. Application fee: $40 ($50 for international students). Electronic applications accepted. *Financial support:* In 2016–17, 8 research assistantships, 2 teaching assistantships were awarded; fellowships with tuition reimbursements, career-related internships or fieldwork, and Federal Work-Study also available. Support available to part-time students. Financial award application deadline: 4/1; financial award applicants required to submit FAFSA. *Unit head:* Dr. Frank Liu, Department Chair, 479-575-6197, Fax: 479-575-5339, E-mail: frankliu@uark.edu. *Application contact:* Dr. Gordon Beavers, Graduate Coordinator, 479-575-6040, Fax: 479-575-5339, E-mail: gordonb@uark.edu.
Website: http://www.csce.uark.edu/

University of Bridgeport, School of Engineering, Departments of Computer Science and Computer Engineering, Bridgeport, CT 06604. Offers computer engineering (MS); computer science (MS); computer science and engineering (PhD). *Degree requirements:* For master's, thesis optional; for doctorate, comprehensive exam, thesis/dissertation. *Entrance requirements:* Additional exam requirements/recommendations for international students: Recommended—TOEFL (minimum score 550 paper-based; 80 iBT), IELTS (minimum score 6.5). Electronic applications accepted. *Expenses:* Contact institution.

The University of British Columbia, Faculty of Applied Science, Department of Electrical and Computer Engineering, Vancouver, BC V6T 1Z4, Canada. Offers M Eng, MA Sc, PhD. *Program availability:* Part-time. *Degree requirements:* For master's, thesis (for some programs); for doctorate, thesis/dissertation. *Entrance requirements:* Additional exam requirements/recommendations for international students: Required—TOEFL, IELTS. Application fee: $100 Canadian dollars ($162 Canadian dollars for international students). Electronic applications accepted. *Expenses:* $4,802 per year tuition and fees, $8,436 per year international. *Financial support:* Fellowships, research assistantships, teaching assistantships, career-related internships or fieldwork, institutionally sponsored loans, scholarships/grants, and tuition waivers (full and partial) available. *Faculty research:* Applied electromagnetics, biomedical engineering, communications and signal processing, computer and software engineering, power engineering, robotics, solid-state, systems and control. *Application contact:* Ross Sheppard, Graduate Admissions Coordinator, 604-822-6190, E-mail: help@ece.ubc.ca.
Website: https://www.ece.ubc.ca/

University of Calgary, Faculty of Graduate Studies, Schulich School of Engineering, Department of Electrical and Computer Engineering, Calgary, AB T2N 1N4, Canada. Offers M Eng, M Sc, PhD. *Program availability:* Part-time. *Degree requirements:* For master's, thesis (for M Sc); for doctorate, thesis/dissertation, candidacy exam. *Entrance requirements:* For master's, minimum GPA of 3.0; for doctorate, minimum GPA of 3.5. Additional exam requirements/recommendations for international students: Required—TOEFL (minimum score 550 paper-based; 80 iBT) or IELTS (minimum score 7). Electronic applications accepted. *Faculty research:* Biomedical and bioelectrics, telecommunications and signal processing, software and computer engineering, power and control, microelectronics and instrumentation.

University of California, Davis, College of Engineering, Program in Electrical and Computer Engineering, Davis, CA 95616. Offers MS, PhD. Terminal master's awarded for partial completion of doctoral program. *Degree requirements:* For master's, comprehensive exam (for some programs), thesis (for some programs); for doctorate, thesis/dissertation, preliminary and qualifying exams, thesis defense. *Entrance requirements:* For master's, GRE General Test, minimum GPA of 3.2; for doctorate, GRE, minimum graduate GPA of 3.5. Additional exam requirements/recommendations for international students: Required—TOEFL (minimum score 550 paper-based). Electronic applications accepted.

University of California, Riverside, Graduate Division, Department of Computer Science and Engineering, Computer Engineering Program, Riverside, CA 92521. Offers MS. *Faculty:* 9 full-time (0 women). *Students:* 36 full-time (13 women), 35 international. 119 applicants, 48% accepted, 24 enrolled. In 2016, 25 master's awarded. *Degree requirements:* For master's, comprehensive exam, project, or thesis. *Entrance requirements:* For master's, GRE General Test (minimum score of 1100 or 300 for new format), minimum GPA of 3.2 in junior/senior years of undergraduate study (last two years). Additional exam requirements/recommendations for international students: Required—TOEFL (minimum score 550 paper-based; 80 iBT), IELTS (minimum score 7). *Application deadline:* For fall admission, 5/1 for domestic students, 3/1 for international students. Application fee: $0 ($100 for international students). Electronic applications accepted. *Expenses:* Tuition, state resident: full-time $16,666. Tuition, nonresident: full-time $31,768. *Required fees:* $11,055.54 per quarter. $3685.18 per quarter. Tuition and fees vary according to campus/location and program. *Financial support:* Scholarships/grants available. Financial award application deadline: 1/1; financial award applicants required to submit FAFSA. *Unit head:* Dr. Walid Najjar, Director, 951-827-5639, Fax: 951-827-4643, E-mail: najjar@cs.ucr.edu. *Application contact:* Madie Heersink, Graduate Student Affairs Officer, 951-827-5639, Fax: 951-827-4643, E-mail: madie@cs.ucr.edu.
Website: http://www.cen.ucr.edu

University of California, San Diego, Graduate Division, Department of Computer Science and Engineering, La Jolla, CA 92093. Offers computer engineering (MS, PhD); computer science (MS, PhD). *Students:* 602 full-time (127 women), 76 part-time (13 women). 4,193 applicants, 18% accepted, 293 enrolled. In 2016, 102 master's, 15 doctorates awarded. Terminal master's awarded for partial completion of doctoral program. *Degree requirements:* For master's, comprehensive exam (for some

programs), thesis (for some programs), comprehensive exam or thesis; for doctorate, comprehensive exam, thesis/dissertation, 1-quarter teaching assistantship. *Entrance requirements:* For master's and doctorate, GRE General Test, GRE Subject Test (recommended). Additional exam requirements/recommendations for international students: Required—TOEFL (minimum score 550 paper-based; 80 iBT), IELTS (minimum score 7). *Application deadline:* For fall admission, 12/14 for domestic students. Application fee: $105 ($125 for international students). Electronic applications accepted. *Expenses:* Tuition, state resident: full-time $11,220. Tuition, nonresident: full-time $26,322. *Required fees:* $1864. *Financial support:* Fellowships, research assistantships, teaching assistantships, career-related internships or fieldwork, and scholarships/grants available. Financial award applicants required to submit FAFSA. *Faculty research:* Artificial intelligence and machine learning, bioinformatics, computer architecture and compilers, visual computing, computer graphics, computer vision, databases and information management, embedded systems and software, high-performance computing, human-computer interaction, programming systems, security and cryptography, software engineering, systems and networking, ubiquitous computing and social dynamics, VLSI/CAD. *Unit head:* Dean Tullsen, Chair, 858-534-6181, E-mail: dtullsen@ucsd.edu. *Application contact:* Julie Connor, Graduate Coordinator, 858-534-8872, E-mail: gradinfo@cs.ucsd.edu.
Website: http://cse.ucsd.edu

University of California, San Diego, Graduate Division, Department of Electrical and Computer Engineering, La Jolla, CA 92093. Offers applied ocean science (MS, PhD); applied physics (MS, PhD); communication theory and systems (MS, PhD); computer engineering (MS, PhD); electronic circuits and systems (MS, PhD); intelligent systems, robotics and control (MS, PhD); medical devices and systems (MS, PhD); nanoscale devices and systems (MS, PhD); photonics (MS, PhD); signal and image processing (MS, PhD). *Students:* 612 full-time (119 women), 39 part-time (8 women). 2,885 applicants, 25% accepted, 269 enrolled. In 2016, 147 master's, 43 doctorates awarded. Terminal master's awarded for partial completion of doctoral program. *Degree requirements:* For master's, comprehensive exam (for some programs), thesis (for some programs); for doctorate, comprehensive exam, thesis/dissertation. *Entrance requirements:* For master's and doctorate, GRE General Test, minimum GPA of 3.0, resume or curriculum vitae (recommended). Additional exam requirements/recommendations for international students: Required—TOEFL (minimum score 550 paper-based; 80 iBT), IELTS (minimum score 7), PTE (minimum score 65). *Application deadline:* For fall admission, 12/13 for domestic students. Application fee: $105 ($125 for international students). Electronic applications accepted. *Expenses:* Tuition, state resident: full-time $11,220. Tuition, nonresident: full-time $26,322. *Required fees:* $1864. *Financial support:* Fellowships, research assistantships, teaching assistantships, scholarships/grants, traineeships, and unspecified assistantships available. Financial award applicants required to submit FAFSA. *Faculty research:* Applied ocean science; applied physics; communication theory and systems; computer engineering; electronic circuits and systems; intelligent systems, robotics and control; medical devices and systems; nanoscale devices and systems; photonics; signal and image processing. *Unit head:* Truong Nguyen, Chair, 858-822-5554, E-mail: nguyent@ece.ucsd.edu. *Application contact:* Melanie Lynn, Graduate Admissions Coordinator, 858-822-3213, E-mail: ecegradapps@ece.ucsd.edu.
Website: http://ece.ucsd.edu/

University of California, Santa Barbara, Graduate Division, College of Engineering, Department of Computer Science, Santa Barbara, CA 93106-5110. Offers computer science (MS, PhD), including cognitive science (PhD), computational science and engineering (PhD), technology and society (PhD). Terminal master's awarded for partial completion of doctoral program. *Degree requirements:* For master's, comprehensive exam (for some programs), thesis (for some programs), project (for some programs); for doctorate, thesis/dissertation. *Entrance requirements:* For master's and doctorate, GRE. Additional exam requirements/recommendations for international students: Required—TOEFL (minimum score 600 paper-based; 100 iBT), IELTS (minimum score 7). Electronic applications accepted. *Faculty research:* Algorithms and theory, computational science and engineering, computer architecture, database and information systems, machine learning and data mining, networking, operating systems and distributed systems, programming languages and software engineering, security and cryptography, social computing, visual computing and interaction.

University of California, Santa Barbara, Graduate Division, College of Engineering, Department of Electrical and Computer Engineering, Santa Barbara, CA 93106-2014. Offers communications, control and signal processing (MS, PhD); computer engineering (MS, PhD); electronics and photonics (MS, PhD); MS/PhD. *Degree requirements:* For master's, comprehensive exam, thesis; for doctorate, thesis/dissertation. *Entrance requirements:* For master's and doctorate, GRE General Test. Additional exam requirements/recommendations for international students: Required—TOEFL (minimum score 550 paper-based; 80 iBT), IELTS (minimum score 7). Electronic applications accepted. *Faculty research:* Communications, signal processing, computer engineering, control, electronics and photonics.

University of California, Santa Cruz, Jack Baskin School of Engineering, Department of Computer Engineering, Santa Cruz, CA 95064. Offers computer engineering (MS, PhD). *Program availability:* Part-time. *Faculty:* 22 full-time (5 women), 6 part-time/adjunct (1 woman). *Students:* 128 full-time (24 women), 14 part-time (3 women); includes 24 minority (1 Black or African American, non-Hispanic/Latino; 1 American Indian or Alaska Native, non-Hispanic/Latino; 9 Asian, non-Hispanic/Latino; 10 Hispanic/Latino; 3 Native Hawaiian or other Pacific Islander, non-Hispanic/Latino), 82 international. 231 applicants, 56% accepted, 50 enrolled. In 2016, 17 master's, 3 doctorates awarded. Terminal master's awarded for partial completion of doctoral program. *Degree requirements:* For master's, thesis; for doctorate, thesis/dissertation, oral qualifying exams. *Entrance requirements:* For master's and doctorate, GRE General Test. Additional exam requirements/recommendations for international students: Required—TOEFL (minimum score 570 paper-based; 89 iBT); Recommended—IELTS (minimum score 8). *Application deadline:* For fall admission, 1/3 for domestic and international students. Application fee: $105 ($125 for international students). Electronic applications accepted. *Financial support:* In 2016–17, 63 students received support, including 13 fellowships (averaging $18,000 per year), 74 research assistantships (averaging $20,043 per year), 102 teaching assistantships (averaging $20,052 per year); institutionally sponsored loans and tuition waivers (full and partial) also available. Financial award application deadline: 1/3; financial award applicants required to submit FAFSA. *Faculty research:* Computer-aided design of digital systems, networks, robotics and control, sensing and interaction. *Unit head:* Martine Schlag, Chair/Professor, E-mail: martine@soe.ucsc.edu. *Application contact:* Emily Gregg, Graduate Student Advisor, 831-459-2576, E-mail: bsoe-ga@rt.ucsc.edu.
Website: https://www.soe.ucsc.edu/departments/computer-engineering

University of Central Florida, College of Engineering and Computer Science, Department of Electrical Engineering and Computer Science, Program in Computer Engineering, Orlando, FL 32816. Offers MS Cp E, PhD. *Program availability:* Part-time, evening/weekend. *Students:* 92 full-time (19 women), 26 part-time (5 women); includes 22 minority (3 Black or African American, non-Hispanic/Latino; 10 Asian, non-Hispanic/Latino; 7 Hispanic/Latino; 2 Two or more races, non-Hispanic/Latino), 75 international.

Average age 29. 92 applicants, 78% accepted, 30 enrolled. In 2016, 14 master's, 7 doctorates awarded. *Degree requirements:* For master's, thesis or alternative; for doctorate, thesis/dissertation, departmental qualifying exam, candidacy exam. *Entrance requirements:* For master's, GRE General Test, minimum GPA of 3.0 in last 60 hours; for doctorate, GRE General Test, minimum GPA of 3.5 in last 60 hours. Additional exam requirements/recommendations for international students: Required—TOEFL. *Application deadline:* For fall admission, 7/15 for domestic students; for spring admission, 12/1 for domestic students. Application fee: $30. Electronic applications accepted. *Expenses:* Tuition, state resident: part-time $288.16 per credit hour. Tuition, nonresident: part-time $1071.31 per credit hour. *Financial support:* In 2016–17, 36 students received support, including 5 fellowships with partial tuition reimbursements available (averaging $16,200 per year), 28 research assistantships with partial tuition reimbursements available (averaging $11,735 per year), 14 teaching assistantships with partial tuition reimbursements available (averaging $9,140 per year); tuition waivers (partial) also available. Financial award application deadline: 3/1; financial award applicants required to submit FAFSA. *Unit head:* Dr. Zhihua Qu, Chair, 407-823-5976, Fax: 407-823-5835, E-mail: qu@ucf.edu. *Application contact:* Assistant Director, Graduate Admissions, 407-823-2766, Fax: 407-823-6442, E-mail: gradadmissions@ucf.edu.
Website: http://www.ece.ucf.edu/

University of Cincinnati, Graduate School, College of Engineering and Applied Science, Department of Electrical Engineering and Computing Systems, Program in Computer Engineering, Cincinnati, OH 45221. Offers MS. *Degree requirements:* For master's, thesis. *Entrance requirements:* For master's, GRE General Test. Additional exam requirements/recommendations for international students: Required—TOEFL (minimum score 550 paper-based). Electronic applications accepted. *Expenses:* Tuition, area resident: Full-time $12,790; part-time $389 per credit hour. Tuition, state resident: full-time $13,290; part-time $419 per credit hour. Tuition, nonresident: full-time $24,532; part-time $976 per credit hour. *International tuition:* $24,832 full-time. *Required fees:* $3958; $140 per credit hour. Tuition and fees vary according to course load, degree level, program and reciprocity agreements. *Faculty research:* Digital signal processing, large-scale systems, picture processing.

University of Cincinnati, Graduate School, College of Engineering and Applied Science, Department of Electrical Engineering and Computing Systems, Program in Computer Science and Engineering, Cincinnati, OH 45221. Offers PhD. *Degree requirements:* For doctorate, thesis/dissertation. *Entrance requirements:* For doctorate, GRE General Test. Additional exam requirements/recommendations for international students: Required—TOEFL. *Expenses:* Tuition, area resident: Full-time $12,790; part-time $389 per credit hour. Tuition, state resident: full-time $13,290; part-time $419 per credit hour. Tuition, nonresident: full-time $24,532; part-time $976 per credit hour. *International tuition:* $24,832 full-time. *Required fees:* $3958; $140 per credit hour. Tuition and fees vary according to course load, degree level, program and reciprocity agreements.

University of Colorado Boulder, Graduate School, College of Engineering and Applied Science, Department of Electrical, Computer and Energy Engineering, Boulder, CO 80309. Offers ME, MS, PhD. *Faculty:* 40 full-time (7 women). *Students:* 312 full-time (66 women), 42 part-time (8 women); includes 30 minority (3 Black or African American, non-Hispanic/Latino; 12 Asian, non-Hispanic/Latino; 10 Hispanic/Latino; 5 Two or more races, non-Hispanic/Latino), 230 international. Average age 27. 858 applicants, 40% accepted, 128 enrolled. In 2016, 68 master's, 18 doctorates awarded. Terminal master's awarded for partial completion of doctoral program. *Degree requirements:* For master's, thesis or alternative; for doctorate, one foreign language, thesis/dissertation, departmental qualifying exam. *Entrance requirements:* For master's, GRE General Test, minimum undergraduate GPA of 3.0; for doctorate, GRE General Test, minimum undergraduate GPA of 3.5. *Application deadline:* For fall admission, 1/15 for domestic and international students; for spring admission, 9/1 for domestic and international students. Applications are processed on a rolling basis. Application fee: $60 ($80 for international students). Electronic applications accepted. Application fee is waived when completed online. *Financial support:* In 2016–17, 528 students received support, including 139 fellowships (averaging $8,551 per year), 97 research assistantships with full and partial tuition reimbursements available (averaging $37,877 per year), 30 teaching assistantships with full and partial tuition reimbursements available (averaging $17,238 per year); institutionally sponsored loans, scholarships/grants, health care benefits, and unspecified assistantships also available. Financial award application deadline: 1/15; financial award applicants required to submit FAFSA. *Faculty research:* Electrical engineering/electronics, electromagnetic propagation, solid state electronics, electromagnetics, circuits and systems. *Total annual research expenditures:* $10.8 million. *Application contact:* E-mail: ecegrad@colorado.edu.
Website: http://ecee.colorado.edu

University of Dayton, Department of Electrical and Computer Engineering, Dayton, OH 45469. Offers computer engineering (MS); electrical engineering (MSEE, PhD). *Program availability:* Part-time. *Faculty:* 17 full-time (0 women), 16 part-time/adjunct (2 women). *Students:* 145 full-time (30 women), 14 part-time (4 women); includes 10 minority (2 Black or African American, non-Hispanic/Latino; 6 Asian, non-Hispanic/Latino; 2 Two or more races, non-Hispanic/Latino), 100 international. Average age 28. 82 applicants, 22% accepted. In 2016, 88 master's, 8 doctorates awarded. *Degree requirements:* For master's, thesis optional; for doctorate, variable foreign language requirement, thesis/dissertation. *Entrance requirements:* For master's, minimum GPA of 3.2, 3 letters of recommendation, bachelor's degree, transcripts; for doctorate, minimum GPA of 3.2, master's degree, transcripts, 3 letters of recommendation. Additional exam requirements/recommendations for international students: Required—TOEFL (minimum score 550 paper-based; 80 iBT). *Application deadline:* For fall admission, 8/1 for domestic students, 5/1 priority date for international students; for spring admission, 11/1 priority date for international students. Applications are processed on a rolling basis. Application fee: $0 ($50 for international students). Electronic applications accepted. *Expenses:* $890 per credit hour (for MS), $970 per credit hour (for PhD); $25 registration fee. *Financial support:* In 2016–17, 17 research assistantships with full tuition reimbursements (averaging $12,500 per year), 30 teaching assistantships with full tuition reimbursements (averaging $10,000 per year) were awarded; institutionally sponsored loans, health care benefits, and unspecified assistantships also available. Financial award application deadline: 3/1; financial award applicants required to submit FAFSA. *Faculty research:* Electrical engineering, video processing, leaky wave antennas, thin film research. *Unit head:* Dr. Guru Subramanyam, Chair, 937-229-3188, Fax: 937-229-4529, E-mail: gsubramanyam1@udayton.edu. *Application contact:* E-mail: graduateadmission@udayton.edu.
Website: https://www.udayton.edu/engineering/departments/electrical_and_computer/index.php

University of Delaware, College of Engineering, Department of Electrical and Computer Engineering, Newark, DE 19716. Offers MSECE, PhD. *Program availability:* Part-time, online learning. Terminal master's awarded for partial completion of doctoral program. *Degree requirements:* For master's, thesis optional; for doctorate, thesis/dissertation. *Entrance requirements:* For master's, GRE General Test; for doctorate, GRE General Test, qualifying exam. Additional exam requirements/recommendations for international students: Required—TOEFL. Electronic applications accepted. *Faculty research:* HIV evolution during dynamic therapy, compressive sensing in imaging, sensor, networks, and UWB radios, computer network time synchronization, silicon spintronics, devices and imaging in the high-terahertz band.

University of Denver, Daniel Felix Ritchie School of Engineering and Computer Science, Department of Electrical and Computer Engineering, Denver, CO 80208. Offers computer engineering (MS); electrical and computer engineering (PhD); electrical engineering (MS); engineering (MS); mechatronic systems engineering (MS, PhD). *Program availability:* Part-time, evening/weekend. *Faculty:* 13 full-time (1 woman). *Students:* 6 full-time (1 woman), 61 part-time (13 women); includes 6 minority (2 Black or African American, non-Hispanic/Latino; 1 Asian, non-Hispanic/Latino; 2 Hispanic/Latino; 1 Two or more races, non-Hispanic/Latino), 36 international. Average age 30. 56 applicants, 61% accepted, 14 enrolled. In 2016, 39 master's, 5 doctorates awarded. Terminal master's awarded for partial completion of doctoral program. *Degree requirements:* For master's, thesis optional, proficiency in high- or low-level computer language; for doctorate, comprehensive exam, thesis/dissertation, proficiency in high- or low-level computer language. *Entrance requirements:* For master's, GRE General Test, bachelor's degree, transcripts, personal statement, resume or curriculum vitae, three letters of recommendation; for doctorate, GRE General Test, master's degree, transcripts, personal statement, resume or curriculum vitae, three letters of recommendation. Additional exam requirements/recommendations for international students: Required—TOEFL (minimum score 550 paper-based; 80 iBT). *Application deadline:* For fall admission, 2/1 priority date for domestic and international students. Applications are processed on a rolling basis. Application fee: $65. Electronic applications accepted. *Expenses:* $29,022 per year full-time. *Financial support:* In 2016–17, 39 students received support, including 9 research assistantships with tuition reimbursements available (averaging $11,897 per year), 1 teaching assistantship with tuition reimbursement available (averaging $17,496 per year); Federal Work-Study, scholarships/grants, and unspecified assistantships also available. Financial award application deadline: 2/15; financial award applicants required to submit FAFSA. *Faculty research:* Mechatronic systems, unmanned systems, service robotics, smart grid, sensor fusion. *Total annual research expenditures:* $1.5 million. *Unit head:* Dr. Kimon Valavanis, Professor/Chair, 303-871-2586, Fax: 303-871-2194, E-mail: kimon.valavanis@du.edu. *Application contact:* Molly Dunn, Assistant to the Chair, 303-871-6618, Fax: 303-871-2194, E-mail: molly.dunn@du.edu.
Website: http://ritchieschool.du.edu/departments/ece/

University of Detroit Mercy, College of Engineering and Science, Detroit, MI 48221. Offers chemistry (MS); civil and environmental engineering (DE); electrical and computer engineering (ME); electrical engineering (DE); engineering management (M Eng Mgt); environmental engineering (MEE); mechanical engineering (MME, DE); product development (MS); software engineering (MSSE); teaching of mathematics (MATM). *Program availability:* Part-time, evening/weekend. *Degree requirements:* For doctorate, thesis/dissertation. Electronic applications accepted. Application fee is waived when completed online. *Expenses:* Contact institution.

University of Florida, Graduate School, Herbert Wertheim College of Engineering and College of Liberal Arts and Sciences, Department of Computer and Information Science and Engineering, Gainesville, FL 32611. Offers computer engineering (ME, MS, PhD); computer science (MS); digital arts and sciences (MS). *Program availability:* Part-time, online learning. Terminal master's awarded for partial completion of doctoral program. *Degree requirements:* For master's, comprehensive exam, thesis optional; for doctorate, comprehensive exam, thesis/dissertation. *Entrance requirements:* For master's and doctorate, minimum GPA of 3.0. Additional exam requirements/recommendations for international students: Required—TOEFL (minimum score 550 paper-based; 80 iBT), IELTS (minimum score 6). Electronic applications accepted. *Faculty research:* Computer systems and computer networking; high-performance computing and algorithm; database and machine learning; computer graphics, vision, and intelligent systems; human center computing and digital art.

University of Florida, Graduate School, Herbert Wertheim College of Engineering, Department of Electrical and Computer Engineering, Gainesville, FL 32611. Offers ME, MS, PhD, JD/MS, MSM/MS. *Program availability:* Part-time, online learning. Terminal master's awarded for partial completion of doctoral program. *Degree requirements:* For master's, comprehensive exam (for some programs), thesis (for some programs); for doctorate, comprehensive exam, thesis/dissertation. *Entrance requirements:* For master's, minimum GPA of 3.0; for doctorate, minimum GPA of 3.5. Additional exam requirements/recommendations for international students: Required—TOEFL (minimum score 550 paper-based; 80 iBT), IELTS (minimum score 6). Electronic applications accepted. *Faculty research:* Computer engineering, devices, electromagnetics and energy systems, electronics and signals and systems.

University of Houston–Clear Lake, School of Science and Computer Engineering, Program in Computer Engineering, Houston, TX 77058-1002. Offers MS. *Program availability:* Part-time, evening/weekend. *Entrance requirements:* For master's, GRE General Test. Additional exam requirements/recommendations for international students: Required—TOEFL (minimum score 550 paper-based).

University of Idaho, College of Graduate Studies, College of Engineering, Department of Electrical and Computer Engineering, Moscow, ID 83844. Offers computer engineering (M Engr, MS); electrical engineering (M Engr, MS, PhD). *Faculty:* 13 full-time, 2 part-time/adjunct. *Students:* 30 full-time (5 women), 52 part-time (5 women). Average age 32. In 2016, 25 master's, 1 doctorate awarded. *Entrance requirements:* For master's and doctorate, minimum GPA of 3.0. *Application deadline:* For fall admission, 8/1 for domestic students; for spring admission, 12/15 for domestic students. Applications are processed on a rolling basis. Application fee: $60. Electronic applications accepted. *Expenses:* Tuition, state resident: full-time $6460; part-time $414 per credit hour. Tuition, nonresident: full-time $21,268; part-time $1237 per credit hour. *Required fees:* $2070; $60 per credit hour. Full-time tuition and fees vary according to course load and reciprocity agreements. *Financial support:* Fellowships, research assistantships, teaching assistantships, career-related internships or fieldwork, and Federal Work-Study available. Financial award applicants required to submit FAFSA. *Faculty research:* Microelectronics, laser electrophotography, intelligent systems research, advanced transportation technologies. *Unit head:* Dr. Mohsen Guizani, Chair, 208-885-6554, E-mail: info@ece.uidaho.edu. *Application contact:* Sean Scoggin, Graduate Recruitment Coordinator, 208-885-4001, Fax: 208-885-4406, E-mail: graduateadmissions@uidaho.edu.
Website: https://www.uidaho.edu/engr/departments/ece

University of Illinois at Chicago, College of Engineering, Department of Electrical and Computer Engineering, Chicago, IL 60607-7128. Offers MS, PhD. *Program availability:* Part-time. *Degree requirements:* For master's, thesis or alternative; for doctorate, thesis/dissertation, departmental qualifying exam. *Entrance requirements:* For master's, minimum GPA of 2.75, BS in related field; for doctorate, GRE General Test, minimum GPA of 2.75, MS in related field. Additional exam requirements/recommendations for international students: Required—TOEFL. Electronic applications accepted. *Expenses:* Contact institution. *Faculty research:* Bioelectronics and biomimetics, computer engineering, device physics and electronics, information systems.

University of Illinois at Urbana–Champaign, Graduate College, College of Engineering, Department of Electrical and Computer Engineering, Champaign, IL 61820. Offers MS, PhD, MS/MBA.

The University of Iowa, Graduate College, College of Engineering, Department of Electrical and Computer Engineering, Iowa City, IA 52242-1316. Offers MS, PhD. *Program availability:* Part-time. *Faculty:* 18 full-time (4 women), 4 part-time/adjunct (0 women). *Students:* 51 full-time (13 women), 13 part-time (2 women); includes 6 minority (2 Asian, non-Hispanic/Latino; 2 Hispanic/Latino; 2 Two or more races, non-Hispanic/Latino), 42 international. Average age 28. 130 applicants, 18% accepted, 15 enrolled. In 2016, 7 master's, 7 doctorates awarded. *Degree requirements:* For master's, comprehensive exam, thesis optional; for doctorate, comprehensive exam, thesis/dissertation, qualifying exam. *Entrance requirements:* For master's and doctorate, GRE. Additional exam requirements/recommendations for international students: Required—TOEFL (minimum score 550 paper-based; 81 iBT), IELTS (minimum score 7). *Application deadline:* For fall admission, 2/1 priority date for domestic students, 2/1 for international students; for spring admission, 12/1 for domestic students; for summer admission, 4/15 for domestic students. Applications are processed on a rolling basis. Application fee: $60 ($100 for international students). Electronic applications accepted. *Financial support:* In 2016–17, 54 students received support, including 2 fellowships with full tuition reimbursements available (averaging $25,500 per year), 39 research assistantships with full and partial tuition reimbursements available (averaging $22,981 per year), 13 teaching assistantships with full and partial tuition reimbursements available (averaging $18,809 per year); scholarships/grants and unspecified assistantships also available. Financial award application deadline: 2/1; financial award applicants required to submit FAFSA. *Faculty research:* Applied optics and nanotechnology, compressive sensing, computational genomics, database management systems, large-scale intelligent and control systems, medical image processing, VLSI design and test. *Total annual research expenditures:* $6.3 million. *Unit head:* Dr. Er-Wei Bai, Department Executive Officer, 319-335-5949, Fax: 319-335-6028, E-mail: er-wei-bai@uiowa.edu. *Application contact:* Cathy Kern, Secretary, 319-335-5197, Fax: 319-335-6028, E-mail: ece@engineering.uiowa.edu.
Website: https://ece.engineering.uiowa.edu

The University of Kansas, Graduate Studies, School of Engineering, Program in Computer Engineering, Lawrence, KS 66045. Offers MS. *Program availability:* Part-time. *Students:* 5 full-time (1 woman), 4 part-time (2 women), 5 international. Average age 26. 16 applicants, 44% accepted, 2 enrolled. In 2016, 4 master's awarded. *Entrance requirements:* For master's, GRE, minimum GPA of 3.0, official transcript, three recommendations, statement of academic objectives, resume. Additional exam requirements/recommendations for international students: Required—TOEFL or IELTS. *Application deadline:* For fall admission, 12/15 priority date for domestic and international students; for spring admission, 10/1 for domestic and international students. Application fee: $65 ($85 for international students). Electronic applications accepted. *Financial support:* Fellowships, research assistantships, teaching assistantships, career-related internships or fieldwork, scholarships/grants, and unspecified assistantships available. Financial award application deadline: 12/15. *Faculty research:* Communication systems and networking, computer systems design, interactive intelligent systems, radar systems and remote sensing, bioinformatics. *Unit head:* Victor Frost, Chair, 785-864-4833, E-mail: vsfrost@ku.edu. *Application contact:* Pam Shadoin, Graduate Admissions Contact, 785-864-4487, E-mail: eecs_graduate@ku.edu.
Website: http://www.eecs.ku.edu/

University of Louisiana at Lafayette, College of Engineering, Center for Advanced Computer Studies, Lafayette, LA 70504. Offers computer engineering (MS, PhD); computer science (MS, PhD). *Program availability:* Part-time. Terminal master's awarded for partial completion of doctoral program. *Degree requirements:* For master's, thesis or alternative; for doctorate, comprehensive exam, thesis/dissertation, final oral exam. *Entrance requirements:* For master's, GRE General Test, minimum GPA of 2.75; for doctorate, GRE General Test, minimum GPA of 3.0. Additional exam requirements/recommendations for international students: Required—TOEFL. Electronic applications accepted.

University of Louisiana at Lafayette, College of Engineering, Department of Electrical and Computer Engineering, Lafayette, LA 70504. Offers computer engineering (MS, PhD); telecommunications (MSTC). *Degree requirements:* For master's, thesis or alternative; for doctorate, comprehensive exam, thesis/dissertation, final oral exam. *Entrance requirements:* For master's, GRE General Test, minimum GPA of 2.75. Additional exam requirements/recommendations for international students: Required—TOEFL (minimum score 550 paper-based). Electronic applications accepted.

University of Louisville, J. B. Speed School of Engineering, Department of Computer Engineering and Computer Science, Louisville, KY 40292-0001. Offers computer engineering and computer science (M Eng, MS, PhD); data mining (Certificate); network and information security (Certificate). *Accreditation:* ABET (one or more programs are accredited). *Program availability:* Part-time, 100% online, blended/hybrid learning. *Students:* 76 full-time (24 women), 81 part-time (16 women); includes 17 minority (5 Black or African American, non-Hispanic/Latino; 7 Asian, non-Hispanic/Latino; 2 Hispanic/Latino; 3 Two or more races, non-Hispanic/Latino), 54 international. Average age 31. 80 applicants, 46% accepted, 29 enrolled. In 2016, 17 master's, 1 doctorate, 1 other advanced degree awarded. *Degree requirements:* For master's, thesis optional, minimum GPA of 3.0; for doctorate, comprehensive exam, thesis/dissertation, minimum GPA of 3.0. *Entrance requirements:* For master's, GRE, two letters of recommendation, personal statement; for doctorate, GRE, two letters of recommendation, official final transcripts; for Certificate, undergraduate degree. Additional exam requirements/recommendations for international students: Required—TOEFL (minimum score 550 paper-based; 80 iBT), IELTS (minimum score 6.5). *Application deadline:* For fall admission, 5/1 priority date for international students; for spring admission, 11/1 priority date for international students; for summer admission, 3/1 priority date for international students. Applications are processed on a rolling basis. Application fee: $60. Electronic applications accepted. *Expenses:* Tuition, state resident: full-time $12,246; part-time $681 per credit hour. Tuition, nonresident: full-time $25,486; part-time $1417 per credit hour. *Required fees:* $196. Tuition and fees vary according to program and reciprocity agreements. *Financial support:* In 2016–17, 2 fellowships with full tuition reimbursements (averaging $22,000 per year) were awarded; research assistantships with full tuition reimbursements, teaching assistantships with full tuition reimbursements, scholarships/grants, health care benefits, and tuition waivers also available. Financial award application deadline: 1/1. *Faculty research:* Software systems engineering, information security and forensics, multimedia and vision, mobile and distributed computing, intelligent systems. *Total annual research expenditures:* $740,736. *Unit head:* Dr. Adel S. Elmaghraby, Chair, 502-852-6304, Fax: 502-852-4713, E-mail: adel@louisville.edu. *Application contact:* Dr. Mehmed Kantardzic, Director of Graduate Studies, 502-852-3703, E-mail: mehmed.kantardzic@louisville.edu.
Website: http://louisville.edu/speed/computer

University of Louisville, J. B. Speed School of Engineering, Department of Electrical and Computer Engineering, Louisville, KY 40292-0001. Offers M Eng, MS, PhD. *Accreditation:* ABET (one or more programs are accredited). *Students:* 47 full-time (5

women), 26 part-time (3 women); includes 6 minority (1 Black or African American, non-Hispanic/Latino; 1 Asian, non-Hispanic/Latino; 4 Hispanic/Latino), 36 international. Average age 29. 70 applicants, 29% accepted, 14 enrolled. In 2016, 6 master's, 2 doctorates awarded. *Degree requirements:* For master's, thesis optional; for doctorate, comprehensive exam, thesis/dissertation. *Entrance requirements:* For master's and doctorate, GRE General Test, two letters of recommendation, official transcripts. Additional exam requirements/recommendations for international students: Required—TOEFL (minimum score 550 paper-based; 80 iBT), IELTS (minimum score 6.5). *Application deadline:* For fall admission, 5/1 priority date for international students; for spring admission, 11/1 priority date for international students; for summer admission, 3/1 priority date for international students. Applications are processed on a rolling basis. Application fee: $60. Electronic applications accepted. *Expenses:* Tuition, state resident: full-time $12,246; part-time $681 per credit hour. Tuition, nonresident: full-time $25,486; part-time $1417 per credit hour. *Required fees:* $196. Tuition and fees vary according to program and reciprocity agreements. *Financial support:* In 2016–17, 2 fellowships with full tuition reimbursements (averaging $20,000 per year) were awarded; research assistantships with full tuition reimbursements, teaching assistantships with full tuition reimbursements, scholarships/grants, health care benefits, and tuition waivers (full) also available. Financial award application deadline: 1/1; financial award applicants required to submit FAFSA. *Faculty research:* Nanotechnology; microfabrication; computer engineering; control, communication and signal processing; electronic devices and systems. *Total annual research expenditures:* $1.8 million. *Unit head:* Alpenhaar Bruce, Chair, 502-852-1554, E-mail: bruce.alphenaar@louisville.edu. *Application contact:* John Naber, Director of Graduate Studies, 502-852-7910, E-mail: john.naber@louisville.edu.
Website: http://www.louisville.edu/speed/electrical/

University of Maine, Graduate School, College of Engineering, Department of Electrical and Computer Engineering, Orono, ME 04469. Offers computer engineering (MS); electrical engineering (MS, PhD). *Program availability:* Part-time. *Faculty:* 12 full-time (1 woman), 1 part-time/adjunct (0 women). *Students:* 18 full-time (1 woman), 5 part-time (1 woman); includes 1 minority (Hispanic/Latino), 14 international. Average age 27. 35 applicants, 71% accepted, 5 enrolled. In 2016, 9 master's, 1 doctorate awarded. Terminal master's awarded for partial completion of doctoral program. *Degree requirements:* For master's, thesis (for some programs); for doctorate, comprehensive exam, thesis/dissertation. *Entrance requirements:* For master's and doctorate, GRE General Test. Additional exam requirements/recommendations for international students: Required—TOEFL. *Application deadline:* For fall admission, 2/1 priority date for domestic students. Applications are processed on a rolling basis. Application fee: $65. Electronic applications accepted. *Expenses:* Tuition, state resident: full-time $7524; part-time $2508 per credit. Tuition, nonresident: full-time $24,498; part-time $8166 per credit. *Required fees:* $1148; $571 per credit. *Financial support:* In 2016–17, 11 students received support, including 1 fellowship (averaging $20,000 per year), 4 research assistantships with full tuition reimbursements available (averaging $22,800 per year), 6 teaching assistantships with full tuition reimbursements available (averaging $14,600 per year); Federal Work-Study, institutionally sponsored loans, and tuition waivers (full and partial) also available. Financial award application deadline: 3/1. *Faculty research:* Microwave acoustic sensors, semiconductor devices and fabrication, high performance computing, instrumentation and industrial automation, wireless communication. *Total annual research expenditures:* $2 million. *Unit head:* Dr. Donald Hummels, Chair, 207-581-2244. *Application contact:* Scott G. Delcourt, Assistant Vice President for Graduate Studies and Senior Associate Dean, 207-581-3291, Fax: 207-581-3232, E-mail: graduate@maine.edu.
Website: http://www.ece.umaine.edu/

University of Manitoba, Faculty of Graduate Studies, Faculty of Engineering, Department of Electrical and Computer Engineering, Winnipeg, MB R3T 2N2, Canada. Offers M Eng, M Sc, PhD. *Degree requirements:* For master's, thesis; for doctorate, thesis/dissertation.

University of Maryland, Baltimore County, The Graduate School, College of Engineering and Information Technology, Department of Computer Science and Electrical Engineering, Program in Computer Engineering, Baltimore, MD 21250. Offers MS, PhD. *Program availability:* Part-time. *Faculty:* 14 full-time (3 women), 1 part-time/adjunct. *Students:* 30 full-time (4 women), 13 part-time (4 women); includes 2 minority (1 Black or African American, non-Hispanic/Latino; 1 Asian, non-Hispanic/Latino), 24 international. Average age 28. 61 applicants, 67% accepted, 13 enrolled. In 2016, 5 master's, 1 doctorate awarded. *Degree requirements:* For master's, comprehensive exam (for some programs), thesis or alternative; for doctorate, comprehensive exam, thesis/dissertation. *Entrance requirements:* For master's, GRE General Test, strong background in computer engineering, computer science, and math courses; for doctorate, GRE General Test, MS in computer science (strongly recommended); strong background in computer engineering, computer science, and mathematics courses. Additional exam requirements/recommendations for international students: Required—TOEFL (minimum score 550 paper-based; 80 iBT). *Application deadline:* For fall admission, 6/1 for domestic students, 1/1 for international students; for spring admission, 11/1 for domestic students, 6/1 for international students. Applications are processed on a rolling basis. Application fee: $70. Electronic applications accepted. *Expenses:* Contact institution. *Financial support:* In 2016–17, 1 fellowship, 10 research assistantships with full tuition reimbursements (averaging $18,000 per year), 6 teaching assistantships with full tuition reimbursements (averaging $18,000 per year) were awarded; career-related internships or fieldwork, Federal Work-Study, scholarships/grants, health care benefits, tuition waivers (partial), and unspecified assistantships also available. Support available to part-time students. Financial award application deadline: 6/30; financial award applicants required to submit FAFSA. *Faculty research:* Communication and signal processing, photonics and micro electronics, sensor systems, signal processing architectures, VLSI design and test. *Unit head:* Dr. Anupam Joshi, Professor and Chair, 410-455-3500, Fax: 410-455-3969, E-mail: joshi@cs.umbc.edu. *Application contact:* Dr. Mohamed Younis, Professor and Graduate Program Director, 410-455-3500, Fax: 410-455-3969, E-mail: younis@umbc.edu.
Website: http://www.csee.umbc.edu/

★ **University of Maryland, College Park,** Academic Affairs, A. James Clark School of Engineering, Department of Electrical and Computer Engineering, College Park, MD 20742. Offers electrical and computer engineering (M Eng, MS, PhD); electrical engineering (MS, PhD); telecommunications (MS). *Program availability:* Part-time, evening/weekend, online learning. *Degree requirements:* For master's, thesis optional; for doctorate, thesis/dissertation, oral exam, qualifying exam. *Entrance requirements:* For master's and doctorate, GRE General Test, 3 letters of recommendation. Electronic applications accepted. *Faculty research:* Communications and control, electrophysics, micro-electronics, robotics, computer engineering.

See Display below and Close-Up on page 429.

University of Massachusetts Amherst, Graduate School, College of Engineering, Department of Electrical and Computer Engineering, Amherst, MA 01003. Offers MSECE, PhD. *Program availability:* Part-time. Terminal master's awarded for partial completion of doctoral program. *Degree requirements:* For master's, thesis or alternative; for doctorate, comprehensive exam, thesis/dissertation. *Entrance requirements:* For master's and doctorate, GRE General Test. Additional exam requirements/recommendations for international students: Required—TOEFL (minimum score 550 paper-based; 80 iBT), IELTS (minimum score 6.5). Electronic applications accepted.

University of Massachusetts Dartmouth, Graduate School, College of Engineering, Department of Electrical and Computer Engineering, North Dartmouth, MA 02747-2300. Offers acoustics (Postbaccalaureate Certificate); communications (Postbaccalaureate Certificate); computer engineering (MS, PhD); computing infrastructure (Postbaccalaureate Certificate); digital security signal processing (Postbaccalaureate Certificate); electrical engineering (MS, PhD). *Program availability:* Part-time. *Faculty:* 15 full-time (3 women), 1 part-time/adjunct (0 women). *Students:* 31 full-time (8 women), 45 part-time (5 women); includes 8 minority (2 Black or African American, non-Hispanic/Latino; 2 Asian, non-Hispanic/Latino; 2 Hispanic/Latino; 2 Two or more races, non-Hispanic/Latino), 39 international. Average age 28. 101 applicants, 57% accepted, 23 enrolled. In 2016, 25 master's, 3 doctorates, 3 other advanced degrees awarded. Terminal master's awarded for partial completion of doctoral program. *Degree requirements:* For master's, thesis or project; for doctorate, comprehensive exam, thesis/dissertation. *Entrance requirements:* For master's, GRE (UMass Dartmouth electrical/computer engineering bachelor's degree recipients are exempt), statement of purpose (minimum of 300 words), resume, 3 letters of recommendation, official transcripts; for doctorate, GRE (UMass Dartmouth electrical/computer engineering degree recipients are exempt), statement of purpose (minimum of 300 words), resume, 3 letters of recommendation, official transcripts; for Postbaccalaureate Certificate, statement of purpose (minimum of 300 words), resume, official transcripts. Additional exam requirements/recommendations for international students: Required—TOEFL (minimum score 550 paper-based; 80 iBT). *Application deadline:* For fall admission, 2/15 priority date for domestic students, 1/15 priority date for international students; for spring admission, 11/1 priority date for domestic students, 10/1 priority date for international students. Application fee: $60. Electronic applications accepted. *Expenses:* Tuition, state resident: full-time $14,994; part-time $624.75 per credit. Tuition, nonresident: full-time $27,068; part-time $1127.83 per credit. *Required fees:* $405; $25.88 per credit. Tuition and fees vary according to course load and reciprocity agreements. *Financial support:* In 2016–17, 5 fellowships (averaging $5,143 per year), 14 research assistantships (averaging $10,724 per year), 11 teaching assistantships (averaging $14,705 per year) were awarded; unspecified assistantships and instructional assistantships, doctoral support also available. Financial award application deadline: 3/1; financial award applicants required to submit FAFSA. *Faculty research:* Computer engineering, cyber security, acoustics, signals and systems, electromagnetics, electronics and solid-state devices, marine systems, photonics. *Total annual research expenditures:* $2.6 million. *Unit head:* Hong Liu, Graduate Program Director, 508-999-8514, Fax: 508-999-8489, E-mail: hliu@umassd.edu. *Application contact:* Steven Briggs, Director of Marketing and Recruitment for Graduate Studies, 508-999-8604, Fax: 508-999-8183, E-mail: graduate@umassd.edu.
Website: http://www.umassd.edu/engineering/ece/graduate

University of Massachusetts Lowell, Francis College of Engineering, Department of Electrical and Computer Engineering, Program in Computer Engineering, Lowell, MA 01854. Offers MS Eng, PhD. *Degree requirements:* For master's, thesis optional.

University of Memphis, Graduate School, Herff College of Engineering, Department of Electrical and Computer Engineering, Memphis, TN 38103. Offers computer engineering (MS, PhD); electrical engineering (MS, PhD); imaging and signal processing (Graduate Certificate). *Faculty:* 12 full-time (1 woman). *Students:* 12 full-time (4 women), 12 part-time (5 women); includes 1 minority (Two or more races, non-Hispanic/Latino), 18 international. Average age 26. 52 applicants, 67% accepted, 4 enrolled. In 2016, 19 master's awarded. *Degree requirements:* For master's, comprehensive exam, thesis or alternative; for doctorate, comprehensive exam, thesis/dissertation. *Entrance requirements:* For master's and doctorate, GRE General Test, MAT, or GMAT, three letters of recommendation. Additional exam requirements/recommendations for international students: Required—TOEFL (minimum score 550 paper-based; 79 iBT). *Application deadline:* For fall admission, 8/1 for domestic students; for spring admission, 12/1 for domestic students. Application fee: $35 ($60 for international students). Electronic applications accepted. *Expenses:* $5,231.50 per semester full-time in-state, $9,623.50 full-time out-of-state. *Financial support:* In 2016–17, 4 students received support, including 9 research assistantships (averaging $15,120 per year), 16 teaching assistantships (averaging $11,038 per year); fellowships, career-related internships or fieldwork, Federal Work-Study, scholarships/grants, and unspecified assistantships also available. Financial award application deadline: 2/1; financial award applicants required to submit FAFSA. *Faculty research:* Image processing, imaging sensors, biomedical systems, intelligent systems. *Unit head:* Dr. Russell Deaton, Chair/Professor, 901-678-2175, Fax: 901-678-5469. *Application contact:* Dr. Aaron Robinson, Coordinator of Graduate Studies, 901-678-4996, Fax: 901-678-5469, E-mail: alrobins@memphis.edu.
Website: http://www.memphis.edu/eece/

University of Miami, Graduate School, College of Engineering, Department of Electrical and Computer Engineering, Coral Gables, FL 33124. Offers MSECE, PhD. *Program availability:* Part-time. *Degree requirements:* For master's, thesis (for some programs); for doctorate, comprehensive exam, thesis/dissertation, dissertation proposal defense. *Entrance requirements:* For master's, GRE General Test, minimum GPA of 3.0; for doctorate, GRE General Test, minimum undergraduate GPA of 3.3, graduate 3.5. Additional exam requirements/recommendations for international students: Required—TOEFL (minimum score 550 paper-based; 59 iBT), IELTS (minimum score 7). Electronic applications accepted. *Faculty research:* Computer network, image processing, database systems, digital signal processing, machine intelligence.

University of Michigan, College of Engineering, Department of Computer Science and Engineering, Ann Arbor, MI 48109. Offers MS, MSE, PhD. *Students:* 328 full-time (51 women), 5 part-time (3 women). 1,801 applicants, 15% accepted, 85 enrolled. In 2016, 86 master's, 30 doctorates awarded. *Expenses:* Tuition, state resident: full-time $21,466; part-time $1152 per credit hour. Tuition, nonresident: full-time $43,346; part-time $2367 per credit hour. Part-time tuition and fees vary according to course load, degree level and program. *Faculty research:* Solid state electronics and optics; communications, control, signal process; sensors and integrated circuitry; software systems; artificial intelligence; hardware systems. *Total annual research expenditures:* $27.3 million. *Unit head:* Prof. Peter Chen, Interim Chair, 734-763-4472, E-mail: pmchen@umich.edu. *Application contact:* Ashley Andreae, Graduate Programs Coordinator, 734-647-1807, E-mail: smash@umich.edu.
Website: http://eecs.umich.edu/cse/

University of Michigan, College of Engineering, Department of Electrical and Computer Engineering, Ann Arbor, MI 48109. Offers MS, MSE, PhD. *Students:* 743 full-time (151 women), 17 part-time (4 women). 2,454 applicants, 30% accepted, 331 enrolled. In 2016, 202 master's, 53 doctorates awarded. *Expenses:* Tuition, state resident: full-time $21,466; part-time $1152 per credit hour. Tuition, nonresident: full-time $43,346; part-time $2367 per credit hour. Part-time tuition and fees vary according to course load, degree level and program. *Faculty research:* Solid state electronics and optics; communications, control, signal process; sensors and integrated circuitry; software systems; artificial intelligence; hardware systems. *Total annual research expenditures:* $41.2 million. *Unit head:* Prof. Khalil Najafi, Department Chair, 734-764-

3317, Fax: 734-763-1503, E-mail: najafi@umich.edu. *Application contact:* Jose-Antonio Rubio, Graduate Program Coordinator, 734-764-9387, E-mail: jadrubio@umich.edu.
Website: http://eecs.umich.edu/ece/

University of Michigan–Dearborn, College of Engineering and Computer Science, MSE Program in Computer Engineering, Dearborn, MI 48128. Offers MSE. *Program availability:* Part-time, evening/weekend, 100% online. *Faculty:* 20 full-time (2 women), 12 part-time/adjunct (0 women). *Students:* 16 full-time (4 women), 37 part-time (6 women); includes 8 minority (1 Black or African American, non-Hispanic/Latino; 4 Asian, non-Hispanic/Latino; 1 Hispanic/Latino; 2 Two or more races, non-Hispanic/Latino), 23 international. Average age 26. 48 applicants, 69% accepted, 19 enrolled. In 2016, 9 master's awarded. *Degree requirements:* For master's, thesis optional. *Entrance requirements:* For master's, bachelor's degree in electrical and/or computer engineering with minimum overall GPA of 3.0. Additional exam requirements/recommendations for international students: Required—TOEFL (minimum score 560 paper-based; 84 iBT), IELTS (minimum score 6.5). *Application deadline:* For fall admission, 8/1 for domestic students, 5/1 for international students; for winter admission, 12/1 for domestic students, 9/1 for international students; for spring admission, 4/1 for domestic students, 1/1 for international students. Applications are processed on a rolling basis. Application fee: $60. Electronic applications accepted. *Expenses:* Tuition, state resident: full-time $13,118; part-time $2280 per term. Tuition, nonresident: full-time $21,816; part-time $3771 per term. *Required fees:* $866; $658 per unit. $329 per term. Tuition and fees vary according to program. *Financial support:* In 2016–17, 3 students received support. Research assistantships, teaching assistantships, scholarships/grants, unspecified assistantships, and non-resident tuition scholarships available. Financial award application deadline: 3/1; financial award applicants required to submit FAFSA. *Faculty research:* Pattern recognition, machine vision, fuzzy systems, vehicle electronics and wireless communications. *Unit head:* Dr. Paul Richardson, Chair, 313-593-5560, E-mail: richarpc@umich.edu. *Application contact:* Office of Graduate Studies, 313-583-6321, E-mail: umd-graduatestudies@umich.edu.
Website: http://umdearborn.edu/cecs/ECE/grad_prog/index.php

University of Michigan–Dearborn, College of Engineering and Computer Science, PhD Program in Electrical and Computer Engineering, Dearborn, MI 48128. Offers PhD. *Program availability:* Part-time, evening/weekend. *Degree requirements:* For doctorate, thesis/dissertation. *Entrance requirements:* For doctorate, GRE, bachelor's or master's degree in electrical or computer engineering or closely-related field. Additional exam requirements/recommendations for international students: Required—TOEFL (minimum score 560 paper-based; 84 iBT), IELTS (minimum score 6.5). Electronic applications accepted. *Expenses:* Tuition, state resident: full-time $13,118; part-time $2280 per term. Tuition, nonresident: full-time $21,816; part-time $3771 per term. *Required fees:* $866; $658 per unit. $329 per term. Tuition and fees vary according to program. *Faculty research:* Fuzzy systems and applications, machine vision, pattern recognition and machine intelligence, vehicle electronics, wireless communications.

University of Minnesota, Duluth, Graduate School, Swenson College of Science and Engineering, Department of Electrical and Computer Engineering, Duluth, MN 55812-2496. Offers MSECE. *Program availability:* Part-time. *Degree requirements:* For master's, thesis. *Entrance requirements:* Additional exam requirements/recommendations for international students: Recommended—TOEFL, IELTS, TWE. *Faculty research:* Biomedical instrumentation, transportation systems, computer hardware and software, signal processing, optical communications.

University of Minnesota, Twin Cities Campus, College of Science and Engineering, Department of Computer Science and Engineering, Minneapolis, MN 55455-0213. Offers computer science (MCS, MS, PhD); data science (MS); software engineering (MSSE). *Program availability:* Part-time. Terminal master's awarded for partial completion of doctoral program. *Degree requirements:* For doctorate, thesis/dissertation. *Entrance requirements:* For master's and doctorate, GRE General Test. Additional exam requirements/recommendations for international students: Required—TOEFL. Electronic applications accepted. *Faculty research:* Computer architecture, bioinformatics and computational biology, data mining, graphics and visualization, high performance computing, human-computer interaction, networks, software systems, theory, artificial intelligence.

University of Minnesota, Twin Cities Campus, College of Science and Engineering, Department of Electrical and Computer Engineering, Minneapolis, MN 55455-0213. Offers MSEE, PhD. *Program availability:* Part-time. *Degree requirements:* For master's, thesis or alternative; for doctorate, thesis/dissertation. *Entrance requirements:* Additional exam requirements/recommendations for international students: Required—TOEFL (minimum score 550 paper-based). Electronic applications accepted. *Faculty research:* Signal processing, micro and nano structures, computers, controls, power electronics.

University of Missouri–Kansas City, School of Computing and Engineering, Kansas City, MO 64110-2499. Offers civil engineering (MS); computer and electrical engineering (PhD); computer science (MS), including bioinformatics, software engineering, telecommunications networking; computer science and informatics (PhD); computing (PhD); electrical engineering (MS); engineering (PhD); engineering and construction management (Graduate Certificate); mechanical engineering (MS); telecommunications and computer networking (PhD). PhD (interdisciplinary) offered through the School of Graduate Studies. *Program availability:* Part-time. *Faculty:* 45 full-time (6 women), 26 part-time/adjunct (4 women). *Students:* 473 full-time (155 women), 207 part-time (42 women); includes 24 minority (10 Black or African American, non-Hispanic/Latino; 10 Asian, non-Hispanic/Latino; 4 Hispanic/Latino), 581 international. Average age 25. 1,143 applicants, 44% accepted, 227 enrolled. In 2016, 446 master's, 2 other advanced degrees awarded. *Degree requirements:* For doctorate, thesis/dissertation. *Entrance requirements:* For master's, GRE General Test, minimum GPA of 3.0, 3 letters of recommendation from professors; for doctorate, GRE General Test, minimum GPA of 3.5. Additional exam requirements/recommendations for international students: Required—TOEFL (minimum score 550 paper-based; 80 iBT). *Application deadline:* For fall admission, 1/15 priority date for domestic students, 1/15 for international students. Applications are processed on a rolling basis. Application fee: $45 ($50 for international students). *Financial support:* In 2016–17, 37 research assistantships with partial tuition reimbursements (averaging $15,679 per year), 47 teaching assistantships with partial tuition reimbursements (averaging $16,830 per year) were awarded; career-related internships or fieldwork, Federal Work-Study, scholarships/grants, tuition waivers (partial), and unspecified assistantships also available. Support available to part-time students. Financial award application deadline: 3/1; financial award applicants required to submit FAFSA. *Faculty research:* Algorithms, bioinformatics and medical informatics, biomechanics/biomaterials, civil engineering materials, networking and telecommunications, thermal science. *Unit head:* Dr. Kevin Z. Truman, Dean, 816-235-2399, Fax: 816-235-5159. *Application contact:* 816-235-2399, Fax: 816-235-5159.
Website: http://sce.umkc.edu

University of Nebraska–Lincoln, Graduate College, College of Arts and Sciences and College of Engineering, Department of Computer Science and Engineering, Lincoln, NE 68588. Offers bioinformatics (MS, PhD); computer engineering (MS, PhD); computer science (MS, PhD); information technology (PhD). *Degree requirements:* For master's, thesis optional; for doctorate, comprehensive exam, thesis/dissertation. *Entrance* *requirements:* For master's and doctorate, GRE General Test. Additional exam requirements/recommendations for international students: Required—TOEFL (minimum score 600 paper-based). Electronic applications accepted. *Faculty research:* Software engineering, geo- and bio-informatics, scientific computation, secure communication.

University of Nevada, Las Vegas, Graduate College, Howard R. Hughes College of Engineering, Department of Electrical and Computer Engineering, Las Vegas, NV 89154-4026. Offers MS, PhD, MS/MS, MS/PhD. *Program availability:* Part-time. *Faculty:* 17 full-time (3 women). *Students:* 29 full-time (8 women), 19 part-time (1 woman); includes 16 minority (1 Black or African American, non-Hispanic/Latino; 7 Asian, non-Hispanic/Latino; 7 Hispanic/Latino; 1 Two or more races, non-Hispanic/Latino), 23 international. Average age 29. 37 applicants, 54% accepted, 9 enrolled. In 2016, 9 master's, 6 doctorates awarded. *Degree requirements:* For master's, comprehensive exam (for some programs), thesis (for some programs), project; for doctorate, comprehensive exam, thesis/dissertation. *Entrance requirements:* For master's, GRE General Test, bachelor's degree with minimum GPA 3.0; statement of purpose; 3 letters of recommendation; for doctorate, GRE General Test, 3 letters of recommendation; statement of purpose; bachelor's degree with minimum GPA of 3.5/master's degree with minimum GPA of 3.2. Additional exam requirements/recommendations for international students: Required—TOEFL (minimum score 550 paper-based; 80 iBT), IELTS (minimum score 7). *Application deadline:* For fall admission, 2/1 for domestic students; for spring admission, 10/1 for domestic students. Application fee: $60 ($95 for international students). Electronic applications accepted. *Expenses:* $269.25 per credit, $792 per 3-credit course; $9,634 per year resident; $23,274 per year non-resident; $7,094 fees non-resident (7 credits or more); $1,307 annual health insurance fee. *Financial support:* In 2016–17, 9 research assistantships with partial tuition reimbursements (averaging $16,408 per year), 21 teaching assistantships with partial tuition reimbursements (averaging $13,310 per year) were awarded; institutionally sponsored loans, scholarships/grants, health care benefits, and unspecified assistantships also available. Financial award application deadline: 3/15. *Faculty research:* Computer engineering, power engineering, semiconductor and nanotechnology, electronics and VLSI, telecommunications and control, electromagnetics and plasma. *Total annual research expenditures:* $1.6 million. *Unit head:* Dr. Yingtao Jiang, Chair/Professor, 702-895-2533, Fax: 702-895-4075, E-mail: yingtao.jiang@unlv.edu. *Application contact:* Dr. Robert Schill, Graduate Coordinator, 702-895-1526, Fax: 702-895-4075, E-mail: robert.schill@unlv.edu.
Website: http://ece.unlv.edu/

University of Nevada, Reno, Graduate School, College of Engineering, Department of Computer Science and Engineering, Reno, NV 89557. Offers MS, PhD. Terminal master's awarded for partial completion of doctoral program. *Degree requirements:* For master's, thesis optional; for doctorate, thesis/dissertation. *Entrance requirements:* For master's, GRE General Test, minimum GPA of 2.75; for doctorate, GRE General Test, minimum GPA of 3.0. Additional exam requirements/recommendations for international students: Required—TOEFL (minimum score 500 paper-based; 61 iBT), IELTS (minimum score 6). Electronic applications accepted. *Faculty research:* Evolutionary computing systems, computer vision/virtual reality, software engineering.

University of New Brunswick Fredericton, School of Graduate Studies, Faculty of Engineering, Department of Electrical and Computer Engineering, Fredericton, NB E3B 5A3, Canada. Offers M Eng, M Sc E, PhD. *Program availability:* Part-time. *Degree requirements:* For master's, thesis, research proposal; 10 courses (for M Eng); for doctorate, comprehensive exam, thesis/dissertation, research proposal. *Entrance requirements:* For master's, minimum GPA of 3.3; references; for doctorate, M Sc; minimum GPA of 3.3; previous transcripts; references. Additional exam requirements/recommendations for international students: Required—TOEFL (minimum score 580 paper-based; 93 iBT), IELTS (minimum score 7), TWE (minimum score 4). Electronic applications accepted. *Faculty research:* Biomedical engineering, communications, robotics and control systems, electromagnetic systems, embedded systems, optical fiber systems, sustainable energy and power systems, power electronics, image and signal processing, software systems, electronics and digital systems.

University of New Haven, Graduate School, Tagliatela College of Engineering, Program in Electrical Engineering, West Haven, CT 06516. Offers control systems (MS); digital signal processing and communication (MS); electrical and computer engineering (MS); electrical engineering (MS). *Program availability:* Part-time, evening/weekend. *Students:* 99 full-time (33 women), 22 part-time (3 women); includes 4 minority (2 Black or African American, non-Hispanic/Latino; 1 Asian, non-Hispanic/Latino; 1 Two or more races, non-Hispanic/Latino), 114 international. Average age 25. 346 applicants, 59% accepted, 13 enrolled. In 2016, 116 master's awarded. *Degree requirements:* For master's, thesis or alternative. *Entrance requirements:* For master's, bachelor's degree in electrical engineering. Additional exam requirements/recommendations for international students: Required—TOEFL (minimum score 75 iBT), IELTS, PTE (minimum score 50). *Application deadline:* Applications are processed on a rolling basis. Application fee: $50. Electronic applications accepted. Application fee is waived when completed online. *Expenses: Tuition:* Full-time $15,660; part-time $870 per credit hour. *Required fees:* $200; $85 per term. Tuition and fees vary according to program. *Financial support:* Research assistantships with partial tuition reimbursements, teaching assistantships with partial tuition reimbursements, career-related internships or fieldwork, Federal Work-Study, scholarships/grants, and unspecified assistantships available. Support available to part-time students. Financial award applicants required to submit FAFSA. *Unit head:* Dr. Bijan Karimi, Coordinator, 203-932-7164, E-mail: bkarimi@newhaven.edu. *Application contact:* Michelle Mason, Director of Graduate Enrollment, 203-932-7067, E-mail: mmason@newhaven.edu.
Website: http://www.newhaven.edu/9592/

University of New Mexico, Graduate Studies, School of Engineering, Programs in Computer Engineering, Albuquerque, NM 87131-2039. Offers MS, PhD. *Program availability:* Part-time, evening/weekend, online learning. *Faculty:* 11 full-time (2 women), 1 (woman) part-time/adjunct. *Students:* 32 full-time (7 women), 31 part-time (3 women); includes 10 minority (1 Black or African American, non-Hispanic/Latino; 1 Asian, non-Hispanic/Latino; 7 Hispanic/Latino; 1 Two or more races, non-Hispanic/Latino), 32 international. Average age 29. 59 applicants, 24% accepted, 14 enrolled. In 2016, 14 master's, 7 doctorates awarded. Terminal master's awarded for partial completion of doctoral program. *Degree requirements:* For master's, thesis; for doctorate, comprehensive exam, thesis/dissertation. *Entrance requirements:* For master's, GRE General Test, minimum GPA of 3.0; for doctorate, GRE General Test, minimum GPA of 3.5. Additional exam requirements/recommendations for international students: Required—TOEFL (minimum score 550 paper-based; 79 iBT). *Application deadline:* For fall admission, 6/15 for domestic students, 2/15 for international students; for spring admission, 11/1 for domestic students, 6/15 for international students. Application fee: $50. Electronic applications accepted. *Financial support:* Fellowships, research assistantships, teaching assistantships, scholarships/grants, health care benefits, and unspecified assistantships available. Financial award application deadline: 2/15; financial award applicants required to submit FAFSA. *Faculty research:* Bioengineering, computational intelligence, computer architecture and VLSI design, computer graphics and vision, computer networks and systems, image processing. *Unit head:* Dr. Chaouki T. Abdallah, Chair, 505-277-0298, Fax: 505-277-1439, E-mail: chaouki@ece.unm.edu. *Application contact:* Elmyra Grelle, Coordinator, 505-277-2600, Fax: 505-277-1439, E-mail: egrelle@ece.unm.edu.
Website: http://www.ece.unm.edu/

University of New Mexico, Graduate Studies, School of Engineering, Programs in Electrical and Computer Engineering, Albuquerque, NM 87131-2039. Offers MS, PhD. *Program availability:* Part-time, evening/weekend, online learning. *Faculty:* 16 full-time (3 women), 5 part-time/adjunct (2 women). *Students:* 115 full-time (17 women), 153 part-time (31 women); includes 51 minority (1 Black or African American, non-Hispanic/Latino; 1 American Indian or Alaska Native, non-Hispanic/Latino; 6 Asian, non-Hispanic/Latino; 41 Hispanic/Latino; 2 Two or more races, non-Hispanic/Latino), 110 international. Average age 31. 299 applicants, 28% accepted, 49 enrolled. In 2016, 31 master's, 11 doctorates awarded. Terminal master's awarded for partial completion of doctoral program. *Degree requirements:* For master's, thesis; for doctorate, comprehensive exam, thesis/dissertation. *Entrance requirements:* For master's, GRE General Test, minimum GPA of 3.0; for doctorate, GRE General Test, minimum GPA of 3.5. Additional exam requirements/recommendations for international students: Required—TOEFL (minimum score 550 paper-based; 79 iBT). *Application deadline:* For fall admission, 6/15 for domestic students, 2/15 for international students; for spring admission, 11/1 for domestic students, 6/15 for international students. Application fee: $50. Electronic applications accepted. *Financial support:* Fellowships with tuition reimbursements, research assistantships with tuition reimbursements, teaching assistantships with tuition reimbursements, scholarships/grants, health care benefits, and unspecified assistantships available. *Faculty research:* Applied electromagnetics, biomedical engineering, communications, image processing, microelectronics, optoelectronics, signal processing, systems and controls. *Unit head:* Dr. Chaouki T. Abdallah, Chair, 505-277-0298, Fax: 505-277-1439, E-mail: chaouki@ece.unm.edu. *Application contact:* Elmyra Grelle, Coordinator, 505-277-2600, Fax: 505-277-1439, E-mail: egrelle@ece.unm.edu.
Website: http://www.ece.unm.edu/

The University of North Carolina at Charlotte, William States Lee College of Engineering, Department of Electrical and Computer Engineering, Charlotte, NC 28223-0001. Offers electrical engineering (MSEE, PhD). *Program availability:* Part-time, evening/weekend. *Faculty:* 27 full-time (2 women). *Students:* 191 full-time (48 women), 44 part-time (9 women); includes 8 minority (5 Black or African American, non-Hispanic/Latino; 2 Asian, non-Hispanic/Latino; 1 Hispanic/Latino), 205 international. Average age 26. 700 applicants, 52% accepted, 76 enrolled. In 2016, 107 master's, 10 doctorates awarded. *Degree requirements:* For master's, thesis, project, or exam; for doctorate, comprehensive exam, thesis/dissertation. *Entrance requirements:* For master's, GRE, undergraduate degree in electrical and computer engineering or a closely-related field of engineering or sciences; minimum undergraduate GPA of 3.0; letters of recommendation; statement of purpose; for doctorate, GRE General Test, master's degree in electrical and/or computer engineering or a closely-allied field demonstrating strong academic background for performing research in a chosen area of interest; minimum undergraduate and master's-level GPA of 3.5; letters of recommendation; statement of purpose. Additional exam requirements/recommendations for international students: Required—TOEFL (minimum score 523 paper-based, 70 iBT) or IELTS (6.5). *Application deadline:* For fall admission, 1/15 for domestic and international students; for spring admission, 7/15 for domestic and international students. Applications are processed on a rolling basis. Application fee: $75. Electronic applications accepted. *Expenses:* Contact institution. *Financial support:* In 2016–17, 65 students received support, including 26 research assistantships (averaging $8,720 per year), 39 teaching assistantships (averaging $6,013 per year); career-related internships or fieldwork, institutionally sponsored loans, scholarships/grants, and unspecified assistantships also available. Support available to part-time students. Financial award application deadline: 3/1; financial award applicants required to submit FAFSA. *Total annual research expenditures:* $1.7 million. *Unit head:* Dr. Asis Nasipuri, Chair, 704-687-8418, E-mail: anasipur@uncc.edu. *Application contact:* Kathy B. Giddings, Director of Graduate Admissions, 704-687-5503, Fax: 704-687-1668, E-mail: gradadm@uncc.edu.
Website: http://ece.uncc.edu/

University of North Texas, Robert B. Toulouse School of Graduate Studies, Denton, TX 76203-5459. Offers accounting (MS); applied anthropology (MA, MS); applied behavior analysis (Certificate); applied geography (MA); applied technology and performance improvement (M Ed, MS); art education (MA); art history (MA); art museum education (Certificate); arts leadership (Certificate); audiology (Au D); behavior analysis (MS); behavioral science (PhD); biochemistry and molecular biology (MS); biology (MA, MS); biomedical engineering (MS); business analysis (MS); chemistry (MS); clinical health psychology (PhD); communication studies (MA, MS); computer engineering (MS); computer science (MS); counseling (M Ed, MS), including clinical mental health counseling (MS), college and university counseling, elementary school counseling, secondary school counseling; creative writing (MA); criminal justice (MS); curriculum and instruction (M Ed); decision sciences (MBA); design (MA, MFA), including fashion design (MFA), innovation studies, interior design (MFA); early childhood studies (MS); economics (MS); educational leadership (M Ed, Ed D); educational psychology (MS, PhD), including family studies (MS), gifted and talented (MS), human development (MS), learning and cognition (MS), research, measurement and evaluation (MS); electrical engineering (MS); emergency management (MPA); engineering technology (MS); English (MA); English as a second language (MA); environmental science (MS); finance (MBA, MS); financial management (MPA); French (MA); health services management (MBA); higher education (M Ed, Ed D); history (MA, MS); hospitality management (MS); human resources management (MPA); information science (MS); information systems (PhD); information technologies (MBA); interdisciplinary studies (MA, MS); international studies (MA); international sustainable tourism (MS); jazz studies (MM); journalism (MA, MJ, Graduate Certificate), including interactive and virtual digital communication (Graduate Certificate), narrative journalism (Graduate Certificate), public relations (Graduate Certificate); kinesiology (MS); linguistics (MA); local government management (MPA); logistics (PhD); logistics and supply chain management (MBA); long-term care, senior housing, and aging services (MA); management (PhD); marketing (MBA); mathematics (MA, MS); mechanical and energy engineering (MS, PhD); music (MA), including ethnomusicology, music theory, musicology, performance; music composition (PhD); music education (MM Ed, PhD); nonprofit management (MPA); operations and supply chain management (MBA); performance (MM, DMA); philosophy (MA); political science (MA); professional and technical communication (MA); radio, television and film (MA, MFA); rehabilitation counseling (Certificate); sociology (MA); Spanish (MA); special education (M Ed); speech-language pathology (MA); strategic management (MBA); studio art (MFA); teaching (M Ed); MBA/MS. *Program availability:* Part-time, evening/weekend, online learning. Terminal master's awarded for partial completion of doctoral program. *Degree requirements:* For master's, variable foreign language requirement, comprehensive exam (for some programs), thesis (for some programs); for doctorate, variable foreign language requirement, comprehensive exam (for some programs), thesis/dissertation; for other advanced degree, variable foreign language requirement, comprehensive exam (for some programs). *Entrance requirements:* For master's and doctorate, GRE, GMAT. Additional exam requirements/recommendations for international students: Required—TOEFL (minimum score 550 paper-based; 79 iBT). Electronic applications accepted.

Computer Engineering

University of Notre Dame, Graduate School, College of Engineering, Department of Computer Science and Engineering, Notre Dame, IN 46556. Offers MSCSE, PhD. Terminal master's awarded for partial completion of doctoral program. *Degree requirements:* For master's, comprehensive exam; for doctorate, thesis/dissertation, candidacy exam. *Entrance requirements:* For master's and doctorate, GRE General Test. Additional exam requirements/recommendations for international students: Required—TOEFL (minimum score 600 paper-based; 80 iBT). Electronic applications accepted. *Faculty research:* Algorithms and theory of computer science, artificial intelligence, behavior-based robotics, biometrics, computer vision.

University of Oklahoma, Gallogly College of Engineering, School of Electrical and Computer Engineering, Program in Electrical and Computer Engineering, Norman, OK 73019. Offers MS, PhD. *Program availability:* Part-time. *Students:* 83 full-time (15 women), 53 part-time (12 women); includes 14 minority (2 Black or African American, non-Hispanic/Latino; 1 American Indian or Alaska Native, non-Hispanic/Latino; 5 Asian, non-Hispanic/Latino; 5 Hispanic/Latino; 1 Two or more races, non-Hispanic/Latino), 88 international. Average age 29. 102 applicants, 35% accepted, 22 enrolled. In 2016, 23 master's, 15 doctorates awarded. Terminal master's awarded for partial completion of doctoral program. *Degree requirements:* For master's, comprehensive exam (for some programs), thesis (for some programs); for doctorate, thesis/dissertation, general exam. *Entrance requirements:* For master's and doctorate, GRE, minimum GPA of 3.0. Additional exam requirements/recommendations for international students: Required—TOEFL (minimum score 79 iBT) or IELTS (minimum score 6.5). *Application deadline:* For fall admission, 4/1 for domestic students, 3/1 for international students; for spring admission, 11/1 for domestic students, 10/1 for international students. Applications are processed on a rolling basis. Application fee: $50 ($100 for international students). Electronic applications accepted. *Expenses:* Tuition, state resident: full-time $4886; part-time $203.60 per credit hour. Tuition, nonresident: full-time $18,989; part-time $791.20 per credit hour. *Required fees:* $3283; $126.25 per credit hour. $126.50 per semester. *Financial support:* In 2016–17, 111 students received support. Fellowships with full and partial tuition reimbursements available, research assistantships with full and partial tuition reimbursements available, teaching assistantships with full and partial tuition reimbursements available, career-related internships or fieldwork, scholarships/grants, and health care benefits available. Financial award application deadline: 6/1; financial award applicants required to submit FAFSA. *Faculty research:* Biomedical imaging, radar engineering, semiconductor devices, intelligent transportation systems, signals and systems. *Unit head:* Dr. J.R. Cruz, Director, 405-325-8131, Fax: 405-325-7066, E-mail: jcruz@ou.edu. *Application contact:* Lisa Wilkins, Graduate Programs Assistant III, 405-325-4285, Fax: 405-325-7066, E-mail: lawikins@ou.edu.
Website: http://www.ou.edu/coe/ece.html

University of Ottawa, Faculty of Graduate and Postdoctoral Studies, Faculty of Engineering, Ottawa-Carleton Institute for Electrical and Computer Engineering, Ottawa, ON K1N 6N5, Canada. Offers M Eng, MA Sc, PhD. *Degree requirements:* For master's, thesis or alternative, project; for doctorate, comprehensive exam, thesis/dissertation. *Entrance requirements:* For master's, honors degree or equivalent, minimum B average; for doctorate, minimum A- average. Electronic applications accepted. *Faculty research:* CAD, distributed systems.

University of Pittsburgh, Swanson School of Engineering, Department of Electrical and Computer Engineering, Pittsburgh, PA 15260. Offers computer engineering (MS, PhD); electrical and computer engineering (MS, PhD). *Program availability:* Part-time, 100% online. *Faculty:* 21 full-time (3 women), 8 part-time/adjunct (1 woman). *Students:* 142 full-time (31 women), 38 part-time (7 women); includes 13 minority (4 Black or African American, non-Hispanic/Latino; 3 Asian, non-Hispanic/Latino; 3 Hispanic/Latino; 1 Native Hawaiian or other Pacific Islander, non-Hispanic/Latino; 2 Two or more races, non-Hispanic/Latino), 113 international. 891 applicants, 20% accepted, 55 enrolled. In 2016, 35 master's, 14 doctorates awarded. Terminal master's awarded for partial completion of doctoral program. *Degree requirements:* For doctorate, comprehensive exam, thesis/dissertation, final oral exams. *Entrance requirements:* For master's and doctorate, GRE General Test, minimum GPA of 3.0. Additional exam requirements/recommendations for international students: Required—TOEFL (minimum score 550 paper-based; 80 iBT). *Application deadline:* For fall admission, 3/1 priority date for domestic and international students; for spring admission, 7/1 priority date for domestic and international students. Applications are processed on a rolling basis. Application fee: $50. Electronic applications accepted. *Expenses:* $24,962 full-time per academic year in-state tuition, $41,222 full-time per academic year out-of-state tuition; $830 mandatory fees per academic year. *Financial support:* In 2016–17, 16 fellowships with full tuition reimbursements (averaging $30,720 per year), 61 research assistantships with full tuition reimbursements (averaging $27,396 per year), 25 teaching assistantships with full tuition reimbursements (averaging $26,328 per year) were awarded; scholarships/grants and tuition waivers (full) also available. Financial award application deadline: 3/1. *Faculty research:* Computer engineering, image processing, signal processing, electro-optic devices, controls/power. *Total annual research expenditures:* $8.8 million. *Unit head:* Dr. Alan D. George, Chairman, 412-624-8000, Fax: 412-624-8003, E-mail: alan.george@pitt.edu. *Application contact:* Rama Bazaz, Director, 412-624-9800, Fax: 412-624-9808, E-mail: ssoeadm@pitt.edu.
Website: http://www.engineering.pitt.edu/Departments/Electrical-Computer/

University of Puerto Rico, Mayagüez Campus, Graduate Studies, College of Engineering, Computer Science and Engineering Program, Mayagüez, PR 00681-9000. Offers PhD. *Program availability:* Part-time. *Faculty:* 10 full-time (1 woman). *Students:* 36 full-time (4 women), 9 part-time (1 woman); includes 37 minority (all Hispanic/Latino), 6 international. Average age 25. 13 applicants, 85% accepted, 5 enrolled. *Degree requirements:* For doctorate, one foreign language, comprehensive exam, thesis/dissertation. *Entrance requirements:* For doctorate, GRE General Test, BS in engineering or science; undergraduate courses in data structures, programming language, calculus III and linear algebra, or the equivalent. *Application deadline:* For fall admission, 2/15 for domestic and international students; for spring admission, 9/15 for domestic and international students. Applications are processed on a rolling basis. Application fee: $25. Electronic applications accepted. *Expenses: Tuition, area resident:* Full-time $2466. *International tuition:* $7166 full-time. *Required fees:* $210. One-time fee: $5 full-time. Tuition and fees vary according to course level, campus/location, program and student level. *Financial support:* In 2016–17, 12 students received support, including 7 research assistantships with full and partial tuition reimbursements available (averaging $1,919 per year), 11 teaching assistantships with full and partial tuition reimbursements available (averaging $5,252 per year); unspecified assistantships also available. *Faculty research:* Big data analysis, parallel and distributor processing, mobile computing and networking, remote sensing, channel capacity. *Unit head:* Bienvenido Velez, Ph.D., Acting Director, 787-832-4040 Ext. 5827, Fax: 787-833-3331, E-mail: bienvenido.velez@upr.edu. *Application contact:* Alida Minguela, Administrative Assistant, 787-832-4040 Ext. 5217, Fax: 787-833-3331, E-mail: alida@ece.uprm.edu.
Website: http://cse.uprm.edu/

University of Puerto Rico, Mayagüez Campus, Graduate Studies, College of Engineering, Department of Electrical and Computer Engineering, Mayagüez, PR 00681-9000. Offers computer engineering (ME, MS); computing and information

sciences and engineering (PhD); electrical engineering (ME, MS). *Program availability:* Part-time. *Faculty:* 48 full-time (6 women). *Students:* 45 full-time (6 women), 8 part-time (3 women); includes 45 minority (all Hispanic/Latino), 5 international. Average age 25. 30 applicants, 83% accepted, 18 enrolled. In 2016, 12 master's awarded. Terminal master's awarded for partial completion of doctoral program. *Degree requirements:* For master's, one foreign language, comprehensive exam, thesis; for doctorate, one foreign language, comprehensive exam, thesis/dissertation. *Entrance requirements:* For master's and doctorate, proficiency in English and Spanish; BS in electrical or computer engineering, or equivalent; minimum GPA of 3.0. *Application deadline:* For fall admission, 2/15 for domestic and international students; for spring admission, 9/15 for domestic and international students. Applications are processed on a rolling basis. Application fee: $25. Electronic applications accepted. *Expenses: Tuition, area resident:* Full-time $2466. *International tuition:* $7166 full-time. *Required fees:* $210. One-time fee: $5 full-time. Tuition and fees vary according to course level, campus/location, program and student level. *Financial support:* In 2016–17, 50 students received support, including 41 research assistantships with full and partial tuition reimbursements available (averaging $3,442 per year), 26 teaching assistantships with full and partial tuition reimbursements available (averaging $4,149 per year); unspecified assistantships also available. *Faculty research:* Digital signal processing, power electronics, microwave ocean emissivity, parallel and distributed computing, microwave remote sensing. *Unit head:* Jose Colom-Ustaris, Ph.D., Department Head, 787-832-4040 Ext. 3086, Fax: 787-831-7564, E-mail: jose.colom1@upr.edu. *Application contact:* Claribel Lorenzo, Administrative Secretary V, 787-832-4040 Ext. 3821, E-mail: claribel.lorenzo@upr.edu.
Website: https://ece.uprm.edu/

University of Regina, Faculty of Graduate Studies and Research, Faculty of Engineering and Applied Science, Program in Electronic Systems Engineering, Regina, SK S4S 0A2, Canada. Offers M Eng, MA Sc, PhD. *Program availability:* Part-time. *Faculty:* 7 full-time (1 woman), 24 part-time/adjunct (0 women). *Students:* 12 full-time (1 woman), 5 part-time (0 women). 101 applicants, 8% accepted. In 2016, 13 master's, 2 doctorates awarded. *Degree requirements:* For master's, thesis, project, report; for doctorate, thesis/dissertation. *Entrance requirements:* For doctorate, master's degree. Additional exam requirements/recommendations for international students: Required—TOEFL (minimum score 550 paper-based; 80 iBT), IELTS (minimum score 6.5), PTE (minimum score 59). *Application deadline:* For fall admission, 3/31 for domestic and international students; for winter admission, 7/31 for domestic and international students; for spring admission, 11/30 for domestic and international students. Application fee: $100. Electronic applications accepted. *Expenses:* Contact institution. *Financial support:* In 2016–17, 14 fellowships (averaging $6,286 per year), 12 teaching assistantships (averaging $2,521 per year) were awarded; career-related internships or fieldwork and scholarships/grants also available. Financial award application deadline: 6/15. *Faculty research:* Local area networks, digital and data communications systems design, telecommunications and computer networks, image processing, radio frequency (RF) and microwave engineering. *Unit head:* Dr. Amr Henni, Associate Dean, Research and Graduate Studies, 306-585-4960, Fax: 306-585-4855, E-mail: amr.henni@uregina.ca. *Application contact:* Dr. Abdul Bais, Graduate Coordinator, 306-585-4701, Fax: 306-585-4855, E-mail: abdul.bais@uregina.ca.
Website: http://www.uregina.ca/engineering/

University of Rhode Island, Graduate School, College of Engineering, Department of Electrical, Computer and Biomedical Engineering, Kingston, RI 02881. Offers acoustics and underwater acoustics (MS, PhD); biomedical engineering (MS, PhD); circuits and devices (MS); communication theory (MS, PhD); computer architectures and digital systems (MS, PhD); computer networks (MS, PhD); digital signal processing (MS); embedded systems and computer applications (MS, PhD); fault-tolerant computing (MS, PhD); materials and optics (MS, PhD); systems theory (MS, PhD). *Program availability:* Part-time. *Faculty:* 22 full-time (3 women). *Students:* 27 full-time (5 women), 17 part-time (3 women); includes 6 minority (1 American Indian or Alaska Native, non-Hispanic/Latino; 3 Asian, non-Hispanic/Latino; 1 Hispanic/Latino; 1 Two or more races, non-Hispanic/Latino), 21 international. In 2016, 8 master's, 7 doctorates awarded. *Degree requirements:* For master's, comprehensive exam (for some programs), thesis optional; for doctorate, comprehensive exam, thesis/dissertation. *Entrance requirements:* For master's and doctorate, GRE, 2 letters of recommendation (3 for international applicants). Additional exam requirements/recommendations for international students: Required—TOEFL. *Application deadline:* For fall admission, 7/15 for domestic students, 2/1 for international students; for spring admission, 11/15 for domestic students, 7/15 for international students; for summer admission, 4/15 for domestic students. Application fee: $65. Electronic applications accepted. *Expenses:* Tuition, state resident: full-time $11,796; part-time $655 per credit. Tuition, nonresident: full-time $24,206; part-time $1345 per credit. *Required fees:* $1546; $44 per credit. One-time fee: $155 full-time; $35 part-time. *Financial support:* In 2016–17, 11 research assistantships with tuition reimbursements (averaging $9,825 per year), 4 teaching assistantships with tuition reimbursements (averaging $8,681 per year) were awarded. Financial award application deadline: 7/15; financial award applicants required to submit FAFSA. *Unit head:* Dr. Godi Fischer, Chair, 401-874-5879, Fax: 401-782-6422, E-mail: fischer@ele.uri.edu. *Application contact:* Dr. Frederick J. Vetter, Graduate Director, 401-874-5141, E-mail: vetter@ele.uri.edu.
Website: http://www.ele.uri.edu/

University of Rochester, Hajim School of Engineering and Applied Sciences, Department of Electrical and Computer Engineering, Rochester, NY 14627. Offers MS, PhD. *Faculty:* 19 full-time (1 woman). *Students:* 122 full-time (19 women), 1 part-time (0 women); includes 5 minority (2 Black or African American, non-Hispanic/Latino; 2 Asian, non-Hispanic/Latino; 1 Hispanic/Latino), 94 international. Average age 26. 543 applicants, 41% accepted, 43 enrolled. In 2016, 57 master's, 11 doctorates awarded. Terminal master's awarded for partial completion of doctoral program. *Degree requirements:* For master's, comprehensive exam, thesis, final exam; for doctorate, thesis/dissertation, qualifying exam. *Entrance requirements:* For master's and doctorate, GRE. Additional exam requirements/recommendations for international students: Required—TOEFL. *Application deadline:* For fall admission, 1/15 for domestic students. Application fee: $60. Electronic applications accepted. *Expenses:* $1,538 per credit hour. *Financial support:* In 2016–17, 130 students received support, including 2 fellowships with full tuition reimbursements available (averaging $27,600 per year), 54 research assistantships with full tuition reimbursements available (averaging $27,600 per year), 42 teaching assistantships with full and partial tuition reimbursements available (averaging $2,500 per year); tuition waivers (full and partial) also available. *Faculty research:* Bio-informatics, communications, signal processing, digital audio, image processing, medical imaging. *Unit head:* Mark Bocko, Chair, 585-275-4879. *Application contact:* Michele Foster, Administrative Assistant/Graduate Program Coordinator, 585-275-4054, E-mail: michele.foster@rochester.edu.
Website: http://www.ece.rochester.edu/graduate/index.html

University of Rochester, Hajim School of Engineering and Applied Sciences, Master of Science in Technical Entrepreneurship and Management Program, Rochester, NY 14642. Offers biomedical engineering (MS); chemical engineering (MS); computer science (MS); electrical and computer engineering (MS); energy and the environment (MS); materials science (MS); mechanical engineering (MS); optics (MS). Program

offered in collaboration with the Simon School of Business. *Program availability:* Part-time. *Students:* 42 full-time (13 women), 6 part-time (3 women); includes 7 minority (1 Black or African American, non-Hispanic/Latino; 1 Asian, non-Hispanic/Latino; 4 Hispanic/Latino; 1 Two or more races, non-Hispanic/Latino), 28 international. Average age 24. 245 applicants, 65% accepted, 29 enrolled. In 2016, 31 master's awarded. *Degree requirements:* For master's, comprehensive exam, final exam. *Entrance requirements:* For master's, GRE or GMAT, 3 letters of recommendation; personal statement; official transcript; bachelor's degree (or equivalent for international students) in engineering, science, or mathematics. Additional exam requirements/recommendations for international students: Required—TOEFL (minimum score 600 paper-based; 100 iBT). *Application deadline:* For fall admission, 2/1 for domestic and international students. Application fee: $60. Electronic applications accepted. *Expenses:* $1,800 per credit. *Financial support:* In 2016–17, 45 students received support. Career-related internships or fieldwork and scholarships/grants available. Support available to part-time students. Financial award application deadline: 2/1. *Faculty research:* High efficiency solar cells, macromolecular self-assembly, digital signal processing, memory hierarchy management, molecular and physical mechanisms in cell migration, optical imaging systems. *Unit head:* Duncan T. Moore, Vice Provost for Entrepreneurship, 585-275-5248, Fax: 585-473-6745, E-mail: duncan.moore@rochester.edu. *Application contact:* Andrea Barrett, Executive Director, 585-276-3407, Fax: 585-276-2357, E-mail: andrea.barrett@rochester.edu.
Website: http://www.rochester.edu/team

University of San Diego, Shiley-Marcos School of Engineering, San Diego, CA 92110-2492. Offers cyber security engineering (MS). *Faculty:* 1 full-time (0 women). *Students:* 3 part-time (0 women); includes 1 minority (Asian, non-Hispanic/Latino). 17 applicants, 82% accepted, 3 enrolled. *Degree requirements:* For master's, capstone course. *Entrance requirements:* Additional exam requirements/recommendations for international students: Required—TOEFL (minimum score 120 iBT). *Application deadline:* For fall admission, 8/2 for domestic students; for spring admission, 11/7 for domestic students; for summer admission, 4/11 for domestic students. Application fee: $45. *Unit head:* Dr. Chell Roberts, Dean, 619-260-4627, E-mail: croberts@sandiego.edu. *Application contact:* Monica Mahon, Associate Director of Graduate Admissions, 619-260-4524, Fax: 619-260-4158, E-mail: grads@sandiego.edu.
Website: http://www.sandiego.edu/engineering/

University of South Alabama, College of Engineering, Department of Electrical and Computer Engineering, Mobile, AL 36688. Offers computer engineering (MSEE); electrical engineering (MSEE). *Program availability:* Part-time. *Faculty:* 9 full-time (0 women). *Students:* 47 full-time (13 women), 6 part-time (1 woman); includes 5 minority (3 Black or African American, non-Hispanic/Latino; 1 Native Hawaiian or other Pacific Islander, non-Hispanic/Latino; 1 Two or more races, non-Hispanic/Latino), 42 international. Average age 25. 104 applicants, 55% accepted, 7 enrolled. In 2016, 88 master's awarded. *Degree requirements:* For master's, comprehensive exam, thesis or project. *Entrance requirements:* For master's, GRE General Test, BS in engineering, minimum GPA of 3.0. Additional exam requirements/recommendations for international students: Required—TOEFL (minimum score 550 paper-based; 79 iBT). *Application deadline:* For fall admission, 7/1 priority date for domestic students, 6/1 priority date for international students; for spring admission, 12/1 priority date for domestic students, 11/1 priority date for international students; for summer admission, 5/1 priority date for domestic students, 4/1 priority date for international students. Applications are processed on a rolling basis. Application fee: $35. Electronic applications accepted. *Expenses:* Contact institution. *Financial support:* Fellowships, research assistantships, teaching assistantships, career-related internships or fieldwork, institutionally sponsored loans, scholarships/grants, and unspecified assistantships available. Support available to part-time students. Financial award application deadline: 5/31; financial award applicants required to submit FAFSA. *Faculty research:* Plasma characterization, oil polluted contaminants, target detection and tracking, space propulsion applications, electrical and computer engineering. *Unit head:* Dr. Hulya Kirkici, Department Chair, 251-460-6117, Fax: 251-460-6028, E-mail: hkirkici@southalabama.edu. *Application contact:* Brenda Poole, Academic Records Specialist, 251-460-6140, Fax: 251-460-6343, E-mail: engineering@southalabama.edu.
Website: http://www.southalabama.edu/colleges/engineering/ece/index.html

University of South Carolina, The Graduate School, College of Engineering and Computing, Department of Computer Science and Engineering, Columbia, SC 29208. Offers computer science and engineering (ME, MS, PhD); software engineering (MS). *Program availability:* Part-time, evening/weekend, online learning. *Degree requirements:* For master's, comprehensive exam, thesis (for some programs); for doctorate, comprehensive exam, thesis/dissertation. *Entrance requirements:* For master's and doctorate, GRE General Test. Additional exam requirements/recommendations for international students: Required—TOEFL (minimum score 570 paper-based). Electronic applications accepted. *Faculty research:* Computer security, computer vision, artificial intelligence, multiagent systems, bioinformatics.

University of Southern California, Graduate School, Viterbi School of Engineering, Department of Computer Science, Los Angeles, CA 90089. Offers computer networks (MS); computer science (MS, PhD); computer security (MS); game development (MS); high performance computing and simulations (MS); human language technology (MS); intelligent robotics (MS); multimedia and creative technologies (MS); software engineering (MS). *Program availability:* Part-time, evening/weekend, online learning. *Entrance requirements:* For master's and doctorate, GRE General Test. Additional exam requirements/recommendations for international students: Required—TOEFL. Electronic applications accepted. *Faculty research:* Databases, computer graphics and computer vision, software engineering, networks and security, robotics, multimedia and virtual reality.

University of Southern California, Graduate School, Viterbi School of Engineering, Ming Hsieh Department of Electrical Engineering, Los Angeles, CA 90089. Offers computer engineering (MS, PhD); electric power (MS); electrical engineering (MS, PhD, Engr); engineering technology commercialization (Graduate Certificate); multimedia and creative technologies (MS); telecommunications (MS); VLSI design (MS); wireless health technology (MS). *Program availability:* Part-time, online learning. Terminal master's awarded for partial completion of doctoral program. *Degree requirements:* For master's, thesis optional; for doctorate, thesis/dissertation. *Entrance requirements:* For master's and doctorate, GRE General Test. Additional exam requirements/recommendations for international students: Recommended—TOEFL. Electronic applications accepted. *Faculty research:* Communications, computer engineering and networks, control systems, integrated circuits and systems, electromagnetics and energy conversion, micro electro-mechanical systems and nanotechnology, photonics and quantum electronics, plasma research, signal and image processing.

University of South Florida, College of Engineering, Department of Computer Science and Engineering, Tampa, FL 33620-9951. Offers computer engineering (MSCP); computer science (MSCS); computer science and engineering (PhD). *Program availability:* Part-time. *Faculty:* 21 full-time (3 women). *Students:* 182 full-time (41 women), 43 part-time (11 women); includes 20 minority (4 Black or African American, non-Hispanic/Latino; 7 Asian, non-Hispanic/Latino; 8 Hispanic/Latino; 1 Two or more races, non-Hispanic/Latino), 171 international. Average age 27. 566 applicants, 43%

accepted, 67 enrolled. In 2016, 41 master's, 10 doctorates awarded. Terminal master's awarded for partial completion of doctoral program. *Degree requirements:* For master's, comprehensive exam, thesis or alternative; for doctorate, comprehensive exam, thesis/dissertation, teaching of at least one undergraduate computer science and engineering course. *Entrance requirements:* For master's, GRE General Test, minimum GPA of 3.0 in last 60 hours of coursework, three letters of recommendation, statement of purpose; for doctorate, GRE General Test, minimum GPA of 3.0 in last 60 hours of coursework, three letters of recommendation, statement of purpose that includes three areas of research interest. Additional exam requirements/recommendations for international students: Required—TOEFL (minimum score 550 paper-based; 79 iBT) or IELTS (minimum score 6.5). *Application deadline:* For fall admission, 2/15 for domestic and international students; for spring admission, 10/15 for domestic students, 9/15 for international students. Application fee: $30. Electronic applications accepted. *Expenses:* Tuition, state resident: full-time $7766; part-time $431.43 per credit hour. Tuition, nonresident: full-time $15,789; part-time $877.17 per credit hour. Required fees: $37 per term. *Financial support:* In 2016–17, 26 students received support, including 30 research assistantships with tuition reimbursements available (averaging $14,942 per year), 35 teaching assistantships with tuition reimbursements available (averaging $14,003 per year); unspecified assistantships also available. Financial award application deadline: 1/1; financial award applicants required to submit FAFSA. *Faculty research:* Artificial intelligence/intelligence systems; computational biology and bioinformatics; computer vision and pattern recognition; databases; distributed systems; graphics; information systems (networks) and location-aware information systems; robotics (biomorphic robotics and robot perception and action); software security; VLSI, computer architecture, and parallel processing. *Total annual research expenditures:* $1.2 million. *Unit head:* Dr. Lawrence Hall, Professor and Department Chair, 813-974-4195, Fax: 813-974-5094, E-mail: hall@cse.usf.edu. *Application contact:* Dr. Srivinas Katkoori, Associate Professor and Graduate Program Director, 813-974-5737, Fax: 813-974-5094, E-mail: katkoori@cse.usf.edu.
Website: http://www.cse.usf.edu/

The University of Tennessee, Graduate School, Tickle College of Engineering, Department of Electrical Engineering and Computer Science, Program in Computer Engineering, Knoxville, TN 37996. Offers MS, PhD. *Program availability:* Part-time. *Faculty:* 7 full-time (2 women). *Students:* 34 full-time (6 women), 5 part-time (1 woman); includes 1 minority (Asian, non-Hispanic/Latino), 23 international. Average age 27. 84 applicants, 20% accepted, 16 enrolled. In 2016, 6 master's, 9 doctorates awarded. *Degree requirements:* For master's, thesis or alternative; for doctorate, comprehensive exam, thesis/dissertation. *Entrance requirements:* For master's, GRE General Test (for MS students pursuing research thesis), minimum GPA of 2.7 (for U.S. degree holders), 3.0 (for international degree holders); 3 references; personal statement; for doctorate, GRE General Test, minimum GPA of 3.0 on previous graduate course work; 3 references; personal statement. Additional exam requirements/recommendations for international students: Required—TOEFL (minimum score 550 paper-based). *Application deadline:* For fall admission, 2/1 priority date for domestic and international students; for spring admission, 6/15 for domestic and international students. Applications are processed on a rolling basis. Application fee: $35. Electronic applications accepted. *Financial support:* In 2016–17, 33 students received support, including 1 fellowship with full tuition reimbursement available (averaging $25,000 per year), 23 research assistantships with full tuition reimbursements available (averaging $21,288 per year), 6 teaching assistantships with full tuition reimbursements available (averaging $18,866 per year); career-related internships or fieldwork, Federal Work-Study, institutionally sponsored loans, health care benefits, and unspecified assistantships also available. Financial award application deadline: 2/1; financial award applicants required to submit FAFSA. *Unit head:* Dr. Leon Tolbert, Head, 865-974-3461, Fax: 865-974-5483, E-mail: tolbert@utk.edu. *Application contact:* Dr. Jens Gregor, Associate Head, 865-974-4399, Fax: 865-974-5483, E-mail: jgregor@utk.edu.
Website: http://www.eecs.utk.edu

The University of Texas at Arlington, Graduate School, College of Engineering, Department of Computer Science and Engineering, Arlington, TX 76019. Offers computer engineering (MS, PhD); computer science (MS, PhD); mathematical sciences, computer science (PhD); software engineering (MS). *Program availability:* Part-time, online learning. Terminal master's awarded for partial completion of doctoral program. *Degree requirements:* For master's, comprehensive exam (for some programs), thesis; for doctorate, comprehensive exam, thesis/dissertation. *Entrance requirements:* For master's, GRE General Test, minimum GPA of 3.0 (3.2 in computer science-related classes); for doctorate, GRE General Test, minimum GPA of 3.5. Additional exam requirements/recommendations for international students: Required—TOEFL (minimum score 550 paper-based; 92 iBT), IELTS (minimum score 6.5). *Application deadline:* For fall admission, 6/1 for domestic students, 5/1 for international students; for spring admission, 12/1 for domestic students, 10/1 for international students. Applications are processed on a rolling basis. Application fee: $35 ($50 for international students). *Financial support:* Fellowships with full tuition reimbursements, research assistantships with partial tuition reimbursements, teaching assistantships with partial tuition reimbursements, career-related internships or fieldwork, and scholarships/grants available. Financial award application deadline: 6/1; financial award applicants required to submit FAFSA. *Faculty research:* Algorithms, homeland security, mobile pervasive computing, high performance computing bio information. *Unit head:* Dr. Fillia Makedon, Chairman, 817-272-3605, E-mail: makedon@uta.edu. *Application contact:* Dr. Bahram Khalili, Graduate Advisor, 817-272-5407, Fax: 817-272-3784, E-mail: khalili@uta.edu.
Website: http://www.cse.uta.edu/

The University of Texas at Austin, Graduate School, Cockrell School of Engineering, Department of Electrical and Computer Engineering, Austin, TX 78712-1111. Offers MS, PhD. *Program availability:* Part-time. *Entrance requirements:* For master's, GRE General Test, minimum GPA of 3.3 in upper-division course work; for doctorate, GRE General Test. Electronic applications accepted.

The University of Texas at Dallas, Erik Jonson School of Engineering and Computer Science, Department of Electrical Engineering, Richardson, TX 75080. Offers computer engineering (MS, PhD); electrical engineering (MSEE, PhD); telecommunications engineering (MSTE, PhD). *Program availability:* Part-time, evening/weekend. *Faculty:* 47 full-time (4 women), 5 part-time/adjunct (0 women). *Students:* 648 full-time (178 women), 196 part-time (50 women); includes 40 minority (1 Black or African American, non-Hispanic/Latino; 23 Asian, non-Hispanic/Latino; 11 Hispanic/Latino; 5 Two or more races, non-Hispanic/Latino), 744 international. Average age 27. 2,663 applicants, 34% accepted, 287 enrolled. In 2016, 292 master's, 41 doctorates awarded. *Degree requirements:* For master's, thesis or major design project; for doctorate, thesis/dissertation. *Entrance requirements:* For master's, GRE General Test, minimum GPA of 3.0 in related bachelor's degree; for doctorate, GRE General Test, minimum GPA of 3.5. Additional exam requirements/recommendations for international students: Required—TOEFL (minimum score 550 paper-based). *Application deadline:* For fall admission, 7/15 for domestic students, 5/1 priority date for international students; for spring admission, 11/15 for domestic students, 9/1 priority date for international students. Applications are processed on a rolling basis. Application fee: $50 ($100 for international students). Electronic applications accepted. *Expenses:* Tuition, state resident: full-time $12,418; part-time $690 per semester hour. Tuition, nonresident: full-time $24,150;

part-time $1342 per semester hour. Tuition and fees vary according to course load. *Financial support:* In 2016–17, 234 students received support, including 12 fellowships (averaging $1,267 per year), 128 research assistantships with partial tuition reimbursements available (averaging $23,845 per year), 76 teaching assistantships with partial tuition reimbursements available (averaging $17,289 per year); Federal Work-Study, institutionally sponsored loans, scholarships/grants, unspecified assistantships, and cooperative positions also available. Support available to part-time students. Financial award application deadline: 4/30; financial award applicants required to submit FAFSA. *Faculty research:* Semiconductor device manufacturing, photonics devices and systems, signal processing and language technology, nano-fabrication, energy efficient digital systems. *Unit head:* Dr. Lawrence Overzet, Department Head, 972-883-6755, Fax: 972-883-2710, E-mail: overzet@utdallas.edu. *Application contact:* 972-883-6755, Fax: 972-883-2710, E-mail: eegrad_assist@utdallas.edu.
Website: http://www.ee.utdallas.edu

The University of Texas at El Paso, Graduate School, College of Engineering, Department of Electrical and Computer Engineering, El Paso, TX 79968-0001. Offers computer engineering (MS); electrical and computer engineering (PhD); electrical engineering (MS). *Program availability:* Part-time, evening/weekend. Terminal master's awarded for partial completion of doctoral program. *Degree requirements:* For master's, thesis optional; for doctorate, thesis/dissertation. *Entrance requirements:* For master's, GRE General Test, minimum GPA of 3.0; for doctorate, GRE General Test, minimum graduate GPA of 3.0. Additional exam requirements/recommendations for international students: Required—TOEFL. Electronic applications accepted. *Faculty research:* Signal and image processing, computer architecture, fiber optics, computational electromagnetics, electronic displays and thin films.

The University of Texas at San Antonio, College of Engineering, Department of Electrical and Computer Engineering, San Antonio, TX 78249-0617. Offers advanced materials engineering (MS); computer engineering (MS); electrical engineering (MSEE, PhD). *Program availability:* Part-time. *Faculty:* 26 full-time (4 women), 3 part-time/adjunct (0 women). *Students:* 122 full-time (31 women), 100 part-time (22 women); includes 46 minority (4 Black or African American, non-Hispanic/Latino; 10 Asian, non-Hispanic/Latino; 30 Hispanic/Latino; 1 Native Hawaiian or other Pacific Islander, non-Hispanic/Latino; 1 Two or more races, non-Hispanic/Latino), 131 international. Average age 28. 233 applicants, 73% accepted, 50 enrolled. In 2016, 115 master's, 15 doctorates awarded. Terminal master's awarded for partial completion of doctoral program. *Degree requirements:* For master's, comprehensive exam, thesis (for some programs); for doctorate, comprehensive exam, thesis/dissertation. *Entrance requirements:* For master's, GRE General Test, bachelor's degree in electrical or computer engineering from ABET-accredited institution of higher education or related field; minimum GPA of 3.0 on the last 60 semester credit hours of undergraduate studies; for doctorate, GRE General Test, master's degree or minimum GPA of 3.3 in last 60 semester credit hours of undergraduate level coursework in electrical engineering; statement of purpose. Additional exam requirements/recommendations for international students: Required—TOEFL (minimum score 550 paper-based; 79 iBT), IELTS (minimum score 6.5). *Application deadline:* For fall admission, 7/1 for domestic students, 4/1 for international students; for spring admission, 11/1 for domestic students, 9/1 for international students. Applications are processed on a rolling basis. Application fee: $45 ($80 for international students). Electronic applications accepted. *Financial support:* Unspecified assistantships available. Financial award application deadline: 3/31. *Faculty research:* Computer engineering, digital signal processing, systems and controls, communications, electronics materials and devices, electric power engineering. *Total annual research expenditures:* $3.9 million. *Unit head:* Dr. Chunjiang Qian, Department Chair/Professor, 210-458-7928, E-mail: chunjiang.qian@utsa.edu.
Website: http://ece.utsa.edu/

University of Toronto, School of Graduate Studies, Faculty of Applied Science and Engineering, Department of Electrical and Computer Engineering, Toronto, ON M5S 1A1, Canada. Offers M Eng, MA Sc, PhD. *Program availability:* Part-time. *Degree requirements:* For master's, thesis (for some programs), oral thesis defense (MA Sc); for doctorate, thesis/dissertation, qualifying exam, thesis defense. *Entrance requirements:* For master's, four-year degree in electrical or computer engineering, minimum B average, 2 letters of reference; for doctorate, minimum B+ average, MA Sc in electrical or computer engineering, 2 letters of reference. Additional exam requirements/recommendations for international students: Required—TOEFL (minimum score 580 paper-based; 93 iBT). Electronic applications accepted.

University of Victoria, Faculty of Graduate Studies, Faculty of Engineering, Department of Electrical and Computer Engineering, Victoria, BC V8W 2Y2, Canada. Offers M Eng, MA Sc, PhD. *Degree requirements:* For master's, thesis; for doctorate, thesis/dissertation, candidacy exam. *Entrance requirements:* For master's, GRE (recommended), bachelor's degree in engineering; for doctorate, GRE (recommended), master's degree. Additional exam requirements/recommendations for international students: Required—TOEFL (minimum score 575 paper-based), IELTS (minimum score 7). Electronic applications accepted. *Faculty research:* Communications and computers; electromagnetics, microwaves, and optics; electronics; power systems, signal processing, and control.

University of Virginia, School of Engineering and Applied Science, Department of Electrical and Computer Engineering, Program in Computer Engineering, Charlottesville, VA 22903. Offers ME, MS, PhD. *Program availability:* Online learning. *Students:* 45 full-time (9 women), 2 part-time (0 women); includes 5 minority (1 Black or African American, non-Hispanic/Latino; 2 Asian, non-Hispanic/Latino; 1 Hispanic/Latino; 1 Two or more races, non-Hispanic/Latino), 38 international. Average age 25. 94 applicants, 28% accepted, 16 enrolled. In 2016, 11 master's awarded. Terminal master's awarded for partial completion of doctoral program. *Degree requirements:* For master's, thesis (for some programs); for doctorate, comprehensive exam, thesis/dissertation. *Entrance requirements:* For master's, GRE General Test, 3 letters of recommendation; for doctorate, GRE General Test, 3 letters of recommendation; essay. Additional exam requirements/recommendations for international students: Required—TOEFL (minimum score 650 paper-based; 90 iBT), IELTS (minimum score 7). *Application deadline:* For fall admission, 8/1 for domestic students, 4/1 for international students; for winter admission, 12/1 for domestic students, 8/1 for international students; for spring admission, 5/1 for domestic students, 1/1 for international students. Applications are processed on a rolling basis. Application fee: $60. Electronic applications accepted. *Expenses:* Tuition, state resident: full-time $15,026; part-time $834 per credit hour. Tuition, nonresident: full-time $25,168; part-time $1378 per credit hour. *Required fees:* $2654. *Financial support:* Fellowships, research assistantships, and teaching assistantships available. Financial award application deadline: 1/15; financial award applicants required to submit FAFSA. *Faculty research:* Computer architecture, VLSI, switching theory, operating systems, real-time and embedded systems, compiler, software systems and software engineering, fault-tolerant computing and reliability engineering. *Unit head:* Joanne Bechta Dugan, Director, Computer Engineering Program, 434-924-3198, Fax: 434-924-8818, E-mail: compe@virginia.edu. *Application contact:* Pamela M. Norris, Associate Dean for Research and Graduate Programs, 434-243-7683, Fax: 434-982-3044, E-mail: pamela@virginia.edu.
Website: http://www.cpe.virginia.edu/grads/

University of Washington, Bothell, Program in Computing and Software Systems, Bothell, WA 98011. Offers MS. *Program availability:* Part-time, evening/weekend. *Degree requirements:* For master's, comprehensive exam (for some programs), thesis optional. *Entrance requirements:* For master's, GRE. Additional exam requirements/recommendations for international students: Required—TOEFL (minimum score 580 paper-based; 92 iBT) or IELTS (minimum score 7). Electronic applications accepted. *Expenses:* Contact institution. *Faculty research:* Computer science, software engineering, computer graphics, parallel and distributed systems, computer vision.

University of Washington, Tacoma, Graduate Programs, Program in Computing and Software Systems, Tacoma, WA 98402-3100. Offers MS. *Program availability:* Part-time. *Degree requirements:* For master's, capstone project/thesis or 15 credits elective coursework. *Entrance requirements:* For master's, GRE, personal statement, resume, transcripts, 3 recommendations. Additional exam requirements/recommendations for international students: Required—TOEFL (minimum score 580 paper-based; 92 iBT), IELTS (minimum score 7). Electronic applications accepted. *Faculty research:* Data stream analysis, formal methods, data mining, robotic systems, software development processes.

University of Waterloo, Graduate Studies, Faculty of Engineering, Department of Electrical and Computer Engineering, Waterloo, ON N2L 3G1, Canada. Offers M Eng, MA Sc, PhD. *Program availability:* Part-time. *Degree requirements:* For master's, research paper or thesis; for doctorate, comprehensive exam, thesis/dissertation. *Entrance requirements:* For master's, honors degree, minimum B+ average; for doctorate, master's degree, minimum A- average. Additional exam requirements/recommendations for international students: Required—TOEFL, IELTS, PTE. Electronic applications accepted. *Faculty research:* Communications, computers, systems and control, silicon devices, power engineering.

The University of Western Ontario, Faculty of Graduate Studies, Physical Sciences Division, Faculty of Engineering, London, ON N6A 5B8, Canada. Offers chemical and biochemical engineering (ME Sc, PhD); civil and environmental engineering (M Eng, ME Sc, PhD); electrical and computer engineering (M Eng, ME Sc, PhD); mechanical and materials engineering (M Eng, ME Sc, PhD). *Program availability:* Part-time. Terminal master's awarded for partial completion of doctoral program. *Degree requirements:* For master's, thesis; for doctorate, thesis/dissertation. *Entrance requirements:* For master's, minimum B average; for doctorate, minimum B+ average. *Faculty research:* Wind, geotechnical, chemical reactor engineering, applied electrostatics, biochemical engineering.

University of Wisconsin–Milwaukee, Graduate School, College of Engineering and Applied Science, Program in Engineering, Milwaukee, WI 53201-0413. Offers biomedical engineering (MS); civil engineering (MS, PhD); computer science (PhD); electrical and computer engineering (MS); electrical engineering (PhD); engineering mechanics (MS); industrial and management engineering (MS); industrial engineering (PhD); manufacturing engineering (MS); materials (PhD); materials engineering (MS); mechanical engineering (MS). *Program availability:* Part-time. *Students:* 199 full-time (52 women), 156 part-time (32 women); includes 27 minority (2 Black or African American, non-Hispanic/Latino; 15 Asian, non-Hispanic/Latino; 3 Hispanic/Latino; 7 Two or more races, non-Hispanic/Latino), 244 international. Average age 30. 396 applicants, 61% accepted, 102 enrolled. In 2016, 72 master's, 26 doctorates awarded. *Degree requirements:* For master's, comprehensive exam (for some programs), thesis or alternative; for doctorate, comprehensive exam, thesis/dissertation, internship. *Entrance requirements:* For master's, GRE, minimum GPA of 2.75; for doctorate, GRE, minimum GPA of 3.5. Additional exam requirements/recommendations for international students: Required—TOEFL (minimum score 550 paper-based; 79 iBT), IELTS (minimum score 6.5). *Application deadline:* For fall admission, 1/1 priority date for domestic students; for spring admission, 9/1 for domestic students. Applications are processed on a rolling basis. Application fee: $56 ($96 for international students). *Financial support:* In 2016–17, 3 fellowships, 55 research assistantships, 77 teaching assistantships were awarded; career-related internships or fieldwork, Federal Work-Study, unspecified assistantships, and project assistantships also available. Support available to part-time students. Financial award application deadline: 4/15. *Unit head:* David Yu, Representative, 414-229-6169, E-mail: yu@uwm.edu. *Application contact:* Betty Warras, General Information Contact, 414-229-6169, Fax: 414-229-6967, E-mail: bwarras@uwm.edu.
Website: http://www4.uwm.edu/ceas/academics/graduate_programs/

Villanova University, College of Engineering, Department of Electrical and Computer Engineering, Program in Computer Engineering, Villanova, PA 19085-1699. Offers computer architectures (Certificate); computer engineering (MSCPE); intelligent control systems (Certificate). *Program availability:* Part-time, evening/weekend. *Degree requirements:* For master's, thesis optional. *Entrance requirements:* For master's, GRE General Test (for applicants with degrees from foreign universities), BEE, minimum GPA of 3.0. Additional exam requirements/recommendations for international students: Required—TOEFL (minimum score 600 paper-based; 100 iBT). Electronic applications accepted. *Faculty research:* Expert systems, computer vision, neural networks, image processing, computer architectures.

Virginia Polytechnic Institute and State University, Graduate School, College of Engineering, Blacksburg, VA 24061. Offers aerospace engineering (ME, MS, PhD); biological systems engineering (ME, MS, PhD); biomedical engineering (MS, PhD); chemical engineering (ME, MS, PhD); civil engineering (ME, MS, PhD); computer engineering (ME, MS, PhD); computer science (MS, PhD); electrical engineering (ME, PhD); engineering education (PhD); engineering mechanics (ME, MS, PhD); environmental engineering (MS); environmental science and engineering (MS); industrial and systems engineering (ME, MS, PhD); materials science and engineering (ME, MS, PhD); mechanical engineering (ME, MS, PhD); mining and minerals engineering (PhD); mining engineering (ME, MS); nuclear engineering (MS, PhD); ocean engineering (MS); systems engineering (ME, MS). *Faculty:* 400 full-time (73 women), 3 part-time/adjunct (2 women). *Students:* 1,949 full-time (487 women), 393 part-time (69 women); includes 251 minority (56 Black or African American, non-Hispanic/Latino; 3 American Indian or Alaska Native, non-Hispanic/Latino; 87 Asian, non-Hispanic/Latino; 70 Hispanic/Latino; 35 Two or more races, non-Hispanic/Latino), 1,354 international. Average age 27. 4,903 applicants, 19% accepted, 569 enrolled. In 2016, 364 master's, 200 doctorates awarded. *Degree requirements:* For master's, comprehensive exam (for some programs), thesis (for some programs); for doctorate, comprehensive exam (for some programs), thesis/dissertation (for some programs). *Entrance requirements:* For master's and doctorate, GRE/GMAT. Additional exam requirements/recommendations for international students: Required—TOEFL (minimum score 80 iBT). *Application deadline:* For fall admission, 8/1 for domestic students, 4/1 for international students; for spring admission, 1/1 for domestic students, 9/1 for international students. Applications are processed on a rolling basis. Application fee: $75. Electronic applications accepted. *Expenses:* Tuition, state resident: full-time $12,467; part-time $692.50 per credit hour. Tuition, nonresident: full-time $25,095; part-time $1394.25 per credit hour. *Required fees:* $2669; $491.50 per semester. Tuition and fees vary according to course load, campus/location and program. *Financial support:* In 2016–17, 160 fellowships with full tuition reimbursements (averaging $7,387 per year), 872 research assistantships with full tuition reimbursements (averaging $22,329 per year), 313 teaching assistantships with full tuition reimbursements (averaging $18,714

per year) were awarded. Financial award application deadline: 3/1; financial award applicants required to submit FAFSA. *Total annual research expenditures:* $91.8 million. *Unit head:* Dr. Julia Ross, Dean, 540-231-9752, Fax: 540-231-3031, E-mail: deaneng@vt.edu. *Application contact:* Linda Perkins, Executive Assistant, 540-231-9752, Fax: 540-231-3031, E-mail: lperkins@vt.edu.
Website: http://www.eng.vt.edu/

Virginia Polytechnic Institute and State University, VT Online, Blacksburg, VA 24061. Offers advanced transportation systems (Certificate); aerospace engineering (MS); agricultural and life sciences (MSLFS); business information systems (Graduate Certificate); career and technical education (MS); civil engineering (MS); computer engineering (M Eng, MS); decision support systems (Graduate Certificate); eLearning leadership (MA); electrical engineering (M Eng, MS); engineering administration (MEA); environmental engineering (Certificate); environmental politics and policy (Graduate Certificate); environmental sciences and engineering (MS); foundations of political analysis (Graduate Certificate); health product risk management (Graduate Certificate); industrial and systems engineering (MS); information policy and society (Graduate Certificate); information security (Graduate Certificate); information technology (MIT); instructional technology (MA); integrative STEM education (MA Ed); liberal arts (Graduate Certificate); life sciences: health product risk management (MS); natural resources (MNR, Graduate Certificate); networking (Graduate Certificate); nonprofit and nongovernmental organization management (Graduate Certificate); ocean engineering (MS); political science (MA); security studies (Graduate Certificate); software development (Graduate Certificate). *Expenses:* Tuition, state resident: full-time $12,467; part-time $692.50 per credit hour. Tuition, nonresident: full-time $25,095; part-time $1394.25 per credit hour. *Required fees:* $2669; $491.50 per semester. Tuition and fees vary according to course load, campus/location and program.

Washington State University, Voiland College of Engineering and Architecture, School of Electrical Engineering and Computer Science, Pullman, WA 99164-2752. Offers computer engineering (MS); computer science (MS); electrical engineering (MS); electrical engineering and computer science (PhD); electrical power engineering (MS). MS programs in computer engineering, computer science and electrical engineering also offered at Tri-Cities campus; MS in electrical power engineering offered at the Global (online) campus. *Program availability:* Part-time. *Degree requirements:* For master's, comprehensive exam (for some programs), thesis or alternative; for doctorate, comprehensive exam, thesis/dissertation. *Entrance requirements:* For master's and doctorate, GRE General Test, minimum GPA of 3.0, 3 letters of recommendation, statement of purpose, transcripts. Additional exam requirements/recommendations for international students: Required—TOEFL (minimum score 580 paper-based). *Faculty research:* Software engineering, networks, distributed computing, computer engineering, electrophysics, artificial intelligence, bioinformatics and computational biology, computer graphics, communications, control systems, signal processing, power systems, microelectronics, algorithms.

Washington University in St. Louis, School of Engineering and Applied Science, Department of Computer Science and Engineering, St. Louis, MO 63130-4899. Offers computer engineering (MS, PhD); computer science (MS, PhD); computer science and engineering (M Eng). *Program availability:* Part-time. Terminal master's awarded for partial completion of doctoral program. *Degree requirements:* For master's, thesis optional; for doctorate, thesis/dissertation. *Entrance requirements:* For doctorate, GRE General Test. Additional exam requirements/recommendations for international students: Required—TOEFL. Electronic applications accepted. *Faculty research:* Artificial intelligence, computational genomics, computer and systems architecture, media and machines, networking and communication, software systems.

Wayne State University, College of Engineering, Department of Electrical and Computer Engineering, Detroit, MI 48202. Offers computer engineering (MS, PhD); electrical engineering (MS, PhD). *Faculty:* 22. *Students:* 247 full-time (54 women), 41 part-time (3 women); includes 16 minority (2 Black or African American, non-Hispanic/Latino; 11 Asian, non-Hispanic/Latino; 3 Two or more races, non-Hispanic/Latino), 250 international. Average age 26. 689 applicants, 50% accepted, 100 enrolled. In 2016, 73 master's, 3 doctorates awarded. *Degree requirements:* For master's, thesis; for doctorate, thesis/dissertation. *Entrance requirements:* For master's, GRE (if BS is not from ABET-accredited university), BS from ABET-accredited university; for doctorate, GRE (if BS is not from ABET-accredited university), minimum master's GPA of 3.6. Additional exam requirements/recommendations for international students: Required—TOEFL (minimum score 550 paper-based; 79 iBT), TWE (minimum score 5.5), Michigan English Language Assessment Battery (minimum score 85); Recommended—IELTS (minimum score 6.5). *Application deadline:* For fall admission, 6/1 priority date for domestic students, 5/1 priority date for international students; for winter admission, 10/1 priority date for domestic students, 9/1 priority date for international students; for spring admission, 2/1 priority date for domestic students, 1/1 priority date for international students. Applications are processed on a rolling basis. Application fee: $50. Electronic applications accepted. *Expenses:* $18,871 per year resident tuition and fees, $36,065 per year non-resident tuition and fees. *Financial support:* In 2016–17, 43 students received support, including 3 fellowships with tuition reimbursements available (averaging $16,000 per year), 9 research assistantships with tuition reimbursements available (averaging $18,419 per year), 16 teaching assistantships with tuition reimbursements available (averaging $19,237 per year); scholarships/grants, health care benefits, and unspecified assistantships also available. Support available to part-time students. Financial award applicants required to submit FAFSA. *Faculty research:* Computer systems, smart sensors and nanotechnology, communication systems and imaging, optics and photonics, biomedical electronics. *Total annual research expenditures:* $1.7 million. *Unit head:* Dr. Mohammed Ismail Elnaggar, Department Chair, E-mail: gd8686@wayne.edu. *Application contact:* Eric Eric Scimeca, Graduate Program Coordinator, 313-577-0412, E-mail: eric.scimeca@wayne.edu.
Website: http://engineering.wayne.edu/ece/

Weber State University, College of Engineering, Applied Science and Technology, Ogden, UT 84408-1001. Offers computer engineering (MS). *Expenses:* Tuition, state resident: full-time $4389; part-time $1548.87 per credit hour. Tuition, nonresident: full-time $13,169; part-time $9294.56 per credit hour. *Required fees:* $782; $575.46 per credit hour. $9.50 per term. Tuition and fees vary according to course level and program.

Unit head: Dr. David L. Ferro, Dean, 801-626-6303, E-mail: dferro@weber.edu. *Application contact:* Scott Teichert, Director of Admissions, 801-626-7670, Fax: 801-626-6045, E-mail: scottteichert@weber.edu.
Website: http://www.weber.edu/east

Western Michigan University, Graduate College, College of Engineering and Applied Sciences, Department of Electrical and Computer Engineering, Kalamazoo, MI 49008. Offers computer engineering (MSE); electrical and computer engineering (PhD); electrical engineering (MSE). *Program availability:* Part-time. *Degree requirements:* For master's, thesis optional.

West Virginia University, Statler College of Engineering and Mineral Resources, Lane Department of Computer Science and Electrical Engineering, Program in Computer Engineering, Morgantown, WV 26506. Offers PhD. *Degree requirements:* For doctorate, comprehensive exam, thesis/dissertation. *Entrance requirements:* For doctorate, GRE General Test, minimum GPA of 3.0, letters of recommendation. Additional exam requirements/recommendations for international students: Required—TOEFL. *Faculty research:* Software engineering, microprocessor applications, microelectronic systems, fault tolerance, advanced computer architectures and networks.

Wichita State University, Graduate School, College of Engineering, Department of Electrical Engineering and Computer Science, Wichita, KS 67260. Offers computer networking (MS); computer science (MS); electrical engineering (MS); electrical engineering and computer science (PhD). *Program availability:* Part-time, evening/weekend. *Unit head:* Dr. John Watkins, Chair, 316-978-3156, Fax: 316-978-5408, E-mail: john.watkins@wichita.edu. *Application contact:* Jordan Oleson, Admissions Coordinator, 316-978-3095, Fax: 316-978-3253, E-mail: jordan.oleson@wichita.edu.
Website: http://www.wichita.edu/eecs

Worcester Polytechnic Institute, Graduate Studies and Research, Department of Electrical and Computer Engineering, Worcester, MA 01609-2280. Offers electrical and computer engineering (Advanced Certificate, Graduate Certificate); electrical engineering (M Eng, MS, PhD). *Program availability:* Part-time, evening/weekend. *Faculty:* 17 full-time (1 woman), 18 part-time/adjunct (4 women). *Students:* 107 full-time (14 women), 136 part-time (16 women); includes 42 minority (9 Black or African American, non-Hispanic/Latino; 19 Asian, non-Hispanic/Latino; 14 Hispanic/Latino), 91 international. 483 applicants, 47% accepted, 70 enrolled. In 2016, 111 master's, 10 doctorates awarded. Terminal master's awarded for partial completion of doctoral program. *Degree requirements:* For master's, thesis optional; for doctorate, comprehensive exam, thesis/dissertation. *Entrance requirements:* For master's, GRE (recommended), 3 letters of recommendation; for doctorate, GRE, 3 letters of recommendation, statement of purpose. Additional exam requirements/recommendations for international students: Required—TOEFL (minimum score 563 paper-based; 84 iBT), IELTS (minimum score 7), GRE. *Application deadline:* For fall admission, 1/1 priority date for domestic students, 1/1 for international students; for spring admission, 10/1 priority date for domestic students, 10/1 for international students. Applications are processed on a rolling basis. Application fee: $70. Electronic applications accepted. *Financial support:* Research assistantships, teaching assistantships, career-related internships or fieldwork, institutionally sponsored loans, scholarships/grants, and unspecified assistantships available. Financial award application deadline: 1/1; financial award applicants required to submit FAFSA. *Unit head:* Dr. Yehia Massoud, Department Head, 508-831-5231, Fax: 508-831-5491, E-mail: massoud@wpi.edu. *Application contact:* Dr. Kaveh Pahlavan, Graduate Coordinator, 508-831-5231, Fax: 508-831-5491, E-mail: kaveh@wpi.edu.
Website: http://www.wpi.edu/academics/ece

Wright State University, Graduate School, College of Engineering and Computer Science, Department of Computer Science and Engineering, Computer Engineering Program, Dayton, OH 45435. Offers MSCE. *Degree requirements:* For master's, thesis optional. *Entrance requirements:* For master's, GRE General Test, minimum GPA of 3.0 in major, 2.7 overall. Additional exam requirements/recommendations for international students: Required—TOEFL. Application fee: $25. *Expenses:* Tuition, state resident: full-time $9952; part-time $622 per credit hour. Tuition, nonresident: full-time $16,960; part-time $1060 per credit hour. *Financial support:* Fellowships, research assistantships, and teaching assistantships available. Support available to part-time students. Financial award application deadline: 3/31; financial award applicants required to submit FAFSA. *Faculty research:* Networking and digital communications, parallel and concurrent computing, robotics and control, computer vision, optical computing. *Unit head:* Dr. Forouzan Golshani, Chair, 937-775-5131, Fax: 937-775-5133, E-mail: cse-dept@wright.edu. *Application contact:* Dr. Jay E. Dejongh, Graduate Program Director, 937-775-5136, Fax: 937-775-5133, E-mail: jay.dejongh@wright.edu.

Wright State University, Graduate School, College of Engineering and Computer Science, Department of Computer Science and Engineering, Program in Computer Science and Engineering, Dayton, OH 45435. Offers MSCE, PhD. *Degree requirements:* For doctorate, thesis/dissertation, candidacy and general exams. *Entrance requirements:* For doctorate, GRE General Test, minimum GPA of 3.3. Additional exam requirements/recommendations for international students: Required—TOEFL. Application fee: $25. *Expenses:* Tuition, state resident: full-time $9952; part-time $622 per credit hour. Tuition, nonresident: full-time $16,960; part-time $1060 per credit hour. *Financial support:* Application deadline: 3/31. *Unit head:* Dr. Thomas Sudkamp, Director, 937-775-5118, Fax: 937-775-5133, E-mail: thomas.sudkamp@wright.edu. *Application contact:* John Kimble, Associate Director of Graduate Admissions and Records, 937-775-2957, Fax: 937-775-2453, E-mail: john.kimble@wright.edu.

Youngstown State University, Graduate School, College of Science, Technology, Engineering and Mathematics, Department of Electrical and Computer Engineering, Youngstown, OH 44555-0001. Offers computer engineering (MSE); electrical engineering (MSE). *Program availability:* Part-time, evening/weekend. *Degree requirements:* For master's, thesis optional. *Entrance requirements:* For master's, minimum GPA of 2.75 in field. Additional exam requirements/recommendations for international students: Required—TOEFL. *Faculty research:* Computer-aided design, power systems, electromagnetic energy conversion, sensors, control systems.

Electrical Engineering

Air Force Institute of Technology, Graduate School of Engineering and Management, Department of Electrical and Computer Engineering, Dayton, OH 45433-7765. Offers computer engineering (MS, PhD); computer systems/science (MS); electrical engineering (MS, PhD); electro-optics (MS, PhD). *Accreditation:* ABET (one or more programs are accredited). *Program availability:* Part-time. *Degree requirements:* For master's, thesis; for doctorate, thesis/dissertation. *Entrance requirements:* For master's and doctorate, GRE General Test, minimum GPA of 3.0, U.S. citizenship. *Faculty research:* Remote sensing, information survivability, microelectronics, computer networks, artificial intelligence.

Alfred University, Graduate School, College of Ceramics, Inamori School of Engineering, Alfred, NY 14802. Offers biomaterials engineering (MS); ceramic engineering (MS, PhD); electrical engineering (MS); glass science (MS, PhD); materials

science and engineering (MS, PhD); mechanical engineering (MS). *Program availability:* Part-time. *Faculty:* 18 full-time (1 woman). *Students:* 26 full-time (6 women), 16 part-time (4 women); includes 1 minority (Hispanic/Latino), 12 international. Average age 27. 14 applicants, 79% accepted, 10 enrolled. In 2016, 13 master's, 5 doctorates awarded. *Degree requirements:* For master's, thesis; for doctorate, thesis/dissertation. *Entrance requirements:* Additional exam requirements/recommendations for international students: Required—TOEFL (minimum score 590 paper-based; 90 iBT), IELTS (minimum score 6.5). *Application deadline:* For fall admission, 3/1 priority date for domestic students, 3/15 for international students; for spring admission, 10/1 priority date for domestic students, 10/1 for international students. Applications are processed on a rolling basis. Application fee: $60. Electronic applications accepted. *Expenses:* Contact institution. *Financial support:* Fellowships with full tuition reimbursements, research assistantships with full tuition reimbursements, teaching assistantships with full tuition reimbursements, tuition waivers (full and partial), and unspecified assistantships available. Financial award application deadline: 8/1; financial award applicants required to submit FAFSA. *Faculty research:* X-ray diffraction, biomaterials and polymers, thin-film processing, electronic and optical ceramics, solid-state chemistry. *Unit head:* Dr. Alistair N. Cormack, Dean, 607-871-2422, E-mail: cormack@alfred.edu. *Application contact:* Sara Love, Coordinator of Graduate Admissions, 607-871-2115, Fax: 607-871-2198, E-mail: gradinquiry@alfred.edu.
Website: http://engineering.alfred.edu/grad/

The American University in Cairo, School of Sciences and Engineering, Cairo, Egypt. Offers biotechnology (MS); chemistry (MS); computer science (MS); computing (M Comp); construction engineering (M Eng, MS); electronics and communications engineering (M Eng); environmental engineering (MS); environmental system design (M Eng); mechanical engineering (M Eng, MS); nanotechnology (MS); physics (MS); robotics, control and smart systems (MS); sciences and engineering (PhD); sustainable development (MS, Graduate Diploma). *Program availability:* Part-time, evening/weekend. *Faculty:* 43 full-time (4 women), 12 part-time/adjunct (1 woman). *Students:* 50 full-time (21 women), 262 part-time (128 women), 13 international. Average age 28. 193 applicants, 46% accepted, 55 enrolled. In 2016, 71 master's, 5 doctorates awarded. *Degree requirements:* For master's, comprehensive exam (for some programs), thesis (for some programs); for doctorate, comprehensive exam (for some programs), thesis/dissertation. *Entrance requirements:* Additional exam requirements/recommendations for international students: Required—TOEFL (minimum score 450 paper-based; 45 iBT), IELTS (minimum score 5). *Application deadline:* For fall admission, 2/1 priority date for domestic and international students; for spring admission, 10/15 priority date for domestic and international students. Applications are processed on a rolling basis. Application fee: $80. Electronic applications accepted. *Expenses:* Contact institution. *Financial support:* Fellowships with partial tuition reimbursements, scholarships/grants, and unspecified assistantships available. Financial award application deadline: 3/10. *Faculty research:* Construction, mechanical and electronics engineering, physics, computer science, biotechnology and nanotechnology. *Unit head:* Dr. Hassan El Fawal, Dean, 20-2-2615-2926, E-mail: hassan.elfawal@aucegypt.edu. *Application contact:* Maha Hegazi, Director for Graduate Admissions, 20-2-2615-1462, E-mail: mahahegazi@aucegypt.edu.
Website: http://www.aucegypt.edu/sse/Pages/default.aspx

American University of Beirut, Graduate Programs, Faculty of Engineering and Architecture, 11-0236, Lebanon. Offers applied energy (ME); civil engineering (PhD); electrical and computer engineering (PhD); energy studies (MS); engineering management (MEM); environmental and water resources (ME); environmental technology (MSES); mechanical engineering (ME, PhD); urban design (MUD); urban planning and policy (MUPP). *Program availability:* Part-time, evening/weekend, 100% online. *Faculty:* 99 full-time (22 women), 1 part-time/adjunct (0 women). *Students:* 308 full-time (143 women), 86 part-time (39 women). Average age 26. 430 applicants, 69% accepted, 125 enrolled. In 2016, 103 master's, 7 doctorates awarded. Terminal master's awarded for partial completion of doctoral program. *Degree requirements:* For master's, comprehensive exam, thesis optional; for doctorate, comprehensive exam, thesis/dissertation. *Entrance requirements:* For doctorate, GRE. Additional exam requirements/recommendations for international students: Required—TOEFL (minimum score 573 paper-based; 88 iBT); Recommended—IELTS (minimum score 7). *Application deadline:* For fall admission, 2/10 priority date for domestic and international students; for spring admission, 11/2 priority date for domestic students, 11/2 for international students. Application fee: $50. Electronic applications accepted. *Expenses:* Contact institution. *Financial support:* In 2016–17, 22 students received support, including 94 fellowships with full tuition reimbursements available (averaging $18,200 per year), 44 research assistantships with full tuition reimbursements available (averaging $7,596 per year), 124 teaching assistantships with full tuition reimbursements available (averaging $1,056 per year); career-related internships or fieldwork, Federal Work-Study, institutionally sponsored loans, scholarships/grants, traineeships, health care benefits, tuition waivers, and unspecified assistantships also available. Support available to part-time students. Financial award application deadline: 12/20. *Total annual research expenditures:* $1.5 million. *Unit head:* Prof. Alan Shihadeh, Interim Dean, 961-1350000 Ext. 3400, Fax: 961-1744462, E-mail: as20@aub.edu.lb. *Application contact:* Dr. Salim Kanaan, Director, Admissions Office, 961-1350000 Ext. 2594, Fax: 961-1750775, E-mail: sk00@aub.edu.lb.
Website: http://www.aub.edu.lb/fea/fea_home/Pages/index.aspx

American University of Sharjah, Graduate Programs, Sharjah, United Arab Emirates. Offers accounting (MS); business (EMBA, MBA); chemical engineering (MS Ch E); civil engineering (MSCE); computer engineering (MS); electrical engineering (MSEE); engineering systems management (MS); mathematics (MS); mechanical engineering (MSME); mechatronics engineering (MS); teaching English to speakers of other languages (MA); translation and interpreting (MA); urban planning (MUP). *Program availability:* Part-time, evening/weekend. *Degree requirements:* For master's, thesis (for some programs). *Entrance requirements:* For master's, GMAT (for MBA). Additional exam requirements/recommendations for international students: Required—TOEFL (minimum score 550 paper-based; 80 iBT), TWE (minimum score 5); Recommended—IELTS (minimum score 6.5). Electronic applications accepted. *Faculty research:* Water pollution, management and waste water treatment, energy and sustainability, air pollution, Islamic finance, family business and small and medium enterprises.

Arizona State University at the Tempe campus, Ira A. Fulton Schools of Engineering, School of Electrical, Computer and Energy Engineering, Tempe, AZ 85287-5706. Offers electrical engineering (MS, MSE, PhD); nuclear power generation (Graduate Certificate). *Program availability:* Part-time, evening/weekend, online learning. Terminal master's awarded for partial completion of doctoral program. *Degree requirements:* For master's, thesis and defense (MS); comprehensive exams (MSE); interactive Program of Study (iPOS) submitted before completing 50 percent of required credit hours; for doctorate, comprehensive exam, thesis/dissertation, interactive Program of Study (iPOS) submitted before completing 50 percent of required credit hours. *Entrance requirements:* For master's, GRE, minimum GPA of 3.0 in last 2 years of work leading to bachelor's degree, 3.5 if from non-ABET accredited school; for doctorate, GRE, master's degree with minimum GPA of 3.5 or 3.6 in last 2 years of ABET-accredited undergraduate program. Additional exam requirements/recommendations for international students: Required—TOEFL, IELTS, or PTE. Electronic applications accepted. *Expenses:* Contact institution. *Faculty research:* Power and energy systems, signal processing and communications, solid state devices and modeling, wireless communications and circuits, photovoltaics, biosignatures discovery automation, flexible electronics, nanostructures.

Auburn University, Graduate School, Ginn College of Engineering, Department of Electrical and Computer Engineering, Auburn University, AL 36849. Offers MEE, MS, PhD. *Program availability:* Part-time. *Faculty:* 22 full-time (0 women), 4 part-time/adjunct (0 women). *Students:* 93 full-time (18 women), 42 part-time (3 women); includes 3 minority (1 Black or African American, non-Hispanic/Latino; 1 Asian, non-Hispanic/Latino; 1 Hispanic/Latino), 105 international. Average age 26. 240 applicants, 53% accepted, 27 enrolled. In 2016, 49 master's, 18 doctorates awarded. *Degree requirements:* For master's, comprehensive exam, thesis (for some programs); for doctorate, thesis/dissertation. *Entrance requirements:* For master's and doctorate, GRE General Test, GRE Subject Test. *Application deadline:* Applications are processed on a rolling basis. Application fee: $50 ($60 for international students). Electronic applications accepted. *Expenses:* Tuition, state resident: full-time $9072; part-time $504 per credit hour. Tuition, nonresident: full-time $27,216; part-time $1512 per credit hour. *Required fees:* $812 per semester. Tuition and fees vary according to degree level and program. *Financial support:* Fellowships, research assistantships, teaching assistantships, and Federal Work-Study available. Support available to part-time students. Financial award application deadline: 3/15; financial award applicants required to submit FAFSA. *Faculty research:* Power systems, energy conversion, electronics, electromagnetics, digital systems. *Unit head:* Dr. Mark Nelms, Head, 334-844-1830. *Application contact:* Dr. George Flowers, Dean of the Graduate School, 334-844-2125.
Website: http://www.eng.auburn.edu/ee/

Baylor University, Graduate School, School of Engineering and Computer Science, Department of Electrical and Computer Engineering, Waco, TX 76798. Offers MS, PhD. *Faculty:* 15 full-time (1 woman). *Students:* 38 full-time (7 women), 4 part-time (0 women); includes 3 minority (1 Black or African American, non-Hispanic/Latino; 1 Asian, non-Hispanic/Latino; 1 Two or more races, non-Hispanic/Latino), 19 international. Average age 25. 34 applicants, 38% accepted, 13 enrolled. In 2016, 6 master's, 2 doctorates awarded. Terminal master's awarded for partial completion of doctoral program. *Degree requirements:* For master's, thesis (for some programs); for doctorate, comprehensive exam, thesis/dissertation. *Entrance requirements:* For master's and doctorate, GRE. Additional exam requirements/recommendations for international students: Required—TOEFL (minimum score 550 paper-based; 100 iBT). *Application deadline:* For fall admission, 2/15 for domestic and international students; for spring admission, 12/1 for domestic and international students. Applications are processed on a rolling basis. Application fee: $50. Electronic applications accepted. *Expenses:* $1,583 per hour tuition, $174 per semester fees. *Financial support:* In 2016–17, 18 students received support, including 28 research assistantships with full tuition reimbursements available (averaging $21,500 per year), 16 teaching assistantships with full tuition reimbursements available (averaging $16,000 per year); fellowships, scholarships/grants, health care benefits, and unspecified assistantships also available. Financial award application deadline: 4/15. *Faculty research:* Biosensors, microwave frequency signals, wearable sensors, optoelectronic devices, energy efficient power electronics. *Unit head:* Dr. Kwang Y. Lee, Chair, 254-710-4817, Fax: 254-710-3010, E-mail: kwang_y_lee@baylor.edu. *Application contact:* Dr. B. Randall Jean, Graduate Director, 254-710-4194, Fax: 254-710-3010.
Website: http://www.ecs.baylor.edu/ece/

Binghamton University, State University of New York, Graduate School, Thomas J. Watson School of Engineering and Applied Science, Department of Electrical and Computer Engineering, Binghamton, NY 13902-6000. Offers M Eng, MS, PhD. *Program availability:* Part-time, evening/weekend, online learning. *Faculty:* 18 full-time (1 woman), 4 part-time/adjunct (0 women). *Students:* 110 full-time (23 women), 98 part-time (8 women); includes 17 minority (6 Black or African American, non-Hispanic/Latino; 7 Asian, non-Hispanic/Latino; 4 Hispanic/Latino), 136 international. Average age 27. 421 applicants, 66% accepted, 80 enrolled. In 2016, 72 master's, 7 doctorates awarded. *Degree requirements:* For master's, thesis (for some programs); for doctorate, comprehensive exam, thesis/dissertation. *Entrance requirements:* For master's and doctorate, GRE General Test. Additional exam requirements/recommendations for international students: Required—TOEFL (minimum score 550 paper-based; 80 iBT). *Application deadline:* Applications are processed on a rolling basis. Application fee: $75. Electronic applications accepted. *Expenses:* Contact institution. *Financial support:* In 2016–17, 56 students received support, including 28 research assistantships with full tuition reimbursements available (averaging $16,500 per year), 21 teaching assistantships with full tuition reimbursements available (averaging $16,500 per year); career-related internships or fieldwork, Federal Work-Study, institutionally sponsored loans, scholarships/grants, health care benefits, tuition waivers (full and partial), and unspecified assistantships also available. Financial award applicants required to submit FAFSA. *Unit head:* Ellen Tilden, Coordinator of Graduate Programs, 607-777-2873, E-mail: etilden@binghamton.edu. *Application contact:* Ben Balkaya, Assistant Dean and Director, 607-777-2151, Fax: 607-777-2501, E-mail: balkaya@binghamton.edu.

Boise State University, College of Engineering, Department of Electrical and Computer Engineering, Boise, ID 83725. Offers M Engr, MS, PhD. *Program availability:* Part-time. *Faculty:* 14. *Students:* 28 full-time (7 women), 23 part-time (0 women); includes 4 minority (3 Asian, non-Hispanic/Latino; 1 Hispanic/Latino), 23 international. Average age 30. 60 applicants, 45% accepted, 9 enrolled. In 2016, 9 master's awarded. Terminal master's awarded for partial completion of doctoral program. *Degree requirements:* For master's, comprehensive exam, thesis (for some programs); for doctorate, thesis/dissertation. *Entrance requirements:* For master's, GRE General Test, minimum GPA of 3.0. Additional exam requirements/recommendations for international students: Required—TOEFL (minimum score 550 paper-based; 80 iBT), IELTS (minimum score 6). *Application deadline:* For fall admission, 2/1 priority date for domestic and international students. Application fee: $65 ($95 for international students). Electronic applications accepted. *Expenses:* Tuition, state resident: full-time $6058; part-time $358 per credit hour. Tuition, nonresident: full-time $20,108; part-time $608 per credit hour. *Required fees:* $2108. Tuition and fees vary according to program. *Financial support:* In 2016–17, 11 students received support, including 17 research assistantships (averaging $10,214 per year); scholarships/grants and unspecified assistantships also available. Financial award application deadline: 2/1; financial award applicants required to submit FAFSA. *Unit head:* Dr. Nader Rafia, Department Chair, 208-426-3711, E-mail: nrafia@boisestate.edu. *Application contact:* Hao Chen, Graduate Program Coordinator, 208-426-1020, E-mail: haochen@boisestate.edu.
Website: http://coen.boisestate.edu/ece/

Boston University, College of Engineering, Department of Electrical and Computer Engineering, Boston, MA 02215. Offers computer engineering (M Eng, MS, PhD). *Program availability:* Part-time. *Students:* 305 full-time (77 women), 98 part-time (22 women); includes 31 minority (3 Black or African American, non-Hispanic/Latino; 19 Asian, non-Hispanic/Latino; 9 Hispanic/Latino), 296 international. Average age 25. 1,219 applicants, 25% accepted, 142 enrolled. In 2016, 133 master's, 17 doctorates awarded. Terminal master's awarded for partial completion of doctoral program. *Degree requirements:* For master's, thesis (for some programs); for doctorate, comprehensive

exam, thesis/dissertation. *Entrance requirements:* For master's and doctorate, GRE General Test. Additional exam requirements/recommendations for international students: Required—TOEFL (minimum score 90 iBT), IELTS (minimum score 7). *Financial support:* Application deadline: 1/1. *Faculty research:* Communications and computer networks; signal, image, video, and multimedia processing; solid-state materials, devices, and photonics; systems, control, and reliable computing; VLSI, computer engineering and high-performance computing. *Unit head:* Dr. William C. Karl, Interim Chairman, 617-353-9880, Fax: 617-353-6440, E-mail: wckarl@bu.edu.
Website: http://www.bu.edu/ece/

Bradley University, The Graduate School, Caterpillar College of Engineering and Technology, Department of Electrical and Computer Engineering, Peoria, IL 61625-0002. Offers MSEE. *Program availability:* Part-time, evening/weekend. *Degree requirements:* For master's, comprehensive exam. *Entrance requirements:* For master's, GRE, minimum GPA of 3.0. Additional exam requirements/recommendations for international students: Required—TOEFL (minimum score 550 paper-based; 79 iBT), IELTS (minimum score 6.5). *Application deadline:* For fall admission, 5/15 priority date for domestic and international students; for spring admission, 10/15 priority date for domestic and international students. Applications are processed on a rolling basis. Application fee: $40 ($50 for international students). Electronic applications accepted. *Expenses: Tuition:* Full-time $7650; part-time $850 per credit. *Required fees:* $50 per credit. One-time fee: $100 full-time. *Financial support:* Research assistantships with full and partial tuition reimbursements, teaching assistantships, scholarships/grants, tuition waivers (partial), and unspecified assistantships available. Support available to part-time students. Financial award application deadline: 4/1. *Unit head:* In Soo Ahn, Chair, 309-677-2734, E-mail: isa@bradley.edu. *Application contact:* Kayla Carroll, Director of International Admissions and Student Services, 309-677-2375, E-mail: klcarroll@fsmail.bradley.edu.
Website: http://www.bradley.edu/academic/departments/electrical/

Brigham Young University, Graduate Studies, Ira A. Fulton College of Engineering and Technology, Department of Electrical and Computer Engineering, Provo, UT 84602. Offers MS, PhD. *Faculty:* 23 full-time (1 woman). *Students:* 100 full-time (9 women); includes 2 minority (1 Asian, non-Hispanic/Latino; 1 Hispanic/Latino), 19 international. Average age 27. 59 applicants, 63% accepted, 27 enrolled. In 2016, 10 master's, 6 doctorates awarded. *Degree requirements:* For master's, thesis; for doctorate, comprehensive exam, thesis/dissertation. *Entrance requirements:* For master's and doctorate, GRE General Test, minimum GPA of 3.2 in last 60 hours of course work. Additional exam requirements/recommendations for international students: Required—TOEFL (minimum score 580 paper-based; 85 iBT). *Application deadline:* For fall admission, 1/15 for domestic and international students; for winter admission, 8/15 for domestic and international students. Application fee: $50. Electronic applications accepted. *Expenses: Tuition:* Full-time $6680; part-time $393 per credit. Tuition and fees vary according to course load, program and student's religious affiliation. *Financial support:* In 2016–17, 168 students received support, including 5 fellowships with full tuition reimbursements available (averaging $20,250 per year), 140 research assistantships with full tuition reimbursements available (averaging $5,415 per year), 47 teaching assistantships with full tuition reimbursements available (averaging $5,340 per year); scholarships/grants also available. Financial award application deadline: 5/15; financial award applicants required to submit FAFSA. *Faculty research:* Microwave earth remote sensing, configurable computing and embedded systems, MEMS semiconductors, integrated electro-optics, multiple-agent intelligent coordinated control systems for unmanned air vehicles. *Total annual research expenditures:* $3.5 million. *Unit head:* Dr. Brent E. Nelson, Chair, 801-422-4012, Fax: 801-422-0201, E-mail: nelson@ee.byu.edu. *Application contact:* Janalyn L. Mergist, Graduate Secretary, 801-422-4013, Fax: 801-422-0201, E-mail: janalyn@ee.byu.edu.
Website: http://www.ee.byu.edu/

Brown University, Graduate School, School of Engineering, Program in Electrical Sciences and Computer Engineering, Providence, RI 02912. Offers Sc M, PhD. *Degree requirements:* For doctorate, thesis/dissertation, preliminary exam.

Bucknell University, Graduate Studies, College of Engineering, Department of Electrical Engineering, Lewisburg, PA 17837. Offers MSEE. *Program availability:* Part-time. *Degree requirements:* For master's, thesis. *Entrance requirements:* For master's, GRE General Test, minimum GPA of 3.0. Additional exam requirements/recommendations for international students: Required—TOEFL (minimum score 600 paper-based).

California Institute of Technology, Division of Engineering and Applied Science, Option in Electrical Engineering, Pasadena, CA 91125-0001. Offers MS, PhD, Engr. *Degree requirements:* For doctorate, thesis/dissertation. Electronic applications accepted. *Faculty research:* Solid-state electronics, power electronics, communications, controls, submillimeter-wave integrated circuits.

California Polytechnic State University, San Luis Obispo, College of Engineering, Department of Electrical Engineering, San Luis Obispo, CA 93407. Offers MS. *Program availability:* Part-time. *Faculty:* 11 full-time (4 women). *Students:* 36 full-time (2 women), 13 part-time (1 woman); includes 16 minority (7 Asian, non-Hispanic/Latino; 7 Hispanic/Latino; 2 Two or more races, non-Hispanic/Latino), 10 international. Average age 24. 69 applicants, 26% accepted, 13 enrolled. In 2016, 34 master's awarded. *Degree requirements:* For master's, comprehensive exam (for some programs), thesis (for some programs). *Entrance requirements:* For master's, GRE. Additional exam requirements/recommendations for international students: Required—TOEFL (minimum score 80 iBT). *Application deadline:* For fall admission, 3/1 for domestic and international students. Applications are processed on a rolling basis. Application fee: $55. Electronic applications accepted. *Expenses:* Tuition, state resident: full-time $6738; part-time $3906 per year. Tuition, nonresident: full-time $15,666; part-time $8370 per year. *Required fees:* $3603; $3141 per unit. $1047 per term. *Financial support:* Fellowships, research assistantships, teaching assistantships, career-related internships or fieldwork, scholarships/grants, and unspecified assistantships available. Financial award application deadline: 3/2; financial award applicants required to submit FAFSA. *Faculty research:* Communications, systems design and analysis, control systems, electronic devices, microprocessors. *Unit head:* Dr. Jane Zhang, Graduate Coordinator, 805-756-7528, E-mail: jzhang@calpoly.edu.
Website: http://www.ee.calpoly.edu/

California State Polytechnic University, Pomona, Program in Electrical Engineering, Pomona, CA 91768-2557. Offers communication systems (MSEE). *Program availability:* Part-time, evening/weekend. *Students:* 15 full-time (3 women), 56 part-time (7 women); includes 31 minority (1 American Indian or Alaska Native, non-Hispanic/Latino; 21 Asian, non-Hispanic/Latino; 9 Hispanic/Latino), 14 international. Average age 27. 27 applicants, 96% accepted, 15 enrolled. In 2016, 34 master's awarded. *Entrance requirements:* Additional exam requirements/recommendations for international students: Required—TOEFL. *Application deadline:* Applications are processed on a rolling basis. Application fee: $55. Electronic applications accepted. *Expenses:* Contact institution. *Financial support:* Application deadline: 3/2; applicants required to submit FAFSA. *Unit head:* Dr. Halima M. El Naga, Graduate Coordinator, 909-869-2515, Fax: 909-869-4687, E-mail: helnaga@cpp.edu. *Application contact:* Andrew M. Wright,

Director of Admissions, 909-869-3130, Fax: 909-869-4529, E-mail: awright@cpp.edu.
Website: http://www.cpp.edu/~engineering/ECE/msee.shtml

California State University, Chico, Office of Graduate Studies, College of Engineering, Computer Science, and Construction Management, Electrical and Computer Engineering Department, Option in Electronics Engineering, Chico, CA 95929-0722. Offers electronic engineering (MS). *Students:* 10 full-time (4 women), 11 part-time (6 women); includes 14 minority (all Asian, non-Hispanic/Latino). 64 applicants, 75% accepted, 9 enrolled. In 2016, 15 master's awarded. *Degree requirements:* For master's, thesis or project plan. *Entrance requirements:* For master's, GRE General Test, 2 letters of recommendation, statement of purpose, resume. Additional exam requirements/recommendations for international students: Required—TOEFL (minimum score 550 paper-based; 80 iBT), IELTS (minimum score 6.5), PTE (minimum score 59). *Application deadline:* For fall admission, 3/1 priority date for domestic students, 3/1 for international students; for spring admission, 9/15 priority date for domestic students, 9/15 for international students. Application fee: $55. Electronic applications accepted. *Financial support:* Application deadline: 3/1; applicants required to submit FAFSA. *Unit head:* Dr. Chuen Hsu, Chair, 530-898-5343, Fax: 530-898-4956, E-mail: elce@csuchico.edu. *Application contact:* Judy L. Morris, Graduate Admissions Coordinator, 530-898-5416, Fax: 530-898-3342, E-mail: jlmorris@csuchico.edu.

California State University, Fresno, Division of Research and Graduate Studies, Lyles College of Engineering, Department of Electrical and Computer Engineering, Fresno, CA 93740-8027. Offers computer engineering (MSE); electrical engineering (MSE). *Program availability:* Part-time, evening/weekend. *Degree requirements:* For master's, thesis or alternative. *Entrance requirements:* For master's, GRE General Test, minimum GPA of 2.7. Additional exam requirements/recommendations for international students: Required—TOEFL. *Application deadline:* For fall admission, 5/1 for domestic and international students; for spring admission, 10/1 for domestic and international students. Applications are processed on a rolling basis. Application fee: $55. Electronic applications accepted. *Financial support:* Career-related internships or fieldwork, Federal Work-Study, and scholarships/grants available. Support available to part-time students. Financial award application deadline: 3/1; financial award applicants required to submit FAFSA. *Faculty research:* Research in electromagnetic devices. *Unit head:* Dr. Reza Raeisi, Chair, 559-278-6038, Fax: 559-278-6297, E-mail: rraeisi@csufresno.edu. *Application contact:* Dr. Nagy Bengiamin, Graduate Program Coordinator, 559-278-8339.
Website: http://www.fresnostate.edu/engineering/elec-computer/

California State University, Fullerton, Graduate Studies, College of Engineering and Computer Science, Department of Electrical Engineering, Fullerton, CA 92834-9480. Offers electrical engineering (MS); systems engineering (MS). *Program availability:* Part-time. *Degree requirements:* For master's, comprehensive exam, project or thesis. *Entrance requirements:* For master's, GRE General Test, GRE Subject Test, minimum undergraduate GPA of 2.5, 3.0 graduate. Application fee: $55. *Expenses:* Tuition, state resident: full-time $3369; part-time $1953 per unit. Tuition, nonresident: full-time $3915; part-time $2499 per unit. Tuition and fees vary according to course load, degree level and program. *Financial support:* Career-related internships or fieldwork, Federal Work-Study, institutionally sponsored loans, and scholarships/grants available. Support available to part-time students. Financial award application deadline: 3/1; financial award applicants required to submit FAFSA. *Unit head:* Dr. Mostafa Shiva, Chair, 657-278-3013. *Application contact:* Admissions/Applications, 657-278-2371.

California State University, Long Beach, Graduate Studies, College of Engineering, Department of Electrical Engineering, Long Beach, CA 90840. Offers MSEE. *Program availability:* Part-time. *Degree requirements:* For master's, comprehensive exam or thesis. *Entrance requirements:* Additional exam requirements/recommendations for international students: Required—TOEFL. *Application deadline:* For fall admission, 3/1 for domestic students. Application fee: $55. Electronic applications accepted. *Financial support:* Teaching assistantships, career-related internships or fieldwork, Federal Work-Study, institutionally sponsored loans, scholarships/grants, and unspecified assistantships available. Financial award application deadline: 3/2. *Faculty research:* Health care systems, VLSI, communications, CAD/CAM. *Unit head:* Hen-Geul Yeh, Chair, 562-985-5102.

California State University, Los Angeles, Graduate Studies, College of Engineering, Computer Science, and Technology, Department of Electrical and Computer Engineering, Los Angeles, CA 90032-8530. Offers electrical engineering (MS). *Program availability:* Part-time, evening/weekend. *Degree requirements:* For master's, comprehensive exam or thesis. *Entrance requirements:* For master's, GRE General Test, GRE Subject Test. Additional exam requirements/recommendations for international students: Required—TOEFL (minimum score 550 paper-based). Electronic applications accepted.

California State University, Northridge, Graduate Studies, College of Engineering and Computer Science, Department of Electrical and Computer Engineering, Northridge, CA 91330. Offers electrical engineering (MS). *Program availability:* Part-time, evening/weekend. *Faculty:* 19 full-time (14 women), 17 part-time/adjunct (13 women). *Students:* 82 full-time (19 women), 61 part-time (12 women); includes 14 minority (8 Asian, non-Hispanic/Latino; 5 Hispanic/Latino; 1 Native Hawaiian or other Pacific Islander, non-Hispanic/Latino), 101 international. Average age 27. 312 applicants, 42% accepted, 40 enrolled. *Degree requirements:* For master's, thesis or alternative. *Entrance requirements:* For master's, GRE General Test, minimum GPA of 2.75. Additional exam requirements/recommendations for international students: Required—TOEFL. *Application deadline:* For fall admission, 11/30 for domestic students. Application fee: $55. *Expenses:* Tuition, state resident: full-time $4152. *Financial support:* Application deadline: 3/1. *Faculty research:* Reflector antenna study. *Unit head:* Dr. George Law, Chair, 818-677-2190, E-mail: ece@csun.edu.
Website: http://www.ecs.csun.edu/ece/index.html

California State University, Sacramento, Office of Graduate Studies, College of Engineering and Computer Science, Department of Electrical and Electronic Engineering, Sacramento, CA 95819. Offers MS. *Program availability:* Part-time, evening/weekend. *Students:* 52 full-time (17 women), 67 part-time (16 women); includes 99 minority (6 Black or African American, non-Hispanic/Latino; 90 Asian, non-Hispanic/Latino; 3 Hispanic/Latino). Average age 28. In 2016, 46 master's awarded. *Degree requirements:* For master's, thesis or comprehensive exam, writing proficiency exam. *Entrance requirements:* For master's, minimum GPA of 3.0 in last 60 units of the BS in electrical and electronic engineering or equivalent, 3.25 in electrical and electronic engineering major or equivalent major. Additional exam requirements/recommendations for international students: Required—TOEFL (minimum score 550 paper-based; 80 iBT). *Application deadline:* For fall admission, 3/1 for domestic and international students; for spring admission, 9/15 for domestic students, 9/30 for international students. Applications are processed on a rolling basis. Application fee: $55. Electronic applications accepted. *Expenses:* $4,302 full-time tuition and fees per semester, $2,796 part-time. *Financial support:* Research assistantships, teaching assistantships, career-related internships or fieldwork, and Federal Work-Study available. Support available to part-time students. Financial award application deadline: 3/1; financial award applicants required to submit FAFSA. *Unit head:* Dr. Thomas Matthews, Chair, 916-278-6873, E-mail: matthews@ecs.csus.edu. *Application contact:* Jose Martinez, Graduate

Electrical Engineering

Admissions Supervisor, 916-278-7871, E-mail: martinj@skymail.csus.edu.
Website: http://www.ecs.csus.edu/eee

Capitol Technology University, Graduate Programs, Laurel, MD 20708-9759. Offers business administration (MBA); computer science (MS); electrical engineering (MS); information and telecommunications systems management (MS); information architecture (MS); network security (MS). *Program availability:* Part-time, evening/weekend, online learning. *Entrance requirements:* For master's, minimum GPA of 3.0. Electronic applications accepted.

Carleton University, Faculty of Graduate Studies, Faculty of Engineering and Design, Ottawa-Carleton Institute for Electrical Engineering, Department of Electronics, Ottawa, ON K1S 5B6, Canada. Offers electrical engineering (M Eng, MA Sc, PhD). *Degree requirements:* For master's, thesis optional; for doctorate, comprehensive exam, thesis/dissertation. *Entrance requirements:* For master's, honors degree; for doctorate, MA Sc or M Eng. Additional exam requirements/recommendations for international students: Required—TOEFL.

Carleton University, Faculty of Graduate Studies, Faculty of Engineering and Design, Ottawa-Carleton Institute for Electrical Engineering, Department of Systems and Computer Engineering, Ottawa, ON K1S 5B6, Canada. Offers electrical engineering (MA Sc, PhD); information and systems science (M Sc); technology innovation management (M Eng, MA Sc). PhD program offered jointly with University of Ottawa. *Degree requirements:* For master's, thesis optional. *Entrance requirements:* For master's, honors degree. Additional exam requirements/recommendations for international students: Required—TOEFL. *Faculty research:* Design manufacturing management; network design, protocols, and performance; software engineering; wireless and satellite communications.

Carnegie Mellon University, Carnegie Institute of Technology, Department of Electrical and Computer Engineering, Pittsburgh, PA 15213-3891. Offers MS, PhD. *Program availability:* Part-time. *Degree requirements:* For master's, thesis; for doctorate, thesis/dissertation, qualifying exam, teaching experience. *Entrance requirements:* For master's and doctorate, GRE General Test. Additional exam requirements/recommendations for international students: Required—TOEFL. *Faculty research:* Computer-aided design, solid-state devices, VLSI, processing, robotics and controls, signal processing, data systems storage.

Case Western Reserve University, School of Graduate Studies, Case School of Engineering, Department of Electrical Engineering and Computer Science, Cleveland, OH 44106. Offers computer engineering (MS, PhD); computing and information sciences (MS, PhD); electrical engineering (MS, PhD); systems and control engineering (MS, PhD). *Program availability:* Part-time, evening/weekend, online only, 100% online. *Faculty:* 32 full-time (3 women). *Students:* 188 full-time (42 women), 14 part-time (3 women); includes 7 minority (1 Black or African American, non-Hispanic/Latino; 5 Asian, non-Hispanic/Latino; 1 Hispanic/Latino), 152 international. In 2016, 25 master's, 26 doctorates awarded. Terminal master's awarded for partial completion of doctoral program. *Degree requirements:* For master's, thesis; for doctorate, thesis/dissertation, qualifying exam, teaching experience. *Entrance requirements:* For master's and doctorate, GRE General Test. Additional exam requirements/recommendations for international students: Required—TOEFL. *Application deadline:* For fall admission, 2/1 for domestic students; for spring admission, 11/1 for domestic students. Applications are processed on a rolling basis. Application fee: $50. *Expenses: Tuition:* Full-time $42,576; part-time $1774 per credit hour. *Required fees:* $34. Tuition and fees vary according to course load and program. *Financial support:* In 2016–17, 1 fellowship with tuition reimbursement, 63 research assistantships with tuition reimbursements, 10 teaching assistantships were awarded; career-related internships or fieldwork, Federal Work-Study, and institutionally sponsored loans also available. Support available to part-time students. Financial award application deadline: 3/1; financial award applicants required to submit FAFSA. *Faculty research:* Micro-/nano-systems; robotics and haptics; applied artificial intelligence; automation; computer-aided design and testing of digital systems. *Total annual research expenditures:* $4.9 million. *Unit head:* Dr. Kenneth Loparo, Department Chair, 216-368-4115, E-mail: kal4@case.edu. *Application contact:* Kimberly Yurchick, Student Affairs Specialist, 216-368-2920, Fax: 216-368-2801, E-mail: ksy4@case.edu.
Website: http://eecs.cwru.edu/

The Catholic University of America, School of Engineering, Department of Electrical Engineering and Computer Science, Washington, DC 20064. Offers computer science (MSCS, PhD); electrical engineering (MEE, PhD). *Program availability:* Part-time. *Faculty:* 10 full-time (2 women), 7 part-time/adjunct (1 woman). *Students:* 13 full-time (2 women), 40 part-time (11 women); includes 6 minority (1 Black or African American, non-Hispanic/Latino; 1 Asian, non-Hispanic/Latino; 4 Two or more races, non-Hispanic/Latino), 35 international. Average age 33. 40 applicants, 63% accepted, 12 enrolled. In 2016, 7 master's, 10 doctorates awarded. *Degree requirements:* For master's, thesis or alternative; for doctorate, comprehensive exam, thesis/dissertation, oral exams. *Entrance requirements:* For master's and doctorate, statement of purpose, official copies of academic transcripts, three letters of recommendation. Additional exam requirements/recommendations for international students: Required—TOEFL (minimum score 550 paper-based; 80 iBT). *Application deadline:* For fall admission, 7/15 priority date for domestic students, 7/1 for international students; for spring admission, 11/15 priority date for domestic students, 11/1 for international students. Applications are processed on a rolling basis. Application fee: $55. Electronic applications accepted. *Expenses:* $43,380 per year; $1,170 per credit; $200 per semester part-time fees. *Financial support:* Fellowships, research assistantships, teaching assistantships, Federal Work-Study, scholarships/grants, tuition waivers (full and partial), and unspecified assistantships available. Financial award application deadline: 2/1; financial award applicants required to submit FAFSA. *Faculty research:* Signal and image processing, computer communications, robotics, intelligent controls, bio-electromagnetics. *Total annual research expenditures:* $455,269. *Unit head:* Dr. Ozlem Kilic, Chair, 202-319-5879, Fax: 202-319-5195, E-mail: regalia@cua.edu. *Application contact:* Director of Graduate Admissions, 202-319-5057, Fax: 202-319-6533, E-mail: cua-admissions@cua.edu.
Website: http://eecs.cua.edu/

The Citadel, The Military College of South Carolina, Citadel Graduate College, School of Engineering, Department of Electrical and Computer Engineering, Charleston, SC 29409. Offers computer engineering (Graduate Certificate); electrical engineering (MS). *Program availability:* Part-time, evening/weekend. *Students:* 1 part-time. 2 applicants, 50% accepted. *Degree requirements:* For master's, 30 hours of coursework with minimum GPA of 3.0 on hours earned at The Citadel. *Entrance requirements:* For master's, GRE, 2 letters of recommendation; official transcript of baccalaureate degree from an ABET accredited engineering program or approved alternative. Additional exam requirements/recommendations for international students: Required—TOEFL (minimum score 550 paper-based; 79 iBT). *Application deadline:* Applications are processed on a rolling basis. Application fee: $40. Electronic applications accepted. *Expenses:* Tuition, state resident: full-time $5121; part-time $569 per credit hour. Tuition, nonresident: full-time $8613; part-time $957 per credit hour. *Required fees:* $90 per term. *Financial support:* Fellowships and unspecified assistantships available. Support available to part-time students. Financial award application deadline: 7/1; financial award applicants required to submit FAFSA. *Unit head:* Dr. Robert J. Barsanti, Jr., Department Head, 843-953-7593, E-mail: robert.barsanti@citadel.edu. *Application contact:* Dr. Tara Hornor, Associate Provost for Planning, Assessment and Evaluation/Dean of Enrollment Management, 843-953-5089, E-mail: cgc@citadel.edu.
Website: http://www.citadel.edu/root/ece

City College of the City University of New York, Graduate School, Grove School of Engineering, Department of Electrical Engineering, New York, NY 10031-9198. Offers ME, MS, PhD. PhD program offered jointly with Graduate School and University Center of the City University of New York. *Program availability:* Part-time. *Degree requirements:* For master's, thesis optional; for doctorate, one foreign language, comprehensive exam, thesis/dissertation. *Entrance requirements:* For master's and doctorate, GRE General Test. Additional exam requirements/recommendations for international students: Required—TOEFL (minimum score 500 paper-based; 61 iBT). Tuition and fees vary according to course load, degree level and program. *Faculty research:* Optical electronics, microwaves, communication, signal processing, control systems.

Clarkson University, Wallace H. Coulter School of Engineering, Department of Electrical and Computer Engineering, Potsdam, NY 13699. Offers electrical and computer engineering (PhD); electrical engineering (ME, MS). *Program availability:* Part-time, evening/weekend. *Faculty:* 33 full-time (8 women), 7 part-time/adjunct (1 woman). *Students:* 45 full-time (6 women), 24 part-time (2 women); includes 8 minority (1 Black or African American, non-Hispanic/Latino; 5 Asian, non-Hispanic/Latino; 2 Hispanic/Latino), 25 international. 60 applicants, 47% accepted, 14 enrolled. In 2016, 14 master's, 3 doctorates awarded. *Degree requirements:* For master's, thesis (for some programs), thesis or project (for MS); project (for ME); for doctorate, comprehensive exam, thesis/dissertation. *Entrance requirements:* For master's and doctorate, GRE. Additional exam requirements/recommendations for international students: Required—TOEFL (minimum score 550 paper-based, 80 iBT) or IELTS (6.5). *Application deadline:* Applications are processed on a rolling basis. Application fee: $50. Electronic applications accepted. *Expenses: Tuition:* Full-time $23,400; part-time $1300 per credit hour. Tuition and fees vary according to campus/location and program. *Financial support:* Scholarships/grants and unspecified assistantships available. *Unit head:* Dr. David Crouse, Chair of Electrical and Computer Engineering, 315-268-6529, E-mail: dcrouse@clarkson.edu. *Application contact:* Dan Capogna, Graduate Admissions Contact, 518-631-9910, E-mail: graduate@clarkson.edu.
Website: http://graduate.clarkson.edu

Clarkson University, Wallace H. Coulter School of Engineering, Master's Programs in Energy Systems, Schenectady, NY 12308. Offers business of energy (Advanced Certificate); electrical engineering (ME), including power engineering; energy systems (MS). *Program availability:* Part-time, evening/weekend. *Students:* 5 full-time (3 women), 3 part-time (0 women); includes 1 minority (Asian, non-Hispanic/Latino). 7 applicants, 43% accepted, 3 enrolled. In 2016, 1 degree awarded. *Degree requirements:* For master's, project. *Entrance requirements:* Additional exam requirements/recommendations for international students: Required—TOEFL (minimum score 550 paper-based, 80 iBT) or IELTS (6.5). *Application deadline:* Applications are processed on a rolling basis. Application fee: $50. Electronic applications accepted. *Expenses: Tuition:* Full-time $23,400; part-time $1300 per credit hour. Tuition and fees vary according to campus/location and program. *Financial support:* Scholarships/grants available. *Unit head:* Robert Kozik, Associate Dean of Engineering, 518-631-9881, E-mail: bkozik@clarkson.edu. *Application contact:* Dan Capogna, Graduate Admissions Contact, 518-631-9910, E-mail: graduate@clarkson.edu.

Clemson University, Graduate School, College of Engineering, Computing and Applied Sciences, Holcombe Department of Electrical and Computer Engineering, Program in Electrical Engineering, Clemson, SC 29634. Offers M Engr, MS, PhD. *Program availability:* Part-time, blended/hybrid learning. *Faculty:* 25 full-time (2 women), 3 part-time/adjunct (0 women). *Students:* 132 full-time (26 women), 16 part-time (4 women); includes 4 minority (1 Black or African American, non-Hispanic/Latino; 2 Asian, non-Hispanic/Latino; 1 Two or more races, non-Hispanic/Latino), 115 international. Average age 26. 429 applicants, 11% accepted, 25 enrolled. In 2016, 34 master's, 7 doctorates awarded. *Degree requirements:* For master's, comprehensive exam (for some programs), thesis or alternative; for doctorate, comprehensive exam, thesis/dissertation, departmental qualifying exam. *Entrance requirements:* For master's and doctorate, GRE General Test, unofficial transcripts, letters of recommendation. Additional exam requirements/recommendations for international students: Required—TOEFL (minimum score 95 iBT), IELTS (minimum score 7). *Application deadline:* For fall admission, 1/15 priority date for domestic students, 4/15 for international students; for spring admission, 9/15 priority date for domestic students, 9/15 for international students. Applications are processed on a rolling basis. Application fee: $80 ($90 for international students). Electronic applications accepted. *Expenses:* $4,841 per semester full-time resident, $9,640 per semester full-time non-resident, $612 per credit hour part-time resident, $1,223 per credit hour part-time non-resident. *Financial support:* In 2016–17, 114 students received support, including 8 fellowships with partial tuition reimbursements available (averaging $8,105 per year), 56 research assistantships with partial tuition reimbursements available (averaging $21,114 per year), 37 teaching assistantships with partial tuition reimbursements available (averaging $16,291 per year); unspecified assistantships also available. Financial award application deadline: 1/15. *Faculty research:* Cognitive radios; organic electronics/polymer-based devices, micro-optics and nano-photonics. *Unit head:* Dr. Daniel Noneaker, Department Chair, 864-656-0100, E-mail: dnoneak@clemson.edu. *Application contact:* Dr. Harlan Russell, Graduate Program Coordinator, 864-656-7214, E-mail: harlanr@clemson.edu.
Website: https://www.clemson.edu/cecas/departments/ece/index.html

Cleveland State University, College of Graduate Studies, Fenn College of Engineering, Department of Electrical and Computer Engineering, Cleveland, OH 44115. Offers electrical engineering (MS, D Eng); software engineering (MS). *Program availability:* Part-time, evening/weekend. *Faculty:* 15 full-time (2 women), 1 part-time/adjunct (0 women). *Students:* 209 full-time (36 women), 163 part-time (33 women); includes 17 minority (4 Black or African American, non-Hispanic/Latino; 13 Asian, non-Hispanic/Latino), 297 international. Average age 25. 1,083 applicants, 44% accepted, 89 enrolled. In 2016, 171 master's, 2 doctorates awarded. Terminal master's awarded for partial completion of doctoral program. *Degree requirements:* For master's, thesis optional; for doctorate, comprehensive exam, thesis/dissertation, qualifying and candidacy exams. *Entrance requirements:* For master's, GRE General Test (minimum score 650 quantitative), minimum GPA of 2.75; for doctorate, GRE General Test (minimum quantitative score in 80th percentile), minimum GPA of 3.25. Additional exam requirements/recommendations for international students: Required—TOEFL (minimum score 550 paper-based; 78 iBT) or IELTS (minimum score 6.0). *Application deadline:* For fall admission, 7/1 priority date for domestic students, 5/15 for international students; for spring admission, 11/15 for domestic students, 11/1 for international students; for summer admission, 4/1 for domestic students, 3/15 for international students. Applications are processed on a rolling basis. Application fee: $40. Electronic applications accepted. *Expenses:* Contact institution. *Financial support:* In 2016–17, 31 students received support, including 23 research assistantships with tuition reimbursements available (averaging $4,242 per year), 8 teaching assistantships with tuition reimbursements available (averaging $4,242 per year); career-related internships

or fieldwork, scholarships/grants, and unspecified assistantships also available. Financial award applicants required to submit FAFSA. *Faculty research:* Computer networks, computer security and privacy, mobile computing, distributed computing, software engineering, knowledge-based control systems, artificial intelligence, digital communications, MEMS, sensors, power systems, power electronics. *Total annual research expenditures:* $484,362. *Unit head:* Dr. Chansu Yu, Chairperson, 216-687-2584, Fax: 216-687-5405, E-mail: f.xiong@csuohio.edu. *Application contact:* Deborah L. Brown, Interim Assistant Director, Graduate Admissions, 216-523-7572, Fax: 216-687-9214, E-mail: d.l.brown@csuohio.edu.
Website: http://www.csuohio.edu/ece

Colorado School of Mines, Office of Graduate Studies, Department of Electrical Engineering and Computer Science, Golden, CO 80401. Offers computer science (MS, PhD); electrical engineering (MS, PhD). *Program availability:* Part-time. *Degree requirements:* For master's, thesis (for some programs); for doctorate, comprehensive exam, thesis/dissertation. *Entrance requirements:* For master's and doctorate, GRE General Test. Additional exam requirements/recommendations for international students: Required—TOEFL (minimum score 550 paper-based; 80 iBT). Electronic applications accepted. *Expenses:* Tuition, state resident: full-time $15,690. Tuition, nonresident: full-time $34,020. *Required fees:* $2152. Tuition and fees vary according to course load.

Colorado State University, Walter Scott, Jr. College of Engineering, Department of Electrical and Computer Engineering, Fort Collins, CO 80523-1373. Offers computer engineering (ME, MS, PhD); electrical engineering (ME, MS, PhD). *Program availability:* Part-time, evening/weekend, 100% online. *Faculty:* 28 full-time (4 women), 7 part-time/adjunct (3 women). *Students:* 60 full-time (8 women), 158 part-time (33 women); includes 11 minority (7 Asian, non-Hispanic/Latino; 3 Hispanic/Latino; 1 Two or more races, non-Hispanic/Latino), 167 international. Average age 27. 159 applicants, 98% accepted, 36 enrolled. In 2016, 58 master's, 16 doctorates awarded. *Degree requirements:* For master's, comprehensive exam (for some programs), thesis (for some programs); for doctorate, comprehensive exam, thesis/dissertation. *Entrance requirements:* For master's and doctorate, GRE, minimum GPA of 3.0; transcripts; resume; 3 letters of reference. Additional exam requirements/recommendations for international students: Required—PTE (minimum score 58), TOEFL (minimum score 80 iBT) or IELTS (6.5). *Application deadline:* For fall admission, 2/1 for domestic and international students; for spring admission, 9/1 for domestic and international students. Applications are processed on a rolling basis. Application fee: $60 ($70 for international students). Electronic applications accepted. *Expenses:* Contact institution. *Financial support:* In 2016–17, 65 students received support, including 4 fellowships (averaging $40,281 per year), 48 research assistantships (averaging $26,285 per year), 9 teaching assistantships (averaging $15,781 per year); career-related internships or fieldwork, scholarships/grants, traineeships, and unspecified assistantships also available. Financial award application deadline: 2/1. *Faculty research:* Communications and signal processing; controls and robotics; electromagnetics and remote sensing; electric power and energy systems; lasers, optics and applications. *Total annual research expenditures:* $9.7 million. *Unit head:* Dr. Anthony Maciejewski, Department Head, 970-491-6600, Fax: 970-491-2249, E-mail: aam@colostate.edu. *Application contact:* Katya Stewart-Sweeney, Graduate Advisor, 970-491-7850, Fax: 970-491-2249, E-mail: katyas@colostate.edu.
Website: http://www.engr.colostate.edu/ece/

Colorado Technical University Aurora, Program in Electrical Engineering, Aurora, CO 80014. Offers MS.

Colorado Technical University Colorado Springs, Graduate Studies, Program in Electrical Engineering, Colorado Springs, CO 80907. Offers MSEE. *Program availability:* Part-time, evening/weekend, online learning. *Degree requirements:* For master's, thesis or alternative. *Faculty research:* Electronic systems design, communication systems design.

Columbia University, Fu Foundation School of Engineering and Applied Science, Department of Electrical Engineering, New York, NY 10027. Offers computer engineering (MS); electrical engineering (MS, Eng Sc D, PhD). PhD offered through the Graduate School of Arts and Sciences. *Program availability:* Part-time, online learning. *Degree requirements:* For doctorate, thesis/dissertation, qualifying exam. *Entrance requirements:* For master's and doctorate, GRE General Test. Additional exam requirements/recommendations for international students: Required—TOEFL, IELTS, PTE. Electronic applications accepted. *Faculty research:* Media informatics and signal processing, integrated circuits and cyberphysical systems, communications systems and networking, nanoscale electronics and photonics, systems biology and neuroengineering.

Concordia University, School of Graduate Studies, Faculty of Engineering and Computer Science, Department of Electrical and Computer Engineering, Montréal, QC H3G 1M8, Canada. Offers M Eng, MA Sc, PhD. *Degree requirements:* For master's, thesis optional; for doctorate, comprehensive exam, thesis/dissertation. *Faculty research:* Computer communications and protocols, circuits and systems, graph theory, VLSI systems, microelectronics.

Cooper Union for the Advancement of Science and Art, Albert Nerken School of Engineering, New York, NY 10003. Offers chemical engineering (ME); civil engineering (ME); electrical engineering (ME); mechanical engineering (ME). *Program availability:* Part-time. *Faculty:* 27 full-time (1 woman), 15 part-time/adjunct (2 women). *Students:* 36 full-time (5 women), 39 part-time (8 women); includes 34 minority (3 Black or African American, non-Hispanic/Latino; 16 Asian, non-Hispanic/Latino; 5 Hispanic/Latino; 10 Two or more races, non-Hispanic/Latino), 3 international. Average age 24. 59 applicants, 75% accepted, 34 enrolled. In 2016, 25 master's awarded. *Degree requirements:* For master's, thesis (for some programs). *Entrance requirements:* For master's, BE or BS in an engineering discipline; official copies of school transcripts including secondary (high school), college and university work; two letters of recommendation; resume. Additional exam requirements/recommendations for international students: Required—TOEFL (minimum score 600 paper-based; 100 iBT). *Application deadline:* For fall admission, 3/31 for domestic and international students. Application fee: $75. Electronic applications accepted. *Expenses:* Tuition: Full-time $16,055; part-time $1235 per credit. *Required fees:* $925 per semester. One-time fee: $250. Tuition and fees vary according to course load. *Financial support:* In 2016–17, 70 students received support, including 4 fellowships with tuition reimbursements available (averaging $11,000 per year); career-related internships or fieldwork, tuition waivers (full and partial), and tuition scholarships offered to exceptional students also available. Support available to part-time students. Financial award application deadline: 5/1; financial award applicants required to submit FAFSA. *Faculty research:* Civil infrastructure, imaging and sensing technology, biomedical engineering, encryption technology, process engineering. *Unit head:* Richard Stock, Acting Dean of Albert Nerken School of Engineering, 212-353-4285, E-mail: stock@cooper.edu. *Application contact:* Chabeli Lajara, Administrative Assistant, 212-353-4120, E-mail: admissions@cooper.edu.
Website: http://cooper.edu/engineering

Cornell University, Graduate School, Graduate Fields of Engineering, Field of Electrical and Computer Engineering, Ithaca, NY 14853. Offers computer engineering (M Eng, PhD); electrical engineering (M Eng, PhD); electrical systems (M Eng, PhD); electrophysics (M Eng, PhD). *Degree requirements:* For doctorate, comprehensive exam, thesis/dissertation. *Entrance requirements:* For master's, GRE General Test, 2 letters of recommendation; for doctorate, GRE General Test, 3 letters of recommendation. Additional exam requirements/recommendations for international students: Required—TOEFL (minimum score 600 paper-based; 77 iBT). Electronic applications accepted. *Faculty research:* Communications, information theory, signal processing and power control, computer engineering, microelectromechanical systems and nanotechnology.

Dalhousie University, Faculty of Engineering, Department of Electrical and Computer Engineering, Halifax, NS B3J 1Z1, Canada. Offers M Eng, MA Sc, PhD. *Degree requirements:* For master's, thesis; for doctorate, thesis/dissertation. *Entrance requirements:* Additional exam requirements/recommendations for international students: Required—TOEFL, IELTS, CANTEST, CAEL, or Michigan English Language Assessment Battery. Electronic applications accepted. *Faculty research:* Communications, computer engineering, power engineering, electronics, systems engineering.

Drexel University, College of Engineering, Department of Electrical and Computer Engineering, Program in Electrical Engineering, Philadelphia, PA 19104-2875. Offers MSEE. *Program availability:* Part-time, evening/weekend. *Faculty:* 34 full-time (4 women), 4 part-time/adjunct (0 women). *Students:* 116 full-time (21 women), 53 part-time (9 women); includes 20 minority (8 Black or African American, non-Hispanic/Latino; 8 Asian, non-Hispanic/Latino; 1 Hispanic/Latino; 3 Two or more races, non-Hispanic/Latino), 90 international. Average age 28. In 2016, 73 master's awarded. Terminal master's awarded for partial completion of doctoral program. *Degree requirements:* For master's, thesis (for some programs). *Application deadline:* For fall admission, 8/21 for domestic students. Applications are processed on a rolling basis. Application fee: $50. Electronic applications accepted. *Expenses:* Tuition: Full-time $32,184; part-time $1192 per credit hour. *Required fees:* $280. Tuition and fees vary according to campus/location and program. *Financial support:* Research assistantships, teaching assistantships, career-related internships or fieldwork, and unspecified assistantships available. Financial award application deadline: 2/1. *Unit head:* Dr. Nihat M. Bilgutay, Head, 215-895-6806, Fax: 215-895-1695, E-mail: bilgutay@ece.drexel.edu. *Application contact:* Director of Graduate Admissions, 215-895-6700, Fax: 215-895-5939, E-mail: enroll@drexel.edu.

Duke University, Graduate School, Pratt School of Engineering, Department of Electrical and Computer Engineering, Durham, NC 27708. Offers MS, PhD, JD/MS. Terminal master's awarded for partial completion of doctoral program. *Degree requirements:* For doctorate, thesis/dissertation. *Entrance requirements:* For master's and doctorate, GRE General Test. Additional exam requirements/recommendations for international students: Required—TOEFL (minimum score 90 iBT), IELTS (minimum score 7). Electronic applications accepted. *Faculty research:* Architecture and networking; biological applications circuits and systems; nanosystems, devices and materials; quantum computing and photonics; sensing and signals visualization; waves and metamaterials.

See Display below and Close-Up on page 425.

Duke University, Graduate School, Pratt School of Engineering, Master of Engineering Program, Durham, NC 27708-0271. Offers biomedical engineering (M Eng); civil engineering (M Eng); electrical and computer engineering (M Eng); environmental engineering (M Eng); materials science and engineering (M Eng); mechanical engineering (M Eng); photonics and optical sciences (M Eng). *Program availability:* Part-time. *Entrance requirements:* For master's, GRE General Test, resume, 3 letters of recommendation, statement of purpose, transcripts. Additional exam requirements/recommendations for international students: Required—TOEFL.

École Polytechnique de Montréal, Graduate Programs, Department of Electrical and Computer Engineering, Montréal, QC H3C 3A7, Canada. Offers automation (M Eng, M Sc A, PhD); computer science (M Eng, M Sc A, PhD); electrical engineering (DESS); electrotechnology (M Eng, M Sc A, PhD); microelectronics (M Eng, M Sc A, PhD); microwave technology (M Eng, M Sc A, PhD). *Program availability:* Part-time, evening/weekend. *Degree requirements:* For master's, one foreign language, thesis; for doctorate, one foreign language, thesis/dissertation. *Entrance requirements:* For master's, minimum GPA of 2.75; for doctorate, minimum GPA of 3.0. *Faculty research:* Microwaves, telecommunications, software engineering.

Embry-Riddle Aeronautical University–Daytona, Department of Electrical, Computer, Software and Systems Engineering, Daytona Beach, FL 32114-3900. Offers computer engineering (MS); cybersecurity engineering (MS); electrical engineering (MSECE); electrical engineering and computer science (PhD), including electrical, computer, software, and systems engineering; software engineering (MSSE); systems engineering (MS). *Program availability:* Part-time. *Faculty:* 13 full-time (1 woman), 1 part-time/adjunct (0 women). *Students:* 63 full-time (17 women), 8 part-time (3 women); includes 6 minority (1 Black or African American, non-Hispanic/Latino; 1 Asian, non-Hispanic/Latino; 1 Hispanic/Latino; 3 Two or more races, non-Hispanic/Latino), 41 international. Average age 25. 93 applicants, 45% accepted, 21 enrolled. In 2016, 30 master's awarded. *Degree requirements:* For master's, thesis or alternative; for doctorate, thesis/dissertation. *Entrance requirements:* For master's, GRE (for some programs); for doctorate, GRE. Additional exam requirements/recommendations for international students: Required—TOEFL (minimum score 550 paper-based, 79 iBT) or IELTS (6). *Application deadline:* For fall admission, 3/1 priority date for domestic students; for spring admission, 11/1 priority date for domestic students; for summer admission, 4/1 priority date for domestic students. Applications are processed on a rolling basis. Application fee: $50. Electronic applications accepted. *Expenses:* Tuition: Full-time $16,296; part-time $1358 per credit hour. *Required fees:* $1294; $647 per semester. One-time fee: $100 full-time. Tuition and fees vary according to course load, degree level and program. *Financial support:* Research assistantships, teaching assistantships, career-related internships or fieldwork, scholarships/grants, unspecified assistantships, and on-campus employment available. Financial award application deadline: 3/15; financial award applicants required to submit FAFSA. *Faculty research:* Cybersecurity and assured systems engineering, radar, unmanned and autonomous systems, modeling and simulation, cyber-physical systems. *Unit head:* Timothy Wilson, PhD, Professor of Electrical and Computer Engineering/Chair, Department of Electrical, Computer, Software and Systems Engineering, 386-226-6100, E-mail: timothy.wilson@erau.edu. *Application contact:* Graduate Admissions, 386-226-6176, Fax: 386-226-7070, E-mail: graduate.admissions@erau.edu.
Website: https://daytonabeach.erau.edu/college-engineering/electrical-computer-software-systems/index.html

Fairfield University, School of Engineering, Fairfield, CT 06824. Offers database management (CAS); electrical and computer engineering (MS); information security (CAS); management of technology (MS); mechanical engineering (MS); network technology (CAS); software engineering (MS); Web application development (CAS).

DUKE UNIVERSITY

Electrical & Computer Engineering M.S. and Ph.D.

Why Duke?

Duke's Pratt School of Engineering students work in a supportive, close-knit community which gives them ample opportunities to:

- publish with their faculty adviser,

- present research at professional conferences,

- work in a highly collaborative, cross-disciplinary environment, &

- make significant contributions to their field.

Our Electrical and Computer Engineering Department is ranked seventh in faculty scholarly productivity.

Research Areas

Graduate students and faculty collaborate in cutting edge research in these areas:

- architecture & networking

- biological applications circuits & systems

- nanosystems, devices & materials

- quantum computing & photonics

- sensing & signals visualization

- waves & metamaterials

Why Durham, NC?

Duke is located in the Research Triangle region of North Carolina which is known for having the highest concentration of Ph.D.'s and M.D.'s in the world.

Durham is a vibrant, culturally rich city with affordable housing and a warm climate.

Professor Steve Cummer (at left) with a research scientist

Duke

PRATT SCHOOL of ENGINEERING

ece.duke.edu

For more information see our website or contact us:
dgs@ee.duke.edu
1 919 660 5245

Program availability: Part-time, evening/weekend. *Faculty:* 7 full-time (1 woman), 15 part-time/adjunct (2 women). *Students:* 104 full-time (31 women), 56 part-time (15 women); includes 17 minority (8 Black or African American, non-Hispanic/Latino; 5 Asian, non-Hispanic/Latino; 4 Hispanic/Latino), 108 international. Average age 28. 193 applicants, 63% accepted, 20 enrolled. In 2016, 173 master's awarded. *Degree requirements:* For master's, capstone course. *Entrance requirements:* For master's, resume, 2 recommendations. Additional exam requirements/recommendations for international students: Required—TOEFL (minimum score 550 paper-based; 80 iBT) or IELTS (minimum score 6.5). *Application deadline:* For fall admission, 5/15 for international students; for spring admission, 10/15 for international students. Applications are processed on a rolling basis. Application fee: $60. Electronic applications accepted. *Expenses:* $800 per credit hour. *Financial support:* In 2016–17, 27 students received support. Scholarships/grants and unspecified assistantships available. Financial award applicants required to submit FAFSA. *Faculty research:* Artificial intelligence and information visualization, natural language processing, thermofluids, microwaves and electromagnetics, micro-/nano-manufacturing. *Unit head:* Dr. Bruce Berdanier, Dean, 203-254-4147, Fax: 203-254-4013, E-mail: bberdanier@fairfield.edu. *Application contact:* Marianne Gumpper, Director of Graduate and Continuing Studies Admission, 203-254-4184, Fax: 203-254-4073, E-mail: gradadmis@fairfield.edu.
Website: http://www.fairfield.edu/soe

Fairleigh Dickinson University, Metropolitan Campus, University College: Arts, Sciences, and Professional Studies, School of Computer Sciences and Engineering, Program in Electrical Engineering, Teaneck, NJ 07666-1914. Offers MSEE. *Entrance requirements:* For master's, GRE General Test.

Florida Agricultural and Mechanical University, Division of Graduate Studies, Research, and Continuing Education, FAMU-FSU College of Engineering, Department of Electrical and Computer Engineering, Tallahassee, FL 32307-3200. Offers electrical engineering (MS, PhD). *Degree requirements:* For master's, comprehensive exam, thesis, conference paper; for doctorate, comprehensive exam, thesis/dissertation, publishable paper. *Entrance requirements:* For master's, GRE General Test, minimum GPA of 3.0; for doctorate, minimum GPA of 3.3. Additional exam requirements/recommendations for international students: Required—TOEFL (minimum score 550 paper-based). *Faculty research:* Electromagnetics, computer security, advanced power systems, sensor systems.

Florida Atlantic University, College of Engineering and Computer Science, Department of Computer and Electrical Engineering and Computer Science, Boca Raton, FL 33431-0991. Offers bioengineering (MS); computer engineering (MS, PhD); computer science (MS, PhD); electrical engineering (MS, PhD). *Program availability:* Part-time, evening/weekend. *Faculty:* 23 full-time (5 women), 1 part-time/adjunct (0 women). *Students:* 103 full-time (30 women), 127 part-time (30 women); includes 77 minority (15 Black or African American, non-Hispanic/Latino; 10 Asian, non-Hispanic/Latino; 46 Hispanic/Latino; 6 Two or more races, non-Hispanic/Latino), 74 international. Average age 32. 215 applicants, 51% accepted, 85 enrolled. In 2016, 45 master's, 5 doctorates awarded. Terminal master's awarded for partial completion of doctoral program. *Degree requirements:* For master's, thesis optional; for doctorate, thesis/dissertation, qualifying exam. *Entrance requirements:* For master's, GRE General Test, minimum GPA of 3.0; for doctorate, GRE General Test, master's degree, minimum GPA of 3.5. Additional exam requirements/recommendations for international students: Required—TOEFL (minimum score 500 paper-based; 61 iBT), IELTS (minimum score 6). *Application deadline:* For fall admission, 7/1 priority date for domestic students, 2/15 for international students; for spring admission, 11/1 for domestic students, 7/15 for international students. Applications are processed on a rolling basis. Application fee: $30. *Expenses:* Tuition, state resident: full-time $7392; part-time $369.82 per credit hour. Tuition, nonresident: full-time $19,432; part-time $1024.81 per credit hour. *Financial support:* Fellowships, research assistantships with partial tuition reimbursements, teaching assistantships with full tuition reimbursements, career-related internships or fieldwork, and Federal Work-Study available. Support available to part-time students. Financial award application deadline: 4/1; financial award applicants required to submit FAFSA. *Faculty research:* VLSI and neural networks, communication networks, software engineering, computer architecture, multimedia and video processing. *Unit head:* Jean Mangiaracina, 561-297-3855, E-mail: jmangiar@fau.edu.
Website: http://www.ceecs.fau.edu/

Florida Institute of Technology, College of Engineering, Program in Electrical Engineering, Melbourne, FL 32901-6975. Offers MS, PhD. *Program availability:* Part-time. *Students:* 88 full-time (18 women), 41 part-time (4 women); includes 9 minority (1 Black or African American, non-Hispanic/Latino; 6 Asian, non-Hispanic/Latino; 2 Hispanic/Latino), 101 international. Average age 28. 491 applicants, 54% accepted, 55 enrolled. In 2016, 77 master's, 5 doctorates awarded. *Degree requirements:* For master's, comprehensive exam (for some programs), thesis optional, 30 credit hours; for doctorate, comprehensive exam, thesis/dissertation, significant original research, publication in professional journal of conference proceedings, minimum of 48 credit hours after master's degree. *Entrance requirements:* For master's, GRE, bachelor's degree from ABET-accredited program; for doctorate, GRE, 3 letters of recommendation, resume, statement of objectives, on-campus interview (highly recommended). Additional exam requirements/recommendations for international students: Required—TOEFL (minimum score 550 paper-based; 79 iBT). *Application deadline:* For fall admission, 4/1 for international students; for spring admission, 9/30 for international students. Applications are processed on a rolling basis. Electronic applications accepted. *Expenses: Tuition:* Full-time $22,338; part-time $1241 per credit hour. *Required fees:* $250. Tuition and fees vary according to degree level, campus/location and program. *Financial support:* Career-related internships or fieldwork, institutionally sponsored loans, tuition waivers (partial), unspecified assistantships, and tuition remissions available. Support available to part-time students. Financial award application deadline: 3/1; financial award applicants required to submit FAFSA. *Faculty research:* Electro-optics, electromagnetics, microelectronics, communications, computer architecture, neural networks. *Unit head:* Dr. Samuel P. Kozaitis, Department Head, 321-674-8060, Fax: 321-674-8192, E-mail: kozaitis@fit.edu. *Application contact:* Cheryl A. Brown, Associate Director of Graduate Admissions, 321-674-7581, Fax: 321-723-9468, E-mail: cbrown@fit.edu.
Website: http://coe.fit.edu/ee/

Florida Institute of Technology, Extended Studies Division, Melbourne, FL 32901-6975. Offers acquisition and contract management (MS); aerospace engineering (MS); business administration (MBA, DBA); computer information systems (MS); computer science (MS); electrical engineering (MS); engineering management (MS); human resources management (MS); logistics management (MS), including humanitarian and disaster relief logistics; management (MS), including acquisition and contract management, e-business, human resources management, information systems, logistics management, management, transportation management; material acquisition management (MS); mechanical engineering (MS); operations research (MS); project management (MS), including information systems, operations research; public administration (MPA); quality management (MS); software engineering (MS); space systems (MS); space systems management (MS); supply chain management (MS);

systems management (MS), including information systems, operations research; technology management (MS). *Program availability:* Part-time, evening/weekend, online learning. *Faculty:* 10 full-time (3 women), 122 part-time/adjunct (29 women). *Students:* 131 full-time (58 women), 997 part-time (348 women); includes 389 minority (231 Black or African American, non-Hispanic/Latino; 9 American Indian or Alaska Native, non-Hispanic/Latino; 26 Asian, non-Hispanic/Latino; 99 Hispanic/Latino; 3 Native Hawaiian or other Pacific Islander, non-Hispanic/Latino; 21 Two or more races, non-Hispanic/Latino), 53 international. Average age 36. 962 applicants, 48% accepted, 323 enrolled. In 2016, 403 master's awarded. *Degree requirements:* For master's, comprehensive exam (for some programs). *Entrance requirements:* For master's, GMAT or resume showing 8 years of supervised experience, minimum GPA of 3.0, 2 letters of recommendation, resume. Additional exam requirements/recommendations for international students: Required—TOEFL (minimum score 550 paper-based; 79 iBT). *Application deadline:* For fall admission, 4/1 for international students; for spring admission, 9/30 for international students. Applications are processed on a rolling basis. Electronic applications accepted. *Expenses:* Contact institution. *Financial support:* Application deadline: 3/1; applicants required to submit FAFSA. *Unit head:* Dr. Theodore R. Richardson, III, Dean, 321-674-8123, Fax: 321-674-7597, E-mail: trichardson@fit.edu. *Application contact:* Carolyn Farrior, Director of Graduate Admissions, Online Learning and Off-Campus Programs, 321-674-7118, Fax: 321-674-8216, E-mail: cfarrior@fit.edu.
Website: http://es.fit.edu

Florida International University, College of Engineering and Computing, Department of Electrical and Computer Engineering, Miami, FL 33175. Offers computer engineering (MS); electrical engineering (MS, PhD). *Program availability:* Part-time, evening/weekend. *Faculty:* 27 full-time (3 women), 10 part-time/adjunct (0 women). *Students:* 139 full-time (25 women), 55 part-time (9 women); includes 65 minority (11 Black or African American, non-Hispanic/Latino; 7 Asian, non-Hispanic/Latino; 46 Hispanic/Latino; 1 Native Hawaiian or other Pacific Islander, non-Hispanic/Latino), 114 international. Average age 29. 271 applicants, 43% accepted, 47 enrolled. In 2016, 57 master's, 15 doctorates awarded. Terminal master's awarded for partial completion of doctoral program. *Degree requirements:* For master's, thesis optional; for doctorate, comprehensive exam, thesis/dissertation. *Entrance requirements:* For master's, minimum undergraduate GPA of 3.0 in upper-level coursework, resume, letters of recommendation, letter of intent; for doctorate, GRE General Test, minimum graduate GPA of 3.3, resume, letters of recommendation, letter of intent. Additional exam requirements/recommendations for international students: Required—TOEFL (minimum score 550 paper-based; 80 iBT). *Application deadline:* For fall admission, 6/1 for domestic students, 4/1 for international students; for spring admission, 10/1 for domestic students, 9/1 for international students. Applications are processed on a rolling basis. Application fee: $30. Electronic applications accepted. *Expenses:* Tuition, state resident: full-time $8912; part-time $446 per credit hour. Tuition, nonresident: full-time $21,393; part-time $992 per credit hour. *Required fees:* $2185; $195 per semester. Tuition and fees vary according to program. *Financial support:* Institutionally sponsored loans, scholarships/grants, and unspecified assistantships available. Financial award application deadline: 3/1; financial award applicants required to submit FAFSA. *Unit head:* Dr. Shekhar Bhansali, Chair, 305-348-4439, Fax: 305-348-3707, E-mail: sbhansa@fiu.edu. *Application contact:* Sara-Michelle Lemus, Engineering Admissions Officer, 305-348-1890, Fax: 305-348-7441, E-mail: grad_eng@fiu.edu.
Website: http://cec.fiu.edu

Florida State University, The Graduate School, FAMU-FSU College of Engineering, Department of Electrical and Computer Engineering, Tallahassee, FL 32306. Offers electrical engineering (MS, PhD). *Program availability:* Part-time. *Faculty:* 22 full-time (3 women), 4 part-time/adjunct (2 women). *Students:* 93 full-time (14 women); includes 15 minority (8 Black or African American, non-Hispanic/Latino; 3 Asian, non-Hispanic/Latino; 3 Hispanic/Latino; 1 Two or more races, non-Hispanic/Latino), 63 international. Average age 26. 147 applicants, 58% accepted, 26 enrolled. In 2016, 19 master's, 7 doctorates awarded. *Degree requirements:* For master's, comprehensive exam (for some programs), thesis (for some programs); for doctorate, thesis/dissertation, preliminary exam, qualifying exam. *Entrance requirements:* For master's, GRE General Test, minimum GPA of 3.0, BS in electrical engineering; for doctorate, GRE General Test, minimum graduate GPA of 3.3, MS in electrical engineering. Additional exam requirements/recommendations for international students: Required—TOEFL (minimum score 550 paper-based; 80 iBT); Recommended—IELTS. *Application deadline:* For fall admission, 3/1 for domestic and international students; for spring admission, 11/1 for domestic and international students; for summer admission, 3/1 for domestic and international students. Applications are processed on a rolling basis. Application fee: $30. Electronic applications accepted. *Expenses:* Tuition, state resident: full-time $7263; part-time $403.51 per credit hour. Tuition, nonresident: full-time $18,087; part-time $1004.85 per credit hour. *Required fees:* $1365; $75.81 per credit hour. $20 per semester. Tuition and fees vary according to campus/location. *Financial support:* In 2016–17, 2 fellowships with full tuition reimbursements, 28 research assistantships with full tuition reimbursements, 18 teaching assistantships with full tuition reimbursements were awarded; career-related internships or fieldwork, institutionally sponsored loans, scholarships/grants, tuition waivers (full), and unspecified assistantships also available. Financial award application deadline: 3/1; financial award applicants required to submit FAFSA. *Faculty research:* Electromagnetics, digital signal processing, computer systems, image processing, laser optics. *Total annual research expenditures:* $2 million. *Unit head:* Dr. Simon Foo, Chair and Professor, 850-410-6474, Fax: 850-410-6479, E-mail: foo@eng.famu.fsu.edu. *Application contact:* Melissa Jackson, Graduate Program Coordinator, 850-410-6454, Fax: 850-410-6479, E-mail: ecegrad@eng.famu.fsu.edu.
Website: http://www.eng.famu.fsu.edu/ece/

Gannon University, School of Graduate Studies, College of Engineering and Business, School of Engineering and Computer Science, Program in Electrical and Computer Engineering, Erie, PA 16541-0001. Offers MSEE, MSES. *Program availability:* Part-time, evening/weekend. *Students:* 76 full-time (16 women), 29 part-time (4 women); includes 1 minority (Asian, non-Hispanic/Latino), 101 international. Average age 25. 267 applicants, 58% accepted, 17 enrolled. In 2016, 94 master's awarded. *Degree requirements:* For master's, thesis (for some programs), oral exam (for some programs), design project (for some programs). *Entrance requirements:* For master's, bachelor's degree in electrical or computer engineering from an ABET-accredited program or its equivalent with minimum GPA of 2.5, transcripts, 3 letters of recommendation. Additional exam requirements/recommendations for international students: Required—TOEFL (minimum score 79 iBT). *Application deadline:* Applications are processed on a rolling basis. Application fee: $25. Electronic applications accepted. Application fee is waived when completed online. *Expenses: Tuition:* Full-time $17,370. *Required fees:* $550. Tuition and fees vary according to course load and program. *Financial support:* Federal Work-Study available. Financial award application deadline: 7/1; financial award applicants required to submit FAFSA. *Unit head:* Dr. Wookwon Lee, Chair, 814-871-7630, E-mail: lee023@gannon.edu. *Application contact:* Bridget Philip, Director of Graduate Admissions, 814-871-7412, E-mail: graduate@gannon.edu.

George Mason University, Volgenau School of Engineering, Department of Electrical and Computer Engineering, Fairfax, VA 22030. Offers computer engineering (MS); electrical and computer engineering (PhD, Certificate). MS programs offered jointly with Old Dominion University, University of Virginia, Virginia Commonwealth University, and Virginia Polytechnic Institute and State University. *Faculty:* 34 full-time (5 women), 42 part-time/adjunct (3 women). *Students:* 208 full-time (58 women), 196 part-time (38 women); includes 82 minority (24 Black or African American, non-Hispanic/Latino; 28 Asian, non-Hispanic/Latino; 22 Hispanic/Latino; 1 Native Hawaiian or other Pacific Islander, non-Hispanic/Latino; 7 Two or more races, non-Hispanic/Latino), 193 international. Average age 29. 353 applicants, 82% accepted, 107 enrolled. In 2016, 168 master's, 11 doctorates, 54 other advanced degrees awarded. *Degree requirements:* For master's, thesis optional; for doctorate, comprehensive exam, thesis or scholarly paper. *Entrance requirements:* For master's, GRE, personal goals statement; 2 official copies of transcripts; self-evaluation form; 3 letters of recommendation; resume; official bank statement; photocopy of passport; proof of financial support; for doctorate, GRE (waived for GMU electrical and computer engineering master's graduates with minimum GPA of 3.0), personal goals statement; 2 official copies of transcripts; self-evaluation form; 3 letters of recommendation; resume; official bank statement; photocopy of passport; proof of financial support. Additional exam requirements/recommendations for international students: Required—TOEFL (minimum score 575 paper-based; 88 iBT), IELTS (minimum score 6.5), PTE (minimum score 59). *Application deadline:* For fall admission, 1/15 priority date for domestic students. Application fee: $75 ($80 for international students). Electronic applications accepted. *Expenses:* Contact institution. *Financial support:* In 2016–17, 71 students received support, including 2 fellowships (averaging $10,814 per year), 29 research assistantships with tuition reimbursements available (averaging $17,506 per year), 42 teaching assistantships with tuition reimbursements available (averaging $11,959 per year); career-related internships or fieldwork, Federal Work-Study, scholarships/grants, unspecified assistantships, and health care benefits (for full-time research or teaching assistantship recipients) also available. Support available to part-time students. Financial award application deadline: 3/1; financial award applicants required to submit FAFSA. *Faculty research:* Communication networks, signal processing, system failure diagnosis, multiprocessors, material processing using microwave energy. *Total annual research expenditures:* $2.3 million. *Unit head:* Monson Hayes, Chair, 703-993-1570, Fax: 703-993-1601, E-mail: hayes@gmu.edu. *Application contact:* Jammie Chang, Academic Program Coordinator, 703-993-1570, Fax: 703-993-1601, E-mail: jchangn@gmu.edu.
Website: http://ece.gmu.edu/

The George Washington University, School of Engineering and Applied Science, Department of Electrical and Computer Engineering, Washington, DC 20052. Offers electrical engineering (MS, PhD); telecommunication and computers (MS). *Program availability:* Part-time, evening/weekend. *Faculty:* 26 full-time (2 women). *Students:* 191 full-time (43 women), 67 part-time (56 women); includes 19 minority (9 Black or African American, non-Hispanic/Latino; 7 Asian, non-Hispanic/Latino; 3 Hispanic/Latino), 218 international. Average age 27. 545 applicants, 88% accepted, 103 enrolled. In 2016, 48 master's, 7 doctorates, 1 other advanced degree awarded. *Degree requirements:* For master's, thesis optional; for doctorate, comprehensive exam, thesis/dissertation, dissertation defense, qualifying exam. *Entrance requirements:* For master's, appropriate bachelor's degree, minimum GPA of 3.0; for doctorate, GRE (if highest earned degree is BS), appropriate bachelor's or master's degree, minimum GPA of 3.3; for other advanced degree, appropriate master's degree, minimum GPA of 3.0. Additional exam requirements/recommendations for international students: Required—TOEFL or The George Washington University English as a Foreign Language Test. *Application deadline:* For fall admission, 3/1 priority date for domestic students; for spring admission, 10/1 for domestic students. Applications are processed on a rolling basis. Application fee: $75. *Financial support:* In 2016–17, 39 students received support. Fellowships with tuition reimbursements available, research assistantships, teaching assistantships with tuition reimbursements available, career-related internships or fieldwork, and institutionally sponsored loans available. Financial award application deadline: 3/1; financial award applicants required to submit FAFSA. *Faculty research:* Computer graphics, multimedia systems. *Unit head:* Prof. Ahmed Louri, Chair, 202-994-5905, E-mail: louri@gwu.edu. *Application contact:* Adina Lav, Marketing, Recruiting and Admissions, 202-994-5827, Fax: 202-994-0909, E-mail: engineering@gwu.edu.
Website: http://www.ece.gwu.edu/

Georgia Institute of Technology, Graduate Studies, College of Engineering, School of Electrical and Computer Engineering, Atlanta, GA 30332-0001. Offers MS, PhD. *Program availability:* Part-time, online learning. Terminal master's awarded for partial completion of doctoral program. *Degree requirements:* For master's, thesis optional; for doctorate, comprehensive exam, thesis/dissertation. *Entrance requirements:* For master's and doctorate, GRE General Test. Additional exam requirements/recommendations for international students: Required—TOEFL (minimum score 550 paper-based; 79 iBT). Electronic applications accepted. *Expenses:* Contact institution. *Faculty research:* Telecommunications, computer systems, microelectronics, optical engineering, digital signal processing.

Georgia Southern University, Jack N. Averitt College of Graduate Studies, Allen E. Paulson College of Engineering and Information Technology, Program in Electrical and Electronic Systems, Statesboro, GA 30458. Offers MSAE. *Students:* 16 full-time (3 women), 1 part-time (0 women); includes 4 minority (3 Black or African American, non-Hispanic/Latino; 1 Hispanic/Latino), 9 international. Average age 25. 32 applicants, 69% accepted, 7 enrolled. In 2016, 3 master's awarded. *Degree requirements:* For master's, thesis optional. *Entrance requirements:* For master's, GRE, minimum GPA of 2.75. Additional exam requirements/recommendations for international students: Required—TOEFL (minimum score 550 paper-based; 80 iBT), IELTS (minimum score 6). *Application deadline:* For fall admission, 2/1 for domestic students; for spring admission, 10/1 for domestic students. Application fee: $50. Electronic applications accepted. *Expenses:* Tuition, state resident: full-time $7236; part-time $277 per semester hour. Tuition, nonresident: full-time $27,118; part-time $1105 per semester hour. *Required fees:* $2092. *Financial support:* Unspecified assistantships available. Financial award application deadline: 4/20; financial award applicants required to submit FAFSA. *Faculty research:* Programming, artificial intelligence, web systems, data mining, database systems. *Unit head:* Dr. Biswanath Samanta, Program Chair, 912-478-0334, E-mail: bsamanta@georgiasouthern.edu.

The Graduate Center, City University of New York, Graduate Studies, Program in Engineering, New York, NY 10016-4039. Offers biomedical engineering (PhD); chemical engineering (PhD); civil engineering (PhD); electrical engineering (PhD); mechanical engineering (PhD). *Degree requirements:* For doctorate, thesis/dissertation. *Entrance requirements:* For doctorate, GRE General Test. Additional exam requirements/recommendations for international students: Required—TOEFL. Electronic applications accepted.

Grand Valley State University, Padnos College of Engineering and Computing, School of Engineering, Allendale, MI 49401-9403. Offers electrical and computer engineering (MSE); manufacturing operations (MSE); mechanical engineering (MSE); product design and manufacturing engineering (MSE). *Program availability:* Part-time, evening/weekend. *Faculty:* 16 full-time (3 women). *Students:* 29 full-time (8 women), 38 part-time (5 women); includes 5 minority (2 Black or African American, non-Hispanic/Latino; 1 Asian, non-Hispanic/Latino; 2 Hispanic/Latino), 37 international. Average age 26. 129

applicants, 58% accepted, 23 enrolled. In 2016, 24 master's awarded. *Degree requirements:* For master's, project or thesis. *Entrance requirements:* For master's, engineering degree, minimum GPA of 3.0, resume, 3 confidential letters of recommendation, 1-2 page essay, base of underlying relevant knowledge/evidence from academic records or relevant wok experience. Additional exam requirements/ recommendations for international students: Required—TOEFL (minimum score 80 iBT) or IELTS (6.5). *Application deadline:* Applications are processed on a rolling basis. Application fee: $30. Electronic applications accepted. *Expenses:* $661 per credit hour. *Financial support:* In 2016–17, 32 students received support, including 8 fellowships; career-related internships or fieldwork, Federal Work-Study, institutionally sponsored loans, scholarships/grants, and unspecified assistantships also available. *Faculty research:* Digital signal processing, computer aided design, computer aided manufacturing, manufacturing simulation, biomechanics, product design. *Total annual research expenditures:* $300,000. *Unit head:* Dr. Wael Mokhtar, Director, 616-331-6015, Fax: 616-331-7215, E-mail: mokhtarw@gvsu.edu. *Application contact:* Dr. Shabbir Choudhuri, Graduate Program Director, 616-331-6845, Fax: 616-331-7215, E-mail: choudhus@gvsu.edu.
Website: http://www.engineer.gvsu.edu/

Harvard University, Graduate School of Arts and Sciences, Harvard John A. Paulson School of Engineering and Applied Sciences, Cambridge, MA 02138. Offers applied mathematics (PhD); applied physics (PhD); computational science and engineering (ME, SM); computer science (PhD); design engineering (MDE); engineering science (ME), including electrical engineering (ME, SM, PhD); engineering sciences (SM, PhD), including bioengineering (PhD), electrical engineering (ME, SM, PhD), environmental science and engineering (PhD), materials science and mechanical engineering (PhD). MDE offered in collaboration with Graduate School of Design. *Program availability:* Part-time. *Faculty:* 80 full-time (13 women), 47 part-time/adjunct (10 women). *Students:* 459 full-time (135 women), 19 part-time (7 women); includes 79 minority (2 Black or African American, non-Hispanic/Latino; 49 Asian, non-Hispanic/Latino; 15 Hispanic/Latino; 1 Native Hawaiian or other Pacific Islander, non-Hispanic/Latino; 12 Two or more races, non-Hispanic/Latino), 233 international. Average age 27. 2,486 applicants, 11% accepted, 126 enrolled. In 2016, 37 master's, 48 doctorates awarded. Terminal master's awarded for partial completion of doctoral program. *Degree requirements:* For master's, thesis (for ME); for doctorate, comprehensive exam, thesis/dissertation. *Entrance requirements:* For master's and doctorate, GRE General Test, GRE Subject Test (recommended), 3 letters of recommendation. Additional exam requirements/ recommendations for international students: Required—TOEFL (minimum score 80 iBT). *Application deadline:* For fall admission, 12/15 priority date for domestic and international students. Application fee: $105. Electronic applications accepted. *Expenses:* $43,296 full-time tuition, $3,718 fees. *Financial support:* In 2016–17, 394 students received support, including 86 fellowships with full tuition reimbursements available (averaging $26,424 per year), 258 research assistantships with tuition reimbursements available (averaging $35,232 per year), 106 teaching assistantships with tuition reimbursements available (averaging $6,313 per year); health care benefits also available. *Faculty research:* Applied mathematics, applied physics, computer science and electrical engineering, environmental engineering, mechanical and biomedical engineering. *Total annual research expenditures:* $50.1 million. *Unit head:* Francis J. Doyle, III, Dean, 617-495-5829, Fax: 617-495-5264, E-mail: dean@seas.harvard.edu. *Application contact:* Office of Admissions and Financial Aid, 617-495-5315, E-mail: admissions@seas.harvard.edu.
Website: http://www.seas.harvard.edu/

Howard University, College of Engineering, Architecture, and Computer Sciences, School of Engineering and Computer Science, Department of Electrical Engineering, Washington, DC 20059-0002. Offers M Eng, PhD. Offered through the Graduate School of Arts and Sciences. *Program availability:* Part-time. *Degree requirements:* For master's, thesis (for some programs), qualifying exam; for doctorate, thesis/dissertation, preliminary exam. *Entrance requirements:* For master's, GRE General Test, bachelor's degree in electrical engineering, minimum GPA of 3.0; for doctorate, GRE General Test, minimum GPA of 3.0. Additional exam requirements/recommendations for international students: Required—TOEFL. Electronic applications accepted. *Faculty research:* Solid-state electronics, antennas and microwaves, communications and signal processing, controls and power systems, nanotechnology.

Illinois Institute of Technology, Graduate College, Armour College of Engineering, Department of Electrical and Computer Engineering, Chicago, IL 60616. Offers biomedical imaging and signals (MAS); computer engineering (MS, PhD); electrical engineering (MS, PhD); electricity markets (MAS); network engineering (MAS); power engineering (MAS); telecommunications and software engineering (MAS); VLSI and microelectronics (MAS); MS/MS. *Program availability:* Part-time, evening/weekend, online learning. Terminal master's awarded for partial completion of doctoral program. *Degree requirements:* For master's, comprehensive exam (for some programs), thesis (for some programs); for doctorate, comprehensive exam, thesis/dissertation. *Entrance requirements:* For master's and doctorate, GRE General Test (minimum score 1100 Quantitative and Verbal, 3.5 Analytical Writing), minimum undergraduate GPA of 3.0. Additional exam requirements/recommendations for international students: Required—TOEFL (minimum score 550 paper-based; 80 iBT); Recommended—IELTS (minimum score 5.5). Electronic applications accepted. *Faculty research:* Communication systems, wireless networks, computer systems, computer networks, wireless security, cloud computing and micro-electronics; electromagnetics and electronics; power and control systems; signal and image processing.

Indiana University–Purdue University Fort Wayne, College of Engineering, Technology, and Computer Science, Department of Electrical and Computer Engineering, Fort Wayne, IN 46805-1499. Offers computer engineering (MSE); electrical engineering (MSE); systems engineering (MSE). *Program availability:* Part-time. *Entrance requirements:* For master's, minimum GPA of 3.0, bachelor's degree in engineering discipline. Additional exam requirements/recommendations for international students: Required—TOEFL (minimum score 550 paper-based; 79 iBT); Recommended—TWE. Electronic applications accepted.

Indiana University–Purdue University Indianapolis, School of Engineering and Technology, Department of Electrical and Computer Engineering, Indianapolis, IN 46202. Offers electrical and computer engineering (MS, PhD); engineering (MSE). *Faculty:* 17 full-time (4 women), 5 part-time/adjunct. *Students:* 89 full-time (18 women), 66 part-time (15 women); includes 9 minority (4 Black or African American, non-Hispanic/Latino; 4 Asian, non-Hispanic/Latino; 1 Hispanic/Latino), 123 international. Average age 26. 173 applicants, 58% accepted, 49 enrolled. In 2016, 58 master's awarded. *Degree requirements:* For master's, thesis optional; for doctorate, thesis/dissertation. *Entrance requirements:* For master's, GRE, minimum GPA of 3.0, three recommendation letters, statement of purpose/intent; for doctorate, GRE, minimum GPA of 3.0, three recommendation letters, statement of purpose/intent, curriculum vitae. Additional exam requirements/recommendations for international students: Required—TOEFL; Recommended—IELTS, TSE. Application fee: $55 ($65 for international students). Electronic applications accepted. *Expenses:* $382 resident tuition per credit hour; $1,100 non-resident tuition per credit hour; $215-370 per term mandatory fees. *Financial support:* In 2016–17, 31 students received support. Fellowships, research assistantships, teaching assistantships, scholarships/grants, tuition waivers, and unspecified assistantships available. Financial award application deadline: 1/2. *Faculty research:* Modeling and control of advanced vehicle systems; data analytics and parallel processing; robotics and automation; 3-D imaging algorithms and image processing; signal/video processing and analysis; power electronics an renewable energy. *Total annual research expenditures:* $1 million. *Unit head:* Dr. Brian King, Chair, Department of Electrical and Computer Engineering, 317-274-9723, E-mail: briking@iupui.edu. *Application contact:* Sherrie Tucker, ECE Graduate Program Coordinator, 317-278-9726, E-mail: ecegrad@iupui.edu.
Website: http://www.engr.iupui.edu/departments/ece/

Instituto Tecnológico y de Estudios Superiores de Monterrey, Campus Chihuahua, Graduate Programs, Chihuahua, Mexico. Offers computer systems engineering (Ingeniero); electrical engineering (Ingeniero); electromechanical engineering (Ingeniero); electronic engineering (Ingeniero); engineering administration (MEA); industrial engineering (MIE, Ingeniero); international trade (MIT); mechanical engineering (Ingeniero).

Instituto Tecnológico y de Estudios Superiores de Monterrey, Campus Monterrey, Graduate and Research Division, Programs in Engineering, Monterrey, Mexico. Offers applied statistics (M Eng); artificial intelligence (PhD); automation engineering (M Eng); chemical engineering (M Eng); civil engineering (M Eng); electrical engineering (M Eng); electronic engineering (M Eng); environmental engineering (M Eng); industrial engineering (M Eng, PhD); manufacturing engineering (M Eng); mechanical engineering (M Eng); systems and quality engineering (M Eng). M Eng program offered jointly with University of Waterloo; PhD in industrial engineering with Texas A&M University. *Program availability:* Part-time, evening/weekend. Terminal master's awarded for partial completion of doctoral program. *Degree requirements:* For master's, one foreign language, thesis; for doctorate, one foreign language, thesis/dissertation. *Entrance requirements:* For master's, EXADEP; for doctorate, GRE, master's degree in related field. Additional exam requirements/recommendations for international students: Required—TOEFL. *Faculty research:* Flexible manufacturing cells, materials, statistical methods, environmental prevention, control and evaluation.

Inter American University of Puerto Rico, Bayamón Campus, Graduate School, Bayamón, PR 00957. Offers biology (MS), including environmental sciences and ecology, molecular biotechnology; electrical engineering (ME), including control system, potence system; human resources (MBA); mechanical engineering (ME, MS), including aerospace, energy. *Program availability:* Part-time, evening/weekend. *Faculty:* 12 full-time (5 women), 4 part-time/adjunct (2 women). *Students:* 7 full-time (5 women), 115 part-time (69 women); includes 119 minority (1 Black or African American, non-Hispanic/Latino; 118 Hispanic/Latino). Average age 28. 94 applicants, 72% accepted, 56 enrolled. In 2016, 22 master's awarded. *Degree requirements:* For master's, comprehensive exam, research project. *Entrance requirements:* For master's, EXADEP, GRE General Test, letters of recommendation. *Application deadline:* For fall admission, 7/1 for domestic students, 5/1 priority date for international students; for winter admission, 11/15 priority date for domestic and international students; for spring admission, 2/15 priority date for domestic and international students. Application fee: $31. *Expenses: Tuition:* Part-time $207 per credit. *Required fees:* $328 per semester. *Unit head:* Prof. Juan F. Martinez, Chancellor, 787-279-1200 Ext. 2295, Fax: 787-279-2205, E-mail: jmartinez@bayamon.inter.edu. *Application contact:* Aurelis Baez, Director of Student Services, 787-279-1912 Ext. 2017, Fax: 787-279-2205, E-mail: abaez@bayamon.inter.edu.

International Technological University, Program in Electrical Engineering, San Jose, CA 95134. Offers MSEE, PhD. *Program availability:* Part-time, evening/weekend. *Degree requirements:* For master's, thesis or capstone project; for doctorate, comprehensive exam, thesis/dissertation. *Entrance requirements:* For master's, 3 semesters of calculus, minimum GPA of 2.5. Additional exam requirements/ recommendations for international students: Required—TOEFL, IELTS. Electronic applications accepted.

Iowa State University of Science and Technology, Department of Electrical and Computer Engineering, Ames, IA 50011. Offers computer engineering (M Eng, MS, PhD); electrical engineering (M Eng, MS, PhD). *Degree requirements:* For master's, thesis or alternative; for doctorate, thesis/dissertation. *Entrance requirements:* For master's and doctorate, GRE General Test. Additional exam requirements/ recommendations for international students: Required—TOEFL (minimum score 570 paper-based; 79 iBT), IELTS (minimum score 6.5). *Application deadline:* For fall admission, 1/15 priority date for domestic and international students; for spring admission, 9/15 for domestic and international students. Application fee: $40 ($90 for international students). Electronic applications accepted. *Application contact:* Vicky Thorland-Oster, Application Contact, 515-294-8403, E-mail: ecegrad@iastate.edu.
Website: http://www.ece.iastate.edu/

Johns Hopkins University, Engineering Program for Professionals, Part-time Program in Electrical and Computer Engineering, Baltimore, MD 21218. Offers communications and networking (MS); electrical and computer engineering (Graduate Certificate, Post-Master's Certificate); photonics (MS). *Program availability:* Part-time, evening/weekend, 100% online, blended/hybrid learning. *Faculty:* 48 part-time/adjunct (2 women). *Students:* 5 full-time (0 women), 303 part-time (52 women); includes 63 minority (11 Black or African American, non-Hispanic/Latino; 24 Asian, non-Hispanic/Latino; 24 Hispanic/Latino; 4 Two or more races, non-Hispanic/Latino). Average age 28. 108 applicants, 68% accepted, 53 enrolled. In 2016, 78 master's, 2 other advanced degrees awarded. *Degree requirements:* For master's and other advanced degree, thesis optional. *Entrance requirements:* Additional exam requirements/recommendations for international students: Required—TOEFL (minimum score 600 paper-based; 100 iBT). *Application deadline:* Applications are processed on a rolling basis. Application fee: $0. Electronic applications accepted. *Unit head:* Dr. Brian Jennison, Program Chair, 443-778-6421, E-mail: brian.jennison@jhuapl.edu. *Application contact:* Doug Schiller, Admissions Director, 410-516-2300, Fax: 410-579-8049, E-mail: schiller@jhu.edu.
Website: http://www.ep.jhu.edu/

Johns Hopkins University, G. W. C. Whiting School of Engineering, Department of Electrical and Computer Engineering, Baltimore, MD 21218. Offers MSE, PhD. *Faculty:* 23 full-time (4 women), 4 part-time/adjunct (1 woman). *Students:* 146 full-time (29 women), 3 part-time (0 women); includes 12 minority (6 Black or African American, non-Hispanic/Latino; 4 Asian, non-Hispanic/Latino; 2 Two or more races, non-Hispanic/Latino), 106 international. Average age 26. 394 applicants, 37% accepted, 51 enrolled. In 2016, 20 master's, 13 doctorates awarded. Terminal master's awarded for partial completion of doctoral program. *Degree requirements:* For master's, thesis optional; for doctorate, thesis/dissertation, qualifying and oral exams, seminar. *Entrance requirements:* For master's and doctorate, GRE General Test, transcripts, 3 letters of recommendation, statement of purpose. Additional exam requirements/ recommendations for international students: Required—TOEFL (minimum score 600 paper-based, 100 iBT) or IELTS (7). *Application deadline:* For fall admission, 12/18 for domestic and international students. Application fee: $75. Electronic applications accepted. *Financial support:* In 2016–17, 88 students received support, including 20 fellowships with full tuition reimbursements available (averaging $27,996 per year), 68 research assistantships with full tuition reimbursements available (averaging $27,996

per year); teaching assistantships with full tuition reimbursements available, career-related internships or fieldwork, Federal Work-Study, institutionally sponsored loans, scholarships/grants, health care benefits, tuition waivers (partial), and unspecified assistantships also available. Financial award application deadline: 12/15. *Faculty research:* Microsystems, neuromorphics and brain-machines interface; acoustics, speech and language processing; photonics, bio photonics and optoelectronics; signal processing and imaging science and technology; networks, controls and systems. *Total annual research expenditures:* $16.1 million. *Unit head:* Dr. Ralph Etienne-Cummings, Chair, 410-516-7031, Fax: 410-516-5566, E-mail: retienne@jhu.edu. *Application contact:* Debbie Race, Academic Program Administrator, 410-516-4808, Fax: 410-516-5566, E-mail: drace@jhu.edu.
Website: http://www.ece.jhu.edu/

Kansas State University, Graduate School, College of Engineering, Department of Electrical and Computer Engineering, Manhattan, KS 66506. Offers electrical engineering (MS), including bioengineering, communication systems, design of computer systems, electrical engineering, energy and power systems, integrated circuits and devices, real time embedded systems, renewable energy, signal processing. *Program availability:* Part-time, evening/weekend, online learning. *Faculty:* 21 full-time (4 women), 1 (woman) part-time/adjunct. *Students:* 47 full-time (11 women), 51 part-time (5 women); includes 13 minority (6 Black or African American, non-Hispanic/Latino; 6 Asian, non-Hispanic/Latino; 1 Two or more races, non-Hispanic/Latino), 40 international. Average age 31. 146 applicants, 29% accepted, 17 enrolled. In 2016, 16 master's, 5 doctorates awarded. *Degree requirements:* For master's, thesis or alternative, final exam; for doctorate, thesis/dissertation, final exam, preliminary exams. *Entrance requirements:* For master's, GRE General Test, bachelor's degree in electrical engineering or computer science, minimum GPA of 3.0; for doctorate, GRE General Test. Additional exam requirements/recommendations for international students: Required—TOEFL (minimum score 600 paper-based; 85 iBT). *Application deadline:* For fall admission, 1/1 priority date for domestic and international students; for spring admission, 8/1 priority date for domestic and international students. Applications are processed on a rolling basis. Application fee: $50 ($75 for international students). Electronic applications accepted. *Expenses:* Tuition, state resident: full-time $9670. Tuition, nonresident: full-time $21,828. *Required fees:* $862. *Financial support:* In 2016–17, 40 students received support, including 22 research assistantships with tuition reimbursements available (averaging $12,100 per year), 18 teaching assistantships with full tuition reimbursements available (averaging $12,220 per year); career-related internships or fieldwork, institutionally sponsored loans, and scholarships/grants also available. Support available to part-time students. Financial award application deadline: 3/1; financial award applicants required to submit FAFSA. *Faculty research:* Energy systems and renewable energy, computer systems and real time embedded systems, communication systems and signal processing, integrated circuits and devices, bioengineering. *Total annual research expenditures:* $1.3 million. *Unit head:* Dr. Don Gruenbacher, Head, 785-532-5600, Fax: 785-532-1188, E-mail: grue@k-state.edu. *Application contact:* Dr. Andrew Rys, Graduate Program Director, 785-532-4665, Fax: 785-532-1188, E-mail: andrys@k-state.edu.
Website: http://www.ece.k-state.edu/

Kennesaw State University, Southern Polytechnic College of Engineering and Engineering Technology, Department of Electrical and Computer Engineering Technology, Kennesaw, GA 30144. Offers electrical engineering technology (MS). *Program availability:* Part-time, evening/weekend. *Degree requirements:* For master's, thesis. *Entrance requirements:* For master's, GRE (minimum scores: 147 Verbal, 147 Quantitative, 3.5 Analytical), minimum GPA of 2.7. Additional exam requirements/recommendations for international students: Required—TOEFL (minimum score 550 paper-based; 79 iBT), IELTS (minimum score 6.5). Electronic applications accepted. *Faculty research:* Analog and digital communications, computer networking, analog and low power electronics design, control systems and digital signal processing, instrumentation (medical and industrial), biomedical signal analysis, biomedical imaging, renewable energy systems, electronics, power distribution, power electronics.

Kettering University, Graduate School, Electrical and Computer Engineering Department, Flint, MI 48504. Offers engineering (MS). *Program availability:* Part-time, evening/weekend, online learning. *Degree requirements:* For master's, thesis optional. *Entrance requirements:* Additional exam requirements/recommendations for international students: Required—TOEFL (minimum score 550 paper-based; 79 iBT). Electronic applications accepted. *Faculty research:* Electric power trains, batteries, motor control, haptics.

Lakehead University, Graduate Studies, Faculty of Engineering, Thunder Bay, ON P7B 5E1, Canada. Offers control engineering (M Sc Engr); electrical/computer engineering (M Sc Engr); environmental engineering (M Sc Engr). *Program availability:* Part-time. *Degree requirements:* For master's, thesis. *Entrance requirements:* For master's, bachelor's degree in chemical, electrical or mechanical engineering, minimum B average. Additional exam requirements/recommendations for international students: Required—TOEFL. *Faculty research:* Pulp and paper, adaptive/process control, robust/interactive learning control, vibration control.

Lamar University, College of Graduate Studies, College of Engineering, Phillip M. Drayer Department of Electrical Engineering, Beaumont, TX 77710. Offers ME, MES, DE. *Program availability:* Part-time. *Faculty:* 9 full-time (0 women). *Students:* 52 full-time (3 women), 32 part-time (5 women); includes 6 minority (1 Black or African American, non-Hispanic/Latino; 5 Asian, non-Hispanic/Latino), 75 international. Average age 26. 64 applicants, 98% accepted, 17 enrolled. In 2016, 110 master's, 1 doctorate awarded. *Degree requirements:* For master's, thesis (for some programs); for doctorate, thesis/dissertation. *Entrance requirements:* For master's and doctorate, GRE General Test. Additional exam requirements/recommendations for international students: Required—TOEFL (minimum score 550 paper-based; 79 iBT), IELTS (minimum score 6.5). *Application deadline:* For fall admission, 8/10 for domestic students, 7/1 for international students; for spring admission, 1/5 for domestic students, 12/1 for international students. Applications are processed on a rolling basis. Application fee: $25 ($50 for international students). Electronic applications accepted. *Expenses:* $8,134 in-state full-time, $5,574 in-state part-time; $15,604 out-of-state full-time, $10,554 out-of-state part-time per year. *Financial support:* Fellowships with partial tuition reimbursements, research assistantships with partial tuition reimbursements, teaching assistantships with partial tuition reimbursements, and tuition waivers (partial) available. Financial award application deadline: 4/1; financial award applicants required to submit FAFSA. *Faculty research:* Video processing, photonics, VLSI design, computer networking. *Unit head:* Dr. Harley Ross Myler, Chair, 409-880-8746, Fax: 409-880-8121. *Application contact:* Deidre Mayer, Interim Director, Admissions and Academic Services, 409-880-8888, Fax: 409-880-7419, E-mail: gradmissions@lamar.edu.
Website: http://engineering.lamar.edu/electrical

Lawrence Technological University, College of Engineering, Southfield, MI 48075-1058. Offers architectural engineering (MS); automotive engineering (MS); biomedical engineering (MS); civil engineering (MA, MS, PhD), including environmental engineering (MS), geotechnical engineering (MS), structural engineering (MS), transportation engineering (MS), water resource engineering (MS); construction engineering management (MA); electrical and computer engineering (MS); engineering management

(MA); engineering technology (MS); fire engineering (MS); industrial engineering (MS), including healthcare; manufacturing systems (ME); mechanical engineering (MS, DE, PhD), including manufacturing (DE), solid mechanics (MS), thermal-fluids (MS); mechatronic systems engineering (MS). *Program availability:* Part-time, evening/weekend. *Faculty:* 24 full-time (5 women), 26 part-time/adjunct (2 women). *Students:* 22 full-time (7 women), 588 part-time (81 women); includes 23 minority (11 Black or African American, non-Hispanic/Latino; 4 Asian, non-Hispanic/Latino; 7 Hispanic/Latino; 1 Two or more races, non-Hispanic/Latino), 469 international. Average age 27. 1,186 applicants, 39% accepted, 99 enrolled. In 2016, 293 master's, 3 doctorates awarded. Terminal master's awarded for partial completion of doctoral program. *Degree requirements:* For master's, thesis optional; for doctorate, comprehensive exam, thesis/dissertation optional. *Entrance requirements:* Additional exam requirements/recommendations for international students: Required—TOEFL (minimum score 550 paper-based; 79 iBT), IELTS (minimum score 6.5). *Application deadline:* For fall admission, 5/22 for international students; for spring admission, 10/11 for international students; for summer admission, 2/16 for international students. Applications are processed on a rolling basis. Application fee: $50. Electronic applications accepted. *Expenses: Tuition:* Full-time $14,868; part-time $1062 per credit. *Required fees:* $75 per semester. Tuition and fees vary according to campus/location. *Financial support:* In 2016–17, 25 students received support, including 5 research assistantships with full tuition reimbursements available; unspecified assistantships also available. Financial award application deadline: 4/1; financial award applicants required to submit FAFSA. *Faculty research:* Carbon fiber reinforced polymer reinforced concrete structures; low impact storm water management solutions; vehicle battery energy management; wireless communication; entrepreneurial mindset and engineering. *Total annual research expenditures:* $1.7 million. *Unit head:* Dr. Nabil Grace, Dean, 248-204-2500, Fax: 248-204-2509, E-mail: engrdean@ltu.edu. *Application contact:* Jane Rohrback, Director of Admissions, 248-204-3160, Fax: 248-204-2228, E-mail: admissions@ltu.edu.
Website: http://www.ltu.edu/engineering/index.asp

Lehigh University, P.C. Rossin College of Engineering and Applied Science, Department of Electrical and Computer Engineering, Bethlehem, PA 18015. Offers electrical engineering (MS, PhD); wireless network engineering (MS). *Program availability:* Part-time. *Faculty:* 21 full-time (4 women). *Students:* 82 full-time (14 women), 8 part-time (1 woman); includes 1 minority (Hispanic/Latino), 74 international. Average age 25. 324 applicants, 33% accepted, 29 enrolled. In 2016, 12 master's, 8 doctorates awarded. Terminal master's awarded for partial completion of doctoral program. *Degree requirements:* For master's, thesis optional; for doctorate, thesis/dissertation, qualifying or comprehensive exam for all 1st year PhD's; general exam 7 months or more prior to completion/dissertation defense. *Entrance requirements:* For master's and doctorate, GRE General Test, BS in field or related field. Additional exam requirements/recommendations for international students: Required—TOEFL (minimum score 79 iBT), IELTS (minimum score 6.5). *Application deadline:* For fall admission, 4/1 for domestic and international students; for spring admission, 11/1 for domestic and international students. Application fee: $75. Electronic applications accepted. Application fee is waived when completed online. *Expenses:* $1,420 per credit hour. *Financial support:* In 2016–17, 50 students received support, including 6 fellowships with full tuition reimbursements available (averaging $28,140 per year), 35 research assistantships with full tuition reimbursements available (averaging $28,140 per year), 7 teaching assistantships with full tuition reimbursements available (averaging $21,530 per year). Financial award application deadline: 1/15. *Faculty research:* Nanostructures/nanodevices, terahertz generation, analog devices, mixed mode design and signal circuits, optoelectronic sensors, micro-fabrication technology and design, packaging/reliability of microsensors, coding and networking information theory, radio frequency, wireless and optical wireless communication, wireless networks. *Total annual research expenditures:* $2.8 million. *Unit head:* Dr. Svetlana Tatic-Lucic, Interim Chair, 610-758-4069, Fax: 610-758-6279, E-mail: svt2@lehigh.edu. *Application contact:* Diane Hubinsky, Graduate Coordinator, 610-758-4072, Fax: 610-758-6279, E-mail: dih2@lehigh.edu.
Website: http://www.ece.lehigh.edu/

Louisiana State University and Agricultural & Mechanical College, Graduate School, College of Engineering, Division of Electrical and Computer Engineering, Baton Rouge, LA 70803. Offers MSEE, PhD.

Louisiana Tech University, Graduate School, College of Engineering and Science, Department of Electrical Engineering, Ruston, LA 71272. Offers MS, PhD. *Program availability:* Part-time. Terminal master's awarded for partial completion of doctoral program. *Degree requirements:* For master's, thesis; for doctorate, thesis/dissertation. *Entrance requirements:* For master's, GRE General Test, minimum GPA of 3.0 in last 60 hours; for doctorate, minimum graduate GPA of 3.25 (with MS) or GRE General Test. Additional exam requirements/recommendations for international students: Required—TOEFL. *Application deadline:* For fall admission, 8/1 for domestic students; for spring admission, 2/1 for domestic students. Applications are processed on a rolling basis. Application fee: $20 ($30 for international students). *Financial support:* Fellowships, research assistantships, teaching assistantships, Federal Work-Study, and unspecified assistantships available. Financial award application deadline: 4/1. *Faculty research:* Communications, computers and microprocessors, electrical and power systems, pattern recognition, robotics. *Unit head:* Dr. Davis Harbour, Program Chair, 318-257-4715, Fax: 318-255-4922. *Application contact:* Marilyn J. Robinson, Assistant to the Dean, 318-257-2924, Fax: 318-257-4487.
Website: http://coes.latech.edu/ee/

Loyola Marymount University, College of Science and Engineering, Program in Electrical Engineering, Los Angeles, CA 90045-2659. Offers electrical engineering (MS). *Entrance requirements:* Additional exam requirements/recommendations for international students: Required—TOEFL. Electronic applications accepted.

Manhattan College, Graduate Programs, School of Engineering, Program in Electrical Engineering, Riverdale, NY 10471. Offers MS. *Program availability:* Part-time, evening/weekend. *Degree requirements:* For master's, thesis or alternative. *Entrance requirements:* For master's, GRE (recommended), minimum GPA of 3.0. Additional exam requirements/recommendations for international students: Required—TOEFL (minimum score 550 paper-based; 80 iBT), IELTS (minimum score 6). *Application deadline:* For fall admission, 8/10 priority date for domestic students, 8/10 for international students; for spring admission, 1/7 for domestic and international students. Applications are processed on a rolling basis. Application fee: $60. *Financial support:* Teaching assistantships with partial tuition reimbursements, career-related internships or fieldwork, Federal Work-Study, scholarships/grants, unspecified assistantships, and laboratory assistantships available. Support available to part-time students. Financial award application deadline: 2/1. *Faculty research:* Multimedia tools, neural networks, robotic control systems, magnetic resonance imaging, telemedicine, computer-based instruction. *Unit head:* Dr. George Giakos, Chairperson, 718-862-7154, Fax: 718-862-7162, E-mail: george.giakos@manhattan.edu.
Website: https://manhattan.edu/academics/graduate-programs/electrical-engineering.php

Marquette University, Graduate School, College of Engineering, Department of Electrical and Computer Engineering, Milwaukee, WI 53201-1881. Offers digital signal

processing (Certificate); electric machines, drives, and controls (Certificate); electrical and computer engineering (MS, PhD); microwaves and antennas (Certificate); sensors and smart systems (Certificate). *Program availability:* Part-time, evening/weekend. *Faculty:* 15 full-time (2 women), 4 part-time/adjunct (0 women). *Students:* 24 full-time (3 women), 25 part-time (7 women); includes 4 minority (2 Black or African American, non-Hispanic/Latino; 2 Hispanic/Latino), 25 international. Average age 27. 108 applicants, 63% accepted, 14 enrolled. In 2016, 14 master's, 6 doctorates awarded. Terminal master's awarded for partial completion of doctoral program. *Degree requirements:* For master's, comprehensive exam (for some programs), thesis optional; for doctorate, thesis/dissertation, dissertation defense, qualifying exam. *Entrance requirements:* For master's, GRE General Test (recommended), official transcripts from all current and previous colleges/universities except Marquette, three letters of recommendation; for doctorate, GRE General Test, minimum GPA of 3.0, official transcripts from all current and previous colleges/universities except Marquette, three letters of recommendation, statement of purpose, submission of any English language publications authored by applicant (strongly recommended). Additional exam requirements/recommendations for international students: Required—TOEFL (minimum score 530 paper-based). *Application deadline:* For fall admission, 7/15 priority date for domestic students; for spring admission, 11/15 for domestic students. Applications are processed on a rolling basis. Application fee: $50. Electronic applications accepted. *Financial support:* Fellowships, research assistantships, teaching assistantships, scholarships/grants, health care benefits, tuition waivers (partial), and unspecified assistantships available. Support available to part-time students. Financial award application deadline: 2/15. *Faculty research:* Electric machines, drives, and controls; applied solid-state electronics; computers and signal processing; microwaves and antennas; solid state devices and acoustic wave sensors. *Total annual research expenditures:* $947,209. *Unit head:* Dr. Edwin E. Yaz, Chair, 414-288-6820, Fax: 414-288-5579. *Application contact:* Dr. Fabien Josse, 414-288-6789.
Website: http://www.marquette.edu/engineering/electrical_computer/grad.shtml

Massachusetts Institute of Technology, School of Engineering, Department of Electrical Engineering and Computer Science, Cambridge, MA 02139. Offers computer science (PhD, Sc D, ECS); computer science and engineering (PhD, Sc D); computer science and molecular biology (M Eng); electrical engineering (PhD, Sc D, EE); electrical engineering and computer science (M Eng, SM, PhD, Sc D); SM/MBA. *Faculty:* 116 full-time (18 women). *Students:* 864 full-time (210 women), 3 part-time (1 woman); includes 225 minority (11 Black or African American, non-Hispanic/Latino; 142 Asian, non-Hispanic/Latino; 50 Hispanic/Latino; 22 Two or more races, non-Hispanic/Latino), 406 international. Average age 26. 2,773 applicants, 8% accepted, 128 enrolled. In 2016, 236 master's, 87 doctorates awarded. *Degree requirements:* For master's and other advanced degree, thesis; for doctorate, comprehensive exam, thesis/dissertation. *Entrance requirements:* Additional exam requirements/recommendations for international students: Required—TOEFL, IELTS. *Application deadline:* For fall admission, 12/15 for domestic and international students. Application fee: $75. Electronic applications accepted. *Expenses: Tuition:* Full-time $46,400; part-time $725 per credit. One-time fee: $312 full-time. Full-time tuition and fees vary according to course load and program. *Financial support:* In 2016–17, 825 students received support, including fellowships (averaging $39,000 per year), 526 research assistantships (averaging $36,900 per year), 175 teaching assistantships (averaging $37,500 per year); Federal Work-Study, institutionally sponsored loans, scholarships/grants, traineeships, health care benefits, unspecified assistantships, and resident tutors also available. Support available to part-time students. Financial award application deadline: 5/1; financial award applicants required to submit FAFSA. *Faculty research:* Information systems, circuits, biomedical sciences and engineering, computer science: artificial intelligence, systems, theory. *Total annual research expenditures:* $108.1 million. *Unit head:* Prof. Anantha P. Chandrakasan, Department Head, 617-253-4600, Fax: 617-258-7254, E-mail: hq@eecs.mit.edu. *Application contact:* Graduate Admissions, 617-253-4603, E-mail: grad-ap@eecs.mit.edu.
Website: http://www.eecs.mit.edu/

McGill University, Faculty of Graduate and Postdoctoral Studies, Faculty of Engineering, Department of Electrical and Computer Engineering, Montréal, QC H3A 2T5, Canada. Offers M Eng, PhD.

McMaster University, School of Graduate Studies, Faculty of Engineering, Department of Electrical and Computer Engineering, Hamilton, ON L8S 4M2, Canada. Offers electrical engineering (M Eng, MA Sc, PhD). *Degree requirements:* For master's, thesis; for doctorate, comprehensive exam, thesis/dissertation. *Entrance requirements:* Additional exam requirements/recommendations for international students: Required—TOEFL (minimum score 550 paper-based). *Faculty research:* Robust and blind adaptive filtering, topics in statistical signal processing, local and metropolitan area networks, smart antennas, embedded wireless communications.

McNeese State University, Doré School of Graduate Studies, College of Engineering and Engineering Technology, Department of Engineering, Master of Engineering Program, Lake Charles, LA 70609. Offers chemical engineering (M Eng); civil engineering (M Eng); electrical engineering (M Eng); engineering management (M Eng); mechanical engineering (M Eng). *Program availability:* Part-time, evening/weekend. *Degree requirements:* For master's, thesis or alternative. *Entrance requirements:* For master's, GRE, baccalaureate degree, minimum overall GPA of 3.0. Additional exam requirements/recommendations for international students: Required—TOEFL (minimum score 560 paper-based; 83 iBT).

Memorial University of Newfoundland, School of Graduate Studies, Faculty of Engineering and Applied Science, St. John's, NL A1C 5S7, Canada. Offers civil engineering (M Eng, PhD); electrical and computer engineering (M Eng, PhD); mechanical engineering (M Eng, PhD); ocean and naval architecture engineering (M Eng, PhD). *Program availability:* Part-time. *Degree requirements:* For master's, thesis; for doctorate, comprehensive exam, thesis/dissertation, oral thesis defense. *Entrance requirements:* For master's, 2nd class degree; for doctorate, master's degree in engineering. Electronic applications accepted. *Faculty research:* Engineering analysis, environmental and hydrotechnical studies, manufacturing and robotics, mechanics, structures and materials.

Mercer University, Graduate Studies, Macon Campus, School of Engineering, Macon, GA 31207. Offers biomedical engineering (MSE); computer engineering (MSE); electrical engineering (MSE); engineering management (MSE); environmental engineering (MSE); environmental systems (MS); mechanical engineering (MSE); software engineering (MSE); software systems (MS); technical communications management (MS); technical management (MS). *Program availability:* Part-time-only, evening/weekend, online learning. *Faculty:* 21 full-time (5 women), 1 part-time/adjunct (0 women). *Students:* 44 full-time (9 women), 60 part-time (12 women); includes 14 minority (3 Black or African American, non-Hispanic/Latino; 1 American Indian or Alaska Native, non-Hispanic/Latino; 4 Asian, non-Hispanic/Latino; 3 Hispanic/Latino; 3 Two or more races, non-Hispanic/Latino), 2 international. Average age 27. In 2016, 64 master's awarded. *Degree requirements:* For master's, thesis or alternative. *Entrance requirements:* For master's, GRE (minimum score 300), minimum undergraduate GPA of 3.0. Additional exam requirements/recommendations for international students: Required—TOEFL (minimum score 550 paper-based; 80 iBT). *Application deadline:* For fall admission, 4/1 priority date for domestic and international students; for spring admission, 11/1 priority date for domestic and international students. Applications are processed on a rolling basis. Application fee: $75. *Expenses:* $865 per credit hour. *Financial support:* Applicants required to submit FAFSA. *Faculty research:* Designing prostheses and orthotics, oxygen transfer and limitations in biological systems, low-cost groundwater development, lung airway and transport, autonomous mobile robots. *Unit head:* Dr. Laura W. Lackey, Dean, 478-301-4106, Fax: 478-301-5593, E-mail: lackey_l@mercer.edu. *Application contact:* Dr. Richard O. Mines, Jr., Program Director, 478-301-2347, Fax: 478-301-5433, E-mail: mines_ro@mercer.edu.
Website: http://engineering.mercer.edu/

Miami University, College of Engineering and Computing, Department of Electrical and Computer Engineering, Oxford, OH 45056. Offers MS. *Students:* 16 full-time (3 women), 1 part-time (0 women), 11 international. Average age 25. *Expenses:* Tuition, state resident: full-time $12,890; part-time $564 per credit hour. Tuition, nonresident: full-time $29,604; part-time $1260 per credit hour. *Required fees:* $638. Part-time tuition and fees vary according to course load and program. *Unit head:* Dr. Q. Herb Zhou, Chair, 513-523-0740, E-mail: zhouq@miamioh.edu. *Application contact:* 513-529-0340, E-mail: cecgrad@miamioh.edu.
Website: http://miamioh.edu/cec/academics/departments/ece/

Michigan State University, The Graduate School, College of Engineering, Department of Electrical and Computer Engineering, East Lansing, MI 48824. Offers electrical engineering (MS, PhD). *Entrance requirements:* Additional exam requirements/recommendations for international students: Required—TOEFL. Electronic applications accepted.

Michigan Technological University, Graduate School, College of Engineering, Department of Electrical and Computer Engineering, Houghton, MI 49931. Offers advanced electric power engineering (Graduate Certificate); automotive systems and controls (Graduate Certificate); computer engineering (MS, PhD); electrical engineering (MS, PhD). *Program availability:* Part-time, online learning. *Faculty:* 44 full-time, 9 part-time/adjunct. *Students:* 197 full-time (28 women), 51 part-time; includes 11 minority (3 Black or African American, non-Hispanic/Latino; 2 Asian, non-Hispanic/Latino; 6 Hispanic/Latino), 205 international. Average age 27. 804 applicants, 36% accepted, 70 enrolled. In 2016, 100 master's, 4 doctorates, 56 other advanced degrees awarded. Terminal master's awarded for partial completion of doctoral program. *Degree requirements:* For master's, comprehensive exam (for some programs), thesis (for some programs); for doctorate, comprehensive exam, thesis/dissertation. *Entrance requirements:* For master's and doctorate, GRE, statement of purpose, personal statement, official transcripts, 2 letters of recommendation; for Graduate Certificate, statement of purpose, personal statement, official transcripts. Additional exam requirements/recommendations for international students: Required—TOEFL (recommended minimum score 100 iBT) or IELTS (recommended minimum score of 7.0). *Application deadline:* For fall admission, 2/15 priority date for domestic and international students; for spring admission, 8/15 priority date for domestic and international students. Applications are processed on a rolling basis. Electronic applications accepted. *Expenses:* Contact institution. *Financial support:* In 2016–17, 155 students received support, including 8 fellowships with tuition reimbursements available (averaging $15,242 per year), 26 research assistantships with tuition reimbursements available (averaging $15,242 per year), 20 teaching assistantships with tuition reimbursements available (averaging $15,242 per year); career-related internships or fieldwork, Federal Work-Study, scholarships/grants, health care benefits, unspecified assistantships, and cooperative program also available. Financial award applicants required to submit FAFSA. *Faculty research:* Electrical power systems, optics and photonics, embedded computing systems, computer networks, communication and information theory. *Total annual research expenditures:* $2.4 million. *Unit head:* Dr. Daniel R. Fuhrmann, Department Chair, 906-487-2550, Fax: 906-487-2949, E-mail: fuhrmann@mtu.edu. *Application contact:* Dr. John Pakkala, Graduate Academic Advisor, 906-487-2550, Fax: 906-487-2949, E-mail: jepakkal@mtu.edu.
Website: http://www.mtu.edu/ece/

Mississippi State University, Bagley College of Engineering, Department of Electrical and Computer Engineering, Mississippi State, MS 39762. Offers MS, PhD. *Program availability:* Part-time, blended/hybrid learning. *Faculty:* 19 full-time (2 women). *Students:* 53 full-time (10 women), 39 part-time (1 woman); includes 10 minority (6 Black or African American, non-Hispanic/Latino; 2 Asian, non-Hispanic/Latino; 2 Hispanic/Latino), 39 international. Average age 32. 142 applicants, 43% accepted, 25 enrolled. In 2016, 13 master's, 6 doctorates awarded. Terminal master's awarded for partial completion of doctoral program. *Degree requirements:* For master's, comprehensive exam, thesis optional; for doctorate, comprehensive exam, thesis/dissertation, written exam, oral preliminary exam. *Entrance requirements:* For master's, GRE (for graduates from program not accredited by EAC/ABET), minimum GPA of 3.0 on BS; for doctorate, GRE (for graduates from program not accredited by EAC/ABET), minimum GPA of 3.5 on BS or MS. Additional exam requirements/recommendations for international students: Required—TOEFL (minimum score 550 paper-based; 79 iBT); Recommended—IELTS (minimum score 6.5). *Application deadline:* For fall admission, 7/1 for domestic students, 5/1 for international students; for spring admission, 11/1 for domestic students, 9/1 for international students. Applications are processed on a rolling basis. Application fee: $60. Electronic applications accepted. *Expenses:* Tuition, state resident: full-time $7670; part-time $852.50 per credit hour. Tuition, nonresident: full-time $20,790; part-time $2310.50 per credit hour. Part-time tuition and fees vary according to course load. *Financial support:* In 2016–17, 17 research assistantships with full tuition reimbursements (averaging $18,824 per year), 19 teaching assistantships with full tuition reimbursements (averaging $16,011 per year) were awarded; Federal Work-Study, institutionally sponsored loans, scholarships/grants, and unspecified assistantships also available. Financial award application deadline: 4/1; financial award applicants required to submit FAFSA. *Faculty research:* Digital computing, power, controls, communication systems, microelectronics. *Total annual research expenditures:* $12.7 million. *Unit head:* Dr. Nicholas H. Younan, Jr., Professor and Department Head, 662-325-3912, Fax: 662-325-2298, E-mail: ece-head@ece.msstate.edu. *Application contact:* Doretta Martin, Senior Admissions Assistant, 662-325-9514, E-mail: dmartin@grad.msstate.edu.
Website: http://www.ece.msstate.edu/

Missouri University of Science and Technology, Graduate School, Department of Electrical and Computer Engineering, Rolla, MO 65409. Offers computer engineering (MS, DE, PhD); electrical engineering (MS, DE, PhD). *Program availability:* Part-time, evening/weekend. Terminal master's awarded for partial completion of doctoral program. *Degree requirements:* For master's, thesis optional; for doctorate, comprehensive exam, thesis/dissertation, departmental qualifying exam. *Entrance requirements:* For master's, GRE General Test (minimum score 1100 verbal and quantitative, writing 4.5); for doctorate, GRE General Test (minimum score: verbal and quantitative 1100, writing 3.5). Additional exam requirements/recommendations for international students: Required—TOEFL (minimum score 550 paper-based). Electronic applications accepted. *Faculty research:* Power systems, computer/communication networks, intelligent control/robotics, robust control, nanotechnologies.

Montana State University, The Graduate School, College of Engineering, Department of Electrical and Computer Engineering, Bozeman, MT 59717. Offers electrical engineering (MS); engineering (PhD), including electrical and computer engineering option. *Program availability:* Part-time. *Degree requirements:* For master's, comprehensive exam, thesis (for some programs); for doctorate, comprehensive exam, thesis/dissertation. *Entrance requirements:* For master's, GRE, BS in electrical or computer engineering or related field; for doctorate, GRE, MS in electrical or computer engineering or related field. Additional exam requirements/recommendations for international students: Required—TOEFL (minimum score 550 paper-based). Electronic applications accepted. *Faculty research:* Optics and optoelectonics, communications and signal processing, microfabrication, complex systems and control, energy systems.

Montana Tech of The University of Montana, Electrical Engineering Program, Butte, MT 59701-8997. Offers MS. *Program availability:* Part-time. *Faculty:* 4 full-time (0 women). *Students:* 5 full-time (1 woman), 2 part-time (1 woman); includes 1 minority (Asian, non-Hispanic/Latino), 2 international. Average age 25. 5 applicants, 40% accepted. In 2016, 3 master's awarded. *Degree requirements:* For master's, comprehensive exam (for some programs), thesis optional. *Entrance requirements:* For master's, minimum GPA of 3.0. Additional exam requirements/recommendations for international students: Required—TOEFL (minimum score 545 paper-based; 78 iBT), IELTS (minimum score 6.5). *Application deadline:* For fall admission, 4/1 priority date for domestic students, 3/1 priority date for international students; for spring admission, 10/1 priority date for domestic students, 6/1 priority date for international students. Applications are processed on a rolling basis. Application fee: $50. Electronic applications accepted. *Expenses:* Tuition, state resident: full-time $2901; part-time $1450.68 per degree program. Tuition, nonresident: full-time $8432; part-time $4215.84 per degree program. *Required fees:* $668; $354 per degree program. Tuition and fees vary according to course load and program. *Financial support:* In 2016–17, 3 students received support, including 5 teaching assistantships with partial tuition reimbursements available (averaging $4,000 per year); research assistantships with full tuition reimbursements available, career-related internships or fieldwork, tuition waivers (full and partial), and unspecified assistantships also available. Financial award application deadline: 4/1. *Faculty research:* Energy grid modernization, battery diagnostics instrumentation, wind turbine research, improving energy efficiency. *Unit head:* Dr. Daniel Trudnowski, Professor, 406-496-4681, Fax: 406-496-4849, E-mail: dtrudnowski@mtech.edu. *Application contact:* Daniel Stirling, Administrator, Graduate School, 406-496-4304, Fax: 406-496-4710, E-mail: gradschool@mtech.edu.
Website: http://www.mtech.edu/academics/gradschool/degreeprograms/degrees-electrical-engineering.htm

Morgan State University, School of Graduate Studies, Clarence M. Mitchell, Jr. School of Engineering, Baltimore, MD 21251. Offers civil engineering (M Eng, D Eng); electrical and computer engineering (M Eng, MS, D Eng); industrial and systems engineering (M Eng, D Eng); transportation (MS). *Program availability:* Part-time, evening/weekend. *Degree requirements:* For master's, thesis, comprehensive exam or equivalent; for doctorate, thesis/dissertation, comprehensive exam or equivalent. *Entrance requirements:* For master's, GRE, minimum undergraduate GPA of 2.5; for doctorate, GRE, minimum GPA of 3.0. Additional exam requirements/recommendations for international students: Required—TOEFL (minimum score 550 paper-based).

Naval Postgraduate School, Departments and Academic Groups, Department of Electrical and Computer Engineering, Monterey, CA 93943-5216. Offers computer engineering (MS); electrical engineer (EE); electrical engineering (PhD); engineering acoustics (MS); engineering science (MS). Program only open to commissioned officers of the United States and friendly nations and selected United States federal civilian employees. *Accreditation:* ABET (one or more programs are accredited). *Program availability:* Part-time, online learning. *Degree requirements:* For master's and EE, thesis (for some programs), capstone project or research/dissertation paper (for some programs); for doctorate, thesis/dissertation. *Faculty research:* Theory and design of digital communication systems; behavior modeling for detection, identification, prediction and reaction in artificial intelligence (AI) systems solutions; waveform design for target class discrimination with closed-loop radar; iterative technique for system identification with adaptive signal design.

Naval Postgraduate School, Departments and Academic Groups, Space Systems Academic Group, Monterey, CA 93943. Offers applied physics (MS); astronautical engineering (MS); computer science (MS); electrical engineering (MS); mechanical engineering (MS); space systems (Engr); space systems operations (MS). Program only open to commissioned officers of the United States and friendly nations and selected United States federal civilian employees. *Program availability:* Part-time. *Degree requirements:* For master's and Engr, thesis; for doctorate, thesis/dissertation. *Faculty research:* Military applications for space; space reconnaissance and remote sensing; radiation-hardened electronics for space; design, construction and operations of small satellites; satellite communications systems.

Naval Postgraduate School, Departments and Academic Groups, Undersea Warfare Academic Group, Monterey, CA 93943. Offers applied mathematics (MS); applied physics (MS); applied science (MS), including acoustics, operations research, physical oceanography, signal processing; electrical engineering (MS); engineering acoustics (MS, PhD); engineering science (MS), including electrical engineering, mechanical engineering; mechanical engineer (ME); mechanical engineering (MS, MSME); meteorology (MS); operations research (MS); physical oceanography (MS). Program only open to commissioned officers of the United States and friendly nations and selected United States federal civilian employees. *Program availability:* Part-time. *Degree requirements:* For master's, thesis. *Faculty research:* Unmanned/autonomous vehicles, sea mines and countermeasures, submarine warfare in the twentieth and twenty-first centuries.

New Jersey Institute of Technology, Newark College of Engineering, Newark, NJ 07102. Offers biomedical engineering (MS, PhD); chemical engineering (MS, PhD); computer engineering (MS, PhD); electrical engineering (MS, PhD); engineering management (MS); environmental engineering (PhD); healthcare systems management (MS); industrial engineering (MS, PhD); Internet engineering (MS); manufacturing engineering (MS); mechanical engineering (MS, PhD); occupational safety and health engineering (MS); pharmaceutical bioprocessing (MS); pharmaceutical engineering (MS); pharmaceutical systems management (MS); power and energy systems (MS); telecommunications (MS); transportation (MS, PhD). *Program availability:* Part-time, evening/weekend. *Faculty:* 146 full-time (21 women), 119 part-time/adjunct (10 women). *Students:* 804 full-time (191 women), 550 part-time (129 women); includes 357 minority (82 Black or African American, non-Hispanic/Latino; 1 American Indian or Alaska Native, non-Hispanic/Latino; 138 Asian, non-Hispanic/Latino; 114 Hispanic/Latino; 22 Two or more races, non-Hispanic/Latino), 675 international. Average age 27. 2,959 applicants, 51% accepted, 442 enrolled. In 2016, 595 master's, 29 doctorates awarded. Terminal master's awarded for partial completion of doctoral program. *Degree requirements:* For master's, thesis optional; for doctorate, thesis/dissertation. *Entrance requirements:* For master's, GRE General Test; for doctorate, GRE General Test, minimum graduate GPA of 3.5. Additional exam requirements/recommendations for international students: Required—TOEFL (minimum score 550 paper-based; 79 iBT). *Application deadline:* For fall admission, 6/1 priority date for domestic students, 5/1 priority date for international students; for spring admission, 11/15 priority date for domestic and international students. Applications are processed on a rolling basis. Application fee: $75. Electronic applications accepted. *Expenses:* Contact institution. *Financial support:* In 2016–17, 172 students received support, including 1 fellowship (averaging $1,528 per year), 79 research assistantships (averaging $13,336 per year), 92 teaching assistantships (averaging $20,619 per year); scholarships/grants also available. Financial award application deadline: 1/15. *Faculty research:* Nonlinear signal processing, intelligent medical image analysis, calibration issues in coherent localization, computer-aided design, neural network for tool wear measurement. *Total annual research expenditures:* $11.1 million. *Unit head:* Dr. Moshe Kam, Dean, 973-596-5534, E-mail: moshe.kam@njit.edu. *Application contact:* Stephen Eck, Director of Admissions, 973-596-3300, Fax: 973-596-3461, E-mail: admissions@njit.edu.
Website: http://engineering.njit.edu/

New Mexico Institute of Mining and Technology, Center for Graduate Studies, Department of Electrical Engineering, Socorro, NM 87801. Offers MS. *Entrance requirements:* Additional exam requirements/recommendations for international students: Required—TOEFL (minimum score 540 paper-based). Electronic applications accepted.

New Mexico State University, College of Engineering, Klipsch School of Electrical and Computer Engineering, Las Cruces, NM 88003. Offers MSEE, PhD, Graduate Certificate. *Program availability:* Part-time, evening/weekend, 100% online. *Faculty:* 18 full-time (1 woman), 1 part-time/adjunct (0 women). *Students:* 73 full-time (11 women), 44 part-time (10 women); includes 30 minority (4 Black or African American, non-Hispanic/Latino; 1 American Indian or Alaska Native, non-Hispanic/Latino; 1 Asian, non-Hispanic/Latino; 22 Hispanic/Latino; 2 Two or more races, non-Hispanic/Latino), 55 international. Average age 30. 125 applicants, 48% accepted, 26 enrolled. In 2016, 37 master's, 6 doctorates awarded. Terminal master's awarded for partial completion of doctoral program. *Degree requirements:* For master's, thesis (for some programs), final oral or written exam; for doctorate, comprehensive exam, thesis/dissertation, qualifying exam. *Entrance requirements:* For master's, GRE, minimum GPA of 3.0; for doctorate, minimum GPA of 3.0. Additional exam requirements/recommendations for international students: Required—TOEFL (minimum score 550 paper-based; 79 iBT), IELTS (minimum score 6.5). *Application deadline:* For fall admission, 3/1 priority date for domestic and international students; for spring admission, 8/1 priority date for domestic and international students. Applications are processed on a rolling basis. Application fee: $40 ($50 for international students). Electronic applications accepted. *Expenses:* Tuition, state resident: full-time $4086. Tuition, nonresident: full-time $14,254. *Required fees:* $853. Tuition and fees vary according to course load. *Financial support:* In 2016–17, 66 students received support, including 1 fellowship (averaging $4,088 per year), 23 research assistantships (averaging $13,395 per year), 20 teaching assistantships (averaging $11,971 per year); career-related internships or fieldwork, Federal Work-Study, scholarships/grants, traineeships, health care benefits, and unspecified assistantships also available. Support available to part-time students. Financial award application deadline: 3/1. *Faculty research:* Image and digital signal processing, energy systems, wireless communications, analog and mixed-signal VLSI design, electro-optics. *Total annual research expenditures:* $1.5 million. *Unit head:* Dr. Satishkuma Ranade, Department Head, 575-646-3115, Fax: 575-646-1435, E-mail: sranade@nmsu.edu. *Application contact:* 575-646-3115, Fax: 575-646-1435, E-mail: eceoffice@nmsu.edu.
Website: http://ece.nmsu.edu

New York Institute of Technology, School of Engineering and Computing Sciences, Department of Electrical and Computer Engineering, Old Westbury, NY 11568-8000. Offers MS. *Program availability:* Part-time, evening/weekend. *Faculty:* 10 full-time (2 women), 8 part-time/adjunct (all women). *Students:* 193 full-time (38 women), 74 part-time (17 women); includes 22 minority (9 Black or African American, non-Hispanic/Latino; 7 Asian, non-Hispanic/Latino; 6 Hispanic/Latino), 233 international. Average age 24. 627 applicants, 65% accepted, 57 enrolled. In 2016, 175 master's awarded. *Degree requirements:* For master's, thesis or alternative. *Entrance requirements:* For master's, BS in electrical or computer engineering or closely-related field; minimum undergraduate GPA of 2.85. Additional exam requirements/recommendations for international students: Required—TOEFL (minimum score 79 iBT), IELTS (minimum score 6). *Application deadline:* For fall admission, 7/1 for domestic students, 6/1 for international students; for spring admission, 12/1 for domestic and international students. Applications are processed on a rolling basis. Application fee: $50. Electronic applications accepted. *Expenses:* $1,215 per credit. *Financial support:* Fellowships with partial tuition reimbursements, teaching assistantships with partial tuition reimbursements, career-related internships or fieldwork, Federal Work-Study, scholarships/grants, tuition waivers (full and partial), and unspecified assistantships available. Support available to part-time students. Financial award application deadline: 3/1; financial award applicants required to submit FAFSA. *Faculty research:* Securing inter-vehicular networks with time and driver identity considerations; security of mobile devices and wireless networks; implantable wireless system to study gastric neurophysiology; model-based software for configuring single switch scanning systems; family-based framework of quality assurance for biomedical ontologies. *Unit head:* Dr. Yoshikazu Saito, Department Chairperson, 212-261-1650, Fax: 516-686-7439, E-mail: ysaito@nyit.edu. *Application contact:* Alice Dolitsky, Director, Graduate Admissions, 516-686-7520, Fax: 516-686-1116, E-mail: nyitgrad@nyit.edu.
Website: http://www.nyit.edu/engineering/electrical_and_computer_engineering

New York University, Polytechnic School of Engineering, Department of Electrical and Computer Engineering, Major in Electrical Engineering, New York, NY 10012-1019. Offers MS, PhD. *Program availability:* Part-time, evening/weekend, online learning. *Degree requirements:* For master's, comprehensive exam (for some programs), thesis (for some programs); for doctorate, comprehensive exam, thesis/dissertation, qualifying exam. *Entrance requirements:* For master's, BS in electrical engineering; for doctorate, MS in electrical engineering. Additional exam requirements/recommendations for international students: Required—TOEFL (minimum score 550 paper-based; 80 iBT); Recommended—IELTS (minimum score 6.5). Electronic applications accepted.

Norfolk State University, School of Graduate Studies, School of Science and Technology, Program in Electronics Engineering, Norfolk, VA 23504. Offers MS.

North Carolina Agricultural and Technical State University, School of Graduate Studies, College of Engineering, Department of Electrical and Computer Engineering, Greensboro, NC 27411. Offers electrical engineering (MSEE, PhD), including communications and signal processing, computer engineering, electronic and optical materials and devices, power systems and control. *Program availability:* Part-time. *Degree requirements:* For master's, project, thesis defense; for doctorate, thesis/dissertation. *Entrance requirements:* For master's, GRE General Test, GRE Subject Test, minimum GPA of 2.8; for doctorate, GRE General Test, minimum GPA of 3.0. *Faculty research:* Semiconductor compounds, VLSI design, image processing, optical systems and devices, fault-tolerant computing.

North Carolina Agricultural and Technical State University, School of Graduate Studies, School of Technology, Department of Electronics, Computer, and Information Technology, Greensboro, NC 27411. Offers electronics and computer technology (MSIT, MSTM); information technology (MSIT, MSTM).

Electrical Engineering

North Carolina State University, Graduate School, College of Engineering, Department of Electrical and Computer Engineering, Program in Electrical Engineering, Raleigh, NC 27695. Offers MS, PhD. *Degree requirements:* For master's, thesis (for some programs); for doctorate, thesis/dissertation. *Entrance requirements:* For master's and doctorate, GRE. Additional exam requirements/recommendations for international students: Required—TOEFL (minimum score 575 paper-based). Electronic applications accepted. *Faculty research:* Microwave devices, wireless communications, nanoelectronics and photonics, robotic and mechatronics, power electronics.

North Dakota State University, College of Graduate and Interdisciplinary Studies, College of Engineering, Department of Electrical and Computer Engineering, Fargo, ND 58102. Offers ME, MS, PhD. *Program availability:* Part-time. Terminal master's awarded for partial completion of doctoral program. *Degree requirements:* For master's, comprehensive exam, thesis; for doctorate, comprehensive exam, thesis/dissertation. *Entrance requirements:* Additional exam requirements/recommendations for international students: Required—TOEFL (minimum score 525 paper-based; 71 iBT). Electronic applications accepted. *Faculty research:* Computers, power and control systems, microwaves, communications and signal processing, bioengineering.

Northeastern University, College of Engineering, Boston, MA 02115-5096. Offers bioengineering (MS, PhD); chemical engineering (MS, PhD); civil engineering (MS, PhD); computer engineering (PhD); computer systems engineering (MS); electrical and computer engineering (MS); electrical and computer engineering leadership (MS); electrical engineering (PhD); energy systems (MS); engineering and public policy (MS); engineering management (MS, Certificate); environmental engineering (MS); industrial engineering (MS, PhD); information assurance (PhD); information systems (MS); interdisciplinary engineering (PhD); mechanical engineering (PhD); operations research (MS); telecommunication systems management (MS). *Program availability:* Part-time, online learning. *Faculty:* 202 full-time (59 women), 53 part-time/adjunct (9 women). *Students:* 2,982 full-time (954 women), 192 part-time (38 women). In 2016, 851 master's, 74 doctorates awarded. Application fee: $75. Electronic applications accepted. *Expenses:* $1,471 per credit. *Financial support:* Fellowships, research assistantships, teaching assistantships, career-related internships or fieldwork, scholarships/grants, health care benefits, tuition waivers, and unspecified assistantships available. Support available to part-time students. Financial award applicants required to submit FAFSA. *Unit head:* Dr. Nadine Aubry, Dean, College of Engineering. *Application contact:* Jeffery Hengel, Director of Graduate Admissions, 617-373-2711, E-mail: j.hengel@northeastern.edu.
Website: http://www.coe.neu.edu/academics/graduate-school-engineering

Northern Arizona University, Graduate College, College of Engineering, Forestry, and Natural Sciences, Programs in Engineering, Flagstaff, AZ 86011. Offers civil engineering (M Eng, MSE); computer science (MSE); electrical and computer engineering (M Eng, MSE); engineering (M Eng, MSE); environmental engineering (M Eng, MSE); mechanical engineering (M Eng, MSE). *Program availability:* Part-time, online learning. *Degree requirements:* For master's, thesis. *Entrance requirements:* For master's, GRE General Test. Additional exam requirements/recommendations for international students: Required—TOEFL (minimum score 550 paper-based; 80 iBT), IELTS (minimum score 7). Electronic applications accepted. *Expenses:* Tuition, state resident: full-time $8971; part-time $444 per credit hour. Tuition, nonresident: full-time $20,958; part-time $1164 per credit hour. *Required fees:* $1018; $644 per credit hour. Tuition and fees vary according to course load, campus/location and program.

Northern Illinois University, Graduate School, College of Engineering and Engineering Technology, Department of Electrical Engineering, De Kalb, IL 60115-2854. Offers MS. *Program availability:* Part-time, evening/weekend. *Faculty:* 9 full-time (0 women). *Students:* 23 full-time (10 women), 16 part-time (7 women); includes 6 minority (2 Black or African American, non-Hispanic/Latino; 3 Hispanic/Latino; 1 Two or more races, non-Hispanic/Latino), 28 international. Average age 26. 139 applicants, 55% accepted, 9 enrolled. In 2016, 41 master's awarded. *Degree requirements:* For master's, comprehensive exam, thesis optional. *Entrance requirements:* For master's, GRE General Test, minimum GPA of 2.75. Additional exam requirements/recommendations for international students: Required—TOEFL (minimum score 550 paper-based). *Application deadline:* For fall admission, 6/1 for domestic students, 5/1 for international students; for spring admission, 11/1 for domestic students, 10/1 for international students. Applications are processed on a rolling basis. Application fee: $40. Electronic applications accepted. *Financial support:* In 2016–17, 3 research assistantships with full tuition reimbursements, 20 teaching assistantships with full tuition reimbursements were awarded; fellowships with full tuition reimbursements, career-related internships or fieldwork, Federal Work-Study, scholarships/grants, tuition waivers (full), and staff assistantships also available. Support available to part-time students. Financial award applicants required to submit FAFSA. *Faculty research:* Digital signal processing, optics, nano-electronic devices, VLSI. *Unit head:* Dr. Donald S. Zinger, Interim Chair, 815-753-1290, Fax: 815-753-1289, E-mail: dzinger@niu.edu. *Application contact:* Graduate School Office, 815-753-0395, E-mail: gradsch@niu.edu.
Website: http://www.niu.edu/ee/

Northwestern Polytechnic University, School of Engineering, Fremont, CA 94539-7482. Offers computer engineering (DCE); computer science (MS); computer systems engineering (MS); electrical engineering (MS). *Program availability:* Part-time, evening/weekend. *Degree requirements:* For master's, thesis optional; for doctorate, thesis/dissertation. *Entrance requirements:* For master's, minimum GPA of 3.0. Additional exam requirements/recommendations for international students: Required—TOEFL (minimum score 550 paper-based; 79 iBT). *Faculty research:* Computer networking, database design, Internet technology, software engineering, digital signal processing.

Northwestern University, McCormick School of Engineering and Applied Science, Department of Electrical Engineering and Computer Science, Evanston, IL 60208. Offers computer engineering (MS, PhD); computer science (MS, PhD); electrical engineering (MS, PhD); information technology (MS). MS and PhD admissions and degrees offered through The Graduate School. *Program availability:* Part-time. Terminal master's awarded for partial completion of doctoral program. *Degree requirements:* For master's, comprehensive exam (for some programs), thesis optional; for doctorate, comprehensive exam, thesis/dissertation. *Entrance requirements:* For master's and doctorate, GRE General Test. Additional exam requirements/recommendations for international students: Required—TOEFL (minimum score 577 paper-based; 90 iBT), IELTS (minimum score 7). Electronic applications accepted. *Faculty research:* Solid state and photonics; computing, algorithms, and applications; computer engineering and systems; cognitive systems; graphics and interactive media; signals and systems.

Oakland University, Graduate Study and Lifelong Learning, School of Engineering and Computer Science, Department of Electrical and Computer Engineering, Rochester, MI 48309-4401. Offers electrical and computer engineering (MS, PhD); embedded systems (MS); mechatronics (MS). *Program availability:* Part-time, evening/weekend. *Entrance requirements:* For master's, minimum GPA of 3.0. Additional exam requirements/recommendations for international students: Required—TOEFL (minimum score 550 paper-based). Electronic applications accepted. *Expenses:* Contact institution.

The Ohio State University, Graduate School, College of Engineering, Department of Electrical and Computer Engineering, Columbus, OH 43210. Offers electrical and computer engineering (MS, PhD); electrical engineering (MS, PhD). *Program availability:* Part-time. *Faculty:* 62. *Students:* 421 full-time (78 women), 33 part-time (11 women); includes 6 minority (all Two or more races, non-Hispanic/Latino), 344 international. Average age 25. In 2016, 151 master's, 42 doctorates awarded. Terminal master's awarded for partial completion of doctoral program. *Degree requirements:* For master's, thesis optional; for doctorate, thesis/dissertation. *Entrance requirements:* For master's, GRE General Test (for all graduates of foreign universities and for applicants if undergraduate GPA below 3.2); for doctorate, GRE General Test (for all graduates of foreign universities and for applicants if graduate work GPA is below 3.5). Additional exam requirements/recommendations for international students: Required—TOEFL (minimum score 580 paper-based; 92 iBT); Recommended—IELTS (minimum score 7.5). *Application deadline:* For fall admission, 11/30 priority date for domestic and international students. Applications are processed on a rolling basis. Application fee: $60 ($70 for international students). Electronic applications accepted. *Financial support:* Fellowships with full tuition reimbursements, research assistantships with full tuition reimbursements, teaching assistantships with full tuition reimbursements, career-related internships or fieldwork, Federal Work-Study, institutionally sponsored loans, scholarships/grants, traineeships, health care benefits, and unspecified assistantships available. Support available to part-time students. *Unit head:* Dr. Joel T. Johnson, Chair, 614-292-1563, E-mail: johnson.1374@osu.edu. *Application contact:* Electrical and Computer Engineering Graduate Program, 614-292-2572, Fax: 614-292-7596, E-mail: ecegrad@ece.osu.edu.
Website: http://ece.osu.edu/

Ohio University, Graduate College, Russ College of Engineering and Technology, School of Electrical Engineering and Computer Science, Athens, OH 45701-2979. Offers electrical engineering (MS); electrical engineering and computer science (PhD). *Degree requirements:* For master's, comprehensive exam (for some programs), thesis; for doctorate, comprehensive exam, thesis/dissertation, qualifying exams. *Entrance requirements:* For master's, GRE, BSEE or BSCS, minimum GPA of 3.0; for doctorate, GRE, MSEE or MSCS, minimum GPA of 3.0. Additional exam requirements/recommendations for international students: Required—TOEFL (minimum score 550 paper-based; 80 iBT) or IELTS (minimum score 6.5). *Application deadline:* For fall admission, 2/1 priority date for domestic students, 1/1 priority date for international students; for winter admission, 6/1 priority date for domestic students, 5/1 priority date for international students; for spring admission, 8/15 priority date for domestic students, 7/15 priority date for international students. Applications are processed on a rolling basis. Application fee: $50 ($55 for international students). Electronic applications accepted. *Financial support:* Research assistantships with full tuition reimbursements, teaching assistantships with full tuition reimbursements, Federal Work-Study, institutionally sponsored loans, scholarships/grants, and unspecified assistantships available. Financial award applicants required to submit FAFSA. *Faculty research:* Avionics, networking/communications, intelligent distribution, real-time computing, control systems, optical properties of semiconductors. *Unit head:* Dr. David Juedes, Chair, 740-593-1566, Fax: 740-593-0007, E-mail: juedes@ohio.edu. *Application contact:* Dr. Douglas Lawrence, Graduate Chair, 740-593-1578, Fax: 740-593-0007, E-mail: lawrencd@ohio.edu.
Website: http://www.ohio.edu/eecs

Oklahoma Christian University, Graduate School of Engineering and Computer Science, Oklahoma City, OK 73136-1100. Offers electrical and computer engineering (MSE); engineering management (MSE); mechanical engineering (MSE); software engineering (MSCS, MSE). *Program availability:* Part-time. *Faculty:* 8 full-time (1 woman), 7 part-time/adjunct (0 women). *Students:* 187 full-time (27 women), 85 part-time (12 women). Average age 25. 255 applicants, 33% accepted, 69 enrolled. In 2016, 188 master's awarded. *Entrance requirements:* Additional exam requirements/recommendations for international students: Required—TOEFL (minimum score 550 paper-based). *Application deadline:* Applications are processed on a rolling basis. Application fee: $25. Electronic applications accepted. *Expenses:* Contact institution. *Unit head:* Mary Ann Brown, Director for Graduate School Engineering, 405-425-5579. *Application contact:* Angie Ricketts, Admissions Counselor, 405-425-5587, E-mail: angie.ricketts@oc.edu.
Website: http://www.oc.edu/academics/graduate/engineering/

Oklahoma State University, College of Engineering, Architecture and Technology, School of Electrical and Computer Engineering, Stillwater, OK 74078. Offers MS, PhD. *Program availability:* Online learning. *Faculty:* 22 full-time (2 women). *Students:* 53 full-time (12 women), 48 part-time (11 women); includes 8 minority (1 Black or African American, non-Hispanic/Latino; 2 Asian, non-Hispanic/Latino; 4 Hispanic/Latino; 1 Two or more races, non-Hispanic/Latino), 69 international. Average age 28. 285 applicants, 18% accepted, 24 enrolled. In 2016, 88 master's, 11 doctorates awarded. *Degree requirements:* For master's, thesis or alternative; for doctorate, comprehensive exam, thesis/dissertation. *Entrance requirements:* For master's and doctorate, GRE or GMAT. Additional exam requirements/recommendations for international students: Required—TOEFL (minimum score 550 paper-based; 79 iBT). *Application deadline:* For fall admission, 3/1 priority date for international students; for spring admission, 8/1 priority date for international students. Applications are processed on a rolling basis. Application fee: $40 ($75 for international students). Electronic applications accepted. *Expenses:* Tuition, state resident: full-time $3775; part-time $209.70 per credit hour. Tuition, nonresident: full-time $14,851; part-time $825.05 per credit hour. *Required fees:* $2027; $112.60 per credit hour. Tuition and fees vary according to campus/location. *Financial support:* In 2016–17, 18 research assistantships (averaging $10,061 per year), 21 teaching assistantships (averaging $6,318 per year) were awarded; career-related internships or fieldwork, Federal Work-Study, scholarships/grants, health care benefits, tuition waivers (partial), and unspecified assistantships also available. Support available to part-time students. Financial award application deadline: 3/1; financial award applicants required to submit FAFSA. *Unit head:* Dr. Jeffrey Young, Department Head, 405-744-5151, Fax: 405-744-9198, E-mail: jl.young@okstate.edu. *Application contact:* Dr. R. G. Ramakumar, Graduate Coordinator, 405-744-5157, Fax: 405-744-9198, E-mail: ramakum@okstate.edu.
Website: http://www.ece.okstate.edu

Old Dominion University, Frank Batten College of Engineering and Technology, Graduate Program in Electrical and Computer Engineering, Norfolk, VA 23529. Offers ME, MS, D Eng, PhD. *Program availability:* Part-time, online learning. *Faculty:* 23 full-time (2 women), 1 part-time/adjunct (0 women). *Students:* 24 full-time (6 women), 62 part-time (12 women); includes 14 minority (7 Black or African American, non-Hispanic/Latino; 4 Asian, non-Hispanic/Latino; 2 Hispanic/Latino; 1 Two or more races, non-Hispanic/Latino), 40 international. Average age 30. 63 applicants, 63% accepted, 9 enrolled. In 2016, 16 master's, 5 doctorates awarded. *Degree requirements:* For master's, comprehensive exam (for some programs), thesis (for some programs); for doctorate, thesis/dissertation, candidacy exam, diagnostic exam. *Entrance requirements:* For master's, GRE, two letters of recommendation, resume, personal statement of objectives; for doctorate, GRE, three letters of recommendation, resume, personal statement of objectives. Additional exam requirements/recommendations for international students: Required—TOEFL (minimum score 550 paper-based; 79 iBT), IELTS. *Application deadline:* For fall admission, 6/1 for domestic students, 4/15 for international students; for spring admission, 11/1 for domestic students, 10/1 for

international students. Applications are processed on a rolling basis. Application fee: $50. Electronic applications accepted. *Expenses:* Tuition, state resident: full-time $8604; part-time $478 per credit hour. Tuition, nonresident: full-time $21,510; part-time $1195 per credit hour. *Required fees:* $66 per semester. Tuition and fees vary according to campus/location, program and reciprocity agreements. *Financial support:* In 2016–17, 26 research assistantships with full and partial tuition reimbursements (averaging $15,000 per year), 27 teaching assistantships with full and partial tuition reimbursements (averaging $15,000 per year) were awarded; scholarships/grants and unspecified assistantships also available. Financial award application deadline: 2/15. *Faculty research:* Cyber-physical systems, communications and networking, computer vision, computational modeling, controls, security and hardware, medical/biological systems, methods, and devices, bioelectrics, medical image processing, plasma medicine, signal processing for medical and biological systems, solid state and physical electronics, photovoltaics, plasma processing, thin films and nanotechnology. *Total annual research expenditures:* $2.3 million. *Unit head:* Dr. Chunsheng Xin, Graduate Program Director, 757-683-5294, Fax: 757-683-3220, E-mail: cxin@odu.edu.
Website: http://www.odu.edu/ece/

Oregon Health & Science University, School of Medicine, Graduate Programs in Medicine, Department of Computer Science and Engineering, Portland, OR 97239-3098. Offers computer science and engineering (MS, PhD); electrical engineering (MS, PhD). *Program availability:* Part-time. *Faculty:* 7 full-time (2 women), 1 part-time/adjunct (0 women). *Students:* 10 full-time (3 women), 14 part-time (5 women); includes 3 minority (all Asian, non-Hispanic/Latino), 10 international. Average age 33. 10 applicants, 3 enrolled. In 2016, 5 master's, 1 doctorate awarded. Terminal master's awarded for partial completion of doctoral program. *Degree requirements:* For master's, thesis (for some programs); for doctorate, comprehensive exam, thesis/dissertation, qualifying exam. *Entrance requirements:* For master's and doctorate, GRE General Test (minimum scores: 153 Verbal/148 Quantitative/4.5 Analytical). Additional exam requirements/recommendations for international students: Required—IELTS or TOEFL. *Application deadline:* For fall admission, 7/15 for domestic students, 5/15 for international students; for winter admission, 10/15 for domestic students, 9/15 for international students; for spring admission, 1/15 for domestic students, 12/15 for international students. Applications are processed on a rolling basis. Application fee: $70. Electronic applications accepted. *Financial support:* Health care benefits, tuition waivers (full), and full-tuition and stipends (for PhD students) available. Financial award applicants required to submit FAFSA. *Faculty research:* Natural language processing, speech signal processing, computational biology, autism spectrum disorders, hearing and speaking disorders. *Unit head:* Dr. Peter Heeman, Program Director, 503-748-1635, E-mail: heemanp@ohsu.edu. *Application contact:* Pat Dickerson, Administrative Coordinator, 503-748-1635, E-mail: dickersp@ohsu.edu.

Oregon State University, College of Engineering, Program in Electrical and Computer Engineering, Corvallis, OR 97331. Offers analog and mixed signal (M Eng, MS, PhD); artificial intelligence and machine learning (M Eng, MS, PhD); communications and signal processing (M Eng, MS, PhD); computer systems (M Eng, MS, PhD); energy systems (M Eng, MS, PhD); materials and devices (M Eng, MS, PhD); radio frequencies/microwaves/optoelectronics (M Eng, MS, PhD). *Faculty:* 58 full-time (9 women), 3 part-time/adjunct (1 woman). *Students:* 202 full-time (26 women), 31 part-time (9 women); includes 11 minority (9 Asian, non-Hispanic/Latino; 2 Two or more races, non-Hispanic/Latino), 182 international. Average age 28. 535 applicants, 11% accepted, 49 enrolled. In 2016, 52 master's, 8 doctorates awarded. *Entrance requirements:* For master's and doctorate, GRE. Additional exam requirements/recommendations for international students: Required—TOEFL (minimum score 600 paper-based; 80 iBT), IELTS (minimum score 7). *Application deadline:* For fall admission, 1/15 for domestic students. Application fee: $75 ($85 for international students). *Expenses:* $14,130 resident full-time tuition, $23,769 non-resident. *Financial support:* Application deadline: 1/15. *Unit head:* V. John Mathews, Professor and School Head. *Application contact:* Graduate Coordinator, 541-737-7234, E-mail: eecs.gradinfo@oregonstate.edu.
Website: http://eecs.oregonstate.edu/current-students/graduate/ece-program

Oregon State University, College of Engineering, Program in Materials Science, Corvallis, OR 97331. Offers chemical engineering (MS, PhD); chemistry (MS, PhD); civil engineering (MS, PhD); electrical and computer engineering (MS, PhD); forest products (MS, PhD); mathematics (MS, PhD); mechanical engineering (MS, PhD); nuclear engineering (MS); physics (MS, PhD). *Faculty:* 52 full-time (12 women), 3 part-time/adjunct (0 women). *Students:* 34 full-time (8 women), 10 part-time (3 women); includes 7 minority (4 Hispanic/Latino; 3 Two or more races, non-Hispanic/Latino), 15 international. Average age 30. 78 applicants, 24% accepted, 10 enrolled. In 2016, 7 master's, 6 doctorates awarded. *Degree requirements:* For master's, thesis or alternative. *Entrance requirements:* For master's and doctorate, GRE. Additional exam requirements/recommendations for international students: Required—TOEFL (minimum score 80 iBT), IELTS (minimum score 6.5). *Application deadline:* For fall admission, 8/1 for domestic students, 4/1 for international students; for winter admission, 12/1 for domestic students, 7/1 for international students; for spring admission, 2/1 for domestic students, 10/1 for international students; for summer admission, 5/1 for domestic students, 1/1 for international students. Application fee: $75 ($85 for international students). *Expenses:* $14,130 resident full-time tuition, $23,769 non-resident. *Financial support:* Fellowships, research assistantships, teaching assistantships, Federal Work-Study, and institutionally sponsored loans available. Support available to part-time students. Financial award application deadline: 1/15. *Unit head:* Dr. Harriet Nembhard, School Head. *Application contact:* Jean Robinson, Advisor, E-mail: jean.robinson@oregonstate.edu.
Website: http://matsci.oregonstate.edu/

Penn State Harrisburg, Graduate School, School of Science, Engineering and Technology, Middletown, PA 17057. Offers computer science (MS); electrical engineering (M Eng, MS); engineering management (MPS); engineering science (M Eng); environmental engineering (M Eng); environmental pollution control (MEPC, MS); structural engineering (Certificate). *Program availability:* Part-time, evening/weekend. *Unit head:* Dr. Mukund S. Kulkarni, Chancellor, 717-948-6105, Fax: 717-948-6452. *Application contact:* Robert W. Coffman, Jr., Director of Enrollment Management, Admissions, 717-948-6250, Fax: 717-948-6325, E-mail: hbgadmit@psu.edu.
Website: https://harrisburg.psu.edu/science-engineering-technology

Penn State University Park, Graduate School, College of Engineering, Department of Electrical Engineering, University Park, PA 16802. Offers M Eng, MS, PhD. *Unit head:* Dr. Amr S. Elnashai, Dean, 814-865-7537, Fax: 814-863-4749. *Application contact:* Lori Hawn, Director, Graduate Student Services, 814-865-1795, Fax: 814-863-4627, E-mail: l-gswww@lists.psu.edu.
Website: http://ee.psu.edu/

Penn State University Park, Graduate School, College of Engineering, Department of Electrical Engineering and Computer Science, University Park, PA 16802. Offers computer science and engineering (M Eng, MS, PhD). *Unit head:* Dr. Amr S. Elnashai, Dean, 814-865-7537, Fax: 814-863-4749. *Application contact:* Lori Hawn, Director, Graduate Student Services, 814-865-1795, Fax: 814-863-4627, E-mail: l-gswww@lists.psu.edu.
Website: http://eecs.psu.edu/

Pittsburg State University, Graduate School, College of Technology, Department of Engineering Technology, Pittsburg, KS 66762. Offers electrical engineering technology (MET); general engineering technology (MET); manufacturing engineering technology (MET); mechanical engineering technology (MET); plastics engineering technology (MET). *Program availability:* Part-time, 100% online, blended/hybrid learning. *Students:* 59 (9 women); includes 3 minority (2 Black or African American, non-Hispanic/Latino; 1 Asian, non-Hispanic/Latino), 35 international. In 2016, 42 master's awarded. *Degree requirements:* For master's, thesis optional. *Entrance requirements:* Additional exam requirements/recommendations for international students: Required—TOEFL (minimum score 550 paper-based; 79 iBT), IELTS (minimum score 6.5), PTE (minimum score 51). *Application deadline:* For fall admission, 7/15 for domestic students, 6/1 for international students; for spring admission, 12/15 for domestic students, 10/15 for international students; for summer admission, 5/15 for domestic students, 4/1 for international students. Applications are processed on a rolling basis. Application fee: $35 ($60 for international students). Electronic applications accepted. *Expenses:* Contact institution. *Financial support:* In 2016–17, 4 teaching assistantships with full tuition reimbursements (averaging $5,500 per year) were awarded. Financial award application deadline: 2/1; financial award applicants required to submit FAFSA. *Unit head:* Greg Murray, Chairperson, 620-235-4384. *Application contact:* Lisa Allen, Assistant Director of Graduate and Continuing Studies, 620-235-4218, Fax: 620-235-4219, E-mail: lallen@pittstate.edu.
Website: http://www.pittstate.edu/department/engineering-tech/

Polytechnic University of Puerto Rico, Graduate School, Hato Rey, PR 00918. Offers business administration (MBA), including computer information systems, general management, management of information systems, management of international enterprises; civil engineering (ME, MS); computer engineering (ME, MS); computer science (MCS, MS); electrical engineering (ME, MS); engineering management (MEM); environmental management (MEM); landscape architecture (M Land Arch); manufacturing competitiveness (MMC, MS); manufacturing engineering (ME, MS); mechanical engineering (M Mech E). *Program availability:* Part-time, evening/weekend. *Entrance requirements:* For master's, 3 letters of recommendation.

Portland State University, Graduate Studies, Maseeh College of Engineering and Computer Science, Department of Electrical and Computer Engineering, Portland, OR 97207-0751. Offers M Eng, MS, PhD. *Program availability:* Part-time, evening/weekend. *Faculty:* 22 full-time (2 women), 10 part-time/adjunct (1 woman). *Students:* 186 full-time (47 women), 134 part-time (25 women); includes 34 minority (2 Black or African American, non-Hispanic/Latino; 18 Asian, non-Hispanic/Latino; 8 Hispanic/Latino; 6 Two or more races, non-Hispanic/Latino), 203 international. Average age 29. 465 applicants, 38% accepted, 113 enrolled. In 2016, 127 master's, 7 doctorates awarded. *Degree requirements:* For master's, variable foreign language requirement, oral exam; for doctorate, one foreign language, comprehensive exam, thesis/dissertation, oral and written exams. *Entrance requirements:* For master's, GRE, minimum GPA of 2.75; for doctorate, GRE General Test, GRE Subject Test, master's degree in electrical engineering or related field, 3 reference letters, statement of purpose, writing sample. Additional exam requirements/recommendations for international students: Required—TOEFL (minimum score 550 paper-based; 80 iBT). *Application deadline:* For fall admission, 2/1 for domestic and international students; for winter admission, 8/15 for domestic and international students; for spring admission, 11/1 for domestic and international students. Application fee: $65. *Expenses:* Contact institution. *Financial support:* In 2016–17, 12 research assistantships with tuition reimbursements (averaging $9,339 per year), 25 teaching assistantships with tuition reimbursements (averaging $3,226 per year) were awarded; career-related internships or fieldwork, Federal Work-Study, scholarships/grants, and unspecified assistantships also available. Support available to part-time students. Financial award application deadline: 3/1; financial award applicants required to submit FAFSA. *Faculty research:* Optics and laser systems, design automation, VLSI design, computer systems, power electronics. *Total annual research expenditures:* $1.5 million. *Unit head:* Dr. James McNames, Chair, 503-725-5390, Fax: 503-725-3807, E-mail: mcnames@ece.pdx.edu. *Application contact:* Melisa Cehajic, Graduate Coordinator, 503-725-3002, Fax: 503-725-3807, E-mail: melisa@pdx.edu.
Website: http://www.pdx.edu/ece/

Prairie View A&M University, College of Engineering, Prairie View, TX 77446. Offers computer information systems (MSCIS); computer science (MSCS); electrical engineering (MSEE, PhDEE); general engineering (MS Engr). *Program availability:* Part-time, evening/weekend. *Faculty:* 27 full-time (7 women), 2 part-time/adjunct (both women). *Students:* 171 full-time (45 women), 50 part-time (17 women); includes 89 minority (70 Black or African American, non-Hispanic/Latino; 16 Asian, non-Hispanic/Latino; 3 Hispanic/Latino), 115 international. Average age 30. 155 applicants, 94% accepted, 85 enrolled. In 2016, 43 master's, 3 doctorates awarded. *Degree requirements:* For master's, thesis optional; for doctorate, comprehensive exam, thesis/dissertation. *Entrance requirements:* For master's, GRE General Test (minimum score of 900), bachelor's degree in engineering from ABET-accredited institution; for doctorate, minimum GPA of 3.0. Additional exam requirements/recommendations for international students: Required—TOEFL (minimum score 550 paper-based; 79 iBT). *Application deadline:* For fall admission, 5/1 priority date for domestic and international students; for spring admission, 10/1 priority date for domestic students, 9/1 priority date for international students; for summer admission, 3/1 priority date for domestic students, 2/1 priority date for international students. Applications are processed on a rolling basis. Application fee: $50. Electronic applications accepted. *Expenses:* Tuition, state resident: full-time $4362; part-time $273.48 per credit hour. Tuition, nonresident: full-time $12,390; part-time $534.10 per credit hour. *Required fees:* $2782; $178.26 per credit hour. *Financial support:* In 2016–17, 1 fellowship with full tuition reimbursement (averaging $14,000 per year), 33 research assistantships with full and partial tuition reimbursements (averaging $17,260 per year), 3 teaching assistantships with full and partial tuition reimbursements (averaging $15,000 per year) were awarded; career-related internships or fieldwork, institutionally sponsored loans, scholarships/grants, health care benefits, tuition waivers (full), and unspecified assistantships also available. Financial award application deadline: 4/1; financial award applicants required to submit FAFSA. *Faculty research:* Electrical and computer engineering: big data analysis, wireless communications, bioinformatics and computational biology, space radiation; computer science: cloud computing, cyber security; chemical engineering: thermochemical processing of biofuel, photochemical modeling; civil and environmental engineering: environmental sustainability, water resources, structure; mechanical engineering: thermal science, nanocomposites, computational fluid dynamics. *Unit head:* Dr. Kendall T. Harris, Dean, 936-261-9900, Fax: 936-261-9868, E-mail: tharris@pvamu.edu. *Application contact:* Pauline Walker, Administrative Assistant II, Research and Graduate Studies, 936-261-3521, Fax: 936-261-3529, E-mail: gradadmissions@pvamu.edu.

Princeton University, Graduate School, School of Engineering and Applied Science, Department of Electrical Engineering, Princeton, NJ 08544-1019. Offers M Eng, PhD. Terminal master's awarded for partial completion of doctoral program. *Degree requirements:* For doctorate, thesis/dissertation, general exam. *Entrance requirements:* For master's, GRE General Test, 3 letters of recommendation; for doctorate, GRE General Test, official transcript(s), 3 letters of recommendation, personal statement.

Additional exam requirements/recommendations for international students: Required—TOEFL. Electronic applications accepted. *Faculty research:* Computer engineering, electronic materials and devices, information sciences and systems, optics and optical electronics.

Purdue University, College of Engineering, School of Electrical and Computer Engineering, West Lafayette, IN 47907-2035. Offers MSECE, PhD. MS and PhD degree programs in biomedical engineering offered jointly with School of Mechanical Engineering and School of Chemical Engineering. *Program availability:* Part-time, online learning. *Faculty:* 129. *Students:* 675. In 2016, 127 master's, 80 doctorates awarded. Terminal master's awarded for partial completion of doctoral program. *Degree requirements:* For master's, thesis optional; for doctorate, thesis/dissertation. *Entrance requirements:* For master's and doctorate, GRE General Test, minimum GPA of 3.25. *Application deadline:* For fall admission, 12/15 priority date for domestic and international students; for spring admission, 9/15 for domestic and international students. Application fee: $60 ($75 for international students). Electronic applications accepted. *Financial support:* Fellowships with full and partial tuition reimbursements, research assistantships with full and partial tuition reimbursements, teaching assistantships with full and partial tuition reimbursements, scholarships/grants, health care benefits, and unspecified assistantships available. Financial award application deadline: 12/15. *Faculty research:* Automatic control, biomedical imaging and sensing, communications, networking, signal and image processing, computer engineering, education, fields and optics, microelectronics and nanotechnology, power and energy systems, VLSI and circuit design. *Unit head:* Ragu Balakrishnan, Head/Professor, E-mail: ragu@ecn.purdue.edu. *Application contact:* Debra Bowman, Graduate Admissions, E-mail: ecegrad@purdue.edu.
Website: https://engineering.purdue.edu/ECE

Purdue University Northwest, Graduate Studies Office, School of Engineering, Mathematics, and Science, Department of Engineering, Hammond, IN 46323-2094. Offers computer engineering (MSE); electrical engineering (MSE); engineering (MS); mechanical engineering (MSE). *Program availability:* Evening/weekend. *Entrance requirements:* Additional exam requirements/recommendations for international students: Required—TOEFL.

Queen's University at Kingston, School of Graduate Studies, Faculty of Applied Science, Department of Electrical and Computer Engineering, Kingston, ON K7L 3N6, Canada. Offers M Eng, M Sc, M Sc Eng, PhD. *Program availability:* Part-time. *Degree requirements:* For master's, thesis optional; for doctorate, comprehensive exam, thesis/dissertation. *Entrance requirements:* Additional exam requirements/recommendations for international students: Required—TOEFL (minimum score 580 paper-based). *Faculty research:* Communications and signal processing systems, computer engineering systems.

Rensselaer at Hartford, Department of Engineering, Program in Electrical Engineering, Hartford, CT 06120-2991. Offers ME, MS. *Program availability:* Part-time, evening/weekend. *Degree requirements:* For master's, thesis optional. *Entrance requirements:* For master's, GRE. Additional exam requirements/recommendations for international students: Required—TOEFL (minimum score 600 paper-based; 100 iBT).

Rensselaer Polytechnic Institute, Graduate School, School of Engineering, Program in Electrical Engineering, Troy, NY 12180-3590. Offers M Eng, MS, D Eng, PhD. *Faculty:* 40 full-time (7 women), 1 part-time/adjunct (0 women). *Students:* 89 full-time (13 women), 5 part-time (2 women). 350 applicants, 28% accepted, 26 enrolled. In 2016, 9 master's, 22 doctorates awarded. Terminal master's awarded for partial completion of doctoral program. *Degree requirements:* For master's, thesis (for some programs); for doctorate, thesis/dissertation. *Entrance requirements:* For master's and doctorate, GRE. Additional exam requirements/recommendations for international students: Required—TOEFL (minimum score 570 paper-based; 88 iBT), IELTS (minimum score 6.5), PTE (minimum score 60). *Application deadline:* For fall admission, 1/1 priority date for domestic and international students; for spring admission, 8/15 priority date for domestic and international students. Applications are processed on a rolling basis. Application fee: $75. Electronic applications accepted. *Expenses: Tuition:* Full-time $49,520; part-time $2060 per credit hour. *Required fees:* $2617. *Financial support:* In 2016–17, research assistantships (averaging $22,000 per year), teaching assistantships (averaging $22,000 per year) were awarded; fellowships also available. Financial award application deadline: 1/1. *Faculty research:* Communications, information, and signals and systems; computer engineering, hardware, and architecture; computer networking; control, robotics, and automation; energy sources and systems; image science: computer vision, image processing, and geographic information science; microelectronics, photonics, VLSI, and mixed-signal design; plasma science and electromagnetics. *Total annual research expenditures:* $8.6 million. *Unit head:* Dr. Hussein Abouzeid, Graduate Program Director, 518-276-6534, E-mail: gpd@ecse.rpi.edu. *Application contact:* Office of Graduate Admissions, 518-276-6216, E-mail: gradadmissions@rpi.edu.
Website: http://www.ecse.rpi.edu/

Rice University, Graduate Programs, George R. Brown School of Engineering, Department of Electrical and Computer Engineering, Houston, TX 77251-1892. Offers bioengineering (MS, PhD); circuits, controls, and communication systems (MS, PhD); computer science and engineering (MS, PhD); electrical engineering (MEE); lasers, microwaves, and solid-state electronics (MS, PhD); MBA/MEE. *Program availability:* Part-time. *Degree requirements:* For master's, thesis (for some programs); for doctorate, thesis/dissertation. *Entrance requirements:* For master's and doctorate, GRE General Test, GRE Subject Test, minimum GPA of 3.0. Additional exam requirements/recommendations for international students: Required—TOEFL (minimum score 600 paper-based; 90 iBT). Electronic applications accepted. *Faculty research:* Physical electronics, systems, computer engineering, bioengineering.

Rochester Institute of Technology, Graduate Enrollment Services, Kate Gleason College of Engineering, Electrical and Microelectronic Engineering Department, MS Program in Electrical Engineering, Rochester, NY 14623-5603. Offers MS. *Program availability:* Part-time, evening/weekend. *Students:* 150 full-time (32 women), 60 part-time (15 women); includes 9 minority (7 Asian, non-Hispanic/Latino; 2 Hispanic/Latino), 149 international. Average age 24. 397 applicants, 57% accepted, 62 enrolled. In 2016, 63 master's awarded. *Degree requirements:* For master's, thesis or alternative. *Entrance requirements:* For master's, GRE, baccalaureate degree from accredited university in engineering or related field, official transcripts, minimum GPA of 3.0, two letters of reference. Additional exam requirements/recommendations for international students: Required—TOEFL (minimum score 550 paper-based; 79 iBT), IELTS (minimum score 6.5), PTE (minimum score 58). *Application deadline:* For fall admission, 2/15 priority date for domestic and international students; for spring admission, 12/15 priority date for domestic and international students. Applications are processed on a rolling basis. Application fee: $60. Electronic applications accepted. *Expenses:* $1,742 per credit hour. *Financial support:* In 2016–17, 111 students received support. Research assistantships with partial tuition reimbursements available, teaching assistantships with partial tuition reimbursements available, career-related internships or fieldwork, scholarships/grants, and unspecified assistantships available. Support available to part-time students. Financial award applicants required to submit FAFSA. *Faculty research:* Analog and RF; digital and computer systems; electromagnetics, microwaves, and antennas; energy systems; image, video and computer vision; multi-agent bio-robotics; robotics and control systems; wireless communications. *Unit head:* Dr. Jayanti Venkatraman, Graduate Program Director, 585-475-2143, E-mail: jnveee@rit.edu. *Application contact:* Diane Ellison, Associate Vice President, Graduate Enrollment Services, 585-475-2229, Fax: 585-475-7164, E-mail: gradinfo@rit.edu.
Website: https://www.rit.edu/kgcoe/electrical/graduate-ms/overview

Rochester Institute of Technology, Graduate Enrollment Services, Kate Gleason College of Engineering, Electrical and Microelectronic Engineering Department, MS Program in Microelectronic Engineering, Rochester, NY 14623. Offers MS. *Program availability:* Part-time. *Students:* 14 full-time (5 women), 5 part-time (1 woman); includes 1 minority (Asian, non-Hispanic/Latino), 11 international. Average age 24. 22 applicants, 41% accepted, 6 enrolled. In 2016, 4 master's awarded. *Degree requirements:* For master's, thesis. *Entrance requirements:* For master's, GRE, minimum GPA of 3.0 (recommended). Additional exam requirements/recommendations for international students: Required—TOEFL (minimum score 550 paper-based; 79 iBT), IELTS (minimum score 6.5), PTE (minimum score 58). *Application deadline:* For fall admission, 2/15 priority date for domestic and international students; for spring admission, 12/15 priority date for domestic and international students. Applications are processed on a rolling basis. Application fee: $60. Electronic applications accepted. *Expenses:* $1,742 per credit hour. *Financial support:* In 2016–17, 16 students received support. Research assistantships with partial tuition reimbursements available, teaching assistantships with partial tuition reimbursements available, career-related internships or fieldwork, scholarships/grants, and unspecified assistantships available. Support available to part-time students. Financial award applicants required to submit FAFSA. *Faculty research:* Thin-film electronics and photonics; FinFET manufacturing, process and devices; Gallium Nitride materials, optoelectronics, lasers; tunneling devices, TFETs, nanofabrication; nanomaterials, MEMS, sensors and beyond. *Unit head:* Dr. Robert Pearson, Graduate Program Director, 585-475-2923, Fax: 585-475-5845, E-mail: robert.pearson@rit.edu. *Application contact:* Diane Ellison, Associate Vice President, Graduate Enrollment Services, 585-475-2229, Fax: 585-475-7164, E-mail: gradinfo@rit.edu.
Website: http://www.rit.edu/kgcoe/microelectronic/ms/overview

Rose-Hulman Institute of Technology, Faculty of Engineering and Applied Sciences, Department of Electrical and Computer Engineering, Terre Haute, IN 47803-3999. Offers electrical and computer engineering (M Eng); electrical engineering (MS); systems engineering and management (MS). *Program availability:* Part-time. *Faculty:* 18 full-time (2 women), 1 (woman) part-time/adjunct. *Students:* 7 full-time (3 women), 7 part-time (0 women), 12 international. Average age 25. 17 applicants, 65% accepted, 3 enrolled. In 2016, 7 master's awarded. *Degree requirements:* For master's, thesis (for some programs). *Entrance requirements:* For master's, GRE, minimum GPA of 3.0. Additional exam requirements/recommendations for international students: Required—TOEFL (minimum score 580 paper-based; 92 iBT). *Application deadline:* For fall admission, 2/1 priority date for domestic students. Applications are processed on a rolling basis. Application fee: $0. Electronic applications accepted. *Expenses: Tuition:* Full-time $43,122. *Financial support:* In 2016–17, 14 students received support. Fellowships with tuition reimbursements available, research assistantships with tuition reimbursements available, institutionally sponsored loans, scholarships/grants, and tuition waivers (full and partial) available. *Faculty research:* VLSI, power systems, analog electronics, communications, electromagnetics. *Total annual research expenditures:* $84,698. *Unit head:* Dr. Mario Simoni, Chairman, 812-877-8341, Fax: 812-877-8895, E-mail: simoni@rose-hulman.edu. *Application contact:* Dr. Azad Siahmakoun, Associate Dean of the Faculty, 812-877-8400, Fax: 812-877-8061, E-mail: siahmako@rose-hulman.edu.
Website: http://www.rose-hulman.edu/academics/academic-departments/electrical-computer-engineering.aspx

Rowan University, Graduate School, College of Engineering, Department of Electrical Engineering, Glassboro, NJ 08028-1701. Offers MS. Electronic applications accepted.

Royal Military College of Canada, Division of Graduate Studies and Research, Engineering Division, Department of Electrical and Computer Engineering, Kingston, ON K7K 7B4, Canada. Offers computer engineering (M Eng, PhD); electrical engineering (M Eng, PhD); software engineering (M Eng, PhD). *Degree requirements:* For master's, thesis; for doctorate, comprehensive exam, thesis/dissertation. *Entrance requirements:* For master's, honours degree with second-class standing in the appropriate field; for doctorate, master's degree. Electronic applications accepted.

Rutgers University–New Brunswick, Graduate School-New Brunswick, Department of Electrical and Computer Engineering, Piscataway, NJ 08854-8097. Offers communications and solid-state electronics (MS, PhD); computer engineering (MS, PhD); control systems (MS, PhD); digital signal processing (MS, PhD). *Program availability:* Part-time. Terminal master's awarded for partial completion of doctoral program. *Degree requirements:* For master's, thesis or alternative; for doctorate, thesis/dissertation. *Entrance requirements:* For master's and doctorate, GRE General Test. Additional exam requirements/recommendations for international students: Required—TOEFL. Electronic applications accepted. *Faculty research:* Communication and information processing, wireless information networks, micro-vacuum devices, machine vision, VLSI design.

St. Cloud State University, School of Graduate Studies, College of Science and Engineering, Department of Electrical and Computer Engineering, St. Cloud, MN 56301-4498. Offers electrical engineering (MS). *Degree requirements:* For master's, thesis or alternative. *Entrance requirements:* For master's, GRE General Test, minimum GPA of 2.75. Additional exam requirements/recommendations for international students: Required—Michigan English Language Assessment Battery; Recommended—TOEFL (minimum score 550 paper-based), IELTS (minimum score 6.5). Electronic applications accepted.

St. Mary's University, School of Science, Engineering and Technology, Program in Electrical Engineering, San Antonio, TX 78228-8507. Offers MS. *Program availability:* Part-time, evening/weekend. *Faculty:* 2 full-time (0 women). *Students:* 4 full-time (0 women), 3 part-time (0 women), 4 international. Average age 33. 32 applicants, 28% accepted, 2 enrolled. In 2016, 3 master's awarded. *Degree requirements:* For master's, thesis or project. *Entrance requirements:* For master's, GRE (minimum quantitative score of 148), bachelor's degree in electrical engineering, computer engineering or closely-related discipline; minimum undergraduate GPA of 3.0; written statement of purpose; two letters of recommendation; official transcripts. Additional exam requirements/recommendations for international students: Required—TOEFL (minimum score 550 paper-based; 80 iBT), IELTS (minimum score 6.5). *Application deadline:* For fall admission, 7/1 for domestic students; for spring admission, 11/15 for domestic students; for summer admission, 4/1 for domestic students. Applications are processed on a rolling basis. Application fee: $0. Electronic applications accepted. *Expenses: Tuition:* Full-time $15,600; part-time $865 per credit hour. *Required fees:* $148 per semester. *Financial support:* Research assistantships, career-related internships or fieldwork, Federal Work-Study, institutionally sponsored loans, scholarships/grants, health care benefits, and stipends available. Financial award application deadline: 3/31; financial award applicants required to submit FAFSA. *Faculty research:* Sequencing, scheduling and professional ethics. *Unit head:* Dr. Djaffer Ibaroudene, Graduate

Program Director, 210-431-2050, E-mail: dibaroudene@stmarytx.edu.
Website: https://www.stmarytx.edu/academics/set/graduate/electrical-engineering/

San Diego State University, Graduate and Research Affairs, College of Engineering, Department of Electrical and Computer Engineering, San Diego, CA 92182. Offers electrical engineering (MS). *Program availability:* Evening/weekend. *Entrance requirements:* For master's, GRE General Test. Additional exam requirements/ recommendations for international students: Required—TOEFL. Electronic applications accepted. *Faculty research:* Ultra-high speed integral circuits and systems, naval command control and ocean surveillance, signal processing and analysis.

San Francisco State University, Division of Graduate Studies, College of Science and Engineering, School of Engineering, San Francisco, CA 94132-1722. Offers embedded electrical and computer systems (MS); energy systems (MS); structural/earthquake engineering (MS). *Program availability:* Part-time. *Application deadline:* Applications are processed on a rolling basis. Electronic applications accepted. *Expenses:* Tuition, state resident: full-time $6738. Tuition, nonresident: full-time $15,666. *Required fees:* $1012. Tuition and fees vary according to degree level and program. *Unit head:* Dr. Wenshen Pong, Director, 415-338-7738, Fax: 415-338-0525, E-mail: wspong@sfsu.edu. *Application contact:* Dr. Hamid Shahnasser, Graduate Coordinator, 415-338-2124, Fax: 415-338-0525, E-mail: hamid@sfsu.edu.
Website: http://engineering.sfsu.edu/

Santa Clara University, School of Engineering, Santa Clara, CA 95053. Offers applied mathematics (MS); bioengineering (MS); civil engineering (MS); computer science and engineering (MS, PhD); electrical engineering (MS, PhD); engineering (Engineer); engineering management and leadership (MS); mechanical engineering (MS, PhD); software engineering (MS); sustainable energy (MS). *Program availability:* Part-time, evening/weekend. *Faculty:* 66 full-time (22 women), 59 part-time/adjunct (12 women). *Students:* 449 full-time (188 women), 315 part-time (114 women); includes 197 minority (3 Black or African American, non-Hispanic/Latino; 144 Asian, non-Hispanic/Latino; 33 Hispanic/Latino; 1 Native Hawaiian or other Pacific Islander, non-Hispanic/Latino; 16 Two or more races, non-Hispanic/Latino), 418 international. Average age 28. 1,217 applicants, 45% accepted, 293 enrolled. In 2016, 466 master's awarded. *Entrance requirements:* For master's, GRE, transcript; for doctorate, GRE, master's degree or equivalent, 3 letters of recommendation, statement of purpose; for Engineer, master's degree. Additional exam requirements/recommendations for international students: Required—TOEFL (minimum score 79 iBT) or IELTS (6.5). *Application deadline:* For fall admission, 4/1 for domestic and international students; for winter admission, 9/9 for domestic students, 9/2 for international students; for spring admission, 2/17 for domestic students, 12/9 for international students. Application fee: $60. Electronic applications accepted. *Expenses:* $928 per unit. *Financial support:* Fellowships, research assistantships, teaching assistantships, career-related internships or fieldwork, Federal Work-Study, scholarships/grants, traineeships, health care benefits, tuition waivers, and unspecified assistantships available. Support available to part-time students. Financial award applicants required to submit FAFSA. *Unit head:* Dr. Alfonso Ortega, Dean. *Application contact:* Stacey Tinker, Director of Admissions and Marketing, 408-554-4313, Fax: 408-554-4323, E-mail: stinker@scu.edu.
Website: http://www.scu.edu/engineering/graduate/

South Dakota School of Mines and Technology, Graduate Division, Program in Electrical Engineering, Rapid City, SD 57701-3995. Offers MS. *Program availability:* Part-time. *Degree requirements:* For master's, thesis. *Entrance requirements:* Additional exam requirements/recommendations for international students: Required—TOEFL (minimum score 520 paper-based; 68 iBT), TWE. Electronic applications accepted.

South Dakota State University, Graduate School, College of Engineering, Department of Electrical Engineering and Computer Science, Brookings, SD 57007. Offers electrical engineering (PhD); engineering (MS). *Program availability:* Part-time. *Degree requirements:* For master's, thesis (for some programs), oral exam; for doctorate, comprehensive exam, thesis/dissertation, oral exam. *Entrance requirements:* For master's and doctorate, GRE. Additional exam requirements/recommendations for international students: Required—TOEFL (minimum score 575 paper-based). *Faculty research:* Image processing, communications, power systems, electronic materials and devices, nanotechnology, photovoltaics.

Southern Illinois University Carbondale, Graduate School, College of Engineering, Department of Electrical and Computer Engineering, Carbondale, IL 62901-4701. Offers MS, PhD, JD/MS. *Degree requirements:* For master's, comprehensive exam, thesis. *Entrance requirements:* For master's, GRE, minimum GPA of 2.7; for doctorate, GRE, minimum GPA of 3.25. Additional exam requirements/recommendations for international students: Required—TOEFL. *Faculty research:* Circuits and power systems, communications and signal processing, controls and systems, electromagnetics and optics, electronics instrumentation and bioengineering.

Southern Illinois University Carbondale, Graduate School, College of Engineering, Program in Engineering Science, Carbondale, IL 62901-4701. Offers engineering science (PhD), including civil and environmental engineering, electrical and computer engineering, mechanical engineering and energy processes, mining and mineral resources engineering. *Degree requirements:* For doctorate, thesis/dissertation. *Entrance requirements:* For doctorate, GRE General Test, minimum GPA of 3.5. Additional exam requirements/recommendations for international students: Required—TOEFL.

Southern Illinois University Edwardsville, Graduate School, School of Engineering, Department of Electrical and Computer Engineering, Edwardsville, IL 62026. Offers electrical engineering (MS). *Program availability:* Part-time, evening/weekend. *Degree requirements:* For master's, thesis (for some programs), research paper, final exam. *Entrance requirements:* For master's, minimum undergraduate GPA of 2.75 in engineering, mathematics, and science courses. Additional exam requirements/ recommendations for international students: Required—TOEFL (minimum score 550 paper-based; 79 iBT), IELTS (minimum score 6.5). Electronic applications accepted.

Southern Methodist University, Bobby B. Lyle School of Engineering, Department of Electrical Engineering, Dallas, TX 75275-0338. Offers applied science (MS); electrical engineering (MSEE, PhD); telecommunications (MS). *Program availability:* Part-time, evening/weekend, online learning. Terminal master's awarded for partial completion of doctoral program. *Degree requirements:* For master's, thesis optional; for doctorate, thesis/dissertation, oral and written qualifying exams, oral final exam. *Entrance requirements:* For master's, GRE General Test, minimum GPA of 3.0 in last 2 years; bachelor's degree in engineering, mathematics, or sciences; for doctorate, preliminary counseling exam, minimum GPA of 3.0, bachelor's degree in related field. Additional exam requirements/recommendations for international students: Required—TOEFL. Electronic applications accepted. *Faculty research:* Mobile communications, optical communications, digital signal processing, photonics.

Stanford University, School of Engineering, Department of Electrical Engineering, Stanford, CA 94305-2004. Offers MS, PhD. Terminal master's awarded for partial completion of doctoral program. *Degree requirements:* For doctorate, thesis/ dissertation. *Entrance requirements:* For master's and doctorate, GRE General Test. Additional exam requirements/recommendations for international students: Required—TOEFL. Electronic applications accepted. *Expenses: Tuition:* Full-time $47,331. *Required fees:* $609.

State University of New York at New Paltz, Graduate School, School of Science and Engineering, Department of Electrical and Computer Engineering, New Paltz, NY 12561. Offers electrical engineering (MS). *Program availability:* Part-time, evening/ weekend. *Students:* 23 full-time (10 women), 27 part-time (9 women); includes 2 minority (1 Black or African American, non-Hispanic/Latino; 1 Asian, non-Hispanic/ Latino), 47 international. 79 applicants, 63% accepted, 5 enrolled. In 2016, 94 master's awarded. *Degree requirements:* For master's, comprehensive exam, thesis optional. *Entrance requirements:* For master's, minimum GPA of 3.0. Additional exam requirements/recommendations for international students: Required—TOEFL (minimum score 550 paper-based; 80 iBT), IELTS (minimum score 6.5). *Application deadline:* Applications are processed on a rolling basis. Application fee: $50. Electronic applications accepted. *Financial support:* In 2016–17, 15 fellowships with partial tuition reimbursements (averaging $1,360 per year) were awarded. *Unit head:* Dr. Damodaran Radhakrishnan, Program Coordinator, 845-257-3772, E-mail: damu@newpaltz.edu.
Website: http://www.engr.newpaltz.edu/

Stevens Institute of Technology, Graduate School, Charles V. Schaefer Jr. School of Engineering and Science, Department of Electrical and Computer Engineering, Program in Electrical Engineering, Hoboken, NJ 07030. Offers autonomous robotics (Certificate); electrical engineering (M Eng, PhD, Certificate), including computer architecture and digital systems (M Eng), microelectronics and photonics science and technology (M Eng), signal processing for communications (M Eng), telecommunications systems engineering (M Eng), wireless communications (M Eng, Certificate). *Program availability:* Part-time, evening/weekend. *Students:* 190 full-time (47 women), 31 part-time (5 women); includes 14 minority (6 Black or African American, non-Hispanic/Latino; 8 Asian, non-Hispanic/Latino), 181 international. Average age 25. 851 applicants, 59% accepted, 93 enrolled. In 2016, 152 master's, 6 doctorates awarded. *Degree requirements:* For master's, thesis optional, minimum B average in major field and overall; for doctorate, comprehensive exam (for some programs), thesis/dissertation; for Certificate, minimum B average. *Entrance requirements:* Additional exam requirements/ recommendations for international students: Required—TOEFL (minimum score 74 iBT), IELTS (minimum score 6). *Application deadline:* For fall admission, 6/1 for domestic students, 4/15 for international students; for spring admission, 11/30 for domestic students, 11/1 for international students. Applications are processed on a rolling basis. Application fee: $65. Electronic applications accepted. *Expenses:* Contact institution. *Financial support:* Fellowships, research assistantships, teaching assistantships, career-related internships or fieldwork, Federal Work-Study, scholarships/grants, and unspecified assistantships available. Financial award application deadline: 2/15; financial award applicants required to submit FAFSA. *Unit head:* Cristina Comaniciu, Program Director, 201-216-5606, Fax: 201-216-8246, E-mail: ccomanic@stevens.edu. *Application contact:* Graduate Admissions, 888-783-8367, Fax: 888-511-1306, E-mail: graduate@stevens.edu.

Stevens Institute of Technology, Graduate School, Charles V. Schaefer Jr. School of Engineering and Science, Department of Mechanical Engineering, Program in Integrated Product Development, Hoboken, NJ 07030. Offers armament engineering (M Eng); computer and electrical engineering (M Eng); manufacturing technologies (M Eng); systems reliability and design (M Eng). *Program availability:* Part-time, evening/weekend. *Students:* 15 applicants. In 2016, 2 master's awarded. *Degree requirements:* For master's, thesis optional, minimum B average in major field and overall. *Entrance requirements:* Additional exam requirements/recommendations for international students: Required—TOEFL (minimum score 74 iBT), IELTS (minimum score 6). *Application deadline:* For fall admission, 6/1 for domestic students, 4/15 for international students; for spring admission, 11/30 for domestic students, 11/1 for international students. Applications are processed on a rolling basis. Application fee: $65. Electronic applications accepted. *Expenses:* Contact institution. *Financial support:* Fellowships, research assistantships, teaching assistantships, career-related internships or fieldwork, Federal Work-Study, scholarships/grants, and unspecified assistantships available. Financial award application deadline: 2/15; financial award applicants required to submit FAFSA. *Unit head:* Dr. Frank Fisher, Interim Department Director, 201-216-8913, Fax: 201-216-8315, E-mail: ffisher@stevens.edu. *Application contact:* Graduate Admissions, 888-783-8367, Fax: 888-511-1306, E-mail: graduate@stevens.edu.

Stevens Institute of Technology, Graduate School, Charles V. Schaefer Jr. School of Engineering and Science, Interdisciplinary Program in Microelectronics and Photonics, Hoboken, NJ 07030. Offers M Eng, MS, PhD. *Program availability:* Part-time, evening/ weekend. *Faculty:* 3 full-time (0 women). *Degree requirements:* For master's, thesis optional, minimum B average in major field and overall; for doctorate, comprehensive exam (for some programs), thesis/dissertation. *Entrance requirements:* Additional exam requirements/recommendations for international students: Required—TOEFL (minimum score 74 iBT), IELTS (minimum score 6). *Application deadline:* For fall admission, 6/1 for domestic students, 4/15 for international students; for spring admission, 11/30 for domestic students, 11/1 for international students. Applications are processed on a rolling basis. Application fee: $65. Electronic applications accepted. *Expenses:* Contact institution. *Financial support:* Fellowships, research assistantships, teaching assistantships, career-related internships or fieldwork, Federal Work-Study, scholarships/grants, and unspecified assistantships available. Financial award application deadline: 2/15; financial award applicants required to submit FAFSA. *Unit head:* Dr. Keith G. Sheppard, Interim Dean, 201-216-5260, Fax: 201-216-8372, E-mail: keith.sheppard@stevens.edu. *Application contact:* Graduate Admissions, 888-783-8367, Fax: 888-511-1306, E-mail: graduate@stevens.edu.

Stony Brook University, State University of New York, Graduate School, College of Engineering and Applied Sciences, Department of Electrical and Computer Engineering, Program in Electrical Engineering, Stony Brook, NY 11794. Offers MS, PhD. *Faculty:* 27 full-time (6 women), 13 part-time/adjunct (5 women). *Students:* 92 full-time (24 women), 23 part-time (4 women); includes 15 minority (3 Black or African American, non-Hispanic/Latino; 9 Asian, non-Hispanic/Latino; 3 Hispanic/Latino), 87 international. 419 applicants, 50% accepted, 35 enrolled. In 2016, 46 master's, 15 doctorates awarded. *Degree requirements:* For doctorate, thesis/dissertation. *Entrance requirements:* For doctorate, GRE, two official transcripts, letters of recommendation. Additional exam requirements/recommendations for international students: Required—TOEFL (minimum score 90 iBT). *Application deadline:* For fall admission, 1/15 for domestic students; for spring admission, 10/1 for domestic students. Application fee: $100. *Expenses:* Contact institution. *Financial support:* Research assistantships and teaching assistantships available. *Total annual research expenditures:* $3.7 million. *Unit head:* Prof. Petar M. Djuric, Chair, 631-632-8420, Fax: 631-632-8494, E-mail: petar.djuric@stonybrook.edu. *Application contact:* Susan Hayden, Coordinator, 631-632-8400, Fax: 631-632-8494, E-mail: susan.hayden@stonybrook.edu.

Syracuse University, College of Engineering and Computer Science, CAS Program in Microwave Engineering, Syracuse, NY 13244. Offers CAS. *Program availability:* Part-time. *Degree requirements:* For CAS, thesis. *Entrance requirements:* For degree, GRE General Test, personal statement, official transcripts, resume. Additional exam requirements/recommendations for international students: Required—TOEFL (minimum

score 100 iBT). *Application deadline:* For fall admission, 7/1 priority date for domestic students, 6/1 priority date for international students; for spring admission, 11/15 priority date for domestic students, 10/15 priority date for international students. Applications are processed on a rolling basis. Application fee: $75. Electronic applications accepted. *Expenses: Tuition:* Full-time $25,974; part-time $1443 per credit hour. *Required fees:* $802; $50 per course. Tuition and fees vary according to course load and program. *Financial support:* Application deadline: 1/1. *Faculty research:* Microwave theory, microwave circuit behavior, microwave filters and transistor amplifiers, wireless communication, electrical engineering. *Unit head:* Dr. Kishan Mehrotra, Professor and Chair, Department of Electrical Engineering and Computer Science, 315-443-2811, E-mail: mehrotra@syr.edu. *Application contact:* Brenda Flowers, Information Contact, 315-443-4408, E-mail: bflowers@syr.edu.
Website: http://eng-cs.syr.edu/

Syracuse University, College of Engineering and Computer Science, MS Program in Electrical Engineering, Syracuse, NY 13244. Offers MS. *Program availability:* Part-time. *Students:* Average age 24. In 2016, 48 master's awarded. *Degree requirements:* For master's, thesis optional. *Entrance requirements:* For master's, GRE General Test, three letters of recommendation, personal statement, resume, official transcripts. Additional exam requirements/recommendations for international students: Required—TOEFL (minimum score 100 iBT). *Application deadline:* For fall admission, 7/1 priority date for domestic students, 6/1 priority date for international students; for spring admission, 10/1 priority date for domestic students, 11/1 priority date for international students. Applications are processed on a rolling basis. Application fee: $75. Electronic applications accepted. *Expenses: Tuition:* Full-time $25,974; part-time $1443 per credit hour. *Required fees:* $802; $50 per course. Tuition and fees vary according to course load and program. *Financial support:* Fellowships with full tuition reimbursements, research assistantships with tuition reimbursements, teaching assistantships with tuition reimbursements, scholarships/grants, and tuition waivers (partial) available. Financial award application deadline: 1/1; financial award applicants required to submit FAFSA. *Faculty research:* Methods of engineering analysis, electromagnetic fields, electromechanical devices. *Unit head:* Dr. Prasanta Ghosh, Program Director, 315-443-4440, Fax: 315-443-2583, E-mail: pkghosh@syr.edu. *Application contact:* Kathleen Joyce, Director of Graduate Recruitment, 315-443-2219, E-mail: topgrads@syr.edu.
Website: http://eng-cs.syr.edu/

Syracuse University, College of Engineering and Computer Science, PhD Program in Electrical and Computer Engineering, Syracuse, NY 13244. Offers PhD. *Program availability:* Part-time. *Students:* Average age 29. In 2016, 12 doctorates awarded. *Degree requirements:* For doctorate, comprehensive exam, thesis/dissertation. *Entrance requirements:* For doctorate, GRE General Test, three letters of recommendation, personal statement, resume, official transcripts. Additional exam requirements/recommendations for international students: Required—TOEFL (minimum score 100 iBT). *Application deadline:* For fall admission, 7/1 priority date for domestic students, 6/1 priority date for international students; for spring admission, 11/1 priority date for domestic students, 10/1 priority date for international students. Applications are processed on a rolling basis. Application fee: $75. Electronic applications accepted. *Expenses: Tuition:* Full-time $25,974; part-time $1443 per credit hour. *Required fees:* $802; $50 per course. Tuition and fees vary according to course load and program. *Financial support:* Fellowships with full tuition reimbursements, research assistantships with tuition reimbursements, and teaching assistantships with tuition reimbursements available. Financial award application deadline: 1/1. *Faculty research:* Electrical engineering, computer engineering hardware. *Unit head:* Dr. Qinru Qiu, Professor, Computer Engineering/Program Director, Electrical Engineering and Computer Science, 315-443-1836, E-mail: qiqiu@syr.edu. *Application contact:* Kathleen Joyce, Assistant Dean, 315-443-2219, E-mail: bflowers@syr.edu.
Website: http://eng-cs.syr.edu/

Temple University, College of Engineering, Department of Electrical and Computer Engineering, Philadelphia, PA 19122-6096. Offers electrical and computer engineering (PhD); electrical engineering (MSEE). *Program availability:* Part-time, evening/weekend. *Faculty:* 13 full-time (3 women), 4 part-time/adjunct (0 women). *Students:* 39 full-time (10 women), 9 part-time (0 women); includes 5 minority (1 Black or African American, non-Hispanic/Latino; 3 Asian, non-Hispanic/Latino; 1 Hispanic/Latino), 29 international. 66 applicants, 65% accepted, 18 enrolled. In 2016, 15 master's awarded. Terminal master's awarded for partial completion of doctoral program. *Degree requirements:* For master's, thesis optional; for doctorate, thesis/dissertation, preliminary exam, dissertation proposal and defense. *Entrance requirements:* For master's, GRE General Test, minimum GPA of 3.0; BS in engineering from ABET-accredited or equivalent institution; resume; goals statement; three letters of reference; official transcripts; for doctorate, GRE General Test, minimum GPA of 3.0; MS in engineering from ABET-accredited or equivalent institution (preferred); resume; goals statement; three letters of reference; official transcripts. Additional exam requirements/recommendations for international students: Required—TOEFL (minimum score 550 paper-based; 79 iBT), IELTS (minimum score 6.5), PTE (minimum score 53). *Application deadline:* For fall admission, 3/1 priority date for domestic and international students; for spring admission, 11/1 priority date for domestic students, 8/1 priority date for international students. Applications are processed on a rolling basis. Application fee: $60. Electronic applications accepted. *Expenses:* $995 per credit hour in-state tuition; $1,319 per credit hour out-of-state tuition. *Financial support:* In 2016–17, 21 students received support, including 1 fellowship with tuition reimbursement available, 7 research assistantships with tuition reimbursements available, 13 teaching assistantships with tuition reimbursements available; Federal Work-Study, institutionally sponsored loans, scholarships/grants, health care benefits, and unspecified assistantships also available. Financial award application deadline: 3/1; financial award applicants required to submit FAFSA. *Faculty research:* Embedded systems and system-on-a-chip design, intelligent interactive multimedia, intrusion detection, multisensory fusion, speaker identification, speech processing, visualization and fault detection in multicasting networks. *Unit head:* Dr. Li Bai, Chair, 215-204-6616, Fax: 215-204-6936, E-mail: lbai@temple.edu. *Application contact:* Leslie Levin, Director, Admissions and Graduate Student Services, 215-204-7800, Fax: 215-204-6936, E-mail: gradengr@temple.edu.
Website: http://engineering.temple.edu/department/electrical-computer-engineering

Temple University, College of Engineering, PhD in Engineering Program, Philadelphia, PA 19122-6096. Offers bioengineering (PhD); civil engineering (PhD); electrical engineering (PhD); environmental engineering (PhD); mechanical engineering (PhD). *Program availability:* Part-time, evening/weekend. *Faculty:* 67 full-time (13 women), 11 part-time/adjunct (1 woman). *Students:* 32 full-time (11 women), 7 part-time (2 women); includes 10 minority (3 Black or African American, non-Hispanic/Latino; 5 Asian, non-Hispanic/Latino; 1 Hispanic/Latino; 1 Two or more races, non-Hispanic/Latino), 19 international. 11 applicants, 64% accepted, 3 enrolled. In 2016, 6 doctorates awarded. *Degree requirements:* For doctorate, thesis/dissertation, preliminary exam, dissertation proposal and defense. *Entrance requirements:* For doctorate, GRE, minimum undergraduate GPA of 3.0; MS in engineering from ABET-accredited or equivalent institution (preferred); resume; goals statement; three letters of reference; official transcripts. Additional exam requirements/recommendations for international students: Required—TOEFL (minimum score 550 paper-based; 79 iBT), IELTS (minimum score 6.5), PTE (minimum score 53). *Application deadline:* For fall admission, 1/15 priority date for domestic and international students; for spring admission, 11/1 priority date for domestic students, 8/1 priority date for international students. Applications are processed on a rolling basis. Application fee: $60. Electronic applications accepted. *Expenses:* $995 per credit hour in-state tuition; $1,319 per credit hour out-of-state. *Financial support:* Fellowships with tuition reimbursements, research assistantships with tuition reimbursements, teaching assistantships with tuition reimbursements, Federal Work-Study, scholarships/grants, health care benefits, and unspecified assistantships available. Financial award application deadline: 3/1; financial award applicants required to submit FAFSA. *Faculty research:* Advanced/computer-aided manufacturing and advanced materials processing; bioengineering; computer engineering; construction engineering and management; dynamics, controls, and systems; energy and environmental science; engineering physics and engineering mathematics; green engineering; signal processing and communication; transportation engineering; water resources, hydrology, and environmental engineering. *Unit head:* Dr. Saroj Biswas, Associate Dean, College of Engineering, 215-204-8403, E-mail: sbiswas@temple.edu. *Application contact:* Leslie Levin, Director, Admissions and Graduate Student Services, 215-204-7800, Fax: 215-204-6936, E-mail: gradengr@temple.edu.
Website: http://engineering.temple.edu/additional-programs/phd-engineering

See Display on page 63 and Close-Up on page 83.

Tennessee State University, The School of Graduate Studies and Research, College of Engineering, Nashville, TN 37209-1561. Offers biomedical engineering (ME); civil engineering (ME); computer and information systems engineering (MS, PhD); electrical engineering (ME); environmental engineering (ME); manufacturing engineering (ME); mathematical sciences (MS); mechanical engineering (ME). *Program availability:* Part-time, evening/weekend. *Degree requirements:* For master's, project; for doctorate, comprehensive exam, thesis/dissertation. *Entrance requirements:* For doctorate, minimum GPA of 3.3. *Faculty research:* Robotics, intelligent systems, human-computer interaction software systems, biomedical engineering, signal/image processing, probabilistic design, intelligent manufacturing, cooperative mobile robots, condition based maintenance, sensor fusion.

Tennessee Technological University, College of Graduate Studies, College of Engineering, Department of Electrical and Computer Engineering, Cookeville, TN 38505. Offers MS. *Program availability:* Part-time. *Faculty:* 19 full-time (0 women). *Students:* 11 full-time (1 woman), 17 part-time (1 woman); includes 2 minority (both Two or more races, non-Hispanic/Latino), 16 international. Average age 27. 114 applicants, 46% accepted, 6 enrolled. In 2016, 8 master's awarded. *Degree requirements:* For master's, thesis. *Entrance requirements:* For master's, GRE. Additional exam requirements/recommendations for international students: Required—TOEFL (minimum score 550 paper-based; 79 iBT), IELTS (minimum score 5.5), PTE (minimum score 53), or TOEIC (Test of English as an International Communication). *Application deadline:* For fall admission, 8/1 for domestic students, 5/1 for international students; for spring admission, 12/1 for domestic students, 10/1 for international students; for summer admission, 5/1 for domestic students, 2/1 for international students. Applications are processed on a rolling basis. Application fee: $35 ($40 for international students). Electronic applications accepted. *Expenses:* Tuition, state resident: full-time $9375; part-time $534 per credit hour. Tuition, nonresident: full-time $22,443; part-time $1260 per credit hour. *Financial support:* In 2016–17, 8 research assistantships (averaging $7,650 per year), 12 teaching assistantships (averaging $7,500 per year) were awarded; fellowships and career-related internships or fieldwork also available. Financial award application deadline: 4/1. *Faculty research:* Control, digital, and power systems. *Unit head:* Dr. R. Wayne Johnson, Chairperson, 931-372-3397, Fax: 931-372-3436, E-mail: wjohnson@tntech.edu. *Application contact:* Shelia K. Kendrick, Coordinator of Graduate Studies, 931-372-3808, Fax: 931-372-3497, E-mail: skendrick@tntech.edu.

Texas A&M University, College of Engineering, Department of Electrical and Computer Engineering, College Station, TX 77843. Offers computer engineering (M Eng, MS, PhD); electrical engineering (M Eng, MS, PhD). *Faculty:* 72. *Students:* 590 full-time (109 women), 112 part-time (20 women); includes 29 minority (3 Black or African American, non-Hispanic/Latino; 14 Asian, non-Hispanic/Latino; 9 Hispanic/Latino; 1 Native Hawaiian or other Pacific Islander, non-Hispanic/Latino; 2 Two or more races, non-Hispanic/Latino), 625 international. Average age 27. 1,958 applicants, 27% accepted, 217 enrolled. In 2016, 207 master's, 42 doctorates awarded. *Degree requirements:* For master's, thesis (MS); for doctorate, thesis/dissertation. *Entrance requirements:* For master's and doctorate, GRE General Test. Additional exam requirements/recommendations for international students: Required—TOEFL (minimum score 550 paper-based; 80 iBT), IELTS (minimum score 6), PTE (minimum score 53). *Application deadline:* For fall admission, 1/1 for domestic students, 2/1 for international students; for spring admission, 10/1 for domestic students, 8/1 for international students. Application fee: $50 ($90 for international students). *Expenses:* Contact institution. *Financial support:* In 2016–17, 448 students received support, including 24 fellowships with tuition reimbursements available (averaging $11,557 per year), 182 research assistantships with tuition reimbursements available (averaging $5,334 per year), 124 teaching assistantships with tuition reimbursements available (averaging $6,551 per year); career-related internships or fieldwork, institutionally sponsored loans, scholarships/grants, traineeships, health care benefits, tuition waivers (full and partial), and unspecified assistantships also available. Support available to part-time students. Financial award application deadline: 3/15; financial award applicants required to submit FAFSA. *Faculty research:* Solid-state, electric power systems, and communications engineering. *Unit head:* Dr. Miroslav M. Begovic, Department Head, 979-862-1553, E-mail: begovic@ece.tamu.edu. *Application contact:* Tammy Carda, Senior Academic Advisor II, 979-845-7467, E-mail: t-carda@tamu.edu.
Website: http://engineering.tamu.edu/electrical/

Texas A&M University–Kingsville, College of Graduate Studies, Frank H. Dotterweich College of Engineering, Department of Electrical Engineering and Computer Science, Program in Electrical Engineering, Kingsville, TX 78363. Offers ME, MS. *Degree requirements:* For master's, variable foreign language requirement, comprehensive exam, thesis (for some programs). *Entrance requirements:* For master's, GRE (minimum score of 145 quantitative revised score, 800 quantitative and verbal old score), MAT, GMAT. Additional exam requirements/recommendations for international students: Required—TOEFL (minimum score 550 paper-based; 79 iBT). Electronic applications accepted.

Texas State University, The Graduate College, College of Science and Engineering, Program in Engineering, San Marcos, TX 78666. Offers electrical engineering (MS); industrial engineering (MS); manufacturing engineering (MS). *Program availability:* Part-time. *Faculty:* 15 full-time (2 women), 2 part-time/adjunct (0 women). *Students:* 49 full-time (15 women), 10 part-time (3 women); includes 7 minority (3 Asian, non-Hispanic/Latino; 3 Hispanic/Latino; 1 Two or more races, non-Hispanic/Latino), 45 international. Average age 28. 163 applicants, 43% accepted, 30 enrolled. *Degree requirements:* For master's, comprehensive exam, thesis (for some programs), thesis or research project. *Entrance requirements:* For master's, GRE (minimum preferred scores of 285 overall, 135 verbal, 150 quantitative), baccalaureate degree from regionally-accredited university in engineering, computer science, physics, technology, or closely-related field with minimum GPA of 3.0 on last 60 undergraduate semester hours; resume or curriculum vitae; 2 letters of recommendation; statement of purpose. Additional exam requirements/recommendations for international students: Required—TOEFL (minimum score 550 paper-based; 78 iBT), IELTS (minimum score 6.5). *Application deadline:* For fall admission, 2/15 priority date for domestic students, 2/1 priority date for international students. Application fee: $40 ($90 for international students). Electronic applications accepted. *Expenses:* $4,851 per semester. *Financial support:* In 2016–17, 25 students received support, including 15 research assistantships (averaging $14,047 per year), 19 teaching assistantships (averaging $13,572 per year); Federal Work-Study, institutionally sponsored loans, scholarships/grants, and unspecified assistantships also available. Support available to part-time students. Financial award application deadline: 3/1; financial award applicants required to submit FAFSA. *Faculty research:* Building a regional energy and educational network; recruitment and retention of female undergraduates in engineering and computer science; fostering nanotechnology environment, health, safety awareness; low-cost flexible graphene-based digital beam forming phased-array antennas engaging, sustaining and empowering women and minorities in STEM. *Total annual research expenditures:* $854,198. *Unit head:* Dr. Vishu Viswanathan, Graduate Advisor, 512-245-1826, Fax: 512-245-8365, E-mail: vishu.viswanathan@txstate.edu. *Application contact:* Dr. Andrea Golato, Dean of Graduate School, 512-245-2581, Fax: 512-245-8365, E-mail: gradcollege@txstate.edu. Website: http://www.engineering.txstate.edu/Programs/Graduate.html

Texas Tech University, Graduate School, Edward E. Whitacre Jr. College of Engineering, Department of Electrical and Computer Engineering, Lubbock, TX 79409-3102. Offers electrical engineering (MSEE, PhD). *Program availability:* Part-time. *Faculty:* 29 full-time (4 women), 5 part-time/adjunct (1 woman). *Students:* 119 full-time (24 women), 29 part-time (6 women); includes 15 minority (6 Black or African American, non-Hispanic/Latino; 3 Asian, non-Hispanic/Latino; 3 Hispanic/Latino; 3 Two or more races, non-Hispanic/Latino), 97 international. Average age 28. 340 applicants, 42% accepted, 44 enrolled. In 2016, 101 master's, 9 doctorates awarded. *Degree requirements:* For master's, comprehensive exam, thesis (for some programs); for doctorate, comprehensive exam, thesis/dissertation. *Entrance requirements:* For master's and doctorate, GRE (Verbal and Quantitative), minimum GPA of 3.0, statement of purpose, 3 letters of recommendation, resume. Additional exam requirements/recommendations for international students: Required—TOEFL (minimum score 550 paper-based; 79 iBT). *Application deadline:* For fall admission, 6/1 priority date for domestic students, 1/15 priority date for international students; for spring admission, 9/1 priority date for domestic students, 6/15 priority date for international students. Applications are processed on a rolling basis. Application fee: $75. Electronic applications accepted. *Expenses:* $325 per credit hour full-time resident tuition, $733 per credit hour full-time non-resident tuition; $53.75 per credit hour fee plus $608 per term fee. *Financial support:* In 2016–17, 136 students received support, including 115 fellowships (averaging $4,395 per year), 82 research assistantships (averaging $17,620 per year), 24 teaching assistantships (averaging $13,794 per year); scholarships/grants, health care benefits, tuition waivers (partial), and unspecified assistantships also available. Financial award application deadline: 4/15; financial award applicants required to submit FAFSA. *Faculty research:* Pulsed power and power electronics, wide band-gap power semiconductors, nano-photonics and nano-technology, neural imaging and image analysis, renewable power integration and smart grid technology, RF amplifiers, radar & microwave technology, cyber security, MEMS, biomedical instrumentation, genomics. *Total annual research expenditures:* $5.4 million. *Unit head:* Dr. Michael Gunter Giesselmann, Chair, 806-834-6841, Fax: 806-742-1245, E-mail: michael.giesselmann@ttu.edu. *Application contact:* Jackie Charlebois, Supervisor, Graduate Admissions, 806-742-3533, Fax: 806-742-1245, E-mail: jackie.charlebois@ttu.edu.
Website: http://www.depts.ttu.edu/ece/

Tufts University, Graduate School of Arts and Sciences, Graduate Certificate Programs, Microwave and Wireless Engineering Program, Medford, MA 02155. Offers Certificate. *Program availability:* Part-time, evening/weekend. Electronic applications accepted. *Expenses:* Tuition: Full-time $49,892; part-time $1248 per credit hour. *Required fees:* $844. Full-time tuition and fees vary according to degree level, program and student level. Part-time tuition and fees vary according to course load.

Tufts University, School of Engineering, Department of Electrical and Computer Engineering, Medford, MA 02155. Offers bioengineering (ME, MS), including signals and systems; electrical engineering (MS, PhD). *Program availability:* Part-time. Terminal master's awarded for partial completion of doctoral program. *Degree requirements:* For master's, thesis or alternative; for doctorate, thesis/dissertation. *Entrance requirements:* For master's and doctorate, GRE General Test. Additional exam requirements/recommendations for international students: Required—TOEFL (minimum score 550 paper-based; 80 iBT), IELTS (minimum score 6.5). Electronic applications accepted. *Expenses:* Tuition: Full-time $49,892; part-time $1248 per credit hour. *Required fees:* $844. Full-time tuition and fees vary according to degree level, program and student level. Part-time tuition and fees vary according to course load. *Faculty research:* Communication theory, networks, protocol, and transmission technology; simulation and modeling; digital processing technology; image and signal processing for security and medical applications; integrated circuits and VLSI.

Tuskegee University, Graduate Programs, College of Engineering, Department of Electrical Engineering, Tuskegee, AL 36088. Offers MSEE. *Degree requirements:* For master's, thesis or alternative. *Entrance requirements:* For master's, GRE General Test, GRE Subject Test. Additional exam requirements/recommendations for international students: Required—TOEFL (minimum score 500 paper-based). *Faculty research:* Photovoltaic insulation, automatic guidance and control, wind energy.

Universidad de las Américas Puebla, Division of Graduate Studies, School of Engineering, Program in Electronic Engineering, Puebla, Mexico. Offers MS. *Program availability:* Part-time, evening/weekend. *Faculty research:* Telecommunications, data processing, digital systems.

Universidad del Turabo, Graduate Programs, School of Engineering, Gurabo, PR 00778-3030. Offers computer engineering (M Eng); electrical engineering (M Eng); mechanical engineering (M Eng); telecommunications and network systems administration (M Eng). *Students:* 14 full-time (0 women), 46 part-time (7 women); all minorities (all Hispanic/Latino). Average age 34. 74 applicants, 41% accepted, 20 enrolled. In 2016, 13 master's awarded. *Entrance requirements:* For master's, GRE, EXADEP or GMAT, interview, essay, official transcript, recommendation letters. *Application deadline:* Applications are processed on a rolling basis. Application fee: $25. Electronic applications accepted. *Financial support:* Institutionally sponsored loans available. Financial award applicants required to submit FAFSA. *Unit head:* Hector Rodriguez, Dean, 787-743-7979 Ext. 4144. *Application contact:* Diriee Rodriguez, Admissions Director, 787-743-7979 Ext. 4453, E-mail: admisiones-ut@suagm.edu. Website: http://ut.suagm.edu/es/engineering

Université de Moncton, Faculty of Engineering, Program in Electrical Engineering, Moncton, NB E1A 3E9, Canada. Offers M Sc A. *Degree requirements:* For master's, thesis, proficiency in French. *Faculty research:* Telecommunications, electronics and instrumentation, analog and digital electronics, electronic control of machines, energy systems, electronic design.

Université de Sherbrooke, Faculty of Engineering, Department of Electrical Engineering and Computer Engineering, Sherbrooke, QC J1K 2R1, Canada. Offers electrical engineering (M Sc A, PhD). *Degree requirements:* For master's, one foreign language, thesis; for doctorate, comprehensive exam, thesis/dissertation. *Entrance requirements:* For master's, bachelor's degree in engineering or equivalent. Electronic applications accepted. *Faculty research:* Minielectronics, biomedical engineering, digital signal prolonging and telecommunications, software engineering and artificial intelligence.

Université du Québec à Trois-Rivières, Graduate Programs, Program in Electrical Engineering, Trois-Rivières, QC G9A 5H7, Canada. Offers M Sc A, PhD. *Program availability:* Part-time. *Degree requirements:* For master's, thesis; for doctorate, thesis/dissertation. *Entrance requirements:* For master's, appropriate bachelor's degree, proficiency in French; for doctorate, appropriate master's degree, proficiency in French. *Faculty research:* Industrial electronics.

Université Laval, Faculty of Sciences and Engineering, Department of Electrical and Computer Engineering, Programs in Electrical Engineering, Québec, QC G1K 7P4, Canada. Offers M Sc, PhD. Terminal master's awarded for partial completion of doctoral program. *Degree requirements:* For master's, thesis (for some programs); for doctorate, thesis/dissertation. *Entrance requirements:* For master's and doctorate, knowledge of French and English. Electronic applications accepted.

University at Buffalo, the State University of New York, Graduate School, School of Engineering and Applied Sciences, Department of Electrical Engineering, Buffalo, NY 14260. Offers ME, MS, PhD. *Program availability:* Part-time. Terminal master's awarded for partial completion of doctoral program. *Degree requirements:* For master's, comprehensive exam (for some programs), thesis or exam; for doctorate, comprehensive exam, thesis/dissertation. *Entrance requirements:* For master's and doctorate, GRE General Test. Additional exam requirements/recommendations for international students: Required—TOEFL (minimum score 550 paper-based; 79 iBT). Electronic applications accepted. *Faculty research:* High power electronics and plasmas, electronic materials signal and image processing, photonics and communications, optics, nanoelectronics.

See Display below and Close-Up on page 427.

The University of Akron, Graduate School, College of Engineering, Department of Electrical and Computer Engineering, Akron, OH 44325. Offers engineering (PhD). *Program availability:* Evening/weekend. *Faculty:* 17 full-time (2 women), 4 part-time/adjunct (1 woman). *Students:* 82 full-time (13 women), 4 part-time (1 woman); includes 1 minority (Two or more races, non-Hispanic/Latino), 80 international. Average age 27. 106 applicants, 52% accepted, 25 enrolled. In 2016, 17 master's, 3 doctorates awarded. *Degree requirements:* For master's, oral comprehensive exam or thesis; for doctorate, one foreign language, thesis/dissertation, candidacy exam, qualifying exam. *Entrance requirements:* For master's, GRE, minimum GPA of 2.75, three letters of recommendation, statement of purpose; for doctorate, GRE, minimum GPA of 3.0 with bachelor's degree, 3.5 with master's degree; three letters of recommendation; statement of purpose; resume. Additional exam requirements/recommendations for international students: Required—TOEFL (minimum score 550 paper-based; 79 iBT), IELTS (minimum score 6.5). *Application deadline:* Applications are processed on a rolling basis. Application fee: $45 ($70 for international students). Electronic applications accepted. *Expenses:* Tuition, state resident: full-time $8618; part-time $359 per credit hour. Tuition, nonresident: full-time $17,149; part-time $715 per credit hour. *Required fees:* $1652. *Financial support:* In 2016–17, 49 research assistantships with full and partial tuition reimbursements, 18 teaching assistantships with full tuition reimbursements were awarded. *Faculty research:* Computational electromagnetics and nondestructive testing, control systems, sensors and actuators applications and networks, alternative energy systems and hybrid vehicles, analog integrated circuit (IC) design, embedded systems. *Total annual research expenditures:* $1.5 million. *Unit head:* Dr. Joan Carletta, Interim Chair, 330-972-5993, E-mail: carlett@uakron.edu. *Application contact:* Dr. Hamid Bahrami, Graduate Director, 330-972-7940, E-mail: hrb@uakron.edu.
Website: http://www.uakron.edu/engineering/ECE/

The University of Alabama, Graduate School, College of Engineering, Department of Electrical and Computer Engineering, Tuscaloosa, AL 35487-0286. Offers electrical engineering (MS, PhD). *Program availability:* Part-time, online learning. *Faculty:* 23 full-time (4 women). *Students:* 54 full-time (8 women), 10 part-time (1 woman); includes 1 minority (Hispanic/Latino), 47 international. Average age 27. 82 applicants, 39% accepted, 17 enrolled. In 2016, 8 master's, 8 doctorates awarded. *Degree requirements:* For master's, thesis or alternative; for doctorate, one foreign language, comprehensive exam, thesis/dissertation. *Entrance requirements:* For master's, GRE (for students from non ABET-accredited schools), minimum GPA of 3.0 in last 60 hours of course work or overall; for doctorate, GRE (for students from non ABET-accredited schools), minimum GPA of 3.0 overall. Additional exam requirements/recommendations for international students: Required—TOEFL (minimum score 550 paper-based). *Application deadline:* For fall admission, 7/1 priority date for domestic students, 1/15 priority date for international students; for spring admission, 11/1 priority date for domestic students, 6/1 priority date for international students. Applications are processed on a rolling basis. Application fee: $50 ($60 for international students). Electronic applications accepted. *Expenses:* Tuition, state resident: full-time $10,470. Tuition, nonresident: full-time $26,950. *Financial support:* In 2016–17, 1 fellowship with full tuition reimbursement (averaging $15,000 per year), 14 research assistantships with full tuition reimbursements (averaging $14,000 per year), 6 teaching assistantships with full tuition reimbursements (averaging $11,025 per year) were awarded; health care benefits and unspecified assistantships also available. *Faculty research:* Devices and materials, electromechanical systems, embedded systems. *Total annual research expenditures:* $1.9 million. *Unit head:* Dr. Tim Haskew, Department Head, 205-348-1766, Fax: 205-348-6959, E-mail: thaskew@eng.ua.edu. *Application contact:* Steve Shepard, Graduate Program Coordinator/Professor, 205-348-1650, Fax: 205-348-6419, E-mail: sshepard@eng.ua.edu.
Website: http://ece.eng.ua.edu

The University of Alabama at Birmingham, School of Engineering, Program in Electrical Engineering, Birmingham, AL 35294. Offers computer engineering (PhD); electrical engineering (MSEE). *Program availability:* Part-time. *Faculty:* 10 full-time, 5 part-time/adjunct. *Students:* 10 full-time (2 women), 12 part-time (2 women); includes 18 minority (1 Black or African American, non-Hispanic/Latino; 15 Asian, non-Hispanic/Latino; 1 Hispanic/Latino; 1 Two or more races, non-Hispanic/Latino). Average age 29. 36 applicants, 83% accepted, 15 enrolled. In 2016, 9 master's awarded. *Degree requirements:* For master's, comprehensive exam, thesis (for some programs); for doctorate, comprehensive exam, thesis/dissertation. *Entrance requirements:* For master's, GRE, minimum GPA of 3.0 in all junior and senior electrical and computer engineering and mathematics courses attempted, letters of evaluation. Additional exam requirements/recommendations for international students: Required—TOEFL (minimum score 80 iBT), IELTS (minimum score 6.5). *Application deadline:* For fall admission, 7/1 for domestic and international students; for spring admission, 11/1 for domestic and international students; for summer admission, 4/1 for domestic and international

Electrical Engineering

students. Applications are processed on a rolling basis. Application fee: $50 ($60 for international students). Electronic applications accepted. *Expenses:* $396 per hour resident tuition; $935 per hour non-resident tuition; $150 per course online course fee. *Financial support:* In 2016–17, 18 students received support, including 3 research assistantships with full and partial tuition reimbursements available (averaging $15,960 per year), 14 teaching assistantships (averaging $5,520 per year); unspecified assistantships also available. *Total annual research expenditures:* $1,370. *Unit head:* Dr. Murat Tanik, Chair, 205-934-8440, Fax: 205-975-3337, E-mail: mtanik@uab.edu. *Application contact:* Holly Hebard, Director of Graduate School Operations, 205-934-8227, Fax: 205-934-8413, E-mail: gradschool@uab.edu.
Website: https://www.uab.edu/engineering/home/graduate#msee

The University of Alabama in Huntsville, School of Graduate Studies, College of Engineering, Department of Electrical and Computer Engineering, Huntsville, AL 35899. Offers computer engineering (MSE, PhD); electrical engineering (MSE, PhD), including optics and photonics technology (MSE); optical science and engineering (PhD); software engineering (MSSE). *Program availability:* Part-time, evening/weekend. *Degree requirements:* For master's, comprehensive exam, thesis or alternative, oral and written exams; for doctorate, comprehensive exam, thesis/dissertation, oral and written exams. *Entrance requirements:* For master's, GRE General Test, appropriate bachelor's degree, minimum GPA of 3.0; for doctorate, GRE General Test, minimum GPA of 3.0. Additional exam requirements/recommendations for international students: Required—TOEFL (minimum score 500 paper-based; 80 iBT), IELTS (minimum score 6.5). Electronic applications accepted. *Expenses:* Tuition, state resident: full-time $9834; part-time $600 per credit hour. Tuition, nonresident: full-time $21,830; part-time $1325 per credit hour. *Faculty research:* Advanced computer architecture and systems, fault tolerant computing and verification, computational electro-magnetics, nano-photonics and plasmonics, micro electro-mechanical (MEMS) systems.

University of Alaska Fairbanks, College of Engineering and Mines, Department of Electrical and Computer Engineering, Fairbanks, AK 99775-5915. Offers electrical engineering (MEE, MS). *Program availability:* Part-time. *Faculty:* 9 full-time (2 women). *Students:* 18 full-time (5 women), 4 part-time (1 woman); includes 1 minority (Hispanic/Latino), 9 international. Average age 26. 21 applicants, 57% accepted, 8 enrolled. In 2016, 2 master's awarded. *Degree requirements:* For master's, comprehensive exam. *Entrance requirements:* For master's, GRE General Test, bachelor's degree from accredited institution with minimum cumulative undergraduate and major GPA of 3.0. Additional exam requirements/recommendations for international students: Required—TOEFL (minimum score 550 paper-based; 79 iBT), IELTS (minimum score 6.5). *Application deadline:* For fall admission, 6/1 for domestic students, 3/1 for international students; for spring admission, 10/15 for domestic students, 9/1 for international students. Applications are processed on a rolling basis. Application fee: $60. Electronic applications accepted. *Expenses:* $533 per credit resident tuition, $673 per semester resident fees; $1,088 per credit non-resident tuition, $835 per semester non-resident fees. *Financial support:* In 2016–17, 7 research assistantships with full tuition reimbursements (averaging $12,563 per year), 9 teaching assistantships with full tuition reimbursements (averaging $7,023 per year) were awarded; fellowships with full tuition reimbursements, career-related internships or fieldwork, Federal Work-Study, scholarships/grants, health care benefits, and unspecified assistantships also available. Support available to part-time students. Financial award application deadline: 7/1; financial award applicants required to submit FAFSA. *Faculty research:* Geomagnetically-induced currents in power lines, electromagnetic wave propagation, laser radar systems, bioinformatics, distributed sensor networks. *Unit head:* Dr. Charles Mayer, Chair, 907-474-7137, Fax: 907-474-5135, E-mail: uaf-cem-ece-dept@alaska.edu. *Application contact:* Mary Kreta, Director of Admissions, 907-474-7500, Fax:

907-474-7097, E-mail: admissions@uaf.edu.
Website: http://cem.uaf.edu/ece/

University of Alberta, Faculty of Graduate Studies and Research, Department of Electrical and Computer Engineering, Edmonton, AB T6G 2E1, Canada. Offers communications (M Eng, M Sc, PhD); computer engineering (M Eng, M Sc, PhD); electromagnetics (M Eng, M Sc, PhD); nanotechnology and microdevices (M Eng, M Sc, PhD); power/power electronics (M Eng, M Sc, PhD); systems (M Eng, M Sc, PhD). Terminal master's awarded for partial completion of doctoral program. *Degree requirements:* For master's, thesis; for doctorate, thesis/dissertation. *Entrance requirements:* Additional exam requirements/recommendations for international students: Required—TOEFL. Electronic applications accepted. *Faculty research:* Controls, communications, microelectronics, electromagnetics.

The University of Arizona, College of Engineering, Department of Electrical and Computer Engineering, Tucson, AZ 85721. Offers MS, PhD. *Program availability:* Part-time. *Degree requirements:* For master's, thesis (for some programs); for doctorate, thesis/dissertation. *Entrance requirements:* For master's, GRE General Test, 3 letters of recommendation, statement of purpose; for doctorate, GRE General Test, master's degree in related field, 3 letters of recommendation, statement of purpose. Additional exam requirements/recommendations for international students: Required—TOEFL (minimum score 550 paper-based; 79 iBT). Electronic applications accepted. *Faculty research:* Communication systems, control systems, signal processing, computer-aided logic.

University of Arkansas, Graduate School, College of Engineering, Department of Electrical Engineering, Fayetteville, AR 72701. Offers electrical engineering (MSEE, PhD); telecommunications engineering (MS Tc E). In 2016, 24 master's, 4 doctorates awarded. *Degree requirements:* For master's, thesis optional; for doctorate, one foreign language, thesis/dissertation. *Entrance requirements:* For master's and doctorate, GRE General Test. *Application deadline:* For fall admission, 4/1 for international students; for spring admission, 10/1 for international students. Applications are processed on a rolling basis. Application fee: $40 ($50 for international students). Electronic applications accepted. *Financial support:* In 2016–17, 48 research assistantships, 8 teaching assistantships were awarded; fellowships with tuition reimbursements, career-related internships or fieldwork, and Federal Work-Study also available. Support available to part-time students. Financial award application deadline: 4/1; financial award applicants required to submit FAFSA. *Unit head:* Dr. Juan Balda, Department Chair, 479-575-3005, Fax: 479-575-7967, E-mail: jbalda@uark.edu. *Application contact:* Dr. Hameed Naseem, Graduate Coordinator, 479-575-6581, E-mail: hnaseem@uark.edu.
Website: http://www.eleg.uark.edu/

University of Bridgeport, School of Engineering, Department of Electrical Engineering, Bridgeport, CT 06604. Offers MS. *Program availability:* Part-time, evening/weekend. Terminal master's awarded for partial completion of doctoral program. *Degree requirements:* For master's, thesis optional. *Entrance requirements:* Additional exam requirements/recommendations for international students: Recommended—TOEFL (minimum score 550 paper-based; 80 iBT), IELTS (minimum score 6.5). Electronic applications accepted. *Expenses:* Contact institution.

The University of British Columbia, Faculty of Applied Science, Department of Electrical and Computer Engineering, Vancouver, BC V6T 1Z4, Canada. Offers M Eng, MA Sc, PhD. *Program availability:* Part-time. *Degree requirements:* For master's, thesis (for some programs); for doctorate, thesis/dissertation. *Entrance requirements:* Additional exam requirements/recommendations for international students: Required—TOEFL, IELTS. Application fee: $100 Canadian dollars ($162 Canadian dollars for international students). Electronic applications accepted. *Expenses:* $4,802 per year tuition and fees, $8,436 per year international. *Financial support:* Fellowships, research

assistantships, teaching assistantships, career-related internships or fieldwork, institutionally sponsored loans, scholarships/grants, and tuition waivers (full and partial) available. *Faculty research:* Applied electromagnetics, biomedical engineering, communications and signal processing, computer and software engineering, power engineering, robotics, solid-state, systems and control. *Application contact:* Ross Sheppard, Graduate Admissions Coordinator, 604-822-6190, E-mail: help@ece.ubc.ca.
Website: https://www.ece.ubc.ca/

University of Calgary, Faculty of Graduate Studies, Schulich School of Engineering, Department of Electrical and Computer Engineering, Calgary, AB T2N 1N4, Canada. Offers M Eng, M Sc, PhD. *Program availability:* Part-time. *Degree requirements:* For master's, thesis (for M Sc); for doctorate, thesis/dissertation, candidacy exam. *Entrance requirements:* For master's, minimum GPA of 3.0; for doctorate, minimum GPA of 3.5. Additional exam requirements/recommendations for international students: Required—TOEFL (minimum score 550 paper-based; 80 iBT) or IELTS (minimum score 7). Electronic applications accepted. *Faculty research:* Biomedical and bioelectrics, telecommunications and signal processing, software and computer engineering, power and control, microelectronics and instrumentation.

University of California, Berkeley, Graduate Division, College of Engineering, Department of Electrical Engineering and Computer Sciences, Berkeley, CA 94720-1500. Offers computer science (MS, PhD); electrical engineering (M Eng, MS, PhD). *Students:* 580 full-time (124 women); includes 146 minority (11 Black or African American, non-Hispanic/Latino; 110 Asian, non-Hispanic/Latino; 25 Hispanic/Latino), 329 international. Average age 27. 4,215 applicants, 142 enrolled. In 2016, 89 master's, 78 doctorates awarded. Terminal master's awarded for partial completion of doctoral program. *Degree requirements:* For master's, comprehensive exam (for some programs), thesis (for some programs), comprehensive exam or thesis; for doctorate, thesis/dissertation, qualifying exam. *Entrance requirements:* For master's and doctorate, GRE General Test, minimum GPA of 3.0, 3 letters of recommendation. Additional exam requirements/recommendations for international students: Required—TOEFL (minimum score 570 paper-based; 90 iBT). *Application deadline:* For fall admission, 12/15 for domestic students. Application fee: $105 ($125 for international students). Electronic applications accepted. *Financial support:* Fellowships, research assistantships, teaching assistantships, scholarships/grants, and unspecified assistantships available. Financial award applicants required to submit FAFSA. *Unit head:* Prof. Jitendra Malik, Chair, 510-642-3214, E-mail: eecs-chair@eecs.berkeley.edu. *Application contact:* Admission Assistant, 510-642-3068, Fax: 510-642-7644, E-mail: gradadmissions@eecs.berkeley.edu.
Website: http://eecs.berkeley.edu

University of California, Davis, College of Engineering, Program in Electrical and Computer Engineering, Davis, CA 95616. Offers MS, PhD. Terminal master's awarded for partial completion of doctoral program. *Degree requirements:* For master's, comprehensive exam (for some programs), thesis (for some programs); for doctorate, thesis/dissertation, preliminary and qualifying exams, thesis defense. *Entrance requirements:* For master's, GRE General Test, minimum GPA of 3.2; for doctorate, GRE, minimum graduate GPA of 3.5. Additional exam requirements/recommendations for international students: Required—TOEFL (minimum score 550 paper-based). Electronic applications accepted.

University of California, Irvine, Henry Samueli School of Engineering, Department of Electrical Engineering and Computer Science, Irvine, CA 92697. Offers electrical engineering and computer science (MS, PhD); networked systems (MS, PhD). *Program availability:* Part-time. *Students:* 305 full-time (77 women), 22 part-time (7 women); includes 21 minority (18 Asian, non-Hispanic/Latino; 1 Hispanic/Latino; 2 Two or more races, non-Hispanic/Latino), 280 international. Average age 26. 1,808 applicants, 21% accepted, 105 enrolled. In 2016, 109 master's, 15 doctorates awarded. Terminal master's awarded for partial completion of doctoral program. *Degree requirements:* For doctorate, thesis/dissertation. *Entrance requirements:* For master's and doctorate, GRE General Test, minimum GPA of 3.0, 3 letters of recommendation. Additional exam requirements/recommendations for international students: Required—TOEFL (minimum score 550 paper-based). *Application deadline:* For fall admission, 1/15 priority date for domestic students, 1/15 for international students. Applications are processed on a rolling basis. Application fee: $105 ($125 for international students). Electronic applications accepted. *Financial support:* Fellowships, research assistantships with full tuition reimbursements, teaching assistantships, institutionally sponsored loans, traineeships, health care benefits, and unspecified assistantships available. Financial award application deadline: 3/1; financial award applicants required to submit FAFSA. *Faculty research:* Optics and electronic devices and circuits, signal processing, communications, machine vision, power electronics. *Unit head:* Prof. H. Kumar Wickramasinghe, Chair, 949-824-2213, E-mail: hkwick@uci.edu. *Application contact:* Jean Bennett, Director of Graduate Student Affairs, 949-824-6475, Fax: 949-824-8200, E-mail: jean.bennett@uci.edu.
Website: http://www.eng.uci.edu/dept/eecs

University of California, Los Angeles, Graduate Division, Henry Samueli School of Engineering and Applied Science, Department of Electrical Engineering, Los Angeles, CA 90095-1594. Offers MS, PhD. *Faculty:* 47 full-time (7 women), 12 part-time/adjunct (0 women). *Students:* 554 full-time (111 women); includes 54 minority (1 Black or African American, non-Hispanic/Latino; 1 American Indian or Alaska Native, non-Hispanic/Latino; 44 Asian, non-Hispanic/Latino; 7 Hispanic/Latino; 1 Two or more races, non-Hispanic/Latino), 463 international. 1,962 applicants, 23% accepted, 187 enrolled. In 2016, 152 master's, 37 doctorates awarded. *Degree requirements:* For master's, comprehensive exam or thesis; for doctorate, thesis/dissertation, qualifying exams. *Entrance requirements:* For master's, GRE General Test, minimum GPA of 3.0; for doctorate, GRE General Test, minimum GPA of 3.25. Additional exam requirements/recommendations for international students: Required—TOEFL (minimum score 560 paper-based; 87 iBT), IELTS (minimum score 7). *Application deadline:* For fall admission, 12/15 for domestic and international students. Application fee: $105 ($125 for international students). Electronic applications accepted. *Financial support:* In 2016–17, 238 fellowships, 440 research assistantships, 114 teaching assistantships were awarded; career-related internships or fieldwork, Federal Work-Study, institutionally sponsored loans, and tuition waivers (full and partial) also available. Financial award application deadline: 12/15; financial award applicants required to submit FAFSA. *Faculty research:* Circuits and embedded systems, physical and wave electronics, signals and systems. *Total annual research expenditures:* $23.3 million. *Unit head:* Dr. Gregory J. Pottie, Chair, 310-825-8150, E-mail: pottie@ee.ucla.edu. *Application contact:* Deeona Columbia, Student Affairs Officer, 310-825-7574, E-mail: deeona@seas.ucla.edu.
Website: http://www.ee.ucla.edu/

University of California, Merced, Graduate Division, School of Engineering, Merced, CA 95343. Offers biological engineering and small scale technologies (MS, PhD); electrical engineering and computer science (MS, PhD); environmental systems (MS, PhD); mechanical engineering (MS); mechanical engineering and applied mechanics (PhD). *Faculty:* 44 full-time (7 women). *Students:* 170 full-time (52 women), 2 part-time (0 women); includes 34 minority (2 Black or African American, non-Hispanic/Latino; 11 Asian, non-Hispanic/Latino; 14 Hispanic/Latino; 2 Native Hawaiian or other Pacific Islander, non-Hispanic/Latino; 5 Two or more races, non-Hispanic/Latino), 99 international. Average age 28. 307 applicants, 35% accepted, 46 enrolled. In 2016, 15 master's, 12 doctorates awarded. Terminal master's awarded for partial completion of doctoral program. *Degree requirements:* For master's, variable foreign language requirement, comprehensive exam, thesis or alternative; for doctorate, variable foreign language requirement, comprehensive exam, thesis/dissertation. *Entrance requirements:* For master's and doctorate, GRE. Additional exam requirements/recommendations for international students: Required—TOEFL (minimum score 550 paper-based; 80 iBT); Recommended—IELTS (minimum score 7). *Application deadline:* For fall admission, 1/15 priority date for domestic and international students. Applications are processed on a rolling basis. Application fee: $90 ($110 for international students). Electronic applications accepted. *Expenses:* Contact institution. *Financial support:* In 2016–17, 150 students received support, including 16 fellowships with full tuition reimbursements available (averaging $19,088 per year), 45 research assistantships with full tuition reimbursements available (averaging $18,389 per year), 89 teaching assistantships with full tuition reimbursements available (averaging $19,249 per year); scholarships/grants, traineeships, and health care benefits also available. Financial award application deadline: 1/15. *Faculty research:* Water resources, biotechnology, renewable energy, big data, cyber-physical systems. *Total annual research expenditures:* $3.3 million. *Unit head:* Dr. Mark Matsumoto, Dean, Fax: 209-228-4047, E-mail: mmatsumoto@ucmerced.edu. *Application contact:* Tsu Ya, Director of Admissions and Academic Services, 209-228-4521, Fax: 209-228-6906, E-mail: tya@ucmerced.edu.

University of California, Riverside, Graduate Division, Department of Electrical Engineering, Riverside, CA 92521-0102. Offers electrical engineering (MS, PhD), including computer engineering (MS), control and robotics (PhD). Terminal master's awarded for partial completion of doctoral program. *Degree requirements:* For master's, thesis optional; for doctorate, thesis/dissertation, qualifying exams. *Entrance requirements:* For master's and doctorate, GRE General Test, minimum GPA of 3.25. Additional exam requirements/recommendations for international students: Required—TOEFL (minimum score 550 paper-based; 80 iBT). Electronic applications accepted. *Expenses:* Tuition, state resident: full-time $16,666. Tuition, nonresident: full-time $31,768. *Required fees:* $11,055.54 per quarter. $3685.18 per quarter. Tuition and fees vary according to campus/location and program. *Faculty research:* Solid state devices, integrated circuits, signal processing.

University of California, San Diego, Graduate Division, Department of Electrical and Computer Engineering, La Jolla, CA 92093. Offers applied ocean science (MS, PhD); applied physics (MS, PhD); communication theory and systems (MS, PhD); computer engineering (MS, PhD); electronic circuits and systems (MS, PhD); intelligent systems, robotics and control (MS, PhD); medical devices and systems (MS, PhD); nanoscale devices and systems (MS, PhD); photonics (MS, PhD); signal and image processing (MS, PhD). *Students:* 612 full-time (119 women), 39 part-time (8 women). 2,885 applicants, 25% accepted, 269 enrolled. In 2016, 147 master's, 43 doctorates awarded. Terminal master's awarded for partial completion of doctoral program. *Degree requirements:* For master's, comprehensive exam (for some programs), thesis (for some programs); for doctorate, comprehensive exam, thesis/dissertation. *Entrance requirements:* For master's and doctorate, GRE General Test, minimum GPA of 3.0, resume or curriculum vitae (recommended). Additional exam requirements/recommendations for international students: Required—TOEFL (minimum score 550 paper-based; 80 iBT), IELTS (minimum score 7), PTE (minimum score 65). *Application deadline:* For fall admission, 12/13 for domestic students. Application fee: $105 ($125 for international students). Electronic applications accepted. *Expenses:* Tuition, state resident: full-time $11,220. Tuition, nonresident: full-time $26,322. *Required fees:* $1864. *Financial support:* Fellowships, research assistantships, teaching assistantships, scholarships/grants, traineeships, and unspecified assistantships available. Financial award applicants required to submit FAFSA. *Faculty research:* Applied ocean science; applied physics; communication theory and systems; computer engineering; electronic circuits and systems; intelligent systems, robotics and control; medical devices and systems; nanoscale devices and systems; photonics; signal and image processing. *Unit head:* Truong Nguyen, Chair, 858-822-5554, E-mail: nguyent@ece.ucsd.edu. *Application contact:* Melanie Lynn, Graduate Admissions Coordinator, 858-822-3213, E-mail: ecegradapps@ece.ucsd.edu.
Website: http://ece.ucsd.edu/

University of California, Santa Barbara, Graduate Division, College of Engineering, Department of Electrical and Computer Engineering, Santa Barbara, CA 93106-2014. Offers communications, control and signal processing (MS, PhD); computer engineering (MS, PhD); electronics and photonics (MS, PhD); MS/PhD. *Degree requirements:* For master's, comprehensive exam, thesis; for doctorate, thesis/dissertation. *Entrance requirements:* For master's and doctorate, GRE General Test. Additional exam requirements/recommendations for international students: Required—TOEFL (minimum score 550 paper-based; 80 iBT), IELTS (minimum score 7). Electronic applications accepted. *Faculty research:* Communications, signal processing, computer engineering, control, electronics and photonics.

University of California, Santa Cruz, Jack Baskin School of Engineering, Department of Electrical Engineering, Santa Cruz, CA 95064. Offers MS, PhD. *Faculty:* 11 full-time (0 women), 4 part-time/adjunct (0 women). *Students:* 96 full-time (12 women), 10 part-time (1 woman); includes 11 minority (1 Black or African American, non-Hispanic/Latino; 6 Asian, non-Hispanic/Latino; 3 Hispanic/Latino; 1 Native Hawaiian or other Pacific Islander, non-Hispanic/Latino), 74 international. 306 applicants, 57% accepted, 44 enrolled. In 2016, 22 master's, 8 doctorates awarded. Terminal master's awarded for partial completion of doctoral program. *Degree requirements:* For master's, thesis or comprehensive exam; for doctorate, thesis/dissertation, qualifying exam. *Entrance requirements:* For master's and doctorate, GRE General Test. Additional exam requirements/recommendations for international students: Required—TOEFL (minimum score 570 paper-based; 89 iBT); Recommended—IELTS (minimum score 8). *Application deadline:* For fall admission, 1/3 for domestic and international students. Application fee: $105 ($125 for international students). Electronic applications accepted. *Financial support:* In 2016–17, 27 students received support, including 14 fellowships (averaging $19,494 per year), 48 research assistantships (averaging $20,043 per year), 20 teaching assistantships (averaging $20,052 per year); institutionally sponsored loans and tuition waivers (full and partial) also available. Financial award application deadline: 1/3; financial award applicants required to submit FAFSA. *Faculty research:* Photonics and electronics, signal processing and communications, remote sensing, nanotechnology. *Unit head:* Joel Kubby, Chair/Professor, E-mail: jkubby@soe.ucsc.edu. *Application contact:* Lisa Slater, Graduate Student Advisor, 831-459-3609, E-mail: bsoe-ga@rt.ucsc.edu.
Website: https://www.soe.ucsc.edu/departments/electrical-engineering

University of Central Florida, College of Engineering and Computer Science, Department of Electrical Engineering and Computer Science, Program in Electrical Engineering, Orlando, FL 32816. Offers electrical engineering (MSEE, PhD). *Program availability:* Part-time, evening/weekend. *Students:* 165 full-time (34 women), 45 part-time (7 women); includes 33 minority (5 Black or African American, non-Hispanic/Latino; 10 Asian, non-Hispanic/Latino; 18 Hispanic/Latino), 134 international. Average age 29.

277 applicants, 74% accepted, 60 enrolled. In 2016, 53 master's, 16 doctorates awarded. *Degree requirements:* For master's, thesis or alternative; for doctorate, thesis/dissertation, departmental qualifying exam, candidacy exam. *Entrance requirements:* For master's, GRE General Test, minimum GPA of 3.0 in last 60 hours; for doctorate, GRE General Test, minimum GPA of 3.5 in last 60 hours. Additional exam requirements/recommendations for international students: Required—TOEFL. *Application deadline:* For fall admission, 7/15 for domestic students; for spring admission, 12/1 for domestic students. Application fee: $30. Electronic applications accepted. *Expenses:* Tuition, state resident: part-time $288.16 per credit hour. Tuition, nonresident: part-time $1071.31 per credit hour. *Financial support:* In 2016–17, 89 students received support, including 21 fellowships with partial tuition reimbursements available (averaging $9,075 per year), 60 research assistantships with partial tuition reimbursements available (averaging $12,151 per year), 36 teaching assistantships with partial tuition reimbursements available (averaging $10,298 per year); tuition waivers (partial) also available. Financial award application deadline: 3/1; financial award applicants required to submit FAFSA. *Unit head:* Dr. Zhihua Qu, Chair, 407-823-5976, Fax: 407-823-5835, E-mail: qu@ucf.edu. *Application contact:* Assistant Director, Graduate Admissions, 407-823-2766, Fax: 407-823-6442, E-mail: gradadmissions@ucf.edu.
Website: http://web.eecs.ucf.edu/

University of Central Oklahoma, The Jackson College of Graduate Studies, College of Mathematics and Science, Department of Engineering and Physics, Edmond, OK 73034-5209. Offers biomedical engineering (MS); electrical engineering (MS); mechanical systems (MS); physics (MS). *Program availability:* Part-time. *Degree requirements:* For master's, thesis optional. *Entrance requirements:* For master's, GRE, 24 hours of course work in physics or equivalent, mathematics through differential equations, minimum GPA of 2.75 overall and 3.0 in last 60 hours attempted. Additional exam requirements/recommendations for international students: Required—TOEFL (minimum score 550 paper-based). Electronic applications accepted.

University of Cincinnati, Graduate School, College of Engineering and Applied Science, Department of Electrical Engineering and Computing Systems, Program in Electrical Engineering, Cincinnati, OH 45221. Offers MS, PhD. *Degree requirements:* For master's, thesis; for doctorate, thesis/dissertation. *Entrance requirements:* For master's and doctorate, GRE General Test. Additional exam requirements/recommendations for international students: Required—TOEFL (minimum score 550 paper-based). *Expenses: Tuition, area resident:* Full-time $12,790; part-time $389 per credit hour. Tuition, state resident: full-time $13,290; part-time $419 per credit hour. Tuition, nonresident: full-time $24,532; part-time $976 per credit hour. *International tuition:* $24,832 full-time. *Required fees:* $3958; $140 per credit hour. Tuition and fees vary according to course load, degree level, program and reciprocity agreements. *Faculty research:* Integrated circuits and optical devices, charge-coupled devices, photosensitive devices.

University of Colorado Boulder, Graduate School, College of Engineering and Applied Science, Department of Electrical, Computer and Energy Engineering, Boulder, CO 80309. Offers ME, MS, PhD. *Faculty:* 40 full-time (7 women). *Students:* 312 full-time (66 women), 42 part-time (8 women); includes 30 minority (3 Black or African American, non-Hispanic/Latino; 12 Asian, non-Hispanic/Latino; 10 Hispanic/Latino; 5 Two or more races, non-Hispanic/Latino), 230 international. Average age 27. 858 applicants, 40% accepted, 128 enrolled. In 2016, 68 master's, 18 doctorates awarded. Terminal master's awarded for partial completion of doctoral program. *Degree requirements:* For master's, thesis or alternative; for doctorate, one foreign language, thesis/dissertation, departmental qualifying exam. *Entrance requirements:* For master's, GRE General Test, minimum undergraduate GPA of 3.0; for doctorate, GRE General Test, minimum undergraduate GPA of 3.5. *Application deadline:* For fall admission, 1/15 for domestic and international students; for spring admission, 9/1 for domestic and international students. Applications are processed on a rolling basis. Application fee: $60 ($80 for international students). Electronic applications accepted. Application fee is waived when completed online. *Financial support:* In 2016–17, 528 students received support, including 139 fellowships (averaging $8,551 per year), 97 research assistantships with full and partial tuition reimbursements available (averaging $37,877 per year), 30 teaching assistantships with full and partial tuition reimbursements available (averaging $17,238 per year); institutionally sponsored loans, scholarships/grants, health care benefits, and unspecified assistantships also available. Financial award application deadline: 1/15; financial award applicants required to submit FAFSA. *Faculty research:* Electrical engineering/electronics, electromagnetic propagation, solid state electronics, electromagnetics, circuits and systems. *Total annual research expenditures:* $10.8 million. *Application contact:* E-mail: ecegrad@colorado.edu.
Website: http://ecee.colorado.edu

University of Colorado Colorado Springs, College of Engineering and Applied Science, Department of Electrical and Computer Engineering, Colorado Springs, CO 80918. Offers electrical engineering (MS). *Program availability:* Part-time, evening/weekend. *Faculty:* 9 full-time (2 women), 2 part-time/adjunct (0 women). *Students:* 7 full-time (1 woman), 40 part-time (7 women); includes 8 minority (3 Asian, non-Hispanic/Latino; 4 Hispanic/Latino; 1 Two or more races, non-Hispanic/Latino), 16 international. Average age 30. 34 applicants, 74% accepted, 7 enrolled. In 2016, 17 master's awarded. *Degree requirements:* For master's, thesis (for some programs), final oral exam or thesis. *Entrance requirements:* For master's, GRE (minimum score of 1200 combined on verbal and quantitative), minimum GPA of 3.0, BS or course work in electrical engineering. Additional exam requirements/recommendations for international students: Required—TOEFL (minimum score 550 paper-based; 78 iBT), IELTS (minimum score 6). *Application deadline:* For fall admission, 4/1 for international students; for spring admission, 10/1 for international students. Applications are processed on a rolling basis. Application fee: $60 ($100 for international students). Electronic applications accepted. *Expenses:* Contact institution. *Financial support:* In 2016–17, 4 students received support. Career-related internships or fieldwork, Federal Work-Study, scholarships/grants, and unspecified assistantships available. Support available to part-time students. Financial award application deadline: 3/1; financial award applicants required to submit FAFSA. *Faculty research:* Micro heater array development, testing and testable design of digital and analog circuits, boards, and systems, linear and nonlinear adaptive filtering; dynamic system modeling, state estimation and control, computer architecture and design, wireless communication systems, DSP algorithm development for communication systems, sensor networks, statistical signal processing, real-time digital signal processing, microwave and RF systems, traveling-wave tubes. *Total annual research expenditures:* $554,264. *Unit head:* Dr. T. S. Kalkur, Chair, 719-255-3147, Fax: 719-255-3589. *Application contact:* Eva Wynhorst, Program Assistant, 719-255-3548, Fax: 719-255-3589, E-mail: ewynhors@uccs.edu.
Website: http://www.uccs.edu/~ece/

University of Colorado Denver, College of Engineering and Applied Science, Department of Electrical Engineering, Denver, CO 80217. Offers MS, EASPh D. *Program availability:* Part-time, evening/weekend. *Faculty:* 10 full-time (0 women), 8 part-time/adjunct (1 woman). *Students:* 45 full-time (8 women), 20 part-time (2 women); includes 9 minority (1 Black or African American, non-Hispanic/Latino; 3 Asian, non-Hispanic/Latino; 3 Hispanic/Latino; 1 Native Hawaiian or other Pacific Islander, non-Hispanic/Latino; 1 Two or more races, non-Hispanic/Latino), 38 international. Average age 27. 131 applicants, 55% accepted, 11 enrolled. In 2016, 38 master's awarded. *Degree requirements:* For master's, thesis or project, 30 credit hours; for doctorate, thesis/dissertation, 60 credit hours beyond master's work (30 of which are for dissertation research). *Entrance requirements:* For master's and doctorate, GRE, three letters of recommendation, personal statement. Additional exam requirements/recommendations for international students: Required—TOEFL (minimum score 550 paper-based; 80 iBT), TOEFL (minimum score 600 paper-based) for EAS PhD; Recommended—IELTS (minimum score 6.8). *Application deadline:* For fall admission, 5/1 for domestic students, 4/15 for international students; for spring admission, 10/1 for domestic students, 9/15 for international students. Application fee: $50 ($75 for international students). Electronic applications accepted. *Expenses:* Contact institution. *Financial support:* In 2016–17, 6 students received support. Fellowships, research assistantships, teaching assistantships, career-related internships or fieldwork, Federal Work-Study, institutionally sponsored loans, scholarships/grants, traineeships, and unspecified assistantships available. Financial award application deadline: 4/1; financial award applicants required to submit FAFSA. *Faculty research:* Communication and signal processing, embedded systems, electromagnetic fields and matter, energy and power systems, photonics and biomedical imaging. *Unit head:* Dr. Stephen Gedney, Chair, 303-352-3744, E-mail: stephen.gedney@ucdenver.edu. *Application contact:* Annie Bennett, Program Assistant, 303-556-8108, E-mail: annie.bennett@ucdenver.edu.
Website: http://www.ucdenver.edu/academics/colleges/Engineering/Programs/Electrical-Engineering/Pages/ElectricalEngineering.aspx

University of Colorado Denver, College of Engineering and Applied Science, Master of Engineering Program, Denver, CO 80217-3364. Offers civil engineering (M Eng), including civil engineering, geographic information systems, transportation systems; electrical engineering (M Eng); mechanical engineering (M Eng). *Program availability:* Part-time. *Students:* 35 full-time (9 women), 23 part-time (7 women); includes 5 minority (1 American Indian or Alaska Native, non-Hispanic/Latino; 2 Hispanic/Latino; 2 Two or more races, non-Hispanic/Latino), 11 international. Average age 31. 75 applicants, 63% accepted, 13 enrolled. In 2016, 17 master's awarded. *Degree requirements:* For master's, comprehensive exam, 27 credit hours of course work, 3 credit hours of report or thesis work. *Entrance requirements:* For master's, GRE (for those with GPA below 2.75), transcripts, references, statement of purpose. Additional exam requirements/recommendations for international students: Required—TOEFL (minimum score 537 paper-based; 75 iBT); Recommended—IELTS (minimum score 6.5). *Application deadline:* For fall admission, 4/1 for domestic students, 3/1 for international students; for spring admission, 10/1 for domestic students, 9/15 for international students. Applications are processed on a rolling basis. Application fee: $50 ($75 for international students). Electronic applications accepted. *Expenses:* Contact institution. *Financial support:* In 2016–17, 120 students received support. Fellowships, research assistantships, teaching assistantships, Federal Work-Study, institutionally sponsored loans, scholarships/grants, traineeships, and unspecified assistantships available. Financial award application deadline: 4/1; financial award applicants required to submit FAFSA. *Faculty research:* Civil, electrical and mechanical engineering. *Application contact:* Graduate School Admissions, 303-315-2179, E-mail: ceasgaapplications@ucdenver.edu.
Website: http://www.ucdenver.edu/academics/colleges/Engineering/admissions/Masters/Pages/MastersAdmissions.aspx

University of Connecticut, Graduate School, School of Engineering, Department of Electrical and Computer Engineering, Field of Electrical Engineering, Storrs, CT 06269. Offers MS, PhD. Terminal master's awarded for partial completion of doctoral program. *Degree requirements:* For master's, comprehensive exam; for doctorate, thesis/dissertation. *Entrance requirements:* For master's and doctorate, GRE General Test. Additional exam requirements/recommendations for international students: Required—TOEFL (minimum score 550 paper-based). Electronic applications accepted.

University of Dayton, Department of Electrical and Computer Engineering, Dayton, OH 45469. Offers computer engineering (MS); electrical engineering (MSEE, PhD). *Program availability:* Part-time. *Faculty:* 17 full-time (0 women), 16 part-time/adjunct (2 women). *Students:* 145 full-time (30 women), 14 part-time (4 women); includes 10 minority (2 Black or African American, non-Hispanic/Latino; 6 Asian, non-Hispanic/Latino; 2 Two or more races, non-Hispanic/Latino), 100 international. Average age 28. 82 applicants, 22% accepted. In 2016, 88 master's, 8 doctorates awarded. *Degree requirements:* For master's, thesis optional; for doctorate, variable foreign language requirement, thesis/dissertation. *Entrance requirements:* For master's, minimum GPA of 3.2, 3 letters of recommendation, bachelor's degree, transcripts; for doctorate, minimum GPA of 3.2, master's degree, transcripts, 3 letters of recommendation. Additional exam requirements/recommendations for international students: Required—TOEFL (minimum score 550 paper-based; 80 iBT). *Application deadline:* For fall admission, 8/1 for domestic students, 5/1 priority date for international students; for spring admission, 11/1 priority date for international students. Applications are processed on a rolling basis. Application fee: $0 ($50 for international students). Electronic applications accepted. *Expenses:* $890 per credit hour (for MS), $970 per credit hour (for PhD); $25 registration fee. *Financial support:* In 2016–17, 17 research assistantships with full tuition reimbursements (averaging $12,500 per year), 30 teaching assistantships with full tuition reimbursements (averaging $10,000 per year) were awarded; institutionally sponsored loans, health care benefits, and unspecified assistantships also available. Financial award application deadline: 3/1; financial award applicants required to submit FAFSA. *Faculty research:* Electrical engineering, video processing, leaky wave antennas, thin film research. *Unit head:* Dr. Guru Subramanyam, Chair, 937-229-3188, Fax: 937-229-4529, E-mail: gsubramanyam1@udayton.edu. *Application contact:* E-mail: graduateadmission@udayton.edu.
Website: https://www.udayton.edu/engineering/departments/electrical_and_computer/index.php

University of Delaware, College of Engineering, Department of Electrical and Computer Engineering, Newark, DE 19716. Offers MSECE, PhD. *Program availability:* Part-time, online learning. Terminal master's awarded for partial completion of doctoral program. *Degree requirements:* For master's, thesis optional; for doctorate, thesis/dissertation. *Entrance requirements:* For master's, GRE General Test; for doctorate, GRE General Test, qualifying exam. Additional exam requirements/recommendations for international students: Required—TOEFL. Electronic applications accepted. *Faculty research:* HIV evolution during dynamic therapy, compressive sensing in imaging, sensor, networks, and UWB radios, computer network time synchronization, silicon spintronics, devices and imaging in the high-terahertz band.

University of Denver, Daniel Felix Ritchie School of Engineering and Computer Science, Department of Electrical and Computer Engineering, Denver, CO 80208. Offers computer engineering (MS); electrical and computer engineering (PhD); electrical engineering (MS); engineering (MS); mechatronic systems engineering (MS, PhD). *Program availability:* Part-time, evening/weekend. *Faculty:* 13 full-time (1 woman). *Students:* 6 full-time (1 woman), 61 part-time (13 women); includes 6 minority (2 Black or African American, non-Hispanic/Latino; 1 Asian, non-Hispanic/Latino; 2 Hispanic/Latino; 1 Two or more races, non-Hispanic/Latino), 36 international. Average age 30. 56

applicants, 61% accepted, 14 enrolled. In 2016, 39 master's, 5 doctorates awarded. Terminal master's awarded for partial completion of doctoral program. *Degree requirements:* For master's, thesis optional, proficiency in high- or low-level computer language; for doctorate, comprehensive exam, thesis/dissertation, proficiency in high- or low-level computer language. *Entrance requirements:* For master's, GRE General Test, bachelor's degree, transcripts, personal statement, resume or curriculum vitae, three letters of recommendation; for doctorate, GRE General Test, master's degree, transcripts, personal statement, resume or curriculum vitae, three letters of recommendation. Additional exam requirements/recommendations for international students: Required—TOEFL (minimum score 550 paper-based; 80 iBT). *Application deadline:* For fall admission, 2/1 priority date for domestic and international students. Applications are processed on a rolling basis. Application fee: $65. Electronic applications accepted. *Expenses:* $29,022 per year full-time. *Financial support:* In 2016–17, 39 students received support, including 9 research assistantships with tuition reimbursements available (averaging $11,897 per year), 1 teaching assistantship with tuition reimbursement available (averaging $17,496 per year); Federal Work-Study, scholarships/grants, and unspecified assistantships also available. Financial award application deadline: 2/15; financial award applicants required to submit FAFSA. *Faculty research:* Mechatronic systems, unmanned systems, service robotics, smart grid, sensor fusion. *Total annual research expenditures:* $1.5 million. *Unit head:* Dr. Kimon Valavanis, Professor/Chair, 303-871-2586, Fax: 303-871-2194, E-mail: kimon.valavanis@du.edu. *Application contact:* Molly Dunn, Assistant to the Chair, 303-871-6618, Fax: 303-871-2194, E-mail: molly.dunn@du.edu.
Website: http://ritchieschool.du.edu/departments/ece/

University of Detroit Mercy, College of Engineering and Science, Detroit, MI 48221. Offers chemistry (MS); civil and environmental engineering (DE); electrical and computer engineering (ME); electrical engineering (DE); engineering management (M Eng Mgt); environmental engineering (MEE); mechanical engineering (MME, DE); product development (MS); software engineering (MSSE); teaching of mathematics (MATM). *Program availability:* Part-time, evening/weekend. *Degree requirements:* For doctorate, thesis/dissertation. Electronic applications accepted. Application fee is waived when completed online. *Expenses:* Contact institution.

University of Florida, Graduate School, Herbert Wertheim College of Engineering, Department of Electrical and Computer Engineering, Gainesville, FL 32611. Offers ME, MS, PhD, JD/MS, MSM/MS. *Program availability:* Part-time, online learning. Terminal master's awarded for partial completion of doctoral program. *Degree requirements:* For master's, comprehensive exam (for some programs), thesis (for some programs); for doctorate, comprehensive exam, thesis/dissertation. *Entrance requirements:* For master's, minimum GPA of 3.0; for doctorate, minimum GPA of 3.5. Additional exam requirements/recommendations for international students: Required—TOEFL (minimum score 550 paper-based; 80 iBT), IELTS (minimum score 6). Electronic applications accepted. *Faculty research:* Computer engineering, devices, electromagnetics and energy systems, electronics and signals and systems.

University of Hawaii at Manoa, Graduate Division, College of Engineering, Department of Electrical Engineering, Honolulu, HI 96822. Offers MS, PhD. *Program availability:* Part-time. *Degree requirements:* For master's, comprehensive exam, thesis; for doctorate, comprehensive exam, thesis/dissertation. *Entrance requirements:* For master's and doctorate, GRE General Test. Additional exam requirements/recommendations for international students: Required—TOEFL (minimum score 540 paper-based; 76 iBT), IELTS (minimum score 5). *Faculty research:* Computers and artificial intelligence, communication and networking, control theory, physical electronics, VLSI design, micromillimeter waves.

University of Houston, Cullen College of Engineering, Department of Electrical and Computer Engineering, Houston, TX 77204. Offers electrical engineering (MEE, MSEE, PhD). *Program availability:* Part-time. Terminal master's awarded for partial completion of doctoral program. *Degree requirements:* For master's, thesis (for some programs); for doctorate, comprehensive exam, thesis/dissertation. *Entrance requirements:* For master's and doctorate, GRE General Test. Additional exam requirements/recommendations for international students: Required—TOEFL (minimum score 580 paper-based; 92 iBT). Electronic applications accepted. *Faculty research:* Applied electromagnetics and microelectronics, signal and image processing, biomedical engineering, geophysical applications, control engineering.

University of Idaho, College of Graduate Studies, College of Engineering, Department of Electrical and Computer Engineering, Moscow, ID 83844. Offers computer engineering (M Engr, MS); electrical engineering (M Engr, MS, PhD). *Faculty:* 13 full-time, 2 part-time/adjunct. *Students:* 30 full-time (5 women), 52 part-time (5 women). Average age 32. In 2016, 25 master's, 1 doctorate awarded. *Entrance requirements:* For master's and doctorate, minimum GPA of 3.0. *Application deadline:* For fall admission, 8/1 for domestic students; for spring admission, 12/15 for domestic students. Applications are processed on a rolling basis. Application fee: $60. Electronic applications accepted. *Expenses:* Tuition, state resident: full-time $6460; part-time $414 per credit hour. Tuition, nonresident: full-time $21,268; part-time $1237 per credit hour. *Required fees:* $2070; $60 per credit hour. Full-time tuition and fees vary according to course load and reciprocity agreements. *Financial support:* Fellowships, research assistantships, teaching assistantships, career-related internships or fieldwork, and Federal Work-Study available. Financial award applicants required to submit FAFSA. *Faculty research:* Microelectronics, laser electrophotography, intelligent systems research, advanced transportation technologies. *Unit head:* Dr. Mohsen Guizani, Chair, 208-885-6554, E-mail: info@ece.uidaho.edu. *Application contact:* Sean Scoggin, Graduate Recruitment Coordinator, 208-885-4001, Fax: 208-885-4406, E-mail: graduateadmissions@uidaho.edu.
Website: https://www.uidaho.edu/engr/departments/ece

University of Illinois at Chicago, College of Engineering, Department of Electrical and Computer Engineering, Chicago, IL 60607-7128. Offers MS, PhD. *Program availability:* Part-time. *Degree requirements:* For master's, thesis or alternative; for doctorate, thesis/dissertation, departmental qualifying exam. *Entrance requirements:* For master's, minimum GPA of 2.75, BS in related field; for doctorate, GRE General Test, minimum GPA of 2.75, MS in related field. Additional exam requirements/recommendations for international students: Required—TOEFL. Electronic applications accepted. *Expenses:* Contact institution. *Faculty research:* Bioelectronics and biomimetics, computer engineering, device physics and electronics, information systems.

University of Illinois at Urbana–Champaign, Graduate College, College of Engineering, Department of Electrical and Computer Engineering, Champaign, IL 61820. Offers MS, PhD, MS/MBA.

The University of Iowa, Graduate College, College of Engineering, Department of Electrical and Computer Engineering, Iowa City, IA 52242-1316. Offers MS, PhD. *Program availability:* Part-time. *Faculty:* 18 full-time (4 women), 4 part-time/adjunct (0 women). *Students:* 51 full-time (13 women), 13 part-time (2 women); includes 6 minority (2 Asian, non-Hispanic/Latino; 2 Hispanic/Latino; 2 Two or more races, non-Hispanic/Latino), 42 international. Average age 28. 130 applicants, 18% accepted, 15 enrolled. In 2016, 7 master's, 7 doctorates awarded. *Degree requirements:* For master's, comprehensive exam, thesis optional; for doctorate, comprehensive exam, thesis/

dissertation, qualifying exam. *Entrance requirements:* For master's and doctorate, GRE. Additional exam requirements/recommendations for international students: Required—TOEFL (minimum score 550 paper-based; 81 iBT), IELTS (minimum score 7). *Application deadline:* For fall admission, 2/1 priority date for domestic students, 2/1 for international students; for spring admission, 12/1 for domestic students; for summer admission, 4/15 for domestic students. Applications are processed on a rolling basis. Application fee: $60 ($100 for international students). Electronic applications accepted. *Financial support:* In 2016–17, 54 students received support, including 2 fellowships with full tuition reimbursements available (averaging $25,500 per year), 39 research assistantships with full and partial tuition reimbursements available (averaging $22,981 per year), 13 teaching assistantships with full and partial tuition reimbursements available (averaging $18,809 per year); scholarships/grants and unspecified assistantships also available. Financial award application deadline: 2/1; financial award applicants required to submit FAFSA. *Faculty research:* Applied optics and nanotechnology, compressive sensing, computational genomics, database management systems, large-scale intelligent and control systems, medical image processing, VLSI design and test. *Total annual research expenditures:* $6.3 million. *Unit head:* Dr. Er-Wei Bai, Department Executive Officer, 319-335-5949, Fax: 319-335-6028, E-mail: er-wei-bai@uiowa.edu. *Application contact:* Cathy Kern, Secretary, 319-335-5197, Fax: 319-335-6028, E-mail: ece@engineering.uiowa.edu.
Website: https://ece.engineering.uiowa.edu

The University of Kansas, Graduate Studies, School of Engineering, Program in Electrical Engineering, Lawrence, KS 66045. Offers MS, PhD. *Program availability:* Part-time. *Students:* 58 full-time (11 women), 17 part-time (5 women); includes 4 minority (1 Black or African American, non-Hispanic/Latino; 2 Asian, non-Hispanic/Latino; 1 Hispanic/Latino), 52 international. Average age 27. 87 applicants, 61% accepted, 16 enrolled. In 2016, 22 master's, 6 doctorates awarded. Terminal master's awarded for partial completion of doctoral program. *Entrance requirements:* For master's, GRE, minimum GPA of 3.0, official transcript, three recommendations, statement of academic objectives, resume; for doctorate, GRE, minimum GPA of 3.5, official transcript, three recommendations, statement of academic objectives, resume. Additional exam requirements/recommendations for international students: Required—TOEFL, IELTS. *Application deadline:* For fall admission, 12/15 priority date for domestic and international students; for spring admission, 10/1 for domestic and international students. Application fee: $65 ($85 for international students). Electronic applications accepted. *Financial support:* Fellowships, research assistantships, teaching assistantships, career-related internships or fieldwork, scholarships/grants, and unspecified assistantships available. Financial award application deadline: 12/15. *Faculty research:* Communication systems and networking, computer systems design, radar systems and remote sensing. *Unit head:* Victor Frost, Chair, 785-864-4833, E-mail: vsfrost@ku.edu. *Application contact:* Pam Shadoin, Graduate Admissions Contact, 785-864-4487, E-mail: pshadoin@ku.edu.
Website: http://www.eecs.ku.edu/prospective_students/graduate/masters#electrical_engineering

University of Kentucky, Graduate School, College of Engineering, Program in Electrical Engineering, Lexington, KY 40506-0032. Offers MSEE, PhD. *Degree requirements:* For master's, comprehensive exam, thesis optional; for doctorate, one foreign language, comprehensive exam, thesis/dissertation. *Entrance requirements:* For master's, GRE General Test, minimum undergraduate GPA of 2.75; for doctorate, GRE General Test, minimum undergraduate GPA of 3.0. Additional exam requirements/recommendations for international students: Required—TOEFL (minimum score 550 paper-based). Electronic applications accepted. *Faculty research:* Signal processing, systems, and control; electromagnetic field theory; power electronics and machines; computer engineering and VLSI; materials and devices.

University of Louisville, J. B. Speed School of Engineering, Department of Electrical and Computer Engineering, Louisville, KY 40292-0001. Offers M Eng, MS, PhD. *Accreditation:* ABET (one or more programs are accredited). *Students:* 47 full-time (5 women), 26 part-time (3 women); includes 6 minority (1 Black or African American, non-Hispanic/Latino; 1 Asian, non-Hispanic/Latino; 4 Hispanic/Latino), 36 international. Average age 29. 70 applicants, 29% accepted, 14 enrolled. In 2016, 6 master's, 2 doctorates awarded. *Degree requirements:* For master's, thesis optional; for doctorate, comprehensive exam, thesis/dissertation. *Entrance requirements:* For master's and doctorate, GRE General Test, two letters of recommendation, official transcripts. Additional exam requirements/recommendations for international students: Required—TOEFL (minimum score 550 paper-based; 80 iBT), IELTS (minimum score 6.5). *Application deadline:* For fall admission, 5/1 priority date for international students; for spring admission, 11/1 priority date for international students; for summer admission, 3/1 priority date for international students. Applications are processed on a rolling basis. Application fee: $60. Electronic applications accepted. *Expenses:* Tuition, state resident: full-time $12,246; part-time $681 per credit hour. Tuition, nonresident: full-time $25,486; part-time $1417 per credit hour. *Required fees:* $196. Tuition and fees vary according to program and reciprocity agreements. *Financial support:* In 2016–17, 2 fellowships with full tuition reimbursements (averaging $20,000 per year) were awarded; research assistantships with full tuition reimbursements, teaching assistantships with full tuition reimbursements, scholarships/grants, health care benefits, and tuition waivers (full) also available. Financial award application deadline: 1/1; financial award applicants required to submit FAFSA. *Faculty research:* Nanotechnology; microfabrication; computer engineering; control, communication and signal processing; electronic devices and systems. *Total annual research expenditures:* $1.8 million. *Unit head:* Alpenhaar Bruce, Chair, 502-852-1554, E-mail: bruce.alphenaar@louisville.edu. *Application contact:* John Naber, Director of Graduate Studies, 502-852-7910, E-mail: john.naber@louisville.edu.
Website: http://www.louisville.edu/speed/electrical/

University of Maine, Graduate School, College of Engineering, Department of Electrical and Computer Engineering, Orono, ME 04469. Offers computer engineering (MS); electrical engineering (MS, PhD). *Program availability:* Part-time. *Faculty:* 12 full-time (1 woman), 1 part-time/adjunct (0 women). *Students:* 18 full-time (1 woman), 5 part-time (1 woman); includes 1 minority (Hispanic/Latino), 14 international. Average age 27. 35 applicants, 71% accepted, 5 enrolled. In 2016, 9 master's, 1 doctorate awarded. Terminal master's awarded for partial completion of doctoral program. *Degree requirements:* For master's, thesis (for some programs); for doctorate, comprehensive exam, thesis/dissertation. *Entrance requirements:* For master's and doctorate, GRE General Test. Additional exam requirements/recommendations for international students: Required—TOEFL. *Application deadline:* For fall admission, 2/1 priority date for domestic students. Applications are processed on a rolling basis. Application fee: $65. Electronic applications accepted. *Expenses:* Tuition, state resident: full-time $7524; part-time $2508 per credit. Tuition, nonresident: full-time $24,498; part-time $8166 per credit. *Required fees:* $1148; $571 per credit. *Financial support:* In 2016–17, 11 students received support, including 1 fellowship (averaging $20,000 per year), 4 research assistantships with full tuition reimbursements available (averaging $22,800 per year), 6 teaching assistantships with full tuition reimbursements available (averaging $14,600 per year); Federal Work-Study, institutionally sponsored loans, and tuition waivers (full and partial) also available. Financial award application deadline: 3/1. *Faculty research:* Microwave acoustic sensors, semiconductor devices and fabrication,

Electrical Engineering

high performance computing, instrumentation and industrial automation, wireless communication. *Total annual research expenditures:* $2 million. *Unit head:* Dr. Donald Hummels, Chair, 207-581-2244. *Application contact:* Scott G. Delcourt, Assistant Vice President for Graduate Studies and Senior Associate Dean, 207-581-3291, Fax: 207-581-3232, E-mail: graduate@maine.edu.
Website: http://www.ece.umaine.edu/

The University of Manchester, School of Electrical and Electronic Engineering, Manchester, United Kingdom. Offers M Phil, PhD.

University of Manitoba, Faculty of Graduate Studies, Faculty of Engineering, Department of Electrical and Computer Engineering, Winnipeg, MB R3T 2N2, Canada. Offers M Eng, M Sc, PhD. *Degree requirements:* For master's, thesis; for doctorate, thesis/dissertation.

University of Maryland, Baltimore County, The Graduate School, College of Engineering and Information Technology, Department of Computer Science and Electrical Engineering, Program in Electrical Engineering, Baltimore, MD 21227. Offers MS, PhD. *Program availability:* Part-time. *Faculty:* 14 full-time (3 women). *Students:* 41 full-time (9 women), 19 part-time (4 women); includes 12 minority (6 Black or African American, non-Hispanic/Latino; 4 Asian, non-Hispanic/Latino; 2 Hispanic/Latino), 31 international. Average age 31. 82 applicants, 63% accepted, 15 enrolled. In 2016, 4 master's, 6 doctorates awarded. *Degree requirements:* For master's, thesis optional; for doctorate, comprehensive exam, thesis/dissertation. *Entrance requirements:* For master's and doctorate, GRE General Test, BS from ABET-accredited undergraduate program in electrical engineering or strong background in computer science, mathematics, physics, or other areas of engineering or science. Additional exam requirements/recommendations for international students: Required—TOEFL (minimum score 550 paper-based; 80 iBT). *Application deadline:* For fall admission, 6/1 for domestic students, 1/1 for international students; for spring admission, 11/1 for domestic students, 6/1 for international students. Applications are processed on a rolling basis. Application fee: $70. Electronic applications accepted. *Expenses:* Contact institution. *Financial support:* In 2016–17, 1 fellowship with full tuition reimbursement (averaging $23,000 per year), 16 research assistantships with full tuition reimbursements (averaging $18,000 per year), 8 teaching assistantships with full tuition reimbursements (averaging $18,000 per year) were awarded; career-related internships or fieldwork, Federal Work-Study, scholarships/grants, health care benefits, tuition waivers (partial), and unspecified assistantships also available. Support available to part-time students. Financial award application deadline: 6/30; financial award applicants required to submit FAFSA. *Faculty research:* Communication and signal processing, photonics and micro electronics, sensor systems, signal processing architectures, VLSI design and test. *Unit head:* Dr. Anupam Joshi, Professor and Chair, 410-455-3500, Fax: 410-455-3969, E-mail: joshi@cs.umbc.edu. *Application contact:* Dr. Mohamed Younis, Professor and Graduate Program Director, 410-455-3500, Fax: 410-455-3969, E-mail: younis@umbc.edu.
Website: http://www.csee.umbc.edu/

★ **University of Maryland, College Park,** Academic Affairs, A. James Clark School of Engineering, Department of Electrical and Computer Engineering, Electrical Engineering Program, College Park, MD 20742. Offers MS, PhD. *Degree requirements:* For master's, thesis or alternative; for doctorate, thesis/dissertation, oral exam, qualifying exam. *Entrance requirements:* For master's and doctorate, GRE General Test, minimum GPA of 3.0. Electronic applications accepted.
See Display on page 389 and Close-Up on page 429.

University of Massachusetts Amherst, Graduate School, College of Engineering, Department of Electrical and Computer Engineering, Amherst, MA 01003. Offers MSECE, PhD. *Program availability:* Part-time. Terminal master's awarded for partial completion of doctoral program. *Degree requirements:* For master's, thesis or alternative; for doctorate, comprehensive exam, thesis/dissertation. *Entrance requirements:* For master's and doctorate, GRE General Test. Additional exam requirements/recommendations for international students: Required—TOEFL (minimum score 550 paper-based; 80 iBT), IELTS (minimum score 6.5). Electronic applications accepted.

University of Massachusetts Dartmouth, Graduate School, College of Engineering, Department of Electrical and Computer Engineering, North Dartmouth, MA 02747-2300. Offers acoustics (Postbaccalaureate Certificate); communications (Postbaccalaureate Certificate); computer engineering (MS, PhD); computing infrastructure (Postbaccalaureate Certificate); digital security signal processing (Postbaccalaureate Certificate); electrical engineering (MS, PhD). *Program availability:* Part-time. *Faculty:* 15 full-time (3 women), 1 part-time/adjunct (0 women). *Students:* 31 full-time (8 women), 45 part-time (5 women); includes 8 minority (2 Black or African American, non-Hispanic/Latino; 2 Asian, non-Hispanic/Latino; 2 Hispanic/Latino; 2 Two or more races, non-Hispanic/Latino), 39 international. Average age 28. 101 applicants, 57% accepted, 23 enrolled. In 2016, 25 master's, 3 doctorates, 3 other advanced degrees awarded. Terminal master's awarded for partial completion of doctoral program. *Degree requirements:* For master's, thesis or project; for doctorate, comprehensive exam, thesis/dissertation. *Entrance requirements:* For master's, GRE (UMass Dartmouth electrical/computer engineering bachelor's degree recipients are exempt), statement of purpose (minimum of 300 words), resume, 3 letters of recommendation, official transcripts; for doctorate, GRE (UMass Dartmouth electrical/computer engineering degree recipients are exempt), statement of purpose (minimum of 300 words), resume, 3 letters of recommendation, official transcripts; for Postbaccalaureate Certificate, statement of purpose (minimum of 300 words), resume, official transcripts. Additional exam requirements/recommendations for international students: Required—TOEFL (minimum score 550 paper-based; 80 iBT). *Application deadline:* For fall admission, 2/15 priority date for domestic students, 1/15 priority date for international students; for spring admission, 11/1 priority date for domestic students, 10/1 priority date for international students. Application fee: $60. Electronic applications accepted. *Expenses:* Tuition, state resident: full-time $14,994; part-time $624.75 per credit. Tuition, nonresident: full-time $27,068; part-time $1127.83 per credit. *Required fees:* $405; $25.88 per credit. Tuition and fees vary according to course load and reciprocity agreements. *Financial support:* In 2016–17, 5 fellowships (averaging $5,143 per year), 14 research assistantships (averaging $10,724 per year), 11 teaching assistantships (averaging $14,705 per year) were awarded; unspecified assistantships and instructional assistantships, doctoral support also available. Financial award application deadline: 3/1; financial award applicants required to submit FAFSA. *Faculty research:* Computer engineering, cyber security, acoustics, signals and systems, electromagnetics, electronics and solid-state devices, marine systems, photonics. *Total annual research expenditures:* $2.6 million. *Unit head:* Hong Liu, Graduate Program Director, 508-999-8514, Fax: 508-999-8489, E-mail: hliu@umassd.edu. *Application contact:* Steven Briggs, Director of Marketing and Recruitment for Graduate Studies, 508-999-8604, Fax: 508-999-8183, E-mail: graduate@umassd.edu.
Website: http://www.umassd.edu/engineering/ece/graduate

University of Massachusetts Lowell, Francis College of Engineering, Department of Electrical and Computer Engineering, Program in Electrical Engineering, Lowell, MA 01854. Offers MS Eng, PhD. *Program availability:* Part-time, evening/weekend. Terminal master's awarded for partial completion of doctoral program. *Degree requirements:* For master's, thesis; for doctorate, 2 foreign languages, thesis/dissertation. *Entrance requirements:* For master's and doctorate, GRE General Test.

University of Memphis, Graduate School, Herff College of Engineering, Department of Electrical and Computer Engineering, Memphis, TN 38103. Offers computer engineering (MS, PhD); electrical engineering (MS, PhD); imaging and signal processing (Graduate Certificate). *Faculty:* 12 full-time (1 woman). *Students:* 12 full-time (4 women), 12 part-time (5 women); includes 1 minority (Two or more races, non-Hispanic/Latino), 18 international. Average age 26. 52 applicants, 67% accepted, 4 enrolled. In 2016, 19 master's awarded. *Degree requirements:* For master's, comprehensive exam, thesis or alternative; for doctorate, comprehensive exam, thesis/dissertation. *Entrance requirements:* For master's and doctorate, GRE General Test, MAT, or GMAT, three letters of recommendation. Additional exam requirements/recommendations for international students: Required—TOEFL (minimum score 550 paper-based; 79 iBT). *Application deadline:* For fall admission, 8/1 for domestic students; for spring admission, 12/1 for domestic students. Application fee: $35 ($60 for international students). Electronic applications accepted. *Expenses:* $5,231.50 per semester full-time in-state, $9,623.50 full-time out-of-state. *Financial support:* In 2016–17, 4 students received support, including 9 research assistantships (averaging $15,120 per year), 16 teaching assistantships (averaging $11,038 per year); fellowships, career-related internships or fieldwork, Federal Work-Study, scholarships/grants, and unspecified assistantships also available. Financial award application deadline: 2/1; financial award applicants required to submit FAFSA. *Faculty research:* Image processing, imaging sensors, biomedical systems, intelligent systems. *Unit head:* Dr. Russell Deaton, Chair/Professor, 901-678-2175, Fax: 901-678-5469. *Application contact:* Dr. Aaron Robinson, Coordinator of Graduate Studies, 901-678-4996, Fax: 901-678-5469, E-mail: alrobins@memphis.edu.
Website: http://www.memphis.edu/eece/

University of Miami, Graduate School, College of Engineering, Department of Electrical and Computer Engineering, Coral Gables, FL 33124. Offers MSECE, PhD. *Program availability:* Part-time. *Degree requirements:* For master's, thesis (for some programs); for doctorate, comprehensive exam, thesis/dissertation, dissertation proposal defense. *Entrance requirements:* For master's, GRE General Test, minimum GPA of 3.0; for doctorate, GRE General Test, minimum undergraduate GPA of 3.3, graduate 3.5. Additional exam requirements/recommendations for international students: Required—TOEFL (minimum score 550 paper-based; 59 iBT), IELTS (minimum score 7). Electronic applications accepted. *Faculty research:* Computer network, image processing, database systems, digital signal processing, machine intelligence.

University of Michigan, College of Engineering, Department of Electrical and Computer Engineering, Ann Arbor, MI 48109. Offers MS, MSE, PhD. *Students:* 743 full-time (151 women), 17 part-time (4 women). 2,454 applicants, 30% accepted, 331 enrolled. In 2016, 202 master's, 53 doctorates awarded. *Expenses:* Tuition, state resident: full-time $21,466; part-time $1152 per credit hour. Tuition, nonresident: full-time $43,346; part-time $2367 per credit hour. Part-time tuition and fees vary according to course load, degree level and program. *Faculty research:* Solid state electronics and optics; communications, control, signal process; sensors and integrated circuitry; software systems; artificial intelligence; hardware systems. *Total annual research expenditures:* $41.2 million. *Unit head:* Prof. Khalil Najafi, Department Chair, 734-764-3317, Fax: 734-763-1503, E-mail: najafi@umich.edu. *Application contact:* Jose-Antonio Rubio, Graduate Program Coordinator, 734-764-9387, E-mail: jadrubio@umich.edu.
Website: http://eecs.umich.edu/ece/

University of Michigan–Dearborn, College of Engineering and Computer Science, MSE Program in Electrical Engineering, Dearborn, MI 48128. Offers MSE. *Program availability:* Part-time, evening/weekend, 100% online. *Faculty:* 20 full-time (2 women), 12 part-time/adjunct (0 women). *Students:* 34 full-time (8 women), 128 part-time (21 women); includes 25 minority (7 Black or African American, non-Hispanic/Latino; 12 Asian, non-Hispanic/Latino; 3 Hispanic/Latino; 3 Two or more races, non-Hispanic/Latino), 62 international. Average age 27. 127 applicants, 72% accepted, 58 enrolled. In 2016, 73 master's awarded. *Degree requirements:* For master's, thesis optional. *Entrance requirements:* For master's, bachelor's degree in electrical and/or computer engineering with minimum overall GPA of 3.0. Additional exam requirements/recommendations for international students: Required—TOEFL (minimum score 560 paper-based; 84 iBT), IELTS (minimum score 6.5). *Application deadline:* For fall admission, 8/1 for domestic students, 5/1 for international students; for winter admission, 12/1 for domestic students, 9/1 for international students; for spring admission, 4/1 for domestic students, 1/1 for international students. Applications are processed on a rolling basis. Application fee: $60. Electronic applications accepted. *Expenses:* Tuition, state resident: full-time $13,118; part-time $2280 per term. Tuition, nonresident: full-time $21,816; part-time $3771 per term. *Required fees:* $866; $658 per unit. $329 per term. Tuition and fees vary according to program. *Financial support:* Research assistantships, teaching assistantships, scholarships/grants, unspecified assistantships, and non-resident tuition scholarships available. Support available to part-time students. Financial award application deadline: 3/1; financial award applicants required to submit FAFSA. *Faculty research:* Pattern recognition, machine vision, fuzzy systems, vehicle electronics and wireless communications. *Unit head:* Dr. Paul Richardson, Chair, 313-593-5560, E-mail: richarpc@umich.edu. *Application contact:* Office of Graduate Studies, 313-583-6321, E-mail: umd-graduatestudies@umich.edu.
Website: http://umdearborn.edu/cecs/ECE/grad_prog/index.php

University of Michigan–Dearborn, College of Engineering and Computer Science, PhD Program in Electrical and Computer Engineering, Dearborn, MI 48128. Offers PhD. *Program availability:* Part-time, evening/weekend. *Degree requirements:* For doctorate, thesis/dissertation. *Entrance requirements:* For doctorate, GRE, bachelor's or master's degree in electrical or computer engineering or closely-related field. Additional exam requirements/recommendations for international students: Required—TOEFL (minimum score 560 paper-based; 84 iBT), IELTS (minimum score 6.5). Electronic applications accepted. *Expenses:* Tuition, state resident: full-time $13,118; part-time $2280 per term. Tuition, nonresident: full-time $21,816; part-time $3771 per term. *Required fees:* $866; $658 per unit. $329 per term. Tuition and fees vary according to program. *Faculty research:* Fuzzy systems and applications, machine vision, pattern recognition and machine intelligence, vehicle electronics, wireless communications.

University of Minnesota, Duluth, Graduate School, Swenson College of Science and Engineering, Department of Electrical and Computer Engineering, Duluth, MN 55812-2496. Offers MSECE. *Program availability:* Part-time. *Degree requirements:* For master's, thesis. *Entrance requirements:* Additional exam requirements/recommendations for international students: Recommended—TOEFL, IELTS, TWE. *Faculty research:* Biomedical instrumentation, transportation systems, computer hardware and software, signal processing, optical communications.

University of Minnesota, Twin Cities Campus, College of Science and Engineering, Department of Electrical and Computer Engineering, Minneapolis, MN 55455-0213. Offers MSEE, PhD. *Program availability:* Part-time. *Degree requirements:* For master's, thesis or alternative; for doctorate, thesis/dissertation. *Entrance requirements:* Additional exam requirements/recommendations for international students: Required—TOEFL (minimum score 550 paper-based). Electronic applications accepted. *Faculty research:* Signal processing, micro and nano structures, computers, controls, power electronics.

University of Missouri, Office of Research and Graduate Studies, College of Engineering, Department of Electrical and Computer Engineering, Columbia, MO 65211. Offers MS, PhD. *Faculty:* 23 full-time (4 women), 2 part-time/adjunct (0 women). *Students:* 63 full-time (13 women), 81 part-time (13 women). *Degree requirements:* For master's, thesis or alternative; for doctorate, thesis/dissertation. *Entrance requirements:* For master's, GRE General Test, minimum GPA of 3.0; for doctorate, GRE General Test, GRE Subject Test, minimum GPA of 3.0. Additional exam requirements/recommendations for international students: Required—TOEFL (minimum score 550 paper-based; 80 iBT). *Application deadline:* For fall admission, 2/15 priority date for domestic and international students; for winter admission, 9/1 priority date for domestic and international students. Applications are processed on a rolling basis. Application fee: $75 ($90 for international students). Electronic applications accepted. *Expenses:* Tuition, state resident: full-time $6347; part-time $352.60 per credit hour. Tuition, nonresident: full-time $17,379; part-time $965.50 per credit hour. *Required fees:* $1035. Tuition and fees vary according to course load, campus/location and program. *Financial support:* Fellowships, research assistantships, teaching assistantships, institutionally sponsored loans, scholarships/grants, traineeships, health care benefits, and unspecified assistantships available. Support available to part-time students.
Website: http://engineering.missouri.edu/ece/degree-programs/

University of Missouri–Kansas City, School of Computing and Engineering, Kansas City, MO 64110-2499. Offers civil engineering (MS); computer and electrical engineering (PhD); computer science (MS), including bioinformatics, software engineering, telecommunications networking; computer science and informatics (PhD); computing (PhD); electrical engineering (MS); engineering (PhD); engineering and construction management (Graduate Certificate); mechanical engineering (MS); telecommunications and computer networking (PhD). PhD (interdisciplinary) offered through the School of Graduate Studies. *Program availability:* Part-time. *Faculty:* 45 full-time (6 women), 26 part-time/adjunct (4 women). *Students:* 473 full-time (155 women), 207 part-time (42 women); includes 24 minority (10 Black or African American, non-Hispanic/Latino; 10 Asian, non-Hispanic/Latino; 4 Hispanic/Latino), 581 international. Average age 25. 1,143 applicants, 44% accepted, 227 enrolled. In 2016, 446 master's, 2 other advanced degrees awarded. *Degree requirements:* For doctorate, thesis/dissertation. *Entrance requirements:* For master's, GRE General Test, minimum GPA of 3.0, 3 letters of recommendation from professors; for doctorate, GRE General Test, minimum GPA of 3.5. Additional exam requirements/recommendations for international students: Required—TOEFL (minimum score 550 paper-based; 80 iBT). *Application deadline:* For fall admission, 1/15 priority date for domestic students, 1/15 for international students. Applications are processed on a rolling basis. Application fee: $45 ($50 for international students). *Financial support:* In 2016–17, 37 research assistantships with partial tuition reimbursements (averaging $15,679 per year), 47 teaching assistantships with partial tuition reimbursements (averaging $16,830 per year) were awarded; career-related internships or fieldwork, Federal Work-Study, scholarships/grants, tuition waivers (partial), and unspecified assistantships also available. Support available to part-time students. Financial award application deadline: 3/1; financial award applicants required to submit FAFSA. *Faculty research:* Algorithms, bioinformatics and medical informatics, biomechanics/biomaterials, civil engineering materials, networking and telecommunications, thermal science. *Unit head:* Dr. Kevin Z. Truman, Dean, 816-235-2399, Fax: 816-235-5159. *Application contact:* 816-235-2399, Fax: 816-235-5159.
Website: http://sce.umkc.edu/

University of Nebraska–Lincoln, Graduate College, College of Engineering, Department of Electrical Engineering, Lincoln, NE 68588. Offers MS, PhD. *Degree requirements:* For master's, thesis optional; for doctorate, comprehensive exam, thesis/dissertation. *Entrance requirements:* For master's and doctorate, GRE General Test. Additional exam requirements/recommendations for international students: Required—TOEFL (minimum score 550 paper-based). Electronic applications accepted. *Faculty research:* Electromagnetics, communications, biomedical digital signal processing, electrical breakdown of gases, optical properties of microelectronic materials.

University of Nevada, Las Vegas, Graduate College, Howard R. Hughes College of Engineering, Department of Electrical and Computer Engineering, Las Vegas, NV 89154-4026. Offers MS, PhD, MS/MS, MS/PhD. *Program availability:* Part-time. *Faculty:* 17 full-time (3 women). *Students:* 29 full-time (8 women), 19 part-time (1 woman); includes 16 minority (1 Black or African American, non-Hispanic/Latino; 7 Asian, non-Hispanic/Latino; 7 Hispanic/Latino; 1 Two or more races, non-Hispanic/Latino), 23 international. Average age 29. 37 applicants, 54% accepted, 9 enrolled. In 2016, 9 master's, 6 doctorates awarded. *Degree requirements:* For master's, comprehensive exam (for some programs), thesis (for some programs), project; for doctorate, comprehensive exam, thesis/dissertation. *Entrance requirements:* For master's, GRE General Test, bachelor's degree with minimum GPA 3.0; statement of purpose; 3 letters of recommendation; for doctorate, GRE General Test, 3 letters of recommendation; statement of purpose; bachelor's degree with minimum GPA of 3.5/master's degree with minimum GPA of 3.2. Additional exam requirements/recommendations for international students: Required—TOEFL (minimum score 550 paper-based; 80 iBT), IELTS (minimum score 7). *Application deadline:* For fall admission, 2/1 for domestic students; for spring admission, 10/1 for domestic students. Application fee: $60 ($95 for international students). Electronic applications accepted. *Expenses:* $269.25 per credit, $792 per 3-credit course; $9,634 per year resident; $23,274 per year non-resident; $7,094 fees non-resident (7 credits or more); $1,307 annual health insurance fee. *Financial support:* In 2016–17, 9 research assistantships with partial tuition reimbursements (averaging $16,408 per year), 21 teaching assistantships with partial tuition reimbursements (averaging $13,310 per year) were awarded; institutionally sponsored loans, scholarships/grants, health care benefits, and unspecified assistantships also available. Financial award application deadline: 3/15. *Faculty research:* Computer engineering, power engineering, semiconductor and nanotechnology, electronics and VLSI, telecommunications and control, electromagnetics and plasma. *Total annual research expenditures:* $1.6 million. *Unit head:* Dr. Yingtao Jiang, Chair/Professor, 702-895-2533, Fax: 702-895-4075, E-mail: yingtao.jiang@unlv.edu. *Application contact:* Dr. Robert Schill, Graduate Coordinator, 702-895-1526, Fax: 702-895-4075, E-mail: robert.schill@unlv.edu.
Website: http://ece.unlv.edu/

University of Nevada, Reno, Graduate School, College of Engineering, Department of Electrical Engineering, Reno, NV 89557. Offers MS, PhD. Terminal master's awarded for partial completion of doctoral program. *Degree requirements:* For master's, thesis optional; for doctorate, thesis/dissertation. *Entrance requirements:* For master's, GRE General Test, minimum GPA of 2.75; for doctorate, GRE General Test, minimum GPA of 3.0. Additional exam requirements/recommendations for international students: Required—TOEFL (minimum score 500 paper-based; 61 iBT), IELTS (minimum score 6). Electronic applications accepted. *Faculty research:* Acoustics, neural networking, synthetic aperture radar simulation, optical fiber communications and sensors.

University of New Brunswick Fredericton, School of Graduate Studies, Faculty of Engineering, Department of Electrical and Computer Engineering, Fredericton, NB E3B 5A3, Canada. Offers M Eng, M Sc E, PhD. *Program availability:* Part-time. *Degree requirements:* For master's, thesis, research proposal; 10 courses (for M Eng); for doctorate, comprehensive exam, thesis/dissertation, research proposal. *Entrance requirements:* For master's, minimum GPA of 3.3; references; for doctorate, M Sc; minimum GPA of 3.3; previous transcripts; references. Additional exam requirements/recommendations for international students: Required—TOEFL (minimum score 580 paper-based; 93 iBT), IELTS (minimum score 7), TWE (minimum score 4). Electronic applications accepted. *Faculty research:* Biomedical engineering, communications, robotics and control systems, electromagnetic systems, embedded systems, optical fiber systems, sustainable energy and power systems, power electronics, image and signal processing, software systems, electronics and digital systems.

University of New Hampshire, Graduate School, College of Engineering and Physical Sciences, Department of Electrical and Computer Engineering, Durham, NH 03824. Offers electrical and computer engineering (MS); electrical engineering (M Engr, PhD). *Program availability:* Part-time, evening/weekend. *Degree requirements:* For master's, thesis or alternative; for doctorate, thesis/dissertation. *Entrance requirements:* For master's and doctorate, GRE (for non-U.S. university bachelor's degree holders). Additional exam requirements/recommendations for international students: Required—TOEFL (minimum score 550 paper-based; 80 iBT). Electronic applications accepted. *Faculty research:* Biomedical engineering, communications systems and information theory, digital systems, illumination engineering.

University of New Haven, Graduate School, Tagliatela College of Engineering, Program in Electrical Engineering, West Haven, CT 06516. Offers control systems (MS); digital signal processing and communication (MS); electrical and computer engineering (MS); electrical engineering (MS). *Program availability:* Part-time, evening/weekend. *Students:* 99 full-time (33 women), 22 part-time (3 women); includes 4 minority (2 Black or African American, non-Hispanic/Latino; 1 Asian, non-Hispanic/Latino; 1 Two or more races, non-Hispanic/Latino), 114 international. Average age 25. 346 applicants, 59% accepted, 13 enrolled. In 2016, 116 master's awarded. *Degree requirements:* For master's, thesis or alternative. *Entrance requirements:* For master's, bachelor's degree in electrical engineering. Additional exam requirements/recommendations for international students: Required—TOEFL (minimum score 75 iBT), IELTS, PTE (minimum score 50). *Application deadline:* Applications are processed on a rolling basis. Application fee: $50. Electronic applications accepted. Application fee is waived when completed online. *Expenses: Tuition:* Full-time $15,660; part-time $870 per credit hour. *Required fees:* $200; $85 per term. Tuition and fees vary according to program. *Financial support:* Research assistantships with partial tuition reimbursements, teaching assistantships with partial tuition reimbursements, career-related internships or fieldwork, Federal Work-Study, scholarships/grants, and unspecified assistantships available. Support available to part-time students. Financial award applicants required to submit FAFSA. *Unit head:* Dr. Bijan Karimi, Coordinator, 203-932-7164, E-mail: bkarimi@newhaven.edu. *Application contact:* Michelle Mason, Director of Graduate Enrollment, 203-932-7067, E-mail: mmason@newhaven.edu.
Website: http://www.newhaven.edu/9592/

University of New Mexico, Graduate Studies, School of Engineering, Programs in Electrical and Computer Engineering, Albuquerque, NM 87131-2039. Offers MS, PhD. *Program availability:* Part-time, evening/weekend, online learning. *Faculty:* 16 full-time (3 women), 5 part-time/adjunct (2 women). *Students:* 115 full-time (17 women), 153 part-time (31 women); includes 51 minority (1 Black or African American, non-Hispanic/Latino; 1 American Indian or Alaska Native, non-Hispanic/Latino; 6 Asian, non-Hispanic/Latino; 41 Hispanic/Latino; 2 Two or more races, non-Hispanic/Latino), 110 international. Average age 31. 299 applicants, 28% accepted, 49 enrolled. In 2016, 31 master's, 11 doctorates awarded. Terminal master's awarded for partial completion of doctoral program. *Degree requirements:* For master's, thesis; for doctorate, comprehensive exam, thesis/dissertation. *Entrance requirements:* For master's, GRE General Test, minimum GPA of 3.0; for doctorate, GRE General Test, minimum GPA of 3.5. Additional exam requirements/recommendations for international students: Required—TOEFL (minimum score 550 paper-based; 79 iBT). *Application deadline:* For fall admission, 6/15 for domestic students, 2/15 for international students; for spring admission, 11/1 for domestic students, 6/15 for international students. Application fee: $50. Electronic applications accepted. *Financial support:* Fellowships with tuition reimbursements, research assistantships with tuition reimbursements, teaching assistantships with tuition reimbursements, scholarships/grants, health care benefits, and unspecified assistantships available. *Faculty research:* Applied electromagnetics, biomedical engineering, communications, image processing, microelectronics, optoelectronics, signal processing, systems and controls. *Unit head:* Dr. Chaouki T. Abdallah, Chair, 505-277-0298, Fax: 505-277-1439, E-mail: chaouki@ece.unm.edu. *Application contact:* Elmyra Grelle, Coordinator, 505-277-2600, Fax: 505-277-1439, E-mail: egrelle@ece.unm.edu.
Website: http://www.ece.unm.edu/

The University of North Carolina at Charlotte, William States Lee College of Engineering, Department of Electrical and Computer Engineering, Charlotte, NC 28223-0001. Offers electrical engineering (MSEE, PhD). *Program availability:* Part-time, evening/weekend. *Faculty:* 27 full-time (2 women). *Students:* 191 full-time (48 women), 44 part-time (9 women); includes 8 minority (5 Black or African American, non-Hispanic/Latino; 2 Asian, non-Hispanic/Latino; 1 Hispanic/Latino), 205 international. Average age 26. 700 applicants, 52% accepted, 76 enrolled. In 2016, 107 master's, 10 doctorates awarded. *Degree requirements:* For master's, thesis, project, or exam; for doctorate, comprehensive exam, thesis/dissertation. *Entrance requirements:* For master's, GRE, undergraduate degree in electrical and computer engineering or a closely-related field of engineering or sciences; minimum undergraduate GPA of 3.0; letters of recommendation; statement of purpose; for doctorate, GRE General Test, master's degree in electrical and/or computer engineering or a closely-allied field demonstrating strong academic background for performing research in a chosen area of interest; minimum undergraduate and master's-level GPA of 3.5; letters of recommendation; statement of purpose. Additional exam requirements/recommendations for international students: Required—TOEFL (minimum score 523 paper-based, 70 iBT) or IELTS (6.5). *Application deadline:* For fall admission, 1/15 for domestic and international students; for spring admission, 7/15 for domestic and international students. Applications are processed on a rolling basis. Application fee: $75. Electronic applications accepted. *Expenses:* Contact institution. *Financial support:* In 2016–17, 65 students received support, including 26 research assistantships (averaging $8,720 per year), 39 teaching assistantships (averaging $6,013 per year); career-related internships or fieldwork, institutionally sponsored loans, scholarships/grants, and unspecified assistantships also available. Support available to part-time students. Financial award application deadline: 3/1; financial award applicants required to submit FAFSA. *Total annual research expenditures:* $1.7 million. *Unit head:* Dr. Asis Nasipuri, Chair, 704-687-8418, E-mail: anasipur@uncc.edu. *Application contact:* Kathy B. Giddings, Director of Graduate Admissions, 704-687-5503, Fax: 704-687-1668, E-mail: gradadm@uncc.edu.
Website: http://ece.uncc.edu/

Electrical Engineering

University of North Dakota, Graduate School, School of Engineering and Mines, Department of Electrical Engineering, Grand Forks, ND 58202. Offers M Engr, MS, PhD. *Program availability:* Part-time. *Degree requirements:* For master's, comprehensive exam, thesis or alternative. *Entrance requirements:* For master's, GRE General Test, minimum GPA of 3.0 (MS), 2.5 (M Engr). Additional exam requirements/recommendations for international students: Required—TOEFL (minimum score 550 paper-based; 79 iBT), IELTS (minimum score 6.5). *Application deadline:* For fall admission, 8/1 priority date for domestic students, 5/1 priority date for international students; for spring admission, 12/1 priority date for domestic students, 9/1 priority date for international students. Applications are processed on a rolling basis. Application fee: $35. Electronic applications accepted. *Financial support:* Fellowships with full and partial tuition reimbursements, research assistantships with full and partial tuition reimbursements, teaching assistantships with full and partial tuition reimbursements, Federal Work-Study, institutionally sponsored loans, scholarships/grants, health care benefits, tuition waivers (full and partial), and unspecified assistantships available. Support available to part-time students. Financial award application deadline: 3/15; financial award applicants required to submit FAFSA. *Faculty research:* Controls and robotics, signal processing, energy conversion, microwaves, computer engineering. *Unit head:* Dr. Naima Kaabouch, Graduate Director, 701-777-4460, Fax: 701-777-4838, E-mail: naimakaabouch@mail.und.edu. *Application contact:* Staci Wells, Admissions Associate, 701-777-2945, Fax: 701-777-3619, E-mail: staci.wells@gradschool.und.edu. Website: http://www.und.nodak.edu/dept/sem/ee/

University of North Florida, College of Computing, Engineering, and Construction, School of Engineering, Jacksonville, FL 32224. Offers MSCE, MSEE, MSME. *Program availability:* Part-time. *Faculty:* 19 full-time (1 woman). *Students:* 15 full-time (4 women), 34 part-time (6 women); includes 10 minority (2 Asian, non-Hispanic/Latino; 5 Hispanic/Latino; 3 Two or more races, non-Hispanic/Latino), 13 international. Average age 28. 43 applicants, 63% accepted, 17 enrolled. In 2016, 14 master's awarded. *Application deadline:* For fall admission, 8/1 priority date for domestic students, 5/1 for international students; for spring admission, 12/1 priority date for domestic students, 10/1 for international students; for summer admission, 3/15 priority date for domestic students, 2/1 for international students. Application fee: $30. Tuition and fees vary according to course load, campus/location and program. *Financial support:* In 2016–17, 30 students received support, including 11 research assistantships (averaging $3,925 per year), 8 teaching assistantships (averaging $2,552 per year); Federal Work-Study, scholarships/grants, tuition waivers, and unspecified assistantships also available. Financial award application deadline: 4/1; financial award applicants required to submit FAFSA. *Total annual research expenditures:* $804,835. *Unit head:* Dr. Murat Tiryakioglu, Director, 904-620-1393, E-mail: m.tiryakioglu@unf.edu. *Application contact:* Dr. Amanda Pascale, Director, The Graduate School, 904-320-1360, Fax: 904-620-1362, E-mail: graduateschool@unf.edu.
Website: http://www.unf.edu/ccec/engineering/

University of North Texas, Robert B. Toulouse School of Graduate Studies, Denton, TX 76203-5459. Offers accounting (MS); applied anthropology (MA, MS); applied behavior analysis (Certificate); applied geography (MA); applied technology and performance improvement (M Ed, MS); art education (MA); art history (MA); art museum education (Certificate); arts leadership (Certificate); audiology (Au D); behavior analysis (MS); behavioral science (PhD); biochemistry and molecular biology (MS); biology (MA, MS); biomedical engineering (MS); business analysis (MS); chemistry (MS); clinical health psychology (PhD); communication studies (MA, MS); computer engineering (MS); computer science (MS); counseling (M Ed, MS), including clinical mental health counseling (MS), college and university counseling, elementary school counseling, secondary school counseling; creative writing (MA); criminal justice (MS); curriculum and instruction (M Ed); decision sciences (MBA); design (MA, MFA), including fashion design (MFA), innovation studies, interior design (MFA); early childhood studies (MS); economics (MS); educational leadership (M Ed, Ed D); educational psychology (MS, PhD), including family studies (MS), gifted and talented (MS), human development (MS), learning and cognition (MS), research, measurement and evaluation (MS); electrical engineering (MS); emergency management (MPA); engineering technology (MS); English (MA); English as a second language (MA); environmental science (MS); finance (MBA, MS); financial management (MPA); French (MA); health services management (MBA); higher education (M Ed, Ed D); history (MA, MS); hospitality management (MS); human resources management (MPA); information science (MS); information systems (PhD); information technologies (MBA); interdisciplinary studies (MA, MS); international studies (MA); international sustainable tourism (MS); jazz studies (MM); journalism (MA, MJ, Graduate Certificate), including interactive and virtual digital communication (Graduate Certificate), narrative journalism (Graduate Certificate), public relations (Graduate Certificate); kinesiology (MS); linguistics (MA); local government management (MPA); logistics (PhD); logistics and supply chain management (MBA); long-term care, senior housing, and aging services (MA); management (PhD); marketing (MBA); mathematics (MA, MS); mechanical and energy engineering (MS, PhD); music (MA), including ethnomusicology, music theory, musicology, performance; music composition (PhD); music education (MM Ed, PhD); nonprofit management (MPA); operations and supply chain management (MBA); performance (MM, DMA); philosophy (MA); political science (MA); professional and technical communication (MA); radio, television and film (MA, MFA); rehabilitation counseling (Certificate); sociology (MA); Spanish (MA); special education (M Ed); speech-language pathology (MA); strategic management (MBA); studio art (MFA); teaching (M Ed); MBA/MS. *Program availability:* Part-time, evening/weekend, online learning. Terminal master's awarded for partial completion of doctoral program. *Degree requirements:* For master's, variable foreign language requirement, comprehensive exam (for some programs), thesis (for some programs); for doctorate, variable foreign language requirement, comprehensive exam (for some programs), thesis/dissertation; for other advanced degree, variable foreign language requirement, comprehensive exam (for some programs). *Entrance requirements:* For master's and doctorate, GRE, GMAT. Additional exam requirements/recommendations for international students: Required—TOEFL (minimum score 550 paper-based; 79 iBT). Electronic applications accepted.

University of Notre Dame, Graduate School, College of Engineering, Department of Electrical Engineering, Notre Dame, IN 46556. Offers MSEE, PhD. Terminal master's awarded for partial completion of doctoral program. *Degree requirements:* For master's, comprehensive exam; for doctorate, thesis/dissertation, candidacy exam. *Entrance requirements:* For master's and doctorate, GRE General Test. Additional exam requirements/recommendations for international students: Required—TOEFL (minimum score 600 paper-based; 80 iBT). Electronic applications accepted. *Faculty research:* Electronic properties of materials and devices, signal and imaging processing, communication theory, control theory and applications, optoelectronics.

University of Oklahoma, Gallogly College of Engineering, School of Electrical and Computer Engineering, Program in Electrical and Computer Engineering, Norman, OK 73019. Offers MS, PhD. *Program availability:* Part-time. *Students:* 83 full-time (15 women), 53 part-time (12 women); includes 14 minority (2 Black or African American, non-Hispanic/Latino; 1 American Indian or Alaska Native, non-Hispanic/Latino; 5 Asian, non-Hispanic/Latino; 5 Hispanic/Latino; 1 Two or more races, non-Hispanic/Latino), 88 international. Average age 29. 102 applicants, 35% accepted, 22 enrolled. In 2016, 23 master's, 15 doctorates awarded. Terminal master's awarded for partial completion of

doctoral program. *Degree requirements:* For master's, comprehensive exam (for some programs), thesis (for some programs); for doctorate, thesis/dissertation, general exam. *Entrance requirements:* For master's and doctorate, GRE, minimum GPA of 3.0. Additional exam requirements/recommendations for international students: Required—TOEFL (minimum score 79 iBT) or IELTS (minimum score 6.5). *Application deadline:* For fall admission, 4/1 for domestic students, 3/1 for international students; for spring admission, 11/1 for domestic students, 10/1 for international students. Applications are processed on a rolling basis. Application fee: $50 ($100 for international students). Electronic applications accepted. *Expenses:* Tuition, state resident: full-time $4886; part-time $203.60 per credit hour. Tuition, nonresident: full-time $18,989; part-time $791.20 per credit hour. *Required fees:* $3283; $126.25 per credit hour. $126.50 per semester. *Financial support:* In 2016–17, 111 students received support. Fellowships with full and partial tuition reimbursements available, research assistantships with full and partial tuition reimbursements available, teaching assistantships with full and partial tuition reimbursements available, career-related internships or fieldwork, scholarships/grants, and health care benefits available. Financial award application deadline: 6/1; financial award applicants required to submit FAFSA. *Faculty research:* Biomedical imaging, radar engineering, semiconductor devices, intelligent transportation systems, signals and systems. *Unit head:* Dr. J.R. Cruz, Director, 405-325-8131, Fax: 405-325-7066, E-mail: jcruz@ou.edu. *Application contact:* Lisa Wilkins, Graduate Programs Assistant III, 405-325-4285, Fax: 405-325-7066, E-mail: lawikins@ou.edu.
Website: http://www.ou.edu/coe/ece.html

University of Ottawa, Faculty of Graduate and Postdoctoral Studies, Faculty of Engineering, Ottawa-Carleton Institute for Electrical and Computer Engineering, Ottawa, ON K1N 6N5, Canada. Offers M Eng, MA Sc, PhD. *Degree requirements:* For master's, thesis or alternative, project; for doctorate, comprehensive exam, thesis/dissertation. *Entrance requirements:* For master's, honors degree or equivalent, minimum B average; for doctorate, minimum A- average. Electronic applications accepted. *Faculty research:* CAD, distributed systems.

University of Pennsylvania, School of Engineering and Applied Science, Department of Electrical and Systems Engineering, Philadelphia, PA 19104. Offers MSE, PhD. *Program availability:* Part-time. *Faculty:* 25 full-time (2 women), 6 part-time/adjunct (0 women). *Students:* 188 full-time (50 women), 53 part-time (20 women); includes 18 minority (10 Asian, non-Hispanic/Latino; 7 Hispanic/Latino; 1 Two or more races, non-Hispanic/Latino), 184 international. Average age 25. 1,060 applicants, 35% accepted, 170 enrolled. In 2016, 84 master's, 7 doctorates awarded. *Degree requirements:* For master's, comprehensive exam, thesis optional; for doctorate, comprehensive exam, thesis/dissertation. *Entrance requirements:* For master's and doctorate, GRE. Additional exam requirements/recommendations for international students: Required—TOEFL (minimum score 100 iBT), IELTS (minimum score 7). *Application deadline:* For fall admission, 3/15 priority date for domestic and international students. Application fee: $80. Electronic applications accepted. *Expenses:* Tuition: Full-time $31,068; part-time $5762 per course. *Required fees:* $3200; $336 per course. Full-time tuition and fees vary according to degree level, program and student level. Part-time tuition and fees vary according to course load, degree level and program. *Faculty research:* Circuits and computer engineering, information decision systems, nano-devices and nano-systems. *Application contact:* William Fenton, Assistant Director of Graduate Admissions, 215-898-4542, Fax: 215-573-5577, E-mail: gradstudies@seas.upenn.edu.

University of Pittsburgh, Swanson School of Engineering, Department of Electrical and Computer Engineering, Pittsburgh, PA 15260. Offers computer engineering (MS, PhD); electrical and computer engineering (MS, PhD). *Program availability:* Part-time, 100% online. *Faculty:* 21 full-time (3 women), 8 part-time/adjunct (1 woman). *Students:* 142 full-time (31 women), 38 part-time (7 women); includes 13 minority (4 Black or African American, non-Hispanic/Latino; 3 Asian, non-Hispanic/Latino; 3 Hispanic/Latino; 1 Native Hawaiian or other Pacific Islander, non-Hispanic/Latino; 2 Two or more races, non-Hispanic/Latino), 113 international. 891 applicants, 20% accepted, 55 enrolled. In 2016, 35 master's, 14 doctorates awarded. Terminal master's awarded for partial completion of doctoral program. *Degree requirements:* For doctorate, comprehensive exam, thesis/dissertation, final oral exams. *Entrance requirements:* For master's and doctorate, GRE General Test, minimum GPA of 3.0. Additional exam requirements/recommendations for international students: Required—TOEFL (minimum score 550 paper-based; 80 iBT). *Application deadline:* For fall admission, 3/1 priority date for domestic and international students; for spring admission, 7/1 priority date for domestic and international students. Applications are processed on a rolling basis. Application fee: $50. Electronic applications accepted. *Expenses:* $24,962 full-time per academic year in-state tuition, $41,222 full-time per academic year out-of-state tuition; $830 mandatory fees per academic year. *Financial support:* In 2016–17, 16 fellowships with full tuition reimbursements (averaging $30,720 per year), 61 research assistantships with full tuition reimbursements (averaging $27,396 per year), 25 teaching assistantships with full tuition reimbursements (averaging $26,328 per year) were awarded; scholarships/grants and tuition waivers (full) also available. Financial award application deadline: 3/1. *Faculty research:* Computer engineering, image processing, signal processing, electro-optic devices, controls/power. *Total annual research expenditures:* $8.8 million. *Unit head:* Dr. Alan D. George, Chairman, 412-624-8000, Fax: 412-624-8003, E-mail: alan.george@pitt.edu. *Application contact:* Rama Bazaz, Director, 412-624-9800, Fax: 412-624-9808, E-mail: ssoeadm@pitt.edu.
Website: http://www.engineering.pitt.edu/Departments/Electrical-Computer/

University of Portland, School of Engineering, Portland, OR 97203-5798. Offers biomedical engineering (MBME); civil engineering (ME); computer science (ME); electrical engineering (ME); mechanical engineering (ME). *Program availability:* Part-time, evening/weekend. *Degree requirements:* For master's, thesis optional. *Entrance requirements:* For master's, GRE General Test, minimum GPA of 3.0, 3 letters of recommendation, resume, statement of goals, official transcripts. Additional exam requirements/recommendations for international students: Required—TOEFL (minimum score 550 paper-based; 80 iBT), IELTS (minimum score 7). *Expenses:* Contact institution.

University of Puerto Rico, Mayagüez Campus, Graduate Studies, College of Engineering, Department of Electrical and Computer Engineering, Mayagüez, PR 00681-9000. Offers computer engineering (ME, MS); computing and information sciences and engineering (PhD); electrical engineering (ME, MS). *Program availability:* Part-time. *Faculty:* 48 full-time (6 women). *Students:* 45 full-time (6 women), 8 part-time (3 women); includes 45 minority (all Hispanic/Latino), 5 international. Average age 25. 30 applicants, 83% accepted, 18 enrolled. In 2016, 12 master's awarded. Terminal master's awarded for partial completion of doctoral program. *Degree requirements:* For master's, one foreign language, comprehensive exam, thesis; for doctorate, one foreign language, comprehensive exam, thesis/dissertation. *Entrance requirements:* For master's and doctorate, proficiency in English and Spanish; BS in electrical or computer engineering, or equivalent; minimum GPA of 3.0. *Application deadline:* For fall admission, 2/15 for domestic and international students; for spring admission, 9/15 for domestic and international students. Applications are processed on a rolling basis. Application fee: $25. Electronic applications accepted. *Expenses: Tuition, area resident:* Full-time $2466. *International tuition:* $7166 full-time. *Required fees:* $210. One-time fee: $5 full-time. Tuition and fees vary according to course level, campus/location,

program and student level. *Financial support:* In 2016–17, 50 students received support, including 41 research assistantships with full and partial tuition reimbursements available (averaging $3,442 per year), 26 teaching assistantships with full and partial tuition reimbursements available (averaging $4,149 per year); unspecified assistantships also available. *Faculty research:* Digital signal processing, power electronics, microwave ocean emissivity, parallel and distributed computing, microwave remote sensing. *Unit head:* Jose Colom-Ustaris, Ph.D., Department Head, 787-832-4040 Ext. 3086, Fax: 787-831-7564, E-mail: jose.colom1@upr.edu. *Application contact:* Claribel Lorenzo, Administrative Secretary V, 787-832-4040 Ext. 3821, E-mail: claribel.lorenzo@upr.edu.
Website: https://ece.uprm.edu/

University of Rhode Island, Graduate School, College of Engineering, Department of Electrical, Computer and Biomedical Engineering, Kingston, RI 02881. Offers acoustics and underwater acoustics (MS, PhD); biomedical engineering (MS, PhD); circuits and devices (MS); communication theory (MS, PhD); computer architectures and digital systems (MS, PhD); computer networks (MS, PhD); digital signal processing (MS); embedded systems and computer applications (MS, PhD); fault-tolerant computing (MS, PhD); materials and optics (MS, PhD); systems theory (MS, PhD). *Program availability:* Part-time. *Faculty:* 22 full-time (3 women). *Students:* 27 full-time (5 women), 17 part-time (3 women); includes 6 minority (1 American Indian or Alaska Native, non-Hispanic/Latino; 3 Asian, non-Hispanic/Latino; 1 Hispanic/Latino; 1 Two or more races, non-Hispanic/Latino), 21 international. In 2016, 8 master's, 7 doctorates awarded. *Degree requirements:* For master's, comprehensive exam (for some programs), thesis optional; for doctorate, comprehensive exam, thesis/dissertation. *Entrance requirements:* For master's and doctorate, GRE, 2 letters of recommendation (3 for international applicants). Additional exam requirements/recommendations for international students: Required—TOEFL. *Application deadline:* For fall admission, 7/15 for domestic students, 2/1 for international students; for spring admission, 11/15 for domestic students, 7/15 for international students; for summer admission, 4/15 for domestic students. Application fee: $65. Electronic applications accepted. *Expenses:* Tuition, state resident: full-time $11,796; part-time $655 per credit. Tuition, nonresident: full-time $24,206; part-time $1345 per credit. *Required fees:* $1546; $44 per credit. One-time fee: $155 full-time; $35 part-time. *Financial support:* In 2016–17, 11 research assistantships with tuition reimbursements (averaging $9,825 per year), 4 teaching assistantships with tuition reimbursements (averaging $8,681 per year) were awarded. Financial award application deadline: 7/15; financial award applicants required to submit FAFSA. *Unit head:* Dr. Godi Fischer, Chair, 401-874-5879, Fax: 401-782-6422, E-mail: fischer@ele.uri.edu. *Application contact:* Dr. Frederick J. Vetter, Graduate Director, 401-874-5141, E-mail: vetter@ele.uri.edu.
Website: http://www.ele.uri.edu/

University of Rochester, Hajim School of Engineering and Applied Sciences, Department of Electrical and Computer Engineering, Rochester, NY 14627. Offers MS, PhD. *Faculty:* 19 full-time (1 woman). *Students:* 122 full-time (19 women), 1 part-time (0 women); includes 5 minority (2 Black or African American, non-Hispanic/Latino; 2 Asian, non-Hispanic/Latino; 1 Hispanic/Latino), 94 international. Average age 26. 543 applicants, 41% accepted, 43 enrolled. In 2016, 57 master's, 11 doctorates awarded. Terminal master's awarded for partial completion of doctoral program. *Degree requirements:* For master's, comprehensive exam, thesis, final exam; for doctorate, thesis/dissertation, qualifying exam. *Entrance requirements:* For master's and doctorate, GRE. Additional exam requirements/recommendations for international students: Required—TOEFL. *Application deadline:* For fall admission, 1/15 for domestic students. Application fee: $60. Electronic applications accepted. *Expenses:* $1,538 per credit hour. *Financial support:* In 2016–17, 130 students received support, including 2 fellowships with full tuition reimbursements available (averaging $27,600 per year), 54 research assistantships with full tuition reimbursements available (averaging $27,600 per year), 42 teaching assistantships with full and partial tuition reimbursements available (averaging $2,500 per year); tuition waivers (full and partial) also available. *Faculty research:* Bio-informatics, communications, signal processing, digital audio, image processing, medical imaging. *Unit head:* Mark Bocko, Chair, 585-275-4879. *Application contact:* Michele Foster, Administrative Assistant/Graduate Program Coordinator, 585-275-4054, E-mail: michele.foster@rochester.edu.
Website: http://www.ece.rochester.edu/graduate/index.html

University of Rochester, Hajim School of Engineering and Applied Sciences, Master of Science in Technical Entrepreneurship and Management Program, Rochester, NY 14642. Offers biomedical engineering (MS); chemical engineering (MS); computer science (MS); electrical and computer engineering (MS); energy and the environment (MS); materials science (MS); mechanical engineering (MS); optics (MS). Program offered in collaboration with the Simon School of Business. *Program availability:* Part-time. *Students:* 42 full-time (13 women), 6 part-time (3 women); includes 7 minority (1 Black or African American, non-Hispanic/Latino; 1 Asian, non-Hispanic/Latino; 4 Hispanic/Latino; 1 Two or more races, non-Hispanic/Latino), 28 international. Average age 24. 245 applicants, 65% accepted, 29 enrolled. In 2016, 31 master's awarded. *Degree requirements:* For master's, comprehensive exam, final exam. *Entrance requirements:* For master's, GRE or GMAT, 3 letters of recommendation; personal statement; official transcript; bachelor's degree (or equivalent for international students) in engineering, science, or mathematics. Additional exam requirements/recommendations for international students: Required—TOEFL (minimum score 600 paper-based; 100 iBT). *Application deadline:* For fall admission, 2/1 for domestic and international students. Application fee: $60. Electronic applications accepted. *Expenses:* $1,800 per credit. *Financial support:* In 2016–17, 45 students received support. Career-related internships or fieldwork and scholarships/grants available. Support available to part-time students. Financial award application deadline: 2/1. *Faculty research:* High efficiency solar cells, macromolecular self-assembly, digital signal processing, memory hierarchy management, molecular and physical mechanisms in cell migration, optical imaging systems. *Unit head:* Duncan T. Moore, Vice Provost for Entrepreneurship, 585-275-5248, Fax: 585-473-6745, E-mail: duncan.moore@rochester.edu. *Application contact:* Andrea Barrett, Executive Director, 585-276-3407, Fax: 585-276-2357, E-mail: andrea.barrett@rochester.edu.
Website: http://www.rochester.edu/team

University of St. Thomas, Graduate Studies, School of Engineering, St. Paul, MN 55105-1096. Offers data science (MS); electrical engineering (MS); information technology (MS); manufacturing engineering (MS); manufacturing systems (Certificate); mechanical engineering (MS); medical device development (Certificate); regulatory science (MS); software engineering (MS); software management (MS); systems engineering (MS); technology leadership (Certificate); technology management (MS). *Accreditation:* ABET (one or more programs are accredited). *Entrance requirements:* For master's, resume, official transcripts. Additional exam requirements/recommendations for international students: Required—TOEFL (minimum score 550 paper-based). *Application deadline:* For fall admission, 8/1 priority date for domestic students; for spring admission, 1/1 priority date for domestic students. Applications are processed on a rolling basis. Application fee: $50. Electronic applications accepted. *Expenses:* Contact institution. *Financial support:* Fellowships, research assistantships, institutionally sponsored loans, and scholarships/grants available. Support available to part-time students. Financial award application deadline: 4/1; financial award applicants required to submit FAFSA. *Unit head:* Don Weinkauf, Dean, 651-962-5760, Fax: 651-962-6419, E-mail: dhweinkauf@stthomas.edu. *Application contact:* Tina M. Hansen, Graduate Program Manager, 651-962-5755, Fax: 651-962-6419, E-mail: tina.hansen@stthomas.edu.
Website: http://www.stthomas.edu/engineering/

University of Saskatchewan, College of Graduate Studies and Research, College of Engineering, Electrical Engineering Program, Saskatoon, SK S7N 5A9, Canada. Offers M Eng, M Sc, PhD, PGD. *Program availability:* Part-time. *Degree requirements:* For master's, thesis (for some programs), 30 credits (for M Eng); thesis and 12 credits (for MS); for doctorate, comprehensive exam, thesis/dissertation, qualifying exam, 18 credits; for PGD, 30 credits. *Entrance requirements:* For master's and doctorate, GRE. Additional exam requirements/recommendations for international students: Required—TOEFL, TOEFL (minimum iBT score of 80), IELTS (6.5), CanTEST (4.5), or PTE (59). Electronic applications accepted. *Faculty research:* Artificial neural networks and fuzzy logic, biomedical microdevices, computer engineering, control systems, digital signal processing, electrical machines and power magnetics, embedded systems, high aspect ratio micro patterning, instrumentation and microprocessor applications, multimedia and video signal processing, optoelectronics and photonics, power system protection and control, power system reliability economics, renewable energy applications, thin films.

University of South Alabama, College of Engineering, Department of Electrical and Computer Engineering, Mobile, AL 36688. Offers computer engineering (MSEE); electrical engineering (MSEE). *Program availability:* Part-time. *Faculty:* 9 full-time (0 women). *Students:* 47 full-time (13 women), 6 part-time (1 woman); includes 5 minority (3 Black or African American, non-Hispanic/Latino; 1 Native Hawaiian or other Pacific Islander, non-Hispanic/Latino; 1 Two or more races, non-Hispanic/Latino), 42 international. Average age 25. 104 applicants, 55% accepted, 7 enrolled. In 2016, 88 master's awarded. *Degree requirements:* For master's, comprehensive exam, thesis or project. *Entrance requirements:* For master's, GRE General Test, BS in engineering, minimum GPA of 3.0. Additional exam requirements/recommendations for international students: Required—TOEFL (minimum score 550 paper-based; 79 iBT). *Application deadline:* For fall admission, 7/1 priority date for domestic students, 6/1 priority date for international students; for spring admission, 12/1 priority date for domestic students, 11/1 priority date for international students; for summer admission, 5/1 priority date for domestic students, 4/1 priority date for international students. Applications are processed on a rolling basis. Application fee: $35. Electronic applications accepted. *Expenses:* Contact institution. *Financial support:* Fellowships, research assistantships, teaching assistantships, career-related internships or fieldwork, institutionally sponsored loans, scholarships/grants, and unspecified assistantships available. Support available to part-time students. Financial award application deadline: 5/31; financial award applicants required to submit FAFSA. *Faculty research:* Plasma characterization, oil polluted contaminants, target detection and tracking, space propulsion applications, electrical and computer engineering. *Unit head:* Dr. Hulya Kirkici, Department Chair, 251-460-6117, Fax: 251-460-6028, E-mail: hkirkici@southalabama.edu. *Application contact:* Brenda Poole, Academic Records Specialist, 251-460-6140, Fax: 251-460-6343, E-mail: engineering@southalabama.edu.
Website: http://www.southalabama.edu/colleges/engineering/ece/index.html

University of South Carolina, The Graduate School, College of Engineering and Computing, Department of Electrical Engineering, Columbia, SC 29208. Offers ME, MS, PhD. *Program availability:* Part-time, evening/weekend, online learning. *Degree requirements:* For master's, comprehensive exam, thesis (for some programs); for doctorate, comprehensive exam, thesis/dissertation, qualifying exam. *Entrance requirements:* For master's and doctorate, GRE General Test. Additional exam requirements/recommendations for international students: Required—TOEFL (minimum score 570 paper-based; 88 iBT). Electronic applications accepted. *Faculty research:* Microelectronics, photonics, wireless communications, signal integrity, energy and control systems.

University of Southern California, Graduate School, Viterbi School of Engineering, Ming Hsieh Department of Electrical Engineering, Los Angeles, CA 90089. Offers computer engineering (MS, PhD); electric power (MS); electrical engineering (MS, PhD, Engr); engineering technology commercialization (Graduate Certificate); multimedia and creative technologies (MS); telecommunications (MS); VLSI design (MS); wireless health technology (MS). *Program availability:* Part-time, online learning. Terminal master's awarded for partial completion of doctoral program. *Degree requirements:* For master's, thesis optional; for doctorate, thesis/dissertation. *Entrance requirements:* For master's and doctorate, GRE General Test. Additional exam requirements/recommendations for international students: Recommended—TOEFL. Electronic applications accepted. *Faculty research:* Communications, computer engineering and networks, control systems, integrated circuits and systems, electromagnetics and energy conversion, micro electro-mechanical systems and nanotechnology, photonics and quantum electronics, plasma research, signal and image processing.

University of South Florida, College of Engineering, Department of Electrical Engineering, Tampa, FL 33620-9951. Offers MSEE, PhD. *Program availability:* Part-time, online learning. *Faculty:* 30 full-time (3 women), 1 part-time/adjunct (0 women). *Students:* 315 full-time (57 women), 66 part-time (9 women); includes 31 minority (9 Black or African American, non-Hispanic/Latino; 10 Asian, non-Hispanic/Latino; 11 Hispanic/Latino; 1 Two or more races, non-Hispanic/Latino), 315 international. Average age 26. 537 applicants, 61% accepted, 102 enrolled. In 2016, 129 master's, 12 doctorates awarded. Terminal master's awarded for partial completion of doctoral program. *Degree requirements:* For master's, comprehensive exam, thesis or alternative; for doctorate, comprehensive exam, thesis/dissertation. *Entrance requirements:* For master's, minimum GPA of 3.0 in last 60 hours of coursework, three letters of recommendation; for doctorate, GRE General Test, minimum GPA of 3.0 in last 60 hours of coursework, three letters of recommendation, statement of purpose. Additional exam requirements/recommendations for international students: Required—TOEFL (minimum score 550 paper-based; 79 iBT) or IELTS (minimum score 6.5). *Application deadline:* For fall admission, 2/15 for domestic and international students; for spring admission, 10/15 for domestic students, 9/15 for international students; for summer admission, 2/15 for domestic students, 1/15 for international students. Application fee: $30. Electronic applications accepted. *Expenses:* Tuition, state resident: full-time $7766; part-time $431.43 per credit hour. Tuition, nonresident: full-time $15,789; part-time $877.17 per credit hour. *Required fees:* $37 per term. *Financial support:* In 2016–17, 44 students received support, including 57 research assistantships (averaging $12,357 per year), 41 teaching assistantships with tuition reimbursements available (averaging $13,528 per year). Financial award applicants required to submit FAFSA. *Faculty research:* Wireless communication and signal processing, surface science, wireless and microwave information systems (WAMI), in vivo Wireless Information Networking (iWINLAB), personalized interactive experiences (PIE), Smart Grid power systems, defense and intelligence. *Total annual research expenditures:* $2.7 million. *Unit head:* Dr. Thomas Weller, Professor and Department Chair, 813-974-2740, E-mail: weller@usf.edu. *Application contact:* Dr. Andrew Hoff, Associate Professor and Graduate Program Director, 813-974-4958, Fax: 813-974-5250, E-mail: hoff@usf.edu.
Website: http://ee.eng.usf.edu/

Electrical Engineering

The University of Tennessee, Graduate School, Tickle College of Engineering, Department of Electrical Engineering and Computer Science, Program in Electrical Engineering, Knoxville, TN 37996. Offers MS, PhD. *Program availability:* Part-time. *Faculty:* 24 full-time (5 women), 2 part-time/adjunct (0 women). *Students:* 146 full-time (36 women), 12 part-time (1 woman); includes 7 minority (1 Black or African American, non-Hispanic/Latino; 3 Asian, non-Hispanic/Latino; 2 Hispanic/Latino; 1 Two or more races, non-Hispanic/Latino), 110 international. Average age 28. 253 applicants, 21% accepted, 41 enrolled. In 2016, 13 master's, 19 doctorates awarded. *Degree requirements:* For master's, thesis or alternative; for doctorate, comprehensive exam, thesis/dissertation. *Entrance requirements:* For master's, GRE General Test (for MS students pursuing research thesis), minimum GPA of 2.7 (for U.S. degree holders), 3.0 (for international degree holders); 3 references; personal statement; for doctorate, GRE General Test, minimum GPA of 3.0 on previous graduate coursework; 3 references; personal statement. Additional exam requirements/recommendations for international students: Required—TOEFL (minimum score 550 paper-based). *Application deadline:* For fall admission, 2/1 priority date for domestic and international students; for spring admission, 6/15 for domestic and international students. Applications are processed on a rolling basis. Application fee: $35. Electronic applications accepted. *Financial support:* In 2016–17, 134 students received support, including 13 fellowships with full tuition reimbursements available (averaging $28,294 per year), 78 research assistantships with full tuition reimbursements available (averaging $23,751 per year), 32 teaching assistantships with full tuition reimbursements available (averaging $20,470 per year); career-related internships or fieldwork, Federal Work-Study, institutionally sponsored loans, health care benefits, and unspecified assistantships also available. Financial award application deadline: 2/1; financial award applicants required to submit FAFSA. *Unit head:* Dr. Leon Tolbert, Head, 865-974-3461, Fax: 865-974-5483, E-mail: tolbert@utk.edu. *Application contact:* Dr. Jens Gregor, Associate Head, 865-974-4399, Fax: 865-974-5483, E-mail: jgregor@utk.edu.
Website: http://www.eecs.utk.edu

The University of Tennessee at Chattanooga, Program in Engineering, Chattanooga, TN 37403. Offers automotive systems (MS Engr); chemical engineering (MS Engr); civil engineering (MS Engr); computational engineering (MS Engr); electrical engineering (MS Engr); industrial engineering (MS Engr); mechanical engineering (MS Engr). *Program availability:* Part-time. *Faculty:* 21 full-time (2 women), 2 part-time/adjunct (1 woman). *Students:* 21 full-time (5 women), 26 part-time (7 women); includes 11 minority (4 Black or African American, non-Hispanic/Latino; 5 Asian, non-Hispanic/Latino; 1 Hispanic/Latino; 1 Two or more races, non-Hispanic/Latino), 18 international. Average age 28. 30 applicants, 83% accepted, 14 enrolled. In 2016, 25 master's awarded. *Degree requirements:* For master's, comprehensive exam, thesis or alternative, engineering project. *Entrance requirements:* For master's, GRE General Test, minimum undergraduate GPA of 2.7 or 3.0 in last two years of undergraduate coursework. Additional exam requirements/recommendations for international students: Required—TOEFL (minimum score 550 paper-based; 79 iBT), IELTS (minimum score 6). *Application deadline:* For fall admission, 6/15 priority date for domestic students, 7/1 for international students; for spring admission, 11/1 priority date for domestic students, 11/1 for international students. Applications are processed on a rolling basis. Application fee: $35 ($40 for international students). Electronic applications accepted. *Expenses:* $9,876 full-time in-state; $25,994 full-time out-of-state; $450 per credit part-time in-state; $1,345 per credit part-time out-of-state. *Financial support:* In 2016–17, 6 research assistantships, 5 teaching assistantships were awarded; career-related internships or fieldwork, scholarships/grants, health care benefits, and unspecified assistantships also available. Support available to part-time students. Financial award application deadline: 7/1. *Faculty research:* Quality control and reliability engineering, financial management, thermal science, energy conservation, structural analysis. *Total annual research expenditures:* $921,122. *Unit head:* Dr. Daniel Pack, Dean, 423-425-2256, Fax: 423-425-5311, E-mail: daniel-pack@utc.edu. *Application contact:* Dr. Joanne Romagni, Dean of the Graduate School, 423-425-4478, Fax: 423-425-5223, E-mail: joanne-romagni@utc.edu.
Website: http://www.utc.edu/college-engineering-computer-science/graduate-programs/msengr.php

The University of Texas at Arlington, Graduate School, College of Engineering, Department of Electrical Engineering, Arlington, TX 76019. Offers M Engr, MS, PhD. *Program availability:* Part-time, evening/weekend, online learning. Terminal master's awarded for partial completion of doctoral program. *Degree requirements:* For master's, thesis optional; for doctorate, comprehensive exam, thesis/dissertation, written diagnostic exam. *Entrance requirements:* For master's, GRE General Test, minimum GPA of 3.25; for doctorate, GRE General Test, minimum GPA of 3.5. Additional exam requirements/recommendations for international students: Required—TOEFL (minimum score 560 paper-based); Recommended—TWE (minimum score 4). *Application deadline:* For fall admission, 6/1 for domestic students, 4/1 for international students; for spring admission, 10/15 for domestic students, 9/15 for international students. Applications are processed on a rolling basis. Application fee: $35 ($50 for international students). *Financial support:* Fellowships, research assistantships, teaching assistantships, Federal Work-Study, institutionally sponsored loans, scholarships/grants, and unspecified assistantships available. Financial award application deadline: 6/1; financial award applicants required to submit FAFSA. *Faculty research:* Nanotech and microelectromechanical systems (MEMS), digital image processing, telecommunications and optics, energy systems and power electronics, VLSI and semiconductors. *Unit head:* Dr. Jonathan Bredow, Chair, 817-272-3266, Fax: 817-272-2253, E-mail: jbredow@uta.edu. *Application contact:* Dr. William E. Dillon, Graduate Adviser, 817-272-2671, Fax: 817-272-1509, E-mail: eedept@uta.edu.
Website: http://www.ee.uta.edu/ee

The University of Texas at Austin, Graduate School, Cockrell School of Engineering, Department of Electrical and Computer Engineering, Austin, TX 78712-1111. Offers MS, PhD. *Program availability:* Part-time. *Entrance requirements:* For master's, GRE General Test, minimum GPA of 3.3 in upper-division course work; for doctorate, GRE General Test. Electronic applications accepted.

The University of Texas at Dallas, Erik Jonson School of Engineering and Computer Science, Department of Electrical Engineering, Richardson, TX 75080. Offers computer engineering (MS, PhD); electrical engineering (MSEE, PhD); telecommunications engineering (MSTE, PhD). *Program availability:* Part-time, evening/weekend. *Faculty:* 47 full-time (4 women), 5 part-time/adjunct (0 women). *Students:* 648 full-time (178 women), 196 part-time (50 women); includes 40 minority (1 Black or African American, non-Hispanic/Latino; 23 Asian, non-Hispanic/Latino; 11 Hispanic/Latino; 5 Two or more races, non-Hispanic/Latino), 744 international. Average age 27. 2,663 applicants, 34% accepted, 287 enrolled. In 2016, 292 master's, 41 doctorates awarded. *Degree requirements:* For master's, thesis or major design project; for doctorate, thesis/dissertation. *Entrance requirements:* For master's, GRE General Test, minimum GPA of 3.0 in related bachelor's degree; for doctorate, GRE General Test, minimum GPA of 3.5. Additional exam requirements/recommendations for international students: Required—TOEFL (minimum score 550 paper-based). *Application deadline:* For fall admission, 7/15 for domestic students, 5/1 priority date for international students; for spring admission, 11/15 for domestic students, 9/1 priority date for international students. Applications are processed on a rolling basis. Application fee: $50 ($100 for international students). Electronic applications accepted. *Expenses:* Tuition, state resident: full-time $12,418; part-time $690 per semester hour. Tuition, nonresident: full-time $24,150; part-time $1342 per semester hour. Tuition and fees vary according to course load. *Financial support:* In 2016–17, 234 students received support, including 12 fellowships (averaging $1,267 per year), 128 research assistantships with partial tuition reimbursements available (averaging $23,845 per year), 76 teaching assistantships with partial tuition reimbursements available (averaging $17,289 per year); Federal Work-Study, institutionally sponsored loans, scholarships/grants, unspecified assistantships, and cooperative positions also available. Support available to part-time students. Financial award application deadline: 4/30; financial award applicants required to submit FAFSA. *Faculty research:* Semiconductor device manufacturing, photonics devices and systems, signal processing and language technology, nano-fabrication, energy efficient digital systems. *Unit head:* Dr. Lawrence Overzet, Department Head, 972-883-6755, Fax: 972-883-2710, E-mail: overzet@utdallas.edu. *Application contact:* 972-883-6755, Fax: 972-883-2710, E-mail: eegrad_assist@utdallas.edu.
Website: http://www.ee.utdallas.edu

The University of Texas at El Paso, Graduate School, College of Engineering, Department of Electrical and Computer Engineering, El Paso, TX 79968-0001. Offers computer engineering (MS); electrical and computer engineering (PhD); electrical engineering (MS). *Program availability:* Part-time, evening/weekend. Terminal master's awarded for partial completion of doctoral program. *Degree requirements:* For master's, thesis optional; for doctorate, thesis/dissertation. *Entrance requirements:* For master's, GRE General Test, minimum GPA of 3.0; for doctorate, GRE General Test, minimum graduate GPA of 3.0. Additional exam requirements/recommendations for international students: Required—TOEFL. Electronic applications accepted. *Faculty research:* Signal and image processing, computer architecture, fiber optics, computational electromagnetics, electronic displays and thin films.

The University of Texas at San Antonio, College of Engineering, Department of Electrical and Computer Engineering, San Antonio, TX 78249-0617. Offers advanced materials engineering (MS); computer engineering (MS); electrical engineering (MSEE, PhD). *Program availability:* Part-time. *Faculty:* 26 full-time (4 women), 3 part-time/adjunct (0 women). *Students:* 122 full-time (31 women), 100 part-time (22 women); includes 46 minority (4 Black or African American, non-Hispanic/Latino; 10 Asian, non-Hispanic/Latino; 30 Hispanic/Latino; 1 Native Hawaiian or other Pacific Islander, non-Hispanic/Latino; 1 Two or more races, non-Hispanic/Latino), 131 international. Average age 28. 233 applicants, 73% accepted, 50 enrolled. In 2016, 115 master's, 15 doctorates awarded. Terminal master's awarded for partial completion of doctoral program. *Degree requirements:* For master's, comprehensive exam, thesis (for some programs); for doctorate, comprehensive exam, thesis/dissertation. *Entrance requirements:* For master's, GRE General Test, bachelor's degree in electrical or computer engineering from ABET-accredited institution of higher education or related field; minimum GPA of 3.0 on the last 60 semester credit hours of undergraduate studies; for doctorate, GRE General Test, master's degree or minimum GPA of 3.3 in last 60 semester credit hours of undergraduate level coursework in electrical engineering; statement of purpose. Additional exam requirements/recommendations for international students: Required—TOEFL (minimum score 550 paper-based; 79 iBT), IELTS (minimum score 6.5). *Application deadline:* For fall admission, 7/1 for domestic students, 4/1 for international students; for spring admission, 11/1 for domestic students, 9/1 for international students. Applications are processed on a rolling basis. Application fee: $45 ($80 for international students). Electronic applications accepted. *Financial support:* Unspecified assistantships available. Financial award application deadline: 3/31. *Faculty research:* Computer engineering, digital signal processing, systems and controls, communications, electronics materials and devices, electric power engineering. *Total annual research expenditures:* $3.9 million. *Unit head:* Dr. Chunjiang Qian, Department Chair/Professor, 210-458-7928, E-mail: chunjiang.qian@utsa.edu.
Website: http://ece.utsa.edu/

The University of Texas at Tyler, College of Engineering, Department of Electrical Engineering, Tyler, TX 75799-0001. Offers MS. *Program availability:* Part-time, evening/weekend. *Degree requirements:* For master's, comprehensive exam (for some programs). *Entrance requirements:* For master's, GRE General Test, bachelor's degree in electrical engineering. Additional exam requirements/recommendations for international students: Required—TOEFL. *Faculty research:* Electronics, digital sign processing, real time systems electromagnetic fields, semiconductor modeling.

The University of Texas Rio Grande Valley, College of Engineering and Computer Science, Department of Electrical Engineering, Edinburg, TX 78539. Offers MS. Tuition and fees vary according to course load and program.

University of the District of Columbia, School of Engineering and Applied Sciences, Program in Electrical Engineering, Washington, DC 20008-1175. Offers MSEE.

The University of Toledo, College of Graduate Studies, College of Engineering, Department of Electrical Engineering and Computer Science, Toledo, OH 43606-3390. Offers computer science (MS, PhD); electrical engineering (MS, PhD). *Program availability:* Part-time, evening/weekend. *Degree requirements:* For master's, thesis or alternative; for doctorate, thesis/dissertation, qualifying exam. *Entrance requirements:* For master's, GRE General Test, minimum GPA of 3.0; for doctorate, GRE General Test, minimum GPA of 3.3. Additional exam requirements/recommendations for international students: Required—TOEFL (minimum score 550 paper-based; 80 iBT). Electronic applications accepted. *Faculty research:* Communication and signal processing, high performance computing systems, intelligent systems, power electronics and energy systems, RF and microwave systems, sensors and medical devices, solid state devices.

University of Toronto, School of Graduate Studies, Faculty of Applied Science and Engineering, Department of Electrical and Computer Engineering, Toronto, ON M5S 1A1, Canada. Offers M Eng, MA Sc, PhD. *Program availability:* Part-time. *Degree requirements:* For master's, thesis (for some programs), oral thesis defense (MA Sc); for doctorate, thesis/dissertation, qualifying exam, thesis defense. *Entrance requirements:* For master's, four-year degree in electrical or computer engineering, minimum B average, 2 letters of reference; for doctorate, minimum B+ average, MA Sc in electrical or computer engineering, 2 letters of reference. Additional exam requirements/recommendations for international students: Required—TOEFL (minimum score 580 paper-based; 93 iBT). Electronic applications accepted.

The University of Tulsa, Graduate School, College of Engineering and Natural Sciences, Department of Electrical and Computer Engineering, Tulsa, OK 74104-3189. Offers computer engineering (ME, MSE, PhD); electrical engineering (ME, MSE). *Program availability:* Part-time. *Faculty:* 6 full-time (0 women). *Students:* 34 full-time (4 women), 4 part-time (0 women); includes 3 minority (1 Black or African American, non-Hispanic/Latino; 1 Asian, non-Hispanic/Latino; 1 Hispanic/Latino), 8 international. Average age 26. 51 applicants, 39% accepted, 13 enrolled. In 2016, 4 master's awarded. Terminal master's awarded for partial completion of doctoral program. *Degree requirements:* For master's, comprehensive exam (for some programs), design report (ME), thesis (MS); for doctorate, comprehensive exam, thesis/dissertation. *Entrance requirements:* For master's, GRE General Test. Additional exam requirements/recommendations for international students: Required—TOEFL (minimum score 550

paper-based; 80 iBT), IELTS (minimum score 6). *Application deadline:* Applications are processed on a rolling basis. Application fee: $55. Electronic applications accepted. *Expenses: Tuition:* Full-time $22,230; part-time $1235 per credit hour. *Required fees:* $990 per semester. Tuition and fees vary according to course load. *Financial support:* In 2016–17, 22 students received support, including 1 fellowship with tuition reimbursement available (averaging $1,250 per year), 16 research assistantships with full tuition reimbursements available (averaging $14,614 per year), 5 teaching assistantships with full tuition reimbursements available (averaging $13,509 per year); career-related internships or fieldwork, Federal Work-Study, scholarships/grants, health care benefits, tuition waivers (full and partial), and unspecified assistantships also available. Support available to part-time students. Financial award application deadline: 2/1; financial award applicants required to submit FAFSA. *Faculty research:* VLSI microprocessors, intelligent systems, electromagnetics, intrusion detection systems, digital electronics. *Total annual research expenditures:* $492,694. *Unit head:* Dr. Kaveh Ashenayi, Chairperson, 918-631-3278, Fax: 918-631-3344, E-mail: kash@utulsa.edu. *Application contact:* Dr. Heng-Ming Tai, Adviser, 918-631-3271, Fax: 918-631-3344, E-mail: tai@utulsa.edu.
Website: http://engineering.utulsa.edu/academics/electrical-and-computer-engineering/

University of Utah, Graduate School, College of Engineering, Department of Electrical and Computer Engineering, Salt Lake City, UT 84112. Offers electrical and computer engineering (MS, PhD); electrical engineering (ME); MS/MBA. *Program availability:* Part-time. *Faculty:* 25 full-time (2 women), 10 part-time/adjunct (1 woman). *Students:* 163 full-time (35 women), 53 part-time (5 women); includes 11 minority (7 Asian, non-Hispanic/Latino; 3 Hispanic/Latino; 1 Two or more races, non-Hispanic/Latino), 142 international. Average age 28. 395 applicants, 51% accepted, 61 enrolled. In 2016, 45 master's, 8 doctorates awarded. Terminal master's awarded for partial completion of doctoral program. *Degree requirements:* For master's, comprehensive exam (for some programs), thesis (for some programs); for doctorate, comprehensive exam, thesis/dissertation. *Entrance requirements:* For master's, GRE General Test, minimum GPA of 3.2; for doctorate, GRE General Test, minimum GPA of 3.5. Additional exam requirements/recommendations for international students: Required—TOEFL (minimum score 600 paper-based; 100 iBT); Recommended—IELTS (minimum score 7.5). *Application deadline:* For fall admission, 1/15 for domestic and international students; for spring admission, 10/1 for domestic students. Application fee: $10 ($25 for international students). *Expenses:* Contact institution. *Financial support:* In 2016–17, 103 students received support, including 2 fellowships with full tuition reimbursements available (averaging $25,000 per year), 71 research assistantships with full tuition reimbursements available (averaging $22,165 per year), 30 teaching assistantships with full tuition reimbursements available (averaging $19,948 per year); Federal Work-Study, institutionally sponsored loans, health care benefits, and unspecified assistantships also available. Financial award application deadline: 1/15; financial award applicants required to submit FAFSA. *Faculty research:* Semiconductors, VLSI design, control systems, electromagnetics and applied optics, communication theory and digital signal processing, power systems. *Total annual research expenditures:* $6.8 million. *Unit head:* Dr. Gianluca Lazzi, Chair, 801-581-6942, Fax: 801-581-5281, E-mail: lazzi@utah.edu. *Application contact:* Holly Cox, Administrative Manager, 801-581-3843, Fax: 801-581-5281, E-mail: h.cox@utah.edu.
Website: http://www.ece.utah.edu/

University of Vermont, Graduate College, College of Engineering and Mathematics, Department of Electrical Engineering, Burlington, VT 05405. Offers MS, PhD. *Degree requirements:* For master's, thesis or alternative; for doctorate, one foreign language, thesis/dissertation. *Entrance requirements:* For master's, GRE General Test. Additional exam requirements/recommendations for international students: Required—TOEFL (minimum score 550 paper-based; 80 iBT). Electronic applications accepted. *Expenses:* Tuition, state resident: full-time $5814. Tuition, nonresident: full-time $14,670.

University of Victoria, Faculty of Graduate Studies, Faculty of Engineering, Department of Electrical and Computer Engineering, Victoria, BC V8W 2Y2, Canada. Offers M Eng, MA Sc, PhD. *Degree requirements:* For master's, thesis; for doctorate, thesis/dissertation, candidacy exam. *Entrance requirements:* For master's, GRE (recommended), bachelor's degree in engineering; for doctorate, GRE (recommended), master's degree. Additional exam requirements/recommendations for international students: Required—TOEFL (minimum score 575 paper-based), IELTS (minimum score 7). Electronic applications accepted. *Faculty research:* Communications and computers; electromagnetics, microwaves, and optics; electronics; power systems, signal processing, and control.

University of Virginia, School of Engineering and Applied Science, Department of Electrical and Computer Engineering, Program in Electrical Engineering, Charlottesville, VA 22903. Offers ME, MS, PhD. *Students:* 128 full-time (33 women), 12 part-time (3 women); includes 11 minority (2 Black or African American, non-Hispanic/Latino; 6 Asian, non-Hispanic/Latino; 2 Hispanic/Latino; 1 Two or more races, non-Hispanic/Latino), 103 international. Average age 26. 360 applicants, 24% accepted, 39 enrolled. In 2016, 9 master's, 14 doctorates awarded. *Degree requirements:* For doctorate, thesis/dissertation. *Entrance requirements:* For master's, GRE General Test, 3 letters of recommendation; for doctorate, GRE General Test, 3 letters of recommendation; essay. Additional exam requirements/recommendations for international students: Required—TOEFL (minimum score 650 paper-based; 100 iBT), IELTS (minimum score 7). *Application deadline:* For fall admission, 8/1 for domestic students, 1/15 for international students; for winter admission, 12/1 for domestic students, 8/1 for international students; for spring admission, 5/1 for domestic students. Applications are processed on a rolling basis. Application fee: $60. Electronic applications accepted. *Expenses:* Tuition, state resident: full-time $15,026; part-time $834 per credit hour. Tuition, nonresident: full-time $25,168; part-time $1378 per credit hour. *Required fees:* $2654. *Financial support:* Fellowships, research assistantships, and teaching assistantships available. Financial award application deadline: 1/15; financial award applicants required to submit FAFSA. *Unit head:* John C. Lach, Chair, 434-924-3960, Fax: 434-924-8818, E-mail: jlach@virginia.edu. *Application contact:* Graduate Program Director, 434-924-3960, Fax: 434-924-8818, E-mail: eceinfo@virginia.edu.
Website: http://www.ece.virginia.edu/curriculum/grads/ee.html

University of Washington, Graduate School, College of Engineering, Department of Electrical Engineering, Seattle, WA 98195-2500. Offers electrical engineering (MS, PhD); electrical engineering and nanotechnology (PhD). *Program availability:* Part-time, evening/weekend. *Faculty:* 45 full-time (9 women). *Students:* 242 full-time (67 women), 117 part-time (18 women); includes 70 minority (3 Black or African American, non-Hispanic/Latino; 50 Asian, non-Hispanic/Latino; 12 Hispanic/Latino; 5 Two or more races, non-Hispanic/Latino), 163 international. 1,327 applicants, 12% accepted, 91 enrolled. In 2016, 70 master's, 30 doctorates awarded. Terminal master's awarded for partial completion of doctoral program. *Degree requirements:* For master's, thesis optional; for doctorate, thesis/dissertation, qualifying, general, and final exams. *Entrance requirements:* For master's and doctorate, GRE General Test (recommended minimum Quantitative score of 160), minimum GPA of 3.5 (recommended); resume or curriculum vitae, statement of purpose, 3 letters of recommendation, undergraduate and graduate transcripts. Additional exam requirements/recommendations for international students: Required—TOEFL (minimum score 600 paper-based; 92 iBT). *Application deadline:* For fall admission, 12/15 for domestic and international students. Applications are processed on a rolling basis. Application fee: $85. Electronic applications accepted. *Expenses:* Contact institution. *Financial support:* In 2016–17, 168 students received support, including 13 fellowships with full tuition reimbursements available (averaging $2,556 per year), 98 research assistantships with full tuition reimbursements available (averaging $2,463 per year), 57 teaching assistantships with full tuition reimbursements available (averaging $2,463 per year); career-related internships or fieldwork, Federal Work-Study, institutionally sponsored loans, and health care benefits also available. Financial award application deadline: 12/15; financial award applicants required to submit FAFSA. *Faculty research:* Computing and networking, photonics and nano-devices, power and energy systems, robotics and controls, data sciences and biosystems. *Total annual research expenditures:* $19 million. *Unit head:* Dr. Radha Poovendran, Professor/Chair, 206-543-6515, Fax: 206-543-3842, E-mail: chair@ee.washington.edu. *Application contact:* Brenda Larson, Graduate Program Lead Academic Counselor, 206-616-1351, Fax: 206-543-3842, E-mail: brenda@ee.washington.edu.
Website: http://www.ee.washington.edu/

University of Waterloo, Graduate Studies, Faculty of Engineering, Department of Electrical and Computer Engineering, Waterloo, ON N2L 3G1, Canada. Offers M Eng, MA Sc, PhD. *Program availability:* Part-time. *Degree requirements:* For master's, research paper or thesis; for doctorate, comprehensive exam, thesis/dissertation. *Entrance requirements:* For master's, honors degree, minimum B+ average; for doctorate, master's degree, minimum A- average. Additional exam requirements/recommendations for international students: Required—TOEFL, IELTS, PTE. Electronic applications accepted. *Faculty research:* Communications, computers, systems and control, silicon devices, power engineering.

The University of Western Ontario, Faculty of Graduate Studies, Physical Sciences Division, Faculty of Engineering, London, ON N6A 5B8, Canada. Offers chemical and biochemical engineering (ME Sc, PhD); civil and environmental engineering (M Eng, ME Sc, PhD); electrical and computer engineering (M Eng, ME Sc, PhD); mechanical and materials engineering (M Eng, ME Sc, PhD). *Program availability:* Part-time. Terminal master's awarded for partial completion of doctoral program. *Degree requirements:* For master's, thesis; for doctorate, thesis/dissertation. *Entrance requirements:* For master's, minimum B average; for doctorate, minimum B+ average. *Faculty research:* Wind, geotechnical, chemical reactor engineering, applied electrostatics, biochemical engineering.

University of Windsor, Faculty of Graduate Studies, Faculty of Engineering, Department of Electrical and Computer Engineering, Windsor, ON N9B 3P4, Canada. Offers electrical engineering (M Eng, MA Sc, PhD). *Program availability:* Part-time. *Degree requirements:* For master's, thesis; for doctorate, comprehensive exam, thesis/dissertation. *Entrance requirements:* For master's, minimum B average; for doctorate, master's degree, minimum B+ average. Additional exam requirements/recommendations for international students: Required—TOEFL (minimum score 600 paper-based). Electronic applications accepted. *Faculty research:* Systems, signals, power.

University of Wisconsin–Madison, Graduate School, College of Engineering, Department of Electrical and Computer Engineering, Madison, WI 53706. Offers electrical engineering (MS, PhD); machine learning and signal processing (MS). *Faculty:* 41 full-time (8 women). *Students:* 262 full-time (35 women), 53 part-time (9 women); includes 18 minority (1 Black or African American, non-Hispanic/Latino; 10 Asian, non-Hispanic/Latino; 5 Hispanic/Latino; 2 Two or more races, non-Hispanic/Latino), 201 international. Average age 28. 1,236 applicants, 19% accepted, 62 enrolled. In 2016, 93 master's, 29 doctorates awarded. Terminal master's awarded for partial completion of doctoral program. *Degree requirements:* For master's, thesis or alternative; for doctorate, comprehensive exam, thesis/dissertation, exam. *Entrance requirements:* For master's and doctorate, GRE General Test, bachelor's degree; minimum GPA of 3.0 on last 60 semester hours. Additional exam requirements/recommendations for international students: Required—TOEFL (minimum score 580 paper-based; 92 iBT), IELTS (minimum score 7). *Application deadline:* For fall admission, 12/15 for domestic and international students. Application fee: $75 ($81 for international students). Electronic applications accepted. *Expenses:* $13,157 per year in-state tuition and fees; $26,484 per year out-of-state tuition and fees. *Financial support:* In 2016–17, 182 students received support, including 17 fellowships with full tuition reimbursements available, 124 research assistantships with full tuition reimbursements available, 36 teaching assistantships with full tuition reimbursements available; career-related internships or fieldwork, Federal Work-Study, institutionally sponsored loans, health care benefits, unspecified assistantships, and project assistantships also available. Support available to part-time students. Financial award application deadline: 12/1; financial award applicants required to submit FAFSA. *Faculty research:* Applied physics; computer engineering; power engineering; systems engineering. *Total annual research expenditures:* $15.4 million. *Unit head:* Prof. John Booske, Chair, 608-890-0804, E-mail: office@ece.wisc.edu. *Application contact:* Michael Radloff, Student Services Coordinator, 608-890-2756, E-mail: ecegradadmission@engr.wisc.edu.
Website: https://www.engr.wisc.edu/department/electrical-computer-engineering/

University of Wisconsin–Milwaukee, Graduate School, College of Engineering and Applied Science, Program in Engineering, Milwaukee, WI 53201-0413. Offers biomedical engineering (MS); civil engineering (MS, PhD); computer science (PhD); electrical and computer engineering (MS); electrical engineering (PhD); engineering mechanics (MS); industrial and management engineering (MS); industrial engineering (PhD); manufacturing engineering (MS); materials (PhD); materials engineering (MS); mechanical engineering (MS). *Program availability:* Part-time. *Students:* 199 full-time (52 women), 156 part-time (32 women); includes 27 minority (2 Black or African American, non-Hispanic/Latino; 15 Asian, non-Hispanic/Latino; 3 Hispanic/Latino; 7 Two or more races, non-Hispanic/Latino), 244 international. Average age 30. 396 applicants, 61% accepted, 102 enrolled. In 2016, 72 master's, 26 doctorates awarded. *Degree requirements:* For master's, comprehensive exam (for some programs), thesis or alternative; for doctorate, comprehensive exam, thesis/dissertation, internship. *Entrance requirements:* For master's, GRE, minimum GPA of 2.75; for doctorate, GRE, minimum GPA of 3.5. Additional exam requirements/recommendations for international students: Required—TOEFL (minimum score 550 paper-based; 79 iBT), IELTS (minimum score 6.5). *Application deadline:* For fall admission, 1/1 priority date for domestic students; for spring admission, 9/1 for domestic students. Applications are processed on a rolling basis. Application fee: $56 ($96 for international students). *Financial support:* In 2016–17, 3 fellowships, 55 research assistantships, 77 teaching assistantships were awarded; career-related internships or fieldwork, Federal Work-Study, unspecified assistantships, and project assistantships also available. Support available to part-time students. Financial award application deadline: 4/15. *Unit head:* David Yu, Representative, 414-229-6169, E-mail: yu@uwm.edu. *Application contact:* Betty Warras, General Information Contact, 414-229-6169, Fax: 414-229-6967, E-mail: bwarras@uwm.edu.
Website: http://www4.uwm.edu/ceas/academics/graduate_programs/

University of Wyoming, College of Engineering and Applied Sciences, Department of Electrical and Computer Engineering, Laramie, WY 82071. Offers electrical engineering (MS, PhD). *Program availability:* Part-time. *Degree requirements:* For master's, thesis (for some programs); for doctorate, comprehensive exam, thesis/dissertation, dissertation proposal/presentation. *Entrance requirements:* For master's, GRE General Test, minimum undergraduate GPA of 3.0; for doctorate, GRE General Test, minimum GPA of 3.0. Additional exam requirements/recommendations for international students: Required—TOEFL (minimum score 550 paper-based; 79 iBT). Electronic applications accepted. *Faculty research:* Robotics and controls, signal and image processing, power electronics, power systems, computer networks, wind energy.

Utah State University, School of Graduate Studies, College of Engineering, Department of Electrical and Computer Engineering, Logan, UT 84322. Offers electrical engineering (ME, MS, PhD). *Program availability:* Part-time. *Degree requirements:* For master's, thesis (for some programs); for doctorate, comprehensive exam, thesis/dissertation. *Entrance requirements:* For master's, GRE General Test, minimum GPA of 3.0, BS in electrical engineering, 3 recommendation letters; for doctorate, GRE General Test, minimum GPA of 3.0, MS in electrical engineering, 3 recommendation letters. Additional exam requirements/recommendations for international students: Required—TOEFL. Electronic applications accepted. *Faculty research:* Parallel processing, networking, control systems, digital signal processing, communications.

Vanderbilt University, School of Engineering, Department of Electrical Engineering and Computer Science, Program in Electrical Engineering, Nashville, TN 37240-1001. Offers M Eng, MS, PhD. MS and PhD offered through the Graduate School. *Program availability:* Part-time. Terminal master's awarded for partial completion of doctoral program. *Degree requirements:* For master's, thesis; for doctorate, comprehensive exam, thesis/dissertation. *Entrance requirements:* For master's and doctorate, GRE General Test, 3 letters of recommendation. Additional exam requirements/recommendations for international students: Required—TOEFL. Electronic applications accepted. *Expenses:* Tuition: Part-time $1854 per credit hour. *Faculty research:* Robotics, microelectronics, signal and image processing, VLSI, solid-state sensors, radiation effects and reliability.

Villanova University, College of Engineering, Department of Electrical and Computer Engineering, Program in Electrical Engineering, Villanova, PA 19085-1699. Offers electric power systems (Certificate); electrical engineering (MSEE); electro mechanical systems (Certificate); high frequency systems (Certificate); intelligent control systems (Certificate); wireless and digital communications (Certificate). *Program availability:* Part-time, evening/weekend. *Degree requirements:* For master's, thesis optional. *Entrance requirements:* For master's, GRE General Test (for applicants with degrees from foreign universities), BEE, minimum GPA of 3.0. Additional exam requirements/recommendations for international students: Required—TOEFL (minimum score 600 paper-based; 100 iBT). *Faculty research:* Signal processing, communications, antennas, devices.

Virginia Polytechnic Institute and State University, Graduate School, College of Engineering, Blacksburg, VA 24061. Offers aerospace engineering (ME, MS, PhD); biological systems engineering (ME, MS, PhD); biomedical engineering (MS, PhD); chemical engineering (ME, MS, PhD); civil engineering (ME, MS, PhD); computer engineering (ME, MS, PhD); computer science (MS, PhD); electrical engineering (ME, PhD); engineering education (PhD); engineering mechanics (ME, MS, PhD); environmental engineering (MS); environmental science and engineering (MS); industrial and systems engineering (ME, MS, PhD); materials science and engineering (ME, MS, PhD); mechanical engineering (ME, MS, PhD); mining and minerals engineering (PhD); mining engineering (ME, MS); nuclear engineering (MS, PhD); ocean engineering (MS); systems engineering (ME, MS). *Faculty:* 400 full-time (73 women), 3 part-time/adjunct (2 women). *Students:* 1,949 full-time (487 women), 393 part-time (69 women); includes 251 minority (56 Black or African American, non-Hispanic/Latino; 3 American Indian or Alaska Native, non-Hispanic/Latino; 87 Asian, non-Hispanic/Latino; 70 Hispanic/Latino; 35 Two or more races, non-Hispanic/Latino), 1,354 international. Average age 27. 4,903 applicants, 19% accepted, 569 enrolled. In 2016, 364 master's, 200 doctorates awarded. *Degree requirements:* For master's, comprehensive exam (for some programs), thesis (for some programs); for doctorate, comprehensive exam (for some programs), thesis/dissertation (for some programs). *Entrance requirements:* For master's and doctorate, GRE/GMAT. Additional exam requirements/recommendations for international students: Required—TOEFL (minimum score 80 iBT). *Application deadline:* For fall admission, 8/1 for domestic students, 4/1 for international students; for spring admission, 1/1 for domestic students, 9/1 for international students. Applications are processed on a rolling basis. Application fee: $75. Electronic applications accepted. *Expenses:* Tuition, state resident: full-time $12,467; part-time $692.50 per credit hour. Tuition, nonresident: full-time $25,095; part-time $1394.25 per credit hour. *Required fees:* $2669; $491.50 per semester. Tuition and fees vary according to course load, campus/location and program. *Financial support:* In 2016–17, 160 fellowships with full tuition reimbursements (averaging $7,387 per year), 872 research assistantships with full tuition reimbursements (averaging $22,329 per year), 313 teaching assistantships with full tuition reimbursements (averaging $18,714 per year) were awarded. Financial award application deadline: 3/1; financial award applicants required to submit FAFSA. *Total annual research expenditures:* $91.8 million. *Unit head:* Dr. Julia Ross, Dean, 540-231-9752, Fax: 540-231-3031, E-mail: deaneng@vt.edu. *Application contact:* Linda Perkins, Executive Assistant, 540-231-9752, Fax: 540-231-3031, E-mail: lperkins@vt.edu.
Website: http://www.eng.vt.edu/

Virginia Polytechnic Institute and State University, VT Online, Blacksburg, VA 24061. Offers advanced transportation systems (Certificate); aerospace engineering (MS); agricultural and life sciences (MSLFS); business information systems (Graduate Certificate); career and technical education (MS); civil engineering (MS); computer engineering (M Eng, MS); decision support systems (Graduate Certificate); eLearning leadership (MA); electrical engineering (M Eng, MS); engineering administration (MEA); environmental engineering (Certificate); environmental politics and policy (Graduate Certificate); environmental sciences and engineering (MS); foundations of political analysis (Graduate Certificate); health product risk management (Graduate Certificate); industrial and systems engineering (MS); information policy and society (Graduate Certificate); information security (Graduate Certificate); information technology (MIT); instructional technology (MA); integrative STEM education (MA Ed); liberal arts (Graduate Certificate); life sciences: health product risk management (MS); natural resources (MNR, Graduate Certificate); networking (Graduate Certificate); nonprofit and nongovernmental organization management (Graduate Certificate); ocean engineering (MS); political science (MA); security studies (Graduate Certificate); software development (Graduate Certificate). *Expenses:* Tuition, state resident: full-time $12,467; part-time $692.50 per credit hour. Tuition, nonresident: full-time $25,095; part-time $1394.25 per credit hour. *Required fees:* $2669; $491.50 per semester. Tuition and fees vary according to course load, campus/location and program.

Washington State University, Voiland College of Engineering and Architecture, School of Electrical Engineering and Computer Science, Pullman, WA 99164-2752. Offers computer engineering (MS); computer science (MS); electrical engineering (MS); electrical engineering and computer science (PhD); electrical power engineering (MS). MS programs in computer engineering, computer science and electrical engineering also offered at Tri-Cities campus; MS in electrical power engineering offered at the Global (online) campus. *Program availability:* Part-time. *Degree requirements:* For

master's, comprehensive exam (for some programs), thesis or alternative; for doctorate, comprehensive exam, thesis/dissertation. *Entrance requirements:* For master's and doctorate, GRE General Test, minimum GPA of 3.0, 3 letters of recommendation, statement of purpose, transcripts. Additional exam requirements/recommendations for international students: Required—TOEFL (minimum score 580 paper-based). *Faculty research:* Software engineering, networks, distributed computing, computer engineering, electrophysics, artificial intelligence, bioinformatics and computational biology, computer graphics, communications, control systems, signal processing, power systems, microelectronics, algorithms.

Wayne State University, College of Engineering, Department of Electrical and Computer Engineering, Detroit, MI 48202. Offers computer engineering (MS, PhD); electrical engineering (MS, PhD). *Faculty:* 22. *Students:* 247 full-time (54 women), 41 part-time (3 women); includes 16 minority (2 Black or African American, non-Hispanic/Latino; 11 Asian, non-Hispanic/Latino; 3 Two or more races, non-Hispanic/Latino), 250 international. Average age 26. 689 applicants, 50% accepted, 100 enrolled. In 2016, 73 master's, 3 doctorates awarded. *Degree requirements:* For master's, thesis; for doctorate, thesis/dissertation. *Entrance requirements:* For master's, GRE (if BS is not from ABET-accredited university), BS from ABET-accredited university; for doctorate, GRE (if BS is not from ABET-accredited university), minimum master's GPA of 3.6. Additional exam requirements/recommendations for international students: Required—TOEFL (minimum score 550 paper-based; 79 iBT), TWE (minimum score 5.5), Michigan English Language Assessment Battery (minimum score 85); Recommended—IELTS (minimum score 6.5). *Application deadline:* For fall admission, 6/1 priority date for domestic students, 5/1 priority date for international students; for winter admission, 10/1 priority date for domestic students, 9/1 priority date for international students; for spring admission, 2/1 priority date for domestic students, 1/1 priority date for international students. Applications are processed on a rolling basis. Application fee: $50. Electronic applications accepted. *Expenses:* $18,871 per year resident tuition and fees, $36,065 per year non-resident tuition and fees. *Financial support:* In 2016–17, 43 students received support, including 3 fellowships with tuition reimbursements available (averaging $16,000 per year), 9 research assistantships with tuition reimbursements available (averaging $18,419 per year), 16 teaching assistantships with tuition reimbursements available (averaging $19,237 per year); scholarships/grants, health care benefits, and unspecified assistantships also available. Support available to part-time students. Financial award applicants required to submit FAFSA. *Faculty research:* Computer systems, smart sensors and nanotechnology, communication systems and imaging, optics and photonics, biomedical electronics. *Total annual research expenditures:* $1.7 million. *Unit head:* Dr. Mohammed Ismail Elnaggar, Department Chair, E-mail: gd8686@wayne.edu. *Application contact:* Eric Eric Scimeca, Graduate Program Coordinator, 313-577-0412, E-mail: eric.scimeca@wayne.edu.
Website: http://engineering.wayne.edu/ece/

Western Michigan University, Graduate College, College of Engineering and Applied Sciences, Department of Electrical and Computer Engineering, Kalamazoo, MI 49008. Offers computer engineering (MSE); electrical and computer engineering (PhD); electrical engineering (MSE). *Program availability:* Part-time. *Degree requirements:* For master's, thesis optional.

Western New England University, College of Engineering, Department of Electrical Engineering, Springfield, MA 01119. Offers electrical engineering (MSEE); mechatronics (MSEE). *Program availability:* Part-time, evening/weekend. *Faculty:* 9 full-time (0 women). *Students:* 26 part-time (7 women); includes 1 minority (Two or more races, non-Hispanic/Latino), 15 international. Average age 27. 128 applicants, 30% accepted, 9 enrolled. In 2016, 10 master's awarded. *Degree requirements:* For master's, comprehensive exam, thesis optional. *Entrance requirements:* For master's, official transcript, bachelor's degree in engineering or related field, two recommendations, resume. Additional exam requirements/recommendations for international students: Required—TOEFL (minimum score 79 iBT). *Application deadline:* Applications are processed on a rolling basis. Application fee: $30. Electronic applications accepted. *Expenses:* Contact institution. *Financial support:* Application deadline: 4/15; applicants required to submit FAFSA. *Faculty research:* Superconductors, microwave cooking, computer voice output, digital filters, computer engineering. *Unit head:* Dr. Neeraj J. Magotra, Chair, 413-782-1274, E-mail: neeraj.magotra@wne.edu. *Application contact:* Matthew Fox, Director of Admissions for Graduate Students and Adult Learners, 413-782-1410, Fax: 413-782-1777, E-mail: study@wne.edu.
Website: http://www1.wne.edu/academics/graduate/electrical-engineering.cfm

West Virginia University, Statler College of Engineering and Mineral Resources, Lane Department of Computer Science and Electrical Engineering, Program in Electrical Engineering, Morgantown, WV 26506. Offers MSEE, PhD. Terminal master's awarded for partial completion of doctoral program. *Degree requirements:* For master's, thesis or alternative; for doctorate, comprehensive exam, thesis/dissertation. *Entrance requirements:* For master's and doctorate, GRE General Test, minimum GPA of 3.0, letters of recommendation. Additional exam requirements/recommendations for international students: Required—TOEFL. *Faculty research:* Power and control systems, communications and signal processing, electromechanical systems, microelectronics and photonics.

Wichita State University, Graduate School, College of Engineering, Department of Electrical Engineering and Computer Science, Wichita, KS 67260. Offers computer networking (MS); computer science (MS); electrical engineering (MS); electrical engineering and computer science (PhD). *Program availability:* Part-time, evening/weekend. *Unit head:* Dr. John Watkins, Chair, 316-978-3156, Fax: 316-978-5408, E-mail: john.watkins@wichita.edu. *Application contact:* Jordan Oleson, Admissions Coordinator, 316-978-3095, Fax: 316-978-3253, E-mail: jordan.oleson@wichita.edu.
Website: http://www.wichita.edu/eecs

Widener University, Graduate Programs in Engineering, Program in Electrical Engineering, Chester, PA 19013. Offers M Eng. *Program availability:* Part-time, evening/weekend. *Students:* 3 full-time (0 women), 2 part-time (0 women), 3 international. Average age 30. In 2016, 1 master's awarded. *Degree requirements:* For master's, thesis optional. *Application deadline:* For fall admission, 8/1 priority date for domestic students; for spring admission, 12/1 for domestic students. Applications are processed on a rolling basis. Application fee: $0. Electronic applications accepted. Tuition and fees vary according to degree level and program. *Financial support:* Teaching assistantships with full tuition reimbursements and unspecified assistantships available. Financial award application deadline: 3/15. *Faculty research:* Signal and image processing, electromagnetics, telecommunications and computer network. *Unit head:* Rudolph Treichel, Assistant Dean/Director of Graduate Programs, 610-499-1294, Fax: 610-499-4059, E-mail: rjtreichel@widener.edu.

Wilkes University, College of Graduate and Professional Studies, College of Science and Engineering, Department of Electrical Engineering and Physics, Wilkes-Barre, PA 18766-0002. Offers bioengineering (MS); electrical engineering (MSEE). *Program availability:* Part-time. *Students:* 13 full-time (5 women), 13 part-time (4 women); includes 3 minority (1 Black or African American, non-Hispanic/Latino; 1 Asian, non-Hispanic/Latino; 1 Hispanic/Latino), 9 international. Average age 26. In 2016, 5 master's awarded. *Entrance requirements:* For master's, GRE General Test. Additional exam requirements/recommendations for international students: Required—TOEFL (minimum

score 550 paper-based; 79 iBT). *Application deadline:* Applications are processed on a rolling basis. Application fee: $45 ($65 for international students). Electronic applications accepted. Tuition and fees vary according to degree level and program. *Financial support:* Unspecified assistantships available. Financial award application deadline: 3/1; financial award applicants required to submit FAFSA. *Unit head:* Dr. William Hudson, Dean, 570-408-4600, Fax: 570-408-7846, E-mail: william.hudson@wilkes.edu. *Application contact:* Director of Graduate Enrollment, 570-408-4234, Fax: 570-408-7846.
Website: http://www.wilkes.edu/academics/colleges/science-and-engineering/engineering-physics/electrical-engineering-physics/index.aspx

Worcester Polytechnic Institute, Graduate Studies and Research, Department of Electrical and Computer Engineering, Worcester, MA 01609-2280. Offers electrical and computer engineering (Advanced Certificate, Graduate Certificate); electrical engineering (M Eng, MS, PhD). *Program availability:* Part-time, evening/weekend. *Faculty:* 17 full-time (1 woman), 18 part-time/adjunct (4 women). *Students:* 107 full-time (14 women), 136 part-time (16 women); includes 42 minority (9 Black or African American, non-Hispanic/Latino; 19 Asian, non-Hispanic/Latino; 14 Hispanic/Latino), 91 international. 483 applicants, 47% accepted, 70 enrolled. In 2016, 111 master's, 10 doctorates awarded. Terminal master's awarded for partial completion of doctoral program. *Degree requirements:* For master's, thesis optional; for doctorate, comprehensive exam, thesis/dissertation. *Entrance requirements:* For master's, GRE (recommended), 3 letters of recommendation; for doctorate, GRE, 3 letters of recommendation, statement of purpose. Additional exam requirements/recommendations for international students: Required—TOEFL (minimum score 563 paper-based; 84 iBT), IELTS (minimum score 7), GRE. *Application deadline:* For fall admission, 1/1 priority date for domestic students, 1/1 for international students; for spring admission, 10/1 priority date for domestic students, 10/1 for international students. Applications are processed on a rolling basis. Application fee: $70. Electronic applications accepted. *Financial support:* Research assistantships, teaching assistantships, career-related internships or fieldwork, institutionally sponsored loans, scholarships/grants, and unspecified assistantships available. Financial award application deadline: 1/1; financial award applicants required to submit FAFSA. *Unit head:* Dr. Yehia Massoud, Department Head, 508-831-5231, Fax: 508-831-5491, E-mail: massoud@wpi.edu. *Application contact:* Dr. Kaveh Pahlavan, Graduate Coordinator, 508-831-5231, Fax: 508-831-5491, E-mail: kaveh@wpi.edu.
Website: http://www.wpi.edu/academics/ece

Wright State University, Graduate School, College of Engineering and Computer Science, Department of Electrical Engineering, Dayton, OH 45435. Offers MSEE. *Program availability:* Part-time, evening/weekend. *Degree requirements:* For master's, thesis or course option alternative. *Entrance requirements:* Additional exam requirements/recommendations for international students: Required—TOEFL. *Application deadline:* Applications are processed on a rolling basis. Application fee: $25. *Expenses:* Tuition, state resident: full-time $9952; part-time $622 per credit hour. Tuition, nonresident: full-time $16,960; part-time $1060 per credit hour. *Financial support:* Fellowships, research assistantships, teaching assistantships, and unspecified assistantships available. Support available to part-time students. Financial award application deadline: 3/1; financial award applicants required to submit FAFSA. *Faculty research:* Robotics, circuit design, power electronics, image processing, communication systems. *Unit head:* Dr. Fred D. Garber, Chair, 937-775-5037, Fax: 937-775-5009, E-mail: fred.garber@wright.edu. *Application contact:* Dr. Lang Hong, Graduate Program Director, 937-775-5037, Fax: 937-775-5009, E-mail: lang.hong@wright.edu.
Website: https://engineering-computer-science.wright.edu/electrical-engineering

Yale University, Graduate School of Arts and Sciences, School of Engineering and Applied Science, Department of Electrical Engineering, New Haven, CT 06520. Offers MS, PhD. Terminal master's awarded for partial completion of doctoral program. *Degree requirements:* For doctorate, thesis/dissertation, exam. *Entrance requirements:* For master's and doctorate, GRE General Test. Additional exam requirements/recommendations for international students: Required—TOEFL. *Faculty research:* Signal processing, control, and communications; digital systems and computer engineering; microelectronics and photonics; nanotechnology; computers, sensors, and networking.

Youngstown State University, Graduate School, College of Science, Technology, Engineering and Mathematics, Department of Electrical and Computer Engineering, Youngstown, OH 44555-0001. Offers computer engineering (MSE); electrical engineering (MSE). *Program availability:* Part-time, evening/weekend. *Degree requirements:* For master's, thesis optional. *Entrance requirements:* For master's, minimum GPA of 2.75 in field. Additional exam requirements/recommendations for international students: Required—TOEFL. *Faculty research:* Computer-aided design, power systems, electromagnetic energy conversion, sensors, control systems.

DUKE UNIVERSITY
Department of Electrical and Computer Engineering

Programs of Study

Graduate study in the Department of Electrical and Computer Engineering (ECE) is intended to prepare students for leadership roles in academia, industry, and government that require creative technical problem-solving skills. The Department offers both Ph.D. and M.S. degree programs, with opportunities for study in a broad spectrum of areas within the disciplines of electrical and computer engineering. Research and course offerings in the Department are organized into four areas of specialization: computer engineering; information physics; microelectronics, photonics, and nanotechnology; and signal and information processing. Interdisciplinary programs are also available that connect the above programs with those in other engineering departments and computer science, the natural sciences, and the Medical School. Students in the Department may also be involved in research conducted in one of the Duke centers, e.g., the Fitzpatrick Institute for Photonics or the Center for Metamaterials and Intregrated Plasmonics. Under a reciprocal agreement with neighboring universities, a student may elect to enroll in some courses offered at the University of North Carolina at Chapel Hill and North Carolina State University in Raleigh. Since an important criterion for admitting new students is the match between student and faculty research interests, prospective students are encouraged to indicate in which Departmental specialization areas they are interested when applying.

Research Facilities

The ECE Department currently occupies approximately 47,000 square feet in two buildings: the Fitzpatrick Center for Interdisciplinary Engineering, Medicine and Applied Sciences (FCIEMAS) and Hudson Hall. CIEMAS houses cross-disciplinary activities involving the Pratt School and its partners in the fields of bioengineering, photonics, microsystems integration, sensing and simulation, and materials science and materials engineering. This comprehensive facility provides extensive fabrication and test laboratories, Departmental offices, teaching labs, and other lab support spaces as well as direct access to a café. In addition, the Shared Materials Instrumentation Facility (SMiF), a state-of-the-art clean room for nanotechnology research, is housed on its main floor. Hudson Hall is the oldest of the buildings in the engineering complex. It was built in 1948 when the Engineering School moved to Duke's West Campus and was known as Old Red. An annex was built onto the back of the building in 1972, and in 1992, the building was expanded again and renamed Hudson Hall to honor Fitzgerald S. (Jerry) Hudson E'46. Hudson Hall is home to all four departments in the Pratt School of Engineering, as well as the school's laboratories, computing facilities, offices, and classrooms.

Financial Aid

Financial support is available for the majority of Ph.D. students. Graduate fellowships for the first two semesters of study provide a stipend, registration fees, and full tuition. Beyond this initial period, most students receive research assistantships funded by faculty research grants, which, together with financial aid, cover their full registration fees, tuition, and stipend until completion of the Ph.D. degree.

Cost of Study

For the 2017–18 academic year, 9-month tuition for master's students is $51,480 and 12-month tuition for Ph.D. student is $55,040. The Graduate School estimates the cost of room, board, local transportation, and personal and miscellaneous costs to be approximately $2,204/month in 2017–18.

Living and Housing Costs

Due to renovations, Duke University will not offer on-campus housing to graduate students in the 2017–18 academic year. A wide variety of options for off-campus housing near the engineering complex and in the greater Durham area are available; the estimated average cost of housing for the 2017–18 academic year (9 months) is $8,658.

Student Group

In the 2017–18 academic year a total of 289 graduate students are enrolled, of whom 169 are doctoral students and 120 are master's students.

Location

Located in the rolling central Piedmont area of North Carolina, the Duke University campus is widely regarded as one of the most beautiful in the nation. The four-season climate is mild, but winter skiing is available in the North Carolina mountains a few hours' drive to the west, and ocean recreation is a similar distance away to the east. Duke is readily accessible by Interstates 85 and 40 and from Raleigh-Durham International Airport, which is about a 20-minute drive from the campus via Interstate 40 and the Durham expressway.

The University and The Department

Trinity College, founded in 1859, was selected by James B. Duke as the major recipient of a 1924 endowment that enabled a university to be organized around the college and to be named for Washington B. Duke, the family patriarch. A department of engineering was established at Trinity College in 1910, and the Department of Electrical Engineering was formed in 1920. Its name changed to the Department of Electrical and Computer Engineering in 1996. Duke University remains a privately supported university, with more than 14,000 students in degree programs.

Applying

Admission to the Department is based on a review of previous education and experience, the applicant's statement of intent, letters of evaluation, standardized test scores (GRE and TOEFL), and grade point average. The application deadline for spring admission (Ph.D. only) is October 1. December 1 is the priority deadline for submission of Ph.D. applications for admission and financial award for the fall semester. January 1 is the priority deadline for submission of M.S. applications for admission. Fall applications for both programs are accepted through February 28 but are guaranteed review only if submitted by the priority deadline.

Correspondence and Information

Andrew D. Hilton, Assistant Professor of the Practice and
    Managing Director of Graduate Studies
Department of Electrical and Computer Engineering
Pratt School of Engineering, Box 90291
Duke University
Durham, North Carolina 27708-0291
Phone: 919-660-5245
E-mail: dgs@ee.duke.edu
Website: http://www.ee.duke.edu

THE FACULTY AND THEIR RESEARCH

Tyler K. Bletsch, Assistant Professor of the Practice; D.Phil., North Carolina State. Software security, power aware computing, embedded systems, robotics, engineering education.

John A. Board, Bass Fellow and Associate Professor of ECE and Computer Science; D.Phil., Oxford. High performance scientific computing and simulation, novel computer architectures, cluster computing and parallel processing, ubiquitous computing.

David J. Brady, Bass Fellow and Michael J. Fitzpatrick Professor; Ph.D., Caltech. Computational optical sensor systems, hyperspectral microscopy, Raman spectroscopy for tissue chemometrics, optical coherence sensors and infrared spectral filters.

Martin A. Brooke, Associate Professor; Ph.D., USC. Integrated analog CMOS circuit design, integrated nanoscale systems, mixed signal VLSI design, sensing and sensor systems, optical imaging and communications, analog and power electronics, electronic circuit assembly and testing.

April S. Brown, John Cocke Professor; D.Sc., Cornell. Nanomaterial manufacturing and characterization, sensing and sensor systems, nanoscale/microscale computing systems, integrated nanoscale systems.

Robert Calderbank, Charles S. Snyder Professor of Computer Science and Professor of ECE and Math; Ph.D., Caltech. Computer engineering, computer architecture, information theory.

Lawrence Carin, Duke Vice Provost for Research and Professor of ECE; Ph.D., Maryland, College Park, Homeland security, sensing and sensor systems, signal processing, land mine detection.

Krishnendu Chakrabarty, William H. Younger Professor and Executive Director of Graduate Studies; Ph.D., Michigan. Computer engineering, nanoscale/microscale computing systems, self-assembled computer architecture, micro-electronic mechanical machines, failure analysis, integrated nanoscale systems, microsystems.

Duke University

Yiran Chen, Associate Professor; Ph.D., Purdue. Nonvolatile memory and storage systems, neuromorphic computing, and mobile applications.

Leslie M. Collins, Professor; Ph.D., Michigan. Sensing and sensor systems, homeland security, land mine detection, neural prosthesis, geophysics, signal processing.

Steven A. Cummer, Professor; Ph.D., Stanford. Geophysics, photonics, atmospheric science, metamaterials, electromagnetics.

Richard B. Fair, Lord-Chandran Professor; Ph.D., Duke. Computer engineering, sensing and sensor systems, electronic devices, integrated nanoscale systems, medical diagnostics, microsystems, semiconductors.

Aaron D. Franklin, Associate Professor; Ph.D., Purdue. Low-dimensional nanoelectronics, carbon nanotube (CNT) transistors, device scaling, transport studies, advanced integration approaches.

Michael E. Gehm, Associate Professor; Ph.D., Duke. Computational sensor systems, spectroscopy, spectral imaging, computational mass spectrometry, adaptive sensors, mmW and THz imaging, rapid prototyping of optical components, general optical physics.

Jeffrey T. Glass, Professor of ECE and Hogg Family Director of Engineering Management and Entrepreneurship; Ph.D., Virginia. Micro-electronic mechanical machines, engineering management, entrepreneurship, social entrepreneurship, sensing and sensor systems, materials.

Michael R. Gustafson, Associate Professor of the Practice; Ph.D., Duke. Engineering education, electronic circuit assembly and testing, electronic devices.

Kris Hauser, Associate Professor; Ph.D., Stanford. Robot motion planning and control, semiautonomous robots, integrating perception and planning, automated vehicle collision avoidance, robotic manipulation, robot-assisted medicine, legged locomotion.

Andrew D. Hilton, Assistant Professor of the Practice and Co-Director of Graduate Studies; Ph.D., Pennsylvania. Processor micro-architecture, latency tolerance, energy efficient computation, architectural simulation and sampling methodologies, architectural support for security.

Lisa G. Huettel, Professor of the Practice, Associate Chair, and Director of Undergraduate Studies; Ph.D., Duke. Sensing and sensor systems, engineering education, signal processing, distributed systems.

William T. Joines, Professor; Ph.D., Duke. Photonics, electromagnetics, electromagnetic field and wave interactions with materials and structures.

Nan M. Jokerst, J. A. Jones Professor; Ph.D., USC. Photonics, sensing and sensor systems, nanomaterial manufacturing and characterization, semiconductors, integrated nanoscale systems, microsystems.

Jungsang Kim, Professor; Ph.D., Stanford. Photonics, micro-electronic mechanical machines, sensing and sensor systems, semiconductors, quantum information, integrated nanoscale systems.

Jeffrey L. Krolik, Professor; Ph.D., Toronto (Canada). Sensing and sensor systems, signal processing, acoustics, medical imaging, homeland security, electromagnetics, antennas.

Benjamin C. Lee, Associate Professor of ECE and Computer Science; Ph.D., Harvard. Scalable technologies, power-efficient computer architectures, high-performance applications.

Hai (Helen) Li, Clare Boothe Luce Associate Professor; Ph.D., Purdue. Brain-inspired computing systems and neuromorphic design, memory design and architecture based on conventional and emerging technologies, and device/circuit/architecture co-design for low power and high performance.

Xin Li, Professor; Ph.D., Carnegie Mellon. Integrated circuits, signal processing, and data analytics.

Qing H. Liu, Professor; Ph.D., Illinois at Urbana-Champaign. Electromagnetics, antennas, medical imaging, photonics, acoustics, computational electromagnetics.

Hisham Z. Massoud, Professor; Ph.D., Stanford. Nanomaterial manufacturing and characterization, nanoscale/microscale computing systems, computer engineering, engineering education, electronic devices, manufacturing, semiconductors, microsystems.

Maiken H. Mikkelsen, Nortel Networks Assistant Professor; Ph.D., California, Santa Barbara. Nanophysics, experimental condensed matter physics, spintronics, nanophotonics, and quantum information science.

Loren W. Nolte, Professor; Ph.D., Michigan. Sensing and sensor systems, medical imaging, signal processing.

Douglas P. Nowacek, Repass-Rodgers University Associate Professor of Conservation Technology and Associate Professor of ECE; Ph.D., MIT/Woods Hole Oceanographic Institution. Acoustics, micro-electronic mechanical machines.

Willie J. Padilla, Professor; Ph.D., California, San Diego. Experimental condensed matter physics, infrared, optical and magneto-optical properties of novel materials, fourier transform, terahertz time domain spectroscopy.

Miroslav Pajic, Assistant Professor; Ph.D., Pennsylvania. Design and analysis of cyber-physical systems, real-time and embedded systems, distributed/networked control systems, high-confidence medical device systems.

Henry D. Pfister, Associate Professor; Ph.D., California, San Diego. Information theory, channel coding, and iterative information processing with applications in wireless communications, data storage, and signal processing.

Galen Reeves, Assistant Professor of ECE and Statistical Science; Ph.D., Berkeley. Signal processing, statistics, information theory, machine learning, compressive sensing.

Cynthia D. Rudin, Associate Professor of ECE and Computer Science; Ph.D., Princeton. Machine learning, data mining, applied statistics, and knowledge discovery (Big Data).

Guillermo Sapiro, Edmund T. Pratt, Jr. School Professor; D.Sc., Technion, Haifa (Israel). Image and video processing, computer graphics, computational vision, biomedical imaging, cryotomography of viruses.

David R. Smith, William Bevan Professor; Ph.D., California, San Diego. Photonics, metamaterials, electromagnetic, plasmonics.

Daniel J. Sorin, Professor; Ph.D., Wisconsin–Madison. Computer engineering, computer architecture, fault tolerance, reliability.

Adrienne D. Stiff-Roberts, Associate Professor; Ph.D., Michigan. Nanomaterial manufacturing and characterization, semiconductor photonic devices, photonics, nanoscience.

Stacy L. Tantum, Associate Professor of the Practice; Ph.D., Duke. Signal detection and estimation theory, statistical signal processing, pattern recognition and machine learning, remote sensing, matched-field processing, ocean acoustics.

Kishor S. Trivedi; Hudson Professor of ECE and Professor of Computer Science; Ph.D., Illinois at Urbana-Champaign. Computer engineering, failure analysis, fault tolerance, reliability, computer architecture.

ECE Student, Duke Pratt School of Engineering.

Hudson Hall, Duke Pratt School of Engineering.

UNIVERSITY AT BUFFALO, STATE UNIVERSITY OF NEW YORK

School of Engineering and Applied Sciences
Department of Electrical Engineering

University at Buffalo
Department of Electrical Engineering
School of Engineering and Applied Sciences

Programs of Study

The Department of Electrical Engineering at the University at Buffalo (UB) offers courses of study leading to the Master of Science (M.S.), Master of Engineering (M.E.), and Doctor of Philosophy (Ph.D.). Each of the graduate programs allows students to specialize in numerous areas of interest. The M.S. and Ph.D. degrees can be earned in the fields of communications and signal processing, solid state electronics, optics and photonics, and energy systems.

The M.S. in Electrical Engineering degree program comprises an appropriate academic core and a cohesive set of advanced courses, culminating in a thesis, or comprehensive examination (duration: 1–2 years).

The M.E. degree with a specialization in production management augments the scientific knowledge of the electrical engineer with the skills of a manager. The goal of the program is to provide skills to meet the challenges of managing technical teams in highly competitive corporate environments.

The Ph.D. program provides an advanced level of study and training for the development of research-level scholars with expertise in human factors, operations research, or production systems (duration: 4–6 years). Distinctive to the program is the flexibility in course work— students may follow a prescribed path (course flowsheets are available for each research area) or customize their own under the guidance of faculty.

Graduates pursue careers in wide-ranging industries, which include research and development, product design, manufacturing operations, service, technical sales, marketing, consulting, education, and policy-making. Many students are able to leverage their experience through research assistantships with faculty or through internships in industry, to land their first job after completion of the degree.

Research Facilities

In 2011, the Department of Electrical Engineering (EE) moved into Davis Hall, a new green building with state-of-the-art research laboratory facilities, teaching labs, and lecture halls, designed to support collaboration among faculty and students within the department, across the university, and with other institutions. The new building houses ergonomically designed office spaces, conference rooms, smart rooms, and a brand new, Class 1000 cleanroom (approximately 5,000 square feet). Davis Hall is home to the following research laboratories:

- Wireless Communication Systems and Networks Lab
- Secure Communications Lab
- Signal Processing and Communication Electronics Lab
- Cognitive Communications and Networking Lab
- Testing and Characterization Lab
- SMALL (Sensors + Microactuators Learning Lab)
- Electronic Materials Lab
- Analog VLSI and Sensors Laboratory
- Advanced Spectroscopic Evaluation Laboratory
- Nanophotonics and Nonlinear Optics Lab
- Underwater Communications and Networking Lab
- Advanced Power Sources Lab
- Nano-Optics and Biophotonics
- Embedded Systems Lab

Additional EE facilities across campus include the Energy Systems Institute and the Multidisciplinary Nano- and Microsystems lab.

Financial Aid

Graduate students may apply for a variety of fellowships and scholarships including teaching assistantships (TA), student assistantships (SA), tuition scholarships (TS), or research assistantships (RA). TA, SA, and TS awards are made to students via a department-wide selection process while RA awards are made directly by individual professors. On-campus employment is also available for domestic and international students. Several fellowships and scholarships are available.

Cost of Study

Annual costs related to enrollment and study, including tuition, special fees, book, and thesis costs total $15,000. Additional cost of study information is available online at http://financialaid.buffalo.edu/costs/gradcost.php.

Living and Housing Costs

UB does not provide graduate student housing; however, there are numerous affordable housing options available in the nearby area. A reasonable figure that a single or married student should allow for housing, food, and moderate entertainment in order to live at a local standard ranges from $15,000–$20,000. Buffalo boasts a variety of affordable housing and entertainment options given the area's reasonable cost of living.

Student Group

The number of students engaged in EE graduate work totals approximately 400 (300 in master's programs/100 in Ph.D. programs). The group breaks down as follows: 25 percent female/75 percent male; 85 percent international/15 percent domestic; and 90 percent full-time/10 percent part-time).

EE has a variety of clubs, organizations, and activities that enhance engineering education outside the classroom, including Graduate Student Association, Society of Women Engineer, Society of Hispanic Professional Engineers, and others. The diversity and number of organizations reflects the students' wide range of professional interests.

Student Outcomes

UB EE graduates have been hired for jobs in their field of study by Alcatel Lucent, AMD, Boeing, Cisco, Ford, General Electric, General Motors, Google, Hewlett-Packard, IBM, Intel, Lockheed Martin, Micron, Moog, Motorola, NASA, National Grid, Nokia, Qualcomm, Rockwell, Texas Instruments, U.S. Department of Defense, U.S. Department of Energy, and many others. Ph.D. graduates have also pursued careers as faculty in academia.

Location

The Buffalo–Niagara region is a major metropolitan area with a diverse blend of communities, each with its own distinct character. The region is known for a welcoming nature and spirited loyalty. Notable aspects include affordable living, four distinct seasons, smart economic growth, widely accessible arts and culture, major league sports, an international airport, and close proximity to the U.S.–Canada border.

The University

A member of the prestigious Association of American Universities, the University at Buffalo ranks first among the nation's research-intensive public universities. UB Engineering is New York State's largest and most comprehensive public school of engineering. Ranked in the top 15 percent of the nation's 300 engineering schools, UB Engineering offers a wide variety of excellent instruction, research opportunities, resources, and facilities to its students. The Department of Electrical

University at Buffalo, State University of New York

Engineering has been cited as among the nation's best by *U.S. News & World Report* in its annual ranking of "America's Best Graduate Schools" and specialty rankings.

Applying

Students may apply for fall or spring admission. The deadline for fall admission is February 1, and the deadline for spring is September 15. Admission decisions are usually made on or before March 31 for fall admission and on or before October 31 for spring admission.

Students seeking admission apply via Gradmit, UB's online application system at www.gradmit.buffalo.edu. In addition to an excellent undergraduate academic record, faculty consider demonstrated practical engineering experience and leadership skills. Other criteria for admission include: GRE scores and TOEFL scores (TOEFL for international), a baccalaureate degree in engineering or a related technical field; a minimum 3.0 grade point average (on a 4.0 scale) for all undergraduate work during the last two years of the applicant's studies; and prerequisite knowledge/skills in mathematics through the level of multivariate calculus, probability and statistics considered from a calculus point of view, and computer programming.

Correspondence and Information

Graduate Admissions
230 Davis Hall
Department of Electrical Engineering
University at Buffalo State University of New York
Buffalo, New York 14260
Phone: 716-645-3117
Fax: 716-645-3656
E-mail: eegrad@buffalo.edu
Website: http://engineering.buffalo.edu/electrical/grad

THE FACULTY

Signals, Communications and Networking Research Group:
Adly Fam
Josep M. Jornet
Michael Langberg
Nicholas Mastronarde
Mehrdad Soumekh
Weifeng Su
Zhi Sun
Leslie Ying

Solid State Electronics Research Group:
Jonathan Bird
Ping C Cheng
Erik Einarsson
Liesl Folks
Huamin Li
Vladimir Mitin
Kwang Oh
Arindam Sanyal
Uttam Singisetti
Chu Ryang Wie

Optics & Photonics Research Group
Edward Furlani
Qiaoqiang Gan
Natalia Litchinitser
Pao-Lo Liu
Peter Liu

Energy Systems Research Group:
Kevin Burke
HyungSeon Oh
Xiu Yao
Jennifer Zirnheld

Electrical Engineering graduate students in the lab (boat) of the Extreme Environment Communications Lab on Lake Erie.

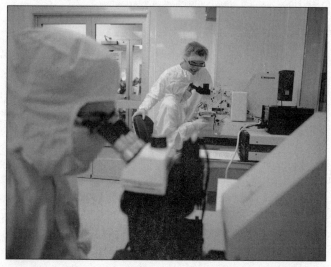

Electrical Engineering graduate students at work in UB's Class 1000 Cleanroom.

UNIVERSITY OF MARYLAND, COLLEGE PARK

A. James Clark School of Engineering
Department of Electrical and Computer Engineering

 For more information, visit http://petersons.to/umaryland-ece

DEPARTMENT OF
ELECTRICAL & COMPUTER
ENGINEERING

Programs of Study

The Department of Electrical and Computer Engineering (ECE) at the University of Maryland (UMD) offers highly ranked Master of Science (M.S.) and Doctor of Philosophy (Ph.D.) programs in electrical engineering. Both programs are designed with a focus on research, and are supported by over 30 specialized state-of-the-art research labs. The M.S. program offers students the option of completing theses or scholarly papers, while the doctoral program requires students to pass oral Ph.D. research proposal examinations in addition to their dissertation.

The Department covers a wide spectrum of activities in the following areas:

- Communications and networking
- Signal processing
- Control, robotics, and dynamical systems
- Computer engineering
- Optics and photonics
- Circuits and systems
- Electronic materials and devices
- Bioelectronics and systems
- Applied electromagnetics

The ECE Department also offers a combined B.S./M.S. program to students with exceptional academics and faculty mentor recommendations. The program is tailored to the needs of the individual student, taking his or her career goals and interests into account.

The Master of Engineering (M.Eng.) degree is distinct from the research-focused M.S. in ECE. This program requires successful completion of 10 approved courses (30 credits total). Neither a thesis nor a scholarly paper is required. This program is managed by the Office of Advanced Engineering Education.

The Office of Advanced Engineering also offers a Graduate Certificate in Engineering (CGEN) degree. The program requires completion of four approved courses (12 credits total) with an ECE focus.

The ECE Department offers a Master's in Telecommunications program in conjunction with the Department of Electrical and Computer Engineering and the Robert H. Smith School of Business. The program combines innovative and state-of-the-art technical courses with instruction in management, regulatory, and public policy in order to develop students into top-rate professionals who are able to succeed in a constantly changing industry. The cross-disciplinary curriculum was developed with the guidance of industry leaders.

Research

The Clark School of Engineering conducts over $107 million in research annually, including over $42 million within the ECE department alone. Students have access to the latest in research and instructional technology at the School's more than 130 laboratories and 23 research centers. The School has many outstanding partnerships with corporations and government agencies, including Lockheed Martin, Cisco, NASA, the National Institutes of Health (NIH), and the Army Research Laboratory.

The ECE department has one of the strongest electrical engineering research programs in the nation. ECE students have access to 15 teaching laboratories, nearly 50 labs dedicated to electrical and computer engineering, and a number of additional university research institutes and centers.

ECE professors specialize in a wide variety of research areas, including communications and networking; signal processing; control, robotics, and dynamical systems; computer engineering; optics and photonics; circuits and systems; electronic materials and devices; bioelectronics and systems; and applied electromagnetics.

Financial Aid

The ECE department offers various types of financial aid to exceptionally qualified applicants, including graduate fellowships, graduate teaching assistantships, and graduate research assistantships. If applicants indicate that they wish to be considered for financial aid and submit all their application materials by December 16, they will be considered for all available forms of funding. Most financial aid offers are made before April 15. U.S. students interested in receiving Federal support should complete the FAFSA by the February 15 priority deadline.

The University of Maryland and the Clark School of Engineering offer a variety of competitive engineering scholarships that are awarded for academic merit and financial need. Graduate assistantships provide students with skills in research, pedagogy, leadership, and academic administration, in addition to financial assistance.

In addition, the UMD graduate school offers the following graduate fellowships: The Graduate School Summer Research Fellowship, Kulkarni Summer Research Fellowship, Graduate Dean's Dissertation Fellowship, and Wylie Dissertation Fellowship.

Cost of Study

For the 2016–17 academic year, graduate tuition was $651 per credit for Maryland residents and $1,404 per credit for nonresidents. There is no cap or flat rate for tuition. There is a mandatory flat-rate fee of $427.50 for part-time students (1–8 credits) or $769 for full-time students (9 or more credits).

Complete details regarding graduate tuition and fees are available at https://bursar.umd.edu/t_grd1617.html.

Student Group

The A. James Clark School of Engineering serves nearly 4,500 students through education, research, and technology entrepreneurship opportunities. In fall 2015, more than 300 graduate students enrolled in the ECE department. Approximately 90 M.S. students and 290 Ph.D. students currently participate in the program.

Students in the Clark School have access to close to 200 high-tech centers, laboratories, consortia, and major projects. Within the Clark School, the Department of Electrical and Computer Engineering has many close affiliations with research institutes and national laboratories, providing students with many opportunities for team-oriented interdisciplinary research.

Notable alumni of the Clark School include a former director of NASA, co-founder of Sirius Satellite Radio, and deputy secretary of the U.S. Department of Defense.

University of Maryland, College Park

The Faculty

Faculty members within the Department of Electrical and Computer Engineering and Clark School of Engineering are nationally recognized as highly respected leaders in their fields. Many faculty members are IEEE Fellows, ACM Fellows, and OSA Fellows. Many others hold joint appointments with different research institutes, such as with the Institute for Systems Research (ISR) and the University of Maryland Institute for Advanced Computer Studies (UMAICS).

For example, Dr. Armand Makowski has held a joint appointment with the Institute for Systems Research since 1985. He is also a cofounder of the Center for Satellite and Hybrid Communication Networks at NASA.

Dr. Gilmer Blankenship is an IEEE Fellow with over 25 years of research in control system science, and has published more than 120 papers and reports in his areas of specialty. Dr. Pamela Abshire has been named one of the "brilliant women in tech" by InTheCapital.com, and has been awarded the Kent Teaching Award.

Led by 89 full-time and affiliate faculty members and 50 research faculty and postdoctoral candidates, the research programs within ECE cover a wide spectrum of activities. A complete listing of faculty members and their areas of research can be found at http://www.ece.umd.edu/faculty.

Location

UMD is located just outside of Washington, DC, and is only a short drive from Baltimore or Annapolis, Maryland. The city of College Park prides itself on being a safe, vibrant, and prosperous community. Students can take advantage of the area's many cultural attractions, including the College Park Aviation Museum, Clarice Smith Performing Arts Center, and Goddard Space Flight Center. The College Park Airport is the world's oldest continually operating airport, founded in 1909.

Maryland's proximity to Washington, D.C., offers unique research opportunities with national and government laboratories such as NASA's Goddard Space Flight Center, the National Institutes of Health, the National Institute of Standards and Technology, and the Army and Navy Research Labs. No other engineering program in the U.S. can provide such proximity and access to national laboratories, the federal government, and the Department of Defense.

The University and The School of Engineering

The University of Maryland has a rich and storied past, with origins traced back to 1856. Today, UMD is a nationally recognized university dedicated to furthering research and academics designed to train tomorrow's leaders to face the most difficult global challenges.

The University of Maryland has been ranked among the best in the nation for a variety of categories, including teaching, academics, service learning, diversity, and affordability. The Princeton Review named UMD among the best values in education, and *Kiplinger's* named the school fifth in affordability among public universities.

U.S. News & World Report collectively ranks the graduate programs at the A. James Clark School of Engineering as 18th in the nation. The Institute of Higher Education and Center for World-Class Universities has named the school 11th in the world among all engineering programs. The Academic Ranking of World Universities poll has named the Clark School 14th in the world for academic research.

Admissions Requirements and Application Information

For admission to the graduate programs in Electrical and Computer Engineering, applicants should hold an undergraduate degree in electrical or computer engineering or a related field (math, computer science, physics, or other areas of engineering) and have an overall grade point average of 3.5 (B+) or better. In exceptional cases, students with a lower GPA may also be admitted. Other criteria include overall academic record, strength of recommendations, GRE scores, and adequacy of preparation. Applicants are competitively judged by a faculty committee.

A completed application consists of the following materials: application form; $75 application fee; statement of purpose; resume/CV; 3 letters of recommendation; GRE scores (general test only); official transcripts; and TOEFL, IELTS, or PTE scores (international applicants only). Applications will not be reviewed until all materials have been received.

Applications and all supporting materials must be received by: December 16 for priority consideration for financial support; March 15 for international applicants; and May 16 for U.S. citizens and permanent residents. Applications are not accepted for spring or summer admission.

Applications are to be submitted online via the Graduate School website at http://gradschool.umd.edu/admissions/application-process/step-step-guide-applying.

Correspondence and Information

ECE Graduate Studies Office
2434 A.V. Williams Building
E-mail: ecegradstudies@umd.edu
Phone: 301-405-3681

Section 10
Energy and Power Engineering

This section contains a directory of institutions offering graduate work in energy and power engineering. Additional information about programs listed in the directory may be obtained by writing directly to the dean of a graduate school or chair of a department at the address given in the directory.

For programs offering related work, see also in this book *Computer Science and Information Technology, Engineering and Applied Sciences, Industrial Engineering,* and *Mechanical Engineering and Mechanics.* In another guide in this series:

Graduate Programs in the Physical Sciences, Mathematics, Agricultural Sciences, the Environment & Natural Resources
See *Physics* and *Mathematical Sciences*

CONTENTS

Program Directories

Energy and Power Engineering

Appalachian State University, Cratis D. Williams Graduate School, Department of Sustainable Technology and the Built Environment, Boone, NC 28608. Offers appropriate technology (MS); renewable energy engineering (MS). *Program availability:* Part-time. *Degree requirements:* For master's, comprehensive exam, thesis optional. *Entrance requirements:* For master's, GRE General Test, 3 letters of recommendation. Additional exam requirements/recommendations for international students: Required—TOEFL (minimum score 550 paper-based; 79 iBT), IELTS (minimum score 6.5). *Application deadline:* For fall admission, 3/15 priority date for domestic students, 2/1 for international students; for spring admission, 11/1 for domestic students, 7/1 for international students. Applications are processed on a rolling basis. Application fee: $55. Electronic applications accepted. *Expenses:* Tuition, state resident: full-time $4744. Tuition, nonresident: full-time $17,913. Full-time tuition and fees vary according to program. *Financial support:* Fellowships, research assistantships, teaching assistantships, career-related internships or fieldwork, Federal Work-Study, institutionally sponsored loans, scholarships/grants, and unspecified assistantships available. Financial award application deadline: 4/1; financial award applicants required to submit FAFSA. *Faculty research:* Wind power, biofuels, green construction, solar energy production. *Unit head:* Dr. Jeff Tiller, Chair, 828-262-6351, E-mail: tillerjs@appstate.edu. *Application contact:* Dr. Marie Hoepfl, Graduate Program Director, 828-262-3122, E-mail: hoepflmc@appstate.edu.
Website: http://www.tec.appstate.edu

Arizona State University at the Tempe campus, Ira A. Fulton Schools of Engineering, School for Engineering of Matter, Transport and Energy, Tempe, AZ 85281. Offers aerospace engineering (MS, PhD); chemical engineering (MS, PhD); materials science and engineering (MS, PhD); mechanical engineering (MS, PhD); solar energy engineering and commercialization (PSM). *Program availability:* Part-time, evening/weekend, online learning. Terminal master's awarded for partial completion of doctoral program. *Degree requirements:* For master's, thesis and oral defense (MS); applied project or comprehensive exam (MSE); interactive Program of Study (iPOS) submitted before completing 50 percent of required credit hours; for doctorate, comprehensive exam, thesis/dissertation, interactive Program of Study (iPOS) submitted before completing 50 percent of required credit hours. *Entrance requirements:* For master's, GRE, minimum GPA of 3.0 or equivalent in last 2 years of work leading to bachelor's degree; for doctorate, GRE, minimum GPA of 3.0 in last 2 years of work leading to bachelor's degree. Additional exam requirements/recommendations for international students: Required—TOEFL, IELTS, or PTE. Electronic applications accepted. *Expenses:* Contact institution. *Faculty research:* Electronic materials and packaging, materials for energy (batteries), adaptive/intelligent materials and structures, multiscale fluid mechanics, membranes, therapeutics and bioseparations, flexible structures, nanostructured materials, and micro/nano transport.

Carnegie Mellon University, Carnegie Institute of Technology, Department of Civil and Environmental Engineering, Pittsburgh, PA 15213. Offers advanced infrastructure systems (MS, PhD); advanced infrastructure systems technology development and application (MS); air quality engineering and science (MS); civil and environmental engineering (MS, PhD); civil and environmental engineering/engineering and public policy (PhD); civil engineering (MS, PhD); computational mechanics (MS, PhD); computational modeling and monitoring for resilient structural and material systems (MS); energy infrastructure systems (MS); environmental engineering (MS, PhD); environmental management and science (MS, PhD); IT-based sustainable global infrastructure and construction management (MS); sustainability and green design (MS); water quality engineering and science (MS). *Program availability:* Part-time. *Faculty:* 23 full-time (5 women), 12 part-time/adjunct (3 women). *Students:* 230 full-time (87 women), 4 part-time (0 women); includes 17 minority (4 Black or African American, non-Hispanic/Latino; 12 Asian, non-Hispanic/Latino; 1 Two or more races, non-Hispanic/Latino), 179 international. Average age 25. 653 applicants, 60% accepted, 107 enrolled. In 2016, 145 master's, 15 doctorates awarded. Terminal master's awarded for partial completion of doctoral program. *Degree requirements:* For master's, thesis optional; for doctorate, comprehensive exam, thesis/dissertation, two-part qualifying exam, public defense of dissertation. *Entrance requirements:* For master's, GRE General Test, BS in engineering, science or mathematics; for doctorate, GRE General Test, BS or MS in engineering, science or mathematics. Additional exam requirements/recommendations for international students: Required—TOEFL (minimum score 84 iBT) or IELTS (6.0). *Application deadline:* For fall admission, 1/5 priority date for domestic and international students; for spring admission, 9/15 priority date for domestic and international students. Applications are processed on a rolling basis. Application fee: $65. Electronic applications accepted. *Expenses:* Contact institution. *Financial support:* In 2016–17, 129 students received support. Fellowships with tuition reimbursements available, research assistantships with tuition reimbursements available, scholarships/grants, tuition waivers (full and partial), unspecified assistantships, and service assistantships available. Financial award application deadline: 1/5. *Faculty research:* Advanced infrastructure systems; environmental engineering, sustainability, and science; mechanics, materials, and computing. *Total annual research expenditures:* $7.4 million. *Unit head:* Dr. David A. Dzombak, Professor and Department Head, 412-268-2941, Fax: 412-268-7813, E-mail: dzombak@cmu.edu. *Application contact:* David A. Vey, Graduate Admissions Manager, 412-268-2292, Fax: 412-268-7813, E-mail: dvey@andrew.cmu.edu.
Website: http://www.cmu.edu/cee/

Carnegie Mellon University, Mellon College of Science, Department of Chemistry, Pittsburgh, PA 15213-3891. Offers atmospheric chemistry (PhD); bioinorganic chemistry (PhD); bioorganic chemistry and chemical biology (PhD); biophysical chemistry (PhD); catalysis (PhD); green and environmental chemistry (PhD); materials and nanoscience (PhD); renewable energy (PhD); sensors, probes, and imaging (PhD); spectroscopy and single molecule analysis (PhD); theoretical and computational chemistry (PhD). *Program availability:* Part-time. Terminal master's awarded for partial completion of doctoral program. *Degree requirements:* For doctorate, thesis/dissertation, departmental qualifying and oral exams, teaching experience. *Entrance requirements:* For doctorate, GRE General Test, GRE Subject Test. Additional exam requirements/recommendations for international students: Required—TOEFL. Electronic applications accepted. *Faculty research:* Physical and theoretical chemistry, chemical synthesis, biophysical/bioinorganic chemistry.

The Catholic University of America, School of Engineering, Department of Mechanical Engineering, Washington, DC 20064. Offers energy and environment (MME); general (MME); mechanical engineering (MSE, PhD). *Program availability:* Part-time. *Faculty:* 9 full-time (0 women), 7 part-time/adjunct (0 women). *Students:* 7 full-time (1 woman), 12 part-time (2 women); includes 4 minority (3 Black or African American, non-Hispanic/Latino; 1 Two or more races, non-Hispanic/Latino), 8 international. Average age 32. 26 applicants, 85% accepted, 9 enrolled. In 2016, 16 master's, 1 doctorate awarded. Terminal master's awarded for partial completion of doctoral program. *Degree requirements:* For master's, thesis (for some programs); for doctorate, comprehensive exam, thesis/dissertation. *Entrance requirements:* For master's and doctorate, statement of purpose, official copies of academic transcripts, three letters of recommendation. Additional exam requirements/recommendations for international students: Required—TOEFL (minimum score 550 paper-based; 80 iBT). *Application deadline:* For fall admission, 7/15 priority date for domestic students, 7/1 for international students; for spring admission, 11/15 priority date for domestic students, 11/1 for international students. Applications are processed on a rolling basis. Application fee: $55. Electronic applications accepted. *Expenses:* $43,380 per year; $1,170 per credit; $200 per semester part-time fees. *Financial support:* Fellowships, research assistantships, teaching assistantships, Federal Work-Study, scholarships/grants, tuition waivers (full and partial), and unspecified assistantships available. Financial award application deadline: 2/1; financial award applicants required to submit FAFSA. *Faculty research:* Energy and environment, acoustics and vibration, bio fabrication and lab-on-chip, experimental mechanics, smart materials. *Total annual research expenditures:* $243,170. *Unit head:* Dr. Sen Nieh, Chair, 202-319-5170, Fax: 202-319-5173, E-mail: nieh@cua.edu. *Application contact:* Director of Graduate Admissions, 202-319-5057, Fax: 202-319-6533, E-mail: cua-admissions@cua.edu.
Website: http://mechanical.cua.edu/

Clarkson University, Wallace H. Coulter School of Engineering, Master's Programs in Energy Systems, Schenectady, NY 12308. Offers business of energy (Advanced Certificate); electrical engineering (ME), including power engineering; energy systems (MS). *Program availability:* Part-time, evening/weekend. *Students:* 5 full-time (3 women), 3 part-time (0 women); includes 1 minority (Asian, non-Hispanic/Latino). 7 applicants, 43% accepted, 3 enrolled. In 2016, 1 degree awarded. *Degree requirements:* For master's, project. *Entrance requirements:* Additional exam requirements/recommendations for international students: Required—TOEFL (minimum score 550 paper-based, 80 iBT) or IELTS (6.5). *Application deadline:* Applications are processed on a rolling basis. Application fee: $50. Electronic applications accepted. *Expenses: Tuition:* Full-time $23,400; part-time $1300 per credit hour. Tuition and fees vary according to campus/location and program. *Financial support:* Scholarships/grants available. *Unit head:* Robert Kozik, Associate Dean of Engineering, 518-631-9881, E-mail: bkozik@clarkson.edu. *Application contact:* Dan Capogna, Graduate Admissions Contact, 518-631-9910, E-mail: graduate@clarkson.edu.

Cornell University, Graduate School, Graduate Fields of Agriculture and Life Sciences and Graduate Fields of Engineering, Field of Biological and Environmental Engineering, Ithaca, NY 14853. Offers bioenergy and integrated energy systems (M Eng, MPS, MS, PhD); biological engineering (M Eng, MPS, MS, PhD); bioprocess engineering (M Eng, MPS, MS, PhD); ecohydrology (M Eng, MPS, MS, PhD); environmental engineering (M Eng, MPS, MS, PhD); environmental management (MPS); food engineering (M Eng, MPS, MS, PhD); industrial biotechnology (M Eng, MPS, MS, PhD); nanobiotechnology (M Eng, MPS, MS, PhD); sustainable systems (M Eng, MPS, MS, PhD); synthetic biology (MS); syntheticbiology (M Eng, MPS, PhD). Terminal master's awarded for partial completion of doctoral program. *Degree requirements:* For master's, thesis (MS); for doctorate, comprehensive exam, thesis/dissertation. *Entrance requirements:* For master's, letters of recommendation (3 for MS, 2 for M Eng and MPS); for doctorate, GRE General Test, 3 letters of recommendation. Additional exam requirements/recommendations for international students: Required—TOEFL (minimum score 550 paper-based; 77 iBT). Electronic applications accepted. *Faculty research:* Biological and food engineering, environmental, soil and water engineering, international agricultural engineering, structures and controlled environments, machine systems and energy.

Florida State University, The Graduate School, FAMU-FSU College of Engineering, Department of Mechanical Engineering, Tallahassee, FL 32310-6046. Offers mechanical engineering (MS, PhD); sustainable energy (MS). *Program availability:* Part-time. *Faculty:* 26 full-time (3 women), 4 part-time/adjunct (1 woman). *Students:* 79 full-time (8 women); includes 16 minority (7 Black or African American, non-Hispanic/Latino; 1 American Indian or Alaska Native, non-Hispanic/Latino; 1 Asian, non-Hispanic/Latino; 3 Hispanic/Latino; 4 Two or more races, non-Hispanic/Latino), 25 international. Average age 25. 115 applicants, 46% accepted, 23 enrolled. In 2016, 19 master's, 6 doctorates awarded. Terminal master's awarded for partial completion of doctoral program. *Degree requirements:* For master's, thesis optional, 30 credit hours (24 coursework, 6 research); for doctorate, thesis/dissertation, 45 credit hours (21 coursework, 24 research). *Entrance requirements:* For master's and doctorate, GRE General Test (minimum scores: Verbal 150, Quantitative 155), minimum GPA of 3.0, official transcripts, resume, personal statement, 3 letters of recommendation. Additional exam requirements/recommendations for international students: Required—TOEFL (minimum score 550 paper-based; 80 iBT), IELTS (minimum score 6.5), Michigan English Language Assessment Battery (minimum score 77). *Application deadline:* For fall admission, 4/1 for domestic and international students; for spring admission, 11/1 for domestic and international students. Applications are processed on a rolling basis. Application fee: $30. Electronic applications accepted. *Expenses:* Tuition, state resident: full-time $7263; part-time $403.51 per credit hour. Tuition, nonresident: full-time $18,087; part-time $1004.85 per credit hour. *Required fees:* $1365; $75.81 per credit hour. $20 per semester. Tuition and fees vary according to campus/location. *Financial support:* In 2016–17, 3 fellowships with full tuition reimbursements, 45 research assistantships with full tuition reimbursements, 23 teaching assistantships with full tuition reimbursements (averaging $4,364 per year) were awarded; career-related internships or fieldwork, institutionally sponsored loans, scholarships/grants, health care benefits, tuition waivers (full), and unspecified assistantships also available. Support available to part-time students. Financial award application deadline: 3/1; financial award applicants required to submit FAFSA. *Faculty research:* Aero-propulsion, superconductivity, smart materials, nanomaterials, intelligent robotic systems, robotic locomotion, sustainable energy. *Total annual research expenditures:* $8.5 million. *Unit head:* Dr. Emmanuel Collins, Chair, 850-410-6373, Fax: 850-410-6337, E-mail: ecollins@eng.famu.fsu.edu. *Application contact:* Chase Pedersen, Coordinator of Graduate Studies, 850-410-6196, Fax: 850-410-6337, E-mail: cvpedersen@fsu.edu.
Website: http://www.eng.famu.fsu.edu/me/

Georgia Southern University, Jack N. Averitt College of Graduate Studies, Allen E. Paulson College of Engineering and Information Technology, Department of Mechanical Engineering, Program in Engineering/Energy Science, Statesboro, GA 30458. Offers MSAE. *Program availability:* Part-time. *Students:* 11 full-time (0 women), 7 part-time (2 women); includes 8 minority (5 Black or African American, non-Hispanic/Latino; 1 Asian, non-Hispanic/Latino; 2 Hispanic/Latino), 4 international. Average age 27. 19 applicants, 84% accepted, 2 enrolled. In 2016, 2 master's awarded. *Degree requirements:* For master's, thesis optional. *Entrance requirements:* Additional exam requirements/recommendations for international students: Required—TOEFL (minimum score 550 paper-based; 80 iBT), IELTS (minimum score 6). *Application deadline:* For fall admission, 3/1 priority date for domestic students; for spring admission, 11/1 for domestic students. Applications are processed on a rolling basis. Application fee: $50. Electronic applications accepted. *Expenses:* Tuition, state resident: full-time $7236; part-time $277 per semester hour. Tuition, nonresident: full-time $27,118; part-time $1105 per semester hour. *Required fees:* $2092. *Financial support:* In 2016–17, 2 students received support. Unspecified assistantships available. Financial award application deadline: 4/20; financial award applicants required to submit FAFSA. *Faculty research:* Renewable energy and engines, bio mechatronics, digital surface imaging, smart materials, nanocomposite material science. *Unit head:* Dr. Yaukim Kalaani, Chair, 912-478-0006, Fax: 912-478-0537, E-mail: yalkalanni@georgiasouthern.edu.

Instituto Tecnologico de Santo Domingo, Graduate School, Area of Basic And Environmental Sciences, Santo Domingo, Dominican Republic. Offers environmental science (M En S), including environmental education, environmental management, marine resources, natural resources management; mathematics (MS, PhD); renewable energy technology (MS, Certificate).

Inter American University of Puerto Rico, Bayamón Campus, Graduate School, Bayamón, PR 00957. Offers biology (MS), including environmental sciences and ecology, molecular biotechnology; electrical engineering (ME), including control system, potence system; human resources (MBA); mechanical engineering (ME, MS), including aerospace, energy. *Program availability:* Part-time, evening/weekend. *Faculty:* 12 full-time (5 women), 4 part-time/adjunct (2 women). *Students:* 7 full-time (5 women), 115 part-time (69 women); includes 119 minority (1 Black or African American, non-Hispanic/Latino; 118 Hispanic/Latino). Average age 28. 94 applicants, 72% accepted, 56 enrolled. In 2016, 22 master's awarded. *Degree requirements:* For master's, comprehensive exam, research project. *Entrance requirements:* For master's, EXADEP, GRE General Test, letters of recommendation. *Application deadline:* For fall admission, 7/1 for domestic students, 5/1 priority date for international students; for winter admission, 11/15 priority date for domestic and international students; for spring admission, 2/15 priority date for domestic and international students. Application fee: $31. *Expenses: Tuition:* Part-time $207 per credit. *Required fees:* $328 per semester. *Unit head:* Prof. Juan F. Martinez, Chancellor, 787-279-1200 Ext. 2295, Fax: 787-279-2205, E-mail: jmartinez@bayamon.inter.edu. *Application contact:* Aurelis Baez, Director of Student Services, 787-279-1912 Ext. 2017, Fax: 787-279-2205, E-mail: abaez@bayamon.inter.edu.

Kansas State University, Graduate School, College of Engineering, Department of Electrical and Computer Engineering, Manhattan, KS 66506. Offers electrical engineering (MS), including bioengineering, communication systems, design of computer systems, electrical engineering, energy and power systems, integrated circuits and devices, real time embedded systems, renewable energy, signal processing. *Program availability:* Part-time, evening/weekend, online learning. *Faculty:* 21 full-time (4 women), 1 (woman) part-time/adjunct. *Students:* 47 full-time (11 women), 51 part-time (5 women); includes 13 minority (6 Black or African American, non-Hispanic/Latino; 6 Asian, non-Hispanic/Latino; 1 Two or more races, non-Hispanic/Latino), 40 international. Average age 31. 146 applicants, 29% accepted, 17 enrolled. In 2016, 16 master's, 5 doctorates awarded. *Degree requirements:* For master's, thesis or alternative, final exam; for doctorate, thesis/dissertation, final exam, preliminary exams. *Entrance requirements:* For master's, GRE General Test, bachelor's degree in electrical engineering or computer science, minimum GPA of 3.0; for doctorate, GRE General Test. Additional exam requirements/recommendations for international students: Required—TOEFL (minimum score 600 paper-based; 85 iBT). *Application deadline:* For fall admission, 1/1 priority date for domestic and international students; for spring admission, 8/1 priority date for domestic and international students. Applications are processed on a rolling basis. Application fee: $50 ($75 for international students). Electronic applications accepted. *Expenses:* Tuition, state resident: full-time $9670. Tuition, nonresident: full-time $21,828. *Required fees:* $862. *Financial support:* In 2016–17, 40 students received support, including 22 research assistantships with tuition reimbursements available (averaging $12,100 per year), 18 teaching assistantships with full tuition reimbursements available (averaging $12,220 per year); career-related internships or fieldwork, institutionally sponsored loans, and scholarships/grants also available. Support available to part-time students. Financial award application deadline: 3/1; financial award applicants required to submit FAFSA. *Faculty research:* Energy systems and renewable energy, computer systems and real time embedded systems, communication systems and signal processing, integrated circuits and devices, bioengineering. *Total annual research expenditures:* $1.3 million. *Unit head:* Dr. Don Gruenbacher, Head, 785-532-5600, Fax: 785-532-1188, E-mail: grue@k-state.edu. *Application contact:* Dr. Andrew Rys, Graduate Program Director, 785-532-4665, Fax: 785-532-1188, E-mail: andrys@k-state.edu.
Website: http://www.ece.k-state.edu/

Lehigh University, P.C. Rossin College of Engineering and Applied Science, Program in Energy Systems Engineering, Bethlehem, PA 18015. Offers M Eng. *Program availability:* Part-time. *Faculty:* 1 full-time (0 women), 2 part-time/adjunct (0 women). *Students:* 5 full-time (0 women), 6 part-time (2 women); includes 2 minority (both Hispanic/Latino), 2 international. Average age 29. 14 applicants, 71% accepted, 5 enrolled. In 2016, 11 master's awarded. *Entrance requirements:* For master's, GRE. Additional exam requirements/recommendations for international students: Required—TOEFL (minimum score 79 iBT). *Application deadline:* For fall admission, 5/15 for domestic and international students. Application fee: $75. *Expenses:* $1,420 per credit. *Financial support:* Scholarships/grants available. Financial award application deadline: 1/15. *Unit head:* Prof. Ramesh Shankar, Director, 610-758-3529, E-mail: ras816@lehigh.edu. *Application contact:* Wendy A. Vohar, Graduate Coordinator, 610-758-3650, E-mail: waa3@lehigh.edu.
Website: http://www.lehigh.edu/esei

New Jersey Institute of Technology, Newark College of Engineering, Newark, NJ 07102. Offers biomedical engineering (MS, PhD); chemical engineering (MS, PhD); computer engineering (MS, PhD); electrical engineering (MS, PhD); engineering management (MS); environmental engineering (PhD); healthcare systems management (MS); industrial engineering (MS, PhD); Internet engineering (MS); manufacturing engineering (MS); mechanical engineering (MS, PhD); occupational safety and health engineering (MS); pharmaceutical bioprocessing (MS); pharmaceutical engineering (MS); pharmaceutical systems management (MS); power and energy systems (MS); telecommunications (MS); transportation (MS, PhD). *Program availability:* Part-time, evening/weekend. *Faculty:* 146 full-time (21 women), 119 part-time/adjunct (10 women). *Students:* 804 full-time (191 women), 550 part-time (129 women); includes 357 minority (82 Black or African American, non-Hispanic/Latino; 1 American Indian or Alaska Native, non-Hispanic/Latino; 138 Asian, non-Hispanic/Latino; 114 Hispanic/Latino; 22 Two or more races, non-Hispanic/Latino), 675 international. Average age 27. 2,959 applicants, 51% accepted, 442 enrolled. In 2016, 595 master's, 29 doctorates awarded. Terminal master's awarded for partial completion of doctoral program. *Degree requirements:* For master's, thesis optional; for doctorate, thesis/dissertation. *Entrance requirements:* For master's, GRE General Test; for doctorate, GRE General Test, minimum graduate GPA of 3.5. Additional exam requirements/recommendations for international students: Required—TOEFL (minimum score 550 paper-based; 79 iBT). *Application deadline:* For fall admission, 6/1 priority date for domestic students, 5/1 priority date for international students; for spring admission, 11/15 priority date for domestic and international students. Applications are processed on a rolling basis. Application fee: $75. Electronic applications accepted. *Expenses:* Contact institution. *Financial support:* In 2016–17, 172 students received support, including 1 fellowship (averaging $1,528 per year), 79 research assistantships (averaging $13,336 per year), 92 teaching assistantships (averaging $20,619 per year); scholarships/grants also available. Financial award application deadline: 1/15. *Faculty research:* Nonlinear signal processing, intelligent medical image analysis, calibration issues in coherent localization, computer-aided design, neural network for tool wear measurement. *Total annual research expenditures:* $11.1 million. *Unit head:* Dr. Moshe Kam, Dean, 973-596-5534, E-mail: moshe.kam@njit.edu. *Application contact:* Stephen Eck, Director of Admissions, 973-596-3300, Fax: 973-596-3461, E-mail: admissions@njit.edu.
Website: http://engineering.njit.edu/

New York Institute of Technology, School of Engineering and Computing Sciences, Department of Energy Management, Old Westbury, NY 11568-8000. Offers energy management (MS); energy technology (Advanced Certificate); environmental management (Advanced Certificate); facilities management (Advanced Certificate); infrastructure security management (Advanced Certificate). *Program availability:* Part-time, evening/weekend, 100% online, blended/hybrid learning. *Faculty:* 1 full-time (0 women), 5 part-time/adjunct (0 women). *Students:* 53 full-time (7 women), 56 part-time (8 women); includes 20 minority (5 Black or African American, non-Hispanic/Latino; 1 American Indian or Alaska Native, non-Hispanic/Latino; 5 Asian, non-Hispanic/Latino; 9 Hispanic/Latino), 60 international. Average age 28. 167 applicants, 77% accepted, 33 enrolled. In 2016, 54 master's, 3 other advanced degrees awarded. *Degree requirements:* For master's, thesis or alternative. *Entrance requirements:* For master's and Advanced Certificate, BS; minimum undergraduate GPA of 2.85. Additional exam requirements/recommendations for international students: Required—TOEFL (minimum score 79 iBT), IELTS (minimum score 6). *Application deadline:* For fall admission, 7/1 for domestic students, 6/1 for international students; for spring admission, 12/1 for domestic and international students. Applications are processed on a rolling basis. Application fee: $50. Electronic applications accepted. *Expenses:* $1,215 per credit. *Financial support:* Fellowships with partial tuition reimbursements, teaching assistantships with partial tuition reimbursements, career-related internships or fieldwork, Federal Work-Study, scholarships/grants, tuition waivers (full and partial), and unspecified assistantships available. Support available to part-time students. Financial award application deadline: 3/1; financial award applicants required to submit FAFSA. *Faculty research:* Alternative energy systems; energy policy, master planning, and auditing; facilities management; lighting technology; cogeneration; utility rate structures; smart homes; monitoring systems; building information modeling; sustainability. *Unit head:* Dr. Robert Amundsen, Department Chair, 516-686-7578, E-mail: ramundse@nyit.edu. *Application contact:* Alice Dolitsky, Director, Graduate Admissions, 516-686-7520, Fax: 516-686-1116, E-mail: nyitgrad@nyit.edu.
Website: http://www.nyit.edu/degrees/energy_management_ms

North Carolina Agricultural and Technical State University, School of Graduate Studies, College of Engineering, Department of Electrical and Computer Engineering, Greensboro, NC 27411. Offers electrical engineering (MSEE, PhD), including communications and signal processing, computer engineering, electronic and optical materials and devices, power systems and control. *Program availability:* Part-time. *Degree requirements:* For master's, project, thesis defense; for doctorate, thesis/dissertation. *Entrance requirements:* For master's, GRE General Test, GRE Subject Test, minimum GPA of 2.8; for doctorate, GRE General Test, minimum GPA of 3.0. *Faculty research:* Semiconductor compounds, VLSI design, image processing, optical systems and devices, fault-tolerant computing.

Northeastern University, College of Engineering, Boston, MA 02115-5096. Offers bioengineering (MS, PhD); chemical engineering (MS, PhD); civil engineering (MS, PhD); computer engineering (PhD); computer systems engineering (MS); electrical and computer engineering (MS); electrical and computer engineering leadership (MS); electrical engineering (PhD); energy systems (MS); engineering and public policy (MS); engineering management (MS, Certificate); environmental engineering (MS); industrial engineering (MS, PhD); information assurance (PhD); information systems (MS); interdisciplinary engineering (PhD); mechanical engineering (PhD); operations research (MS); telecommunication systems management (MS). *Program availability:* Part-time, online learning. *Faculty:* 202 full-time (59 women), 53 part-time/adjunct (9 women). *Students:* 2,982 full-time (954 women), 192 part-time (38 women). In 2016, 851 master's, 74 doctorates awarded. Application fee: $75. Electronic applications accepted. *Expenses:* $1,471 per credit. *Financial support:* Fellowships, research assistantships, teaching assistantships, career-related internships or fieldwork, scholarships/grants, health care benefits, tuition waivers, and unspecified assistantships available. Support available to part-time students. Financial award applicants required to submit FAFSA. *Unit head:* Dr. Nadine Aubry, Dean, College of Engineering. *Application contact:* Jeffery Hengel, Director of Graduate Admissions, 617-373-2711, E-mail: j.hengel@northeastern.edu.
Website: http://www.coe.neu.edu/academics/graduate-school-engineering

San Francisco State University, Division of Graduate Studies, College of Science and Engineering, School of Engineering, San Francisco, CA 94132-1722. Offers embedded electrical and computer systems (MS); energy systems (MS); structural/earthquake engineering (MS). *Program availability:* Part-time. *Application deadline:* Applications are processed on a rolling basis. Electronic applications accepted. *Expenses:* Tuition, state resident: full-time $6738. Tuition, nonresident: full-time $15,666. *Required fees:* $1012. Tuition and fees vary according to degree level and program. *Unit head:* Dr. Wenshen Pong, Director, 415-338-7738, Fax: 415-338-0525, E-mail: wspong@sfsu.edu. *Application contact:* Dr. Hamid Shahnasser, Graduate Coordinator, 415-338-2124, Fax: 415-338-0525, E-mail: hamid@sfsu.edu.
Website: http://engineering.sfsu.edu/

Santa Clara University, School of Engineering, Santa Clara, CA 95053. Offers applied mathematics (MS); bioengineering (MS); civil engineering (MS); computer science and engineering (MS, PhD); electrical engineering (MS, PhD); engineering (Engineer); engineering management and leadership (MS); mechanical engineering (MS, PhD); software engineering (MS); sustainable energy (MS). *Program availability:* Part-time, evening/weekend. *Faculty:* 66 full-time (22 women), 59 part-time/adjunct (12 women). *Students:* 449 full-time (188 women), 315 part-time (114 women); includes 197 minority (3 Black or African American, non-Hispanic/Latino; 144 Asian, non-Hispanic/Latino; 33 Hispanic/Latino; 1 Native Hawaiian or other Pacific Islander, non-Hispanic/Latino; 16 Two or more races, non-Hispanic/Latino), 418 international. Average age 28. 1,217 applicants, 45% accepted, 293 enrolled. In 2016, 466 master's awarded. *Entrance requirements:* For master's, GRE, transcript; for doctorate, GRE, master's degree or equivalent, 3 letters of recommendation, statement of purpose; for Engineer, master's degree. Additional exam requirements/recommendations for international students: Required—TOEFL (minimum score 79 iBT) or IELTS (6.5). *Application deadline:* For fall admission, 4/1 for domestic and international students; for winter admission, 9/9 for domestic students, 9/2 for international students; for spring admission, 2/17 for domestic students, 12/9 for international students. Application fee: $60. Electronic applications accepted. *Expenses:* $928 per unit. *Financial support:* Fellowships, research assistantships, teaching assistantships, career-related internships or fieldwork, Federal

Energy and Power Engineering

Work-Study, scholarships/grants, traineeships, health care benefits, tuition waivers, and unspecified assistantships available. Support available to part-time students. Financial award applicants required to submit FAFSA. *Unit head:* Dr. Alfonso Ortega, Dean. *Application contact:* Stacey Tinker, Director of Admissions and Marketing, 408-554-4313, Fax: 408-554-4323, E-mail: stinker@scu.edu.
Website: http://www.scu.edu/engineering/graduate/

Southern Illinois University Carbondale, Graduate School, College of Engineering, Program in Engineering Science, Carbondale, IL 62901-4701. Offers engineering science (PhD), including civil and environmental engineering, electrical and computer engineering, mechanical engineering and energy processes, mining and mineral resources engineering. *Degree requirements:* For doctorate, thesis/dissertation. *Entrance requirements:* For doctorate, GRE General Test, minimum GPA of 3.5. Additional exam requirements/recommendations for international students: Required—TOEFL.

Stanford University, School of Earth, Energy and Environmental Sciences, Department of Energy Resources Engineering, Stanford, CA 94305-2004. Offers energy resources engineering (MS, PhD, Eng); petroleum engineering (MS, PhD). Terminal master's awarded for partial completion of doctoral program. *Degree requirements:* For doctorate, thesis/dissertation; for Eng, thesis. *Entrance requirements:* For master's, doctorate, and Eng, GRE General Test. Additional exam requirements/recommendations for international students: Required—TOEFL. Electronic applications accepted. *Expenses: Tuition:* Full-time $47,331. *Required fees:* $609.

Stanford University, School of Engineering, Department of Civil and Environmental Engineering, Stanford, CA 94305-2004. Offers atmosphere and energy (MS, PhD); construction (MS), including construction engineering and management, design-construction integration, sustainable design and construction; environmental engineering and science (MS, PhD, Eng); environmental fluid mechanics and hydrology (PhD); geomechanics (MS); structural engineering (MS). Terminal master's awarded for partial completion of doctoral program. *Degree requirements:* For doctorate, thesis/dissertation, qualifying exam; for Eng, thesis. *Entrance requirements:* For master's, doctorate, and Eng, GRE General Test. Additional exam requirements/recommendations for international students: Required—TOEFL. Electronic applications accepted. *Expenses: Tuition:* Full-time $47,331. *Required fees:* $609.

Syracuse University, College of Engineering and Computer Science, MS Program in Energy Systems Engineering, Syracuse, NY 13244. Offers energy systems engineering (MS), including alternative energy, electric energy, thermal energy. *Program availability:* Part-time. *Students:* Average age 23. *Entrance requirements:* For master's, GRE, BS, three letters of recommendation, official transcripts, resume, personal statement. *Application deadline:* For fall admission, 7/1 priority date for domestic students, 6/1 priority date for international students; for spring admission, 11/15 priority date for domestic students, 10/15 priority date for international students. Applications are processed on a rolling basis. Application fee: $75. Electronic applications accepted. *Expenses: Tuition:* Full-time $25,974; part-time $1443 per credit hour. *Required fees:* $802; $50 per course. Tuition and fees vary according to course load and program. *Financial support:* Fellowships, research assistantships, and teaching assistantships available. *Faculty research:* Energy consumption, conservation, conversion and creation. *Unit head:* Prof. H. E Khalifa, Professor, 315-443-1286, E-mail: hekhalif@syr.edu. *Application contact:* Kathleen Joyce, Assistant Dean, 315-443-2219, E-mail: topgrads@syr.edu.
Website: http://eng-cs.syr.edu/

Texas A&M University–Kingsville, College of Graduate Studies, Frank H. Dotterweich College of Engineering, Program in Sustainable Energy Systems Engineering, Kingsville, TX 78363. Offers PhD. *Degree requirements:* For doctorate, variable foreign language requirement, comprehensive exam, thesis/dissertation (for some programs). *Entrance requirements:* For doctorate, GRE, MAT, GMAT, bachelor's or master's degree in engineering or science, curriculum vitae, official transcripts, statement of purpose, three letters of recommendation. Additional exam requirements/recommendations for international students: Required—TOEFL (minimum score 550 paper-based; 79 iBT). Electronic applications accepted.

Texas Tech University, Graduate School, Interdisciplinary Programs, Lubbock, TX 79409. Offers arid land studies (MS); biotechnology (MS); interdisciplinary studies (MA, MS); museum science (MA); wind science and engineering (PhD); JD/MS. *Program availability:* Part-time. *Faculty:* 10 full-time (4 women). *Students:* 122 full-time (56 women), 83 part-time (46 women); includes 78 minority (25 Black or African American, non-Hispanic/Latino; 1 American Indian or Alaska Native, non-Hispanic/Latino; 2 Asian, non-Hispanic/Latino; 41 Hispanic/Latino; 1 Native Hawaiian or other Pacific Islander, non-Hispanic/Latino; 8 Two or more races, non-Hispanic/Latino), 32 international. Average age 29. 114 applicants, 71% accepted, 60 enrolled. In 2016, 55 master's, 1 doctorate awarded. Terminal master's awarded for partial completion of doctoral program. *Degree requirements:* For master's, comprehensive exam (for some programs), thesis (for some programs); for doctorate, comprehensive exam, thesis/dissertation (for some programs). *Entrance requirements:* Additional exam requirements/recommendations for international students: Required—TOEFL (minimum score 550 paper-based; 79 iBT), IELTS (minimum score 6.5), PTE (minimum score 60), Cambridge Advanced (B), Cambridge Proficiency (C), ELS English for Academic Purposes (Level 112). *Application deadline:* For fall admission, 6/1 priority date for domestic students, 1/15 priority date for international students; for spring admission, 9/1 priority date for domestic students, 6/15 priority date for international students. Applications are processed on a rolling basis. Application fee: $75. Electronic applications accepted. *Expenses: Tuition:* state resident: full-time $7200; part-time $300 per credit hour. Tuition, nonresident: full-time $16,992; part-time $708 per credit hour. *Required fees:* $2428; $50.50 per credit hour. $608 per semester. Tuition and fees vary according to program. *Financial support:* In 2016–17, 116 students received support, including 107 fellowships (averaging $4,360 per year), 10 research assistantships (averaging $10,619 per year), 7 teaching assistantships (averaging $9,152 per year); scholarships/grants and unspecified assistantships also available. Financial award application deadline: 4/15; financial award applicants required to submit FAFSA. *Total annual research expenditures:* $2 million. *Unit head:* Dr. Mark Sheridan, Vice Provost for Graduate and Postdoctoral Affairs/Dean of the Graduate School, 806-742-2787, Fax: 806-742-1746, E-mail: mark.sheridan@ttu.edu. *Application contact:* Amanda Wysinger, Academic Advisor, 806-834-0822, Fax: 806-742-4038, E-mail: amanda.wysinger@ttu.edu.
Website: http://www.depts.ttu.edu/gradschool/about/INDS/index.php

Universidad Autonoma de Guadalajara, Graduate Programs, Guadalajara, Mexico. Offers administrative law and justice (LL M); advertising and corporate communications (MA); architecture (M Arch); business (MBA); computational science (MCC); education (Ed M, Ed D); English-Spanish translation (MA); entrepreneurship and management (MBA); integrated management of digital animation (MA); international business (MIB); international corporate law (LL M); internet technologies (MS); manufacturing systems (MMS); occupational health (MS); philosophy (MA, PhD); power electronics (MS); quality systems (MQS); renewable energy (MS); social evaluation of projects (MBA); strategic market research (MBA); tax law (MA); teaching mathematics (MA).

University of Alberta, Faculty of Graduate Studies and Research, Department of Electrical and Computer Engineering, Edmonton, AB T6G 2E1, Canada. Offers communications (M Eng, M Sc, PhD); computer engineering (M Eng, M Sc, PhD); electromagnetics (M Eng, M Sc, PhD); nanotechnology and microdevices (M Eng, M Sc, PhD); power/power electronics (M Eng, M Sc, PhD); systems (M Eng, M Sc, PhD). Terminal master's awarded for partial completion of doctoral program. *Degree requirements:* For master's, thesis; for doctorate, thesis/dissertation. *Entrance requirements:* Additional exam requirements/recommendations for international students: Required—TOEFL. Electronic applications accepted. *Faculty research:* Controls, communications, microelectronics, electromagnetics.

University of Calgary, Faculty of Graduate Studies, Schulich School of Engineering, Department of Chemical and Petroleum Engineering, Calgary, AB T2N 1N4, Canada. Offers chemical engineering (M Eng, M Sc, PhD); energy and environment engineering (M Eng, M Sc, PhD); energy and environmental systems (M Eng, M Sc, PhD); environmental engineering (M Eng, M Sc, PhD); petroleum engineering (M Eng, M Sc, PhD); reservoir characterization (M Eng, M Sc). *Program availability:* Part-time. *Degree requirements:* For master's, thesis (for some programs); for doctorate, comprehensive exam, thesis/dissertation, candidacy exam. *Entrance requirements:* For master's, minimum GPA of 3.0 or equivalent; for doctorate, minimum GPA of 3.5 or equivalent. Additional exam requirements/recommendations for international students: Required—TOEFL (minimum score 550 paper-based; 80 iBT), IELTS (minimum score 7). Electronic applications accepted. *Faculty research:* Environmental engineering, biomedical engineering modeling, simulation and control, petroleum recovery and reservoir engineering, phase equilibria and transport properties.

University of Calgary, Faculty of Graduate Studies, Schulich School of Engineering, Department of Civil Engineering, Calgary, AB T2N 1N4, Canada. Offers avalanche mechanics (M Sc, PhD); civil engineering (M Eng, M Sc, PhD); energy and environment engineering (M Eng, M Sc, PhD); environmental engineering (M Eng, M Sc, PhD); geotechnical engineering (M Eng, M Sc, PhD); materials science (M Eng, M Sc, PhD); project management (M Eng, M Sc, PhD); structures and solid mechanics (M Eng, M Sc, PhD); transportation engineering (M Eng, M Sc, PhD); water resources (M Eng, M Sc, PhD). *Program availability:* Part-time. *Degree requirements:* For master's, thesis; for doctorate, thesis/dissertation, written and oral candidacy exam. *Entrance requirements:* For master's, minimum GPA of 3.0; for doctorate, minimum GPA of 3.5. Additional exam requirements/recommendations for international students: Required—TOEFL (minimum score 580 paper-based; 93 iBT), IELTS (minimum score 7). Electronic applications accepted. *Faculty research:* Geotechnical engineering, energy and environment, transportation, project management, structures and solid mechanics.

University of Colorado Colorado Springs, College of Engineering and Applied Science, Program in General Engineering, Colorado Springs, CO 80918. Offers energy engineering (ME); engineering management (ME); information assurance (ME); software engineering (ME); space operations (ME); systems engineering (ME). *Program availability:* Part-time, evening/weekend, blended/hybrid learning. *Faculty:* 1 full-time (0 women), 15 part-time/adjunct (6 women). *Students:* 18 full-time (3 women), 166 part-time (34 women); includes 36 minority (6 Black or African American, non-Hispanic/Latino; 8 Asian, non-Hispanic/Latino; 12 Hispanic/Latino; 10 Two or more races, non-Hispanic/Latino), 57 international. Average age 36. 89 applicants, 72% accepted, 41 enrolled. In 2016, 21 master's, 8 doctorates awarded. *Degree requirements:* For master's, thesis, portfolio, or project; for doctorate, comprehensive exam, thesis/dissertation. *Entrance requirements:* For master's, GRE (minimum score of 148 new grading scale on quantitative portion if undergraduate GPA is less than 3.0); for doctorate, GRE (minimum score of 148 new grading scale on the quantitative portion if the applicant has not graduated from a program of recognized standing), minimum GPA of 3.3 in the bachelor's or master's degree program attempted. Additional exam requirements/recommendations for international students: Required—TOEFL (minimum score 80 iBT), IELTS (minimum score 6). *Application deadline:* For fall admission, 7/1 for domestic students, 6/1 for international students; for spring admission, 11/1 for domestic and international students; for summer admission, 4/15 for domestic and international students. Applications are processed on a rolling basis. Application fee: $60 ($100 for international students). Electronic applications accepted. *Expenses:* Contact institution. *Financial support:* In 2016–17, 28 students received support. Federal Work-Study, scholarships/grants, traineeships, and unspecified assistantships available. Support available to part-time students. Financial award application deadline: 3/1; financial award applicants required to submit FAFSA. *Unit head:* Dr. Ramaswami Dandapani, Dean, 719-255-3543, Fax: 719-255-3542, E-mail: rdan@cas.uccs.edu. *Application contact:* Dawn House, Coordinator, 719-255-3246, E-mail: dhouse@uccs.edu.

University of Illinois at Urbana–Champaign, Graduate College, College of Engineering, Department of Nuclear, Plasma, and Radiological Engineering, Urbana, IL 61801. Offers energy systems (M Eng); nuclear, plasma, and radiological engineering (MS, PhD). Terminal master's awarded for partial completion of doctoral program.

The University of Iowa, Graduate College, College of Engineering, Department of Mechanical Engineering, Iowa City, IA 52242-1316. Offers energy systems (MS, PhD); engineering design (MS, PhD); fluid dynamics (MS, PhD); materials and manufacturing (MS, PhD); wind energy (MS, PhD). *Faculty:* 16 full-time (0 women). *Students:* 37 full-time (4 women), 12 part-time (0 women); includes 1 minority (Black or African American, non-Hispanic/Latino), 30 international. Average age 29. 75 applicants, 13% accepted, 2 enrolled. In 2016, 6 master's, 5 doctorates awarded. Terminal master's awarded for partial completion of doctoral program. *Degree requirements:* For master's, oral exam or thesis; for doctorate, comprehensive exam, thesis/dissertation. *Entrance requirements:* For master's and doctorate, GRE (minimum Verbal score of 153, Quantitative 151), minimum undergraduate GPA of 3.0. Additional exam requirements/recommendations for international students: Required—TOEFL (minimum score 600 paper-based; 100 iBT), IELTS (minimum score 7). *Application deadline:* For fall admission, 1/15 for domestic and international students; for spring admission, 9/1 for domestic and international students; for summer admission, 1/15 for domestic and international students. Application fee: $60 ($100 for international students). Electronic applications accepted. *Financial support:* In 2016–17, 56 students received support, including 37 research assistantships with full tuition reimbursements available (averaging $22,981 per year), 19 teaching assistantships with full tuition reimbursements available (averaging $18,809 per year); traineeships and unspecified assistantships also available. Financial award applicants required to submit FAFSA. *Faculty research:* Computer simulation methodology, biomechanics, metal casting, dynamics, laser processing, system reliability, ship hydrodynamics, solid mechanics, fluid dynamics, energy, human modeling and Nano technology. *Total annual research expenditures:* $9.1 million. *Unit head:* Dr. Ching-Long Lin, Departmental Executive Officer, 319-335-5673, Fax: 319-335-5669, E-mail: ching-long-lin@uiowa.edu. *Application contact:* Tara Hoadley, Academic Program Specialist, 319-335-5939, Fax: 319-335-5669, E-mail: mech_eng@engineering.uiowa.edu.
Website: https://mie.engineering.uiowa.edu

University of Massachusetts Lowell, Francis College of Engineering, Program in Energy Engineering, Lowell, MA 01854. Offers MS Eng, PhD. *Degree requirements:* For master's, thesis optional. *Entrance requirements:* For master's, GRE General Test.

Additional exam requirements/recommendations for international students: Required—TOEFL.

University of Memphis, Graduate School, Herff College of Engineering, Department of Mechanical Engineering, Memphis, TN 38103. Offers power systems (MS). *Program availability:* Part-time. *Faculty:* 7 full-time (0 women). *Students:* 6 full-time (0 women), 2 part-time (0 women); includes 2 minority (1 Asian, non-Hispanic/Latino; 1 Two or more races, non-Hispanic/Latino), 3 international. Average age 26. 17 applicants, 65% accepted, 2 enrolled. In 2016, 2 master's awarded. Terminal master's awarded for partial completion of doctoral program. *Degree requirements:* For master's, comprehensive exam, thesis or alternative; for doctorate, comprehensive exam, thesis/dissertation. *Entrance requirements:* For master's, GRE General Test, MAT, GMAT, BS in mechanical engineering, minimum undergraduate GPA of 3.0, three letters of recommendation; for doctorate, GRE, BS in mechanical engineering, minimum undergraduate GPA of 3.0, three letters of recommendation; for Graduate Certificate, letter of intent, two letters of recommendation. Additional exam requirements/recommendations for international students: Required—TOEFL (minimum score 550 paper-based; 79 iBT). *Application deadline:* For fall admission, 8/1 for domestic students; for spring admission, 12/1 for domestic students. Application fee: $35 ($60 for international students). *Expenses:* $5,231.50 per semester full-time in-state, $9,623.50 full-time out-of-state. *Financial support:* In 2016–17, 6 students received support, including 1 research assistantship with full tuition reimbursement available (averaging $26,000 per year), 10 teaching assistantships with full tuition reimbursements available (averaging $19,500 per year); fellowships with full tuition reimbursements available, career-related internships or fieldwork, Federal Work-Study, scholarships/grants, and unspecified assistantships also available. Financial award application deadline: 2/1; financial award applicants required to submit FAFSA. *Faculty research:* Computational fluid dynamics, computational mechanics, integrated design, nondestructive testing, operations research. *Unit head:* Dr. Sumanta Acharya, Chair, 901-678-2173, Fax: 901-678-5459. *Application contact:* Dr. Teong Tan, Graduate Studies Coordinator, 901-678-3264, Fax: 901-678-5459, E-mail: ttan@memphis.edu.
Website: http://www.memphis.edu/me/

University of Michigan, College of Engineering, Department of Integrative Systems and Design, Ann Arbor, MI 48109. Offers automotive engineering (M Eng); design science (MS, PhD); energy systems engineering (M Eng, MS); global automotive and manufacturing engineering (M Eng); manufacturing engineering (M Eng, D Eng); pharmaceutical engineering (M Eng); robotics and autonomous vehicles (M Eng); systems engineering and design (M Eng); MBA/M Eng; MSE/MS. *Program availability:* Part-time, online learning. *Students:* 147 full-time (33 women), 234 part-time (39 women). 315 applicants, 8% accepted, 13 enrolled. In 2016, 158 master's, 2 doctorates awarded. Terminal master's awarded for partial completion of doctoral program. *Degree requirements:* For master's, capstone project; for doctorate, thesis/dissertation. *Entrance requirements:* For master's, GRE; for doctorate, GRE, 2 years of work experience. Additional exam requirements/recommendations for international students: Required—TOEFL (minimum score 560 paper-based). *Application deadline:* Applications are processed on a rolling basis. Electronic applications accepted. *Expenses:* Tuition, state resident: full-time $21,466; part-time $1152 per credit hour. Tuition, nonresident: full-time $43,346; part-time $2367 per credit hour. Part-time tuition and fees vary according to course load, degree level and program. *Financial support:* Fellowships, research assistantships with full tuition reimbursements, teaching assistantships with full tuition reimbursements, career-related internships or fieldwork, scholarships/grants, and unspecified assistantships available. Financial award applicants required to submit FAFSA. *Faculty research:* Automotive engineering, design science, energy systems engineering, engineering sustainable systems, financial engineering, global automotive and manufacturing engineering, integrated microsystems, manufacturing engineering, pharmaceutical engineering, robotics and autonomous vehicles. *Total annual research expenditures:* $292,225. *Unit head:* Prof. Panos Papalambros, Department Chair, 734-647-8401, E-mail: pyp@umich.edu. *Application contact:* Kathy Bishar, Senior Graduate Coordinator, 734-764-3312, E-mail: kbishar@umich.edu.
Website: http://www.isd.engin.umich.edu

University of Michigan–Dearborn, College of Engineering and Computer Science, MSE Program in Energy Systems Engineering, Dearborn, MI 48128. Offers MSE. *Program availability:* Part-time, evening/weekend, 100% online. *Faculty:* 1 full-time (0 women). *Students:* 2 full-time (0 women), 19 part-time (3 women); includes 3 minority (2 Black or African American, non-Hispanic/Latino; 1 Hispanic/Latino), 3 international. Average age 26. 29 applicants, 52% accepted, 8 enrolled. In 2016, 3 master's awarded. *Entrance requirements:* Additional exam requirements/recommendations for international students: Required—TOEFL (minimum score 560 paper-based; 84 iBT), IELTS (minimum score 6.5). *Application deadline:* For fall admission, 8/1 for domestic students, 5/1 for international students; for winter admission, 12/1 for domestic students, 9/1 for international students; for spring admission, 4/1 for domestic students, 1/1 for international students. Applications are processed on a rolling basis. Application fee: $60. Electronic applications accepted. *Expenses:* Tuition, state resident: full-time $13,118; part-time $2280 per term. Tuition, nonresident: full-time $21,816; part-time $3771 per term. *Required fees:* $866; $658 per unit. $329 per term. Tuition and fees vary according to program. *Financial support:* Scholarships/grants, unspecified assistantships, and non-resident tuition scholarships available. Support available to part-time students. Financial award application deadline: 3/1; financial award applicants required to submit FAFSA. *Faculty research:* Solar cell materials, energy cost and policy, power distribution, power management and fuel cells. *Unit head:* Dr. Taehyung Kim, Director/Professor, 313-583-6736, E-mail: taehyung@umich.edu. *Application contact:* Office of Graduate Studies, 313-583-6321, E-mail: umd-graduatestudies@umich.edu.
Website: http://umdearborn.edu/cecs/IDP/mse_ese/index.php

The University of North Carolina at Charlotte, William States Lee College of Engineering, Department of Engineering Technology and Construction Management, Charlotte, NC 28223-0001. Offers applied energy (Graduate Certificate); applied energy and electromechanical systems (MS); construction and facilities management (MS); fire protection and administration (MS). *Program availability:* Part-time. *Faculty:* 26 full-time (5 women). *Students:* 46 full-time (8 women), 19 part-time (1 woman); includes 9 minority (4 Black or African American, non-Hispanic/Latino; 2 Asian, non-Hispanic/Latino; 3 Hispanic/Latino), 31 international. Average age 27. 71 applicants, 83% accepted, 24 enrolled. In 2016, 34 master's awarded. *Degree requirements:* For master's, thesis, capstone, or comprehensive exam. *Entrance requirements:* For master's, GRE, minimum undergraduate GPA of 3.0, recommendations, statistics, integral and differential calculus (for students pursuing fire protection concentration or applied energy and electromechanical systems program); for Graduate Certificate, bachelor's degree in engineering, engineering technology, construction management or a closely-related technical or scientific field; undergraduate coursework of at least 3 semesters in engineering analysis or calculus; minimum GPA of 3.0. Additional exam requirements/recommendations for international students: Required—TOEFL (minimum score 523 paper-based, 70 iBT) or IELTS (6.5). *Application deadline:* For fall admission, 3/1 priority date for domestic and international students; for spring admission, 10/1 priority date for domestic and international students. Applications are processed on a

rolling basis. Application fee: $75. Electronic applications accepted. *Expenses:* Contact institution. *Financial support:* In 2016–17, 22 students received support, including 22 research assistantships (averaging $8,235 per year); career-related internships or fieldwork, institutionally sponsored loans, scholarships/grants, and unspecified assistantships also available. Support available to part-time students. Financial award application deadline: 3/1; financial award applicants required to submit FAFSA. *Total annual research expenditures:* $1.5 million. *Unit head:* Dr. Anthony Brizendine, Chair, 704-687-5050, E-mail: albrizen@uncc.edu. *Application contact:* Kathy B. Giddings, Director of Graduate Admissions, 704-687-5503, Fax: 704-687-1668, E-mail: gradadm@uncc.edu.
Website: http://et.uncc.edu/

The University of North Carolina at Charlotte, William States Lee College of Engineering, Department of Systems Engineering and Engineering Management, Charlotte, NC 28223-0001. Offers energy analytics (Graduate Certificate); engineering management (MSEM); Lean Six Sigma (Graduate Certificate); logistics and supply chains (Graduate Certificate); systems analytics (Graduate Certificate). *Program availability:* Part-time, evening/weekend, 100% online, blended/hybrid learning. *Faculty:* 9 full-time (1 woman), 2 part-time/adjunct (1 woman). *Students:* 22 full-time (10 women), 61 part-time (12 women); includes 13 minority (7 Black or African American, non-Hispanic/Latino; 1 Asian, non-Hispanic/Latino; 4 Hispanic/Latino; 1 Two or more races, non-Hispanic/Latino), 29 international. Average age 30. 210 applicants, 56% accepted, 31 enrolled. In 2016, 44 master's, 5 other advanced degrees awarded. *Degree requirements:* For master's, project or thesis. *Entrance requirements:* For master's, GRE or GMAT, bachelor's degree in engineering or a closely-related technical or scientific field, or in business, provided relevant technical course requirements have been met; undergraduate coursework in engineering economics, calculus, or statistics; minimum GPA of 3.0; for Graduate Certificate, bachelor's degree in engineering or closely-related technical or scientific field, or bachelor's degree in business, provided relevant technical course requirements have been met; minimum GPA of 3.0; undergraduate coursework in engineering economics, calculus, and statistics; written description of work experience. Additional exam requirements/recommendations for international students: Required—TOEFL (minimum score 523 paper-based, 70 iBT) or IELTS (6.5). *Application deadline:* For fall admission, 3/1 priority date for domestic and international students; for spring admission, 10/1 priority date for domestic and international students; for summer admission, 4/1 priority date for domestic and international students. Applications are processed on a rolling basis. Application fee: $75. Electronic applications accepted. *Expenses:* Contact institution. *Financial support:* In 2016–17, 2 students received support, including 2 research assistantships (averaging $13,750 per year); career-related internships or fieldwork, institutionally sponsored loans, scholarships/grants, and unspecified assistantships also available. Support available to part-time students. Financial award application deadline: 3/1; financial award applicants required to submit FAFSA. *Total annual research expenditures:* $196,680. *Unit head:* Dr. Simon M. Hsiang, Chair, 704-687-1958, E-mail: shsiang1@uncc.edu. *Application contact:* Kathy B. Giddings, Director of Graduate Admissions, 704-687-5503, Fax: 704-687-1668, E-mail: gradadm@uncc.edu.
Website: http://seem.uncc.edu/

University of North Texas, Robert B. Toulouse School of Graduate Studies, Denton, TX 76203-5459. Offers accounting (MS); applied anthropology (MA, MS); applied behavior analysis (Certificate); applied geography (MA); applied technology and performance improvement (M Ed, MS); art education (MA); art history (MA); art museum education (Certificate); arts leadership (Certificate); audiology (Au D); behavior analysis (MS); behavioral science (PhD); biochemistry and molecular biology (MS); biology (MA, MS); biomedical engineering (MS); business analysis (MS); chemistry (MS); clinical health psychology (PhD); communication studies (MA, MS); computer engineering (MS); computer science (MS); counseling (M Ed, MS), including clinical mental health counseling (MS), college and university counseling, elementary school counseling, secondary school counseling; creative writing (MA); criminal justice (MS); curriculum and instruction (M Ed); decision sciences (MBA); design (MA, MFA), including fashion design (MFA), innovation studies, interior design (MFA); early childhood studies (MS); economics (MS); educational leadership (M Ed, Ed D); educational psychology (MS, PhD), including family studies (MS), gifted and talented (MS), human development (MS), learning and cognition (MS), research, measurement and evaluation (MS); electrical engineering (MS); emergency management (MPA); engineering technology (MS); English (MA); English as a second language (MA); environmental science (MS); finance (MBA, MS); financial management (MPA); French (MA); health services management (MBA); higher education (M Ed, Ed D); history (MA, MS); hospitality management (MS); human resources management (MPA); information science (MS); information systems (PhD); information technologies (MBA); interdisciplinary studies (MA, MS); international studies (MA); international sustainable tourism (MS); jazz studies (MM); journalism (MA, MJ, Graduate Certificate), including interactive and virtual digital communication (Graduate Certificate), narrative journalism (Graduate Certificate), public relations (Graduate Certificate); kinesiology (MS); linguistics (MA); local government management (MPA); logistics (PhD); logistics and supply chain management (MBA); long-term care, senior housing, and aging services (MA); management (PhD); marketing (MBA); mathematics (MA, MS); mechanical and energy engineering (MS, PhD); music (MA), including ethnomusicology, music theory, musicology, performance; music composition (PhD); music education (MM Ed, PhD); nonprofit management (MPA); operations and supply chain management (MBA); performance (MM, DMA); philosophy (MA); political science (MA); professional and technical communication (MA); radio, television and film (MA, MFA); rehabilitation counseling (Certificate); sociology (MA); Spanish (MA); special education (M Ed); speech-language pathology (MA); strategic management (MBA); studio art (MFA); teaching (M Ed); MBA/MS. *Program availability:* Part-time, evening/weekend, online learning. Terminal master's awarded for partial completion of doctoral program. *Degree requirements:* For master's, variable foreign language requirement, comprehensive exam (for some programs), thesis (for some programs); for doctorate, variable foreign language requirement, comprehensive exam (for some programs), thesis/dissertation; for other advanced degree, variable foreign language requirement, comprehensive exam (for some programs). *Entrance requirements:* For master's and doctorate, GRE, GMAT. Additional exam requirements/recommendations for international students: Required—TOEFL (minimum score 550 paper-based; 79 iBT). Electronic applications accepted.

University of Puerto Rico, Mayagüez Campus, Graduate Studies, College of Engineering, Department of Mechanical Engineering, Mayagüez, PR 00681-9000. Offers mechanical engineering (ME, MS, PhD), including aerospace and unmanned vehivles (ME), automation/mechatronics, bioengineering, cae and design, fluid mechanics, heat transfer/energy systems, manufacturing, mechanics of materials, micro and nano engineering. *Program availability:* Part-time. *Faculty:* 22 full-time (4 women), 1 part-time/adjunct (0 women). *Students:* 34 full-time (4 women), 8 part-time (2 women); includes 38 minority (all Hispanic/Latino), 3 international. Average age 25. 22 applicants, 100% accepted, 7 enrolled. In 2016, 17 master's awarded. Terminal master's awarded for partial completion of doctoral program. *Degree requirements:* For master's, one foreign language, comprehensive exam, thesis; for doctorate, one foreign language, comprehensive exam, thesis/dissertation. *Entrance requirements:* For master's, BS in mechanical engineering or its equivalent; for doctorate, GRE, BS or MS in mechanical

engineering or its equivalent; minimum GPA of 3.0. Additional exam requirements/recommendations for international students: Required—TOEFL (minimum score 80 paper-based; 80 iBT). *Application deadline:* For fall admission, 2/15 for domestic and international students; for spring admission, 9/15 for domestic and international students. Applications are processed on a rolling basis. Application fee: $25. Electronic applications accepted. *Expenses: Tuition, area resident:* Full-time $2466. *International tuition:* $7166 full-time. *Required fees:* $210. One-time fee: $5 full-time. Tuition and fees vary according to course level, campus/location, program and student level. *Financial support:* In 2016–17, 39 students received support, including 26 research assistantships with full and partial tuition reimbursements available (averaging $3,801 per year), 30 teaching assistantships with full and partial tuition reimbursements available (averaging $3,293 per year); unspecified assistantships also available. *Faculty research:* Computational fluid dynamics, thermal sciences, mechanical design, material health, microfluidics. *Unit head:* Paul Sundaram, Ph.D., Chairperson, 787-832-4040 Ext. 3659, Fax: 787-265-3817, E-mail: paul.sundaram@upr.edu. *Application contact:* Yolanda Perez, Academic Orientation Officer, 787-832-4040 Ext. 2362, Fax: 787-265-3817, E-mail: yolanda.perez4@upr.edu.
Website: https://wordpress.uprm.edu/inme/

University of Rochester, Hajim School of Engineering and Applied Sciences, Program in Alternative Energy, Rochester, NY 14627. Offers MS. *Students:* 5 full-time (2 women), 1 part-time (0 women), 5 international. Average age 25. 8 applicants, 100% accepted, 3 enrolled. In 2016, 6 master's awarded. *Degree requirements:* For master's, comprehensive exam, thesis, final exam. *Entrance requirements:* For master's, GRE. Additional exam requirements/recommendations for international students: Required—TOEFL (minimum score 600 paper-based; 100 iBT). *Application deadline:* For fall admission, 3/1 for domestic and international students. Application fee: $60. Electronic applications accepted. *Expenses:* $1,538 per credit. *Financial support:* In 2016–17, 3 students received support. Tuition waivers (partial) available. Financial award application deadline: 4/15. *Faculty research:* Solar cells, fuel dells, biofuels, nuclear fusion, nanotechnology. *Unit head:* Matthew Yates, Chair, 585-273-2335, E-mail: myates@che.rochester.edu. *Application contact:* Vicki Heberling, Coordinator, 585-275-4913, E-mail: victoria.heberling@rochester.edu.
Website: http://www.che.rochester.edu/graduate/alternative.html

The University of Tennessee, Graduate School, Tickle College of Engineering, Bredesen Center for Interdisciplinary Research and Graduate Education, Knoxville, TN 37996. Offers energy science and engineering (PhD). *Students:* 52 full-time (21 women); includes 5 minority (2 Asian, non-Hispanic/Latino; 2 Hispanic/Latino; 1 Two or more races, non-Hispanic/Latino), 13 international. Average age 27. 77 applicants, 40% accepted, 24 enrolled. In 2016, 2 doctorates awarded. *Degree requirements:* For doctorate, comprehensive exam, thesis/dissertation, qualifying examination. *Entrance requirements:* For doctorate, GRE General Test, research interest letter, resume/curriculum vitae, 3 letters of recommendation. Additional exam requirements/recommendations for international students: Required—TOEFL (minimum score 550 paper-based). *Application deadline:* For fall admission, 1/31 for domestic and international students. Applications are processed on a rolling basis. Application fee: $35. Electronic applications accepted. *Financial support:* In 2016–17, 52 students received support, including 52 fellowships with full tuition reimbursements available (averaging $28,000 per year); health care benefits also available. Financial award application deadline: 1/31. *Faculty research:* Biomass processing for biofuels, cellulosic ethanol, and lignin repurposing; applied photosynthesis; nuclear fusion, reactor design and modeling; design and distribution of wind power; development of photovoltaic materials; fuel cell and battery design for energy conversion and storage; development of next generation SMART grid systems and novel grid management tools; climate change modeling, environmental, and planetary sciences as they relate to energy usage. *Unit head:* Dr. Lee Riedinger, Director, 865-974-7999, Fax: 865-974-9482, E-mail: lrieding@utk.edu. *Application contact:* Dr. Lee Riedinger, Director, 865-974-7999, Fax: 865-974-9482, E-mail: lrieding@utk.edu.
Website: http://bredesencenter.utk.edu/

The University of Tennessee at Chattanooga, Engineering Management and Technology Program, Chattanooga, TN 37403. Offers construction management (Graduate Certificate); engineering management (MS); fundamentals of engineering management (Graduate Certificate); leadership and ethics (Graduate Certificate); logistics and supply chain management (Graduate Certificate); power systems management (Graduate Certificate); project and technology management (Graduate Certificate); quality management (Graduate Certificate). *Program availability:* 100% online, blended/hybrid learning. *Faculty:* 6 full-time (1 woman). *Students:* 14 full-time (3 women), 49 part-time (11 women); includes 17 minority (10 Black or African American, non-Hispanic/Latino; 2 Asian, non-Hispanic/Latino; 3 Hispanic/Latino; 2 Two or more races, non-Hispanic/Latino), 8 international. Average age 33. 29 applicants, 93% accepted, 15 enrolled. In 2016, 36 master's, 7 other advanced degrees awarded. *Degree requirements:* For master's, thesis. *Entrance requirements:* For master's, GRE General Test, letters of recommendation; minimum undergraduate GPA of 2.7 overall or 3.0 in final two years. Additional exam requirements/recommendations for international students: Required—TOEFL (minimum score 550 paper-based; 79 iBT), IELTS (minimum score 6). *Application deadline:* For fall admission, 6/15 priority date for domestic students, 7/1 for international students; for spring admission, 11/1 priority date for domestic students, 11/1 for international students. Applications are processed on a rolling basis. Application fee: $35 ($40 for international students). Electronic applications accepted. *Expenses:* $9,876 full-time in-state; $25,994 full-time out-of-state; $450 per credit part-time in-state; $1,345 per credit part-time out-of-state. *Financial support:* In 2016–17, 4 research assistantships were awarded; teaching assistantships, career-related internships or fieldwork, scholarships/grants, and unspecified assistantships also available. Support available to part-time students. Financial award application deadline: 7/1; financial award applicants required to submit FAFSA. *Faculty research:* Plant layout design, lean manufacturing, Six Sigma, value management, product development. *Unit head:* Dr. Neslihan Alp, Department Head, 423-425-4032, Fax: 423-425-5818, E-mail: neslihan-alp@utc.edu. *Application contact:* Dr. Joanne Romagni, Dean of the Graduate School, 423-425-4478, Fax: 423-425-5223, E-mail: joanne-romagni@utc.edu.
Website: http://www.utc.edu/college-engineering-computer-science/programs/engineering-management-and-technology/index.php#li03

Washington State University, Voiland College of Engineering and Architecture, School of Electrical Engineering and Computer Science, Pullman, WA 99164-2752. Offers computer engineering (MS); computer science (MS); electrical engineering (MS); electrical engineering and computer science (PhD); electrical power engineering (MS). MS programs in computer engineering, computer science and electrical engineering also offered at Tri-Cities campus; MS in electrical power engineering offered at the Global (online) campus. *Program availability:* Part-time. *Degree requirements:* For master's, comprehensive exam (for some programs), thesis or alternative; for doctorate, comprehensive exam, thesis/dissertation. *Entrance requirements:* For master's and doctorate, GRE General Test, minimum GPA of 3.0, 3 letters of recommendation, statement of purpose, transcripts. Additional exam requirements/recommendations for international students: Required—TOEFL (minimum score 580 paper-based). *Faculty research:* Software engineering, networks, distributed computing, computer engineering, electrophysics, artificial intelligence, bioinformatics and computational biology, computer graphics, communications, control systems, signal processing, power systems, microelectronics, algorithms.

Wayne State University, College of Engineering, Alternative Energy Technology Program, Detroit, MI 48202. Offers MS, Graduate Certificate. *Faculty:* 9. *Students:* 2 part-time (0 women). Average age 29. 26 applicants, 38% accepted, 1 enrolled. In 2016, 1 master's, 1 other advanced degree awarded. *Degree requirements:* For master's, thesis optional. *Entrance requirements:* For master's, bachelor's degree in engineering; minimum GPA of 3.0 or significant professional experience; for Graduate Certificate, bachelor's degree in engineering; minimum GPA of 2.7 or significant professional experience. Additional exam requirements/recommendations for international students: Required—TOEFL (minimum score 550 paper-based; 79 iBT), Michigan English Language Assessment Battery (minimum score 85); Recommended—IELTS (minimum score 6.5). *Application deadline:* For fall admission, 6/1 priority date for domestic students, 5/1 priority date for international students; for winter admission, 10/1 priority date for domestic students, 9/1 priority date for international students; for spring admission, 2/1 priority date for domestic students, 1/1 priority date for international students; for summer admission, 2/1 priority date for domestic students, 1/1 priority date for international students. Applications are processed on a rolling basis. Application fee: $50. Electronic applications accepted. *Expenses:* $18,871 per year resident tuition and fees, $36,065 per year non-resident tuition and fees. *Financial support:* Scholarships/grants available. Support available to part-time students. Financial award applicants required to submit FAFSA. *Unit head:* Dr. Gene Y. Liao, Program Director, 313-577-8078, E-mail: geneliao@wayne.edu. *Application contact:* Ellen Cope, Graduate Program Coordinator, 313-577-0409, Fax: 313-577-3810, E-mail: escope@wayne.edu.
Website: http://engineering.wayne.edu/aet/index.php

Worcester Polytechnic Institute, Graduate Studies and Research, Programs in Interdisciplinary Studies, Worcester, MA 01609-2280. Offers bioscience administration (MS); impact engineering (MS); manufacturing engineering management (MS); power systems management (MS); social science (PhD); systems modeling (MS). *Program availability:* Part-time, evening/weekend. *Faculty:* 1 part-time/adjunct (0 women). *Students:* 5 full-time (2 women), 54 part-time (21 women); includes 14 minority (3 Black or African American, non-Hispanic/Latino; 5 Asian, non-Hispanic/Latino; 5 Hispanic/Latino; 1 Two or more races, non-Hispanic/Latino), 4 international. 18 applicants, 89% accepted, 8 enrolled. *Degree requirements:* For master's, thesis; for doctorate, comprehensive exam, thesis/dissertation. *Entrance requirements:* For master's and doctorate, 3 letters of recommendation. Additional exam requirements/recommendations for international students: Required—TOEFL (minimum score 563 paper-based; 84 iBT), IELTS (minimum score 7). *Application deadline:* For fall admission, 1/1 priority date for domestic students, 1/1 for international students; for spring admission, 10/1 priority date for domestic students, 10/1 for international students. Applications are processed on a rolling basis. Application fee: $70. Electronic applications accepted. *Financial support:* Institutionally sponsored loans, scholarships/grants, and unspecified assistantships available. Financial award application deadline: 1/1; financial award applicants required to submit FAFSA. *Unit head:* Dr. Fred J. Looft, Head, 508-831-5231, Fax: 508-831-5491, E-mail: fjlooft@wpi.edu. *Application contact:* Lynne Dougherty, Administrative Assistant, 508-831-5301, Fax: 508-831-5717, E-mail: grad@wpi.edu.

Nuclear Engineering

Air Force Institute of Technology, Graduate School of Engineering and Management, Department of Engineering Physics, Dayton, OH 45433-7765. Offers applied physics (MS, PhD); electro-optics (MS, PhD); materials science (PhD); nuclear engineering (MS, PhD); space physics (MS). *Program availability:* Part-time. *Degree requirements:* For master's, thesis; for doctorate, thesis/dissertation. *Entrance requirements:* For master's and doctorate, GRE General Test, minimum GPA of 3.0, U.S. citizenship. *Faculty research:* High-energy lasers, space physics, nuclear weapon effects, semiconductor physics.

Arizona State University at the Tempe campus, Ira A. Fulton Schools of Engineering, School of Electrical, Computer and Energy Engineering, Tempe, AZ 85287-5706. Offers electrical engineering (MS, MSE, PhD); nuclear power generation (Graduate Certificate). *Program availability:* Part-time, evening/weekend, online learning. Terminal master's awarded for partial completion of doctoral program. *Degree requirements:* For master's, thesis and defense (MS); comprehensive exams (MSE); interactive Program of Study (iPOS) submitted before completing 50 percent of required credit hours; for doctorate, comprehensive exam, thesis/dissertation, interactive Program of Study (iPOS) submitted before completing 50 percent of required credit hours. *Entrance requirements:* For master's, GRE, minimum GPA of 3.0 in last 2 years of work leading to bachelor's degree, 3.5 if from non-ABET accredited school; for doctorate, GRE, master's degree with minimum GPA of 3.5 or 3.6 in last 2 years of ABET-accredited undergraduate program. Additional exam requirements/recommendations for international students: Required—TOEFL, IELTS, or PTE. Electronic applications accepted. *Expenses:* Contact institution. *Faculty research:* Power and energy systems, signal processing and communications, solid state devices and modeling, wireless communications and circuits, photovoltaics, biosignatures discovery automation, flexible electronics, nanostructures.

Colorado School of Mines, Office of Graduate Studies, Department of Physics, Golden, CO 80401. Offers applied physics (MS, PhD); materials science (MS, PhD); nuclear engineering (ME, MS, PhD). *Program availability:* Part-time. *Degree requirements:* For master's, thesis (for some programs); for doctorate, comprehensive exam, thesis/dissertation. *Entrance requirements:* For master's and doctorate, GRE General Test, GRE Subject Test. Additional exam requirements/recommendations for international students: Required—TOEFL (minimum score 550 paper-based; 80 iBT). Electronic applications accepted. *Expenses:* Tuition, state resident: full-time $15,690. Tuition, nonresident: full-time $34,020. *Required fees:* $2152. Tuition and fees vary according to course load. *Faculty research:* Light scattering, low-energy nuclear physics, high fusion plasma diagnostics, laser operations, mathematical physics.

École Polytechnique de Montréal, Graduate Programs, Institute of Nuclear Engineering, Montréal, QC H3C 3A7, Canada. Offers nuclear engineering (M Eng, PhD, DESS); nuclear engineering, socio-economics of energy (M Sc A). *Degree requirements:* For master's, one foreign language, thesis; for doctorate, one foreign language, thesis/dissertation. *Entrance requirements:* For master's, minimum GPA of 2.75; for doctorate, minimum GPA of 3.0. *Faculty research:* Nuclear technology, thermohydraulics.

Georgia Institute of Technology, Graduate Studies, College of Engineering, George W. Woodruff School of Mechanical Engineering, Nuclear and Radiological Engineering and Medical Physics Programs, Atlanta, GA 30332-0001. Offers medical physics (MS, MSMP); nuclear and radiological engineering (PhD); nuclear engineering (MSNE). *Program availability:* Part-time, online learning. Terminal master's awarded for partial completion of doctoral program. *Degree requirements:* For master's, thesis optional; for doctorate, comprehensive exam, thesis/dissertation. *Entrance requirements:* For master's and doctorate, GRE General Test, minimum GPA of 3.0. Additional exam requirements/recommendations for international students: Required—TOEFL (minimum score 580 paper-based; 94 iBT). Electronic applications accepted. *Faculty research:* Reactor physics, nuclear materials, plasma physics, radiation detection, radiological assessment.

Idaho State University, Office of Graduate Studies, College of Science and Engineering, Nuclear Engineering and Health Physics Department, Pocatello, ID 83209. Offers nuclear science and engineering (MS, PhD). *Program availability:* Part-time. *Degree requirements:* For master's, comprehensive exam (for some programs), thesis, seminar; for doctorate, comprehensive exam, thesis/dissertation, oral and written exams at the end of 1st year. *Entrance requirements:* For master's, GRE; for doctorate, master's degree in engineering, physics, geosciences, or math; 3 letters of recommendation. Additional exam requirements/recommendations for international students: Required—TOEFL (minimum score 550 paper-based; 80 iBT). Electronic applications accepted.

Kansas State University, Graduate School, College of Engineering, Department of Mechanical and Nuclear Engineering, Manhattan, KS 66506. Offers mechanical engineering (MS); nuclear engineering (PhD). *Faculty:* 22 full-time (3 women). *Students:* 59 full-time (11 women), 12 part-time (2 women); includes 6 minority (1 Black or African American, non-Hispanic/Latino; 2 Asian, non-Hispanic/Latino; 3 Hispanic/Latino), 34 international. Average age 27. 106 applicants, 25% accepted, 21 enrolled. In 2016, 6 master's, 3 doctorates awarded. *Degree requirements:* For master's, thesis optional; for doctorate, comprehensive exam, thesis/dissertation. *Entrance requirements:* For master's, GRE General Test; for doctorate, GRE General Test, master's degree in mechanical engineering; minimum GPA of 3.0 overall or last 60 hours in calculus-based engineering or related program. Additional exam requirements/recommendations for international students: Required—TOEFL (minimum score 550 paper-based; 79 iBT). *Application deadline:* For fall and spring admission, 12/1 priority date for domestic and international students. Applications are processed on a rolling basis. Application fee: $50 ($75 for international students). Electronic applications accepted. *Expenses:* Tuition, state resident: full-time $9670. Tuition, nonresident: full-time $21,828. *Required fees:* $862. *Financial support:* In 2016–17, 20 research assistantships (averaging $22,700 per year), 17 teaching assistantships with full and partial tuition reimbursements (averaging $21,000 per year) were awarded; career-related internships or fieldwork, institutionally sponsored loans, and scholarships/grants also available. Support available to part-time students. Financial award application deadline: 3/1; financial award applicants required to submit FAFSA. *Faculty research:* Radiation detection and protection, heat and mass transfer, machine design, control systems, nuclear reactor physics and engineering. *Total annual research expenditures:* $1.5 million. *Unit head:* Dr. William Dunn, Head, 785-532-5610, Fax: 785-532-7057, E-mail: dunn@k-state.edu. *Application contact:* Dr. Steve Eckels, Graduate Program Director, 785-532-5610, Fax: 785-532-7057, E-mail: eckels@k-state.edu.
Website: http://www.mne.k-state.edu/

Massachusetts Institute of Technology, School of Engineering, Department of Nuclear Science and Engineering, Cambridge, MA 02139. Offers SM, PhD, Sc D, NE. *Faculty:* 16 full-time (3 women), 1 part-time/adjunct (0 women). *Students:* 110 full-time (25 women); includes 11 minority (2 Black or African American, non-Hispanic/Latino; 1 American Indian or Alaska Native, non-Hispanic/Latino; 3 Asian, non-Hispanic/Latino; 3 Hispanic/Latino; 2 Two or more races, non-Hispanic/Latino), 57 international. Average age 26. 173 applicants, 26% accepted, 26 enrolled. In 2016, 15 master's, 13 doctorates awarded. *Degree requirements:* For master's and NE, thesis; for doctorate, comprehensive exam, thesis/dissertation. *Entrance requirements:* For master's, doctorate, and NE, GRE General Test. Additional exam requirements/recommendations for international students: Required—TOEFL, IELTS. *Application deadline:* For fall admission, 12/15 for domestic and international students. Application fee: $75. Electronic applications accepted. *Expenses: Tuition:* Full-time $46,400; part-time $725 per credit. One-time fee: $312 full-time. Full-time tuition and fees vary according to course load and program. *Financial support:* In 2016–17, 100 students received support, including fellowships (averaging $37,900 per year), 66 research assistantships (averaging $37,000 per year), 4 teaching assistantships (averaging $39,000 per year); Federal Work-Study, institutionally sponsored loans, scholarships/grants, traineeships, health care benefits, unspecified assistantships, and resident tutors also available. Support available to part-time students. Financial award application deadline: 5/1; financial award applicants required to submit FAFSA. *Faculty research:* Advanced fission reactor engineering and innovation; nuclear fuel cycle technology and economics; plasma physics and fusion engineering; advanced computation and simulation; materials in extreme environments; radiation sources, detection, and measurement; quantum engineering; nuclear systems engineering, design, management and policy. *Total annual research expenditures:* $19.2 million. *Unit head:* Prof. Dennis Whyte, Department Head, 617-253-7522, E-mail: nse-info@mit.edu. *Application contact:* Academic Programs Administrator, 617-253-3814, E-mail: brandyb@mit.edu.
Website: http://web.mit.edu/nse/

McMaster University, School of Graduate Studies, Faculty of Engineering, Department of Engineering Physics, Hamilton, ON L8S 4M2, Canada. Offers engineering physics (M Eng, MA Sc, PhD); nuclear engineering (PhD). *Degree requirements:* For master's, thesis or alternative; for doctorate, comprehensive exam, thesis/dissertation. *Entrance requirements:* For master's, minimum B average in engineering, mathematics, or physical sciences. Additional exam requirements/recommendations for international students: Required—TOEFL (minimum score 550 paper-based). *Faculty research:* Non-thermal plasmas for pollution control and electrostatic precipitation, bulk and thin film luminescent materials, devices and systems for optical fiber communications, physics and applications of III-V materials and devices, defect spectroscopy in semiconductors.

Missouri University of Science and Technology, Graduate School, Department of Mining and Nuclear Engineering, Rolla, MO 65409. Offers mining engineering (MS, DE, PhD); nuclear engineering (MS, DE, PhD). *Degree requirements:* For master's, thesis optional; for doctorate, comprehensive exam. *Entrance requirements:* For master's, GRE (minimum score 600 quantitative, 3 writing); for doctorate, GRE (minimum score: quantitative 600, writing 3.5). Additional exam requirements/recommendations for international students: Required—TOEFL (minimum score 550 paper-based). Electronic applications accepted. *Faculty research:* Mine health and safety, nuclear radiation transport, modeling of mining operations, radiation effects, blasting.

North Carolina State University, Graduate School, College of Engineering, Department of Nuclear Engineering, Raleigh, NC 27695. Offers MNE, MS, PhD. *Degree requirements:* For master's, thesis (for some programs); for doctorate, thesis/dissertation. *Entrance requirements:* For master's, bachelor's degree in engineering or GRE; for doctorate, engineering degree or GRE. Electronic applications accepted. *Faculty research:* Computational reactor engineering, plasma applications, waste management, materials, radiation applications and measurement.

The Ohio State University, Graduate School, College of Engineering, Department of Mechanical and Aerospace Engineering, Program in Nuclear Engineering, Columbus, OH 43210. Offers MS, PhD. *Faculty:* 7. *Students:* 39 full-time (9 women), 1 part-time (0 women), 18 international. Average age 25. In 2016, 10 master's, 4 doctorates awarded. *Degree requirements:* For master's, thesis optional; for doctorate, thesis/dissertation. *Entrance requirements:* For master's and doctorate, GRE. Additional exam requirements/recommendations for international students: Required—TOEFL (minimum score 550 paper-based; 79 iBT), Michigan English Language Assessment Battery (minimum score 82); Recommended—IELTS (minimum score 7). *Application deadline:* For fall admission, 11/30 priority date for domestic and international students; for spring admission, 10/1 for domestic and international students. Applications are processed on a rolling basis. Application fee: $60 ($70 for international students). Electronic applications accepted. *Financial support:* Fellowships with tuition reimbursements, research assistantships with tuition reimbursements, teaching assistantships with tuition reimbursements, career-related internships or fieldwork, Federal Work-Study, and institutionally sponsored loans available. Support available to part-time students. *Unit head:* Dr. Jeffrey Bons, Graduate Studies Committee Chair, 614-292-8414, E-mail: bons.2@osu.edu. *Application contact:* Janeen Sands, Graduate Programs Coordinator, 614-247-6605, Fax: 614-292-5746, E-mail: nuclear@osu.edu.
Website: http://mae.osu.edu/nuclear

Oregon State University, College of Engineering, Program in Nuclear Engineering, Corvallis, OR 97331. Offers application of nuclear techniques (M Eng, MS, PhD); arms control technology (M Eng, MS, PhD); nuclear instrumentation and applications (M Eng, MS, PhD); nuclear medicine (M Eng, MS, PhD); nuclear power generation (M Eng, PhD); nuclear reactor engineering (M Eng, MS, PhD); nuclear systems design and modeling (M Eng, MS, PhD); nuclear waste management (M Eng, MS, PhD); numerical methods for reactor analysis (M Eng); radiation shielding (M Eng). *Faculty:* 12 full-time (4 women), 2 part-time/adjunct (1 woman). *Students:* 49 full-time (4 women), 9 part-time (0 women); includes 12 minority (1 Black or African American, non-Hispanic/Latino; 3 Asian, non-Hispanic/Latino; 4 Hispanic/Latino; 4 Two or more races, non-Hispanic/Latino), 6 international. Average age 26. 73 applicants, 48% accepted, 21 enrolled. In 2016, 8 master's, 6 doctorates awarded. *Entrance requirements:* For master's and doctorate, GRE. Additional exam requirements/recommendations for international students: Required—TOEFL (minimum score 80 iBT), IELTS (minimum score 6.5). *Application deadline:* For fall admission, 2/1 priority date for domestic and international students. Application fee: $75 ($85 for international students). *Expenses:* $14,130 resident full-time tuition, $23,769 non-resident. *Financial support:* Application deadline: 2/1. *Unit head:* Dr. Kathryn Higley, Department Head/Professor. *Application contact:* Nuclear Engineering Advisor, 541-737-2343, E-mail: nuc_engr@ne.oregonstate.edu.
Website: http://ne.oregonstate.edu/nuclear-engineering-program

Penn State University Park, Graduate School, College of Engineering, Department of Mechanical and Nuclear Engineering, University Park, PA 16802. Offers mechanical engineering (MS, PhD); nuclear engineering (M Eng, MS, PhD). *Unit head:* Dr. Amr S. Elnashai, Dean, 814-865-7537, Fax: 814-863-4749. *Application contact:* Lori Hawn, Director, Graduate Student Services, 814-865-1795, Fax: 814-863-4627, E-mail: l-gswww@lists.psu.edu.
Website: http://mne.psu.edu/

Purdue University, College of Engineering, School of Nuclear Engineering, West Lafayette, IN 47907-2017. Offers MS, MSNE, PhD. *Program availability:* Part-time. *Faculty:* 25. *Students:* 53. In 2016, 12 master's, 8 doctorates awarded. Terminal master's awarded for partial completion of doctoral program. *Degree requirements:* For master's, thesis optional; for doctorate, thesis/dissertation. *Entrance requirements:* For master's, GRE General Test, minimum GPA of 3.2; for doctorate, GRE General Test, minimum GPA of 3.5. *Application deadline:* For fall admission, 1/15 priority date for domestic and international students; for spring admission, 9/30 for domestic and international students. Applications are processed on a rolling basis. Application fee: $60 ($75 for international students). Electronic applications accepted. *Financial support:* Fellowships with full and partial tuition reimbursements, research assistantships with full and partial tuition reimbursements, teaching assistantships with full and partial tuition reimbursements, career-related internships or fieldwork, scholarships/grants, and unspecified assistantships available. Support available to part-time students. Financial award applicants required to submit FAFSA. *Faculty research:* Applied intelligent systems, bioelectrics and electro physics, materials under extreme environment, fuel cycle and waste management, hydrogen and fuel cell, nuclear systems simulation, reactor physics, thermal hydraulics and reactor safety. *Application contact:* Tiffany Stergar, Academic Program Administrator, E-mail: nuclss@purdue.edu.
Website: https://engineering.purdue.edu/NE

Rensselaer Polytechnic Institute, Graduate School, School of Engineering, Program in Nuclear Engineering, Troy, NY 12180-3590. Offers M Eng, MS, D Eng, PhD. *Faculty:* 48 full-time (7 women), 1 part-time/adjunct (0 women). *Students:* 27 full-time (5 women), 1 part-time (0 women). 30 applicants, 43% accepted, 4 enrolled. In 2016, 1 master's, 4 doctorates awarded. Terminal master's awarded for partial completion of doctoral program. *Degree requirements:* For master's, thesis (for some programs); for doctorate, thesis/dissertation. *Entrance requirements:* For master's and doctorate, GRE. Additional exam requirements/recommendations for international students: Required—TOEFL (minimum score 600 paper-based; 100 iBT), IELTS (minimum score 7), PTE (minimum score 68). *Application deadline:* For fall admission, 1/1 priority date for domestic and international students; for spring admission, 8/15 priority date for domestic and international students. Applications are processed on a rolling basis. Application fee: $75. Electronic applications accepted. *Expenses: Tuition:* Full-time $49,520; part-time $2060 per credit hour. *Required fees:* $2617. *Financial support:* In 2016–17, research assistantships (averaging $22,000 per year), teaching assistantships (averaging $22,000 per year) were awarded; fellowships also available. Financial award application deadline: 1/1. *Faculty research:* Design, dynamics and vibrations, fissions systems and radiation transport, fluid mechanics (computational, theoretical, and experimental), heat transfer and energy conversion, manufacturing, medical imaging and health physics, multiscale/computational modeling, nanostructured materials and properties, nuclear physics/nuclear reactor, propulsion. *Total annual research expenditures:* $3.4 million. *Unit head:* Dr. Theo Borca-Tasciuc, Graduate Program Director, 518-276-2627, E-mail: borcat@rpi.edu. *Application contact:* Office of Graduate Admissions, 518-276-6216, E-mail: gradadmissions@rpi.edu.
Website: http://mane.rpi.edu/

Nuclear Engineering

Royal Military College of Canada, Division of Graduate Studies and Research, Engineering Division, Program in Nuclear Engineering, Kingston, ON K7K 7B4, Canada. Offers M Eng, MA Sc, PhD. *Degree requirements:* For master's, thesis; for doctorate, comprehensive exam, thesis/dissertation. *Entrance requirements:* For master's, honours degree with second-class standing; for doctorate, master's degree. Electronic applications accepted.

Royal Military College of Canada, Division of Graduate Studies and Research, Engineering Division, Program in Nuclear Science, Kingston, ON K7K 7B4, Canada. Offers M Sc, PhD. *Degree requirements:* For master's, thesis; for doctorate, comprehensive exam, thesis/dissertation. *Entrance requirements:* For master's, honour's degree with second-class standing; for doctorate, master's degree. Electronic applications accepted.

Stevens Institute of Technology, Graduate School, Charles V. Schaefer Jr. School of Engineering and Science, Department of Mechanical Engineering, Hoboken, NJ 07030. Offers additive manufacturing (Certificate); advanced manufacturing (Certificate); air pollution technology (Certificate); computational fluid mechanics and heat transfer (Certificate); design and production management (Certificate); integrated product development (M Eng), including armament engineering, computer and electrical engineering, manufacturing technologies, systems reliability and design; mechanical engineering (M Eng, PhD); medical devices (Certificate); nuclear power engineering (Certificate); ordnance engineering (Certificate); pharmaceutical manufacturing (M Eng, MS, Certificate); power generation (Certificate); product architecture and engineering (M Eng); robotics and control (Certificate); structural analysis and design (Certificate); vibration and noise control (Certificate). *Program availability:* Part-time, evening/weekend. *Faculty:* 28 full-time (2 women), 15 part-time/adjunct (1 woman). *Students:* 141 full-time (27 women), 83 part-time (18 women); includes 27 minority (3 Black or African American, non-Hispanic/Latino; 1 American Indian or Alaska Native, non-Hispanic/Latino; 21 Asian, non-Hispanic/Latino; 2 Hispanic/Latino), 111 international. Average age 26. 569 applicants, 48% accepted, 61 enrolled. In 2016, 132 master's, 4 doctorates, 71 other advanced degrees awarded. Terminal master's awarded for partial completion of doctoral program. *Degree requirements:* For master's, thesis optional, minimum B average in major field and overall; for doctorate, comprehensive exam (for some programs), thesis/dissertation; for other advanced degree, minimum B average. *Entrance requirements:* Additional exam requirements/recommendations for international students: Required—TOEFL (minimum score 74 iBT), IELTS (minimum score 6). *Application deadline:* For fall admission, 6/1 for domestic students, 4/15 for international students; for spring admission, 11/30 for domestic students, 11/1 for international students. Applications are processed on a rolling basis. Application fee: $65. Electronic applications accepted. *Expenses:* Contact institution. *Financial support:* Fellowships, research assistantships, teaching assistantships, career-related internships or fieldwork, Federal Work-Study, scholarships/grants, and unspecified assistantships available. Financial award application deadline: 2/15; financial award applicants required to submit FAFSA. *Faculty research:* Nanotechnology, sustainable energy, fluid systems, materials, design, and manufacturing, robotics. *Unit head:* Dr. Frank Fisher, Director, 201-216-8913, Fax: 201-216-8315, E-mail: ffisher@stevens.edu. *Application contact:* Graduate Admissions, 888-783-8367, Fax: 888-511-1306, E-mail: graduate@stevens.edu.

Texas A&M University, College of Engineering, Department of Nuclear Engineering, College Station, TX 77843. Offers health physics (MS); nuclear engineering (M Eng, MS, PhD). *Faculty:* 17. *Students:* 116 full-time (19 women), 23 part-time (3 women); includes 27 minority (3 Black or African American, non-Hispanic/Latino; 1 American Indian or Alaska Native, non-Hispanic/Latino; 3 Asian, non-Hispanic/Latino; 18 Hispanic/Latino; 2 Two or more races, non-Hispanic/Latino), 29 international. Average age 28. 91 applicants, 66% accepted, 30 enrolled. In 2016, 25 master's, 21 doctorates awarded. *Degree requirements:* For master's, thesis or alternative; for doctorate, thesis/dissertation, departmental qualifying exams. *Entrance requirements:* For master's and doctorate, GRE General Test, 3 letters of recommendation. Additional exam requirements/recommendations for international students: Required—TOEFL (minimum score 550 paper-based; 80 iBT), IELTS (minimum score 6), PTE (minimum score 53). *Application deadline:* For fall admission, 12/1 for domestic and international students; for spring admission, 9/1 for domestic and international students. Applications are processed on a rolling basis. Application fee: $50 ($90 for international students). Electronic applications accepted. *Expenses:* Contact institution. *Financial support:* In 2016–17, 107 students received support, including 22 fellowships with tuition reimbursements available (averaging $15,452 per year), 77 research assistantships with tuition reimbursements available (averaging $7,913 per year), 21 teaching assistantships with tuition reimbursements available (averaging $11,493 per year); career-related internships or fieldwork, institutionally sponsored loans, scholarships/grants, traineeships, health care benefits, tuition waivers (full and partial), and unspecified assistantships also available. Support available to part-time students. Financial award application deadline: 3/15; financial award applicants required to submit FAFSA. *Unit head:* Dr. Yassin A. Hassan, Head, 979-845-7090, E-mail: y-hassan@tamu.edu. *Application contact:* Robb Jenson, Graduate Program Coordinator, 979-458-2072, E-mail: robb.jenson@tamu.edu.
Website: https://engineering.tamu.edu/nuclear

University of California, Berkeley, Graduate Division, College of Engineering, Department of Nuclear Engineering, Berkeley, CA 94720-1730. Offers M Eng, MS, PhD. *Students:* 75 full-time (27 women); includes 12 minority (2 Black or African American, non-Hispanic/Latino; 5 Asian, non-Hispanic/Latino; 5 Hispanic/Latino), 17 international. Average age 27. 119 applicants, 22 enrolled. In 2016, 14 master's, 9 doctorates awarded. Terminal master's awarded for partial completion of doctoral program. *Degree requirements:* For master's, comprehensive exam (for some programs), thesis (for some programs), project or thesis; for doctorate, thesis/dissertation, oral exam. *Entrance requirements:* For master's and doctorate, GRE General Test, minimum GPA of 3.0, 3 letters of recommendation. Additional exam requirements/recommendations for international students: Required—TOEFL (minimum score 570 paper-based; 90 iBT). *Application deadline:* For fall admission, 12/15 for domestic students. Application fee: $105 ($125 for international students). Electronic applications accepted. *Financial support:* Fellowships, research assistantships, teaching assistantships, health care benefits, and unspecified assistantships available. *Faculty research:* Applied nuclear reactions and instrumentation, fission reactor engineering, fusion reactor technology, nuclear waste and materials management, radiation protection and environmental effects. *Unit head:* Prof. Karl A. van Bibber, Chair, 510-642-4077, Fax: 510-643-9685. *Application contact:* 510-642-5760, Fax: 510-643-9685, E-mail: admissions@nuc.berkeley.edu.
Website: http://www.nuc.berkeley.edu

University of Cincinnati, Graduate School, College of Engineering and Applied Science, Department of Mechanical and Materials Engineering, Cincinnati, OH 45221. Offers industrial engineering (PhD); mechanical engineering (MS, PhD); nuclear engineering (PhD); MBA/MS. *Program availability:* Part-time, evening/weekend. Terminal master's awarded for partial completion of doctoral program. *Degree requirements:* For doctorate, thesis/dissertation. *Entrance requirements:* For master's and doctorate, GRE General Test. Additional exam requirements/recommendations for

international students: Required—TOEFL (minimum score 575 paper-based). Electronic applications accepted. *Expenses: Tuition, area resident:* Full-time $12,790; part-time $389 per credit hour. Tuition, state resident: full-time $13,290; part-time $419 per credit hour. Tuition, nonresident: full-time $24,532; part-time $976 per credit hour. *International tuition:* $24,832 full-time. *Required fees:* $3958; $140 per credit hour. Tuition and fees vary according to course load, degree level, program and reciprocity agreements.

University of Florida, Graduate School, Herbert Wertheim College of Engineering, Department of Materials Science and Engineering, Nuclear Engineering Program, Gainesville, FL 32611. Offers imaging science and technology (PhD); nuclear engineering sciences (ME, MS, PhD). *Program availability:* Part-time. Terminal master's awarded for partial completion of doctoral program. *Degree requirements:* For master's, comprehensive exam, thesis; for doctorate, comprehensive exam, thesis/dissertation. *Entrance requirements:* For master's and doctorate, minimum GPA of 3.0. Additional exam requirements/recommendations for international students: Required—TOEFL (minimum score 550 paper-based; 80 iBT), IELTS (minimum score 6). Electronic applications accepted. *Faculty research:* Nuclear materials, radiation detection, thermal hydraulics, reactor physics and transport, generation 4 reactor technology.

University of Idaho, College of Graduate Studies, College of Engineering, Program in Nuclear Engineering, Moscow, ID 83844-2282. Offers M Engr, MS, PhD. *Faculty:* 5 full-time, 1 part-time/adjunct. *Students:* 11 full-time, 9 part-time. Average age 36. In 2016, 2 master's, 2 doctorates awarded. *Degree requirements:* For master's, thesis or alternative; for doctorate, thesis/dissertation. *Entrance requirements:* For master's and doctorate, minimum GPA of 3.0. Additional exam requirements/recommendations for international students: Required—TOEFL. *Application deadline:* For fall admission, 8/1 for domestic students; for spring admission, 12/15 for domestic students. Applications are processed on a rolling basis. Application fee: $60. Electronic applications accepted. *Expenses:* Tuition, state resident: full-time $6460; part-time $414 per credit hour. Tuition, nonresident: full-time $21,268; part-time $1237 per credit hour. *Required fees:* $2070; $60 per credit hour. Full-time tuition and fees vary according to course load and reciprocity agreements. *Financial support:* Applicants required to submit FAFSA. *Unit head:* Dr. Larry Stauffer, Dean, 208-282-6479, E-mail: deanengr@uidaho.edu. *Application contact:* Sean Scoggin, Graduate Recruiter, 208-885-4723, E-mail: graduateadmissions@uidaho.edu.

University of Illinois at Urbana–Champaign, Graduate College, College of Engineering, Department of Nuclear, Plasma, and Radiological Engineering, Urbana, IL 61801. Offers energy systems (M Eng); nuclear, plasma, and radiological engineering (MS, PhD). Terminal master's awarded for partial completion of doctoral program.

The University of Manchester, School of Mechanical, Aerospace and Civil Engineering, Manchester, United Kingdom. Offers advanced manufacturing technology (M Ent); aerospace engineering (M Phil, M Sc, PhD); civil engineering (M Phil, M Sc, PhD); environmental engineering (M Phil, PhD); management of projects (M Phil, M Sc, PhD); mechanical engineering (M Phil, M Sc, PhD); mechanical engineering design (M Ent); nuclear engineering (M Phil, D Eng, PhD).

University of Maryland, College Park, Academic Affairs, A. James Clark School of Engineering, Department of Materials Science and Engineering, Nuclear Engineering Program, College Park, MD 20742. Offers ME, MS, PhD. *Program availability:* Part-time, evening/weekend, online learning. *Degree requirements:* For master's, thesis optional; for doctorate, variable foreign language requirement, thesis/dissertation, oral exam. *Entrance requirements:* For master's and doctorate, GRE General Test, minimum GPA of 3.0. Additional exam requirements/recommendations for international students: Required—TOEFL. Electronic applications accepted. *Faculty research:* Reliability and risk assessment, heat transfer and two-phase flow, reactor safety analysis, nuclear reactor, radiation/polymers.

University of Massachusetts Lowell, Francis College of Engineering, Program in Energy Engineering, Lowell, MA 01854. Offers MS Eng, PhD. *Degree requirements:* For master's, thesis optional. *Entrance requirements:* For master's, GRE General Test. Additional exam requirements/recommendations for international students: Required—TOEFL.

University of Michigan, College of Engineering, Department of Nuclear Engineering and Radiological Sciences, Ann Arbor, MI 48109. Offers nuclear engineering (Nuc E); nuclear engineering and radiological sciences (MSE, PhD); nuclear science (MS, PhD). *Students:* 127 full-time (22 women). 149 applicants, 44% accepted, 46 enrolled. In 2016, 29 master's, 15 doctorates awarded. Terminal master's awarded for partial completion of doctoral program. *Degree requirements:* For master's, thesis optional; for doctorate, thesis/dissertation, oral defense of dissertation, preliminary exams. *Entrance requirements:* For master's and doctorate, GRE General Test. Additional exam requirements/recommendations for international students: Required—TOEFL. *Application deadline:* Applications are processed on a rolling basis. Electronic applications accepted. *Expenses:* Tuition, state resident: full-time $21,466; part-time $1152 per credit hour. Tuition, nonresident: full-time $43,346; part-time $2367 per credit hour. Part-time tuition and fees vary according to course load, degree level and program. *Financial support:* Fellowships, research assistantships, teaching assistantships, career-related internships or fieldwork, institutionally sponsored loans, scholarships/grants, traineeships, health care benefits, and unspecified assistantships available. *Faculty research:* Radiation safety, environmental sciences, medical physics, fission systems and radiation transport, materials, plasmas and fusion, radiation measurements and imaging. *Total annual research expenditures:* $20.7 million. *Unit head:* Dr. Ronald Gilgenbach, Department Chair, 734-763-1261, Fax: 734-763-4540, E-mail: rongilg@umich.edu. *Application contact:* Garnette Roberts, Graduate Program Coordinator, 734-615-8810, Fax: 734-763-4540, E-mail: ners-grad-admissions@umich.edu.
Website: http://www.engin.umich.edu/ners

University of Missouri, Office of Research and Graduate Studies, College of Engineering, Nuclear Engineering Program, Columbia, MO 65211. Offers environmental and regulatory compliance (MS, PhD); nuclear engineering (Certificate). *Students:* 21 full-time (6 women), 6 part-time (0 women). *Degree requirements:* For master's, research project; for doctorate, thesis/dissertation. *Entrance requirements:* For master's and doctorate, GRE General Test. Additional exam requirements/recommendations for international students: Required—TOEFL (minimum score 500 paper-based; 61 iBT). *Application deadline:* For fall admission, 3/1 priority date for domestic and international students; for winter admission, 10/1 priority date for domestic students, 9/1 priority date for international students. Application fee: $75 ($90 for international students). Electronic applications accepted. *Expenses:* Tuition, state resident: full-time $6347; part-time $352.60 per credit hour. Tuition, nonresident: full-time $17,379; part-time $965.50 per credit hour. *Required fees:* $1035. Tuition and fees vary according to course load, campus/location and program. *Financial support:* Fellowships with tuition reimbursements, research assistantships with tuition reimbursements, teaching assistantships with tuition reimbursements, institutionally sponsored loans, scholarships/grants, health care benefits, and unspecified assistantships available. Support available to part-time students.
Website: http://engineering.missouri.edu/nuclear/

University of Nevada, Las Vegas, Graduate College, Howard R. Hughes College of Engineering, Department of Mechanical Engineering, Las Vegas, NV 89154-4027. Offers aerospace engineering (MS); biomedical engineering (MS); materials and nuclear engineering (MS); mechanical engineering (MS, PhD); nuclear criticality safety (Certificate); nuclear safeguards and security (Certificate). *Program availability:* Part-time. *Faculty:* 16 full-time (2 women), 3 part-time/adjunct (1 woman). *Students:* 47 full-time (13 women), 21 part-time (4 women); includes 15 minority (1 American Indian or Alaska Native, non-Hispanic/Latino; 6 Asian, non-Hispanic/Latino; 3 Hispanic/Latino; 5 Two or more races, non-Hispanic/Latino), 16 international. Average age 30. 68 applicants, 54% accepted, 15 enrolled. In 2016, 10 master's, 3 doctorates, 4 other advanced degrees awarded. *Degree requirements:* For master's, thesis optional, design project; for doctorate, comprehensive exam, thesis/dissertation. *Entrance requirements:* For master's, GRE General Test, statement of purpose; 2 letters of recommendation; for doctorate, GRE General Test, 3 letters of recommendation; statement of purpose; bachelor's degree with minimum GPA of 3.5/master's degree with minimum GPA of 3.3. Additional exam requirements/recommendations for international students: Required—TOEFL (minimum score 550 paper-based; 80 iBT), IELTS (minimum score 7). *Application deadline:* For fall admission, 8/1 for domestic students, 5/1 for international students; for spring admission, 12/1 for domestic students, 10/1 for international students. Application fee: $60 ($95 for international students). Electronic applications accepted. *Expenses:* $269.25 per credit, $792 per 3-credit course; $9,634 per year resident; $23,274 per year non-resident; $7,094 fees non-resident (7 credits or more); $1,307 annual health insurance fee. *Financial support:* In 2016–17, 1 fellowship with partial tuition reimbursement (averaging $15,000 per year), 13 research assistantships with partial tuition reimbursements (averaging $17,115 per year), 27 teaching assistantships with partial tuition reimbursements (averaging $16,172 per year) were awarded; institutionally sponsored loans, scholarships/grants, health care benefits, and unspecified assistantships also available. Financial award application deadline: 3/15. *Faculty research:* Dynamics and control systems; energy systems including renewable and nuclear; computational fluid and solid mechanics; structures, materials and manufacturing; vibrations and acoustics. *Total annual research expenditures:* $4.5 million. *Unit head:* Dr. Brendan O'Toole, Chair/Professor, 702-895-3885, Fax: 702-895-3936, E-mail: brendan.otoole@unlv.edu. *Application contact:* Dr. Hui Zhao, Graduate Coordinator, 702-895-1463, Fax: 702-895-3936, E-mail: hui.zhao@unlv.edu.
Website: http://me.unlv.edu/

University of New Mexico, Graduate Studies, School of Engineering, Program in Nuclear Engineering, Albuquerque, NM 87131-2039. Offers MS, PhD. *Program availability:* Part-time, online learning. *Faculty:* 26 full-time (2 women), 1 part-time/adjunct (0 women). *Students:* 3 full-time (0 women), 8 part-time (2 women). Average age 32. 20 applicants, 30% accepted, 5 enrolled. In 2016, 6 master's, 4 doctorates awarded. Terminal master's awarded for partial completion of doctoral program. *Degree requirements:* For master's, thesis (for some programs); for doctorate, comprehensive exam, thesis/dissertation. *Entrance requirements:* For master's, GRE General Test, minimum GPA of 3.0, 3 letters of recommendation, letter of intent; for doctorate, GRE General Test, 3 letters of recommendation, letter of intent. Additional exam requirements/recommendations for international students: Required—TOEFL. *Application deadline:* For fall admission, 1/15 priority date for domestic students, 3/1 for international students; for spring admission, 7/15 priority date for domestic students, 8/1 for international students. Application fee: $50. Electronic applications accepted. *Financial support:* Research assistantships, scholarships/grants, health care benefits, and tuition waivers (full) available. Financial award application deadline: 3/1; financial award applicants required to submit FAFSA. *Faculty research:* Plasma science, space power, thermal hydraulics, radiation measurement and protection, fusion plasma measurements, medical physics, nuclear criticality safety, radiation measurements and protection, radiation transport modeling and simulation, Monte Carlo methods. *Unit head:* Dr. Anil Prinja, Associate Chair, 505-277-5431, Fax: 505-277-5433, E-mail: tward@unm.edu. *Application contact:* Jocelyn White, Coordinator/Program Advisor, 505-277-5606, Fax: 505-277-5433, E-mail: jowhite@unm.edu.
Website: http://ne.unm.edu/programs-and-degrees/graduate/index.html

University of South Carolina, The Graduate School, College of Engineering and Computing, Department of Nuclear Engineering, Columbia, SC 29208. Offers ME, MS, PhD. *Program availability:* Part-time, evening/weekend, online learning. *Degree requirements:* For master's, thesis (for some programs); for doctorate, thesis/dissertation. *Entrance requirements:* For master's and doctorate, GRE General Test. Additional exam requirements/recommendations for international students: Required—TOEFL (minimum score 600 paper-based; 100 iBT). Electronic applications accepted.

The University of Tennessee, Graduate School, Tickle College of Engineering, Department of Nuclear Engineering, Program in Nuclear Engineering, Knoxville, TN 37996. Offers MS, PhD. *Program availability:* Part-time. *Faculty:* 29 full-time (5 women), 19 part-time/adjunct (0 women). *Students:* 99 full-time (15 women), 24 part-time (2 women); includes 14 minority (2 Black or African American, non-Hispanic/Latino; 1 Asian, non-Hispanic/Latino; 9 Hispanic/Latino; 2 Two or more races, non-Hispanic/Latino), 17 international. Average age 31. 88 applicants, 67% accepted, 35 enrolled. In 2016, 33 master's, 13 doctorates awarded. *Degree requirements:* For master's, thesis or alternative; for doctorate, comprehensive exam, thesis/dissertation. *Entrance requirements:* For master's, GRE General Test (for MS students pursuing research thesis), minimum GPA of 2.7 (for U.S. degree holders), 3.0 (for international degree holders); for doctorate, GRE General Test, minimum GPA of 3.0 on previous graduate course work. Additional exam requirements/recommendations for international students: Required—TOEFL (minimum score 550 paper-based). *Application deadline:* For fall admission, 2/1 priority date for domestic and international students; for spring admission, 6/15 for domestic students, 5/15 for international students. Applications are processed on a rolling basis. Application fee: $35. Electronic applications accepted. *Financial support:* In 2016–17, 81 students received support, including 5 fellowships with full tuition reimbursements available (averaging $26,760 per year), 54 research assistantships with full tuition reimbursements available (averaging $28,816 per year), 14 teaching assistantships with full tuition reimbursements available (averaging $23,972 per year); career-related internships or fieldwork, Federal Work-Study, institutionally sponsored loans, health care benefits, and unspecified assistantships also available. Financial award application deadline: 2/1; financial award applicants required to submit FAFSA. *Faculty research:* Heat transfer and fluid dynamics; instrumentation, sensors and controls; nuclear materials and nuclear security; radiological engineering; reactor system design and safety. *Unit head:* Dr. J. Wesley Hines, Head, 865-974-2525, Fax: 865-974-0668, E-mail: jhines2@utk.edu. *Application contact:* Dr. Masood Parang, Associate Dean of Student Affairs, 865-974-2454, Fax: 865-974-9871, E-mail: mparang@utk.edu.

University of Utah, Graduate School, College of Engineering, Department of Civil and Environmental Engineering, Program in Nuclear Engineering, Salt Lake City, UT 84112. Offers MS, PhD. *Program availability:* Part-time. *Faculty:* 2 full-time (1 woman). *Students:* 16 full-time (3 women), 2 part-time (0 women); includes 5 minority (2 Hispanic/Latino; 3 Two or more races, non-Hispanic/Latino), 1 international. Average age 31. 26 applicants, 27% accepted, 4 enrolled. In 2016, 8 master's, 2 doctorates awarded. Terminal master's awarded for partial completion of doctoral program. *Degree requirements:* For master's, comprehensive exam, thesis (for some programs); for doctorate, comprehensive exam, thesis/dissertation, qualifying exam. *Entrance requirements:* For master's and doctorate, GRE General Test, minimum GPA of 3.0. Additional exam requirements/recommendations for international students: Required—TOEFL (minimum score 550 paper-based; 80 iBT). *Application deadline:* For fall admission, 1/1 for domestic students, 12/1 for international students; for spring admission, 10/1 for domestic students, 9/1 for international students. Applications are processed on a rolling basis. Application fee: $10 ($25 for international students). Electronic applications accepted. *Expenses:* Contact institution. *Financial support:* In 2016–17, 20 students received support, including 9 fellowships with full tuition reimbursements available (averaging $23,800 per year), 7 research assistantships with full tuition reimbursements available (averaging $22,247 per year), 1 teaching assistantship with full tuition reimbursement available (averaging $22,200 per year); traineeships, health care benefits, and unspecified assistantships also available. Financial award application deadline: 12/15; financial award applicants required to submit FAFSA. *Faculty research:* Material damage, energy, forensics. *Total annual research expenditures:* $379,000. *Unit head:* Dr. Michael Barber, Interim Chair, 801-581-6931, Fax: 801-585-5477, E-mail: barber@civil.utah.edu. *Application contact:* Bonnie Ogden, Academic Advisor, 801-581-6678, Fax: 801-585-5477, E-mail: bonnie.ogden@utah.edu.
Website: http://www.nuclear.utah.edu/

University of Wisconsin–Madison, Graduate School, College of Engineering, Department of Engineering Physics, Madison, WI 53706. Offers engineering mechanics (MS, PhD); nuclear engineering and engineering physics (MS, PhD). *Program availability:* Part-time, online learning. *Faculty:* 21 full-time (3 women). *Students:* 116 full-time (19 women), 10 part-time (2 women); includes 17 minority (3 Black or African American, non-Hispanic/Latino; 5 Asian, non-Hispanic/Latino; 8 Hispanic/Latino; 1 Two or more races, non-Hispanic/Latino), 23 international. Average age 26. 162 applicants, 55% accepted, 25 enrolled. In 2016, 29 master's, 11 doctorates awarded. Terminal master's awarded for partial completion of doctoral program. *Degree requirements:* For master's, thesis optional, 30 credits of technical courses; oral exam; minimum GPA of 3.0; for doctorate, thesis/dissertation, minimum of 51 credits; minimum GPA of 3.0. *Entrance requirements:* For master's and doctorate, GRE General Test, minimum GPA of 3.0 in last 60 hours, appropriate bachelor's degree. Additional exam requirements/recommendations for international students: Required—TOEFL (minimum score 580 paper-based; 92 iBT), IELTS (minimum score 7). *Application deadline:* For fall admission, 12/31 priority date for domestic and international students. Application fee: $75 ($81 for international students). Electronic applications accepted. *Expenses:* $13,157 per year in-state tuition and fees; $26,484 per year out-of-state tuition and fees. *Financial support:* In 2016–17, 119 students received support, including 5 fellowships with full tuition reimbursements available (averaging $29,628 per year), 93 research assistantships with full tuition reimbursements available (averaging $23,175 per year), 19 teaching assistantships with full tuition reimbursements available (averaging $14,941 per year); career-related internships or fieldwork, Federal Work-Study, institutionally sponsored loans, unspecified assistantships, and project assistantships also available. Support available to part-time students. Financial award application deadline: 12/1; financial award applicants required to submit FAFSA. *Faculty research:* Bio-/micro-/nano-mechanics; astronautics; fission reactor engineering; fusion science and technology; radiation sciences; mechanics of materials. *Total annual research expenditures:* $14.1 million. *Unit head:* Dr. Douglass Henderson, Chair, 608-263-1646, Fax: 608-263-7451, E-mail: dlhender@wisc.edu. *Application contact:* Sara Hladilek, Student Services Coordinator, 608-263-1795, Fax: 608-263-7451, E-mail: shladilek@wisc.edu.
Website: http://www.engr.wisc.edu/ep/

Virginia Commonwealth University, Graduate School, School of Engineering, Department of Mechanical and Nuclear Engineering, Richmond, VA 23284-9005. Offers MS, PhD. *Entrance requirements:* For master's and doctorate, GRE. Additional exam requirements/recommendations for international students: Required—TOEFL (minimum score 600 paper-based; 100 iBT). *Application deadline:* For fall admission, 2/1 priority date for domestic students; for spring admission, 11/15 for domestic students. Application fee: $50. Electronic applications accepted. *Financial support:* Applicants required to submit FAFSA. *Unit head:* Dr. Rosalyn S. Hobson, Associate Dean for Graduate Studies, 804-828-8308, Fax: 804-827-7030, E-mail: rhobson@vcu.edu. *Application contact:* Dr. Karla M. Mossi, Director, Graduate Programs, 804-827-5275, E-mail: kmmossi@vcu.edu.
Website: http://mechanical-and-nuclear.egr.vcu.edu/

Virginia Polytechnic Institute and State University, Graduate School, College of Engineering, Blacksburg, VA 24061. Offers aerospace engineering (ME, MS, PhD); biological systems engineering (ME, MS, PhD); biomedical engineering (MS, PhD); chemical engineering (ME, MS, PhD); civil engineering (ME, MS, PhD); computer engineering (ME, MS, PhD); computer science (MS, PhD); electrical engineering (ME, PhD); engineering education (PhD); engineering mechanics (ME, MS, PhD); environmental engineering (MS); environmental science and engineering (MS); industrial and systems engineering (ME, MS, PhD); materials science and engineering (ME, MS, PhD); mechanical engineering (ME, MS, PhD); mining and minerals engineering (PhD); mining engineering (ME, MS); nuclear engineering (MS, PhD); ocean engineering (MS); systems engineering (ME, MS). *Faculty:* 400 full-time (73 women), 3 part-time/adjunct (2 women). *Students:* 1,949 full-time (487 women), 393 part-time (69 women); includes 251 minority (56 Black or African American, non-Hispanic/Latino; 3 American Indian or Alaska Native, non-Hispanic/Latino; 87 Asian, non-Hispanic/Latino; 70 Hispanic/Latino; 35 Two or more races, non-Hispanic/Latino), 1,354 international. Average age 27. 4,903 applicants, 19% accepted, 569 enrolled. In 2016, 364 master's, 200 doctorates awarded. *Degree requirements:* For master's, comprehensive exam (for some programs), thesis (for some programs); for doctorate, comprehensive exam (for some programs), thesis/dissertation (for some programs). *Entrance requirements:* For master's and doctorate, GRE/GMAT. Additional exam requirements/recommendations for international students: Required—TOEFL (minimum score 80 iBT). *Application deadline:* For fall admission, 8/1 for domestic students, 4/1 for international students; for spring admission, 1/1 for domestic students, 9/1 for international students. Applications are processed on a rolling basis. Application fee: $75. Electronic applications accepted. *Expenses:* Tuition, state resident: full-time $12,467; part-time $692.50 per credit hour. Tuition, nonresident: full-time $25,095; part-time $1394.25 per credit hour. *Required fees:* $2669; $491.50 per semester. Tuition and fees vary according to course load, campus/location and program. *Financial support:* In 2016–17, 160 fellowships with full tuition reimbursements (averaging $7,387 per year), 872 research assistantships with full tuition reimbursements (averaging $22,329 per year), 313 teaching assistantships with full tuition reimbursements (averaging $18,714 per year) were awarded. Financial award application deadline: 3/1; financial award applicants required to submit FAFSA. *Total annual research expenditures:* $91.8 million. *Unit head:* Dr. Julia Ross, Dean, 540-231-9752, Fax: 540-231-3031, E-mail: deaneng@vt.edu. *Application contact:* Linda Perkins, Executive Assistant, 540-231-9752, Fax: 540-231-3031, E-mail: lperkins@vt.edu.
Website: http://www.eng.vt.edu/

Section 11
Engineering Design

This section contains a directory of institutions offering graduate work in engineering design. Additional information about programs listed in the directory may be obtained by writing directly to the dean of a graduate school or chair of a department at the address given in the directory.

For programs offering related work, see also in this book *Aerospace/Aeronautical Engineering; Agricultural Engineering and Bioengineering; Biomedical Engineering and Biotechnology; Computer Science and Information Technology; Electrical and Computer Engineering; Energy and Power Engineering; Engineering and Applied Sciences; Industrial Engineering; Management of Engineering and Technology;* and *Mechanical Engineering and Mechanics.* In another guide in this series:

Graduate Programs in the Biological/Biomedical Sciences & Health-Related Medical Professions
See *Biological and Biomedical Sciences*

CONTENTS

Engineering Design

Harvard University, Graduate School of Arts and Sciences, Harvard John A. Paulson School of Engineering and Applied Sciences, Cambridge, MA 02138. Offers applied mathematics (PhD); applied physics (PhD); computational science and engineering (ME, SM); computer science (PhD); design engineering (MDE); engineering science (ME), including electrical engineering (ME, SM, PhD); engineering sciences (SM, PhD), including bioengineering (PhD), electrical engineering (ME, SM, PhD), environmental science and engineering (PhD), materials science and mechanical engineering (PhD). MDE offered in collaboration with Graduate School of Design. *Program availability:* Part-time. *Faculty:* 80 full-time (13 women), 47 part-time/adjunct (10 women). *Students:* 459 full-time (135 women), 19 part-time (7 women); includes 79 minority (2 Black or African American, non-Hispanic/Latino; 49 Asian, non-Hispanic/Latino; 15 Hispanic/Latino; 1 Native Hawaiian or other Pacific Islander, non-Hispanic/Latino; 12 Two or more races, non-Hispanic/Latino), 233 international. Average age 27. 2,486 applicants, 11% accepted, 126 enrolled. In 2016, 37 master's, 48 doctorates awarded. Terminal master's awarded for partial completion of doctoral program. *Degree requirements:* For master's, thesis (for ME); for doctorate, comprehensive exam, thesis/dissertation. *Entrance requirements:* For master's and doctorate, GRE General Test, GRE Subject Test (recommended), 3 letters of recommendation. Additional exam requirements/recommendations for international students: Required—TOEFL (minimum score 80 iBT). *Application deadline:* For fall admission, 12/15 priority date for domestic and international students. Application fee: $105. Electronic applications accepted. *Expenses:* $43,296 full-time tuition, $3,718 fees. *Financial support:* In 2016–17, 394 students received support, including 86 fellowships with full tuition reimbursements available (averaging $26,424 per year), 258 research assistantships with tuition reimbursements available (averaging $35,232 per year), 106 teaching assistantships with tuition reimbursements available (averaging $6,313 per year); health care benefits also available. *Faculty research:* Applied mathematics, applied physics, computer science and electrical engineering, environmental engineering, mechanical and biomedical engineering. *Total annual research expenditures:* $50.1 million. *Unit head:* Francis J. Doyle, III, Dean, 617-495-5829, Fax: 617-495-5264, E-mail: dean@seas.harvard.edu. *Application contact:* Office of Admissions and Financial Aid, 617-495-5315, E-mail: admissions@seas.harvard.edu.
Website: http://www.seas.harvard.edu/

Northwestern University, McCormick School of Engineering and Applied Science, Department of Mechanical Engineering, MS in Product Design and Development Management Program, Evanston, IL 60208. Offers MS. *Program availability:* Part-time, evening/weekend. *Entrance requirements:* Additional exam requirements/recommendations for international students: Required—TOEFL (minimum score 100 iBT), IELTS (minimum score 7). Electronic applications accepted.

Northwestern University, McCormick School of Engineering and Applied Science, Segal Design Institute, MS in Engineering Design and Innovation Program, Evanston, IL 60208. Offers MS. *Entrance requirements:* For master's, GRE General Test, 2 letters of recommendation, portfolio, statement of purpose. Additional exam requirements/recommendations for international students: Required—TOEFL (minimum score 550 paper-based; 80 iBT) or IELTS (minimum score 7). Electronic applications accepted.

Ohio Dominican University, Division of Business, Columbus, OH 43219-2099. Offers business administration (MBA), including accounting, data analytics, finance, leadership, risk management, sport management; healthcare administration (MS); sport management (MS). *Accreditation:* ACBSP. *Program availability:* Part-time, evening/weekend, 100% online, blended/hybrid learning. *Faculty:* 11 full-time (5 women), 22 part-time/adjunct (8 women). *Students:* 80 full-time (34 women), 128 part-time (68 women); includes 63 minority (40 Black or African American, non-Hispanic/Latino; 2 American Indian or Alaska Native, non-Hispanic/Latino; 7 Asian, non-Hispanic/Latino; 6 Hispanic/Latino; 2 Native Hawaiian or other Pacific Islander, non-Hispanic/Latino; 6 Two or more races, non-Hispanic/Latino), 9 international. Average age 31. 91 applicants, 53% accepted, 37 enrolled. *Degree requirements:* For master's, thesis or alternative. *Entrance requirements:* Additional exam requirements/recommendations for international students: Required—TOEFL (minimum score 550 paper-based), IELTS (minimum score 6.5). *Application deadline:* For fall admission, 8/15 for domestic students, 6/10 for international students; for spring admission, 1/4 for domestic students, 11/2 for international students; for summer admission, 5/30 for domestic students. Applications are processed on a rolling basis. Application fee: $25. Electronic applications accepted. *Expenses:* Contact institution. *Financial support:* Applicants required to submit FAFSA. *Unit head:* Dr. Kenneth C. Fah, Chair, 614-251-4566, E-mail: fahk@ohiodominican.edu. *Application contact:* John W. Naughton, Director for Graduate Admissions, 614-251-4721, Fax: 614-251-6654, E-mail: grad@ohiodominican.edu. Website: http://www.ohiodominican.edu/academics/graduate/mba

Penn State University Park, Graduate School, College of Engineering, School of Engineering Design, Technology, and Professional Programs, University Park, PA 16802. Offers engineering design (M Eng, MS). *Degree requirements:* For master's, thesis (MS); internship or scholarly paper (M Eng). *Unit head:* Dr. Amr S. Elnashai, Dean, 814-865-7537, Fax: 814-863-4749. *Application contact:* Lori Hawn, Director, Graduate Student Services, 814-865-1795, Fax: 814-863-4627, E-mail: l-gswww@lists.psu.edu.
Website: http://sedtapp.psu.edu/

Rochester Institute of Technology, Graduate Enrollment Services, Kate Gleason College of Engineering, Design, Development and Manufacturing Department, Rochester, NY 14623-5603. Offers manufacturing leadership (MS); product development (MS). *Program availability:* Part-time-only, evening/weekend, 100% online, blended/hybrid learning. *Students:* 1 (woman) full-time, 68 part-time (6 women); includes 8 minority (2 Black or African American, non-Hispanic/Latino; 2 Asian, non-Hispanic/Latino; 3 Hispanic/Latino; 1 Two or more races, non-Hispanic/Latino), 1 international. Average age 37. 25 applicants, 64% accepted, 12 enrolled. In 2016, 14 master's awarded. *Degree requirements:* For master's, thesis or alternative, capstone. *Entrance requirements:* For master's, minimum GPA of 2.5, 2 years of related work experience. Additional exam requirements/recommendations for international students: Required—PTE (minimum score 58), TOEFL (minimum score 550 paper-based, 79 iBT) or IELTS (minimum score 6.5). *Application deadline:* Applications are processed on a rolling basis. Application fee: $60. Electronic applications accepted. *Expenses:* $1,742 per credit hour. *Financial support:* Scholarships/grants available. Support available to part-time students. Financial award applicants required to submit FAFSA. *Faculty research:* Systems engineering; project management; lean product development and lean manufacturing; decision analysis; modeling and simulation; supply chain management. *Unit head:* Mark Smith, Director, 585-475-7102, Fax: 585-475-7955, E-mail: mark.smith@rit.edu. *Application contact:* Diane Ellison, Associate Vice President, Graduate Enrollment Services, 585-475-2229, Fax: 585-475-7164, E-mail: gradinfo@rit.edu.
Website: https://www.rit.edu/kgcoe/

San Diego State University, Graduate and Research Affairs, College of Engineering, Department of Mechanical Engineering, San Diego, CA 92182. Offers engineering sciences and applied mechanics (PhD); manufacture and design (MS); mechanical engineering (MS). PhD offered jointly with University of California, San Diego and Department of Aerospace Engineering and Engineering Mechanics. *Program availability:* Evening/weekend. *Degree requirements:* For master's, comprehensive exam (for some programs), thesis (for some programs); for doctorate, thesis/dissertation. *Entrance requirements:* For master's, GRE General Test; for doctorate, GRE, 3 letters of recommendation. Additional exam requirements/recommendations for international students: Required—TOEFL. Electronic applications accepted. *Faculty research:* Energy analysis and diagnosis, seawater pump design, space-related research.

Stanford University, School of Engineering, Department of Mechanical Engineering, Program in Product Design, Stanford, CA 94305-2004. Offers MS. *Entrance requirements:* For master's, GRE General Test, undergraduate degree in engineering, math or sciences. Additional exam requirements/recommendations for international students: Required—TOEFL. *Expenses: Tuition:* Full-time $47,331. *Required fees:* $609.

Stevens Institute of Technology, Graduate School, Charles V. Schaefer Jr. School of Engineering and Science, Department of Mechanical Engineering, Program in Product Architecture and Engineering, Hoboken, NJ 07030. Offers M Eng. *Program availability:* Part-time, evening/weekend. *Students:* 1 full-time (0 women), 1 part-time (0 women); includes 1 minority (Asian, non-Hispanic/Latino). Average age 27. 21 applicants, 19% accepted, 1 enrolled. In 2016, 5 master's awarded. *Degree requirements:* For master's, thesis optional, minimum B average in major field and overall. *Entrance requirements:* Additional exam requirements/recommendations for international students: Required—TOEFL (minimum score 74 iBT), IELTS (minimum score 6). *Application deadline:* For fall admission, 6/1 for domestic students, 4/15 for international students; for spring admission, 11/30 for domestic students, 11/1 for international students. Applications are processed on a rolling basis. Application fee: $65. Electronic applications accepted. *Expenses:* Contact institution. *Financial support:* Fellowships, research assistantships, teaching assistantships, career-related internships or fieldwork, Federal Work-Study, scholarships/grants, and unspecified assistantships available. Financial award application deadline: 2/15; financial award applicants required to submit FAFSA. *Unit head:* John Nastasi, Director, 201-216-3582, Fax: 201-216-8963, E-mail: jnastasi@stevens.edu. *Application contact:* Graduate Admissions, 888-783-8367, Fax: 888-511-1306, E-mail: graduate@stevens.edu.

University of Michigan, College of Engineering, Department of Integrative Systems and Design, Ann Arbor, MI 48109. Offers automotive engineering (M Eng); design science (MS, PhD); energy systems engineering (M Eng, MS); global automotive and manufacturing engineering (M Eng); manufacturing engineering (M Eng, D Eng); pharmaceutical engineering (M Eng); robotics and autonomous vehicles (M Eng); systems engineering and design (M Eng); MBA/M Eng; MSE/MS. *Program availability:* Part-time, online learning. *Students:* 147 full-time (33 women), 234 part-time (39 women). 315 applicants, 8% accepted, 13 enrolled. In 2016, 158 master's, 2 doctorates awarded. Terminal master's awarded for partial completion of doctoral program. *Degree requirements:* For master's, capstone project; for doctorate, thesis/dissertation. *Entrance requirements:* For master's, GRE; for doctorate, GRE, 2 years of work experience. Additional exam requirements/recommendations for international students: Required—TOEFL (minimum score 560 paper-based). *Application deadline:* Applications are processed on a rolling basis. Electronic applications accepted. *Expenses:* Tuition, state resident: full-time $21,466; part-time $1152 per credit hour. Tuition, nonresident: full-time $43,346; part-time $2367 per credit hour. Part-time tuition and fees vary according to course load, degree level and program. *Financial support:* Fellowships, research assistantships with full tuition reimbursements, teaching assistantships with full tuition reimbursements, career-related internships or fieldwork, scholarships/grants, and unspecified assistantships available. Financial award applicants required to submit FAFSA. *Faculty research:* Automotive engineering, design science, energy systems engineering, engineering sustainable systems, financial engineering, global automotive and manufacturing engineering, integrated microsystems, manufacturing engineering, pharmaceutical engineering, robotics and autonomous vehicles. *Total annual research expenditures:* $292,225. *Unit head:* Prof. Panos Papalambros, Department Chair, 734-647-8401, E-mail: pyp@umich.edu. *Application contact:* Kathy Bishar, Senior Graduate Coordinator, 734-764-3312, E-mail: kbishar@umich.edu.
Website: http://www.isd.engin.umich.edu

Worcester Polytechnic Institute, Graduate Studies and Research, Foisie Business School, Worcester, MA 01609-2280. Offers information technology (MS), including information security management; management (Graduate Certificate); marketing and technological innovation (MS); operations design and leadership (MS); technology (MBA, MS). *Accreditation:* AACSB. *Program availability:* Part-time, evening/weekend, 100% online, blended/hybrid learning. *Faculty:* 20 full-time (12 women), 16 part-time/adjunct (1 woman). *Students:* 237 full-time (139 women), 186 part-time (67 women); includes 35 minority (4 Black or African American, non-Hispanic/Latino; 17 Asian, non-Hispanic/Latino; 12 Hispanic/Latino; 2 Two or more races, non-Hispanic/Latino), 221 international. 645 applicants, 62% accepted, 144 enrolled. In 2016, 150 master's awarded. *Degree requirements:* For master's, thesis optional. *Entrance requirements:* For master's, GMAT (MBA); GMAT or GRE General Test (MS), statement of purpose, 3 letters of recommendation, resume; for Graduate Certificate, GMAT or GRE General Test, statement of purpose, 3 letters of recommendation. Additional exam requirements/recommendations for international students: Required—TOEFL (minimum score 563 paper-based; 84 iBT), IELTS (minimum score 7). *Application deadline:* For fall admission, 6/1 priority date for domestic and international students; for spring admission, 11/1 priority date for domestic students, 10/1 priority date for international students. Applications are processed on a rolling basis. Application fee: $70. Electronic applications accepted. *Financial support:* Career-related internships or fieldwork, institutionally sponsored loans, scholarships/grants, and unspecified assistantships available. Financial award application deadline: 6/1; financial award applicants required to submit FAFSA. *Unit head:* Melissa Terrio, Executive Director, 508-831-4665, Fax: 508-831-4665, E-mail: biz@wpi.edu. *Application contact:* Eileen Dagostino, Recruiting Operations Coordinator, 508-831-4665, Fax: 508-831-5720, E-mail: edag@wpi.edu.
Website: https://www.wpi.edu/academics/business

Section 12
Engineering Physics

This section contains a directory of institutions offering graduate work in engineering physics. Additional information about programs listed in the directory may be obtained by writing directly to the dean of a graduate school or chair of a department at the address given in the directory.

For programs offering related work, see also in this book *Electrical and Computer Engineering, Energy and Power Engineering (Nuclear Engineering), Engineering and Applied Sciences,* and *Materials Sciences and Engineering.* In the other guides in this series:

Graduate Programs in the Biological/Biomedical Sciences & Health-Related Medical Professions
See *Biophysics* and *Health Sciences (Medical Physics)*
Graduate Programs in the Physical Sciences, Mathematics, Agricultural Sciences, the Environment & Natural Resources
See *Physics*

CONTENTS

Program Directory

Engineering Physics

Air Force Institute of Technology, Graduate School of Engineering and Management, Department of Engineering Physics, Dayton, OH 45433-7765. Offers applied physics (MS, PhD); electro-optics (MS, PhD); materials science (PhD); nuclear engineering (MS, PhD); space physics (MS). *Program availability:* Part-time. *Degree requirements:* For master's, thesis; for doctorate, thesis/dissertation. *Entrance requirements:* For master's and doctorate, GRE General Test, minimum GPA of 3.0, U.S. citizenship. *Faculty research:* High-energy lasers, space physics, nuclear weapon effects, semiconductor physics.

Cornell University, Graduate School, Graduate Fields of Engineering, Field of Applied Physics, Ithaca, NY 14853. Offers applied physics (PhD); engineering physics (M Eng). *Degree requirements:* For doctorate, comprehensive exam, thesis/dissertation, written exams. *Entrance requirements:* For master's, GRE General Test, 3 letters of recommendation; for doctorate, GRE General Test, GRE Subject Test (physics), GRE Writing Assessment, 3 letters of recommendation. Additional exam requirements/ recommendations for international students: Required—TOEFL (minimum score 600 paper-based; 77 iBT). Electronic applications accepted. *Faculty research:* Quantum and nonlinear optics, plasma physics, solid state physics, condensed matter physics and nanotechnology, electron and X-ray spectroscopy.

École Polytechnique de Montréal, Graduate Programs, Department of Engineering Physics, Montréal, QC H3C 3A7, Canada. Offers optical engineering (M Eng, M Sc A, PhD); solid-state physics and engineering (M Eng, M Sc A, PhD). *Program availability:* Part-time. *Degree requirements:* For master's, one foreign language, thesis; for doctorate, one foreign language, thesis/dissertation. *Entrance requirements:* For master's, minimum GPA of 2.75; for doctorate, minimum GPA of 3.0. *Faculty research:* Optics, thin-film physics, laser spectroscopy, plasmas, photonic devices.

Embry-Riddle Aeronautical University–Daytona, Department of Physical Sciences, Daytona Beach, FL 32114-3900. Offers engineering physics (MS, PhD). *Program availability:* Part-time. *Faculty:* 11 full-time (1 woman). *Students:* 36 full-time (11 women), 2 part-time (both women); includes 5 minority (1 Black or African American, non-Hispanic/Latino; 2 Hispanic/Latino; 2 Two or more races, non-Hispanic/Latino), 12 international. Average age 26. 32 applicants, 50% accepted, 9 enrolled. In 2016, 7 master's awarded. *Degree requirements:* For master's, thesis optional; for doctorate, comprehensive exam, thesis/dissertation. *Entrance requirements:* For doctorate, GRE. Additional exam requirements/recommendations for international students: Required— TOEFL (minimum score 550 paper-based, 79 iBT) or IELTS (6). *Application deadline:* For fall admission, 3/1 priority date for domestic students; for spring admission, 11/1 priority date for domestic students; for summer admission, 4/1 priority date for domestic students. Applications are processed on a rolling basis. Application fee: $50. Electronic applications accepted. *Expenses: Tuition:* Full-time $16,296; part-time $1358 per credit hour. *Required fees:* $1294; $647 per semester. One-time fee: $100 full-time. Tuition and fees vary according to course load, degree level and program. *Financial support:* Research assistantships, teaching assistantships, career-related internships or fieldwork, scholarships/grants, traineeships, unspecified assistantships, and on-campus employment available. Financial award application deadline: 3/15; financial award applicants required to submit FAFSA. *Faculty research:* Spacecraft instrumentation; spacecraft systems engineering; spacecraft power and thermal control; space robotics/ autonomous systems; remote sensing. *Unit head:* Terry Oswalt, PhD, Professor of Engineering Physics/Chair, Department of Physical Sciences, 386-226-6100, E-mail: terry.oswalt@erau.edu. *Application contact:* Graduate Admissions, 386-226-6176, E-mail: graduate.admissions@erau.edu.
Website: http://daytonabeach.erau.edu/college-arts-sciences/physical-sciences/index.html

George Mason University, College of Science, Department of Physics and Astronomy, Fairfax, VA 22030. Offers applied and engineering physics (MS); computational science and informatics (PhD). *Faculty:* 38 full-time (12 women), 10 part-time/adjunct (0 women). *Students:* 26 full-time (4 women), 25 part-time (4 women); includes 8 minority (3 Black or African American, non-Hispanic/Latino; 2 Hispanic/Latino; 3 Two or more races, non-Hispanic/Latino), 11 international. Average age 31. 47 applicants, 57% accepted, 16 enrolled. In 2016, 9 master's, 10 doctorates awarded. *Degree requirements:* For master's, thesis optional; for doctorate, comprehensive exam, thesis/dissertation. *Entrance requirements:* For master's and doctorate, GRE, baccalaureate degree in related field with minimum GPA of 3.0 in last 60 credit hours; 3 letters of recommendation; expanded goals statement; resume; 2 copies of official transcripts. Additional exam requirements/recommendations for international students: Required— TOEFL (minimum score 575 paper-based; 88 iBT), IELTS (minimum score 6.5), PTE (minimum score 59). Application fee: $75 ($80 for international students). Electronic applications accepted. *Expenses:* Tuition, state resident: full-time $10,628; part-time $443 per credit. Tuition, nonresident: full-time $29,306; part-time $1221 per credit. *Required fees:* $3096; $129 per credit. Tuition and fees vary according to program. *Financial support:* In 2016–17, 27 students received support, including 15 research assistantships with tuition reimbursements available (averaging $19,214 per year), 12 teaching assistantships with tuition reimbursements available (averaging $17,562 per year); career-related internships or fieldwork, Federal Work-Study, scholarships/grants, unspecified assistantships, and health care benefits (for full-time research or teaching assistantship recipients) also available. Support available to part-time students. Financial award application deadline: 3/1; financial award applicants required to submit FAFSA. *Faculty research:* Particle and nuclear physics; computational statistics; astronomy, astrophysics, and space and planetary science; astronomy and physics education; atomic physics; biophysics and neuroscience; optical physics; fundamental theoretical studies; multidimensional data analysis. *Total annual research expenditures:* $3.2 million. *Unit head:* Dr. Paul So, 709-993-4377, E-mail: paso@gmu.edu. *Application contact:* Executive Assistant, 703-993-1280, E-mail: physics@gmu.edu.

McMaster University, School of Graduate Studies, Faculty of Engineering, Department of Engineering Physics, Hamilton, ON L8S 4M2, Canada. Offers engineering physics (M Eng, MA Sc, PhD); nuclear engineering (PhD). *Degree requirements:* For master's, thesis or alternative; for doctorate, comprehensive exam, thesis/dissertation. *Entrance requirements:* For master's, minimum B average in engineering, mathematics, or physical sciences. Additional exam requirements/recommendations for international students: Required—TOEFL (minimum score 550 paper-based). *Faculty research:* Non-thermal plasmas for pollution control and electrostatic precipitation, bulk and thin film luminescent materials, devices and systems for optical fiber communications, physics and applications of III-V materials and devices, defect spectroscopy in semiconductors.

Rensselaer Polytechnic Institute, Graduate School, School of Engineering, Program in Engineering Physics, Troy, NY 12180-3590. Offers MS, PhD. *Program availability:* Part-time. *Faculty:* 48 full-time (7 women), 1 part-time/adjunct (0 women). *Students:* 1 part-time (0 women). 3 applicants, 67% accepted. Terminal master's awarded for partial completion of doctoral program. *Degree requirements:* For master's, thesis (for some programs); for doctorate, thesis/dissertation. *Entrance requirements:* For master's and

doctorate, GRE. Additional exam requirements/recommendations for international students: Required—TOEFL (minimum score 600 paper-based; 100 iBT), IELTS (minimum score 7), PTE (minimum score 68). *Application deadline:* For fall admission, 1/1 priority date for domestic and international students; for spring admission, 8/15 priority date for domestic and international students. Applications are processed on a rolling basis. Application fee: $75. Electronic applications accepted. *Expenses: Tuition:* Full-time $49,520; part-time $2060 per credit hour. *Required fees:* $2617. *Financial support:* In 2016–17, 1 student received support, including research assistantships (averaging $22,000 per year), teaching assistantships (averaging $22,000 per year); fellowships also available. Financial award application deadline: 1/1. *Faculty research:* Applied radiation, radiation transport, medical physics, multiphase phenomena, sonoluminescence, fusion plasma engineering. *Total annual research expenditures:* $1.6 million. *Unit head:* Dr. Theo Borca-Tasciuc, Graduate Program Director, 518-276-2627, E-mail: borcat@rpi.edu. *Application contact:* Graduate Admissions, 518-276-6216, E-mail: gradadmissions@rpi.edu.
Website: http://mane.rpi.edu/

Stanford University, School of Humanities and Sciences, Department of Applied Physics, Stanford, CA 94305-2004. Offers applied and engineering physics (MS); applied physics (PhD). Terminal master's awarded for partial completion of doctoral program. *Degree requirements:* For doctorate, thesis/dissertation. *Entrance requirements:* For master's and doctorate, GRE General Test, GRE Subject Test. Additional exam requirements/recommendations for international students: Required— TOEFL. Electronic applications accepted. *Expenses: Tuition:* Full-time $47,331. *Required fees:* $609.

University of California, San Diego, Graduate Division, Department of Mechanical and Aerospace Engineering, Program in Engineering Physics, La Jolla, CA 92093. Offers MS, PhD. *Students:* 21 full-time (3 women). 24 applicants, 54% accepted, 9 enrolled. In 2016, 1 master's, 4 doctorates awarded. *Degree requirements:* For master's, comprehensive exam (for some programs), thesis (for some programs), comprehensive exam or thesis; for doctorate, comprehensive exam, thesis/dissertation. *Entrance requirements:* For master's and doctorate, GRE General Test, minimum GPA of 3.0. Additional exam requirements/recommendations for international students: Required— TOEFL (minimum score 550 paper-based; 80 iBT), IELTS (minimum score 7). *Application deadline:* For fall admission, 12/14 for domestic students. Application fee: $105 ($125 for international students). Electronic applications accepted. *Expenses:* Tuition, state resident: full-time $11,220. Tuition, nonresident: full-time $26,322. *Required fees:* $1864. *Financial support:* Fellowships, research assistantships, teaching assistantships, scholarships/grants, and unspecified assistantships available. Financial award applicants required to submit FAFSA. *Faculty research:* Experimental, theoretical, and computational programs addressing turbulent flows; mechanics of two-phase flow; rheology of suspensions; laminar and turbulent combustion; chemical kinetics of combustion systems. *Unit head:* Vitali Nesterenko, Chair, 858-534-0113, E-mail: mae-chair-l@ucsd.edu. *Application contact:* Lydia Ramirez, Graduate Coordinator, 858-534-4387, E-mail: mae-gradadm-l@ucsd.edu.
Website: http://maeweb.ucsd.edu/

University of Central Oklahoma, The Jackson College of Graduate Studies, College of Mathematics and Science, Department of Engineering and Physics, Edmond, OK 73034-5209. Offers biomedical engineering (MS); electrical engineering (MS); mechanical systems (MS); physics (MS). *Program availability:* Part-time. *Degree requirements:* For master's, thesis optional. *Entrance requirements:* For master's, GRE, 24 hours of course work in physics or equivalent, mathematics through differential equations, minimum GPA of 2.75 overall and 3.0 in last 60 hours attempted. Additional exam requirements/recommendations for international students: Required—TOEFL (minimum score 550 paper-based). Electronic applications accepted.

University of Oklahoma, College of Arts and Sciences, Department of Physics and Astronomy, Norman, OK 73019. Offers engineering physics (MS); physics (MS, PhD). *Program availability:* Part-time. *Faculty:* 30 full-time (1 woman). *Students:* 52 full-time (8 women), 32 part-time (9 women); includes 3 minority (1 Asian, non-Hispanic/Latino; 2 Hispanic/Latino), 39 international. Average age 27. 86 applicants, 24% accepted, 21 enrolled. In 2016, 11 master's, 6 doctorates awarded. Terminal master's awarded for partial completion of doctoral program. *Degree requirements:* For master's, comprehensive exam, thesis (for some programs); for doctorate, comprehensive exam, thesis/dissertation (for some programs). *Entrance requirements:* Additional exam requirements/recommendations for international students: Required—TOEFL (minimum score 79 iBT) or IELTS (minimum score 6.5). *Application deadline:* For fall admission, 4/1 for domestic students, 5/31 for international students; for spring admission, 11/15 for international students; for summer admission, 11/1 for domestic students. Application fee: $50 ($100 for international students). Electronic applications accepted. *Expenses:* Tuition, state resident: full-time $4886; part-time $203.60 per credit hour. Tuition, nonresident: full-time $18,989; part-time $791.20 per credit hour. *Required fees:* $3283; $126.25 per credit hour. $126.50 per semester. *Financial support:* In 2016–17, 79 students received support, including 27 research assistantships with tuition reimbursements available (averaging $15,699 per year), 53 teaching assistantships with tuition reimbursements available (averaging $14,689 per year); fellowships, institutionally sponsored loans, scholarships/grants, health care benefits, and unspecified assistantships also available. Financial award application deadline: 6/1; financial award applicants required to submit FAFSA. *Faculty research:* Astrophysics; atomic, molecular, and optical physics; high energy physics; condensed matter physics. *Total annual research expenditures:* $3.1 million. *Unit head:* Dr. Gregory A. Parker, Chair, 405-325-3961, Fax: 405-325-7557, E-mail: office@nhn.ou.edu. *Application contact:* Dr. Lloyd Bumm, Professor, 405-325-6053, Fax: 405-325-7557, E-mail: grad@nhn.ou.edu.
Website: http://www.nhn.ou.edu

University of Oklahoma, Gallogly College of Engineering, Department of Engineering Physics, Norman, OK 73019. Offers MS, PhD. *Students:* 4 full-time (0 women), 5 part-time (0 women), 7 international. Average age 27. 3 applicants. In 2016, 3 master's awarded. Terminal master's awarded for partial completion of doctoral program. *Degree requirements:* For master's, thesis or alternative, departmental qualifying exam; for doctorate, thesis/dissertation, comprehensive, departmental qualifying, oral, and written exams. *Entrance requirements:* For master's and doctorate, GRE General Test, GRE Subject Test (physics), previous course work in physics. Additional exam requirements/ recommendations for international students: Required—TOEFL (minimum score 100 iBT) or IELTS (minimum score 7). *Application deadline:* For fall admission, 3/1 for domestic and international students; for spring admission, 10/1 for domestic students, 9/1 for international students. Applications are processed on a rolling basis. Application fee: $50 ($100 for international students). Electronic applications accepted. *Expenses:* Tuition, state resident: full-time $4886; part-time $203.60 per credit hour. Tuition, nonresident: full-time $18,989; part-time $791.20 per credit hour. *Required fees:* $3283;

$126.25 per credit hour. $126.50 per semester. *Financial support:* In 2016–17, 8 students received support. Scholarships/grants, health care benefits, tuition waivers (full), and unspecified assistantships available. Financial award application deadline: 6/1; financial award applicants required to submit FAFSA. *Faculty research:* Electronic materials; characterization and device fabrication; scanning probe microscopy; high field magneto transport and magneto-optics; laser applications in chemical reaction dynamics. *Unit head:* Dr. Mike Santos, Chair in Engineering Physics/Professor of Physics, 405-325-3961, E-mail: ephys@nhn.ou.edu.
Website: http://www.ou.edu/content/coe/ephysics/grad.html

University of Saskatchewan, College of Graduate Studies and Research, College of Arts and Science, Department of Physics and Engineering Physics, Saskatoon, SK S7N 5A2, Canada. Offers M Sc, PhD. *Degree requirements:* For master's, thesis; for doctorate, comprehensive exam (for some programs), thesis/dissertation. *Entrance requirements:* Additional exam requirements/recommendations for international students: Required—TOEFL (minimum score 80 iBT); Recommended—IELTS (minimum score 6.5). Electronic applications accepted.

The University of Tulsa, Graduate School, College of Engineering and Natural Sciences, Department of Physics and Engineering Physics, Tulsa, OK 74104-3189. Offers engineering physics (MS); physics (MS, PhD). *Program availability:* Part-time. *Faculty:* 8 full-time (0 women). *Students:* 9 full-time (2 women), 5 part-time (1 woman); includes 2 minority (1 American Indian or Alaska Native, non-Hispanic/Latino; 1 Two or more races, non-Hispanic/Latino), 11 international. Average age 30. 59 applicants, 31% accepted, 1 enrolled. In 2016, 1 doctorate awarded. Terminal master's awarded for partial completion of doctoral program. *Degree requirements:* For master's, thesis; for doctorate, comprehensive exam, thesis/dissertation. *Entrance requirements:* For master's, GRE General Test. Additional exam requirements/recommendations for international students: Required—TOEFL (minimum score 550 paper-based; 80 iBT), IELTS (minimum score 6). *Application deadline:* Applications are processed on a rolling basis. Application fee: $55. Electronic applications accepted. *Expenses: Tuition:* Full-time $22,230; part-time $1235 per credit hour. *Required fees:* $990 per semester. Tuition and fees vary according to course load. *Financial support:* In 2016–17, 14 students received support, including 6 fellowships with tuition reimbursements available (averaging $4,572 per year), 5 research assistantships with full tuition reimbursements available (averaging $7,818 per year), 10 teaching assistantships with full tuition reimbursements available (averaging $11,796 per year); career-related internships or fieldwork, Federal Work-Study, scholarships/grants, health care benefits, tuition waivers (full and partial), and unspecified assistantships also available. Support available to part-time students. Financial award application deadline: 2/1. *Total annual research expenditures:* $285,393. *Unit head:* Dr. George Miller, Program Chair, 918-631-3021, Fax: 918-631-2995, E-mail: george-miller@utulsa.edu. *Application contact:* Dr. Sanwu Wang, Advisor, 918-631-3022, Fax: 918-631-2995, E-mail: sanwu-wang@utulsa.edu. Website: http://engineering.utulsa.edu/academics/physics-and-engineering-physics/

University of Virginia, School of Engineering and Applied Science, Program in Engineering Physics, Charlottesville, VA 22903. Offers ME, MS, PhD. *Program availability:* Online learning. *Students:* 8 full-time (3 women); includes 1 minority (Asian, non-Hispanic/Latino), 3 international. Average age 27. 2 applicants, 50% accepted. In 2016, 1 master's, 2 doctorates awarded. *Degree requirements:* For master's, comprehensive exam; for doctorate, comprehensive exam, thesis/dissertation. *Entrance requirements:* For master's and doctorate, GRE General Test, 3 recommendations. Additional exam requirements/recommendations for international students: Required—TOEFL. *Application deadline:* For fall admission, 1/15 for domestic and international students. Applications are processed on a rolling basis. Application fee: $60. Electronic applications accepted. *Expenses:* Tuition, state resident: full-time $15,026; part-time $834 per credit hour. Tuition, nonresident: full-time $25,168; part-time $1378 per credit hour. *Required fees:* $2654. *Financial support:* Fellowships, research assistantships, and teaching assistantships available. Financial award application deadline: 2/1; financial award applicants required to submit FAFSA. *Faculty research:* Continuum and rarefied gas dynamics, ultracentrifuge isotope enrichment, solid-state physics, atmospheric physics, atomic collisions. *Unit head:* Petra Reinke, Co-Chair, 434-924-7237, Fax: 434-982-5660, E-mail: pr6e@virginia.edu.
Website: http://www.virginia.edu/ep/

University of Wisconsin–Madison, Graduate School, College of Engineering, Department of Engineering Physics, Madison, WI 53706. Offers engineering mechanics (MS, PhD); nuclear engineering and engineering physics (MS, PhD). *Program availability:* Part-time, online learning. *Faculty:* 21 full-time (3 women). *Students:* 116 full-time (19 women), 10 part-time (2 women); includes 17 minority (3 Black or African American, non-Hispanic/Latino; 5 Asian, non-Hispanic/Latino; 8 Hispanic/Latino; 1 Two or more races, non-Hispanic/Latino), 23 international. Average age 26. 162 applicants, 55% accepted, 25 enrolled. In 2016, 29 master's, 11 doctorates awarded. Terminal master's awarded for partial completion of doctoral program. *Degree requirements:* For master's, thesis optional, 30 credits of technical courses; oral exam; minimum GPA of 3.0; for doctorate, thesis/dissertation, minimum of 51 credits; minimum GPA of 3.0. *Entrance requirements:* For master's and doctorate, GRE General Test, minimum GPA of 3.0 in last 60 hours, appropriate bachelor's degree. Additional exam requirements/recommendations for international students: Required—TOEFL (minimum score 580 paper-based; 92 iBT), IELTS (minimum score 7). *Application deadline:* For fall admission, 12/31 priority date for domestic and international students. Application fee: $75 ($81 for international students). Electronic applications accepted. *Expenses:* $13,157 per year in-state tuition and fees; $26,484 per year out-of-state tuition and fees. *Financial support:* In 2016–17, 119 students received support, including 5 fellowships with full tuition reimbursements available (averaging $29,628 per year), 93 research assistantships with full tuition reimbursements available (averaging $23,175 per year), 19 teaching assistantships with full tuition reimbursements available (averaging $14,941 per year); career-related internships or fieldwork, Federal Work-Study, institutionally sponsored loans, unspecified assistantships, and project assistantships also available. Support available to part-time students. Financial award application deadline: 12/1; financial award applicants required to submit FAFSA. *Faculty research:* Bio-/micro-/nano-mechanics; astronautics; fission reactor engineering; fusion science and technology; radiation sciences; mechanics of materials. *Total annual research expenditures:* $14.1 million. *Unit head:* Dr. Douglass Henderson, Chair, 608-263-1646, Fax: 608-263-7451, E-mail: dlhender@wisc.edu. *Application contact:* Sara Hladilek, Student Services Coordinator, 608-263-1795, Fax: 608-263-7451, E-mail: shladilek@wisc.edu. Website: http://www.engr.wisc.edu/ep/

Yale University, Graduate School of Arts and Sciences, School of Engineering and Applied Science, Department of Applied Physics, New Haven, CT 06520. Offers MS, PhD. Terminal master's awarded for partial completion of doctoral program. *Degree requirements:* For doctorate, thesis/dissertation, area exam. *Entrance requirements:* For master's and doctorate, GRE General Test. Additional exam requirements/recommendations for international students: Required—TOEFL. *Faculty research:* Condensed-matter physics, optical physics, materials science.

Section 13
Geological, Mineral/Mining, and Petroleum Engineering

This section contains a directory of institutions offering graduate work in geological, mineral/mining, and petroleum engineering. Additional information about programs listed in the directory may be obtained by writing directly to the dean of a graduate school or chair of a department at the address given in the directory.

For programs offering related work, see also in this book *Chemical Engineering, Civil and Environmental Engineering, Electrical and Computer Engineering, Energy and Power Engineering, Engineering and Applied Sciences, Management of Engineering and Technology,* and *Materials Sciences and Engineering.* In another guide in this series:

Graduate Programs in the Physical Sciences, Mathematics, Agricultural Sciences, the Environment & Natural Resources
See *Geosciences* and *Marine Sciences and Oceanography*

CONTENTS

Program Directories

Geological Engineering

Arizona State University at the Tempe campus, College of Liberal Arts and Sciences, School of Earth and Space Exploration, Tempe, AZ 85287-1404. Offers astrophysics (MS, PhD); exploration systems design (PhD); geological sciences (MS, PhD). PhD in exploration systems design is offered in collaboration with the Ira A. Fulton School of Engineering. Terminal master's awarded for partial completion of doctoral program. *Degree requirements:* For master's, thesis, interactive Program of Study (iPOS) submitted before completing 50 percent of required credit hours; for doctorate, thesis/dissertation, interactive Program of Study (iPOS) submitted before completing 50 percent of required credit hours. *Entrance requirements:* For master's and doctorate, GRE, minimum GPA of 3.0 or equivalent in last 2 years of work leading to bachelor's degree. Additional exam requirements/recommendations for international students: Required—TOEFL, IELTS, or PTE. Electronic applications accepted.

Colorado School of Mines, Office of Graduate Studies, Department of Geology and Geological Engineering, Golden, CO 80401. Offers geochemistry (MS, PMS, PhD); geological engineering (ME, MS, PhD); geology (MS, PhD). *Program availability:* Part-time. *Degree requirements:* For master's, thesis (for some programs); for doctorate, comprehensive exam, thesis/dissertation. *Entrance requirements:* For master's and doctorate, GRE General Test. Additional exam requirements/recommendations for international students: Required—TOEFL (minimum score 550 paper-based; 80 iBT). Electronic applications accepted. *Expenses:* Tuition, state resident: full-time $15,690. Tuition, nonresident: full-time $34,020. *Required fees:* $2152. Tuition and fees vary according to course load. *Faculty research:* Predictive sediment modeling, petrophysics, aquifer-contaminant flow modeling, water-rock interactions, geotechnical engineering.

Colorado School of Mines, Office of Graduate Studies, Department of Geophysics, Golden, CO 80401-1887. Offers geophysical engineering (ME, MS, PhD); geophysics (MS, PhD); hydrology (MS, PhD); mineral exploration and mining geosciences (PMS). *Program availability:* Part-time. *Degree requirements:* For master's, thesis (for some programs); for doctorate, comprehensive exam, thesis/dissertation. *Entrance requirements:* For master's and doctorate, GRE General Test. Additional exam requirements/recommendations for international students: Required—TOEFL (minimum score 550 paper-based; 80 iBT). Electronic applications accepted. *Expenses:* Tuition, state resident: full-time $15,690. Tuition, nonresident: full-time $34,020. *Required fees:* $2152. Tuition and fees vary according to course load. *Faculty research:* Seismic exploration, gravity and geomagnetic fields, electrical mapping and sounding, bore hole measurements, environmental physics.

Missouri University of Science and Technology, Graduate School, Department of Geological Sciences and Engineering, Rolla, MO 65409. Offers geological engineering (MS, DE, PhD); geology and geophysics (MS, PhD), including geochemistry, geology, geophysics, groundwater and environmental geology; petroleum engineering (MS, DE, PhD). *Program availability:* Part-time. *Degree requirements:* For master's, thesis optional; for doctorate, comprehensive exam, thesis/dissertation. *Entrance requirements:* For master's, GRE General Test (minimum score 600 quantitative, writing 3.5), minimum GPA of 3.0 in last 4 semesters; for doctorate, GRE General Test (minimum scores: Quantitative 600, Writing 3.5). Additional exam requirements/recommendations for international students: Required—TOEFL (minimum score 550 paper-based). Electronic applications accepted. *Faculty research:* Digital image processing and geographic information systems, mineralogy, igneous and sedimentary petrology-geochemistry, sedimentology groundwater hydrology and contaminant transport.

Montana Tech of The University of Montana, Geosciences Programs, Butte, MT 59701-8997. Offers geochemistry (MS); geological engineering (MS); geology (MS); geophysical engineering (MS); hydrogeological engineering (MS); hydrogeology (MS). *Program availability:* Part-time. *Faculty:* 17 full-time (5 women), 6 part-time/adjunct (2 women). *Students:* 25 full-time (8 women), 13 part-time (4 women); includes 5 minority (3 Black or African American, non-Hispanic/Latino; 2 Hispanic/Latino), 8 international. Average age 28. 24 applicants, 50% accepted, 10 enrolled. In 2016, 12 master's awarded. *Degree requirements:* For master's, comprehensive exam (for some programs), thesis (for some programs). *Entrance requirements:* For master's, GRE General Test, minimum GPA of 3.0. Additional exam requirements/recommendations for international students: Required—TOEFL (minimum score 545 paper-based; 78 iBT), IELTS (minimum score 6.5). *Application deadline:* For fall admission, 4/1 priority date for domestic students, 3/1 priority date for international students; for spring admission, 10/1 priority date for domestic students, 7/1 priority date for international students. Applications are processed on a rolling basis. Application fee: $50. Electronic applications accepted. *Expenses:* Tuition, state resident: full-time $2901; part-time $1450.68 per degree program. Tuition, nonresident: full-time $8432; part-time $4215.84 per degree program. *Required fees:* $668; $354 per degree program. Tuition and fees vary according to course load and program. *Financial support:* In 2016–17, 15 students received support, including 10 teaching assistantships with partial tuition reimbursements available (averaging $5,000 per year); research assistantships with partial tuition reimbursements available, career-related internships or fieldwork, tuition waivers (full and partial), and unspecified assistantships also available. Financial award application deadline: 4/1; financial award applicants required to submit FAFSA. *Faculty research:* Water resource development, seismic processing, petroleum reservoir characterization, environmental geochemistry, geologic mapping. *Unit head:* Dr. Larry Smith, Department Head, 406-496-4859, Fax: 406-496-4260, E-mail: lsmith@mtech.edu. *Application contact:* Daniel Stirling, Administrator, Graduate School, 406-496-4304, Fax: 406-496-4710, E-mail: gradschool@mtech.edu.
Website: http://www.mtech.edu/academics/gradschool/degreeprograms/degrees.htm

New Mexico Institute of Mining and Technology, Center for Graduate Studies, Department of Mineral Engineering, Socorro, NM 87801. Offers explosives engineering (MS); geotechnical engineering (MS); mining engineering (MS). *Degree requirements:* For master's, thesis. *Entrance requirements:* Additional exam requirements/recommendations for international students: Required—TOEFL (minimum score 540 paper-based). *Faculty research:* Drilling and blasting, geological engineering, mine design, applied mineral exploration, rock mechanics.

New Mexico State University, College of Engineering, Department of Civil and Geological Engineering, Las Cruces, NM 88003. Offers civil and geological engineering (MSCE, PhD); environmental engineering (MS Env E). *Program availability:* Part-time. *Faculty:* 13 full-time (3 women). *Students:* 54 full-time (16 women), 16 part-time (4 women); includes 18 minority (2 Black or African American, non-Hispanic/Latino; 3 American Indian or Alaska Native, non-Hispanic/Latino; 1 Asian, non-Hispanic/Latino; 11 Hispanic/Latino; 1 Two or more races, non-Hispanic/Latino), 35 international. Average age 30. 64 applicants, 48% accepted, 17 enrolled. In 2016, 19 master's, 3 doctorates awarded. *Degree requirements:* For master's, thesis (for some programs); for doctorate, comprehensive exam, thesis/dissertation, qualifying exam. *Entrance requirements:* For master's and doctorate, BS in engineering, minimum GPA of 3.0. Additional exam requirements/recommendations for international students: Required—TOEFL (minimum score 550 paper-based; 79 iBT), IELTS (minimum score 6.5). *Application deadline:* For fall admission, 4/1 priority date for domestic and international students; for spring admission, 9/1 priority date for domestic and international students. Applications are processed on a rolling basis. Application fee: $40 ($50 for international students). Electronic applications accepted. *Expenses:* Tuition, state resident: full-time $4086. Tuition, nonresident: full-time $14,254. *Required fees:* $853. Tuition and fees vary according to course load. *Financial support:* In 2016–17, 61 students received support, including 5 fellowships (averaging $2,853 per year), 27 research assistantships (averaging $13,824 per year), 23 teaching assistantships (averaging $8,051 per year); career-related internships or fieldwork, Federal Work-Study, scholarships/grants, traineeships, health care benefits, and unspecified assistantships also available. Support available to part-time students. Financial award application deadline: 3/1. *Faculty research:* Structural engineering, water resources engineering, environmental engineering, geotechnical engineering, transportation. *Total annual research expenditures:* $3.1 million. *Unit head:* Dr. David Jauregui, Department Head, 575-646-3801, Fax: 575-646-6049, E-mail: jauregui@nmsu.edu. *Application contact:* Elvia Cisneros, Administrative Assistant, 575-646-3801, Fax: 575-646-6049, E-mail: civil@nmsu.edu.
Website: http://ce.nmsu.edu

South Dakota School of Mines and Technology, Graduate Division, Department of Geology and Geological Engineering, Rapid City, SD 57701-3995. Offers geology and geological engineering (MS, PhD); paleontology (MS). *Program availability:* Part-time. *Degree requirements:* For master's, thesis; for doctorate, thesis/dissertation. *Entrance requirements:* For master's and doctorate, GRE General Test, GRE Subject Test. Additional exam requirements/recommendations for international students: Required—TOEFL (minimum score 520 paper-based; 68 iBT), TWE. Electronic applications accepted. *Faculty research:* Contaminants in soil, nitrate leaching, environmental changes, fracture formations, greenhouse effect.

The University of Akron, Graduate School, Buchtel College of Arts and Sciences, Department of Geosciences, Akron, OH 44325. Offers earth science (MS); engineering geology (MS); environmental geology (MS); geology (MS). *Program availability:* Part-time. *Faculty:* 7 full-time (1 woman), 4 part-time/adjunct (0 women). *Students:* 32 full-time (11 women), 2 part-time (0 women); includes 1 minority (Black or African American, non-Hispanic/Latino), 16 international. Average age 27. 38 applicants, 66% accepted, 11 enrolled. In 2016, 22 master's awarded. *Degree requirements:* For master's, comprehensive exam, thesis, seminar, proficiency exam. *Entrance requirements:* For master's, minimum GPA of 2.75, three letters of recommendation, statement of purpose. Additional exam requirements/recommendations for international students: Required—TOEFL (minimum score 550 paper-based; 79 iBT), IELTS (minimum score 6.5). *Application deadline:* Applications are processed on a rolling basis. Application fee: $45 ($70 for international students). Electronic applications accepted. *Expenses:* Tuition, state resident: full-time $8618; part-time $359 per credit hour. Tuition, nonresident: full-time $17,149; part-time $715 per credit hour. *Required fees:* $1652. *Financial support:* In 2016–17, 1 research assistantship with full tuition reimbursement, 21 teaching assistantships with full and partial tuition reimbursements were awarded; instructional support assistantships also available. *Faculty research:* Terrestrial environmental change, karst hydrogeology, lacustrine paleo environments, environmental magnetism and geophysics. *Total annual research expenditures:* $509,174. *Unit head:* Dr. Stephen Weeks, Interim Chair, 330-972-6954, E-mail: scw@uakron.edu. *Application contact:* Dr. John Peck, Director of Graduate Studies, 330-972-7659, E-mail: jpeck@uakron.edu.
Website: http://www.uakron.edu/geology/

University of Alaska Anchorage, School of Engineering, Program in Arctic Engineering, Anchorage, AK 99508. Offers MS. *Program availability:* Part-time, evening/weekend. *Degree requirements:* For master's, thesis or alternative, engineering project report. *Entrance requirements:* For master's, bachelor's degree in engineering. Additional exam requirements/recommendations for international students: Required—TOEFL (minimum score 550 paper-based). *Faculty research:* Load-bearing ice, control of drifting snow, permafrost and foundations, frozen ground engineering.

University of Alaska Fairbanks, College of Engineering and Mines, Department of Mining and Geological Engineering, Fairbanks, AK 99775-5800. Offers geological engineering (MS); mineral preparation engineering (MS); mining engineering (MS). *Program availability:* Part-time. *Faculty:* 7 full-time (1 woman). *Students:* 4 full-time (1 woman), 4 part-time (0 women); includes 2 minority (1 American Indian or Alaska Native, non-Hispanic/Latino; 1 Two or more races, non-Hispanic/Latino), 5 international. Average age 31. 7 applicants, 43% accepted, 2 enrolled. In 2016, 2 master's awarded. *Degree requirements:* For master's, comprehensive exam, oral defense of project or thesis. *Entrance requirements:* For master's, GRE General Test (for geological engineering), bachelor's degree from accredited institution with minimum cumulative undergraduate and major GPA of 3.0. Additional exam requirements/recommendations for international students: Required—TOEFL (minimum score 550 paper-based; 79 iBT), IELTS (minimum score 6.5). *Application deadline:* For fall admission, 6/1 for domestic students, 3/1 for international students; for spring admission, 10/15 for domestic students, 9/1 for international students. Applications are processed on a rolling basis. Application fee: $60. Electronic applications accepted. *Expenses:* $533 per credit resident tuition, $673 per semester resident fees; $1,088 per credit non-resident tuition, $835 per semester non-resident fees. *Financial support:* In 2016–17, 1 research assistantship with full tuition reimbursement (averaging $16,834 per year), 2 teaching assistantships with full tuition reimbursements (averaging $7,302 per year) were awarded; fellowships with full tuition reimbursements, career-related internships or fieldwork, Federal Work-Study, scholarships/grants, health care benefits, and unspecified assistantships also available. Support available to part-time students. Financial award application deadline: 7/1; financial award applicants required to submit FAFSA. *Faculty research:* Underground mining in permafrost, testing of ultra clean diesel, slope stability, fractal and mathematical morphology, soil and rock mechanics. *Unit head:* Dr. Margaret Darrow, Chair, 907-474-7388, Fax: 907-474-6635, E-mail: cem.mingeo@alaska.edu. *Application contact:* Mary Kreta, Director of Admissions, 907-474-7500, Fax: 907-474-7097, E-mail: admissions@uaf.edu.
Website: http://cem.uaf.edu/mingeo

The University of Arizona, College of Engineering, Department of Mining and Geological Engineering, Tucson, AZ 85721. Offers mining and geological engineering (MS, PhD); mining engineering (Certificate), including mine health and safety, mine information and production technology, rock mechanics. *Program availability:* Part-time, online learning. *Degree requirements:* For master's, thesis; for doctorate, thesis/dissertation. *Entrance requirements:* For master's, GRE General Test, 3 letters of recommendation; for doctorate, GRE General Test, 3 letters of recommendation, statements of purpose. Additional exam requirements/recommendations for international students: Required—TOEFL (minimum score 550 paper-based; 79 iBT).

Electronic applications accepted. *Faculty research:* Geomechanics, mineral processing, information technology, automation, geosensing.

The University of British Columbia, Faculty of Science, Department of Earth, Ocean and Atmospheric Sciences, Vancouver, BC V6T 1Z4, Canada. Offers atmospheric science (M Sc, PhD); geological engineering (M Eng, MA Sc, PhD); geological sciences (M Sc, PhD); geophysics (M Sc, MA Sc, PhD); oceanography (M Sc, PhD). *Degree requirements:* For master's, one foreign language, thesis (for some programs); for doctorate, one foreign language, comprehensive exam, thesis/dissertation. *Entrance requirements:* Additional exam requirements/recommendations for international students: Required—TOEFL. Application fee: $100 Canadian dollars ($162 Canadian dollars for international students). *Expenses:* $4,802 per year tuition and fees, $8,436 per year international (for M Sc, MA Sc, and PhD); $5,835 per year tuition and fees, $18,900 per year international (for M Eng). *Financial support:* Fellowships, research assistantships, teaching assistantships, Federal Work-Study, institutionally sponsored loans, scholarships/grants, tuition waivers (full and partial), and unspecified assistantships available. *Faculty research:* Oceans and atmosphere, environmental earth science, hydro geology, mineral deposits, geophysics. *Application contact:* Audrey Van Slyck, Graduate Program Coordinator, 604-822-2713, Fax: 604-822-6088, E-mail: gradsec@eos.ubc.ca.
Website: https://www.eoas.ubc.ca/

University of Hawaii at Manoa, Graduate Division, School of Ocean and Earth Science and Technology, Department of Geology and Geophysics, Honolulu, HI 96822. Offers high-pressure geophysics and geochemistry (MS, PhD); hydrogeology and engineering geology (MS, PhD); marine geology and geophysics (MS, PhD); planetary geosciences and remote sensing (MS, PhD); seismology and solid-earth geophysics (MS, PhD); volcanology, petrology, and geochemistry (MS, PhD). *Program availability:* Part-time. Terminal master's awarded for partial completion of doctoral program. *Degree requirements:* For master's, thesis optional; for doctorate, comprehensive exam, thesis/dissertation. *Entrance requirements:* For master's and doctorate, GRE General Test, minimum GPA of 3.0. Additional exam requirements/recommendations for international students: Required—TOEFL (minimum score 580 paper-based; 92 iBT), IELTS (minimum score 5).

University of Idaho, College of Graduate Studies, College of Engineering, Department of Civil Engineering, Moscow, ID 83844. Offers civil engineering (M Engr, MS, PhD); engineering management (M Engr); geological engineering (MS). *Faculty:* 17 full-time, 3 part-time/adjunct. *Students:* 19 full-time, 64 part-time. Average age 34. In 2016, 31 master's, 2 doctorates awarded. *Entrance requirements:* For master's and doctorate, minimum GPA of 3.0. Additional exam requirements/recommendations for international students: Required—TOEFL. *Application deadline:* For fall admission, 8/1 for domestic students; for spring admission, 12/15 for domestic students. Applications are processed on a rolling basis. Application fee: $60. Electronic applications accepted. *Expenses:* Tuition, state resident: full-time $6460; part-time $414 per credit hour. Tuition, nonresident: full-time $21,268; part-time $1237 per credit hour. *Required fees:* $2070; $60 per credit hour. Full-time tuition and fees vary according to course load and reciprocity agreements. *Financial support:* Fellowships, research assistantships, teaching assistantships, and career-related internships or fieldwork available. Financial award applicants required to submit FAFSA. *Unit head:* Patricia Colberg, Department Chair, 208-885-6782, E-mail: civilengr@uidaho.edu. *Application contact:* Sean Scoggin, Graduate Recruitment Coordinator, 208-885-4001, Fax: 208-885-4406, E-mail: graduateadmissions@uidaho.edu.
Website: http://www.uidaho.edu/engr/ce/

University of Minnesota, Twin Cities Campus, College of Science and Engineering, Department of Civil, Environmental, and Geo-Engineering, Minneapolis, MN 55455-0213. Offers civil engineering (MCE, MS, PhD); geological engineering (M Geo E, MS); stream restoration science and engineering (Certificate). *Program availability:* Part-time. *Degree requirements:* For master's, thesis optional; for doctorate, thesis/dissertation. *Entrance requirements:* For master's and doctorate, GRE General Test. Additional exam requirements/recommendations for international students: Required—TOEFL. Electronic applications accepted. *Faculty research:* Environmental engineering, geomechanics, structural engineering, transportation, water resources.

University of Nevada, Reno, Graduate School, College of Science, Mackay School of Earth Sciences and Engineering, Department of Geological Sciences and Engineering, Program in Geological Engineering, Reno, NV 89557. Offers MS, PhD. Terminal master's awarded for partial completion of doctoral program. *Degree requirements:* For master's, thesis optional; for doctorate, thesis/dissertation. *Entrance requirements:* For master's and doctorate, GRE General Test, minimum GPA of 2.75. Additional exam requirements/recommendations for international students: Required—TOEFL (minimum score 500 paper-based; 61 iBT), IELTS (minimum score 6). Electronic applications accepted. *Faculty research:* Reclamation, remediation, restoration.

University of North Dakota, Graduate School, School of Engineering and Mines, Department of Geological Engineering, Grand Forks, ND 58202. Offers MS, PhD. *Degree requirements:* For master's, thesis. *Entrance requirements:* For master's, GRE General Test. Additional exam requirements/recommendations for international students: Required—TOEFL (minimum score 550 paper-based; 79 iBT), IELTS (minimum score 6.5). *Application deadline:* For fall admission, 8/1 priority date for domestic and international students; for spring admission, 12/1 priority date for domestic and international students. Applications are processed on a rolling basis. Application fee: $35. Electronic applications accepted. *Financial support:* Fellowships with full and partial tuition reimbursements, research assistantships with full and partial tuition reimbursements, teaching assistantships with full and partial tuition reimbursements, Federal Work-Study, scholarships/grants, health care benefits, tuition waivers (full and partial), and unspecified assistantships available. Support available to part-time students. Financial award applicants required to submit FAFSA. *Unit head:* Dr. Scott Korom, Graduate Director, 701-777-6156, E-mail: scottkorom@mail.nodak.edu. *Application contact:* Staci Wells, Admissions Associate, 701-777-2945, Fax: 701-777-3619, E-mail: staci.wells@gradschool.und.edu.

University of Oklahoma, Mewbourne College of Earth and Energy, Mewbourne School of Petroleum and Geological Engineering, Program in Geological Engineering, Norman, OK 73019-1003. Offers MS, PhD. *Program availability:* Part-time. *Students:* 1 full-time (0 women), 4 part-time (2 women), all international. Average age 30. 5 applicants, 20% accepted, 1 enrolled. Terminal master's awarded for partial completion of doctoral program. *Degree requirements:* For master's, variable foreign language requirement, comprehensive exam (for some programs), thesis (for some programs); for doctorate, variable foreign language requirement, comprehensive exam, thesis/dissertation. *Entrance requirements:* For master's and doctorate, GRE, minimum GPA of 3.2, three letters of recommendation, statement of purpose, resume/curriculum vitae. Additional exam requirements/recommendations for international students: Required—TOEFL (minimum score 79 iBT) or IELTS (minimum score 6.5). *Application deadline:* For fall admission, 3/1 for domestic and international students; for spring admission, 9/1 for domestic and international students. Application fee: $50 ($100 for international students). Electronic applications accepted. *Expenses:* Tuition, state resident: full-time $4886; part-time $203.60 per credit hour. Tuition, nonresident: full-time $18,989; part-time $791.20 per credit hour. *Required fees:* $3283; $126.25 per credit hour. $126.50 per semester. *Financial support:* In 2016–17, 3 students received support. Unspecified assistantships available. Financial award application deadline: 6/1; financial award applicants required to submit FAFSA. *Faculty research:* Geomechanics applied to petroleum and geothermal reservoir development, reaction fluid flow in fractures. *Unit head:* Dr. Deepak Devegowda, Associate Professor and Graduate Liaison, 405-325-3081, Fax: 405-325-7477, E-mail: deepak.devegowda@ou.edu. *Application contact:* Sheriee Parnell, Graduate Programs Coordinator, 405-325-6821, Fax: 405-325-7477, E-mail: sheriee@ou.edu.
Website: http://mpge.ou.edu

University of Saskatchewan, College of Graduate Studies and Research, College of Engineering, Civil and Geological Engineering Program, Saskatoon, SK S7N 5A9, Canada. Offers M Eng, M Sc, PhD. *Program availability:* Part-time. *Degree requirements:* For master's, thesis (for some programs), 30 credits (for M Eng); thesis and 12 credits (for MS); for doctorate, comprehensive exam, thesis/dissertation, qualifying exam, 18 credits. *Entrance requirements:* For master's, GRE, minimum GPA of 5.0 on an 8.0 scale; for doctorate, GRE. Additional exam requirements/recommendations for international students: Required—TOEFL, TOEFL (minimum iBT score of 80), IELTS (6.5), CanTEST (4.5), or PTE (59). Electronic applications accepted. *Faculty research:* Geotechnical/geo-environmental engineering, structural engineering, water resources engineering, civil engineering materials, environmental/sanitary engineering, hydrogeology, rock mechanics and mining, transportation engineering.

University of Utah, Graduate School, College of Mines and Earth Sciences, Department of Geology and Geophysics, Salt Lake City, UT 84112. Offers environmental engineering (ME, MS, PhD); geological engineering (ME, MS, PhD); geology (MS, PhD); geophysics (MS, PhD). *Faculty:* 32 full-time (8 women), 4 part-time/adjunct (2 women). *Students:* 54 full-time (21 women), 26 part-time (11 women); includes 6 minority (1 American Indian or Alaska Native, non-Hispanic/Latino; 4 Hispanic/Latino; 1 Two or more races, non-Hispanic/Latino), 16 international. Average age 30. 228 applicants, 14% accepted, 22 enrolled. In 2016, 18 master's, 3 doctorates awarded. Terminal master's awarded for partial completion of doctoral program. *Degree requirements:* For master's, comprehensive exam, thesis; for doctorate, thesis/dissertation, qualifying exam (written and oral). *Entrance requirements:* For master's and doctorate, GRE General Test, minimum GPA of 3.25. Additional exam requirements/recommendations for international students: Required—TOEFL (minimum score 500 paper-based; 61 iBT). *Application deadline:* For fall admission, 1/15 priority date for domestic and international students. Application fee: $55 ($65 for international students). Electronic applications accepted. *Expenses:* Tuition, state resident: full-time $7011; part-time $3918.24 per credit hour. Tuition, nonresident: full-time $22,154; part-time $11,665.42 per credit hour. *Financial support:* In 2016–17, 62 students received support, including 14 fellowships with full tuition reimbursements available (averaging $17,500 per year), 32 research assistantships with full tuition reimbursements available (averaging $23,000 per year), 16 teaching assistantships with full tuition reimbursements available (averaging $17,500 per year); career-related internships or fieldwork, institutionally sponsored loans, scholarships/grants, health care benefits, unspecified assistantships, and stipends also available. Financial award application deadline: 1/15; financial award applicants required to submit FAFSA. *Faculty research:* Igneous, metamorphic, and sedimentary petrology; stratigraphy; paleoclimatology; hydrology; seismology. *Total annual research expenditures:* $4.1 million. *Unit head:* Dr. John Bartley, Chair, 801-585-1670, Fax: 801-581-7065, E-mail: john.bartley@utah.edu. *Application contact:* Dr. Gabriel J. Bowen, Director of Graduate Studies, 801-585-7925, Fax: 801-581-7065, E-mail: gabe.bowen@utah.edu.
Website: http://www.earth.utah.edu/

University of Wisconsin–Madison, Graduate School, College of Engineering, Geological Engineering Program, Madison, WI 53706. Offers MS, PhD. *Program availability:* Part-time. *Faculty:* 28 full-time (6 women). *Students:* 12 full-time (2 women), 1 part-time (0 women); includes 1 minority (Two or more races, non-Hispanic/Latino), 5 international. Average age 25. 23 applicants, 48% accepted, 5 enrolled. In 2016, 2 master's, 2 doctorates awarded. *Degree requirements:* For master's, minimum of 30 credits; minimum GPA of 3.0; for doctorate, comprehensive exam, thesis/dissertation, minimum of 51 credits; minimum GPA of 3.0. *Entrance requirements:* For master's and doctorate, GRE, BS; minimum GPA of 3.0. Additional exam requirements/recommendations for international students: Required—TOEFL (minimum score 580 paper-based; 92 iBT), IELTS (minimum score 7). *Application deadline:* For fall admission, 12/15 priority date for domestic and international students; for spring admission, 9/1 for domestic and international students. Application fee: $75 ($81 for international students). Electronic applications accepted. *Expenses:* $13,157 per year in-state tuition and fees; $26,484 per year out-of-state tuition and fees. *Financial support:* In 2016–17, 13 students received support. Fellowships with full tuition reimbursements available, research assistantships with full tuition reimbursements available, teaching assistantships with full tuition reimbursements available, Federal Work-Study, scholarships/grants, and unspecified assistantships available. Support available to part-time students. Financial award application deadline: 12/1; financial award applicants required to submit FAFSA. *Faculty research:* Constitutive models for geomaterials, rock fracture, in situ stress determination, environmental geotechnics, site remediation. *Unit head:* William Likos, Chair, 608-890-2662, Fax: 608-263-2453, E-mail: likos@wisc.edu. *Application contact:* Cheryl Loschko, Student Services Coordinator, 608-890-2420, E-mail: loschko@wisc.edu.
Website: https://www.engr.wisc.edu/department/civil-environmental-engineering/academics/ms-phd-geological-engineering/

Mineral/Mining Engineering

Colorado School of Mines, Office of Graduate Studies, Department of Geophysics, Golden, CO 80401-1887. Offers geophysical engineering (ME, MS, PhD); geophysics (MS, PhD); hydrology (MS, PhD); mineral exploration and mining geosciences (PMS). *Program availability:* Part-time. *Degree requirements:* For master's, thesis (for some programs); for doctorate, comprehensive exam, thesis/dissertation. *Entrance requirements:* For master's and doctorate, GRE General Test. Additional exam requirements/recommendations for international students: Required—TOEFL (minimum score 550 paper-based; 80 iBT). Electronic applications accepted. *Expenses:* Tuition, state resident: full-time $15,690. Tuition, nonresident: full-time $34,020. *Required fees:* $2152. Tuition and fees vary according to course load. *Faculty research:* Seismic exploration, gravity and geomagnetic fields, electrical mapping and sounding, bore hole measurements, environmental physics.

Colorado School of Mines, Office of Graduate Studies, Department of Mining Engineering, Golden, CO 80401. Offers mining and earth systems engineering (MS); mining engineering (PhD); underground construction and tunneling (MS, PhD). *Program availability:* Part-time. *Degree requirements:* For master's, thesis (for some programs); for doctorate, comprehensive exam, thesis/dissertation. *Entrance requirements:* For master's and doctorate, GRE General Test. Additional exam requirements/recommendations for international students: Required—TOEFL (minimum score 550 paper-based; 80 iBT). Electronic applications accepted. *Expenses:* Tuition, state resident: full-time $15,690. Tuition, nonresident: full-time $34,020. *Required fees:* $2152. Tuition and fees vary according to course load. *Faculty research:* Mine evaluation and planning, geostatistics, mining robotics, water jet cutting, rock mechanics.

Dalhousie University, Faculty of Engineering, Department of Mineral Resource Engineering, Halifax, NS B3J 1Z1, Canada. Offers mineral resource engineering (M Eng, MA Sc, PhD). *Degree requirements:* For master's, thesis; for doctorate, thesis/dissertation. *Entrance requirements:* Additional exam requirements/recommendations for international students: Required—TOEFL, IELTS, CANTEST, CAEL, or Michigan English Language Assessment Battery. Electronic applications accepted. *Faculty research:* Mining technology, environmental impact, petroleum engineering, mine waste management, rock mechanics.

Laurentian University, School of Graduate Studies and Research, Programme in Geology (Earth Sciences), Sudbury, ON P3E 2C6, Canada. Offers geology (M Sc); mineral deposits and precambrian geology (PhD); mineral exploration (M Sc). *Program availability:* Part-time. *Degree requirements:* For master's, thesis. *Entrance requirements:* For master's, honors degree with second class or better. *Faculty research:* Localization and metallogenesis of Ni-Cu-(PGE) sulfide mineralization in the Thompson Nickel Belt, mapping lithology and ore-grade and monitoring dissolved organic carbon in lakes using remote sensing, global reefs, volcanic effects on VMS deposits.

Laurentian University, School of Graduate Studies and Research, School of Engineering, Sudbury, ON P3E 2C6, Canada. Offers mineral resources engineering (M Eng, MA Sc); natural resources engineering (PhD). *Program availability:* Part-time. *Faculty research:* Mining engineering, rock mechanics (tunneling, rockbursts, rock support), metallurgy (mineral processing, hydro and pyrometallurgy), simulations and remote mining, simulations and scheduling.

McGill University, Faculty of Graduate and Postdoctoral Studies, Faculty of Engineering, Department of Mining and Materials Engineering, Montréal, QC H3A 2T5, Canada. Offers materials engineering (M Eng, PhD); mining engineering (M Eng, M Sc, PhD, Diploma).

Missouri University of Science and Technology, Graduate School, Department of Mining and Nuclear Engineering, Rolla, MO 65409. Offers mining engineering (MS, DE, PhD); nuclear engineering (MS, DE, PhD). *Degree requirements:* For master's, thesis optional; for doctorate, comprehensive exam. *Entrance requirements:* For master's, GRE (minimum score 600 quantitative, 3 writing); for doctorate, GRE (minimum score: quantitative 600, writing 3.5). Additional exam requirements/recommendations for international students: Required—TOEFL (minimum score 550 paper-based). Electronic applications accepted. *Faculty research:* Mine health and safety, nuclear radiation transport, modeling of mining operations, radiation effects, blasting.

Montana Tech of The University of Montana, Department of Metallurgical/Mineral Processing Engineering, Butte, MT 59701-8997. Offers MS. *Program availability:* Part-time. *Faculty:* 6 full-time (0 women). *Students:* 6 full-time (4 women), 2 part-time (0 women); includes 2 minority (both Black or African American, non-Hispanic/Latino), 3 international. 4 applicants, 75% accepted, 3 enrolled. In 2016, 2 master's awarded. *Degree requirements:* For master's, comprehensive exam (for some programs), thesis optional. *Entrance requirements:* For master's, GRE General Test, minimum GPA of 3.0. Additional exam requirements/recommendations for international students: Required—TOEFL (minimum score 545 paper-based; 78 iBT), IELTS (minimum score 6.5). *Application deadline:* For fall admission, 4/1 priority date for domestic students, 3/1 priority date for international students; for spring admission, 10/1 priority date for domestic students, 6/1 priority date for international students. Applications are processed on a rolling basis. Application fee: $50. Electronic applications accepted. *Expenses:* Tuition, state resident: full-time $2901; part-time $1450.68 per degree program. Tuition, nonresident: full-time $8432; part-time $4215.84 per degree program. *Required fees:* $668; $354 per degree program. Tuition and fees vary according to course load and program. *Financial support:* In 2016–17, 4 students received support, including 2 teaching assistantships with partial tuition reimbursements available (averaging $5,000 per year); research assistantships with partial tuition reimbursements available, career-related internships or fieldwork, tuition waivers (full and partial), and unspecified assistantships also available. Financial award application deadline: 4/1; financial award applicants required to submit FAFSA. *Faculty research:* Stabilizing hazardous waste, decontamination of metals by melt refining, ultraviolet enhancement of stabilization reactions, extractive metallurgy, fuel cells. *Unit head:* Dr. Courtney Young, Department Head, 406-496-4158, Fax: 406-496-4664, E-mail: cyoung@mtech.edu. *Application contact:* Daniel Stirling, Administrator, Graduate School, 406-496-4304, Fax: 406-496-4710, E-mail: gradschool@mtech.edu.
Website: http://www.mtech.edu/academics/gradschool/degreeprograms/degrees-metallurgical.htm

Montana Tech of The University of Montana, Mining Engineering Program, Butte, MT 59701-8997. Offers MS. *Program availability:* Part-time. *Faculty:* 4 full-time (0 women). *Students:* 6 full-time (2 women), 1 part-time (0 women), 4 international. Average age 26. 9 applicants, 67% accepted, 6 enrolled. In 2016, 3 master's awarded. *Degree requirements:* For master's, thesis optional. *Entrance requirements:* For master's, minimum GPA of 3.0. Additional exam requirements/recommendations for international students: Required—TOEFL (minimum score 545 paper-based; 78 iBT), IELTS (minimum score 6.5). *Application deadline:* For fall admission, 4/1 priority date for domestic students, 3/1 priority date for international students; for spring admission, 10/1 priority date for domestic students, 6/1 priority date for international students. Applications are processed on a rolling basis. Application fee: $50. Electronic applications accepted. *Expenses:* Tuition, state resident: full-time $2901; part-time $1450.68 per degree program. Tuition, nonresident: full-time $8432; part-time $4215.84 per degree program. *Required fees:* $668; $354 per degree program. Tuition and fees vary according to course load and program. *Financial support:* In 2016–17, 2 students received support, including 2 teaching assistantships with partial tuition reimbursements available (averaging $4,000 per year); research assistantships, career-related internships or fieldwork, tuition waivers (full and partial), and unspecified assistantships also available. Financial award application deadline: 4/1; financial award applicants required to submit FAFSA. *Faculty research:* Geostatistics, geotechnics, mine planning, economic models, equipment selection. *Unit head:* Dr. Scott Rosenthal, Department Head, 406-496-4867, Fax: 406-496-4260, E-mail: srosenthal@mtech.edu. *Application contact:* Daniel Stirling, Administrator, Graduate School, 406-496-4304, Fax: 406-496-4710, E-mail: gradschool@mtech.edu.
Website: http://www.mtech.edu/academics/gradschool/degreeprograms/degrees-mining-engineering.htm

New Mexico Institute of Mining and Technology, Center for Graduate Studies, Department of Mineral Engineering, Socorro, NM 87801. Offers explosives engineering (MS); geotechnical engineering (MS); mining engineering (MS). *Degree requirements:* For master's, thesis. *Entrance requirements:* Additional exam requirements/recommendations for international students: Required—TOEFL (minimum score 540 paper-based). *Faculty research:* Drilling and blasting, geological engineering, mine design, applied mineral exploration, rock mechanics.

Penn State University Park, Graduate School, College of Earth and Mineral Sciences, John and Willie Leone Family Department of Energy and Mineral Engineering, University Park, PA 16802. Offers MS, PhD. *Unit head:* Dr. William E. Easterling, III, Dean, 814-865-7482, Fax: 814-863-7708. *Application contact:* Lori Hawn, Director, Graduate Student Services, 814-865-1795, Fax: 814-863-4627, E-mail: l-gswww@lists.psu.edu.
Website: http://eme.psu.edu/

Queen's University at Kingston, School of Graduate Studies, Faculty of Applied Science, Department of Mining Engineering, Kingston, ON K7L 3N6, Canada. Offers M Eng, M Sc, M Sc Eng, PhD. *Program availability:* Part-time. *Degree requirements:* For master's, thesis optional; for doctorate, comprehensive exam, thesis/dissertation. *Entrance requirements:* Additional exam requirements/recommendations for international students: Required—TOEFL (minimum score 550 paper-based). Electronic applications accepted. *Faculty research:* Rock mechanics, drilling, ventilation/environmental control, gold extraction.

South Dakota School of Mines and Technology, Graduate Division, Department of Mining Engineering and Management, Rapid City, SD 57701-3995. Offers mining engineering (MS). *Program availability:* Part-time. *Entrance requirements:* For master's, GRE General Test. Additional exam requirements/recommendations for international students: Required—TOEFL (minimum score 520 paper-based; 68 iBT), TWE. Electronic applications accepted.

Southern Illinois University Carbondale, Graduate School, College of Engineering, Department of Mining and Mineral Resources Engineering, Carbondale, IL 62901-4701. Offers mining engineering (MS). *Degree requirements:* For master's, comprehensive exam, thesis. *Entrance requirements:* For master's, GRE (recommended), minimum GPA of 2.7. Additional exam requirements/recommendations for international students: Required—TOEFL. *Faculty research:* Rock mechanics and ground control, mine subsidence, mine systems analysis, fine coal cleaning, surface mine reclamation.

Southern Illinois University Carbondale, Graduate School, College of Engineering, Program in Engineering Science, Carbondale, IL 62901-4701. Offers engineering science (PhD), including civil and environmental engineering, electrical and computer engineering, mechanical engineering and energy processes, mining and mineral resources engineering. *Degree requirements:* For doctorate, thesis/dissertation. *Entrance requirements:* For doctorate, GRE General Test, minimum GPA of 3.5. Additional exam requirements/recommendations for international students: Required—TOEFL.

Université du Québec en Abitibi-Témiscamingue, Graduate Programs, Program in Engineering, Rouyn-Noranda, QC J9X 5E4, Canada. Offers engineering (ME); mineral engineering (ME); mining engineering (DESS).

Université Laval, Faculty of Sciences and Engineering, Department of Mining, Metallurgical and Materials Engineering, Programs in Mining Engineering, Québec, QC G1K 7P4, Canada. Offers M Sc, PhD. Terminal master's awarded for partial completion of doctoral program. *Degree requirements:* For master's, thesis; for doctorate, comprehensive exam, thesis/dissertation. *Entrance requirements:* For master's and doctorate, knowledge of French and English. Electronic applications accepted.

University of Alaska Fairbanks, College of Engineering and Mines, Department of Mining and Geological Engineering, Fairbanks, AK 99775-5800. Offers geological engineering (MS); mineral preparation engineering (MS); mining engineering (MS). *Program availability:* Part-time. *Faculty:* 7 full-time (1 woman). *Students:* 4 full-time (1 woman), 4 part-time (0 women); includes 2 minority (1 American Indian or Alaska Native, non-Hispanic/Latino; 1 Two or more races, non-Hispanic/Latino), 5 international. Average age 31. 7 applicants, 43% accepted, 2 enrolled. In 2016, 2 master's awarded. *Degree requirements:* For master's, comprehensive exam, oral defense of project or thesis. *Entrance requirements:* For master's, GRE General Test (for geological engineering), bachelor's degree from accredited institution with minimum cumulative undergraduate and major GPA of 3.0. Additional exam requirements/recommendations for international students: Required—TOEFL (minimum score 550 paper-based; 79 iBT), IELTS (minimum score 6.5). *Application deadline:* For fall admission, 6/1 for domestic students, 3/1 for international students; for spring admission, 10/15 for domestic students, 9/1 for international students. Applications are processed on a rolling basis. Application fee: $60. Electronic applications accepted. *Expenses:* $533 per credit resident tuition, $673 per semester resident fees; $1,088 per credit non-resident tuition, $835 per semester non-resident fees. *Financial support:* In 2016–17, 1 research assistantship with full tuition reimbursement (averaging $16,834 per year), 2 teaching assistantships with full tuition reimbursements (averaging $7,302 per year) were awarded; fellowships with full tuition reimbursements, career-related internships or fieldwork, Federal Work-Study, scholarships/grants, health care benefits, and unspecified assistantships also available. Support available to part-time students. Financial award application deadline: 7/1; financial award applicants required to submit FAFSA. *Faculty research:* Underground mining in permafrost, testing of ultra clean diesel, slope stability, fractal and mathematical morphology, soil and rock mechanics. *Unit head:* Dr. Margaret Darrow, Chair, 907-474-7388, Fax: 907-474-6635, E-mail: cem.mingeo@alaska.edu. *Application contact:* Mary Kreta, Director of Admissions, 907-474-7500, Fax: 907-474-7097, E-mail: admissions@uaf.edu.
Website: http://cem.uaf.edu/mingeo

University of Alberta, Faculty of Graduate Studies and Research, Department of Civil and Environmental Engineering, Edmonton, AB T6G 2E1, Canada. Offers construction engineering and management (M Eng, M Sc, PhD); environmental engineering (M Eng, M Sc, PhD); environmental science (M Sc, PhD); geoenvironmental engineering (M Eng, M Sc, PhD); geotechnical engineering (M Eng, M Sc, PhD); mining engineering (M Eng, M Sc, PhD); petroleum engineering (M Eng, M Sc, PhD); structural engineering (M Eng, M Sc, PhD); water resources (M Eng, M Sc, PhD). *Program availability:* Part-time, online learning. *Degree requirements:* For master's, thesis (for some programs); for doctorate, thesis/dissertation. *Entrance requirements:* For master's, minimum GPA of 3.0 in last 2 years of undergraduate studies; for doctorate, minimum GPA of 3.0. Additional exam requirements/recommendations for international students: Required—TOEFL (minimum score 550 paper-based). Electronic applications accepted. *Faculty research:* Mining.

The University of Arizona, College of Engineering, Department of Mining and Geological Engineering, Tucson, AZ 85721. Offers mining and geological engineering (MS, PhD); mining engineering (Certificate), including mine health and safety, mine information and production technology, rock mechanics. *Program availability:* Part-time, online learning. *Degree requirements:* For master's, thesis; for doctorate, thesis/dissertation. *Entrance requirements:* For master's, GRE General Test, 3 letters of recommendation; for doctorate, GRE General Test, 3 letters of recommendation, statements of purpose. Additional exam requirements/recommendations for international students: Required—TOEFL (minimum score 550 paper-based; 79 iBT). Electronic applications accepted. *Faculty research:* Geomechanics, mineral processing, information technology, automation, geosensing.

The University of British Columbia, Faculty of Applied Science, Department of Mining Engineering, Vancouver, BC V6T 1Z4, Canada. Offers M Eng, MA Sc, PhD. *Degree requirements:* For master's, thesis; for doctorate, thesis/dissertation. *Entrance requirements:* Additional exam requirements/recommendations for international students: Required—TOEFL, IELTS. *Application deadline:* For spring admission, 11/1 for international students. Application fee: $100 ($162 for international students). Electronic applications accepted. *Expenses:* $4,802 per year tuition and fees, $8,436 per year international (for MA Sc and PhD); $5,835 per year tuition and fees, $18,900 per year international (for M Eng). *Financial support:* Fellowships, research assistantships, teaching assistantships, and career-related internships or fieldwork available. *Faculty research:* Advanced mining methods and automation, rock mechanics, mine economics, operations research, mine waste management, environmental aspects of mining, process control, fine particle processing, surface chemistry. *Application contact:* Maria Lui, Graduate Program Staff, 604-822-2540, E-mail: gradprogram@mining.ubc.ca.
Website: http://mining.ubc.ca/graduate/

University of Kentucky, Graduate School, College of Engineering, Program in Mining Engineering, Lexington, KY 40506-0032. Offers MME, MS Min, PhD. *Degree requirements:* For master's, comprehensive exam, thesis optional; for doctorate, one foreign language, comprehensive exam, thesis/dissertation. *Entrance requirements:* For master's, GRE General Test, minimum undergraduate GPA of 2.75; for doctorate, GRE General Test, minimum undergraduate GPA of 3.0. Additional exam requirements/recommendations for international students: Required—TOEFL (minimum score 550 paper-based). Electronic applications accepted. *Faculty research:* Benefication of fine and ultrafine particles, operation research in mining and mineral processing, land reclamation.

University of Nevada, Reno, Graduate School, College of Science, Mackay School of Earth Sciences and Engineering, Department of Mining Engineering, Reno, NV 89557. Offers MS. *Degree requirements:* For master's, thesis optional. *Entrance requirements:* For master's, GRE, minimum GPA of 2.75. Additional exam requirements/recommendations for international students: Required—TOEFL (minimum score 500 paper-based; 61 iBT), IELTS (minimum score 6). Electronic applications accepted. *Faculty research:* Mine ventilation, rock mechanics, mine design.

The University of Texas at Austin, Graduate School, Cockrell School of Engineering, Department of Petroleum and Geosystems Engineering, Program in Energy and Earth Resources, Austin, TX 78712-1111. Offers MA. *Degree requirements:* For master's, thesis, seminar. *Entrance requirements:* For master's, GRE General Test. Additional exam requirements/recommendations for international students: Required—TOEFL. Electronic applications accepted.

University of Utah, Graduate School, College of Mines and Earth Sciences, Department of Mining Engineering, Salt Lake City, UT 84112. Offers ME, MS, PhD. *Program availability:* Part-time. *Faculty:* 4 full-time (0 women), 1 part-time/adjunct (0 women). *Students:* 9 full-time (3 women), 2 part-time (1 woman); includes 1 minority (Two or more races, non-Hispanic/Latino), 1 international. Average age 30. 24 applicants, 21% accepted, 3 enrolled. In 2016, 1 master's, 7 doctorates awarded. *Degree requirements:* For master's, comprehensive exam (for some programs), thesis (for some programs); for doctorate, one foreign language, comprehensive exam, thesis/dissertation. *Entrance requirements:* For master's, minimum undergraduate GPA of 3.0; for doctorate, GRE General Test, minimum undergraduate GPA of 3.0. Additional exam requirements/recommendations for international students: Required—TOEFL (minimum score 550 paper-based; 80 iBT). *Application deadline:* For fall admission, 4/1 for domestic and international students; for spring admission, 11/1 priority date for domestic students, 11/1 for international students. Application fee: $55 ($65 for international students). Electronic applications accepted. *Expenses:* Contact institution. *Financial support:* In 2016–17, 10 students received support, including 4 fellowships with tuition reimbursements available (averaging $24,000 per year), 4 research assistantships with tuition reimbursements available (averaging $24,000 per year), 1 teaching assistantship with tuition reimbursement available (averaging $24,000 per year); career-related internships or fieldwork, institutionally sponsored loans, health care benefits, and unspecified assistantships also available. Support available to part-time students. Financial award application deadline: 4/15. *Faculty research:* Blasting, underground coal mine design and operations, rock mechanics, mine ventilation, 2-D and 3-D visualization, mine automation, mine safety. *Total annual research expenditures:* $324,354. *Unit head:* Dr. Michael Gordon Nelson, Chair, 801-585-3064, Fax: 801-585-5410, E-mail: mike.nelson@utah.edu. *Application contact:* Pam Hofmann, Administrative Manager, 801-581-7198, Fax: 801-585-5410, E-mail: pam.hofmann@utah.edu.
Website: http://www.mining.utah.edu/

Virginia Polytechnic Institute and State University, Graduate School, College of Engineering, Blacksburg, VA 24061. Offers aerospace engineering (ME, MS, PhD); biological systems engineering (ME, MS, PhD); biomedical engineering (MS, PhD); chemical engineering (ME, MS, PhD); civil engineering (ME, MS, PhD); computer engineering (ME, MS, PhD); computer science (MS, PhD); electrical engineering (ME, PhD); engineering education (PhD); engineering mechanics (ME, MS, PhD); environmental engineering (MS); environmental science and engineering (MS); industrial and systems engineering (ME, MS, PhD); materials science and engineering (ME, MS, PhD); mechanical engineering (ME, MS, PhD); mining and minerals engineering (PhD); mining engineering (ME, MS); nuclear engineering (MS, PhD); ocean engineering (MS); systems engineering (ME, MS). *Faculty:* 400 full-time (73 women), 3 part-time/adjunct (2 women). *Students:* 1,949 full-time (487 women), 393 part-time (69 women); includes 251 minority (56 Black or African American, non-Hispanic/Latino; 3 American Indian or Alaska Native, non-Hispanic/Latino; 87 Asian, non-Hispanic/Latino; 70 Hispanic/Latino; 35 Two or more races, non-Hispanic/Latino), 1,354 international. Average age 27. 4,903 applicants, 19% accepted, 569 enrolled. In 2016, 364 master's, 200 doctorates awarded. *Degree requirements:* For master's, comprehensive exam (for some programs), thesis (for some programs); for doctorate, comprehensive exam (for some programs), thesis/dissertation (for some programs). *Entrance requirements:* For master's and doctorate, GRE/GMAT. Additional exam requirements/recommendations for international students: Required—TOEFL (minimum score 80 iBT). *Application deadline:* For fall admission, 8/1 for domestic students, 4/1 for international students; for spring admission, 1/1 for domestic students, 9/1 for international students. Applications are processed on a rolling basis. Application fee: $75. Electronic applications accepted. *Expenses:* Tuition, state resident: full-time $12,467; part-time $692.50 per credit hour. Tuition, nonresident: full-time $25,095; part-time $1394.25 per credit hour. *Required fees:* $2669; $491.50 per semester. Tuition and fees vary according to course load, campus/location and program. *Financial support:* In 2016–17, 160 fellowships with full tuition reimbursements (averaging $7,387 per year), 872 research assistantships with full tuition reimbursements (averaging $22,329 per year), 313 teaching assistantships with full tuition reimbursements (averaging $18,714 per year) were awarded. Financial award application deadline: 3/1; financial award applicants required to submit FAFSA. *Total annual research expenditures:* $91.8 million. *Unit head:* Dr. Julia Ross, Dean, 540-231-9752, Fax: 540-231-3031, E-mail: deaneng@vt.edu. *Application contact:* Linda Perkins, Executive Assistant, 540-231-9752, Fax: 540-231-3031, E-mail: lperkins@vt.edu.
Website: http://www.eng.vt.edu/

West Virginia University, Statler College of Engineering and Mineral Resources, Department of Mining Engineering, Morgantown, WV 26506. Offers MS Min E, PhD. *Program availability:* Part-time. *Degree requirements:* For master's, thesis; for doctorate, comprehensive exam, thesis/dissertation. *Entrance requirements:* For master's, minimum GPA of 3.0; for doctorate, GRE General Test, MS in mineral engineering, minimum GPA of 3.5. Additional exam requirements/recommendations for international students: Required—TOEFL. *Faculty research:* Mine safety.

Petroleum Engineering

Colorado School of Mines, Office of Graduate Studies, Department of Petroleum Engineering, Golden, CO 80401. Offers petroleum engineering (ME, MS, PhD); petroleum reservoir systems (PMS). *Program availability:* Part-time. *Degree requirements:* For master's, thesis (for some programs); for doctorate, comprehensive exam, thesis/dissertation. *Entrance requirements:* For master's and doctorate, GRE General Test. Additional exam requirements/recommendations for international students: Required—TOEFL (minimum score 550 paper-based; 80 iBT). Electronic applications accepted. *Expenses:* Tuition, state resident: full-time $15,690. Tuition, nonresident: full-time $34,020. *Required fees:* $2152. Tuition and fees vary according to course load. *Faculty research:* Dynamic rock mechanics, deflagration theory, geostatistics, geochemistry, petrophysics.

Louisiana State University and Agricultural & Mechanical College, Graduate School, College of Engineering, Department of Petroleum Engineering, Baton Rouge, LA 70803. Offers MS Pet E, PhD.

Missouri University of Science and Technology, Graduate School, Department of Geological Sciences and Engineering, Rolla, MO 65409. Offers geological engineering (MS, DE, PhD); geology and geophysics (MS, PhD), including geochemistry, geology, geophysics, groundwater and environmental geology; petroleum engineering (MS, DE, PhD). *Program availability:* Part-time. *Degree requirements:* For master's, thesis optional; for doctorate, comprehensive exam, thesis/dissertation. *Entrance requirements:* For master's, GRE General Test (minimum score 600 quantitative, writing 3.5), minimum GPA of 3.0 in last 4 semesters; for doctorate, GRE General Test (minimum scores: Quantitative 600, Writing 3.5). Additional exam requirements/recommendations for international students: Required—TOEFL (minimum score 550 paper-based). Electronic applications accepted. *Faculty research:* Digital image processing and geographic information systems, mineralogy, igneous and sedimentary petrology-geochemistry, sedimentology groundwater hydrology and contaminant transport.

Montana Tech of The University of Montana, Department of Petroleum Engineering, Butte, MT 59701-8997. Offers MS. *Program availability:* Part-time, evening/weekend. *Faculty:* 8 full-time (2 women), 1 part-time/adjunct (0 women). *Students:* 7 full-time (0 women), 1 part-time (0 women); includes 1 minority (American Indian or Alaska Native, non-Hispanic/Latino), 2 international. 23 applicants, 9% accepted, 2 enrolled. In 2016, 4 master's awarded. *Degree requirements:* For master's, comprehensive exam, thesis optional. *Entrance requirements:* For master's, minimum GPA of 3.0. Additional exam requirements/recommendations for international students: Required—TOEFL (minimum score 545 paper-based; 78 iBT), IELTS (minimum score 6.5). *Application deadline:* For fall admission, 4/1 priority date for domestic students, 3/1 priority date for international students; for spring admission, 10/1 priority date for domestic students, 6/1 priority date for international students. Applications are processed on a rolling basis. Application fee: $50. Electronic applications accepted. *Expenses:* Tuition, state resident: full-time $2901; part-time $1450.68 per degree program. Tuition, nonresident: full-time $8432; part-time $4215.84 per degree program. *Required fees:* $668; $354 per degree program. Tuition and fees vary according to course load and program. *Financial support:* In 2016–17, 6 students received support, including 5 teaching assistantships with partial tuition reimbursements available (averaging $4,800 per year); research assistantships, career-related internships or fieldwork, institutionally sponsored loans, tuition waivers (full and partial), and unspecified assistantships also available. Financial award application deadline: 4/1; financial award applicants required to submit FAFSA. *Faculty research:* Reservoir characterization, simulations, near well bore problems, environmental waste. *Unit head:* Burt Todd, Head, 406-496-4834, Fax: 406-496-4417, E-mail: btodd@mtech.edu. *Application contact:* Daniel Stirling, Administrator, Graduate School, 406-496-4304, Fax: 406-496-4710, E-mail: gradschool@mtech.edu.
Website: http://www.mtech.edu/academics/gradschool/degreeprograms/degrees-petroleum-engineering.htm

New Mexico Institute of Mining and Technology, Center for Graduate Studies, Department of Petroleum and Natural Gas Engineering, Socorro, NM 87801. Offers petroleum engineering (MS, PhD). *Degree requirements:* For master's, thesis optional; for doctorate, thesis/dissertation. *Entrance requirements:* For master's, GRE General Test; for doctorate, GRE General Test, GRE Subject Test. Additional exam requirements/recommendations for international students: Required—TOEFL (minimum score 540 paper-based). *Faculty research:* Enhanced recovery processes, drilling and production, reservoir evaluation, produced water management, wettability and phase behavior.

Petroleum Engineering

Texas A&M University, College of Engineering, Department of Petroleum Engineering, College Station, TX 77843. Offers M Eng, MS, PhD. *Program availability:* Part-time, online learning. *Faculty:* 34. *Students:* 257 full-time (47 women), 142 part-time (24 women); includes 70 minority (7 Black or African American, non-Hispanic/Latino; 1 American Indian or Alaska Native, non-Hispanic/Latino; 23 Asian, non-Hispanic/Latino; 33 Hispanic/Latino; 6 Two or more races, non-Hispanic/Latino), 205 international. Average age 29. 465 applicants, 21% accepted, 73 enrolled. In 2016, 100 master's, 14 doctorates awarded. *Degree requirements:* For master's, comprehensive exam, thesis (MS); for doctorate, comprehensive exam, thesis/dissertation. *Entrance requirements:* For master's and doctorate, GRE General Test. Additional exam requirements/recommendations for international students: Required—TOEFL (minimum score 550 paper-based; 80 iBT), IELTS (minimum score 6), PTE (minimum score 53). *Application deadline:* For fall admission, 12/15 for domestic students; for spring admission, 9/1 for domestic students; for summer admission, 11/1 for domestic students. Applications are processed on a rolling basis. Application fee: $50 ($90 for international students). Electronic applications accepted. *Expenses:* Contact institution. *Financial support:* In 2016–17, 248 students received support, including 6 fellowships with tuition reimbursements available (averaging $18,667 per year), 139 research assistantships with tuition reimbursements available (averaging $5,861 per year), 53 teaching assistantships with tuition reimbursements available (averaging $8,513 per year); career-related internships or fieldwork, institutionally sponsored loans, scholarships/grants, traineeships, health care benefits, tuition waivers (full and partial), and unspecified assistantships also available. Support available to part-time students. Financial award application deadline: 3/15; financial award applicants required to submit FAFSA. *Faculty research:* Drilling and well stimulation, well completions and well performance, reservoir modeling and reservoir description, reservoir simulation, improved/enhanced recovery. *Unit head:* Dr. A. Daniel Hill, Department Head, 979-845-2244, E-mail: dan.hill@pe.tamu.edu. *Application contact:* Graduate Advisor, 979-847-9095, E-mail: graduate_program@pe.tamu.edu.
Website: http://engineering.tamu.edu/petroleum

Texas A&M University–Kingsville, College of Graduate Studies, Frank H. Dotterweich College of Engineering, Wayne H. King Department of Chemical and Natural Gas Engineering, Program in Natural Gas Engineering, Kingsville, TX 78363. Offers ME, MS. *Degree requirements:* For master's, variable foreign language requirement, comprehensive exam, thesis (for some programs). *Entrance requirements:* For master's, GRE (minimum quantitative score of 150, verbal 145), MAT, GMAT, minimum GPA of 2.7. Additional exam requirements/recommendations for international students: Required—TOEFL (minimum score 550 paper-based; 79 iBT). Electronic applications accepted.

Texas Tech University, Graduate School, Edward E. Whitacre Jr. College of Engineering, Bob L. Herd Department of Petroleum Engineering, Lubbock, TX 79409. Offers MSPE, PhD. *Program availability:* Part-time. *Faculty:* 10 full-time (0 women), 2 part-time/adjunct (0 women). *Students:* 67 full-time (8 women), 18 part-time (2 women); includes 4 minority (2 Black or African American, non-Hispanic/Latino; 1 Hispanic/Latino; 1 Two or more races, non-Hispanic/Latino), 76 international. Average age 30. 211 applicants, 24% accepted, 18 enrolled. In 2016, 12 master's, 3 doctorates awarded. *Degree requirements:* For master's, comprehensive exam, thesis (for some programs); for doctorate, comprehensive exam, thesis/dissertation, qualifying exam, proposal defense exam. *Entrance requirements:* For master's, GRE (Verbal and Quantitative), Graduate Certificate in petroleum engineering (for non-petroleum students); for doctorate, GRE (Verbal and Quantitative). Additional exam requirements/recommendations for international students: Required—TOEFL (minimum score 550 paper-based; 79 iBT), IELTS (minimum score 6.5). *Application deadline:* For fall admission, 6/1 priority date for domestic students, 1/15 priority date for international students; for spring admission, 9/1 priority date for domestic students, 6/15 priority date for international students. Applications are processed on a rolling basis. Application fee: $75. Electronic applications accepted. *Expenses:* $325 per credit hour full-time resident tuition, $733 per credit hour full-time non-resident tuition; $53.75 per credit hour fee plus $608 per term fee. *Financial support:* In 2016–17, 60 students received support, including 55 fellowships (averaging $1,791 per year), 10 research assistantships (averaging $12,899 per year), 24 teaching assistantships (averaging $22,244 per year); scholarships/grants, tuition waivers (partial), and unspecified assistantships also available. Financial award application deadline: 5/22; financial award applicants required to submit FAFSA. *Faculty research:* Development of conventional/unconventional oil and gas resources; enhanced oil recovery processes; oil and gas reserves definitions and economics; drilling and completion practices; production engineering and stimulation including latest in hydraulic fracturing technology. *Total annual research expenditures:* $705,050. *Unit head:* Dr. Marshall C. Watson, Chair, 806-742-1801, Fax: 806-742-3502, E-mail: marshall.watson@ttu.edu. *Application contact:* Dr. Habib K. Menouar, Graduate Advisor, 806-834-3452, Fax: 806-742-3502, E-mail: habib.menouar@ttu.edu.
Website: http://www.pe.ttu.edu/

University of Alaska Fairbanks, College of Engineering and Mines, Department of Petroleum Engineering, Fairbanks, AK 99775. Offers MS. *Program availability:* Part-time. *Faculty:* 5 full-time (0 women). *Students:* 10 full-time (1 woman), 12 part-time (1 woman); includes 1 minority (Black or African American, non-Hispanic/Latino), 15 international. Average age 29. 53 applicants, 11% accepted, 1 enrolled. In 2016, 10 master's awarded. *Degree requirements:* For master's, comprehensive exam, oral defense of project or thesis. *Entrance requirements:* For master's, bachelor's degree in engineering or the natural sciences with minimum cumulative undergraduate and major GPA of 3.0. Additional exam requirements/recommendations for international students: Required—TOEFL (minimum score 550 paper-based; 79 iBT), IELTS (minimum score 6.5). *Application deadline:* For fall admission, 6/1 for domestic students, 3/1 for international students; for spring admission, 10/15 for domestic students, 9/1 for international students. Applications are processed on a rolling basis. Application fee: $60. Electronic applications accepted. *Expenses:* $533 per credit resident tuition, $673 per semester resident fees; $1,088 per credit non-resident tuition, $835 per semester non-resident fees. *Financial support:* In 2016–17, 1 research assistantship with full tuition reimbursement (averaging $6,202 per year), 6 teaching assistantships with full tuition reimbursements (averaging $6,542 per year) were awarded; fellowships with full tuition reimbursements, career-related internships or fieldwork, Federal Work-Study, scholarships/grants, health care benefits, and unspecified assistantships also available. Support available to part-time students. Financial award application deadline: 7/1; financial award applicants required to submit FAFSA. *Faculty research:* Gas-to-liquid transportation hydraulics and issues, carbon sequestration, enhanced oil recovery, reservoir engineering, coal bed methane. *Unit head:* Dr. Abhijit Dandekar, Chair, 907-474-7734, Fax: 907-474-5912, E-mail: uaf-pete-dept@alaska.edu. *Application contact:* Mary Kreta, Director of Admissions, 907-474-7500, Fax: 907-474-7097, E-mail: admissions@uaf.edu.
Website: http://cem.uaf.edu/pete/

University of Alberta, Faculty of Graduate Studies and Research, Department of Civil and Environmental Engineering, Edmonton, AB T6G 2E1, Canada. Offers construction engineering and management (M Eng, M Sc, PhD); environmental engineering (M Eng, M Sc, PhD); environmental science (M Sc, PhD); geoenvironmental engineering (M Eng, M Sc, PhD); geotechnical engineering (M Eng, M Sc, PhD); mining engineering (M Eng, M Sc, PhD); petroleum engineering (M Eng, M Sc, PhD); structural engineering (M Eng, M Sc, PhD); water resources (M Eng, M Sc, PhD). *Program availability:* Part-time, online learning. *Degree requirements:* For master's, thesis (for some programs); for doctorate, thesis/dissertation. *Entrance requirements:* For master's, minimum GPA of 3.0 in last 2 years of undergraduate studies; for doctorate, minimum GPA of 3.0. Additional exam requirements/recommendations for international students: Required—TOEFL (minimum score 550 paper-based). Electronic applications accepted. *Faculty research:* Mining.

University of Calgary, Faculty of Graduate Studies, Schulich School of Engineering, Department of Chemical and Petroleum Engineering, Calgary, AB T2N 1N4, Canada. Offers chemical engineering (M Eng, M Sc, PhD); energy and environment engineering (M Eng, M Sc, PhD); energy and environmental systems (M Eng, M Sc, PhD); environmental engineering (M Eng, M Sc, PhD); petroleum engineering (M Eng, M Sc, PhD); reservoir characterization (M Eng, M Sc). *Program availability:* Part-time. *Degree requirements:* For master's, thesis (for some programs); for doctorate, comprehensive exam, thesis/dissertation, candidacy exam. *Entrance requirements:* For master's, minimum GPA of 3.0 or equivalent; for doctorate, minimum GPA of 3.5 or equivalent. Additional exam requirements/recommendations for international students: Required—TOEFL (minimum score 550 paper-based; 80 iBT), IELTS (minimum score 7). Electronic applications accepted. *Faculty research:* Environmental engineering, biomedical engineering modeling, simulation and control, petroleum recovery and reservoir engineering, phase equilibria and transport properties.

University of Houston, Cullen College of Engineering, Department of Chemical and Biomolecular Engineering, Houston, TX 77204. Offers chemical engineering (MCHE, PhD); petroleum engineering (M Pet E). *Program availability:* Part-time. Terminal master's awarded for partial completion of doctoral program. *Entrance requirements:* For master's and doctorate, GRE General Test. Additional exam requirements/recommendations for international students: Required—TOEFL (minimum score 550 paper-based; 79 iBT), IELTS (minimum score 6.5). *Faculty research:* Chemical engineering.

The University of Kansas, Graduate Studies, School of Engineering, Program in Chemical and Petroleum Engineering, Lawrence, KS 66045. Offers chemical and petroleum engineering (PhD); chemical engineering (MS); petroleum engineering (MS); petroleum management (Certificate). *Program availability:* Part-time. *Students:* 46 full-time (16 women), 3 part-time (0 women); includes 1 minority (Two or more races, non-Hispanic/Latino), 36 international. Average age 26. 135 applicants, 11% accepted, 5 enrolled. In 2016, 4 master's, 5 doctorates, 6 other advanced degrees awarded. *Entrance requirements:* For master's, GRE General Test, minimum GPA of 3.0, resume, personal statement, transcripts, three letters of recommendation; for doctorate, GRE General Test, minimum GPA of 3.5, resume, personal statement, transcripts, three letters of recommendation. Additional exam requirements/recommendations for international students: Required—TOEFL or IELTS. *Application deadline:* For fall admission, 12/15 priority date for domestic and international students; for spring admission, 8/31 priority date for domestic and international students. Application fee: $65 ($85 for international students). Electronic applications accepted. *Financial support:* Fellowships, research assistantships, teaching assistantships, career-related internships or fieldwork, Federal Work-Study, scholarships/grants, traineeships, and unspecified assistantships available. Financial award application deadline: 12/15; financial award applicants required to submit FAFSA. *Faculty research:* Enhanced oil recovery, catalysis and kinetics, electrochemical engineering, biomedical engineering, semiconductor materials processing. *Unit head:* Laurence Weatherley, Chair, 785-864-3553, E-mail: lweather@ku.edu. *Application contact:* Graduate Admission Contact, 785-864-2900, E-mail: cpegrad@ku.edu.
Website: http://www.cpe.engr.ku.edu

The University of Kansas, Graduate Studies, School of Engineering, Program in Petroleum Engineering, Lawrence, KS 66045. Offers petroleum engineering (MS); petroleum management (Certificate). *Program availability:* Part-time. *Students:* 8 full-time (4 women), 1 part-time (0 women), 7 international. Average age 26. 56 applicants. In 2016, 3 master's, 6 other advanced degrees awarded. *Entrance requirements:* For master's, GRE, resume, personal statement, transcripts, three letters of recommendation. Additional exam requirements/recommendations for international students: Required—TOEFL, GRE or IELTS. *Application deadline:* For fall admission, 12/15 priority date for domestic and international students; for spring admission, 8/31 priority date for domestic and international students. Application fee: $65 ($85 for international students). Electronic applications accepted. *Financial support:* Research assistantships, teaching assistantships, Federal Work-Study, scholarships/grants, and unspecified assistantships available. Financial award application deadline: 12/15. *Unit head:* Laurence Weatherley, Chair, 785-864-3553, E-mail: lweather@ku.edu. *Application contact:* Graduate Admission Contact, 785-864-2900, E-mail: cpegrad@ku.edu.
Website: http://www.cpe.engr.ku.edu/

University of Louisiana at Lafayette, College of Engineering, Department of Petroleum Engineering, Lafayette, LA 70504. Offers MSE. *Program availability:* Evening/weekend. *Degree requirements:* For master's, comprehensive exam, thesis or alternative. *Entrance requirements:* For master's, GRE General Test, minimum GPA of 2.85. Electronic applications accepted.

University of Oklahoma, Mewbourne College of Earth and Energy, Mewbourne School of Petroleum and Geological Engineering, Program in Natural Gas Engineering and Management, Norman, OK 73019-1003. Offers natural gas engineering and management (MS); natural gas technology (Graduate Certificate). *Program availability:* Part-time. *Students:* 6 full-time (0 women), 12 part-time (1 woman); includes 1 minority (Hispanic/Latino), 12 international. Average age 30. 9 applicants, 67% accepted, 4 enrolled. In 2016, 7 master's awarded. Terminal master's awarded for partial completion of doctoral program. *Degree requirements:* For master's, variable foreign language requirement, comprehensive exam (for some programs), thesis (for some programs). *Entrance requirements:* For master's, GRE, minimum GPA of 3.2, three letters of recommendation, statement of purpose, resume/curriculum vitae. Additional exam requirements/recommendations for international students: Required—TOEFL (minimum score 79 iBT) or IELTS (minimum score 6.5). *Application deadline:* For fall admission, 3/1 for domestic and international students; for spring admission, 9/1 for domestic and international students. Application fee: $50 ($100 for international students). Electronic applications accepted. *Expenses:* Tuition, state resident: full-time $4886; part-time $203.60 per credit hour. Tuition, nonresident: full-time $18,989; part-time $791.20 per credit hour. *Required fees:* $3283; $126.25 per credit hour. $126.50 per semester. *Financial support:* In 2016–17, 6 students received support. Unspecified assistantships available. Financial award application deadline: 6/1; financial award applicants required to submit FAFSA. *Faculty research:* Natural gas processing, field production technology, oil/gas project management. *Unit head:* Dr. Suresh Sharma, Director of Natural Gas and Management Programs, 405-325-5928, Fax: 405-325-7477, E-mail: ssharma@ou.edu. *Application contact:* Sheriee Parnell, Graduate Programs Coordinator, 405-325-6821, Fax: 405-325-7477, E-mail: sheriee@ou.edu.
Website: http://mpge.ou.edu

University of Oklahoma, Mewbourne College of Earth and Energy, Mewbourne School of Petroleum and Geological Engineering, Program in Petroleum Engineering, Norman, OK 73019-1003. Offers MS, PhD. *Program availability:* Part-time. *Students:* 85 full-time (13 women), 45 part-time (10 women); includes 6 minority (2 Black or African American, non-Hispanic/Latino; 3 Asian, non-Hispanic/Latino; 1 Two or more races, non-Hispanic/Latino), 107 international. Average age 28. 207 applicants, 11% accepted, 20 enrolled. In 2016, 21 master's, 6 doctorates awarded. Terminal master's awarded for partial completion of doctoral program. *Degree requirements:* For master's, variable foreign language requirement, comprehensive exam (for some programs), thesis (for some programs); for doctorate, variable foreign language requirement, comprehensive exam, thesis/dissertation. *Entrance requirements:* For master's and doctorate, GRE General Test, minimum GPA of 3.2, three letters of recommendation, statement of purpose, resume/curriculum vitae. Additional exam requirements/recommendations for international students: Required—TOEFL (minimum score 79 iBT) or IELTS (minimum score 6.5). *Application deadline:* For fall admission, 3/1 for domestic and international students; for spring admission, 9/1 for domestic and international students. Application fee: $50 ($100 for international students). Electronic applications accepted. *Expenses:* Tuition, state resident: full-time $4886; part-time $203.60 per credit hour. Tuition, nonresident: full-time $18,989; part-time $791.20 per credit hour. *Required fees:* $3283; $126.25 per credit hour. $126.50 per semester. *Financial support:* In 2016–17, 91 students received support. Unspecified assistantships available. Financial award application deadline: 6/1; financial award applicants required to submit FAFSA. *Faculty research:* Unconventional oil, reservoir, oil and gas processing, flow assurance and mitigation in reservoirs. *Unit head:* Dr. Deepak Devegowda, Associate Professor and Graduate Liaison, 405-325-3081, Fax: 405-325-7477, E-mail: deepak.devegowda@ou.edu. *Application contact:* Sheriee Parnell, Graduate Programs Coordinator, 405-325-6821, Fax: 405-325-7477, E-mail: sheriee@ou.edu.
Website: http://mpge.ou.edu

University of Pittsburgh, Swanson School of Engineering, Department of Chemical and Petroleum Engineering, Pittsburgh, PA 15260. Offers chemical engineering (MS Ch E, PhD); petroleum engineering (MSPE); MS Ch E/MSPE. *Program availability:* Part-time, 100% online. *Faculty:* 22 full-time (4 women), 12 part-time/adjunct (1 woman). *Students:* 106 full-time (36 women), 11 part-time (3 women); includes 11 minority (4 Black or African American, non-Hispanic/Latino; 3 Asian, non-Hispanic/Latino; 1 Hispanic/Latino; 3 Two or more races, non-Hispanic/Latino), 73 international. 336 applicants, 45% accepted, 42 enrolled. In 2016, 25 master's, 10 doctorates awarded. Terminal master's awarded for partial completion of doctoral program. *Degree requirements:* For doctorate, comprehensive exam, thesis/dissertation, final oral exams. *Entrance requirements:* For master's and doctorate, GRE General Test, minimum GPA of 3.0. Additional exam requirements/recommendations for international students: Required—TOEFL (minimum score 550 paper-based; 80 iBT). *Application deadline:* For fall admission, 3/1 priority date for domestic and international students; for spring admission, 7/1 priority date for domestic and international students. Applications are processed on a rolling basis. Application fee: $50. Electronic applications accepted. *Expenses:* $24,962 full-time per academic year in-state tuition, $41,222 full-time per academic year out-of-state tuition; $830 mandatory fees per academic year. *Financial support:* In 2016–17, 10 fellowships with full tuition reimbursements (averaging $30,720 per year), 33 research assistantships with full tuition reimbursements (averaging $27,396 per year), 29 teaching assistantships with full tuition reimbursements (averaging $26,328 per year) were awarded; scholarships/grants, traineeships, and tuition waivers (full) also available. Financial award application deadline: 3/1. *Faculty research:* Biotechnology, polymers, catalysis, energy and environment, computational modeling. *Total annual research expenditures:* $10 million. *Unit head:* Dr. Steven R. Little, Chairman, 412-624-9614, Fax: 412-624-9639, E-mail: srlittle@pitt.edu. *Application contact:* Rama Bazaz, Director, 412-624-9800, Fax: 412-624-9808, E-mail: ssoeadm@pitt.edu.
Website: http://www.engineering.pitt.edu/Departments/Chemical-Petroleum

University of Regina, Faculty of Graduate Studies and Research, Faculty of Engineering and Applied Science, Program in Petroleum Systems Engineering, Regina, SK S4S 0A2, Canada. Offers M Eng, MA Sc, PhD. *Program availability:* Part-time. *Faculty:* 7 full-time (0 women), 24 part-time/adjunct (0 women). *Students:* 52 full-time (15 women), 2 part-time (1 woman). 137 applicants, 8% accepted. In 2016, 25 master's, 3 doctorates awarded. *Degree requirements:* For master's, thesis, project, report; for doctorate, thesis/dissertation. *Entrance requirements:* For doctorate, master's degree. Additional exam requirements/recommendations for international students: Required—TOEFL (minimum score 550 paper-based; 80 iBT), IELTS (minimum score 6.5), PTE (minimum score 59). *Application deadline:* For fall admission, 3/31 for domestic and international students; for winter admission, 7/31 for domestic and international students; for spring admission, 11/30 for domestic and international students. Application fee: $100. Electronic applications accepted. *Expenses:* Contact institution. *Financial support:* In 2016–17, 16 fellowships (averaging $6,313 per year), 13 teaching assistantships (averaging $2,548 per year) were awarded; career-related internships or fieldwork and scholarships/grants also available. Financial award application deadline: 6/15. *Faculty research:* Enhanced oil recovery, production engineering, reservoir engineering, surface thermodynamics, geostatistics. *Unit head:* Dr. Amr Henni, Associate Dean, Research and Graduate Studies, 306-585-4960, Fax: 306-585-4855, E-mail: amr.henni@uregina.ca. *Application contact:* Dr. Na Jia, Graduate Coordinator, 306-337-3287, Fax: 306-585-4855, E-mail: na.jia@uregina.ca.
Website: http://www.uregina.ca/engineering/

University of Southern California, Graduate School, Viterbi School of Engineering, Mork Family Department of Chemical Engineering and Materials Science, Los Angeles, CA 90089. Offers chemical engineering (MS, PhD, Engr); geoscience technologies (MS); materials engineering (MS); materials science (MS, PhD, Engr); petroleum engineering (MS, PhD, Engr); smart oilfield technologies (MS, Graduate Certificate). Terminal master's awarded for partial completion of doctoral program. *Degree requirements:* For master's, thesis optional; for doctorate, thesis/dissertation. *Entrance requirements:* For master's and doctorate, GRE General Test. Additional exam requirements/recommendations for international students: Recommended—TOEFL. Electronic applications accepted. *Expenses:* Contact institution. *Faculty research:* Heterogeneous materials and porous media, statistical mechanics, molecular simulation, polymer science and engineering, advanced materials, reaction engineering and catalysis, membrane processes and separation, biochemical engineering, cell culture, bioreactor modeling, petroleum engineering.

The University of Texas at Austin, Graduate School, Cockrell School of Engineering, Department of Petroleum and Geosystems Engineering, Austin, TX 78712-1111. Offers energy and earth resources (MA); petroleum engineering (MS, PhD). *Program availability:* Evening/weekend, online learning. *Entrance requirements:* For master's and doctorate, GRE General Test. Electronic applications accepted.

The University of Tulsa, Graduate School, College of Engineering and Natural Sciences, McDougall School of Petroleum Engineering, Tulsa, OK 74104-3189. Offers ME, MSE, PhD. *Program availability:* Part-time. *Faculty:* 13 full-time (0 women). *Students:* 59 full-time (7 women), 29 part-time (6 women), 78 international. Average age 27. 380 applicants, 14% accepted, 10 enrolled. In 2016, 27 master's, 4 doctorates awarded. Terminal master's awarded for partial completion of doctoral program. *Degree requirements:* For master's, thesis (MSE); for doctorate, comprehensive exam, thesis/dissertation. *Entrance requirements:* For master's and doctorate, GRE General Test. Additional exam requirements/recommendations for international students: Required—TOEFL (minimum score 550 paper-based; 80 iBT), IELTS (minimum score 6). *Application deadline:* Applications are processed on a rolling basis. Application fee: $55. Electronic applications accepted. *Expenses: Tuition:* Full-time $22,230; part-time $1235 per credit hour. *Required fees:* $990 per semester. Tuition and fees vary according to course load. *Financial support:* In 2016–17, 56 students received support, including 20 fellowships with full tuition reimbursements available (averaging $4,988 per year), 46 research assistantships with full tuition reimbursements available (averaging $12,946 per year), 17 teaching assistantships with full tuition reimbursements available (averaging $12,471 per year); career-related internships or fieldwork, Federal Work-Study, scholarships/grants, health care benefits, tuition waivers (full and partial), and unspecified assistantships also available. Support available to part-time students. Financial award application deadline: 2/1; financial award applicants required to submit FAFSA. *Faculty research:* Artificial lift, drilling, multiphase flow in pipes, separation technology, horizontal well technology, reservoir characterization, well testing, reservoir simulation, unconventional natural gas. *Total annual research expenditures:* $8.3 million. *Unit head:* Dr. Mustafa Onur, Chairperson, 918-631-3059, Fax: 915-631-2059, E-mail: mustafa-onur@utulsa.edu. *Application contact:* Dr. Rami Younis, Adviser, 918-631-2426, Fax: 918-631-5142, E-mail: rami-younis@utulsa.edu.
Website: http://engineering.utulsa.edu/academics/petroleum-engineering/

University of Utah, Graduate School, College of Engineering, Department of Chemical Engineering, Salt Lake City, UT 84112. Offers chemical engineering (MS, PhD); petroleum engineering (MS); MS/MBA. *Program availability:* Part-time, evening/weekend, online learning. *Faculty:* 14 full-time (2 women), 10 part-time/adjunct (2 women). *Students:* 75 full-time (17 women), 35 part-time (6 women); includes 13 minority (3 Black or African American, non-Hispanic/Latino; 5 Asian, non-Hispanic/Latino; 4 Hispanic/Latino; 1 Two or more races, non-Hispanic/Latino), 54 international. Average age 28. 210 applicants, 17% accepted, 29 enrolled. In 2016, 20 master's, 15 doctorates awarded. *Degree requirements:* For master's, comprehensive exam, thesis (for some programs); for doctorate, comprehensive exam, thesis/dissertation. *Entrance requirements:* For master's, GRE General Test, minimum GPA of 3.0; for doctorate, GRE General Test, minimum GPA of 3.0, degree or course work in chemical engineering. Additional exam requirements/recommendations for international students: Required—TOEFL (minimum score 550 paper-based; 80 iBT), IELTS (minimum score 6.5). *Application deadline:* For fall admission, 1/15 priority date for domestic and international students; for spring admission, 10/1 priority date for domestic and international students; for summer admission, 2/1 priority date for domestic and international students. Applications are processed on a rolling basis. Application fee: $0 ($15 for international students). Electronic applications accepted. *Expenses:* Contact institution. *Financial support:* In 2016–17, 53 students received support, including 5 fellowships with full tuition reimbursements available (averaging $25,450 per year), 41 research assistantships with full tuition reimbursements available (averaging $24,444 per year), 6 teaching assistantships (averaging $6,848 per year); Federal Work-Study, institutionally sponsored loans, scholarships/grants, and unspecified assistantships also available. Financial award application deadline: 4/15; financial award applicants required to submit FAFSA. *Faculty research:* Drug delivery, fossil fuel and biomass combustion and gasification, oil and gas reservoir characteristics and management, multi-scale simulation, micro-scale synthesis. *Unit head:* Dr. Milind D. Deo, Chair, 801-581-6915, Fax: 801-585-9291, E-mail: milind.deo@utah.edu. *Application contact:* Cynthia Ruiz, Graduate Coordinator, 801-587-3610, Fax: 801-585-9291, E-mail: cynthia.ruiz@chemeng.utah.edu.
Website: http://www.che.utah.edu/

University of Wyoming, College of Engineering and Applied Sciences, Department of Chemical and Petroleum Engineering, Program in Petroleum Engineering, Laramie, WY 82071. Offers MS, PhD. *Program availability:* Part-time. Terminal master's awarded for partial completion of doctoral program. *Degree requirements:* For master's, thesis; for doctorate, thesis/dissertation. *Entrance requirements:* For master's and doctorate, GRE General Test, minimum GPA of 3.0. Additional exam requirements/recommendations for international students: Required—TOEFL (minimum score 600 paper-based). Electronic applications accepted. *Faculty research:* Oil recovery methods, oil production, coal bed methane.

West Virginia University, Statler College of Engineering and Mineral Resources, Department of Petroleum and Natural Gas Engineering, Morgantown, WV 26506. Offers MSPNGE, PhD. *Program availability:* Part-time. *Degree requirements:* For master's, thesis; for doctorate, thesis/dissertation. *Entrance requirements:* For master's, minimum GPA of 3.0, BS or equivalent in petroleum or natural gas engineering; for doctorate, minimum GPA of 3.0, BS or MS in petroleum engineering from an ABET accredited or an internationally recognized petroleum engineering program or equivalent. Additional exam requirements/recommendations for international students: Required—TOEFL. *Faculty research:* Gas reservoir engineering, well logging, environment artificial intelligence.

Section 14
Industrial Engineering

This section contains a directory of institutions offering graduate work in industrial engineering. Additional information about programs listed in the directory may be obtained by writing directly to the dean of a graduate school or chair of a department at the address given in the directory.

For programs offering related work, see also in this book *Computer Science and Information Technology, Electrical and Computer Engineering, Energy and Power Engineering, Engineering and Applied Sciences,* and *Management of Engineering and Technology.* In the other guides in this series:

Graduate Programs in the Physical Sciences, Mathematics, Agricultural Sciences, the Environment & Natural Resources
See *Mathematical Sciences*
Graduate Programs in Business, Education, Information Studies, Law & Social Work
See *Business Administration and Management*

CONTENTS

Program Directories

Automotive Engineering

Clemson University, Graduate School, College of Engineering, Computing and Applied Sciences, Department of Automotive Engineering, Greenville, SC 29607. Offers MS, PhD. *Faculty:* 13 full-time (0 women), 4 part-time/adjunct (0 women). *Students:* 178 full-time (34 women), 9 part-time (1 woman); includes 5 minority (1 Black or African American, non-Hispanic/Latino; 3 Asian, non-Hispanic/Latino; 1 Hispanic/Latino), 139 international. Average age 25. 599 applicants, 18% accepted, 81 enrolled. In 2016, 61 master's, 7 doctorates awarded. *Degree requirements:* For master's, industrial internship; for doctorate, comprehensive exam, thesis/dissertation. *Entrance requirements:* For master's and doctorate, GRE General Test, unofficial transcripts, letters of recommendation. Additional exam requirements/recommendations for international students: Required—TOEFL (minimum score 80 iBT), IELTS (minimum score 7). *Application deadline:* For fall admission, 1/15 priority date for domestic students, 4/30 priority date for international students; for spring admission, 9/1 for domestic and international students. Applications are processed on a rolling basis. Application fee: $80 ($90 for international students). Electronic applications accepted. *Expenses:* $5,928 per semester resident, $13,128 per semester non-resident, $786 per semester hour resident, $1,812 per semester hour non-resident. *Financial support:* In 2016–17, 62 students received support, including 26 fellowships with partial tuition reimbursements available (averaging $13,901 per year), 31 research assistantships with partial tuition reimbursements available (averaging $21,794 per year), 23 teaching assistantships with partial tuition reimbursements available (averaging $20,521 per year); career-related internships or fieldwork also available. Financial award application deadline: 1/15. *Faculty research:* Advanced powertrains, automotive systems integration, manufacturing and materials, vehicle performance, vehicle-to-vehicle and vehicle-infrastructure integration. *Total annual research expenditures:* $4.2 million. *Unit head:* Dr. Zoran Filipi, Chair and Executive Director, 864-283-7222, E-mail: zfilipi@clemson.edu. *Application contact:* Dr. Beshah Ayalew, Graduate Coordinator, 864-283-7228, E-mail: beshah@clemson.edu.
Website: https://www.clemson.edu/cecas/departments/automotive-engineering/

College for Creative Studies, Graduate Programs, Detroit, MI 48202-4034. Offers color and materials design (MFA); integrated design (MFA); interaction design (MFA); transportation design (MFA). *Accreditation:* NASAD.

Lawrence Technological University, College of Engineering, Southfield, MI 48075-1058. Offers architectural engineering (MS); automotive engineering (MS); biomedical engineering (MS); civil engineering (MA, MS, PhD), including environmental engineering (MS), geotechnical engineering (MS), structural engineering (MS), transportation engineering (MS), water resource engineering (MS); construction engineering management (MA); electrical and computer engineering (MS); engineering management (MA); engineering technology (MS); fire engineering (MS); industrial engineering (MS), including healthcare; manufacturing systems (ME); mechanical engineering (MS, DE, PhD), including manufacturing (DE), solid mechanics (MS), thermal-fluids (MS); mechatronic systems engineering (MS). *Program availability:* Part-time, evening/weekend. *Faculty:* 24 full-time (5 women), 26 part-time/adjunct (2 women). *Students:* 22 full-time (7 women), 588 part-time (81 women); includes 23 minority (11 Black or African American, non-Hispanic/Latino; 4 Asian, non-Hispanic/Latino; 7 Hispanic/Latino; 1 Two or more races, non-Hispanic/Latino), 469 international. Average age 27. 1,186 applicants, 39% accepted, 99 enrolled. In 2016, 293 master's, 3 doctorates awarded. Terminal master's awarded for partial completion of doctoral program. *Degree requirements:* For master's, thesis optional; for doctorate, comprehensive exam, thesis/dissertation optional. *Entrance requirements:* Additional exam requirements/recommendations for international students: Required—TOEFL (minimum score 550 paper-based; 79 iBT), IELTS (minimum score 6.5). *Application deadline:* For fall admission, 5/22 for international students; for spring admission, 10/11 for international students; for summer admission, 2/16 for international students. Applications are processed on a rolling basis. Application fee: $50. Electronic applications accepted. *Expenses: Tuition:* Full-time $14,868; part-time $1062 per credit. *Required fees:* $75 per semester. Tuition and fees vary according to campus/location. *Financial support:* In 2016–17, 25 students received support, including 5 research assistantships with full tuition reimbursements available; unspecified assistantships also available. Financial award application deadline: 4/1; financial award applicants required to submit FAFSA. *Faculty research:* Carbon fiber reinforced polymer reinforced concrete structures; low impact storm water management solutions; vehicle battery energy management; wireless communication; entrepreneurial mindset and engineering. *Total annual research expenditures:* $1.7 million. *Unit head:* Dr. Nabil Grace, Dean, 248-204-2500, Fax: 248-204-2509, E-mail: engrdean@ltu.edu. *Application contact:* Jane Rohrback, Director of Admissions, 248-204-3160, Fax: 248-204-2228, E-mail: admissions@ltu.edu.
Website: http://www.ltu.edu/engineering/index.asp

Michigan Technological University, Graduate School, College of Engineering, Department of Electrical and Computer Engineering, Houghton, MI 49931. Offers advanced electric power engineering (Graduate Certificate); automotive systems and controls (Graduate Certificate); computer engineering (MS, PhD); electrical engineering (MS, PhD). *Program availability:* Part-time, online learning. *Faculty:* 44 full-time, 9 part-time/adjunct. *Students:* 197 full-time (28 women), 51 part-time; includes 11 minority (3 Black or African American, non-Hispanic/Latino; 2 Asian, non-Hispanic/Latino; 6 Hispanic/Latino), 205 international. Average age 27. 804 applicants, 36% accepted, 70 enrolled. In 2016, 100 master's, 4 doctorates, 56 other advanced degrees awarded. Terminal master's awarded for partial completion of doctoral program. *Degree requirements:* For master's, comprehensive exam (for some programs), thesis (for some programs); for doctorate, comprehensive exam, thesis/dissertation. *Entrance requirements:* For master's and doctorate, GRE, statement of purpose, personal statement, official transcripts, 2 letters of recommendation; for Graduate Certificate, statement of purpose, personal statement, official transcripts. Additional exam requirements/recommendations for international students: Required—TOEFL (recommended minimum score 100 iBT) or IELTS (recommended minimum score of 7.0). *Application deadline:* For fall admission, 2/15 priority date for domestic and international students; for spring admission, 8/15 priority date for domestic and international students. Applications are processed on a rolling basis. Electronic applications accepted. *Expenses:* Contact institution. *Financial support:* In 2016–17, 155 students received support, including 8 fellowships with tuition reimbursements available (averaging $15,242 per year), 26 research assistantships with tuition reimbursements available (averaging $15,242 per year), 20 teaching assistantships with tuition reimbursements available (averaging $15,242 per year); career-related internships or fieldwork, Federal Work-Study, scholarships/grants, health care benefits, unspecified assistantships, and cooperative program also available. Financial award applicants required to submit FAFSA. *Faculty research:* Electrical power systems, optics and photonics, embedded computing systems, computer networks, communication and information theory. *Total annual research expenditures:* $2.4 million. *Unit head:* Dr. Daniel R. Fuhrmann, Department Chair, 906-487-2550, Fax: 906-487-2949, E-mail: fuhrmann@mtu.edu. *Application contact:* Dr. John Pakkala, Graduate Academic Advisor, 906-487-2550, Fax: 906-487-2949, E-mail: jepakkal@mtu.edu.
Website: http://www.mtu.edu/ece/

Michigan Technological University, Graduate School, College of Engineering, Department of Mechanical Engineering-Engineering Mechanics, Houghton, MI 49931. Offers automotive systems and controls (Graduate Certificate); engineering mechanics (MS); hybrid electric drive vehicle engineering (Graduate Certificate); mechanical engineering (MS); mechanical engineering-engineering mechanics (PhD). *Program availability:* Part-time, evening/weekend, 100% online, blended/hybrid learning. *Faculty:* 84 full-time, 60 part-time/adjunct. *Students:* 300 full-time, 82 part-time; includes 7 minority (3 Asian, non-Hispanic/Latino; 3 Hispanic/Latino; 1 Two or more races, non-Hispanic/Latino), 295 international. Average age 26. 1,544 applicants, 18% accepted, 104 enrolled. In 2016, 102 master's, 11 doctorates, 7 other advanced degrees awarded. Terminal master's awarded for partial completion of doctoral program. *Degree requirements:* For master's, thesis (for some programs); for doctorate, comprehensive exam, thesis/dissertation. *Entrance requirements:* For master's, GRE (Michigan Tech and online students exempt), statement of purpose, personal statement, official transcripts, 2 letters of recommendation, resume/curriculum vitae; for doctorate, GRE (Michigan Tech and online students exempt), MS (preferred), statement of purpose, official transcripts, 2 letters of recommendation, resume/curriculum vitae; for Graduate Certificate, statement of purpose, official transcripts, BS in engineering. Additional exam requirements/recommendations for international students: Required—TOEFL (minimum score 90 iBT) or IELTS (minimum score 7.0). *Application deadline:* For fall admission, 3/1 priority date for domestic and international students; for spring admission, 8/1 priority date for domestic and international students. Applications are processed on a rolling basis. Electronic applications accepted. *Expenses:* Contact institution. *Financial support:* In 2016–17, 247 students received support, including 14 fellowships with tuition reimbursements available (averaging $15,242 per year), 37 research assistantships with tuition reimbursements available (averaging $15,242 per year), 31 teaching assistantships with tuition reimbursements available (averaging $15,242 per year); career-related internships or fieldwork, Federal Work-Study, scholarships/grants, health care benefits, unspecified assistantships, and cooperative program also available. Financial award applicants required to submit FAFSA. *Faculty research:* Mobility and autonomy, complex systems and controls, multi-scale materials and mechanics, thermo-fluids and energy conversion, human-centered engineering. *Total annual research expenditures:* $5.3 million. *Unit head:* Dr. William W. Predebon, Chair, 906-487-2551, Fax: 906-487-2822, E-mail: wwpredeb@mtu.edu. *Application contact:* Julie Foster, Graduate Program Assistant, 906-487-3611, Fax: 906-487-2822, E-mail: jafoster@mtu.edu.
Website: http://www.mtu.edu/mechanical/

Minnesota State University Mankato, College of Graduate Studies and Research, College of Science, Engineering and Technology, Department of Automotive and Manufacturing Engineering Technology, Mankato, MN 56001. Offers manufacturing engineering technology (MS). *Students:* 8 full-time (all women), 22 part-time (3 women). *Degree requirements:* For master's, comprehensive exam, thesis. *Entrance requirements:* For master's, minimum GPA of 2.75 during previous 2 years. Additional exam requirements/recommendations for international students: Required—TOEFL (minimum score 525 paper-based). *Application deadline:* For fall admission, 7/1 priority date for domestic students; for spring admission, 11/1 for domestic students. Applications are processed on a rolling basis. Application fee: $40. Electronic applications accepted. *Financial support:* Research assistantships with full tuition reimbursements, teaching assistantships with full tuition reimbursements, and unspecified assistantships available. Financial award application deadline: 3/15; financial award applicants required to submit FAFSA. *Unit head:* Dr. Bruce Jones, Chair, 507-389-6700, Fax: 507-389-5002, E-mail: bruce.jones@mnsu.edu.
Website: http://cset.mnsu.edu/amet/

University of Michigan, College of Engineering, Department of Integrative Systems and Design, Ann Arbor, MI 48109. Offers automotive engineering (M Eng); design science (MS, PhD); energy systems engineering (M Eng, MS); global automotive and manufacturing engineering (M Eng); manufacturing engineering (M Eng, D Eng); pharmaceutical engineering (M Eng); robotics and autonomous vehicles (M Eng); systems engineering and design (M Eng); MBA/M Eng; MSE/MS. *Program availability:* Part-time, online learning. *Students:* 147 full-time (33 women), 234 part-time (39 women). 315 applicants, 8% accepted, 13 enrolled. In 2016, 158 master's, 2 doctorates awarded. Terminal master's awarded for partial completion of doctoral program. *Degree requirements:* For master's, capstone project; for doctorate, thesis/dissertation. *Entrance requirements:* For master's, GRE; for doctorate, GRE, 2 years of work experience. Additional exam requirements/recommendations for international students: Required—TOEFL (minimum score 560 paper-based). *Application deadline:* Applications are processed on a rolling basis. Electronic applications accepted. *Expenses:* Tuition, state resident: full-time $21,466; part-time $1152 per credit hour. Tuition, nonresident: full-time $43,346; part-time $2367 per credit hour. Part-time tuition and fees vary according to course load, degree level and program. *Financial support:* Fellowships, research assistantships with full tuition reimbursements, teaching assistantships with full tuition reimbursements, career-related internships or fieldwork, scholarships/grants, and unspecified assistantships available. Financial award applicants required to submit FAFSA. *Faculty research:* Automotive engineering, design science, energy systems engineering, engineering sustainable systems, financial engineering, global automotive and manufacturing engineering, integrated microsystems, manufacturing engineering, pharmaceutical engineering, robotics and autonomous vehicles. *Total annual research expenditures:* $292,225. *Unit head:* Prof. Panos Papalambros, Department Chair, 734-647-8401, E-mail: pyp@umich.edu. *Application contact:* Kathy Bishar, Senior Graduate Coordinator, 734-764-3312, E-mail: kbishar@umich.edu.
Website: http://www.isd.engin.umich.edu

University of Michigan–Dearborn, College of Engineering and Computer Science, MSE Program in Automotive Systems Engineering, Dearborn, MI 48128. Offers MSE. *Program availability:* Part-time, evening/weekend, 100% online. *Faculty:* 1 full-time (0 women). *Students:* 99 full-time (5 women), 99 part-time (9 women); includes 15 minority (4 Black or African American, non-Hispanic/Latino; 6 Asian, non-Hispanic/Latino; 5 Hispanic/Latino), 140 international. Average age 26. 320 applicants, 43% accepted, 74 enrolled. In 2016, 77 master's awarded. *Degree requirements:* For master's, thesis optional. *Entrance requirements:* For master's, BS or equivalent degree in engineering from ABET-accredited program with minimum cumulative GPA of 3.0. Additional exam requirements/recommendations for international students: Required—TOEFL (minimum score 560 paper-based; 84 iBT), IELTS (minimum score 6.5). *Application deadline:* For fall admission, 8/1 priority date for domestic students, 5/1 for international students; for winter admission, 12/1 priority date for domestic students, 9/1 for international students; for spring admission, 4/1 priority date for domestic students, 1/1 for international

students. Applications are processed on a rolling basis. Application fee: $60. Electronic applications accepted. *Expenses:* Tuition, state resident: full-time $13,118; part-time $2280 per term. Tuition, nonresident: full-time $21,816; part-time $3771 per term. *Required fees:* $866; $658 per unit. $329 per term. Tuition and fees vary according to program. *Financial support:* Research assistantships, scholarships/grants, unspecified assistantships, and non-resident tuition scholarships available. Financial award application deadline: 3/1; financial award applicants required to submit FAFSA. *Faculty research:* Performance of lightweight automotive materials, stamping, hydroforming, tailor-welded blanking, automotive composites processing and design, thermoplastic matrix composites, injection molding. *Unit head:* Dr. Ben Li, Chair, 313-593-5241, E-mail: benqli@umich.edu. *Application contact:* Office of Graduate Studies, 313-583-6321, E-mail: umd-graduatestudies@umich.edu.
Website: https://umdearborn.edu/cecs/departments/interdisciplinary-programs/mse-automotive-systems-engineering

University of Michigan–Dearborn, College of Engineering and Computer Science, PhD Program in Automotive Systems Engineering, Dearborn, MI 48128. Offers PhD. *Program availability:* Part-time, evening/weekend. *Faculty:* 1 full-time (0 women). *Students:* 12 part-time (2 women); includes 3 minority (all Asian, non-Hispanic/Latino), 7 international. Average age 32. 17 applicants, 24% accepted, 3 enrolled. In 2016, 1 doctorate awarded. *Degree requirements:* For doctorate, thesis/dissertation. *Entrance requirements:* For doctorate, GRE. Additional exam requirements/recommendations for international students: Required—TOEFL (minimum score 560 paper-based; 84 iBT), IELTS (minimum score 6.5). *Application deadline:* For fall admission, 2/15 for domestic and international students. Application fee: $60. Electronic applications accepted. *Expenses:* Tuition, state resident: full-time $13,118; part-time $2280 per term. Tuition, nonresident: full-time $21,816; part-time $3771 per term. *Required fees:* $866; $658 per unit. $329 per term. Tuition and fees vary according to program. *Financial support:* Research assistantships, teaching assistantships, scholarships/grants, and unspecified assistantships available. Financial award application deadline: 3/1; financial award applicants required to submit FAFSA. *Faculty research:* Circuits and electronics, controls, signal processing, fluids. *Unit head:* Dr. Yi Lu Murphey, Director/Professor, 313-593-5290, E-mail: yilu@umich.edu. *Application contact:* Office of Graduate Studies, 313-583-6321, E-mail: umd-graduatestudies@umich.edu.
Website: https://umdearborn.edu/cecs/departments/interdisciplinary-programs/phd-automotive-systems-engineering

The University of Tennessee at Chattanooga, Program in Engineering, Chattanooga, TN 37403. Offers automotive systems (MS Engr); chemical engineering (MS Engr); civil engineering (MS Engr); computational engineering (MS Engr); electrical engineering (MS Engr); industrial engineering (MS Engr); mechanical engineering (MS Engr). *Program availability:* Part-time. *Faculty:* 21 full-time (2 women), 2 part-time/adjunct (1 woman). *Students:* 21 full-time (5 women), 26 part-time (7 women); includes 11 minority (4 Black or African American, non-Hispanic/Latino; 5 Asian, non-Hispanic/Latino; 1 Hispanic/Latino; 1 Two or more races, non-Hispanic/Latino), 18 international. Average age 28. 30 applicants, 83% accepted, 14 enrolled. In 2016, 25 master's awarded. *Degree requirements:* For master's, comprehensive exam, thesis or alternative, engineering project. *Entrance requirements:* For master's, GRE General Test, minimum undergraduate GPA of 2.7 or 3.0 in last two years of undergraduate coursework. Additional exam requirements/recommendations for international students: Required—TOEFL (minimum score 550 paper-based; 79 iBT), IELTS (minimum score 6). *Application deadline:* For fall admission, 6/15 priority date for domestic students, 7/1 for international students; for spring admission, 11/1 priority date for domestic students, 11/1 for international students. Applications are processed on a rolling basis. Application fee: $35 ($40 for international students). Electronic applications accepted. *Expenses:* $9,876 full-time in-state; $25,994 full-time out-of-state; $450 per credit part-time in-state; $1,345 per credit part-time out-of-state. *Financial support:* In 2016–17, 6 research assistantships, 5 teaching assistantships were awarded; career-related internships or fieldwork, scholarships/grants, health care benefits, and unspecified assistantships also available. Support available to part-time students. Financial award application deadline: 7/1. *Faculty research:* Quality control and reliability engineering, financial management, thermal science, energy conservation, structural analysis. *Total annual research expenditures:* $921,122. *Unit head:* Dr. Daniel Pack, Dean, 423-425-2256, Fax: 423-425-5311, E-mail: daniel-pack@utc.edu. *Application contact:* Dr. Joanne Romagni, Dean of the Graduate School, 423-425-4478, Fax: 423-425-5223, E-mail: joanne-romagni@utc.edu.
Website: http://www.utc.edu/college-engineering-computer-science/graduate-programs/msengr.php

University of Wisconsin–Madison, Graduate School, College of Engineering, Department of Mechanical Engineering, Madison, WI 53706-1380. Offers mechanical engineering (MS, PhD), including automotive engineering (MS). *Program availability:* Part-time, online learning. *Faculty:* 31 full-time (5 women). *Students:* 183 full-time (22 women), 36 part-time (2 women); includes 33 minority (3 Black or African American, non-Hispanic/Latino; 1 American Indian or Alaska Native, non-Hispanic/Latino; 9 Asian, non-Hispanic/Latino; 19 Hispanic/Latino; 1 Two or more races, non-Hispanic/Latino), 96 international. Average age 28. 609 applicants, 21% accepted, 45 enrolled. In 2016, 61 master's, 15 doctorates awarded. Terminal master's awarded for partial completion of doctoral program. *Degree requirements:* For master's, thesis optional, 30 credits; minimum GPA of 3.0; for doctorate, thesis/dissertation, qualifying exam, preliminary exam, final oral defense, 42 formal course credits, 18 thesis credits, minimum GPA of 3.25. *Entrance requirements:* For master's, GRE, BS in mechanical engineering or related field, minimum GPA of 3.2 in last 60 hours of course work; for doctorate, GRE, BS in mechanical engineering or related field, minimum undergraduate GPA of 3.2 in last 60 hours of course work. Additional exam requirements/recommendations for international students: Required—TOEFL (minimum score 580 paper-based; 92 iBT), IELTS (minimum score 7). *Application deadline:* For fall admission, 1/1 for domestic and international students; for spring admission, 10/1 for domestic and international students; for summer admission, 12/15 for domestic and international students. Applications are processed on a rolling basis. Application fee: $75 ($81 for international students). Electronic applications accepted. *Expenses:* $13,157 per year in-state tuition and fees; $26,484 per year out-of-state tuition and fees. *Financial support:* In 2016–17, 136 students received support, including 9 fellowships with full tuition reimbursements available, 76 research assistantships with full tuition reimbursements available, 49 teaching assistantships with full tuition reimbursements available; career-related internships or fieldwork, institutionally sponsored loans, scholarships/grants, traineeships, health care benefits, and unspecified assistantships also available. Financial award application deadline: 12/1; financial award applicants required to submit FAFSA. *Faculty research:* Polymer engineering; robotics/electromechanical system control; advanced manufacturing and prototype processes; computational mechanics; thermal-fluid systems; engine and vehicle systems. *Total annual research expenditures:* $10.6 million. *Unit head:* Jaal B. Ghandhi, Chair, 608-263-1684, E-mail: jaal.ghandhi@wisc.edu. *Application contact:* Sara Hladilek, Student Services Coordinator, 608-262-8617, E-mail: shladilek@wisc.edu.
Website: http://www.engr.wisc.edu/me/

Wayne State University, College of Engineering, Program in Electric-Drive Vehicle Engineering, Detroit, MI 48202. Offers MS, Graduate Certificate. *Degree requirements:* For master's, thesis optional. *Entrance requirements:* For master's, bachelor's degree in engineering from accredited institution with minimum GPA of 3.0, significant professional experience, or enrollment in electric-drive vehicle engineering Graduate Certificate program; for Graduate Certificate, bachelor's degree in engineering from accredited institution with minimum GPA of 2.7 or significant professional experience. Additional exam requirements/recommendations for international students: Required—TOEFL (minimum score 550 paper-based; 79 iBT), TWE (minimum score 5.5), Michigan English Language Assessment Battery (minimum score 85); Recommended—IELTS (minimum score 6.5). *Application deadline:* For fall admission, 6/1 priority date for domestic students, 5/1 priority date for international students; for winter admission, 10/1 priority date for domestic students, 9/1 priority date for international students; for spring admission, 2/1 priority date for domestic students, 1/1 priority date for international students. Applications are processed on a rolling basis. Application fee: $0. Electronic applications accepted. *Expenses:* Contact institution. *Financial support:* Scholarships/grants and unspecified assistantships available. Financial award application deadline: 3/31; financial award applicants required to submit FAFSA. *Unit head:* Dr. Ece Yaprak, Division Chair, 313-577-8075, E-mail: yaprak@eng.wayne.edu.
Website: http://engineering.wayne.edu/eve/index.php

Industrial/Management Engineering

American University of Armenia, Graduate Programs, Yerevan, Armenia. Offers business administration (MBA); computer and information science (MS), including business management, design and manufacturing, energy (ME, MS), industrial engineering and systems management; economics (MS); industrial engineering and systems management (ME), including business, computer aided design/manufacturing, energy (ME, MS), information technology; law (LL M); political science and international affairs (MPSIA); public health (MPH); teaching English as a foreign language (MA). *Program availability:* Part-time, evening/weekend. *Degree requirements:* For master's, thesis (for some programs), capstone/project. *Entrance requirements:* For master's, GRE, GMAT, or LSAT. Additional exam requirements/recommendations for international students: Recommended—TOEFL (minimum score 79 iBT), IELTS (minimum score 6.5). *Faculty research:* Microfinance, finance (rural/development, international, corporate), firm life cycle theory, TESOL, language proficiency testing, public policy, administrative law, economic development, cryptography, artificial intelligence, energy efficiency/renewable energy, computer-aided design/manufacturing, health financing, tuberculosis control, mother/child health, preventive ophthalmology, post-earthquake psychopathological investigations, tobacco control, environmental health risk assessments.

Arizona State University at the Tempe campus, Ira A. Fulton Schools of Engineering, School of Computing, Informatics, and Decision Systems Engineering, Tempe, AZ 85287-8809. Offers computer engineering (MS, PhD); computer science (MCS, MS, PhD); industrial engineering (MS, PhD); software engineering (MS). *Program availability:* Part-time, evening/weekend, online learning. Terminal master's awarded for partial completion of doctoral program. *Degree requirements:* For master's, comprehensive exam (for some programs), portfolio (MCS); interactive Program of Study (iPOS) submitted before completing 50 percent of required credit hours; for doctorate, comprehensive exam, thesis/dissertation, interactive Program of Study (iPOS) submitted before completing 50 percent of required credit hours. *Entrance requirements:* For master's, GRE, minimum GPA of 3.0 or equivalent in last 2 years of work leading to bachelor's degree; for doctorate, GRE, minimum GPA of 3.0 in last 2 years of work leading to bachelor's degree. Additional exam requirements/recommendations for international students: Required—TOEFL, IELTS, or PTE. Electronic applications accepted. *Expenses:* Contact institution. *Faculty research:* Artificial intelligence, cyberphysical and embedded systems, health informatics, information assurance and security, information management/multimedia/visualization, network science, personalized learning/educational games, production logistics, software and systems engineering, statistical modeling and data mining.

Auburn University, Graduate School, Ginn College of Engineering, Department of Industrial and Systems Engineering, Auburn University, AL 36849. Offers MISE, MS, PhD, Graduate Certificate. *Program availability:* Part-time. *Faculty:* 13 full-time (1 woman), 2 part-time/adjunct (1 woman). *Students:* 79 full-time (19 women), 45 part-time (8 women); includes 9 minority (6 Black or African American, non-Hispanic/Latino; 2 Asian, non-Hispanic/Latino; 1 Two or more races, non-Hispanic/Latino), 78 international. Average age 29. 279 applicants, 34% accepted, 39 enrolled. In 2016, 63 master's, 6 doctorates, 14 other advanced degrees awarded. *Degree requirements:* For master's, thesis (MS); for doctorate, thesis/dissertation. *Entrance requirements:* For master's and doctorate, GRE General Test. *Application deadline:* Applications are processed on a rolling basis. Application fee: $50 ($60 for international students). *Expenses:* Tuition, state resident: full-time $9072; part-time $504 per credit hour. Tuition, nonresident: full-time $27,216; part-time $1512 per credit hour. *Required fees:* $812 per semester. Tuition and fees vary according to degree level and program. *Financial support:* Fellowships, research assistantships, teaching assistantships, and Federal Work-Study available. Support available to part-time students. Financial award application deadline: 3/15; financial award applicants required to submit FAFSA. *Unit head:* John Evans, Chair, 334-844-1400. *Application contact:* Dr. George Flowers, Dean of the Graduate School, 334-844-2125.
Website: http://www.eng.auburn.edu/insy/

Binghamton University, State University of New York, Graduate School, Thomas J. Watson School of Engineering and Applied Science, Department of Systems Science and Industrial Engineering, Binghamton, NY 13902-6000. Offers executive health systems (MS); industrial and systems engineering (M Eng); systems science and industrial engineering (MS, PhD). MS in executive health systems also offered in Manhattan. *Program availability:* Part-time, evening/weekend, online learning. *Faculty:* 21 full-time (4 women), 4 part-time/adjunct (0 women). *Students:* 221 full-time (65 women), 125 part-time (40 women); includes 54 minority (18 Black or African American, non-Hispanic/Latino; 20 Asian, non-Hispanic/Latino; 16 Hispanic/Latino), 238 international. Average age 28. 468 applicants, 88% accepted, 117 enrolled. In 2016, 109 master's, 11 doctorates awarded. *Degree requirements:* For master's, thesis; for doctorate, thesis/dissertation. *Entrance requirements:* For master's and doctorate, GRE

General Test. Additional exam requirements/recommendations for international students: Required—TOEFL (minimum score 550 paper-based; 80 iBT). *Application deadline:* For fall admission, 4/1 priority date for domestic and international students; for spring admission, 11/15 priority date for domestic and international students. Applications are processed on a rolling basis. Application fee: $75. Electronic applications accepted. *Expenses:* Contact institution. *Financial support:* In 2016–17, 97 students received support, including 1 fellowship with full tuition reimbursement available (averaging $10,000 per year), 45 research assistantships with full tuition reimbursements available (averaging $16,500 per year), 13 teaching assistantships with full tuition reimbursements available (averaging $16,500 per year); career-related internships or fieldwork, Federal Work-Study, institutionally sponsored loans, scholarships/grants, health care benefits, tuition waivers (full and partial), and unspecified assistantships also available. Financial award application deadline: 2/1; financial award applicants required to submit FAFSA. *Faculty research:* Problem restructuring, protein modeling. *Unit head:* Ellen Tilden, Coordinator of Graduate Studies, 607-777-2873, E-mail: etilden@binghamton.edu. *Application contact:* Ben Balkaya, Assistant Dean and Director, 607-777-2151, Fax: 607-777-2501, E-mail: balkaya@binghamton.edu.
Website: http://www.ssie.binghamton.edu

Bradley University, The Graduate School, Caterpillar College of Engineering and Technology, Department of Industrial and Manufacturing Engineering and Technology, Peoria, IL 61625-0002. Offers industrial engineering (MS); manufacturing engineering (MS). *Program availability:* Part-time, evening/weekend. *Degree requirements:* For master's, comprehensive exam, project. *Entrance requirements:* Additional exam requirements/recommendations for international students: Required—TOEFL (minimum score 550 paper-based; 79 iBT), IELTS (minimum score 6.5). *Application deadline:* For fall admission, 5/15 priority date for domestic and international students; for spring admission, 10/15 priority date for domestic and international students. Applications are processed on a rolling basis. Application fee: $40 ($50 for international students). Electronic applications accepted. *Expenses: Tuition:* Full-time $7650; part-time $850 per credit. *Required fees:* $50 per credit. One-time fee: $100 full-time. *Financial support:* Research assistantships with full and partial tuition reimbursements, scholarships/grants, tuition waivers (partial), and unspecified assistantships available. Support available to part-time students. Financial award application deadline: 4/1. *Unit head:* Dr. Joseph Chen, Chair, 309-677-2740, E-mail: jchen@bradley.edu. *Application contact:* Kayla Carroll, Director of International Admission and Student Services, 309-677-2375, E-mail: klcarroll@fsmail.bradley.edu.
Website: http://www.bradley.edu/academic/departments/imet/

Buffalo State College, State University of New York, The Graduate School, Faculty of Applied Science and Education, Department of Technology, Program in Industrial Technology, Buffalo, NY 14222-1095. Offers MS. *Degree requirements:* For master's, thesis or project. *Entrance requirements:* For master's, minimum GPA of 2.5. Additional exam requirements/recommendations for international students: Required—TOEFL (minimum score 550 paper-based).

California Polytechnic State University, San Luis Obispo, College of Engineering, Department of Industrial Engineering, San Luis Obispo, CA 93407. Offers MS. *Program availability:* Part-time. *Faculty:* 4 full-time (1 woman). *Students:* 4 full-time (1 woman); includes 2 minority (1 Asian, non-Hispanic/Latino; 1 Two or more races, non-Hispanic/Latino), 1 international. Average age 22. 21 applicants, 19% accepted, 1 enrolled. In 2016, 9 master's awarded. *Degree requirements:* For master's, comprehensive exam (for some programs), thesis (for some programs). *Entrance requirements:* For master's, GRE. Additional exam requirements/recommendations for international students: Required—TOEFL (minimum score 80 iBT). *Application deadline:* For fall admission, 3/1 for domestic and international students. Applications are processed on a rolling basis. Application fee: $55. Electronic applications accepted. *Expenses:* Tuition, state resident: full-time $6738; part-time $3906 per year. Tuition, nonresident: full-time $15,666; part-time $8370 per year. *Required fees:* $3603; $3141 per unit. $1047 per term. *Financial support:* Fellowships, research assistantships, teaching assistantships, career-related internships or fieldwork, Federal Work-Study, institutionally sponsored loans, and scholarships/grants available. Support available to part-time students. Financial award application deadline: 3/2; financial award applicants required to submit FAFSA. *Faculty research:* Operations research, simulation, project management, supply chain and logistics, quality engineering. *Unit head:* Dr. Jon Pan, Graduate Coordinator, 805-756-2540, E-mail: pan@calpoly.edu.
Website: http://www.ime.calpoly.edu/programs/graduate/

California State University, East Bay, Office of Graduate Studies, College of Business and Economics, MBA Program, Hayward, CA 94542-3000. Offers entrepreneurship (MBA), including small business management; finance (MBA); global innovators (MBA); human resources and organizational behavior (MBA), including human resources/personnel management; information technology management (MBA), including computer information systems; marketing management (MBA), including marketing; operations and supply chain management (MBA); strategy and international business (MBA). *Accreditation:* AACSB. *Program availability:* Part-time, evening/weekend. *Students:* 137 full-time (75 women), 168 part-time (80 women); includes 71 minority (8 Black or African American, non-Hispanic/Latino; 55 Asian, non-Hispanic/Latino; 4 Hispanic/Latino; 2 Native Hawaiian or other Pacific Islander, non-Hispanic/Latino; 2 Two or more races, non-Hispanic/Latino), 70 international. Average age 32. 385 applicants, 48% accepted, 83 enrolled. In 2016, 148 master's awarded. *Degree requirements:* For master's, comprehensive exam or thesis. *Entrance requirements:* For master's, GMAT (minimum 20th percentile verbal and quantitative section), bachelor's degree, minimum GPA of 2.75. Additional exam requirements/recommendations for international students: Required—TOEFL (minimum score 550 paper-based; 79 iBT). *Application deadline:* For fall admission, 6/30 for domestic and international students. Applications are processed on a rolling basis. Application fee: $55. Electronic applications accepted. *Expenses:* Contact institution. *Financial support:* Career-related internships or fieldwork, Federal Work-Study, institutionally sponsored loans, and scholarships/grants available. Support available to part-time students. Financial award application deadline: 3/2; financial award applicants required to submit FAFSA. *Unit head:* Xinjian Lu, Associate Dean, 510-855-3290, E-mail: xinjian.lu@csueastbay.edu. *Application contact:* Dr. Donna Wiley, Interim Associate Vice President for Academic Programs and Graduate Studies, 510-885-3716, Fax: 510-885-4777, E-mail: donna.wiley@csueastbay.edu.
Website: http://www20.csueastbay.edu/ecat/graduate-chapters/g-buad.html#mba

California State University, Fresno, Division of Research and Graduate Studies, Jordan College of Agricultural Sciences and Technology, Department of Industrial Technology, Fresno, CA 93740-8027. Offers MS. *Program availability:* Part-time, evening/weekend. *Degree requirements:* For master's, comprehensive exam (for some programs), thesis (for some programs). *Entrance requirements:* For master's, GRE General Test, minimum GPA of 2.5. Additional exam requirements/recommendations for international students: Required—TOEFL. *Application deadline:* For fall admission, 5/1 priority date for domestic and international students; for spring admission, 10/1 for domestic and international students. Applications are processed on a rolling basis. Application fee: $55. Electronic applications accepted. *Financial support:* Career-related internships or fieldwork, Federal Work-Study, and scholarships/grants available. Support available to part-time students. Financial award application deadline: 3/1; financial award applicants required to submit FAFSA. *Faculty research:* Fuels/pollution, energy, outdoor storage methods. *Unit head:* Dr. Athanasios Alexandrou, Chair, 559-278-1951, Fax: 559-278-5081, E-mail: aalexandrou@csufresno.edu. *Application contact:* Dr. Balaji Seth, Coordinator, 559-278-2333, Fax: 559-278-5081, E-mail: balajis@csufresno.edu.
Website: http://fresnostate.edu/jcast/indtech/

California State University, Northridge, Graduate Studies, College of Engineering and Computer Science, Department of Manufacturing Systems Engineering and Management, Northridge, CA 91330. Offers engineering automation (MS); engineering management (MS); manufacturing systems engineering (MS); materials engineering (MS). *Program availability:* Online learning. *Faculty:* 8 full-time (7 women), 21 part-time/adjunct (16 women). *Students:* 124 full-time (29 women), 94 part-time (19 women); includes 27 minority (1 American Indian or Alaska Native, non-Hispanic/Latino; 11 Asian, non-Hispanic/Latino; 13 Hispanic/Latino; 2 Two or more races, non-Hispanic/Latino), 145 international. Average age 27. 302 applicants, 33% accepted, 45 enrolled. *Entrance requirements:* For master's, GRE (if cumulative undergraduate GPA less than 3.0). *Application deadline:* For fall admission, 3/30 for domestic students; for spring admission, 9/30 for domestic students. Application fee: $55. *Expenses:* Tuition, state resident: full-time $4152. *Unit head:* Ahmad Sarfaraz, Chair, 818-677-2167.
Website: http://www.csun.edu/~msem/

Central Washington University, Graduate Studies and Research, College of Education and Professional Studies, Department of Industrial and Engineering Technology, Ellensburg, WA 98926. Offers engineering technology (MS). *Program availability:* Part-time. *Degree requirements:* For master's, thesis or alternative. *Entrance requirements:* For master's, minimum GPA of 3.0. Additional exam requirements/recommendations for international students: Required—TOEFL (minimum score 550 paper-based; 79 iBT), IELTS (minimum score 6.5). Electronic applications accepted.

Clemson University, Graduate School, College of Engineering, Computing and Applied Sciences, Department of Industrial Engineering, Clemson, SC 29634. Offers M Engr, MS, PhD. *Program availability:* Part-time, 100% online. *Faculty:* 17 full-time (4 women). *Students:* 59 full-time (20 women), 101 part-time (18 women); includes 18 minority (5 Black or African American, non-Hispanic/Latino; 4 Asian, non-Hispanic/Latino; 7 Hispanic/Latino; 1 Native Hawaiian or other Pacific Islander, non-Hispanic/Latino; 1 Two or more races, non-Hispanic/Latino), 62 international. Average age 31. 414 applicants, 20% accepted, 23 enrolled. In 2016, 89 master's, 6 doctorates awarded. Terminal master's awarded for partial completion of doctoral program. *Median time to degree:* Of those who began their doctoral program in fall 2008, 92% received their degree in 8 years or less. *Degree requirements:* For master's, thesis or alternative; for doctorate, comprehensive exam, thesis/dissertation. *Entrance requirements:* For master's and doctorate, GRE General Test, unofficial transcripts, letters of recommendation. Additional exam requirements/recommendations for international students: Required—TOEFL (minimum score 80 iBT), IELTS (minimum score 6.5). *Application deadline:* For fall admission, 4/1 for domestic students, 1/1 for international students. Applications are processed on a rolling basis. Application fee: $80 ($90 for international students). Electronic applications accepted. *Expenses:* $4,841 per semester full-time resident, $9,640 per semester full-time non-resident, $612 per credit hour part-time resident, $1,223 per credit hour part-time non-resident. *Financial support:* In 2016–17, 45 students received support, including 1 fellowship with partial tuition reimbursement available (averaging $9,640 per year), 25 research assistantships with partial tuition reimbursements available (averaging $19,901 per year), 17 teaching assistantships with partial tuition reimbursements available (averaging $18,093 per year); career-related internships or fieldwork and unspecified assistantships also available. Financial award application deadline: 4/1. *Faculty research:* System optimization, health care engineering, human factors and safety, human-computer interaction, quality. *Total annual research expenditures:* $1.7 million. *Unit head:* Dr. J. Cole Smith, Department Chair, 864-656-4716, E-mail: jcsmith@clemson.edu. *Application contact:* Dr. B. Rae Cho, Graduate Coordinator, 864-656-1874, E-mail: bcho@clemson.edu.
Website: https://www.clemson.edu/cecas/departments/ie/index.html

Cleveland State University, College of Graduate Studies, Fenn College of Engineering, Department of Industrial and Manufacturing Engineering, Cleveland, OH 44115. Offers MS, D Eng. *Program availability:* Part-time. *Faculty:* 5 full-time (0 women), 2 part-time/adjunct (0 women). *Students:* 6 applicants, 33% accepted. Terminal master's awarded for partial completion of doctoral program. *Degree requirements:* For master's, thesis or alternative; for doctorate, thesis/dissertation, candidacy and qualifying exams. *Entrance requirements:* For master's, GRE General Test, minimum GPA of 2.75; for doctorate, GRE General Test, minimum GPA of 3.25. Additional exam requirements/recommendations for international students: Required—TOEFL (minimum score 550 paper-based; 78 iBT). *Application deadline:* For fall admission, 7/1 priority date for domestic students, 5/15 priority date for international students; for spring admission, 11/15 for domestic students, 11/1 priority date for international students; for summer admission, 4/1 for domestic students, 3/15 for international students. Applications are processed on a rolling basis. Application fee: $40. Electronic applications accepted. *Expenses:* Tuition, state resident: full-time $9565. Tuition, nonresident: full-time $17,980. Tuition and fees vary according to program. *Financial support:* In 2016–17, 4 research assistantships with tuition reimbursements (averaging $3,550 per year), 2 teaching assistantships with tuition reimbursements (averaging $3,725 per year) were awarded; fellowships, career-related internships or fieldwork, institutionally sponsored loans, tuition waivers (partial), and unspecified assistantships also available. Support available to part-time students. Financial award applicants required to submit FAFSA. *Faculty research:* Modeling of manufacturing systems, statistical process control, computerized production planning and facilities design, cellular manufacturing, artificial intelligence and sensors. *Unit head:* Dr. Joseph A. Svestka, Chairperson, 216-687-4662, Fax: 216-687-9330, E-mail: j.svestka@csuohio.edu. *Application contact:* Shirley A. Love, Administrative Services Coordinator, 216-687-2044, Fax: 216-687-9330, E-mail: s.love@csuohio.edu.

Colorado State University, Walter Scott, Jr. College of Engineering, Department of Mechanical Engineering, Fort Collins, CO 80523-1374. Offers industrial engineering (PhD); mechanical engineering (ME, MS, PhD). *Program availability:* Part-time, evening/weekend, 100% online, blended/hybrid learning. *Faculty:* 29 full-time (4 women), 6 part-time/adjunct (0 women). *Students:* 49 full-time (5 women), 66 part-time (8 women); includes 10 minority (1 Asian, non-Hispanic/Latino; 5 Hispanic/Latino; 4 Two or more races, non-Hispanic/Latino), 26 international. Average age 27. 105 applicants, 40% accepted, 28 enrolled. In 2016, 13 master's, 11 doctorates awarded. Terminal master's awarded for partial completion of doctoral program. *Degree requirements:* For master's, thesis, thesis defense; for doctorate, thesis/dissertation, oral qualifying exam, preliminary exam, dissertation defense. *Entrance requirements:* For master's, GRE (minimum scores of 150 Verbal, 155 Quantitative, 3.5 Analytical), bachelor's degree in engineering, science, or engineering-related field; minimum GPA of 3.0; successful completion of undergraduate courses in calculus, ordinary differential equations, and calculus-based physics; for doctorate, GRE (minimum scores of 150 Verbal, 155 Quantitative, 3.5 Analytical), bachelor's degree in engineering, science, or engineering-related field; minimum GPA of 3.25; successful completion of undergraduate courses in calculus, ordinary differential equations, and calculus-based physics. Additional exam requirements/recommendations for international students: Required—TOEFL (minimum score 550 paper-based, 80 iBT) or IELTS (6.5). *Application deadline:* For fall admission, 1/15 priority date for domestic and international students; for spring admission, 8/1 priority date for domestic and international students. Application fee: $60 ($70 for international students). Electronic applications accepted. *Expenses:* Contact institution. *Financial support:* In 2016–17, 3 fellowships with full and partial tuition reimbursements (averaging $53,671 per year), 29 research assistantships with full and partial tuition reimbursements (averaging $20,927 per year), 29 teaching assistantships with full and partial tuition reimbursements (averaging $15,797 per year) were awarded; scholarships/grants and health care benefits also available. Financial award application deadline: 4/1. *Faculty research:* Computational fluid dynamics and high performance computing, energy, health, materials, robotics. *Total annual research expenditures:* $7.3 million. *Unit head:* Dr. Susan James, Professor and Department Head, 970-491-0924, Fax: 970-491-3827, E-mail: susan.james@engr.colostate.edu. Website: http://www.engr.colostate.edu/me/

Colorado State University–Pueblo, College of Education, Engineering and Professional Studies, Department of Engineering, Pueblo, CO 81001-4901. Offers industrial and systems engineering (MS). *Degree requirements:* For master's, thesis optional. *Entrance requirements:* For master's, GRE General Test. Additional exam requirements/recommendations for international students: Required—TOEFL (minimum score 500 paper-based). *Faculty research:* Nanotechnology, applied operations, research transportation, decision analysis.

Columbia University, Fu Foundation School of Engineering and Applied Science, Department of Industrial Engineering and Operations Research, New York, NY 10027. Offers financial engineering (MS); industrial engineering and operations research (MS, Eng Sc D, PhD); management science and engineering (MS); MS/MBA. *Program availability:* Part-time, evening/weekend, online learning. *Degree requirements:* For doctorate, thesis/dissertation, oral and written qualifying exams. *Entrance requirements:* For master's and doctorate, GRE General Test. Additional exam requirements/recommendations for international students: Required—TOEFL, IELTS, PTE. Electronic applications accepted. *Faculty research:* Applied probability and optimization; financial engineering, modeling risk including credit risk and systemic risk, asset allocation, portfolio execution, behavioral finance, agent-based model in finance; revenue management; management and optimization of service systems, call centers, capacity allocation in healthcare systems, inventory control for vaccines; energy, smart grids, demand shaping, managing renewable energy sources, energy-aware scheduling.

Concordia University, School of Graduate Studies, Faculty of Engineering and Computer Science, Department of Mechanical and Industrial Engineering, Montréal, QC H3G 1M8, Canada. Offers industrial engineering (M Eng, MA Sc, PhD); mechanical engineering (M Eng, MA Sc, PhD, Certificate). M Eng in composites program offered jointly with École Polytechnique de Montréal. *Degree requirements:* For master's, variable foreign language requirement, thesis or alternative; for doctorate, comprehensive exam, thesis/dissertation. *Faculty research:* Mechanical systems, fluid control systems, thermofluids engineering and robotics, industrial control systems.

Cornell University, Graduate School, Graduate Fields of Agriculture and Life Sciences and Graduate Fields of Engineering, Field of Biological and Environmental Engineering, Ithaca, NY 14853. Offers bioenergy and integrated energy systems (M Eng, MPS, MS, PhD); biological engineering (M Eng, MPS, MS, PhD); bioprocess engineering (M Eng, MPS, MS, PhD); ecohydrology (M Eng, MPS, MS, PhD); environmental engineering (M Eng, MPS, MS, PhD); environmental management (MPS); food engineering (M Eng, MPS, MS, PhD); industrial biotechnology (M Eng, MPS, MS, PhD); nanobiotechnology (M Eng, MPS, MS, PhD); sustainable systems (M Eng, MPS, MS, PhD); synthetic biology (MS); syntheticbiology (M Eng, MPS, PhD). Terminal master's awarded for partial completion of doctoral program. *Degree requirements:* For master's, thesis (MS); for doctorate, comprehensive exam, thesis/dissertation. *Entrance requirements:* For master's, letters of recommendation (3 for MS, 2 for M Eng and MPS); for doctorate, GRE General Test, 3 letters of recommendation. Additional exam requirements/recommendations for international students: Required—TOEFL (minimum score 550 paper-based; 77 iBT). Electronic applications accepted. *Faculty research:* Biological and food engineering, environmental, soil and water engineering, international agricultural engineering, structures and controlled environments, machine systems and energy.

Cornell University, Graduate School, Graduate Fields of Engineering, Field of Operations Research and Information Engineering, Ithaca, NY 14853. Offers applied probability and statistics (PhD); manufacturing systems engineering (PhD); mathematical programming (PhD); operations research and industrial engineering (M Eng). *Degree requirements:* For doctorate, comprehensive exam, thesis/dissertation. *Entrance requirements:* For master's and doctorate, GRE General Test, 3 letters of recommendation. Additional exam requirements/recommendations for international students: Required—TOEFL (minimum score 600 paper-based; 100 iBT). Electronic applications accepted. *Faculty research:* Mathematical programming and combinatorial optimization, statistics, stochastic processes, mathematical finance, simulation, manufacturing, e-commerce.

Dalhousie University, Faculty of Engineering, Department of Industrial Engineering, Halifax, NS B3J 2X4, Canada. Offers M Eng, MA Sc, PhD. *Degree requirements:* For master's, thesis; for doctorate, thesis/dissertation. *Entrance requirements:* Additional exam requirements/recommendations for international students: Required—TOEFL, IELTS, CANTEST, CAEL, or Michigan English Language Assessment Battery. Electronic applications accepted. *Faculty research:* Industrial ergonomics, operations research, production manufacturing systems, scheduling stochastic models.

Eastern Kentucky University, The Graduate School, College of Business and Technology, Department of Technology, Program in Industrial Technology, Richmond, KY 40475-3102. Offers MS. *Program availability:* Part-time. *Entrance requirements:* For master's, GRE General Test, minimum GPA of 2.5. *Faculty research:* Quality control, dental implants, manufacturing technology.

École Polytechnique de Montréal, Graduate Programs, Department of Mathematics and Industrial Engineering, Montréal, QC H3C 3A7, Canada. Offers ergonomy (M Eng, M Sc A, DESS); mathematical method in CA engineering (M Eng, M Sc A, PhD); operational research (M Eng, M Sc A, PhD); production (M Eng, M Sc A); technology management (M Eng, M Sc A). DESS program offered jointly with HEC Montreal and Université de Montréal. *Program availability:* Part-time. *Degree requirements:* For master's, one foreign language, thesis. *Entrance requirements:* For master's, minimum GPA of 2.75. *Faculty research:* Use of computers in organizations.

Florida Agricultural and Mechanical University, Division of Graduate Studies, Research, and Continuing Education, FAMU-FSU College of Engineering, Department of Industrial and Manufacturing Engineering, Tallahassee, FL 32307-3200. Offers industrial engineering (MS, PhD). *Degree requirements:* For master's, thesis optional. *Entrance requirements:* For master's, GRE General Test, minimum GPA of 3.0. Additional exam requirements/recommendations for international students: Required—TOEFL (minimum score 550 paper-based). *Faculty research:* Design for environmentally conscious manufacturing, affordable composite manufacturing, integrated product and process design, precision machining research.

Florida State University, The Graduate School, FAMU-FSU College of Engineering, Department of Industrial and Manufacturing Engineering, Tallahassee, FL 32306. Offers industrial engineering (MS, PhD). *Faculty:* 14 full-time (1 woman), 1 (woman) part-time/adjunct. *Students:* 49 full-time (15 women); includes 10 minority (5 Black or African American, non-Hispanic/Latino; 1 Asian, non-Hispanic/Latino; 4 Hispanic/Latino), 28 international. Average age 24. 76 applicants, 36% accepted, 11 enrolled. In 2016, 41 master's, 4 doctorates awarded. *Degree requirements:* For master's, thesis, proposal presentation, progress presentation, defense presentation; for doctorate, thesis/dissertation, preliminary exam, proposal exam, defense exam. *Entrance requirements:* For master's, GRE General Test (minimum new score of 146 Verbal and 155 Quantitative), minimum GPA of 3.0; for doctorate, GRE General Test (minimum new score of 146 Verbal and 155 Quantitative), minimum GPA of 3.0 (without MS in industrial engineering), 3.4 (with MS in industrial engineering). Additional exam requirements/recommendations for international students: Required—TOEFL (minimum score 550 paper-based; 80 iBT); Recommended—IELTS (minimum score 6.5). *Application deadline:* For fall admission, 3/1 for domestic and international students; for spring admission, 11/1 for domestic and international students; for summer admission, 1/1 for domestic and international students. Applications are processed on a rolling basis. Application fee: $30. Electronic applications accepted. *Expenses:* Tuition, state resident: full-time $7263; part-time $403.51 per credit hour. Tuition, nonresident: full-time $18,087; part-time $1004.85 per credit hour. *Required fees:* $1365; $75.81 per credit hour. $20 per semester. Tuition and fees vary according to campus/location. *Financial support:* In 2016–17, 57 students received support, including 5 fellowships with full tuition reimbursements available, 19 research assistantships with full tuition reimbursements available, 10 teaching assistantships with full tuition reimbursements available; tuition waivers (full) and unspecified assistantships also available. Financial award application deadline: 3/1; financial award applicants required to submit FAFSA. *Faculty research:* Precision manufacturing, composite manufacturing, green manufacturing, applied optimization, simulation. *Total annual research expenditures:* $2.2 million. *Unit head:* Dr. Okenwa Okoli, Chair/Professor/Associate Director, 850-410-6352, Fax: 850-410-6342, E-mail: okoli@eng.famu.fsu.edu. *Application contact:* Shedric Triplett, Graduate Studies Assistant, 850-410-6582, Fax: 850-410-6342, E-mail: striplett@fsu.edu.
Website: http://www.eng.famu.fsu.edu/departments/industrial/

Georgia Institute of Technology, Graduate Studies, College of Engineering, H. Milton Stewart School of Industrial and Systems Engineering, Program in Industrial and Systems Engineering, Atlanta, GA 30332-0001. Offers industrial engineering (MS, PhD). *Program availability:* Part-time, online learning. Terminal master's awarded for partial completion of doctoral program. *Degree requirements:* For master's, thesis optional; for doctorate, comprehensive exam, thesis/dissertation. *Entrance requirements:* For master's and doctorate, GRE General Test. Additional exam requirements/recommendations for international students: Required—TOEFL (minimum score 550 paper-based; 79 iBT). Electronic applications accepted. *Faculty research:* Computer-integrated manufacturing systems, materials handling systems, production and distribution.

Illinois State University, Graduate School, College of Applied Science and Technology, Department of Technology, Normal, IL 61790-2200. Offers MS. *Degree requirements:* For master's, thesis or alternative. *Entrance requirements:* For master's, GRE General Test, minimum GPA of 2.8. *Faculty research:* Illinois Manufacturing Extension Center Field Office hosting, model for the professional development of K-12 technology education teachers, Illinois State University Illinois Mathematics and Science Partnership, Illinois University council for career and technical education.

Indiana University–Purdue University Fort Wayne, College of Engineering, Technology, and Computer Science, Program in Technology, Fort Wayne, IN 46805-1499. Offers facilities/construction management (MS); industrial technology/manufacturing (MS); information technology/advanced computer applications (MS). *Program availability:* Part-time. *Entrance requirements:* For master's, minimum GPA of 3.0. Additional exam requirements/recommendations for international students: Required—TOEFL (minimum score 550 paper-based; 79 iBT), TWE. Electronic applications accepted.

Instituto Tecnologico de Santo Domingo, Graduate School, Area of Engineering, Santo Domingo, Dominican Republic. Offers construction administration (MS, Certificate); data telecommunications (M Eng, MS, Certificate); industrial engineering (M Eng, Certificate); industrial management (M Mgmt); information technology (Certificate); maintenance engineering (M Eng); occupational hazard prevention (M Mgmt); production management (Certificate); quantitative methods (Certificate); sanitary and environmental engineering (M Eng); structural engineering (M Eng); systems engineering and electronic data processing (Certificate); transportation (Certificate).

Instituto Tecnológico y de Estudios Superiores de Monterrey, Campus Chihuahua, Graduate Programs, Chihuahua, Mexico. Offers computer systems engineering (Ingeniero); electrical engineering (Ingeniero); electromechanical engineering (Ingeniero); electronic engineering (Ingeniero); engineering administration (MEA); industrial engineering (MIE, Ingeniero); international trade (MIT); mechanical engineering (Ingeniero).

Instituto Tecnológico y de Estudios Superiores de Monterrey, Campus Ciudad de México, Virtual University Division, Ciudad de Mexico, Mexico. Offers administration of information technologies (MA); computer sciences (MA); education (MA, PhD); educational technology (MA); environmental engineering (MA); environmental systems (MA); humanistic studies (MA); industrial engineering (MA); international business for Latin America (MA); quality systems (MA); quality systems and productivity (MA). *Program availability:* Part-time, evening/weekend, online learning. *Entrance requirements:* For master's and doctorate, Instituto entrance exam. Additional exam requirements/recommendations for international students: Required—TOEFL.

Instituto Tecnológico y de Estudios Superiores de Monterrey, Campus Laguna, Graduate School, Torreón, Mexico. Offers business administration (MBA); industrial engineering (MIE); management information systems (MS). *Program availability:* Part-time. *Entrance requirements:* For master's, GMAT. *Faculty research:* Computer communications from home to the university.

Instituto Tecnológico y de Estudios Superiores de Monterrey, Campus Monterrey, Graduate and Research Division, Programs in Engineering, Monterrey, Mexico. Offers applied statistics (M Eng); artificial intelligence (PhD); automation engineering (M Eng); chemical engineering (M Eng); civil engineering (M Eng); electrical engineering (M Eng); electronic engineering (M Eng); environmental engineering (M Eng); industrial engineering (M Eng, PhD); manufacturing engineering (M Eng); mechanical engineering (M Eng); systems and quality engineering (M Eng). M Eng program offered jointly with University of Waterloo; PhD in industrial engineering with Texas A&M University. *Program availability:* Part-time, evening/weekend. Terminal master's awarded for partial completion of doctoral program. *Degree requirements:* For master's, one foreign language, thesis; for doctorate, one foreign language, thesis/dissertation. *Entrance requirements:* For master's, EXADEP; for doctorate, GRE, master's degree in related field. Additional exam requirements/recommendations for international students:

Industrial/Management Engineering

Required—TOEFL. *Faculty research:* Flexible manufacturing cells, materials, statistical methods, environmental prevention, control and evaluation.

Iowa State University of Science and Technology, Department of Industrial and Manufacturing Systems Engineering, Ames, IA 50011. Offers industrial engineering (M Eng, MS, PhD); operations research (MS); systems engineering (M Eng). *Degree requirements:* For master's, thesis or alternative; for doctorate, thesis/dissertation. *Entrance requirements:* For master's and doctorate, GRE General Test. Additional exam requirements/recommendations for international students: Required—TOEFL (minimum score 550 paper-based; 79 iBT), IELTS (minimum score 6.5). *Application deadline:* For fall admission, 1/15 priority date for international students; for spring admission, 7/15 priority date for international students. Application fee: $60 ($90 for international students). Electronic applications accepted. *Faculty research:* Economic modeling, valuation techniques, robotics, digital controls, systems reliability. *Application contact:* Deborah McDonough, Application Contact, 515-294-0129, Fax: 515-294-3524, E-mail: imsegradprogram@iastate.edu.
Website: http://www.imse.iastate.edu

Kansas State University, Graduate School, College of Engineering, Department of Industrial and Manufacturing Systems Engineering, Manhattan, KS 66506. Offers engineering management (MEM); industrial engineering (MS); operations research (MS). *Program availability:* Part-time, online learning. *Faculty:* 10 full-time (2 women), 1 part-time/adjunct (0 women). *Students:* 34 full-time (8 women), 51 part-time (6 women); includes 17 minority (5 Black or African American, non-Hispanic/Latino; 4 Asian, non-Hispanic/Latino; 4 Hispanic/Latino; 4 Two or more races, non-Hispanic/Latino), 25 international. Average age 30. 62 applicants, 56% accepted, 10 enrolled. In 2016, 27 master's, 3 doctorates awarded. *Degree requirements:* For master's, thesis or alternative; for doctorate, thesis/dissertation. *Entrance requirements:* For master's, GRE General Test (minimum score of 750 old version, 159 new format on Quantitative portion of exam), bachelor's degree in engineering, mathematics, or physical science; for doctorate, GRE General Test (minimum score of 770 old version, 164 new format on Quantitative portion of exam), master's degree in engineering or industrial manufacturing. Additional exam requirements/recommendations for international students: Required—PTE (minimum score 58), TOEFL (minimum score 550 paper-based; 79 iBT) or IELTS (minimum score 6.5). *Application deadline:* For fall admission, 6/1 priority date for domestic students, 12/1 priority date for international students; for spring admission, 11/1 priority date for domestic students, 8/1 priority date for international students. Applications are processed on a rolling basis. Application fee: $50 ($75 for international students). Electronic applications accepted. *Expenses:* Tuition, state resident: full-time $9670. Tuition, nonresident: full-time $21,828. *Required fees:* $862. *Financial support:* In 2016–17, 12 research assistantships (averaging $12,442 per year), 9 teaching assistantships with full tuition reimbursements (averaging $14,111 per year) were awarded; Federal Work-Study, institutionally sponsored loans, and scholarships/grants also available. Support available to part-time students. Financial award application deadline: 3/1; financial award applicants required to submit FAFSA. *Faculty research:* Industrial engineering, ergonomics, healthcare systems engineering, manufacturing processes, operations research, engineering management. *Total annual research expenditures:* $2.6 million. *Unit head:* Dr. Bradley Kramer, Head, 785-532-5606, Fax: 785-532-3738, E-mail: bradleyk@k-state.edu. *Application contact:* Dr. David Ben-Arieh, Chair of Graduate Committee, 785-532-5606, Fax: 785-532-3738, E-mail: imse@k-state.edu.
Website: http://www.imse.k-state.edu/

Lamar University, College of Graduate Studies, College of Engineering, Department of Industrial Engineering, Beaumont, TX 77710. Offers engineering management (MEM); industrial engineering (ME, MES, DE). *Faculty:* 10 full-time (2 women), 1 part-time/adjunct (0 women). *Students:* 111 full-time (13 women), 57 part-time (6 women); includes 2 minority (1 Black or African American, non-Hispanic/Latino; 1 Asian, non-Hispanic/Latino), 163 international. Average age 25. 153 applicants, 86% accepted, 26 enrolled. In 2016, 77 master's, 3 doctorates awarded. *Degree requirements:* For doctorate, thesis/dissertation. *Entrance requirements:* For master's and doctorate, GRE General Test. Additional exam requirements/recommendations for international students: Required—TOEFL (minimum score 550 paper-based; 79 iBT), IELTS (minimum score 6.5). *Application deadline:* For fall admission, 8/10 for domestic students, 7/1 for international students; for spring admission, 1/5 for domestic students, 12/1 for international students. Applications are processed on a rolling basis. Application fee: $25 ($50 for international students). Electronic applications accepted. *Expenses:* $8,134 in-state full-time, $5,574 in-state part-time; $15,604 out-of-state full-time, $10,554 out-of-state part-time per year. *Financial support:* Fellowships, research assistantships, and teaching assistantships available. Financial award application deadline: 4/1; financial award applicants required to submit FAFSA. *Faculty research:* Process simulation, total quality management, ergonomics and safety, scheduling. *Unit head:* Dr. Brian Craig, Chair, 409-880-8804, Fax: 409-880-8121. *Application contact:* Deidre Mayer, Interim Director, Admissions and Academic Services, 409-880-8888, Fax: 409-880-7419, E-mail: gradmissions@lamar.edu.
Website: http://engineering.lamar.edu/industrial

Lawrence Technological University, College of Engineering, Southfield, MI 48075-1058. Offers architectural engineering (MS); automotive engineering (MS); biomedical engineering (MS); civil engineering (MA, MS, PhD), including environmental engineering (MS), geotechnical engineering (MS), structural engineering (MS), transportation engineering (MS), water resource engineering (MS); construction engineering management (MA); electrical and computer engineering (MS); engineering management (MA); engineering technology (MS); fire engineering (MS); industrial engineering (MS), including healthcare; manufacturing systems (ME); mechanical engineering (MS, DE, PhD), including manufacturing (DE), solid mechanics (MS), thermal-fluids (MS); mechatronic systems engineering (MS). *Program availability:* Part-time, evening/weekend. *Faculty:* 24 full-time (5 women), 26 part-time/adjunct (2 women). *Students:* 22 full-time (7 women), 588 part-time (81 women); includes 23 minority (11 Black or African American, non-Hispanic/Latino; 4 Asian, non-Hispanic/Latino; 7 Hispanic/Latino; 1 Two or more races, non-Hispanic/Latino), 469 international. Average age 27. 1,186 applicants, 39% accepted, 99 enrolled. In 2016, 293 master's, 3 doctorates awarded. Terminal master's awarded for partial completion of doctoral program. *Degree requirements:* For master's, thesis optional; for doctorate, comprehensive exam, thesis/dissertation optional. *Entrance requirements:* Additional exam requirements/recommendations for international students: Required—TOEFL (minimum score 550 paper-based; 79 iBT), IELTS (minimum score 6.5). *Application deadline:* For fall admission, 5/22 for international students; for spring admission, 10/11 for international students; for summer admission, 2/16 for international students. Applications are processed on a rolling basis. Application fee: $50. Electronic applications accepted. *Expenses:* Tuition: Full-time $14,868; part-time $1062 per credit. *Required fees:* $75 per semester. Tuition and fees vary according to campus/location. *Financial support:* In 2016–17, 25 students received support, including 5 research assistantships with full tuition reimbursements available; unspecified assistantships also available. Financial award application deadline: 4/1; financial award applicants required to submit FAFSA. *Faculty research:* Carbon fiber reinforced polymer reinforced concrete structures; low impact storm water management solutions; vehicle battery energy management; wireless communication; entrepreneurial mindset and engineering. *Total annual research expenditures:* $1.7 million. *Unit head:* Dr. Nabil Grace, Dean, 248-204-2500, Fax: 248-204-2509, E-mail: engrdean@ltu.edu. *Application contact:* Jane Rohrback, Director of Admissions, 248-204-3160, Fax: 248-204-2228, E-mail: admissions@ltu.edu.
Website: http://www.ltu.edu/engineering/index.asp

Lehigh University, P.C. Rossin College of Engineering and Applied Science, Department of Industrial and Systems Engineering, Bethlehem, PA 18015. Offers analytical finance (MS); industrial and systems engineering (M Eng, MS, PhD); management science and engineering (M Eng, MS); MBA/E. *Program availability:* Part-time, 100% online, classroom live. *Faculty:* 19 full-time (2 women), 3 part-time/adjunct (0 women). *Students:* 102 full-time (28 women), 7 part-time (3 women); includes 1 minority (Asian, non-Hispanic/Latino), 103 international. Average age 25. 375 applicants, 35% accepted, 39 enrolled. In 2016, 36 master's, 8 doctorates awarded. Terminal master's awarded for partial completion of doctoral program. *Degree requirements:* For master's, thesis (MS); project (M Eng); for doctorate, comprehensive exam, thesis/dissertation. *Entrance requirements:* For master's and doctorate, GRE General Test. Additional exam requirements/recommendations for international students: Required—TOEFL (minimum score 550 paper-based; 79 iBT), IELTS (minimum score 6.5). *Application deadline:* For fall admission, 7/15 for domestic and international students; for spring admission, 12/1 for domestic and international students. Application fee: $75. Electronic applications accepted. *Expenses:* $1,420 per credit hour. *Financial support:* In 2016–17, 33 students received support, including 2 fellowships with full tuition reimbursements available (averaging $20,490 per year), 18 research assistantships with full tuition reimbursements available (averaging $20,490 per year), 11 teaching assistantships with full tuition reimbursements available (averaging $21,105 per year); unspecified assistantships also available. Financial award application deadline: 1/15. *Faculty research:* Mathematical optimization; logistics and service systems, stochastic processes and simulation; computational optimization and high performance computing; financial engineering and robust optimization; machine learning and data mining. *Total annual research expenditures:* $1.7 million. *Unit head:* Dr. Tamas Terlaky, Chair, 610-758-4050, Fax: 610-758-4886, E-mail: terlaky@lehigh.edu. *Application contact:* Rita Frey, Graduate Coordinator, 610-758-4051, Fax: 610-758-4886, E-mail: ise@lehigh.edu.
Website: http://www.lehigh.edu/ise

Louisiana Tech University, Graduate School, College of Engineering and Science, Department of Industrial Engineering, Ruston, LA 71272. Offers MS. *Entrance requirements:* For master's, GRE. Additional exam requirements/recommendations for international students: Required—TOEFL (minimum score 550 paper-based; 80 iBT). *Financial support:* Unspecified assistantships available. *Unit head:* Dr. Jun-Ing Ker, Program Chair, 318-257-2963, Fax: 318-257-2562, E-mail: ker@latech.edu. *Application contact:* Marilyn J. Robinson, Assistant to the Dean, 318-257-2924, Fax: 318-257-4487.
Website: http://coes.latech.edu/industrial-engineering/

Mississippi State University, Bagley College of Engineering, Department of Industrial and Systems Engineering, Mississippi State, MS 39762. Offers human factors and ergonomics (MS); industrial and systems engineering (PhD); industrial systems (MS); management systems (MS); manufacturing systems (MS); operations research (MS). *Program availability:* Part-time, blended/hybrid learning. *Faculty:* 12 full-time (1 woman). *Students:* 25 full-time (5 women), 59 part-time (13 women); includes 18 minority (6 Black or African American, non-Hispanic/Latino; 5 Asian, non-Hispanic/Latino; 6 Hispanic/Latino; 1 Native Hawaiian or other Pacific Islander, non-Hispanic/Latino), 21 international. Average age 35. 72 applicants, 32% accepted, 11 enrolled. In 2016, 11 master's, 7 doctorates awarded. *Degree requirements:* For master's, comprehensive exam (for some programs), thesis optional, comprehensive oral or written exam; for doctorate, comprehensive exam, thesis/dissertation, candidacy exam. *Entrance requirements:* For master's, GRE (for graduates from program not accredited by EAC/ABET), minimum GPA of 3.0 on junior and senior years; for doctorate, GRE (for graduates from program not accredited by EAC/ABET), minimum GPA of 3.5 on master's degree and junior and senior years of BS. Additional exam requirements/recommendations for international students: Required—TOEFL (minimum score 550 paper-based; 79 iBT); Recommended—IELTS (minimum score 6.5). *Application deadline:* For fall admission, 7/1 for domestic students, 5/1 for international students; for spring admission, 11/1 for domestic students, 9/1 for international students. Applications are processed on a rolling basis. Application fee: $60. Electronic applications accepted. *Expenses:* Tuition, state resident: full-time $7670; part-time $852.50 per credit hour. Tuition, nonresident: full-time $20,790; part-time $2310.50 per credit hour. Part-time tuition and fees vary according to course load. *Financial support:* In 2016–17, 12 research assistantships with full tuition reimbursements (averaging $16,360 per year), 3 teaching assistantships with full tuition reimbursements (averaging $17,014 per year) were awarded; Federal Work-Study, institutionally sponsored loans, and unspecified assistantships also available. Financial award application deadline: 4/1; financial award applicants required to submit FAFSA. *Faculty research:* Operations research, ergonomics, production systems, management systems, transportation. *Total annual research expenditures:* $4.4 million. *Unit head:* Dr. John Usher, Professor/Department Head, 662-325-7624, Fax: 662-325-7618, E-mail: usher@ise.msstate.edu. *Application contact:* Doretta Martin, Senior Admissions Assistant, 662-325-9514, E-mail: dmartin@grad.msstate.edu.
Website: http://www.ise.msstate.edu/

Montana State University, The Graduate School, College of Engineering, Department of Mechanical and Industrial Engineering, Bozeman, MT 59717. Offers engineering (PhD), including industrial engineering, mechanical engineering; industrial and management engineering (MS); mechanical engineering (MS). *Program availability:* Part-time. *Degree requirements:* For master's, comprehensive exam, thesis, oral exams; for doctorate, comprehensive exam, thesis/dissertation, qualifying exam. *Entrance requirements:* For master's, GRE, official transcript, minimum GPA of 3.0, demonstrated potential for success, statement of goals, three letters of recommendation, proof of funds affidavit; for doctorate, minimum undergraduate GPA of 3.0, 3.2 graduate; three letters of recommendation; statement of objectives. Additional exam requirements/recommendations for international students: Required—TOEFL or IELTS. Electronic applications accepted. *Faculty research:* Human factors engineering, energy, design and manufacture, systems modeling, materials and structures, measurement systems.

Montana Tech of The University of Montana, Project Engineering and Management Program, Butte, MT 59701-8997. Offers MPEM. *Program availability:* Part-time, evening/weekend, online learning. *Faculty:* 1 full-time (0 women), 8 part-time/adjunct (2 women). *Students:* 10 part-time (5 women); includes 2 minority (both Black or African American, non-Hispanic/Latino). Average age 28. 10 applicants, 90% accepted, 5 enrolled. In 2016, 4 master's awarded. *Degree requirements:* For master's, comprehensive exam, final project presentation. *Entrance requirements:* For master's, minimum GPA of 3.0. Additional exam requirements/recommendations for international students: Required—TOEFL (minimum score 550 paper-based; 80 iBT), IELTS (minimum score 7). *Application deadline:* For fall admission, 4/1 priority date for domestic students, 3/1 priority date for international students; for spring admission, 10/1 priority date for domestic students, 8/1 priority date for international students. Applications are processed on a rolling basis. Application fee: $50. Electronic applications accepted. *Expenses:* Tuition, state resident: full-time $2901; part-time

$1450.68 per degree program. Tuition, nonresident: full-time $8432; part-time $4215.84 per degree program. *Required fees:* $668; $354 per degree program. Tuition and fees vary according to course load and program. *Financial support:* Application deadline: 4/1; applicants required to submit FAFSA. *Unit head:* Dr. Kumar Ganesan, Director, 406-496-4239, Fax: 406-496-4650, E-mail: kganesan@mtech.edu. *Application contact:* Daniel Stirling, Administrator, Graduate School, 406-496-4304, Fax: 406-496-4710, E-mail: gradschoo@mtech.edu.
Website: https://www.mtech.edu/academics/gradschool/distancelearning/distancelearning-pem.htm

Morehead State University, Graduate Programs, College of Science and Technology, Department of Industrial and Engineering Technology, Morehead, KY 40351. Offers career and technical education (MS); engineering technology (MS). *Program availability:* Part-time, evening/weekend. *Degree requirements:* For master's, completion and defense of thesis or written and oral comprehensive exit exams. *Entrance requirements:* For master's, GRE, minimum undergraduate GPA of 3.0 in major. Additional exam requirements/recommendations for international students: Required—TOEFL (minimum score 500 paper-based). Electronic applications accepted.

Morgan State University, School of Graduate Studies, Clarence M. Mitchell, Jr. School of Engineering, Baltimore, MD 21251. Offers civil engineering (M Eng, D Eng); electrical and computer engineering (M Eng, MS, D Eng); industrial and systems engineering (M Eng, D Eng); transportation (MS). *Program availability:* Part-time, evening/weekend. *Degree requirements:* For master's, thesis, comprehensive exam or equivalent; for doctorate, thesis/dissertation, comprehensive exam or equivalent. *Entrance requirements:* For master's, GRE, minimum undergraduate GPA of 2.5; for doctorate, GRE, minimum GPA of 3.0. Additional exam requirements/recommendations for international students: Required—TOEFL (minimum score 550 paper-based).

New Jersey Institute of Technology, Newark College of Engineering, Newark, NJ 07102. Offers biomedical engineering (MS, PhD); chemical engineering (MS, PhD); computer engineering (MS, PhD); electrical engineering (MS, PhD); engineering management (MS); environmental engineering (PhD); healthcare systems management (MS); industrial engineering (MS, PhD); Internet engineering (MS); manufacturing engineering (MS); mechanical engineering (MS, PhD); occupational safety and health engineering (MS); pharmaceutical bioprocessing (MS); pharmaceutical engineering (MS); pharmaceutical systems management (MS); power and energy systems (MS); telecommunications (MS); transportation (MS, PhD). *Program availability:* Part-time, evening/weekend. *Faculty:* 146 full-time (21 women), 119 part-time/adjunct (10 women). *Students:* 804 full-time (191 women), 550 part-time (129 women); includes 357 minority (82 Black or African American, non-Hispanic/Latino; 1 American Indian or Alaska Native, non-Hispanic/Latino; 138 Asian, non-Hispanic/Latino; 114 Hispanic/Latino; 22 Two or more races, non-Hispanic/Latino), 675 international. Average age 27. 2,959 applicants, 51% accepted, 442 enrolled. In 2016, 595 master's, 29 doctorates awarded. Terminal master's awarded for partial completion of doctoral program. *Degree requirements:* For master's, thesis optional; for doctorate, thesis/dissertation. *Entrance requirements:* For master's, GRE General Test; for doctorate, GRE General Test, minimum graduate GPA of 3.5. Additional exam requirements/recommendations for international students: Required—TOEFL (minimum score 550 paper-based; 79 iBT). *Application deadline:* For fall admission, 6/1 priority date for domestic students, 5/1 priority date for international students; for spring admission, 11/15 priority date for domestic and international students. Applications are processed on a rolling basis. Application fee: $75. Electronic applications accepted. *Expenses:* Contact institution. *Financial support:* In 2016–17, 172 students received support, including 1 fellowship (averaging $1,528 per year), 79 research assistantships (averaging $13,336 per year), 92 teaching assistantships (averaging $20,619 per year); scholarships/grants also available. Financial award application deadline: 1/15. *Faculty research:* Nonlinear signal processing, intelligent medical image analysis, calibration issues in coherent localization, computer-aided design, neural network for tool wear measurement. *Total annual research expenditures:* $11.1 million. *Unit head:* Dr. Moshe Kam, Dean, 973-596-5534, E-mail: moshe.kam@njit.edu. *Application contact:* Stephen Eck, Director of Admissions, 973-596-3300, Fax: 973-596-3461, E-mail: admissions@njit.edu.
Website: http://engineering.njit.edu/

New Mexico State University, College of Engineering, Department of Industrial Engineering, Las Cruces, NM 88003. Offers industrial engineering (MSIE, PhD); systems engineering (Graduate Certificate). *Program availability:* Part-time-only, evening/weekend, 100% online. *Faculty:* 6 full-time (3 women). *Students:* 40 full-time (9 women), 87 part-time (23 women); includes 48 minority (9 Black or African American, non-Hispanic/Latino; 1 American Indian or Alaska Native, non-Hispanic/Latino; 2 Asian, non-Hispanic/Latino; 32 Hispanic/Latino; 4 Two or more races, non-Hispanic/Latino), 30 international. Average age 33. 96 applicants, 55% accepted, 38 enrolled. In 2016, 48 master's, 3 doctorates, 2 other advanced degrees awarded. *Degree requirements:* For master's, thesis optional; for doctorate, comprehensive exam, thesis/dissertation, qualifying exam. *Entrance requirements:* Additional exam requirements/recommendations for international students: Required—TOEFL (minimum score 550 paper-based; 79 iBT), IELTS (minimum score 6.5). *Application deadline:* For fall admission, 7/1 priority date for domestic students, 3/1 for international students; for spring admission, 11/1 for domestic students, 10/1 for international students. Applications are processed on a rolling basis. Application fee: $40 ($50 for international students). Electronic applications accepted. *Expenses:* Tuition, state resident: full-time $4086. Tuition, nonresident: full-time $14,254. *Required fees:* $853. Tuition and fees vary according to course load. *Financial support:* In 2016–17, 33 students received support, including 1 research assistantship (averaging $16,964 per year), 5 teaching assistantships (averaging $15,712 per year); career-related internships or fieldwork, Federal Work-Study, scholarships/grants, traineeships, health care benefits, and unspecified assistantships also available. Support available to part-time students. Financial award application deadline: 3/1. *Faculty research:* Operations research, simulation, manufacturing engineering, systems engineering, applied statistics. *Total annual research expenditures:* $154,041. *Unit head:* Dr. Edward Pines, Department Head, 575-646-4923, Fax: 575-646-2976, E-mail: epines@nmsu.edu. *Application contact:* 575-646-4923, Fax: 575-646-2976, E-mail: ie@nmsu.edu.
Website: http://ie.nmsu.edu

New York University, Polytechnic School of Engineering, Department of Technology Management, Major in Industrial Engineering, New York, NY 10012-1019. Offers MS. *Program availability:* Part-time, evening/weekend, online learning. *Degree requirements:* For master's, comprehensive exam (for some programs), thesis (for some programs). *Entrance requirements:* For master's, BE or BS in engineering, physics, chemistry, mathematical sciences, or biological sciences, or MBA. Additional exam requirements/recommendations for international students: Required—TOEFL (minimum score 550 paper-based; 80 iBT); Recommended—IELTS (minimum score 6.5). Electronic applications accepted.

North Carolina Agricultural and Technical State University, School of Graduate Studies, College of Engineering, Department of Industrial and Systems Engineering, Greensboro, NC 27411. Offers industrial engineering (MSIE, PhD). *Program availability:* Part-time. *Degree requirements:* For master's, thesis, project; for doctorate, thesis/dissertation. *Entrance requirements:* For master's, GRE General Test (recommended); for doctorate, GRE General Test, degree in engineering, BS in industrial engineering from ABET-accredited program with minimum cumulative credit point average of 3.7 or MS in discipline related to industrial engineering from college or university recognized by a regional or general accrediting agency with minimum cumulative GPA of 3.3. Additional exam requirements/recommendations for international students: Required—TOEFL (minimum score 550 paper-based; 79 iBT). *Faculty research:* Human-machine systems engineering, management systems engineering, operations research and systems analysis, production systems engineering.

North Carolina State University, Graduate School, College of Engineering, Edward P. Fitts Department of Industrial and Systems Engineering, Raleigh, NC 27695. Offers industrial engineering (MIE, MS, PhD). PhD offered jointly with North Carolina Agricultural and Technical State University, The University of North Carolina at Charlotte. *Program availability:* Part-time. Terminal master's awarded for partial completion of doctoral program. *Degree requirements:* For master's, thesis optional; for doctorate, thesis/dissertation. *Entrance requirements:* For master's, GRE General Test, minimum GPA of 3.0; for doctorate, GRE General Test. Additional exam requirements/recommendations for international students: Required—TOEFL. Electronic applications accepted.

North Dakota State University, College of Graduate and Interdisciplinary Studies, College of Engineering, Department of Industrial and Manufacturing Engineering, Fargo, ND 58102. Offers industrial and manufacturing engineering (PhD); industrial engineering and management (MS); manufacturing engineering (MS). *Program availability:* Part-time. *Degree requirements:* For doctorate, comprehensive exam, thesis/dissertation. *Entrance requirements:* For master's, GRE General Test, bachelor's degree in engineering; for doctorate, GRE General Test, master's degree in engineering. Additional exam requirements/recommendations for international students: Required—TOEFL (minimum score 550 paper-based; 79 iBT), TWE (minimum score 4). Electronic applications accepted. *Faculty research:* Electronics manufacturing, quality engineering, manufacturing process science, healthcare, lean manufacturing.

Northeastern University, College of Engineering, Boston, MA 02115-5096. Offers bioengineering (MS, PhD); chemical engineering (MS, PhD); civil engineering (MS, PhD); computer engineering (PhD); computer systems engineering (MS); electrical and computer engineering (MS); electrical and computer engineering leadership (MS); electrical engineering (PhD); energy systems (MS); engineering and public policy (MS); engineering management (MS, Certificate); environmental engineering (MS); industrial engineering (MS, PhD); information assurance (PhD); information systems (MS); interdisciplinary engineering (PhD); mechanical engineering (PhD); operations research (MS); telecommunication systems management (MS). *Program availability:* Part-time, online learning. *Faculty:* 202 full-time (59 women), 53 part-time/adjunct (9 women). *Students:* 2,982 full-time (954 women), 192 part-time (38 women). In 2016, 851 master's, 74 doctorates awarded. Application fee: $75. Electronic applications accepted. *Expenses:* $1,471 per credit. *Financial support:* Fellowships, research assistantships, teaching assistantships, career-related internships or fieldwork, scholarships/grants, health care benefits, tuition waivers, and unspecified assistantships available. Support available to part-time students. Financial award applicants required to submit FAFSA. *Unit head:* Dr. Nadine Aubry, Dean, College of Engineering. *Application contact:* Jeffery Hengel, Director of Graduate Admissions, 617-373-2711, E-mail: j.hengel@northeastern.edu.
Website: http://www.coe.neu.edu/academics/graduate-school-engineering

Northern Illinois University, Graduate School, College of Engineering and Engineering Technology, Department of Industrial Engineering, De Kalb, IL 60115-2854. Offers MS. *Program availability:* Part-time. *Faculty:* 4 full-time (1 woman), 1 part-time/adjunct (0 women). *Students:* 92 full-time (10 women), 77 part-time (9 women); includes 15 minority (3 Black or African American, non-Hispanic/Latino; 5 Asian, non-Hispanic/Latino; 6 Hispanic/Latino; 1 Two or more races, non-Hispanic/Latino), 134 international. Average age 26. 231 applicants, 56% accepted, 38 enrolled. In 2016, 41 master's awarded. *Degree requirements:* For master's, comprehensive exam, thesis optional. *Entrance requirements:* For master's, GRE General Test, minimum GPA of 2.75. Additional exam requirements/recommendations for international students: Required—TOEFL (minimum score 550 paper-based). *Application deadline:* For fall admission, 6/1 for domestic students, 5/1 for international students; for spring admission, 11/1 for domestic students, 10/1 for international students. Applications are processed on a rolling basis. Application fee: $40. Electronic applications accepted. *Financial support:* In 2016–17, 22 research assistantships, 28 teaching assistantships were awarded; fellowships, Federal Work-Study, scholarships/grants, tuition waivers (full), and staff assistantships also available. Support available to part-time students. Financial award applicants required to submit FAFSA. *Faculty research:* Assembly robots, engineering ethics, quality cost models, data mining. *Unit head:* Dr. Purushothaman Damodaran, Chair, 815-753-1349, Fax: 815-753-0823. *Application contact:* Graduate School Office, 815-753-0395, E-mail: gradsch@niu.edu.
Website: http://www.niu.edu/isye

Northwestern University, McCormick School of Engineering and Applied Science, Department of Industrial Engineering and Management Sciences, Evanston, IL 60208. Offers analytics (MS); engineering management (MEM); industrial engineering and management science (MS, PhD). MS and PhD admissions and degrees offered through The Graduate School. Terminal master's awarded for partial completion of doctoral program. *Degree requirements:* For master's, comprehensive exam; for doctorate, comprehensive exam, thesis/dissertation. *Entrance requirements:* For master's and doctorate, GRE General Test. Additional exam requirements/recommendations for international students: Required—TOEFL (minimum score 577 paper-based; 90 iBT), IELTS (minimum score 7). Electronic applications accepted. *Faculty research:* Financial engineering, healthcare engineering, humanitarian systems, optimization, organization behavior and technology management, production and logistics, social and organizational networks, statistics for enterprise engineering, stochastic modeling and simulation.

The Ohio State University, Graduate School, College of Engineering, Department of Integrated Systems Engineering, Columbus, OH 43210. Offers industrial and systems engineering (MS, PhD). *Faculty:* 21. *Students:* 89 full-time (21 women), 5 part-time (1 woman), 68 international. Average age 27. In 2016, 33 master's, 9 doctorates awarded. *Degree requirements:* For master's, thesis optional; for doctorate, thesis/dissertation. *Entrance requirements:* For master's and doctorate, GRE General Test (desired minimum scores: Quantitative 166, Verbal 153, Analytical Writing 4.5). Additional exam requirements/recommendations for international students: Required—TOEFL (minimum score 550 paper-based; 79 iBT), Michigan English Language Assessment Battery (minimum score 82); Recommended—IELTS (minimum score 7). *Application deadline:* For fall admission, 12/13 priority date for domestic students, 11/30 priority date for international students; for spring admission, 12/4 for domestic students, 10/1 for international students; for summer admission, 2/1 for domestic and international students. Applications are processed on a rolling basis. Application fee: $60 ($70 for international students). Electronic applications accepted. *Financial support:* Fellowships with tuition reimbursements, research assistantships with tuition reimbursements, teaching assistantships with tuition reimbursements, career-related internships or fieldwork, Federal Work-Study, institutionally sponsored loans, and unspecified

assistantships available. Support available to part-time students. *Unit head:* Dr. Philip J. Smith, Chair, 614-292-4120, E-mail: smith.131@osu.edu. *Application contact:* Dr. Jerald Brevik, Graduate Studies Chair, 614-292-0177, Fax: 614-292-7852, E-mail: brevik.1@osu.edu.
Website: http://ise.osu.edu/

Ohio University, Graduate College, Russ College of Engineering and Technology, Department of Industrial and Systems Engineering, Athens, OH 45701-2979. Offers M Eng Mgt, MS. *Program availability:* Part-time, evening/weekend. *Degree requirements:* For master's, comprehensive exam (for some programs), thesis optional, research project. *Entrance requirements:* For master's, GRE General Test. Additional exam requirements/recommendations for international students: Required—TOEFL (minimum score 550 paper-based; 80 iBT) or IELTS (minimum score 6.5). *Application deadline:* For fall admission, 3/1 priority date for domestic and international students; for winter admission, 9/1 priority date for domestic and international students; for spring admission, 1/1 priority date for domestic and international students. Applications are processed on a rolling basis. Application fee: $50 ($55 for international students). Electronic applications accepted. *Financial support:* Research assistantships with full tuition reimbursements, Federal Work-Study, institutionally sponsored loans, tuition waivers (full), and unspecified assistantships available. Financial award application deadline: 2/15; financial award applicants required to submit FAFSA. *Faculty research:* Software systems integration, human factors and ergonomics. *Unit head:* Dr. Robert P. Judd, Chairman, 740-593-0106, Fax: 740-593-0778, E-mail: judd@ohio.edu. *Application contact:* Dr. Gursel Suer, Graduate Chairman, 740-593-1542, Fax: 740-593-0778, E-mail: suer@ohio.edu.
Website: http://www.ohio.edu/industrial/

Ohio University, Graduate College, Russ College of Engineering and Technology, Program in Mechanical and Systems Engineering, Athens, OH 45701-2979. Offers industrial and systems engineering (MS); mechanical and systems engineering (PhD). *Degree requirements:* For doctorate, comprehensive exam, thesis/dissertation. *Entrance requirements:* For doctorate, GRE General Test, MS in engineering or related field. Additional exam requirements/recommendations for international students: Required—TOEFL (minimum score 550 paper-based; 80 iBT) or IELTS (minimum score 6.5). *Application deadline:* For fall admission, 3/15 priority date for domestic and international students. Applications are processed on a rolling basis. Application fee: $50 ($55 for international students). Electronic applications accepted. *Financial support:* Research assistantships with full tuition reimbursements, Federal Work-Study, institutionally sponsored loans, and unspecified assistantships available. Financial award application deadline: 3/15; financial award applicants required to submit FAFSA. *Faculty research:* Material processing, expert systems, environmental geotechnical manufacturing, thermal systems, robotics. *Unit head:* Dr. Dennis Irwin, Dean, 740-593-1474, Fax: 740-593-0659, E-mail: irwind@ohio.edu. *Application contact:* Dr. Shawn Ostermann, Associate Dean, 740-593-1482, Fax: 740-593-0659, E-mail: ostermann@ohio.edu.
Website: http://www.ohio.edu/engineering/msephd/

Oklahoma State University, College of Engineering, Architecture and Technology, School of Industrial Engineering and Management, Stillwater, OK 74078. Offers MS, PhD. *Program availability:* Online learning. *Faculty:* 14 full-time (4 women). *Students:* 98 full-time (11 women), 138 part-time (26 women); includes 18 minority (5 Black or African American, non-Hispanic/Latino; 2 Asian, non-Hispanic/Latino; 6 Hispanic/Latino; 5 Two or more races, non-Hispanic/Latino), 114 international. Average age 29. 364 applicants, 25% accepted, 67 enrolled. In 2016, 69 master's, 5 doctorates awarded. *Degree requirements:* For master's, creative component or thesis; for doctorate, comprehensive exam, thesis/dissertation. *Entrance requirements:* For master's and doctorate, GRE or GMAT. Additional exam requirements/recommendations for international students: Required—TOEFL (minimum score 550 paper-based; 79 iBT). *Application deadline:* For fall admission, 3/1 priority date for international students; for spring admission, 8/1 priority date for international students. Applications are processed on a rolling basis. Application fee: $40 ($75 for international students). Electronic applications accepted. *Expenses:* Tuition, state resident: full-time $3775; part-time $209.70 per credit hour. Tuition, nonresident: full-time $14,851; part-time $825.05 per credit hour. *Required fees:* $2027; $112.60 per credit hour. Tuition and fees vary according to campus/location. *Financial support:* In 2016–17, 12 research assistantships (averaging $8,253 per year), 27 teaching assistantships (averaging $7,819 per year) were awarded; career-related internships or fieldwork, Federal Work-Study, scholarships/grants, health care benefits, tuition waivers (partial), and unspecified assistantships also available. Support available to part-time students. Financial award application deadline: 3/1; financial award applicants required to submit FAFSA. *Unit head:* Dr. Sunderesh Heragu, Head, 405-744-6055, Fax: 405-744-4654, E-mail: sunderesh.heragu@okstate.edu. *Application contact:* Dr. Baski Balasundaram, Director of Graduate Program, 405-744-6055, Fax: 405-744-4654, E-mail: baski@okstate.edu.
Website: http://iem.okstate.edu/

Oregon State University, College of Engineering, Program in Industrial Engineering, Corvallis, OR 97331. Offers advanced manufacturing (M Eng, MS, PhD); engineering management (M Eng); human systems engineering (M Eng, MS, PhD); information systems engineering (M Eng, MS, PhD). *Program availability:* 100% online. *Faculty:* 52 full-time (12 women), 3 part-time/adjunct (0 women). *Students:* 75 full-time (18 women), 28 part-time (11 women); includes 14 minority (1 American Indian or Alaska Native, non-Hispanic/Latino; 7 Asian, non-Hispanic/Latino; 4 Hispanic/Latino; 2 Two or more races, non-Hispanic/Latino), 56 international. Average age 29. 158 applicants, 33% accepted, 35 enrolled. In 2016, 19 master's, 3 doctorates awarded. *Entrance requirements:* For master's and doctorate, GRE. Additional exam requirements/recommendations for international students: Required—TOEFL (minimum score 80 iBT), IELTS (minimum score 6.5). *Application deadline:* For fall admission, 8/1 for domestic students, 4/1 for international students; for winter admission, 12/1 for domestic students, 7/1 for international students; for spring admission, 2/1 for domestic students, 10/1 for international students; for summer admission, 5/1 for domestic students, 1/1 for international students. Application fee: $75 ($85 for international students). *Expenses:* $14,130 resident full-time tuition, $23,769 non-resident. *Financial support:* Application deadline: 1/15. *Unit head:* Dr. Harriet Nembhard, School Head. *Application contact:* Jean Robinson, Advisor, E-mail: jean.robinson@oregonstate.edu.
Website: http://mime.oregonstate.edu/academics/grad/ie

Penn State University Park, Graduate School, College of Engineering, Department of Industrial and Manufacturing Engineering, University Park, PA 16802. Offers industrial engineering (MS, PhD). *Unit head:* Dr. Amr S. Elnashai, Dean, 814-865-7537, Fax: 814-863-4749. *Application contact:* Lori Hawn, Director, Graduate Student Services, 814-865-1795, Fax: 814-863-4627, E-mail: l-gswww@lists.psu.edu.
Website: http://ie.psu.edu/

Purdue University, College of Engineering, School of Industrial Engineering, West Lafayette, IN 47907-2023. Offers MS, MSIE, PhD. *Program availability:* Part-time, online learning. *Faculty:* 38. *Students:* 287. In 2016, 52 master's, 13 doctorates awarded. Terminal master's awarded for partial completion of doctoral program. *Degree requirements:* For master's, thesis optional; for doctorate, thesis/dissertation. *Entrance requirements:* For master's and doctorate, GRE General Test, minimum GPA of 3.2. *Application deadline:* For fall admission, 1/5 for domestic and international students; for spring admission, 9/15 for domestic and international students. Applications are processed on a rolling basis. Application fee: $60 ($75 for international students). Electronic applications accepted. *Financial support:* Fellowships with full and partial tuition reimbursements, research assistantships with full and partial tuition reimbursements, teaching assistantships with full and partial tuition reimbursements, scholarships/grants, health care benefits, and unspecified assistantships available. Financial award applicants required to submit FAFSA. *Faculty research:* Cognition and decision making, next generation products and services, computational industrial engineering, complex systems and networks. *Unit head:* Dr. Abhijit Deshmukh, Head/Professor of Industrial Engineering, E-mail: abhi@purdue.edu. *Application contact:* Cheryl Barnhart, Graduate Program Administrator, E-mail: iego@purdue.edu.
Website: https://engineering.purdue.edu/IE

Rensselaer Polytechnic Institute, Graduate School, School of Engineering, Program in Decision Sciences and Engineering Systems, Troy, NY 12180-3590. Offers PhD. *Faculty:* 2 full-time (both women). *Students:* 18 full-time (6 women). 27 applicants, 30% accepted, 5 enrolled. In 2016, 2 doctorates awarded. Terminal master's awarded for partial completion of doctoral program. *Degree requirements:* For doctorate, thesis/dissertation. *Entrance requirements:* For doctorate, GRE. Additional exam requirements/recommendations for international students: Required—TOEFL (minimum score 570 paper-based; 88 iBT), IELTS (minimum score 6.5), PTE (minimum score 60). *Application deadline:* For fall admission, 1/1 priority date for domestic students, 1/1 for international students; for spring admission, 8/15 for domestic and international students. Applications are processed on a rolling basis. Application fee: $75. Electronic applications accepted. *Expenses: Tuition:* Full-time $49,520; part-time $2060 per credit hour. *Required fees:* $2617. *Financial support:* In 2016–17, research assistantships (averaging $22,000 per year), teaching assistantships (averaging $22,000 per year) were awarded; fellowships also available. Financial award application deadline: 1/1. *Faculty research:* Agent-based modeling, computational optimization, data mining, decision analysis, decision technologies, human factors engineering, logistics, network optimization and analysis, scheduling, simulation modeling, statistical analysis, stochastic programming. *Total annual research expenditures:* $40,810. *Unit head:* Dr. Tom Sharkey, Graduate Program Director, 518-276-2958, E-mail: sharkt@rpi.edu. *Application contact:* Office of Graduate Admissions, 518-276-6216, E-mail: gradadmissions@rpi.edu.
Website: http://ise.rpi.edu/

Rensselaer Polytechnic Institute, Graduate School, School of Engineering, Program in Industrial and Management Engineering, Troy, NY 12180-3590. Offers M Eng, MS. *Program availability:* Part-time. *Faculty:* 9 full-time (0 women), 1 part-time/adjunct (0 women). *Students:* 2 full-time (0 women). 60 applicants, 12% accepted, 2 enrolled. In 2016, 1 master's awarded. *Degree requirements:* For master's, thesis (for some programs). *Entrance requirements:* For master's, GRE. Additional exam requirements/recommendations for international students: Required—TOEFL (minimum score 570 paper-based; 88 iBT), IELTS (minimum score 6.5), PTE (minimum score 60). *Application deadline:* For fall admission, 1/1 priority date for domestic and international students; for spring admission, 8/15 priority date for domestic and international students. Applications are processed on a rolling basis. Application fee: $75. Electronic applications accepted. *Expenses: Tuition:* Full-time $49,520; part-time $2060 per credit hour. *Required fees:* $2617. *Financial support:* In 2016–17, teaching assistantships (averaging $22,000 per year) were awarded. Financial award application deadline: 1/1. *Faculty research:* Bayesian decision systems; database systems; decision technologies for adaptive supply chains; maritime safety systems; materials flow logistics; network optimization, simulated based optimization; social networks/data mining, soft computing/computational optimization; statistical forecasting/exploratory data analysis; stochastic processes in supply chains. *Total annual research expenditures:* $232,257. *Unit head:* Dr. Bill Foley, Graduate Program Director, 518-276-2886, E-mail: foleyw@rpi.edu. *Application contact:* Office of Graduate Admissions, 518-276-6216, E-mail: gradadmissions@rpi.edu.
Website: http://ise.rpi.edu/

Rochester Institute of Technology, Graduate Enrollment Services, Kate Gleason College of Engineering, Industrial and Systems Engineering Department, ME Program in Industrial and Systems Engineering, Rochester, NY 14623-5603. Offers ME. *Program availability:* Part-time. *Students:* 7 full-time (3 women), 9 part-time (1 woman), 10 international. Average age 25. 77 applicants, 25% accepted, 4 enrolled. In 2016, 14 master's awarded. *Degree requirements:* For master's, thesis or alternative, capstone project. *Entrance requirements:* For master's, minimum GPA of 3.0 (recommended). Additional exam requirements/recommendations for international students: Required—TOEFL (minimum score 580 paper-based; 90 iBT), IELTS (minimum score 6), PTE (minimum score 58). *Application deadline:* For fall admission, 2/15 priority date for domestic and international students; for spring admission, 12/15 priority date for domestic and international students. Applications are processed on a rolling basis. Application fee: $60. Electronic applications accepted. *Expenses:* $1,742 per credit hour. *Financial support:* In 2016–17, 1 student received support. Research assistantships with partial tuition reimbursements available, teaching assistantships with partial tuition reimbursements available, career-related internships or fieldwork, scholarships/grants, and unspecified assistantships available. Support available to part-time students. Financial award applicants required to submit FAFSA. *Faculty research:* Advanced manufacturing, engineering education, ergonomics and human factors, healthcare delivery systems, operations research and simulation, systems engineering, production and logistics, sustainable engineering. *Unit head:* Dr. Marcos Esterman, Associate Professor, 585-475-2598, E-mail: mxeeie@rit.edu. *Application contact:* Diane Ellison, Associate Vice President, Graduate Enrollment Services, 585-475-2229, Fax: 585-475-7164, E-mail: gradinfo@rit.edu.
Website: http://www.rit.edu/kgcoe/ise/program/ms-industrial-systems-engineering/master-engineering-industrial-and-systems-engineering

Rochester Institute of Technology, Graduate Enrollment Services, Kate Gleason College of Engineering, Industrial and Systems Engineering Department, MS Program in Industrial and Systems Engineering, Rochester, NY 14623-5603. Offers MS. *Program availability:* Part-time. *Students:* 34 full-time (6 women), 5 part-time (0 women); includes 2 minority (both Black or African American, non-Hispanic/Latino), 33 international. Average age 24. 246 applicants, 29% accepted, 17 enrolled. In 2016, 8 master's awarded. *Degree requirements:* For master's, thesis. *Entrance requirements:* For master's, GRE, minimum GPA of 3.0 (recommended). Additional exam requirements/recommendations for international students: Required—TOEFL (minimum score 580 paper-based; 90 iBT), IELTS (minimum score 6.5), PTE (minimum score 58). *Application deadline:* For fall admission, 2/15 priority date for domestic and international students; for spring admission, 12/15 priority date for domestic and international students. Applications are processed on a rolling basis. Application fee: $60. Electronic applications accepted. *Expenses:* $1,742 per credit hour. *Financial support:* In 2016–17, 29 students received support. Research assistantships with partial tuition reimbursements available, teaching assistantships with partial tuition reimbursements available, career-related internships or fieldwork, scholarships/grants, and unspecified assistantships available. Support available to part-time students. Financial award applicants required to submit FAFSA. *Faculty research:* Advanced manufacturing;

health care systems engineering, data analytics, operations research, and simulation; supply chain and logistics systems; biomechanics, ergonomics, safety, and rehabilitation. *Unit head:* Dr. Marcos Esterman, Associate Professor, 585-475-2598, E-mail: mxeeie@rit.edu. *Application contact:* Diane Ellison, Associate Vice President, Graduate Enrollment Services, 585-475-2229, Fax: 585-475-7164, E-mail: gradinfo@rit.edu.
Website: http://www.rit.edu/kgcoe/ise/program/master-science-degrees/master-science-industrial-and-systems-engineering

Rutgers University–New Brunswick, Graduate School-New Brunswick, Department of Industrial and Systems Engineering, Piscataway, NJ 08854-8097. Offers industrial and systems engineering (MS, PhD); information technology (MS); manufacturing systems engineering (MS); quality and reliability engineering (MS). *Program availability:* Part-time, evening/weekend. Terminal master's awarded for partial completion of doctoral program. *Degree requirements:* For master's, thesis or alternative, seminar; for doctorate, comprehensive exam, thesis/dissertation. *Entrance requirements:* For master's and doctorate, GRE General Test. Additional exam requirements/recommendations for international students: Required—TOEFL. *Faculty research:* Production and manufacturing systems, quality and reliability engineering, systems engineering and aviation safety.

St. Mary's University, School of Science, Engineering and Technology, Program in Industrial Engineering, San Antonio, TX 78228-8507. Offers MS. *Program availability:* Part-time, evening/weekend. *Faculty:* 4 full-time (0 women), 4 part-time/adjunct. *Students:* 6 full-time (2 women), 5 part-time (1 woman); includes 2 minority (both Hispanic/Latino), 7 international. Average age 26. 34 applicants, 24% accepted, 1 enrolled. In 2016, 5 master's awarded. *Degree requirements:* For master's, project or thesis. *Entrance requirements:* For master's, GRE (minimum quantitative score of 148), BS in computer engineering, electrical engineering, or closely-related discipline; minimum GPA of 3.0; written statement of purpose indicating applicant's interests and objectives; two letters of recommendation. Additional exam requirements/recommendations for international students: Required—TOEFL (minimum score 550 paper-based; 80 iBT), IELTS (minimum score 6). *Application deadline:* For fall admission, 7/1 for domestic students; for spring admission, 11/15 for domestic students; for summer admission, 4/1 for domestic students. Applications are processed on a rolling basis. Application fee: $0. Electronic applications accepted. *Expenses:* Tuition: Full-time $15,600; part-time $865 per credit hour. *Required fees:* $148 per semester. *Financial support:* Career-related internships or fieldwork, Federal Work-Study, institutionally sponsored loans, scholarships/grants, and health care benefits available. Financial award application deadline: 3/31; financial award applicants required to submit FAFSA. *Faculty research:* Supply chain, lean production, engineering ethics, manufacturing engineering, human factors and ergonomics. *Unit head:* Dr. Rafael Moras, Director, 210-431-2017, E-mail: rmoras@stmarytx.edu.
Website: https://www.stmarytx.edu/academics/set/graduate/industrial-engineering/

South Dakota State University, Graduate School, College of Engineering, Department of Engineering Technology and Management, Brookings, SD 57007. Offers industrial management (MS). *Degree requirements:* For master's, comprehensive exam, thesis (for some programs), oral exam. *Entrance requirements:* Additional exam requirements/recommendations for international students: Required—TOEFL (minimum score 575 paper-based). *Faculty research:* Query, economic development, statistical process control, foreign business plans, operations management.

Southern Illinois University Edwardsville, Graduate School, School of Engineering, Department of Mechanical and Industrial Engineering, Program in Industrial Engineering, Edwardsville, IL 62026. Offers MS. *Program availability:* Part-time, evening/weekend. *Degree requirements:* For master's, thesis (for some programs), final exam. *Entrance requirements:* For master's, GRE (for applicants whose degree is from non-ABET accredited institution). Additional exam requirements/recommendations for international students: Required—TOEFL (minimum score 550 paper-based; 79 iBT), IELTS (minimum score 6.5). Electronic applications accepted.

Stanford University, School of Engineering, Department of Management Science and Engineering, Stanford, CA 94305-2004. Offers MS, PhD. Terminal master's awarded for partial completion of doctoral program. *Degree requirements:* For doctorate, thesis/dissertation, qualification procedure. *Entrance requirements:* For master's and doctorate, GRE General Test. Additional exam requirements/recommendations for international students: Required—TOEFL. Electronic applications accepted. *Expenses:* Tuition: Full-time $47,331. *Required fees:* $609.

Texas A&M University, College of Engineering, Department of Industrial and Systems Engineering, College Station, TX 77843. Offers engineering systems management (MS); industrial engineering (M Eng, MS, PhD). *Program availability:* Part-time, online learning. *Faculty:* 22. *Students:* 228 full-time (52 women), 62 part-time (21 women); includes 34 minority (3 Black or African American, non-Hispanic/Latino; 14 Asian, non-Hispanic/Latino; 15 Hispanic/Latino; 2 Two or more races, non-Hispanic/Latino), 222 international. Average age 26. 967 applicants, 20% accepted, 110 enrolled. In 2016, 97 master's, 11 doctorates awarded. *Degree requirements:* For master's, comprehensive exam (for some programs), thesis optional; for doctorate, comprehensive exam, thesis/dissertation. *Entrance requirements:* For master's and doctorate, GRE General Test. Additional exam requirements/recommendations for international students: Required—TOEFL (minimum score 550 paper-based; 80 iBT), IELTS (minimum score 6), PTE (minimum score 53). *Application deadline:* For fall admission, 6/1 priority date for domestic students, 3/1 priority date for international students; for spring admission, 8/1 priority date for domestic and international students. Applications are processed on a rolling basis. Application fee: $50 ($90 for international students). Electronic applications accepted. *Expenses:* Contact institution. *Financial support:* In 2016–17, 165 students received support, including 7 fellowships with tuition reimbursements available (averaging $14,315 per year), 62 research assistantships with tuition reimbursements available (averaging $5,401 per year), 31 teaching assistantships with tuition reimbursements available (averaging $8,551 per year); career-related internships or fieldwork, institutionally sponsored loans, scholarships/grants, traineeships, health care benefits, tuition waivers (full and partial), and unspecified assistantships also available. Support available to part-time students. Financial award application deadline: 3/15; financial award applicants required to submit FAFSA. *Faculty research:* Manufacturing systems, computer integration, operations research, logistics, simulation. *Unit head:* Dr. Cesar O. Malave, Head, 979-845-5535, Fax: 979-458-4299, E-mail: malave@tamu.edu. *Application contact:* Erin Roady, Graduate Program Coordinator, 979-845-5536, Fax: 979-458-4299, E-mail: erinroady@tamu.edu.
Website: http://engineering.tamu.edu/industrial

Texas A&M University–Kingsville, College of Graduate Studies, Frank H. Dotterweich College of Engineering, Department of Mechanical and Industrial Engineering, Program in Industrial Engineering, Kingsville, TX 78363. Offers ME, MS. *Degree requirements:* For master's, variable foreign language requirement, comprehensive exam, thesis (for some programs). *Entrance requirements:* For master's, GRE (minimum overall old score of 900-1000 depending on GPA), MAT, GMAT. Additional exam requirements/recommendations for international students: Required—TOEFL (minimum score 550 paper-based; 79 iBT). Electronic applications accepted.

Texas Southern University, School of Science and Technology, Department of Industrial Technology, Houston, TX 77004-4584. Offers MS. *Degree requirements:* For master's, comprehensive exam. *Entrance requirements:* For master's, GRE General Test, minimum GPA of 2.5. Additional exam requirements/recommendations for international students: Required—TOEFL. Electronic applications accepted.

Texas State University, The Graduate College, College of Science and Engineering, Program in Engineering, San Marcos, TX 78666. Offers electrical engineering (MS); industrial engineering (MS); manufacturing engineering (MS). *Program availability:* Part-time. *Faculty:* 15 full-time (2 women), 2 part-time/adjunct (0 women). *Students:* 49 full-time (15 women), 10 part-time (3 women); includes 7 minority (3 Asian, non-Hispanic/Latino; 3 Hispanic/Latino; 1 Two or more races, non-Hispanic/Latino), 45 international. Average age 28. 163 applicants, 43% accepted, 30 enrolled. *Degree requirements:* For master's, comprehensive exam, thesis (for some programs), thesis or research project. *Entrance requirements:* For master's, GRE (minimum preferred scores of 285 overall, 135 verbal, 150 quantitative), baccalaureate degree from regionally-accredited university in engineering, computer science, physics, technology, or closely-related field with minimum GPA of 3.0 on last 60 undergraduate semester hours; resume or curriculum vitae; 2 letters of recommendation; statement of purpose. Additional exam requirements/recommendations for international students: Required—TOEFL (minimum score 550 paper-based; 78 iBT), IELTS (minimum score 6.5). *Application deadline:* For fall admission, 2/15 priority date for domestic students, 2/1 priority date for international students. Application fee: $40 ($90 for international students). Electronic applications accepted. *Expenses:* $4,851 per semester. *Financial support:* In 2016–17, 25 students received support, including 15 research assistantships (averaging $14,047 per year), 19 teaching assistantships (averaging $13,572 per year); Federal Work-Study, institutionally sponsored loans, scholarships/grants, and unspecified assistantships also available. Support available to part-time students. Financial award application deadline: 3/1; financial award applicants required to submit FAFSA. *Faculty research:* Building a regional energy and educational network; recruitment and retention of female undergraduates in engineering and computer science; fostering nanotechnology environment, health, safety awareness; low-cost flexible graphene-based digital beam forming phased-array antennas engaging, sustaining and empowering women and minorities in STEM. *Total annual research expenditures:* $854,198. *Unit head:* Dr. Vishu Viswanathan, Graduate Advisor, 512-245-1826, Fax: 512-245-8365, E-mail: vishu.viswanathan@txstate.edu. *Application contact:* Dr. Andrea Golato, Dean of Graduate School, 512-245-2581, Fax: 512-245-8365, E-mail: gradcollege@txstate.edu.
Website: http://www.engineering.txstate.edu/Programs/Graduate.html

Texas Tech University, Graduate School, Edward E. Whitacre Jr. College of Engineering, Department of Industrial, Manufacturing, and Systems Engineering, Lubbock, TX 79409-3061. Offers industrial engineering (MSIE, PhD); systems and engineering management (MSSEM, PhD). *Program availability:* Part-time, 100% online, blended/hybrid learning. *Faculty:* 13 full-time (2 women). *Students:* 90 full-time (15 women), 97 part-time (14 women); includes 25 minority (9 Black or African American, non-Hispanic/Latino; 1 American Indian or Alaska Native, non-Hispanic/Latino; 2 Asian, non-Hispanic/Latino; 11 Hispanic/Latino; 2 Two or more races, non-Hispanic/Latino), 102 international. Average age 32. 376 applicants, 38% accepted, 48 enrolled. In 2016, 43 master's, 7 doctorates awarded. Terminal master's awarded for partial completion of doctoral program. *Degree requirements:* For master's, comprehensive exam, thesis optional; for doctorate, comprehensive exam, thesis/dissertation. *Entrance requirements:* For master's and doctorate, GRE (Verbal and Quantitative). Additional exam requirements/recommendations for international students: Required—TOEFL (minimum score 550 paper-based; 79 iBT). *Application deadline:* For fall admission, 6/1 priority date for domestic students, 1/15 priority date for international students; for spring admission, 9/1 priority date for domestic students, 6/15 priority date for international students. Applications are processed on a rolling basis. Application fee: $75. Electronic applications accepted. *Expenses:* $325 per credit hour full-time resident tuition, $733 per credit hour full-time non-resident tuition; $53.75 per credit hour fee plus $608 per term fee. *Financial support:* In 2016–17, 73 students received support, including 71 fellowships (averaging $2,464 per year), 9 research assistantships (averaging $15,691 per year), 21 teaching assistantships (averaging $21,474 per year); scholarships/grants, tuition waivers (partial), and unspecified assistantships also available. Financial award application deadline: 2/1; financial award applicants required to submit FAFSA. *Faculty research:* Ergonomics and human factors engineering, manufacturing systems, operations research, statistics and quality assurance, systems and engineering management. *Total annual research expenditures:* $282,884. *Unit head:* Dr. Hong-Chao Zhang, Interim Chair, 806-742-3543, E-mail: hong-chao.zhang@ttu.edu. *Application contact:* Dr. Jennifer Cross, Associate Professor, 806-742-3543, Fax: 806-742-3411, E-mail: jennifer.cross@ttu.edu.
Website: http://www.ie.ttu.edu/

Universidad de las Américas Puebla, Division of Graduate Studies, School of Engineering, Program in Industrial Engineering, Puebla, Mexico. Offers industrial engineering (MS); production management (M Adm). *Program availability:* Part-time, evening/weekend. *Degree requirements:* For master's, one foreign language, thesis. *Faculty research:* Textile industry, quality control.

Université de Moncton, Faculty of Engineering, Program in Industrial Engineering, Moncton, NB E1A 3E9, Canada. Offers M Sc A. *Degree requirements:* For master's, thesis, proficiency in French. *Faculty research:* Production systems, optimization, simulation and expert systems, modeling and warehousing systems, quality control.

Université du Québec à Trois-Rivières, Graduate Programs, Program in Industrial Engineering, Trois-Rivières, QC G9A 5H7, Canada. Offers M Sc, DESS. *Entrance requirements:* For degree, appropriate bachelor's degree, proficiency in French. *Faculty research:* Production.

Université Laval, Faculty of Sciences and Engineering, Programs in Industrial Engineering, Québec, QC G1K 7P4, Canada. Offers Diploma. *Program availability:* Part-time. *Entrance requirements:* For degree, knowledge of French. Electronic applications accepted.

University at Buffalo, the State University of New York, Graduate School, School of Engineering and Applied Sciences, Department of Industrial and Systems Engineering, Buffalo, NY 14260. Offers ME, MS, PhD. *Program availability:* Part-time, online learning. Terminal master's awarded for partial completion of doctoral program. *Degree requirements:* For master's, comprehensive exam (for some programs), thesis or alternative; for doctorate, thesis/dissertation. *Entrance requirements:* For master's and doctorate, GRE General Test. Additional exam requirements/recommendations for international students: Required—TOEFL (minimum score 550 paper-based; 79 iBT). Electronic applications accepted. *Faculty research:* Ergonomics, operations research, production systems, human factors.

The University of Alabama in Huntsville, School of Graduate Studies, College of Engineering, Department of Industrial and Systems Engineering and Engineering Management, Huntsville, AL 35899. Offers engineering management (MSE, PhD); industrial engineering (MSE, PhD); operations research (MSOR); systems engineering (MSE, PhD). *Program availability:* Part-time, evening/weekend, online learning. *Degree requirements:* For master's, comprehensive exam, thesis or alternative, oral and written exams; for doctorate, comprehensive exam, thesis/dissertation, oral and written exams. *Entrance requirements:* For master's and doctorate, GRE General Test, minimum GPA of 3.0. Additional exam requirements/recommendations for international students: Required—TOEFL (minimum score 500 paper-based; 80 iBT), IELTS (minimum score 6.5). Electronic applications accepted. *Expenses:* Tuition, state resident: full-time $9834; part-time $600 per credit hour. Tuition, nonresident: full-time $21,830; part-time $1325 per credit hour. *Faculty research:* Systems engineering process, electronic manufacturing, heuristic manufacturing, teams and team development.

The University of Arizona, College of Engineering, Department of Systems and Industrial Engineering, Tucson, AZ 85721. Offers engineering management (Graduate Certificate); industrial engineering (MS); systems and industrial engineering (MS, PhD); systems engineering (MS, PhD, Graduate Certificate). *Program availability:* Part-time, online learning. *Degree requirements:* For doctorate, thesis/dissertation. *Entrance requirements:* For master's, GRE General Test (minimum score: 500 Verbal, 700 Quantitative), 3 letters of recommendation; for doctorate, GRE General Test (minimum score: 500 Verbal, 700 Quantitative), minimum GPA of 3.5, 3 letters of recommendation, letter of intent. Additional exam requirements/recommendations for international students: Required—TOEFL (minimum score 575 paper-based; 80 iBT). Electronic applications accepted. *Faculty research:* Optimization, systems theory, logistics, transportation, embedded systems.

University of Arkansas, Graduate School, College of Engineering, Department of Industrial Engineering, Program in Industrial Engineering, Fayetteville, AR 72701. Offers MSE, MSIE, PhD. *Students:* 61 applicants, 59% accepted. In 2016, 13 master's, 3 doctorates awarded. *Degree requirements:* For master's, thesis optional; for doctorate, one foreign language, thesis/dissertation. *Application deadline:* For fall admission, 4/1 for international students; for spring admission, 10/1 for international students. Applications are processed on a rolling basis. Application fee: $40 ($50 for international students). Electronic applications accepted. *Financial support:* In 2016–17, 32 research assistantships were awarded; fellowships, teaching assistantships, career-related internships or fieldwork, and Federal Work-Study also available. Support available to part-time students. Financial award application deadline: 4/1; financial award applicants required to submit FAFSA. *Unit head:* Dr. Ed Pohl, Department Chairperson, 479-575-3157, Fax: 479-575-8431, E-mail: epohl@uark.edu. *Application contact:* Dr. Justin Chimka, Graduate Coordinator, 479-575-7392, E-mail: jchimka@uark.edu.
Website: http://www.ineg.uark.edu/

University of California, Berkeley, Graduate Division, College of Engineering, Department of Industrial Engineering and Operations Research, Berkeley, CA 94720-1500. Offers decision analytics (M Eng); industrial engineering and operations research (M Eng, MS, PhD). *Program availability:* Part-time, evening/weekend. *Students:* 125 full-time (48 women), 25 part-time (9 women); includes 21 minority (20 Asian, non-Hispanic/Latino; 1 Hispanic/Latino), 112 international. Average age 27. 625 applicants, 94 enrolled. In 2016, 82 master's, 10 doctorates awarded. Terminal master's awarded for partial completion of doctoral program. *Degree requirements:* For master's, comprehensive exam (for some programs), thesis (for some programs), comprehensive exam or thesis (MS); for doctorate, thesis/dissertation, qualifying exam. *Entrance requirements:* For master's and doctorate, GRE General Test, minimum GPA of 3.0, 3 letters of recommendation. Additional exam requirements/recommendations for international students: Required—TOEFL (minimum score 570 paper-based; 90 iBT). *Application deadline:* For fall admission, 12/2 for domestic students. Application fee: $105 ($125 for international students). Electronic applications accepted. *Financial support:* Fellowships, research assistantships, teaching assistantships, career-related internships or fieldwork, Federal Work-Study, tuition waivers (full and partial), and unspecified assistantships available. Financial award applicants required to submit FAFSA. *Faculty research:* Mathematical programming, robotics and manufacturing, linear and nonlinear optimization, production planning and scheduling, queuing theory. *Unit head:* Prof. Ken Goldberg, Chair, 510-642-5484, Fax: 510-642-1403, E-mail: gradadm@ieor.berkeley.edu. *Application contact:* 510-642-5485, Fax: 510-642-1403, E-mail: gradadm@ieor.berkeley.edu.
Website: http://www.ieor.berkeley.edu/

University of Central Florida, College of Engineering and Computer Science, Department of Industrial Engineering and Management Systems, Orlando, FL 32816. Offers MSIE, PhD, Certificate. *Program availability:* Part-time, evening/weekend. *Faculty:* 16 full-time (3 women), 10 part-time/adjunct (0 women). *Students:* 69 full-time (20 women), 159 part-time (58 women); includes 76 minority (19 Black or African American, non-Hispanic/Latino; 14 Asian, non-Hispanic/Latino; 40 Hispanic/Latino; 3 Two or more races, non-Hispanic/Latino), 47 international. Average age 32. 204 applicants, 65% accepted, 72 enrolled. In 2016, 101 master's, 13 doctorates, 19 other advanced degrees awarded. *Degree requirements:* For master's, thesis or alternative; for doctorate, thesis/dissertation, departmental qualifying exam, candidacy exam. *Entrance requirements:* For master's, GRE General Test, minimum GPA of 3.0 in last 60 hours of course work; for doctorate, minimum GPA of 3.5 in last 60 hours of course work. Additional exam requirements/recommendations for international students: Required—TOEFL. *Application deadline:* For fall admission, 7/15 for domestic students; for spring admission, 12/1 for domestic students. Application fee: $30. Electronic applications accepted. *Expenses:* Tuition, state resident: part-time $288.16 per credit hour. Tuition, nonresident: part-time $1071.31 per credit hour. *Financial support:* In 2016–17, 22 students received support, including 11 fellowships with partial tuition reimbursements available (averaging $8,382 per year), 6 research assistantships with partial tuition reimbursements available (averaging $7,545 per year), 9 teaching assistantships with partial tuition reimbursements available (averaging $12,122 per year); career-related internships or fieldwork, Federal Work-Study, institutionally sponsored loans, tuition waivers (partial), and unspecified assistantships also available. Financial award application deadline: 3/1; financial award applicants required to submit FAFSA. *Unit head:* Dr. Waldemar Karwowski, Chair, 407-823-0042, E-mail: wkar@ucf.edu. *Application contact:* Assistant Director, Graduate Admissions, 407-823-2766, Fax: 407-823-6442, E-mail: gradadmissions@ucf.edu.
Website: http://iems.ucf.edu/

University of Cincinnati, Graduate School, College of Engineering and Applied Science, Department of Mechanical and Materials Engineering, Cincinnati, OH 45221. Offers industrial engineering (PhD); mechanical engineering (MS, PhD); nuclear engineering (PhD); MBA/MS. *Program availability:* Part-time, evening/weekend. Terminal master's awarded for partial completion of doctoral program. *Degree requirements:* For doctorate, thesis/dissertation. *Entrance requirements:* For master's and doctorate, GRE General Test. Additional exam requirements/recommendations for international students: Required—TOEFL (minimum score 575 paper-based). Electronic applications accepted. *Expenses: Tuition, area resident:* Full-time $12,790; part-time $389 per credit hour. Tuition, state resident: full-time $13,290; part-time $419 per credit hour. Tuition, nonresident: full-time $24,532; part-time $976 per credit hour. *International tuition:* $24,832 full-time. *Required fees:* $3958; $140 per credit hour. Tuition and fees vary according to course load, degree level, program and reciprocity agreements.

University of Florida, Graduate School, Herbert Wertheim College of Engineering, Department of Industrial and Systems Engineering, Gainesville, FL 32611. Offers industrial and systems engineering (ME, MS, PhD, Engr); quantitative finance (PhD). *Program availability:* Part-time, evening/weekend, online learning. Terminal master's awarded for partial completion of doctoral program. *Degree requirements:* For master's, thesis (for some programs); for doctorate, comprehensive exam (for some programs), thesis/dissertation (for some programs). *Entrance requirements:* For master's and doctorate, minimum GPA of 3.0; for Engr, GRE General Test. Additional exam requirements/recommendations for international students: Required—TOEFL (minimum score 550 paper-based; 80 iBT), IELTS (minimum score 6). Electronic applications accepted. *Faculty research:* Operations research; financial engineering; logistics and supply chain management; energy, healthcare, and transportation applications of operations research.

University of Houston, Cullen College of Engineering, Department of Industrial Engineering, Houston, TX 77204. Offers MIE, PhD. *Program availability:* Part-time. Terminal master's awarded for partial completion of doctoral program. *Degree requirements:* For master's, thesis (for some programs); for doctorate, thesis/dissertation, departmental qualifying exam. *Entrance requirements:* For master's and doctorate, GRE General Test. Additional exam requirements/recommendations for international students: Required—TOEFL; Recommended—IELTS. Electronic applications accepted.

University of Illinois at Chicago, College of Engineering, Department of Mechanical and Industrial Engineering, Program in Industrial Engineering, Chicago, IL 60607-7128. Offers industrial engineering (MS); industrial engineering and operations research (PhD). *Program availability:* Part-time. *Degree requirements:* For doctorate, thesis/dissertation. *Entrance requirements:* For doctorate, GRE General Test, minimum GPA of 2.75. Additional exam requirements/recommendations for international students: Required—TOEFL. Electronic applications accepted. *Expenses:* Contact institution. *Faculty research:* Manufacturing information systems and manufacturing control, supply chain, logistics, optimization quality control, haptics and virtual reality, industrial automation, safety and reliability engineering, diagnostics, prognostics, controls and statistical modeling.

University of Illinois at Urbana–Champaign, Graduate College, College of Engineering, Department of Industrial and Enterprise Systems Engineering, Urbana, IL 61801. Offers industrial engineering (MS, PhD); systems and entrepreneurial engineering (MS, PhD); MBA/MS.

University of Illinois at Urbana–Champaign, Graduate College, College of Engineering, Department of Mechanical Science and Engineering, Champaign, IL 61820. Offers mechanical engineering (MS, PhD); theoretical and applied mechanics (MS, PhD). Terminal master's awarded for partial completion of doctoral program. *Entrance requirements:* Additional exam requirements/recommendations for international students: Required—TOEFL (minimum score 613 paper-based; 103 iBT), IELTS (minimum score 7).

The University of Iowa, Graduate College, College of Engineering, Department of Industrial Engineering, Iowa City, IA 52242-1316. Offers engineering design and manufacturing (MS, PhD); healthcare systems (MS, PhD); human factors (MS, PhD); information and engineering management (MS, PhD); operations research (MS, PhD); wind energy (MS, PhD). *Faculty:* 11 full-time (1 woman), 1 part-time/adjunct (0 women). *Students:* 15 full-time (2 women), 6 part-time (0 women); includes 2 minority (1 Asian, non-Hispanic/Latino; 1 Two or more races, non-Hispanic/Latino), 11 international. Average age 29. 68 applicants, 9% accepted, 5 enrolled. In 2016, 4 master's, 3 doctorates awarded. Terminal master's awarded for partial completion of doctoral program. *Degree requirements:* For master's, thesis optional, exam; for doctorate, comprehensive exam, thesis/dissertation, final defense exam. *Entrance requirements:* For master's and doctorate, GRE (minimum Verbal score of 153, Quantitative 151), minimum undergraduate GPA of 3.0. Additional exam requirements/recommendations for international students: Required—TOEFL (minimum score 600 paper-based; 100 iBT), IELTS (minimum score 7). *Application deadline:* For fall admission, 7/15 for domestic students, 4/15 for international students; for spring admission, 12/1 for domestic students, 10/1 for international students; for summer admission, 4/15 for domestic students, 3/1 for international students. Applications are processed on a rolling basis. Application fee: $60 ($100 for international students). Electronic applications accepted. *Financial support:* In 2016–17, 21 students received support, including 1 fellowship with partial tuition reimbursement available (averaging $25,500 per year), 15 research assistantships with full tuition reimbursements available (averaging $22,981 per year), 5 teaching assistantships with full tuition reimbursements available (averaging $18,809 per year); career-related internships or fieldwork, scholarships/grants, and unspecified assistantships also available. Support available to part-time students. Financial award applicants required to submit FAFSA. *Faculty research:* Operations research, informatics, human factors engineering, healthcare systems, bio-manufacturing, manufacturing systems, renewable energy, human-machine interactions. *Total annual research expenditures:* $6.3 million. *Unit head:* Dr. Ching-Long Lin, Department Executive Officer, 319-335-5673, Fax: 319-335-5669, E-mail: ching-long-lin@uiowa.edu. *Application contact:* Tara Hoadley, Academic Program Specialist, 319-335-5939, Fax: 319-335-5669, E-mail: indeng@engineering.uiowa.edu.
Website: https://mie.engineering.uiowa.edu

University of Louisville, J. B. Speed School of Engineering, Department of Industrial Engineering, Louisville, KY 40292-0001. Offers engineering management (M Eng); industrial engineering (M Eng, MS, PhD); logistics and distribution (Certificate). *Accreditation:* ABET (one or more programs are accredited). *Program availability:* 100% online. *Faculty:* 7 full-time (4 women), 5 part-time/adjunct (2 women). *Students:* 68 full-time (19 women), 129 part-time (22 women); includes 25 minority (10 Black or African American, non-Hispanic/Latino; 1 American Indian or Alaska Native, non-Hispanic/Latino; 6 Asian, non-Hispanic/Latino; 3 Hispanic/Latino; 5 Two or more races, non-Hispanic/Latino), 86 international. Average age 32. 93 applicants, 44% accepted, 25 enrolled. In 2016, 33 master's, 3 doctorates awarded. *Degree requirements:* For master's and Certificate, thesis optional; for doctorate, comprehensive exam, thesis/dissertation. *Entrance requirements:* For master's and doctorate, GRE General Test, two letters of recommendation, official transcripts. Additional exam requirements/recommendations for international students: Required—TOEFL (minimum score 550 paper-based; 80 iBT), IELTS (minimum score 6.5). *Application deadline:* For fall admission, 5/1 priority date for international students; for spring admission, 11/1 priority date for international students; for summer admission, 3/1 priority date for international students. Applications are processed on a rolling basis. Application fee: $60. Electronic applications accepted. *Expenses:* Tuition, state resident: full-time $12,246; part-time $681 per credit hour. Tuition, nonresident: full-time $25,486; part-time $1417 per credit hour. *Required fees:* $196. Tuition and fees vary according to program and reciprocity agreements. *Financial support:* In 2016–17, 2 fellowships with full tuition reimbursements (averaging $22,000 per year) were awarded; research assistantships with full tuition reimbursements, teaching assistantships with full tuition reimbursements, scholarships/grants, health care benefits, and tuition waivers (full) also available. Financial award application deadline: 1/1; financial award applicants required to submit FAFSA. *Faculty research:* Optimization, computer simulation, logistics and distribution, ergonomics and human factors, advanced manufacturing process. *Total annual research expenditures:* $620,986. *Unit head:* Dr. Suraj M. Alexander, Chair, 502-852-

6342, E-mail: usher@louisville.edu. *Application contact:* Lihui Bai, Director of Graduate Studies, 502-852-1416, E-mail: lihui.bai@louisville.edu.
Website: http://www.louisville.edu/speed/industrial/

University of Manitoba, Faculty of Graduate Studies, Faculty of Engineering, Department of Mechanical and Manufacturing Engineering, Winnipeg, MB R3T 2N2, Canada. Offers M Eng, M Sc, PhD. *Degree requirements:* For master's, thesis; for doctorate, thesis/dissertation.

University of Massachusetts Amherst, Graduate School, College of Engineering, Department of Mechanical and Industrial Engineering, Amherst, MA 01003. Offers industrial engineering and operations research (MS, PhD); mechanical engineering (MSME, PhD). *Program availability:* Part-time. Terminal master's awarded for partial completion of doctoral program. *Degree requirements:* For master's, thesis or alternative; for doctorate, comprehensive exam, thesis/dissertation. *Entrance requirements:* For master's and doctorate, GRE General Test. Additional exam requirements/recommendations for international students: Required—TOEFL (minimum score 550 paper-based; 80 iBT), IELTS (minimum score 6.5). Electronic applications accepted.

University of Massachusetts Dartmouth, Graduate School, College of Engineering, Department of Mechanical Engineering, North Dartmouth, MA 02747-2300. Offers industrial and systems engineering (MS); mechanical engineering (MS). *Program availability:* Part-time. *Faculty:* 10 full-time (1 woman). *Students:* 18 full-time (0 women), 12 part-time (0 women); includes 2 minority (both Two or more races, non-Hispanic/Latino), 15 international. Average age 25. 57 applicants, 51% accepted, 11 enrolled. In 2016, 12 master's awarded. *Degree requirements:* For master's, thesis, project or oral exam. *Entrance requirements:* For master's, GRE (UMass Dartmouth mechanical engineering bachelor's degree recipients are exempt), statement of purpose (minimum of 300 words), resume, 3 letters of recommendation, official transcripts. Additional exam requirements/recommendations for international students: Required—TOEFL (minimum score 533 paper-based; 72 iBT). *Application deadline:* For fall admission, 2/15 priority date for domestic students, 1/15 priority date for international students; for spring admission, 11/15 priority date for domestic students, 10/15 priority date for international students. Application fee: $60. Electronic applications accepted. *Expenses:* Tuition, state resident: full-time $14,994; part-time $624.75 per credit. Tuition, nonresident: full-time $27,068; part-time $1127.83 per credit. *Required fees:* $405; $25.88 per credit. Tuition and fees vary according to course load and reciprocity agreements. *Financial support:* In 2016–17, 2 research assistantships (averaging $5,596 per year), 7 teaching assistantships (averaging $6,818 per year) were awarded; institutionally sponsored loans, scholarships/grants, and unspecified assistantships also available. Support available to part-time students. Financial award application deadline: 3/1; financial award applicants required to submit FAFSA. *Faculty research:* Biopreservation, renewable energy, fluid structure interaction, buoyant flows, high performance heat exchanges, mechanics of biomaterials, composite materials, computational mechanics. *Total annual research expenditures:* $1.1 million. *Unit head:* Wenzhen Juang, Graduate Program Director, Mechanical Engineering, 508-910-6568, E-mail: whuang@umassd.edu. *Application contact:* Steven Briggs, Director of Marketing and Recruitment for Graduate Studies, 508-999-8604, Fax: 508-999-8183, E-mail: graduate@umassd.edu.
Website: http://www.umassd.edu/engineering/mne/graduate

University of Massachusetts Dartmouth, Graduate School, College of Engineering, Program in Engineering and Applied Science, North Dartmouth, MA 02747-2300. Offers applied mechanics and materials (PhD); computational science and engineering (PhD); computer science and information systems (PhD); engineering and applied science (PhD); industrial and systems engineering (PhD). *Program availability:* Part-time. *Students:* 23 full-time (7 women), 8 part-time (3 women); includes 2 minority (both Black or African American, non-Hispanic/Latino), 15 international. Average age 31. 14 applicants, 79% accepted, 7 enrolled. *Degree requirements:* For doctorate, comprehensive exam, thesis/dissertation. *Entrance requirements:* For doctorate, GRE, statement of purpose (minimum of 300 words), resume, 3 letters of recommendation, official transcripts. Additional exam requirements/recommendations for international students: Required—TOEFL (minimum score 550 paper-based; 79 iBT). *Application deadline:* For fall admission, 2/15 priority date for domestic students, 1/15 priority date for international students; for spring admission, 11/15 priority date for domestic students, 10/15 priority date for international students. Application fee: $60. Electronic applications accepted. *Expenses:* Tuition, state resident: full-time $14,994; part-time $624.75 per credit. Tuition, nonresident: full-time $27,068; part-time $1127.83 per credit. *Required fees:* $405; $25.88 per credit. Tuition and fees vary according to course load and reciprocity agreements. *Financial support:* In 2016–17, 11 fellowships (averaging $16,591 per year), 12 research assistantships (averaging $5,160 per year) were awarded; institutionally sponsored loans, scholarships/grants, and doctoral support also available. Support available to part-time students. Financial award application deadline: 3/1; financial award applicants required to submit FAFSA. *Faculty research:* Tissue/cell engineering, bio transport sensors/networks, marine systems biomimetic materials, composite/polymeric materials, resilient infrastructure robotics, renewable energy. *Total annual research expenditures:* $253,000. *Unit head:* Gaurav Khanna, Graduate Program Director, Engineering and Applied Science, 508-910-6605, Fax: 508-999-9115, E-mail: gkhanna@umassd.edu. *Application contact:* Steven Briggs, Director of Marketing and Recruitment for Graduate Studies, 508-999-8604, Fax: 508-999-8183, E-mail: graduate@umassd.edu.
Website: http://www.umassd.edu/engineering/graduate/doctoraldegreeprograms/egrandappliedsciencephd/

University of Massachusetts Lowell, College of Health Sciences, Department of Work Environment, Lowell, MA 01854. Offers cleaner production and pollution prevention (Sc D). *Accreditation:* ABET. *Program availability:* Part-time. Terminal master's awarded for partial completion of doctoral program. *Degree requirements:* For doctorate, thesis/dissertation. *Entrance requirements:* For doctorate, GRE General Test. Additional exam requirements/recommendations for international students: Required—TOEFL.

University of Miami, Graduate School, College of Engineering, Department of Industrial Engineering, Coral Gables, FL 33124. Offers environmental health and safety (MS); ergonomics (PhD); industrial engineering (MSIE, PhD); management of technology (MS); occupational ergonomics and safety (MS, MSOES), including environmental health and safety (MS), occupational ergonomics and safety (MSOES); MBA/MSIE. *Program availability:* Part-time. *Degree requirements:* For master's, thesis (for some programs); for doctorate, comprehensive exam, thesis/dissertation. *Entrance requirements:* For master's and doctorate, GRE General Test, minimum GPA of 3.0. Additional exam requirements/recommendations for international students: Required—TOEFL (minimum score 550 paper-based). *Faculty research:* Logistics, supply chain management, industrial applications of biomechanics and ergonomics, technology management, back pain, aging, operations research, manufacturing, safety, human reliability, energy assessment.

University of Michigan, College of Engineering, Department of Industrial and Operations Engineering, Ann Arbor, MI 48109. Offers MS, MSE, PhD, MBA/MS, MBA/MSE. *Accreditation:* ABET. *Program availability:* Part-time. *Students:* 184 full-time (52 women), 18 part-time (5 women). 608 applicants, 35% accepted, 100 enrolled. In 2016, 90 master's, 13 doctorates awarded. Terminal master's awarded for partial completion of doctoral program. *Degree requirements:* For doctorate, oral defense of dissertation, preliminary exams, qualifying exam. *Entrance requirements:* For master's and doctorate, GRE General Test. Additional exam requirements/recommendations for international students: Required—TOEFL. *Application deadline:* Applications are processed on a rolling basis. Electronic applications accepted. *Expenses:* Tuition, state resident: full-time $21,466; part-time $1152 per credit hour. Tuition, nonresident: full-time $43,346; part-time $2367 per credit hour. Part-time tuition and fees vary according to course load, degree level and program. *Financial support:* Fellowships, research assistantships, teaching assistantships, Federal Work-Study, institutionally sponsored loans, scholarships/grants, traineeships, health care benefits, and unspecified assistantships available. Financial award applicants required to submit FAFSA. *Faculty research:* Production/distribution/logistics, financial engineering and enterprise systems, ergonomics (physical and cognitive), stochastic processes, linear and nonlinear optimization, operations research. *Total annual research expenditures:* $6.1 million. *Unit head:* Mark Daskin, Department Chair, 734-764-9410, Fax: 734-764-3451, E-mail: msdaskin@umich.edu. *Application contact:* Matt Irelan, Graduate Student Advisor/Program Coordinator, 734-764-6480, Fax: 734-764-3451, E-mail: mirelan@umich.edu.
Website: http://www.engin.umich.edu/ioe

University of Michigan–Dearborn, College of Engineering and Computer Science, MSE Program in Industrial and Systems Engineering, Dearborn, MI 48128. Offers MSE. *Program availability:* Part-time, evening/weekend, 100% online. *Faculty:* 15 full-time (2 women), 6 part-time/adjunct (2 women). *Students:* 60 full-time (14 women), 37 part-time (11 women); includes 8 minority (2 Black or African American, non-Hispanic/Latino; 1 Asian, non-Hispanic/Latino; 3 Hispanic/Latino; 1 Native Hawaiian or other Pacific Islander, non-Hispanic/Latino; 1 Two or more races, non-Hispanic/Latino), 73 international. Average age 25. 214 applicants, 57% accepted, 45 enrolled. In 2016, 23 master's awarded. *Entrance requirements:* For master's, bachelor's degree in engineering, a physical science, computer science, or applied mathematics. Additional exam requirements/recommendations for international students: Required—TOEFL (minimum score 560 paper-based; 84 iBT), IELTS (minimum score 6.5). *Application deadline:* For fall admission, 8/1 for domestic students, 5/1 for international students; for winter admission, 12/1 for domestic students, 9/1 for international students; for spring admission, 4/1 for domestic students, 1/1 for international students. Applications are processed on a rolling basis. Application fee: $60. Electronic applications accepted. *Expenses:* Tuition, state resident: full-time $13,118; part-time $2280 per term. Tuition, nonresident: full-time $21,816; part-time $3771 per term. *Required fees:* $866; $658 per unit. $329 per term. Tuition and fees vary according to program. *Financial support:* Research assistantships, teaching assistantships, scholarships/grants, and non-resident tuition scholarships available. Support available to part-time students. Financial award application deadline: 3/1; financial award applicants required to submit FAFSA. *Faculty research:* Integrated design and manufacturing, operations research and decision science, human factors and ergonomics. *Unit head:* Dr. Armen Zakarian, Chair, 313-593-5361, Fax: 313-593-3692, E-mail: zakarian@umich.edu. *Application contact:* Office of Graduate Studies, 313-583-6321, E-mail: umd-graduatestudies@umich.edu.
Website: https://umdearborn.edu/cecs/departments/industrial-and-manufacturing-systems-engineering/graduate-programs/mse-industrial-systems-engineering

University of Michigan–Dearborn, College of Engineering and Computer Science, PhD Program in Industrial and Systems Engineering, Dearborn, MI 48128. Offers PhD. *Program availability:* Part-time, evening/weekend. *Degree requirements:* For doctorate, thesis/dissertation, qualifying and prelimiary examinations. *Entrance requirements:* For doctorate, master's degree in engineering or closely-related field. Additional exam requirements/recommendations for international students: Required—TOEFL (minimum score 560 paper-based; 84 iBT), IELTS (minimum score 6.5). Electronic applications accepted. *Expenses:* Tuition, state resident: full-time $13,118; part-time $2280 per term. Tuition, nonresident: full-time $21,816; part-time $3771 per term. *Required fees:* $866; $658 per unit. $329 per term. Tuition and fees vary according to program.

University of Minnesota, Twin Cities Campus, College of Science and Engineering, Department of Industrial and Systems Engineering, Minneapolis, MN 55455-0213. Offers MS, PhD. *Program availability:* Part-time. *Degree requirements:* For doctorate, thesis/dissertation. *Entrance requirements:* For master's, GRE General Test, minimum GPA of 3.0; for doctorate, GRE General Test. Additional exam requirements/recommendations for international students: Required—TOEFL. Electronic applications accepted. *Faculty research:* Operations research, supply chains and logistics, health care, revenue management, transportation, service and manufacturing operations.

University of Missouri, Office of Research and Graduate Studies, College of Engineering, Department of Industrial and Manufacturing Systems Engineering, Columbia, MO 65211. Offers ME, MS, PhD. *Faculty:* 9 full-time (1 woman). *Students:* 14 full-time (5 women), 19 part-time (7 women). *Degree requirements:* For master's, thesis or alternative; for doctorate, thesis/dissertation. *Entrance requirements:* For master's and doctorate, GRE General Test, minimum GPA of 3.0. Additional exam requirements/recommendations for international students: Required—TOEFL (minimum score 550 paper-based; 80 iBT). *Application deadline:* For fall admission, 3/1 priority date for domestic and international students; for winter admission, 9/15 priority date for domestic and international students. Applications are processed on a rolling basis. Application fee: $75 ($90 for international students). Electronic applications accepted. *Expenses:* Tuition, state resident: full-time $6347; part-time $352.60 per credit hour. Tuition, nonresident: full-time $17,379; part-time $965.50 per credit hour. *Required fees:* $1035. Tuition and fees vary according to course load, campus/location and program. *Financial support:* Fellowships, research assistantships, teaching assistantships, institutionally sponsored loans, traineeships, health care benefits, and unspecified assistantships available. Support available to part-time students.
Website: http://engineering.missouri.edu/imse/degree-programs/

University of Nebraska–Lincoln, Graduate College, College of Engineering, Department of Industrial and Management Systems Engineering, Lincoln, NE 68588. Offers engineering management (M Eng); industrial and management systems engineering (MS, PhD); manufacturing systems engineering (MS). *Program availability:* Online learning. *Degree requirements:* For master's, thesis optional; for doctorate, comprehensive exam, thesis/dissertation. *Entrance requirements:* For master's and doctorate, GRE. Additional exam requirements/recommendations for international students: Required—TOEFL (minimum score 525 paper-based). Electronic applications accepted. *Faculty research:* Ergonomics, occupational safety, quality control, industrial packaging, facility design.

University of New Haven, Graduate School, Tagliatela College of Engineering, Program in Industrial Engineering, West Haven, CT 06516. Offers industrial engineering (MSIE); quality engineering (Graduate Certificate); MBA/MSIE. *Program availability:* Part-time, evening/weekend. *Students:* 80 full-time (8 women), 12 part-time (2 women); includes 2 minority (1 Black or African American, non-Hispanic/Latino; 1 Hispanic/Latino), 80 international. Average age 25. 236 applicants, 68% accepted, 24 enrolled. In 2016, 16 master's, 23 other advanced degrees awarded. *Degree requirements:* For master's, project. *Entrance requirements:* For master's, bachelor's degree in engineering. Additional exam requirements/recommendations for international students: Required—TOEFL (minimum score 75 iBT), IELTS, PTE (minimum score 50).

Industrial/Management Engineering

Application deadline: Applications are processed on a rolling basis. Application fee: $50. Electronic applications accepted. Application fee is waived when completed online. *Expenses: Tuition:* Full-time $15,660; part-time $870 per credit hour. *Required fees:* $200; $85 per term. Tuition and fees vary according to program. *Financial support:* Research assistantships with partial tuition reimbursements, teaching assistantships with partial tuition reimbursements, career-related internships or fieldwork, Federal Work-Study, scholarships/grants, and unspecified assistantships available. Support available to part-time students. Financial award applicants required to submit FAFSA. *Unit head:* Dr. Ali Montazer, Program Director, 203-932-7050, E-mail: amontazer@newhaven.edu. *Application contact:* Michelle Mason, Director of Graduate Enrollment, 203-932-7067, E-mail: mmason@newhaven.edu.
Website: http://www.newhaven.edu/9595/

University of Oklahoma, Gallogly College of Engineering, School of Industrial and Systems Engineering, Norman, OK 73019. Offers data science and analytics (MS); industrial and systems engineering (MS, PhD). *Faculty:* 16 full-time (3 women). *Students:* 49 full-time (13 women), 21 part-time (8 women); includes 9 minority (3 Black or African American, non-Hispanic/Latino; 2 Asian, non-Hispanic/Latino; 1 Hispanic/Latino; 3 Two or more races, non-Hispanic/Latino), 51 international. Average age 27. 131 applicants, 24% accepted, 15 enrolled. In 2016, 19 master's, 4 doctorates awarded. *Degree requirements:* For master's, comprehensive exam, thesis or alternative, 30 units with thesis, 33 without thesis; for doctorate, comprehensive exam, thesis/dissertation, 90 units. *Entrance requirements:* For master's and doctorate, GRE, BS in engineering, mathematics or equivalent. Additional exam requirements/recommendations for international students: Required—TOEFL (minimum score 79 iBT) or IELTS (minimum score 6.5). *Application deadline:* For fall admission, 6/1 priority date for domestic students, 4/1 for international students; for spring admission, 10/15 priority date for domestic students, 9/1 for international students. Applications are processed on a rolling basis. Application fee: $50 ($100 for international students). Electronic applications accepted. *Expenses:* Tuition, state resident: full-time $4886; part-time $203.60 per credit hour. Tuition, nonresident: full-time $18,989; part-time $791.20 per credit hour. *Required fees:* $3283; $126.25 per credit hour. $126.50 per semester. *Financial support:* In 2016–17, 30 students received support, including 11 research assistantships with full tuition reimbursements available (averaging $12,961 per year), 11 teaching assistantships with full tuition reimbursements available (averaging $11,160 per year); Federal Work-Study, institutionally sponsored loans, scholarships/grants, and health care benefits also available. Financial award application deadline: 6/1; financial award applicants required to submit FAFSA. *Faculty research:* Manufacturing metrology, cyber-physical-social systems, engineering design, ergonomics, data science and analytics. *Total annual research expenditures:* $527,601. *Unit head:* Dr. Shivakumar Raman, Professor/Interim Director, 405-819-3710, Fax: 405-325-7555, E-mail: raman@ou.edu. *Application contact:* Dr. Janet Allen, Chair/Graduate Liaison, 405-550-3969, Fax: 405-325-7555, E-mail: janet.allen@ou.edu.
Website: http://www.ou.edu/coe/ise.html

University of Pittsburgh, Swanson School of Engineering, Department of Industrial Engineering, Pittsburgh, PA 15260. Offers MSIE, PhD. *Program availability:* Part-time, 100% online. *Faculty:* 16 full-time (3 women), 13 part-time/adjunct (4 women). *Students:* 67 full-time (18 women), 15 part-time (5 women); includes 6 minority (1 Black or African American, non-Hispanic/Latino; 2 Asian, non-Hispanic/Latino; 3 Hispanic/Latino), 62 international. 393 applicants, 42% accepted, 40 enrolled. In 2016, 40 master's, 5 doctorates awarded. Terminal master's awarded for partial completion of doctoral program. *Degree requirements:* For doctorate, comprehensive exam, thesis/dissertation, final oral exams. *Entrance requirements:* For master's and doctorate, GRE General Test, minimum GPA of 3.0. Additional exam requirements/recommendations for international students: Required—TOEFL (minimum score 550 paper-based; 80 iBT). *Application deadline:* For fall admission, 3/1 priority date for domestic and international students; for spring admission, 7/1 priority date for domestic and international students. Applications are processed on a rolling basis. Application fee: $50. Electronic applications accepted. *Expenses:* $24,962 full-time per academic year in-state tuition, $41,222 full-time per academic year out-of-state tuition; $830 mandatory fees per academic year. *Financial support:* In 2016–17, 5 fellowships with full tuition reimbursements (averaging $30,720 per year), 22 research assistantships with full tuition reimbursements (averaging $27,396 per year), 13 teaching assistantships with full tuition reimbursements (averaging $26,328 per year) were awarded; scholarships/grants and tuition waivers (full) also available. Financial award application deadline: 3/1. *Faculty research:* Operations research, engineering management, computational intelligence, manufacturing, information systems. *Total annual research expenditures:* $4.6 million. *Unit head:* Dr. Bopaya Bidanda, Chairman, 412-624-9830, Fax: 412-624-9831, E-mail: bidanda@pitt.edu. *Application contact:* Rama Bazaz, Director, 412-624-9800, Fax: 412-624-9808, E-mail: ssoeadm@pitt.edu.
Website: http://www.engineering.pitt.edu/Departments/Industrial/

University of Puerto Rico, Mayagüez Campus, Graduate Studies, College of Engineering, Department of Industrial Engineering, Mayagüez, PR 00681-9000. Offers ME, MS. *Program availability:* Part-time. *Faculty:* 21 full-time (11 women). *Students:* 28 full-time (14 women), 9 part-time (5 women); includes 32 minority (all Hispanic/Latino), 2 international. Average age 25. 13 applicants, 62% accepted, 5 enrolled. In 2016, 8 master's awarded. *Degree requirements:* For master's, one foreign language, comprehensive exam, thesis, project. *Entrance requirements:* For master's, minimum GPA of 2.5; proficiency in English and Spanish; BS in engineering. Additional exam requirements/recommendations for international students: Required—TOEFL (minimum score 80 paper-based; 80 iBT). *Application deadline:* For fall admission, 2/15 for domestic and international students; for spring admission, 9/15 for domestic and international students. Applications are processed on a rolling basis. Application fee: $25. Electronic applications accepted. *Expenses: Tuition, area resident:* Full-time $2466. *International tuition:* $7166 full-time. *Required fees:* $210. One-time fee: $5 full-time. Tuition and fees vary according to course level, campus/location, program and student level. *Financial support:* In 2016–17, 20 students received support, including 13 research assistantships with full and partial tuition reimbursements available (averaging $3,811 per year), 11 teaching assistantships with full and partial tuition reimbursements available (averaging $3,351 per year); unspecified assistantships also available. *Faculty research:* Systems thinking and systems integration, facilities design, engineering analysis methods, lean logistics, lead data-based biological discovery. *Unit head:* Viviana I. Cesani, Ph.D., Department Head, 787-832-4040 Ext. 3819, Fax: 787-265-3820, E-mail: vivianai.cesani@upr.edu. *Application contact:* Griselys Rosado, Academic Advisor, 787-832-4040 Ext. 3204, Fax: 787-265-3820, E-mail: griselys.rosado@upr.edu.
Website: http://engineering.uprm.edu/inin/

University of Regina, Faculty of Graduate Studies and Research, Faculty of Engineering and Applied Science, Program in Industrial Systems Engineering, Regina, SK S4S 0A2, Canada. Offers M Eng, MA Sc, PhD. *Program availability:* Part-time. *Faculty:* 10 full-time (0 women), 24 part-time/adjunct (0 women). *Students:* 29 full-time (5 women), 5 part-time (0 women). 114 applicants, 16% accepted. In 2016, 14 master's, 2 doctorates awarded. *Degree requirements:* For master's, thesis, project, report; for doctorate, thesis/dissertation. *Entrance requirements:* For doctorate, master's degree. Additional exam requirements/recommendations for international students: Required—TOEFL (minimum score 550 paper-based; 80 iBT), IELTS (minimum score 6.5), PTE (minimum score 59). *Application deadline:* For fall admission, 3/31 for domestic and international students; for winter admission, 7/31 for domestic and international students; for spring admission, 11/30 for domestic and international students. Application fee: $100. Electronic applications accepted. *Expenses:* Contact institution. *Financial support:* In 2016–17, 11 fellowships (averaging $6,364 per year), 10 teaching assistantships (averaging $2,537 per year) were awarded; career-related internships or fieldwork and scholarships/grants also available. Financial award application deadline: 6/15. *Faculty research:* Stochastic systems simulation, metallurgy of welding, computer-aided engineering, finite element method of engineering systems, manufacturing systems. *Unit head:* Dr. Amr Henni, Associate Dean, Research and Graduate Studies, 306-585-4960, Fax: 306-585-4855, E-mail: amr.henni@uregina.ca. *Application contact:* Dr. Rene Mayorga, Graduate Coordinator, 306-585-4726, Fax: 306-585-4822, E-mail: rene.mayorga@uregina.ca.
Website: http://www.uregina.ca/engineering/

University of Southern California, Graduate School, Viterbi School of Engineering, Daniel J. Epstein Department of Industrial and Systems Engineering, Los Angeles, CA 90089. Offers digital supply chain management (MS); engineering management (MS); engineering technology communication (Graduate Certificate); health systems operations (Graduate Certificate); industrial and systems engineering (MS, PhD, Engr); manufacturing engineering (MS); operations research engineering (MS); optimization and supply chain management (Graduate Certificate); product development engineering (MS); safety systems and security (MS); systems architecting and engineering (MS, Graduate Certificate); systems safety and security (Graduate Certificate); transportation systems (Graduate Certificate); MS/MBA. *Program availability:* Part-time, evening/weekend, online learning. Terminal master's awarded for partial completion of doctoral program. *Degree requirements:* For master's, thesis optional; for doctorate, thesis/dissertation. *Entrance requirements:* For master's and doctorate, GRE General Test. Additional exam requirements/recommendations for international students: Recommended—TOEFL. Electronic applications accepted. *Faculty research:* Health systems, music cognition and retrieval, transportation and logistics, manufacturing and automation, engineering systems design, risk and economic analysis.

University of South Florida, College of Engineering, Department of Industrial and Management Systems Engineering, Tampa, FL 33620-9951. Offers engineering management (MSEM); industrial engineering (MSIE, PhD); information technology (MSIT). *Program availability:* Part-time, online learning. *Faculty:* 13 full-time (3 women). *Students:* 119 full-time (22 women), 85 part-time (19 women); includes 27 minority (4 Black or African American, non-Hispanic/Latino; 7 Asian, non-Hispanic/Latino; 15 Hispanic/Latino; 1 Two or more races, non-Hispanic/Latino), 135 international. Average age 27. 420 applicants, 36% accepted, 50 enrolled. In 2016, 63 master's, 9 doctorates awarded. Terminal master's awarded for partial completion of doctoral program. *Degree requirements:* For master's, comprehensive exam, thesis (for some programs); for doctorate, comprehensive exam, thesis/dissertation, 2 tools of research as specified by dissertation committee. *Entrance requirements:* For master's, GRE General Test, BS in engineering (or equivalent) with minimum GPA of 3.0 in last 60 hours of coursework, letter of recommendation, resume; for doctorate, GRE General Test, minimum GPA of 3.0 in last 60 hours of undergraduate/graduate coursework, three letters of recommendation, statement of purpose, strong background in scientific and engineering principles. Additional exam requirements/recommendations for international students: Required—TOEFL (minimum score 550 paper-based; 79 iBT) or IELTS (minimum score 6.5). *Application deadline:* For fall admission, 2/15 for domestic and international students; for spring admission, 10/15 for domestic students, 9/15 for international students; for summer admission, 2/15 for domestic students, 1/15 for international students. Application fee: $30. Electronic applications accepted. *Expenses:* Tuition, state resident: full-time $7766; part-time $431.43 per credit hour. Tuition, nonresident: full-time $15,789; part-time $877.17 per credit hour. *Required fees:* $37 per term. *Financial support:* In 2016–17, 31 students received support, including 20 research assistantships with partial tuition reimbursements available (averaging $16,748 per year), 11 teaching assistantships with partial tuition reimbursements available (averaging $15,000 per year); tuition waivers (partial) also available. Financial award applicants required to submit FAFSA. *Faculty research:* Healthcare, healthcare systems, public health policies, energy and environment, manufacturing, logistics, transportation. *Total annual research expenditures:* $253,139. *Unit head:* Dr. Tapas K. Das, Professor and Department Chair, 813-974-5585, Fax: 813-974-5953, E-mail: das@usf.edu. *Application contact:* Dr. Alex Savachkin, Associate Professor and Graduate Director, 813-974-5577, Fax: 813-974-5953, E-mail: alexs@usf.edu.
Website: http://imse.eng.usf.edu

University of South Florida, Innovative Education, Tampa, FL 33620-9951. Offers adult, career and higher education (Graduate Certificate), including college teaching, leadership in developing human resources, leadership in higher education; Africana studies (Graduate Certificate), including diasporas and health disparities, genocide and human rights; aging studies (Graduate Certificate), including gerontology; art research (Graduate Certificate), including museum studies; business foundations (Graduate Certificate); chemical and biomedical engineering (Graduate Certificate), including materials science and engineering, water, health and sustainability; child and family studies (Graduate Certificate), including positive behavior support; civil and industrial engineering (Graduate Certificate), including transportation systems analysis; community and family health (Graduate Certificate), including maternal and child health, social marketing and public health, violence and injury: prevention and intervention, women's health; criminology (Graduate Certificate), including criminal justice administration; educational measurement and research (Graduate Certificate), including evaluation; English (Graduate Certificate), including comparative literary studies, creative writing, professional and technical communication; entrepreneurship (Graduate Certificate); environmental health (Graduate Certificate), including safety management; epidemiology and biostatistics (Graduate Certificate), including applied biostatistics, biostatistics, concepts and tools of epidemiology, epidemiology, epidemiology of infectious diseases; geography, environment and planning (Graduate Certificate), including community development, environmental policy and management, geographical information systems; geology (Graduate Certificate), including hydrogeology; global health (Graduate Certificate), including disaster management, global health and Latin American and Caribbean studies, global health practice, humanitarian assistance, infection control; government and international affairs (Graduate Certificate), including Cuban studies, globalization studies; health policy and management (Graduate Certificate), including health management and leadership, public health policy and programs; hearing specialist: early intervention (Graduate Certificate); industrial and management systems engineering (Graduate Certificate), including systems engineering, technology management; information studies (Graduate Certificate), including school library media specialist; information systems/decision sciences (Graduate Certificate), including analytics and business intelligence; instructional technology (Graduate Certificate), including distance education, Florida digital/virtual educator, instructional design, multimedia design, Web design; internal medicine, bioethics and medical humanities (Graduate Certificate), including biomedical ethics; Latin American and Caribbean studies (Graduate Certificate); mass communications (Graduate Certificate), including multimedia journalism; mathematics and statistics (Graduate Certificate), including mathematics; medicine (Graduate

Certificate), including aging and neuroscience, bioinformatics, biotechnology, brain fitness and memory management, clinical investigation, health informatics, health sciences, integrative weight management, intellectual property, medicine and gender, metabolic and nutritional medicine, metabolic cardiology, pharmacy sciences; national and competitive intelligence (Graduate Certificate); psychological and social foundations (Graduate Certificate), including career counseling, college teaching, diversity in education, mental health counseling, school counseling; public affairs (Graduate Certificate), including nonprofit management, public management, research administration; public health (Graduate Certificate), including environmental health, health equity, public health generalist, translational research in adolescent behavioral health; public health practices (Graduate Certificate), including planning for healthy communities; rehabilitation and mental health counseling (Graduate Certificate), including integrative mental health care, marriage and family therapy, rehabilitation technology; secondary education (Graduate Certificate), including ESOL, foreign language education: culture and content, foreign language education: professional; social work (Graduate Certificate), including geriatric social work/clinical gerontology; special education (Graduate Certificate), including autism spectrum disorder, disabilities education: severe/profound; world languages (Graduate Certificate), including teaching English as a second language (TESL) or foreign language. *Expenses:* Tuition, state resident: full-time $7766; part-time $431.43 per credit hour. Tuition, nonresident: full-time $15,789; part-time $877.17 per credit hour. *Required fees:* $37 per term. *Unit head:* Kathy Barnes, Interdisciplinary Programs Coordinator, 813-974-8031, Fax: 813-974-7061, E-mail: barnesk@usf.edu. *Application contact:* Karen Tylinski, Metro Initiatives, 813-974-9943, Fax: 813-974-7061, E-mail: ktylinsk@usf.edu.
Website: http://www.usf.edu/innovative-education/

The University of Tennessee, Graduate School, Tickle College of Engineering, Department of Industrial and Systems Engineering, Knoxville, TN 37966. Offers engineering management (MS); industrial engineering (MS, PhD); reliability and maintainability engineering (MS); MS/MBA. *Program availability:* Part-time, online learning. *Faculty:* 13 full-time (2 women), 5 part-time/adjunct (0 women). *Students:* 90 full-time (20 women), 67 part-time (10 women); includes 18 minority (4 Black or African American, non-Hispanic/Latino; 7 Asian, non-Hispanic/Latino; 6 Hispanic/Latino; 1 Two or more races, non-Hispanic/Latino); 55 international. Average age 37. 103 applicants, 64% accepted, 23 enrolled. In 2016, 26 master's, 7 doctorates awarded. *Degree requirements:* For master's, thesis or alternative; for doctorate, comprehensive exam, thesis/dissertation. *Entrance requirements:* For master's, GRE General Test (for MS students pursuing research thesis), minimum GPA of 2.7 (for U.S. degree holders), 3.0 (for international degree holders); for doctorate, GRE General Test, minimum GPA of 3.0 on previous graduate course work. Additional exam requirements/recommendations for international students: Required—TOEFL (minimum score 550 paper-based). *Application deadline:* For fall admission, 2/1 priority date for domestic and international students; for spring admission, 6/15 for domestic and international students. Applications are processed on a rolling basis. Application fee: $35. Electronic applications accepted. *Financial support:* In 2016–17, 36 students received support, including 4 fellowships with full tuition reimbursements available (averaging $25,000 per year), 21 research assistantships with full tuition reimbursements available (averaging $18,799 per year), 10 teaching assistantships with full tuition reimbursements available (averaging $18,783 per year); career-related internships or fieldwork, Federal Work-Study, institutionally sponsored loans, health care benefits, and unspecified assistantships also available. Financial award application deadline: 2/1; financial award applicants required to submit FAFSA. *Faculty research:* Defense-oriented supply chain modeling; dependability and reliability of large computer networks; design of lean, reliable systems; new product development; operations research in the automotive industry. *Total annual research expenditures:* $1 million. *Unit head:* Dr. John Kobza, Department Head, 865-974-3333, Fax: 865-974-0588, E-mail: jkobza@utk.edu. *Application contact:* Dr. Alberto Garcia-Diaz, Professor, 865-974-7647, E-mail: agd@utk.edu.
Website: http://www.engr.utk.edu/ie/

The University of Tennessee, The University of Tennessee Space Institute, Tullahoma, TN 37388. Offers aerospace engineering (MS, PhD); biomedical engineering (MS, PhD); engineering science (MS, PhD); industrial and systems engineering/engineering management (MS, PhD); mechanical engineering (MS, PhD); physics (MS, PhD). *Program availability:* Part-time, blended/hybrid learning. Terminal master's awarded for partial completion of doctoral program. *Degree requirements:* For doctorate, one foreign language, thesis/dissertation. *Entrance requirements:* Additional exam requirements/recommendations for international students: Required—TOEFL (minimum score 550 paper-based; 80 iBT), IELTS (minimum score 6.5). Electronic applications accepted. *Expenses:* Contact institution. *Faculty research:* Fluid mechanics/aerodynamics, chemical and electric propulsion and laser diagnostics, computational mechanics and simulations, carbon fiber production and composite materials.

The University of Tennessee at Chattanooga, Program in Engineering, Chattanooga, TN 37403. Offers automotive systems (MS Engr); chemical engineering (MS Engr); civil engineering (MS Engr); computational engineering (MS Engr); electrical engineering (MS Engr); industrial engineering (MS Engr); mechanical engineering (MS Engr). *Program availability:* Part-time. *Faculty:* 21 full-time (2 women), 2 part-time/adjunct (1 woman). *Students:* 21 full-time (5 women), 26 part-time (7 women); includes 11 minority (4 Black or African American, non-Hispanic/Latino; 5 Asian, non-Hispanic/Latino; 1 Hispanic/Latino; 1 Two or more races, non-Hispanic/Latino), 18 international. Average age 28. 30 applicants, 83% accepted, 14 enrolled. In 2016, 25 master's awarded. *Degree requirements:* For master's, comprehensive exam, thesis or alternative, engineering project. *Entrance requirements:* For master's, GRE General Test, minimum undergraduate GPA of 2.7 or 3.0 in last two years of undergraduate coursework. Additional exam requirements/recommendations for international students: Required—TOEFL (minimum score 550 paper-based; 79 iBT), IELTS (minimum score 6). *Application deadline:* For fall admission, 6/15 priority date for domestic students, 7/1 for international students; for spring admission, 11/1 priority date for domestic students, 11/1 for international students. Applications are processed on a rolling basis. Application fee: $35 ($40 for international students). Electronic applications accepted. *Expenses:* $9,876 full-time in-state; $25,994 full-time out-of-state; $450 per credit part-time in-state; $1,345 per credit part-time out-of-state. *Financial support:* In 2016–17, 6 research assistantships, 5 teaching assistantships were awarded; career-related internships or fieldwork, scholarships/grants, health care benefits, and unspecified assistantships also available. Support available to part-time students. Financial award application deadline: 7/1. *Faculty research:* Quality control and reliability engineering, financial management, thermal science, energy conservation, structural analysis. *Total annual research expenditures:* $921,122. *Unit head:* Dr. Daniel Pack, Dean, 423-425-2256, Fax: 423-425-5311, E-mail: daniel-pack@utc.edu. *Application contact:* Dr. Joanne Romagni, Dean of the Graduate School, 423-425-4478, Fax: 423-425-5223, E-mail: joanne-romagni@utc.edu.
Website: http://www.utc.edu/college-engineering-computer-science/graduate-programs/msengr.php

The University of Texas at Arlington, Graduate School, College of Engineering, Department of Industrial and Manufacturing Systems Engineering, Arlington, TX 76019.

Offers engineering management (MS); industrial engineering (MS, PhD); logistics (MS); systems engineering (MS). *Program availability:* Part-time, evening/weekend, online learning. Terminal master's awarded for partial completion of doctoral program. *Degree requirements:* For master's, comprehensive exam, thesis optional; for doctorate, comprehensive exam, thesis/dissertation. *Entrance requirements:* For master's and doctorate, GRE General Test, minimum GPA of 3.0. Additional exam requirements/recommendations for international students: Required—TOEFL (minimum score 550 paper-based). *Application deadline:* For fall admission, 6/6 for domestic students, 4/4 for international students; for spring admission, 10/15 for domestic students, 9/5 for international students. Applications are processed on a rolling basis. Application fee: $35 ($50 for international students). *Financial support:* Fellowships, research assistantships, teaching assistantships, career-related internships or fieldwork, Federal Work-Study, institutionally sponsored loans, scholarships/grants, and unspecified assistantships available. Financial award application deadline: 6/1; financial award applicants required to submit FAFSA. *Faculty research:* Manufacturing, healthcare logistics, environmental systems, operations research, statistics. *Unit head:* Dr. Donald H. Liles, Chair, 817-272-3092, Fax: 817-272-3406, E-mail: dliles@uta.edu. *Application contact:* Dr. Sheik Imrhan, Graduate Advisor, 817-272-3167, Fax: 817-272-3406, E-mail: imrhan@uta.edu.
Website: http://ie.uta.edu/

The University of Texas at Austin, Graduate School, Cockrell School of Engineering, Department of Mechanical Engineering, Program in Operations Research and Industrial Engineering, Austin, TX 78712-1111. Offers MS, PhD. *Entrance requirements:* For master's and doctorate, GRE General Test. Additional exam requirements/recommendations for international students: Required—TOEFL.

The University of Texas at El Paso, Graduate School, College of Engineering, Department of Industrial Engineering, El Paso, TX 79968-0001. Offers industrial engineering (MS); manufacturing engineering (MS); systems engineering (MS, Certificate). *Program availability:* Part-time, evening/weekend. *Degree requirements:* For master's, thesis optional. *Entrance requirements:* For master's, GRE General Test, minimum GPA of 3.0 in major. Additional exam requirements/recommendations for international students: Required—TOEFL. Electronic applications accepted. *Faculty research:* Computer vision, automated inspection, simulation and modeling.

The University of Toledo, College of Graduate Studies, College of Engineering, Department of Mechanical, Industrial, and Manufacturing Engineering, Toledo, OH 43606-3390. Offers industrial engineering (MS, PhD); mechanical engineering (MS, PhD). *Program availability:* Part-time, online learning. *Degree requirements:* For master's, thesis optional; for doctorate, thesis/dissertation, qualifying exam. *Entrance requirements:* For master's, GRE General Test, minimum GPA of 3.0; for doctorate, GRE General Test, minimum GPA of 3.3. Additional exam requirements/recommendations for international students: Required—TOEFL (minimum score 550 paper-based; 80 iBT). Electronic applications accepted. *Faculty research:* Computational and experimental thermal sciences, manufacturing process and systems, mechanics, materials, design, quality and management engineering systems.

University of Toronto, School of Graduate Studies, Faculty of Applied Science and Engineering, Department of Mechanical and Industrial Engineering, Toronto, ON M5S 1A1, Canada. Offers M Eng, MA Sc, PhD. *Program availability:* Part-time. *Degree requirements:* For master's, thesis (for some programs), oral exam/thesis defense (MA Sc); for doctorate, thesis/dissertation, thesis defense, qualifying examination. *Entrance requirements:* For master's, GRE (recommended), minimum B+ average in last 2 years of undergraduate study, 2 letters of reference, resume, Canadian citizenship or permanent residency (M Eng); for doctorate, GRE (recommended), minimum B+ average, 2 letters of reference, resume. Additional exam requirements/recommendations for international students: Required—TOEFL (minimum score 580 paper-based), Michigan English Language Assessment Battery (minimum score 85), IELTS (minimum score 7), or COPE (minimum score 4). Electronic applications accepted.

University of Washington, Graduate School, College of Engineering, Department of Industrial and Systems Engineering, Seattle, WA 98195. Offers MISE, MS, PhD. *Program availability:* Part-time, online learning. *Faculty:* 10 full-time (5 women). *Students:* 60 full-time (25 women), 45 part-time (15 women); includes 29 minority (3 Black or African American, non-Hispanic/Latino; 15 Asian, non-Hispanic/Latino; 8 Hispanic/Latino; 3 Two or more races, non-Hispanic/Latino), 39 international. 273 applicants, 34% accepted, 33 enrolled. In 2016, 35 master's, 4 doctorates awarded. Terminal master's awarded for partial completion of doctoral program. *Degree requirements:* For master's, thesis optional; for doctorate, comprehensive exam, thesis/dissertation, qualifying, general, and final exams. *Entrance requirements:* For master's, GRE General Test, minimum GPA of 3.0; bachelor's degree in engineering, math, or science; transcripts; letters of recommendation; resume; statement of objectives; for doctorate, GRE General Test, minimum GPA of 3.0; master's degree in engineering, math, or science (preferred); transcripts; letters of recommendation; resume; statement of objectives. Additional exam requirements/recommendations for international students: Required—TOEFL (minimum score 580 paper-based; 92 iBT); Recommended—IELTS (minimum score 7). *Application deadline:* For fall admission, 1/1 priority date for domestic students, 1/1 for international students. Applications are processed on a rolling basis. Application fee: $85. Electronic applications accepted. *Expenses:* Contact institution. *Financial support:* In 2016–17, 32 students received support, including 22 research assistantships with full tuition reimbursements available (averaging $2,394 per year), 10 teaching assistantships with full tuition reimbursements available (averaging $2,394 per year); fellowships, career-related internships or fieldwork, scholarships/grants, traineeships, and tuition waivers (full) also available. Financial award application deadline: 2/1; financial award applicants required to submit FAFSA. *Faculty research:* Manufacturing, systems engineering and integration, optimization, human factors, virtual reality, quality and reliability, large-scale assembly, supply chain management, health systems engineering. *Total annual research expenditures:* $1 million. *Unit head:* Dr. Linda Ng Boyle, Professor/Chair, 206-543-1427, Fax: 206-685-3072, E-mail: linda@uw.edu. *Application contact:* Jennifer W. Tsai, Academic Counselor, 206-543-5041, Fax: 206-685-3072, E-mail: ieadvise@uw.edu.
Website: http://depts.washington.edu/ie/

University of Windsor, Faculty of Graduate Studies, Faculty of Engineering, Department of Industrial and Manufacturing Systems Engineering, Windsor, ON N9B 3P4, Canada. Offers industrial engineering (M Eng, MA Sc); manufacturing systems engineering (PhD). *Program availability:* Part-time. *Degree requirements:* For master's, thesis; for doctorate, comprehensive exam, thesis/dissertation. *Entrance requirements:* For master's, minimum B average; for doctorate, master's degree, minimum B average. Additional exam requirements/recommendations for international students: Required—TOEFL (minimum score 560 paper-based). Electronic applications accepted. *Faculty research:* Human factors, operations research.

University of Wisconsin–Madison, Graduate School, College of Engineering, Department of Industrial and Systems Engineering, Madison, WI 53706. Offers industrial engineering (MS, PhD), including human factors and health systems engineering (MS), systems engineering and analytics (MS). *Program availability:* Part-time. *Faculty:* 18 full-time (5 women). *Students:* 94 full-time (37 women), 6 part-time (2 women); includes 2

minority (both Black or African American, non-Hispanic/Latino), 73 international. Average age 26. 463 applicants, 22% accepted, 35 enrolled. In 2016, 28 master's, 13 doctorates awarded. Terminal master's awarded for partial completion of doctoral program. *Degree requirements:* For master's, thesis optional, 30 credits; minimum GPA of 3.0; for doctorate, comprehensive exam, thesis/dissertation, minimum of 32 credits; minimum GPA of 3.0. *Entrance requirements:* For master's and doctorate, GRE General Test, minimum GPA of 3.0, BS in engineering or equivalent, course work in computer programming and statistics. Additional exam requirements/recommendations for international students: Required—TOEFL (minimum score 580 paper-based; 92 iBT), IELTS (minimum score 7). *Application deadline:* For fall admission, 1/1 for domestic and international students; for spring admission, 10/1 for domestic and international students; for summer admission, 2/1 for domestic and international students. Application fee: $75 ($81 for international students). Electronic applications accepted. *Expenses:* $13,157 per year in-state tuition and fees; $26,484 per year out-of-state tuition and fees. *Financial support:* In 2016–17, 50 students received support, including 1 fellowship with full tuition reimbursement available, 30 research assistantships with full tuition reimbursements available, 14 teaching assistantships with full tuition reimbursements available; career-related internships or fieldwork, Federal Work-Study, institutionally sponsored loans, scholarships/grants, traineeships, health care benefits, and unspecified assistantships also available. Financial award application deadline: 12/1; financial award applicants required to submit FAFSA. *Faculty research:* Operations research; human factors and ergonomics; health systems engineering; manufacturing and production systems. *Total annual research expenditures:* $12.5 million. *Unit head:* Dr. Jeff Lindroth, Chair, 608-890-1931, Fax: 608-262-8454, E-mail: linderoth@wisc.edu. *Application contact:* Pam Peterson, Student Services Coordinator, 608-263-4025, Fax: 608-262-8454, E-mail: prpeterson@wisc.edu.
Website: http://www.engr.wisc.edu/department/industrial-systems-engineering/

University of Wisconsin–Milwaukee, Graduate School, College of Engineering and Applied Science, Program in Engineering, Milwaukee, WI 53201-0413. Offers biomedical engineering (MS); civil engineering (MS, PhD); computer science (PhD); electrical and computer engineering (MS); electrical engineering (PhD); engineering mechanics (MS); industrial and management engineering (MS); industrial engineering (PhD); manufacturing engineering (MS); materials (PhD); materials engineering (MS); mechanical engineering (MS). *Program availability:* Part-time. *Students:* 199 full-time (52 women), 156 part-time (32 women); includes 27 minority (2 Black or African American, non-Hispanic/Latino; 15 Asian, non-Hispanic/Latino; 3 Hispanic/Latino; 7 Two or more races, non-Hispanic/Latino), 244 international. Average age 30. 396 applicants, 61% accepted, 102 enrolled. In 2016, 72 master's, 26 doctorates awarded. *Degree requirements:* For master's, comprehensive exam (for some programs), thesis or alternative; for doctorate, comprehensive exam, thesis/dissertation, internship. *Entrance requirements:* For master's, GRE, minimum GPA of 2.75; for doctorate, GRE, minimum GPA of 3.5. Additional exam requirements/recommendations for international students: Required—TOEFL (minimum score 550 paper-based; 79 iBT), IELTS (minimum score 6.5). *Application deadline:* For fall admission, 1/1 priority date for domestic students; for spring admission, 9/1 for domestic students. Applications are processed on a rolling basis. Application fee: $56 ($96 for international students). *Financial support:* In 2016–17, 3 fellowships, 55 research assistantships, 77 teaching assistantships were awarded; career-related internships or fieldwork, Federal Work-Study, unspecified assistantships, and project assistantships also available. Support available to part-time students. Financial award application deadline: 4/15. *Unit head:* David Yu, Representative, 414-229-6169, E-mail: yu@uwm.edu. *Application contact:* Betty Warras, General Information Contact, 414-229-6169, Fax: 414-229-6967, E-mail: bwarras@uwm.edu.
Website: http://www4.uwm.edu/ceas/academics/graduate_programs/

University of Wisconsin–Stout, Graduate School, College of Management, Program in Risk Control, Menomonie, WI 54751. Offers MS. *Program availability:* Part-time. *Degree requirements:* For master's, thesis. *Entrance requirements:* For master's, minimum GPA of 3.0. Additional exam requirements/recommendations for international students: Required—TOEFL (minimum score 500 paper-based; 61 iBT). Electronic applications accepted. *Faculty research:* Environmental microbiology, water supply safety, facilities planning, industrial ventilation, bioterrorist.

Virginia Polytechnic Institute and State University, Graduate School, College of Engineering, Blacksburg, VA 24061. Offers aerospace engineering (ME, MS, PhD); biological systems engineering (ME, MS, PhD); biomedical engineering (MS, PhD); chemical engineering (ME, MS, PhD); civil engineering (ME, MS, PhD); computer engineering (ME, MS, PhD); computer science (MS, PhD); electrical engineering (ME, PhD); engineering education (PhD); engineering mechanics (ME, MS, PhD); environmental engineering (MS); environmental science and engineering (MS); industrial and systems engineering (ME, MS, PhD); materials science and engineering (ME, MS, PhD); mechanical engineering (ME, MS, PhD); mining and minerals engineering (PhD); mining engineering (ME, MS); nuclear engineering (MS, PhD); ocean engineering (MS); systems engineering (ME, MS). *Faculty:* 400 full-time (73 women), 3 part-time/adjunct (2 women). *Students:* 1,949 full-time (487 women), 393 part-time (69 women); includes 251 minority (56 Black or African American, non-Hispanic/Latino; 3 American Indian or Alaska Native, non-Hispanic/Latino; 87 Asian, non-Hispanic/Latino; 70 Hispanic/Latino; 35 Two or more races, non-Hispanic/Latino), 1,354 international. Average age 27. 4,903 applicants, 19% accepted, 569 enrolled. In 2016, 364 master's, 200 doctorates awarded. *Degree requirements:* For master's, comprehensive exam (for some programs), thesis (for some programs); for doctorate, comprehensive exam (for some programs), thesis/dissertation (for some programs). *Entrance requirements:* For master's and doctorate, GRE/GMAT. Additional exam requirements/recommendations for international students: Required—TOEFL (minimum score 80 iBT). *Application deadline:* For fall admission, 8/1 for domestic students, 4/1 for international students; for spring admission, 1/1 for domestic students, 9/1 for international students. Applications are processed on a rolling basis. Application fee: $75. Electronic applications accepted. *Expenses:* Tuition, state resident: full-time $12,467; part-time $692.50 per credit hour. Tuition, nonresident: full-time $25,095; part-time $1394.25 per credit hour. *Required fees:* $2669; $491.50 per semester. Tuition and fees vary according to course load, campus/location and program. *Financial support:* In 2016–17, 160 fellowships with full tuition reimbursements (averaging $7,387 per year), 872 research assistantships with full tuition reimbursements (averaging $22,329 per year), 313 teaching assistantships with full tuition reimbursements (averaging $18,714 per year) were awarded. Financial award application deadline: 3/1; financial award applicants required to submit FAFSA. *Total annual research expenditures:* $91.8 million. *Unit head:* Dr. Julia Ross, Dean, 540-231-9752, Fax: 540-231-3031, E-mail: deaneng@vt.edu. *Application contact:* Linda Perkins, Executive Assistant, 540-231-9752, Fax: 540-231-3031, E-mail: lperkins@vt.edu. Website: http://www.eng.vt.edu/

Virginia Polytechnic Institute and State University, VT Online, Blacksburg, VA 24061. Offers advanced transportation systems (Certificate); aerospace engineering (MS); agricultural and life sciences (MSLFS); business information systems (Graduate Certificate); career and technical education (MS); civil engineering (MS); computer engineering (M Eng, MS); decision support systems (Graduate Certificate); eLearning leadership (MA); electrical engineering (M Eng, MS); engineering administration (MEA); environmental engineering (Certificate); environmental politics and policy (Graduate Certificate); environmental sciences and engineering (MS); foundations of political analysis (Graduate Certificate); health product risk management (Graduate Certificate); industrial and systems engineering (MS); information policy and society (Graduate Certificate); information security (Graduate Certificate); information technology (MIT); instructional technology (MA); integrative STEM education (MA Ed); liberal arts (Graduate Certificate); life sciences: health product risk management (MS); natural resources (MNR, Graduate Certificate); networking (Graduate Certificate); nonprofit and nongovernmental organization management (Graduate Certificate); ocean engineering (MS); political science (MA); security studies (Graduate Certificate); software development (Graduate Certificate). *Expenses:* Tuition, state resident: full-time $12,467; part-time $692.50 per credit hour. Tuition, nonresident: full-time $25,095; part-time $1394.25 per credit hour. *Required fees:* $2669; $491.50 per semester. Tuition and fees vary according to course load, campus/location and program.

Wayne State University, College of Engineering, Department of Industrial and Systems Engineering, Detroit, MI 48202. Offers data science and business analytics (MS); engineering management (MS); industrial engineering (MS, PhD); manufacturing engineering (MS); systems engineering (Certificate). *Faculty:* 10. *Students:* 313 full-time (37 women), 140 part-time (26 women); includes 37 minority (16 Black or African American, non-Hispanic/Latino; 15 Asian, non-Hispanic/Latino; 3 Hispanic/Latino; 3 Two or more races, non-Hispanic/Latino), 340 international. Average age 28. 1,171 applicants, 42% accepted, 105 enrolled. In 2016, 117 master's, 5 doctorates awarded. *Degree requirements:* For master's, thesis (for some programs); for doctorate, thesis/dissertation. *Entrance requirements:* For master's, BS from ABET-accredited institution; for doctorate, MS in industrial engineering or operations research with minimum graduate GPA of 3.5; for Certificate, BS in engineering or other technical field from ABET-accredited institution, full-time work experience as practicing engineer or technical leader. Additional exam requirements/recommendations for international students: Required—TOEFL (minimum score 550 paper-based; 79 iBT), TWE (minimum score 5.5), Michigan English Language Assessment Battery (minimum score 85); Recommended—IELTS (minimum score 6.5). *Application deadline:* For fall admission, 6/1 priority date for domestic students, 5/1 priority date for international students; for winter admission, 10/1 priority date for domestic students, 9/1 priority date for international students; for spring admission, 2/1 priority date for domestic students, 1/1 priority date for international students. Applications are processed on a rolling basis. Application fee: $50. Electronic applications accepted. *Expenses:* $18,871 per year resident tuition and fees, $36,065 per year non-resident tuition and fees. *Financial support:* In 2016–17, 118 students received support, including 2 fellowships with tuition reimbursements available (averaging $16,000 per year), 4 research assistantships with tuition reimbursements available (averaging $18,883 per year), 12 teaching assistantships with tuition reimbursements available (averaging $19,177 per year); scholarships/grants, tuition waivers (full), and unspecified assistantships also available. Financial award applicants required to submit FAFSA. *Faculty research:* Healthcare systems engineering, product design and development, quality and reliability engineering, supply chain management and logistics. *Total annual research expenditures:* $3.2 million. *Unit head:* Dr. Leslie Monplaisir, Associate Professor/Chair, 313-577-3821, Fax: 313-577-8833, E-mail: leslie.monplaisir@wayne.edu. *Application contact:* Eric Scimeca, Graduate Program Coordinator, 313-577-0412, E-mail: eric.scimeca@wayne.edu. Website: http://engineering.wayne.edu/ise/

Western Michigan University, Graduate College, College of Engineering and Applied Sciences, Department of Industrial and Entrepreneurial Engineering and Engineering Management, Kalamazoo, MI 49008. Offers engineering management (MS); industrial engineering (MSE, PhD). *Degree requirements:* For master's, thesis optional.

Western New England University, College of Engineering, Program in Industrial Engineering, Springfield, MA 01119. Offers MS. *Program availability:* Part-time, evening/weekend. *Degree requirements:* For master's, comprehensive exam, thesis optional. *Entrance requirements:* For master's, bachelor's degree in engineering or related field, two letters of recommendation, resume, transcript. Additional exam requirements/recommendations for international students: Required—TOEFL (minimum score 79 iBT). Electronic applications accepted. *Expenses:* Contact institution. *Faculty research:* Project scheduling, flexible manufacturing systems, facility layout, energy management.

West Virginia University, Statler College of Engineering and Mineral Resources, Department of Industrial and Management Systems Engineering, Program in Industrial Engineering, Morgantown, WV 26506. Offers engineering (MSE); industrial engineering (MSIE, PhD). *Program availability:* Part-time. *Degree requirements:* For master's, thesis or alternative; for doctorate, comprehensive exam, thesis/dissertation. *Entrance requirements:* For master's, GRE General Test, minimum GPA of 3.0 Regular; 2.75 Provisional; for doctorate, GRE General Test, minimum GPA of 3.5. Additional exam requirements/recommendations for international students: Required—TOEFL (minimum score 550 paper-based; 80 iBT). Electronic applications accepted. *Faculty research:* Production planning and control, quality control, robotics and CIMS, ergonomics, castings.

Wichita State University, Graduate School, College of Engineering, Department of Industrial and Manufacturing Engineering, Wichita, KS 67260. Offers engineering management (MEM); industrial engineering (MS, PhD). *Program availability:* Part-time. In 2016, 37 master's, 3 doctorates awarded. *Entrance requirements:* Additional exam requirements/recommendations for international students: Required—TOEFL. *Financial support:* Teaching assistantships available. *Unit head:* Dr. Krishna Krishnan, Chair, 316-978-3425, Fax: 316-978-3742, E-mail: krishna.krishnan@wichita.edu. *Application contact:* Jordan Oleson, Admissions Coordinator, 316-978-3095, Fax: 316-978-3253, E-mail: jordan.oleson@wichita.edu.
Website: http://www.wichita.edu/ime

Wright State University, Graduate School, College of Engineering and Computer Science, Department of Biomedical, Industrial and Human Factors Engineering, Dayton, OH 45435. Offers biomedical engineering (MS); industrial and human factors engineering (MS). *Program availability:* Part-time. *Degree requirements:* For master's, thesis or course option alternative. *Entrance requirements:* Additional exam requirements/recommendations for international students: Required—TOEFL. *Application deadline:* For fall admission, 5/30 for domestic students. Application fee: $25. *Expenses:* Tuition, state resident: full-time $9952; part-time $622 per credit hour. Tuition, nonresident: full-time $16,960; part-time $1060 per credit hour. *Financial support:* Fellowships, research assistantships, teaching assistantships, Federal Work-Study, institutionally sponsored loans, and unspecified assistantships available. Support available to part-time students. Financial award application deadline: 3/15; financial award applicants required to submit FAFSA. *Faculty research:* Medical imaging, functional electrical stimulation, implantable aids, man-machine interfaces, expert systems. *Unit head:* Dr. S. Narayanan, Chair, 937-775-5044, Fax: 937-775-7364, E-mail: sundaram.narayanan@wright.edu. *Application contact:* John Kimble, Associate Director of Graduate Admissions and Records, 937-775-2957, Fax: 937-775-2453, E-mail: john.kimble@wright.edu.
Website: https://engineering-computer-science.wright.edu/biomedical-industrial-and-human-factors-engineering

Youngstown State University, Graduate School, College of Science, Technology, Engineering and Mathematics, Department of Industrial and Systems Engineering, Youngstown, OH 44555-0001. Offers MSE.

Manufacturing Engineering

American University of Armenia, Graduate Programs, Yerevan, Armenia. Offers business administration (MBA); computer and information science (MS), including business management, design and manufacturing, energy (ME, MS), industrial engineering and systems management; economics (MS); industrial engineering and systems management (ME), including business, computer aided design/manufacturing, energy (ME, MS), information technology; law (LL M); political science and international affairs (MPSIA); public health (MPH); teaching English as a foreign language (MA). *Program availability:* Part-time, evening/weekend. *Degree requirements:* For master's, thesis (for some programs), capstone/project. *Entrance requirements:* For master's, GRE, GMAT, or LSAT. Additional exam requirements/recommendations for international students: Recommended—TOEFL (minimum score 79 iBT), IELTS (minimum score 6.5). *Faculty research:* Microfinance, finance (rural/development, international, corporate), firm life cycle theory, TESOL, language proficiency testing, public policy, administrative law, economic development, cryptography, artificial intelligence, energy efficiency/renewable energy, computer-aided design/manufacturing, health financing, tuberculosis control, mother/child health, preventive ophthalmology, post-earthquake psychopathological investigations, tobacco control, environmental health risk assessments.

Arizona State University at the Tempe campus, Ira A. Fulton Schools of Engineering, The Polytechnic School, Program in Engineering Technology, Mesa, AZ 85212. Offers manufacturing engineering technology (MS). *Program availability:* Part-time, evening/weekend. *Degree requirements:* For master's, thesis or applied project and oral defense, final examination, interactive Program of Study (iPOS) submitted before completing 50 percent of required credit hours. *Entrance requirements:* For master's, bachelor's degree with minimum of 30 credit hours or equivalent in a technology area including course work applicable to the concentration being sought and minimum of 16 credit hours of math and science; industrial experience beyond bachelor's degree (recommended). Additional exam requirements/recommendations for international students: Required—TOEFL, IELTS, or PTE. Electronic applications accepted. *Faculty research:* Manufacturing modeling and simulation &ITsmart&RO and composite materials, optimization of turbine engines, machinability and manufacturing processes design, fuel cells and other alternative energy sources.

Boston University, College of Engineering, Department of Mechanical Engineering, Boston, MA 02215. Offers manufacturing engineering (M Eng, MS); mechanical engineering (PhD); MS/MBA. *Program availability:* Part-time, 100% online, blended/hybrid learning. *Students:* 164 full-time (30 women), 40 part-time (8 women); includes 27 minority (15 Asian, non-Hispanic/Latino; 5 Hispanic/Latino; 2 Native Hawaiian or other Pacific Islander, non-Hispanic/Latino; 5 Two or more races, non-Hispanic/Latino), 89 international. Average age 26. 498 applicants, 37% accepted, 84 enrolled. In 2016, 65 master's, 11 doctorates awarded. Terminal master's awarded for partial completion of doctoral program. *Degree requirements:* For master's, thesis (for some programs); for doctorate, comprehensive exam, thesis/dissertation. *Entrance requirements:* For master's and doctorate, GRE General Test. Additional exam requirements/recommendations for international students: Required—TOEFL (minimum score 90 iBT), IELTS (minimum score 7). *Faculty research:* Acoustics, ultrasound, and vibrations; biomechanics; dynamics, control, and robotics; energy and thermofluid sciences; MEMS and nanotechnology. *Unit head:* Dr. Alice White, Chairperson, 617-353-2814, Fax: 617-353-5866, E-mail: aew1@bu.edu.
Website: http://www.bu.edu/me/

Bradley University, The Graduate School, Caterpillar College of Engineering and Technology, Department of Industrial and Manufacturing Engineering and Technology, Peoria, IL 61625-0002. Offers industrial engineering (MS); manufacturing engineering (MS). *Program availability:* Part-time, evening/weekend. *Degree requirements:* For master's, comprehensive exam, project. *Entrance requirements:* Additional exam requirements/recommendations for international students: Required—TOEFL (minimum score 550 paper-based; 79 iBT), IELTS (minimum score 6.5). *Application deadline:* For fall admission, 5/15 priority date for domestic and international students; for spring admission, 10/15 priority date for domestic and international students. Applications are processed on a rolling basis. Application fee: $40 ($50 for international students). Electronic applications accepted. *Expenses:* Tuition: Full-time $7650; part-time $850 per credit. *Required fees:* $50 per credit. One-time fee: $100 full-time. *Financial support:* Research assistantships with full and partial tuition reimbursements, scholarships/grants, tuition waivers (partial), and unspecified assistantships available. Support available to part-time students. Financial award application deadline: 4/1. *Unit head:* Dr. Joseph Chen, Chair, 309-677-2740, E-mail: jchen@bradley.edu. *Application contact:* Kayla Carroll, Director of International Admission and Student Services, 309-677-2375, E-mail: klcarroll@fsmail.bradley.edu.
Website: http://www.bradley.edu/academic/departments/imet/

Brigham Young University, Graduate Studies, Ira A. Fulton College of Engineering and Technology, School of Technology, Provo, UT 84602. Offers construction management (MS); information technology (MS); manufacturing engineering technology (MS); technology and engineering education (MS). *Faculty:* 25 full-time (0 women), 3 part-time/adjunct (0 women). *Students:* 36 full-time (4 women); includes 5 minority (2 American Indian or Alaska Native, non-Hispanic/Latino; 2 Asian, non-Hispanic/Latino; 1 Hispanic/Latino). Average age 29. 14 applicants, 100% accepted, 13 enrolled. In 2016, 11 master's awarded. *Degree requirements:* For master's, thesis. *Entrance requirements:* For master's, GRE General Test; GMAT or GRE (for construction management emphasis), minimum GPA of 3.0 in last 60 hours of course work. Additional exam requirements/recommendations for international students: Required—TOEFL (minimum score 580 paper-based; 85 iBT). *Application deadline:* For fall admission, 2/15 for domestic and international students; for winter admission, 9/10 for domestic students, 9/15 for international students; for spring admission, 2/15 for domestic and international students; for summer admission, 2/15 for domestic and international students. Application fee: $50. Electronic applications accepted. *Expenses:* Tuition: Full-time $6680; part-time $393 per credit. Tuition and fees vary according to course load, program and student's religious affiliation. *Financial support:* In 2016–17, 28 students received support, including 3 research assistantships (averaging $18,288 per year), 11 teaching assistantships (averaging $7,500 per year); scholarships/grants also available. *Faculty research:* Information assurance and security, HEI and databases, manufacturing materials, processes and systems, innovation in construction management scheduling and delivery methods. *Total annual research expenditures:* $844,333. *Unit head:* Dr. Barry M. Lunt, Director, 801-422-6300, Fax: 801-422-0490, E-mail: blunt@byu.edu. *Application contact:* Clifton Farnsworth, Graduate Coordinator, 801-422-6494, Fax: 801-422-0490, E-mail: clifton_farnsworth@byu.edu.
Website: http://www.et.byu.edu/sot/

California State University, Northridge, Graduate Studies, College of Engineering and Computer Science, Department of Manufacturing Systems Engineering and Management, Northridge, CA 91330. Offers engineering automation (MS); engineering management (MS); manufacturing systems engineering (MS); materials engineering (MS). *Program availability:* Online learning. *Faculty:* 8 full-time (7 women), 21 part-time/adjunct (16 women). *Students:* 124 full-time (29 women), 94 part-time (19 women); includes 27 minority (1 American Indian or Alaska Native, non-Hispanic/Latino; 11 Asian, non-Hispanic/Latino; 13 Hispanic/Latino; 2 Two or more races, non-Hispanic/Latino), 145 international. Average age 27. 302 applicants, 33% accepted, 45 enrolled. *Entrance requirements:* For master's, GRE (if cumulative undergraduate GPA less than 3.0). *Application deadline:* For fall admission, 3/30 for domestic students; for spring admission, 9/30 for domestic students. Application fee: $55. *Expenses:* Tuition, state resident: full-time $4152. *Unit head:* Ahmad Sarfaraz, Chair, 818-677-2167.
Website: http://www.csun.edu/~msem/

The Citadel, The Military College of South Carolina, Citadel Graduate College, School of Engineering, Department of Mechanical Engineering, Charleston, SC 29409. Offers aeronautical engineering (Graduate Certificate); composites engineering (Graduate Certificate); manufacturing engineering (Graduate Certificate); mechanical engineering (MS); mechatronics engineering (Graduate Certificate); power and energy (Graduate Certificate). *Program availability:* Part-time, evening/weekend. *Students:* 1 part-time; minority (Asian, non-Hispanic/Latino). 1 applicant, 100% accepted, 1 enrolled. *Degree requirements:* For master's, 30 hours of coursework with minimum GPA of 3.0 on hours earned at The Citadel. *Entrance requirements:* For master's, GRE, 2 letters of recommendation; official transcript of baccalaureate degree from an ABET accredited engineering program or approved alternative. Additional exam requirements/recommendations for international students: Required—TOEFL (minimum score 550 paper-based; 79 iBT). *Application deadline:* Applications are processed on a rolling basis. Application fee: $40. Electronic applications accepted. *Expenses:* Tuition, state resident: full-time $5121; part-time $569 per credit hour. Tuition, nonresident: full-time $8613; part-time $957 per credit hour. *Required fees:* $90 per term. *Financial support:* Fellowships and unspecified assistantships available. Support available to part-time students. Financial award application deadline: 7/1; financial award applicants required to submit FAFSA. *Unit head:* Dr. Robert J. Rabb, Department Head, 843-953-0520, E-mail: rrabb@citadel.edu. *Application contact:* Dr. Tara Hornor, Associate Provost for Planning, Assessment and Evaluation/Dean of Enrollment Management, 843-953-5089, E-mail: cgc@citadel.edu.
Website: http://www.citadel.edu/root/me

Clemson University, Graduate School, College of Agriculture, Forestry and Life Sciences, Department of Food, Nutrition and Packaging Sciences, Program in Packaging Science, Clemson, SC 29634. Offers MS. *Program availability:* Part-time. *Faculty:* 24 full-time (9 women), 1 part-time/adjunct (0 women). *Students:* 4 full-time (1 woman), 1 part-time (0 women), 2 international. Average age 31. 11 applicants, 27% accepted, 2 enrolled. In 2016, 8 master's awarded. *Degree requirements:* For master's, thesis. *Entrance requirements:* For master's, GRE General Test, unofficial transcripts, letters of recommendation. Additional exam requirements/recommendations for international students: Required—TOEFL (minimum score 80 iBT), IELTS (minimum score 6.5). *Application deadline:* For fall admission, 6/1 for domestic students, 4/15 for international students. Applications are processed on a rolling basis. Application fee: $80 ($90 for international students). Electronic applications accepted. *Expenses:* $5,617 per semester full-time resident, $11,194 per semester full-time non-resident, $697 per credit hour part-time resident, $1,392 per credit hour part-time non-resident. *Financial support:* In 2016–17, 8 students received support, including 1 research assistantship with partial tuition reimbursement available (averaging $9,083 per year), 3 teaching assistantships with partial tuition reimbursements available (averaging $14,000 per year). Financial award application deadline: 2/15. *Unit head:* Dr. E. Jeffery Rhodehamel, Department Chair, 864-656-1211, Fax: 864-656-0331, E-mail: jrhode@clemson.edu. *Application contact:* Dr. Paul Dawson, Graduate Coordinator, 864-656-1138, E-mail: pdawson@clemson.edu.
Website: https://www.clemson.edu/cafls/departments/fnps/degrees/packaging-science-ms/index.html

Cornell University, Graduate School, Graduate Fields of Engineering, Field of Operations Research and Information Engineering, Ithaca, NY 14853. Offers applied probability and statistics (PhD); manufacturing systems engineering (PhD); mathematical programming (PhD); operations research and industrial engineering (M Eng). *Degree requirements:* For doctorate, comprehensive exam, thesis/dissertation. *Entrance requirements:* For master's and doctorate, GRE General Test, 3 letters of recommendation. Additional exam requirements/recommendations for international students: Required—TOEFL (minimum score 600 paper-based; 100 iBT). Electronic applications accepted. *Faculty research:* Mathematical programming and combinatorial optimization, statistics, stochastic processes, mathematical finance, simulation, manufacturing, e-commerce.

Eastern Kentucky University, The Graduate School, College of Business and Technology, Department of Technology, Richmond, KY 40475-3102. Offers industrial education (MS), including occupational training and development, technical administration, technology education; industrial technology (MS). *Program availability:* Part-time, evening/weekend. *Entrance requirements:* For master's, GRE General Test, minimum GPA of 2.5. *Faculty research:* Lunar excavation, computer networking, integrating academic and vocational education.

East Tennessee State University, School of Graduate Studies, College of Business and Technology, Department of Engineering Technology, Surveying and Digital Media, Johnson City, TN 37614. Offers MS, Postbaccalaureate Certificate. *Program availability:* Part-time. *Degree requirements:* For master's, comprehensive exam, thesis optional, capstone. *Entrance requirements:* For master's, bachelor's degree in technical or related area, minimum GPA of 3.0; for Postbaccalaureate Certificate, minimum GPA of 2.5, three letters of recommendation. Additional exam requirements/recommendations for international students: Required—TOEFL (minimum score 550 paper-based; 79 iBT). Electronic applications accepted. *Faculty research:* Computer-integrated manufacturing, alternative energy, sustainability, CAD/CAM, organizational change.

Florida State University, The Graduate School, FAMU-FSU College of Engineering, Department of Industrial and Manufacturing Engineering, Tallahassee, FL 32306. Offers industrial engineering (MS, PhD). *Faculty:* 14 full-time (1 woman), 1 (woman) part-time/adjunct. *Students:* 49 full-time (15 women); includes 10 minority (5 Black or African American, non-Hispanic/Latino; 1 Asian, non-Hispanic/Latino; 4 Hispanic/Latino), 28 international. Average age 24. 76 applicants, 36% accepted, 11 enrolled. In 2016, 41 master's, 4 doctorates awarded. *Degree requirements:* For master's, thesis, proposal presentation, progress presentation, defense presentation; for doctorate, thesis/dissertation, preliminary exam, proposal exam, defense exam. *Entrance requirements:* For master's, GRE General Test (minimum new score of 146 Verbal and 155 Quantitative), minimum GPA of 3.0; for doctorate, GRE General Test (minimum new score of 146 Verbal and 155 Quantitative), minimum GPA of 3.0 (without MS in industrial engineering), 3.4 (with MS in industrial engineering). Additional exam requirements/

recommendations for international students: Required—TOEFL (minimum score 550 paper-based; 80 iBT); Recommended—IELTS (minimum score 6.5). *Application deadline:* For fall admission, 3/1 for domestic and international students; for spring admission, 11/1 for domestic and international students; for summer admission, 1/1 for domestic and international students. Applications are processed on a rolling basis. Application fee: $30. Electronic applications accepted. *Expenses:* Tuition, state resident: full-time $7263; part-time $403.51 per credit hour. Tuition, nonresident: full-time $18,087; part-time $1004.85 per credit hour. *Required fees:* $1365; $75.81 per credit hour. $20 per semester. Tuition and fees vary according to campus/location. *Financial support:* In 2016–17, 57 students received support, including 5 fellowships with full tuition reimbursements available, 19 research assistantships with full tuition reimbursements available, 10 teaching assistantships with full tuition reimbursements available; tuition waivers (full) and unspecified assistantships also available. Financial award application deadline: 3/1; financial award applicants required to submit FAFSA. *Faculty research:* Precision manufacturing, composite manufacturing, green manufacturing, applied optimization, simulation. *Total annual research expenditures:* $2.2 million. *Unit head:* Dr. Okenwa Okoli, Chair/Professor/Associate Director, 850-410-6352, Fax: 850-410-6342, E-mail: okoli@eng.famu.fsu.edu. *Application contact:* Shedric Triplett, Graduate Studies Assistant, 850-410-6582, Fax: 850-410-6342, E-mail: striplett@fsu.edu.
Website: http://www.eng.famu.fsu.edu/departments/industrial/

Georgia Southern University, Jack N. Averitt College of Graduate Studies, Allen E. Paulson College of Engineering and Information Technology, Department of Mechanical Engineering, Statesboro, GA 30460. Offers engineering and manufacturing management (Graduate Certificate); engineering/energy science (MSAE); engineering/engineering management (MSAE); engineering/mechatronics (MSAE); occupational safety and environmental compliance (Graduate Certificate). *Program availability:* Part-time, evening/weekend. *Students:* 43 full-time (7 women), 20 part-time (5 women); includes 23 minority (18 Black or African American, non-Hispanic/Latino; 2 Asian, non-Hispanic/Latino; 3 Hispanic/Latino), 15 international. Average age 27. 40 applicants, 83% accepted, 13 enrolled. In 2016, 15 master's awarded. *Degree requirements:* For master's, comprehensive exam, thesis optional. *Entrance requirements:* For master's, GRE. Additional exam requirements/recommendations for international students: Required—TOEFL (minimum score 550 paper-based; 80 iBT), IELTS (minimum score 6). *Application deadline:* For fall admission, 3/1 priority date for domestic and international students; for spring admission, 10/1 priority date for domestic students, 10/1 for international students. Applications are processed on a rolling basis. Application fee: $50. Electronic applications accepted. *Expenses:* Tuition, state resident: full-time $7236; part-time $277 per semester hour. Tuition, nonresident: full-time $27,118; part-time $1105 per semester hour. *Required fees:* $2092. *Financial support:* In 2016–17, 3 students received support, including 4 research assistantships with partial tuition reimbursements available (averaging $7,200 per year), teaching assistantships with partial tuition reimbursements available (averaging $7,200 per year); Federal Work-Study, scholarships/grants, tuition waivers (partial), and unspecified assistantships also available. Financial award application deadline: 4/15; financial award applicants required to submit FAFSA. *Faculty research:* Interdisciplinary research in computational mechanics, experimental and computational biofuel combustion and tribology, mechatronics and control, thermomechanical and thermofluid finite element modeling, information technology, analysis and design of antennas for wireless communications, wireless energy harvest, propagation modeling, RFID, wireless sensors, GPS/GNSS, metamaterials, finite element modeling of bioinstrumentation, embedded systems. *Total annual research expenditures:* $81,085. *Unit head:* Dr. Brian Vlcek, Chair, 912-478-5761, Fax: 912-478-1455, E-mail: bvlcek@georgiasouthern.edu.

Grand Valley State University, Padnos College of Engineering and Computing, School of Engineering, Allendale, MI 49401-9403. Offers electrical and computer engineering (MSE); manufacturing operations (MSE); mechanical engineering (MSE); product design and manufacturing engineering (MSE). *Program availability:* Part-time, evening/weekend. *Faculty:* 16 full-time (3 women). *Students:* 29 full-time (8 women), 38 part-time (5 women); includes 5 minority (2 Black or African American, non-Hispanic/Latino; 1 Asian, non-Hispanic/Latino; 2 Hispanic/Latino), 37 international. Average age 26. 129 applicants, 58% accepted, 23 enrolled. In 2016, 24 master's awarded. *Degree requirements:* For master's, project or thesis. *Entrance requirements:* For master's, engineering degree, minimum GPA of 3.0, resume, 3 confidential letters of recommendation, 1-2 page essay, base of underlying relevant knowledge/evidence from academic records or relevant wok experience. Additional exam requirements/recommendations for international students: Required—TOEFL (minimum score 80 iBT) or IELTS (6.5). *Application deadline:* Applications are processed on a rolling basis. Application fee: $30. Electronic applications accepted. *Expenses:* $661 per credit hour. *Financial support:* In 2016–17, 32 students received support, including 8 fellowships; career-related internships or fieldwork, Federal Work-Study, institutionally sponsored loans, scholarships/grants, and unspecified assistantships also available. *Faculty research:* Digital signal processing, computer aided design, computer aided manufacturing, manufacturing simulation, biomechanics, product design. *Total annual research expenditures:* $300,000. *Unit head:* Dr. Wael Mokhtar, Director, 616-331-6015, Fax: 616-331-7215, E-mail: mokhtarw@gvsu.edu. *Application contact:* Dr. Shabbir Choudhuri, Graduate Program Director, 616-331-6845, Fax: 616-331-7215, E-mail: choudhus@gvsu.edu.
Website: http://www.engineer.gvsu.edu/

Illinois Institute of Technology, Graduate College, Armour College of Engineering, Department of Mechanical, Materials and Aerospace Engineering, Chicago, IL 60616. Offers manufacturing engineering (MAS, MS); materials science and engineering (MAS, MS, PhD); mechanical and aerospace engineering (MAS, MS, PhD), including economics (MS), energy (MS), environment (MS). *Program availability:* Part-time, evening/weekend, online learning. Terminal master's awarded for partial completion of doctoral program. *Degree requirements:* For master's, comprehensive exam (for some programs), thesis (for some programs); for doctorate, comprehensive exam, thesis/dissertation. *Entrance requirements:* For master's and doctorate, GRE General Test (minimum score 1000 Quantitative and Verbal, 3.0 Analytical Writing), minimum undergraduate GPA of 3.0. Additional exam requirements/recommendations for international students: Required—TOEFL (minimum score 550 paper-based; 80 iBT). Electronic applications accepted. *Faculty research:* Fluid dynamics, metallurgical and materials engineering, solids and structures, computational mechanics, computer added design and manufacturing, thermal sciences, dynamic analysis and control of complex systems.

Instituto Tecnológico y de Estudios Superiores de Monterrey, Campus Monterrey, Graduate and Research Division, Programs in Engineering, Monterrey, Mexico. Offers applied statistics (M Eng); artificial intelligence (PhD); automation engineering (M Eng); chemical engineering (M Eng); civil engineering (M Eng); electrical engineering (M Eng); electronic engineering (M Eng); environmental engineering (M Eng); industrial engineering (M Eng, PhD); manufacturing engineering (M Eng); mechanical engineering (M Eng); systems and quality engineering (M Eng). M Eng program offered jointly with University of Waterloo; PhD in industrial engineering with Texas A&M University. *Program availability:* Part-time, evening/weekend. Terminal master's awarded for partial completion of doctoral program. *Degree requirements:* For master's, one foreign language, thesis; for doctorate, one foreign language, thesis/dissertation. *Entrance requirements:* For master's, EXADEP; for doctorate, GRE, master's degree in related field. Additional exam requirements/recommendations for international students: Required—TOEFL. *Faculty research:* Flexible manufacturing cells, materials, statistical methods, environmental prevention, control and evaluation.

Kansas State University, Graduate School, College of Engineering, Department of Industrial and Manufacturing Systems Engineering, Manhattan, KS 66506. Offers engineering management (MEM); industrial engineering (MS); operations research (MS). *Program availability:* Part-time, online learning. *Faculty:* 10 full-time (2 women), 1 part-time/adjunct (0 women). *Students:* 34 full-time (8 women), 51 part-time (6 women); includes 17 minority (5 Black or African American, non-Hispanic/Latino; 4 Asian, non-Hispanic/Latino; 4 Hispanic/Latino; 4 Two or more races, non-Hispanic/Latino), 25 international. Average age 30. 62 applicants, 56% accepted, 10 enrolled. In 2016, 27 master's, 3 doctorates awarded. *Degree requirements:* For master's, thesis or alternative; for doctorate, thesis/dissertation. *Entrance requirements:* For master's, GRE General Test (minimum score of 750 old version, 159 new format on Quantitative portion of exam), bachelor's degree in engineering, mathematics, or physical science; for doctorate, GRE General Test (minimum score of 770 old version, 164 new format on Quantitative portion of exam), master's degree in engineering or industrial manufacturing. Additional exam requirements/recommendations for international students: Required—PTE (minimum score 58), TOEFL (minimum score 550 paper-based; 79 iBT) or IELTS (minimum score 6.5). *Application deadline:* For fall admission, 6/1 priority date for domestic students, 12/1 priority date for international students; for spring admission, 11/1 priority date for domestic students, 8/1 priority date for international students. Applications are processed on a rolling basis. Application fee: $50 ($75 for international students). Electronic applications accepted. *Expenses:* Tuition, state resident: full-time $9670. Tuition, nonresident: full-time $21,828. *Required fees:* $862. *Financial support:* In 2016–17, 12 research assistantships (averaging $12,442 per year), 9 teaching assistantships with full tuition reimbursements (averaging $14,111 per year) were awarded; Federal Work-Study, institutionally sponsored loans, and scholarships/grants also available. Support available to part-time students. Financial award application deadline: 3/1; financial award applicants required to submit FAFSA. *Faculty research:* Industrial engineering, ergonomics, healthcare systems engineering, manufacturing processes, operations research, engineering management. *Total annual research expenditures:* $2.6 million. *Unit head:* Dr. Bradley Kramer, Head, 785-532-5606, Fax: 785-532-3738, E-mail: bradleyk@k-state.edu. *Application contact:* Dr. David Ben-Arieh, Chair of Graduate Committee, 785-532-5606, Fax: 785-532-3738, E-mail: imse@k-state.edu.
Website: http://www.imse.k-state.edu/

Kettering University, Graduate School, Department of Industrial and Manufacturing Engineering, Flint, MI 48504. Offers engineering (MS). *Program availability:* Part-time, evening/weekend, online learning. *Degree requirements:* For master's, thesis optional. *Entrance requirements:* Additional exam requirements/recommendations for international students: Required—TOEFL (minimum score 550 paper-based; 79 iBT). Electronic applications accepted. *Faculty research:* Failure analysis, gestural controls.

Lawrence Technological University, College of Engineering, Southfield, MI 48075-1058. Offers architectural engineering (MS); automotive engineering (MS); biomedical engineering (MS); civil engineering (MA, MS, PhD), including environmental engineering (MS), geotechnical engineering (MS), structural engineering (MS), transportation engineering (MS), water resource engineering (MS); construction engineering management (MA); electrical and computer engineering (MS); engineering management (MA); engineering technology (MS); fire engineering (MS); industrial engineering (MS), including healthcare; manufacturing systems (ME); mechanical engineering (MS, DE, PhD), including manufacturing (DE), solid mechanics (MS), thermal-fluids (MS); mechatronic systems engineering (MS). *Program availability:* Part-time, evening/weekend. *Faculty:* 24 full-time (5 women), 26 part-time/adjunct (2 women). *Students:* 22 full-time (7 women), 588 part-time (81 women); includes 23 minority (11 Black or African American, non-Hispanic/Latino; 4 Asian, non-Hispanic/Latino; 7 Hispanic/Latino; 1 Two or more races, non-Hispanic/Latino), 469 international. Average age 27. 1,186 applicants, 39% accepted, 99 enrolled. In 2016, 293 master's, 3 doctorates awarded. Terminal master's awarded for partial completion of doctoral program. *Degree requirements:* For master's, thesis optional; for doctorate, comprehensive exam, thesis/dissertation optional. *Entrance requirements:* Additional exam requirements/recommendations for international students: Required—TOEFL (minimum score 550 paper-based; 79 iBT), IELTS (minimum score 6.5). *Application deadline:* For fall admission, 5/22 for international students; for spring admission, 10/11 for international students; for summer admission, 2/16 for international students. Applications are processed on a rolling basis. Application fee: $50. Electronic applications accepted. *Expenses: Tuition:* Full-time $14,868; part-time $1062 per credit. *Required fees:* $75 per semester. Tuition and fees vary according to campus/location. *Financial support:* In 2016–17, 25 students received support, including 5 research assistantships with full tuition reimbursements available; unspecified assistantships also available. Financial award application deadline: 4/1; financial award applicants required to submit FAFSA. *Faculty research:* Carbon fiber reinforced polymer reinforced concrete structures; low impact storm water management solutions; vehicle battery energy management; wireless communication; entrepreneurial mindset and engineering. *Total annual research expenditures:* $1.7 million. *Unit head:* Dr. Nabil Grace, Dean, 248-204-2500, Fax: 248-204-2509, E-mail: engrdean@ltu.edu. *Application contact:* Jane Rohrback, Director of Admissions, 248-204-3160, Fax: 248-204-2228, E-mail: admissions@ltu.edu.
Website: http://www.ltu.edu/engineering/index.asp

Lehigh University, P.C. Rossin College of Engineering and Applied Science, Program in Manufacturing Systems Engineering, Bethlehem, PA 18015. Offers MS, MBA/E. *Program availability:* Part-time, blended/hybrid learning. *Faculty:* 2 full-time (0 women), 2 part-time/adjunct (0 women). *Students:* 5 full-time (0 women), 15 part-time (5 women); includes 3 minority (1 Asian, non-Hispanic/Latino; 2 Hispanic/Latino), 5 international. Average age 30. 10 applicants, 90% accepted, 6 enrolled. In 2016, 8 master's awarded. *Degree requirements:* For master's, comprehensive exam, project or thesis. *Entrance requirements:* For master's, GRE General Test, minimum GPA of 2.75. Additional exam requirements/recommendations for international students: Required—TOEFL (minimum score 620 paper-based; 85 iBT). *Application deadline:* For fall admission, 7/15 priority date for domestic students, 7/15 for international students; for spring admission, 12/1 priority date for domestic students, 12/1 for international students. Applications are processed on a rolling basis. Application fee: $75. Electronic applications accepted. *Expenses:* $1,420 per credit. *Faculty research:* Manufacturing systems design, development, and implementation; accounting and management; agile/lean systems; supply chain issues; sustainable systems design; product design; development of applications for novel materials. *Unit head:* Dr. Keith M. Gardiner, Director, 610-758-5070, Fax: 610-758-6527, E-mail: kg03@lehigh.edu. *Application contact:* Carolyn C. Jones, Graduate Coordinator, 610-758-5157, Fax: 610-758-6527, E-mail: ccj1@lehigh.edu.
Website: https://mse.lehigh.edu/

Massachusetts Institute of Technology, School of Engineering, Department of Mechanical Engineering, Cambridge, MA 02139. Offers manufacturing (M Eng);

mechanical engineering (SM, PhD, Sc D, Mech E); naval architecture and marine engineering (SM, PhD, Sc D); naval engineering (Naval E); ocean engineering (SM, PhD, Sc D); oceanographic engineering (SM, PhD, Sc D); SM/MBA. *Faculty:* 70 full-time (9 women), 1 part-time/adjunct (0 women). *Students:* 567 full-time (159 women), 1 part-time (0 women); includes 94 minority (6 Black or African American, non-Hispanic/Latino; 1 American Indian or Alaska Native, non-Hispanic/Latino; 41 Asian, non-Hispanic/Latino; 32 Hispanic/Latino; 14 Two or more races, non-Hispanic/Latino), 275 international. Average age 27. 1,345 applicants, 14% accepted, 127 enrolled. In 2016, 123 master's, 65 doctorates, 10 other advanced degrees awarded. Terminal master's awarded for partial completion of doctoral program. *Degree requirements:* For master's, thesis; for doctorate, comprehensive exam, thesis/dissertation; for other advanced degree, comprehensive exam, thesis. *Entrance requirements:* For master's, doctorate, and other advanced degree, GRE General Test. Additional exam requirements/recommendations for international students: Required—TOEFL, IELTS. *Application deadline:* For fall and spring admission, 12/15 for domestic and international students. Application fee: $75. Electronic applications accepted. *Expenses: Tuition:* Full-time $46,400; part-time $725 per credit. One-time fee: $312 full-time. Full-time tuition and fees vary according to course load and program. *Financial support:* In 2016–17, 466 students received support, including fellowships (averaging $36,000 per year), 338 research assistantships (averaging $36,300 per year), 62 teaching assistantships (averaging $39,300 per year); Federal Work-Study, institutionally sponsored loans, scholarships/grants, traineeships, health care benefits, unspecified assistantships, and resident tutors also available. Support available to part-time students. Financial award application deadline: 5/1; financial award applicants required to submit FAFSA. *Faculty research:* Mechanics: modeling, experimentation and computation; design, manufacturing, and product development; controls, instrumentation, and robotics; energy science and engineering; ocean science and engineering; bioengineering; micro- and Nano-engineering. *Total annual research expenditures:* $55.6 million. *Unit head:* Prof. Gang Chen, Department Head, 617-253-2201, Fax: 617-258-6156, E-mail: mehq@mit.edu. *Application contact:* 617-253-2291, E-mail: megradoffice@mit.edu.
Website: http://meche.mit.edu/

Michigan State University, The Graduate School, College of Agriculture and Natural Resources, School of Packaging, East Lansing, MI 48824. Offers MS, PhD. *Entrance requirements:* Additional exam requirements/recommendations for international students: Required—TOEFL. Electronic applications accepted.

Minnesota State University Mankato, College of Graduate Studies and Research, College of Science, Engineering and Technology, Department of Automotive and Manufacturing Engineering Technology, Mankato, MN 56001. Offers manufacturing engineering technology (MS). *Students:* 8 full-time (all women), 22 part-time (3 women). *Degree requirements:* For master's, comprehensive exam, thesis. *Entrance requirements:* For master's, minimum GPA of 2.75 during previous 2 years. Additional exam requirements/recommendations for international students: Required—TOEFL (minimum score 525 paper-based). *Application deadline:* For fall admission, 7/1 priority date for domestic students; for spring admission, 11/1 for domestic students. Applications are processed on a rolling basis. Application fee: $40. Electronic applications accepted. *Financial support:* Research assistantships with full tuition reimbursements, teaching assistantships with full tuition reimbursements, and unspecified assistantships available. Financial award application deadline: 3/15; financial award applicants required to submit FAFSA. *Unit head:* Dr. Bruce Jones, Chair, 507-389-6700, Fax: 507-389-5002, E-mail: bruce.jones@mnsu.edu.
Website: http://cset.mnsu.edu/amet/

Missouri University of Science and Technology, Graduate School, Department of Engineering Management and Systems Engineering, Rolla, MO 65409. Offers engineering management (MS, DE, PhD); manufacturing engineering (M Eng, MS); systems engineering (MS, PhD). *Degree requirements:* For master's, thesis optional; for doctorate, comprehensive exam. *Entrance requirements:* For master's, GRE (minimum score 1150 verbal and quantitative, 4.5 writing); for doctorate, GRE (minimum score: 1100 verbal and quantitative, 3.5 writing). Additional exam requirements/recommendations for international students: Required—TOEFL (minimum score 580 paper-based). Electronic applications accepted. *Faculty research:* Management of technology, industrial engineering, manufacturing engineering, packaging engineering, quality engineering.

New Jersey Institute of Technology, Newark College of Engineering, Newark, NJ 07102. Offers biomedical engineering (MS, PhD); chemical engineering (MS, PhD); computer engineering (MS, PhD); electrical engineering (MS, PhD); engineering management (MS); environmental engineering (PhD); healthcare systems management (MS); industrial engineering (MS, PhD); Internet engineering (MS); manufacturing engineering (MS); mechanical engineering (MS, PhD); occupational safety and health engineering (MS); pharmaceutical bioprocessing (MS); pharmaceutical engineering (MS); pharmaceutical systems management (MS); power and energy systems (MS); telecommunications (MS); transportation (MS, PhD). *Program availability:* Part-time, evening/weekend. *Faculty:* 146 full-time (21 women), 119 part-time/adjunct (10 women). *Students:* 804 full-time (191 women), 550 part-time (129 women); includes 357 minority (82 Black or African American, non-Hispanic/Latino; 1 American Indian or Alaska Native, non-Hispanic/Latino; 138 Asian, non-Hispanic/Latino; 114 Hispanic/Latino; 22 Two or more races, non-Hispanic/Latino), 675 international. Average age 27. 2,959 applicants, 51% accepted, 442 enrolled. In 2016, 595 master's, 29 doctorates awarded. Terminal master's awarded for partial completion of doctoral program. *Degree requirements:* For master's, thesis optional; for doctorate, thesis/dissertation. *Entrance requirements:* For master's, GRE General Test; for doctorate, GRE General Test, minimum graduate GPA of 3.5. Additional exam requirements/recommendations for international students: Required—TOEFL (minimum score 550 paper-based; 79 iBT). *Application deadline:* For fall admission, 6/1 priority date for domestic students, 5/1 priority date for international students; for spring admission, 11/15 priority date for domestic and international students. Applications are processed on a rolling basis. Application fee: $75. Electronic applications accepted. *Expenses:* Contact institution. *Financial support:* In 2016–17, 172 students received support, including 1 fellowship (averaging $1,528 per year), 79 research assistantships (averaging $13,336 per year), 92 teaching assistantships (averaging $20,619 per year); scholarships/grants also available. Financial award application deadline: 1/15. *Faculty research:* Nonlinear signal processing, intelligent medical image analysis, calibration issues in coherent localization, computer-aided design, neural network for tool wear measurement. *Total annual research expenditures:* $11.1 million. *Unit head:* Dr. Moshe Kam, Dean, 973-596-5534, E-mail: moshe.kam@njit.edu. *Application contact:* Stephen Eck, Director of Admissions, 973-596-3300, Fax: 973-596-3461, E-mail: admissions@njit.edu.
Website: http://engineering.njit.edu/

New York University, Polytechnic School of Engineering, Department of Technology Management, Major in Manufacturing Engineering, New York, NY 10012-1019. Offers MS. *Program availability:* Part-time, evening/weekend, online learning. *Degree requirements:* For master's, comprehensive exam (for some programs), thesis (for some programs). *Entrance requirements:* For master's, BE or BS in engineering, physics, chemistry, mathematical sciences, or biological sciences, or MBA. Additional exam requirements/recommendations for international students: Required—TOEFL (minimum score 550 paper-based; 80 iBT); Recommended—IELTS (minimum score 6.5). Electronic applications accepted.

North Carolina State University, Graduate School, College of Engineering, Integrated Manufacturing Systems Engineering Institute, Raleigh, NC 27695. Offers MIMS. *Program availability:* Part-time. *Degree requirements:* For master's, thesis optional. *Entrance requirements:* For master's, GRE. Additional exam requirements/recommendations for international students: Required—TOEFL. Electronic applications accepted. *Faculty research:* Mechatronics, manufacturing systems modeling, systems integration product and process engineering, logistics.

North Dakota State University, College of Graduate and Interdisciplinary Studies, College of Engineering, Department of Industrial and Manufacturing Engineering, Fargo, ND 58102. Offers industrial and manufacturing engineering (PhD); industrial engineering and management (MS); manufacturing engineering (MS). *Program availability:* Part-time. *Degree requirements:* For doctorate, comprehensive exam, thesis/dissertation. *Entrance requirements:* For master's, GRE General Test, bachelor's degree in engineering; for doctorate, GRE General Test, master's degree in engineering. Additional exam requirements/recommendations for international students: Required—TOEFL (minimum score 550 paper-based; 79 iBT), TWE (minimum score 4). Electronic applications accepted. *Faculty research:* Electronics manufacturing, quality engineering, manufacturing process science, healthcare, lean manufacturing.

Oregon Institute of Technology, Program in Manufacturing Engineering Technology, Klamath Falls, OR 97601-8801. Offers MS. *Program availability:* Part-time, online learning. *Degree requirements:* For master's, one foreign language, project. *Entrance requirements:* For master's, GRE General Test. Electronic applications accepted.

Oregon State University, College of Engineering, Program in Industrial Engineering, Corvallis, OR 97331. Offers advanced manufacturing (M Eng, MS, PhD); engineering management (M Eng); human systems engineering (M Eng, MS, PhD); information systems engineering (M Eng, MS, PhD). *Program availability:* 100% online. *Faculty:* 52 full-time (12 women), 3 part-time/adjunct (0 women). *Students:* 75 full-time (18 women), 28 part-time (11 women); includes 14 minority (1 American Indian or Alaska Native, non-Hispanic/Latino; 7 Asian, non-Hispanic/Latino; 4 Hispanic/Latino; 2 Two or more races, non-Hispanic/Latino), 56 international. Average age 29. 158 applicants, 33% accepted, 35 enrolled. In 2016, 19 master's, 3 doctorates awarded. *Entrance requirements:* For master's and doctorate, GRE. Additional exam requirements/recommendations for international students: Required—TOEFL (minimum score 80 iBT), IELTS (minimum score 6.5). *Application deadline:* For fall admission, 8/1 for domestic students, 4/1 for international students; for winter admission, 12/1 for domestic students, 7/1 for international students; for spring admission, 2/1 for domestic students, 10/1 for international students; for summer admission, 5/1 for domestic students, 1/1 for international students. Application fee: $75 ($85 for international students). *Expenses:* $14,130 resident full-time tuition, $23,769 non-resident. *Financial support:* Application deadline: 1/15. *Unit head:* Dr. Harriet Nembhard, School Head. *Application contact:* Jean Robinson, Advisor, E-mail: jean.robinson@oregonstate.edu.
Website: http://mime.oregonstate.edu/academics/grad/ie

Pittsburg State University, Graduate School, College of Technology, Department of Engineering Technology, Pittsburg, KS 66762. Offers electrical engineering technology (MET); general engineering technology (MET); manufacturing engineering technology (MET); mechanical engineering technology (MET); plastics engineering technology (MET). *Program availability:* Part-time, 100% online, blended/hybrid learning. *Students:* 59 (9 women); includes 3 minority (2 Black or African American, non-Hispanic/Latino; 1 Asian, non-Hispanic/Latino), 35 international. In 2016, 42 master's awarded. *Degree requirements:* For master's, thesis optional. *Entrance requirements:* Additional exam requirements/recommendations for international students: Required—TOEFL (minimum score 550 paper-based; 79 iBT), IELTS (minimum score 6.5), PTE (minimum score 51). *Application deadline:* For fall admission, 7/15 for domestic students, 6/1 for international students; for spring admission, 12/15 for domestic students, 10/15 for international students; for summer admission, 5/15 for domestic students, 4/1 for international students. Applications are processed on a rolling basis. Application fee: $35 ($60 for international students). Electronic applications accepted. *Expenses:* Contact institution. *Financial support:* In 2016–17, 4 teaching assistantships with full tuition reimbursements (averaging $5,500 per year) were awarded. Financial award application deadline: 2/1; financial award applicants required to submit FAFSA. *Unit head:* Greg Murray, Chairperson, 620-235-4384. *Application contact:* Lisa Allen, Assistant Director of Graduate and Continuing Studies, 620-235-4218, Fax: 620-235-4219, E-mail: lallen@pittstate.edu.
Website: http://www.pittstate.edu/department/engineering-tech/

Polytechnic University of Puerto Rico, Graduate School, Hato Rey, PR 00918. Offers business administration (MBA), including computer information systems, general management, management of information systems, management of international enterprises; civil engineering (ME, MS); computer engineering (ME, MS); computer science (MCS, MS); electrical engineering (ME, MS); engineering management (MEM); environmental management (MEM); landscape architecture (M Land Arch); manufacturing competitiveness (MMC, MS); manufacturing engineering (ME, MS); mechanical engineering (M Mech E). *Program availability:* Part-time, evening/weekend. *Entrance requirements:* For master's, 3 letters of recommendation.

Portland State University, Graduate Studies, Maseeh College of Engineering and Computer Science, Department of Engineering and Technology Management, Portland, OR 97207-0751. Offers engineering and technology management (M Eng); engineering management (MS); manufacturing engineering (ME); manufacturing management (M Eng); systems science/engineering management (PhD); MS/MBA; MS/MS. *Program availability:* Part-time, evening/weekend. *Faculty:* 6 full-time (1 woman), 5 part-time/adjunct (0 women). *Students:* 53 full-time (19 women), 75 part-time (34 women); includes 18 minority (3 Black or African American, non-Hispanic/Latino; 11 Asian, non-Hispanic/Latino; 3 Hispanic/Latino; 1 Two or more races, non-Hispanic/Latino), 73 international. Average age 36. 76 applicants, 50% accepted, 20 enrolled. In 2016, 34 master's, 4 doctorates awarded. *Degree requirements:* For master's, thesis optional; for doctorate, one foreign language, comprehensive exam, thesis/dissertation, oral and written exams. *Entrance requirements:* For master's, minimum GPA of 2.75 undergraduate or 3.0 graduate (at least 12 credits); minimum 4 years of experience in engineering or related discipline; 3 letters of recommendation; background in probability/statistics, differential equations, computer programming and linear algebra; for doctorate, GRE General Test (minimum combined score of 1100 for verbal and quantitative), minimum GPA of 3.0 undergraduate, 3.25 graduate. Additional exam requirements/recommendations for international students: Required—TOEFL (minimum score 550 paper-based; 80 iBT). *Application deadline:* For fall admission, 4/1 for domestic students, 3/1 for international students; for winter admission, 9/1 for domestic students, 7/1 for international students; for spring admission, 11/1 for domestic students, 9/1 for international students; for summer admission, 2/1 for domestic students, 12/1 for international students. Application fee: $65. Electronic applications accepted. *Expenses:* Contact institution. *Financial support:* In 2016–17, 7 research assistantships with tuition reimbursements (averaging $2,885 per year), 3 teaching assistantships with tuition reimbursements (averaging $1,176 per year) were awarded; career-related internships or fieldwork, Federal Work-Study, scholarships/grants, and unspecified assistantships

also available. Support available to part-time students. Financial award application deadline: 3/1; financial award applicants required to submit FAFSA. *Faculty research:* Scheduling, hierarchical decision modeling, operations research, knowledge-based information systems. *Total annual research expenditures:* $323,951. *Unit head:* Dr. Timothy Anderson, Chair, 503-725-4668, Fax: 503-725-4667, E-mail: tim.anderson@pdx.edu. *Application contact:* Shawn Wall, Department Manager, 503-725-4661, E-mail: shawnw@pdx.edu.
Website: http://www.pdx.edu/engineering-technology-management/

Rochester Institute of Technology, Graduate Enrollment Services, College of Applied Science and Technology, School of Engineering Technology, MS Program in Manufacturing and Mechanical Systems Integration, Rochester, NY 14623. Offers MS. *Program availability:* Part-time, evening/weekend. *Students:* 46 full-time (9 women), 17 part-time (1 woman); includes 2 minority (1 Asian, non-Hispanic/Latino; 1 Two or more races, non-Hispanic/Latino), 52 international. Average age 25. 78 applicants, 88% accepted, 27 enrolled. In 2016, 18 master's awarded. *Degree requirements:* For master's, thesis (for some programs). *Entrance requirements:* For master's, GRE, minimum GPA of 3.0 (recommended). Additional exam requirements/recommendations for international students: Required—TOEFL (minimum score 550 paper-based; 79 iBT), IELTS (minimum score 6.5), PTE (minimum score 58). *Application deadline:* Applications are processed on a rolling basis. Application fee: $60. Electronic applications accepted. *Expenses:* $1,742 per credit hour. *Financial support:* In 2016–17, 44 students received support. Research assistantships with partial tuition reimbursements available, teaching assistantships with partial tuition reimbursements available, career-related internships or fieldwork, scholarships/grants, and unspecified assistantships available. Support available to part-time students. Financial award applicants required to submit FAFSA. *Faculty research:* Advanced manufacturing in electronics/photonics including materials and reliability development; complex rheological fluid spray research and development; system dynamics modeling and control using computer aided engineering; automation (robotics) using cyber-physical systems; the Internet of Things, and cloud computing; applications-focused plastics and polymer composites research. *Unit head:* Dr. James Lee, Program Director, 585-475-2899, E-mail: jhleme@rit.edu. *Application contact:* Diane Ellison, Associate Vice President, Graduate Enrollment Services, 585-475-2229, Fax: 585-475-7164, E-mail: gradinfo@rit.edu.
Website: http://www.rit.edu/cast/mmet/graduate-programs/ms-in-manufacturing-and-mechanical-systems-integration

Rochester Institute of Technology, Graduate Enrollment Services, College of Applied Science and Technology, School of Engineering Technology, MS Program in Packaging Science, Rochester, NY 14623. Offers MS. *Program availability:* Part-time. *Students:* 34 full-time (12 women), 11 part-time (2 women); includes 2 minority (1 Black or African American, non-Hispanic/Latino; 1 Asian, non-Hispanic/Latino), 40 international. Average age 26. 34 applicants, 53% accepted, 9 enrolled. In 2016, 15 master's awarded. *Degree requirements:* For master's, thesis or project. *Entrance requirements:* For master's, minimum GPA of 3.0 (recommended). Additional exam requirements/recommendations for international students: Required—TOEFL (minimum score 550 paper-based; 79 iBT), IELTS (minimum score 6.5), PTE (minimum score 58). *Application deadline:* Applications are processed on a rolling basis. Application fee: $60. Electronic applications accepted. *Expenses:* $1,742 per credit hour. *Financial support:* In 2016–17, 43 students received support. Research assistantships with partial tuition reimbursements available, teaching assistantships with partial tuition reimbursements available, career-related internships or fieldwork, scholarships/grants, and unspecified assistantships available. Support available to part-time students. Financial award applicants required to submit FAFSA. *Faculty research:* Protective packaging, modeling and mapping of the packaged products in supply chain; packaging design; shelf life extension of food and pharmaceutical products, interaction between packaging materials and packaged goods; design of bioplastic packaging materials for aerobic and anaerobic end of life scenarios; development and evaluation of active and intelligent packaging components. *Unit head:* Deanna Jacobs, Chair, 585-475-6801, E-mail: dmjipk@rit.edu. *Application contact:* Diane Ellison, Associate Vice President, Graduate Enrollment Services, 585-475-2229, Fax: 585-475-7164, E-mail: gradinfo@rit.edu.
Website: http://www.rit.edu/cast/packaging/

Rochester Institute of Technology, Graduate Enrollment Services, Kate Gleason College of Engineering, Design, Development and Manufacturing Department, Rochester, NY 14623-5603. Offers manufacturing leadership (MS); product development (MS). *Program availability:* Part-time-only, evening/weekend, 100% online, blended/hybrid learning. *Students:* 1 (woman) full-time, 68 part-time (6 women); includes 8 minority (2 Black or African American, non-Hispanic/Latino; 2 Asian, non-Hispanic/Latino; 3 Hispanic/Latino; 1 Two or more races, non-Hispanic/Latino), 1 international. Average age 37. 25 applicants, 64% accepted, 12 enrolled. In 2016, 14 master's awarded. *Degree requirements:* For master's, thesis or alternative, capstone. *Entrance requirements:* For master's, minimum GPA of 2.5, 2 years of related work experience. Additional exam requirements/recommendations for international students: Required—PTE (minimum score 58), TOEFL (minimum score 550 paper-based, 79 iBT) or IELTS (minimum score 6.5). *Application deadline:* Applications are processed on a rolling basis. Application fee: $60. Electronic applications accepted. *Expenses:* $1,742 per credit hour. *Financial support:* Scholarships/grants available. Support available to part-time students. Financial award applicants required to submit FAFSA. *Faculty research:* Systems engineering; project management; lean product development and lean manufacturing; decision analysis; modeling and simulation; supply chain management. *Unit head:* Mark Smith, Director, 585-475-7102, Fax: 585-475-7955, E-mail: mark.smith@rit.edu. *Application contact:* Diane Ellison, Associate Vice President, Graduate Enrollment Services, 585-475-2229, Fax: 585-475-7164, E-mail: gradinfo@rit.edu.
Website: https://www.rit.edu/kgcoe/

Rochester Institute of Technology, Graduate Enrollment Services, Kate Gleason College of Engineering, Electrical and Microelectronic Engineering Department, ME Program in Microelectronic Manufacturing Engineering, Rochester, NY 14623. Offers ME. *Program availability:* Part-time, evening/weekend, 100% online. *Students:* 5 full-time (2 women), 5 part-time (1 woman); includes 2 minority (both Asian, non-Hispanic/Latino), 6 international. Average age 30. 13 applicants, 62% accepted, 6 enrolled. In 2016, 4 master's awarded. *Degree requirements:* For master's, thesis or alternative. *Entrance requirements:* For master's, minimum GPA of 3.0 (recommended). Additional exam requirements/recommendations for international students: Required—TOEFL (minimum score 550 paper-based; 79 iBT), IELTS (minimum score 6.5), PTE (minimum score 28). *Application deadline:* For fall admission, 2/15 priority date for domestic and international students. Applications are processed on a rolling basis. Application fee: $60. Electronic applications accepted. *Expenses:* $1,742 per credit hour (classroom), $993 per credit hour (online). *Financial support:* In 2016–17, 3 students received support. Research assistantships with partial tuition reimbursements available, teaching assistantships with partial tuition reimbursements available, career-related internships or fieldwork, scholarships/grants, and unspecified assistantships available. Support available to part-time students. Financial award applicants required to submit FAFSA. *Faculty research:* Microlithography and design of experiments; electronic materials for microelectronic photovoltaics devices; semiconductor nanolithography materials and systems; thin film deposition and etching. *Unit head:* Dr. Robert Pearson, Graduate Program Director, 585-475-2923, Fax: 585-475-5845, E-mail: robert.pearson@rit.edu. *Application contact:* Diane Ellison, Associate Vice President, Graduate Enrollment Services, 585-475-2229, Fax: 585-475-7164, E-mail: gradinfo@rit.edu.
Website: http://www.rit.edu/kgcoe/program/microelectronic-engineering-1

Rochester Institute of Technology, Graduate Enrollment Services, Kate Gleason College of Engineering, Industrial and Systems Engineering Department, Rochester, NY 14623. Offers engineering management (ME); industrial and systems engineering (ME, MS); sustainable engineering (ME, MS). *Program availability:* Part-time. *Students:* 76 full-time (20 women), 26 part-time (7 women); includes 10 minority (3 Black or African American, non-Hispanic/Latino; 2 Asian, non-Hispanic/Latino; 4 Hispanic/Latino; 1 Two or more races, non-Hispanic/Latino), 56 international. Average age 25. 563 applicants, 28% accepted, 28 enrolled. In 2016, 46 master's awarded. *Degree requirements:* For master's, thesis (for some programs). *Entrance requirements:* For master's, GRE, minimum GPA of 3.0 (recommended). Additional exam requirements/recommendations for international students: Required—PTE (minimum score 58), TOEFL (minimum score 550 paper-based, 79 iBT) or IELTS (minimum score 6.5). *Application deadline:* For fall admission, 2/15 priority date for domestic and international students; for spring admission, 12/15 priority date for domestic and international students. Applications are processed on a rolling basis. Application fee: $60. Electronic applications accepted. *Expenses:* $1,742 per credit hour. *Financial support:* In 2016–17, 36 students received support. Research assistantships with partial tuition reimbursements available, teaching assistantships with partial tuition reimbursements available, career-related internships or fieldwork, scholarships/grants, and unspecified assistantships available. Support available to part-time students. Financial award applicants required to submit FAFSA. *Faculty research:* Advanced manufacturing; health systems; statistics/analytics; supply chain, production and logistics systems; systems engineering/product life-cycle management; lean manufacturing; renewable and alternative energies; grid optimization and Smart Grid applications; sanitation, water supply, soil fertility; off grid energy applications; human centered design. *Unit head:* Dr. Scott Grasman, Department Head, 585-475-2598, Fax: 585-475-2520, E-mail: ise@rit.edu. *Application contact:* Diane Ellison, Associate Vice President, Graduate Enrollment Services, 585-475-2229, Fax: 585-475-7164, E-mail: gradinfo@rit.edu.
Website: http://www.rit.edu/kgcoe/ise/

Southern Methodist University, Bobby B. Lyle School of Engineering, Department of Mechanical Engineering, Dallas, TX 75205. Offers manufacturing systems management (MS); mechanical engineering (MSME, PhD); packaging of electronic and optical devices (MS). *Program availability:* Part-time, evening/weekend, online learning. Terminal master's awarded for partial completion of doctoral program. *Degree requirements:* For master's, thesis optional; for doctorate, thesis/dissertation, oral and written qualifying exams, oral final exam. *Entrance requirements:* For master's, GRE General Test, minimum GPA of 3.0 in last 2 years; bachelor's degree in engineering, mathematics, or sciences; for doctorate, preliminary counseling exam, minimum graduate GPA of 3.0, bachelor's degree in related field. Additional exam requirements/recommendations for international students: Required—TOEFL. *Faculty research:* Design, systems, and controls; thermal and fluid sciences.

Stevens Institute of Technology, Graduate School, Charles V. Schaefer Jr. School of Engineering and Science, Department of Mechanical Engineering, Program in Integrated Product Development, Hoboken, NJ 07030. Offers armament engineering (M Eng); computer and electrical engineering (M Eng); manufacturing technologies (M Eng); systems reliability and design (M Eng). *Program availability:* Part-time, evening/weekend. *Students:* 15 applicants. In 2016, 2 master's awarded. *Degree requirements:* For master's, thesis optional, minimum B average in major field and overall. *Entrance requirements:* Additional exam requirements/recommendations for international students: Required—TOEFL (minimum score 74 iBT), IELTS (minimum score 6). *Application deadline:* For fall admission, 6/1 for domestic students, 4/15 for international students; for spring admission, 11/30 for domestic students, 11/1 for international students. Applications are processed on a rolling basis. Application fee: $65. Electronic applications accepted. *Expenses:* Contact institution. *Financial support:* Fellowships, research assistantships, teaching assistantships, career-related internships or fieldwork, Federal Work-Study, scholarships/grants, and unspecified assistantships available. Financial award application deadline: 2/15; financial award applicants required to submit FAFSA. *Unit head:* Dr. Frank Fisher, Interim Department Director, 201-216-8913, Fax: 201-216-8315, E-mail: ffisher@stevens.edu. *Application contact:* Graduate Admissions, 888-783-8367, Fax: 888-511-1306, E-mail: graduate@stevens.edu.

Tennessee State University, The School of Graduate Studies and Research, College of Engineering, Nashville, TN 37209-1561. Offers biomedical engineering (ME); civil engineering (ME); computer and information systems engineering (MS, PhD); electrical engineering (ME); environmental engineering (ME); manufacturing engineering (ME); mathematical sciences (MS); mechanical engineering (ME). *Program availability:* Part-time, evening/weekend. *Degree requirements:* For master's, project; for doctorate, comprehensive exam, thesis/dissertation. *Entrance requirements:* For doctorate, minimum GPA of 3.3. *Faculty research:* Robotics, intelligent systems, human-computer interaction software systems, biomedical engineering, signal/image processing, probabilistic design, intelligent manufacturing, cooperative mobile robots, condition based maintenance, sensor fusion.

Texas A&M University, College of Engineering, Department of Engineering Technology and Industrial Distribution, College Station, TX 77843. Offers industrial distribution (MID); technical management (METM). *Faculty:* 31. *Students:* 119 full-time (16 women), 2 part-time (1 woman); includes 36 minority (11 Black or African American, non-Hispanic/Latino; 2 Asian, non-Hispanic/Latino; 18 Hispanic/Latino; 5 Two or more races, non-Hispanic/Latino), 5 international. Average age 36. 62 applicants, 98% accepted, 60 enrolled. In 2016, 67 master's awarded. *Entrance requirements:* Additional exam requirements/recommendations for international students: Required—TOEFL (minimum score 550 paper-based; 80 iBT), IELTS (minimum score 6), PTE (minimum score 53). *Application deadline:* For fall admission, 3/1 priority date for domestic and international students; for winter admission, 11/1 for domestic and international students; for spring admission, 8/1 priority date for domestic and international students. Applications are processed on a rolling basis. Application fee: $50 ($90 for international students). Electronic applications accepted. *Expenses:* Contact institution. *Financial support:* In 2016–17, 71 students received support. Application deadline: 3/15; applicants required to submit FAFSA. *Unit head:* Dr. Reza Langari, Department Head, 979-862-4945, E-mail: rlangari@tamu.edu. *Application contact:* Graduate Admissions, 979-458-0427, E-mail: graduate-admissions@tamu.edu.
Website: http://engineering.tamu.edu/etid

Texas State University, The Graduate College, College of Science and Engineering, Program in Engineering, San Marcos, TX 78666. Offers electrical engineering (MS); industrial engineering (MS); manufacturing engineering (MS). *Program availability:* Part-time. *Faculty:* 15 full-time (2 women), 2 part-time/adjunct (0 women). *Students:* 49 full-time (15 women), 10 part-time (3 women); includes 7 minority (3 Asian, non-Hispanic/Latino; 3 Hispanic/Latino; 1 Two or more races, non-Hispanic/Latino), 45 international. Average age 28. 163 applicants, 43% accepted, 30 enrolled. *Degree requirements:* For master's, comprehensive exam, thesis (for some programs), thesis or research project. *Entrance requirements:* For master's, GRE (minimum preferred scores of 285 overall, 135 verbal, 150 quantitative), baccalaureate degree from regionally-accredited university in engineering, computer science, physics, technology, or closely-related field with minimum GPA of 3.0 on last 60 undergraduate semester hours; resume or curriculum vitae; 2 letters of recommendation; statement of purpose. Additional exam requirements/recommendations for international students: Required—TOEFL (minimum score 550 paper-based; 78 iBT), IELTS (minimum score 6.5). *Application deadline:* For fall admission, 2/15 priority date for domestic students, 2/1 priority date for international students. Application fee: $40 ($90 for international students). Electronic applications accepted. *Expenses:* $4,851 per semester. *Financial support:* In 2016–17, 25 students received support, including 15 research assistantships (averaging $14,047 per year), 19 teaching assistantships (averaging $13,572 per year); Federal Work-Study, institutionally sponsored loans, scholarships/grants, and unspecified assistantships also available. Support available to part-time students. Financial award application deadline: 3/1; financial award applicants required to submit FAFSA. *Faculty research:* Building a regional energy and educational network; recruitment and retention of female undergraduates in engineering and computer science; fostering nanotechnology environment, health, safety awareness; low-cost flexible graphene-based digital beam forming phased-array antennas engaging, sustaining and empowering women and minorities in STEM. *Total annual research expenditures:* $854,198. *Unit head:* Dr. Vishu Viswanathan, Graduate Advisor, 512-245-1826, Fax: 512-245-8365, E-mail: vishu.viswanathan@txstate.edu. *Application contact:* Dr. Andrea Golato, Dean of Graduate School, 512-245-2581, Fax: 512-245-8365, E-mail: gradcollege@txstate.edu. Website: http://www.engineering.txstate.edu/Programs/Graduate.html

Texas Tech University, Graduate School, Edward E. Whitacre Jr. College of Engineering, Department of Industrial, Manufacturing, and Systems Engineering, Lubbock, TX 79409-3061. Offers industrial engineering (MSIE, PhD); systems and engineering management (MSSEM, PhD). *Program availability:* Part-time, 100% online, blended/hybrid learning. *Faculty:* 13 full-time (2 women). *Students:* 90 full-time (15 women), 97 part-time (14 women); includes 25 minority (9 Black or African American, non-Hispanic/Latino; 1 American Indian or Alaska Native, non-Hispanic/Latino; 2 Asian, non-Hispanic/Latino; 11 Hispanic/Latino; 2 Two or more races, non-Hispanic/Latino), 102 international. Average age 32. 376 applicants, 38% accepted, 48 enrolled. In 2016, 43 master's, 7 doctorates awarded. Terminal master's awarded for partial completion of doctoral program. *Degree requirements:* For master's, comprehensive exam, thesis optional; for doctorate, comprehensive exam, thesis/dissertation. *Entrance requirements:* For master's and doctorate, GRE (Verbal and Quantitative). Additional exam requirements/recommendations for international students: Required—TOEFL (minimum score 550 paper-based; 79 iBT). *Application deadline:* For fall admission, 6/1 priority date for domestic students, 1/15 priority date for international students; for spring admission, 9/1 priority date for domestic students, 6/15 priority date for international students. Applications are processed on a rolling basis. Application fee: $75. Electronic applications accepted. *Expenses:* $325 per credit hour full-time resident tuition, $733 per credit hour full-time non-resident tuition; $53.75 per credit hour fee plus $608 per term fee. *Financial support:* In 2016–17, 73 students received support, including 71 fellowships (averaging $2,464 per year), 9 research assistantships (averaging $15,691 per year), 21 teaching assistantships (averaging $21,474 per year); scholarships/grants, tuition waivers (partial), and unspecified assistantships also available. Financial award application deadline: 2/1; financial award applicants required to submit FAFSA. *Faculty research:* Ergonomics and human factors engineering, manufacturing systems, operations research, statistics and quality assurance, systems and engineering management. *Total annual research expenditures:* $282,884. *Unit head:* Dr. Hong-Chao Zhang, Interim Chair, 806-742-3543, E-mail: hong-chao.zhang@ttu.edu. *Application contact:* Dr. Jennifer Cross, Associate Professor, 806-742-3543, Fax: 806-742-3411, E-mail: jennifer.cross@ttu.edu.
Website: http://www.ie.ttu.edu/

Tufts University, Graduate School of Arts and Sciences, Graduate Certificate Programs, Manufacturing Engineering Program, Medford, MA 02155. Offers Certificate. *Program availability:* Part-time, evening/weekend. Electronic applications accepted. *Expenses:* Tuition: Full-time $49,892; part-time $1248 per credit hour. *Required fees:* $844. Full-time tuition and fees vary according to degree level, program and student level. Part-time tuition and fees vary according to course load.

Universidad Autonoma de Guadalajara, Graduate Programs, Guadalajara, Mexico. Offers administrative law and justice (LL M); advertising and corporate communications (MA); architecture (M Arch); business (MBA); computational science (MCC); education (Ed M, Ed D); English-Spanish translation (MA); entrepreneurship and management (MBA); integrated management of digital animation (MA); international business (MIB); international corporate law (LL M); internet technologies (MS); manufacturing systems (MMS); occupational health (MS); philosophy (MA, PhD); power electronics (MS); quality systems (MQS); renewable energy (MS); social evaluation of projects (MBA); strategic market research (MBA); tax law (MA); teaching mathematics (MA).

Universidad de las Américas Puebla, Division of Graduate Studies, School of Engineering, Program in Manufacturing Administration, Puebla, Mexico. Offers MS. *Faculty research:* Operations research, construction.

University of Calgary, Faculty of Graduate Studies, Schulich School of Engineering, Department of Mechanical and Manufacturing Engineering, Calgary, AB T2N 1N4, Canada. Offers M Eng, M Sc, PhD. *Program availability:* Part-time. *Degree requirements:* For master's, thesis (for some programs); for doctorate, thesis/dissertation, candidacy exam. *Entrance requirements:* For master's, minimum GPA of 3.0; for doctorate, minimum GPA of 3.3. Additional exam requirements/recommendations for international students: Required—TOEFL (minimum score 550 paper-based; 80 iBT), IELTS (minimum score 7). *Faculty research:* Thermofluids, solid mechanics, materials, biomechanics, manufacturing.

University of California, Irvine, Henry Samueli School of Engineering, Program in Materials and Manufacturing Technology, Irvine, CA 92697. Offers engineering (MS, PhD). *Program availability:* Part-time. *Students:* 20 full-time (9 women), 1 part-time (0 women); includes 3 minority (all Asian, non-Hispanic/Latino), 16 international. Average age 27. 28 applicants, 68% accepted, 5 enrolled. In 2016, 8 master's, 1 doctorate awarded. *Entrance requirements:* For master's and doctorate, GRE General Test, 3 letters of recommendation, minimum GPA of 3.0. Additional exam requirements/recommendations for international students: Required—TOEFL (minimum score 550 paper-based). *Application deadline:* For fall admission, 1/15 priority date for domestic students, 1/15 for international students. Applications are processed on a rolling basis. Application fee: $105 ($125 for international students). Electronic applications accepted. *Financial support:* Fellowships with tuition reimbursements, research assistantships with full tuition reimbursements, teaching assistantships with tuition reimbursements, institutionally sponsored loans, traineeships, health care benefits, and unspecified assistantships available. Financial award application deadline: 3/1; financial award applicants required to submit FAFSA. *Faculty research:* Advanced materials, microelectronic and photonic devices and packaging, biomedical devices, MEMS, thin film materials, nanotechnology. *Application contact:* Connie Cheng, Assistant Director of Graduate Student Affairs, 949-824-3562, Fax: 949-824-8200, E-mail: connie.cheng@

uci.edu.
Website: http://www.eng.uci.edu/

University of California, Los Angeles, Graduate Division, Henry Samueli School of Engineering and Applied Science, Department of Mechanical and Aerospace Engineering, Program in Manufacturing Engineering, Los Angeles, CA 90095-1597. Offers MS. *Students:* 8 applicants. *Degree requirements:* For master's, comprehensive exam or thesis. *Entrance requirements:* For master's, GRE General Test, minimum GPA of 3.0. Additional exam requirements/recommendations for international students: Required—TOEFL (minimum score 560 paper-based; 87 iBT), IELTS (minimum score 7). *Application deadline:* For fall admission, 12/1 for domestic and international students. Application fee: $105 ($125 for international students). Electronic applications accepted. *Financial support:* Fellowships, research assistantships, teaching assistantships, Federal Work-Study, institutionally sponsored loans, and tuition waivers (full and partial) available. Financial award application deadline: 12/1; financial award applicants required to submit FAFSA. *Unit head:* Dr. Christopher S. Lynch, Chair, 310-825-7660, E-mail: cslynch@seas.ucla.edu. *Application contact:* Angie Castillo, Student Affairs Officer, 310-825-7793, Fax: 310-206-4830, E-mail: angie@seas.ucla.edu.
Website: http://www.mae.ucla.edu/

The University of Iowa, Graduate College, College of Engineering, Department of Industrial Engineering, Iowa City, IA 52242-1316. Offers engineering design and manufacturing (MS, PhD); healthcare systems (MS, PhD); human factors (MS, PhD); information and engineering management (MS, PhD); operations research (MS, PhD); wind energy (MS, PhD). *Faculty:* 11 full-time (1 woman), 1 part-time/adjunct (0 women). *Students:* 15 full-time (2 women), 6 part-time (0 women); includes 2 minority (1 Asian, non-Hispanic/Latino; 1 Two or more races, non-Hispanic/Latino), 11 international. Average age 29. 68 applicants, 9% accepted, 5 enrolled. In 2016, 4 master's, 3 doctorates awarded. Terminal master's awarded for partial completion of doctoral program. *Degree requirements:* For master's, thesis optional, exam; for doctorate, comprehensive exam, thesis/dissertation, final defense exam. *Entrance requirements:* For master's and doctorate, GRE (minimum Verbal score of 153, Quantitative 151), minimum undergraduate GPA of 3.0. Additional exam requirements/recommendations for international students: Required—TOEFL (minimum score 600 paper-based; 100 iBT), IELTS (minimum score 7). *Application deadline:* For fall admission, 7/15 for domestic students, 4/15 for international students; for spring admission, 12/1 for domestic students, 10/1 for international students; for summer admission, 4/15 for domestic students, 3/1 for international students. Applications are processed on a rolling basis. Application fee: $60 ($100 for international students). Electronic applications accepted. *Financial support:* In 2016–17, 21 students received support, including 1 fellowship with partial tuition reimbursement available (averaging $25,500 per year), 15 research assistantships with full tuition reimbursements available (averaging $22,981 per year), 5 teaching assistantships with full tuition reimbursements available (averaging $18,809 per year); career-related internships or fieldwork, scholarships/grants, and unspecified assistantships also available. Support available to part-time students. Financial award applicants required to submit FAFSA. *Faculty research:* Operations research, informatics, human factors engineering, healthcare systems, bio-manufacturing, manufacturing systems, renewable energy, human-machine interactions. *Total annual research expenditures:* $6.3 million. *Unit head:* Dr. Ching-Long Lin, Department Executive Officer, 319-335-5673, Fax: 319-335-5669, E-mail: ching-long-lin@uiowa.edu. *Application contact:* Tara Hoadley, Academic Program Specialist, 319-335-5939, Fax: 319-335-5669, E-mail: indeng@engineering.uiowa.edu.
Website: https://mie.engineering.uiowa.edu

The University of Iowa, Graduate College, College of Engineering, Department of Mechanical Engineering, Iowa City, IA 52242-1316. Offers energy systems (MS, PhD); engineering design (MS, PhD); fluid dynamics (MS, PhD); materials and manufacturing (MS, PhD); wind energy (MS, PhD). *Faculty:* 16 full-time (0 women). *Students:* 37 full-time (4 women), 12 part-time (0 women); includes 1 minority (Black or African American, non-Hispanic/Latino), 30 international. Average age 29. 75 applicants, 13% accepted, 2 enrolled. In 2016, 6 master's, 5 doctorates awarded. Terminal master's awarded for partial completion of doctoral program. *Degree requirements:* For master's, oral exam or thesis; for doctorate, comprehensive exam, thesis/dissertation. *Entrance requirements:* For master's and doctorate, GRE (minimum Verbal score of 153, Quantitative 151), minimum undergraduate GPA of 3.0. Additional exam requirements/recommendations for international students: Required—TOEFL (minimum score 600 paper-based; 100 iBT), IELTS (minimum score 7). *Application deadline:* For fall admission, 1/15 for domestic and international students; for spring admission, 9/1 for domestic and international students; for summer admission, 1/15 for domestic and international students. Application fee: $60 ($100 for international students). Electronic applications accepted. *Financial support:* In 2016–17, 56 students received support, including 37 research assistantships with full tuition reimbursements available (averaging $22,981 per year), 19 teaching assistantships with full tuition reimbursements available (averaging $18,809 per year); traineeships and unspecified assistantships also available. Financial award applicants required to submit FAFSA. *Faculty research:* Computer simulation methodology, biomechanics, metal casting, dynamics, laser processing, system reliability, ship hydrodynamics, solid mechanics, fluid dynamics, energy, human modeling and Nano technology. *Total annual research expenditures:* $9.1 million. *Unit head:* Dr. Ching-Long Lin, Departmental Executive Officer, 319-335-5673, Fax: 319-335-5669, E-mail: ching-long-lin@uiowa.edu. *Application contact:* Tara Hoadley, Academic Program Specialist, 319-335-5939, Fax: 319-335-5669, E-mail: mech_eng@engineering.uiowa.edu.
Website: https://mie.engineering.uiowa.edu

University of Kentucky, Graduate School, College of Engineering, Program in Manufacturing Systems Engineering, Lexington, KY 40506-0032. Offers MSMSE. *Degree requirements:* For master's, comprehensive exam. *Entrance requirements:* For master's, GRE General Test, minimum undergraduate GPA of 2.75. Additional exam requirements/recommendations for international students: Required—TOEFL (minimum score 550 paper-based). Electronic applications accepted. *Faculty research:* Manufacturing processes and equipment, manufacturing systems and control, computer-aided design and manufacturing, automation in manufacturing, electric manufacturing and packaging.

University of Manitoba, Faculty of Graduate Studies, Faculty of Engineering, Department of Mechanical and Manufacturing Engineering, Winnipeg, MB R3T 2N2, Canada. Offers M Eng, M Sc, PhD. *Degree requirements:* For master's, thesis; for doctorate, thesis/dissertation.

University of Maryland, College Park, Academic Affairs, A. James Clark School of Engineering, Department of Mechanical Engineering, College Park, MD 20742. Offers electronic packaging and reliability (MS, PhD); manufacturing and design (MS, PhD); mechanics and materials (MS, PhD); reliability engineering (M Eng, MS, PhD); thermal and fluid sciences (MS, PhD). *Program availability:* Part-time, evening/weekend, online learning. *Degree requirements:* For master's, thesis optional; for doctorate, thesis/dissertation, qualifying exam. *Entrance requirements:* For master's, GRE General Test, 3 letters of recommendation; for doctorate, GRE General Test, minimum GPA of 3.0. Additional exam requirements/recommendations for international students: Required—

TOEFL. Electronic applications accepted. *Faculty research:* Injection molding, electronic packaging, fluid mechanics, product engineering.

University of Michigan, College of Engineering, Department of Integrative Systems and Design, Ann Arbor, MI 48109. Offers automotive engineering (M Eng); design science (MS, PhD); energy systems engineering (M Eng, MS); global automotive and manufacturing engineering (M Eng); manufacturing engineering (M Eng, D Eng); pharmaceutical engineering (M Eng); robotics and autonomous vehicles (M Eng); systems engineering and design (M Eng); MBA/M Eng; MSE/MS. *Program availability:* Part-time, online learning. *Students:* 147 full-time (33 women), 234 part-time (39 women). 315 applicants, 8% accepted, 13 enrolled. In 2016, 158 master's, 2 doctorates awarded. Terminal master's awarded for partial completion of doctoral program. *Degree requirements:* For master's, capstone project; for doctorate, thesis/dissertation. *Entrance requirements:* For master's, GRE; for doctorate, GRE, 2 years of work experience. Additional exam requirements/recommendations for international students: Required—TOEFL (minimum score 560 paper-based). *Application deadline:* Applications are processed on a rolling basis. Electronic applications accepted. *Expenses:* Tuition, state resident: full-time $21,466; part-time $1152 per credit hour. Tuition, nonresident: full-time $43,346; part-time $2367 per credit hour. Part-time tuition and fees vary according to course load, degree level and program. *Financial support:* Fellowships, research assistantships with full tuition reimbursements, teaching assistantships with full tuition reimbursements, career-related internships or fieldwork, scholarships/grants, and unspecified assistantships available. Financial award applicants required to submit FAFSA. *Faculty research:* Automotive engineering, design science, energy systems engineering, engineering sustainable systems, financial engineering, global automotive and manufacturing engineering, integrated microsystems, manufacturing engineering, pharmaceutical engineering, robotics and autonomous vehicles. *Total annual research expenditures:* $292,225. *Unit head:* Prof. Panos Papalambros, Department Chair, 734-647-8401, E-mail: pyp@umich.edu. *Application contact:* Kathy Bishar, Senior Graduate Coordinator, 734-764-3312, E-mail: kbishar@umich.edu.
Website: http://www.isd.engin.umich.edu

University of Michigan–Dearborn, College of Engineering and Computer Science, MSE Program in Manufacturing Systems Engineering, Dearborn, MI 48128. Offers MSE. *Program availability:* Part-time, evening/weekend, 100% online. *Faculty:* 4 full-time (0 women). *Students:* 4 full-time (0 women), 10 part-time (3 women); includes 4 minority (1 Black or African American, non-Hispanic/Latino; 1 Asian, non-Hispanic/Latino; 2 Hispanic/Latino), 7 international. Average age 26. 27 applicants, 41% accepted, 5 enrolled. In 2016, 2 master's awarded. *Degree requirements:* For master's, thesis optional. *Entrance requirements:* For master's, BS in engineering or a physical science from accredited program with minimum B average. Additional exam requirements/recommendations for international students: Required—TOEFL (minimum score 560 paper-based; 84 iBT), IELTS (minimum score 6.5). *Application deadline:* For fall admission, 8/1 priority date for domestic students, 5/1 priority date for international students; for winter admission, 12/1 priority date for domestic students, 9/1 priority date for international students; for spring admission, 4/1 priority date for domestic students, 1/1 priority date for international students. Applications are processed on a rolling basis. Application fee: $60. Electronic applications accepted. *Expenses:* Tuition, state resident: full-time $13,118; part-time $2280 per term. Tuition, nonresident: full-time $21,816; part-time $3771 per term. *Required fees:* $866; $658 per unit. $329 per term. Tuition and fees vary according to program. *Financial support:* Scholarships/grants and unspecified assistantships available. Support available to part-time students. Financial award application deadline: 3/1; financial award applicants required to submit FAFSA. *Faculty research:* Advanced manufacturing processes, supply chain management, quality systems, manufacturing and assembly systems. *Unit head:* Dr. Armen Zakarian, Director/Professor, 313-593-5361, E-mail: zakarian@umich.edu. *Application contact:* Office of Graduate Studies, 313-583-6321, E-mail: umd-graduatestudies@umich.edu.
Website: http://umdearborn.edu/cecs/IDP/mse_mse/index.php

University of Missouri, Office of Research and Graduate Studies, College of Engineering, Department of Industrial and Manufacturing Systems Engineering, Columbia, MO 65211. Offers ME, MS, PhD. *Faculty:* 9 full-time (1 woman). *Students:* 14 full-time (5 women), 19 part-time (7 women). *Degree requirements:* For master's, thesis or alternative; for doctorate, thesis/dissertation. *Entrance requirements:* For master's and doctorate, GRE General Test, minimum GPA of 3.0. Additional exam requirements/recommendations for international students: Required—TOEFL (minimum score 550 paper-based; 80 iBT). *Application deadline:* For fall admission, 3/1 priority date for domestic and international students; for winter admission, 9/15 priority date for domestic and international students. Applications are processed on a rolling basis. Application fee: $75 ($90 for international students). Electronic applications accepted. *Expenses:* Tuition, state resident: full-time $6347; part-time $352.60 per credit hour. Tuition, nonresident: full-time $17,379; part-time $965.50 per credit hour. *Required fees:* $1035. Tuition and fees vary according to course load, campus/location and program. *Financial support:* Fellowships, research assistantships, teaching assistantships, institutionally sponsored loans, traineeships, health care benefits, and unspecified assistantships available. Support available to part-time students.
Website: http://engineering.missouri.edu/imse/degree-programs/

University of Nebraska–Lincoln, Graduate College, College of Engineering, Department of Industrial and Management Systems Engineering, Lincoln, NE 68588. Offers engineering management (M Eng); industrial and management systems engineering (MS, PhD); manufacturing systems engineering (MS). *Program availability:* Online learning. *Degree requirements:* For master's, thesis optional; for doctorate, comprehensive exam, thesis/dissertation. *Entrance requirements:* For master's and doctorate, GRE. Additional exam requirements/recommendations for international students: Required—TOEFL (minimum score 525 paper-based). Electronic applications accepted. *Faculty research:* Ergonomics, occupational safety, quality control, industrial packaging, facility design.

University of New Mexico, Graduate Studies, School of Engineering, Manufacturing Engineering Program, Albuquerque, NM 87131. Offers MEME, MBA/MEME. *Program availability:* Part-time. *Faculty:* 1 full-time (0 women). *Students:* 3 full-time (1 woman), 1 part-time (0 women); includes 1 minority (Hispanic/Latino), 2 international. Average age 26. 7 applicants, 57% accepted, 3 enrolled. In 2016, 5 master's awarded. *Degree requirements:* For master's, 500 hours of relevant industry experience (paid or unpaid). *Entrance requirements:* For master's, GRE General Test (minimum combined score: 300), minimum GPA of 3.0. Additional exam requirements/recommendations for international students: Required—TOEFL (minimum score 550 paper-based; 79 iBT). *Application deadline:* For fall admission, 7/30 priority date for domestic students, 3/1 for international students; for spring admission, 11/30 priority date for domestic students, 8/1 for international students. Application fee: $50. Electronic applications accepted. *Financial support:* Teaching assistantships, career-related internships or fieldwork, and health care benefits available. Support available to part-time students. Financial award application deadline: 3/1; financial award applicants required to submit FAFSA. *Faculty research:* Robotics, automation control and machine vision, microsystems and microgrippers, semiconductor manufacturing and metrology, cross-training and operations of technicians and engineers. *Unit head:* Dr. John E. Wood, Director, 505-272-7000, Fax: 505-272-7152, E-mail: jw@unm.edu. *Application contact:* Arden L. Ballantine, Information Contact, 505-272-7000, Fax: 505-272-7152, E-mail: aballant@unm.edu.
Website: http://www.mfg.unm.edu/

University of Puerto Rico, Mayagüez Campus, Graduate Studies, College of Engineering, Department of Mechanical Engineering, Mayagüez, PR 00681-9000. Offers mechanical engineering (ME, MS, PhD), including aerospace and unmanned vehivles (ME), automation/mechatronics, bioengineering, cae and design, fluid mechanics, heat transfer/energy systems, manufacturing, mechanics of materials, micro and nano engineering. *Program availability:* Part-time. *Faculty:* 22 full-time (4 women), 1 part-time/adjunct (0 women). *Students:* 34 full-time (4 women), 8 part-time (2 women); includes 38 minority (all Hispanic/Latino), 3 international. Average age 25. 22 applicants, 100% accepted, 7 enrolled. In 2016, 17 master's awarded. Terminal master's awarded for partial completion of doctoral program. *Degree requirements:* For master's, one foreign language, comprehensive exam, thesis; for doctorate, one foreign language, comprehensive exam, thesis/dissertation. *Entrance requirements:* For master's, BS in mechanical engineering or its equivalent; for doctorate, GRE, BS or MS in mechanical engineering or its equivalent; minimum GPA of 3.0. Additional exam requirements/recommendations for international students: Required—TOEFL (minimum score 80 paper-based; 80 iBT). *Application deadline:* For fall admission, 2/15 for domestic and international students; for spring admission, 9/15 for domestic and international students. Applications are processed on a rolling basis. Application fee: $25. Electronic applications accepted. *Expenses: Tuition, area resident:* Full-time $2466. *International tuition:* $7166 full-time. *Required fees:* $210. One-time fee: $5 full-time. Tuition and fees vary according to course level, campus/location, program and student level. *Financial support:* In 2016–17, 39 students received support, including 26 research assistantships with full and partial tuition reimbursements available (averaging $3,801 per year), 30 teaching assistantships with full and partial tuition reimbursements available (averaging $3,293 per year); unspecified assistantships also available. *Faculty research:* Computational fluid dynamics, thermal sciences, mechanical design, material health, microfluidics. *Unit head:* Paul Sundaram, Ph.D., Chairperson, 787-832-4040 Ext. 3659, Fax: 787-265-3817, E-mail: paul.sundaram@upr.edu. *Application contact:* Yolanda Perez, Academic Orientation Officer, 787-832-4040 Ext. 2362, Fax: 787-265-3817, E-mail: yolanda.perez4@upr.edu.
Website: https://wordpress.uprm.edu/inme/

University of St. Thomas, Graduate Studies, School of Engineering, St. Paul, MN 55105-1096. Offers data science (MS); electrical engineering (MS); information technology (MS); manufacturing engineering (MS); manufacturing systems (Certificate); mechanical engineering (MS); medical device development (Certificate); regulatory science (MS); software engineering (MS); software management (MS); systems engineering (MS); technology leadership (Certificate); technology management (MS). *Accreditation:* ABET (one or more programs are accredited). *Entrance requirements:* For master's, resume, official transcripts. Additional exam requirements/recommendations for international students: Required—TOEFL (minimum score 550 paper-based). *Application deadline:* For fall admission, 8/1 priority date for domestic students; for spring admission, 1/1 priority date for domestic students. Applications are processed on a rolling basis. Application fee: $50. Electronic applications accepted. *Expenses:* Contact institution. *Financial support:* Fellowships, research assistantships, institutionally sponsored loans, and scholarships/grants available. Support available to part-time students. Financial award application deadline: 4/1; financial award applicants required to submit FAFSA. *Unit head:* Don Weinkauf, Dean, 651-962-5760, Fax: 651-962-6419, E-mail: dhweinkauf@stthomas.edu. *Application contact:* Tina M. Hansen, Graduate Program Manager, 651-962-5755, Fax: 651-962-6419, E-mail: tina.hansen@stthomas.edu.
Website: http://www.stthomas.edu/engineering/

University of Southern California, Graduate School, Viterbi School of Engineering, Daniel J. Epstein Department of Industrial and Systems Engineering, Los Angeles, CA 90089. Offers digital supply chain management (MS); engineering management (MS); engineering technology communication (Graduate Certificate); health systems operations (Graduate Certificate); industrial and systems engineering (MS, PhD, Engr); manufacturing engineering (MS); operations research engineering (MS); optimization and supply chain management (Graduate Certificate); product development engineering (MS); safety systems and security (MS); systems architecting and engineering (MS, Graduate Certificate); systems safety and security (Graduate Certificate); transportation systems (Graduate Certificate); MS/MBA. *Program availability:* Part-time, evening/weekend, online learning. Terminal master's awarded for partial completion of doctoral program. *Degree requirements:* For master's, thesis optional; for doctorate, thesis/dissertation. *Entrance requirements:* For master's and doctorate, GRE General Test. Additional exam requirements/recommendations for international students: Recommended—TOEFL. Electronic applications accepted. *Faculty research:* Health systems, music cognition and retrieval, transportation and logistics, manufacturing and automation, engineering systems design, risk and economic analysis.

The University of Texas at El Paso, Graduate School, College of Engineering, Department of Industrial Engineering, El Paso, TX 79968-0001. Offers industrial engineering (MS); manufacturing engineering (MS); systems engineering (MS, Certificate). *Program availability:* Part-time, evening/weekend. *Degree requirements:* For master's, thesis optional. *Entrance requirements:* For master's, GRE General Test, minimum GPA of 3.0 in major. Additional exam requirements/recommendations for international students: Required—TOEFL. Electronic applications accepted. *Faculty research:* Computer vision, automated inspection, simulation and modeling.

The University of Texas at San Antonio, College of Engineering, Department of Mechanical Engineering, San Antonio, TX 78249-0617. Offers advanced manufacturing and enterprise engineering (MS); mechanical engineering (MS, PhD). *Program availability:* Part-time, evening/weekend. *Faculty:* 21 full-time (2 women), 3 part-time/adjunct (0 women). *Students:* 73 full-time (12 women), 52 part-time (9 women); includes 41 minority (2 Black or African American, non-Hispanic/Latino; 10 Asian, non-Hispanic/Latino; 25 Hispanic/Latino; 4 Two or more races, non-Hispanic/Latino), 49 international. Average age 30. 114 applicants, 68% accepted, 30 enrolled. In 2016, 32 master's, 4 doctorates awarded. Terminal master's awarded for partial completion of doctoral program. *Degree requirements:* For master's, comprehensive exam, thesis; for doctorate, comprehensive exam, thesis/dissertation. *Entrance requirements:* For master's, GRE General Test, bachelor's degree in mechanical engineering or related field from accredited institution of higher education; for doctorate, GRE General Test, master's degree in mechanical engineering, or exceptionally outstanding undergraduate record in mechanical engineering or related field; minimum GPA of 3.33. Additional exam requirements/recommendations for international students: Required—TOEFL (minimum score 550 paper-based; 79 iBT), IELTS (minimum score 6.5). *Application deadline:* For fall admission, 7/1 for domestic students, 4/1 for international students; for spring admission, 11/1 for domestic students, 9/1 for international students. Applications are processed on a rolling basis. Application fee: $45 ($80 for international students). Electronic applications accepted. *Expenses:* Contact institution. *Financial support:* In 2016–17, 25 students received support, including 10 fellowships with partial tuition reimbursements available (averaging $25,000 per year), 8 research assistantships

(averaging $15,665 per year), 27 teaching assistantships (averaging $10,000 per year); career-related internships or fieldwork and unspecified assistantships also available. Financial award application deadline: 10/1. *Faculty research:* Mechanics and materials, advanced manufacturing, wind turbine, computational fluid dynamics, robotics, biomechanics, wind energy. *Total annual research expenditures:* $2.4 million. *Unit head:* Dr. Hai-Chao Han, Department Chair/Professor, 210-458-6021, E-mail: hai-chao.han@utsa.edu.
Website: http://engineering.utsa.edu/me/

The University of Texas Rio Grande Valley, College of Engineering and Computer Science, Department of Manufacturing and Industrial Engineering, Edinburg, TX 78539. Offers engineering management (MS); manufacturing engineering (MS); systems engineering (MS). Tuition and fees vary according to course load and program.

University of Toronto, School of Graduate Studies, Advanced Design and Manufacturing Institute, Toronto, ON M5S 1A1, Canada. Offers M Eng. Program offered jointly with McMaster University, Queen's University, and The University of Western Ontario; available only to Canadian citizens and permanent residents of Canada. *Program availability:* Part-time. *Entrance requirements:* For master's, honours bachelor's degree in engineering with grades equivalent to a mid-B or better. Additional exam requirements/recommendations for international students: Required—TOEFL (minimum score 580 paper-based; 93 iBT), TWE (minimum score 4). Electronic applications accepted.

University of Windsor, Faculty of Graduate Studies, Faculty of Engineering, Department of Industrial and Manufacturing Systems Engineering, Windsor, ON N9B 3P4, Canada. Offers industrial engineering (M Eng, MA Sc); manufacturing systems engineering (PhD). *Program availability:* Part-time. *Degree requirements:* For master's, thesis; for doctorate, comprehensive exam, thesis/dissertation. *Entrance requirements:* For master's, minimum B average; for doctorate, master's degree, minimum B average. Additional exam requirements/recommendations for international students: Required—TOEFL (minimum score 560 paper-based). Electronic applications accepted. *Faculty research:* Human factors, operations research.

University of Wisconsin–Madison, Graduate School, College of Engineering, Manufacturing Systems Engineering Program, Madison, WI 53706. Offers MS. *Program availability:* Part-time. *Faculty:* 7 full-time (0 women). *Students:* 23 full-time (3 women), 5 part-time (1 woman); includes 1 minority (Asian, non-Hispanic/Latino), 25 international. Average age 26. 70 applicants, 21% accepted, 7 enrolled. In 2016, 23 master's awarded. *Degree requirements:* For master's, thesis (for some programs), minimum of 30 credits; independent research projects; minimum GPA of 3.0. *Entrance requirements:* For master's, GRE General Test, BS in engineering or physical sciences coupled with industry experience; minimum GPA of 3.0; 2 years of relevant industry experience or project work. Additional exam requirements/recommendations for international students: Required—TOEFL (minimum score 580 paper-based; 92 iBT), IELTS (minimum score 7). *Application deadline:* For fall admission, 1/1 for domestic and international students. Application fee: $75 ($81 for international students). Electronic applications accepted. *Expenses:* $13,157 per year in-state tuition and fees; $26,484 per year out-of-state tuition and fees. *Financial support:* Fellowships with full tuition reimbursements, research assistantships with full tuition reimbursements, teaching assistantships with full tuition reimbursements, career-related internships or fieldwork, institutionally sponsored loans, health care benefits, and unspecified assistantships available. Financial award application deadline: 12/1; financial award applicants required to submit FAFSA. *Faculty research:* Advanced manufacturing, computer-aided manufacturing, rapid prototyping, lead time reduction, quick response manufacturing. *Unit head:* Prof. Frank E. Pfefferkorn, Director, 608-263-2668, E-mail: mse@engr.wisc.edu. *Application contact:* Pam Peterson, Student Status Coordinator, 608-263-4025, Fax: 608-262-8454, E-mail: prpeterson@wisc.edu.
Website: https://www.engr.wisc.edu/academics/graduate-academics/manufacturing-systems-engineering/

University of Wisconsin–Milwaukee, Graduate School, College of Engineering and Applied Science, Program in Engineering, Milwaukee, WI 53201-0413. Offers biomedical engineering (MS); civil engineering (MS, PhD); computer science (PhD); electrical and computer engineering (MS); electrical engineering (PhD); engineering mechanics (MS); industrial and management engineering (MS); industrial engineering (PhD); manufacturing engineering (MS); materials (PhD); materials engineering (MS); mechanical engineering (MS). *Program availability:* Part-time. *Students:* 199 full-time (52 women), 156 part-time (32 women); includes 27 minority (2 Black or African American, non-Hispanic/Latino; 15 Asian, non-Hispanic/Latino; 3 Hispanic/Latino; 7 Two or more races, non-Hispanic/Latino), 244 international. Average age 30. 396 applicants, 61% accepted, 102 enrolled. In 2016, 72 master's, 26 doctorates awarded. *Degree requirements:* For master's, comprehensive exam (for some programs), thesis or alternative; for doctorate, comprehensive exam, thesis/dissertation, internship. *Entrance requirements:* For master's, GRE, minimum GPA of 2.75; for doctorate, GRE, minimum GPA of 3.5. Additional exam requirements/recommendations for international students: Required—TOEFL (minimum score 550 paper-based; 79 iBT), IELTS (minimum score 6.5). *Application deadline:* For fall admission, 1/1 priority date for domestic students; for spring admission, 9/1 for domestic students. Applications are processed on a rolling basis. Application fee: $56 ($96 for international students). *Financial support:* In 2016–17, 3 fellowships, 55 research assistantships, 77 teaching assistantships were awarded; career-related internships or fieldwork, Federal Work-Study, unspecified assistantships, and project assistantships also available. Support available to part-time students. Financial award application deadline: 4/15. *Unit head:* David Yu, Representative, 414-229-6169, E-mail: yu@uwm.edu. *Application contact:* Betty Warras, General Information Contact, 414-229-6169, Fax: 414-229-6967, E-mail: bwarras@uwm.edu.
Website: http://www4.uwm.edu/ceas/academics/graduate_programs/

University of Wisconsin–Stout, Graduate School, College of Science, Technology, Engineering and Mathematics, Program in Manufacturing Engineering, Menomonie, WI 54751. Offers MS. *Program availability:* Online learning. *Degree requirements:* For master's, thesis. *Entrance requirements:* For master's, minimum GPA of 3.0. Additional exam requirements/recommendations for international students: Required—TOEFL (minimum score 500 paper-based; 61 iBT). Electronic applications accepted. *Faculty research:* General ceramics patents, metal matrix composites, solidification processing, high temperature processing.

Villanova University, College of Engineering, Department of Mechanical Engineering, Villanova, PA 19085-1699. Offers electro-mechanical systems (Certificate); machinery dynamics (Certificate); mechanical engineering (MSME); nonlinear dynamics and control (Certificate); thermofluid systems (Certificate). *Program availability:* Part-time, evening/weekend, online learning. *Degree requirements:* For master's, thesis optional. *Entrance requirements:* For master's, GRE General Test (for applicants with degrees from foreign universities), BME, minimum GPA of 3.0. Additional exam requirements/recommendations for international students: Required—TOEFL (minimum score 600 paper-based; 100 iBT). Electronic applications accepted. *Faculty research:* Composite materials, power plant systems, fluid mechanics, automated manufacturing, dynamic analysis.

Wayne State University, College of Engineering, Department of Industrial and Systems Engineering, Detroit, MI 48202. Offers data science and business analytics (MS); engineering management (MS); industrial engineering (MS, PhD); manufacturing engineering (MS); systems engineering (Certificate). *Faculty:* 10. *Students:* 313 full-time (37 women), 140 part-time (26 women); includes 37 minority (16 Black or African American, non-Hispanic/Latino; 15 Asian, non-Hispanic/Latino; 3 Hispanic/Latino; 3 Two or more races, non-Hispanic/Latino), 340 international. Average age 28. 1,171 applicants, 42% accepted, 105 enrolled. In 2016, 117 master's, 5 doctorates awarded. *Degree requirements:* For master's, thesis (for some programs); for doctorate, thesis/dissertation. *Entrance requirements:* For master's, BS from ABET-accredited institution; for doctorate, MS in industrial engineering or operations research with minimum graduate GPA of 3.5; for Certificate, BS in engineering or other technical field from ABET-accredited institution, full-time work experience as practicing engineer or technical leader. Additional exam requirements/recommendations for international students: Required—TOEFL (minimum score 550 paper-based; 79 iBT), TWE (minimum score 5.5), Michigan English Language Assessment Battery (minimum score 85); Recommended—IELTS (minimum score 6.5). *Application deadline:* For fall admission, 6/1 priority date for domestic students, 5/1 priority date for international students; for winter admission, 10/1 priority date for domestic students, 9/1 priority date for international students; for spring admission, 2/1 priority date for domestic students, 1/1 priority date for international students. Applications are processed on a rolling basis. Application fee: $50. Electronic applications accepted. *Expenses:* $18,871 per year resident tuition and fees, $36,065 per year non-resident tuition and fees. *Financial support:* In 2016–17, 118 students received support, including 2 fellowships with tuition reimbursements available (averaging $16,000 per year), 4 research assistantships with tuition reimbursements available (averaging $18,883 per year), 12 teaching assistantships with tuition reimbursements available (averaging $19,177 per year); scholarships/grants, tuition waivers (full), and unspecified assistantships also available. Financial award applicants required to submit FAFSA. *Faculty research:* Healthcare systems engineering, product design and development, quality and reliability engineering, supply chain management and logistics. *Total annual research expenditures:* $3.2 million. *Unit head:* Dr. Leslie Monplaisir, Associate Professor/Chair, 313-577-3821, Fax: 313-577-8833, E-mail: leslie.monplaisir@wayne.edu. *Application contact:* Eric Scimeca, Graduate Program Coordinator, 313-577-0412, E-mail: eric.scimeca@wayne.edu.
Website: http://engineering.wayne.edu/ise/

Western Illinois University, School of Graduate Studies, College of Business and Technology, Program in Engineering Technology Leadership, Macomb, IL 61455-1390. Offers MS. *Program availability:* Part-time. *Students:* 16 full-time (3 women), 9 part-time (3 women); includes 2 minority (both Hispanic/Latino), 19 international. Average age 26. 26 applicants, 65% accepted, 12 enrolled. In 2016, 19 master's awarded. *Degree requirements:* For master's, thesis or alternative. *Entrance requirements:* Additional exam requirements/recommendations for international students: Required—TOEFL (minimum score 550 paper-based; 80 iBT). *Application deadline:* Applications are processed on a rolling basis. Application fee: $30. Electronic applications accepted. *Financial support:* In 2016–17, 6 students received support, including 5 teaching assistantships with full tuition reimbursements available; unspecified assistantships also available. Financial award applicants required to submit FAFSA. *Unit head:* Dr. Ray Diez, Chairperson, 309-298-1091. *Application contact:* Dr. Nancy Parsons, Associate Provost and Director of Graduate Studies, 309-298-1806, Fax: 309-298-2345, E-mail: grad-office@wiu.edu.
Website: http://wiu.edu/engrtech

Western Michigan University, Graduate College, College of Engineering and Applied Sciences, Department of Engineering Design, Manufacturing, and Management Systems, Kalamazoo, MI 49008. Offers MS.

Western New England University, College of Engineering, Master's Program in Engineering Management, Springfield, MA 01119. Offers business and engineering information systems (MSEM); general engineering management (MSEM); production and manufacturing systems (MSEM); quality engineering (MSEM); MSEM/MBA. *Program availability:* Part-time, evening/weekend, online learning. *Faculty:* 6 full-time. *Students:* 46 part-time (6 women); includes 5 minority (1 Black or African American, non-Hispanic/Latino; 1 Asian, non-Hispanic/Latino; 3 Hispanic/Latino), 13 international. Average age 31. 151 applicants, 29% accepted, 9 enrolled. In 2016, 28 master's awarded. *Degree requirements:* For master's, thesis optional. *Entrance requirements:* For master's, official transcript, bachelor's degree in engineering or related field, two recommendations, resume. Additional exam requirements/recommendations for international students: Required—TOEFL (minimum score 79 iBT). *Application deadline:* Applications are processed on a rolling basis. Application fee: $30. Electronic applications accepted. *Expenses:* Contact institution. *Financial support:* Application deadline: 4/15; applicants required to submit FAFSA. *Unit head:* Dr. Thomas Keyser, Chair and Professor, 413-782-1210, E-mail: thomas.keyser@wne.edu. *Application contact:* Matthew Fox, Director of Admissions for Graduate Students and Adult Learners, 413-782-1410, Fax: 413-782-1777, E-mail: study@wne.edu.
Website: http://www1.wne.edu/academics/graduate/engineering-management.cfm

Wichita State University, Graduate School, College of Engineering, Department of Industrial and Manufacturing Engineering, Wichita, KS 67260. Offers engineering management (MEM); industrial engineering (MS, PhD). *Program availability:* Part-time. In 2016, 37 master's, 3 doctorates awarded. *Entrance requirements:* Additional exam requirements/recommendations for international students: Required—TOEFL. *Financial support:* Teaching assistantships available. *Unit head:* Dr. Krishna Krishnan, Chair, 316-978-3425, Fax: 316-978-3742, E-mail: krishna.krishnan@wichita.edu. *Application contact:* Jordan Oleson, Admissions Coordinator, 316-978-3095, Fax: 316-978-3253, E-mail: jordan.oleson@wichita.edu.
Website: http://www.wichita.edu/ime

Worcester Polytechnic Institute, Graduate Studies and Research, Department of Mechanical Engineering, Program in Manufacturing Engineering, Worcester, MA 01609-2280. Offers MS, PhD. *Program availability:* Part-time, evening/weekend. *Students:* 21 full-time (3 women), 22 part-time (3 women); includes 10 minority (2 Black or African American, non-Hispanic/Latino; 2 Asian, non-Hispanic/Latino; 4 Hispanic/Latino; 2 Two or more races, non-Hispanic/Latino), 12 international. 38 applicants, 74% accepted, 17 enrolled. In 2016, 11 master's awarded. *Degree requirements:* For master's, thesis optional; for doctorate, comprehensive exam, thesis/dissertation, research proposal. *Entrance requirements:* For master's and doctorate, GRE (recommended), 3 letters of recommendation. Additional exam requirements/recommendations for international students: Required—TOEFL (minimum score 563 paper-based; 84 iBT), IELTS (minimum score 7), GRE. *Application deadline:* For fall admission, 1/1 priority date for domestic and international students; for spring admission, 10/1 priority date for domestic and international students. Applications are processed on a rolling basis. Application fee: $70. Electronic applications accepted. *Financial support:* Research assistantships, teaching assistantships, career-related internships or fieldwork, institutionally sponsored loans, scholarships/grants, and unspecified assistantships available. Financial award application deadline: 1/1; financial award applicants required to submit FAFSA. *Unit head:* Dr. Richard Sisson, Director, 508-831-6088, Fax: 508-831-5673, E-mail: rong@

wpi.edu. *Application contact:* GlorieAnn Minnich, Graduate Secretary, 508-831-6088, Fax: 508-831-5673, E-mail: gkminnich@wpi.edu.
Website: http://www.wpi.edu/academics/mfe

Worcester Polytechnic Institute, Graduate Studies and Research, Programs in Interdisciplinary Studies, Worcester, MA 01609-2280. Offers bioscience administration (MS); impact engineering (MS); manufacturing engineering management (MS); power systems management (MS); social science (PhD); systems modeling (MS). *Program availability:* Part-time, evening/weekend. *Faculty:* 1 part-time/adjunct (0 women). *Students:* 5 full-time (2 women), 54 part-time (21 women); includes 14 minority (3 Black or African American, non-Hispanic/Latino; 5 Asian, non-Hispanic/Latino; 5 Hispanic/Latino; 1 Two or more races, non-Hispanic/Latino), 4 international. 18 applicants, 89% accepted, 8 enrolled. *Degree requirements:* For master's, thesis; for doctorate, comprehensive exam, thesis/dissertation. *Entrance requirements:* For master's and doctorate, 3 letters of recommendation. Additional exam requirements/recommendations for international students: Required—TOEFL (minimum score 563 paper-based; 84 iBT), IELTS (minimum score 7). *Application deadline:* For fall admission, 1/1 priority date for domestic students, 1/1 for international students; for spring admission, 10/1 priority date for domestic students, 10/1 for international students. Applications are processed on a rolling basis. Application fee: $70. Electronic applications accepted. *Financial support:* Institutionally sponsored loans, scholarships/grants, and unspecified assistantships available. Financial award application deadline: 1/1; financial award applicants required to submit FAFSA. *Unit head:* Dr. Fred J. Looft, Head, 508-831-5231, Fax: 508-831-5491, E-mail: fjlooft@wpi.edu. *Application contact:* Lynne Dougherty, Administrative Assistant, 508-831-5301, Fax: 508-831-5717, E-mail: grad@wpi.edu.

Pharmaceutical Engineering

New Jersey Institute of Technology, Newark College of Engineering, Newark, NJ 07102. Offers biomedical engineering (MS, PhD); chemical engineering (MS, PhD); computer engineering (MS, PhD); electrical engineering (MS, PhD); engineering management (MS); environmental engineering (PhD); healthcare systems management (MS); industrial engineering (MS, PhD); Internet engineering (MS); manufacturing engineering (MS); mechanical engineering (MS, PhD); occupational safety and health engineering (MS); pharmaceutical bioprocessing (MS); pharmaceutical engineering (MS); pharmaceutical systems management (MS); power and energy systems (MS); telecommunications (MS); transportation (MS, PhD). *Program availability:* Part-time, evening/weekend. *Faculty:* 146 full-time (21 women), 119 part-time/adjunct (10 women). *Students:* 804 full-time (191 women), 550 part-time (129 women); includes 357 minority (82 Black or African American, non-Hispanic/Latino; 1 American Indian or Alaska Native, non-Hispanic/Latino; 138 Asian, non-Hispanic/Latino; 114 Hispanic/Latino; 22 Two or more races, non-Hispanic/Latino), 675 international. Average age 27. 2,959 applicants, 51% accepted, 442 enrolled. In 2016, 595 master's, 29 doctorates awarded. Terminal master's awarded for partial completion of doctoral program. *Degree requirements:* For master's, thesis optional; for doctorate, thesis/dissertation. *Entrance requirements:* For master's, GRE General Test; for doctorate, GRE General Test, minimum graduate GPA of 3.5. Additional exam requirements/recommendations for international students: Required—TOEFL (minimum score 550 paper-based; 79 iBT). *Application deadline:* For fall admission, 6/1 priority date for domestic students, 5/1 priority date for international students; for spring admission, 11/15 priority date for domestic and international students. Applications are processed on a rolling basis. Application fee: $75. Electronic applications accepted. *Expenses:* Contact institution. *Financial support:* In 2016–17, 172 students received support, including 1 fellowship (averaging $1,528 per year), 79 research assistantships (averaging $13,336 per year), 92 teaching assistantships (averaging $20,619 per year); scholarships/grants also available. Financial award application deadline: 1/15. *Faculty research:* Nonlinear signal processing, intelligent medical image analysis, calibration issues in coherent localization, computer-aided design, neural network for tool wear measurement. *Total annual research expenditures:* $11.1 million. *Unit head:* Dr. Moshe Kam, Dean, 973-596-5534, E-mail: moshe.kam@njit.edu. *Application contact:* Stephen Eck, Director of Admissions, 973-596-3300, Fax: 973-596-3461, E-mail: admissions@njit.edu.
Website: http://engineering.njit.edu/

University of Michigan, College of Engineering, Department of Integrative Systems and Design, Ann Arbor, MI 48109. Offers automotive engineering (M Eng); design science (MS, PhD); energy systems engineering (M Eng, MS); global automotive and manufacturing engineering (M Eng); manufacturing engineering (M Eng, D Eng); pharmaceutical engineering (M Eng); robotics and autonomous vehicles (M Eng); systems engineering and design (M Eng); MBA/M Eng; MSE/MS. *Program availability:* Part-time, online learning. *Students:* 147 full-time (33 women), 234 part-time (39 women). 315 applicants, 8% accepted, 13 enrolled. In 2016, 158 master's, 2 doctorates awarded. Terminal master's awarded for partial completion of doctoral program. *Degree requirements:* For master's, capstone project; for doctorate, thesis/dissertation. *Entrance requirements:* For master's, GRE; for doctorate, GRE, 2 years of work experience. Additional exam requirements/recommendations for international students: Required—TOEFL (minimum score 560 paper-based). *Application deadline:* Applications are processed on a rolling basis. Electronic applications accepted. *Expenses:* Tuition, state resident: full-time $21,466; part-time $1152 per credit hour. Tuition, nonresident: full-time $43,346; part-time $2367 per credit hour. Part-time tuition and fees vary according to course load, degree level and program. *Financial support:* Fellowships, research assistantships with full tuition reimbursements, teaching assistantships with full tuition reimbursements, career-related internships or fieldwork, scholarships/grants, and unspecified assistantships available. Financial award applicants required to submit FAFSA. *Faculty research:* Automotive engineering, design science, energy systems engineering, engineering sustainable systems, financial engineering, global automotive and manufacturing engineering, integrated microsystems, manufacturing engineering, pharmaceutical engineering, robotics and autonomous vehicles. *Total annual research expenditures:* $292,225. *Unit head:* Prof. Panos Papalambros, Department Chair, 734-647-8401, E-mail: pyp@umich.edu. *Application contact:* Kathy Bishar, Senior Graduate Coordinator, 734-764-3312, E-mail: kbishar@umich.edu.
Website: http://www.isd.engin.umich.edu

Reliability Engineering

Arizona State University at the Tempe campus, Ira A. Fulton Schools of Engineering, ASU Engineering Online Programs, Tempe, AZ 85287. Offers construction (MS); embedded systems (M Eng); enterprise systems innovation and management (MSE); modeling and simulation (M Eng); quality and reliability engineering (M Eng); software engineering (MSE); systems engineering (M Eng).

University of Maryland, College Park, Academic Affairs, A. James Clark School of Engineering, Department of Mechanical Engineering, Reliability Engineering Program, College Park, MD 20742. Offers M Eng, MS, PhD. *Program availability:* Part-time, evening/weekend, online learning. *Degree requirements:* For master's, thesis optional; for doctorate, thesis/dissertation. *Entrance requirements:* For master's, GRE General Test, 3 letters of recommendation; for doctorate, GRE General Test, minimum GPA of 3.0. Additional exam requirements/recommendations for international students: Required—TOEFL. Electronic applications accepted. *Faculty research:* Electron linear acceleration, x-ray and imaging.

The University of Tennessee, Graduate School, Tickle College of Engineering, Department of Chemical and Biomolecular Engineering, Knoxville, TN 37996. Offers chemical engineering (MS, PhD); reliability and maintainability engineering (MS); MS/MBA. *Program availability:* Part-time. *Faculty:* 32 full-time (5 women). *Students:* 53 full-time (16 women), 2 part-time (0 women); includes 7 minority (2 Black or African American, non-Hispanic/Latino; 3 Hispanic/Latino; 2 Two or more races, non-Hispanic/Latino), 24 international. Average age 26. 82 applicants, 30% accepted, 10 enrolled. In 2016, 4 master's, 7 doctorates awarded. *Degree requirements:* For master's, thesis or alternative; for doctorate, comprehensive exam, thesis/dissertation. *Entrance requirements:* For master's, GRE General Test (for MS students pursuing research thesis), minimum GPA of 2.7 (for U.S. degree holders), 3.0 (for international degree holders); for doctorate, GRE General Test, minimum GPA of 3.0 on previous graduate course work. Additional exam requirements/recommendations for international students: Required—TOEFL (minimum score 550 paper-based). *Application deadline:* For fall admission, 2/1 priority date for domestic and international students; for spring admission, 6/15 for domestic and international students. Applications are processed on a rolling basis. Application fee: $35. Electronic applications accepted. *Financial support:* In 2016–17, 51 students received support, including 3 fellowships (averaging $25,333 per year), 28 research assistantships with full tuition reimbursements available (averaging $25,846 per year), 15 teaching assistantships with full tuition reimbursements available (averaging $24,126 per year); career-related internships or fieldwork, Federal Work-Study, institutionally sponsored loans, health care benefits, and unspecified assistantships also available. Financial award application deadline: 2/1; financial award applicants required to submit FAFSA. *Faculty research:* Bio-fuels; engineering of soft, functional and structural materials; fuel cells and energy storage devices; molecular and cellular bioengineering; molecular modeling and simulations. *Total annual research expenditures:* $3.9 million. *Unit head:* Dr. Bamin Khomami, Head, 865-974-2421, Fax: 865-974-7076, E-mail: bkhomami@utk.edu. *Application contact:* Dr. Paul Frymier, Graduate Program Coordinator, 865-974-4961, Fax: 865-974-7076, E-mail: pdf@utk.edu.
Website: http://www.engr.utk.edu/cbe/

The University of Tennessee, Graduate School, Tickle College of Engineering, Department of Electrical Engineering and Computer Science, Knoxville, TN 37996. Offers computer engineering (MS, PhD); computer science (MS, PhD); electrical engineering (MS, PhD); reliability and maintainability engineering (MS); MS/MBA. *Program availability:* Part-time. *Faculty:* 59 full-time (10 women), 5 part-time/adjunct (2 women). *Students:* 242 full-time (56 women), 32 part-time (4 women); includes 15 minority (2 Black or African American, non-Hispanic/Latino; 8 Asian, non-Hispanic/Latino; 3 Hispanic/Latino; 2 Two or more races, non-Hispanic/Latino), 160 international. Average age 28. 484 applicants, 20% accepted, 79 enrolled. In 2016, 27 master's, 34 doctorates awarded. *Degree requirements:* For master's, thesis or alternative; for doctorate, comprehensive exam, thesis/dissertation. *Entrance requirements:* For master's, GRE General Test (for MS students pursuing research thesis), minimum GPA of 2.7 (for U.S. degree holders), 3.0 (for international degree holders); 3 references; personal statement; for doctorate, GRE General Test, minimum GPA of 3.0 on previous graduate course work; 3 references; personal statement. Additional exam requirements/recommendations for international students: Required—TOEFL (minimum score 550 paper-based). *Application deadline:* For fall admission, 2/1 priority date for domestic and international students; for spring admission, 6/15 for domestic and international students. Applications are processed on a rolling basis. Application fee: $35. Electronic applications accepted. *Financial support:* In 2016–17, 223 students received support, including 17 fellowships with full tuition reimbursements available (averaging $27,519 per year), 129 research assistantships with full tuition reimbursements available (averaging $23,383 per year), 58 teaching assistantships with full tuition reimbursements available (averaging $19,508 per year); career-related internships or fieldwork, Federal Work-Study, institutionally sponsored loans, health care benefits, and unspecified assistantships also available. Financial award application deadline: 2/1; financial award applicants required to submit FAFSA. *Faculty research:* Artificial intelligence and visualization; microelectronics, mixed-signal electronics, VLSI, embedded systems; scientific and distributed computing; computer vision, robotics, and image processing; power electronics, power systems, communications. *Total annual research expenditures:* $17.5 million. *Unit head:* Dr. Leon Tolbert, Head, 865-974-3461, Fax: 865-974-5483, E-mail: tolbert@utk.edu. *Application contact:* Dr. Jens Gregor, Associate Head, 865-974-4399, Fax: 865-974-5483, E-mail: jgregor@utk.edu.
Website: http://www.eecs.utk.edu

The University of Tennessee, Graduate School, Tickle College of Engineering, Department of Industrial and Systems Engineering, Knoxville, TN 37966. Offers engineering management (MS); industrial engineering (MS, PhD); reliability and maintainability engineering (MS); MS/MBA. *Program availability:* Part-time, online learning. *Faculty:* 13 full-time (2 women), 5 part-time/adjunct (0 women). *Students:* 90

full-time (20 women), 67 part-time (10 women); includes 18 minority (4 Black or African American, non-Hispanic/Latino; 7 Asian, non-Hispanic/Latino; 6 Hispanic/Latino; 1 Two or more races, non-Hispanic/Latino), 55 international. Average age 37. 103 applicants, 64% accepted, 23 enrolled. In 2016, 26 master's, 7 doctorates awarded. *Degree requirements:* For master's, thesis or alternative; for doctorate, comprehensive exam, thesis/dissertation. *Entrance requirements:* For master's, GRE General Test (for MS students pursuing research thesis), minimum GPA of 2.7 (for U.S. degree holders), 3.0 (for international degree holders); for doctorate, GRE General Test, minimum GPA of 3.0 on previous graduate course work. Additional exam requirements/recommendations for international students: Required—TOEFL (minimum score 550 paper-based). *Application deadline:* For fall admission, 2/1 priority date for domestic and international students; for spring admission, 6/15 for domestic and international students. Applications are processed on a rolling basis. Application fee: $35. Electronic applications accepted. *Financial support:* In 2016–17, 36 students received support, including 4 fellowships with full tuition reimbursements available (averaging $25,000 per year), 21 research assistantships with full tuition reimbursements available (averaging $18,799 per year), 10 teaching assistantships with full tuition reimbursements available (averaging $18,783 per year); career-related internships or fieldwork, Federal Work-Study, institutionally sponsored loans, health care benefits, and unspecified assistantships also available. Financial award application deadline: 2/1; financial award applicants required to submit FAFSA. *Faculty research:* Defense-oriented supply chain modeling; dependability and reliability of large computer networks; design of lean, reliable systems; new product development; operations research in the automotive industry. *Total annual research expenditures:* $1 million. *Unit head:* Dr. John Kobza, Department Head, 865-974-3333, Fax: 865-974-0588, E-mail: jkobza@utk.edu. *Application contact:* Dr. Alberto Garcia-Diaz, Professor, 865-974-7647, E-mail: agd@utk.edu.
Website: http://www.engr.utk.edu/ie/

The University of Tennessee, Graduate School, Tickle College of Engineering, Department of Materials Science and Engineering, Knoxville, TN 37996-2200. Offers materials science and engineering (MS, PhD); polymer engineering (MS, PhD); reliability and maintainability engineering (MS); MS/MBA. *Program availability:* Part-time. *Faculty:* 28 full-time (4 women), 10 part-time/adjunct (2 women). *Students:* 78 full-time (21 women), 6 part-time (2 women); includes 6 minority (1 Black or African American, non-Hispanic/Latino; 2 Asian, non-Hispanic/Latino; 3 Hispanic/Latino), 37 international. Average age 29. 138 applicants, 17% accepted, 17 enrolled. In 2016, 19 master's, 11 doctorates awarded. *Degree requirements:* For master's, thesis or alternative; for doctorate, comprehensive exam, thesis/dissertation. *Entrance requirements:* For master's, GRE General Test (for MS students pursuing research thesis), minimum GPA of 2.7 (for U.S. degree holders), 3.0 (for international degree holders); 3 references; for doctorate, GRE General Test, minimum GPA of 3.0 on

previous graduate course work; 3 references. Additional exam requirements/recommendations for international students: Required—TOEFL (minimum score 550 paper-based). *Application deadline:* For fall admission, 2/1 priority date for domestic and international students; for spring admission, 6/15 for domestic and international students. Applications are processed on a rolling basis. Application fee: $35. Electronic applications accepted. *Financial support:* In 2016–17, 77 students received support, including 9 fellowships with full tuition reimbursements available (averaging $30,278 per year), 50 research assistantships with full tuition reimbursements available (averaging $23,100 per year), 16 teaching assistantships with full tuition reimbursements available (averaging $21,291 per year); career-related internships or fieldwork, Federal Work-Study, institutionally sponsored loans, health care benefits, and unspecified assistantships also available. Financial award application deadline: 2/1; financial award applicants required to submit FAFSA. *Faculty research:* Biomaterials; functional materials electronic, magnetic and optical; high temperature materials; mechanical behavior of materials; neutron materials science. *Total annual research expenditures:* $8.8 million. *Unit head:* Dr. Veerle Keppens, Head, 865-974-5336, Fax: 865-974-4115, E-mail: vkeppens@utk.edu. *Application contact:* Dr. Roberto S. Benson, Associate Head, 865-974-5347, Fax: 865-974-4115, E-mail: rbenson1@utk.edu.
Website: http://www.engr.utk.edu/mse

The University of Tennessee, Graduate School, Tickle College of Engineering, Department of Nuclear Engineering, Program in Reliability and Maintainability Engineering, Knoxville, TN 37996. Offers MS. *Students:* 13 part-time (3 women); includes 3 minority (1 Black or African American, non-Hispanic/Latino; 1 Asian, non-Hispanic/Latino; 1 Hispanic/Latino). Average age 34. 3 applicants, 33% accepted, 1 enrolled. In 2016, 3 master's awarded. *Degree requirements:* For master's, thesis or alternative. *Entrance requirements:* For master's, GRE General Test (for MS students pursuing research thesis), minimum GPA of 2.7 (for U.S. degree holders), 3.0 (for international degree holders). Additional exam requirements/recommendations for international students: Required—TOEFL (minimum score 550 paper-based). *Application deadline:* For fall admission, 2/1 priority date for domestic and international students; for spring admission, 6/15 for domestic and international students. Applications are processed on a rolling basis. Application fee: $35. Electronic applications accepted. *Financial support:* Career-related internships or fieldwork, Federal Work-Study, institutionally sponsored loans, health care benefits, and unspecified assistantships available. Financial award application deadline: 2/1; financial award applicants required to submit FAFSA. *Unit head:* Dr. J. Wesley Hines, Head, 865-974-2525, Fax: 865-974-0668, E-mail: jhines2@utk.edu. *Application contact:* Dr. Masood Parang, Associate Dean of Student Affairs, 865-974-2454, Fax: 865-974-9871, E-mail: mparang@utk.edu.
Website: http://www.engr.utk.edu/rme/

Safety Engineering

Embry-Riddle Aeronautical University–Prescott, Program in Safety Science, Prescott, AZ 86301-3720. Offers aviation safety (MSSS). *Program availability:* Part-time. *Faculty:* 4 full-time (0 women), 1 part-time/adjunct (0 women). *Students:* 27 full-time (7 women); includes 3 minority (1 Black or African American, non-Hispanic/Latino; 2 Two or more races, non-Hispanic/Latino), 9 international. Average age 32. 29 applicants, 69% accepted, 9 enrolled. In 2016, 20 master's awarded. *Degree requirements:* For master's, research project, capstone, or thesis. *Entrance requirements:* For master's, GRE (taken within the last 5 years), transcripts, statement of objectives, references, resume. Additional exam requirements/recommendations for international students: Required—TOEFL (minimum score 550 paper-based, 79 iBT) or IELTS (6). *Application deadline:* For fall admission, 1/15 priority date for domestic students; for spring admission, 11/1 priority date for domestic students; for summer admission, 4/1 priority date for domestic students. Applications are processed on a rolling basis. Application fee: $50. Electronic applications accepted. *Expenses: Tuition:* Full-time $16,296; part-time $1358 per credit hour. *Required fees:* $1234; $617 per semester. One-time fee: $100 full-time. Tuition and fees vary according to course load. *Financial support:* Research assistantships, career-related internships or fieldwork, scholarships/grants, and unspecified assistantships available. Financial award application deadline: 3/15; financial award applicants required to submit FAFSA. *Faculty research:* Wildlife Strike Database, Website maintenance, expansion of graphics applications to Web search for general aviation. *Unit head:* Archie Dickey, PhD, Dean, College of Arts and Sciences, E-mail: archie.dickey@erau.edu. *Application contact:* Graduate Admissions, 928-777-6600, E-mail: prescott@erau.edu.
Website: http://prescott.erau.edu/degrees/master/safety-science/index.html

Florida Institute of Technology, College of Aeronautics, Program in Applied Aviation Safety, Melbourne, FL 32901-6975. Offers MSA. *Program availability:* Part-time. *Students:* 6 full-time (1 woman), 1 part-time (0 women); includes 1 minority (Hispanic/Latino), 5 international. Average age 26. 10 applicants, 50% accepted, 1 enrolled. In 2016, 2 master's awarded. *Degree requirements:* For master's, thesis, 36 credit hours. *Entrance requirements:* For master's, GRE, 3 letters of recommendation, resume, statement of objectives. Additional exam requirements/recommendations for international students: Required—TOEFL (minimum score 550 paper-based; 79 iBT). *Application deadline:* Applications are processed on a rolling basis. Electronic applications accepted. *Expenses: Tuition:* Full-time $22,338; part-time $1241 per credit hour. *Required fees:* $250. Tuition and fees vary according to degree level, campus/location and program. *Financial support:* Applicants required to submit FAFSA. *Unit head:* Dr. Korhan Oyman, Dean, 321-674-8971, E-mail: koyman@fit.edu. *Application contact:* Cheryl A. Brown, Associate Director of Graduate Admissions, 321-674-7581, Fax: 321-723-9468, E-mail: cbrown@fit.edu.
Website: http://www.fit.edu/programs/8205/msa-aviation-applied-aviation-safety#.VUDm_k10ypo

Indiana University Bloomington, School of Public Health, Department of Applied Health Science, Bloomington, IN 47405. Offers behavioral, social, and community health (MPH); family health (MPH); health behavior (PhD); nutrition science (MS); professional health education (MPH); public health administration (MPH); safety management (MS); school and college health education (MS). *Accreditation:* CEPH (one or more programs are accredited). *Degree requirements:* For master's, thesis optional; for doctorate, comprehensive exam, thesis/dissertation. *Entrance requirements:* For master's, GRE (for MS in nutrition science), 3 recommendations; for doctorate, GRE, 3 recommendations. Additional exam requirements/recommendations for international students: Required—TOEFL (minimum score 550 paper-based; 80 iBT). Electronic applications accepted. *Faculty research:* Cancer education, HIV/AIDS and drug education, public health, parent-child interactions, safety education, obesity, public health policy, public health administration, school health, health education, human development, nutrition, human sexuality, chronic disease, early childhood health.

Murray State University, College of Health Sciences and Human Services, Program in Occupational Safety and Health, Murray, KY 42071. Offers environmental science (MS); industrial hygiene (MS); safety management (MS). *Accreditation:* ABET. *Program availability:* Part-time. *Degree requirements:* For master's, comprehensive exam, thesis optional, professional internship. Electronic applications accepted. *Faculty research:* Light effects on plant growth, ergonomics, toxic effects of pets' pesticides, traffic safety.

New Jersey Institute of Technology, Newark College of Engineering, Newark, NJ 07102. Offers biomedical engineering (MS, PhD); chemical engineering (MS, PhD); computer engineering (MS, PhD); electrical engineering (MS, PhD); engineering management (MS); environmental engineering (PhD); healthcare systems management (MS); industrial engineering (MS, PhD); Internet engineering (MS); manufacturing engineering (MS); mechanical engineering (MS, PhD); occupational safety and health engineering (MS); pharmaceutical bioprocessing (MS); pharmaceutical engineering (MS); pharmaceutical systems management (MS); power and energy systems (MS); telecommunications (MS); transportation (MS, PhD). *Program availability:* Part-time, evening/weekend. *Faculty:* 146 full-time (21 women), 119 part-time/adjunct (10 women). *Students:* 804 full-time (191 women), 550 part-time (129 women); includes 357 minority (82 Black or African American, non-Hispanic/Latino; 1 American Indian or Alaska Native, non-Hispanic/Latino; 138 Asian, non-Hispanic/Latino; 114 Hispanic/Latino; 22 Two or more races, non-Hispanic/Latino), 675 international. Average age 27. 2,959 applicants, 51% accepted, 442 enrolled. In 2016, 595 master's, 29 doctorates awarded. Terminal master's awarded for partial completion of doctoral program. *Degree requirements:* For master's, thesis optional; for doctorate, thesis/dissertation. *Entrance requirements:* For master's, GRE General Test; for doctorate, GRE General Test, minimum graduate GPA of 3.5. Additional exam requirements/recommendations for international students: Required—TOEFL (minimum score 550 paper-based; 79 iBT). *Application deadline:* For fall admission, 6/1 priority date for domestic students, 5/1 priority date for international students; for spring admission, 11/15 priority date for domestic and international students. Applications are processed on a rolling basis. Application fee: $75. Electronic applications accepted. *Expenses:* Contact institution. *Financial support:* In 2016–17, 172 students received support, including 1 fellowship (averaging $1,528 per year), 79 research assistantships (averaging $13,336 per year), 92 teaching assistantships (averaging $20,619 per year); scholarships/grants also available. Financial award application deadline: 1/15. *Faculty research:* Nonlinear signal processing, intelligent medical image analysis, calibration issues in coherent localization, computer-aided design, neural network for tool wear measurement. *Total annual research expenditures:* $11.1 million. *Unit head:* Dr. Moshe Kam, Dean, 973-596-5534, E-mail: moshe.kam@njit.edu. *Application contact:* Stephen Eck, Director of Admissions, 973-596-3300, Fax: 973-596-3461, E-mail: admissions@njit.edu.
Website: http://engineering.njit.edu/

Rochester Institute of Technology, Graduate Enrollment Services, College of Applied Science and Technology, School of Engineering Technology, MS Program in Environmental, Health and Safety Management, Rochester, NY 14623. Offers MS. *Program availability:* Part-time, evening/weekend, 100% online, blended/hybrid learning. *Students:* 22 full-time (8 women), 16 part-time (5 women); includes 6 minority (2 Black or African American, non-Hispanic/Latino; 1 Asian, non-Hispanic/Latino; 3 Hispanic/Latino), 10 international. Average age 31. 53 applicants, 40% accepted, 14 enrolled. In 2016, 11 master's awarded. *Degree requirements:* For master's, thesis or alternative. *Entrance requirements:* For master's, minimum GPA of 3.0 (recommended). Additional exam requirements/recommendations for international students: Required—TOEFL (minimum score 570 paper-based; 88 iBT), IELTS (minimum score 6.5), PTE (minimum score 61). *Application deadline:* Applications are processed on a rolling basis. Application fee: $60. Electronic applications accepted. *Expenses:* $1,742 per credit hour. *Financial support:* In 2016–17, 13 students received support. Research assistantships with partial tuition reimbursements available, teaching assistantships with

partial tuition reimbursements available, career-related internships or fieldwork, scholarships/grants, and unspecified assistantships available. Support available to part-time students. Financial award applicants required to submit FAFSA. *Faculty research:* Design and implementation of integrated management systems for environmental sustainability, health and safety (ESHS); multidimensional corporate sustainability; global resilience and disaster science. *Unit head:* Joseph Rosenbeck, Graduate Program Director, 585-475-6469, E-mail: jmrcem@rit.edu. *Application contact:* Diane Ellison, Associate Vice President, Graduate Enrollment Services, 585-475-2229, Fax: 585-475-7164, E-mail: gradinfo@rit.edu.
Website: https://www.rit.edu/cast/cetems/ms-environmental-health-safety-management

University of Minnesota, Duluth, Graduate School, Swenson College of Science and Engineering, Department of Mechanical and Industrial Engineering, Duluth, MN 55812-2496. Offers engineering management (MSEM); environmental health and safety (MEHS). *Program availability:* Part-time, evening/weekend, online learning. *Degree requirements:* For master's, comprehensive exam, thesis or alternative, capstone design project (MSEM), field project (MEHS). *Entrance requirements:* For master's, GRE (MEHS), interview (MEHS), letters of recommendation. Additional exam requirements/recommendations for international students: Required—TOEFL (minimum score 550 paper-based). *Faculty research:* Transportation, ergonomics, toxicology, supply chain management, automation and robotics.

University of Southern California, Graduate School, Viterbi School of Engineering, Daniel J. Epstein Department of Industrial and Systems Engineering, Los Angeles, CA 90089. Offers digital supply chain management (MS); engineering management (MS); engineering technology communication (Graduate Certificate); health systems operations (Graduate Certificate); industrial and systems engineering (MS, PhD, Engr); manufacturing engineering (MS); operations research engineering (MS); optimization and supply chain management (Graduate Certificate); product development engineering (MS); safety systems and security (MS); systems architecting and engineering (MS, Graduate Certificate); systems safety and security (Graduate Certificate); transportation systems (Graduate Certificate); MS/MBA. *Program availability:* Part-time, evening/weekend, online learning. Terminal master's awarded for partial completion of doctoral program. *Degree requirements:* For master's, thesis optional; for doctorate, thesis/dissertation. *Entrance requirements:* For master's and doctorate, GRE General Test. Additional exam requirements/recommendations for international students: Recommended—TOEFL. Electronic applications accepted. *Faculty research:* Health systems, music cognition and retrieval, transportation and logistics, manufacturing and automation, engineering systems design, risk and economic analysis.

West Virginia University, Statler College of Engineering and Mineral Resources, Department of Industrial and Management Systems Engineering, Program in Safety Management, Morgantown, WV 26506. Offers MS. *Degree requirements:* For master's, comprehensive exam, thesis optional. *Entrance requirements:* For master's, minimum GPA of 3.0 for regular admission; 2.75 for provisional. Additional exam requirements/recommendations for international students: Required—TOEFL (minimum score 550 paper-based; 80 iBT). Electronic applications accepted.

Systems Engineering

Air Force Institute of Technology, Graduate School of Engineering and Management, Department of Aeronautics and Astronautics, Dayton, OH 45433-7765. Offers aeronautical engineering (MS, PhD); astronautical engineering (MS, PhD); materials science (MS, PhD); space operations (MS); systems engineering (MS, PhD). *Accreditation:* ABET (one or more programs are accredited). *Program availability:* Part-time. *Degree requirements:* For master's, thesis; for doctorate, thesis/dissertation. *Entrance requirements:* For master's and doctorate, GRE General Test, minimum GPA of 3.0, U.S. citizenship. *Faculty research:* Computational fluid dynamics, experimental aerodynamics, computational structural mechanics, experimental structural mechanics, aircraft and spacecraft stability and control.

Arizona State University at the Tempe campus, Ira A. Fulton Schools of Engineering, ASU Engineering Online Programs, Tempe, AZ 85287. Offers construction (MS); embedded systems (M Eng); enterprise systems innovation and management (MSE); modeling and simulation (M Eng); quality and reliability engineering (M Eng); software engineering (MSE); systems engineering (M Eng).

Auburn University, Graduate School, Ginn College of Engineering, Department of Industrial and Systems Engineering, Auburn University, AL 36849. Offers MISE, MS, PhD, Graduate Certificate. *Program availability:* Part-time. *Faculty:* 13 full-time (1 woman), 2 part-time/adjunct (1 woman). *Students:* 79 full-time (19 women), 45 part-time (8 women); includes 9 minority (6 Black or African American, non-Hispanic/Latino; 2 Asian, non-Hispanic/Latino; 1 Two or more races, non-Hispanic/Latino), 78 international. Average age 29. 279 applicants, 34% accepted, 39 enrolled. In 2016, 63 master's, 6 doctorates, 14 other advanced degrees awarded. *Degree requirements:* For master's, thesis (MS); for doctorate, thesis/dissertation. *Entrance requirements:* For master's and doctorate, GRE General Test. *Application deadline:* Applications are processed on a rolling basis. Application fee: $50 ($60 for international students). *Expenses:* Tuition, state resident: full-time $9072; part-time $504 per credit hour. Tuition, nonresident: full-time $27,216; part-time $1512 per credit hour. *Required fees:* $812 per semester. Tuition and fees vary according to degree level and program. *Financial support:* Fellowships, research assistantships, teaching assistantships, and Federal Work-Study available. Support available to part-time students. Financial award application deadline: 3/15; financial award applicants required to submit FAFSA. *Unit head:* John Evans, Chair, 334-844-1400. *Application contact:* Dr. George Flowers, Dean of the Graduate School, 334-844-2125.
Website: http://www.eng.auburn.edu/insy/

Boston University, College of Engineering, Division of Systems Engineering, Brookline, MA 02446. Offers systems engineering (M Eng, MS, PhD), including engineering practice (M Eng). *Program availability:* Part-time. *Students:* 59 full-time (20 women), 3 part-time (1 woman); includes 4 minority (3 Asian, non-Hispanic/Latino; 1 Hispanic/Latino), 48 international. Average age 25. 175 applicants, 27% accepted, 20 enrolled. In 2016, 16 master's, 7 doctorates awarded. Terminal master's awarded for partial completion of doctoral program. *Degree requirements:* For master's, thesis (for some programs); for doctorate, comprehensive exam, thesis/dissertation. *Entrance requirements:* For master's and doctorate, GRE General Test. Additional exam requirements/recommendations for international students: Required—TOEFL (minimum score 90 iBT), IELTS (minimum score 7). *Faculty research:* Communication, network, sensing, and information systems; control systems, automation, and robotics; discrete event, queuing, hybrid, and complex systems; optimization and algorithms; production, service, distribution, and energy systems. *Unit head:* Dr. Christos Cassandras, Division Head, 617-353-7154, Fax: 617-353-5548, E-mail: cgc@bu.edu.
Website: http://www.bu.edu/se/

California Institute of Technology, Division of Engineering and Applied Science, Option in Control and Dynamical Systems, Pasadena, CA 91125-0001. Offers MS, PhD. *Degree requirements:* For doctorate, thesis/dissertation. *Faculty research:* Robustness, multivariable and nonlinear systems, optimal control, decentralized control, modeling and system identification for robust control.

California State Polytechnic University, Pomona, Program in Systems Engineering, Pomona, CA 91768-2557. Offers MS. *Program availability:* Part-time, evening/weekend. *Students:* 8 part-time (4 women); includes 4 minority (2 Asian, non-Hispanic/Latino; 1 Hispanic/Latino; 1 Two or more races, non-Hispanic/Latino), 2 international. Average age 29. 6 applicants, 83% accepted, 4 enrolled. *Entrance requirements:* Additional exam requirements/recommendations for international students: Required—TOEFL. *Application deadline:* Applications are processed on a rolling basis. Application fee: $55. Electronic applications accepted. *Expenses:* Contact institution. *Financial support:* Application deadline: 3/2. *Unit head:* Dr. Kamran Abedini, Professor/Coordinator, 909-869-2569, Fax: 909-869-2564, E-mail: kabedini@cpp.edu. *Application contact:* Andrew M. Wright, Director of Admissions, 909-869-3130, Fax: 909-869-4529, E-mail: awright@cpp.edu.
Website: https://www.cpp.edu/~ceu/degree-programs/systems-engineering/index.shtml

California State University, Fullerton, Graduate Studies, College of Engineering and Computer Science, Department of Electrical Engineering, Fullerton, CA 92834-9480. Offers electrical engineering (MS); systems engineering (MS). *Program availability:* Part-time. *Degree requirements:* For master's, comprehensive exam, project or thesis. *Entrance requirements:* For master's, GRE General Test, GRE Subject Test, minimum undergraduate GPA of 2.5, 3.0 graduate. Application fee: $55. *Expenses:* Tuition, state resident: full-time $3369; part-time $1953 per unit. Tuition, nonresident: full-time $3915; part-time $2499 per unit. Tuition and fees vary according to course load, degree level and program. *Financial support:* Career-related internships or fieldwork, Federal Work-Study, institutionally sponsored loans, and scholarships/grants available. Support available to part-time students. Financial award application deadline: 3/1; financial award applicants required to submit FAFSA. *Unit head:* Dr. Mostafa Shiva, Chair, 657-278-3013. *Application contact:* Admissions/Applications, 657-278-2371.

California State University, Northridge, Graduate Studies, College of Engineering and Computer Science, Department of Manufacturing Systems Engineering and Management, Northridge, CA 91330. Offers engineering automation (MS); engineering management (MS); manufacturing systems engineering (MS); materials engineering (MS). *Program availability:* Online learning. *Faculty:* 8 full-time (7 women), 21 part-time/adjunct (16 women). *Students:* 124 full-time (29 women), 94 part-time (19 women); includes 27 minority (1 American Indian or Alaska Native, non-Hispanic/Latino; 11 Asian, non-Hispanic/Latino; 13 Hispanic/Latino; 2 Two or more races, non-Hispanic/Latino), 145 international. Average age 27. 302 applicants, 33% accepted, 45 enrolled. *Entrance requirements:* For master's, GRE (if cumulative undergraduate GPA less than 3.0). *Application deadline:* For fall admission, 3/30 for domestic students; for spring admission, 9/30 for domestic students. Application fee: $55. *Expenses:* Tuition, state resident: full-time $4152. *Unit head:* Ahmad Sarfaraz, Chair, 818-677-2167.
Website: http://www.csun.edu/~msem/

Carleton University, Faculty of Graduate Studies, Faculty of Engineering and Design, Ottawa-Carleton Institute for Electrical Engineering, Department of Systems and Computer Engineering, Ottawa, ON K1S 5B6, Canada. Offers electrical engineering (MA Sc, PhD); information and systems science (M Sc); technology innovation management (M Eng, MA Sc). PhD program offered jointly with University of Ottawa. *Degree requirements:* For master's, thesis optional. *Entrance requirements:* For master's, honors degree. Additional exam requirements/recommendations for international students: Required—TOEFL. *Faculty research:* Design manufacturing management; network design, protocols, and performance; software engineering; wireless and satellite communications.

Carnegie Mellon University, Carnegie Institute of Technology, Information Networking Institute, Pittsburgh, PA 15213. Offers information networking (MS); information security (MS); information technology - information security (MS); information technology - mobility (MS); information technology - software management (MS). *Degree requirements:* For master's, thesis optional. *Entrance requirements:* For master's, GRE General Test, bachelor's degree in computer science, computer engineering, or electrical engineering, or related technology degree; programming skills (C/C++ fluency for some programs). Additional exam requirements/recommendations for international students: Required—TOEFL. *Faculty research:* Computer forensics and incident response; dependable systems, embedded systems, mobile systems, and sensor networks; computer and information networks, network and information security, human and socio-economic factors in secure system design; wireless sensor networks, survivable embedded systems, signal processing/compression; strategic management, international strategic management, group dynamics and decision-making structures, simulated competitive environments.

Case Western Reserve University, School of Graduate Studies, Case School of Engineering, Department of Electrical Engineering and Computer Science, Cleveland, OH 44106. Offers computer engineering (MS, PhD); computing and information sciences (MS, PhD); electrical engineering (MS, PhD); systems and control engineering (MS, PhD). *Program availability:* Part-time, evening/weekend, online only, 100% online. *Faculty:* 32 full-time (3 women). *Students:* 188 full-time (42 women), 14 part-time (3 women); includes 7 minority (1 Black or African American, non-Hispanic/Latino; 5 Asian, non-Hispanic/Latino; 1 Hispanic/Latino), 152 international. In 2016, 25 master's, 26 doctorates awarded. Terminal master's awarded for partial completion of doctoral program. *Degree requirements:* For master's, thesis; for doctorate, thesis/dissertation, qualifying exam, teaching experience. *Entrance requirements:* For master's and doctorate, GRE General Test. Additional exam requirements/recommendations for international students: Required—TOEFL. *Application deadline:* For fall admission, 2/1 for domestic students; for spring admission, 11/1 for domestic students. Applications are processed on a rolling basis. Application fee: $50. *Expenses: Tuition:* Full-time $42,576; part-time $1774 per credit hour. *Required fees:* $34. Tuition and fees vary according to course load and program. *Financial support:* In 2016–17, 1 fellowship with tuition reimbursement, 63 research assistantships with tuition reimbursements, 10 teaching assistantships were awarded; career-related internships or fieldwork, Federal Work-Study, and institutionally sponsored loans also available. Support available to part-time students. Financial award application deadline: 3/1; financial award applicants required to submit FAFSA. *Faculty research:* Micro-/nano-systems; robotics and haptics; applied artificial intelligence; automation; computer-aided design and testing of digital systems. *Total annual research expenditures:* $4.9 million. *Unit head:* Dr. Kenneth Loparo,

Department Chair, 216-368-4115, E-mail: kal4@case.edu. *Application contact:* Kimberly Yurchick, Student Affairs Specialist, 216-368-2920, Fax: 216-368-2801, E-mail: ksy4@case.edu.
Website: http://eecs.cwru.edu/

The Catholic University of America, School of Engineering, Program in Engineering Management, Washington, DC 20064. Offers engineering management (MSE, Certificate), including engineering management and organization (MSE), project and systems engineering management (MSE), technology management (MSE); program management (Certificate); systems engineering and management of information technology (Certificate). *Program availability:* Part-time. *Faculty:* 3 part-time/adjunct (0 women). *Students:* 14 full-time (2 women), 11 part-time (3 women); includes 2 minority (both Two or more races, non-Hispanic/Latino), 20 international. Average age 30. 35 applicants, 54% accepted, 11 enrolled. In 2016, 26 master's awarded. *Degree requirements:* For master's, minimum GPA of 3.0. *Entrance requirements:* For master's and Certificate, statement of purpose, official copies of academic transcripts, two letters of recommendation. Additional exam requirements/recommendations for international students: Required—TOEFL (minimum score 550 paper-based; 80 iBT). *Application deadline:* For fall admission, 7/15 priority date for domestic students, 7/1 for international students; for spring admission, 11/15 priority date for domestic students, 11/1 for international students. Applications are processed on a rolling basis. Application fee: $55. Electronic applications accepted. *Expenses:* $43,380 per year; $1,170 per credit; $200 per semester part-time fees. *Financial support:* Fellowships, research assistantships, teaching assistantships, Federal Work-Study, scholarships/grants, tuition waivers (full and partial), and unspecified assistantships available. Financial award application deadline: 2/1; financial award applicants required to submit FAFSA. *Faculty research:* Engineering management and organization, project and systems engineering management, technology management. *Unit head:* Melvin G. Williams, Jr., Director, 202-319-5191, Fax: 202-319-6860, E-mail: williamsme@cua.edu. *Application contact:* Director of Graduate Admissions, 202-319-5057, Fax: 202-319-6533, E-mail: cua-admissions@cua.edu.
Website: http://engrmgmt.cua.edu/

The Citadel, The Military College of South Carolina, Citadel Graduate College, School of Engineering, Department of Engineering Leadership and Program Management, Charleston, SC 29409. Offers project management (MS); systems engineering management (Graduate Certificate); technical program management (Graduate Certificate); technical project management (Graduate Certificate). *Program availability:* Part-time, evening/weekend. *Faculty:* 2 full-time (0 women), 6 part-time/adjunct (0 women). *Students:* 5 full-time (2 women), 85 part-time (37 women); includes 21 minority (10 Black or African American, non-Hispanic/Latino; 1 American Indian or Alaska Native, non-Hispanic/Latino; 2 Asian, non-Hispanic/Latino; 6 Hispanic/Latino; 1 Native Hawaiian or other Pacific Islander, non-Hispanic/Latino; 1 Two or more races, non-Hispanic/Latino), 1 international. 65 applicants, 98% accepted, 38 enrolled. In 2016, 35 master's, 45 other advanced degrees awarded. *Entrance requirements:* For master's, GRE or GMAT, minimum of one year of professional experience or permission from department head; two letters of reference; resume detailing previous work; for Graduate Certificate, one-page letter of intent; resume detailing previous work. Additional exam requirements/recommendations for international students: Required—TOEFL (minimum score 550 paper-based; 79 iBT). *Application deadline:* Applications are processed on a rolling basis. Application fee: $40. Electronic applications accepted. *Expenses:* Tuition, state resident: full-time $5121; part-time $569 per credit hour. Tuition, nonresident: full-time $8613; part-time $957 per credit hour. *Required fees:* $90 per term. *Financial support:* Fellowships and unspecified assistantships available. Support available to part-time students. Financial award application deadline: 7/1; financial award applicants required to submit FAFSA. *Unit head:* Dr. Charles O. Skipper, Department Head, 843-953-9811, E-mail: charles.skipper@citadel.edu. *Application contact:* Dr. Keith Plemmons, Associate Professor, 843-953-7677, E-mail: keith.plemmons@citadel.edu.
Website: http://www.citadel.edu/pmgt/

Clarkson University, Wallace H. Coulter School of Engineering, Program in Engineering and Management Systems, Schenectady, NY 12308. Offers business of energy (Advanced Certificate); engineering and management systems (MS). *Program availability:* Part-time, evening/weekend, 100% online, blended/hybrid learning. *Students:* 10 full-time (5 women), 24 part-time (8 women); includes 5 minority (1 Black or African American, non-Hispanic/Latino; 3 Asian, non-Hispanic/Latino; 1 Hispanic/Latino), 1 international. 21 applicants, 57% accepted, 9 enrolled. In 2016, 8 master's, 12 other advanced degrees awarded. *Entrance requirements:* Additional exam requirements/recommendations for international students: Required—TOEFL (minimum score 550 paper-based, 80 iBT) or IELTS (6.5). *Application deadline:* Applications are processed on a rolling basis. Application fee: $50. Electronic applications accepted. *Expenses: Tuition:* Full-time $23,400; part-time $1300 per credit hour. Tuition and fees vary according to campus/location and program. *Financial support:* Scholarships/grants available. *Unit head:* Robert Kozik, Associate Dean of Engineering, 518-631-9881, E-mail: bkozik@clarkson.edu. *Application contact:* Dan Capogna, Graduate Admissions Contact, 518-631-9910, E-mail: graduate@clarkson.edu.
Website: http://graduate.clarkson.edu

Colorado State University, Walter Scott, Jr. College of Engineering, Program in Systems Engineering, Fort Collins, CO 80523. Offers ME, MS, PhD. *Degree requirements:* For doctorate, thesis/dissertation. *Entrance requirements:* For master's, GRE General Test, minimum GPA of 3.0; for doctorate, GRE General Test, TOEFL, minimum GPA of 3.0. Electronic applications accepted. *Expenses:* Tuition, state resident: full-time $9628. Tuition, nonresident: full-time $23,603. *Required fees:* $2253; $528.14 per credit hour. $264.07 per semester. Tuition and fees vary according to course load and program. *Faculty research:* Robotic assembly, dynamics of robots, controls, manufacturability of mechanical devices and systems.

Colorado State University–Pueblo, College of Education, Engineering and Professional Studies, Department of Engineering, Pueblo, CO 81001-4901. Offers industrial and systems engineering (MS). *Degree requirements:* For master's, thesis optional. *Entrance requirements:* For master's, GRE General Test. Additional exam requirements/recommendations for international students: Required—TOEFL (minimum score 500 paper-based). *Faculty research:* Nanotechnology, applied operations, research transportation, decision analysis.

Colorado Technical University Aurora, Program in Systems Engineering, Aurora, CO 80014. Offers MS.

Colorado Technical University Colorado Springs, Graduate Studies, Program in Systems Engineering, Colorado Springs, CO 80907. Offers MS.

Concordia University, School of Graduate Studies, Faculty of Engineering and Computer Science, Concordia Institute for Information Systems Engineering (CIISE), Montréal, QC H3G 1M8, Canada. Offers 3D graphics and game development (Certificate); information and systems engineering (PhD); information systems security (M Eng, MA Sc); quality systems engineering (M Eng, MA Sc); service engineering and network management (Certificate).

Cornell University, Graduate School, Graduate Fields of Engineering, Field of Systems Engineering, Ithaca, NY 14853. Offers M Eng, PhD. *Degree requirements:* For master's, thesis. *Entrance requirements:* For master's, GRE General Test. Additional exam requirements/recommendations for international students: Required—TOEFL (minimum score 600 paper-based; 77 iBT). *Faculty research:* Space systems, systems engineering of mechanical and aerospace systems, multi-echelon inventory theory, math modeling of complex systems, chain supply integration.

Embry-Riddle Aeronautical University–Daytona, Department of Human Factors, Daytona Beach, FL 32114-3900. Offers human factors (PhD). *Program availability:* Part-time. *Faculty:* 7 full-time (2 women). *Students:* 42 full-time (19 women), 1 (woman) part-time; includes 9 minority (2 Black or African American, non-Hispanic/Latino; 1 American Indian or Alaska Native, non-Hispanic/Latino; 6 Two or more races, non-Hispanic/Latino), 5 international. Average age 26. 57 applicants, 32% accepted, 16 enrolled. In 2016, 6 master's awarded. *Degree requirements:* For master's, thesis or alternative; for doctorate, comprehensive exam, thesis/dissertation. *Entrance requirements:* For doctorate, GRE. Additional exam requirements/recommendations for international students: Required—TOEFL (minimum score 550 paper-based, 79 iBT) or IELTS (6). *Application deadline:* For fall admission, 3/1 priority date for domestic students; for spring admission, 11/1 priority date for domestic students; for summer admission, 4/1 priority date for domestic students. Applications are processed on a rolling basis. Application fee: $50. Electronic applications accepted. *Expenses: Tuition:* Full-time $16,296; part-time $1358 per credit hour. *Required fees:* $1294; $647 per semester. One-time fee: $100 full-time. Tuition and fees vary according to course load, degree level and program. *Financial support:* Research assistantships, teaching assistantships, career-related internships or fieldwork, scholarships/grants, unspecified assistantships, and on-campus employment available. Financial award application deadline: 3/15; financial award applicants required to submit FAFSA. *Unit head:* Scott Shappell, PhD, Professor/Department Chair, E-mail: scott.shappell@erau.edu. *Application contact:* Graduate Admissions, 800-862-2416, E-mail: graduate.admissions@erau.edu.
Website: http://daytonabeach.erau.edu/college-arts-sciences/human-factors/index.html

Embry-Riddle Aeronautical University–Daytona, Program in Unmanned and Autonomous Systems Engineering, Daytona Beach, FL 32114-3900. Offers systems engineering (MSUASE); technical (MSUASE); unmanned aircraft systems (MSUASE). *Program availability:* Part-time. *Degree requirements:* For master's, thesis optional. *Entrance requirements:* Additional exam requirements/recommendations for international students: Required—TOEFL (minimum score 550 paper-based; 79 iBT), IELTS (minimum score 6), TOEFL or IELTS accepted. Electronic applications accepted. *Expenses: Tuition:* Full-time $16,296; part-time $1358 per credit hour. *Required fees:* $1294; $647 per semester. One-time fee: $100 full-time. Tuition and fees vary according to course load, degree level and program.

Embry-Riddle Aeronautical University–Worldwide, Department of Aeronautics, Graduate Studies, Daytona Beach, FL 32114-3900. Offers aeronautics (MSA); aeronautics and design (MS); aviation maintenance (MAM); aviation/aerospace management (MS); education (MS); human factors (MS, MSHFS), including aerospace (MSHFS), systems engineering (MSHFS); occupational safety management (MS); operations (MS); safety/emergency response (MS); small unmanned aircraft system (SUAS) operation (MS); space systems (MS); unmanned aerospace systems (MS). *Program availability:* Part-time, evening/weekend, 100% online, blended/hybrid learning, EagleVision Classroom (between classrooms), EagleVision Home (faculty and students at home), and a blend of Classroom or Home. *Faculty:* 34 full-time (9 women), 146 part-time/adjunct (20 women). *Students:* 865 full-time (156 women), 998 part-time (163 women); includes 434 minority (179 Black or African American, non-Hispanic/Latino; 7 American Indian or Alaska Native, non-Hispanic/Latino; 65 Asian, non-Hispanic/Latino; 71 Hispanic/Latino; 4 Native Hawaiian or other Pacific Islander, non-Hispanic/Latino; 108 Two or more races, non-Hispanic/Latino), 128 international. Average age 37. In 2016, 572 master's awarded. *Degree requirements:* For master's, comprehensive exam (for some programs), thesis (for some programs), thesis or capstone project. *Entrance requirements:* For master's, GRE (for MSHFS). Additional exam requirements/recommendations for international students: Required—TOEFL (minimum score 550 paper-based, 79 iBT) or IELTS (6). *Application deadline:* Applications are processed on a rolling basis. Application fee: $50. Electronic applications accepted. *Expenses:* $620 per credit (for civilians), $530 per credit (for military). *Financial support:* Career-related internships or fieldwork and scholarships/grants available. Financial award applicants required to submit FAFSA. *Faculty research:* Aerodynamics statistical design and educational development. *Unit head:* Ian R. McAndrew, PhD, Department Chair, E-mail: ian.mcandrew@erau.edu. *Application contact:* Worldwide Campus, 800-522-6787, E-mail: worldwide@erau.edu.
Website: http://worldwide.erau.edu/colleges/aeronautics/department-aeronautics-graduate-studies/

Embry-Riddle Aeronautical University–Worldwide, Department of Decision Sciences, Daytona Beach, FL 32114-3900. Offers aviation and aerospace (MSPM); aviation/aerospace management (MSEM); financial management (MSEM, MSPM); general management (MSPM); global management (MSPM); human resources management (MSPM); information systems (MSPM); leadership (MSEM, MSPM); logistics and supply chain management (MSEM, MSLSCM, MSPM); management (MSEM, MSPM); project management (MSEM); systems engineering (MSEM, MSPM); technical management (MSPM). *Program availability:* Part-time, evening/weekend, 100% online, blended/hybrid learning, EagleVision is a virtual classroom that combines Web video conferencing and a learning management system. EagleVision Classroom (between classrooms), EagleVision Home (faculty and students at home), and a blend of Classroom or Home. *Degree requirements:* For master's, comprehensive exam (for some programs), thesis (for some programs). *Entrance requirements:* Additional exam requirements/recommendations for international students: Required—TOEFL (minimum score 550 paper-based; 79 iBT), IELTS (minimum score 6), TOEFL or IELTS accepted. Electronic applications accepted. *Expenses:* Contact institution.

Embry-Riddle Aeronautical University–Worldwide, Department of Engineering Sciences, Daytona Beach, FL 32114-3900. Offers aerospace engineering (MS); systems engineering (M Sys E), including engineering management, technical. *Program availability:* Part-time, evening/weekend, 100% online, blended/hybrid learning. *Entrance requirements:* For master's, GRE required for MSAE. Additional exam requirements/recommendations for international students: Required—TOEFL (minimum score 550 paper-based; 79 iBT), IELTS (minimum score 6), TOEFL or IELTS accepted. Electronic applications accepted. *Expenses:* Contact institution.

Florida Institute of Technology, College of Engineering, Program in Systems Engineering, Melbourne, FL 32901-6975. Offers MS, PhD. *Program availability:* Part-time. *Students:* 15 full-time (2 women), 45 part-time (4 women); includes 15 minority (2 Black or African American, non-Hispanic/Latino; 2 Asian, non-Hispanic/Latino; 11 Hispanic/Latino), 15 international. Average age 31. 43 applicants, 42% accepted, 5 enrolled. In 2016, 21 master's awarded. *Degree requirements:* For master's, comprehensive exam (for some programs), thesis optional, 30 credit hours; for doctorate, comprehensive exam, thesis/dissertation, 24 credit hours of coursework, 24 credit hours of research, technical paper presented at recognized conference. *Entrance requirements:* For master's, GRE, minimum GPA of 3.0, 3 letters of recommendation, resume, bachelor's degree in engineering from ABET-accredited program, statement of objectives; for doctorate, GRE (minimum score of 315), minimum GPA of 3.5, 3 letters of

recommendation, resume, statement of objectives. Additional exam requirements/recommendations for international students: Required—TOEFL (minimum score 550 paper-based; 79 iBT). *Application deadline:* For fall admission, 4/1 for international students; for spring admission, 9/30 for international students. Applications are processed on a rolling basis. Electronic applications accepted. *Expenses: Tuition:* Full-time $22,338; part-time $1241 per credit hour. *Required fees:* $250. Tuition and fees vary according to degree level, campus/location and program. *Financial support:* Career-related internships or fieldwork, institutionally sponsored loans, unspecified assistantships, and tuition remissions available. Support available to part-time students. Financial award application deadline: 3/1; financial award applicants required to submit FAFSA. *Faculty research:* System/software engineering, simulation and analytical modeling, project management, multimedia tools, quality. *Unit head:* Dr. Muzaffar A. Shaikh, Department Head, 321-674-7132, Fax: 321-674-7136, E-mail: mshaikh@fit.edu. *Application contact:* Cheryl A. Brown, Associate Director of Graduate Admissions, 321-674-7581, Fax: 321-723-9468, E-mail: cbrown@fit.edu.
Website: http://coe.fit.edu/se/

George Mason University, Volgenau School of Engineering, Department of Systems Engineering and Operations Research, Fairfax, VA 22030. Offers operations research (MS); systems engineering and operations research (PhD, Certificate). MS programs offered jointly with Old Dominion University, University of Virginia, Virginia Commonwealth University, and Virginia Polytechnic Institute and State University. *Faculty:* 20 full-time (5 women), 13 part-time/adjunct (0 women). *Students:* 33 full-time (9 women), 101 part-time (24 women); includes 36 minority (7 Black or African American, non-Hispanic/Latino; 19 Asian, non-Hispanic/Latino; 5 Hispanic/Latino; 5 Two or more races, non-Hispanic/Latino), 11 international. Average age 32. 91 applicants, 79% accepted, 35 enrolled. In 2016, 38 master's, 3 doctorates, 10 other advanced degrees awarded. *Degree requirements:* For master's, thesis optional; for doctorate, comprehensive exam, thesis/dissertation, qualifying exams. *Entrance requirements:* For master's, GRE General Test, BS in related field; minimum GPA of 3.0; 3 letters of recommendation; 2 official transcripts; expanded goals statement; proof of financial support; photocopy of passport; official bank statement; multivariable calculus, applied probability, statistics and a computer language course; self evaluation form; for doctorate, GRE, MS with minimum GPA of 3.5; BS with minimum GPA of 3.0 in systems or operational research; 2 official transcripts; 3 letters of recommendation; resume; expanded goals statement; self evaluation form; photocopy of passport; official bank statement; proof of financial support; for Certificate, personal goals statement; 2 official transcripts; self-evaluation form; letter of recommendation; resume; official bank statement; photocopy of passport; proof of financial support; baccalaureate degree in related field. Additional exam requirements/recommendations for international students: Required—TOEFL (minimum score 575 paper-based; 88 iBT), IELTS (minimum score 6.5), PTE (minimum score 59). *Application deadline:* For fall admission, 1/15 priority date for domestic students. Application fee: $75 ($80 for international students). Electronic applications accepted. *Expenses:* Contact institution. *Financial support:* In 2016–17, 13 students received support, including 4 research assistantships with tuition reimbursements available (averaging $18,458 per year), 9 teaching assistantships with tuition reimbursements available (averaging $13,778 per year); career-related internships or fieldwork, Federal Work-Study, scholarships/grants, unspecified assistantships, and health care benefits (for full-time research or teaching assistantship recipients) also available. Support available to part-time students. Financial award application deadline: 3/1; financial award applicants required to submit FAFSA. *Faculty research:* Requirements engineering, signal processing, systems architecture, data fusion. *Total annual research expenditures:* $531,974. *Unit head:* Ariela Sofer, Chair, 703-993-1692, Fax: 703-993-1521, E-mail: asofer@gmu.edu. *Application contact:* Andy Loerch, Associate Chair, Graduate Information, 703-993-1657, E-mail: aloerch@gmu.edu.
Website: http://seor.gmu.edu

Georgetown University, Graduate School of Arts and Sciences, School of Continuing Studies, Washington, DC 20057. Offers American studies (MALS); Catholic studies (MALS); classical civilizations (MALS); emergency and disaster management (MPS); ethics and the professions (MALS); global strategic communications (MPS); hospitality management (MPS); human resources management (MPS); humanities (MALS); individualized study (MALS); integrated marketing communications (MPS); international affairs (MALS); Islam and Muslim-Christian relations (MALS); journalism (MPS); liberal studies (DLS); literature and society (MALS); medieval and early modern European studies (MALS); public relations and corporate communications (MPS); real estate (MPS); religious studies (MALS); social and public policy (MALS); sports industry management (MPS); systems engineering management (MPS); technology management (MPS); the theory and practice of American democracy (MALS); urban and regional planning (MPS); visual culture (MALS). MPS in systems engineering management offered jointly with Stevens Institute of Technology. *Entrance requirements:* Additional exam requirements/recommendations for international students: Required—TOEFL.

The George Washington University, School of Engineering and Applied Science, Department of Engineering Management and Systems Engineering, Washington, DC 20052. Offers system engineering (PhD). *Program availability:* Part-time, evening/weekend. *Faculty:* 12 full-time (2 women). *Students:* 102 full-time (36 women), 735 part-time (235 women); includes 319 minority (171 Black or African American, non-Hispanic/Latino; 2 American Indian or Alaska Native, non-Hispanic/Latino; 94 Asian, non-Hispanic/Latino; 41 Hispanic/Latino; 4 Native Hawaiian or other Pacific Islander, non-Hispanic/Latino; 7 Two or more races, non-Hispanic/Latino), 57 international. Average age 37. 594 applicants, 69% accepted, 201 enrolled. In 2016, 211 master's, 41 doctorates, 11 other advanced degrees awarded. *Degree requirements:* For master's, thesis optional; for doctorate, one foreign language, thesis/dissertation, final and qualifying exams, submission of articles; for other advanced degree, professional project. *Entrance requirements:* For master's, appropriate bachelor's degree, minimum GPA of 2.7, second-semester calculus; for doctorate, appropriate master's degree, minimum GPA of 3.5, 2 letters of recommendation; for other advanced degree, appropriate master's degree, minimum GPA of 3.4. Additional exam requirements/recommendations for international students: Required—TOEFL or The George Washington University English as a Foreign Language Test. *Application deadline:* For fall admission, 3/1 for domestic students; for spring admission, 10/1 for domestic students. Applications are processed on a rolling basis. Application fee: $75. *Financial support:* In 2016–17, 35 students received support. Fellowships with tuition reimbursements available, research assistantships, teaching assistantships with tuition reimbursements available, career-related internships or fieldwork, and institutionally sponsored loans available. Financial award application deadline: 3/1; financial award applicants required to submit FAFSA. *Faculty research:* Artificial intelligence and expert systems, human factors engineering and systems analysis. *Total annual research expenditures:* $421,800. *Unit head:* Dr. Thomas Mazzuchi, Chair, 202-994-4892, E-mail: mazzu@gwu.edu. *Application contact:* Adina Lav, Marketing, Recruiting and Admissions, 202-994-5827, Fax: 202-994-0909, E-mail: engineering@gwu.edu.
Website: http://www.seas.gwu.edu/department-engineering-management-systems-engineering

Georgia Institute of Technology, Graduate Studies, College of Engineering, Professional Master's in Applied Systems Engineering Program, Atlanta, GA 30332-0001. Offers PMS. *Program availability:* Part-time. *Degree requirements:* For master's, capstone project. *Entrance requirements:* Additional exam requirements/recommendations for international students: Required—TOEFL (minimum score 550 paper-based; 79 iBT). Electronic applications accepted.

Georgia Southern University, Jack N. Averitt College of Graduate Studies, Allen E. Paulson College of Engineering and Information Technology, Program in Electrical and Electronic Systems, Statesboro, GA 30458. Offers MSAE. *Students:* 16 full-time (3 women), 1 part-time (0 women); includes 4 minority (3 Black or African American, non-Hispanic/Latino; 1 Hispanic/Latino), 9 international. Average age 25. 32 applicants, 69% accepted, 7 enrolled. In 2016, 3 master's awarded. *Degree requirements:* For master's, thesis optional. *Entrance requirements:* For master's, GRE, minimum GPA of 2.75. Additional exam requirements/recommendations for international students: Required—TOEFL (minimum score 550 paper-based; 80 iBT), IELTS (minimum score 6). *Application deadline:* For fall admission, 2/1 for domestic students; for spring admission, 10/1 for domestic students. Application fee: $50. Electronic applications accepted. *Expenses:* Tuition, state resident: full-time $7236; part-time $277 per semester hour. Tuition, nonresident: full-time $27,118; part-time $1105 per semester hour. *Required fees:* $2092. *Financial support:* Unspecified assistantships available. Financial award application deadline: 4/20; financial award applicants required to submit FAFSA. *Faculty research:* Programming, artificial intelligence, web systems, data mining, database systems. *Unit head:* Dr. Biswanath Samanta, Program Chair, 912-478-0334, E-mail: bsamanta@georgiasouthern.edu.

Harrisburg University of Science and Technology, Program in Information Systems Engineering and Management, Harrisburg, PA 17101. Offers analytics (MS); digital government (MS); digital health (MS); entrepreneurship (MS); information security (MS); software engineering and systems development (MS). *Program availability:* Part-time, evening/weekend. *Faculty:* 9 full-time (0 women), 1 (woman) part-time/adjunct. *Students:* 1,031 full-time (264 women), 35 part-time (10 women); includes 2 minority (1 Black or African American, non-Hispanic/Latino; 1 Asian, non-Hispanic/Latino), 1,060 international. In 2016, 83 master's awarded. *Degree requirements:* For master's, thesis optional. *Entrance requirements:* For master's, baccalaureate degree. Additional exam requirements/recommendations for international students: Required—TOEFL (minimum score 520 paper-based; 80 iBT); Recommended—IELTS (minimum score 6). *Application deadline:* Applications are processed on a rolling basis. Application fee: $0. Electronic applications accepted. *Expenses: Tuition:* Full-time $4800; part-time $800 per semester hour. *Financial support:* In 2016–17, 2 students received support. Teaching assistantships available. Financial award applicants required to submit FAFSA. *Faculty research:* Healthcare Informatics, material analysis, enterprise systems, circuit design, enterprise architectures. *Unit head:* Dr. Amjad Umar, Director and Professor, 717-901-5141, Fax: 717-901-3141, E-mail: aumar@harrisburgu.edu.

Indiana University Bloomington, School of Informatics and Computing, Program in Intelligent Systems Engineering, Bloomington, IN 47405-7000. Offers PhD. *Program availability:* Part-time. *Faculty:* 13 full-time (3 women). *Students:* 19. Average age 30. 31 applicants, 19 enrolled. *Degree requirements:* For doctorate, thesis/dissertation, qualifying exam. *Entrance requirements:* For doctorate, GRE, statement of purpose, curriculum vitae, 3 letters of recommendation, transcripts. Additional exam requirements/recommendations for international students: Required—TOEFL. *Application deadline:* Applications are processed on a rolling basis. Application fee: $55 ($65 for international students). Electronic applications accepted. *Financial support:* Fellowships, research assistantships, scholarships/grants, health care benefits, and unspecified assistantships available. *Faculty research:* Data mining, data modeling, computer networks, biophysics, biocomplexity, high performance computing, large scale computing, parallel and distributed computing, bioengineering, systems biology, computational, toxicology, experimental imaging analysis, medical modeling and data analysis, cyberinfrastructure, neuroengineering, 3D pranging, nanoengineering, high performance hardware, computer engineering, intelligent systems multimedia. *Unit head:* Geoffrey Fox, Chair, 812-856-7977, E-mail: gcf@indiana.edu. *Application contact:* Rebecca Winkle, Director of Graduate Administration, 812-855-2917, E-mail: isegrad@indiana.edu.

Indiana University–Purdue University Fort Wayne, College of Engineering, Technology, and Computer Science, Department of Electrical and Computer Engineering, Fort Wayne, IN 46805-1499. Offers computer engineering (MSE); electrical engineering (MSE); systems engineering (MSE). *Program availability:* Part-time. *Entrance requirements:* For master's, minimum GPA of 3.0, bachelor's degree in engineering discipline. Additional exam requirements/recommendations for international students: Required—TOEFL (minimum score 550 paper-based; 79 iBT); Recommended—TWE. Electronic applications accepted.

Instituto Tecnológico y de Estudios Superiores de Monterrey, Campus Chihuahua, Graduate Programs, Chihuahua, Mexico. Offers computer systems engineering (Ingeniero); electrical engineering (Ingeniero); electromechanical engineering (Ingeniero); electronic engineering (Ingeniero); engineering administration (MEA); industrial engineering (MIE, Ingeniero); international trade (MIT); mechanical engineering (Ingeniero).

Instituto Tecnológico y de Estudios Superiores de Monterrey, Campus Monterrey, Graduate and Research Division, Programs in Engineering, Monterrey, Mexico. Offers applied statistics (M Eng); artificial intelligence (PhD); automation engineering (M Eng); chemical engineering (M Eng); civil engineering (M Eng); electrical engineering (M Eng); electronic engineering (M Eng); environmental engineering (M Eng); industrial engineering (M Eng, PhD); manufacturing engineering (M Eng); mechanical engineering (M Eng); systems and quality engineering (M Eng). M Eng program offered jointly with University of Waterloo; PhD in industrial engineering with Texas A&M University. *Program availability:* Part-time, evening/weekend. Terminal master's awarded for partial completion of doctoral program. *Degree requirements:* For master's, one foreign language, thesis; for doctorate, one foreign language, thesis/dissertation. *Entrance requirements:* For master's, EXADEP; for doctorate, GRE, master's degree in related field. Additional exam requirements/recommendations for international students: Required—TOEFL. *Faculty research:* Flexible manufacturing cells, materials, statistical methods, environmental prevention, control and evaluation.

Iowa State University of Science and Technology, Program in Systems Engineering, Ames, IA 50011. Offers M Eng. *Entrance requirements:* Additional exam requirements/recommendations for international students: Required—TOEFL (minimum score 550 paper-based; 79 iBT), IELTS (minimum score 6.5). *Application deadline:* Applications are processed on a rolling basis. Application fee: $60 ($90 for international students). Electronic applications accepted. *Unit head:* Laurie Hoifeldt, Application Contact, 515-294-4702, E-mail: systems-eng@iastate.edu. *Application contact:* Holly Twedt, Application Contact, 515-294-4702.
Website: http://www.elo.iastate.edu/graduate-degrees/systems-engineering-masters-degree-online/

Johns Hopkins University, Engineering Program for Professionals, Part-time Program in Systems Engineering, Baltimore, MD 21218. Offers MS, MSE, Graduate Certificate,

Post-Master's Certificate. *Accreditation:* ABET. *Program availability:* Part-time, evening/weekend, 100% online, blended/hybrid learning. *Faculty:* 50 part-time/adjunct (10 women). *Students:* 5 full-time (1 woman), 483 part-time (117 women); includes 100 minority (22 Black or African American, non-Hispanic/Latino; 1 American Indian or Alaska Native, non-Hispanic/Latino; 28 Asian, non-Hispanic/Latino; 42 Hispanic/Latino; 7 Two or more races, non-Hispanic/Latino), 6 international. Average age 32. 152 applicants, 64% accepted, 64 enrolled. In 2016, 280 master's, 95 other advanced degrees awarded. *Degree requirements:* For master's and other advanced degree, thesis optional. *Entrance requirements:* Additional exam requirements/recommendations for international students: Required—TOEFL (minimum score 600 paper-based; 100 iBT). *Application deadline:* Applications are processed on a rolling basis. Application fee: $0. Electronic applications accepted. *Unit head:* Dr. Ronald R. Luman, Program Chair, 443-778-5239, E-mail: ronald.luman@jhuapl.edu. *Application contact:* Doug Schiller, Admissions Director, 410-516-2300, Fax: 410-579-8049, E-mail: schiller@jhu.edu.
Website: http://www.ep.jhu.edu/

Kennesaw State University, Southern Polytechnic College of Engineering and Engineering Technology, Department of Systems and Industrial Engineering, Kennesaw, GA 30144. Offers quality assurance (MS); systems engineering (MS, Graduate Certificate). *Program availability:* Part-time, evening/weekend, online learning. *Degree requirements:* For master's, thesis optional. *Entrance requirements:* For master's, GRE. Additional exam requirements/recommendations for international students: Required—TOEFL (minimum score 550 paper-based; 79 iBT), IELTS (minimum score 6.5). Electronic applications accepted. *Faculty research:* Supply chain and logistics reliability, maintainability system analysis, design optimization, engineering education.

Lehigh University, P.C. Rossin College of Engineering and Applied Science, Department of Industrial and Systems Engineering, Bethlehem, PA 18015. Offers analytical finance (MS); industrial and systems engineering (M Eng, MS, PhD); management science and engineering (M Eng, MS); MBA/E. *Program availability:* Part-time, 100% online, classroom live. *Faculty:* 19 full-time (2 women), 3 part-time/adjunct (0 women). *Students:* 102 full-time (28 women), 7 part-time (3 women); includes 1 minority (Asian, non-Hispanic/Latino), 103 international. Average age 25. 375 applicants, 35% accepted, 39 enrolled. In 2016, 36 master's, 8 doctorates awarded. Terminal master's awarded for partial completion of doctoral program. *Degree requirements:* For master's, thesis (MS); project (M Eng); for doctorate, comprehensive exam, thesis/dissertation. *Entrance requirements:* For master's and doctorate, GRE General Test. Additional exam requirements/recommendations for international students: Required—TOEFL (minimum score 550 paper-based; 79 iBT), IELTS (minimum score 6.5). *Application deadline:* For fall admission, 7/15 for domestic and international students; for spring admission, 12/1 for domestic and international students. Application fee: $75. Electronic applications accepted. *Expenses:* $1,420 per credit hour. *Financial support:* In 2016–17, 33 students received support, including 2 fellowships with full tuition reimbursements available (averaging $20,490 per year), 18 research assistantships with full tuition reimbursements available (averaging $20,490 per year), 11 teaching assistantships with full tuition reimbursements available (averaging $21,105 per year); unspecified assistantships also available. Financial award application deadline: 1/15. *Faculty research:* Mathematical optimization; logistics and service systems, stochastic processes and simulation; computational optimization and high performance computing; financial engineering and robust optimization; machine learning and data mining. *Total annual research expenditures:* $1.7 million. *Unit head:* Dr. Tamas Terlaky, Chair, 610-758-4050, Fax: 610-758-4886, E-mail: terlaky@lehigh.edu. *Application contact:* Rita Frey, Graduate Coordinator, 610-758-4051, Fax: 610-758-4886, E-mail: ise@lehigh.edu.
Website: http://www.lehigh.edu/ise

Lehigh University, P.C. Rossin College of Engineering and Applied Science, Program in Manufacturing Systems Engineering, Bethlehem, PA 18015. Offers MS, MBA/E. *Program availability:* Part-time, blended/hybrid learning. *Faculty:* 2 full-time (0 women), 2 part-time/adjunct (0 women). *Students:* 5 full-time (0 women), 15 part-time (5 women); includes 3 minority (1 Asian, non-Hispanic/Latino; 2 Hispanic/Latino), 5 international. Average age 30. 10 applicants, 90% accepted, 6 enrolled. In 2016, 8 master's awarded. *Degree requirements:* For master's, comprehensive exam, project or thesis. *Entrance requirements:* For master's, GRE General Test, minimum GPA of 2.75. Additional exam requirements/recommendations for international students: Required—TOEFL (minimum score 620 paper-based; 85 iBT). *Application deadline:* For fall admission, 7/15 priority date for domestic students, 7/15 for international students; for spring admission, 12/1 priority date for domestic students, 12/1 for international students. Applications are processed on a rolling basis. Application fee: $75. Electronic applications accepted. *Expenses:* $1,420 per credit. *Faculty research:* Manufacturing systems design, development, and implementation; accounting and management; agile/lean systems; supply chain issues; sustainable systems design; product design; development of applications for novel materials. *Unit head:* Dr. Keith M. Gardiner, Director, 610-758-5070, Fax: 610-758-6527, E-mail: kg03@lehigh.edu. *Application contact:* Carolyn C. Jones, Graduate Coordinator, 610-758-5157, Fax: 610-758-6527, E-mail: ccj1@lehigh.edu.
Website: https://mse.lehigh.edu/

Loyola Marymount University, College of Business Administration, MBA/MS Program in Systems Engineering, Los Angeles, CA 90045. Offers MBA/MS. *Program availability:* Part-time. *Students:* 5 full-time (2 women), 2 part-time (1 woman); includes 3 minority (1 Black or African American, non-Hispanic/Latino; 2 Hispanic/Latino). Average age 37. 1 applicant. *Entrance requirements:* Additional exam requirements/recommendations for international students: Required—TOEFL (minimum score 600 paper-based; 100 iBT). *Application deadline:* For fall admission, 7/15 for domestic students; for spring admission, 12/15 for domestic students. Application fee: $50. Electronic applications accepted. *Expenses:* Contact institution. *Financial support:* In 2016–17, 3 students received support. Career-related internships or fieldwork, institutionally sponsored loans, scholarships/grants, and unspecified assistantships available. Financial award application deadline: 6/30; financial award applicants required to submit FAFSA. *Unit head:* Dr. Frederick S. Brown, Director, 310-338-7878, E-mail: fbrown@lmu.edu. *Application contact:* Chake H. Kouyoumjian, Associate Dean of Graduate Studies, 310-338-2721, E-mail: ckouyoum@lmu.edu.
Website: http://cse.lmu.edu/graduateprograms/systemsengineering/systemsengineeringandleadershipprogramdualdegreemsandmba/#d.en.124341

Loyola Marymount University, College of Science and Engineering, Department of Systems Engineering and Engineering Management, Program in Healthcare Systems Engineering, Los Angeles, CA 90045-2659. Offers MS. *Students:* 10 full-time (5 women), 1 (woman) part-time; includes 7 minority (1 Black or African American, non-Hispanic/Latino; 3 Asian, non-Hispanic/Latino; 2 Hispanic/Latino; 1 Two or more races, non-Hispanic/Latino), 1 international. Average age 27. *Entrance requirements:* For master's, bachelor's degree in science and engineering, minimum cumulative GPA of 3.0, 3 letters of recommendation, essay. Additional exam requirements/recommendations for international students: Required—TOEFL. *Application deadline:* Applications are processed on a rolling basis. Application fee: $50. Electronic

applications accepted. *Financial support:* In 2016–17, 6 students received support. *Unit head:* Dr. Frederick S. Brown. *Application contact:* Chake H. Kouyoumjian, Associate Dean of Graduate Studies, 310-338-2721, E-mail: ckouyoum@lmu.edu.
Website: http://cse.lmu.edu/graduateprograms/systemsengineering/msdegreeprograminhealthcaresystemsengineering

Loyola Marymount University, College of Science and Engineering, Department of Systems Engineering and Engineering Management, Program in System Engineering Leadership, Los Angeles, CA 90045-2659. Offers MS/MBA. *Students:* 5 full-time (2 women), 2 part-time (1 woman); includes 3 minority (1 Black or African American, non-Hispanic/Latino; 2 Hispanic/Latino). Average age 37. 1 applicant. *Entrance requirements:* Additional exam requirements/recommendations for international students: Required—TOEFL (minimum score 600 paper-based; 100 iBT). *Application deadline:* For fall admission, 7/15 for domestic students; for spring admission, 12/15 for domestic students. Applications are processed on a rolling basis. Application fee: $50. Electronic applications accepted. *Financial support:* In 2016–17, 3 students received support. Scholarships/grants and unspecified assistantships available. Support available to part-time students. Financial award application deadline: 6/30; financial award applicants required to submit FAFSA. *Unit head:* Dr. Frederick S. Brown, Graduate Director, 310-338-7878, E-mail: fbrown@lmu.edu. *Application contact:* Chake H. Kouyoumjian, Associate Dean for Graduate Studies, 310-338-2721, E-mail: ckouyoum@lmu.edu.
Website: http://cse.lmu.edu/graduateprograms/systemsengineering/systemsengineeringandleadershipprogramdualdegreemsandmba/#d.en.124341

Loyola Marymount University, College of Science and Engineering, Department of Systems Engineering and Engineering Management, Program in Systems Engineering, Los Angeles, CA 90045. Offers MS. *Students:* 21 full-time (4 women), 3 part-time (2 women); includes 9 minority (1 Black or African American, non-Hispanic/Latino; 5 Asian, non-Hispanic/Latino; 3 Hispanic/Latino), 6 international. Average age 32. 27 applicants, 78% accepted, 6 enrolled. In 2016, 37 master's awarded. *Entrance requirements:* For master's, personal statement, resume, letters of recommendation. Additional exam requirements/recommendations for international students: Required—TOEFL (minimum score 550 paper-based; 80 iBT). *Application deadline:* For fall admission, 7/15 for domestic students; for spring admission, 12/15 for domestic students. Applications are processed on a rolling basis. Application fee: $50. Electronic applications accepted. *Financial support:* In 2016–17, 3 students received support. Scholarships/grants and unspecified assistantships available. Support available to part-time students. Financial award application deadline: 6/30; financial award applicants required to submit FAFSA. *Unit head:* Dr. Frederick S. Brown, Program Director, 310-338-7878, E-mail: fbrown@lmu.edu. *Application contact:* Chake H. Kouyoumjian, Associate Dean of Graduate Studies, 310-338-2721, E-mail: ckouyoum@lmu.edu.
Website: http://cse.lmu.edu/graduateprograms/systemsengineering/

Massachusetts Institute of Technology, School of Engineering, Institute for Data, Systems, and Society, Cambridge, MA 02139. Offers social and engineering systems (PhD); technology and policy (SM). *Faculty:* 4 full-time (2 women). *Students:* 112 full-time (43 women), 1 part-time; includes 15 minority (1 Black or African American, non-Hispanic/Latino; 8 Asian, non-Hispanic/Latino; 3 Hispanic/Latino; 3 Two or more races, non-Hispanic/Latino), 54 international. Average age 27. 659 applicants, 18% accepted, 84 enrolled. In 2016, 82 master's, 8 doctorates awarded. *Degree requirements:* For master's, thesis; for doctorate, comprehensive exam, thesis/dissertation. *Entrance requirements:* For doctorate, GRE General Test. Additional exam requirements/recommendations for international students: Required—IELTS. *Application deadline:* For fall admission, 12/15 for domestic and international students. Application fee: $75. Electronic applications accepted. *Expenses: Tuition:* Full-time $46,400; part-time $725 per credit. One-time fee: $312 full-time. Full-time tuition and fees vary according to course load and program. *Financial support:* In 2016–17, 97 students received support, including fellowships (averaging $38,400 per year), 66 research assistantships (averaging $36,100 per year), 8 teaching assistantships (averaging $38,300 per year); Federal Work-Study, institutionally sponsored loans, traineeships, health care benefits, unspecified assistantships, and resident tutors also available. Support available to part-time students. Financial award application deadline: 5/1; financial award applicants required to submit FAFSA. *Faculty research:* Information theory and decision systems; sociotechnical systems; statistics and data science; network science; critical infrastructures; health care delivery; humans and technology; policy and standards; social behavior; uncertainty, risk, and dynamics. *Total annual research expenditures:* $9.5 million. *Unit head:* Munther A. Dahleh, Department Head, 617-253-3300, E-mail: idss-info@mit.edu. *Application contact:* 617-253-1182, E-mail: idss_academic_office@mit.edu.
Website: http://idss.mit.edu/

Massachusetts Institute of Technology, School of Engineering, System Design and Management Program, Cambridge, MA 02139-4307. Offers engineering and management (SM). Offered jointly with MIT Sloan School of Management. *Students:* 147 full-time (45 women); includes 22 minority (2 Black or African American, non-Hispanic/Latino; 11 Asian, non-Hispanic/Latino; 7 Hispanic/Latino; 2 Two or more races, non-Hispanic/Latino), 86 international. Average age 32. 261 applicants, 36% accepted, 79 enrolled. In 2016, 73 master's awarded. *Degree requirements:* For master's, thesis. Application fee: $75. *Expenses: Tuition:* Full-time $46,400; part-time $725 per credit. One-time fee: $312 full-time. Full-time tuition and fees vary according to course load and program. *Financial support:* In 2016–17, 45 students received support, including 8 fellowships (averaging $40,500 per year), 11 research assistantships (averaging $28,400 per year), 22 teaching assistantships (averaging $29,800 per year); Federal Work-Study, institutionally sponsored loans, scholarships/grants, traineeships, health care benefits, unspecified assistantships, and graduate resident tutors also available. Financial award application deadline: 5/1; financial award applicants required to submit FAFSA. *Faculty research:* Humans and technology; information theory and decision systems; sociotechnical systems; policy and standards; social behavior; uncertainty, risk, and dynamics. *Application contact:* Information Contact, 617-425-2432, Fax: 617-253-1462, E-mail: sdm@mit.edu.

Mississippi State University, Bagley College of Engineering, Department of Industrial and Systems Engineering, Mississippi State, MS 39762. Offers human factors and ergonomics (MS); industrial and systems engineering (PhD); industrial systems (MS); management systems (MS); manufacturing systems (MS); operations research (MS). *Program availability:* Part-time, blended/hybrid learning. *Faculty:* 12 full-time (1 woman). *Students:* 25 full-time (5 women), 59 part-time (13 women); includes 18 minority (6 Black or African American, non-Hispanic/Latino; 5 Asian, non-Hispanic/Latino; 6 Hispanic/Latino; 1 Native Hawaiian or other Pacific Islander, non-Hispanic/Latino), 21 international. Average age 35. 72 applicants, 32% accepted, 11 enrolled. In 2016, 11 master's, 7 doctorates awarded. *Degree requirements:* For master's, comprehensive exam (for some programs), thesis optional, comprehensive oral or written exam; for doctorate, comprehensive exam, thesis/dissertation, candidacy exam. *Entrance requirements:* For master's, GRE (for graduates from program not accredited by EAC/ABET), minimum GPA of 3.0 on junior and senior years; for doctorate, GRE (for graduates from program not accredited by EAC/ABET), minimum GPA of 3.5 on master's degree and junior and senior years of BS. Additional exam requirements/

recommendations for international students: Required—TOEFL (minimum score 550 paper-based; 79 iBT); Recommended—IELTS (minimum score 6.5). *Application deadline:* For fall admission, 7/1 for domestic students, 5/1 for international students; for spring admission, 11/1 for domestic students, 9/1 for international students. Applications are processed on a rolling basis. Application fee: $60. Electronic applications accepted. *Expenses:* Tuition, state resident: full-time $7670; part-time $852.50 per credit hour. Tuition, nonresident: full-time $20,790; part-time $2310.50 per credit hour. Part-time tuition and fees vary according to course load. *Financial support:* In 2016–17, 12 research assistantships with full tuition reimbursements (averaging $16,360 per year), 3 teaching assistantships with full tuition reimbursements (averaging $17,014 per year) were awarded; Federal Work-Study, institutionally sponsored loans, and unspecified assistantships also available. Financial award application deadline: 4/1; financial award applicants required to submit FAFSA. *Faculty research:* Operations research, ergonomics, production systems, management systems, transportation. *Total annual research expenditures:* $4.4 million. *Unit head:* Dr. John Usher, Professor/Department Head, 662-325-7624, Fax: 662-325-7618, E-mail: usher@ise.msstate.edu. *Application contact:* Doretta Martin, Senior Admissions Assistant, 662-325-9514, E-mail: dmartin@grad.msstate.edu.
Website: http://www.ise.msstate.edu/

Missouri University of Science and Technology, Graduate School, Department of Engineering Management and Systems Engineering, Rolla, MO 65409. Offers engineering management (MS, DE, PhD); manufacturing engineering (M Eng, MS); systems engineering (MS, PhD). *Degree requirements:* For master's, thesis optional; for doctorate, comprehensive exam. *Entrance requirements:* For master's, GRE (minimum score 1150 verbal and quantitative, 4.5 writing); for doctorate, GRE (minimum score: 1100 verbal and quantitative, 3.5 writing). Additional exam requirements/recommendations for international students: Required—TOEFL (minimum score 580 paper-based). Electronic applications accepted. *Faculty research:* Management of technology, industrial engineering, manufacturing engineering, packaging engineering, quality engineering.

Naval Postgraduate School, Departments and Academic Groups, Department of Systems Engineering, Monterey, CA 93943. Offers engineering systems (MS); product development (MS); systems engineering (MS, PhD, Certificate); systems engineering analysis (MS, PhD); systems engineering management (MS, PhD). Program only open to commissioned officers of the United States and friendly nations and selected United States federal civilian employees. *Accreditation:* ABET. *Program availability:* Part-time. *Degree requirements:* For master's, thesis (for some programs), internal project, capstone project, or research/dissertation paper (for some programs); for doctorate, thesis/dissertation (for some programs), internal project, capstone project, or research/dissertation paper (for some programs). *Faculty research:* Net-centric enterprise systems/services, artificial intelligence (AI) systems engineering, unconventional weapons of mass destruction, complex systems engineering, risk-benefit analysis.

New Mexico Institute of Mining and Technology, Center for Graduate Studies, Department of Mechanical Engineering, Socorro, NM 87801. Offers explosives engineering (MS); fluid and thermal sciences (MS); mechatronics systems engineering (MS); solid mechanics (MS). *Degree requirements:* For master's, thesis (for some programs). *Entrance requirements:* For master's, GRE General Test. Additional exam requirements/recommendations for international students: Required—TOEFL (minimum score 540 paper-based). *Faculty research:* Vibrations, fluid-structure interactions.

New Mexico State University, College of Engineering, Department of Industrial Engineering, Las Cruces, NM 88003. Offers industrial engineering (MSIE, PhD); systems engineering (Graduate Certificate). *Program availability:* Part-time-only, evening/weekend, 100% online. *Faculty:* 6 full-time (3 women). *Students:* 40 full-time (9 women), 87 part-time (23 women); includes 48 minority (9 Black or African American, non-Hispanic/Latino; 1 American Indian or Alaska Native, non-Hispanic/Latino; 2 Asian, non-Hispanic/Latino; 32 Hispanic/Latino; 4 Two or more races, non-Hispanic/Latino), 30 international. Average age 33. 96 applicants, 55% accepted, 38 enrolled. In 2016, 48 master's, 3 doctorates, 2 other advanced degrees awarded. *Degree requirements:* For master's, thesis optional; for doctorate, comprehensive exam, thesis/dissertation, qualifying exam. *Entrance requirements:* Additional exam requirements/recommendations for international students: Required—TOEFL (minimum score 550 paper-based; 79 iBT), IELTS (minimum score 6.5). *Application deadline:* For fall admission, 7/1 priority date for domestic students, 3/1 for international students; for spring admission, 11/1 for domestic students, 10/1 for international students. Applications are processed on a rolling basis. Application fee: $40 ($50 for international students). Electronic applications accepted. *Expenses:* Tuition, state resident: full-time $4086. Tuition, nonresident: full-time $14,254. *Required fees:* $853. Tuition and fees vary according to course load. *Financial support:* In 2016–17, 33 students received support, including 1 research assistantship (averaging $16,964 per year), 5 teaching assistantships (averaging $15,712 per year); career-related internships or fieldwork, Federal Work-Study, scholarships/grants, traineeships, health care benefits, and unspecified assistantships also available. Support available to part-time students. Financial award application deadline: 3/1. *Faculty research:* Operations research, simulation, manufacturing engineering, systems engineering, applied statistics. *Total annual research expenditures:* $154,041. *Unit head:* Dr. Edward Pines, Department Head, 575-646-4923, Fax: 575-646-2976, E-mail: epines@nmsu.edu. *Application contact:* 575-646-4923, Fax: 575-646-2976, E-mail: ie@nmsu.edu.
Website: http://ie.nmsu.edu

New York University, Polytechnic School of Engineering, Department of Electrical and Computer Engineering, Major in Systems Engineering, New York, NY 10012-1019. Offers MS. *Program availability:* Part-time, evening/weekend, online learning. *Degree requirements:* For master's, comprehensive exam (for some programs), thesis (for some programs). *Entrance requirements:* For master's, BS in electrical engineering. Additional exam requirements/recommendations for international students: Required—TOEFL (minimum score 550 paper-based; 80 iBT); Recommended—IELTS (minimum score 6.5). Electronic applications accepted.

North Carolina Agricultural and Technical State University, School of Graduate Studies, College of Engineering, Department of Industrial and Systems Engineering, Greensboro, NC 27411. Offers industrial engineering (MSIE, PhD). *Program availability:* Part-time. *Degree requirements:* For master's, thesis, project; for doctorate, thesis/dissertation. *Entrance requirements:* For master's, GRE General Test (recommended); for doctorate, GRE General Test, degree in engineering, BS in industrial engineering from ABET-accredited program with minimum cumulative credit point average of 3.7 or MS in discipline related to industrial engineering from college or university recognized by a regional or general accrediting agency with minimum cumulative GPA of 3.3. Additional exam requirements/recommendations for international students: Required—TOEFL (minimum score 550 paper-based; 79 iBT). *Faculty research:* Human-machine systems engineering, management systems engineering, operations research and systems analysis, production systems engineering.

Northeastern University, College of Engineering, Boston, MA 02115-5096. Offers bioengineering (MS, PhD); chemical engineering (MS, PhD); civil engineering (MS, PhD); computer engineering (PhD); computer systems engineering (MS); electrical and computer engineering (MS); electrical and computer engineering leadership (MS); electrical engineering (PhD); energy systems (MS); engineering and public policy (MS); engineering management (MS, Certificate); environmental engineering (MS); industrial engineering (MS, PhD); information assurance (PhD); information systems (MS); interdisciplinary engineering (PhD); mechanical engineering (PhD); operations research (MS); telecommunication systems management (MS). *Program availability:* Part-time, online learning. *Faculty:* 202 full-time (59 women), 53 part-time/adjunct (9 women). *Students:* 2,982 full-time (954 women), 192 part-time (38 women). In 2016, 851 master's, 74 doctorates awarded. Application fee: $75. Electronic applications accepted. *Expenses:* $1,471 per credit. *Financial support:* Fellowships, research assistantships, teaching assistantships, career-related internships or fieldwork, scholarships/grants, health care benefits, tuition waivers, and unspecified assistantships available. Support available to part-time students. Financial award applicants required to submit FAFSA. *Unit head:* Dr. Nadine Aubry, Dean, College of Engineering. *Application contact:* Jeffery Hengel, Director of Graduate Admissions, 617-373-2711, E-mail: j.hengel@northeastern.edu.
Website: http://www.coe.neu.edu/academics/graduate-school-engineering

Oakland University, Graduate Study and Lifelong Learning, School of Engineering and Computer Science, Department of Industrial and Systems Engineering, Rochester, MI 48309-4401. Offers engineering management (MS); industrial and systems engineering (MS); productivity improvement (Graduate Certificate); systems engineering (PhD).

The Ohio State University, Graduate School, College of Engineering, Department of Integrated Systems Engineering, Columbus, OH 43210. Offers industrial and systems engineering (MS, PhD). *Faculty:* 21. *Students:* 89 full-time (21 women), 5 part-time (1 woman), 68 international. Average age 27. In 2016, 33 master's, 9 doctorates awarded. *Degree requirements:* For master's, thesis optional; for doctorate, thesis/dissertation. *Entrance requirements:* For master's and doctorate, GRE General Test (desired minimum scores: Quantitative 166, Verbal 153, Analytical Writing 4.5). Additional exam requirements/recommendations for international students: Required—TOEFL (minimum score 550 paper-based; 79 iBT), Michigan English Language Assessment Battery (minimum score 82); Recommended—IELTS (minimum score 7). *Application deadline:* For fall admission, 12/13 priority date for domestic students, 11/30 priority date for international students; for spring admission, 12/4 for domestic students, 10/1 for international students; for summer admission, 2/1 for domestic and international students. Applications are processed on a rolling basis. Application fee: $60 ($70 for international students). Electronic applications accepted. *Financial support:* Fellowships with tuition reimbursements, research assistantships with tuition reimbursements, teaching assistantships with tuition reimbursements, career-related internships or fieldwork, Federal Work-Study, institutionally sponsored loans, and unspecified assistantships available. Support available to part-time students. *Unit head:* Dr. Philip J. Smith, Chair, 614-292-4120, E-mail: smith.131@osu.edu. *Application contact:* Dr. Jerald Brevik, Graduate Studies Chair, 614-292-0177, Fax: 614-292-7852, E-mail: brevik.1@osu.edu.
Website: http://ise.osu.edu/

Ohio University, Graduate College, Russ College of Engineering and Technology, Department of Industrial and Systems Engineering, Athens, OH 45701-2979. Offers M Eng Mgt, MS. *Program availability:* Part-time, evening/weekend. *Degree requirements:* For master's, comprehensive exam (for some programs), thesis optional, research project. *Entrance requirements:* For master's, GRE General Test. Additional exam requirements/recommendations for international students: Required—TOEFL (minimum score 550 paper-based; 80 iBT) or IELTS (minimum score 6.5). *Application deadline:* For fall admission, 3/1 priority date for domestic and international students; for winter admission, 9/1 priority date for domestic and international students; for spring admission, 1/1 priority date for domestic and international students. Applications are processed on a rolling basis. Application fee: $50 ($55 for international students). Electronic applications accepted. *Financial support:* Research assistantships with full tuition reimbursements, Federal Work-Study, institutionally sponsored loans, tuition waivers (full), and unspecified assistantships available. Financial award application deadline: 2/15; financial award applicants required to submit FAFSA. *Faculty research:* Software systems integration, human factors and ergonomics. *Unit head:* Dr. Robert P. Judd, Chairman, 740-593-0106, Fax: 740-593-0778, E-mail: judd@ohio.edu. *Application contact:* Dr. Gursel Suer, Graduate Chairman, 740-593-1542, Fax: 740-593-0778, E-mail: suer@ohio.edu.
Website: http://www.ohio.edu/industrial/

Old Dominion University, Frank Batten College of Engineering and Technology, Program in Engineering Management and Systems Engineering, Norfolk, VA 23529. Offers D Eng, PhD. *Program availability:* Part-time, evening/weekend, 100% online, blended/hybrid learning. *Faculty:* 14 full-time (2 women), 12 part-time/adjunct (2 women). *Students:* 1 (woman) full-time, 14 part-time (4 women); includes 5 minority (1 Black or African American, non-Hispanic/Latino; 2 Asian, non-Hispanic/Latino; 2 Hispanic/Latino). Average age 46. 3 applicants, 67% accepted, 2 enrolled. In 2016, 2 doctorates awarded. *Degree requirements:* For doctorate, thesis/dissertation, candidacy exam, project. *Entrance requirements:* For doctorate, GRE, resume, letters of recommendation, minimum GPA of 3.0, interview. Additional exam requirements/recommendations for international students: Required—TOEFL (minimum score 550 paper-based; 79 iBT). *Application deadline:* For fall admission, 6/1 priority date for domestic students, 4/15 for international students; for spring admission, 11/1 priority date for domestic students, 2/1 for international students. Applications are processed on a rolling basis. Application fee: $50. Electronic applications accepted. *Expenses:* Tuition, state resident: full-time $8604; part-time $478 per credit hour. Tuition, nonresident: full-time $21,510; part-time $1195 per credit hour. *Required fees:* $66 per semester. Tuition and fees vary according to campus/location, program and reciprocity agreements. *Financial support:* In 2016–17, 22 students received support, including 5 research assistantships with full tuition reimbursements available (averaging $23,250 per year), 12 teaching assistantships with full tuition reimbursements available (averaging $23,250 per year); career-related internships or fieldwork and tuition waivers (full and partial) also available. Support available to part-time students. Financial award application deadline: 2/15; financial award applicants required to submit FAFSA. *Faculty research:* Project management, systems engineering, modeling and simulation, virtual collaboration environments, multidisciplinary designs, human systems engineering, decision analysis. *Total annual research expenditures:* $729,085. *Unit head:* Dr. Andres Sousa-Poza, Department Chair, 757-683-4558, Fax: 757-683-5640, E-mail: enmagpd@odu.edu. *Application contact:* Dr. Patrick Hester, Graduate Program Director, 757-683-4558, Fax: 757-683-5640, E-mail: enmagpd@odu.edu.
Website: http://eng.odu.edu/enma/

Old Dominion University, Frank Batten College of Engineering and Technology, Program in Systems Engineering, Norfolk, VA 23529. Offers ME. *Program availability:* Part-time, evening/weekend, online learning. *Faculty:* 14 full-time (2 women), 12 part-time/adjunct (2 women). *Students:* 2 full-time (0 women), 30 part-time (4 women); includes 15 minority (9 Black or African American, non-Hispanic/Latino; 3 Asian, non-Hispanic/Latino; 2 Hispanic/Latino; 1 Two or more races, non-Hispanic/Latino), 1 international. Average age 34. 16 applicants, 81% accepted, 11 enrolled. In 2016, 18 master's awarded. *Degree requirements:* For master's, comprehensive exam, project. *Entrance requirements:* For master's, GRE, minimum GPA of 3.0. Additional exam

requirements/recommendations for international students: Required—TOEFL (minimum score 550 paper-based; 79 iBT). *Application deadline:* For fall admission, 6/1 priority date for domestic students, 4/15 for international students; for spring admission, 11/1 priority date for domestic students, 2/1 for international students. Applications are processed on a rolling basis. Application fee: $50. Electronic applications accepted. *Expenses:* $478 per credit. *Financial support:* In 2016–17, 22 students received support, including 5 research assistantships with full tuition reimbursements available (averaging $23,250 per year), 12 teaching assistantships with full tuition reimbursements available (averaging $23,250 per year); career-related internships or fieldwork, scholarships/grants, and tuition waivers (full and partial) also available. Support available to part-time students. Financial award application deadline: 2/15; financial award applicants required to submit FAFSA. *Faculty research:* System of systems engineering, complex systems, optimization. *Total annual research expenditures:* $729,085. *Unit head:* Dr. Andres Sousa-Poza, Chair, 757-683-4558, Fax: 757-683-5640, E-mail: asousapo@odu.edu. *Application contact:* Dr. Pilar Pazos, Graduate Program Director, 757-683-5540, Fax: 757-683-5640, E-mail: enmagpd@odu.edu.
Website: http://eng.odu.edu/enma/academics/systemsengr.shtml

Oregon State University, College of Engineering, Program in Industrial Engineering, Corvallis, OR 97331. Offers advanced manufacturing (M Eng, MS, PhD); engineering management (M Eng); human systems engineering (M Eng, MS, PhD); information systems engineering (M Eng, MS, PhD). *Program availability:* 100% online. *Faculty:* 52 full-time (12 women), 3 part-time/adjunct (0 women). *Students:* 75 full-time (18 women), 28 part-time (11 women); includes 14 minority (1 American Indian or Alaska Native, non-Hispanic/Latino; 7 Asian, non-Hispanic/Latino; 4 Hispanic/Latino; 2 Two or more races, non-Hispanic/Latino), 56 international. Average age 29. 158 applicants, 33% accepted, 35 enrolled. In 2016, 19 master's, 3 doctorates awarded. *Entrance requirements:* For master's and doctorate, GRE. Additional exam requirements/recommendations for international students: Required—TOEFL (minimum score 80 iBT), IELTS (minimum score 6.5). *Application deadline:* For fall admission, 8/1 for domestic students, 4/1 for international students; for winter admission, 12/1 for domestic students, 7/1 for international students; for spring admission, 2/1 for domestic students, 10/1 for international students; for summer admission, 5/1 for domestic students, 1/1 for international students. Application fee: $75 ($85 for international students). *Expenses:* $14,130 resident full-time tuition, $23,769 non-resident. *Financial support:* Application deadline: 1/15. *Unit head:* Dr. Harriet Nembhard, School Head. *Application contact:* Jean Robinson, Advisor, E-mail: jean.robinson@oregonstate.edu.
Website: http://mime.oregonstate.edu/academics/grad/ie

Penn State Great Valley, Graduate Studies, Engineering Division, Malvern, PA 19355-1488. Offers engineering management (MEM); software engineering (MSE); systems engineering (M Eng, Certificate). *Unit head:* Dr. James A. Nemes, Chancellor, 610-648-3202 Ext. 610, Fax: 610-725-5296, E-mail: cse1@psu.edu. *Application contact:* JoAnn Kelly, Director of Admissions, 610-648-3315, Fax: 610-725-5296, E-mail: jek2@psu.edu.
Website: http://greatvalley.psu.edu/academics/masters-degrees/systems-engineering

Regis University, College of Computer and Information Sciences, Denver, CO 80221-1099. Offers agile technologies (Certificate); cybersecurity (Certificate); data science (M Sc); database administration with Oracle (Certificate); database development (Certificate); database technologies (M Sc); enterprise Java software development (Certificate); enterprise resource planning (Certificate); executive information technology (Certificate); health care informatics (Certificate); health care informatics and information management (M Sc); information assurance (M Sc); information assurance policy management (Certificate); information technology management (M Sc); mobile software development (Certificate); software engineering (M Sc, Certificate); software engineering and database technology (M Sc); storage area networks (Certificate); systems engineering (M Sc, Certificate). *Program availability:* Part-time, evening/weekend, 100% online, blended/hybrid learning. *Faculty:* 11 full-time (3 women), 30 part-time/adjunct (10 women). *Students:* 341 full-time (95 women), 318 part-time (98 women); includes 186 minority (56 Black or African American, non-Hispanic/Latino; 2 American Indian or Alaska Native, non-Hispanic/Latino; 48 Asian, non-Hispanic/Latino; 63 Hispanic/Latino; 17 Two or more races, non-Hispanic/Latino), 57 international. Average age 37. 342 applicants, 79% accepted, 174 enrolled. In 2016, 192 master's awarded. *Degree requirements:* For master's, thesis (for some programs), final research project. *Entrance requirements:* For master's, official transcript reflecting baccalaureate degree awarded from regionally-accredited college or university, 2 years of related experience, resume, interview. Additional exam requirements/recommendations for international students: Required—TOEFL (minimum score 550 paper-based; 82 iBT). *Application deadline:* For fall admission, 8/15 priority date for domestic students, 7/13 for international students; for winter admission, 10/10 priority date for domestic students, 9/8 for international students; for spring admission, 1/10 priority date for domestic students, 11/17 for international students; for summer admission, 5/1 priority date for domestic students. Applications are processed on a rolling basis. Application fee: $75. Electronic applications accepted. *Expenses:* $730 per credit hour. *Financial support:* Scholarships/grants available. Financial award application deadline: 4/15; financial award applicants required to submit FAFSA. *Faculty research:* Information policy, knowledge management, software architectures, data science. *Unit head:* Shari Plantz-Masters, Academic Dean. *Application contact:* Cate Clark, Director of Admissions, 303-458-4900, Fax: 303-964-5534, E-mail: ruadmissions@regis.edu.
Website: http://regis.edu/CCIS.aspx

Rensselaer Polytechnic Institute, Graduate School, School of Engineering, Program in Computer and Systems Engineering, Troy, NY 12180-3590. Offers M Eng, MS, D Eng, PhD. *Faculty:* 39 full-time (7 women), 1 part-time/adjunct (0 women). *Students:* 13 full-time (4 women), 2 part-time (0 women), 10 international. Average age 27. 49 applicants, 24% accepted, 5 enrolled. In 2016, 2 master's, 1 doctorate awarded. Terminal master's awarded for partial completion of doctoral program. *Degree requirements:* For master's, thesis (for some programs); for doctorate, thesis/dissertation. *Entrance requirements:* For master's and doctorate, GRE. Additional exam requirements/recommendations for international students: Required—TOEFL (minimum score 570 paper-based; 88 iBT), IELTS (minimum score 6.5), PTE (minimum score 60). *Application deadline:* For fall admission, 1/1 priority date for domestic and international students; for spring admission, 8/15 priority date for domestic and international students. Applications are processed on a rolling basis. Application fee: $75. Electronic applications accepted. *Expenses:* Tuition: Full-time $49,520; part-time $2060 per credit hour. *Required fees:* $2617. *Financial support:* In 2016–17, research assistantships (averaging $22,000 per year), teaching assistantships (averaging $22,000 per year) were awarded; fellowships also available. Financial award application deadline: 1/1. *Faculty research:* Communications, information, and signals and systems; computer engineering, hardware, and architecture; computer networking; control, robotics, and automation; energy sources and systems; image science: computer vision, image processing, and geographic information science; microelectronics, photonics, VLSI, and mixed-signal design; plasma science and electromagnetics. *Unit head:* Dr. Ken Vastola, Graduate Program Director, 518-576-6074, E-mail: gpd@ecse.rpi.edu. *Application contact:* Office of Graduate Admissions, 518-276-6216, E-mail: gradadmissions@

rpi.edu.
Website: http://www.ecse.rpi.edu/

Rensselaer Polytechnic Institute, Graduate School, School of Engineering, Program in Decision Sciences and Engineering Systems, Troy, NY 12180-3590. Offers PhD. *Faculty:* 2 full-time (both women). *Students:* 18 full-time (6 women). 27 applicants, 30% accepted, 5 enrolled. In 2016, 2 doctorates awarded. Terminal master's awarded for partial completion of doctoral program. *Degree requirements:* For doctorate, thesis/dissertation. *Entrance requirements:* For doctorate, GRE. Additional exam requirements/recommendations for international students: Required—TOEFL (minimum score 570 paper-based; 88 iBT), IELTS (minimum score 6.5), PTE (minimum score 60). *Application deadline:* For fall admission, 1/1 priority date for domestic students, 1/1 for international students; for spring admission, 8/15 for domestic and international students. Applications are processed on a rolling basis. Application fee: $75. Electronic applications accepted. *Expenses:* Tuition: Full-time $49,520; part-time $2060 per credit hour. *Required fees:* $2617. *Financial support:* In 2016–17, research assistantships (averaging $22,000 per year), teaching assistantships (averaging $22,000 per year) were awarded; fellowships also available. Financial award application deadline: 1/1. *Faculty research:* Agent-based modeling, computational optimization, data mining, decision analysis, decision technologies, human factors engineering, logistics, network optimization and analysis, scheduling, simulation modeling, statistical analysis, stochastic programming. *Total annual research expenditures:* $40,810. *Unit head:* Dr. Tom Sharkey, Graduate Program Director, 518-276-2958, E-mail: sharkt@rpi.edu. *Application contact:* Office of Graduate Admissions, 518-276-6216, E-mail: gradadmissions@rpi.edu.
Website: http://ise.rpi.edu/

Rensselaer Polytechnic Institute, Graduate School, School of Engineering, Program in Systems Engineering and Technology Management, Troy, NY 12180-3590. Offers M Eng. *Program availability:* Part-time. *Faculty:* 9 full-time (0 women), 1 part-time/adjunct (0 women). *Students:* 13 part-time (3 women). 7 applicants, 29% accepted. *Degree requirements:* For master's, thesis (for some programs). *Entrance requirements:* For master's, GRE. Additional exam requirements/recommendations for international students: Required—TOEFL (minimum score 570 paper-based; 88 iBT), IELTS (minimum score 6.5), PTE (minimum score 60). *Application deadline:* For fall admission, 1/1 priority date for domestic and international students; for spring admission, 8/15 priority date for domestic and international students. Applications are processed on a rolling basis. Application fee: $75. Electronic applications accepted. *Expenses:* Tuition: Full-time $49,520; part-time $2060 per credit hour. *Required fees:* $2617. *Financial support:* Career-related internships or fieldwork and institutionally sponsored loans available. Financial award application deadline: 1/1. *Total annual research expenditures:* $853,423. *Unit head:* Dr. Bill Foley, Graduate Program Director, 518-276-4009, E-mail: foleyw@rpi.edu. *Application contact:* Graduate Admissions, 518-276-6216, E-mail: gradadmissions@rpi.edu.
Website: http://ise.rpi.edu/

Rochester Institute of Technology, Graduate Enrollment Services, Kate Gleason College of Engineering, Design, Development and Manufacturing Department, MS Program in Product Development, Rochester, NY 14623. Offers MS. *Program availability:* Part-time, evening/weekend, 100% online. *Students:* 1 (woman) full-time, 45 part-time (4 women); includes 4 minority (1 Black or African American, non-Hispanic/Latino; 1 Asian, non-Hispanic/Latino; 2 Hispanic/Latino), 1 international. Average age 37. 17 applicants, 59% accepted, 8 enrolled. In 2016, 6 master's awarded. *Degree requirements:* For master's, capstone project. *Entrance requirements:* For master's, undergraduate degree in engineering or related field, minimum GPA of 3.0, 2 years of experience in product development. Additional exam requirements/recommendations for international students: Required—TOEFL (minimum score 550 paper-based; 79 iBT), IELTS (minimum score 6.5), PTE (minimum score 58). *Application deadline:* Applications are processed on a rolling basis. Application fee: $60. Electronic applications accepted. *Expenses:* $1,742 per credit hour. *Financial support:* Scholarships/grants available. Support available to part-time students. Financial award applicants required to submit FAFSA. *Faculty research:* Systems engineering, lean product development, decision analysis, agile methods, project management. *Unit head:* Mark Smith, Graduate Program Director, 585-475-7971, Fax: 585-475-4080, E-mail: mpdmail@rit.edu. *Application contact:* Diane Ellison, Associate Vice President, Graduate Enrollment Services, 585-475-2229, Fax: 585-475-7164, E-mail: gradinfo@rit.edu.
Website: https://www.rit.edu/kgcoe/mpd/

Rochester Institute of Technology, Graduate Enrollment Services, Kate Gleason College of Engineering, Industrial and Systems Engineering Department, ME Program in Industrial and Systems Engineering, Rochester, NY 14623-5603. Offers ME. *Program availability:* Part-time. *Students:* 7 full-time (3 women), 9 part-time (1 woman), 10 international. Average age 25. 77 applicants, 25% accepted, 4 enrolled. In 2016, 14 master's awarded. *Degree requirements:* For master's, thesis or alternative, capstone project. *Entrance requirements:* For master's, minimum GPA of 3.0 (recommended). Additional exam requirements/recommendations for international students: Required—TOEFL (minimum score 580 paper-based; 90 iBT), IELTS (minimum score 6), PTE (minimum score 58). *Application deadline:* For fall admission, 2/15 priority date for domestic and international students; for spring admission, 12/15 priority date for domestic and international students. Applications are processed on a rolling basis. Application fee: $60. Electronic applications accepted. *Expenses:* $1,742 per credit hour. *Financial support:* In 2016–17, 1 student received support. Research assistantships with partial tuition reimbursements available, teaching assistantships with partial tuition reimbursements available, career-related internships or fieldwork, scholarships/grants, and unspecified assistantships available. Support available to part-time students. Financial award applicants required to submit FAFSA. *Faculty research:* Advanced manufacturing, engineering education, ergonomics and human factors, healthcare delivery systems, operations research and simulation, systems engineering, production and logistics, sustainable engineering. *Unit head:* Dr. Marcos Esterman, Associate Professor, 585-475-2598, E-mail: mxeeie@rit.edu. *Application contact:* Diane Ellison, Associate Vice President, Graduate Enrollment Services, 585-475-2229, Fax: 585-475-7164, E-mail: gradinfo@rit.edu.
Website: http://www.rit.edu/kgcoe/ise/program/ms-industrial-systems-engineering/master-engineering-industrial-and-systems-engineering

Rochester Institute of Technology, Graduate Enrollment Services, Kate Gleason College of Engineering, Industrial and Systems Engineering Department, MS Program in Industrial and Systems Engineering, Rochester, NY 14623-5603. Offers MS. *Program availability:* Part-time. *Students:* 34 full-time (6 women), 5 part-time (0 women); includes 2 minority (both Black or African American, non-Hispanic/Latino), 33 international. Average age 24. 246 applicants, 29% accepted, 17 enrolled. In 2016, 8 master's awarded. *Degree requirements:* For master's, thesis. *Entrance requirements:* For master's, GRE, minimum GPA of 3.0 (recommended). Additional exam requirements/recommendations for international students: Required—TOEFL (minimum score 580 paper-based; 90 iBT), IELTS (minimum score 6.5), PTE (minimum score 58). *Application deadline:* For fall admission, 2/15 priority date for domestic and international students; for spring admission, 12/15 priority date for domestic and international

students. Applications are processed on a rolling basis. Application fee: $60. Electronic applications accepted. *Expenses:* $1,742 per credit hour. *Financial support:* In 2016–17, 29 students received support. Research assistantships with partial tuition reimbursements available, teaching assistantships with partial tuition reimbursements available, career-related internships or fieldwork, scholarships/grants, and unspecified assistantships available. Support available to part-time students. Financial award applicants required to submit FAFSA. *Faculty research:* Advanced manufacturing; health care systems engineering, data analytics, operations research, and simulation; supply chain and logistics systems; biomechanics, ergonomics, safety, and rehabilitation. *Unit head:* Dr. Marcos Esterman, Associate Professor, 585-475-2598, E-mail: mxeeie@rit.edu. *Application contact:* Diane Ellison, Associate Vice President, Graduate Enrollment Services, 585-475-2229, Fax: 585-475-7164, E-mail: gradinfo@rit.edu.
Website: http://www.rit.edu/kgcoe/ise/program/master-science-degrees/master-science-industrial-and-systems-engineering

Rochester Institute of Technology, Graduate Enrollment Services, Kate Gleason College of Engineering, Microsystems Engineering Department, PhD Program in Microsystems Engineering, Rochester, NY 14623-5603. Offers PhD. *Program availability:* Part-time. *Students:* 40 full-time (8 women), 2 part-time (0 women); includes 1 minority (Hispanic/Latino), 26 international. Average age 29. 31 applicants, 35% accepted, 8 enrolled. In 2016, 4 doctorates awarded. *Degree requirements:* For doctorate, comprehensive exam, thesis/dissertation. *Entrance requirements:* For doctorate, GRE, minimum GPA of 3.0 (recommended). Additional exam requirements/recommendations for international students: Required—TOEFL (minimum score 600 paper-based; 100 iBT), IELTS (minimum score 6.5), PTE (minimum score 68). *Application deadline:* For fall admission, 1/15 priority date for domestic and international students. Applications are processed on a rolling basis. Application fee: $60. Electronic applications accepted. *Expenses:* $1,742 per credit hour. *Financial support:* In 2016–17, 47 students received support. Fellowships, research assistantships with full tuition reimbursements available, teaching assistantships with full tuition reimbursements available, career-related internships or fieldwork, scholarships/grants, health care benefits, and unspecified assistantships available. Support available to part-time students. Financial award applicants required to submit FAFSA. *Faculty research:* Semiconductor microelectronics and nanoelectronics; photovoltaics, solar cells, and energy; photonics and integrated silicon photonics; nanobiodevices and materials; microfluidics and micromechanical systems. *Unit head:* Dr. Bruce Smith, Director, 585-475-2058, E-mail: bwsemc@rit.edu. *Application contact:* Diane Ellison, Associate Vice President, Graduate Enrollment Services, 585-475-2229, Fax: 585-475-7164, E-mail: gradinfo@rit.edu.
Website: http://www.rit.edu/kgcoe/program/microsystems-engineering

Rose-Hulman Institute of Technology, Faculty of Engineering and Applied Sciences, Department of Electrical and Computer Engineering, Terre Haute, IN 47803-3999. Offers electrical and computer engineering (M Eng); electrical engineering (MS); systems engineering and management (MS). *Program availability:* Part-time. *Faculty:* 18 full-time (2 women), 1 (woman) part-time/adjunct. *Students:* 7 full-time (3 women), 7 part-time (0 women), 12 international. Average age 25. 17 applicants, 65% accepted, 3 enrolled. In 2016, 7 master's awarded. *Degree requirements:* For master's, thesis (for some programs). *Entrance requirements:* For master's, GRE, minimum GPA of 3.0. Additional exam requirements/recommendations for international students: Required—TOEFL (minimum score 580 paper-based; 92 iBT). *Application deadline:* For fall admission, 2/1 priority date for domestic students. Applications are processed on a rolling basis. Application fee: $0. Electronic applications accepted. *Expenses: Tuition:* Full-time $43,122. *Financial support:* In 2016–17, 14 students received support. Fellowships with tuition reimbursements available, research assistantships with tuition reimbursements available, institutionally sponsored loans, scholarships/grants, and tuition waivers (full and partial) available. *Faculty research:* VLSI, power systems, analog electronics, communications, electromagnetics. *Total annual research expenditures:* $84,698. *Unit head:* Dr. Mario Simoni, Chairman, 812-877-8341, Fax: 812-877-8895, E-mail: simoni@rose-hulman.edu. *Application contact:* Dr. Azad Siahmakoun, Associate Dean of the Faculty, 812-877-8400, Fax: 812-877-8061, E-mail: siahmako@rose-hulman.edu.
Website: http://www.rose-hulman.edu/academics/academic-departments/electrical-computer-engineering.aspx

Rutgers University–New Brunswick, Graduate School-New Brunswick, Department of Industrial and Systems Engineering, Piscataway, NJ 08854-8097. Offers industrial and systems engineering (MS, PhD); information technology (MS); manufacturing systems engineering (MS); quality and reliability engineering (MS). *Program availability:* Part-time, evening/weekend. Terminal master's awarded for partial completion of doctoral program. *Degree requirements:* For master's, thesis or alternative, seminar; for doctorate, comprehensive exam, thesis/dissertation. *Entrance requirements:* For master's and doctorate, GRE General Test. Additional exam requirements/recommendations for international students: Required—TOEFL. *Faculty research:* Production and manufacturing systems, quality and reliability engineering, systems engineering and aviation safety.

Simon Fraser University, Office of Graduate Studies and Postdoctoral Fellows, Faculty of Applied Sciences, School of Mechatronic Systems Engineering, Burnaby, BC V5A 1S6, Canada. Offers MA Sc, PhD. *Faculty:* 17 full-time (2 women). *Students:* 99 full-time (22 women). 99 applicants, 27% accepted, 20 enrolled. In 2016, 12 master's, 13 doctorates awarded. *Degree requirements:* For master's, one foreign language, thesis; for doctorate, one foreign language, comprehensive exam, thesis/dissertation. *Entrance requirements:* Additional exam requirements/recommendations for international students: Required—TOEFL (minimum score 580 paper-based; 93 iBT), IELTS (minimum score 7), TWE (minimum score 5). *Application deadline:* For fall admission, 9/15 for domestic and international students; for spring admission, 1/15 for domestic and international students; for summer admission, 6/14 for domestic and international students. Application fee: $90 ($125 for international students). Electronic applications accepted. *Financial support:* In 2016–17, 58 students received support, including 36 fellowships (averaging $3,250 per year); research assistantships, teaching assistantships, and scholarships/grants also available. *Faculty research:* Intelligent systems and smart materials, micro-electro mechanical systems (MEMS), biomedical engineering, thermal engineering, alternative energy. *Unit head:* Dr. Mehrdad Moallem, Graduate Program Chair, 778-782-8156, E-mail: mse-grad-chair@sfu.ca. *Application contact:* Jennifer Coffey, Graduate Program Assistant, 778-782-8456, E-mail: msedept@sfu.ca.
Website: http://www.sfu.ca/mechatronics.html

Southern Methodist University, Bobby B. Lyle School of Engineering, Department of Engineering Management, Information, and Systems, Dallas, TX 75275. Offers engineering management (MSEM, DE); information engineering and management (MSIEM); operations research (MS, PhD); systems engineering (MS, PhD). *Program availability:* Part-time, evening/weekend, online learning. Terminal master's awarded for partial completion of doctoral program. *Degree requirements:* For master's, thesis optional; for doctorate, thesis/dissertation, oral and written qualifying exams. *Entrance requirements:* For master's, minimum GPA of 3.0 in last 2 years; bachelor's degree in engineering, mathematics, sciences, or technical area; for doctorate, GRE General Test (operations research, engineering management), bachelor's degree in related field. Additional exam requirements/recommendations for international students: Required—TOEFL. *Faculty research:* Telecommunications, decision systems, information engineering, operations research, software.

Southern Methodist University, Bobby B. Lyle School of Engineering, Program in Datacenter Systems Engineering, Dallas, TX 75275. Offers MS. *Program availability:* Part-time, online learning. *Entrance requirements:* For master's, BS in one of the engineering disciplines, computer science, one of the quantitative sciences or mathematics; minimum of two years of college-level mathematics including one year of college-level calculus.

Stevens Institute of Technology, Graduate School, Charles V. Schaefer Jr. School of Engineering and Science, Department of Electrical and Computer Engineering, Program in Networked Information Systems, Hoboken, NJ 07030. Offers MS, Certificate. *Program availability:* Part-time, evening/weekend. *Students:* 3 full-time (0 women), 9 part-time (1 woman); includes 2 minority (1 Black or African American, non-Hispanic/Latino; 1 Two or more races, non-Hispanic/Latino), 3 international. Average age 31. 59 applicants, 59% accepted, 14 enrolled. In 2016, 10 master's, 3 other advanced degrees awarded. *Degree requirements:* For master's, thesis optional, minimum B average in major field and overall; for Certificate, minimum B average. *Entrance requirements:* Additional exam requirements/recommendations for international students: Required—TOEFL (minimum score 74 iBT), IELTS (minimum score 6). *Application deadline:* For fall admission, 6/1 for domestic students, 4/15 for international students; for spring admission, 11/30 for domestic students, 11/1 for international students. Applications are processed on a rolling basis. Application fee: $65. Electronic applications accepted. *Expenses:* Contact institution. *Financial support:* Fellowships, research assistantships, teaching assistantships, career-related internships or fieldwork, Federal Work-Study, scholarships/grants, and unspecified assistantships available. Financial award application deadline: 2/15; financial award applicants required to submit FAFSA. *Unit head:* Yingying Chen, Program Director, 201-216-8066, Fax: 201-216-8246, E-mail: yingying.chen@stevens.edu. *Application contact:* Graduate Admissions, 888-783-8367, Fax: 201-511-1306, E-mail: graduate@stevens.edu.

Stevens Institute of Technology, Graduate School, School of Systems and Enterprises, Program in Systems Engineering, Hoboken, NJ 07030. Offers systems and supportability engineering (Certificate); systems engineering (M Eng, PhD); systems engineering and architecting (Certificate); systems engineering management (Certificate); systems engineering of embedded/cyber-physical systems (Certificate); systems engineering security (Certificate). *Program availability:* Part-time, evening/weekend. *Students:* 44 full-time (12 women), 155 part-time (33 women); includes 21 minority (6 Black or African American, non-Hispanic/Latino; 15 Asian, non-Hispanic/Latino), 26 international. Average age 34. 127 applicants, 61% accepted, 28 enrolled. In 2016, 124 master's, 9 doctorates, 134 other advanced degrees awarded. *Degree requirements:* For master's, thesis optional, minimum B average in major field and overall; for doctorate, comprehensive exam (for some programs), thesis/dissertation; for Certificate, minimum B average. *Entrance requirements:* Additional exam requirements/recommendations for international students: Required—TOEFL (minimum score 74 iBT), IELTS (minimum score 6). *Application deadline:* For fall admission, 6/1 for domestic students, 4/15 for international students; for spring admission, 11/30 for domestic students, 11/1 for international students. Applications are processed on a rolling basis. Application fee: $65. Electronic applications accepted. *Expenses:* Contact institution. *Financial support:* Fellowships, research assistantships, teaching assistantships, career-related internships or fieldwork, Federal Work-Study, scholarships/grants, and unspecified assistantships available. Financial award application deadline: 2/15; financial award applicants required to submit FAFSA. *Unit head:* Dr. Jon Wade, Director, E-mail: jon.wade@stevens.edu. *Application contact:* Graduate Admissions, 888-783-8367, Fax: 888-511-1306, E-mail: graduate@stevens.edu.
Website: https://www.stevens.edu/school-systems-enterprises/masters-degree-programs/systems-engineering

Stony Brook University, State University of New York, Graduate School, College of Engineering and Applied Sciences, Department of Computer Science, Program in Information Systems Engineering, Stony Brook, NY 11794. Offers MS. *Entrance requirements:* Additional exam requirements/recommendations for international students: Required—TOEFL. *Application deadline:* For fall admission, 1/15 for domestic students; for spring admission, 10/1 for domestic students. Application fee: $100. *Expenses:* Contact institution. *Unit head:* Prof. Arie Kaufman, Chair, 631-632-8470, Fax: 631-632-8334, E-mail: arie.kaufman@stonybrook.edu.

Tennessee State University, The School of Graduate Studies and Research, College of Engineering, Nashville, TN 37209-1561. Offers biomedical engineering (ME); civil engineering (ME); computer and information systems engineering (MS, PhD); electrical engineering (ME); environmental engineering (ME); manufacturing engineering (ME); mathematical sciences (MS); mechanical engineering (ME). *Program availability:* Part-time, evening/weekend. *Degree requirements:* For master's, project; for doctorate, comprehensive exam, thesis/dissertation. *Entrance requirements:* For doctorate, minimum GPA of 3.3. *Faculty research:* Robotics, intelligent systems, human-computer interaction software systems, biomedical engineering, signal/image processing, probabilistic design, intelligent manufacturing, cooperative mobile robots, condition based maintenance, sensor fusion.

Texas A&M University–Kingsville, College of Graduate Studies, Frank H. Dotterweich College of Engineering, Program in Sustainable Energy Systems Engineering, Kingsville, TX 78363. Offers PhD. *Degree requirements:* For doctorate, variable foreign language requirement, comprehensive exam, thesis/dissertation (for some programs). *Entrance requirements:* For doctorate, GRE, MAT, GMAT, bachelor's or master's degree in engineering or science, curriculum vitae, official transcripts, statement of purpose, three letters of recommendation. Additional exam requirements/recommendations for international students: Required—TOEFL (minimum score 550 paper-based; 79 iBT). Electronic applications accepted.

Texas Tech University, Graduate School, Edward E. Whitacre Jr. College of Engineering, Department of Industrial, Manufacturing, and Systems Engineering, Lubbock, TX 79409-3061. Offers industrial engineering (MSIE, PhD); systems and engineering management (MSSEM, PhD). *Program availability:* Part-time, 100% online, blended/hybrid learning. *Faculty:* 13 full-time (2 women). *Students:* 90 full-time (15 women), 97 part-time (14 women); includes 25 minority (9 Black or African American, non-Hispanic/Latino; 1 American Indian or Alaska Native, non-Hispanic/Latino; 2 Asian, non-Hispanic/Latino; 11 Hispanic/Latino; 2 Two or more races, non-Hispanic/Latino), 102 international. Average age 32. 376 applicants, 38% accepted, 48 enrolled. In 2016, 43 master's, 7 doctorates awarded. Terminal master's awarded for partial completion of doctoral program. *Degree requirements:* For master's, comprehensive exam, thesis optional; for doctorate, comprehensive exam, thesis/dissertation. *Entrance requirements:* For master's and doctorate, GRE (Verbal and Quantitative). Additional exam requirements/recommendations for international students: Required—TOEFL (minimum score 550 paper-based; 79 iBT). *Application deadline:* For fall admission, 6/1 priority date for domestic students, 1/15 priority date for international students; for spring

admission, 9/1 priority date for domestic students, 6/15 priority date for international students. Applications are processed on a rolling basis. Application fee: $75. Electronic applications accepted. *Expenses:* $325 per credit hour full-time resident tuition, $733 per credit hour full-time non-resident tuition; $53.75 per credit hour fee plus $608 per term fee. *Financial support:* In 2016–17, 73 students received support, including 71 fellowships (averaging $2,464 per year), 9 research assistantships (averaging $15,691 per year), 21 teaching assistantships (averaging $21,474 per year); scholarships/grants, tuition waivers (partial), and unspecified assistantships also available. Financial award application deadline: 2/1; financial award applicants required to submit FAFSA. *Faculty research:* Ergonomics and human factors engineering, manufacturing systems, operations research, statistics and quality assurance, systems and engineering management. *Total annual research expenditures:* $282,884. *Unit head:* Dr. Hong-Chao Zhang, Interim Chair, 806-742-3543, E-mail: hong-chao.zhang@ttu.edu. *Application contact:* Dr. Jennifer Cross, Associate Professor, 806-742-3543, Fax: 806-742-3411, E-mail: jennifer.cross@ttu.edu.
Website: http://www.ie.ttu.edu/

The University of Alabama in Huntsville, School of Graduate Studies, College of Engineering, Department of Industrial and Systems Engineering and Engineering Management, Huntsville, AL 35899. Offers engineering management (MSE, PhD); industrial engineering (MSE, PhD); operations research (MSOR); systems engineering (MSE, PhD). *Program availability:* Part-time, evening/weekend, online learning. *Degree requirements:* For master's, comprehensive exam, thesis or alternative, oral and written exams; for doctorate, comprehensive exam, thesis/dissertation, oral and written exams. *Entrance requirements:* For master's and doctorate, GRE General Test, minimum GPA of 3.0. Additional exam requirements/recommendations for international students: Required—TOEFL (minimum score 500 paper-based; 80 iBT), IELTS (minimum score 6.5). Electronic applications accepted. *Expenses:* Tuition, state resident: full-time $9834; part-time $600 per credit hour. Tuition, nonresident: full-time $21,830; part-time $1325 per credit hour. *Faculty research:* Systems engineering process, electronic manufacturing, heuristic manufacturing, teams and team development.

University of Alberta, Faculty of Graduate Studies and Research, Department of Electrical and Computer Engineering, Edmonton, AB T6G 2E1, Canada. Offers communications (M Eng, M Sc, PhD); computer engineering (M Eng, M Sc, PhD); electromagnetics (M Eng, M Sc, PhD); nanotechnology and microdevices (M Eng, M Sc, PhD); power/power electronics (M Eng, M Sc, PhD); systems (M Eng, M Sc, PhD). Terminal master's awarded for partial completion of doctoral program. *Degree requirements:* For master's, thesis; for doctorate, thesis/dissertation. *Entrance requirements:* Additional exam requirements/recommendations for international students: Required—TOEFL. Electronic applications accepted. *Faculty research:* Controls, communications, microelectronics, electromagnetics.

The University of Arizona, College of Engineering, Department of Systems and Industrial Engineering, Tucson, AZ 85721. Offers engineering management (Graduate Certificate); industrial engineering (MS); systems and industrial engineering (MS, PhD); systems engineering (MS, PhD, Graduate Certificate). *Program availability:* Part-time, online learning. *Degree requirements:* For doctorate, thesis/dissertation. *Entrance requirements:* For master's, GRE General Test (minimum score: 500 Verbal, 700 Quantitative), 3 letters of recommendation; for doctorate, GRE General Test (minimum score: 500 Verbal, 700 Quantitative), minimum GPA of 3.5, 3 letters of recommendation, letter of intent. Additional exam requirements/recommendations for international students: Required—TOEFL (minimum score 575 paper-based; 80 iBT). Electronic applications accepted. *Faculty research:* Optimization, systems theory, logistics, transportation, embedded systems.

University of Arkansas at Little Rock, Graduate School, George W. Donaghey College of Engineering and Information Technology, Department of Systems Engineering, Little Rock, AR 72204-1099. Offers MS, PhD, Graduate Certificate.

University of California, Merced, Graduate Division, School of Engineering, Merced, CA 95343. Offers biological engineering and small scale technologies (MS, PhD); electrical engineering and computer science (MS, PhD); environmental systems (MS, PhD); mechanical engineering (MS); mechanical engineering and applied mechanics (PhD). *Faculty:* 44 full-time (7 women). *Students:* 170 full-time (52 women), 2 part-time (0 women); includes 34 minority (2 Black or African American, non-Hispanic/Latino; 11 Asian, non-Hispanic/Latino; 14 Hispanic/Latino; 2 Native Hawaiian or other Pacific Islander, non-Hispanic/Latino; 5 Two or more races, non-Hispanic/Latino), 99 international. Average age 28. 307 applicants, 35% accepted, 46 enrolled. In 2016, 15 master's, 12 doctorates awarded. Terminal master's awarded for partial completion of doctoral program. *Degree requirements:* For master's, variable foreign language requirement, comprehensive exam, thesis or alternative; for doctorate, variable foreign language requirement, comprehensive exam, thesis/dissertation. *Entrance requirements:* For master's and doctorate, GRE. Additional exam requirements/recommendations for international students: Required—TOEFL (minimum score 550 paper-based; 80 iBT); Recommended—IELTS (minimum score 7). *Application deadline:* For fall admission, 1/15 priority date for domestic and international students. Applications are processed on a rolling basis. Application fee: $90 ($110 for international students). Electronic applications accepted. *Expenses:* Contact institution. *Financial support:* In 2016–17, 150 students received support, including 16 fellowships with full tuition reimbursements available (averaging $19,088 per year), 45 research assistantships with full tuition reimbursements available (averaging $18,389 per year), 89 teaching assistantships with full tuition reimbursements available (averaging $19,249 per year); scholarships/grants, traineeships, and health care benefits also available. Financial award application deadline: 1/15. *Faculty research:* Water resources, biotechnology, renewable energy, big data, cyber-physical systems. *Total annual research expenditures:* $3.3 million. *Unit head:* Dr. Mark Matsumoto, Dean, Fax: 209-228-4047, E-mail: mmatsumoto@ucmerced.edu. *Application contact:* Tsu Ya, Director of Admissions and Academic Services, 209-228-4521, Fax: 209-228-6906, E-mail: tya@ucmerced.edu.

University of Colorado Colorado Springs, College of Engineering and Applied Science, Program in General Engineering, Colorado Springs, CO 80918. Offers energy engineering (ME); engineering management (ME); information assurance (ME); software engineering (ME); space operations (ME); systems engineering (ME). *Program availability:* Part-time, evening/weekend, blended/hybrid learning. *Faculty:* 1 full-time (0 women), 15 part-time/adjunct (6 women). *Students:* 18 full-time (3 women), 166 part-time (34 women); includes 36 minority (6 Black or African American, non-Hispanic/Latino; 8 Asian, non-Hispanic/Latino; 12 Hispanic/Latino; 10 Two or more races, non-Hispanic/Latino), 57 international. Average age 36. 89 applicants, 72% accepted, 41 enrolled. In 2016, 21 master's, 8 doctorates awarded. *Degree requirements:* For master's, thesis, portfolio, or project; for doctorate, comprehensive exam, thesis/dissertation. *Entrance requirements:* For master's, GRE (minimum score of 148 new grading scale on quantitative portion if undergraduate GPA is less than 3.0); for doctorate, GRE (minimum score of 148 new grading scale on the quantitative portion if the applicant has not graduated from a program of recognized standing), minimum GPA of 3.3 in the bachelor's or master's degree program attempted. Additional exam requirements/recommendations for international students: Required—TOEFL (minimum score 80 iBT), IELTS (minimum score 6). *Application deadline:* For fall admission, 7/1 for domestic students, 6/1 for international students; for spring admission, 11/1 for domestic and international students; for summer admission, 4/15 for domestic and international students. Applications are processed on a rolling basis. Application fee: $60 ($100 for international students). Electronic applications accepted. *Expenses:* Contact institution. *Financial support:* In 2016–17, 28 students received support. Federal Work-Study, scholarships/grants, traineeships, and unspecified assistantships available. Support available to part-time students. Financial award application deadline: 3/1; financial award applicants required to submit FAFSA. *Unit head:* Dr. Ramaswami Dandapani, Dean, 719-255-3543, Fax: 719-255-3542, E-mail: rdan@cas.uccs.edu. *Application contact:* Dawn House, Coordinator, 719-255-3246, E-mail: dhouse@uccs.edu.

University of Florida, Graduate School, Herbert Wertheim College of Engineering, Department of Industrial and Systems Engineering, Gainesville, FL 32611. Offers industrial and systems engineering (ME, MS, PhD, Engr); quantitative finance (PhD). *Program availability:* Part-time, evening/weekend, online learning. Terminal master's awarded for partial completion of doctoral program. *Degree requirements:* For master's, thesis (for some programs); for doctorate, comprehensive exam (for some programs), thesis/dissertation (for some programs). *Entrance requirements:* For master's and doctorate, minimum GPA of 3.0; for Engr, GRE General Test. Additional exam requirements/recommendations for international students: Required—TOEFL (minimum score 550 paper-based; 80 iBT), IELTS (minimum score 6). Electronic applications accepted. *Faculty research:* Operations research; financial engineering; logistics and supply chain management; energy, healthcare, and transportation applications of operations research.

University of Houston–Clear Lake, School of Science and Computer Engineering, Program in System Engineering, Houston, TX 77058-1002. Offers MS. *Entrance requirements:* Additional exam requirements/recommendations for international students: Required—TOEFL (minimum score 550 paper-based).

University of Illinois at Urbana–Champaign, Graduate College, College of Engineering, Department of Industrial and Enterprise Systems Engineering, Urbana, IL 61801. Offers industrial engineering (MS, PhD); systems and entrepreneurial engineering (MS, PhD); MBA/MS.

University of Maryland, Baltimore County, The Graduate School, Program in Systems Engineering, Baltimore, MD 21227. Offers MS, Postbaccalaureate Certificate. *Program availability:* Part-time. *Faculty:* 1 full-time (0 women). *Students:* 5 full-time (2 women), 35 part-time (5 women); includes 13 minority (7 Black or African American, non-Hispanic/Latino; 4 Asian, non-Hispanic/Latino; 2 Hispanic/Latino), 4 international. Average age 33. 24 applicants, 54% accepted, 10 enrolled. In 2016, 21 master's, 4 other advanced degrees awarded. *Degree requirements:* For master's, comprehensive exam (for some programs), thesis optional. *Entrance requirements:* For master's, undergraduate degree in engineering or information technology; minimum undergraduate GPA of 3.0. Additional exam requirements/recommendations for international students: Required—TOEFL (minimum score 550 paper-based; 80 iBT), GRE General Test. *Application deadline:* For fall admission, 7/1 for domestic and international students; for spring admission, 12/1 for domestic and international students. Applications are processed on a rolling basis. Application fee: $70. Electronic applications accepted. *Expenses:* Tuition, state resident: full-time $13,294. Tuition, nonresident: full-time $20,286. *Financial support:* In 2016–17, 1 research assistantship (averaging $18,000 per year) was awarded; career-related internships or fieldwork, Federal Work-Study, scholarships/grants, health care benefits, tuition waivers (partial), and unspecified assistantships also available. Support available to part-time students. Financial award application deadline: 6/30; financial award applicants required to submit FAFSA. *Faculty research:* Systems architecture design, modeling and simulation, design and risk analysis, system integrations test, management and engineering projects. *Unit head:* Dr. Anupam Joshi, Professor and Chair, 410-455-3500, Fax: 410-455-3969, E-mail: joshi@umbc.edu. *Application contact:* Dr. Thomas M. Moore, Lecturer/Graduate Program Director, 410-455-1151, E-mail: mooretg@umbc.edu.
Website: http://www.umbc.edu/se/

University of Maryland, College Park, Academic Affairs, A. James Clark School of Engineering, Systems Engineering Program, College Park, MD 20742. Offers M Eng, MS. *Program availability:* Part-time, evening/weekend. *Degree requirements:* For master's, thesis optional. *Entrance requirements:* For master's, GRE General Test, minimum GPA of 3.0. Electronic applications accepted. *Faculty research:* Automation, computer, information, manufacturing, and process systems.

University of Massachusetts Dartmouth, Graduate School, College of Engineering, Department of Mechanical Engineering, North Dartmouth, MA 02747-2300. Offers industrial and systems engineering (MS); mechanical engineering (MS). *Program availability:* Part-time. *Faculty:* 10 full-time (1 woman). *Students:* 18 full-time (0 women), 12 part-time (0 women); includes 2 minority (both Two or more races, non-Hispanic/Latino), 15 international. Average age 25. 57 applicants, 51% accepted, 11 enrolled. In 2016, 12 master's awarded. *Degree requirements:* For master's, thesis, project or oral exam. *Entrance requirements:* For master's, GRE (UMass Dartmouth mechanical engineering bachelor's degree recipients are exempt), statement of purpose (minimum of 300 words), resume, 3 letters of recommendation, official transcripts. Additional exam requirements/recommendations for international students: Required—TOEFL (minimum score 533 paper-based; 72 iBT). *Application deadline:* For fall admission, 2/15 priority date for domestic students, 1/15 priority date for international students; for spring admission, 11/15 priority date for domestic students, 10/15 priority date for international students. Application fee: $60. Electronic applications accepted. *Expenses:* Tuition, state resident: full-time $14,994; part-time $624.75 per credit. Tuition, nonresident: full-time $27,068; part-time $1127.83 per credit. *Required fees:* $405; $25.88 per credit. Tuition and fees vary according to course load and reciprocity agreements. *Financial support:* In 2016–17, 2 research assistantships (averaging $5,596 per year), 7 teaching assistantships (averaging $6,818 per year) were awarded; institutionally sponsored loans, scholarships/grants, and unspecified assistantships also available. Support available to part-time students. Financial award application deadline: 3/1; financial award applicants required to submit FAFSA. *Faculty research:* Biopreservation, renewable energy, fluid structure interaction, buoyant flows, high performance heat exchanges, mechanics of biomaterials, composite materials, computational mechanics. *Total annual research expenditures:* $1.1 million. *Unit head:* Wenzhen Juang, Graduate Program Director, Mechanical Engineering, 508-910-6568, E-mail: whuang@umassd.edu. *Application contact:* Steven Briggs, Director of Marketing and Recruitment for Graduate Studies, 508-999-8604, Fax: 508-999-8183, E-mail: graduate@umassd.edu.
Website: http://www.umassd.edu/engineering/mne/graduate

University of Massachusetts Dartmouth, Graduate School, College of Engineering, Program in Engineering and Applied Science, North Dartmouth, MA 02747-2300. Offers applied mechanics and materials (PhD); computational science and engineering (PhD); computer science and information systems (PhD); engineering and applied science (PhD); industrial and systems engineering (PhD). *Program availability:* Part-time. *Students:* 23 full-time (7 women), 8 part-time (3 women); includes 2 minority (both Black or African American, non-Hispanic/Latino), 15 international. Average age 31. 14 applicants, 79% accepted, 7 enrolled. *Degree requirements:* For doctorate, comprehensive exam, thesis/dissertation. *Entrance requirements:* For doctorate, GRE,

statement of purpose (minimum of 300 words), resume, 3 letters of recommendation, official transcripts. Additional exam requirements/recommendations for international students: Required—TOEFL (minimum score 550 paper-based; 79 iBT). *Application deadline:* For fall admission, 2/15 priority date for domestic students, 1/15 priority date for international students; for spring admission, 11/15 priority date for domestic students, 10/15 priority date for international students. Application fee: $60. Electronic applications accepted. *Expenses:* Tuition, state resident: full-time $14,994; part-time $624.75 per credit. Tuition, nonresident: full-time $27,068; part-time $1127.83 per credit. *Required fees:* $405; $25.88 per credit. Tuition and fees vary according to course load and reciprocity agreements. *Financial support:* In 2016–17, 11 fellowships (averaging $16,591 per year), 12 research assistantships (averaging $5,160 per year) were awarded; institutionally sponsored loans, scholarships/grants, and doctoral support also available. Support available to part-time students. Financial award application deadline: 3/1; financial award applicants required to submit FAFSA. *Faculty research:* Tissue/cell engineering, bio transport sensors/networks, marine systems biomimetic materials, composite/polymeric materials, resilient infrastructure robotics, renewable energy. *Total annual research expenditures:* $253,000. *Unit head:* Gaurav Khanna, Graduate Program Director, Engineering and Applied Science, 508-910-6605, Fax: 508-999-9115, E-mail: gkhanna@umassd.edu. *Application contact:* Steven Briggs, Director of Marketing and Recruitment for Graduate Studies, 508-999-8604, Fax: 508-999-8183, E-mail: graduate@umassd.edu.
Website: http://www.umassd.edu/engineering/graduate/doctoraldegreeprograms/egrandappliedsciencephd/

University of Michigan, College of Engineering, Department of Integrative Systems and Design, Ann Arbor, MI 48109. Offers automotive engineering (M Eng); design science (MS, PhD); energy systems engineering (M Eng, MS); global automotive and manufacturing engineering (M Eng); manufacturing engineering (M Eng, D Eng); pharmaceutical engineering (M Eng); robotics and autonomous vehicles (M Eng); systems engineering and design (M Eng); MBA/M Eng; MSE/MS. *Program availability:* Part-time, online learning. *Students:* 147 full-time (33 women), 234 part-time (39 women). 315 applicants, 8% accepted, 13 enrolled. In 2016, 158 master's, 2 doctorates awarded. Terminal master's awarded for partial completion of doctoral program. *Degree requirements:* For master's, capstone project; for doctorate, thesis/dissertation. *Entrance requirements:* For master's, GRE; for doctorate, GRE, 2 years of work experience. Additional exam requirements/recommendations for international students: Required—TOEFL (minimum score 560 paper-based). *Application deadline:* Applications are processed on a rolling basis. Electronic applications accepted. *Expenses:* Tuition, state resident: full-time $21,466; part-time $1152 per credit hour. Tuition, nonresident: full-time $43,346; part-time $2367 per credit hour. Part-time tuition and fees vary according to course load, degree level and program. *Financial support:* Fellowships, research assistantships with full tuition reimbursements, teaching assistantships with full tuition reimbursements, career-related internships or fieldwork, scholarships/grants, and unspecified assistantships available. Financial award applicants required to submit FAFSA. *Faculty research:* Automotive engineering, design science, energy systems engineering, engineering sustainable systems, financial engineering, global automotive and manufacturing engineering, integrated microsystems, manufacturing engineering, pharmaceutical engineering, robotics and autonomous vehicles. *Total annual research expenditures:* $292,225. *Unit head:* Prof. Panos Papalambros, Department Chair, 734-647-8401, E-mail: pyp@umich.edu. *Application contact:* Kathy Bishar, Senior Graduate Coordinator, 734-764-3312, E-mail: kbishar@umich.edu.
Website: http://www.isd.engin.umich.edu

University of Michigan–Dearborn, College of Engineering and Computer Science, MSE Program in Industrial and Systems Engineering, Dearborn, MI 48128. Offers MSE. *Program availability:* Part-time, evening/weekend, 100% online. *Faculty:* 15 full-time (2 women), 6 part-time/adjunct (2 women). *Students:* 60 full-time (14 women), 37 part-time (11 women); includes 8 minority (2 Black or African American, non-Hispanic/Latino; 1 Asian, non-Hispanic/Latino; 3 Hispanic/Latino; 1 Native Hawaiian or other Pacific Islander, non-Hispanic/Latino; 1 Two or more races, non-Hispanic/Latino), 73 international. Average age 25. 214 applicants, 57% accepted, 45 enrolled. In 2016, 23 master's awarded. *Entrance requirements:* For master's, bachelor's degree in engineering, a physical science, computer science, or applied mathematics. Additional exam requirements/recommendations for international students: Required—TOEFL (minimum score 560 paper-based; 84 iBT), IELTS (minimum score 6.5). *Application deadline:* For fall admission, 8/1 for domestic students, 5/1 for international students; for winter admission, 12/1 for domestic students, 9/1 for international students; for spring admission, 4/1 for domestic students, 1/1 for international students. Applications are processed on a rolling basis. Application fee: $60. Electronic applications accepted. *Expenses:* Tuition, state resident: full-time $13,118; part-time $2280 per term. Tuition, nonresident: full-time $21,816; part-time $3771 per term. *Required fees:* $866; $658 per unit. $329 per term. Tuition and fees vary according to program. *Financial support:* Research assistantships, teaching assistantships, scholarships/grants, and non-resident tuition scholarships available. Support available to part-time students. Financial award application deadline: 3/1; financial award applicants required to submit FAFSA. *Faculty research:* Integrated design and manufacturing, operations research and decision science, human factors and ergonomics. *Unit head:* Dr. Armen Zakarian, Chair, 313-593-5361, Fax: 313-593-3692, E-mail: zakarian@umich.edu. *Application contact:* Office of Graduate Studies, 313-583-6321, E-mail: umd-graduatestudies@umich.edu.
Website: https://umdearborn.edu/cecs/departments/industrial-and-manufacturing-systems-engineering/graduate-programs/mse-industrial-systems-engineering

University of Michigan–Dearborn, College of Engineering and Computer Science, PhD Program in Industrial and Systems Engineering, Dearborn, MI 48128. Offers PhD. *Program availability:* Part-time, evening/weekend. *Degree requirements:* For doctorate, thesis/dissertation, qualifying and prelimiary examinations. *Entrance requirements:* For doctorate, master's degree in engineering or closely-related field. Additional exam requirements/recommendations for international students: Required—TOEFL (minimum score 560 paper-based; 84 iBT), IELTS (minimum score 6.5). Electronic applications accepted. *Expenses:* Tuition, state resident: full-time $13,118; part-time $2280 per term. Tuition, nonresident: full-time $21,816; part-time $3771 per term. *Required fees:* $866; $658 per unit. $329 per term. Tuition and fees vary according to program.

University of Michigan–Dearborn, College of Engineering and Computer Science, PhD Program in Information Systems Engineering, Dearborn, MI 48128. Offers PhD. *Program availability:* Part-time, evening/weekend. *Faculty:* 1 full-time (0 women). *Students:* 3 full-time (0 women), 15 part-time (2 women); includes 1 minority (Black or African American, non-Hispanic/Latino), 13 international. Average age 31. 26 applicants, 27% accepted, 3 enrolled. In 2016, 1 doctorate awarded. *Degree requirements:* For doctorate, thesis/dissertation. *Entrance requirements:* For doctorate, GRE. Additional exam requirements/recommendations for international students: Required—TOEFL (minimum score 560 paper-based; 84 iBT), IELTS (minimum score 6.5). *Application deadline:* For fall admission, 2/15 priority date for domestic and international students. Application fee: $60. Electronic applications accepted. *Expenses:* Tuition, state resident: full-time $13,118; part-time $2280 per term. Tuition, nonresident: full-time $21,816; part-time $3771 per term. *Required fees:* $866; $658 per unit. $329 per term. Tuition and fees vary according to program. *Financial support:* Research assistantships, scholarships/grants, and unspecified assistantships available. Financial award application deadline: 3/1; financial award applicants required to submit FAFSA. *Faculty research:* Database systems, networks, software engineering, circuits and electronics, signal processing. *Unit head:* Dr. Yi Lu Murphey, Director/Professor, 313-593-5290, E-mail: yilu@umich.edu. *Application contact:* Office of Graduate Studies, 313-583-6321, E-mail: umd-graduatestudies@umich.edu.
Website: http://umdearborn.edu/cecs/IDP/phd_ise/index.php

University of Nebraska at Omaha, Graduate Studies, College of Information Science and Technology, Department of Computer Science, Omaha, NE 68182. Offers artificial intelligence (Certificate); communication networks (Certificate); computer science (MA, MS); computer science education (MS, Certificate); software engineering (Certificate); system and architecture (Certificate). *Program availability:* Part-time, evening/weekend. *Faculty:* 13 full-time (4 women). *Students:* 73 full-time (19 women), 44 part-time (15 women); includes 8 minority (3 Asian, non-Hispanic/Latino; 1 Hispanic/Latino; 4 Two or more races, non-Hispanic/Latino), 87 international. Average age 27. 132 applicants, 59% accepted, 33 enrolled. In 2016, 58 master's awarded. *Degree requirements:* For master's, comprehensive exam, thesis (for some programs). *Entrance requirements:* For master's, GRE General Test, minimum GPA of 3.0, prior course work in computer science, official transcripts, resume, 2 letters of recommendation; for Certificate, minimum GPA of 3.0, resume. Additional exam requirements/recommendations for international students: Required—TOEFL, IELTS, PTE. *Application deadline:* For fall admission, 7/1 priority date for domestic and international students; for spring admission, 11/1 priority date for domestic and international students; for summer admission, 3/1 for domestic and international students. Applications are processed on a rolling basis. Application fee: $45. Electronic applications accepted. *Financial support:* In 2016–17, 16 students received support, including 16 research assistantships with tuition reimbursements available; teaching assistantships with tuition reimbursements available, Federal Work-Study, institutionally sponsored loans, scholarships/grants, health care benefits, tuition waivers (full), and unspecified assistantships also available. Support available to part-time students. Financial award application deadline: 3/1; financial award applicants required to submit FAFSA. *Unit head:* Dr. Qiuming Zhu, Chairperson, 402-554-2341, E-mail: graduate@unomaha.edu. *Application contact:* Dr. Azad Azadmanesh, Graduate Program Chair, 402-554-2341, E-mail: graduate@unomaha.edu.

University of New Hampshire, Graduate School, College of Engineering and Physical Sciences, Department of Mechanical Engineering, Durham, NH 03824. Offers materials science (MS, PhD); mechanical engineering (M Engr, MS, PhD); systems engineering (PhD). *Program availability:* Part-time. *Degree requirements:* For master's, thesis or alternative; for doctorate, thesis/dissertation. *Entrance requirements:* For master's and doctorate, GRE. Additional exam requirements/recommendations for international students: Required—TOEFL (minimum score 550 paper-based; 80 iBT). Electronic applications accepted. *Faculty research:* Solid mechanics, dynamics, materials science, dynamic systems, automatic control.

University of New Mexico, Graduate Studies, School of Engineering, Program in Nanoscience and Microsystems Engineering, Albuquerque, NM 87131. Offers MS, PhD. *Program availability:* Part-time. *Faculty:* 10 full-time (2 women), 1 (woman) part-time/adjunct. *Students:* 31 full-time (7 women), 20 part-time (7 women); includes 11 minority (3 Black or African American, non-Hispanic/Latino; 1 Asian, non-Hispanic/Latino; 4 Hispanic/Latino; 3 Two or more races, non-Hispanic/Latino), 7 international. Average age 33. 28 applicants, 50% accepted, 11 enrolled. In 2016, 6 master's, 5 doctorates awarded. *Degree requirements:* For master's, comprehensive exam, thesis; for doctorate, comprehensive exam, thesis/dissertation. *Entrance requirements:* For master's and doctorate, GRE. Additional exam requirements/recommendations for international students: Required—TOEFL. *Application deadline:* For fall admission, 7/30 for domestic students, 2/1 for international students; for spring admission, 11/30 for domestic students, 6/1 for international students. Applications are processed on a rolling basis. Application fee: $50. Electronic applications accepted. *Financial support:* Research assistantships with full tuition reimbursements and teaching assistantships with full tuition reimbursements available. *Unit head:* Dr. Abhaya Datye, Professor, 505-277-0477, Fax: 505-277-1024, E-mail: datye@unm.edu. *Application contact:* Heather Elizabeth Armstrong, Program Specialist, 505-277-6824, Fax: 505-277-1024, E-mail: heathera@unm.edu.
Website: http://nsms.unm.edu

The University of North Carolina at Charlotte, William States Lee College of Engineering, Department of Civil and Environmental Engineering, Charlotte, NC 28223-0001. Offers civil engineering (MSCE); infrastructure and environmental systems (PhD), including infrastructure and environmental systems design. *Program availability:* Part-time, evening/weekend. *Faculty:* 24 full-time (4 women). *Students:* 56 full-time (16 women), 37 part-time (14 women); includes 13 minority (4 Black or African American, non-Hispanic/Latino; 3 Asian, non-Hispanic/Latino; 6 Hispanic/Latino), 37 international. Average age 31. 110 applicants, 56% accepted, 18 enrolled. In 2016, 19 master's, 11 doctorates awarded. *Degree requirements:* For master's, comprehensive exam (for some programs), thesis, project, or comprehensive exam; for doctorate, comprehensive exam, thesis/dissertation. *Entrance requirements:* For master's, GRE, undergraduate degree in civil and environmental engineering or a closely-related field; minimum undergraduate GPA of 3.0; for doctorate, GRE General Test, equivalent to U.S. baccalaureate or master's degree from regionally-accredited college or university in engineering, earth science and geology, chemical and biological sciences or a related field with minimum undergraduate GPA of 3.2, graduate 3.5. Additional exam requirements/recommendations for international students: Required—TOEFL (minimum score 523 paper-based, 70 iBT) or IELTS (6.5). *Application deadline:* For fall admission, 3/1 priority date for domestic and international students; for spring admission, 10/1 priority date for domestic and international students; for summer admission, 4/1 priority date for domestic and international students. Applications are processed on a rolling basis. Application fee: $75. Electronic applications accepted. *Expenses:* Contact institution. *Financial support:* In 2016–17, 36 students received support, including 2 fellowships (averaging $30,183 per year), 22 research assistantships (averaging $12,465 per year), 12 teaching assistantships (averaging $4,856 per year); career-related internships or fieldwork, institutionally sponsored loans, scholarships/grants, and unspecified assistantships also available. Support available to part-time students. Financial award application deadline: 3/1; financial award applicants required to submit FAFSA. *Total annual research expenditures:* $2.9 million. *Unit head:* Dr. John L. Daniels, Chair, 704-687-1219, E-mail: jodaniel@uncc.edu. *Application contact:* Kathy B. Giddings, Director of Graduate Admissions, 704-687-5503, Fax: 704-687-1668, E-mail: gradadm@uncc.edu.
Website: http://cee.uncc.edu/

The University of North Carolina at Charlotte, William States Lee College of Engineering, Department of Systems Engineering and Engineering Management, Charlotte, NC 28223-0001. Offers energy analytics (Graduate Certificate); engineering management (MSEM); Lean Six Sigma (Graduate Certificate); logistics and supply chains (Graduate Certificate); systems analytics (Graduate Certificate). *Program availability:* Part-time, evening/weekend, 100% online, blended/hybrid learning. *Faculty:* 9 full-time (1 woman), 2 part-time/adjunct (1 woman). *Students:* 22 full-time (10 women),

61 part-time (12 women); includes 13 minority (7 Black or African American, non-Hispanic/Latino; 1 Asian, non-Hispanic/Latino; 4 Hispanic/Latino; 1 Two or more races, non-Hispanic/Latino), 29 international. Average age 30. 210 applicants, 56% accepted, 31 enrolled. In 2016, 44 master's, 5 other advanced degrees awarded. *Degree requirements:* For master's, project or thesis. *Entrance requirements:* For master's, GRE or GMAT, bachelor's degree in engineering or a closely-related technical or scientific field, or in business, provided relevant technical course requirements have been met; undergraduate coursework in engineering economics, calculus, or statistics; minimum GPA of 3.0; for Graduate Certificate, bachelor's degree in engineering or closely-related technical or scientific field, or bachelor's degree in business, provided relevant technical course requirements have been met; minimum GPA of 3.0; undergraduate coursework in engineering economics, calculus, and statistics; written description of work experience. Additional exam requirements/recommendations for international students: Required—TOEFL (minimum score 523 paper-based, 70 iBT) or IELTS (6.5). *Application deadline:* For fall admission, 3/1 priority date for domestic and international students; for spring admission, 10/1 priority date for domestic and international students; for summer admission, 4/1 priority date for domestic and international students. Applications are processed on a rolling basis. Application fee: $75. Electronic applications accepted. *Expenses:* Contact institution. *Financial support:* In 2016–17, 2 students received support, including 2 research assistantships (averaging $13,750 per year); career-related internships or fieldwork, institutionally sponsored loans, scholarships/grants, and unspecified assistantships also available. Support available to part-time students. Financial award application deadline: 3/1; financial award applicants required to submit FAFSA. *Total annual research expenditures:* $196,680. *Unit head:* Dr. Simon M. Hsiang, Chair, 704-687-1958, E-mail: shsiang1@uncc.edu. *Application contact:* Kathy B. Giddings, Director of Graduate Admissions, 704-687-5503, Fax: 704-687-1668, E-mail: gradadm@uncc.edu.
Website: http://seem.uncc.edu/

University of Pennsylvania, School of Engineering and Applied Science, Department of Electrical and Systems Engineering, Philadelphia, PA 19104. Offers MSE, PhD. *Program availability:* Part-time. *Faculty:* 25 full-time (2 women), 6 part-time/adjunct (0 women). *Students:* 188 full-time (50 women), 53 part-time (20 women); includes 18 minority (10 Asian, non-Hispanic/Latino; 7 Hispanic/Latino; 1 Two or more races, non-Hispanic/Latino), 184 international. Average age 25. 1,060 applicants, 35% accepted, 170 enrolled. In 2016, 84 master's, 7 doctorates awarded. *Degree requirements:* For master's, comprehensive exam, thesis optional; for doctorate, comprehensive exam, thesis/dissertation. *Entrance requirements:* For master's and doctorate, GRE. Additional exam requirements/recommendations for international students: Required—TOEFL (minimum score 100 iBT), IELTS (minimum score 7). *Application deadline:* For fall admission, 3/15 priority date for domestic and international students. Application fee: $80. Electronic applications accepted. *Expenses: Tuition:* Full-time $31,068; part-time $5762 per course. *Required fees:* $3200; $336 per course. Full-time tuition and fees vary according to degree level, program and student level. Part-time tuition and fees vary according to course load, degree level and program. *Faculty research:* Circuits and computer engineering, information decision systems, nano-devices and nano-systems. *Application contact:* William Fenton, Assistant Director of Graduate Admissions, 215-898-4542, Fax: 215-573-5577, E-mail: gradstudies@seas.upenn.edu.

University of Pennsylvania, School of Engineering and Applied Science, Program in Embedded Systems, Philadelphia, PA 19104. Offers MSE. *Students:* 28 full-time (3 women), 22 part-time (9 women); includes 3 minority (all Asian, non-Hispanic/Latino), 42 international. Average age 25. 234 applicants, 16% accepted, 33 enrolled. Application fee: $80. *Expenses: Tuition:* Full-time $31,068; part-time $5762 per course. *Required fees:* $3200; $336 per course. Full-time tuition and fees vary according to degree level, program and student level. Part-time tuition and fees vary according to course load, degree level and program. *Faculty research:* Embedded control systems, model based design and verification, real time operating systems, implementation of embedded systems. *Unit head:* Dr. Rahul Mangharam, Director, E-mail: rahulm@seas.upenn.edu. *Application contact:* William Fenton, Assistant Director of Graduate Admissions, 215-898-4542, Fax: 215-573-5577, E-mail: gradstudies@seas.upenn.edu.
Website: http://www.cis.upenn.edu/prospective-students/graduate/embs.php

University of Regina, Faculty of Graduate Studies and Research, Faculty of Engineering and Applied Science, Program in Industrial Systems Engineering, Regina, SK S4S 0A2, Canada. Offers M Eng, MA Sc, PhD. *Program availability:* Part-time. *Faculty:* 10 full-time (0 women), 24 part-time/adjunct (0 women). *Students:* 29 full-time (5 women), 5 part-time (0 women). 114 applicants, 16% accepted. In 2016, 14 master's, 2 doctorates awarded. *Degree requirements:* For master's, thesis, project, report; for doctorate, thesis/dissertation. *Entrance requirements:* For doctorate, master's degree. Additional exam requirements/recommendations for international students: Required—TOEFL (minimum score 550 paper-based; 80 iBT), IELTS (minimum score 6.5), PTE (minimum score 59). *Application deadline:* For fall admission, 3/31 for domestic and international students; for winter admission, 7/31 for domestic and international students; for spring admission, 11/30 for domestic and international students. Application fee: $100. Electronic applications accepted. *Expenses:* Contact institution. *Financial support:* In 2016–17, 11 fellowships (averaging $6,364 per year), 10 teaching assistantships (averaging $2,537 per year) were awarded; career-related internships or fieldwork and scholarships/grants also available. Financial award application deadline: 6/15. *Faculty research:* Stochastic systems simulation, metallurgy of welding, computer-aided engineering, finite element method of engineering systems, manufacturing systems. *Unit head:* Dr. Amr Henni, Associate Dean, Research and Graduate Studies, 306-585-4960, Fax: 306-585-4855, E-mail: amr.henni@uregina.ca. *Application contact:* Dr. Rene Mayorga, Graduate Coordinator, 306-585-4726, Fax: 306-585-4822, E-mail: rene.mayorga@uregina.ca.
Website: http://www.uregina.ca/engineering/

University of Regina, Faculty of Graduate Studies and Research, Faculty of Engineering and Applied Science, Program in Petroleum Systems Engineering, Regina, SK S4S 0A2, Canada. Offers M Eng, MA Sc, PhD. *Program availability:* Part-time. *Faculty:* 7 full-time (0 women), 24 part-time/adjunct (0 women). *Students:* 52 full-time (15 women), 2 part-time (1 woman). 137 applicants, 8% accepted. In 2016, 25 master's, 3 doctorates awarded. *Degree requirements:* For master's, thesis, project, report; for doctorate, thesis/dissertation. *Entrance requirements:* For doctorate, master's degree. Additional exam requirements/recommendations for international students: Required—TOEFL (minimum score 550 paper-based; 80 iBT), IELTS (minimum score 6.5), PTE (minimum score 59). *Application deadline:* For fall admission, 3/31 for domestic and international students; for winter admission, 7/31 for domestic and international students; for spring admission, 11/30 for domestic and international students. Application fee: $100. Electronic applications accepted. *Expenses:* Contact institution. *Financial support:* In 2016–17, 16 fellowships (averaging $6,313 per year), 13 teaching assistantships (averaging $2,548 per year) were awarded; career-related internships or fieldwork and scholarships/grants also available. Financial award application deadline: 6/15. *Faculty research:* Enhanced oil recovery, production engineering, reservoir engineering, surface thermodynamics, geostatistics. *Unit head:* Dr. Amr Henni, Associate Dean, Research and Graduate Studies, 306-585-4960, Fax: 306-585-4855, E-mail: amr.henni@uregina.ca. *Application contact:* Dr. Na Jia, Graduate Coordinator, 306-337-3287, Fax: 306-585-4855, E-mail: na.jia@uregina.ca.
Website: http://www.uregina.ca/engineering/

University of Regina, Faculty of Graduate Studies and Research, Faculty of Engineering and Applied Science, Program in Process Systems Engineering, Regina, SK S4S 0A2, Canada. Offers M Eng, MA Sc. *Program availability:* Part-time. *Faculty:* 2 full-time (0 women), 24 part-time/adjunct (0 women). *Students:* 25 full-time (7 women), 1 (woman) part-time. 58 applicants, 21% accepted. In 2016, 6 master's awarded. *Degree requirements:* For master's, thesis, project, report. *Entrance requirements:* Additional exam requirements/recommendations for international students: Required—TOEFL (minimum score 550 paper-based; 80 iBT), IELTS (minimum score 6.5), PTE (minimum score 59). *Application deadline:* For fall admission, 3/31 for domestic and international students; for winter admission, 7/31 for domestic and international students; for spring admission, 11/30 for domestic and international students. Application fee: $100. Electronic applications accepted. *Expenses:* Contact institution. *Financial support:* In 2016–17, 6 fellowships (averaging $6,333 per year), 5 teaching assistantships (averaging $2,550 per year) were awarded; career-related internships or fieldwork and scholarships/grants also available. Financial award application deadline: 6/15. *Faculty research:* Membrane separation technologies, advanced reaction engineering, advanced transport phenomena, advanced heat transfer, advanced mass transfer. *Unit head:* Dr. Amr Henni, Associate Dean, Research and Graduate Studies, 306-585-4960, Fax: 306-585-4855, E-mail: amr.henni@uregina.ca. *Application contact:* Dr. Hussameldin Ibrahim, Graduate Coordinator, 306-337-3347, Fax: 306-585-4855, E-mail: hussameldin.ibrahim@uregina.ca.
Website: http://www.uregina.ca/engineering/

University of St. Thomas, Graduate Studies, School of Engineering, St. Paul, MN 55105-1096. Offers data science (MS); electrical engineering (MS); information technology (MS); manufacturing engineering (MS); manufacturing systems (Certificate); mechanical engineering (MS); medical device development (Certificate); regulatory science (MS); software engineering (MS); software management (MS); systems engineering (MS); technology leadership (Certificate); technology management (MS). *Accreditation:* ABET (one or more programs are accredited). *Entrance requirements:* For master's, resume, official transcripts. Additional exam requirements/recommendations for international students: Required—TOEFL (minimum score 550 paper-based). *Application deadline:* For fall admission, 8/1 priority date for domestic students; for spring admission, 1/1 priority date for domestic students. Applications are processed on a rolling basis. Application fee: $50. Electronic applications accepted. *Expenses:* Contact institution. *Financial support:* Fellowships, research assistantships, institutionally sponsored loans, and scholarships/grants available. Support available to part-time students. Financial award application deadline: 4/1; financial award applicants required to submit FAFSA. *Unit head:* Don Weinkauf, Dean, 651-962-5760, Fax: 651-962-6419, E-mail: dhweinkauf@stthomas.edu. *Application contact:* Tina M. Hansen, Graduate Program Manager, 651-962-5755, Fax: 651-962-6419, E-mail: tina.hansen@stthomas.edu.
Website: http://www.stthomas.edu/engineering/

University of South Alabama, College of Engineering, Program in Systems Engineering, Mobile, AL 36688. Offers D Sc. *Students:* 10 full-time (3 women), 3 part-time (0 women); includes 1 minority (Black or African American, non-Hispanic/Latino), 2 international. Average age 34. 8 applicants, 88% accepted, 5 enrolled. In 2016, 1 doctorate awarded. *Degree requirements:* For doctorate, thesis/dissertation, qualifying examination. *Entrance requirements:* For doctorate, GRE, MS in engineering, minimum graduate GPA of 3.0. Additional exam requirements/recommendations for international students: Required—TOEFL (minimum score 550 paper-based; 79 iBT). *Application deadline:* For fall admission, 7/1 priority date for domestic students, 6/1 priority date for international students; for spring admission, 12/1 priority date for domestic students, 11/1 priority date for international students; for summer admission, 5/1 priority date for domestic students, 4/1 priority date for international students. Application fee: $35. Electronic applications accepted. *Expenses:* Contact institution. *Financial support:* Fellowships, research assistantships, teaching assistantships, career-related internships or fieldwork, Federal Work-Study, institutionally sponsored loans, scholarships/grants, and unspecified assistantships available. Support available to part-time students. Financial award application deadline: 5/31; financial award applicants required to submit FAFSA. *Unit head:* Dr. Robert Cloutier, Systems Engineering Chair, 251-341-7993, Fax: 251-460-6343, E-mail: rcloutier@southalabama.edu. *Application contact:* Brenda Poole, Academic Records Specialist, 251-460-6140, Fax: 251-460-6343, E-mail: engineering@southalabama.edu.
Website: http://www.southalabama.edu/colleges/engineering/dsc-se/index.html

University of Southern California, Graduate School, Viterbi School of Engineering, Daniel J. Epstein Department of Industrial and Systems Engineering, Los Angeles, CA 90089. Offers digital supply chain management (MS); engineering management (MS); engineering technology communication (Graduate Certificate); health systems operations (Graduate Certificate); industrial and systems engineering (MS, PhD, Engr); manufacturing engineering (MS); operations research engineering (MS); optimization and supply chain management (Graduate Certificate); product development engineering (MS); safety systems and security (MS); systems architecting and engineering (MS, Graduate Certificate); systems safety and security (Graduate Certificate); transportation systems (Graduate Certificate); MS/MBA. *Program availability:* Part-time, evening/weekend, online learning. Terminal master's awarded for partial completion of doctoral program. *Degree requirements:* For master's, thesis optional; for doctorate, thesis/dissertation. *Entrance requirements:* For master's and doctorate, GRE General Test. Additional exam requirements/recommendations for international students: Recommended—TOEFL. Electronic applications accepted. *Faculty research:* Health systems, music cognition and retrieval, transportation and logistics, manufacturing and automation, engineering systems design, risk and economic analysis.

University of South Florida, Innovative Education, Tampa, FL 33620-9951. Offers adult, career and higher education (Graduate Certificate), including college teaching, leadership in developing human resources, leadership in higher education; Africana studies (Graduate Certificate), including diasporas and health disparities, genocide and human rights; aging studies (Graduate Certificate), including gerontology; art research (Graduate Certificate), including museum studies; business foundations (Graduate Certificate); chemical and biomedical engineering (Graduate Certificate), including materials science and engineering, water, health and sustainability; child and family studies (Graduate Certificate), including positive behavior support; civil and industrial engineering (Graduate Certificate), including transportation systems analysis; community and family health (Graduate Certificate), including maternal and child health, social marketing and public health, violence and injury: prevention and intervention, women's health; criminology (Graduate Certificate), including criminal justice administration; educational measurement and research (Graduate Certificate), including evaluation; English (Graduate Certificate), including comparative literary studies, creative writing, professional and technical communication; entrepreneurship (Graduate Certificate); environmental health (Graduate Certificate), including safety management; epidemiology and biostatistics (Graduate Certificate), including applied biostatistics, biostatistics, concepts and tools of epidemiology, epidemiology, epidemiology of infectious diseases; geography, environment and planning (Graduate Certificate),

including community development, environmental policy and management, geographical information systems; geology (Graduate Certificate), including hydrogeology; global health (Graduate Certificate), including disaster management, global health and Latin American and Caribbean studies, global health practice, humanitarian assistance, infection control; government and international affairs (Graduate Certificate), including Cuban studies, globalization studies; health policy and management (Graduate Certificate), including health management and leadership, public health policy and programs; hearing specialist: early intervention (Graduate Certificate); industrial and management systems engineering (Graduate Certificate), including systems engineering, technology management; information studies (Graduate Certificate), including school library media specialist; information systems/decision sciences (Graduate Certificate), including analytics and business intelligence; instructional technology (Graduate Certificate), including distance education, Florida digital/virtual educator, instructional design, multimedia design, Web design; internal medicine, bioethics and medical humanities (Graduate Certificate), including biomedical ethics; Latin American and Caribbean studies (Graduate Certificate); mass communications (Graduate Certificate), including multimedia journalism; mathematics and statistics (Graduate Certificate), including mathematics; medicine (Graduate Certificate), including aging and neuroscience, bioinformatics, biotechnology, brain fitness and memory management, clinical investigation, health informatics, health sciences, integrative weight management, intellectual property, medicine and gender, metabolic and nutritional medicine, metabolic cardiology, pharmacy sciences; national and competitive intelligence (Graduate Certificate); psychological and social foundations (Graduate Certificate), including career counseling, college teaching, diversity in education, mental health counseling, school counseling; public affairs (Graduate Certificate), including nonprofit management, public management, research administration; public health (Graduate Certificate), including environmental health, health equity, public health generalist, translational research in adolescent behavioral health; public health practices (Graduate Certificate), including planning for healthy communities; rehabilitation and mental health counseling (Graduate Certificate), including integrative mental health care, marriage and family therapy, rehabilitation technology; secondary education (Graduate Certificate), including ESOL, foreign language education: culture and content, foreign language education: professional; social work (Graduate Certificate), including geriatric social work/clinical gerontology; special education (Graduate Certificate), including autism spectrum disorder, disabilities education: severe/profound; world languages (Graduate Certificate), including teaching English as a second language (TESL) or foreign language. *Expenses:* Tuition, state resident: full-time $7766; part-time $431.43 per credit hour. Tuition, nonresident: full-time $15,789; part-time $877.17 per credit hour. *Required fees:* $37 per term. *Unit head:* Kathy Barnes, Interdisciplinary Programs Coordinator, 813-974-8031, Fax: 813-974-7061, E-mail: barnesk@usf.edu. *Application contact:* Karen Tylinski, Metro Initiatives, 813-974-9943, Fax: 813-974-7061, E-mail: ktylinsk@usf.edu.
Website: http://www.usf.edu/innovative-education/

The University of Texas at Arlington, Graduate School, College of Engineering, Department of Industrial and Manufacturing Systems Engineering, Program in Systems Engineering, Arlington, TX 76019. Offers MS. *Unit head:* Dr. Donald H. Liles, Chair, 817-272-3092, Fax: 817-272-3406, E-mail: dliles@uta.edu. *Application contact:* Dr. Sheik Imrhan, Graduate Advisor, 817-272-3167, Fax: 817-272-3406, E-mail: imrhan@uta.edu.

The University of Texas at Dallas, Erik Jonson School of Engineering and Computer Science, Department of Systems Engineering, Richardson, TX 75080. Offers systems engineering and management (MS). *Program availability:* Part-time, evening/weekend. *Faculty:* 2 full-time (0 women), 1 part-time/adjunct (0 women). *Students:* 73 full-time (10 women), 65 part-time (11 women); includes 32 minority (11 Black or African American, non-Hispanic/Latino; 11 Asian, non-Hispanic/Latino; 10 Hispanic/Latino), 75 international. Average age 31. 213 applicants, 34% accepted, 47 enrolled. In 2016, 28 master's awarded. *Degree requirements:* For master's, thesis or major design project. *Entrance requirements:* For master's, GRE General Test, minimum GPA of 3.0 in related bachelor's degree. Additional exam requirements/recommendations for international students: Required—TOEFL (minimum score 550 paper-based). *Application deadline:* For fall admission, 7/15 for domestic students, 5/1 priority date for international students; for spring admission, 11/15 for domestic students, 9/1 priority date for international students. Applications are processed on a rolling basis. Application fee: $50 ($100 for international students). Electronic applications accepted. *Expenses:* Tuition, state resident: full-time $12,418; part-time $690 per semester hour. Tuition, nonresident: full-time $24,150; part-time $1342 per semester hour. Tuition and fees vary according to course load. *Financial support:* In 2016–17, 19 students received support, including 1 teaching assistantship with partial tuition reimbursement available (averaging $16,650 per year); fellowships, research assistantships with partial tuition reimbursements available, Federal Work-Study, institutionally sponsored loans, scholarships/grants, unspecified assistantships, and cooperative positions also available. Support available to part-time students. Financial award application deadline: 4/30; financial award applicants required to submit FAFSA. *Unit head:* Dr. Steve Yurkovich, Head, 972-883-2305. *Application contact:* Leiane Davis, Administrative Associate, 972-883-6851, Fax: 972-883-2813, E-mail: leiane.davis@utdallas.edu.
Website: http://ecs.utdallas.edu/SYSE/

The University of Texas at Dallas, Naveen Jindal School of Management, Program in Organizations, Strategy and International Management, Richardson, TX 75080. Offers business administration (MBA); executive business administration (EMBA); global leadership (EMBA); healthcare management (MS); healthcare management for physicians (EMBA); innovation and entrepreneurship (MS); international management studies (MS, PhD); management and administrative sciences (MS); management science (PhD); project management (EMBA, MS); systems engineering and management (MS); MS/MBA. *Program availability:* Part-time, evening/weekend. *Faculty:* 29 full-time (7 women), 29 part-time/adjunct (5 women). *Students:* 524 full-time (189 women), 860 part-time (374 women); includes 452 minority (112 Black or African American, non-Hispanic/Latino; 3 American Indian or Alaska Native, non-Hispanic/Latino; 207 Asian, non-Hispanic/Latino; 85 Hispanic/Latino; 45 Two or more races, non-Hispanic/Latino), 317 international. Average age 34. 1,763 applicants, 37% accepted, 420 enrolled. In 2016, 521 master's, 13 doctorates awarded. *Degree requirements:* For doctorate, thesis/dissertation. *Entrance requirements:* For master's and doctorate, GMAT. Additional exam requirements/recommendations for international students: Required—TOEFL (minimum score 550 paper-based). *Application deadline:* For fall admission, 7/15 for domestic students, 5/1 priority date for international students; for spring admission, 11/15 for domestic students, 9/1 priority date for international students. Applications are processed on a rolling basis. Application fee: $50 ($100 for international students). Electronic applications accepted. *Expenses:* Tuition, state resident: full-time $12,418; part-time $690 per semester hour. Tuition, nonresident: full-time $24,150; part-time $1342 per semester hour. Tuition and fees vary according to course load. *Financial support:* In 2016–17, 385 students received support, including 21 research assistantships with partial tuition reimbursements available (averaging $25,698 per year), 68 teaching assistantships with partial tuition reimbursements available (averaging $16,973 per year); Federal Work-Study, institutionally sponsored loans, scholarships/grants, and unspecified assistantships also available. Support available to part-time students. Financial award application deadline: 4/30; financial award applicants required to submit FAFSA. *Faculty research:* International accounting, international trade and finance, economic development, international economics. *Unit head:* Dr. Seung-Hyun Lee, Area Coordinator, 972-883-6267, Fax: 972-883-5977, E-mail: sxl029100@utdallas.edu. *Application contact:* Maria Hasenhuttl, Assistant Area Coordinator, 972-883-5898, Fax: 972-883-5977, E-mail: maria.hasenhuttl@utdallas.edu.
Website: http://jindal.utdallas.edu/osim/

The University of Texas at El Paso, Graduate School, College of Engineering, Department of Industrial Engineering, El Paso, TX 79968-0001. Offers industrial engineering (MS); manufacturing engineering (MS); systems engineering (MS, Certificate). *Program availability:* Part-time, evening/weekend. *Degree requirements:* For master's, thesis optional. *Entrance requirements:* For master's, GRE General Test, minimum GPA of 3.0 in major. Additional exam requirements/recommendations for international students: Required—TOEFL. Electronic applications accepted. *Faculty research:* Computer vision, automated inspection, simulation and modeling.

The University of Texas Rio Grande Valley, College of Engineering and Computer Science, Department of Manufacturing and Industrial Engineering, Edinburg, TX 78539. Offers engineering management (MS); manufacturing engineering (MS); systems engineering (MS). Tuition and fees vary according to course load and program.

University of Utah, Graduate School, David Eccles School of Business, Department of Operations and Information Systems, Salt Lake City, UT 84112. Offers information systems (MS, Graduate Certificate), including business intelligence and analytics, IT security, product and process management, software and systems architecture. *Program availability:* Part-time, evening/weekend, 100% online, blended/hybrid learning. *Faculty:* 12 full-time (5 women), 7 part-time/adjunct (0 women). *Students:* 143 full-time (43 women), 107 part-time (28 women); includes 127 minority (1 Black or African American, non-Hispanic/Latino; 120 Asian, non-Hispanic/Latino; 3 Hispanic/Latino; 3 Two or more races, non-Hispanic/Latino), 123 international. Average age 29. 334 applicants, 72% accepted, 127 enrolled. In 2016, 96 master's awarded. *Degree requirements:* For master's, capstone project. *Entrance requirements:* For master's, GMAT/GRE, minimum undergraduate GPA of 3.0, 2 letters of recommendation, personal statement, professional resume. Additional exam requirements/recommendations for international students: Required—TOEFL (minimum score 550 paper-based; 80 iBT), IELTS (minimum score 6.5). *Application deadline:* For fall admission, 7/28 for domestic students, 3/1 for international students; for spring admission, 12/7 for domestic students, 8/16 for international students. Applications are processed on a rolling basis. Application fee: $55 ($65 for international students). Electronic applications accepted. *Expenses:* Contact institution. *Financial support:* In 2016–17, 75 students received support, including 7 teaching assistantships (averaging $5,000 per year); fellowships with partial tuition reimbursements available, tuition waivers (partial), and unspecified assistantships also available. Financial award application deadline: 3/31; financial award applicants required to submit FAFSA. *Faculty research:* Business intelligence and analytics, software and system architecture, product and process management, IT security, Web and data mining, applications and management of IT in healthcare. *Unit head:* Dr. Bradden Blair, Director of the IS Programs, 801-587-9489, Fax: 801-581-3666, E-mail: b.blair@eccles.utah.edu. *Application contact:* Raven Clissold, Admissions Coordinator, 801-587-5838, Fax: 801-581-3666, E-mail: raven.clissold@eccles.utah.edu.
Website: http://msis.eccles.utah.edu

University of Virginia, School of Engineering and Applied Science, Department of Systems and Information Engineering, Charlottesville, VA 22903. Offers ME, MS, PhD, ME/MBA. *Program availability:* Online learning. *Faculty:* 20 full-time (3 women). *Students:* 62 full-time (13 women), 9 part-time (2 women); includes 10 minority (1 Black or African American, non-Hispanic/Latino; 5 Asian, non-Hispanic/Latino; 2 Hispanic/Latino; 2 Two or more races, non-Hispanic/Latino), 43 international. Average age 28. 147 applicants, 38% accepted, 26 enrolled. In 2016, 47 master's, 5 doctorates awarded. *Degree requirements:* For master's, comprehensive exam (for some programs); for doctorate, comprehensive exam, thesis/dissertation. *Entrance requirements:* For master's, GRE General Test, 3 letters of recommendation; for doctorate, GRE General Test, 3 letters of recommendation; essay. Additional exam requirements/recommendations for international students: Required—TOEFL (minimum score 650 paper-based; 90 iBT), IELTS (minimum score 7). *Application deadline:* For fall admission, 8/1 for domestic students, 4/1 for international students; for winter admission, 12/1 for domestic students, 8/1 for international students; for spring admission, 5/1 for domestic students, 1/1 for international students. Applications are processed on a rolling basis. Application fee: $60. Electronic applications accepted. *Expenses:* Tuition, state resident: full-time $15,026; part-time $834 per credit hour. Tuition, nonresident: full-time $25,168; part-time $1378 per credit hour. *Required fees:* $2654. *Financial support:* Fellowships, research assistantships, and teaching assistantships available. Financial award application deadline: 1/15; financial award applicants required to submit FAFSA. *Faculty research:* Systems integration, human factors, computational statistics and simulation, risk and decision analysis, optimization and control. *Unit head:* Barry Horowitz, Chair, 434-924-5393, Fax: 434-982-2972, E-mail: bh8e@virginia.edu. *Application contact:* Jayne Weber, Degree Coordinator, 434-924-6473, Fax: 434-982-2972, E-mail: jef2f@virginia.edu.
Website: http://www.sys.virginia.edu/

University of Waterloo, Graduate Studies, Faculty of Engineering, Department of Systems Design Engineering, Waterloo, ON N2L 3G1, Canada. Offers M Eng, MA Sc, PhD. *Program availability:* Part-time. *Degree requirements:* For master's, research project or thesis; for doctorate, comprehensive exam, thesis/dissertation. *Entrance requirements:* For master's, honors degree, minimum B average, resume; for doctorate, master's degree, minimum A- average. Additional exam requirements/recommendations for international students: Required—TOEFL, IELTS, PTE. Electronic applications accepted. *Faculty research:* Ergonomics, human factors and biomedical engineering, modeling and simulation, pattern analysis, machine intelligence and robotics.

University of Wisconsin–Madison, Graduate School, College of Engineering, Department of Industrial and Systems Engineering, Madison, WI 53706. Offers industrial engineering (MS, PhD), including human factors and health systems engineering (MS), systems engineering and analytics (MS). *Program availability:* Part-time. *Faculty:* 18 full-time (5 women). *Students:* 94 full-time (37 women), 6 part-time (2 women); includes 2 minority (both Black or African American, non-Hispanic/Latino), 73 international. Average age 26. 463 applicants, 22% accepted, 35 enrolled. In 2016, 28 master's, 13 doctorates awarded. Terminal master's awarded for partial completion of doctoral program. *Degree requirements:* For master's, thesis optional, 30 credits; minimum GPA of 3.0; for doctorate, comprehensive exam, thesis/dissertation, minimum of 32 credits; minimum GPA of 3.0. *Entrance requirements:* For master's and doctorate, GRE General Test, minimum GPA of 3.0, BS in engineering or equivalent, course work in computer programming and statistics. Additional exam requirements/recommendations for international students: Required—TOEFL (minimum score 580 paper-based; 92 iBT), IELTS (minimum score 7). *Application deadline:* For fall admission, 1/1 for domestic and international students; for spring admission, 10/1 for domestic and international students; for summer admission, 2/1 for domestic and international students. Application fee: $75 ($81 for international students). Electronic applications accepted. *Expenses:*

$13,157 per year in-state tuition and fees; $26,484 per year out-of-state tuition and fees. *Financial support:* In 2016–17, 50 students received support, including 1 fellowship with full tuition reimbursement available, 30 research assistantships with full tuition reimbursements available, 14 teaching assistantships with full tuition reimbursements available; career-related internships or fieldwork, Federal Work-Study, institutionally sponsored loans, scholarships/grants, traineeships, health care benefits, and unspecified assistantships also available. Financial award application deadline: 12/1; financial award applicants required to submit FAFSA. *Faculty research:* Operations research; human factors and ergonomics; health systems engineering; manufacturing and production systems. *Total annual research expenditures:* $12.5 million. *Unit head:* Dr. Jeff Lindroth, Chair, 608-890-1931, Fax: 608-262-8454, E-mail: linderoth@wisc.edu. *Application contact:* Pam Peterson, Student Services Coordinator, 608-263-4025, Fax: 608-262-8454, E-mail: prpeterson@wisc.edu.
Website: http://www.engr.wisc.edu/department/industrial-systems-engineering/

Virginia Polytechnic Institute and State University, Graduate School, College of Engineering, Blacksburg, VA 24061. Offers aerospace engineering (ME, MS, PhD); biological systems engineering (ME, MS, PhD); biomedical engineering (MS, PhD); chemical engineering (ME, MS, PhD); civil engineering (ME, MS, PhD); computer engineering (ME, MS, PhD); computer science (MS, PhD); electrical engineering (ME, PhD); engineering education (PhD); engineering mechanics (ME, MS, PhD); environmental engineering (MS); environmental science and engineering (MS); industrial and systems engineering (ME, MS, PhD); materials science and engineering (ME, MS, PhD); mechanical engineering (ME, MS, PhD); mining and minerals engineering (PhD); mining engineering (ME, MS); nuclear engineering (MS, PhD); ocean engineering (MS); systems engineering (ME, MS). *Faculty:* 400 full-time (73 women), 3 part-time/adjunct (2 women). *Students:* 1,949 full-time (487 women), 393 part-time (69 women); includes 251 minority (56 Black or African American, non-Hispanic/Latino; 3 American Indian or Alaska Native, non-Hispanic/Latino; 87 Asian, non-Hispanic/Latino; 70 Hispanic/Latino; 35 Two or more races, non-Hispanic/Latino), 1,354 international. Average age 27. 4,903 applicants, 19% accepted, 569 enrolled. In 2016, 364 master's, 200 doctorates awarded. *Degree requirements:* For master's, comprehensive exam (for some programs), thesis (for some programs); for doctorate, comprehensive exam (for some programs), thesis/dissertation (for some programs). *Entrance requirements:* For master's and doctorate, GRE/GMAT. Additional exam requirements/recommendations for international students: Required—TOEFL (minimum score 80 iBT). *Application deadline:* For fall admission, 8/1 for domestic students, 4/1 for international students; for spring admission, 1/1 for domestic students, 9/1 for international students. Applications are processed on a rolling basis. Application fee: $75. Electronic applications accepted. *Expenses:* Tuition, state resident: full-time $12,467; part-time $692.50 per credit hour. Tuition, nonresident: full-time $25,095; part-time $1394.25 per credit hour. *Required fees:* $2669; $491.50 per semester. Tuition and fees vary according to course load, campus/location and program. *Financial support:* In 2016–17, 160 fellowships with full tuition reimbursements (averaging $7,387 per year), 872 research assistantships with full tuition reimbursements (averaging $22,329 per year), 313 teaching assistantships with full tuition reimbursements (averaging $18,714 per year) were awarded. Financial award application deadline: 3/1; financial award applicants required to submit FAFSA. *Total annual research expenditures:* $91.8 million. *Unit head:* Dr. Julia Ross, Dean, 540-231-9752, Fax: 540-231-3031, E-mail: deaneng@vt.edu. *Application contact:* Linda Perkins, Executive Assistant, 540-231-9752, Fax: 540-231-3031, E-mail: lperkins@vt.edu.
Website: http://www.eng.vt.edu/

Virginia Polytechnic Institute and State University, VT Online, Blacksburg, VA 24061. Offers advanced transportation systems (Certificate); aerospace engineering (MS); agricultural and life sciences (MSLFS); business information systems (Graduate Certificate); career and technical education (MS); civil engineering (MS); computer engineering (M Eng, MS); decision support systems (Graduate Certificate); eLearning leadership (MA); electrical engineering (M Eng, MS); engineering administration (MEA); environmental engineering (Certificate); environmental politics and policy (Graduate Certificate); environmental sciences and engineering (MS); foundations of political analysis (Graduate Certificate); health product risk management (Graduate Certificate); industrial and systems engineering (MS); information policy and society (Graduate Certificate); information security (Graduate Certificate); information technology (MIT); instructional technology (MA); integrative STEM education (MA Ed); liberal arts (Graduate Certificate); life sciences: health product risk management (MS); natural resources (MNR, Graduate Certificate); networking (Graduate Certificate); nonprofit and nongovernmental organization management (Graduate Certificate); ocean engineering (MS); political science (MA); security studies (Graduate Certificate); software development (Graduate Certificate). *Expenses:* Tuition, state resident: full-time $12,467; part-time $692.50 per credit hour. Tuition, nonresident: full-time $25,095; part-time $1394.25 per credit hour. *Required fees:* $2669; $491.50 per semester. Tuition and fees vary according to course load, campus/location and program.

Wayne State University, College of Engineering, Department of Industrial and Systems Engineering, Detroit, MI 48202. Offers data science and business analytics (MS); engineering management (MS); industrial engineering (MS, PhD); manufacturing engineering (MS); systems engineering (Certificate). *Faculty:* 10. *Students:* 313 full-time (37 women), 140 part-time (26 women); includes 37 minority (16 Black or African American, non-Hispanic/Latino; 15 Asian, non-Hispanic/Latino; 3 Hispanic/Latino; 3 Two or more races, non-Hispanic/Latino), 340 international. Average age 28. 1,171 applicants, 42% accepted, 105 enrolled. In 2016, 117 master's, 5 doctorates awarded. *Degree requirements:* For master's, thesis (for some programs); for doctorate, thesis/dissertation. *Entrance requirements:* For master's, BS from ABET-accredited institution; for doctorate, MS in industrial engineering or operations research with minimum graduate GPA of 3.5; for Certificate, BS in engineering or other technical field from ABET-accredited institution, full-time work experience as practicing engineer or technical leader. Additional exam requirements/recommendations for international students: Required—TOEFL (minimum score 550 paper-based; 79 iBT), TWE (minimum score 5.5), Michigan English Language Assessment Battery (minimum score 85); Recommended—IELTS (minimum score 6.5). *Application deadline:* For fall admission, 6/1 priority date for domestic students, 5/1 priority date for international students; for winter admission, 10/1 priority date for domestic students, 9/1 priority date for international students; for spring admission, 2/1 priority date for domestic students, 1/1 priority date for international students. Applications are processed on a rolling basis. Application fee: $50. Electronic applications accepted. *Expenses:* $18,871 per year resident tuition and fees, $36,065 per year non-resident tuition and fees. *Financial support:* In 2016–17, 118 students received support, including 2 fellowships with tuition reimbursements available (averaging $16,000 per year), 4 research assistantships with tuition reimbursements available (averaging $18,883 per year), 12 teaching assistantships with tuition reimbursements available (averaging $19,177 per year); scholarships/grants, tuition waivers (full), and unspecified assistantships also available. Financial award applicants required to submit FAFSA. *Faculty research:* Healthcare systems engineering, product design and development, quality and reliability engineering, supply chain management and logistics. *Total annual research expenditures:* $3.2 million. *Unit head:* Dr. Leslie Monplaisir, Associate Professor/Chair, 313-577-3821, Fax: 313-577-8833, E-mail: leslie.monplaisir@wayne.edu. *Application contact:* Eric Scimeca, Graduate Program Coordinator, 313-577-0412, E-mail: eric.scimeca@wayne.edu.
Website: http://engineering.wayne.edu/ise/

Worcester Polytechnic Institute, Graduate Studies and Research, Program in Systems Engineering, Worcester, MA 01609-2280. Offers MS, Graduate Certificate. *Program availability:* Part-time, evening/weekend, online only, 100% online. *Students:* 7 full-time (6 women), 161 part-time (31 women); includes 39 minority (8 Black or African American, non-Hispanic/Latino; 1 American Indian or Alaska Native, non-Hispanic/Latino; 19 Asian, non-Hispanic/Latino; 6 Hispanic/Latino; 5 Two or more races, non-Hispanic/Latino), 1 international. 97 applicants, 84% accepted, 63 enrolled. In 2016, 87 master's awarded. *Entrance requirements:* For master's, 3 letters of recommendation. Additional exam requirements/recommendations for international students: Required—TOEFL (minimum score 563 paper-based; 84 iBT), IELTS (minimum score 7). *Application deadline:* For fall admission, 1/1 for domestic and international students; for spring admission, 10/1 for domestic and international students. Applications are processed on a rolling basis. Application fee: $70. Electronic applications accepted. *Financial support:* Research assistantships and teaching assistantships available. Financial award application deadline: 1/1; financial award applicants required to submit FAFSA. *Unit head:* Don Gelosh, Director, E-mail: dsgelosh@wpi.edu. *Application contact:* Lynne Dougherty, Administrative Assistant, 508-831-5301, Fax: 508-831-5717, E-mail: grad@wpi.edu.
Website: http://cpe.wpi.edu/online/systems.html

Section 15
Management of Engineering and Technology

This section contains a directory of institutions offering graduate work in management of engineering and technology. Additional information about programs listed in the directory may be obtained by writing directly to the dean of a graduate school or chair of a department at the address given in the directory.

For programs offering related work, in the other guides in this series:

Graduate Programs in the Humanities, Arts & Social Sciences

See *Applied Arts and Design, Architecture, Economics,* and *Sociology, Anthropology, and Archaeology*

Graduate Programs in the Biological/Biomedical Sciences & Health-Related Medical Professions

See *Biophysics (Radiation Biology); Ecology, Environmental Biology, and Evolutionary Biology;* and *Health Services (Health Services Management and Hospital Administration)*

Graduate Programs in Business, Education, Information Studies, Law & Social Work

See *Business Administration and Management* and *Law*

CONTENTS

Program Directories

Construction Management

The American University in Dubai, Graduate Programs, Dubai, United Arab Emirates. Offers construction management (MS); education (M Ed); finance (MBA); generalist (MBA); marketing (MBA). *Program availability:* Part-time, evening/weekend. *Degree requirements:* For master's, thesis optional. *Entrance requirements:* For master's, GMAT (for MBA); GRE (for M Ed and MS), minimum undergraduate GPA of 3.0, official transcripts, two reference forms, curriculum vitae/resume, statement of career objectives, work experience. Additional exam requirements/recommendations for international students: Required—TOEFL (minimum score 550 paper-based; 79 iBT). Electronic applications accepted.

Arizona State University at the Tempe campus, Ira A. Fulton Schools of Engineering, ASU Engineering Online Programs, Tempe, AZ 85287. Offers construction (MS); embedded systems (M Eng); enterprise systems innovation and management (MSE); modeling and simulation (M Eng); quality and reliability engineering (M Eng); software engineering (MSE); systems engineering (M Eng).

Arizona State University at the Tempe campus, Ira A. Fulton Schools of Engineering, School of Sustainable Engineering and the Built Environment, Tempe, AZ 85287-5306. Offers civil, environmental and sustainable engineering (MS, MSE, PhD); construction engineering (MSE); construction management (MS, PhD). *Program availability:* Part-time, evening/weekend, online learning. Terminal master's awarded for partial completion of doctoral program. *Degree requirements:* For master's, thesis optional, comprehensive exams (MSE); interactive Program of Study (iPOS) submitted before completing 50 percent of required credit hours; for doctorate, comprehensive exam, thesis/dissertation, interactive Program of Study (iPOS) submitted before completing 50 percent of required credit hours. *Entrance requirements:* For master's, GRE, minimum GPA of 3.0 or equivalent in last 2 years of work leading to bachelor's degree; for doctorate, GRE, minimum GPA of 3.0 in last 2 years of work leading to bachelor's degree, 3.2 in all graduate-level coursework with master's degree; 3 letters of recommendation; resume/curriculum vitae; letter of intent; thesis (if applicable); statement of research interests. Additional exam requirements/recommendations for international students: Required—TOEFL, IELTS, or PTE. Electronic applications accepted. *Expenses:* Contact institution. *Faculty research:* Water purification, transportation (safety and materials), construction management, environmental biotechnology, environmental nanotechnology, earth systems engineering and management, SMART innovations, project performance metrics, and underground infrastructure.

Brigham Young University, Graduate Studies, Ira A. Fulton College of Engineering and Technology, School of Technology, Provo, UT 84602. Offers construction management (MS); information technology (MS); manufacturing engineering technology (MS); technology and engineering education (MS). *Faculty:* 25 full-time (0 women), 3 part-time/adjunct (0 women). *Students:* 36 full-time (4 women); includes 5 minority (2 American Indian or Alaska Native, non-Hispanic/Latino; 2 Asian, non-Hispanic/Latino; 1 Hispanic/Latino). Average age 29. 14 applicants, 100% accepted, 13 enrolled. In 2016, 11 master's awarded. *Degree requirements:* For master's, thesis. *Entrance requirements:* For master's, GRE General Test; GMAT or GRE (for construction management emphasis), minimum GPA of 3.0 in last 60 hours of course work. Additional exam requirements/recommendations for international students: Required—TOEFL (minimum score 580 paper-based; 85 iBT). *Application deadline:* For fall admission, 2/15 for domestic and international students; for winter admission, 9/10 for domestic students, 9/15 for international students; for spring admission, 2/15 for domestic and international students; for summer admission, 2/15 for domestic and international students. Application fee: $50. Electronic applications accepted. *Expenses: Tuition:* Full-time $6680; part-time $393 per credit. Tuition and fees vary according to course load, program and student's religious affiliation. *Financial support:* In 2016–17, 28 students received support, including 3 research assistantships (averaging $18,288 per year), 11 teaching assistantships (averaging $7,500 per year); scholarships/grants also available. *Faculty research:* Information assurance and security, HEI and databases, manufacturing materials, processes and systems, innovation in construction management scheduling and delivery methods. *Total annual research expenditures:* $844,333. *Unit head:* Dr. Barry M. Lunt, Director, 801-422-6300, Fax: 801-422-0490, E-mail: blunt@byu.edu. *Application contact:* Clifton Farnsworth, Graduate Coordinator, 801-422-6494, Fax: 801-422-0490, E-mail: clifton_farnsworth@byu.edu. Website: http://www.et.byu.edu/sot/

California Baptist University, Program in Business Administration, Riverside, CA 92504-3206. Offers accounting (MBA); construction management (MBA); healthcare management (MBA); management (MBA). *Accreditation:* ACBSP. *Program availability:* Part-time, evening/weekend, 100% online, blended/hybrid learning. *Faculty:* 14 full-time (3 women), 10 part-time/adjunct (1 woman). *Students:* 105 full-time (48 women), 122 part-time (63 women); includes 101 minority (23 Black or African American, non-Hispanic/Latino; 1 American Indian or Alaska Native, non-Hispanic/Latino; 10 Asian, non-Hispanic/Latino; 59 Hispanic/Latino; 2 Native Hawaiian or other Pacific Islander, non-Hispanic/Latino; 6 Two or more races, non-Hispanic/Latino), 54 international. Average age 29. 136 applicants, 65% accepted, 62 enrolled. In 2016, 71 master's awarded. *Degree requirements:* For master's, interdisciplinary capstone project. *Entrance requirements:* For master's, GMAT, minimum GPA of 2.5; two recommendations; comprehensive essay; resume; interview. Additional exam requirements/recommendations for international students: Required—TOEFL (minimum score 80 iBT). *Application deadline:* For fall admission, 8/1 priority date for domestic students, 7/1 for international students; for spring admission, 12/1 priority date for domestic students, 11/1 for international students. Applications are processed on a rolling basis. Application fee: $45. Electronic applications accepted. *Expenses:* Contact institution. *Financial support:* In 2016–17, 38 students received support. Federal Work-Study and scholarships/grants available. Financial award applicants required to submit CSS PROFILE or FAFSA. *Faculty research:* Behavioral economics, economic indicators, marketing ethics, international business, microfinance. *Unit head:* Dr. Steve Strombeck, Interim Dean, School of Business, 951-343-4701, Fax: 951-343-4361, E-mail: sstrombeck@calbaptist.edu. *Application contact:* Stephanie Fluitt, Graduate Admissions Counselor, 951-343-4696, E-mail: sfluitt@calbaptist.edu. Website: http://www.calbaptist.edu/mba/about/

California State University, Chico, Office of Graduate Studies, College of Engineering, Computer Science, and Construction Management, Chico, CA 95929-0722. Offers MS. *Program availability:* Part-time, online learning. *Faculty:* 59 full-time (12 women), 37 part-time/adjunct (4 women). *Students:* 28 full-time (6 women), 47 part-time (13 women); includes 56 minority (55 Asian, non-Hispanic/Latino; 1 Hispanic/Latino). 89 applicants, 74% accepted, 12 enrolled. In 2016, 34 master's awarded. *Degree requirements:* For master's, thesis or project. *Entrance requirements:* For master's, GRE. Additional exam requirements/recommendations for international students: Required—TOEFL (minimum score 550 paper-based; 80 iBT), IELTS (minimum score 6.5), PTE (minimum score 59). *Application deadline:* For fall admission, 3/1 priority date for domestic students, 3/1 for

international students; for spring admission, 9/15 priority date for domestic students, 9/15 for international students. Application fee: $55. Electronic applications accepted. *Financial support:* Fellowships, research assistantships, teaching assistantships, career-related internships or fieldwork, Federal Work-Study, scholarships/grants, and traineeships available. Support available to part-time students. Financial award application deadline: 3/1; financial award applicants required to submit FAFSA. *Unit head:* Ricardo Jacquez, Dean, 530-898-5963, Fax: 530-898-4070, E-mail: ecc@csuchico.edu. *Application contact:* Judy L. Rice, Graduate Admissions Counselor, 530-898-5416, Fax: 530-898-3342, E-mail: jlrice@csuchico.edu. Website: http://www.csuchico.edu/ecc/

California State University, East Bay, Office of Graduate Studies, College of Science, School of Engineering, Program in Construction Management, Hayward, CA 94542-3000. Offers MS. *Students:* 7 full-time (4 women), 57 part-time (12 women); includes 17 minority (5 Black or African American, non-Hispanic/Latino; 7 Asian, non-Hispanic/Latino; 3 Hispanic/Latino; 2 Two or more races, non-Hispanic/Latino), 28 international. Average age 31. 145 applicants, 48% accepted, 19 enrolled. In 2016, 16 master's awarded. *Degree requirements:* For master's, comprehensive exam (for some programs), research project or exam. *Entrance requirements:* For master's, GRE or GMAT, baccalaureate degree from accredited university with minimum overall GPA of 2.5; relevant work experience; college algebra and trigonometry or equivalent level math courses; personal statement; resume; two letters of recommendation. Additional exam requirements/recommendations for international students: Required—TOEFL (minimum score 550 paper-based; 79 iBT). *Application deadline:* For fall admission, 6/30 for domestic and international students. Applications are processed on a rolling basis. Application fee: $55. Electronic applications accepted. *Financial support:* Federal Work-Study and institutionally sponsored loans available. Support available to part-time students. Financial award application deadline: 3/2; financial award applicants required to submit FAFSA. *Unit head:* Dr. Saeid Motavalli, Department Chair/Graduate Advisor, 510-885-4481, E-mail: saeid.motavalli@csueastbay.edu. *Application contact:* Dr. Donna Wiley, Interim Associate Vice President for Academic Programs and Graduate Studies, 510-885-3716, Fax: 510-885-4777, E-mail: donna.wiley@csueastbay.edu. Website: http://www20.csueastbay.edu/csci/departments/engineering/

California State University, Northridge, Graduate Studies, College of Engineering and Computer Science, Department of Civil Engineering and Construction Management, Northridge, CA 91330. Offers engineering (MS), including structural engineering. *Program availability:* Part-time, evening/weekend. *Faculty:* 8 full-time (6 women), 14 part-time/adjunct (all women). *Students:* 20 full-time (6 women), 45 part-time (7 women); includes 29 minority (1 Black or African American, non-Hispanic/Latino; 9 Asian, non-Hispanic/Latino; 17 Hispanic/Latino; 2 Two or more races, non-Hispanic/Latino), 7 international. Average age 28. 71 applicants, 52% accepted, 23 enrolled. *Degree requirements:* For master's, thesis. *Entrance requirements:* Additional exam requirements/recommendations for international students: Required—TOEFL. *Application deadline:* For fall admission, 11/30 for domestic students. Application fee: $55. *Expenses:* Tuition, state resident: full-time $4152. *Financial support:* Teaching assistantships available. Financial award application deadline: 3/1. *Faculty research:* Composite study. *Unit head:* Dr. Nazaret Dermendjian, Chair, 818-677-2166. Website: http://www.csun.edu/~ceam/

Carnegie Mellon University, Carnegie Institute of Technology, Department of Civil and Environmental Engineering, Pittsburgh, PA 15213. Offers advanced infrastructure systems (MS, PhD); advanced infrastructure systems technology development and application (MS); air quality engineering and science (MS); civil and environmental engineering (MS, PhD); civil and environmental engineering/engineering and public policy (PhD); civil engineering (MS, PhD); computational mechanics (MS, PhD); computational modeling and monitoring for resilient structural and material systems (MS); energy infrastructure systems (MS); environmental engineering (MS, PhD); environmental management and science (MS, PhD); IT-based sustainable global infrastructure and construction management (MS); sustainability and green design (MS); water quality engineering and science (MS). *Program availability:* Part-time. *Faculty:* 23 full-time (5 women), 12 part-time/adjunct (3 women). *Students:* 230 full-time (87 women), 4 part-time (0 women); includes 17 minority (4 Black or African American, non-Hispanic/Latino; 12 Asian, non-Hispanic/Latino; 1 Two or more races, non-Hispanic/Latino), 179 international. Average age 25. 653 applicants, 60% accepted, 107 enrolled. In 2016, 145 master's, 15 doctorates awarded. Terminal master's awarded for partial completion of doctoral program. *Degree requirements:* For master's, thesis optional; for doctorate, comprehensive exam, thesis/dissertation, two-part qualifying exam, public defense of dissertation. *Entrance requirements:* For master's, GRE General Test, BS in engineering, science or mathematics; for doctorate, GRE General Test, BS or MS in engineering, science or mathematics. Additional exam requirements/recommendations for international students: Required—TOEFL (minimum score 84 iBT) or IELTS (6.0). *Application deadline:* For fall admission, 1/5 priority date for domestic and international students; for spring admission, 9/15 priority date for domestic and international students. Applications are processed on a rolling basis. Application fee: $65. Electronic applications accepted. *Expenses:* Contact institution. *Financial support:* In 2016–17, 129 students received support. Fellowships with tuition reimbursements available, research assistantships with tuition reimbursements available, scholarships/grants, tuition waivers (full and partial), unspecified assistantships, and service assistantships available. Financial award application deadline: 1/5. *Faculty research:* Advanced infrastructure systems; environmental engineering, sustainability, and science; mechanics, materials, and computing. *Total annual research expenditures:* $7.4 million. *Unit head:* Dr. David A. Dzombak, Professor and Department Head, 412-268-2941, Fax: 412-268-7813, E-mail: dzombak@cmu.edu. *Application contact:* David A. Vey, Graduate Admissions Manager, 412-268-2292, Fax: 412-268-7813, E-mail: dvey@andrew.cmu.edu. Website: http://www.cmu.edu/cee/

Carnegie Mellon University, College of Fine Arts, School of Architecture, Pittsburgh, PA 15213-3891. Offers architecture (MSA); architecture, engineering, and construction management (PhD); building performance and diagnostics (MS, PhD); computational design (MS, PhD); engineering construction management (MSA); tangible interaction design (MTID); urban design (MUD). Terminal master's awarded for partial completion of doctoral program. *Degree requirements:* For doctorate, thesis/dissertation. *Entrance requirements:* For master's and doctorate, GRE General Test. Additional exam requirements/recommendations for international students: Required—TOEFL.

Central Connecticut State University, School of Graduate Studies, School of Engineering, Science and Technology, Department of Manufacturing and Construction Management, New Britain, CT 06050-4010. Offers construction management (MS, Certificate); environmental and occupational safety (Certificate); lean manufacturing and Six Sigma (Certificate); supply chain and logistics (Certificate); technology management (MS). *Program availability:* Part-time, evening/weekend. *Faculty:* 7 full-time (0 women),

3 part-time/adjunct (0 women). *Students:* 23 full-time (6 women), 88 part-time (21 women); includes 29 minority (11 Black or African American, non-Hispanic/Latino; 7 Asian, non-Hispanic/Latino; 10 Hispanic/Latino; 1 Two or more races, non-Hispanic/Latino), 12 international. Average age 34. 79 applicants, 68% accepted, 32 enrolled. In 2016, 43 master's, 4 other advanced degrees awarded. *Degree requirements:* For master's, comprehensive exam, special project; for Certificate, qualifying exam. *Entrance requirements:* For master's, minimum undergraduate GPA of 2.7. Additional exam requirements/recommendations for international students: Required—TOEFL (minimum score 550 paper-based; 79 iBT). *Application deadline:* For fall admission, 8/1 for domestic students, 5/1 for international students; for spring admission, 11/1 for domestic and international students. Applications are processed on a rolling basis. Application fee: $50. Electronic applications accepted. *Expenses: Tuition, area resident:* Full-time $6497; part-time $606 per credit. Tuition, state resident: full-time $9748; part-time $622 per credit. Tuition, nonresident: full-time $18,102; part-time $622 per credit. *Required fees:* $4459; $246 per credit. *Financial support:* In 2016–17, 10 students received support. Career-related internships or fieldwork, Federal Work-Study, scholarships/grants, and unspecified assistantships available. Support available to part-time students. Financial award application deadline: 3/1; financial award applicants required to submit FAFSA. *Faculty research:* All aspects of middle management, technical supervision in the workplace. *Unit head:* Dr. Ravindra Thamma, Chair, 860-832-1830, E-mail: kovelj@ccsu.edu. *Application contact:* Patricia Gardner, Associate Director of Graduate Studies, 860-832-2350, Fax: 860-832-2362.
Website: http://www.ccsu.edu/mcm/

Clemson University, Graduate School, College of Architecture, Arts, and Humanities, Department of Construction Science and Management, Clemson, SC 29634-0507. Offers MCSM, Certificate. *Program availability:* Part-time, blended/hybrid learning. *Faculty:* 7 full-time (2 women), 1 part-time/adjunct (0 women). *Students:* 13 full-time (4 women), 12 part-time (1 woman), 12 international. Average age 28. 85 applicants, 34% accepted, 9 enrolled. In 2016, 11 master's awarded. *Degree requirements:* For master's, thesis optional. *Entrance requirements:* For master's, GRE General Test, unofficial transcripts, letters of recommendation. Additional exam requirements/recommendations for international students: Required—TOEFL (minimum score 80 iBT), IELTS (minimum score 6.5). *Application deadline:* Applications are processed on a rolling basis. Application fee: $80 ($90 for international students). Electronic applications accepted. *Expenses:* $4,841 per semester full-time resident, $9,640 per semester full-time non-resident, $612 per credit hour part-time resident, $1,223 per credit hour part-time non-resident. *Financial support:* Career-related internships or fieldwork and unspecified assistantships available. Financial award application deadline: 3/1. *Faculty research:* Construction best practices, productivity improvement, women's issues in construction, construction project management. *Total annual research expenditures:* $45,609. *Unit head:* Dr. Roger Liska, Chair and Professor, 864-656-3878, E-mail: riggor@clemson.edu. *Application contact:* Dr. Shima Clarke, Professor and Graduate Coordinator, 864-656-4498, E-mail: shimac@clemson.edu.
Website: http://www.clemson.edu/caah/csm/

Colorado State University, College of Health and Human Sciences, Department of Construction Management, Fort Collins, CO 80523-1584. Offers MS. *Faculty:* 5 full-time (1 woman). *Students:* 15 full-time (5 women), 13 part-time (2 women); includes 2 minority (1 Black or African American, non-Hispanic/Latino; 1 Hispanic/Latino), 20 international. Average age 30. 66 applicants, 42% accepted, 13 enrolled. In 2016, 8 master's awarded. *Degree requirements:* For master's, thesis optional, professional paper (for some programs); submit article for journal or proceedings with faculty advisor. *Entrance requirements:* For master's, GRE, minimum undergraduate GPA of 3.0 or five years of professional experience; undergraduate degree in a related discipline including construction, engineering, architecture or business; three letters of recommendation; official transcripts; resume; statement of purpose. Additional exam requirements/recommendations for international students: Required—TOEFL (minimum score 550 paper-based; 80 iBT), IELTS (minimum score 6.5). *Application deadline:* For fall admission, 2/1 priority date for domestic and international students. Applications are processed on a rolling basis. Application fee: $60 ($70 for international students). Electronic applications accepted. *Expenses:* Tuition, state resident: full-time $9628. Tuition, nonresident: full-time $23,603. *Required fees:* $2253; $528.14 per credit hour. $264.07 per semester. Tuition and fees vary according to course load and program. *Financial support:* In 2016–17, 4 research assistantships with full and partial tuition reimbursements (averaging $12,481 per year), 8 teaching assistantships with full and partial tuition reimbursements (averaging $15,075 per year) were awarded; scholarships/grants and unspecified assistantships also available. Financial award application deadline: 3/1. *Faculty research:* Project management; sustainability; heavy civil/transportation infrastructure/asset management; performance measurement and improvement; building information modeling (BIM). *Total annual research expenditures:* $240,854. *Unit head:* Dr. Mostafa Khattab, Department Head, 970-491-7353, Fax: 970-491-2473, E-mail: mostafa.khattab@colostate.edu. *Application contact:* Dr. Mehmet Ozbek, Associate Professor and Graduate Program Coordinator, 970-491-7353, Fax: 970-491-2473, E-mail: cminfo@colostate.edu.
Website: http://www.cm.chhs.colostate.edu/

Columbia University, Fu Foundation School of Engineering and Applied Science, Department of Civil Engineering and Engineering Mechanics, New York, NY 10027. Offers civil engineering (MS, Eng Sc D, PhD); construction engineering and management (MS); engineering mechanics (MS, Eng Sc D, PhD). *Program availability:* Part-time, online learning. Terminal master's awarded for partial completion of doctoral program. *Degree requirements:* For doctorate, thesis/dissertation, qualifying exam. *Entrance requirements:* For master's and doctorate, GRE General Test. Additional exam requirements/recommendations for international students: Required—TOEFL, IELTS, PTE. Electronic applications accepted. *Faculty research:* Structural dynamics, structural health and monitoring, fatigue and fracture mechanics, geo-environmental engineering, multiscale science and engineering.

Columbia University, School of Continuing Education, Program in Construction Administration, New York, NY 10027. Offers MS. *Program availability:* Part-time, evening/weekend. *Degree requirements:* For master's, minimum GPA of 3.0 or internship. *Entrance requirements:* For master's, bachelor's degree, minimum GPA of 3.0. Additional exam requirements/recommendations for international students: Recommended—TOEFL. Electronic applications accepted.

Drexel University, Goodwin College of Professional Studies, School of Technology and Professional Studies, Philadelphia, PA 19104-2875. Offers construction management (MS); creativity and innovation (MS); engineering technology (MS); food science (MS); hospitality management (MS); professional studies: creativity studies (MS); professional studies: e-learning leadership (MS); professional studies: homeland security management (MS); project management (MS); property management (MS); sport management (MS). *Program availability:* Part-time, evening/weekend. *Faculty:* 37 full-time (14 women). *Students:* 13 full-time, 462 part-time; includes 133 minority (86 Black or African American, non-Hispanic/Latino; 24 Asian, non-Hispanic/Latino; 23 Hispanic/Latino). In 2016, 88 master's awarded. *Entrance requirements:* Additional exam requirements/recommendations for international students: Required—TOEFL, IELTS. *Application deadline:* For fall admission, 9/1 for domestic students; for winter admission, 12/1 for domestic students; for spring admission, 3/1 for domestic students. Applications are processed on a rolling basis. Application fee: $75. Electronic applications accepted. Application fee is waived when completed online. *Expenses: Tuition:* Full-time $32,184; part-time $1192 per credit hour. *Required fees:* $280. Tuition and fees vary according to campus/location and program. *Financial support:* Applicants required to submit FAFSA. *Unit head:* Dr. William F. Lynch, Dean, 215-895-2159, E-mail: goodwin@drexel.edu. *Application contact:* Matthew Gray, Manager, Recruitment and Enrollment, 215-895-6255, Fax: 215-895-2153, E-mail: mdg67@drexel.edu.
Website: http://drexel.edu/grad/programs/goodwin/

East Carolina University, Graduate School, College of Engineering and Technology, Department of Construction Management, Greenville, NC 27858-4353. Offers MCM. *Students:* 7 full-time (1 woman), 23 part-time (3 women); includes 5 minority (3 Black or African American, non-Hispanic/Latino; 1 Hispanic/Latino; 1 Two or more races, non-Hispanic/Latino), 2 international. Average age 35. 21 applicants, 52% accepted, 8 enrolled. In 2016, 8 master's awarded. *Unit head:* Dr. Syed M. Ahmed, Chair, 252-328-6958, E-mail: ahmeds@ecu.edu. *Application contact:* Dean of Graduate School, 252-328-6012, Fax: 252-328-6071, E-mail: gradschool@ecu.edu.

Eastern Michigan University, Graduate School, College of Technology, School of Visual and Built Environments, Programs in Construction Management, Ypsilanti, MI 48197. Offers construction (Certificate); construction management (MS); project leadership (Certificate); sustainable construction (Certificate). *Program availability:* Part-time, evening/weekend, online learning. *Students:* 18 full-time (1 woman), 12 part-time (3 women); includes 5 minority (2 Black or African American, non-Hispanic/Latino; 1 Asian, non-Hispanic/Latino; 2 Two or more races, non-Hispanic/Latino), 17 international. Average age 30. 49 applicants, 61% accepted, 9 enrolled. In 2016, 4 master's, 1 other advanced degree awarded. *Entrance requirements:* Additional exam requirements/recommendations for international students: Required—TOEFL. *Application deadline:* Applications are processed on a rolling basis. Application fee: $45. *Financial support:* Fellowships, research assistantships with full tuition reimbursements, teaching assistantships with full tuition reimbursements, career-related internships or fieldwork, Federal Work-Study, institutionally sponsored loans, scholarships/grants, tuition waivers (partial), and unspecified assistantships available. Support available to part-time students. Financial award applicants required to submit FAFSA. *Application contact:* Dr. Suleiman Ashur, Director, 734-487-0354, Fax: 734-487-8755, E-mail: sashur@emich.edu.

Florida International University, College of Engineering and Computing, School of Construction, Miami, FL 33175. Offers construction management (MS, PMS). *Program availability:* Part-time, evening/weekend. *Faculty:* 9 full-time (1 woman), 7 part-time/adjunct (0 women). *Students:* 35 full-time (15 women), 44 part-time (12 women); includes 39 minority (6 Black or African American, non-Hispanic/Latino; 1 Asian, non-Hispanic/Latino; 31 Hispanic/Latino; 1 Two or more races, non-Hispanic/Latino), 24 international. Average age 31. 118 applicants, 43% accepted, 20 enrolled. In 2016, 35 master's awarded. *Degree requirements:* For master's, thesis optional. *Entrance requirements:* For master's, minimum GPA of 3.0 in upper-level course work. Additional exam requirements/recommendations for international students: Required—TOEFL (minimum score 550 paper-based; 80 iBT). *Application deadline:* For fall admission, 6/1 for domestic students, 4/1 for international students; for spring admission, 10/1 for domestic students, 9/1 for international students. Applications are processed on a rolling basis. Application fee: $30. Electronic applications accepted. *Expenses:* Tuition, state resident: full-time $8912; part-time $446 per credit hour. Tuition, nonresident: full-time $21,393; part-time $992 per credit hour. *Required fees:* $2185; $195 per semester. Tuition and fees vary according to program. *Financial support:* In 2016–17, 5 students received support. Institutionally sponsored loans, scholarships/grants, and unspecified assistantships available. Financial award application deadline: 3/1; financial award applicants required to submit FAFSA. *Faculty research:* Information technology, construction organizations, contracts and partnerships in construction, construction education, concrete technology. *Unit head:* Dr. Irtishad Ahmad, Director, 305-348-3172, Fax: 305-348-6255, E-mail: ahmadi@fiu.edu. *Application contact:* Sara-Michelle Lemus, Engineering Admissions Officer, 305-348-1890, Fax: 305-348-7441, E-mail: grad_eng@fiu.edu.
Website: http://cec.fiu.edu

Georgia Southern University, Jack N. Averitt College of Graduate Studies, Allen E. Paulson College of Engineering and Information Technology, Program in Civil Engineering and Construction Management, Statesboro, GA 30458. Offers MSAE. *Students:* 11 full-time (2 women), 4 part-time (1 woman); includes 4 minority (3 Black or African American, non-Hispanic/Latino; 1 Asian, non-Hispanic/Latino), 7 international. Average age 29. 9 applicants, 100% accepted, 7 enrolled. *Entrance requirements:* For master's, bachelor's degree in engineering, information technology, or a scientific discipline; minimum cumulative GPA of 2.75. Additional exam requirements/recommendations for international students: Required—TOEFL. Electronic applications accepted. *Expenses:* Tuition, state resident: full-time $7236; part-time $277 per semester hour. Tuition, nonresident: full-time $27,118; part-time $1105 per semester hour. *Required fees:* $2092. *Financial support:* Applicants required to submit FAFSA. *Unit head:* Dr. David Williams, Associate Dean, 912-478-4848, E-mail: dwilliams@georgiasouthern.edu.
Website: http://ceit.georgiasouthern.edu/cecm/

Illinois Institute of Technology, Graduate College, Armour College of Engineering, Department of Civil, Architectural and Environmental Engineering, Chicago, IL 60616. Offers architectural engineering (M Arch E); civil engineering (MS, PhD), including architectural engineering (MS), construction engineering and management (MS), geoenvironmental engineering (MS), geotechnical engineering (MS), structural engineering (MS), transportation engineering (MS); construction engineering and management (MCEM); environmental engineering (M Env E, MS, PhD); geoenvironmental engineering (M Geoenv E); geotechnical engineering (MGE); infrastructure engineering and management (MPW); structural engineering (MSE); transportation engineering (M Trans E). *Program availability:* Part-time, evening/weekend, online learning. Terminal master's awarded for partial completion of doctoral program. *Degree requirements:* For master's, thesis (for some programs); for doctorate, comprehensive exam, thesis/dissertation. *Entrance requirements:* For master's, GRE General Test (minimum score 900 Quantitative and Verbal, 2.5 Analytical Writing), minimum undergraduate GPA of 3.0; for doctorate, GRE General Test (minimum score 1000 Quantitative and Verbal, 3.0 Analytical Writing), minimum undergraduate GPA of 3.0. Additional exam requirements/recommendations for international students: Required—TOEFL (minimum score 550 paper-based; 80 iBT). Electronic applications accepted. *Faculty research:* Structural, architectural, geotechnical and geoenvironmental engineering; construction engineering and management; transportation engineering; environmental engineering and public works.

Indiana University–Purdue University Fort Wayne, College of Engineering, Technology, and Computer Science, Program in Technology, Fort Wayne, IN 46805-1499. Offers facilities/construction management (MS); industrial technology/manufacturing (MS); information technology/advanced computer applications (MS). *Program availability:* Part-time. *Entrance requirements:* For master's, minimum GPA of 3.0. Additional exam requirements/recommendations for international students:

Required—TOEFL (minimum score 550 paper-based; 79 iBT), TWE. Electronic applications accepted.

Instituto Tecnologico de Santo Domingo, Graduate School, Area of Engineering, Santo Domingo, Dominican Republic. Offers construction administration (MS, Certificate); data telecommunications (M Eng, MS, Certificate); industrial engineering (M Eng, Certificate); industrial management (M Mgmt); information technology (Certificate); maintenance engineering (M Eng); occupational hazard prevention (M Mgmt); production management (Certificate); quantitative methods (Certificate); sanitary and environmental engineering (M Eng); structural engineering (M Eng); systems engineering and electronic data processing (Certificate); transportation (Certificate).

Kennesaw State University, College of Architecture and Construction Management, Department of Construction Management, Marietta, GA 30060. Offers MS. *Program availability:* Part-time, evening/weekend. *Degree requirements:* For master's, comprehensive exam, thesis or alternative. *Entrance requirements:* For master's, GMAT or GRE, 3 reference forms, minimum GPA of 2.75. Additional exam requirements/recommendations for international students: Required—TOEFL (minimum score 550 paper-based; 79 iBT), IELTS (minimum score 6.5). Electronic applications accepted. *Faculty research:* Environmental construction and green building techniques, risk management, bidding strategies in construction, construction worker safety, building automation and performance measurements.

Louisiana State University and Agricultural & Mechanical College, Graduate School, College of Engineering, Department of Construction Management, Baton Rouge, LA 70803. Offers MS, PhD.

Marquette University, Graduate School, College of Engineering, Department of Civil and Environmental Engineering, Milwaukee, WI 53201-1881. Offers construction engineering and management (MS, PhD, Certificate); environmental engineering (MS, PhD); structural design (Certificate); structural engineering and structural mechanics (MS, PhD); transportation (Certificate); transportation engineering and materials (MS, PhD); waste and wastewater treatment processes (Certificate); water resources engineering (Certificate). *Program availability:* Part-time, evening/weekend. *Faculty:* 17 full-time (2 women), 2 part-time/adjunct (0 women). *Students:* 27 full-time (8 women), 6 part-time (0 women); includes 5 minority (1 Asian, non-Hispanic/Latino; 2 Hispanic/Latino; 2 Two or more races, non-Hispanic/Latino), 13 international. Average age 28. 70 applicants, 56% accepted, 9 enrolled. In 2016, 8 master's, 5 doctorates awarded. Terminal master's awarded for partial completion of doctoral program. *Degree requirements:* For master's, comprehensive exam (for some programs), thesis or alternative; for doctorate, thesis/dissertation. *Entrance requirements:* For master's, GRE General Test (recommended), minimum GPA of 3.0, official transcripts from all current and previous colleges/universities except Marquette, three letters of recommendation; for doctorate, GRE General Test, minimum GPA of 3.0, official transcripts from all current and previous colleges/universities except Marquette, three letters of recommendation, brief statement of purpose, submission of any English language publications authored by applicant (strongly recommended). Additional exam requirements/recommendations for international students: Required—TOEFL (minimum score 530 paper-based). *Application deadline:* For fall admission, 6/1 priority date for domestic students. Applications are processed on a rolling basis. Application fee: $50. Electronic applications accepted. *Financial support:* Fellowships, research assistantships, teaching assistantships, scholarships/grants, health care benefits, tuition waivers (partial), and unspecified assistantships available. Support available to part-time students. Financial award application deadline: 2/15. *Faculty research:* Highway safety, highway performance, and intelligent transportation systems; surface mount technology; watershed management. *Total annual research expenditures:* $480,876. *Unit head:* Dr. Christopher Foley, Chair, 414-288-5741. *Application contact:* Dr. Stephen M. Heinrich, Director of Graduate Studies, 414-288-5466.
Website: http://www.marquette.edu/civil-environmental-engineering/

Michigan State University, The Graduate School, College of Agriculture and Natural Resources and College of Social Science, School of Planning, Design and Construction, East Lansing, MI 48824. Offers construction management (MS, PhD); environmental design (MA); interior design and facilities management (MA); international planning studies (MIPS); urban and regional planning (MURP). *Degree requirements:* For master's, thesis or alternative. *Entrance requirements:* Additional exam requirements/recommendations for international students: Required—TOEFL. Electronic applications accepted.

Milwaukee School of Engineering, Rader School of Business, Program in Construction and Business Management, Milwaukee, WI 53202-3109. Offers MS. *Program availability:* Evening/weekend, online learning. *Faculty:* 1 full-time (0 women), 2 part-time/adjunct (0 women). *Students:* 1 full-time (0 women), 3 part-time (1 woman); includes 1 minority (Black or African American, non-Hispanic/Latino), 1 international. Average age 26. 4 applicants, 25% accepted. In 2016, 2 master's awarded. *Degree requirements:* For master's, thesis, capstone project. *Entrance requirements:* For master's, GRE or GMAT if GPA is less than 2.8, BS in related field, official transcripts, two letters of recommendation, personal essay. Additional exam requirements/recommendations for international students: Required—TOEFL (minimum score 90 iBT), IELTS (minimum score 6.5). *Application deadline:* Applications are processed on a rolling basis. Application fee: $0. Electronic applications accepted. *Expenses: Tuition:* Full-time $31,440; part-time $655 per credit. *Financial support:* In 2016–17, 1 student received support. Career-related internships or fieldwork, institutionally sponsored loans, scholarships/grants, and tuition waivers (full) available. Financial award application deadline: 3/15; financial award applicants required to submit FAFSA. *Unit head:* Gene Wright, Director, 414-277-2286, Fax: 414-277-7479, E-mail: wright@msoe.edu. *Application contact:* Ian Dahlinghaus, Graduate Admissions Counselor, 414-277-7208, E-mail: dahlinghaus@msoe.edu.
Website: http://www.msoe.edu/community/academics/business/page/1296/construction-and-business-management-overview

Missouri State University, Graduate College, College of Business Administration, Department of Technology and Construction Management, Springfield, MO 65897. Offers project management (MS). *Program availability:* Part-time. *Faculty:* 4 full-time (0 women), 2 part-time/adjunct (1 woman). *Students:* 28 full-time (9 women), 52 part-time (15 women); includes 15 minority (5 Black or African American, non-Hispanic/Latino; 1 Asian, non-Hispanic/Latino; 5 Hispanic/Latino; 4 Two or more races, non-Hispanic/Latino), 14 international. Average age 35. 40 applicants, 48% accepted, 11 enrolled. In 2016, 27 master's awarded. *Degree requirements:* For master's, thesis or alternative. *Entrance requirements:* For master's, GRE or GMAT, minimum GPA of 2.75. Additional exam requirements/recommendations for international students: Required—TOEFL (minimum score 550 paper-based; 79 iBT), IELTS (minimum score 6). *Application deadline:* For fall admission, 7/20 priority date for domestic students, 5/1 for international students; for spring admission, 12/20 priority date for domestic students, 9/1 for international students; for summer admission, 5/20 priority date for domestic students. Applications are processed on a rolling basis. Application fee: $35 ($50 for international students). Electronic applications accepted. *Expenses:* Tuition, state resident: full-time $5830. Tuition, nonresident: full-time $10,708. *Required fees:* $1130. Tuition and fees vary according to class time, course level, course load and program. *Financial support:* Federal Work-Study, institutionally sponsored loans, scholarships/grants, and unspecified assistantships available. Financial award application deadline: 3/31; financial award applicants required to submit FAFSA. *Unit head:* Dr. Richard N. Callahan, Department Head, 417-836-5121, Fax: 417-836-8556, E-mail: indmgt@missouristate.edu. *Application contact:* Michael Edwards, Coordinator of Graduate Admissions, 417-836-5330, Fax: 417-836-6200, E-mail: michaeledwards@missouristate.edu.
Website: http://tcm.missouristate.edu/

New England Institute of Technology, Program in Construction Management, East Greenwich, RI 02818. Offers MS. *Program availability:* Part-time-only, evening/weekend, 100% online, blended/hybrid learning. *Entrance requirements:* Additional exam requirements/recommendations for international students: Required—TOEFL. *Application deadline:* Applications are processed on a rolling basis. Application fee: $25. Electronic applications accepted. *Expenses:* $480 per credit tuition, $50 registration fee, $155 student fee, $100 administrative fee. *Financial support:* Applicants required to submit FAFSA. *Application contact:* Michael Caruso, Director of Admissions, 800-736-7744 Ext. 3411, Fax: 401-886-0868, E-mail: mcaruso@neit.edu.
Website: http://www.neit.edu/Programs/Masters-Degree-Programs/Construction-Management-Masters-Degree

NewSchool of Architecture and Design, Program in Construction Management, San Diego, CA 92101-6634. Offers MCM. *Program availability:* Part-time, online learning. *Degree requirements:* For master's, thesis. *Entrance requirements:* For master's, GRE/GMAT. Additional exam requirements/recommendations for international students: Required—TOEFL, IELTS. Electronic applications accepted.

New York University, Polytechnic School of Engineering, Department of Civil and Urban Engineering, Major in Construction Management, New York, NY 10012-1019. Offers MS. *Degree requirements:* For master's, comprehensive exam (for some programs), thesis (for some programs). *Entrance requirements:* Additional exam requirements/recommendations for international students: Required—TOEFL (minimum score 550 paper-based; 80 iBT); Recommended—IELTS (minimum score 6.5). Electronic applications accepted.

New York University, Polytechnic School of Engineering, Department of Technology Management, New York, NY 10012-1019. Offers construction management (Advanced Certificate); electronic business management (Advanced Certificate); entrepreneurship (Advanced Certificate); human resources management (Advanced Certificate); industrial engineering (MS); information management (Advanced Certificate); management (MS); management of technology (MS); manufacturing engineering (MS); organizational behavior (MS, Advanced Certificate); project management (Advanced Certificate); technology management (MBA, PhD, Advanced Certificate); telecommunications management (Advanced Certificate). *Program availability:* Part-time, evening/weekend. *Degree requirements:* For master's, comprehensive exam (for some programs), thesis (for some programs); for doctorate, comprehensive exam, thesis/dissertation. *Entrance requirements:* For master's, GMAT, minimum B average in undergraduate course work. Additional exam requirements/recommendations for international students: Required—TOEFL (minimum score 550 paper-based; 80 iBT); Recommended—IELTS (minimum score 6.5). Electronic applications accepted. *Faculty research:* Global innovation and research and development strategy, managing emerging technologies, technology and development, service design and innovation, tech entrepreneurship and commercialization, sustainable and clean-tech innovation, impacts of information technology upon individuals, organizations and society.

New York University, School of Continuing and Professional Studies, Schack Institute of Real Estate, Program in Construction Management, New York, NY 10012-1019. Offers MS, Advanced Certificate. *Program availability:* Part-time, evening/weekend. *Degree requirements:* For master's, thesis, capstone project. *Entrance requirements:* For master's, GRE or GMAT (only upon request), bachelor's degree, resume with relevant professional work, internship or volunteer experience, two letters of recommendation, statement of purpose. Additional exam requirements/recommendations for international students: Required—TOEFL (minimum score 600 paper-based; 100 iBT), IELTS (minimum score 7). Electronic applications accepted.

North Carolina Agricultural and Technical State University, School of Graduate Studies, School of Technology, Department of Construction Management and Occupational Safety and Health, Greensboro, NC 27411. Offers construction management (MSTM); environmental and occupational safety (MSTM); occupational safety and health (MSTM).

North Dakota State University, College of Graduate and Interdisciplinary Studies, College of Engineering, Department of Construction Management and Engineering, Fargo, ND 58102. Offers construction management (MCM, MS, Graduate Certificate). *Entrance requirements:* Additional exam requirements/recommendations for international students: Required—TOEFL (minimum score 525 paper-based; 71 iBT). Electronic applications accepted.

Norwich University, College of Graduate and Continuing Studies, Master of Business Administration Program, Northfield, VT 05663. Offers construction management (MBA); energy management (MBA); finance (MBA); logistics (MBA); organizational leadership (MBA); project management (MBA); supply chain management (MBA). *Accreditation:* ACBSP. *Program availability:* Evening/weekend, online only, mostly all online with a week-long residency requirement. *Faculty:* 24 part-time/adjunct (5 women). *Students:* 228 full-time (54 women); includes 54 minority (23 Black or African American, non-Hispanic/Latino; 1 American Indian or Alaska Native, non-Hispanic/Latino; 6 Asian, non-Hispanic/Latino; 20 Hispanic/Latino; 1 Native Hawaiian or other Pacific Islander, non-Hispanic/Latino; 3 Two or more races, non-Hispanic/Latino), 2 international. Average age 36. 74 applicants, 100% accepted, 57 enrolled. In 2016, 135 master's awarded. *Degree requirements:* For master's, comprehensive exam. *Entrance requirements:* For master's, minimum undergraduate GPA of 2.75. Additional exam requirements/recommendations for international students: Required—TOEFL (minimum score 550 paper-based; 80 iBT), IELTS (minimum score 6.5). *Application deadline:* For fall admission, 8/14 for domestic and international students; for winter admission, 11/13 for domestic and international students; for spring admission, 2/12 for domestic and international students; for summer admission, 6/5 for domestic and international students. Electronic applications accepted. *Expenses:* Contact institution. *Financial support:* In 2016–17, 113 students received support. Scholarships/grants available. Financial award application deadline: 8/4; financial award applicants required to submit FAFSA. *Unit head:* Dr. Jose Cordova, Program Director, 802-485-2567, Fax: 802-485-2533, E-mail: jcordova@norwich.edu. *Application contact:* Admissions Advisor, 800-460-5597 Ext. 3376, Fax: 802-485-2533, E-mail: mba@online.norwich.edu.
Website: https://online.norwich.edu/degree-programs/masters/master-business-administration/overview

Norwich University, College of Graduate and Continuing Studies, Master of Civil Engineering Program, Northfield, VT 05663. Offers construction management (MCE); environmental (MCE); geotechnical (MCE); structural (MCE). *Program availability:* Evening/weekend, online only, mostly all online with a week-long residency requirement. *Faculty:* 1 full-time (0 women), 11 part-time/adjunct (1 woman). *Students:* 70 full-time (17 women); includes 28 minority (16 Black or African American, non-Hispanic/Latino; 4

Asian, non-Hispanic/Latino; 5 Hispanic/Latino; 1 Native Hawaiian or other Pacific Islander, non-Hispanic/Latino; 2 Two or more races, non-Hispanic/Latino), 1 international. Average age 36. 35 applicants, 97% accepted, 18 enrolled. In 2016, 63 master's awarded. *Degree requirements:* For master's, capstone. *Entrance requirements:* For master's, minimum undergraduate GPA of 2.75. Additional exam requirements/recommendations for international students: Required—TOEFL (minimum score 550 paper-based; 80 iBT), IELTS (minimum score 6.5). *Application deadline:* For fall admission, 8/14 for domestic and international students; for spring admission, 2/12 for domestic and international students. Electronic applications accepted. *Expenses:* Contact institution. *Financial support:* In 2016–17, 10 students received support. Scholarships/grants available. Financial award application deadline: 8/4; financial award applicants required to submit FAFSA. *Unit head:* Dr. Thomas Descoteaux, Program Director, 802-485-2730, Fax: 802-485-2533, E-mail: tdescote@norwich.edu. *Application contact:* Admissions Advisor, 800-460-5597 Ext. 3369, Fax: 802-485-2533, E-mail: mce@online.norwich.edu.
Website: https://online.norwich.edu/degree-programs/masters/master-civil-engineering/overview

Philadelphia University, College of Architecture and the Built Environment, Program in Construction Management, Philadelphia, PA 19144. Offers MS.

Pittsburg State University, Graduate School, College of Technology, Department of Technology and Workforce Learning, Pittsburg, KS 66762. Offers career and technical education (MS); human resource development (MS); technology (MS), including automotive technology, construction management, graphic design, graphics management, innovation in technology, personnel development, technology management, workforce learning; workforce development and education (Ed S). *Program availability:* Part-time, evening/weekend, 100% online, blended/hybrid learning. *Students:* 171 (79 women); includes 20 minority (4 Black or African American, non-Hispanic/Latino; 5 American Indian or Alaska Native, non-Hispanic/Latino; 2 Asian, non-Hispanic/Latino; 4 Hispanic/Latino; 5 Two or more races, non-Hispanic/Latino), 61 international. In 2016, 62 master's, 2 other advanced degrees awarded. *Degree requirements:* For master's, thesis or alternative; for Ed S, thesis optional. *Entrance requirements:* Additional exam requirements/recommendations for international students: Required—TOEFL (minimum score 520 paper-based; 68 iBT), IELTS (minimum score 6), PTE (minimum score 47). *Application deadline:* For fall admission, 7/15 for domestic students, 6/1 for international students; for spring admission, 12/15 for domestic students, 10/15 for international students; for summer admission, 5/15 for domestic students, 4/1 for international students. Applications are processed on a rolling basis. Application fee: $35 ($60 for international students). Electronic applications accepted. *Expenses:* Contact institution. *Financial support:* In 2016–17, 8 teaching assistantships with full tuition reimbursements (averaging $5,500 per year) were awarded; career-related internships or fieldwork also available. Financial award application deadline: 2/1; financial award applicants required to submit FAFSA. *Unit head:* Dr. John Iley, Chairperson, 620-235-4373, E-mail: jiley@pittstate.edu. *Application contact:* Lisa Allen, Assistant Director of Graduate and Continuing Studies, 620-235-4218, Fax: 620-235-4219, E-mail: lallen@pittstate.edu.

Polytechnic University of Puerto Rico, Miami Campus, Graduate School, Miami, FL 33166. Offers accounting (MBA); business administration (MBA); construction management (MEM); environmental management (MEM); finance (MBA); human resources management (MBA); logistics and supply chain management (MBA); management of international enterprises (MBA); manufacturing management (MEM); marketing management (MBA); project management (MBA). *Program availability:* Part-time, evening/weekend, online learning. *Entrance requirements:* For master's, minimum GPA of 3.0. Electronic applications accepted.

Polytechnic University of Puerto Rico, Orlando Campus, Graduate School, Orlando, FL 32825. Offers accounting (MBA); business administration (MBA); construction management (MEM); engineering management (MEM); environmental management (MEM); finance (MBA); human resources management (MBA); management of international enterprises (MBA); management of technology (MBA); manufacturing management (MEM). *Program availability:* Part-time, evening/weekend, online learning. *Entrance requirements:* For master's, minimum GPA of 3.0. Additional exam requirements/recommendations for international students: Recommended—TOEFL. Electronic applications accepted.

Purdue University, Graduate School, College of Technology, Department of Building Construction Management, West Lafayette, IN 47907. Offers MS. *Program availability:* Online learning. *Faculty:* 11 full-time (1 woman). *Students:* 15 full-time (9 women), 8 part-time (0 women); includes 3 minority (1 Black or African American, non-Hispanic/Latino; 2 Hispanic/Latino), 12 international. Average age 31. 69 applicants, 36% accepted, 13 enrolled. In 2016, 6 master's awarded. *Entrance requirements:* For master's, GRE, BS/BA with minimum GPA of 3.0. Additional exam requirements/recommendations for international students: Required—TOEFL (minimum score 550 paper-based; 77 iBT); Recommended—TWE. *Application deadline:* For fall admission, 4/1 for domestic and international students; for spring admission, 10/1 for domestic students, 9/1 for international students; for summer admission, 4/1 for domestic students, 2/15 for international students. Application fee: $60 ($75 for international students). Electronic applications accepted. *Financial support:* Fellowships, research assistantships, and teaching assistantships available. *Unit head:* Robert F. Cox, Head, 765-494-2465. *Application contact:* Dawn F. Lamb, Graduate Chair, 765-496-1077, E-mail: dflamb@purdue.edu.
Website: http://www.tech.purdue.edu/bcm/

South Dakota School of Mines and Technology, Graduate Division, Program in Construction Engineering Management, Rapid City, SD 57701-3995. Offers MS. *Program availability:* Part-time, evening/weekend, online learning. *Entrance requirements:* For master's, GRE General Test. Additional exam requirements/recommendations for international students: Required—TOEFL (minimum score 520 paper-based; 68 iBT). Electronic applications accepted.

State University of New York College of Environmental Science and Forestry, Department of Sustainable Construction Management and Engineering, Syracuse, NY 13210-2779. Offers construction management (MPS, MS, PhD); sustainable construction (MPS, MS, PhD); wood science (MPS, MS, PhD). *Students:* 8 full-time (5 women), 4 part-time (1 woman); includes 1 minority (Hispanic/Latino), 5 international. Average age 29. 5 applicants, 80% accepted, 1 enrolled. In 2016, 1 master's awarded. *Degree requirements:* For master's, thesis (for some programs); for doctorate, comprehensive exam, thesis/dissertation. *Entrance requirements:* For master's and doctorate, GRE General Test, minimum GPA of 3.0. Additional exam requirements/recommendations for international students: Required—TOEFL (minimum score 550 paper-based; 80 iBT), IELTS (minimum score 6). *Application deadline:* For fall admission, 2/1 priority date for domestic and international students; for spring admission, 11/1 priority date for domestic and international students. Applications are processed on a rolling basis. Application fee: $60. *Expenses:* Tuition, state resident: full-time $10,870; part-time $453 per credit. Tuition, nonresident: full-time $22,210; part-time $925 per credit. *Required fees:* $1075; $89.22 per credit. *Financial support:* In 2016–17, 2 students received support. Application deadline: 6/30; applicants required to submit FAFSA. *Unit head:* Dr. Susan E. Anagnost, Chair, 315-470-6880, Fax: 315-470-

6879, E-mail: seanagno@esf.edu. *Application contact:* Scott Shannon, Associate Provost for Instruction/Dean of the Graduate School, 315-470-6599, Fax: 315-470-6879, E-mail: esfgrad@esf.edu.
Website: http://www.esf.edu/scme/

Stevens Institute of Technology, Graduate School, Charles V. Schaefer Jr. School of Engineering and Science, Department of Civil, Environmental, and Ocean Engineering, Program in Construction Management, Hoboken, NJ 07030. Offers construction management (MS, Certificate), including construction accounting/estimating (Certificate), construction engineering (Certificate), construction law/disputes (Certificate), construction/quality management (Certificate). *Program availability:* Part-time, evening/weekend. *Students:* 50 full-time (21 women), 22 part-time (6 women); includes 3 minority (all Black or African American, non-Hispanic/Latino), 49 international. Average age 25. 157 applicants, 72% accepted, 28 enrolled. In 2016, 39 master's, 15 other advanced degrees awarded. *Degree requirements:* For master's, thesis optional, minimum B average in major field and overall; for Certificate, minimum B average. *Entrance requirements:* Additional exam requirements/recommendations for international students: Required—TOEFL (minimum score 74 iBT), IELTS (minimum score 6). *Application deadline:* For fall admission, 6/1 for domestic students, 4/15 for international students; for spring admission, 11/30 for domestic students, 11/1 for international students. Applications are processed on a rolling basis. Application fee: $65. Electronic applications accepted. *Expenses:* Contact institution. *Financial support:* Fellowships, research assistantships, teaching assistantships, career-related internships or fieldwork, Federal Work-Study, scholarships/grants, and unspecified assistantships available. Financial award application deadline: 2/15; financial award applicants required to submit FAFSA. *Unit head:* Dr. Linda Thomas, Director, 201-216-5681, E-mail: lthomas2@stevens.edu. *Application contact:* Graduate Admission, 888-783-8367, Fax: 888-511-1306, E-mail: graduate@stevens.edu.

Texas A&M University, College of Architecture, Department of Construction Science, College Station, TX 77843. Offers construction management (MS). *Students:* 34 full-time (14 women), 3 part-time (0 women); includes 4 minority (2 Asian, non-Hispanic/Latino; 2 Hispanic/Latino), 30 international. Average age 26. 88 applicants, 39% accepted, 17 enrolled. In 2016, 50 master's awarded. *Degree requirements:* For master's, comprehensive exam. *Entrance requirements:* For master's, GRE General Test, 3 recommendation letters, resume, statement of research interest, minimum undergraduate GPA of 3.0 in last 60 hours of applicant's undergraduate degree. Additional exam requirements/recommendations for international students: Required—TOEFL (minimum score 550 paper-based; 80 iBT), IELTS (minimum score 6), PTE (minimum score 53). *Application deadline:* For fall admission, 2/15 for domestic and international students. Applications are processed on a rolling basis. Application fee: $50 ($90 for international students). Electronic applications accepted. *Expenses:* Contact institution. *Financial support:* In 2016–17, 33 students received support, including 7 fellowships with tuition reimbursements available (averaging $1,143 per year), 10 research assistantships with tuition reimbursements available (averaging $2,020 per year), 8 teaching assistantships with tuition reimbursements available (averaging $3,003 per year); career-related internships or fieldwork, institutionally sponsored loans, scholarships/grants, traineeships, health care benefits, tuition waivers (full and partial), and unspecified assistantships also available. Support available to part-time students. Financial award application deadline: 3/15; financial award applicants required to submit FAFSA. *Faculty research:* Advanced project management, construction operation, construction productivity and labor, facility management, information technology in construction, law and risk management, sustainability. *Unit head:* Prof. Joe Horlen, Head, 979-458-3477, E-mail: jhorlen@tamu.edu. *Application contact:* Ben Bigelow, Graduate Program Coordinator, 979-458-4457, E-mail: bbigelow@arch.tamu.edu.
Website: http://cosc.arch.tamu.edu/

Universidad de las Américas Puebla, Division of Graduate Studies, School of Engineering, Program in Construction Management, Puebla, Mexico. Offers M Adm. *Program availability:* Part-time, evening/weekend. *Degree requirements:* For master's, one foreign language, thesis. *Faculty research:* Building structures, budget, project management.

University of Alaska Fairbanks, College of Engineering and Mines, Department of Civil and Environmental Engineering, Fairbanks, AK 99775-5900. Offers civil engineering (MS); design and construction management (Graduate Certificate); environmental engineering (PhD). *Program availability:* Part-time. *Faculty:* 9 full-time (3 women), 1 part-time/adjunct (0 women). *Students:* 10 full-time (3 women), 8 part-time (3 women); includes 4 minority (1 Black or African American, non-Hispanic/Latino; 2 Asian, non-Hispanic/Latino; 1 Two or more races, non-Hispanic/Latino), 2 international. Average age 29. 14 applicants, 43% accepted, 3 enrolled. In 2016, 9 master's, 1 other advanced degree awarded. *Degree requirements:* For master's, comprehensive exam, thesis (for some programs), oral defense of project or thesis; for doctorate, comprehensive exam, thesis/dissertation. *Entrance requirements:* For master's, bachelor's degree from accredited institution with minimum cumulative undergraduate and major GPA of 3.0. Additional exam requirements/recommendations for international students: Required—TOEFL (minimum score 550 paper-based; 79 iBT), IELTS (minimum score 6.5). *Application deadline:* For fall admission, 6/1 for domestic students, 3/1 for international students; for spring admission, 10/15 for domestic students, 9/1 for international students. Applications are processed on a rolling basis. Application fee: $60. Electronic applications accepted. *Expenses:* $533 per credit resident tuition, $673 per semester resident fees; $1,088 per credit non-resident tuition, $835 per semester non-resident fees. *Financial support:* In 2016–17, 5 research assistantships with full tuition reimbursements (averaging $4,248 per year), 6 teaching assistantships with full tuition reimbursements (averaging $5,781 per year) were awarded; fellowships with full tuition reimbursements, career-related internships or fieldwork, Federal Work-Study, scholarships/grants, health care benefits, and unspecified assistantships also available. Support available to part-time students. Financial award application deadline: 7/1; financial award applicants required to submit FAFSA. *Faculty research:* Soils, structures, culvert thawing with solar power, pavement drainage, contaminant hydrogeology. *Unit head:* Dr. Leroy Hulsey, Department Chair, 907-474-7241, Fax: 907-474-6087, E-mail: fycee@uaf.edu. *Application contact:* Mary Kreta, Director of Admissions, 907-474-7500, Fax: 907-474-7097, E-mail: admissions@uaf.edu.
Website: http://cem.uaf.edu/cee

University of Arkansas at Little Rock, Graduate School, George W. Donaghey College of Engineering and Information Technology, Department of Construction Management and Civil and Construction Engineering, Little Rock, AR 72204-1099. Offers construction management (MS).

University of California, Berkeley, UC Berkeley Extension, Certificate Programs in Engineering, Construction and Facilities Management, Berkeley, CA 94720-1500. Offers construction management (Certificate); HVAC (Certificate); integrated circuit design and techniques (online) (Certificate). *Program availability:* Online learning.

University of Denver, Daniels College of Business, Franklin L. Burns School of Real Estate and Construction Management, Denver, CO 80208. Offers real estate and the built environment (MBA, MS). *Program availability:* Part-time, evening/weekend. *Faculty:* 7 full-time (1 woman), 7 part-time/adjunct (1 woman). *Students:* 19 full-time (1

woman), 68 part-time (19 women); includes 19 minority (2 Black or African American, non-Hispanic/Latino; 4 Asian, non-Hispanic/Latino; 7 Hispanic/Latino; 6 Two or more races, non-Hispanic/Latino), 3 international. Average age 35. 62 applicants, 90% accepted, 39 enrolled. In 2016, 30 master's awarded. *Entrance requirements:* For master's, GRE General Test or GMAT, bachelor's degree, transcripts, essays, resume, interview. Additional exam requirements/recommendations for international students: Required—TOEFL (minimum score 570 paper-based; 88 iBT), TWE. *Application deadline:* For fall admission, 11/15 priority date for domestic and international students; for spring admission, 10/1 priority date for domestic and international students. Applications are processed on a rolling basis. Application fee: $100. Electronic applications accepted. *Expenses:* $43,458 per year full-time. *Financial support:* In 2016–17, 54 students received support, including 2 teaching assistantships with tuition reimbursements available (averaging $1,492 per year); Federal Work-Study, institutionally sponsored loans, scholarships/grants, and unspecified assistantships also available. Support available to part-time students. Financial award application deadline: 2/15; financial award applicants required to submit FAFSA. *Unit head:* Dr. Barbara Jackson, Associate Professor and Director, 303-871-3470, Fax: 303-871-2971, E-mail: barbara.jackson@du.edu.
Website: https://daniels.du.edu/burns-school/

University of Florida, Graduate School, College of Design, Construction and Planning, Doctoral Program in Design, Construction and Planning, Gainesville, FL 32611. Offers construction management (PhD); design, construction and planning (PhD); geographic information systems (PhD); historic preservation (PhD); interior design (PhD); landscape architecture (PhD); urban and regional planning (PhD). *Degree requirements:* For doctorate, thesis/dissertation. *Entrance requirements:* For doctorate, GRE General Test, minimum GPA of 3.0. Additional exam requirements/recommendations for international students: Required—TOEFL (minimum score 550 paper-based; 80 iBT), IELTS (minimum score 6). Electronic applications accepted. *Faculty research:* Architecture, building construction, urban and regional planning.

University of Florida, Graduate School, College of Design, Construction and Planning, M.E. Rinker, Sr. School of Construction Management, Gainesville, FL 32611. Offers construction management (MSCM); fire and emergency services (MFES); historic preservation (MSCM); international construction (MICM), including historic preservation; sustainable construction (MSCM); sustainable design (MSCM). *Program availability:* Part-time, online learning. *Degree requirements:* For master's, thesis. *Entrance requirements:* For master's, GRE General Test, minimum GPA of 3.0. Additional exam requirements/recommendations for international students: Required—TOEFL (minimum score 550 paper-based; 80 iBT), IELTS (minimum score 6). Electronic applications accepted. *Faculty research:* Safety, affordable housing, construction management, environmental issues, sustainable construction.

University of Houston, College of Technology, Department of Engineering Technology, Houston, TX 77204. Offers construction management (MS); engineering technology (MS); network communications (M Tech). *Program availability:* Part-time. *Degree requirements:* For master's, project or thesis (most programs). *Entrance requirements:* For master's, GRE. Additional exam requirements/recommendations for international students: Required—TOEFL (minimum score 550 paper-based; 79 iBT). Electronic applications accepted.

The University of Kansas, Graduate Studies, School of Engineering, Program in Construction Management, Lawrence, KS 66045. Offers MCM. *Program availability:* Part-time, evening/weekend. *Students:* 6 full-time (1 woman), 2 part-time (0 women). Average age 28. 18 applicants, 22% accepted, 2 enrolled. *Entrance requirements:* For master's, GRE, two letters of recommendation, statement of purpose, resume. Additional exam requirements/recommendations for international students: Required—TOEFL or IELTS. *Application deadline:* For fall admission, 7/31 for domestic students, 5/15 for international students; for spring admission, 12/30 for domestic students, 10/15 for international students; for summer admission, 5/15 for domestic students. Application fee: $65 ($85 for international students). Electronic applications accepted. *Financial support:* Career-related internships or fieldwork available. Financial award application deadline: 2/7. *Faculty research:* Construction engineering, construction management. *Unit head:* David Darwin, Chair, 785-864-3827, Fax: 785-864-5631, E-mail: daved@ku.edu. *Application contact:* Susan Scott, Administrative Assistant, 785-864-3826, E-mail: sbscott@ku.edu.
Website: http://ceae.ku.edu/overview-6

University of Nevada, Las Vegas, Graduate College, Howard R. Hughes College of Engineering, Department of Engineering, Las Vegas, NV 89154-4054. Offers construction management (MS); solar and renewable energy (Certificate). *Program availability:* Part-time. *Students:* 4 full-time (0 women), 4 part-time (1 woman); includes 2 minority (1 Black or African American, non-Hispanic/Latino; 1 Asian, non-Hispanic/Latino), 3 international. Average age 31. 20 applicants, 65% accepted, 3 enrolled. In 2016, 2 other advanced degrees awarded. *Entrance requirements:* Additional exam requirements/recommendations for international students: Required—TOEFL (minimum score 550 paper-based; 80 iBT), IELTS (minimum score 7). *Application deadline:* Applications are processed on a rolling basis. Application fee: $60 ($95 for international students). Electronic applications accepted. *Expenses:* $269.25 per credit, $792 per 3-credit course; $9,634 per year resident; $23,274 per year non-resident; $7,094 fees non-resident (7 credits or more); $1,307 annual health insurance fee. *Financial support:* In 2016–17, 3 teaching assistantships with partial tuition reimbursements (averaging $10,000 per year) were awarded; institutionally sponsored loans, scholarships/grants, health care benefits, and unspecified assistantships also available. Financial award application deadline: 3/15.

University of New Mexico, Graduate Studies, School of Engineering, Program in Civil Engineering, Albuquerque, NM 87131-0001. Offers civil engineering (M Eng, MSCE); construction management (MCM); engineering (PhD). *Program availability:* Part-time. *Faculty:* 17 full-time (3 women), 2 part-time/adjunct (1 woman). *Students:* 23 full-time (5 women), 35 part-time (14 women); includes 18 minority (2 American Indian or Alaska Native, non-Hispanic/Latino; 1 Asian, non-Hispanic/Latino; 12 Hispanic/Latino; 3 Two or more races, non-Hispanic/Latino), 17 international. Average age 32. 55 applicants, 31% accepted, 16 enrolled. In 2016, 20 master's, 4 doctorates awarded. Terminal master's awarded for partial completion of doctoral program. *Degree requirements:* For master's, comprehensive exam, thesis (for some programs); for doctorate, comprehensive exam, thesis/dissertation. *Entrance requirements:* For master's, GRE General Test (for MSCE and M Eng); GRE or GMAT (for MCM), minimum GPA of 3.0; for doctorate, GRE General Test, minimum GPA of 3.0. Additional exam requirements/recommendations for international students: Required—TOEFL (minimum score 550 paper-based; 80 iBT), IELTS (minimum score 6.5). *Application deadline:* For fall admission, 7/15 for domestic students, 3/1 for international students; for spring admission, 11/10 for domestic students, 8/1 for international students. Applications are processed on a rolling basis. Application fee: $50. Electronic applications accepted. *Financial support:* Research assistantships with tuition reimbursements, teaching assistantships with tuition reimbursements, scholarships/grants, health care benefits, and unspecified assistantships available. Support available to part-time students. Financial award application deadline: 3/1; financial award applicants required to submit FAFSA. *Faculty research:* Integrating design and construction, project delivery methods, sustainable design and construction, leadership and management in construction, project management and project supervision, production management and improvement. *Total annual research expenditures:* $4.2 million. *Unit head:* Dr. John C. Stormont, Chair, 505-277-2722, Fax: 505-277-1988, E-mail: jcstorm@unm.edu. *Application contact:* Missy Garoza, Professional Academic Advisor, 505-277-2722, Fax: 505-277-1988, E-mail: civil@unm.edu.
Website: http://civil.unm.edu

University of New Mexico, Graduate Studies, School of Engineering, Program in Construction Management, Albuquerque, NM 87131. Offers MCM. *Program availability:* Part-time. *Faculty:* 2 full-time (0 women). *Students:* 1 (woman) full-time, 2 part-time (1 woman); includes 2 minority (both Hispanic/Latino). Average age 26. 12 applicants, 17% accepted, 1 enrolled. In 2016, 2 master's awarded. *Degree requirements:* For master's, comprehensive exam, thesis optional. *Entrance requirements:* For master's, GMAT (minimum score 500) or GRE (minimum score 294 combined verbal and quantitative), minimum GPA of 3.0; courses in statistics, elements of calculus, engineering economy, and construction contracting. Additional exam requirements/recommendations for international students: Required—TOEFL (minimum score 550 paper-based; 80 iBT), IELTS (minimum score 6.5). *Application deadline:* For fall admission, 7/15 for domestic students, 3/1 for international students; for spring admission, 11/10 for domestic students, 8/1 for international students. Applications are processed on a rolling basis. Application fee: $50. Electronic applications accepted. *Financial support:* Scholarships/grants, health care benefits, and unspecified assistantships available. Support available to part-time students. Financial award application deadline: 3/1; financial award applicants required to submit FAFSA. *Faculty research:* Applied industry research and training, integration of the design/construction continuum, leadership in project management, life-cycle costing, production management and productivity management, project delivery methods, sustainable asset management, sustainable design and construction. *Unit head:* Dr. John C. Stormont, Chair, 505-277-2722, Fax: 505-277-1988, E-mail: jcstorm@unm.edu. *Application contact:* Missy Garoza, Professional Academic Advisor, 505-277-2722, Fax: 505-277-1988, E-mail: civil@unm.edu.
Website: http://civil.unm.edu

The University of North Carolina at Charlotte, William States Lee College of Engineering, Department of Engineering Technology and Construction Management, Charlotte, NC 28223-0001. Offers applied energy (Graduate Certificate); applied energy and electromechanical systems (MS); construction and facilities management (MS); fire protection and administration (MS). *Program availability:* Part-time. *Faculty:* 26 full-time (5 women). *Students:* 46 full-time (8 women), 19 part-time (1 woman); includes 9 minority (4 Black or African American, non-Hispanic/Latino; 2 Asian, non-Hispanic/Latino; 3 Hispanic/Latino), 31 international. Average age 27. 71 applicants, 83% accepted, 24 enrolled. In 2016, 34 master's awarded. *Degree requirements:* For master's, thesis, capstone, or comprehensive exam. *Entrance requirements:* For master's, GRE, minimum undergraduate GPA of 3.0, recommendations, statistics; integral and differential calculus (for students pursuing fire protection concentration or applied energy and electromechanical systems program); for Graduate Certificate, bachelor's degree in engineering, engineering technology, construction management or a closely-related technical or scientific field; undergraduate coursework of at least 3 semesters in engineering analysis or calculus; minimum GPA of 3.0. Additional exam requirements/recommendations for international students: Required—TOEFL (minimum score 523 paper-based, 70 iBT) or IELTS (6.5). *Application deadline:* For fall admission, 3/1 priority date for domestic and international students; for spring admission, 10/1 priority date for domestic and international students. Applications are processed on a rolling basis. Application fee: $75. Electronic applications accepted. *Expenses:* Contact institution. *Financial support:* In 2016–17, 22 students received support, including 22 research assistantships (averaging $8,235 per year); career-related internships or fieldwork, institutionally sponsored loans, scholarships/grants, and unspecified assistantships also available. Support available to part-time students. Financial award application deadline: 3/1; financial award applicants required to submit FAFSA. *Total annual research expenditures:* $1.5 million. *Unit head:* Dr. Anthony Brizendine, Chair, 704-687-5050, E-mail: albrizen@uncc.edu. *Application contact:* Kathy B. Giddings, Director of Graduate Admissions, 704-687-5503, Fax: 704-687-1668, E-mail: gradadm@uncc.edu.
Website: http://et.uncc.edu/

University of North Florida, Coggin College of Business, MBA Program, Jacksonville, FL 32224. Offers accounting (MBA); construction management (MBA); e-commerce (MBA); economics (MBA); finance (MBA); human resource management (MBA); international business (MBA); logistics (MBA); management applications (MBA). *Accreditation:* AACSB. *Program availability:* Part-time, evening/weekend. *Faculty:* 16 full-time (4 women), 1 (woman) part-time/adjunct. *Students:* 105 full-time (50 women), 162 part-time (68 women); includes 57 minority (14 Black or African American, non-Hispanic/Latino; 1 American Indian or Alaska Native, non-Hispanic/Latino; 17 Asian, non-Hispanic/Latino; 18 Hispanic/Latino; 7 Two or more races, non-Hispanic/Latino), 41 international. Average age 28. 231 applicants, 46% accepted, 84 enrolled. In 2016, 114 master's awarded. *Entrance requirements:* For master's, GMAT or GRE, U.S. bachelor's degree from regionally-accredited university or equivalent foreign degree. Additional exam requirements/recommendations for international students: Required—TOEFL (minimum score 550 paper-based; 79 iBT). *Application deadline:* For fall admission, 8/1 priority date for domestic students, 5/1 for international students; for spring admission, 12/1 priority date for domestic students, 10/1 for international students; for summer admission, 4/29 priority date for domestic students, 2/1 for international students. Application fee: $30. Tuition and fees vary according to course load, campus/location and program. *Financial support:* In 2016–17, 22 students received support, including 1 research assistantship (averaging $2,501 per year); teaching assistantships, Federal Work-Study, and tuition waivers (partial) also available. Support available to part-time students. Financial award application deadline: 4/1; financial award applicants required to submit FAFSA. *Faculty research:* Performance measures, costing, and inventory issues in logistics and supply chain management; inter-organizational systems; international management and marketing practices; e-commerce; organizational learning and socialization processes. *Total annual research expenditures:* $17,654. *Unit head:* Dr. Parvez Ahmed, Graduate Program Director, 904-620-1678, E-mail: pahmed@unf.edu. *Application contact:* Amy Bishop, MSM Advisor, 904-620-2575, Fax: 904-620-2832, E-mail: coggin.students@unf.edu.
Website: http://www.unf.edu/graduateschool/academics/programs/MBA.aspx

University of Oklahoma, College of Architecture, Haskell and Irene Lemon Division of Construction Science, Norman, OK 73019. Offers construction science (MCM); planning, design, and construction (PhD), including construction science. *Program availability:* Part-time, evening/weekend. *Students:* 16 full-time (3 women), 7 part-time (3 women); includes 6 minority (5 Hispanic/Latino; 1 Two or more races, non-Hispanic/Latino), 9 international. Average age 30. 22 applicants, 55% accepted, 8 enrolled. Terminal master's awarded for partial completion of doctoral program. *Degree requirements:* For master's, thesis optional, special project; for doctorate, thesis/dissertation. *Entrance requirements:* For master's, minimum GPA of 3.5. Additional exam requirements/recommendations for international students: Required—TOEFL (minimum score 79 iBT) or IELTS (minimum score 6.5). Application fee: $50 ($100 for international students). Electronic applications accepted. *Expenses:* Tuition, state

resident: full-time $4886; part-time $203.60 per credit hour. Tuition, nonresident: full-time $18,989; part-time $791.20 per credit hour. *Required fees:* $3283; $126.25 per credit hour. $126.50 per semester. *Financial support:* In 2016–17, 22 students received support, including 8 research assistantships with full and partial tuition reimbursements available (averaging $10,372 per year), 1 teaching assistantship with full and partial tuition reimbursement available (averaging $13,500 per year); fellowships with full and partial tuition reimbursements available, career-related internships or fieldwork, and scholarships/grants also available. Financial award application deadline: 6/1; financial award applicants required to submit FAFSA. *Faculty research:* Lean construction, construction safety, building information modeling, construction risk management, structures. *Unit head:* Lisa Holliday, Interim Director, 405-325-9464, E-mail: lisaholliday@ou.edu. *Application contact:* Anthony Perrenoud, Graduate Liaison, 405-325-2674, E-mail: perrenoud@ou.edu.
Website: http://www.ou.edu/content/architecture/construction_science.html

University of Southern California, Graduate School, Viterbi School of Engineering, Sonny Astani Department of Civil Engineering, Los Angeles, CA 90089. Offers applied mechanics (MS); civil engineering (MS, PhD); computer-aided engineering (ME, Graduate Certificate); construction management (MCM); engineering technology commercialization (Graduate Certificate); environmental engineering (MS, PhD); environmental quality management (ME); structural design (ME); sustainable cities (Graduate Certificate); transportation systems (MS, Graduate Certificate); water and waste management (MS). *Program availability:* Part-time, evening/weekend. Terminal master's awarded for partial completion of doctoral program. *Degree requirements:* For master's, thesis optional; for doctorate, thesis/dissertation. *Entrance requirements:* For master's and doctorate, GRE General Test. Additional exam requirements/recommendations for international students: Recommended—TOEFL. Electronic applications accepted. *Faculty research:* Geotechnical engineering, transportation engineering, structural engineering, construction management, environmental engineering, water resources.

The University of Tennessee at Chattanooga, Engineering Management and Technology Program, Chattanooga, TN 37403. Offers construction management (Graduate Certificate); engineering management (MS); fundamentals of engineering management (Graduate Certificate); leadership and ethics (Graduate Certificate); logistics and supply chain management (Graduate Certificate); power systems management (Graduate Certificate); project and technology management (Graduate Certificate); quality management (Graduate Certificate). *Program availability:* 100% online, blended/hybrid learning. *Faculty:* 6 full-time (1 woman). *Students:* 14 full-time (3 women), 49 part-time (11 women); includes 17 minority (10 Black or African American, non-Hispanic/Latino; 2 Asian, non-Hispanic/Latino; 3 Hispanic/Latino; 2 Two or more races, non-Hispanic/Latino), 8 international. Average age 33. 29 applicants, 93% accepted, 15 enrolled. In 2016, 36 master's, 7 other advanced degrees awarded. *Degree requirements:* For master's, thesis. *Entrance requirements:* For master's, GRE General Test, letters of recommendation; minimum undergraduate GPA of 2.7 overall or 3.0 in final two years. Additional exam requirements/recommendations for international students: Required—TOEFL (minimum score 550 paper-based; 79 iBT), IELTS (minimum score 6). *Application deadline:* For fall admission, 6/15 priority date for domestic students, 7/1 for international students; for spring admission, 11/1 priority date for domestic students, 11/1 for international students. Applications are processed on a rolling basis. Application fee: $35 ($40 for international students). Electronic applications accepted. *Expenses:* $9,876 full-time in-state; $25,994 full-time out-of-state; $450 per credit part-time in-state; $1,345 per credit part-time out-of-state. *Financial support:* In 2016–17, 4 research assistantships were awarded; teaching assistantships, career-related internships or fieldwork, scholarships/grants, and unspecified assistantships also available. Support available to part-time students. Financial award application deadline: 7/1; financial award applicants required to submit FAFSA. *Faculty research:* Plant layout design, lean manufacturing, Six Sigma, value management, product development. *Unit head:* Dr. Neslihan Alp, Department Head, 423-425-4032, Fax: 423-425-5818, E-mail: neslihan-alp@utc.edu. *Application contact:* Dr. Joanne Romagni, Dean of the Graduate School, 423-425-4478, Fax: 423-425-5223, E-mail: joanne-romagni@utc.edu.
Website: http://www.utc.edu/college-engineering-computer-science/programs/engineering-management-and-technology/index.php#li03

The University of Texas at Arlington, Graduate School, College of Engineering, Department of Civil Engineering, Arlington, TX 76019. Offers civil engineering (M Engr, MS, PhD); construction management (MCM). *Program availability:* Part-time, evening/weekend, online learning. Terminal master's awarded for partial completion of doctoral program. *Degree requirements:* For master's, comprehensive exam, thesis (for some programs), oral and written exams; for doctorate, comprehensive exam, thesis/dissertation, oral and written defense of dissertation. *Entrance requirements:* For master's, GRE General Test, minimum GPA of 3.0 in last 60 hours of undergraduate course work; for doctorate, GRE General Test, minimum GPA of 3.5. Additional exam requirements/recommendations for international students: Required—TOEFL. *Application deadline:* For fall admission, 6/6 for domestic students, 4/4 for international students; for spring admission, 10/15 for domestic students, 9/5 for international students. Applications are processed on a rolling basis. Application fee: $35 ($50 for international students). Electronic applications accepted. *Financial support:* Fellowships with partial tuition reimbursements, research assistantships with partial tuition reimbursements, teaching assistantships with partial tuition reimbursements, career-related internships or fieldwork, Federal Work-Study, scholarships/grants, tuition waivers (partial), and unspecified assistantships available. Financial award application deadline: 6/1; financial award applicants required to submit FAFSA. *Faculty research:* Environmental and water resources structures, geotechnical, transportation. *Unit head:* Dr. Ali Abolmaali, Chair, 817-272-5055, Fax: 817-272-2630, E-mail: abolmaali@uta.edu. *Application contact:* Dr. Stephen Mattingly, Graduate Advisor, 817-272-2201, Fax: 817-272-2630, E-mail: mattingly@uta.edu.
Website: http://www.uta.edu/ce/

The University of Texas at El Paso, Graduate School, College of Engineering, Department of Civil Engineering, El Paso, TX 79968-0001. Offers civil engineering (MS, PhD); construction management (MS, Certificate); environmental engineering (MEENE, MSENE). *Program availability:* Part-time, evening/weekend. *Degree requirements:* For master's, comprehensive exam, thesis optional; for doctorate, comprehensive exam, thesis/dissertation. *Entrance requirements:* For master's, GRE, minimum GPA of 3.0; for doctorate, GRE. Additional exam requirements/recommendations for international students: Required—TOEFL. Electronic applications accepted. *Faculty research:* Non-destructive testing for geotechnical and pavement applications, transportation systems, wastewater treatment systems, air quality, linear and non-linear modeling of structures, structural reliability.

University of Washington, Graduate School, College of Built Environments, Department of Construction Management, Seattle, WA 98195. Offers MSCM. *Program availability:* Part-time, evening/weekend. *Degree requirements:* For master's, thesis or alternative. *Entrance requirements:* For master's, GRE General Test, minimum GPA of 3.0. Additional exam requirements/recommendations for international students:

Required—TOEFL. Electronic applications accepted. *Faculty research:* Business practices, delivery methods, materials, productivity.

University of Wisconsin–Stout, Graduate School, College of Science, Technology, Engineering and Mathematics, Program in Construction Management, Menomonie, WI 54751. Offers MS. *Entrance requirements:* For master's, bachelor's degree in construction or a construction-related field from accredited institution, minimum GPA of 3.0, resume.

Virginia Polytechnic Institute and State University, Graduate School, College of Architecture and Urban Studies, Blacksburg, VA 24061. Offers architecture (MS Arch); architecture and design research (PhD); building/construction science and management (MS); creative technologies (MFA); environmental design and planning (PhD); landscape architecture (MLA); planning, governance, and globalization (PhD); public administration (MPA); public administration/public affairs (PhD, Certificate); public and international affairs (MPIA); urban and regional planning (MURP). *Accreditation:* ASLA (one or more programs are accredited). *Faculty:* 136 full-time (53 women). *Students:* 371 full-time (185 women), 210 part-time (104 women); includes 118 minority (49 Black or African American, non-Hispanic/Latino; 1 American Indian or Alaska Native, non-Hispanic/Latino; 30 Asian, non-Hispanic/Latino; 32 Hispanic/Latino; 6 Two or more races, non-Hispanic/Latino), 137 international. Average age 31. 566 applicants, 55% accepted, 160 enrolled. In 2016, 137 master's, 24 doctorates awarded. *Degree requirements:* For master's, comprehensive exam (for some programs), thesis (for some programs); for doctorate, comprehensive exam (for some programs), thesis/dissertation (for some programs). *Entrance requirements:* For master's and doctorate, GRE/GMAT. Additional exam requirements/recommendations for international students: Required—TOEFL (minimum score 80 iBT). *Application deadline:* For fall admission, 8/1 for domestic students, 4/1 for international students; for spring admission, 1/1 for domestic students, 9/1 for international students. Applications are processed on a rolling basis. Application fee: $75. Electronic applications accepted. *Expenses:* Tuition, state resident: full-time $12,467; part-time $692.50 per credit hour. Tuition, nonresident: full-time $25,095; part-time $1394.25 per credit hour. *Required fees:* $2669; $491.50 per semester. Tuition and fees vary according to course load, campus/location and program. *Financial support:* In 2016–17, 11 research assistantships with full tuition reimbursements (averaging $19,474 per year), 45 teaching assistantships with full tuition reimbursements (averaging $16,014 per year) were awarded. Financial award application deadline: 3/1; financial award applicants required to submit FAFSA. *Total annual research expenditures:* $3.6 million. *Unit head:* Dr. A. J. Davis, Dean, 540-231-6416, Fax: 540-231-6332, E-mail: davisa@vt.edu. *Application contact:* Christine Mattsson-Coon, Executive Assistant, 540-231-6416, Fax: 540-231-6332, E-mail: cmattsso@vt.edu.
Website: http://www.caus.vt.edu/

Wentworth Institute of Technology, Master of Science in Construction Management Program, Boston, MA 02115-5998. Offers MS. *Program availability:* Part-time-only, evening/weekend, 100% online, blended/hybrid learning. *Faculty:* 38 part-time/adjunct (11 women). *Students:* 1 (woman) full-time, 50 part-time (13 women); includes 11 minority (6 Black or African American, non-Hispanic/Latino; 1 American Indian or Alaska Native, non-Hispanic/Latino; 1 Hispanic/Latino; 3 Two or more races, non-Hispanic/Latino). Average age 30. 46 applicants, 83% accepted, 27 enrolled. In 2016, 23 master's awarded. *Degree requirements:* For master's, thesis optional, capstone. *Entrance requirements:* For master's, two recommendations from employer; current resume; bachelor's degree in construction management or a bachelor's degree with competencies in construction and a statement of purpose; minimum GPA of 3.0. Additional exam requirements/recommendations for international students: Recommended—TOEFL (minimum score 525 paper-based). *Application deadline:* For fall admission, 8/1 for domestic and international students; for spring admission, 12/20 for domestic and international students. Applications are processed on a rolling basis. Application fee: $50. Electronic applications accepted. *Expenses:* Contact institution. *Financial support:* Scholarships/grants available. Support available to part-time students. Financial award application deadline: 8/1; financial award applicants required to submit FAFSA. *Unit head:* Philip Hammond, Director of Graduate Programs, 617-989-4594, Fax: 617-989-4399, E-mail: hammondp1@wit.edu. *Application contact:* Martha Sheehan, Director of Admissions and Marketing, 617-989-4661, Fax: 617-989-4399, E-mail: sheehanm@wit.edu.
Website: http://www.wit.edu/continuinged/programs/construction-mgmt-masters.html

Western Carolina University, Graduate School, Kimmel School of Construction Management and Technology, Department of Construction Management, Cullowhee, NC 28723. Offers MCM. *Program availability:* Part-time, evening/weekend, online learning. *Entrance requirements:* For master's, GRE or GMAT, appropriate undergraduate degree, resume, letters of recommendation, work experience. Additional exam requirements/recommendations for international students: Required—TOEFL (minimum score 550 paper-based; 79 iBT). *Expenses:* Tuition, state resident: full-time $2174. Tuition, nonresident: full-time $7377. *Required fees:* $1442. Part-time tuition and fees vary according to course load. *Faculty research:* Hazardous waste management, energy management and conservation, engineering materials, refrigeration and air conditioning systems.

Worcester Polytechnic Institute, Graduate Studies and Research, Department of Civil and Environmental Engineering, Worcester, MA 01609-2280. Offers civil and environmental engineering (Advanced Certificate, Graduate Certificate); civil engineering (ME, MS, PhD); construction project management (MS); environmental engineering (M Eng, MS); master builder (M Eng). *Program availability:* Part-time, evening/weekend, blended/hybrid learning. *Faculty:* 10 full-time (0 women), 4 part-time/adjunct (0 women). *Students:* 31 full-time (15 women), 20 part-time (8 women); includes 5 minority (1 Black or African American, non-Hispanic/Latino; 1 American Indian or Alaska Native, non-Hispanic/Latino; 1 Hispanic/Latino; 2 Two or more races, non-Hispanic/Latino), 19 international. 111 applicants, 58% accepted, 13 enrolled. In 2016, 20 master's, 6 doctorates awarded. *Degree requirements:* For master's, thesis optional; for doctorate, comprehensive exam, thesis/dissertation. *Entrance requirements:* For master's, GRE (recommended), 3 letters of recommendation; for doctorate, GRE (recommended), 3 letters of recommendation, statement of purpose. Additional exam requirements/recommendations for international students: Required—TOEFL (minimum score 563 paper-based; 84 iBT), IELTS (minimum score 7), GRE. *Application deadline:* For fall admission, 1/1 priority date for domestic and international students; for spring admission, 10/1 priority date for domestic and international students. Applications are processed on a rolling basis. Application fee: $70. Electronic applications accepted. *Financial support:* Research assistantships, teaching assistantships, career-related internships or fieldwork, institutionally sponsored loans, scholarships/grants, and unspecified assistantships available. Financial award application deadline: 1/1; financial award applicants required to submit FAFSA. *Unit head:* Dr. Tahar El-Korchi, Interim Head, 508-831-5530, Fax: 508-831-5808, E-mail: tek@wpi.edu. *Application contact:* Dr. Rajib Mallick, Graduate Coordinator, 508-831-5530, Fax: 508-831-5808, E-mail: rajib@wpi.edu.
Website: http://www.wpi.edu/academics/cee

Energy Management and Policy

American University of Armenia, Graduate Programs, Yerevan, Armenia. Offers business administration (MBA); computer and information science (MS), including business management, design and manufacturing, energy (ME, MS), industrial engineering and systems management; economics (MS); industrial engineering and systems management (ME), including business, computer aided design/manufacturing, energy (ME, MS), information technology; law (LL M); political science and international affairs (MPSIA); public health (MPH); teaching English as a foreign language (MA). *Program availability:* Part-time, evening/weekend. *Degree requirements:* For master's, thesis (for some programs), capstone/project. *Entrance requirements:* For master's, GRE, GMAT, or LSAT. Additional exam requirements/recommendations for international students: Recommended—TOEFL (minimum score 79 iBT), IELTS (minimum score 6.5). *Faculty research:* Microfinance, finance (rural/development, international, corporate), firm life cycle theory, TESOL, language proficiency testing, public policy, administrative law, economic development, cryptography, artificial intelligence, energy efficiency/renewable energy, computer-aided design/manufacturing, health financing, tuberculosis control, mother/child health, preventive ophthalmology, post-earthquake psychopathological investigations, tobacco control, environmental health risk assessments.

Boston University, Graduate School of Arts and Sciences, Department of Earth and Environment, Boston, MA 02215. Offers earth and environment (PhD); earth sciences (MA, PhD); energy and environment (MA); geography (MA, PhD); global development policy (MA); international relations and environmental policy (MA); remote sensing and geospatial sciences (MA). *Students:* 66 full-time (30 women), 3 part-time (1 woman); includes 4 minority (1 Asian, non-Hispanic/Latino; 3 Hispanic/Latino), 31 international. Average age 27. 163 applicants, 35% accepted, 18 enrolled. In 2016, 11 master's, 13 doctorates awarded. Terminal master's awarded for partial completion of doctoral program. *Degree requirements:* For master's, comprehensive exam (for some programs), thesis (for some programs); for doctorate, comprehensive exam, thesis/dissertation. *Entrance requirements:* For master's and doctorate, GRE General Test, 3 letters of recommendation, official transcripts, personal statement, writing sample (for geography). Additional exam requirements/recommendations for international students: Required—TOEFL (minimum score 550 paper-based; 84 iBT). *Application deadline:* For fall admission, 1/31 for domestic and international students; for winter admission, 10/15 for domestic and international students. Application fee: $95. Electronic applications accepted. *Financial support:* In 2016–17, 39 students received support, including 4 fellowships with full tuition reimbursements available (averaging $21,500 per year), 14 research assistantships with full tuition reimbursements available (averaging $21,500 per year), 15 teaching assistantships with full tuition reimbursements available (averaging $21,500 per year); Federal Work-Study, scholarships/grants, traineeships, and health care benefits also available. Financial award application deadline: 1/31. *Faculty research:* Biogeosciences, climate and surface processes; energy, environment and society; geographical sciences; geology, geochemistry and geophysics. *Unit head:* David Marchant, Chair, 617-353-3236, E-mail: marchant@bu.edu. *Application contact:* Alissa Beideck, Graduate Program Coordinator, 617-353-2529, Fax: 617-353-8399, E-mail: abeideck@bu.edu.
Website: http://www.bu.edu/earth/

Colorado State University, Warner College of Natural Resources, Department of Ecosystem Science and Sustainability, Fort Collins, CO 80523-1476. Offers greenhouse gas management and accounting (MGMA); watershed science (MS). *Faculty:* 9 full-time (2 women), 3 part-time/adjunct (2 women). *Students:* 14 full-time (8 women), 13 part-time (8 women); includes 5 minority (3 Hispanic/Latino; 2 Two or more races, non-Hispanic/Latino), 2 international. Average age 28. 34 applicants, 47% accepted, 11 enrolled. In 2016, 4 master's awarded. *Degree requirements:* For master's, thesis (for some programs), internship. *Entrance requirements:* For master's, GRE (70th percentile or higher), minimum GPA of 3.0. Additional exam requirements/recommendations for international students: Required—TOEFL (minimum score 550 paper-based; 80 iBT), IELTS (minimum score 6.5). *Application deadline:* For fall admission, 2/1 priority date for domestic and international students. Application fee: $60 ($70 for international students). Electronic applications accepted. *Expenses:* Contact institution. *Financial support:* In 2016–17, 9 students received support, including 1 fellowship (averaging $61,080 per year), 4 research assistantships (averaging $23,138 per year), 7 teaching assistantships (averaging $13,932 per year). *Faculty research:* Watershed/snow/alpine/land use hydrology, geographic information systems and remote sensing, greenhouse gas emissions, climate change, environmental accounting. *Total annual research expenditures:* $2.2 million. *Unit head:* Dr. John Moore, Department Head, 970-491-5589, Fax: 970-491-1965, E-mail: john.moore@colostate.edu. *Application contact:* Nikki Foxley, Graduate Admissions Coordinator, 970-491-5589, Fax: 970-491-1965, E-mail: nikki.foxley@colostate.edu.
Website: http://warnercnr.colostate.edu/departments/ess

Duke University, The Fuqua School of Business, The Duke MBA-Cross Continent Program, Durham, NC 27708-0586. Offers business administration (MBA); energy and environment (MBA); entrepreneurship and innovation (MBA); finance (MBA); health sector management (Certificate); marketing (MBA); strategy (MBA). *Faculty:* 88 full-time (19 women), 50 part-time/adjunct (9 women). *Students:* 214 full-time (74 women); includes 58 minority (13 Black or African American, non-Hispanic/Latino; 35 Asian, non-Hispanic/Latino; 10 Hispanic/Latino), 35 international. Average age 30. In 2016, 105 master's awarded. *Entrance requirements:* For master's, GMAT or GRE, transcripts, essays, resume, recommendation letters, letter of company support, interview. *Application deadline:* For fall admission, 10/12 priority date for domestic and international students; for winter admission, 2/7 priority date for domestic and international students; for spring admission, 5/3 priority date for domestic and international students; for summer admission, 5/31 for domestic and international students. Applications are processed on a rolling basis. Application fee: $225. Electronic applications accepted. *Expenses:* Contact institution. *Financial support:* In 2016–17, 49 students received support. Institutionally sponsored loans and scholarships/grants available. Financial award applicants required to submit FAFSA. *Unit head:* Mohan Venkatachalam, Senior Associate Dean, Executive Programs, 919-660-7859, E-mail: mohan.venkatachalam@duke.edu. *Application contact:* Sharon Thompson, Assistant Dean, Office of Admissions, 919-660-7705, Fax: 919-681-8026, E-mail: admissions-info@fuqua.duke.edu.
Website: http://www.fuqua.duke.edu/programs/duke_mba/cross_continent/

Duke University, The Fuqua School of Business, The Duke MBA-Daytime Program, Durham, NC 27708-0586. Offers academic excellence in finance (Certificate); business administration (MBA); decision sciences (MBA); energy and environment (MBA); energy finance (MBA); entrepreneurship and innovation (MBA); finance (MBA); financial analysis (MBA); health sector management (Certificate); leadership and ethics (MBA); management (MBA); marketing (MBA); operations management (MBA); social entrepreneurship (MBA); strategy (MBA). *Faculty:* 88 full-time (19 women), 50 part-time/

adjunct (9 women). *Students:* 897 full-time (310 women); includes 174 minority (39 Black or African American, non-Hispanic/Latino; 3 American Indian or Alaska Native, non-Hispanic/Latino; 75 Asian, non-Hispanic/Latino; 51 Hispanic/Latino; 1 Native Hawaiian or other Pacific Islander, non-Hispanic/Latino; 5 Two or more races, non-Hispanic/Latino), 343 international. Average age 28. In 2016, 440 master's awarded. *Entrance requirements:* For master's, GMAT or GRE, transcripts, essays, resume, recommendation letters, interview. *Application deadline:* For fall admission, 9/13 for domestic and international students; for winter admission, 10/13 for domestic and international students; for spring admission, 1/4 for domestic and international students; for summer admission, 3/20 for domestic and international students. Application fee: $225. Electronic applications accepted. *Expenses:* $66,717 (first-year tuition and fees). *Financial support:* In 2016–17, 415 students received support. Institutionally sponsored loans and scholarships/grants available. Financial award applicants required to submit FAFSA. *Unit head:* Russ Morgan, Senior Associate Dean for Full-time Programs, 919-660-2931, Fax: 919-684-8742, E-mail: ruskin.morgan@duke.edu. *Application contact:* Sharon Thompson, Assistant Dean, Office of Admissions, 919-660-7705, Fax: 919-681-8026, E-mail: admissions-info@fuqua.duke.edu.
Website: http://www.fuqua.duke.edu/daytime-mba/

Duke University, The Fuqua School of Business, The Duke MBA-Global Executive Program, Durham, NC 27708-0586. Offers business administration (MBA); energy and environment (MBA); entrepreneurship and innovation (MBA); finance (MBA); health sector management (Certificate); marketing (MBA); strategy (MBA). *Faculty:* 88 full-time (19 women), 50 part-time/adjunct (9 women). *Students:* 48 full-time (14 women); includes 18 minority (3 Black or African American, non-Hispanic/Latino; 11 Asian, non-Hispanic/Latino; 4 Hispanic/Latino), 10 international. Average age 39. In 2016, 27 master's awarded. *Entrance requirements:* For master's, transcripts, essays, resume, recommendation letters, letter of company support, interview. *Application deadline:* For fall admission, 10/12 priority date for domestic and international students; for winter admission, 12/7 priority date for domestic and international students; for spring admission, 3/20 priority date for domestic and international students; for summer admission, 5/31 for domestic and international students. Applications are processed on a rolling basis. Application fee: $225. Electronic applications accepted. *Expenses:* Contact institution. *Financial support:* In 2016–17, 22 students received support. Institutionally sponsored loans and scholarships/grants available. Financial award applicants required to submit FAFSA. *Unit head:* Mohan Venkatachalam, Senior Associate Dean, Executive Programs, 919-660-7859, E-mail: mohan.venkatachalam@duke.edu. *Application contact:* Sharon Thompson, Assistant Dean, Office of Admissions, 919-660-7705, Fax: 919-681-8026, E-mail: admissions-info@fuqua.duke.edu.
Website: http://www.fuqua.duke.edu/programs/duke_mba/global-executive/

Duke University, The Fuqua School of Business, The Duke MBA-Weekend Executive Program, Durham, NC 27708-0586. Offers business administration (MBA); energy and environment (MBA); entrepreneurship and innovation (MBA); finance (MBA); health sector management (Certificate); marketing (MBA); strategy (MBA). *Faculty:* 88 full-time (19 women), 50 part-time/adjunct (9 women). *Students:* 190 full-time (43 women); includes 75 minority (11 Black or African American, non-Hispanic/Latino; 3 American Indian or Alaska Native, non-Hispanic/Latino; 48 Asian, non-Hispanic/Latino; 12 Hispanic/Latino; 1 Two or more races, non-Hispanic/Latino), 26 international. Average age 35. In 2016, 87 master's awarded. *Entrance requirements:* For master's, GMAT or GRE, transcripts, essays, resume, recommendation letters, letter of company support, interview. *Application deadline:* For fall admission, 8/30 priority date for domestic and international students; for winter admission, 10/12 priority date for domestic and international students; for spring admission, 2/7 priority date for domestic and international students; for summer admission, 3/20 for domestic and international students. Applications are processed on a rolling basis. Application fee: $225. Electronic applications accepted. *Expenses:* Contact institution. *Financial support:* In 2016–17, 33 students received support. Institutionally sponsored loans and scholarships/grants available. Financial award applicants required to submit FAFSA. *Unit head:* Mohan Venkatachalam, Senior Associate Dean, Executive Programs, 919-660-7859, E-mail: mohan.venkatachalam@duke.edu. *Application contact:* Sharon Thompson, Assistant Dean, Office of Admissions, 919-660-7705, Fax: 919-681-8026, E-mail: admissions-info@fuqua.duke.edu.
Website: http://www.fuqua.duke.edu/programs/duke_mba/weekend_executive/

Eastern Illinois University, Graduate School, Lumpkin College of Business and Applied Sciences, School of Technology, Program in Sustainable Energy, Charleston, IL 61920. Offers MS, MS/MBA, MS/MS. *Program availability:* Part-time, evening/weekend. *Degree requirements:* For master's, comprehensive exam. *Entrance requirements:* For master's, GMAT or GRE. Additional exam requirements/recommendations for international students: Required—TOEFL (minimum score 500 paper-based; 61 iBT), IELTS (minimum score 6). Electronic applications accepted.

Franklin Pierce University, Graduate and Professional Studies, Rindge, NH 03461-0060. Offers curriculum and instruction (M Ed); elementary education (MS Ed); emerging network technologies (Graduate Certificate); energy and sustainability studies (MBA, Graduate Certificate); health administration (MBA, Graduate Certificate); human resource management (MBA, Graduate Certificate); information technology (MBA); leadership (MBA); nursing education (MS); nursing leadership (MS); physical therapy (DPT); physician assistant studies (MPAS); special education (M Ed); sports management (MBA). *Accreditation:* APTA. *Program availability:* Part-time, 100% online, blended/hybrid learning. *Faculty:* 47 full-time (36 women), 165 part-time/adjunct (108 women). *Students:* 380 full-time (226 women), 245 part-time (158 women); includes 52 minority (13 Black or African American, non-Hispanic/Latino; 2 American Indian or Alaska Native, non-Hispanic/Latino; 14 Asian, non-Hispanic/Latino; 22 Hispanic/Latino; 1 Native Hawaiian or other Pacific Islander, non-Hispanic/Latino), 13 international. Average age 29. 1,995 applicants, 28% accepted, 267 enrolled. In 2016, 120 master's, 86 doctorates awarded. *Degree requirements:* For master's, concentrated original research projects; student teaching; fieldwork and/or internship; leadership project; PRAXIS I and II (for M Ed); for doctorate, concentrated original research projects, clinical fieldwork and/or internship, leadership project. *Entrance requirements:* For master's, minimum GPA of 2.5, 3 letters of recommendation; competencies in accounting, economics, statistics, and computer skills through life experience or undergraduate coursework (for MBA); certification/e-portfolio, minimum C grade in all education courses (for M Ed); license to practice as RN (for MS); for doctorate, GRE, 80 hours of observation/work in PT settings; completion of anatomy, chemistry, physics, and statistics; minimum GPA of 3.0. Additional exam requirements/recommendations for international students: Required—TOEFL (minimum score 550 paper-based; 61 iBT). *Application deadline:* Applications are processed on a rolling basis. Application fee: $0. Electronic applications accepted. *Expenses: Tuition:* Full-time $15,960; part-time $665 per credit hour. Tuition and fees vary according to program. *Financial support:* Teaching assistantships with tuition reimbursements, career-related internships or fieldwork, and unspecified assistantships available. Support available to part-time students. Financial award applicants required to submit FAFSA. *Faculty research:* Evidence-based practice in sports physical therapy, human resource management in economic crisis, leadership in nursing, innovation in sports facility management, differentiated learning and understanding by design. *Unit head:* Dr. Maria Altobello, Dean, 603-647-3509, Fax: 603-229-4580, E-mail: altobellom@franklinpierce.edu. *Application contact:* Graduate Studies, 800-325-1090, Fax: 603-626-4815, E-mail: cgps@franklinpierce.edu. Website: http://www.franklinpierce.edu/academics/gradstudies/index.htm

Indiana University Bloomington, School of Public and Environmental Affairs, Environmental Science Programs, Bloomington, IN 47405. Offers applied ecology (MSES); energy (MSES); environmental chemistry, toxicology, and risk assessment (MSES); environmental science (PhD); hazardous materials management (Certificate); specialized environmental science (MSES); water resources (MSES); JD/MSES; MSES/MA; MSES/MPA; MSES/MS. *Program availability:* Part-time. Terminal master's awarded for partial completion of doctoral program. *Degree requirements:* For master's, capstone or thesis; internship; for doctorate, comprehensive exam, thesis/dissertation. *Entrance requirements:* For master's, GRE General Test or GMAT, official transcripts, 3 letters of recommendation, resume, personal statement; for doctorate, GRE General Test or LSAT, official transcripts, 3 letters of recommendation, resume or curriculum vitae, statement of purpose. Additional exam requirements/recommendations for international students: Required—TOEFL (minimum score 600 paper-based; 96 iBT); Recommended—IELTS (minimum score 7). Electronic applications accepted. *Faculty research:* Applied ecology, bio-geochemistry, toxicology, wetlands ecology, environmental microbiology, forest ecology, environmental chemistry.

Indiana University Bloomington, School of Public and Environmental Affairs, Public Affairs Programs, Bloomington, IN 47405. Offers economic development (MPA); energy (MPA); environmental policy (PhD); environmental policy and natural resource management (MPA); information systems (MPA); international development (MPA); local government management (MPA); nonprofit management (MPA, Certificate); policy analysis (MPA); public budgeting and financial management (Certificate); public finance (PhD); public financial administration (MPA); public management (MPA, PhD, Certificate); public policy analysis (PhD); social entrepreneurship (Certificate); specialized public affairs (MPA); sustainability and sustainable development (MPA); JD/MPA; MPA/MA; MPA/MIS; MPA/MLS; MSES/MPA. *Accreditation:* NASPAA (one or more programs are accredited). *Program availability:* Part-time. *Degree requirements:* For master's, capstone, internship; for doctorate, comprehensive exam, thesis/dissertation. *Entrance requirements:* For master's, GRE General Test or GMAT, official transcripts, 3 letters of recommendation, resume, personal statement; for doctorate, GRE General Test, official transcripts, 3 letters of recommendation, statement of purpose. Additional exam requirements/recommendations for international students: Required—TOEFL (minimum score 600 paper-based; 96 iBT); Recommended—IELTS (minimum score 7). Electronic applications accepted. *Faculty research:* International development, environmental policy and resource management, policy analysis, public finance, public management, urban management, nonprofit management, energy policy, social policy, public finance.

Instituto Tecnologico de Santo Domingo, Graduate School, Area of Basic And Environmental Sciences, Santo Domingo, Dominican Republic. Offers environmental science (M En S), including environmental education, environmental management, marine resources, natural resources management; mathematics (MS, PhD); renewable energy technology (MS, Certificate).

Johns Hopkins University, Zanvyl Krieger School of Arts and Sciences, Advanced Academic Programs, Program in Environmental Sciences and Policy, Washington, DC 20036. Offers energy policy and climate (MS); environmental sciences (MS); geographic information systems (MS, Certificate). *Program availability:* Part-time, evening/weekend, online learning. *Degree requirements:* For master's, thesis (for some programs). *Entrance requirements:* For master's, minimum GPA of 3.0, coursework in chemistry and calculus. Additional exam requirements/recommendations for international students: Required—TOEFL (minimum score 100 iBT). Electronic applications accepted.

Kansas State University, Graduate School, College of Engineering, Department of Electrical and Computer Engineering, Manhattan, KS 66506. Offers electrical engineering (MS), including bioengineering, communication systems, design of computer systems, electrical engineering, energy and power systems, integrated circuits and devices, real time embedded systems, renewable energy, signal processing. *Program availability:* Part-time, evening/weekend, online learning. *Faculty:* 21 full-time (4 women), 1 (woman) part-time/adjunct. *Students:* 47 full-time (11 women), 51 part-time (5 women); includes 13 minority (6 Black or African American, non-Hispanic/Latino; 6 Asian, non-Hispanic/Latino; 1 Two or more races, non-Hispanic/Latino), 40 international. Average age 31. 146 applicants, 29% accepted, 17 enrolled. In 2016, 16 master's, 5 doctorates awarded. *Degree requirements:* For master's, thesis or alternative, final exam; for doctorate, thesis/dissertation, final exam, preliminary exams. *Entrance requirements:* For master's, GRE General Test, bachelor's degree in electrical engineering or computer science, minimum GPA of 3.0; for doctorate, GRE General Test. Additional exam requirements/recommendations for international students: Required—TOEFL (minimum score 600 paper-based; 85 iBT). *Application deadline:* For fall admission, 1/1 priority date for domestic and international students; for spring admission, 8/1 priority date for domestic and international students. Applications are processed on a rolling basis. Application fee: $50 ($75 for international students). Electronic applications accepted. *Expenses:* Tuition, state resident: full-time $9670. Tuition, nonresident: full-time $21,828. *Required fees:* $862. *Financial support:* In 2016–17, 40 students received support, including 22 research assistantships with tuition reimbursements available (averaging $12,100 per year), 18 teaching assistantships with full tuition reimbursements available (averaging $12,220 per year); career-related internships or fieldwork, institutionally sponsored loans, and scholarships/grants also available. Support available to part-time students. Financial award application deadline: 3/1; financial award applicants required to submit FAFSA. *Faculty research:* Energy systems and renewable energy, computer systems and real time embedded systems, communication systems and signal processing, integrated circuits and devices, bioengineering. *Total annual research expenditures:* $1.3 million. *Unit head:* Dr. Don Gruenbacher, Head, 785-532-5600, Fax: 785-532-1188, E-mail: grue@k-state.edu. *Application contact:* Dr. Andrew Rys, Graduate Program Director, 785-532-4665, Fax: 785-532-1188, E-mail: andrys@k-state.edu.
Website: http://www.ece.k-state.edu/

Michigan Technological University, Graduate School, College of Sciences and Arts, Department of Social Sciences, Houghton, MI 49931. Offers environmental and energy policy (MS, PhD); industrial archaeology (MS); industrial heritage and archaeology (PhD). *Faculty:* 31 full-time (15 women), 20 part-time/adjunct (5 women). *Students:* 18 full-time (10 women), 14 part-time (5 women); includes 2 minority (both American Indian or Alaska Native, non-Hispanic/Latino), 7 international. Average age 36. 66 applicants, 17% accepted, 7 enrolled. In 2016, 13 master's, 3 doctorates awarded. Terminal master's awarded for partial completion of doctoral program. *Degree requirements:* For master's, thesis; for doctorate, comprehensive exam, thesis/dissertation. *Entrance requirements:* For master's and doctorate, GRE, statement of purpose, official

transcripts, 3 letters of recommendation, writing sample, resume/curriculum vitae. Additional exam requirements/recommendations for international students: Required—TOEFL (recommended minimum score 100 iBT) or IELTS. *Application deadline:* For fall admission, 1/15 priority date for domestic students, 2/1 priority date for international students; for spring admission, 10/1 for domestic students. Applications are processed on a rolling basis. Application fee: $0. Electronic applications accepted. *Expenses:* Tuition, state resident: full-time $16,290; part-time $905 per credit. Tuition, nonresident: full-time $16,290; part-time $905 per credit. *Required fees:* $248; $124 per term. Tuition and fees vary according to course load and program. *Financial support:* In 2016–17, 22 students received support, including 2 fellowships with full tuition reimbursements available (averaging $15,242 per year), 5 research assistantships with full tuition reimbursements available (averaging $15,242 per year), 10 teaching assistantships with full tuition reimbursements available (averaging $15,242 per year); career-related internships or fieldwork, scholarships/grants, health care benefits, unspecified assistantships, and cooperative program also available. Financial award application deadline: 1/15. *Faculty research:* Industrial archeology, mining history, environmental and energy policy, land-use policy, environmental decision-making, sustainability. *Total annual research expenditures:* $984,488. *Unit head:* Dr. Hugh S. Gorman, Chair, 906-487-2116, E-mail: hsgorman@mtu.edu. *Application contact:* Amy Spahn, Office Assistant, 906-487-2113, Fax: 906-487-2284, E-mail: gradadms@mtu.edu.
Website: http://www.mtu.edu/social-sciences/

New York Institute of Technology, School of Engineering and Computing Sciences, Department of Energy Management, Old Westbury, NY 11568-8000. Offers energy management (MS); energy technology (Advanced Certificate); environmental management (Advanced Certificate); facilities management (Advanced Certificate); infrastructure security management (Advanced Certificate). *Program availability:* Part-time, evening/weekend, 100% online, blended/hybrid learning. *Faculty:* 1 full-time (0 women), 5 part-time/adjunct (0 women). *Students:* 53 full-time (7 women), 56 part-time (8 women); includes 20 minority (5 Black or African American, non-Hispanic/Latino; 1 American Indian or Alaska Native, non-Hispanic/Latino; 5 Asian, non-Hispanic/Latino; 9 Hispanic/Latino), 60 international. Average age 28. 167 applicants, 77% accepted, 33 enrolled. In 2016, 54 master's, 3 other advanced degrees awarded. *Degree requirements:* For master's, thesis or alternative. *Entrance requirements:* For master's and Advanced Certificate, BS; minimum undergraduate GPA of 2.85. Additional exam requirements/recommendations for international students: Required—TOEFL (minimum score 79 iBT), IELTS (minimum score 6). *Application deadline:* For fall admission, 7/1 for domestic students, 6/1 for international students; for spring admission, 12/1 for domestic and international students. Applications are processed on a rolling basis. Application fee: $50. Electronic applications accepted. *Expenses:* $1,215 per credit. *Financial support:* Fellowships with partial tuition reimbursements, teaching assistantships with partial tuition reimbursements, career-related internships or fieldwork, Federal Work-Study, scholarships/grants, tuition waivers (full and partial), and unspecified assistantships available. Support available to part-time students. Financial award application deadline: 3/1; financial award applicants required to submit FAFSA. *Faculty research:* Alternative energy systems; energy policy, master planning, and auditing; facilities management; lighting technology; cogeneration; utility rate structures; smart homes; monitoring systems; building information modeling; sustainability. *Unit head:* Dr. Robert Amundsen, Department Chair, 516-686-7578, E-mail: ramundse@nyit.edu. *Application contact:* Alice Dolitsky, Director, Graduate Admissions, 516-686-7520, Fax: 516-686-1116, E-mail: nyitgrad@nyit.edu.
Website: http://www.nyit.edu/degrees/energy_management_ms

New York University, School of Continuing and Professional Studies, Center for Global Affairs, New York, NY 10012-1019. Offers global affairs (MS), including environment/energy policy, human rights and international law, international development and humanitarian assistance, international relations, peace building, private sector, transnational security; global energy (Advanced Certificate); peacebuilding (Advanced Certificate); transnational security (Advanced Certificate). *Program availability:* Part-time, evening/weekend. *Degree requirements:* For master's, thesis. *Entrance requirements:* For master's, GRE or GMAT (only upon request), bachelor's degree, resume with relevant professional work, internship or volunteer experience, two letters of recommendation, statement of purpose. Additional exam requirements/recommendations for international students: Required—TOEFL (minimum score 600 paper-based; 100 iBT), IELTS (minimum score 7). Electronic applications accepted.

Norwich University, College of Graduate and Continuing Studies, Master of Business Administration Program, Northfield, VT 05663. Offers construction management (MBA); energy management (MBA); finance (MBA); logistics (MBA); organizational leadership (MBA); project management (MBA); supply chain management (MBA). *Accreditation:* ACBSP. *Program availability:* Evening/weekend, online only, mostly all online with a week-long residency requirement. *Faculty:* 24 part-time/adjunct (5 women). *Students:* 228 full-time (54 women); includes 54 minority (23 Black or African American, non-Hispanic/Latino; 1 American Indian or Alaska Native, non-Hispanic/Latino; 6 Asian, non-Hispanic/Latino; 20 Hispanic/Latino; 1 Native Hawaiian or other Pacific Islander, non-Hispanic/Latino; 3 Two or more races, non-Hispanic/Latino), 2 international. Average age 36. 74 applicants, 100% accepted, 57 enrolled. In 2016, 135 master's awarded. *Degree requirements:* For master's, comprehensive exam. *Entrance requirements:* For master's, minimum undergraduate GPA of 2.75. Additional exam requirements/recommendations for international students: Required—TOEFL (minimum score 550 paper-based; 80 iBT), IELTS (minimum score 6.5). *Application deadline:* For fall admission, 8/14 for domestic and international students; for winter admission, 11/13 for domestic and international students; for spring admission, 2/12 for domestic and international students; for summer admission, 6/5 for domestic and international students. Electronic applications accepted. *Expenses:* Contact institution. *Financial support:* In 2016–17, 113 students received support. Scholarships/grants available. Financial award application deadline: 8/4; financial award applicants required to submit FAFSA. *Unit head:* Dr. Jose Cordova, Program Director, 802-485-2567, Fax: 802-485-2533, E-mail: jcordova@norwich.edu. *Application contact:* Admissions Advisor, 800-460-5597 Ext. 3376, Fax: 802-485-2533, E-mail: mba@online.norwich.edu.
Website: https://online.norwich.edu/degree-programs/masters/master-business-administration/overview

Oklahoma Baptist University, Program in Business Administration, Shawnee, OK 74804. Offers business administration (MBA); energy management (MBA). *Accreditation:* ACBSP. *Program availability:* Online learning.

Oklahoma City University, Meinders School of Business, Oklahoma City, OK 73106-1402. Offers business (MBA, MSA); computer science (MS); energy legal studies (MS); energy management (MS); JD/MBA. *Program availability:* Part-time, evening/weekend, 100% online. *Faculty:* 17 full-time (3 women), 5 part-time/adjunct (1 woman). *Students:* 170 full-time (68 women), 218 part-time (90 women); includes 82 minority (17 Black or African American, non-Hispanic/Latino; 10 American Indian or Alaska Native, non-Hispanic/Latino; 16 Asian, non-Hispanic/Latino; 24 Hispanic/Latino; 15 Two or more races, non-Hispanic/Latino), 103 international. Average age 30. 592 applicants, 50% accepted, 138 enrolled. In 2016, 171 master's awarded. *Degree requirements:* For master's, practicum/capstone. *Entrance requirements:* For master's, undergraduate degree from accredited institution, minimum GPA of 3.0, essay, letters of

Energy Management and Policy

recommendation. Additional exam requirements/recommendations for international students: Required—TOEFL (minimum score 550 paper-based; 80 iBT). *Application deadline:* Applications are processed on a rolling basis. Application fee: $50. Electronic applications accepted. *Expenses:* Contact institution. *Financial support:* In 2016–17, 262 students received support. Career-related internships or fieldwork, Federal Work-Study, institutionally sponsored loans, scholarships/grants, and tuition waivers (full and partial) available. Support available to part-time students. Financial award application deadline: 6/1; financial award applicants required to submit FAFSA. *Faculty research:* Group support systems, leadership, decision models in accounting. *Unit head:* Dr. Steve Agee, Dean, 405-208-5275, Fax: 405-208-5008, E-mail: sagee@okcu.edu. *Application contact:* Michael Harrington, Director of Graduate Admission, 800-633-7242, Fax: 405-208-5916, E-mail: gadmissions@okcu.edu.
Website: http://msb.okcu.edu

Rice University, Graduate Programs, School of Social Sciences, Department of Economics, Houston, TX 77251-1892. Offers economics (PhD); energy economics (MEECON). *Degree requirements:* For doctorate, comprehensive exam, thesis/dissertation. *Entrance requirements:* For doctorate, GRE. Additional exam requirements/recommendations for international students: Required—TOEFL (minimum score 600 paper-based; 90 iBT). Electronic applications accepted.

Samford University, Howard College of Arts and Sciences, Birmingham, AL 35229. Offers energy management and policy (MSEM); JD/MSEM. *Program availability:* Part-time, evening/weekend. *Faculty:* 6 full-time (3 women), 3 part-time/adjunct (0 women). *Students:* 7 full-time (2 women), 4 part-time; includes 1 minority (Black or African American, non-Hispanic/Latino), 7 international. Average age 27. In 2016, 14 master's awarded. *Entrance requirements:* For master's, GRE General Test (minimum score 295 combined) or MAT (minimum score 396), minimum GPA of 2.5 with 3 years of work experience or 3.0 for a recent college graduate. Additional exam requirements/recommendations for international students: Required—TOEFL (minimum score 90 iBT); Recommended—IELTS (minimum score 6.5). *Application deadline:* For fall admission, 8/1 for domestic and international students; for winter admission, 12/1 for domestic and international students; for spring admission, 12/1 for domestic and international students; for summer admission, 5/1 for domestic and international students. Applications are processed on a rolling basis. Application fee: $35. *Expenses:* Tuition: Full-time $18,530; part-time $789 per credit hour. *Required fees:* $610. Tuition and fees vary according to course load, degree level, program and student level. *Financial support:* Application deadline: 3/1; applicants required to submit FAFSA. *Faculty research:* Mosquito fish as an environmental model for pollutants, PCB contamination, environmental epidemiology and toxicology, geographic information systems, geology and natural resource management, energy management, chemical and biological analysis of water, aquatic biomonitoring. *Unit head:* Tim Hall, Dean of Howard College of Arts and Sciences, E-mail: thall5@samford.edu. *Application contact:* Dr. Ronald N. Hunsinger, Professor/Chair, Biological and Environmental Sciences, 205-726-2944, Fax: 205-726-2479, E-mail: rnhunsin@samford.edu.
Website: http://howard.samford.edu/

Tulane University, A. B. Freeman School of Business, New Orleans, LA 70118-5669. Offers accounting (M Acct); analytics (MBA); banking and financial services (M Fin); energy (M Fin, MBA); entrepreneurship (MBA); finance (MBA, PhD); international business (MBA); international management (MBA); strategic management and leadership (MBA); JD/M Acct; JD/MBA; MBA/M Acc; MBA/MA; MBA/MD; MBA/ME; MBA/MPH. *Accreditation:* AACSB. *Program availability:* Part-time, evening/weekend. *Faculty:* 46 full-time (11 women), 36 part-time/adjunct (3 women). *Students:* 488 full-time (240 women), 414 part-time (198 women); includes 81 minority (31 Black or African American, non-Hispanic/Latino; 1 American Indian or Alaska Native, non-Hispanic/Latino; 17 Asian, non-Hispanic/Latino; 29 Hispanic/Latino; 3 Two or more races, non-Hispanic/Latino), 575 international. Average age 27. 2,038 applicants, 71% accepted, 511 enrolled. In 2016, 694 master's, 9 doctorates awarded. Terminal master's awarded for partial completion of doctoral program. *Degree requirements:* For master's, one foreign language, comprehensive exam (for some programs); for doctorate, one foreign language, comprehensive exam, thesis/dissertation. *Entrance requirements:* For master's and doctorate, GMAT or GRE, interview. Additional exam requirements/recommendations for international students: Required—TOEFL or IELTS. *Application deadline:* For fall admission, 11/1 priority date for domestic and international students; for winter admission, 1/6 for domestic and international students; for spring admission, 3/1 priority date for domestic and international students; for summer admission, 5/5 for domestic students. Applications are processed on a rolling basis. Application fee: $125. Electronic applications accepted. *Expenses:* Contact institution. *Financial support:* In 2016–17, 153 students received support. Fellowships with tuition reimbursements available, research assistantships, teaching assistantships, career-related internships or fieldwork, Federal Work-Study, tuition waivers (full and partial), and unspecified assistantships available. Support available to part-time students. Financial award application deadline: 4/15; financial award applicants required to submit FAFSA. *Faculty research:* Corporate finance, managerial accounting and financial reporting, strategic management and leadership, consumer behavior and decision making, organizational behavior and human resource management. *Unit head:* Ira Solomon, PhD, Dean, 504-865-5407, Fax: 504-865-5491, E-mail: businessdean@tulane.edu. *Application contact:* Melissa Booth, Director of Graduate Admissions and Financial Aid, 800-223-5402, E-mail: freeman.admissions@tulane.edu.
Website: http://www.freeman.tulane.edu

Université du Québec, Institut National de la Recherche Scientifique, Graduate Programs, Centre for Energie Materiaux Telecommunications, Varennes, QC G1K 9A9, Canada. Offers energy and materials science (M Sc, PhD); telecommunications (M Sc, PhD). *Program availability:* Part-time. *Faculty:* 36 full-time. *Students:* 185 full-time (47 women), 10 part-time (2 women), 154 international. Average age 31. 27 applicants, 78% accepted, 13 enrolled. In 2016, 13 master's, 23 doctorates awarded. *Degree requirements:* For master's, thesis (for some programs); for doctorate, thesis/dissertation. *Entrance requirements:* For master's, appropriate bachelor's degree, proficiency in French; for doctorate, appropriate master's degree, proficiency in French. *Application deadline:* For fall admission, 3/30 for domestic and international students; for winter admission, 11/1 for domestic and international students; for spring admission, 3/1 for domestic and international students. Application fee: $45. Electronic applications accepted. *Financial support:* In 2016–17, fellowships (averaging $16,500 per year) were awarded; research assistantships and scholarships/grants also available. *Faculty research:* New energy sources, plasmas, telecommunications, advanced materials, ultrafast photonics. *Unit head:* Federico Rosei, Director, 450-228-6905, E-mail: rosei@emt.inrs.ca. *Application contact:* Sylvie Richard, Registrar, 418-654-2518, Fax: 418-654-3858, E-mail: sylvie.richard@adm.inrs.ca.
Website: http://www.emt.inrs.ca

University of Calgary, Faculty of Graduate Studies, Schulich School of Engineering, Department of Chemical and Petroleum Engineering, Calgary, AB T2N 1N4, Canada. Offers chemical engineering (M Eng, M Sc, PhD); energy and environment engineering (M Eng, M Sc, PhD); energy and environmental systems (M Eng, M Sc, PhD); environmental engineering (M Eng, M Sc, PhD); petroleum engineering (M Eng, M Sc, PhD); reservoir characterization (M Eng, M Sc). *Program availability:* Part-time. *Degree*

requirements: For master's, thesis (for some programs); for doctorate, comprehensive exam, thesis/dissertation, candidacy exam. *Entrance requirements:* For master's, minimum GPA of 3.0 or equivalent; for doctorate, minimum GPA of 3.5 or equivalent. Additional exam requirements/recommendations for international students: Required—TOEFL (minimum score 550 paper-based; 80 iBT), IELTS (minimum score 7). Electronic applications accepted. *Faculty research:* Environmental engineering, biomedical engineering modeling, simulation and control, petroleum recovery and reservoir engineering, phase equilibria and transport properties.

University of California, Berkeley, Graduate Division, College of Natural Resources, Group in Energy and Resources, Berkeley, CA 94720-1500. Offers MA, MS, PhD. *Students:* 55 full-time (27 women); includes 19 minority (2 Black or African American, non-Hispanic/Latino; 1 American Indian or Alaska Native, non-Hispanic/Latino; 8 Asian, non-Hispanic/Latino; 8 Hispanic/Latino), 7 international. Average age 31. 314 applicants, 11 enrolled. In 2016, 15 master's, 14 doctorates awarded. *Degree requirements:* For master's, project or thesis; for doctorate, one foreign language, thesis/dissertation, qualifying exam. *Entrance requirements:* For master's and doctorate, GRE General Test, minimum GPA of 3.0, 3 letters of recommendation. *Application deadline:* For fall admission, 12/5 for domestic students. Application fee: $105 ($125 for international students). Electronic applications accepted. *Financial support:* Fellowships, research assistantships, teaching assistantships, institutionally sponsored loans, health care benefits, and unspecified assistantships available. *Faculty research:* Technical, economic, environmental, and institutional aspects of energy conservation in residential and commercial buildings; international patterns of energy use; renewable energy sources; assessment of valuation of energy and environmental resources pricing. *Unit head:* Prof. Harrison Fraker, Chair, 510-642-1640, E-mail: ergdeskb@berkeley.edu. *Application contact:* Kay Burns, Student Affairs Officer, 510-642-8859, E-mail: erggrad@berkeley.edu.
Website: http://erg.berkeley.edu/

University of California, San Diego, Graduate Division, School of Global Policy and Strategy, Master of Public Policy Program, La Jolla, CA 92093. Offers American policy in global context (MPP); business, government and regulation (MPP); energy and environmental policy (MPP); health policy (MPP); program design and evaluation (MPP); security policy (MPP). *Faculty:* 33 full-time (9 women), 20 part-time/adjunct (4 women). *Students:* 300 full-time (150 women). 460 applicants, 120 enrolled. *Entrance requirements:* For master's, GMAT or GRE General Test. Additional exam requirements/recommendations for international students: Required—TOEFL (minimum score 90 iBT), IELTS (minimum score 7). *Application deadline:* For fall admission, 1/15 for domestic and international students. Applications are processed on a rolling basis. Application fee: $105 ($125 for international students). Electronic applications accepted. *Expenses:* Contact institution. *Financial support:* Fellowships, research assistantships, teaching assistantships, career-related internships or fieldwork, scholarships/grants, and unspecified assistantships available. Financial award application deadline: 1/15. *Unit head:* Sonja Steinbrech, Director of Enrollment, 858-534-7162, E-mail: ssteinbrech@ucsd.edu. *Application contact:* Admissions Representative, 858-534-5914, E-mail: gps-apply@uscd.edu.
Website: http://gps.ucsd.edu/academics/mpp.html

University of Colorado Denver, Business School, Program in Global Energy Management, Denver, CO 80217. Offers MS. *Program availability:* Online learning. *Students:* 54 full-time (13 women), 4 part-time (2 women); includes 13 minority (4 Black or African American, non-Hispanic/Latino; 8 Hispanic/Latino; 1 Two or more races, non-Hispanic/Latino), 6 international. Average age 35. 28 applicants, 82% accepted, 16 enrolled. In 2016, 32 master's awarded. *Degree requirements:* For master's, 36 semester credit hours. *Entrance requirements:* For master's, GMAT if less than three years of experience in the energy industry (waived for students already holding a graduate degree), minimum of 5 years' experience in energy industry; resume; letters of recommendation; essays. Additional exam requirements/recommendations for international students: Required—TOEFL (minimum score 525 paper-based; 71 iBT); Recommended—IELTS (minimum score 6). *Application deadline:* For fall admission, 6/1 for domestic and international students; for winter admission, 12/1 for domestic and international students; for spring admission, 12/1 for domestic and international students. Application fee: $50 ($75 for international students). Electronic applications accepted. *Expenses:* Contact institution. *Financial support:* In 2016–17, 6 students received support. Fellowships, research assistantships, teaching assistantships, Federal Work-Study, institutionally sponsored loans, scholarships/grants, and traineeships available. Financial award application deadline: 4/1; financial award applicants required to submit FAFSA. *Unit head:* Jim Marchiori, Executive Director of Global Energy Management, 303-315-8436, E-mail: gem@ucdenver.edu. *Application contact:* Michele Motley, Graduate Advisor, Global Energy Management Program, 303-315-8066, E-mail: michelle.motley@ucdenver.edu.
Website: http://www.ucdenver.edu/academics/colleges/business/degrees/ms/gem/Pages/Overview.aspx

University of Delaware, Center for Energy and Environmental Policy, Newark, DE 19716. Offers energy and environmental policy (MA, MEEP, PhD); urban affairs and public policy (PhD), including technology, environment, and society. *Degree requirements:* For master's, analytical paper or thesis; for doctorate, comprehensive exam, thesis/dissertation. *Entrance requirements:* For master's, GRE General Test, minimum GPA of 3.0; for doctorate, GRE General Test, minimum GPA of 3.5. Additional exam requirements/recommendations for international students: Required—TOEFL. Electronic applications accepted. *Faculty research:* Sustainable development, renewable energy, climate change, environmental policy, environmental justice, disaster policy.

University of Illinois at Urbana–Champaign, Graduate College, College of Agricultural, Consumer and Environmental Sciences, Program in Bioenergy, Champaign, IL 61820. Offers PSM. Applications accepted for Fall semester only.

University of Mary, Gary Tharaldson School of Business, Bismarck, ND 58504-9652. Offers business administration (MBA); energy management (MBA, MS); executive (MBA, MS); health care (MBA, MS); human resource management (MBA); project management (MBA, MPM); virtuous leadership (MBA, MPM, MS). *Program availability:* Part-time, evening/weekend. *Entrance requirements:* For master's, minimum GPA of 2.5. Additional exam requirements/recommendations for international students: Required—TOEFL (minimum score 550 paper-based; 80 iBT). Electronic applications accepted.

University of Phoenix–Bay Area Campus, School of Business, San Jose, CA 95134-1805. Offers accountancy (MS); accounting (MBA); business administration (MBA, DBA); energy management (MBA); global management (MBA); health care management (MBA); human resource management (MBA); human resources management (MM); management (MM); marketing (MBA); organizational leadership (DM); project management (MBA); public administration (MPA); technology management (MBA). *Accreditation:* ACBSP. *Program availability:* Evening/weekend, online learning. *Degree requirements:* For master's, thesis (for some programs). *Entrance requirements:* For master's, minimum undergraduate GPA of 3.0, 3 years of work experience. Additional exam requirements/recommendations for international students: Required—TOEFL (minimum score 550 paper-based; 79 iBT). Electronic applications accepted.

University of Phoenix–Online Campus, School of Business, Phoenix, AZ 85034-7209. Offers accountancy (MS); accounting (MBA, Certificate); business administration (MBA); energy management (MBA); global management (MBA); health care management (MBA); human resource management (MBA, Certificate); human resources management (MM); management (MM); marketing (MBA, Certificate); project management (MBA, Certificate); public administration (MBA, MM); technology management (MBA). *Program availability:* Evening/weekend, online learning. *Entrance requirements:* Additional exam requirements/recommendations for international students: Required—TOEFL, TOEIC (Test of English as an International Communication), Berlitz Online English Proficiency Exam, PTE, or IELTS. Electronic applications accepted. *Expenses:* Contact institution.

University of Phoenix–Phoenix Campus, School of Business, Tempe, AZ 85282-2371. Offers accounting (MBA, MS, Certificate); business administration (MBA); energy management (MBA); global management (MBA); health care management (MBA); human resource management (MBA, Certificate); management (MM); marketing (MBA); project management (MBA); technology management (MBA). *Program availability:* Evening/weekend, online learning. *Entrance requirements:* Additional exam requirements/recommendations for international students: Required—TOEFL, TOEIC (Test of English as an International Communication), Berlitz Online English Proficiency Exam, PTE, or IELTS. Electronic applications accepted. *Expenses:* Contact institution.

University of Phoenix–Southern California Campus, School of Business, Costa Mesa, CA 92626. Offers accounting (MBA); business administration (MBA); energy management (MBA); global management (MBA); health care management (MBA); human resource management (MBA); management (MM); marketing (MBA); project management (MBA); technology management (MBA). *Program availability:* Evening/weekend, online learning. *Entrance requirements:* Additional exam requirements/recommendations for international students: Required—TOEFL, TOEIC (Test of English as an International Communication), Berlitz Online English Proficiency Exam, PTE, or IELTS. Electronic applications accepted. *Expenses:* Contact institution.

University of Pittsburgh, Graduate School of Public and International Affairs, Master of Public Administration Program, Pittsburgh, PA 15260. Offers energy and environment (MPA); governance and international public management (MPA); policy research and analysis (MPA); public and nonprofit management (MPA); urban affairs and planning (MPA); JD/MPA; MPH/MPA; MSIS/MPA; MSW/MPA. *Accreditation:* NASPAA. *Program availability:* Part-time, evening/weekend. *Faculty:* 34 full-time (12 women), 17 part-time/ adjunct (5 women). *Students:* 93 full-time (66 women), 21 part-time (16 women); includes 8 minority (4 Black or African American, non-Hispanic/Latino; 1 Asian, non-Hispanic/Latino; 3 Hispanic/Latino), 61 international. Average age 26. 200 applicants, 81% accepted, 49 enrolled. In 2016, 62 master's awarded. *Degree requirements:* For master's, thesis optional, capstone seminar. *Entrance requirements:* For master's, GRE General Test or GMAT, 2 letters of recommendation, resume, undergraduate transcripts, personal statement. Additional exam requirements/recommendations for international students: Required—TOEFL (minimum score 80 iBT); Recommended— IELTS (minimum score 7). *Application deadline:* For fall admission, 2/1 priority date for domestic students, 1/15 for international students; for spring admission, 11/1 for domestic students, 8/1 for international students. Application fee: $50. Electronic applications accepted. *Expenses:* $22,578 per year in-state; $36,734 per year out-of-state. *Financial support:* In 2016–17, 10 students received support, including 2 research assistantships with full tuition reimbursements available (averaging $14,620 per year); fellowships with full tuition reimbursements available, career-related internships or fieldwork, scholarships/grants, health care benefits, and unspecified assistantships also available. Financial award application deadline: 2/1; financial award applicants required to submit FAFSA. *Faculty research:* Urban affairs and planning, governance and international public management, nonprofit management, policy research and analysis, energy and environmental policy. *Total annual research expenditures:* $1.3 million. *Unit head:* Dr. John T.S. Keeler, Dean, 412-648-7605, Fax: 412-648-2605, E-mail: keeler@ pitt.edu. *Application contact:* Dr. Michael T. Rizzi, Director of Student Services, 412-648-7640, Fax: 412-648-7641, E-mail: rizzim@pitt.edu.
Website: http://www.gspia.pitt.edu/

University of Rochester, Hajim School of Engineering and Applied Sciences, Master of Science in Technical Entrepreneurship and Management Program, Rochester, NY 14642. Offers biomedical engineering (MS); chemical engineering (MS); computer science (MS); electrical and computer engineering (MS); energy and the environment (MS); materials science (MS); mechanical engineering (MS); optics (MS). Program offered in collaboration with the Simon School of Business. *Program availability:* Part-time. *Students:* 42 full-time (13 women), 6 part-time (3 women); includes 7 minority (1 Black or African American, non-Hispanic/Latino; 1 Asian, non-Hispanic/Latino; 4 Hispanic/Latino; 1 Two or more races, non-Hispanic/Latino), 28 international. Average age 24. 245 applicants, 65% accepted, 29 enrolled. In 2016, 31 master's awarded. *Degree requirements:* For master's, comprehensive exam, final exam. *Entrance requirements:* For master's, GRE or GMAT, 3 letters of recommendation; personal statement; official transcript; bachelor's degree (or equivalent for international students) in engineering, science, or mathematics. Additional exam requirements/ recommendations for international students: Required—TOEFL (minimum score 600 paper-based; 100 iBT). *Application deadline:* For fall admission, 2/1 for domestic and international students. Application fee: $60. Electronic applications accepted. *Expenses:* $1,800 per credit. *Financial support:* In 2016–17, 45 students received support. Career-related internships or fieldwork and scholarships/grants available. Support available to part-time students. Financial award application deadline: 2/1. *Faculty research:* High

efficiency solar cells, macromolecular self-assembly, digital signal processing, memory hierarchy management, molecular and physical mechanisms in cell migration, optical imaging systems. *Unit head:* Duncan T. Moore, Vice Provost for Entrepreneurship, 585-275-5248, Fax: 585-473-6745, E-mail: duncan.moore@rochester.edu. *Application contact:* Andrea Barrett, Executive Director, 585-276-3407, Fax: 585-276-2357, E-mail: andrea.barrett@rochester.edu.
Website: http://www.rochester.edu/team

University of San Francisco, College of Arts and Sciences, Energy Systems Management Program, San Francisco, CA 94117-1080. Offers MS. *Program availability:* Part-time, evening/weekend. *Entrance requirements:* For master's, GRE. *Application deadline:* For fall admission, 2/1 for domestic students. *Expenses:* Tuition: Full-time $23,310; part-time $1295 per credit. Tuition and fees vary according to course load, degree level, campus/location and program. *Unit head:* Mark Landerghini, Information Contact, 415-422-5101, Fax: 415-422-2217, E-mail: asgraduate@usfca.edu. *Application contact:* Dr. Maggie Winslow, Program Manager, 415-422-5987, E-mail: mwinslow@ usfca.edu.
Website: https://www.usfca.edu/arts-sciences/graduate-programs/energy-systems-management

The University of Texas at Tyler, College of Business and Technology, Program in Business Administration, Tyler, TX 75799-0001. Offers cyber security (MBA); engineering management (MBA); general management (MBA); healthcare management (MBA); internal assurance and consulting (MBA); marketing (MBA); oil, gas and energy (MBA); organizational development (MBA); quality management (MBA). *Accreditation:* AACSB. *Program availability:* Part-time, online learning. *Entrance requirements:* Additional exam requirements/recommendations for international students: Required— TOEFL (minimum score 550 paper-based). *Faculty research:* General business, inventory control, institutional markets, service marketing, product distribution, accounting fraud, financial reporting and recognition.

The University of Tulsa, Graduate School, Collins College of Business, Online Program in Energy Business, Tulsa, OK 74104-3189. Offers MEB. *Program availability:* Part-time, evening/weekend, online only, 100% online. *Students:* 3 full-time (0 women), 99 part-time (16 women); includes 14 minority (5 Black or African American, non-Hispanic/Latino; 2 American Indian or Alaska Native, non-Hispanic/Latino; 1 Asian, non-Hispanic/Latino; 4 Hispanic/Latino; 2 Two or more races, non-Hispanic/Latino), 3 international. Average age 35. 35 applicants, 46% accepted, 12 enrolled. In 2016, 37 master's awarded. *Degree requirements:* For master's, thesis optional. *Entrance requirements:* For master's, GMAT. Additional exam requirements/recommendations for international students: Required—TOEFL (minimum score 577 paper-based; 91 iBT), IELTS (minimum score 6.5). *Application deadline:* For fall admission, 7/1 for domestic students. Applications are processed on a rolling basis. Application fee: $55. Electronic applications accepted. *Expenses:* Tuition: Full-time $22,230; part-time $1235 per credit hour. *Required fees:* $990 per semester. Tuition and fees vary according to course load. *Financial support:* Fellowships with tuition reimbursements, career-related internships or fieldwork, Federal Work-Study, institutionally sponsored loans, scholarships/grants, health care benefits, and tuition waivers available. Support available to part-time students. Financial award applicants required to submit FAFSA. *Unit head:* Dr. Ralph Jackson, Associate Dean, 918-631-2242, Fax: 918-631-2142, E-mail: ralph-jackson@ utulsa.edu. *Application contact:* Ashley Chapa, Marketing Manager, 918-631-2680, Fax: 918-631-2142, E-mail: graduate-business@utulsa.edu.

Vermont Law School, Graduate and Professional Programs, Master's Programs, South Royalton, VT 05068-0096. Offers American legal studies (LL M); energy law (LL M); energy regulation and law (MERL); environmental law (LL M); environmental law and policy (MELP); food and agriculture law (LL M); food and agriculture law and policy (MFALP); JD/MELP; JD/MERL; JD/MFALP. *Program availability:* Part-time, 100% online, blended/hybrid learning. *Entrance requirements:* Additional exam requirements/ recommendations for international students: Required—TOEFL. *Application deadline:* For fall admission, 3/1 priority date for domestic students. Applications are processed on a rolling basis. Application fee: $60. *Expenses:* Tuition: Full-time $47,998. *Financial support:* Fellowships with full tuition reimbursements, career-related internships or fieldwork, Federal Work-Study, institutionally sponsored loans, scholarships/grants, and tuition waivers (partial) available. Support available to part-time students. Financial award application deadline: 3/1; financial award applicants required to submit FAFSA. *Faculty research:* Environment and new economy; takings; international environmental law; interaction among science, law, and environmental policy; climate change and the law. *Unit head:* Marc B. Mihaly, President and Dean, 802-831-1237, Fax: 802-763-2490. *Application contact:* John D. Miller, Jr., Vice President for Enrollment Management, Marketing and Communications, 802-831-1239, Fax: 802-831-1174, E-mail: admiss@ vermontlaw.edu.
Website: http://www.vermontlaw.edu/Academics/degrees/masters

Waynesburg University, Graduate and Professional Studies, Canonsburg, PA 15370. Offers business (MBA), including energy management, finance, health systems, human resources, leadership, market development; counseling (MA), including addictions counseling, clinical mental health; counselor education and supervision (PhD); criminal investigation (MA); education (M Ed), including autism, curriculum and instruction, educational leadership, online teaching; nursing (MSN), including administration, education, informatics; nursing practice (DNP); special education (M Ed); technology (M Ed); MSN/MBA. *Accreditation:* AACN. *Program availability:* Part-time, evening/ weekend. *Degree requirements:* For doctorate, thesis/dissertation. *Entrance requirements:* Additional exam requirements/recommendations for international students: Required—TOEFL. Electronic applications accepted.

Engineering Management

Air Force Institute of Technology, Graduate School of Engineering and Management, Department of Systems and Engineering Management, Dayton, OH 45433-7765. Offers cost analysis (MS); environmental and engineering management (MS); environmental engineering science (MS); information resource/systems management (MS). *Accreditation:* ABET. *Program availability:* Part-time. *Degree requirements:* For master's, thesis. *Entrance requirements:* For master's, GRE, GMAT, minimum GPA of 3.0.

American University of Beirut, Graduate Programs, Faculty of Engineering and Architecture, 11-0236, Lebanon. Offers applied energy (ME); civil engineering (PhD); electrical and computer engineering (PhD); energy studies (MS); engineering management (MEM); environmental and water resources (ME); environmental technology (MSES); mechanical engineering (ME, PhD); urban design (MUD); urban planning and policy (MUPP). *Program availability:* Part-time, evening/weekend, 100% online. *Faculty:* 99 full-time (22 women), 1 part-time/adjunct (0 women). *Students:* 308

full-time (143 women), 86 part-time (39 women). Average age 26. 430 applicants, 69% accepted, 125 enrolled. In 2016, 103 master's, 7 doctorates awarded. Terminal master's awarded for partial completion of doctoral program. *Degree requirements:* For master's, comprehensive exam, thesis optional; for doctorate, comprehensive exam, thesis/ dissertation. *Entrance requirements:* For doctorate, GRE. Additional exam requirements/recommendations for international students: Required—TOEFL (minimum score 573 paper-based; 88 iBT); Recommended—IELTS (minimum score 7). *Application deadline:* For fall admission, 2/10 priority date for domestic and international students; for spring admission, 11/2 priority date for domestic students, 11/2 for international students. Application fee: $50. Electronic applications accepted. *Expenses:* Contact institution. *Financial support:* In 2016–17, 22 students received support, including 94 fellowships with full tuition reimbursements available (averaging $18,200 per year), 44 research assistantships with full tuition reimbursements available (averaging $7,596 per year), 124 teaching assistantships with full tuition

reimbursements available (averaging $1,056 per year); career-related internships or fieldwork, Federal Work-Study, institutionally sponsored loans, scholarships/grants, traineeships, health care benefits, tuition waivers, and unspecified assistantships also available. Support available to part-time students. Financial award application deadline: 12/20. *Total annual research expenditures:* $1.5 million. *Unit head:* Prof. Alan Shihadeh, Interim Dean, 961-1350000 Ext. 3400, Fax: 961-1744462, E-mail: as20@aub.edu.lb. *Application contact:* Dr. Salim Kanaan, Director, Admissions Office, 961-1350000 Ext. 2594, Fax: 961-1750775, E-mail: sk00@aub.edu.lb.
Website: http://www.aub.edu.lb/fea/fea_home/Pages/index.aspx

American University of Sharjah, Graduate Programs, Sharjah, United Arab Emirates. Offers accounting (MS); business (EMBA, MBA); chemical engineering (MS Ch E); civil engineering (MSCE); computer engineering (MS); electrical engineering (MSEE); engineering systems management (MS); mathematics (MS); mechanical engineering (MSME); mechatronics engineering (MS); teaching English to speakers of other languages (MA); translation and interpreting (MA); urban planning (MUP). *Program availability:* Part-time, evening/weekend. *Degree requirements:* For master's, thesis (for some programs). *Entrance requirements:* For master's, GMAT (for MBA). Additional exam requirements/recommendations for international students: Required—TOEFL (minimum score 550 paper-based; 80 iBT), TWE (minimum score 5); Recommended—IELTS (minimum score 6.5). Electronic applications accepted. *Faculty research:* Water pollution, management and waste water treatment, energy and sustainability, air pollution, Islamic finance, family business and small and medium enterprises.

Arkansas State University, Graduate School, College of Engineering, State University, AR 72467. Offers engineering (MS Eng); engineering management (MEM). *Program availability:* Part-time. *Degree requirements:* For master's, comprehensive exam. *Entrance requirements:* For master's, GRE, appropriate bachelor's degree, official transcript, letters of recommendation, resume, immunization records. Additional exam requirements/recommendations for international students: Required—TOEFL (minimum score 550 paper-based; 79 iBT), IELTS (minimum score 6), PTE (minimum score 56). Electronic applications accepted. *Expenses:* Contact institution.

California State Polytechnic University, Pomona, Program in Engineering Management, Pomona, CA 91768-2557. Offers MS. *Program availability:* Part-time, evening/weekend. *Students:* 3 full-time (1 woman), 39 part-time (10 women); includes 15 minority (4 Asian, non-Hispanic/Latino; 8 Hispanic/Latino; 3 Two or more races, non-Hispanic/Latino), 13 international. Average age 29. 15 applicants, 100% accepted, 12 enrolled. In 2016, 15 master's awarded. *Entrance requirements:* Additional exam requirements/recommendations for international students: Required—TOEFL. *Application deadline:* Applications are processed on a rolling basis. Application fee: $55. Electronic applications accepted. *Expenses:* Contact institution. *Financial support:* Application deadline: 3/2; applicants required to submit FAFSA. *Unit head:* Dr. Kamran Abedini, Chair/Graduate Coordinator, 909-869-2569, Fax: 909-869-2564, E-mail: kabedini@cpp.edu. *Application contact:* Andrew M. Wright, Director of Admissions, 909-869-3130, Fax: 909-869-4529, E-mail: awright@cpp.edu.
Website: http://www.cpp.edu/~engineering/IME/grad.shtml

California State University, East Bay, Office of Graduate Studies, College of Science, School of Engineering, Program in Engineering Management, Hayward, CA 94542-3000. Offers MS. *Students:* 19 full-time (10 women), 51 part-time (14 women); includes 4 minority (1 Asian, non-Hispanic/Latino; 2 Hispanic/Latino; 1 Two or more races, non-Hispanic/Latino), 59 international. Average age 27. 219 applicants, 34% accepted, 16 enrolled. In 2016, 25 master's awarded. *Degree requirements:* For master's, comprehensive exam (for some programs), research project or exam. *Entrance requirements:* For master's, GRE or GMAT, minimum GPA of 2.5, personal statement, two letters of recommendation, resume, college algebra/trigonometry or equivalent. Additional exam requirements/recommendations for international students: Required—TOEFL (minimum score 550 paper-based). *Application deadline:* For fall admission, 6/30 for domestic and international students. Application fee: $55. Electronic applications accepted. *Financial support:* Federal Work-Study and institutionally sponsored loans available. Support available to part-time students. Financial award application deadline: 3/2; financial award applicants required to submit FAFSA. *Unit head:* Dr. Saeid Motavalli, Department Chair/Graduate Advisor, 510-885-4481, E-mail: saeid.motavalli@csueastbay.edu. *Application contact:* Dr. Donna Wiley, Interim Associate Vice President for Academic Programs and Graduate Studies, 510-885-3716, Fax: 510-885-4777, E-mail: donna.wiley@csueastbay.edu.
Website: http://www20.csueastbay.edu/csci/departments/engineering/

California State University, Long Beach, Graduate Studies, College of Engineering, Department of Mechanical and Aerospace Engineering, Long Beach, CA 90840. Offers aerospace engineering (MSAE); engineering and industrial applied mathematics (PhD); interdisciplinary engineering (MSE); management engineering (MSE); mechanical engineering (MSME). *Program availability:* Part-time. *Entrance requirements:* Additional exam requirements/recommendations for international students: Required—TOEFL. *Application deadline:* For fall admission, 7/1 for domestic students. Application fee: $55. Electronic applications accepted. *Financial support:* Career-related internships or fieldwork, Federal Work-Study, institutionally sponsored loans, scholarships/grants, and unspecified assistantships available. Financial award application deadline: 3/2. *Faculty research:* Unsteady turbulent flows, solar energy, energy conversion, CAD/CAM, computer-assisted instruction. *Unit head:* Jalal Torabzadeh, Chair, 562-985-4398.

California State University Maritime Academy, Graduate Studies, Vallejo, CA 94590. Offers transportation and engineering management (MS), including engineering management, humanitarian disaster management, transportation. *Program availability:* Evening/weekend, online only, 100% online. *Faculty:* 16 part-time/adjunct (2 women). *Students:* 49 full-time (10 women); includes 11 minority (2 Black or African American, non-Hispanic/Latino; 5 Asian, non-Hispanic/Latino; 2 Hispanic/Latino; 2 Native Hawaiian or other Pacific Islander, non-Hispanic/Latino), 1 international. Average age 32. 29 applicants, 93% accepted, 26 enrolled. In 2016, 24 master's awarded. *Degree requirements:* For master's, minimum GPA of 3.0 in 10 required courses including capstone course and project. *Entrance requirements:* For master's, GMAT/GRE (for applicants with fewer than five years of post-baccalaureate professional experience), equivalent of four-year U.S. bachelor's degree with minimum GPA of 2.5 during last two years (60 semester units or 90 quarter units) of coursework in degree program. Additional exam requirements/recommendations for international students: Required—TOEFL (minimum score 550 paper-based). *Application deadline:* Applications are processed on a rolling basis. Application fee: $55. Electronic applications accepted. *Expenses:* Contact institution. *Financial support:* Applicants required to submit FAFSA. *Unit head:* Dr. Jim Burns, Dean, Graduate Studies. *Application contact:* Kathy Arnold, Program Coordinator, 707-654-1271, Fax: 707-654-1158, E-mail: karnold@csum.edu.
Website: http://www.csum.edu/web/industry/graduate-studies

California State University, Northridge, Graduate Studies, College of Engineering and Computer Science, Department of Manufacturing Systems Engineering and Management, Northridge, CA 91330. Offers engineering automation (MS); engineering management (MS); manufacturing systems engineering (MS); materials engineering (MS). *Program availability:* Online learning. *Faculty:* 8 full-time (7 women), 21 part-time/adjunct (16 women). *Students:* 124 full-time (29 women), 94 part-time (19 women); includes 27 minority (1 American Indian or Alaska Native, non-Hispanic/Latino; 11 Asian, non-Hispanic/Latino; 13 Hispanic/Latino; 2 Two or more races, non-Hispanic/Latino), 145 international. Average age 27. 302 applicants, 33% accepted, 45 enrolled. *Entrance requirements:* For master's, GRE (if cumulative undergraduate GPA less than 3.0). *Application deadline:* For fall admission, 3/30 for domestic students; for spring admission, 9/30 for domestic students. Application fee: $55. *Expenses:* Tuition, state resident: full-time $4152. *Unit head:* Ahmad Sarfaraz, Chair, 818-677-2167.
Website: http://www.csun.edu/~msem/

Case Western Reserve University, School of Graduate Studies, Case School of Engineering, The Institute for Management and Engineering, Cleveland, OH 44106. Offers MEM. *Students:* 70 full-time (15 women), 2 part-time (0 women); includes 14 minority (3 Black or African American, non-Hispanic/Latino; 8 Asian, non-Hispanic/Latino; 2 Hispanic/Latino; 1 Two or more races, non-Hispanic/Latino), 33 international. In 2016, 59 master's awarded. *Entrance requirements:* Additional exam requirements/recommendations for international students: Required—TOEFL, IELTS (minimum score 7.5). *Application deadline:* For fall admission, 5/1 for domestic students, 2/1 for international students. *Expenses: Tuition:* Full-time $42,576; part-time $1774 per credit hour. *Required fees:* $34. Tuition and fees vary according to course load and program. *Unit head:* Mindy Bairel, Interim Executive Director, 216-368-0637, Fax: 216-368-0144, E-mail: mmb149@case.edu. *Application contact:* Ramona David, Program Assistant, 216-368-0596, Fax: 216-368-0144, E-mail: rxd47@cwru.edu.
Website: http://www.mem.case.edu

The Catholic University of America, School of Engineering, Program in Engineering Management, Washington, DC 20064. Offers engineering management (MSE, Certificate), including engineering management and organization (MSE), project and systems engineering management (MSE), technology management (MSE); program management (Certificate); systems engineering and management of information technology (Certificate). *Program availability:* Part-time. *Faculty:* 3 part-time/adjunct (0 women). *Students:* 14 full-time (2 women), 11 part-time (3 women); includes 2 minority (both Two or more races, non-Hispanic/Latino), 20 international. Average age 30. 35 applicants, 54% accepted, 11 enrolled. In 2016, 26 master's awarded. *Degree requirements:* For master's, minimum GPA of 3.0. *Entrance requirements:* For master's and Certificate, statement of purpose, official copies of academic transcripts, two letters of recommendation. Additional exam requirements/recommendations for international students: Required—TOEFL (minimum score 550 paper-based; 80 iBT). *Application deadline:* For fall admission, 7/15 priority date for domestic students, 7/1 for international students; for spring admission, 11/15 priority date for domestic students, 11/1 for international students. Applications are processed on a rolling basis. Application fee: $55. Electronic applications accepted. *Expenses:* $43,380 per year; $1,170 per credit; $200 per semester part-time fees. *Financial support:* Fellowships, research assistantships, teaching assistantships, Federal Work-Study, scholarships/grants, tuition waivers (full and partial), and unspecified assistantships available. Financial award application deadline: 2/1; financial award applicants required to submit FAFSA. *Faculty research:* Engineering management and organization, project and systems engineering management, technology management. *Unit head:* Melvin G. Williams, Jr., Director, 202-319-5191, Fax: 202-319-6860, E-mail: williamsme@cua.edu. *Application contact:* Director of Graduate Admissions, 202-319-5057, Fax: 202-319-6533, E-mail: cua-admissions@cua.edu.
Website: http://engrmgmt.cua.edu/

Central Michigan University, Central Michigan University Global Campus, Program in Administration, Mount Pleasant, MI 48859. Offers acquisitions administration (MSA, Certificate); engineering management administration (MSA, Certificate); general administration (MSA, Certificate); health services administration (MSA, Certificate); human resources administration (MSA, Certificate); information resource management (MSA); information resource management administration (Certificate); international administration (MSA, Certificate); leadership (MSA, Certificate); philanthropy and fundraising administration (MSA, Certificate); public administration (MSA, Certificate); recreation and park administration (MSA); research administration (MSA, Certificate). *Program availability:* Part-time, evening/weekend, online learning. *Faculty:* 21 full-time (5 women), 168 part-time/adjunct (43 women). *Students:* 3,059 (1,741 women); includes 1,392 minority (1,003 Black or African American, non-Hispanic/Latino; 27 American Indian or Alaska Native, non-Hispanic/Latino; 93 Asian, non-Hispanic/Latino; 49 Hispanic/Latino; 10 Native Hawaiian or other Pacific Islander, non-Hispanic/Latino; 210 Two or more races, non-Hispanic/Latino). Average age 38. In 2016, 289 master's awarded. *Entrance requirements:* For master's, minimum GPA of 2.7 in major. *Application deadline:* Applications are processed on a rolling basis. Application fee: $50. Electronic applications accepted. *Financial support:* Scholarships/grants available. Support available to part-time students. Financial award applicants required to submit FAFSA. *Unit head:* Dr. Patricia Chase, Director, 989-774-6525, E-mail: chase1pb@cmich.edu. *Application contact:* 877-268-4636, E-mail: cmuglobal@cmich.edu.

The Citadel, The Military College of South Carolina, Citadel Graduate College, School of Engineering, Department of Engineering Leadership and Program Management, Charleston, SC 29409. Offers project management (MS); systems engineering management (Graduate Certificate); technical program management (Graduate Certificate); technical project management (Graduate Certificate). *Program availability:* Part-time, evening/weekend. *Faculty:* 2 full-time (0 women), 6 part-time/adjunct (0 women). *Students:* 5 full-time (2 women), 85 part-time (37 women); includes 21 minority (10 Black or African American, non-Hispanic/Latino; 1 American Indian or Alaska Native, non-Hispanic/Latino; 2 Asian, non-Hispanic/Latino; 6 Hispanic/Latino; 1 Native Hawaiian or other Pacific Islander, non-Hispanic/Latino; 1 Two or more races, non-Hispanic/Latino), 1 international. 65 applicants, 98% accepted, 38 enrolled. In 2016, 35 master's, 45 other advanced degrees awarded. *Entrance requirements:* For master's, GRE or GMAT, minimum of one year of professional experience or permission from department head; two letters of reference; resume detailing previous work; for Graduate Certificate, one-page letter of intent; resume detailing previous work. Additional exam requirements/recommendations for international students: Required—TOEFL (minimum score 550 paper-based; 79 iBT). *Application deadline:* Applications are processed on a rolling basis. Application fee: $40. Electronic applications accepted. *Expenses:* Tuition, state resident: full-time $5121; part-time $569 per credit hour. Tuition, nonresident: full-time $8613; part-time $957 per credit hour. *Required fees:* $90 per term. *Financial support:* Fellowships and unspecified assistantships available. Support available to part-time students. Financial award application deadline: 7/1; financial award applicants required to submit FAFSA. *Unit head:* Dr. Charles O. Skipper, Department Head, 843-953-9811, E-mail: charles.skipper@citadel.edu. *Application contact:* Dr. Keith Plemmons, Associate Professor, 843-953-7677, E-mail: keith.plemmons@citadel.edu.
Website: http://www.citadel.edu/pmgt/

Clarkson University, Program in Engineering Management, Potsdam, NY 13699. Offers MS. *Program availability:* Part-time-only, evening/weekend, blended/hybrid learning. *Faculty:* 2 full-time (0 women), 11 part-time/adjunct (1 woman). *Students:* 2 full-time (0 women), 142 part-time (34 women); includes 25 minority (4 Black or African American, non-Hispanic/Latino; 11 Asian, non-Hispanic/Latino; 9 Hispanic/Latino; 1 Two or more races, non-Hispanic/Latino), 7 international. 90 applicants, 74% accepted, 67 enrolled. In 2016, 65 master's awarded. *Degree requirements:* For master's, project. *Entrance requirements:* For master's, GRE or GMAT. Additional exam requirements/

recommendations for international students: Required—TOEFL (minimum score 550 paper-based, 80 iBT) or IELTS (6.5). *Application deadline:* Applications are processed on a rolling basis. Application fee: $50. Electronic applications accepted. *Expenses:* $1,504 per credit. *Financial support:* Scholarships/grants available. *Unit head:* Mike Walsh, Associate Vice President of Graduate Business Development, 518-631-9846, E-mail: mwalsh@clarkson.edu. *Application contact:* Dan Capogna, Graduate Admissions Contact, 518-631-9910, E-mail: graduate@clarkson.edu.
Website: http://graduate.clarkson.edu

Colorado School of Mines, Office of Graduate Studies, Department of Economics and Business, Golden, CO 80401. Offers engineering and technology management (MS); mineral economics (PhD); operations research and engineering (PhD). *Program availability:* Part-time. *Degree requirements:* For master's, thesis (for some programs); for doctorate, comprehensive exam, thesis/dissertation. *Entrance requirements:* For master's and doctorate, GRE General Test. Additional exam requirements/recommendations for international students: Required—TOEFL (minimum score 550 paper-based; 80 iBT). Electronic applications accepted. *Expenses:* Tuition, state resident: full-time $15,690. Tuition, nonresident: full-time $34,020. *Required fees:* $2152. Tuition and fees vary according to course load. *Faculty research:* International trade, resource and environmental economics, energy economics, operations research.

Cornell University, Graduate School, Graduate Fields of Engineering, Field of Civil and Environmental Engineering, Ithaca, NY 14853. Offers engineering management (M Eng, MS, PhD); environmental engineering (M Eng, MS, PhD); environmental fluid mechanics and hydrology (M Eng, MS, PhD); environmental systems engineering (M Eng, MS, PhD); geotechnical engineering (M Eng, MS, PhD); remote sensing (M Eng, MS, PhD); structural engineering (M Eng, MS, PhD); structural mechanics (M Eng, MS); transportation engineering (MS, PhD); transportation systems engineering (M Eng); water resource systems (M Eng, MS, PhD). Terminal master's awarded for partial completion of doctoral program. *Degree requirements:* For master's, thesis (MS); for doctorate, comprehensive exam, thesis/dissertation. *Entrance requirements:* For master's and doctorate, GRE General Test (recommended), 2 letters of recommendation. Additional exam requirements/recommendations for international students: Required—TOEFL (minimum score 600 paper-based; 77 iBT). Electronic applications accepted. *Faculty research:* Environmental engineering, geotechnical engineering, remote sensing, environmental fluid mechanics and hydrology, structural engineering.

Dallas Baptist University, College of Business, Business Administration Program, Dallas, TX 75211-9299. Offers accounting (MBA); business communication (MBA); conflict resolution management (MBA); entrepreneurship (MBA); finance (MBA); health care management (MBA); international business (MBA); leading the non-profit organization (MBA); management (MBA); management information systems (MBA); marketing (MBA); project management (MBA); technology and engineering management (MBA). *Accreditation:* ACBSP. *Program availability:* Part-time, evening/weekend, 100% online, blended/hybrid learning. *Application deadline:* Applications are processed on a rolling basis. Application fee: $25. Electronic applications accepted. Application fee is waived when completed online. *Expenses: Tuition:* Full-time $15,408; part-time $856 per credit hour. *Required fees:* $400 per semester. Tuition and fees vary according to course load and degree level. *Unit head:* Dr. Sandra Reid, Chair of Graduate Business Programs, 214-333-5280, E-mail: sandra@dbu.edu. *Application contact:* Bobby Soto, Director of Admissions, 214-333-5242, E-mail: graduate@dbu.edu.
Website: http://www3.dbu.edu/graduate/mba.asp

Dartmouth College, Thayer School of Engineering, Program in Engineering Management, Hanover, NH 03755. Offers MEM. Program offered in conjunction with Tuck School of Business. *Degree requirements:* For master's, capstone experience. *Entrance requirements:* For master's, GRE General Test. Additional exam requirements/recommendations for international students: Required—TOEFL. *Application deadline:* For fall admission, 1/1 priority date for domestic students. Applications are processed on a rolling basis. Application fee: $45. *Expenses:* Contact institution. *Financial support:* Fellowships, teaching assistantships, career-related internships or fieldwork, Federal Work-Study, institutionally sponsored loans, scholarships/grants, health care benefits, and tuition waivers (full and partial) available. Financial award application deadline: 1/15; financial award applicants required to submit CSS PROFILE. *Unit head:* Geoffrey G. Parker, Director, 603-646-9075, Fax: 603-646-2580, E-mail: geoffrey.g.parker@dartmouth.edu. *Application contact:* Candace S. Potter, Graduate Admissions and Financial Aid Administrator, 603-646-3844, Fax: 603-646-1620, E-mail: candace.s.potter@dartmouth.edu.
Website: http://engineering.dartmouth.edu/academics/graduate/mem

Drexel University, College of Engineering, Program in Engineering Management, Philadelphia, PA 19104-2875. Offers MS, Certificate. *Program availability:* Part-time, evening/weekend, online learning. *Faculty:* 1 (woman) full-time, 6 part-time/adjunct (1 woman). *Students:* 1 (woman) full-time, 52 part-time (15 women); includes 8 minority (5 Black or African American, non-Hispanic/Latino; 1 Asian, non-Hispanic/Latino; 2 Hispanic/Latino), 3 international. Average age 32. In 2016, 27 master's, 8 other advanced degrees awarded. *Degree requirements:* For master's, thesis optional. *Entrance requirements:* For master's, minimum GPA of 3.0. Additional exam requirements/recommendations for international students: Required—TOEFL. *Application deadline:* For fall admission, 8/21 for domestic students. Applications are processed on a rolling basis. Application fee: $50. Electronic applications accepted. *Expenses: Tuition:* Full-time $32,184; part-time $1192 per credit hour. *Required fees:* $280. Tuition and fees vary according to campus/location and program. *Financial support:* Application deadline: 2/1. *Faculty research:* Quality, operations research and management, ergonomics, applied statistics. *Unit head:* Dr. Steve Smith, Director, 215-895-5809. *Application contact:* Director of Graduate Admissions, 215-895-6700, Fax: 215-895-5939, E-mail: enroll@drexel.edu.

Duke University, Graduate School, Pratt School of Engineering, Distributed Master of Engineering Management Program (d-MEMP), Durham, NC 27708-0271. Offers MEM. *Program availability:* Part-time, evening/weekend, online learning. *Entrance requirements:* For master's, GRE General Test, resume, 3 letters of recommendation, statement of purpose, transcripts. Additional exam requirements/recommendations for international students: Required—TOEFL. Electronic applications accepted. *Expenses:* Contact institution. *Faculty research:* Entrepreneurship, innovation and product development, project management, operations and supply chain management, financial engineering.

Duke University, Graduate School, Pratt School of Engineering, Master of Engineering Management Program, Durham, NC 27708-0271. Offers MEM. *Program availability:* Part-time, online learning. *Entrance requirements:* For master's, GRE General Test, resume, 3 letters of recommendation, statement of purpose, transcripts. Additional exam requirements/recommendations for international students: Required—TOEFL. Electronic applications accepted. *Expenses:* Contact institution. *Faculty research:* Entrepreneurship, innovation and product development, project management, operations and supply chain management, financial engineering.

Eastern Michigan University, Graduate School, College of Technology, School of Engineering Technology, Program in Engineering Management, Ypsilanti, MI 48197. Offers MS. *Program availability:* Part-time, evening/weekend, online learning. *Students:* 27 full-time (7 women), 59 part-time (11 women); includes 9 minority (4 Black or African American, non-Hispanic/Latino; 1 American Indian or Alaska Native, non-Hispanic/Latino; 1 Asian, non-Hispanic/Latino; 2 Hispanic/Latino; 1 Two or more races, non-Hispanic/Latino), 26 international. Average age 33. 70 applicants, 51% accepted, 18 enrolled. In 2016, 26 master's awarded. *Entrance requirements:* Additional exam requirements/recommendations for international students: Required—TOEFL. *Application deadline:* Applications are processed on a rolling basis. Application fee: $45. *Financial support:* Fellowships, research assistantships with full tuition reimbursements, teaching assistantships with full tuition reimbursements, career-related internships or fieldwork, Federal Work-Study, institutionally sponsored loans, scholarships/grants, tuition waivers (partial), and unspecified assistantships available. Support available to part-time students. Financial award applicants required to submit FAFSA. *Application contact:* Dr. Bryan Booker, Program Coordinator, 734-487-2040, Fax: 734-487-8755, E-mail: bbooker1@emich.edu.

Embry-Riddle Aeronautical University–Worldwide, Department of Engineering Sciences, Daytona Beach, FL 32114-3900. Offers aerospace engineering (MS); systems engineering (M Sys E), including engineering management, technical. *Program availability:* Part-time, evening/weekend, 100% online, blended/hybrid learning. *Entrance requirements:* For master's, GRE required for MSAE. Additional exam requirements/recommendations for international students: Required—TOEFL (minimum score 550 paper-based; 79 iBT), IELTS (minimum score 6), TOEFL or IELTS accepted. Electronic applications accepted. *Expenses:* Contact institution.

Florida Institute of Technology, College of Engineering, Program in Engineering Management, Melbourne, FL 32901-6975. Offers MS. *Program availability:* Part-time. *Students:* 35 full-time (7 women), 14 part-time (2 women); includes 3 minority (1 Black or African American, non-Hispanic/Latino; 1 Asian, non-Hispanic/Latino; 1 Hispanic/Latino), 38 international. Average age 26. 229 applicants, 52% accepted, 18 enrolled. In 2016, 11 master's awarded. *Degree requirements:* For master's, comprehensive exam (for some programs), thesis optional, 30 credit hours. *Entrance requirements:* For master's, GRE (minimum score of 300), BS in engineering from ABET-accredited program, minimum GPA of 3.0, 3 letters of recommendation, resume, statement of objectives. Additional exam requirements/recommendations for international students: Required—TOEFL (minimum score 550 paper-based; 79 iBT). *Application deadline:* Applications are processed on a rolling basis. Application fee: $50. Electronic applications accepted. *Expenses: Tuition:* Full-time $22,338; part-time $1241 per credit hour. *Required fees:* $250. Tuition and fees vary according to degree level, campus/location and program. *Financial support:* Application deadline: 3/1; applicants required to submit FAFSA. *Unit head:* Dr. Muzaffar A. Shaikh, Department Head, 321-674-7132, E-mail: mshaikh@fit.edu. *Application contact:* Cheryl A. Brown, Associate Director of Graduate Admissions, 321-674-7581, Fax: 321-723-9468, E-mail: cbrown@fit.edu.
Website: http://coe.fit.edu/se

Florida Institute of Technology, Extended Studies Division, Melbourne, FL 32901-6975. Offers acquisition and contract management (MS); aerospace engineering (MS); business administration (MBA, DBA); computer information systems (MS); computer science (MS); electrical engineering (MS); engineering management (MS); human resources management (MS); logistics management (MS), including humanitarian and disaster relief logistics; management (MS), including acquisition and contract management, e-business, human resources management, information systems, logistics management, management, transportation management; material acquisition management (MS); mechanical engineering (MS); operations research (MS); project management (MS), including information systems, operations research; public administration (MPA); quality management (MS); software engineering (MS); space systems (MS); space systems management (MS); supply chain management (MS); systems management (MS), including information systems, operations research; technology management (MS). *Program availability:* Part-time, evening/weekend, online learning. *Faculty:* 10 full-time (3 women), 122 part-time/adjunct (29 women). *Students:* 131 full-time (58 women), 997 part-time (348 women); includes 389 minority (231 Black or African American, non-Hispanic/Latino; 9 American Indian or Alaska Native, non-Hispanic/Latino; 26 Asian, non-Hispanic/Latino; 99 Hispanic/Latino; 3 Native Hawaiian or other Pacific Islander, non-Hispanic/Latino; 21 Two or more races, non-Hispanic/Latino), 53 international. Average age 36. 962 applicants, 48% accepted, 323 enrolled. In 2016, 403 master's awarded. *Degree requirements:* For master's, comprehensive exam (for some programs). *Entrance requirements:* For master's, GMAT or resume showing 8 years of supervised experience, minimum GPA of 3.0, 2 letters of recommendation, resume. Additional exam requirements/recommendations for international students: Required—TOEFL (minimum score 550 paper-based; 79 iBT). *Application deadline:* For fall admission, 4/1 for international students; for spring admission, 9/30 for international students. Applications are processed on a rolling basis. Electronic applications accepted. *Expenses:* Contact institution. *Financial support:* Application deadline: 3/1; applicants required to submit FAFSA. *Unit head:* Dr. Theodore R. Richardson, III, Dean, 321-674-8123, Fax: 321-674-7597, E-mail: trichardson@fit.edu. *Application contact:* Carolyn Farrior, Director of Graduate Admissions, Online Learning and Off-Campus Programs, 321-674-7118, Fax: 321-674-8216, E-mail: cfarrior@fit.edu.
Website: http://es.fit.edu

Florida International University, College of Engineering and Computing, Department of Engineering Management, Miami, FL 33199. Offers MS. *Accreditation:* CAHME. *Program availability:* Part-time, evening/weekend. *Faculty:* 1 full-time (0 women), 3 part-time/adjunct (1 woman). *Students:* 86 full-time (22 women), 42 part-time (18 women); includes 60 minority (10 Black or African American, non-Hispanic/Latino; 1 American Indian or Alaska Native, non-Hispanic/Latino; 1 Asian, non-Hispanic/Latino; 48 Hispanic/Latino), 51 international. Average age 30. 135 applicants, 44% accepted, 36 enrolled. In 2016, 91 master's awarded. *Entrance requirements:* For master's, GRE, minimum GPA of 3.0. Additional exam requirements/recommendations for international students: Required—TOEFL (minimum score 550 paper-based; 80 iBT). *Application deadline:* For fall admission, 6/1 for domestic students, 4/1 for international students; for spring admission, 10/1 for domestic students, 9/1 for international students. Applications are processed on a rolling basis. Application fee: $30. Electronic applications accepted. *Expenses:* Tuition, state resident: full-time $8912; part-time $446 per credit hour. Tuition, nonresident: full-time $21,393; part-time $992 per credit hour. *Required fees:* $2185; $195 per semester. Tuition and fees vary according to program. *Financial support:* Institutionally sponsored loans and scholarships/grants available. Financial award application deadline: 3/1; financial award applicants required to submit FAFSA. *Unit head:* Dr. Chin-Sheng Chen, Director, 305-348-7527, E-mail: chenc@fiu.edu. *Application contact:* Sara-Michelle Lemus, Engineering Admissions Officer, 305-348-1890, Fax: 305-348-7441, E-mail: grad_eng@fiu.edu.

Gannon University, School of Graduate Studies, College of Engineering and Business, School of Engineering and Computer Science, Program in Engineering Management, Erie, PA 16541-0001. Offers MSEM. *Program availability:* Part-time, evening/weekend. *Students:* 51 full-time (10 women), 13 part-time (0 women), 58 international. Average

age 26. 166 applicants, 62% accepted, 9 enrolled. In 2016, 25 master's awarded. *Entrance requirements:* For master's, bachelor's degree in engineering from an ABET-accredited program or its equivalent with minimum GPA of 2.5, transcripts, 3 letters of recommendation. Additional exam requirements/recommendations for international students: Required—TOEFL (minimum score 79 iBT). *Application deadline:* Applications are processed on a rolling basis. Application fee: $25. Electronic applications accepted. Application fee is waived when completed online. *Expenses: Tuition:* Full-time $17,370. *Required fees:* $550. Tuition and fees vary according to course load and program. *Financial support:* Federal Work-Study available. Financial award application deadline: 7/1; financial award applicants required to submit FAFSA. *Unit head:* Dr. Mahesh Aggarwal, Chair, 814-871-7629, E-mail: aggarwal001@gannon.edu. *Application contact:* Bridget Philip, Director of Graduate Admissions, 814-871-7412, E-mail: graduate@gannon.edu.

The George Washington University, School of Engineering and Applied Science, Department of Engineering Management and Systems Engineering, Washington, DC 20052. Offers system engineering (PhD). *Program availability:* Part-time, evening/weekend. *Faculty:* 12 full-time (2 women). *Students:* 102 full-time (36 women), 735 part-time (235 women); includes 319 minority (171 Black or African American, non-Hispanic/Latino; 2 American Indian or Alaska Native, non-Hispanic/Latino; 94 Asian, non-Hispanic/Latino; 41 Hispanic/Latino; 4 Native Hawaiian or other Pacific Islander, non-Hispanic/Latino; 7 Two or more races, non-Hispanic/Latino), 57 international. Average age 37. 594 applicants, 69% accepted, 201 enrolled. In 2016, 211 master's, 41 doctorates, 11 other advanced degrees awarded. *Degree requirements:* For master's, thesis optional; for doctorate, one foreign language, thesis/dissertation, final and qualifying exams, submission of articles; for other advanced degree, professional project. *Entrance requirements:* For master's, appropriate bachelor's degree, minimum GPA of 2.7, second-semester calculus; for doctorate, appropriate master's degree, minimum GPA of 3.5, 2 letters of recommendation; for other advanced degree, appropriate master's degree, minimum GPA of 3.4. Additional exam requirements/recommendations for international students: Required—TOEFL or The George Washington University English as a Foreign Language Test. *Application deadline:* For fall admission, 3/1 for domestic students; for spring admission, 10/1 for domestic students. Applications are processed on a rolling basis. Application fee: $75. *Financial support:* In 2016–17, 35 students received support. Fellowships with tuition reimbursements available, research assistantships, teaching assistantships with tuition reimbursements available, career-related internships or fieldwork, and institutionally sponsored loans available. Financial award application deadline: 3/1; financial award applicants required to submit FAFSA. *Faculty research:* Artificial intelligence and expert systems, human factors engineering and systems analysis. *Total annual research expenditures:* $421,800. *Unit head:* Dr. Thomas Mazzuchi, Chair, 202-994-4892, E-mail: mazzu@gwu.edu. *Application contact:* Adina Lav, Marketing, Recruiting and Admissions, 202-994-5827, Fax: 202-994-0909, E-mail: engineering@gwu.edu.
Website: http://www.seas.gwu.edu/department-engineering-management-systems-engineering

Georgia Southern University, Jack N. Averitt College of Graduate Studies, Allen E. Paulson College of Engineering and Information Technology, Department of Mechanical Engineering, Program in Engineering/Engineering Management, Statesboro, GA 30458. Offers MSAE. *Students:* 13 full-time (3 women), 10 part-time (2 women); includes 10 minority (8 Black or African American, non-Hispanic/Latino; 1 Asian, non-Hispanic/Latino; 1 Hispanic/Latino), 2 international. Average age 27. 10 applicants, 80% accepted, 5 enrolled. In 2016, 8 master's awarded. *Degree requirements:* For master's, thesis optional. *Entrance requirements:* For master's, GRE. Additional exam requirements/recommendations for international students: Required—TOEFL (minimum score 550 paper-based; 80 iBT), IELTS (minimum score 6). *Application deadline:* For fall admission, 3/1 priority date for domestic students; for spring admission, 11/1 for domestic students. Applications are processed on a rolling basis. Application fee: $50. Electronic applications accepted. *Expenses:* Tuition, state resident: full-time $7236; part-time $277 per semester hour. Tuition, nonresident: full-time $27,118; part-time $1105 per semester hour. *Required fees:* $2092. *Financial support:* Unspecified assistantships available. Financial award application deadline: 4/20; financial award applicants required to submit FAFSA. *Faculty research:* Business intelligence, data mining and analytics, e-commerce, industrial economics, business continuity and disaster recovery. *Unit head:* Dr. Biswanath Samanta, Chair, 912-478-0334, Fax: 912-478-1455, E-mail: bsamanta@georgiasouthern.edu.

Indiana Tech, Program in Engineering Management, Fort Wayne, IN 46803-1297. Offers MSE. *Program availability:* Part-time, evening/weekend, online only, 100% online. *Entrance requirements:* For master's, BS in a technical field, minimum GPA of 2.5, one undergraduate course each in accounting and finance. Electronic applications accepted.

Instituto Tecnológico y de Estudios Superiores de Monterrey, Campus Chihuahua, Graduate Programs, Chihuahua, Mexico. Offers computer systems engineering (Ingeniero); electrical engineering (Ingeniero); electromechanical engineering (Ingeniero); electronic engineering (Ingeniero); engineering administration (MEA); industrial engineering (MIE, Ingeniero); international trade (MIT); mechanical engineering (Ingeniero).

International Technological University, Program in Engineering Management, San Jose, CA 95134. Offers MSEM. *Program availability:* Part-time, evening/weekend. *Degree requirements:* For master's, thesis or capstone project. *Entrance requirements:* Additional exam requirements/recommendations for international students: Required—TOEFL, IELTS. Electronic applications accepted.

Johns Hopkins University, Engineering Program for Professionals, Part-time Program in Engineering Management, Baltimore, MD 21218. Offers MEM. *Program availability:* Part-time, evening/weekend, 100% online, blended/hybrid learning. *Students:* 2 full-time (0 women), 52 part-time (16 women); includes 10 minority (1 Black or African American, non-Hispanic/Latino; 4 Asian, non-Hispanic/Latino; 4 Hispanic/Latino; 1 Native Hawaiian or other Pacific Islander, non-Hispanic/Latino), 4 international. Average age 28. 44 applicants, 66% accepted, 16 enrolled. In 2016, 1 master's awarded. *Entrance requirements:* Additional exam requirements/recommendations for international students: Required—TOEFL (minimum score 600 paper-based; 100 iBT). *Unit head:* Dr. Daniel Horn, Assistant Dean, 410-516-2300, Fax: 410-579-8049, E-mail: dhorn@jhu.edu. *Application contact:* Doug Schiller, Admissions Director, 410-516-2300, Fax: 410-579-8049, E-mail: schiller@jhu.edu.

Johns Hopkins University, G. W. C. Whiting School of Engineering, Master of Science in Engineering Management Program, Baltimore, MD 21218. Offers biomaterials (MSEM); civil engineering (MSEM); communications science (MSEM); computer science (MSEM); environmental systems analysis, economics and public policy (MSEM); fluid mechanics (MSEM); materials science and engineering (MSEM); mechanical engineering (MSEM); mechanics and materials (MSEM); nano-biotechnology (MSEM); nanomaterials and nanotechnology (MSEM); operations research (MSEM); probability and statistics (MSEM); smart product and device design (MSEM). *Faculty:* 7 full-time (4 women), 1 part-time/adjunct (0 women). *Students:* 35 full-time (14 women), 8 part-time (3 women); includes 7 minority (4 Asian, non-Hispanic/Latino; 3 Hispanic/Latino), 26 international. Average age 24. 228 applicants, 28% accepted, 25 enrolled. In 2016, 18 master's awarded. *Entrance requirements:* For master's, GRE, 3 letters of recommendation, statement of purpose, transcripts. Additional exam requirements/recommendations for international students: Required—TOEFL (minimum score 600 paper-based, 100 iBT) or IELTS (7). *Application deadline:* For fall admission, 2/1 for domestic and international students. Application fee: $75. Electronic applications accepted. *Financial support:* Fellowships and health care benefits available. *Unit head:* Dr. Pamela Sheff, Director, 410-516-7056, Fax: 410-516-4880, E-mail: pamsheff@gmail.com. *Application contact:* Richard Helman, Director of Graduate Admissions, 410-516-8174, Fax: 410-516-0780, E-mail: graduateadmissions@jhu.edu.
Website: http://engineering.jhu.edu/msem/

Kansas State University, Graduate School, College of Engineering, Department of Industrial and Manufacturing Systems Engineering, Manhattan, KS 66506. Offers engineering management (MEM); industrial engineering (MS); operations research (MS). *Program availability:* Part-time, online learning. *Faculty:* 10 full-time (2 women), 1 part-time/adjunct (0 women). *Students:* 34 full-time (8 women), 51 part-time (6 women); includes 17 minority (5 Black or African American, non-Hispanic/Latino; 4 Asian, non-Hispanic/Latino; 4 Hispanic/Latino; 4 Two or more races, non-Hispanic/Latino), 25 international. Average age 30. 62 applicants, 56% accepted, 10 enrolled. In 2016, 27 master's, 3 doctorates awarded. *Degree requirements:* For master's, thesis or alternative; for doctorate, thesis/dissertation. *Entrance requirements:* For master's, GRE General Test (minimum score of 750 old version, 159 new format on Quantitative portion of exam), bachelor's degree in engineering, mathematics, or physical science; for doctorate, GRE General Test (minimum score of 770 old version, 164 new format on Quantitative portion of exam), master's degree in engineering or industrial manufacturing. Additional exam requirements/recommendations for international students: Required—PTE (minimum score 58), TOEFL (minimum score 550 paper-based; 79 iBT) or IELTS (minimum score 6.5). *Application deadline:* For fall admission, 6/1 priority date for domestic students, 12/1 priority date for international students; for spring admission, 11/1 priority date for domestic students, 8/1 priority date for international students. Applications are processed on a rolling basis. Application fee: $50 ($75 for international students). Electronic applications accepted. *Expenses:* Tuition, state resident: full-time $9670. Tuition, nonresident: full-time $21,828. *Required fees:* $862. *Financial support:* In 2016–17, 12 research assistantships (averaging $12,442 per year), 9 teaching assistantships with full tuition reimbursements (averaging $14,111 per year) were awarded; Federal Work-Study, institutionally sponsored loans, and scholarships/grants also available. Support available to part-time students. Financial award application deadline: 3/1; financial award applicants required to submit FAFSA. *Faculty research:* Industrial engineering, ergonomics, healthcare systems engineering, manufacturing processes, operations research, engineering management. *Total annual research expenditures:* $2.6 million. *Unit head:* Dr. Bradley Kramer, Head, 785-532-5606, Fax: 785-532-3738, E-mail: bradleyk@k-state.edu. *Application contact:* Dr. David Ben-Arieh, Chair of Graduate Committee, 785-532-5606, Fax: 785-532-3738, E-mail: imse@k-state.edu.
Website: http://www.imse.k-state.edu/

Kettering University, Graduate School, Department of Business, Flint, MI 48504. Offers MBA, MS. *Accreditation:* ACBSP. *Program availability:* Part-time, evening/weekend, online learning. *Entrance requirements:* Additional exam requirements/recommendations for international students: Required—TOEFL (minimum score 550 paper-based; 79 iBT). Electronic applications accepted.

Lamar University, College of Graduate Studies, College of Engineering, Department of Industrial Engineering, Beaumont, TX 77710. Offers engineering management (MEM); industrial engineering (ME, MES, DE). *Faculty:* 10 full-time (2 women), 1 part-time/adjunct (0 women). *Students:* 111 full-time (13 women), 57 part-time (6 women); includes 2 minority (1 Black or African American, non-Hispanic/Latino; 1 Asian, non-Hispanic/Latino), 163 international. Average age 25. 153 applicants, 86% accepted, 26 enrolled. In 2016, 77 master's, 3 doctorates awarded. *Degree requirements:* For doctorate, thesis/dissertation. *Entrance requirements:* For master's and doctorate, GRE General Test. Additional exam requirements/recommendations for international students: Required—TOEFL (minimum score 550 paper-based; 79 iBT), IELTS (minimum score 6.5). *Application deadline:* For fall admission, 8/10 for domestic students, 7/1 for international students; for spring admission, 1/5 for domestic students, 12/1 for international students. Applications are processed on a rolling basis. Application fee: $25 ($50 for international students). Electronic applications accepted. *Expenses:* $8,134 in-state full-time, $5,574 in-state part-time; $15,604 out-of-state full-time, $10,554 out-of-state part-time per year. *Financial support:* Fellowships, research assistantships, and teaching assistantships available. Financial award application deadline: 4/1; financial award applicants required to submit FAFSA. *Faculty research:* Process simulation, total quality management, ergonomics and safety, scheduling. *Unit head:* Dr. Brian Craig, Chair, 409-880-8804, Fax: 409-880-8121. *Application contact:* Deidre Mayer, Interim Director, Admissions and Academic Services, 409-880-8888, Fax: 409-880-7419, E-mail: gradmissions@lamar.edu.
Website: http://engineering.lamar.edu/industrial

Lawrence Technological University, College of Engineering, Southfield, MI 48075-1058. Offers architectural engineering (MS); automotive engineering (MS); biomedical engineering (MS); civil engineering (MA, MS, PhD), including environmental engineering (MS), geotechnical engineering (MS), structural engineering (MS), transportation engineering (MS), water resource engineering (MS); construction engineering management (MA); electrical and computer engineering (MS); engineering management (MA); engineering technology (MS); fire engineering (MS); industrial engineering (MS), including healthcare; manufacturing systems (ME); mechanical engineering (MS, DE, PhD), including manufacturing (DE), solid mechanics (MS), thermal-fluids (MS); mechatronic systems engineering (MS). *Program availability:* Part-time, evening/weekend. *Faculty:* 24 full-time (5 women), 26 part-time/adjunct (2 women). *Students:* 22 full-time (7 women), 588 part-time (81 women); includes 23 minority (11 Black or African American, non-Hispanic/Latino; 4 Asian, non-Hispanic/Latino; 7 Hispanic/Latino; 1 Two or more races, non-Hispanic/Latino), 469 international. Average age 27. 1,186 applicants, 39% accepted, 99 enrolled. In 2016, 293 master's, 3 doctorates awarded. Terminal master's awarded for partial completion of doctoral program. *Degree requirements:* For master's, thesis optional; for doctorate, comprehensive exam, thesis/dissertation optional. *Entrance requirements:* Additional exam requirements/recommendations for international students: Required—TOEFL (minimum score 550 paper-based; 79 iBT), IELTS (minimum score 6.5). *Application deadline:* For fall admission, 5/22 for international students; for spring admission, 10/11 for international students; for summer admission, 2/16 for international students. Applications are processed on a rolling basis. Application fee: $50. Electronic applications accepted. *Expenses: Tuition:* Full-time $14,868; part-time $1062 per credit. *Required fees:* $75 per semester. Tuition and fees vary according to campus/location. *Financial support:* In 2016–17, 25 students received support, including 5 research assistantships with full tuition reimbursements available; unspecified assistantships also available. Financial award application deadline: 4/1; financial award applicants required to submit FAFSA. *Faculty research:* Carbon fiber reinforced polymer reinforced concrete structures; low impact storm water management solutions; vehicle battery energy management; wireless communication; entrepreneurial mindset and engineering. *Total annual research expenditures:* $1.7 million. *Unit head:* Dr. Nabil Grace, Dean, 248-204-2500,

Fax: 248-204-2509, E-mail: engrdean@ltu.edu. *Application contact:* Jane Rohrback, Director of Admissions, 248-204-3160, Fax: 248-204-2228, E-mail: admissions@ltu.edu. Website: http://www.ltu.edu/engineering/index.asp

Lehigh University, P.C. Rossin College of Engineering and Applied Science, Department of Industrial and Systems Engineering, Bethlehem, PA 18015. Offers analytical finance (MS); industrial and systems engineering (M Eng, MS, PhD); management science and engineering (M Eng, MS); MBA/E. *Program availability:* Part-time, 100% online, classroom live. *Faculty:* 19 full-time (2 women), 3 part-time/adjunct (0 women). *Students:* 102 full-time (28 women), 7 part-time (3 women); includes 1 minority (Asian, non-Hispanic/Latino), 103 international. Average age 25. 375 applicants, 35% accepted, 39 enrolled. In 2016, 36 master's, 8 doctorates awarded. Terminal master's awarded for partial completion of doctoral program. *Degree requirements:* For master's, thesis (MS); project (M Eng); for doctorate, comprehensive exam, thesis/dissertation. *Entrance requirements:* For master's and doctorate, GRE General Test. Additional exam requirements/recommendations for international students: Required—TOEFL (minimum score 550 paper-based; 79 iBT), IELTS (minimum score 6.5). *Application deadline:* For fall admission, 7/15 for domestic and international students; for spring admission, 12/1 for domestic and international students. Application fee: $75. Electronic applications accepted. *Expenses:* $1,420 per credit hour. *Financial support:* In 2016–17, 33 students received support, including 2 fellowships with full tuition reimbursements available (averaging $20,490 per year), 18 research assistantships with full tuition reimbursements available (averaging $20,490 per year), 11 teaching assistantships with full tuition reimbursements available (averaging $21,105 per year); unspecified assistantships also available. Financial award application deadline: 1/15. *Faculty research:* Mathematical optimization; logistics and service systems, stochastic processes and simulation; computational optimization and high performance computing; financial engineering and robust optimization; machine learning and data mining. *Total annual research expenditures:* $1.7 million. *Unit head:* Dr. Tamas Terlaky, Chair, 610-758-4050, Fax: 610-758-4886, E-mail: terlaky@lehigh.edu. *Application contact:* Rita Frey, Graduate Coordinator, 610-758-4051, Fax: 610-758-4886, E-mail: ise@lehigh.edu.

Website: http://www.lehigh.edu/ise

LeTourneau University, Graduate Programs, Longview, TX 75607-7001. Offers business (MBA); counseling (MA), including licensed professional counselor, marriage and family therapy, school counseling; curriculum and instruction (M Ed); educational administration (M Ed); engineering (ME, MS); engineering management (MEM); health care administration (MS); marriage and family therapy (MA); psychology (MA); strategic leadership (MSL); teacher leadership (M Ed); teaching and learning (M Ed). *Program availability:* Part-time, 100% online, blended/hybrid learning. *Faculty:* 24 full-time (7 women), 40 part-time/adjunct (15 women). *Students:* 82 full-time (48 women), 428 part-time (331 women); includes 234 minority (138 Black or African American, non-Hispanic/Latino; 5 American Indian or Alaska Native, non-Hispanic/Latino; 5 Asian, non-Hispanic/Latino; 50 Hispanic/Latino; 36 Two or more races, non-Hispanic/Latino), 15 international. Average age 37. 257 applicants, 60% accepted, 141 enrolled. In 2016, 136 master's awarded. *Degree requirements:* For master's, thesis (for some programs). *Entrance requirements:* Additional exam requirements/recommendations for international students: Required—TOEFL. *Application deadline:* For fall admission, 8/22 for domestic students, 8/29 for international students; for winter admission, 10/10 for domestic students; for spring admission, 1/2 for domestic students, 1/10 for international students; for summer admission, 5/1 for domestic and international students. Applications are processed on a rolling basis. Electronic applications accepted. *Expenses:* $10,890-$18,450 tuition per year (depending on program). *Financial support:* Research assistantships, institutionally sponsored loans, and unspecified assistantships available. Financial award applicants required to submit FAFSA. *Application contact:* Chris Fontaine, Assistant Vice President for Enrollment Services and Global Admissions, 903-233-4312, E-mail: chrisfontaine@letu.edu.
Website: http://www.letu.edu

Long Island University–LIU Post, College of Management, Brookville, NY 11548-1300. Offers accountancy (MS); finance (MBA); information systems (MS); international business (MBA); management (MBA); management engineering (MS); marketing (MBA); taxation (MS); technical project management (MS); JD/MBA. *Accreditation:* AACSB. *Program availability:* Part-time, 100% online, blended/hybrid learning. *Faculty:* 35 full-time (12 women), 25 part-time/adjunct (6 women). *Students:* 153 full-time (61 women), 68 part-time (22 women); includes 44 minority (8 Black or African American, non-Hispanic/Latino; 24 Asian, non-Hispanic/Latino; 11 Hispanic/Latino; 1 Two or more races, non-Hispanic/Latino), 79 international. 429 applicants, 58% accepted, 74 enrolled. In 2016, 124 master's awarded. *Degree requirements:* For master's, thesis (for some programs). *Entrance requirements:* For master's, GMAT, GRE, or LSAT. Additional exam requirements/recommendations for international students: Required—PTE, TOEFL (minimum score 550 paper-based, 75 iBT) or IELTS. *Application deadline:* Applications are processed on a rolling basis. Application fee: $50. Electronic applications accepted. *Expenses: Tuition:* Full-time $28,272; part-time $1178 per credit. *Required fees:* $451 per term. Tuition and fees vary according to degree level and program. *Financial support:* In 2016–17, 68 students received support. Career-related internships or fieldwork, Federal Work-Study, institutionally sponsored loans, and scholarships/grants available. Support available to part-time students. Financial award application deadline: 2/15; financial award applicants required to submit FAFSA. *Faculty research:* Finance and sustainability, innovation and intellectual property rights, marketing: data analytics and business intelligence, social networking local and international. *Unit head:* Dr. Robert M. Valli, Dean, 516-299-4192, E-mail: rob.valli@liu.edu. *Application contact:* Carol Zerah, Director of Graduate and International Admissions, 516-299-2900, Fax: 516-299-2137, E-mail: post-enroll@liu.edu.
Website: http://liu.edu/CWPost/Academics/Schools/COM

Loyola Marymount University, College of Science and Engineering, Department of Systems Engineering and Engineering Management, Program in System Engineering Leadership, Los Angeles, CA 90045-2659. Offers MS/MBA. *Students:* 5 full-time (2 women), 2 part-time (1 woman); includes 3 minority (1 Black or African American, non-Hispanic/Latino; 2 Hispanic/Latino). Average age 37. 1 applicant. *Entrance requirements:* Additional exam requirements/recommendations for international students: Required—TOEFL (minimum score 600 paper-based; 100 iBT). *Application deadline:* For fall admission, 7/15 for domestic students; for spring admission, 12/15 for domestic students. Applications are processed on a rolling basis. Application fee: $50. Electronic applications accepted. *Financial support:* In 2016–17, 3 students received support. Scholarships/grants and unspecified assistantships available. Support available to part-time students. Financial award application deadline: 6/30; financial award applicants required to submit FAFSA. *Unit head:* Dr. Frederick S. Brown, Graduate Director, 310-338-7878, E-mail: fbrown@lmu.edu. *Application contact:* Chake H. Kouyoumjian, Associate Dean for Graduate Studies, 310-338-2721, E-mail: ckouyoum@lmu.edu.
Website: http://cse.lmu.edu/graduateprograms/systemsengineering/systemsengineeringandleadershipprogramdualdegreemsandmba/#d.en.124341

Marquette University, Graduate School, College of Engineering, Department of Mechanical Engineering, Milwaukee, WI 53201-1881. Offers engineering innovation (Certificate); engineering management (MSEM); mechanical engineering (MS, PhD); new product and process development (Certificate). *Program availability:* Part-time, evening/weekend. *Faculty:* 17 full-time (0 women), 4 part-time/adjunct (0 women). *Students:* 25 full-time (1 woman), 33 part-time (3 women); includes 7 minority (1 Black or African American, non-Hispanic/Latino; 2 Asian, non-Hispanic/Latino; 3 Hispanic/Latino; 1 Two or more races, non-Hispanic/Latino), 10 international. Average age 27. 51 applicants, 69% accepted, 8 enrolled. In 2016, 12 master's awarded. Terminal master's awarded for partial completion of doctoral program. *Degree requirements:* For master's, comprehensive exam, thesis (for some programs); for doctorate, comprehensive exam, thesis/dissertation, qualifying exam. *Entrance requirements:* For master's, GRE General Test, minimum GPA of 3.0, official transcripts from all current and previous colleges/universities except Marquette, three letters of recommendation; for doctorate, GRE General Test, minimum GPA of 3.0, official transcripts from all current and previous colleges/universities except Marquette, three letters of recommendation, statement of purpose, copies of any published work. Additional exam requirements/recommendations for international students: Required—TOEFL (minimum score 530 paper-based). *Application deadline:* For fall admission, 8/1 priority date for domestic students; for spring admission, 1/1 priority date for domestic students. Applications are processed on a rolling basis. Application fee: $50. Electronic applications accepted. *Financial support:* Fellowships, research assistantships, teaching assistantships, scholarships/grants, tuition waivers (partial), and unspecified assistantships available. Support available to part-time students. Financial award application deadline: 2/15. *Faculty research:* Computer-integrated manufacturing, energy conversion, simulation modeling and optimization, applied mechanics, metallurgy. *Total annual research expenditures:* $620,063. *Unit head:* Dr. Kyuil Kim, Chair, 414-288-7259, Fax: 414-288-7790. *Application contact:* Dr. John Borg.
Website: http://www.marquette.edu/engineering/mechanical/grad.shtml

Marshall University, Academic Affairs Division, College of Information Technology and Engineering, Program in Engineering, Huntington, WV 25755. Offers engineering (MSME); engineering management (MSE); environmental engineering (MSE); transportation and infrastructure engineering (MSE). *Program availability:* Part-time, evening/weekend. *Degree requirements:* For master's, final project, oral exam. *Entrance requirements:* For master's, GMAT or GRE General Test, minimum undergraduate GPA of 2.75.

Massachusetts Institute of Technology, School of Engineering, System Design and Management Program, Cambridge, MA 02139-4307. Offers engineering and management (SM). Offered jointly with MIT Sloan School of Management. *Students:* 147 full-time (45 women); includes 22 minority (2 Black or African American, non-Hispanic/Latino; 11 Asian, non-Hispanic/Latino; 7 Hispanic/Latino; 2 Two or more races, non-Hispanic/Latino), 86 international. Average age 32. 261 applicants, 36% accepted, 79 enrolled. In 2016, 73 master's awarded. *Degree requirements:* For master's, thesis. Application fee: $75. *Expenses: Tuition:* Full-time $46,400; part-time $725 per credit. One-time fee: $312 full-time. Full-time tuition and fees vary according to course load and program. *Financial support:* In 2016–17, 45 students received support, including 8 fellowships (averaging $40,500 per year), 11 research assistantships (averaging $28,400 per year), 22 teaching assistantships (averaging $29,800 per year); Federal Work-Study, institutionally sponsored loans, scholarships/grants, traineeships, health care benefits, unspecified assistantships, and graduate resident tutors also available. Financial award application deadline: 5/1; financial award applicants required to submit FAFSA. *Faculty research:* Humans and technology; information theory and decision systems; sociotechnical systems; policy and standards; social behavior; uncertainty, risk, and dynamics. *Application contact:* Information Contact, 617-425-2432, Fax: 617-253-1462, E-mail: sdm@mit.edu.

McNeese State University, Doré School of Graduate Studies, College of Engineering and Engineering Technology, Department of Engineering, Master of Engineering Program, Lake Charles, LA 70609. Offers chemical engineering (M Eng); civil engineering (M Eng); electrical engineering (M Eng); engineering management (M Eng); mechanical engineering (M Eng). *Program availability:* Part-time, evening/weekend. *Degree requirements:* For master's, thesis or alternative. *Entrance requirements:* For master's, GRE, baccalaureate degree, minimum overall GPA of 3.0. Additional exam requirements/recommendations for international students: Required—TOEFL (minimum score 560 paper-based; 83 iBT).

Mercer University, Graduate Studies, Macon Campus, School of Engineering, Macon, GA 31207. Offers biomedical engineering (MSE); computer engineering (MSE); electrical engineering (MSE); engineering management (MSE); environmental engineering (MSE); environmental systems (MS); mechanical engineering (MSE); software engineering (MSE); software systems (MS); technical communications management (MS); technical management (MS). *Program availability:* Part-time-only, evening/weekend, online learning. *Faculty:* 21 full-time (5 women), 1 part-time/adjunct (0 women). *Students:* 44 full-time (9 women), 60 part-time (12 women); includes 14 minority (3 Black or African American, non-Hispanic/Latino; 1 American Indian or Alaska Native, non-Hispanic/Latino; 4 Asian, non-Hispanic/Latino; 3 Hispanic/Latino; 3 Two or more races, non-Hispanic/Latino), 2 international. Average age 27. In 2016, 64 master's awarded. *Degree requirements:* For master's, thesis or alternative. *Entrance requirements:* For master's, GRE (minimum score 300), minimum undergraduate GPA of 3.0. Additional exam requirements/recommendations for international students: Required—TOEFL (minimum score 550 paper-based; 80 iBT). *Application deadline:* For fall admission, 4/1 priority date for domestic and international students; for spring admission, 11/1 priority date for domestic and international students. Applications are processed on a rolling basis. Application fee: $75. *Expenses:* $865 per credit hour. *Financial support:* Applicants required to submit FAFSA. *Faculty research:* Designing prostheses and orthotics, oxygen transfer and limitations in biological systems, low-cost groundwater development, lung airway and transport, autonomous mobile robots. *Unit head:* Dr. Laura W. Lackey, Dean, 478-301-4106, Fax: 478-301-5593, E-mail: lackey_l@mercer.edu. *Application contact:* Dr. Richard O. Mines, Jr., Program Director, 478-301-2347, Fax: 478-301-5433, E-mail: mines_ro@mercer.edu.
Website: http://engineering.mercer.edu/

Merrimack College, School of Science and Engineering, North Andover, MA 01845-5800. Offers athletic training (MS); civil engineering (MS); community health education (MS); computer science (MS); data science (MS); exercise and sport science (MS); health and wellness management (MS); mechanical engineering (MS), including engineering management. *Program availability:* Part-time, evening/weekend, 100% online. *Faculty:* 16 full-time, 2 part-time/adjunct. *Students:* 88 full-time (32 women), 13 part-time (6 women); includes 6 minority (4 Hispanic/Latino; 2 Two or more races, non-Hispanic/Latino), 39 international. Average age 25. 156 applicants, 67% accepted, 59 enrolled. In 2016, 46 master's awarded. *Degree requirements:* For master's, comprehensive exam, thesis optional, internship or capstone (for some programs). *Entrance requirements:* For master's, official college transcripts, resume, personal statement, 2 recommendations. Additional exam requirements/recommendations for international students: Required—TOEFL (minimum score 84 iBT), IELTS (minimum score 6.5), PTE (minimum score 56). *Application deadline:* For fall admission, 8/14 for domestic students, 7/14 for international students; for spring admission, 1/10 for domestic students, 12/10 for international students; for summer admission, 5/10 for

domestic students, 4/10 for international students. Applications are processed on a rolling basis. Application fee: $0. Electronic applications accepted. *Expenses:* Contact institution. *Financial support:* Fellowships with full tuition reimbursements, career-related internships or fieldwork, scholarships/grants, and health care benefits available. Support available to part-time students. Financial award application deadline: 5/1; financial award applicants required to submit FAFSA. *Faculty research:* Viral genomics and evolution (biology), robotics (mechanical engineering), knot theory (mathematics), computer graphics and network security (computer science), water management (civil engineering). *Application contact:* Allison Pena, Graduate Admissions Counselor, 978-837-3563, E-mail: penaa@merrimack.edu.
Website: http://www.merrimack.edu/academics/graduate/

Middle Tennessee State University, College of Graduate Studies, College of Basic and Applied Sciences, Program in Professional Science, Murfreesboro, TN 37132. Offers actuarial sciences (MS); biostatistics (MS); biotechnology (MS); engineering management (MS); health care informatics (MS). *Program availability:* Part-time, evening/weekend, online learning. *Degree requirements:* For master's, comprehensive exam. *Entrance requirements:* For master's, GRE. Additional exam requirements/recommendations for international students: Required—TOEFL (minimum score 525 paper-based; 71 iBT) or IELTS (minimum score 6).

Milwaukee School of Engineering, Rader School of Business, Program in Engineering Management, Milwaukee, WI 53202-3109. Offers MS. *Program availability:* Part-time, evening/weekend. *Faculty:* 2 full-time (1 woman), 8 part-time/adjunct (4 women). *Students:* 8 full-time (1 woman), 41 part-time (9 women); includes 7 minority (1 Black or African American, non-Hispanic/Latino; 2 Asian, non-Hispanic/Latino; 4 Hispanic/Latino), 4 international. Average age 24. 22 applicants, 45% accepted, 7 enrolled. In 2016, 9 master's awarded. *Degree requirements:* For master's, thesis, thesis defense or capstone project. *Entrance requirements:* For master's, GRE General Test or GMAT if undergraduate GPA less than 2.8, BS in engineering, engineering technology, science, business, management, or related area; 2 letters of recommendation. Additional exam requirements/recommendations for international students: Required—TOEFL (minimum score 90 iBT), IELTS (minimum score 6.5). *Application deadline:* Applications are processed on a rolling basis. Application fee: $0. Electronic applications accepted. *Expenses: Tuition:* Full-time $31,440; part-time $655 per credit. *Financial support:* Career-related internships or fieldwork, institutionally sponsored loans, scholarships/grants, traineeships, and tuition waivers (partial) available. Financial award application deadline: 3/15; financial award applicants required to submit FAFSA. *Faculty research:* Operations, project management, quality marketing. *Unit head:* Gene Wright, Director, 414-277-2286, Fax: 414-277-2487, E-mail: wright@msoe.edu. *Application contact:* Ian Dahlinghaus, Graduate Program Associate, 414-277-7208, E-mail: dahlinghaus@msoe.edu.
Website: http://www.msoe.edu/community/academics/business/page/1300/engineering-management-overview

Milwaukee School of Engineering, Rader School of Business, Program in STEM Leadership, Milwaukee, WI 53202-3109. Offers MBA. *Program availability:* Part-time. *Students:* 2 part-time (both women). Average age 29. 1 applicant. In 2016, 1 master's awarded. *Entrance requirements:* For master's, GRE or GMAT if GPA is below 3.0, official transcripts, two letters of recommendation, personal essay, minimum GPA of 3.0. Additional exam requirements/recommendations for international students: Required—TOEFL (minimum score 90 iBT), IELTS (minimum score 6.5). *Application deadline:* Applications are processed on a rolling basis. Electronic applications accepted. *Expenses: Tuition:* Full-time $31,440; part-time $655 per credit. *Financial support:* Institutionally sponsored loans available. Financial award application deadline: 3/15; financial award applicants required to submit FAFSA. *Unit head:* Dr. Kathy S. Faggiani, Director, 414-277-2711, E-mail: faggiani@msoe.edu. *Application contact:* Ian Dahlinghaus, Graduate Program Associate, 414-277-7208, E-mail: dahlinghaus@msoe.edu.
Website: http://www.msoe.edu/academics/business-graduate/master-of-business-administration-in-stem-leadership/

Missouri University of Science and Technology, Graduate School, Department of Engineering Management and Systems Engineering, Rolla, MO 65409. Offers engineering management (MS, DE, PhD); manufacturing engineering (M Eng, MS); systems engineering (MS, PhD). *Degree requirements:* For master's, thesis optional; for doctorate, comprehensive exam. *Entrance requirements:* For master's, GRE (minimum score 1150 verbal and quantitative, 4.5 writing); for doctorate, GRE (minimum score: 1100 verbal and quantitative, 3.5 writing). Additional exam requirements/recommendations for international students: Required—TOEFL (minimum score 580 paper-based). Electronic applications accepted. *Faculty research:* Management of technology, industrial engineering, manufacturing engineering, packaging engineering, quality engineering.

Naval Postgraduate School, Departments and Academic Groups, Department of Systems Engineering, Monterey, CA 93943. Offers engineering systems (MS); product development (MS); systems engineering (MS, PhD, Certificate); systems engineering analysis (MS, PhD); systems engineering management (MS, PhD). Program only open to commissioned officers of the United States and friendly nations and selected United States federal civilian employees. *Accreditation:* ABET. *Program availability:* Part-time. *Degree requirements:* For master's, thesis (for some programs), internal project, capstone project, or research/dissertation paper (for some programs); for doctorate, thesis/dissertation (for some programs), internal project, capstone project, or research/dissertation paper (for some programs). *Faculty research:* Net-centric enterprise systems/services, artificial intelligence (AI) systems engineering, unconventional weapons of mass destruction, complex systems engineering, risk-benefit analysis.

New Jersey Institute of Technology, Newark College of Engineering, Newark, NJ 07102. Offers biomedical engineering (MS, PhD); chemical engineering (MS, PhD); computer engineering (MS, PhD); electrical engineering (MS, PhD); engineering management (MS); environmental engineering (PhD); healthcare systems management (MS); industrial engineering (MS, PhD); Internet engineering (MS); manufacturing engineering (MS); mechanical engineering (MS, PhD); occupational safety and health engineering (MS); pharmaceutical bioprocessing (MS); pharmaceutical engineering (MS); pharmaceutical systems management (MS); power and energy systems (MS); telecommunications (MS); transportation (MS, PhD). *Program availability:* Part-time, evening/weekend. *Faculty:* 146 full-time (21 women), 119 part-time/adjunct (10 women). *Students:* 804 full-time (191 women), 550 part-time (129 women); includes 357 minority (82 Black or African American, non-Hispanic/Latino; 1 American Indian or Alaska Native, non-Hispanic/Latino; 138 Asian, non-Hispanic/Latino; 114 Hispanic/Latino; 22 Two or more races, non-Hispanic/Latino), 675 international. Average age 27. 2,959 applicants, 51% accepted, 442 enrolled. In 2016, 595 master's, 29 doctorates awarded. Terminal master's awarded for partial completion of doctoral program. *Degree requirements:* For master's, thesis optional; for doctorate, thesis/dissertation. *Entrance requirements:* For master's, GRE General Test; for doctorate, GRE General Test, minimum graduate GPA of 3.5. Additional exam requirements/recommendations for international students: Required—TOEFL (minimum score 550 paper-based; 79 iBT). *Application deadline:* For fall admission, 6/1 priority date for domestic students, 5/1 priority date for international students; for spring admission, 11/15 priority date for domestic and international students. Applications are processed on a rolling basis. Application fee: $75. Electronic applications accepted. *Expenses:* Contact institution. *Financial support:* In 2016–17, 172 students received support, including 1 fellowship (averaging $1,528 per year), 79 research assistantships (averaging $13,336 per year), 92 teaching assistantships (averaging $20,619 per year); scholarships/grants also available. Financial award application deadline: 1/15. *Faculty research:* Nonlinear signal processing, intelligent medical image analysis, calibration issues in coherent localization, computer-aided design, neural network for tool wear measurement. *Total annual research expenditures:* $11.1 million. *Unit head:* Dr. Moshe Kam, Dean, 973-596-5534, E-mail: moshe.kam@njit.edu. *Application contact:* Stephen Eck, Director of Admissions, 973-596-3300, Fax: 973-596-3461, E-mail: admissions@njit.edu.
Website: http://engineering.njit.edu/

New Mexico Institute of Mining and Technology, Center for Graduate Studies, Department of Management, Socorro, NM 87801. Offers STEM education (MEM). *Program availability:* Part-time.

Northeastern University, College of Engineering, Boston, MA 02115-5096. Offers bioengineering (MS, PhD); chemical engineering (MS, PhD); civil engineering (MS, PhD); computer engineering (PhD); computer systems engineering (MS); electrical and computer engineering (MS); electrical and computer engineering leadership (MS); electrical engineering (PhD); energy systems (MS); engineering and public policy (MS); engineering management (MS, Certificate); environmental engineering (MS); industrial engineering (MS, PhD); information assurance (PhD); information systems (MS); interdisciplinary engineering (PhD); mechanical engineering (PhD); operations research (MS); telecommunication systems management (MS). *Program availability:* Part-time, online learning. *Faculty:* 202 full-time (59 women), 53 part-time/adjunct (9 women). *Students:* 2,982 full-time (954 women), 192 part-time (38 women). In 2016, 851 master's, 74 doctorates awarded. Application fee: $75. Electronic applications accepted. *Expenses:* $1,471 per credit. *Financial support:* Fellowships, research assistantships, teaching assistantships, career-related internships or fieldwork, scholarships/grants, health care benefits, tuition waivers, and unspecified assistantships available. Support available to part-time students. Financial award applicants required to submit FAFSA. *Unit head:* Dr. Nadine Aubry, Dean, College of Engineering. *Application contact:* Jeffery Hengel, Director of Graduate Admissions, 617-373-2711, E-mail: j.hengel@northeastern.edu.
Website: http://www.coe.neu.edu/academics/graduate-school-engineering

Northwestern University, McCormick School of Engineering and Applied Science, Department of Industrial Engineering and Management Sciences, Master's in Engineering Management Program, Evanston, IL 60208. Offers MEM. *Program availability:* Part-time, evening/weekend. *Entrance requirements:* For master's, 3 years of work experience. Additional exam requirements/recommendations for international students: Required—TOEFL (minimum score 100 iBT), IELTS (minimum score 7). Electronic applications accepted. *Expenses:* Contact institution.

Northwestern University, McCormick School of Engineering and Applied Science, MMM Program, Evanston, IL 60208. Offers design innovation (MBA, MS). *Entrance requirements:* For master's, GMAT or GRE, transcripts, two letters of recommendation, resume, evaluative interview report, work experience, two core essays, interest essay, video essay. Additional exam requirements/recommendations for international students: Required—TOEFL, IELTS. *Expenses:* Contact institution.

Oakland University, Graduate Study and Lifelong Learning, School of Engineering and Computer Science, Department of Industrial and Systems Engineering, Rochester, MI 48309-4401. Offers engineering management (MS); industrial and systems engineering (MS); productivity improvement (Graduate Certificate); systems engineering (PhD).

Oklahoma Christian University, Graduate School of Engineering and Computer Science, Oklahoma City, OK 73136-1100. Offers electrical and computer engineering (MSE); engineering management (MSE); mechanical engineering (MSE); software engineering (MSCS, MSE). *Program availability:* Part-time. *Faculty:* 8 full-time (1 woman), 7 part-time/adjunct (0 women). *Students:* 187 full-time (27 women), 85 part-time (12 women). Average age 25. 255 applicants, 33% accepted, 69 enrolled. In 2016, 188 master's awarded. *Entrance requirements:* Additional exam requirements/recommendations for international students: Required—TOEFL (minimum score 550 paper-based). *Application deadline:* Applications are processed on a rolling basis. Application fee: $25. Electronic applications accepted. *Expenses:* Contact institution. *Unit head:* Mary Ann Brown, Director for Graduate School Engineering, 405-425-5579. *Application contact:* Angie Ricketts, Admissions Counselor, 405-425-5587, E-mail: angie.ricketts@oc.edu.
Website: http://www.oc.edu/academics/graduate/engineering/

Old Dominion University, Frank Batten College of Engineering and Technology, Program in Engineering Management and Systems Engineering, Norfolk, VA 23529. Offers D Eng, PhD. *Program availability:* Part-time, evening/weekend, 100% online, blended/hybrid learning. *Faculty:* 14 full-time (2 women), 12 part-time/adjunct (2 women). *Students:* 1 (woman) full-time, 14 part-time (4 women); includes 5 minority (1 Black or African American, non-Hispanic/Latino; 2 Asian, non-Hispanic/Latino; 2 Hispanic/Latino). Average age 46. 3 applicants, 67% accepted, 2 enrolled. In 2016, 2 doctorates awarded. *Degree requirements:* For doctorate, thesis/dissertation, candidacy exam, project. *Entrance requirements:* For doctorate, GRE, resume, letters of recommendation, minimum GPA of 3.0, interview. Additional exam requirements/recommendations for international students: Required—TOEFL (minimum score 550 paper-based; 79 iBT). *Application deadline:* For fall admission, 6/1 priority date for domestic students, 4/15 for international students; for spring admission, 11/1 priority date for domestic students, 2/1 for international students. Applications are processed on a rolling basis. Application fee: $50. Electronic applications accepted. *Expenses:* Tuition, state resident: full-time $8604; part-time $478 per credit hour. Tuition, nonresident: full-time $21,510; part-time $1195 per credit hour. *Required fees:* $66 per semester. Tuition and fees vary according to campus/location, program and reciprocity agreements. *Financial support:* In 2016–17, 22 students received support, including 5 research assistantships with full tuition reimbursements available (averaging $23,250 per year), 12 teaching assistantships with full tuition reimbursements available (averaging $23,250 per year); career-related internships or fieldwork and tuition waivers (full and partial) also available. Support available to part-time students. Financial award application deadline: 2/15; financial award applicants required to submit FAFSA. *Faculty research:* Project management, systems engineering, modeling and simulation, virtual collaboration environments, multidisciplinary designs, human systems engineering, decision analysis. *Total annual research expenditures:* $729,085. *Unit head:* Dr. Andres Sousa-Poza, Department Chair, 757-683-4558, Fax: 757-683-5640, E-mail: enmagpd@odu.edu. *Application contact:* Dr. Patrick Hester, Graduate Program Director, 757-683-4558, Fax: 757-683-5640, E-mail: enmagpd@odu.edu.
Website: http://eng.odu.edu/enma/

Oregon State University, College of Engineering, Program in Industrial Engineering, Corvallis, OR 97331. Offers advanced manufacturing (M Eng, MS, PhD); engineering management (M Eng); human systems engineering (M Eng, MS, PhD); information systems engineering (M Eng, MS, PhD). *Program availability:* 100% online. *Faculty:* 52 full-time (12 women), 3 part-time/adjunct (0 women). *Students:* 75 full-time (18 women),

28 part-time (11 women); includes 14 minority (1 American Indian or Alaska Native, non-Hispanic/Latino; 7 Asian, non-Hispanic/Latino; 4 Hispanic/Latino; 2 Two or more races, non-Hispanic/Latino), 56 international. Average age 29. 158 applicants, 33% accepted, 35 enrolled. In 2016, 19 master's, 3 doctorates awarded. *Entrance requirements:* For master's and doctorate, GRE. Additional exam requirements/recommendations for international students: Required—TOEFL (minimum score 80 iBT), IELTS (minimum score 6.5). *Application deadline:* For fall admission, 8/1 for domestic students, 4/1 for international students; for winter admission, 12/1 for domestic students, 7/1 for international students; for spring admission, 2/1 for domestic students, 10/1 for international students; for summer admission, 5/1 for domestic students, 1/1 for international students. Application fee: $75 ($85 for international students). *Expenses:* $14,130 resident full-time tuition, $23,769 non-resident. *Financial support:* Application deadline: 1/15. *Unit head:* Dr. Harriet Nembhard, School Head. *Application contact:* Jean Robinson, Advisor, E-mail: jean.robinson@oregonstate.edu.
Website: http://mime.oregonstate.edu/academics/grad/ie

Penn State Great Valley, Graduate Studies, Engineering Division, Malvern, PA 19355-1488. Offers engineering management (MEM); software engineering (MSE); systems engineering (M Eng, Certificate). *Unit head:* Dr. James A. Nemes, Chancellor, 610-648-3202 Ext. 610, Fax: 610-725-5296, E-mail: cse1@psu.edu. *Application contact:* JoAnn Kelly, Director of Admissions, 610-648-3315, Fax: 610-725-5296, E-mail: jek2@psu.edu.
Website: http://greatvalley.psu.edu/academics/masters-degrees/systems-engineering

Penn State Harrisburg, Graduate School, School of Science, Engineering and Technology, Middletown, PA 17057. Offers computer science (MS); electrical engineering (M Eng, MS); engineering management (MPS); engineering science (M Eng); environmental engineering (M Eng); environmental pollution control (MEPC, MS); structural engineering (Certificate). *Program availability:* Part-time, evening/weekend. *Unit head:* Dr. Mukund S. Kulkarni, Chancellor, 717-948-6105, Fax: 717-948-6452. *Application contact:* Robert W. Coffman, Jr., Director of Enrollment Management, Admissions, 717-948-6250, Fax: 717-948-6325, E-mail: hbgadmit@psu.edu.
Website: https://harrisburg.psu.edu/science-engineering-technology

Point Park University, School of Arts and Sciences, Department of Natural Science and Engineering Technology, Pittsburgh, PA 15222-1984. Offers engineering management (MS); environmental studies (MS). *Program availability:* Part-time, evening/weekend. *Degree requirements:* For master's, comprehensive exam (for some programs), thesis or alternative. *Entrance requirements:* For master's, minimum QPA of 2.75, 2 letters of recommendation, minimum B average in engineering technology or a related field, official undergraduate transcript, statement of intent, resume. Additional exam requirements/recommendations for international students: Required—TOEFL. Electronic applications accepted.

Polytechnic University of Puerto Rico, Graduate School, Hato Rey, PR 00918. Offers business administration (MBA), including computer information systems, general management, management of information systems, management of international enterprises; civil engineering (ME, MS); computer engineering (ME, MS); computer science (MCS, MS); electrical engineering (ME, MS); engineering management (MEM); environmental management (MEM); landscape architecture (M Land Arch); manufacturing competitiveness (MMC, MS); manufacturing engineering (ME, MS); mechanical engineering (M Mech E). *Program availability:* Part-time, evening/weekend. *Entrance requirements:* For master's, 3 letters of recommendation.

Polytechnic University of Puerto Rico, Orlando Campus, Graduate School, Orlando, FL 32825. Offers accounting (MBA); business administration (MBA); construction management (MEM); engineering management (MEM); environmental management (MEM); finance (MBA); human resources management (MBA); management of international enterprises (MBA); management of technology (MBA); manufacturing management (MEM). *Program availability:* Part-time, evening/weekend, online learning. *Entrance requirements:* For master's, minimum GPA of 3.0. Additional exam requirements/recommendations for international students: Recommended—TOEFL. Electronic applications accepted.

Portland State University, Graduate Studies, College of Liberal Arts and Sciences, Systems Science Program, Portland, OR 97207-0751. Offers computational intelligence (Certificate); computer modeling and simulation (Certificate); systems science (MS); systems science/anthropology (PhD); systems science/business administration (PhD); systems science/civil engineering (PhD); systems science/economics (PhD); systems science/engineering management (PhD); systems science/general (PhD); systems science/mathematical sciences (PhD); systems science/mechanical engineering (PhD); systems science/psychology (PhD); systems science/sociology (PhD). *Faculty:* 2 full-time (0 women), 3 part-time/adjunct (1 woman). *Students:* 12 full-time (3 women), 21 part-time (5 women); includes 5 minority (1 Black or African American, non-Hispanic/Latino; 2 Hispanic/Latino; 2 Two or more races, non-Hispanic/Latino). Average age 39. 16 applicants, 69% accepted, 9 enrolled. In 2016, 4 master's, 6 doctorates awarded. *Degree requirements:* For master's, comprehensive exam (for some programs), thesis optional; for doctorate, variable foreign language requirement, comprehensive exam (for some programs), thesis/dissertation. *Entrance requirements:* For master's, GRE/GMAT (recommended), minimum GPA of 3.0 undergraduate or graduate work, 2 letters of recommendation, statement of interest; for doctorate, GMAT, GRE General Test, minimum GPA of 3.0 undergraduate, 3.25 graduate; 2 letters of recommendation; statement of interest. Additional exam requirements/recommendations for international students: Required—TOEFL (minimum score 550 paper-based; 80 iBT). *Application deadline:* For fall admission, 1/15 for domestic and international students; for spring admission, 11/1 for domestic students. Application fee: $65. Electronic applications accepted. *Expenses:* Contact institution. *Financial support:* In 2016–17, 2 research assistantships with tuition reimbursements (averaging $7,830 per year) were awarded; teaching assistantships, career-related internships or fieldwork, Federal Work-Study, scholarships/grants, and unspecified assistantships also available. Support available to part-time students. Financial award application deadline: 3/1; financial award applicants required to submit FAFSA. *Faculty research:* Systems theory and methodology, artificial intelligence neural networks, information theory, nonlinear dynamics/chaos, modeling and simulation. *Unit head:* Dr. Wayne Wakeland, Chair, 503-725-4975, E-mail: wakeland@pdx.edu.
Website: http://www.pdx.edu/sysc/

Portland State University, Graduate Studies, Maseeh College of Engineering and Computer Science, Department of Civil and Environmental Engineering, Portland, OR 97207-0751. Offers civil and environmental engineering (M Eng, MS, PhD); civil and environmental engineering management (M Eng); environmental sciences and resources (PhD); systems science (PhD). *Program availability:* Part-time, evening/weekend. *Faculty:* 27 full-time (5 women), 4 part-time/adjunct (2 women). *Students:* 50 full-time (11 women), 51 part-time (14 women); includes 10 minority (1 Black or African American, non-Hispanic/Latino; 1 Asian, non-Hispanic/Latino; 3 Hispanic/Latino; 5 Two or more races, non-Hispanic/Latino), 43 international. Average age 31. 89 applicants, 61% accepted, 26 enrolled. In 2016, 28 master's, 1 doctorate awarded. *Degree requirements:* For master's, comprehensive exam (for some programs), thesis (for some programs); for doctorate, one foreign language, comprehensive exam, thesis/dissertation, oral and written exams. *Entrance requirements:* For master's, BS in an engineering field, science, or closely-related area with minimum GPA of 3.0; for doctorate, MS in an engineering field, science, or closely-related area. Additional exam requirements/recommendations for international students: Required—TOEFL (minimum score 550 paper-based). *Application deadline:* For fall admission, 1/4 priority date for domestic and international students; for winter admission, 9/1 for domestic and international students; for spring admission, 11/1 for domestic and international students. Applications are processed on a rolling basis. Application fee: $65. *Expenses:* Contact institution. *Financial support:* In 2016–17, 21 research assistantships with tuition reimbursements (averaging $5,959 per year), 16 teaching assistantships with tuition reimbursements (averaging $6,096 per year) were awarded; career-related internships or fieldwork, Federal Work-Study, scholarships/grants, and unspecified assistantships also available. Support available to part-time students. Financial award application deadline: 3/1; financial award applicants required to submit FAFSA. *Faculty research:* Structures, water resources, geotechnical engineering, environmental engineering, transportation. *Total annual research expenditures:* $2.6 million. *Unit head:* Dr. Chris Monsere, Chair, 503-725-9746, Fax: 503-725-4298, E-mail: monserec@cecs.pdx.edu. *Application contact:* Ariel Lewis, Department Manager, 503-725-4244, Fax: 503-725-4298, E-mail: ariel.lewis@pdx.edu.
Website: http://www.pdx.edu/cee/

Portland State University, Graduate Studies, Maseeh College of Engineering and Computer Science, Department of Engineering and Technology Management, Portland, OR 97207-0751. Offers engineering and technology management (M Eng); engineering management (MS); manufacturing engineering (ME); manufacturing management (M Eng); systems science/engineering management (PhD); MS/MBA; MS/MS. *Program availability:* Part-time, evening/weekend. *Faculty:* 6 full-time (1 woman), 5 part-time/adjunct (0 women). *Students:* 53 full-time (19 women), 75 part-time (34 women); includes 18 minority (3 Black or African American, non-Hispanic/Latino; 11 Asian, non-Hispanic/Latino; 3 Hispanic/Latino; 1 Two or more races, non-Hispanic/Latino), 73 international. Average age 36. 76 applicants, 50% accepted, 20 enrolled. In 2016, 34 master's, 4 doctorates awarded. *Degree requirements:* For master's, thesis optional; for doctorate, one foreign language, comprehensive exam, thesis/dissertation, oral and written exams. *Entrance requirements:* For master's, minimum GPA of 2.75 undergraduate or 3.0 graduate (at least 12 credits); minimum 4 years of experience in engineering or related discipline; 3 letters of recommendation; background in probability/statistics, differential equations, computer programming and linear algebra; for doctorate, GRE General Test (minimum combined score of 1100 for verbal and quantitative), minimum GPA of 3.0 undergraduate, 3.25 graduate. Additional exam requirements/recommendations for international students: Required—TOEFL (minimum score 550 paper-based; 80 iBT). *Application deadline:* For fall admission, 4/1 for domestic students, 3/1 for international students; for winter admission, 9/1 for domestic students, 7/1 for international students; for spring admission, 11/1 for domestic students, 9/1 for international students; for summer admission, 2/1 for domestic students, 12/1 for international students. Application fee: $65. Electronic applications accepted. *Expenses:* Contact institution. *Financial support:* In 2016–17, 7 research assistantships with tuition reimbursements (averaging $2,885 per year), 3 teaching assistantships with tuition reimbursements (averaging $1,176 per year) were awarded; career-related internships or fieldwork, Federal Work-Study, scholarships/grants, and unspecified assistantships also available. Support available to part-time students. Financial award application deadline: 3/1; financial award applicants required to submit FAFSA. *Faculty research:* Scheduling, hierarchical decision modeling, operations research, knowledge-based information systems. *Total annual research expenditures:* $323,951. *Unit head:* Dr. Timothy Anderson, Chair, 503-725-4668, Fax: 503-725-4667, E-mail: tim.anderson@pdx.edu. *Application contact:* Shawn Wall, Department Manager, 503-725-4661, E-mail: shawnw@pdx.edu.
Website: http://www.pdx.edu/engineering-technology-management/

Rensselaer Polytechnic Institute, Graduate School, Lally School of Management, Troy, NY 12180-3590. Offers MBA, MS, PhD, MS/MBA. *Accreditation:* AACSB. *Program availability:* Part-time, evening/weekend. *Faculty:* 35 full-time (10 women), 7 part-time/adjunct (0 women). *Students:* 172 full-time (84 women). 1,019 applicants, 38% accepted, 104 enrolled. In 2016, 79 master's, 7 doctorates awarded. *Degree requirements:* For doctorate, thesis/dissertation. *Entrance requirements:* For master's and doctorate, GMAT or GRE. Additional exam requirements/recommendations for international students: Required—TOEFL (minimum score 570 paper-based; 88 iBT), IELTS (minimum score 6.5), PTE (minimum score 60). *Application deadline:* For fall admission, 1/1 priority date for domestic and international students; for spring admission, 8/15 priority date for domestic and international students. Applications are processed on a rolling basis. Application fee: $75. Electronic applications accepted. *Expenses:* Contact institution. *Financial support:* In 2016–17, 64 students received support. Scholarships/grants available. Financial award application deadline: 1/1; financial award applicants required to submit FAFSA. *Faculty research:* Business analytics, quantitative finance and risk analytics, management, supply chain management, technology commercialization and entrepreneurship. *Total annual research expenditures:* $639,851. *Unit head:* Dr. Gina O'Connor, Associate Dean, Lally School of Management, 518-276-6842, E-mail: oconng@rpi.edu. *Application contact:* Office of Graduate Admissions, 518-276-6216, E-mail: gradadmissions@rpi.edu.
Website: http://lallyschool.rpi.edu/

Robert Morris University, School of Engineering, Mathematics and Science, Moon Township, PA 15108-1189. Offers engineering management (MS). *Program availability:* Part-time, evening/weekend. *Faculty:* 7 full-time (1 woman). *Students:* 17 part-time (6 women); includes 2 minority (1 Asian, non-Hispanic/Latino; 1 Hispanic/Latino), 6 international. Average age 36. 40 applicants, 28% accepted, 4 enrolled. In 2016, 20 master's awarded. *Entrance requirements:* For master's, letters of recommendation. Additional exam requirements/recommendations for international students: Required—TOEFL (minimum score 550 paper-based; 79 iBT). *Application deadline:* For fall admission, 7/1 priority date for domestic and international students; for spring admission, 11/1 priority date for domestic and international students. Applications are processed on a rolling basis. Application fee: $35. Electronic applications accepted. *Expenses:* $870 per credit (for master's degree). *Financial support:* Federal Work-Study, institutionally sponsored loans, and unspecified assistantships available. Financial award application deadline: 5/1; financial award applicants required to submit FAFSA. *Unit head:* Dr. Maria V. Kalevitch, Dean, 412-397-4020, Fax: 412-397-2472, E-mail: kalevitch@rmu.edu.
Website: http://www.rmu.edu/web/cms/schools/sems/

Rochester Institute of Technology, Graduate Enrollment Services, Kate Gleason College of Engineering, Design, Development and Manufacturing Department, MS Program in Product Development, Rochester, NY 14623. Offers MS. *Program availability:* Part-time, evening/weekend, 100% online. *Students:* 1 (woman) full-time, 45 part-time (4 women); includes 4 minority (1 Black or African American, non-Hispanic/Latino; 1 Asian, non-Hispanic/Latino; 2 Hispanic/Latino), 1 international. Average age 37. 17 applicants, 59% accepted, 8 enrolled. In 2016, 6 master's awarded. *Degree requirements:* For master's, capstone project. *Entrance requirements:* For master's, undergraduate degree in engineering or related field, minimum GPA of 3.0, 2 years of experience in product development. Additional exam requirements/recommendations for international students: Required—TOEFL (minimum score 550 paper-based; 79 iBT),

IELTS (minimum score 6.5), PTE (minimum score 58). *Application deadline:* Applications are processed on a rolling basis. Application fee: $60. Electronic applications accepted. *Expenses:* $1,742 per credit hour. *Financial support:* Scholarships/grants available. Support available to part-time students. Financial award applicants required to submit FAFSA. *Faculty research:* Systems engineering, lean product development, decision analysis, agile methods, project management. *Unit head:* Mark Smith, Graduate Program Director, 585-475-7971, Fax: 585-475-4080, E-mail: mpdmail@rit.edu. *Application contact:* Diane Ellison, Associate Vice President, Graduate Enrollment Services, 585-475-2229, Fax: 585-475-7164, E-mail: gradinfo@rit.edu.
Website: https://www.rit.edu/kgcoe/mpd/

Rochester Institute of Technology, Graduate Enrollment Services, Kate Gleason College of Engineering, Industrial and Systems Engineering Department, ME Program in Engineering Management, Rochester, NY 14623-5603. Offers ME. *Program availability:* Part-time. *Students:* 24 full-time (5 women), 7 part-time (3 women); includes 6 minority (1 Black or African American, non-Hispanic/Latino; 2 American Indian or Alaska Native, non-Hispanic/Latino; 3 Hispanic/Latino), 7 international. Average age 27. 221 applicants, 19% accepted, 5 enrolled. In 2016, 19 master's awarded. *Degree requirements:* For master's, thesis or alternative, capstone. *Entrance requirements:* For master's, minimum GPA of 3.0 (recommended). Additional exam requirements/recommendations for international students: Required—TOEFL (minimum score 580 paper-based; 90 iBT), IELTS (minimum score 6.5), PTE (minimum score 58). *Application deadline:* For fall admission, 2/15 priority date for domestic and international students; for spring admission, 12/15 priority date for domestic and international students. Applications are processed on a rolling basis. Application fee: $60. Electronic applications accepted. *Expenses:* $1,742 per credit hour. *Financial support:* Research assistantships with partial tuition reimbursements, teaching assistantships with partial tuition reimbursements, career-related internships or fieldwork, scholarships/grants, and unspecified assistantships available. Support available to part-time students. Financial award applicants required to submit FAFSA. *Faculty research:* Systems engineering/product development; lean manufacturing; operations research and simulation; production and logistics; project management. *Unit head:* Dr. Marcos Esterman, Associate Professor, 585-475-2598, E-mail: mxeeie@rit.edu. *Application contact:* Diane Ellison, Associate Vice President, Graduate Enrollment Services, 585-475-2229, Fax: 585-475-7164, E-mail: gradinfo@rit.edu.
Website: http://www.rit.edu/kgcoe/ise/program/master-engineering-degrees/master-engineering-engineering-management

Rose-Hulman Institute of Technology, Faculty of Engineering and Applied Sciences, Department of Engineering Management, Terre Haute, IN 47803-3999. Offers M Eng, MS. *Program availability:* Part-time, evening/weekend. *Faculty:* 7 full-time (2 women). *Students:* 20 full-time (5 women), 10 part-time (3 women); includes 4 minority (1 Black or African American, non-Hispanic/Latino; 1 Asian, non-Hispanic/Latino; 1 Hispanic/Latino; 1 Two or more races, non-Hispanic/Latino), 14 international. Average age 24. 29 applicants, 93% accepted, 19 enrolled. In 2016, 11 master's awarded. *Degree requirements:* For master's, integrated project. *Entrance requirements:* For master's, GRE, minimum GPA of 3.0. Additional exam requirements/recommendations for international students: Required—TOEFL (minimum score 580 paper-based; 92 iBT). *Application deadline:* For fall admission, 2/1 priority date for domestic students. Applications are processed on a rolling basis. Application fee: $0. Electronic applications accepted. *Expenses: Tuition:* Full-time $43,122. *Financial support:* In 2016–17, 27 students received support. Fellowships with tuition reimbursements available available. *Faculty research:* Systems engineering, technical entrepreneurship, project management, organizational development and management, manufacturing and supply chain, marketing and new product development. *Total annual research expenditures:* $12,700. *Unit head:* Dr. Craig Downing, Chairman, 812-877-8822, Fax: 812-877-8878, E-mail: craig.downing@rose-hulman.edu. *Application contact:* Dr. Azad Siahmakoun, Associate Dean of the Faculty, 812-877-8400, Fax: 812-877-8061, E-mail: siahmako@rose-hulman.edu.
Website: http://www.rose-hulman.edu/academics/academic-departments/engineering-management.aspx

St. Cloud State University, School of Graduate Studies, College of Science and Engineering, Program in Engineering Management, St. Cloud, MN 56301-4498. Offers MEM. *Degree requirements:* For master's, thesis or alternative. *Entrance requirements:* For master's, GRE General Test, minimum GPA of 2.75. Additional exam requirements/recommendations for international students: Required—Michigan English Language Assessment Battery; Recommended—TOEFL (minimum score 550 paper-based), IELTS (minimum score 6.5). Electronic applications accepted.

Saint Martin's University, Office of Graduate Studies, Program in Engineering Management, Lacey, WA 98503. Offers M Eng Mgt. *Program availability:* Part-time. *Faculty:* 3 full-time (0 women), 2 part-time/adjunct (0 women). *Students:* 6 full-time (1 woman), 3 part-time (0 women); includes 3 minority (1 Black or African American, non-Hispanic/Latino; 1 Asian, non-Hispanic/Latino; 1 Hispanic/Latino), 4 international. Average age 30. 13 applicants, 31% accepted, 1 enrolled. In 2016, 8 master's awarded. *Degree requirements:* For master's, comprehensive exam (for some programs), thesis optional. *Entrance requirements:* For master's, engineering license examination, minimum GPA of 2.8. Additional exam requirements/recommendations for international students: Required—TOEFL (minimum score 550 paper-based; 79 iBT); Recommended—IELTS (minimum score 6.5). *Application deadline:* For fall admission, 4/1 priority date for domestic and international students; for spring admission, 11/1 priority date for domestic and international students. Applications are processed on a rolling basis. Application fee: $50. Electronic applications accepted. *Expenses: Tuition:* Full-time $13,800; part-time $1150 per credit hour. *Required fees:* $720; $60 per credit hour. Tuition and fees vary according to course level and program. *Financial support:* Fellowships, research assistantships, and Federal Work-Study available. Support available to part-time students. Financial award application deadline: 3/1; financial award applicants required to submit FAFSA. *Faculty research:* Highway safety management, transportation, hydraulics, database structure. *Unit head:* Dr. David Olwell, Dean, Hal and Inge Marcus School of Engineering, 360-688-2731, Fax: 360-438-4522, E-mail: dolwell@stmartin.edu. *Application contact:* Casey Caronna, Administrative Assistant, 360-412-6128, E-mail: ccaronna@stmartin.edu.
Website: https://www.stmartin.edu

St. Mary's University, School of Science, Engineering and Technology, Program in Engineering Systems Management, San Antonio, TX 78228-8507. Offers MS. *Program availability:* Part-time, evening/weekend, online learning. *Faculty:* 4 full-time (0 women), 5 part-time/adjunct (0 women). *Students:* 3 full-time (2 women), 4 part-time (0 women); includes 2 minority (both Hispanic/Latino), 3 international. Average age 33. 24 applicants, 42% accepted, 4 enrolled. In 2016, 14 master's awarded. *Degree requirements:* For master's, thesis or project. *Entrance requirements:* For master's, GRE (minimum quantitative score of 148), BS in computer engineering, electrical engineering, or closely-related discipline; minimum GPA of 3.0; written statement of purpose indicating applicant's interests and objectives; two letters of recommendation. Additional exam requirements/recommendations for international students: Required—TOEFL (minimum score 550 paper-based; 80 iBT), IELTS (minimum score 6). *Application deadline:* For fall admission, 7/1 for domestic students; for spring admission, 11/15 for domestic students; for summer admission, 4/1 for domestic students. Applications are processed on a rolling basis. Application fee: $0. Electronic applications accepted. *Expenses: Tuition:* Full-time $15,600; part-time $865 per credit hour. *Required fees:* $148 per semester. *Financial support:* Career-related internships or fieldwork, Federal Work-Study, institutionally sponsored loans, scholarships/grants, and health care benefits available. Financial award application deadline: 3/31; financial award applicants required to submit FAFSA. *Faculty research:* Supply chain, financial factors in supply chains, engineering ethics, high technology and society, lean production. *Unit head:* Dr. Rafael Moras, Director, 210-431-2017, E-mail: rmoras@stmarytx.edu.
Website: https://www.stmarytx.edu/academics/set/graduate/engineering-systems-management/

Santa Clara University, School of Engineering, Santa Clara, CA 95053. Offers applied mathematics (MS); bioengineering (MS); civil engineering (MS); computer science and engineering (MS, PhD); electrical engineering (MS, PhD); engineering (Engineer); engineering management and leadership (MS); mechanical engineering (MS, PhD); software engineering (MS); sustainable energy (MS). *Program availability:* Part-time, evening/weekend. *Faculty:* 66 full-time (22 women), 59 part-time/adjunct (12 women). *Students:* 449 full-time (188 women), 315 part-time (114 women); includes 197 minority (3 Black or African American, non-Hispanic/Latino; 144 Asian, non-Hispanic/Latino; 33 Hispanic/Latino; 1 Native Hawaiian or other Pacific Islander, non-Hispanic/Latino; 16 Two or more races, non-Hispanic/Latino), 418 international. Average age 28. 1,217 applicants, 45% accepted, 293 enrolled. In 2016, 466 master's awarded. *Entrance requirements:* For master's, GRE, transcript; for doctorate, GRE, master's degree or equivalent, 3 letters of recommendation, statement of purpose; for Engineer, master's degree. Additional exam requirements/recommendations for international students: Required—TOEFL (minimum score 79 iBT) or IELTS (6.5). *Application deadline:* For fall admission, 4/1 for domestic and international students; for winter admission, 9/9 for domestic students, 9/2 for international students; for spring admission, 2/17 for domestic students, 12/9 for international students. Application fee: $60. Electronic applications accepted. *Expenses:* $928 per unit. *Financial support:* Fellowships, research assistantships, teaching assistantships, career-related internships or fieldwork, Federal Work-Study, scholarships/grants, traineeships, health care benefits, tuition waivers, and unspecified assistantships available. Support available to part-time students. Financial award applicants required to submit FAFSA. *Unit head:* Dr. Alfonso Ortega, Dean. *Application contact:* Stacey Tinker, Director of Admissions and Marketing, 408-554-4313, Fax: 408-554-4323, E-mail: stinker@scu.edu.
Website: http://www.scu.edu/engineering/graduate/

South Dakota School of Mines and Technology, Graduate Division, Program in Construction Engineering Management, Rapid City, SD 57701-3995. Offers MS. *Program availability:* Part-time, evening/weekend, online learning. *Entrance requirements:* For master's, GRE General Test. Additional exam requirements/recommendations for international students: Required—TOEFL (minimum score 520 paper-based; 68 iBT). Electronic applications accepted.

South Dakota School of Mines and Technology, Graduate Division, Program in Engineering Management, Rapid City, SD 57701-3995. Offers MS. Program offered jointly with The University of South Dakota. *Program availability:* Part-time, online learning. *Entrance requirements:* For master's, GMAT. Additional exam requirements/recommendations for international students: Required—TOEFL, TWE. Electronic applications accepted.

Southern Illinois University Carbondale, Graduate School, College of Engineering, Program in Quality Engineering Management, Carbondale, IL 62901-4701. Offers quality engineering and management (MS). *Degree requirements:* For master's, comprehensive exam, thesis. *Entrance requirements:* For master's, minimum GPA of 2.7. Additional exam requirements/recommendations for international students: Required—TOEFL. *Faculty research:* Computer-aided manufacturing, robotics, quality assurance.

Southern Methodist University, Bobby B. Lyle School of Engineering, Department of Engineering Management, Information, and Systems, Dallas, TX 75275. Offers engineering management (MSEM, DE); information engineering and management (MSIEM); operations research (MS, PhD); systems engineering (MS, PhD). *Program availability:* Part-time, evening/weekend, online learning. Terminal master's awarded for partial completion of doctoral program. *Degree requirements:* For master's, thesis optional; for doctorate, thesis/dissertation, oral and written qualifying exams. *Entrance requirements:* For master's, minimum GPA of 3.0 in last 2 years; bachelor's degree in engineering, mathematics, sciences, or technical area; for doctorate, GRE General Test (operations research, engineering management), bachelor's degree in related field. Additional exam requirements/recommendations for international students: Required—TOEFL. *Faculty research:* Telecommunications, decision systems, information engineering, operations research, software.

Stanford University, School of Engineering, Department of Management Science and Engineering, Stanford, CA 94305-2004. Offers MS, PhD. Terminal master's awarded for partial completion of doctoral program. *Degree requirements:* For doctorate, thesis/dissertation, qualification procedure. *Entrance requirements:* For master's and doctorate, GRE General Test. Additional exam requirements/recommendations for international students: Required—TOEFL. Electronic applications accepted. *Expenses: Tuition:* Full-time $47,331. *Required fees:* $609.

Stevens Institute of Technology, Graduate School, School of Business, Program in Business Administration, Hoboken, NJ 07030. Offers business intelligence and analytics (MBA); engineering management (MBA); finance (MBA); information systems (MBA); innovation and entrepreneurship (MBA); marketing (MBA); pharmaceutical management (MBA); project management (MBA, Certificate); technology management (MBA); telecommunications management (MBA). *Accreditation:* AACSB. *Program availability:* Part-time, evening/weekend. *Students:* 35 full-time (15 women), 181 part-time (79 women); includes 53 minority (10 Black or African American, non-Hispanic/Latino; 2 American Indian or Alaska Native, non-Hispanic/Latino; 36 Asian, non-Hispanic/Latino; 5 Hispanic/Latino), 30 international. Average age 32. 215 applicants, 53% accepted, 61 enrolled. In 2016, 61 master's awarded. *Degree requirements:* For master's, thesis optional, minimum B average in major field and overall; for Certificate, minimum B average. *Entrance requirements:* Additional exam requirements/recommendations for international students: Required—TOEFL (minimum score 74 iBT), IELTS (minimum score 6). *Application deadline:* For fall admission, 6/1 for domestic students, 4/15 for international students; for spring admission, 11/30 for domestic students, 11/1 for international students. Applications are processed on a rolling basis. Application fee: $65. Electronic applications accepted. *Expenses:* Contact institution. *Financial support:* Fellowships, research assistantships, teaching assistantships, career-related internships or fieldwork, Federal Work-Study, scholarships/grants, and unspecified assistantships available. Financial award application deadline: 2/15; financial award applicants required to submit FAFSA. *Unit head:* Dr. Gregory Prastacos, Dean, 201-216-8366, E-mail: gprastac@stevens.edu. *Application contact:* Graduate Admissions, 888-783-8367, Fax: 888-511-1306, E-mail: graduate@stevens.edu.
Website: https://www.stevens.edu/school-business/masters-programs/mbaemba

Stevens Institute of Technology, Graduate School, School of Systems and Enterprises, Program in Engineering Management, Hoboken, NJ 07030. Offers M Eng, PhD, Certificate. *Program availability:* Part-time, evening/weekend. *Students:* 83 full-time (28 women), 38 part-time (8 women); includes 10 minority (3 Black or African American, non-Hispanic/Latino; 4 Asian, non-Hispanic/Latino; 3 Hispanic/Latino), 71 international. Average age 26. 326 applicants, 64% accepted, 51 enrolled. In 2016, 58 master's, 1 doctorate, 6 other advanced degrees awarded. *Degree requirements:* For master's, thesis optional, minimum B average in major field and overall; for doctorate, comprehensive exam (for some programs), thesis/dissertation; for Certificate, minimum B average. *Entrance requirements:* Additional exam requirements/recommendations for international students: Required—TOEFL (minimum score 74 iBT), IELTS (minimum score 6). *Application deadline:* For fall admission, 6/1 for domestic students, 4/15 for international students; for spring admission, 11/30 for domestic students, 11/1 for international students. Applications are processed on a rolling basis. Application fee: $65. Electronic applications accepted. *Expenses:* Contact institution. *Financial support:* Fellowships, research assistantships, teaching assistantships, career-related internships or fieldwork, Federal Work-Study, scholarships/grants, and unspecified assistantships available. Financial award application deadline: 2/15; financial award applicants required to submit FAFSA. *Unit head:* Dr. Jose Ramirez-Marquez, Director, 201-216-8003, Fax: 201-216-5080, E-mail: jmarquez@stevens.edu. *Application contact:* Graduate Admissions, 888-783-8367, Fax: 888-511-1306, E-mail: graduate@stevens.edu.
Website: https://www.stevens.edu/school-systems-enterprises

Syracuse University, College of Engineering and Computer Science, MS Program in Engineering Management, Syracuse, NY 13244. Offers MS. *Program availability:* Part-time. *Students:* Average age 25. *Entrance requirements:* For master's, GRE, three letters of recommendation, personal statement, resume, official transcripts. Additional exam requirements/recommendations for international students: Required—TOEFL (minimum score 100 iBT). *Application deadline:* For fall admission, 7/1 priority date for domestic students, 6/1 priority date for international students; for spring admission, 10/1 priority date for domestic students, 11/1 priority date for international students. Applications are processed on a rolling basis. Application fee: $75. Electronic applications accepted. *Expenses:* Tuition: Full-time $25,974; part-time $1443 per credit hour. *Required fees:* $802; $50 per course. Tuition and fees vary according to course load and program. *Financial support:* Fellowships, research assistantships, and teaching assistantships available. Financial award application deadline: 1/1. *Faculty research:* Industrial energy systems, engineering education, design methodologies, second-law analysis. *Unit head:* Fred Carranti, Program Director, 315-443-4346, E-mail: carranti@syr.edu. *Application contact:* Kathleen Joyce, Assistant Dean, 315-443-2219, E-mail: topgrads@syr.edu.
Website: http://eng-cs.syr.edu/

Tarleton State University, College of Graduate Studies, College of Science and Technology, Department of Engineering Technology, Stephenville, TX 76402. Offers quality and engineering management (MS). *Program availability:* Part-time, evening/weekend, 100% online. *Faculty:* 1 (woman) full-time, 1 part-time/adjunct (0 women). *Students:* 11 full-time (0 women), 30 part-time (7 women); includes 10 minority (3 Black or African American, non-Hispanic/Latino; 7 Hispanic/Latino). 19 applicants, 95% accepted, 14 enrolled. In 2016, 5 master's awarded. *Degree requirements:* For master's, comprehensive exam, thesis optional. *Entrance requirements:* For master's, GRE General Test, minimum GPA of 3.0. Additional exam requirements/recommendations for international students: Required—TOEFL (minimum score 550 paper-based; 80 iBT). *Application deadline:* For fall admission, 8/15 for domestic students; for spring admission, 1/7 for domestic students. Applications are processed on a rolling basis. Application fee: $45 ($145 for international students). Electronic applications accepted. *Expenses:* $3,672 tuition; $2,437 fees. *Financial support:* Applicants required to submit FAFSA. *Unit head:* Billy Gray, Department Head, 254-968-9374, E-mail: bgray@tarleton.edu. *Application contact:* Information Contact, 254-968-9104, Fax: 254-968-9670, E-mail: gradoffice@tarleton.edu.
Website: http://www.tarleton.edu/degrees/masters/ms-quality-engineering-management/

Temple University, College of Engineering, Program in Engineering Management, Philadelphia, PA 19122-6096. Offers MS, Certificate. Program jointly offered with Fox School of Business and Management. *Program availability:* Part-time, evening/weekend, 100% online, blended/hybrid learning. *Faculty:* 2 full-time (0 women), 2 part-time/adjunct (1 woman). *Students:* 8 full-time (3 women), 27 part-time (6 women); includes 8 minority (3 Black or African American, non-Hispanic/Latino; 1 Asian, non-Hispanic/Latino; 3 Hispanic/Latino; 1 Two or more races, non-Hispanic/Latino), 7 international. 48 applicants, 79% accepted, 21 enrolled. In 2016, 4 master's, 15 other advanced degrees awarded. *Entrance requirements:* For master's, GRE, minimum GPA of 3.0; BS in engineering from ABET-accredited or equivalent institution or related degree; resume; goals statement; three letters of reference; official transcripts. Additional exam requirements/recommendations for international students: Required—TOEFL (minimum score 550 paper-based; 79 iBT), IELTS (minimum score 6.5), PTE (minimum score 53). *Application deadline:* For fall admission, 3/1 priority date for domestic and international students; for spring admission, 11/1 priority date for domestic students, 8/1 priority date for international students. Applications are processed on a rolling basis. Application fee: $60. Electronic applications accepted. *Expenses:* $995 per credit hour in-state tuition; $1,319 per credit hour out-of-state. *Financial support:* Federal Work-Study and scholarships/grants available. Financial award application deadline: 3/1; financial award applicants required to submit FAFSA. *Unit head:* Dr. Thomas Edwards, Director, Engineering Management Program, 215-204-7794, E-mail: tuc56565@temple.edu. *Application contact:* Leslie Levin, Director, Admissions and Graduate Student Services, 215-204-7800, Fax: 215-204-6936, E-mail: gradengr@temple.edu.
Website: http://engineering.temple.edu/department/engineering-management

Texas A&M University, College of Engineering, Department of Industrial and Systems Engineering, College Station, TX 77843. Offers engineering systems management (MS); industrial engineering (M Eng, MS, PhD). *Program availability:* Part-time, online learning. *Faculty:* 22. *Students:* 228 full-time (52 women), 62 part-time (21 women); includes 34 minority (3 Black or African American, non-Hispanic/Latino; 14 Asian, non-Hispanic/Latino; 15 Hispanic/Latino; 2 Two or more races, non-Hispanic/Latino), 222 international. Average age 26. 967 applicants, 20% accepted, 110 enrolled. In 2016, 97 master's, 11 doctorates awarded. *Degree requirements:* For master's, comprehensive exam (for some programs), thesis optional; for doctorate, comprehensive exam, thesis/dissertation. *Entrance requirements:* For master's and doctorate, GRE General Test. Additional exam requirements/recommendations for international students: Required—TOEFL (minimum score 550 paper-based; 80 iBT), IELTS (minimum score 6), PTE (minimum score 53). *Application deadline:* For fall admission, 6/1 priority date for domestic students, 3/1 priority date for international students; for spring admission, 8/1 priority date for domestic and international students. Applications are processed on a rolling basis. Application fee: $50 ($90 for international students). Electronic applications accepted. *Expenses:* Contact institution. *Financial support:* In 2016–17, 165 students received support, including 7 fellowships with tuition reimbursements available (averaging $14,315 per year), 62 research assistantships with tuition reimbursements available (averaging $5,401 per year), 31 teaching assistantships with tuition reimbursements available (averaging $8,551 per year); career-related internships or fieldwork, institutionally sponsored loans, scholarships/grants, traineeships, health care benefits, tuition waivers (full and partial), and unspecified assistantships also available. Support available to part-time students. Financial award application deadline: 3/15; financial award applicants required to submit FAFSA. *Faculty research:* Manufacturing systems, computer integration, operations research, logistics, simulation. *Unit head:* Dr. Cesar O. Malave, Head, 979-845-5535, Fax: 979-458-4299, E-mail: malave@tamu.edu. *Application contact:* Erin Roady, Graduate Program Coordinator, 979-845-5536, Fax: 979-458-4299, E-mail: erinroady@tamu.edu.
Website: http://engineering.tamu.edu/industrial

Texas Tech University, Graduate School, Edward E. Whitacre Jr. College of Engineering, Department of Industrial, Manufacturing, and Systems Engineering, Lubbock, TX 79409-3061. Offers industrial engineering (MSIE, PhD); systems and engineering management (MSSEM, PhD). *Program availability:* Part-time, 100% online, blended/hybrid learning. *Faculty:* 13 full-time (2 women). *Students:* 90 full-time (15 women), 97 part-time (14 women); includes 25 minority (9 Black or African American, non-Hispanic/Latino; 1 American Indian or Alaska Native, non-Hispanic/Latino; 2 Asian, non-Hispanic/Latino; 11 Hispanic/Latino; 2 Two or more races, non-Hispanic/Latino), 102 international. Average age 32. 376 applicants, 38% accepted, 48 enrolled. In 2016, 43 master's, 7 doctorates awarded. Terminal master's awarded for partial completion of doctoral program. *Degree requirements:* For master's, comprehensive exam, thesis optional; for doctorate, comprehensive exam, thesis/dissertation. *Entrance requirements:* For master's and doctorate, GRE (Verbal and Quantitative). Additional exam requirements/recommendations for international students: Required—TOEFL (minimum score 550 paper-based; 79 iBT). *Application deadline:* For fall admission, 6/1 priority date for domestic students, 1/15 priority date for international students; for spring admission, 9/1 priority date for domestic students, 6/15 priority date for international students. Applications are processed on a rolling basis. Application fee: $75. Electronic applications accepted. *Expenses:* $325 per credit hour full-time resident tuition, $733 per credit hour full-time non-resident tuition; $53.75 per credit hour fee plus $608 per term fee. *Financial support:* In 2016–17, 73 students received support, including 71 fellowships (averaging $2,464 per year), 9 research assistantships (averaging $15,691 per year), 21 teaching assistantships (averaging $21,474 per year); scholarships/grants, tuition waivers (partial), and unspecified assistantships also available. Financial award application deadline: 2/1; financial award applicants required to submit FAFSA. *Faculty research:* Ergonomics and human factors engineering, manufacturing systems, operations research, statistics and quality assurance, systems and engineering management. Total annual research expenditures: $282,884. *Unit head:* Dr. Hong-Chao Zhang, Interim Chair, 806-742-3543, E-mail: hong-chao.zhang@ttu.edu. *Application contact:* Dr. Jennifer Cross, Associate Professor, 806-742-3543, Fax: 806-742-3411, E-mail: jennifer.cross@ttu.edu.
Website: http://www.ie.ttu.edu/

Tufts University, School of Engineering, The Gordon Institute, Medford, MA 02155. Offers engineering management (MSEM); innovation and management (MS). *Program availability:* Part-time. *Entrance requirements:* Additional exam requirements/recommendations for international students: Required—TOEFL (minimum score 550 paper-based; 80 iBT), IELTS (minimum score 6.5). Electronic applications accepted. *Expenses:* Contact institution. *Faculty research:* Engineering management, engineering leadership.

Université de Sherbrooke, Faculty of Engineering, Programs in Engineering Management, Sherbrooke, QC J1K 2R1, Canada. Offers M Eng, Diploma. *Program availability:* Part-time, evening/weekend. *Entrance requirements:* For master's and Diploma, bachelor's degree in engineering, 1 year of practical experience. Electronic applications accepted.

The University of Alabama at Birmingham, School of Engineering, Program in Mechanical Engineering, Birmingham, AL 35294. Offers advanced safety engineering and management (M Eng); mechanical engineering (MSME). *Faculty:* 8 full-time, 2 part-time/adjunct. *Students:* 44 full-time (5 women), 10 part-time (2 women); includes 2 minority (1 Black or African American, non-Hispanic/Latino; 1 Asian, non-Hispanic/Latino), 8 international. Average age 27. 22 applicants, 73% accepted, 2 enrolled. In 2016, 9 master's awarded. *Degree requirements:* For master's, thesis (for some programs). *Entrance requirements:* For master's, GRE (minimum 50th percentile ranking on Quantitative Reasoning and Verbal Reasoning sections), minimum B average overall or over last 60 semester hours of earned credit. Additional exam requirements/recommendations for international students: Required—TOEFL (minimum score 80 iBT). *Application deadline:* For fall admission, 7/1 for domestic students; for spring admission, 11/1 for domestic students; for summer admission, 4/1 for domestic students. Applications are processed on a rolling basis. Application fee: $50 ($60 for international students). Electronic applications accepted. *Expenses:* $396 per hour resident tuition; $935 per hour non-resident tuition; $150 per course online course fee. *Financial support:* In 2016–17, 18 students received support, including 1 fellowship with full tuition reimbursement available (averaging $10,000 per year), 7 research assistantships with full tuition reimbursements available (averaging $22,000 per year), 10 teaching assistantships (averaging $2,500 per year). Total annual research expenditures: $2 million. *Unit head:* Dr. David Littlefield, Graduate Program Director, 205-934-8460, E-mail: littlefield@uab.edu. *Application contact:* Holly Hebard, Director of Graduate School Operations, 205-934-8227, Fax: 205-934-8413, E-mail: gradschool@uab.edu.
Website: http://www.uab.edu/engineering/home/departments-research/me/graduate

University of Alaska Anchorage, School of Engineering, Program in Engineering Management, Anchorage, AK 99508. Offers MS. *Program availability:* Part-time, evening/weekend. *Degree requirements:* For master's, comprehensive exam (for some programs), thesis optional. *Entrance requirements:* For master's, BS in engineering or science, work experience in engineering or science. Additional exam requirements/recommendations for international students: Required—TOEFL (minimum score 550 paper-based). *Faculty research:* Engineering economy, long-range forecasting, multicriteria design making, project management process and training.

University of Alaska Anchorage, School of Engineering, Program in Science Management, Anchorage, AK 99508. Offers MS. *Program availability:* Part-time, evening/weekend. *Degree requirements:* For master's, comprehensive exam (for some programs), thesis (for some programs). *Entrance requirements:* For master's, GRE General Test, BS in engineering or scientific field. Additional exam requirements/recommendations for international students: Required—TOEFL (minimum score 550 paper-based). *Faculty research:* Engineering economy, long-range forecasting, multicriteria decision making, project management process and training.

University of Alberta, Faculty of Graduate Studies and Research, Department of Mechanical Engineering, Edmonton, AB T6G 2E1, Canada. Offers engineering management (M Eng); mechanical engineering (M Eng, M Sc, PhD); MBA/M Eng. *Program availability:* Part-time. *Degree requirements:* For master's, thesis; for doctorate, thesis/dissertation. *Entrance requirements:* For master's and doctorate, minimum GPA of 7.0 on a 9.0 scale. Additional exam requirements/recommendations for international students: Required—TOEFL (minimum score 580 paper-based). *Faculty research:*

Combustion and environmental issues, advanced materials, computational fluid dynamics, biomedical, acoustics and vibrations.

The University of Arizona, College of Engineering, Department of Systems and Industrial Engineering, Tucson, AZ 85721. Offers engineering management (Graduate Certificate); industrial engineering (MS); systems and industrial engineering (MS, PhD); systems engineering (MS, PhD, Graduate Certificate). *Program availability:* Part-time, online learning. *Degree requirements:* For doctorate, thesis/dissertation. *Entrance requirements:* For master's, GRE General Test (minimum score: 500 Verbal, 700 Quantitative), 3 letters of recommendation; for doctorate, GRE General Test (minimum score: 500 Verbal, 700 Quantitative), minimum GPA of 3.5, 3 letters of recommendation, letter of intent. Additional exam requirements/recommendations for international students: Required—TOEFL (minimum score 575 paper-based; 80 iBT). Electronic applications accepted. *Faculty research:* Optimization, systems theory, logistics, transportation, embedded systems.

University of California, Berkeley, Graduate Division, College of Engineering, Department of Civil and Environmental Engineering, Berkeley, CA 94720-1500. Offers engineering and project management (M Eng, MS, PhD); environmental engineering (M Eng, MS, PhD); geoengineering (M Eng, MS, PhD); structural engineering, mechanics and materials (M Eng, MS, PhD); transportation engineering (M Eng, MS, PhD); M Arch/MS; MCP/MS; MPP/MS. *Students:* 360 full-time (143 women); includes 71 minority (15 Black or African American, non-Hispanic/Latino; 39 Asian, non-Hispanic/Latino; 17 Hispanic/Latino), 148 international. Average age 27. 1,086 applicants, 185 enrolled. In 2016, 188 master's, 26 doctorates awarded. Terminal master's awarded for partial completion of doctoral program. *Degree requirements:* For master's, comprehensive exam (for some programs), thesis (for some programs), comprehensive exam or thesis (MS); for doctorate, thesis/dissertation, qualifying exam. *Entrance requirements:* For master's, GRE General Test, minimum GPA of 3.0, 3 letters of recommendation; for doctorate, GRE General Test, minimum GPA of 3.5, 3 letters of recommendation. Additional exam requirements/recommendations for international students: Required—TOEFL (minimum score 570 paper-based; 90 iBT). *Application deadline:* For fall admission, 12/16 for domestic students. Application fee: $105 ($125 for international students). Electronic applications accepted. *Financial support:* Applicants required to submit FAFSA. *Unit head:* Prof. Robert Harley, Chair, 510-643-8739, Fax: 510-643-5264, E-mail: chair@ce.berkeley.edu. *Application contact:* Shelly Okimoto, Graduate Advisor, 510-642-6464, Fax: 510-643-5264, E-mail: aao@ce.berkeley.edu.
Website: http://www.ce.berkeley.edu/

University of California, Irvine, Henry Samueli School of Engineering, Program in Engineering Management, Irvine, CA 92697. Offers MS. Program offered jointly with the Paul Merage School of Business. *Students:* 15 full-time (7 women); includes 3 minority (all Asian, non-Hispanic/Latino), 11 international. Average age 24. 250 applicants, 22% accepted, 15 enrolled. In 2016, 15 master's awarded. *Application deadline:* For fall admission, 1/15 priority date for domestic students. Applications are processed on a rolling basis. Application fee: $105 ($125 for international students). *Application contact:* Jean Bennett, Director of Graduate Student Affairs, 949-824-6475, Fax: 949-824-8200, E-mail: jean.bennett@uci.edu.
Website: http://www.eng.uci.edu/admissions/graduate/programs-and-concentrations/engineering-management

University of Colorado Boulder, Graduate School, College of Engineering and Applied Science, Engineering Management Program, Boulder, CO 80309. Offers ME. *Students:* 79 full-time (20 women), 100 part-time (15 women); includes 35 minority (6 Black or African American, non-Hispanic/Latino; 9 Asian, non-Hispanic/Latino; 14 Hispanic/Latino; 6 Two or more races, non-Hispanic/Latino), 12 international. Average age 34. 74 applicants, 59% accepted, 31 enrolled. *Entrance requirements:* For master's, minimum undergraduate GPA of 3.0. *Application deadline:* For fall admission, 3/15 for domestic students, 1/15 for international students; for spring admission, 10/15 for domestic students, 8/5 for international students. Application fee: $60 ($80 for international students). Electronic applications accepted. Application fee is waived when completed online. *Financial support:* In 2016–17, 48 students received support, including 6 fellowships (averaging $3,117 per year), 1 research assistantship with full and partial tuition reimbursement available (averaging $12,836 per year); institutionally sponsored loans, scholarships/grants, health care benefits, and unspecified assistantships also available. Financial award applicants required to submit FAFSA. *Faculty research:* Quality and process, research and development, operations and logistics. *Total annual research expenditures:* $249. *Application contact:* E-mail: emp@colorado.edu.
Website: http://engineeringanywhere.colorado.edu/emp

University of Colorado Colorado Springs, College of Engineering and Applied Science, Program in General Engineering, Colorado Springs, CO 80918. Offers energy engineering (ME); engineering management (ME); information assurance (ME); software engineering (ME); space operations (ME); systems engineering (ME). *Program availability:* Part-time, evening/weekend, blended/hybrid learning. *Faculty:* 1 full-time (0 women), 15 part-time/adjunct (6 women). *Students:* 18 full-time (3 women), 166 part-time (34 women); includes 36 minority (6 Black or African American, non-Hispanic/Latino; 8 Asian, non-Hispanic/Latino; 12 Hispanic/Latino; 10 Two or more races, non-Hispanic/Latino), 57 international. Average age 36. 89 applicants, 72% accepted, 41 enrolled. In 2016, 21 master's, 8 doctorates awarded. *Degree requirements:* For master's, thesis, portfolio, or project; for doctorate, comprehensive exam, thesis/dissertation. *Entrance requirements:* For master's, GRE (minimum score of 148 new grading scale on quantitative portion if undergraduate GPA is less than 3.0); for doctorate, GRE (minimum score of 148 new grading scale on the quantitative portion if the applicant has not graduated from a program of recognized standing), minimum GPA of 3.3 in the bachelor's or master's degree program attempted. Additional exam requirements/recommendations for international students: Required—TOEFL (minimum score 80 iBT), IELTS (minimum score 6). *Application deadline:* For fall admission, 7/1 for domestic students, 6/1 for international students; for spring admission, 11/1 for domestic and international students; for summer admission, 4/15 for domestic and international students. Applications are processed on a rolling basis. Application fee: $60 ($100 for international students). Electronic applications accepted. *Expenses:* Contact institution. *Financial support:* In 2016–17, 28 students received support. Federal Work-Study, scholarships/grants, traineeships, and unspecified assistantships available. Support available to part-time students. Financial award application deadline: 3/1; financial award applicants required to submit FAFSA. *Unit head:* Dr. Ramaswami Dandapani, Dean, 719-255-3543, Fax: 719-255-3542, E-mail: rdan@cas.uccs.edu. *Application contact:* Dawn House, Coordinator, 719-255-3246, E-mail: dhouse@uccs.edu.

University of Dayton, Department of Engineering Management and Systems, Dayton, OH 45469. Offers engineering management (MSEM); management science (MSMS). *Program availability:* Part-time, evening/weekend, blended/hybrid learning. *Faculty:* 4 full-time (1 woman), 9 part-time/adjunct (1 woman). *Students:* 40 full-time (8 women), 23 part-time (7 women); includes 8 minority (4 Black or African American, non-Hispanic/Latino; 1 Asian, non-Hispanic/Latino; 1 Hispanic/Latino; 2 Two or more races, non-Hispanic/Latino), 18 international. Average age 31. 205 applicants, 16% accepted. In 2016, 27 master's awarded. *Degree requirements:* For master's, 7 core courses/5 electives (for MSEM); 4 core courses/8 electives (for MSMS); capstone project. *Entrance requirements:* For master's, minimum GPA of 3.0; undergraduate degree from accredited program in engineering, engineering technology, math or science (for engineering management); undergraduate degree with at least three semesters of analytic geometry and calculus, and linear algebra background (for management science). Additional exam requirements/recommendations for international students: Required—TOEFL (minimum score 550 paper-based; 80 iBT). *Application deadline:* Applications are processed on a rolling basis. Application fee: $0 ($50 for international students). Electronic applications accepted. *Expenses:* $890 per credit hour, $25 registration fee. *Financial support:* Application deadline: 3/1; applicants required to submit FAFSA. *Faculty research:* Modeling and simulation analysis, statistical experimental design, reliability and maintainability, operations research modeling, engineering education. *Total annual research expenditures:* $135,000. *Unit head:* Dr. Edward Mykytka, Chair, 937-229-2238, E-mail: emykytka1@udayton.edu. *Application contact:* 937-229-4462, E-mail: graduateadmission@udayton.edu.
Website: http://www.udayton.edu/engineering/departments/engineering_management_and_systems

University of Denver, Daniel Felix Ritchie School of Engineering and Computer Science, Department of Mechanical and Materials Engineering, Denver, CO 80208. Offers bioengineering (MS); engineering (MS, PhD), including management (MS); materials science (MS, PhD); mechanical engineering (MS, PhD). *Program availability:* Part-time. *Faculty:* 11 full-time (1 woman), 2 part-time/adjunct (both women). *Students:* 2 full-time (0 women), 27 part-time (7 women); includes 6 minority (1 Asian, non-Hispanic/Latino; 5 Hispanic/Latino), 13 international. Average age 28. 57 applicants, 79% accepted, 13 enrolled. In 2016, 11 master's, 5 doctorates awarded. Terminal master's awarded for partial completion of doctoral program. *Degree requirements:* For master's, thesis optional; for doctorate, comprehensive exam, thesis/dissertation. *Entrance requirements:* For master's, GRE General Test, bachelor's degree, transcripts, personal statement, resume or curriculum vitae, two letters of recommendation; for doctorate, GRE General Test, master's degree, transcripts, personal statement, resume or curriculum vitae, two letters of recommendation. Additional exam requirements/recommendations for international students: Required—TOEFL (minimum score 550 paper-based; 80 iBT). *Application deadline:* For fall admission, 2/1 priority date for domestic and international students. Applications are processed on a rolling basis. Application fee: $65. Electronic applications accepted. *Expenses:* $29,022 per year full-time. *Financial support:* In 2016–17, 15 students received support, including 4 research assistantships with tuition reimbursements available (averaging $11,667 per year), 5 teaching assistantships with tuition reimbursements available (averaging $12,084 per year); Federal Work-Study, institutionally sponsored loans, scholarships/grants, health care benefits, and unspecified assistantships also available. Financial award application deadline: 2/15; financial award applicants required to submit FAFSA. *Faculty research:* Cardiac biomechanics, novel high voltage/temperature materials and structures, high speed stereo radiography, musculoskeletal modeling, composites. *Total annual research expenditures:* $996,915. *Unit head:* Dr. Matt Gordon, Professor and Chair, 303-871-3580, Fax: 303-871-4450, E-mail: matthew.gordon@du.edu. *Application contact:* Yvonne Petitt, Assistant to the Chair, 303-871-2107, Fax: 303-871-4450, E-mail: yvonne.petitt@du.edu.
Website: http://ritchieschool.du.edu/departments/mme/

University of Detroit Mercy, College of Engineering and Science, Detroit, MI 48221. Offers chemistry (MS); civil and environmental engineering (DE); electrical and computer engineering (ME); electrical engineering (DE); engineering management (M Eng Mgt); environmental engineering (MEE); mechanical engineering (MME, DE); product development (MS); software engineering (MSSE); teaching of mathematics (MATM). *Program availability:* Part-time, evening/weekend. *Degree requirements:* For doctorate, thesis/dissertation. Electronic applications accepted. Application fee is waived when completed online. *Expenses:* Contact institution.

University of Idaho, College of Graduate Studies, College of Engineering, Department of Civil Engineering, Moscow, ID 83844. Offers civil engineering (M Engr, MS, PhD); engineering management (M Engr); geological engineering (MS). *Faculty:* 17 full-time, 3 part-time/adjunct. *Students:* 19 full-time, 64 part-time. Average age 34. In 2016, 31 master's, 2 doctorates awarded. *Entrance requirements:* For master's and doctorate, minimum GPA of 3.0. Additional exam requirements/recommendations for international students: Required—TOEFL. *Application deadline:* For fall admission, 8/1 for domestic students; for spring admission, 12/15 for domestic students. Applications are processed on a rolling basis. Application fee: $60. Electronic applications accepted. *Expenses:* Tuition, state resident: full-time $6460; part-time $414 per credit hour. Tuition, nonresident: full-time $21,268; part-time $1237 per credit hour. *Required fees:* $2070; $60 per credit hour. Full-time tuition and fees vary according to course load and reciprocity agreements. *Financial support:* Fellowships, research assistantships, teaching assistantships, and career-related internships or fieldwork available. Financial award applicants required to submit FAFSA. *Unit head:* Patricia Colberg, Department Chair, 208-885-6782, E-mail: civilengr@uidaho.edu. *Application contact:* Sean Scoggin, Graduate Recruitment Coordinator, 208-885-4001, Fax: 208-885-4406, E-mail: graduateadmissions@uidaho.edu.
Website: http://www.uidaho.edu/engr/ce/

The University of Kansas, Graduate Studies, School of Engineering, Program in Engineering Management, Overland Park, KS 66213. Offers MS, Certificate. *Program availability:* Part-time, evening/weekend, online learning. *Students:* 4 full-time (0 women), 86 part-time (16 women); includes 17 minority (4 Black or African American, non-Hispanic/Latino; 9 Asian, non-Hispanic/Latino; 3 Hispanic/Latino; 1 Two or more races, non-Hispanic/Latino), 12 international. Average age 32. 34 applicants, 50% accepted, 12 enrolled. In 2016, 30 master's awarded. *Entrance requirements:* For master's, minimum GPA of 3.0, 2 years of industrial experience, BS in engineering or related science. Additional exam requirements/recommendations for international students: Required—TOEFL (minimum score 600 paper-based, 100 iBT) or IELTS. Application fee: $65 ($85 for international students). Electronic applications accepted. *Faculty research:* Project management, systems analysis, high performance teams, manufacturing systems, strategic analysis. *Unit head:* Herbert R. Tuttle, Director, 913-897-8561, E-mail: htuttle@ku.edu. *Application contact:* Jennifer Keleher-Price, Program Advisor, 913-897-8560, E-mail: jkeleher-price@ku.edu.
Website: http://emgt.ku.edu/

University of Louisiana at Lafayette, College of Engineering, Department of Engineering and Technology Management, Lafayette, LA 70504. Offers MSET. *Program availability:* Part-time, evening/weekend. *Degree requirements:* For master's, comprehensive exam, thesis or alternative. *Entrance requirements:* For master's, GRE General Test, minimum GPA of 2.85. Additional exam requirements/recommendations for international students: Required—TOEFL (minimum score 550 paper-based). Electronic applications accepted. *Faculty research:* Mathematical programming, production management forecasting.

University of Louisville, J. B. Speed School of Engineering, Department of Industrial Engineering, Louisville, KY 40292-0001. Offers engineering management (M Eng); industrial engineering (M Eng, MS, PhD); logistics and distribution (Certificate). *Accreditation:* ABET (one or more programs are accredited). *Program availability:* 100% online. *Faculty:* 7 full-time (4 women), 5 part-time/adjunct (2 women). *Students:* 68 full-

time (19 women), 129 part-time (22 women); includes 25 minority (10 Black or African American, non-Hispanic/Latino; 1 American Indian or Alaska Native, non-Hispanic/Latino; 6 Asian, non-Hispanic/Latino; 3 Hispanic/Latino; 5 Two or more races, non-Hispanic/Latino), 86 international. Average age 32. 93 applicants, 44% accepted, 25 enrolled. In 2016, 33 master's, 3 doctorates awarded. *Degree requirements:* For master's and Certificate, thesis optional; for doctorate, comprehensive exam, thesis/dissertation. *Entrance requirements:* For master's and doctorate, GRE General Test, two letters of recommendation, official transcripts. Additional exam requirements/recommendations for international students: Required—TOEFL (minimum score 550 paper-based; 80 iBT), IELTS (minimum score 6.5). *Application deadline:* For fall admission, 5/1 priority date for international students; for spring admission, 11/1 priority date for international students; for summer admission, 3/1 priority date for international students. Applications are processed on a rolling basis. Application fee: $60. Electronic applications accepted. *Expenses:* Tuition, state resident: full-time $12,246; part-time $681 per credit hour. Tuition, nonresident: full-time $25,486; part-time $1417 per credit hour. *Required fees:* $196. Tuition and fees vary according to program and reciprocity agreements. *Financial support:* In 2016–17, 2 fellowships with full tuition reimbursements (averaging $22,000 per year) were awarded; research assistantships with full tuition reimbursements, teaching assistantships with full tuition reimbursements, scholarships/grants, health care benefits, and tuition waivers (full) also available. Financial award application deadline: 1/1; financial award applicants required to submit FAFSA. *Faculty research:* Optimization, computer simulation, logistics and distribution, ergonomics and human factors, advanced manufacturing process. *Total annual research expenditures:* $620,986. *Unit head:* Dr. Suraj M. Alexander, Chair, 502-852-6342, E-mail: usher@louisville.edu. *Application contact:* Lihui Bai, Director of Graduate Studies, 502-852-1416, E-mail: lihui.bai@louisville.edu.
Website: http://www.louisville.edu/speed/industrial/

University of Management and Technology, Program in Engineering Management, Arlington, VA 22209-1609. Offers MS.

The University of Manchester, School of Mechanical, Aerospace and Civil Engineering, Manchester, United Kingdom. Offers advanced manufacturing technology (M Ent); aerospace engineering (M Phil, M Sc, PhD); civil engineering (M Phil, M Sc, PhD); environmental engineering (M Phil, PhD); management of projects (M Phil, M Sc, PhD); mechanical engineering (M Phil, M Sc, PhD); mechanical engineering design (M Ent); nuclear engineering (M Phil, D Eng, PhD).

University of Maryland, Baltimore County, The Graduate School, Program in Engineering Management, Baltimore, MD 21227. Offers MS, Postbaccalaureate Certificate. *Program availability:* Part-time. *Faculty:* 2 full-time (0 women), 3 part-time/adjunct (0 women). *Students:* 16 full-time (4 women), 49 part-time (13 women); includes 16 minority (9 Black or African American, non-Hispanic/Latino; 3 Asian, non-Hispanic/Latino; 2 Hispanic/Latino; 2 Two or more races, non-Hispanic/Latino), 16 international. Average age 32. 77 applicants, 65% accepted, 21 enrolled. In 2016, 42 master's, 13 other advanced degrees awarded. *Degree requirements:* For master's, comprehensive exam (for some programs), thesis optional. *Entrance requirements:* For master's, BS in engineering, computer science, mathematics, physics, chemistry, or other physical sciences; two letters of recommendation (for international students). Additional exam requirements/recommendations for international students: Required—TOEFL (minimum score 550 paper-based; 80 iBT), GRE General Test. *Application deadline:* For fall admission, 7/1 for domestic and international students; for spring admission, 12/1 for domestic and international students. Applications are processed on a rolling basis. Application fee: $70. Electronic applications accepted. *Expenses:* Tuition, state resident: full-time $13,294. Tuition, nonresident: full-time $20,286. *Financial support:* Career-related internships or fieldwork, Federal Work-Study, scholarships/grants, health care benefits, and unspecified assistantships available. Support available to part-time students. Financial award application deadline: 6/30; financial award applicants required to submit FAFSA. *Faculty research:* Regulatory engineering, environmental engineering, systems engineering, advanced manufacturing, chemical engineering. *Unit head:* Dr. Anupam Joshi, Professor and Chair, 410-455-3500, Fax: 410-455-3969, E-mail: joshi@umbc.edu. *Application contact:* Dr. Thomas M. Moore, Lecturer/Graduate Program Director, 410-455-1151, E-mail: mooretg@umbc.edu.

University of Michigan–Dearborn, College of Engineering and Computer Science, MS Program in Engineering Management, Dearborn, MI 48128. Offers MS. *Program availability:* Part-time, evening/weekend, 100% online. *Faculty:* 8 full-time (2 women), 4 part-time/adjunct (0 women). *Students:* 8 full-time (1 woman), 123 part-time (26 women); includes 23 minority (4 Black or African American, non-Hispanic/Latino; 9 Asian, non-Hispanic/Latino; 8 Hispanic/Latino; 2 Two or more races, non-Hispanic/Latino), 22 international. Average age 30. 83 applicants, 60% accepted, 38 enrolled. In 2016, 21 master's awarded. *Entrance requirements:* Additional exam requirements/recommendations for international students: Required—TOEFL (minimum score 560 paper-based; 84 iBT), IELTS (minimum score 6.5). *Application deadline:* For fall admission, 8/1 for domestic students, 5/1 for international students; for winter admission, 12/1 for domestic students, 9/1 for international students; for spring admission, 4/1 for domestic students, 1/1 for international students. Applications are processed on a rolling basis. Application fee: $60. Electronic applications accepted. *Expenses:* Tuition, state resident: full-time $13,118; part-time $2280 per term. Tuition, nonresident: full-time $21,816; part-time $3771 per term. *Required fees:* $866; $658 per unit. $329 per term. Tuition and fees vary according to program. *Financial support:* Scholarships/grants, unspecified assistantships, and non-resident tuition scholarships available. Support available to part-time students. Financial award application deadline: 3/1; financial award applicants required to submit FAFSA. *Faculty research:* Integrated design, operations research and decision science, supply chain management, engineering management. *Unit head:* Dr. Armen Zakarian, Chair, 313-593-5361, Fax: 313-593-3692, E-mail: zakarian@umich.edu. *Application contact:* Office of Graduate Studies, 313-583-6321, E-mail: umd-graduatestudies@umich.edu.
Website: https://umdearborn.edu/cecs/departments/industrial-and-manufacturing-systems-engineering/graduate-programs/ms-engineering-management

University of Minnesota, Duluth, Graduate School, Swenson College of Science and Engineering, Department of Mechanical and Industrial Engineering, Duluth, MN 55812-2496. Offers engineering management (MSEM); environmental health and safety (MEHS). *Program availability:* Part-time, evening/weekend, online learning. *Degree requirements:* For master's, comprehensive exam, thesis or alternative, capstone design project (MSEM), field project (MEHS). *Entrance requirements:* For master's, GRE (MEHS), interview (MEHS), letters of recommendation. Additional exam requirements/recommendations for international students: Required—TOEFL (minimum score 550 paper-based). *Faculty research:* Transportation, ergonomics, toxicology, supply chain management, automation and robotics.

University of Missouri–Kansas City, School of Computing and Engineering, Kansas City, MO 64110-2499. Offers civil engineering (MS); computer and electrical engineering (PhD); computer science (MS), including bioinformatics, software engineering, telecommunications networking; computer science and informatics (PhD); computing (PhD); electrical engineering (MS); engineering (PhD); engineering and construction management (Graduate Certificate); mechanical engineering (MS); telecommunications and computer networking (PhD). PhD (interdisciplinary) offered through the School of Graduate Studies. *Program availability:* Part-time. *Faculty:* 45 full-time (6 women), 26 part-time/adjunct (4 women). *Students:* 473 full-time (155 women), 207 part-time (42 women); includes 24 minority (10 Black or African American, non-Hispanic/Latino; 10 Asian, non-Hispanic/Latino; 4 Hispanic/Latino), 581 international. Average age 25. 1,143 applicants, 44% accepted, 227 enrolled. In 2016, 446 master's, 2 other advanced degrees awarded. *Degree requirements:* For doctorate, thesis/dissertation. *Entrance requirements:* For master's, GRE General Test, minimum GPA of 3.0, 3 letters of recommendation from professors; for doctorate, GRE General Test, minimum GPA of 3.5. Additional exam requirements/recommendations for international students: Required—TOEFL (minimum score 550 paper-based; 80 iBT). *Application deadline:* For fall admission, 1/15 priority date for domestic students, 1/15 for international students. Applications are processed on a rolling basis. Application fee: $45 ($50 for international students). *Financial support:* In 2016–17, 37 research assistantships with partial tuition reimbursements (averaging $15,679 per year), 47 teaching assistantships with partial tuition reimbursements (averaging $16,830 per year) were awarded; career-related internships or fieldwork, Federal Work-Study, scholarships/grants, tuition waivers (partial), and unspecified assistantships also available. Support available to part-time students. Financial award application deadline: 3/1; financial award applicants required to submit FAFSA. *Faculty research:* Algorithms, bioinformatics and medical informatics, biomechanics/biomaterials, civil engineering materials, networking and telecommunications, thermal science. *Unit head:* Dr. Kevin Z. Truman, Dean, 816-235-2399, Fax: 816-235-5159. *Application contact:* 816-235-2399, Fax: 816-235-5159.
Website: http://sce.umkc.edu/

University of Nebraska–Lincoln, Graduate College, College of Engineering, Department of Industrial and Management Systems Engineering, Lincoln, NE 68588. Offers engineering management (M Eng); industrial and management systems engineering (MS, PhD); manufacturing systems engineering (MS). *Program availability:* Online learning. *Degree requirements:* For master's, thesis optional; for doctorate, comprehensive exam, thesis/dissertation. *Entrance requirements:* For master's and doctorate, GRE. Additional exam requirements/recommendations for international students: Required—TOEFL (minimum score 525 paper-based). Electronic applications accepted. *Faculty research:* Ergonomics, occupational safety, quality control, industrial packaging, facility design.

University of New Brunswick Fredericton, School of Graduate Studies, Faculty of Business Administration, Fredericton, NB E3B 5A3, Canada. Offers business administration (MBA); engineering management (MBA); entrepreneurship (MBA); sports and recreation management (MBA); MBA/LL B. *Program availability:* Part-time. *Degree requirements:* For master's, thesis optional. *Entrance requirements:* For master's, GMAT (minimum score 550), minimum GPA of 3.0; 3-5 years of work experience; 3 letters of reference with at least one academic reference. Additional exam requirements/recommendations for international students: Required—TOEFL (minimum score 580 paper-based; 92 iBT) or IELTS (minimum score 7). Electronic applications accepted. *Faculty research:* Entrepreneurship, finance, law, sport and recreation management, engineering management.

University of New Haven, Graduate School, Tagliatela College of Engineering, Program in Engineering and Operations Management, West Haven, CT 06516. Offers engineering and operations management (MS); engineering management (MS); Lean Six Sigma (Graduate Certificate). *Program availability:* Part-time. *Students:* 32 full-time (8 women), 33 part-time (3 women); includes 6 minority (3 Black or African American, non-Hispanic/Latino; 2 Asian, non-Hispanic/Latino; 1 Hispanic/Latino), 31 international. Average age 30. 141 applicants, 68% accepted, 26 enrolled. In 2016, 58 master's awarded. *Entrance requirements:* Additional exam requirements/recommendations for international students: Required—TOEFL (minimum score 75 iBT), IELTS, PTE (minimum score 50). *Application deadline:* Applications are processed on a rolling basis. Application fee: $50. Electronic applications accepted. Application fee is waived when completed online. *Expenses: Tuition:* Full-time $15,660; part-time $870 per credit hour. *Required fees:* $200; $85 per term. Tuition and fees vary according to program. *Unit head:* Dr. Ali Montazer, Program Director, 203-932-7050, E-mail: amontazer@newhaven.edu. *Application contact:* Michelle Mason, Director of Graduate Enrollment, 203-932-7067, E-mail: mmason@newhaven.edu.
Website: http://www.newhaven.edu/88389/

University of New Orleans, Graduate School, College of Engineering, Program in Engineering Management, New Orleans, LA 70148. Offers MS. *Degree requirements:* For master's, thesis optional. *Entrance requirements:* For master's, GRE General Test, minimum GPA of 3.0. Additional exam requirements/recommendations for international students: Required—TOEFL (minimum score 550 paper-based; 79 iBT). Electronic applications accepted.

The University of North Carolina at Charlotte, William States Lee College of Engineering, Department of Systems Engineering and Engineering Management, Charlotte, NC 28223-0001. Offers energy analytics (Graduate Certificate); engineering management (MSEM); Lean Six Sigma (Graduate Certificate); logistics and supply chains (Graduate Certificate); systems analytics (Graduate Certificate). *Program availability:* Part-time, evening/weekend, 100% online, blended/hybrid learning. *Faculty:* 9 full-time (1 woman), 2 part-time/adjunct (1 woman). *Students:* 22 full-time (10 women), 61 part-time (12 women); includes 13 minority (7 Black or African American, non-Hispanic/Latino; 1 Asian, non-Hispanic/Latino; 4 Hispanic/Latino; 1 Two or more races, non-Hispanic/Latino), 29 international. Average age 30. 210 applicants, 56% accepted, 31 enrolled. In 2016, 44 master's, 5 other advanced degrees awarded. *Degree requirements:* For master's, project or thesis. *Entrance requirements:* For master's, GRE or GMAT, bachelor's degree in engineering or a closely-related technical or scientific field, or in business, provided relevant technical course requirements have been met; undergraduate coursework in engineering economics, calculus, or statistics; minimum GPA of 3.0; for Graduate Certificate, bachelor's degree in engineering or closely-related technical or scientific field, or bachelor's degree in business, provided relevant technical course requirements have been met; minimum GPA of 3.0; undergraduate coursework in engineering economics, calculus, and statistics; written description of work experience. Additional exam requirements/recommendations for international students: Required—TOEFL (minimum score 523 paper-based, 70 iBT) or IELTS (6.5). *Application deadline:* For fall admission, 3/1 priority date for domestic and international students; for spring admission, 10/1 priority date for domestic and international students; for summer admission, 4/1 priority date for domestic and international students. Applications are processed on a rolling basis. Application fee: $75. Electronic applications accepted. *Expenses:* Contact institution. *Financial support:* In 2016–17, 2 students received support, including 2 research assistantships (averaging $13,750 per year); career-related internships or fieldwork, institutionally sponsored loans, scholarships/grants, and unspecified assistantships also available. Support available to part-time students. Financial award application deadline: 3/1; financial award applicants required to submit FAFSA. *Total annual research expenditures:* $196,680. *Unit head:* Dr. Simon M. Hsiang, Chair, 704-687-1958, E-mail: shsiang1@uncc.edu. *Application contact:* Kathy B. Giddings, Director of Graduate Admissions, 704-687-5503, Fax: 704-687-1668, E-mail: gradadm@uncc.edu.
Website: http://seem.uncc.edu/

Engineering Management

University of Ottawa, Faculty of Graduate and Postdoctoral Studies, Faculty of Engineering, Engineering Management Program, Ottawa, ON K1N 6N5, Canada. Offers engineering management (M Eng); information technology (Certificate); project management (Certificate). *Degree requirements:* For master's, thesis or alternative. *Entrance requirements:* For master's and Certificate, honors degree or equivalent, minimum B average. Electronic applications accepted.

University of Puerto Rico, Mayagüez Campus, Graduate Studies, College of Engineering, Department of Civil Engineering and Surveying, Mayagüez, PR 00681-9000. Offers civil engineering (ME, MS, PhD), including construction engineering and management (ME, MS), environmental engineering, geotechnical engineering (ME, MS), structural engineering, transportation engineering. *Program availability:* Part-time. *Faculty:* 37 full-time (7 women), 2 part-time/adjunct (0 women). *Students:* 118 full-time (37 women), 9 part-time (2 women); includes 110 minority (all Hispanic/Latino), 17 international. Average age 25. 35 applicants, 94% accepted, 16 enrolled. In 2016, 26 master's, 2 doctorates awarded. Terminal master's awarded for partial completion of doctoral program. *Degree requirements:* For master's, one foreign language, thesis; for doctorate, one foreign language, comprehensive exam, thesis/dissertation, qualifying exams. *Entrance requirements:* For master's, proficiency in English and Spanish; BS in civil engineering or its equivalent; for doctorate, proficiency in English and Spanish. *Application deadline:* For fall admission, 2/15 for domestic and international students; for spring admission, 9/15 for domestic and international students. Applications are processed on a rolling basis. Application fee: $25. Electronic applications accepted. *Expenses: Tuition, area resident:* Full-time $2466. *International tuition:* $7166 full-time. *Required fees:* $210. One-time fee: $5 full-time. Tuition and fees vary according to course level, campus/location, program and student level. *Financial support:* In 2016–17, 89 students received support, including 74 research assistantships with full and partial tuition reimbursements available (averaging $3,171 per year), 38 teaching assistantships with full and partial tuition reimbursements available (averaging $3,107 per year); unspecified assistantships also available. *Faculty research:* Structural design, concrete structure, finite elements, dynamic analysis, transportation, soils. *Unit head:* Ismael Pagan, Prof., Director, 787-832-4040 Ext. 3815, Fax: 787-833-8260, E-mail: ismael.pagan@upr.edu. *Application contact:* Myriam Hernandez, Administrative Officer III, 787-832-4040 Ext. 3815, Fax: 787-833-8260, E-mail: myriam.hernandez1@upr.edu.
Website: http://engineering.uprm.edu/inci/

University of Regina, Faculty of Graduate Studies and Research, Kenneth Levene Graduate School of Business, Program in Business Administration, Regina, SK S4S 0A2, Canada. Offers business foundations (PGD); engineering management (MBA); executive business administration (EMBA); international business (MBA); leadership (M Admin); organizational leadership (Master's Certificate); project management (Master's Certificate); public safety management (MBA). *Program availability:* Part-time, evening/weekend. *Faculty:* 43 full-time (15 women), 6 part-time/adjunct (0 women). *Students:* 42 full-time (19 women), 21 part-time (12 women). 65 applicants, 48% accepted. In 2016, 57 master's, 13 other advanced degrees awarded. *Degree requirements:* For master's, project (for some programs). *Entrance requirements:* For master's, GMAT, three years of relevant work experience, four-year undergraduate degree; for other advanced degree, GMAT (for PGD), four-year undergraduate degree and two years of relevant work experience (for Master's Certificate); three years' work experience (for PGD). Additional exam requirements/recommendations for international students: Required—TOEFL (minimum score 580 paper-based; 80 iBT), IELTS (minimum score 6.5), PTE (minimum score 59). *Application deadline:* Applications are processed on a rolling basis. Application fee: $100. Electronic applications accepted. *Expenses:* Contact institution. *Financial support:* In 2016–17, 6 fellowships (averaging $6,000 per year), 7 teaching assistantships (averaging $2,501 per year) were awarded; career-related internships or fieldwork and scholarships/grants also available. Financial award application deadline: 6/15. *Faculty research:* Business policy and strategy, production and operations management, human behavior in organizations, financial management, social issues in business. *Unit head:* Dr. Andrew Gaudes, Dean, 306-585-4162, Fax: 306-585-5361, E-mail: andrew.gaudes@uregina.ca. *Application contact:* Ronald Camp, Graduate Programs, 306-337-2387, Fax: 306-585-5361, E-mail: ronald.camp@uregina.ca.
Website: http://www.uregina.ca/business/levene/

University of St. Thomas, Graduate Studies, School of Engineering, St. Paul, MN 55105-1096. Offers data science (MS); electrical engineering (MS); information technology (MS); manufacturing engineering (MS); manufacturing systems (Certificate); mechanical engineering (MS); medical device development (Certificate); regulatory science (MS); software engineering (MS); software management (MS); systems engineering (MS); technology leadership (Certificate); technology management (MS). *Accreditation:* ABET (one or more programs are accredited). *Entrance requirements:* For master's, resume, official transcripts. Additional exam requirements/recommendations for international students: Required—TOEFL (minimum score 550 paper-based). *Application deadline:* For fall admission, 8/1 priority date for domestic students; for spring admission, 1/1 priority date for domestic students. Applications are processed on a rolling basis. Application fee: $50. Electronic applications accepted. *Expenses:* Contact institution. *Financial support:* Fellowships, research assistantships, institutionally sponsored loans, and scholarships/grants available. Support available to part-time students. Financial award application deadline: 4/1; financial award applicants required to submit FAFSA. *Unit head:* Don Weinkauf, Dean, 651-962-5760, Fax: 651-962-6419, E-mail: dhweinkauf@stthomas.edu. *Application contact:* Tina M. Hansen, Graduate Program Manager, 651-962-5755, Fax: 651-962-6419, E-mail: tina.hansen@stthomas.edu.
Website: http://www.stthomas.edu/engineering/

University of Southern California, Graduate School, Viterbi School of Engineering, Daniel J. Epstein Department of Industrial and Systems Engineering, Los Angeles, CA 90089. Offers digital supply chain management (MS); engineering management (MS); engineering technology communication (Graduate Certificate); health systems operations (Graduate Certificate); industrial and systems engineering (MS, PhD, Engr); manufacturing engineering (MS); operations research engineering (MS); optimization and supply chain management (Graduate Certificate); product development engineering (MS); safety systems and security (MS); systems architecting and engineering (MS, Graduate Certificate); systems safety and security (Graduate Certificate); transportation systems (Graduate Certificate); MS/MBA. *Program availability:* Part-time, evening/weekend, online learning. Terminal master's awarded for partial completion of doctoral program. *Degree requirements:* For master's, thesis optional; for doctorate, thesis/dissertation. *Entrance requirements:* For master's and doctorate, GRE General Test. Additional exam requirements/recommendations for international students: Recommended—TOEFL. Electronic applications accepted. *Faculty research:* Health systems, music cognition and retrieval, transportation and logistics, manufacturing and automation, engineering systems design, risk and economic analysis.

University of Southern California, Graduate School, Viterbi School of Engineering, Department of Aerospace and Mechanical Engineering, Los Angeles, CA 90089. Offers aerospace and mechanical engineering: computational fluid and solid mechanics (MS); aerospace and mechanical engineering: dynamics and control (MS); aerospace engineering (MS, PhD, Engr), including aerospace engineering (PhD, Engr); green technologies (MS); mechanical engineering (MS, PhD, Engr), including energy conversion (MS), mechanical engineering (PhD, Engr), nuclear power (MS); product development engineering (MS). *Program availability:* Part-time, evening/weekend, online learning. Terminal master's awarded for partial completion of doctoral program. *Degree requirements:* For master's, thesis optional; for doctorate, thesis/dissertation. *Entrance requirements:* For master's, doctorate, and Engr, GRE General Test. Additional exam requirements/recommendations for international students: Recommended—TOEFL. Electronic applications accepted. *Faculty research:* Mechanics and materials, aerodynamics of air/ground vehicles, gas dynamics, aerosols, astronautics and space science, geophysical and microgravity flows, planetary physics, power MEMs and MEMS vacuum pumps, heat transfer and combustion.

University of Southern Indiana, Graduate Studies, Romain College of Business, Program in Business Administration, Evansville, IN 47712-3590. Offers accounting (MBA); business administration (MBA); data analytics (MBA); engineering management (MBA); health administration (MBA); human resources (MBA). *Accreditation:* AACSB. *Program availability:* Part-time, evening/weekend, 100% online, blended/hybrid learning. *Faculty:* 22 full-time (4 women), 2 part-time/adjunct (0 women). *Students:* 149 full-time (70 women), 64 part-time (29 women); includes 25 minority (17 Black or African American, non-Hispanic/Latino; 1 Asian, non-Hispanic/Latino; 5 Hispanic/Latino; 2 Two or more races, non-Hispanic/Latino), 5 international. Average age 32. In 2016, 36 master's awarded. *Entrance requirements:* For master's, GMAT or GRE, minimum GPA of 2.5, resume, 3 professional references. Additional exam requirements/recommendations for international students: Required—TOEFL (minimum score 550 paper-based; 79 iBT), IELTS (minimum score 6). *Application deadline:* For fall admission, 8/1 for domestic students, 3/1 priority date for international students. Applications are processed on a rolling basis. Application fee: $40. Electronic applications accepted. *Expenses:* Tuition, state resident: full-time $8497. Tuition, nonresident: full-time $16,691. *Required fees:* $500. *Financial support:* In 2016–17, 8 students received support. Federal Work-Study, scholarships/grants, tuition waivers (full and partial), and unspecified assistantships available. Financial award application deadline: 3/1; financial award applicants required to submit FAFSA. *Unit head:* Dr. Jack E. Smothers, Program Director, 812-461-5248, E-mail: jesmothers@usi.edu. *Application contact:* Michelle Simmons, MBA Program Assistant, 812-464-1926, Fax: 812-465-1044, E-mail: masimmons3@usi.edu.
Website: http://www.usi.edu/business/mba

University of South Florida, College of Engineering, Department of Industrial and Management Systems Engineering, Tampa, FL 33620-9951. Offers engineering management (MSEM); industrial engineering (MSIE, PhD); information technology (MSIT). *Program availability:* Part-time, online learning. *Faculty:* 13 full-time (3 women). *Students:* 119 full-time (22 women), 85 part-time (19 women); includes 27 minority (4 Black or African American, non-Hispanic/Latino; 7 Asian, non-Hispanic/Latino; 15 Hispanic/Latino; 1 Two or more races, non-Hispanic/Latino), 135 international. Average age 27. 420 applicants, 36% accepted, 50 enrolled. In 2016, 63 master's, 9 doctorates awarded. Terminal master's awarded for partial completion of doctoral program. *Degree requirements:* For master's, comprehensive exam, thesis (for some programs); for doctorate, comprehensive exam, thesis/dissertation, 2 tools of research as specified by dissertation committee. *Entrance requirements:* For master's, GRE General Test, BS in engineering (or equivalent) with minimum GPA of 3.0 in last 60 hours of coursework, letter of recommendation, resume; for doctorate, GRE General Test, minimum GPA of 3.0 in last 60 hours of undergraduate/graduate coursework, three letters of recommendation, statement of purpose, strong background in scientific and engineering principles. Additional exam requirements/recommendations for international students: Required—TOEFL (minimum score 550 paper-based; 79 iBT) or IELTS (minimum score 6.5). *Application deadline:* For fall admission, 2/15 for domestic and international students; for spring admission, 10/15 for domestic students, 9/15 for international students; for summer admission, 2/15 for domestic students, 1/15 for international students. Application fee: $30. Electronic applications accepted. *Expenses:* Tuition, state resident: full-time $7766; part-time $431.43 per credit hour. Tuition, nonresident: full-time $15,789; part-time $877.17 per credit hour. *Required fees:* $37 per term. *Financial support:* In 2016–17, 31 students received support, including 20 research assistantships with partial tuition reimbursements available (averaging $16,748 per year), 11 teaching assistantships with partial tuition reimbursements available (averaging $15,000 per year); tuition waivers (partial) also available. Financial award applicants required to submit FAFSA. *Faculty research:* Healthcare, healthcare systems, public health policies, energy and environment, manufacturing, logistics, transportation. *Total annual research expenditures:* $253,139. *Unit head:* Dr. Tapas K. Das, Professor and Department Chair, 813-974-5585, Fax: 813-974-5953, E-mail: das@usf.edu. *Application contact:* Dr. Alex Savachkin, Associate Professor and Graduate Director, 813-974-5577, Fax: 813-974-5953, E-mail: alexs@usf.edu.
Website: http://imse.eng.usf.edu

The University of Tennessee, Graduate School, Tickle College of Engineering, Department of Industrial and Systems Engineering, Knoxville, TN 37966. Offers engineering management (MS); industrial engineering (MS, PhD); reliability and maintainability engineering (MS); MS/MBA. *Program availability:* Part-time, online learning. *Faculty:* 13 full-time (2 women), 5 part-time/adjunct (0 women). *Students:* 90 full-time (20 women), 67 part-time (10 women); includes 18 minority (4 Black or African American, non-Hispanic/Latino; 7 Asian, non-Hispanic/Latino; 6 Hispanic/Latino; 1 Two or more races, non-Hispanic/Latino), 55 international. Average age 37. 103 applicants, 64% accepted, 23 enrolled. In 2016, 26 master's, 7 doctorates awarded. *Degree requirements:* For master's, thesis or alternative; for doctorate, comprehensive exam, thesis/dissertation. *Entrance requirements:* For master's, GRE General Test (for MS students pursuing research thesis), minimum GPA of 2.7 (for U.S. degree holders), 3.0 (for international degree holders); for doctorate, GRE General Test, minimum GPA of 3.0 on previous graduate course work. Additional exam requirements/recommendations for international students: Required—TOEFL (minimum score 550 paper-based). *Application deadline:* For fall admission, 2/1 priority date for domestic and international students; for spring admission, 6/15 for domestic and international students. Applications are processed on a rolling basis. Application fee: $35. Electronic applications accepted. *Financial support:* In 2016–17, 36 students received support, including 4 fellowships with full tuition reimbursements available (averaging $25,000 per year), 21 research assistantships with full tuition reimbursements available (averaging $18,799 per year), 10 teaching assistantships with full tuition reimbursements available (averaging $18,783 per year); career-related internships or fieldwork, Federal Work-Study, institutionally sponsored loans, health care benefits, and unspecified assistantships also available. Financial award application deadline: 2/1; financial award applicants required to submit FAFSA. *Faculty research:* Defense-oriented supply chain modeling; dependability and reliability of large computer networks; design of lean, reliable systems; new product development; operations research in the automotive industry. *Total annual research expenditures:* $1 million. *Unit head:* Dr. John Kobza, Department Head, 865-974-3333, Fax: 865-974-0588, E-mail: jkobza@utk.edu. *Application contact:* Dr. Alberto Garcia-Diaz, Professor, 865-974-7647, E-mail: agd@utk.edu.
Website: http://www.engr.utk.edu/ie/

The University of Tennessee, The University of Tennessee Space Institute, Tullahoma, TN 37388. Offers aerospace engineering (MS, PhD); biomedical engineering (MS, PhD); engineering science (MS, PhD); industrial and systems engineering/engineering management (MS, PhD); mechanical engineering (MS, PhD); physics (MS, PhD). *Program availability:* Part-time, blended/hybrid learning. Terminal master's awarded for partial completion of doctoral program. *Degree requirements:* For doctorate, one foreign language, thesis/dissertation. *Entrance requirements:* Additional exam requirements/recommendations for international students: Required—TOEFL (minimum score 550 paper-based; 80 iBT), IELTS (minimum score 6.5). Electronic applications accepted. *Expenses:* Contact institution. *Faculty research:* Fluid mechanics/aerodynamics, chemical and electric propulsion and laser diagnostics, computational mechanics and simulations, carbon fiber production and composite materials.

The University of Tennessee at Chattanooga, Engineering Management and Technology Program, Chattanooga, TN 37403. Offers construction management (Graduate Certificate); engineering management (MS); fundamentals of engineering management (Graduate Certificate); leadership and ethics (Graduate Certificate); logistics and supply chain management (Graduate Certificate); power systems management (Graduate Certificate); project and technology management (Graduate Certificate); quality management (Graduate Certificate). *Program availability:* 100% online, blended/hybrid learning. *Faculty:* 6 full-time (1 woman). *Students:* 14 full-time (3 women), 49 part-time (11 women); includes 17 minority (10 Black or African American, non-Hispanic/Latino; 2 Asian, non-Hispanic/Latino; 3 Hispanic/Latino; 2 Two or more races, non-Hispanic/Latino), 8 international. Average age 33. 29 applicants, 93% accepted, 15 enrolled. In 2016, 36 master's, 7 other advanced degrees awarded. *Degree requirements:* For master's, thesis. *Entrance requirements:* For master's, GRE General Test, letters of recommendation; minimum undergraduate GPA of 2.7 overall or 3.0 in final two years. Additional exam requirements/recommendations for international students: Required—TOEFL (minimum score 550 paper-based; 79 iBT), IELTS (minimum score 6). *Application deadline:* For fall admission, 6/15 priority date for domestic students, 7/1 for international students; for spring admission, 11/1 priority date for domestic students, 11/1 for international students. Applications are processed on a rolling basis. Application fee: $35 ($40 for international students). Electronic applications accepted. *Expenses:* $9,876 full-time in-state; $25,994 full-time out-of-state; $450 per credit part-time in-state; $1,345 per credit part-time out-of-state. *Financial support:* In 2016–17, 4 research assistantships were awarded; teaching assistantships, career-related internships or fieldwork, scholarships/grants, and unspecified assistantships also available. Support available to part-time students. Financial award application deadline: 7/1; financial award applicants required to submit FAFSA. *Faculty research:* Plant layout design, lean manufacturing, Six Sigma, value management, product development. *Unit head:* Dr. Neslihan Alp, Department Head, 423-425-4032, Fax: 423-425-5818, E-mail: neslihan-alp@utc.edu. *Application contact:* Dr. Joanne Romagni, Dean of the Graduate School, 423-425-4478, Fax: 423-425-5223, E-mail: joanne-romagni@utc.edu.
Website: http://www.utc.edu/college-engineering-computer-science/programs/engineering-management-and-technology/index.php#li03

The University of Texas at Arlington, Graduate School, College of Engineering, Department of Industrial and Manufacturing Systems Engineering, Program in Engineering Management, Arlington, TX 76019. Offers MS. *Program availability:* Part-time, evening/weekend, online learning. *Degree requirements:* For master's, comprehensive exam, thesis optional. *Entrance requirements:* For master's, GRE, 3 years of full-time work experience, minimum GPA of 3.0. Additional exam requirements/recommendations for international students: Required—TOEFL (minimum score 550 paper-based). *Application deadline:* For fall admission, 6/6 for domestic students, 4/4 for international students; for spring admission, 10/15 for domestic students, 9/5 for international students. Application fee: $35 ($50 for international students). *Financial support:* Fellowships, research assistantships, teaching assistantships, career-related internships or fieldwork, Federal Work-Study, institutionally sponsored loans, scholarships/grants, and unspecified assistantships available. Financial award application deadline: 6/1; financial award applicants required to submit FAFSA. *Unit head:* Dr. Donald H. Liles, Chair, 817-272-3092, Fax: 817-272-3406, E-mail: dliles@uta.edu. *Application contact:* Dr. Sheik Imrhan, Graduate Advisor, 817-272-3167, Fax: 817-272-3406, E-mail: imrhan@uta.edu.
Website: http://ie.uta.edu/

The University of Texas at Tyler, College of Business and Technology, Program in Business Administration, Tyler, TX 75799-0001. Offers cyber security (MBA); engineering management (MBA); general management (MBA); healthcare management (MBA); internal assurance and consulting (MBA); marketing (MBA); oil, gas and energy (MBA); organizational development (MBA); quality management (MBA). *Accreditation:* AACSB. *Program availability:* Part-time, online learning. *Entrance requirements:* Additional exam requirements/recommendations for international students: Required—TOEFL (minimum score 550 paper-based). *Faculty research:* General business, inventory control, institutional markets, service marketing, product distribution, accounting fraud, financial reporting and recognition.

The University of Texas Rio Grande Valley, College of Engineering and Computer Science, Department of Manufacturing and Industrial Engineering, Edinburg, TX 78539. Offers engineering management (MS); manufacturing engineering (MS); systems engineering (MS). Tuition and fees vary according to course load and program.

University of Waterloo, Graduate Studies, Faculty of Engineering, Department of Management Sciences, Waterloo, ON N2L 3G1, Canada. Offers applied operations research (MA Sc, MMS, PhD); information systems (MA Sc, MMS, PhD); management of technology (MA Sc, MMS, PhD). *Program availability:* Part-time, online learning. *Degree requirements:* For master's, research paper or thesis; for doctorate, comprehensive exam, thesis/dissertation. *Entrance requirements:* For master's, GMAT or GRE, honors degree, minimum B average, resume; for doctorate, GMAT or GRE, master's degree, minimum A- average, resume. Additional exam requirements/recommendations for international students: Required—TOEFL, IELTS, PTE. Electronic applications accepted. *Faculty research:* Operations research, manufacturing systems, scheduling, information systems.

Valparaiso University, Graduate School and Continuing Education, College of Business, Valparaiso, IN 46383. Offers business administration (MBA); business intelligence (Certificate); engineering management (Certificate); entrepreneurship (Certificate); finance (Certificate); general business (Certificate); management (Certificate); marketing (Certificate); sustainability (Certificate); JD/MBA; MSN/MBA. *Accreditation:* AACSB. *Program availability:* Part-time, evening/weekend, online learning. *Entrance requirements:* For master's, GMAT, GRE, minimum GPA of 3.0. Additional exam requirements/recommendations for international students: Required—TOEFL (minimum score 550 paper-based; 80 iBT), IELTS (minimum score 6). Electronic applications accepted. *Expenses:* Contact institution.

Virginia Polytechnic Institute and State University, VT Online, Blacksburg, VA 24061. Offers advanced transportation systems (Certificate); aerospace engineering (MS); agricultural and life sciences (MSLFS); business information systems (Graduate Certificate); career and technical education (MS); civil engineering (MS); computer engineering (M Eng, MS); decision support systems (Graduate Certificate); eLearning leadership (MA); electrical engineering (M Eng, MS); engineering administration (MEA); environmental engineering (Certificate); environmental politics and policy (Graduate Certificate); environmental sciences and engineering (MS); foundations of political analysis (Graduate Certificate); health product risk management (Graduate Certificate); industrial and systems engineering (MS); information policy and society (Graduate Certificate); information security (Graduate Certificate); information technology (MIT); instructional technology (MA); integrative STEM education (MA Ed); liberal arts (Graduate Certificate); life sciences: health product risk management (MS); natural resources (MNR, Graduate Certificate); networking (Graduate Certificate); nonprofit and nongovernmental organization management (Graduate Certificate); ocean engineering (MS); political science (MA); security studies (Graduate Certificate); software development (Graduate Certificate). *Expenses:* Tuition, state resident: full-time $12,467; part-time $692.50 per credit hour. Tuition, nonresident: full-time $25,095; part-time $1394.25 per credit hour. *Required fees:* $2669; $491.50 per semester. Tuition and fees vary according to course load, campus/location and program.

Washington State University, Voiland College of Engineering and Architecture, Program in Engineering and Technology Management, Pullman, WA 99164-2785. Offers METM, Certificate. Program offered through the Global (online) campus. *Program availability:* Part-time, evening/weekend, online learning. *Degree requirements:* For master's, one foreign language, comprehensive exam (for some programs). *Entrance requirements:* Additional exam requirements/recommendations for international students: Required—TOEFL. Electronic applications accepted. *Faculty research:* Constraints management, Six Sigma quality management, supply chain management, project management, construction management, systems engineering management, manufacturing leadership.

Wayne State University, College of Engineering, Department of Industrial and Systems Engineering, Detroit, MI 48202. Offers data science and business analytics (MS); engineering management (MS); industrial engineering (MS, PhD); manufacturing engineering (MS); systems engineering (Certificate). *Faculty:* 10. *Students:* 313 full-time (37 women), 140 part-time (26 women); includes 37 minority (16 Black or African American, non-Hispanic/Latino; 15 Asian, non-Hispanic/Latino; 3 Hispanic/Latino; 3 Two or more races, non-Hispanic/Latino), 340 international. Average age 28. 1,171 applicants, 42% accepted, 105 enrolled. In 2016, 117 master's, 5 doctorates awarded. *Degree requirements:* For master's, thesis (for some programs); for doctorate, thesis/dissertation. *Entrance requirements:* For master's, BS from ABET-accredited institution; for doctorate, MS in industrial engineering or operations research with minimum graduate GPA of 3.5; for Certificate, BS in engineering or other technical field from ABET-accredited institution, full-time work experience as practicing engineer or technical leader. Additional exam requirements/recommendations for international students: Required—TOEFL (minimum score 550 paper-based; 79 iBT), TWE (minimum score 5.5), Michigan English Language Assessment Battery (minimum score 85); Recommended—IELTS (minimum score 6.5). *Application deadline:* For fall admission, 6/1 priority date for domestic students, 5/1 priority date for international students; for winter admission, 10/1 priority date for domestic students, 9/1 priority date for international students; for spring admission, 2/1 priority date for domestic students, 1/1 priority date for international students. Applications are processed on a rolling basis. Application fee: $50. Electronic applications accepted. *Expenses:* $18,871 per year resident tuition and fees, $36,065 per year non-resident tuition and fees. *Financial support:* In 2016–17, 118 students received support, including 2 fellowships with tuition reimbursements available (averaging $16,000 per year), 4 research assistantships with tuition reimbursements available (averaging $18,883 per year), 12 teaching assistantships with tuition reimbursements available (averaging $19,177 per year); scholarships/grants, tuition waivers (full), and unspecified assistantships also available. Financial award applicants required to submit FAFSA. *Faculty research:* Healthcare systems engineering, product design and development, quality and reliability engineering, supply chain management and logistics. *Total annual research expenditures:* $3.2 million. *Unit head:* Dr. Leslie Monplaisir, Associate Professor/Chair, 313-577-3821, Fax: 313-577-8833, E-mail: leslie.monplaisir@wayne.edu. *Application contact:* Eric Scimeca, Graduate Program Coordinator, 313-577-0412, E-mail: eric.scimeca@wayne.edu.
Website: http://engineering.wayne.edu/ise/

Western Michigan University, Graduate College, College of Engineering and Applied Sciences, Department of Industrial and Entrepreneurial Engineering and Engineering Management, Kalamazoo, MI 49008. Offers engineering management (MS); industrial engineering (MSE, PhD). *Degree requirements:* For master's, thesis optional.

Western New England University, College of Engineering, Master's Program in Engineering Management, Springfield, MA 01119. Offers business and engineering information systems (MSEM); general engineering management (MSEM); production and manufacturing systems (MSEM); quality engineering (MSEM); MSEM/MBA. *Program availability:* Part-time, evening/weekend, online learning. *Faculty:* 6 full-time. *Students:* 46 part-time (6 women); includes 5 minority (1 Black or African American, non-Hispanic/Latino; 1 Asian, non-Hispanic/Latino; 3 Hispanic/Latino), 13 international. Average age 31. 151 applicants, 29% accepted, 9 enrolled. In 2016, 28 master's awarded. *Degree requirements:* For master's, thesis optional. *Entrance requirements:* For master's, official transcript, bachelor's degree in engineering or related field, two recommendations, resume. Additional exam requirements/recommendations for international students: Required—TOEFL (minimum score 79 iBT). *Application deadline:* Applications are processed on a rolling basis. Application fee: $30. Electronic applications accepted. *Expenses:* Contact institution. *Financial support:* Application deadline: 4/15; applicants required to submit FAFSA. *Unit head:* Dr. Thomas Keyser, Chair and Professor, 413-782-1210, E-mail: thomas.keyser@wne.edu. *Application contact:* Matthew Fox, Director of Admissions for Graduate Students and Adult Learners, 413-782-1410, Fax: 413-782-1777, E-mail: study@wne.edu.
Website: http://www1.wne.edu/academics/graduate/engineering-management.cfm

Western New England University, College of Engineering, PhD Program in Engineering Management, Springfield, MA 01119. Offers PhD. *Program availability:* Part-time, evening/weekend. *Faculty:* 6 full-time. *Students:* 14 part-time (3 women); includes 2 minority (1 Asian, non-Hispanic/Latino; 1 Hispanic/Latino), 7 international. Average age 37. 11 applicants, 27% accepted. In 2016, 2 doctorates awarded. *Degree requirements:* For doctorate, comprehensive exam, thesis/dissertation. *Entrance requirements:* For doctorate, GRE, official transcript, bachelor's or master's degree in engineering or related field, two letters of recommendation, minimum GPA of 3.5. Additional exam requirements/recommendations for international students: Required—TOEFL (minimum score 550 paper-based; 79 iBT). *Application deadline:* For fall admission, 1/15 priority date for domestic students. Applications are processed on a rolling basis. Application fee: $30. Electronic applications accepted. *Expenses:* $1,280 per credit. *Financial support:* In 2016–17, 6 fellowships with tuition reimbursements were awarded. Financial award application deadline: 4/15; financial award applicants required to submit FAFSA. *Unit head:* Dr. Thomas Keyser, Chair and Professor, 413-782-1210, E-mail: thomas.keyser@wne.edu. *Application contact:* Matthew Fox, Director of Admissions for Graduate Students and Adult Learners, 413-782-1410, Fax: 413-782-1777, E-mail: study@wne.edu.
Website: http://www1.wne.edu/academics/graduate/engineering-management-phd.cfm

Engineering Management

Wichita State University, Graduate School, College of Engineering, Department of Industrial and Manufacturing Engineering, Wichita, KS 67260. Offers engineering management (MEM); industrial engineering (MS, PhD). *Program availability:* Part-time. In 2016, 37 master's, 3 doctorates awarded. *Entrance requirements:* Additional exam requirements/recommendations for international students: Required—TOEFL. *Financial support:* Teaching assistantships available. *Unit head:* Dr. Krishna Krishnan, Chair, 316-978-3425, Fax: 316-978-3742, E-mail: krishna.krishnan@wichita.edu. *Application contact:* Jordan Oleson, Admissions Coordinator, 316-978-3095, Fax: 316-978-3253, E-mail: jordan.oleson@wichita.edu.
Website: http://www.wichita.edu/ime

Widener University, Graduate Programs in Engineering, Program in Engineering Management, Chester, PA 19013. Offers M Eng. *Program availability:* Part-time, evening/weekend. *Students:* 1 (woman) full-time, 1 part-time (0 women), 1 international. Average age 26. In 2016, 1 master's awarded. *Degree requirements:* For master's, thesis optional. *Application deadline:* For fall admission, 8/1 priority date for domestic students; for spring admission, 12/1 for domestic students. Applications are processed on a rolling basis. Application fee: $0. Electronic applications accepted. Tuition and fees vary according to degree level and program. *Financial support:* Application deadline: 3/15. *Unit head:* Rudolph Treichel, Assistant Dean/Director of Graduate Programs, 610-499-1294, Fax: 610-499-4059, E-mail: rjtreichel@widener.edu.

Wilkes University, College of Graduate and Professional Studies, College of Science and Engineering, Department of Mechanical Engineering and Engineering Management, Wilkes-Barre, PA 18766-0002. Offers engineering management (MS); mechanical engineering (MS). *Program availability:* Part-time. *Students:* 15 full-time (0 women), 12 part-time (0 women); includes 3 minority (1 Hispanic/Latino; 2 Two or more races, non-Hispanic/Latino), 15 international. Average age 27. In 2016, 18 master's awarded. *Application deadline:* Applications are processed on a rolling basis. Application fee: $45 ($65 for international students). Electronic applications accepted. Tuition and fees vary according to degree level and program. *Financial support:* Institutionally sponsored loans and unspecified assistantships available. *Unit head:* Dr. William Hudson, Dean, 570-408-4600, Fax: 570-408-7860, E-mail: william.hudson@wilkes.edu. *Application contact:* Director of Graduate Enrollment, 570-408-4234, Fax: 570-408-7846.
Website: http://www.wilkes.edu/academics/colleges/science-and-engineering/mechanical-engineering-engineering-management-applied-and-engineering-sciences/

Ergonomics and Human Factors

Arizona State University at the Tempe campus, Ira A. Fulton Schools of Engineering, The Polytechnic School, Programs in Technology Management, Mesa, AZ 85212. Offers aviation management and human factors (MS); environmental technology management (MS); global technology and development (MS); graphic information technology (MS); management of technology (MS). *Program availability:* Part-time, evening/weekend, online learning. *Degree requirements:* For master's, thesis or applied project and oral defense; interactive Program of Study (iPOS) submitted before completing 50 percent of required credit hours. *Entrance requirements:* For master's, GRE, minimum GPA of 3.0 or equivalent in last 2 years of work leading to bachelor's degree. Additional exam requirements/recommendations for international students: Required—TOEFL, IELTS, or PTE. Electronic applications accepted. *Faculty research:* Digital imaging, digital publishing, Internet development/e-commerce, information aviation human factors, pilot selection, databases, multimedia, commercial digital photography, digital workflow, computer graphics modeling and animation, information design, sociotechnology, visual and technical literacy, environmental management, quality management, project management, industrial ethics, hazardous materials, environmental chemistry.

Bentley University, Graduate School of Business, Program in Human Factors in Information Design, Waltham, MA 02452-4705. Offers MSHFID. *Program availability:* Part-time, evening/weekend, 100% online, blended/hybrid learning. *Faculty:* 71 full-time (25 women), 33 part-time/adjunct (15 women). *Students:* 28 full-time (22 women), 69 part-time (52 women); includes 13 minority (2 Black or African American, non-Hispanic/Latino; 7 Asian, non-Hispanic/Latino; 3 Hispanic/Latino; 1 Two or more races, non-Hispanic/Latino), 15 international. Average age 33. 61 applicants, 79% accepted, 30 enrolled. In 2016, 47 master's awarded. *Entrance requirements:* For master's, GMAT or GRE General Test, current resume; two letters of recommendation; official copies of all university level transcripts. Additional exam requirements/recommendations for international students: Required—TOEFL (minimum score 600 paper-based; 100 iBT), IELTS (minimum score 7), or PTE. *Application deadline:* Applications are processed on a rolling basis. Application fee: $50. Electronic applications accepted. *Expenses:* $4,225 per course, $480 fee per year. *Financial support:* In 2016–17, 17 students received support. Scholarships/grants and unspecified assistantships available. Financial award application deadline: 6/1; financial award applicants required to submit FAFSA. *Faculty research:* Usability engineering; ethnography; human-computer interaction; virtual reality; user experience. *Unit head:* Dr. William M. Gribbons, Professor, 781-891-2926, E-mail: wgribbons@bentley.edu. *Application contact:* Sharon Hill, Assistant Dean/Director of Graduate Admissions, 781-891-2108, Fax: 781-891-2464, E-mail: bentleygraduateadmissions@bentley.edu.
Website: http://www.bentley.edu/graduate/ms-programs/masters-human-factors-information-design

California State University, Long Beach, Graduate Studies, College of Liberal Arts, Department of Psychology, Long Beach, CA 90840. Offers human factors (MS); industrial/organizational psychology (MS); psychology (MA). *Program availability:* Part-time, evening/weekend. *Degree requirements:* For master's, comprehensive exam, thesis. *Entrance requirements:* For master's, GRE General Test, GRE Subject Test. *Application deadline:* For fall admission, 3/1 for domestic students. Applications are processed on a rolling basis. Application fee: $55. Electronic applications accepted. *Financial support:* Federal Work-Study, institutionally sponsored loans, and scholarships/grants available. Financial award application deadline: 3/2. *Faculty research:* Physiological psychology, social and personality psychology, community-clinical psychology, industrial-organizational psychology, developmental psychology. *Unit head:* David J. Whitney, Chair, 562-985-5001, Fax: 562-985-8004. *Application contact:* Dr. Mark Wiley, Associate Dean, 562-985-5381, Fax: 562-985-2463, E-mail: mwiley@csulb.edu.

The Catholic University of America, School of Arts and Sciences, Department of Psychology, Washington, DC 20064. Offers applied experimental psychology (PhD); clinical psychology (PhD); general psychology (MA); human development psychology (PhD); human factors (MA); MA/JD. MA/JD offered jointly with Columbus School of Law. *Accreditation:* APA (one or more programs are accredited). *Program availability:* Part-time. *Faculty:* 11 full-time (6 women), 5 part-time/adjunct (2 women). *Students:* 40 full-time (26 women), 36 part-time (29 women); includes 19 minority (3 Black or African American, non-Hispanic/Latino; 5 Asian, non-Hispanic/Latino; 4 Hispanic/Latino; 7 Two or more races, non-Hispanic/Latino), 8 international. Average age 28. 230 applicants, 27% accepted, 23 enrolled. In 2016, 15 master's, 6 doctorates awarded. *Degree requirements:* For master's, comprehensive exam, thesis (for some programs); for doctorate, comprehensive exam, thesis/dissertation. *Entrance requirements:* For master's, GRE General Test, statement of purpose, official copies of academic transcripts, three letters of recommendation; for doctorate, GRE General Test, GRE Subject Test, statement of purpose, official copies of academic transcripts, three letters of recommendation. Additional exam requirements/recommendations for international students: Required—TOEFL (minimum score 550 paper-based; 80 iBT). *Application deadline:* For fall admission, 7/15 priority date for domestic students, 7/1 for international students; for spring admission, 11/15 priority date for domestic students, 11/1 for international students. Applications are processed on a rolling basis. Application fee: $55. Electronic applications accepted. *Expenses:* $42,850 per year; $1,170 per credit; $200 per semester part-time fees. *Financial support:* Fellowships, research assistantships, teaching assistantships, Federal Work-Study, scholarships/grants, tuition waivers (full and partial), and unspecified assistantships available. Financial award application deadline: 2/1; financial award applicants required to submit FAFSA. *Faculty research:* Clinical psychology, applied cognitive science, psychopathology, cognitive neuroscience, psychotherapy. *Total annual research expenditures:* $936,581. *Unit head:* Dr. Marc M. Sebrechts, Chair, 202-319-5750, Fax: 202-319-6263, E-mail: sebrechts@cua.edu. *Application contact:* Director of Graduate Admissions, 202-319-5057, Fax: 202-319-6533, E-mail: cua-admissions@cua.edu.
Website: http://psychology.cua.edu/

Clemson University, Graduate School, College of Behavioral, Social and Health Sciences, Department of Psychology, Program in Human Factors Psychology, Clemson, SC 29634. Offers PhD. *Faculty:* 29 full-time (11 women), 1 (woman) part-time/adjunct. *Students:* 17 full-time (7 women); includes 1 minority (Two or more races, non-Hispanic/Latino). Average age 27. 31 applicants, 10% accepted, 3 enrolled. In 2016, 1 doctorate awarded. *Degree requirements:* For doctorate, comprehensive exam, thesis/dissertation. *Entrance requirements:* For doctorate, GRE General Test, unofficial transcripts, letters of recommendation, statement of intent. Additional exam requirements/recommendations for international students: Required—TOEFL (minimum score 80 iBT), IELTS (minimum score 6.5). *Application deadline:* For fall admission, 1/15 priority date for domestic and international students. Application fee: $80 ($90 for international students). Electronic applications accepted. *Expenses:* $5,617 per semester full-time resident, $11,194 per semester full-time non-resident, $697 per credit hour part-time resident, $1,392 per credit hour part-time non-resident. *Financial support:* In 2016–17, 14 students received support, including 1 fellowship with partial tuition reimbursement available (averaging $5,000 per year), 2 research assistantships with partial tuition reimbursements available (averaging $17,768 per year), 15 teaching assistantships with partial tuition reimbursements available (averaging $13,733 per year); career-related internships or fieldwork also available. Financial award application deadline: 1/15. *Faculty research:* Transportation safety, human factors in health care, human-computer interaction, ergonomics, vision and visual performance. *Unit head:* Dr. Patrick Raymark, Chair, 864-656-4715, Fax: 864-656-0358, E-mail: praymar@clemson.edu. *Application contact:* Dr. Robert Sinclair, Graduate Program Coordinator, 864-656-3931, E-mail: rsincla@clemson.edu.
Website: http://www.clemson.edu/cbshs/departments/psychology/graduate/hfphd.html

Colorado State University, College of Veterinary Medicine and Biomedical Sciences, Department of Environmental and Radiological Health Sciences, Fort Collins, CO 80523-1681. Offers environmental health (MS, PhD), including environmental health and safety (MS), epidemiology, ergonomics, industrial hygiene, toxicology; radiological health sciences (MS, PhD), including health physics (MS); toxicology (MS, PhD). *Faculty:* 35 full-time (17 women), 4 part-time/adjunct (2 women). *Students:* 103 full-time (47 women), 53 part-time (33 women); includes 27 minority (6 Black or African American, non-Hispanic/Latino; 1 American Indian or Alaska Native, non-Hispanic/Latino; 6 Asian, non-Hispanic/Latino; 10 Hispanic/Latino; 4 Two or more races, non-Hispanic/Latino), 16 international. Average age 29. 108 applicants, 82% accepted, 55 enrolled. In 2016, 29 master's, 5 doctorates awarded. Terminal master's awarded for partial completion of doctoral program. *Degree requirements:* For master's, comprehensive exam (for some programs), thesis (for some programs); for doctorate, comprehensive exam (for some programs), thesis/dissertation (for some programs). *Entrance requirements:* For master's, GRE or MCAT, minimum GPA of 3.0, bachelor's degree, resume or curriculum vitae, official transcripts, written statement, 3 letters of recommendation; for doctorate, GRE, minimum GPA of 3.0, MS or proof of research, resume or curriculum vitae, official transcripts, written statement, 3 letters of recommendation. Additional exam requirements/recommendations for international students: Required—TOEFL (minimum score 550 paper-based; 80 iBT), IELTS (minimum score 6.5). *Application deadline:* For fall admission, 7/1 for domestic students, 5/1 for international students; for spring admission, 11/1 for domestic students, 9/1 for international students. Application fee: $60 ($70 for international students). Electronic applications accepted. *Expenses:* Contact institution. *Financial support:* In 2016–17, 4 students received support, including 14 fellowships with full and partial tuition reimbursements available (averaging $43,336 per year), 18 research assistantships with full and partial tuition reimbursements available (averaging $22,712 per year), 3 teaching assistantships with full and partial tuition reimbursements available (averaging $13,932 per year); traineeships also available. Financial award application deadline: 2/1; financial award applicants required to submit FAFSA. *Faculty research:* Air pollution, radiation physics, treatment of occupational illness and injuries, DNA damage and repair. *Total annual research expenditures:* $9.7 million. *Unit head:* Dr. Jac Nickoloff, Department Head, 970-491-6674, E-mail: j.nickoloff@colostate.edu. *Application contact:* Toni Brown, Graduate Coordinator, 970-491-5003, E-mail: toni.m.brown@colostate.edu.
Website: http://csu-cvmbs.colostate.edu/academics/erhs/Pages/graduate-studies.aspx

Cornell University, Graduate School, Graduate Fields of Human Ecology, Field of Design and Environmental Analysis, Ithaca, NY 14853. Offers applied research in human-environment relations (MS); facilities planning and management (MS); housing and design (MS); human factors and ergonomics (MS); human-environment relations (MS); interior design (MA, MPS). *Degree requirements:* For master's, thesis. *Entrance requirements:* For master's, GRE General Test, portfolio or slides of recent work; bachelor's degree in interior design, architecture or related design discipline; 2 letters of recommendation. Additional exam requirements/recommendations for international students: Required—TOEFL (minimum score 600 paper-based; 105 iBT). Electronic applications accepted. *Faculty research:* Facility planning and management, environmental psychology, housing, interior design, ergonomics and human factors.

Embry-Riddle Aeronautical University–Daytona, Department of Human Factors, Daytona Beach, FL 32114-3900. Offers human factors (PhD). *Program availability:* Part-time. *Faculty:* 7 full-time (2 women). *Students:* 42 full-time (19 women), 1 (woman) part-time; includes 9 minority (2 Black or African American, non-Hispanic/Latino; 1 American Indian or Alaska Native, non-Hispanic/Latino; 6 Two or more races, non-Hispanic/Latino), 5 international. Average age 26. 57 applicants, 32% accepted, 16 enrolled. In 2016, 6 master's awarded. *Degree requirements:* For master's, thesis or alternative; for doctorate, comprehensive exam, thesis/dissertation. *Entrance requirements:* For doctorate, GRE. Additional exam requirements/recommendations for international students: Required—TOEFL (minimum score 550 paper-based, 79 iBT) or IELTS (6). *Application deadline:* For fall admission, 3/1 priority date for domestic students; for spring admission, 11/1 priority date for domestic students; for summer admission, 4/1 priority date for domestic students. Applications are processed on a rolling basis. Application fee: $50. Electronic applications accepted. *Expenses: Tuition:* Full-time $16,296; part-time $1358 per credit hour. *Required fees:* $1294; $647 per semester. One-time fee: $100 full-time. Tuition and fees vary according to course load, degree level and program. *Financial support:* Research assistantships, teaching assistantships, career-related internships or fieldwork, scholarships/grants, unspecified assistantships, and on-campus employment available. Financial award application deadline: 3/15; financial award applicants required to submit FAFSA. *Unit head:* Scott Shappell, PhD, Professor/Department Chair, E-mail: scott.shappell@erau.edu. *Application contact:* Graduate Admissions, 800-862-2416, E-mail: graduate.admissions@erau.edu.
Website: http://daytonabeach.erau.edu/college-arts-sciences/human-factors/index.html

Florida Institute of Technology, College of Aeronautics, Program in Aviation Human Factors, Melbourne, FL 32901-6975. Offers MS. *Program availability:* Part-time. *Students:* 7 full-time (2 women), 1 part-time, 2 international. Average age 25. 13 applicants, 69% accepted, 4 enrolled. In 2016, 2 master's awarded. *Degree requirements:* For master's, thesis optional, minimum of 36 credit hours. *Entrance requirements:* For master's, GRE General Test, 3 letters of recommendation, statement of objectives, resume. Additional exam requirements/recommendations for international students: Required—TOEFL (minimum score 550 paper-based; 79 iBT). *Application deadline:* Applications are processed on a rolling basis. Electronic applications accepted. *Expenses: Tuition:* Full-time $22,338; part-time $1241 per credit hour. *Required fees:* $250. Tuition and fees vary according to degree level, campus/location and program. *Financial support:* Applicants required to submit FAFSA. *Unit head:* Dr. Korhan Oyman, Dean, 321-674-8971, Fax: 321-674-8059, E-mail: koyman@fit.edu. *Application contact:* Cheryl A. Brown, Associate Director of Graduate Admissions, 321-674-7581, Fax: 321-723-9468, E-mail: cbrown@fit.edu.
Website: http://www.fit.edu/programs/8229/ms-aviation-human-factors#.VT_URE10ypo

Florida Institute of Technology, College of Aeronautics, Program in Human Factors in Aeronautics, Melbourne, FL 32901-6975. Offers MS. *Program availability:* Part-time, evening/weekend, online only, 100% online. *Students:* 3 full-time (0 women), 16 part-time (4 women); includes 2 minority (1 Asian, non-Hispanic/Latino; 1 Hispanic/Latino), 1 international. Average age 36. 15 applicants, 20% accepted, 3 enrolled. In 2016, 10 master's awarded. *Degree requirements:* For master's, thesis, 36 credit hours. *Entrance requirements:* For master's, GRE, 3 letters of recommendation, resume, statement of objectives. Additional exam requirements/recommendations for international students: Required—TOEFL (minimum score 550 paper-based; 79 iBT). *Application deadline:* Applications are processed on a rolling basis. Electronic applications accepted. *Expenses: Tuition:* Full-time $22,338; part-time $1241 per credit hour. *Required fees:* $250. Tuition and fees vary according to degree level, campus/location and program. *Unit head:* Dr. Korhan Oyman, Dean, 321-674-8971, Fax: 321-674-8059, E-mail: koyman@fit.edu. *Application contact:* Cheryl A. Brown, Associate Director of Graduate Admissions, 321-674-7581, Fax: 321-723-9468, E-mail: cbrown@fit.edu.
Website: http://coa.fit.edu

Florida Institute of Technology, School of Human-Centered Design, Innovation and Art, Melbourne, FL 32901-6975. Offers human-centered design (MS, PhD). *Program availability:* Part-time, evening/weekend. *Faculty:* 3 full-time (0 women). *Students:* 9 full-time (2 women), 4 part-time (1 woman); includes 3 minority (1 Black or African American, non-Hispanic/Latino; 1 Asian, non-Hispanic/Latino; 1 Two or more races, non-Hispanic/Latino), 6 international. Average age 35. 21 applicants, 57% accepted, 4 enrolled. In 2016, 4 master's, 1 doctorate awarded. *Degree requirements:* For master's, comprehensive exam (for some programs), thesis or final exam, professional oriented project; for doctorate, comprehensive exam, thesis/dissertation, publication in journal. *Entrance requirements:* For master's, GRE (minimum score of 1100), undergraduate degree with minimum GPA of 3.2; three letters of recommendation; statement of objectives; resume; for doctorate, GRE, master's degree with minimum cumulative GPA of 3.2; transcripts; three letters of recommendation; statement of objectives; resume. Additional exam requirements/recommendations for international students: Required—TOEFL (minimum score 600 paper-based; 100 iBT). *Application deadline:* For fall admission, 4/1 for international students; for spring admission, 9/30 for international students. Applications are processed on a rolling basis. Electronic applications accepted. *Expenses: Tuition:* Full-time $22,338; part-time $1241 per credit hour. *Required fees:* $250. Tuition and fees vary according to degree level, campus/location and program. *Financial support:* In 2016–17, 5 research assistantships with partial tuition reimbursements were awarded; career-related internships or fieldwork, institutionally sponsored loans, tuition waivers (partial), unspecified assistantships, and tuition remissions also available. Financial award application deadline: 3/1; financial award applicants required to submit FAFSA. *Faculty research:* Cognitive engineering, advanced interaction media, complexity analysis in human-centered design, life-critical systems, human-centered organization design and management, modeling and simulation. *Unit head:* Dr. Guy Boy, Director, 321-674-7631, Fax: 321-984-8461, E-mail: gboy@fit.edu. *Application contact:* Cheryl A. Brown, Associate Director of Graduate Admissions, 321-674-7581, Fax: 321-723-9468, E-mail: cbrown@fit.edu.
Website: http://research.fit.edu/hcdi/

Georgia Institute of Technology, Graduate Studies, College of Computing, Program in Human-Centered Computing, Atlanta, GA 30332-0001. Offers MS, PhD. *Program availability:* Part-time. *Degree requirements:* For doctorate, comprehensive exam, thesis/dissertation, research project, teaching requirement. *Entrance requirements:* For doctorate, GRE General Test. Additional exam requirements/recommendations for international students: Required—TOEFL (minimum score 600 paper-based; 100 iBT). Electronic applications accepted.

Indiana University Bloomington, School of Public Health, Department of Kinesiology, Bloomington, IN 47405. Offers applied sport science (MS); athletic administration/sport management (MS); athletic training (MS); biomechanics (MS); ergonomics (MS); exercise physiology (MS); human performance (PhD), including biomechanics, exercise physiology, motor learning/control, sport management; motor learning/control (MS); physical activity (MPH); physical activity, fitness and wellness (MS). *Program availability:* Part-time. Terminal master's awarded for partial completion of doctoral program. *Degree requirements:* For master's, thesis optional; for doctorate, variable foreign language requirement, comprehensive exam, thesis/dissertation. *Entrance requirements:* For master's, GRE General Test, minimum GPA of 2.8; for doctorate, GRE General Test, minimum graduate GPA of 3.5, undergraduate 3.0. Additional exam requirements/recommendations for international students: Required—TOEFL (minimum score 80 iBT). *Faculty research:* Exercise physiology and biochemistry, sports biomechanics, human motor control, adaptation of fitness and exercise to special populations.

Michigan Technological University, Graduate School, College of Sciences and Arts, Department of Cognitive and Learning Sciences, Houghton, MI 49931. Offers applied cognitive science and human factors (MS, PhD); applied science education (MS); post-secondary STEM education (Graduate Certificate). *Program availability:* Part-time, blended/hybrid learning. *Faculty:* 24 full-time (9 women), 11 part-time/adjunct (3 women). *Students:* 12 full-time (8 women), 21 part-time (10 women); includes 2 minority (1 Black or African American, non-Hispanic/Latino; 1 Two or more races, non-Hispanic/Latino), 3 international. Average age 35. 46 applicants, 20% accepted, 5 enrolled. In 2016, 6 master's, 4 doctorates awarded. Terminal master's awarded for partial completion of doctoral program. *Degree requirements:* For master's, comprehensive exam (for some programs), thesis (for some programs); for doctorate, comprehensive exam, thesis/dissertation, applied internship experience. *Entrance requirements:* For master's, GRE (for applied cognitive science and human factors program only), statement of purpose, personal statement, official transcripts, 3 letters of recommendation, resume/curriculum vitae; for doctorate, GRE, statement of purpose, personal statement, official transcripts, 3 letters of recommendation, resume/curriculum vitae. Additional exam requirements/recommendations for international students: Required—TOEFL (recommended minimum score 90 iBT) or IELTS. *Application deadline:* For fall admission, 2/15 priority date for domestic and international students. Applications are processed on a rolling basis. Electronic applications accepted. *Expenses:* Tuition, state resident: full-time $16,290; part-time $905 per credit. Tuition, nonresident: full-time $16,290; part-time $905 per credit. *Required fees:* $248; $124 per term. Tuition and fees vary according to course load and program. *Financial support:* In 2016–17, 14 students received support, including 2 fellowships (averaging $15,242 per year), 7 research assistantships with tuition reimbursements available (averaging $15,242 per year), teaching assistantships (averaging $15,242 per year); career-related internships or fieldwork, Federal Work-Study, scholarships/grants, health care benefits, unspecified assistantships, and adjunct instructor positions also available. Financial award applicants required to submit FAFSA. *Faculty research:* Physical ergonomics, applied science education, applied cognitive science, human factors, educational technology cognitive modeling. *Total annual research expenditures:* $308,969. *Unit head:* Dr. Susan L. Amato-Henderson, Chair, 906-487-2536, Fax: 906-487-2468, E-mail: slamato@mtu.edu. *Application contact:* Carol T. Wingerson, Senior Staff Assistant, 906-487-2328, Fax: 906-487-2284, E-mail: gradadms@mtu.edu.
Website: http://www.mtu.edu/cls/

Mississippi State University, Bagley College of Engineering, Department of Industrial and Systems Engineering, Mississippi State, MS 39762. Offers human factors and ergonomics (MS); industrial and systems engineering (PhD); industrial systems (MS); management systems (MS); manufacturing systems (MS); operations research (MS). *Program availability:* Part-time, blended/hybrid learning. *Faculty:* 12 full-time (1 woman). *Students:* 25 full-time (5 women), 59 part-time (13 women); includes 18 minority (6 Black or African American, non-Hispanic/Latino; 5 Asian, non-Hispanic/Latino; 6 Hispanic/Latino; 1 Native Hawaiian or other Pacific Islander, non-Hispanic/Latino), 21 international. Average age 35. 72 applicants, 32% accepted, 11 enrolled. In 2016, 11 master's, 7 doctorates awarded. *Degree requirements:* For master's, comprehensive exam (for some programs), thesis optional, comprehensive oral or written exam; for doctorate, comprehensive exam, thesis/dissertation, candidacy exam. *Entrance requirements:* For master's, GRE (for graduates from program not accredited by EAC/ABET), minimum GPA of 3.0 on junior and senior years; for doctorate, GRE (for graduates from program not accredited by EAC/ABET), minimum GPA of 3.5 on master's degree and junior and senior years of BS. Additional exam requirements/recommendations for international students: Required—TOEFL (minimum score 550 paper-based; 79 iBT); Recommended—IELTS (minimum score 6.5). *Application deadline:* For fall admission, 7/1 for domestic students, 5/1 for international students; for spring admission, 11/1 for domestic students, 9/1 for international students. Applications are processed on a rolling basis. Application fee: $60. Electronic applications accepted. *Expenses:* Tuition, state resident: full-time $7670; part-time $852.50 per credit hour. Tuition, nonresident: full-time $20,790; part-time $2310.50 per credit hour. Part-time tuition and fees vary according to course load. *Financial support:* In 2016–17, 12 research assistantships with full tuition reimbursements (averaging $16,360 per year), 3 teaching assistantships with full tuition reimbursements (averaging $17,014 per year) were awarded; Federal Work-Study, institutionally sponsored loans, and unspecified assistantships also available. Financial award application deadline: 4/1; financial award applicants required to submit FAFSA. *Faculty research:* Operations research, ergonomics, production systems, management systems, transportation. *Total annual research expenditures:* $4.4 million. *Unit head:* Dr. John Usher, Professor/Department Head, 662-325-7624, Fax: 662-325-7618, E-mail: usher@ise.msstate.edu. *Application contact:* Doretta Martin, Senior Admissions Assistant, 662-325-9514, E-mail: dmartin@grad.msstate.edu.
Website: http://www.ise.msstate.edu/

Missouri Western State University, Program in Applied Science, St. Joseph, MO 64507-2294. Offers chemistry (MAS); engineering technology management (MAS); human factors and usability testing (MAS); industrial life science (MAS); sport and fitness management (MAS). *Accreditation:* AACSB. *Program availability:* Part-time. *Students:* 41 full-time (18 women), 27 part-time (11 women); includes 7 minority (6 Black or African American, non-Hispanic/Latino; 1 Two or more races, non-Hispanic/Latino), 15 international. Average age 29. 43 applicants, 88% accepted, 30 enrolled. In 2016, 34 master's awarded. *Entrance requirements:* Additional exam requirements/recommendations for international students: Recommended—TOEFL (minimum score 79 iBT), IELTS (minimum score 6). *Application deadline:* For fall admission, 7/15 for domestic and international students; for spring admission, 10/1 for domestic and international students; for summer admission, 3/15 for domestic students. Applications are processed on a rolling basis. Application fee: $50. Electronic applications accepted. *Expenses:* Tuition, state resident: full-time $6548; part-time $327.39 per credit hour. Tuition, nonresident: full-time $11,848; part-time $592.39 per credit hour. *Required fees:* $542; $99 per credit hour. $176 per semester. One-time fee: $50. Tuition and fees vary according to course load and program. *Financial support:* Scholarships/grants and unspecified assistantships available. Support available to part-time students. *Unit head:* Dr. Benjamin D. Caldwell, Dean of the Graduate School, 816-271-4394, Fax: 816-271-4525, E-mail: graduate@missouriwestern.edu.

New York University, Graduate School of Arts and Science, Department of Environmental Medicine, New York, NY 10012-1019. Offers environmental health sciences (MS, PhD), including biostatistics (PhD), environmental hygiene (MS), epidemiology (PhD), ergonomics and biomechanics (PhD), exposure assessment and health effects (PhD), molecular toxicology/carcinogenesis (PhD), toxicology. *Program availability:* Part-time. Terminal master's awarded for partial completion of doctoral program. *Degree requirements:* For master's, thesis or alternative; for doctorate, one foreign language, thesis/dissertation, oral and written exams. *Entrance requirements:*

Ergonomics and Human Factors

For master's and doctorate, GRE General Test, minimum GPA of 3.0; bachelor's degree in biological, physical, or engineering science. Additional exam requirements/recommendations for international students: Required—TOEFL.

North Carolina State University, Graduate School, College of Humanities and Social Sciences, Department of Psychology, Raleigh, NC 27695. Offers developmental psychology (PhD); ergonomics and experimental psychology (PhD); industrial/organizational psychology (PhD); psychology in the public interest (PhD); school psychology (PhD). *Accreditation:* APA. *Degree requirements:* For doctorate, comprehensive exam, thesis/dissertation. *Entrance requirements:* For doctorate, GRE General Test, GRE Subject Test (industrial/organizational psychology), MAT (recommended), minimum GPA of 3.0 in major. Electronic applications accepted. *Faculty research:* Cognitive and social development (human factors, families, the workplace, community issues and health, aging).

Old Dominion University, College of Sciences, Doctoral Program in Psychology, Norfolk, VA 23529. Offers applied psychological sciences (PhD); human factors psychology (PhD); industrial/organizational psychology (PhD). *Faculty:* 28 full-time (12 women), 11 part-time/adjunct (9 women). *Students:* 47 full-time (26 women); includes 4 minority (1 Black or African American, non-Hispanic/Latino; 3 Hispanic/Latino). Average age 25. 74 applicants, 14% accepted, 9 enrolled. In 2016, 3 doctorates awarded. *Degree requirements:* For doctorate, comprehensive exam, thesis/dissertation, candidacy exam. *Entrance requirements:* For doctorate, GRE General Test, GRE Subject Test, 3 recommendation letters. Additional exam requirements/recommendations for international students: Required—TOEFL. *Application deadline:* For winter admission, 1/5 for domestic and international students. Application fee: $50. Electronic applications accepted. *Expenses:* $478 per credit hour in-state; $1,195 per credit hour out-of-state. *Financial support:* In 2016–17, 40 students received support, including 5 research assistantships with full tuition reimbursements available (averaging $15,000 per year), 35 teaching assistantships with full tuition reimbursements available (averaging $15,000 per year). Financial award application deadline: 1/15. *Faculty research:* Human factors, industrial psychology, organizational psychology, applied psychological sciences (health, developmental, community, quantitative). *Total annual research expenditures:* $978,563. *Unit head:* Dr. Debra A. Major, Graduate Program Director, 757-683-4235, Fax: 757-683-5087, E-mail: dmajor@odu.edu. *Application contact:* William Heffelfinger, Director of Graduate Admissions, 757-683-5554, Fax: 757-683-3255, E-mail: gradadmit@odu.edu.
Website: http://www.odu.edu/psychology/

Purdue University, Graduate School, College of Health and Human Sciences, School of Health Sciences, West Lafayette, IN 47907. Offers health physics (MS, PhD); medical physics (MS, PhD); occupational and environmental health science (MS, PhD), including aerosol deposition and lung disease, ergonomics, exposure and risk assessment, indoor air quality and bioaerosols (PhD), liver/lung toxicology; radiation biology (PhD); toxicology (PhD); MS/PhD. *Program availability:* Part-time. *Faculty:* 12 full-time (4 women), 1 part-time/adjunct. *Students:* 37 full-time (16 women), 5 part-time (1 woman); includes 6 minority (2 Black or African American, non-Hispanic/Latino; 2 Asian, non-Hispanic/Latino; 1 Hispanic/Latino; 1 Two or more races, non-Hispanic/Latino), 9 international. Average age 28. 57 applicants, 65% accepted, 15 enrolled. In 2016, 10 master's, 4 doctorates awarded. *Degree requirements:* For master's, thesis optional; for doctorate, one foreign language, thesis/dissertation. *Entrance requirements:* For master's and doctorate, GRE General Test, minimum undergraduate GPA of 3.0 or equivalent. Additional exam requirements/recommendations for international students: Required—TOEFL (minimum score 550 paper-based; 77 iBT); Recommended—TWE. *Application deadline:* For fall admission, 5/15 for domestic and international students; for spring admission, 10/15 for domestic and international students. Applications are processed on a rolling basis. Application fee: $60 ($75 for international students). Electronic applications accepted. *Financial support:* In 2016–17, fellowships with tuition reimbursements (averaging $14,400 per year), research assistantships with tuition reimbursements (averaging $12,000 per year), teaching assistantships with tuition reimbursements (averaging $12,000 per year) were awarded; career-related internships or fieldwork and traineeships also available. Support available to part-time students. Financial award applicants required to submit FAFSA. *Faculty research:* Environmental toxicology, industrial hygiene, radiation dosimetry. *Unit head:* Dr. Wei Zheng, Head, 765-494-1419, E-mail: wz18@purdue.edu. *Application contact:* Karen E. Walker, Graduate Contact, 765-494-1419, E-mail: kwalker@purdue.edu.
Website: http://www.healthsciences.purdue.edu/

Tufts University, School of Engineering, Department of Mechanical Engineering, Medford, MA 02155. Offers bioengineering (ME, MS), including bioinformatics, biomechanical systems and devices, signals and systems; bioinformatics (MS); human factors (MS); mechanical engineering (ME, MS, PhD). *Program availability:* Part-time. Terminal master's awarded for partial completion of doctoral program. *Degree requirements:* For master's, thesis; for doctorate, thesis/dissertation. *Entrance requirements:* For master's and doctorate, GRE General Test. Additional exam requirements/recommendations for international students: Required—TOEFL (minimum score 550 paper-based; 80 iBT), IELTS (minimum score 6.5). Electronic applications accepted. *Expenses: Tuition:* Full-time $49,892; part-time $1248 per credit hour. *Required fees:* $844. Full-time tuition and fees vary according to degree level, program and student level. Part-time tuition and fees vary according to course load. *Faculty research:* Applied mechanics, biomaterials, controls/robotics, design/systems, human factors.

Université de Montréal, Faculty of Medicine, Programs in Ergonomics, Montréal, QC H3C 3J7, Canada. Offers occupational therapy (DESS). Program offered jointly with École Polytechnique de Montréal.

Université du Québec à Montréal, Graduate Programs, Program in Ergonomics in Occupational Health and Safety, Montréal, QC H3C 3P8, Canada. Offers Diploma. *Program availability:* Part-time. *Entrance requirements:* For degree, appropriate bachelor's degree or equivalent, proficiency in French.

The University of Alabama, Graduate School, College of Human Environmental Sciences, Program in Human Environmental Science, Tuscaloosa, AL 35487. Offers interactive technology (MS); quality management (MS); restaurant and meeting management (MS); rural community health (MS); sport management (MS). *Program availability:* Part-time, evening/weekend, online learning. *Faculty:* 52 full-time (38 women), 3 part-time/adjunct (2 women). *Students:* 213 full-time (138 women), 392 part-time (278 women); includes 142 minority (105 Black or African American, non-Hispanic/Latino; 3 American Indian or Alaska Native, non-Hispanic/Latino; 4 Asian, non-Hispanic/Latino; 17 Hispanic/Latino; 2 Native Hawaiian or other Pacific Islander, non-Hispanic/Latino; 11 Two or more races, non-Hispanic/Latino), 5 international. Average age 33. 400 applicants, 74% accepted, 232 enrolled. In 2016, 230 master's awarded. *Degree requirements:* For master's, comprehensive exam. *Entrance requirements:* For master's, GRE (for some specializations), minimum GPA of 3.0. Additional exam requirements/recommendations for international students: Required—TOEFL. *Application deadline:* For fall admission, 7/1 for domestic students; for spring admission, 11/1 for domestic students; for summer admission, 4/15 for domestic students. Applications are processed on a rolling basis. Application fee: $50 ($60 for international students). Electronic applications accepted. *Expenses:* Tuition, state resident: full-time $10,470. Tuition, nonresident: full-time $26,950. *Financial support:* In 2016–17, 2 teaching assistantships with full tuition reimbursements were awarded. Financial award application deadline: 7/1. *Faculty research:* Rural health, hospitality management, sport management, interactive technology, consumer quality management, environmental health and safety. *Unit head:* Dr. Milla D. Boschung, Dean, 205-348-6250, Fax: 205-348-1786, E-mail: mboschun@ches.ua.edu. *Application contact:* Dr. Stuart Usdan, Associate Dean, 205-348-6150, Fax: 205-348-3789, E-mail: susdan@ches.ua.edu.
Website: http://www.ches.ua.edu/programs-of-study.html

University of Cincinnati, Graduate School, College of Medicine, Graduate Programs in Biomedical Sciences, Department of Environmental Health, Cincinnati, OH 45221. Offers environmental and industrial hygiene (MS, PhD); environmental and occupational medicine (MS); environmental genetics and molecular toxicology (MS, PhD); epidemiology and biostatistics (MS, PhD); occupational safety and ergonomics (MS, PhD). *Accreditation:* ABET (one or more programs are accredited); CEPH. Terminal master's awarded for partial completion of doctoral program. *Degree requirements:* For master's, thesis; for doctorate, thesis/dissertation, qualifying exam. *Entrance requirements:* For master's, GRE General Test, bachelor's degree in science; for doctorate, GRE General Test. Additional exam requirements/recommendations for international students: Required—TOEFL (minimum score 600 paper-based; 100 iBT). Electronic applications accepted. *Expenses: Tuition, area resident:* Full-time $12,790; part-time $389 per credit hour. Tuition, state resident: full-time $13,290; part-time $419 per credit hour. Tuition, nonresident: full-time $24,532; part-time $976 per credit hour. *International tuition:* $24,832 full-time. *Required fees:* $3958; $140 per credit hour. Tuition and fees vary according to course load, degree level, program and reciprocity agreements. *Faculty research:* Carcinogens and mutagenesis, pulmonary studies, reproduction and development.

The University of Iowa, Graduate College, College of Engineering, Department of Industrial Engineering, Iowa City, IA 52242-1316. Offers engineering design and manufacturing (MS, PhD); healthcare systems (MS, PhD); human factors (MS, PhD); information and engineering management (MS, PhD); operations research (MS, PhD); wind energy (MS, PhD). *Faculty:* 11 full-time (1 woman), 1 part-time/adjunct (0 women). *Students:* 15 full-time (2 women), 6 part-time (0 women); includes 2 minority (1 Asian, non-Hispanic/Latino; 1 Two or more races, non-Hispanic/Latino), 11 international. Average age 29. 68 applicants, 9% accepted, 5 enrolled. In 2016, 4 master's, 3 doctorates awarded. Terminal master's awarded for partial completion of doctoral program. *Degree requirements:* For master's, thesis optional, exam; for doctorate, comprehensive exam, thesis/dissertation, final defense exam. *Entrance requirements:* For master's and doctorate, GRE (minimum Verbal score of 153, Quantitative 151), minimum undergraduate GPA of 3.0. Additional exam requirements/recommendations for international students: Required—TOEFL (minimum score 600 paper-based; 100 iBT), IELTS (minimum score 7). *Application deadline:* For fall admission, 7/15 for domestic students, 4/15 for international students; for spring admission, 12/1 for domestic students, 10/1 for international students; for summer admission, 4/15 for domestic students, 3/1 for international students. Applications are processed on a rolling basis. Application fee: $60 ($100 for international students). Electronic applications accepted. *Financial support:* In 2016–17, 21 students received support, including 1 fellowship with partial tuition reimbursement available (averaging $25,500 per year), 15 research assistantships with full tuition reimbursements available (averaging $22,981 per year), 5 teaching assistantships with full tuition reimbursements available (averaging $18,809 per year); career-related internships or fieldwork, scholarships/grants, and unspecified assistantships also available. Support available to part-time students. Financial award applicants required to submit FAFSA. *Faculty research:* Operations research, informatics, human factors engineering, healthcare systems, bio-manufacturing, manufacturing systems, renewable energy, human-machine interactions. *Total annual research expenditures:* $6.3 million. *Unit head:* Dr. Ching-Long Lin, Department Executive Officer, 319-335-5673, Fax: 319-335-5669, E-mail: ching-long-lin@uiowa.edu. *Application contact:* Tara Hoadley, Academic Program Specialist, 319-335-5939, Fax: 319-335-5669, E-mail: indeng@engineering.uiowa.edu.
Website: https://mie.engineering.uiowa.edu

The University of Iowa, Graduate College, College of Public Health, Department of Occupational and Environmental Health, Iowa City, IA 52242-1316. Offers agricultural safety and health (MS, PhD); ergonomics (MPH); industrial hygiene (MS, PhD); occupational and environmental health (MPH, MS, PhD, Certificate); MS/MA; MS/MS. *Accreditation:* ABET (one or more programs are accredited); CEPH. *Degree requirements:* For master's, thesis optional, exam; for doctorate, comprehensive exam, thesis/dissertation. *Entrance requirements:* For master's and doctorate, GRE General Test, minimum GPA of 3.0. Additional exam requirements/recommendations for international students: Required—TOEFL (minimum score 600 paper-based; 100 iBT). Electronic applications accepted.

University of Miami, Graduate School, College of Engineering, Department of Industrial Engineering, Program in Occupational Ergonomics and Safety, Coral Gables, FL 33124. Offers environmental health and safety (MS); occupational ergonomics and safety (MSOES). *Program availability:* Part-time. *Degree requirements:* For master's, thesis optional. *Entrance requirements:* For master's, GRE General Test, minimum GPA of 3.0. Additional exam requirements/recommendations for international students: Required—TOEFL (minimum score 550 paper-based). Electronic applications accepted. *Faculty research:* Noise, heat stress, water pollution.

University of Wisconsin–Madison, Graduate School, College of Engineering, Department of Industrial and Systems Engineering, Madison, WI 53706. Offers industrial engineering (MS, PhD), including human factors and health systems engineering (MS), systems engineering and analytics (MS). *Program availability:* Part-time. *Faculty:* 18 full-time (5 women). *Students:* 94 full-time (37 women), 6 part-time (2 women); includes 2 minority (both Black or African American, non-Hispanic/Latino), 73 international. Average age 26. 463 applicants, 22% accepted, 35 enrolled. In 2016, 28 master's, 13 doctorates awarded. Terminal master's awarded for partial completion of doctoral program. *Degree requirements:* For master's, thesis optional, 30 credits; minimum GPA of 3.0; for doctorate, comprehensive exam, thesis/dissertation, minimum of 32 credits; minimum GPA of 3.0. *Entrance requirements:* For master's and doctorate, GRE General Test, minimum GPA of 3.0, BS in engineering or equivalent, course work in computer programming and statistics. Additional exam requirements/recommendations for international students: Required—TOEFL (minimum score 580 paper-based; 92 iBT), IELTS (minimum score 7). *Application deadline:* For fall admission, 1/1 for domestic and international students; for spring admission, 10/1 for domestic and international students; for summer admission, 2/1 for domestic and international students. Application fee: $75 ($81 for international students). Electronic applications accepted. *Expenses:* $13,157 per year in-state tuition and fees; $26,484 per year out-of-state tuition and fees. *Financial support:* In 2016–17, 50 students received support, including 1 fellowship with full tuition reimbursement available, 30 research assistantships with full tuition reimbursements available, 14 teaching assistantships with full tuition reimbursements available; career-related internships or fieldwork, Federal Work-Study, institutionally sponsored loans, scholarships/grants, traineeships, health care benefits, and unspecified assistantships also available. Financial award application deadline: 12/1; financial award applicants required to submit FAFSA. *Faculty research:* Operations

research; human factors and ergonomics; health systems engineering; manufacturing and production systems. *Total annual research expenditures:* $12.5 million. *Unit head:* Dr. Jeff Lindroth, Chair, 608-890-1931, Fax: 608-262-8454, E-mail: linderoth@wisc.edu. *Application contact:* Pam Peterson, Student Services Coordinator, 608-263-4025, Fax: 608-262-8454, E-mail: prpeterson@wisc.edu.
Website: http://www.engr.wisc.edu/department/industrial-systems-engineering/

University of Wisconsin–Milwaukee, Graduate School, College of Health Sciences, Department of Occupational Science and Technology, Milwaukee, WI 53201-0413. Offers assistive technology and design (MS); ergonomics (MS). *Accreditation:* AOTA. *Students:* 92 full-time (84 women), 4 part-time (3 women); includes 7 minority (3 Asian, non-Hispanic/Latino; 1 Hispanic/Latino; 3 Two or more races, non-Hispanic/Latino). Average age 26. 90 applicants, 40% accepted, 32 enrolled. In 2016, 34 master's awarded. *Degree requirements:* For master's, thesis or alternative. *Entrance requirements:* Additional exam requirements/recommendations for international students: Required—TOEFL (minimum score 550 paper-based; 79 iBT), IELTS (minimum score 6.5). *Application deadline:* For fall admission, 1/1 priority date for domestic students; for spring admission, 9/1 for domestic students. Applications are processed on a rolling basis. Application fee: $56 ($75 for international students). *Financial support:* Fellowships, research assistantships, teaching assistantships, and unspecified assistantships available. Support available to part-time students. Financial award application deadline: 4/15. *Unit head:* Jay Kapellusch, PhD, Department Chair, 414-229-5292, Fax: 414-229-2619, E-mail: kap@uwm.edu. *Application contact:* Bhagwant S. Sindhu, PhD, Graduate Program Coordinator, 414-229-1180, Fax: 414-229-5100, E-mail: sindhu@uwm.edu.
Website: http://uwm.edu/healthsciences/academics/occupational-science-technology/

Wright State University, Graduate School, College of Engineering and Computer Science, Department of Biomedical, Industrial and Human Factors Engineering, Dayton, OH 45435. Offers biomedical engineering (MS); industrial and human factors engineering (MS). *Program availability:* Part-time. *Degree requirements:* For master's, thesis or course option alternative. *Entrance requirements:* Additional exam requirements/recommendations for international students: Required—TOEFL. *Application deadline:* For fall admission, 5/30 for domestic students. Application fee: $25. *Expenses:* Tuition, state resident: full-time $9952; part-time $622 per credit hour. Tuition, nonresident: full-time $16,960; part-time $1060 per credit hour. *Financial support:* Fellowships, research assistantships, teaching assistantships, Federal Work-Study, institutionally sponsored loans, and unspecified assistantships available. Support available to part-time students. Financial award application deadline: 3/15; financial award applicants required to submit FAFSA. *Faculty research:* Medical imaging, functional electrical stimulation, implantable aids, man-machine interfaces, expert systems. *Unit head:* Dr. S. Narayanan, Chair, 937-775-5044, Fax: 937-775-7364, E-mail: sundaram.narayanan@wright.edu. *Application contact:* John Kimble, Associate Director of Graduate Admissions and Records, 937-775-2957, Fax: 937-775-2453, E-mail: john.kimble@wright.edu.
Website: https://engineering-computer-science.wright.edu/biomedical-industrial-and-human-factors-engineering

Wright State University, Graduate School, College of Science and Mathematics, Department of Psychology, Program in Human Factors and Industrial/Organizational Psychology, Dayton, OH 45435. Offers MS, PhD. *Degree requirements:* For master's, thesis; for doctorate, thesis/dissertation. *Expenses:* Tuition, state resident: full-time $9952; part-time $622 per credit hour. Tuition, nonresident: full-time $16,960; part-time $1060 per credit hour. *Unit head:* Dr. Dan Weber, Director, 937-775-2391, Fax: 937-775-3347, E-mail: dan.weber@wright.edu. *Application contact:* Dr. Dan Weber, Director, 937-775-2391, Fax: 937-775-3347, E-mail: dan.weber@wright.edu.

Management of Technology

Air Force Institute of Technology, Graduate School of Engineering and Management, Department of Operational Sciences, Dayton, OH 45433-7765. Offers logistics management (MS); operations research (MS, PhD); space operations (MS). *Program availability:* Part-time. *Degree requirements:* For master's, thesis; for doctorate, thesis/dissertation. *Entrance requirements:* For doctorate, GRE General Test, minimum GPA of 3.0, U.S. citizenship. *Faculty research:* Optimization, simulation, combat modeling and analysis, reliability and maintainability, resource scheduling.

Arizona State University at the Tempe campus, Ira A. Fulton Schools of Engineering, The Polytechnic School, Programs in Technology Management, Mesa, AZ 85212. Offers aviation management and human factors (MS); environmental technology management (MS); global technology and development (MS); graphic information technology (MS); management of technology (MS). *Program availability:* Part-time, evening/weekend, online learning. *Degree requirements:* For master's, thesis or applied project and oral defense; interactive Program of Study (iPOS) submitted before completing 50 percent of required credit hours. *Entrance requirements:* For master's, GRE, minimum GPA of 3.0 or equivalent in last 2 years of work leading to bachelor's degree. Additional exam requirements/recommendations for international students: Required—TOEFL, IELTS, or PTE. Electronic applications accepted. *Faculty research:* Digital imaging, digital publishing, Internet development/e-commerce, information aviation human factors, pilot selection, databases, multimedia, commercial digital photography, digital workflow, computer graphics modeling and animation, information design, sociotechnology, visual and technical literacy, environmental management, quality management, project management, industrial ethics, hazardous materials, environmental chemistry.

Athabasca University, Faculty of Business, Edmonton, AB T5L 4W1, Canada. Offers business administration (MBA); information technology management (MBA), including policing concentration; innovative management (DBA); management (GDM); project management (MBA, GDM). *Program availability:* Part-time, evening/weekend, online learning. *Degree requirements:* For master's, thesis or alternative, applied project. *Entrance requirements:* For master's, 3-8 years of managerial experience, 3 years with undergraduate degree, 5 years' managerial experience with professional designation, 8-10 years' management experience (on exception). Electronic applications accepted. *Expenses:* Contact institution. *Faculty research:* Human resources, project management, operations research, information technology management, corporate stewardship, energy management.

Boston University, Metropolitan College, Department of Administrative Sciences, Boston, MA 02215. Offers applied business analytics (MS); economic development and tourism management (MSAS); enterprise risk management (MS); financial management (MS); global marketing management (MS); innovation and technology (MSAS); insurance management (MSM); project management (MS); supply chain management (MS). *Accreditation:* AACSB. *Program availability:* Part-time, evening/weekend, online learning. *Faculty:* 15 full-time (3 women), 22 part-time/adjunct (3 women). *Students:* 301 full-time (146 women), 934 part-time (501 women); includes 237 minority (81 Black or African American, non-Hispanic/Latino; 5 American Indian or Alaska Native, non-Hispanic/Latino; 60 Asian, non-Hispanic/Latino; 76 Hispanic/Latino; 1 Native Hawaiian or other Pacific Islander, non-Hispanic/Latino; 14 Two or more races, non-Hispanic/Latino), 514 international. Average age 31. 593 applicants, 69% accepted, 260 enrolled. In 2016, 263 master's awarded. *Degree requirements:* For master's, thesis optional. *Entrance requirements:* For master's, 1 year of work experience, minimum GPA of 3.0. Additional exam requirements/recommendations for international students: Required—TOEFL (minimum score 84 iBT). *Application deadline:* Applications are processed on a rolling basis. Application fee: $80. Electronic applications accepted. *Expenses:* Contact institution. *Financial support:* In 2016–17, 15 students received support, including 14 research assistantships (averaging $8,400 per year); career-related internships or fieldwork, Federal Work-Study, and unspecified assistantships also available. *Faculty research:* International business, innovative process. *Unit head:* Dr. John Sullivan, Chair, 617-353-3016, E-mail: adminsc@bu.edu. *Application contact:* Fiona Niven, Administrative Sciences Department, 617-353-3016, E-mail: adminsc@bu.edu.
Website: http://www.bu.edu/met/academic-community/departments/administrative-sciences/

California Lutheran University, Graduate Studies, School of Management, Thousand Oaks, CA 91360-2787. Offers business (IMBA); computer science (MS); econometrics (MBA); economics (MS); entrepreneurship (MBA, Certificate); finance (MBA, Certificate); financial planning (MBA, Certificate); information systems and technology (MS); information technology management (MBA, Certificate); international business (MBA, Certificate); management and organization behavior (MBA); management and organizational behavior (Certificate); marketing (MBA, Certificate); microeconomics (MBA); nonprofit and social enterprise (MBA); public policy and administration (MPPA). *Program availability:* Part-time, evening/weekend, 100% online, blended/hybrid learning. *Faculty:* 25 full-time (10 women), 36 part-time/adjunct (12 women). *Students:* 427 full-time (172 women), 189 part-time (87 women); includes 120 minority (14 Black or African American, non-Hispanic/Latino; 2 American Indian or Alaska Native, non-Hispanic/Latino; 19 Asian, non-Hispanic/Latino; 37 Hispanic/Latino; 48 Two or more races, non-Hispanic/Latino), 338 international. Average age 30. 591 applicants, 64% accepted, 131 enrolled. In 2016, 305 master's awarded. *Entrance requirements:* For master's, GMAT, interview, minimum GPA of 3.0. *Application deadline:* Applications are processed on a rolling basis. Application fee: $50. Electronic applications accepted. *Expenses:* Contact institution. *Unit head:* Dr. Gerhard Apfelthaler, Dean, 805-493-3360. *Application contact:* 805-493-3325, Fax: 805-493-3861, E-mail: clugrad@callutheran.edu.
Website: http://www.callutheran.edu/management/

California State University, Los Angeles, Graduate Studies, College of Engineering, Computer Science, and Technology, Department of Technology, Los Angeles, CA 90032-8530. Offers industrial and technical studies (MA). *Program availability:* Part-time, evening/weekend. *Entrance requirements:* For master's, minimum GPA of 2.5. Additional exam requirements/recommendations for international students: Required—TOEFL (minimum score 550 paper-based).

Cambridge College, School of Management, Cambridge, MA 02138-5304. Offers business negotiation and conflict resolution (M Mgt); general business (M Mgt); health care informatics (M Mgt); health care management (M Mgt); leadership in human and organizational dynamics (M Mgt); non-profit and public organization management (M Mgt); small business development (M Mgt); technology management (M Mgt). *Program availability:* Part-time, evening/weekend. *Degree requirements:* For master's, thesis, seminars. *Entrance requirements:* For master's, resume, 2 professional references. Additional exam requirements/recommendations for international students: Required—TOEFL (minimum score 550 paper-based; 79 iBT), Michigan English Language Assessment Battery (minimum score 85); Recommended—IELTS (minimum score 6). Electronic applications accepted. *Expenses:* Contact institution. *Faculty research:* Negotiation, mediation and conflict resolution; leadership; management of diverse organizations; case studies and simulation methodologies for management education, digital as a second language: social networking for digital immigrants, non-profit and public management.

Capella University, School of Business and Technology, Doctoral Programs in Technology, Minneapolis, MN 55402. Offers general information technology (PhD); global operations and supply chain management (DBA); information assurance and security (PhD); information technology education (PhD); information technology management (DBA, PhD).

Capella University, School of Business and Technology, Master's Programs in Technology, Minneapolis, MN 55402. Offers enterprise software architecture (MS); general information systems and technology management (MS); global operations and supply chain management (MBA); information assurance and security (MS); information technology management (MBA); network management (MS).

Carleton University, Faculty of Graduate Studies, Faculty of Engineering and Design, Ottawa-Carleton Institute for Electrical Engineering, Department of Systems and Computer Engineering, Program in Technology Innovation Management, Ottawa, ON K1S 5B6, Canada. Offers M Eng, MA Sc. *Degree requirements:* For master's, thesis optional. *Entrance requirements:* For master's, honors degree. Additional exam requirements/recommendations for international students: Required—TOEFL.

The Catholic University of America, School of Engineering, Program in Engineering Management, Washington, DC 20064. Offers engineering management (MSE, Certificate), including engineering management and organization (MSE), project and systems engineering management (MSE), technology management (MSE); program management (Certificate); systems engineering and management of information technology (Certificate). *Program availability:* Part-time. *Faculty:* 3 part-time/adjunct (0 women). *Students:* 14 full-time (2 women), 11 part-time (3 women); includes 2 minority (both Two or more races, non-Hispanic/Latino), 20 international. Average age 30. 35 applicants, 54% accepted, 11 enrolled. In 2016, 26 master's awarded. *Degree requirements:* For master's, minimum GPA of 3.0. *Entrance requirements:* For master's and Certificate, statement of purpose, official copies of academic transcripts, two letters of recommendation. Additional exam requirements/recommendations for international students: Required—TOEFL (minimum score 550 paper-based; 80 iBT). *Application deadline:* For fall admission, 7/15 priority date for domestic students, 7/1 for international students; for spring admission, 11/15 priority date for domestic students, 11/1 for international students. Applications are processed on a rolling basis. Application fee: $55. Electronic applications accepted. *Expenses:* $43,380 per year; $1,170 per credit; $200 per semester part-time fees. *Financial support:* Fellowships, research

assistantships, teaching assistantships, Federal Work-Study, scholarships/grants, tuition waivers (full and partial), and unspecified assistantships available. Financial award application deadline: 2/1; financial award applicants required to submit FAFSA. *Faculty research:* Engineering management and organization, project and systems engineering management, technology management. *Unit head:* Melvin G. Williams, Jr., Director, 202-319-5191, Fax: 202-319-6860, E-mail: williamsme@cua.edu. *Application contact:* Director of Graduate Admissions, 202-319-5057, Fax: 202-319-6533, E-mail: cua-admissions@cua.edu.
Website: http://engrmgmt.cua.edu/

Central Connecticut State University, School of Graduate Studies, School of Engineering, Science and Technology, Department of Manufacturing and Construction Management, New Britain, CT 06050-4010. Offers construction management (MS, Certificate); environmental and occupational safety (Certificate); lean manufacturing and Six Sigma (Certificate); supply chain and logistics (Certificate); technology management (MS). *Program availability:* Part-time, evening/weekend. *Faculty:* 7 full-time (0 women), 3 part-time/adjunct (0 women). *Students:* 23 full-time (6 women), 88 part-time (21 women); includes 29 minority (11 Black or African American, non-Hispanic/Latino; 7 Asian, non-Hispanic/Latino; 10 Hispanic/Latino; 1 Two or more races, non-Hispanic/Latino), 12 international. Average age 34. 79 applicants, 68% accepted, 32 enrolled. In 2016, 43 master's, 4 other advanced degrees awarded. *Degree requirements:* For master's, comprehensive exam, special project; for Certificate, qualifying exam. *Entrance requirements:* For master's, minimum undergraduate GPA of 2.7. Additional exam requirements/recommendations for international students: Required—TOEFL (minimum score 550 paper-based; 79 iBT). *Application deadline:* For fall admission, 8/1 for domestic students, 5/1 for international students; for spring admission, 11/1 for domestic and international students. Applications are processed on a rolling basis. Application fee: $50. Electronic applications accepted. *Expenses: Tuition, area resident:* Full-time $6497; part-time $606 per credit. Tuition, state resident: full-time $9748; part-time $622 per credit. Tuition, nonresident: full-time $18,102; part-time $622 per credit. *Required fees:* $4459; $246 per credit. *Financial support:* In 2016–17, 10 students received support. Career-related internships or fieldwork, Federal Work-Study, scholarships/grants, and unspecified assistantships available. Support available to part-time students. Financial award application deadline: 3/1; financial award applicants required to submit FAFSA. *Faculty research:* All aspects of middle management, technical supervision in the workplace. *Unit head:* Dr. Ravindra Thamma, Chair, 860-832-1830, E-mail: kovelj@ccsu.edu. *Application contact:* Patricia Gardner, Associate Director of Graduate Studies, 860-832-2350, Fax: 860-832-2362.
Website: http://www.ccsu.edu/mcm/

Champlain College, Graduate Studies, Burlington, VT 05402-0670. Offers business (MBA); digital forensic science (MS); early childhood education (M Ed); emergent media (MFA, MS); executive leadership (MS); health care administration (MS); information security operations (MS); law (MS); mediation and applied conflict studies (MS). MS in emergent media program held in Shanghai. *Program availability:* Part-time, online learning. *Degree requirements:* For master's, capstone project. *Entrance requirements:* Additional exam requirements/recommendations for international students: Required—TOEFL (minimum score 550 paper-based; 80 iBT). Electronic applications accepted.

City University of Seattle, Graduate Division, School of Management, Seattle, WA 98121. Offers accounting (Certificate); change leadership (MBA, Certificate); computer systems (MS); finance (Certificate); financial management (MBA); general management (MBA); general management-Europe (MBA); global marketing (MBA); human resources management (Certificate); individualized study (MBA); information security (MS); information systems (MBA); leadership (MA); marketing (MBA, Certificate); project management (MBA, MS, Certificate); sustainable business (Certificate); technology management (MBA, Certificate). *Program availability:* Part-time, evening/weekend, online learning. *Degree requirements:* For master's, comprehensive exam (for some programs), thesis (for some programs). *Entrance requirements:* For master's, baccalaureate degree or equivalent from an accredited or otherwise recognized institution. Additional exam requirements/recommendations for international students: Required—TOEFL (minimum score 567 paper-based; 87 iBT); Recommended—IELTS. Electronic applications accepted.

Coleman University, Program in Business and Technology Management, San Diego, CA 92123. Offers MS. *Program availability:* Evening/weekend, online learning. *Entrance requirements:* For master's, bachelor's degree, minimum GPA of 3.0. Additional exam requirements/recommendations for international students: Required—TOEFL (minimum score 500 paper-based).

Colorado School of Mines, Office of Graduate Studies, Department of Economics and Business, Golden, CO 80401. Offers engineering and technology management (MS); mineral economics (PhD); operations research and engineering (PhD). *Program availability:* Part-time. *Degree requirements:* For master's, thesis (for some programs); for doctorate, comprehensive exam, thesis/dissertation. *Entrance requirements:* For master's and doctorate, GRE General Test. Additional exam requirements/recommendations for international students: Required—TOEFL (minimum score 550 paper-based; 80 iBT). Electronic applications accepted. *Expenses:* Tuition, state resident: full-time $15,690. Tuition, nonresident: full-time $34,020. *Required fees:* $2152. Tuition and fees vary according to course load. *Faculty research:* International trade, resource and environmental economics, energy economics, operations research.

Colorado Technical University Aurora, Programs in Business Administration and Management, Aurora, CO 80014. Offers accounting (MBA); business administration (MBA); business administration and management (EMBA); finance (MBA); human resource management (MBA); marketing (MBA); mediation and dispute resolution (MBA); operations management (MBA); project management (MBA); technology management (MBA). *Program availability:* Part-time, evening/weekend. *Degree requirements:* For master's, thesis or alternative. *Entrance requirements:* For master's, minimum undergraduate GPA of 3.0, resume.

Colorado Technical University Colorado Springs, Graduate Studies, Program in Management, Colorado Springs, CO 80907. Offers accounting (MBA, MSA); business administration (MBA); finance (MBA); human resources management (MBA); logistics/supply chain management (MBA); management (DM); marketing (MBA); mediation and dispute resolution (MBA); operations management (MBA); project management (MBA); technology management (MBA). *Accreditation:* ACBSP. *Program availability:* Part-time, evening/weekend, online learning. *Degree requirements:* For master's, thesis or alternative; for doctorate, thesis/dissertation. *Entrance requirements:* For doctorate, minimum graduate GPA of 3.0, 5 years of related work experience. *Faculty research:* Sexual harassment, performance evaluation, critical thinking.

Columbia University, School of Continuing Education, Program in Technology Management, New York, NY 10027. Offers Exec MS. *Program availability:* Part-time, evening/weekend. *Entrance requirements:* For master's, minimum undergraduate GPA of 3.0. Additional exam requirements/recommendations for international students: Required—American Language Program placement test. Electronic applications accepted. *Faculty research:* Information systems, management.

Dallas Baptist University, College of Business, Business Administration Program, Dallas, TX 75211-9299. Offers accounting (MBA); business communication (MBA); conflict resolution management (MBA); entrepreneurship (MBA); finance (MBA); health care management (MBA); international business (MBA); leading the non-profit organization (MBA); management (MBA); management information systems (MBA); marketing (MBA); project management (MBA); technology and engineering management (MBA). *Accreditation:* ACBSP. *Program availability:* Part-time, evening/weekend, 100% online, blended/hybrid learning. *Application deadline:* Applications are processed on a rolling basis. Application fee: $25. Electronic applications accepted. Application fee is waived when completed online. *Expenses: Tuition:* Full-time $15,408; part-time $856 per credit hour. *Required fees:* $400 per semester. Tuition and fees vary according to course load and degree level. *Unit head:* Dr. Sandra Reid, Chair of Graduate Business Programs, 214-333-5280, E-mail: sandra@dbu.edu. *Application contact:* Bobby Soto, Director of Admissions, 214-333-5242, E-mail: graduate@dbu.edu.
Website: http://www3.dbu.edu/graduate/mba.asp

DePaul University, College of Computing and Digital Media, Chicago, IL 60604. Offers animation (MA, MFA); business information technology (MS); cinema (MFA); cinema production (MS); computational finance (MS); computer and information sciences (PhD); computer game development (MS); computer information and network security (MS); computer science (MS); e-commerce technology (MS); health informatics (MS); human-computer interaction (MS); information systems (MS); information technology project management (MS); network engineering and management (MS); predictive analytics (MS); screenwriting (MFA); software engineering (MS); JD/MS. *Program availability:* Part-time, evening/weekend, online learning. *Degree requirements:* For master's, thesis (for some programs); for doctorate, comprehensive exam, thesis/dissertation. *Entrance requirements:* For master's, GRE or GMAT (for MS in computational finance only), bachelor's degree, resume (MS in predictive analytics only), IT experience (MS in information technology project management only), portfolio review (all MFA programs and MA in animation); for doctorate, GRE, master's degree in computer science. Additional exam requirements/recommendations for international students: Required—TOEFL (minimum score 590 paper-based; 80 iBT), IELTS (minimum score 6.5), PTE (minimum score 53). Electronic applications accepted. *Expenses:* Contact institution. *Faculty research:* Data mining, computer science, human-computer interaction, security, animation and film.

East Carolina University, Graduate School, College of Engineering and Technology, Department of Technology Systems, Greenville, NC 27858-4353. Offers computer network professional (Certificate); information assurance (Certificate); Lean Six Sigma Black Belt (Certificate); network technology (MS), including computer networking management, digital communications technology, information security, Web technologies; occupational safety (MS); technology management (PhD); technology systems (MS), including industrial distribution and logistics, manufacturing systems, performance improvement, quality systems; Website developer (Certificate). *Students:* 23 full-time (1 woman), 199 part-time (55 women); includes 59 minority (39 Black or African American, non-Hispanic/Latino; 3 American Indian or Alaska Native, non-Hispanic/Latino; 4 Asian, non-Hispanic/Latino; 10 Hispanic/Latino; 3 Two or more races, non-Hispanic/Latino), 5 international. Average age 38. 85 applicants, 87% accepted, 61 enrolled. In 2016, 23 master's awarded. *Entrance requirements:* For master's and Certificate, GRE General Test or MAT, minimum GPA of 2.5; for doctorate, GRE General Test, related work experience. *Application deadline:* For fall admission, 6/1 priority date for domestic students. Applications are processed on a rolling basis. Application fee: $50. *Financial support:* Application deadline: 6/1. *Unit head:* Dr. Tijjani Mohammed, Chair, 252-328-9668, E-mail: mohammedt@ecu.edu. *Application contact:* Dean of Graduate School, 252-328-6012, Fax: 252-328-6071, E-mail: gradschool@ecu.edu.

Eastern Michigan University, Graduate School, College of Technology, Program in Technology, Ypsilanti, MI 48197. Offers PhD. *Program availability:* Part-time, evening/weekend. *Students:* 11 full-time (8 women), 51 part-time (23 women); includes 13 minority (10 Black or African American, non-Hispanic/Latino; 2 Asian, non-Hispanic/Latino; 1 Hispanic/Latino), 19 international. Average age 42. 27 applicants, 22% accepted, 4 enrolled. In 2016, 10 doctorates awarded. *Degree requirements:* For doctorate, comprehensive exam, thesis/dissertation. *Entrance requirements:* For doctorate, GRE. Additional exam requirements/recommendations for international students: Required—TOEFL. *Application deadline:* For fall admission, 5/15 priority date for domestic students, 2/15 priority date for international students; for winter admission, 10/15 priority date for domestic students, 9/1 priority date for international students; for summer admission, 3/15 priority date for domestic students, 3/1 priority date for international students. Applications are processed on a rolling basis. Application fee: $45. *Financial support:* Fellowships, research assistantships with tuition reimbursements, teaching assistantships with tuition reimbursements, career-related internships or fieldwork, Federal Work-Study, institutionally sponsored loans, scholarships/grants, tuition waivers (partial), and unspecified assistantships available. Support available to part-time students. Financial award applicants required to submit FAFSA. *Application contact:* Dr. John Dugger, Advisor, 734-487-0354, Fax: 734-487-0843, E-mail: cot_phd@emich.edu.

École Polytechnique de Montréal, Graduate Programs, Department of Mathematics and Industrial Engineering, Montréal, QC H3C 3A7, Canada. Offers ergonomy (M Eng, M Sc A, DESS); mathematical method in CA engineering (M Eng, M Sc A, PhD); operational research (M Eng, M Sc A, PhD); production (M Eng, M Sc A); technology management (M Eng, M Sc A). DESS program offered jointly with HEC Montreal and Université de Montréal. *Program availability:* Part-time. *Degree requirements:* For master's, one foreign language, thesis. *Entrance requirements:* For master's, minimum GPA of 2.75. *Faculty research:* Use of computers in organizations.

Embry-Riddle Aeronautical University–Worldwide, Department of Decision Sciences, Daytona Beach, FL 32114-3900. Offers aviation and aerospace (MSPM); aviation/aerospace management (MSEM); financial management (MSEM, MSPM); general management (MSPM); global management (MSPM); human resources management (MSPM); information systems (MSPM); leadership (MSEM, MSPM); logistics and supply chain management (MSEM, MSLSCM, MSPM); management (MSEM, MSPM); project management (MSEM); systems engineering (MSEM, MSPM); technical management (MSPM). *Program availability:* Part-time, evening/weekend, 100% online, blended/hybrid learning, EagleVision is a virtual classroom that combines Web video conferencing and a learning management system. EagleVision Classroom (between classrooms), EagleVision Home (faculty and students at home), and a blend of Classroom or Home. *Degree requirements:* For master's, comprehensive exam (for some programs), thesis (for some programs). *Entrance requirements:* Additional exam requirements/recommendations for international students: Required—TOEFL (minimum score 550 paper-based; 79 iBT), IELTS (minimum score 6), TOEFL or IELTS accepted. Electronic applications accepted. *Expenses:* Contact institution.

Embry-Riddle Aeronautical University–Worldwide, Department of Technology Management, Daytona Beach, FL 32114-3900. Offers information security and assurance (MS), including information assurance in a global context, information systems security, protecting business intelligence; management information systems (MS), including business intelligence siness and analytics, information security and assurance, information systems project management. *Program availability:* Part-time, evening/weekend, 100% online, blended/hybrid learning, EagleVision is a virtual classroom that combines Web video conferencing and a learning management system. EagleVision Classroom (between classrooms), EagleVision Home (faculty and students at home), and a blend of Classroom or Home. *Entrance requirements:* Additional exam requirements/recommendations for international students: Required—TOEFL (minimum score 550 paper-based; 79 iBT), IELTS (minimum score 6), TOEFL or IELTS accepted. Electronic applications accepted. *Expenses:* Contact institution.

Excelsior College, School of Business and Technology, Albany, NY 12203-5159. Offers business administration (MBA); cybersecurity management (MBA, Graduate Certificate); general business management (MS); health care management (MBA); human performance technology (MBA); human resource management (MS); human resources management (MBA); leadership (MBA, MS); mediation and arbitration (MBA, MS); social media management (MBA); technology management (MBA). *Program availability:* Part-time, evening/weekend, online learning. *Faculty:* 25 part-time/adjunct (9 women). *Students:* 1,801 part-time (487 women); includes 775 minority (424 Black or African American, non-Hispanic/Latino; 5 American Indian or Alaska Native, non-Hispanic/Latino; 58 Asian, non-Hispanic/Latino; 209 Hispanic/Latino; 15 Native Hawaiian or other Pacific Islander, non-Hispanic/Latino; 64 Two or more races, non-Hispanic/Latino), 11 international. Average age 39. In 2016, 288 master's awarded. *Application deadline:* Applications are processed on a rolling basis. Application fee: $50. Electronic applications accepted. *Expenses: Tuition:* Part-time $645 per credit. *Required fees:* $265 per credit. *Financial support:* Scholarships/grants available. *Unit head:* Dr. Lifang Shih, Dean, 888-647-2388. *Application contact:* Admissions, 888-647-2388 Ext. 133, Fax: 518-464-8777, E-mail: admissions@excelsior.edu.

Fairfield University, School of Engineering, Fairfield, CT 06824. Offers database management (CAS); electrical and computer engineering (MS); information security (CAS); management of technology (MS); mechanical engineering (MS); network technology (CAS); software engineering (MS); Web application development (CAS). *Program availability:* Part-time, evening/weekend. *Faculty:* 7 full-time (1 woman), 15 part-time/adjunct (2 women). *Students:* 104 full-time (31 women), 56 part-time (15 women); includes 17 minority (8 Black or African American, non-Hispanic/Latino; 5 Asian, non-Hispanic/Latino; 4 Hispanic/Latino), 108 international. Average age 28. 193 applicants, 63% accepted, 20 enrolled. In 2016, 173 master's awarded. *Degree requirements:* For master's, capstone course. *Entrance requirements:* For master's, resume, 2 recommendations. Additional exam requirements/recommendations for international students: Required—TOEFL (minimum score 550 paper-based; 80 iBT) or IELTS (minimum score 6.5). *Application deadline:* For fall admission, 5/15 for international students; for spring admission, 10/15 for international students. Applications are processed on a rolling basis. Application fee: $60. Electronic applications accepted. *Expenses:* $800 per credit hour. *Financial support:* In 2016–17, 27 students received support. Scholarships/grants and unspecified assistantships available. Financial award applicants required to submit FAFSA. *Faculty research:* Artificial intelligence and information visualization, natural language processing, thermofluids, microwaves and electromagnetics, micro-/nano-manufacturing. *Unit head:* Dr. Bruce Berdanier, Dean, 203-254-4147, Fax: 203-254-4013, E-mail: bberdanier@fairfield.edu. *Application contact:* Marianne Gumpper, Director of Graduate and Continuing Studies Admission, 203-254-4184, Fax: 203-254-4073, E-mail: gradadmis@fairfield.edu.
Website: http://www.fairfield.edu/soe

Fairleigh Dickinson University, College at Florham, Silberman College of Business, Departments of Management, Marketing, and Entrepreneurial Studies, Program in Management, Madison, NJ 07940-1099. Offers evolving technology (Certificate); management (MBA); MBA/MA.

Florida Institute of Technology, Extended Studies Division, Melbourne, FL 32901-6975. Offers acquisition and contract management (MS); aerospace engineering (MS); business administration (MBA, DBA); computer information systems (MS); computer science (MS); electrical engineering (MS); engineering management (MS); human resources management (MS); logistics management (MS), including humanitarian and disaster relief logistics; management (MS), including acquisition and contract management, e-business, human resources management, information systems, logistics management, management, transportation management; material acquisition management (MS); mechanical engineering (MS); operations research (MS); project management (MS), including information systems, operations research; public administration (MPA); quality management (MS); software engineering (MS); space systems (MS); space systems management (MS); supply chain management (MS); systems management (MS), including information systems, operations research; technology management (MS). *Program availability:* Part-time, evening/weekend, online learning. *Faculty:* 10 full-time (3 women), 122 part-time/adjunct (29 women). *Students:* 131 full-time (58 women), 997 part-time (348 women); includes 389 minority (231 Black or African American, non-Hispanic/Latino; 9 American Indian or Alaska Native, non-Hispanic/Latino; 26 Asian, non-Hispanic/Latino; 99 Hispanic/Latino; 3 Native Hawaiian or other Pacific Islander, non-Hispanic/Latino; 21 Two or more races, non-Hispanic/Latino), 53 international. Average age 36. 962 applicants, 48% accepted, 323 enrolled. In 2016, 403 master's awarded. *Degree requirements:* For master's, comprehensive exam (for some programs). *Entrance requirements:* For master's, GMAT or resume showing 8 years of supervised experience, minimum GPA of 3.0, 2 letters of recommendation, resume. Additional exam requirements/recommendations for international students: Required—TOEFL (minimum score 550 paper-based; 79 iBT). *Application deadline:* For fall admission, 4/1 for international students; for spring admission, 9/30 for international students. Applications are processed on a rolling basis. Electronic applications accepted. *Expenses:* Contact institution. *Financial support:* Application deadline: 3/1; applicants required to submit FAFSA. *Unit head:* Dr. Theodore R. Richardson, III, Dean, 321-674-8123, Fax: 321-674-7597, E-mail: trichardson@fit.edu. *Application contact:* Carolyn Farrior, Director of Graduate Admissions, Online Learning and Off-Campus Programs, 321-674-7118, Fax: 321-674-8216, E-mail: cfarrior@fit.edu.
Website: http://es.fit.edu

George Mason University, School of Business, Program in Technology Management, Fairfax, VA 22030. Offers MS. *Faculty:* 6 full-time (1 woman). *Students:* 16 full-time (5 women); includes 8 minority (3 Black or African American, non-Hispanic/Latino; 4 Asian, non-Hispanic/Latino; 1 Two or more races, non-Hispanic/Latino), 1 international. Average age 38. In 2016, 26 master's awarded. *Entrance requirements:* For master's, GMAT/GRE, resume; official transcripts; 2 professional letters of recommendation; professional essay; expanded goals statement; interview. Additional exam requirements/recommendations for international students: Required—TOEFL (minimum score 575 paper-based; 88 iBT), IELTS (minimum score 6.5), PTE (minimum score 59). Application fee: $75 ($80 for international students). Electronic applications accepted. *Expenses:* Contact institution. *Financial support:* Career-related internships or fieldwork, Federal Work-Study, and scholarships/grants available. Financial award application deadline: 3/1; financial award applicants required to submit FAFSA. *Faculty research:* Leadership careers in technology-oriented businesses, achieving success in the technology marketplace, emphasizing technology leadership and management, technology innovation, commercialization, methods and approaches of systems thinking. *Unit head:* Kumar Mehta, Director, 703-993-9412, E-mail: kmehta1@gmu.edu. *Application contact:* Jacky Buchy, Assistant Dean, Graduate Enrollment, 703-993-1856, Fax: 703-993-1778, E-mail: jbuchy@gmu.edu.
Website: http://business.gmu.edu/masters-in-technology-management/

Georgetown University, Graduate School of Arts and Sciences, School of Continuing Studies, Washington, DC 20057. Offers American studies (MALS); Catholic studies (MALS); classical civilizations (MALS); emergency and disaster management (MPS); ethics and the professions (MALS); global strategic communications (MPS); hospitality management (MPS); human resources management (MPS); humanities (MALS); individualized study (MALS); integrated marketing communications (MPS); international affairs (MALS); Islam and Muslim-Christian relations (MALS); journalism (MPS); liberal studies (DLS); literature and society (MALS); medieval and early modern European studies (MALS); public relations and corporate communications (MPS); real estate (MPS); religious studies (MALS); social and public policy (MALS); sports industry management (MPS); systems engineering management (MPS); technology management (MPS); the theory and practice of American democracy (MALS); urban and regional planning (MPS); visual culture (MALS). MPS in systems engineering management offered jointly with Stevens Institute of Technology. *Entrance requirements:* Additional exam requirements/recommendations for international students: Required—TOEFL.

The George Washington University, School of Business, Department of Information Systems and Technology Management, Washington, DC 20052. Offers information and decision systems (PhD); information systems (MSIST); information systems development (MSIST); information systems management (MBA); information systems project management (MSIST); management information systems (MSIST); management of science, technology, and innovation (MBA, PhD). Programs also offered in Ashburn and Arlington, VA. *Program availability:* Part-time, evening/weekend, online learning. *Faculty:* 13 full-time (4 women). *Students:* 114 full-time (55 women), 74 part-time (30 women); includes 50 minority (15 Black or African American, non-Hispanic/Latino; 28 Asian, non-Hispanic/Latino; 6 Hispanic/Latino; 1 Two or more races, non-Hispanic/Latino), 103 international. Average age 28. 345 applicants, 66% accepted, 67 enrolled. In 2016, 105 master's awarded. *Entrance requirements:* For master's, GMAT. Additional exam requirements/recommendations for international students: Required—TOEFL. *Application deadline:* For fall admission, 4/1 priority date for domestic students; for spring admission, 10/1 for domestic students. Applications are processed on a rolling basis. Application fee: $75. *Financial support:* In 2016–17, 35 students received support. Fellowships, teaching assistantships, career-related internships or fieldwork, Federal Work-Study, institutionally sponsored loans, and tuition waivers available. Financial award application deadline: 4/1. *Faculty research:* Expert systems, decision support systems. *Unit head:* Richard Donnelly, Chair, 202-994-7155, E-mail: rgd@gwu.edu. *Application contact:* Christopher Storer, Executive Director, Graduate Admissions, 202-994-1212, E-mail: gwmba@gwu.edu.

Golden Gate University, Ageno School of Business, San Francisco, CA 94105-2968. Offers accounting (MBA); business administration (EMBA, MBA, PMBA, DBA); business analytics (MS); finance (MBA, MS, Certificate); financial planning (MS, Certificate); healthcare information systems (Certificate); human resource management (MBA, MS); human resources management (Certificate); information systems (MS); information technology (MBA); information technology management (Certificate); integrated marketing and communications (MS, Certificate); international business (MBA); management (MBA); marketing (MBA, MS, Certificate); operations supply chain management (Certificate); psychology (MA, Certificate); public administration (EMPA); public relations (MS, Certificate); technical market analysis (Certificate); JD/MBA. *Program availability:* Part-time, evening/weekend. *Faculty:* 18 full-time (3 women), 117 part-time/adjunct (44 women). *Students:* 458 full-time (254 women), 664 part-time (331 women); includes 346 minority (75 Black or African American, non-Hispanic/Latino; 2 American Indian or Alaska Native, non-Hispanic/Latino; 132 Asian, non-Hispanic/Latino; 105 Hispanic/Latino; 9 Native Hawaiian or other Pacific Islander, non-Hispanic/Latino; 23 Two or more races, non-Hispanic/Latino), 354 international. Average age 34. 905 applicants, 83% accepted, 165 enrolled. In 2016, 350 master's, 2 doctorates awarded. *Degree requirements:* For doctorate, thesis/dissertation, qualifying examination. *Entrance requirements:* For master's, GMAT (for MBA), minimum GPA of 2.5 (MS). Additional exam requirements/recommendations for international students: Required—TOEFL (minimum score 550 paper-based; 79 iBT). *Application deadline:* For fall admission, 5/15 for domestic and international students; for winter admission, 1/15 for domestic and international students; for spring admission, 9/15 for domestic and international students. Applications are processed on a rolling basis. Application fee: $70 ($110 for international students). Electronic applications accepted. *Expenses:* Contact institution. *Financial support:* In 2016–17, 372 students received support. Career-related internships or fieldwork, Federal Work-Study, institutionally sponsored loans, and scholarships/grants available. Support available to part-time students. Financial award applicants required to submit FAFSA. *Unit head:* Dr. Gordon Swartz, Dean, 415-442-7027, Fax: 415-442-6579, E-mail: gswartz@ggu.edu. *Application contact:* Angela Melero, Enrollment Services, 415-442-7800, Fax: 415-442-7807, E-mail: info@ggu.edu.
Website: http://www.ggu.edu/programs/business-and-management

Harrisburg University of Science and Technology, Program in Project Management, Harrisburg, PA 17101. Offers information technology (MS). *Program availability:* Part-time, evening/weekend. *Faculty:* 2 full-time (0 women), 11 part-time/adjunct (1 woman). *Students:* 863 full-time (358 women), 15 part-time (7 women); includes 6 minority (3 Black or African American, non-Hispanic/Latino; 3 Asian, non-Hispanic/Latino), 868 international. In 2016, 17 master's awarded. *Degree requirements:* For master's, thesis optional. *Entrance requirements:* For master's, baccalaureate degree. Additional exam requirements/recommendations for international students: Required—TOEFL (minimum score 520 paper-based; 80 iBT); Recommended—IELTS (minimum score 6). *Application deadline:* Applications are processed on a rolling basis. Application fee: $0. Electronic applications accepted. *Expenses: Tuition:* Full-time $4800; part-time $800 per semester hour. *Financial support:* Applicants required to submit FAFSA. *Faculty research:* Strategic planning, organizational development. *Unit head:* Dr. Thomas Sheives, Program Lead/Associate Professor, 717-901-5158, E-mail: tsheives@harrisburgu.edu.

Harvard University, Graduate School of Arts and Sciences, Program in Information, Technology and Management, Cambridge, MA 02138. Offers PhD.

Harvard University, Harvard Business School, Doctoral Programs in Management, Boston, MA 02163. Offers accounting and management (DBA); business economics (PhD); health policy management (PhD); management (DBA); marketing (DBA); organizational behavior (PhD); science, technology and management (PhD); strategy (DBA); technology and operations management (DBA). *Degree requirements:* For doctorate, comprehensive exam (for some programs), thesis/dissertation. *Entrance requirements:* For doctorate, GRE General Test or GMAT. Additional exam requirements/recommendations for international students: Required—TOEFL.

Herzing University Online, Program in Business Administration, Menomonee Falls, WI 53051. Offers accounting (MBA); business administration (MBA); business management (MBA); healthcare management (MBA); human resources (MBA); marketing (MBA);

project management (MBA); technology management (MBA). *Program availability:* Online learning.

Idaho State University, Office of Graduate Studies, College of Technology, Department of Human Resource Training and Development, Pocatello, ID 83209-8380. Offers MTD. *Program availability:* Part-time, evening/weekend. *Degree requirements:* For master's, comprehensive exam, thesis optional, statistical procedures. *Entrance requirements:* For master's, GRE or MAT, minimum GPA of 3.0 in upper-division courses. Additional exam requirements/recommendations for international students: Required—TOEFL (minimum score 550 paper-based; 80 iBT). Electronic applications accepted. *Faculty research:* Learning styles, instructional methodology, leadership administration.

Illinois State University, Graduate School, College of Applied Science and Technology, Department of Technology, Normal, IL 61790-2200. Offers MS. *Degree requirements:* For master's, thesis or alternative. *Entrance requirements:* For master's, GRE General Test, minimum GPA of 2.8. *Faculty research:* Illinois Manufacturing Extension Center Field Office hosting, model for the professional development of K-12 technology education teachers, Illinois State University Illinois Mathematics and Science Partnership, Illinois University council for career and technical education.

Indiana State University, College of Graduate and Professional Studies, College of Technology, Department of Applied Engineering and Technology Management, Terre Haute, IN 47809. Offers technology management (MS); MA/MS. *Accreditation:* NCATE (one or more programs are accredited). *Entrance requirements:* For master's, bachelor's degree in industrial technology or related field. Additional exam requirements/recommendations for international students: Required—TOEFL. Electronic applications accepted.

Indiana State University, College of Graduate and Professional Studies, Program in Technology Management, Terre Haute, IN 47809. Offers PhD. Program part of consortium with North Carolina Agricultural and Technical University, University of Central Missouri, Bowling Green State University, and East Carolina University. *Program availability:* Online learning. *Degree requirements:* For doctorate, thesis/dissertation. *Entrance requirements:* For doctorate, GRE or GMAT, minimum graduate GPA of 3.5, 6000 hours of occupational experience. Electronic applications accepted. *Faculty research:* Production management, quality control, human resource development, construction project management, lean manufacturing.

Indiana University–Purdue University Indianapolis, School of Engineering and Technology, MS in Technology Program, Indianapolis, IN 46202. Offers applied data management and analytics (MS); facilities management (MS); information security and assurance (MS); motorsports (MS); organizational leadership (MS); technical communication (MS). *Program availability:* Online learning.

Instituto Centroamericano de Administración de Empresas, Graduate Programs, La Garita, Costa Rica. Offers agribusiness management (MIAM); business administration (EMBA); finance (MBA); real estate management (MGREM); sustainable development (MBA); technology (MBA). *Degree requirements:* For master's, comprehensive exam, essay. *Entrance requirements:* For master's, GMAT or GRE General Test, fluency in Spanish, interview, letters of recommendation, minimum 1 year of work experience. Additional exam requirements/recommendations for international students: Recommended—TOEFL. Electronic applications accepted. *Faculty research:* Competitiveness, production.

Instituto Tecnológico y de Estudios Superiores de Monterrey, Campus Cuernavaca, Programs in Information Science, Temixco, Mexico. Offers administration of information technology (MATI); computer science (MCC, DCC); information technology (MTI).

Instituto Tecnológico y de Estudios Superiores de Monterrey, Campus Irapuato, Graduate Programs, Irapuato, Mexico. Offers administration (MBA); administration of information technology (MAIT); administration of telecommunications (MAT); architecture (M Arch); computer science (MCS); education (M Ed); educational administration (MEA); educational innovation and technology (DEIT); educational technology (MET); electronic commerce (MBA); environmental administration and planning (MEAP); environmental systems (MES); finances (MBA); humanistic studies (MHS); international management for Latin American executives (MIMLAE); library and information science (MLIS); manufacturing quality management (MMQM); marketing research (MBA).

Iona College, Hagan School of Business, Department of Information Systems, New Rochelle, NY 10801-1890. Offers accounting and information systems (MS); business continuity and risk management (AC); information systems (MBA, MS, PMC); project management (MS). *Program availability:* Part-time, evening/weekend. *Faculty:* 6 full-time (1 woman), 1 part-time/adjunct (0 women). *Students:* 6 full-time (4 women), 14 part-time (5 women); includes 4 minority (1 Black or African American, non-Hispanic/Latino; 1 American Indian or Alaska Native, non-Hispanic/Latino; 2 Hispanic/Latino), 6 international. Average age 30. 14 applicants, 100% accepted, 6 enrolled. In 2016, 12 master's awarded. *Entrance requirements:* For master's, GMAT, 2 letters of recommendation, minimum GPA of 3.0; for other advanced degree, GMAT, minimum GPA of 3.0. Additional exam requirements/recommendations for international students: Required—TOEFL (minimum score 550 paper-based; 80 iBT), IELTS (minimum score 6.5). *Application deadline:* For fall admission, 8/15 priority date for domestic students, 8/1 priority date for international students; for winter admission, 11/15 priority date for domestic students, 11/1 priority date for international students; for spring admission, 2/15 priority date for domestic students, 2/1 priority date for international students; for summer admission, 5/15 priority date for domestic students, 5/1 priority date for international students. Applications are processed on a rolling basis. Application fee: $50. Electronic applications accepted. *Expenses:* Contact institution. *Financial support:* In 2016–17, 9 students received support. Scholarships/grants, tuition waivers (partial), and unspecified assistantships available. Support available to part-time students. Financial award application deadline: 4/15; financial award applicants required to submit FAFSA. *Faculty research:* Fuzzy sets, risk management, computer security, competence set analysis, investment strategies. *Unit head:* Dr. Shoshana Altschuller, Department Chair, 914-637-7726, E-mail: saltschuller@iona.edu. *Application contact:* Katelyn Brunck, Director of MBA Admissions, 914-633-2451, Fax: 914-633-2277, E-mail: kbrunck@iona.edu.
Website: http://www.iona.edu/Academics/Hagan-School-of-Business/Departments/Information-Systems/Graduate-Programs.aspx

Johns Hopkins University, Engineering Program for Professionals, Part-time Program in Technical Management, Baltimore, MD 21218. Offers MS, Graduate Certificate, Post-Master's Certificate. *Program availability:* Part-time, evening/weekend, 100% online, blended/hybrid learning. *Faculty:* 30 part-time/adjunct (7 women). *Students:* 4 full-time (1 woman), 107 part-time (35 women); includes 21 minority (11 Black or African American, non-Hispanic/Latino; 3 Asian, non-Hispanic/Latino; 5 Hispanic/Latino; 1 Native Hawaiian or other Pacific Islander, non-Hispanic/Latino; 1 Two or more races, non-Hispanic/Latino), 6 international. Average age 36. 34 applicants, 68% accepted, 11 enrolled. In 2016, 46 master's, 1 other advanced degree awarded. *Entrance requirements:* Additional exam requirements/recommendations for international students: Required—TOEFL (minimum score 600 paper-based; 100 iBT). *Application deadline:* Applications are processed on a rolling basis. Application fee: $0. Electronic applications accepted. *Unit head:* Dr. Timothy Collins, Program Chair, 240-228-6350, E-mail: timothy.collins@jhuapl.edu. *Application contact:* Doug Schiller, Admissions Director, 410-516-2300, Fax: 410-579-8049, E-mail: schiller@jhu.edu.
Website: http://www.ep.jhu.edu/

Kansas State University, Graduate School, College of Technology and Aviation, Salina, KS 67401. Offers MT. *Program availability:* Part-time, evening/weekend, 100% online. *Faculty:* 4 full-time (1 woman), 1 part-time/adjunct (0 women). *Students:* 4 full-time (1 woman), 8 part-time (4 women); includes 2 minority (both Two or more races, non-Hispanic/Latino), 2 international. Average age 35. 6 applicants, 33% accepted, 1 enrolled. In 2016, 1 master's awarded. *Entrance requirements:* For master's, GRE. Additional exam requirements/recommendations for international students: Required—TOEFL (minimum score 550 paper-based; 79 iBT), IELTS (minimum score 6.5), TWE, or PTE. *Application deadline:* For fall admission, 3/1 for domestic students, 1/1 for international students; for spring admission, 10/1 for domestic students, 8/1 for international students. Application fee: $50 ($75 for international students). Electronic applications accepted. *Expenses:* Tuition, state resident: full-time $9670. Tuition, nonresident: full-time $21,828. *Required fees:* $862. *Total annual research expenditures:* $12.4 million. *Unit head:* Dr. Verna Fitzsimmons, Dean, 785-826-2601, E-mail: vfitzsimmons@ksu.edu. *Application contact:* Dr. Don Von Bergen, Graduate Program Director, 785-826-2904, E-mail: salgrad@k-state.edu.
Website: http://polytechnic.k-state.edu/

La Salle University, School of Arts and Sciences, Program in Information Technology Leadership, Philadelphia, PA 19141-1199. Offers information technology leadership (MS); software project leadership (Certificate). *Program availability:* Online learning. *Faculty:* 1 (woman) full-time, 2 part-time/adjunct (0 women). *Students:* 1 (woman) full-time, 10 part-time (2 women); includes 5 minority (4 Black or African American, non-Hispanic/Latino; 1 Asian, non-Hispanic/Latino). Average age 33. 5 applicants, 100% accepted, 4 enrolled. In 2016, 4 master's, 3 other advanced degrees awarded. *Degree requirements:* For master's, capstone course. *Entrance requirements:* For master's, GRE, GMAT, or MAT, two letters of recommendation; background in computer science or equivalent other training; professional resume; interview; for Certificate, two letters of recommendation; background in computer science or equivalent other training; professional resume; interview. Additional exam requirements/recommendations for international students: Required—TOEFL. *Application deadline:* For fall admission, 8/15 priority date for domestic students, 7/15 for international students; for spring admission, 12/15 priority date for domestic students, 11/15 for international students; for summer admission, 4/15 priority date for domestic students, 3/15 for international students. Applications are processed on a rolling basis. Application fee: $35. Electronic applications accepted. Application fee is waived when completed online. *Expenses:* Contact institution. *Financial support:* In 2016–17, 4 students received support. Scholarships/grants available. Support available to part-time students. Financial award application deadline: 8/31; financial award applicants required to submit FAFSA. *Unit head:* Margaret M. McCoey, Director, 215-951-1136, Fax: 215-951-1805, E-mail: itleader@lasalle.edu. *Application contact:* Elizabeth Heenan, Director, Graduate and Adult Enrollment, 215-951-1100, Fax: 215-951-1462, E-mail: heenan@lasalle.edu.
Website: http://www.lasalle.edu/information-technology-leadership/

Lewis University, College of Business, Graduate School of Management, Program in Business Administration, Romeoville, IL 60446. Offers accounting (MBA); custom elective option (MBA); e-business (MBA); finance (MBA); healthcare management (MBA); human resources management (MBA); international business (MBA); management information systems (MBA); marketing (MBA); project management (MBA); technology and operations management (MBA). *Program availability:* Part-time, evening/weekend. *Students:* 145 full-time (72 women), 213 part-time (123 women); includes 101 minority (46 Black or African American, non-Hispanic/Latino; 2 American Indian or Alaska Native, non-Hispanic/Latino; 7 Asian, non-Hispanic/Latino; 41 Hispanic/Latino; 1 Native Hawaiian or other Pacific Islander, non-Hispanic/Latino; 4 Two or more races, non-Hispanic/Latino), 47 international. Average age 31. In 2016, 99 master's awarded. *Degree requirements:* For master's, comprehensive exam. *Entrance requirements:* For master's, interview, bachelor's degree, resume, 2 recommendations. Additional exam requirements/recommendations for international students: Required—TOEFL (minimum score 550 paper-based). *Application deadline:* For fall admission, 8/15 priority date for domestic students, 5/1 priority date for international students; for spring admission, 11/15 priority date for international students. Applications are processed on a rolling basis. Application fee: $40. Electronic applications accepted. *Expenses: Tuition:* Full-time $13,860; part-time $770 per credit hour. *Required fees:* $75 per semester. Tuition and fees vary according to degree level and program. *Financial support:* Career-related internships or fieldwork, Federal Work-Study, scholarships/grants, and unspecified assistantships available. Financial award application deadline: 5/1; financial award applicants required to submit FAFSA. *Unit head:* Dr. Maureen Culleeney, Academic Program Director, 815-838-0500 Ext. 5631, E-mail: culleema@lewisu.edu. *Application contact:* Michele Ryan, Director of Admission, 815-838-0500 Ext. 5384, E-mail: gsm@lewisu.edu.

Liberty University, School of Business, Lynchburg, VA 24515. Offers accounting (MBA, MS); business administration (MBA); criminal justice (MBA); cyber security (MS); executive leadership (MA); information systems (MS), including information assurance, technology management; international business (MBA, DBA); leadership (DBA); marketing (MBA, MS, DBA), including digital marketing and advertising (MS), project management (MS), public relations (MS), sports marketing and media (MS); project management (MBA, DBA); public administration (MBA); public relations (MBA). *Program availability:* Part-time, online learning. *Students:* 1,458 full-time (807 women), 4,188 part-time (2,041 women); includes 1,372 minority (1,060 Black or African American, non-Hispanic/Latino; 19 American Indian or Alaska Native, non-Hispanic/Latino; 85 Asian, non-Hispanic/Latino; 75 Hispanic/Latino; 10 Native Hawaiian or other Pacific Islander, non-Hispanic/Latino; 123 Two or more races, non-Hispanic/Latino), 124 international. Average age 35. 5,424 applicants, 45% accepted, 1242 enrolled. In 2016, 1,859 master's, 87 other advanced degrees awarded. *Entrance requirements:* For master's, minimum undergraduate GPA of 3.0, 15 hours of upper-level business courses. Additional exam requirements/recommendations for international students: Required—TOEFL (minimum score 600 paper-based; 100 iBT). *Application deadline:* Applications are processed on a rolling basis. Application fee: $50. Electronic applications accepted. *Expenses:* Contact institution. *Financial support:* Applicants required to submit FAFSA. *Unit head:* Dr. Scott Hicks, Dean, 434-592-4808, Fax: 434-582-2366, E-mail: smhicks@liberty.edu. *Application contact:* Jay Bridge, Director of Graduate Admissions, 800-424-9595, Fax: 800-628-7977, E-mail: gradadmissions@liberty.edu.
Website: http://www.liberty.edu/academics/business/index.cfm?PID-149

Lipscomb University, College of Computing and Technology, Nashville, TN 37204-3951. Offers data science (MS); information technology (MS), including data science, information security, information technology management, software engineering; software engineering (MS). *Program availability:* Part-time, evening/weekend. *Faculty:* 7 full-time (0 women), 6 part-time/adjunct (1 woman). *Students:* 21 full-time (10 women), 10 part-time (3 women); includes 9 minority (5 Black or African American, non-Hispanic/Latino; 4 Asian, non-Hispanic/Latino), 1 international. Average age 34. 47 applicants,

49% accepted, 12 enrolled. In 2016, 26 degrees awarded. *Degree requirements:* For master's, capstone project. *Entrance requirements:* For master's, GRE, 2 references, transcripts, resume, personal statement. Additional exam requirements/recommendations for international students: Required—TOEFL (minimum score 570 paper-based; 80 iBT). *Application deadline:* Applications are processed on a rolling basis. Application fee: $50 ($75 for international students). Electronic applications accepted. *Expenses:* $1,226 per hour. *Financial support:* Scholarships/grants and employer agreements available. Financial award applicants required to submit FAFSA. *Unit head:* Dr. Fortune S. Mhlanga, Dean, 615-966-5073, E-mail: fortune.mhlanga@lipscomb.edu. *Application contact:* Brett Ramsey, Enrollment Management Specialist, 615-966-1193, E-mail: brett.ramsey@lipscomb.edu.
Website: http://www.lipscomb.edu/technology/

London Metropolitan University, Graduate Programs, London, United Kingdom. Offers applied psychology (M Sc); architecture (MA); biomedical science (M Sc); blood science (M Sc); cancer pharmacology (M Sc); computer networking and cyber security (M Sc); computing and information systems (M Sc); conference interpreting (MA); counter-terrorism studies (M Sc); creative, digital and professional writing (MA); crime, violence and prevention (M Sc); criminology (M Sc); curating contemporary art (MA); data analytics (M Sc); digital media (MA); early childhood studies (MA); education (MA, Ed D); financial services law, regulation and compliance (LL M); food science (M Sc); forensic psychology (M Sc); health and social care management and policy (M Sc); human nutrition (M Sc); human resource management (MA); human rights and international conflict (MA); information technology (M Sc); intelligence and security studies (M Sc); international oil, gas and energy law (LL M); international relations (MA); interpreting (MA); learning and teaching in higher education (MA); legal practice (LL M); media and entertainment law (LL M); organizational and consumer psychology (M Sc); psychological therapy (M Sc); psychology of mental health (M Sc); public health (M Sc); public policy and management (MPA); security studies (M Sc); social work (M Sc); spatial planning and urban design (MA); sports therapy (M Sc); supporting older children and young people with dyslexia (MA); teaching languages (MA), including Arabic, English; translation (MA); woman and child abuse (MA).

Marist College, Graduate Programs, School of Computer Science and Mathematics, Poughkeepsie, NY 12601-1387. Offers computer science/software development (MS); information systems (MS, Adv C); technology management (MS). *Program availability:* Part-time, evening/weekend, online learning. *Entrance requirements:* For master's, resume. Additional exam requirements/recommendations for international students: Required—TOEFL (minimum score 550 paper-based; 80 iBT); Recommended—IELTS (minimum score 6.5). Electronic applications accepted. *Faculty research:* Data quality, artificial intelligence, imaging, analysis of algorithms, distributed systems and applications.

Marist College, Graduate Programs, School of Management and School of Computer Science and Mathematics, Program in Technology Management, Poughkeepsie, NY 12601-1387. Offers MS. *Program availability:* Part-time, evening/weekend, online learning. *Entrance requirements:* For master's, GMAT or GRE, minimum undergraduate GPA of 3.0, 2 letters of recommendation, resume, professional experience. Additional exam requirements/recommendations for international students: Required—TOEFL (minimum score 550 paper-based; 80 iBT); Recommended—IELTS (minimum score 6.5). Electronic applications accepted.

Marquette University, Graduate School, College of Engineering, Department of Biomedical Engineering, Milwaukee, WI 53201-1881. Offers biocomputing (ME); bioimaging (ME); bioinstrumentation (ME); bioinstrumentation/computers (MS, PhD); biomechanics (ME); biomechanics/biomaterials (MS, PhD); biorehabilitation (ME); functional imaging (PhD); healthcare technologies management (MS); rehabilitation bioengineering (PhD); systems physiology (MS, PhD). *Program availability:* Part-time, evening/weekend. *Faculty:* 17 full-time (6 women), 8 part-time/adjunct (4 women). *Students:* 37 full-time (14 women), 16 part-time (6 women); includes 8 minority (1 Black or African American, non-Hispanic/Latino; 6 Asian, non-Hispanic/Latino; 1 Hispanic/Latino), 6 international. Average age 26. 83 applicants, 59% accepted, 14 enrolled. In 2016, 15 master's, 4 doctorates awarded. Terminal master's awarded for partial completion of doctoral program. *Degree requirements:* For master's, comprehensive exam, thesis; for doctorate, comprehensive exam, thesis/dissertation, dissertation defense, qualifying exam. *Entrance requirements:* For master's, GRE General Test, minimum GPA of 3.0, official transcripts from all current and previous colleges/universities except Marquette, three letters of recommendation, brief statement of purpose that includes proposed area of research specialization, interview with program director (for ME), one year of post-baccalaureate professional work experience; for doctorate, GRE General Test, minimum GPA of 3.0, official transcripts from all current and previous colleges/universities except Marquette, three letters of recommendation, brief statement of purpose that includes proposed area of research specialization. Additional exam requirements/recommendations for international students: Required—TOEFL (minimum score 530 paper-based). *Application deadline:* For fall admission, 2/15 priority date for domestic students; for spring admission, 11/15 priority date for domestic students. Applications are processed on a rolling basis. Application fee: $50. Electronic applications accepted. *Financial support:* Fellowships, research assistantships, teaching assistantships, scholarships/grants, health care benefits, tuition waivers (partial), and unspecified assistantships available. Support available to part-time students. Financial award application deadline: 2/15. *Faculty research:* Cell and organ physiology, signal processing, gait analysis, orthopedic rehabilitation engineering, telemedicine. *Total annual research expenditures:* $2.1 million. *Unit head:* Dr. Lars Olson, Interim Chair, 414-288-3539. *Application contact:* Dr. Robert Scheidt, 414-288-6125.
Website: http://www.marquette.edu/engineering/biomedical/

Marshall University, Academic Affairs Division, College of Information Technology and Engineering, Division of Applied Science and Technology, Program in Technology Management, Huntington, WV 25755. Offers MS. *Program availability:* Part-time, evening/weekend. *Degree requirements:* For master's, final project, oral exam. *Entrance requirements:* For master's, GRE General Test or GMAT, minimum undergraduate GPA of 2.5.

Mercer University, Graduate Studies, Macon Campus, School of Engineering, Macon, GA 31207. Offers biomedical engineering (MSE); computer engineering (MSE); electrical engineering (MSE); engineering management (MSE); environmental engineering (MSE); environmental systems (MS); mechanical engineering (MSE); software engineering (MSE); software systems (MS); technical communications management (MS); technical management (MS). *Program availability:* Part-time-only, evening/weekend, online learning. *Faculty:* 21 full-time (5 women), 1 part-time/adjunct (0 women). *Students:* 44 full-time (9 women), 60 part-time (12 women); includes 14 minority (3 Black or African American, non-Hispanic/Latino; 1 American Indian or Alaska Native, non-Hispanic/Latino; 4 Asian, non-Hispanic/Latino; 3 Hispanic/Latino; 3 Two or more races, non-Hispanic/Latino), 2 international. Average age 27. In 2016, 64 master's awarded. *Degree requirements:* For master's, thesis or alternative. *Entrance requirements:* For master's, GRE (minimum score 300), minimum undergraduate GPA of 3.0. Additional exam requirements/recommendations for international students: Required—TOEFL (minimum score 550 paper-based; 80 iBT). *Application deadline:* For fall admission, 4/1 priority date for domestic and international students; for spring admission, 11/1 priority date for domestic and international students. Applications are processed on a rolling basis. Application fee: $75. *Expenses:* $865 per credit hour. *Financial support:* Applicants required to submit FAFSA. *Faculty research:* Designing prostheses and orthotics, oxygen transfer and limitations in biological systems, low-cost groundwater development, lung airway and transport, autonomous mobile robots. *Unit head:* Dr. Laura W. Lackey, Dean, 478-301-4106, Fax: 478-301-5593, E-mail: lackey_l@mercer.edu. *Application contact:* Dr. Richard O. Mines, Jr., Program Director, 478-301-2347, Fax: 478-301-5433, E-mail: mines_ro@mercer.edu.
Website: http://engineering.mercer.edu/

Murray State University, College of Science, Engineering and Technology, Program in Management of Technology, Murray, KY 42071. Offers MS. *Program availability:* Part-time, evening/weekend. *Degree requirements:* For master's, comprehensive exam. *Entrance requirements:* Additional exam requirements/recommendations for international students: Required—TOEFL or IELTS. *Faculty research:* Environmental, hydrology, groundworks.

New Jersey Institute of Technology, Martin Tuchman School of Management, Newark, NJ 07102. Offers business administration (MBA); business data science (PhD); finance for managers (Certificate); international business (MS); management (MS); management essentials (Certificate); management of technology (Certificate). *Accreditation:* AACSB. *Program availability:* Part-time, evening/weekend. *Faculty:* 29 full-time (9 women), 21 part-time/adjunct (3 women). *Students:* 90 full-time (35 women), 147 part-time (53 women); includes 104 minority (30 Black or African American, non-Hispanic/Latino; 30 Asian, non-Hispanic/Latino; 38 Hispanic/Latino; 6 Two or more races, non-Hispanic/Latino), 57 international. Average age 31. 385 applicants, 52% accepted, 80 enrolled. In 2016, 81 master's, 11 other advanced degrees awarded. Terminal master's awarded for partial completion of doctoral program. *Degree requirements:* For master's, thesis optional. *Entrance requirements:* For doctorate, GRE General Test, minimum graduate GPA of 3.5. Additional exam requirements/recommendations for international students: Required—TOEFL (minimum score 550 paper-based; 79 iBT). *Application deadline:* For fall admission, 6/1 priority date for domestic students, 5/1 priority date for international students; for spring admission, 11/15 priority date for domestic and international students. Applications are processed on a rolling basis. Application fee: $75. Electronic applications accepted. *Expenses:* Contact institution. *Financial support:* In 2016–17, 7 students received support, including 3 research assistantships (averaging $9,088 per year), 4 teaching assistantships (averaging $19,250 per year); fellowships, career-related internships or fieldwork, Federal Work-Study, institutionally sponsored loans, and unspecified assistantships also available. Financial award application deadline: 1/15. *Faculty research:* Manufacturing systems analysis, earnings management, knowledge-based view of the firm, data envelopment analysis, human factors in human/machine systems. *Unit head:* Dr. Reggie Caudill, Interim Dean, 973-596-5856, Fax: 973-596-3074, E-mail: reggie.j.caudill@njit.edu. *Application contact:* Stephen Eck, Director of Admissions, 973-596-3300, Fax: 973-596-3461, E-mail: admissions@njit.edu.
Website: http://management.njit.edu

New York University, Polytechnic School of Engineering, Department of Finance and Risk Engineering, New York, NY 10012-1019. Offers financial engineering (MS, Advanced Certificate), including capital markets (MS), computational finance (MS), financial technology (MS); financial technology management (Advanced Certificate); organizational behavior (Advanced Certificate); risk management (Advanced Certificate); technology management (Advanced Certificate). MS program also offered in Manhattan. *Program availability:* Part-time, evening/weekend. *Degree requirements:* For master's, comprehensive exam (for some programs), thesis (for some programs). *Entrance requirements:* For master's, GMAT, minimum B average in undergraduate course work. Additional exam requirements/recommendations for international students: Required—TOEFL (minimum score 550 paper-based; 80 iBT); Recommended—IELTS (minimum score 6.5). Electronic applications accepted. *Faculty research:* Optimal control theory, general modeling and analysis, risk parity optimality, a new algorithmic approach to entangled political economy.

New York University, Polytechnic School of Engineering, Department of Technology Management, Major in Management of Technology, New York, NY 10012-1019. Offers MS. Program also offered in Manhattan. *Degree requirements:* For master's, comprehensive exam (for some programs), thesis (for some programs). *Entrance requirements:* For master's, GMAT, minimum B average in undergraduate course work. Additional exam requirements/recommendations for international students: Required—TOEFL (minimum score 550 paper-based; 80 iBT); Recommended—IELTS (minimum score 6.5). Electronic applications accepted.

New York University, Polytechnic School of Engineering, Department of Technology Management, Major in Technology Management, New York, NY 10012-1019. Offers MBA, PhD. *Entrance requirements:* Additional exam requirements/recommendations for international students: Required—TOEFL (minimum score 550 paper-based; 80 iBT); Recommended—IELTS (minimum score 6.5). Electronic applications accepted.

North Carolina Agricultural and Technical State University, School of Graduate Studies, School of Technology, Department of Manufacturing Systems, Greensboro, NC 27411. Offers manufacturing (MSTM). *Program availability:* Part-time, evening/weekend. *Degree requirements:* For master's, comprehensive exam, thesis or alternative, qualifying exam. *Entrance requirements:* For master's, GRE General Test, minimum GPA of 3.0.

North Carolina State University, Graduate School, College of Textiles, Program in Textile Technology Management, Raleigh, NC 27695. Offers PhD. *Degree requirements:* For doctorate, one foreign language, thesis/dissertation, cumulative exams. *Entrance requirements:* For doctorate, GRE or GMAT. Electronic applications accepted. *Faculty research:* Niche markets, supply chain, globalization, logistics.

Northern Kentucky University, Office of Graduate Programs, College of Informatics, Program in Computer Information Technology, Highland Heights, KY 41099. Offers MSCIT. *Program availability:* Part-time, evening/weekend. *Degree requirements:* For master's, comprehensive exam (for some programs), thesis or alternative. *Entrance requirements:* For master's, GRE (waived for undergraduates with GPA greater than 3.0 from a STEM discipline), resume, transcripts. Additional exam requirements/recommendations for international students: Required—TOEFL (minimum score 79 iBT); Recommended—IELTS (minimum score 6.5). Electronic applications accepted. *Faculty research:* Data privacy, security, cloud computing, social networks, intrusion detection.

Notre Dame de Namur University, Division of Academic Affairs, School of Business and Management, Program in Business Administration, Belmont, CA 94002-1908. Offers business administration (MBA); entrepreneurship (MBA); finance (MBA); human resource management (MBA); marketing (MBA); media and promotion (MBA); technology and operations management (MBA). *Accreditation:* ACBSP. *Program availability:* Part-time, evening/weekend. *Entrance requirements:* For master's, minimum GPA of 2.5. Additional exam requirements/recommendations for international students: Required—TOEFL (minimum score 550 paper-based; 79 iBT). Electronic applications accepted.

Management of Technology

Pacific States University, College of Business, Los Angeles, CA 90010. Offers accounting (MBA); finance (MBA); international business (MBA, DBA); management of information technology (MBA); real estate management (MBA). *Program availability:* Part-time, evening/weekend, online learning. *Degree requirements:* For doctorate, comprehensive exam, thesis/dissertation. *Entrance requirements:* For master's, minimum undergraduate GPA of 2.5 during last 90 hours of course work. Additional exam requirements/recommendations for international students: Required—TOEFL (minimum score 500 paper-based; 61 iBT), IELTS (minimum score 5.5).

Pittsburg State University, Graduate School, College of Technology, Department of Technology and Workforce Learning, Pittsburg, KS 66762. Offers career and technical education (MS); human resource development (MS); technology (MS), including automotive technology, construction management, graphic design, graphics management, innovation in technology, personnel development, technology management, workforce learning; workforce development and education (Ed S). *Program availability:* Part-time, evening/weekend, 100% online, blended/hybrid learning. *Students:* 171 (79 women); includes 20 minority (4 Black or African American, non-Hispanic/Latino; 5 American Indian or Alaska Native, non-Hispanic/Latino; 2 Asian, non-Hispanic/Latino; 4 Hispanic/Latino; 5 Two or more races, non-Hispanic/Latino), 61 international. In 2016, 62 master's, 2 other advanced degrees awarded. *Degree requirements:* For master's, thesis or alternative; for Ed S, thesis optional. *Entrance requirements:* Additional exam requirements/recommendations for international students: Required—TOEFL (minimum score 520 paper-based; 68 iBT), IELTS (minimum score 6), PTE (minimum score 47). *Application deadline:* For fall admission, 7/15 for domestic students, 6/1 for international students; for spring admission, 12/15 for domestic students, 10/15 for international students; for summer admission, 5/15 for domestic students, 4/1 for international students. Applications are processed on a rolling basis. Application fee: $35 ($60 for international students). Electronic applications accepted. *Expenses:* Contact institution. *Financial support:* In 2016–17, 8 teaching assistantships with full tuition reimbursements (averaging $5,500 per year) were awarded; career-related internships or fieldwork also available. Financial award application deadline: 2/1; financial award applicants required to submit FAFSA. *Unit head:* Dr. John Iley, Chairperson, 620-235-4373, E-mail: jiley@pittstate.edu. *Application contact:* Lisa Allen, Assistant Director of Graduate and Continuing Studies, 620-235-4218, Fax: 620-235-4219, E-mail: lallen@pittstate.edu.

Polytechnic University of Puerto Rico, Graduate School, Hato Rey, PR 00918. Offers business administration (MBA), including computer information systems, general management, management of information systems, management of international enterprises; civil engineering (ME, MS); computer engineering (ME, MS); computer science (MCS, MS); electrical engineering (ME, MS); engineering management (MEM); environmental management (MEM); landscape architecture (M Land Arch); manufacturing competitiveness (MMC, MS); manufacturing engineering (ME, MS); mechanical engineering (M Mech E). *Program availability:* Part-time, evening/weekend. *Entrance requirements:* For master's, 3 letters of recommendation.

Polytechnic University of Puerto Rico, Orlando Campus, Graduate School, Orlando, FL 32825. Offers accounting (MBA); business administration (MBA); construction management (MEM); engineering management (MEM); environmental management (MEM); finance (MBA); human resources management (MBA); management of international enterprises (MBA); management of technology (MBA); manufacturing management (MEM). *Program availability:* Part-time, evening/weekend, online learning. *Entrance requirements:* For master's, minimum GPA of 3.0. Additional exam requirements/recommendations for international students: Recommended—TOEFL. Electronic applications accepted.

Portland State University, Graduate Studies, Maseeh College of Engineering and Computer Science, Department of Engineering and Technology Management, Portland, OR 97207-0751. Offers engineering and technology management (M Eng); engineering management (MS); manufacturing engineering (ME); manufacturing management (M Eng); systems science/engineering management (PhD); MS/MBA; MS/MS. *Program availability:* Part-time, evening/weekend. *Faculty:* 6 full-time (1 woman), 5 part-time/adjunct (0 women). *Students:* 53 full-time (19 women), 75 part-time (34 women); includes 18 minority (3 Black or African American, non-Hispanic/Latino; 11 Asian, non-Hispanic/Latino; 3 Hispanic/Latino; 1 Two or more races, non-Hispanic/Latino), 73 international. Average age 36. 76 applicants, 50% accepted, 20 enrolled. In 2016, 34 master's, 4 doctorates awarded. *Degree requirements:* For master's, thesis optional; for doctorate, one foreign language, comprehensive exam, thesis/dissertation, oral and written exams. *Entrance requirements:* For master's, minimum GPA of 2.75 undergraduate or 3.0 graduate (at least 12 credits); minimum 4 years of experience in engineering or related discipline; 3 letters of recommendation; background in probability/statistics, differential equations, computer programming and linear algebra; for doctorate, GRE General Test (minimum combined score of 1100 for verbal and quantitative), minimum GPA of 3.0 undergraduate, 3.25 graduate. Additional exam requirements/recommendations for international students: Required—TOEFL (minimum score 550 paper-based; 80 iBT). *Application deadline:* For fall admission, 4/1 for domestic students, 3/1 for international students; for winter admission, 9/1 for domestic students, 7/1 for international students; for spring admission, 11/1 for domestic students, 9/1 for international students; for summer admission, 2/1 for domestic students, 12/1 for international students. Application fee: $65. Electronic applications accepted. *Expenses:* Contact institution. *Financial support:* In 2016–17, 7 research assistantships with tuition reimbursements (averaging $2,885 per year), 3 teaching assistantships with tuition reimbursements (averaging $1,176 per year) were awarded; career-related internships or fieldwork, Federal Work-Study, scholarships/grants, and unspecified assistantships also available. Support available to part-time students. Financial award application deadline: 3/1; financial award applicants required to submit FAFSA. *Faculty research:* Scheduling, hierarchical decision modeling, operations research, knowledge-based information systems. *Total annual research expenditures:* $323,951. *Unit head:* Dr. Timothy Anderson, Chair, 503-725-4668, Fax: 503-725-4667, E-mail: tim.anderson@pdx.edu. *Application contact:* Shawn Wall, Department Manager, 503-725-4661, E-mail: shawnw@pdx.edu.
Website: http://www.pdx.edu/engineering-technology-management/

Purdue University, Graduate School, College of Technology, Department of Technology Leadership and Innovation, West Lafayette, IN 47907. Offers leadership (MS, PhD); organizational leadership (MS); technology innovation (MS). *Program availability:* Part-time, evening/weekend, online learning. *Faculty:* 24 full-time (6 women). *Students:* 44 full-time (20 women), 93 part-time (39 women); includes 29 minority (11 Black or African American, non-Hispanic/Latino; 6 Asian, non-Hispanic/Latino; 10 Hispanic/Latino; 1 Native Hawaiian or other Pacific Islander, non-Hispanic/Latino; 1 Two or more races, non-Hispanic/Latino), 18 international. Average age 35. 68 applicants, 78% accepted, 38 enrolled. In 2016, 22 master's awarded. *Entrance requirements:* For master's, GRE General Test, minimum GPA of 3.0. Additional exam requirements/recommendations for international students: Required—TOEFL (minimum score 550 paper-based; 77 iBT); Recommended—TWE. *Application deadline:* For fall admission, 4/1 for domestic and international students; for spring admission, 10/1 for domestic students, 9/1 for international students. Applications are processed on a rolling basis. Application fee: $60 ($75 for international students). Electronic applications

accepted. *Financial support:* Fellowships and teaching assistantships available. Support available to part-time students. Financial award applicants required to submit FAFSA. *Unit head:* Dr. Ragu R. Athinarayanan, Dean, 765-494-0940, E-mail: rathinar@purdue.edu. *Application contact:* Jill S. Albrecht, Secretary/Placement Coordinator, 765-494-5599, E-mail: jsalbrecht@purdue.edu.
Website: http://www.tech.purdue.edu/TLI/

Rensselaer Polytechnic Institute, Graduate School, Lally School of Management, Program in Management, Troy, NY 12180-3590. Offers MBA, MS, PhD. *Program availability:* Part-time. *Faculty:* 35 full-time (10 women), 7 part-time/adjunct (0 women). *Students:* 40 full-time (18 women), 8 part-time (3 women). 238 applicants, 36% accepted, 15 enrolled. In 2016, 24 master's, 7 doctorates awarded. *Degree requirements:* For doctorate, thesis/dissertation. *Entrance requirements:* For master's and doctorate, GMAT or GRE. Additional exam requirements/recommendations for international students: Required—TOEFL (minimum score 570 paper-based; 88 iBT), IELTS (minimum score 6.5), PTE (minimum score 60), TOEFL (minimum score 600 paper-based; 100 iBT), IELTS (minimum score 7.0), or PTE (minimum score 68) for PhD. *Application deadline:* For fall admission, 1/1 priority date for domestic and international students; for spring admission, 8/15 priority date for domestic and international students. Applications are processed on a rolling basis. Application fee: $75. Electronic applications accepted. *Expenses:* Tuition: Full-time $49,520; part-time $2060 per credit hour. *Required fees:* $2617. *Financial support:* In 2016–17, research assistantships (averaging $22,000 per year), teaching assistantships (averaging $22,000 per year) were awarded; fellowships and scholarships/grants also available. Financial award application deadline: 1/1; financial award applicants required to submit FAFSA. *Faculty research:* Business analytics; finance, financial engineering and risk analytics; innovation and technological entrepreneurship; management; management of information systems; new product development and marketing; supply chain management; technology commercialization and entrepreneurship; accounting; information systems; marketing; operations management; organization behavior; strategic management. *Unit head:* Dr. Gina O'Connor, Associate Dean, Lally School of Management, 518-276-6842, E-mail: oconng@rpi.edu. *Application contact:* Office of Graduate Admissions, 518-276-6216, E-mail: gradadmissions@rpi.edu.
Website: https://lallyschool.rpi.edu/programs/graduate-programs

Rollins College, Crummer Graduate School of Business, Winter Park, FL 32789-4499. Offers business administration (EDBA); entrepreneurship (MBA); finance (MBA); international business (MBA); management (MBA); marketing (MBA); operations and technology management (MBA). *Accreditation:* AACSB. *Program availability:* Part-time, evening/weekend, online learning. *Faculty:* 22 full-time (5 women), 4 part-time/adjunct (3 women). *Students:* 254 full-time (105 women), 83 part-time (36 women); includes 63 minority (15 Black or African American, non-Hispanic/Latino; 9 Asian, non-Hispanic/Latino; 35 Hispanic/Latino; 4 Two or more races, non-Hispanic/Latino), 48 international. Average age 31. 360 applicants, 74% accepted, 207 enrolled. In 2016, 159 master's awarded. *Degree requirements:* For master's, minimum GPA of 2.85; for doctorate, thesis/dissertation, minimum GPA of 3.0. *Entrance requirements:* For master's, GMAT or GRE, official transcripts, two letters of recommendation, essay, current resume/curriculum vitae, interview; for doctorate, official transcripts, two letters of recommendation, essays, current resume/curriculum vitae, interview. Additional exam requirements/recommendations for international students: Required—TOEFL (minimum score 100 iBT) or IELTS (minimum score 7). *Application deadline:* Applications are processed on a rolling basis. Application fee: $50. Electronic applications accepted. *Expenses:* Contact institution. *Financial support:* In 2016–17, 125 students received support. Federal Work-Study and scholarships/grants available. Support available to part-time students. Financial award applicants required to submit FAFSA. *Faculty research:* Sustainability, world financial markets, international business, market research, strategic marketing. *Unit head:* Deborah Crown, Dean, 407-646-2249, Fax: 407-646-1550, E-mail: dcrown@rollins.edu. *Application contact:* Maralyn E. Graham, Admissions Coordinator, 407-646-2405, Fax: 407-646-1550, E-mail: mbaadmissions@rollins.edu.
Website: http://www.rollins.edu/mba/

Rutgers University–Newark, Rutgers Business School–Newark and New Brunswick, Doctoral Programs in Management, Newark, NJ 07102. Offers accounting (PhD); accounting information systems (PhD); economics (PhD); finance (PhD); individualized study (PhD); information technology (PhD); international business (PhD); management science (PhD); marketing science (PhD); organizational management (PhD); science, technology and management (PhD); supply chain management (PhD). *Degree requirements:* For doctorate, comprehensive exam, thesis/dissertation. *Entrance requirements:* For doctorate, GRE or GMAT. Additional exam requirements/recommendations for international students: Required—TOEFL (minimum score 550 paper-based; 79 iBT). Electronic applications accepted.

Ryerson University, School of Graduate Studies, Ted Rogers School of Management, Toronto, ON M5B 2K3, Canada. Offers global business administration (MBA); management (MSM); management of technology and innovation (MBA).

St. Ambrose University, College of Arts and Sciences, Program in Information Technology Management, Davenport, IA 52803-2898. Offers MSITM. *Program availability:* Part-time. *Degree requirements:* For master's, thesis (for some programs), practica. *Entrance requirements:* For master's, GRE or GMAT, minimum GPA of 2.8. Additional exam requirements/recommendations for international students: Required—TOEFL. Electronic applications accepted.

Seton Hall University, Stillman School of Business, Programs in Business Administration, South Orange, NJ 07079-2697. Offers accounting (MBA); entrepreneurship (Certificate); finance (MBA, Certificate); information technology management (MBA); international business (MBA); management (MBA); marketing (MBA); sport management (MBA); supply chain management (MBA, Certificate). *Program availability:* Part-time, evening/weekend. *Degree requirements:* For master's, 20 hours of community service (Social Responsibility Project). *Entrance requirements:* For master's, GMAT or CPA, GRE (waived based on work experience or advanced degree from AACSB institution), MS in business discipline, professional degree (MD, JD, PhD, DVM, DDS, CPA, etc.), minimum undergraduate GPA of 3.0. Additional exam requirements/recommendations for international students: Required—TOEFL (minimum score 607 paper-based; 102 iBT), IELTS (minimum score 6), PTE. Electronic applications accepted. *Expenses:* Contact institution. *Faculty research:* Sport, hedge funds, executive compensation, social media, legal studies.

Simon Fraser University, Office of Graduate Studies and Postdoctoral Fellows, Faculty of Business Administration, Vancouver, BC V6B 5K3, Canada. Offers business administration (EMBA, PhD, Graduate Diploma); finance (M Sc); management of technology (MBA); management of technology/biotechnology (MBA). *Program availability:* Online learning. *Faculty:* 91 full-time (33 women). *Students:* 554 full-time (252 women), 161 part-time (58 women). 928 applicants, 45% accepted, 279 enrolled. In 2016, 178 master's, 3 doctorates, 78 other advanced degrees awarded. *Degree requirements:* For master's, thesis (for some programs); for doctorate, comprehensive exam, thesis/dissertation. *Entrance requirements:* For master's, GMAT, minimum GPA of 3.0 (on scale of 4.33) or 3.33 based on last 60 credits of undergraduate courses; for doctorate, minimum GPA of 3.5 (on scale of 4.33); for Graduate Diploma, minimum GPA

of 2.5 (on scale of 4.33) or 2.67 based on last 60 credits of undergraduate courses. Additional exam requirements/recommendations for international students: Recommended—TOEFL (minimum score 580 paper-based; 93 iBT), IELTS (minimum score 7), TWE (minimum score 5). *Application deadline:* For fall admission, 4/2 for domestic students; for winter admission, 10/1 for domestic students; for spring admission, 2/2 for domestic students. Application fee: $90 ($125 for international students). *Expenses:* Contact institution. *Financial support:* In 2016–17, 71 students received support, including 9 fellowships (averaging $6,139 per year), teaching assistantships (averaging $5,608 per year); research assistantships, career-related internships or fieldwork, and scholarships/grants also available. *Faculty research:* Accounting, management and organizational studies, technology and operations management, finance, international business. *Unit head:* Dr. Ian McCarthy, Associate Dean, Graduate Programs, 778-782-9255, Fax: 778-782-4920, E-mail: grad-business@sfu.ca. *Application contact:* Graduate Secretary, 778-782-5013, Fax: 778-782-5122, E-mail: grad-business@sfu.ca.
Website: http://beedie.sfu.ca/graduate/index.php

South Dakota School of Mines and Technology, Graduate Division, Program in Engineering Management, Rapid City, SD 57701-3995. Offers MS. Program offered jointly with The University of South Dakota. *Program availability:* Part-time, online learning. *Entrance requirements:* For master's, GMAT. Additional exam requirements/recommendations for international students: Required—TOEFL, TWE. Electronic applications accepted.

Southeast Missouri State University, School of Graduate Studies, Department of Polytechnic Studies, Cape Girardeau, MO 63701-4799. Offers MS. *Program availability:* Part-time, evening/weekend, online learning. *Faculty:* 13 full-time (3 women). *Students:* 107 full-time (32 women), 44 part-time (11 women); includes 5 minority (3 Black or African American, non-Hispanic/Latino; 1 Asian, non-Hispanic/Latino; 1 Hispanic/Latino), 127 international. Average age 27. 185 applicants, 66% accepted, 33 enrolled. In 2016, 65 master's awarded. *Degree requirements:* For master's, comprehensive exam (for some programs), thesis or alternative. *Entrance requirements:* Additional exam requirements/recommendations for international students: Required—TOEFL (minimum score 550 paper-based; 79 iBT), IELTS (minimum score 6), PTE (minimum score 53). *Application deadline:* For fall admission, 8/1 for domestic students, 5/1 for international students; for spring admission, 11/1 for domestic students, 10/1 for international students. Applications are processed on a rolling basis. Application fee: $30 ($40 for international students). Electronic applications accepted. *Expenses:* Tuition, state resident: full-time $3130; part-time $260.80 per credit hour. Tuition, nonresident: full-time $5842; part-time $486.80 per credit hour. *Required fees:* $33.70 per credit hour. *Financial support:* In 2016–17, 95 students received support. Career-related internships or fieldwork, Federal Work-Study, scholarships/grants, traineeships, tuition waivers (full), and unspecified assistantships available. Financial award application deadline: 6/30; financial award applicants required to submit FAFSA. *Faculty research:* Mechanical engineering, electrical engineering, industrial systems, networking. *Total annual research expenditures:* $25,000. *Unit head:* Dr. Brad Deken, Department Chair, 573-651-2104, Fax: 573-986-6174, E-mail: bdeken@semo.edu. *Application contact:* Dr. Khaled Bawahen, Graduate Coordinator, 573-986-7478, Fax: 573-986-6174, E-mail: kbawaneh@semo.edu.
Website: http://www.semo.edu/polytech/

State University of New York Polytechnic Institute, Program in Business Administration in Technology Management, Utica, NY 13502. Offers accounting and finance (MBA); business management (MBA); health services management (MBA); human resource management (MBA); marketing management (MBA). *Program availability:* Part-time, online learning. *Degree requirements:* For master's, capstone course. *Entrance requirements:* For master's, GMAT, resume, one letter of reference. Additional exam requirements/recommendations for international students: Required—TOEFL (minimum score 550 paper-based; 79 iBT), IELTS (minimum score 6.5). Electronic applications accepted. *Faculty research:* Technology management, writing schools, leadership, new products.

Stevens Institute of Technology, Graduate School, School of Business, Doctoral Program in Technology Management, Hoboken, NJ 07030. Offers information management (PhD); technology management (PhD); telecommunications management (PhD). *Program availability:* Part-time, evening/weekend, online learning. *Students:* 10 full-time (3 women), 4 part-time (1 woman); includes 1 minority (American Indian or Alaska Native, non-Hispanic/Latino), 10 international. Average age 30. In 2016, 1 doctorate awarded. *Degree requirements:* For doctorate, comprehensive exam (for some programs), thesis/dissertation. *Entrance requirements:* Additional exam requirements/recommendations for international students: Required—TOEFL (minimum score 74 iBT), IELTS (minimum score 6). *Application deadline:* For fall admission, 6/1 for domestic students, 4/15 for international students; for spring admission, 11/30 for domestic students, 11/1 for international students. Applications are processed on a rolling basis. Application fee: $65. Electronic applications accepted. *Expenses:* Contact institution. *Financial support:* Fellowships, research assistantships, teaching assistantships, career-related internships or fieldwork, Federal Work-Study, scholarships/grants, and unspecified assistantships available. Financial award application deadline: 2/15; financial award applicants required to submit FAFSA. *Unit head:* Dr. Thomas Lechler, Director, 201-216-8174, Fax: 201-216-5385, E-mail: tlechler@stevens.edu. *Application contact:* Graduate Admissions, 888-783-8367, Fax: 888-511-1306, E-mail: graduate@stevens.edu.
Website: https://www.stevens.edu/school-business/phd-business-administration

Stevens Institute of Technology, Graduate School, School of Business, Program in Business Administration for Experienced Professionals, Hoboken, NJ 07030. Offers business administration (EMBA); technology management (EMBA). *Program availability:* Part-time, evening/weekend. *Students:* 3 full-time (1 woman), 32 part-time (9 women); includes 11 minority (3 Black or African American, non-Hispanic/Latino; 8 Asian, non-Hispanic/Latino), 1 international. Average age 36. 20 applicants, 100% accepted, 10 enrolled. In 2016, 12 master's awarded. *Degree requirements:* For master's, thesis optional, minimum B average in major field and overall. *Entrance requirements:* Additional exam requirements/recommendations for international students: Required—TOEFL (minimum score 74 iBT), IELTS (minimum score 6). *Application deadline:* For fall admission, 6/1 for domestic students, 4/15 for international students; for spring admission, 11/30 for domestic students, 11/1 for international students. Applications are processed on a rolling basis. Application fee: $65. Electronic applications accepted. *Expenses:* Contact institution. *Financial support:* Fellowships, research assistantships, teaching assistantships, career-related internships or fieldwork, Federal Work-Study, scholarships/grants, and unspecified assistantships available. Financial award application deadline: 2/15; financial award applicants required to submit FAFSA. *Unit head:* Dr. Gregory Prastacos, Dean, 201-216-5366, E-mail: gprastac@stevens.edu. *Application contact:* Graduate Admissions, 888-783-8367, Fax: 888-511-1306, E-mail: graduate@stevens.edu.
Website: https://www.stevens.edu/school-business/masters-programs/mbaemba

Stevens Institute of Technology, Graduate School, School of Business, Program in Management, Hoboken, NJ 07030. Offers general management (MS); global innovation management (MS); human resource management (MS); information management (MS); project management (MS); technology commercialization (MS); technology management (MS). *Program availability:* Part-time, evening/weekend. *Students:* 83 full-time (28 women), 82 part-time (36 women); includes 30 minority (6 Black or African American, non-Hispanic/Latino; 1 American Indian or Alaska Native, non-Hispanic/Latino; 21 Asian, non-Hispanic/Latino; 2 Hispanic/Latino), 73 international. Average age 29. 381 applicants, 64% accepted, 53 enrolled. In 2016, 66 master's awarded. *Degree requirements:* For master's, thesis optional, minimum B average in major field and overall. *Entrance requirements:* Additional exam requirements/recommendations for international students: Required—TOEFL (minimum score 74 iBT), IELTS (minimum score 6). *Application deadline:* For fall admission, 6/1 for domestic students, 4/15 for international students; for spring admission, 11/30 for domestic students, 11/1 for international students. Applications are processed on a rolling basis. Application fee: $65. Electronic applications accepted. *Expenses:* Contact institution. *Financial support:* Fellowships, research assistantships, teaching assistantships, career-related internships or fieldwork, Federal Work-Study, scholarships/grants, and unspecified assistantships available. Financial award application deadline: 2/15; financial award applicants required to submit FAFSA. *Unit head:* Brian Rothschild, Director, 201-216-3677, E-mail: brian.rothschild@stevens.edu. *Application contact:* Graduate Admissions, 888-783-8367, Fax: 888-511-1306, E-mail: graduate@stevens.edu.
Website: https://www.stevens.edu/school-business/masters-programs/management

Stevens Institute of Technology, Graduate School, School of Business, Program in Technology Management for Experienced Professionals, Hoboken, NJ 07030. Offers MS, Certificate. *Program availability:* Part-time, evening/weekend, online learning. *Students:* 20 applicants, 100% accepted, 10 enrolled. *Degree requirements:* For master's, thesis optional, minimum B average in major field and overall; for Certificate, minimum B average. *Entrance requirements:* Additional exam requirements/recommendations for international students: Required—TOEFL (minimum score 74 iBT), IELTS (minimum score 6). *Application deadline:* For fall admission, 6/1 for domestic students, 4/15 for international students; for spring admission, 11/30 for domestic students, 11/1 for international students. Applications are processed on a rolling basis. Application fee: $65. Electronic applications accepted. *Expenses: Tuition:* Full-time $33,328; part-time $1501 per credit. *Required fees:* $1186; $566 per credit. $283 per semester. *Financial support:* Fellowships, research assistantships, teaching assistantships, career-related internships or fieldwork, Federal Work-Study, scholarships/grants, and unspecified assistantships available. Financial award application deadline: 2/15; financial award applicants required to submit FAFSA. *Unit head:* Dr. Gregory Prastacos, Dean, 201-216-8366, E-mail: gprastac@stevens.edu. *Application contact:* Graduate Admissions, 888-783-8367, Fax: 888-511-1306, E-mail: graduate@stevens.edu.

Stevens Institute of Technology, Graduate School, School of Business, Program in Telecommunications Management, Hoboken, NJ 07030. Offers business (MS); global innovation management (MS); management of wireless networks (MS); online security, technology and business (MS); project management (MS); technical management (MS); telecommunications management (PhD, Certificate). *Program availability:* Part-time, evening/weekend. *Students:* 1 full-time (0 women), 38 part-time (8 women); includes 5 minority (3 Black or African American, non-Hispanic/Latino; 2 Asian, non-Hispanic/Latino), 1 international. Average age 38. In 2016, 14 master's, 2 other advanced degrees awarded. *Degree requirements:* For master's, thesis optional, minimum B average in major field and overall; for doctorate, comprehensive exam (for some programs), thesis/dissertation; for Certificate, minimum B average. *Entrance requirements:* Additional exam requirements/recommendations for international students: Required—TOEFL (minimum score 74 iBT), IELTS (minimum score 6). *Application deadline:* For fall admission, 6/1 for domestic students, 4/15 for international students; for spring admission, 11/30 for domestic students, 11/1 for international students. Applications are processed on a rolling basis. Application fee: $65. Electronic applications accepted. *Expenses:* Contact institution. *Financial support:* Fellowships, research assistantships, teaching assistantships, career-related internships or fieldwork, Federal Work-Study, scholarships/grants, health care benefits, and unspecified assistantships available. Financial award application deadline: 2/15; financial award applicants required to submit FAFSA. *Unit head:* Dr. Gregory Prastacos, Dean, 201-216-8366, E-mail: gprastac@stevens.edu. *Application contact:* Graduate Admission, 888-783-8367, Fax: 888-511-1306, E-mail: graduate@stevens.edu.
Website: https://www.stevens.edu/school-business/masters-programs/network-communication-management-services

Stevenson University, Program in Business and Technology Management, Owings Mills, MD 21117. Offers emerging technology (MS); innovative leadership (MS). *Program availability:* Part-time, online only, 100% online. *Faculty:* 1 full-time (0 women), 13 part-time/adjunct (3 women). *Students:* 17 full-time (7 women), 118 part-time (62 women); includes 66 minority (58 Black or African American, non-Hispanic/Latino; 1 American Indian or Alaska Native, non-Hispanic/Latino; 4 Asian, non-Hispanic/Latino; 3 Hispanic/Latino). Average age 32. 52 applicants, 73% accepted, 24 enrolled. In 2016, 55 master's awarded. *Degree requirements:* For master's, capstone course. *Entrance requirements:* For master's, bachelor's degree from regionally-accredited institution, official college transcripts from all previous academic work, minimum cumulative GPA of 3.0 in past academic work, personal statement (250-350 words). *Application deadline:* Applications are processed on a rolling basis. Application fee: $0. Electronic applications accepted. *Expenses:* $670 per credit hour. *Financial support:* Unspecified assistantships available. Financial award applicants required to submit FAFSA. *Unit head:* Steven Engorn, Coordinator, 443-352-4220, Fax: 443-394-0538, E-mail: sengorn@stevenson.edu. *Application contact:* Tonia Cristino, Assistant Director, Recruitment and Admissions, 443-352-4058, Fax: 443-394-0538, E-mail: tcristino@stevenson.edu.
Website: http://www.stevenson.edu

Stony Brook University, State University of New York, Graduate School, College of Engineering and Applied Sciences, Department of Technology and Society, Program in Global Operations Management, Stony Brook, NY 11794. Offers MS. *Program availability:* Online learning. *Entrance requirements:* For master's, GRE. Additional exam requirements/recommendations for international students: Required—TOEFL (minimum score 85 iBT), IELTS (minimum score 6.5). *Application deadline:* For fall admission, 1/15 for domestic students; for spring admission, 10/1 for domestic students. Electronic applications accepted. *Expenses:* Contact institution. *Unit head:* Dr. David Ferguson, Chairman, 631-632-8763, E-mail: david.ferguson@stonybrook.edu. *Application contact:* Marypat Taveras, Coordinator, 631-632-8762, Fax: 631-632-7809, E-mail: marypat.taveras@stonybrook.edu.
Website: http://www.stonybrook.edu/est/graduate/elearn.shtml

Texas A&M University, College of Engineering, Department of Engineering Technology and Industrial Distribution, College Station, TX 77843. Offers industrial distribution (MID); technical management (METM). *Faculty:* 31. *Students:* 119 full-time (16 women), 2 part-time (1 woman); includes 36 minority (11 Black or African American, non-Hispanic/Latino; 2 Asian, non-Hispanic/Latino; 18 Hispanic/Latino; 5 Two or more races, non-Hispanic/Latino), 5 international. Average age 36. 62 applicants, 98% accepted, 60 enrolled. In 2016, 67 master's awarded. *Entrance requirements:* Additional exam requirements/recommendations for international students: Required—

TOEFL (minimum score 550 paper-based; 80 iBT), IELTS (minimum score 6), PTE (minimum score 53). *Application deadline:* For fall admission, 3/1 priority date for domestic and international students; for winter admission, 11/1 for domestic and international students; for spring admission, 8/1 priority date for domestic and international students. Applications are processed on a rolling basis. Application fee: $50 ($90 for international students). Electronic applications accepted. *Expenses:* Contact institution. *Financial support:* In 2016–17, 71 students received support. Application deadline: 3/15; applicants required to submit FAFSA. *Unit head:* Dr. Reza Langari, Department Head, 979-862-4945, E-mail: rlangari@tamu.edu. *Application contact:* Graduate Admissions, 979-458-0427, E-mail: graduate-admissions@tamu.edu. Website: http://engineering.tamu.edu/etid

Texas A&M University–Commerce, College of Science and Engineering, Commerce, TX 75429-3011. Offers biological science (MS); chemistry (MS); computational linguistics (Graduate Certificate); computational science (MS); computer science (MS); environmental science (Graduate Certificate); mathematics (MS); physics (MS); technology management (MS). *Program availability:* Part-time, 100% online, blended/hybrid learning. *Faculty:* 44 full-time (4 women), 15 part-time/adjunct (0 women). *Students:* 427 full-time (166 women), 276 part-time (130 women); includes 80 minority (26 Black or African American, non-Hispanic/Latino; 1 American Indian or Alaska Native, non-Hispanic/Latino; 14 Asian, non-Hispanic/Latino; 32 Hispanic/Latino; 7 Two or more races, non-Hispanic/Latino), 452 international. Average age 28. 1,103 applicants, 53% accepted, 282 enrolled. In 2016, 303 master's awarded. *Degree requirements:* For master's, comprehensive exam, thesis optional. *Entrance requirements:* For master's, GRE, official transcripts, letters of recommendation, resume, statement of goals. Additional exam requirements/recommendations for international students: Required—TOEFL (minimum score 550 paper-based; 79 iBT), IELTS (minimum score 6). *Application deadline:* For fall admission, 6/1 priority date for international students; for spring admission, 10/15 priority date for international students; for summer admission, 3/15 priority date for international students. Applications are processed on a rolling basis. Application fee: $50 ($75 for international students). Electronic applications accepted. *Expenses:* Tuition, state resident: full-time $3630. Tuition, nonresident: full-time $10,974. *Required fees:* $2146. Tuition and fees vary according to course load, degree level and program. *Financial support:* In 2016–17, 211 students received support, including 11 research assistantships with partial tuition reimbursements available (averaging $8,000 per year), 41 teaching assistantships with partial tuition reimbursements available (averaging $8,000 per year); scholarships/grants, health care benefits, and unspecified assistantships also available. Financial award application deadline: 5/1; financial award applicants required to submit FAFSA. *Faculty research:* Regenerative medicine, catalytic materials and processes, nuclear theory/astrophysics, image processing/recognition. *Total annual research expenditures:* $1.1 million. *Unit head:* Dr. Brent L. Donham, Dean, 903-886-5390, Fax: 903-886-5199, E-mail: brent.donham@tamuc.edu. *Application contact:* Shaine L. Marsden, Graduate Recruiter, 903-886-5775, E-mail: shaine.marsden@tamuc.edu.
Website: http://www.tamuc.edu/academics/graduateSchool/programs/sciences/default.aspx

Texas State University, The Graduate College, College of Science and Engineering, Program in Technology Management, San Marcos, TX 78666. Offers MS. *Program availability:* Part-time, evening/weekend. *Faculty:* 8 full-time (1 woman). *Students:* 16 full-time (4 women), 17 part-time; includes 9 minority (2 Black or African American, non-Hispanic/Latino; 7 Hispanic/Latino), 13 international. Average age 28. 45 applicants, 56% accepted, 9 enrolled. In 2016, 5 master's awarded. *Degree requirements:* For master's, comprehensive exam, thesis optional. *Entrance requirements:* For master's, baccalaureate degree from regionally-accredited university with minimum GPA of 2.75 on last 60 undergraduate semester hours. Additional exam requirements/recommendations for international students: Required—TOEFL (minimum score 550 paper-based; 78 iBT), IELTS (minimum score 6.5). *Application deadline:* For fall admission, 2/1 priority date for domestic and international students; for spring admission, 10/15 for domestic students, 10/1 for international students; for summer admission, 4/15 for domestic students, 3/15 for international students. Applications are processed on a rolling basis. Application fee: $40 ($90 for international students). Electronic applications accepted. *Expenses:* $4,851 per semester. *Financial support:* In 2016–17, 13 students received support, including 2 research assistantships (averaging $13,600 per year), 4 teaching assistantships (averaging $13,780 per year); career-related internships or fieldwork, Federal Work-Study, and institutionally sponsored loans also available. Support available to part-time students. Financial award application deadline: 3/1; financial award applicants required to submit FAFSA. *Faculty research:* Measuring information content of the artifacts of early design, evaluation of pavement preservation and maintenance activities-general airports, assessing the effect of gravity on the property of materials, methodology for collaborative ontology development for service-oriented manufacturing enterprises, assembly tolerance analysis for wheel stack, concrete based on Portland limestone cement with limestone content greater than 15%, improving crack sealant application methods. *Total annual research expenditures:* $148,473. *Unit head:* Dr. Andy Batey, Graduate Advisor, 512-245-2137, E-mail: ab08@txstate.edu. *Application contact:* Dr. Andrea Golato, Dean of the Graduate College, 512-245-2581, E-mail: gradcollege@txstate.edu.
Website: http://www.txstate.edu/technology/degrees-programs/graduate.html

Towson University, Program in e-Business and Technology Management, Towson, MD 21252-0001. Offers project, program and portfolio management (Postbaccalaureate Certificate); supply chain management (MS, Postbaccalaureate Certificate). *Students:* 2 full-time (1 woman), 22 part-time (8 women); includes 7 minority (3 Black or African American, non-Hispanic/Latino; 1 Asian, non-Hispanic/Latino; 3 Two or more races, non-Hispanic/Latino), 2 international. *Entrance requirements:* For master's and Postbaccalaureate Certificate, GRE or GMAT, bachelor's degree in relevant field and/or three years of post-bachelor's experience working in supply chain related areas; minimum cumulative GPA of 3.0; resume; 2 reference letters. Additional exam requirements/recommendations for international students: Required—TOEFL (minimum score 550 paper-based). *Application deadline:* Applications are processed on a rolling basis. Application fee: $45. Electronic applications accepted. *Expenses:* Tuition, state resident: full-time $7580; part-time $379 per unit. Tuition, nonresident: full-time $15,700; part-time $785 per unit. *Required fees:* $2480. *Unit head:* Dr. Tobin Porterfield, Director, 410-704-3265, E-mail: tporterfield@towson.edu. *Application contact:* Coverley Beidleman, Assistant Director of Graduate Admissions, 410-704-2113, Fax: 410-704-3030, E-mail: grads@towson.edu.
Website: http://www.towson.edu/cbe/departments/ebusiness/grad/

University at Albany, State University of New York, School of Business, MBA Programs, Albany, NY 12222. Offers business administration (MBA); cyber security (MBA); entrepreneurship (MBA); finance (MBA); human resource information systems (MBA); information technology management (MBA); marketing (MBA); JD/MBA. JD/MBA offered with Albany Law School. *Program availability:* Part-time, evening/weekend. *Faculty:* 25 full-time (8 women), 4 part-time/adjunct (1 woman). *Students:* 92 full-time (39 women), 192 part-time (77 women); includes 63 minority (12 Black or African American, non-Hispanic/Latino; 1 American Indian or Alaska Native, non-Hispanic/Latino; 32 Asian, non-Hispanic/Latino; 13 Hispanic/Latino; 5 Two or more races, non-Hispanic/Latino), 27 international. Average age 25. 217 applicants, 73% accepted, 119 enrolled. In 2016, 122 master's awarded. *Degree requirements:* For master's, thesis (for some programs), field or research project. *Entrance requirements:* For master's, GMAT, minimum undergraduate GPA of 3.0; 3 letters of recommendation; resume; statement of goals. Additional exam requirements/recommendations for international students: Required—TOEFL (minimum score 100 iBT); Recommended—IELTS (minimum score 7). *Application deadline:* For fall admission, 4/1 priority date for domestic students, 3/1 for international students; for spring admission, 12/1 for domestic students; for summer admission, 5/1 for domestic students. Applications are processed on a rolling basis. Application fee: $75. Electronic applications accepted. *Expenses:* $16,274 Full-Time MBA per year; $696 Part-Time MBA per credit hour. *Financial support:* In 2016–17, 20 students received support, including 20 fellowships with partial tuition reimbursements available (averaging $6,500 per year); research assistantships, teaching assistantships, and unspecified assistantships also available. Financial award application deadline: 4/1; financial award applicants required to submit FAFSA. *Faculty research:* Cyber security, entrepreneurship, human resource information systems, information technology management, finance, marketing. *Total annual research expenditures:* $136,000. *Unit head:* Dr. Hany A. Shawky, Interim Dean, 518-956-8337, E-mail: hshawky@albany.edu. *Application contact:* Zina Mega Lawrence, Assistant Dean of Graduate Student Services, 518-956-8320, Fax: 518-442-4042, E-mail: zlawrence@albany.edu.
Website: http://graduatebusiness.albany.edu/

University of Advancing Technology, Master of Science Program in Technology, Tempe, AZ 85283-1042. Offers advancing computer science (MS); emerging technologies (MS); game production and management (MS); information assurance (MS); technology leadership (MS). *Degree requirements:* For master's, project or thesis. *Entrance requirements:* Additional exam requirements/recommendations for international students: Required—TOEFL (minimum score 550 paper-based). Electronic applications accepted. *Faculty research:* Artificial intelligence, fractals, organizational management.

The University of Alabama in Huntsville, School of Graduate Studies, College of Business Administration, Programs in Business and Management, Huntsville, AL 35899. Offers business analytics (MSMS); federal contracting and procurement management (Certificate); human resource management (MSM); management (MBA), including acquisition management, entrepreneurship, federal contract accounting, finance, human resource management, logistics and supply chain management, marketing, project management; supply chain management (Certificate); technology and innovation management (Certificate). *Accreditation:* AACSB. *Program availability:* Part-time, evening/weekend. *Degree requirements:* For master's, comprehensive exam, thesis or alternative. *Entrance requirements:* For master's, GMAT (minimum score 500), minimum AACSB index of 1080. Additional exam requirements/recommendations for international students: Required—TOEFL (minimum score 550 paper-based; 80 iBT), IELTS (minimum score 6.5). Electronic applications accepted. *Expenses:* Tuition, state resident: full-time $9834; part-time $600 per credit hour. Tuition, nonresident: full-time $21,830; part-time $1325 per credit hour. *Faculty research:* Supply chain management, management of research and development, international marketing and branding, organizational behavior and human resource management, social networks and computational economics.

University of Bridgeport, School of Engineering, Department of Technology Management, Bridgeport, CT 06604. Offers MS, PhD. *Degree requirements:* For master's, thesis optional. *Entrance requirements:* Additional exam requirements/recommendations for international students: Recommended—TOEFL (minimum score 550 paper-based; 80 iBT), IELTS (minimum score 6.5). Electronic applications accepted. *Expenses:* Contact institution.

University of California, Los Angeles, Graduate Division, UCLA Anderson School of Management, Los Angeles, CA 90095-1481. Offers accounting (PhD); behavioral decision making (PhD); business administration (EMBA, MBA); decisions, operations, and technology management (PhD); finance (PhD); financial engineering (MFE); global economics and management (PhD); management and organizations (PhD); marketing (PhD); strategy and policy (PhD); DDS/MBA; MBA/JD; MBA/MD; MBA/MLAS; MBA/MLIS; MBA/MN; MBA/MPH; MBA/MPP; MBA/MSCS; MBA/MURP. *Accreditation:* AACSB. *Program availability:* Part-time, evening/weekend. *Faculty:* 90 full-time (20 women), 98 part-time/adjunct (19 women). *Students:* 865 full-time (263 women), 1,201 part-time (337 women); includes 710 minority (48 Black or African American, non-Hispanic/Latino; 1 American Indian or Alaska Native, non-Hispanic/Latino; 505 Asian, non-Hispanic/Latino; 88 Hispanic/Latino; 4 Native Hawaiian or other Pacific Islander, non-Hispanic/Latino; 64 Two or more races, non-Hispanic/Latino), 451 international. Average age 31. 5,643 applicants, 26% accepted, 881 enrolled. In 2016, 807 master's, 7 doctorates awarded. *Degree requirements:* For master's, comprehensive exam, field consulting project; internship (for MBA); thesis/dissertation (for MFE); for doctorate, comprehensive exam, thesis/dissertation, oral and written qualifying exams. *Entrance requirements:* For master's, GMAT or GRE, 4-year bachelor's degree or equivalent; 2 letters of recommendation; essays (1 for MBA, 2 for FEMBA and MFE); 4-8 years of full-time work experience (for FEMBA); minimum eight years of work experience with at least three years at management level (for EMBA); for doctorate, GMAT or GRE, bachelor's degree from college or university of fully-recognized standing, minimum B average during junior and senior years of undergraduate years, 3 letters of recommendation, statement of purpose. Additional exam requirements/recommendations for international students: Required—TOEFL (minimum score 560 paper-based; 87 iBT), IELTS (minimum score 7). *Application deadline:* For fall admission, 10/6 priority date for domestic and international students; for winter admission, 1/5 for domestic and international students; for spring admission, 4/12 for domestic and international students. Applications are processed on a rolling basis. Application fee: $200. Electronic applications accepted. *Expenses:* Contact institution. *Financial support:* In 2016–17, 633 students received support, including 455 fellowships (averaging $30,253 per year); research assistantships with partial tuition reimbursements available, teaching assistantships with partial tuition reimbursements available, career-related internships or fieldwork, institutionally sponsored loans, and scholarships/grants also available. Support available to part-time students. *Faculty research:* Finance/global economics, entrepreneurship, accounting, human resources/organizational behavior, marketing, behavioral decision making. *Total annual research expenditures:* $1.1 million. *Unit head:* Dr. Judy D. Olian, Dean/Chair in Management, 310-825-7982, Fax: 310-206-2073, E-mail: judy.olian@anderson.ucla.edu. *Application contact:* Alex Lawrence, Assistant Dean and Director of MBA Admissions, 310-825-6944, Fax: 310-825-8582, E-mail: mba.admissions@anderson.ucla.edu.
Website: http://www.anderson.ucla.edu/

University of California, Santa Barbara, Graduate Division, College of Engineering, Program in Technology Management, Santa Barbara, CA 93106-2014. Offers MTM.

University of California, Santa Cruz, Jack Baskin School of Engineering, Department of Technology Management, Santa Cruz, CA 95064. Offers PhD. *Faculty:* 9 full-time (1 woman). *Students:* 9 full-time (5 women), 2 part-time (1 woman), 7 international. 29 applicants, 28% accepted, 4 enrolled. Terminal master's awarded for partial completion of doctoral program. *Degree requirements:* For doctorate, thesis/dissertation, 2 seminars. *Entrance requirements:* For doctorate, GRE General Test; GRE Subject Test preferably in computer science, engineering, physics, or mathematics (highly

recommended). Additional exam requirements/recommendations for international students: Required—TOEFL (minimum score 570 paper-based; 89 iBT); Recommended—IELTS (minimum score 8). *Application deadline:* For fall admission, 1/3 for domestic and international students. Application fee: $105 ($125 for international students). Electronic applications accepted. *Financial support:* In 2016–17, 9 students received support, including 5 fellowships (averaging $18,000 per year), 6 research assistantships (averaging $20,043 per year), 15 teaching assistantships (averaging $20,052 per year); institutionally sponsored loans and tuition waivers (full and partial) also available. Financial award application deadline: 1/3; financial award applicants required to submit FAFSA. *Faculty research:* Integration of information systems, technology, and business management. *Unit head:* John Musacchio, Chair, 831-459-1385, E-mail: johnm@soe.ucsc.edu. *Application contact:* Will Suh, Graduate Student Advisor, 831-459-2332, E-mail: bsoe-ga@rt.ucsc.edu.
Website: https://www.soe.ucsc.edu/departments/technology-management

University of Central Missouri, The Graduate School, Warrensburg, MO 64093. Offers accountancy (MA); accounting (MBA); applied mathematics (MS); aviation safety (MA); biology (MS); business administration (MBA); career and technical education leadership (MS); college student personnel administration (MS); communication (MA); computer science (MS); counseling (MS); criminal justice (MS); educational leadership (Ed D); educational technology (MS); elementary and early childhood education (MSE); English (MA); environmental studies (MA); finance (MBA); history (MA); human services/educational technology (Ed S); human services/learning resources (Ed S); human services/professional counseling (Ed S); industrial hygiene (MS); industrial management (MS); information systems (MBA); information technology (MS); kinesiology (MS); library science and information services (MS); literacy education (MSE); marketing (MBA); mathematics (MS); music (MA); occupational safety management (MS); psychology (MS); rural family nursing (MS); school administration (MSE); social gerontology (MS); sociology (MA); special education (MSE); speech language pathology (MS); superintendency (Ed S); teaching (MAT); teaching English as a second language (MA); technology (MS); technology management (PhD); theatre (MA). *Program availability:* Part-time, 100% online, blended/hybrid learning. *Degree requirements:* For master's and Ed S, comprehensive exam (for some programs), thesis (for some programs). *Entrance requirements:* Additional exam requirements/recommendations for international students: Required—TOEFL (minimum score 550 paper-based; 79 iBT). Electronic applications accepted.

University of Colorado Denver, Business School, Master of Business Administration Program, Denver, CO 80217. Offers bioinnovation and entrepreneurship (MBA); business intelligence (MBA); business strategy (MBA); business to business marketing (MBA); business to consumer marketing (MBA); change management (MBA); corporate financial management (MBA); enterprise technology management (MBA); entrepreneurship (MBA); health administration (MBA), including financial management, health administration, health information technologies, international health management and policy; human resources management (MBA); international business (MBA); investment management (MBA); managing for sustainability (MBA); sports and entertainment management (MBA). *Accreditation:* AACSB. *Program availability:* Part-time, evening/weekend, 100% online, blended/hybrid learning. *Students:* 544 full-time (210 women), 112 part-time (22 women); includes 99 minority (15 Black or African American, non-Hispanic/Latino; 4 American Indian or Alaska Native, non-Hispanic/Latino; 38 Asian, non-Hispanic/Latino; 36 Hispanic/Latino; 6 Two or more races, non-Hispanic/Latino), 22 international. Average age 32. 335 applicants, 73% accepted, 179 enrolled. In 2016, 251 master's awarded. *Degree requirements:* For master's, 48 semester hours, including 30 of core courses, 3 in international business, and 15 in electives from over 50 other business courses. *Entrance requirements:* For master's, GMAT, resume, official transcripts, essay, two letters of recommendation, financial statements (for international applicants). Additional exam requirements/recommendations for international students: Required—TOEFL (minimum score 560 paper-based; 83 iBT); Recommended—IELTS (minimum score 6.5). *Application deadline:* For fall admission, 4/15 priority date for domestic students, 3/15 priority date for international students; for spring admission, 10/15 priority date for domestic students, 9/15 priority date for international students; for summer admission, 2/15 priority date for domestic students, 1/15 priority date for international students. Applications are processed on a rolling basis. Application fee: $50 ($75 for international students). Electronic applications accepted. *Expenses:* Contact institution. *Financial support:* In 2016–17, 171 students received support. Fellowships, research assistantships, teaching assistantships, Federal Work-Study, institutionally sponsored loans, scholarships/grants, traineeships, and unspecified assistantships available. Financial award application deadline: 4/1; financial award applicants required to submit FAFSA. *Faculty research:* Marketing, management, entrepreneurship, finance, health administration. *Unit head:* Woodrow Eckard, MBA Director, 303-315-8470, E-mail: woody.eckard@ucdenver.edu. *Application contact:* Shelly Townley, Admissions Director, Graduate Programs, 303-315-8202, E-mail: shelly.townley@ucdenver.edu.
Website: http://www.ucdenver.edu/academics/colleges/business/degrees/mba/Pages/MBA.aspx

University of Colorado Denver, Business School, Program in Information Systems, Denver, CO 80217. Offers accounting and information systems audit and control (MS); business intelligence systems (MS); digital health entrepreneurship (MS); enterprise risk management (MS); enterprise technology management (MS); geographic information systems (MS); health information technology (MS); technology innovation and entrepreneurship (MS); Web and mobile computing (MS). *Program availability:* Part-time, evening/weekend, online learning. *Students:* 110 full-time (44 women), 33 part-time (11 women); includes 19 minority (1 Black or African American, non-Hispanic/Latino; 8 Asian, non-Hispanic/Latino; 6 Hispanic/Latino; 4 Two or more races, non-Hispanic/Latino), 79 international. Average age 29. 140 applicants, 71% accepted, 38 enrolled. In 2016, 50 master's awarded. *Degree requirements:* For master's, 30 credit hours. *Entrance requirements:* For master's, GMAT, resume, essay, two letters of recommendation, financial statements (for international applicants). Additional exam requirements/recommendations for international students: Required—TOEFL (minimum score 525 paper-based; 71 iBT); Recommended—IELTS (minimum score 6.5). *Application deadline:* For fall admission, 4/15 priority date for domestic students, 3/15 priority date for international students; for spring admission, 10/15 priority date for domestic students, 9/15 priority date for international students; for summer admission, 2/15 priority date for domestic students, 1/15 priority date for international students. Applications are processed on a rolling basis. Application fee: $50 ($75 for international students). Electronic applications accepted. *Expenses:* Contact institution. *Financial support:* In 2016–17, 24 students received support. Fellowships, research assistantships, teaching assistantships, Federal Work-Study, institutionally sponsored loans, scholarships/grants, and traineeships available. Financial award application deadline: 4/1; financial award applicants required to submit FAFSA. *Faculty research:* Human-computer interaction, expert systems, database management, electronic commerce, object-oriented software development. *Unit head:* Dr. Jahangir Karimi, Director of Information Systems Programs, 303-315-8430, E-mail: jahangir.karimi@ucdenver.edu. *Application contact:* 303-315-8200, E-mail: bschool.admissions@ucdenver.edu.
Website: http://www.ucdenver.edu/academics/colleges/business/degrees/ms/IS/Pages/Information-Systems.aspx

University of Colorado Denver, Business School, Program in Management and Organization, Denver, CO 80217. Offers business strategy (MS); change and innovation (MS); enterprise technology management (MS); entrepreneurship and innovation (MS); global management (MS); leadership (MS); managing for sustainability (MS); managing human resources (MS); sports and entertainment management (MS). *Accreditation:* AACSB. *Program availability:* Part-time, evening/weekend, online learning. *Students:* 20 full-time (13 women), 17 part-time (10 women); includes 6 minority (3 Black or African American, non-Hispanic/Latino; 1 American Indian or Alaska Native, non-Hispanic/Latino; 1 Hispanic/Latino; 1 Two or more races, non-Hispanic/Latino), 6 international. Average age 33. 24 applicants, 58% accepted, 6 enrolled. In 2016, 19 master's awarded. *Degree requirements:* For master's, 30 semester hours (12 of required courses, 12 of management electives, and 6 of free electives). *Entrance requirements:* For master's, GMAT, resume, two letters of recommendation, essay, financial statements (for international applicants). Additional exam requirements/recommendations for international students: Required—TOEFL (minimum score 525 paper-based; 71 iBT); Recommended—IELTS (minimum score 6.5). *Application deadline:* For fall admission, 4/15 priority date for domestic students, 3/15 priority date for international students; for spring admission, 10/15 priority date for domestic students, 9/15 priority date for international students; for summer admission, 2/15 priority date for domestic students, 1/15 priority date for international students. Applications are processed on a rolling basis. Application fee: $50 ($75 for international students). Electronic applications accepted. *Expenses:* Contact institution. *Financial support:* In 2016–17, 7 students received support. Fellowships, research assistantships, teaching assistantships, Federal Work-Study, institutionally sponsored loans, scholarships/grants, and traineeships available. Financial award application deadline: 4/1; financial award applicants required to submit FAFSA. *Faculty research:* Human resource management, management of catastrophe, turnaround strategies. *Unit head:* Dr. Kenneth Bettenhausen, Associate Professor/Director of MS in Management, 303-315-8425, E-mail: kenneth.bettenhausen@ucdenver.edu. *Application contact:* 303-315-8200, E-mail: bschool.admissions@ucdenver.edu.
Website: http://www.ucdenver.edu/academics/colleges/business/degrees/ms/management/Pages/Management.aspx

University of Dallas, Satish and Yasmin Gupta College of Business, Irving, TX 75062-4736. Offers accounting (MBA, MS); business administration (DBA); business analytics (MS); business management (MBA); corporate finance (MBA); cybersecurity (MS); finance (MS); financial services (MBA); global business (MBA, MS); health services management (MBA); human resource management (MBA); information and technology management (MS); information assurance (MBA); information technology (MBA); information technology service management (MBA); marketing management (MBA); organization development (MBA); project management (MBA); sports and entertainment management (MBA); strategic leadership (MBA); supply chain management (MBA). *Accreditation:* AACSB. *Program availability:* Part-time, evening/weekend, online learning. *Entrance requirements:* Additional exam requirements/recommendations for international students: Required—TOEFL. Electronic applications accepted. *Expenses:* Contact institution.

University of Delaware, Alfred Lerner College of Business and Economics, Department of Accounting and Management Information Systems and Department of Electrical and Computer Engineering, Program in Information Systems and Technology Management, Newark, DE 19716. Offers MS. *Program availability:* Part-time, evening/weekend. *Entrance requirements:* For master's, GRE or GMAT, 2 letters of recommendation, resume, minimum GPA of 2.75. Additional exam requirements/recommendations for international students: Required—TOEFL (minimum score 600 paper-based). *Faculty research:* Security, developer trust, XML.

University of Idaho, College of Graduate Studies, College of Engineering, Department of Engineering, Moscow, ID 83844. Offers biological engineering (M Engr, MS, PhD); technology management (MS). *Faculty:* 8 full-time. *Students:* 1 full-time, 25 part-time. Average age 42. In 2016, 6 master's, 1 doctorate awarded. *Entrance requirements:* For master's, minimum GPA of 3.0. Additional exam requirements/recommendations for international students: Required—TOEFL. *Application deadline:* Applications are processed on a rolling basis. Application fee: $60. Electronic applications accepted. *Expenses:* Tuition, state resident: full-time $6460; part-time $414 per credit hour. Tuition, nonresident: full-time $21,268; part-time $1237 per credit hour. *Required fees:* $2070; $60 per credit hour. Full-time tuition and fees vary according to course load and reciprocity agreements. *Financial support:* Applicants required to submit FAFSA. *Unit head:* Dr. Larry Stauffer, Dean, 208-885-6479. *Application contact:* Stephanie Thomas, Graduate Recruitment Coordinator, 208-885-4001, Fax: 208-885-4406, E-mail: gadms@uidaho.edu.
Website: http://www.uidaho.edu/engr/

University of Illinois at Urbana–Champaign, Graduate College, College of Agricultural, Consumer and Environmental Sciences, Department of Agricultural and Biological Engineering, Champaign, IL 61820. Offers agricultural and biological engineering (MS, PhD); technical systems management (MS, PSM).

University of Illinois at Urbana–Champaign, Graduate College, College of Business, Department of Business Administration, Champaign, IL 61820. Offers business administration (MS, PhD); technology management (MS). *Accreditation:* AACSB. *Expenses:* Contact institution.

University of Massachusetts Dartmouth, Graduate School, Charlton College of Business, Department of Decision and Information Sciences, North Dartmouth, MA 02747-2300. Offers healthcare management (MS); technology management (MS). *Program availability:* Part-time, 100% online, blended/hybrid learning. *Faculty:* 13 full-time (5 women), 3 part-time/adjunct (0 women). *Students:* 17 full-time (9 women), 22 part-time (15 women); includes 8 minority (1 Black or African American, non-Hispanic/Latino; 4 Asian, non-Hispanic/Latino; 2 Hispanic/Latino; 1 Two or more races, non-Hispanic/Latino), 15 international. Average age 33. 38 applicants, 79% accepted, 19 enrolled. *Degree requirements:* For master's, thesis or project (for healthcare management). *Entrance requirements:* For master's, GMAT, statement of purpose (minimum 300 words), resume, official transcripts, 2 letters of recommendation. Additional exam requirements/recommendations for international students: Required—TOEFL (minimum score 533 paper-based; 72 iBT). *Application deadline:* For fall admission, 7/1 priority date for domestic students, 6/1 priority date for international students; for spring admission, 11/15 priority date for domestic students, 10/15 priority date for international students. Application fee: $60. Electronic applications accepted. *Expenses:* Tuition, state resident: full-time $14,994; part-time $624.75 per credit. Tuition, nonresident: full-time $27,068; part-time $1127.83 per credit. *Required fees:* $405; $25.88 per credit. Tuition and fees vary according to course load and reciprocity agreements. *Financial support:* Institutionally sponsored loans, scholarships/grants, and unspecified assistantships available. Financial award application deadline: 3/1; financial award applicants required to submit FAFSA. *Faculty research:* Healthcare management and policy, process management, supply chain management, project team work processes in project management, technology-mediated learning, the use of IT in organizations, leadership in health systems, decision models for adaptation of the

advanced manufacturing technologies, revenue management and dynamic pricing. *Unit head:* Melissa Pacheco, Assistant Dean of Graduate Programs, 508-999-8543, Fax: 508-999-8646, E-mail: mpacheco@umassd.edu. *Application contact:* Steven Briggs, Director of Marketing and Recruitment for Graduate Studies, 508-999-8604, Fax: 508-999-8183, E-mail: graduate@umassd.edu.
Website: http://www.umassd.edu/charlton/programs/graduate/

University of Miami, Graduate School, College of Engineering, Department of Industrial Engineering, Coral Gables, FL 33124. Offers environmental health and safety (MS); ergonomics (PhD); industrial engineering (MSIE, PhD); management of technology (MS); occupational ergonomics and safety (MS, MSOES), including environmental health and safety (MS), occupational ergonomics and safety (MSOES); MBA/MSIE. *Program availability:* Part-time. *Degree requirements:* For master's, thesis (for some programs); for doctorate, comprehensive exam, thesis/dissertation. *Entrance requirements:* For master's and doctorate, GRE General Test, minimum GPA of 3.0. Additional exam requirements/recommendations for international students: Required—TOEFL (minimum score 550 paper-based). *Faculty research:* Logistics, supply chain management, industrial applications of biomechanics and ergonomics, technology management, back pain, aging, operations research, manufacturing, safety, human reliability, energy assessment.

University of Minnesota, Twin Cities Campus, College of Science and Engineering, Technological Leadership Institute, Program in Management of Technology, Minneapolis, MN 55455-0213. Offers MSMOT. *Program availability:* Evening/weekend. *Degree requirements:* For master's, thesis, capstone project. *Entrance requirements:* For master's, 5 years of work experience in high-tech company, preferably in Twin Cities area; demonstrated technological leadership ability. Additional exam requirements/recommendations for international students: Required—TOEFL (minimum score 580 paper-based; 90 iBT). Electronic applications accepted. *Expenses:* Contact institution. *Faculty research:* Operations management, strategic management, technology foresight, marketing, business analysis.

University of New Mexico, Anderson School of Management, Department of Finance, International, Technology and Entrepreneurship, Albuquerque, NM 87131. Offers entrepreneurship (MBA); finance (MBA); international management (MBA); international management in Latin America (MBA); management of technology (MBA). *Program availability:* Part-time, evening/weekend. *Faculty:* 15 full-time (2 women), 5 part-time/adjunct (0 women). In 2016, 41 master's awarded. *Entrance requirements:* For master's, GMAT or GRE, minimum GPA of 3.0 on last 60 hours of coursework; bachelor's degree from regionally-accredited college or university in U.S. or its equivalent in another country. Additional exam requirements/recommendations for international students: Required—TOEFL (minimum score 550 paper-based; 79 iBT), IELTS (minimum score 6.5). *Application deadline:* For fall admission, 4/1 priority date for domestic and international students; for spring admission, 10/1 priority date for domestic and international students. Applications are processed on a rolling basis. Application fee: $50. Electronic applications accepted. *Expenses:* Contact institution. *Financial support:* In 2016–17, 12 fellowships (averaging $15,441 per year), 12 research assistantships with partial tuition reimbursements (averaging $16,707 per year) were awarded; career-related internships or fieldwork, Federal Work-Study, scholarships/grants, and unspecified assistantships also available. Support available to part-time students. Financial award application deadline: 6/1; financial award applicants required to submit FAFSA. *Faculty research:* Corporate finance, investments, management in Latin America, management of technology, entrepreneurship. *Unit head:* Dr. Sul Kassicieh, Chair, 505-277-6471, E-mail: sul@unm.edu. *Application contact:* Lisa Beauchene, Student Recruitment Specialist, 505-277-6471, E-mail: andersonadvising@unm.edu.
Website: https://www.mgt.unm.edu/fite/default.asp?mm=faculty

University of Phoenix–Atlanta Campus, College of Information Systems and Technology, Sandy Springs, GA 30350-4147. Offers information systems (MIS); technology management (MBA). *Program availability:* Evening/weekend. *Degree requirements:* For master's, thesis (for some programs). *Entrance requirements:* For master's, 3 years of work experience, minimum undergraduate GPA of 3.0. Additional exam requirements/recommendations for international students: Required—TOEFL (minimum score 550 paper-based; 79 iBT). Electronic applications accepted.

University of Phoenix–Augusta Campus, College of Information Systems and Technology, Augusta, GA 30909-4583. Offers information systems (MIS); technology management (MBA).

University of Phoenix–Bay Area Campus, School of Business, San Jose, CA 95134-1805. Offers accountancy (MS); accounting (MBA); business administration (MBA, DBA); energy management (MBA); global management (MBA); health care management (MBA); human resource management (MBA); human resources management (MM); management (MM); marketing (MBA); organizational leadership (DM); project management (MBA); public administration (MPA); technology management (MBA). *Accreditation:* ACBSP. *Program availability:* Evening/weekend, online learning. *Degree requirements:* For master's, thesis (for some programs). *Entrance requirements:* For master's, minimum undergraduate GPA of 3.0, 3 years of work experience. Additional exam requirements/recommendations for international students: Required—TOEFL (minimum score 550 paper-based; 79 iBT). Electronic applications accepted.

University of Phoenix–Central Valley Campus, College of Information Systems and Technology, Fresno, CA 93720-1552. Offers information systems (MIS); technology management (MBA).

University of Phoenix–Charlotte Campus, College of Information Systems and Technology, Charlotte, NC 28273-3409. Offers information systems (MIS); information systems management (MISM); technology management (MBA). *Program availability:* Evening/weekend. *Degree requirements:* For master's, thesis (for some programs). *Entrance requirements:* For master's, minimum undergraduate GPA of 3.0, 3 years work experience. Additional exam requirements/recommendations for international students: Required—TOEFL (minimum score 550 paper-based; 79 iBT). Electronic applications accepted.

University of Phoenix–Colorado Campus, College of Information Systems and Technology, Lone Tree, CO 80124-5453. Offers e-business (MBA); management (MIS); technology management (MBA). *Program availability:* Evening/weekend, online learning. *Degree requirements:* For master's, thesis (for some programs). *Entrance requirements:* For master's, minimum undergraduate GPA of 3.0, 3 years of work experience. Additional exam requirements/recommendations for international students: Required—TOEFL (minimum score 550 paper-based; 79 iBT). Electronic applications accepted.

University of Phoenix–Colorado Springs Downtown Campus, College of Information Systems and Technology, Colorado Springs, CO 80903. Offers technology management (MBA). *Program availability:* Evening/weekend. *Degree requirements:* For master's, thesis (for some programs). *Entrance requirements:* For master's, minimum undergraduate GPA of 3.0, 3 years of work experience. Additional exam requirements/recommendations for international students: Required—TOEFL (minimum score 550 paper-based; 79 iBT). Electronic applications accepted.

University of Phoenix–Columbus Georgia Campus, College of Information Systems and Technology, Columbus, GA 31909. Offers e-business (MBA); information systems (MIS); technology management (MBA). *Program availability:* Evening/weekend, online learning. *Degree requirements:* For master's, thesis (for some programs). *Entrance requirements:* For master's, minimum undergraduate GPA of 3.0, 3 years of work experience. Additional exam requirements/recommendations for international students: Required—TOEFL (minimum score 550 paper-based; 79 iBT). Electronic applications accepted.

University of Phoenix–Dallas Campus, College of Information Systems and Technology, Dallas, TX 75251. Offers e-business (MBA); information systems (MIS); technology management (MBA). *Program availability:* Evening/weekend. *Degree requirements:* For master's, thesis (for some programs). *Entrance requirements:* For master's, minimum undergraduate GPA of 3.0, 3 years of work experience. Additional exam requirements/recommendations for international students: Required—TOEFL (minimum score 550 paper-based; 79 iBT). Electronic applications accepted.

University of Phoenix–Hawaii Campus, College of Information Systems and Technology, Honolulu, HI 96813-3800. Offers information systems (MIS); technology management (MBA). *Program availability:* Evening/weekend. *Degree requirements:* For master's, thesis (for some programs). *Entrance requirements:* For master's, minimum undergraduate GPA of 3.0, 3 years of work experience. Additional exam requirements/recommendations for international students: Required—TOEFL (minimum score 550 paper-based; 79 iBT). Electronic applications accepted.

University of Phoenix–Houston Campus, College of Information Systems and Technology, Houston, TX 77079-2004. Offers e-business (MBA); information systems (MIS); technology management (MBA). *Program availability:* Evening/weekend, online learning. *Degree requirements:* For master's, comprehensive exam (for some programs), thesis. *Entrance requirements:* For master's, minimum undergraduate GPA of 3.0, 3 years of work experience. Additional exam requirements/recommendations for international students: Required—TOEFL (minimum score 550 paper-based; 79 iBT). Electronic applications accepted.

University of Phoenix–Jersey City Campus, College of Information Systems and Technology, Jersey City, NJ 07310. Offers information systems (MIS); technology management (MBA). *Program availability:* Online learning.

University of Phoenix–Las Vegas Campus, College of Information Systems and Technology, Las Vegas, NV 89135. Offers information systems (MIS); technology management (MBA). *Program availability:* Evening/weekend. *Degree requirements:* For master's, thesis (for some programs). *Entrance requirements:* For master's, minimum undergraduate GPA of 3.0, 3 years of work experience. Additional exam requirements/recommendations for international students: Required—TOEFL (minimum score 550 paper-based; 79 iBT). Electronic applications accepted.

University of Phoenix–New Mexico Campus, College of Information Systems and Technology, Albuquerque, NM 87113-1570. Offers e-business (MBA); information systems (MS); technology management (MBA). *Program availability:* Evening/weekend. *Degree requirements:* For master's, thesis (for some programs). *Entrance requirements:* For master's, minimum undergraduate GPA of 3.0, 3 years of work experience. Additional exam requirements/recommendations for international students: Required—TOEFL (minimum score 550 paper-based; 79 iBT). Electronic applications accepted.

University of Phoenix–Online Campus, School of Business, Phoenix, AZ 85034-7209. Offers accountancy (MS); accounting (MBA, Certificate); business administration (MBA); energy management (MBA); global management (MBA); health care management (MBA); human resource management (MBA, Certificate); human resources management (MM); management (MM); marketing (MBA, Certificate); project management (MBA, Certificate); public administration (MBA, MM); technology management (MBA). *Program availability:* Evening/weekend, online learning. *Entrance requirements:* Additional exam requirements/recommendations for international students: Required—TOEFL, TOEIC (Test of English as an International Communication), Berlitz Online English Proficiency Exam, PTE, or IELTS. Electronic applications accepted. *Expenses:* Contact institution.

University of Phoenix–Phoenix Campus, School of Business, Tempe, AZ 85282-2371. Offers accounting (MBA, MS, Certificate); business administration (MBA); energy management (MBA); global management (MBA); health care management (MBA); human resource management (MBA, Certificate); management (MM); marketing (MBA); project management (MBA); technology management (MBA). *Program availability:* Evening/weekend, online learning. *Entrance requirements:* Additional exam requirements/recommendations for international students: Required—TOEFL, TOEIC (Test of English as an International Communication), Berlitz Online English Proficiency Exam, PTE, or IELTS. Electronic applications accepted. *Expenses:* Contact institution.

University of Phoenix–Sacramento Valley Campus, College of Information Systems and Technology, Sacramento, CA 95833-4334. Offers management (MIS); technology management (MBA). *Program availability:* Evening/weekend. *Degree requirements:* For master's, thesis (for some programs). *Entrance requirements:* For master's, minimum undergraduate GPA of 3.0, 3 years work experience. Additional exam requirements/recommendations for international students: Required—TOEFL (minimum score 550 paper-based; 79 iBT). Electronic applications accepted.

University of Phoenix–San Antonio Campus, College of Information Systems and Technology, San Antonio, TX 78230. Offers information systems (MIS); technology management (MBA).

University of Phoenix–San Diego Campus, College of Information Systems and Technology, San Diego, CA 92123. Offers management (MIS); technology management (MBA). *Program availability:* Evening/weekend. *Degree requirements:* For master's, thesis (for some programs). *Entrance requirements:* For master's, minimum undergraduate GPA of 3.0, 3 years work experience. Additional exam requirements/recommendations for international students: Required—TOEFL (minimum score 550 paper-based; 79 iBT). Electronic applications accepted.

University of Phoenix–Southern Arizona Campus, College of Information Systems and Technology, Tucson, AZ 85711. Offers information systems (MIS); technology management (MBA). *Program availability:* Evening/weekend. *Degree requirements:* For master's, thesis (for some programs). *Entrance requirements:* For master's, minimum undergraduate GPA of 3.0, 3 years of work experience. Additional exam requirements/recommendations for international students: Required—TOEFL (minimum score 550 paper-based; 79 iBT). Electronic applications accepted.

University of Phoenix–Southern California Campus, School of Business, Costa Mesa, CA 92626. Offers accounting (MBA); business administration (MBA); energy management (MBA); global management (MBA); health care management (MBA); human resource management (MBA); management (MM); marketing (MBA); project management (MBA); technology management (MBA). *Program availability:* Evening/weekend, online learning. *Entrance requirements:* Additional exam requirements/recommendations for international students: Required—TOEFL, TOEIC (Test of English as an International Communication), Berlitz Online English Proficiency Exam, PTE, or IELTS. Electronic applications accepted. *Expenses:* Contact institution.

University of Phoenix–Utah Campus, School of Business, Salt Lake City, UT 84123-4642. Offers accounting (MBA); business administration (MBA); global management (MBA); human resource management (MBA, MM); management (MM); marketing (MBA); technology management (MBA). *Accreditation:* ACBSP. *Program availability:* Evening/weekend. *Degree requirements:* For master's, thesis (for some programs). *Entrance requirements:* For master's, minimum undergraduate GPA of 3.0, 3 years of work experience. Additional exam requirements/recommendations for international students: Required—TOEFL (minimum score 550 paper-based; 79 iBT). Electronic applications accepted.

University of Portland, Dr. Robert B. Pamplin, Jr. School of Business, Portland, OR 97203-5798. Offers entrepreneurship (MBA); finance (MBA, MS); health care management (MBA); marketing (MBA); nonprofit management (EMBA); operations and technology management (MBA, MS); sustainability (MBA). *Accreditation:* AACSB. *Program availability:* Part-time, evening/weekend. *Entrance requirements:* For master's, GMAT, minimum GPA of 3.0, resume, 2 letters of recommendation. Additional exam requirements/recommendations for international students: Required—TOEFL (minimum score 570 paper-based; 89 iBT), IELTS (minimum score 7). *Expenses:* Contact institution.

University of St. Thomas, Graduate Studies, School of Engineering, St. Paul, MN 55105-1096. Offers data science (MS); electrical engineering (MS); information technology (MS); manufacturing engineering (MS); manufacturing systems (Certificate); mechanical engineering (MS); medical device development (Certificate); regulatory science (MS); software engineering (MS); software management (MS); systems engineering (MS); technology leadership (Certificate); technology management (MS). *Accreditation:* ABET (one or more programs are accredited). *Entrance requirements:* For master's, resume, official transcripts. Additional exam requirements/recommendations for international students: Required—TOEFL (minimum score 550 paper-based). *Application deadline:* For fall admission, 8/1 priority date for domestic students; for spring admission, 1/1 priority date for domestic students. Applications are processed on a rolling basis. Application fee: $50. Electronic applications accepted. *Expenses:* Contact institution. *Financial support:* Fellowships, research assistantships, institutionally sponsored loans, and scholarships/grants available. Support available to part-time students. Financial award application deadline: 4/1; financial award applicants required to submit FAFSA. *Unit head:* Don Weinkauf, Dean, 651-962-5760, Fax: 651-962-6419, E-mail: dhweinkauf@stthomas.edu. *Application contact:* Tina M. Hansen, Graduate Program Manager, 651-962-5755, Fax: 651-962-6419, E-mail: tina.hansen@stthomas.edu.
Website: http://www.stthomas.edu/engineering/

University of South Florida, Innovative Education, Tampa, FL 33620-9951. Offers adult, career and higher education (Graduate Certificate), including college teaching, leadership in developing human resources, leadership in higher education; Africana studies (Graduate Certificate), including diasporas and health disparities, genocide and human rights; aging studies (Graduate Certificate), including gerontology; art research (Graduate Certificate), including museum studies; business foundations (Graduate Certificate); chemical and biomedical engineering (Graduate Certificate), including materials science and engineering, water, health and sustainability; child and family studies (Graduate Certificate), including positive behavior support; civil and industrial engineering (Graduate Certificate), including transportation systems analysis; community and family health (Graduate Certificate), including maternal and child health, social marketing and public health, violence and injury: prevention and intervention, women's health; criminology (Graduate Certificate), including criminal justice administration; educational measurement and research (Graduate Certificate), including evaluation; English (Graduate Certificate), including comparative literary studies, creative writing, professional and technical communication; entrepreneurship (Graduate Certificate); environmental health (Graduate Certificate), including safety management; epidemiology and biostatistics (Graduate Certificate), including applied biostatistics, biostatistics, concepts and tools of epidemiology, epidemiology, epidemiology of infectious diseases; geography, environment and planning (Graduate Certificate), including community development, environmental policy and management, geographical information systems; geology (Graduate Certificate), including hydrogeology; global health (Graduate Certificate), including disaster management, global health and Latin American and Caribbean studies, global health practice, humanitarian assistance, infection control; government and international affairs (Graduate Certificate), including Cuban studies, globalization studies; health policy and management (Graduate Certificate), including health management and leadership, public health policy and programs; hearing specialist: early intervention (Graduate Certificate); industrial and management systems engineering (Graduate Certificate), including systems engineering, technology management; information studies (Graduate Certificate), including school library media specialist; information systems/decision sciences (Graduate Certificate), including analytics and business intelligence; instructional technology (Graduate Certificate), including distance education, Florida digital/virtual educator, instructional design, multimedia design, Web design; internal medicine, bioethics and medical humanities (Graduate Certificate), including biomedical ethics; Latin American and Caribbean studies (Graduate Certificate); mass communications (Graduate Certificate), including multimedia journalism; mathematics and statistics (Graduate Certificate), including mathematics; medicine (Graduate Certificate), including aging and neuroscience, bioinformatics, biotechnology, brain fitness and memory management, clinical investigation, health informatics, health sciences, integrative weight management, intellectual property, medicine and gender, metabolic and nutritional medicine, metabolic cardiology, pharmacy sciences; national and competitive intelligence (Graduate Certificate); psychological and social foundations (Graduate Certificate), including career counseling, college teaching, diversity in education, mental health counseling, school counseling; public affairs (Graduate Certificate), including nonprofit management, public management, research administration; public health (Graduate Certificate), including environmental health, health equity, public health generalist, translational research in adolescent behavioral health; public health practices (Graduate Certificate), including planning for healthy communities; rehabilitation and mental health counseling (Graduate Certificate), including integrative mental health care, marriage and family therapy, rehabilitation technology; secondary education (Graduate Certificate), including ESOL, foreign language education: culture and content, foreign language education: professional; social work (Graduate Certificate), including geriatric social work/clinical gerontology; special education (Graduate Certificate), including autism spectrum disorder, disabilities education: severe/profound; world languages (Graduate Certificate), including teaching English as a second language (TESL) or foreign language. *Expenses:* Tuition, state resident: full-time $7766; part-time $431.43 per credit hour. Tuition, nonresident: full-time $15,789; part-time $877.17 per credit hour. *Required fees:* $37 per term. *Unit head:* Kathy Barnes, Interdisciplinary Programs Coordinator, 813-974-8031, Fax: 813-974-7061, E-mail: barnesk@usf.edu. *Application contact:* Karen Tylinski, Metro Initiatives, 813-974-9943, Fax: 813-974-7061, E-mail: ktylinsk@usf.edu.
Website: http://www.usf.edu/innovative-education/

The University of Texas at Dallas, Naveen Jindal School of Management, Program in Information Systems and Operations Management, Richardson, TX 75080. Offers business analytics (MS); information technology and management (MS); supply chain management (MS). *Program availability:* Part-time, evening/weekend. *Faculty:* 19 full-time (0 women), 37 part-time/adjunct (11 women). *Students:* 1,577 full-time (577 women), 457 part-time (189 women); includes 136 minority (21 Black or African American, non-Hispanic/Latino; 83 Asian, non-Hispanic/Latino; 19 Hispanic/Latino; 13 Two or more races, non-Hispanic/Latino), 1,795 international. Average age 27. 3,354 applicants, 66% accepted, 931 enrolled. In 2016, 787 master's awarded. *Degree requirements:* For master's, thesis optional. *Entrance requirements:* For master's, GMAT. Additional exam requirements/recommendations for international students: Required—TOEFL (minimum score 550 paper-based). *Application deadline:* For fall admission, 7/15 for domestic students, 5/1 priority date for international students; for spring admission, 11/15 for domestic students, 9/1 priority date for international students. Applications are processed on a rolling basis. Application fee: $50 ($100 for international students). Electronic applications accepted. *Expenses:* Tuition, state resident: full-time $12,418; part-time $690 per semester hour. Tuition, nonresident: full-time $24,150; part-time $1342 per semester hour. Tuition and fees vary according to course load. *Financial support:* In 2016–17, 473 students received support, including 5 research assistantships with partial tuition reimbursements available (averaging $14,880 per year), 48 teaching assistantships with partial tuition reimbursements available (averaging $10,122 per year); career-related internships or fieldwork, Federal Work-Study, institutionally sponsored loans, scholarships/grants, and unspecified assistantships also available. Support available to part-time students. Financial award application deadline: 4/30; financial award applicants required to submit FAFSA. *Faculty research:* Technology marketing, measuring information work productivity, electronic commerce, decision support systems, data quality. *Unit head:* Dr. Milind Dawande, Area Coordinator, 972-883-2793, E-mail: milind@utdallas.edu. *Application contact:* Dr. Ozalp Ozer, PhD Area Coordinator, 972-883-2316, E-mail: oozer@utdallas.edu.
Website: http://jindal.utdallas.edu/isom/

The University of Texas at San Antonio, College of Business, Department of Information Systems and Cyber Security, San Antonio, TX 78249-0617. Offers cyber security (MSIT); information technology (MS, PhD); management of technology (MBA); technology entrepreneurship and management (Certificate). *Program availability:* Part-time, evening/weekend. *Faculty:* 10 full-time (2 women), 4 part-time/adjunct (0 women). *Students:* 70 full-time (19 women), 73 part-time (21 women); includes 38 minority (6 Black or African American, non-Hispanic/Latino; 6 Asian, non-Hispanic/Latino; 24 Hispanic/Latino; 2 Two or more races, non-Hispanic/Latino), 38 international. Average age 30. 141 applicants, 59% accepted, 55 enrolled. In 2016, 45 master's, 1 doctorate, 6 other advanced degrees awarded. *Degree requirements:* For master's, comprehensive exam (for some programs), thesis optional; for doctorate, comprehensive exam, thesis/dissertation. *Entrance requirements:* For master's and doctorate, GMAT/GRE, official transcripts, statement of purpose, letters of recommendation. Additional exam requirements/recommendations for international students: Required—TOEFL (minimum score 550 paper-based; 79 iBT), IELTS (minimum score 6.5). *Application deadline:* For fall admission, 7/1 for domestic students, 4/1 for international students; for spring admission, 11/1 for domestic students, 9/1 for international students. Applications are processed on a rolling basis. Application fee: $45 ($80 for international students). Electronic applications accepted. *Expenses:* Contact institution. *Financial support:* In 2016–17, 15 students received support, including 1 fellowship with full tuition reimbursement available (averaging $25,000 per year), 10 research assistantships with tuition reimbursements available (averaging $9,000 per year), 12 teaching assistantships with tuition reimbursements available (averaging $9,000 per year); scholarships/grants, health care benefits, and unspecified assistantships also available. Support available to part-time students. Financial award application deadline: 2/15. *Faculty research:* Cyber security, digital forensics, economics of information systems, information systems privacy, information technology adoption. *Total annual research expenditures:* $650,902. *Unit head:* Dr. Yoris A. Au, Chair/Associate Professor, 210-458-6300, Fax: 210-458-6305, E-mail: yoris.au@utsa.edu.
Website: http://business.utsa.edu/directory/index.aspx?DepID-16

University of Toronto, Faculty of Medicine, Program in Management of Innovation, Toronto, ON M5S 1A1, Canada. Offers MMI. *Entrance requirements:* For master's, GMAT, minimum B+ average, 2 reference letters, resume/curriculum vitae. Additional exam requirements/recommendations for international students: Required—TOEFL (minimum score 580 paper-based; 93 iBT), TWE (minimum score 5). Electronic applications accepted.

University of Virginia, McIntire School of Commerce, Program in Management of Information Technology, Charlottesville, VA 22903. Offers MS. *Program availability:* Evening/weekend. *Entrance requirements:* For master's, GMAT, 2 recommendation letters. bachelor's degree, interview. Additional exam requirements/recommendations for international students: Required—TOEFL (minimum score 620 paper-based). Electronic applications accepted. *Expenses:* Contact institution.

University of Washington, Graduate School, Michael G. Foster School of Business, Seattle, WA 98195-3200. Offers auditing and assurance (MP Acc); business administration (MBA, PhD); entrepreneurship (MS); executive business administration (MBA); global executive business administration (MBA); information systems (MSIS); supply chain management (MSSCM); taxation (MP Acc); technology management (MBA); JD/MBA; MBA/MAIS; MBA/MHA. *Accreditation:* AACSB. *Program availability:* Part-time, evening/weekend. Terminal master's awarded for partial completion of doctoral program. *Degree requirements:* For doctorate, comprehensive exam, thesis/dissertation. *Entrance requirements:* For master's and doctorate, GMAT, GRE. Additional exam requirements/recommendations for international students: Required—TOEFL (minimum score 600 paper-based; 100 iBT). Electronic applications accepted. *Expenses:* Contact institution. *Faculty research:* Finance, marketing, organizational behavior, information technology, strategy.

University of Waterloo, Graduate Studies, Faculty of Engineering, Conrad Business, Entrepreneurship and Technology Center, Waterloo, ON N2L 3G1, Canada. Offers MBET. *Entrance requirements:* For master's, honors degree. Additional exam requirements/recommendations for international students: Required—TOEFL (minimum score 90 iBT), IELTS (minimum score 7), PTE (minimum score 63). Electronic applications accepted.

University of Waterloo, Graduate Studies, Faculty of Engineering, Department of Management Sciences, Waterloo, ON N2L 3G1, Canada. Offers applied operations research (MA Sc, MMS, PhD); information systems (MA Sc, MMS, PhD); management of technology (MA Sc, MMS, PhD). *Program availability:* Part-time, online learning. *Degree requirements:* For master's, research paper or thesis; for doctorate, comprehensive exam, thesis/dissertation. *Entrance requirements:* For master's, GMAT or GRE, honors degree, minimum B average, resume; for doctorate, GMAT or GRE, master's degree, minimum A- average, resume. Additional exam requirements/recommendations for international students: Required—TOEFL, IELTS, PTE. Electronic applications accepted. *Faculty research:* Operations research, manufacturing systems, scheduling, information systems.

University of Wisconsin–Madison, Graduate School, Wisconsin School of Business, Wisconsin Full-Time MBA Program, Madison, WI 53706. Offers applied security analysis (MBA); arts administration (MBA); brand and product management (MBA); corporate finance and investment banking (MBA); marketing research (MBA);

operations and technology management (MBA); real estate (MBA); risk management and insurance (MBA); strategic human resource management (MBA); supply chain management (MBA). *Faculty:* 125 full-time (32 women), 48 part-time/adjunct (11 women). *Students:* 197 full-time (73 women); includes 30 minority (11 Black or African American, non-Hispanic/Latino; 9 Asian, non-Hispanic/Latino; 10 Hispanic/Latino), 42 international. Average age 29. 728 applicants, 26% accepted, 99 enrolled. In 2016, 100 master's awarded. *Entrance requirements:* For master's, GMAT or GRE, bachelor's or equivalent degree, 2 years of work experience, essay, letter of recommendation, resume. Additional exam requirements/recommendations for international students: Required—TOEFL (minimum score 100 iBT), IELTS (minimum score 7.5). *Application deadline:* For fall admission, 9/28 for domestic students, 11/1 for international students; for winter admission, 11/2 for domestic students, 12/16 for international students; for spring admission, 1/11 for domestic students, 2/24 for international students; for summer admission, 3/1 for domestic students, 4/14 for international students. Applications are processed on a rolling basis. Application fee: $75 ($81 for international students). Electronic applications accepted. *Expenses:* $7,947 per semester resident tuition, $2,430 fees; $16,082 per semester resident tuition, $2,830 fees. *Financial support:* In 2016–17, 178 students received support, including 8 fellowships with full tuition reimbursements available (averaging $56,413 per year), 23 research assistantships with full tuition reimbursements available (averaging $42,151 per year), 51 teaching assistantships with full tuition reimbursements available (averaging $39,963 per year); scholarships/grants, health care benefits, and unspecified assistantships also available. Financial award application deadline: 4/11. *Faculty research:* Forms of competition and outcomes in dual distribution systems; explaining the accuracy of revised forecasts; supply chain planning for random demand surges; advanced demand information in a multi-product system; the effects of presentation salience and measurement subjectivity on nonprofessional investors' fair value judgments. *Unit head:* Prof. Ella Mae Matsumura, Associate Dean, Full-time MBA Program, 608-262-9731, E-mail: ematsumura@bus.wisc.edu. *Application contact:* Mary Lewitzke, Assistant Director of Admissions and Recruiting, Full-time MBA Program, 608-262-4000, E-mail: mlewitzke@bus.wisc.edu.
Website: http://www.bus.wisc.edu/mba

University of Wisconsin–Milwaukee, Graduate School, Lubar School of Business, MS and Certificate Business Programs, Milwaukee, WI 53201-0413. Offers business analytics (Graduate Certificate); enterprise resource planning (Graduate Certificate); information technology management (MS); investment management (Graduate Certificate); nonprofit management (Graduate Certificate); nonprofit management and leadership (MS); state and local taxation (Graduate Certificate). *Students:* 174 full-time (83 women), 157 part-time (64 women); includes 69 minority (23 Black or African American, non-Hispanic/Latino; 27 Asian, non-Hispanic/Latino; 6 Hispanic/Latino; 13 Two or more races, non-Hispanic/Latino), 65 international. Average age 32. 281 applicants, 56% accepted, 116 enrolled. In 2016, 171 master's, 34 other advanced degrees awarded. *Entrance requirements:* Additional exam requirements/recommendations for international students: Required—TOEFL (minimum score 550 paper-based; 79 iBT), IELTS (minimum score 6.5). *Application deadline:* Applications are processed on a rolling basis. Application fee: $56 ($96 for international students). Electronic applications accepted. *Financial support:* In 2016–17, 12 teaching assistantships were awarded; fellowships, research assistantships, health care benefits, unspecified assistantships, and project assistantships also available. Financial award applicants required to submit FAFSA. *Application contact:* General Information Contact, 414-229-4982, Fax: 414-229-6967, E-mail: gradschool@uwm.edu.

Walsh College of Accountancy and Business Administration, Graduate Programs, Program in Information Technology Leadership, Troy, MI 48083. Offers chief information officer (MS); chief security officer (MS); program management office (MS). *Program availability:* Part-time, evening/weekend. *Faculty:* 9 full-time (6 women), 14 part-time/adjunct (7 women). *Students:* 21 (11 women); includes 3 minority (2 Black or African American, non-Hispanic/Latino; 1 American Indian or Alaska Native, non-Hispanic/Latino), 4 international. Average age 34. 7 applicants, 100% accepted, 4 enrolled. In 2016, 4 master's awarded. *Entrance requirements:* For master's, minimum overall cumulative GPA of 2.75 from all colleges previously attended. Additional exam requirements/recommendations for international students: Required—TOEFL (minimum score 550 paper-based, 79 iBT), IELTS (6.5), Michigan English Language Assessment Battery, or MTELP. *Application deadline:* Applications are processed on a rolling basis. Application fee: $35. Electronic applications accepted. *Expenses:* $740 per credit hour, $125 registration fee per semester. *Financial support:* In 2016–17, 2 students received support. Career-related internships or fieldwork and scholarships/grants available. Financial award application deadline: 6/30; financial award applicants required to submit FAFSA. *Faculty research:* Business intelligence, data and decision-making, cyber security, project management, mobile technologies. *Unit head:* Dr. Barbara Ciaramitaro, Chair, Information Technology and Decision Sciences, 248-823-1635, Fax: 248-689-0920, E-mail: bciara2@walshcollege.edu. *Application contact:* Heather Rigby, Director, Admissions and Academic Advising, 248-823-1610, Fax: 248-689-0938, E-mail: hrigby@walshcollege.edu.
Website: http://www.walshcollege.edu/MSITL

Washington State University, Voiland College of Engineering and Architecture, Program in Engineering and Technology Management, Pullman, WA 99164-2785. Offers METM, Certificate. Program offered through the Global (online) campus. *Program availability:* Part-time, evening/weekend, online learning. *Degree requirements:* For master's, one foreign language, comprehensive exam (for some programs). *Entrance requirements:* Additional exam requirements/recommendations for international students: Required—TOEFL. Electronic applications accepted. *Faculty research:* Constraints management, Six Sigma quality management, supply chain management, project management, construction management, systems engineering management, manufacturing leadership.

Webster University, George Herbert Walker School of Business and Technology, Department of Management, St. Louis, MO 63119-3194. Offers business and organizational security management (MA); digital marketing management (Graduate Certificate); government contracting (Graduate Certificate); health administration (MHA); health care management (MA); health services management (MA); human resources development (MA); human resources management (MA); information technology management (MA, MS); management (D Mgt); management and leadership (MA); marketing (MA); nonprofit leadership (MA); nonprofit revenue development (Graduate Certificate); organizational development (Graduate Certificate); procurement and acquisitions management (MA); public administration (MPA); space systems operations management (MS). *Program availability:* Part-time, evening/weekend, online learning. *Degree requirements:* For master's, thesis (for some programs); for doctorate, thesis/dissertation, written exam. *Entrance requirements:* For doctorate, GMAT, 3 years of work experience, MBA. Additional exam requirements/recommendations for international students: Required—TOEFL. *Application deadline:* Applications are processed on a rolling basis. Application fee: $25 ($50 for international students). *Expenses: Tuition:* Full-time $21,900; part-time $730 per credit hour. Tuition and fees vary according to campus/location and program. *Financial support:* Federal Work-Study available. Support available to part-time students. Financial award application deadline: 4/1; financial award applicants required to submit FAFSA. *Unit head:* Barrett Baebler, Chair, 314-246-7940, E-mail: baeblerb@webster.edu. *Application contact:* Sarah Nandor, Director, Graduate and Transfer Admissions, 314-968-7109, E-mail: gadmit@webster.edu.

Wentworth Institute of Technology, Online Master of Science in Technology Management Program, Boston, MA 02115-5998. Offers MS. *Program availability:* Part-time-only, evening/weekend, online only, 100% online. *Faculty:* 17 part-time/adjunct (6 women). *Students:* 30 part-time (8 women); includes 11 minority (4 Black or African American, non-Hispanic/Latino; 5 Asian, non-Hispanic/Latino; 2 Hispanic/Latino). Average age 32. 19 applicants, 89% accepted, 14 enrolled. In 2016, 10 master's awarded. *Degree requirements:* For master's, thesis optional, capstone. *Entrance requirements:* For master's, resume, official transcripts, two professional recommendations, BA or BS, one year of professional experience in a technical role and/or technical organization, statement of purpose, minimum GPA of 3.0. Additional exam requirements/recommendations for international students: Recommended—TOEFL (minimum score 525 paper-based). *Application deadline:* For fall admission, 8/1 for domestic and international students; for spring admission, 12/20 for domestic and international students. Applications are processed on a rolling basis. Application fee: $50. Electronic applications accepted. *Expenses:* Contact institution. *Financial support:* Scholarships/grants available. Support available to part-time students. Financial award application deadline: 8/1; financial award applicants required to submit FAFSA. *Unit head:* Philip Hammond, Director of Graduate Programs, 617-989-4594, Fax: 617-989-4399, E-mail: hammondp1@wit.edu. *Application contact:* Martha Sheehan, Director of Admissions and Marketing, 617-989-4661, Fax: 617-989-4399, E-mail: sheehanm@wit.edu.
Website: http://www.wit.edu/continuinged/online/programs/technology.mgmt.masters

Western Kentucky University, Graduate Studies, Ogden College of Science and Engineering, Department of Architectural and Manufacturing Sciences, Bowling Green, KY 42101. Offers technology management (MS).

Wilfrid Laurier University, Faculty of Graduate and Postdoctoral Studies, School of Business and Economics, Department of Business, Waterloo, ON N2L 3C5, Canada. Offers accounting (PhD); finance (M Fin); financial economics (PhD); marketing (PhD); operations and supply chain management (PhD); organizational behavior and human resource management (M Sc); organizational behaviour and human resource management (PhD); supply chain management (M Sc); technology management (EMTM). *Accreditation:* AACSB. *Program availability:* Part-time, evening/weekend. *Degree requirements:* For master's, thesis optional; for doctorate, comprehensive exam, thesis/dissertation. *Entrance requirements:* For master's, GMAT, 4-year honors degree with minimum B+ average; for doctorate, GMAT, master's degree, minimum B+ average. Additional exam requirements/recommendations for international students: Required—TOEFL (minimum score 89 iBT). Electronic applications accepted. *Faculty research:* Financial economics, management and organizational behavior, operations and supply chain management.

Operations Research

Air Force Institute of Technology, Graduate School of Engineering and Management, Department of Operational Sciences, Dayton, OH 45433-7765. Offers logistics management (MS); operations research (MS, PhD); space operations (MS). *Program availability:* Part-time. *Degree requirements:* For master's, thesis; for doctorate, thesis/dissertation. *Entrance requirements:* For doctorate, GRE General Test, minimum GPA of 3.0, U.S. citizenship. *Faculty research:* Optimization, simulation, combat modeling and analysis, reliability and maintainability, resource scheduling.

Bowling Green State University, Graduate College, College of Arts and Sciences, Department of Computer Science, Bowling Green, OH 43403. Offers computer science (MS), including operations research, parallel and distributed computing, software engineering. *Program availability:* Part-time. *Degree requirements:* For master's, thesis or alternative. *Entrance requirements:* For master's, GRE General Test. Additional exam requirements/recommendations for international students: Required—TOEFL. *Application deadline:* For fall admission, 2/1 priority date for domestic students; for spring admission, 11/15 priority date for domestic students. Application fee: $30. Electronic applications accepted. *Financial support:* Research assistantships with full tuition reimbursements, teaching assistantships with full tuition reimbursements, career-related internships or fieldwork, tuition waivers (full and partial), and unspecified assistantships available. Financial award applicants required to submit FAFSA. *Faculty research:* Artificial intelligence, real time and concurrent programming languages, behavioral aspects of computing, network protocols. *Unit head:* Dr. Rob Green,

Graduate Coordinator, 419-372-8782, E-mail: csgradstudies@bgsu.edu. *Application contact:* Dr. Ron Lancaster, Graduate Coordinator, 419-372-8697.

Capella University, School of Business and Technology, Master's Programs in Business, Minneapolis, MN 55402. Offers accounting (MBA); business analysis (MS); business intelligence (MBA); entrepreneurship (MBA); finance (MBA); general business administration (MBA); general human resource management (MS); general leadership (MS); health care management (MBA); human resource management (MBA); marketing (MBA); project management (MBA, MS). *Accreditation:* ACBSP.

Carnegie Mellon University, Tepper School of Business, Program in Operations Research, Pittsburgh, PA 15213-3891. Offers PhD. *Degree requirements:* For doctorate, thesis/dissertation. *Entrance requirements:* For doctorate, GMAT or GRE General Test.

Case Western Reserve University, Weatherhead School of Management, Department of Operations, Cleveland, OH 44106. Offers operations and supply chain management (MSM); operations research (PhD); MBA/MSM. *Program availability:* Part-time. *Degree requirements:* For doctorate, thesis/dissertation. *Entrance requirements:* For master's, GRE General Test; for doctorate, GMAT, GRE General Test. *Expenses: Tuition:* Full-time $42,576; part-time $1774 per credit hour. *Required fees:* $34. Tuition and fees vary according to course load and program. *Faculty research:* Mathematical finance, mathematical programming, scheduling, stochastic optimization, environmental/energy models.

Claremont Graduate University, Graduate Programs, Institute of Mathematical Sciences, Claremont, CA 91711-6160. Offers computational and systems biology (PhD); computational mathematics and numerical analysis (MA, MS); computational science (PhD); engineering and industrial applied mathematics (PhD); mathematics (PhD); operations research and statistics (MA, MS); physical applied mathematics (MA, MS); pure mathematics (MA, MS); scientific computing (MA, MS); systems and control theory (MA, MS). PhD programs offered jointly with San Diego State University and California State University, Long Beach. *Program availability:* Part-time. *Faculty:* 5 full-time (1 woman), 3 part-time/adjunct (0 women). *Students:* 45 full-time (15 women), 40 part-time (17 women); includes 22 minority (3 Black or African American, non-Hispanic/Latino; 9 Asian, non-Hispanic/Latino; 9 Hispanic/Latino; 1 Two or more races, non-Hispanic/Latino), 34 international. Average age 32. In 2016, 11 master's, 16 doctorates awarded. Terminal master's awarded for partial completion of doctoral program. *Entrance requirements:* For master's and doctorate, GRE General Test. Additional exam requirements/recommendations for international students: Required—TOEFL (minimum score 75 iBT). *Application deadline:* For fall admission, 2/1 priority date for domestic and international students. Applications are processed on a rolling basis. Application fee: $80. Electronic applications accepted. *Expenses: Tuition:* Full-time $44,328; part-time $1847 per unit. *Required fees:* $600; $300 per semester. Tuition and fees vary according to course load and program. *Financial support:* Fellowships, research assistantships, Federal Work-Study, institutionally sponsored loans, scholarships/grants, and tuition waivers (full and partial) available. Support available to part-time students. Financial award application deadline: 2/15; financial award applicants required to submit FAFSA. *Unit head:* John Angus, Director, 909-607-3376, E-mail: john.angus@cgu.edu. *Application contact:* Jake Campbell, Assistant Director of Admissions, 909-607-3024, E-mail: jake.campbell@cgu.edu.
Website: https://www.cgu.edu/school/institute-of-mathematical-sciences/

The College of William and Mary, Faculty of Arts and Sciences, Department of Computer Science, Program in Computational Operations Research, Williamsburg, VA 23187-8795. Offers MS. *Program availability:* Part-time. *Faculty:* 6 full-time (2 women), 1 part-time/adjunct (0 women). *Students:* 21 full-time (9 women); includes 8 minority (1 Black or African American, non-Hispanic/Latino; 7 Asian, non-Hispanic/Latino), 7 international. Average age 23. 26 applicants, 73% accepted, 14 enrolled. In 2016, 10 master's awarded. *Degree requirements:* For master's, comprehensive exam, research project. *Entrance requirements:* For master's, GRE General Test, minimum GPA of 3.0. Additional exam requirements/recommendations for international students: Required—TOEFL. *Application deadline:* For fall admission, 3/1 priority date for domestic students, 3/15 priority date for international students; for spring admission, 11/1 for domestic and international students. Applications are processed on a rolling basis. Application fee: $45. Electronic applications accepted. *Expenses:* Contact institution. *Financial support:* In 2016–17, 13 students received support, including 2 fellowships (averaging $2,000 per year), 7 teaching assistantships with full tuition reimbursements available (averaging $13,995 per year); scholarships/grants, tuition waivers (full), and unspecified assistantships also available. Financial award application deadline: 3/1; financial award applicants required to submit FAFSA. *Faculty research:* Metaheuristics, reliability, optimization, statistics, networks. *Unit head:* Dr. Rex Kincaid, Professor, 757-221-2038, E-mail: rrkinc@math.wm.edu. *Application contact:* Vanessa Godwin, Administrative Director, 757-221-3455, Fax: 757-221-1717, E-mail: cor@cs.wm.edu.
Website: http://www.wm.edu/as/mathematics/graduate/cor/index.php

Colorado School of Mines, Office of Graduate Studies, Department of Economics and Business, Golden, CO 80401. Offers engineering and technology management (MS); mineral economics (PhD); operations research and engineering (PhD). *Program availability:* Part-time. *Degree requirements:* For master's, thesis (for some programs); for doctorate, comprehensive exam, thesis/dissertation. *Entrance requirements:* For master's and doctorate, GRE General Test. Additional exam requirements/recommendations for international students: Required—TOEFL (minimum score 550 paper-based; 80 iBT). Electronic applications accepted. *Expenses:* Tuition, state resident: full-time $15,690. Tuition, nonresident: full-time $34,020. *Required fees:* $2152. Tuition and fees vary according to course load. *Faculty research:* International trade, resource and environmental economics, energy economics, operations research.

Columbia University, Fu Foundation School of Engineering and Applied Science, Department of Industrial Engineering and Operations Research, New York, NY 10027. Offers financial engineering (MS); industrial engineering and operations research (MS, Eng Sc D, PhD); management science and engineering (MS); MS/MBA. *Program availability:* Part-time, evening/weekend, online learning. *Degree requirements:* For doctorate, thesis/dissertation, oral and written qualifying exams. *Entrance requirements:* For master's and doctorate, GRE General Test. Additional exam requirements/recommendations for international students: Required—TOEFL, IELTS, PTE. Electronic applications accepted. *Faculty research:* Applied probability and optimization; financial engineering, modeling risk including credit risk and systemic risk, asset allocation, portfolio execution, behavioral finance, agent-based model in finance; revenue management; management and optimization of service systems, call centers, capacity allocation in healthcare systems, inventory control for vaccines; energy, smart grids, demand shaping, managing renewable energy sources, energy-aware scheduling.

Cornell University, Graduate School, Graduate Fields of Engineering, Field of Operations Research and Information Engineering, Ithaca, NY 14853. Offers applied probability and statistics (PhD); manufacturing systems engineering (PhD); mathematical programming (PhD); operations research and industrial engineering (M Eng). *Degree requirements:* For doctorate, comprehensive exam, thesis/dissertation. *Entrance requirements:* For master's and doctorate, GRE General Test, 3 letters of recommendation. Additional exam requirements/recommendations for international students: Required—TOEFL (minimum score 600 paper-based; 100 iBT). Electronic applications accepted. *Faculty research:* Mathematical programming and combinatorial optimization, statistics, stochastic processes, mathematical finance, simulation, manufacturing, e-commerce.

École Polytechnique de Montréal, Graduate Programs, Department of Mathematics and Industrial Engineering, Montréal, QC H3C 3A7, Canada. Offers ergonomy (M Eng, M Sc A, DESS); mathematical method in CA engineering (M Eng, M Sc A, PhD); operational research (M Eng, M Sc A, PhD); production (M Eng, M Sc A); technology management (M Eng, M Sc A). DESS program offered jointly with HEC Montreal and Université de Montréal. *Program availability:* Part-time. *Degree requirements:* For master's, one foreign language, thesis. *Entrance requirements:* For master's, minimum GPA of 2.75. *Faculty research:* Use of computers in organizations.

Florida Institute of Technology, College of Science, Program in Operations Research, Melbourne, FL 32901-6975. Offers MS, PhD. *Program availability:* Part-time, evening/weekend. *Students:* 27 full-time (11 women), 41 part-time (8 women); includes 13 minority (4 Black or African American, non-Hispanic/Latino; 1 Asian, non-Hispanic/Latino; 7 Hispanic/Latino; 1 Two or more races, non-Hispanic/Latino), 20 international. Average age 33. 49 applicants, 45% accepted, 5 enrolled. In 2016, 11 master's awarded. Terminal master's awarded for partial completion of doctoral program. *Degree requirements:* For master's, comprehensive exam (for some programs), thesis or final exam, 30 credit hours; for doctorate, comprehensive exam, 42 credit hours, virtual written grant proposal and oral defense, written dissertation and oral defense, dissertation research, written qualifying exam. *Entrance requirements:* For master's, undergraduate degree in science or engineering with substantial mathematics background; for doctorate, master's degree in operations research or equivalent, resume, 3 letters of recommendations, statement of objectives. Additional exam requirements/recommendations for international students: Required—TOEFL (minimum score 550 paper-based; 79 iBT). *Application deadline:* Applications are processed on a rolling basis. Application fee: $50. Electronic applications accepted. *Expenses: Tuition:* Full-time $22,338; part-time $1241 per credit hour. *Required fees:* $250. Tuition and fees vary according to degree level, campus/location and program. *Financial support:* In 2016–17, 1 student received support. Research assistantships with tuition reimbursements available, teaching assistantships with tuition reimbursements available, career-related internships or fieldwork, and tuition remissions available. Financial award application deadline: 3/1; financial award applicants required to submit FAFSA. *Faculty research:* Numerical computation, applied statistics, simulation, optimization, scheduling, decision analysis, queuing processes. *Unit head:* Dr. Ugur Abdulla, Chair, 321-674-7483, Fax: 321-674-7412, E-mail: abdulla@fit.edu. *Application contact:* Cheryl A. Brown, Associate Director of Graduate Admissions, 321-674-7581, Fax: 321-723-9468, E-mail: cbrown@fit.edu.
Website: http://cos.fit.edu/math/or/

Florida Institute of Technology, Extended Studies Division, Melbourne, FL 32901-6975. Offers acquisition and contract management (MS); aerospace engineering (MS); business administration (MBA, DBA); computer information systems (MS); computer science (MS); electrical engineering (MS); engineering management (MS); human resources management (MS); logistics management (MS), including humanitarian and disaster relief logistics; management (MS), including acquisition and contract management, e-business, human resources management, information systems, logistics management, management, transportation management; material acquisition management (MS); mechanical engineering (MS); operations research (MS); project management (MS), including information systems, operations research; public administration (MPA); quality management (MS); software engineering (MS); space systems (MS); space systems management (MS); supply chain management (MS); systems management (MS), including information systems, operations research; technology management (MS). *Program availability:* Part-time, evening/weekend, online learning. *Faculty:* 10 full-time (3 women), 122 part-time/adjunct (29 women). *Students:* 131 full-time (58 women), 997 part-time (348 women); includes 389 minority (231 Black or African American, non-Hispanic/Latino; 9 American Indian or Alaska Native, non-Hispanic/Latino; 26 Asian, non-Hispanic/Latino; 99 Hispanic/Latino; 3 Native Hawaiian or other Pacific Islander, non-Hispanic/Latino; 21 Two or more races, non-Hispanic/Latino), 53 international. Average age 36. 962 applicants, 48% accepted, 323 enrolled. In 2016, 403 master's awarded. *Degree requirements:* For master's, comprehensive exam (for some programs). *Entrance requirements:* For master's, GMAT or resume showing 8 years of supervised experience, minimum GPA of 3.0, 2 letters of recommendation, resume. Additional exam requirements/recommendations for international students: Required—TOEFL (minimum score 550 paper-based; 79 iBT). *Application deadline:* For fall admission, 4/1 for international students; for spring admission, 9/30 for international students. Applications are processed on a rolling basis. Electronic applications accepted. *Expenses:* Contact institution. *Financial support:* Application deadline: 3/1; applicants required to submit FAFSA. *Unit head:* Dr. Theodore R. Richardson, III, Dean, 321-674-8123, Fax: 321-674-7597, E-mail: trichardson@fit.edu. *Application contact:* Carolyn Farrior, Director of Graduate Admissions, Online Learning and Off-Campus Programs, 321-674-7118, Fax: 321-674-8216, E-mail: cfarrior@fit.edu.
Website: http://es.fit.edu

George Mason University, Volgenau School of Engineering, Department of Systems Engineering and Operations Research, Fairfax, VA 22030. Offers operations research (MS); systems engineering and operations research (PhD, Certificate). MS programs offered jointly with Old Dominion University, University of Virginia, Virginia Commonwealth University, and Virginia Polytechnic Institute and State University. *Faculty:* 20 full-time (5 women), 13 part-time/adjunct (0 women). *Students:* 33 full-time (9 women), 101 part-time (24 women); includes 36 minority (7 Black or African American, non-Hispanic/Latino; 19 Asian, non-Hispanic/Latino; 5 Hispanic/Latino; 5 Two or more races, non-Hispanic/Latino), 11 international. Average age 32. 91 applicants, 79% accepted, 35 enrolled. In 2016, 38 master's, 3 doctorates, 10 other advanced degrees awarded. *Degree requirements:* For master's, thesis optional; for doctorate, comprehensive exam, thesis/dissertation, qualifying exams. *Entrance requirements:* For master's, GRE General Test, BS in related field; minimum GPA of 3.0; 3 letters of recommendation; 2 official transcripts; expanded goals statement; proof of financial support; photocopy of passport; official bank statement; multivariable calculus, applied probability, statistics and a computer language course; self evaluation form; for doctorate, GRE, MS with minimum GPA of 3.5; BS with minimum GPA of 3.0 in systems or operational research; 2 official transcripts; 3 letters of recommendation; resume; expanded goals statement; self evaluation form; photocopy of passport; official bank statement; proof of financial support; for Certificate, personal goals statement; 2 official transcripts; self-evaluation form; letter of recommendation; resume; official bank statement; photocopy of passport; proof of financial support; baccalaureate degree in related field. Additional exam requirements/recommendations for international students: Required—TOEFL (minimum score 575 paper-based; 88 iBT), IELTS (minimum score 6.5), PTE (minimum score 59). *Application deadline:* For fall admission, 1/15 priority date for domestic students. Application fee: $75 ($80 for international students). Electronic applications accepted. *Expenses:* Contact institution. *Financial support:* In 2016–17, 13 students received support, including 4 research assistantships with tuition reimbursements available (averaging $18,458 per year), 9 teaching assistantships with tuition reimbursements available (averaging $13,778 per year); career-related internships or fieldwork, Federal Work-Study, scholarships/grants, unspecified assistantships, and health care benefits (for full-time research or teaching assistantship recipients) also available. Support available to part-time students. Financial award application deadline: 3/1; financial award applicants required to submit FAFSA. *Faculty research:* Requirements engineering, signal processing, systems architecture, data fusion. *Total annual research expenditures:* $531,974. *Unit head:* Ariela Sofer, Chair, 703-993-1692, Fax: 703-993-1521, E-mail: asofer@gmu.edu. *Application contact:* Andy Loerch, Associate Chair, Graduate Information, 703-993-1657, E-mail: aloerch@gmu.edu.
Website: http://seor.gmu.edu

Georgia Institute of Technology, Graduate Studies, College of Engineering, H. Milton Stewart School of Industrial and Systems Engineering, Program in Operations Research, Atlanta, GA 30332-0001. Offers MS, PhD. *Program availability:* Part-time, online learning. *Degree requirements:* For doctorate, comprehensive exam. *Entrance requirements:* For master's and doctorate, GRE General Test. Additional exam requirements/recommendations for international students: Required—TOEFL (minimum score 550 paper-based; 79 iBT). Electronic applications accepted. *Faculty research:* Linear and nonlinear deterministic models in operations research, mathematical statistics, design of experiments.

Georgia State University, J. Mack Robinson College of Business, Department of Managerial Sciences, Atlanta, GA 30302-3083. Offers business analysis (MBA, MS);

entrepreneurship (MBA); human resources management (MBA, MS); operations management (MBA, MS); organization behavior/human resource management (PhD); organization management (MBA); organizational change (MS); strategic management (PhD). *Accreditation:* AACSB. *Program availability:* Part-time, evening/weekend. *Faculty:* 25 full-time (11 women). *Students:* 30 full-time (20 women), 10 part-time (4 women); includes 14 minority (11 Black or African American, non-Hispanic/Latino; 1 Asian, non-Hispanic/Latino; 1 Hispanic/Latino; 1 Two or more races, non-Hispanic/Latino), 12 international. Average age 31. 79 applicants, 30% accepted, 13 enrolled. In 2016, 23 master's, 2 doctorates awarded. *Degree requirements:* For doctorate, comprehensive exam, thesis/dissertation. *Entrance requirements:* For master's, GRE or GMAT, transcripts from all institutions attended, resume, essays; for doctorate, GMAT, three letters of recommendation, personal statement, transcripts from all institutions attended, resume. Additional exam requirements/recommendations for international students: Required—TOEFL (minimum score 610 paper-based; 101 iBT), IELTS (minimum score 7). *Application deadline:* For fall admission, 5/1 priority date for domestic students, 2/1 priority date for international students; for spring admission, 9/15 priority date for domestic students, 4/1 priority date for international students. Applications are processed on a rolling basis. Application fee: $50. Electronic applications accepted. *Expenses:* Tuition, state resident: full-time $6876; part-time $382 per credit hour. Tuition, nonresident: full-time $22,374; part-time $1243 per credit hour. *Required fees:* $2128; $1064 per term. Part-time tuition and fees vary according to course load and program. *Financial support:* Research assistantships, teaching assistantships, scholarships/grants, tuition waivers, and unspecified assistantships available. Financial award applicants required to submit FAFSA. *Faculty research:* Entrepreneurship and innovation; strategy process; workplace interactions, relationships, and processes; leadership and culture; supply chain management. *Unit head:* Dr. Pamela S. Barr, Interim Chair, 404-413-7525, Fax: 404-413-7571. *Application contact:* Toby McChesney, Assistant Dean for Graduate Recruiting and Student Services, 404-413-7167, Fax: 404-413-7162, E-mail: rcbgradadmissions@gsu.edu.
Website: http://mgmt.robinson.gsu.edu/

HEC Montreal, School of Business Administration, Master of Science Programs in Administration, Program in Business Analytics, Montréal, QC H3T 2A7, Canada. Offers M Sc. All courses are given in English. *Students:* 22 full-time (3 women), 13 part-time (4 women). 14 applicants, 64% accepted, 9 enrolled. In 2016, 1 master's awarded. *Degree requirements:* For master's, one foreign language, thesis. *Entrance requirements:* For master's, Test de francais international (TFI) with minimum score of 850 (for those who have never studied in French), BBA, undergraduate degree in another field, degree deemed equivalent by program director and minimum GPA of 3.0 on 4.3 scale. *Application deadline:* For fall admission, 3/15 for domestic and international students; for winter admission, 9/15 for domestic and international students. Application fee: $86. Electronic applications accepted. *Expenses: Tuition, area resident:* Part-time $77.80 Canadian dollars per credit. Tuition, state resident: full-time $2797 Canadian dollars; part-time $240.92 Canadian dollars per credit. Tuition, nonresident: full-time $8673 Canadian dollars; part-time $531.43 Canadian dollars per credit. *International tuition:* $19,131 Canadian dollars full-time. *Required fees:* $1699 Canadian dollars; $40.58 Canadian dollars per credit. $67.32 Canadian dollars per term. Tuition and fees vary according to degree level and program. *Financial support:* Research assistantships, teaching assistantships, and scholarships/grants available. Financial award application deadline: 9/2. *Unit head:* Dr. Marie-Helene Jobin, Director, 514-340-6283, E-mail: marie-helene.jobin@hec.ca. *Application contact:* Marianne de Moura, Administrative Director, 514-340-7106, Fax: 514-340-6411, E-mail: marianne.de-moura@hec.ca.
Website: http://www.hec.ca/programmes/maitrises/maitrise-analytique-affaires/index.html

Idaho State University, Office of Graduate Studies, College of Science and Engineering, Mechanical Engineering Department, Pocatello, ID 83209-8060. Offers measurement and control engineering (MS); mechanical engineering (MS). *Program availability:* Part-time. *Degree requirements:* For master's, comprehensive exam (for some programs), 2 semesters of seminar; thesis or project. *Entrance requirements:* For master's, GRE. Additional exam requirements/recommendations for international students: Required—TOEFL (minimum score 550 paper-based; 80 iBT). Electronic applications accepted. *Faculty research:* Modeling and identification of biomedical systems, intelligent systems and adaptive control, active flow control of turbo machinery, validation of advanced computational codes for thermal fluid interactions, development of methodologies for the assessment of passive safety system performance in advanced reactors, alternative energy research (wind, solar, hydrogen).

Indiana University–Purdue University Fort Wayne, College of Arts and Sciences, Department of Mathematical Sciences, Fort Wayne, IN 46805-1499. Offers applied mathematics (MS); applied statistics (Certificate); mathematics (MS); operations research (MS); teaching (MAT). *Program availability:* Part-time, evening/weekend. *Entrance requirements:* For master's, minimum GPA of 3.0, major or minor in mathematics, three letters of recommendation. Additional exam requirements/recommendations for international students: Required—TOEFL (minimum score 550 paper-based; 79 iBT); Recommended—TWE. Electronic applications accepted. *Faculty research:* Eves' Theorem, paired-placements for student teaching, holomorphic maps.

Iowa State University of Science and Technology, Department of Industrial and Manufacturing Systems Engineering, Ames, IA 50011. Offers industrial engineering (M Eng, MS, PhD); operations research (MS); systems engineering (M Eng). *Degree requirements:* For master's, thesis or alternative; for doctorate, thesis/dissertation. *Entrance requirements:* For master's and doctorate, GRE General Test. Additional exam requirements/recommendations for international students: Required—TOEFL (minimum score 550 paper-based; 79 iBT), IELTS (minimum score 6.5). *Application deadline:* For fall admission, 1/15 priority date for international students; for spring admission, 7/15 priority date for international students. Application fee: $60 ($90 for international students). Electronic applications accepted. *Faculty research:* Economic modeling, valuation techniques, robotics, digital controls, systems reliability. *Application contact:* Deborah McDonough, Application Contact, 515-294-0129, Fax: 515-294-3524, E-mail: imsegradprogram@iastate.edu.
Website: http://www.imse.iastate.edu

Johns Hopkins University, G. W. C. Whiting School of Engineering, Department of Applied Mathematics and Statistics, Baltimore, MD 21218. Offers computational medicine (PhD); discrete mathematics (MA, MSE, PhD); financial mathematics (MSE); operations research/optimization (MA, MSE, PhD); statistics/probability (MA, MSE, PhD). *Faculty:* 26 full-time (5 women), 1 part-time/adjunct (0 women). *Students:* 154 full-time (66 women), 12 part-time (5 women); includes 8 minority (1 Black or African American, non-Hispanic/Latino; 3 Asian, non-Hispanic/Latino; 2 Hispanic/Latino; 2 Two or more races, non-Hispanic/Latino), 142 international. Average age 24. 1,239 applicants, 25% accepted, 64 enrolled. In 2016, 51 master's, 6 doctorates awarded. Terminal master's awarded for partial completion of doctoral program. *Degree requirements:* For master's, thesis (for some programs); for doctorate, thesis/dissertation, oral exam, introductory exam. *Entrance requirements:* For master's and doctorate, GRE General Test, 3 letters of recommendation, statement of purpose, transcripts. Additional exam requirements/recommendations for international students: Required—TOEFL (minimum score 600 paper-based; 100 iBT), IELTS (minimum score 7). *Application deadline:* For fall admission, 1/15 for domestic and international students; for spring admission, 9/15 for domestic and international students. Application fee: $75. Electronic applications accepted. *Financial support:* In 2016–17, 40 students received support, including 15 fellowships with full tuition reimbursements available (averaging $25,398 per year), 6 research assistantships with full tuition reimbursements available (averaging $23,004 per year), 19 teaching assistantships with full tuition reimbursements available (averaging $23,004 per year); Federal Work-Study, health care benefits, and tuition waivers (full and partial) also available. Financial award application deadline: 1/15; financial award applicants required to submit FAFSA. *Faculty research:* Matrix and numerical analysis, differential equation modeling, optimization & operations research, probability and statistics, discrete mathematics, financial mathematics. *Total annual research expenditures:* $1.9 million. *Unit head:* Dr. Laurent Younes, Chair, 410-516-5103, Fax: 410-516-7459, E-mail: laurent.younes@jhu.edu. *Application contact:* Kristin Bechtel, Academic Program Coordinator, 410-516-7198, Fax: 410-516-7459, E-mail: kbechtel@jhu.edu.
Website: http://engineering.jhu.edu/ams

Johns Hopkins University, G. W. C. Whiting School of Engineering, Master of Science in Engineering Management Program, Baltimore, MD 21218. Offers biomaterials (MSEM); civil engineering (MSEM); communications science (MSEM); computer science (MSEM); environmental systems analysis, economics and public policy (MSEM); fluid mechanics (MSEM); materials science and engineering (MSEM); mechanical engineering (MSEM); mechanics and materials (MSEM); nanobiotechnology (MSEM); nanomaterials and nanotechnology (MSEM); operations research (MSEM); probability and statistics (MSEM); smart product and device design (MSEM). *Faculty:* 7 full-time (4 women), 1 part-time/adjunct (0 women). *Students:* 35 full-time (14 women), 8 part-time (3 women); includes 7 minority (4 Asian, non-Hispanic/Latino; 3 Hispanic/Latino), 26 international. Average age 24. 228 applicants, 28% accepted, 25 enrolled. In 2016, 18 master's awarded. *Entrance requirements:* For master's, GRE, 3 letters of recommendation, statement of purpose, transcripts. Additional exam requirements/recommendations for international students: Required—TOEFL (minimum score 600 paper-based, 100 iBT) or IELTS (7). *Application deadline:* For fall admission, 2/1 for domestic and international students. Application fee: $75. Electronic applications accepted. *Financial support:* Fellowships and health care benefits available. *Unit head:* Dr. Pamela Sheff, Director, 410-516-7056, Fax: 410-516-4880, E-mail: pamsheff@gmail.com. *Application contact:* Richard Helman, Director of Graduate Admissions, 410-516-8174, Fax: 410-516-0780, E-mail: graduateadmissions@jhu.edu.
Website: http://engineering.jhu.edu/msem/

Kansas State University, Graduate School, College of Engineering, Department of Industrial and Manufacturing Systems Engineering, Manhattan, KS 66506. Offers engineering management (MEM); industrial engineering (MS); operations research (MS). *Program availability:* Part-time, online learning. *Faculty:* 10 full-time (2 women), 1 part-time/adjunct (0 women). *Students:* 34 full-time (8 women), 51 part-time (6 women); includes 17 minority (5 Black or African American, non-Hispanic/Latino; 4 Asian, non-Hispanic/Latino; 4 Hispanic/Latino; 4 Two or more races, non-Hispanic/Latino), 25 international. Average age 30. 62 applicants, 56% accepted, 10 enrolled. In 2016, 27 master's, 3 doctorates awarded. *Degree requirements:* For master's, thesis or alternative; for doctorate, thesis/dissertation. *Entrance requirements:* For master's, GRE General Test (minimum score of 750 old version, 159 new format on Quantitative portion of exam), bachelor's degree in engineering, mathematics, or physical science; for doctorate, GRE General Test (minimum score of 770 old version, 164 new format on Quantitative portion of exam), master's degree in engineering or industrial manufacturing. Additional exam requirements/recommendations for international students: Required—PTE (minimum score 58), TOEFL (minimum score 550 paper-based; 79 iBT) or IELTS (minimum score 6.5). *Application deadline:* For fall admission, 6/1 priority date for domestic students, 12/1 priority date for international students; for spring admission, 11/1 priority date for domestic students, 8/1 priority date for international students. Applications are processed on a rolling basis. Application fee: $50 ($75 for international students). Electronic applications accepted. *Expenses:* Tuition, state resident: full-time $9670. Tuition, nonresident: full-time $21,828. *Required fees:* $862. *Financial support:* In 2016–17, 12 research assistantships (averaging $12,442 per year), 9 teaching assistantships with full tuition reimbursements (averaging $14,111 per year) were awarded; Federal Work-Study, institutionally sponsored loans, and scholarships/grants also available. Support available to part-time students. Financial award application deadline: 3/1; financial award applicants required to submit FAFSA. *Faculty research:* Industrial engineering, ergonomics, healthcare systems engineering, manufacturing processes, operations research, engineering management. *Total annual research expenditures:* $2.6 million. *Unit head:* Dr. Bradley Kramer, Head, 785-532-5606, Fax: 785-532-3738, E-mail: bradleyk@k-state.edu. *Application contact:* Dr. David Ben-Arieh, Chair of Graduate Committee, 785-532-5606, Fax: 785-532-3738, E-mail: imse@k-state.edu.
Website: http://www.imse.k-state.edu/

Massachusetts Institute of Technology, Operations Research Center, Cambridge, MA 02139. Offers SM, PhD. *Faculty:* 48 full-time (9 women). *Students:* 86 full-time (21 women); includes 8 minority (7 Asian, non-Hispanic/Latino; 1 Two or more races, non-Hispanic/Latino), 48 international. Average age 26. 335 applicants, 9% accepted, 20 enrolled. In 2016, 5 master's, 9 doctorates awarded. Terminal master's awarded for partial completion of doctoral program. *Degree requirements:* For master's, thesis; for doctorate, comprehensive exam, thesis/dissertation. *Entrance requirements:* For master's and doctorate, GRE General Test. Additional exam requirements/recommendations for international students: Required—TOEFL, IELTS. *Application deadline:* For fall admission, 12/15 for domestic and international students. Application fee: $75. Electronic applications accepted. *Expenses: Tuition:* Full-time $46,400; part-time $725 per credit. One-time fee: $312 full-time. Full-time tuition and fees vary according to course load and program. *Financial support:* In 2016–17, 81 students received support, including 5 fellowships (averaging $45,400 per year), 62 research assistantships (averaging $38,100 per year), 11 teaching assistantships (averaging $39,600 per year); Federal Work-Study, institutionally sponsored loans, scholarships/grants, traineeships, health care benefits, unspecified assistantships, and resident tutors also available. Support available to part-time students. Financial award application deadline: 5/1; financial award applicants required to submit FAFSA. *Faculty research:* Probability; optimization; statistics; stochastic processes; analytics. *Unit head:* Dr. Dimitris J. Bertsimas, Co-Director, 617-253-3601, Fax: 617-258-9214, E-mail: orc_staff@mit.edu. *Application contact:* Laura A. Rose, Graduate Admissions Coordinator, 617-253-9303, E-mail: lrose@mit.edu.
Website: http://orc.mit.edu/

Mississippi State University, Bagley College of Engineering, Department of Industrial and Systems Engineering, Mississippi State, MS 39762. Offers human factors and ergonomics (MS); industrial and systems engineering (PhD); industrial systems (MS); management systems (MS); manufacturing systems (MS); operations research (MS). *Program availability:* Part-time, blended/hybrid learning. *Faculty:* 12 full-time (1 woman). *Students:* 25 full-time (5 women), 59 part-time (13 women); includes 18 minority (6 Black or African American, non-Hispanic/Latino; 5 Asian, non-Hispanic/Latino; 6 Hispanic/Latino; 1 Native Hawaiian or other Pacific Islander, non-Hispanic/Latino), 21

international. Average age 35. 72 applicants, 32% accepted, 11 enrolled. In 2016, 11 master's, 7 doctorates awarded. *Degree requirements:* For master's, comprehensive exam (for some programs), thesis optional, comprehensive oral or written exam; for doctorate, comprehensive exam, thesis/dissertation, candidacy exam. *Entrance requirements:* For master's, GRE (for graduates from program not accredited by EAC/ABET), minimum GPA of 3.0 on junior and senior years; for doctorate, GRE (for graduates from program not accredited by EAC/ABET), minimum GPA of 3.5 on master's degree and junior and senior years of BS. Additional exam requirements/recommendations for international students: Required—TOEFL (minimum score 550 paper-based; 79 iBT); Recommended—IELTS (minimum score 6.5). *Application deadline:* For fall admission, 7/1 for domestic students, 5/1 for international students; for spring admission, 11/1 for domestic students, 9/1 for international students. Applications are processed on a rolling basis. Application fee: $60. Electronic applications accepted. *Expenses:* Tuition, state resident: full-time $7670; part-time $852.50 per credit hour. Tuition, nonresident: full-time $20,790; part-time $2310.50 per credit hour. Part-time tuition and fees vary according to course load. *Financial support:* In 2016–17, 12 research assistantships with full tuition reimbursements (averaging $16,360 per year), 3 teaching assistantships with full tuition reimbursements (averaging $17,014 per year) were awarded; Federal Work-Study, institutionally sponsored loans, and unspecified assistantships also available. Financial award application deadline: 4/1; financial award applicants required to submit FAFSA. *Faculty research:* Operations research, ergonomics, production systems, management systems, transportation. *Total annual research expenditures:* $4.4 million. *Unit head:* Dr. John Usher, Professor/Department Head, 662-325-7624, Fax: 662-325-7618, E-mail: usher@ise.msstate.edu. *Application contact:* Doretta Martin, Senior Admissions Assistant, 662-325-9514, E-mail: dmartin@grad.msstate.edu.
Website: http://www.ise.msstate.edu/

Naval Postgraduate School, Departments and Academic Groups, Department of Operations Research, Monterey, CA 93943. Offers applied science (MS), including operations research; cost estimating analysis (MS); human systems integration (MS); operations research (MS, PhD); systems analysis (MS). Program only open to commissioned officers of the United States and friendly nations and selected United States federal civilian employees. *Program availability:* Part-time. *Degree requirements:* For master's, thesis (for some programs); for doctorate, thesis/dissertation. *Faculty research:* Next generation network science, performance analysis of ground solider mobile ad-hoc networks, irregular warfare methods and tools, human social cultural behavior modeling, large-scale optimization.

Naval Postgraduate School, Departments and Academic Groups, Undersea Warfare Academic Group, Monterey, CA 93943. Offers applied mathematics (MS); applied physics (MS); applied science (MS), including acoustics, operations research, physical oceanography, signal processing; electrical engineering (MS); engineering acoustics (MS, PhD); engineering science (MS), including electrical engineering, mechanical engineering; mechanical engineer (ME); mechanical engineering (MS, MSME); meteorology (MS); operations research (MS); physical oceanography (MS). Program only open to commissioned officers of the United States and friendly nations and selected United States federal civilian employees. *Program availability:* Part-time. *Degree requirements:* For master's, thesis. *Faculty research:* Unmanned/autonomous vehicles, sea mines and countermeasures, submarine warfare in the twentieth and twenty-first centuries.

New Mexico Institute of Mining and Technology, Center for Graduate Studies, Department of Mathematics, Socorro, NM 87801. Offers applied and industrial mathematics (PhD); industrial mathematics (MS); mathematics (MS); operations research and statistics (MS). *Degree requirements:* For master's, thesis optional; for doctorate, thesis/dissertation. *Entrance requirements:* For master's, GRE General Test. Additional exam requirements/recommendations for international students: Required—TOEFL (minimum score 540 paper-based). *Faculty research:* Applied mathematics, differential equations, industrial mathematics, numerical analysis, stochastic processes.

North Carolina State University, Graduate School, College of Engineering and College of Physical and Mathematical Sciences, Program in Operations Research, Raleigh, NC 27695. Offers MOR, MS, PhD. *Program availability:* Part-time. *Degree requirements:* For master's, thesis (for some programs), thesis (MS); for doctorate, thesis/dissertation, comprehensive oral and written exams. *Entrance requirements:* For master's, GRE General Test, minimum GPA of 2.7; for doctorate, GRE General Test, minimum GPA of 3.0. Additional exam requirements/recommendations for international students: Required—TOEFL. Electronic applications accepted. *Faculty research:* Queuing analysis, simulation, inventory theory, supply chain management, mathematical programming.

North Carolina State University, Graduate School, Institute for Advanced Analytics, Raleigh, NC 27695. Offers analytics (MS). *Entrance requirements:* For master's, GRE General Test. Additional exam requirements/recommendations for international students: Required—TOEFL. Electronic applications accepted.

Northeastern University, College of Engineering, Boston, MA 02115-5096. Offers bioengineering (MS, PhD); chemical engineering (MS, PhD); civil engineering (MS, PhD); computer engineering (PhD); computer systems engineering (MS); electrical and computer engineering (MS); electrical and computer engineering leadership (MS); electrical engineering (PhD); energy systems (MS); engineering and public policy (MS); engineering management (MS, Certificate); environmental engineering (MS); industrial engineering (MS, PhD); information assurance (PhD); information systems (MS); interdisciplinary engineering (PhD); mechanical engineering (PhD); operations research (MS); telecommunication systems management (MS). *Program availability:* Part-time, online learning. *Faculty:* 202 full-time (59 women), 53 part-time/adjunct (9 women). *Students:* 2,982 full-time (954 women), 192 part-time (38 women). In 2016, 851 master's, 74 doctorates awarded. Application fee: $75. Electronic applications accepted. *Expenses:* $1,471 per credit. *Financial support:* Fellowships, research assistantships, teaching assistantships, career-related internships or fieldwork, scholarships/grants, health care benefits, tuition waivers, and unspecified assistantships available. Support available to part-time students. Financial award applicants required to submit FAFSA. *Unit head:* Dr. Nadine Aubry, Dean, College of Engineering. *Application contact:* Jeffery Hengel, Director of Graduate Admissions, 617-373-2711, E-mail: j.hengel@northeastern.edu.
Website: http://www.coe.neu.edu/academics/graduate-school-engineering

Northeastern University, College of Science, Boston, MA 02115-5096. Offers applied mathematics (MS); bioinformatics (MS); biology (PhD); biotechnology (MS); chemistry (MS, PhD); ecology, evolution, and marine biology (PhD); marine biology (MS); mathematics (MS, PhD); network science (PhD); operations research (MSOR); physics (MS, PhD); psychology (PhD). *Program availability:* Part-time. *Faculty:* 217 full-time (76 women), 58 part-time/adjunct (20 women). *Students:* 578 full-time (268 women), 63 part-time (27 women). In 2016, 121 master's, 50 doctorates awarded. Terminal master's awarded for partial completion of doctoral program. *Degree requirements:* For master's, comprehensive exam (for some programs), thesis; for doctorate, comprehensive exam (for some programs), thesis/dissertation. *Entrance requirements:* For master's, GRE General Test. *Application deadline:* Applications are processed on a rolling basis. Application fee: $75. Electronic applications accepted. *Expenses:* Contact institution.

Financial support: Fellowships with tuition reimbursements, research assistantships with tuition reimbursements, teaching assistantships with tuition reimbursements, career-related internships or fieldwork, scholarships/grants, health care benefits, tuition waivers (full and partial), and unspecified assistantships available. Support available to part-time students. Financial award applicants required to submit FAFSA. *Unit head:* Dr. Kenneth Henderson, Dean. *Application contact:* Graduate Student Services, 617-373-4275, E-mail: gradcos@northeastern.edu.
Website: http://www.northeastern.edu/cos/

The Ohio State University, Graduate School, Max M. Fisher College of Business, Program in Business Operational Excellence, Columbus, OH 43210. Offers MBOE. *Program availability:* Online learning. *Students:* 44 full-time (15 women). Average age 41. In 2016, 27 master's awarded. *Entrance requirements:* For master's, GMAT if undergraduate GPA is below a 3.0, bachelor's degree from accredited university; at least 3-5 years of successful work experience in which managing processes are part of the job; recommendation by an executive sponsor. Additional exam requirements/recommendations for international students: Required—TOEFL (minimum score 550 paper-based; 79 iBT), Michigan English Language Assessment Battery (minimum score 82); Recommended—IELTS (minimum score 7). *Application deadline:* For fall and spring admission, 6/30 priority date for domestic and international students. Application fee: $60 ($70 for international students). *Unit head:* Beth Miller, Program Director, 614-292-8575, E-mail: miller.6148@osu.edu. *Application contact:* Graduate and Professional Admissions, 614-292-9444, Fax: 614-292-3895, E-mail: gpadmissions@osu.edu.
Website: http://fisher.osu.edu/mboe

Princeton University, Graduate School, School of Engineering and Applied Science, Department of Operations Research and Financial Engineering, Princeton, NJ 08544-1019. Offers M Eng, MSE, PhD. Terminal master's awarded for partial completion of doctoral program. *Degree requirements:* For master's, thesis (MSE); for doctorate, thesis/dissertation, general exam. *Entrance requirements:* For master's and doctorate, GRE General Test, official transcript(s), 3 letters of recommendation, personal statement. Additional exam requirements/recommendations for international students: Required—TOEFL. Electronic applications accepted. *Faculty research:* Applied and computational mathematics; financial mathematics; optimization, queuing theory, and machine learning; statistics and stochastic analysis; transportation and logistics.

Rutgers University–New Brunswick, Graduate School-New Brunswick, Program in Operations Research, Piscataway, NJ 08854-8097. Offers PhD. *Program availability:* Part-time. *Degree requirements:* For doctorate, comprehensive exam, thesis/dissertation, qualifying exam. *Entrance requirements:* For doctorate, GRE General Test, GRE Subject Test. Electronic applications accepted. *Faculty research:* Mathematical programming, combinatorial optimization, graph theory, stochastic modeling, queuing theory.

Simon Fraser University, Office of Graduate Studies and Postdoctoral Fellows, Faculty of Science, Department of Mathematics, Burnaby, BC V5A 1S6, Canada. Offers applied and computational mathematics (M Sc, PhD); mathematics (M Sc, PhD); operations research (M Sc, PhD). *Faculty:* 39 full-time (9 women). *Students:* 68 full-time (17 women). 74 applicants, 42% accepted, 14 enrolled. In 2016, 8 master's, 3 doctorates awarded. *Degree requirements:* For master's, thesis or alternative; for doctorate, comprehensive exam, thesis/dissertation. *Entrance requirements:* For master's, GRE General Test, GRE Subject Test (mathematics), minimum GPA of 3.0 (on scale of 4.33) or 3.33 based on last 60 credits of undergraduate courses; for doctorate, GRE General Test, GRE Subject Test (mathematics), minimum GPA of 3.5 (on scale of 4.33). Additional exam requirements/recommendations for international students: Recommended—TOEFL (minimum score 580 paper-based; 93 iBT), IELTS (minimum score 7), TWE (minimum score 5). *Application deadline:* For fall admission, 2/1 for domestic and international students. Application fee: $90 Canadian dollars ($125 Canadian dollars for international students). Electronic applications accepted. *Financial support:* In 2016–17, 34 students received support, including 19 fellowships (averaging $5,474 per year), teaching assistantships (averaging $5,608 per year); research assistantships and scholarships/grants also available. Support available to part-time students. *Faculty research:* Computer algebra, discrete mathematics, fluid dynamics, nonlinear partial differential equations and variation methods, numerical analysis and scientific computing. *Unit head:* Dr. Manfred Trummer, Chair, 778-782-3378, Fax: 778-782-4947, E-mail: math-gsc@sfu.ca. *Application contact:* Sofia Leposavic, Graduate Secretary, 778-782-3059, Fax: 778-782-4947, E-mail: mathgsec@sfu.ca.
Website: http://www.math.sfu.ca/

Southern Illinois University Edwardsville, Graduate School, College of Arts and Sciences, Department of Mathematics and Statistics, Program in Statistics and Operations Research, Edwardsville, IL 62026. Offers MS. *Program availability:* Part-time. *Degree requirements:* For master's, thesis (for some programs), special project. *Entrance requirements:* Additional exam requirements/recommendations for international students: Required—TOEFL (minimum score 550 paper-based, 79 iBT), IELTS (minimum score 6.5), Michigan Test of English Language Proficiency or PTE. Electronic applications accepted.

Southern Methodist University, Bobby B. Lyle School of Engineering, Department of Engineering Management, Information, and Systems, Dallas, TX 75275. Offers engineering management (MSEM, DE); information engineering and management (MSIEM); operations research (MS, PhD); systems engineering (MS, PhD). *Program availability:* Part-time, evening/weekend, online learning. Terminal master's awarded for partial completion of doctoral program. *Degree requirements:* For master's, thesis optional; for doctorate, thesis/dissertation, oral and written qualifying exams. *Entrance requirements:* For master's, minimum GPA of 3.0 in last 2 years; bachelor's degree in engineering, mathematics, sciences, or technical area; for doctorate, GRE General Test (operations research, engineering management), bachelor's degree in related field. Additional exam requirements/recommendations for international students: Required—TOEFL. *Faculty research:* Telecommunications, decision systems, information engineering, operations research, software.

The University of Alabama in Huntsville, School of Graduate Studies, College of Engineering, Department of Industrial and Systems Engineering and Engineering Management, Huntsville, AL 35899. Offers engineering management (MSE, PhD); industrial engineering (MSE, PhD); operations research (MSOR); systems engineering (MSE, PhD). *Program availability:* Part-time, evening/weekend, online learning. *Degree requirements:* For master's, comprehensive exam, thesis or alternative, oral and written exams; for doctorate, comprehensive exam, thesis/dissertation, oral and written exams. *Entrance requirements:* For master's and doctorate, GRE General Test, minimum GPA of 3.0. Additional exam requirements/recommendations for international students: Required—TOEFL (minimum score 500 paper-based; 80 iBT), IELTS (minimum score 6.5). Electronic applications accepted. *Expenses:* Tuition, state resident: full-time $9834; part-time $600 per credit hour. Tuition, nonresident: full-time $21,830; part-time $1325 per credit hour. *Faculty research:* Systems engineering process, electronic manufacturing, heuristic manufacturing, teams and team development.

University of Arkansas, Graduate School, College of Engineering, Department of Industrial Engineering, Fayetteville, AR 72701. Offers industrial engineering (MSE, MSIE, PhD); operations management (MS); operations research (MSE, MSOR).

Operations Research

Faculty: 10 full-time (1 woman), 26 part-time/adjunct (1 woman). *Students:* 198 applicants, 83% accepted. In 2016, 227 master's, 3 doctorates awarded. *Degree requirements:* For master's, thesis optional; for doctorate, one foreign language, thesis/dissertation. *Application deadline:* For fall admission, 4/1 for international students; for spring admission, 10/1 for international students. Applications are processed on a rolling basis. Application fee: $40 ($50 for international students). Electronic applications accepted. *Financial support:* In 2016–17, 34 research assistantships were awarded; fellowships, teaching assistantships, career-related internships or fieldwork, and Federal Work-Study also available. Support available to part-time students. Financial award application deadline: 4/1; financial award applicants required to submit FAFSA. *Unit head:* Dr. Ed Pohl, Departmental Chair, 479-575-3157, Fax: 479-575-8431, E-mail: epohl@uark.edu. *Application contact:* Dr. Justin Chimka, Graduate Coordinator, 479-575-6756, E-mail: jchimka@uark.edu.
Website: http://www.ineg.uark.edu

The University of British Columbia, Sauder School of Business, Master of Business Analytics Program, Vancouver, BC V6T 1Z2, Canada. Offers MSBA. *Degree requirements:* For master's, course work and industry project. *Entrance requirements:* For master's, GMAT or GRE, strong quantitative or analytical background, bachelor's degree or recognized equivalent from an accredited university-level institution, minimum of B+ average in undergraduate upper-level course work. Additional exam requirements/recommendations for international students: Required—TOEFL, IELTS or Michigan English Language Assessment Battery. Application fee: $138. Electronic applications accepted. *Expenses:* $28,460 tuition, $42,006 international; $1,024 Sauder building fee. *Financial support:* Scholarships/grants available. *Faculty research:* Operations and logistics. *Unit head:* Robert Helsley, Dean, 604-822-8559, Fax: 604-822-8468.
Website: http://www.sauder.ubc.ca/Programs/Master_of_Business_Analytics

University of California, Berkeley, Graduate Division, College of Engineering, Department of Industrial Engineering and Operations Research, Berkeley, CA 94720-1500. Offers decision analytics (M Eng); industrial engineering and operations research (M Eng, MS, PhD). *Program availability:* Part-time, evening/weekend. *Students:* 125 full-time (48 women), 25 part-time (9 women); includes 21 minority (20 Asian, non-Hispanic/Latino; 1 Hispanic/Latino), 112 international. Average age 27. 625 applicants, 94 enrolled. In 2016, 82 master's, 10 doctorates awarded. Terminal master's awarded for partial completion of doctoral program. *Degree requirements:* For master's, comprehensive exam (for some programs), thesis (for some programs), comprehensive exam or thesis (MS); for doctorate, thesis/dissertation, qualifying exam. *Entrance requirements:* For master's and doctorate, GRE General Test, minimum GPA of 3.0, 3 letters of recommendation. Additional exam requirements/recommendations for international students: Required—TOEFL (minimum score 570 paper-based; 90 iBT). *Application deadline:* For fall admission, 12/2 for domestic students. Application fee: $105 ($125 for international students). Electronic applications accepted. *Financial support:* Fellowships, research assistantships, teaching assistantships, career-related internships or fieldwork, Federal Work-Study, tuition waivers (full and partial), and unspecified assistantships available. Financial award applicants required to submit FAFSA. *Faculty research:* Mathematical programming, robotics and manufacturing, linear and nonlinear optimization, production planning and scheduling, queuing theory. *Unit head:* Prof. Ken Goldberg, Chair, 510-642-5484, Fax: 510-642-1403, E-mail: gradadm@ieor.berkeley.edu. *Application contact:* 510-642-5485, Fax: 510-642-1403, E-mail: gradadm@ieor.berkeley.edu.
Website: http://www.ieor.berkeley.edu/

University of Colorado Denver, College of Liberal Arts and Sciences, Department of Mathematical and Statistical Sciences, Denver, CO 80217. Offers applied mathematics (MS, PhD), including applied mathematics, applied probability (MS), applied statistics (MS), computational biology, computational mathematics (PhD), discrete mathematics, finite geometry (PhD), mathematics education (PhD), mathematics of engineering and science (MS), numerical analysis, operations research (MS), optimization and operations research (PhD), probability (PhD), statistics (PhD). *Program availability:* Part-time. *Faculty:* 20 full-time (3 women), 4 part-time/adjunct (0 women). *Students:* 49 full-time (22 women), 10 part-time (4 women); includes 11 minority (1 Black or African American, non-Hispanic/Latino; 1 American Indian or Alaska Native, non-Hispanic/Latino; 3 Asian, non-Hispanic/Latino; 5 Hispanic/Latino; 1 Two or more races, non-Hispanic/Latino), 12 international. Average age 32. 88 applicants, 66% accepted, 12 enrolled. In 2016, 13 master's, 2 doctorates awarded. *Degree requirements:* For master's, comprehensive exam, thesis optional, 30 hours of course work with minimum GPA of 3.0; for doctorate, comprehensive exam, thesis/dissertation, 42 hours of course work with minimum GPA of 3.25. *Entrance requirements:* For master's, GRE General Test; GRE Subject Test in math (recommended), 30 hours of course work in mathematics (24 of which must be upper-division mathematics), bachelor's degree with minimum GPA of 3.0; for doctorate, GRE General Test; GRE Subject Test in math (recommended), 30 hours of course work in mathematics (24 of which must be upper-division mathematics), master's degree with minimum GPA of 3.25. Additional exam requirements/recommendations for international students: Required—TOEFL (minimum score 537 paper-based; 75 iBT); Recommended—IELTS (minimum score 6.5). *Application deadline:* For fall admission, 4/1 for domestic and international students; for spring admission, 10/1 for domestic and international students; for summer admission, 4/1 for domestic and international students. Application fee: $50 ($75 for international students). Electronic applications accepted. *Expenses:* Tuition, state resident: full-time $11,006; part-time $474 per credit. Tuition, nonresident: full-time $28,212; part-time $1264 per credit hour. *Required fees:* $256 per semester. One-time fee: $94.32. Tuition and fees vary according to campus/location and program. *Financial support:* In 2016–17, 35 students received support. Fellowships with partial tuition reimbursements available, research assistantships with full tuition reimbursements available, teaching assistantships with full tuition reimbursements available, Federal Work-Study, institutionally sponsored loans, scholarships/grants, and traineeships available. Financial award application deadline: 4/1; financial award applicants required to submit FAFSA. *Faculty research:* Computational mathematics, computational biology, discrete mathematics and geometry, probability and statistics, optimization. *Unit head:* Dr. Michael Ferrara, Graduate Chair, 303-315-1705, E-mail: michael.ferrara@ucdenver.edu. *Application contact:* Julie Blunck, Program Assistant, 303-315-1743, E-mail: julie.blunck@ucdenver.edu.
Website: http://www.ucdenver.edu/academics/colleges/CLAS/Departments/math/Pages/MathStats.aspx

University of Delaware, College of Agriculture and Natural Resources, Department of Food and Resource Economics, Operations Research Program, Newark, DE 19716. Offers MS. *Program availability:* Part-time. *Degree requirements:* For master's, thesis, oral exam. *Entrance requirements:* For master's, GRE General Test, 3 letters of recommendation, program language/s, engineering calculus. Additional exam requirements/recommendations for international students: Required—TOEFL. Electronic applications accepted. *Faculty research:* Simulation and modeling-production scheduling and optimization, agricultural production and resource economics, transportation engineering, statistical quality control.

University of Illinois at Chicago, College of Engineering, Department of Mechanical and Industrial Engineering, Program in Industrial Engineering, Chicago, IL 60607-7128.

Offers industrial engineering (MS); industrial engineering and operations research (PhD). *Program availability:* Part-time. *Degree requirements:* For doctorate, thesis/dissertation. *Entrance requirements:* For doctorate, GRE General Test, minimum GPA of 2.75. Additional exam requirements/recommendations for international students: Required—TOEFL. Electronic applications accepted. *Expenses:* Contact institution. *Faculty research:* Manufacturing information systems and manufacturing control, supply chain, logistics, optimization quality control, haptics and virtual reality, industrial automation, safety and reliability engineering, diagnostics, prognostics, controls and statistical modeling.

The University of Iowa, Graduate College, College of Engineering, Department of Industrial Engineering, Iowa City, IA 52242-1316. Offers engineering design and manufacturing (MS, PhD); healthcare systems (MS, PhD); human factors (MS, PhD); information and engineering management (MS, PhD); operations research (MS, PhD); wind energy (MS, PhD). *Faculty:* 11 full-time (1 woman), 1 part-time/adjunct (0 women). *Students:* 15 full-time (2 women), 6 part-time (0 women); includes 2 minority (1 Asian, non-Hispanic/Latino; 1 Two or more races, non-Hispanic/Latino), 11 international. Average age 29. 68 applicants, 9% accepted, 5 enrolled. In 2016, 4 master's, 3 doctorates awarded. Terminal master's awarded for partial completion of doctoral program. *Degree requirements:* For master's, thesis optional, exam; for doctorate, comprehensive exam, thesis/dissertation, final defense exam. *Entrance requirements:* For master's and doctorate, GRE (minimum Verbal score of 153, Quantitative 151), minimum undergraduate GPA of 3.0. Additional exam requirements/recommendations for international students: Required—TOEFL (minimum score 600 paper-based; 100 iBT), IELTS (minimum score 7). *Application deadline:* For fall admission, 7/15 for domestic students, 4/15 for international students; for spring admission, 12/1 for domestic students, 10/1 for international students; for summer admission, 4/15 for domestic students, 3/1 for international students. Applications are processed on a rolling basis. Application fee: $60 ($100 for international students). Electronic applications accepted. *Financial support:* In 2016–17, 21 students received support, including 1 fellowship with partial tuition reimbursement available (averaging $25,500 per year), 15 research assistantships with full tuition reimbursements available (averaging $22,981 per year), 5 teaching assistantships with full tuition reimbursements available (averaging $18,809 per year); career-related internships or fieldwork, scholarships/grants, and unspecified assistantships also available. Support available to part-time students. Financial award applicants required to submit FAFSA. *Faculty research:* Operations research, informatics, human factors engineering, healthcare systems, bio-manufacturing, manufacturing systems, renewable energy, human-machine interactions. *Total annual research expenditures:* $6.3 million. *Unit head:* Dr. Ching-Long Lin, Department Executive Officer, 319-335-5673, Fax: 319-335-5669, E-mail: ching-long-lin@uiowa.edu. *Application contact:* Tara Hoadley, Academic Program Specialist, 319-335-5939, Fax: 319-335-5669, E-mail: indeng@engineering.uiowa.edu.
Website: https://mie.engineering.uiowa.edu

University of Massachusetts Amherst, Graduate School, College of Engineering, Department of Mechanical and Industrial Engineering, Amherst, MA 01003. Offers industrial engineering and operations research (MS, PhD); mechanical engineering (MSME, PhD). *Program availability:* Part-time. Terminal master's awarded for partial completion of doctoral program. *Degree requirements:* For master's, thesis or alternative; for doctorate, comprehensive exam, thesis/dissertation. *Entrance requirements:* For master's and doctorate, GRE General Test. Additional exam requirements/recommendations for international students: Required—TOEFL (minimum score 550 paper-based; 80 iBT), IELTS (minimum score 6.5). Electronic applications accepted.

University of Michigan, College of Engineering, Department of Industrial and Operations Engineering, Ann Arbor, MI 48109. Offers MS, MSE, PhD, MBA/MS, MBA/MSE. *Accreditation:* ABET. *Program availability:* Part-time. *Students:* 184 full-time (52 women), 18 part-time (5 women). 608 applicants, 35% accepted, 100 enrolled. In 2016, 90 master's, 13 doctorates awarded. Terminal master's awarded for partial completion of doctoral program. *Degree requirements:* For doctorate, oral defense of dissertation, preliminary exams, qualifying exam. *Entrance requirements:* For master's and doctorate, GRE General Test. Additional exam requirements/recommendations for international students: Required—TOEFL. *Application deadline:* Applications are processed on a rolling basis. Electronic applications accepted. *Expenses:* Tuition, state resident: full-time $21,466; part-time $1152 per credit hour. Tuition, nonresident: full-time $43,346; part-time $2367 per credit hour. Part-time tuition and fees vary according to course load, degree level and program. *Financial support:* Fellowships, research assistantships, teaching assistantships, Federal Work-Study, institutionally sponsored loans, scholarships/grants, traineeships, health care benefits, and unspecified assistantships available. Financial award applicants required to submit FAFSA. *Faculty research:* Production/distribution/logistics, financial engineering and enterprise systems, ergonomics (physical and cognitive), stochastic processes, linear and nonlinear optimization, operations research. *Total annual research expenditures:* $6.1 million. *Unit head:* Mark Daskin, Department Chair, 734-764-9410, Fax: 734-764-3451, E-mail: msdaskin@umich.edu. *Application contact:* Matt Irelan, Graduate Student Advisor/Program Coordinator, 734-764-6480, Fax: 734-764-3451, E-mail: mirelan@umich.edu.
Website: http://www.engin.umich.edu/ioe

The University of North Carolina at Chapel Hill, Graduate School, College of Arts and Sciences, Department of Operations Research, Chapel Hill, NC 27599. Offers MS, PhD. *Degree requirements:* For master's, comprehensive exam; for doctorate, comprehensive exam, thesis/dissertation. *Entrance requirements:* For master's and doctorate, GRE General Test, minimum GPA of 3.0.

University of Southern California, Graduate School, Viterbi School of Engineering, Daniel J. Epstein Department of Industrial and Systems Engineering, Los Angeles, CA 90089. Offers digital supply chain management (MS); engineering management (MS); engineering technology communication (Graduate Certificate); health systems operations (Graduate Certificate); industrial and systems engineering (MS, PhD, Engr); manufacturing engineering (MS); operations research engineering (MS); optimization and supply chain management (Graduate Certificate); product development engineering (MS); safety systems and security (MS); systems architecting and engineering (MS, Graduate Certificate); systems safety and security (Graduate Certificate); transportation systems (Graduate Certificate); MS/MBA. *Program availability:* Part-time, evening/weekend, online learning. Terminal master's awarded for partial completion of doctoral program. *Degree requirements:* For master's, thesis optional; for doctorate, thesis/dissertation. *Entrance requirements:* For master's and doctorate, GRE General Test. Additional exam requirements/recommendations for international students: Recommended—TOEFL. Electronic applications accepted. *Faculty research:* Health systems, music cognition and retrieval, transportation and logistics, manufacturing and automation, engineering systems design, risk and economic analysis.

The University of Texas at Austin, Graduate School, Cockrell School of Engineering, Department of Mechanical Engineering, Program in Operations Research and Industrial Engineering, Austin, TX 78712-1111. Offers MS, PhD. *Entrance requirements:* For master's and doctorate, GRE General Test. Additional exam requirements/recommendations for international students: Required—TOEFL.

University of Waterloo, Graduate Studies, Faculty of Engineering, Department of Management Sciences, Waterloo, ON N2L 3G1, Canada. Offers applied operations research (MA Sc, MMS, PhD); information systems (MA Sc, MMS, PhD); management of technology (MA Sc, MMS, PhD). *Program availability:* Part-time, online learning. *Degree requirements:* For master's, research paper or thesis; for doctorate, comprehensive exam, thesis/dissertation. *Entrance requirements:* For master's, GMAT or GRE, honors degree, minimum B average, resume; for doctorate, GMAT or GRE, master's degree, minimum A- average, resume. Additional exam requirements/recommendations for international students: Required—TOEFL, IELTS, PTE. Electronic applications accepted. *Faculty research:* Operations research, manufacturing systems, scheduling, information systems.

Technology and Public Policy

Arizona State University at the Tempe campus, College of Liberal Arts and Sciences, Program in Science and Technology Policy, Tempe, AZ 85287-6505. Offers MS. Fall admission only. *Degree requirements:* For master's, thesis or alternative, internship, applied project, interactive Program of Study (iPOS) submitted before completing 50 percent of required credit hours. *Entrance requirements:* For master's, GRE, bachelor's degree (or equivalent) or graduate degree from regionally-accredited college or university or of recognized standing; minimum GPA of 3.0 or equivalent in last 2 years of work leading to bachelor's degree; 3 letters of recommendation; personal statement; current resume. Additional exam requirements/recommendations for international students: Required—TOEFL, IELTS, or PTE. Electronic applications accepted. *Expenses:* Contact institution.

Carnegie Mellon University, Carnegie Institute of Technology, Department of Civil and Environmental Engineering, Pittsburgh, PA 15213. Offers advanced infrastructure systems (MS, PhD); advanced infrastructure systems technology development and application (MS); air quality engineering and science (MS); civil and environmental engineering (MS, PhD); civil and environmental engineering/engineering and public policy (PhD); civil engineering (MS, PhD); computational mechanics (MS, PhD); computational modeling and monitoring for resilient structural and material systems (MS); energy infrastructure systems (MS); environmental engineering (MS, PhD); environmental management and science (MS, PhD); IT-based sustainable global infrastructure and construction management (MS); sustainability and green design (MS); water quality engineering and science (MS). *Program availability:* Part-time. *Faculty:* 23 full-time (5 women), 12 part-time/adjunct (3 women). *Students:* 230 full-time (87 women), 4 part-time (0 women); includes 17 minority (4 Black or African American, non-Hispanic/Latino; 12 Asian, non-Hispanic/Latino; 1 Two or more races, non-Hispanic/Latino), 179 international. Average age 25. 653 applicants, 60% accepted, 107 enrolled. In 2016, 145 master's, 15 doctorates awarded. Terminal master's awarded for partial completion of doctoral program. *Degree requirements:* For master's, thesis optional; for doctorate, comprehensive exam, thesis/dissertation, two-part qualifying exam, public defense of dissertation. *Entrance requirements:* For master's, GRE General Test, BS in engineering, science or mathematics; for doctorate, GRE General Test, BS or MS in engineering, science or mathematics. Additional exam requirements/recommendations for international students: Required—TOEFL (minimum score 84 iBT) or IELTS (6.0). *Application deadline:* For fall admission, 1/5 priority date for domestic and international students; for spring admission, 9/15 priority date for domestic and international students. Applications are processed on a rolling basis. Application fee: $65. Electronic applications accepted. *Expenses:* Contact institution. *Financial support:* In 2016–17, 129 students received support. Fellowships with tuition reimbursements available, research assistantships with tuition reimbursements available, scholarships/grants, tuition waivers (full and partial), unspecified assistantships, and service assistantships available. Financial award application deadline: 1/5. *Faculty research:* Advanced infrastructure systems; environmental engineering, sustainability, and science; mechanics, materials, and computing. *Total annual research expenditures:* $7.4 million. *Unit head:* Dr. David A. Dzombak, Professor and Department Head, 412-268-2941, Fax: 412-268-7813, E-mail: dzombak@cmu.edu. *Application contact:* David A. Vey, Graduate Admissions Manager, 412-268-2292, Fax: 412-268-7813, E-mail: dvey@andrew.cmu.edu.
Website: http://www.cmu.edu/cee/

Carnegie Mellon University, Carnegie Institute of Technology, Department of Engineering and Public Policy, Pittsburgh, PA 15213-3891. Offers PhD. *Degree requirements:* For doctorate, thesis/dissertation. *Entrance requirements:* For doctorate, GRE General Test, BS in physical sciences or engineering. Additional exam requirements/recommendations for international students: Required—TOEFL. *Faculty research:* Issues in energy and environmental policy, IT and telecommunications policy, risk analysis and communication, management of technological innovation, security and engineered civil systems.

Eastern Michigan University, Graduate School, College of Technology, School of Technology and Professional Services Management, Program in Technology Studies, Ypsilanti, MI 48197. Offers MS. *Program availability:* Part-time, evening/weekend, online learning. *Students:* 9 full-time (0 women), 84 part-time (13 women); includes 15 minority (9 Black or African American, non-Hispanic/Latino; 1 American Indian or Alaska Native, non-Hispanic/Latino; 1 Asian, non-Hispanic/Latino; 2 Hispanic/Latino; 2 Two or more races, non-Hispanic/Latino), 5 international. Average age 38. 35 applicants, 80% accepted, 23 enrolled. In 2016, 51 master's awarded. *Degree requirements:* For master's, thesis optional. *Entrance requirements:* For master's, GRE General Test, minimum GPA of 2.6. Additional exam requirements/recommendations for international students: Required—TOEFL. *Application deadline:* Applications are processed on a rolling basis. Application fee: $45. *Financial support:* Fellowships, research assistantships with full tuition reimbursements, teaching assistantships with full tuition reimbursements, career-related internships or fieldwork, Federal Work-Study, institutionally sponsored loans, scholarships/grants, tuition waivers (partial), and unspecified assistantships available. Support available to part-time students. Financial award applicants required to submit FAFSA. *Application contact:* Dr. Denise Pilato, Program Coordinator, 734-487-1161, Fax: 734-487-7690, E-mail: denise.pilato@emich.edu.

The George Washington University, Elliott School of International Affairs, Program in International Science and Technology Policy, Washington, DC 20052. Offers MA, Graduate Certificate. *Program availability:* Part-time. *Students:* 16 full-time (5 women), 12 part-time (5 women); includes 4 minority (all Asian, non-Hispanic/Latino), 3 international. Average age 28. 23 applicants, 87% accepted, 10 enrolled. In 2016, 11 master's awarded. *Degree requirements:* For master's, one foreign language, capstone project. *Entrance requirements:* For master's, GRE General Test. Additional exam requirements/recommendations for international students: Required—TOEFL (minimum score 100 iBT), IELTS (minimum score 7). *Application deadline:* For fall admission, 1/15 priority date for domestic and international students; for spring admission, 10/1 for domestic students. Application fee: $75. Electronic applications accepted. *Financial support:* In 2016–17, 15 students received support. Fellowships with partial tuition reimbursements available, Federal Work-Study, and scholarships/grants available. Financial award application deadline: 1/15; financial award applicants required to submit FAFSA. *Faculty research:* Science policy, space policy, risk assessment, technology transfer, energy policy. *Unit head:* Prof. Allison Macfarlane, Director, 202-994-7292, E-mail: cistp@gwu.edu. *Application contact:* Nicole A. Campbell, Director of Graduate Admissions, 202-994-7050, Fax: 202-994-9537, E-mail: esiagrad@gwu.edu.
Website: http://elliott.gwu.edu/international-science-and-technology-policy

Massachusetts Institute of Technology, School of Engineering, Institute for Data, Systems, and Society, Cambridge, MA 02139. Offers social and engineering systems (PhD); technology and policy (SM). *Faculty:* 4 full-time (2 women). *Students:* 112 full-time (43 women), 1 part-time; includes 15 minority (1 Black or African American, non-Hispanic/Latino; 8 Asian, non-Hispanic/Latino; 3 Hispanic/Latino; 3 Two or more races, non-Hispanic/Latino), 54 international. Average age 27. 659 applicants, 18% accepted, 84 enrolled. In 2016, 82 master's, 8 doctorates awarded. *Degree requirements:* For master's, thesis; for doctorate, comprehensive exam, thesis/dissertation. *Entrance requirements:* For doctorate, GRE General Test. Additional exam requirements/recommendations for international students: Required—IELTS. *Application deadline:* For fall admission, 12/15 for domestic and international students. Application fee: $75. Electronic applications accepted. *Expenses: Tuition:* Full-time $46,400; part-time $725 per credit. One-time fee: $312 full-time. Full-time tuition and fees vary according to course load and program. *Financial support:* In 2016–17, 97 students received support, including fellowships (averaging $38,400 per year), 66 research assistantships (averaging $36,100 per year), 8 teaching assistantships (averaging $38,300 per year); Federal Work-Study, institutionally sponsored loans, traineeships, health care benefits, unspecified assistantships, and resident tutors also available. Support available to part-time students. Financial award application deadline: 5/1; financial award applicants required to submit FAFSA. *Faculty research:* Information theory and decision systems; sociotechnical systems; statistics and data science; network science; critical infrastructures; health care delivery; humans and technology; policy and standards; social behavior; uncertainty, risk, and dynamics. *Total annual research expenditures:* $9.5 million. *Unit head:* Munther A. Dahleh, Department Head, 617-253-3300, E-mail: idss-info@mit.edu. *Application contact:* 617-253-1182, E-mail: idss_academic_office@mit.edu.
Website: http://idss.mit.edu/

Massachusetts Institute of Technology, School of Humanities, Arts, and Social Sciences, Program in Science, Technology, and Society, Cambridge, MA 02139. Offers history, anthropology, and science, technology and society (PhD). *Faculty:* 13 full-time (5 women). *Students:* 31 full-time (22 women); includes 5 minority (1 American Indian or Alaska Native, non-Hispanic/Latino; 2 Asian, non-Hispanic/Latino; 2 Hispanic/Latino), 8 international. Average age 31. 160 applicants, 5% accepted, 5 enrolled. In 2016, 3 doctorates awarded. *Degree requirements:* For doctorate, one foreign language, comprehensive exam, thesis/dissertation. *Entrance requirements:* For doctorate, GRE General Test. Additional exam requirements/recommendations for international students: Required—TOEFL, IELTS. *Application deadline:* For fall admission, 12/15 for domestic and international students. Application fee: $75. Electronic applications accepted. *Expenses: Tuition:* Full-time $46,400; part-time $725 per credit. One-time fee: $312 full-time. Full-time tuition and fees vary according to course load and program. *Financial support:* In 2016–17, 30 students received support, including 21 fellowships (averaging $38,600 per year), 1 research assistantship (averaging $39,300 per year), 4 teaching assistantships (averaging $40,200 per year); Federal Work-Study, institutionally sponsored loans, scholarships/grants, traineeships, health care benefits, unspecified assistantships, and resident tutors also available. Support available to part-time students. Financial award application deadline: 5/1; financial award applicants required to submit FAFSA. *Faculty research:* History of science; history of technology; sociology of science and technology; anthropology of science and technology; science, technology, and society. *Total annual research expenditures:* $186,000. *Unit head:* Prof. Jenniger Light, Program Director, 617-253-4062, Fax: 617-258-8118, E-mail: stsprogram@mit.edu. *Application contact:* 617-253-9759, E-mail: hasts@mit.edu.
Website: http://sts-program.mit.edu/

Rensselaer Polytechnic Institute, Graduate School, School of Humanities, Arts, and Social Sciences, Program in Science and Technology Studies, Troy, NY 12180-3590. Offers MS, PhD. *Faculty:* 14 full-time (4 women), 2 part-time/adjunct (0 women). *Students:* 19 full-time (10 women), 1 (woman) part-time. 20 applicants, 60% accepted, 4 enrolled. In 2016, 1 master's, 6 doctorates awarded. Terminal master's awarded for partial completion of doctoral program. *Degree requirements:* For master's, thesis (for some programs); for doctorate, comprehensive exam, thesis/dissertation. *Entrance requirements:* For master's and doctorate, GRE. Additional exam requirements/recommendations for international students: Required—TOEFL (minimum score 600 paper-based; 100 iBT), IELTS (minimum score 7), PTE (minimum score 68). *Application deadline:* For fall admission, 1/1 priority date for domestic and international students; for spring admission, 8/15 priority date for domestic and international students. Applications are processed on a rolling basis. Application fee: $75. Electronic applications accepted. *Expenses: Tuition:* Full-time $49,520; part-time $2060 per credit hour. *Required fees:* $2617. *Financial support:* In 2016–17, research assistantships (averaging $22,000 per year), teaching assistantships (averaging $22,000 per year) were awarded; fellowships also available. Financial award application deadline: 1/1. *Faculty research:* Policy studies, science studies, technology studies. *Unit head:* Dr. Abby Kinchy, Graduate Program Director, 518-276-6980, E-mail: kincha@rpi.edu. *Application contact:* Office of Graduate Admissions, 518-276-6216, E-mail: gradadmissions@rpi.edu.
Website: http://www.sts.rpi.edu/pl/graduate-programs-sts

Rochester Institute of Technology, Graduate Enrollment Services, College of Liberal Arts, Department of Public Policy, MS Program in Science, Technology and Public Policy, Rochester, NY 14623. Offers MS. *Program availability:* Part-time. *Students:* 1 (woman) full-time, 2 part-time (1 woman). Average age 27. 5 applicants, 20% accepted, 1 enrolled. In 2016, 2 master's awarded. *Degree requirements:* For master's, thesis. *Entrance requirements:* For master's, GRE, minimum GPA of 3.0 (recommended). Additional exam requirements/recommendations for international students: Required—TOEFL (minimum score 570 paper-based; 88 iBT), IELTS (minimum score 6.5), PTE (minimum score 61). *Application deadline:* For fall admission, 2/15 priority date for domestic and international students; for spring admission, 12/15 priority date for domestic and international students. Applications are processed on a rolling basis.

Technology and Public Policy

Application fee: $60. Electronic applications accepted. *Expenses:* $1,742 per credit hour. *Financial support:* In 2016–17, 4 students received support. Research assistantships with partial tuition reimbursements available, teaching assistantships with partial tuition reimbursements available, career-related internships or fieldwork, scholarships/grants, and unspecified assistantships available. Support available to part-time students. Financial award applicants required to submit FAFSA. *Faculty research:* Environmental management, innovation, and policy; technological innovation, environmental economics and policy; alternative energy and climate change; cybersecurity economics and Internet policy; e-democracy and digital government. *Unit head:* Franz Foltz, Graduate Program Director, 585-475-5368, E-mail: fafgsh@rit.edu. *Application contact:* Diane Ellison, Associate Vice President, Graduate Enrollment Services, 585-475-2229, Fax: 585-475-7164, E-mail: gradinfo@rit.edu.
Website: http://www.rit.edu/cla/publicpolicy/academics/science-technology-and-public-policy-ms

St. Cloud State University, School of Graduate Studies, College of Science and Engineering, Department of Environmental and Technological Studies, St. Cloud, MN 56301-4498. Offers MS. *Degree requirements:* For master's, thesis or alternative. *Entrance requirements:* For master's, minimum GPA of 2.75. Additional exam requirements/recommendations for international students: Required—TOEFL (minimum score 550 paper-based), Michigan English Language Assessment Battery; Recommended—IELTS (minimum score 6.5). Electronic applications accepted.

Stony Brook University, State University of New York, Graduate School, College of Engineering and Applied Sciences, Department of Technology and Society, Program in Technology, Policy, and Innovation, Stony Brook, NY 11794-3760. Offers PhD. *Program availability:* Part-time. *Faculty:* 14 full-time (5 women), 15 part-time/adjunct (4 women). *Students:* 20 full-time (9 women), 6 part-time (4 women); includes 8 minority (3 Black or African American, non-Hispanic/Latino; 4 Asian, non-Hispanic/Latino; 1 Two or more races, non-Hispanic/Latino), 11 international. 107 applicants, 56% accepted, 21 enrolled. In 2016, 2 doctorates awarded. *Degree requirements:* For doctorate, comprehensive exam, thesis/dissertation, qualifying examination, preliminary examination. *Entrance requirements:* For doctorate, GRE General Test, minimum undergraduate GPA of 3.0, curriculum vitae. Additional exam requirements/recommendations for international students: Required—TOEFL (minimum score 85 iBT), IELTS (minimum score 6.5). *Application deadline:* For fall admission, 1/15 for domestic and international students; for spring admission, 10/1 for domestic students. Application fee: $100. *Expenses:* Contact institution. *Total annual research expenditures:* $2.4 million. *Unit head:* Dr. David Ferguson, Chair, 631-632-8763, E-mail: david.ferguson@stonybrook.edu. *Application contact:* Marypat Taveras, Coordinator, 631-632-8762, Fax: 631-632-7809, E-mail: marypat.taveras@stonybrook.edu.
Website: http://www.stonybrook.edu/est/graduate/phd.shtml

University of Minnesota, Twin Cities Campus, Graduate School, Hubert H. Humphrey School of Public Affairs, Program in Science, Technology, and Environmental Policy, Minneapolis, MN 55455. Offers MS, JD/MS. *Program availability:* Part-time. *Degree requirements:* For master's, thesis. *Entrance requirements:* For master's, GRE General Test, undergraduate training in the biological or physical sciences or engineering, minimum undergraduate GPA of 3.0. Additional exam requirements/recommendations for international students: Required—TOEFL (minimum score 600 paper-based; 100 iBT), IELTS (minimum score 7). Electronic applications accepted. *Expenses:* Contact institution. *Faculty research:* Economics, history, philosophy, and politics of science and technology; organization and management of science and technology.

University of South Africa, College of Human Sciences, Pretoria, South Africa. Offers adult education (M Ed); African languages (MA, PhD); African politics (MA, PhD); Afrikaans (MA, PhD); ancient history (MA, PhD); ancient Near Eastern studies (MA, PhD); anthropology (MA, PhD); applied linguistics (MA); Arabic (MA, PhD); archaeology (MA); art history (MA); Biblical archaeology (MA); Biblical studies (M Th, D Th, PhD); Christian spirituality (M Th, D Th); church history (M Th, D Th); classical studies (MA, PhD); clinical psychology (MA); communication (MA, PhD); comparative education (M Ed, Ed D); consulting psychology (D Admin, D Com, PhD); curriculum studies (M Ed, Ed D); development studies (M Admin, MA, D Admin, PhD); didactics (M Ed, Ed D); education (M Tech); education management (M Ed, Ed D); educational psychology (M Ed); English (MA); environmental education (M Ed); French (MA, PhD); German (MA, PhD); Greek (MA); guidance and counseling (M Ed); health studies (MA, PhD), including health sciences education (MA), health services management (MA), medical and surgical nursing science (critical care general) (MA), midwifery and neonatal nursing science (MA), trauma and emergency care (MA); history (MA, PhD); history of education (Ed D); inclusive education (M Ed, Ed D); information and communications technology policy and regulation (MA); information science (MA, MIS, PhD); international politics (MA, PhD); Islamic studies (MA, PhD); Italian (MA, PhD); Judaica (MA, PhD); linguistics (MA, PhD); mathematical education (M Ed); mathematics education (MA); missiology (M Th, D Th); modern Hebrew (MA, PhD); musicology (MA, MMus, D Mus, PhD); natural science education (M Ed); New Testament (M Th, D Th); Old Testament (D Th); pastoral therapy (M Th, D Th); philosophy (MA); philosophy of education (M Ed, Ed D); politics (MA, PhD); Portuguese (MA, PhD); practical theology (M Th, D Th); psychology (MA, MS, PhD); psychology of education (M Ed, Ed D); public health (MA); religious studies (MA, D Th, PhD); Romance languages (MA); Russian (MA, PhD); Semitic languages (MA, PhD); social behavior studies in HIV/AIDS (MA); social science (mental health) (MA); social science in development studies (MA); social science in psychology (MA); social science in social work (MA); social science in sociology (MA); social work (MSW, DSW, PhD); socio-education (M Ed, Ed D); sociolinguistics (MA); sociology (MA, PhD); Spanish (MA, PhD); systematic theology (M Th, D Th); TESOL (teaching English to speakers of other languages) (MA); theological ethics (M Th, D Th); theory of literature (MA, PhD); urban ministries (D Th); urban ministry (M Th).

The University of Texas at Austin, Graduate School, McCombs School of Business, Program in Technology Commercialization, Austin, TX 78712-1111. Offers MS. Twelve-month program, beginning in May, with classes held every other Friday and Saturday. *Program availability:* Evening/weekend, online learning. *Degree requirements:* For master's, year-long global teaming project. *Entrance requirements:* For master's, GRE General Test or GMAT. Additional exam requirements/recommendations for international students: Required—TOEFL (minimum score 550 paper-based; 79 iBT). Electronic applications accepted. *Expenses:* Contact institution. *Faculty research:* Technology transfer; entrepreneurship; commercialization; research, development and innovation.

Section 16
Materials Sciences and Engineering

This section contains a directory of institutions offering graduate work in materials sciences and engineering, Additional information about programs may be obtained by writing directly to the dean of a graduate school or chair of a department at the address given in the directory.

For programs offering related work, see also in this book *Agricultural Engineering and Bioengineering, Biomedical Engineering and Biotechnology, Engineering and Applied Sciences,* and *Geological, Mineral/Mining, and Petroleum Engineering.* In another guide in this series:

Graduate Programs in the Physical Sciences, Mathematics, Agricultural Sciences, the Environment & Natural Resources
See *Chemistry* and *Geosciences*

CONTENTS

Program Directories

Ceramic Sciences and Engineering

Alfred University, Graduate School, College of Ceramics, Inamori School of Engineering, Alfred, NY 14802. Offers biomaterials engineering (MS); ceramic engineering (MS, PhD); electrical engineering (MS); glass science (MS, PhD); materials science and engineering (MS, PhD); mechanical engineering (MS). *Program availability:* Part-time. *Faculty:* 18 full-time (1 woman). *Students:* 26 full-time (6 women), 16 part-time (4 women); includes 1 minority (Hispanic/Latino), 12 international. Average age 27. 14 applicants, 79% accepted, 10 enrolled. In 2016, 13 master's, 5 doctorates awarded. *Degree requirements:* For master's, thesis; for doctorate, thesis/dissertation. *Entrance requirements:* Additional exam requirements/recommendations for international students: Required—TOEFL (minimum score 590 paper-based; 90 iBT), IELTS (minimum score 6.5). *Application deadline:* For fall admission, 3/1 priority date for domestic students, 3/15 for international students; for spring admission, 10/1 priority date for domestic students, 10/1 for international students. Applications are processed on a rolling basis. Application fee: $60. Electronic applications accepted. *Expenses:* Contact institution. *Financial support:* Fellowships with full tuition reimbursements, research assistantships with full tuition reimbursements, teaching assistantships with full tuition reimbursements, tuition waivers (full and partial), and unspecified assistantships available. Financial award application deadline: 8/1; financial award applicants required to submit FAFSA. *Faculty research:* X-ray diffraction, biomaterials and polymers, thin-film processing, electronic and optical ceramics, solid-state chemistry. *Unit head:* Dr. Alistair N. Cormack, Dean, 607-871-2422, E-mail: cormack@alfred.edu. *Application contact:* Sara Love, Coordinator of Graduate Admissions, 607-871-2115, Fax: 607-871-2198, E-mail: gradinquiry@alfred.edu.
Website: http://engineering.alfred.edu/grad/

Missouri University of Science and Technology, Graduate School, Department of Materials Science and Engineering, Rolla, MO 65409. Offers ceramic engineering (MS, DE, PhD); metallurgical engineering (MS, PhD). *Degree requirements:* For master's, thesis optional; for doctorate, comprehensive exam. *Entrance requirements:* For master's, GRE (minimum combined score 1100, 600 verbal, 3.5 writing); for doctorate, GRE (minimum score: quantitative 600, writing 3.5). Additional exam requirements/recommendations for international students: Required—TOEFL (minimum score 570 paper-based). Electronic applications accepted.

Electronic Materials

Colorado School of Mines, Office of Graduate Studies, Department of Metallurgical and Materials Engineering, Golden, CO 80401. Offers materials science (MS, PhD); metallurgical and materials engineering (ME, MS, PhD). *Program availability:* Part-time. *Degree requirements:* For master's, thesis (for some programs); for doctorate, comprehensive exam, thesis/dissertation. *Entrance requirements:* For master's and doctorate, GRE General Test. Additional exam requirements/recommendations for international students: Required—TOEFL (minimum score 550 paper-based; 80 iBT). Electronic applications accepted. *Expenses:* Tuition, state resident: full-time $15,690. Tuition, nonresident: full-time $34,020. *Required fees:* $2152. Tuition and fees vary according to course load.

Princeton University, Princeton Institute for the Science and Technology of Materials (PRISM), Princeton, NJ 08544-1019. Offers materials (PhD).

University of Arkansas, Graduate School, Interdisciplinary Program in Microelectronics and Photonics, Fayetteville, AR 72701. Offers MS, PhD. In 2016, 8 master's, 3 doctorates awarded. *Degree requirements:* For doctorate, thesis/dissertation. *Application deadline:* For fall admission, 4/1 for international students; for spring admission, 10/1 for international students. Applications are processed on a rolling basis. Application fee: $40 ($50 for international students). Electronic applications accepted. *Financial support:* In 2016–17, 25 research assistantships, 4 teaching assistantships were awarded; fellowships with tuition reimbursements also available. Financial award application deadline: 4/1; financial award applicants required to submit FAFSA. *Unit head:* Dr. Rick Wise, Head, 479-575-2875, Fax: 479-575-4580, E-mail: rickwise@uark.edu. *Application contact:* Graduate Admissions, 479-575-6246, Fax: 479-575-5908, E-mail: gradinfo@uark.edu.
Website: http://microep.uark.edu

Materials Engineering

Alabama Agricultural and Mechanical University, School of Graduate Studies, College of Engineering, Technology, and Physical Sciences, Department of Mechanical and Civil Engineering, Huntsville, AL 35811. Offers material engineering (M Eng), including civil engineering, mechanical engineering. *Expenses:* Tuition, nonresident: part-time $826 per credit hour. Full-time tuition and fees vary according to course load and program. *Unit head:* Mohamed Seif, Chair, 256-372-5889, E-mail: mohamed.seif@aamu.edu.

Arizona State University at the Tempe campus, Ira A. Fulton Schools of Engineering, School for Engineering of Matter, Transport and Energy, Tempe, AZ 85281. Offers aerospace engineering (MS, PhD); chemical engineering (MS, PhD); materials science and engineering (MS, PhD); mechanical engineering (MS, PhD); solar energy engineering and commercialization (PSM). *Program availability:* Part-time, evening/weekend, online learning. Terminal master's awarded for partial completion of doctoral program. *Degree requirements:* For master's, thesis and oral defense (MS); applied project or comprehensive exam (MSE); interactive Program of Study (iPOS) submitted before completing 50 percent of required credit hours; for doctorate, comprehensive exam, thesis/dissertation, interactive Program of Study (iPOS) submitted before completing 50 percent of required credit hours. *Entrance requirements:* For master's, GRE, minimum GPA of 3.0 or equivalent in last 2 years of work leading to bachelor's degree; for doctorate, GRE, minimum GPA of 3.0 in last 2 years of work leading to bachelor's degree. Additional exam requirements/recommendations for international students: Required—TOEFL, IELTS, or PTE. Electronic applications accepted. *Expenses:* Contact institution. *Faculty research:* Electronic materials and packaging, materials for energy (batteries), adaptive/intelligent materials and structures, multiscale fluid mechanics, membranes, therapeutics and bioseparations, flexible structures, nanostructured materials, and micro/nano transport.

Auburn University, Graduate School, Ginn College of Engineering, Department of Mechanical Engineering, Program in Materials Engineering, Auburn University, AL 36849. Offers M Mtl E, MS, PhD. *Faculty:* 38 full-time (1 woman), 1 part-time/adjunct (0 women). *Students:* 34 full-time (9 women), 12 part-time (3 women); includes 2 minority (1 Black or African American, non-Hispanic/Latino; 1 Asian, non-Hispanic/Latino), 36 international. Average age 27. 62 applicants, 44% accepted, 11 enrolled. In 2016, 3 master's, 5 doctorates awarded. *Degree requirements:* For master's, thesis (MS), oral exam; for doctorate, one foreign language, thesis/dissertation. *Entrance requirements:* For master's and doctorate, GRE General Test. *Application deadline:* Applications are processed on a rolling basis. Application fee: $50 ($60 for international students). Electronic applications accepted. *Expenses:* Tuition, state resident: full-time $9072; part-time $504 per credit hour. Tuition, nonresident: full-time $27,216; part-time $1512 per credit hour. *Required fees:* $812 per semester. Tuition and fees vary according to degree level and program. *Financial support:* Fellowships, research assistantships, teaching assistantships, and Federal Work-Study available. Support available to part-time students. Financial award application deadline: 3/15; financial award applicants required to submit FAFSA. *Faculty research:* Smart materials. *Unit head:* Dr. Bryan Chin, Head, 334-844-3322. *Application contact:* Dr. George Flowers, Dean of the Graduate School, 334-844-2125.
Website: http://www.eng.auburn.edu/matl/

Binghamton University, State University of New York, Graduate School, Thomas J. Watson School of Engineering and Applied Science and Harpur College of Arts and Sciences, Materials Science and Engineering Program, Binghamton, NY 13902-6000. Offers MS, PhD. *Program availability:* Part-time, online learning. *Faculty:* 3 full-time (0 women). *Students:* 14 full-time (2 women), 33 part-time (12 women); includes 3 minority (all Asian, non-Hispanic/Latino), 37 international. Average age 28. 101 applicants, 42% accepted, 8 enrolled. In 2016, 7 master's, 2 doctorates awarded. *Degree requirements:* For master's, thesis; for doctorate, comprehensive exam, thesis/dissertation. *Entrance requirements:* For master's and doctorate, GRE General Test. Additional exam requirements/recommendations for international students: Required—TOEFL (minimum score 550 paper-based; 80 iBT). *Application deadline:* Applications are processed on a rolling basis. Application fee: $75. Electronic applications accepted. *Expenses:* Contact institution. *Financial support:* In 2016–17, 31 students received support, including 21 research assistantships with full tuition reimbursements available (averaging $17,500 per year), 10 teaching assistantships with full tuition reimbursements available (averaging $17,500 per year); fellowships, career-related internships or fieldwork, Federal Work-Study, institutionally sponsored loans, scholarships/grants, health care benefits, tuition waivers (full and partial), and unspecified assistantships also available. Financial award application deadline: 2/1; financial award applicants required to submit FAFSA. *Unit head:* Ellen Tilden, Coordinator of Graduate Programs, 607-777-2873, E-mail: etilden@binghamton.edu. *Application contact:* Ben Balkaya, Assistant Dean and Director, 607-777-2151, Fax: 607-777-2501, E-mail: balkaya@binghamton.edu.
Website: https://www.binghamton.edu/me/grad/materials-science.html

Boise State University, College of Engineering, Micron School of Materials Science and Engineering, Boise, ID 83725. Offers materials science and engineering (M Engr, MS, PhD). *Faculty:* 16. *Students:* 37 full-time (13 women), 6 part-time (3 women); includes 6 minority (5 Asian, non-Hispanic/Latino; 1 Hispanic/Latino), 8 international. Average age 29. 61 applicants, 36% accepted, 7 enrolled. In 2016, 10 master's, 1 doctorate awarded. Terminal master's awarded for partial completion of doctoral program. *Degree requirements:* For master's, comprehensive exam, thesis (for some programs). *Entrance requirements:* For master's, GRE General Test. Additional exam requirements/recommendations for international students: Required—TOEFL (minimum score 550 paper-based; 80 iBT), IELTS (minimum score 6). *Application deadline:* For fall admission, 1/15 priority date for domestic and international students. Application fee: $65 ($95 for international students). Electronic applications accepted. *Expenses:* Tuition, state resident: full-time $6058; part-time $358 per credit hour. Tuition, nonresident: full-time $20,108; part-time $608 per credit hour. *Required fees:* $2108. Tuition and fees vary according to program. *Financial support:* In 2016–17, 6 students received support, including 32 research assistantships (averaging $8,599 per year); scholarships/grants and unspecified assistantships also available. Financial award application deadline: 1/15; financial award applicants required to submit FAFSA. *Unit head:* Dr. Janet Callahan, Department Chair, 208-426-5983, E-mail: janetcallahan@boisestate.edu. *Application contact:* Dr. David Estrada, Graduate Program Coordinator, 208-426-5693, E-mail: daveestrada@boisestate.edu.
Website: http://coen.boisestate.edu/mse/degreeprograms/

Boston University, College of Engineering, Division of Materials Science and Engineering, Brookline, MA 02446. Offers materials science and engineering (M Eng, MS, PhD). *Program availability:* Part-time. *Students:* 69 full-time (26 women), 15 part-time (6 women); includes 8 minority (5 Asian, non-Hispanic/Latino; 3 Hispanic/Latino), 53 international. Average age 25. 271 applicants, 30% accepted, 29 enrolled. In 2016, 28 master's, 7 doctorates awarded. Terminal master's awarded for partial completion of doctoral program. *Degree requirements:* For master's, thesis (for some programs); for doctorate, comprehensive exam, thesis/dissertation. *Entrance requirements:* For master's and doctorate, GRE General Test. Additional exam requirements/recommendations for international students: Required—TOEFL (minimum score 90 iBT), IELTS (minimum score 7). *Financial support:* Application deadline: 1/1. *Faculty research:* Biomaterials, electronic and photonic materials, materials for energy and environment, nanomaterials. *Unit head:* Dr. David Bishop, Division Head, 617-353-8899,

Fax: 617-353-5548, E-mail: djb1@bu.edu.
Website: http://www.bu.edu/mse/

California State University, Northridge, Graduate Studies, College of Engineering and Computer Science, Department of Manufacturing Systems Engineering and Management, Northridge, CA 91330. Offers engineering automation (MS); engineering management (MS); manufacturing systems engineering (MS); materials engineering (MS). *Program availability:* Online learning. *Faculty:* 8 full-time (7 women), 21 part-time/adjunct (16 women). *Students:* 124 full-time (29 women), 94 part-time (19 women); includes 27 minority (1 American Indian or Alaska Native, non-Hispanic/Latino; 11 Asian, non-Hispanic/Latino; 13 Hispanic/Latino; 2 Two or more races, non-Hispanic/Latino), 145 international. Average age 27. 302 applicants, 33% accepted, 45 enrolled. *Entrance requirements:* For master's, GRE (if cumulative undergraduate GPA less than 3.0). *Application deadline:* For fall admission, 3/30 for domestic students; for spring admission, 9/30 for domestic students. Application fee: $55. *Expenses:* Tuition, state resident: full-time $4152. *Unit head:* Ahmad Sarfaraz, Chair, 818-677-2167.
Website: http://www.csun.edu/~msem/

Carleton University, Faculty of Graduate Studies, Faculty of Engineering and Design, Department of Mechanical and Aerospace Engineering, Ottawa, ON K1S 5B6, Canada. Offers aerospace engineering (M Eng, MA Sc, PhD); materials engineering (M Eng, MA Sc); mechanical engineering (M Eng, MA Sc, PhD). *Degree requirements:* For master's, thesis optional; for doctorate, thesis/dissertation. *Entrance requirements:* For master's, honors degree; for doctorate, MA Sc or M Eng. Additional exam requirements/recommendations for international students: Required—TOEFL. *Faculty research:* Thermal fluids engineering, heat transfer, vehicle engineering.

Carnegie Mellon University, Carnegie Institute of Technology, Department of Materials Science and Engineering, Pittsburgh, PA 15213-3891. Offers MS, PhD. *Program availability:* Part-time. Terminal master's awarded for partial completion of doctoral program. *Degree requirements:* For master's, exam; for doctorate, thesis/dissertation, qualifying exam. *Entrance requirements:* For master's and doctorate, GRE General Test. Additional exam requirements/recommendations for international students: Required—TOEFL. *Faculty research:* Materials characterization, process metallurgy, high strength alloys, growth kinetics, ceramics.

Case Western Reserve University, School of Graduate Studies, Case School of Engineering, Department of Materials Science and Engineering, Cleveland, OH 44106. Offers materials science and engineering (MS, PhD). *Program availability:* Part-time, online learning. *Faculty:* 12 full-time (1 woman). *Students:* 34 full-time (9 women), 6 part-time (2 women); includes 5 minority (1 Black or African American, non-Hispanic/Latino; 2 Asian, non-Hispanic/Latino; 1 Hispanic/Latino; 1 Two or more races, non-Hispanic/Latino), 18 international. In 2016, 4 master's, 5 doctorates awarded. Terminal master's awarded for partial completion of doctoral program. *Degree requirements:* For master's, thesis (for some programs); for doctorate, thesis/dissertation, qualifying exam, teaching experience. *Entrance requirements:* For master's and doctorate, GRE General Test. Additional exam requirements/recommendations for international students: Required—TOEFL. *Application deadline:* For fall admission, 2/15 priority date for domestic students; for spring admission, 9/15 for domestic students. Applications are processed on a rolling basis. Application fee: $50. *Expenses: Tuition:* Full-time $42,576; part-time $1774 per credit hour. *Required fees:* $34. Tuition and fees vary according to course load and program. *Financial support:* In 2016–17, 1 fellowship with tuition reimbursement, 29 research assistantships with tuition reimbursements were awarded; teaching assistantships also available. Financial award application deadline: 4/30; financial award applicants required to submit FAFSA. *Faculty research:* Surface hardening of steels and other alloys, chemistry and structure of surfaces, microstructural and mechanical property characterization, materials for energy applications, thermodynamics and kinetics of materials, performance and reliability of materials. *Total annual research expenditures:* $3.6 million. *Unit head:* Dr. Frank Ernst, Department Chair, 216-368-0611, Fax: 216-368-4224, E-mail: emse.info@case.edu. *Application contact:* Theresa Claytor, Student Affairs Coordinator, 216-368-8555, Fax: 216-368-8555, E-mail: esme.info@case.edu.
Website: http://engineering.case.edu/emse/

The Catholic University of America, School of Engineering, Department of Materials Science and Engineering, Washington, DC 20064. Offers MS. *Program availability:* Part-time. *Faculty:* 1 part-time/adjunct (0 women). *Students:* 11 full-time (6 women), 2 part-time (both women); includes 3 minority (1 Asian, non-Hispanic/Latino; 2 Two or more races, non-Hispanic/Latino), 10 international. Average age 27. 9 applicants, 78% accepted, 3 enrolled. In 2016, 3 master's awarded. *Degree requirements:* For master's, thesis optional. *Entrance requirements:* For master's, GRE (minimum score 1250), minimum GPA of 3.0, statement of purpose, official copies of academic transcripts. Additional exam requirements/recommendations for international students: Required—TOEFL (minimum score 550 paper-based; 80 iBT). *Application deadline:* For fall admission, 7/15 for domestic students, 7/1 for international students; for spring admission, 11/15 for domestic students, 11/1 for international students. Applications are processed on a rolling basis. Application fee: $55. Electronic applications accepted. *Expenses:* $43,380 per year; $1,170 per credit; $200 per semester part-time fees. *Financial support:* Fellowships, research assistantships, teaching assistantships, Federal Work-Study, scholarships/grants, tuition waivers (full and partial), and unspecified assistantships available. Financial award application deadline: 2/1; financial award applicants required to submit FAFSA. *Faculty research:* Nanotechnology, biomaterials, magnetic and optical materials, glass, ceramics, and metallurgy processing and instrumentation. *Unit head:* Dr. Biprodas Dutta, Director, 202-319-5535, Fax: 202-319-4469, E-mail: duttab@cua.edu. *Application contact:* Director of Graduate Admissions, 202-319-5057, Fax: 202-319-6533, E-mail: cua-admissions@cua.edu.
Website: http://materialsscience.cua.edu/

Clarkson University, Wallace H. Coulter School of Engineering, Program in Materials Science and Engineering, Potsdam, NY 13699. Offers PhD. *Students:* 5 full-time (1 woman); includes 1 minority (Asian, non-Hispanic/Latino), 2 international. 23 applicants, 35% accepted. *Degree requirements:* For doctorate, comprehensive exam, thesis/dissertation. *Entrance requirements:* For doctorate, GRE. Additional exam requirements/recommendations for international students: Required—TOEFL (minimum score 550 paper-based, 80 iBT) or IELTS (6.5). *Application deadline:* Applications are processed on a rolling basis. Application fee: $50. Electronic applications accepted. *Expenses: Tuition:* Full-time $23,400; part-time $1300 per credit hour. Tuition and fees vary according to campus/location and program. *Financial support:* Scholarships/grants and unspecified assistantships available. *Unit head:* Dr. Marilyn Freeman, Director of Materials Science and Engineering, 315-268-2316, E-mail: mfreeman@clarkson.edu. *Application contact:* Dan Capogna, Graduate Admissions Contact, 518-631-9910, E-mail: graduate@clarkson.edu.
Website: http://graduate.clarkson.edu

Clemson University, Graduate School, College of Engineering, Computing and Applied Sciences, Department of Materials Science and Engineering, Clemson, SC 29634. Offers MS, PhD. *Program availability:* Part-time. *Faculty:* 17 full-time (2 women), 2 part-time/adjunct (0 women). *Students:* 44 full-time (10 women), 9 part-time (2 women); includes 3 minority (1 Asian, non-Hispanic/Latino; 2 Hispanic/Latino), 26 international. Average age 27. 120 applicants, 21% accepted, 10 enrolled. In 2016, 5 master's, 10 doctorates awarded. Terminal master's awarded for partial completion of doctoral program. *Degree requirements:* For master's, thesis; for doctorate, comprehensive exam, thesis/dissertation. *Entrance requirements:* For master's and doctorate, GRE General Test, unofficial transcripts, letters of recommendation. Additional exam requirements/recommendations for international students: Required—TOEFL (minimum score 80 iBT), IELTS (minimum score 6.5). *Application deadline:* For fall admission, 2/1 priority date for domestic and international students; for spring admission, 9/1 priority date for domestic and international students. Applications are processed on a rolling basis. Application fee: $80 ($90 for international students). Electronic applications accepted. *Expenses:* $4,841 per semester full-time resident, $9,640 per semester full-time non-resident, $612 per credit hour part-time resident, $1,223 per credit hour part-time non-resident. *Financial support:* In 2016–17, 63 students received support, including 7 fellowships with partial tuition reimbursements available (averaging $7,071 per year), 22 research assistantships with partial tuition reimbursements available (averaging $20,409 per year), 1 teaching assistantship with partial tuition reimbursement available (averaging $15,000 per year); career-related internships or fieldwork and unspecified assistantships also available. Financial award application deadline: 2/1. *Total annual research expenditures:* $2.9 million. *Unit head:* Dr. Rajendra Bordia, Department Chair, 864-656-5228, E-mail: rbordia@clemson.edu. *Application contact:* Dr. Kyle Brinkman, Graduate Program Coordinator, 864-656-1405, E-mail: ksbrink@clemson.edu.
Website: https://www.clemson.edu/cecas/departments/mse/index.html

The College of William and Mary, Faculty of Arts and Sciences, Department of Applied Science, Williamsburg, VA 23185. Offers accelerator science (PhD); applied mathematics (PhD); applied mechanics (PhD); applied robotics (PhD); applied science (MS); atmospheric and environmental science (PhD); computational neuroscience (PhD); interface, thin film and surface science (PhD); lasers and optics (PhD); magnetic resonance (PhD); materials science and engineering (PhD); mathematical and computational biology (PhD); medical imaging (PhD); nanotechnology (PhD); neuroscience (PhD); non-destructive evaluation (PhD); polymer chemistry (PhD); remote sensing (PhD). *Program availability:* Part-time. *Faculty:* 8 full-time (2 women), 2 part-time/adjunct (0 women). *Students:* 30 full-time (11 women), 4 part-time (0 women); includes 16 minority (2 Black or African American, non-Hispanic/Latino; 12 Asian, non-Hispanic/Latino; 2 Hispanic/Latino), 12 international. Average age 28. 37 applicants, 27% accepted, 7 enrolled. In 2016, 6 doctorates awarded. Terminal master's awarded for partial completion of doctoral program. *Degree requirements:* For master's, comprehensive exam, thesis; for doctorate, comprehensive exam, thesis/dissertation, 4 core courses. *Entrance requirements:* For master's and doctorate, GRE General Test, GRE Subject Test. Additional exam requirements/recommendations for international students: Required—TOEFL, IELTS. *Application deadline:* For fall admission, 2/3 priority date for domestic students, 2/3 for international students; for spring admission, 10/15 priority date for domestic students, 10/14 for international students. Applications are processed on a rolling basis. Application fee: $45. Electronic applications accepted. *Expenses:* Contact institution. *Financial support:* In 2016–17, 7 students received support, including 27 research assistantships (averaging $25,000 per year), 1 teaching assistantship (averaging $9,500 per year); fellowships, scholarships/grants, health care benefits, tuition waivers (full), and unspecified assistantships also available. Financial award application deadline: 4/15; financial award applicants required to submit FAFSA. *Faculty research:* Computational biology, non-destructive evaluation, neurophysiology, laser spectroscopy, nanotechnology. *Total annual research expenditures:* $536,220. *Unit head:* Dr. Christopher Del Negro, Chair, 757-221-7808, Fax: 757-221-2050, E-mail: cadeln@wm.edu. *Application contact:* Lianne Rios Ashburne, Graduate Program Coordinator, 757-221-2563, Fax: 757-221-2050, E-mail: lrashburne@wm.edu.
Website: http://www.wm.edu/as/appliedscience

Colorado School of Mines, Office of Graduate Studies, Department of Metallurgical and Materials Engineering, Golden, CO 80401. Offers materials science (MS, PhD); metallurgical and materials engineering (ME, MS, PhD). *Program availability:* Part-time. *Degree requirements:* For master's, thesis (for some programs); for doctorate, comprehensive exam, thesis/dissertation. *Entrance requirements:* For master's and doctorate, GRE General Test. Additional exam requirements/recommendations for international students: Required—TOEFL (minimum score 550 paper-based; 80 iBT). Electronic applications accepted. *Expenses:* Tuition, state resident: full-time $15,690. Tuition, nonresident: full-time $34,020. *Required fees:* $2152. Tuition and fees vary according to course load.

Columbia University, Fu Foundation School of Engineering and Applied Science, Department of Applied Physics and Applied Mathematics, New York, NY 10027. Offers applied mathematics (MS, Eng Sc D, PhD); applied physics (MS, Eng Sc D, PhD); materials science and engineering (MS, Eng Sc D, PhD); medical physics (MS). *Program availability:* Part-time, online learning. Terminal master's awarded for partial completion of doctoral program. *Degree requirements:* For master's, comprehensive exam; for doctorate, thesis/dissertation, qualifying exam. *Entrance requirements:* For master's, GRE General Test, GRE Subject Test (strongly recommended); for doctorate, GRE General Test, GRE Subject Test (applied physics). Additional exam requirements/recommendations for international students: Required—TOEFL, IELTS, PTE. Electronic applications accepted. *Faculty research:* Plasma physics and fusion energy; optical and laser physics; atmospheric, oceanic and earth physics; applied mathematics; solid state science and processing of materials, their properties, and their structure; medical physics.

Cornell University, Graduate School, Graduate Fields of Engineering, Field of Materials Science and Engineering, Ithaca, NY 14853. Offers materials engineering (M Eng, PhD); materials science (M Eng, PhD). *Degree requirements:* For doctorate, comprehensive exam, thesis/dissertation. *Entrance requirements:* For master's and doctorate, GRE General Test, 3 letters of recommendation. Additional exam requirements/recommendations for international students: Required—TOEFL (minimum score 550 paper-based; 77 iBT). Electronic applications accepted. *Faculty research:* Ceramics, complex fluids, glass, metals, polymers semiconductors.

Dalhousie University, Faculty of Engineering, Department of Materials Engineering, Halifax, NS B3H 1Z1, Canada. Offers M Eng, MA Sc, PhD. *Degree requirements:* For master's, thesis; for doctorate, thesis/dissertation. *Entrance requirements:* Additional exam requirements/recommendations for international students: Required—TOEFL, IELTS, CANTEST, CAEL, or Michigan English Language Assessment Battery. Electronic applications accepted. *Faculty research:* Ceramic and metal matrix composites, electron microscopy, electrolysis in molten salt, fracture mechanics, electronic materials.

Dartmouth College, Thayer School of Engineering, Program in Materials Sciences and Engineering, Hanover, NH 03755. Offers MS, PhD. *Degree requirements:* For master's, thesis; for doctorate, thesis/dissertation, candidacy oral exam. *Entrance requirements:* For master's and doctorate, GRE General Test. *Application deadline:* For fall admission, 1/1 priority date for domestic students. Application fee: $45. *Financial support:* Fellowships, research assistantships, teaching assistantships, career-related internships or fieldwork, Federal Work-Study, institutionally sponsored loans, and tuition waivers (full and partial) available. Financial award application deadline: 1/15. *Faculty research:* Electronic and magnetic materials, microstructural evolution, biomaterials and

nanostructures, laser-material interactions, nanocomposites. *Total annual research expenditures:* $5.9 million. *Unit head:* Dr. Joseph J. Helbie, Dean, 603-646-2238, Fax: 603-646-2580, E-mail: joseph.j.helbie@dartmouth.edu. *Application contact:* Candace S. Potter, Graduate Admissions Administrator, 603-646-3844, Fax: 603-646-1620, E-mail: candace.s.potter@dartmouth.edu.
Website: http://engineering.dartmouth.edu/

Drexel University, College of Engineering, Department of Materials Engineering, Philadelphia, PA 19104-2875. Offers MS, PhD. *Program availability:* Part-time, evening/weekend. *Faculty:* 19 full-time (5 women). *Students:* 70 full-time (26 women), 5 part-time (0 women); includes 14 minority (4 Black or African American, non-Hispanic/Latino; 2 American Indian or Alaska Native, non-Hispanic/Latino; 5 Asian, non-Hispanic/Latino; 3 Hispanic/Latino), 24 international. Average age 26. In 2016, 17 master's, 14 doctorates awarded. Terminal master's awarded for partial completion of doctoral program. *Degree requirements:* For master's, thesis or alternative; for doctorate, thesis/dissertation. *Entrance requirements:* For master's, minimum GPA of 3.0; for doctorate, minimum GPA of 3.0, MS. Additional exam requirements/recommendations for international students: Required—TOEFL. *Application deadline:* For fall admission, 8/21 for domestic students. Applications are processed on a rolling basis. Application fee: $50. Electronic applications accepted. *Expenses: Tuition:* Full-time $32,184; part-time $1192 per credit hour. *Required fees:* $280. Tuition and fees vary according to campus/location and program. *Financial support:* Research assistantships, teaching assistantships, career-related internships or fieldwork, and unspecified assistantships available. Financial award application deadline: 2/1. *Faculty research:* Composite science; polymer and biomedical engineering; solidification; near net shape processing, including powder metallurgy. *Unit head:* Dr. Roger Doherty, Acting Head, 215-895-2330. *Application contact:* Director of Graduate Admissions, 215-895-6700, Fax: 215-895-5939, E-mail: enroll@drexel.edu.

Duke University, Graduate School, Pratt School of Engineering, Master of Engineering Program, Durham, NC 27708-0271. Offers biomedical engineering (M Eng); civil engineering (M Eng); electrical and computer engineering (M Eng); environmental engineering (M Eng); materials science and engineering (M Eng); mechanical engineering (M Eng); photonics and optical sciences (M Eng). *Program availability:* Part-time. *Entrance requirements:* For master's, GRE General Test, resume, 3 letters of recommendation, statement of purpose, transcripts. Additional exam requirements/recommendations for international students: Required—TOEFL.

Florida International University, College of Engineering and Computing, Department of Mechanical and Materials Engineering, Miami, FL 33199. Offers materials science and engineering (MS, PhD); mechanical engineering (MS, PhD). *Program availability:* Part-time, evening/weekend. *Faculty:* 17 full-time (2 women), 6 part-time/adjunct (0 women). *Students:* 54 full-time (14 women), 27 part-time (3 women); includes 23 minority (5 Black or African American, non-Hispanic/Latino; 17 Hispanic/Latino; 1 Two or more races, non-Hispanic/Latino), 49 international. Average age 30. 105 applicants, 49% accepted, 12 enrolled. In 2016, 16 master's, 7 doctorates awarded. Terminal master's awarded for partial completion of doctoral program. *Degree requirements:* For master's, thesis or alternative; for doctorate, comprehensive exam, thesis/dissertation. *Entrance requirements:* For master's, GRE (depending on program), 3 letters of recommendation, minimum undergraduate GPA of 3.0 in upper-level course work; for doctorate, GRE (minimum combined score of 1150, verbal 450, quantitative 650), minimum undergraduate GPA of 3.0 in upper-level coursework with BS, 3.3 with MS; 3 letters of recommendation; letter of intent. Additional exam requirements/recommendations for international students: Required—TOEFL (minimum score 550 paper-based; 80 iBT) or IELTS (minimum score 6.5). *Application deadline:* For fall admission, 6/1 for domestic students, 4/1 for international students; for spring admission, 10/1 for domestic students, 9/1 for international students. Applications are processed on a rolling basis. Application fee: $30. Electronic applications accepted. *Expenses:* Tuition, state resident: full-time $8912; part-time $446 per credit hour. Tuition, nonresident: full-time $21,393; part-time $992 per credit hour. *Required fees:* $2185; $195 per semester. Tuition and fees vary according to program. *Financial support:* Institutionally sponsored loans, scholarships/grants, and unspecified assistantships available. Financial award application deadline: 3/1; financial award applicants required to submit FAFSA. *Faculty research:* Mechanics and materials, fluid/thermal/energy, design and manufacturing, materials science engineering. *Unit head:* Dr. Ibrahim Tansel, Chair, 305-348-3304, Fax: 305-348-6007, E-mail: tanseli@fiu.edu. *Application contact:* Sara-Michelle Lemus, Engineering Admissions Officer, 305-348-7442, Fax: 305-348-7441, E-mail: grad_eng@fiu.edu.
Website: http://cec.fiu.edu

Florida State University, The Graduate School, Materials Science and Engineering Program, Tallahassee, FL 32310. Offers MS, PhD. *Faculty:* 37 full-time (6 women). *Students:* 19 full-time (8 women); includes 1 minority (Hispanic/Latino), 14 international. Average age 28. 27 applicants, 26% accepted, 4 enrolled. In 2016, 3 master's awarded. Terminal master's awarded for partial completion of doctoral program. *Degree requirements:* For master's, thesis; for doctorate, comprehensive exam, thesis/dissertation. *Entrance requirements:* For master's and doctorate, GRE General Test (minimum new format 55th percentile Verbal, 75th percentile Quantitative, old version 1100 combined Verbal and Quantitative), minimum GPA of 3.0, 3 letters of recommendation. Additional exam requirements/recommendations for international students: Required—TOEFL (minimum score 80 iBT). *Application deadline:* For fall admission, 5/1 for domestic and international students; for spring admission, 9/1 for domestic and international students; for summer admission, 1/1 for domestic and international students. Applications are processed on a rolling basis. Application fee: $30. Electronic applications accepted. *Expenses:* Tuition, state resident: full-time $7263; part-time $403.51 per credit hour. Tuition, nonresident: full-time $18,087; part-time $1004.85 per credit hour. *Required fees:* $1365; $75.81 per credit hour. $20 per semester. Tuition and fees vary according to campus/location. *Financial support:* In 2016–17, 18 students received support, including 18 research assistantships with full tuition reimbursements available (averaging $23,104 per year); partial payment of required health insurance also available. Financial award application deadline: 12/15. *Faculty research:* Magnetism and magnetic materials, composites, superconductors, polymers, computations, nanotechnology. *Unit head:* Prof. Eric Hellstrom, Director, 850-645-7489, Fax: 850-645-7754, E-mail: hellstrom@asc.magnet.fsu.edu. *Application contact:* Judy Gardner, Admissions Coordinator, 850-645-8980, Fax: 850-645-9123, E-mail: jdgardner@fsu.edu.
Website: http://materials.fsu.edu

Georgia Institute of Technology, Graduate Studies, College of Engineering, School of Materials Science and Engineering, Atlanta, GA 30332-0001. Offers MS, PhD. *Program availability:* Part-time. Terminal master's awarded for partial completion of doctoral program. *Degree requirements:* For master's, thesis optional; for doctorate, comprehensive exam, thesis/dissertation, teaching assignment. *Entrance requirements:* For master's and doctorate, GRE General Test. Additional exam requirements/recommendations for international students: Required—TOEFL (minimum score 620 paper-based; 105 iBT). Electronic applications accepted. *Faculty research:* Nanomaterials, biomaterials, computational materials science, mechanical behavior, advanced engineering materials.

Illinois Institute of Technology, Graduate College, Armour College of Engineering, Department of Mechanical, Materials and Aerospace Engineering, Chicago, IL 60616. Offers manufacturing engineering (MAS, MS); materials science and engineering (MAS, MS, PhD); mechanical and aerospace engineering (MAS, MS, PhD), including economics (MS), energy (MS), environment (MS). *Program availability:* Part-time, evening/weekend, online learning. Terminal master's awarded for partial completion of doctoral program. *Degree requirements:* For master's, comprehensive exam (for some programs), thesis (for some programs); for doctorate, comprehensive exam, thesis/dissertation. *Entrance requirements:* For master's and doctorate, GRE General Test (minimum score 1000 Quantitative and Verbal, 3.0 Analytical Writing), minimum undergraduate GPA of 3.0. Additional exam requirements/recommendations for international students: Required—TOEFL (minimum score 550 paper-based; 80 iBT). Electronic applications accepted. *Faculty research:* Fluid dynamics, metallurgical and materials engineering, solids and structures, computational mechanics, computer added design and manufacturing, thermal sciences, dynamic analysis and control of complex systems.

Instituto Tecnológico y de Estudios Superiores de Monterrey, Campus Estado de México, Professional and Graduate Division, Estado de Mexico, Mexico. Offers administration of information technologies (MITA); architecture (M Arch); business administration (GMBA, MBA); computer sciences (MCS, PhD); education (M Ed); educational institution administration (MAD); educational technology and innovation (PhD); electronic commerce (MEC); environmental systems (MS); finance (MAF); humanistic studies (MHS); information sciences and knowledge management (MISKM); information systems (MS); manufacturing systems (MS); marketing (MEM); quality systems and productivity (MS); science and materials engineering (PhD); telecommunications management (MTM). *Program availability:* Part-time, online learning. *Degree requirements:* For master's, one foreign language, thesis (for some programs); for doctorate, one foreign language, thesis/dissertation. *Entrance requirements:* For master's, E-PAEP 500, interview; for doctorate, E-PAEP 500, research proposal. Additional exam requirements/recommendations for international students: Required—TOEFL (minimum score 550 paper-based). *Faculty research:* Surface treatments by plasmas, mechanical properties, robotics, graphical computing, mechatronics security protocols.

Iowa State University of Science and Technology, Department of Materials Science and Engineering, Ames, IA 50011. Offers M Eng, MS, PhD. *Entrance requirements:* For master's and doctorate, GRE General Test. Additional exam requirements/recommendations for international students: Required—TOEFL (minimum score 550 paper-based; 79 iBT), IELTS (minimum score 6.5). *Application deadline:* For fall admission, 1/15 priority date for domestic and international students; for spring admission, 8/15 priority date for domestic and international students. Application fee: $60 ($90 for international students). Electronic applications accepted. *Financial support:* Teaching assistantships, scholarships/grants, health care benefits, and unspecified assistantships available. *Application contact:* Patrick Morton, Director of Graduate Education, 515-294-1214, Fax: 515-294-5444, E-mail: gradmse@iastate.edu.
Website: http://www.mse.iastate.edu

Johns Hopkins University, Engineering Program for Professionals, Part-time Program in Materials Science and Engineering, Baltimore, MD 21218. Offers nanotechnology (M Mat SE). *Program availability:* Part-time, evening/weekend. *Faculty:* 2 part-time/adjunct (1 woman). *Students:* 3 full-time (2 women), 16 part-time (3 women); includes 4 minority (2 Black or African American, non-Hispanic/Latino; 1 Asian, non-Hispanic/Latino; 1 Hispanic/Latino). Average age 28. 6 applicants, 83% accepted, 5 enrolled. In 2016, 5 master's awarded. *Entrance requirements:* Additional exam requirements/recommendations for international students: Required—TOEFL (minimum score 600 paper-based; 100 iBT). *Application deadline:* Applications are processed on a rolling basis. Application fee: $0. Electronic applications accepted. *Unit head:* Dr. James Spicer, Program Chair, 410-516-8524, E-mail: spicer@jhu.edu. *Application contact:* Doug Schiller, Admissions Director, 410-516-2300, Fax: 410-579-8049, E-mail: schiller@jhu.edu.
Website: http://www.ep.jhu.edu

Johns Hopkins University, G. W. C. Whiting School of Engineering, Department of Materials Science and Engineering, Baltimore, MD 21218. Offers M Mat SE, MSE, PhD. *Faculty:* 17 full-time (4 women), 2 part-time/adjunct (1 woman). *Students:* 70 full-time (23 women), 2 part-time (0 women); includes 14 minority (1 Black or African American, non-Hispanic/Latino; 8 Asian, non-Hispanic/Latino; 3 Hispanic/Latino; 2 Two or more races, non-Hispanic/Latino), 30 international. Average age 26. 243 applicants, 19% accepted, 21 enrolled. In 2016, 23 master's, 9 doctorates awarded. Terminal master's awarded for partial completion of doctoral program. *Degree requirements:* For master's, thesis; for doctorate, thesis/dissertation, oral exam, thesis defense. *Entrance requirements:* For master's and doctorate, GRE General Test, 2 letters of recommendation, statement of purpose, transcripts. Additional exam requirements/recommendations for international students: Required—TOEFL (minimum score 600 paper-based, 100 iBT) or IELTS (7). *Application deadline:* For fall admission, 12/15 priority date for domestic and international students; for spring admission, 10/17 priority date for domestic and international students. Application fee: $75. Electronic applications accepted. *Financial support:* In 2016–17, 70 students received support, including 9 fellowships with full tuition reimbursements available (averaging $30,200 per year), 55 research assistantships with full tuition reimbursements available (averaging $30,200 per year), teaching assistantships with full tuition reimbursements available (averaging $30,200 per year); Federal Work-Study, institutionally sponsored loans, health care benefits, tuition waivers (full), and unspecified assistantships also available. Financial award application deadline: 3/15. *Faculty research:* Biomaterials; computational materials science; materials for energy; nanomaterials; optoelectronic and magnetic materials; structural materials. *Total annual research expenditures:* $8.3 million. *Unit head:* Dr. Jonah Erlebacher, Chair, 410-516-6141, Fax: 410-516-5293, E-mail: jonah.erlebacher@jhu.edu. *Application contact:* Jeanine Majewski, Academic Coordinator, 410-516-8760, Fax: 410-516-5293, E-mail: dmse-gradadmissions@jhu.edu.
Website: http://engineering.jhu.edu/materials/

Johns Hopkins University, G. W. C. Whiting School of Engineering, Master of Science in Engineering Management Program, Baltimore, MD 21218. Offers biomaterials (MSEM); civil engineering (MSEM); communications science (MSEM); computer science (MSEM); environmental systems analysis, economics and public policy (MSEM); fluid mechanics (MSEM); materials science and engineering (MSEM); mechanical engineering (MSEM); mechanics and materials (MSEM); nano-biotechnology (MSEM); nanomaterials and nanotechnology (MSEM); operations research (MSEM); probability and statistics (MSEM); smart product and device design (MSEM). *Faculty:* 7 full-time (4 women), 1 part-time/adjunct (0 women). *Students:* 35 full-time (14 women), 8 part-time (3 women); includes 7 minority (4 Asian, non-Hispanic/Latino; 3 Hispanic/Latino), 26 international. Average age 24. 228 applicants, 28% accepted, 25 enrolled. In 2016, 18 master's awarded. *Entrance requirements:* For master's, GRE, 3 letters of recommendation, statement of purpose, transcripts. Additional exam requirements/recommendations for international students: Required—TOEFL (minimum score 600 paper-based, 100 iBT) or IELTS (7). *Application deadline:*

For fall admission, 2/1 for domestic and international students. Application fee: $75. Electronic applications accepted. *Financial support:* Fellowships and health care benefits available. *Unit head:* Dr. Pamela Sheff, Director, 410-516-7056, Fax: 410-516-4880, E-mail: pamsheff@gmail.com. *Application contact:* Richard Helman, Director of Graduate Admissions, 410-516-8174, Fax: 410-516-0780, E-mail: graduateadmissions@jhu.edu.
Website: http://engineering.jhu.edu/msem/

Lehigh University, P.C. Rossin College of Engineering and Applied Science, Department of Materials Science and Engineering, Bethlehem, PA 18015. Offers materials science and engineering (M Eng, MS, PhD); photonics (MS); polymer science/engineering (M Eng, MS, PhD); MBA/E. *Program availability:* Part-time. *Faculty:* 15 full-time (3 women). *Students:* 23 full-time (4 women), 4 part-time (2 women); includes 3 minority (2 Asian, non-Hispanic/Latino; 1 Two or more races, non-Hispanic/Latino), 8 international. Average age 27. 143 applicants, 6% accepted, 4 enrolled. In 2016, 4 master's, 8 doctorates awarded. *Degree requirements:* For master's, thesis; for doctorate, comprehensive exam, thesis/dissertation. *Entrance requirements:* For master's and doctorate, GRE General Test, minimum GPA of 3.0. Additional exam requirements/recommendations for international students: Required—TOEFL (minimum score 487 paper-based; 85 iBT), IELTS (minimum score 6.5). *Application deadline:* For fall admission, 1/15 priority date for domestic students, 1/15 for international students; for spring admission, 12/1 priority date for domestic students, 12/1 for international students. Applications are processed on a rolling basis. Application fee: $75. Electronic applications accepted. *Expenses:* $1,420 per credit hour. *Financial support:* In 2016–17, 25 students received support, including 3 fellowships with tuition reimbursements available (averaging $21,105 per year), 19 research assistantships with tuition reimbursements available (averaging $28,140 per year), 6 teaching assistantships with tuition reimbursements available (averaging $21,530 per year); scholarships/grants and health care benefits also available. Financial award application deadline: 1/15. *Faculty research:* Metals, ceramics, crystals, polymers, fatigue crack propagation, biomaterials. *Total annual research expenditures:* $3.1 million. *Unit head:* Dr. Wojciech Misiolek, Chairperson, 610-758-4252, Fax: 610-758-4244, E-mail: wzm2@lehigh.edu. *Application contact:* Lisa Carreras Arechiga, Graduate Administrative Coordinator, 610-758-4222, Fax: 610-758-4244, E-mail: lia4@lehigh.edu.
Website: http://www.lehigh.edu/~inmatsci/

Massachusetts Institute of Technology, School of Engineering, Department of Civil and Environmental Engineering, Cambridge, MA 02139. Offers biological oceanography (PhD, Sc D); chemical oceanography (PhD, Sc D); civil and environmental engineering (M Eng, SM, PhD, Sc D); civil and environmental systems (PhD, Sc D); civil engineering (PhD, Sc D, CE); civil engineering and computation (PhD); coastal engineering (PhD, Sc D); construction engineering and management (PhD, Sc D); environmental biology (PhD, Sc D); environmental chemistry (PhD, Sc D); environmental engineering (PhD, Sc D); environmental engineering and computation (PhD); environmental fluid mechanics (PhD, Sc D); geotechnical and geoenvironmental engineering (PhD, Sc D); hydrology (PhD, Sc D); information technology (PhD, Sc D); oceanographic engineering (PhD, Sc D); structures and materials (PhD, Sc D); transportation (PhD, Sc D); SM/MBA. *Faculty:* 35 full-time (6 women). *Students:* 192 full-time (64 women); includes 25 minority (2 Black or African American, non-Hispanic/Latino; 11 Asian, non-Hispanic/Latino; 8 Hispanic/Latino; 4 Two or more races, non-Hispanic/Latino), 113 international. Average age 27. 530 applicants, 20% accepted, 77 enrolled. In 2016, 56 master's, 16 doctorates, 1 other advanced degree awarded. *Degree requirements:* For master's, thesis; for doctorate, comprehensive exam, thesis/dissertation; for CE, comprehensive exam, thesis. *Entrance requirements:* For master's, doctorate, and CE, GRE General Test. Additional exam requirements/recommendations for international students: Required—TOEFL, IELTS. *Application deadline:* For fall admission, 12/15 for domestic and international students. Application fee: $75. Electronic applications accepted. *Expenses: Tuition:* Full-time $46,400; part-time $725 per credit. One-time fee: $312 full-time. Full-time tuition and fees vary according to course load and program. *Financial support:* In 2016–17, 150 students received support, including fellowships (averaging $41,900 per year), 124 research assistantships (averaging $36,900 per year), 9 teaching assistantships (averaging $36,900 per year); Federal Work-Study, institutionally sponsored loans, scholarships/grants, traineeships, health care benefits, unspecified assistantships, and resident tutors also available. Support available to part-time students. Financial award application deadline: 5/1; financial award applicants required to submit FAFSA. *Faculty research:* Environmental chemistry, environmental fluid mechanics and coastal engineering, environmental microbiology, geotechnical engineering and geomechanics, hydrology and hydro climatology, infrastructure systems, mechanics of materials and structures, transportation systems. *Total annual research expenditures:* $25 million. *Unit head:* Prof. Markus Buehler, Department Head, 617-253-7101. *Application contact:* 617-253-7119, E-mail: cee-admissions@mit.edu.
Website: http://cee.mit.edu/

Massachusetts Institute of Technology, School of Engineering, Department of Materials Science and Engineering, Cambridge, MA 02139. Offers archaeological materials (PhD, Sc D); materials engineering (Mat E); materials science and engineering (SM, PhD, Sc D). *Faculty:* 32 full-time (10 women). *Students:* 170 full-time (43 women); includes 29 minority (1 Black or African American, non-Hispanic/Latino; 17 Asian, non-Hispanic/Latino; 6 Hispanic/Latino; 5 Two or more races, non-Hispanic/Latino), 93 international. Average age 26. 463 applicants, 12% accepted, 28 enrolled. In 2016, 5 master's, 39 doctorates awarded. *Degree requirements:* For master's, thesis; for doctorate, comprehensive exam, thesis/dissertation; for Mat E, comprehensive exam, thesis. *Entrance requirements:* For master's and doctorate, GRE General Test. Additional exam requirements/recommendations for international students: Required—IELTS. *Application deadline:* For fall admission, 12/1 for domestic and international students. Application fee: $75. Electronic applications accepted. *Expenses: Tuition:* Full-time $46,400; part-time $725 per credit. One-time fee: $312 full-time. Full-time tuition and fees vary according to course load and program. *Financial support:* In 2016–17, 159 students received support, including fellowships (averaging $34,000 per year), 103 research assistantships (averaging $37,500 per year), 16 teaching assistantships (averaging $39,800 per year); Federal Work-Study, institutionally sponsored loans, scholarships/grants, traineeships, health care benefits, unspecified assistantships, and resident tutors also available. Support available to part-time students. Financial award application deadline: 5/1; financial award applicants required to submit FAFSA. *Faculty research:* Thermodynamics and kinetics of materials; structure, processing and properties of materials; electronic, structural and biological materials engineering; computational materials science; materials in energy, medicine, nanotechnology and the environment. *Total annual research expenditures:* $25.5 million. *Unit head:* Prof. Christopher Schuh, Department Head, 617-253-3300, Fax: 617-252-1775, E-mail: dmse@mit.edu. *Application contact:* 617-253-3302, E-mail: dmse-admissions@mit.edu.
Website: http://dmse.mit.edu/

McGill University, Faculty of Graduate and Postdoctoral Studies, Faculty of Engineering, Department of Civil Engineering and Applied Mechanics, Montréal, QC H3A 2T5, Canada. Offers environmental engineering (M Eng, M Sc, PhD); fluid mechanics (M Sc); fluid mechanics and hydraulic engineering (M Eng, PhD); materials engineering (M Eng, PhD); rehabilitation of urban infrastructure (M Eng, PhD); soil behavior (M Eng, PhD); soil mechanics and foundations (M Eng, PhD); structures and structural mechanics (M Eng, PhD); water resources (M Sc); water resources engineering (M Eng, PhD).

McGill University, Faculty of Graduate and Postdoctoral Studies, Faculty of Engineering, Department of Mining and Materials Engineering, Montréal, QC H3A 2T5, Canada. Offers materials engineering (M Eng, PhD); mining engineering (M Eng, M Sc, PhD, Diploma).

McMaster University, School of Graduate Studies, Faculty of Engineering, Department of Materials Science and Engineering, Hamilton, ON L8S 4M2, Canada. Offers materials engineering (M Eng, MA Sc, PhD); materials science (M Eng, PhD). *Degree requirements:* For master's, thesis; for doctorate, comprehensive exam, thesis/dissertation. *Entrance requirements:* Additional exam requirements/recommendations for international students: Required—TOEFL (minimum score 550 paper-based). *Faculty research:* Localized corrosion of metals and alloys, electron microscopy, polymer synthesis and characterization, polymer reaction kinetics and engineering, polymer process modeling.

Michigan State University, The Graduate School, College of Engineering, Department of Chemical Engineering and Materials Science, East Lansing, MI 48824. Offers chemical engineering (MS, PhD); materials science and engineering (MS, PhD). *Entrance requirements:* Additional exam requirements/recommendations for international students: Required—TOEFL. Electronic applications accepted.

Michigan Technological University, Graduate School, College of Engineering, Department of Materials Science and Engineering, Houghton, MI 49931. Offers MS, PhD. *Program availability:* Part-time, online learning. *Faculty:* 32 full-time, 18 part-time/adjunct. *Students:* 33 full-time (12 women), 4 part-time, 26 international. Average age 26. 199 applicants, 25% accepted, 10 enrolled. In 2016, 4 master's, 3 doctorates awarded. Terminal master's awarded for partial completion of doctoral program. *Degree requirements:* For master's, comprehensive exam (for some programs), thesis (for some programs); for doctorate, comprehensive exam, thesis/dissertation. *Entrance requirements:* For master's and doctorate, GRE (domestic students from ABET-accredited programs exempt), statement of purpose, personal statement, official transcripts, 3 letters of recommendation. Additional exam requirements/recommendations for international students: Required—TOEFL (recommended minimum score 79 iBT) or IELTS, GRE. *Application deadline:* For fall admission, 2/1 priority date for domestic and international students; for spring admission, 8/15 priority date for domestic and international students. Applications are processed on a rolling basis. Electronic applications accepted. *Expenses:* Contact institution. *Financial support:* In 2016–17, 27 students received support, including 3 fellowships with tuition reimbursements available (averaging $15,242 per year), 14 research assistantships with tuition reimbursements available (averaging $15,242 per year), teaching assistantships with tuition reimbursements available (averaging $15,242 per year); career-related internships or fieldwork, Federal Work-Study, scholarships/grants, health care benefits, unspecified assistantships, and cooperative program also available. Financial award applicants required to submit FAFSA. *Faculty research:* Structure/property/processing relationships, microstructural characterization, alloy design, electronic/magnetic/photonic materials, materials and manufacturing processes. *Total annual research expenditures:* $3 million. *Unit head:* Dr. Stephen L. Kampe, Chair, 906-487-2036, Fax: 906-487-2934, E-mail: kampe@mtu.edu. *Application contact:* Stephen A. Hackney, Associate Department Chair for Graduate Studies, 906-487-2170, Fax: 906-487-2934, E-mail: hackney@mtu.edu.
Website: http://www.mtu.edu/materials/

New Jersey Institute of Technology, College of Science and Liberal Arts, Newark, NJ 07102. Offers applied mathematics (MS); applied physics (M Sc, PhD); applied statistics (MS, Certificate); biology (MS, PhD); biostatistics (MS); chemistry (MS, PhD); computational biology (MS); environmental and sustainability policy (MS); environmental science (MS, PhD); history (MA, MAT); materials science and engineering (MS, PhD); mathematical and computational finance (MS); mathematics science (PhD); pharmaceutical chemistry (MS); practice of technical communications (Certificate); professional and technical communications (MS). *Program availability:* Part-time, evening/weekend. *Faculty:* 166 full-time (39 women), 87 part-time/adjunct (32 women). *Students:* 196 full-time (71 women), 68 part-time (33 women); includes 55 minority (15 Black or African American, non-Hispanic/Latino; 19 Asian, non-Hispanic/Latino; 15 Hispanic/Latino; 6 Two or more races, non-Hispanic/Latino), 140 international. Average age 28. 504 applicants, 64% accepted, 65 enrolled. In 2016, 81 master's, 18 doctorates, 1 other advanced degree awarded. Terminal master's awarded for partial completion of doctoral program. *Degree requirements:* For master's, thesis optional; for doctorate, thesis/dissertation. *Entrance requirements:* For master's, GRE General Test; for doctorate, GRE General Test, minimum graduate GPA of 3.5. Additional exam requirements/recommendations for international students: Required—TOEFL (minimum score 550 paper-based; 79 iBT). *Application deadline:* For fall admission, 6/1 priority date for domestic students, 5/1 priority date for international students; for spring admission, 11/15 priority date for domestic and international students. Applications are processed on a rolling basis. Application fee: $75. Electronic applications accepted. *Expenses:* Contact institution. *Financial support:* In 2016–17, 106 students received support, including 32 research assistantships (averaging $17,108 per year), 74 teaching assistantships (averaging $21,368 per year); fellowships, scholarships/grants, traineeships, and unspecified assistantships also available. Financial award application deadline: 1/15. *Faculty research:* Biophotonics and bioimaging, morphogenetic patterning, embryogenesis, biological fluid dynamics, applied research in the mathematical sciences. *Unit head:* Dr. Kevin Belfield, Dean, 973-596-3676, Fax: 973-565-0586, E-mail: kevin.d.belfield@njit.edu. *Application contact:* Stephen Eck, Director of Admissions, 973-596-3300, Fax: 973-596-3461, E-mail: admissions@njit.edu.
Website: http://csla.njit.edu/

New Mexico Institute of Mining and Technology, Center for Graduate Studies, Department of Materials Engineering, Socorro, NM 87801. Offers MS, PhD. *Degree requirements:* For master's, thesis; for doctorate, thesis/dissertation. *Entrance requirements:* For master's, GRE General Test; for doctorate, GRE General Test, GRE Subject Test. Additional exam requirements/recommendations for international students: Required—TOEFL (minimum score 540 paper-based). *Faculty research:* Thin films, ceramics, damage studies from radiation, corrosion shock.

North Carolina State University, Graduate School, College of Engineering, Department of Materials Science and Engineering, Raleigh, NC 27695. Offers MMSE, MS, PhD. PhD offered jointly with The University of North Carolina at Charlotte. *Degree requirements:* For master's, thesis; for doctorate, thesis/dissertation. Electronic applications accepted. *Faculty research:* Processing and properties of wide band gap semiconductors, ferroelectric thin-film materials, ductility of nanocrystalline materials, computational materials science, defects in silicon-based devices.

Northwestern University, McCormick School of Engineering and Applied Science, Department of Materials Science and Engineering, Evanston, IL 60208. Offers integrated computational materials engineering (Certificate); materials science and engineering (MS, PhD). Admissions and degrees offered through The Graduate School. *Program availability:* Part-time. Terminal master's awarded for partial completion of doctoral program. *Degree requirements:* For master's, thesis optional, oral thesis defense; for doctorate, comprehensive exam, thesis/dissertation, oral defense of dissertation, preliminary evaluation, qualifying exam. *Entrance requirements:* For master's and doctorate, GRE General Test. Additional exam requirements/ recommendations for international students: Required—TOEFL (minimum score 577 paper-based; 90 iBT), IELTS (minimum score 7). Electronic applications accepted. *Faculty research:* Art conservation science; biomaterials; ceramics; composites; energy; magnetic materials; materials for electronics and photonics; materials synthesis and processing; materials theory, computation, and design; metals; nanomaterials; polymers, self-assembly, and surfaces and interfaces.

The Ohio State University, Graduate School, College of Engineering, Department of Materials Science and Engineering, Columbus, OH 43210. Offers materials science and engineering (MS, PhD); welding engineering (MS, PhD). *Faculty:* 37. *Students:* 141 full-time (37 women), 47 part-time (9 women); includes 17 minority (9 Asian, non-Hispanic/ Latino; 8 Hispanic/Latino), 53 international. Average age 28. In 2016, 41 master's, 18 doctorates awarded. *Degree requirements:* For master's, thesis; for doctorate, thesis/ dissertation. *Entrance requirements:* For master's and doctorate, GRE (for graduates of foreign universities and holders of non-engineering degrees). Additional exam requirements/recommendations for international students: Required—TOEFL (minimum score 550 paper-based; 79 iBT), Michigan English Language Assessment Battery (minimum score 82); Recommended—IELTS (minimum score 7). *Application deadline:* For fall admission, 12/13 priority date for domestic students, 11/30 priority date for international students; for spring admission, 12/14 for domestic students, 11/12 for international students; for summer admission, 5/15 for domestic students, 4/14 for international students. Applications are processed on a rolling basis. Application fee: $60 ($70 for international students). Electronic applications accepted. *Financial support:* Fellowships with tuition reimbursements, research assistantships with tuition reimbursements, teaching assistantships, career-related internships or fieldwork, scholarships/grants, and unspecified assistantships available. *Faculty research:* Computational materials modeling, biomaterials, metallurgy, ceramics, advanced alloys/ composites. *Unit head:* Dr. Peter Anderson, Chair, 614-292-6255, E-mail: anderson.1@osu.edu. *Application contact:* Mark Cooper, Graduate Studies Coordinator, 614-292-7280, Fax: 614-292-1357, E-mail: mse@osu.edu.
Website: http://mse.osu.edu/

Oklahoma State University, College of Engineering, Architecture and Technology, School of Materials Science and Engineering, Stillwater, OK 74078. Offers MS, PhD. *Faculty:* 7 full-time (0 women). *Students:* 3 full-time (1 woman), 17 part-time (5 women); includes 3 minority (1 Asian, non-Hispanic/Latino; 2 Two or more races, non-Hispanic/ Latino), 13 international. Average age 28. 16 applicants, 38% accepted, 5 enrolled. *Entrance requirements:* Additional exam requirements/recommendations for international students: Required—TOEFL. *Application deadline:* For fall admission, 3/1 for domestic students; for spring admission, 8/1 for domestic students. Application fee: $40 ($75 for international students). Electronic applications accepted. *Expenses:* Tuition, state resident: full-time $3775; part-time $209.70 per credit hour. Tuition, nonresident: full-time $14,851; part-time $825.05 per credit hour. *Required fees:* $2027; $112.60 per credit hour. Tuition and fees vary according to campus/location. *Financial support:* In 2016–17, 13 research assistantships (averaging $18,193 per year), 4 teaching assistantships (averaging $10,229 per year) were awarded. *Unit head:* Dr. Raj N. Singh, Head, 918-594-8650, E-mail: rajns@okstate.edu.
Website: http://mse.okstate.edu/

Penn State University Park, Graduate School, Intercollege Graduate Programs, Intercollege Graduate Program in Materials Science and Engineering, University Park, PA 16802. Offers MS, PhD. *Financial support:* Fellowships available. *Unit head:* Dr. Regina Vasilatos-Younken, Dean, 814-865-2516, Fax: 814-863-4627. *Application contact:* Lori Hawn, Director, Graduate Student Services, 814-865-1795, Fax: 814-863-4627, E-mail: l-gswww@lists.psu.edu.
Website: http://matse.psu.edu/graduate

Purdue University, College of Engineering, School of Materials Engineering, West Lafayette, IN 47907-2045. Offers MSMSE, PhD. *Program availability:* Part-time. *Faculty:* 52. *Students:* 142. In 2016, 7 master's, 8 doctorates awarded. *Degree requirements:* For master's, thesis optional; for doctorate, thesis/dissertation. *Entrance requirements:* For master's and doctorate, GRE (highly recommended), minimum GPA of 3.0. Additional exam requirements/recommendations for international students: Required—GRE. *Application deadline:* For fall admission, 1/1 for domestic and international students. Applications are processed on a rolling basis. Application fee: $60 ($75 for international students). Electronic applications accepted. *Financial support:* Fellowships with full and partial tuition reimbursements, research assistantships with full and partial tuition reimbursements, teaching assistantships with full and partial tuition reimbursements, career-related internships or fieldwork, scholarships/grants, health care benefits, and unspecified assistantships available. Support available to part-time students. Financial award applicants required to submit FAFSA. *Faculty research:* Processing, characterization, properties, and modeling of metals, electronics, ceramics, biomaterials, polymers/soft matter and composites. *Unit head:* Dr. David Bahr, Head and Professor of Materials Engineering, E-mail: dfbahr@purdue.edu. *Application contact:* Vicki Cline, Academic Program Administrator, E-mail: msegrad@purdue.edu.
Website: https://engineering.purdue.edu/MSE

Rensselaer Polytechnic Institute, Graduate School, School of Engineering, Program in Materials Science and Engineering, Troy, NY 12180-3590. Offers M Eng, MS, D Eng, PhD. *Faculty:* 17 full-time (3 women), 1 part-time/adjunct (0 women). *Students:* 43 full-time (14 women), 6 part-time (2 women). 159 applicants, 19% accepted, 9 enrolled. In 2016, 3 master's, 6 doctorates awarded. Terminal master's awarded for partial completion of doctoral program. *Degree requirements:* For master's, thesis; for doctorate, comprehensive exam, thesis/dissertation. *Entrance requirements:* For master's and doctorate, GRE. Additional exam requirements/recommendations for international students: Required—TOEFL (minimum score 600 paper-based; 100 iBT), IELTS (minimum score 7), PTE (minimum score 68). *Application deadline:* For fall admission, 1/1 priority date for domestic and international students; for spring admission, 8/15 priority date for domestic and international students. Applications are processed on a rolling basis. Application fee: $75. Electronic applications accepted. *Expenses: Tuition:* Full-time $49,520; part-time $2060 per credit hour. *Required fees:* $2617. *Financial support:* In 2016–17, research assistantships with full tuition reimbursements (averaging $22,000 per year), teaching assistantships with full tuition reimbursements (averaging $22,000 per year) were awarded; fellowships also available. Financial award application deadline: 1/1. *Faculty research:* Advanced processing and synthesis, composites, computational materials, corrosion/electrochemical materials, electronic materials, glasses/ceramics, materials characterization, materials for energy, materials/biology interface, metals, nanomaterials, polymeric materials. *Total annual research expenditures:* $2.6 million. *Unit head:* Dr. Liping Huang, Graduate Program Director, 518-276-2174, E-mail: huangl5@rpi.edu. *Application contact:* Office of Graduate Admissions, 518-276-6216, E-mail: gradadmissions@rpi.edu.
Website: http://mse.rpi.edu/graduate

Rochester Institute of Technology, Graduate Enrollment Services, College of Science, School of Chemistry and Materials Science, MS Program in Materials Science and Engineering, Rochester, NY 14623-5603. Offers MS. Offered jointly with Kate Gleason College of Engineering. *Program availability:* Part-time, evening/weekend. *Students:* 13 full-time (2 women), 4 part-time (1 woman); includes 2 minority (1 Black or African American, non-Hispanic/Latino; 1 Asian, non-Hispanic/Latino), 10 international. Average age 25. 41 applicants, 59% accepted, 8 enrolled. In 2016, 8 master's awarded. *Degree requirements:* For master's, thesis or project. *Entrance requirements:* For master's, GRE or GMAT, minimum GPA of 3.0 (recommended). Additional exam requirements/recommendations for international students: Required—TOEFL (minimum score 575 paper-based; 90 iBT), IELTS (minimum score 6.5), PTE (minimum score 62). *Application deadline:* Applications are processed on a rolling basis. Electronic applications accepted. *Expenses:* $1,742 per credit hour. *Financial support:* In 2016–17, 11 students received support. Research assistantships with partial tuition reimbursements available, teaching assistantships with partial tuition reimbursements available, career-related internships or fieldwork, scholarships/grants, and unspecified assistantships available. Support available to part-time students. Financial award applicants required to submit FAFSA. *Faculty research:* Magnetism and magnetic materials, photovoltaics and batteries, electronic materials, functional nanomaterials, 3D printing and additive manufacturing. *Unit head:* Casey Miller, Director, 585-475-4148, E-mail: cwmsch@rit.edu. *Application contact:* Diane Ellison, Associate Vice President, Graduate Enrollment Services, 585-475-2229, Fax: 585-475-7164, E-mail: gradinfo@rit.edu.
Website: https://www.rit.edu/cos/cmse/

Rutgers University–New Brunswick, Graduate School-New Brunswick, Program in Materials Science and Engineering, Piscataway, NJ 08854-8097. Offers MS, PhD. *Program availability:* Part-time. *Degree requirements:* For master's, thesis; for doctorate, comprehensive exam, thesis/dissertation. *Entrance requirements:* For master's and doctorate, GRE General Test. Additional exam requirements/recommendations for international students: Recommended—TOEFL. Electronic applications accepted. *Faculty research:* Ceramic processing, nanostructured materials, electrical and structural ceramics, fiber optics.

South Dakota School of Mines and Technology, Graduate Division, Doctoral Program in Materials Engineering and Science, Rapid City, SD 57701-3995. Offers PhD. *Program availability:* Part-time. *Degree requirements:* For doctorate, thesis/dissertation. *Entrance requirements:* For doctorate, GRE General Test, minimum graduate GPA of 3.0, 3 letters of recommendation. Additional exam requirements/recommendations for international students: Required—TOEFL (minimum score 520 paper-based; 68 iBT), TWE. Electronic applications accepted.

South Dakota School of Mines and Technology, Graduate Division, Master's Program in Materials Engineering and Science, Rapid City, SD 57701-3995. Offers MS. *Degree requirements:* For master's, thesis (for some programs). *Entrance requirements:* For master's, GRE General Test. Additional exam requirements/recommendations for international students: Required—TOEFL (minimum score 520 paper-based; 68 iBT), TWE. Electronic applications accepted.

Southern Methodist University, Dedman College of Humanities and Sciences, Department of Chemistry, Dallas, TX 75275-0314. Offers chemistry (MS, PhD); materials science and engineering (MS, PhD). Terminal master's awarded for partial completion of doctoral program. *Degree requirements:* For master's, thesis; for doctorate, comprehensive exam, thesis/dissertation. *Entrance requirements:* For master's, GRE General Test, bachelor's degree in chemistry, minimum GPA of 3.0; for doctorate, GRE General Test, bachelor's degree in chemistry or closely-related field, minimum GPA of 3.0. Additional exam requirements/recommendations for international students: Required—TOEFL (minimum score 550 paper-based; 80 iBT). Electronic applications accepted. *Faculty research:* Materials/polymer, medicinal/bioorganic, theoretical and computational, organic/inorganic/organometallic synthesis, inorganic polymer chemistry.

Stanford University, School of Engineering, Department of Materials Science and Engineering, Stanford, CA 94305-2004. Offers MS, PhD, Engr. Terminal master's awarded for partial completion of doctoral program. *Degree requirements:* For doctorate, thesis/dissertation; for Engr, thesis. *Entrance requirements:* For master's, doctorate, and Engr, GRE General Test. Additional exam requirements/recommendations for international students: Required—TOEFL. Electronic applications accepted. *Expenses: Tuition:* Full-time $47,331. *Required fees:* $609.

Stevens Institute of Technology, Graduate School, Charles V. Schaefer Jr. School of Engineering and Science, Department of Chemical Engineering and Materials Science, Program in Materials Science and Engineering, Hoboken, NJ 07030. Offers M Eng, PhD. *Program availability:* Part-time, evening/weekend. *Students:* 81 full-time (21 women), 2 part-time (1 woman), 79 international. Average age 25. 261 applicants, 61% accepted, 35 enrolled. In 2016, 36 master's awarded. *Degree requirements:* For master's, thesis optional, minimum B average in major field and overall; for doctorate, comprehensive exam (for some programs), thesis/dissertation. *Entrance requirements:* Additional exam requirements/recommendations for international students: Required—TOEFL (minimum score 74 iBT), IELTS (minimum score 6). *Application deadline:* For fall admission, 6/1 for domestic students, 4/15 for international students; for spring admission, 11/30 for domestic students, 11/1 for international students. Applications are processed on a rolling basis. Application fee: $65. Electronic applications accepted. *Expenses:* Contact institution. *Financial support:* Fellowships, research assistantships, teaching assistantships, career-related internships or fieldwork, Federal Work-Study, scholarships/grants, and unspecified assistantships available. Financial award application deadline: 2/15; financial award applicants required to submit FAFSA. *Unit head:* Dr. Henry Du, Director, 201-216-5262, Fax: 201-216-8306, E-mail: hdu@stevens.edu. *Application contact:* Graduate Admissions, 888-783-8367, Fax: 888-511-1306, E-mail: graduate@stevens.edu.

Stony Brook University, State University of New York, Graduate School, College of Engineering and Applied Sciences, Department of Materials Science and Engineering, Stony Brook, NY 11794-2275. Offers MS, PhD. *Faculty:* 18 full-time (5 women), 10 part-time/adjunct (3 women). *Students:* 113 full-time (39 women), 20 part-time (10 women); includes 20 minority (5 Black or African American, non-Hispanic/Latino; 10 Asian, non-Hispanic/Latino; 4 Hispanic/Latino; 1 Two or more races, non-Hispanic/Latino), 84 international. Average age 26. 202 applicants, 49% accepted, 33 enrolled. In 2016, 26 master's, 13 doctorates awarded. *Degree requirements:* For master's, thesis or alternative; for doctorate, comprehensive exam, thesis/dissertation. *Entrance requirements:* For master's and doctorate, GRE General Test, minimum undergraduate GPA of 3.0. Additional exam requirements/recommendations for international students: Required—TOEFL (minimum score 90 iBT). *Application deadline:* For fall admission, 1/15 for domestic students; for spring admission, 10/1 for domestic students. Application fee: $100. *Expenses:* Contact institution. *Financial support:* In 2016–17, 2 fellowships, 21 research assistantships, 19 teaching assistantships were awarded. *Faculty research:* Crystal growth, crystallography, semiconductors, synchrotron X-rays or radiation, fuel cells. *Total annual research expenditures:* $3.4 million. *Unit head:* Dr. Michael Dudley, Chairman, 631-632-8500, Fax: 631-632-8052, E-mail: michael.dudley@stonybrook.edu. *Application contact:* Rosa DiLiberto, Coordinator, 631-632-4986, E-mail: rosa.diliberto@stonybrook.edu.
Website: http://www.stonybrook.edu/commcms/matscieng/index.html

Texas A&M University, College of Engineering, Department of Materials Science and Engineering, College Station, TX 77843. Offers M Eng, MS, PhD. *Faculty:* 16. *Students:* 119 full-time (36 women), 14 part-time (2 women); includes 17 minority (1 Black or African American, non-Hispanic/Latino; 7 Asian, non-Hispanic/Latino; 5 Hispanic/Latino; 4 Two or more races, non-Hispanic/Latino), 91 international. Average age 28. 265 applicants, 29% accepted, 25 enrolled. In 2016, 12 master's, 10 doctorates awarded. *Degree requirements:* For master's, thesis (MS); for doctorate, thesis/dissertation. *Entrance requirements:* For master's and doctorate, GRE General Test. Additional exam requirements/recommendations for international students: Required—TOEFL (minimum score 550 paper-based; 80 iBT), IELTS (minimum score 6), PTE (minimum score 53). *Application deadline:* For fall admission, 2/28 for domestic and international students; for spring admission, 7/31 for domestic students, 6/1 for international students. Application fee: $50 ($90 for international students). *Expenses:* Contact institution. *Financial support:* In 2016–17, 119 students received support, including 17 fellowships with tuition reimbursements available (averaging $17,522 per year), 83 research assistantships with tuition reimbursements available (averaging $6,669 per year), 15 teaching assistantships with tuition reimbursements available (averaging $8,718 per year); career-related internships or fieldwork, institutionally sponsored loans, scholarships/grants, traineeships, health care benefits, tuition waivers (full and partial), and unspecified assistantships also available. Support available to part-time students. Financial award application deadline: 3/15; financial award applicants required to submit FAFSA. *Faculty research:* Innovative design methods, pavement distress characterization, materials property, characterization and modeling recyclable materials. *Unit head:* Ibrahim Karaman, Department Head, 979-862-3923, E-mail: ikaraman@tamu.edu. *Application contact:* Mildan Radovic, Associate Department Head, 979-845-5114, E-mail: mradovic@tamu.edu.
Website: http://engineering.tamu.edu/materials

Texas State University, The Graduate College, College of Science and Engineering, PhD Program in Materials Science, Engineering, and Commercialization, San Marcos, TX 78666. Offers PhD. *Faculty:* 14 full-time (5 women), 4 part-time/adjunct (1 woman). *Students:* 30 full-time (11 women), 4 part-time (1 woman); includes 5 minority (3 Black or African American, non-Hispanic/Latino; 1 Asian, non-Hispanic/Latino; 1 Hispanic/Latino), 17 international. Average age 32. 36 applicants, 39% accepted, 8 enrolled. In 2016, 6 doctorates awarded. *Degree requirements:* For doctorate, comprehensive exam, thesis/dissertation. *Entrance requirements:* For doctorate, GRE (for applicants who have not received a master's degree from a U.S. institution), baccalaureate and master's degree from regionally-accredited college or university in biology, chemistry, engineering, materials science, physics, technology, or closely-related field with minimum GPA of 3.5 in graduate work; statement of purpose; 3 letters of recommendation; curriculum vitae or resume. Additional exam requirements/recommendations for international students: Required—TOEFL (minimum score 550 paper-based; 78 iBT); Recommended—IELTS (minimum score 6.5). *Application deadline:* For fall admission, 2/1 priority date for domestic and international students. Application fee: $40 ($90 for international students). Electronic applications accepted. *Expenses:* $4,851 per semester. *Financial support:* In 2016–17, 20 students received support, including 15 research assistantships (averaging $29,374 per year), 16 teaching assistantships (averaging $37,652 per year); scholarships/grants, health care benefits, and unspecified assistantships also available. Support available to part-time students. Financial award application deadline: 3/1; financial award applicants required to submit FAFSA. *Faculty research:* Micro power chip prototype development; applied epitaxial materials; Spin-dependent transport at oxide interfaces grown by molecular beam epitaxy. *Total annual research expenditures:* $455,774. *Unit head:* Dr. Jennifer Irvin, PhD Program Director, 512-245-7875, Fax: 512-245-8365, E-mail: ji12@txstate.edu. *Application contact:* Dr. Andrea Golato, Dean of Graduate School, 512-245-2581, Fax: 512-245-8365, E-mail: gradcollege@txstate.edu.
Website: http://www.msec.txstate.edu/

Tuskegee University, Graduate Programs, College of Engineering, Department of Materials Science and Engineering, Tuskegee, AL 36088. Offers PhD. *Entrance requirements:* Additional exam requirements/recommendations for international students: Required—TOEFL (minimum score 500 paper-based).

The University of Alabama, Graduate School, College of Engineering, Department of Metallurgical and Materials Engineering, Tuscaloosa, AL 35487. Offers MS Met E, PhD. PhD offered jointly with The University of Alabama at Birmingham. *Faculty:* 11 full-time (3 women). *Students:* 14 full-time (5 women), 2 part-time (0 women); includes 1 minority (Black or African American, non-Hispanic/Latino), 7 international. Average age 27. 20 applicants, 20% accepted, 1 enrolled. In 2016, 5 master's, 1 doctorate awarded. *Degree requirements:* For master's, thesis or alternative; for doctorate, thesis/dissertation. *Entrance requirements:* For master's, GRE General Test, minimum GPA of 3.0 in last 60 hours; for doctorate, GRE General Test, minimum graduate GPA of 3.0, graduate degree. Additional exam requirements/recommendations for international students: Required—TOEFL (minimum score 550 paper-based). *Application deadline:* For fall admission, 7/1 for domestic students, 5/1 priority date for international students. Applications are processed on a rolling basis. Application fee: $50 ($60 for international students). Electronic applications accepted. *Expenses:* Tuition, state resident: full-time $10,470. Tuition, nonresident: full-time $26,950. *Financial support:* In 2016–17, 3 fellowships (averaging $15,000 per year), 14 research assistantships (averaging $14,700 per year), 6 teaching assistantships (averaging $12,250 per year) were awarded; Federal Work-Study and unspecified assistantships also available. *Faculty research:* Thermodynamics, molten metals processing, casting and solidification, mechanical properties of materials, thin films and nanostructures, electrochemistry, corrosion and alloy development. *Total annual research expenditures:* $3.2 million. *Unit head:* Dr. Mark Weaver, Head/Professor, 205-348-7073, Fax: 205-348-2164, E-mail: mweaver@eng.ua.edu. *Application contact:* Dr. Greg B. Thompson, Associate Professor, 205-348-1589, Fax: 205-348-2164, E-mail: sgupta@eng.ua.edu.
Website: http://www.eng.ua.edu/~mtedept/

The University of Alabama at Birmingham, School of Engineering, Program in Materials Engineering, Birmingham, AL 35294. Offers MS Mt E, PhD. PhD offered jointly with The University of Alabama (Tuscaloosa). *Faculty:* 8 full-time (3 women), 1 part-time/adjunct. *Students:* 5 full-time (3 women); includes 2 minority (both Hispanic/Latino). Average age 28. 15 applicants, 87% accepted, 4 enrolled. In 2016, 7 master's, 3 doctorates awarded. *Degree requirements:* For master's, comprehensive exam, thesis (for some programs), project/thesis; for doctorate, comprehensive exam, thesis/dissertation. *Entrance requirements:* For master's and doctorate, GRE General Test (minimum quantitative score of 148/170 [600/800 on the old scale], verbal score of 153/180 [500/800 on the old scale], and 3/6 on the analytical writing), minimum GPA of 3.0 on all undergraduate degree major courses attempted. Additional exam requirements/recommendations for international students: Required—TOEFL (minimum score 80 iBT), TWE (minimum score 3.5). *Application deadline:* For fall admission, 7/1 for domestic and international students; for spring admission, 11/1 for domestic and international students; for summer admission, 4/1 for domestic and international students. Applications are processed on a rolling basis. Application fee: $50 ($60 for international students). Electronic applications accepted. *Expenses:* $396 per hour resident tuition; $935 per hour non-resident tuition; $150 per course online course fee. *Financial support:* In 2016–17, 23 students received support, including 2 fellowships with full tuition reimbursements available (averaging $21,456 per year), 20 research assistantships with full tuition reimbursements available (averaging $21,456 per year); unspecified assistantships also available. *Faculty research:* Casting metallurgy, microgravity solidification, thin film techniques, ceramics/glass processing, biomedical materials processing. *Total annual research expenditures:* $1.4 million. *Unit head:* Dr. Charles Monroe, Graduate Program Director, 205-975-4128, E-mail: camonroe@uab.edu. *Application contact:* Holly Hebard, Director of Graduate School Operations, 205-934-8227, Fax: 205-934-8413, E-mail: gradschool@uab.edu.
Website: https://www.uab.edu/engineering/home/departments-research/mse/grad

University of Alberta, Faculty of Graduate Studies and Research, Department of Chemical and Materials Engineering, Edmonton, AB T6G 2E1, Canada. Offers chemical engineering (M Eng, M Sc, PhD); materials engineering (M Eng, M Sc, PhD); process control (M Eng, M Sc, PhD); welding (M Eng). *Program availability:* Part-time, online learning. Terminal master's awarded for partial completion of doctoral program. *Degree requirements:* For master's, thesis; for doctorate, thesis/dissertation. *Faculty research:* Advanced materials and polymers, catalytic and reaction engineering, mineral processing, physical metallurgy, fluid mechanics.

The University of Arizona, College of Engineering, Department of Materials Science and Engineering, Tucson, AZ 85721. Offers MS, PhD. *Program availability:* Part-time. *Degree requirements:* For master's, thesis (for some programs); for doctorate, comprehensive exam, thesis/dissertation. *Entrance requirements:* For master's and doctorate, GRE General Test, 3 letters of recommendation, statement of purpose. Additional exam requirements/recommendations for international students: Required—TOEFL (minimum score 550 paper-based; 79 iBT). Electronic applications accepted. *Faculty research:* High-technology ceramics, optical materials, electronic materials, chemical metallurgy, science of materials.

The University of British Columbia, Faculty of Applied Science, Department of Materials Engineering, Vancouver, BC V6T 1Z4, Canada. Offers M Sc, MA Sc, PhD. *Degree requirements:* For master's, comprehensive exam, thesis; for doctorate, comprehensive exam, thesis/dissertation. *Entrance requirements:* Additional exam requirements/recommendations for international students: Required—TOEFL. *Application deadline:* For winter admission, 7/15 for domestic and international students; for summer admission, 11/1 for domestic and international students. Application fee: $100 Canadian dollars ($162 Canadian dollars for international students). Electronic applications accepted. *Expenses:* $4,802 per year tuition and fees, $8,436 per year international. *Financial support:* Fellowships, research assistantships, teaching assistantships, career-related internships or fieldwork, Federal Work-Study, institutionally sponsored loans, and scholarships/grants available. *Faculty research:* Electroslag melting, mathematical modeling, solidification and hydrometallurgy. *Application contact:* Michelle Tierney, Graduate Program Assistant, 604-822-4878, Fax: 604-822-3619, E-mail: gradsec@mtrl.ubc.ca.
Website: http://mtrl.ubc.ca/

University of California, Berkeley, Graduate Division, College of Engineering, Department of Materials Science and Engineering, Berkeley, CA 94720-1500. Offers engineering science (M Eng, MS, PhD). *Faculty:* 15 full-time. *Students:* 116 full-time (38 women); includes 34 minority (4 Black or African American, non-Hispanic/Latino; 1 American Indian or Alaska Native, non-Hispanic/Latino; 17 Asian, non-Hispanic/Latino; 12 Hispanic/Latino), 61 international. Average age 27. 522 applicants, 50 enrolled. In 2016, 23 master's, 18 doctorates awarded. Terminal master's awarded for partial completion of doctoral program. *Degree requirements:* For master's, comprehensive exam (for some programs), thesis (for some programs), comprehensive exam or thesis (MS); for doctorate, comprehensive exam, thesis/dissertation, qualifying exam. *Entrance requirements:* For master's and doctorate, GRE General Test, minimum GPA of 3.0, 3 letters of recommendation. Additional exam requirements/recommendations for international students: Required—TOEFL (minimum score 570 paper-based; 90 iBT). *Application deadline:* For fall admission, 12/5 for domestic students. Application fee: $105 ($125 for international students). Electronic applications accepted. *Financial support:* Fellowships, research assistantships, teaching assistantships, and unspecified assistantships available. Financial award applicants required to submit FAFSA. *Faculty research:* Ceramics, biomaterials, structural, electronic, magnetic and optical materials. *Unit head:* Prof. Mark D. Asta, Chair, 510-642-0716, Fax: 510-643-5792, E-mail: msessa@berkeley.edu. *Application contact:* 510-642-0716, Fax: 510-643-5792, E-mail: msessa@berkeley.edu.
Website: http://www.mse.berkeley.edu/

University of California, Davis, College of Engineering, Program in Materials Science and Engineering, Davis, CA 95616. Offers MS, PhD. Terminal master's awarded for partial completion of doctoral program. *Degree requirements:* For master's, comprehensive exam (for some programs), thesis (for some programs); for doctorate, comprehensive exam, thesis/dissertation. *Entrance requirements:* Additional exam requirements/recommendations for international students: Required—TOEFL (minimum score 550 paper-based).

University of California, Irvine, Henry Samueli School of Engineering, Department of Chemical Engineering and Materials Science, Irvine, CA 92697. Offers chemical and biochemical engineering (MS, PhD); materials science and engineering (MS, PhD). *Program availability:* Part-time. *Students:* 141 full-time (60 women), 14 part-time (5 women); includes 42 minority (4 Black or African American, non-Hispanic/Latino; 29 Asian, non-Hispanic/Latino; 7 Hispanic/Latino; 2 Two or more races, non-Hispanic/Latino), 71 international. Average age 26. 595 applicants, 23% accepted, 41 enrolled. In 2016, 47 master's, 11 doctorates awarded. Terminal master's awarded for partial completion of doctoral program. *Degree requirements:* For doctorate, thesis/dissertation. *Entrance requirements:* For master's and doctorate, GRE General Test, minimum GPA of 3.0, 3 letters of recommendation. Additional exam requirements/recommendations for international students: Required—TOEFL (minimum score 550 paper-based). *Application deadline:* For fall admission, 1/15 priority date for domestic students, 1/15 for international students. Applications are processed on a rolling basis. Application fee: $105 ($125 for international students). Electronic applications accepted. *Financial support:* Fellowships with tuition reimbursements, research assistantships with full tuition reimbursements, teaching assistantships with tuition reimbursements, institutionally sponsored loans, traineeships, health care benefits, and unspecified assistantships available. Financial award application deadline: 3/1; financial award applicants required to submit FAFSA. *Faculty research:* Molecular biotechnology, nanobiomaterials, biophotonics, synthesis, super plasticity and mechanical behavior, characterization of advanced and nanostructural materials. *Unit head:* Prof. Vasan Venugopalan, Chair, 949-824-5802, Fax: 949-824-2541, E-mail: vvenugop@uci.edu. *Application contact:* Grace Chau, Academic Program and Graduate Admission Coordinator, 949-824-3887, Fax: 949-824-2541, E-mail: chaug@uci.edu.
Website: http://www.eng.uci.edu/dept/chems

University of California, Irvine, Henry Samueli School of Engineering, Program in Materials and Manufacturing Technology, Irvine, CA 92697. Offers engineering (MS, PhD). *Program availability:* Part-time. *Students:* 20 full-time (9 women), 1 part-time (0 women); includes 3 minority (all Asian, non-Hispanic/Latino), 16 international. Average age 27. 28 applicants, 68% accepted, 5 enrolled. In 2016, 8 master's, 1 doctorate awarded. *Entrance requirements:* For master's and doctorate, GRE General Test, 3

letters of recommendation, minimum GPA of 3.0. Additional exam requirements/recommendations for international students: Required—TOEFL (minimum score 550 paper-based). *Application deadline:* For fall admission, 1/15 priority date for domestic students, 1/15 for international students. Applications are processed on a rolling basis. Application fee: $105 ($125 for international students). Electronic applications accepted. *Financial support:* Fellowships with tuition reimbursements, research assistantships with full tuition reimbursements, teaching assistantships with tuition reimbursements, institutionally sponsored loans, traineeships, health care benefits, and unspecified assistantships available. Financial award application deadline: 3/1; financial award applicants required to submit FAFSA. *Faculty research:* Advanced materials, microelectronic and photonic devices and packaging, biomedical devices, MEMS, thin film materials, nanotechnology. *Application contact:* Connie Cheng, Assistant Director of Graduate Student Affairs, 949-824-3562, Fax: 949-824-8200, E-mail: connie.cheng@uci.edu.
Website: http://www.eng.uci.edu/

University of California, Los Angeles, Graduate Division, Henry Samueli School of Engineering and Applied Science, Department of Materials Science and Engineering, Los Angeles, CA 90095-1595. Offers MS, PhD. *Faculty:* 14 full-time (2 women), 4 part-time/adjunct (0 women). *Students:* 177 full-time (51 women); includes 35 minority (1 Black or African American, non-Hispanic/Latino; 26 Asian, non-Hispanic/Latino; 6 Hispanic/Latino; 2 Two or more races, non-Hispanic/Latino), 113 international. 345 applicants, 53% accepted, 60 enrolled. In 2016, 24 master's, 20 doctorates awarded. *Degree requirements:* For master's, comprehensive exam or thesis; for doctorate, thesis/dissertation, qualifying exams. *Entrance requirements:* For master's, GRE General Test, minimum GPA of 3.0; for doctorate, GRE General Test, minimum GPA of 3.25. Additional exam requirements/recommendations for international students: Required—TOEFL (minimum score 560 paper-based; 87 iBT), IELTS (minimum score 7). *Application deadline:* For fall admission, 11/30 for domestic and international students. Application fee: $105 ($125 for international students). Electronic applications accepted. *Financial support:* In 2016–17, 93 fellowships, 126 research assistantships, 51 teaching assistantships were awarded; Federal Work-Study, institutionally sponsored loans, and tuition waivers (full and partial) also available. Financial award application deadline: 11/30; financial award applicants required to submit FAFSA. *Faculty research:* Ceramics and ceramic processing, electronic and optical materials, structural materials. *Total annual research expenditures:* $7 million. *Unit head:* Dr. Dwight C. Streit, Chair, 310-825-7011, E-mail: streit@ucla.edu. *Application contact:* Patti Barrera, Student Affairs Officer, 310-825-8916, E-mail: patti@seas.ucla.edu.
Website: http://www.mse.ucla.edu

University of California, Riverside, Graduate Division, Materials Science and Engineering Program, Riverside, CA 92521. Offers MS. *Entrance requirements:* For master's, GRE. Additional exam requirements/recommendations for international students: Required—TOEFL (minimum score 550 paper-based; 80 iBT). Electronic applications accepted. *Expenses:* Tuition, state resident: full-time $16,666. Tuition, nonresident: full-time $31,768. *Required fees:* $11,055.54 per quarter. $3685.18 per quarter. Tuition and fees vary according to campus/location and program.

University of California, Santa Barbara, Graduate Division, College of Engineering, Department of Materials, Santa Barbara, CA 93106-5050. Offers MS, PhD, MS/PhD. Terminal master's awarded for partial completion of doctoral program. *Degree requirements:* For master's, variable foreign language requirement, comprehensive exam, thesis; for doctorate, variable foreign language requirement, comprehensive exam, thesis/dissertation. *Entrance requirements:* For master's and doctorate, GRE General Test. Additional exam requirements/recommendations for international students: Required—TOEFL (minimum score 600 paper-based; 100 iBT), IELTS (minimum score 7). Electronic applications accepted. *Faculty research:* Electronic and photonic materials, inorganic materials, macromolecular and biomolecular materials, structural materials.

University of Central Florida, College of Engineering and Computer Science, Department of Materials Science and Engineering, Orlando, FL 32816. Offers MSMSE, PhD. *Students:* 47 full-time (19 women), 7 part-time (3 women); includes 7 minority (2 Asian, non-Hispanic/Latino; 4 Hispanic/Latino; 1 Two or more races, non-Hispanic/Latino), 32 international. Average age 28. 82 applicants, 49% accepted, 14 enrolled. In 2016, 12 master's, 3 doctorates awarded. *Degree requirements:* For master's, thesis or alternative; for doctorate, thesis/dissertation, candidacy exam, departmental qualifying exam. *Entrance requirements:* Additional exam requirements/recommendations for international students: Required—TOEFL. *Application deadline:* For fall admission, 7/15 for domestic students; for spring admission, 12/1 for domestic students. Application fee: $30. Electronic applications accepted. *Expenses:* Tuition, state resident: part-time $288.16 per credit hour. Tuition, nonresident: part-time $1071.31 per credit hour. *Financial support:* In 2016–17, 42 students received support, including 9 fellowships with tuition reimbursements available (averaging $7,178 per year), 42 research assistantships (averaging $12,060 per year), 7 teaching assistantships (averaging $11,382 per year). Financial award application deadline: 3/1; financial award applicants required to submit FAFSA. *Unit head:* Dr. Sudipta Seal, Interim Chair, 407-823-5277, E-mail: sseal@ucf.edu. *Application contact:* Assistant Director, Graduate Admissions, 407-823-2766, Fax: 407-823-6442, E-mail: gradadmissions@ucf.edu.
Website: http://mse.ucf.edu/

University of Cincinnati, Graduate School, College of Engineering and Applied Science, Department of Mechanical and Materials Engineering, Program in Materials Science and Engineering, Cincinnati, OH 45221. Offers MS, PhD. *Program availability:* Evening/weekend. *Degree requirements:* For master's, thesis optional; for doctorate, one foreign language, comprehensive exam, thesis/dissertation, oral English proficiency exam. *Entrance requirements:* For master's and doctorate, GRE General Test, BS in related field, minimum undergraduate GPA of 3.0. Additional exam requirements/recommendations for international students: Required—TOEFL. Electronic applications accepted. *Expenses: Tuition, area resident:* Full-time $12,790; part-time $389 per credit hour. Tuition, state resident: full-time $13,290; part-time $419 per credit hour. Tuition, nonresident: full-time $24,532; part-time $976 per credit hour. *International tuition:* $24,832 full-time. *Required fees:* $3958; $140 per credit hour. Tuition and fees vary according to course load, degree level, program and reciprocity agreements. *Faculty research:* Polymer characterization, surface analysis, and adhesion; mechanical behavior of high-temperature materials; composites; electrochemistry of materials.

University of Connecticut, Graduate School, School of Engineering, Department of Metallurgy and Materials Engineering, Storrs, CT 06269. Offers M Eng. Terminal master's awarded for partial completion of doctoral program. *Degree requirements:* For master's, comprehensive exam, thesis or alternative. *Entrance requirements:* For master's, GRE General Test, GRE Subject Test. Additional exam requirements/recommendations for international students: Required—TOEFL (minimum score 550 paper-based). Electronic applications accepted.

University of Dayton, Department of Materials Engineering, Dayton, OH 45469. Offers MS Mat E, DE, PhD. *Program availability:* Part-time, evening/weekend, blended/hybrid learning. *Faculty:* 4 full-time (0 women), 9 part-time/adjunct (0 women). *Students:* 50 full-time (16 women), 13 part-time (3 women); includes 8 minority (3 Black or African American, non-Hispanic/Latino; 3 Asian, non-Hispanic/Latino; 2 Hispanic/Latino), 18 international. Average age 29. 67 applicants, 37% accepted. In 2016, 33 master's, 6 doctorates awarded. Terminal master's awarded for partial completion of doctoral program. *Degree requirements:* For master's, thesis optional; for doctorate, comprehensive exam, thesis/dissertation, departmental qualifying exam. *Entrance requirements:* Additional exam requirements/recommendations for international students: Required—TOEFL (minimum score 550 paper-based; 80 iBT). *Application deadline:* For fall admission, 8/1 priority date for domestic students, 5/1 priority date for international students; for spring admission, 11/1 priority date for international students. Applications are processed on a rolling basis. Application fee: $0 ($50 for international students). Electronic applications accepted. *Expenses:* $890 per credit hour (for MS), $970 per credit hour (for PhD); $25 registration fee. *Financial support:* In 2016–17, 6 research assistantships with full tuition reimbursements (averaging $13,500 per year) were awarded; Federal Work-Study, institutionally sponsored loans, health care benefits, and unspecified assistantships also available. Support available to part-time students. Financial award application deadline: 3/1; financial award applicants required to submit FAFSA. *Faculty research:* Nano-materials, composite materials, carbon materials, 3D printed metals and plastics, 2D nano-materials. *Unit head:* Dr. Charles Browning, Chair/Interim Graduate Program Director, 937-229-2679, E-mail: cbrowning1@udayton.edu.
Website: https://www.udayton.edu/engineering/departments/chemical_and_materials/index.php

University of Delaware, College of Engineering, Department of Materials Science and Engineering, Newark, DE 19716. Offers MMSE, PhD. Terminal master's awarded for partial completion of doctoral program. *Degree requirements:* For master's, thesis; for doctorate, thesis/dissertation. *Entrance requirements:* For master's and doctorate, GRE General Test, 3 letters of recommendation, minimum GPA of 3.2. Additional exam requirements/recommendations for international students: Required—TOEFL. Electronic applications accepted. *Faculty research:* Thin films and self assembly, drug delivery and tissue engineering, biomaterials and nanocomposites, semiconductor and oxide interfaces, electronic and magnetic materials.

University of Denver, Daniel Felix Ritchie School of Engineering and Computer Science, Department of Mechanical and Materials Engineering, Denver, CO 80208. Offers bioengineering (MS); engineering (MS, PhD), including management (MS); materials science (MS, PhD); mechanical engineering (MS, PhD). *Program availability:* Part-time. *Faculty:* 11 full-time (1 woman), 2 part-time/adjunct (both women). *Students:* 2 full-time (0 women), 27 part-time (7 women); includes 6 minority (1 Asian, non-Hispanic/Latino; 5 Hispanic/Latino), 13 international. Average age 28. 57 applicants, 79% accepted, 13 enrolled. In 2016, 11 master's, 5 doctorates awarded. Terminal master's awarded for partial completion of doctoral program. *Degree requirements:* For master's, thesis optional; for doctorate, comprehensive exam, thesis/dissertation. *Entrance requirements:* For master's, GRE General Test, bachelor's degree, transcripts, personal statement, resume or curriculum vitae, two letters of recommendation; for doctorate, GRE General Test, master's degree, transcripts, personal statement, resume or curriculum vitae, two letters of recommendation. Additional exam requirements/recommendations for international students: Required—TOEFL (minimum score 550 paper-based; 80 iBT). *Application deadline:* For fall admission, 2/1 priority date for domestic and international students. Applications are processed on a rolling basis. Application fee: $65. Electronic applications accepted. *Expenses:* $29,022 per year full-time. *Financial support:* In 2016–17, 15 students received support, including 4 research assistantships with tuition reimbursements available (averaging $11,667 per year), 5 teaching assistantships with tuition reimbursements available (averaging $12,084 per year); Federal Work-Study, institutionally sponsored loans, scholarships/grants, health care benefits, and unspecified assistantships also available. Financial award application deadline: 2/15; financial award applicants required to submit FAFSA. *Faculty research:* Cardiac biomechanics, novel high voltage/temperature materials and structures, high speed stereo radiography, musculoskeletal modeling, composites. *Total annual research expenditures:* $996,915. *Unit head:* Dr. Matt Gordon, Professor and Chair, 303-871-3580, Fax: 303-871-4450, E-mail: matthew.gordon@du.edu. *Application contact:* Yvonne Petitt, Assistant to the Chair, 303-871-2107, Fax: 303-871-4450, E-mail: yvonne.petitt@du.edu.
Website: http://ritchieschool.du.edu/departments/mme/

University of Florida, Graduate School, Herbert Wertheim College of Engineering, Department of Materials Science and Engineering, Gainesville, FL 32611. Offers material science and engineering (MS), including clinical and translational science; materials science and engineering (ME, PhD); nuclear engineering (ME, PhD), including imaging science and technology (PhD), nuclear engineering sciences (ME, MS, PhD); nuclear engineering (MS), including nuclear engineering sciences (ME, MS, PhD); JD/MS. *Program availability:* Part-time, online learning. Terminal master's awarded for partial completion of doctoral program. *Degree requirements:* For master's, comprehensive exam, thesis; for doctorate, comprehensive exam, thesis/dissertation. *Entrance requirements:* For master's and doctorate, minimum GPA of 3.0. Additional exam requirements/recommendations for international students: Required—TOEFL (minimum score 550 paper-based; 80 iBT), IELTS (minimum score 6). Electronic applications accepted. *Faculty research:* Polymeric system, biomaterials and biomimetics; inorganic and organic electronic materials; functional ceramic materials for energy systems and microelectronic applications; advanced metallic systems for aerospace, transportation and biological applications; nuclear materials.

University of Illinois at Chicago, College of Engineering, Department of Civil and Materials Engineering, Chicago, IL 60607-7128. Offers MS, PhD. *Program availability:* Evening/weekend. *Degree requirements:* For master's, thesis (for some programs); for doctorate, thesis/dissertation, preliminary and qualifying exams. *Entrance requirements:* For master's and doctorate, GRE General Test, minimum GPA of 3.0. Additional exam requirements/recommendations for international students: Required—TOEFL. Electronic applications accepted. *Expenses:* Contact institution. *Faculty research:* Integrated fiber optic, acoustic emission and MEMS-based sensors development; monitoring the state of repaired and strengthened structures; development of weigh-in-motion (WIM) systems; image processing techniques for characterization of concrete entrained air bubble systems.

University of Illinois at Urbana–Champaign, Graduate College, College of Engineering, Department of Materials Science and Engineering, Champaign, IL 61820. Offers M Eng, MS, PhD, MS/MBA, PhD/MBA.

The University of Iowa, Graduate College, College of Engineering, Department of Mechanical Engineering, Iowa City, IA 52242-1316. Offers energy systems (MS, PhD); engineering design (MS, PhD); fluid dynamics (MS, PhD); materials and manufacturing (MS, PhD); wind energy (MS, PhD). *Faculty:* 16 full-time (0 women). *Students:* 37 full-time (4 women), 12 part-time (0 women); includes 1 minority (Black or African American, non-Hispanic/Latino), 30 international. Average age 29. 75 applicants, 13% accepted, 2 enrolled. In 2016, 6 master's, 5 doctorates awarded. Terminal master's awarded for partial completion of doctoral program. *Degree requirements:* For master's, oral exam or thesis; for doctorate, comprehensive exam, thesis/dissertation. *Entrance requirements:* For master's and doctorate, GRE (minimum Verbal score of 153, Quantitative 151), minimum undergraduate GPA of 3.0. Additional exam requirements/recommendations for international students: Required—TOEFL (minimum score 600 paper-based; 100

iBT), IELTS (minimum score 7). *Application deadline:* For fall admission, 1/15 for domestic and international students; for spring admission, 9/1 for domestic and international students; for summer admission, 1/15 for domestic and international students. Application fee: $60 ($100 for international students). Electronic applications accepted. *Financial support:* In 2016–17, 56 students received support, including 37 research assistantships with full tuition reimbursements available (averaging $22,981 per year), 19 teaching assistantships with full tuition reimbursements available (averaging $18,809 per year); traineeships and unspecified assistantships also available. Financial award applicants required to submit FAFSA. *Faculty research:* Computer simulation methodology, biomechanics, metal casting, dynamics, laser processing, system reliability, ship hydrodynamics, solid mechanics, fluid dynamics, energy, human modeling and Nano technology. *Total annual research expenditures:* $9.1 million. *Unit head:* Dr. Ching-Long Lin, Departmental Executive Officer, 319-335-5673, Fax: 319-335-5669, E-mail: ching-long-lin@uiowa.edu. *Application contact:* Tara Hoadley, Academic Program Specialist, 319-335-5939, Fax: 319-335-5669, E-mail: mech_eng@engineering.uiowa.edu.
Website: https://mie.engineering.uiowa.edu

University of Kentucky, Graduate School, College of Engineering, Program in Materials Science and Engineering, Lexington, KY 40506-0032. Offers MS, PhD. *Degree requirements:* For master's, comprehensive exam, thesis optional; for doctorate, comprehensive exam, thesis/dissertation. *Entrance requirements:* For master's, GRE General Test, minimum undergraduate GPA of 2.75; for doctorate, GRE General Test, minimum undergraduate GPA of 3.0. Additional exam requirements/recommendations for international students: Required—TOEFL (minimum score 550 paper-based). Electronic applications accepted. *Faculty research:* Physical and mechanical metallurgy, computational material engineering, polymers and composites, high-temperature ceramics, powder metallurgy.

University of Maryland, College Park, Academic Affairs, A. James Clark School of Engineering, Department of Materials Science and Engineering, Materials Science and Engineering Program, College Park, MD 20742. Offers MS, PhD. *Program availability:* Part-time, evening/weekend, online learning. *Degree requirements:* For master's, comprehensive exam, thesis optional, research paper; for doctorate, thesis/dissertation, oral exam. *Entrance requirements:* For master's and doctorate, GRE General Test, minimum B+ average in undergraduate course work. Additional exam requirements/recommendations for international students: Required—TOEFL. Electronic applications accepted.

University of Maryland, College Park, Academic Affairs, A. James Clark School of Engineering, Department of Mechanical Engineering, College Park, MD 20742. Offers electronic packaging and reliability (MS, PhD); manufacturing and design (MS, PhD); mechanics and materials (MS, PhD); reliability engineering (M Eng, MS, PhD); thermal and fluid sciences (MS, PhD). *Program availability:* Part-time, evening/weekend, online learning. *Degree requirements:* For master's, thesis optional; for doctorate, thesis/dissertation, qualifying exam. *Entrance requirements:* For master's, GRE General Test, 3 letters of recommendation; for doctorate, GRE General Test, minimum GPA of 3.0. Additional exam requirements/recommendations for international students: Required—TOEFL. Electronic applications accepted. *Faculty research:* Injection molding, electronic packaging, fluid mechanics, product engineering.

University of Michigan, College of Engineering, Department of Materials Science and Engineering, Ann Arbor, MI 48109. Offers MS, PhD. *Program availability:* Part-time. *Students:* 169 full-time (58 women), 3 part-time (2 women). 604 applicants, 20% accepted, 49 enrolled. In 2016, 31 master's, 33 doctorates awarded. *Degree requirements:* For master's, thesis, oral defense of thesis; for doctorate, thesis/dissertation, oral defense of dissertation, written exam. *Entrance requirements:* For master's and doctorate, GRE General Test. Additional exam requirements/recommendations for international students: Required—TOEFL. *Application deadline:* Applications are processed on a rolling basis. Electronic applications accepted. *Expenses:* Tuition, state resident: full-time $21,466; part-time $1152 per credit hour. Tuition, nonresident: full-time $43,346; part-time $2367 per credit hour. Part-time tuition and fees vary according to course load, degree level and program. *Financial support:* Fellowships, research assistantships, and teaching assistantships available. Financial award applicants required to submit FAFSA. *Faculty research:* Soft materials (polymers, biomaterials), computational materials science, structural materials, electronic and optical materials, nanocomposite materials. *Total annual research expenditures:* $18.5 million. *Unit head:* Amit Misra, Department Chair, 734-763-2445, E-mail: amitmis@umich.edu. *Application contact:* Renee Hilgendorf, Graduate Program Coordinator, 734-763-9790, E-mail: reneeh@umich.edu.
Website: http://www.mse.engin.umich.edu

University of Minnesota, Twin Cities Campus, College of Science and Engineering, Department of Chemical Engineering and Materials Science, Program in Materials Science and Engineering, Minneapolis, MN 55455-0132. Offers M Mat SE, MS Mat SE, PhD. *Program availability:* Part-time. Terminal master's awarded for partial completion of doctoral program. *Degree requirements:* For master's, thesis; for doctorate, thesis/dissertation. *Entrance requirements:* For master's and doctorate, GRE General Test. Additional exam requirements/recommendations for international students: Required—TOEFL. Electronic applications accepted. *Faculty research:* Ceramics and metals; coating processes and interfacial engineering; crystal growth and design; polymers; electronic, photonic and magnetic materials.

University of Nebraska–Lincoln, Graduate College, College of Engineering, Department of Mechanical and Materials Engineering, Lincoln, NE 68588-0526. Offers biomedical engineering (PhD); engineering mechanics (MS); materials engineering (PhD); mechanical engineering (MS), including materials science engineering, metallurgical engineering; mechanical engineering and applied mechanics (PhD); MS/MS. MS/MS offered with University of Rouen-France. *Degree requirements:* For master's, thesis optional; for doctorate, comprehensive exam, thesis/dissertation. *Entrance requirements:* For master's and doctorate, GRE General Test. Additional exam requirements/recommendations for international students: Required—TOEFL (minimum score 550 paper-based). Electronic applications accepted. *Faculty research:* Medical robotics, rehabilitation dynamics, and design; combustion, fluid mechanics, and heat transfer; nano-materials, manufacturing, and devices; fiber, tissue, bio-polymer, and adaptive composites; blast, impact, fracture, and failure; electro-active and magnetic materials and devices; functional materials, design, and added manufacturing; materials characterization, modeling, and computational simulation.

University of Nevada, Las Vegas, Graduate College, Howard R. Hughes College of Engineering, Department of Mechanical Engineering, Las Vegas, NV 89154-4027. Offers aerospace engineering (MS); biomedical engineering (MS); materials and nuclear engineering (MS); mechanical engineering (MS, PhD); nuclear criticality safety (Certificate); nuclear safeguards and security (Certificate). *Program availability:* Part-time. *Faculty:* 16 full-time (2 women), 3 part-time/adjunct (1 woman). *Students:* 47 full-time (13 women), 21 part-time (4 women); includes 15 minority (1 American Indian or Alaska Native, non-Hispanic/Latino; 6 Asian, non-Hispanic/Latino; 3 Hispanic/Latino; 5 Two or more races, non-Hispanic/Latino), 16 international. Average age 30. 68 applicants, 54% accepted, 15 enrolled. In 2016, 10 master's, 3 doctorates, 4 other advanced degrees awarded. *Degree requirements:* For master's, thesis optional, design

project; for doctorate, comprehensive exam, thesis/dissertation. *Entrance requirements:* For master's, GRE General Test, statement of purpose; 2 letters of recommendation; for doctorate, GRE General Test, 3 letters of recommendation; statement of purpose; bachelor's degree with minimum GPA of 3.5/master's degree with minimum GPA of 3.3. Additional exam requirements/recommendations for international students: Required—TOEFL (minimum score 550 paper-based; 80 iBT), IELTS (minimum score 7). *Application deadline:* For fall admission, 8/1 for domestic students, 5/1 for international students; for spring admission, 12/1 for domestic students, 10/1 for international students. Application fee: $60 ($95 for international students). Electronic applications accepted. *Expenses:* $269.25 per credit, $792 per 3-credit course; $9,634 per year resident; $23,274 per year non-resident; $7,094 fees non-resident (7 credits or more); $1,307 annual health insurance fee. *Financial support:* In 2016–17, 1 fellowship with partial tuition reimbursement (averaging $15,000 per year), 13 research assistantships with partial tuition reimbursements (averaging $17,115 per year), 27 teaching assistantships with partial tuition reimbursements (averaging $16,172 per year) were awarded; institutionally sponsored loans, scholarships/grants, health care benefits, and unspecified assistantships also available. Financial award application deadline: 3/15. *Faculty research:* Dynamics and control systems; energy systems including renewable and nuclear; computational fluid and solid mechanics; structures, materials and manufacturing; vibrations and acoustics. *Total annual research expenditures:* $4.5 million. *Unit head:* Dr. Brendan O'Toole, Chair/Professor, 702-895-3885, Fax: 702-895-3936, E-mail: brendan.otoole@unlv.edu. *Application contact:* Dr. Hui Zhao, Graduate Coordinator, 702-895-1463, Fax: 702-895-3936, E-mail: hui.zhao@unlv.edu.
Website: http://me.unlv.edu/

University of Nevada, Reno, Graduate School, College of Engineering, Department of Chemical and Materials Engineering, Program in Materials Science and Engineering, Reno, NV 89557. Offers MS, PhD. Terminal master's awarded for partial completion of doctoral program. *Degree requirements:* For master's, thesis; for doctorate, one foreign language, thesis/dissertation. *Entrance requirements:* For master's, minimum GPA of 2.75; for doctorate, GRE, minimum GPA of 3.0. Additional exam requirements/recommendations for international students: Required—TOEFL (minimum score 500 paper-based; 61 iBT), IELTS (minimum score 6). Electronic applications accepted. *Faculty research:* Hydrometallurgy, applied surface chemistry, mineral processing, mineral bioprocessing, ceramics.

University of Pennsylvania, School of Engineering and Applied Science, Department of Materials Science and Engineering, Philadelphia, PA 19104. Offers MSE, PhD. *Program availability:* Part-time. *Faculty:* 14 full-time (3 women), 2 part-time/adjunct (1 woman). *Students:* 99 full-time (24 women), 20 part-time (4 women); includes 3 minority (2 Hispanic/Latino; 1 Two or more races, non-Hispanic/Latino), 84 international. Average age 24. 517 applicants, 24% accepted, 84 enrolled. In 2016, 54 master's, 11 doctorates awarded. *Degree requirements:* For master's, comprehensive exam, thesis optional; for doctorate, comprehensive exam, thesis/dissertation. *Entrance requirements:* For master's and doctorate, GRE. Additional exam requirements/recommendations for international students: Required—TOEFL (minimum score 100 iBT), IELTS (minimum score 7). *Application deadline:* For fall admission, 3/15 priority date for domestic and international students; for spring admission, 11/1 priority date for domestic students, 10/1 priority date for international students. Application fee: $80. Electronic applications accepted. *Expenses:* Tuition: Full-time $31,068; part-time $5762 per course. *Required fees:* $3200; $336 per course. Full-time tuition and fees vary according to degree level, program and student level. Part-time tuition and fees vary according to course load, degree level and program. *Faculty research:* Biomaterials, ceramics, electronic and optical properties, nanostructured materials, semiconductors. *Application contact:* William Fenton, Assistant Director of Graduate Admissions, 215-898-4542, Fax: 215-573-5577, E-mail: gradstudies@seas.upenn.edu.
Website: http://www.mse.seas.upenn.edu/current-students/masters/index.php

University of Puerto Rico, Mayagüez Campus, Graduate Studies, College of Engineering, Department of Mechanical Engineering, Mayagüez, PR 00681-9000. Offers mechanical engineering (ME, MS, PhD), including aerospace and unmanned vehivles (ME), automation/mechatronics, bioengineering, cae and design, fluid mechanics, heat transfer/energy systems, manufacturing, mechanics of materials, micro and nano engineering. *Program availability:* Part-time. *Faculty:* 22 full-time (4 women), 1 part-time/adjunct (0 women). *Students:* 34 full-time (4 women), 8 part-time (2 women); includes 38 minority (all Hispanic/Latino), 3 international. Average age 25. 22 applicants, 100% accepted, 7 enrolled. In 2016, 17 master's awarded. Terminal master's awarded for partial completion of doctoral program. *Degree requirements:* For master's, one foreign language, comprehensive exam, thesis; for doctorate, one foreign language, comprehensive exam, thesis/dissertation. *Entrance requirements:* For master's, BS in mechanical engineering or its equivalent; for doctorate, GRE, BS or MS in mechanical engineering or its equivalent; minimum GPA of 3.0. Additional exam requirements/recommendations for international students: Required—TOEFL (minimum score 80 paper-based; 80 iBT). *Application deadline:* For fall admission, 2/15 for domestic and international students; for spring admission, 9/15 for domestic and international students. Applications are processed on a rolling basis. Application fee: $25. Electronic applications accepted. *Expenses:* Tuition, area resident: Full-time $2466. International tuition: $7166 full-time. *Required fees:* $210. One-time fee: $5 full-time. Tuition and fees vary according to course level, campus/location, program and student level. *Financial support:* In 2016–17, 39 students received support, including 26 research assistantships with full and partial tuition reimbursements available (averaging $3,801 per year), 30 teaching assistantships with full and partial tuition reimbursements available (averaging $3,293 per year); unspecified assistantships also available. *Faculty research:* Computational fluid dynamics, thermal sciences, mechanical design, material health, microfluidics. *Unit head:* Paul Sundaram, Ph.D., Chairperson, 787-832-4040 Ext. 3659, Fax: 787-265-3817, E-mail: paul.sundaram@upr.edu. *Application contact:* Yolanda Perez, Academic Orientation Officer, 787-832-4040 Ext. 2362, Fax: 787-265-3817, E-mail: yolanda.perez4@upr.edu.
Website: https://wordpress.uprm.edu/inme/

University of Southern California, Graduate School, Viterbi School of Engineering, Mork Family Department of Chemical Engineering and Materials Science, Los Angeles, CA 90089. Offers chemical engineering (MS, PhD, Engr); geoscience technologies (MS); materials engineering (MS); materials science (MS, PhD, Engr); petroleum engineering (MS, PhD, Engr); smart oilfield technologies (MS, Graduate Certificate). Terminal master's awarded for partial completion of doctoral program. *Degree requirements:* For master's, thesis optional; for doctorate, thesis/dissertation. *Entrance requirements:* For master's and doctorate, GRE General Test. Additional exam requirements/recommendations for international students: Recommended—TOEFL. Electronic applications accepted. *Expenses:* Contact institution. *Faculty research:* Heterogeneous materials and porous media, statistical mechanics, molecular simulation, polymer science and engineering, advanced materials, reaction engineering and catalysis, membrane processes and separation, biochemical engineering, cell culture, bioreactor modeling, petroleum engineering.

University of South Florida, College of Engineering, Department of Civil and Environmental Engineering, Tampa, FL 33620-9951. Offers civil engineering (MCE, MSCE, PhD), including geotechnical engineering, materials science and engineering, structures engineering, transportation engineering, water resources; environmental engineering (MEVE, MSEV, PhD), including engineering for international development (MSEV). *Program availability:* Part-time. *Faculty:* 20 full-time (5 women). *Students:* 117 full-time (41 women), 63 part-time (18 women); includes 33 minority (7 Black or African American, non-Hispanic/Latino; 2 Asian, non-Hispanic/Latino; 20 Hispanic/Latino; 4 Two or more races, non-Hispanic/Latino), 84 international. Average age 28. 250 applicants, 52% accepted, 51 enrolled. In 2016, 55 master's, 13 doctorates awarded. Terminal master's awarded for partial completion of doctoral program. *Degree requirements:* For master's, comprehensive exam, thesis (for some programs); for doctorate, comprehensive exam, thesis/dissertation. *Entrance requirements:* For master's, GRE General Test, minimum GPA of 3.0 in major, letters of reference, statement of purpose; for doctorate, GRE General Test, letters of recommendation, statement of purpose, resume. Additional exam requirements/recommendations for international students: Required—TOEFL (minimum score 550 paper-based; 79 iBT) or IELTS (minimum score 6.5). *Application deadline:* For fall admission, 2/15 for domestic students, 2/15 priority date for international students; for spring admission, 10/15 for domestic students, 9/15 priority date for international students. Application fee: $30. Electronic applications accepted. *Expenses:* Tuition, state resident: full-time $7766; part-time $431.43 per credit hour. Tuition, nonresident: full-time $15,789; part-time $877.17 per credit hour. *Required fees:* $37 per term. *Financial support:* In 2016–17, 36 students received support, including 44 research assistantships (averaging $14,123 per year), 21 teaching assistantships with tuition reimbursements available (averaging $15,329 per year). *Faculty research:* Environmental and water resources engineering, geotechnics and geoenvironmental systems, structures and materials systems, transportation systems. *Total annual research expenditures:* $3.7 million. *Unit head:* Dr. Manjriker Gunaratne, Professor and Department Chair, 813-974-5818, Fax: 813-974-2957, E-mail: gunaratn@usf.edu. *Application contact:* Dr. Sarina J. Ergas, Professor and Graduate Program Coordinator, 813-974-1119, Fax: 813-974-2957, E-mail: sergas@usf.edu. Website: http://www.usf.edu/engineering/cee/

University of South Florida, Innovative Education, Tampa, FL 33620-9951. Offers adult, career and higher education (Graduate Certificate), including college teaching, leadership in developing human resources, leadership in higher education; Africana studies (Graduate Certificate), including diasporas and health disparities, genocide and human rights; aging studies (Graduate Certificate), including gerontology; art research (Graduate Certificate), including museum studies; business foundations (Graduate Certificate); chemical and biomedical engineering (Graduate Certificate), including materials science and engineering, water, health and sustainability; child and family studies (Graduate Certificate), including positive behavior support; civil and industrial engineering (Graduate Certificate), including transportation systems analysis; community and family health (Graduate Certificate), including maternal and child health, social marketing and public health, violence and injury: prevention and intervention, women's health; criminology (Graduate Certificate), including criminal justice administration; educational measurement and research (Graduate Certificate), including evaluation; English (Graduate Certificate), including comparative literary studies, creative writing, professional and technical communication; entrepreneurship (Graduate Certificate); environmental health (Graduate Certificate), including safety management; epidemiology and biostatistics (Graduate Certificate), including applied biostatistics, biostatistics, concepts and tools of epidemiology, epidemiology, epidemiology of infectious diseases; geography, environment and planning (Graduate Certificate), including community development, environmental policy and management, geographical information systems; geology (Graduate Certificate), including hydrogeology; global health (Graduate Certificate), including disaster management, global health and Latin American and Caribbean studies, global health practice, humanitarian assistance, infection control; government and international affairs (Graduate Certificate), including Cuban studies, globalization studies; health policy and management (Graduate Certificate), including health management and leadership, public health policy and programs; hearing specialist: early intervention (Graduate Certificate); industrial and management systems engineering (Graduate Certificate), including systems engineering, technology management; information studies (Graduate Certificate), including school library media specialist; information systems/decision sciences (Graduate Certificate), including analytics and business intelligence; instructional technology (Graduate Certificate), including distance education, Florida digital/virtual educator, instructional design, multimedia design, Web design; internal medicine, bioethics and medical humanities (Graduate Certificate), including biomedical ethics; Latin American and Caribbean studies (Graduate Certificate); mass communications (Graduate Certificate), including multimedia journalism; mathematics and statistics (Graduate Certificate), including mathematics; medicine (Graduate Certificate), including aging and neuroscience, bioinformatics, biotechnology, brain fitness and memory management, clinical investigation, health informatics, health sciences, integrative weight management, intellectual property, medicine and gender, metabolic and nutritional medicine, metabolic cardiology, pharmacy sciences; national and competitive intelligence (Graduate Certificate); psychological and social foundations (Graduate Certificate), including career counseling, college teaching, diversity in education, mental health counseling, school counseling; public affairs (Graduate Certificate), including nonprofit management, public management, research administration; public health (Graduate Certificate), including environmental health, health equity, public health generalist, translational research in adolescent behavioral health; public health practices (Graduate Certificate), including planning for healthy communities; rehabilitation and mental health counseling (Graduate Certificate), including integrative mental health care, marriage and family therapy, rehabilitation technology; secondary education (Graduate Certificate), including ESOL, foreign language education: culture and content, foreign language education: professional; social work (Graduate Certificate), including geriatric social work/clinical gerontology; special education (Graduate Certificate), including autism spectrum disorder, disabilities education: severe/profound; world languages (Graduate Certificate), including teaching English as a second language (TESL) or foreign language. *Expenses:* Tuition, state resident: full-time $7766; part-time $431.43 per credit hour. Tuition, nonresident: full-time $15,789; part-time $877.17 per credit hour. *Required fees:* $37 per term. *Unit head:* Kathy Barnes, Interdisciplinary Programs Coordinator, 813-974-8031, Fax: 813-974-7061, E-mail: barnesk@usf.edu. *Application contact:* Karen Tylinski, Metro Initiatives, 813-974-9943, Fax: 813-974-7061, E-mail: ktylinsk@usf.edu. Website: http://www.usf.edu/innovative-education/

The University of Tennessee, Graduate School, Tickle College of Engineering, Department of Materials Science and Engineering, Program in Materials Science and Engineering, Knoxville, TN 37996. Offers MS, PhD. *Faculty:* 26 full-time (3 women), 10 part-time/adjunct (2 women). *Students:* 78 full-time (21 women), 6 part-time (2 women); includes 6 minority (1 Black or African American, non-Hispanic/Latino; 2 Asian, non-Hispanic/Latino; 3 Hispanic/Latino), 37 international. Average age 29. 138 applicants, 17% accepted, 17 enrolled. In 2016, 19 master's, 10 doctorates awarded. *Degree requirements:* For master's, thesis or alternative; for doctorate, comprehensive exam, thesis/dissertation. *Entrance requirements:* For master's, GRE General Test (for MS students pursuing research thesis), minimum GPA of 2.7 (for U.S. degree holders), 3.0 (for international degree holders); 3 references; for doctorate, GRE General Test, minimum GPA of 3.0 on previous graduate course work; 3 references. Additional exam

requirements/recommendations for international students: Required—TOEFL (minimum score 550 paper-based). *Application deadline:* For fall admission, 2/1 priority date for domestic and international students; for spring admission, 6/15 for domestic and international students. Applications are processed on a rolling basis. Application fee: $35. Electronic applications accepted. *Financial support:* In 2016–17, 77 students received support, including 9 fellowships with full tuition reimbursements available (averaging $30,278 per year), 50 research assistantships with full tuition reimbursements available (averaging $23,100 per year), 16 teaching assistantships with full tuition reimbursements available (averaging $21,291 per year); career-related internships or fieldwork, Federal Work-Study, institutionally sponsored loans, health care benefits, and unspecified assistantships also available. Financial award application deadline: 2/1; financial award applicants required to submit FAFSA. *Faculty research:* Biomaterials; functional materials electronic, magnetic and optical; high temperature materials; mechanical behavior of materials; neutron materials science. *Unit head:* Dr. Veerle Keppens, Head, 865-974-5336, Fax: 865-974-4115, E-mail: vkeppens@utk.edu. *Application contact:* Dr. Roberto S. Benson, Associate Head, 865-974-5347, Fax: 865-974-4115, E-mail: rbenson1@utk.edu. Website: http://www.engr.utk.edu/mse

The University of Texas at Arlington, Graduate School, College of Engineering, Department of Materials Science and Engineering, Arlington, TX 76019. Offers M Engr, MS, PhD. Terminal master's awarded for partial completion of doctoral program. *Degree requirements:* For master's, comprehensive exam (for some programs), thesis optional; for doctorate, comprehensive exam, thesis/dissertation optional. *Entrance requirements:* For master's, GRE General Test, minimum GPA of 3.0; for doctorate, GRE General Test, minimum GPA of 3.5. Additional exam requirements/recommendations for international students: Required—TOEFL (minimum score 550 paper-based; 79 iBT), IELTS. *Application deadline:* For fall admission, 6/1 for domestic students, 4/1 for international students; for spring admission, 10/15 for domestic students, 9/15 for international students. Applications are processed on a rolling basis. Application fee: $35 ($50 for international students). *Financial support:* Fellowships, research assistantships, teaching assistantships, scholarships/grants, and unspecified assistantships available. Financial award application deadline: 6/1; financial award applicants required to submit FAFSA. *Faculty research:* Electronic materials, conductive polymer, composites biomaterial, structural materials. *Unit head:* Dr. Eric Jones, Associate Dean for Graduate Studies. *Application contact:* Dr. Eric Jones, Associate Dean for Graduate Studies. Website: http://www.uta.edu/mse

The University of Texas at Austin, Graduate School, Cockrell School of Engineering, Program in Materials Science and Engineering, Austin, TX 78712-1111. Offers MS, PhD. *Program availability:* Part-time. *Degree requirements:* For master's, thesis (for some programs); for doctorate, thesis/dissertation. *Entrance requirements:* For master's and doctorate, GRE General Test. Additional exam requirements/recommendations for international students: Required—TOEFL (minimum score 550 paper-based). Electronic applications accepted.

The University of Texas at Dallas, Erik Jonson School of Engineering and Computer Science, Department of Materials Science and Engineering, Richardson, TX 75080. Offers MS, PhD. *Program availability:* Part-time, evening/weekend. *Faculty:* 15 full-time (2 women). *Students:* 58 full-time (14 women), 4 part-time (2 women); includes 9 minority (2 Black or African American, non-Hispanic/Latino; 4 Asian, non-Hispanic/Latino; 2 Hispanic/Latino; 1 Two or more races, non-Hispanic/Latino), 38 international. Average age 28. 116 applicants, 37% accepted, 15 enrolled. In 2016, 13 master's, 6 doctorates awarded. *Degree requirements:* For master's, thesis or major design project; for doctorate, thesis/dissertation. *Entrance requirements:* For master's, GRE General Test, minimum GPA of 3.0 in related bachelor's degree; for doctorate, GRE General Test, minimum GPA of 3.5. Additional exam requirements/recommendations for international students: Required—TOEFL (minimum score 550 paper-based). *Application deadline:* For fall admission, 7/15 for domestic students, 5/1 priority date for international students; for spring admission, 11/15 for domestic students, 9/1 priority date for international students. Applications are processed on a rolling basis. Application fee: $50 ($100 for international students). Electronic applications accepted. *Expenses:* Tuition, state resident: full-time $12,418; part-time $690 per semester hour. Tuition, nonresident: full-time $24,150; part-time $1342 per semester hour. Tuition and fees vary according to course load. *Financial support:* In 2016–17, 56 students received support, including 3 fellowships (averaging $2,067 per year), 48 research assistantships with partial tuition reimbursements available (averaging $25,391 per year), 5 teaching assistantships with partial tuition reimbursements available (averaging $21,600 per year); career-related internships or fieldwork, Federal Work-Study, institutionally sponsored loans, scholarships/grants, and unspecified assistantships also available. Support available to part-time students. Financial award application deadline: 4/30; financial award applicants required to submit FAFSA. *Faculty research:* Graphene-based semiconducting materials, neuro-inspired computational paradigms, electronic materials with emphasis on dielectrics, energy harvesting (photovoltaics, lithium-ion batteries), biosensors and hydrogen storage materials. *Unit head:* Dr. Yves Chabal, Department Head, 972-883-5751, Fax: 972-883-5725, E-mail: chabal@utdallas.edu. *Application contact:* Dr. Julia Hsu, Associate Department Head, 972-883-5789, Fax: 972-883-5725, E-mail: jwhsu@utdallas.edu. Website: http://mse.utdallas.edu/

The University of Texas at El Paso, Graduate School, College of Engineering, Department of Metallurgical and Materials Engineering, El Paso, TX 79968-0001. Offers materials science and engineering (PhD); metallurgical and materials engineering (MS). *Program availability:* Part-time, evening/weekend. *Degree requirements:* For master's, thesis. *Entrance requirements:* For master's, GRE General Test. Additional exam requirements/recommendations for international students: Required—TOEFL. Electronic applications accepted.

The University of Texas at El Paso, Graduate School, Interdisciplinary Program in Materials Science and Engineering, El Paso, TX 79968-0001. Offers PhD. *Program availability:* Part-time, evening/weekend. *Degree requirements:* For doctorate, thesis/dissertation. *Entrance requirements:* For doctorate, GRE, letters of recommendation. Additional exam requirements/recommendations for international students: Required—TOEFL; Recommended—IELTS. Electronic applications accepted.

The University of Texas at San Antonio, College of Engineering, Department of Electrical and Computer Engineering, San Antonio, TX 78249-0617. Offers advanced materials engineering (MS); computer engineering (MS); electrical engineering (MSEE, PhD). *Program availability:* Part-time. *Faculty:* 26 full-time (4 women), 3 part-time/adjunct (0 women). *Students:* 122 full-time (31 women), 100 part-time (22 women); includes 46 minority (4 Black or African American, non-Hispanic/Latino; 10 Asian, non-Hispanic/Latino; 30 Hispanic/Latino; 1 Native Hawaiian or other Pacific Islander, non-Hispanic/Latino; 1 Two or more races, non-Hispanic/Latino), 131 international. Average age 28. 233 applicants, 73% accepted, 50 enrolled. In 2016, 115 master's, 15 doctorates awarded. Terminal master's awarded for partial completion of doctoral program. *Degree requirements:* For master's, comprehensive exam, thesis (for some programs); for doctorate, comprehensive exam, thesis/dissertation. *Entrance requirements:* For master's, GRE General Test, bachelor's degree in electrical or

computer engineering from ABET-accredited institution of higher education or related field; minimum GPA of 3.0 on the last 60 semester credit hours of undergraduate studies; for doctorate, GRE General Test, master's degree or minimum GPA of 3.3 in last 60 semester credit hours of undergraduate level coursework in electrical engineering; statement of purpose. Additional exam requirements/recommendations for international students: Required—TOEFL (minimum score 550 paper-based; 79 iBT), IELTS (minimum score 6.5). *Application deadline:* For fall admission, 7/1 for domestic students, 4/1 for international students; for spring admission, 11/1 for domestic students, 9/1 for international students. Applications are processed on a rolling basis. Application fee: $45 ($80 for international students). Electronic applications accepted. *Financial support:* Unspecified assistantships available. Financial award application deadline: 3/31. *Faculty research:* Computer engineering, digital signal processing, systems and controls, communications, electronics materials and devices, electric power engineering. *Total annual research expenditures:* $3.9 million. *Unit head:* Dr. Chunjiang Qian, Department Chair/Professor, 210-458-7928, E-mail: chunjiang.qian@utsa.edu.
Website: http://ece.utsa.edu/

University of Toronto, School of Graduate Studies, Faculty of Applied Science and Engineering, Department of Materials Science and Engineering, Toronto, ON M5S 1A1, Canada. Offers M Eng, MA Sc, PhD. *Program availability:* Part-time. *Degree requirements:* For master's, thesis (for some programs), oral presentation/thesis defense (MA Sc), qualifying exam; for doctorate, thesis/dissertation. *Entrance requirements:* For master's, BA Sc or B Sc in materials science and engineering, 2 letters of reference; for doctorate, MA Sc or equivalent, 2 letters of reference, minimum B+ average in last 2 years. Additional exam requirements/recommendations for international students: Required—TOEFL (minimum score 580 paper-based), TWE (minimum score 4). Electronic applications accepted.

University of Utah, Graduate School, College of Engineering, Department of Materials Science and Engineering, Salt Lake City, UT 84112. Offers MS, PhD. *Faculty:* 8 full-time (0 women), 2 part-time/adjunct (1 woman). *Students:* 21 full-time (9 women), 7 part-time (2 women), 11 international. Average age 29. 61 applicants, 5% accepted, 3 enrolled. In 2016, 3 master's, 4 doctorates awarded. *Degree requirements:* For master's, thesis; for doctorate, thesis/dissertation. *Entrance requirements:* For master's and doctorate, GRE General Test, minimum GPA of 3.0. Additional exam requirements/recommendations for international students: Required—TOEFL (minimum score 570 paper-based; 88 iBT), IELTS (minimum score 7). *Application deadline:* For fall admission, 1/15 for domestic students, 12/15 for international students. Application fee: $0 ($15 for international students). Electronic applications accepted. *Expenses:* Contact institution. *Financial support:* In 2016–17, 1 student received support, including 1 fellowship with full tuition reimbursement available (averaging $26,780 per year), 16 research assistantships with full tuition reimbursements available (averaging $23,000 per year); teaching assistantships with full tuition reimbursements available also available. Financial award application deadline: 2/1; financial award applicants required to submit FAFSA. *Faculty research:* Solid oxide fuel cells, computational nanostructures, solar cells, Nano sensors, batteries: renewable energy. *Total annual research expenditures:* $3.3 million. *Unit head:* Dr. Feng Liu, Chair, 801-581-6863, Fax: 801-581-4816, E-mail: fliu@eng.utah.edu. *Application contact:* Marcie Leek, Academic Advisor, 801-581-6863, Fax: 801-581-4816, E-mail: marcie.leek@utah.edu.
Website: http://www.mse.utah.edu/

University of Washington, Graduate School, College of Engineering, Department of Materials Science and Engineering, Seattle, WA 98195-2120. Offers applied materials science and engineering (MS); materials science and engineering (MS, PhD). *Program availability:* Part-time. *Faculty:* 13 full-time (2 women). *Students:* 97 full-time (28 women), 19 part-time (5 women); includes 21 minority (1 Black or African American, non-Hispanic/Latino; 12 Asian, non-Hispanic/Latino; 5 Hispanic/Latino; 1 Native Hawaiian or other Pacific Islander, non-Hispanic/Latino; 2 Two or more races, non-Hispanic/Latino), 40 international. 505 applicants, 21% accepted, 49 enrolled. In 2016, 41 master's, 12 doctorates awarded. Terminal master's awarded for partial completion of doctoral program. *Degree requirements:* For master's, comprehensive exam, final presentation; for doctorate, comprehensive exam, thesis/dissertation, qualifying evaluation, general and final exams. *Entrance requirements:* For master's and doctorate, GRE General Test, minimum GPA of 3.0, resume/curriculum vitae, letters of recommendation, statement of purpose, transcripts. Additional exam requirements/recommendations for international students: Required—TOEFL (minimum score 580 paper-based; 92 iBT). *Application deadline:* For fall admission, 1/2 for domestic and international students. Application fee: $85. Electronic applications accepted. *Expenses:* Contact institution. *Financial support:* In 2016–17, 49 students received support, including 3 fellowships with full tuition reimbursements available (averaging $2,800 per year), 34 research assistantships with full tuition reimbursements available (averaging $2,398 per year), 12 teaching assistantships with full tuition reimbursements available (averaging $2,398 per year); career-related internships or fieldwork, Federal Work-Study, institutionally sponsored loans, scholarships/grants, health care benefits, unspecified assistantships, and stipend supplements also available. Financial award application deadline: 1/1; financial award applicants required to submit FAFSA. *Faculty research:* Synthesis/structure/property and processing, biomaterials and biomimetics, materials chemistry and characterization, optical and electronic materials. *Total annual research expenditures:* $6.3 million. *Unit head:* Dr. Fumio Ohuchi, Professor/Chair, 206-685-8272, Fax: 206-543-3100, E-mail: ohuchi@uw.edu. *Application contact:* Karen Wetterhahn, Academic Counselor, 206-543-2740, Fax: 206-543-3100, E-mail: karenlw@uw.edu.
Website: http://depts.washington.edu/mse/

The University of Western Ontario, Faculty of Graduate Studies, Physical Sciences Division, Faculty of Engineering, London, ON N6A 5B8, Canada. Offers chemical and biochemical engineering (ME Sc, PhD); civil and environmental engineering (M Eng, ME Sc, PhD); electrical and computer engineering (M Eng, ME Sc, PhD); mechanical and materials engineering (M Eng, ME Sc, PhD). *Program availability:* Part-time. Terminal master's awarded for partial completion of doctoral program. *Degree requirements:* For master's, thesis; for doctorate, thesis/dissertation. *Entrance requirements:* For master's, minimum B average; for doctorate, minimum B+ average. *Faculty research:* Wind, geotechnical, chemical reactor engineering, applied electrostatics, biochemical engineering.

University of Windsor, Faculty of Graduate Studies, Faculty of Engineering, Department of Mechanical, Automotive, and Materials Engineering, Windsor, ON N9B 3P4, Canada. Offers engineering materials (M Eng, MA Sc, PhD); mechanical engineering (M Eng, MA Sc, PhD). *Program availability:* Part-time. *Degree requirements:* For master's, thesis; for doctorate, comprehensive exam, thesis/dissertation. *Entrance requirements:* For master's, minimum B average; for doctorate, master's degree, minimum B average. Additional exam requirements/recommendations for international students: Required—TOEFL (minimum score 600 paper-based). Electronic applications accepted. *Faculty research:* Thermofluids, applied mechanics, materials engineering.

University of Wisconsin–Madison, Graduate School, College of Engineering, Department of Materials Science and Engineering, Madison, WI 53706. Offers MS, PhD. *Program availability:* Part-time. *Faculty:* 16 full-time (3 women). *Students:* 110 full-time (24 women), 7 part-time (2 women); includes 13 minority (1 Black or African American, non-Hispanic/Latino; 2 Asian, non-Hispanic/Latino; 6 Hispanic/Latino; 4 Two or more races, non-Hispanic/Latino), 65 international. Average age 27. 559 applicants, 10% accepted, 17 enrolled. In 2016, 17 master's, 16 doctorates awarded. Terminal master's awarded for partial completion of doctoral program. *Degree requirements:* For master's, thesis, minimum of 30 credits; for doctorate, comprehensive exam, thesis/dissertation, minimum of 51 credits. *Entrance requirements:* For master's and doctorate, GRE General Test, BS in physical sciences or engineering; minimum GPA of 3.0. Additional exam requirements/recommendations for international students: Required—TOEFL (minimum score 580 paper-based; 92 iBT), IELTS (minimum score 7). *Application deadline:* For fall admission, 1/1 for domestic and international students; for spring admission, 10/1 for domestic students, 10/15 for international students. Application fee: $75 ($81 for international students). Electronic applications accepted. *Expenses:* $13,157 per year in-state tuition and fees; $26,484 per year out-of-state tuition and fees. *Financial support:* In 2016–17, 79 students received support, including 4 fellowships with full tuition reimbursements available, 65 research assistantships with full tuition reimbursements available, 9 teaching assistantships with full tuition reimbursements available; career-related internships or fieldwork, traineeships, health care benefits, tuition waivers (full), and unspecified assistantships also available. Financial award application deadline: 12/1; financial award applicants required to submit FAFSA. *Faculty research:* Thin film deposition, electron microscopy, computational materials science, mechanics and materials design. *Total annual research expenditures:* $10.5 million. *Unit head:* Dr. Paul Voyles, Chair, 608-265-6740, Fax: 608-262-8353, E-mail: paul.voyles@wisc.edu. *Application contact:* Michael Radloff, Student Services Coordinator, 608-890-2756, E-mail: radloff2@wisc.edu.
Website: https://www.engr.wisc.edu/department/materials-science-engineering/academics/ms/

University of Wisconsin–Milwaukee, Graduate School, College of Engineering and Applied Science, Program in Engineering, Milwaukee, WI 53201-0413. Offers biomedical engineering (MS); civil engineering (MS, PhD); computer science (PhD); electrical and computer engineering (MS); electrical engineering (PhD); engineering mechanics (MS); industrial and management engineering (MS); industrial engineering (PhD); manufacturing engineering (MS); materials (PhD); materials engineering (MS); mechanical engineering (MS). *Program availability:* Part-time. *Students:* 199 full-time (52 women), 156 part-time (32 women); includes 27 minority (2 Black or African American, non-Hispanic/Latino; 15 Asian, non-Hispanic/Latino; 3 Hispanic/Latino; 7 Two or more races, non-Hispanic/Latino), 244 international. Average age 30. 396 applicants, 61% accepted, 102 enrolled. In 2016, 72 master's, 26 doctorates awarded. *Degree requirements:* For master's, comprehensive exam (for some programs), thesis or alternative; for doctorate, comprehensive exam, thesis/dissertation, internship. *Entrance requirements:* For master's, GRE, minimum GPA of 2.75; for doctorate, GRE, minimum GPA of 3.5. Additional exam requirements/recommendations for international students: Required—TOEFL (minimum score 550 paper-based; 79 iBT), IELTS (minimum score 6.5). *Application deadline:* For fall admission, 1/1 priority date for domestic students; for spring admission, 9/1 for domestic students. Applications are processed on a rolling basis. Application fee: $56 ($96 for international students). *Financial support:* In 2016–17, 3 fellowships, 55 research assistantships, 77 teaching assistantships were awarded; career-related internships or fieldwork, Federal Work-Study, unspecified assistantships, and project assistantships also available. Support available to part-time students. Financial award application deadline: 4/15. *Unit head:* David Yu, Representative, 414-229-6169, E-mail: yu@uwm.edu. *Application contact:* Betty Warras, General Information Contact, 414-229-6169, Fax: 414-229-6967, E-mail: bwarras@uwm.edu.
Website: http://www4.uwm.edu/ceas/academics/graduate_programs/

Virginia Polytechnic Institute and State University, Graduate School, College of Engineering, Blacksburg, VA 24061. Offers aerospace engineering (ME, MS, PhD); biological systems engineering (ME, MS, PhD); biomedical engineering (MS, PhD); chemical engineering (ME, MS, PhD); civil engineering (ME, MS, PhD); computer engineering (ME, MS, PhD); computer science (MS, PhD); electrical engineering (ME, PhD); engineering education (PhD); engineering mechanics (ME, MS, PhD); environmental engineering (MS); environmental science and engineering (MS); industrial and systems engineering (ME, MS, PhD); materials science and engineering (ME, MS, PhD); mechanical engineering (ME, MS, PhD); mining and minerals engineering (PhD); mining engineering (ME, MS); nuclear engineering (MS, PhD); ocean engineering (MS); systems engineering (ME, MS). *Faculty:* 400 full-time (73 women), 3 part-time/adjunct (2 women). *Students:* 1,949 full-time (487 women), 393 part-time (69 women); includes 251 minority (56 Black or African American, non-Hispanic/Latino; 3 American Indian or Alaska Native, non-Hispanic/Latino; 87 Asian, non-Hispanic/Latino; 70 Hispanic/Latino; 35 Two or more races, non-Hispanic/Latino), 1,354 international. Average age 27. 4,903 applicants, 19% accepted, 569 enrolled. In 2016, 364 master's, 200 doctorates awarded. *Degree requirements:* For master's, comprehensive exam (for some programs), thesis (for some programs); for doctorate, comprehensive exam (for some programs), thesis/dissertation (for some programs). *Entrance requirements:* For master's and doctorate, GRE/GMAT. Additional exam requirements/recommendations for international students: Required—TOEFL (minimum score 80 iBT). *Application deadline:* For fall admission, 8/1 for domestic students, 4/1 for international students; for spring admission, 1/1 for domestic students, 9/1 for international students. Applications are processed on a rolling basis. Application fee: $75. Electronic applications accepted. *Expenses:* Tuition, state resident: full-time $12,467; part-time $692.50 per credit hour. Tuition, nonresident: full-time $25,095; part-time $1394.25 per credit hour. *Required fees:* $2669; $491.50 per semester. Tuition and fees vary according to course load, campus/location and program. *Financial support:* In 2016–17, 160 fellowships with full tuition reimbursements (averaging $7,387 per year), 872 research assistantships with full tuition reimbursements (averaging $22,329 per year), 313 teaching assistantships with full tuition reimbursements (averaging $18,714 per year) were awarded. Financial award application deadline: 3/1; financial award applicants required to submit FAFSA. *Total annual research expenditures:* $91.8 million. *Unit head:* Dr. Julia Ross, Dean, 540-231-9752, Fax: 540-231-3031, E-mail: deaneng@vt.edu. *Application contact:* Linda Perkins, Executive Assistant, 540-231-9752, Fax: 540-231-3031, E-mail: lperkins@vt.edu.
Website: http://www.eng.vt.edu/

Washington State University, Voiland College of Engineering and Architecture, School of Mechanical and Materials Engineering, Pullman, WA 99164-2920. Offers materials science and engineering (MS, PhD); mechanical engineering (MS, PhD). MS programs also offered at Tri-Cities campus. *Program availability:* Part-time. Terminal master's awarded for partial completion of doctoral program. *Degree requirements:* For master's, comprehensive exam, thesis; for doctorate, comprehensive exam, thesis/dissertation, preliminary exam. *Entrance requirements:* For master's, GRE, bachelor's degree, minimum GPA of 3.0, resume, statement of purpose, 3 letters of recommendation, official transcripts, Student Interest Profile form; for doctorate, GRE, bachelor's degree, minimum GPA of 3.4, resume, statement of purpose, 3 letters of recommendation, official transcripts, Student Interest Profile form. Additional exam requirements/recommendations for international students: Required—TOEFL (minimum score 500 paper-based), IELTS. Electronic applications accepted. *Faculty research:* Multiscale modeling and characterization of materials; advanced energy; bioengineering;

engineering education and curricular innovation; modeling and visualization in the areas of product realization, materials, and processes.

Worcester Polytechnic Institute, Graduate Studies and Research, Department of Mechanical Engineering, Program in Materials Science and Engineering, Worcester, MA 01609-2280. Offers MS, PhD. *Program availability:* Part-time, evening/weekend. *Students:* 67 full-time (24 women), 3 part-time (1 woman); includes 5 minority (2 Hispanic/Latino; 3 Two or more races, non-Hispanic/Latino), 47 international. 129 applicants, 77% accepted, 20 enrolled. In 2016, 30 master's, 2 doctorates awarded. *Degree requirements:* For master's, thesis; for doctorate, comprehensive exam, thesis/dissertation. *Entrance requirements:* For master's and doctorate, GRE (recommended), 3 letters of recommendation. Additional exam requirements/recommendations for international students: Required—TOEFL (minimum score 563 paper-based; 84 iBT), IELTS (minimum score 7), GRE. *Application deadline:* For fall admission, 1/1 priority date for domestic students, 1/1 for international students; for spring admission, 10/1 priority date for domestic students, 10/1 for international students. Applications are processed on a rolling basis. Application fee: $70. Electronic applications accepted. *Financial support:* Research assistantships, teaching assistantships, career-related internships or fieldwork, institutionally sponsored loans, scholarships/grants, and unspecified assistantships available. Financial award application deadline: 1/1; financial award applicants required to submit FAFSA. *Unit head:* Dr. Richard D. Sisson, Jr., Director, 508-831-5633, Fax: 508-831-5178, E-mail: sisson@wpi.edu. *Application contact:* Rita Shilansky, Graduate Secretary, 508-831-5633, Fax: 508-831-5178, E-mail: rita@wpi.edu.
Website: http://www.wpi.edu/academics/mte

Wright State University, Graduate School, College of Engineering and Computer Science, Department of Mechanical and Materials Engineering, Dayton, OH 45435. Offers aerospace systems engineering (MSE); materials science and engineering (MSE); mechanical engineering (MSE); renewable ande clean energy (MSE). *Degree requirements:* For master's, thesis or course option alternative. *Entrance requirements:* Additional exam requirements/recommendations for international students: Required—TOEFL. Application fee: $25. *Expenses:* Tuition, state resident: full-time $9952; part-time $622 per credit hour. Tuition, nonresident: full-time $16,960; part-time $1060 per credit hour. *Financial support:* Fellowships, research assistantships, teaching assistantships, and unspecified assistantships available. Support available to part-time students. Financial award application deadline: 3/15; financial award applicants required to submit FAFSA. *Unit head:* Dr. George P.G. Huang, Chair, 937-775-5040, Fax: 937-775-5009, E-mail: george.huang@wright.edu. *Application contact:* John Kimble, Associate Director of Graduate Admissions and Records, 937-775-2957, Fax: 937-775-2453, E-mail: john.kimble@wright.edu.
Website: https://engineering-computer-science.wright.edu/mechanical-and-materials-engineering

Materials Sciences

Air Force Institute of Technology, Graduate School of Engineering and Management, Department of Aeronautics and Astronautics, Dayton, OH 45433-7765. Offers aeronautical engineering (MS, PhD); astronautical engineering (MS, PhD); materials science (MS, PhD); space operations (MS); systems engineering (MS, PhD). *Accreditation:* ABET (one or more programs are accredited). *Program availability:* Part-time. *Degree requirements:* For master's, thesis; for doctorate, thesis/dissertation. *Entrance requirements:* For master's and doctorate, GRE General Test, minimum GPA of 3.0, U.S. citizenship. *Faculty research:* Computational fluid dynamics, experimental aerodynamics, computational structural mechanics, experimental structural mechanics, aircraft and spacecraft stability and control.

Air Force Institute of Technology, Graduate School of Engineering and Management, Department of Engineering Physics, Dayton, OH 45433-7765. Offers applied physics (MS, PhD); electro-optics (MS, PhD); materials science (PhD); nuclear engineering (MS, PhD); space physics (MS). *Program availability:* Part-time. *Degree requirements:* For master's, thesis; for doctorate, thesis/dissertation. *Entrance requirements:* For master's and doctorate, GRE General Test, minimum GPA of 3.0, U.S. citizenship. *Faculty research:* High-energy lasers, space physics, nuclear weapon effects, semiconductor physics.

Alabama Agricultural and Mechanical University, School of Graduate Studies, College of Engineering, Technology, and Physical Sciences, Department of Physics, Chemistry and Mathematics, Huntsville, AL 35811. Offers physics (MS, PhD), including materials science (PhD), optics/lasers (PhD), space science (PhD). *Program availability:* Part-time, evening/weekend. *Degree requirements:* For doctorate, thesis/dissertation. *Entrance requirements:* For master's and doctorate, GRE General Test. Additional exam requirements/recommendations for international students: Required—TOEFL (minimum score 500 paper-based; 61 iBT). *Application deadline:* For fall admission, 5/1 for domestic students. Applications are processed on a rolling basis. Application fee: $25. Electronic applications accepted. *Expenses:* Tuition, nonresident: part-time $826 per credit hour. Full-time tuition and fees vary according to course load and program. *Financial support:* Fellowships with tuition reimbursements, research assistantships with tuition reimbursements, teaching assistantships with tuition reimbursements, career-related internships or fieldwork, and Federal Work-Study available. Financial award application deadline: 4/1. *Unit head:* Dr. Mohan Aggarwal, Chair, 256-372-8132.

Alfred University, Graduate School, College of Ceramics, Inamori School of Engineering, Alfred, NY 14802. Offers biomaterials engineering (MS); ceramic engineering (MS, PhD); electrical engineering (MS); glass science (MS, PhD); materials science and engineering (MS, PhD); mechanical engineering (MS). *Program availability:* Part-time. *Faculty:* 18 full-time (1 woman). *Students:* 26 full-time (6 women), 16 part-time (4 women); includes 1 minority (Hispanic/Latino), 12 international. Average age 27. 14 applicants, 79% accepted, 10 enrolled. In 2016, 13 master's, 5 doctorates awarded. *Degree requirements:* For master's, thesis; for doctorate, thesis/dissertation. *Entrance requirements:* Additional exam requirements/recommendations for international students: Required—TOEFL (minimum score 590 paper-based; 90 iBT), IELTS (minimum score 6.5). *Application deadline:* For fall admission, 3/1 priority date for domestic students, 3/15 for international students; for spring admission, 10/1 priority date for domestic students, 10/1 for international students. Applications are processed on a rolling basis. Application fee: $60. Electronic applications accepted. *Expenses:* Contact institution. *Financial support:* Fellowships with full tuition reimbursements, research assistantships with full tuition reimbursements, teaching assistantships with full tuition reimbursements, tuition waivers (full and partial), and unspecified assistantships available. Financial award application deadline: 8/1; financial award applicants required to submit FAFSA. *Faculty research:* X-ray diffraction, biomaterials and polymers, thin-film processing, electronic and optical ceramics, solid-state chemistry. *Unit head:* Dr. Alistair N. Cormack, Dean, 607-871-2422, E-mail: cormack@alfred.edu. *Application contact:* Sara Love, Coordinator of Graduate Admissions, 607-871-2115, Fax: 607-871-2198, E-mail: gradinquiry@alfred.edu.
Website: http://engineering.alfred.edu/grad/

Arizona State University at the Tempe campus, Ira A. Fulton Schools of Engineering, School for Engineering of Matter, Transport and Energy, Tempe, AZ 85281. Offers aerospace engineering (MS, PhD); chemical engineering (MS, PhD); materials science and engineering (MS, PhD); mechanical engineering (MS, PhD); solar energy engineering and commercialization (PSM). *Program availability:* Part-time, evening/weekend, online learning. Terminal master's awarded for partial completion of doctoral program. *Degree requirements:* For master's, thesis and oral defense (MS); applied project or comprehensive exam (MSE); interactive Program of Study (iPOS) submitted before completing 50 percent of required credit hours; for doctorate, comprehensive exam, thesis/dissertation, interactive Program of Study (iPOS) submitted before completing 50 percent of required credit hours. *Entrance requirements:* For master's, GRE, minimum GPA of 3.0 or equivalent in last 2 years of work leading to bachelor's degree; for doctorate, GRE, minimum GPA of 3.0 in last 2 years of work leading to bachelor's degree. Additional exam requirements/recommendations for international students: Required—TOEFL, IELTS, or PTE. Electronic applications accepted. *Expenses:* Contact institution. *Faculty research:* Electronic materials and packaging, materials for energy (batteries), adaptive/intelligent materials and structures, multiscale fluid mechanics, membranes, therapeutics and bioseparations, flexible structures, nanostructured materials, and micro/nano transport.

Binghamton University, State University of New York, Graduate School, Thomas J. Watson School of Engineering and Applied Science and Harpur College of Arts and Sciences, Materials Science and Engineering Program, Binghamton, NY 13902-6000. Offers MS, PhD. *Program availability:* Part-time, online learning. *Faculty:* 3 full-time (0 women). *Students:* 14 full-time (2 women), 33 part-time (12 women); includes 3 minority (all Asian, non-Hispanic/Latino), 37 international. Average age 28. 101 applicants, 42% accepted, 8 enrolled. In 2016, 7 master's, 2 doctorates awarded. *Degree requirements:* For master's, thesis; for doctorate, comprehensive exam, thesis/dissertation. *Entrance requirements:* For master's and doctorate, GRE General Test. Additional exam requirements/recommendations for international students: Required—TOEFL (minimum score 550 paper-based; 80 iBT). *Application deadline:* Applications are processed on a rolling basis. Application fee: $75. Electronic applications accepted. *Expenses:* Contact institution. *Financial support:* In 2016–17, 31 students received support, including 21 research assistantships with full tuition reimbursements available (averaging $17,500 per year), 10 teaching assistantships with full tuition reimbursements available (averaging $17,500 per year); fellowships, career-related internships or fieldwork, Federal Work-Study, institutionally sponsored loans, scholarships/grants, health care benefits, tuition waivers (full and partial), and unspecified assistantships also available. Financial award application deadline: 2/1; financial award applicants required to submit FAFSA. *Unit head:* Ellen Tilden, Coordinator of Graduate Programs, 607-777-2873, E-mail: etilden@binghamton.edu. *Application contact:* Ben Balkaya, Assistant Dean and Director, 607-777-2151, Fax: 607-777-2501, E-mail: balkaya@binghamton.edu.
Website: https://www.binghamton.edu/me/grad/materials-science.html

Boston University, College of Engineering, Division of Materials Science and Engineering, Brookline, MA 02446. Offers materials science and engineering (M Eng, MS, PhD). *Program availability:* Part-time. *Students:* 69 full-time (26 women), 15 part-time (6 women); includes 8 minority (5 Asian, non-Hispanic/Latino; 3 Hispanic/Latino), 53 international. Average age 25. 271 applicants, 30% accepted, 29 enrolled. In 2016, 28 master's, 7 doctorates awarded. Terminal master's awarded for partial completion of doctoral program. *Degree requirements:* For master's, thesis (for some programs); for doctorate, comprehensive exam, thesis/dissertation. *Entrance requirements:* For master's and doctorate, GRE General Test. Additional exam requirements/recommendations for international students: Required—TOEFL (minimum score 90 iBT), IELTS (minimum score 7). *Financial support:* Application deadline: 1/1. *Faculty research:* Biomaterials, electronic and photonic materials, materials for energy and environment, nanomaterials. *Unit head:* Dr. David Bishop, Division Head, 617-353-8899, Fax: 617-353-5548, E-mail: djb1@bu.edu.
Website: http://www.bu.edu/mse/

Brown University, Graduate School, School of Engineering, Program in Materials Science and Engineering, Providence, RI 02912. Offers Sc M, PhD. *Degree requirements:* For doctorate, thesis/dissertation, preliminary exam.

California Institute of Technology, Division of Engineering and Applied Science, Option in Materials Science, Pasadena, CA 91125-0001. Offers MS, PhD. *Degree requirements:* For doctorate, thesis/dissertation. *Faculty research:* Mechanical properties, physical properties, kinetics of phase transformations, metastable phases, transmission electron microscopy.

Carnegie Mellon University, Carnegie Institute of Technology, Department of Materials Science and Engineering, Pittsburgh, PA 15213-3891. Offers MS, PhD. *Program availability:* Part-time. Terminal master's awarded for partial completion of doctoral program. *Degree requirements:* For master's, exam; for doctorate, thesis/dissertation, qualifying exam. *Entrance requirements:* For master's and doctorate, GRE General Test. Additional exam requirements/recommendations for international students: Required—TOEFL. *Faculty research:* Materials characterization, process metallurgy, high strength alloys, growth kinetics, ceramics.

Case Western Reserve University, School of Graduate Studies, Case School of Engineering, Department of Materials Science and Engineering, Cleveland, OH 44106. Offers materials science and engineering (MS, PhD). *Program availability:* Part-time, online learning. *Faculty:* 12 full-time (1 woman). *Students:* 34 full-time (9 women), 6 part-time (2 women); includes 5 minority (1 Black or African American, non-Hispanic/Latino; 2 Asian, non-Hispanic/Latino; 1 Hispanic/Latino; 1 Two or more races, non-Hispanic/Latino), 18 international. In 2016, 4 master's, 5 doctorates awarded. Terminal master's awarded for partial completion of doctoral program. *Degree requirements:* For master's, thesis (for some programs); for doctorate, thesis/dissertation, qualifying exam, teaching experience. *Entrance requirements:* For master's and doctorate, GRE General Test. Additional exam requirements/recommendations for international students: Required—TOEFL. *Application deadline:* For fall admission, 2/15 priority date for domestic students; for spring admission, 9/15 for domestic students. Applications are processed on a rolling basis. Application fee: $50. *Expenses: Tuition:* Full-time $42,576; part-time $1774 per credit hour. *Required fees:* $34. Tuition and fees vary according to course load and program. *Financial support:* In 2016–17, 1 fellowship with tuition reimbursement, 29 research assistantships with tuition reimbursements were awarded;

teaching assistantships also available. Financial award application deadline: 4/30; financial award applicants required to submit FAFSA. *Faculty research:* Surface hardening of steels and other alloys, chemistry and structure of surfaces, microstructural and mechanical property characterization, materials for energy applications, thermodynamics and kinetics of materials, performance and reliability of materials. *Total annual research expenditures:* $3.6 million. *Unit head:* Dr. Frank Ernst, Department Chair, 216-368-0611, Fax: 216-368-4224, E-mail: emse.info@case.edu. *Application contact:* Theresa Claytor, Student Affairs Coordinator, 216-368-8555, Fax: 216-368-8555, E-mail: esme.info@case.edu.
Website: http://engineering.case.edu/emse/

The Catholic University of America, School of Engineering, Department of Materials Science and Engineering, Washington, DC 20064. Offers MS. *Program availability:* Part-time. *Faculty:* 1 part-time/adjunct (0 women). *Students:* 11 full-time (6 women), 2 part-time (both women); includes 3 minority (1 Asian, non-Hispanic/Latino; 2 Two or more races, non-Hispanic/Latino), 10 international. Average age 27. 9 applicants, 78% accepted, 3 enrolled. In 2016, 3 master's awarded. *Degree requirements:* For master's, thesis optional. *Entrance requirements:* For master's, GRE (minimum score 1250), minimum GPA of 3.0, statement of purpose, official copies of academic transcripts. Additional exam requirements/recommendations for international students: Required—TOEFL (minimum score 550 paper-based; 80 iBT). *Application deadline:* For fall admission, 7/15 for domestic students, 7/1 for international students; for spring admission, 11/15 for domestic students, 11/1 for international students. Applications are processed on a rolling basis. Application fee: $55. Electronic applications accepted. *Expenses:* $43,380 per year; $1,170 per credit; $200 per semester part-time fees. *Financial support:* Fellowships, research assistantships, teaching assistantships, Federal Work-Study, scholarships/grants, tuition waivers (full and partial), and unspecified assistantships available. Financial award application deadline: 2/1; financial award applicants required to submit FAFSA. *Faculty research:* Nanotechnology, biomaterials, magnetic and optical materials, glass, ceramics, and metallurgy processing and instrumentation. *Unit head:* Dr. Biprodas Dutta, Director, 202-319-5535, Fax: 202-319-4469, E-mail: duttab@cua.edu. *Application contact:* Director of Graduate Admissions, 202-319-5057, Fax: 202-319-6533, E-mail: cua-admissions@cua.edu.
Website: http://materialsscience.cua.edu/

Central Michigan University, College of Graduate Studies, College of Science and Technology, Department of Physics, Program in the Science of Advanced Materials, Mount Pleasant, MI 48859. Offers PhD. *Degree requirements:* For doctorate, comprehensive exam, thesis/dissertation. *Entrance requirements:* For doctorate, GRE. Electronic applications accepted. *Faculty research:* Electronic properties of nanomaterials, polymers for energy and for environmental applications, inorganic materials synthesis, magnetic properties from first-principles, and nano devices for biomedical applications and environmental remediation.

Clarkson University, Wallace H. Coulter School of Engineering, Program in Materials Science and Engineering, Potsdam, NY 13699. Offers PhD. *Students:* 5 full-time (1 woman); includes 1 minority (Asian, non-Hispanic/Latino), 2 international. 23 applicants, 35% accepted. *Degree requirements:* For doctorate, comprehensive exam, thesis/dissertation. *Entrance requirements:* For doctorate, GRE. Additional exam requirements/recommendations for international students: Required—TOEFL (minimum score 550 paper-based, 80 iBT) or IELTS (6.5). *Application deadline:* Applications are processed on a rolling basis. Application fee: $50. Electronic applications accepted. *Expenses: Tuition:* Full-time $23,400; part-time $1300 per credit hour. Tuition and fees vary according to campus/location and program. *Financial support:* Scholarships/grants and unspecified assistantships available. *Unit head:* Dr. Marilyn Freeman, Director of Materials Science and Engineering, 315-268-2316, E-mail: mfreeman@clarkson.edu. *Application contact:* Dan Capogna, Graduate Admissions Contact, 518-631-9910, E-mail: graduate@clarkson.edu.
Website: http://graduate.clarkson.edu

Clemson University, Graduate School, College of Engineering, Computing and Applied Sciences, Department of Materials Science and Engineering, Clemson, SC 29634. Offers MS, PhD. *Program availability:* Part-time. *Faculty:* 17 full-time (2 women), 2 part-time/adjunct (0 women). *Students:* 44 full-time (10 women), 9 part-time (2 women); includes 3 minority (1 Asian, non-Hispanic/Latino; 2 Hispanic/Latino), 26 international. Average age 27. 120 applicants, 21% accepted, 10 enrolled. In 2016, 5 master's, 10 doctorates awarded. Terminal master's awarded for partial completion of doctoral program. *Degree requirements:* For master's, thesis; for doctorate, comprehensive exam, thesis/dissertation. *Entrance requirements:* For master's and doctorate, GRE General Test, unofficial transcripts, letters of recommendation. Additional exam requirements/recommendations for international students: Required—TOEFL (minimum score 80 iBT), IELTS (minimum score 6.5). *Application deadline:* For fall admission, 2/1 priority date for domestic and international students; for spring admission, 9/1 priority date for domestic and international students. Applications are processed on a rolling basis. Application fee: $80 ($90 for international students). Electronic applications accepted. *Expenses:* $4,841 per semester full-time resident, $9,640 per semester full-time non-resident, $612 per credit hour part-time resident, $1,223 per credit hour part-time non-resident. *Financial support:* In 2016–17, 63 students received support, including 7 fellowships with partial tuition reimbursements available (averaging $7,071 per year), 22 research assistantships with partial tuition reimbursements available (averaging $20,409 per year), 1 teaching assistantship with partial tuition reimbursement available (averaging $15,000 per year); career-related internships or fieldwork and unspecified assistantships also available. Financial award application deadline: 2/1. *Total annual research expenditures:* $2.9 million. *Unit head:* Dr. Rajendra Bordia, Department Chair, 864-656-5228, E-mail: rbordia@clemson.edu. *Application contact:* Dr. Kyle Brinkman, Graduate Program Coordinator, 864-656-1405, E-mail: ksbrink@clemson.edu.
Website: https://www.clemson.edu/cecas/departments/mse/index.html

The College of William and Mary, Faculty of Arts and Sciences, Department of Applied Science, Williamsburg, VA 23185. Offers accelerator science (PhD); applied mathematics (PhD); applied mechanics (PhD); applied robotics (PhD); applied science (MS); atmospheric and environmental science (PhD); computational neuroscience (PhD); interface, thin film and surface science (PhD); lasers and optics (PhD); magnetic resonance (PhD); materials science and engineering (PhD); mathematical and computational biology (PhD); medical imaging (PhD); nanotechnology (PhD); neuroscience (PhD); non-destructive evaluation (PhD); polymer chemistry (PhD); remote sensing (PhD). *Program availability:* Part-time. *Faculty:* 8 full-time (2 women), 2 part-time/adjunct (0 women). *Students:* 30 full-time (11 women), 4 part-time (0 women); includes 16 minority (2 Black or African American, non-Hispanic/Latino; 12 Asian, non-Hispanic/Latino; 2 Hispanic/Latino), 12 international. Average age 28. 37 applicants, 27% accepted, 7 enrolled. In 2016, 6 doctorates awarded. Terminal master's awarded for partial completion of doctoral program. *Degree requirements:* For master's, comprehensive exam, thesis; for doctorate, comprehensive exam, thesis/dissertation, 4 core courses. *Entrance requirements:* For master's and doctorate, GRE General Test, GRE Subject Test. Additional exam requirements/recommendations for international students: Required—TOEFL, IELTS. *Application deadline:* For fall admission, 2/3 priority date for domestic students, 2/3 for international students; for spring admission, 10/15 priority date for domestic students, 10/14 for international students. Applications are processed on a rolling basis. Application fee: $45. Electronic applications accepted. *Expenses:* Contact institution. *Financial support:* In 2016–17, 7 students received support, including 27 research assistantships (averaging $25,000 per year), 1 teaching assistantship (averaging $9,500 per year); fellowships, scholarships/grants, health care benefits, tuition waivers (full), and unspecified assistantships also available. Financial award application deadline: 4/15; financial award applicants required to submit FAFSA. *Faculty research:* Computational biology, non-destructive evaluation, neurophysiology, laser spectroscopy, nanotechnology. *Total annual research expenditures:* $536,220. *Unit head:* Dr. Christopher Del Negro, Chair, 757-221-7808, Fax: 757-221-2050, E-mail: cadeln@wm.edu. *Application contact:* Lianne Rios Ashburne, Graduate Program Coordinator, 757-221-2563, Fax: 757-221-2050, E-mail: lrashburne@wm.edu.
Website: http://www.wm.edu/as/appliedscience

Colorado School of Mines, Office of Graduate Studies, Department of Metallurgical and Materials Engineering, Golden, CO 80401. Offers materials science (MS, PhD); metallurgical and materials engineering (ME, MS, PhD). *Program availability:* Part-time. *Degree requirements:* For master's, thesis (for some programs); for doctorate, comprehensive exam, thesis/dissertation. *Entrance requirements:* For master's and doctorate, GRE General Test. Additional exam requirements/recommendations for international students: Required—TOEFL (minimum score 550 paper-based; 80 iBT). Electronic applications accepted. *Expenses:* Tuition, state resident: full-time $15,690. Tuition, nonresident: full-time $34,020. *Required fees:* $2152. Tuition and fees vary according to course load.

Columbia University, Fu Foundation School of Engineering and Applied Science, Department of Applied Physics and Applied Mathematics, New York, NY 10027. Offers applied mathematics (MS, Eng Sc D, PhD); applied physics (MS, Eng Sc D, PhD); materials science and engineering (MS, Eng Sc D, PhD); medical physics (MS). *Program availability:* Part-time, online learning. Terminal master's awarded for partial completion of doctoral program. *Degree requirements:* For master's, comprehensive exam; for doctorate, thesis/dissertation, qualifying exam. *Entrance requirements:* For master's, GRE General Test, GRE Subject Test (strongly recommended); for doctorate, GRE General Test, GRE Subject Test (applied physics). Additional exam requirements/recommendations for international students: Required—TOEFL, IELTS, PTE. Electronic applications accepted. *Faculty research:* Plasma physics and fusion energy; optical and laser physics; atmospheric, oceanic and earth physics; applied mathematics; solid state science and processing of materials, their properties, and their structure; medical physics.

Cornell University, Graduate School, Graduate Fields of Engineering, Field of Materials Science and Engineering, Ithaca, NY 14853. Offers materials engineering (M Eng, PhD); materials science (M Eng, PhD). *Degree requirements:* For doctorate, comprehensive exam, thesis/dissertation. *Entrance requirements:* For master's and doctorate, GRE General Test, 3 letters of recommendation. Additional exam requirements/recommendations for international students: Required—TOEFL (minimum score 550 paper-based; 77 iBT). Electronic applications accepted. *Faculty research:* Ceramics, complex fluids, glass, metals, polymers semiconductors.

Dartmouth College, Thayer School of Engineering, Program in Materials Sciences and Engineering, Hanover, NH 03755. Offers MS, PhD. *Degree requirements:* For master's, thesis; for doctorate, thesis/dissertation, candidacy oral exam. *Entrance requirements:* For master's and doctorate, GRE General Test. *Application deadline:* For fall admission, 1/1 priority date for domestic students. Application fee: $45. *Financial support:* Fellowships, research assistantships, teaching assistantships, career-related internships or fieldwork, Federal Work-Study, institutionally sponsored loans, and tuition waivers (full and partial) available. Financial award application deadline: 1/15. *Faculty research:* Electronic and magnetic materials, microstructural evolution, biomaterials and nanostructures, laser-material interactions, nanocomposites. *Total annual research expenditures:* $5.9 million. *Unit head:* Dr. Joseph J. Helbie, Dean, 603-646-2238, Fax: 603-646-2580, E-mail: joseph.j.helbie@dartmouth.edu. *Application contact:* Candace S. Potter, Graduate Admissions Administrator, 603-646-3844, Fax: 603-646-1620, E-mail: candace.s.potter@dartmouth.edu.
Website: http://engineering.dartmouth.edu/

Duke University, Graduate School, Pratt School of Engineering, Department of Mechanical Engineering and Materials Science, Durham, NC 27708. Offers materials science (MS, PhD); mechanical engineering (MS, PhD); JD/MS. Terminal master's awarded for partial completion of doctoral program. *Degree requirements:* For master's, thesis optional; for doctorate, thesis/dissertation. *Entrance requirements:* For master's and doctorate, GRE General Test. Additional exam requirements/recommendations for international students: Required—TOEFL (minimum score 90 iBT), IELTS (minimum score 7). Electronic applications accepted.

Duke University, Graduate School, Pratt School of Engineering, Master of Engineering Program, Durham, NC 27708-0271. Offers biomedical engineering (M Eng); civil engineering (M Eng); electrical and computer engineering (M Eng); environmental engineering (M Eng); materials science and engineering (M Eng); mechanical engineering (M Eng); photonics and optical sciences (M Eng). *Program availability:* Part-time. *Entrance requirements:* For master's, GRE General Test, resume, 3 letters of recommendation, statement of purpose, transcripts. Additional exam requirements/recommendations for international students: Required—TOEFL.

Florida International University, College of Engineering and Computing, Department of Mechanical and Materials Engineering, Miami, FL 33199. Offers materials science and engineering (MS, PhD); mechanical engineering (MS, PhD). *Program availability:* Part-time, evening/weekend. *Faculty:* 17 full-time (2 women), 6 part-time/adjunct (0 women). *Students:* 54 full-time (14 women), 27 part-time (3 women); includes 23 minority (5 Black or African American, non-Hispanic/Latino; 17 Hispanic/Latino; 1 Two or more races, non-Hispanic/Latino), 49 international. Average age 30. 105 applicants, 49% accepted, 12 enrolled. In 2016, 16 master's, 7 doctorates awarded. Terminal master's awarded for partial completion of doctoral program. *Degree requirements:* For master's, thesis or alternative; for doctorate, comprehensive exam, thesis/dissertation. *Entrance requirements:* For master's, GRE (depending on program), 3 letters of recommendation, minimum undergraduate GPA of 3.0 in upper-level course work; for doctorate, GRE (minimum combined score of 1150, verbal 450, quantitative 650), minimum undergraduate GPA of 3.0 in upper-level coursework with BS, 3.3 with MS; 3 letters of recommendation; letter of intent. Additional exam requirements/recommendations for international students: Required—TOEFL (minimum score 550 paper-based; 80 iBT) or IELTS (minimum score 6.5). *Application deadline:* For fall admission, 6/1 for domestic students, 4/1 for international students; for spring admission, 10/1 for domestic students, 9/1 for international students. Applications are processed on a rolling basis. Application fee: $30. Electronic applications accepted. *Expenses:* Tuition, state resident: full-time $8912; part-time $446 per credit hour. Tuition, nonresident: full-time $21,393; part-time $992 per credit hour. *Required fees:* $2185; $195 per semester. Tuition and fees vary according to program. *Financial support:* Institutionally sponsored loans, scholarships/grants, and unspecified assistantships available. Financial award application deadline: 3/1; financial award applicants required to submit FAFSA. *Faculty research:* Mechanics and materials, fluid/thermal/energy, design and manufacturing, materials science engineering. *Unit head:*

Dr. Ibrahim Tansel, Chair, 305-348-3304, Fax: 305-348-6007, E-mail: tanseli@fiu.edu. *Application contact:* Sara-Michelle Lemus, Engineering Admissions Officer, 305-348-7442, Fax: 305-348-7441, E-mail: grad_eng@fiu.edu.
Website: http://cec.fiu.edu

Florida State University, The Graduate School, College of Arts and Sciences, Department of Chemistry and Biochemistry, Tallahassee, FL 32306-4390. Offers analytical chemistry (MS, PhD); biochemistry (MS, PhD); inorganic chemistry (MS, PhD); materials chemistry (PhD); organic chemistry (MS, PhD); physical chemistry (MS, PhD). *Faculty:* 40 full-time (6 women), 4 part-time/adjunct (2 women). *Students:* 152 full-time (42 women), 5 part-time (3 women); includes 32 minority (8 Black or African American, non-Hispanic/Latino; 9 Asian, non-Hispanic/Latino; 11 Hispanic/Latino; 1 Native Hawaiian or other Pacific Islander, non-Hispanic/Latino; 3 Two or more races, non-Hispanic/Latino), 59 international. Average age 28. 182 applicants, 47% accepted, 31 enrolled. In 2016, 12 master's, 11 doctorates awarded. Terminal master's awarded for partial completion of doctoral program. *Degree requirements:* For master's, thesis (for some programs); for doctorate, thesis/dissertation. *Entrance requirements:* For master's and doctorate, GRE General Test (minimum scores: 150 verbal, 151 quantitative; 1100 total on the old scale), minimum GPA of 3.1 in undergraduate course work. Additional exam requirements/recommendations for international students: Required—TOEFL (minimum score 90 iBT). *Application deadline:* For fall admission, 12/15 priority date for domestic and international students. Application fee: $30. Electronic applications accepted. *Expenses:* Tuition, state resident: full-time $7263; part-time $403.51 per credit hour. Tuition, nonresident: full-time $18,087; part-time $1004.85 per credit hour. *Required fees:* $1365; $75.81 per credit hour. $20 per semester. Tuition and fees vary according to campus/location. *Financial support:* In 2016–17, 157 students received support, including 4 fellowships with full tuition reimbursements available (averaging $22,000 per year), 57 research assistantships with full tuition reimbursements available (averaging $22,809 per year), 91 teaching assistantships with full tuition reimbursements available (averaging $22,809 per year). Financial award application deadline: 12/15; financial award applicants required to submit FAFSA. *Faculty research:* Bioanalytical chemistry, including separations, microfluidics, petrol omics; materials chemistry, including magnets, polymers, catalysts, nanomaterials; spectroscopy, including NMR and EPR, ultrafast, Raman, and mass spectrometry; organic synthesis, natural products, photochemistry, and supramolecular chemistry; biochemistry, with focus on structural biology, metabolomics, and anticancer drugs. *Total annual research expenditures:* $3.5 million. *Unit head:* Dr. Timothy Logan, Chairman, 850-644-3810, Fax: 850-644-8281, E-mail: gradinfo@chem.fsu.edu. *Application contact:* Dr. Geoffrey Strouse, Associate Chair for Graduate Studies, 850-445-9042, Fax: 850-644-8281, E-mail: gradinfo@chem.fsu.edu.
Website: http://www.chem.fsu.edu/

Florida State University, The Graduate School, College of Arts and Sciences, Department of Scientific Computing, Tallahassee, FL 32306-4120. Offers computational science (MS, PhD), including atmospheric science (PhD), biochemistry (PhD), biological science (PhD), computational science (PhD), geological science (PhD), materials science (PhD), physics (PhD). *Program availability:* Part-time. *Faculty:* 14 full-time (2 women). *Students:* 37 full-time (6 women), 3 part-time (1 woman); includes 7 minority (3 Asian, non-Hispanic/Latino; 2 Hispanic/Latino; 2 Two or more races, non-Hispanic/Latino), 12 international. Average age 27. 40 applicants, 28% accepted, 6 enrolled. In 2016, 9 master's, 7 doctorates awarded. Terminal master's awarded for partial completion of doctoral program. *Degree requirements:* For master's, thesis (for some programs); for doctorate, comprehensive exam, thesis/dissertation. *Entrance requirements:* For master's and doctorate, GRE General Test, knowledge of at least one object-oriented computing language, 3 letters of recommendation, resume, statement of purpose. Additional exam requirements/recommendations for international students: Required—TOEFL (minimum score 550 paper-based; 80 iBT). *Application deadline:* For fall admission, 1/15 for domestic and international students. Application fee: $30. Electronic applications accepted. *Expenses:* Tuition, state resident: full-time $7263; part-time $403.51 per credit hour. Tuition, nonresident: full-time $18,087; part-time $1004.85 per credit hour. *Required fees:* $1365; $75.81 per credit hour. $20 per semester. Tuition and fees vary according to campus/location. *Financial support:* In 2016–17, 33 students received support, including 10 research assistantships with full tuition reimbursements available (averaging $26,670 per year), 23 teaching assistantships with full tuition reimbursements available (averaging $23,000 per year); scholarships/grants, health care benefits, tuition waivers (full), and unspecified assistantships also available. Financial award application deadline: 1/15. *Faculty research:* Morphometrics, mathematical and systems biology, mining proteomic and metabolic data, computational materials research, advanced 4-D Var data-assimilation methods in dynamic meteorology and oceanography, computational fluid dynamics, astrophysics. *Total annual research expenditures:* $500,000. *Unit head:* Dr. Gordon Erlebacher, Chair, 850-644-7024, E-mail: gerlebacher@fsu.edu. *Application contact:* David Amwake, Administrative Specialist, 850-644-2273, Fax: 850-644-0098, E-mail: damwake@fsu.edu.
Website: http://www.sc.fsu.edu

Florida State University, The Graduate School, Materials Science and Engineering Program, Tallahassee, FL 32310. Offers MS, PhD. *Faculty:* 37 full-time (6 women). *Students:* 19 full-time (8 women); includes 1 minority (Hispanic/Latino), 14 international. Average age 28. 27 applicants, 26% accepted, 4 enrolled. In 2016, 3 master's awarded. Terminal master's awarded for partial completion of doctoral program. *Degree requirements:* For master's, thesis; for doctorate, comprehensive exam, thesis/dissertation. *Entrance requirements:* For master's and doctorate, GRE General Test (minimum new format 55th percentile Verbal, 75th percentile Quantitative, old version 1100 combined Verbal and Quantitative), minimum GPA of 3.0, 3 letters of recommendation. Additional exam requirements/recommendations for international students: Required—TOEFL (minimum score 80 iBT). *Application deadline:* For fall admission, 5/1 for domestic and international students; for spring admission, 9/1 for domestic and international students; for summer admission, 1/1 for domestic and international students. Applications are processed on a rolling basis. Application fee: $30. Electronic applications accepted. *Expenses:* Tuition, state resident: full-time $7263; part-time $403.51 per credit hour. Tuition, nonresident: full-time $18,087; part-time $1004.85 per credit hour. *Required fees:* $1365; $75.81 per credit hour. $20 per semester. Tuition and fees vary according to campus/location. *Financial support:* In 2016–17, 18 students received support, including 18 research assistantships with full tuition reimbursements available (averaging $23,104 per year); partial payment of required health insurance also available. Financial award application deadline: 12/15. *Faculty research:* Magnetism and magnetic materials, composites, superconductors, polymers, computations, nanotechnology. *Unit head:* Prof. Eric Hellstrom, Director, 850-645-7489, Fax: 850-645-7754, E-mail: hellstrom@asc.magnet.fsu.edu. *Application contact:* Judy Gardner, Admissions Coordinator, 850-645-8980, Fax: 850-645-9123, E-mail: jdgardner@fsu.edu.
Website: http://materials.fsu.edu

Georgetown University, Graduate School of Arts and Sciences, Department of Chemistry, Washington, DC 20057. Offers analytical chemistry (PhD); biochemistry (PhD); computational chemistry (PhD); inorganic chemistry (PhD); materials chemistry (PhD); organic chemistry (PhD); theoretical chemistry (PhD). Terminal master's awarded for partial completion of doctoral program. *Degree requirements:* For doctorate, comprehensive exam, thesis/dissertation. *Entrance requirements:* For doctorate, GRE General Test. Additional exam requirements/recommendations for international students: Required—TOEFL.

The George Washington University, Columbian College of Arts and Sciences, Department of Chemistry, Washington, DC 20052. Offers analytical chemistry (MS, PhD); inorganic chemistry (MS, PhD); materials science (MS, PhD); organic chemistry (MS, PhD); physical chemistry (MS, PhD). *Program availability:* Part-time, evening/weekend. *Faculty:* 17 full-time (5 women). *Students:* 28 full-time (13 women), 18 part-time (10 women); includes 3 minority (1 Asian, non-Hispanic/Latino; 2 Hispanic/Latino), 13 international. Average age 27. 89 applicants, 52% accepted, 15 enrolled. In 2016, 2 master's, 6 doctorates awarded. Terminal master's awarded for partial completion of doctoral program. *Degree requirements:* For master's, comprehensive exam, thesis or alternative; for doctorate, thesis/dissertation, general exam. *Entrance requirements:* For master's and doctorate, GRE General Test, interview, minimum GPA of 3.0. Additional exam requirements/recommendations for international students: Required—TOEFL (minimum score 550 paper-based; 80 iBT). *Application deadline:* For fall admission, 1/15 priority date for domestic and international students; for spring admission, 9/1 priority date for domestic and international students. Applications are processed on a rolling basis. Application fee: $75. Electronic applications accepted. *Financial support:* In 2016–17, 27 students received support. Fellowships with tuition reimbursements available, research assistantships, teaching assistantships with tuition reimbursements available, Federal Work-Study, and tuition waivers available. Financial award application deadline: 1/15. *Unit head:* Dr. Michael King, Chair, 202-994-6488. *Application contact:* Information Contact, 202-994-6121, E-mail: gwchem@gwu.edu.
Website: http://chemistry.columbian.gwu.edu/

Harvard University, Graduate School of Arts and Sciences, Harvard John A. Paulson School of Engineering and Applied Sciences, Cambridge, MA 02138. Offers applied mathematics (PhD); applied physics (PhD); computational science and engineering (ME, SM); computer science (PhD); design engineering (MDE); engineering science (ME), including electrical engineering (ME, SM, PhD); engineering sciences (SM, PhD), including bioengineering (PhD), electrical engineering (ME, SM, PhD), environmental science and engineering (PhD), materials science and mechanical engineering (PhD). MDE offered in collaboration with Graduate School of Design. *Program availability:* Part-time. *Faculty:* 80 full-time (13 women), 47 part-time/adjunct (10 women). *Students:* 459 full-time (135 women), 19 part-time (7 women); includes 79 minority (2 Black or African American, non-Hispanic/Latino; 49 Asian, non-Hispanic/Latino; 15 Hispanic/Latino; 1 Native Hawaiian or other Pacific Islander, non-Hispanic/Latino; 12 Two or more races, non-Hispanic/Latino), 233 international. Average age 27. 2,486 applicants, 11% accepted, 126 enrolled. In 2016, 37 master's, 48 doctorates awarded. Terminal master's awarded for partial completion of doctoral program. *Degree requirements:* For master's, thesis (for ME); for doctorate, comprehensive exam, thesis/dissertation. *Entrance requirements:* For master's and doctorate, GRE General Test, GRE Subject Test (recommended), 3 letters of recommendation. Additional exam requirements/recommendations for international students: Required—TOEFL (minimum score 80 iBT). *Application deadline:* For fall admission, 12/15 priority date for domestic and international students. Application fee: $105. Electronic applications accepted. *Expenses:* $43,296 full-time tuition, $3,718 fees. *Financial support:* In 2016–17, 394 students received support, including 86 fellowships with full tuition reimbursements available (averaging $26,424 per year), 258 research assistantships with tuition reimbursements available (averaging $35,232 per year), 106 teaching assistantships with tuition reimbursements available (averaging $6,313 per year); health care benefits also available. *Faculty research:* Applied mathematics, applied physics, computer science and electrical engineering, environmental engineering, mechanical and biomedical engineering. *Total annual research expenditures:* $50.1 million. *Unit head:* Francis J. Doyle, III, Dean, 617-495-5829, Fax: 617-495-5264, E-mail: dean@seas.harvard.edu. *Application contact:* Office of Admissions and Financial Aid, 617-495-5315, E-mail: admissions@seas.harvard.edu.
Website: http://www.seas.harvard.edu/

Illinois Institute of Technology, Graduate College, Armour College of Engineering, Department of Mechanical, Materials and Aerospace Engineering, Chicago, IL 60616. Offers manufacturing engineering (MAS, MS); materials science and engineering (MAS, MS, PhD); mechanical and aerospace engineering (MAS, MS, PhD), including economics (MS), energy (MS), environment (MS). *Program availability:* Part-time, evening/weekend, online learning. Terminal master's awarded for partial completion of doctoral program. *Degree requirements:* For master's, comprehensive exam (for some programs), thesis (for some programs); for doctorate, comprehensive exam, thesis/dissertation. *Entrance requirements:* For master's and doctorate, GRE General Test (minimum score 1000 Quantitative and Verbal, 3.0 Analytical Writing), minimum undergraduate GPA of 3.0. Additional exam requirements/recommendations for international students: Required—TOEFL (minimum score 550 paper-based; 80 iBT). Electronic applications accepted. *Faculty research:* Fluid dynamics, metallurgical and materials engineering, solids and structures, computational mechanics, computer added design and manufacturing, thermal sciences, dynamic analysis and control of complex systems.

Illinois Institute of Technology, Graduate College, College of Science, Department of Chemistry, Chicago, IL 60616. Offers analytical chemistry (MAS); chemistry (MAS, MS, PhD); materials chemistry (MAS), including inorganic, organic, or polymeric materials. *Program availability:* Part-time, evening/weekend, online learning. Terminal master's awarded for partial completion of doctoral program. *Degree requirements:* For master's, comprehensive exam, thesis (for some programs); for doctorate, comprehensive exam, thesis/dissertation. *Entrance requirements:* For master's, GRE General Test (minimum score 300 Quantitative and Verbal, 2.5 Analytical Writing), minimum undergraduate GPA of 3.0; for doctorate, GRE General Test (minimum score 310 Quantitative and Verbal, 3.0 Analytical Writing), GRE Subject Test, minimum undergraduate GPA of 3.0. Additional exam requirements/recommendations for international students: Required—TOEFL (minimum score 550 paper-based; 80 iBT); Recommended—IELTS. Electronic applications accepted. *Faculty research:* Materials science, biological chemistry, synthetic chemistry, computational chemistry, energy, sensor science and technology, scholarship of teaching and learning.

Indiana University Bloomington, University Graduate School, College of Arts and Sciences, Department of Chemistry, Bloomington, IN 47405. Offers analytical chemistry (PhD); chemical biology (PhD); chemistry (MAT); inorganic chemistry (PhD); materials chemistry (PhD); organic chemistry (PhD); physical chemistry (PhD); MSES/MS. Terminal master's awarded for partial completion of doctoral program. *Degree requirements:* For master's, thesis; for doctorate, thesis/dissertation. *Entrance requirements:* For master's and doctorate, GRE General Test, GRE Subject Test. Additional exam requirements/recommendations for international students: Required—TOEFL. Electronic applications accepted. *Faculty research:* Synthesis of complex natural products, organic reaction mechanisms, organic electrochemistry, transitive-metal chemistry, solid-state and surface chemistry.

Instituto Tecnológico y de Estudios Superiores de Monterrey, Campus Estado de México, Professional and Graduate Division, Estado de Mexico, Mexico. Offers administration of information technologies (MITA); architecture (M Arch); business administration (GMBA, MBA); computer sciences (MCS, PhD); education (M Ed); educational institution administration (MAD); educational technology and innovation (PhD); electronic commerce (MEC); environmental systems (MS); finance (MAF); humanistic studies (MHS); information sciences and knowledge management (MISKM); information systems (MS); manufacturing systems (MS); marketing (MEM); quality systems and productivity (MS); science and materials engineering (PhD); telecommunications management (MTM). *Program availability:* Part-time, online learning. *Degree requirements:* For master's, one foreign language, thesis (for some programs); for doctorate, one foreign language, thesis/dissertation. *Entrance requirements:* For master's, E-PAEP 500, interview; for doctorate, E-PAEP 500, research proposal. Additional exam requirements/recommendations for international students: Required—TOEFL (minimum score 550 paper-based). *Faculty research:* Surface treatments by plasmas, mechanical properties, robotics, graphical computing, mechatronics security protocols.

Iowa State University of Science and Technology, Department of Materials Science and Engineering, Ames, IA 50011. Offers M Eng, MS, PhD. *Entrance requirements:* For master's and doctorate, GRE General Test. Additional exam requirements/recommendations for international students: Required—TOEFL (minimum score 550 paper-based; 79 iBT), IELTS (minimum score 6.5). *Application deadline:* For fall admission, 1/15 priority date for domestic and international students; for spring admission, 8/15 priority date for domestic and international students. Application fee: $60 ($90 for international students). Electronic applications accepted. *Financial support:* Teaching assistantships, scholarships/grants, health care benefits, and unspecified assistantships available. *Application contact:* Patrick Morton, Director of Graduate Education, 515-294-1214, Fax: 515-294-5444, E-mail: gradmse@iastate.edu.
Website: http://www.mse.iastate.edu

Jackson State University, Graduate School, College of Science, Engineering and Technology, Department of Civil and Environmental Engineering and Industrial Systems and Technology, Jackson, MS 39217. Offers civil engineering (MS, PhD); coastal engineering (MS, PhD); environmental engineering (MS, PhD); hazardous materials management (MS); technology education (MS Ed). *Program availability:* Part-time, evening/weekend. *Degree requirements:* For master's, comprehensive exam, thesis or alternative. *Entrance requirements:* For master's, GRE General Test. Additional exam requirements/recommendations for international students: Required—TOEFL (minimum score 520 paper-based; 67 iBT). *Application deadline:* For fall admission, 3/1 priority date for domestic students, 3/1 for international students; for spring admission, 10/1 for domestic and international students. Applications are processed on a rolling basis. Application fee: $25. *Expenses:* Tuition, state resident: full-time $7141. Tuition, nonresident: full-time $17,494. *Required fees:* $1080. Tuition and fees vary according to class time, course level, course load, degree level, campus/location, program and student level. *Financial support:* Career-related internships or fieldwork, Federal Work-Study, scholarships/grants, and unspecified assistantships available. Support available to part-time students. Financial award application deadline: 3/1; financial award applicants required to submit FAFSA. *Unit head:* Dr. Farshad Amini, Chair, 601-979-3913, Fax: 601-979-3238, E-mail: famini@jsums.edu. *Application contact:* Fatoumatta Sisay, Manager of Graduate Admissions, 601-979-0342, Fax: 601-979-4325, E-mail: fatoumatta.sisay@jsums.edu.
Website: http://www.jsums.edu/ceeist/

Johns Hopkins University, Engineering Program for Professionals, Part-time Program in Materials Science and Engineering, Baltimore, MD 21218. Offers nanotechnology (M Mat SE). *Program availability:* Part-time, evening/weekend. *Faculty:* 2 part-time/adjunct (1 woman). *Students:* 3 full-time (2 women), 16 part-time (3 women); includes 4 minority (2 Black or African American, non-Hispanic/Latino; 1 Asian, non-Hispanic/Latino; 1 Hispanic/Latino). Average age 28. 6 applicants, 83% accepted, 5 enrolled. In 2016, 5 master's awarded. *Entrance requirements:* Additional exam requirements/recommendations for international students: Required—TOEFL (minimum score 600 paper-based; 100 iBT). *Application deadline:* Applications are processed on a rolling basis. Application fee: $0. Electronic applications accepted. *Unit head:* Dr. James Spicer, Program Chair, 410-516-8524, E-mail: spicer@jhu.edu. *Application contact:* Doug Schiller, Admissions Director, 410-516-2300, Fax: 410-579-8049, E-mail: schiller@jhu.edu.
Website: http://www.ep.jhu.edu

Johns Hopkins University, G. W. C. Whiting School of Engineering, Department of Materials Science and Engineering, Baltimore, MD 21218. Offers M Mat SE, MSE, PhD. *Faculty:* 17 full-time (4 women), 2 part-time/adjunct (1 woman). *Students:* 70 full-time (23 women), 2 part-time (0 women); includes 14 minority (1 Black or African American, non-Hispanic/Latino; 8 Asian, non-Hispanic/Latino; 3 Hispanic/Latino; 2 Two or more races, non-Hispanic/Latino), 30 international. Average age 26. 243 applicants, 19% accepted, 21 enrolled. In 2016, 23 master's, 9 doctorates awarded. Terminal master's awarded for partial completion of doctoral program. *Degree requirements:* For master's, thesis; for doctorate, thesis/dissertation, oral exam, thesis defense. *Entrance requirements:* For master's and doctorate, GRE General Test, 2 letters of recommendation, statement of purpose, transcripts. Additional exam requirements/recommendations for international students: Required—TOEFL (minimum score 600 paper-based, 100 iBT) or IELTS (7). *Application deadline:* For fall admission, 12/15 priority date for domestic and international students; for spring admission, 10/17 priority date for domestic and international students. Application fee: $75. Electronic applications accepted. *Financial support:* In 2016–17, 70 students received support, including 9 fellowships with full tuition reimbursements available (averaging $30,200 per year), 55 research assistantships with full tuition reimbursements available (averaging $30,200 per year), teaching assistantships with full tuition reimbursements available (averaging $30,200 per year); Federal Work-Study, institutionally sponsored loans, health care benefits, tuition waivers (full), and unspecified assistantships also available. Financial award application deadline: 3/15. *Faculty research:* Biomaterials; computational materials science; materials for energy; nanomaterials; optoelectronic and magnetic materials; structural materials. *Total annual research expenditures:* $8.3 million. *Unit head:* Dr. Jonah Erlebacher, Chair, 410-516-6141, Fax: 410-516-5293, E-mail: jonah.erlebacher@jhu.edu. *Application contact:* Jeanine Majewski, Academic Coordinator, 410-516-8760, Fax: 410-516-5293, E-mail: dmse-gradadmissions@jhu.edu.
Website: http://engineering.jhu.edu/materials/

Johns Hopkins University, G. W. C. Whiting School of Engineering, Master of Science in Engineering Management Program, Baltimore, MD 21218. Offers biomaterials (MSEM); civil engineering (MSEM); communications science (MSEM); computer science (MSEM); environmental systems analysis, economics and public policy (MSEM); fluid mechanics (MSEM); materials science and engineering (MSEM); mechanical engineering (MSEM); mechanics and materials (MSEM); nano-biotechnology (MSEM); nanomaterials and nanotechnology (MSEM); operations research (MSEM); probability and statistics (MSEM); smart product and device design (MSEM). *Faculty:* 7 full-time (4 women), 1 part-time/adjunct (0 women). *Students:* 35 full-time (14 women), 8 part-time (3 women); includes 7 minority (4 Asian, non-Hispanic/Latino; 3 Hispanic/Latino), 26 international. Average age 24. 228 applicants, 28% accepted, 25 enrolled. In 2016, 18 master's awarded. *Entrance requirements:* For master's, GRE, 3 letters of recommendation, statement of purpose, transcripts. Additional exam requirements/recommendations for international students: Required—TOEFL (minimum score 600 paper-based, 100 iBT) or IELTS (7). *Application deadline:* For fall admission, 2/1 for domestic and international students. Application fee: $75. Electronic applications accepted. *Financial support:* Fellowships and health care benefits available. *Unit head:* Dr. Pamela Sheff, Director, 410-516-7056, Fax: 410-516-4880, E-mail: pamsheff@gmail.com. *Application contact:* Richard Helman, Director of Graduate Admissions, 410-516-8174, Fax: 410-516-0780, E-mail: graduateadmissions@jhu.edu.
Website: http://engineering.jhu.edu/msem/

Lehigh University, P.C. Rossin College of Engineering and Applied Science, Department of Materials Science and Engineering, Bethlehem, PA 18015. Offers materials science and engineering (M Eng, MS, PhD); photonics (MS); polymer science/engineering (M Eng, MS, PhD); MBA/E. *Program availability:* Part-time. *Faculty:* 15 full-time (3 women). *Students:* 23 full-time (4 women), 4 part-time (2 women); includes 3 minority (2 Asian, non-Hispanic/Latino; 1 Two or more races, non-Hispanic/Latino), 8 international. Average age 27. 143 applicants, 6% accepted, 4 enrolled. In 2016, 4 master's, 8 doctorates awarded. *Degree requirements:* For master's, thesis; for doctorate, comprehensive exam, thesis/dissertation. *Entrance requirements:* For master's and doctorate, GRE General Test, minimum GPA of 3.0. Additional exam requirements/recommendations for international students: Required—TOEFL (minimum score 487 paper-based; 85 iBT), IELTS (minimum score 6.5). *Application deadline:* For fall admission, 1/15 priority date for domestic students, 1/15 for international students; for spring admission, 12/1 priority date for domestic students, 12/1 for international students. Applications are processed on a rolling basis. Application fee: $75. Electronic applications accepted. *Expenses:* $1,420 per credit hour. *Financial support:* In 2016–17, 25 students received support, including 3 fellowships with tuition reimbursements available (averaging $21,105 per year), 19 research assistantships with tuition reimbursements available (averaging $28,140 per year), 6 teaching assistantships with tuition reimbursements available (averaging $21,530 per year); scholarships/grants and health care benefits also available. Financial award application deadline: 1/15. *Faculty research:* Metals, ceramics, crystals, polymers, fatigue crack propagation, biomaterials. *Total annual research expenditures:* $3.1 million. *Unit head:* Dr. Wojciech Misiolek, Chairperson, 610-758-4252, Fax: 610-758-4244, E-mail: wzm2@lehigh.edu. *Application contact:* Lisa Carreras Arechiga, Graduate Administrative Coordinator, 610-758-4222, Fax: 610-758-4244, E-mail: lia4@lehigh.edu.
Website: http://www.lehigh.edu/~inmatsci/

Massachusetts Institute of Technology, School of Engineering, Department of Materials Science and Engineering, Cambridge, MA 02139. Offers archaeological materials (PhD, Sc D); materials engineering (Mat E); materials science and engineering (SM, PhD, Sc D). *Faculty:* 32 full-time (10 women). *Students:* 170 full-time (43 women); includes 29 minority (1 Black or African American, non-Hispanic/Latino; 17 Asian, non-Hispanic/Latino; 6 Hispanic/Latino; 5 Two or more races, non-Hispanic/Latino), 93 international. Average age 26. 463 applicants, 12% accepted, 28 enrolled. In 2016, 5 master's, 39 doctorates awarded. *Degree requirements:* For master's, thesis; for doctorate, comprehensive exam, thesis/dissertation; for Mat E, comprehensive exam, thesis. *Entrance requirements:* For master's and doctorate, GRE General Test. Additional exam requirements/recommendations for international students: Required—IELTS. *Application deadline:* For fall admission, 12/1 for domestic and international students. Application fee: $75. Electronic applications accepted. *Expenses: Tuition:* Full-time $46,400; part-time $725 per credit. One-time fee: $312 full-time. Full-time tuition and fees vary according to course load and program. *Financial support:* In 2016–17, 159 students received support, including fellowships (averaging $34,000 per year), 103 research assistantships (averaging $37,500 per year), 16 teaching assistantships (averaging $39,800 per year); Federal Work-Study, institutionally sponsored loans, scholarships/grants, traineeships, health care benefits, unspecified assistantships, and resident tutors also available. Support available to part-time students. Financial award application deadline: 5/1; financial award applicants required to submit FAFSA. *Faculty research:* Thermodynamics and kinetics of materials; structure, processing and properties of materials; electronic, structural and biological materials engineering; computational materials science; materials in energy, medicine, nanotechnology and the environment. *Total annual research expenditures:* $25.5 million. *Unit head:* Prof. Christopher Schuh, Department Head, 617-253-3300, Fax: 617-252-1775, E-mail: dmse@mit.edu. *Application contact:* 617-253-3302, E-mail: dmse-admissions@mit.edu.
Website: http://dmse.mit.edu/

McMaster University, School of Graduate Studies, Faculty of Engineering, Department of Materials Science and Engineering, Hamilton, ON L8S 4M2, Canada. Offers materials engineering (M Eng, MA Sc, PhD); materials science (M Eng, PhD). *Degree requirements:* For master's, thesis; for doctorate, comprehensive exam, thesis/dissertation. *Entrance requirements:* Additional exam requirements/recommendations for international students: Required—TOEFL (minimum score 550 paper-based). *Faculty research:* Localized corrosion of metals and alloys, electron microscopy, polymer synthesis and characterization, polymer reaction kinetics and engineering, polymer process modeling.

Michigan State University, The Graduate School, College of Engineering, Department of Chemical Engineering and Materials Science, East Lansing, MI 48824. Offers chemical engineering (MS, PhD); materials science and engineering (MS, PhD). *Entrance requirements:* Additional exam requirements/recommendations for international students: Required—TOEFL. Electronic applications accepted.

Missouri State University, Graduate College, College of Natural and Applied Sciences, Department of Physics, Astronomy, and Materials Science, Springfield, MO 65897. Offers materials science (MS); natural and applied science (MNAS), including physics (MNAS, MS Ed); secondary education (MS Ed), including physics (MNAS, MS Ed). *Program availability:* Part-time. *Faculty:* 9 full-time (0 women). *Students:* 17 full-time (2 women), 3 part-time (0 women), 15 international. Average age 26. 36 applicants, 44% accepted, 7 enrolled. In 2016, 5 master's awarded. *Degree requirements:* For master's, comprehensive exam, thesis. *Entrance requirements:* For master's, GRE (MS, MNAS), minimum undergraduate GPA of 3.0 (MS and MNAS), 9-12 teaching certification (MS Ed). Additional exam requirements/recommendations for international students: Required—TOEFL (minimum score 550 paper-based; 79 iBT), IELTS (minimum score 6). *Application deadline:* For fall admission, 7/20 priority date for domestic students, 5/1 for international students; for spring admission, 12/20 priority date for domestic students, 9/1 for international students. Applications are processed on a rolling basis. Application fee: $35 ($50 for international students). Electronic applications accepted. *Expenses:* Tuition, state resident: full-time $5830. Tuition, nonresident: full-time $10,708. *Required fees:* $1130. Tuition and fees vary according to class time, course level, course load and program. *Financial support:* In 2016–17, 6 research assistantships with full tuition reimbursements (averaging $10,672 per year), 11 teaching assistantships with full tuition reimbursements (averaging $10,672 per year) were awarded; Federal Work-Study, institutionally sponsored loans, scholarships/grants, and unspecified assistantships also available. Financial award application deadline: 3/31; financial award applicants required to submit FAFSA. *Faculty research:* Nanocomposites,

ferroelectricity, infrared focal plane array sensors, biosensors, pulsating stars. *Unit head:* Dr. David Cornelison, Department Head, 417-836-4467, Fax: 417-836-6226, E-mail: physics@missouristate.edu. *Application contact:* Michael Edwards, Coordinator of Graduate Admissions, 417-836-5330, Fax: 417-836-6200, E-mail: michaeledwards@missouristate.edu.
Website: http://physics.missouristate.edu/

Montana Tech of The University of Montana, Program in Materials Science, Butte, MT 59701-8997. Offers PhD. *Faculty:* 11 full-time (1 woman), 3 part-time/adjunct (0 women). *Students:* 8 full-time (0 women), 5 part-time (2 women), 2 international. Average age 29. 9 applicants, 56% accepted, 5 enrolled. *Degree requirements:* For doctorate, thesis/dissertation optional. *Entrance requirements:* Additional exam requirements/recommendations for international students: Required—TOEFL (minimum score 600 paper-based; 90 iBT), IELTS (minimum score 7). *Application deadline:* For fall admission, 4/1 for domestic students, 6/1 for international students; for spring admission, 9/1 for domestic and international students. Application fee: $50. *Expenses:* Tuition, state resident: full-time $2901; part-time $1450.68 per degree program. Tuition, nonresident: full-time $8432; part-time $4215.84 per degree program. *Required fees:* $668; $354 per degree program. Tuition and fees vary according to course load and program. *Financial support:* In 2016–17, 4 research assistantships with full tuition reimbursements (averaging $24,000 per year) were awarded; teaching assistantships, Federal Work-Study, health care benefits, tuition waivers (full), and unspecified assistantships also available. Financial award applicants required to submit FAFSA. *Unit head:* Dr. Jerry Downey, Associate Professor, Metallurgical and Materials Engineering, 406-496-4578, Fax: 406-496-4723, E-mail: jdowney@mtech.edu. *Application contact:* Daniel Stirling, Administrator, Graduate School, 406-496-4304, Fax: 406-496-4723, E-mail: gradschool@mtech.edu.
Website: http://www.mtmatsci.org/

New Jersey Institute of Technology, College of Science and Liberal Arts, Newark, NJ 07102. Offers applied mathematics (MS); applied physics (M Sc, PhD); applied statistics (MS, Certificate); biology (MS, PhD); biostatistics (MS); chemistry (MS, PhD); computational biology (MS); environmental and sustainability policy (MS); environmental science (MS, PhD); history (MA, MAT); materials science and engineering (MS, PhD); mathematical and computational finance (MS); mathematics science (PhD); pharmaceutical chemistry (MS); practice of technical communications (Certificate); professional and technical communications (MS). *Program availability:* Part-time, evening/weekend. *Faculty:* 166 full-time (39 women), 87 part-time/adjunct (32 women). *Students:* 196 full-time (71 women), 68 part-time (33 women); includes 55 minority (15 Black or African American, non-Hispanic/Latino; 19 Asian, non-Hispanic/Latino; 15 Hispanic/Latino; 6 Two or more races, non-Hispanic/Latino), 140 international. Average age 28. 504 applicants, 64% accepted, 65 enrolled. In 2016, 81 master's, 18 doctorates, 1 other advanced degree awarded. Terminal master's awarded for partial completion of doctoral program. *Degree requirements:* For master's, thesis optional; for doctorate, thesis/dissertation. *Entrance requirements:* For master's, GRE General Test; for doctorate, GRE General Test, minimum graduate GPA of 3.5. Additional exam requirements/recommendations for international students: Required—TOEFL (minimum score 550 paper-based; 79 iBT). *Application deadline:* For fall admission, 6/1 priority date for domestic students, 5/1 priority date for international students; for spring admission, 11/15 priority date for domestic and international students. Applications are processed on a rolling basis. Application fee: $75. Electronic applications accepted. *Expenses:* Contact institution. *Financial support:* In 2016–17, 106 students received support, including 32 research assistantships (averaging $17,108 per year), 74 teaching assistantships (averaging $21,368 per year); fellowships, scholarships/grants, traineeships, and unspecified assistantships also available. Financial award application deadline: 1/15. *Faculty research:* Biophotonics and bioimaging, morphogenetic patterning, embryogenesis, biological fluid dynamics, applied research in the mathematical sciences. *Unit head:* Dr. Kevin Belfield, Dean, 973-596-3676, Fax: 973-565-0586, E-mail: kevin.d.belfield@njit.edu. *Application contact:* Stephen Eck, Director of Admissions, 973-596-3300, Fax: 973-596-3461, E-mail: admissions@njit.edu.
Website: http://csla.njit.edu/

Norfolk State University, School of Graduate Studies, School of Science and Technology, Department of Chemistry, Norfolk, VA 23504. Offers materials science (MS). *Entrance requirements:* Additional exam requirements/recommendations for international students: Required—TOEFL (minimum score 500 paper-based).

North Carolina State University, Graduate School, College of Engineering, Department of Materials Science and Engineering, Raleigh, NC 27695. Offers MMSE, MS, PhD. PhD offered jointly with The University of North Carolina at Charlotte. *Degree requirements:* For master's, thesis; for doctorate, thesis/dissertation. Electronic applications accepted. *Faculty research:* Processing and properties of wide band gap semiconductors, ferroelectric thin-film materials, ductility of nanocrystalline materials, computational materials science, defects in silicon-based devices.

North Dakota State University, College of Graduate and Interdisciplinary Studies, Interdisciplinary Program in Materials and Nanotechnology, Fargo, ND 58102. Offers MS, PhD. *Entrance requirements:* For doctorate, GRE General Test. Additional exam requirements/recommendations for international students: Required—TOEFL (minimum score 525 paper-based; 71 iBT).

Northwestern University, McCormick School of Engineering and Applied Science, Department of Civil and Environmental Engineering, Evanston, IL 60208-3109. Offers environmental engineering and science (MS, PhD); geotechnical engineering (MS, PhD); mechanics of materials and solids (MS, PhD); project management (MS); structural engineering and materials (MS, PhD); transportation systems analysis and planning (MS, PhD). MS and PhD admissions and degrees offered through The Graduate School. *Program availability:* Part-time. Terminal master's awarded for partial completion of doctoral program. *Degree requirements:* For master's, comprehensive exam (for some programs), thesis (for some programs); for doctorate, comprehensive exam, thesis/dissertation. *Entrance requirements:* For master's and doctorate, GRE General Test, minimum 2 letters of recommendation, transcripts from all academic institutions attended. Additional exam requirements/recommendations for international students: Required—TOEFL (minimum score 577 paper-based; 90 iBT), IELTS (minimum score 7). Electronic applications accepted. *Faculty research:* Environmental engineering and science, geotechnics, mechanics, materials, structures, and transportation systems analysis and planning.

Northwestern University, McCormick School of Engineering and Applied Science, Department of Materials Science and Engineering, Evanston, IL 60208. Offers integrated computational materials engineering (Certificate); materials science and engineering (MS, PhD). Admissions and degrees offered through The Graduate School. *Program availability:* Part-time. Terminal master's awarded for partial completion of doctoral program. *Degree requirements:* For master's, thesis optional, oral thesis defense; for doctorate, comprehensive exam, thesis/dissertation, oral defense of dissertation, preliminary evaluation, qualifying exam. *Entrance requirements:* For master's and doctorate, GRE General Test. Additional exam requirements/recommendations for international students: Required—TOEFL (minimum score 577 paper-based; 90 iBT), IELTS (minimum score 7). Electronic applications accepted. *Faculty research:* Art conservation science; biomaterials; ceramics; composites; energy; magnetic materials; materials for electronics and photonics; materials synthesis and processing; materials theory, computation, and design; metals; nanomaterials; polymers, self-assembly, and surfaces and interfaces.

The Ohio State University, Graduate School, College of Engineering, Department of Materials Science and Engineering, Columbus, OH 43210. Offers materials science and engineering (MS, PhD); welding engineering (MS, PhD). *Faculty:* 37. *Students:* 141 full-time (37 women), 47 part-time (9 women); includes 17 minority (9 Asian, non-Hispanic/Latino; 8 Hispanic/Latino), 53 international. Average age 28. In 2016, 41 master's, 18 doctorates awarded. *Degree requirements:* For master's, thesis; for doctorate, thesis/dissertation. *Entrance requirements:* For master's and doctorate, GRE (for graduates of foreign universities and holders of non-engineering degrees). Additional exam requirements/recommendations for international students: Required—TOEFL (minimum score 550 paper-based; 79 iBT), Michigan English Language Assessment Battery (minimum score 82); Recommended—IELTS (minimum score 7). *Application deadline:* For fall admission, 12/13 priority date for domestic students, 11/30 priority date for international students; for spring admission, 12/14 for domestic students, 11/12 for international students; for summer admission, 5/15 for domestic students, 4/14 for international students. Applications are processed on a rolling basis. Application fee: $60 ($70 for international students). Electronic applications accepted. *Financial support:* Fellowships with tuition reimbursements, research assistantships with tuition reimbursements, teaching assistantships, career-related internships or fieldwork, scholarships/grants, and unspecified assistantships available. *Faculty research:* Computational materials modeling, biomaterials, metallurgy, ceramics, advanced alloys/composites. *Unit head:* Dr. Peter Anderson, Chair, 614-292-6255, E-mail: anderson.1@osu.edu. *Application contact:* Mark Cooper, Graduate Studies Coordinator, 614-292-7280, Fax: 614-292-1357, E-mail: mse@osu.edu.
Website: http://mse.osu.edu/

Oklahoma State University, College of Engineering, Architecture and Technology, School of Materials Science and Engineering, Stillwater, OK 74078. Offers MS, PhD. *Faculty:* 7 full-time (0 women). *Students:* 3 full-time (1 woman), 17 part-time (5 women); includes 3 minority (1 Asian, non-Hispanic/Latino; 2 Two or more races, non-Hispanic/Latino), 13 international. Average age 28. 16 applicants, 38% accepted, 5 enrolled. *Entrance requirements:* Additional exam requirements/recommendations for international students: Required—TOEFL. *Application deadline:* For fall admission, 3/1 for domestic students; for spring admission, 8/1 for domestic students. Application fee: $40 ($75 for international students). Electronic applications accepted. *Expenses:* Tuition, state resident: full-time $3775; part-time $209.70 per credit hour. Tuition, nonresident: full-time $14,851; part-time $825.05 per credit hour. *Required fees:* $2027; $112.60 per credit hour. Tuition and fees vary according to campus/location. *Financial support:* In 2016–17, 13 research assistantships (averaging $18,193 per year), 4 teaching assistantships (averaging $10,229 per year) were awarded. *Unit head:* Dr. Raj N. Singh, Head, 918-594-8650, E-mail: rajns@okstate.edu.
Website: http://mse.okstate.edu/

Oregon State University, College of Engineering, Program in Materials Science, Corvallis, OR 97331. Offers chemical engineering (MS, PhD); chemistry (MS, PhD); civil engineering (MS, PhD); electrical and computer engineering (MS, PhD); forest products (MS, PhD); mathematics (MS, PhD); mechanical engineering (MS, PhD); nuclear engineering (MS); physics (MS, PhD). *Faculty:* 52 full-time (12 women), 3 part-time/adjunct (0 women). *Students:* 34 full-time (8 women), 10 part-time (3 women); includes 7 minority (4 Hispanic/Latino; 3 Two or more races, non-Hispanic/Latino), 15 international. Average age 30. 78 applicants, 24% accepted, 10 enrolled. In 2016, 7 master's, 6 doctorates awarded. *Degree requirements:* For master's, thesis or alternative. *Entrance requirements:* For master's and doctorate, GRE. Additional exam requirements/recommendations for international students: Required—TOEFL (minimum score 80 iBT), IELTS (minimum score 6.5). *Application deadline:* For fall admission, 8/1 for domestic students, 4/1 for international students; for winter admission, 12/1 for domestic students, 7/1 for international students; for spring admission, 2/1 for domestic students, 10/1 for international students; for summer admission, 5/1 for domestic students, 1/1 for international students. Application fee: $75 ($85 for international students). *Expenses:* $14,130 resident full-time tuition, $23,769 non-resident. *Financial support:* Fellowships, research assistantships, teaching assistantships, Federal Work-Study, and institutionally sponsored loans available. Support available to part-time students. Financial award application deadline: 1/15. *Unit head:* Dr. Harriet Nembhard, School Head. *Application contact:* Jean Robinson, Advisor, E-mail: jean.robinson@oregonstate.edu.
Website: http://matsci.oregonstate.edu/

Oregon State University, College of Science, Program in Chemistry, Corvallis, OR 97331. Offers analytical chemistry (MA, MS, PhD); inorganic chemistry (MA, MS, PhD); materials chemistry (MA, MS, PhD); nuclear chemistry (MA, MS, PhD); organic chemistry (MA, MS, PhD); physical chemistry (MA, MS, PhD). *Faculty:* 21 full-time (6 women), 1 part-time/adjunct (0 women). *Students:* 120 full-time (43 women), 1 (woman) part-time; includes 14 minority (1 Black or African American, non-Hispanic/Latino; 4 Asian, non-Hispanic/Latino; 6 Hispanic/Latino; 3 Two or more races, non-Hispanic/Latino), 52 international. Average age 28. 70 applicants, 36% accepted, 24 enrolled. In 2016, 7 master's, 12 doctorates awarded. Terminal master's awarded for partial completion of doctoral program. *Degree requirements:* For master's, thesis (for some programs); for doctorate, thesis/dissertation. *Entrance requirements:* For master's and doctorate, GRE, minimum GPA of 3.0 in last 90 hours of course work. Additional exam requirements/recommendations for international students: Required—TOEFL (minimum score 80 iBT), IELTS (minimum score 6.5). *Application deadline:* For fall admission, 1/15 for domestic and international students. Application fee: $75 ($85 for international students). *Expenses:* Tuition, state resident: full-time $12,150; part-time $450 per credit. Tuition, nonresident: full-time $21,789; part-time $807 per credit. *Required fees:* $1651; $1507 per credit. One-time fee: $350. Tuition and fees vary according to course load, campus/location and program. *Financial support:* Fellowships, research assistantships, and teaching assistantships available. Support available to part-time students. *Faculty research:* Solid state chemistry, enzyme reaction mechanisms, structure and dynamics of gas molecules, chemiluminescence, nonlinear optical spectroscopy. *Unit head:* Dr. Rich G. Carter, Professor/Chair. *Application contact:* Sarah Burton, Chemistry Advisor, 541-737-6808, E-mail: chemadm@chem.oregonstate.edu.
Website: http://chemistry.oregonstate.edu/

Penn State University Park, Graduate School, Intercollege Graduate Programs, Intercollege Graduate Program in Materials Science and Engineering, University Park, PA 16802. Offers MS, PhD. *Financial support:* Fellowships available. *Unit head:* Dr. Regina Vasilatos-Younken, Dean, 814-865-2516, Fax: 814-863-4627. *Application contact:* Lori Hawn, Director, Graduate Student Services, 814-865-1795, Fax: 814-863-4627, E-mail: l-gswww@lists.psu.edu.
Website: http://matse.psu.edu/graduate

Princeton University, Princeton Institute for the Science and Technology of Materials (PRISM), Princeton, NJ 08544-1019. Offers materials (PhD).

Rensselaer Polytechnic Institute, Graduate School, School of Engineering, Program in Materials Science and Engineering, Troy, NY 12180-3590. Offers M Eng, MS, D Eng, PhD. *Faculty:* 17 full-time (3 women), 1 part-time/adjunct (0 women). *Students:* 43 full-time (14 women), 6 part-time (2 women). 159 applicants, 19% accepted, 9 enrolled. In

2016, 3 master's, 6 doctorates awarded. Terminal master's awarded for partial completion of doctoral program. *Degree requirements:* For master's, thesis; for doctorate, comprehensive exam, thesis/dissertation. *Entrance requirements:* For master's and doctorate, GRE. Additional exam requirements/recommendations for international students: Required—TOEFL (minimum score 600 paper-based; 100 iBT), IELTS (minimum score 7), PTE (minimum score 68). *Application deadline:* For fall admission, 1/1 priority date for domestic and international students; for spring admission, 8/15 priority date for domestic and international students. Applications are processed on a rolling basis. Application fee: $75. Electronic applications accepted. *Expenses: Tuition:* Full-time $49,520; part-time $2060 per credit hour. *Required fees:* $2617. *Financial support:* In 2016–17, research assistantships with full tuition reimbursements (averaging $22,000 per year), teaching assistantships with full tuition reimbursements (averaging $22,000 per year) were awarded; fellowships also available. Financial award application deadline: 1/1. *Faculty research:* Advanced processing and synthesis, composites, computational materials, corrosion/electrochemical materials, electronic materials, glasses/ceramics, materials characterization, materials for energy, materials/biology interface, metals, nanomaterials, polymeric materials. *Total annual research expenditures:* $2.6 million. *Unit head:* Dr. Liping Huang, Graduate Program Director, 518-276-2174, E-mail: huangl5@rpi.edu. *Application contact:* Office of Graduate Admissions, 518-276-6216, E-mail: gradadmissions@rpi.edu.
Website: http://mse.rpi.edu/graduate

Rice University, Graduate Programs, George R. Brown School of Engineering, Department of Mechanical Engineering and Materials Science, Houston, TX 77251-1892. Offers materials science (MMS, MS, PhD); mechanical engineering (MME, MS, PhD); MBA/ME. *Program availability:* Part-time. Terminal master's awarded for partial completion of doctoral program. *Degree requirements:* For master's, comprehensive exam, thesis; for doctorate, comprehensive exam, thesis/dissertation. *Entrance requirements:* For master's and doctorate, GRE General Test, minimum GPA of 3.0. Additional exam requirements/recommendations for international students: Required—TOEFL (minimum score 600 paper-based; 90 iBT), IELTS (minimum score 7). Electronic applications accepted. *Faculty research:* Heat transfer, biomedical engineering, fluid dynamics, aero-astronautics, control systems/robotics, materials science.

Rochester Institute of Technology, Graduate Enrollment Services, College of Science, School of Chemistry and Materials Science, MS Program in Materials Science and Engineering, Rochester, NY 14623-5603. Offers MS. Offered jointly with Kate Gleason College of Engineering. *Program availability:* Part-time, evening/weekend. *Students:* 13 full-time (2 women), 4 part-time (1 woman); includes 2 minority (1 Black or African American, non-Hispanic/Latino; 1 Asian, non-Hispanic/Latino), 10 international. Average age 25. 41 applicants, 59% accepted, 8 enrolled. In 2016, 8 master's awarded. *Degree requirements:* For master's, thesis or project. *Entrance requirements:* For master's, GRE or GMAT, minimum GPA of 3.0 (recommended). Additional exam requirements/recommendations for international students: Required—TOEFL (minimum score 575 paper-based; 90 iBT), IELTS (minimum score 6.5), PTE (minimum score 62). *Application deadline:* Applications are processed on a rolling basis. Electronic applications accepted. *Expenses:* $1,742 per credit hour. *Financial support:* In 2016–17, 11 students received support. Research assistantships with partial tuition reimbursements available, teaching assistantships with partial tuition reimbursements available, career-related internships or fieldwork, scholarships/grants, and unspecified assistantships available. Support available to part-time students. Financial award applicants required to submit FAFSA. *Faculty research:* Magnetism and magnetic materials, photovoltaics and batteries, electronic materials, functional nanomaterials, 3D printing and additive manufacturing. *Unit head:* Casey Miller, Director, 585-475-4148, E-mail: cwmsch@rit.edu. *Application contact:* Diane Ellison, Associate Vice President, Graduate Enrollment Services, 585-475-2229, Fax: 585-475-7164, E-mail: gradinfo@rit.edu.
Website: https://www.rit.edu/cos/cmse/

Royal Military College of Canada, Division of Graduate Studies and Research, Engineering Division, Program in Chemical and Materials Science, Kingston, ON K7K 7B4, Canada. Offers M Sc, PhD. *Degree requirements:* For master's, thesis; for doctorate, comprehensive exam, thesis/dissertation. *Entrance requirements:* For master's, honours degree with second-class standing; for doctorate, master's degree. Electronic applications accepted.

Rutgers University–New Brunswick, Graduate School-New Brunswick, Program in Materials Science and Engineering, Piscataway, NJ 08854-8097. Offers MS, PhD. *Program availability:* Part-time. *Degree requirements:* For master's, thesis; for doctorate, comprehensive exam, thesis/dissertation. *Entrance requirements:* For master's and doctorate, GRE General Test. Additional exam requirements/recommendations for international students: Recommended—TOEFL. Electronic applications accepted. *Faculty research:* Ceramic processing, nanostructured materials, electrical and structural ceramics, fiber optics.

School of the Art Institute of Chicago, Graduate Division, Department of Fiber and Material Studies, Chicago, IL 60603-3103. Offers MFA. *Accreditation:* NASAD. *Entrance requirements:* Additional exam requirements/recommendations for international students: Required—TOEFL, IELTS.

South Dakota School of Mines and Technology, Graduate Division, Doctoral Program in Materials Engineering and Science, Rapid City, SD 57701-3995. Offers PhD. *Program availability:* Part-time. *Degree requirements:* For doctorate, thesis/dissertation. *Entrance requirements:* For doctorate, GRE General Test, minimum graduate GPA of 3.0, 3 letters of recommendation. Additional exam requirements/recommendations for international students: Required—TOEFL (minimum score 520 paper-based; 68 iBT), TWE. Electronic applications accepted.

South Dakota School of Mines and Technology, Graduate Division, Master's Program in Materials Engineering and Science, Rapid City, SD 57701-3995. Offers MS. *Degree requirements:* For master's, thesis (for some programs). *Entrance requirements:* For master's, GRE General Test. Additional exam requirements/recommendations for international students: Required—TOEFL (minimum score 520 paper-based; 68 iBT), TWE. Electronic applications accepted.

Southern Methodist University, Dedman College of Humanities and Sciences, Department of Chemistry, Dallas, TX 75275-0314. Offers chemistry (MS, PhD); materials science and engineering (MS, PhD). Terminal master's awarded for partial completion of doctoral program. *Degree requirements:* For master's, thesis; for doctorate, comprehensive exam, thesis/dissertation. *Entrance requirements:* For master's, GRE General Test, bachelor's degree in chemistry, minimum GPA of 3.0; for doctorate, GRE General Test, bachelor's degree in chemistry or closely-related field, minimum GPA of 3.0. Additional exam requirements/recommendations for international students: Required—TOEFL (minimum score 550 paper-based; 80 iBT). Electronic applications accepted. *Faculty research:* Materials/polymer, medicinal/bioorganic, theoretical and computational, organic/inorganic/organometallic synthesis, inorganic polymer chemistry.

Stanford University, School of Engineering, Department of Materials Science and Engineering, Stanford, CA 94305-2004. Offers MS, PhD, Engr. Terminal master's awarded for partial completion of doctoral program. *Degree requirements:* For doctorate, thesis/dissertation; for Engr, thesis. *Entrance requirements:* For master's, doctorate, and Engr, GRE General Test. Additional exam requirements/recommendations for international students: Required—TOEFL. Electronic applications accepted. *Expenses: Tuition:* Full-time $47,331. *Required fees:* $609.

State University of New York College of Environmental Science and Forestry, Department of Paper and Bioprocess Engineering, Syracuse, NY 13210-2779. Offers biomaterials engineering (MS, PhD); bioprocess engineering (MPS, MS, PhD); bioprocessing (Advanced Certificate); paper science and engineering (MPS, MS, PhD); sustainable engineering management (MPS). *Faculty:* 13 full-time (2 women), 4 part-time/adjunct (0 women). *Students:* 28 full-time (14 women), 3 part-time (2 women); includes 1 minority (Asian, non-Hispanic/Latino), 19 international. Average age 29. 19 applicants, 89% accepted, 6 enrolled. In 2016, 6 master's, 1 doctorate, 4 other advanced degrees awarded. *Degree requirements:* For master's, thesis; for doctorate, comprehensive exam, thesis/dissertation; for Advanced Certificate, 15 credit hours. *Entrance requirements:* For master's and doctorate, GRE General Test, minimum GPA of 3.0; for Advanced Certificate, BS, calculus plus science major. Additional exam requirements/recommendations for international students: Required—TOEFL (minimum score 550 paper-based; 80 iBT), IELTS (minimum score 6). *Application deadline:* For fall admission, 2/1 priority date for domestic and international students; for spring admission, 11/1 priority date for domestic and international students. Applications are processed on a rolling basis. Application fee: $60. *Expenses:* Tuition, state resident: full-time $10,870; part-time $453 per credit. Tuition, nonresident: full-time $22,210; part-time $925 per credit. *Required fees:* $1075; $89.22 per credit. *Financial support:* In 2016–17, 14 students received support. Application deadline: 6/30; applicants required to submit FAFSA. *Faculty research:* Sustainable products and processes, biorefinery, pulping and papermaking, nanocellulose, bioconversions, process control and modeling. *Unit head:* Dr. Gary M. Scott, Chair, 315-470-6501, Fax: 315-470-6945, E-mail: gscott@esf.edu. *Application contact:* Scott Shannon, Associate Provost and Dean, Instruction and Graduate Studies, 315-470-6599, Fax: 315-470-6978, E-mail: esfgrad@esf.edu.
Website: http://www.esf.edu/pbe/

Stevens Institute of Technology, Graduate School, Charles V. Schaefer Jr. School of Engineering and Science, Department of Chemical Engineering and Materials Science, Program in Materials Science and Engineering, Hoboken, NJ 07030. Offers M Eng, PhD. *Program availability:* Part-time, evening/weekend. *Students:* 81 full-time (21 women), 2 part-time (1 woman), 79 international. Average age 25. 261 applicants, 61% accepted, 35 enrolled. In 2016, 36 master's awarded. *Degree requirements:* For master's, thesis optional, minimum B average in major field and overall; for doctorate, comprehensive exam (for some programs), thesis/dissertation. *Entrance requirements:* Additional exam requirements/recommendations for international students: Required—TOEFL (minimum score 74 iBT), IELTS (minimum score 6). *Application deadline:* For fall admission, 6/1 for domestic students, 4/15 for international students; for spring admission, 11/30 for domestic students, 11/1 for international students. Applications are processed on a rolling basis. Application fee: $65. Electronic applications accepted. *Expenses:* Contact institution. *Financial support:* Fellowships, research assistantships, teaching assistantships, career-related internships or fieldwork, Federal Work-Study, scholarships/grants, and unspecified assistantships available. Financial award application deadline: 2/15; financial award applicants required to submit FAFSA. *Unit head:* Dr. Henry Du, Director, 201-216-5262, Fax: 201-216-8306, E-mail: hdu@stevens.edu. *Application contact:* Graduate Admissions, 888-783-8367, Fax: 888-511-1306, E-mail: graduate@stevens.edu.

Stony Brook University, State University of New York, Graduate School, College of Engineering and Applied Sciences, Department of Materials Science and Engineering, Stony Brook, NY 11794-2275. Offers MS, PhD. *Faculty:* 18 full-time (5 women), 10 part-time/adjunct (3 women). *Students:* 113 full-time (39 women), 20 part-time (10 women); includes 20 minority (5 Black or African American, non-Hispanic/Latino; 10 Asian, non-Hispanic/Latino; 4 Hispanic/Latino; 1 Two or more races, non-Hispanic/Latino), 84 international. Average age 26. 202 applicants, 49% accepted, 33 enrolled. In 2016, 26 master's, 13 doctorates awarded. *Degree requirements:* For master's, thesis or alternative; for doctorate, comprehensive exam, thesis/dissertation. *Entrance requirements:* For master's and doctorate, GRE General Test, minimum undergraduate GPA of 3.0. Additional exam requirements/recommendations for international students: Required—TOEFL (minimum score 90 iBT). *Application deadline:* For fall admission, 1/15 for domestic students; for spring admission, 10/1 for domestic students. Application fee: $100. *Expenses:* Contact institution. *Financial support:* In 2016–17, 2 fellowships, 21 research assistantships, 19 teaching assistantships were awarded. *Faculty research:* Crystal growth, crystallography, semiconductors, synchrotron X-rays or radiation, fuel cells. *Total annual research expenditures:* $3.4 million. *Unit head:* Dr. Michael Dudley, Chairman, 631-632-8500, Fax: 631-632-8052, E-mail: michael.dudley@stonybrook.edu. *Application contact:* Rosa DiLiberto, Coordinator, 631-632-4986, E-mail: rosa.diliberto@stonybrook.edu.
Website: http://www.stonybrook.edu/commcms/matscieng/index.html

Texas A&M University, College of Engineering, Department of Materials Science and Engineering, College Station, TX 77843. Offers M Eng, MS, PhD. *Faculty:* 16. *Students:* 119 full-time (36 women), 14 part-time (2 women); includes 17 minority (1 Black or African American, non-Hispanic/Latino; 7 Asian, non-Hispanic/Latino; 5 Hispanic/Latino; 4 Two or more races, non-Hispanic/Latino), 91 international. Average age 28. 265 applicants, 29% accepted, 25 enrolled. In 2016, 12 master's, 10 doctorates awarded. *Degree requirements:* For master's, thesis (MS); for doctorate, thesis/dissertation. *Entrance requirements:* For master's and doctorate, GRE General Test. Additional exam requirements/recommendations for international students: Required—TOEFL (minimum score 550 paper-based; 80 iBT), IELTS (minimum score 6), PTE (minimum score 53). *Application deadline:* For fall admission, 2/28 for domestic and international students; for spring admission, 7/31 for domestic students, 6/1 for international students. Application fee: $50 ($90 for international students). *Expenses:* Contact institution. *Financial support:* In 2016–17, 119 students received support, including 17 fellowships with tuition reimbursements available (averaging $17,522 per year), 83 research assistantships with tuition reimbursements available (averaging $6,669 per year), 15 teaching assistantships with tuition reimbursements available (averaging $8,718 per year); career-related internships or fieldwork, institutionally sponsored loans, scholarships/grants, traineeships, health care benefits, tuition waivers (full and partial), and unspecified assistantships also available. Support available to part-time students. Financial award application deadline: 3/15; financial award applicants required to submit FAFSA. *Faculty research:* Innovative design methods, pavement distress characterization, materials property, characterization and modeling recyclable materials. *Unit head:* Ibrahim Karaman, Department Head, 979-862-3923, E-mail: ikaraman@tamu.edu. *Application contact:* Mildan Radovic, Associate Department Head, 979-845-5114, E-mail: mradovic@tamu.edu.
Website: http://engineering.tamu.edu/materials

Texas State University, The Graduate College, College of Science and Engineering, PhD Program in Materials Science, Engineering, and Commercialization, San Marcos, TX 78666. Offers PhD. *Faculty:* 14 full-time (5 women), 4 part-time/adjunct (1 woman). *Students:* 30 full-time (11 women), 4 part-time (1 woman); includes 5 minority (3 Black or African American, non-Hispanic/Latino; 1 Asian, non-Hispanic/Latino; 1 Hispanic/

Latino), 17 international. Average age 32. 36 applicants, 39% accepted, 8 enrolled. In 2016, 6 doctorates awarded. *Degree requirements:* For doctorate, comprehensive exam, thesis/dissertation. *Entrance requirements:* For doctorate, GRE (for applicants who have not received a master's degree from a U.S. institution), baccalaureate and master's degree from regionally-accredited college or university in biology, chemistry, engineering, materials science, physics, technology, or closely-related field with minimum GPA of 3.5 in graduate work; statement of purpose; 3 letters of recommendation; curriculum vitae or resume. Additional exam requirements/recommendations for international students: Required—TOEFL (minimum score 550 paper-based; 78 iBT); Recommended—IELTS (minimum score 6.5). *Application deadline:* For fall admission, 2/1 priority date for domestic and international students. Application fee: $40 ($90 for international students). Electronic applications accepted. *Expenses:* $4,851 per semester. *Financial support:* In 2016–17, 20 students received support, including 15 research assistantships (averaging $29,374 per year), 16 teaching assistantships (averaging $37,652 per year); scholarships/grants, health care benefits, and unspecified assistantships also available. Support available to part-time students. Financial award application deadline: 3/1; financial award applicants required to submit FAFSA. *Faculty research:* Micro power chip prototype development; applied epitaxial materials; Spin-dependent transport at oxide interfaces grown by molecular beam epitaxy. *Total annual research expenditures:* $455,774. *Unit head:* Dr. Jennifer Irvin, PhD Program Director, 512-245-7875, Fax: 512-245-8365, E-mail: ji12@txstate.edu. *Application contact:* Dr. Andrea Golato, Dean of Graduate School, 512-245-2581, Fax: 512-245-8365, E-mail: gradcollege@txstate.edu.
Website: http://www.msec.txstate.edu/

Texas State University, The Graduate College, College of Science and Engineering, Program in Material Physics, San Marcos, TX 78666. Offers MS. *Program availability:* Part-time. *Faculty:* 12 full-time (3 women), 1 part-time/adjunct (0 women). *Students:* 3 full-time; includes 1 minority (Hispanic/Latino), 1 international. Average age 26. 9 applicants, 44% accepted, 1 enrolled. In 2016, 1 master's awarded. *Degree requirements:* For master's, comprehensive exam, thesis. *Entrance requirements:* For master's, baccalaureate degree from regionally-accredited university with minimum GPA of 2.75 on last 60 undergraduate semester hours, statement of purpose, resume/curriculum vitae, 3 letters of recommendation. Additional exam requirements/recommendations for international students: Required—TOEFL (minimum score 550 paper-based; 78 iBT), IELTS (minimum score 6.5). *Application deadline:* For fall admission, 2/15 priority date for domestic and international students; for spring admission, 10/15 for domestic students, 10/1 for international students. Applications are processed on a rolling basis. Application fee: $40 ($90 for international students). Electronic applications accepted. *Expenses:* $4,851 per semester. *Financial support:* In 2016–17, 3 students received support, including 1 research assistantship (averaging $18,500 per year), 1 teaching assistantship (averaging $13,849 per year); Federal Work-Study, institutionally sponsored loans, scholarships/grants, health care benefits, and unspecified assistantships also available. Support available to part-time students. Financial award application deadline: 3/1; financial award applicants required to submit FAFSA. *Faculty research:* Thermal transport in diamond films electronics thermal management, first solar materials characterization. *Total annual research expenditures:* $502,984. *Unit head:* Dr. Edwin Piner, Graduate Advisor, 512-245-7049, Fax: 512-245-8233, E-mail: ep26@txstate.edu. *Application contact:* Dr. Andrea Golato, Dean of Graduate School, 512-245-2581, Fax: 512-245-8365, E-mail: gradcollege@txstate.edu.
Website: http://www.txstate.edu/physics/students/graduates/graduate-programs.html

Trent University, Graduate Studies, Program in Materials Science, Peterborough, ON K9J 7B8, Canada. Offers M Sc.

Université du Québec, Institut National de la Recherche Scientifique, Graduate Programs, Centre for Energie Materiaux Telecommunications, Varennes, QC G1K 9A9, Canada. Offers energy and materials science (M Sc, PhD); telecommunications (M Sc, PhD). *Program availability:* Part-time. *Faculty:* 36 full-time. *Students:* 185 full-time (47 women), 10 part-time (2 women), 154 international. Average age 31. 27 applicants, 78% accepted, 13 enrolled. In 2016, 13 master's, 23 doctorates awarded. *Degree requirements:* For master's, thesis (for some programs); for doctorate, thesis/dissertation. *Entrance requirements:* For master's, appropriate bachelor's degree, proficiency in French; for doctorate, appropriate master's degree, proficiency in French. *Application deadline:* For fall admission, 3/30 for domestic and international students; for winter admission, 11/1 for domestic and international students; for spring admission, 3/1 for domestic and international students. Application fee: $45. Electronic applications accepted. *Financial support:* In 2016–17, fellowships (averaging $16,500 per year) were awarded; research assistantships and scholarships/grants also available. *Faculty research:* New energy sources, plasmas, telecommunications, advanced materials, ultrafast photonics. *Unit head:* Federico Rosei, Director, 450-228-6905, E-mail: rosei@emt.inrs.ca. *Application contact:* Sylvie Richard, Registrar, 418-654-2518, Fax: 418-654-3858, E-mail: sylvie.richard@adm.inrs.ca.
Website: http://www.emt.inrs.ca

The University of Alabama, Graduate School, College of Engineering and College of Arts and Sciences, Tri-Campus Materials Science PhD Program, Tuscaloosa, AL 35487. Offers PhD. Program offered jointly with The University of Alabama at Birmingham and The University of Alabama in Huntsville. *Students:* 23 full-time (4 women), 3 part-time (1 woman); includes 5 minority (3 Black or African American, non-Hispanic/Latino; 1 Hispanic/Latino; 1 Two or more races, non-Hispanic/Latino), 11 international. Average age 27. 23 applicants, 43% accepted, 6 enrolled. In 2016, 8 doctorates awarded. *Degree requirements:* For doctorate, comprehensive exam, thesis/dissertation. *Entrance requirements:* For doctorate, GRE General Test. Additional exam requirements/recommendations for international students: Required—TOEFL (minimum score 550 paper-based). *Application deadline:* For fall admission, 2/28 priority date for domestic and international students; for spring admission, 10/30 priority date for domestic students, 9/30 priority date for international students. Applications are processed on a rolling basis. Application fee: $50 ($60 for international students). Electronic applications accepted. *Expenses:* Tuition, state resident: full-time $10,470. Tuition, nonresident: full-time $26,950. *Financial support:* In 2016–17, 4 research assistantships with full tuition reimbursements (averaging $19,500 per year) were awarded; career-related internships or fieldwork and unspecified assistantships also available. Financial award application deadline: 2/28. *Faculty research:* Magnetic multilayers, metals casting, molecular electronics, conducting polymers, metals physics, electrodeposition. *Unit head:* Dr. Greg Thompson, Campus Coordinator, 205-348-1589, E-mail: gthompson@eng.ua.edu. *Application contact:* Dr. David A. Francko, Dean, 205-348-8280, Fax: 205-348-0400, E-mail: dfrancko@ua.edu.

The University of Alabama in Huntsville, School of Graduate Studies, College of Engineering, Department of Chemical and Materials Engineering, Huntsville, AL 35899. Offers biotechnology science and engineering (PhD); chemical and materials engineering (MSE); materials science (PhD); mechanical engineering (PhD), including chemical engineering. *Program availability:* Part-time, evening/weekend. *Degree requirements:* For master's, comprehensive exam, thesis or alternative, oral and written exams; for doctorate, comprehensive exam, thesis/dissertation. *Entrance requirements:* For master's, GRE General Test, appropriate bachelor's degree, minimum GPA of 3.0; for doctorate, GRE General Test, minimum GPA of 3.0. Additional exam requirements/recommendations for international students: Required—TOEFL (minimum score 500 paper-based; 80 iBT), IELTS (minimum score 6.5). Electronic applications accepted. *Expenses:* Tuition, state resident: full-time $9834; part-time $600 per credit hour. Tuition, nonresident: full-time $21,830; part-time $1325 per credit hour. *Faculty research:* Ultrathin films for optical, sensor and biological applications; materials processing including low gravity; hypergolic reactants; computational fluid dynamics; biofuels and renewable resources.

The University of Alabama in Huntsville, School of Graduate Studies, College of Science, Department of Chemistry, Huntsville, AL 35899. Offers biotechnology science and engineering (PhD); chemistry (MS); education (MS); materials science (MS, PhD). *Program availability:* Part-time, evening/weekend. *Degree requirements:* For master's, comprehensive exam, thesis or alternative, oral and written exams. *Entrance requirements:* For master's, GRE General Test, minimum GPA of 3.0. Additional exam requirements/recommendations for international students: Required—TOEFL (minimum score 550 paper-based; 80 iBT), IELTS (minimum score 6.5). Electronic applications accepted. *Expenses:* Tuition, state resident: full-time $9834; part-time $600 per credit hour. Tuition, nonresident: full-time $21,830; part-time $1325 per credit hour. *Faculty research:* Natural products drug discovery, protein biochemistry, macromolecular biophysics, polymer synthesis, surface modification and analysis of materials.

The University of Arizona, College of Engineering, Department of Materials Science and Engineering, Tucson, AZ 85721. Offers MS, PhD. *Program availability:* Part-time. *Degree requirements:* For master's, thesis (for some programs); for doctorate, comprehensive exam, thesis/dissertation. *Entrance requirements:* For master's and doctorate, GRE General Test, 3 letters of recommendation, statement of purpose. Additional exam requirements/recommendations for international students: Required—TOEFL (minimum score 550 paper-based; 79 iBT). Electronic applications accepted. *Faculty research:* High-technology ceramics, optical materials, electronic materials, chemical metallurgy, science of materials.

University of Calgary, Faculty of Graduate Studies, Schulich School of Engineering, Department of Civil Engineering, Calgary, AB T2N 1N4, Canada. Offers avalanche mechanics (M Sc, PhD); civil engineering (M Eng, M Sc, PhD); energy and environment engineering (M Eng, M Sc, PhD); environmental engineering (M Eng, M Sc, PhD); geotechnical engineering (M Eng, M Sc, PhD); materials science (M Eng, M Sc, PhD); project management (M Eng, M Sc, PhD); structures and solid mechanics (M Eng, M Sc, PhD); transportation engineering (M Eng, M Sc, PhD); water resources (M Eng, M Sc, PhD). *Program availability:* Part-time. *Degree requirements:* For master's, thesis; for doctorate, thesis/dissertation, written and oral candidacy exam. *Entrance requirements:* For master's, minimum GPA of 3.0; for doctorate, minimum GPA of 3.5. Additional exam requirements/recommendations for international students: Required—TOEFL (minimum score 580 paper-based; 93 iBT), IELTS (minimum score 7). Electronic applications accepted. *Faculty research:* Geotechnical engineering, energy and environment, transportation, project management, structures and solid mechanics.

University of California, Berkeley, Graduate Division, College of Engineering, Department of Materials Science and Engineering, Berkeley, CA 94720-1500. Offers engineering science (M Eng, MS, PhD). *Faculty:* 15 full-time. *Students:* 116 full-time (38 women); includes 34 minority (4 Black or African American, non-Hispanic/Latino; 1 American Indian or Alaska Native, non-Hispanic/Latino; 17 Asian, non-Hispanic/Latino; 12 Hispanic/Latino), 61 international. Average age 27. 522 applicants, 50 enrolled. In 2016, 23 master's, 18 doctorates awarded. Terminal master's awarded for partial completion of doctoral program. *Degree requirements:* For master's, comprehensive exam (for some programs), thesis (for some programs), comprehensive exam or thesis (MS); for doctorate, comprehensive exam, thesis/dissertation, qualifying exam. *Entrance requirements:* For master's and doctorate, GRE General Test, minimum GPA of 3.0, 3 letters of recommendation. Additional exam requirements/recommendations for international students: Required—TOEFL (minimum score 570 paper-based; 90 iBT). *Application deadline:* For fall admission, 12/5 for domestic students. Application fee: $105 ($125 for international students). Electronic applications accepted. *Financial support:* Fellowships, research assistantships, teaching assistantships, and unspecified assistantships available. Financial award applicants required to submit FAFSA. *Faculty research:* Ceramics, biomaterials, structural, electronic, magnetic and optical materials. *Unit head:* Prof. Mark D. Asta, Chair, 510-642-0716, Fax: 510-643-5792, E-mail: msessa@berkeley.edu. *Application contact:* 510-642-0716, Fax: 510-643-5792, E-mail: msessa@berkeley.edu.
Website: http://www.mse.berkeley.edu/

University of California, Davis, College of Engineering, Program in Materials Science and Engineering, Davis, CA 95616. Offers MS, PhD. Terminal master's awarded for partial completion of doctoral program. *Degree requirements:* For master's, comprehensive exam (for some programs), thesis (for some programs); for doctorate, comprehensive exam, thesis/dissertation. *Entrance requirements:* Additional exam requirements/recommendations for international students: Required—TOEFL (minimum score 550 paper-based).

University of California, Irvine, Henry Samueli School of Engineering, Department of Chemical Engineering and Materials Science, Irvine, CA 92697. Offers chemical and biochemical engineering (MS, PhD); materials science and engineering (MS, PhD). *Program availability:* Part-time. *Students:* 141 full-time (60 women), 14 part-time (5 women); includes 42 minority (4 Black or African American, non-Hispanic/Latino; 29 Asian, non-Hispanic/Latino; 7 Hispanic/Latino; 2 Two or more races, non-Hispanic/Latino), 71 international. Average age 26. 595 applicants, 23% accepted, 41 enrolled. In 2016, 47 master's, 11 doctorates awarded. Terminal master's awarded for partial completion of doctoral program. *Degree requirements:* For doctorate, thesis/dissertation. *Entrance requirements:* For master's and doctorate, GRE General Test, minimum GPA of 3.0, 3 letters of recommendation. Additional exam requirements/recommendations for international students: Required—TOEFL (minimum score 550 paper-based). *Application deadline:* For fall admission, 1/15 priority date for domestic students, 1/15 for international students. Applications are processed on a rolling basis. Application fee: $105 ($125 for international students). Electronic applications accepted. *Financial support:* Fellowships with tuition reimbursements, research assistantships with full tuition reimbursements, teaching assistantships with tuition reimbursements, institutionally sponsored loans, traineeships, health care benefits, and unspecified assistantships available. Financial award application deadline: 3/1; financial award applicants required to submit FAFSA. *Faculty research:* Molecular biotechnology, nanobiomaterials, biophotonics, synthesis, super plasticity and mechanical behavior, characterization of advanced and nanostructural materials. *Unit head:* Prof. Vasan Venugopalan, Chair, 949-824-5802, Fax: 949-824-2541, E-mail: vvenugop@uci.edu. *Application contact:* Grace Chau, Academic Program and Graduate Admission Coordinator, 949-824-3887, Fax: 949-824-2541, E-mail: chaug@uci.edu.
Website: http://www.eng.uci.edu/dept/chems

University of California, Irvine, School of Physical Sciences and Department of Physics and Astronomy, Program in Chemical and Materials Physics (CHAMP), Irvine, CA 92697. Offers MS, PhD. *Students:* 53 full-time (11 women); includes 17 minority (1 American Indian or Alaska Native, non-Hispanic/Latino; 10 Asian, non-Hispanic/Latino; 3 Hispanic/Latino; 3 Two or more races, non-Hispanic/Latino), 12 international. Average age 27. 46 applicants, 50% accepted, 9 enrolled. In 2016, 10 master's, 11 doctorates awarded. *Degree requirements:* For doctorate, thesis/dissertation. *Entrance requirements:* For master's and doctorate, GRE General Test, GRE Subject Test, minimum GPA of 3.0. *Application deadline:* For fall admission, 1/15 priority date for domestic students, 1/15 for international students. Applications are processed on a rolling basis. Application fee: $105 ($125 for international students). Electronic applications accepted. *Financial support:* Fellowships, research assistantships with full tuition reimbursements, teaching assistantships, institutionally sponsored loans, traineeships, health care benefits, and unspecified assistantships available. Financial award application deadline: 3/1; financial award applicants required to submit FAFSA. *Unit head:* A.J. Shaka, Co-Director, 949-824-8509, E-mail: ajshaka@uci.edu. *Application contact:* Jaime M. Albano, Student Affairs Manager, 949-824-4261, Fax: 949-824-8571, E-mail: jmalbano@uci.edu.

University of California, Los Angeles, Graduate Division, Henry Samueli School of Engineering and Applied Science, Department of Materials Science and Engineering, Los Angeles, CA 90095-1595. Offers MS, PhD. *Faculty:* 14 full-time (2 women), 4 part-time/adjunct (0 women). *Students:* 177 full-time (51 women); includes 35 minority (1 Black or African American, non-Hispanic/Latino; 26 Asian, non-Hispanic/Latino; 6 Hispanic/Latino; 2 Two or more races, non-Hispanic/Latino), 113 international. 345 applicants, 53% accepted, 60 enrolled. In 2016, 24 master's, 20 doctorates awarded. *Degree requirements:* For master's, comprehensive exam or thesis; for doctorate, thesis/dissertation, qualifying exams. *Entrance requirements:* For master's, GRE General Test, minimum GPA of 3.0; for doctorate, GRE General Test, minimum GPA of 3.25. Additional exam requirements/recommendations for international students: Required—TOEFL (minimum score 560 paper-based; 87 iBT), IELTS (minimum score 7). *Application deadline:* For fall admission, 11/30 for domestic and international students. Application fee: $105 ($125 for international students). Electronic applications accepted. *Financial support:* In 2016–17, 93 fellowships, 126 research assistantships, 51 teaching assistantships were awarded; Federal Work-Study, institutionally sponsored loans, and tuition waivers (full and partial) also available. Financial award application deadline: 11/30; financial award applicants required to submit FAFSA. *Faculty research:* Ceramics and ceramic processing, electronic and optical materials, structural materials. *Total annual research expenditures:* $7 million. *Unit head:* Dr. Dwight C. Streit, Chair, 310-825-7011, E-mail: streit@ucla.edu. *Application contact:* Patti Barrera, Student Affairs Officer, 310-825-8916, E-mail: patti@seas.ucla.edu.
Website: http://www.mse.ucla.edu

University of California, Riverside, Graduate Division, Materials Science and Engineering Program, Riverside, CA 92521. Offers MS. *Entrance requirements:* For master's, GRE. Additional exam requirements/recommendations for international students: Required—TOEFL (minimum score 550 paper-based; 80 iBT). Electronic applications accepted. *Expenses:* Tuition, state resident: full-time $16,666. Tuition, nonresident: full-time $31,768. *Required fees:* $11,055.54 per quarter. $3685.18 per quarter. Tuition and fees vary according to campus/location and program.

University of California, San Diego, Graduate Division, Program in Materials Science and Engineering, La Jolla, CA 92093. Offers MS, PhD. *Students:* 212 full-time (66 women), 10 part-time (2 women). 446 applicants, 53% accepted, 68 enrolled. In 2016, 27 master's, 19 doctorates awarded. *Degree requirements:* For master's, comprehensive exam (for some programs), thesis (for some programs), thesis or comprehensive exam; for doctorate, comprehensive exam, thesis/dissertation. *Entrance requirements:* For master's and doctorate, GRE General Test, minimum GPA of 3.2. Additional exam requirements/recommendations for international students: Required—TOEFL (minimum score 550 paper-based; 80 iBT), IELTS (minimum score 7). *Application deadline:* For fall admission, 1/4 for domestic students. Application fee: $105 ($125 for international students). Electronic applications accepted. *Expenses:* Tuition, state resident: full-time $11,220. Tuition, nonresident: full-time $26,322. *Required fees:* $1864. *Financial support:* Fellowships, research assistantships, and teaching assistantships available. Financial award applicants required to submit FAFSA. *Faculty research:* Magnetic and nano-materials, structural materials, electronic materials and interfaces, biomaterials, energy materials and applications. *Unit head:* Prabhakar Banderu, Director, 858-534-5325, E-mail: pbandaru@ucsd.edu. *Application contact:* Katherine Hamilton, Graduate Coordinator, 858-534-7715, E-mail: kahamilton@ucsd.edu.
Website: http://matsci.ucsd.edu/

University of California, Santa Barbara, Graduate Division, College of Engineering, Department of Materials, Santa Barbara, CA 93106-5050. Offers MS, PhD, MS/PhD. Terminal master's awarded for partial completion of doctoral program. *Degree requirements:* For master's, variable foreign language requirement, comprehensive exam, thesis; for doctorate, variable foreign language requirement, comprehensive exam, thesis/dissertation. *Entrance requirements:* For master's and doctorate, GRE General Test. Additional exam requirements/recommendations for international students: Required—TOEFL (minimum score 600 paper-based; 100 iBT), IELTS (minimum score 7). Electronic applications accepted. *Faculty research:* Electronic and photonic materials, inorganic materials, macromolecular and biomolecular materials, structural materials.

University of Central Florida, College of Engineering and Computer Science, Department of Materials Science and Engineering, Orlando, FL 32816. Offers MSMSE, PhD. *Students:* 47 full-time (19 women), 7 part-time (3 women); includes 7 minority (2 Asian, non-Hispanic/Latino; 4 Hispanic/Latino; 1 Two or more races, non-Hispanic/Latino), 32 international. Average age 28. 82 applicants, 49% accepted, 14 enrolled. In 2016, 12 master's, 3 doctorates awarded. *Degree requirements:* For master's, thesis or alternative; for doctorate, thesis/dissertation, candidacy exam, departmental qualifying exam. *Entrance requirements:* Additional exam requirements/recommendations for international students: Required—TOEFL. *Application deadline:* For fall admission, 7/15 for domestic students; for spring admission, 12/1 for domestic students. Application fee: $30. Electronic applications accepted. *Expenses:* Tuition, state resident: part-time $288.16 per credit hour. Tuition, nonresident: part-time $1071.31 per credit hour. *Financial support:* In 2016–17, 42 students received support, including 9 fellowships with tuition reimbursements available (averaging $7,178 per year), 42 research assistantships (averaging $12,060 per year), 7 teaching assistantships (averaging $11,382 per year). Financial award application deadline: 3/1; financial award applicants required to submit FAFSA. *Unit head:* Dr. Sudipta Seal, Interim Chair, 407-823-5277, E-mail: sseal@ucf.edu. *Application contact:* Assistant Director, Graduate Admissions, 407-823-2766, Fax: 407-823-6442, E-mail: gradadmissions@ucf.edu.
Website: http://mse.ucf.edu/

University of Cincinnati, Graduate School, College of Engineering and Applied Science, Department of Mechanical and Materials Engineering, Program in Materials Science and Engineering, Cincinnati, OH 45221. Offers MS, PhD. *Program availability:* Evening/weekend. *Degree requirements:* For master's, thesis optional; for doctorate, one foreign language, comprehensive exam, thesis/dissertation, oral English proficiency exam. *Entrance requirements:* For master's and doctorate, GRE General Test, BS in related field, minimum undergraduate GPA of 3.0. Additional exam requirements/recommendations for international students: Required—TOEFL. Electronic applications accepted. *Expenses: Tuition, area resident:* Full-time $12,790; part-time $389 per credit hour. Tuition, state resident: full-time $13,290; part-time $419 per credit hour. Tuition,

nonresident: full-time $24,532; part-time $976 per credit hour. *International tuition:* $24,832 full-time. *Required fees:* $3958; $140 per credit hour. Tuition and fees vary according to course load, degree level, program and reciprocity agreements. *Faculty research:* Polymer characterization, surface analysis, and adhesion; mechanical behavior of high-temperature materials; composites; electrochemistry of materials.

University of Connecticut, Graduate School, School of Engineering, Department of Chemical, Materials and Biomolecular Engineering, Field of Materials Science and Engineering, Storrs, CT 06269. Offers MS, PhD. Terminal master's awarded for partial completion of doctoral program. *Degree requirements:* For master's, comprehensive exam; for doctorate, thesis/dissertation. *Entrance requirements:* For master's and doctorate, GRE General Test, GRE Subject Test. Additional exam requirements/recommendations for international students: Required—TOEFL (minimum score 550 paper-based). Electronic applications accepted.

University of Connecticut, Institute of Materials Science, Storrs, CT 06269. Offers MS, PhD.

University of Delaware, College of Engineering, Department of Materials Science and Engineering, Newark, DE 19716. Offers MMSE, PhD. Terminal master's awarded for partial completion of doctoral program. *Degree requirements:* For master's, thesis; for doctorate, thesis/dissertation. *Entrance requirements:* For master's and doctorate, GRE General Test, 3 letters of recommendation, minimum GPA of 3.2. Additional exam requirements/recommendations for international students: Required—TOEFL. Electronic applications accepted. *Faculty research:* Thin films and self assembly, drug delivery and tissue engineering, biomaterials and nanocomposites, semiconductor and oxide interfaces, electronic and magnetic materials.

University of Denver, Daniel Felix Ritchie School of Engineering and Computer Science, Department of Mechanical and Materials Engineering, Denver, CO 80208. Offers bioengineering (MS); engineering (MS, PhD), including management (MS); materials science (MS, PhD); mechanical engineering (MS, PhD). *Program availability:* Part-time. *Faculty:* 11 full-time (1 woman), 2 part-time/adjunct (both women). *Students:* 2 full-time (0 women), 27 part-time (7 women); includes 6 minority (1 Asian, non-Hispanic/Latino; 5 Hispanic/Latino), 13 international. Average age 28. 57 applicants, 79% accepted, 13 enrolled. In 2016, 11 master's, 5 doctorates awarded. Terminal master's awarded for partial completion of doctoral program. *Degree requirements:* For master's, thesis optional; for doctorate, comprehensive exam, thesis/dissertation. *Entrance requirements:* For master's, GRE General Test, bachelor's degree, transcripts, personal statement, resume or curriculum vitae, two letters of recommendation; for doctorate, GRE General Test, master's degree, transcripts, personal statement, resume or curriculum vitae, two letters of recommendation. Additional exam requirements/recommendations for international students: Required—TOEFL (minimum score 550 paper-based; 80 iBT). *Application deadline:* For fall admission, 2/1 priority date for domestic and international students. Applications are processed on a rolling basis. Application fee: $65. Electronic applications accepted. *Expenses:* $29,022 per year full-time. *Financial support:* In 2016–17, 15 students received support, including 4 research assistantships with tuition reimbursements available (averaging $11,667 per year), 5 teaching assistantships with tuition reimbursements available (averaging $12,084 per year); Federal Work-Study, institutionally sponsored loans, scholarships/grants, health care benefits, and unspecified assistantships also available. Financial award application deadline: 2/15; financial award applicants required to submit FAFSA. *Faculty research:* Cardiac biomechanics, novel high voltage/temperature materials and structures, high speed stereo radiography, musculoskeletal modeling, composites. *Total annual research expenditures:* $996,915. *Unit head:* Dr. Matt Gordon, Professor and Chair, 303-871-3580, Fax: 303-871-4450, E-mail: matthew.gordon@du.edu. *Application contact:* Yvonne Petitt, Assistant to the Chair, 303-871-2107, Fax: 303-871-4450, E-mail: yvonne.petitt@du.edu.
Website: http://ritchieschool.du.edu/departments/mme/

University of Florida, Graduate School, Herbert Wertheim College of Engineering, Department of Materials Science and Engineering, Gainesville, FL 32611. Offers material science and engineering (MS), including clinical and translational science; materials science and engineering (ME, PhD); nuclear engineering (ME, PhD), including imaging science and technology (PhD), nuclear engineering sciences (ME, MS, PhD); nuclear engineering (MS), including nuclear engineering sciences (ME, MS, PhD); JD/MS. *Program availability:* Part-time, online learning. Terminal master's awarded for partial completion of doctoral program. *Degree requirements:* For master's, comprehensive exam, thesis; for doctorate, comprehensive exam, thesis/dissertation. *Entrance requirements:* For master's and doctorate, minimum GPA of 3.0. Additional exam requirements/recommendations for international students: Required—TOEFL (minimum score 550 paper-based; 80 iBT), IELTS (minimum score 6). Electronic applications accepted. *Faculty research:* Polymeric system, biomaterials and biomimetics; inorganic and organic electronic materials; functional ceramic materials for energy systems and microelectronic applications; advanced metallic systems for aerospace, transportation and biological applications; nuclear materials.

University of Idaho, College of Graduate Studies, College of Engineering, Department of Chemical and Materials Engineering, Moscow, ID 83844. Offers chemical engineering (M Engr, MS, PhD); materials science and engineering (MS, PhD); metallurgical engineering (MS). *Faculty:* 10 full-time, 2 part-time/adjunct. *Students:* 16 full-time, 7 part-time. Average age 31. In 2016, 7 master's, 1 doctorate awarded. *Entrance requirements:* For master's and doctorate, GRE, minimum GPA of 3.0. *Application deadline:* For fall admission, 8/1 for domestic students; for spring admission, 12/15 for domestic students. Applications are processed on a rolling basis. Application fee: $60. Electronic applications accepted. *Expenses:* Tuition, state resident: full-time $6460; part-time $414 per credit hour. Tuition, nonresident: full-time $21,268; part-time $1237 per credit hour. *Required fees:* $2070; $60 per credit hour. Full-time tuition and fees vary according to course load and reciprocity agreements. *Financial support:* Fellowships, research assistantships, and teaching assistantships available. Financial award applicants required to submit FAFSA. *Faculty research:* Geothermal energy utilization, alcohol production from agriculture waste material, energy conservation in pulp and paper mills. *Unit head:* Dr. Eric Aston, Department Chair, 208-885-7572, E-mail: che@uidaho.edu. *Application contact:* Sean Scoggin, Graduate Recruitment Coordinator, 208-885-4001, Fax: 208-885-4406, E-mail: graduateadmissions@uidaho.edu.
Website: https://www.uidaho.edu/engr/departments/cme

University of Illinois at Urbana–Champaign, Graduate College, College of Engineering, Department of Materials Science and Engineering, Champaign, IL 61820. Offers M Eng, MS, PhD, MS/MBA, PhD/MBA.

University of Kentucky, Graduate School, College of Engineering, Program in Materials Science and Engineering, Lexington, KY 40506-0032. Offers MS, PhD. *Degree requirements:* For master's, comprehensive exam, thesis optional; for doctorate, comprehensive exam, thesis/dissertation. *Entrance requirements:* For master's, GRE General Test, minimum undergraduate GPA of 2.75; for doctorate, GRE General Test, minimum undergraduate GPA of 3.0. Additional exam requirements/recommendations for international students: Required—TOEFL (minimum score 550 paper-based). Electronic applications accepted. *Faculty research:* Physical and mechanical metallurgy, computational material engineering, polymers and composites, high-temperature ceramics, powder metallurgy.

The University of Manchester, School of Chemistry, Manchester, United Kingdom. Offers biological chemistry (PhD); chemistry (M Ent, M Phil, M Sc, D Ent, PhD); inorganic chemistry (PhD); materials chemistry (PhD); nanoscience (PhD); nuclear fission (PhD); organic chemistry (PhD); physical chemistry (PhD); theoretical chemistry (PhD).

The University of Manchester, School of Materials, Manchester, United Kingdom. Offers advanced aerospace materials engineering (M Sc); advanced metallic systems (PhD); biomedical materials (M Phil, M Sc, PhD); ceramics and glass (M Phil, M Sc, PhD); composite materials (M Sc, PhD); corrosion and protection (M Phil, M Sc, PhD); materials (M Phil, PhD); metallic materials (M Phil, M Sc, PhD); nanostructural materials (M Phil, M Sc, PhD); paper science (M Phil, M Sc, PhD); polymer science and engineering (M Phil, M Sc, PhD); technical textiles (M Sc); textile design, fashion and management (M Phil, M Sc, PhD); textile science and technology (M Phil, M Sc, PhD); textiles (M Phil, PhD); textiles and fashion (M Ent).

University of Maryland, College Park, Academic Affairs, A. James Clark School of Engineering, Department of Materials Science and Engineering, Materials Science and Engineering Program, College Park, MD 20742. Offers MS, PhD. *Program availability:* Part-time, evening/weekend, online learning. *Degree requirements:* For master's, comprehensive exam, thesis optional, research paper; for doctorate, thesis/dissertation, oral exam. *Entrance requirements:* For master's and doctorate, GRE General Test, minimum B+ average in undergraduate course work. Additional exam requirements/recommendations for international students: Required—TOEFL. Electronic applications accepted.

University of Michigan, College of Engineering, Department of Materials Science and Engineering, Ann Arbor, MI 48109. Offers MS, PhD. *Program availability:* Part-time. *Students:* 169 full-time (58 women), 3 part-time (2 women). 604 applicants, 20% accepted, 49 enrolled. In 2016, 31 master's, 33 doctorates awarded. *Degree requirements:* For master's, thesis, oral defense of thesis; for doctorate, thesis/dissertation, oral defense of dissertation, written exam. *Entrance requirements:* For master's and doctorate, GRE General Test. Additional exam requirements/recommendations for international students: Required—TOEFL. *Application deadline:* Applications are processed on a rolling basis. Electronic applications accepted. *Expenses:* Tuition, state resident: full-time $21,466; part-time $1152 per credit hour. Tuition, nonresident: full-time $43,346; part-time $2367 per credit hour. Part-time tuition and fees vary according to course load, degree level and program. *Financial support:* Fellowships, research assistantships, and teaching assistantships available. Financial award applicants required to submit FAFSA. *Faculty research:* Soft materials (polymers, biomaterials), computational materials science, structural materials, electronic and optical materials, nanocomposite materials. *Total annual research expenditures:* $18.5 million. *Unit head:* Amit Misra, Department Chair, 734-763-2445, E-mail: amitmis@umich.edu. *Application contact:* Renee Hilgendorf, Graduate Program Coordinator, 734-763-9790, E-mail: reneeh@umich.edu.
Website: http://www.mse.engin.umich.edu

University of Michigan, Rackham Graduate School, College of Literature, Science, and the Arts, Department of Chemistry, Ann Arbor, MI 48109-1055. Offers analytical (PhD); chemical biology (PhD); inorganic (PhD); materials (PhD); organic (PhD); physical (PhD). *Degree requirements:* For doctorate, comprehensive exam, thesis/dissertation, oral defense of dissertation, organic cumulative proficiency exams. *Entrance requirements:* For doctorate, GRE General Test, GRE Subject Test (recommended), 3 letters of recommendation. Additional exam requirements/recommendations for international students: Required—TOEFL (minimum score 560 paper-based; 84 iBT). Electronic applications accepted. *Expenses:* Tuition, state resident: full-time $21,466; part-time $1152 per credit hour. Tuition, nonresident: full-time $43,346; part-time $2367 per credit hour. Part-time tuition and fees vary according to course load, degree level and program. *Faculty research:* Biological catalysis, protein engineering, chemical sensors, de novo metalloprotein design, supramolecular architecture.

University of Minnesota, Twin Cities Campus, College of Science and Engineering, Department of Chemical Engineering and Materials Science, Program in Materials Science and Engineering, Minneapolis, MN 55455-0132. Offers M Mat SE, MS Mat SE, PhD. *Program availability:* Part-time. Terminal master's awarded for partial completion of doctoral program. *Degree requirements:* For master's, thesis; for doctorate, thesis/dissertation. *Entrance requirements:* For master's and doctorate, GRE General Test. Additional exam requirements/recommendations for international students: Required—TOEFL. Electronic applications accepted. *Faculty research:* Ceramics and metals; coating processes and interfacial engineering; crystal growth and design; polymers; electronic, photonic and magnetic materials.

University of Mississippi Medical Center, School of Graduate Studies in the Health Sciences, Program in Biomedical Materials Science, Jackson, MS 39216-4505. Offers MS, PhD. Terminal master's awarded for partial completion of doctoral program. *Degree requirements:* For master's, thesis; for doctorate, comprehensive exam, thesis/dissertation. *Entrance requirements:* For master's, GRE, BS; for doctorate, GRE, BS, MS (preferred). Additional exam requirements/recommendations for international students: Required—TOEFL (minimum score 105 iBT). Electronic applications accepted. *Faculty research:* Tissue engineering, fatigue life prediction, metallurgy and alloy development, dental implant design and testing, ceramics, materials for dental applications.

University of Nebraska–Lincoln, Graduate College, College of Arts and Sciences, Department of Chemistry, Lincoln, NE 68588. Offers analytical chemistry (PhD); biochemistry (PhD); chemistry (MS); inorganic chemistry (PhD); materials chemistry (PhD); organic chemistry (PhD); physical chemistry (PhD). *Degree requirements:* For master's, one foreign language, thesis optional, departmental qualifying exam; for doctorate, one foreign language, comprehensive exam, thesis/dissertation, departmental qualifying exams. *Entrance requirements:* For master's and doctorate, GRE. Additional exam requirements/recommendations for international students: Required—TOEFL (minimum score 550 paper-based). Electronic applications accepted. *Faculty research:* Bioorganic and bioinorganic chemistry, biophysical and bioanalytical chemistry, structure-function of DNA and proteins, organometallics, mass spectrometry.

University of New Brunswick Fredericton, School of Graduate Studies, Faculty of Engineering, Department of Civil Engineering, Fredericton, NB E3B 5A3, Canada. Offers construction engineering and management (M Eng, M Sc E, PhD); environmental engineering (M Eng, M Sc E, PhD); environmental studies (M Eng); geotechnical engineering (M Eng, M Sc E, PhD); groundwater/hydrology (M Eng, M Sc E, PhD); materials (M Eng, M Sc E, PhD); pavements (M Eng, M Sc E, PhD); structures (M Eng, M Sc E, PhD); transportation (M Eng, M Sc E, PhD). *Program availability:* Part-time. *Degree requirements:* For master's, thesis; for doctorate, comprehensive exam, thesis/dissertation, qualifying exam; 27 credit hours of courses. *Entrance requirements:* For master's, minimum GPA of 3.0; B Sc E in civil engineering or related engineering degree; for doctorate, minimum GPA of 3.0; graduate degree in engineering or applied science. Additional exam requirements/recommendations for international students: Required—IELTS (minimum score 7.5), TWE (minimum score 4), Michigan English Language Assessment Battery (minimum score 85) or CanTest (minimum score 4.5); Recommended—TOEFL (minimum score 580 paper-based). Electronic applications accepted. *Faculty research:* Construction engineering and management; engineering materials and infrastructure renewal; highway and pavement research; structures and solid mechanics; geotechnical and geoenvironmental engineering; structure interaction; transportation and planning; environment, solid waste management; structural engineering; water and environmental engineering.

University of New Hampshire, Graduate School, College of Engineering and Physical Sciences, Department of Mechanical Engineering, Durham, NH 03824. Offers materials science (MS, PhD); mechanical engineering (M Engr, MS, PhD); systems engineering (PhD). *Program availability:* Part-time. *Degree requirements:* For master's, thesis or alternative; for doctorate, thesis/dissertation. *Entrance requirements:* For master's and doctorate, GRE. Additional exam requirements/recommendations for international students: Required—TOEFL (minimum score 550 paper-based; 80 iBT). Electronic applications accepted. *Faculty research:* Solid mechanics, dynamics, materials science, dynamic systems, automatic control.

University of New Hampshire, Graduate School, College of Engineering and Physical Sciences, Program in Materials Science, Durham, NH 03824. Offers MS, PhD. *Degree requirements:* For master's, thesis or alternative. *Entrance requirements:* For master's, GRE. Additional exam requirements/recommendations for international students: Required—TOEFL (minimum score 550 paper-based; 80 iBT). Electronic applications accepted.

University of Pennsylvania, School of Engineering and Applied Science, Department of Materials Science and Engineering, Philadelphia, PA 19104. Offers MSE, PhD. *Program availability:* Part-time. *Faculty:* 14 full-time (3 women), 2 part-time/adjunct (1 woman). *Students:* 99 full-time (24 women), 20 part-time (4 women); includes 3 minority (2 Hispanic/Latino; 1 Two or more races, non-Hispanic/Latino), 84 international. Average age 24. 517 applicants, 24% accepted, 84 enrolled. In 2016, 54 master's, 11 doctorates awarded. *Degree requirements:* For master's, comprehensive exam, thesis optional; for doctorate, comprehensive exam, thesis/dissertation. *Entrance requirements:* For master's and doctorate, GRE. Additional exam requirements/recommendations for international students: Required—TOEFL (minimum score 100 iBT), IELTS (minimum score 7). *Application deadline:* For fall admission, 3/15 priority date for domestic and international students; for spring admission, 11/1 priority date for domestic students, 10/1 priority date for international students. Application fee: $80. Electronic applications accepted. *Expenses: Tuition:* Full-time $31,068; part-time $5762 per course. *Required fees:* $3200; $336 per course. Full-time tuition and fees vary according to degree level, program and student level. Part-time tuition and fees vary according to course load, degree level and program. *Faculty research:* Biomaterials, ceramics, electronic and optical properties, nanostructured materials, semiconductors. *Application contact:* William Fenton, Assistant Director of Graduate Admissions, 215-898-4542, Fax: 215-573-5577, E-mail: gradstudies@seas.upenn.edu.
Website: http://www.mse.seas.upenn.edu/current-students/masters/index.php

University of Pittsburgh, Swanson School of Engineering, Department of Mechanical Engineering and Materials Science, Pittsburgh, PA 15260. Offers MSME, MSNE, PhD. *Program availability:* Part-time, 100% online. *Faculty:* 29 full-time (1 woman), 24 part-time/adjunct (2 women). *Students:* 131 full-time (17 women), 97 part-time (20 women); includes 12 minority (3 Black or African American, non-Hispanic/Latino; 4 Asian, non-Hispanic/Latino; 4 Hispanic/Latino; 1 Two or more races, non-Hispanic/Latino), 99 international. 604 applicants, 41% accepted, 60 enrolled. In 2016, 85 master's, 17 doctorates awarded. Terminal master's awarded for partial completion of doctoral program. *Degree requirements:* For doctorate, comprehensive exam, thesis/dissertation, final oral exams. *Entrance requirements:* For master's and doctorate, minimum GPA of 3.0. Additional exam requirements/recommendations for international students: Required—TOEFL (minimum score 550 paper-based; 80 iBT). *Application deadline:* For fall admission, 3/1 priority date for domestic and international students; for spring admission, 7/1 priority date for domestic and international students. Applications are processed on a rolling basis. Application fee: $50. Electronic applications accepted. *Expenses:* $24,962 full-time per academic year in-state tuition, $41,222 full-time per academic year out-of-state tuition; $830 mandatory fees per academic year. *Financial support:* In 2016–17, 7 fellowships with full tuition reimbursements (averaging $30,720 per year), 30 research assistantships with full tuition reimbursements (averaging $27,396 per year), 33 teaching assistantships with full tuition reimbursements (averaging $26,328 per year) were awarded; scholarships/grants and tuition waivers (full) also available. Financial award application deadline: 3/1. *Faculty research:* Smart materials and structure solid mechanics, computational fluid dynamics, multiphase bio-fluid dynamics, mechanical vibration analysis. *Total annual research expenditures:* $7.9 million. *Unit head:* Dr. Brian Gleeson, Chairman, 412-624-1185, Fax: 412-624-4846, E-mail: bgleeson@pitt.edu. *Application contact:* Rama Bazaz, Director, 412-624-9800, Fax: 412-624-9808, E-mail: ssoeadm@pitt.edu.
Website: http://www.engineering.pitt.edu/Departments/MEMS/

University of Puerto Rico, Mayagüez Campus, Graduate Studies, College of Arts and Sciences, Department of Chemistry, Mayagüez, PR 00681-9000. Offers applied chemistry (MS, PhD), including biophysical chemistry (PhD), chemistry of materials (PhD), environmental chemistry (PhD). *Program availability:* Part-time. *Faculty:* 18 full-time (8 women). *Students:* 67 full-time (40 women); includes 52 minority (all Hispanic/Latino), 15 international. Average age 25. 11 applicants, 82% accepted, 6 enrolled. In 2016, 1 master's, 7 doctorates awarded. Terminal master's awarded for partial completion of doctoral program. *Degree requirements:* For master's, one foreign language, comprehensive exam, thesis; for doctorate, one foreign language, comprehensive exam, thesis/dissertation. *Entrance requirements:* For master's, GRE General Test or minimum GPA of 2.0, BS in chemistry or the equivalent; minimum GPA of 2.8; for doctorate, GRE General Test or minimum GPA of 2.0. *Application deadline:* For fall admission, 2/15 for domestic and international students; for spring admission, 9/15 for domestic and international students. Applications are processed on a rolling basis. Application fee: $25. Electronic applications accepted. *Expenses: Tuition, area resident:* Full-time $2466. *International tuition:* $7166 full-time. *Required fees:* $210. One-time fee: $5 full-time. Tuition and fees vary according to course level, campus/location, program and student level. *Financial support:* In 2016–17, 57 students received support, including 30 research assistantships with full and partial tuition reimbursements available (averaging $5,167 per year), 37 teaching assistantships with full and partial tuition reimbursements available (averaging $5,132 per year); unspecified assistantships also available. *Faculty research:* Synthesis of heterocyclic moieties, protein structure and function, chemistry of explosives, bio-nanocomposites, process analytical technology. *Unit head:* Enrique Melendez, Ph.D., Director, 787-832-4040 Ext. 3122, Fax: 787-265-3849, E-mail: enrique.melendez@upr.edu. *Application contact:* Francheska Becerra, Graduate Student Affairs Officer I, 787-832-4040 Ext. 2434, Fax: 787-265-3849, E-mail: graduatechem@uprm.edu.
Website: http://www.uprm.edu/chemistry/

University of Rochester, Hajim School of Engineering and Applied Sciences, Master of Science in Technical Entrepreneurship and Management Program, Rochester, NY 14642. Offers biomedical engineering (MS); chemical engineering (MS); computer

science (MS); electrical and computer engineering (MS); energy and the environment (MS); materials science (MS); mechanical engineering (MS); optics (MS). Program offered in collaboration with the Simon School of Business. *Program availability:* Part-time. *Students:* 42 full-time (13 women), 6 part-time (3 women); includes 7 minority (1 Black or African American, non-Hispanic/Latino; 1 Asian, non-Hispanic/Latino; 4 Hispanic/Latino; 1 Two or more races, non-Hispanic/Latino), 28 international. Average age 24. 245 applicants, 65% accepted, 29 enrolled. In 2016, 31 master's awarded. *Degree requirements:* For master's, comprehensive exam, final exam. *Entrance requirements:* For master's, GRE or GMAT, 3 letters of recommendation; personal statement; official transcript; bachelor's degree (or equivalent for international students) in engineering, science, or mathematics. Additional exam requirements/recommendations for international students: Required—TOEFL (minimum score 600 paper-based; 100 iBT). *Application deadline:* For fall admission, 2/1 for domestic and international students. Application fee: $60. Electronic applications accepted. *Expenses:* $1,800 per credit. *Financial support:* In 2016–17, 45 students received support. Career-related internships or fieldwork and scholarships/grants available. Support available to part-time students. Financial award application deadline: 2/1. *Faculty research:* High efficiency solar cells, macromolecular self-assembly, digital signal processing, memory hierarchy management, molecular and physical mechanisms in cell migration, optical imaging systems. *Unit head:* Duncan T. Moore, Vice Provost for Entrepreneurship, 585-275-5248, Fax: 585-473-6745, E-mail: duncan.moore@rochester.edu. *Application contact:* Andrea Barrett, Executive Director, 585-276-3407, Fax: 585-276-2357, E-mail: andrea.barrett@rochester.edu.
Website: http://www.rochester.edu/team

University of Rochester, Hajim School of Engineering and Applied Sciences, Program in Materials Science, Rochester, NY 14627. Offers MS, PhD. *Students:* 40 full-time (10 women), 1 (woman) part-time; includes 2 minority (1 American Indian or Alaska Native, non-Hispanic/Latino; 1 Two or more races, non-Hispanic/Latino), 33 international. Average age 25. 142 applicants, 47% accepted, 16 enrolled. In 2016, 8 master's, 3 doctorates awarded. Terminal master's awarded for partial completion of doctoral program. *Degree requirements:* For master's, comprehensive exam, thesis, final exam; for doctorate, thesis/dissertation, qualifying exam. *Entrance requirements:* For master's and doctorate, GRE, 3 recommendation letters, curriculum vitae, personal statement. Additional exam requirements/recommendations for international students: Required—TOEFL (minimum score 600 paper-based; 100 iBT). *Application deadline:* For fall admission, 1/15 for domestic and international students. Application fee: $60. Electronic applications accepted. *Expenses:* $1,538 per credit. *Financial support:* In 2016–17, 16 students received support, including 5 fellowships (averaging $24,000 per year); tuition waivers (full and partial) also available. Financial award application deadline: 1/15. *Unit head:* Lewis J. Rothberg, Director, 585-273-4725, E-mail: lewis.rothberg@rochester.edu. *Application contact:* Gina Eagan, Administrative Assistant, 585-275-1626, E-mail: gina.eagan@rochester.edu.
Website: http://www.rochester.edu/college/matsci/

University of Southern California, Graduate School, Viterbi School of Engineering, Mork Family Department of Chemical Engineering and Materials Science, Los Angeles, CA 90089. Offers chemical engineering (MS, PhD, Engr); geoscience technologies (MS); materials engineering (MS); materials science (MS, PhD, Engr); petroleum engineering (MS, PhD, Engr); smart oilfield technologies (MS, Graduate Certificate). Terminal master's awarded for partial completion of doctoral program. *Degree requirements:* For master's, thesis optional; for doctorate, thesis/dissertation. *Entrance requirements:* For master's and doctorate, GRE General Test. Additional exam requirements/recommendations for international students: Recommended—TOEFL. Electronic applications accepted. *Expenses:* Contact institution. *Faculty research:* Heterogeneous materials and porous media, statistical mechanics, molecular simulation, polymer science and engineering, advanced materials, reaction engineering and catalysis, membrane processes and separation, biochemical engineering, cell culture, bioreactor modeling, petroleum engineering.

University of South Florida, Innovative Education, Tampa, FL 33620-9951. Offers adult, career and higher education (Graduate Certificate), including college teaching, leadership in developing human resources, leadership in higher education; Africana studies (Graduate Certificate), including diasporas and health disparities, genocide and human rights; aging studies (Graduate Certificate), including gerontology; art research (Graduate Certificate), including museum studies; business foundations (Graduate Certificate); chemical and biomedical engineering (Graduate Certificate), including materials science and engineering, water, health and sustainability; child and family studies (Graduate Certificate), including positive behavior support; civil and industrial engineering (Graduate Certificate), including transportation systems analysis; community and family health (Graduate Certificate), including maternal and child health, social marketing and public health, violence and injury: prevention and intervention, women's health; criminology (Graduate Certificate), including criminal justice administration; educational measurement and research (Graduate Certificate), including evaluation; English (Graduate Certificate), including comparative literary studies, creative writing, professional and technical communication; entrepreneurship (Graduate Certificate); environmental health (Graduate Certificate), including safety management; epidemiology and biostatistics (Graduate Certificate), including applied biostatistics, biostatistics, concepts and tools of epidemiology, epidemiology, epidemiology of infectious diseases; geography, environment and planning (Graduate Certificate), including community development, environmental policy and management, geographical information systems; geology (Graduate Certificate), including hydrogeology; global health (Graduate Certificate), including disaster management, global health and Latin American and Caribbean studies, global health practice, humanitarian assistance, infection control; government and international affairs (Graduate Certificate), including Cuban studies, globalization studies; health policy and management (Graduate Certificate), including health management and leadership, public health policy and programs; hearing specialist: early intervention (Graduate Certificate); industrial and management systems engineering (Graduate Certificate), including systems engineering, technology management; information studies (Graduate Certificate), including school library media specialist; information systems/decision sciences (Graduate Certificate), including analytics and business intelligence; instructional technology (Graduate Certificate), including distance education, Florida digital/virtual educator, instructional design, multimedia design, Web design; internal medicine, bioethics and medical humanities (Graduate Certificate), including biomedical ethics; Latin American and Caribbean studies (Graduate Certificate); mass communications (Graduate Certificate), including multimedia journalism; mathematics and statistics (Graduate Certificate), including mathematics; medicine (Graduate Certificate), including aging and neuroscience, bioinformatics, biotechnology, brain fitness and memory management, clinical investigation, health informatics, health sciences, integrative weight management, intellectual property, medicine and gender, metabolic and nutritional medicine, metabolic cardiology, pharmacy sciences; national and competitive intelligence (Graduate Certificate); psychological and social foundations (Graduate Certificate), including career counseling, college teaching, diversity in education, mental health counseling, school counseling; public affairs (Graduate Certificate), including nonprofit management, public management, research administration; public health (Graduate Certificate), including environmental health, health equity, public health generalist, translational research in adolescent behavioral health; public health practices (Graduate Certificate), including planning for healthy communities; rehabilitation and mental health counseling (Graduate Certificate), including integrative mental health care, marriage and family therapy, rehabilitation technology; secondary education (Graduate Certificate), including ESOL, foreign language education: culture and content, foreign language education: professional; social work (Graduate Certificate), including geriatric social work/clinical gerontology; special education (Graduate Certificate), including autism spectrum disorder, disabilities education: severe/profound; world languages (Graduate Certificate), including teaching English as a second language (TESL) or foreign language. *Expenses:* Tuition, state resident: full-time $7766; part-time $431.43 per credit hour. Tuition, nonresident: full-time $15,789; part-time $877.17 per credit hour. *Required fees:* $37 per term. *Unit head:* Kathy Barnes, Interdisciplinary Programs Coordinator, 813-974-8031, Fax: 813-974-7061, E-mail: barnesk@usf.edu. *Application contact:* Karen Tylinski, Metro Initiatives, 813-974-9943, Fax: 813-974-7061, E-mail: ktylinsk@usf.edu.
Website: http://www.usf.edu/innovative-education/

The University of Tennessee, Graduate School, Tickle College of Engineering, Department of Materials Science and Engineering, Program in Materials Science and Engineering, Knoxville, TN 37996. Offers MS, PhD. *Faculty:* 26 full-time (3 women), 10 part-time/adjunct (2 women). *Students:* 78 full-time (21 women), 6 part-time (2 women); includes 6 minority (1 Black or African American, non-Hispanic/Latino; 2 Asian, non-Hispanic/Latino; 3 Hispanic/Latino), 37 international. Average age 29. 138 applicants, 17% accepted, 17 enrolled. In 2016, 19 master's, 10 doctorates awarded. *Degree requirements:* For master's, thesis or alternative; for doctorate, comprehensive exam, thesis/dissertation. *Entrance requirements:* For master's, GRE General Test (for MS students pursuing research thesis), minimum GPA of 2.7 (for U.S. degree holders), 3.0 (for international degree holders); 3 references; for doctorate, GRE General Test, minimum GPA of 3.0 on previous graduate course work; 3 references. Additional exam requirements/recommendations for international students: Required—TOEFL (minimum score 550 paper-based). *Application deadline:* For fall admission, 2/1 priority date for domestic and international students; for spring admission, 6/15 for domestic and international students. Applications are processed on a rolling basis. Application fee: $35. Electronic applications accepted. *Financial support:* In 2016–17, 77 students received support, including 9 fellowships with full tuition reimbursements available (averaging $30,278 per year), 50 research assistantships with full tuition reimbursements available (averaging $23,100 per year), 16 teaching assistantships with full tuition reimbursements available (averaging $21,291 per year); career-related internships or fieldwork, Federal Work-Study, institutionally sponsored loans, health care benefits, and unspecified assistantships also available. Financial award application deadline: 2/1; financial award applicants required to submit FAFSA. *Faculty research:* Biomaterials; functional materials electronic, magnetic and optical; high temperature materials; mechanical behavior of materials; neutron materials science. *Unit head:* Dr. Veerle Keppens, Head, 865-974-5336, Fax: 865-974-4115, E-mail: vkeppens@utk.edu. *Application contact:* Dr. Roberto S. Benson, Associate Head, 865-974-5347, Fax: 865-974-4115, E-mail: rbenson1@utk.edu.
Website: http://www.engr.utk.edu/mse

The University of Texas at Arlington, Graduate School, College of Engineering, Department of Materials Science and Engineering, Arlington, TX 76019. Offers M Engr, MS, PhD. Terminal master's awarded for partial completion of doctoral program. *Degree requirements:* For master's, comprehensive exam (for some programs), thesis optional; for doctorate, comprehensive exam, thesis/dissertation optional. *Entrance requirements:* For master's, GRE General Test, minimum GPA of 3.0; for doctorate, GRE General Test, minimum GPA of 3.5. Additional exam requirements/recommendations for international students: Required—TOEFL (minimum score 550 paper-based; 79 iBT), IELTS. *Application deadline:* For fall admission, 6/1 for domestic students, 4/1 for international students; for spring admission, 10/15 for domestic students, 9/15 for international students. Applications are processed on a rolling basis. Application fee: $35 ($50 for international students). *Financial support:* Fellowships, research assistantships, teaching assistantships, scholarships/grants, and unspecified assistantships available. Financial award application deadline: 6/1; financial award applicants required to submit FAFSA. *Faculty research:* Electronic materials, conductive polymer, composites biomaterial, structural materials. *Unit head:* Dr. Eric Jones, Associate Dean for Graduate Studies. *Application contact:* Dr. Eric Jones, Associate Dean for Graduate Studies.
Website: http://www.uta.edu/mse

The University of Texas at Austin, Graduate School, Cockrell School of Engineering, Program in Materials Science and Engineering, Austin, TX 78712-1111. Offers MS, PhD. *Program availability:* Part-time. *Degree requirements:* For master's, thesis (for some programs); for doctorate, thesis/dissertation. *Entrance requirements:* For master's and doctorate, GRE General Test. Additional exam requirements/recommendations for international students: Required—TOEFL (minimum score 550 paper-based). Electronic applications accepted.

The University of Texas at Dallas, Erik Jonson School of Engineering and Computer Science, Department of Materials Science and Engineering, Richardson, TX 75080. Offers MS, PhD. *Program availability:* Part-time, evening/weekend. *Faculty:* 15 full-time (2 women). *Students:* 58 full-time (14 women), 4 part-time (2 women); includes 9 minority (2 Black or African American, non-Hispanic/Latino; 4 Asian, non-Hispanic/Latino; 2 Hispanic/Latino; 1 Two or more races, non-Hispanic/Latino), 38 international. Average age 28. 116 applicants, 37% accepted, 15 enrolled. In 2016, 13 master's, 6 doctorates awarded. *Degree requirements:* For master's, thesis or major design project; for doctorate, thesis/dissertation. *Entrance requirements:* For master's, GRE General Test, minimum GPA of 3.0 in related bachelor's degree; for doctorate, GRE General Test, minimum GPA of 3.5. Additional exam requirements/recommendations for international students: Required—TOEFL (minimum score 550 paper-based). *Application deadline:* For fall admission, 7/15 for domestic students, 5/1 priority date for international students; for spring admission, 11/15 for domestic students, 9/1 priority date for international students. Applications are processed on a rolling basis. Application fee: $50 ($100 for international students). Electronic applications accepted. *Expenses:* Tuition, state resident: full-time $12,418; part-time $690 per semester hour. Tuition, nonresident: full-time $24,150; part-time $1342 per semester hour. Tuition and fees vary according to course load. *Financial support:* In 2016–17, 56 students received support, including 3 fellowships (averaging $2,067 per year), 48 research assistantships with partial tuition reimbursements available (averaging $25,391 per year), 5 teaching assistantships with partial tuition reimbursements available (averaging $21,600 per year); career-related internships or fieldwork, Federal Work-Study, institutionally sponsored loans, scholarships/grants, and unspecified assistantships also available. Support available to part-time students. Financial award application deadline: 4/30; financial award applicants required to submit FAFSA. *Faculty research:* Graphene-based semiconducting materials, neuro-inspired computational paradigms, electronic materials with emphasis on dielectrics, energy harvesting (photovoltaics, lithium-ion batteries), biosensors and hydrogen storage materials. *Unit head:* Dr. Yves Chabal, Department Head, 972-883-5751, Fax: 972-883-5725, E-mail: chabal@utdallas.edu. *Application contact:* Dr. Julia Hsu, Associate Department Head, 972-883-5789, Fax:

972-883-5725, E-mail: jwhsu@utdallas.edu.
Website: http://mse.utdallas.edu/

The University of Texas at El Paso, Graduate School, College of Engineering, Department of Metallurgical and Materials Engineering, El Paso, TX 79968-0001. Offers materials science and engineering (PhD); metallurgical and materials engineering (MS). *Program availability:* Part-time, evening/weekend. *Degree requirements:* For master's, thesis. *Entrance requirements:* For master's, GRE General Test. Additional exam requirements/recommendations for international students: Required—TOEFL. Electronic applications accepted.

The University of Texas at El Paso, Graduate School, Interdisciplinary Program in Materials Science and Engineering, El Paso, TX 79968-0001. Offers PhD. *Program availability:* Part-time, evening/weekend. *Degree requirements:* For doctorate, thesis/dissertation. *Entrance requirements:* For doctorate, GRE, letters of recommendation. Additional exam requirements/recommendations for international students: Required—TOEFL; Recommended—IELTS. Electronic applications accepted.

The University of Toledo, College of Graduate Studies, College of Natural Sciences and Mathematics, Department of Physics and Astronomy, Toledo, OH 43606-3390. Offers photovoltaics (PSM); physics (MS, PhD), including astrophysics (PhD), materials science, medical physics (PhD); MS/PhD. *Degree requirements:* For master's, thesis; for doctorate, thesis/dissertation, departmental qualifying exam. *Entrance requirements:* For master's and doctorate, GRE General Test, GRE Subject Test, minimum cumulative point-hour ratio of 2.7 for all previous academic work, three letters of recommendation, statement of purpose, transcripts from all prior institutions attended. Additional exam requirements/recommendations for international students: Required—TOEFL (minimum score 550 paper-based; 80 iBT). Electronic applications accepted. *Faculty research:* Atomic physics, solid-state physics, materials science, astrophysics.

University of Toronto, School of Graduate Studies, Faculty of Applied Science and Engineering, Department of Materials Science and Engineering, Toronto, ON M5S 1A1, Canada. Offers M Eng, MA Sc, PhD. *Program availability:* Part-time. *Degree requirements:* For master's, thesis (for some programs), oral presentation/thesis defense (MA Sc), qualifying exam; for doctorate, thesis/dissertation. *Entrance requirements:* For master's, BA Sc or B Sc in materials science and engineering, 2 letters of reference; for doctorate, MA Sc or equivalent, 2 letters of reference, minimum B+ average in last 2 years. Additional exam requirements/recommendations for international students: Required—TOEFL (minimum score 580 paper-based), TWE (minimum score 4). Electronic applications accepted.

University of Utah, Graduate School, College of Engineering, Department of Materials Science and Engineering, Salt Lake City, UT 84112. Offers MS, PhD. *Faculty:* 8 full-time (0 women), 2 part-time/adjunct (1 woman). *Students:* 21 full-time (9 women), 7 part-time (2 women), 11 international. Average age 29. 61 applicants, 5% accepted, 3 enrolled. In 2016, 3 master's, 4 doctorates awarded. *Degree requirements:* For master's, thesis; for doctorate, thesis/dissertation. *Entrance requirements:* For master's and doctorate, GRE General Test, minimum GPA of 3.0. Additional exam requirements/recommendations for international students: Required—TOEFL (minimum score 570 paper-based; 88 iBT), IELTS (minimum score 7). *Application deadline:* For fall admission, 1/15 for domestic students, 12/15 for international students. Application fee: $0 ($15 for international students). Electronic applications accepted. *Expenses:* Contact institution. *Financial support:* In 2016–17, 1 student received support, including 1 fellowship with full tuition reimbursement available (averaging $26,780 per year), 16 research assistantships with full tuition reimbursements available (averaging $23,000 per year); teaching assistantships with full tuition reimbursements available also available. Financial award application deadline: 2/1; financial award applicants required to submit FAFSA. *Faculty research:* Solid oxide fuel cells, computational nanostructures, solar cells, Nano sensors, batteries: renewable energy. *Total annual research expenditures:* $3.3 million. *Unit head:* Dr. Feng Liu, Chair, 801-581-6863, Fax: 801-581-4816, E-mail: fliu@eng.utah.edu. *Application contact:* Marcie Leek, Academic Advisor, 801-581-6863, Fax: 801-581-4816, E-mail: marcie.leek@utah.edu.
Website: http://www.mse.utah.edu/

University of Vermont, Graduate College, College of Engineering and Mathematics, Program in Materials Science, Burlington, VT 05405. Offers MS, PhD. *Degree requirements:* For master's, thesis or alternative; for doctorate, thesis/dissertation. *Entrance requirements:* For master's and doctorate, GRE General Test. Additional exam requirements/recommendations for international students: Required—TOEFL (minimum score 550 paper-based; 80 iBT). Electronic applications accepted. *Expenses:* Tuition, state resident: full-time $5814. Tuition, nonresident: full-time $14,670.

University of Virginia, School of Engineering and Applied Science, Department of Materials Science and Engineering, Charlottesville, VA 22903. Offers materials science (MMSE, MS, PhD). *Program availability:* Part-time, online learning. *Faculty:* 16 full-time (2 women). *Students:* 77 full-time (23 women), 1 (woman) part-time; includes 9 minority (6 Asian, non-Hispanic/Latino; 1 Hispanic/Latino; 2 Two or more races, non-Hispanic/Latino), 23 international. Average age 26. 112 applicants, 24% accepted, 16 enrolled. In 2016, 12 master's, 7 doctorates awarded. Terminal master's awarded for partial completion of doctoral program. *Degree requirements:* For master's, comprehensive exam, thesis (for some programs); for doctorate, comprehensive exam, thesis/dissertation. *Entrance requirements:* For master's and doctorate, GRE General Test, three recommendations. Additional exam requirements/recommendations for international students: Required—TOEFL. *Application deadline:* For fall admission, 1/15 for domestic and international students. Applications are processed on a rolling basis. Application fee: $60. Electronic applications accepted. *Expenses:* Tuition, state resident: full-time $15,026; part-time $834 per credit hour. Tuition, nonresident: full-time $25,168; part-time $1378 per credit hour. *Required fees:* $2654. *Financial support:* Fellowships, research assistantships, and teaching assistantships available. Financial award application deadline: 1/15; financial award applicants required to submit FAFSA. *Faculty research:* Environmental effects on material behavior, electronic materials, metals, polymers, tribology. *Unit head:* John R. Scully, Interim Department Chair, 434-982-5786, Fax: 434-982-5799, E-mail: jrs8d@virginia.edu. *Application contact:* Pamela M. Norris, Associate Dean for Research and Graduate Programs, 434-243-7683, Fax: 434-982-3044, E-mail: pamela@cs.virginia.edu.
Website: http://www.virginia.edu/ms/

University of Washington, Graduate School, College of Engineering, Department of Materials Science and Engineering, Seattle, WA 98195-2120. Offers applied materials science and engineering (MS); materials science and engineering (MS, PhD). *Program availability:* Part-time. *Faculty:* 13 full-time (2 women). *Students:* 97 full-time (28 women), 19 part-time (5 women); includes 21 minority (1 Black or African American, non-Hispanic/Latino; 12 Asian, non-Hispanic/Latino; 5 Hispanic/Latino; 1 Native Hawaiian or other Pacific Islander, non-Hispanic/Latino; 2 Two or more races, non-Hispanic/Latino), 40 international. 505 applicants, 21% accepted, 49 enrolled. In 2016, 41 master's, 12 doctorates awarded. Terminal master's awarded for partial completion of doctoral program. *Degree requirements:* For master's, comprehensive exam, final presentation; for doctorate, comprehensive exam, thesis/dissertation, qualifying evaluation, general and final exams. *Entrance requirements:* For master's and doctorate, GRE General Test, minimum GPA of 3.0, resume/curriculum vitae, letters of recommendation, statement of purpose, transcripts. Additional exam requirements/recommendations for international students: Required—TOEFL (minimum score 580 paper-based; 92 iBT). *Application deadline:* For fall admission, 1/2 for domestic and international students. Application fee: $85. Electronic applications accepted. *Expenses:* Contact institution. *Financial support:* In 2016–17, 49 students received support, including 3 fellowships with full tuition reimbursements available (averaging $2,800 per year), 34 research assistantships with full tuition reimbursements available (averaging $2,398 per year), 12 teaching assistantships with full tuition reimbursements available (averaging $2,398 per year); career-related internships or fieldwork, Federal Work-Study, institutionally sponsored loans, scholarships/grants, health care benefits, unspecified assistantships, and stipend supplements also available. Financial award application deadline: 1/1; financial award applicants required to submit FAFSA. *Faculty research:* Synthesis/structure/property and processing, biomaterials and biomimetics, materials chemistry and characterization, optical and electronic materials. *Total annual research expenditures:* $6.3 million. *Unit head:* Dr. Fumio Ohuchi, Professor/Chair, 206-685-8272, Fax: 206-543-3100, E-mail: ohuchi@uw.edu. *Application contact:* Karen Wetterhahn, Academic Counselor, 206-543-2740, Fax: 206-543-3100, E-mail: karenlw@uw.edu.
Website: http://depts.washington.edu/mse/

Vanderbilt University, School of Engineering, Interdisciplinary Program in Materials Science, Nashville, TN 37240-1001. Offers M Eng, MS, PhD. *Program availability:* Part-time. Terminal master's awarded for partial completion of doctoral program. *Degree requirements:* For master's, thesis; for doctorate, thesis/dissertation. *Entrance requirements:* For master's and doctorate, GRE General Test. Electronic applications accepted. *Expenses:* *Tuition:* Part-time $1854 per credit hour. *Faculty research:* Nanostructure materials, materials physics, surface and interface science, materials synthesis, biomaterials.

Virginia Polytechnic Institute and State University, Graduate School, College of Engineering, Blacksburg, VA 24061. Offers aerospace engineering (ME, MS, PhD); biological systems engineering (ME, MS, PhD); biomedical engineering (MS, PhD); chemical engineering (ME, MS, PhD); civil engineering (ME, MS, PhD); computer engineering (ME, MS, PhD); computer science (MS, PhD); electrical engineering (ME, PhD); engineering education (PhD); engineering mechanics (ME, MS, PhD); environmental engineering (MS); environmental science and engineering (MS); industrial and systems engineering (ME, MS, PhD); materials science and engineering (ME, MS, PhD); mechanical engineering (ME, MS, PhD); mining and minerals engineering (PhD); mining engineering (ME, MS); nuclear engineering (MS, PhD); ocean engineering (MS); systems engineering (ME, MS). *Faculty:* 400 full-time (73 women), 3 part-time/adjunct (2 women). *Students:* 1,949 full-time (487 women), 393 part-time (69 women); includes 251 minority (56 Black or African American, non-Hispanic/Latino; 3 American Indian or Alaska Native, non-Hispanic/Latino; 87 Asian, non-Hispanic/Latino; 70 Hispanic/Latino; 35 Two or more races, non-Hispanic/Latino), 1,354 international. Average age 27. 4,903 applicants, 19% accepted, 569 enrolled. In 2016, 364 master's, 200 doctorates awarded. *Degree requirements:* For master's, comprehensive exam (for some programs), thesis (for some programs); for doctorate, comprehensive exam (for some programs), thesis/dissertation (for some programs). *Entrance requirements:* For master's and doctorate, GRE/GMAT. Additional exam requirements/recommendations for international students: Required—TOEFL (minimum score 80 iBT). *Application deadline:* For fall admission, 8/1 for domestic students, 4/1 for international students; for spring admission, 1/1 for domestic students, 9/1 for international students. Applications are processed on a rolling basis. Application fee: $75. Electronic applications accepted. *Expenses:* Tuition, state resident: full-time $12,467; part-time $692.50 per credit hour. Tuition, nonresident: full-time $25,095; part-time $1394.25 per credit hour. *Required fees:* $2669; $491.50 per semester. Tuition and fees vary according to course load, campus/location and program. *Financial support:* In 2016–17, 160 fellowships with full tuition reimbursements (averaging $7,387 per year), 872 research assistantships with full tuition reimbursements (averaging $22,329 per year), 313 teaching assistantships with full tuition reimbursements (averaging $18,714 per year) were awarded. Financial award application deadline: 3/1; financial award applicants required to submit FAFSA. *Total annual research expenditures:* $91.8 million. *Unit head:* Dr. Julia Ross, Dean, 540-231-9752, Fax: 540-231-3031, E-mail: deaneng@vt.edu. *Application contact:* Linda Perkins, Executive Assistant, 540-231-9752, Fax: 540-231-3031, E-mail: lperkins@vt.edu.
Website: http://www.eng.vt.edu/

Washington State University, Voiland College of Engineering and Architecture, School of Mechanical and Materials Engineering, Pullman, WA 99164-2920. Offers materials science and engineering (MS, PhD); mechanical engineering (MS, PhD). MS programs also offered at Tri-Cities campus. *Program availability:* Part-time. Terminal master's awarded for partial completion of doctoral program. *Degree requirements:* For master's, comprehensive exam, thesis; for doctorate, comprehensive exam, thesis/dissertation, preliminary exam. *Entrance requirements:* For master's, GRE, bachelor's degree, minimum GPA of 3.0, resume, statement of purpose, 3 letters of recommendation, official transcripts, Student Interest Profile form; for doctorate, GRE, bachelor's degree, minimum GPA of 3.4, resume, statement of purpose, 3 letters of recommendation, official transcripts, Student Interest Profile form. Additional exam requirements/recommendations for international students: Required—TOEFL (minimum score 500 paper-based), IELTS. Electronic applications accepted. *Faculty research:* Multiscale modeling and characterization of materials; advanced energy; bioengineering; engineering education and curricular innovation; modeling and visualization in the areas of product realization, materials, and processes.

Washington University in St. Louis, School of Engineering and Applied Science, Department of Mechanical Engineering and Materials Science, St. Louis, MO 63130-4899. Offers aerospace engineering (MS, PhD); materials science (MS); mechanical engineering (M Eng, MS, PhD). *Program availability:* Part-time. Terminal master's awarded for partial completion of doctoral program. *Degree requirements:* For master's, thesis optional; for doctorate, thesis/dissertation optional. *Entrance requirements:* For master's, GRE; for doctorate, GRE General Test, departmental qualifying exam. *Faculty research:* Aerosols science and technology, applied mechanics, biomechanics and biomedical engineering, design, dynamic systems, combustion science, composite materials, materials science.

Wayne State University, College of Engineering, Department of Chemical Engineering and Materials Science, Detroit, MI 48202. Offers chemical engineering (MS, PhD); materials science and engineering (MS, PhD, Graduate Certificate), including materials science and engineering (MS, PhD), polymer engineering (Graduate Certificate). *Program availability:* Part-time. *Faculty:* 11. *Students:* 44 full-time (12 women), 23 part-time (6 women); includes 3 minority (1 Black or African American, non-Hispanic/Latino; 2 Asian, non-Hispanic/Latino), 40 international. Average age 26. 230 applicants, 31% accepted, 18 enrolled. In 2016, 12 master's, 5 doctorates awarded. *Degree requirements:* For master's, thesis optional; for doctorate, thesis/dissertation. *Entrance requirements:* For master's, three letters of recommendation (at least two from the applicant's academic institution); personal statement; resume; for doctorate, GRE, three letters of recommendation (at least two from the applicant's academic institution); personal statement; resume; for Graduate Certificate, bachelor's degree in engineering, chemistry, or physics. Additional exam requirements/recommendations for international students: Required—TOEFL (minimum score 550 paper-based; 79 iBT), TWE (minimum score 5.5), Michigan English Language Assessment Battery (minimum score 85); Recommended—IELTS (minimum score 6.5). *Application deadline:* For fall admission, 3/1 priority date for domestic and international students; for winter admission, 10/1 priority date for domestic students, 9/1 priority date for international students; for spring admission, 2/1 priority date for domestic and international students; for summer admission, 2/1 priority date for domestic and international students. Application fee: $50. Electronic applications accepted. *Expenses:* $18,871 per year resident tuition and fees, $36,065 per year non-resident tuition and fees. *Financial support:* In 2016–17, 26 students received support, including 7 fellowships with tuition reimbursements available (averaging $14,884 per year), 10 research assistantships with tuition reimbursements available (averaging $19,546 per year), 12 teaching assistantships with tuition reimbursements available (averaging $19,017 per year); scholarships/grants, health care benefits, and unspecified assistantships also available. Support available to part-time students. Financial award applicants required to submit FAFSA. *Faculty research:* Thermodynamics and transport properties of polymer solutions; processing, rheology, and separation of polymers; heterogeneous catalysts; surface science of catalyst and polymeric materials; laser-based imaging of chemical species and reactions; environmental transport and management of hazardous waste; process design and synthesis based on waste minimization, biocatalysis in multiphase systems, biomaterials and tissue engineering. *Total annual research expenditures:* $1.6 million. *Unit head:* Dr. Guangzhao Mao, Professor and Chair, 313-577-3804, E-mail: gzmao@eng.wayne.edu. *Application contact:* Ellen Cope, Graduate Program Coordinator, E-mail: escope@wayne.edu. Website: http://engineering.wayne.edu/che/

Worcester Polytechnic Institute, Graduate Studies and Research, Department of Mechanical Engineering, Program in Materials Process Engineering, Worcester, MA 01609-2280. Offers MS. *Program availability:* Part-time, evening/weekend. *Students:* 2 full-time (1 woman), 7 part-time (1 woman); includes 3 minority (1 Black or African American, non-Hispanic/Latino; 1 Native Hawaiian or other Pacific Islander, non-Hispanic/Latino; 1 Two or more races, non-Hispanic/Latino), 2 international. 7 applicants, 100% accepted, 3 enrolled. In 2016, 1 master's awarded. *Degree requirements:* For master's, thesis optional. *Entrance requirements:* For master's, GRE (recommended), 3 letters of recommendation. Additional exam requirements/recommendations for international students: Required—TOEFL (minimum score 563 paper-based; 84 iBT), IELTS (minimum score 7), GRE. *Application deadline:* For fall admission, 1/1 priority date for domestic and international students; for spring admission, 10/1 priority date for domestic and international students. Applications are processed on a rolling basis. Application fee: $70. Electronic applications accepted. *Financial support:* Research assistantships and teaching assistantships available. Financial award application deadline: 1/1; financial award applicants required to submit FAFSA. *Unit head:* Dr. Richard D. Sisson, Jr., Director, 508-831-5633, Fax: 508-831-

5178, E-mail: sisson@wpi.edu. *Application contact:* Rita Shilansky, Graduate Secretary, 508-831-5633, Fax: 508-831-5178, E-mail: rita@wpi.edu. Website: http://www.wpi.edu/academics/mpe

Worcester Polytechnic Institute, Graduate Studies and Research, Department of Mechanical Engineering, Program in Materials Science and Engineering, Worcester, MA 01609-2280. Offers MS, PhD. *Program availability:* Part-time, evening/weekend. *Students:* 67 full-time (24 women), 3 part-time (1 woman); includes 5 minority (2 Hispanic/Latino; 3 Two or more races, non-Hispanic/Latino), 47 international. 129 applicants, 77% accepted, 20 enrolled. In 2016, 30 master's, 2 doctorates awarded. *Degree requirements:* For master's, thesis; for doctorate, comprehensive exam, thesis/dissertation. *Entrance requirements:* For master's and doctorate, GRE (recommended), 3 letters of recommendation. Additional exam requirements/recommendations for international students: Required—TOEFL (minimum score 563 paper-based; 84 iBT), IELTS (minimum score 7), GRE. *Application deadline:* For fall admission, 1/1 priority date for domestic students, 1/1 for international students; for spring admission, 10/1 priority date for domestic students, 10/1 for international students. Applications are processed on a rolling basis. Application fee: $70. Electronic applications accepted. *Financial support:* Research assistantships, teaching assistantships, career-related internships or fieldwork, institutionally sponsored loans, scholarships/grants, and unspecified assistantships available. Financial award application deadline: 1/1; financial award applicants required to submit FAFSA. *Unit head:* Dr. Richard D. Sisson, Jr., Director, 508-831-5633, Fax: 508-831-5178, E-mail: sisson@wpi.edu. *Application contact:* Rita Shilansky, Graduate Secretary, 508-831-5633, Fax: 508-831-5178, E-mail: rita@wpi.edu. Website: http://www.wpi.edu/academics/mte

Wright State University, Graduate School, College of Engineering and Computer Science, Department of Mechanical and Materials Engineering, Dayton, OH 45435. Offers aerospace systems engineering (MSE); materials science and engineering (MSE); mechanical engineering (MSE); renewable ande clean energy (MSE). *Degree requirements:* For master's, thesis or course option alternative. *Entrance requirements:* Additional exam requirements/recommendations for international students: Required—TOEFL. Application fee: $25. *Expenses:* Tuition, state resident: full-time $9952; part-time $622 per credit hour. Tuition, nonresident: full-time $16,960; part-time $1060 per credit hour. *Financial support:* Fellowships, research assistantships, teaching assistantships, and unspecified assistantships available. Support available to part-time students. Financial award application deadline: 3/15; financial award applicants required to submit FAFSA. *Unit head:* Dr. George P.G. Huang, Chair, 937-775-5040, Fax: 937-775-5009, E-mail: george.huang@wright.edu. *Application contact:* John Kimble, Associate Director of Graduate Admissions and Records, 937-775-2957, Fax: 937-775-2453, E-mail: john.kimble@wright.edu. Website: https://engineering-computer-science.wright.edu/mechanical-and-materials-engineering

Metallurgical Engineering and Metallurgy

Colorado School of Mines, Office of Graduate Studies, Department of Metallurgical and Materials Engineering, Golden, CO 80401. Offers materials science (MS, PhD); metallurgical and materials engineering (ME, MS, PhD). *Program availability:* Part-time. *Degree requirements:* For master's, thesis (for some programs); for doctorate, comprehensive exam, thesis/dissertation. *Entrance requirements:* For master's and doctorate, GRE General Test. Additional exam requirements/recommendations for international students: Required—TOEFL (minimum score 550 paper-based; 80 iBT). Electronic applications accepted. *Expenses:* Tuition, state resident: full-time $15,690. Tuition, nonresident: full-time $34,020. *Required fees:* $2152. Tuition and fees vary according to course load.

Michigan Technological University, Graduate School, College of Engineering, Department of Materials Science and Engineering, Houghton, MI 49931. Offers MS, PhD. *Program availability:* Part-time, online learning. *Faculty:* 32 full-time, 18 part-time/adjunct. *Students:* 33 full-time (12 women), 4 part-time, 26 international. Average age 26. 199 applicants, 25% accepted, 10 enrolled. In 2016, 4 master's, 3 doctorates awarded. Terminal master's awarded for partial completion of doctoral program. *Degree requirements:* For master's, comprehensive exam (for some programs), thesis (for some programs); for doctorate, comprehensive exam, thesis/dissertation. *Entrance requirements:* For master's and doctorate, GRE (domestic students from ABET-accredited programs exempt), statement of purpose, personal statement, official transcripts, 3 letters of recommendation. Additional exam requirements/recommendations for international students: Required—TOEFL (recommended minimum score 79 iBT) or IELTS, GRE. *Application deadline:* For fall admission, 2/1 priority date for domestic and international students; for spring admission, 8/15 priority date for domestic and international students. Applications are processed on a rolling basis. Electronic applications accepted. *Expenses:* Contact institution. *Financial support:* In 2016–17, 27 students received support, including 3 fellowships with tuition reimbursements available (averaging $15,242 per year), 14 research assistantships with tuition reimbursements available (averaging $15,242 per year), teaching assistantships with tuition reimbursements available (averaging $15,242 per year); career-related internships or fieldwork, Federal Work-Study, scholarships/grants, health care benefits, unspecified assistantships, and cooperative program also available. Financial award applicants required to submit FAFSA. *Faculty research:* Structure/property/processing relationships, microstructural characterization, alloy design, electronic/magnetic/photonic materials, materials and manufacturing processes. *Total annual research expenditures:* $3 million. *Unit head:* Dr. Stephen L. Kampe, Chair, 906-487-2036, Fax: 906-487-2934, E-mail: kampe@mtu.edu. *Application contact:* Stephen A. Hackney, Associate Department Chair for Graduate Studies, 906-487-2170, Fax: 906-487-2934, E-mail: hackney@mtu.edu. Website: http://www.mtu.edu/materials/

Missouri University of Science and Technology, Graduate School, Department of Materials Science and Engineering, Rolla, MO 65409. Offers ceramic engineering (MS, DE, PhD); metallurgical engineering (MS, PhD). *Degree requirements:* For master's, thesis optional; for doctorate, comprehensive exam. *Entrance requirements:* For master's, GRE (minimum combined score 1100, 600 verbal, 3.5 writing); for doctorate, GRE (minimum score: quantitative 600, writing 3.5). Additional exam requirements/recommendations for international students: Required—TOEFL (minimum score 570 paper-based). Electronic applications accepted.

Montana Tech of The University of Montana, Department of Metallurgical/Mineral Processing Engineering, Butte, MT 59701-8997. Offers MS. *Program availability:* Part-time. *Faculty:* 6 full-time (0 women). *Students:* 6 full-time (4 women), 2 part-time (0 women); includes 2 minority (both Black or African American, non-Hispanic/Latino), 3

international. 4 applicants, 75% accepted, 3 enrolled. In 2016, 2 master's awarded. *Degree requirements:* For master's, comprehensive exam (for some programs), thesis optional. *Entrance requirements:* For master's, GRE General Test, minimum GPA of 3.0. Additional exam requirements/recommendations for international students: Required—TOEFL (minimum score 545 paper-based; 78 iBT), IELTS (minimum score 6.5). *Application deadline:* For fall admission, 4/1 priority date for domestic students, 3/1 priority date for international students; for spring admission, 10/1 priority date for domestic students, 6/1 priority date for international students. Applications are processed on a rolling basis. Application fee: $50. Electronic applications accepted. *Expenses:* Tuition, state resident: full-time $2901; part-time $1450.68 per degree program. Tuition, nonresident: full-time $8432; part-time $4215.84 per degree program. *Required fees:* $668; $354 per degree program. Tuition and fees vary according to course load and program. *Financial support:* In 2016–17, 4 students received support, including 2 teaching assistantships with partial tuition reimbursements available (averaging $5,000 per year); research assistantships with partial tuition reimbursements available, career-related internships or fieldwork, tuition waivers (full and partial), and unspecified assistantships also available. Financial award application deadline: 4/1; financial award applicants required to submit FAFSA. *Faculty research:* Stabilizing hazardous waste, decontamination of metals by melt refining, ultraviolet enhancement of stabilization reactions, extractive metallurgy, fuel cells. *Unit head:* Dr. Courtney Young, Department Head, 406-496-4158, Fax: 406-496-4664, E-mail: cyoung@mtech.edu. *Application contact:* Daniel Stirling, Administrator, Graduate School, 406-496-4304, Fax: 406-496-4710, E-mail: gradschool@mtech.edu. Website: http://www.mtech.edu/academics/gradschool/degreeprograms/degrees-metallurgical.htm

The Ohio State University, Graduate School, College of Engineering, Department of Materials Science and Engineering, Program in Welding Engineering, Columbus, OH 43210. Offers MS, PhD. *Program availability:* Part-time, online learning. *Students:* 32 full-time (8 women), 45 part-time (8 women); includes 12 minority (7 Asian, non-Hispanic/Latino; 5 Hispanic/Latino), 9 international. Average age 32. In 2016, 13 master's, 5 doctorates awarded. *Degree requirements:* For master's, thesis optional; for doctorate, thesis/dissertation. *Entrance requirements:* For master's and doctorate, GRE General Test (for all with undergraduate GPA less than 3.0 or with a non-ABET accredited degree). Additional exam requirements/recommendations for international students: Required—TOEFL (minimum score 550 paper-based; 79 iBT), Michigan English Language Assessment Battery (minimum score 82); Recommended—IELTS (minimum score 7). *Application deadline:* For fall admission, 12/1 priority date for domestic students, 11/30 priority date for international students. Applications are processed on a rolling basis. Application fee: $60 ($70 for international students). Electronic applications accepted. *Financial support:* Fellowships with tuition reimbursements, research assistantships with tuition reimbursements, teaching assistantships with tuition reimbursements, Federal Work-Study, and institutionally sponsored loans available. Support available to part-time students. *Unit head:* Dr. Antonio Ramirez Londono, Graduate Studies Committee Chair, 614-292-8662, E-mail: ramirezlondono.1@osu.edu. *Application contact:* Mark Cooper, Graduate Studies Coordinator, 614-292-7280, Fax: 614-292-1537, E-mail: cooper.73@osu.edu. Website: http://engineering.osu.edu/graduate/welding

Université Laval, Faculty of Sciences and Engineering, Department of Mining, Metallurgical and Materials Engineering, Programs in Metallurgical Engineering, Québec, QC G1K 7P4, Canada. Offers M Sc, PhD. Terminal master's awarded for partial completion of doctoral program. *Degree requirements:* For master's, thesis; for doctorate, comprehensive exam, thesis/dissertation. *Entrance requirements:* For master's and doctorate, knowledge of French and English. Electronic applications accepted.

The University of Alabama, Graduate School, College of Engineering, Department of Metallurgical and Materials Engineering, Tuscaloosa, AL 35487. Offers MS Met E, PhD. PhD offered jointly with The University of Alabama at Birmingham. *Faculty:* 11 full-time (3 women). *Students:* 14 full-time (5 women), 2 part-time (0 women); includes 1 minority (Black or African American, non-Hispanic/Latino), 7 international. Average age 27. 20 applicants, 20% accepted, 1 enrolled. In 2016, 5 master's, 1 doctorate awarded. *Degree requirements:* For master's, thesis or alternative; for doctorate, thesis/dissertation. *Entrance requirements:* For master's, GRE General Test, minimum GPA of 3.0 in last 60 hours; for doctorate, GRE General Test, minimum graduate GPA of 3.0, graduate degree. Additional exam requirements/recommendations for international students: Required—TOEFL (minimum score 550 paper-based). *Application deadline:* For fall admission, 7/1 for domestic students, 5/1 priority date for international students. Applications are processed on a rolling basis. Application fee: $50 ($60 for international students). Electronic applications accepted. *Expenses:* Tuition, state resident: full-time $10,470. Tuition, nonresident: full-time $26,950. *Financial support:* In 2016–17, 3 fellowships (averaging $15,000 per year), 14 research assistantships (averaging $14,700 per year), 6 teaching assistantships (averaging $12,250 per year) were awarded; Federal Work-Study and unspecified assistantships also available. *Faculty research:* Thermodynamics, molten metals processing, casting and solidification, mechanical properties of materials, thin films and nanostructures, electrochemistry, corrosion and alloy development. *Total annual research expenditures:* $3.2 million. *Unit head:* Dr. Mark Weaver, Head/Professor, 205-348-7073, Fax: 205-348-2164, E-mail: mweaver@eng.ua.edu. *Application contact:* Dr. Greg B. Thompson, Associate Professor, 205-348-1589, Fax: 205-348-2164, E-mail: sgupta@eng.ua.edu.
Website: http://www.eng.ua.edu/~mtedept/

University of Connecticut, Graduate School, School of Engineering, Department of Metallurgy and Materials Engineering, Storrs, CT 06269. Offers M Eng. Terminal master's awarded for partial completion of doctoral program. *Degree requirements:* For master's, comprehensive exam, thesis or alternative. *Entrance requirements:* For master's, GRE General Test, GRE Subject Test. Additional exam requirements/recommendations for international students: Required—TOEFL (minimum score 550 paper-based). Electronic applications accepted.

University of Idaho, College of Graduate Studies, College of Engineering, Department of Chemical and Materials Engineering, Moscow, ID 83844. Offers chemical engineering (M Engr, MS, PhD); materials science and engineering (MS, PhD); metallurgical engineering (MS). *Faculty:* 10 full-time, 2 part-time/adjunct. *Students:* 16 full-time, 7 part-time. Average age 31. In 2016, 7 master's, 1 doctorate awarded. *Entrance requirements:* For master's and doctorate, GRE, minimum GPA of 3.0. *Application deadline:* For fall admission, 8/1 for domestic students; for spring admission, 12/15 for domestic students. Applications are processed on a rolling basis. Application fee: $60. Electronic applications accepted. *Expenses:* Tuition, state resident: full-time $6460; part-time $414 per credit hour. Tuition, nonresident: full-time $21,268; part-time $1237 per credit hour. *Required fees:* $2070; $60 per credit hour. Full-time tuition and fees vary according to course load and reciprocity agreements. *Financial support:* Fellowships, research assistantships, and teaching assistantships available. Financial award applicants required to submit FAFSA. *Faculty research:* Geothermal energy utilization, alcohol production from agriculture waste material, energy conservation in pulp and paper mills. *Unit head:* Dr. Eric Aston, Department Chair, 208-885-7572, E-mail: che@uidaho.edu. *Application contact:* Sean Scoggin, Graduate Recruitment Coordinator, 208-885-4001, Fax: 208-885-4406, E-mail: graduateadmissions@uidaho.edu.
Website: https://www.uidaho.edu/engr/departments/cme

The University of Manchester, School of Materials, Manchester, United Kingdom. Offers advanced aerospace materials engineering (M Sc); advanced metallic systems (PhD); biomedical materials (M Phil, M Sc, PhD); ceramics and glass (M Phil, M Sc, PhD); composite materials (M Sc, PhD); corrosion and protection (M Phil, M Sc, PhD); materials (M Phil, PhD); metallic materials (M Phil, M Sc, PhD); nanostructural materials (M Phil, M Sc, PhD); paper science (M Phil, M Sc, PhD); polymer science and engineering (M Phil, M Sc, PhD); technical textiles (M Sc); textile design, fashion and management (M Phil, M Sc, PhD); textile science and technology (M Phil, M Sc, PhD); textiles (M Phil, PhD); textiles and fashion (M Ent).

University of Nebraska–Lincoln, Graduate College, College of Engineering, Department of Mechanical and Materials Engineering, Lincoln, NE 68588-0526. Offers biomedical engineering (PhD); engineering mechanics (MS); materials engineering (PhD); mechanical engineering (MS), including materials science engineering, metallurgical engineering; mechanical engineering and applied mechanics (PhD); MS/MS. MS/MS offered with University of Rouen-France. *Degree requirements:* For master's, thesis optional; for doctorate, comprehensive exam, thesis/dissertation. *Entrance requirements:* For master's and doctorate, GRE General Test. Additional exam requirements/recommendations for international students: Required—TOEFL (minimum score 550 paper-based). Electronic applications accepted. *Faculty research:* Medical robotics, rehabilitation dynamics, and design; combustion, fluid mechanics, and heat transfer; nano-materials, manufacturing, and devices; fiber, tissue, bio-polymer, and adaptive composites; blast, impact, fracture, and failure; electro-active and magnetic materials and devices; functional materials, design, and added manufacturing; materials characterization, modeling, and computational simulation.

University of Nevada, Reno, Graduate School, College of Engineering, Department of Chemical and Materials Engineering, Program in Materials Science and Engineering, Reno, NV 89557. Offers MS, PhD. Terminal master's awarded for partial completion of doctoral program. *Degree requirements:* For master's, thesis; for doctorate, one foreign language, thesis/dissertation. *Entrance requirements:* For master's, minimum GPA of 2.75; for doctorate, GRE, minimum GPA of 3.0. Additional exam requirements/recommendations for international students: Required—TOEFL (minimum score 500 paper-based; 61 iBT), IELTS (minimum score 6). Electronic applications accepted. *Faculty research:* Hydrometallurgy, applied surface chemistry, mineral processing, mineral bioprocessing, ceramics.

The University of Texas at El Paso, Graduate School, College of Engineering, Department of Metallurgical and Materials Engineering, El Paso, TX 79968-0001. Offers materials science and engineering (PhD); metallurgical and materials engineering (MS). *Program availability:* Part-time, evening/weekend. *Degree requirements:* For master's, thesis. *Entrance requirements:* For master's, GRE General Test. Additional exam requirements/recommendations for international students: Required—TOEFL. Electronic applications accepted.

University of Utah, Graduate School, College of Mines and Earth Sciences, Department of Metallurgical Engineering, Salt Lake City, UT 84112. Offers ME, MS, PhD. *Program availability:* Part-time. *Faculty:* 17 full-time (1 woman), 1 part-time/adjunct (0 women). *Students:* 45 full-time (6 women), 5 part-time (2 women); includes 6 minority (4 Asian, non-Hispanic/Latino; 2 Hispanic/Latino), 31 international. Average age 27. 34 applicants, 62% accepted, 8 enrolled. In 2016, 7 master's, 6 doctorates awarded. Terminal master's awarded for partial completion of doctoral program. *Degree requirements:* For master's, thesis; for doctorate, comprehensive exam, thesis/dissertation. *Entrance requirements:* For master's and doctorate, GRE General Test, minimum GPA of 3.0. Additional exam requirements/recommendations for international students: Required—TOEFL (minimum score 530 paper-based; 71 iBT) or IELTS (minimum score 5.5). *Application deadline:* For fall admission, 4/1 priority date for domestic students, 2/1 priority date for international students; for spring admission, 11/1 priority date for domestic students, 9/1 priority date for international students; for summer admission, 3/15 priority date for domestic students, 1/15 priority date for international students. Application fee: $55 ($65 for international students). Electronic applications accepted. *Expenses:* Contact institution. *Financial support:* In 2016–17, 60 students received support, including 4 fellowships with full tuition reimbursements available (averaging $20,000 per year), 55 research assistantships with full tuition reimbursements available (averaging $24,000 per year); institutionally sponsored loans also available. Financial award application deadline: 5/31; financial award applicants required to submit FAFSA. *Faculty research:* Physical metallurgy, mathematical modeling, mineral processing, chemical metallurgy nanoscience and technology. *Total annual research expenditures:* $4.1 million. *Unit head:* Dr. Manoranjan Misra, Chair, 801-587-9769, Fax: 801-581-4937, E-mail: mano.misra@utah.edu. *Application contact:* Sara J. Wilson, Administrative Manager, 801-581-6386, Fax: 801-581-4937, E-mail: sara.j.wilson@utah.edu.
Website: http://www.metallurgy.utah.edu/

Polymer Science and Engineering

Auburn University, Graduate School, Ginn College of Engineering, Department of Polymer and Fiber Engineering, Auburn University, AL 36849. Offers MS, PhD. *Faculty:* 5 full-time (1 woman). *Students:* 5 full-time (2 women), 1 part-time (0 women), 5 international. Average age 26. 19 applicants, 26% accepted, 2 enrolled. In 2016, 3 master's, 1 doctorate awarded. *Degree requirements:* For master's, thesis optional. Application fee: $50 ($60 for international students). *Expenses:* Tuition, state resident: full-time $9072; part-time $504 per credit hour. Tuition, nonresident: full-time $27,216; part-time $1512 per credit hour. *Required fees:* $812 per semester. Tuition and fees vary according to degree level and program. *Financial support:* Unspecified assistantships available. *Unit head:* Maria Auad, Interim Head, 334-844-5452. *Application contact:* Dr. George Flowers, Dean of the Graduate School, 334-844-2125.
Website: http://eng.auburn.edu/research/centers/polymer-and-fiber/

California Polytechnic State University, San Luis Obispo, College of Science and Mathematics, Department of Chemistry and Biochemistry, San Luis Obispo, CA 93407. Offers polymers and coating science (MS). *Program availability:* Part-time. *Faculty:* 3 full-time (0 women). *Students:* 2 full-time (0 women), 5 part-time (2 women); includes 3 minority (2 Asian, non-Hispanic/Latino; 1 Hispanic/Latino). Average age 23. 7 applicants, 43% accepted, 2 enrolled. In 2016, 11 master's awarded. *Degree requirements:* For master's, comprehensive exam (for some programs), thesis (for some programs). *Entrance requirements:* For master's, GRE. Additional exam requirements/recommendations for international students: Required—TOEFL (minimum score 80 iBT). *Application deadline:* For fall admission, 4/1 for domestic and international students. Applications are processed on a rolling basis. Application fee: $55. Electronic applications accepted. *Expenses:* Tuition, state resident: full-time $6738; part-time $3906 per year. Tuition, nonresident: full-time $15,666; part-time $8370 per year. *Required fees:* $3603; $3141 per unit. $1047 per term. *Financial support:* Fellowships, research assistantships, career-related internships or fieldwork, Federal Work-Study, and scholarships/grants available. Support available to part-time students. Financial award application deadline: 3/2; financial award applicants required to submit FAFSA. *Faculty research:* Polymer physical chemistry and analysis, polymer synthesis, coatings formulation. *Unit head:* Dr. Raymond Fernando, Graduate Coordinator, E-mail: rhfernan@calpoly.edu.
Website: http://www.chemistry.calpoly.edu/

Carnegie Mellon University, Carnegie Institute of Technology, Department of Chemical Engineering and Department of Chemistry, Program in Colloids, Polymers and Surfaces, Pittsburgh, PA 15213-3891. Offers MS. *Program availability:* Part-time, evening/weekend. *Entrance requirements:* For master's, GRE General Test, GRE Subject Test. Additional exam requirements/recommendations for international students: Required—TOEFL. *Faculty research:* Surface phenomena, polymer rheology, solubilization phenomena, colloid transport phenomena, polymer synthesis.

Case Western Reserve University, School of Graduate Studies, Case School of Engineering, Department of Macromolecular Science and Engineering, Cleveland, OH 44106. Offers MS, PhD, MD/PhD. *Program availability:* Part-time. *Faculty:* 13 full-time (2 women). *Students:* 79 full-time (33 women), 12 part-time (5 women); includes 9 minority (4 Black or African American, non-Hispanic/Latino; 4 Asian, non-Hispanic/Latino; 1 Two or more races, non-Hispanic/Latino), 66 international. In 2016, 16 master's, 16 doctorates awarded. Terminal master's awarded for partial completion of doctoral program. *Degree requirements:* For master's, thesis; for doctorate, thesis/dissertation, qualifying exam, teaching experience. *Entrance requirements:* For master's and doctorate, GRE General Test. Additional exam requirements/recommendations for international students: Required—TOEFL. *Application deadline:* For fall admission, 2/28 priority date for domestic students; for spring admission, 10/1 priority date for domestic students. Applications are processed on a rolling basis. Application fee: $50. *Expenses: Tuition:* Full-time $42,576; part-time $1774 per credit hour. *Required fees:* $34. Tuition and fees vary according to course load and program. *Financial support:* In 2016–17, 3 fellowships, 48 research assistantships with tuition reimbursements were awarded. Financial award applicants required to submit FAFSA. *Faculty research:* Synthesis and molecular design; processing, modeling and simulation, structure-property relationships. *Total annual research expenditures:* $4 million. *Unit head:* Dr. David Schiraldi, Department Chair, 216-368-4243, Fax: 216-368-4202, E-mail: das44@case.edu. *Application contact:* Theresa Claytor, Student Affairs Coordinator, 216-368-8555, Fax: 216-368-8555, E-mail: theresa.claytor@case.edu.
Website: http://polymers.case.edu

The College of William and Mary, Faculty of Arts and Sciences, Department of Applied Science, Williamsburg, VA 23185. Offers accelerator science (PhD); applied mathematics (PhD); applied mechanics (PhD); applied robotics (PhD); applied science

(MS); atmospheric and environmental science (PhD); computational neuroscience (PhD); interface, thin film and surface science (PhD); lasers and optics (PhD); magnetic resonance (PhD); materials science and engineering (PhD); mathematical and computational biology (PhD); medical imaging (PhD); nanotechnology (PhD); neuroscience (PhD); non-destructive evaluation (PhD); polymer chemistry (PhD); remote sensing (PhD). *Program availability:* Part-time. *Faculty:* 8 full-time (2 women), 2 part-time/adjunct (0 women). *Students:* 30 full-time (11 women), 4 part-time (0 women); includes 16 minority (2 Black or African American, non-Hispanic/Latino; 12 Asian, non-Hispanic/Latino; 2 Hispanic/Latino), 12 international. Average age 28. 37 applicants, 27% accepted, 7 enrolled. In 2016, 6 doctorates awarded. Terminal master's awarded for partial completion of doctoral program. *Degree requirements:* For master's, comprehensive exam, thesis; for doctorate, comprehensive exam, thesis/dissertation, 4 core courses. *Entrance requirements:* For master's and doctorate, GRE General Test, GRE Subject Test. Additional exam requirements/recommendations for international students: Required—TOEFL, IELTS. *Application deadline:* For fall admission, 2/3 priority date for domestic students, 2/3 for international students; for spring admission, 10/15 priority date for domestic students, 10/14 for international students. Applications are processed on a rolling basis. Application fee: $45. Electronic applications accepted. *Expenses:* Contact institution. *Financial support:* In 2016–17, 7 students received support, including 27 research assistantships (averaging $25,000 per year), 1 teaching assistantship (averaging $9,500 per year); fellowships, scholarships/grants, health care benefits, tuition waivers (full), and unspecified assistantships also available. Financial award application deadline: 4/15; financial award applicants required to submit FAFSA. *Faculty research:* Computational biology, non-destructive evaluation, neurophysiology, laser spectroscopy, nanotechnology. *Total annual research expenditures:* $536,220. *Unit head:* Dr. Christopher Del Negro, Chair, 757-221-7808, Fax: 757-221-2050, E-mail: cadeln@wm.edu. *Application contact:* Lianne Rios Ashburne, Graduate Program Coordinator, 757-221-2563, Fax: 757-221-2050, E-mail: lrashburne@wm.edu. Website: http://www.wm.edu/as/appliedscience

Cornell University, Graduate School, Graduate Fields of Engineering, Field of Chemical Engineering, Ithaca, NY 14853. Offers advanced materials processing (M Eng, MS, PhD); applied mathematics and computational methods (M Eng, MS, PhD); biochemical engineering (M Eng, MS, PhD); chemical reaction engineering (M Eng, MS, PhD); classical and statistical thermodynamics (M Eng, MS, PhD); fluid dynamics, rheology and biorheology (M Eng, MS, PhD); heat and mass transfer (M Eng, MS, PhD); kinetics and catalysis (M Eng, MS, PhD); polymers (M Eng, MS, PhD); surface science (M Eng, MS, PhD). *Degree requirements:* For master's, thesis (MS); for doctorate, comprehensive exam, thesis/dissertation. *Entrance requirements:* For master's and doctorate, GRE General Test, 2 letters of recommendation. Additional exam requirements/recommendations for international students: Required—TOEFL (minimum score 600 paper-based; 77 iBT). Electronic applications accepted. *Faculty research:* Biochemical, biomedical and metabolic engineering; fluid and polymer dynamics; surface science and chemical kinetics; electronics materials; microchemical systems and nanotechnology.

Cornell University, Graduate School, Graduate Fields of Human Ecology, Field of Fiber Science and Apparel Design, Ithaca, NY 14853. Offers apparel design (MA, MPS); fiber science (MS, PhD); polymer science (MS, PhD); textile science (MS, PhD). *Degree requirements:* For master's, thesis (MA, MS), project paper (MPS); for doctorate, comprehensive exam, thesis/dissertation. *Entrance requirements:* For master's, GRE General Test, 2 letters of recommendation, portfolio (for functional apparel design); for doctorate, GRE General Test, 2 letters of recommendation. Additional exam requirements/recommendations for international students: Required—TOEFL (minimum score 600 paper-based; 77 iBT). Electronic applications accepted. *Faculty research:* Apparel design, consumption, mass customization, 3-D body scanning.

Eastern Michigan University, Graduate School, College of Technology, School of Engineering Technology, Programs in Polymers and Coatings Technology, Ypsilanti, MI 48197. Offers MS, Postbaccalaureate Certificate. *Program availability:* Part-time, evening/weekend, online learning. *Students:* 12 full-time (3 women), 5 part-time (1 woman); includes 1 minority (Asian, non-Hispanic/Latino), 11 international. Average age 26. 17 applicants, 71% accepted, 7 enrolled. In 2016, 5 master's awarded. *Degree requirements:* For master's, thesis optional. *Entrance requirements:* For master's, GRE General Test, BS in chemistry, minimum GPA of 2.6. Additional exam requirements/recommendations for international students: Required—TOEFL. *Application deadline:* Applications are processed on a rolling basis. Application fee: $45. *Financial support:* Fellowships, research assistantships with full tuition reimbursements, teaching assistantships with full tuition reimbursements, career-related internships or fieldwork, Federal Work-Study, institutionally sponsored loans, scholarships/grants, tuition waivers (partial), and unspecified assistantships available. Support available to part-time students. Financial award applicants required to submit FAFSA. *Application contact:* Dr. Vijay Mannari, Program Coordinator, 734-487-2040, Fax: 734-487-8755, E-mail: vmannari@emich.edu.

Lehigh University, P.C. Rossin College of Engineering and Applied Science and College of Arts and Sciences, Center for Polymer Science and Engineering, Bethlehem, PA 18015. Offers M Eng, MS, PhD. *Program availability:* Part-time, evening/weekend, 100% online, blended/hybrid learning. *Faculty:* 24 full-time (4 women). *Students:* 5 full-time (4 women), 22 part-time (5 women); includes 8 minority (1 Black or African American, non-Hispanic/Latino; 6 Asian, non-Hispanic/Latino; 1 Native Hawaiian or other Pacific Islander, non-Hispanic/Latino), 4 international. Average age 31. 48 applicants, 21% accepted, 6 enrolled. In 2016, 4 master's awarded. Terminal master's awarded for partial completion of doctoral program. *Degree requirements:* For master's, thesis (for some programs); for doctorate, thesis/dissertation. *Entrance requirements:* For master's and doctorate, GRE General Test. Additional exam requirements/recommendations for international students: Required—TOEFL (minimum score 487 paper-based; 85 iBT), IELTS (minimum score 6.5). *Application deadline:* For fall admission, 7/15 for domestic students, 1/15 for international students; for spring admission, 12/1 for domestic and international students. Applications are processed on a rolling basis. Application fee: $75. Electronic applications accepted. *Expenses:* $1,420 per credit. *Financial support:* In 2016–17, 1 student received support, including 1 research assistantship (averaging $27,106 per year); teaching assistantships, scholarships/grants, and health care benefits also available. Financial award application deadline: 1/15. *Faculty research:* Polymer colloids, polymer coatings, blends and composites, polymer interfaces, emulsion polymer. *Unit head:* Dr. Raymond A. Pearson, Director, 610-758-3857, Fax: 610-758-3526, E-mail: rp02@lehigh.edu. *Application contact:* James E. Roberts, Chair, Polymer Education Committee, 610-758-4841, Fax: 610-758-6536, E-mail: jer1@lehigh.edu. Website: http://www.lehigh.edu/~inpcreng/academics/graduate/polymerscieng.html

Lehigh University, P.C. Rossin College of Engineering and Applied Science, Department of Materials Science and Engineering, Bethlehem, PA 18015. Offers materials science and engineering (M Eng, MS, PhD); photonics (MS); polymer science/engineering (M Eng, MS, PhD); MBA/E. *Program availability:* Part-time. *Faculty:* 15 full-time (3 women). *Students:* 23 full-time (4 women), 4 part-time (2 women); includes 3 minority (2 Asian, non-Hispanic/Latino; 1 Two or more races, non-Hispanic/Latino), 8 international. Average age 27. 143 applicants, 6% accepted, 4 enrolled. In 2016, 4

master's, 8 doctorates awarded. *Degree requirements:* For master's, thesis; for doctorate, comprehensive exam, thesis/dissertation. *Entrance requirements:* For master's and doctorate, GRE General Test, minimum GPA of 3.0. Additional exam requirements/recommendations for international students: Required—TOEFL (minimum score 487 paper-based; 85 iBT), IELTS (minimum score 6.5). *Application deadline:* For fall admission, 1/15 priority date for domestic students, 1/15 for international students; for spring admission, 12/1 priority date for domestic students, 12/1 for international students. Applications are processed on a rolling basis. Application fee: $75. Electronic applications accepted. *Expenses:* $1,420 per credit hour. *Financial support:* In 2016–17, 25 students received support, including 3 fellowships with tuition reimbursements available (averaging $21,105 per year), 19 research assistantships with tuition reimbursements available (averaging $28,140 per year), 6 teaching assistantships with tuition reimbursements available (averaging $21,530 per year); scholarships/grants and health care benefits also available. Financial award application deadline: 1/15. *Faculty research:* Metals, ceramics, crystals, polymers, fatigue crack propagation, biomaterials. *Total annual research expenditures:* $3.1 million. *Unit head:* Dr. Wojciech Misiolek, Chairperson, 610-758-4252, Fax: 610-758-4244, E-mail: wzm2@lehigh.edu. *Application contact:* Lisa Carreras Arechiga, Graduate Administrative Coordinator, 610-758-4222, Fax: 610-758-4244, E-mail: lia4@lehigh.edu. Website: http://www.lehigh.edu/~inmatsci/

North Carolina State University, Graduate School, College of Textiles, Program in Fiber and Polymer Science, Raleigh, NC 27695. Offers PhD. *Degree requirements:* For doctorate, one foreign language, thesis/dissertation, cumulative exams. *Entrance requirements:* For doctorate, GRE. Electronic applications accepted. *Faculty research:* Polymer science, fiber mechanics, medical textiles, nanotechnology.

North Dakota State University, College of Graduate and Interdisciplinary Studies, College of Science and Mathematics, Department of Coatings and Polymeric Materials, Fargo, ND 58102. Offers MS, PhD. *Program availability:* Part-time. Terminal master's awarded for partial completion of doctoral program. *Degree requirements:* For master's, thesis, cumulative exams; for doctorate, comprehensive exam, thesis/dissertation, cumulative exams. *Entrance requirements:* For master's and doctorate, BS in chemistry or chemical engineering, minimum GPA of 3.0. Additional exam requirements/recommendations for international students: Required—TOEFL (minimum score 550 paper-based). Electronic applications accepted. *Faculty research:* Nanomaterials, combinatorial materials science.

Pittsburg State University, Graduate School, College of Arts and Sciences, Department of Chemistry, Pittsburg, KS 66762. Offers chemistry (MS); polymer chemistry (MS). *Students:* 20 (8 women); includes 1 minority (Hispanic/Latino), 14 international. In 2016, 4 master's awarded. *Degree requirements:* For master's, comprehensive exam (for some programs), thesis or alternative. *Entrance requirements:* Additional exam requirements/recommendations for international students: Required—TOEFL (minimum score 520 paper-based; 68 iBT), IELTS (minimum score 6), PTE (minimum score 47). *Application deadline:* For fall admission, 7/15 for domestic students, 6/1 for international students; for spring admission, 12/15 for domestic students, 10/15 for international students; for summer admission, 5/15 for domestic students, 4/1 for international students. Applications are processed on a rolling basis. Application fee: $35 ($60 for international students). Electronic applications accepted. *Expenses:* Contact institution. *Financial support:* In 2016–17, 6 research assistantships with partial tuition reimbursements (averaging $5,000 per year), 4 teaching assistantships with full tuition reimbursements (averaging $5,500 per year) were awarded; career-related internships or fieldwork, Federal Work-Study, and unspecified assistantships also available. Financial award application deadline: 2/1; financial award applicants required to submit FAFSA. *Unit head:* Dr. Petar Dvornic, Chairperson, 620-235-4748, Fax: 620-235-4003, E-mail: pdvornic@pittstate.edu. *Application contact:* Lisa Allen, Assistant Director of Graduate and Continuing Studies, 620-235-4223, Fax: 620-235-4219, E-mail: lallen@pittstate.edu. Website: http://www.pittstate.edu/department/chemistry/

Pittsburg State University, Graduate School, College of Technology, Department of Engineering Technology, Pittsburg, KS 66762. Offers electrical engineering technology (MET); general engineering technology (MET); manufacturing engineering technology (MET); mechanical engineering technology (MET); plastics engineering technology (MET). *Program availability:* Part-time, 100% online, blended/hybrid learning. *Students:* 59 (9 women); includes 3 minority (2 Black or African American, non-Hispanic/Latino; 1 Asian, non-Hispanic/Latino), 35 international. In 2016, 42 master's awarded. *Degree requirements:* For master's, thesis optional. *Entrance requirements:* Additional exam requirements/recommendations for international students: Required—TOEFL (minimum score 550 paper-based; 79 iBT), IELTS (minimum score 6.5), PTE (minimum score 51). *Application deadline:* For fall admission, 7/15 for domestic students, 6/1 for international students; for spring admission, 12/15 for domestic students, 10/15 for international students; for summer admission, 5/15 for domestic students, 4/1 for international students. Applications are processed on a rolling basis. Application fee: $35 ($60 for international students). Electronic applications accepted. *Expenses:* Contact institution. *Financial support:* In 2016–17, 4 teaching assistantships with full tuition reimbursements (averaging $5,500 per year) were awarded. Financial award application deadline: 2/1; financial award applicants required to submit FAFSA. *Unit head:* Greg Murray, Chairperson, 620-235-4384. *Application contact:* Lisa Allen, Assistant Director of Graduate and Continuing Studies, 620-235-4218, Fax: 620-235-4219, E-mail: lallen@pittstate.edu. Website: http://www.pittstate.edu/department/engineering-tech/

Stevens Institute of Technology, Graduate School, Charles V. Schaefer Jr. School of Engineering and Science, Department of Chemistry, Chemical Biology and Biomedical Engineering, Hoboken, NJ 07030. Offers analytical chemistry (Certificate), including analytical chemistry; bioinformatics (Certificate), including bioinformatics; biomedical chemistry (Certificate), including biomedical chemistry; biomedical engineering (M Eng, PhD); chemical biology (MS, PhD, Certificate), including chemical physiology (Certificate); chemical physiology (Certificate), including polymer chemistry; chemistry (MS, PhD); polymer chemistry (Certificate). *Program availability:* Part-time, evening/weekend, online learning. *Faculty:* 27 full-time (11 women), 9 part-time/adjunct (2 women). *Students:* 86 full-time (36 women), 18 part-time (11 women); includes 14 minority (4 Black or African American, non-Hispanic/Latino; 7 Asian, non-Hispanic/Latino; 3 Hispanic/Latino), 58 international. Average age 27. 311 applicants, 37% accepted, 33 enrolled. In 2016, 28 master's, 6 doctorates, 6 other advanced degrees awarded. Terminal master's awarded for partial completion of doctoral program. *Degree requirements:* For master's, thesis optional, minimum B average in major field and overall; for doctorate, comprehensive exam (for some programs), thesis/dissertation; for Certificate, minimum B average. *Entrance requirements:* Additional exam requirements/recommendations for international students: Required—TOEFL (minimum score 74 iBT), IELTS (minimum score 6). *Application deadline:* Applications are processed on a rolling basis. Application fee: $65. Electronic applications accepted. *Expenses:* Contact institution. *Financial support:* Fellowships, research assistantships, teaching assistantships, career-related internships or fieldwork, Federal Work-Study, scholarships/grants, and unspecified assistantships available. Financial award application deadline: 2/15; financial award applicants required to submit FAFSA. *Faculty* *research:* Polymerization engineering, methods of instrumental analysis, medicinal chemistry, structural chemistry, protein trafficking, proteomics. *Unit head:* Dr. Peter Tolias, Interim Director, 201-216-8253, Fax: 201-216-8196, E-mail: ptolias@stevens.edu. *Application contact:* Graduate Admissions, 888-783-8367, Fax: 888-511-1306, E-mail: graduate@stevens.edu.

The University of Akron, Graduate School, College of Polymer Science and Polymer Engineering, Department of Polymer Engineering, Akron, OH 44325. Offers MS, PhD. *Program availability:* Part-time, evening/weekend. *Faculty:* 9 full-time (2 women), 3 part-time/adjunct (0 women). *Students:* 124 full-time (44 women), 19 part-time (6 women); includes 10 minority (1 Black or African American, non-Hispanic/Latino; 4 Asian, non-Hispanic/Latino; 3 Hispanic/Latino; 2 Two or more races, non-Hispanic/Latino), 110 international. Average age 25. 137 applicants, 49% accepted, 44 enrolled. In 2016, 20 master's, 7 doctorates awarded. *Degree requirements:* For master's, thesis; for doctorate, one foreign language, thesis/dissertation, candidacy exam. *Entrance requirements:* For master's and doctorate, GRE, bachelor's degree in engineering or physical science, minimum GPA of 3.0, three letters of recommendation, statement of purpose. Additional exam requirements/recommendations for international students: Required—TOEFL (minimum score 550 paper-based; 79 iBT), IELTS (minimum score 6.5). *Application deadline:* For fall admission, 1/15 priority date for domestic and international students. Application fee: $45 ($70 for international students). Electronic applications accepted. *Expenses:* Tuition, state resident: full-time $8618; part-time $359 per credit hour. Tuition, nonresident: full-time $17,149; part-time $715 per credit hour. *Required fees:* $1652. *Financial support:* In 2016–17, 78 research assistantships with full tuition reimbursements were awarded. *Faculty research:* Processing and properties of multi-functional polymeric materials, nanomaterials and nanocomposites, micro- and nano-scale materials processing, novel self-assembled polymeric materials for energy applications, coating materials and coating technology. *Total annual research expenditures:* $4 million. *Unit head:* Dr. Sadhan Jana, Chair, 330-972-8293, E-mail: janas@uakron.edu. *Application contact:* Sarah Thorley, Coordinator of Academic Programs, 330-972-8845, E-mail: sarah3@uakron.edu. Website: http://www.uakron.edu/dpe/

The University of Akron, Graduate School, College of Polymer Science and Polymer Engineering, Department of Polymer Science, Akron, OH 44325. Offers MS, PhD. *Program availability:* Part-time, evening/weekend. *Faculty:* 19 full-time (2 women), 3 part-time/adjunct (0 women). *Students:* 203 full-time (61 women), 11 part-time (3 women); includes 9 minority (5 Black or African American, non-Hispanic/Latino; 1 American Indian or Alaska Native, non-Hispanic/Latino; 2 Asian, non-Hispanic/Latino; 1 Hispanic/Latino), 173 international. Average age 25. 120 applicants, 66% accepted, 67 enrolled. In 2016, 33 master's, 25 doctorates awarded. Terminal master's awarded for partial completion of doctoral program. *Degree requirements:* For master's, thesis; for doctorate, one foreign language, thesis/dissertation, cumulative exam, seminars. *Entrance requirements:* For master's and doctorate, GRE, minimum GPA of 3.0, three letters of recommendation, statement of purpose. Additional exam requirements/recommendations for international students: Required—TOEFL (minimum score 550 paper-based; 79 iBT), IELTS (minimum score 6.5). *Application deadline:* For fall admission, 12/1 priority date for domestic students, 12/15 priority date for international students. Application fee: $45 ($70 for international students). Electronic applications accepted. *Expenses:* Tuition, state resident: full-time $8618; part-time $359 per credit hour. Tuition, nonresident: full-time $17,149; part-time $715 per credit hour. *Required fees:* $1652. *Financial support:* In 2016–17, 4 fellowships with full tuition reimbursements, 136 research assistantships with full and partial tuition reimbursements were awarded. *Faculty research:* Synthesis of polymers, structure of polymers, physical properties of polymers, engineering and technological properties of polymers, elastomers. *Total annual research expenditures:* $8.5 million. *Unit head:* Dr. Coleen Pugh, Chair, 330-972-6614, E-mail: cpugh@uakron.edu. *Application contact:* Melissa Bowman, Coordinator, Academic Programs, 330-972-7532, E-mail: mb8@uakron.edu. Website: http://www.uakron.edu/dps/

University of Connecticut, Institute of Materials Science, Polymer Program, Storrs, CT 06269-3136. Offers polymer science and engineering (MS, PhD). *Program availability:* Part-time. Terminal master's awarded for partial completion of doctoral program. *Degree requirements:* For master's, thesis (for some programs); for doctorate, one foreign language, comprehensive exam, thesis/dissertation. *Entrance requirements:* For master's and doctorate, GRE General Test. Additional exam requirements/recommendations for international students: Required—TOEFL (minimum score 550 paper-based; 80 iBT), IELTS (minimum score 6.5). Electronic applications accepted.

The University of Manchester, School of Materials, Manchester, United Kingdom. Offers advanced aerospace materials engineering (M Sc); advanced metallic systems (PhD); biomedical materials (M Phil, M Sc, PhD); ceramics and glass (M Phil, M Sc, PhD); composite materials (M Sc, PhD); corrosion and protection (M Phil, M Sc, PhD); materials (M Phil, PhD); metallic materials (M Phil, M Sc, PhD); nanostructural materials (M Phil, M Sc, PhD); paper science (M Phil, M Sc, PhD); polymer science and engineering (M Phil, M Sc, PhD); technical textiles (M Sc); textile design, fashion and management (M Phil, M Sc, PhD); textile science and technology (M Phil, M Sc, PhD); textiles (M Phil, PhD); textiles and fashion (M Ent).

University of Massachusetts Amherst, Graduate School, College of Natural Sciences, Department of Polymer Science and Engineering, Amherst, MA 01003. Offers MS, PhD. Terminal master's awarded for partial completion of doctoral program. *Degree requirements:* For master's, thesis or alternative; for doctorate, comprehensive exam, thesis/dissertation. *Entrance requirements:* For master's and doctorate, GRE General Test. Additional exam requirements/recommendations for international students: Required—TOEFL (minimum score 550 paper-based; 80 iBT), IELTS (minimum score 6.5). Electronic applications accepted.

University of Massachusetts Lowell, College of Sciences, Department of Chemistry, Program in Polymer Science, Lowell, MA 01854. Offers PhD. Electronic applications accepted.

University of Massachusetts Lowell, Francis College of Engineering, Department of Plastics Engineering, Lowell, MA 01854. Offers plastics engineering (MS Eng, PhD), including coatings and adhesives (MS Eng). *Program availability:* Part-time. Terminal master's awarded for partial completion of doctoral program. *Degree requirements:* For master's, thesis optional; for doctorate, comprehensive exam, thesis/dissertation. *Entrance requirements:* For master's and doctorate, GRE General Test. Additional exam requirements/recommendations for international students: Required—TOEFL.

University of Missouri–Kansas City, College of Arts and Sciences, Department of Chemistry, Kansas City, MO 64110-2499. Offers analytical chemistry (PhD); inorganic chemistry (PhD); organic chemistry (PhD); physical chemistry (PhD); polymer chemistry (MS, PhD). PhD (interdisciplinary) offered through the School of Graduate Studies. *Program availability:* Part-time, evening/weekend. *Faculty:* 15 full-time (2 women), 1 part-time/adjunct (0 women). *Students:* 2 full-time (1 woman), 4 part-time (1 woman); includes 1 minority (Black or African American, non-Hispanic/Latino), 1 international. Average age 42. 36 applicants, 28% accepted, 2 enrolled. In 2016, 7 master's awarded. *Degree requirements:* For master's, thesis (for some programs); for doctorate, thesis/

dissertation. *Entrance requirements:* For master's, equivalent of American Chemical Society approved bachelor's degree in chemistry; for doctorate, GRE General Test, equivalent of American Chemical Society approved bachelor's degree in chemistry. Additional exam requirements/recommendations for international students: Required—TOEFL (minimum score 550 paper-based; 80 iBT), TWE. *Application deadline:* For fall admission, 4/15 for domestic and international students; for spring admission, 10/15 for domestic and international students. Applications are processed on a rolling basis. Application fee: $45 ($50 for international students). Electronic applications accepted. *Financial support:* In 2016–17, 17 teaching assistantships with partial tuition reimbursements (averaging $18,058 per year) were awarded; research assistantships with partial tuition reimbursements, Federal Work-Study, institutionally sponsored loans, and scholarships/grants also available. Support available to part-time students. Financial award application deadline: 3/1; financial award applicants required to submit FAFSA. *Faculty research:* Molecular spectroscopy, characterization and synthesis of materials and compounds, computational chemistry, natural products, drug delivery systems and anti-tumor agents. *Unit head:* Dr. Kathleen V. Kilway, Chair, 816-235-2289, Fax: 816-235-5502, E-mail: kilwayk@umkc.edu. *Application contact:* Graduate Recruiting Committee, 816-235-2272, Fax: 816-235-5502, E-mail: umkc-chemdept@umkc.edu.

University of Southern Mississippi, Graduate School, College of Science and Technology, School of Polymers and High Performance Materials, Hattiesburg, MS 39406. Offers polymer science and engineering (MS, PhD), including polymer science and engineering (PhD). Terminal master's awarded for partial completion of doctoral program. *Degree requirements:* For master's, comprehensive exam, thesis; for doctorate, comprehensive exam, thesis/dissertation, original proposal. *Entrance requirements:* For master's, GRE General Test, minimum GPA of 2.75; for doctorate, GRE General Test, minimum GPA of 3.5. Additional exam requirements/recommendations for international students: Required—TOEFL, IELTS. *Application deadline:* For fall admission, 3/1 priority date for domestic students, 3/1 for international students. Applications are processed on a rolling basis. Application fee: $60. Electronic applications accepted. *Expenses:* Tuition, area resident: Full-time $15,708; part-time $437 per credit hour. *Financial support:* Fellowships, research assistantships with full tuition reimbursements, teaching assistantships with full tuition reimbursements, Federal Work-Study, scholarships/grants, health care benefits, and unspecified assistantships available. Financial award application deadline: 3/15; financial award applicants required to submit FAFSA. *Faculty research:* Water-soluble polymers; polymer composites; coatings; solid-state, laser-initiated polymerization. *Unit head:* Dr. Jeffery Wiggins, Director, 601-266-4868, Fax: 601-266-6178. Website: https://www.usm.edu/polymer

The University of Tennessee, Graduate School, Tickle College of Engineering, Department of Materials Science and Engineering, Program in Polymer Engineering, Knoxville, TN 37996. Offers MS, PhD. *Faculty:* 2 full-time (1 woman). In 2016, 1 doctorate awarded. *Degree requirements:* For master's, thesis or alternative; for doctorate, comprehensive exam, thesis/dissertation. *Entrance requirements:* For master's, GRE General Test (for MS students pursuing research thesis), minimum GPA of 2.7 (for U.S. degree holders), 3.0 (for international degree holders); 3 references; for doctorate, GRE General Test, minimum GPA of 3.0 on previous graduate course work; 3 references. Additional exam requirements/recommendations for international students: Required—TOEFL (minimum score 550 paper-based). *Application deadline:* For fall admission, 2/1 priority date for domestic and international students; for spring admission, 6/15 for domestic and international students. Applications are processed on a rolling basis. Application fee: $35. Electronic applications accepted. *Financial support:* Fellowships with full tuition reimbursements, research assistantships with full tuition reimbursements, teaching assistantships with full tuition reimbursements, career-related internships or fieldwork, Federal Work-Study, institutionally sponsored loans, health care benefits, and unspecified assistantships available. Financial award application deadline: 2/1; financial award applicants required to submit FAFSA. *Faculty research:* Polymer chemistry, processing, and characterization. *Unit head:* Dr. Veerle Keppens, Head, 865-974-5336, Fax: 865-974-4115, E-mail: vkeppens@utk.edu. *Application contact:* Dr. Roberto S. Benson, Associate Head, 865-974-5347, Fax: 865-974-4115, E-mail: rbenson1@utk.edu. Website: http://www.engr.utk.edu/mse

Wayne State University, College of Engineering, Department of Chemical Engineering and Materials Science, Detroit, MI 48202. Offers chemical engineering (MS, PhD); materials science and engineering (MS, PhD, Graduate Certificate), including materials science and engineering (MS, PhD), polymer engineering (Graduate Certificate). *Program availability:* Part-time. *Faculty:* 11. *Students:* 44 full-time (12 women), 23 part-time (6 women); includes 3 minority (1 Black or African American, non-Hispanic/Latino; 2 Asian, non-Hispanic/Latino), 40 international. Average age 26. 230 applicants, 31% accepted, 18 enrolled. In 2016, 12 master's, 5 doctorates awarded. *Degree requirements:* For master's, thesis optional; for doctorate, thesis/dissertation. *Entrance requirements:* For master's, three letters of recommendation (at least two from the applicant's academic institution); personal statement; resume; for doctorate, GRE, three letters of recommendation (at least two from the applicant's academic institution); personal statement; resume; for Graduate Certificate, bachelor's degree in engineering, chemistry, or physics. Additional exam requirements/recommendations for international students: Required—TOEFL (minimum score 550 paper-based; 79 iBT), TWE (minimum score 5.5), Michigan English Language Assessment Battery (minimum score 85); Recommended—IELTS (minimum score 6.5). *Application deadline:* For fall admission, 3/1 priority date for domestic and international students; for winter admission, 10/1 priority date for domestic students, 9/1 priority date for international students; for spring admission, 2/1 priority date for domestic and international students; for summer admission, 2/1 priority date for domestic and international students. Application fee: $50. Electronic applications accepted. *Expenses:* $18,871 per year resident tuition and fees, $36,065 per year non-resident tuition and fees. *Financial support:* In 2016–17, 26 students received support, including 7 fellowships with tuition reimbursements available (averaging $14,884 per year), 10 research assistantships with tuition reimbursements available (averaging $19,546 per year), 12 teaching assistantships with tuition reimbursements available (averaging $19,017 per year); scholarships/grants, health care benefits, and unspecified assistantships also available. Support available to part-time students. Financial award applicants required to submit FAFSA. *Faculty research:* Thermodynamics and transport properties of polymer solutions; processing, rheology, and separation of polymers; heterogeneous catalysts; surface science of catalyst and polymeric materials; laser-based imaging of chemical species and reactions; environmental transport and management of hazardous waste; process design and synthesis based on waste minimization, biocatalysis in multiphase systems, biomaterials and tissue engineering. *Total annual research expenditures:* $1.6 million. *Unit head:* Dr. Guangzhao Mao, Professor and Chair, 313-577-3804, E-mail: gzmao@eng.wayne.edu. *Application contact:* Ellen Cope, Graduate Program Coordinator, E-mail: escope@wayne.edu. Website: http://engineering.wayne.edu/che/

Section 17
Mechanical Engineering and Mechanics

This section contains a directory of institutions offering graduate work in mechanical engineering and mechanics. Additional information about programs listed in the directory may be obtained by writing directly to the dean of a graduate school or chair of a department at the address given in the directory.

For programs offering related work, see also in this book *Engineering and Applied Sciences, Management of Engineering and Technology,* and *Materials Sciences and Engineering.* In another guide in this series:
Graduate Programs in the Physical Sciences, Mathematics, Agricultural Sciences, the Environment & Natural Resources
See *Geosciences* and *Physics*

CONTENTS

Mechanical Engineering

Alfred University, Graduate School, College of Ceramics, Inamori School of Engineering, Alfred, NY 14802. Offers biomaterials engineering (MS); ceramic engineering (MS, PhD); electrical engineering (MS); glass science (MS, PhD); materials science and engineering (MS, PhD); mechanical engineering (MS). *Program availability:* Part-time. *Faculty:* 18 full-time (1 woman). *Students:* 26 full-time (6 women), 16 part-time (4 women); includes 1 minority (Hispanic/Latino), 12 international. Average age 27. 14 applicants, 79% accepted, 10 enrolled. In 2016, 13 master's, 5 doctorates awarded. *Degree requirements:* For master's, thesis; for doctorate, thesis/dissertation. *Entrance requirements:* Additional exam requirements/recommendations for international students: Required—TOEFL (minimum score 590 paper-based; 90 iBT), IELTS (minimum score 6.5). *Application deadline:* For fall admission, 3/1 priority date for domestic students, 3/15 for international students; for spring admission, 10/1 priority date for domestic students, 10/1 for international students. Applications are processed on a rolling basis. Application fee: $60. Electronic applications accepted. *Expenses:* Contact institution. *Financial support:* Fellowships with full tuition reimbursements, research assistantships with full tuition reimbursements, teaching assistantships with full tuition reimbursements, tuition waivers (full and partial), and unspecified assistantships available. Financial award application deadline: 8/1; financial award applicants required to submit FAFSA. *Faculty research:* X-ray diffraction, biomaterials and polymers, thin-film processing, electronic and optical ceramics, solid-state chemistry. *Unit head:* Dr. Alistair N. Cormack, Dean, 607-871-2422, E-mail: cormack@alfred.edu. *Application contact:* Sara Love, Coordinator of Graduate Admissions, 607-871-2115, Fax: 607-871-2198, E-mail: gradinquiry@alfred.edu.
Website: http://engineering.alfred.edu/grad/

The American University in Cairo, School of Sciences and Engineering, Cairo, Egypt. Offers biotechnology (MS); chemistry (MS); computer science (MS); computing (M Comp); construction engineering (M Eng, MS); electronics and communications engineering (M Eng); environmental engineering (MS); environmental system design (M Eng); mechanical engineering (M Eng, MS); nanotechnology (MS); physics (MS); robotics, control and smart systems (MS); sciences and engineering (PhD); sustainable development (MS, Graduate Diploma). *Program availability:* Part-time, evening/weekend. *Faculty:* 43 full-time (4 women), 12 part-time/adjunct (1 woman). *Students:* 50 full-time (21 women), 262 part-time (128 women), 13 international. Average age 28. 193 applicants, 46% accepted, 55 enrolled. In 2016, 71 master's, 5 doctorates awarded. *Degree requirements:* For master's, comprehensive exam (for some programs), thesis (for some programs); for doctorate, comprehensive exam (for some programs), thesis/dissertation. *Entrance requirements:* Additional exam requirements/recommendations for international students: Required—TOEFL (minimum score 450 paper-based; 45 iBT), IELTS (minimum score 5). *Application deadline:* For fall admission, 2/1 priority date for domestic and international students; for spring admission, 10/15 priority date for domestic and international students. Applications are processed on a rolling basis. Application fee: $80. Electronic applications accepted. *Expenses:* Contact institution. *Financial support:* Fellowships with partial tuition reimbursements, scholarships/grants, and unspecified assistantships available. Financial award application deadline: 3/10. *Faculty research:* Construction, mechanical and electronics engineering, physics, computer science, biotechnology and nanotechnology. *Unit head:* Dr. Hassan El Fawal, Dean, 20-2-2615-2926, E-mail: hassan.elfawal@aucegypt.edu. *Application contact:* Maha Hegazi, Director for Graduate Admissions, 20-2-2615-1462, E-mail: mahahegazi@aucegypt.edu.
Website: http://www.aucegypt.edu/sse/Pages/default.aspx

American University of Beirut, Graduate Programs, Faculty of Engineering and Architecture, 11-0236, Lebanon. Offers applied energy (ME); civil engineering (PhD); electrical and computer engineering (PhD); energy studies (MS); engineering management (MEM); environmental and water resources (ME); environmental technology (MSES); mechanical engineering (ME, PhD); urban design (MUD); urban planning and policy (MUPP). *Program availability:* Part-time, evening/weekend, 100% online. *Faculty:* 99 full-time (22 women), 1 part-time/adjunct (0 women). *Students:* 308 full-time (143 women), 86 part-time (39 women). Average age 26. 430 applicants, 69% accepted, 125 enrolled. In 2016, 103 master's, 7 doctorates awarded. Terminal master's awarded for partial completion of doctoral program. *Degree requirements:* For master's, comprehensive exam, thesis optional; for doctorate, comprehensive exam, thesis/dissertation. *Entrance requirements:* For doctorate, GRE. Additional exam requirements/recommendations for international students: Required—TOEFL (minimum score 573 paper-based; 88 iBT); Recommended—IELTS (minimum score 7). *Application deadline:* For fall admission, 2/10 priority date for domestic and international students; for spring admission, 11/2 priority date for domestic students, 11/2 for international students. Application fee: $50. Electronic applications accepted. *Expenses:* Contact institution. *Financial support:* In 2016–17, 22 students received support, including 94 fellowships with full tuition reimbursements available (averaging $18,200 per year), 44 research assistantships with full tuition reimbursements available (averaging $7,596 per year), 124 teaching assistantships with full tuition reimbursements available (averaging $1,056 per year); career-related internships or fieldwork, Federal Work-Study, institutionally sponsored loans, scholarships/grants, traineeships, health care benefits, tuition waivers, and unspecified assistantships also available. Support available to part-time students. Financial award application deadline: 12/20. Total annual research expenditures: $1.5 million. *Unit head:* Prof. Alan Shihadeh, Interim Dean, 961-1350000 Ext. 3400, Fax: 961-1744462, E-mail: as20@aub.edu.lb. *Application contact:* Dr. Salim Kanaan, Director, Admissions Office, 961-1350000 Ext. 2594, Fax: 961-1750775, E-mail: sk00@aub.edu.lb.
Website: http://www.aub.edu.lb/fea/fea_home/Pages/index.aspx

American University of Sharjah, Graduate Programs, Sharjah, United Arab Emirates. Offers accounting (MS); business (EMBA, MBA); chemical engineering (MS Ch E); civil engineering (MSCE); computer engineering (MS); electrical engineering (MSEE); engineering systems management (MS); mathematics (MS); mechanical engineering (MSME); mechatronics engineering (MS); teaching English to speakers of other languages (MA); translation and interpreting (MA); urban planning (MUP). *Program availability:* Part-time, evening/weekend. *Degree requirements:* For master's, thesis (for some programs). *Entrance requirements:* For master's, GMAT (for MBA). Additional exam requirements/recommendations for international students: Required—TOEFL (minimum score 550 paper-based; 80 iBT), TWE (minimum score 5); Recommended—IELTS (minimum score 6.5). Electronic applications accepted. *Faculty research:* Water pollution, management and waste water treatment, energy and sustainability, air pollution, Islamic finance, family business and small and medium enterprises.

Arizona State University at the Tempe campus, Ira A. Fulton Schools of Engineering, The Polytechnic School, Program in Engineering Technology, Mesa, AZ 85212. Offers manufacturing engineering technology (MS). *Program availability:* Part-time, evening/weekend. *Degree requirements:* For master's, thesis or applied project and oral defense, final examination, interactive Program of Study (iPOS) submitted before completing 50 percent of required credit hours. *Entrance requirements:* For master's, bachelor's degree with minimum of 30 credit hours or equivalent in a technology area including course work applicable to the concentration being sought and minimum of 16 credit hours of math and science; industrial experience beyond bachelor's degree (recommended). Additional exam requirements/recommendations for international students: Required—TOEFL, IELTS, or PTE. Electronic applications accepted. *Faculty research:* Manufacturing modeling and simulation &ITsmart&RO and composite materials, optimization of turbine engines, machinability and manufacturing processes design, fuel cells and other alternative energy sources.

Arizona State University at the Tempe campus, Ira A. Fulton Schools of Engineering, School for Engineering of Matter, Transport and Energy, Tempe, AZ 85281. Offers aerospace engineering (MS, PhD); chemical engineering (MS, PhD); materials science and engineering (MS, PhD); mechanical engineering (MS, PhD); solar energy engineering and commercialization (PSM). *Program availability:* Part-time, evening/weekend, online learning. Terminal master's awarded for partial completion of doctoral program. *Degree requirements:* For master's, thesis and oral defense (MS); applied project or comprehensive exam (MSE); interactive Program of Study (iPOS) submitted before completing 50 percent of required credit hours; for doctorate, comprehensive exam, thesis/dissertation, interactive Program of Study (iPOS) submitted before completing 50 percent of required credit hours. *Entrance requirements:* For master's, GRE, minimum GPA of 3.0 or equivalent in last 2 years of work leading to bachelor's degree; for doctorate, GRE, minimum GPA of 3.0 in last 2 years of work leading to bachelor's degree. Additional exam requirements/recommendations for international students: Required—TOEFL, IELTS, or PTE. Electronic applications accepted. *Expenses:* Contact institution. *Faculty research:* Electronic materials and packaging, materials for energy (batteries), adaptive/intelligent materials and structures, multiscale fluid mechanics, membranes, therapeutics and bioseparations, flexible structures, nanostructured materials, and micro/nano transport.

Auburn University, Graduate School, Ginn College of Engineering, Department of Mechanical Engineering, Auburn University, AL 36849. Offers M Mtl E, MME, MS, PhD. *Program availability:* Part-time. *Faculty:* 38 full-time (1 woman), 1 part-time/adjunct (0 women). *Students:* 121 full-time (23 women), 73 part-time (8 women); includes 8 minority (3 Black or African American, non-Hispanic/Latino; 2 Asian, non-Hispanic/Latino; 3 Hispanic/Latino), 129 international. Average age 26. 244 applicants, 50% accepted, 51 enrolled. In 2016, 28 master's, 12 doctorates awarded. *Degree requirements:* For master's, thesis (for some programs); for doctorate, one foreign language, thesis/dissertation. *Entrance requirements:* For master's and doctorate, GRE General Test. *Application deadline:* Applications are processed on a rolling basis. Application fee: $50 ($60 for international students). *Expenses:* Tuition, state resident: full-time $9072; part-time $504 per credit hour. Tuition, nonresident: full-time $27,216; part-time $1512 per credit hour. Required fees: $812 per semester. Tuition and fees vary according to degree level and program. *Financial support:* Fellowships, research assistantships, teaching assistantships, and Federal Work-Study available. Support available to part-time students. Financial award application deadline: 3/15; financial award applicants required to submit FAFSA. *Faculty research:* Engineering mechanics, experimental mechanics, engineering design, engineering acoustics, engineering optics. *Unit head:* Dr. Jeff Suhling, Chair, 334-844-3332. *Application contact:* Dr. George Flowers, Dean of the Graduate School, 334-844-2125.
Website: http://www.eng.auburn.edu/me/

Baylor University, Graduate School, School of Engineering and Computer Science, Department of Mechanical Engineering, Waco, TX 76798. Offers biomedical engineering (MSBME); engineering (ME); mechanical engineering (MS, PhD). *Program availability:* Part-time. *Faculty:* 13 full-time (2 women). *Students:* 30 full-time (3 women), 1 part-time (0 women); includes 4 minority (1 Black or African American, non-Hispanic/Latino; 1 Asian, non-Hispanic/Latino; 2 Hispanic/Latino), 10 international. 20 applicants, 35% accepted, 3 enrolled. In 2016, 8 master's awarded. *Degree requirements:* For master's, thesis (for some programs), 33 coursework credits or 6 project credits and 27 coursework credits (for ME); for doctorate, thesis/dissertation (for some programs). *Entrance requirements:* For master's, GRE. Additional exam requirements/recommendations for international students: Required—TOEFL (minimum score 550 paper-based; 80 iBT), IELTS (minimum score 6.5), PTE (minimum score 58). *Application deadline:* For fall admission, 2/15 priority date for domestic and international students; for winter admission, 12/1 priority date for domestic and international students; for summer admission, 5/1 priority date for domestic students. Application fee: $50. Electronic applications accepted. *Expenses:* Tuition: Full-time $28,494; part-time $1583 per credit hour. Required fees: $167 per credit hour. Tuition and fees vary according to course load and program. *Financial support:* In 2016–17, 15 students received support, including 8 research assistantships with full tuition reimbursements available (averaging $15,000 per year), 7 teaching assistantships with full tuition reimbursements available (averaging $15,000 per year). Financial award application deadline: 2/15. *Unit head:* Dr. Dennis L. O'Neal, Dean, 254-710-3871, Fax: 254-710-3839, E-mail: dennis_oneal@baylor.edu. *Application contact:* Dr. Carolyn Skurla, Associate Professor and Graduate Program Director, 254-710-7371, Fax: 254-710-3360, E-mail: carolyn_skurla@baylor.edu.
Website: http://www.ecs.baylor.edu/mechanicalengineering/

Binghamton University, State University of New York, Graduate School, Thomas J. Watson School of Engineering and Applied Science, Department of Mechanical Engineering, Binghamton, NY 13902-6000. Offers M Eng, MS, PhD. *Program availability:* Part-time, evening/weekend, online learning. *Faculty:* 23 full-time (3 women), 6 part-time/adjunct (0 women). *Students:* 46 full-time (7 women), 45 part-time (6 women); includes 10 minority (8 Asian, non-Hispanic/Latino; 1 Hispanic/Latino; 1 Native Hawaiian or other Pacific Islander, non-Hispanic/Latino), 56 international. Average age 26. 192 applicants, 64% accepted, 31 enrolled. In 2016, 40 master's, 5 doctorates awarded. *Degree requirements:* For master's, thesis (for some programs); for doctorate, comprehensive exam, thesis/dissertation. *Entrance requirements:* For master's and doctorate, GRE General Test. Additional exam requirements/recommendations for international students: Required—TOEFL (minimum score 550 paper-based; 80 iBT). *Application deadline:* Applications are processed on a rolling basis. Application fee: $75. Electronic applications accepted. *Expenses:* Contact institution. *Financial support:* In 2016–17, 51 students received support, including 21 research assistantships with full tuition reimbursements available (averaging $16,500 per year), 15 teaching assistantships with full tuition reimbursements available (averaging $16,500 per year); fellowships, career-related internships or fieldwork, Federal Work-Study, institutionally sponsored loans, scholarships/grants, health care benefits, tuition waivers (full and partial), and unspecified assistantships also available. Financial award application deadline: 2/1; financial award applicants required to submit FAFSA. *Unit head:* Timothy Singler, Graduate Director, 607-777-4330, E-mail: singler@

binghamton.edu. *Application contact:* Ben Balkaya, Assistant Dean and Director, 607-777-2151, Fax: 607-777-2501, E-mail: balkaya@binghamton.edu.

Boise State University, College of Engineering, Department of Mechanical and Biomedical Engineering, Boise, ID 83725. Offers mechanical engineering (M Engr, MS). *Program availability:* Part-time. *Faculty:* 16. *Students:* 8 full-time (2 women), 1 part-time (0 women); includes 1 minority (Asian, non-Hispanic/Latino), 2 international. Average age 25. 19 applicants, 58% accepted, 6 enrolled. In 2016, 4 master's awarded. *Degree requirements:* For master's, comprehensive exam, thesis (for some programs). *Entrance requirements:* For master's, GRE General Test, minimum GPA of 3.0. Additional exam requirements/recommendations for international students: Required—TOEFL (minimum score 550 paper-based; 80 iBT), IELTS (minimum score 6). *Application deadline:* For fall admission, 3/15 priority date for domestic and international students. Application fee: $65 ($95 for international students). Electronic applications accepted. *Expenses:* Tuition, state resident: full-time $6058; part-time $358 per credit hour. Tuition, nonresident: full-time $20,108; part-time $608 per credit hour. *Required fees:* $2108. Tuition and fees vary according to program. *Financial support:* In 2016–17, 3 students received support, including 2 research assistantships (averaging $7,596 per year), 1 teaching assistantship (averaging $11,108 per year); scholarships/grants and unspecified assistantships also available. Financial award application deadline: 3/15; financial award applicants required to submit FAFSA. *Unit head:* Dr. Don Plumlee, Department Chair, 208-426-3575, E-mail: dplumlee@boisestate.edu. *Application contact:* Dr. John Gardner, Graduate Coordinator, 208-426-5702, E-mail: jgardner@boisestate.edu.
Website: http://coen.boisestate.edu/mbe/students/graduate-students/

Boston University, College of Engineering, Department of Mechanical Engineering, Boston, MA 02215. Offers manufacturing engineering (M Eng, MS); mechanical engineering (PhD); MS/MBA. *Program availability:* Part-time, 100% online, blended/hybrid learning. *Students:* 164 full-time (30 women), 40 part-time (8 women); includes 27 minority (15 Asian, non-Hispanic/Latino; 5 Hispanic/Latino; 2 Native Hawaiian or other Pacific Islander, non-Hispanic/Latino; 5 Two or more races, non-Hispanic/Latino), 89 international. Average age 26. 498 applicants, 37% accepted, 84 enrolled. In 2016, 65 master's, 11 doctorates awarded. Terminal master's awarded for partial completion of doctoral program. *Degree requirements:* For master's, thesis (for some programs); for doctorate, comprehensive exam, thesis/dissertation. *Entrance requirements:* For master's and doctorate, GRE General Test. Additional exam requirements/recommendations for international students: Required—TOEFL (minimum score 90 iBT), IELTS (minimum score 7). *Faculty research:* Acoustics, ultrasound, and vibrations; biomechanics; dynamics, control, and robotics; energy and thermofluid sciences; MEMS and nanotechnology. *Unit head:* Dr. Alice White, Chairperson, 617-353-2814, Fax: 617-353-5866, E-mail: aew1@bu.edu.
Website: http://www.bu.edu/me/

Bradley University, The Graduate School, Caterpillar College of Engineering and Technology, Department of Mechanical Engineering, Peoria, IL 61625-0002. Offers MSME. *Program availability:* Part-time, evening/weekend. *Degree requirements:* For master's, comprehensive exam, thesis optional. *Entrance requirements:* Additional exam requirements/recommendations for international students: Required—TOEFL (minimum score 550 paper-based; 79 iBT), IELTS (minimum score 6.5). *Application deadline:* For fall admission, 5/15 priority date for domestic and international students; for spring admission, 10/15 priority date for domestic and international students. Applications are processed on a rolling basis. Application fee: $40 ($50 for international students). Electronic applications accepted. *Expenses: Tuition:* Full-time $7650; part-time $850 per credit. *Required fees:* $50 per credit. One-time fee: $100 full-time. *Financial support:* Research assistantships with full and partial tuition reimbursements, teaching assistantships, scholarships/grants, tuition waivers (partial), and unspecified assistantships available. Support available to part-time students. Financial award application deadline: 4/1. *Faculty research:* Ground-coupled heat pumps, robotic end-effectors, power plant optimization. *Unit head:* Dr. Paul Mehta, Chairperson, 309-677-2754. *Application contact:* Kayla Carroll, Director of International Admissions and Student Services, 309-677-2375, E-mail: klcarroll@fsmail.bradley.edu.
Website: http://www.bradley.edu/academic/departments/mechanical/

Brigham Young University, Graduate Studies, Ira A. Fulton College of Engineering and Technology, Department of Mechanical Engineering, Provo, UT 84602. Offers MS, PhD. *Faculty:* 26 full-time (1 woman), 5 part-time/adjunct (1 woman). *Students:* 117 full-time (9 women); includes 3 minority (1 American Indian or Alaska Native, non-Hispanic/Latino; 1 Asian, non-Hispanic/Latino; 1 Hispanic/Latino), 5 international. Average age 27. 71 applicants, 65% accepted, 31 enrolled. In 2016, 24 master's, 5 doctorates awarded. Terminal master's awarded for partial completion of doctoral program. *Degree requirements:* For master's, thesis; for doctorate, comprehensive exam, thesis/dissertation. *Entrance requirements:* For master's and doctorate, GRE General Test, minimum GPA of 3.0 in undergraduate degree course work, 3 letters of recommendation, personal statement of intent, resume. Additional exam requirements/recommendations for international students: Required—TOEFL (minimum score 580 paper-based; 85 iBT), IELTS (minimum score 7). *Application deadline:* For fall admission, 1/15 for domestic and international students; for winter admission, 9/1 for domestic and international students. Application fee: $50. Electronic applications accepted. *Expenses: Tuition:* Full-time $6680; part-time $393 per credit. Tuition and fees vary according to course load, program and student's religious affiliation. *Financial support:* In 2016–17, 160 students received support, including 16 fellowships with full and partial tuition reimbursements available (averaging $15,828 per year), 264 research assistantships with full and partial tuition reimbursements available (averaging $12,852 per year), 14 teaching assistantships with full and partial tuition reimbursements available (averaging $12,660 per year); scholarships/grants also available. Financial award application deadline: 3/1; financial award applicants required to submit FAFSA. *Faculty research:* Computational and experimental fluid mechanics, dynamic and mechatronic systems and controls, product design and development, manufacturing systems and processes, materials and bio-mechanics. *Total annual research expenditures:* $4.7 million. *Unit head:* Dr. Daniel Maynes, Chair, 801-422-2625, Fax: 801-422-0516, E-mail: maynes@byu.edu. *Application contact:* Janelle Harkness, Graduate Advisor, 801-422-1650, Fax: 801-422-0516, E-mail: jharkness@byu.edu.
Website: http://me.byu.edu

Brown University, Graduate School, School of Engineering, Program in Mechanics of Solids and Structures, Providence, RI 02912. Offers Sc M, PhD. *Degree requirements:* For doctorate, thesis/dissertation, preliminary exam.

Bucknell University, Graduate Studies, College of Engineering, Department of Mechanical Engineering, Lewisburg, PA 17837. Offers MSME. *Program availability:* Part-time. *Degree requirements:* For master's, thesis. *Entrance requirements:* For master's, GRE General Test, minimum GPA of 3.0. Additional exam requirements/recommendations for international students: Required—TOEFL (minimum score 600 paper-based). *Faculty research:* Heat pump performance, microprocessors in heat engine testing, computer-aided design.

California Baptist University, Program in Mechanical Engineering, Riverside, CA 92504-3206. Offers MS. *Program availability:* Part-time. *Faculty:* 7 full-time (2 women). *Students:* 4 full-time (0 women); includes 1 minority (Asian, non-Hispanic/Latino), 1 international. Average age 24. 14 applicants, 71% accepted, 10 enrolled. *Entrance requirements:* For master's, minimum undergraduate GPA of 3.0, bachelor's transcripts, three letters of recommendation, essay, resume, interview. Additional exam requirements/recommendations for international students: Required—TOEFL (minimum score 80 iBT). *Application deadline:* For fall admission, 8/1 priority date for domestic students, 7/1 priority date for international students; for spring admission, 12/1 priority date for domestic students, 11/1 priority date for international students. Applications are processed on a rolling basis. Application fee: $45. Electronic applications accepted. *Expenses:* Contact institution. *Financial support:* Federal Work-Study and scholarships/grants available. Financial award applicants required to submit CSS PROFILE or FAFSA. *Faculty research:* Conduction, internal mixed convection, absorption refrigeration, biomechanics, dynamics. *Unit head:* Dr. Ziliang Zhou, Assistant Dean, College of Engineering, 951-343-4681, E-mail: zzhou@calbaptist.edu. *Application contact:* Felicia Tasabia, Administrative Assistant, 951-343-4972, E-mail: ftasabia@calbaptist.edu.

California Institute of Technology, Division of Engineering and Applied Science, Option in Mechanical Engineering, Pasadena, CA 91125-0001. Offers MS, PhD, Engr. *Degree requirements:* For doctorate, thesis/dissertation. *Faculty research:* Design, mechanics, thermal and fluids engineering, jet propulsion.

California Polytechnic State University, San Luis Obispo, College of Engineering, Department of Mechanical Engineering, San Luis Obispo, CA 93407. Offers MS. *Program availability:* Part-time. *Faculty:* 8 full-time (2 women). *Students:* 19 full-time (4 women), 7 part-time (0 women); includes 10 minority (6 Asian, non-Hispanic/Latino; 2 Hispanic/Latino; 2 Two or more races, non-Hispanic/Latino), 1 international. Average age 25. 45 applicants, 42% accepted, 7 enrolled. In 2016, 26 master's awarded. *Degree requirements:* For master's, comprehensive exam (for some programs), thesis (for some programs). *Entrance requirements:* For master's, GRE. Additional exam requirements/recommendations for international students: Required—TOEFL (minimum score 80 iBT). *Application deadline:* For fall admission, 1/1 for domestic and international students. Applications are processed on a rolling basis. Electronic applications accepted. *Expenses:* Tuition, state resident: full-time $6738; part-time $3906 per year. Tuition, nonresident: full-time $15,666; part-time $8370 per year. *Required fees:* $3603; $3141 per unit. $1047 per term. *Financial support:* Fellowships, research assistantships, teaching assistantships, career-related internships or fieldwork, Federal Work-Study, and scholarships/grants available. Support available to part-time students. Financial award application deadline: 3/2; financial award applicants required to submit FAFSA. *Faculty research:* Mechatronics, robotics, thermosciences, mechanics and stress analysis, composite materials. *Unit head:* Dr. Saeed Niku, Graduate Coordinator, 805-756-1376, E-mail: sniku@calpoly.edu.
Website: http://me.calpoly.edu

California State Polytechnic University, Pomona, Program in Mechanical Engineering, Pomona, CA 91768-2557. Offers MS. *Program availability:* Part-time, evening/weekend. *Students:* 8 full-time (1 woman), 64 part-time (7 women); includes 46 minority (1 Black or African American, non-Hispanic/Latino; 24 Asian, non-Hispanic/Latino; 18 Hispanic/Latino; 3 Two or more races, non-Hispanic/Latino), 11 international. Average age 27. 22 applicants, 100% accepted, 17 enrolled. In 2016, 14 master's awarded. *Entrance requirements:* Additional exam requirements/recommendations for international students: Required—TOEFL. *Application deadline:* Applications are processed on a rolling basis. Application fee: $55. Electronic applications accepted. *Expenses:* Contact institution. *Financial support:* Application deadline: 3/2; applicants required to submit FAFSA. *Unit head:* Dr. Henry Xue, Graduate Coordinator, 909-869-4304, Fax: 909-869-4341, E-mail: hxue@cpp.edu. *Application contact:* Andrew M. Wright, Director of Admissions, 909-869-3130, Fax: 909-869-4529, E-mail: awright@cpp.edu.
Website: http://www.cpp.edu/~engineering/ME/masters.shtml

California State University, Fresno, Division of Research and Graduate Studies, Lyles College of Engineering, Department of Mechanical Engineering, Fresno, CA 93740-8027. Offers MS. *Program availability:* Part-time. *Degree requirements:* For master's, thesis or alternative. *Entrance requirements:* For master's, GRE General Test, minimum GPA of 2.7. Additional exam requirements/recommendations for international students: Required—TOEFL. *Application deadline:* For fall admission, 5/1 for domestic and international students; for spring admission, 10/1 for domestic and international students. Applications are processed on a rolling basis. Application fee: $55. Electronic applications accepted. *Financial support:* Career-related internships or fieldwork, Federal Work-Study, and scholarships/grants available. Support available to part-time students. Financial award application deadline: 3/1; financial award applicants required to submit FAFSA. *Faculty research:* Flowmeter calibration, digital camera calibration. *Unit head:* Dr. Gemunu Happawana, Chair, 559-278-6832, Fax: 559-278-6759, E-mail: ghappawana@csufresno.edu. *Application contact:* Dr. Maziar Ghazinejad, Graduate Program Coordinator, 559-278-0382, Fax: 559-278-6759, E-mail: mghazinejad@csufresno.edu.
Website: http://www.fresnostate.edu/engineering/mechanical-engineering/

California State University, Fullerton, Graduate Studies, College of Engineering and Computer Science, Department of Mechanical Engineering, Fullerton, CA 92834-9480. Offers MS. *Program availability:* Part-time. *Degree requirements:* For master's, comprehensive exam, project or thesis. *Entrance requirements:* For master's, minimum undergraduate GPA of 2.5. Application fee: $55. *Expenses:* Tuition, state resident: full-time $3369; part-time $1953 per unit. Tuition, nonresident: full-time $3915; part-time $2499 per unit. Tuition and fees vary according to course load, degree level and program. *Financial support:* Career-related internships or fieldwork, Federal Work-Study, institutionally sponsored loans, and scholarships/grants available. Support available to part-time students. Financial award application deadline: 3/1; financial award applicants required to submit FAFSA. *Unit head:* Dr. Roberta E. Rikli, Chair, 657-278-3014. *Application contact:* Admissions/Applications, 657-278-2371.

California State University, Long Beach, Graduate Studies, College of Engineering, Department of Mechanical and Aerospace Engineering, Long Beach, CA 90840. Offers aerospace engineering (MSAE); engineering and industrial applied mathematics (PhD); interdisciplinary engineering (MSE); management engineering (MSE); mechanical engineering (MSME). *Program availability:* Part-time. *Entrance requirements:* Additional exam requirements/recommendations for international students: Required—TOEFL. *Application deadline:* For fall admission, 7/1 for domestic students. Application fee: $55. Electronic applications accepted. *Financial support:* Career-related internships or fieldwork, Federal Work-Study, institutionally sponsored loans, scholarships/grants, and unspecified assistantships available. Financial award application deadline: 3/2. *Faculty research:* Unsteady turbulent flows, solar energy, energy conversion, CAD/CAM, computer-assisted instruction. *Unit head:* Jalal Torabzadeh, Chair, 562-985-4398.

California State University, Los Angeles, Graduate Studies, College of Engineering, Computer Science, and Technology, Department of Mechanical Engineering, Los Angeles, CA 90032-8530. Offers MS. *Program availability:* Part-time, evening/weekend. *Degree requirements:* For master's, comprehensive exam or thesis. *Entrance requirements:* For master's, minimum GPA of 2.75. Additional exam requirements/recommendations for international students: Required—TOEFL (minimum score 550 paper-based). Electronic applications accepted. *Faculty research:* Mechanical design, thermal systems, solar-powered vehicle.

California State University, Northridge, Graduate Studies, College of Engineering and Computer Science, Department of Mechanical Engineering, Northridge, CA 91330. Offers MS. *Program availability:* Part-time, evening/weekend. *Faculty:* 10 full-time (8 women), 24 part-time/adjunct (21 women). *Students:* 19 full-time (3 women), 33 part-time (3 women); includes 15 minority (7 Asian, non-Hispanic/Latino; 7 Hispanic/Latino; 1 Two or more races, non-Hispanic/Latino), 10 international. Average age 28. 85 applicants, 26% accepted, 12 enrolled. *Degree requirements:* For master's, thesis or project. *Entrance requirements:* Additional exam requirements/recommendations for international students: Required—TOEFL. *Application deadline:* For fall admission, 11/30 for domestic students. Application fee: $55. *Expenses:* Tuition, state resident: full-time $4152. *Financial support:* Application deadline: 3/1. *Unit head:* Dr. Hamid Johari, Chair, 818-677-2187.
Website: http://www.ecs.csun.edu/me/

California State University, Sacramento, Office of Graduate Studies, College of Engineering and Computer Science, Department of Mechanical Engineering, Sacramento, CA 95819. Offers MS. *Program availability:* Part-time, evening/weekend. *Students:* 68 full-time (24 women), 97 part-time (17 women); includes 122 minority (11 Black or African American, non-Hispanic/Latino; 100 Asian, non-Hispanic/Latino; 11 Hispanic/Latino). Average age 28. 190 applicants, 75% accepted, 43 enrolled. In 2016, 16 master's awarded. *Entrance requirements:* For master's, minimum GPA of 3.0 in upper-division engineering coursework. Additional exam requirements/recommendations for international students: Required—TOEFL (minimum score 550 paper-based; 80 iBT). *Application deadline:* For fall admission, 3/1 for domestic and international students; for spring admission, 9/15 for domestic students, 9/30 for international students. Applications are processed on a rolling basis. Application fee: $55. Electronic applications accepted. *Expenses:* $4,302 full-time tuition and fees per semester, $2,796 part-time. *Financial support:* Research assistantships, teaching assistantships, career-related internships or fieldwork, and Federal Work-Study available. Support available to part-time students. Financial award application deadline: 3/1; financial award applicants required to submit FAFSA. *Unit head:* Dr. Akihiko Kumagai, Graduate Program Coordinator, 916-278-5838, E-mail: kumagaia@ecs.csus.edu. *Application contact:* Jose Martinez, Outreach and Graduate Diversity Coordinator, 916-278-6470, Fax: 916-278-5669, E-mail: martinj@skymail.csus.edu.
Website: http://www.ecs.csus.edu/wcm/me

Carleton University, Faculty of Graduate Studies, Faculty of Engineering and Design, Department of Mechanical and Aerospace Engineering, Ottawa, ON K1S 5B6, Canada. Offers aerospace engineering (M Eng, MA Sc, PhD); materials engineering (M Eng, MA Sc); mechanical engineering (M Eng, MA Sc, PhD). *Degree requirements:* For master's, thesis optional; for doctorate, thesis/dissertation. *Entrance requirements:* For master's, honors degree; for doctorate, MA Sc or M Eng. Additional exam requirements/recommendations for international students: Required—TOEFL. *Faculty research:* Thermal fluids engineering, heat transfer, vehicle engineering.

Carnegie Mellon University, Carnegie Institute of Technology, Department of Mechanical Engineering, Pittsburgh, PA 15213-3891. Offers MS, PhD. *Program availability:* Part-time, evening/weekend. Terminal master's awarded for partial completion of doctoral program. *Degree requirements:* For master's, thesis (for some programs); for doctorate, thesis/dissertation (for some programs), qualifying exam. *Entrance requirements:* For master's and doctorate, GRE General Test. Additional exam requirements/recommendations for international students: Required—TOEFL. *Faculty research:* Combustion, design, fluid, and thermal sciences; computational fluid dynamics; energy and environment; solid mechanics; systems and controls; materials and manufacturing.

Case Western Reserve University, School of Graduate Studies, Case School of Engineering, Department of Mechanical and Aerospace Engineering, Cleveland, OH 44106. Offers MS, PhD, MD/PhD. *Program availability:* Part-time, online learning. *Faculty:* 14 full-time (3 women). *Students:* 91 full-time (16 women), 10 part-time (4 women); includes 8 minority (1 Black or African American, non-Hispanic/Latino; 4 Asian, non-Hispanic/Latino; 3 Hispanic/Latino), 72 international. In 2016, 18 master's, 10 doctorates awarded. *Degree requirements:* For master's, thesis (for some programs); for doctorate, thesis/dissertation, qualifying exam, teaching experience. *Entrance requirements:* For master's and doctorate, GRE General Test. Additional exam requirements/recommendations for international students: Required—TOEFL. *Application deadline:* For fall admission, 7/1 priority date for domestic students. Applications are processed on a rolling basis. Application fee: $50. *Expenses: Tuition:* Full-time $42,576; part-time $1774 per credit hour. *Required fees:* $34. Tuition and fees vary according to course load and program. *Financial support:* In 2016–17, 5 fellowships with tuition reimbursements, 25 research assistantships with tuition reimbursements, 18 teaching assistantships were awarded; institutionally sponsored loans and tuition waivers (full and partial) also available. Financial award application deadline: 3/1; financial award applicants required to submit FAFSA. *Faculty research:* Musculoskeletal biomechanics, combustion diagnostics and computation, mechanical behavior of advanced materials and nanostructures, bio robotics. *Total annual research expenditures:* $5.3 million. *Unit head:* Dr. Robert Gao, Department Chair, 216-368-6045, Fax: 216-368-6445, E-mail: robert.gao@case.edu. *Application contact:* Carla Wilson, Student Affairs Coordinator, 216-368-4580, Fax: 216-368-3007, E-mail: cxw75@case.edu.
Website: http://www.engineering.case.edu/emae

The Catholic University of America, School of Engineering, Department of Mechanical Engineering, Washington, DC 20064. Offers energy and environment (MME); general (MME); mechanical engineering (MSE, PhD). *Program availability:* Part-time. *Faculty:* 9 full-time (0 women), 7 part-time/adjunct (0 women). *Students:* 7 full-time (1 woman), 12 part-time (2 women); includes 4 minority (3 Black or African American, non-Hispanic/Latino; 1 Two or more races, non-Hispanic/Latino), 8 international. Average age 32. 26 applicants, 85% accepted, 9 enrolled. In 2016, 16 master's, 1 doctorate awarded. Terminal master's awarded for partial completion of doctoral program. *Degree requirements:* For master's, thesis (for some programs); for doctorate, comprehensive exam, thesis/dissertation. *Entrance requirements:* For master's and doctorate, statement of purpose, official copies of academic transcripts, three letters of recommendation. Additional exam requirements/recommendations for international students: Required—TOEFL (minimum score 550 paper-based; 80 iBT). *Application deadline:* For fall admission, 7/15 priority date for domestic students, 7/1 for international students; for spring admission, 11/15 priority date for domestic students, 11/1 for international students. Applications are processed on a rolling basis. Application fee: $55. Electronic applications accepted. *Expenses:* $43,380 per year; $1,170 per credit; $200 per semester part-time fees. *Financial support:* Fellowships, research assistantships, teaching assistantships, Federal Work-Study, scholarships/grants, tuition waivers (full and partial), and unspecified assistantships available. Financial award application deadline: 2/1; financial award applicants required to submit FAFSA. *Faculty research:* Energy and environment, acoustics and vibration, bio fabrication and lab-on-chip, experimental mechanics, smart materials. *Total annual research expenditures:* $243,170. *Unit head:* Dr. Sen Nieh, Chair, 202-319-5170, Fax: 202-319-

5173, E-mail: nieh@cua.edu. *Application contact:* Director of Graduate Admissions, 202-319-5057, Fax: 202-319-6533, E-mail: cua-admissions@cua.edu.
Website: http://mechanical.cua.edu/

The Citadel, The Military College of South Carolina, Citadel Graduate College, School of Engineering, Department of Mechanical Engineering, Charleston, SC 29409. Offers aeronautical engineering (Graduate Certificate); composites engineering (Graduate Certificate); manufacturing engineering (Graduate Certificate); mechanical engineering (MS); mechatronics engineering (Graduate Certificate); power and energy (Graduate Certificate). *Program availability:* Part-time, evening/weekend. *Students:* 1 part-time; minority (Asian, non-Hispanic/Latino). 1 applicant, 100% accepted, 1 enrolled. *Degree requirements:* For master's, 30 hours of coursework with minimum GPA of 3.0 on hours earned at The Citadel. *Entrance requirements:* For master's, GRE, 2 letters of recommendation; official transcript of baccalaureate degree from an ABET accredited engineering program or approved alternative. Additional exam requirements/recommendations for international students: Required—TOEFL (minimum score 550 paper-based; 79 iBT). *Application deadline:* Applications are processed on a rolling basis. Application fee: $40. Electronic applications accepted. *Expenses:* Tuition, state resident: full-time $5121; part-time $569 per credit hour. Tuition, nonresident: full-time $8613; part-time $957 per credit hour. *Required fees:* $90 per term. *Financial support:* Fellowships and unspecified assistantships available. Support available to part-time students. Financial award application deadline: 7/1; financial award applicants required to submit FAFSA. *Unit head:* Dr. Robert J. Rabb, Department Head, 843-953-0520, E-mail: rrabb@citadel.edu. *Application contact:* Dr. Tara Hornor, Associate Provost for Planning, Assessment and Evaluation/Dean of Enrollment Management, 843-953-5089, E-mail: cgc@citadel.edu.
Website: http://www.citadel.edu/root/me

City College of the City University of New York, Graduate School, Grove School of Engineering, Department of Mechanical Engineering, New York, NY 10031-9198. Offers ME, MS, PhD. PhD program offered jointly with Graduate School and University Center of the City University of New York. *Program availability:* Part-time. *Degree requirements:* For master's, thesis optional; for doctorate, one foreign language, comprehensive exam, thesis/dissertation. *Entrance requirements:* For master's and doctorate, GRE General Test. Additional exam requirements/recommendations for international students: Required—TOEFL (minimum score 500 paper-based). Tuition and fees vary according to course load, degree level and program. *Faculty research:* Bio-heat and mass transfer, bone mechanics, fracture mechanics, heat transfer in computer parts, mechanisms design.

Clarkson University, Wallace H. Coulter School of Engineering, Department of Mechanical and Aeronautical Engineering, Potsdam, NY 13699. Offers mechanical engineering (ME, MS, PhD). *Program availability:* Part-time, evening/weekend. *Faculty:* 31 full-time (3 women), 12 part-time/adjunct (1 woman). *Students:* 43 full-time (7 women), 60 part-time (11 women); includes 11 minority (3 Black or African American, non-Hispanic/Latino; 1 Asian, non-Hispanic/Latino; 6 Hispanic/Latino; 1 Two or more races, non-Hispanic/Latino), 23 international. 83 applicants, 49% accepted, 18 enrolled. In 2016, 26 master's, 2 doctorates awarded. *Degree requirements:* For master's, thesis (for some programs), thesis or project (for MS); project (for ME); for doctorate, comprehensive exam, thesis/dissertation. *Entrance requirements:* For master's and doctorate, GRE. Additional exam requirements/recommendations for international students: Required—TOEFL (minimum score 550 paper-based, 80 iBT) or IELTS (6.5). *Application deadline:* Applications are processed on a rolling basis. Application fee: $50. Electronic applications accepted. *Expenses: Tuition:* Full-time $23,400; part-time $1300 per credit hour. Tuition and fees vary according to campus/location and program. *Financial support:* Scholarships/grants and unspecified assistantships available. *Unit head:* Dr. Daniel Valentine, Chair of Mechanical and Aeronautical Engineering, 315-268-6586, E-mail: dvalenti@clarkson.edu. *Application contact:* Dan Capogna, Graduate Admissions Contact, 518-631-9910, E-mail: graduate@clarkson.edu.
Website: http://graduate.clarkson.edu

Clemson University, Graduate School, College of Engineering, Computing and Applied Sciences, Department of Mechanical Engineering, Clemson, SC 29634. Offers MS, PhD. *Program availability:* Part-time, evening/weekend, blended/hybrid learning. *Faculty:* 37 full-time (3 women), 1 part-time/adjunct (0 women). *Students:* 144 full-time (31 women), 29 part-time (3 women); includes 8 minority (1 Black or African American, non-Hispanic/Latino; 3 Asian, non-Hispanic/Latino; 3 Hispanic/Latino; 1 Two or more races, non-Hispanic/Latino), 121 international. Average age 26. 593 applicants, 16% accepted, 47 enrolled. In 2016, 72 master's, 17 doctorates awarded. Terminal master's awarded for partial completion of doctoral program. *Degree requirements:* For master's, thesis (for some programs); for doctorate, comprehensive exam, thesis/dissertation. *Entrance requirements:* For master's and doctorate, GRE General Test, unofficial transcripts, letters of recommendation. Additional exam requirements/recommendations for international students: Required—TOEFL (minimum score 80 iBT), IELTS (minimum score 6.5). *Application deadline:* For fall admission, 2/15 for domestic and international students; for spring admission, 9/15 for domestic and international students. Application fee: $80 ($90 for international students). Electronic applications accepted. *Expenses:* $4,841 per semester full-time resident, $9,640 per semester full-time non-resident, $612 per credit hour part-time resident, $1,223 per credit hour part-time non-resident. *Financial support:* In 2016–17, 117 students received support, including 6 fellowships with partial tuition reimbursements available (averaging $7,083 per year), 40 research assistantships with partial tuition reimbursements available (averaging $16,799 per year), 1 teaching assistantship with partial tuition reimbursement available (averaging $24,000 per year); career-related internships or fieldwork, health care benefits, and unspecified assistantships also available. Financial award application deadline: 2/15. *Faculty research:* Engineering design, thermal and fluid sciences, automated manufacturing, dynamical systems and robotics, engineering mechanics and materials. *Total annual research expenditures:* $1.9 million. *Unit head:* Dr. Richard Figliola, Acting Department Chair, 864-656-5635, E-mail: fgliola@clemson.edu. *Application contact:* Dr. Joshua Summers, Graduate Program Coordinator, 864-656-3295, E-mail: jsummer@clemson.edu.
Website: https://www.clemson.edu/cecas/departments/me/

Cleveland State University, College of Graduate Studies, Fenn College of Engineering, Department of Mechanical Engineering, Cleveland, OH 44115. Offers MS, D Eng. *Program availability:* Part-time. *Faculty:* 8 full-time (0 women). *Students:* 53 full-time (5 women), 43 part-time (5 women); includes 7 minority (4 Black or African American, non-Hispanic/Latino; 2 Hispanic/Latino; 1 Two or more races, non-Hispanic/Latino), 45 international. Average age 27. 428 applicants, 21% accepted, 19 enrolled. In 2016, 37 master's, 1 doctorate awarded. *Degree requirements:* For master's, project or thesis; for doctorate, thesis/dissertation, candidacy and qualifying exams. *Entrance requirements:* For master's, GRE General Test, minimum GPA of 3.0; for doctorate, GRE General Test, minimum GPA of 3.25. Additional exam requirements/recommendations for international students: Required—TOEFL (minimum score 550 paper-based; 78 iBT). *Application deadline:* For fall admission, 7/1 priority date for domestic students, 5/15 for international students; for spring admission, 11/15 priority date for domestic students, 11/1 for international students; for summer admission, 4/1 for domestic students, 3/15 for international students. Applications are processed on a

rolling basis. Application fee: $40. Electronic applications accepted. *Expenses:* Tuition, state resident: full-time $9565. Tuition, nonresident: full-time $17,980. Tuition and fees vary according to program. *Financial support:* In 2016–17, 22 students received support, including 9 research assistantships with tuition reimbursements available (averaging $3,480 per year); teaching assistantships with partial tuition reimbursements available, career-related internships or fieldwork, Federal Work-Study, institutionally sponsored loans, and unspecified assistantships also available. Support available to part-time students. Financial award applicants required to submit FAFSA. *Faculty research:* Fluid piezoelectric sensors, laser-optical inspection simulation of forging and forming processes, multiphase flow and heat transfer, turbulent flows. *Unit head:* Dr. William J. Atherton, Interim Chair, 216-687-2595, Fax: 216-687-5375, E-mail: w.atherton@csuohio.edu. *Application contact:* Deborah L. Brown, Interim Assistant Director, Graduate Admissions, 216-523-7572, Fax: 216-687-9214, E-mail: d.l.brown@csuohio.edu.
Website: http://www.csuohio.edu/engineering/mce/

Colorado School of Mines, Office of Graduate Studies, Department of Mechanical Engineering, Golden, CO 80401. Offers mechanical engineering (MS, PhD). *Program availability:* Part-time. *Degree requirements:* For master's, thesis (for some programs); for doctorate, comprehensive exam, thesis/dissertation. *Entrance requirements:* For master's and doctorate, GRE General Test. Additional exam requirements/recommendations for international students: Required—TOEFL (minimum score 550 paper-based; 80 iBT). Electronic applications accepted. *Expenses:* Tuition, state resident: full-time $15,690. Tuition, nonresident: full-time $34,020. *Required fees:* $2152. Tuition and fees vary according to course load. *Faculty research:* Biomechanics; robotics, automation, and design; solid mechanics and materials; thermal science and engineering.

Colorado State University, Walter Scott, Jr. College of Engineering, Department of Mechanical Engineering, Fort Collins, CO 80523-1374. Offers industrial engineering (PhD); mechanical engineering (ME, MS, PhD). *Program availability:* Part-time, evening/weekend, 100% online, blended/hybrid learning. *Faculty:* 29 full-time (4 women), 6 part-time/adjunct (0 women). *Students:* 49 full-time (5 women), 66 part-time (8 women); includes 10 minority (1 Asian, non-Hispanic/Latino; 5 Hispanic/Latino; 4 Two or more races, non-Hispanic/Latino), 26 international. Average age 27. 105 applicants, 40% accepted, 28 enrolled. In 2016, 13 master's, 11 doctorates awarded. Terminal master's awarded for partial completion of doctoral program. *Degree requirements:* For master's, thesis, thesis defense; for doctorate, thesis/dissertation, oral qualifying exam, preliminary exam, dissertation defense. *Entrance requirements:* For master's, GRE (minimum scores of 150 Verbal, 155 Quantitative, 3.5 Analytical), bachelor's degree in engineering, science, or engineering-related field; minimum GPA of 3.0; successful completion of undergraduate courses in calculus, ordinary differential equations, and calculus-based physics; for doctorate, GRE (minimum scores of 150 Verbal, 155 Quantitative, 3.5 Analytical), bachelor's degree in engineering, science, or engineering-related field; minimum GPA of 3.25; successful completion of undergraduate courses in calculus, ordinary differential equations, and calculus-based physics. Additional exam requirements/recommendations for international students: Required—TOEFL (minimum score 550 paper-based, 80 iBT) or IELTS (6.5). *Application deadline:* For fall admission, 1/15 priority date for domestic and international students; for spring admission, 8/1 priority date for domestic and international students. Application fee: $60 ($70 for international students). Electronic applications accepted. *Expenses:* Contact institution. *Financial support:* In 2016–17, 3 fellowships with full and partial tuition reimbursements (averaging $53,671 per year), 29 research assistantships with full and partial tuition reimbursements (averaging $20,927 per year), 29 teaching assistantships with full and partial tuition reimbursements (averaging $15,797 per year) were awarded; scholarships/grants and health care benefits also available. Financial award application deadline: 4/1. *Faculty research:* Computational fluid dynamics and high performance computing, energy, health, materials, robotics. *Total annual research expenditures:* $7.3 million. *Unit head:* Dr. Susan James, Professor and Department Head, 970-491-0924, Fax: 970-491-3827, E-mail: susan.james@engr.colostate.edu.
Website: http://www.engr.colostate.edu/me/

⭐ **Columbia University,** Fu Foundation School of Engineering and Applied Science, Department of Mechanical Engineering, New York, NY 10027. Offers MS, Eng Sc D, PhD. PhD offered through the Graduate School of Arts and Sciences. *Program availability:* Part-time, online learning. *Degree requirements:* For doctorate, thesis/dissertation, qualifying exam. *Entrance requirements:* For master's, GRE General Test, minimum GPA of 3.3; for doctorate, GRE General Test. Additional exam requirements/recommendations for international students: Required—TOEFL, IELTS, PTE. Electronic applications accepted. *Faculty research:* Musculoskeletal biomechanics; nanomechanics, nanomaterials and nanofabrication; manufacturing; optical nanostructure; biofluidic micro systems.
See Close-Up on page 593.

Concordia University, School of Graduate Studies, Faculty of Engineering and Computer Science, Department of Mechanical and Industrial Engineering, Montréal, QC H3G 1M8, Canada. Offers industrial engineering (M Eng, MA Sc, PhD); mechanical engineering (M Eng, MA Sc, PhD, Certificate). M Eng in composites program offered jointly with École Polytechnique de Montréal. *Degree requirements:* For master's, variable foreign language requirement, thesis or alternative; for doctorate, comprehensive exam, thesis/dissertation. *Faculty research:* Mechanical systems, fluid control systems, thermofluids engineering and robotics, industrial control systems.

Cooper Union for the Advancement of Science and Art, Albert Nerken School of Engineering, New York, NY 10003. Offers chemical engineering (ME); civil engineering (ME); electrical engineering (ME); mechanical engineering (ME). *Program availability:* Part-time. *Faculty:* 27 full-time (1 woman), 15 part-time/adjunct (2 women). *Students:* 36 full-time (5 women), 39 part-time (8 women); includes 34 minority (3 Black or African American, non-Hispanic/Latino; 16 Asian, non-Hispanic/Latino; 5 Hispanic/Latino; 10 Two or more races, non-Hispanic/Latino), 3 international. Average age 24. 59 applicants, 75% accepted, 34 enrolled. In 2016, 25 master's awarded. *Degree requirements:* For master's, thesis (for some programs). *Entrance requirements:* For master's, BE or BS in an engineering discipline; official copies of school transcripts including secondary (high school), college and university work; two letters of recommendation; resume. Additional exam requirements/recommendations for international students: Required—TOEFL (minimum score 600 paper-based; 100 iBT). *Application deadline:* For fall admission, 3/31 for domestic and international students. Application fee: $75. Electronic applications accepted. *Expenses: Tuition:* Full-time $16,055; part-time $1235 per credit. *Required fees:* $925 per semester. One-time fee: $250. Tuition and fees vary according to course load. *Financial support:* In 2016–17, 70 students received support, including 4 fellowships with tuition reimbursements available (averaging $11,000 per year); career-related internships or fieldwork, tuition waivers (full and partial), and tuition scholarships offered to exceptional students also available. Support available to part-time students. Financial award application deadline: 5/1; financial award applicants required to submit FAFSA. *Faculty research:* Civil infrastructure, imaging and sensing technology, biomedical engineering, encryption technology, process engineering. *Unit head:* Richard Stock, Acting Dean of Albert Nerken School of Engineering, 212-353-4285, E-mail: stock@cooper.edu. *Application*

contact: Chabeli Lajara, Administrative Assistant, 212-353-4120, E-mail: admissions@cooper.edu.
Website: http://cooper.edu/engineering

Cornell University, Graduate School, Graduate Fields of Engineering, Field of Mechanical Engineering, Ithaca, NY 14853. Offers biomechanical engineering (M Eng, MS, PhD); combustion (M Eng, MS, PhD); energy and power systems (M Eng, MS, PhD); fluid mechanics (M Eng, MS, PhD); heat transfer (M Eng, MS, PhD); materials and manufacturing engineering (M Eng, MS, PhD); mechanical systems and design (M Eng, MS, PhD); multiphase flows (M Eng, MS, PhD). Terminal master's awarded for partial completion of doctoral program. *Degree requirements:* For master's, project (M Eng), thesis (MS); for doctorate, one foreign language, comprehensive exam, thesis/dissertation, 2 semesters of teaching experience. *Entrance requirements:* For master's and doctorate, GRE General Test, 3 letters of recommendation. Additional exam requirements/recommendations for international students: Required—TOEFL (minimum score 550 paper-based; 77 iBT). Electronic applications accepted. *Faculty research:* Combustion and heat transfer, fluid mechanics and computational fluid mechanics, system dynamics and control, biomechanics, manufacturing.

Dalhousie University, Faculty of Engineering, Department of Mechanical Engineering, Halifax, NS B3J 2X4, Canada. Offers M Eng, MA Sc, PhD. *Degree requirements:* For master's, thesis; for doctorate, thesis/dissertation. *Entrance requirements:* Additional exam requirements/recommendations for international students: Required—TOEFL, IELTS, CANTEST, CAEL, or Michigan English Language Assessment Battery. Electronic applications accepted. *Faculty research:* Fluid dynamics and energy, system dynamics, naval architecture, MEMS, space structures.

Dartmouth College, Thayer School of Engineering, Program in Mechanical Engineering, Hanover, NH 03755. Offers MS, PhD. *Degree requirements:* For master's, thesis; for doctorate, thesis/dissertation, candidacy oral exam. *Entrance requirements:* For master's and doctorate, GRE General Test. *Application deadline:* For fall admission, 1/1 priority date for domestic students. Application fee: $45. *Financial support:* Fellowships, research assistantships, teaching assistantships, career-related internships or fieldwork, Federal Work-Study, institutionally sponsored loans, and tuition waivers (full and partial) available. Financial award application deadline: 1/15. *Faculty research:* Tribology, dynamics and control systems, thermal science and energy conversion, fluid mechanics and multi-phase flow, mobile robots. *Total annual research expenditures:* $369,471. *Unit head:* Dr. Joseph J. Helbie, Dean, 603-646-2238, Fax: 603-646-2580, E-mail: joseph.j.helbie@dartmouth.edu. *Application contact:* Candace S. Potter, Graduate Admissions Administrator, 603-646-3844, Fax: 603-646-1620, E-mail: candace.s.potter@dartmouth.edu.
Website: http://engineering.dartmouth.edu/

Drexel University, College of Engineering, Department of Mechanical Engineering and Mechanics, Philadelphia, PA 19104-2875. Offers mechanical engineering (MS, PhD). *Program availability:* Part-time, evening/weekend. *Faculty:* 27 full-time (4 women), 7 part-time/adjunct (0 women). *Students:* 95 full-time (10 women), 49 part-time (3 women); includes 17 minority (4 Black or African American, non-Hispanic/Latino; 8 Asian, non-Hispanic/Latino; 4 Hispanic/Latino; 1 Two or more races, non-Hispanic/Latino), 63 international. Average age 27. In 2016, 50 master's, 10 doctorates awarded. Terminal master's awarded for partial completion of doctoral program. *Degree requirements:* For master's, thesis optional; for doctorate, thesis/dissertation. *Entrance requirements:* For master's, minimum GPA of 3.0, BS in engineering or science; for doctorate, minimum GPA of 3.5, MS in engineering or science. Additional exam requirements/recommendations for international students: Required—TOEFL. *Application deadline:* For fall admission, 8/21 for domestic students. Applications are processed on a rolling basis. Application fee: $50. Electronic applications accepted. *Expenses: Tuition:* Full-time $32,184; part-time $1192 per credit hour. *Required fees:* $280. Tuition and fees vary according to campus/location and program. *Financial support:* Research assistantships, teaching assistantships, and unspecified assistantships available. Financial award application deadline: 2/1. *Faculty research:* Composites, dynamic systems and control, combustion and fuels, biomechanics, mechanics and thermal fluid sciences. *Total annual research expenditures:* $3.7 million. *Unit head:* Dr. Mun Young Choi, Head, 215-895-2284, Fax: 215-895-1478, E-mail: mem@drexel.edu. *Application contact:* Director of Graduate Admissions, 215-895-6700, Fax: 215-895-5939, E-mail: enroll@drexel.edu.

Duke University, Graduate School, Pratt School of Engineering, Department of Mechanical Engineering and Materials Science, Durham, NC 27708. Offers materials science (MS, PhD); mechanical engineering (MS, PhD); JD/MS. Terminal master's awarded for partial completion of doctoral program. *Degree requirements:* For master's, thesis optional; for doctorate, thesis/dissertation. *Entrance requirements:* For master's and doctorate, GRE General Test. Additional exam requirements/recommendations for international students: Required—TOEFL (minimum score 90 iBT), IELTS (minimum score 7). Electronic applications accepted.

Duke University, Graduate School, Pratt School of Engineering, Master of Engineering Program, Durham, NC 27708-0271. Offers biomedical engineering (M Eng); civil engineering (M Eng); electrical and computer engineering (M Eng); environmental engineering (M Eng); materials science and engineering (M Eng); mechanical engineering (M Eng); photonics and optical sciences (M Eng). *Program availability:* Part-time. *Entrance requirements:* For master's, GRE General Test, resume, 3 letters of recommendation, statement of purpose, transcripts. Additional exam requirements/recommendations for international students: Required—TOEFL.

École Polytechnique de Montréal, Graduate Programs, Department of Mechanical Engineering, Montréal, QC H3C 3A7, Canada. Offers aerothermics (M Eng, M Sc A, PhD); applied mechanics (M Eng, M Sc A, PhD); tool design (M Eng, M Sc A, PhD). *Program availability:* Part-time, evening/weekend. *Degree requirements:* For master's, one foreign language, thesis; for doctorate, one foreign language, thesis/dissertation. *Entrance requirements:* For master's, minimum GPA of 2.75; for doctorate, minimum GPA of 3.0. *Faculty research:* Noise control and vibration, fatigue and creep, aerodynamics, composite materials, biomechanics, robotics.

Embry-Riddle Aeronautical University–Daytona, Department of Mechanical Engineering, Daytona Beach, FL 32114-3900. Offers high performance vehicles (MSME); mechanical engineering (PhD); mechanical systems (MSME). *Program availability:* Part-time. *Faculty:* 10 full-time (4 women). *Students:* 47 full-time (6 women), 14 part-time (4 women); includes 11 minority (3 Black or African American, non-Hispanic/Latino; 1 Asian, non-Hispanic/Latino; 1 Hispanic/Latino; 6 Two or more races, non-Hispanic/Latino), 26 international. Average age 26. 53 applicants, 43% accepted, 14 enrolled. In 2016, 19 master's awarded. *Degree requirements:* For master's, thesis optional; for doctorate, comprehensive exam, thesis/dissertation. *Entrance requirements:* For doctorate, GRE. Additional exam requirements/recommendations for international students: Required—TOEFL (minimum score 550 paper-based, 79 iBT) or IELTS (6). *Application deadline:* For fall admission, 3/1 priority date for domestic students; for spring admission, 11/1 priority date for domestic students; for summer admission, 4/1 priority date for domestic students. Applications are processed on a rolling basis. Application fee: $50. Electronic applications accepted. *Expenses: Tuition:* Full-time $16,296; part-time $1358 per credit hour. *Required fees:* $1294; $647 per

semester. One-time fee: $100 full-time. Tuition and fees vary according to course load, degree level and program. *Financial support:* Research assistantships, teaching assistantships, career-related internships or fieldwork, scholarships/grants, unspecified assistantships, and on-campus employment available. Financial award application deadline: 3/15; financial award applicants required to submit FAFSA. *Unit head:* Charles Reinholtz, PhD, Professor and Department Chair, 386-323-8848, E-mail: charles.reinholtz@erau.edu. *Application contact:* Graduate Admissions, 386-226-6176, Fax: 386-226-7070, E-mail: graduate.admissions@erau.edu.
Website: https://daytonabeach.erau.edu/college-engineering/mechanical/index.html

Fairfield University, School of Engineering, Fairfield, CT 06824. Offers database management (CAS); electrical and computer engineering (MS); information security (CAS); management of technology (MS); mechanical engineering (MS); network technology (CAS); software engineering (MS); Web application development (CAS). *Program availability:* Part-time, evening/weekend. *Faculty:* 7 full-time (1 woman), 15 part-time/adjunct (2 women). *Students:* 104 full-time (31 women), 56 part-time (15 women); includes 17 minority (8 Black or African American, non-Hispanic/Latino; 5 Asian, non-Hispanic/Latino; 4 Hispanic/Latino), 108 international. Average age 28. 193 applicants, 63% accepted, 20 enrolled. In 2016, 173 master's awarded. *Degree requirements:* For master's, capstone course. *Entrance requirements:* For master's, resume, 2 recommendations. Additional exam requirements/recommendations for international students: Required—TOEFL (minimum score 550 paper-based; 80 iBT) or IELTS (minimum score 6.5). *Application deadline:* For fall admission, 5/15 for international students; for spring admission, 10/15 for international students. Applications are processed on a rolling basis. Application fee: $60. Electronic applications accepted. *Expenses:* $800 per credit hour. *Financial support:* In 2016–17, 27 students received support. Scholarships/grants and unspecified assistantships available. Financial award applicants required to submit FAFSA. *Faculty research:* Artificial intelligence and information visualization, natural language processing, thermofluids, microwaves and electromagnetics, micro-/nano-manufacturing. *Unit head:* Dr. Bruce Berdanier, Dean, 203-254-4147, Fax: 203-254-4013, E-mail: bberdanier@fairfield.edu. *Application contact:* Marianne Gumpper, Director of Graduate and Continuing Studies Admission, 203-254-4184, Fax: 203-254-4073, E-mail: gradadmis@fairfield.edu.
Website: http://www.fairfield.edu/soe

Florida Agricultural and Mechanical University, Division of Graduate Studies, Research, and Continuing Education, FAMU-FSU College of Engineering, Department of Mechanical Engineering, Tallahassee, FL 32307-3200. Offers MS, PhD. *Degree requirements:* For master's, thesis optional; for doctorate, comprehensive exam, thesis/dissertation. *Entrance requirements:* For master's, GRE General Test, minimum GPA of 3.0. Additional exam requirements/recommendations for international students: Required—TOEFL (minimum score 550 paper-based). *Faculty research:* Fluid mechanical and heat transfer, thermodynamics, dynamics and controls, mechanics and materials.

Florida Atlantic University, College of Engineering and Computer Science, Department of Ocean and Mechanical Engineering, Boca Raton, FL 33431-0991. Offers mechanical engineering (MS, PhD). *Program availability:* Part-time, evening/weekend. *Faculty:* 25 full-time (1 woman), 1 part-time/adjunct (0 women). *Students:* 66 full-time (11 women), 50 part-time (5 women); includes 20 minority (1 Black or African American, non-Hispanic/Latino; 6 Asian, non-Hispanic/Latino; 12 Hispanic/Latino; 1 Two or more races, non-Hispanic/Latino), 51 international. Average age 29. 110 applicants, 65% accepted, 51 enrolled. In 2016, 23 master's, 7 doctorates awarded. Terminal master's awarded for partial completion of doctoral program. *Degree requirements:* For master's, thesis (for some programs); for doctorate, comprehensive exam, thesis/dissertation, qualifying exam. *Entrance requirements:* For master's and doctorate, GRE General Test, minimum GPA of 3.0. Additional exam requirements/recommendations for international students: Required—TOEFL (minimum score 500 paper-based; 61 iBT), IELTS (minimum score 6). *Application deadline:* For fall admission, 7/1 priority date for domestic students, 2/15 for international students; for spring admission, 11/1 for domestic students, 7/15 for international students. Applications are processed on a rolling basis. Application fee: $30. *Expenses:* Tuition, state resident: full-time $7392; part-time $369.82 per credit hour. Tuition, nonresident: full-time $19,432; part-time $1024.81 per credit hour. *Financial support:* Research assistantships, career-related internships or fieldwork, Federal Work-Study, scholarships/grants, and unspecified assistantships available. Financial award application deadline: 1/10; financial award applicants required to submit FAFSA. *Faculty research:* Marine materials and corrosion, ocean structures, marine vehicles, acoustics and vibrations, hydrodynamics, coastal engineering. *Unit head:* Javad Hashemi, Chair, 561-297-3438, E-mail: jhashemi@fau.edu.
Website: http://www.ome.fau.edu/

Florida Institute of Technology, College of Engineering, Program in Mechanical Engineering, Melbourne, FL 32901-6975. Offers MS, PhD. *Program availability:* Part-time. *Students:* 64 full-time (7 women), 27 part-time (3 women); includes 10 minority (1 Black or African American, non-Hispanic/Latino; 3 Asian, non-Hispanic/Latino; 5 Hispanic/Latino; 1 Two or more races, non-Hispanic/Latino), 56 international. Average age 27. 380 applicants, 40% accepted, 33 enrolled. In 2016, 28 master's, 1 doctorate awarded. Terminal master's awarded for partial completion of doctoral program. *Degree requirements:* For master's, thesis, 30 credit hours; for doctorate, comprehensive exam, thesis/dissertation. *Entrance requirements:* For master's, GRE General Test, bachelor's degree from an ABET-accredited program, transcripts; for doctorate, GRE General Test, 3 letters of recommendation, minimum GPA of 3.5, resume, statement of objectives, 18 credit hours at Florida Tech. Additional exam requirements/recommendations for international students: Required—TOEFL (minimum score 550 paper-based; 79 iBT). *Application deadline:* For fall admission, 4/1 for international students; for spring admission, 9/30 for international students. Applications are processed on a rolling basis. Application fee: $0. Electronic applications accepted. *Expenses:* *Tuition:* Full-time $22,338; part-time $1241 per credit hour. *Required fees:* $250. Tuition and fees vary according to degree level, campus/location and program. *Financial support:* Career-related internships or fieldwork, institutionally sponsored loans, tuition waivers (partial), unspecified assistantships, and tuition remissions available. Support available to part-time students. Financial award application deadline: 3/1; financial award applicants required to submit FAFSA. *Faculty research:* Dynamic systems, robotics, and controls; structures, solid mechanics, and materials; thermal-fluid sciences, optical tomography, composite/recycled materials. *Unit head:* Dr. Hamid Hefazi, Department Head, 321-674-7255, Fax: 321-674-8813, E-mail: hhefazi@fit.edu. *Application contact:* Cheryl A. Brown, Associate Director of Graduate Admissions, 321-674-7581, Fax: 321-723-9468, E-mail: cbrown@fit.edu.
Website: http://coe.fit.edu/mae/

Florida Institute of Technology, Extended Studies Division, Melbourne, FL 32901-6975. Offers acquisition and contract management (MS); aerospace engineering (MS); business administration (MBA, DBA); computer information systems (MS); computer science (MS); electrical engineering (MS); engineering management (MS); human resources management (MS); logistics management (MS), including humanitarian and disaster relief logistics; management (MS), including acquisition and contract management, e-business, human resources management, information systems, logistics management, management, transportation management; material acquisition management (MS); mechanical engineering (MS); operations research (MS); project management (MS), including information systems, operations research; public administration (MPA); quality management (MS); software engineering (MS); space systems (MS); space systems management (MS); supply chain management (MS); systems management (MS), including information systems, operations research; technology management (MS). *Program availability:* Part-time, evening/weekend, online learning. *Faculty:* 10 full-time (3 women), 122 part-time/adjunct (29 women). *Students:* 131 full-time (58 women), 997 part-time (348 women); includes 389 minority (231 Black or African American, non-Hispanic/Latino; 9 American Indian or Alaska Native, non-Hispanic/Latino; 26 Asian, non-Hispanic/Latino; 99 Hispanic/Latino; 3 Native Hawaiian or other Pacific Islander, non-Hispanic/Latino; 21 Two or more races, non-Hispanic/Latino), 53 international. Average age 36. 962 applicants, 48% accepted, 323 enrolled. In 2016, 403 master's awarded. *Degree requirements:* For master's, comprehensive exam (for some programs). *Entrance requirements:* For master's, GMAT or resume showing 8 years of supervised experience, minimum GPA of 3.0, 2 letters of recommendation, resume. Additional exam requirements/recommendations for international students: Required—TOEFL (minimum score 550 paper-based; 79 iBT). *Application deadline:* For fall admission, 4/1 for international students; for spring admission, 9/30 for international students. Applications are processed on a rolling basis. Electronic applications accepted. *Expenses:* Contact institution. *Financial support:* Application deadline: 3/1; applicants required to submit FAFSA. *Unit head:* Dr. Theodore R. Richardson, III, Dean, 321-674-8123, Fax: 321-674-7597, E-mail: trichardson@fit.edu. *Application contact:* Carolyn Farrior, Director of Graduate Admissions, Online Learning and Off-Campus Programs, 321-674-7118, Fax: 321-674-8216, E-mail: cfarrior@fit.edu.
Website: http://es.fit.edu

Florida International University, College of Engineering and Computing, Department of Mechanical and Materials Engineering, Miami, FL 33199. Offers materials science and engineering (MS, PhD); mechanical engineering (MS, PhD). *Program availability:* Part-time, evening/weekend. *Faculty:* 17 full-time (2 women), 6 part-time/adjunct (0 women). *Students:* 54 full-time (14 women), 27 part-time (3 women); includes 23 minority (5 Black or African American, non-Hispanic/Latino; 17 Hispanic/Latino; 1 Two or more races, non-Hispanic/Latino), 49 international. Average age 30. 105 applicants, 49% accepted, 12 enrolled. In 2016, 16 master's, 7 doctorates awarded. Terminal master's awarded for partial completion of doctoral program. *Degree requirements:* For master's, thesis or alternative; for doctorate, comprehensive exam, thesis/dissertation. *Entrance requirements:* For master's, GRE (depending on program), 3 letters of recommendation, minimum undergraduate GPA of 3.0 in upper-level course work; for doctorate, GRE (minimum combined score of 1150, verbal 450, quantitative 650), minimum undergraduate GPA of 3.0 in upper-level coursework with BS, 3.3 with MS; 3 letters of recommendation; letter of intent. Additional exam requirements/recommendations for international students: Required—TOEFL (minimum score 550 paper-based; 80 iBT) or IELTS (minimum score 6.5). *Application deadline:* For fall admission, 6/1 for domestic students, 4/1 for international students; for spring admission, 10/1 for domestic students, 9/1 for international students. Applications are processed on a rolling basis. Application fee: $30. Electronic applications accepted. *Expenses:* Tuition, state resident: full-time $8912; part-time $446 per credit hour. Tuition, nonresident: full-time $21,393; part-time $992 per credit hour. *Required fees:* $2185; $195 per semester. Tuition and fees vary according to program. *Financial support:* Institutionally sponsored loans, scholarships/grants, and unspecified assistantships available. Financial award application deadline: 3/1; financial award applicants required to submit FAFSA. *Faculty research:* Mechanics and materials, fluid/thermal/energy, design and manufacturing, materials science engineering. *Unit head:* Dr. Ibrahim Tansel, Chair, 305-348-3304, Fax: 305-348-6007, E-mail: tanseli@fiu.edu. *Application contact:* Sara-Michelle Lemus, Engineering Admissions Officer, 305-348-7442, Fax: 305-348-7441, E-mail: grad_eng@fiu.edu.
Website: http://cec.fiu.edu

Florida State University, The Graduate School, FAMU-FSU College of Engineering, Department of Mechanical Engineering, Tallahassee, FL 32310-6046. Offers mechanical engineering (MS, PhD); sustainable energy (MS). *Program availability:* Part-time. *Faculty:* 26 full-time (3 women), 4 part-time/adjunct (1 woman). *Students:* 79 full-time (8 women); includes 16 minority (7 Black or African American, non-Hispanic/Latino; 1 American Indian or Alaska Native, non-Hispanic/Latino; 1 Asian, non-Hispanic/Latino; 3 Hispanic/Latino; 4 Two or more races, non-Hispanic/Latino), 25 international. Average age 25. 115 applicants, 46% accepted, 23 enrolled. In 2016, 19 master's, 6 doctorates awarded. Terminal master's awarded for partial completion of doctoral program. *Degree requirements:* For master's, thesis optional, 30 credit hours (24 coursework, 6 research); for doctorate, thesis/dissertation, 45 credit hours (21 coursework, 24 research). *Entrance requirements:* For master's and doctorate, GRE General Test (minimum scores: Verbal 150, Quantitative 155), minimum GPA of 3.0, official transcripts, resume, personal statement, 3 letters of recommendation. Additional exam requirements/recommendations for international students: Required—TOEFL (minimum score 550 paper-based; 80 iBT), IELTS (minimum score 6.5), Michigan English Language Assessment Battery (minimum score 77). *Application deadline:* For fall admission, 4/1 for domestic and international students; for spring admission, 11/1 for domestic and international students. Applications are processed on a rolling basis. Application fee: $30. Electronic applications accepted. *Expenses:* Tuition, state resident: full-time $7263; part-time $403.51 per credit hour. Tuition, nonresident: full-time $18,087; part-time $1004.85 per credit hour. *Required fees:* $1365; $75.81 per credit hour. $20 per semester. Tuition and fees vary according to campus/location. *Financial support:* In 2016–17, 3 fellowships with full tuition reimbursements, 45 research assistantships with full tuition reimbursements, 23 teaching assistantships with full tuition reimbursements (averaging $4,364 per year) were awarded; career-related internships or fieldwork, institutionally sponsored loans, scholarships/grants, health care benefits, tuition waivers (full), and unspecified assistantships also available. Support available to part-time students. Financial award application deadline: 3/1; financial award applicants required to submit FAFSA. *Faculty research:* Aero-propulsion, superconductivity, smart materials, nanomaterials, intelligent robotic systems, robotic locomotion, sustainable energy. *Total annual research expenditures:* $8.5 million. *Unit head:* Dr. Emmanuel Collins, Chair, 850-410-6373, Fax: 850-410-6337, E-mail: ecollins@eng.famu.fsu.edu. *Application contact:* Chase Pedersen, Coordinator of Graduate Studies, 850-410-6196, Fax: 850-410-6337, E-mail: cvpedersen@fsu.edu.
Website: http://www.eng.famu.fsu.edu/me/

Gannon University, School of Graduate Studies, College of Engineering and Business, School of Engineering and Computer Science, Program in Mechanical Engineering, Erie, PA 16541-0001. Offers MSME. *Program availability:* Part-time, evening/weekend. *Students:* 110 full-time (9 women), 35 part-time (2 women), 134 international. Average age 25. 242 applicants, 67% accepted, 11 enrolled. In 2016, 40 master's awarded. *Degree requirements:* For master's, comprehensive exam, thesis (for some programs), oral exam (for some programs), design project (for some programs). *Entrance requirements:* For master's, bachelor's degree in mechanical engineering from an ABET-accredited program or its equivalent with minimum GPA of 2.5, transcript, 3 letters of recommendation. Additional exam requirements/recommendations for international students: Required—TOEFL (minimum score 79 iBT). *Application deadline:* Applications are processed on a rolling basis. Application fee: $25. Electronic applications accepted. Application fee is waived when completed online. *Expenses: Tuition:* Full-time $17,370. *Required fees:* $550. Tuition and fees vary according to course load and program. *Financial support:* Federal Work-Study available. Financial award application deadline: 7/1; financial award applicants required to submit FAFSA. *Unit head:* Dr. Mahesh Aggarwal, Chair, 814-871-7629, E-mail: aggarwal001@gannon.edu. *Application contact:* Bridget Philip, Director of Graduate Admissions, 814-871-7412, E-mail: graduate@gannon.edu.

The George Washington University, School of Engineering and Applied Science, Department of Mechanical and Aerospace Engineering, Washington, DC 20052. Offers MS, PhD, App Sc, Engr, Graduate Certificate. *Program availability:* Part-time, evening/weekend. *Faculty:* 22 full-time (4 women). *Students:* 81 full-time (11 women), 71 part-time (10 women); includes 13 minority (2 Black or African American, non-Hispanic/Latino; 4 Asian, non-Hispanic/Latino; 3 Hispanic/Latino; 1 Native Hawaiian or other Pacific Islander, non-Hispanic/Latino; 3 Two or more races, non-Hispanic/Latino), 103 international. Average age 28. 248 applicants, 77% accepted, 42 enrolled. In 2016, 28 master's, 10 doctorates awarded. *Degree requirements:* For master's, thesis optional; for doctorate, thesis/dissertation, final and qualifying exams. *Entrance requirements:* For master's, appropriate bachelor's degree, minimum GPA of 3.0; for doctorate, GRE (if highest earned degree is BS), appropriate bachelor's or master's degree, minimum GPA of 3.4; for other advanced degree, appropriate master's degree, minimum GPA of 3.0. Additional exam requirements/recommendations for international students: Required—TOEFL or The George Washington University English as a Foreign Language Test. *Application deadline:* For fall admission, 3/1 priority date for domestic students; for spring admission, 10/1 for domestic students. Applications are processed on a rolling basis. Application fee: $75. *Financial support:* In 2016–17, 51 students received support. Fellowships with tuition reimbursements available, research assistantships, teaching assistantships with tuition reimbursements available, career-related internships or fieldwork, and institutionally sponsored loans available. Financial award application deadline: 3/1; financial award applicants required to submit FAFSA. *Unit head:* Dr. Michael Plesniak, Chair, 202-994-9800, E-mail: maeng@gwu.edu. *Application contact:* Adina Lav, Marketing, Recruiting and Admissions, 202-994-5827, Fax: 202-994-0909, E-mail: engineering@gwu.edu.

Georgia Institute of Technology, Graduate Studies, College of Engineering, George W. Woodruff School of Mechanical Engineering, Program in Mechanical Engineering, Atlanta, GA 30332-0001. Offers MS, MSME, MSMP, MSNE, PhD. *Program availability:* Part-time, online learning. Terminal master's awarded for partial completion of doctoral program. *Degree requirements:* For master's, thesis; for doctorate, comprehensive exam, thesis/dissertation. *Entrance requirements:* For master's and doctorate, GRE General Test, minimum GPA of 3.3. Additional exam requirements/recommendations for international students: Required—TOEFL (minimum score 580 paper-based; 94 iBT). Electronic applications accepted. *Faculty research:* Automation and mechatronics; computer-aided engineering and design; micro-electronic mechanical systems; heat transfer, combustion and energy systems; fluid mechanics.

Georgia Southern University, Jack N. Averitt College of Graduate Studies, Allen E. Paulson College of Engineering and Information Technology, Department of Mechanical Engineering, Program in Engineering/Mechatronics, Statesboro, GA 30458. Offers MSAE. *Students:* 10 full-time (0 women), 1 part-time (0 women); includes 2 minority (both Black or African American, non-Hispanic/Latino), 3 international. Average age 25. 10 applicants, 80% accepted, 5 enrolled. In 2016, 5 master's awarded. *Degree requirements:* For master's, thesis optional. *Entrance requirements:* Additional exam requirements/recommendations for international students: Required—TOEFL (minimum score 80 iBT). *Application deadline:* For fall admission, 3/1 priority date for domestic students; for spring admission, 11/1 priority date for domestic students. *Expenses:* Tuition, state resident: full-time $7236; part-time $277 per semester hour. Tuition, nonresident: full-time $27,118; part-time $1105 per semester hour. *Required fees:* $2092. *Financial support:* In 2016–17, 1 student received support. Unspecified assistantships available. *Faculty research:* Biomechatronics, electromagnetics, smart antennas, wireless communication systems and networks, wireless sensor and actuator networks. *Unit head:* Dr. Frank Goforth, Chair, 912-478-7583, Fax: 912-478-1455, E-mail: fgoforth@georgiasouthern.edu.

The Graduate Center, City University of New York, Graduate Studies, Program in Engineering, New York, NY 10016-4039. Offers biomedical engineering (PhD); chemical engineering (PhD); civil engineering (PhD); electrical engineering (PhD); mechanical engineering (PhD). *Degree requirements:* For doctorate, thesis/dissertation. *Entrance requirements:* For doctorate, GRE General Test. Additional exam requirements/recommendations for international students: Required—TOEFL. Electronic applications accepted.

Grand Valley State University, Padnos College of Engineering and Computing, School of Engineering, Allendale, MI 49401-9403. Offers electrical and computer engineering (MSE); manufacturing operations (MSE); mechanical engineering (MSE); product design and manufacturing engineering (MSE). *Program availability:* Part-time, evening/weekend. *Faculty:* 16 full-time (3 women). *Students:* 29 full-time (8 women), 38 part-time (5 women); includes 5 minority (2 Black or African American, non-Hispanic/Latino; 1 Asian, non-Hispanic/Latino; 2 Hispanic/Latino), 37 international. Average age 26. 129 applicants, 58% accepted, 23 enrolled. In 2016, 24 master's awarded. *Degree requirements:* For master's, project or thesis. *Entrance requirements:* For master's, engineering degree, minimum GPA of 3.0, resume, 3 confidential letters of recommendation, 1-2 page essay, base of underlying relevant knowledge/evidence from academic records or relevant wok experience. Additional exam requirements/recommendations for international students: Required—TOEFL (minimum score 80 iBT) or IELTS (6.5). *Application deadline:* Applications are processed on a rolling basis. Application fee: $30. Electronic applications accepted. *Expenses:* $661 per credit hour. *Financial support:* In 2016–17, 32 students received support, including 8 fellowships; career-related internships or fieldwork, Federal Work-Study, institutionally sponsored loans, scholarships/grants, and unspecified assistantships also available. *Faculty research:* Digital signal processing, computer aided design, computer aided manufacturing, manufacturing simulation, biomechanics, product design. *Total annual research expenditures:* $300,000. *Unit head:* Dr. Wael Mokhtar, Director, 616-331-6015, Fax: 616-331-7215, E-mail: mokhtarw@gvsu.edu. *Application contact:* Dr. Shabbir Choudhuri, Graduate Program Director, 616-331-6845, Fax: 616-331-7215, E-mail: choudhus@gvsu.edu.
Website: http://www.engineer.gvsu.edu/

Harvard University, Graduate School of Arts and Sciences, Harvard John A. Paulson School of Engineering and Applied Sciences, Cambridge, MA 02138. Offers applied mathematics (PhD); applied physics (PhD); computational science and engineering (ME, SM); computer science (PhD); design engineering (MDE); engineering science (ME), including electrical engineering (ME, SM, PhD); engineering sciences (SM, PhD), including bioengineering (PhD), electrical engineering (ME, SM, PhD), environmental science and engineering (PhD), materials science and mechanical engineering (PhD). MDE offered in collaboration with Graduate School of Design. *Program availability:* Part-time. *Faculty:* 80 full-time (13 women), 47 part-time/adjunct (10 women). *Students:* 459 full-time (135 women), 19 part-time (7 women); includes 79 minority (2 Black or African American, non-Hispanic/Latino; 49 Asian, non-Hispanic/Latino; 15 Hispanic/Latino; 1 Native Hawaiian or other Pacific Islander, non-Hispanic/Latino; 12 Two or more races, non-Hispanic/Latino), 233 international. Average age 27. 2,486 applicants, 11% accepted, 126 enrolled. In 2016, 37 master's, 48 doctorates awarded. Terminal master's awarded for partial completion of doctoral program. *Degree requirements:* For master's, thesis (for ME); for doctorate, comprehensive exam, thesis/dissertation. *Entrance requirements:* For master's and doctorate, GRE General Test, GRE Subject Test (recommended), 3 letters of recommendation. Additional exam requirements/recommendations for international students: Required—TOEFL (minimum score 80 iBT). *Application deadline:* For fall admission, 12/15 priority date for domestic and international students. Application fee: $105. Electronic applications accepted. *Expenses:* $43,296 full-time tuition, $3,718 fees. *Financial support:* In 2016–17, 394 students received support, including 86 fellowships with full tuition reimbursements available (averaging $26,424 per year), 258 research assistantships with tuition reimbursements available (averaging $35,232 per year), 106 teaching assistantships with tuition reimbursements available (averaging $6,313 per year); health care benefits also available. *Faculty research:* Applied mathematics, applied physics, computer science and electrical engineering, environmental engineering, mechanical and biomedical engineering. *Total annual research expenditures:* $50.1 million. *Unit head:* Francis J. Doyle, III, Dean, 617-495-5829, Fax: 617-495-5264, E-mail: dean@seas.harvard.edu. *Application contact:* Office of Admissions and Financial Aid, 617-495-5315, E-mail: admissions@seas.harvard.edu.
Website: http://www.seas.harvard.edu/

Howard University, College of Engineering, Architecture, and Computer Sciences, School of Engineering and Computer Science, Department of Mechanical Engineering, Washington, DC 20059-0002. Offers M Eng, PhD. *Degree requirements:* For master's, comprehensive exam, thesis; for doctorate, one foreign language, comprehensive exam, thesis/dissertation, 2 terms of residency. *Entrance requirements:* For master's and doctorate, GRE General Test, minimum GPA of 3.0. Additional exam requirements/recommendations for international students: Required—TOEFL. Electronic applications accepted. *Faculty research:* The dynamics and control of large flexible space structures, optimization of space structures.

Idaho State University, Office of Graduate Studies, College of Science and Engineering, Mechanical Engineering Department, Pocatello, ID 83209-8060. Offers measurement and control engineering (MS); mechanical engineering (MS). *Program availability:* Part-time. *Degree requirements:* For master's, comprehensive exam (for some programs), 2 semesters of seminar; thesis or project. *Entrance requirements:* For master's, GRE. Additional exam requirements/recommendations for international students: Required—TOEFL (minimum score 550 paper-based; 80 iBT). Electronic applications accepted. *Faculty research:* Modeling and identification of biomedical systems, intelligent systems and adaptive control, active flow control of turbo machinery, validation of advanced computational codes for thermal fluid interactions, development of methodologies for the assessment of passive safety system performance in advanced reactors, alternative energy research (wind, solar, hydrogen).

Illinois Institute of Technology, Graduate College, Armour College of Engineering, Department of Mechanical, Materials and Aerospace Engineering, Chicago, IL 60616. Offers manufacturing engineering (MAS, MS); materials science and engineering (MAS, MS, PhD); mechanical and aerospace engineering (MAS, MS, PhD), including economics (MS), energy (MS), environment (MS). *Program availability:* Part-time, evening/weekend, online learning. Terminal master's awarded for partial completion of doctoral program. *Degree requirements:* For master's, comprehensive exam (for some programs), thesis (for some programs); for doctorate, comprehensive exam, thesis/dissertation. *Entrance requirements:* For master's and doctorate, GRE General Test (minimum score 1000 Quantitative and Verbal, 3.0 Analytical Writing), minimum undergraduate GPA of 3.0. Additional exam requirements/recommendations for international students: Required—TOEFL (minimum score 550 paper-based; 80 iBT). Electronic applications accepted. *Faculty research:* Fluid dynamics, metallurgical and materials engineering, solids and structures, computational mechanics, computer added design and manufacturing, thermal sciences, dynamic analysis and control of complex systems.

Indiana University–Purdue University Fort Wayne, College of Engineering, Technology, and Computer Science, Department of Civil and Mechanical Engineering, Fort Wayne, IN 46805-1499. Offers civil engineering (MSE); mechanical engineering (MSE). *Program availability:* Part-time. *Entrance requirements:* For master's, minimum GPA of 3.0, bachelor's degree in engineering discipline. Additional exam requirements/recommendations for international students: Required—TOEFL (minimum score 550 paper-based; 79 iBT); Recommended—TWE. Electronic applications accepted. *Faculty research:* Continuous space language model, sensor networks, wireless cloud architecture.

Indiana University–Purdue University Indianapolis, School of Engineering and Technology, Department of Mechanical Engineering, Indianapolis, IN 46202. Offers engineering (MSE); mechanical engineering (MSME, PhD). *Program availability:* Part-time. *Faculty:* 17 full-time (2 women), 13 part-time/adjunct. *Students:* 109 full-time (9 women), 74 part-time (9 women); includes 11 minority (3 Black or African American, non-Hispanic/Latino; 4 Asian, non-Hispanic/Latino; 3 Hispanic/Latino; 1 Two or more races, non-Hispanic/Latino), 140 international. Average age 26. 164 applicants, 72% accepted, 67 enrolled. In 2016, 44 master's awarded. *Degree requirements:* For master's, thesis optional; for doctorate, thesis/dissertation. *Entrance requirements:* For master's, GRE, minimum GPA of 3.0, three recommendation letters, statement of purpose/intent; for doctorate, GRE, minimum GPA of 3.0, three recommendation letters, statement of purpose/intent, curriculum vitae. Additional exam requirements/recommendations for international students: Required—TOEFL (minimum score 550 paper-based; 79 iBT); Recommended—IELTS (minimum score 6.5), TSE (minimum score 58). *Application deadline:* For fall admission, 7/1 for domestic students. Application fee: $55 ($65 for international students). Electronic applications accepted. *Expenses:* $382 resident tuition per credit hour; $1,100 non-resident tuition per credit hour; $215-370 per term mandatory fees. *Financial support:* In 2016–17, 45 students received support, including 2 fellowships with full tuition reimbursements available (averaging $17,250 per year), 30 research assistantships with full tuition reimbursements available (averaging $13,000 per year); teaching assistantships, scholarships/grants, tuition waivers (full and partial), and unspecified assistantships also available. Financial award application deadline: 1/1. *Faculty research:* Computational fluid dynamics and finite element methods; heat transfer; composites and materials; biomechanics; and mechatronics. *Total annual research expenditures:* $1.4 million. *Unit head:* Dr. Jie Chen, Chair, Department of Mechanical Engineering, 317-274-9720, E-mail: jchen3@iupui.edu. *Application contact:* Valerie Lim Diemer, Director, Graduate Programs and Admissions, 317-278-4961, E-mail: etinfo@iupui.edu.
Website: http://www.engr.iupui.edu/departments/me/

Instituto Tecnológico y de Estudios Superiores de Monterrey, Campus Chihuahua, Graduate Programs, Chihuahua, Mexico. Offers computer systems engineering (Ingeniero); electrical engineering (Ingeniero); electromechanical engineering (Ingeniero); electronic engineering (Ingeniero); engineering administration (MEA); industrial engineering (MIE, Ingeniero); international trade (MIT); mechanical engineering (Ingeniero).

Instituto Tecnológico y de Estudios Superiores de Monterrey, Campus Monterrey, Graduate and Research Division, Programs in Engineering, Monterrey, Mexico. Offers applied statistics (M Eng); artificial intelligence (PhD); automation engineering (M Eng); chemical engineering (M Eng); civil engineering (M Eng); electrical engineering (M Eng); electronic engineering (M Eng); environmental engineering (M Eng); industrial engineering (M Eng, PhD); manufacturing engineering (M Eng); mechanical engineering (M Eng); systems and quality engineering (M Eng). M Eng program offered jointly with University of Waterloo; PhD in industrial engineering with Texas A&M University. *Program availability:* Part-time, evening/weekend. Terminal master's awarded for partial completion of doctoral program. *Degree requirements:* For master's, one foreign language, thesis; for doctorate, one foreign language, thesis/dissertation. *Entrance requirements:* For master's, EXADEP; for doctorate, GRE, master's degree in related field. Additional exam requirements/recommendations for international students: Required—TOEFL. *Faculty research:* Flexible manufacturing cells, materials, statistical methods, environmental prevention, control and evaluation.

Inter American University of Puerto Rico, Bayamón Campus, Graduate School, Bayamón, PR 00957. Offers biology (MS), including environmental sciences and ecology, molecular biotechnology; electrical engineering (ME), including control system, potence system; human resources (MBA); mechanical engineering (ME, MS), including aerospace, energy. *Program availability:* Part-time, evening/weekend. *Faculty:* 12 full-time (5 women), 4 part-time/adjunct (2 women). *Students:* 7 full-time (5 women), 115 part-time (69 women); includes 119 minority (1 Black or African American, non-Hispanic/Latino; 118 Hispanic/Latino). Average age 28. 94 applicants, 72% accepted, 56 enrolled. In 2016, 22 master's awarded. *Degree requirements:* For master's, comprehensive exam, research project. *Entrance requirements:* For master's, EXADEP, GRE General Test, letters of recommendation. *Application deadline:* For fall admission, 7/1 for domestic students, 5/1 priority date for international students; for winter admission, 11/15 priority date for domestic and international students; for spring admission, 2/15 priority date for domestic and international students. Application fee: $31. *Expenses: Tuition:* Part-time $207 per credit. *Required fees:* $328 per semester. *Unit head:* Prof. Juan F. Martinez, Chancellor, 787-279-1200 Ext. 2295, Fax: 787-279-2205, E-mail: jmartinez@bayamon.inter.edu. *Application contact:* Aurelis Baez, Director of Student Services, 787-279-1912 Ext. 2017, Fax: 787-279-2205, E-mail: abaez@bayamon.inter.edu.

Iowa State University of Science and Technology, Department of Mechanical Engineering, Ames, IA 50011. Offers mechanical engineering (M Eng, MS, PhD); systems engineering (M Eng). *Degree requirements:* For master's, thesis or alternative; for doctorate, thesis/dissertation. *Entrance requirements:* For master's and doctorate, GRE General Test, resume. Additional exam requirements/recommendations for international students: Required—TOEFL (minimum score 570 paper-based; 79 iBT), IELTS (minimum score 6.5). *Application deadline:* For fall admission, 1/10 priority date for domestic and international students; for spring admission, 8/10 priority date for domestic and international students. Application fee: $60 ($90 for international students). Electronic applications accepted. *Application contact:* Hallie Golay, Application Contact, 515-294-0838, Fax: 515-294-6960, E-mail: megradinfo@iastate.edu.
Website: http://www.me.iastate.edu/graduate-program/

Johns Hopkins University, Engineering Program for Professionals, Part-time Program in Mechanical Engineering, Baltimore, MD 21218. Offers MME, Post Master's Certificate. *Program availability:* Part-time, evening/weekend, 100% online, blended/hybrid learning. *Faculty:* 1 full-time (0 women), 8 part-time/adjunct (0 women). *Students:* 102 part-time (23 women); includes 8 minority (1 Black or African American, non-Hispanic/Latino; 1 Asian, non-Hispanic/Latino; 6 Hispanic/Latino). Average age 26. 68 applicants, 69% accepted, 29 enrolled. In 2016, 23 master's awarded. *Entrance requirements:* Additional exam requirements/recommendations for international students: Required—TOEFL (minimum score 600 paper-based; 100 iBT). *Application deadline:* Applications are processed on a rolling basis. Application fee: $0. Electronic applications accepted. *Unit head:* Dr. Gregory Chirikjian, Program Chair, 410-516-7127, E-mail: gchirik1@jhu.edu. *Application contact:* Doug Schiller, Admissions Director, 410-516-2300, Fax: 410-579-8049, E-mail: schiller@jhu.edu.

Johns Hopkins University, G. W. C. Whiting School of Engineering, Department of Mechanical Engineering, Baltimore, MD 21218-2681. Offers MSE, PhD. *Faculty:* 34 full-time (6 women), 9 part-time/adjunct (1 woman). *Students:* 129 full-time (18 women), 10 part-time (1 woman); includes 14 minority (1 Black or African American, non-Hispanic/Latino; 8 Asian, non-Hispanic/Latino; 4 Hispanic/Latino; 1 Two or more races, non-Hispanic/Latino), 85 international. Average age 25. 471 applicants, 24% accepted, 38 enrolled. In 2016, 41 master's, 12 doctorates awarded. Terminal master's awarded for partial completion of doctoral program. *Degree requirements:* For master's, thesis optional; for doctorate, comprehensive exam, thesis/dissertation, oral exam. *Entrance requirements:* For master's and doctorate, GRE General Test, 3 letters of recommendation, statement of purpose, transcripts. Additional exam requirements/recommendations for international students: Required—TOEFL (minimum score 600 paper-based, 100 iBT) or IELTS (7). *Application deadline:* For fall admission, 12/15 priority date for domestic and international students; for spring admission, 10/15 priority date for domestic and international students. Application fee: $25. Electronic applications accepted. *Financial support:* In 2016–17, 90 students received support, including 15 fellowships with full tuition reimbursements available (averaging $30,600 per year), 75 research assistantships with full tuition reimbursements available (averaging $30,600 per year); Federal Work-Study, institutionally sponsored loans, scholarships/grants, health care benefits, tuition waivers (partial), and unspecified assistantships also available. Support available to part-time students. Financial award application deadline: 12/15. *Faculty research:* Mechanical engineering in biology and medicine; energy and the environment; fluid mechanics and heat transfer; mechanics and materials; micro/nanoscale science and technology; systems, controls, and modeling; robotics. *Total annual research expenditures:* $16.6 million. *Unit head:* Dr. Louis Whitcomb, Chair, 410-516-6451, Fax: 410-516-7254, E-mail: llw@jhu.edu. *Application contact:* Mike Bernard, Academic Program Manager, 410-516-7154, Fax: 410-516-7254, E-mail: megrad@jhu.edu.
Website: http://www.me.jhu.edu/

Johns Hopkins University, G. W. C. Whiting School of Engineering, Master of Science in Engineering Management Program, Baltimore, MD 21218. Offers biomaterials (MSEM); civil engineering (MSEM); communications science (MSEM); computer science (MSEM); environmental systems analysis, economics and public policy (MSEM); fluid mechanics (MSEM); materials science and engineering (MSEM); mechanical engineering (MSEM); mechanics and materials (MSEM); nanobiotechnology (MSEM); nanomaterials and nanotechnology (MSEM); operations research (MSEM); probability and statistics (MSEM); smart product and device design (MSEM). *Faculty:* 7 full-time (4 women), 1 part-time/adjunct (0 women). *Students:* 35 full-time (14 women), 8 part-time (3 women); includes 7 minority (4 Asian, non-Hispanic/Latino; 3 Hispanic/Latino), 26 international. Average age 24. 228 applicants, 28% accepted, 25 enrolled. In 2016, 18 master's awarded. *Entrance requirements:* For master's, GRE, 3 letters of recommendation, statement of purpose, transcripts. Additional exam requirements/recommendations for international students: Required—TOEFL (minimum score 600 paper-based, 100 iBT) or IELTS (7). *Application deadline:* For fall admission, 2/1 for domestic and international students. Application fee: $75. Electronic applications accepted. *Financial support:* Fellowships and health care benefits available. *Unit head:* Dr. Pamela Sheff, Director, 410-516-7056, Fax: 410-516-4880, E-mail: pamsheff@gmail.com. *Application contact:* Richard Helman, Director of Graduate Admissions, 410-516-8174, Fax: 410-516-0780, E-mail: graduateadmissions@jhu.edu.
Website: http://engineering.jhu.edu/msem/

Kansas State University, Graduate School, College of Engineering, Department of Mechanical and Nuclear Engineering, Manhattan, KS 66506. Offers mechanical engineering (MS); nuclear engineering (PhD). *Faculty:* 22 full-time (3 women). *Students:* 59 full-time (11 women), 12 part-time (2 women); includes 6 minority (1 Black or African American, non-Hispanic/Latino; 2 Asian, non-Hispanic/Latino; 3 Hispanic/Latino), 34 international. Average age 27. 106 applicants, 25% accepted, 21 enrolled. In 2016, 6 master's, 3 doctorates awarded. *Degree requirements:* For master's, thesis optional; for doctorate, comprehensive exam, thesis/dissertation. *Entrance requirements:* For master's, GRE General Test; for doctorate, GRE General Test, master's degree in mechanical engineering; minimum GPA of 3.0 overall or last 60 hours in calculus-based engineering or related program. Additional exam requirements/recommendations for international students: Required—TOEFL (minimum score 550 paper-based; 79 iBT). *Application deadline:* For fall and spring admission, 12/1 priority date for domestic and international students. Applications are processed on a rolling basis. Application fee: $50 ($75 for international students). Electronic applications accepted. *Expenses:* Tuition, state resident: full-time $9670. Tuition, nonresident: full-time $21,828. *Required fees:* $862. *Financial support:* In 2016–17, 20 research assistantships (averaging $22,700 per year), 17 teaching assistantships with full and partial tuition reimbursements (averaging $21,000 per year) were awarded; career-related internships or fieldwork, institutionally sponsored loans, and scholarships/grants also available. Support available to part-time students. Financial award application deadline: 3/1; financial award applicants required to submit FAFSA. *Faculty research:* Radiation detection and protection, heat and mass transfer, machine design, control systems, nuclear reactor physics and engineering. *Total annual research expenditures:* $1.5 million. *Unit head:* Dr. William Dunn, Head, 785-532-5610, Fax: 785-532-7057, E-mail: dunn@k-state.edu. *Application contact:* Dr. Steve Eckels, Graduate Program Director, 785-532-5610, Fax: 785-532-7057, E-mail: eckels@k-state.edu.
Website: http://www.mne.k-state.edu/

Kettering University, Graduate School, Mechanical Engineering Department, Flint, MI 48504. Offers engineering (MS). *Program availability:* Part-time, evening/weekend, online learning. *Degree requirements:* For master's, thesis optional. *Entrance requirements:* Additional exam requirements/recommendations for international students: Required—TOEFL (minimum score 550 paper-based; 79 iBT). Electronic applications accepted. *Faculty research:* Occupant protection crash safety, biomechanics, alternative energy systems, advanced auto powertrain.

Lamar University, College of Graduate Studies, College of Engineering, Department of Mechanical Engineering, Beaumont, TX 77710. Offers ME, MES, DE. *Program availability:* Part-time. *Faculty:* 10 full-time (1 woman). *Students:* 77 full-time (5 women), 36 part-time (2 women); includes 3 minority (2 Asian, non-Hispanic/Latino; 1 Hispanic/Latino), 106 international. Average age 25. 120 applicants, 78% accepted, 26 enrolled. In 2016, 70 master's, 1 doctorate awarded. Terminal master's awarded for partial completion of doctoral program. *Degree requirements:* For master's, comprehensive exam (for some programs), thesis (for some programs); for doctorate, thesis/dissertation. *Entrance requirements:* For master's and doctorate, GRE General Test. Additional exam requirements/recommendations for international students: Required—TOEFL (minimum score 550 paper-based; 79 iBT), IELTS (minimum score 6.5). *Application deadline:* For fall admission, 8/1 for domestic students, 7/1 for international students; for spring admission, 1/5 for domestic students, 12/1 for international students. Applications are processed on a rolling basis. Application fee: $25 ($50 for international students). Electronic applications accepted. *Expenses:* $8,134 in-state full-time, $5,574 in-state part-time; $15,604 out-of-state full-time, $10,554 out-of-state part-time per year. *Financial support:* Fellowships, research assistantships, teaching assistantships, and tuition waivers (partial) available. Financial award application deadline: 4/1; financial award applicants required to submit FAFSA. *Faculty research:* Materials combustion, mechanical and multiphysics study in micro-electronics, structural instability/reliability, mechanics of micro electronics. *Unit head:* Dr. Hsing-Wei Chu, Chair, 409-880-8094, Fax: 409-880-8121. *Application contact:* Deidre Mayer, Interim Director, Admissions and Academic Services, 409-880-8888, Fax: 409-880-7419, E-mail: gradmissions@lamar.edu.
Website: http://engineering.lamar.edu/mechanical

Lawrence Technological University, College of Engineering, Southfield, MI 48075-1058. Offers architectural engineering (MS); automotive engineering (MS); biomedical engineering (MS); civil engineering (MA, MS, PhD), including environmental engineering (MS), geotechnical engineering (MS), structural engineering (MS), transportation engineering (MS), water resource engineering (MS); construction engineering management (MA); electrical and computer engineering (MS); engineering management (MA); engineering technology (MS); fire engineering (MS); industrial engineering (MS), including healthcare; manufacturing systems (ME); mechanical engineering (MS, DE, PhD), including manufacturing (DE), solid mechanics (MS), thermal-fluids (MS); mechatronic systems engineering (MS). *Program availability:* Part-time, evening/weekend. *Faculty:* 24 full-time (5 women), 26 part-time/adjunct (2 women). *Students:* 22 full-time (7 women), 588 part-time (81 women); includes 23 minority (11 Black or African American, non-Hispanic/Latino; 4 Asian, non-Hispanic/Latino; 7 Hispanic/Latino; 1 Two or more races, non-Hispanic/Latino), 469 international. Average age 27. 1,186 applicants, 39% accepted, 99 enrolled. In 2016, 293 master's, 3 doctorates awarded. Terminal master's awarded for partial completion of doctoral program. *Degree requirements:* For master's, thesis optional; for doctorate, comprehensive exam, thesis/dissertation optional. *Entrance requirements:* Additional exam requirements/recommendations for international students: Required—TOEFL (minimum score 550 paper-based; 79 iBT), IELTS (minimum score 6.5). *Application deadline:* For fall admission, 5/22 for international students; for spring admission, 10/11 for international students; for summer admission, 2/16 for international students. Applications are processed on a rolling basis. Application fee: $50. Electronic applications accepted. *Expenses: Tuition:* Full-time $14,868; part-time $1062 per credit. *Required fees:* $75 per semester. Tuition and fees vary according to campus/location. *Financial support:* In 2016–17, 25 students received support, including 5 research assistantships with full tuition reimbursements available; unspecified assistantships also available. Financial award application deadline: 4/1; financial award applicants required to submit FAFSA. *Faculty research:* Carbon fiber reinforced polymer reinforced concrete structures; low impact storm water management solutions; vehicle battery energy management; wireless communication; entrepreneurial mindset and engineering. *Total annual research expenditures:* $1.7 million. *Unit head:* Dr. Nabil Grace, Dean, 248-204-2500, Fax: 248-204-2509, E-mail: engrdean@ltu.edu. *Application contact:* Jane Rohrback,

Director of Admissions, 248-204-3160, Fax: 248-204-2228, E-mail: admissions@ltu.edu. Website: http://www.ltu.edu/engineering/index.asp

Lehigh University, P.C. Rossin College of Engineering and Applied Science, Department of Mechanical Engineering and Mechanics, Bethlehem, PA 18015. Offers computational and engineering mechanics (MS, PhD); mechanical engineering (M Eng, MS, PhD); MBA/E. *Program availability:* Part-time, 100% online, blended/hybrid learning. *Faculty:* 26 full-time (2 women), 2 part-time/adjunct (1 woman). *Students:* 143 full-time (18 women), 27 part-time (3 women); includes 9 minority (2 Black or African American, non-Hispanic/Latino; 2 Asian, non-Hispanic/Latino; 4 Hispanic/Latino; 1 Native Hawaiian or other Pacific Islander, non-Hispanic/Latino), 100 international. Average age 26. 256 applicants, 35% accepted, 27 enrolled. In 2016, 50 master's, 15 doctorates awarded. Terminal master's awarded for partial completion of doctoral program. *Degree requirements:* For master's, thesis (for MS); for doctorate, thesis/dissertation, general exam. *Entrance requirements:* Additional exam requirements/recommendations for international students: Required—TOEFL (minimum score 550 paper-based; 79 iBT), IELTS (minimum score 6.5), GRE (recommended). *Application deadline:* For fall admission, 7/15 for domestic and international students; for spring admission, 12/1 for domestic and international students. Application fee: $75. Electronic applications accepted. *Expenses:* $1,420 per credit. *Financial support:* In 2016–17, 68 students received support, including 5 fellowships with full tuition reimbursements available (averaging $28,140 per year), 61 research assistantships with full tuition reimbursements available (averaging $25,200 per year), 13 teaching assistantships with full tuition reimbursements available (averaging $28,707 per year); dean's doctoral assistantship also available. Financial award application deadline: 1/15. *Faculty research:* Thermofluids, dynamic systems, CAD/CAM, computational mechanics, solid mechanics. *Total annual research expenditures:* $4 million. *Unit head:* Dr. D. Gary Harlow, Chairman, 610-758-4102, Fax: 610-758-6224, E-mail: dgh0@lehigh.edu. *Application contact:* Allison B. Marsteller, Graduate Coordinator, 610-758-4107, Fax: 610-758-6224, E-mail: alm513@lehigh.edu.
Website: http://www.lehigh.edu/~inmem/

Louisiana State University and Agricultural & Mechanical College, Graduate School, College of Engineering, Department of Mechanical and Industrial Engineering, Baton Rouge, LA 70803. Offers MSME, PhD.

Loyola Marymount University, College of Science and Engineering, Department of Mechanical Engineering, Program in Mechanical Engineering, Los Angeles, CA 90045-2659. Offers MSE. *Students:* 12 full-time (2 women), 4 part-time (1 woman); includes 4 minority (2 Black or African American, non-Hispanic/Latino; 2 Hispanic/Latino), 9 international. Average age 25. 9 applicants, 67% accepted, 3 enrolled. In 2016, 9 master's awarded. *Degree requirements:* For master's, thesis or alternative. *Entrance requirements:* For master's, letters of recommendation, personal statement. Additional exam requirements/recommendations for international students: Required—TOEFL (minimum score 550 paper-based; 80 iBT). *Application deadline:* Applications are processed on a rolling basis. Application fee: $50. Electronic applications accepted. *Financial support:* In 2016–17, 10 students received support, including 4 research assistantships; Federal Work-Study, scholarships/grants, and laboratory assistantships also available. Support available to part-time students. Financial award application deadline: 6/30; financial award applicants required to submit FAFSA. *Unit head:* Dr. Michael Manoogian, Chair, 310-338-2827, E-mail: mmanoogi@lmu.edu. *Application contact:* Chake H. Kouyoumjian, Associate Dean of Graduate Studies, 310-338-2721, E-mail: ckouyoum@lmu.edu.
Website: http://cse.lmu.edu/graduateprograms/mechanicalengineeringgraduateprogram/

Manhattan College, Graduate Programs, School of Engineering, Program in Mechanical Engineering, Riverdale, NY 10471. Offers MS. *Program availability:* Part-time, evening/weekend. *Faculty:* 8 full-time (2 women), 2 part-time/adjunct (0 women). *Students:* 29 full-time (5 women), 8 part-time (0 women); includes 4 minority (1 Black or African American, non-Hispanic/Latino; 3 Hispanic/Latino). Average age 24. 31 applicants, 84% accepted, 20 enrolled. In 2016, 24 master's awarded. *Degree requirements:* For master's, thesis optional. *Entrance requirements:* For master's, GRE (recommended), minimum GPA of 3.0. Additional exam requirements/recommendations for international students: Required—TOEFL (minimum score 550 paper-based; 80 iBT), IELTS (minimum score 6). *Application deadline:* For fall admission, 8/10 priority date for domestic students, 8/10 for international students; for spring admission, 1/7 for domestic and international students. Applications are processed on a rolling basis. Application fee: $60. *Financial support:* In 2016–17, 8 students received support, including 10 teaching assistantships with partial tuition reimbursements available (averaging $7,000 per year); career-related internships or fieldwork, Federal Work-Study, scholarships/grants, and unspecified assistantships also available. Support available to part-time students. Financial award application deadline: 2/1. *Faculty research:* Thermal analysis of rocket thrust chambers, quality of wood, biomechanics/structural analysis of cacti, orthodontic research. *Unit head:* Dr. Bahman Litkouhi, Director, Graduate Program, 718-862-7927, Fax: 718-862-7163, E-mail: mechdept@manhattan.edu. *Application contact:* Kathy Balaj, Information Contact, 718-862-7145, Fax: 718-862-7163, E-mail: kathy.balaj@manhattan.edu.
Website: http://manhattan.edu/academics/engineering

Marquette University, Graduate School, College of Engineering, Department of Mechanical Engineering, Milwaukee, WI 53201-1881. Offers engineering innovation (Certificate); engineering management (MSEM); mechanical engineering (MS, PhD); new product and process development (Certificate). *Program availability:* Part-time, evening/weekend. *Faculty:* 17 full-time (0 women), 4 part-time/adjunct (0 women). *Students:* 25 full-time (1 woman), 33 part-time (3 women); includes 7 minority (1 Black or African American, non-Hispanic/Latino; 2 Asian, non-Hispanic/Latino; 3 Hispanic/Latino; 1 Two or more races, non-Hispanic/Latino), 10 international. Average age 27. 51 applicants, 69% accepted, 8 enrolled. In 2016, 12 master's awarded. Terminal master's awarded for partial completion of doctoral program. *Degree requirements:* For master's, comprehensive exam, thesis (for some programs); for doctorate, comprehensive exam, thesis/dissertation, qualifying exam. *Entrance requirements:* For master's, GRE General Test, minimum GPA of 3.0, official transcripts from all current and previous colleges/universities except Marquette, three letters of recommendation; for doctorate, GRE General Test, minimum GPA of 3.0, official transcripts from all current and previous colleges/universities except Marquette, three letters of recommendation, statement of purpose, copies of any published work. Additional exam requirements/recommendations for international students: Required—TOEFL (minimum score 530 paper-based). *Application deadline:* For fall admission, 8/1 priority date for domestic students; for spring admission, 1/1 priority date for domestic students. Applications are processed on a rolling basis. Application fee: $50. Electronic applications accepted. *Financial support:* Fellowships, research assistantships, teaching assistantships, scholarships/grants, tuition waivers (partial), and unspecified assistantships available. Support available to part-time students. Financial award application deadline: 2/15. *Faculty research:* Computer-integrated manufacturing, energy conversion, simulation modeling and optimization, applied mechanics, metallurgy. *Total annual research expenditures:* $620,063. *Unit head:* Dr. Kyuil Kim, Chair, 414-288-7259, Fax: 414-288-7790.

Application contact: Dr. John Borg.
Website: http://www.marquette.edu/engineering/mechanical/grad.shtml

Massachusetts Institute of Technology, School of Engineering, Department of Mechanical Engineering, Cambridge, MA 02139. Offers manufacturing (M Eng); mechanical engineering (SM, PhD, Sc D, Mech E); naval architecture and marine engineering (SM, PhD, Sc D); naval engineering (Naval E); ocean engineering (SM, PhD, Sc D); oceanographic engineering (SM, PhD, Sc D); SM/MBA. *Faculty:* 70 full-time (9 women), 1 part-time/adjunct (0 women). *Students:* 567 full-time (159 women), 1 part-time (0 women); includes 94 minority (6 Black or African American, non-Hispanic/Latino; 1 American Indian or Alaska Native, non-Hispanic/Latino; 41 Asian, non-Hispanic/Latino; 32 Hispanic/Latino; 14 Two or more races, non-Hispanic/Latino), 275 international. Average age 27. 1,345 applicants, 14% accepted, 127 enrolled. In 2016, 123 master's, 65 doctorates, 10 other advanced degrees awarded. Terminal master's awarded for partial completion of doctoral program. *Degree requirements:* For master's, thesis; for doctorate, comprehensive exam, thesis/dissertation; for other advanced degree, comprehensive exam, thesis. *Entrance requirements:* For master's, doctorate, and other advanced degree, GRE General Test. Additional exam requirements/recommendations for international students: Required—TOEFL, IELTS. *Application deadline:* For fall and spring admission, 12/15 for domestic and international students. Application fee: $75. Electronic applications accepted. *Expenses: Tuition:* Full-time $46,400; part-time $725 per credit. One-time fee: $312 full-time. Full-time tuition and fees vary according to course load and program. *Financial support:* In 2016–17, 466 students received support, including fellowships (averaging $36,000 per year), 338 research assistantships (averaging $36,300 per year), 62 teaching assistantships (averaging $39,300 per year); Federal Work-Study, institutionally sponsored loans, scholarships/grants, traineeships, health care benefits, unspecified assistantships, and resident tutors also available. Support available to part-time students. Financial award application deadline: 5/1; financial award applicants required to submit FAFSA. *Faculty research:* Mechanics: modeling, experimentation and computation; design, manufacturing, and product development; controls, instrumentation, and robotics; energy science and engineering; ocean science and engineering; bioengineering; micro- and Nano-engineering. *Total annual research expenditures:* $55.6 million. *Unit head:* Prof. Gang Chen, Department Head, 617-253-2201, Fax: 617-258-6156, E-mail: mehq@mit.edu. *Application contact:* 617-253-2291, E-mail: megradoffice@mit.edu.
Website: http://meche.mit.edu/

McGill University, Faculty of Graduate and Postdoctoral Studies, Faculty of Engineering, Department of Mechanical Engineering, Montréal, QC H3A 2T5, Canada. Offers aerospace (M Eng); manufacturing management (MMM); mechanical engineering (M Eng, M Sc, PhD).

McMaster University, School of Graduate Studies, Faculty of Engineering, Department of Mechanical Engineering, Hamilton, ON L8S 4M2, Canada. Offers M Eng, MA Sc, PhD. M Eng degree offered as part of the Advanced Design and Manufacturing Institute (ADMI) group collaboration with the University of Toronto, University of Western Ontario, and University of Waterloo. *Degree requirements:* For master's, thesis; for doctorate, comprehensive exam, thesis/dissertation. *Entrance requirements:* Additional exam requirements/recommendations for international students: Required—TOEFL (minimum score 550 paper-based). *Faculty research:* Manufacturing engineering, dimensional metrology, micro-fluidics, multi-phase flow and heat transfer, process modeling simulation.

McNeese State University, Doré School of Graduate Studies, College of Engineering and Engineering Technology, Department of Engineering, Master of Engineering Program, Lake Charles, LA 70609. Offers chemical engineering (M Eng); civil engineering (M Eng); electrical engineering (M Eng); engineering management (M Eng); mechanical engineering (M Eng). *Program availability:* Part-time, evening/weekend. *Degree requirements:* For master's, thesis or alternative. *Entrance requirements:* For master's, GRE, baccalaureate degree, minimum overall GPA of 3.0. Additional exam requirements/recommendations for international students: Required—TOEFL (minimum score 560 paper-based; 83 iBT).

McNeese State University, Doré School of Graduate Studies, College of Engineering and Engineering Technology, Department of Engineering, Pump Reliability Engineering Graduate Certificate Program, Lake Charles, LA 70609. Offers Graduate Certificate. *Entrance requirements:* For degree, GRE, engineering bachelor degree. Additional exam requirements/recommendations for international students: Required—TOEFL (minimum score 560 paper-based).

McNeese State University, Doré School of Graduate Studies, College of Engineering and Engineering Technology, Department of Engineering, Pump Reliability Engineering Postbaccalaureate Certificate Program, Lake Charles, LA 70609. Offers Postbaccalaureate Certificate. *Entrance requirements:* For degree, engineering bachelor degree. Additional exam requirements/recommendations for international students: Required—TOEFL (minimum score 560 paper-based).

Memorial University of Newfoundland, School of Graduate Studies, Faculty of Engineering and Applied Science, St. John's, NL A1C 5S7, Canada. Offers civil engineering (M Eng, PhD); electrical and computer engineering (M Eng, PhD); mechanical engineering (M Eng, PhD); ocean and naval architecture engineering (M Eng, PhD). *Program availability:* Part-time. *Degree requirements:* For master's, thesis; for doctorate, comprehensive exam, thesis/dissertation, oral thesis defense. *Entrance requirements:* For master's, 2nd class degree; for doctorate, master's degree in engineering. Electronic applications accepted. *Faculty research:* Engineering analysis, environmental and hydrotechnical studies, manufacturing and robotics, mechanics, structures and materials.

Mercer University, Graduate Studies, Macon Campus, School of Engineering, Macon, GA 31207. Offers biomedical engineering (MSE); computer engineering (MSE); electrical engineering (MSE); engineering management (MSE); environmental engineering (MSE); environmental systems (MS); mechanical engineering (MSE); software engineering (MSE); software systems (MS); technical communications management (MS); technical management (MS). *Program availability:* Part-time-only, evening/weekend, online learning. *Faculty:* 21 full-time (5 women), 1 part-time/adjunct (0 women). *Students:* 44 full-time (9 women), 60 part-time (12 women); includes 14 minority (3 Black or African American, non-Hispanic/Latino; 1 American Indian or Alaska Native, non-Hispanic/Latino; 4 Asian, non-Hispanic/Latino; 3 Hispanic/Latino; 3 Two or more races, non-Hispanic/Latino), 2 international. Average age 27. In 2016, 64 master's awarded. *Degree requirements:* For master's, thesis or alternative. *Entrance requirements:* For master's, GRE (minimum score 300), minimum undergraduate GPA of 3.0. Additional exam requirements/recommendations for international students: Required—TOEFL (minimum score 550 paper-based; 80 iBT). *Application deadline:* For fall admission, 4/1 priority date for domestic and international students; for spring admission, 11/1 priority date for domestic and international students. Applications are processed on a rolling basis. Application fee: $75. *Expenses:* $865 per credit hour. *Financial support:* Applicants required to submit FAFSA. *Faculty research:* Designing prostheses and orthotics, oxygen transfer and limitations in biological systems, low-cost groundwater development, lung airway and transport, autonomous mobile robots. *Unit head:* Dr. Laura W. Lackey, Dean, 478-301-4106, Fax: 478-301-5593, E-mail:

lackey_l@mercer.edu. *Application contact:* Dr. Richard O. Mines, Jr., Program Director, 478-301-2347, Fax: 478-301-5433, E-mail: mines_ro@mercer.edu.
Website: http://engineering.mercer.edu/

Merrimack College, School of Science and Engineering, North Andover, MA 01845-5800. Offers athletic training (MS); civil engineering (MS); community health education (MS); computer science (MS); data science (MS); exercise and sport science (MS); health and wellness management (MS); mechanical engineering (MS), including engineering management. *Program availability:* Part-time, evening/weekend, 100% online. *Faculty:* 16 full-time, 2 part-time/adjunct. *Students:* 88 full-time (32 women), 13 part-time (6 women); includes 6 minority (4 Hispanic/Latino; 2 Two or more races, non-Hispanic/Latino), 39 international. Average age 25. 156 applicants, 67% accepted, 59 enrolled. In 2016, 46 master's awarded. *Degree requirements:* For master's, comprehensive exam, thesis optional, internship or capstone (for some programs). *Entrance requirements:* For master's, official college transcripts, resume, personal statement, 2 recommendations. Additional exam requirements/recommendations for international students: Required—TOEFL (minimum score 84 iBT), IELTS (minimum score 6.5), PTE (minimum score 56). *Application deadline:* For fall admission, 8/14 for domestic students, 7/14 for international students; for spring admission, 1/10 for domestic students, 12/10 for international students; for summer admission, 5/10 for domestic students, 4/10 for international students. Applications are processed on a rolling basis. Application fee: $0. Electronic applications accepted. *Expenses:* Contact institution. *Financial support:* Fellowships with full tuition reimbursements, career-related internships or fieldwork, scholarships/grants, and health care benefits available. Support available to part-time students. Financial award application deadline: 5/1; financial award applicants required to submit FAFSA. *Faculty research:* Viral genomics and evolution (biology), robotics (mechanical engineering), knot theory (mathematics), computer graphics and network security (computer science), water management (civil engineering). *Application contact:* Allison Pena, Graduate Admissions Counselor, 978-837-3563, E-mail: penaa@merrimack.edu.
Website: http://www.merrimack.edu/academics/graduate/

Miami University, College of Engineering and Computing, Department of Mechanical and Manufacturing Engineering, Oxford, OH 45056. Offers MS. *Students:* 12, 4 international. Average age 23. In 2016, 2 master's awarded. *Expenses:* Tuition, state resident: full-time $12,890; part-time $564 per credit hour. Tuition, nonresident: full-time $29,604; part-time $1260 per credit hour. *Required fees:* $638. Part-time tuition and fees vary according to course load and program. *Unit head:* Dr. Tim Cameron, Chair, 513-529-0713, E-mail: tim.cameron@miamioh.edu. *Application contact:* Dr. James Moller, Graduate Program Director, 513-529-0715, E-mail: mollerjc@miamioh.edu.
Website: http://miamioh.edu/cec/academics/departments/mme/

Michigan State University, The Graduate School, College of Engineering, Department of Mechanical Engineering, East Lansing, MI 48824. Offers engineering mechanics (MS, PhD); mechanical engineering (MS, PhD). *Entrance requirements:* For master's, GRE General Test. Additional exam requirements/recommendations for international students: Required—TOEFL. Electronic applications accepted.

Michigan Technological University, Graduate School, College of Engineering, Department of Mechanical Engineering-Engineering Mechanics, Houghton, MI 49931. Offers automotive systems and controls (Graduate Certificate); engineering mechanics (MS); hybrid electric drive vehicle engineering (Graduate Certificate); mechanical engineering (MS); mechanical engineering-engineering mechanics (PhD). *Program availability:* Part-time, evening/weekend, 100% online, blended/hybrid learning. *Faculty:* 84 full-time, 60 part-time/adjunct. *Students:* 300 full-time, 82 part-time; includes 7 minority (3 Asian, non-Hispanic/Latino; 3 Hispanic/Latino; 1 Two or more races, non-Hispanic/Latino), 295 international. Average age 26. 1,544 applicants, 18% accepted, 104 enrolled. In 2016, 102 master's, 11 doctorates, 7 other advanced degrees awarded. Terminal master's awarded for partial completion of doctoral program. *Degree requirements:* For master's, thesis (for some programs); for doctorate, comprehensive exam, thesis/dissertation. *Entrance requirements:* For master's, GRE (Michigan Tech and online students exempt), statement of purpose, personal statement, official transcripts, 2 letters of recommendation, resume/curriculum vitae; for doctorate, GRE (Michigan Tech and online students exempt), MS (preferred), statement of purpose, official transcripts, 2 letters of recommendation, resume/curriculum vitae; for Graduate Certificate, statement of purpose, official transcripts, BS in engineering. Additional exam requirements/recommendations for international students: Required—TOEFL (minimum score 90 iBT) or IELTS (minimum score 7.0). *Application deadline:* For fall admission, 3/1 priority date for domestic and international students; for spring admission, 8/1 priority date for domestic and international students. Applications are processed on a rolling basis. Electronic applications accepted. *Expenses:* Contact institution. *Financial support:* In 2016–17, 247 students received support, including 14 fellowships with tuition reimbursements available (averaging $15,242 per year), 37 research assistantships with tuition reimbursements available (averaging $15,242 per year), 31 teaching assistantships with tuition reimbursements available (averaging $15,242 per year); career-related internships or fieldwork, Federal Work-Study, scholarships/grants, health care benefits, unspecified assistantships, and cooperative program also available. Financial award applicants required to submit FAFSA. *Faculty research:* Mobility and autonomy, complex systems and controls, multi-scale materials and mechanics, thermo-fluids and energy conversion, human-centered engineering. *Total annual research expenditures:* $5.3 million. *Unit head:* Dr. William W. Predebon, Chair, 906-487-2551, Fax: 906-487-2822, E-mail: wwpredeb@mtu.edu. *Application contact:* Julie Foster, Graduate Program Assistant, 906-487-3611, Fax: 906-487-2822, E-mail: jafoster@mtu.edu.
Website: http://www.mtu.edu/mechanical/

Mississippi State University, Bagley College of Engineering, Department of Mechanical Engineering, Mississippi State, MS 39762. Offers mechanical engineering (MS). *Program availability:* Part-time, blended/hybrid learning. *Faculty:* 17 full-time (2 women), 1 part-time/adjunct (0 women). *Students:* 80 full-time (9 women), 33 part-time (4 women); includes 15 minority (6 Black or African American, non-Hispanic/Latino; 4 Asian, non-Hispanic/Latino; 4 Hispanic/Latino; 1 Two or more races, non-Hispanic/Latino), 31 international. Average age 28. 103 applicants, 42% accepted, 21 enrolled. In 2016, 26 master's, 8 doctorates awarded. *Degree requirements:* For master's, thesis optional, oral exam; for doctorate, thesis/dissertation, qualifying exam, preliminary exam, dissertation defense. *Entrance requirements:* For master's, GRE (for graduates from program not accredited by EAC/ABET), minimum GPA of 2.75; for doctorate, GRE, minimum GPA of 2.75. Additional exam requirements/recommendations for international students: Required—TOEFL (minimum score 550 paper-based; 79 iBT); Recommended—IELTS (minimum score 6.5). *Application deadline:* For fall admission, 7/1 for domestic students, 5/1 for international students; for spring admission, 11/1 for domestic students, 9/1 for international students. Applications are processed on a rolling basis. Application fee: $60. Electronic applications accepted. *Expenses:* Tuition, state resident: full-time $7670; part-time $852.50 per credit hour. Tuition, nonresident: full-time $20,790; part-time $2310.50 per credit hour. Part-time tuition and fees vary according to course load. *Financial support:* In 2016–17, 13 research assistantships with full tuition reimbursements (averaging $17,285 per year), 7 teaching assistantships with full tuition reimbursements (averaging $15,531 per year) were awarded; career-related internships or fieldwork, Federal Work-Study, institutionally sponsored loans, scholarships/grants, and unspecified assistantships also available. Financial award application deadline: 4/1; financial award applicants required to submit FAFSA. *Faculty research:* Fatigue and fracture, heat transfer, fluid dynamics, manufacturing systems, materials. *Total annual research expenditures:* $12.2 million. *Unit head:* Dr. Pedro Mago, Professor/Head, 662-325-6602, Fax: 662-325-7223, E-mail: mago@me.msstate.edu. *Application contact:* Doretta Martin, Senior Admissions Assistant, 662-325-9514, E-mail: dmartin@grad.msstate.edu.
Website: http://www.me.msstate.edu/

Missouri University of Science and Technology, Graduate School, Department of Mechanical and Aerospace Engineering, Rolla, MO 65409. Offers aerospace engineering (MS, PhD); mechanical engineering (MS, DE, PhD). *Program availability:* Part-time, evening/weekend. Terminal master's awarded for partial completion of doctoral program. *Degree requirements:* For master's, thesis optional; for doctorate, comprehensive exam, thesis/dissertation. *Entrance requirements:* For master's, GRE General Test (minimum score 1100 verbal and quantitative, writing 3.5), minimum GPA of 3.0; for doctorate, GRE General Test (minimum score: verbal and quantitative 1100, writing 3.5), minimum GPA of 3.5. Additional exam requirements/recommendations for international students: Required—TOEFL (minimum score 550 paper-based). Electronic applications accepted. *Faculty research:* Dynamics and controls, acoustics, computational fluid dynamics, space mechanics, hypersonics.

Montana State University, The Graduate School, College of Engineering, Department of Mechanical and Industrial Engineering, Bozeman, MT 59717. Offers engineering (PhD), including industrial engineering, mechanical engineering; industrial and management engineering (MS); mechanical engineering (MS). *Program availability:* Part-time. *Degree requirements:* For master's, comprehensive exam, thesis, oral exams; for doctorate, comprehensive exam, thesis/dissertation, qualifying exam. *Entrance requirements:* For master's, GRE, official transcript, minimum GPA of 3.0, demonstrated potential for success, statement of goals, three letters of recommendation, proof of funds affidavit; for doctorate, minimum undergraduate GPA of 3.0, 3.2 graduate; three letters of recommendation; statement of objectives. Additional exam requirements/recommendations for international students: Required—TOEFL or IELTS. Electronic applications accepted. *Faculty research:* Human factors engineering, energy, design and manufacture, systems modeling, materials and structures, measurement systems.

Naval Postgraduate School, Departments and Academic Groups, Department of Mechanical and Aerospace Engineering, Monterey, CA 93943. Offers astronautical engineer (AstE); astronautical engineering (MS); engineering science (MS), including astronautical engineering, mechanical engineering; mechanical and aerospace engineering (PhD); mechanical engineering (MS). Program only open to commissioned officers of the United States and friendly nations and selected United States federal civilian employees. *Accreditation:* ABET (one or more programs are accredited). *Program availability:* Part-time, online learning. *Degree requirements:* For master's, thesis (for some programs), capstone or research/dissertation paper (for some programs); for doctorate, thesis/dissertation; for AstE, thesis. *Faculty research:* Sensors and actuators, new materials and methods, mechanics of materials, laser and material interaction, energy harvesting and storage.

Naval Postgraduate School, Departments and Academic Groups, Space Systems Academic Group, Monterey, CA 93943. Offers applied physics (MS); astronautical engineering (MS); computer science (MS); electrical engineering (MS); mechanical engineering (MS); space systems (Engr); space systems operations (MS). Program only open to commissioned officers of the United States and friendly nations and selected United States federal civilian employees. *Program availability:* Part-time. *Degree requirements:* For master's and Engr, thesis; for doctorate, thesis/dissertation. *Faculty research:* Military applications for space; space reconnaissance and remote sensing; radiation-hardened electronics for space; design, construction and operations of small satellites; satellite communications systems.

Naval Postgraduate School, Departments and Academic Groups, Undersea Warfare Academic Group, Monterey, CA 93943. Offers applied mathematics (MS); applied physics (MS); applied science (MS), including acoustics, operations research, physical oceanography, signal processing; electrical engineering (MS); engineering acoustics (MS, PhD); engineering science (MS), including electrical engineering, mechanical engineering; mechanical engineer (ME); mechanical engineering (MS, MSME); meteorology (MS); operations research (MS); physical oceanography (MS). Program only open to commissioned officers of the United States and friendly nations and selected United States federal civilian employees. *Program availability:* Part-time. *Degree requirements:* For master's, thesis. *Faculty research:* Unmanned/autonomous vehicles, sea mines and countermeasures, submarine warfare in the twentieth and twenty-first centuries.

New Jersey Institute of Technology, Newark College of Engineering, Newark, NJ 07102. Offers biomedical engineering (MS, PhD); chemical engineering (MS, PhD); computer engineering (MS, PhD); electrical engineering (MS, PhD); engineering management (MS); environmental engineering (PhD); healthcare systems management (MS); industrial engineering (MS, PhD); Internet engineering (MS); manufacturing engineering (MS); mechanical engineering (MS, PhD); occupational safety and health engineering (MS); pharmaceutical bioprocessing (MS); pharmaceutical engineering (MS); pharmaceutical systems management (MS); power and energy systems (MS); telecommunications (MS); transportation (MS, PhD). *Program availability:* Part-time, evening/weekend. *Faculty:* 146 full-time (21 women), 119 part-time/adjunct (10 women). *Students:* 804 full-time (191 women), 550 part-time (129 women); includes 357 minority (82 Black or African American, non-Hispanic/Latino; 1 American Indian or Alaska Native, non-Hispanic/Latino; 138 Asian, non-Hispanic/Latino; 114 Hispanic/Latino; 22 Two or more races, non-Hispanic/Latino), 675 international. Average age 27. 2,959 applicants, 51% accepted, 442 enrolled. In 2016, 595 master's, 29 doctorates awarded. Terminal master's awarded for partial completion of doctoral program. *Degree requirements:* For master's, thesis optional; for doctorate, thesis/dissertation. *Entrance requirements:* For master's, GRE General Test; for doctorate, GRE General Test, minimum graduate GPA of 3.5. Additional exam requirements/recommendations for international students: Required—TOEFL (minimum score 550 paper-based; 79 iBT). *Application deadline:* For fall admission, 6/1 priority date for domestic students, 5/1 priority date for international students; for spring admission, 11/15 priority date for domestic and international students. Applications are processed on a rolling basis. Application fee: $75. Electronic applications accepted. *Expenses:* Contact institution. *Financial support:* In 2016–17, 172 students received support, including 1 fellowship (averaging $1,528 per year), 79 research assistantships (averaging $13,336 per year), 92 teaching assistantships (averaging $20,619 per year); scholarships/grants also available. Financial award application deadline: 1/15. *Faculty research:* Nonlinear signal processing, intelligent medical image analysis, calibration issues in coherent localization, computer-aided design, neural network for tool wear measurement. *Total annual research expenditures:* $11.1 million. *Unit head:* Dr. Moshe Kam, Dean, 973-596-5534, E-mail: moshe.kam@njit.edu. *Application contact:* Stephen Eck, Director of Admissions, 973-596-3300, Fax: 973-596-3461, E-mail: admissions@njit.edu.
Website: http://engineering.njit.edu/

New Mexico Institute of Mining and Technology, Center for Graduate Studies, Department of Mechanical Engineering, Socorro, NM 87801. Offers explosives engineering (MS); fluid and thermal sciences (MS); mechatronics systems engineering (MS); solid mechanics (MS). *Degree requirements:* For master's, thesis (for some programs). *Entrance requirements:* For master's, GRE General Test. Additional exam requirements/recommendations for international students: Required—TOEFL (minimum score 540 paper-based). *Faculty research:* Vibrations, fluid-structure interactions.

New Mexico State University, College of Engineering, Department of Mechanical Engineering, Las Cruces, NM 88003. Offers aerospace engineering (MSAE); mechanical engineering (MSME, PhD). *Program availability:* Part-time. *Faculty:* 16 full-time (1 woman). *Students:* 28 full-time (3 women), 12 part-time (2 women); includes 8 minority (7 Hispanic/Latino; 1 Two or more races, non-Hispanic/Latino), 24 international. Average age 28. 81 applicants, 35% accepted, 10 enrolled. In 2016, 14 master's, 6 doctorates awarded. *Degree requirements:* For master's, thesis (for some programs); for doctorate, comprehensive exam, thesis/dissertation, qualifying exam. *Entrance requirements:* For master's and doctorate, GRE, minimum GPA of 3.0. Additional exam requirements/recommendations for international students: Required—TOEFL (minimum score 550 paper-based; 79 iBT), IELTS (minimum score 6.5). *Application deadline:* For fall admission, 5/1 priority date for domestic students, 3/1 for international students; for spring admission, 11/1 for domestic students, 10/1 for international students. Applications are processed on a rolling basis. Application fee: $40 ($50 for international students). Electronic applications accepted. *Expenses:* Tuition, state resident: full-time $4086. Tuition, nonresident: full-time $14,254. *Required fees:* $853. Tuition and fees vary according to course load. *Financial support:* In 2016–17, 33 students received support, including 6 research assistantships (averaging $17,233 per year), 20 teaching assistantships (averaging $16,199 per year); career-related internships or fieldwork, Federal Work-Study, scholarships/grants, traineeships, health care benefits, and unspecified assistantships also available. Support available to part-time students. Financial award application deadline: 3/1. *Faculty research:* Combustion and propulsion, gas dynamics and supersonic flows; experimental and fluid dynamics; nonlinear dynamics and control; robotics and mechatronics; renewable/alternative energy; smart structure and energy harvesting; experimental and computational mechanics; multiscale modeling and nanosystem; micromechanics of materials; aeroelasticity and flutter; design optimization; heat transfer and energy efficiency; polymer and composite materials; thermal and thermomechanical storage. *Total annual research expenditures:* $741,093. *Unit head:* Dr. Ruey-Hung Chen, Department Head, 575-646-1945, Fax: 575-646-6111, E-mail: chenrh@nmsu.edu. *Application contact:* Dr. Young Ho Park, Graduate Program Director, 575-646-3092, Fax: 575-646-6111, E-mail: ypark@nmsu.edu.
Website: http://mae.nmsu.edu/

New York University, Polytechnic School of Engineering, Department of Mechanical and Aerospace Engineering, New York, NY 10012-1019. Offers mechanical engineering (MS, PhD). *Program availability:* Part-time, evening/weekend. *Degree requirements:* For master's, comprehensive exam (for some programs), thesis (for some programs); for doctorate, comprehensive exam, thesis/dissertation. *Entrance requirements:* Additional exam requirements/recommendations for international students: Required—TOEFL (minimum score 550 paper-based; 80 iBT); Recommended—IELTS (minimum score 6.5). Electronic applications accepted. *Faculty research:* Underwater applications of dynamical systems, systems science approaches to understanding variation in state traffic and alcohol policies, development of ankle instability rehabilitation robot, synthetic osteochondral grafts for knee osteoarthritis.

North Carolina Agricultural and Technical State University, School of Graduate Studies, College of Engineering, Department of Mechanical Engineering, Greensboro, NC 27411. Offers MSME, PhD. *Program availability:* Part-time. *Degree requirements:* For master's, thesis, qualifying exam, thesis defense; for doctorate, thesis/dissertation. *Entrance requirements:* For master's, BS in mechanical engineering from accredited institution with minimum overall GPA of 3.0; for doctorate, GRE, MS in mechanical engineering or closely-related field with minimum GPA of 3.3. *Faculty research:* Composites, smart materials and sensors, mechanical systems modeling and finite element analysis, computational fluid dynamics and engine research, design and manufacturing.

North Carolina State University, Graduate School, College of Engineering, Department of Mechanical and Aerospace Engineering, Program in Mechanical Engineering, Raleigh, NC 27695. Offers MS, PhD. *Program availability:* Part-time, online learning. *Degree requirements:* For master's, thesis optional, oral exam; for doctorate, thesis/dissertation, oral and preliminary exams. *Entrance requirements:* For master's and doctorate, GRE General Test. Additional exam requirements/recommendations for international students: Required—TOEFL (minimum score 550 paper-based). Electronic applications accepted. *Faculty research:* Vibration and control, fluid dynamics, thermal sciences, structures and materials, aerodynamics acoustics.

North Dakota State University, College of Graduate and Interdisciplinary Studies, College of Engineering, Department of Mechanical Engineering, Fargo, ND 58102. Offers MS, PhD. *Program availability:* Part-time. *Degree requirements:* For master's, thesis; for doctorate, comprehensive exam, thesis/dissertation. *Entrance requirements:* For master's and doctorate, minimum GPA of 3.0. Additional exam requirements/recommendations for international students: Required—TOEFL (minimum score 550 paper-based). Electronic applications accepted. *Faculty research:* Thermodynamics, finite element analysis, automotive systems, robotics, nanotechnology.

Northeastern University, College of Engineering, Boston, MA 02115-5096. Offers bioengineering (MS, PhD); chemical engineering (MS, PhD); civil engineering (MS, PhD); computer engineering (PhD); computer systems engineering (MS); electrical and computer engineering (MS); electrical and computer engineering leadership (MS); electrical engineering (PhD); energy systems (MS); engineering and public policy (MS); engineering management (MS, Certificate); environmental engineering (MS); industrial engineering (MS, PhD); information assurance (PhD); information systems (MS); interdisciplinary engineering (PhD); mechanical engineering (PhD); operations research (MS); telecommunication systems management (MS). *Program availability:* Part-time, online learning. *Faculty:* 202 full-time (59 women), 53 part-time/adjunct (9 women). *Students:* 2,982 full-time (954 women), 192 part-time (38 women). In 2016, 851 master's, 74 doctorates awarded. Application fee: $75. Electronic applications accepted. *Expenses:* $1,471 per credit. *Financial support:* Fellowships, research assistantships, teaching assistantships, career-related internships or fieldwork, scholarships/grants, health care benefits, tuition waivers, and unspecified assistantships available. Support available to part-time students. Financial award applicants required to submit FAFSA. *Unit head:* Dr. Nadine Aubry, Dean, College of Engineering. *Application contact:* Jeffery Hengel, Director of Graduate Admissions, 617-373-2711, E-mail: j.hengel@northeastern.edu.
Website: http://www.coe.neu.edu/academics/graduate-school-engineering

Northern Arizona University, Graduate College, College of Engineering, Forestry, and Natural Sciences, Programs in Engineering, Flagstaff, AZ 86011. Offers civil engineering (M Eng, MSE); computer science (MSE); electrical and computer engineering (M Eng, MSE); engineering (M Eng, MSE); environmental engineering (M Eng, MSE); mechanical engineering (M Eng, MSE). *Program availability:* Part-time, online learning. *Degree requirements:* For master's, thesis. *Entrance requirements:* For master's, GRE General Test. Additional exam requirements/recommendations for international students: Required—TOEFL (minimum score 550 paper-based; 80 iBT), IELTS (minimum score 7). Electronic applications accepted. *Expenses:* Tuition, state resident: full-time $8971; part-time $444 per credit hour. Tuition, nonresident: full-time $20,958; part-time $1164 per credit hour. *Required fees:* $1018; $644 per credit hour. Tuition and fees vary according to course load, campus/location and program.

Northern Illinois University, Graduate School, College of Engineering and Engineering Technology, Department of Mechanical Engineering, De Kalb, IL 60115-2854. Offers MS. *Program availability:* Part-time. *Faculty:* 9 full-time (0 women). *Students:* 50 full-time (6 women), 31 part-time (1 woman); includes 6 minority (2 Black or African American, non-Hispanic/Latino; 2 Asian, non-Hispanic/Latino; 1 Hispanic/Latino; 1 Two or more races, non-Hispanic/Latino), 46 international. Average age 25. 135 applicants, 40% accepted, 19 enrolled. In 2016, 36 master's awarded. *Degree requirements:* For master's, comprehensive exam, thesis optional. *Entrance requirements:* For master's, GRE General Test, minimum GPA of 2.75. Additional exam requirements/recommendations for international students: Required—TOEFL (minimum score 550 paper-based). *Application deadline:* For fall admission, 6/1 for domestic students, 5/1 for international students; for spring admission, 11/1 for domestic students, 10/1 for international students. Applications are processed on a rolling basis. Application fee: $40. Electronic applications accepted. *Financial support:* In 2016–17, 17 research assistantships with full tuition reimbursements, 32 teaching assistantships with full tuition reimbursements were awarded; fellowships with full tuition reimbursements, Federal Work-Study, scholarships/grants, tuition waivers (full), and staff assistantships also available. Support available to part-time students. Financial award applicants required to submit FAFSA. *Faculty research:* Robotics, nonlinear dynamic systems, piezo mechanics, quartz resonators, sheet metal forming. *Unit head:* Dr. Federico Sciammarella, Interim Chair, 815-753-9970, Fax: 815-753-0416, E-mail: sciammarella@niu.edu. *Application contact:* Graduate School Office, 815-753-0395, E-mail: gradsch@niu.edu.
Website: http://www.niu.edu/me/graduate/

Northwestern University, McCormick School of Engineering and Applied Science, Department of Mechanical Engineering, Evanston, IL 60208. Offers MS, PhD. MS and PhD offered through the Graduate School. *Program availability:* Part-time. Terminal master's awarded for partial completion of doctoral program. *Degree requirements:* For master's, thesis optional; for doctorate, comprehensive exam, thesis/dissertation. *Entrance requirements:* For master's and doctorate, GRE General Test. Additional exam requirements/recommendations for international students: Required—TOEFL (minimum score 577 paper-based; 90 iBT), IELTS (minimum score 7). Electronic applications accepted. *Faculty research:* MEMS/nanotechnology, robotics, virtual design and manufacturing, tribology, microfluidics, computational solid and fluid mechanics, composite materials, nondestructive materials characterization and structural reliability, neuromechanics, biomimetics, energy, sustainability, multiscale simulation.

Oakland University, Graduate Study and Lifelong Learning, School of Engineering and Computer Science, Department of Mechanical Engineering, Rochester, MI 48309-4401. Offers MS, PhD. *Program availability:* Part-time, evening/weekend. *Entrance requirements:* For master's, minimum GPA of 3.0. Additional exam requirements/recommendations for international students: Required—TOEFL (minimum score 550 paper-based). Electronic applications accepted. *Expenses:* Contact institution.

The Ohio State University, Graduate School, College of Engineering, Department of Mechanical and Aerospace Engineering, Columbus, OH 43210. Offers aerospace engineering (MS, PhD); mechanical engineering (MS, PhD); nuclear engineering (MS, PhD). *Faculty:* 69. *Students:* 374 full-time (60 women), 12 part-time (1 woman); includes 27 minority (5 Black or African American, non-Hispanic/Latino; 9 Asian, non-Hispanic/Latino; 6 Hispanic/Latino; 7 Two or more races, non-Hispanic/Latino), 194 international. Average age 25. In 2016, 98 master's, 35 doctorates awarded. *Degree requirements:* For doctorate, thesis/dissertation. *Entrance requirements:* For master's and doctorate, GRE. Additional exam requirements/recommendations for international students: Required—TOEFL (minimum score 550 paper-based; 79 iBT), Michigan English Language Assessment Battery (minimum score 82); Recommended—IELTS (minimum score 7). *Application deadline:* For fall admission, 11/30 priority date for domestic and international students; for spring admission, 10/1 for domestic and international students. Applications are processed on a rolling basis. Application fee: $60 ($70 for international students). Electronic applications accepted. *Financial support:* Fellowships, research assistantships, teaching assistantships, career-related internships or fieldwork, Federal Work-Study, institutionally sponsored loans, and unspecified assistantships available. Support available to part-time students. *Unit head:* Dr. Vish Subramaniam, Chair, 614-292-6096, E-mail: subramaniam.1@osu.edu. *Application contact:* Janeen Sands, Graduate Program Administrator, 614-2[illegible]7-6605, Fax: 614-292-3656, E-mail: maegradadmissions@osu.edu.
Website: http://mae.osu.edu/

Ohio University, Graduate College, Russ College of Engineering and Technology, Department of Mechanical Engineering, Athens, OH 45701-2979. Offers biomedical engineering (MS); mechanical engineering (MS), including CAD/CAM, design, energy, manufacturing, materials, robotics, thermofluids. *Program availability:* Part-time. In 2016, 8 master's awarded. *Degree requirements:* For master's, comprehensive exam (for some programs), thesis. *Entrance requirements:* For master's, GRE, BS in engineering or science, minimum GPA of 2.8. Additional exam requirements/recommendations for international students: Required—TOEFL (minimum score 550 paper-based; 80 iBT) or IELTS (minimum score 6.5). *Application deadline:* For fall admission, 2/15 priority date for domestic and international students. Applications are processed on a rolling basis. Application fee: $50 ($55 for international students). Electronic applications accepted. *Financial support:* Research assistantships with tuition reimbursements, teaching assistantships with tuition reimbursements, career-related internships or fieldwork, Federal Work-Study, institutionally sponsored loans, tuition waivers (full and partial), and unspecified assistantships available. Financial award application deadline: 2/15; financial award applicants required to submit FAFSA. *Faculty research:* Biomedical, energy and the environment, materials and manufacturing, bioengineering. *Unit head:* Dr. Greg Kremer, Chairman, 740-593-1561, Fax: 740-593-0476, E-mail: kremer@bobcat.ent.ohiou.edu. *Application contact:* Dr. Frank F. Kraft, Graduate Chairman, 740-597-1478, Fax: 740-593-0476, E-mail: kraft@ohio.edu.
Website: http://www.ohio.edu/mechanical

Oklahoma Christian University, Graduate School of Engineering and Computer Science, Oklahoma City, OK 73136-1100. Offers electrical and computer engineering (MSE); engineering management (MSE); mechanical engineering (MSE); software engineering (MSCS, MSE). *Program availability:* Part-time. *Faculty:* 8 full-time (1 woman), 7 part-time/adjunct (0 women). *Students:* 187 full-time (27 women), 85 part-time (12 women). Average age 25. 255 applicants, 33% accepted, 69 enrolled. In 2016, 188 master's awarded. *Entrance requirements:* Additional exam requirements/recommendations for international students: Required—TOEFL (minimum score 550 paper-based). *Application deadline:* Applications are processed on a rolling basis. Application fee: $25. Electronic applications accepted. *Expenses:* Contact institution.

Unit head: Mary Ann Brown, Director for Graduate School Engineering, 405-425-5579. *Application contact:* Angie Ricketts, Admissions Counselor, 405-425-5587, E-mail: angie.ricketts@oc.edu.
Website: http://www.oc.edu/academics/graduate/engineering/

Oklahoma State University, College of Engineering, Architecture and Technology, School of Mechanical and Aerospace Engineering, Stillwater, OK 74078. Offers mechanical and aerospace engineering (MS, PhD); mechanical engineering (MS, PhD). *Program availability:* Online learning. *Faculty:* 31 full-time (1 woman), 2 part-time/adjunct (1 woman). *Students:* 27 full-time (5 women), 81 part-time (12 women); includes 13 minority (2 Black or African American, non-Hispanic/Latino; 1 American Indian or Alaska Native, non-Hispanic/Latino; 2 Asian, non-Hispanic/Latino; 8 Two or more races, non-Hispanic/Latino), 49 international. Average age 27. 236 applicants, 10% accepted, 20 enrolled. In 2016, 24 master's, 12 doctorates awarded. *Degree requirements:* For master's, thesis or alternative; for doctorate, comprehensive exam, thesis/dissertation. *Entrance requirements:* For master's and doctorate, GRE or GMAT. Additional exam requirements/recommendations for international students: Required—TOEFL (minimum score 550 paper-based; 79 iBT). *Application deadline:* For fall admission, 3/1 priority date for international students; for spring admission, 8/1 priority date for international students. Applications are processed on a rolling basis. Application fee: $40 ($75 for international students). Electronic applications accepted. *Expenses:* Tuition, state resident: full-time $3775; part-time $209.70 per credit hour. Tuition, nonresident: full-time $14,851; part-time $825.05 per credit hour. *Required fees:* $2027; $112.60 per credit hour. Tuition and fees vary according to campus/location. *Financial support:* In 2016–17, 50 research assistantships (averaging $9,022 per year), 60 teaching assistantships (averaging $5,796 per year) were awarded; career-related internships or fieldwork, Federal Work-Study, scholarships/grants, health care benefits, tuition waivers (partial), and unspecified assistantships also available. Support available to part-time students. Financial award application deadline: 3/1; financial award applicants required to submit FAFSA. *Unit head:* Dr. Daniel E. Fisher, Department Head, 405-744-5900, Fax: 405-744-7873, E-mail: maehead@okstate.edu. *Application contact:* Dr. Charlotte Fore, Manager of Graduate Studies and Research Development, 405-744-5900, Fax: 405-744-7873, E-mail: charlotte.fore@okstate.edu.
Website: http://www.mae.okstate.edu

Old Dominion University, Frank Batten College of Engineering and Technology, Program in Mechanical Engineering, Norfolk, VA 23529. Offers ME, MS, D Eng, PhD. *Program availability:* Part-time, evening/weekend, 100% online, blended/hybrid learning. *Faculty:* 22 full-time (2 women). *Students:* 25 full-time (3 women), 46 part-time (3 women); includes 17 minority (5 Black or African American, non-Hispanic/Latino; 3 Asian, non-Hispanic/Latino; 6 Hispanic/Latino; 3 Two or more races, non-Hispanic/Latino), 24 international. Average age 31. 50 applicants, 76% accepted, 7 enrolled. In 2016, 9 master's, 5 doctorates awarded. *Degree requirements:* For master's, comprehensive exam, thesis optional; for doctorate, thesis/dissertation, candidacy exam. *Entrance requirements:* For master's, GRE, minimum GPA of 3.0; for doctorate, GRE, minimum GPA of 3.5. Additional exam requirements/recommendations for international students: Required—TOEFL (minimum score 550 paper-based). *Application deadline:* For fall admission, 6/1 for domestic students, 2/15 priority date for international students; for spring admission, 11/1 for domestic students, 10/1 for international students. Applications are processed on a rolling basis. Application fee: $50. Electronic applications accepted. *Expenses:* $478 per credit, in-state tuition. *Financial support:* In 2016–17, 12 students received support, including 5 fellowships with partial tuition reimbursements available (averaging $16,000 per year), 11 research assistantships with partial tuition reimbursements available (averaging $15,000 per year), 15 teaching assistantships with partial tuition reimbursements available (averaging $6,400 per year); career-related internships or fieldwork, institutionally sponsored loans, scholarships/grants, and unspecified assistantships also available. Financial award application deadline: 2/15; financial award applicants required to submit FAFSA. *Faculty research:* Computational applied mechanics, manufacturing, experimental stress analysis, systems dynamics and control, mechanical design. *Total annual research expenditures:* $1.8 million. *Unit head:* Dr. Sebastian Bawab, Chair, 757-683-5637, Fax: 757-683-5344, E-mail: sbawab@odu.edu. *Application contact:* Dr. Han Bao, Graduate Program Director, 757-683-4922, Fax: 757-683-3200, E-mail: hbao@aero.odu.edu.
Website: http://www.odu.edu/academics/programs/masters/mechanical-engineering

Oregon State University, College of Engineering, Program in Materials Science, Corvallis, OR 97331. Offers chemical engineering (MS, PhD); chemistry (MS, PhD); civil engineering (MS, PhD); electrical and computer engineering (MS, PhD); forest products (MS, PhD); mathematics (MS, PhD); mechanical engineering (MS, PhD); nuclear engineering (MS); physics (MS, PhD). *Faculty:* 52 full-time (12 women), 3 part-time/adjunct (0 women). *Students:* 34 full-time (8 women), 10 part-time (3 women); includes 7 minority (4 Hispanic/Latino; 3 Two or more races, non-Hispanic/Latino), 15 international. Average age 30. 78 applicants, 24% accepted, 10 enrolled. In 2016, 7 master's, 6 doctorates awarded. *Degree requirements:* For master's, thesis or alternative. *Entrance requirements:* For master's and doctorate, GRE. Additional exam requirements/recommendations for international students: Required—TOEFL (minimum score 80 iBT), IELTS (minimum score 6.5). *Application deadline:* For fall admission, 8/1 for domestic students, 4/1 for international students; for winter admission, 12/1 for domestic students, 7/1 for international students; for spring admission, 2/1 for domestic students, 10/1 for international students; for summer admission, 5/1 for domestic students, 1/1 for international students. Application fee: $75 ($85 for international students). *Expenses:* $14,130 resident full-time tuition, $23,769 non-resident. *Financial support:* Fellowships, research assistantships, teaching assistantships, Federal Work-Study, and institutionally sponsored loans available. Support available to part-time students. Financial award application deadline: 1/15. *Unit head:* Dr. Harriet Nembhard, School Head. *Application contact:* Jean Robinson, Advisor, E-mail: jean.robinson@oregonstate.edu.
Website: http://matsci.oregonstate.edu/

Oregon State University, College of Engineering, Program in Mechanical Engineering, Corvallis, OR 97331. Offers M Eng, MS, PhD. *Program availability:* Part-time. *Faculty:* 44 full-time (7 women), 1 part-time/adjunct (0 women). *Students:* 135 full-time (16 women), 11 part-time (0 women); includes 11 minority (1 Black or African American, non-Hispanic/Latino; 2 Asian, non-Hispanic/Latino; 5 Hispanic/Latino; 3 Two or more races, non-Hispanic/Latino), 67 international. Average age 27. 278 applicants, 26% accepted, 36 enrolled. In 2016, 31 master's, 8 doctorates awarded. *Entrance requirements:* For master's and doctorate, GRE. Additional exam requirements/recommendations for international students: Required—TOEFL (minimum score 80 iBT), IELTS (minimum score 6.5). *Application deadline:* For fall admission, 8/1 for domestic students, 4/1 for international students; for winter admission, 12/1 for domestic students, 7/1 for international students; for spring admission, 2/1 for domestic students, 10/1 for international students; for summer admission, 5/1 for domestic students, 1/1 for international students. Application fee: $75 ($85 for international students). *Expenses:* Contact institution. *Financial support:* Application deadline: 1/15. *Unit head:* Dr. David Cann, Professor and Interim School Head. *Application contact:* Jean Robinson, Mechanical Engineering Advisor, 541-737-9191, E-mail: jean.robinson@oregonstate.edu.
Website: http://mime.oregonstate.edu/academics/grad/me

Penn State University Park, Graduate School, College of Engineering, Department of Mechanical and Nuclear Engineering, University Park, PA 16802. Offers mechanical engineering (MS, PhD); nuclear engineering (M Eng, MS, PhD). *Unit head:* Dr. Amr S. Elnashai, Dean, 814-865-7537, Fax: 814-863-4749. *Application contact:* Lori Hawn, Director, Graduate Student Services, 814-865-1795, Fax: 814-863-4627, E-mail: l-gswww@lists.psu.edu.
Website: http://mne.psu.edu/

Pittsburg State University, Graduate School, College of Technology, Department of Engineering Technology, Pittsburg, KS 66762. Offers electrical engineering technology (MET); general engineering technology (MET); manufacturing engineering technology (MET); mechanical engineering technology (MET); plastics engineering technology (MET). *Program availability:* Part-time, 100% online, blended/hybrid learning. *Students:* 59 (9 women); includes 3 minority (2 Black or African American, non-Hispanic/Latino; 1 Asian, non-Hispanic/Latino), 35 international. In 2016, 42 master's awarded. *Degree requirements:* For master's, thesis optional. *Entrance requirements:* Additional exam requirements/recommendations for international students: Required—TOEFL (minimum score 550 paper-based; 79 iBT), IELTS (minimum score 6.5), PTE (minimum score 51). *Application deadline:* For fall admission, 7/15 for domestic students, 6/1 for international students; for spring admission, 12/15 for domestic students, 10/15 for international students; for summer admission, 5/15 for domestic students, 4/1 for international students. Applications are processed on a rolling basis. Application fee: $35 ($60 for international students). Electronic applications accepted. *Expenses:* Contact institution. *Financial support:* In 2016–17, 4 teaching assistantships with full tuition reimbursements (averaging $5,500 per year) were awarded. Financial award application deadline: 2/1; financial award applicants required to submit FAFSA. *Unit head:* Greg Murray, Chairperson, 620-235-4384. *Application contact:* Lisa Allen, Assistant Director of Graduate and Continuing Studies, 620-235-4218, Fax: 620-235-4219, E-mail: lallen@pittstate.edu.
Website: http://www.pittstate.edu/department/engineering-tech/

Polytechnic University of Puerto Rico, Graduate School, Hato Rey, PR 00918. Offers business administration (MBA), including computer information systems, general management, management of information systems, management of international enterprises; civil engineering (ME, MS); computer engineering (ME, MS); computer science (MCS, MS); electrical engineering (ME, MS); engineering management (MEM); environmental management (MEM); landscape architecture (M Land Arch); manufacturing competitiveness (MMC, MS); manufacturing engineering (ME, MS); mechanical engineering (M Mech E). *Program availability:* Part-time, evening/weekend. *Entrance requirements:* For master's, 3 letters of recommendation.

Portland State University, Graduate Studies, College of Liberal Arts and Sciences, Systems Science Program, Portland, OR 97207-0751. Offers computational intelligence (Certificate); computer modeling and simulation (Certificate); systems science (MS); systems science/anthropology (PhD); systems science/business administration (PhD); systems science/civil engineering (PhD); systems science/economics (PhD); systems science/engineering management (PhD); systems science/general (PhD); systems science/mathematical sciences (PhD); systems science/mechanical engineering (PhD); systems science/psychology (PhD); systems science/sociology (PhD). *Faculty:* 2 full-time (0 women), 3 part-time/adjunct (1 woman). *Students:* 12 full-time (3 women), 21 part-time (5 women); includes 5 minority (1 Black or African American, non-Hispanic/Latino; 2 Hispanic/Latino; 2 Two or more races, non-Hispanic/Latino). Average age 39. 16 applicants, 69% accepted, 9 enrolled. In 2016, 4 master's, 6 doctorates awarded. *Degree requirements:* For master's, comprehensive exam (for some programs), thesis optional; for doctorate, variable foreign language requirement, comprehensive exam (for some programs), thesis/dissertation. *Entrance requirements:* For master's, GRE/GMAT (recommended), minimum GPA of 3.0 undergraduate or graduate work, 2 letters of recommendation, statement of interest; for doctorate, GMAT, GRE General Test, minimum GPA of 3.0 undergraduate, 3.25 graduate; 2 letters of recommendation; statement of interest. Additional exam requirements/recommendations for international students: Required—TOEFL (minimum score 550 paper-based; 80 iBT). *Application deadline:* For fall admission, 1/15 for domestic and international students; for spring admission, 11/1 for domestic students. Application fee: $65. Electronic applications accepted. *Expenses:* Contact institution. *Financial support:* In 2016–17, 2 research assistantships with tuition reimbursements (averaging $7,830 per year) were awarded; teaching assistantships, career-related internships or fieldwork, Federal Work-Study, scholarships/grants, and unspecified assistantships also available. Support available to part-time students. Financial award application deadline: 3/1; financial award applicants required to submit FAFSA. *Faculty research:* Systems theory and methodology, artificial intelligence neural networks, information theory, nonlinear dynamics/chaos, modeling and simulation. *Unit head:* Dr. Wayne Wakeland, Chair, 503-725-4975, E-mail: wakeland@pdx.edu.
Website: http://www.pdx.edu/sysc/

Portland State University, Graduate Studies, Maseeh College of Engineering and Computer Science, Department of Mechanical Engineering, Portland, OR 97207-0751. Offers M Eng, MS, PhD. *Program availability:* Part-time, evening/weekend. *Faculty:* 19 full-time (2 women), 11 part-time/adjunct (3 women). *Students:* 39 full-time (9 women), 38 part-time (5 women); includes 15 minority (2 Black or African American, non-Hispanic/Latino; 9 Asian, non-Hispanic/Latino; 1 Hispanic/Latino; 3 Two or more races, non-Hispanic/Latino), 16 international. Average age 30. 65 applicants, 63% accepted, 24 enrolled. In 2016, 21 master's, 1 doctorate awarded. *Degree requirements:* For master's, thesis or alternative; for doctorate, one foreign language, thesis/dissertation, oral and written exams. *Entrance requirements:* For master's, minimum GPA of 3.0 in upper-division course work, BS in mechanical engineering or allied field, 3 letters of recommendation; for doctorate, GRE General Test, GRE Subject Test, minimum GPA of 3.0 in upper-division course work, 3 letters of recommendation. Additional exam requirements/recommendations for international students: Required—TOEFL (minimum score 550 paper-based; 80 iBT). *Application deadline:* For fall admission, 1/15 priority date for domestic and international students; for winter admission, 9/1 for domestic students, 8/1 for international students; for spring admission, 11/1 for domestic students, 10/1 for international students. Applications are processed on a rolling basis. Application fee: $65. Electronic applications accepted. *Expenses:* Contact institution. *Financial support:* In 2016–17, 12 research assistantships with full tuition reimbursements (averaging $4,273 per year), 21 teaching assistantships with tuition reimbursements (averaging $1,924 per year) were awarded; Federal Work-Study, scholarships/grants, and unspecified assistantships also available. Support available to part-time students. Financial award application deadline: 3/1; financial award applicants required to submit FAFSA. *Faculty research:* Mechanical system modeling, indoor air quality, manufacturing process, computational fluid dynamics, building science. *Total annual research expenditures:* $1.3 million. *Unit head:* Sung Yi, Chair, 503-725-5470, Fax: 503-725-8255, E-mail: syi@pdx.edu. *Application contact:* Tricia Hutchins, Department Manager, 503-725-4291, Fax: 503-725-8255, E-mail: tricia.hutchins@pdx.edu.
Website: http://www.pdx.edu/mme/

Princeton University, Graduate School, School of Engineering and Applied Science, Department of Mechanical and Aerospace Engineering, Princeton, NJ 08544. Offers M Eng, MSE, PhD. Terminal master's awarded for partial completion of doctoral program. *Degree requirements:* For master's, thesis (MSE); for doctorate, thesis/dissertation, general exam. *Entrance requirements:* For master's, GRE General Test, 3 letters of recommendation; for doctorate, GRE General Test, official transcript(s), 3 letters of recommendation, personal statement. Additional exam requirements/recommendations for international students: Required—TOEFL. Electronic applications accepted. *Faculty research:* Bioengineering and bio-mechanics; combustion, energy conversion, and climate; fluid mechanics, dynamics, and control systems; lasers and applied physics; materials and mechanical systems.

Purdue University, College of Engineering, School of Mechanical Engineering, West Lafayette, IN 47907-2088. Offers MS, MSE, MSME, PhD, Certificate. MS and PhD degree programs in biomedical engineering offered jointly with School of Electrical and Computer Engineering and School of Chemical Engineering. *Program availability:* Part-time, online learning. *Faculty:* 113. *Students:* 569. In 2016, 119 master's, 42 doctorates awarded. Terminal master's awarded for partial completion of doctoral program. *Degree requirements:* For master's, thesis optional; for doctorate, thesis/dissertation. *Entrance requirements:* For master's and doctorate, GRE General Test, minimum GPA of 3.2. *Application deadline:* For fall admission, 12/15 for domestic and international students; for spring admission, 11/1 for domestic and international students. Applications are processed on a rolling basis. Application fee: $60 ($75 for international students). Electronic applications accepted. *Financial support:* Fellowships with full and partial tuition reimbursements, research assistantships with full and partial tuition reimbursements, teaching assistantships with full and partial tuition reimbursements, career-related internships or fieldwork, scholarships/grants, health care benefits, and unspecified assistantships available. *Faculty research:* Acoustics, bioengineering, combustion, design, fluid mechanics, heat transfer, manufacturing and materials, mechanics and vibration, nanotechnology, robotics, systems, measurement, and control, thermal systems. *Unit head:* Anil K. Bajaj, Head/Professor. *Application contact:* Julayne Moser, Director of Graduate Programs, E-mail: megradoffice@purdue.edu.
Website: https://engineering.purdue.edu/ME/

Purdue University Northwest, Graduate Studies Office, School of Engineering, Mathematics, and Science, Department of Engineering, Hammond, IN 46323-2094. Offers computer engineering (MSE); electrical engineering (MSE); engineering (MS); mechanical engineering (MSE). *Program availability:* Evening/weekend. *Entrance requirements:* Additional exam requirements/recommendations for international students: Required—TOEFL.

Queen's University at Kingston, School of Graduate Studies, Faculty of Applied Science, Department of Mechanical and Materials Engineering, Kingston, ON K7L 3N6, Canada. Offers M Eng, M Sc, M Sc Eng, PhD. *Program availability:* Part-time. *Degree requirements:* For master's, thesis optional; for doctorate, comprehensive exam, thesis/dissertation. *Entrance requirements:* Additional exam requirements/recommendations for international students: Required—TOEFL. Electronic applications accepted. *Faculty research:* Dynamics and control systems, manufacturing and design, materials and engineering, heat transferring fluid dynamics, energy systems and combustion.

Rensselaer at Hartford, Department of Engineering, Program in Mechanical Engineering, Hartford, CT 06120-2991. Offers ME, MS. *Program availability:* Part-time, evening/weekend. *Degree requirements:* For master's, thesis optional. *Entrance requirements:* For master's, GRE. Additional exam requirements/recommendations for international students: Required—TOEFL (minimum score 600 paper-based; 100 iBT).

Rensselaer Polytechnic Institute, Graduate School, School of Engineering, Program in Mechanical Engineering, Troy, NY 12180-3590. Offers M Eng, MS, D Eng, PhD. *Faculty:* 48 full-time (7 women), 1 part-time/adjunct (0 women). *Students:* 89 full-time (12 women), 64 part-time (10 women). 222 applicants, 36% accepted, 41 enrolled. In 2016, 11 master's, 15 doctorates awarded. *Degree requirements:* For master's, thesis (for some programs); for doctorate, thesis/dissertation. *Entrance requirements:* For master's and doctorate, GRE. Additional exam requirements/recommendations for international students: Required—TOEFL (minimum score 600 paper-based; 100 iBT), IELTS (minimum score 7), PTE (minimum score 68). *Application deadline:* For fall admission, 1/1 priority date for domestic and international students; for spring admission, 8/15 priority date for domestic and international students. Applications are processed on a rolling basis. Application fee: $75. Electronic applications accepted. *Expenses: Tuition:* Full-time $49,520; part-time $2060 per credit hour. *Required fees:* $2617. *Financial support:* In 2016–17, research assistantships (averaging $22,000 per year), teaching assistantships (averaging $22,000 per year) were awarded; fellowships also available. Financial award application deadline: 1/1. *Faculty research:* Advanced nuclear materials; aerodynamics; design; dynamics and vibrations, fission systems and radiation transport; fluid mechanics (computational, theoretical, and experimental); heat transfer and energy conversion; manufacturing, medical imaging and health physics; multiscale/computational modeling; nanostructured materials and properties; nuclear physics/nuclear reactor; propulsion. *Total annual research expenditures:* $7.2 million. *Unit head:* Dr. Theo Borca-Tasciuc, Graduate Program Director, 518-276-2627, E-mail: borcat@rpi.edu. *Application contact:* Office of Graduate Admissions, 518-276-6216, E-mail: gradadmissions@rpi.edu.
Website: http://mane.rpi.edu/

Rice University, Graduate Programs, George R. Brown School of Engineering, Department of Mechanical Engineering and Materials Science, Houston, TX 77251-1892. Offers materials science (MMS, MS, PhD); mechanical engineering (MME, MS, PhD); MBA/ME. *Program availability:* Part-time. Terminal master's awarded for partial completion of doctoral program. *Degree requirements:* For master's, comprehensive exam, thesis; for doctorate, comprehensive exam, thesis/dissertation. *Entrance requirements:* For master's and doctorate, GRE General Test, minimum GPA of 3.0. Additional exam requirements/recommendations for international students: Required—TOEFL (minimum score 600 paper-based; 90 iBT), IELTS (minimum score 7). Electronic applications accepted. *Faculty research:* Heat transfer, biomedical engineering, fluid dynamics, aero-astronautics, control systems/robotics, materials science.

Rochester Institute of Technology, Graduate Enrollment Services, College of Applied Science and Technology, School of Engineering Technology, MS Program in Manufacturing and Mechanical Systems Integration, Rochester, NY 14623. Offers MS. *Program availability:* Part-time, evening/weekend. *Students:* 46 full-time (9 women), 17 part-time (1 woman); includes 2 minority (1 Asian, non-Hispanic/Latino; 1 Two or more races, non-Hispanic/Latino), 52 international. Average age 25. 78 applicants, 88% accepted, 27 enrolled. In 2016, 18 master's awarded. *Degree requirements:* For master's, thesis (for some programs). *Entrance requirements:* For master's, GRE, minimum GPA of 3.0 (recommended). Additional exam requirements/recommendations for international students: Required—TOEFL (minimum score 550 paper-based; 79 iBT), IELTS (minimum score 6.5), PTE (minimum score 58). *Application deadline:* Applications are processed on a rolling basis. Application fee: $60. Electronic applications accepted. *Expenses:* $1,742 per credit hour. *Financial support:* In 2016–17, 44 students received support. Research assistantships with partial tuition reimbursements available, teaching assistantships with partial tuition reimbursements available, career-related internships or fieldwork, scholarships/grants, and unspecified assistantships available. Support available to part-time students. Financial award applicants required to submit FAFSA. *Faculty research:* Advanced manufacturing in electronics/photonics including materials and reliability development; complex rheological fluid spray research and development; system dynamics modeling and control using computer aided engineering; automation (robotics) using cyber-physical systems; the Internet of Things, and cloud computing; applications-focused plastics and polymer composites research. *Unit head:* Dr. James Lee, Program Director, 585-475-2899, E-mail: jhleme@rit.edu. *Application contact:* Diane Ellison, Associate Vice President, Graduate Enrollment Services, 585-475-2229, Fax: 585-475-7164, E-mail: gradinfo@rit.edu.
Website: http://www.rit.edu/cast/mmet/graduate-programs/ms-in-manufacturing-and-mechanical-systems-integration

Rochester Institute of Technology, Graduate Enrollment Services, Kate Gleason College of Engineering, Mechanical Engineering Department, ME Program in Mechanical Engineering, Rochester, NY 14623-5603. Offers ME. *Program availability:* Part-time. *Students:* 97 full-time (10 women), 29 part-time (5 women); includes 7 minority (1 Black or African American, non-Hispanic/Latino; 1 Asian, non-Hispanic/Latino; 4 Hispanic/Latino; 1 Two or more races, non-Hispanic/Latino), 71 international. Average age 24. 229 applicants, 56% accepted, 32 enrolled. In 2016, 59 master's awarded. *Degree requirements:* For master's, thesis or alternative. *Entrance requirements:* For master's, minimum GPA of 3.0 (recommended). Additional exam requirements/recommendations for international students: Required—TOEFL (minimum score 550 paper-based; 79 iBT), IELTS (minimum score 6.5), PTE (minimum score 58). *Application deadline:* For fall admission, 2/15 priority date for domestic and international students; for spring admission, 12/15 priority date for domestic and international students. Applications are processed on a rolling basis. Application fee: $60. Electronic applications accepted. *Expenses:* $1,742 per credit hour. *Financial support:* In 2016–17, 63 students received support. Research assistantships with partial tuition reimbursements available, teaching assistantships with partial tuition reimbursements available, career-related internships or fieldwork, scholarships/grants, and unspecified assistantships available. Support available to part-time students. Financial award applicants required to submit FAFSA. *Faculty research:* Transportation, energy, communications, healthcare, nano-science and engineering, unmanned aircraft systems, biomedical applications. *Unit head:* Dr. Agamemnon Crassidis, Graduate Director, 585-475-5181, E-mail: alceme@rit.edu. *Application contact:* Diane Ellison, Associate Vice President, Graduate Enrollment Services, 585-475-2229, Fax: 585-475-7164, E-mail: gradinfo@rit.edu.
Website: http://www.rit.edu/kgcoe/mechanical/program/graduate-meng/overview

Rochester Institute of Technology, Graduate Enrollment Services, Kate Gleason College of Engineering, Mechanical Engineering Department, MS Program in Mechanical Engineering, Rochester, NY 14623-5603. Offers MS. *Program availability:* Part-time. *Students:* 13 full-time (3 women), 7 part-time (0 women); includes 1 minority (Two or more races, non-Hispanic/Latino), 15 international. Average age 24. 162 applicants, 2% accepted, 2 enrolled. In 2016, 10 master's awarded. *Degree requirements:* For master's, thesis. *Entrance requirements:* For master's, GRE, minimum GPA of 3.0 (recommended). Additional exam requirements/recommendations for international students: Required—TOEFL (minimum score 550 paper-based; 79 iBT), IELTS (minimum score 6.5), PTE (minimum score 58). *Application deadline:* For fall admission, 2/15 priority date for domestic and international students; for spring admission, 12/15 priority date for domestic and international students. Applications are processed on a rolling basis. Application fee: $60. Electronic applications accepted. *Expenses:* $1,742 per credit hour. *Financial support:* In 2016–17, 9 students received support. Research assistantships with partial tuition reimbursements available, teaching assistantships with partial tuition reimbursements available, career-related internships or fieldwork, scholarships/grants, and unspecified assistantships available. Support available to part-time students. Financial award applicants required to submit FAFSA. *Faculty research:* Transportation, energy, communications, healthcare, nano-science and engineering, unmanned aircraft systems, biomedical applications, aerosol mechanics, interface mechanics during rapid evaporation, low SWAP-C inertial navigation systems. *Unit head:* Dr. Agamemnon Crassidis, Graduate Director, 585-475-5181, E-mail: alceme@rit.edu. *Application contact:* Diane Ellison, Associate Vice President, Graduate Enrollment Services, 585-475-2229, Fax: 585-475-7164, E-mail: gradinfo@rit.edu.
Website: http://www.rit.edu/kgcoe/mechanical/program/graduate-ms/overview

Rose-Hulman Institute of Technology, Faculty of Engineering and Applied Sciences, Department of Mechanical Engineering, Terre Haute, IN 47803-3999. Offers M Eng, MS. *Program availability:* Part-time. *Faculty:* 28 full-time (4 women). *Students:* 5 full-time (0 women), 1 part-time (0 women); includes 1 minority (Asian, non-Hispanic/Latino), 4 international. Average age 22. 16 applicants, 63% accepted, 4 enrolled. In 2016, 6 master's awarded. *Degree requirements:* For master's, thesis. *Entrance requirements:* For master's, GRE, minimum GPA of 3.0. Additional exam requirements/recommendations for international students: Required—TOEFL (minimum score 580 paper-based; 92 iBT). *Application deadline:* For fall admission, 2/1 priority date for domestic students. Applications are processed on a rolling basis. Application fee: $0. Electronic applications accepted. *Expenses: Tuition:* Full-time $43,122. *Financial support:* In 2016–17, 5 students received support. Fellowships with tuition reimbursements available, research assistantships with tuition reimbursements available, institutionally sponsored loans, scholarships/grants, and tuition waivers (full and partial) available. *Faculty research:* Finite elements, MEMS, thermodynamics, heat transfer, design methods, noise and vibration analysis. *Total annual research expenditures:* $159,882. *Unit head:* Dr. Lori Olson, Chairman, 812-877-8324, Fax: 812-877-3198, E-mail: olson1@rose-hulman.edu. *Application contact:* Dr. Azad Siahmakoun, Associate Dean of the Faculty, 812-877-8400, Fax: 812-877-8061, E-mail: siahmako@rose-hulman.edu.
Website: http://www.rose-hulman.edu/academics/academic-departments/mechanical-engineering.aspx

Rowan University, Graduate School, College of Engineering, Department of Mechanical Engineering, Glassboro, NJ 08028-1701. Offers MS. Electronic applications accepted.

Royal Military College of Canada, Division of Graduate Studies and Research, Engineering Division, Department of Mechanical Engineering, Kingston, ON K7K 7B4, Canada. Offers M Eng, MA Sc, PhD. *Degree requirements:* For master's, thesis; for doctorate, comprehensive exam, thesis/dissertation. *Entrance requirements:* For master's, honours degree with second-class standing; for doctorate, master's degree. Electronic applications accepted.

Rutgers University–New Brunswick, Graduate School-New Brunswick, Program in Mechanical and Aerospace Engineering, Piscataway, NJ 08854-8097. Offers design and control (MS, PhD); fluid mechanics (MS, PhD); solid mechanics (MS, PhD); thermal sciences (MS, PhD). *Program availability:* Part-time, evening/weekend. *Degree requirements:* For master's, thesis (for some programs); for doctorate, thesis/dissertation. *Entrance requirements:* For master's, GRE General Test, BS in mechanical/aerospace engineering or related field; for doctorate, GRE General Test, MS in mechanical/aerospace engineering or related field. Additional exam requirements/recommendations for international students: Required—TOEFL. Electronic applications accepted. *Faculty research:* Combustion, propulsion, thermal transport, crystal plasticity, optimization, fabrication, nanoidentation.

Mechanical Engineering

St. Cloud State University, School of Graduate Studies, College of Science and Engineering, Program in Mechanical Engineering, St. Cloud, MN 56301-4498. Offers MS. *Degree requirements:* For master's, thesis or alternative. *Entrance requirements:* For master's, GRE General Test, minimum GPA of 2.75. Additional exam requirements/recommendations for international students: Required—Michigan English Language Assessment Battery; Recommended—TOEFL (minimum score 550 paper-based), IELTS (minimum score 6.5). Electronic applications accepted.

Saint Martin's University, Office of Graduate Studies, Program in Mechanical Engineering, Lacey, WA 98503. Offers MME. *Program availability:* Part-time. *Faculty:* 5 full-time (0 women), 1 part-time/adjunct (0 women). *Students:* 10 full-time (5 women), 3 part-time (0 women); includes 4 minority (1 Black or African American, non-Hispanic/Latino; 1 Asian, non-Hispanic/Latino; 2 Two or more races, non-Hispanic/Latino). Average age 28. 10 applicants, 30% accepted, 3 enrolled. In 2016, 1 master's awarded. *Degree requirements:* For master's, thesis optional. *Entrance requirements:* For master's, official transcripts from all colleges and universities attended, three letters of recommendation (preferably from professors, registered engineers or supervisors). Additional exam requirements/recommendations for international students: Required—TOEFL (minimum score 550 paper-based, 79 iBT) or IELTS (minimum score 6.5). *Application deadline:* For fall admission, 4/1 priority date for domestic and international students; for spring admission, 11/1 priority date for domestic and international students. Applications are processed on a rolling basis. Application fee: $50. Electronic applications accepted. *Expenses:* Tuition: Full-time $13,800; part-time $1150 per credit hour. *Required fees:* $720; $60 per credit hour. Tuition and fees vary according to course level and program. *Financial support:* Unspecified assistantships available. Financial award application deadline: 3/1; financial award applicants required to submit FAFSA. *Unit head:* Dr. Shawn Duan, Chair, Mechanical Engineering, 360-688-2745, E-mail: sduan@stmartin.edu. *Application contact:* Casey Caronna, Administrative Assistant, 360-412-6128, E-mail: ccaronna@stmartin.edu.
Website: https://www.stmartin.edu

San Diego State University, Graduate and Research Affairs, College of Engineering, Department of Mechanical Engineering, San Diego, CA 92182. Offers engineering sciences and applied mechanics (PhD); manufacture and design (MS); mechanical engineering (MS). PhD offered jointly with University of California, San Diego and Department of Aerospace Engineering and Engineering Mechanics. *Program availability:* Evening/weekend. *Degree requirements:* For master's, comprehensive exam (for some programs), thesis (for some programs); for doctorate, thesis/dissertation. *Entrance requirements:* For master's, GRE General Test; for doctorate, GRE, 3 letters of recommendation. Additional exam requirements/recommendations for international students: Required—TOEFL. Electronic applications accepted. *Faculty research:* Energy analysis and diagnosis, seawater pump design, space-related research.

Santa Clara University, School of Engineering, Santa Clara, CA 95053. Offers applied mathematics (MS); bioengineering (MS); civil engineering (MS); computer science and engineering (MS, PhD); electrical engineering (MS, PhD); engineering (Engineer); engineering management and leadership (MS); mechanical engineering (MS, PhD); software engineering (MS); sustainable energy (MS). *Program availability:* Part-time, evening/weekend. *Faculty:* 66 full-time (22 women), 59 part-time/adjunct (12 women). *Students:* 449 full-time (188 women), 315 part-time (114 women); includes 197 minority (3 Black or African American, non-Hispanic/Latino; 144 Asian, non-Hispanic/Latino; 33 Hispanic/Latino; 1 Native Hawaiian or other Pacific Islander, non-Hispanic/Latino; 16 Two or more races, non-Hispanic/Latino), 418 international. Average age 28. 1,217 applicants, 45% accepted, 293 enrolled. In 2016, 466 master's awarded. *Entrance requirements:* For master's, GRE, transcript; for doctorate, GRE, master's degree or equivalent, 3 letters of recommendation, statement of purpose; for Engineer, master's degree. Additional exam requirements/recommendations for international students: Required—TOEFL (minimum score 79 iBT) or IELTS (6.5). *Application deadline:* For fall admission, 4/1 for domestic and international students; for winter admission, 9/9 for domestic students, 9/2 for international students; for spring admission, 2/17 for domestic students, 12/9 for international students. Application fee: $60. Electronic applications accepted. *Expenses:* $928 per unit. *Financial support:* Fellowships, research assistantships, teaching assistantships, career-related internships or fieldwork, Federal Work-Study, scholarships/grants, traineeships, health care benefits, tuition waivers, and unspecified assistantships available. Support available to part-time students. Financial award applicants required to submit FAFSA. *Unit head:* Dr. Alfonso Ortega, Dean. *Application contact:* Stacey Tinker, Director of Admissions and Marketing, 408-554-4313, Fax: 408-554-4323, E-mail: stinker@scu.edu.
Website: http://www.scu.edu/engineering/graduate/

Simon Fraser University, Office of Graduate Studies and Postdoctoral Fellows, Faculty of Applied Sciences, School of Mechatronic Systems Engineering, Burnaby, BC V5A 1S6, Canada. Offers MA Sc, PhD. *Faculty:* 17 full-time (2 women). *Students:* 99 full-time (22 women). 99 applicants, 27% accepted, 20 enrolled. In 2016, 12 master's, 13 doctorates awarded. *Degree requirements:* For master's, one foreign language, thesis; for doctorate, one foreign language, comprehensive exam, thesis/dissertation. *Entrance requirements:* Additional exam requirements/recommendations for international students: Required—TOEFL (minimum score 580 paper-based; 93 iBT), IELTS (minimum score 7), TWE (minimum score 5). *Application deadline:* For fall admission, 9/15 for domestic and international students; for spring admission, 1/15 for domestic and international students; for summer admission, 6/14 for domestic and international students. Application fee: $90 ($125 for international students). Electronic applications accepted. *Financial support:* In 2016–17, 58 students received support, including 36 fellowships (averaging $3,250 per year); research assistantships, teaching assistantships, and scholarships/grants also available. *Faculty research:* Intelligent systems and smart materials, micro-electro mechanical systems (MEMS), biomedical engineering, thermal engineering, alternative energy. *Unit head:* Dr. Mehrdad Moallem, Graduate Program Chair, 778-782-8156, E-mail: mse-grad-chair@sfu.ca. *Application contact:* Jennifer Coffey, Graduate Program Assistant, 778-782-8456, E-mail: msedept@sfu.ca.
Website: http://www.sfu.ca/mechatronics.html

South Carolina State University, College of Graduate and Professional Studies, Department of Civil and Mechanical Engineering Technology, Orangeburg, SC 29117-0001. Offers transportation (MS). *Program availability:* Part-time, evening/weekend. *Faculty:* 2 full-time (1 woman), 1 part-time/adjunct (0 women). *Students:* 3 full-time (1 woman), 1 (woman) part-time; all minorities (all Black or African American, non-Hispanic/Latino). Average age 41. 1 applicant, 100% accepted. In 2016, 10 master's awarded. *Degree requirements:* For master's, comprehensive exam, thesis, departmental qualifying exam. *Entrance requirements:* For master's, GRE. Additional exam requirements/recommendations for international students: Recommended—TOEFL. *Application deadline:* For fall admission, 6/15 for domestic and international students; for spring admission, 11/1 for domestic and international students. Application fee: $25. Electronic applications accepted. *Expenses:* Tuition, state resident: full-time $8938; part-time $579 per credit hour. Tuition, nonresident: full-time $19,018; part-time $1139 per credit hour. *Required fees:* $1482; $82 per credit hour. *Financial support:* Fellowships, research assistantships, career-related internships or fieldwork, Federal

Work-Study, scholarships/grants, and unspecified assistantships available. Financial award application deadline: 6/1. *Unit head:* Dr. Stanley Ihekweazu, Chair, 803-536-7117, Fax: 803-516-4607, E-mail: sihekwea@scsu.edu. *Application contact:* Curtis Foskey, Coordinator of Graduate Admission, 803-536-8419, Fax: 803-536-8812, E-mail: cfoskey@scsu.edu.
Website: http://www.scsu.edu/schoolofgraduatestudies.aspx

South Dakota School of Mines and Technology, Graduate Division, Department of Mechanical Engineering, Rapid City, SD 57701-3995. Offers MS, PhD. *Program availability:* Part-time. *Degree requirements:* For master's, thesis (for some programs); for doctorate, thesis/dissertation. *Entrance requirements:* For master's, GRE General Test. Additional exam requirements/recommendations for international students: Required—TOEFL (minimum score 520 paper-based; 68 iBT), TWE. Electronic applications accepted.

South Dakota State University, Graduate School, College of Engineering, Department of Mechanical Engineering, Brookings, SD 57007. Offers agricultural, biosystems and mechanical engineering (PhD); engineering (MS). PhD offered jointly with the Department of Agricultural and Biosystems Engineering. *Program availability:* Part-time. *Degree requirements:* For master's, thesis (for some programs), oral exam. *Entrance requirements:* Additional exam requirements/recommendations for international students: Required—TOEFL (minimum score 525 paper-based; 71 iBT). *Faculty research:* Thermo-fluid science, solid mechanics and dynamics, industrial and quality control engineering, bioenergy.

Southern Illinois University Carbondale, Graduate School, College of Engineering, Department of Mechanical Engineering and Energy Processes, Carbondale, IL 62901-4701. Offers engineering sciences (PhD), including mechanical engineering and energy processes; mechanical engineering (MS). *Degree requirements:* For master's, comprehensive exam, thesis or alternative. *Entrance requirements:* For master's, GRE General Test, minimum GPA of 2.7. Additional exam requirements/recommendations for international students: Required—TOEFL. *Faculty research:* Coal conversion and processing, combustion, materials science and engineering, mechanical system dynamics.

Southern Illinois University Carbondale, Graduate School, College of Engineering, Program in Engineering Science, Carbondale, IL 62901-4701. Offers engineering science (PhD), including civil and environmental engineering, electrical and computer engineering, mechanical engineering and energy processes, mining and mineral resources engineering. *Degree requirements:* For doctorate, thesis/dissertation. *Entrance requirements:* For doctorate, GRE General Test, minimum GPA of 3.5. Additional exam requirements/recommendations for international students: Required—TOEFL.

Southern Illinois University Edwardsville, Graduate School, School of Engineering, Department of Mechanical and Industrial Engineering, Program in Mechanical Engineering, Edwardsville, IL 62026. Offers MS. *Program availability:* Part-time, evening/weekend. *Degree requirements:* For master's, comprehensive exam (for some programs), thesis (for some programs). *Entrance requirements:* Additional exam requirements/recommendations for international students: Required—TOEFL (minimum score 550 paper-based; 79 iBT), IELTS (minimum score 6.5). Electronic applications accepted.

Southern Methodist University, Bobby B. Lyle School of Engineering, Department of Mechanical Engineering, Dallas, TX 75205. Offers manufacturing systems management (MS); mechanical engineering (MSME, PhD); packaging of electronic and optical devices (MS). *Program availability:* Part-time, evening/weekend, online learning. Terminal master's awarded for partial completion of doctoral program. *Degree requirements:* For master's, thesis optional; for doctorate, thesis/dissertation, oral and written qualifying exams, oral final exam. *Entrance requirements:* For master's, GRE General Test, minimum GPA of 3.0 in last 2 years; bachelor's degree in engineering, mathematics, or sciences; for doctorate, preliminary counseling exam, minimum graduate GPA of 3.0, bachelor's degree in related field. Additional exam requirements/recommendations for international students: Required—TOEFL. *Faculty research:* Design, systems, and controls; thermal and fluid sciences.

Stanford University, School of Engineering, Department of Mechanical Engineering, Stanford, CA 94305-2004. Offers biomechanical engineering (MS); mechanical engineering (MS, PhD, Engr); product design (MS). *Degree requirements:* For doctorate, thesis/dissertation; for Engr, thesis. *Entrance requirements:* For master's, GRE General Test, undergraduate degree in engineering, math or sciences; for doctorate and Engr, GRE General Test, MS in engineering, math or sciences. Additional exam requirements/recommendations for international students: Required—TOEFL. *Expenses:* Tuition: Full-time $47,331. *Required fees:* $609.

Stevens Institute of Technology, Graduate School, Charles V. Schaefer Jr. School of Engineering and Science, Department of Mechanical Engineering, Program in Mechanical Engineering, Hoboken, NJ 07030. Offers M Eng, PhD, Eng. *Program availability:* Part-time, evening/weekend. *Students:* 115 full-time (15 women), 62 part-time (9 women); includes 18 minority (3 Black or African American, non-Hispanic/Latino; 1 American Indian or Alaska Native, non-Hispanic/Latino; 12 Asian, non-Hispanic/Latino; 2 Hispanic/Latino), 91 international. Average age 26. 495 applicants, 48% accepted, 50 enrolled. In 2016, 83 master's, 4 doctorates awarded. *Degree requirements:* For master's, thesis optional, minimum B average in major field and overall; for doctorate, comprehensive exam (for some programs), thesis/dissertation; for Eng, minimum B average. *Entrance requirements:* Additional exam requirements/recommendations for international students: Required—TOEFL (minimum score 74 iBT), IELTS (minimum score 6). *Application deadline:* For fall admission, 6/1 for domestic students, 4/15 for international students; for spring admission, 11/30 for domestic students, 11/1 for international students. Applications are processed on a rolling basis. Application fee: $65. Electronic applications accepted. *Expenses:* Contact institution. *Financial support:* Fellowships, research assistantships, teaching assistantships, career-related internships or fieldwork, Federal Work-Study, scholarships/grants, and unspecified assistantships available. Financial award application deadline: 2/15; financial award applicants required to submit FAFSA. *Unit head:* Dr. Frank Fisher, Interim Department Director, 201-216-8913, Fax: 201-216-8315, E-mail: ffisher@stevens.edu. *Application contact:* Graduate Admissions, 888-783-8367, Fax: 888-511-1306, E-mail: graduate@stevens.edu.

Stony Brook University, State University of New York, Graduate School, College of Engineering and Applied Sciences, Department of Mechanical Engineering, Stony Brook, NY 11794-2300. Offers MS, PhD. *Program availability:* Part-time, evening/weekend. *Faculty:* 22 full-time (2 women), 8 part-time/adjunct (1 woman). *Students:* 113 full-time (17 women), 35 part-time (3 women); includes 22 minority (2 Black or African American, non-Hispanic/Latino; 12 Asian, non-Hispanic/Latino; 7 Hispanic/Latino; 1 Two or more races, non-Hispanic/Latino), 89 international. Average age 25. 261 applicants, 44% accepted, 38 enrolled. In 2016, 78 master's, 4 doctorates awarded. Terminal master's awarded for partial completion of doctoral program. *Degree requirements:* For master's, thesis or alternative; for doctorate, comprehensive exam, thesis/dissertation. *Entrance requirements:* For master's, GRE General Test, minimum GPA of 3.0; for doctorate, GRE General Test, minimum GPA of 3.5. Additional exam requirements/

recommendations for international students: Required—TOEFL (minimum score 90 iBT). *Application deadline:* For fall admission, 1/15 for domestic students; for spring admission, 10/1 for domestic students. Application fee: $100. *Expenses:* Contact institution. *Financial support:* In 2016–17, 13 research assistantships, 21 teaching assistantships were awarded; fellowships also available. *Faculty research:* Solid mechanics, composite materials, elastomers or coatings, high temperature coatings, thin films. *Total annual research expenditures:* $2.7 million. *Unit head:* Dr. Jeffrey Q. Ge, Chair, 631-632-8305, Fax: 631-632-8544, E-mail: qiaode.ge@stonybrook.edu. *Application contact:* Dianna Berger, Coordinator, 631-632-8340, Fax: 631-632-8544, E-mail: mechanicaengineeringgraduate@stonybrook.edu.
Website: http://me.eng.sunysb.edu/

Syracuse University, College of Engineering and Computer Science, Programs in Mechanical and Aerospace Engineering, Syracuse, NY 13244. Offers MS, PhD. *Program availability:* Part-time. *Students:* Average age 25. In 2016, 55 master's, 8 doctorates awarded. *Degree requirements:* For master's, project or thesis; for doctorate, comprehensive exam, thesis/dissertation. *Entrance requirements:* For master's and doctorate, GRE General Test, official transcripts, personal statement, three letters of recommendation, resume. Additional exam requirements/recommendations for international students: Required—TOEFL (minimum score 100 iBT). *Application deadline:* For fall admission, 7/1 priority date for domestic students, 6/1 priority date for international students; for spring admission, 11/15 priority date for domestic students, 10/15 priority date for international students. Applications are processed on a rolling basis. Application fee: $75. Electronic applications accepted. *Expenses: Tuition:* Full-time $25,974; part-time $1443 per credit hour. *Required fees:* $802; $50 per course. Tuition and fees vary according to course load and program. *Financial support:* Fellowships with full tuition reimbursements, research assistantships with tuition reimbursements, teaching assistantships with tuition reimbursements, scholarships/grants, and tuition waivers (partial) available. Financial award application deadline: 1/1. *Faculty research:* Solid mechanics and materials, fluid mechanics, thermal sciences, controls and robotics. *Unit head:* Dr. John F. Dannenhoffer, III, Associate Professor/Program Director of Aerospace Engineering, 315-443-3340, E-mail: jfdannen@syr.edu. *Application contact:* Kathleen Joyce, Assistant Dean, 315-443-2219, E-mail: topgrads@syr.edu.
Website: http://eng-cs.syr.edu/

Temple University, College of Engineering, Department of Mechanical Engineering, Philadelphia, PA 19122-6096. Offers MSME. *Program availability:* Part-time, evening/weekend. *Faculty:* 18 full-time (1 woman). *Students:* 16 full-time (3 women), 7 part-time (0 women); includes 1 minority (Hispanic/Latino), 11 international. 79 applicants, 51% accepted, 13 enrolled. In 2016, 6 master's awarded. Terminal master's awarded for partial completion of doctoral program. *Degree requirements:* For master's, thesis optional. *Entrance requirements:* For master's, GRE General Test, minimum GPA of 3.0; BS in engineering from ABET-accredited or equivalent institution; resume; goals statement; three letters of reference; official transcripts. Additional exam requirements/recommendations for international students: Required—TOEFL (minimum score 550 paper-based; 79 iBT), IELTS (minimum score 6.5), PTE (minimum score 53). *Application deadline:* For fall admission, 3/1 priority date for domestic and international students; for spring admission, 11/1 priority date for domestic students, 8/1 priority date for international students. Applications are processed on a rolling basis. Application fee: $60. Electronic applications accepted. *Expenses:* $995 per credit hour in-state tuition; $1,319 per credit hour out-of-state. *Financial support:* In 2016–17, 12 students received support, including 2 fellowships with tuition reimbursements available, 10 teaching assistantships with tuition reimbursements available; research assistantships with tuition reimbursements available, Federal Work-Study, scholarships/grants, health care benefits, and unspecified assistantships also available. Financial award application deadline: 3/1; financial award applicants required to submit FAFSA. *Faculty research:* Renewable and alternative energy, advanced materials, nanotechnology, dynamic systems and controls, thin film photovoltaics, thermal and fluid engineering, biomechanics and bio fluid mechanics. *Unit head:* Dr. Jim Shih Jiun Chen, Chair, 215-204-4305, Fax: 215-204-6936, E-mail: jsjchen@temple.edu. *Application contact:* Leslie Levin, Director, Admissions and Graduate Student Services, 215-204-7800, Fax: 215-204-6936, E-mail: gradengr@temple.edu.
Website: http://engineering.temple.edu/department/mechanical-engineering

Temple University, College of Engineering, PhD in Engineering Program, Philadelphia, PA 19122-6096. Offers bioengineering (PhD); civil engineering (PhD); electrical engineering (PhD); environmental engineering (PhD); mechanical engineering (PhD). *Program availability:* Part-time, evening/weekend. *Faculty:* 67 full-time (13 women), 11 part-time/adjunct (1 woman). *Students:* 32 full-time (11 women), 7 part-time (2 women); includes 10 minority (3 Black or African American, non-Hispanic/Latino; 5 Asian, non-Hispanic/Latino; 1 Hispanic/Latino; 1 Two or more races, non-Hispanic/Latino), 19 international. 11 applicants, 64% accepted, 3 enrolled. In 2016, 6 doctorates awarded. *Degree requirements:* For doctorate, thesis/dissertation, preliminary exam, dissertation proposal and defense. *Entrance requirements:* For doctorate, GRE, minimum undergraduate GPA of 3.0; MS in engineering from ABET-accredited or equivalent institution (preferred); resume; goals statement; three letters of reference; official transcripts. Additional exam requirements/recommendations for international students: Required—TOEFL (minimum score 550 paper-based; 79 iBT), IELTS (minimum score 6.5), PTE (minimum score 53). *Application deadline:* For fall admission, 1/15 priority date for domestic and international students; for spring admission, 11/1 priority date for domestic students, 8/1 priority date for international students. Applications are processed on a rolling basis. Application fee: $60. Electronic applications accepted. *Expenses:* $995 per credit hour in-state tuition; $1,319 per credit hour out-of-state. *Financial support:* Fellowships with tuition reimbursements, research assistantships with tuition reimbursements, teaching assistantships with tuition reimbursements, Federal Work-Study, scholarships/grants, health care benefits, and unspecified assistantships available. Financial award application deadline: 3/1; financial award applicants required to submit FAFSA. *Faculty research:* Advanced/computer-aided manufacturing and advanced materials processing; bioengineering; computer engineering; construction engineering and management; dynamics, controls, and systems; energy and environmental science; engineering physics and engineering mathematics; green engineering; signal processing and communication; transportation engineering; water resources, hydrology, and environmental engineering. *Unit head:* Dr. Saroj Biswas, Associate Dean, College of Engineering, 215-204-8403, E-mail: sbiswas@temple.edu. *Application contact:* Leslie Levin, Director, Admissions and Graduate Student Services, 215-204-7800, Fax: 215-204-6936, E-mail: gradengr@temple.edu.
Website: http://engineering.temple.edu/additional-programs/phd-engineering

See Display on page 63 and Close-Up on page 83.

Tennessee State University, The School of Graduate Studies and Research, College of Engineering, Nashville, TN 37209-1561. Offers biomedical engineering (ME); civil engineering (ME); computer and information systems engineering (MS, PhD); electrical engineering (ME); environmental engineering (ME); manufacturing engineering (ME); mathematical sciences (MS); mechanical engineering (ME). *Program availability:* Part-time, evening/weekend. *Degree requirements:* For master's, project; for doctorate, comprehensive exam, thesis/dissertation. *Entrance requirements:* For doctorate, minimum GPA of 3.3. *Faculty research:* Robotics, intelligent systems, human-computer interaction software systems, biomedical engineering, signal/image processing, probabilistic design, intelligent manufacturing, cooperative mobile robots, condition based maintenance, sensor fusion.

Tennessee Technological University, College of Graduate Studies, College of Engineering, Department of Mechanical Engineering, Cookeville, TN 38505. Offers MS. *Program availability:* Part-time. *Faculty:* 25 full-time (2 women). *Students:* 16 full-time (2 women), 29 part-time (3 women); includes 2 minority (1 Asian, non-Hispanic/Latino; 1 Hispanic/Latino), 21 international. Average age 28. 84 applicants, 43% accepted, 14 enrolled. In 2016, 14 master's awarded. *Degree requirements:* For master's, thesis. *Entrance requirements:* For master's, GRE. Additional exam requirements/recommendations for international students: Required—TOEFL (minimum score 550 paper-based; 79 iBT), IELTS (minimum score 5.5), PTE (minimum score 53), or TOEIC (Test of English as an International Communication). *Application deadline:* For fall admission, 8/1 for domestic students, 5/1 for international students; for spring admission, 12/1 for domestic students, 10/1 for international students; for summer admission, 5/1 for domestic students, 2/1 for international students. Applications are processed on a rolling basis. Application fee: $35 ($40 for international students). Electronic applications accepted. *Expenses:* Tuition, state resident: full-time $9375; part-time $534 per credit hour. Tuition, nonresident: full-time $22,443; part-time $1260 per credit hour. *Financial support:* In 2016–17, 14 research assistantships (averaging $8,190 per year), 17 teaching assistantships (averaging $6,711 per year) were awarded; fellowships also available. Financial award application deadline: 4/1. *Faculty research:* Energy-related systems, design, acoustics and acoustical systems. *Unit head:* Dr. Mohan Rao, Chairperson, 931-372-3254, Fax: 931-372-6340, E-mail: mrao@tntech.edu. *Application contact:* Shelia K. Kendrick, Coordinator of Graduate Studies, 931-372-3808, Fax: 931-372-3497, E-mail: skendrick@tntech.edu.

Texas A&M University, College of Engineering, Department of Mechanical Engineering, College Station, TX 77843. Offers M Eng, MS, PhD. *Faculty:* 60. *Students:* 379 full-time (50 women), 85 part-time (9 women); includes 64 minority (7 Black or African American, non-Hispanic/Latino; 26 Asian, non-Hispanic/Latino; 28 Hispanic/Latino; 3 Two or more races, non-Hispanic/Latino), 268 international. Average age 28. 1,180 applicants, 18% accepted, 109 enrolled. In 2016, 78 master's, 33 doctorates awarded. *Degree requirements:* For master's, thesis (for MS); for doctorate, thesis/dissertation. *Entrance requirements:* For master's, GRE General Test, minimum undergraduate GPA of 3.0; for doctorate, GRE General Test, minimum graduate GPA of 3.5. Additional exam requirements/recommendations for international students: Required—TOEFL (minimum score 570 paper-based; 80 iBT), IELTS (minimum score 6), PTE (minimum score 53). *Application deadline:* For fall admission, 3/1 priority date for domestic students, 3/1 for international students; for winter admission, 11/1 for domestic and international students; for spring admission, 8/1 for domestic and international students. Applications are processed on a rolling basis. Application fee: $50 ($90 for international students). Electronic applications accepted. *Expenses:* Contact institution. *Financial support:* In 2016–17, 355 students received support, including 48 fellowships with tuition reimbursements available (averaging $9,358 per year), 212 research assistantships with tuition reimbursements available (averaging $6,023 per year), 114 teaching assistantships with tuition reimbursements available (averaging $8,329 per year); career-related internships or fieldwork, institutionally sponsored loans, scholarships/grants, traineeships, health care benefits, tuition waivers (full and partial), and unspecified assistantships also available. Support available to part-time students. Financial award application deadline: 3/15; financial award applicants required to submit FAFSA. *Faculty research:* Thermal/fluid sciences, materials/manufacturing and controls systems. *Unit head:* Dr. Andreas A. Polycarpou, Department Head, 979-845-5337, E-mail: apolycarpou@tamu.edu. *Application contact:* Dr. Daniel A. McAdams, Graduate Program Director, 979-862-7834, E-mail: dmcadams@tamu.edu.
Website: http://engineering.tamu.edu/mechanical

Texas A&M University–Kingsville, College of Graduate Studies, Frank H. Dotterweich College of Engineering, Department of Mechanical and Industrial Engineering, Program in Mechanical Engineering, Kingsville, TX 78363. Offers ME, MS. *Degree requirements:* For master's, variable foreign language requirement, comprehensive exam, thesis (for some programs). *Entrance requirements:* For master's, GRE (minimum score quantitative and verbal 950 on old scale), MAT, GMAT, minimum GPA 2.6. Additional exam requirements/recommendations for international students: Required—TOEFL (minimum score 550 paper-based; 79 iBT). Electronic applications accepted.

Texas Tech University, Graduate School, Edward E. Whitacre Jr. College of Engineering, Department of Mechanical Engineering, Lubbock, TX 79409. Offers MSME, PhD. *Program availability:* Part-time. *Faculty:* 45 full-time (7 women). *Students:* 102 full-time (15 women), 25 part-time (4 women); includes 11 minority (1 Black or African American, non-Hispanic/Latino; 5 Asian, non-Hispanic/Latino; 5 Hispanic/Latino), 79 international. Average age 29. 225 applicants, 21% accepted, 25 enrolled. In 2016, 16 master's, 12 doctorates awarded. *Degree requirements:* For master's, comprehensive exam, thesis (for some programs); for doctorate, comprehensive exam, thesis/dissertation. *Entrance requirements:* For master's and doctorate, GRE (Verbal and Quantitative). Additional exam requirements/recommendations for international students: Required—TOEFL (minimum score 550 paper-based; 79 iBT). *Application deadline:* For fall admission, 6/1 priority date for domestic students, 1/15 priority date for international students; for spring admission, 9/1 priority date for domestic students, 6/15 priority date for international students. Applications are processed on a rolling basis. Application fee: $75. Electronic applications accepted. *Expenses:* $325 per credit hour full-time resident tuition, $733 per credit hour full-time non-resident tuition; $53.75 per credit hour fee plus $608 per term fee. *Financial support:* In 2016–17, 119 students received support, including 110 fellowships (averaging $3,156 per year), 46 research assistantships (averaging $16,277 per year), 60 teaching assistantships (averaging $21,822 per year); career-related internships or fieldwork, scholarships/grants, tuition waivers (partial), and unspecified assistantships also available. Financial award application deadline: 4/15; financial award applicants required to submit FAFSA. *Faculty research:* Biomedical engineering, bioengineering, nano- and bio-materials, nonlinear dynamics and controls, turbulence and wind energy, microfluidics, engineering in medicine, advanced propulsion and combustion, advanced computational solids and fluid dynamics. *Total annual research expenditures:* $2.4 million. *Unit head:* Dr. Oliver G. McGee, III, Professor and Chair, 806-834-1565, Fax: 806-742-3540, E-mail: oliver.mcgee@ttu.edu. *Application contact:* Rene Fuentes, Graduate Academic Advisor, 806-834-2335, Fax: 806-742-3540, E-mail: rene.fuentes@ttu.edu.
Website: http://www.depts.ttu.edu/me/

Tufts University, School of Engineering, Department of Mechanical Engineering, Medford, MA 02155. Offers bioengineering (ME, MS), including bioinformatics, biomechanical systems and devices, signals and systems; bioinformatics (MS); human factors (MS); mechanical engineering (ME, MS, PhD). *Program availability:* Part-time. Terminal master's awarded for partial completion of doctoral program. *Degree requirements:* For master's, thesis; for doctorate, thesis/dissertation. *Entrance requirements:* For master's and doctorate, GRE General Test. Additional exam requirements/recommendations for international students: Required—TOEFL (minimum score 550 paper-based; 80 iBT), IELTS (minimum score 6.5). Electronic applications accepted. *Expenses: Tuition:* Full-time $49,892; part-time $1248 per credit hour. *Required fees:* $844. Full-time tuition and fees vary according to degree level, program and student level. Part-time tuition and fees vary according to course load. *Faculty research:* Applied mechanics, biomaterials, controls/robotics, design/systems, human factors.

Tuskegee University, Graduate Programs, College of Engineering, Department of Mechanical Engineering, Tuskegee, AL 36088. Offers MSME. *Degree requirements:* For master's, thesis or alternative. *Entrance requirements:* For master's, GRE General Test, GRE Subject Test. Additional exam requirements/recommendations for international students: Required—TOEFL (minimum score 500 paper-based). *Faculty research:* Superalloys, fatigue and surface machinery, energy management, solar energy.

Universidad del Turabo, Graduate Programs, School of Engineering, Gurabo, PR 00778-3030. Offers computer engineering (M Eng); electrical engineering (M Eng); mechanical engineering (M Eng); telecommunications and network systems administration (M Eng). *Students:* 14 full-time (0 women), 46 part-time (7 women); all minorities (all Hispanic/Latino). Average age 34. 74 applicants, 41% accepted, 20 enrolled. In 2016, 13 master's awarded. *Entrance requirements:* For master's, GRE, EXADEP or GMAT, interview, essay, official transcript, recommendation letters. *Application deadline:* Applications are processed on a rolling basis. Application fee: $25. Electronic applications accepted. *Financial support:* Institutionally sponsored loans available. Financial award applicants required to submit FAFSA. *Unit head:* Hector Rodriguez, Dean, 787-743-7979 Ext. 4144. *Application contact:* Diriee Rodriguez, Admissions Director, 787-743-7979 Ext. 4453, E-mail: admisiones-ut@suagm.edu.
Website: http://ut.suagm.edu/es/engineering

Université de Moncton, Faculty of Engineering, Program in Mechanical Engineering, Moncton, NB E1A 3E9, Canada. Offers M Sc A. *Degree requirements:* For master's, thesis, proficiency in French. *Faculty research:* Composite materials, thermal energy systems, control systems, fluid mechanics and heat transfer, CAD/CAM and robotics.

Université de Sherbrooke, Faculty of Engineering, Department of Mechanical Engineering, Sherbrooke, QC J1K 2R1, Canada. Offers M Sc A, PhD. *Degree requirements:* For master's, one foreign language, thesis; for doctorate, comprehensive exam, thesis/dissertation. *Entrance requirements:* For master's, bachelor's degree in engineering or equivalent; for doctorate, master's degree in engineering or equivalent. Electronic applications accepted. *Faculty research:* Acoustics, aerodynamics, vehicle dynamics, composite materials, heat transfer.

Université Laval, Faculty of Sciences and Engineering, Department of Mechanical Engineering, Programs in Mechanical Engineering, Québec, QC G1K 7P4, Canada. Offers M Sc, PhD. *Program availability:* Part-time. Terminal master's awarded for partial completion of doctoral program. *Degree requirements:* For master's, thesis; for doctorate, comprehensive exam, thesis/dissertation. *Entrance requirements:* For master's and doctorate, knowledge of French. Electronic applications accepted.

University at Buffalo, the State University of New York, Graduate School, School of Engineering and Applied Sciences, Department of Mechanical and Aerospace Engineering, Buffalo, NY 14260. Offers aerospace engineering (MS, PhD); mechanical engineering (MS, PhD). *Program availability:* Part-time. Terminal master's awarded for partial completion of doctoral program. *Degree requirements:* For master's, comprehensive exam, project or thesis; for doctorate, thesis/dissertation. *Entrance requirements:* For master's and doctorate, GRE General Test, GRE Subject Test. Additional exam requirements/recommendations for international students: Required—TOEFL (minimum score 79 iBT). Electronic applications accepted. *Faculty research:* Fluid and thermal sciences, systems and design, mechanics and materials.

The University of Akron, Graduate School, College of Engineering, Department of Mechanical Engineering, Akron, OH 44325. Offers engineering (PhD); mechanical engineering (MS). *Program availability:* Part-time, evening/weekend. *Faculty:* 28 full-time (2 women), 10 part-time/adjunct (0 women). *Students:* 92 full-time (12 women), 29 part-time (4 women); includes 4 minority (1 Asian, non-Hispanic/Latino; 2 Hispanic/Latino; 1 Two or more races, non-Hispanic/Latino), 84 international. Average age 28. 104 applicants, 84% accepted, 24 enrolled. In 2016, 25 master's, 12 doctorates awarded. Terminal master's awarded for partial completion of doctoral program. *Degree requirements:* For master's, thesis optional; for doctorate, one foreign language, thesis/dissertation, candidacy exam, qualifying exam. *Entrance requirements:* For master's, GRE, minimum GPA of 2.75, baccalaureate degree in engineering, three letters of recommendation, statement of purpose; for doctorate, GRE, minimum GPA of 3.0 with bachelor's degree, 3.5 with master's degree; three letters of recommendation; statement of purpose; resume. Additional exam requirements/recommendations for international students: Required—TOEFL (minimum score 550 paper-based; 79 iBT), IELTS (minimum score 6.5). *Application deadline:* Applications are processed on a rolling basis. Application fee: $45 ($70 for international students). Electronic applications accepted. *Expenses:* Tuition, state resident: full-time $8618; part-time $359 per credit hour. Tuition, nonresident: full-time $17,149; part-time $715 per credit hour. *Required fees:* $1652. *Financial support:* In 2016–17, 37 research assistantships with full tuition reimbursements were awarded; instructional support assistantships also available. *Faculty research:* Materials science, tribology and lubrication, vibration and dynamic analysis, solid mechanics, micro and nanoelectromechanical systems (MEMS and NEMS), bio-mechanics. *Total annual research expenditures:* $3.4 million. *Unit head:* Dr. Sergio Felicelli, Chair, 330-972-7367, E-mail: sergio@uakron.edu. *Application contact:* Dr. Xiaosheng Gao, Associate Chair for Graduate Programs, 330-972-2415, E-mail: xgao@uakron.edu.
Website: http://www.uakron.edu/engineering/ME/

The University of Alabama, Graduate School, College of Engineering, Department of Mechanical Engineering, Tuscaloosa, AL 35487. Offers MS, PhD. *Program availability:* Part-time, online learning. *Faculty:* 25 full-time (2 women). *Students:* 64 full-time (5 women), 15 part-time (1 woman); includes 8 minority (4 Black or African American, non-Hispanic/Latino; 1 Asian, non-Hispanic/Latino; 2 Hispanic/Latino; 1 Two or more races, non-Hispanic/Latino), 35 international. Average age 27. 95 applicants, 57% accepted, 24 enrolled. In 2016, 22 master's, 5 doctorates awarded. Terminal master's awarded for partial completion of doctoral program. *Degree requirements:* For master's, comprehensive exam, thesis (for some programs); for doctorate, comprehensive exam, thesis/dissertation. *Entrance requirements:* For master's, GRE General Test, minimum GPA of 3.0; for doctorate, GRE General Test, minimum GPA of 3.0 with MS, 3.3 without MS. Additional exam requirements/recommendations for international students: Required—TOEFL (minimum score 600 paper-based). *Application deadline:* For fall admission, 7/1 priority date for domestic students, 1/15 priority date for international students; for spring admission, 11/1 priority date for domestic students, 6/1 priority date for international students. Applications are processed on a rolling basis. Application fee: $50 ($60 for international students). Electronic applications accepted. *Expenses:* Tuition, state resident: full-time $10,470. Tuition, nonresident: full-time $26,950. *Financial support:* In 2016–17, 32 students received support, including 5 fellowships with full tuition reimbursements available (averaging $18,000 per year), 14 research assistantships with full tuition reimbursements available (averaging $17,500 per year), 13 teaching assistantships with full tuition reimbursements available (averaging $13,000 per year); career-related internships or fieldwork, health care benefits, and unspecified assistantships also available. Financial award application deadline: 3/30. *Faculty research:* Thermal/fluids, robotics, numerical modeling, energy conservation, energy and combustion systems, internal combustion engines, heating, ventilation and air conditioning, medical devices, manufacturing, vehicular systems, controls, acoustics solid mechanics and materials. *Total annual research expenditures:* $2.8 million. *Unit head:* Dr. Kenneth Clark Midkiff, Jr., Professor and Interim Head, 205-348-1645, Fax: 205-348-6419, E-mail: cmidkiff@eng.ua.edu. *Application contact:* Steve Shepard, Graduate Program Coordinator/Professor, 205-348-1650, Fax: 205-348-6419, E-mail: sshepard@eng.ua.edu.
Website: http://www.me.ua.edu

The University of Alabama at Birmingham, School of Engineering, Program in Mechanical Engineering, Birmingham, AL 35294. Offers advanced safety engineering and management (M Eng); mechanical engineering (MSME). *Faculty:* 8 full-time, 2 part-time/adjunct. *Students:* 44 full-time (5 women), 10 part-time (2 women); includes 2 minority (1 Black or African American, non-Hispanic/Latino; 1 Asian, non-Hispanic/Latino), 8 international. Average age 27. 22 applicants, 73% accepted, 2 enrolled. In 2016, 9 master's awarded. *Degree requirements:* For master's, thesis (for some programs). *Entrance requirements:* For master's, GRE (minimum 50th percentile ranking on Quantitative Reasoning and Verbal Reasoning sections), minimum B average overall or over last 60 semester hours of earned credit. Additional exam requirements/recommendations for international students: Required—TOEFL (minimum score 80 iBT). *Application deadline:* For fall admission, 7/1 for domestic students; for spring admission, 11/1 for domestic students; for summer admission, 4/1 for domestic students. Applications are processed on a rolling basis. Application fee: $50 ($60 for international students). Electronic applications accepted. *Expenses:* $396 per hour resident tuition; $935 per hour non-resident tuition; $150 per course online course fee. *Financial support:* In 2016–17, 18 students received support, including 1 fellowship with full tuition reimbursement available (averaging $10,000 per year), 7 research assistantships with full tuition reimbursements available (averaging $22,000 per year), 10 teaching assistantships (averaging $2,500 per year). *Total annual research expenditures:* $2 million. *Unit head:* Dr. David Littlefield, Graduate Program Director, 205-934-8460, E-mail: littlefield@uab.edu. *Application contact:* Holly Hebard, Director of Graduate School Operations, 205-934-8227, Fax: 205-934-8413, E-mail: gradschool@uab.edu.
Website: http://www.uab.edu/engineering/home/departments-research/me/graduate

The University of Alabama in Huntsville, School of Graduate Studies, College of Engineering, Department of Chemical and Materials Engineering, Huntsville, AL 35899. Offers biotechnology science and engineering (PhD); chemical and materials engineering (MSE); materials science (PhD); mechanical engineering (PhD), including chemical engineering. *Program availability:* Part-time, evening/weekend. *Degree requirements:* For master's, comprehensive exam, thesis or alternative, oral and written exams; for doctorate, comprehensive exam, thesis/dissertation. *Entrance requirements:* For master's, GRE General Test, appropriate bachelor's degree, minimum GPA of 3.0; for doctorate, GRE General Test, minimum GPA of 3.0. Additional exam requirements/recommendations for international students: Required—TOEFL (minimum score 500 paper-based; 80 iBT), IELTS (minimum score 6.5). Electronic applications accepted. *Expenses:* Tuition, state resident: full-time $9834; part-time $600 per credit hour. Tuition, nonresident: full-time $21,830; part-time $1325 per credit hour. *Faculty research:* Ultrathin films for optical, sensor and biological applications; materials processing including low gravity; hypergolic reactants; computational fluid dynamics; biofuels and renewable resources.

The University of Alabama in Huntsville, School of Graduate Studies, College of Engineering, Department of Mechanical and Aerospace Engineering, Huntsville, AL 35899. Offers aerospace systems engineering (MS, PhD). *Program availability:* Part-time, evening/weekend. *Degree requirements:* For master's, comprehensive exam, thesis or alternative, oral and written exams; for doctorate, comprehensive exam, thesis/dissertation, oral and written exams. *Entrance requirements:* For master's, GRE General Test, BSE, minimum GPA of 3.0; for doctorate, GRE General Test, minimum GPA of 3.0. Additional exam requirements/recommendations for international students: Required—TOEFL (minimum score 500 paper-based; 80 iBT), IELTS (minimum score 6.5). Electronic applications accepted. *Expenses:* Tuition, state resident: full-time $9834; part-time $600 per credit hour. Tuition, nonresident: full-time $21,830; part-time $1325 per credit hour. *Faculty research:* Rocket propulsion and plasma engineering, materials engineering and solid mechanics, energy conversion, transport, and storage.

University of Alaska Fairbanks, College of Engineering and Mines, Department of Mechanical Engineering, Fairbanks, AK 99775-5905. Offers MS. *Program availability:* Part-time. *Faculty:* 6 full-time (1 woman). *Students:* 8 full-time (2 women), 1 part-time (0 women); includes 1 minority (Hispanic/Latino), 3 international. Average age 26. 11 applicants, 55% accepted, 4 enrolled. In 2016, 5 master's awarded. *Degree requirements:* For master's, comprehensive exam, oral defense of project or thesis. *Entrance requirements:* For master's, GRE General Test, bachelor's degree from accredited institution with minimum cumulative undergraduate and major GPA of 3.0. Additional exam requirements/recommendations for international students: Required—TOEFL (minimum score 550 paper-based; 79 iBT), IELTS (minimum score 6.5). *Application deadline:* For fall admission, 6/1 for domestic students, 3/1 for international students; for spring admission, 10/15 for domestic students, 9/1 for international students. Applications are processed on a rolling basis. Application fee: $60. Electronic applications accepted. *Expenses:* $533 per credit resident tuition, $673 per semester resident fees; $1,088 per credit non-resident tuition, $835 per semester non-resident fees. *Financial support:* In 2016–17, 2 research assistantships with full tuition reimbursements (averaging $12,295 per year), 6 teaching assistantships with full tuition reimbursements (averaging $6,998 per year) were awarded; fellowships with full tuition reimbursements, career-related internships or fieldwork, Federal Work-Study, scholarships/grants, health care benefits, and unspecified assistantships also available. Support available to part-time students. Financial award application deadline: 7/1; financial award applicants required to submit FAFSA. *Faculty research:* Cold regions engineering, fluid mechanics, heat transfer, energy systems, indoor air quality. *Unit head:* Dr. Rorik Peterson, Department Chair, 907-474-7136, Fax: 907-474-6141, E-mail: fymech@uaf.edu. *Application contact:* Mary Kreta, Director of Admissions, 907-474-7500, Fax: 907-474-7097, E-mail: admissions@uaf.edu.
Website: http://cem.uaf.edu/me/

University of Alberta, Faculty of Graduate Studies and Research, Department of Mechanical Engineering, Edmonton, AB T6G 2E1, Canada. Offers engineering management (M Eng); mechanical engineering (M Eng, M Sc, PhD); MBA/M Eng. *Program availability:* Part-time. *Degree requirements:* For master's, thesis; for doctorate, thesis/dissertation. *Entrance requirements:* For master's and doctorate, minimum GPA of 7.0 on a 9.0 scale. Additional exam requirements/recommendations for international students: Required—TOEFL (minimum score 580 paper-based). *Faculty research:* Combustion and environmental issues, advanced materials, computational fluid dynamics, biomedical, acoustics and vibrations.

The University of Arizona, College of Engineering, Department of Aerospace and Mechanical Engineering, Tucson, AZ 85721. Offers aerospace engineering (MS, PhD);

mechanical engineering (MS, PhD). *Program availability:* Part-time. *Degree requirements:* For master's, thesis or alternative; for doctorate, thesis/dissertation. *Entrance requirements:* For master's, GRE General Test, 3 letters of recommendation; for doctorate, GRE General Test, 3 letters of recommendation, statement of purpose. Additional exam requirements/recommendations for international students: Required—TOEFL (minimum score 550 paper-based; 79 iBT). Electronic applications accepted.

University of Arkansas, Graduate School, College of Engineering, Department of Mechanical Engineering, Fayetteville, AR 72701. Offers MSE, MSME, PhD. *Program availability:* Part-time, online learning. *Students:* 40 applicants, 65% accepted. In 2016, 5 master's, 2 doctorates awarded. *Degree requirements:* For master's, thesis optional; for doctorate, one foreign language, thesis/dissertation. *Application deadline:* For fall admission, 4/1 for international students; for spring admission, 10/1 for international students. Applications are processed on a rolling basis. Application fee: $40 ($50 for international students). Electronic applications accepted. *Financial support:* In 2016–17, 16 research assistantships, 1 teaching assistantship were awarded; fellowships, career-related internships or fieldwork, and Federal Work-Study also available. Support available to part-time students. Financial award application deadline: 4/1; financial award applicants required to submit FAFSA. *Unit head:* Dr. Darrin Nutter, Interim Department Head, 479-575-4503, Fax: 479-575-6982, E-mail: dnutter@uark.edu.
Website: http://www.meeg.uark.edu

University of Bridgeport, School of Engineering, Department of Mechanical Engineering, Bridgeport, CT 06604. Offers MS. *Degree requirements:* For master's, thesis optional. *Entrance requirements:* Additional exam requirements/recommendations for international students: Recommended—TOEFL (minimum score 550 paper-based; 80 iBT), IELTS (minimum score 6.5). Electronic applications accepted.

The University of British Columbia, Faculty of Applied Science, Department of Mechanical Engineering, Vancouver, BC V6T 1Z4, Canada. Offers M Eng, MA Sc, PhD. *Degree requirements:* For master's, thesis; for doctorate, comprehensive exam, thesis/dissertation. *Entrance requirements:* For master's, bachelor's degree, minimum B+ average; for doctorate, master's degree, minimum B+ average. Additional exam requirements/recommendations for international students: Required—TOEFL (minimum score 93 iBT), IELTS; Recommended—TWE. *Application deadline:* For fall admission, 6/1 priority date for domestic and international students; for winter admission, 9/1 priority date for domestic and international students. Application fee: $100 Canadian dollars ($162 Canadian dollars for international students). Electronic applications accepted. *Expenses:* $4,802 per year tuition and fees, $8,436 per year international. *Financial support:* Fellowships, research assistantships, and teaching assistantships available. *Faculty research:* Applied mechanics, manufacturing, robotics and controls, thermodynamics and combustion, fluid/aerodynamics, acoustics. *Application contact:* Sarah Karsten, Graduate Program Staff, 604-822-9861, E-mail: admissions@mech.ubc.ca.
Website: http://mech.ubc.ca/graduate/

University of Calgary, Faculty of Graduate Studies, Schulich School of Engineering, Department of Mechanical and Manufacturing Engineering, Calgary, AB T2N 1N4, Canada. Offers M Eng, M Sc, PhD. *Program availability:* Part-time. *Degree requirements:* For master's, thesis (for some programs); for doctorate, thesis/dissertation, candidacy exam. *Entrance requirements:* For master's, minimum GPA of 3.0; for doctorate, minimum GPA of 3.3. Additional exam requirements/recommendations for international students: Required—TOEFL (minimum score 550 paper-based; 80 iBT), IELTS (minimum score 7). *Faculty research:* Thermofluids, solid mechanics, materials, biomechanics, manufacturing.

University of California, Berkeley, Graduate Division, College of Engineering, Department of Mechanical Engineering, Berkeley, CA 94720-1500. Offers M Eng, MS, PhD. *Students:* 391 full-time (94 women); includes 68 minority (3 Black or African American, non-Hispanic/Latino; 42 Asian, non-Hispanic/Latino; 23 Hispanic/Latino), 209 international. Average age 27. 1,308 applicants, 164 enrolled. In 2016, 117 master's, 42 doctorates awarded. Terminal master's awarded for partial completion of doctoral program. *Degree requirements:* For master's, comprehensive exam (for some programs), thesis (for some programs), comprehensive exam or thesis (MS); for doctorate, thesis/dissertation, preliminary and qualifying exams. *Entrance requirements:* For master's and doctorate, GRE General Test, minimum GPA of 3.0, 3 letters of recommendation. Additional exam requirements/recommendations for international students: Required—TOEFL (minimum score 570 paper-based; 90 iBT). *Application deadline:* For fall admission, 12/2 for domestic students. Application fee: $105 ($125 for international students). Electronic applications accepted. *Financial support:* Fellowships, research assistantships, teaching assistantships, health care benefits, and unspecified assistantships available. Financial award applicants required to submit FAFSA. *Unit head:* Prof. Roberto Horowitz, Chair, 510-642-1338, Fax: 510-642-6163, E-mail: mech@me.berkeley.edu. *Application contact:* 510-642-5084, Fax: 510-642-6163, E-mail: mech@me.berkeley.edu.
Website: http://www.me.berkeley.edu/

University of California, Davis, College of Engineering, Program in Mechanical and Aeronautical Engineering, Davis, CA 95616. Offers aeronautical engineering (M Engr, MS, D Engr, PhD, Certificate); mechanical engineering (M Engr, MS, D Engr, PhD, Certificate); M Engr/MBA. *Degree requirements:* For master's, comprehensive exam (for some programs), thesis (for some programs); for doctorate, thesis/dissertation. *Entrance requirements:* For master's and doctorate, GRE General Test, minimum GPA of 3.0. Additional exam requirements/recommendations for international students: Required—TOEFL (minimum score 550 paper-based). Electronic applications accepted.

University of California, Irvine, Henry Samueli School of Engineering, Department of Mechanical and Aerospace Engineering, Irvine, CA 92697. Offers MS, PhD. *Program availability:* Part-time. *Students:* 138 full-time (36 women), 7 part-time (0 women); includes 28 minority (4 Black or African American, non-Hispanic/Latino; 1 American Indian or Alaska Native, non-Hispanic/Latino; 10 Asian, non-Hispanic/Latino; 10 Hispanic/Latino; 3 Two or more races, non-Hispanic/Latino), 84 international. Average age 26. 636 applicants, 20% accepted, 47 enrolled. In 2016, 63 master's, 7 doctorates awarded. Terminal master's awarded for partial completion of doctoral program. *Degree requirements:* For doctorate, thesis/dissertation. *Entrance requirements:* For master's and doctorate, GRE General Test, minimum GPA of 3.0, 3 letters of recommendation. Additional exam requirements/recommendations for international students: Required—TOEFL (minimum score 550 paper-based). *Application deadline:* For fall admission, 1/15 priority date for domestic students, 1/15 for international students. Applications are processed on a rolling basis. Application fee: $105 ($125 for international students). Electronic applications accepted. *Financial support:* Fellowships with tuition reimbursements, research assistantships with full tuition reimbursements, teaching assistantships with tuition reimbursements, institutionally sponsored loans, traineeships, health care benefits, and unspecified assistantships available. Financial award application deadline: 3/1; financial award applicants required to submit FAFSA. *Faculty research:* Thermal and fluid sciences, combustion and propulsion, control systems, robotics, lightweight structures. *Unit head:* Prof. Kenneth Mease, Chair, 949-824-5855, Fax: 949-824-8585, E-mail: kmease@uci.edu. *Application contact:* Prof. Roger Rangel, Graduate Admissions Advisor, 949-824-4033, Fax: 949-824-8585, E-mail: rhrangel@uci.edu.
Website: http://mae.eng.uci.edu/

University of California, Los Angeles, Graduate Division, Henry Samueli School of Engineering and Applied Science, Department of Mechanical and Aerospace Engineering, Program in Mechanical Engineering, Los Angeles, CA 90095-1597. Offers MS, PhD. *Students:* 264 full-time (44 women); includes 66 minority (45 Asian, non-Hispanic/Latino; 14 Hispanic/Latino; 1 Native Hawaiian or other Pacific Islander, non-Hispanic/Latino; 6 Two or more races, non-Hispanic/Latino), 136 international. 790 applicants, 39% accepted, 102 enrolled. In 2016, 70 master's, 23 doctorates awarded. *Degree requirements:* For master's, comprehensive exam or thesis; for doctorate, thesis/dissertation, qualifying exams. *Entrance requirements:* For master's, GRE General Test, minimum GPA of 3.0; for doctorate, GRE General Test, minimum GPA of 3.25. Additional exam requirements/recommendations for international students: Required—TOEFL (minimum score 560 paper-based; 87 iBT), IELTS (minimum score 7). *Application deadline:* For fall admission, 12/1 for domestic and international students. Application fee: $105 ($125 for international students). Electronic applications accepted. *Financial support:* Fellowships, research assistantships, teaching assistantships, Federal Work-Study, institutionally sponsored loans, and tuition waivers (full and partial) available. Financial award application deadline: 12/1; financial award applicants required to submit FAFSA. *Faculty research:* Applied mathematics, applied plasma physics, dynamics, fluid mechanics, heat and mass transfer, design, robotics and manufacturing, nanoelectromechanical/microelectromechanical systems (NEMS/MEMS), structural and solid mechanics, systems and control. *Unit head:* Dr. Christopher S. Lynch, Chair, 310-825-7660, E-mail: cslynch@seas.ucla.edu. *Application contact:* Angie Castillo, Student Affairs Officer, 310-825-7793, Fax: 310-206-4830, E-mail: angie@seas.ucla.edu.
Website: http://www.mae.ucla.edu/

University of California, Merced, Graduate Division, School of Engineering, Merced, CA 95343. Offers biological engineering and small scale technologies (MS, PhD); electrical engineering and computer science (MS, PhD); environmental systems (MS, PhD); mechanical engineering (MS); mechanical engineering and applied mechanics (PhD). *Faculty:* 44 full-time (7 women). *Students:* 170 full-time (52 women), 2 part-time (0 women); includes 34 minority (2 Black or African American, non-Hispanic/Latino; 11 Asian, non-Hispanic/Latino; 14 Hispanic/Latino; 2 Native Hawaiian or other Pacific Islander, non-Hispanic/Latino; 5 Two or more races, non-Hispanic/Latino), 99 international. Average age 28. 307 applicants, 35% accepted, 46 enrolled. In 2016, 15 master's, 12 doctorates awarded. Terminal master's awarded for partial completion of doctoral program. *Degree requirements:* For master's, variable foreign language requirement, comprehensive exam, thesis or alternative; for doctorate, variable foreign language requirement, comprehensive exam, thesis/dissertation. *Entrance requirements:* For master's and doctorate, GRE. Additional exam requirements/recommendations for international students: Required—TOEFL (minimum score 550 paper-based; 80 iBT); Recommended—IELTS (minimum score 7). *Application deadline:* For fall admission, 1/15 priority date for domestic and international students. Applications are processed on a rolling basis. Application fee: $90 ($110 for international students). Electronic applications accepted. *Expenses:* Contact institution. *Financial support:* In 2016–17, 150 students received support, including 16 fellowships with full tuition reimbursements available (averaging $19,088 per year), 45 research assistantships with full tuition reimbursements available (averaging $18,389 per year), 89 teaching assistantships with full tuition reimbursements available (averaging $19,249 per year); scholarships/grants, traineeships, and health care benefits also available. Financial award application deadline: 1/15. *Faculty research:* Water resources, biotechnology, renewable energy, big data, cyber-physical systems. *Total annual research expenditures:* $3.3 million. *Unit head:* Dr. Mark Matsumoto, Dean, Fax: 209-228-4047, E-mail: mmatsumoto@ucmerced.edu. *Application contact:* Tsu Ya, Director of Admissions and Academic Services, 209-228-4521, Fax: 209-228-6906, E-mail: tya@ucmerced.edu.

University of California, Riverside, Graduate Division, Department of Mechanical Engineering, Riverside, CA 92521. Offers MS, PhD. *Program availability:* Part-time. Terminal master's awarded for partial completion of doctoral program. *Degree requirements:* For master's, comprehensive exam or thesis, seminar in mechanical engineering; for doctorate, comprehensive exam, thesis/dissertation, seminar in mechanical engineering. *Entrance requirements:* Additional exam requirements/recommendations for international students: Required—TOEFL (minimum score 550 paper-based; 80 iBT). *Expenses:* Tuition, state resident: full-time $16,666. Tuition, nonresident: full-time $31,768. *Required fees:* $11,055.54 per quarter. $3685.18 per quarter. Tuition and fees vary according to campus/location and program. *Faculty research:* Advanced robotics and machine design, air quality modeling group, computational fluid dynamics, computational mechanics and materials, biomaterials and nanotechnology laboratory.

University of California, San Diego, Graduate Division, Department of Mechanical and Aerospace Engineering, Program in Mechanical Engineering, La Jolla, CA 92093. Offers MS, PhD. *Students:* 181 full-time (37 women), 36 part-time (11 women). 749 applicants, 36% accepted, 77 enrolled. In 2016, 33 master's, 20 doctorates awarded. *Degree requirements:* For master's, comprehensive exam (for some programs), thesis (for some programs), comprehensive exam or thesis; for doctorate, comprehensive exam, thesis/dissertation. *Entrance requirements:* For master's and doctorate, GRE General Test, minimum GPA of 3.0. Additional exam requirements/recommendations for international students: Required—TOEFL (minimum score 550 paper-based; 80 iBT), IELTS (minimum score 7). *Application deadline:* For fall admission, 12/14 for domestic students. Application fee: $105 ($125 for international students). Electronic applications accepted. *Expenses:* Tuition, state resident: full-time $11,220. Tuition, nonresident: full-time $26,322. *Required fees:* $1864. *Financial support:* Fellowships, research assistantships, teaching assistantships, scholarships/grants, and unspecified assistantships available. Financial award applicants required to submit FAFSA. *Faculty research:* Mechatronics, sensor integration, robotics, vehicle design in water/land/air, medical devices. *Unit head:* Vitali Nesterenko, Chair, 858-534-0113, E-mail: mae-chair-l@ucsd.edu. *Application contact:* Lydia Ramirez, Graduate Coordinator, 858-534-4387, E-mail: mae-gradadm-l@ucsd.edu.
Website: http://maeweb.ucsd.edu/

University of California, Santa Barbara, Graduate Division, College of Engineering, Department of Mechanical Engineering, Santa Barbara, CA 93106-5070. Offers bioengineering (PhD); mechanical engineering (MS); MS/PhD. Terminal master's awarded for partial completion of doctoral program. *Degree requirements:* For master's, thesis optional; for doctorate, comprehensive exam, thesis/dissertation. *Entrance requirements:* For master's and doctorate, GRE. Additional exam requirements/recommendations for international students: Required—TOEFL (minimum score 550 paper-based; 80 iBT), IELTS (minimum score 7). Electronic applications accepted. *Faculty research:* Micro/nanoscale technology; bioengineering and systems biology; computational science and engineering, dynamics systems, controls and robotics; thermofluid sciences; solid mechanics, materials, and structures.

University of Central Florida, College of Engineering and Computer Science, Department of Mechanical and Aerospace Engineering, Program in Mechanical Engineering, Orlando, FL 32816. Offers MSME, PhD. *Students:* 143 full-time (15

women), 58 part-time (7 women); includes 53 minority (6 Black or African American, non-Hispanic/Latino; 11 Asian, non-Hispanic/Latino; 29 Hispanic/Latino; 7 Two or more races, non-Hispanic/Latino), 77 international. Average age 28. 235 applicants, 52% accepted, 73 enrolled. In 2016, 30 master's, 14 doctorates awarded. *Degree requirements:* For master's, thesis or alternative; for doctorate, thesis/dissertation, candidacy exam, departmental qualifying exam. *Entrance requirements:* Additional exam requirements/recommendations for international students: Required—TOEFL. *Application deadline:* For fall admission, 7/15 for domestic students; for spring admission, 12/1 for domestic students. Application fee: $30. Electronic applications accepted. *Expenses:* Tuition, state resident: part-time $288.16 per credit hour. Tuition, nonresident: part-time $1071.31 per credit hour. *Financial support:* In 2016–17, 98 students received support, including 29 fellowships with partial tuition reimbursements available (averaging $21,676 per year), 56 research assistantships with partial tuition reimbursements available (averaging $10,413 per year), 37 teaching assistantships with partial tuition reimbursements available (averaging $10,640 per year); career-related internships or fieldwork, institutionally sponsored loans, scholarships/grants, tuition waivers (partial), and unspecified assistantships also available. Financial award application deadline: 3/1; financial award applicants required to submit FAFSA. *Unit head:* Dr. Yoav Peles, Chair, 407-823-2416, Fax: 407-823-0208, E-mail: yoav.peles@ucf.edu. *Application contact:* Assistant Director, Graduate Admissions, 407-823-2766, Fax: 407-823-6442, E-mail: gradadmissions@ucf.edu.
Website: http://mae.ucf.edu/academics/graduate/

University of Central Oklahoma, The Jackson College of Graduate Studies, College of Mathematics and Science, Department of Engineering and Physics, Edmond, OK 73034-5209. Offers biomedical engineering (MS); electrical engineering (MS); mechanical systems (MS); physics (MS). *Program availability:* Part-time. *Degree requirements:* For master's, thesis optional. *Entrance requirements:* For master's, GRE, 24 hours of course work in physics or equivalent, mathematics through differential equations, minimum GPA of 2.75 overall and 3.0 in last 60 hours attempted. Additional exam requirements/recommendations for international students: Required—TOEFL (minimum score 550 paper-based). Electronic applications accepted.

University of Cincinnati, Graduate School, College of Engineering and Applied Science, Department of Mechanical and Materials Engineering, Program in Mechanical Engineering, Cincinnati, OH 45221. Offers MS, PhD. *Program availability:* Evening/weekend. Terminal master's awarded for partial completion of doctoral program. *Degree requirements:* For master's, oral exam or thesis defense; for doctorate, variable foreign language requirement, thesis/dissertation. *Entrance requirements:* For master's and doctorate, GRE General Test. Additional exam requirements/recommendations for international students: Required—TOEFL (minimum score 575 paper-based). Electronic applications accepted. *Expenses: Tuition, area resident:* Full-time $12,790; part-time $389 per credit hour. Tuition, state resident: full-time $13,290; part-time $419 per credit hour. Tuition, nonresident: full-time $24,532; part-time $976 per credit hour. *International tuition:* $24,832 full-time. *Required fees:* $3958; $140 per credit hour. Tuition and fees vary according to course load, degree level, program and reciprocity agreements. *Faculty research:* Signature analysis, structural analysis, energy, design, robotics.

University of Colorado Boulder, Graduate School, College of Engineering and Applied Science, Department of Mechanical Engineering, Boulder, CO 80309. Offers ME, MS, PhD. *Faculty:* 32 full-time (7 women). *Students:* 188 full-time (40 women), 5 part-time (0 women); includes 21 minority (7 Asian, non-Hispanic/Latino; 9 Hispanic/Latino; 5 Two or more races, non-Hispanic/Latino), 63 international. Average age 26. 347 applicants, 48% accepted, 54 enrolled. In 2016, 59 master's, 18 doctorates awarded. Terminal master's awarded for partial completion of doctoral program. *Degree requirements:* For master's, comprehensive exam, thesis optional; for doctorate, comprehensive exam, thesis/dissertation, final and preliminary exams. *Entrance requirements:* For master's and doctorate, minimum undergraduate GPA of 3.0. Additional exam requirements/recommendations for international students: Required—TOEFL. *Application deadline:* For fall admission, 1/15 for domestic and international students; for spring admission, 10/1 for domestic students, 9/1 for international students. Applications are processed on a rolling basis. Application fee: $60 ($80 for international students). Electronic applications accepted. Application fee is waived when completed online. *Financial support:* In 2016–17, 382 students received support, including 131 fellowships (averaging $6,447 per year), 69 research assistantships with full and partial tuition reimbursements available (averaging $37,472 per year), 23 teaching assistantships with full and partial tuition reimbursements available (averaging $41,235 per year); institutionally sponsored loans, scholarships/grants, health care benefits, and unspecified assistantships also available. Financial award application deadline: 1/15; financial award applicants required to submit FAFSA. *Faculty research:* Mechanical engineering, materials engineering, materials: engineering properties, acoustic waves, nanotechnology. *Total annual research expenditures:* $10.9 million. *Application contact:* E-mail: megrad@colorado.edu.
Website: http://www.colorado.edu/mechanical

University of Colorado Colorado Springs, College of Engineering and Applied Science, Department of Mechanical and Aerospace Engineering, Colorado Springs, CO 80918. Offers mechanical engineering (MS). *Program availability:* Part-time, evening/weekend. *Faculty:* 10 full-time (2 women), 1 part-time/adjunct (0 women). *Students:* 8 full-time (2 women), 13 part-time (3 women); includes 3 minority (1 Asian, non-Hispanic/Latino; 1 Hispanic/Latino; 1 Two or more races, non-Hispanic/Latino), 1 international. Average age 27. 24 applicants, 79% accepted, 9 enrolled. In 2016, 11 master's awarded. *Degree requirements:* For master's, thesis or alternative. *Entrance requirements:* For master's, GRE General Test, BS in engineering, applied mathematics or physics from accredited institution with minimum undergraduate GPA of 3.0. Additional exam requirements/recommendations for international students: Required—TOEFL (minimum score 550 paper-based; 80 iBT), IELTS (minimum score 6.5). *Application deadline:* For fall admission, 1/15 for domestic and international students; for spring admission, 8/15 for domestic and international students. Applications are processed on a rolling basis. Application fee: $60 ($100 for international students). Electronic applications accepted. *Expenses:* Contact institution. *Financial support:* In 2016–17, 9 students received support. Research assistantships, teaching assistantships, Federal Work-Study, and unspecified assistantships available. Support available to part-time students. Financial award application deadline: 3/1; financial award applicants required to submit FAFSA. *Faculty research:* Advanced propulsion design and testing, rarefied gas dynamics, microfluidics, micro propulsion and spacecraft-thruster interactions, heat transfer and thermodynamics with application to renewable energy, modeling simulation and control of dynamic systems, tethered spacecraft, theoretical and computational fluid dynamics, thermal fluid sciences with a focus on microscale heat transfer and fluid mechanics, flame characterization using advanced diagnostics. *Total annual research expenditures:* $380,336. *Unit head:* Dr. Peter Gorder, Department Chair, 719-255-3368, E-mail: pgorder@uccs.edu. *Application contact:* Stephanie Vigil, Program Assistant, 719-255-3243, E-mail: svigil5@uccs.edu.
Website: http://eas.uccs.edu/mae/

University of Colorado Denver, College of Engineering and Applied Science, Department of Mechanical Engineering, Denver, CO 80217. Offers mechanical engineering (MS); mechanics (MS); thermal sciences (MS). *Program availability:* Part-time, evening/weekend. *Faculty:* 12 full-time (0 women), 1 (woman) part-time/adjunct. *Students:* 27 full-time (6 women), 15 part-time (3 women); includes 9 minority (1 Black or African American, non-Hispanic/Latino; 6 Hispanic/Latino; 2 Two or more races, non-Hispanic/Latino), 12 international. Average age 28. 44 applicants, 73% accepted, 9 enrolled. In 2016, 13 master's awarded. *Degree requirements:* For master's, comprehensive exam, 30 credit hours, project or thesis. *Entrance requirements:* For master's, GRE, three letters of recommendation, personal statement. Additional exam requirements/recommendations for international students: Required—TOEFL (minimum score 537 paper-based; 75 iBT); Recommended—IELTS (minimum score 6.8). *Application deadline:* For fall admission, 5/1 for domestic students, 4/15 for international students; for spring admission, 10/1 for domestic students, 9/15 for international students. Application fee: $50 ($75 for international students). Electronic applications accepted. *Expenses:* Contact institution. *Financial support:* In 2016–17, 6 students received support. Fellowships, research assistantships, teaching assistantships, career-related internships or fieldwork, Federal Work-Study, institutionally sponsored loans, scholarships/grants, traineeships, and unspecified assistantships available. Financial award application deadline: 4/1; financial award applicants required to submit FAFSA. *Faculty research:* Applied and computational mechanics, bioengineering, energy systems, tribology, micro/mesofluidics and biomechanics, vehicle dynamics. *Unit head:* Dr. Sam Welch, Chair, 303-556-8488, Fax: 303-556-6371, E-mail: sam.welch@ucdenver.edu.
Website: http://www.ucdenver.edu/academics/colleges/Engineering/Programs/Mechanical-Engineering/Pages/MechanicalEngineering.aspx

University of Colorado Denver, College of Engineering and Applied Science, Master of Engineering Program, Denver, CO 80217-3364. Offers civil engineering (M Eng), including civil engineering, geographic information systems, transportation systems; electrical engineering (M Eng); mechanical engineering (M Eng). *Program availability:* Part-time. *Students:* 35 full-time (9 women), 23 part-time (7 women); includes 5 minority (1 American Indian or Alaska Native, non-Hispanic/Latino; 2 Hispanic/Latino; 2 Two or more races, non-Hispanic/Latino), 11 international. Average age 31. 75 applicants, 63% accepted, 13 enrolled. In 2016, 17 master's awarded. *Degree requirements:* For master's, comprehensive exam, 27 credit hours of course work, 3 credit hours of report or thesis work. *Entrance requirements:* For master's, GRE (for those with GPA below 2.75), transcripts, references, statement of purpose. Additional exam requirements/recommendations for international students: Required—TOEFL (minimum score 537 paper-based; 75 iBT); Recommended—IELTS (minimum score 6.5). *Application deadline:* For fall admission, 4/1 for domestic students, 3/1 for international students; for spring admission, 10/1 for domestic students, 9/15 for international students. Applications are processed on a rolling basis. Application fee: $50 ($75 for international students). Electronic applications accepted. *Expenses:* Contact institution. *Financial support:* In 2016–17, 120 students received support. Fellowships, research assistantships, teaching assistantships, Federal Work-Study, institutionally sponsored loans, scholarships/grants, traineeships, and unspecified assistantships available. Financial award application deadline: 4/1; financial award applicants required to submit FAFSA. *Faculty research:* Civil, electrical and mechanical engineering. *Application contact:* Graduate School Admissions, 303-315-2179, E-mail: ceasgaapplications@ucdenver.edu.
Website: http://www.ucdenver.edu/academics/colleges/Engineering/admissions/Masters/Pages/MastersAdmissions.aspx

University of Connecticut, Graduate School, School of Engineering, Department of Mechanical Engineering, Storrs, CT 06269. Offers MS, PhD. Terminal master's awarded for partial completion of doctoral program. *Degree requirements:* For master's, comprehensive exam, thesis or alternative; for doctorate, thesis/dissertation. *Entrance requirements:* For master's and doctorate, GRE General Test, GRE Subject Test. Additional exam requirements/recommendations for international students: Required—TOEFL (minimum score 550 paper-based). Electronic applications accepted.

University of Dayton, Department of Mechanical and Aerospace Engineering, Dayton, OH 45469. Offers aerospace engineering (MSAE, DE, PhD); mechanical engineering (MSME, DE, PhD); renewable and clean energy (MS). *Program availability:* Part-time, blended/hybrid learning. *Faculty:* 17 full-time (3 women), 9 part-time/adjunct (1 woman). *Students:* 143 full-time (19 women), 31 part-time (7 women); includes 14 minority (1 Black or African American, non-Hispanic/Latino; 5 Asian, non-Hispanic/Latino; 4 Hispanic/Latino; 4 Two or more races, non-Hispanic/Latino), 94 international. Average age 28. 432 applicants, 15% accepted. In 2016, 66 master's awarded. *Degree requirements:* For master's, thesis optional; for doctorate, variable foreign language requirement, comprehensive exam, thesis/dissertation, departmental qualifying exam. *Entrance requirements:* For master's, BS in engineering, math, or physics. Additional exam requirements/recommendations for international students: Required—TOEFL (minimum score 550 paper-based; 80 iBT), IELTS (minimum score 6.5). *Application deadline:* Applications are processed on a rolling basis. Application fee: $0 ($50 for international students). Electronic applications accepted. *Expenses:* $890 per credit hour (for MS), $970 per credit hour (for PhD); $25 registration fee. *Financial support:* In 2016–17, 19 research assistantships with full tuition reimbursements (averaging $13,000 per year), 2 teaching assistantships with full tuition reimbursements (averaging $9,150 per year) were awarded; institutionally sponsored loans and health care benefits also available. Support available to part-time students. Financial award application deadline: 3/1; financial award applicants required to submit FAFSA. *Faculty research:* Materials, thermo-fluids, solid mechanics, energy, robotics, design and manufacturing. *Total annual research expenditures:* $1.4 million. *Unit head:* Dr. Kelly Kissock, Chair, 937-229-2999, Fax: 937-229-4766, E-mail: jkissock1@udayton.edu. *Application contact:* Dr. Vinod Jain, Graduate Program Director, 937-229-2992, Fax: 937-229-4766, E-mail: vjain1@udayton.edu.
Website: https://www.udayton.edu/engineering/departments/mechanical_and_aerospace/index.php

University of Delaware, College of Engineering, Department of Mechanical Engineering, Newark, DE 19716. Offers MEM, MSME, PhD. *Program availability:* Part-time. Terminal master's awarded for partial completion of doctoral program. *Degree requirements:* For master's, thesis (for some programs); for doctorate, thesis/dissertation. *Entrance requirements:* For master's and doctorate, GRE General Test. Additional exam requirements/recommendations for international students: Required—TOEFL (minimum score 600 paper-based). Electronic applications accepted. *Faculty research:* Biomedical engineering, clean energy, composites and nanotechnology, robotics and controls, fluid mechanics.

University of Denver, Daniel Felix Ritchie School of Engineering and Computer Science, Department of Mechanical and Materials Engineering, Denver, CO 80208. Offers bioengineering (MS); engineering (MS, PhD), including management (MS); materials science (MS, PhD); mechanical engineering (MS, PhD). *Program availability:* Part-time. *Faculty:* 11 full-time (1 woman), 2 part-time/adjunct (both women). *Students:* 2 full-time (0 women), 27 part-time (7 women); includes 6 minority (1 Asian, non-Hispanic/Latino; 5 Hispanic/Latino), 13 international. Average age 28. 57 applicants, 79% accepted, 13 enrolled. In 2016, 11 master's, 5 doctorates awarded. Terminal master's awarded for partial completion of doctoral program. *Degree requirements:* For master's,

thesis optional; for doctorate, comprehensive exam, thesis/dissertation. *Entrance requirements:* For master's, GRE General Test, bachelor's degree, transcripts, personal statement, resume or curriculum vitae, two letters of recommendation; for doctorate, GRE General Test, master's degree, transcripts, personal statement, resume or curriculum vitae, two letters of recommendation. Additional exam requirements/recommendations for international students: Required—TOEFL (minimum score 550 paper-based; 80 iBT). *Application deadline:* For fall admission, 2/1 priority date for domestic and international students. Applications are processed on a rolling basis. Application fee: $65. Electronic applications accepted. *Expenses:* $29,022 per year full-time. *Financial support:* In 2016–17, 15 students received support, including 4 research assistantships with tuition reimbursements available (averaging $11,667 per year), 5 teaching assistantships with tuition reimbursements available (averaging $12,084 per year); Federal Work-Study, institutionally sponsored loans, scholarships/grants, health care benefits, and unspecified assistantships also available. Financial award application deadline: 2/15; financial award applicants required to submit FAFSA. *Faculty research:* Cardiac biomechanics, novel high voltage/temperature materials and structures, high speed stereo radiography, musculoskeletal modeling, composites. *Total annual research expenditures:* $996,915. *Unit head:* Dr. Matt Gordon, Professor and Chair, 303-871-3580, Fax: 303-871-4450, E-mail: matthew.gordon@du.edu. *Application contact:* Yvonne Petitt, Assistant to the Chair, 303-871-2107, Fax: 303-871-4450, E-mail: yvonne.petitt@du.edu.
Website: http://ritchieschool.du.edu/departments/mme/

University of Detroit Mercy, College of Engineering and Science, Detroit, MI 48221. Offers chemistry (MS); civil and environmental engineering (DE); electrical and computer engineering (ME); electrical engineering (DE); engineering management (M Eng Mgt); environmental engineering (MEE); mechanical engineering (MME, DE); product development (MS); software engineering (MSSE); teaching of mathematics (MATM). *Program availability:* Part-time, evening/weekend. *Degree requirements:* For doctorate, thesis/dissertation. Electronic applications accepted. Application fee is waived when completed online. *Expenses:* Contact institution.

University of Florida, Graduate School, Herbert Wertheim College of Engineering, Department of Mechanical and Aerospace Engineering, Gainesville, FL 32611. Offers aerospace engineering (ME, MS, PhD); mechanical engineering (ME, MS, PhD). *Program availability:* Part-time, online learning. *Degree requirements:* For master's, thesis (for some programs); for doctorate, comprehensive exam, thesis/dissertation. *Entrance requirements:* For master's and doctorate, minimum GPA of 3.0. Additional exam requirements/recommendations for international students: Required—TOEFL (minimum score 550 paper-based; 80 iBT), IELTS (minimum score 6). Electronic applications accepted. *Faculty research:* Thermal sciences, design, controls and robotics, manufacturing, energy transport and utilization.

University of Hawaii at Manoa, Graduate Division, College of Engineering, Department of Mechanical Engineering, Honolulu, HI 96822. Offers MS, PhD. *Program availability:* Part-time. *Degree requirements:* For master's, comprehensive exam, thesis; for doctorate, comprehensive exam, thesis/dissertation. *Entrance requirements:* For master's and doctorate, GRE General Test. Additional exam requirements/recommendations for international students: Required—TOEFL (minimum score 550 paper-based; 79 iBT), IELTS (minimum score 5). *Faculty research:* Materials and manufacturing; mechanics, systems and control; thermal and fluid sciences.

University of Houston, Cullen College of Engineering, Department of Mechanical Engineering, Houston, TX 77204. Offers MME, MSME, PhD. *Program availability:* Part-time. Terminal master's awarded for partial completion of doctoral program. *Degree requirements:* For master's, thesis (for some programs); for doctorate, thesis/dissertation, departmental qualifying exam. *Entrance requirements:* For master's and doctorate, GRE General Test. Additional exam requirements/recommendations for international students: Required—TOEFL.

University of Idaho, College of Graduate Studies, College of Engineering, Department of Mechanical Engineering, Moscow, ID 83844. Offers M Engr, MS, PhD. *Faculty:* 15 full-time. *Students:* 21 full-time, 28 part-time. Average age 31. In 2016, 11 master's, 3 doctorates awarded. *Degree requirements:* For master's, thesis or alternative; for doctorate, thesis/dissertation. *Entrance requirements:* For master's and doctorate, minimum GPA of 3.0. Additional exam requirements/recommendations for international students: Required—TOEFL. *Application deadline:* For fall admission, 8/1 for domestic students; for spring admission, 12/15 for domestic students. Applications are processed on a rolling basis. Application fee: $60. Electronic applications accepted. *Expenses:* Tuition, state resident: full-time $6460; part-time $414 per credit hour. Tuition, nonresident: full-time $21,268; part-time $1237 per credit hour. *Required fees:* $2070; $60 per credit hour. Full-time tuition and fees vary according to course load and reciprocity agreements. *Financial support:* Research assistantships and teaching assistantships available. Financial award applicants required to submit FAFSA. *Faculty research:* Thermodynamics and energy, fluid mechanics and heat transfer, robotics, vibrational characteristics of composite materials, mechanics and materials science. *Unit head:* Dr. Steven Beyerlein, Chair, 208-885-6579, E-mail: medept@uidaho.edu. *Application contact:* Sean Scoggin, Graduate Recruitment Coordinator, 208-885-4732, Fax: 208-885-4406, E-mail: graduateadmissions@uidaho.edu.
Website: https://www.uidaho.edu/engr/departments/me

University of Illinois at Chicago, College of Engineering, Department of Mechanical and Industrial Engineering, Program in Mechanical Engineering, Chicago, IL 60607-7128. Offers fluids engineering (MS, PhD); mechanical analysis and design (MS, PhD); thermomechanical and power engineering (MS, PhD). *Program availability:* Part-time. *Degree requirements:* For master's, thesis. *Entrance requirements:* For master's, GRE General Test, minimum GPA of 2.75. Additional exam requirements/recommendations for international students: Required—TOEFL. Electronic applications accepted. *Expenses:* Contact institution. *Faculty research:* Micro/nanoelectromechanical systems (MEMS/NEMS), micro/nanomanipulation, nanoparticle, nanofluidics, microtransducers and micromechanisms, electrospinning, acoustics, dynamics and vibration, medical imaging and diagnostics, biomechanics and computational mechanics, product design, mechatronics and automatic control, multi-body systems and vehicle dynamics, IC engines, combustors, plasma, combustion, heat transfer, turbulence, multi-phase flows, molecular dynamics and air pollution control.

University of Illinois at Urbana–Champaign, Graduate College, College of Engineering, Department of Mechanical Science and Engineering, Champaign, IL 61820. Offers mechanical engineering (MS, PhD); theoretical and applied mechanics (MS, PhD). Terminal master's awarded for partial completion of doctoral program. *Entrance requirements:* Additional exam requirements/recommendations for international students: Required—TOEFL (minimum score 613 paper-based; 103 iBT), IELTS (minimum score 7).

The University of Iowa, Graduate College, College of Engineering, Department of Mechanical Engineering, Iowa City, IA 52242-1316. Offers energy systems (MS, PhD); engineering design (MS, PhD); fluid dynamics (MS, PhD); materials and manufacturing (MS, PhD); wind energy (MS, PhD). *Faculty:* 16 full-time (0 women). *Students:* 37 full-time (4 women), 12 part-time (0 women); includes 1 minority (Black or African American, non-Hispanic/Latino), 30 international. Average age 29. 75 applicants, 13% accepted, 2

enrolled. In 2016, 6 master's, 5 doctorates awarded. Terminal master's awarded for partial completion of doctoral program. *Degree requirements:* For master's, oral exam or thesis; for doctorate, comprehensive exam, thesis/dissertation. *Entrance requirements:* For master's and doctorate, GRE (minimum Verbal score of 153, Quantitative 151), minimum undergraduate GPA of 3.0. Additional exam requirements/recommendations for international students: Required—TOEFL (minimum score 600 paper-based; 100 iBT), IELTS (minimum score 7). *Application deadline:* For fall admission, 1/15 for domestic and international students; for spring admission, 9/1 for domestic and international students; for summer admission, 1/15 for domestic and international students. Application fee: $60 ($100 for international students). Electronic applications accepted. *Financial support:* In 2016–17, 56 students received support, including 37 research assistantships with full tuition reimbursements available (averaging $22,981 per year), 19 teaching assistantships with full tuition reimbursements available (averaging $18,809 per year); traineeships and unspecified assistantships also available. Financial award applicants required to submit FAFSA. *Faculty research:* Computer simulation methodology, biomechanics, metal casting, dynamics, laser processing, system reliability, ship hydrodynamics, solid mechanics, fluid dynamics, energy, human modeling and Nano technology. *Total annual research expenditures:* $9.1 million. *Unit head:* Dr. Ching-Long Lin, Departmental Executive Officer, 319-335-5673, Fax: 319-335-5669, E-mail: ching-long-lin@uiowa.edu. *Application contact:* Tara Hoadley, Academic Program Specialist, 319-335-5939, Fax: 319-335-5669, E-mail: mech_eng@engineering.uiowa.edu.
Website: https://mie.engineering.uiowa.edu

The University of Kansas, Graduate Studies, School of Engineering, Department of Mechanical Engineering, Lawrence, KS 66045. Offers MS, PhD. *Program availability:* Part-time. *Students:* 36 full-time (6 women), 11 part-time (1 woman); includes 2 minority (1 Asian, non-Hispanic/Latino; 1 Two or more races, non-Hispanic/Latino), 31 international. Average age 26. 115 applicants, 22% accepted, 5 enrolled. In 2016, 11 master's, 1 doctorate awarded. Terminal master's awarded for partial completion of doctoral program. *Entrance requirements:* For master's, GRE, minimum GPA of 3.0, 3 letters of recommendation, official transcript, statement of purpose (one-page maximum); for doctorate, GRE, minimum GPA of 3.5, 3 letters of recommendation, official transcript, statement of purpose (one-page maximum). Additional exam requirements/recommendations for international students: Required—TOEFL or IELTS. *Application deadline:* For fall admission, 12/15 priority date for domestic and international students; for spring admission, 11/1 for domestic students, 9/30 for international students. Application fee: $65 ($85 for international students). Electronic applications accepted. *Financial support:* Fellowships, research assistantships, teaching assistantships, career-related internships or fieldwork, and scholarships/grants available. Financial award application deadline: 12/15. *Faculty research:* Automotive industry, plant operations, manufacturing, power generation, aerospace industry, transportation, bio engineering, oil and gas industry. *Unit head:* Theodore Bergman, Chair, 785-864-3181, E-mail: tlbergman@ku.edu. *Application contact:* Kate Maisch, Graduate Admissions Contact, 785-864-3181, E-mail: kume@ku.edu.
Website: http://www.me.engr.ku.edu/

University of Kentucky, Graduate School, College of Engineering, Program in Mechanical Engineering, Lexington, KY 40506-0032. Offers MSME, PhD. *Degree requirements:* For master's, comprehensive exam, thesis optional; for doctorate, comprehensive exam, thesis/dissertation. *Entrance requirements:* For master's, GRE General Test, minimum undergraduate GPA of 2.75; for doctorate, GRE General Test, minimum undergraduate GPA of 3.0. Additional exam requirements/recommendations for international students: Required—TOEFL (minimum score 550 paper-based). Electronic applications accepted. *Faculty research:* Combustion, computational fluid dynamics, design and systems, manufacturing, thermal and fluid sciences.

University of Louisiana at Lafayette, College of Engineering, Department of Mechanical Engineering, Lafayette, LA 70504. Offers MSE. *Program availability:* Evening/weekend. *Degree requirements:* For master's, comprehensive exam, thesis or alternative. *Entrance requirements:* For master's, GRE General Test, BS in mechanical engineering, minimum GPA of 2.85. Additional exam requirements/recommendations for international students: Required—TOEFL (minimum score 550 paper-based). Electronic applications accepted. *Faculty research:* CAD/CAM, machine design and vibration, thermal science.

University of Louisville, J. B. Speed School of Engineering, Department of Mechanical Engineering, Louisville, KY 40292-0001. Offers M Eng, MS, PhD. *Accreditation:* ABET (one or more programs are accredited). *Faculty:* 16 full-time (2 women), 2 part-time/adjunct (0 women). *Students:* 53 full-time (6 women), 43 part-time (5 women); includes 19 minority (3 Black or African American, non-Hispanic/Latino; 3 Asian, non-Hispanic/Latino; 11 Hispanic/Latino; 2 Two or more races, non-Hispanic/Latino), 14 international. Average age 26. 47 applicants, 53% accepted, 13 enrolled. In 2016, 40 master's awarded. *Degree requirements:* For master's, thesis optional; for doctorate, comprehensive exam, thesis/dissertation. *Entrance requirements:* For master's and doctorate, GRE General Test, two letters of recommendation, official transcripts. Additional exam requirements/recommendations for international students: Required—TOEFL (minimum score 550 paper-based; 80 iBT), IELTS (minimum score 6.5). *Application deadline:* For fall admission, 5/1 priority date for international students; for spring admission, 11/1 priority date for international students; for summer admission, 3/1 priority date for international students. Applications are processed on a rolling basis. Application fee: $60. Electronic applications accepted. *Expenses:* Tuition, state resident: full-time $12,246; part-time $681 per credit hour. Tuition, nonresident: full-time $25,486; part-time $1417 per credit hour. *Required fees:* $196. Tuition and fees vary according to program and reciprocity agreements. *Financial support:* In 2016–17, 2 fellowships with full tuition reimbursements (averaging $22,000 per year) were awarded; research assistantships with full tuition reimbursements, teaching assistantships with full tuition reimbursements, scholarships/grants, health care benefits, and tuition waivers (full) also available. Financial award application deadline: 1/1; financial award applicants required to submit FAFSA. *Faculty research:* Aerospace and automotive engineering, air pollution control, biomechanics and rehabilitation engineering, computer-aided design, micro and nanotechnology. *Total annual research expenditures:* $1 million. *Unit head:* Dr. Kevin Murphy, Jr., Chair, 502-852-6332, Fax: 502-852-6053, E-mail: kdmurp03@louisville.edu. *Application contact:* Peter Quesada, Director of Graduate Studies, 502-852-5981, E-mail: peter.quesada@louisville.edu.
Website: http://www.louisville.edu/speed/mechanical

University of Maine, Graduate School, College of Engineering, Department of Mechanical Engineering, Orono, ME 04469. Offers MS, PSM, PhD. *Faculty:* 14 full-time (2 women), 3 part-time/adjunct (0 women). *Students:* 21 full-time (3 women), 12 part-time (3 women); includes 1 minority (Asian, non-Hispanic/Latino), 16 international. Average age 29. 24 applicants, 79% accepted, 10 enrolled. In 2016, 6 master's, 1 doctorate awarded. *Degree requirements:* For master's, thesis (for some programs); for doctorate, comprehensive exam, thesis/dissertation. *Entrance requirements:* For master's and doctorate, GRE General Test. Additional exam requirements/recommendations for international students: Required—TOEFL (minimum score 80 iBT), IELTS (minimum score 6.5). *Application deadline:* For fall admission, 1/31 for domestic and international students; for spring admission, 7/31 for domestic and

international students. Applications are processed on a rolling basis. Application fee: $65. Electronic applications accepted. *Expenses:* Tuition, state resident: full-time $7524; part-time $2508 per credit. Tuition, nonresident: full-time $24,498; part-time $8166 per credit. *Required fees:* $1148; $571 per credit. *Financial support:* In 2016–17, 22 students received support, including 8 research assistantships with full tuition reimbursements available (averaging $16,200 per year), 7 teaching assistantships with full tuition reimbursements available (averaging $14,800 per year); Federal Work-Study and tuition waivers (full and partial) also available. Financial award application deadline: 3/1. *Faculty research:* Renewable energy, biomechanics and robotics, engineering mechanics, design optimization, thermal sciences. *Total annual research expenditures:* $515,912. *Unit head:* Dr. Senthil Vel, Chair, 207-581-2777, Fax: 207-581-2379, E-mail: senthil.vel@maine.edu. *Application contact:* Scott G. Delcourt, Assistant Vice President for Graduate Studies and Senior Associate Dean, 207-581-3291, Fax: 207-581-3232, E-mail: graduate@maine.edu.
Website: http://umaine.edu/mecheng/

The University of Manchester, School of Mechanical, Aerospace and Civil Engineering, Manchester, United Kingdom. Offers advanced manufacturing technology (M Ent); aerospace engineering (M Phil, M Sc, PhD); civil engineering (M Phil, M Sc, PhD); environmental engineering (M Phil, PhD); management of projects (M Phil, M Sc, PhD); mechanical engineering (M Phil, M Sc, PhD); mechanical engineering design (M Ent); nuclear engineering (M Phil, D Eng, PhD).

University of Manitoba, Faculty of Graduate Studies, Faculty of Engineering, Department of Mechanical and Manufacturing Engineering, Winnipeg, MB R3T 2N2, Canada. Offers M Eng, M Sc, PhD. *Degree requirements:* For master's, thesis; for doctorate, thesis/dissertation.

University of Maryland, Baltimore County, The Graduate School, College of Engineering and Information Technology, Department of Mechanical Engineering, Baltimore, MD 21250. Offers computational thermal fluid dynamics (Postbaccalaureate Certificate); mechanical engineering (MS, PhD); mechatronics (Postbaccalaureate Certificate). *Program availability:* Part-time. *Faculty:* 18 full-time (5 women), 5 part-time/adjunct (0 women). *Students:* 54 full-time (9 women), 21 part-time (5 women); includes 17 minority (6 Black or African American, non-Hispanic/Latino; 6 Asian, non-Hispanic/Latino; 4 Hispanic/Latino; 1 Two or more races, non-Hispanic/Latino), 27 international. Average age 28. 75 applicants, 55% accepted, 14 enrolled. In 2016, 9 master's, 2 doctorates, 4 other advanced degrees awarded. *Degree requirements:* For master's, comprehensive exam (for some programs), thesis (for some programs); for doctorate, comprehensive exam, thesis/dissertation. *Entrance requirements:* Additional exam requirements/recommendations for international students: Required—TOEFL (minimum score 550 paper-based; 80 iBT). *Application deadline:* For fall admission, 6/1 for domestic students, 1/1 for international students; for spring admission, 11/1 for domestic students, 6/1 for international students. Applications are processed on a rolling basis. Application fee: $70. Electronic applications accepted. *Expenses:* Contact institution. *Financial support:* In 2016–17, 3 fellowships with full tuition reimbursements (averaging $18,000 per year), 19 research assistantships with full tuition reimbursements (averaging $16,000 per year), 18 teaching assistantships with full tuition reimbursements (averaging $14,000 per year) were awarded; career-related internships or fieldwork, Federal Work-Study, scholarships/grants, health care benefits, tuition waivers (partial), and unspecified assistantships also available. Support available to part-time students. Financial award application deadline: 6/30; financial award applicants required to submit FAFSA. *Faculty research:* Solid mechanics and materials sciences, thermal/fluids sciences, design-manufacturing and systems, bio-mechanical engineering, engineering education. *Total annual research expenditures:* $1.2 million. *Unit head:* Dr. Charles Eggleton, Professor and Chair, 410-455-3334, Fax: 410-455-1052, E-mail: eggleton@umbc.edu. *Application contact:* Dr. Marc Zupan, Associate Professor/Graduate Program Director, 410-455-6822, Fax: 410-455-1052, E-mail: zupan@umbc.edu.
Website: http://www.me.umbc.edu/

University of Maryland, College Park, Academic Affairs, A. James Clark School of Engineering, Department of Mechanical Engineering, College Park, MD 20742. Offers electronic packaging and reliability (MS, PhD); manufacturing and design (MS, PhD); mechanics and materials (MS, PhD); reliability engineering (M Eng, MS, PhD); thermal and fluid sciences (MS, PhD). *Program availability:* Part-time, evening/weekend, online learning. *Degree requirements:* For master's, thesis optional; for doctorate, thesis/dissertation, qualifying exam. *Entrance requirements:* For master's, GRE General Test, 3 letters of recommendation; for doctorate, GRE General Test, minimum GPA of 3.0. Additional exam requirements/recommendations for international students: Required—TOEFL. Electronic applications accepted. *Faculty research:* Injection molding, electronic packaging, fluid mechanics, product engineering.

University of Massachusetts Amherst, Graduate School, College of Engineering, Department of Mechanical and Industrial Engineering, Amherst, MA 01003. Offers industrial engineering and operations research (MS, PhD); mechanical engineering (MSME, PhD). *Program availability:* Part-time. Terminal master's awarded for partial completion of doctoral program. *Degree requirements:* For master's, thesis or alternative; for doctorate, comprehensive exam, thesis/dissertation. *Entrance requirements:* For master's and doctorate, GRE General Test. Additional exam requirements/recommendations for international students: Required—TOEFL (minimum score 550 paper-based; 80 iBT), IELTS (minimum score 6.5). Electronic applications accepted.

University of Massachusetts Dartmouth, Graduate School, College of Engineering, Department of Mechanical Engineering, North Dartmouth, MA 02747-2300. Offers industrial and systems engineering (MS); mechanical engineering (MS). *Program availability:* Part-time. *Faculty:* 10 full-time (1 woman). *Students:* 18 full-time (0 women), 12 part-time (0 women); includes 2 minority (both Two or more races, non-Hispanic/Latino), 15 international. Average age 25. 57 applicants, 51% accepted, 11 enrolled. In 2016, 12 master's awarded. *Degree requirements:* For master's, thesis, project or oral exam. *Entrance requirements:* For master's, GRE (UMass Dartmouth mechanical engineering bachelor's degree recipients are exempt), statement of purpose (minimum of 300 words), resume, 3 letters of recommendation, official transcripts. Additional exam requirements/recommendations for international students: Required—TOEFL (minimum score 533 paper-based; 72 iBT). *Application deadline:* For fall admission, 2/15 priority date for domestic students, 1/15 priority date for international students; for spring admission, 11/15 priority date for domestic students, 10/15 priority date for international students. Application fee: $60. Electronic applications accepted. *Expenses:* Tuition, state resident: full-time $14,994; part-time $624.75 per credit. Tuition, nonresident: full-time $27,068; part-time $1127.83 per credit. *Required fees:* $405; $25.88 per credit. Tuition and fees vary according to course load and reciprocity agreements. *Financial support:* In 2016–17, 2 research assistantships (averaging $5,596 per year), 7 teaching assistantships (averaging $6,818 per year) were awarded; institutionally sponsored loans, scholarships/grants, and unspecified assistantships also available. Support available to part-time students. Financial award application deadline: 3/1; financial award applicants required to submit FAFSA. *Faculty research:* Biopreservation, renewable energy, fluid structure interaction, buoyant flows, high performance heat exchanges, mechanics of biomaterials, composite materials, computational mechanics. *Total annual research expenditures:* $1.1 million. *Unit head:* Wenzhen Juang, Graduate Program Director, Mechanical Engineering, 508-910-6568, E-mail: whuang@umassd.edu. *Application contact:* Steven Briggs, Director of Marketing and Recruitment for Graduate Studies, 508-999-8604, Fax: 508-999-8183, E-mail: graduate@umassd.edu.
Website: http://www.umassd.edu/engineering/mne/graduate

University of Massachusetts Lowell, Francis College of Engineering, Department of Mechanical Engineering, Lowell, MA 01854. Offers MS Eng, PhD. *Program availability:* Part-time. *Degree requirements:* For master's, thesis or alternative; for doctorate, 2 foreign languages, comprehensive exam, thesis/dissertation. *Entrance requirements:* For master's and doctorate, GRE General Test. Additional exam requirements/recommendations for international students: Required—TOEFL (minimum score 560 paper-based). Electronic applications accepted. *Faculty research:* Composites, heat transfer.

University of Memphis, Graduate School, Herff College of Engineering, Department of Mechanical Engineering, Memphis, TN 38103. Offers power systems (MS). *Program availability:* Part-time. *Faculty:* 7 full-time (0 women). *Students:* 6 full-time (0 women), 2 part-time (0 women); includes 2 minority (1 Asian, non-Hispanic/Latino; 1 Two or more races, non-Hispanic/Latino), 3 international. Average age 26. 17 applicants, 65% accepted, 2 enrolled. In 2016, 2 master's awarded. Terminal master's awarded for partial completion of doctoral program. *Degree requirements:* For master's, comprehensive exam, thesis or alternative; for doctorate, comprehensive exam, thesis/dissertation. *Entrance requirements:* For master's, GRE General Test, MAT, GMAT, BS in mechanical engineering, minimum undergraduate GPA of 3.0, three letters of recommendation; for doctorate, GRE, BS in mechanical engineering, minimum undergraduate GPA of 3.0, three letters of recommendation; for Graduate Certificate, letter of intent, two letters of recommendation. Additional exam requirements/recommendations for international students: Required—TOEFL (minimum score 550 paper-based; 79 iBT). *Application deadline:* For fall admission, 8/1 for domestic students; for spring admission, 12/1 for domestic students. Application fee: $35 ($60 for international students). *Expenses:* $5,231.50 per semester full-time in-state, $9,623.50 full-time out-of-state. *Financial support:* In 2016–17, 6 students received support, including 1 research assistantship with full tuition reimbursement available (averaging $26,000 per year), 10 teaching assistantships with full tuition reimbursements available (averaging $19,500 per year); fellowships with full tuition reimbursements available, career-related internships or fieldwork, Federal Work-Study, scholarships/grants, and unspecified assistantships also available. Financial award application deadline: 2/1; financial award applicants required to submit FAFSA. *Faculty research:* Computational fluid dynamics, computational mechanics, integrated design, nondestructive testing, operations research. *Unit head:* Dr. Sumanta Acharya, Chair, 901-678-2173, Fax: 901-678-5459. *Application contact:* Dr. Teong Tan, Graduate Studies Coordinator, 901-678-3264, Fax: 901-678-5459, E-mail: ttan@memphis.edu.
Website: http://www.memphis.edu/me/

University of Miami, Graduate School, College of Engineering, Department of Mechanical and Aerospace Engineering, Coral Gables, FL 33124. Offers MSME, PhD. *Program availability:* Part-time. *Degree requirements:* For master's, thesis (for some programs); for doctorate, comprehensive exam, thesis/dissertation. *Entrance requirements:* For master's and doctorate, GRE General Test, minimum GPA of 3.0. Additional exam requirements/recommendations for international students: Required—TOEFL (minimum score 550 paper-based). Electronic applications accepted. *Faculty research:* Internal combustion engines, heat transfer, hydrogen energy, controls, fuel cells.

University of Michigan, College of Engineering, Department of Mechanical Engineering, Ann Arbor, MI 48109. Offers MSE, PhD. *Program availability:* Part-time. *Students:* 506 full-time (94 women), 6 part-time (2 women). 1,619 applicants, 25% accepted, 202 enrolled. In 2016, 172 master's, 37 doctorates awarded. Terminal master's awarded for partial completion of doctoral program. *Degree requirements:* For master's, thesis optional; for doctorate, thesis/dissertation, oral defense of dissertation, preliminary and qualifying exams. *Entrance requirements:* For master's, GRE General Test, undergraduate degree in same or relevant field; for doctorate, GRE General Test. Additional exam requirements/recommendations for international students: Required—TOEFL (minimum score 560 paper-based). *Application deadline:* Applications are processed on a rolling basis. Electronic applications accepted. *Expenses:* Tuition, state resident: full-time $21,466; part-time $1152 per credit hour. Tuition, nonresident: full-time $43,346; part-time $2367 per credit hour. Part-time tuition and fees vary according to course load, degree level and program. *Financial support:* Fellowships, research assistantships, teaching assistantships, institutionally sponsored loans, health care benefits, tuition waivers (full), and unspecified assistantships available. *Faculty research:* Design and manufacturing, systems and controls, combustion and heat transfer, materials and solid mechanics, dynamics and vibrations, biosystems, fluid mechanics, microsystems, environmental sustainability's. *Total annual research expenditures:* $31.8 million. *Unit head:* Kon-Well Wang, Department Chair, 734-764-8464, E-mail: kwwang@umich.edu. *Application contact:* Lisa Rogers, Graduate Coordinator, 734-764-0863, E-mail: lisarog@umich.edu.
Website: http://me.engin.umich.edu/

University of Michigan–Dearborn, College of Engineering and Computer Science, Mechanical Engineering (MSE) Program, Dearborn, MI 48128. Offers MSE. *Program availability:* Part-time, evening/weekend, 100% online. *Faculty:* 24 full-time (4 women), 12 part-time/adjunct (2 women). *Students:* 98 full-time (9 women), 194 part-time (23 women); includes 37 minority (3 Black or African American, non-Hispanic/Latino; 1 American Indian or Alaska Native, non-Hispanic/Latino; 15 Asian, non-Hispanic/Latino; 11 Hispanic/Latino; 7 Two or more races, non-Hispanic/Latino), 134 international. Average age 25. 398 applicants, 45% accepted, 106 enrolled. In 2016, 82 master's awarded. *Degree requirements:* For master's, thesis optional. *Entrance requirements:* For master's, BS in mechanical engineering or equivalent from accredited school with minimum GPA of 3.0. Additional exam requirements/recommendations for international students: Required—TOEFL (minimum score 560 paper-based; 84 iBT), IELTS (minimum score 6.5), or Michigan English Language Assessment Battery. *Application deadline:* For fall admission, 8/1 priority date for domestic students, 5/1 for international students; for winter admission, 12/1 priority date for domestic students, 9/1 for international students; for spring admission, 4/1 priority date for domestic students, 1/1 for international students. Applications are processed on a rolling basis. Application fee: $60. Electronic applications accepted. *Expenses:* Tuition, state resident: full-time $13,118; part-time $2280 per term. Tuition, nonresident: full-time $21,816; part-time $3771 per term. *Required fees:* $866; $658 per unit. $329 per term. Tuition and fees vary according to program. *Financial support:* Research assistantships, teaching assistantships, health care benefits, unspecified assistantships, and non-resident tuition scholarships available. Financial award application deadline: 3/1; financial award applicants required to submit FAFSA. *Faculty research:* Materials processing, magneto hydrodynamics flows for energy generation and storage, nanomaterials for energy and biosystems, energy management for automobiles, manufacturing. *Unit head:* Dr. Ben Q. Li, Chair, 313-593-5465, Fax: 313-593-3851, E-mail: benqli@umich.edu. *Application contact:* Office of Graduate Studies, 313-583-6321, E-mail: umd-graduatestudies@

umich.edu.
Website: https://umdearborn.edu/cecs/departments/mechanical-engineering/graduate-programs/mse-mechanical-engineering

University of Michigan–Dearborn, College of Engineering and Computer Science, PhD Program in Mechanical Sciences and Engineering, Dearborn, MI 48128. Offers PhD. *Program availability:* Part-time, evening/weekend. *Degree requirements:* For doctorate, thesis/dissertation. *Entrance requirements:* For doctorate, GRE, bachelor's or master's degree in engineering, applied math, computer science, or physical science. Additional exam requirements/recommendations for international students: Required—TOEFL (minimum score 560 paper-based; 84 iBT), IELTS (minimum score 6.5). *Application deadline:* For fall admission, 2/15 for domestic and international students. Application fee: $60. Electronic applications accepted. *Expenses:* Tuition, state resident: full-time $13,118; part-time $2280 per term. Tuition, nonresident: full-time $21,816; part-time $3771 per term. *Required fees:* $866; $658 per unit. $329 per term. Tuition and fees vary according to program. *Financial support:* Research assistantships, teaching assistantships, scholarships/grants, health care benefits, and unspecified assistantships available. Financial award application deadline: 2/15; financial award applicants required to submit FAFSA. *Unit head:* Dr. Oleg Zikanov, Director, 313-593-3718, E-mail: zikanov@umich.edu. *Application contact:* Office of Graduate Studies Staff, 313-583-6321, E-mail: umd-graduatestudies@umich.edu.
Website: https://umdearborn.edu/cecs/departments/mechanical-engineering/graduate-programs/phd-mechanical-sciences-and-engineering

University of Michigan–Flint, College of Arts and Sciences, Program in Mechanical Engineering, Flint, MI 48502-1950. Offers MSE. *Program availability:* Part-time. *Degree requirements:* For master's, thesis optional. *Entrance requirements:* For master's, GRE, bachelor's degree in mechanical engineering from regionally-accredited college or university, minimum overall undergraduate GPA of 3.0. Additional exam requirements/recommendations for international students: Required—TOEFL (minimum score 84 iBT), IELTS (minimum score 6.5). *Application deadline:* For fall admission, 8/1 for domestic students, 5/1 for international students; for winter admission, 11/15 for domestic students, 8/1 for international students. Applications are processed on a rolling basis. Application fee: $55. Electronic applications accepted. *Financial support:* Federal Work-Study, scholarships/grants, and unspecified assistantships available. Support available to part-time students. Financial award application deadline: 3/1; financial award applicants required to submit FAFSA. *Unit head:* Susie Visser, Program Manager, 810-762-3131, E-mail: vissers@umflint.edu. *Application contact:* Bradley T. Maki, Director of Graduate Admissions, 810-762-3171, Fax: 810-766-6789, E-mail: bmaki@umflint.edu.
Website: https://www.umflint.edu/graduateprograms/master-science-engineering-mse

University of Minnesota, Twin Cities Campus, College of Science and Engineering, Department of Mechanical Engineering, Minneapolis, MN 55455-0213. Offers MSME, PhD. *Program availability:* Part-time. *Degree requirements:* For doctorate, thesis/dissertation. *Entrance requirements:* For master's, GRE General Test, minimum GPA of 3.0; for doctorate, GRE General Test. Additional exam requirements/recommendations for international students: Required—TOEFL. Electronic applications accepted. *Faculty research:* Particle technology, solar energy, controls, heat transfer, fluid power, plasmas, medical devices, bioengineering, nanotechnology, intelligent vehicles.

University of Missouri, Office of Research and Graduate Studies, College of Engineering, Department of Mechanical and Aerospace Engineering, Columbia, MO 65211. Offers MS, PhD. *Faculty:* 33 full-time (0 women), 3 part-time/adjunct (1 woman). *Students:* 47 full-time (7 women), 66 part-time (11 women). *Degree requirements:* For master's, thesis; for doctorate, one foreign language, thesis/dissertation. *Entrance requirements:* For master's and doctorate, GRE General Test, minimum GPA of 3.0. Additional exam requirements/recommendations for international students: Required—TOEFL (minimum score 500 paper-based; 61 iBT). *Application deadline:* For fall admission, 5/31 priority date for domestic and international students; for winter admission, 10/31 priority date for domestic and international students; for spring admission, 4/30 priority date for domestic and international students. Applications are processed on a rolling basis. Application fee: $75 ($90 for international students). Electronic applications accepted. *Expenses:* Tuition, state resident: full-time $6347; part-time $352.60 per credit hour. Tuition, nonresident: full-time $17,379; part-time $965.50 per credit hour. *Required fees:* $1035. Tuition and fees vary according to course load, campus/location and program. *Financial support:* Fellowships, research assistantships, teaching assistantships, institutionally sponsored loans, scholarships/grants, health care benefits, and unspecified assistantships available. Support available to part-time students.
Website: http://engineering.missouri.edu/mae/degree-programs/

University of Missouri–Kansas City, School of Computing and Engineering, Kansas City, MO 64110-2499. Offers civil engineering (MS); computer and electrical engineering (PhD); computer science (MS), including bioinformatics, software engineering, telecommunications networking; computer science and informatics (PhD); computing (PhD); electrical engineering (MS); engineering (PhD); engineering and construction management (Graduate Certificate); mechanical engineering (MS); telecommunications and computer networking (PhD). PhD (interdisciplinary) offered through the School of Graduate Studies. *Program availability:* Part-time. *Faculty:* 45 full-time (6 women), 26 part-time/adjunct (4 women). *Students:* 473 full-time (155 women), 207 part-time (42 women); includes 24 minority (10 Black or African American, non-Hispanic/Latino; 10 Asian, non-Hispanic/Latino; 4 Hispanic/Latino), 581 international. Average age 25. 1,143 applicants, 44% accepted, 227 enrolled. In 2016, 446 master's, 2 other advanced degrees awarded. *Degree requirements:* For doctorate, thesis/dissertation. *Entrance requirements:* For master's, GRE General Test, minimum GPA of 3.0, 3 letters of recommendation from professors; for doctorate, GRE General Test, minimum GPA of 3.5. Additional exam requirements/recommendations for international students: Required—TOEFL (minimum score 550 paper-based; 80 iBT). *Application deadline:* For fall admission, 1/15 priority date for domestic students, 1/15 for international students. Applications are processed on a rolling basis. Application fee: $45 ($50 for international students). *Financial support:* In 2016–17, 37 research assistantships with partial tuition reimbursements (averaging $15,679 per year), 47 teaching assistantships with partial tuition reimbursements (averaging $16,830 per year) were awarded; career-related internships or fieldwork, Federal Work-Study, scholarships/grants, tuition waivers (partial), and unspecified assistantships also available. Support available to part-time students. Financial award application deadline: 3/1; financial award applicants required to submit FAFSA. *Faculty research:* Algorithms, bioinformatics and medical informatics, biomechanics/biomaterials, civil engineering materials, networking and telecommunications, thermal science. *Unit head:* Dr. Kevin Z. Truman, Dean, 816-235-2399, Fax: 816-235-5159. *Application contact:* 816-235-2399, Fax: 816-235-5159.
Website: http://sce.umkc.edu/

University of Nebraska–Lincoln, Graduate College, College of Engineering, Department of Mechanical and Materials Engineering, Lincoln, NE 68588-0526. Offers biomedical engineering (PhD); engineering mechanics (MS); materials engineering (PhD); mechanical engineering (MS), including materials science engineering, metallurgical engineering; mechanical engineering and applied mechanics (PhD); MS/MS. MS/MS offered with University of Rouen-France. *Degree requirements:* For master's, thesis optional; for doctorate, comprehensive exam, thesis/dissertation. *Entrance requirements:* For master's and doctorate, GRE General Test. Additional exam requirements/recommendations for international students: Required—TOEFL (minimum score 550 paper-based). Electronic applications accepted. *Faculty research:* Medical robotics, rehabilitation dynamics, and design; combustion, fluid mechanics, and heat transfer; nano-materials, manufacturing, and devices; fiber, tissue, bio-polymer, and adaptive composites; blast, impact, fracture, and failure; electro-active and magnetic materials and devices; functional materials, design, and added manufacturing; materials characterization, modeling, and computational simulation.

University of Nevada, Las Vegas, Graduate College, Howard R. Hughes College of Engineering, Department of Mechanical Engineering, Las Vegas, NV 89154-4027. Offers aerospace engineering (MS); biomedical engineering (MS); materials and nuclear engineering (MS); mechanical engineering (MS, PhD); nuclear criticality safety (Certificate); nuclear safeguards and security (Certificate). *Program availability:* Part-time. *Faculty:* 16 full-time (2 women), 3 part-time/adjunct (1 woman). *Students:* 47 full-time (13 women), 21 part-time (4 women); includes 15 minority (1 American Indian or Alaska Native, non-Hispanic/Latino; 6 Asian, non-Hispanic/Latino; 3 Hispanic/Latino; 5 Two or more races, non-Hispanic/Latino), 16 international. Average age 30. 68 applicants, 54% accepted, 15 enrolled. In 2016, 10 master's, 3 doctorates, 4 other advanced degrees awarded. *Degree requirements:* For master's, thesis optional, design project; for doctorate, comprehensive exam, thesis/dissertation. *Entrance requirements:* For master's, GRE General Test, statement of purpose; 2 letters of recommendation; for doctorate, GRE General Test, 3 letters of recommendation; statement of purpose; bachelor's degree with minimum GPA of 3.5/master's degree with minimum GPA of 3.3. Additional exam requirements/recommendations for international students: Required—TOEFL (minimum score 550 paper-based; 80 iBT), IELTS (minimum score 7). *Application deadline:* For fall admission, 8/1 for domestic students, 5/1 for international students; for spring admission, 12/1 for domestic students, 10/1 for international students. Application fee: $60 ($95 for international students). Electronic applications accepted. *Expenses:* $269.25 per credit, $792 per 3-credit course; $9,634 per year resident; $23,274 per year non-resident; $7,094 fees non-resident (7 credits or more); $1,307 annual health insurance fee. *Financial support:* In 2016–17, 1 fellowship with partial tuition reimbursement (averaging $15,000 per year), 13 research assistantships with partial tuition reimbursements (averaging $17,115 per year), 27 teaching assistantships with partial tuition reimbursements (averaging $16,172 per year) were awarded; institutionally sponsored loans, scholarships/grants, health care benefits, and unspecified assistantships also available. Financial award application deadline: 3/15. *Faculty research:* Dynamics and control systems; energy systems including renewable and nuclear; computational fluid and solid mechanics; structures, materials and manufacturing; vibrations and acoustics. *Total annual research expenditures:* $4.5 million. *Unit head:* Dr. Brendan O'Toole, Chair/Professor, 702-895-3885, Fax: 702-895-3936, E-mail: brendan.otoole@unlv.edu. *Application contact:* Dr. Hui Zhao, Graduate Coordinator, 702-895-1463, Fax: 702-895-3936, E-mail: hui.zhao@unlv.edu.
Website: http://me.unlv.edu/

University of Nevada, Reno, Graduate School, College of Engineering, Department of Mechanical Engineering, Reno, NV 89557. Offers MS, PhD. Terminal master's awarded for partial completion of doctoral program. *Degree requirements:* For master's, thesis optional; for doctorate, thesis/dissertation. *Entrance requirements:* For master's, GRE General Test, minimum GPA of 2.75; for doctorate, GRE General Test, minimum GPA of 3.0. Additional exam requirements/recommendations for international students: Required—TOEFL (minimum score 500 paper-based; 61 iBT), IELTS (minimum score 6). Electronic applications accepted. *Faculty research:* Composite, solid, fluid, thermal, and smart materials.

University of New Brunswick Fredericton, School of Graduate Studies, Faculty of Engineering, Department of Mechanical Engineering, Fredericton, NB E3B 5A3, Canada. Offers applied mechanics (M Eng, M Sc E, PhD); mechanical engineering (M Eng, M Sc E, PhD). *Program availability:* Part-time. *Degree requirements:* For master's, thesis; for doctorate, comprehensive exam, thesis/dissertation, qualifying exam. *Entrance requirements:* For master's, minimum GPA of 3.0; B Sc E; for doctorate, minimum GPA of 3.0; M Sc E. Additional exam requirements/recommendations for international students: Required—TOEFL (minimum score 580 paper-based; 80 iBT), IELTS (minimum score 7), TWE (minimum score 4), Michigan English Language Assessment Battery (minimum score 85) or CanTest (minimum score 4.5). Electronic applications accepted. *Faculty research:* Acoustics and vibration, biomedical, manufacturing and materials processing, mechatronics and design, nuclear and threat detection, renewable energy systems, robotics and applied mechanics, thermofluids and aerodynamics.

University of New Hampshire, Graduate School, College of Engineering and Physical Sciences, Department of Mechanical Engineering, Durham, NH 03824. Offers materials science (MS, PhD); mechanical engineering (M Engr, MS, PhD); systems engineering (PhD). *Program availability:* Part-time. *Degree requirements:* For master's, thesis or alternative; for doctorate, thesis/dissertation. *Entrance requirements:* For master's and doctorate, GRE. Additional exam requirements/recommendations for international students: Required—TOEFL (minimum score 550 paper-based; 80 iBT). Electronic applications accepted. *Faculty research:* Solid mechanics, dynamics, materials science, dynamic systems, automatic control.

University of New Haven, Graduate School, Tagliatela College of Engineering, Program in Mechanical Engineering, West Haven, CT 06516. Offers MS. *Program availability:* Part-time, evening/weekend. *Students:* 55 full-time (6 women), 15 part-time (0 women), 60 international. Average age 24. 231 applicants, 50% accepted, 15 enrolled. In 2016, 16 master's awarded. *Degree requirements:* For master's, thesis or alternative. *Entrance requirements:* Additional exam requirements/recommendations for international students: Required—TOEFL (minimum score 75 iBT), IELTS, PTE (minimum score 50). *Application deadline:* Applications are processed on a rolling basis. Application fee: $50. Electronic applications accepted. Application fee is waived when completed online. *Expenses: Tuition:* Full-time $15,660; part-time $870 per credit hour. *Required fees:* $200; $85 per term. Tuition and fees vary according to program. *Financial support:* Research assistantships with partial tuition reimbursements, teaching assistantships with partial tuition reimbursements, career-related internships or fieldwork, Federal Work-Study, scholarships/grants, and unspecified assistantships available. Support available to part-time students. Financial award applicants required to submit FAFSA. *Unit head:* Dr. Ravi Gorthala, Program Director, 203-479-4119, E-mail: rgorthala@newhaven.edu. *Application contact:* Michelle Mason, Director of Graduate Enrollment, 203-932-7067, E-mail: mmason@newhaven.edu.
Website: http://www.newhaven.edu/9596/

University of New Mexico, Graduate Studies, School of Engineering, Program in Mechanical Engineering, Albuquerque, NM 87131-2039. Offers MS, PhD. *Program availability:* Part-time. *Faculty:* 9 full-time (1 woman), 1 part-time/adjunct (0 women). *Students:* 39 full-time (6 women), 54 part-time (7 women); includes 29 minority (1 Black or African American, non-Hispanic/Latino; 2 Asian, non-Hispanic/Latino; 26 Hispanic/Latino), 16 international. Average age 29. 62 applicants, 37% accepted, 22 enrolled. In 2016, 16 master's, 2 doctorates awarded. *Degree requirements:* For master's, thesis optional; for doctorate, comprehensive exam, thesis/dissertation. *Entrance*

requirements: For master's and doctorate, GRE. Additional exam requirements/ recommendations for international students: Required—TOEFL (minimum score 550 paper-based; 80 iBT). *Application deadline:* For fall admission, 7/30 for domestic students, 3/1 for international students; for spring admission, 11/30 for domestic students, 8/1 for international students. Applications are processed on a rolling basis. Application fee: $50. Electronic applications accepted. *Financial support:* Fellowships, research assistantships with tuition reimbursements, teaching assistantships with tuition reimbursements, scholarships/grants, health care benefits, and unspecified assistantships available. Financial award application deadline: 3/1; financial award applicants required to submit FAFSA. *Faculty research:* Engineering mechanics and materials (including solid mechanics and materials science), mechanical sciences and engineering (including dynamic systems, controls and robotics), thermal sciences and engineering. *Total annual research expenditures:* $963,606. *Unit head:* Dr. Chris Hall, Chairperson, 505-277-1325, Fax: 505-277-1571, E-mail: cdhall@unm.edu. *Application contact:* Dr. Yu-Lin Shen, Director of Graduate Programs, 505-277-6286, Fax: 505-277-1571, E-mail: shenyl@unm.edu.
Website: http://megrad.unm.edu/

University of New Orleans, Graduate School, College of Engineering, Concentration in Mechanical Engineering, New Orleans, LA 70148. Offers MS. *Degree requirements:* For master's, thesis optional. *Entrance requirements:* For master's, GRE General Test, minimum GPA of 3.0. Additional exam requirements/recommendations for international students: Required—TOEFL (minimum score 550 paper-based; 79 iBT). Electronic applications accepted. *Faculty research:* Two-phase flow instabilities, thermal-hydrodynamic modeling, solar energy, heat transfer from sprays, boundary integral techniques in mechanics.

The University of North Carolina at Charlotte, William States Lee College of Engineering, Department of Mechanical Engineering and Engineering Science, Charlotte, NC 28223-0001. Offers mechanical engineering (MSME, PhD). *Program availability:* Part-time, evening/weekend. *Faculty:* 32 full-time (3 women). *Students:* 130 full-time (11 women), 31 part-time (3 women); includes 2 minority (1 Asian, non-Hispanic/Latino; 1 Hispanic/Latino), 118 international. Average age 26. 274 applicants, 61% accepted, 43 enrolled. In 2016, 31 master's, 5 doctorates awarded. *Degree requirements:* For master's, thesis or comprehensive exam; for doctorate, comprehensive exam, thesis/dissertation. *Entrance requirements:* For master's, GRE, baccalaureate degree from accredited institution in some area of engineering, minimum GPA of 3.0, satisfactory undergraduate preparation in engineering; for doctorate, GRE General Test, master's degree in engineering or a closely-allied field; minimum GPA of 3.5; letters of reference. Additional exam requirements/recommendations for international students: Required—TOEFL (minimum score 523 paper-based, 70 iBT) or IELTS (6.5). *Application deadline:* For fall admission, 3/1 priority date for domestic and international students; for spring admission, 10/1 priority date for domestic and international students. Applications are processed on a rolling basis. Application fee: $75. Electronic applications accepted. *Expenses:* Contact institution. *Financial support:* In 2016–17, 72 students received support, including 2 fellowships (averaging $38,385 per year), 34 research assistantships (averaging $9,768 per year), 36 teaching assistantships (averaging $6,470 per year); career-related internships or fieldwork, institutionally sponsored loans, scholarships/grants, and unspecified assistantships also available. Support available to part-time students. Financial award application deadline: 3/1; financial award applicants required to submit FAFSA. *Total annual research expenditures:* $2.5 million. *Unit head:* Dr. Scott Smith, Department Chair, 704-687-8350, E-mail: kssmith@uncc.edu. *Application contact:* Kathy B. Giddings, Director of Graduate Admissions, 704-687-5503, Fax: 704-687-1668, E-mail: gradadm@uncc.edu.
Website: http://mees.uncc.edu/

University of North Dakota, Graduate School, School of Engineering and Mines, Department of Mechanical Engineering, Grand Forks, ND 58202. Offers M Engr, MS, PhD. *Program availability:* Part-time. *Degree requirements:* For master's, comprehensive exam, thesis or alternative. *Entrance requirements:* For master's, GRE General Test, minimum GPA of 3.0 (MS), 2.5 (M Engr). Additional exam requirements/ recommendations for international students: Required—TOEFL (minimum score 550 paper-based; 79 iBT), IELTS (minimum score 6.5). *Application deadline:* For fall admission, 2/1 priority date for domestic and international students; for spring admission, 10/1 priority date for domestic and international students. Applications are processed on a rolling basis. Application fee: $35. Electronic applications accepted. *Financial support:* Fellowships with full and partial tuition reimbursements, research assistantships with full and partial tuition reimbursements, teaching assistantships with full and partial tuition reimbursements, career-related internships or fieldwork, Federal Work-Study, institutionally sponsored loans, scholarships/grants, health care benefits, tuition waivers (full and partial), and unspecified assistantships available. Support available to part-time students. Financial award application deadline: 3/15; financial award applicants required to submit FAFSA. *Faculty research:* Energy conversion, dynamics, control, manufacturing processes with special emphasis on machining, stress vibration analysis. *Unit head:* Dr. Mathew Cavalli, Director, 701-777-2571, Fax: 701-777-4838, E-mail: mathew.cavalli@mail.und.edu. *Application contact:* Staci Wells, Admissions Associate, 701-777-2945, Fax: 701-777-3619, E-mail: staci.wells@gradschool.und.edu.
Website: http://www.me.und.edu/

University of North Florida, College of Computing, Engineering, and Construction, School of Engineering, Jacksonville, FL 32224. Offers MSCE, MSEE, MSME. *Program availability:* Part-time. *Faculty:* 19 full-time (1 woman). *Students:* 15 full-time (4 women), 34 part-time (6 women); includes 10 minority (2 Asian, non-Hispanic/Latino; 5 Hispanic/Latino; 3 Two or more races, non-Hispanic/Latino), 13 international. Average age 28. 43 applicants, 63% accepted, 17 enrolled. In 2016, 14 master's awarded. *Application deadline:* For fall admission, 8/1 priority date for domestic students, 5/1 for international students; for spring admission, 12/1 priority date for domestic students, 10/1 for international students; for summer admission, 3/15 priority date for domestic students, 2/1 for international students. Application fee: $30. Tuition and fees vary according to course load, campus/location and program. *Financial support:* In 2016–17, 30 students received support, including 11 research assistantships (averaging $3,925 per year), 8 teaching assistantships (averaging $2,552 per year); Federal Work-Study, scholarships/grants, tuition waivers, and unspecified assistantships also available. Financial award application deadline: 4/1; financial award applicants required to submit FAFSA. *Total annual research expenditures:* $804,835. *Unit head:* Dr. Murat Tiryakioglu, Director, 904-620-1393, E-mail: m.tiryakioglu@unf.edu. *Application contact:* Dr. Amanda Pascale, Director, The Graduate School, 904-320-1360, Fax: 904-620-1362, E-mail: graduateschool@unf.edu.
Website: http://www.unf.edu/ccec/engineering/

University of North Texas, Robert B. Toulouse School of Graduate Studies, Denton, TX 76203-5459. Offers accounting (MS); applied anthropology (MA, MS); applied behavior analysis (Certificate); applied geography (MA); applied technology and performance improvement (M Ed, MS); art education (MA); art history (MA); art museum education (Certificate); arts leadership (Certificate); audiology (Au D); behavior analysis (MS); behavioral science (PhD); biochemistry and molecular biology (MS); biology (MA, MS); biomedical engineering (MS); business analysis (MS); chemistry (MS); clinical health psychology (PhD); communication studies (MA, MS); computer engineering (MS); computer science (MS); counseling (M Ed, MS), including clinical mental health counseling (MS), college and university counseling, elementary school counseling, secondary school counseling; creative writing (MA); criminal justice (MS); curriculum and instruction (M Ed); decision sciences (MBA); design (MA, MFA), including fashion design (MFA), innovation studies, interior design (MFA); early childhood studies (MS); economics (MS); educational leadership (M Ed, Ed D); educational psychology (MS, PhD), including family studies (MS), gifted and talented (MS), human development (MS), learning and cognition (MS), research, measurement and evaluation (MS); electrical engineering (MS); emergency management (MPA); engineering technology (MS); English (MA); English as a second language (MA); environmental science (MS); finance (MBA, MS); financial management (MPA); French (MA); health services management (MBA); higher education (M Ed, Ed D); history (MA, MS); hospitality management (MS); human resources management (MPA); information science (MS); information systems (PhD); information technologies (MBA); interdisciplinary studies (MA, MS); international studies (MA); international sustainable tourism (MS); jazz studies (MM); journalism (MA, MJ, Graduate Certificate), including interactive and virtual digital communication (Graduate Certificate), narrative journalism (Graduate Certificate), public relations (Graduate Certificate); kinesiology (MS); linguistics (MA); local government management (MPA); logistics (PhD); logistics and supply chain management (MBA); long-term care, senior housing, and aging services (MA); management (PhD); marketing (MBA); mathematics (MA, MS); mechanical and energy engineering (MS, PhD); music (MA), including ethnomusicology, music theory, musicology, performance; music composition (PhD); music education (MM Ed, PhD); nonprofit management (MPA); operations and supply chain management (MBA); performance (MM, DMA); philosophy (MA); political science (MA); professional and technical communication (MA); radio, television and film (MA, MFA); rehabilitation counseling (Certificate); sociology (MA); Spanish (MA); special education (M Ed); speech-language pathology (MA); strategic management (MBA); studio art (MFA); teaching (M Ed); MBA/MS. *Program availability:* Part-time, evening/weekend, online learning. Terminal master's awarded for partial completion of doctoral program. *Degree requirements:* For master's, variable foreign language requirement, comprehensive exam (for some programs), thesis (for some programs); for doctorate, variable foreign language requirement, comprehensive exam (for some programs), thesis/dissertation; for other advanced degree, variable foreign language requirement, comprehensive exam (for some programs). *Entrance requirements:* For master's and doctorate, GRE, GMAT. Additional exam requirements/ recommendations for international students: Required—TOEFL (minimum score 550 paper-based; 79 iBT). Electronic applications accepted.

University of Notre Dame, Graduate School, College of Engineering, Department of Aerospace and Mechanical Engineering, Notre Dame, IN 46556. Offers aerospace and mechanical engineering (M Eng, PhD); aerospace engineering (MS Aero E); mechanical engineering (MEME, MSME). Terminal master's awarded for partial completion of doctoral program. *Degree requirements:* For master's, comprehensive exam, thesis or alternative; for doctorate, thesis/dissertation, candidacy exam. *Entrance requirements:* For master's and doctorate, GRE General Test. Additional exam requirements/ recommendations for international students: Required—TOEFL (minimum score 600 paper-based; 80 iBT). Electronic applications accepted. *Faculty research:* Aerodynamics/fluid dynamics, design and manufacturing, controls/robotics, solid mechanics or biomechanics/biomaterials.

University of Oklahoma, Gallogly College of Engineering, School of Aerospace and Mechanical Engineering, Program in Mechanical Engineering, Norman, OK 73019. Offers MS, PhD. *Program availability:* Part-time. *Students:* 26 full-time (5 women), 13 part-time (3 women); includes 3 minority (1 Hispanic/Latino; 2 Two or more races, non-Hispanic/Latino), 28 international. Average age 28. 37 applicants, 41% accepted, 9 enrolled. In 2016, 8 master's, 2 doctorates awarded. *Degree requirements:* For master's, comprehensive exam (for some programs), thesis (for some programs); for doctorate, comprehensive exam, thesis/dissertation, general exam. *Entrance requirements:* For master's and doctorate, GRE, letters of reference, resume, statement of purpose. Additional exam requirements/recommendations for international students: Required—TOEFL (minimum score 79 iBT) or IELTS (minimum score 6.5). *Application deadline:* For fall admission, 1/15 for domestic and international students; for spring admission, 9/1 for domestic and international students. Application fee: $50 ($100 for international students). Electronic applications accepted. *Expenses:* Tuition, state resident: full-time $4886; part-time $203.60 per credit hour. Tuition, nonresident: full-time $18,989; part-time $791.20 per credit hour. *Required fees:* $3283; $126.25 per credit hour. $126.50 per semester. *Financial support:* In 2016–17, 36 students received support. Fellowships with full tuition reimbursements available, research assistantships with full tuition reimbursements available, teaching assistantships with full tuition reimbursements available, and scholarships/grants available. Financial award application deadline: 6/1; financial award applicants required to submit FAFSA. *Faculty research:* Composite materials and nanomechanics; robotics; biomechanics; multi-phase flows; engineering design. *Unit head:* Dr. M. Cengiz Altan, Director, 405-325-5011, Fax: 405-325-1088, E-mail: altan@ou.edu. *Application contact:* Kate O'Brien-Hamoush, Student Services Coordinator, 405-325-5013, Fax: 405-325-1088, E-mail: kobrien@ou.edu.
Website: http://www.ou.edu/coe/ame.html

University of Ottawa, Faculty of Graduate and Postdoctoral Studies, Faculty of Engineering, Ottawa-Carleton Institute for Mechanical and Aerospace Engineering, Ottawa, ON K1N 6N5, Canada. Offers M Eng, MA Sc, PhD. MA Sc, M Eng, PhD offered jointly with Carleton University. *Degree requirements:* For master's, thesis or alternative; for doctorate, thesis/dissertation, seminar series, qualifying exam. *Entrance requirements:* For master's, honors degree or equivalent, minimum B average; for doctorate, master's degree, minimum B+ average. Electronic applications accepted. *Faculty research:* Fluid mechanics-heat transfer, solid mechanics, design, manufacturing and control.

University of Pennsylvania, School of Engineering and Applied Science, Department of Mechanical Engineering and Applied Mechanics, Philadelphia, PA 19104. Offers MSE, PhD. *Program availability:* Part-time. *Faculty:* 32 full-time (7 women), 10 part-time/adjunct (0 women). *Students:* 122 full-time (21 women), 40 part-time (7 women); includes 14 minority (1 Black or African American, non-Hispanic/Latino; 4 Asian, non-Hispanic/Latino; 6 Hispanic/Latino; 3 Two or more races, non-Hispanic/Latino), 106 international. Average age 25. 633 applicants, 21% accepted, 66 enrolled. In 2016, 59 master's, 12 doctorates awarded. *Degree requirements:* For master's, comprehensive exam, thesis optional; for doctorate, comprehensive exam, thesis/dissertation. *Entrance requirements:* For master's and doctorate, GRE. Additional exam requirements/ recommendations for international students: Required—TOEFL (minimum score 100 iBT), IELTS (minimum score 7). *Application deadline:* For fall admission, 3/15 priority date for domestic students, 3/15 for international students. Application fee: $80. Electronic applications accepted. *Expenses: Tuition:* Full-time $31,068; part-time $5762 per course. *Required fees:* $3200; $336 per course. Full-time tuition and fees vary according to degree level, program and student level. Part-time tuition and fees vary according to course load, degree level and program. *Faculty research:* Biorobotics, computational mechanics, energy conversion, mechanics of materials, robotics. *Application contact:* William Fenton, Assistant Director of Graduate Admissions, 215-

898-4542, Fax: 215-573-5577, E-mail: gradstudies@seas.upenn.edu.
Website: http://www.me.upenn.edu/prospective-students/masters/masters-degrees.php

University of Pittsburgh, Swanson School of Engineering, Department of Mechanical Engineering and Materials Science, Pittsburgh, PA 15260. Offers MSME, MSNE, PhD. *Program availability:* Part-time, 100% online. *Faculty:* 29 full-time (1 woman), 24 part-time/adjunct (2 women). *Students:* 131 full-time (17 women), 97 part-time (20 women); includes 12 minority (3 Black or African American, non-Hispanic/Latino; 4 Asian, non-Hispanic/Latino; 4 Hispanic/Latino; 1 Two or more races, non-Hispanic/Latino), 99 international. 604 applicants, 41% accepted, 60 enrolled. In 2016, 85 master's, 17 doctorates awarded. Terminal master's awarded for partial completion of doctoral program. *Degree requirements:* For doctorate, comprehensive exam, thesis/dissertation, final oral exams. *Entrance requirements:* For master's and doctorate, minimum GPA of 3.0. Additional exam requirements/recommendations for international students: Required—TOEFL (minimum score 550 paper-based; 80 iBT). *Application deadline:* For fall admission, 3/1 priority date for domestic and international students; for spring admission, 7/1 priority date for domestic and international students. Applications are processed on a rolling basis. Application fee: $50. Electronic applications accepted. *Expenses:* $24,962 full-time per academic year in-state tuition, $41,222 full-time per academic year out-of-state tuition; $830 mandatory fees per academic year. *Financial support:* In 2016–17, 7 fellowships with full tuition reimbursements (averaging $30,720 per year), 30 research assistantships with full tuition reimbursements (averaging $27,396 per year), 33 teaching assistantships with full tuition reimbursements (averaging $26,328 per year) were awarded; scholarships/grants and tuition waivers (full) also available. Financial award application deadline: 3/1. *Faculty research:* Smart materials and structure solid mechanics, computational fluid dynamics, multiphase bio-fluid dynamics, mechanical vibration analysis. *Total annual research expenditures:* $7.9 million. *Unit head:* Dr. Brian Gleeson, Chairman, 412-624-1185, Fax: 412-624-4846, E-mail: bgleeson@pitt.edu. *Application contact:* Rama Bazaz, Director, 412-624-9800, Fax: 412-624-9808, E-mail: ssoeadm@pitt.edu.
Website: http://www.engineering.pitt.edu/Departments/MEMS/

University of Portland, School of Engineering, Portland, OR 97203-5798. Offers biomedical engineering (MBME); civil engineering (ME); computer science (ME); electrical engineering (ME); mechanical engineering (ME). *Program availability:* Part-time, evening/weekend. *Degree requirements:* For master's, thesis optional. *Entrance requirements:* For master's, GRE General Test, minimum GPA of 3.0, 3 letters of recommendation, resume, statement of goals, official transcripts. Additional exam requirements/recommendations for international students: Required—TOEFL (minimum score 550 paper-based; 80 iBT), IELTS (minimum score 7). *Expenses:* Contact institution.

University of Puerto Rico, Mayagüez Campus, Graduate Studies, College of Engineering, Department of Mechanical Engineering, Mayagüez, PR 00681-9000. Offers mechanical engineering (ME, MS, PhD), including aerospace and unmanned vehivles (ME), automation/mechatronics, bioengineering, cae and design, fluid mechanics, heat transfer/energy systems, manufacturing, mechanics of materials, micro and nano engineering. *Program availability:* Part-time. *Faculty:* 22 full-time (4 women), 1 part-time/adjunct (0 women). *Students:* 34 full-time (4 women), 8 part-time (2 women); includes 38 minority (all Hispanic/Latino), 3 international. Average age 25. 22 applicants, 100% accepted, 7 enrolled. In 2016, 17 master's awarded. Terminal master's awarded for partial completion of doctoral program. *Degree requirements:* For master's, one foreign language, comprehensive exam, thesis; for doctorate, one foreign language, comprehensive exam, thesis/dissertation. *Entrance requirements:* For master's, BS in mechanical engineering or its equivalent; for doctorate, GRE, BS or MS in mechanical engineering or its equivalent; minimum GPA of 3.0. Additional exam requirements/recommendations for international students: Required—TOEFL (minimum score 80 paper-based; 80 iBT). *Application deadline:* For fall admission, 2/15 for domestic and international students; for spring admission, 9/15 for domestic and international students. Applications are processed on a rolling basis. Application fee: $25. Electronic applications accepted. *Expenses: Tuition, area resident:* Full-time $2466. *International tuition:* $7166 full-time. *Required fees:* $210. One-time fee: $5 full-time. Tuition and fees vary according to course level, campus/location, program and student level. *Financial support:* In 2016–17, 39 students received support, including 26 research assistantships with full and partial tuition reimbursements available (averaging $3,801 per year), 30 teaching assistantships with full and partial tuition reimbursements available (averaging $3,293 per year); unspecified assistantships also available. *Faculty research:* Computational fluid dynamics, thermal sciences, mechanical design, material health, microfluidics. *Unit head:* Paul Sundaram, Ph.D., Chairperson, 787-832-4040 Ext. 3659, Fax: 787-265-3817, E-mail: paul.sundaram@upr.edu. *Application contact:* Yolanda Perez, Academic Orientation Officer, 787-832-4040 Ext. 2362, Fax: 787-265-3817, E-mail: yolanda.perez4@upr.edu.
Website: https://wordpress.uprm.edu/inme/

University of Rochester, Hajim School of Engineering and Applied Sciences, Department of Mechanical Engineering, Rochester, NY 14627. Offers MS, PhD. *Faculty:* 16 full-time (3 women). *Students:* 39 full-time (9 women), 2 part-time (1 woman); includes 2 minority (1 Hispanic/Latino; 1 Two or more races, non-Hispanic/Latino), 21 international. Average age 26. 105 applicants, 40% accepted, 12 enrolled. In 2016, 4 master's, 4 doctorates awarded. Terminal master's awarded for partial completion of doctoral program. *Degree requirements:* For master's, comprehensive exam, thesis optional, final exam; for doctorate, thesis/dissertation, qualifying exam. *Entrance requirements:* For master's and doctorate, GRE. Additional exam requirements/recommendations for international students: Required—TOEFL (minimum score 600 paper-based; 100 iBT). *Application deadline:* For fall admission, 1/1 for domestic and international students. Application fee: $60. Electronic applications accepted. *Expenses:* $1,538 per credit. *Financial support:* In 2016–17, 38 students received support, including 10 fellowships with full tuition reimbursements available (averaging $29,380 per year), 16 research assistantships (averaging $24,559 per year), 9 teaching assistantships (averaging $14,000 per year); career-related internships or fieldwork, Federal Work-Study, scholarships/grants, and tuition waivers (full and partial) also available. Financial award application deadline: 1/1. *Faculty research:* Fluid and solid mechanics, biomechanics, fusion/plasma, materials science, precision machining and optics manufacturing. *Unit head:* John C. Lambropoulos, Chair, 585-275-4070. *Application contact:* Sarah Ansini, Graduate Program Advisor/Coordinator, 585-275-2849, E-mail: sarah.ansini@rochester.edu.
Website: http://www.me.rochester.edu/graduate/index.html

University of Rochester, Hajim School of Engineering and Applied Sciences, Master of Science in Technical Entrepreneurship and Management Program, Rochester, NY 14642. Offers biomedical engineering (MS); chemical engineering (MS); computer science (MS); electrical and computer engineering (MS); energy and the environment (MS); materials science (MS); mechanical engineering (MS); optics (MS). Program offered in collaboration with the Simon School of Business. *Program availability:* Part-time. *Students:* 42 full-time (13 women), 6 part-time (3 women); includes 7 minority (1 Black or African American, non-Hispanic/Latino; 1 Asian, non-Hispanic/Latino; 4 Hispanic/Latino; 1 Two or more races, non-Hispanic/Latino), 28 international. Average age 24. 245 applicants, 65% accepted, 29 enrolled. In 2016, 31 master's awarded. *Degree requirements:* For master's, comprehensive exam, final exam. *Entrance requirements:* For master's, GRE or GMAT, 3 letters of recommendation; personal statement; official transcript; bachelor's degree (or equivalent for international students) in engineering, science, or mathematics. Additional exam requirements/recommendations for international students: Required—TOEFL (minimum score 600 paper-based; 100 iBT). *Application deadline:* For fall admission, 2/1 for domestic and international students. Application fee: $60. Electronic applications accepted. *Expenses:* $1,800 per credit. *Financial support:* In 2016–17, 45 students received support. Career-related internships or fieldwork and scholarships/grants available. Support available to part-time students. Financial award application deadline: 2/1. *Faculty research:* High efficiency solar cells, macromolecular self-assembly, digital signal processing, memory hierarchy management, molecular and physical mechanisms in cell migration, optical imaging systems. *Unit head:* Duncan T. Moore, Vice Provost for Entrepreneurship, 585-275-5248, Fax: 585-473-6745, E-mail: duncan.moore@rochester.edu. *Application contact:* Andrea Barrett, Executive Director, 585-276-3407, Fax: 585-276-2357, E-mail: andrea.barrett@rochester.edu.
Website: http://www.rochester.edu/team

University of St. Thomas, Graduate Studies, School of Engineering, St. Paul, MN 55105-1096. Offers data science (MS); electrical engineering (MS); information technology (MS); manufacturing engineering (MS); manufacturing systems (Certificate); mechanical engineering (MS); medical device development (Certificate); regulatory science (MS); software engineering (MS); software management (MS); systems engineering (MS); technology leadership (Certificate); technology management (MS). *Accreditation:* ABET (one or more programs are accredited). *Entrance requirements:* For master's, resume, official transcripts. Additional exam requirements/recommendations for international students: Required—TOEFL (minimum score 550 paper-based). *Application deadline:* For fall admission, 8/1 priority date for domestic students; for spring admission, 1/1 priority date for domestic students. Applications are processed on a rolling basis. Application fee: $50. Electronic applications accepted. *Expenses:* Contact institution. *Financial support:* Fellowships, research assistantships, institutionally sponsored loans, and scholarships/grants available. Support available to part-time students. Financial award application deadline: 4/1; financial award applicants required to submit FAFSA. *Unit head:* Don Weinkauf, Dean, 651-962-5760, Fax: 651-962-6419, E-mail: dhweinkauf@stthomas.edu. *Application contact:* Tina M. Hansen, Graduate Program Manager, 651-962-5755, Fax: 651-962-6419, E-mail: tina.hansen@stthomas.edu.
Website: http://www.stthomas.edu/engineering/

University of Saskatchewan, College of Graduate Studies and Research, College of Engineering, Mechanical Engineering Program, Saskatoon, SK S7N 5A9, Canada. Offers M Eng, M Sc, PhD. *Program availability:* Part-time. *Degree requirements:* For master's, thesis (for some programs), 30 credits (for M Eng); thesis and 12 credits (for MS); for doctorate, comprehensive exam, thesis/dissertation, qualifying exam, 18 credits. *Entrance requirements:* For master's and doctorate, GRE. Additional exam requirements/recommendations for international students: Required—TOEFL (minimum iBT score 80), IELTS (6.5), CanTEST (4.5), or PTE (59). Electronic applications accepted. *Faculty research:* Advanced engineering design and manufacturing, advanced materials for clean energy, applied mechanics and machine design, bioengineering, control systems, fluid power, fluid dynamics, material science and metallurgy, robotics, thermal science and energy.

University of South Alabama, College of Engineering, Department of Mechanical Engineering, Mobile, AL 36688. Offers MSME. *Faculty:* 4 full-time (0 women), 1 part-time/adjunct (0 women). *Students:* 14 full-time (1 woman), 4 part-time (0 women); includes 2 minority (both American Indian or Alaska Native, non-Hispanic/Latino), 7 international. Average age 25. 53 applicants, 42% accepted, 6 enrolled. In 2016, 6 master's awarded. *Degree requirements:* For master's, comprehensive exam, project or thesis. *Entrance requirements:* For master's, GRE General Test, BS in engineering, minimum GPA of 3.0. Additional exam requirements/recommendations for international students: Required—TOEFL (minimum score 550 paper-based; 79 iBT). *Application deadline:* For fall admission, 7/1 priority date for domestic students, 6/1 priority date for international students; for spring admission, 12/1 priority date for domestic students, 11/1 priority date for international students; for summer admission, 5/1 priority date for domestic students, 4/1 priority date for international students. Applications are processed on a rolling basis. Application fee: $35. Electronic applications accepted. *Expenses:* Contact institution. *Financial support:* Fellowships, research assistantships, teaching assistantships, career-related internships or fieldwork, Federal Work-Study, institutionally sponsored loans, scholarships/grants, and unspecified assistantships available. Support available to part-time students. Financial award application deadline: 5/31; financial award applicants required to submit FAFSA. *Faculty research:* Composite microstructure - property relationships, transport phenomena in porous media, hybrid micro-fiber/nano-particle composites. *Unit head:* Dr. David Nelson, Department Chair, 251-460-6168, Fax: 251-460-6549, E-mail: danelson@southalabama.edu. *Application contact:* Brenda Poole, Academic Records Specialist, 251-460-6140, Fax: 251-460-6343, E-mail: engineering@southalabama.edu.
Website: http://www.southalabama.edu/colleges/engineering/me/index.html

University of South Carolina, The Graduate School, College of Engineering and Computing, Department of Mechanical Engineering, Columbia, SC 29208. Offers ME, MS, PhD. *Program availability:* Part-time, evening/weekend, online learning. *Degree requirements:* For master's, thesis (for some programs); for doctorate, thesis/dissertation. *Entrance requirements:* For master's and doctorate, GRE General Test. Additional exam requirements/recommendations for international students: Required—TOEFL (minimum score 600 paper-based). Electronic applications accepted. *Faculty research:* Heat exchangers, computer vision measurements in solid mechanics and biomechanics, robot dynamics and control.

University of Southern California, Graduate School, Viterbi School of Engineering, Department of Aerospace and Mechanical Engineering, Los Angeles, CA 90089. Offers aerospace and mechanical engineering: computational fluid and solid mechanics (MS); aerospace and mechanical engineering: dynamics and control (MS); aerospace engineering (MS, PhD, Engr), including aerospace engineering (PhD, Engr); green technologies (MS); mechanical engineering (MS, PhD, Engr), including energy conversion (MS), mechanical engineering (PhD, Engr), nuclear power (MS); product development engineering (MS). *Program availability:* Part-time, evening/weekend, online learning. Terminal master's awarded for partial completion of doctoral program. *Degree requirements:* For master's, thesis optional; for doctorate, thesis/dissertation. *Entrance requirements:* For master's, doctorate, and Engr, GRE General Test. Additional exam requirements/recommendations for international students: Recommended—TOEFL. Electronic applications accepted. *Faculty research:* Mechanics and materials, aerodynamics of air/ground vehicles, gas dynamics, aerosols, astronautics and space science, geophysical and microgravity flows, planetary physics, power MEMs and MEMS vacuum pumps, heat transfer and combustion.

University of South Florida, College of Engineering, Department of Mechanical Engineering, Tampa, FL 33620-9951. Offers mechanical engineering (MME, MSME, PhD), including mechanical engineering (PhD). *Program availability:* Part-time. *Faculty:* 16 full-time (2 women). *Students:* 91 full-time (8 women), 34 part-time (0 women);

includes 14 minority (2 Black or African American, non-Hispanic/Latino; 2 Asian, non-Hispanic/Latino; 9 Hispanic/Latino; 1 Two or more races, non-Hispanic/Latino), 84 international. Average age 26. 228 applicants, 49% accepted, 53 enrolled. In 2016, 32 master's, 10 doctorates awarded. Terminal master's awarded for partial completion of doctoral program. *Degree requirements:* For master's, comprehensive exam, thesis or alternative; for doctorate, comprehensive exam, thesis/dissertation, 2 tools of research as specified by dissertation committee. *Entrance requirements:* For master's, GRE General Test, minimum GPA of 3.0 in last two years of undergraduate coursework from ABET-accredited engineering program; statement of research interests (for MSME); for doctorate, GRE General Test, MS in mechanical engineering or closely-related field (preferred); one-page statement of purpose and research interests. Additional exam requirements/recommendations for international students: Required—TOEFL (minimum score 550 paper-based; 79 iBT) or IELTS (minimum score 6.5). *Application deadline:* For fall admission, 2/15 for domestic and international students; for spring admission, 10/15 for domestic students, 9/15 for international students; for summer admission, 2/15 for domestic students, 1/15 for international students. Application fee: $30. Electronic applications accepted. *Expenses:* Tuition, state resident: full-time $7766; part-time $431.43 per credit hour. Tuition, nonresident: full-time $15,789; part-time $877.17 per credit hour. *Required fees:* $37 per term. *Financial support:* In 2016–17, 14 students received support, including 42 research assistantships with tuition reimbursements available (averaging $12,819 per year), 22 teaching assistantships with partial tuition reimbursements available (averaging $14,017 per year). Financial award applicants required to submit FAFSA. *Faculty research:* Acoustic transducers, cellular mechanotransduction and biomaterials, computational fluid dynamics and heat transfer, computational methods research and education, environmentally benign design and manufacturing, micro/Nano integration, Nano chemical testing, Nanotechnology Research and Education Center (NREC), rehabilitation engineering and electromechanical design, rehabilitation robotics, vibrations/dynamic systems. *Total annual research expenditures:* $2.9 million. *Unit head:* Dr. Rajiv Dubey, Professor and Department Chair, 813-974-5619, Fax: 813-974-3539, E-mail: dubey@usf.edu. *Application contact:* Dr. Delcie Durham, Professor and Graduate Program Director, 813-974-5656, Fax: 813-974-3539, E-mail: drdurham@usf.edu.
Website: http://me.eng.usf.edu/

The University of Tennessee, Graduate School, Tickle College of Engineering, Department of Mechanical, Aerospace and Biomedical Engineering, Program in Mechanical Engineering, Knoxville, TN 37996. Offers MS, PhD, MS/MBA. *Program availability:* Part-time, online learning. *Faculty:* 23 full-time (0 women), 2 part-time/adjunct (0 women). *Students:* 85 full-time (5 women), 20 part-time (1 woman); includes 10 minority (4 Black or African American, non-Hispanic/Latino; 1 American Indian or Alaska Native, non-Hispanic/Latino; 3 Asian, non-Hispanic/Latino; 1 Hispanic/Latino; 1 Two or more races, non-Hispanic/Latino), 39 international. Average age 30. 138 applicants, 32% accepted, 21 enrolled. In 2016, 18 master's, 6 doctorates awarded. *Degree requirements:* For master's, thesis or alternative; for doctorate, comprehensive exam, thesis/dissertation. *Entrance requirements:* For master's, GRE General Test (for MS students pursuing research thesis), minimum GPA of 2.7 (for U.S. degree holders), 3.0 (for international degree holders); 3 references; statement of purpose; for doctorate, GRE General Test, minimum GPA of 3.0 on previous graduate course work; 3 references; statement of purpose. Additional exam requirements/recommendations for international students: Required—TOEFL (minimum score 550 paper-based). *Application deadline:* For fall admission, 2/1 priority date for domestic and international students; for spring admission, 6/15 for domestic and international students. Applications are processed on a rolling basis. Application fee: $35. Electronic applications accepted. *Financial support:* In 2016–17, 67 students received support, including 5 fellowships with full tuition reimbursements available (averaging $26,560 per year), 50 research assistantships with full tuition reimbursements available (averaging $20,080 per year), 40 teaching assistantships with full tuition reimbursements available (averaging $18,979 per year); career-related internships or fieldwork, Federal Work-Study, institutionally sponsored loans, health care benefits, and unspecified assistantships also available. Financial award application deadline: 2/1; financial award applicants required to submit FAFSA. *Faculty research:* Automotive systems and technology; combustion and emissions; alternative fuels; electromechanical actuators; nanomechanics, nanomaterials, and nanotechnology. *Unit head:* Dr. Matthew Mench, Head, 865-974-5115, Fax: 865-974-5274, E-mail: mmench@utk.edu. *Application contact:* Dr. Kivanc Ekici, Associate Professor, Graduate Program Director, 865-974-6016, Fax: 865-974-5274, E-mail: ekici@utk.edu.
Website: http://www.engr.utk.edu/mabe

The University of Tennessee, The University of Tennessee Space Institute, Tullahoma, TN 37388. Offers aerospace engineering (MS, PhD); biomedical engineering (MS, PhD); engineering science (MS, PhD); industrial and systems engineering/engineering management (MS, PhD); mechanical engineering (MS, PhD); physics (MS, PhD). *Program availability:* Part-time, blended/hybrid learning. Terminal master's awarded for partial completion of doctoral program. *Degree requirements:* For doctorate, one foreign language, thesis/dissertation. *Entrance requirements:* Additional exam requirements/recommendations for international students: Required—TOEFL (minimum score 550 paper-based; 80 iBT), IELTS (minimum score 6.5). Electronic applications accepted. *Expenses:* Contact institution. *Faculty research:* Fluid mechanics/aerodynamics, chemical and electric propulsion and laser diagnostics, computational mechanics and simulations, carbon fiber production and composite materials.

The University of Tennessee at Chattanooga, Program in Engineering, Chattanooga, TN 37403. Offers automotive systems (MS Engr); chemical engineering (MS Engr); civil engineering (MS Engr); computational engineering (MS Engr); electrical engineering (MS Engr); industrial engineering (MS Engr); mechanical engineering (MS Engr). *Program availability:* Part-time. *Faculty:* 21 full-time (2 women), 2 part-time/adjunct (1 woman). *Students:* 21 full-time (5 women), 26 part-time (7 women); includes 11 minority (4 Black or African American, non-Hispanic/Latino; 5 Asian, non-Hispanic/Latino; 1 Hispanic/Latino; 1 Two or more races, non-Hispanic/Latino), 18 international. Average age 28. 30 applicants, 83% accepted, 14 enrolled. In 2016, 25 master's awarded. *Degree requirements:* For master's, comprehensive exam, thesis or alternative, engineering project. *Entrance requirements:* For master's, GRE General Test, minimum undergraduate GPA of 2.7 or 3.0 in last two years of undergraduate coursework. Additional exam requirements/recommendations for international students: Required—TOEFL (minimum score 550 paper-based; 79 iBT), IELTS (minimum score 6). *Application deadline:* For fall admission, 6/15 priority date for domestic students, 7/1 for international students; for spring admission, 11/1 priority date for domestic students, 11/1 for international students. Applications are processed on a rolling basis. Application fee: $35 ($40 for international students). Electronic applications accepted. *Expenses:* $9,876 full-time in-state; $25,994 full-time out-of-state; $450 per credit part-time in-state; $1,345 per credit part-time out-of-state. *Financial support:* In 2016–17, 6 research assistantships, 5 teaching assistantships were awarded; career-related internships or fieldwork, scholarships/grants, health care benefits, and unspecified assistantships also available. Support available to part-time students. Financial award application deadline: 7/1. *Faculty research:* Quality control and reliability engineering, financial management, thermal science, energy conservation, structural analysis. *Total annual research expenditures:* $921,122. *Unit head:* Dr. Daniel Pack, Dean, 423-425-2256, Fax: 423-425-5311, E-mail: daniel-pack@utc.edu. *Application contact:* Dr. Joanne Romagni, Dean of the Graduate School, 423-425-4478, Fax: 423-425-5223, E-mail: joanne-romagni@utc.edu.
Website: http://www.utc.edu/college-engineering-computer-science/graduate-programs/msengr.php

The University of Texas at Arlington, Graduate School, College of Engineering, Department of Mechanical and Aerospace Engineering, Program in Mechanical Engineering, Arlington, TX 76019. Offers M Engr, MS, PhD. *Program availability:* Part-time, evening/weekend, online learning. Terminal master's awarded for partial completion of doctoral program. *Degree requirements:* For master's, thesis optional; for doctorate, comprehensive exam, thesis/dissertation. *Entrance requirements:* For master's and doctorate, GRE General Test, minimum GPA of 3.0. Additional exam requirements/recommendations for international students: Required—TOEFL (minimum score 550 paper-based). *Application deadline:* For fall admission, 6/1 for domestic students, 4/1 for international students; for spring admission, 10/5 for domestic students, 9/15 for international students. Applications are processed on a rolling basis. Application fee: $50 ($70 for international students). *Financial support:* Fellowships with partial tuition reimbursements, research assistantships with partial tuition reimbursements, teaching assistantships with partial tuition reimbursements, institutionally sponsored loans, scholarships/grants, health care benefits, and unspecified assistantships available. Financial award application deadline: 6/1; financial award applicants required to submit FAFSA. *Unit head:* Dr. Erian Armanios, Chair, 817-272-2603, Fax: 817-272-5010, E-mail: armanios@uta.edu. *Application contact:* Dr. Albert Tong, Graduate Advisor, 817-272-2297, Fax: 817-272-2952, E-mail: tong@uta.edu.
Website: http://www.mae.uta.edu/

The University of Texas at Austin, Graduate School, Cockrell School of Engineering, Department of Mechanical Engineering, Austin, TX 78712-1111. Offers mechanical engineering (MS, PhD); operations research and industrial engineering (MS, PhD); MBA/MSE; MP Aff/MSE. *Entrance requirements:* For master's and doctorate, GRE General Test. Additional exam requirements/recommendations for international students: Required—TOEFL.

The University of Texas at Dallas, Erik Jonson School of Engineering and Computer Science, Department of Mechanical Engineering, Richardson, TX 75080. Offers MSME, PhD. *Program availability:* Part-time, evening/weekend. *Faculty:* 24 full-time (2 women). *Students:* 156 full-time (14 women), 28 part-time (1 woman); includes 16 minority (7 Asian, non-Hispanic/Latino; 9 Hispanic/Latino), 140 international. Average age 27. 538 applicants, 38% accepted, 57 enrolled. In 2016, 56 master's, 1 doctorate awarded. *Degree requirements:* For master's, thesis or major design project; for doctorate, comprehensive exam, thesis/dissertation, final exam, research project, qualifying exam. *Entrance requirements:* For master's, GRE General Test, minimum GPA of 3.0 in related bachelor's degree; for doctorate, GRE General Test, essay. Additional exam requirements/recommendations for international students: Required—TOEFL (minimum score 550 paper-based). *Application deadline:* For fall admission, 7/15 for domestic students, 5/1 priority date for international students; for spring admission, 11/15 for domestic students, 9/1 priority date for international students. Applications are processed on a rolling basis. Application fee: $50 ($100 for international students). Electronic applications accepted. *Expenses:* Tuition, state resident: full-time $12,418; part-time $690 per semester hour. Tuition, nonresident: full-time $24,150; part-time $1342 per semester hour. Tuition and fees vary according to course load. *Financial support:* In 2016–17, 95 students received support, including 8 fellowships (averaging $7,063 per year), 54 research assistantships with partial tuition reimbursements available (averaging $22,949 per year), 37 teaching assistantships with partial tuition reimbursements available (averaging $16,918 per year); career-related internships or fieldwork, Federal Work-Study, institutionally sponsored loans, scholarships/grants, and unspecified assistantships also available. Support available to part-time students. Financial award application deadline: 4/30; financial award applicants required to submit FAFSA. *Faculty research:* Nano-materials and nano-electronic devices, biomedical devices, nonlinear systems and controls, semiconductor and oxide surfaces, flexible electronics. *Unit head:* Dr. Mario Rotea, Department Head, 972-883-2720, Fax: 972-883-2813, E-mail: rotea@utdallas.edu. *Application contact:* Dr. Hongbing Lu, Associate Department Head, 972-883-4647, Fax: 972-883-2813, E-mail: megrad@utdallas.edu.
Website: http://me.utdallas.edu

The University of Texas at El Paso, Graduate School, College of Engineering, Department of Mechanical Engineering, El Paso, TX 79968-0001. Offers environmental science and engineering (PhD); mechanical engineering (MS). *Program availability:* Part-time. *Degree requirements:* For master's, thesis optional; for doctorate, thesis/dissertation. *Entrance requirements:* For master's, GRE, minimum GPA of 3.0, letter of reference; for doctorate, GRE, minimum GPA of 3.5, letters of reference, BS or equivalent. Additional exam requirements/recommendations for international students: Required—TOEFL; Recommended—IELTS. Electronic applications accepted. *Faculty research:* Aerospace, energy, combustion and propulsion, design engineering, high temperature materials.

The University of Texas at San Antonio, College of Engineering, Department of Mechanical Engineering, San Antonio, TX 78249-0617. Offers advanced manufacturing and enterprise engineering (MS); mechanical engineering (MS, PhD). *Program availability:* Part-time, evening/weekend. *Faculty:* 21 full-time (2 women), 3 part-time/adjunct (0 women). *Students:* 73 full-time (12 women), 52 part-time (9 women); includes 41 minority (2 Black or African American, non-Hispanic/Latino; 10 Asian, non-Hispanic/Latino; 25 Hispanic/Latino; 4 Two or more races, non-Hispanic/Latino), 49 international. Average age 30. 114 applicants, 68% accepted, 30 enrolled. In 2016, 32 master's, 4 doctorates awarded. Terminal master's awarded for partial completion of doctoral program. *Degree requirements:* For master's, comprehensive exam, thesis; for doctorate, comprehensive exam, thesis/dissertation. *Entrance requirements:* For master's, GRE General Test, bachelor's degree in mechanical engineering or related field from accredited institution of higher education; for doctorate, GRE General Test, master's degree in mechanical engineering, or exceptionally outstanding undergraduate record in mechanical engineering or related field; minimum GPA of 3.33. Additional exam requirements/recommendations for international students: Required—TOEFL (minimum score 550 paper-based; 79 iBT), IELTS (minimum score 6.5). *Application deadline:* For fall admission, 7/1 for domestic students, 4/1 for international students; for spring admission, 11/1 for domestic students, 9/1 for international students. Applications are processed on a rolling basis. Application fee: $45 ($80 for international students). Electronic applications accepted. *Expenses:* Contact institution. *Financial support:* In 2016–17, 25 students received support, including 10 fellowships with partial tuition reimbursements available (averaging $25,000 per year), 8 research assistantships (averaging $15,665 per year), 27 teaching assistantships (averaging $10,000 per year); career-related internships or fieldwork and unspecified assistantships also available. Financial award application deadline: 10/1. *Faculty research:* Mechanics and materials, advanced manufacturing, wind turbine, computational fluid dynamics, robotics, biomechanics, wind energy. *Total annual research expenditures:* $2.4 million. *Unit head:* Dr. Hai-Chao Han, Department Chair/Professor, 210-458-6021, E-mail: hai-chao.han@

utsa.edu.

Website: http://engineering.utsa.edu/me/

The University of Texas at Tyler, College of Engineering, Department of Mechanical Engineering, Tyler, TX 75799-0001. Offers MS. *Program availability:* Part-time, evening/weekend. *Degree requirements:* For master's, engineering project. *Entrance requirements:* For master's, GRE or GMAT, bachelor's degree in engineering. *Faculty research:* Mechatronics vibration analysis, fluid dynamics, electronics and instrumentation, manufacturing processes, optics, computational fluid dynamics, signal processing, high voltage related studies, real time systems, semiconductors.

The University of Texas Rio Grande Valley, College of Engineering and Computer Science, Department of Mechanical Engineering, Edinburg, TX 78539. Offers MS. Tuition and fees vary according to course load and program.

The University of Toledo, College of Graduate Studies, College of Engineering, Department of Mechanical, Industrial, and Manufacturing Engineering, Toledo, OH 43606-3390. Offers industrial engineering (MS, PhD); mechanical engineering (MS, PhD). *Program availability:* Part-time, online learning. *Degree requirements:* For master's, thesis optional; for doctorate, thesis/dissertation, qualifying exam. *Entrance requirements:* For master's, GRE General Test, minimum GPA of 3.0; for doctorate, GRE General Test, minimum GPA of 3.3. Additional exam requirements/recommendations for international students: Required—TOEFL (minimum score 550 paper-based; 80 iBT). Electronic applications accepted. *Faculty research:* Computational and experimental thermal sciences, manufacturing process and systems, mechanics, materials, design, quality and management engineering systems.

University of Toronto, School of Graduate Studies, Faculty of Applied Science and Engineering, Department of Mechanical and Industrial Engineering, Toronto, ON M5S 1A1, Canada. Offers M Eng, MA Sc, PhD. *Program availability:* Part-time. *Degree requirements:* For master's, thesis (for some programs), oral exam/thesis defense (MA Sc); for doctorate, thesis/dissertation, thesis defense, qualifying examination. *Entrance requirements:* For master's, GRE (recommended), minimum B+ average in last 2 years of undergraduate study, 2 letters of reference, resume, Canadian citizenship or permanent residency (M Eng); for doctorate, GRE (recommended), minimum B+ average, 2 letters of reference, resume. Additional exam requirements/recommendations for international students: Required—TOEFL (minimum score 580 paper-based), Michigan English Language Assessment Battery (minimum score 85), IELTS (minimum score 7), or COPE (minimum score 4). Electronic applications accepted.

The University of Tulsa, Graduate School, College of Engineering and Natural Sciences, Department of Mechanical Engineering, Tulsa, OK 74104-3189. Offers ME, MSE, PhD. *Program availability:* Part-time. *Faculty:* 13 full-time (0 women). *Students:* 36 full-time (4 women), 14 part-time (3 women), 24 international. Average age 28. 62 applicants, 39% accepted, 12 enrolled. In 2016, 10 master's, 3 doctorates awarded. Terminal master's awarded for partial completion of doctoral program. *Degree requirements:* For master's, thesis (MSE); for doctorate, comprehensive exam, thesis/dissertation. *Entrance requirements:* For master's and doctorate, GRE General Test. Additional exam requirements/recommendations for international students: Required—TOEFL (minimum score 550 paper-based; 80 iBT), IELTS (minimum score 6). *Application deadline:* Applications are processed on a rolling basis. Application fee: $55. Electronic applications accepted. *Expenses: Tuition:* Full-time $22,230; part-time $1235 per credit hour. *Required fees:* $990 per semester. Tuition and fees vary according to course load. *Financial support:* In 2016–17, 40 students received support, including 11 fellowships with full tuition reimbursements available (averaging $4,971 per year), 32 research assistantships with full tuition reimbursements available (averaging $12,668 per year), 13 teaching assistantships with full tuition reimbursements available (averaging $10,610 per year); career-related internships or fieldwork, Federal Work-Study, health care benefits, tuition waivers (full and partial), and unspecified assistantships also available. Support available to part-time students. Financial award application deadline: 2/1; financial award applicants required to submit FAFSA. *Faculty research:* Erosion and corrosion, solid mechanics, composite material, computational fluid dynamics, coiled tubing mechanics. *Total annual research expenditures:* $3.4 million. *Unit head:* Dr. John Henshaw, Chairperson, 918-631-3002, Fax: 918-631-2397, E-mail: john-henshaw@utulsa.edu. *Application contact:* Dr. Siamack A. Shirazi, Adviser, 918-631-3001, Fax: 918-631-2397, E-mail: grad@utulsa.edu.

Website: http://engineering.utulsa.edu/academics/mechanical-engineering/

University of Utah, Graduate School, College of Engineering, Department of Mechanical Engineering, Salt Lake City, UT 84112. Offers MS, PhD, MS/MBA. *Program availability:* Part-time, online learning. *Faculty:* 38 full-time (7 women), 10 part-time/adjunct (1 woman). *Students:* 152 full-time (19 women), 60 part-time (6 women); includes 20 minority (2 Black or African American, non-Hispanic/Latino; 10 Asian, non-Hispanic/Latino; 2 Hispanic/Latino; 6 Two or more races, non-Hispanic/Latino), 63 international. Average age 28. 334 applicants, 58% accepted, 70 enrolled. In 2016, 36 master's, 8 doctorates awarded. Terminal master's awarded for partial completion of doctoral program. *Degree requirements:* For master's, comprehensive exam (for some programs), thesis (for some programs); for doctorate, comprehensive exam, thesis/dissertation, qualifying exam. *Entrance requirements:* For master's and doctorate, GRE General Test, minimum GPA of 3.0, statement of purpose, 3 letters of recommendation, curriculum curriculum vitae/resume, transcripts. Additional exam requirements/recommendations for international students: Required—TOEFL (minimum score 550 paper-based; 80 iBT), IELTS (minimum score 6.5). *Application deadline:* For fall admission, 1/1 priority date for domestic students, 12/1 priority date for international students; for spring admission, 10/1 priority date for domestic students; for summer admission, 2/15 priority date for domestic students. Application fee: $10 ($25 for international students). Electronic applications accepted. *Expenses:* Contact institution. *Financial support:* In 2016–17, 110 students received support, including 9 fellowships with full tuition reimbursements available (averaging $24,000 per year), 63 research assistantships with full tuition reimbursements available (averaging $22,000 per year), 68 teaching assistantships with full and partial tuition reimbursements available (averaging $14,500 per year); institutionally sponsored loans, traineeships, health care benefits, and unspecified assistantships also available. Financial award application deadline: 1/15; financial award applicants required to submit FAFSA. *Faculty research:* Design, ergonomics, manufacturing and systems; robotics, controls and mechatronics; solid mechanics; thermal fluids and energy systems. *Total annual research expenditures:* $2.8 million. *Unit head:* Dr. Timothy Ameel, Chair, 801-585-9730, Fax: 801-585-9826, E-mail: ameel@mech.utah.edu. *Application contact:* Dr. Mathieu Francoeur, Director of Graduate Studies, 801-581-5721, Fax: 801-585-9826, E-mail: mfrancoeur@mech.utah.edu.

Website: http://www.mech.utah.edu/

University of Vermont, Graduate College, College of Engineering and Mathematics, Department of Mechanical Engineering, Burlington, VT 05405. Offers MS, PhD. *Degree requirements:* For master's, thesis; for doctorate, thesis/dissertation. *Entrance requirements:* For master's and doctorate, GRE General Test (for research assistant or teaching assistant funding). Additional exam requirements/recommendations for international students: Required—TOEFL (minimum score 550 paper-based; 80 iBT).

Electronic applications accepted. *Expenses:* Tuition, state resident: full-time $5814. Tuition, nonresident: full-time $14,670.

University of Victoria, Faculty of Graduate Studies, Faculty of Engineering, Department of Mechanical Engineering, Victoria, BC V8W 2Y2, Canada. Offers M Eng, MA Sc, PhD. *Program availability:* Part-time. *Degree requirements:* For master's, thesis (for some programs); for doctorate, thesis/dissertation, candidacy exam. *Entrance requirements:* For master's, minimum B average in undergraduate course work. Additional exam requirements/recommendations for international students: Required—TOEFL (minimum score 575 paper-based), IELTS (minimum score 7). Electronic applications accepted. *Faculty research:* CAD/CAM, energy systems, cryofuels, fuel cell technology, computational mechanics.

University of Virginia, School of Engineering and Applied Science, Department of Mechanical and Aerospace Engineering, Charlottesville, VA 22903. Offers ME, MS, PhD. *Program availability:* Online learning. *Faculty:* 22 full-time (5 women). *Students:* 93 full-time (11 women), 2 part-time (0 women); includes 9 minority (1 Black or African American, non-Hispanic/Latino; 5 Asian, non-Hispanic/Latino; 3 Hispanic/Latino), 42 international. Average age 26. 199 applicants, 35% accepted, 30 enrolled. In 2016, 13 master's, 9 doctorates awarded. *Degree requirements:* For master's, thesis (MS); for doctorate, comprehensive exam, thesis/dissertation. *Entrance requirements:* For master's and doctorate, GRE General Test, 3 letters of recommendation. Additional exam requirements/recommendations for international students: Required—TOEFL (minimum score 650 paper-based; 90 iBT), IELTS (minimum score 7). *Application deadline:* For fall admission, 8/1 for domestic students, 4/1 for international students; for winter admission, 12/1 for domestic students, 8/1 for international students; for spring admission, 5/1 for domestic students, 1/1 for international students. Applications are processed on a rolling basis. Application fee: $60. Electronic applications accepted. *Expenses: Tuition,* state resident: full-time $15,026; part-time $834 per credit hour. Tuition, nonresident: full-time $25,168; part-time $1378 per credit hour. *Required fees:* $2654. *Financial support:* Fellowships, research assistantships, and teaching assistantships available. Financial award application deadline: 1/15; financial award applicants required to submit FAFSA. *Faculty research:* Solid mechanics, dynamical systems and control, thermofluids. *Unit head:* Eroc Loth, Chair, 434-924-7424, Fax: 434-982-2037, E-mail: mae-adm@virginia.edu. *Application contact:* Graduate Secretary, 434-924-7425, Fax: 434-982-2037, E-mail: mae-adm@virginia.edu.

Website: http://www.mae.virginia.edu/NewMAE/

University of Washington, Graduate School, College of Engineering, Department of Mechanical Engineering, Seattle, WA 98195-2600. Offers MSE, MSME, PhD. *Program availability:* Part-time, blended/hybrid learning. *Faculty:* 31 full-time (4 women). *Students:* 143 full-time (31 women), 27 part-time (6 women); includes 50 minority (1 American Indian or Alaska Native, non-Hispanic/Latino; 27 Asian, non-Hispanic/Latino; 10 Hispanic/Latino; 12 Two or more races, non-Hispanic/Latino), 128 international. 671 applicants, 52% accepted, 124 enrolled. In 2016, 64 master's, 15 doctorates awarded. *Degree requirements:* For master's, thesis optional; for doctorate, comprehensive exam, thesis/dissertation, qualifying, general, and final exams. *Entrance requirements:* For master's, GRE General Test (minimum scores: 150 Verbal, 155 Quantitative, and 4.0 Analytical Writing), minimum GPA of 3.0 (overall undergraduate GPA of 3.3 preferred); letters of recommendation; statement of purpose; for doctorate, GRE General Test (minimum scores: 150 Verbal, 155 Quantitative, and 4.0 Analytical Writing), minimum GPA of 3.0 (overall undergraduate GPA of 3.3, graduate 3.5 preferred); letters of recommendation; statement of purpose. Additional exam requirements/recommendations for international students: Required—TOEFL (minimum score 580 paper-based; 92 iBT). *Application deadline:* For fall admission, 12/15 priority date for domestic students, 12/15 for international students; for winter admission, 11/1 for domestic students; for spring admission, 2/1 for domestic students; for summer admission, 4/1 for domestic students. Applications are processed on a rolling basis. Application fee: $85. Electronic applications accepted. *Financial support:* In 2016–17, 126 students received support, including 22 fellowships with partial tuition reimbursements available (averaging $3,283 per year), 72 research assistantships with full tuition reimbursements available (averaging $2,413 per year), 32 teaching assistantships with full tuition reimbursements available (averaging $2,375 per year). Financial award application deadline: 1/15; financial award applicants required to submit FAFSA. *Faculty research:* Environmentally-friendly energy conversion, mechanics and advanced material systems, system and dynamics, bio-health systems. *Total annual research expenditures:* $13 million. *Unit head:* Dr. Per Reinhall, Professor/Chair, 206-543-5090, Fax: 206-685-8047, E-mail: reinhall@uw.edu. *Application contact:* Wanwisa Kisalang, Graduate Academic Adviser, 206-543-7963, Fax: 206-685-8047, E-mail: megrad@uw.edu.

Website: http://www.me.washington.edu

University of Waterloo, Graduate Studies, Faculty of Engineering, Department of Mechanical and Mechatronics Engineering, Waterloo, ON N2L 3G1, Canada. Offers mechanical engineering (M Eng, MA Sc, PhD); mechanical engineering design and manufacturing (M Eng). *Program availability:* Part-time, evening/weekend. *Degree requirements:* For master's, research paper or thesis; for doctorate, comprehensive exam, thesis/dissertation. *Entrance requirements:* For master's, honors degree, minimum B average, resume; for doctorate, master's degree, minimum A- average, resume. Additional exam requirements/recommendations for international students: Required—TOEFL, IELTS, PTE. Electronic applications accepted. *Faculty research:* Fluid mechanics, thermal engineering, solid mechanics, automation and control, materials engineering.

The University of Western Ontario, Faculty of Graduate Studies, Physical Sciences Division, Faculty of Engineering, London, ON N6A 5B8, Canada. Offers chemical and biochemical engineering (ME Sc, PhD); civil and environmental engineering (M Eng, ME Sc, PhD); electrical and computer engineering (M Eng, ME Sc, PhD); mechanical and materials engineering (M Eng, ME Sc, PhD). *Program availability:* Part-time. Terminal master's awarded for partial completion of doctoral program. *Degree requirements:* For master's, thesis; for doctorate, thesis/dissertation. *Entrance requirements:* For master's, minimum B average; for doctorate, minimum B+ average. *Faculty research:* Wind, geotechnical, chemical reactor engineering, applied electrostatics, biochemical engineering.

University of Windsor, Faculty of Graduate Studies, Faculty of Engineering, Department of Mechanical, Automotive, and Materials Engineering, Windsor, ON N9B 3P4, Canada. Offers engineering materials (M Eng, MA Sc, PhD); mechanical engineering (M Eng, MA Sc, PhD). *Program availability:* Part-time. *Degree requirements:* For master's, thesis; for doctorate, comprehensive exam, thesis/dissertation. *Entrance requirements:* For master's, minimum B average; for doctorate, master's degree, minimum B average. Additional exam requirements/recommendations for international students: Required—TOEFL (minimum score 600 paper-based). Electronic applications accepted. *Faculty research:* Thermofluids, applied mechanics, materials engineering.

University of Wisconsin–Madison, Graduate School, College of Engineering, Department of Mechanical Engineering, Madison, WI 53706-1380. Offers mechanical engineering (MS, PhD), including automotive engineering (MS). *Program availability:* Part-time, online learning. *Faculty:* 31 full-time (5 women). *Students:* 183 full-time (22

women), 36 part-time (2 women); includes 33 minority (3 Black or African American, non-Hispanic/Latino; 1 American Indian or Alaska Native, non-Hispanic/Latino; 9 Asian, non-Hispanic/Latino; 19 Hispanic/Latino; 1 Two or more races, non-Hispanic/Latino), 96 international. Average age 28. 609 applicants, 21% accepted, 45 enrolled. In 2016, 61 master's, 15 doctorates awarded. Terminal master's awarded for partial completion of doctoral program. *Degree requirements:* For master's, thesis optional, 30 credits; minimum GPA of 3.0; for doctorate, thesis/dissertation, qualifying exam, preliminary exam, final oral defense, 42 formal course credits, 18 thesis credits, minimum GPA of 3.25. *Entrance requirements:* For master's, GRE, BS in mechanical engineering or related field, minimum GPA of 3.2 in last 60 hours of course work; for doctorate, GRE, BS in mechanical engineering or related field, minimum undergraduate GPA of 3.2 in last 60 hours of course work. Additional exam requirements/recommendations for international students: Required—TOEFL (minimum score 580 paper-based; 92 iBT), IELTS (minimum score 7). *Application deadline:* For fall admission, 1/1 for domestic and international students; for spring admission, 10/1 for domestic and international students; for summer admission, 12/15 for domestic and international students. Applications are processed on a rolling basis. Application fee: $75 ($81 for international students). Electronic applications accepted. *Expenses:* $13,157 per year in-state tuition and fees; $26,484 per year out-of-state tuition and fees. *Financial support:* In 2016–17, 136 students received support, including 9 fellowships with full tuition reimbursements available, 76 research assistantships with full tuition reimbursements available, 49 teaching assistantships with full tuition reimbursements available; career-related internships or fieldwork, institutionally sponsored loans, scholarships/grants, traineeships, health care benefits, and unspecified assistantships also available. Financial award application deadline: 12/1; financial award applicants required to submit FAFSA. *Faculty research:* Polymer engineering; robotics/electromechanical system control; advanced manufacturing and prototype processes; computational mechanics; thermal-fluid systems; engine and vehicle systems. *Total annual research expenditures:* $10.6 million. *Unit head:* Jaal B. Ghandhi, Chair, 608-263-1684, E-mail: jaal.ghandhi@wisc.edu. *Application contact:* Sara Hladilek, Student Services Coordinator, 608-262-8617, E-mail: shladilek@wisc.edu.
Website: http://www.engr.wisc.edu/me/

University of Wisconsin–Milwaukee, Graduate School, College of Engineering and Applied Science, Program in Engineering, Milwaukee, WI 53201-0413. Offers biomedical engineering (MS); civil engineering (MS, PhD); computer science (PhD); electrical and computer engineering (MS); electrical engineering (PhD); engineering mechanics (MS); industrial and management engineering (MS); industrial engineering (PhD); manufacturing engineering (MS); materials (PhD); materials engineering (MS); mechanical engineering (MS). *Program availability:* Part-time. *Students:* 199 full-time (52 women), 156 part-time (32 women); includes 27 minority (2 Black or African American, non-Hispanic/Latino; 15 Asian, non-Hispanic/Latino; 3 Hispanic/Latino; 7 Two or more races, non-Hispanic/Latino), 244 international. Average age 30. 396 applicants, 61% accepted, 102 enrolled. In 2016, 72 master's, 26 doctorates awarded. *Degree requirements:* For master's, comprehensive exam (for some programs), thesis or alternative; for doctorate, comprehensive exam, thesis/dissertation, internship. *Entrance requirements:* For master's, GRE, minimum GPA of 2.75; for doctorate, GRE, minimum GPA of 3.5. Additional exam requirements/recommendations for international students: Required—TOEFL (minimum score 550 paper-based; 79 iBT), IELTS (minimum score 6.5). *Application deadline:* For fall admission, 1/1 priority date for domestic students; for spring admission, 9/1 for domestic students. Applications are processed on a rolling basis. Application fee: $56 ($96 for international students). *Financial support:* In 2016–17, 3 fellowships, 55 research assistantships, 77 teaching assistantships were awarded; career-related internships or fieldwork, Federal Work-Study, unspecified assistantships, and project assistantships also available. Support available to part-time students. Financial award application deadline: 4/15. *Unit head:* David Yu, Representative, 414-229-6169, E-mail: yu@uwm.edu. *Application contact:* Betty Warras, General Information Contact, 414-229-6169, Fax: 414-229-6967, E-mail: bwarras@uwm.edu.
Website: http://www4.uwm.edu/ceas/academics/graduate_programs/

University of Wyoming, College of Engineering and Applied Sciences, Department of Mechanical Engineering, Laramie, WY 82071. Offers MS, PhD. Terminal master's awarded for partial completion of doctoral program. *Degree requirements:* For master's, thesis; for doctorate, thesis/dissertation. *Entrance requirements:* For master's, GRE General Test (minimum score 900), minimum GPA of 3.0; for doctorate, GRE General Test (minimum score: 1000), minimum GPA of 3.0. Additional exam requirements/recommendations for international students: Required—TOEFL (minimum score 550 paper-based). Electronic applications accepted. *Faculty research:* Composite materials, thermal and fluid sciences, continuum mechanics, material science.

Utah State University, School of Graduate Studies, College of Engineering, Department of Mechanical and Aerospace Engineering, Logan, UT 84322. Offers aerospace engineering (MS, PhD); mechanical engineering (ME, MS, PhD). Terminal master's awarded for partial completion of doctoral program. *Degree requirements:* For master's, thesis (for some programs); for doctorate, thesis/dissertation. *Entrance requirements:* For master's, GRE General Test, minimum GPA of 3.0; for doctorate, GRE General Test, minimum GPA of 3.3. Additional exam requirements/recommendations for international students: Required—TOEFL. *Faculty research:* In-space instruments, cryogenic cooling, thermal science, space structures, composite materials.

Vanderbilt University, School of Engineering, Department of Mechanical Engineering, Nashville, TN 37240-1001. Offers M Eng, MS, PhD. MS and PhD offered through the Graduate School. *Program availability:* Part-time. Terminal master's awarded for partial completion of doctoral program. *Degree requirements:* For master's, comprehensive exam, thesis; for doctorate, comprehensive exam, thesis/dissertation. *Entrance requirements:* For master's and doctorate, GRE General Test. Additional exam requirements/recommendations for international students: Required—TOEFL (minimum score 550 paper-based); Recommended—TWE (minimum score 4). Electronic applications accepted. *Expenses: Tuition:* Part-time $1854 per credit hour. *Faculty research:* Active noise and vibration control, robotics, mesoscale and microscale energy conversions, laser diagnostics, combustion.

Villanova University, College of Engineering, Department of Electrical and Computer Engineering, Program in Electrical Engineering, Villanova, PA 19085-1699. Offers electric power systems (Certificate); electrical engineering (MSEE); electro mechanical systems (Certificate); high frequency systems (Certificate); intelligent control systems (Certificate); wireless and digital communications (Certificate). *Program availability:* Part-time, evening/weekend. *Degree requirements:* For master's, thesis optional. *Entrance requirements:* For master's, GRE General Test (for applicants with degrees from foreign universities), BEE, minimum GPA of 3.0. Additional exam requirements/recommendations for international students: Required—TOEFL (minimum score 600 paper-based; 100 iBT). *Faculty research:* Signal processing, communications, antennas, devices.

Villanova University, College of Engineering, Department of Mechanical Engineering, Villanova, PA 19085-1699. Offers electro-mechanical systems (Certificate); machinery dynamics (Certificate); mechanical engineering (MSME); nonlinear dynamics and control (Certificate); thermofluid systems (Certificate). *Program availability:* Part-time, evening/weekend, online learning. *Degree requirements:* For master's, thesis optional. *Entrance requirements:* For master's, GRE General Test (for applicants with degrees from foreign universities), BME, minimum GPA of 3.0. Additional exam requirements/recommendations for international students: Required—TOEFL (minimum score 600 paper-based; 100 iBT). Electronic applications accepted. *Faculty research:* Composite materials, power plant systems, fluid mechanics, automated manufacturing, dynamic analysis.

Virginia Commonwealth University, Graduate School, School of Engineering, Department of Mechanical and Nuclear Engineering, Richmond, VA 23284-9005. Offers MS, PhD. *Entrance requirements:* For master's and doctorate, GRE. Additional exam requirements/recommendations for international students: Required—TOEFL (minimum score 600 paper-based; 100 iBT). *Application deadline:* For fall admission, 2/1 priority date for domestic students; for spring admission, 11/15 for domestic students. Application fee: $50. Electronic applications accepted. *Financial support:* Applicants required to submit FAFSA. *Unit head:* Dr. Rosalyn S. Hobson, Associate Dean for Graduate Studies, 804-828-8308, Fax: 804-827-7030, E-mail: rhobson@vcu.edu. *Application contact:* Dr. Karla M. Mossi, Director, Graduate Programs, 804-827-5275, E-mail: kmmossi@vcu.edu.
Website: http://mechanical-and-nuclear.egr.vcu.edu/

Virginia Polytechnic Institute and State University, Graduate School, College of Engineering, Blacksburg, VA 24061. Offers aerospace engineering (ME, MS, PhD); biological systems engineering (ME, MS, PhD); biomedical engineering (MS, PhD); chemical engineering (ME, MS, PhD); civil engineering (ME, MS, PhD); computer engineering (ME, MS, PhD); computer science (MS, PhD); electrical engineering (ME, PhD); engineering education (PhD); engineering mechanics (ME, MS, PhD); environmental engineering (MS); environmental science and engineering (MS); industrial and systems engineering (ME, MS, PhD); materials science and engineering (ME, MS, PhD); mechanical engineering (ME, MS, PhD); mining and minerals engineering (PhD); mining engineering (ME, MS); nuclear engineering (MS, PhD); ocean engineering (MS); systems engineering (ME, MS). *Faculty:* 400 full-time (73 women), 3 part-time/adjunct (2 women). *Students:* 1,949 full-time (487 women), 393 part-time (69 women); includes 251 minority (56 Black or African American, non-Hispanic/Latino; 3 American Indian or Alaska Native, non-Hispanic/Latino; 87 Asian, non-Hispanic/Latino; 70 Hispanic/Latino; 35 Two or more races, non-Hispanic/Latino), 1,354 international. Average age 27. 4,903 applicants, 19% accepted, 569 enrolled. In 2016, 364 master's, 200 doctorates awarded. *Degree requirements:* For master's, comprehensive exam (for some programs), thesis (for some programs); for doctorate, comprehensive exam (for some programs), thesis/dissertation (for some programs). *Entrance requirements:* For master's and doctorate, GRE/GMAT. Additional exam requirements/recommendations for international students: Required—TOEFL (minimum score 80 iBT). *Application deadline:* For fall admission, 8/1 for domestic students, 4/1 for international students; for spring admission, 1/1 for domestic students, 9/1 for international students. Applications are processed on a rolling basis. Application fee: $75. Electronic applications accepted. *Expenses:* Tuition, state resident: full-time $12,467; part-time $692.50 per credit hour. Tuition, nonresident: full-time $25,095; part-time $1394.25 per credit hour. *Required fees:* $2669; $491.50 per semester. Tuition and fees vary according to course load, campus/location and program. *Financial support:* In 2016–17, 160 fellowships with full tuition reimbursements (averaging $7,387 per year), 872 research assistantships with full tuition reimbursements (averaging $22,329 per year), 313 teaching assistantships with full tuition reimbursements (averaging $18,714 per year) were awarded. Financial award application deadline: 3/1; financial award applicants required to submit FAFSA. *Total annual research expenditures:* $91.8 million. *Unit head:* Dr. Julia Ross, Dean, 540-231-9752, Fax: 540-231-3031, E-mail: deaneng@vt.edu. *Application contact:* Linda Perkins, Executive Assistant, 540-231-9752, Fax: 540-231-3031, E-mail: lperkins@vt.edu.
Website: http://www.eng.vt.edu/

Washington State University, Voiland College of Engineering and Architecture, Engineering and Computer Science Programs, Vancouver Campus, Pullman, WA 99164. Offers MS. *Degree requirements:* For master's, comprehensive exam, thesis optional. *Entrance requirements:* For master's, official transcripts from all colleges and universities attended; one-page statement of purpose; three letters of recommendation. Additional exam requirements/recommendations for international students: Required—TOEFL; Recommended—IELTS. Electronic applications accepted. *Faculty research:* High yield production of bioenergy biofuels and bioproducts, nanomaterials, power systems, microfluidics, atmospheric research.

Washington State University, Voiland College of Engineering and Architecture, School of Mechanical and Materials Engineering, Pullman, WA 99164-2920. Offers materials science and engineering (MS, PhD); mechanical engineering (MS, PhD). MS programs also offered at Tri-Cities campus. *Program availability:* Part-time. Terminal master's awarded for partial completion of doctoral program. *Degree requirements:* For master's, comprehensive exam, thesis; for doctorate, comprehensive exam, thesis/dissertation, preliminary exam. *Entrance requirements:* For master's, GRE, bachelor's degree, minimum GPA of 3.0, resume, statement of purpose, 3 letters of recommendation, official transcripts, Student Interest Profile form; for doctorate, GRE, bachelor's degree, minimum GPA of 3.4, resume, statement of purpose, 3 letters of recommendation, official transcripts, Student Interest Profile form. Additional exam requirements/recommendations for international students: Required—TOEFL (minimum score 500 paper-based), IELTS. Electronic applications accepted. *Faculty research:* Multiscale modeling and characterization of materials; advanced energy; bioengineering; engineering education and curricular innovation; modeling and visualization in the areas of product realization, materials, and processes.

Washington University in St. Louis, School of Engineering and Applied Science, Department of Mechanical Engineering and Materials Science, St. Louis, MO 63130-4899. Offers aerospace engineering (MS, PhD); materials science (MS); mechanical engineering (M Eng, MS, PhD). *Program availability:* Part-time. Terminal master's awarded for partial completion of doctoral program. *Degree requirements:* For master's, thesis optional; for doctorate, thesis/dissertation optional. *Entrance requirements:* For master's, GRE; for doctorate, GRE General Test, departmental qualifying exam. *Faculty research:* Aerosols science and technology, applied mechanics, biomechanics and biomedical engineering, design, dynamic systems, combustion science, composite materials, materials science.

Wayne State University, College of Engineering, Department of Mechanical Engineering, Detroit, MI 48202. Offers MS, PhD. *Faculty:* 10. *Students:* 308 full-time (22 women), 50 part-time (10 women); includes 13 minority (1 Black or African American, non-Hispanic/Latino; 10 Asian, non-Hispanic/Latino; 2 Hispanic/Latino), 305 international. Average age 25. 1,107 applicants, 53% accepted, 135 enrolled. In 2016, 110 master's, 8 doctorates awarded. *Degree requirements:* For master's, thesis optional; for doctorate, thesis/dissertation. *Entrance requirements:* For master's, GRE (if BS is not from ABET-accredited university), minimum undergraduate GPA of 3.0; for doctorate, GRE, minimum graduate or undergraduate upper-division GPA of 3.5, completed undergraduate major or substantial specialized work in proposed doctoral field. Additional exam requirements/recommendations for international students: Required—TOEFL (minimum score 550 paper-based; 79 iBT), TWE (minimum score

5.5), Michigan English Language Assessment Battery (minimum score 85); Recommended—IELTS (minimum score 6.5). *Application deadline:* For fall admission, 6/1 priority date for domestic students, 5/1 priority date for international students; for winter admission, 10/1 priority date for domestic students, 9/1 priority date for international students; for spring admission, 2/1 priority date for domestic students, 1/1 priority date for international students. Applications are processed on a rolling basis. Application fee: $50. Electronic applications accepted. *Expenses:* $18,871 per year resident tuition and fees, $36,065 per year non-resident tuition and fees. *Financial support:* In 2016–17, 68 students received support, including 3 fellowships with tuition reimbursements available (averaging $16,000 per year), 10 research assistantships with tuition reimbursements available (averaging $17,783 per year), 18 teaching assistantships with tuition reimbursements available (averaging $19,177 per year); scholarships/grants and unspecified assistantships also available. Financial award applicants required to submit FAFSA. *Faculty research:* Acoustics and vibrations/noise control, engine combustion and emission controls, advanced materials and structures, computational fluid mechanics, material processing and manufacturing. *Total annual research expenditures:* $966,000. *Unit head:* Dr. Nabil Chalhoub, Chairman/Professor, 313-577-3753, E-mail: ab9714@wayne.edu. *Application contact:* Eric Scimeca, Graduate Program Coordinator, 313-577-0412, E-mail: eric.scimeca@wayne.edu. Website: http://engineering.wayne.edu/me/

Western Michigan University, Graduate College, College of Engineering and Applied Sciences, Department of Mechanical and Aerospace Engineering, Kalamazoo, MI 49008. Offers mechanical engineering (MSE, PhD). *Program availability:* Part-time. *Degree requirements:* For master's, thesis optional; for doctorate, thesis/dissertation.

Western New England University, College of Engineering, Department of Mechanical Engineering, Springfield, MA 01119. Offers mechanical engineering (MSME); mechatronics (MSME). *Program availability:* Part-time, evening/weekend. *Faculty:* 10 full-time (2 women). *Students:* 31 part-time (1 woman), 17 international. Average age 27. 137 applicants, 27% accepted, 9 enrolled. In 2016, 8 master's awarded. *Degree requirements:* For master's, comprehensive exam, thesis optional. *Entrance requirements:* For master's, official transcript, bachelor's degree in engineering or related field, two recommendations, resume. Additional exam requirements/recommendations for international students: Required—TOEFL (minimum score 79 iBT). *Application deadline:* Applications are processed on a rolling basis. Application fee: $30. Electronic applications accepted. *Expenses:* Contact institution. *Financial support:* Application deadline: 4/15; applicants required to submit FAFSA. *Faculty research:* Low-loss fluid mixing, flow separation delay and alleviation, high-lift airfoils, ejector research, compact heat exchangers. *Unit head:* Dr. Said Dini, Chair, 413-782-1498, E-mail: said.dini@wne.edu. *Application contact:* Matthew Fox, Director of Admissions for Graduate Students and Adult Learners, 413-782-1410, Fax: 413-782-1777, E-mail: study@wne.edu.
Website: http://www1.wne.edu/academics/graduate/mechanical-engineering-ms.cfm

West Virginia University, Statler College of Engineering and Mineral Resources, Department of Mechanical and Aerospace Engineering, Program in Mechanical Engineering, Morgantown, WV 26506. Offers MSME, PhD. *Program availability:* Part-time. Terminal master's awarded for partial completion of doctoral program. *Degree requirements:* For master's, thesis; for doctorate, comprehensive exam, thesis/dissertation, qualifying exam, proposal and defense. *Entrance requirements:* For master's and doctorate, GRE Subject Test, minimum GPA of 3.0, 3 references. Additional exam requirements/recommendations for international students: Required—TOEFL. *Faculty research:* Thermal sciences, material sciences, automatic controls, mechanical/structure design.

Wichita State University, Graduate School, College of Engineering, Department of Mechanical Engineering, Wichita, KS 67260. Offers MS, PhD. *Program availability:* Part-time. *Unit head:* Dr. Muhammad M. Rahman, Chair, 316-978-3402, Fax: 316-978-3236, E-mail: muhammad.rahman@wichita.edu. *Application contact:* Jordan Oleson, Admission Coordinator, 316-978-3095, Fax: 316-978-3253, E-mail: jordan.oleson@wichita.edu.
Website: http://www.wichita.edu/mechanical

Widener University, Graduate Programs in Engineering, Program in Mechanical Engineering, Chester, PA 19013. Offers M Eng. *Program availability:* Part-time, evening/weekend. *Students:* 7 part-time (0 women). Average age 27. In 2016, 1 master's awarded. *Degree requirements:* For master's, thesis optional. *Application deadline:* For fall admission, 8/1 priority date for domestic students; for spring admission, 12/1 for domestic students. Applications are processed on a rolling basis. Application fee: $0. Electronic applications accepted. Tuition and fees vary according to degree level and program. *Financial support:* Teaching assistantships with full tuition reimbursements and unspecified assistantships available. Financial award application deadline: 3/15. *Faculty research:* Computational fluid mechanics, thermal and solar engineering, energy conversion, composite materials, solid mechanics. *Unit head:* Rudolph Treichel, Assistant Dean/Director of Graduate Programs, 610-499-1294, Fax: 610-449-4059, E-mail: rjtreichel@widener.edu.

Wilkes University, College of Graduate and Professional Studies, College of Science and Engineering, Department of Mechanical Engineering and Engineering Management, Wilkes-Barre, PA 18766-0002. Offers engineering management (MS); mechanical engineering (MS). *Program availability:* Part-time. *Students:* 15 full-time (0 women), 12 part-time (0 women); includes 3 minority (1 Hispanic/Latino; 2 Two or more races, non-Hispanic/Latino), 15 international. Average age 27. In 2016, 18 master's awarded. *Application deadline:* Applications are processed on a rolling basis. Application fee: $45 ($65 for international students). Electronic applications accepted. Tuition and fees vary according to degree level and program. *Financial support:* Institutionally sponsored loans and unspecified assistantships available. *Unit head:* Dr. William Hudson, Dean, 570-408-4600, Fax: 570-408-7860, E-mail: william.hudson@wilkes.edu. *Application contact:* Director of Graduate Enrollment, 570-408-4234, Fax: 570-408-7846.
Website: http://www.wilkes.edu/academics/colleges/science-and-engineering/mechanical-engineering-engineering-management-applied-and-engineering-sciences/

Worcester Polytechnic Institute, Graduate Studies and Research, Department of Mechanical Engineering, Worcester, MA 01609-2280. Offers manufacturing engineering (MS, PhD); materials process engineering (MS); materials science and engineering (MS, PhD); mechanical engineering (MS, PhD, Graduate Certificate). *Program availability:* Part-time, evening/weekend, 100% online, blended/hybrid learning. *Faculty:* 25 full-time (4 women), 6 part-time/adjunct (2 women). *Students:* 54 full-time (10 women), 98 part-time (10 women); includes 22 minority (2 Black or African American, non-Hispanic/Latino; 8 Asian, non-Hispanic/Latino; 10 Hispanic/Latino; 2 Two or more races, non-Hispanic/Latino), 37 international. 261 applicants, 69% accepted, 74 enrolled. In 2016, 45 master's, 7 doctorates awarded. *Degree requirements:* For master's, thesis optional; for doctorate, comprehensive exam, thesis/dissertation. *Entrance requirements:* For master's, GRE (recommended), BS in mechanical engineering or related field, 3 letters of recommendation, statement of purpose; for doctorate, GRE (recommended), MS in mechanical engineering or related field, 3 letters of recommendation, statement of purpose. Additional exam requirements/recommendations for international students: Required—TOEFL (minimum score 563 paper-based; 84 iBT), IELTS (minimum score 7). *Application deadline:* For fall admission, 1/1 priority date for domestic and international students; for spring admission, 10/1 priority date for domestic and international students. Applications are processed on a rolling basis. Application fee: $70. Electronic applications accepted. *Financial support:* Research assistantships, teaching assistantships, career-related internships or fieldwork, institutionally sponsored loans, scholarships/grants, and unspecified assistantships available. Financial award application deadline: 1/1; financial award applicants required to submit FAFSA. *Unit head:* Dr. Jamal Yagoobi, Interim Head, 508-831-5556, Fax: 508-831-5680, E-mail: jyagoobi@wpi.edu. *Application contact:* Barbara Edilberti, 508-831-5026, Fax: 508-831-5680, E-mail: edilbert@wpi.edu.
Website: http://www.wpi.edu/academics/me

Wright State University, Graduate School, College of Engineering and Computer Science, Department of Mechanical and Materials Engineering, Dayton, OH 45435. Offers aerospace systems engineering (MSE); materials science and engineering (MSE); mechanical engineering (MSE); renewable ande clean energy (MSE). *Degree requirements:* For master's, thesis or course option alternative. *Entrance requirements:* Additional exam requirements/recommendations for international students: Required—TOEFL. Application fee: $25. *Expenses:* Tuition, state resident: full-time $9952; part-time $622 per credit hour. Tuition, nonresident: full-time $16,960; part-time $1060 per credit hour. *Financial support:* Fellowships, research assistantships, teaching assistantships, and unspecified assistantships available. Support available to part-time students. Financial award application deadline: 3/15; financial award applicants required to submit FAFSA. *Unit head:* Dr. George P.G. Huang, Chair, 937-775-5040, Fax: 937-775-5009, E-mail: george.huang@wright.edu. *Application contact:* John Kimble, Associate Director of Graduate Admissions and Records, 937-775-2957, Fax: 937-775-2453, E-mail: john.kimble@wright.edu.
Website: https://engineering-computer-science.wright.edu/mechanical-and-materials-engineering

Yale University, Graduate School of Arts and Sciences, School of Engineering and Applied Science, Department of Mechanical Engineering, New Haven, CT 06520. Offers MS, PhD. Terminal master's awarded for partial completion of doctoral program. *Degree requirements:* For doctorate, thesis/dissertation, exam. *Entrance requirements:* For master's and doctorate, GRE General Test. Additional exam requirements/recommendations for international students: Required—TOEFL. *Faculty research:* Mechanics of fluids, mechanics of solids/material science.

Youngstown State University, Graduate School, College of Science, Technology, Engineering and Mathematics, Department of Mechanical Engineering, Youngstown, OH 44555-0001. Offers MSE. *Program availability:* Part-time, evening/weekend. *Degree requirements:* For master's, thesis optional. *Entrance requirements:* For master's, minimum GPA of 2.75 in field. Additional exam requirements/recommendations for international students: Required—TOEFL. *Faculty research:* Kinematics and dynamics of machines, computational and experimental heat transfer, machine controls and mechanical design.

Mechanics

Brown University, Graduate School, School of Engineering, Program in Mechanics of Solids and Structures, Providence, RI 02912. Offers Sc M, PhD. *Degree requirements:* For doctorate, thesis/dissertation, preliminary exam.

California Institute of Technology, Division of Engineering and Applied Science, Option in Applied Mechanics, Pasadena, CA 91125-0001. Offers MS, PhD. *Degree requirements:* For doctorate, thesis/dissertation. *Faculty research:* Elasticity, mechanics of quasi-static and dynamic fracture, dynamics and mechanical vibrations, stability and control.

Carnegie Mellon University, Carnegie Institute of Technology, Department of Civil and Environmental Engineering, Pittsburgh, PA 15213. Offers advanced infrastructure systems (MS, PhD); advanced infrastructure systems technology development and application (MS); air quality engineering and science (MS); civil and environmental engineering (MS, PhD); civil and environmental engineering/engineering and public policy (PhD); civil engineering (MS, PhD); computational mechanics (MS, PhD); computational modeling and monitoring for resilient structural and material systems (MS); energy infrastructure systems (MS); environmental engineering (MS, PhD); environmental management and science (MS, PhD); IT-based sustainable global infrastructure and construction management (MS); sustainability and green design (MS); water quality engineering and science (MS). *Program availability:* Part-time. *Faculty:* 23 full-time (5 women), 12 part-time/adjunct (3 women). *Students:* 230 full-time (87 women), 4 part-time (0 women); includes 17 minority (4 Black or African American, non-Hispanic/Latino; 12 Asian, non-Hispanic/Latino; 1 Two or more races, non-Hispanic/Latino), 179 international. Average age 25. 653 applicants, 60% accepted, 107 enrolled. In 2016, 145 master's, 15 doctorates awarded. Terminal master's awarded for partial completion of doctoral program. *Degree requirements:* For master's, thesis optional; for doctorate, comprehensive exam, thesis/dissertation, two-part qualifying exam, public defense of dissertation. *Entrance requirements:* For master's, GRE General Test, BS in engineering, science or mathematics; for doctorate, GRE General Test, BS or MS in engineering, science or mathematics. Additional exam requirements/recommendations for international students: Required—TOEFL (minimum score 84 iBT) or IELTS (6.0). *Application deadline:* For fall admission, 1/5 priority date for domestic and international students; for spring admission, 9/15 priority date for domestic and international students. Applications are processed on a rolling basis. Application fee: $65. Electronic applications accepted. *Expenses:* Contact institution. *Financial support:* In 2016–17, 129 students received support. Fellowships with tuition reimbursements available, research assistantships with tuition reimbursements available, scholarships/grants, tuition waivers (full and partial), unspecified assistantships, and service assistantships available. Financial award application deadline: 1/5. *Faculty research:* Advanced infrastructure systems; environmental engineering, sustainability, and science; mechanics, materials, and computing. *Total annual research expenditures:* $7.4 million. *Unit head:* Dr. David A. Dzombak, Professor and Department Head, 412-268-2941, Fax: 412-268-7813, E-mail: dzombak@cmu.edu. *Application contact:* David A. Vey,

Graduate Admissions Manager, 412-268-2292, Fax: 412-268-7813, E-mail: dvey@andrew.cmu.edu.
Website: http://www.cmu.edu/cee/

Columbia University, Fu Foundation School of Engineering and Applied Science, Department of Civil Engineering and Engineering Mechanics, New York, NY 10027. Offers civil engineering (MS, Eng Sc D, PhD); construction engineering and management (MS); engineering mechanics (MS, Eng Sc D, PhD). *Program availability:* Part-time, online learning. Terminal master's awarded for partial completion of doctoral program. *Degree requirements:* For doctorate, thesis/dissertation, qualifying exam. *Entrance requirements:* For master's and doctorate, GRE General Test. Additional exam requirements/recommendations for international students: Required—TOEFL, IELTS, PTE. Electronic applications accepted. *Faculty research:* Structural dynamics, structural health and monitoring, fatigue and fracture mechanics, geo-environmental engineering, multiscale science and engineering.

Cornell University, Graduate School, Graduate Fields of Engineering, Field of Theoretical and Applied Mechanics, Ithaca, NY 14853. Offers advanced composites and structures (M Eng); dynamics and space mechanics (MS, PhD); fluid mechanics (MS, PhD); mechanics of materials (MS, PhD); solid mechanics (MS, PhD). *Degree requirements:* For master's, thesis (MS); for doctorate, one foreign language, comprehensive exam, thesis/dissertation, teaching experience. *Entrance requirements:* For master's and doctorate, GRE General Test, 3 letters of recommendation. Additional exam requirements/recommendations for international students: Required—TOEFL (minimum score 600 paper-based; 77 iBT). Electronic applications accepted. *Faculty research:* Biomathematics, bio-fluids, animal locomotion; non-linear dynamics, celestial mechanics, control; mechanics of materials, computational mechanics; experimental mechanics; non-linear elasticity, granular materials, phase transitions.

Drexel University, College of Engineering, Department of Mechanical Engineering and Mechanics, Philadelphia, PA 19104-2875. Offers mechanical engineering (MS, PhD). *Program availability:* Part-time, evening/weekend. *Faculty:* 27 full-time (4 women), 7 part-time/adjunct (0 women). *Students:* 95 full-time (10 women), 49 part-time (3 women); includes 17 minority (4 Black or African American, non-Hispanic/Latino; 8 Asian, non-Hispanic/Latino; 4 Hispanic/Latino; 1 Two or more races, non-Hispanic/Latino), 63 international. Average age 27. In 2016, 50 master's, 10 doctorates awarded. Terminal master's awarded for partial completion of doctoral program. *Degree requirements:* For master's, thesis optional; for doctorate, thesis/dissertation. *Entrance requirements:* For master's, minimum GPA of 3.0, BS in engineering or science; for doctorate, minimum GPA of 3.5, MS in engineering or science. Additional exam requirements/recommendations for international students: Required—TOEFL. *Application deadline:* For fall admission, 8/21 for domestic students. Applications are processed on a rolling basis. Application fee: $50. Electronic applications accepted. *Expenses: Tuition:* Full-time $32,184; part-time $1192 per credit hour. *Required fees:* $280. Tuition and fees vary according to campus/location and program. *Financial support:* Research assistantships, teaching assistantships, and unspecified assistantships available. Financial award application deadline: 2/1. *Faculty research:* Composites, dynamic systems and control, combustion and fuels, biomechanics, mechanics and thermal fluid sciences. *Total annual research expenditures:* $3.7 million. *Unit head:* Dr. Mun Young Choi, Head, 215-895-2284, Fax: 215-895-1478, E-mail: mem@drexel.edu. *Application contact:* Director of Graduate Admissions, 215-895-6700, Fax: 215-895-5939, E-mail: enroll@drexel.edu.

École Polytechnique de Montréal, Graduate Programs, Department of Mechanical Engineering, Montréal, QC H3C 3A7, Canada. Offers aerothermics (M Eng, M Sc A, PhD); applied mechanics (M Eng, M Sc A, PhD); tool design (M Eng, M Sc A, PhD). *Program availability:* Part-time, evening/weekend. *Degree requirements:* For master's, one foreign language, thesis; for doctorate, one foreign language, thesis/dissertation. *Entrance requirements:* For master's, minimum GPA of 2.75; for doctorate, minimum GPA of 3.0. *Faculty research:* Noise control and vibration, fatigue and creep, aerodynamics, composite materials, biomechanics, robotics.

Georgia Institute of Technology, Graduate Studies, College of Engineering, School of Civil and Environmental Engineering, Program in Engineering Science and Mechanics, Atlanta, GA 30332-0001. Offers MS. Terminal master's awarded for partial completion of doctoral program. *Degree requirements:* For master's, thesis optional. *Entrance requirements:* For master's, GRE. Additional exam requirements/recommendations for international students: Required—TOEFL (minimum score 550 paper-based; 79 iBT). Electronic applications accepted. *Faculty research:* Bioengineering, structural mechanics, solid mechanics, dynamics.

Iowa State University of Science and Technology, Program in Engineering Mechanics, Ames, IA 50011. Offers M Eng, MS, PhD. *Entrance requirements:* For master's and doctorate, GRE. Additional exam requirements/recommendations for international students: Required—TOEFL (minimum score 550 paper-based; 80 iBT), IELTS (minimum score 6.5). *Application deadline:* For fall admission, 1/1 for domestic students; for spring admission, 9/1 for domestic students. Application fee: $60 ($90 for international students). Electronic applications accepted. *Application contact:* Sara Goplin, Application Contact, 515-294-9669, Fax: 515-294-3262, E-mail: aere-info@iastate.edu.
Website: http://www.aere.iastate.edu

Johns Hopkins University, G. W. C. Whiting School of Engineering, Master of Science in Engineering Management Program, Baltimore, MD 21218. Offers biomaterials (MSEM); civil engineering (MSEM); communications science (MSEM); computer science (MSEM); environmental systems analysis, economics and public policy (MSEM); fluid mechanics (MSEM); materials science and engineering (MSEM); mechanical engineering (MSEM); mechanics and materials (MSEM); nano-biotechnology (MSEM); nanomaterials and nanotechnology (MSEM); operations research (MSEM); probability and statistics (MSEM); smart product and device design (MSEM). *Faculty:* 7 full-time (4 women), 1 part-time/adjunct (0 women). *Students:* 35 full-time (14 women), 8 part-time (3 women); includes 7 minority (4 Asian, non-Hispanic/Latino; 3 Hispanic/Latino), 26 international. Average age 24. 228 applicants, 28% accepted, 25 enrolled. In 2016, 18 master's awarded. *Entrance requirements:* For master's, GRE, 3 letters of recommendation, statement of purpose, transcripts. Additional exam requirements/recommendations for international students: Required—TOEFL (minimum score 600 paper-based, 100 iBT) or IELTS (7). *Application deadline:* For fall admission, 2/1 for domestic and international students. Application fee: $75. Electronic applications accepted. *Financial support:* Fellowships and health care benefits available. *Unit head:* Dr. Pamela Sheff, Director, 410-516-7056, Fax: 410-516-4880, E-mail: pamsheff@gmail.com. *Application contact:* Richard Helman, Director of Graduate Admissions, 410-516-8174, Fax: 410-516-0780, E-mail: graduateadmissions@jhu.edu.
Website: http://engineering.jhu.edu/msem/

Lehigh University, P.C. Rossin College of Engineering and Applied Science, Department of Mechanical Engineering and Mechanics, Bethlehem, PA 18015. Offers computational and engineering mechanics (MS, PhD); mechanical engineering (M Eng, MS, PhD); MBA/E. *Program availability:* Part-time, 100% online, blended/hybrid learning. *Faculty:* 26 full-time (2 women), 2 part-time/adjunct (1 woman). *Students:* 143 full-time (18 women), 27 part-time (3 women); includes 9 minority (2 Black or African American, non-Hispanic/Latino; 2 Asian, non-Hispanic/Latino; 4 Hispanic/Latino; 1 Native Hawaiian or other Pacific Islander, non-Hispanic/Latino), 100 international. Average age 26. 256 applicants, 35% accepted, 27 enrolled. In 2016, 50 master's, 15 doctorates awarded. Terminal master's awarded for partial completion of doctoral program. *Degree requirements:* For master's, thesis (for MS); for doctorate, thesis/dissertation, general exam. *Entrance requirements:* Additional exam requirements/recommendations for international students: Required—TOEFL (minimum score 550 paper-based; 79 iBT), IELTS (minimum score 6.5), GRE (recommended). *Application deadline:* For fall admission, 7/15 for domestic and international students; for spring admission, 12/1 for domestic and international students. Application fee: $75. Electronic applications accepted. *Expenses:* $1,420 per credit. *Financial support:* In 2016–17, 68 students received support, including 5 fellowships with full tuition reimbursements available (averaging $28,140 per year), 61 research assistantships with full tuition reimbursements available (averaging $25,200 per year), 13 teaching assistantships with full tuition reimbursements available (averaging $28,707 per year); dean's doctoral assistantship also available. Financial award application deadline: 1/15. *Faculty research:* Thermofluids, dynamic systems, CAD/CAM, computational mechanics, solid mechanics. *Total annual research expenditures:* $4 million. *Unit head:* Dr. D. Gary Harlow, Chairman, 610-758-4102, Fax: 610-758-6224, E-mail: dgh0@lehigh.edu. *Application contact:* Allison B. Marsteller, Graduate Coordinator, 610-758-4107, Fax: 610-758-6224, E-mail: alm513@lehigh.edu.
Website: http://www.lehigh.edu/~inmem/

Louisiana State University and Agricultural & Mechanical College, Graduate School, College of Engineering, Department of Civil and Environmental Engineering, Baton Rouge, LA 70803. Offers environmental engineering (MSCE, PhD); geotechnical engineering (MSCE, PhD); structural engineering and mechanics (MSCE, PhD); transportation engineering (MSCE, PhD); water resources (MSCE, PhD).

McGill University, Faculty of Graduate and Postdoctoral Studies, Faculty of Engineering, Department of Civil Engineering and Applied Mechanics, Montréal, QC H3A 2T5, Canada. Offers environmental engineering (M Eng, M Sc, PhD); fluid mechanics (M Sc); fluid mechanics and hydraulic engineering (M Eng, PhD); materials engineering (M Eng, PhD); rehabilitation of urban infrastructure (M Eng, PhD); soil behavior (M Eng, PhD); soil mechanics and foundations (M Eng, PhD); structures and structural mechanics (M Eng, PhD); water resources (M Sc); water resources engineering (M Eng, PhD).

Michigan State University, The Graduate School, College of Engineering, Department of Mechanical Engineering, East Lansing, MI 48824. Offers engineering mechanics (MS, PhD); mechanical engineering (MS, PhD). *Entrance requirements:* For master's, GRE General Test. Additional exam requirements/recommendations for international students: Required—TOEFL. Electronic applications accepted.

Michigan Technological University, Graduate School, College of Engineering, Department of Mechanical Engineering-Engineering Mechanics, Houghton, MI 49931. Offers automotive systems and controls (Graduate Certificate); engineering mechanics (MS); hybrid electric drive vehicle engineering (Graduate Certificate); mechanical engineering (MS); mechanical engineering-engineering mechanics (PhD). *Program availability:* Part-time, evening/weekend, 100% online, blended/hybrid learning. *Faculty:* 84 full-time, 60 part-time/adjunct. *Students:* 300 full-time, 82 part-time; includes 7 minority (3 Asian, non-Hispanic/Latino; 3 Hispanic/Latino; 1 Two or more races, non-Hispanic/Latino), 295 international. Average age 26. 1,544 applicants, 18% accepted, 104 enrolled. In 2016, 102 master's, 11 doctorates, 7 other advanced degrees awarded. Terminal master's awarded for partial completion of doctoral program. *Degree requirements:* For master's, thesis (for some programs); for doctorate, comprehensive exam, thesis/dissertation. *Entrance requirements:* For master's, GRE (Michigan Tech and online students exempt), statement of purpose, personal statement, official transcripts, 2 letters of recommendation, resume/curriculum vitae; for doctorate, GRE (Michigan Tech and online students exempt), MS (preferred), statement of purpose, official transcripts, 2 letters of recommendation, resume/curriculum vitae; for Graduate Certificate, statement of purpose, official transcripts, BS in engineering. Additional exam requirements/recommendations for international students: Required—TOEFL (minimum score 90 iBT) or IELTS (minimum score 7.0). *Application deadline:* For fall admission, 3/1 priority date for domestic and international students; for spring admission, 8/1 priority date for domestic and international students. Applications are processed on a rolling basis. Electronic applications accepted. *Expenses:* Contact institution. *Financial support:* In 2016–17, 247 students received support, including 14 fellowships with tuition reimbursements available (averaging $15,242 per year), 37 research assistantships with tuition reimbursements available (averaging $15,242 per year), 31 teaching assistantships with tuition reimbursements available (averaging $15,242 per year); career-related internships or fieldwork, Federal Work-Study, scholarships/grants, health care benefits, unspecified assistantships, and cooperative program also available. Financial award applicants required to submit FAFSA. *Faculty research:* Mobility and autonomy, complex systems and controls, multi-scale materials and mechanics, thermo-fluids and energy conversion, human-centered engineering. *Total annual research expenditures:* $5.3 million. *Unit head:* Dr. William W. Predebon, Chair, 906-487-2551, Fax: 906-487-2822, E-mail: wwpredeb@mtu.edu. *Application contact:* Julie Foster, Graduate Program Assistant, 906-487-3611, Fax: 906-487-2822, E-mail: jafoster@mtu.edu.
Website: http://www.mtu.edu/mechanical/

Missouri University of Science and Technology, Graduate School, Department of Civil, Architectural, and Environmental Engineering, Rolla, MO 65409. Offers civil engineering (MS, DE, PhD); construction engineering (MS, DE, PhD); environmental engineering (MS); fluid mechanics (MS, DE, PhD); geotechnical engineering (MS, DE, PhD); hydrology and hydraulic engineering (MS, DE, PhD). *Program availability:* Part-time, evening/weekend. Terminal master's awarded for partial completion of doctoral program. *Degree requirements:* For master's, thesis optional; for doctorate, comprehensive exam, thesis/dissertation. *Entrance requirements:* For master's, GRE General Test (minimum combined score 1100), minimum GPA of 3.0; for doctorate, GRE General Test (minimum score: verbal and quantitative 400, writing 3.5), minimum GPA of 3.0. Additional exam requirements/recommendations for international students: Required—TOEFL (minimum score 550 paper-based). Electronic applications accepted. *Faculty research:* Earthquake engineering, structural optimization and control systems, structural health monitoring/damage detection, soil-structure interaction, soil mechanics and foundation engineering.

Montana State University, The Graduate School, College of Engineering, Department of Civil Engineering, Bozeman, MT 59717. Offers civil engineering (MS); construction engineering management (MCEM); engineering (PhD), including applied mechanics option, civil engineering option. *Program availability:* Part-time. *Degree requirements:* For master's, comprehensive exam, thesis (for some programs); for doctorate, comprehensive exam, thesis/dissertation. *Entrance requirements:* For master's and doctorate, GRE General Test. Additional exam requirements/recommendations for international students: Required—TOEFL (minimum score 550 paper-based). Electronic applications accepted. *Faculty research:* Snow and ice mechanics, biofilm engineering, transportation, structural and geo materials, water resources.

New Mexico Institute of Mining and Technology, Center for Graduate Studies, Department of Mechanical Engineering, Socorro, NM 87801. Offers explosives engineering (MS); fluid and thermal sciences (MS); mechatronics systems engineering (MS); solid mechanics (MS). *Degree requirements:* For master's, thesis (for some programs). *Entrance requirements:* For master's, GRE General Test. Additional exam requirements/recommendations for international students: Required—TOEFL (minimum score 540 paper-based). *Faculty research:* Vibrations, fluid-structure interactions.

Northwestern University, McCormick School of Engineering and Applied Science, Program in Theoretical and Applied Mechanics, Evanston, IL 60208. Offers MS, PhD. Admissions and degrees offered through The Graduate School. Terminal master's awarded for partial completion of doctoral program. *Degree requirements:* For master's, thesis optional; for doctorate, comprehensive exam, thesis/dissertation. *Entrance requirements:* For master's and doctorate, GRE General Test, minimum 2 letters of recommendation, transcripts from all academic institutions attended. Additional exam requirements/recommendations for international students: Required—TOEFL (minimum score 577 paper-based; 90 iBT), IELTS (minimum score 7). Electronic applications accepted. *Faculty research:* Computational mechanics, mechanics in biology and fluids, micro/nanomechanics, multifunctional materials, geomechanics, structural reliability and nondestructive characterization.

Ohio University, Graduate College, Russ College of Engineering and Technology, Department of Civil Engineering, Athens, OH 45701-2979. Offers civil engineering (PhD); construction engineering and management (MS); environmental (MS); geotechnical and geoenvironmental (MS); mechanics (MS); structures (MS); transportation (MS); water resources (MS). *Program availability:* Part-time. *Degree requirements:* For master's, comprehensive exam (for some programs), thesis or alternative; for doctorate, comprehensive exam, thesis/dissertation. *Entrance requirements:* For master's, GRE General Test, minimum GPA of 3.0, 3 letters of recommendation; for doctorate, GRE General Test. Additional exam requirements/recommendations for international students: Required—TOEFL (minimum score 550 paper-based; 80 iBT) or IELTS (minimum score 6.5). *Application deadline:* For fall admission, 5/1 priority date for domestic students, 2/1 priority date for international students; for winter admission, 8/1 priority date for domestic students, 4/1 priority date for international students; for spring admission, 2/1 priority date for domestic students, 7/1 priority date for international students. Applications are processed on a rolling basis. Application fee: $50 ($55 for international students). Electronic applications accepted. *Financial support:* Research assistantships with full tuition reimbursements, teaching assistantships with full tuition reimbursements, Federal Work-Study, institutionally sponsored loans, scholarships/grants, and unspecified assistantships available. Financial award application deadline: 3/15; financial award applicants required to submit FAFSA. *Faculty research:* Noise abatement, materials and environment, highway infrastructure, subsurface investigation (pavements, pipes, bridges). *Unit head:* Dr. Gayle F. Mitchell, Chair, 740-593-0430, Fax: 740-593-0625, E-mail: mitchelg@ohio.edu. *Application contact:* Dr. Shad M. Sargand, Graduate Chair, 740-593-1465, Fax: 740-593-0625, E-mail: sargand@ohio.edu.
Website: http://www.ohio.edu/civil/

Penn State University Park, Graduate School, College of Engineering, Department of Engineering Science and Mechanics, University Park, PA 16802. Offers engineering mechanics (M Eng); engineering science (M Eng); engineering science and mechanics (MS, PhD). *Unit head:* Dr. Amr S. Elnashai, Dean, 814-865-7537, Fax: 814-863-4749. *Application contact:* Lori Hawn, Director, Graduate Student Services, 814-865-1795, Fax: 814-863-4627, E-mail: l-gswww@lists.psu.edu.
Website: http://esm.psu.edu/

Rutgers University–New Brunswick, Graduate School-New Brunswick, Program in Mechanics, Piscataway, NJ 08854-8097. Offers MS, PhD. *Program availability:* Part-time. Terminal master's awarded for partial completion of doctoral program. *Degree requirements:* For master's, thesis optional, qualifying exam; for doctorate, thesis/dissertation, qualifying exam. *Entrance requirements:* For master's and doctorate, GRE General Test, GRE Subject Test (recommended). Additional exam requirements/recommendations for international students: Required—TOEFL. Electronic applications accepted. *Faculty research:* Continuum mechanics, constitutive theory, thermodynamics, visolasticity, liquid crystal theory.

San Diego State University, Graduate and Research Affairs, College of Engineering, Department of Aerospace Engineering and Engineering Mechanics, San Diego, CA 92182. Offers aerospace engineering (MS); engineering mechanics (MS); engineering sciences and applied mechanics (PhD); flight dynamics (MS); fluid dynamics (MS). PhD offered jointly with University of California, San Diego and Department of Mechanical Engineering. Terminal master's awarded for partial completion of doctoral program. *Degree requirements:* For master's, comprehensive exam (for some programs), thesis (for some programs); for doctorate, thesis/dissertation. *Entrance requirements:* For master's, GRE General Test; for doctorate, GRE, 3 letters of recommendation. Additional exam requirements/recommendations for international students: Required—TOEFL. Electronic applications accepted. *Faculty research:* Organized structures in post-stall flow over wings/three dimensional separated flow, airfoil growth effect, probabilities, structural mechanics.

Southern Illinois University Carbondale, Graduate School, College of Engineering, Department of Civil and Environmental Engineering, Carbondale, IL 62901-4701. Offers civil and environmental engineering (ME); civil engineering (MS). *Degree requirements:* For master's, comprehensive exam, thesis. *Entrance requirements:* For master's, GRE, minimum GPA of 2.7. Additional exam requirements/recommendations for international students: Required—TOEFL. *Faculty research:* Composite materials, wastewater treatment, solid waste disposal, slurry transport, geotechnical engineering.

Stanford University, School of Engineering, Department of Civil and Environmental Engineering, Stanford, CA 94305-2004. Offers atmosphere and energy (MS, PhD); construction (MS), including construction engineering and management, design-construction integration, sustainable design and construction; environmental engineering and science (MS, PhD, Eng); environmental fluid mechanics and hydrology (PhD); geomechanics (MS); structural engineering (MS). Terminal master's awarded for partial completion of doctoral program. *Degree requirements:* For doctorate, thesis/dissertation, qualifying exam; for Eng, thesis. *Entrance requirements:* For master's, doctorate, and Eng, GRE General Test. Additional exam requirements/recommendations for international students: Required—TOEFL. Electronic applications accepted. *Expenses: Tuition:* Full-time $47,331. *Required fees:* $609.

The University of Alabama, Graduate School, College of Engineering, Department of Aerospace Engineering and Mechanics, Tuscaloosa, AL 35487. Offers aerospace engineering (MSAEM); engineering science and mechanics (PhD). *Program availability:* Part-time, online learning. *Faculty:* 16 full-time (1 woman). *Students:* 34 full-time (2 women), 33 part-time (5 women); includes 6 minority (2 Asian, non-Hispanic/Latino; 4 Hispanic/Latino), 21 international. Average age 27. 70 applicants, 51% accepted, 21 enrolled. In 2016, 24 master's, 2 doctorates awarded. Terminal master's awarded for partial completion of doctoral program. *Degree requirements:* For master's, comprehensive exam (for some programs), thesis (for some programs); for doctorate, comprehensive exam, thesis/dissertation, 1-year residency. *Entrance requirements:* For master's, GRE, BS in engineering or physics; for doctorate, GRE, BS or MS in engineering or physics. Additional exam requirements/recommendations for international students: Required—TOEFL (minimum score 550 paper-based; 79 iBT). *Application deadline:* For fall admission, 7/15 priority date for domestic students, 2/28 priority date for international students; for spring admission, 12/1 priority date for domestic students, 6/30 priority date for international students. Applications are processed on a rolling basis. Application fee: $50 ($60 for international students). Electronic applications accepted. *Expenses:* Tuition, state resident: full-time $10,470. Tuition, nonresident: full-time $26,950. *Financial support:* In 2016–17, 18 students received support, including fellowships with full tuition reimbursements available (averaging $15,000 per year), research assistantships with full tuition reimbursements available (averaging $20,000 per year), teaching assistantships with full tuition reimbursements available (averaging $14,025 per year); Federal Work-Study, institutionally sponsored loans, scholarships/grants, health care benefits, and unspecified assistantships also available. Financial award application deadline: 2/28. *Faculty research:* Aeronautics, astronautics, solid mechanics, fluid mechanics, computational modeling. *Total annual research expenditures:* $1.5 million. *Unit head:* Dr. John Baker, Professor/Department Head, 205-348-4997, Fax: 205-348-7240, E-mail: john.baker@eng.ua.edu. *Application contact:* Dr. James Paul Hubner, Associate Professor, 205-348-1617, Fax: 208-348-7240, E-mail: phubner@eng.ua.edu.
Website: http://aem.eng.ua.edu/

University of Calgary, Faculty of Graduate Studies, Schulich School of Engineering, Department of Civil Engineering, Calgary, AB T2N 1N4, Canada. Offers avalanche mechanics (M Sc, PhD); civil engineering (M Eng, M Sc, PhD); energy and environment engineering (M Eng, M Sc, PhD); environmental engineering (M Eng, M Sc, PhD); geotechnical engineering (M Eng, M Sc, PhD); materials science (M Eng, M Sc, PhD); project management (M Eng, M Sc, PhD); structures and solid mechanics (M Eng, M Sc, PhD); transportation engineering (M Eng, M Sc, PhD); water resources (M Eng, M Sc, PhD). *Program availability:* Part-time. *Degree requirements:* For master's, thesis; for doctorate, thesis/dissertation, written and oral candidacy exam. *Entrance requirements:* For master's, minimum GPA of 3.0; for doctorate, minimum GPA of 3.5. Additional exam requirements/recommendations for international students: Required—TOEFL (minimum score 580 paper-based; 93 iBT), IELTS (minimum score 7). Electronic applications accepted. *Faculty research:* Geotechnical engineering, energy and environment, transportation, project management, structures and solid mechanics.

University of California, Berkeley, Graduate Division, College of Engineering, Department of Civil and Environmental Engineering, Berkeley, CA 94720-1500. Offers engineering and project management (M Eng, MS, PhD); environmental engineering (M Eng, MS, PhD); geoengineering (M Eng, MS, PhD); structural engineering, mechanics and materials (M Eng, MS, PhD); transportation engineering (M Eng, MS, PhD); M Arch/MS; MCP/MS; MPP/MS. *Students:* 360 full-time (143 women); includes 71 minority (15 Black or African American, non-Hispanic/Latino; 39 Asian, non-Hispanic/Latino; 17 Hispanic/Latino), 148 international. Average age 27. 1,086 applicants, 185 enrolled. In 2016, 188 master's, 26 doctorates awarded. Terminal master's awarded for partial completion of doctoral program. *Degree requirements:* For master's, comprehensive exam (for some programs), thesis (for some programs), comprehensive exam or thesis (MS); for doctorate, thesis/dissertation, qualifying exam. *Entrance requirements:* For master's, GRE General Test, minimum GPA of 3.0, 3 letters of recommendation; for doctorate, GRE General Test, minimum GPA of 3.5, 3 letters of recommendation. Additional exam requirements/recommendations for international students: Required—TOEFL (minimum score 570 paper-based; 90 iBT). *Application deadline:* For fall admission, 12/16 for domestic students. Application fee: $105 ($125 for international students). Electronic applications accepted. *Financial support:* Applicants required to submit FAFSA. *Unit head:* Prof. Robert Harley, Chair, 510-643-8739, Fax: 510-643-5264, E-mail: chair@ce.berkeley.edu. *Application contact:* Shelly Okimoto, Graduate Advisor, 510-642-6464, Fax: 510-643-5264, E-mail: aao@ce.berkeley.edu.
Website: http://www.ce.berkeley.edu/

University of California, Merced, Graduate Division, School of Engineering, Merced, CA 95343. Offers biological engineering and small scale technologies (MS, PhD); electrical engineering and computer science (MS, PhD); environmental systems (MS, PhD); mechanical engineering (MS); mechanical engineering and applied mechanics (PhD). *Faculty:* 44 full-time (7 women). *Students:* 170 full-time (52 women), 2 part-time (0 women); includes 34 minority (2 Black or African American, non-Hispanic/Latino; 11 Asian, non-Hispanic/Latino; 14 Hispanic/Latino; 2 Native Hawaiian or other Pacific Islander, non-Hispanic/Latino; 5 Two or more races, non-Hispanic/Latino), 99 international. Average age 28. 307 applicants, 35% accepted, 46 enrolled. In 2016, 15 master's, 12 doctorates awarded. Terminal master's awarded for partial completion of doctoral program. *Degree requirements:* For master's, variable foreign language requirement, comprehensive exam, thesis or alternative; for doctorate, variable foreign language requirement, comprehensive exam, thesis/dissertation. *Entrance requirements:* For master's and doctorate, GRE. Additional exam requirements/recommendations for international students: Required—TOEFL (minimum score 550 paper-based; 80 iBT); Recommended—IELTS (minimum score 7). *Application deadline:* For fall admission, 1/15 priority date for domestic and international students. Applications are processed on a rolling basis. Application fee: $90 ($110 for international students). Electronic applications accepted. *Expenses:* Contact institution. *Financial support:* In 2016–17, 150 students received support, including 16 fellowships with full tuition reimbursements available (averaging $19,088 per year), 45 research assistantships with full tuition reimbursements available (averaging $18,389 per year), 89 teaching assistantships with full tuition reimbursements available (averaging $19,249 per year); scholarships/grants, traineeships, and health care benefits also available. Financial award application deadline: 1/15. *Faculty research:* Water resources, biotechnology, renewable energy, big data, cyber-physical systems. *Total annual research expenditures:* $3.3 million. *Unit head:* Dr. Mark Matsumoto, Dean, Fax: 209-228-4047, E-mail: mmatsumoto@ucmerced.edu. *Application contact:* Tsu Ya, Director of Admissions and Academic Services, 209-228-4521, Fax: 209-228-6906, E-mail: tya@ucmerced.edu.

University of California, San Diego, Graduate Division, Department of Mechanical and Aerospace Engineering, Program in Applied Mechanics, La Jolla, CA 92093. Offers MS, PhD. *Students:* 9 full-time (0 women). 26 applicants, 19% accepted. In 2016, 2 master's, 2 doctorates awarded. *Degree requirements:* For master's, comprehensive exam (for some programs), thesis (for some programs), comprehensive exam or thesis; for doctorate, comprehensive exam, thesis/dissertation. *Entrance requirements:* For master's and doctorate, GRE General Test, minimum GPA of 3.0. Additional exam requirements/recommendations for international students: Required—TOEFL (minimum score 550 paper-based; 80 iBT), IELTS (minimum score 7). *Application deadline:* For fall admission, 12/14 for domestic students. Application fee: $105 ($125 for international students). Electronic applications accepted. *Expenses:* Tuition, state resident: full-time $11,220. Tuition, nonresident: full-time $26,322. *Required fees:* $1864. *Financial support:* Fellowships, research assistantships, teaching assistantships, scholarships/grants, and unspecified assistantships available. Financial award applicants required to submit FAFSA. *Faculty research:* Interfacial properties, durability, aging, and failure of composites; granular materials, rocks, and centimentious materials; computational methods for materials processing; advanced analytical methods in the theory of elasticity; synthesis, processing, and characterization of advanced ceramics, metals, and composites; shock synthesis and compaction. *Unit head:* Vitali Nesterenko, Chair, 858-534-0113, E-mail: mae-chair-l@ucsd.edu. *Application contact:* Lydia Ramirez, Graduate Coordinator, 858-534-4387, E-mail: mae-gradadm-l@ucsd.edu. Website: http://maeweb.ucsd.edu/

University of Cincinnati, Graduate School, College of Engineering and Applied Science, Department of Aerospace Engineering and Engineering Mechanics, Cincinnati, OH 45221. Offers MS, PhD. *Program availability:* Part-time. Terminal master's awarded for partial completion of doctoral program. *Degree requirements:* For master's, project or thesis; for doctorate, thesis/dissertation. *Entrance requirements:* For master's and doctorate, GRE General Test. Additional exam requirements/recommendations for international students: Required—TOEFL (minimum score 550 paper-based). Electronic applications accepted. *Expenses: Tuition, area resident:* Full-time $12,790; part-time $389 per credit hour. Tuition, state resident: full-time $13,290; part-time $419 per credit hour. Tuition, nonresident: full-time $24,532; part-time $976 per credit hour. *International tuition:* $24,832 full-time. *Required fees:* $3958; $140 per credit hour. Tuition and fees vary according to course load, degree level, program and reciprocity agreements. *Faculty research:* Computational fluid mechanics/propulsion, large space structures, dynamics and guidance of VTOL vehicles.

University of Colorado Denver, College of Engineering and Applied Science, Department of Mechanical Engineering, Denver, CO 80217. Offers mechanical engineering (MS); mechanics (MS); thermal sciences (MS). *Program availability:* Part-time, evening/weekend. *Faculty:* 12 full-time (0 women), 1 (woman) part-time/adjunct. *Students:* 27 full-time (6 women), 15 part-time (3 women); includes 9 minority (1 Black or African American, non-Hispanic/Latino; 6 Hispanic/Latino; 2 Two or more races, non-Hispanic/Latino), 12 international. Average age 28. 44 applicants, 73% accepted, 9 enrolled. In 2016, 13 master's awarded. *Degree requirements:* For master's, comprehensive exam, 30 credit hours, project or thesis. *Entrance requirements:* For master's, GRE, three letters of recommendation, personal statement. Additional exam requirements/recommendations for international students: Required—TOEFL (minimum score 537 paper-based; 75 iBT); Recommended—IELTS (minimum score 6.8). *Application deadline:* For fall admission, 5/1 for domestic students, 4/15 for international students; for spring admission, 10/1 for domestic students, 9/15 for international students. Application fee: $50 ($75 for international students). Electronic applications accepted. *Expenses:* Contact institution. *Financial support:* In 2016–17, 6 students received support. Fellowships, research assistantships, teaching assistantships, career-related internships or fieldwork, Federal Work-Study, institutionally sponsored loans, scholarships/grants, traineeships, and unspecified assistantships available. Financial award application deadline: 4/1; financial award applicants required to submit FAFSA. *Faculty research:* Applied and computational mechanics, bioengineering, energy systems, tribology, micro/mesofluidics and biomechanics, vehicle dynamics. *Unit head:* Dr. Sam Welch, Chair, 303-556-8488, Fax: 303-556-6371, E-mail: sam.welch@ucdenver.edu. Website: http://www.ucdenver.edu/academics/colleges/Engineering/Programs/Mechanical-Engineering/Pages/MechanicalEngineering.aspx

University of Dayton, Department of Civil and Environmental Engineering and Engineering Mechanics, Dayton, OH 45469. Offers engineering mechanics (MSEM); environmental engineering (MSCE); geotechnical engineering (MSCE); structural engineering (MSCE); transportation engineering (MSCE); water resources engineering (MSCE). *Program availability:* Part-time, evening/weekend. *Faculty:* 9 full-time (2 women), 3 part-time/adjunct (1 woman). *Students:* 40 full-time (8 women), 2 part-time (0 women); includes 1 minority (Asian, non-Hispanic/Latino), 30 international. Average age 26. 137 applicants, 17% accepted. In 2016, 14 master's awarded. *Degree requirements:* For master's, thesis optional. *Entrance requirements:* For master's, minimum GPA of 3.0 in undergraduate work. Additional exam requirements/recommendations for international students: Required—TOEFL (minimum score 550 paper-based; 80 iBT); Recommended—IELTS. *Application deadline:* For fall admission, 8/1 priority date for domestic students, 5/1 priority date for international students; for spring admission, 11/1 priority date for international students. Applications are processed on a rolling basis. Application fee: $0 ($50 for international students). Electronic applications accepted. *Expenses:* $890 per credit hour, $25 registration fee. *Financial support:* Research assistantships, institutionally sponsored loans, scholarships/grants, and department-funded awards (averaging $2448 per year) available. Financial award application deadline: 3/1; financial award applicants required to submit FAFSA. *Faculty research:* Vertically-aligned carbon nanotubes infiltrated with temperature-responsive polymers; smart nanocomposite films for self-cleaning and controlled release; bilayer and bulk heterojunction solar cells using liquid crystalline porphyrins as donors by solution processing; DNA damage induced by multiwalled carbon nanotubes in mouse embryonic stem cells. *Total annual research expenditures:* $250,000. *Unit head:* Dr. Donald V. Chase, Chair, 937-229-3847, Fax: 937-229-3491, E-mail: dchase1@udayton.edu. *Application contact:* 937-229-4462, E-mail: graduateadmission@udayton.edu. Website: https://www.udayton.edu/engineering/departments/civil/index.php

University of Illinois at Urbana–Champaign, Graduate College, College of Engineering, Department of Mechanical Science and Engineering, Champaign, IL 61820. Offers mechanical engineering (MS, PhD); theoretical and applied mechanics (MS, PhD). Terminal master's awarded for partial completion of doctoral program. *Entrance requirements:* Additional exam requirements/recommendations for international students: Required—TOEFL (minimum score 613 paper-based; 103 iBT), IELTS (minimum score 7).

University of Maryland, College Park, Academic Affairs, A. James Clark School of Engineering, Department of Mechanical Engineering, College Park, MD 20742. Offers electronic packaging and reliability (MS, PhD); manufacturing and design (MS, PhD); mechanics and materials (MS, PhD); reliability engineering (M Eng, MS, PhD); thermal and fluid sciences (MS, PhD). *Program availability:* Part-time, evening/weekend, online learning. *Degree requirements:* For master's, thesis optional; for doctorate, thesis/dissertation, qualifying exam. *Entrance requirements:* For master's, GRE General Test, 3 letters of recommendation; for doctorate, GRE General Test, minimum GPA of 3.0. Additional exam requirements/recommendations for international students: Required—TOEFL. Electronic applications accepted. *Faculty research:* Injection molding, electronic packaging, fluid mechanics, product engineering.

University of Massachusetts Amherst, Graduate School, College of Engineering, Department of Civil and Environmental Engineering, Amherst, MA 01003. Offers civil engineering (MSCE, PhD); environmental and water resources engineering (MSCE); geotechnical engineering (MSCE); structural engineering and mechanics (MSCE); transportation engineering (MSCE). *Program availability:* Part-time. Terminal master's awarded for partial completion of doctoral program. *Degree requirements:* For master's, thesis or alternative; for doctorate, comprehensive exam, thesis/dissertation. *Entrance requirements:* For master's and doctorate, GRE General Test. Additional exam requirements/recommendations for international students: Required—TOEFL (minimum score 550 paper-based; 80 iBT), IELTS (minimum score 6.5). Electronic applications accepted.

University of Massachusetts Dartmouth, Graduate School, College of Engineering, Program in Engineering and Applied Science, North Dartmouth, MA 02747-2300. Offers applied mechanics and materials (PhD); computational science and engineering (PhD); computer science and information systems (PhD); engineering and applied science (PhD); industrial and systems engineering (PhD). *Program availability:* Part-time. *Students:* 23 full-time (7 women), 8 part-time (3 women); includes 2 minority (both Black or African American, non-Hispanic/Latino), 15 international. Average age 31. 14 applicants, 79% accepted, 7 enrolled. *Degree requirements:* For doctorate, comprehensive exam, thesis/dissertation. *Entrance requirements:* For doctorate, GRE, statement of purpose (minimum of 300 words), resume, 3 letters of recommendation, official transcripts. Additional exam requirements/recommendations for international students: Required—TOEFL (minimum score 550 paper-based; 79 iBT). *Application deadline:* For fall admission, 2/15 priority date for domestic students, 1/15 priority date for international students; for spring admission, 11/15 priority date for domestic students, 10/15 priority date for international students. Application fee: $60. Electronic applications accepted. *Expenses:* Tuition, state resident: full-time $14,994; part-time $624.75 per credit. Tuition, nonresident: full-time $27,068; part-time $1127.83 per credit. *Required fees:* $405; $25.88 per credit. Tuition and fees vary according to course load and reciprocity agreements. *Financial support:* In 2016–17, 11 fellowships (averaging $16,591 per year), 12 research assistantships (averaging $5,160 per year) were awarded; institutionally sponsored loans, scholarships/grants, and doctoral support also available. Support available to part-time students. Financial award application deadline: 3/1; financial award applicants required to submit FAFSA. *Faculty research:* Tissue/cell engineering, bio transport sensors/networks, marine systems biomimetic materials, composite/polymeric materials, resilient infrastructure robotics, renewable energy. *Total annual research expenditures:* $253,000. *Unit head:* Gaurav Khanna, Graduate Program Director, Engineering and Applied Science, 508-910-6605, Fax: 508-999-9115, E-mail: gkhanna@umassd.edu. *Application contact:* Steven Briggs, Director of Marketing and Recruitment for Graduate Studies, 508-999-8604, Fax: 508-999-8183, E-mail: graduate@umassd.edu. Website: http://www.umassd.edu/engineering/graduate/doctoraldegreeprograms/egrandappliedsciencephd/

University of Minnesota, Twin Cities Campus, College of Science and Engineering, Department of Aerospace Engineering and Mechanics, Minneapolis, MN 55455-0213. Offers MS, PhD. *Program availability:* Part-time. *Degree requirements:* For doctorate, thesis/dissertation. *Entrance requirements:* Additional exam requirements/recommendations for international students: Required—TOEFL (minimum score 550 paper-based). Electronic applications accepted. *Faculty research:* Fluid mechanics, solid mechanics and materials, aerospace systems, nanotechnology.

University of Nebraska–Lincoln, Graduate College, College of Engineering, Department of Engineering Mechanics, Lincoln, NE 68588. Offers MS, PhD. *Degree requirements:* For master's, thesis optional; for doctorate, comprehensive exam, thesis/dissertation. *Entrance requirements:* For master's and doctorate, GRE. Additional exam requirements/recommendations for international students: Required—TOEFL (minimum score 550 paper-based). Electronic applications accepted. *Faculty research:* Polymer mechanics, piezoelectric materials, meshless methods, smart materials, fracture mechanics.

University of Nebraska–Lincoln, Graduate College, College of Engineering, Department of Mechanical and Materials Engineering, Lincoln, NE 68588-0526. Offers biomedical engineering (PhD); engineering mechanics (MS); materials engineering (PhD); mechanical engineering (MS), including materials science engineering, metallurgical engineering; mechanical engineering and applied mechanics (PhD); MS/MS. MS/MS offered with University of Rouen-France. *Degree requirements:* For master's, thesis optional; for doctorate, comprehensive exam, thesis/dissertation. *Entrance requirements:* For master's and doctorate, GRE General Test. Additional exam requirements/recommendations for international students: Required—TOEFL (minimum score 550 paper-based). Electronic applications accepted. *Faculty research:* Medical robotics, rehabilitation dynamics, and design; combustion, fluid mechanics, and heat transfer; nano-materials, manufacturing, and devices; fiber, tissue, bio-polymer, and adaptive composites; blast, impact, fracture, and failure; electro-active and magnetic materials and devices; functional materials, design, and added manufacturing; materials characterization, modeling, and computational simulation.

University of New Brunswick Fredericton, School of Graduate Studies, Faculty of Engineering, Department of Mechanical Engineering, Fredericton, NB E3B 5A3, Canada. Offers applied mechanics (M Eng, M Sc E, PhD); mechanical engineering (M Eng, M Sc E, PhD). *Program availability:* Part-time. *Degree requirements:* For master's, thesis; for doctorate, comprehensive exam, thesis/dissertation, qualifying exam. *Entrance requirements:* For master's, minimum GPA of 3.0; B Sc E; for doctorate, minimum GPA of 3.0; M Sc E. Additional exam requirements/recommendations for international students: Required—TOEFL (minimum score 580 paper-based; 80 iBT), IELTS (minimum score 7), TWE (minimum score 4), Michigan English Language Assessment Battery (minimum score 85) or CanTest (minimum score 4.5). Electronic applications accepted. *Faculty research:* Acoustics and vibration, biomedical, manufacturing and materials processing, mechatronics and design, nuclear and threat detection, renewable energy systems, robotics and applied mechanics, thermofluids and aerodynamics.

University of Pennsylvania, School of Engineering and Applied Science, Department of Mechanical Engineering and Applied Mechanics, Philadelphia, PA 19104. Offers MSE, PhD. *Program availability:* Part-time. *Faculty:* 32 full-time (7 women), 10 part-time/adjunct (0 women). *Students:* 122 full-time (21 women), 40 part-time (7 women); includes 14 minority (1 Black or African American, non-Hispanic/Latino; 4 Asian, non-Hispanic/Latino; 6 Hispanic/Latino; 3 Two or more races, non-Hispanic/Latino), 106 international. Average age 25. 633 applicants, 21% accepted, 66 enrolled. In 2016, 59 master's, 12 doctorates awarded. *Degree requirements:* For master's, comprehensive exam, thesis optional; for doctorate, comprehensive exam, thesis/dissertation. *Entrance requirements:* For master's and doctorate, GRE. Additional exam requirements/recommendations for international students: Required—TOEFL (minimum score 100 iBT), IELTS (minimum score 7). *Application deadline:* For fall admission, 3/15 priority date for domestic students, 3/15 for international students. Application fee: $80. Electronic applications accepted. *Expenses:* Tuition: Full-time $31,068; part-time $5762 per course. *Required fees:* $3200; $336 per course. Full-time tuition and fees vary according to degree level, program and student level. Part-time tuition and fees vary according to course load, degree level and program. *Faculty research:* Biorobotics, computational mechanics, energy conversion, mechanics of materials, robotics. *Application contact:* William Fenton, Assistant Director of Graduate Admissions, 215-898-4542, Fax: 215-573-5577, E-mail: gradstudies@seas.upenn.edu. Website: http://www.me.upenn.edu/prospective-students/masters/masters-degrees.php

University of Southern California, Graduate School, Viterbi School of Engineering, Sonny Astani Department of Civil Engineering, Los Angeles, CA 90089. Offers applied mechanics (MS); civil engineering (MS, PhD); computer-aided engineering (ME, Graduate Certificate); construction management (MCM); engineering technology commercialization (Graduate Certificate); environmental engineering (MS, PhD); environmental quality management (ME); structural design (ME); sustainable cities

(Graduate Certificate); transportation systems (MS, Graduate Certificate); water and waste management (MS). *Program availability:* Part-time, evening/weekend. Terminal master's awarded for partial completion of doctoral program. *Degree requirements:* For master's, thesis optional; for doctorate, thesis/dissertation. *Entrance requirements:* For master's and doctorate, GRE General Test. Additional exam requirements/recommendations for international students: Recommended—TOEFL. Electronic applications accepted. *Faculty research:* Geotechnical engineering, transportation engineering, structural engineering, construction management, environmental engineering, water resources.

The University of Texas at Austin, Graduate School, Cockrell School of Engineering, Department of Aerospace Engineering and Engineering Mechanics, Program in Engineering Mechanics, Austin, TX 78712-1111. Offers MS, PhD. *Degree requirements:* For doctorate, one foreign language, thesis/dissertation, qualifying exam. *Entrance requirements:* For master's and doctorate, GRE General Test.

University of Washington, Graduate School, College of Engineering, Department of Civil and Environmental Engineering, Seattle, WA 98195-2700. Offers construction engineering (MSCE, PhD); environmental engineering (MSCE, PhD); geotechnical engineering (MSCE, PhD); hydrology and hydrodynamics (MSCE, PhD); structural engineering and mechanics (MSCE, PhD); transportation engineering (MSCE, PhD). *Program availability:* Part-time, 100% online. *Faculty:* 37 full-time (10 women). *Students:* 239 full-time (97 women), 153 part-time (41 women); includes 71 minority (7 Black or African American, non-Hispanic/Latino; 32 Asian, non-Hispanic/Latino; 22 Hispanic/Latino; 2 Native Hawaiian or other Pacific Islander, non-Hispanic/Latino; 8 Two or more races, non-Hispanic/Latino), 134 international. 782 applicants, 58% accepted, 157 enrolled. In 2016, 132 master's, 13 doctorates awarded. Terminal master's awarded for partial completion of doctoral program. *Degree requirements:* For master's, thesis optional; for doctorate, comprehensive exam, thesis/dissertation, qualifying, general and final exams; completion of degree within 10 years. *Entrance requirements:* For master's, GRE General Test, minimum GPA of 3.0, statement of purpose, letters of recommendation, transcripts; for doctorate, GRE General Test, minimum GPA of 3.5, statement of purpose, letters of recommendation, transcripts, resume. Additional exam requirements/recommendations for international students: Required—TOEFL (minimum score 580 paper-based; 92 iBT); Recommended—IELTS (minimum score 7), TSE. *Application deadline:* For fall admission, 12/15 for domestic and international students. Applications are processed on a rolling basis. Application fee: $85. Electronic applications accepted. *Expenses:* Contact institution. *Financial support:* In 2016–17, 110 students received support, including 10 fellowships with tuition reimbursements available (averaging $2,228 per year), 72 research assistantships with full tuition reimbursements available (averaging $2,351 per year), 28 teaching assistantships with full tuition reimbursements available (averaging $2,387 per year); scholarships/grants also available. Financial award application deadline: 12/15; financial award applicants required to submit FAFSA. *Faculty research:* Structural and geotechnical engineering, transportation and construction engineering, water and environmental engineering. *Total annual research expenditures:* $13.5 million. *Unit head:* Dr. Timothy V. Larson, Professor/Chair, 206-543-6815, Fax: 206-543-1543, E-mail: tlarson@uw.edu. *Application contact:* Melissa Pritchard, Graduate Adviser, 206-543-2574, Fax: 206-543-1543, E-mail: ceginfo@u.washington.edu.
Website: http://www.ce.washington.edu/

University of Wisconsin–Madison, Graduate School, College of Engineering, Department of Engineering Physics, Madison, WI 53706. Offers engineering mechanics (MS, PhD); nuclear engineering and engineering physics (MS, PhD). *Program availability:* Part-time, online learning. *Faculty:* 21 full-time (3 women). *Students:* 116 full-time (19 women), 10 part-time (2 women); includes 17 minority (3 Black or African American, non-Hispanic/Latino; 5 Asian, non-Hispanic/Latino; 8 Hispanic/Latino; 1 Two or more races, non-Hispanic/Latino), 23 international. Average age 26. 162 applicants, 55% accepted, 25 enrolled. In 2016, 29 master's, 11 doctorates awarded. Terminal master's awarded for partial completion of doctoral program. *Degree requirements:* For master's, thesis optional, 30 credits of technical courses; oral exam; minimum GPA of 3.0; for doctorate, thesis/dissertation, minimum of 51 credits; minimum GPA of 3.0. *Entrance requirements:* For master's and doctorate, GRE General Test, minimum GPA of 3.0 in last 60 hours, appropriate bachelor's degree. Additional exam requirements/recommendations for international students: Required—TOEFL (minimum score 580 paper-based; 92 iBT), IELTS (minimum score 7). *Application deadline:* For fall admission, 12/31 priority date for domestic and international students. Application fee: $75 ($81 for international students). Electronic applications accepted. *Expenses:* $13,157 per year in-state tuition and fees; $26,484 per year out-of-state tuition and fees. *Financial support:* In 2016–17, 119 students received support, including 5 fellowships with full tuition reimbursements available (averaging $29,628 per year), 93 research assistantships with full tuition reimbursements available (averaging $23,175 per year), 19 teaching assistantships with full tuition reimbursements available (averaging $14,941 per year); career-related internships or fieldwork, Federal Work-Study, institutionally sponsored loans, unspecified assistantships, and project assistantships also available.

Support available to part-time students. Financial award application deadline: 12/1; financial award applicants required to submit FAFSA. *Faculty research:* Bio-/micro-/nano-mechanics; astronautics; fission reactor engineering; fusion science and technology; radiation sciences; mechanics of materials. *Total annual research expenditures:* $14.1 million. *Unit head:* Dr. Douglass Henderson, Chair, 608-263-1646, Fax: 608-263-7451, E-mail: dlhender@wisc.edu. *Application contact:* Sara Hladilek, Student Services Coordinator, 608-263-1795, Fax: 608-263-7451, E-mail: shladilek@wisc.edu.
Website: http://www.engr.wisc.edu/ep/

University of Wisconsin–Milwaukee, Graduate School, College of Engineering and Applied Science, Program in Engineering, Milwaukee, WI 53201-0413. Offers biomedical engineering (MS); civil engineering (MS, PhD); computer science (PhD); electrical and computer engineering (MS); electrical engineering (PhD); engineering mechanics (MS); industrial and management engineering (MS); industrial engineering (PhD); manufacturing engineering (MS); materials (PhD); materials engineering (MS); mechanical engineering (MS). *Program availability:* Part-time. *Students:* 199 full-time (52 women), 156 part-time (32 women); includes 27 minority (2 Black or African American, non-Hispanic/Latino; 15 Asian, non-Hispanic/Latino; 3 Hispanic/Latino; 7 Two or more races, non-Hispanic/Latino), 244 international. Average age 30. 396 applicants, 61% accepted, 102 enrolled. In 2016, 72 master's, 26 doctorates awarded. *Degree requirements:* For master's, comprehensive exam (for some programs), thesis or alternative; for doctorate, comprehensive exam, thesis/dissertation, internship. *Entrance requirements:* For master's, GRE, minimum GPA of 2.75; for doctorate, GRE, minimum GPA of 3.5. Additional exam requirements/recommendations for international students: Required—TOEFL (minimum score 550 paper-based; 79 iBT), IELTS (minimum score 6.5). *Application deadline:* For fall admission, 1/1 priority date for domestic students; for spring admission, 9/1 for domestic students. Applications are processed on a rolling basis. Application fee: $56 ($96 for international students). *Financial support:* In 2016–17, 3 fellowships, 55 research assistantships, 77 teaching assistantships were awarded; career-related internships or fieldwork, Federal Work-Study, unspecified assistantships, and project assistantships also available. Support available to part-time students. Financial award application deadline: 4/15. *Unit head:* David Yu, Representative, 414-229-6169, E-mail: yu@uwm.edu. *Application contact:* Betty Warras, General Information Contact, 414-229-6169, Fax: 414-229-6967, E-mail: bwarras@uwm.edu.
Website: http://www4.uwm.edu/ceas/academics/graduate_programs/

Virginia Polytechnic Institute and State University, Graduate School, College of Engineering, Blacksburg, VA 24061. Offers aerospace engineering (ME, MS, PhD); biological systems engineering (ME, MS, PhD); biomedical engineering (MS, PhD); chemical engineering (ME, MS, PhD); civil engineering (ME, MS, PhD); computer engineering (ME, MS, PhD); computer science (MS, PhD); electrical engineering (ME, PhD); engineering education (PhD); engineering mechanics (ME, MS, PhD); environmental engineering (MS); environmental science and engineering (MS); industrial and systems engineering (ME, MS, PhD); materials science and engineering (ME, MS, PhD); mechanical engineering (ME, MS, PhD); mining and minerals engineering (PhD); mining engineering (ME, MS); nuclear engineering (MS, PhD); ocean engineering (MS); systems engineering (MS). *Faculty:* 400 full-time (73 women), 3 part-time/adjunct (2 women). *Students:* 1,949 full-time (487 women), 393 part-time (69 women); includes 251 minority (56 Black or African American, non-Hispanic/Latino; 3 American Indian or Alaska Native, non-Hispanic/Latino; 87 Asian, non-Hispanic/Latino; 70 Hispanic/Latino; 35 Two or more races, non-Hispanic/Latino), 1,354 international. Average age 27. 4,903 applicants, 19% accepted, 569 enrolled. In 2016, 364 master's, 200 doctorates awarded. *Degree requirements:* For master's, comprehensive exam (for some programs), thesis (for some programs); for doctorate, comprehensive exam (for some programs), thesis/dissertation (for some programs). *Entrance requirements:* For master's and doctorate, GRE/GMAT. Additional exam requirements/recommendations for international students: Required—TOEFL (minimum score 80 iBT). *Application deadline:* For fall admission, 8/1 for domestic students, 4/1 for international students; for spring admission, 1/1 for domestic students, 9/1 for international students. Applications are processed on a rolling basis. Application fee: $75. Electronic applications accepted. *Expenses:* Tuition, state resident: full-time $12,467; part-time $692.50 per credit hour. Tuition, nonresident: full-time $25,095; part-time $1394.25 per credit hour. *Required fees:* $2669; $491.50 per semester. Tuition and fees vary according to course load, campus/location and program. *Financial support:* In 2016–17, 160 fellowships with full tuition reimbursements (averaging $7,387 per year), 872 research assistantships with full tuition reimbursements (averaging $22,329 per year), 313 teaching assistantships with full tuition reimbursements (averaging $18,714 per year) were awarded. Financial award application deadline: 3/1; financial award applicants required to submit FAFSA. *Total annual research expenditures:* $91.8 million. *Unit head:* Dr. Julia Ross, Dean, 540-231-9752, Fax: 540-231-3031, E-mail: deaneng@vt.edu. *Application contact:* Linda Perkins, Executive Assistant, 540-231-9752, Fax: 540-231-3031, E-mail: lperkins@vt.edu.
Website: http://www.eng.vt.edu/

COLUMBIA UNIVERSITY
Department of Mechanical Engineering

 For more information, visit http:/columbiau-mechanicalengineering

Programs of Study

Columbia University's Department of Mechanical Engineering offers advanced instruction and research opportunities in a variety of areas of current interest in mechanical engineering. The Department offers a full range of graduate degree programs: the Master of Science (M.S.), Doctor of Engineering Science (Eng.Sc.D.), and Doctor of Philosophy (Ph.D.) degrees.

Students who want to earn a master's degree in mechanical engineering can choose from the standard track and other selective specializations including: Energy Systems, Micro/Nanoscale Engineering, and Robotics and Control, with course work approved by an adviser and advisory committee.

The Mechanical Engineering M.S. Express option allows current Columbia Bachelor of Science degree program students with a qualifying GPA to transition into the master's degree program without taking the GRE or TOEFL. This program allows students to do specific long-term course planning, take graduate program courses as seniors, and apply summer research project credits toward the master's degree program, in consultation with an adviser.

Undergraduate students also have the option of the Integrated B.S./M.S. Program. This B.S.-leading-to-M.S. program is open to a select group of Columbia Juniors. Upon admission into the program, students work closely with their faculty advisor to synthesize a two-year program plan that integrates up to 6 points of 4000-level technical elective coursework that simultaneously fulfills half of their B.S. technical elective requirement. This effectively reduces the M.S. program requirement to 24 points.

Students anywhere in the world can pursue a master's degree in mechanical engineering through Columbia's distance-learning program, the Columbia Video Network. Classes in the distance learning graduate program are tailored to students' interests, on topics such as robotics, fluid dynamics, controls, and other graduate-level topics. Prospective students must apply to Columbia's Graduate Engineering Distance Learning Program.

The Mechanical Engineering Department offers two doctoral degree options for post-graduate students: the Doctor of Engineering Science (Eng.Sc.D.) degree program and the Doctor of Philosophy in Mechanical Engineering (Ph.D.) degree program. Both programs help students master specialized areas within the discipline of mechanical engineering.

Columbia's Mechanical Engineer (M.E.) degree program gives mechanical engineering master's degree holders a pathway to more education outside a traditional doctoral degree program. The M.E. degree program blends analytical and applied study in one or more mechanical engineering disciplines.

Research Facilities

Columbia University's mechanical engineering faculty members and students work within the School of Engineering and Applied Science and with other schools to apply engineering to medicine, nanotechnology, materials research, and global climate study. The department has ongoing collaborations with Columbia University Medical Center as well as with the Lamont-Doherty Earth Observatory on the Hudson River, run by Columbia's Earth Institute. Other mechanical engineering interdisciplinary projects involve the Nanoscale Science and Engineering Center and the Materials Research Science and Engineering Center, both operated by Columbia's Center for Integrated Science and Engineering.

The mechanical engineering department hosts more than a dozen labs run by faculty members. The Sustainable Engineering Lab, part of Columbia's Earth Institute, collaborates with governments, NGOs, industry, and other universities to operate energy, irrigation, and public health projects in countries throughout the developing world.

The Robotics and Rehabilitation Lab works with Columbia's medical campus to develop robotic arm and leg exoskeletons for stroke patients with loss of limb control, robotic carts for mobility-impaired infants and toddlers, and tactile feedback shoes for Parkinson's patients.

Research led by the Musculoskeletal Biomechanics Laboratory, a joint effort of the mechanical and biomedical engineering departments, studies cartilage and cellular mechanics as well as cartilage tissue engineering.

Areas of Research

Biomechanics and Soft-Tissue Mechanics Research: Faculty member biomechanics research covers topics such as the electromechanical behavior of cartilage, cervical structure, and function changes during pregnancy; the molecular mechanics of stem-cell differentiation; and clinical inquiries into the role of biomechanics in disease.

Control, Design, Robotics, and Manufacturing Research: The mechanical engineering department conducts diverse robotics, control, and design research on topics from assisted movement for mobility-impaired patients to earthquake damage assessment and laser micromachining processes for industrial manufacturing.

Micro-electromechanical Systems (MEMS) and Nanotechnology Research: Micro-electromechanical Systems (MEMS) and Nanotechnology projects led by mechanical engineering faculty members cover topics such as photonic nanostructures, microcantilever dynamics, carbon nanotube synthesis, and nanoscale bioimaging, among many others.

Bioengineering and Biomechanics Research: Columbia's Department of Mechanical Engineering is known for its research into the mechanics of cartilage and joint function. Other lines in inquiry include techniques for the creation of biofunctional nanoarrays with possible regenerative medicine applications, stem-cell differentiation research, and the potential monitoring of glucose via implantable microelectromechanical systems.

Energy, Fluid Mechanics, and Heat Transfer Research: Studies of energy, heat transfer, and fluid mechanics by mechanical engineering faculty members cover topics that impact the environment, such as the removal of carbon dioxide from the air, and tribology topics including performance improvements to power generation equipment.

Financial Aid

Graduate students in mechanical engineering can apply for The Fu Foundation School of Engineering and Applied Science fellowships that provide funding, research and networking opportunities, and academic prestige. These fellowships include Presidential Distinguished Fellowships; Graduate Minorities in Engineering Fellowships for students of African-American, Hispanic-American, and Native-American heritage; and Special Fellowships for engineering graduate students.

Columbia also offers four National Science Foundation-funded Integrative Graduate Education and Research Training Fellowships for multidisciplinary research and study in four specific fields: information technology, urban infrastructure, multiscale phenomena in soft materials, and biological systems sensing and imaging.

The Columbia Comprehensive Educational Financing Plan pulls together public and private funding sources, lines of credit, payment plans, and other services in conjunction with carefully vetted financial service providers.

Cost of Study

In 2017–18, graduate students enrolled in M.S. and Eng.Sc.D. programs will pay $1,936 per credit, except when a special fee was fixed. Graduate tuition for Ph.D. students is $22,432 per Residence Unit. The Residence Unit—full-time registration for one semester rather than for individual courses (whether or not the student is taking courses)—provides the basis for tuition charges.

Eng.Sc.D. candidates engaged only in research, and who have completed their 12 credits of Doctoral Research Instruction, are assessed a Comprehensive Fee of $2,146 per term by The Fu Foundation School of Engineering and Applied Science.

Ph.D. candidates engaged only in research are assessed $2,146 per term for Matriculation and Facilities by the Graduate School of Arts and Sciences.

There are also fees for facilities, health services, activities, books and course materials, laboratories, etc., which vary depending on the student's course of study and whether they are enrolled full- or part-time.

Faculty

Educational excellence is the central focus of all activities within the Department. Faculty and staff members take great pride in developing a curriculum that prompts students to think deeply, broadly and independently to prepare them to be leaders in engineering and other professions. The dual emphasis on fundamental concepts and design innovation in the curriculum equips graduates to address and solve the most complex technological and societal challenges. Through their passion and dedication, professors and teaching staff apply their expertise toward developing new teaching methods and paradigms that stimulate excitement in both traditional and emerging fields of endeavor and set the highest expectations for students.

A full list of faculty members and their research areas is available online at http://me.columbia.edu/people-by-type/faculty.

The University and The Department

Columbia University in the City of New York, founded in 1754, is currently ranked fourth among national universities by *U.S. News & World Report*. The Princeton Review lists Columbia as a Best Value Private College and rates its library first among American universities. The school also stands out for its socioeconomic diversity and its location in Manhattan's Morningside Heights neighborhood. Notable Columbia alumni include President Barack Obama, former secretary of state Madeleine Albright, and evolutionary biologist Stephen Jay Gould, along with more than 40 Nobel Prize recipients.

Columbia University's Department of Mechanical Engineering is part of the Fu Foundation School of Engineering and Applied Science, originally founded in 1864 as the School of Mines at Columbia College. Today, Columbia's engineering school is a world leader in patents and counts among its patent holdings the MPEG-2 technology that underpins high-definition television. Within the mechanical engineering department, the faculty members lead research on robotics, nanotechnology, energy systems, biomechanics, and other interdisciplinary topics.

Despite the school's high profile and full slate of research, the mechanical engineering graduate program stands out for its low faculty member-to-student ratio of 15 to 1, giving students an opportunity to take meaningful roles in the department's research, academic competitions, and classroom life. Overall, the School of Engineering and Applied Science enrolls some 3,200 graduate students, out of an overall Columbia University student body of approximately 30,000 undergraduate, graduate, and medical students.

Applying

Applicants for admission into the graduate program are required to have completed an undergraduate degree and to furnish an official transcript as part of the admissions application. Ordinarily, the candidate for a graduate degree will have completed an undergraduate course in the same field of engineering in which he or she seeks a graduate degree. However, if the student's interests have changed, it may be necessary to make up basic undergraduate courses essential to graduate study in his or her new field of interest.

A candidate for M.S. or the M.S./Ph.D. track must file an application with Graduate Student Services on the date specified in the academic calendar. Candidates for a doctoral degree must apply for the final examination. If the degree is not earned by the next scheduled time for the issuance of diplomas subsequent to the date of filing, the application must be renewed. Degrees are awarded three times a year: February, May, and October.

Questions about admissions should be directed to Mel Francis (mef2@columbia.edu).

Correspondence and Information

Mechanical Engineering Departmental Office
Columbia University
220 S.W. Mudd Building
500 West 120th Street
New York, New York 10027
United States
Phone: 212-854-2966
Fax: 212-854-3304
E-mail: mef2@columbia.edu
Website: http://me.columbia.edu/graduate-programs

Section 18
Ocean Engineering

This section contains a directory of institutions offering graduate work in ocean engineering. Additional information about programs listed in the directory may be obtained by writing directly to the dean of a graduate school or chair of a department at the address given in the directory.

For programs offering related work, see also in this book *Civil and Environmental Engineering* and *Engineering and Applied Sciences.* In the other guides in this series:

Graduate Programs in the Biological/Biomedical Sciences & Health-Related Medical Professions
  See *Marine Biology*
Graduate Programs in the Physical Sciences, Mathematics, Agricultural Sciences, the Environment & Natural Resources
  See *Environmental Sciences and Management* and *Marine Sciences and Oceanography*

CONTENTS

Program Directory

Ocean Engineering

Florida Atlantic University, College of Engineering and Computer Science, Department of Ocean and Mechanical Engineering, Boca Raton, FL 33431-0991. Offers mechanical engineering (MS, PhD). *Program availability:* Part-time, evening/weekend. *Faculty:* 25 full-time (1 woman), 1 part-time/adjunct (0 women). *Students:* 66 full-time (11 women), 50 part-time (5 women); includes 20 minority (1 Black or African American, non-Hispanic/Latino; 6 Asian, non-Hispanic/Latino; 12 Hispanic/Latino; 1 Two or more races, non-Hispanic/Latino), 51 international. Average age 29. 110 applicants, 65% accepted, 51 enrolled. In 2016, 23 master's, 7 doctorates awarded. Terminal master's awarded for partial completion of doctoral program. *Degree requirements:* For master's, thesis (for some programs); for doctorate, comprehensive exam, thesis/dissertation, qualifying exam. *Entrance requirements:* For master's and doctorate, GRE General Test, minimum GPA of 3.0. Additional exam requirements/recommendations for international students: Required—TOEFL (minimum score 500 paper-based; 61 iBT), IELTS (minimum score 6). *Application deadline:* For fall admission, 7/1 priority date for domestic students, 2/15 for international students; for spring admission, 11/1 for domestic students, 7/15 for international students. Applications are processed on a rolling basis. Application fee: $30. *Expenses:* Tuition, state resident: full-time $7392; part-time $369.82 per credit hour. Tuition, nonresident: full-time $19,432; part-time $1024.81 per credit hour. *Financial support:* Research assistantships, career-related internships or fieldwork, Federal Work-Study, scholarships/grants, and unspecified assistantships available. Financial award application deadline: 1/10; financial award applicants required to submit FAFSA. *Faculty research:* Marine materials and corrosion, ocean structures, marine vehicles, acoustics and vibrations, hydrodynamics, coastal engineering. *Unit head:* Javad Hashemi, Chair, 561-297-3438, E-mail: jhashemi@fau.edu.
Website: http://www.ome.fau.edu/

Florida Institute of Technology, College of Engineering, Program in Ocean Engineering, Melbourne, FL 32901-6975. Offers MS, PhD. *Program availability:* Part-time. *Students:* 22 full-time (7 women), 7 part-time (2 women); includes 2 minority (1 Hispanic/Latino; 1 Two or more races, non-Hispanic/Latino), 15 international. Average age 29. 51 applicants, 43% accepted, 5 enrolled. In 2016, 7 master's, 2 doctorates awarded. *Degree requirements:* For master's, comprehensive exam (for some programs), thesis optional, 30 credit hours (thesis), 33 credit hours (non-thesis) with technical paper; for doctorate, comprehensive exam, thesis/dissertation, research program and publication. *Entrance requirements:* For master's, GRE General Test, 3 letters of recommendation, resume, transcripts, statement of objectives, undergraduate degree in physical sciences or engineering, on-campus interview (highly recommended); for doctorate, GRE General Test, minimum GPA of 3.3, resume, 3 letters of recommendation, statement of objectives. Additional exam requirements/recommendations for international students: Required—TOEFL (minimum score 550 paper-based; 79 iBT). *Application deadline:* Applications are processed on a rolling basis. Application fee: $0. Electronic applications accepted. *Expenses:* Tuition: Full-time $22,338; part-time $1241 per credit hour. *Required fees:* $250. Tuition and fees vary according to degree level, campus/location and program. *Financial support:* Career-related internships or fieldwork, institutionally sponsored loans, tuition waivers (partial), unspecified assistantships, and tuition remissions available. Support available to part-time students. Financial award application deadline: 3/1; financial award applicants required to submit FAFSA. *Faculty research:* Underwater technology, materials and structures, coastal processes and engineering, marine vehicles and ocean systems, naval architecture. *Unit head:* Dr. John Windsor, Program Chair, 321-674-7300, E-mail: jwindsor@fit.edu. *Application contact:* Cheryl A. Brown, Associate Director of Graduate Admission, 321-674-7581, Fax: 321-723-9468, E-mail: cbrown@fit.edu.
Website: http://coe.fit.edu/dmes/

Massachusetts Institute of Technology, School of Engineering, Department of Mechanical Engineering, Cambridge, MA 02139. Offers manufacturing (M Eng); mechanical engineering (SM, PhD, Sc D, Mech E); naval architecture and marine engineering (SM, PhD, Sc D); naval engineering (Naval E); ocean engineering (SM, PhD, Sc D); oceanographic engineering (SM, PhD, Sc D); SM/MBA. *Faculty:* 70 full-time (9 women), 1 part-time/adjunct (0 women). *Students:* 567 full-time (159 women), 1 part-time (0 women); includes 94 minority (6 Black or African American, non-Hispanic/Latino; 1 American Indian or Alaska Native, non-Hispanic/Latino; 41 Asian, non-Hispanic/Latino; 32 Hispanic/Latino; 14 Two or more races, non-Hispanic/Latino), 275 international. Average age 27. 1,345 applicants, 14% accepted, 127 enrolled. In 2016, 123 master's, 65 doctorates, 10 other advanced degrees awarded. Terminal master's awarded for partial completion of doctoral program. *Degree requirements:* For master's, thesis; for doctorate, comprehensive exam, thesis/dissertation; for other advanced degree, comprehensive exam, thesis. *Entrance requirements:* For master's, doctorate, and other advanced degree, GRE General Test. Additional exam requirements/recommendations for international students: Required—TOEFL, IELTS. *Application deadline:* For fall and spring admission, 12/15 for domestic and international students. Application fee: $75. Electronic applications accepted. *Expenses:* Tuition: Full-time $46,400; part-time $725 per credit. One-time fee: $312 full-time. Full-time tuition and fees vary according to course load and program. *Financial support:* In 2016–17, 466 students received support, including fellowships (averaging $36,000 per year), 338 research assistantships (averaging $36,300 per year), 62 teaching assistantships (averaging $39,300 per year); Federal Work-Study, institutionally sponsored loans, scholarships/grants, traineeships, health care benefits, unspecified assistantships, and resident tutors also available. Support available to part-time students. Financial award application deadline: 5/1; financial award applicants required to submit FAFSA. *Faculty research:* Mechanics: modeling, experimentation and computation; design, manufacturing, and product development; controls, instrumentation, and robotics; energy science and engineering; ocean science and engineering; bioengineering; micro- and Nano-engineering. *Total annual research expenditures:* $55.6 million. *Unit head:* Prof. Gang Chen, Department Head, 617-253-2201, Fax: 617-258-6156, E-mail: mehq@mit.edu. *Application contact:* 617-253-2291, E-mail: megradoffice@mit.edu.
Website: http://meche.mit.edu/

Memorial University of Newfoundland, School of Graduate Studies, Faculty of Engineering and Applied Science, St. John's, NL A1C 5S7, Canada. Offers civil engineering (M Eng, PhD); electrical and computer engineering (M Eng, PhD); mechanical engineering (M Eng, PhD); ocean and naval architecture engineering (M Eng, PhD). *Program availability:* Part-time. *Degree requirements:* For master's, thesis; for doctorate, comprehensive exam, thesis/dissertation, oral thesis defense. *Entrance requirements:* For master's, 2nd class degree; for doctorate, master's degree in engineering. Electronic applications accepted. *Faculty research:* Engineering analysis, environmental and hydrotechnical studies, manufacturing and robotics, mechanics, structures and materials.

Oregon State University, College of Engineering, Program in Civil Engineering, Corvallis, OR 97331. Offers civil engineering (M Eng, MS, PhD); coastal and ocean engineering (M Eng, MS, PhD); construction engineering management (M Eng, MS, PhD); engineering education (M Eng, MS, PhD); geomatics (M Eng, MS, PhD); geotechnical engineering (M Eng, MS, PhD); infrastructure materials (M Eng, MS, PhD); structural engineering (M Eng, MS, PhD); transportation engineering (M Eng). *Faculty:* 42 full-time (8 women), 2 part-time/adjunct (0 women). *Students:* 157 full-time (48 women), 10 part-time (3 women); includes 18 minority (7 Asian, non-Hispanic/Latino; 7 Hispanic/Latino; 1 Native Hawaiian or other Pacific Islander, non-Hispanic/Latino; 3 Two or more races, non-Hispanic/Latino), 92 international. Average age 28. 379 applicants, 31% accepted, 50 enrolled. In 2016, 55 master's, 5 doctorates awarded. *Entrance requirements:* For master's and doctorate, GRE. Additional exam requirements/recommendations for international students: Required—TOEFL (minimum score 80 iBT), IELTS (minimum score 6.5). *Application deadline:* For fall admission, 8/1 for domestic students, 4/1 for international students; for winter admission, 12/1 for domestic students, 7/1 for international students; for spring admission, 2/1 for domestic students, 10/1 for international students; for summer admission, 5/1 for domestic students, 1/1 for international students. Application fee: $75 ($85 for international students). *Expenses:* $14,130 resident full-time tuition, $23,769 non-resident. *Financial support:* Application deadline: 1/15. *Unit head:* Dr. Jason Weiss, School Head/Professor. *Application contact:* Shannon Reed, Graduate Program Coordinator, 541-737-4575, E-mail: shannon.reed@oregonstate.edu.
Website: http://cce.oregonstate.edu/graduate-academics

Princeton University, Graduate School, Department of Geosciences, Princeton, NJ 08544-1019. Offers atmospheric and oceanic sciences (PhD); geosciences (PhD); ocean sciences and marine biology (PhD). *Degree requirements:* For doctorate, one foreign language, thesis/dissertation. *Entrance requirements:* For doctorate, GRE General Test. Additional exam requirements/recommendations for international students: Required—TOEFL (minimum score 600 paper-based). Electronic applications accepted. *Faculty research:* Biogeochemistry, climate science, earth history, regional geology and tectonics, solid–earth geophysics.

Stevens Institute of Technology, Graduate School, Charles V. Schaefer Jr. School of Engineering and Science, Department of Civil, Environmental, and Ocean Engineering, Program in Ocean Engineering, Hoboken, NJ 07030. Offers M Eng, PhD. *Program availability:* Part-time, evening/weekend. *Students:* 17 full-time (5 women), 5 part-time (2 women); includes 1 minority (Hispanic/Latino), 13 international. Average age 26. 54 applicants, 70% accepted, 10 enrolled. In 2016, 20 master's, 3 doctorates awarded. *Degree requirements:* For master's, thesis optional, minimum B average in major field and overall; for doctorate, comprehensive exam (for some programs), thesis/dissertation. *Entrance requirements:* Additional exam requirements/recommendations for international students: Required—TOEFL (minimum score 74 iBT), IELTS (minimum score 6). *Application deadline:* For fall admission, 6/1 for domestic students, 4/15 for international students; for spring admission, 11/30 for domestic students, 11/1 for international students. Applications are processed on a rolling basis. Application fee: $65. Electronic applications accepted. *Expenses:* Contact institution. *Financial support:* Fellowships, research assistantships, teaching assistantships, career-related internships or fieldwork, Federal Work-Study, scholarships/grants, and unspecified assistantships available. Financial award application deadline: 2/15; financial award applicants required to submit FAFSA. *Unit head:* Dr. David A. Vaccari, Director, 201-216-5570, Fax: 201-216-8739, E-mail: dvaccari@stevens.edu. *Application contact:* Graduate Admission, 888-783-8367, Fax: 888-511-1306, E-mail: graduate@stevens.edu.

University of Alaska Anchorage, School of Engineering, Program in Civil Engineering, Anchorage, AK 99508. Offers civil engineering (MCE, MS); coastal, ocean, and port engineering (Certificate). *Program availability:* Part-time, evening/weekend. *Degree requirements:* For master's, thesis (for some programs). *Entrance requirements:* For master's, bachelor's degree in engineering. Additional exam requirements/recommendations for international students: Required—TOEFL (minimum score 550 paper-based). *Faculty research:* Structural engineering, engineering education, astronomical observations related to engineering.

University of California, San Diego, Graduate Division, Department of Electrical and Computer Engineering, La Jolla, CA 92093. Offers applied ocean science (MS, PhD); applied physics (MS, PhD); communication theory and systems (MS, PhD); computer engineering (MS, PhD); electronic circuits and systems (MS, PhD); intelligent systems, robotics and control (MS, PhD); medical devices and systems (MS, PhD); nanoscale devices and systems (MS, PhD); photonics (MS, PhD); signal and image processing (MS, PhD). *Students:* 612 full-time (119 women), 39 part-time (8 women). 2,885 applicants, 25% accepted, 269 enrolled. In 2016, 147 master's, 43 doctorates awarded. Terminal master's awarded for partial completion of doctoral program. *Degree requirements:* For master's, comprehensive exam (for some programs), thesis (for some programs); for doctorate, comprehensive exam, thesis/dissertation. *Entrance requirements:* For master's and doctorate, GRE General Test, minimum GPA of 3.0, resume or curriculum vitae (recommended). Additional exam requirements/recommendations for international students: Required—TOEFL (minimum score 550 paper-based; 80 iBT), IELTS (minimum score 7), PTE (minimum score 65). *Application deadline:* For fall admission, 12/13 for domestic students. Application fee: $105 ($125 for international students). Electronic applications accepted. *Expenses:* Tuition, state resident: full-time $11,220. Tuition, nonresident: full-time $26,322. *Required fees:* $1864. *Financial support:* Fellowships, research assistantships, teaching assistantships, scholarships/grants, traineeships, and unspecified assistantships available. Financial award applicants required to submit FAFSA. *Faculty research:* Applied ocean science; applied physics; communication theory and systems; computer engineering; electronic circuits and systems; intelligent systems, robotics and control; medical devices and systems; nanoscale devices and systems; photonics; signal and image processing. *Unit head:* Truong Nguyen, Chair, 858-822-5554, E-mail: nguyent@ece.ucsd.edu. *Application contact:* Melanie Lynn, Graduate Admissions Coordinator, 858-822-3213, E-mail: ecegradapps@ece.ucsd.edu.
Website: http://ece.ucsd.edu/

University of California, San Diego, Graduate Division, Department of Mechanical and Aerospace Engineering, Program in Applied Ocean Science, La Jolla, CA 92093. Offers MS, PhD. *Students:* 2 full-time (1 woman). 11 applicants, 18% accepted. In 2016, 1 master's awarded. *Degree requirements:* For master's, comprehensive exam (for some programs), thesis (for some programs), comprehensive exam or thesis; for doctorate, comprehensive exam, thesis/dissertation. *Entrance requirements:* For master's and doctorate, GRE General Test, minimum GPA of 3.0. Additional exam requirements/recommendations for international students: Required—TOEFL (minimum score 550 paper-based; 80 iBT), IELTS (minimum score 7). *Application deadline:* For fall admission, 12/14 for domestic students. Application fee: $105 ($125 for international students). Electronic applications accepted. *Expenses:* Tuition, state resident: full-time $11,220. Tuition, nonresident: full-time $26,322. *Required fees:* $1864. *Financial*

support: Fellowships, research assistantships, teaching assistantships, scholarships/grants, and unspecified assistantships available. Financial award applicants required to submit FAFSA. *Faculty research:* Water quality in the coastal ocean and subsurface resources; internal waves, gravity currents, wake flows; ocean process modeling. *Unit head:* Vitali Nesterenko, Chair, 858-534-0113, E-mail: mae-chair-l@ucsd.edu. *Application contact:* Lydia Ramirez, Graduate Coordinator, 858-534-4387, E-mail: mae-gradadm-l@ucsd.edu.
Website: http://maeweb.ucsd.edu/

University of Delaware, College of Earth, Ocean, and Environment, School of Marine Science and Policy, Newark, DE 19716. Offers marine policy (MMP); marine studies (MS, PhD), including marine biosciences, oceanography, physical ocean science and engineering; oceanography (PhD).

University of Delaware, College of Engineering, Department of Civil and Environmental Engineering, Newark, DE 19716. Offers environmental engineering (MAS, MCE, PhD); geotechnical engineering (MAS, MCE, PhD); ocean engineering (MAS, MCE, PhD); structural engineering (MAS, MCE, PhD); transportation engineering (MAS, MCE, PhD); water resource engineering (MAS, MCE, PhD). *Program availability:* Part-time. Terminal master's awarded for partial completion of doctoral program. *Degree requirements:* For master's, thesis; for doctorate, thesis/dissertation. *Entrance requirements:* For master's and doctorate, GRE General Test. Additional exam requirements/recommendations for international students: Required—TOEFL. Electronic applications accepted. *Faculty research:* Structural engineering and mechanics; transportation engineering; ocean engineering; soil mechanics and foundation; water resources and environmental engineering.

University of Florida, Graduate School, Herbert Wertheim College of Engineering, Department of Civil and Coastal Engineering, Gainesville, FL 32611. Offers civil engineering (ME, MS, PhD); coastal and oceanographic engineering (ME, MS, PhD); geographic information systems (ME, MS, PhD); hydrologic sciences (ME, MS, PhD); structural engineering (ME, MS); wetland sciences (ME, MS, PhD). *Program availability:* Part-time, online learning. Terminal master's awarded for partial completion of doctoral program. *Degree requirements:* For master's, thesis (for some programs); for doctorate, comprehensive exam, thesis/dissertation. *Entrance requirements:* For master's and doctorate, minimum GPA of 3.0. Additional exam requirements/recommendations for international students: Required—TOEFL (minimum score 550 paper-based; 80 iBT), IELTS (minimum score 6). Electronic applications accepted. *Faculty research:* Traffic congestion mitigation, wind mitigation, sustainable infrastructure materials, improved sensors for in situ measurements, storm surge modeling.

University of Hawaii at Manoa, Graduate Division, School of Ocean and Earth Science and Technology, Department of Ocean and Resources Engineering, Honolulu, HI 96822. Offers MS, PhD. *Accreditation:* ABET (one or more programs are accredited). *Program availability:* Part-time. *Degree requirements:* For master's, thesis optional, exams; for doctorate, comprehensive exam, thesis/dissertation, exams. *Entrance requirements:* For master's and doctorate, GRE General Test. Additional exam requirements/recommendations for international students: Required—TOEFL (minimum score 560 paper-based; 83 iBT), IELTS (minimum score 5). *Faculty research:* Coastal and harbor engineering, near shore environmental ocean engineering, marine structures/naval architecture.

University of Michigan, College of Engineering, Department of Naval Architecture and Marine Engineering, Ann Arbor, MI 48109. Offers MS, MSE, PhD, Mar Eng, Nav Arch, MBA/MSE. *Program availability:* Part-time. *Students:* 85 full-time (19 women), 5 part-time (0 women). 122 applicants, 46% accepted, 33 enrolled. In 2016, 44 master's, 7 doctorates awarded. Terminal master's awarded for partial completion of doctoral program. *Degree requirements:* For master's, thesis (for some programs); for doctorate, comprehensive exam, thesis/dissertation, oral defense of dissertation, written and oral preliminary exams; for other advanced degree, comprehensive exam, thesis, oral defense of thesis. *Entrance requirements:* For doctorate, GRE General Test, master's degree; for other advanced degree, GRE General Test. Additional exam requirements/recommendations for international students: Required—TOEFL. *Application deadline:* Applications are processed on a rolling basis. Electronic applications accepted. *Expenses:* Tuition, state resident: full-time $21,466; part-time $1152 per credit hour. Tuition, nonresident: full-time $43,346; part-time $2367 per credit hour. Part-time tuition and fees vary according to course load, degree level and program. *Financial support:* Fellowships, research assistantships, teaching assistantships, career-related internships or fieldwork, Federal Work-Study, institutionally sponsored loans, scholarships/grants, and unspecified assistantships available. *Faculty research:* System and structural reliability, design and analysis of offshore structures and vehicles, marine systems design, remote sensing of ship wakes and sea surfaces, marine hydrodynamics, nonlinear seakeeping analysis. *Total annual research expenditures:* $11 million. *Unit head:* Jing Sun, Department Chair, 734-615-8061, E-mail: jingsun@umich.edu. *Application contact:* Nathalie Fiveland, Graduate Program Coordinator, 734-936-0566, Fax: 734-936-8820, E-mail: fiveland@umich.edu.
Website: http://www.engin.umich.edu/name

University of New Hampshire, Graduate School, School of Marine Science and Ocean Engineering, Durham, NH 03824. Offers marine biology (MS, PhD); ocean engineering (MS, PhD); ocean mapping (MS, Postbaccalaureate Certificate); oceanography (MS, PhD). *Degree requirements:* For master's, thesis. *Entrance requirements:* Additional exam requirements/recommendations for international students: Required—TOEFL (minimum score 550 paper-based; 80 iBT). Electronic applications accepted.

University of Rhode Island, Graduate School, College of Engineering, Department of Ocean Engineering, Narragansett, RI 02882. Offers acoustics (MS, PhD). *Program availability:* Part-time. *Faculty:* 11 full-time (2 women). *Students:* 26 full-time (7 women), 14 part-time (0 women); includes 3 minority (2 Asian, non-Hispanic/Latino; 1 Hispanic/Latino), 9 international. In 2016, 7 master's, 2 doctorates awarded. *Degree requirements:* For master's, comprehensive exam (for some programs), thesis or

permission of the chair and a total of 30 credits with a minimum of 18 credits of course work in ocean engineering, with one course requiring a paper involving significant independent study and a written comprehensive examination; for doctorate, comprehensive exam, thesis/dissertation. *Entrance requirements:* For master's and doctorate, 2 letters of recommendation. Additional exam requirements/recommendations for international students: Required—TOEFL. *Application deadline:* For fall admission, 7/15 for domestic students, 2/1 for international students; for spring admission, 11/15 for domestic students, 7/15 for international students; for summer admission, 4/15 for domestic students. Application fee: $65. Electronic applications accepted. *Expenses:* Tuition, state resident: full-time $11,796; part-time $655 per credit. Tuition, nonresident: full-time $24,206; part-time $1345 per credit. *Required fees:* $1546; $44 per credit. One-time fee: $155 full-time; $35 part-time. *Financial support:* In 2016–17, 4 research assistantships with tuition reimbursements (averaging $10,237 per year), 3 teaching assistantships with tuition reimbursements (averaging $14,320 per year) were awarded. Financial award application deadline: 2/1; financial award applicants required to submit FAFSA. *Unit head:* Dr. Christopher H. Baxter, Chairman, 401-874-6575, E-mail: baxter@oce.uri.edu. *Application contact:* Graduate Admission, 401-874-2872, E-mail: gradadm@etal.uri.edu.
Website: http://www.oce.uri.edu/

Virginia Polytechnic Institute and State University, Graduate School, College of Engineering, Blacksburg, VA 24061. Offers aerospace engineering (ME, MS, PhD); biological systems engineering (ME, MS, PhD); biomedical engineering (MS, PhD); chemical engineering (ME, MS, PhD); civil engineering (ME, MS, PhD); computer engineering (ME, MS, PhD); computer science (MS, PhD); electrical engineering (ME, PhD); engineering education (PhD); engineering mechanics (ME, MS, PhD); environmental engineering (MS); environmental science and engineering (MS); industrial and systems engineering (ME, MS, PhD); materials science and engineering (ME, MS, PhD); mechanical engineering (ME, MS, PhD); mining and minerals engineering (PhD); mining engineering (ME, MS); nuclear engineering (MS, PhD); ocean engineering (MS); systems engineering (ME, MS). *Faculty:* 400 full-time (73 women), 3 part-time/adjunct (2 women). *Students:* 1,949 full-time (487 women), 393 part-time (69 women); includes 251 minority (56 Black or African American, non-Hispanic/Latino; 3 American Indian or Alaska Native, non-Hispanic/Latino; 87 Asian, non-Hispanic/Latino; 70 Hispanic/Latino; 35 Two or more races, non-Hispanic/Latino), 1,354 international. Average age 27. 4,903 applicants, 19% accepted, 569 enrolled. In 2016, 364 master's, 200 doctorates awarded. *Degree requirements:* For master's, comprehensive exam (for some programs), thesis (for some programs); for doctorate, comprehensive exam (for some programs), thesis/dissertation (for some programs). *Entrance requirements:* For master's and doctorate, GRE/GMAT. Additional exam requirements/recommendations for international students: Required—TOEFL (minimum score 80 iBT). *Application deadline:* For fall admission, 8/1 for domestic students, 4/1 for international students; for spring admission, 1/1 for domestic students, 9/1 for international students. Applications are processed on a rolling basis. Application fee: $75. Electronic applications accepted. *Expenses:* Tuition, state resident: full-time $12,467; part-time $692.50 per credit hour. Tuition, nonresident: full-time $25,095; part-time $1394.25 per credit hour. *Required fees:* $2669; $491.50 per semester. Tuition and fees vary according to course load, campus/location and program. *Financial support:* In 2016–17, 160 fellowships with full tuition reimbursements (averaging $7,387 per year), 872 research assistantships with full tuition reimbursements (averaging $22,329 per year), 313 teaching assistantships with full tuition reimbursements (averaging $18,714 per year) were awarded. Financial award application deadline: 3/1; financial award applicants required to submit FAFSA. *Total annual research expenditures:* $91.8 million. *Unit head:* Dr. Julia Ross, Dean, 540-231-9752, Fax: 540-231-3031, E-mail: deaneng@vt.edu. *Application contact:* Linda Perkins, Executive Assistant, 540-231-9752, Fax: 540-231-3031, E-mail: lperkins@vt.edu.
Website: http://www.eng.vt.edu/

Virginia Polytechnic Institute and State University, VT Online, Blacksburg, VA 24061. Offers advanced transportation systems (Certificate); aerospace engineering (MS); agricultural and life sciences (MSLFS); business information systems (Graduate Certificate); career and technical education (MS); civil engineering (MS); computer engineering (M Eng, MS); decision support systems (Graduate Certificate); eLearning leadership (MA); electrical engineering (M Eng, MS); engineering administration (MEA); environmental engineering (Certificate); environmental politics and policy (Graduate Certificate); environmental sciences and engineering (MS); foundations of political analysis (Graduate Certificate); health product risk management (Graduate Certificate); industrial and systems engineering (MS); information policy and society (Graduate Certificate); information security (Graduate Certificate); information technology (MIT); instructional technology (MA); integrative STEM education (MA Ed); liberal arts (Graduate Certificate); life sciences: health product risk management (MS); natural resources (MNR, Graduate Certificate); networking (Graduate Certificate); nonprofit and nongovernmental organization management (Graduate Certificate); ocean engineering (MS); political science (MA); security studies (Graduate Certificate); software development (Graduate Certificate). *Expenses:* Tuition, state resident: full-time $12,467; part-time $692.50 per credit hour. Tuition, nonresident: full-time $25,095; part-time $1394.25 per credit hour. *Required fees:* $2669; $491.50 per semester. Tuition and fees vary according to course load, campus/location and program.

Woods Hole Oceanographic Institution, MIT/WHOI Joint Program in Oceanography/Applied Ocean Science and Engineering, Woods Hole, MA 02543-1541. Offers applied ocean science and engineering (PhD); biological oceanography (PhD); chemical oceanography (PhD); marine geology and geophysics (PhD); physical oceanography (PhD). Program offered jointly with Massachusetts Institute of Technology. *Degree requirements:* For doctorate, thesis/dissertation. *Entrance requirements:* For doctorate, GRE General Test. Additional exam requirements/recommendations for international students: Required—TOEFL or IELTS. Electronic applications accepted.

Section 19
Paper and Textile Engineering

This section contains a directory of institutions offering graduate work in paper and textile engineering. Additional information about programs listed in the directory may be obtained by writing directly to the dean of a graduate school or chair of a department at the address given in the directory.

For programs offering related work, see also in this book *Engineering and Applied Sciences* and *Materials Sciences and Engineering.* In another guide in this series:

Graduate Programs in the Humanities, Arts & Social Sciences
See *Family and Consumer Sciences (Clothing and Textiles)*

CONTENTS

Program Directories

Paper and Pulp Engineering

Georgia Institute of Technology, Graduate Studies, Multidisciplinary Program in Paper Science and Engineering, Atlanta, GA 30318-5794. Offers MS, PhD. Program offered jointly with School of Chemical and Biomolecular Engineering, School of Chemistry and Biochemistry, School of Materials Science and Engineering, and George W. Woodruff School of Mechanical Engineering. *Program availability:* Part-time. Terminal master's awarded for partial completion of doctoral program. *Degree requirements:* For master's, thesis; for doctorate, comprehensive exam, thesis/dissertation. *Entrance requirements:* For master's and doctorate, GRE General Test. Additional exam requirements/recommendations for international students: Required—TOEFL (minimum score 620 paper-based; 105 iBT). Electronic applications accepted.

North Carolina State University, Graduate School, College of Natural Resources, Department of Wood and Paper Science, Raleigh, NC 27695. Offers MS, MWPS, PhD. *Program availability:* Online learning. *Degree requirements:* For master's, thesis optional; for doctorate, thesis/dissertation. *Entrance requirements:* For master's and doctorate, GRE General Test. Additional exam requirements/recommendations for international students: Required—TOEFL. Electronic applications accepted. *Faculty research:* Pulping, bleaching, recycling, papermaking, drying of wood.

State University of New York College of Environmental Science and Forestry, Department of Paper and Bioprocess Engineering, Syracuse, NY 13210-2779. Offers biomaterials engineering (MS, PhD); bioprocess engineering (MPS, MS, PhD); bioprocessing (Advanced Certificate); paper science and engineering (MPS, MS, PhD); sustainable engineering management (MPS). *Faculty:* 13 full-time (2 women), 4 part-time/adjunct (0 women). *Students:* 28 full-time (14 women), 3 part-time (2 women); includes 1 minority (Asian, non-Hispanic/Latino), 19 international. Average age 29. 19 applicants, 89% accepted, 6 enrolled. In 2016, 6 master's, 1 doctorate, 4 other advanced degrees awarded. *Degree requirements:* For master's, thesis; for doctorate, comprehensive exam, thesis/dissertation; for Advanced Certificate, 15 credit hours. *Entrance requirements:* For master's and doctorate, GRE General Test, minimum GPA of 3.0; for Advanced Certificate, BS, calculus plus science major. Additional exam requirements/recommendations for international students: Required—TOEFL (minimum score 550 paper-based; 80 iBT), IELTS (minimum score 6). *Application deadline:* For fall admission, 2/1 priority date for domestic and international students; for spring admission, 11/1 priority date for domestic and international students. Applications are processed on a rolling basis. Application fee: $60. *Expenses:* Tuition, state resident: full-time $10,870; part-time $453 per credit. Tuition, nonresident: full-time $22,210; part-time $925 per credit. *Required fees:* $1075; $89.22 per credit. *Financial support:* In 2016–17, 14 students received support. Application deadline: 6/30; applicants required to submit FAFSA. *Faculty research:* Sustainable products and processes, biorefinery, pulping and papermaking, nanocellulose, bioconversions, process control and modeling. *Unit head:* Dr. Gary M. Scott, Chair, 315-470-6501, Fax: 315-470-6945, E-mail: gscott@esf.edu. *Application contact:* Scott Shannon, Associate Provost and Dean, Instruction and Graduate Studies, 315-470-6599, Fax: 315-470-6978, E-mail: esfgrad@esf.edu. Website: http://www.esf.edu/pbe/

The University of Manchester, School of Materials, Manchester, United Kingdom. Offers advanced aerospace materials engineering (M Sc); advanced metallic systems (PhD); biomedical materials (M Phil, M Sc, PhD); ceramics and glass (M Phil, M Sc, PhD); composite materials (M Sc, PhD); corrosion and protection (M Phil, M Sc, PhD); materials (M Phil, PhD); metallic materials (M Phil, M Sc, PhD); nanostructural materials (M Phil, M Sc, PhD); paper science (M Phil, M Sc, PhD); polymer science and engineering (M Phil, M Sc, PhD); technical textiles (M Sc); textile design, fashion and management (M Phil, M Sc, PhD); textile science and technology (M Phil, M Sc, PhD); textiles (M Phil, PhD); textiles and fashion (M Ent).

University of Minnesota, Twin Cities Campus, Graduate School, College of Food, Agricultural and Natural Resource Sciences, Program in Natural Resources Science and Management, St. Paul, MN 55108. Offers assessment, monitoring, and geospatial analysis (MS, PhD); economics, policy, management, and society (MS, PhD); forest hydrology and watershed management (MS, PhD); forest products (MS, PhD); forests: biology, ecology, conservation, and management (MS, PhD); natural resources science and management (MS, PhD); paper science and engineering (MS, PhD); recreation resources, tourism, and environmental education (MS, PhD). *Program availability:* Part-time. *Faculty:* 71 full-time (28 women), 52 part-time/adjunct (7 women). *Students:* 79 full-time (46 women), 27 part-time (14 women); includes 11 minority (2 Black or African American, non-Hispanic/Latino; 3 American Indian or Alaska Native, non-Hispanic/Latino; 3 Asian, non-Hispanic/Latino; 3 Hispanic/Latino), 9 international. Average age 31. 63 applicants, 57% accepted, 26 enrolled. In 2016, 19 master's, 3 doctorates awarded. Terminal master's awarded for partial completion of doctoral program. *Degree requirements:* For master's, comprehensive exam, thesis (for some programs); for doctorate, comprehensive exam, thesis/dissertation. *Entrance requirements:* For master's and doctorate, GRE General Test. Additional exam requirements/recommendations for international students: Required—TOEFL (minimum score 550 paper-based; 79 iBT), IELTS (minimum score 6.5). *Application deadline:* For fall admission, 12/16 priority date for domestic and international students; for spring admission, 10/15 for domestic and international students. Applications are processed on a rolling basis. Application fee: $75 ($95 for international students). Electronic applications accepted. *Financial support:* In 2016–17, 5 students received support, including fellowships with full tuition reimbursements available (averaging $40,000 per year), research assistantships with full tuition reimbursements available (averaging $40,000 per year), teaching assistantships with full tuition reimbursements available (averaging $40,000 per year); scholarships/grants, health care benefits, and unspecified assistantships also available. *Faculty research:* Forest hydrology, biology, ecology, conservation, and management; recreation resources and environmental education; wildlife ecology; economics, policy, and society; geographic information systems (GIS); forest products and paper science. *Unit head:* Dr. Mae Davenport, Interim Director of Graduate Studies, 612-624-2721, E-mail: mdaven@umn.edu. *Application contact:* Toni Abts, Graduate Program Coordinator, 612-624-7683, Fax: 612-625-5212, E-mail: twheeler@umn.edu. Website: http://www.nrsm.umn.edu

Western Michigan University, Graduate College, College of Engineering and Applied Sciences, Department of Chemical and Paper Engineering, Kalamazoo, MI 49008. Offers MS, MSE, PhD. *Degree requirements:* For master's, thesis optional; for doctorate, one foreign language, comprehensive exam, thesis/dissertation.

Textile Sciences and Engineering

Cornell University, Graduate School, Graduate Fields of Human Ecology, Field of Fiber Science and Apparel Design, Ithaca, NY 14853. Offers apparel design (MA, MPS); fiber science (MS, PhD); polymer science (MS, PhD); textile science (MS, PhD). *Degree requirements:* For master's, thesis (MA, MS), project paper (MPS); for doctorate, comprehensive exam, thesis/dissertation. *Entrance requirements:* For master's, GRE General Test, 2 letters of recommendation, portfolio (for functional apparel design); for doctorate, GRE General Test, 2 letters of recommendation. Additional exam requirements/recommendations for international students: Required—TOEFL (minimum score 600 paper-based; 77 iBT). Electronic applications accepted. *Faculty research:* Apparel design, consumption, mass customization, 3-D body scanning.

North Carolina State University, Graduate School, College of Textiles, Department of Textile and Apparel Technology and Management, Raleigh, NC 27695. Offers MS, MT. *Degree requirements:* For master's, thesis optional. *Entrance requirements:* For master's, GRE. Electronic applications accepted. *Faculty research:* Textile and apparel products and processes, management systems, nonwovens, process simulation, structure design and analysis.

North Carolina State University, Graduate School, College of Textiles, Department of Textile Engineering, Chemistry, and Science, Program in Textile Chemistry, Raleigh, NC 27695. Offers MS. *Degree requirements:* For master's, thesis optional. *Entrance requirements:* For master's, GRE. Electronic applications accepted. *Faculty research:* Color science, polymer science, dye chemistry, fiber formation, wet processing technology.

North Carolina State University, Graduate School, College of Textiles, Department of Textile Engineering, Chemistry, and Science, Program in Textile Engineering, Raleigh, NC 27695. Offers MS. *Degree requirements:* For master's, thesis optional. *Entrance requirements:* For master's, GRE. Electronic applications accepted. *Faculty research:* Electro-mechanical design, inventory and supply chain control, textile composites, biomedical textile appliations, pollution prevention.

North Carolina State University, Graduate School, College of Textiles, Program in Fiber and Polymer Science, Raleigh, NC 27695. Offers PhD. *Degree requirements:* For doctorate, one foreign language, thesis/dissertation, cumulative exams. *Entrance requirements:* For doctorate, GRE. Electronic applications accepted. *Faculty research:* Polymer science, fiber mechanics, medical textiles, nanotechnology.

Philadelphia University, School of Design and Engineering, PhD Program in Textile Engineering and Sciences, Philadelphia, PA 19144. Offers PhD.

Philadelphia University, School of Design and Engineering, Program in Textile Engineering, Philadelphia, PA 19144. Offers MS. *Program availability:* Part-time. *Degree requirements:* For master's, thesis. *Entrance requirements:* For master's, GRE, minimum GPA of 2.8. Additional exam requirements/recommendations for international students: Required—TOEFL (minimum score 550 paper-based; 79 iBT). Electronic applications accepted.

The University of Texas at Austin, Graduate School, College of Natural Sciences, School of Human Ecology, Program in Textile and Apparel Technology, Austin, TX 78712-1111. Offers MS.

Section 20
Telecommunications

This section contains a directory of institutions offering graduate work in tele-communications. Additional information about programs listed in the directory may be obtained by writing directly to the dean of a graduate school or chair of a department at the address given in the directory.

For programs offering related work, see also in this book *Computer Science and Information Technology* and *Engineering and Applied Sciences*. In the other guides in this series:

Graduate Programs in the Humanities, Arts & Social Sciences
See *Communication and Media*
Graduate Programs in Business, Education, Information Studies, Law & Social Work
See *Business Administration and Management*

CONTENTS

Program Directories

Telecommunications

Ball State University, Graduate School, College of Communication, Information, and Media, Department of Telecommunications, Muncie, IN 47306. Offers telecommunications (MA), including digital storytelling. *Program availability:* Part-time. *Degree requirements:* For master's, thesis or alternative. *Entrance requirements:* For master's, minimum baccalaureate GPA of 2.75 or 3.0 in latter half of baccalaureate. Additional exam requirements/recommendations for international students: Required—TOEFL (minimum score 550 paper-based; 79 iBT), IELTS (minimum score 6.5). Electronic applications accepted.

Boston University, Metropolitan College, Department of Computer Science, Boston, MA 02215. Offers computer information systems (MS), including computer networks, data analytics, database management and business intelligence, health informatics, IT project management, security, Web application development; computer networks (Certificate); computer science (MS); data analytics (Certificate); digital forensics (Certificate); health informatics (Certificate); information technology project management (Certificate); software development (MS); software engineering in health care systems (Certificate); telecommunications (MS), including security. *Program availability:* Part-time, evening/weekend, online learning. *Faculty:* 13 full-time (3 women), 43 part-time/adjunct (3 women). *Students:* 108 full-time (36 women), 1,294 part-time (364 women); includes 428 minority (115 Black or African American, non-Hispanic/Latino; 2 American Indian or Alaska Native, non-Hispanic/Latino; 187 Asian, non-Hispanic/Latino; 98 Hispanic/Latino; 2 Native Hawaiian or other Pacific Islander, non-Hispanic/Latino; 24 Two or more races, non-Hispanic/Latino), 314 international. Average age 33. 463 applicants, 79% accepted, 248 enrolled. In 2016, 311 master's awarded. *Degree requirements:* For master's, thesis optional. *Entrance requirements:* For master's and Certificate, official transcripts from regionally-accredited bachelor's degree program, 3 letters of recommendation, professional resume, personal statement. Additional exam requirements/recommendations for international students: Required—TOEFL (minimum score 84 iBT), IELTS. *Application deadline:* For fall admission, 6/1 priority date for international students; for spring admission, 10/1 priority date for international students. Applications are processed on a rolling basis. Application fee: $85. Electronic applications accepted. *Expenses:* Contact institution. *Financial support:* In 2016–17, 11 research assistantships (averaging $8,400 per year) were awarded; unspecified assistantships also available. Support available to part-time students. Financial award applicants required to submit FAFSA. *Faculty research:* Medical informatics, Web technologies, telecom and networks, security and forensics, software engineering, programming languages, multimedia and artificial intelligence (AI), information systems and IT project management. *Unit head:* Dr. Anatoly Temkin, Chair, 617-353-2566, Fax: 617-353-2367, E-mail: csinfo@bu.edu. *Application contact:* Lesley Moreau, Academic Program Coordinator, 617-353-2566, Fax: 617-353-2367, E-mail: metcs@bu.edu. Website: http://www.bu.edu/csmet/

California Miramar University, Program in Telecommunications Management, San Diego, CA 92108. Offers MST.

Claremont Graduate University, Graduate Programs, Center for Information Systems and Technology, Claremont, CA 91711-6160. Offers cybersecurity and networking (MS); data science and analytics (MS); electronic commerce (PhD); geographic information systems (MS); health informatics (MS); information systems (Certificate); IT strategy and innovation (MS); knowledge management (PhD); systems development (PhD); telecommunications and networking (PhD); MBA/MS. *Program availability:* Part-time. *Faculty:* 8 full-time (1 woman), 1 part-time/adjunct (0 women). *Students:* 60 full-time (18 women), 81 part-time (27 women); includes 34 minority (7 Black or African American, non-Hispanic/Latino; 18 Asian, non-Hispanic/Latino; 7 Hispanic/Latino; 1 Native Hawaiian or other Pacific Islander, non-Hispanic/Latino; 1 Two or more races, non-Hispanic/Latino), 80 international. Average age 35. In 2016, 21 master's, 10 doctorates awarded. *Degree requirements:* For doctorate, comprehensive exam, thesis/dissertation, portfolio. *Entrance requirements:* For master's and doctorate, GMAT, GRE General Test. Additional exam requirements/recommendations for international students: Required—TOEFL (minimum score 75 iBT). *Application deadline:* For fall admission, 2/1 priority date for domestic and international students. Applications are processed on a rolling basis. Application fee: $80. Electronic applications accepted. *Expenses: Tuition:* Full-time $44,328; part-time $1847 per unit. *Required fees:* $600; $300 per semester. Tuition and fees vary according to course load and program. *Financial support:* Fellowships, research assistantships, teaching assistantships, Federal Work-Study, institutionally sponsored loans, and scholarships/grants available. Support available to part-time students. Financial award application deadline: 2/15; financial award applicants required to submit FAFSA. *Faculty research:* Man-machine interaction, organizational aspects of computing, implementation of information systems, information systems practice. *Unit head:* Lorne Olfman, Acting Director, 909-607-3035, E-mail: lorne.olfman@cgu.edu. *Application contact:* Jake Campbell, Senior Assistant Director of Admissions, 909-607-3024, E-mail: jake.campbell@cgu.edu.
Website: https://www.cgu.edu/school/center-for-information-systems-and-technology/

Drexel University, College of Engineering, Department of Electrical and Computer Engineering, Program in Telecommunications Engineering, Philadelphia, PA 19104-2875. Offers MSEE. *Faculty:* 32 full-time (4 women), 3 part-time/adjunct (0 women). *Students:* 10 full-time (6 women), 1 (woman) part-time; includes 1 minority (Asian, non-Hispanic/Latino), 10 international. Average age 23. In 2016, 5 master's awarded. *Entrance requirements:* For master's, BS in electrical engineering or physics, minimum GPA of 3.0. Additional exam requirements/recommendations for international students: Required—TOEFL. *Application deadline:* For fall admission, 8/21 for domestic students. Applications are processed on a rolling basis. Application fee: $50. Electronic applications accepted. *Expenses: Tuition:* Full-time $32,184; part-time $1192 per credit hour. *Required fees:* $280. Tuition and fees vary according to campus/location and program. *Financial support:* Research assistantships, teaching assistantships, and unspecified assistantships available. Financial award application deadline: 2/1. *Unit head:* Dr. Nihat M. Bilgutay, Head, 215-895-6806, Fax: 215-895-1695, E-mail: bilgutay@ece.drexel.edu. *Application contact:* Director of Graduate Admissions, 215-895-6700, Fax: 215-895-5939, E-mail: enroll@drexel.edu.

Fairfield University, School of Engineering, Fairfield, CT 06824. Offers database management (CAS); electrical and computer engineering (MS); information security (CAS); management of technology (MS); mechanical engineering (MS); network technology (CAS); software engineering (MS); Web application development (CAS). *Program availability:* Part-time, evening/weekend. *Faculty:* 7 full-time (1 woman), 15 part-time/adjunct (2 women). *Students:* 104 full-time (31 women), 56 part-time (15 women); includes 17 minority (8 Black or African American, non-Hispanic/Latino; 5 Asian, non-Hispanic/Latino; 4 Hispanic/Latino), 108 international. Average age 28. 193 applicants, 63% accepted, 20 enrolled. In 2016, 173 master's awarded. *Degree requirements:* For master's, capstone course. *Entrance requirements:* For master's, resume, 2 recommendations. Additional exam requirements/recommendations for international students: Required—TOEFL (minimum score 550 paper-based; 80 iBT) or IELTS (minimum score 6.5). *Application deadline:* For fall admission, 5/15 for international students; for spring admission, 10/15 for international students. Applications are processed on a rolling basis. Application fee: $60. Electronic applications accepted. *Expenses:* $800 per credit hour. *Financial support:* In 2016–17, 27 students received support. Scholarships/grants and unspecified assistantships available. Financial award applicants required to submit FAFSA. *Faculty research:* Artificial intelligence and information visualization, natural language processing, thermofluids, microwaves and electromagnetics, micro-/nano-manufacturing. *Unit head:* Dr. Bruce Berdanier, Dean, 203-254-4147, Fax: 203-254-4013, E-mail: bberdanier@fairfield.edu. *Application contact:* Marianne Gumpper, Director of Graduate and Continuing Studies Admission, 203-254-4184, Fax: 203-254-4073, E-mail: gradadmis@fairfield.edu. Website: http://www.fairfield.edu/soe

Florida International University, College of Engineering and Computing, School of Computing and Information Sciences, Miami, FL 33199. Offers computer science (MS, PhD); cybersecurity (MS); data science (MS); information technology (MS); telecommunications and networking (MS). *Program availability:* Part-time, evening/weekend. *Faculty:* 46 full-time (11 women), 28 part-time/adjunct (5 women). *Students:* 145 full-time (39 women), 109 part-time (16 women); includes 124 minority (14 Black or African American, non-Hispanic/Latino; 1 American Indian or Alaska Native, non-Hispanic/Latino; 10 Asian, non-Hispanic/Latino; 97 Hispanic/Latino; 2 Two or more races, non-Hispanic/Latino), 115 international. Average age 29. 407 applicants, 54% accepted, 78 enrolled. In 2016, 90 master's, 8 doctorates awarded. *Degree requirements:* For master's, thesis or alternative; for doctorate, comprehensive exam, thesis/dissertation. *Entrance requirements:* For master's and doctorate, GRE General Test, 3 letters of recommendation, minimum GPA of 3.0. Additional exam requirements/recommendations for international students: Required—TOEFL (minimum score 550 paper-based; 80 iBT). *Application deadline:* For fall admission, 6/1 for domestic students, 4/1 for international students; for spring admission, 10/1 for domestic students, 9/1 for international students. Applications are processed on a rolling basis. Application fee: $30. Electronic applications accepted. *Expenses:* Tuition, state resident: full-time $8912; part-time $446 per credit hour. Tuition, nonresident: full-time $21,393; part-time $992 per credit hour. *Required fees:* $2185; $195 per semester. Tuition and fees vary according to program. *Financial support:* Research assistantships, teaching assistantships, institutionally sponsored loans, scholarships/grants, and unspecified assistantships available. Financial award application deadline: 3/1; financial award applicants required to submit FAFSA. *Faculty research:* Database systems, software engineering, operating systems, networks. *Unit head:* Dr. S. S. Iyengar, Director, 305-348-3947, E-mail: iyengar@cis.fiu.edu. *Application contact:* Sara-Michelle Lemus, Engineering Admissions Officer, 305-348-1890, E-mail: grad_eng@fiu.edu.

Franklin Pierce University, Graduate and Professional Studies, Rindge, NH 03461-0060. Offers curriculum and instruction (M Ed); elementary education (MS Ed); emerging network technologies (Graduate Certificate); energy and sustainability studies (MBA, Graduate Certificate); health administration (MBA, Graduate Certificate); human resource management (MBA, Graduate Certificate); information technology (MBA); leadership (MBA); nursing education (MS); nursing leadership (MS); physical therapy (DPT); physician assistant studies (MPAS); special education (M Ed); sports management (MBA). *Accreditation:* APTA. *Program availability:* Part-time, 100% online, blended/hybrid learning. *Faculty:* 47 full-time (36 women), 165 part-time/adjunct (108 women). *Students:* 380 full-time (226 women), 245 part-time (158 women); includes 52 minority (13 Black or African American, non-Hispanic/Latino; 2 American Indian or Alaska Native, non-Hispanic/Latino; 14 Asian, non-Hispanic/Latino; 22 Hispanic/Latino; 1 Native Hawaiian or other Pacific Islander, non-Hispanic/Latino), 13 international. Average age 29. 1,995 applicants, 28% accepted, 267 enrolled. In 2016, 120 master's, 86 doctorates awarded. *Degree requirements:* For master's, concentrated original research projects; student teaching; fieldwork and/or internship; leadership project; PRAXIS I and II (for M Ed); for doctorate, concentrated original research projects, clinical fieldwork and/or internship, leadership project. *Entrance requirements:* For master's, minimum GPA of 2.5, 3 letters of recommendation; competencies in accounting, economics, statistics, and computer skills through life experience or undergraduate coursework (for MBA); certification/e-portfolio, minimum C grade in all education courses (for M Ed); license to practice as RN (for MS); for doctorate, GRE, 80 hours of observation/work in PT settings; completion of anatomy, chemistry, physics, and statistics; minimum GPA of 3.0. Additional exam requirements/recommendations for international students: Required—TOEFL (minimum score 550 paper-based; 61 iBT). *Application deadline:* Applications are processed on a rolling basis. Application fee: $0. Electronic applications accepted. *Expenses: Tuition:* Full-time $15,960; part-time $665 per credit hour. Tuition and fees vary according to program. *Financial support:* Teaching assistantships with tuition reimbursements, career-related internships or fieldwork, and unspecified assistantships available. Support available to part-time students. Financial award applicants required to submit FAFSA. *Faculty research:* Evidence-based practice in sports physical therapy, human resource management in economic crisis, leadership in nursing, innovation in sports facility management, differentiated learning and understanding by design. *Unit head:* Dr. Maria Altobello, Dean, 603-647-3509, Fax: 603-229-4580, E-mail: altobellom@franklinpierce.edu. *Application contact:* Graduate Studies, 800-325-1090, Fax: 603-626-4815, E-mail: cgps@franklinpierce.edu.
Website: http://www.franklinpierce.edu/academics/gradstudies/index.htm

The George Washington University, School of Engineering and Applied Science, Department of Electrical and Computer Engineering, Washington, DC 20052. Offers electrical engineering (MS, PhD); telecommunication and computers (MS). *Program availability:* Part-time, evening/weekend. *Faculty:* 26 full-time (2 women). *Students:* 191 full-time (43 women), 67 part-time (56 women); includes 19 minority (9 Black or African American, non-Hispanic/Latino; 7 Asian, non-Hispanic/Latino; 3 Hispanic/Latino), 218 international. Average age 27. 545 applicants, 88% accepted, 103 enrolled. In 2016, 48 master's, 7 doctorates, 1 other advanced degree awarded. *Degree requirements:* For master's, thesis optional; for doctorate, comprehensive exam, thesis/dissertation, dissertation defense, qualifying exam. *Entrance requirements:* For master's, appropriate bachelor's degree, minimum GPA of 3.0; for doctorate, GRE (if highest earned degree is BS), appropriate bachelor's or master's degree, minimum GPA of 3.3; for other advanced degree, appropriate master's degree, minimum GPA of 3.0. Additional exam requirements/recommendations for international students: Required—TOEFL or The George Washington University English as a Foreign Language Test. *Application deadline:* For fall admission, 3/1 priority date for domestic students; for spring admission, 10/1 for domestic students. Applications are processed on a rolling basis. Application fee: $75. *Financial support:* In 2016–17, 39 students received support. Fellowships with tuition reimbursements available, research assistantships, teaching assistantships with tuition reimbursements available, career-related internships or fieldwork, and institutionally sponsored loans available. Financial award application deadline: 3/1; financial award applicants required to submit FAFSA. *Faculty research:* Computer graphics, multimedia systems. *Unit head:* Prof. Ahmed Louri, Chair, 202-994-

5905, E-mail: louri@gwu.edu. *Application contact:* Adina Lav, Marketing, Recruiting and Admissions, 202-994-5827, Fax: 202-994-0909, E-mail: engineering@gwu.edu.
Website: http://www.ece.gwu.edu/

Illinois Institute of Technology, Graduate College, Armour College of Engineering, Department of Electrical and Computer Engineering, Chicago, IL 60616. Offers biomedical imaging and signals (MAS); computer engineering (MS, PhD); electrical engineering (MS, PhD); electricity markets (MAS); network engineering (MAS); power engineering (MAS); telecommunications and software engineering (MAS); VLSI and microelectronics (MAS); MS/MS. *Program availability:* Part-time, evening/weekend, online learning. Terminal master's awarded for partial completion of doctoral program. *Degree requirements:* For master's, comprehensive exam (for some programs), thesis (for some programs); for doctorate, comprehensive exam, thesis/dissertation. *Entrance requirements:* For master's and doctorate, GRE General Test (minimum score 1100 Quantitative and Verbal, 3.5 Analytical Writing), minimum undergraduate GPA of 3.0. Additional exam requirements/recommendations for international students: Required—TOEFL (minimum score 550 paper-based; 80 iBT); Recommended—IELTS (minimum score 5.5). Electronic applications accepted. *Faculty research:* Communication systems, wireless networks, computer systems, computer networks, wireless security, cloud computing and micro-electronics; electromagnetics and electronics; power and control systems; signal and image processing.

Illinois Institute of Technology, Graduate College, College of Science, Department of Computer Science, Chicago, IL 60616. Offers business (MCS); computational intelligence (MCS); computer science (MCS, MS, PhD); cyber-physical systems (MCS); data analytics (MCS); data science (MAS); database systems (MCS); distributed and cloud computing (MCS); education (MCS); finance (MCS); information security and assurance (MCS); networking and communications (MCS); software engineering (MCS); telecommunications and software engineering (MAS); MS/MAS. *Program availability:* Part-time, evening/weekend, online learning. Terminal master's awarded for partial completion of doctoral program. *Degree requirements:* For master's, thesis optional; for doctorate, comprehensive exam, thesis/dissertation. *Entrance requirements:* For master's, GRE General Test with minimum scores of 298 Quantitative and Verbal, 3.0 Analytical Writing (for MS); GRE General Test with minimum scores of 292 Quantitative and Verbal, 2.5 Analytical Writing (for MAS), minimum undergraduate GPA of 3.0; for doctorate, GRE General Test (minimum scores: 304 Quantitative and Verbal, 3.5 Analytical Writing), minimum undergraduate GPA of 3.0. Additional exam requirements/recommendations for international students: Required—TOEFL (minimum score 523 paper-based; 70 iBT). Electronic applications accepted. *Faculty research:* Parallel and distributed processing, high-performance computing, computational linguistics, information retrieval, data mining, grid computing.

Instituto Tecnologico de Santo Domingo, Graduate School, Area of Engineering, Santo Domingo, Dominican Republic. Offers construction administration (MS, Certificate); data telecommunications (M Eng, MS, Certificate); industrial engineering (M Eng, Certificate); industrial management (M Mgmt); information technology (Certificate); maintenance engineering (M Eng); occupational hazard prevention (M Mgmt); production management (Certificate); quantitative methods (Certificate); sanitary and environmental engineering (M Eng); structural engineering (M Eng); systems engineering and electronic data processing (Certificate); transportation (Certificate).

Michigan State University, The Graduate School, College of Communication Arts and Sciences, Department of Telecommunication, Information Studies, and Media, East Lansing, MI 48824. Offers digital media arts and technology (MA); information and telecommunication management (MA); information, policy and society (MA); serious game design (MA). *Entrance requirements:* Additional exam requirements/recommendations for international students: Required—TOEFL. Electronic applications accepted.

New Jersey Institute of Technology, Newark College of Engineering, Newark, NJ 07102. Offers biomedical engineering (MS, PhD); chemical engineering (MS, PhD); computer engineering (MS, PhD); electrical engineering (MS, PhD); engineering management (MS); environmental engineering (PhD); healthcare systems management (MS); industrial engineering (MS, PhD); Internet engineering (MS); manufacturing engineering (MS); mechanical engineering (MS, PhD); occupational safety and health engineering (MS); pharmaceutical bioprocessing (MS); pharmaceutical engineering (MS); pharmaceutical systems management (MS); power and energy systems (MS); telecommunications (MS); transportation (MS, PhD). *Program availability:* Part-time, evening/weekend. *Faculty:* 146 full-time (21 women), 119 part-time/adjunct (10 women). *Students:* 804 full-time (191 women), 550 part-time (129 women); includes 357 minority (82 Black or African American, non-Hispanic/Latino; 1 American Indian or Alaska Native, non-Hispanic/Latino; 138 Asian, non-Hispanic/Latino; 114 Hispanic/Latino; 22 Two or more races, non-Hispanic/Latino), 675 international. Average age 27. 2,959 applicants, 51% accepted, 442 enrolled. In 2016, 595 master's, 29 doctorates awarded. Terminal master's awarded for partial completion of doctoral program. *Degree requirements:* For master's, thesis optional; for doctorate, thesis/dissertation. *Entrance requirements:* For master's, GRE General Test; for doctorate, GRE General Test, minimum graduate GPA of 3.5. Additional exam requirements/recommendations for international students: Required—TOEFL (minimum score 550 paper-based; 79 iBT). *Application deadline:* For fall admission, 6/1 priority date for domestic students, 5/1 priority date for international students; for spring admission, 11/15 priority date for domestic and international students. Applications are processed on a rolling basis. Application fee: $75. Electronic applications accepted. *Expenses:* Contact institution. *Financial support:* In 2016–17, 172 students received support, including 1 fellowship (averaging $1,528 per year), 79 research assistantships (averaging $13,336 per year), 92 teaching assistantships (averaging $20,619 per year); scholarships/grants also available. Financial award application deadline: 1/15. *Faculty research:* Nonlinear signal processing, intelligent medical image analysis, calibration issues in coherent localization, computer-aided design, neural network for tool wear measurement. *Total annual research expenditures:* $11.1 million. *Unit head:* Dr. Moshe Kam, Dean, 973-596-5534, E-mail: moshe.kam@njit.edu. *Application contact:* Stephen Eck, Director of Admissions, 973-596-3300, Fax: 973-596-3461, E-mail: admissions@njit.edu.
Website: http://engineering.njit.edu/

Northeastern University, College of Engineering, Boston, MA 02115-5096. Offers bioengineering (MS, PhD); chemical engineering (MS, PhD); civil engineering (MS, PhD); computer engineering (PhD); computer systems engineering (MS); electrical and computer engineering (MS); electrical and computer engineering leadership (MS); electrical engineering (PhD); energy systems (MS); engineering and public policy (MS); engineering management (MS, Certificate); environmental engineering (MS); industrial engineering (MS, PhD); information assurance (PhD); information systems (MS); interdisciplinary engineering (PhD); mechanical engineering (PhD); operations research (MS); telecommunication systems management (MS). *Program availability:* Part-time, online learning. *Faculty:* 202 full-time (59 women), 53 part-time/adjunct (9 women). *Students:* 2,982 full-time (954 women), 192 part-time (38 women). In 2016, 851 master's, 74 doctorates awarded. Application fee: $75. Electronic applications accepted. *Expenses:* $1,471 per credit. *Financial support:* Fellowships, research assistantships, teaching assistantships, career-related internships or fieldwork, scholarships/grants, health care benefits, tuition waivers, and unspecified assistantships available. Support available to part-time students. Financial award applicants required to submit FAFSA. *Unit head:* Dr. Nadine Aubry, Dean, College of Engineering. *Application contact:* Jeffery Hengel, Director of Graduate Admissions, 617-373-2711, E-mail: j.hengel@northeastern.edu.
Website: http://www.coe.neu.edu/academics/graduate-school-engineering

Ohio University, Graduate College, Scripps College of Communication, J. Warren McClure School of Information and Telecommunication Systems, Athens, OH 45701-2979. Offers MCTP. *Program availability:* Part-time. *Degree requirements:* For master's, comprehensive exam (for some programs), thesis (for some programs). *Entrance requirements:* For master's, GRE or GMAT, minimum cumulative GPA of 3.0. Additional exam requirements/recommendations for international students: Required—TOEFL (minimum score 550 paper-based; 80 iBT) or IELTS (minimum score 6.5). *Application deadline:* For fall admission, 2/1 priority date for domestic students, 12/15 priority date for international students. Applications are processed on a rolling basis. Application fee: $50 ($55 for international students). Electronic applications accepted. *Financial support:* Research assistantships with full and partial tuition reimbursements, institutionally sponsored loans, and unspecified assistantships available. Financial award application deadline: 2/1; financial award applicants required to submit FAFSA. *Faculty research:* Voice and data networks, with special emphasis on the interaction of technology and policy issues in the successful design, deployment, and operation of complex networks and information systems. *Unit head:* Philip D. Campbell, Associate Professor and Director, 740-593-4907, Fax: 740-593-4889, E-mail: campbell@ohio.edu. *Application contact:* Dr. Andy Snow, Professor and Associate Director for Graduate Studies, 740-593-0421, Fax: 740-593-4889, E-mail: snowa@ohio.edu.
Website: http://www.ohio.edu/mcclure/

Pace University, Seidenberg School of Computer Science and Information Systems, New York, NY 10038. Offers chief information security officer (APC); computer science (MS, PhD); enterprise analytics (MS); information and communication technology strategy and innovation (APC); information systems (MS, APC); Internet technology (MS); professional studies in computing (DPS); secure software and information engineering (APC); security and information assurance (Certificate); software development and engineering (MS, Certificate); telecommunications systems and networks (MS, Certificate). *Program availability:* Part-time, evening/weekend, online only, 100% online, blended/hybrid learning. *Faculty:* 26 full-time (7 women), 7 part-time/adjunct (2 women). *Students:* 537 full-time (175 women), 303 part-time (85 women); includes 192 minority (79 Black or African American, non-Hispanic/Latino; 3 American Indian or Alaska Native, non-Hispanic/Latino; 53 Asian, non-Hispanic/Latino; 49 Hispanic/Latino; 8 Two or more races, non-Hispanic/Latino), 486 international. Average age 32. 599 applicants, 89% accepted, 248 enrolled. In 2016, 180 master's, 19 doctorates, 1 other advanced degree awarded. *Degree requirements:* For master's, thesis or alternative, capstone course; for doctorate, comprehensive exam (for some programs), thesis/dissertation. *Entrance requirements:* For master's, GRE General Test. Additional exam requirements/recommendations for international students: Required—TOEFL (minimum score 78 iBT), IELTS (minimum score 6.5) or PTE (minimum score 52). *Application deadline:* For fall admission, 8/1 priority date for domestic students, 6/1 for international students; for spring admission, 12/1 for domestic students, 10/1 for international students. Applications are processed on a rolling basis. Application fee: $70. Electronic applications accepted. *Expenses:* Contact institution. *Financial support:* In 2016–17, 45 students received support. Research assistantships, career-related internships or fieldwork, scholarships/grants, and unspecified assistantships available. Support available to part-time students. Financial award application deadline: 2/15; financial award applicants required to submit FAFSA. *Faculty research:* Cyber security/digital forensics; mobile app development; big data/enterprise analytics; artificial intelligence; software development. *Total annual research expenditures:* $314,545. *Unit head:* Dr. Jonathan Hill, Dean, Seidenberg School of Computer Science and Information Systems, 212-346-1864, E-mail: jhill@pace.edu. *Application contact:* Susan Ford-Goldschein, Director of Graduate Admissions, 914-422-4283, Fax: 212-346-1585, E-mail: graduateadmission@pace.edu.
Website: http://www.pace.edu/seidenberg

Rochester Institute of Technology, Graduate Enrollment Services, College of Applied Science and Technology, School of Engineering Technology, MS Program in Telecommunications Engineering Technology, Rochester, NY 14623. Offers MS. *Program availability:* Part-time. *Students:* 79 full-time (16 women), 33 part-time (4 women); includes 4 minority (2 Black or African American, non-Hispanic/Latino; 1 Asian, non-Hispanic/Latino; 1 Hispanic/Latino), 107 international. Average age 25. 203 applicants, 70% accepted, 31 enrolled. In 2016, 26 master's awarded. *Degree requirements:* For master's, thesis or alternative. *Entrance requirements:* For master's, GRE, minimum GPA of 3.0 (recommended). Additional exam requirements/recommendations for international students: Required—TOEFL (minimum score 570 paper-based; 88 iBT), IELTS (minimum score 6.5), PTE (minimum score 61). *Application deadline:* For fall admission, 2/15 priority date for domestic and international students; for spring admission, 12/15 priority date for domestic and international students. Applications are processed on a rolling basis. Application fee: $60. Electronic applications accepted. *Expenses:* $1,742 per credit hour. *Financial support:* In 2016–17, 94 students received support. Research assistantships with partial tuition reimbursements available, teaching assistantships with partial tuition reimbursements available, career-related internships or fieldwork, scholarships/grants, and unspecified assistantships available. Support available to part-time students. Financial award applicants required to submit FAFSA. *Faculty research:* Wireless networks, fiber-optic networks, software-defined networks, telecommunications policy and regulations, network quality of service. *Unit head:* William P. Johnson, Graduate Program Director, 585-475-2140, E-mail: wpjiee@rit.edu. *Application contact:* Diane Ellison, Associate Vice President, Graduate Enrollment Services, 585-475-2229, Fax: 585-475-7164, E-mail: gradinfo@rit.edu.
Website: http://www.rit.edu/cast/ectet/ms-in-telecommunications-engineering-technology.php

Roosevelt University, Graduate Division, College of Arts and Sciences, Department of Computer Science and Telecommunications, Program in Telecommunications, Chicago, IL 60605. Offers MST. *Program availability:* Part-time, evening/weekend. *Entrance requirements:* For master's, GRE. *Faculty research:* Coding theory, mathematical models, network design, simulation models.

Saint Mary's University of Minnesota, Schools of Graduate and Professional Programs, Graduate School of Business and Technology, Information Technology Management Program, Winona, MN 55987-1399. Offers MS. Tuition and fees vary according to degree level and program. *Application contact:* James Callinan, Director of Admissions for Graduate and Professional Programs, 612-728-5185, Fax: 612-728-5121, E-mail: jcallina@smumn.edu.
Website: http://www.smumn.edu/graduate-home/areas-of-study/graduate-school-of-business-technology/ms-in-information-technology-management

Southern Methodist University, Bobby B. Lyle School of Engineering, Department of Electrical Engineering, Dallas, TX 75275-0338. Offers applied science (MS); electrical engineering (MSEE, PhD); telecommunications (MS). *Program availability:* Part-time, evening/weekend, online learning. Terminal master's awarded for partial completion of doctoral program. *Degree requirements:* For master's, thesis optional; for doctorate, thesis/dissertation, oral and written qualifying exams, oral final exam. *Entrance requirements:* For master's, GRE General Test, minimum GPA of 3.0 in last 2 years; bachelor's degree in engineering, mathematics, or sciences; for doctorate, preliminary counseling exam, minimum GPA of 3.0, bachelor's degree in related field. Additional exam requirements/recommendations for international students: Required—TOEFL. Electronic applications accepted. *Faculty research:* Mobile communications, optical communications, digital signal processing, photonics.

State University of New York Polytechnic Institute, Program in Telecommunications, Utica, NY 13502. Offers MS. *Program availability:* Part-time, evening/weekend. *Degree requirements:* For master's, thesis or project. *Entrance requirements:* For master's, GRE General Test, minimum GPA of 3.0, one letter of reference, bachelor's degree in telecommunications or a related field, resume. Additional exam requirements/ recommendations for international students: Required—TOEFL (minimum score 550 paper-based; 79 iBT), IELTS (minimum score 6.5). Electronic applications accepted. *Faculty research:* Cloud security, virtualization, wireless networks, cyber physical system.

Stevens Institute of Technology, Graduate School, School of Business, Program in Telecommunications Management, Hoboken, NJ 07030. Offers business (MS); global innovation management (MS); management of wireless networks (MS); online security, technology and business (MS); project management (MS); technical management (MS); telecommunications management (PhD, Certificate). *Program availability:* Part-time, evening/weekend. *Students:* 1 full-time (0 women), 38 part-time (8 women); includes 5 minority (3 Black or African American, non-Hispanic/Latino; 2 Asian, non-Hispanic/ Latino), 1 international. Average age 38. In 2016, 14 master's, 2 other advanced degrees awarded. *Degree requirements:* For master's, thesis optional, minimum B average in major field and overall; for doctorate, comprehensive exam (for some programs), thesis/dissertation; for Certificate, minimum B average. *Entrance requirements:* Additional exam requirements/recommendations for international students: Required—TOEFL (minimum score 74 iBT), IELTS (minimum score 6). *Application deadline:* For fall admission, 6/1 for domestic students, 4/15 for international students; for spring admission, 11/30 for domestic students, 11/1 for international students. Applications are processed on a rolling basis. Application fee: $65. Electronic applications accepted. *Expenses:* Contact institution. *Financial support:* Fellowships, research assistantships, teaching assistantships, career-related internships or fieldwork, Federal Work-Study, scholarships/grants, health care benefits, and unspecified assistantships available. Financial award application deadline: 2/15; financial award applicants required to submit FAFSA. *Unit head:* Dr. Gregory Prastacos, Dean, 201-216-8366, E-mail: gprastac@stevens.edu. *Application contact:* Graduate Admission, 888-783-8367, Fax: 888-511-1306, E-mail: graduate@stevens.edu.
Website: https://www.stevens.edu/school-business/masters-programs/network-communication-management-services

Stratford University, School of Graduate Studies, Falls Church, VA 22043. Offers accounting (MS); business administration (IMBA, MBA); cyber security (MS); cyber security leadership and policy (MS); digital forensics (MS); enterprise business management (MS); entrepreneurial management (MS); healthcare administration (MS); information systems (MS); international hospitality management (MS); networking and telecommunications (MS); software engineering (MS). *Program availability:* Part-time, evening/weekend, 100% online, blended/hybrid learning. *Students:* 505 full-time (186 women), 172 part-time (88 women); includes 532 minority (165 Black or African American, non-Hispanic/Latino; 18 American Indian or Alaska Native, non-Hispanic/ Latino; 324 Asian, non-Hispanic/Latino; 13 Hispanic/Latino; 10 Native Hawaiian or other Pacific Islander, non-Hispanic/Latino; 2 Two or more races, non-Hispanic/Latino). Average age 27. In 2016, 520 master's awarded. *Degree requirements:* For master's, comprehensive exam, capstone project. *Entrance requirements:* For master's, GRE or GMAT, baccalaureate degree. Additional exam requirements/recommendations for international students: Required—TOEFL (minimum score 79 iBT), IELTS (minimum score 6.5), PTE (minimum score 5). *Application deadline:* Applications are processed on a rolling basis. Application fee: $50. Electronic applications accepted. *Expenses: Tuition:* Full-time $4455; part-time $2227.50 per course. One-time fee: $100. *Financial support:* Federal Work-Study and scholarships/grants available. Financial award applicants required to submit FAFSA. *Unit head:* Dr. Richard R. Shurtz, President, 703-539-6890, Fax: 703-539-6960. *Application contact:* Admissions, 800-444-0804, E-mail: fcadmissions@stratford.edu.

Universidad del Turabo, Graduate Programs, School of Engineering, Program in Telecommunications and Network Systems Administration, Gurabo, PR 00778-3030. Offers M Eng. *Students:* 9 full-time (0 women), 9 part-time (2 women); all minorities (all Hispanic/Latino). Average age 32. 37 applicants, 43% accepted, 9 enrolled. In 2016, 6 master's awarded. *Entrance requirements:* For master's, GRE, EXADEP or GMAT, interview, essay, official transcript, recommendation letters. *Application deadline:* Applications are processed on a rolling basis. Application fee: $25. Electronic applications accepted. *Financial support:* Institutionally sponsored loans available. Financial award applicants required to submit FAFSA. *Unit head:* Hector Rodriguez, Dean, 787-743-7979 Ext. 4144. *Application contact:* Diriee Rodriguez, Admissions Director, 787-743-7979 Ext. 4453, E-mail: admisiones-ut@suagm.edu.
Website: http://ut.suagm.edu/es/engineering

Université du Québec, Institut National de la Recherche Scientifique, Graduate Programs, Centre for Energie Materiaux Telecommunications, Varennes, QC G1K 9A9, Canada. Offers energy and materials science (M Sc, PhD); telecommunications (M Sc, PhD). *Program availability:* Part-time. *Faculty:* 36 full-time. *Students:* 185 full-time (47 women), 10 part-time (2 women), 154 international. Average age 31. 27 applicants, 78% accepted, 13 enrolled. In 2016, 13 master's, 23 doctorates awarded. *Degree requirements:* For master's, thesis (for some programs); for doctorate, thesis/ dissertation. *Entrance requirements:* For master's, appropriate bachelor's degree, proficiency in French; for doctorate, appropriate master's degree, proficiency in French. *Application deadline:* For fall admission, 3/30 for domestic and international students; for winter admission, 11/1 for domestic and international students; for spring admission, 3/1 for domestic and international students. Application fee: $45. Electronic applications accepted. *Financial support:* In 2016–17, fellowships (averaging $16,500 per year) were awarded; research assistantships and scholarships/grants also available. *Faculty research:* New energy sources, plasmas, telecommunications, advanced materials, ultrafast photonics. *Unit head:* Federico Rosei, Director, 450-228-6905, E-mail: rosei@emt.inrs.ca. *Application contact:* Sylvie Richard, Registrar, 418-654-2518, Fax: 418-654-3858, E-mail: sylvie.richard@adm.inrs.ca.
Website: http://www.emt.inrs.ca

University of Alberta, Faculty of Graduate Studies and Research, Department of Electrical and Computer Engineering, Edmonton, AB T6G 2E1, Canada. Offers communications (M Eng, M Sc, PhD); computer engineering (M Eng, M Sc, PhD); electromagnetics (M Eng, M Sc, PhD); nanotechnology and microdevices (M Eng, M Sc, PhD); power/power electronics (M Eng, M Sc, PhD); systems (M Eng, M Sc, PhD). Terminal master's awarded for partial completion of doctoral program. *Degree requirements:* For master's, thesis; for doctorate, thesis/dissertation. *Entrance requirements:* Additional exam requirements/recommendations for international students: Required—TOEFL. Electronic applications accepted. *Faculty research:* Controls, communications, microelectronics, electromagnetics.

University of Arkansas, Graduate School, College of Engineering, Department of Electrical Engineering, Fayetteville, AR 72701. Offers electrical engineering (MSEE, PhD); telecommunications engineering (MS Tc E). In 2016, 24 master's, 4 doctorates awarded. *Degree requirements:* For master's, thesis optional; for doctorate, one foreign language, thesis/dissertation. *Entrance requirements:* For master's and doctorate, GRE General Test. *Application deadline:* For fall admission, 4/1 for international students; for spring admission, 10/1 for international students. Applications are processed on a rolling basis. Application fee: $40 ($50 for international students). Electronic applications accepted. *Financial support:* In 2016–17, 48 research assistantships, 8 teaching assistantships were awarded; fellowships with tuition reimbursements, career-related internships or fieldwork, and Federal Work-Study also available. Support available to part-time students. Financial award application deadline: 4/1; financial award applicants required to submit FAFSA. *Unit head:* Dr. Juan Balda, Department Chair, 479-575-3005, Fax: 479-575-7967, E-mail: jbalda@uark.edu. *Application contact:* Dr. Hameed Naseem, Graduate Coordinator, 479-575-6581, E-mail: hnaseem@uark.edu.
Website: http://www.eleg.uark.edu/

University of California, San Diego, Graduate Division, Department of Electrical and Computer Engineering, La Jolla, CA 92093. Offers applied ocean science (MS, PhD); applied physics (MS, PhD); communication theory and systems (MS, PhD); computer engineering (MS, PhD); electronic circuits and systems (MS, PhD); intelligent systems, robotics and control (MS, PhD); medical devices and systems (MS, PhD); nanoscale devices and systems (MS, PhD); photonics (MS, PhD); signal and image processing (MS, PhD). *Students:* 612 full-time (119 women), 39 part-time (8 women). 2,885 applicants, 25% accepted, 269 enrolled. In 2016, 147 master's, 43 doctorates awarded. Terminal master's awarded for partial completion of doctoral program. *Degree requirements:* For master's, comprehensive exam (for some programs), thesis (for some programs); for doctorate, comprehensive exam, thesis/dissertation. *Entrance requirements:* For master's and doctorate, GRE General Test, minimum GPA of 3.0, resume or curriculum vitae (recommended). Additional exam requirements/ recommendations for international students: Required—TOEFL (minimum score 550 paper-based; 80 iBT), IELTS (minimum score 7), PTE (minimum score 65). *Application deadline:* For fall admission, 12/13 for domestic students. Application fee: $105 ($125 for international students). Electronic applications accepted. *Expenses:* Tuition, state resident: full-time $11,220. Tuition, nonresident: full-time $26,322. *Required fees:* $1864. *Financial support:* Fellowships, research assistantships, teaching assistantships, scholarships/grants, traineeships, and unspecified assistantships available. Financial award applicants required to submit FAFSA. *Faculty research:* Applied ocean science; applied physics; communication theory and systems; computer engineering; electronic circuits and systems; intelligent systems, robotics and control; medical devices and systems; nanoscale devices and systems; photonics; signal and image processing. *Unit head:* Truong Nguyen, Chair, 858-822-5554, E-mail: nguyent@ece.ucsd.edu. *Application contact:* Melanie Lynn, Graduate Admissions Coordinator, 858-822-3213, E-mail: ecegradapps@ece.ucsd.edu.
Website: http://ece.ucsd.edu/

University of California, San Diego, Graduate Division, Program in Wireless Embedded Systems, La Jolla, CA 92093. Offers MAS. *Program availability:* Part-time. *Students:* 47 part-time (6 women). 33 applicants, 88% accepted, 25 enrolled. In 2016, 22 master's awarded. *Degree requirements:* For master's, capstone project. *Entrance requirements:* For master's, GRE General Test (if applicant possesses fewer than 2 years' work experience), 3 letters of recommendation, statement of purpose, resume or curriculum vitae. Additional exam requirements/recommendations for international students: Required—TOEFL (minimum score 550 paper-based; 80 iBT), IELTS (minimum score 7). *Application deadline:* For fall admission, 5/1 priority date for domestic students. Application fee: $105 ($125 for international students). Electronic applications accepted. *Expenses:* Contact institution. *Financial support:* Applicants required to submit FAFSA. *Faculty research:* Systems, software, hardware and communication theory and algorithms. *Unit head:* George Papen, Director, 858-822-1728, E-mail: gpapen@ucsd.edu. *Application contact:* Sally Binney, Graduate Coordinator, 858-246-1463, E-mail: wes-mas@ucsd.edu.
Website: http://maseng.ucsd.edu/wes

University of Colorado Boulder, Graduate School, College of Engineering and Applied Science, Interdisciplinary Telecommunications Program, Boulder, CO 80309. Offers MS, JD/MS, MBA/MS. *Students:* 145 full-time (48 women), 9 part-time (0 women); includes 7 minority (2 Black or African American, non-Hispanic/Latino; 2 Asian, non-Hispanic/Latino; 2 Hispanic/Latino; 1 Two or more races, non-Hispanic/Latino), 127 international. Average age 27. 247 applicants, 48% accepted, 49 enrolled. In 2016, 53 master's awarded. Terminal master's awarded for partial completion of doctoral program. *Degree requirements:* For master's, comprehensive exam, thesis or alternative. *Entrance requirements:* For master's, minimum undergraduate GPA of 3.0. *Application deadline:* For fall admission, 1/30 for domestic and international students; for spring admission, 11/1 for domestic students, 10/1 for international students. Applications are processed on a rolling basis. Application fee: $60 ($80 for international students). Electronic applications accepted. Application fee is waived when completed online. *Financial support:* In 2016–17, 224 students received support, including 106 fellowships (averaging $4,721 per year), 5 research assistantships with full and partial tuition reimbursements available (averaging $49,616 per year), 5 teaching assistantships with full and partial tuition reimbursements available (averaging $38,777 per year); institutionally sponsored loans, scholarships/grants, health care benefits, and unspecified assistantships also available. Financial award applicants required to submit FAFSA. *Faculty research:* Technology, planning, and management of telecommunications systems. *Application contact:* E-mail: itp@colorado.edu.
Website: http://engineeringanywhere.colorado.edu/itp/

University of Florida, Graduate School, College of Journalism and Communications, Program in Mass Communication, Gainesville, FL 32611. Offers international/ intercultural communication (MAMC); journalism (MAMC); mass communication (MAMC, PhD), including clinical translational science (MAMC); public relations (MAMC); science/health communication (MAMC); telecommunication (MAMC). *Accreditation:* ACEJMC. *Entrance requirements:* For master's and doctorate, GRE General Test, minimum GPA of 3.0.

University of Hawaii at Manoa, Graduate Division, College of Social Sciences, School of Communications, Program in Telecommunication and Information Resource Management, Honolulu, HI 96822. Offers Graduate Certificate. *Program availability:* Part-time. *Entrance requirements:* Additional exam requirements/recommendations for international students: Required—TOEFL (minimum score 500 paper-based; 61 iBT), IELTS (minimum score 5).

University of Houston, College of Technology, Department of Engineering Technology, Houston, TX 77204. Offers construction management (MS); engineering technology (MS); network communications (M Tech). *Program availability:* Part-time. *Degree requirements:* For master's, project or thesis (most programs). *Entrance requirements:* For master's, GRE. Additional exam requirements/recommendations for international students: Required—TOEFL (minimum score 550 paper-based; 79 iBT). Electronic applications accepted.

University of Louisiana at Lafayette, College of Engineering, Department of Electrical and Computer Engineering, Program in Telecommunications, Lafayette, LA 70504. Offers MSTC. *Degree requirements:* For master's, thesis or alternative. *Entrance requirements:* For master's, GRE General Test, minimum GPA of 2.75. Additional exam requirements/recommendations for international students: Required—TOEFL (minimum score 550 paper-based). Electronic applications accepted.

University of Maryland, College Park, Academic Affairs, A. James Clark School of Engineering, Department of Electrical and Computer Engineering, Program in Telecommunications, College Park, MD 20742. Offers MS. *Program availability:* Part-time, evening/weekend. *Degree requirements:* For master's, thesis or alternative. *Entrance requirements:* For master's, GRE General Test, minimum GPA of 3.0, professional experience. Additional exam requirements/recommendations for international students: Required—TOEFL. Electronic applications accepted.

University of Massachusetts Dartmouth, Graduate School, College of Engineering, Department of Electrical and Computer Engineering, North Dartmouth, MA 02747-2300. Offers acoustics (Postbaccalaureate Certificate); communications (Postbaccalaureate Certificate); computer engineering (MS, PhD); computing infrastructure (Postbaccalaureate Certificate); digital security signal processing (Postbaccalaureate Certificate); electrical engineering (MS, PhD). *Program availability:* Part-time. *Faculty:* 15 full-time (3 women), 1 part-time/adjunct (0 women). *Students:* 31 full-time (8 women), 45 part-time (5 women); includes 8 minority (2 Black or African American, non-Hispanic/Latino; 2 Asian, non-Hispanic/Latino; 2 Hispanic/Latino; 2 Two or more races, non-Hispanic/Latino), 39 international. Average age 28. 101 applicants, 57% accepted, 23 enrolled. In 2016, 25 master's, 3 doctorates, 3 other advanced degrees awarded. Terminal master's awarded for partial completion of doctoral program. *Degree requirements:* For master's, thesis or project; for doctorate, comprehensive exam, thesis/dissertation. *Entrance requirements:* For master's, GRE (UMass Dartmouth electrical/computer engineering bachelor's degree recipients are exempt), statement of purpose (minimum of 300 words), resume, 3 letters of recommendation, official transcripts; for doctorate, GRE (UMass Dartmouth electrical/computer engineering degree recipients are exempt), statement of purpose (minimum of 300 words), resume, 3 letters of recommendation, official transcripts; for Postbaccalaureate Certificate, statement of purpose (minimum of 300 words), resume, official transcripts. Additional exam requirements/recommendations for international students: Required—TOEFL (minimum score 550 paper-based; 80 iBT). *Application deadline:* For fall admission, 2/15 priority date for domestic students, 1/15 priority date for international students; for spring admission, 11/1 priority date for domestic students, 10/1 priority date for international students. Application fee: $60. Electronic applications accepted. *Expenses:* Tuition, state resident: full-time $14,994; part-time $624.75 per credit. Tuition, nonresident: full-time $27,068; part-time $1127.83 per credit. *Required fees:* $405; $25.88 per credit. Tuition and fees vary according to course load and reciprocity agreements. *Financial support:* In 2016–17, 5 fellowships (averaging $5,143 per year), 14 research assistantships (averaging $10,724 per year), 11 teaching assistantships (averaging $14,705 per year) were awarded; unspecified assistantships and instructional assistantships, doctoral support also available. Financial award application deadline: 3/1; financial award applicants required to submit FAFSA. *Faculty research:* Computer engineering, cyber security, acoustics, signals and systems, electromagnetics, electronics and solid-state devices, marine systems, photonics. *Total annual research expenditures:* $2.6 million. *Unit head:* Hong Liu, Graduate Program Director, 508-999-8514, Fax: 508-999-8489, E-mail: hliu@umassd.edu. *Application contact:* Steven Briggs, Director of Marketing and Recruitment for Graduate Studies, 508-999-8604, Fax: 508-999-8183, E-mail: graduate@umassd.edu.
Website: http://www.umassd.edu/engineering/ece/graduate

University of Missouri–Kansas City, School of Computing and Engineering, Kansas City, MO 64110-2499. Offers civil engineering (MS); computer and electrical engineering (PhD); computer science (MS), including bioinformatics, software engineering, telecommunications networking; computer science and informatics (PhD); computing (PhD); electrical engineering (MS); engineering (PhD); engineering and construction management (Graduate Certificate); mechanical engineering (MS); telecommunications and computer networking (PhD). PhD (interdisciplinary) offered through the School of Graduate Studies. *Program availability:* Part-time. *Faculty:* 45 full-time (6 women), 26 part-time/adjunct (4 women). *Students:* 473 full-time (155 women), 207 part-time (42 women); includes 24 minority (10 Black or African American, non-Hispanic/Latino; 10 Asian, non-Hispanic/Latino; 4 Hispanic/Latino), 581 international. Average age 25. 1,143 applicants, 44% accepted, 227 enrolled. In 2016, 446 master's, 2 other advanced degrees awarded. *Degree requirements:* For doctorate, thesis/dissertation. *Entrance requirements:* For master's, GRE General Test, minimum GPA of 3.0, 3 letters of recommendation from professors; for doctorate, GRE General Test, minimum GPA of 3.5. Additional exam requirements/recommendations for international students: Required—TOEFL (minimum score 550 paper-based; 80 iBT). *Application deadline:* For fall admission, 1/15 priority date for domestic students, 1/15 for international students. Applications are processed on a rolling basis. Application fee: $45 ($50 for international students). *Financial support:* In 2016–17, 37 research assistantships with partial tuition reimbursements (averaging $15,679 per year), 47 teaching assistantships with partial tuition reimbursements (averaging $16,830 per year) were awarded; career-related internships or fieldwork, Federal Work-Study, scholarships/grants, tuition waivers (partial), and unspecified assistantships also available. Support available to part-time students. Financial award application deadline: 3/1; financial award applicants required to submit FAFSA. *Faculty research:* Algorithms, bioinformatics and medical informatics, biomechanics/biomaterials, civil engineering materials, networking and telecommunications, thermal science. *Unit head:* Dr. Kevin Z. Truman, Dean, 816-235-2399, Fax: 816-235-5159. *Application contact:* 816-235-2399, Fax: 816-235-5159.
Website: http://sce.umkc.edu/

The University of North Carolina at Chapel Hill, Graduate School, School of Media and Journalism, Chapel Hill, NC 27599. Offers mass communication (MA, PhD); technology and communication (MA, Certificate); JD/PhD; MA/JD. MA/JD and JD/PhD offered jointly with School of Law. *Accreditation:* ACEJMC (one or more programs are accredited). *Program availability:* Part-time, online learning. *Faculty:* 47 full-time (21 women), 4 part-time/adjunct (2 women). *Students:* 68 full-time (51 women), 59 part-time (42 women); includes 35 minority (10 Black or African American, non-Hispanic/Latino; 4 Asian, non-Hispanic/Latino; 4 Hispanic/Latino; 1 Native Hawaiian or other Pacific Islander, non-Hispanic/Latino; 16 Two or more races, non-Hispanic/Latino), 8 international. Average age 33. 179 applicants, 28% accepted, 42 enrolled. In 2016, 11 master's, 10 doctorates awarded. *Degree requirements:* For master's, comprehensive exam, thesis; for doctorate, comprehensive exam, thesis/dissertation. *Entrance requirements:* For master's and doctorate, GRE General Test, minimum GPA of 3.0. Additional exam requirements/recommendations for international students: Required—TOEFL (minimum score 620 paper-based, 105 iBT) or IELTS (7.5). Application fee: $85. Electronic applications accepted. *Expenses:* $7,094.58 per semester in-state, $15,120.58 per semester out-of-state; $625.42 per credit hour in-state (online), $1,412.42 per credit hour out-of-state (online). *Financial support:* In 2016–17, 55 students received support, including 47 fellowships with full tuition reimbursements available (averaging $17,319 per year), 3 research assistantships with full tuition reimbursements available (averaging $14,000 per year); scholarships/grants and health care benefits also available. Financial award application deadline: 12/5; financial award applicants required to submit FAFSA. *Faculty research:* Media processes and production; legal and regulatory issues in communication; media uses and effects; health communication; political, social, and strategic communication. *Total annual research expenditures:* $1 million. *Unit head:* Susan King, Dean, 919-962-1204, Fax: 919-962-0620, E-mail: susanking@unc.edu. *Application contact:* Casey Hart, Marketing and Instructional Design Coordinator, 919-843-9471, Fax: 919-962-0620, E-mail: mjgrad@unc.edu.
Website: http://mj.unc.edu/

University of Oklahoma, Gallogly College of Engineering, School of Electrical and Computer Engineering, Program in Telecommunications Engineering, Tulsa, OK 74135. Offers MS. *Program availability:* Part-time. *Students:* 5 full-time (1 woman), 6 part-time (0 women), 10 international. Average age 27. 34 applicants, 38% accepted, 2 enrolled. In 2016, 4 master's awarded. Terminal master's awarded for partial completion of doctoral program. *Entrance requirements:* For master's, GRE. Additional exam requirements/recommendations for international students: Required—TOEFL (minimum score 79 iBT) or IELTS (minimum score 6.5). *Application deadline:* For fall admission, 4/1 for international students; for spring admission, 9/1 for international students. Applications are processed on a rolling basis. Application fee: $50 ($100 for international students). Electronic applications accepted. *Expenses:* Tuition, state resident: full-time $4886; part-time $203.60 per credit hour. Tuition, nonresident: full-time $18,989; part-time $791.20 per credit hour. *Required fees:* $3283; $126.25 per credit hour. $126.50 per semester. *Financial support:* In 2016–17, 6 students received support. Research assistantships with full tuition reimbursements available, career-related internships or fieldwork, and health care benefits available. Financial award application deadline: 6/1; financial award applicants required to submit FAFSA. *Faculty research:* Optical networks, wireless networks, network security, quantum cryptography, next generation networks. *Unit head:* Dr. J.R. Cruz, Director, 405-325-8131, Fax: 405-325-7066, E-mail: jcruz@ou.edu. *Application contact:* Renee Wagenblatt, Administrative Assistant II, 918-660-3235, Fax: 918-660-3238, E-mail: rwagenblatt@ou.edu.
Website: http://www.ou.edu/coe/tcom

University of Pittsburgh, School of Information Sciences, Telecommunications and Networking Program, Pittsburgh, PA 15260. Offers information science (PhD), including telecommunications; telecommunications and networking (MST, Certificate). *Program availability:* Part-time, evening/weekend, 100% online. *Faculty:* 4 full-time (0 women), 1 part-time/adjunct (0 women). *Students:* 41 full-time (9 women), 3 part-time (1 woman), 43 international. Average age 26. 131 applicants, 71% accepted, 20 enrolled. In 2016, 28 master's, 3 doctorates awarded. *Degree requirements:* For master's, thesis optional; for doctorate, comprehensive exam, thesis/dissertation. *Entrance requirements:* For master's, GRE, GMAT, bachelor's degree with minimum GPA of 3.0; previous course work in computer programming, calculus, and probability; for doctorate, GRE, GMAT, master's degree; minimum GPA of 3.3; course work in computer programming, differential and integral calculus, probability, and statistics; for Certificate, MSIS, MST from accredited university. Additional exam requirements/recommendations for international students: Required—TOEFL (minimum score 550 paper-based; 80 iBT). *Application deadline:* For fall admission, 1/15 priority date for domestic and international students; for winter admission, 9/15 priority date for domestic students, 6/15 priority date for international students; for spring admission, 9/15 priority date for domestic students, 6/15 priority date for international students; for summer admission, 1/15 priority date for domestic students, 12/15 priority date for international students. Applications are processed on a rolling basis. Application fee: $50. Electronic applications accepted. *Expenses:* $22,628 per year in-state, $37,754 per year out-of-state (fall and spring); $931 per credit in-state, $1,553 per credit out-of-state (summer). *Financial support:* Fellowships with full and partial tuition reimbursements, research assistantships with full and partial tuition reimbursements, teaching assistantships with full and partial tuition reimbursements, career-related internships or fieldwork, institutionally sponsored loans, scholarships/grants, traineeships, health care benefits, and unspecified assistantships available. Financial award application deadline: 1/15; financial award applicants required to submit FAFSA. *Faculty research:* Telecommunication systems, telecommunications policy, network design and management, wireless information systems, network security, cloud computing, big data. *Unit head:* Dr. Martin Weiss, Program Chair, 412-624-9430, Fax: 412-624-5231, E-mail: mbw@pitt.edu. *Application contact:* Shabana Reza, Enrollment Manager, 412-624-3988, Fax: 412-624-5231, E-mail: sreza@sis.pitt.edu.
Website: http://www.ischool.pitt.edu/tele/

University of Southern California, Graduate School, Viterbi School of Engineering, Daniel J. Epstein Department of Industrial and Systems Engineering, Los Angeles, CA 90089. Offers digital supply chain management (MS); engineering management (MS); engineering technology communication (Graduate Certificate); health systems operations (Graduate Certificate); industrial and systems engineering (MS, PhD, Engr); manufacturing engineering (MS); operations research engineering (MS); optimization and supply chain management (Graduate Certificate); product development engineering (MS); safety systems and security (MS); systems architecting and engineering (MS, Graduate Certificate); systems safety and security (Graduate Certificate); transportation systems (Graduate Certificate); MS/MBA. *Program availability:* Part-time, evening/weekend, online learning. Terminal master's awarded for partial completion of doctoral program. *Degree requirements:* For master's, thesis optional; for doctorate, thesis/dissertation. *Entrance requirements:* For master's and doctorate, GRE General Test. Additional exam requirements/recommendations for international students: Recommended—TOEFL. Electronic applications accepted. *Faculty research:* Health systems, music cognition and retrieval, transportation and logistics, manufacturing and automation, engineering systems design, risk and economic analysis.

University of Southern California, Graduate School, Viterbi School of Engineering, Ming Hsieh Department of Electrical Engineering, Los Angeles, CA 90089. Offers computer engineering (MS, PhD); electric power (MS); electrical engineering (MS, PhD, Engr); engineering technology commercialization (Graduate Certificate); multimedia and creative technologies (MS); telecommunications (MS); VLSI design (MS); wireless health technology (MS). *Program availability:* Part-time, online learning. Terminal master's awarded for partial completion of doctoral program. *Degree requirements:* For master's, thesis optional; for doctorate, thesis/dissertation. *Entrance requirements:* For master's and doctorate, GRE General Test. Additional exam requirements/recommendations for international students: Recommended—TOEFL. Electronic applications accepted. *Faculty research:* Communications, computer engineering and networks, control systems, integrated circuits and systems, electromagnetics and energy conversion, micro electro-mechanical systems and nanotechnology, photonics and quantum electronics, plasma research, signal and image processing.

The University of Texas at Dallas, Erik Jonson School of Engineering and Computer Science, Department of Electrical Engineering, Richardson, TX 75080. Offers computer engineering (MS, PhD); electrical engineering (MSEE, PhD); telecommunications engineering (MSTE, PhD). *Program availability:* Part-time, evening/weekend. *Faculty:*

47 full-time (4 women), 5 part-time/adjunct (0 women). *Students:* 648 full-time (178 women), 196 part-time (50 women); includes 40 minority (1 Black or African American, non-Hispanic/Latino; 23 Asian, non-Hispanic/Latino; 11 Hispanic/Latino; 5 Two or more races, non-Hispanic/Latino), 744 international. Average age 27. 2,663 applicants, 34% accepted, 287 enrolled. In 2016, 292 master's, 41 doctorates awarded. *Degree requirements:* For master's, thesis or major design project; for doctorate, thesis/dissertation. *Entrance requirements:* For master's, GRE General Test, minimum GPA of 3.0 in related bachelor's degree; for doctorate, GRE General Test, minimum GPA of 3.5. Additional exam requirements/recommendations for international students: Required—TOEFL (minimum score 550 paper-based). *Application deadline:* For fall admission, 7/15 for domestic students, 5/1 priority date for international students; for spring admission, 11/15 for domestic students, 9/1 priority date for international students. Applications are processed on a rolling basis. Application fee: $50 ($100 for international students). Electronic applications accepted. *Expenses:* Tuition, state resident: full-time $12,418; part-time $690 per semester hour. Tuition, nonresident: full-time $24,150; part-time $1342 per semester hour. Tuition and fees vary according to course load. *Financial support:* In 2016–17, 234 students received support, including 12 fellowships (averaging $1,267 per year), 128 research assistantships with partial tuition reimbursements available (averaging $23,845 per year), 76 teaching assistantships with partial tuition reimbursements available (averaging $17,289 per year); Federal Work-Study, institutionally sponsored loans, scholarships/grants, unspecified assistantships, and cooperative positions also available. Support available to part-time students. Financial award application deadline: 4/30; financial award applicants required to submit FAFSA. *Faculty research:* Semiconductor device manufacturing, photonics devices and systems, signal processing and language technology, nano-fabrication, energy efficient digital systems. *Unit head:* Dr. Lawrence Overzet, Department Head, 972-883-6755, Fax: 972-883-2710, E-mail: overzet@utdallas.edu. *Application contact:* 972-883-6755, Fax: 972-883-2710, E-mail: eegrad_assist@utdallas.edu.
Website: http://www.ee.utdallas.edu

Telecommunications Management

Alaska Pacific University, Graduate Programs, Business Administration Department, Programs in Information and Communication Technology, Anchorage, AK 99508-4672. Offers MBAICT. *Program availability:* Part-time, evening/weekend. *Degree requirements:* For master's, capstone course. *Entrance requirements:* For master's, GMAT or GRE General Test, minimum GPA of 3.0.

Boston University, Metropolitan College, Department of Computer Science, Boston, MA 02215. Offers computer information systems (MS), including computer networks, data analytics, database management and business intelligence, health informatics, IT project management, security, Web application development; computer networks (Certificate); computer science (MS); data analytics (Certificate); digital forensics (Certificate); health informatics (Certificate); information technology project management (Certificate); software development (MS); software engineering in health care systems (Certificate); telecommunications (MS), including security. *Program availability:* Part-time, evening/weekend, online learning. *Faculty:* 13 full-time (3 women), 43 part-time/adjunct (3 women). *Students:* 108 full-time (36 women), 1,294 part-time (364 women); includes 428 minority (115 Black or African American, non-Hispanic/Latino; 2 American Indian or Alaska Native, non-Hispanic/Latino; 187 Asian, non-Hispanic/Latino; 98 Hispanic/Latino; 2 Native Hawaiian or other Pacific Islander, non-Hispanic/Latino; 24 Two or more races, non-Hispanic/Latino), 314 international. Average age 33. 463 applicants, 79% accepted, 248 enrolled. In 2016, 311 master's awarded. *Degree requirements:* For master's, thesis optional. *Entrance requirements:* For master's and Certificate, official transcripts from regionally-accredited bachelor's degree program, 3 letters of recommendation, professional resume, personal statement. Additional exam requirements/recommendations for international students: Required—TOEFL (minimum score 84 iBT), IELTS. *Application deadline:* For fall admission, 6/1 priority date for international students; for spring admission, 10/1 priority date for international students. Applications are processed on a rolling basis. Application fee: $85. Electronic applications accepted. *Expenses:* Contact institution. *Financial support:* In 2016–17, 11 research assistantships (averaging $8,400 per year) were awarded; unspecified assistantships also available. Support available to part-time students. Financial award applicants required to submit FAFSA. *Faculty research:* Medical informatics, Web technologies, telecom and networks, security and forensics, software engineering, programming languages, multimedia and artificial intelligence (AI), information systems and IT project management. *Unit head:* Dr. Anatoly Temkin, Chair, 617-353-2566, Fax: 617-353-2367, E-mail: csinfo@bu.edu. *Application contact:* Lesley Moreau, Academic Program Coordinator, 617-353-2566, Fax: 617-353-2367, E-mail: metcs@bu.edu. Website: http://www.bu.edu/csmet/

California Miramar University, Program in Telecommunications Management, San Diego, CA 92108. Offers MST.

Capitol Technology University, Graduate Programs, Laurel, MD 20708-9759. Offers business administration (MBA); computer science (MS); electrical engineering (MS); information and telecommunications systems management (MS); information architecture (MS); network security (MS). *Program availability:* Part-time, evening/weekend, online learning. *Entrance requirements:* For master's, minimum GPA of 3.0. Electronic applications accepted.

Carnegie Mellon University, Carnegie Institute of Technology, Information Networking Institute, Pittsburgh, PA 15213. Offers information networking (MS); information security (MS); information technology - information security (MS); information technology - mobility (MS); information technology - software management (MS). *Degree requirements:* For master's, thesis optional. *Entrance requirements:* For master's, GRE General Test, bachelor's degree in computer science, computer engineering, or electrical engineering, or related technology degree; programming skills (C/C++ fluency for some programs). Additional exam requirements/recommendations for international students: Required—TOEFL. *Faculty research:* Computer forensics and incident response; dependable systems, embedded systems, mobile systems, and sensor networks; computer and information networks, network and information security, human and socio-economic factors in secure system design; wireless sensor networks, survivable embedded systems, signal processing/compression; strategic management, international strategic management, group dynamics and decision-making structures, simulated competitive environments.

Concordia University, School of Graduate Studies, Faculty of Engineering and Computer Science, Concordia Institute for Information Systems Engineering (CIISE), Montréal, QC H3G 1M8, Canada. Offers 3D graphics and game development (Certificate); information and systems engineering (PhD); information systems security (M Eng, MA Sc); quality systems engineering (M Eng, MA Sc); service engineering and network management (Certificate).

East Carolina University, Graduate School, College of Engineering and Technology, Department of Technology Systems, Greenville, NC 27858-4353. Offers computer network professional (Certificate); information assurance (Certificate); Lean Six Sigma Black Belt (Certificate); network technology (MS), including computer networking management, digital communications technology, information security, Web technologies; occupational safety (MS); technology management (PhD); technology systems (MS), including industrial distribution and logistics, manufacturing systems, performance improvement, quality systems; Website developer (Certificate). *Students:* 23 full-time (1 woman), 199 part-time (55 women); includes 59 minority (39 Black or African American, non-Hispanic/Latino; 3 American Indian or Alaska Native, non-Hispanic/Latino; 4 Asian, non-Hispanic/Latino; 10 Hispanic/Latino; 3 Two or more races, non-Hispanic/Latino), 5 international. Average age 38. 85 applicants, 87% accepted, 61 enrolled. In 2016, 23 master's awarded. *Entrance requirements:* For master's and Certificate, GRE General Test or MAT, minimum GPA of 2.5; for doctorate, GRE General Test, related work experience. *Application deadline:* For fall admission, 6/1 priority date for domestic students. Applications are processed on a rolling basis. Application fee: $50. *Financial support:* Application deadline: 6/1. *Unit head:* Dr. Tijjani Mohammed, Chair, 252-328-9668, E-mail: mohammedt@ecu.edu. *Application contact:* Dean of Graduate School, 252-328-6012, Fax: 252-328-6071, E-mail: gradschool@ecu.edu.

Instituto Tecnológico y de Estudios Superiores de Monterrey, Campus Ciudad de México, School of Design, Engineering and Architecture, Ciudad de Mexico, Mexico. Offers management (MA); telecommunications (MA). *Program availability:* Part-time, evening/weekend, online learning. *Faculty research:* Telecommunications; informatics; technology development; computer systems.

Instituto Tecnológico y de Estudios Superiores de Monterrey, Campus Ciudad Obregón, Program in Administration of Telecommunications, Ciudad Obregón, Mexico. Offers MAT.

Instituto Tecnológico y de Estudios Superiores de Monterrey, Campus Estado de México, Professional and Graduate Division, Estado de Mexico, Mexico. Offers administration of information technologies (MITA); architecture (M Arch); business administration (GMBA, MBA); computer sciences (MCS, PhD); education (M Ed); educational institution administration (MAD); educational technology and innovation (PhD); electronic commerce (MEC); environmental systems (MS); finance (MAF); humanistic studies (MHS); information sciences and knowledge management (MISKM); information systems (MS); manufacturing systems (MS); marketing (MEM); quality systems and productivity (MS); science and materials engineering (PhD); telecommunications management (MTM). *Program availability:* Part-time, online learning. *Degree requirements:* For master's, one foreign language, thesis (for some programs); for doctorate, one foreign language, thesis/dissertation. *Entrance requirements:* For master's, E-PAEP 500, interview; for doctorate, E-PAEP 500, research proposal. Additional exam requirements/recommendations for international students: Required—TOEFL (minimum score 550 paper-based). *Faculty research:* Surface treatments by plasmas, mechanical properties, robotics, graphical computing, mechatronics security protocols.

Instituto Tecnológico y de Estudios Superiores de Monterrey, Campus Irapuato, Graduate Programs, Irapuato, Mexico. Offers administration (MBA); administration of information technology (MAIT); administration of telecommunications (MAT); architecture (M Arch); computer science (MCS); education (M Ed); educational administration (MEA); educational innovation and technology (DEIT); educational technology (MET); electronic commerce (MBA); environmental administration and planning (MEAP); environmental systems (MES); finances (MBA); humanistic studies (MHS); international management for Latin American executives (MIMLAE); library and information science (MLIS); manufacturing quality management (MMQM); marketing research (MBA).

Murray State University, College of Business and Public Affairs, Program in Telecommunications Systems Management, Murray, KY 42071. Offers MS. *Entrance requirements:* For master's, GMAT or GRE. Additional exam requirements/recommendations for international students: Required—TOEFL. *Faculty research:* Network security, emergency management communications, network economies.

New York University, Polytechnic School of Engineering, Department of Technology Management, New York, NY 10012-1019. Offers construction management (Advanced Certificate); electronic business management (Advanced Certificate); entrepreneurship (Advanced Certificate); human resources management (Advanced Certificate); industrial engineering (MS); information management (Advanced Certificate); management (MS); management of technology (MS); manufacturing engineering (MS); organizational behavior (MS, Advanced Certificate); project management (Advanced Certificate); technology management (MBA, PhD, Advanced Certificate); telecommunications management (Advanced Certificate). *Program availability:* Part-time, evening/weekend. *Degree requirements:* For master's, comprehensive exam (for some programs), thesis (for some programs); for doctorate, comprehensive exam, thesis/dissertation. *Entrance requirements:* For master's, GMAT, minimum B average in undergraduate course work. Additional exam requirements/recommendations for international students: Required—TOEFL (minimum score 550 paper-based; 80 iBT); Recommended—IELTS (minimum score 6.5). Electronic applications accepted. *Faculty research:* Global innovation and research and development strategy, managing emerging technologies, technology and development, service design and innovation, tech entrepreneurship and commercialization, sustainable and clean-tech innovation, impacts of information technology upon individuals, organizations and society.

Oklahoma State University, Graduate College, Stillwater, OK 74078. Offers aerospace security (Graduate Certificate); bioenergy and sustainable technology (Graduate Certificate); business data mining (Graduate Certificate); business sustainability (Graduate Certificate); environmental science (MS); international studies (MS); non-profit management (Graduate Certificate); teaching English to speakers of other languages (Graduate Certificate); telecommunications management (MS). Programs are interdisciplinary. *Students:* 50 full-time (28 women), 109 part-time (63 women); includes 23 minority (4 Black or African American, non-Hispanic/Latino; 5 American Indian or Alaska Native, non-Hispanic/Latino; 4 Asian, non-Hispanic/Latino; 4 Hispanic/Latino; 6 Two or more races, non-Hispanic/Latino), 58 international. Average age 29. 363 applicants, 81% accepted, 71 enrolled. In 2016, 56 master's, 9 doctorates awarded. *Degree requirements:* For master's, thesis (for some programs); for doctorate, comprehensive exam, thesis/dissertation. *Entrance requirements:* For master's and doctorate, GRE or GMAT. Additional exam requirements/recommendations for

international students: Required—TOEFL (minimum score 550 paper-based; 79 iBT). *Application deadline:* For fall admission, 3/1 priority date for domestic and international students; for spring admission, 8/1 priority date for domestic and international students. Applications are processed on a rolling basis. Application fee: $40 ($75 for international students). Electronic applications accepted. *Expenses:* Tuition, state resident: full-time $3775; part-time $209.70 per credit hour. Tuition, nonresident: full-time $14,851; part-time $825.05 per credit hour. *Required fees:* $2027; $112.60 per credit hour. Tuition and fees vary according to campus/location. *Financial support:* Research assistantships, career-related internships or fieldwork, Federal Work-Study, scholarships/grants, health care benefits, tuition waivers (partial), and unspecified assistantships available. Support available to part-time students. Financial award application deadline: 3/1; financial award applicants required to submit FAFSA. *Unit head:* Dr. Sheryl Tucker, Dean, 405-744-6368, Fax: 405-744-0355, E-mail: gradi@okstate.edu. *Application contact:* Dr. Susan Mathew, Assistant Director of Graduate Admissions, 405-744-6368, Fax: 405-744-0355, E-mail: gradi@okstate.edu.
Website: http://gradcollege.okstate.edu/

Oklahoma State University, Spears School of Business, Department of Management Science and Information Systems, Stillwater, OK 74078. Offers management information systems (MS); management science and information systems (PhD); telecommunications management (MS). *Program availability:* Part-time, online learning. *Faculty:* 21 full-time (1 woman), 5 part-time/adjunct (2 women). *Students:* 95 full-time (20 women), 67 part-time (19 women); includes 14 minority (1 Black or African American, non-Hispanic/Latino; 2 American Indian or Alaska Native, non-Hispanic/Latino; 3 Asian, non-Hispanic/Latino; 4 Hispanic/Latino; 1 Native Hawaiian or other Pacific Islander, non-Hispanic/Latino; 3 Two or more races, non-Hispanic/Latino), 112 international. Average age 28. 779 applicants, 12% accepted, 56 enrolled. In 2016, 89 master's, 1 doctorate awarded. *Degree requirements:* For master's, thesis or alternative; for doctorate, comprehensive exam, thesis/dissertation. *Entrance requirements:* For master's and doctorate, GRE or GMAT. Additional exam requirements/recommendations for international students: Required—TOEFL (minimum score 550 paper-based; 79 iBT). *Application deadline:* For fall admission, 3/1 priority date for international students; for spring admission, 8/1 priority date for international students. Applications are processed on a rolling basis. Application fee: $40 ($75 for international students). Electronic applications accepted. *Expenses:* Tuition, state resident: full-time $3775; part-time $209.70 per credit hour. Tuition, nonresident: full-time $14,851; part-time $825.05 per credit hour. *Required fees:* $2027; $112.60 per credit hour. Tuition and fees vary according to campus/location. *Financial support:* In 2016–17, 2 research assistantships (averaging $5,500 per year), 18 teaching assistantships (averaging $8,542 per year) were awarded; career-related internships or fieldwork, Federal Work-Study, scholarships/grants, health care benefits, tuition waivers (partial), and unspecified assistantships also available. Support available to part-time students. Financial award application deadline: 3/1; financial award applicants required to submit FAFSA. *Unit head:* Dr. Rick Wilson, Department Head, 405-744-3551, Fax: 405-744-5180, E-mail: rick.wilson@okstate.edu. *Application contact:* Dr. Rathin Sarathy, Graduate Coordinator, 405-744-8646, Fax: 405-744-5180, E-mail: rathin.sarathy@okstate.edu.
Website: http://spears.okstate.edu/msis

San Diego State University, Graduate and Research Affairs, College of Professional Studies and Fine Arts, School of Communication, San Diego, CA 92182. Offers advertising and public relations (MA); critical-cultural studies (MA); interaction studies (MA); intercultural and international studies (MA); new media studies (MA); news and information studies (MA); telecommunications and media management (MA). *Degree requirements:* For master's, thesis. *Entrance requirements:* For master's, GRE General Test, 3 letters of recommendation. Additional exam requirements/recommendations for international students: Required—TOEFL. Electronic applications accepted.

Stevens Institute of Technology, Graduate School, School of Business, Doctoral Program in Technology Management, Hoboken, NJ 07030. Offers information management (PhD); technology management (PhD); telecommunications management (PhD). *Program availability:* Part-time, evening/weekend, online learning. *Students:* 10 full-time (3 women), 4 part-time (1 woman); includes 1 minority (American Indian or Alaska Native, non-Hispanic/Latino), 10 international. Average age 30. In 2016, 1 doctorate awarded. *Degree requirements:* For doctorate, comprehensive exam (for some programs), thesis/dissertation. *Entrance requirements:* Additional exam requirements/recommendations for international students: Required—TOEFL (minimum score 74 iBT), IELTS (minimum score 6). *Application deadline:* For fall admission, 6/1 for domestic students, 4/15 for international students; for spring admission, 11/30 for domestic students, 11/1 for international students. Applications are processed on a rolling basis. Application fee: $65. Electronic applications accepted. *Expenses:* Contact institution. *Financial support:* Fellowships, research assistantships, teaching assistantships, career-related internships or fieldwork, Federal Work-Study, scholarships/grants, and unspecified assistantships available. Financial award application deadline: 2/15; financial award applicants required to submit FAFSA. *Unit head:* Dr. Thomas Lechler, Director, 201-216-8174, Fax: 201-216-5385, E-mail: tlechler@stevens.edu. *Application contact:* Graduate Admissions, 888-783-8367, Fax: 888-511-1306, E-mail: graduate@stevens.edu.
Website: https://www.stevens.edu/school-business/phd-business-administration

Stevens Institute of Technology, Graduate School, School of Business, Program in Business Administration, Hoboken, NJ 07030. Offers business intelligence and analytics (MBA); engineering management (MBA); finance (MBA); information systems (MBA); innovation and entrepreneurship (MBA); marketing (MBA); pharmaceutical management (MBA); project management (MBA, Certificate); technology management (MBA); telecommunications management (MBA). *Accreditation:* AACSB. *Program availability:* Part-time, evening/weekend. *Students:* 35 full-time (15 women), 181 part-time (79 women); includes 53 minority (10 Black or African American, non-Hispanic/Latino; 2 American Indian or Alaska Native, non-Hispanic/Latino; 36 Asian, non-Hispanic/Latino; 5 Hispanic/Latino), 30 international. Average age 32. 215 applicants, 53% accepted, 61 enrolled. In 2016, 61 master's awarded. *Degree requirements:* For master's, thesis optional, minimum B average in major field and overall; for Certificate, minimum B average. *Entrance requirements:* Additional exam requirements/recommendations for international students: Required—TOEFL (minimum score 74 iBT), IELTS (minimum score 6). *Application deadline:* For fall admission, 6/1 for domestic students, 4/15 for international students; for spring admission, 11/30 for domestic students, 11/1 for international students. Applications are processed on a rolling basis. Application fee: $65. Electronic applications accepted. *Expenses:* Contact institution. *Financial support:* Fellowships, research assistantships, teaching assistantships, career-related internships or fieldwork, Federal Work-Study, scholarships/grants, and unspecified assistantships available. Financial award application deadline: 2/15; financial award applicants required to submit FAFSA. *Unit head:* Dr. Gregory Prastacos, Dean, 201-216-8366, E-mail: gprastac@stevens.edu. *Application contact:* Graduate Admissions, 888-783-8367, Fax: 888-511-1306, E-mail: graduate@stevens.edu.
Website: https://www.stevens.edu/school-business/masters-programs/mbaemba

Stevens Institute of Technology, Graduate School, School of Business, Program in Information Systems, Hoboken, NJ 07030. Offers computer science (MS); e-commerce

(MS); enterprise systems (MS); entrepreneurial information technology (MS); information architecture (MS); information management (MS, Certificate); information security (MS); information technology in financial services industry (MS); information technology in the pharmaceutical industry (MS); information technology outsourcing management (MS); project management (MS, Certificate); software engineering (MS); telecommunications (MS). *Program availability:* Part-time, evening/weekend. *Students:* 280 full-time (100 women), 84 part-time (21 women); includes 23 minority (9 Black or African American, non-Hispanic/Latino; 13 Asian, non-Hispanic/Latino; 1 Hispanic/Latino), 283 international. Average age 26. 925 applicants, 62% accepted, 114 enrolled. In 2016, 212 master's, 32 other advanced degrees awarded. *Degree requirements:* For master's, thesis optional, minimum B average in major field and overall; for Certificate, minimum B average. *Entrance requirements:* Additional exam requirements/recommendations for international students: Required—TOEFL (minimum score 74 iBT), IELTS (minimum score 6). *Application deadline:* For fall admission, 6/1 for domestic students, 4/15 for international students; for spring admission, 11/30 for domestic students, 11/1 for international students. Applications are processed on a rolling basis. Application fee: $65. Electronic applications accepted. *Expenses:* Contact institution. *Financial support:* Fellowships, research assistantships, teaching assistantships, career-related internships or fieldwork, Federal Work-Study, scholarships/grants, and unspecified assistantships available. Financial award application deadline: 2/15; financial award applicants required to submit FAFSA. *Unit head:* Dr. Gregory Prastacos, Dean, 201-216-8366, E-mail: gprastac@stevens.edu. *Application contact:* Graduate Admissions, 888-783-8367, Fax: 888-511-1306, E-mail: graduate@stevens.edu.
Website: https://www.stevens.edu/school-business/masters-programs/information-systems

Stevens Institute of Technology, Graduate School, School of Business, Program in Network and Communication Management and Services, Hoboken, NJ 07030. Offers MS. *Program availability:* Part-time, evening/weekend. *Students:* 16 full-time (3 women), 22 part-time (3 women); includes 11 minority (3 Black or African American, non-Hispanic/Latino; 1 American Indian or Alaska Native, non-Hispanic/Latino; 6 Asian, non-Hispanic/Latino; 1 Hispanic/Latino), 14 international. Average age 33. 37 applicants, 68% accepted, 13 enrolled. In 2016, 11 master's awarded. *Degree requirements:* For master's, thesis optional, minimum B average in major field and overall. *Entrance requirements:* Additional exam requirements/recommendations for international students: Required—TOEFL (minimum score 74 iBT), IELTS (minimum score 6). *Application deadline:* For fall admission, 6/1 for domestic students, 4/15 for international students; for spring admission, 9/30 for domestic students, 9/1 for international students. Application fee: $65. *Expenses:* Contact institution. *Financial support:* Fellowships, research assistantships, teaching assistantships, career-related internships or fieldwork, Federal Work-Study, scholarships/grants, and unspecified assistantships available. Financial award application deadline: 2/15; financial award applicants required to submit FAFSA. *Unit head:* Dr. Gregory Prastacos, Dean, 201-216-8366, E-mail: gprastac@stevens.edu. *Application contact:* Graduate Admissions, 888-793-8367, Fax: 888-511-1306, E-mail: graduate@stevens.edu.
Website: http://www.stevens.edu/school-business/masters-programs/network-communication-management-services

Stevens Institute of Technology, Graduate School, School of Business, Program in Telecommunications Management, Hoboken, NJ 07030. Offers business (MS); global innovation management (MS); management of wireless networks (MS); online security, technology and business (MS); project management (MS); technical management (MS); telecommunications management (PhD, Certificate). *Program availability:* Part-time, evening/weekend. *Students:* 1 full-time (0 women), 38 part-time (8 women); includes 5 minority (3 Black or African American, non-Hispanic/Latino; 2 Asian, non-Hispanic/Latino), 1 international. Average age 38. In 2016, 14 master's, 2 other advanced degrees awarded. *Degree requirements:* For master's, thesis optional, minimum B average in major field and overall; for doctorate, comprehensive exam (for some programs), thesis/dissertation; for Certificate, minimum B average. *Entrance requirements:* Additional exam requirements/recommendations for international students: Required—TOEFL (minimum score 74 iBT), IELTS (minimum score 6). *Application deadline:* For fall admission, 6/1 for domestic students, 4/15 for international students; for spring admission, 11/30 for domestic students, 11/1 for international students. Applications are processed on a rolling basis. Application fee: $65. Electronic applications accepted. *Expenses:* Contact institution. *Financial support:* Fellowships, research assistantships, teaching assistantships, career-related internships or fieldwork, Federal Work-Study, scholarships/grants, health care benefits, and unspecified assistantships available. Financial award application deadline: 2/15; financial award applicants required to submit FAFSA. *Unit head:* Dr. Gregory Prastacos, Dean, 201-216-8366, E-mail: gprastac@stevens.edu. *Application contact:* Graduate Admission, 888-783-8367, Fax: 888-511-1306, E-mail: graduate@stevens.edu.
Website: https://www.stevens.edu/school-business/masters-programs/network-communication-management-services

Strayer University, Graduate Studies, Washington, DC 20005-2603. Offers accounting (MS); acquisition (MBA); business administration (MBA); communications technology (MS); educational management (M Ed); finance (MBA); health services administration (MHSA); hospitality and tourism management (MBA); human resource management (MBA); information systems (MS), including computer security management, decision support system management, enterprise resource management, network management, software engineering management, systems development management; management (MBA); management information systems (MS); marketing (MBA); professional accounting (MS), including accounting information systems, controllership, taxation; public administration (MPA); supply chain management (MBA); technology in education (M Ed). Programs also offered at campus locations in Birmingham, AL; Chamblee, GA; Cobb County, GA; Morrow, GA; White Marsh, MD; Charleston, SC; Columbia, SC; Greensboro, NC; Greenville, SC; Lexington, KY; Louisville, KY; Nashville, TN; North Raleigh, NC; Washington, DC. *Accreditation:* ACBSP. *Program availability:* Part-time, evening/weekend, online learning. *Degree requirements:* For master's, thesis. *Entrance requirements:* For master's, GMAT, GRE General Test, bachelor's degree from an accredited college or university, minimum undergraduate GPA of 2.75. Electronic applications accepted.

University of Colorado Boulder, Graduate School, College of Engineering and Applied Science, Interdisciplinary Telecommunications Program, Boulder, CO 80309. Offers MS, JD/MS, MBA/MS. *Students:* 145 full-time (48 women), 9 part-time (0 women); includes 7 minority (2 Black or African American, non-Hispanic/Latino; 2 Asian, non-Hispanic/Latino; 2 Hispanic/Latino; 1 Two or more races, non-Hispanic/Latino), 127 international. Average age 27. 247 applicants, 48% accepted, 49 enrolled. In 2016, 53 master's awarded. Terminal master's awarded for partial completion of doctoral program. *Degree requirements:* For master's, comprehensive exam, thesis or alternative. *Entrance requirements:* For master's, minimum undergraduate GPA of 3.0. *Application deadline:* For fall admission, 1/30 for domestic and international students; for spring admission, 11/1 for domestic students, 10/1 for international students. Applications are processed on a rolling basis. Application fee: $60 ($80 for international students). Electronic applications accepted. Application fee is waived when completed online. *Financial support:* In 2016–17, 224 students received support, including 106

Telecommunications Management

fellowships (averaging $4,721 per year), 5 research assistantships with full and partial tuition reimbursements available (averaging $49,616 per year), 5 teaching assistantships with full and partial tuition reimbursements available (averaging $38,777 per year); institutionally sponsored loans, scholarships/grants, health care benefits, and unspecified assistantships also available. Financial award applicants required to submit FAFSA. *Faculty research:* Technology, planning, and management of telecommunications systems. *Application contact:* E-mail: itp@colorado.edu. Website: http://engineeringanywhere.colorado.edu/itp/

University of South Africa, College of Human Sciences, Pretoria, South Africa. Offers adult education (M Ed); African languages (MA, PhD); African politics (MA, PhD); Afrikaans (MA, PhD); ancient history (MA, PhD); ancient Near Eastern studies (MA, PhD); anthropology (MA, PhD); applied linguistics (MA); Arabic (MA, PhD); archaeology (MA); art history (MA); Biblical archaeology (MA); Biblical studies (M Th, D Th, PhD); Christian spirituality (M Th, D Th); church history (M Th, D Th); classical studies (MA, PhD); clinical psychology (MA); communication (MA, PhD); comparative education (M Ed, Ed D); consulting psychology (D Admin, D Com, PhD); curriculum studies (M Ed, Ed D); development studies (M Admin, MA, D Admin, PhD); didactics (M Ed, Ed D); education (M Tech); education management (M Ed, Ed D); educational psychology (M Ed); English (MA); environmental education (M Ed); French (MA, PhD); German (MA, PhD); Greek (MA); guidance and counseling (M Ed); health studies (MA, PhD), including health sciences education (MA), health services management (MA), medical and surgical nursing science (critical care general) (MA), midwifery and neonatal nursing science (MA), trauma and emergency care (MA); history (MA, PhD); history of education (Ed D); inclusive education (M Ed, Ed D); information and communications technology policy and regulation (MA); information science (MA, MIS, PhD); international politics (MA, PhD); Islamic studies (MA, PhD); Italian (MA, PhD); Judaica (MA, PhD); linguistics (MA, PhD); mathematical education (M Ed); mathematics education (MA); missiology (M Th, D Th); modern Hebrew (MA, PhD); musicology (MA, MMus, D Mus, PhD); natural science education (M Ed); New Testament (M Th, D Th); Old Testament (D Th); pastoral therapy (M Th, D Th); philosophy (MA); philosophy of education (M Ed, Ed D); politics (MA, PhD); Portuguese (MA, PhD); practical theology (M Th, D Th); psychology (MA, MS, PhD); psychology of education (M Ed, Ed D); public health (MA); religious studies (MA, D Th, PhD); Romance languages (MA); Russian (MA, PhD); Semitic languages (MA, PhD); social behavior studies in HIV/AIDS (MA); social science (mental health) (MA); social science in development studies (MA); social science in psychology (MA); social science in social work (MA); social science in sociology (MA); social work (MSW, DSW, PhD); socio-education (M Ed, Ed D); sociolinguistics (MA); sociology (MA, PhD); Spanish (MA, PhD); systematic theology (M Th, D Th); TESOL (teaching English to speakers of other languages) (MA); theological ethics (M Th, D Th); theory of literature (MA, PhD); urban ministries (D Th); urban ministry (M Th).

University of Wisconsin–Stout, Graduate School, College of Science, Technology, Engineering and Mathematics, Program in Information and Communication Technologies, Menomonie, WI 54751. Offers MS. *Program availability:* Part-time, online learning. *Degree requirements:* For master's, thesis. *Entrance requirements:* For master's, minimum GPA of 2.75. Additional exam requirements/recommendations for international students: Required—TOEFL (minimum score 500 paper-based; 61 iBT). Electronic applications accepted.

APPENDIXES

Institutional Changes
Since the 2017 Edition

Following is an alphabetical listing of institutions that have recently closed, merged with other institutions, or changed their names or status. In the case of a name change, the former name appears first, followed by the new name.

Alliant International University–México City (Mexico City, Mexico): *closed.*

The American College (Bryn Mawr, PA): *name changed to The American College of Financial Services.*

Andover Newton Theological School (Newton Centre, MA): *now affiliated with Yale Divinity School.*

Argosy University, Washington DC (Arlington, VA): *name changed to Argosy University, Northern Virginia.*

The Art Institute of Dallas, a campus of South University (Dallas, TX): *name changed to The Art Institute of Dallas, a branch of Miami International University of Art & Design.*

Bard Graduate Center: Decorative Arts, Design History, Material Culture (New York, NY): *name changed to Bard Graduate Center.*

Bexley Hall Episcopal Seminary (Columbus, OH): *merged into a single entry for Bexley Seabury Seminary (Chicago, IL).*

Blessing-Rieman College of Nursing (Quincy, IL): *name changed to Blessing-Rieman College of Nursing & Health Sciences.*

California Maritime Academy (Vallejo, CA): *name changed to California State University Maritime Academy.*

California National University for Advanced Studies (Northridge, CA): *closed.*

California School of Podiatric Medicine at Samuel Merritt University (Oakland, CA): *merged as a unit into Samuel Merritt University (Oakland, CA).*

Calvary Bible College and Theological Seminary (Kansas City, MO): *name changed to Calvary University.*

Carolina Graduate School of Divinity (Greensboro, NC): *closed.*

Centenary College (Hackettstown, NJ): *name changed to Centenary University.*

Charlotte School of Law (Charlotte, NC): *will not be enrolling new students for the fall 2017 term.*

Colorado Heights University (Denver, CO): *closed.*

Colorado Technical University Denver South (Aurora, CO): *name changed to Colorado Technical University Aurora.*

The Commonwealth Medical College (Scranton, PA): *name changed to Geisinger Commonwealth School of Medicine.*

Connecticut College (New London, CT): *will not be accepting graduate program applications for the 2017-18 academic year.*

Daniel Webster College (Nashua, NH): *merged into Southern New Hampshire University (Manchester, NH).*

DeVry College of New York (New York, NY): *name changed to DeVry College of New York–Midtown Manhattan Campus.*

DeVry University (Glendale, AZ): *now a DeVry University center and no longer profiled separately.*

DeVry University (Mesa, AZ): *now a DeVry University center and no longer profiled separately.*

DeVry University (Phoenix, AZ): *name changed to DeVry University–Phoenix Campus.*

DeVry University (Alhambra, CA): *closed.*

DeVry University (Anaheim, CA): *now a DeVry University center and no longer profiled separately.*

DeVry University (Fremont, CA): *name changed to DeVry University–Fremont Campus.*

DeVry University (Long Beach, CA): *name changed to DeVry University–Long Beach Campus.*

DeVry University (Oakland, CA): *now a DeVry University center and no longer profiled separately.*

DeVry University (Oxnard, CA): *closed.*

DeVry University (Palmdale, CA): *now a DeVry University center and no longer profiled separately.*

DeVry University (Pomona, CA): *name changed to DeVry University–Pomona Campus.*

DeVry University (San Diego, CA): *name changed to DeVry University–San Diego Campus.*

DeVry University (Colorado Springs, CO): *now a DeVry University center and no longer profiled separately.*

DeVry University (Jacksonville, FL): *name changed to DeVry University–Jacksonville Campus.*

DeVry University (Miramar, FL): *name changed to DeVry University–Miramar Campus.*

DeVry University (Orlando, FL): *name changed to DeVry University–Orlando Campus.*

DeVry University (Alpharetta, GA): *name changed to DeVry University–Alpharetta Campus.*

DeVry University (Decatur, GA): *name changed to DeVry University–Decatur Campus.*

DeVry University (Duluth, GA): *now a DeVry University center and no longer profiled separately.*

DeVry University (Chicago, IL): *name changed to DeVry University–Chicago Campus.*

DeVry University (Downers Grove, IL): *now a DeVry University center and no longer profiled separately.*

DeVry University (Elgin, IL): *now a DeVry University center and no longer profiled separately.*

DeVry University (Gurnee, IL): *now a DeVry University center and no longer profiled separately.*

DeVry University (Naperville, IL): *now a DeVry University center and no longer profiled separately.*

DeVry University (Tinley Park, IL): *name changed to DeVry University–Tinley Park Campus.*

DeVry University (Merrillville, IN): *now a DeVry University center and no longer profiled separately.*

DeVry University (Henderson, NV): *name changed to DeVry University–Henderson Campus.*

DeVry University (North Brunswick, NJ): *name changed to DeVry University–North Brunswick Campus.*

DeVry University (Paramus, NJ): *now a DeVry University center and no longer profiled separately.*

DeVry University (Charlotte, NC): *name changed to DeVry University–Charlotte Campus.*

DeVry University (Columbus, OH): *name changed to DeVry University–Columbus Campus.*

DeVry University (Seven Hills, OH): *name changed to DeVry University–Seven Hills Campus.*

DeVry University (Fort Washington, PA): *name changed to DeVry University–Ft. Washington Campus.*

DeVry University (King of Prussia, PA): *closed.*

DeVry University (Nashville, TN): *name changed to DeVry University–Nashville Campus.*

DeVry University (Irving, TX): *name changed to DeVry University–Irving Campus.*

DeVry University (Arlington, VA): *name changed to DeVry University–Arlington Campus.*

DeVry University (Chesapeake, VA): *name changed to DeVry University–Chesapeake Campus.*

DeVry University (Manassas, VA): *closed.*

Ellis University (Oakbrook Terrace, IL): *closed.*

Everest University (Largo, FL): *closed.*

Everest University (Largo, FL): *closed.*

Everest University (Orlando, FL): *closed.*

Frank Lloyd Wright School of Architecture (Scottsdale, AZ): *name changed to School of Architecture at Taliesin.*

Hillsdale Free Will Baptist College (Moore, OK): *name changed to Randall University.*

Houston College of Law (Houston, TX): *name changed to South Texas College of Law Houston.*

Humphreys College (Stockton, CA): *name changed to Humphreys University.*

ITT Technical Institute (Indianapolis, IN): *closed.*

John Marshall Law School (Chicago, IL): *name changed to The John Marshall Law School.*

Lakehead University–Orillia (Orillia, ON, Canada): *name changed to Lakehead University.*

Long Island University–Hudson at Rockland (Orangeburg, NY): *merged into a single entry for Long Island University–Hudson (Purchase, NY) by request from the institution.*

Mary Baldwin College (Staunton, VA): *name changed to Mary Baldwin University.*

The Master's College and Seminary (Santa Clarita, CA): *name changed to The Master's University.*

Mayo Graduate School (Rochester, MN): *name changed to Mayo Clinic Graduate School of Biomedical Sciences.*

Mayo Medical School (Rochester, MN): *name changed to Mayo Clinic School of Medicine.*

Mayo School of Health Sciences (Rochester, MN): *name changed to Mayo Clinic School of Health Sciences.*

National College of Natural Medicine (Portland, OR): *name changed to National University of Natural Medicine.*

Oregon College of Art & Craft (Portland, OR): *name changed to Oregon College of Art and Craft.*

Our Lady of the Lake University of San Antonio (San Antonio, TX): *name changed to Our Lady of the Lake University.*

Phillips Graduate Institute (Encino, CA): *name changed to Phillips Graduate University.*

Pinchot University (Seattle, WA): *acquired by Presidio Graduate School (San Francisco, CA).*

Purdue University Northwest (Westville, IN): *merged into a single entry for Purdue University Northwest (Hammond, IN).*

Rabbi Isaac Elchanan Theological Seminary (New York, NY): *merged into Yeshiva University (New York, NY).*

Saint Joseph's College (Rensselaer, IN): *closed.*

School of the Museum of Fine Arts, Boston (Boston, MA): *merged as a unit into Tufts University (Medford, MA).*

Seabury-Western Theological Seminary (Evanston, IL): *name changed to Bexley Seabury Seminary.*

Seminary of the Immaculate Conception (Huntington, NY): *no longer degree granting.*

Summit University (Clarks Summit, PA): *name changed to Clarks Summit University.*

Tennessee Wesleyan College (Athens, TN): *name changed to Tennessee Wesleyan University.*

Texas A&M University at Galveston (Galveston, TX): *merged as a unit into Texas A&M University (College Station, TX).*

Waldorf College (Forest City, IA): *name changed to Waldorf University*

Abbreviations Used in the Guides

The following list includes abbreviations of degree names used in the profiles in the 2017 edition of the guides. Because some degrees (e.g., Doctor of Education) can be abbreviated in more than one way (e.g., D.Ed. or Ed.D.), and because the abbreviations used in the guides reflect the preferences of the individual colleges and universities, the list may include two or more abbreviations for a single degree.

DEGREES

A Mus D	Doctor of Musical Arts
AC	Advanced Certificate
AD	Artist's Diploma
	Doctor of Arts
ADP	Artist's Diploma
Adv C	Advanced Certificate
AGC	Advanced Graduate Certificate
AGSC	Advanced Graduate Specialist Certificate
ALM	Master of Liberal Arts
AM	Master of Arts
AMBA	Accelerated Master of Business Administration
AMRS	Master of Arts in Religious Studies
APC	Advanced Professional Certificate
APMPH	Advanced Professional Master of Public Health
App Sc	Applied Scientist
App Sc D	Doctor of Applied Science
AstE	Astronautical Engineer
ATC	Advanced Training Certificate
Au D	Doctor of Audiology
B Th	Bachelor of Theology
BN	Bachelor of Naturopathy
CAES	Certificate of Advanced Educational Specialization
CAGS	Certificate of Advanced Graduate Studies
CAL	Certificate in Applied Linguistics
CAPS	Certificate of Advanced Professional Studies
CAS	Certificate of Advanced Studies
CASPA	Certificate of Advanced Study in Public Administration
CASR	Certificate in Advanced Social Research
CATS	Certificate of Achievement in Theological Studies
CBHS	Certificate in Basic Health Sciences
CCJA	Certificate in Criminal Justice Administration
CCTS	Certificate in Clinical and Translational Science
CE	Civil Engineer
CEM	Certificate of Environmental Management
CET	Certificate in Educational Technologies
CGS	Certificate of Graduate Studies
Ch E	Chemical Engineer
Clin Sc D	Doctor of Clinical Science
CM	Certificate in Management
CMH	Certificate in Medical Humanities
CMM	Master of Church Ministries
CMS	Certificate in Ministerial Studies
CNM	Certificate in Nonprofit Management
CPASF	Certificate Program for Advanced Study in Finance
CPC	Certificate in Professional Counseling
	Certificate in Publication and Communication
CPH	Certificate in Public Health
CPM	Certificate in Public Management
CPS	Certificate of Professional Studies
CScD	Doctor of Clinical Science
CSD	Certificate in Spiritual Direction
CSS	Certificate of Special Studies
CTS	Certificate of Theological Studies
CURP	Certificate in Urban and Regional Planning
D Admin	Doctor of Administration
D Arch	Doctor of Architecture
D Be	Doctor in Bioethics
D Com	Doctor of Commerce
D Couns	Doctor of Counseling
D Des	Doctorate of Design
D Div	Doctor of Divinity
D Ed	Doctor of Education
D Ed Min	Doctor of Educational Ministry
D Eng	Doctor of Engineering
D Engr	Doctor of Engineering
D Ent	Doctor of Enterprise
D Env	Doctor of Environment
D Law	Doctor of Law
D Litt	Doctor of Letters
D Med Sc	Doctor of Medical Science
D Min	Doctor of Ministry
D Miss	Doctor of Missiology
D Mus	Doctor of Music
D Mus A	Doctor of Musical Arts
D Phil	Doctor of Philosophy
D Prof	Doctor of Professional Studies
D Ps	Doctor of Psychology
D Sc	Doctor of Science
D Sc D	Doctor of Science in Dentistry
D Sc IS	Doctor of Science in Information Systems
D Sc PA	Doctor of Science in Physician Assistant Studies
D Th	Doctor of Theology
D Th P	Doctor of Practical Theology
DA	Doctor of Accounting
	Doctor of Arts
DAH	Doctor of Arts in Humanities
DAOM	Doctorate in Acupuncture and Oriental Medicine
DAT	Doctorate of Athletic Training
	Professional Doctor of Art Therapy
DBA	Doctor of Business Administration
DBH	Doctor of Behavioral Health
DBL	Doctor of Business Leadership
DC	Doctor of Chiropractic
DCC	Doctor of Computer Science
DCD	Doctor of Communications Design
DCL	Doctor of Civil Law
	Doctor of Comparative Law
DCM	Doctor of Church Music
DCN	Doctor of Clinical Nutrition
DCS	Doctor of Computer Science
DDN	Diplôme du Droit Notarial
DDS	Doctor of Dental Surgery
DE	Doctor of Education
	Doctor of Engineering
DED	Doctor of Economic Development
DEIT	Doctor of Educational Innovation and Technology
DEL	Doctor of Executive Leadership
DEM	Doctor of Educational Ministry
DEPD	Diplôme Études Spécialisées
DES	Doctor of Engineering Science
DESS	Diplôme Études Supérieures Spécialisées
DET	Doctor of Educational Technology
DFA	Doctor of Fine Arts
DGP	Diploma in Graduate and Professional Studies
DH Ed	Doctor of Health Education

DH Sc	Doctor of Health Sciences
DHA	Doctor of Health Administration
DHCE	Doctor of Health Care Ethics
DHL	Doctor of Hebrew Letters
DHPE	Doctorate of Health Professionals Education
DHS	Doctor of Health Science
DHSc	Doctor of Health Science
Dip CS	Diploma in Christian Studies
DIT	Doctor of Industrial Technology
	Doctor of Information Technology
DJS	Doctor of Jewish Studies
DLS	Doctor of Liberal Studies
DM	Doctor of Management
	Doctor of Music
DMA	Doctor of Musical Arts
DMD	Doctor of Dental Medicine
DME	Doctor of Manufacturing Management
	Doctor of Music Education
DMEd	Doctor of Music Education
DMFT	Doctor of Marital and Family Therapy
DMH	Doctor of Medical Humanities
DML	Doctor of Modern Languages
DMP	Doctorate in Medical Physics
DMPNA	Doctor of Management Practice in Nurse Anesthesia
DN Sc	Doctor of Nursing Science
DNAP	Doctor of Nurse Anesthesia Practice
DNP	Doctor of Nursing Practice
DNP-A	Doctor of Nursing Practice - Anesthesia
DNS	Doctor of Nursing Science
DO	Doctor of Osteopathy
DOT	Doctor of Occupational Therapy
DPA	Doctor of Public Administration
DPDS	Doctor of Planning and Development Studies
DPH	Doctor of Public Health
DPM	Doctor of Plant Medicine
	Doctor of Podiatric Medicine
DPPD	Doctor of Policy, Planning, and Development
DPS	Doctor of Professional Studies
DPT	Doctor of Physical Therapy
DPTSc	Doctor of Physical Therapy Science
Dr DES	Doctor of Design
Dr NP	Doctor of Nursing Practice
Dr OT	Doctor of Occupational Therapy
Dr PH	Doctor of Public Health
Dr Sc PT	Doctor of Science in Physical Therapy
DrAP	Doctor of Anesthesia Practice
DRSc	Doctor of Regulatory Science
DS	Doctor of Science
DS Sc	Doctor of Social Science
DSJS	Doctor of Science in Jewish Studies
DSL	Doctor of Strategic Leadership
DSS	Doctor of Strategic Security
DSW	Doctor of Social Work
DTL	Doctor of Talmudic Law
	Doctor of Transformational Leadership
DV Sc	Doctor of Veterinary Science
DVM	Doctor of Veterinary Medicine
DWS	Doctor of Worship Studies
EAA	Engineer in Aeronautics and Astronautics
EASPh D	Engineering and Applied Science Doctor of Philosophy
ECS	Engineer in Computer Science
Ed D	Doctor of Education
Ed DCT	Doctor of Education in College Teaching
Ed L D	Doctor of Education Leadership
Ed M	Master of Education
Ed S	Specialist in Education
Ed Sp	Specialist in Education

EDB	Executive Doctorate in Business
EDBA	Executive Doctor of Business Administration
EDM	Executive Doctorate in Management
EE	Electrical Engineer
EJD	Executive Juris Doctor
EMBA	Executive Master of Business Administration
EMFA	Executive Master of Forensic Accounting
EMHA	Executive Master of Health Administration
EMIB	Executive Master of International Business
EML	Executive Master of Leadership
EMPA	Executive Master of Public Administration
EMPL	Executive Master in Public Leadership
EMS	Executive Master of Science
EMTM	Executive Master of Technology Management
Eng	Engineer
Eng Sc D	Doctor of Engineering Science
Engr	Engineer
Exec M Tax	Executive Master of Taxation
Exec MAC	Executive Master of Accounting
Exec Ed D	Executive Doctor of Education
Exec MBA	Executive Master of Business Administration
Exec MPA	Executive Master of Public Administration
Exec MPH	Executive Master of Public Health
Exec MS	Executive Master of Science
Executive Fellows MBA	Executive Fellows Master of Business Administration
G Dip	Graduate Diploma
GBC	Graduate Business Certificate
GDM	Graduate Diploma in Management
GDPA	Graduate Diploma in Public Administration
GDRE	Graduate Diploma in Religious Education
GEMBA	Global Executive Master of Business Administration
GMBA	Global Master of Business Administration
GP LL M	Global Professional Master of Laws
GPD	Graduate Performance Diploma
GSS	Graduate Special Certificate for Students in Special Situations
IEMBA	International Executive Master of Business Administration
IMA	Interdisciplinary Master of Arts
IMBA	International Master of Business Administration
IMES	International Master's in Environmental Studies
Ingeniero	Engineer
JCD	Doctor of Canon Law
JCL	Licentiate in Canon Law
JD	Juris Doctor
JM	Juris Master
JSD	Doctor of Juridical Science
	Doctor of Jurisprudence
	Doctor of the Science of Law
JSM	Master of the Science of Law
L Th	Licenciate in Theology
LL B	Bachelor of Laws
LL CM	Master of Comparative Law
LL D	Doctor of Laws
LL M	Master of Laws
LL M in Tax	Master of Laws in Taxation
LL M CL	Master of Laws in Common Law
M Ac	Master of Accountancy
	Master of Accounting
	Master of Acupuncture
M Ac OM	Master of Acupuncture and Oriental Medicine
M Acc	Master of Accountancy
	Master of Accounting
M Acct	Master of Accountancy
	Master of Accounting

M Accy	Master of Accountancy
M Actg	Master of Accounting
M Acy	Master of Accountancy
M Ad	Master of Administration
M Ad Ed	Master of Adult Education
M Adm	Master of Administration
M Adm Mgt	Master of Administrative Management
M Admin	Master of Administration
M ADU	Master of Architectural Design and Urbanism
M Adv	Master of Advertising
M AEST	Master of Applied Environmental Science and Technology
M Ag	Master of Agriculture
M Ag Ed	Master of Agricultural Education
M Agr	Master of Agriculture
M Anesth Ed	Master of Anesthesiology Education
M App Comp Sc	Master of Applied Computer Science
M App St	Master of Applied Statistics
M Appl Stat	Master of Applied Statistics
M Aq	Master of Aquaculture
M Arc	Master of Architecture
M Arch	Master of Architecture
M Arch I	Master of Architecture I
M Arch II	Master of Architecture II
M Arch E	Master of Architectural Engineering
M Arch H	Master of Architectural History
M Bioethics	Master in Bioethics
M Biomath	Master of Biomathematics
M Ch E	Master of Chemical Engineering
M Chem	Master of Chemistry
M Cl D	Master of Clinical Dentistry
M Cl Sc	Master of Clinical Science
M Comp	Master of Computing
M Comp Sc	Master of Computer Science
M Coun	Master of Counseling
M Dent	Master of Dentistry
M Dent Sc	Master of Dental Sciences
M Des	Master of Design
M Des S	Master of Design Studies
M Div	Master of Divinity
M E Sci	Master of Earth Science
M Ec	Master of Economics
M Econ	Master of Economics
M Ed	Master of Education
M Ed T	Master of Education in Teaching
M En	Master of Engineering
M En S	Master of Environmental Sciences
M Eng	Master of Engineering
M Eng Mgt	Master of Engineering Management
M Engr	Master of Engineering
M Ent	Master of Enterprise
M Env	Master of Environment
M Env Des	Master of Environmental Design
M Env E	Master of Environmental Engineering
M Env Sc	Master of Environmental Science
M Fin	Master of Finance
M FSc	Master of Fisheries Science
M Geo E	Master of Geological Engineering
M Geoenv E	Master of Geoenvironmental Engineering
M Geog	Master of Geography
M Hum	Master of Humanities
M IDST	Master's in Interdisciplinary Studies
M Kin	Master of Kinesiology
M Land Arch	Master of Landscape Architecture
M Litt	Master of Letters
M Mat SE	Master of Material Science and Engineering
M Math	Master of Mathematics
M Mech E	Master of Mechanical Engineering

M Med Sc	Master of Medical Science
M Mgmt	Master of Management
M Mgt	Master of Management
M Min	Master of Ministries
M Mtl E	Master of Materials Engineering
M Mu	Master of Music
M Mus	Master of Music
M Mus Ed	Master of Music Education
M Music	Master of Music
M Nat Sci	Master of Natural Science
M Pet E	Master of Petroleum Engineering
M Pharm	Master of Pharmacy
M Phil	Master of Philosophy
M Phil F	Master of Philosophical Foundations
M Pl	Master of Planning
M Plan	Master of Planning
M Pol	Master of Political Science
M Pr Met	Master of Professional Meteorology
M Prob S	Master of Probability and Statistics
M Psych	Master of Psychology
M Pub	Master of Publishing
M Rel	Master of Religion
M Sc	Master of Science
M Sc A	Master of Science (Applied)
M Sc AC	Master of Science in Applied Computing
M Sc AHN	Master of Science in Applied Human Nutrition
M Sc BMC	Master of Science in Biomedical Communications
M Sc CS	Master of Science in Computer Science
M Sc E	Master of Science in Engineering
M Sc Eng	Master of Science in Engineering
M Sc Engr	Master of Science in Engineering
M Sc F	Master of Science in Forestry
M Sc FE	Master of Science in Forest Engineering
M Sc Geogr	Master of Science in Geography
M Sc N	Master of Science in Nursing
M Sc OT	Master of Science in Occupational Therapy
M Sc P	Master of Science in Planning
M Sc Pl	Master of Science in Planning
M Sc PT	Master of Science in Physical Therapy
M Sc T	Master of Science in Teaching
M SEM	Master of Sustainable Environmental Management
M Serv Soc	Master of Social Service
M Soc	Master of Sociology
M Sp Ed	Master of Special Education
M St	Master of Studies
M Stat	Master of Statistics
M Sys E	Master of Systems Engineering
M Sys Sc	Master of Systems Science
M Tax	Master of Taxation
M Tech	Master of Technology
M Th	Master of Theology
M Tox	Master of Toxicology
M Trans E	Master of Transportation Engineering
M U Ed	Master of Urban Education
M Urb	Master of Urban Planning
M Vet Sc	Master of Veterinary Science
MA	Master of Accounting
	Master of Administration
	Master of Arts
MA Comm	Master of Arts in Communication
MA Ed	Master of Arts in Education
MA Ed/HD	Master of Arts in Education and Human Development
MA Ext	Master of Agricultural Extension
MA Min	Master of Arts in Ministry
MA Past St	Master of Arts in Pastoral Studies
MA Ph	Master of Arts in Philosophy

MA Psych	Master of Arts in Psychology		Master of Arts in Education
MA Sc	Master of Applied Science		Master of Arts in English
MA Sp	Master of Arts (Spirituality)	MAEd	Master of Arts Education
MA Th	Master of Arts in Theology	MAEL	Master of Arts in Educational Leadership
MA-R	Master of Arts (Research)	MAEM	Master of Arts in Educational Ministries
MAA	Master of Administrative Arts	MAEP	Master of Arts in Economic Policy
	Master of Applied Anthropology		Master of Arts in Educational Psychology
	Master of Applied Arts	MAES	Master of Arts in Environmental Sciences
	Master of Arts in Administration	MAET	Master of Arts in English Teaching
MAAA	Master of Arts in Arts Administration	MAF	Master of Arts in Finance
MAAAP	Master of Arts Administration and Policy	MAFE	Master of Arts in Financial Economics
MAAD	Master of Advanced Architectural Design	MAFLL	Master of Arts in Foreign Language and Literature
MAAE	Master of Arts in Art Education	MAFM	Master of Accounting and Financial Management
MAAPPS	Master of Arts in Asia Pacific Policy Studies		
MAAS	Master of Arts in Aging and Spirituality	MAFS	Master of Arts in Family Studies
MAASJ	Master of Arts in Applied Social Justice	MAG	Master of Applied Geography
MAAT	Master of Arts in Applied Theology	MAGS	Master of Arts in Global Service
	Master of Arts in Art Therapy	MAGU	Master of Urban Analysis and Management
MAB	Master of Agribusiness	MAH	Master of Arts in Humanities
MABC	Master of Arts in Biblical Counseling	MAHA	Master of Arts in Humanitarian Assistance
MABE	Master of Arts in Bible Exposition	MAHCM	Master of Arts in Health Care Mission
MABL	Master of Arts in Biblical Languages	MAHG	Master of American History and Government
MABM	Master of Agribusiness Management	MAHL	Master of Arts in Hebrew Letters
MABS	Master of Arts in Biblical Studies	MAHN	Master of Applied Human Nutrition
MABT	Master of Arts in Bible Teaching	MAHR	Master of Applied Historical Research
MAC	Master of Accountancy	MAHS	Master of Arts in Human Services
	Master of Accounting	MAHSR	Master in Applied Health Services Research
	Master of Arts in Communication	MAIA	Master of Arts in International Administration
	Master of Arts in Counseling		Master of Arts in International Affairs
MACC	Master of Arts in Christian Counseling	MAIDM	Master of Arts in Interior Design and Merchandising
	Master of Arts in Clinical Counseling		
MACCT	Master of Accounting	MAIH	Master of Arts in Interdisciplinary Humanities
MACD	Master of Arts in Christian Doctrine	MAIOP	Master of Applied Industrial/Organizational Psychology
MACE	Master of Arts in Christian Education		
MACH	Master of Arts in Church History	MAIPCR	Master of Arts in International Peace and Conflict Management
MACI	Master of Arts in Curriculum and Instruction		
MACIS	Master of Accounting and Information Systems	MAIS	Master of Arts in Intercultural Studies
MACJ	Master of Arts in Criminal Justice		Master of Arts in Interdisciplinary Studies
MACL	Master of Arts in Christian Leadership		Master of Arts in International Studies
	Master of Arts in Community Leadership	MAIT	Master of Administration in Information Technology
MACM	Master of Arts in Christian Ministries		
	Master of Arts in Christian Ministry	MAJ	Master of Arts in Journalism
	Master of Arts in Church Music	MAJ Ed	Master of Arts in Jewish Education
	Master of Arts in Counseling Ministries	MAJCS	Master of Arts in Jewish Communal Service
MACN	Master of Arts in Counseling	MAJE	Master of Arts in Jewish Education
MACO	Master of Arts in Counseling	MAJPS	Master of Arts in Jewish Professional Studies
MAcOM	Master of Acupuncture and Oriental Medicine	MAJS	Master of Arts in Jewish Studies
MACP	Master of Arts in Christian Practice	MAL	Master in Agricultural Leadership
	Master of Arts in Church Planting	MALA	Master of Arts in Liberal Arts
	Master of Arts in Counseling Psychology	MALD	Master of Arts in Law and Diplomacy
MACS	Master of Applied Computer Science	MALER	Master of Arts in Labor and Employment Relations
	Master of Arts in Catholic Studies		
	Master of Arts in Christian Studies	MALL	Master of Arts in Language Learning
MACSE	Master of Arts in Christian School Education	MALP	Master of Arts in Language Pedagogy
MACT	Master of Arts in Communications and Technology	MALS	Master of Arts in Liberal Studies
		MAM	Master of Acquisition Management
MAD	Master in Educational Institution Administration		Master of Agriculture and Management
			Master of Applied Mathematics
	Master of Art and Design		Master of Arts in Management
MADR	Master of Arts in Dispute Resolution		Master of Arts in Ministry
MADS	Master of Animal and Dairy Science		Master of Arts Management
	Master of Applied Disability Studies		Master of Avian Medicine
MAE	Master of Aerospace Engineering	MAMB	Master of Applied Molecular Biology
	Master of Agricultural Economics	MAMC	Master of Arts in Mass Communication
	Master of Agricultural Education		Master of Arts in Ministry and Culture
	Master of Applied Economics		Master of Arts in Ministry for a Multicultural Church
	Master of Architectural Engineering		
	Master of Art Education		Master of Arts in Missional Christianity
		MAME	Master of Arts in Missions/Evangelism

MAMFC	Master of Arts in Marriage and Family Counseling
MAMFT	Master of Arts in Marriage and Family Therapy
MAMHC	Master of Arts in Mental Health Counseling
MAMS	Master of Applied Mathematical Sciences
	Master of Applied Meditation Studies
	Master of Arts in Ministerial Studies
	Master of Arts in Ministry and Spirituality
MAMT	Master of Arts in Mathematics Teaching
MAN	Master of Applied Nutrition
MANT	Master of Arts in New Testament
MAOL	Master of Arts in Organizational Leadership
MAOM	Master of Acupuncture and Oriental Medicine
MAOT	Master of Arts in Old Testament
MAP	Master of Applied Politics
	Master of Applied Psychology
	Master of Arts in Planning
	Master of Psychology
	Master of Public Administration
MAP Min	Master of Arts in Pastoral Ministry
MAPA	Master of Arts in Public Administration
MAPC	Master of Arts in Pastoral Counseling
MAPE	Master of Arts in Physics Education
	Master of Arts in Political Economy
MAPM	Master of Arts in Pastoral Ministry
	Master of Arts in Pastoral Music
	Master of Arts in Practical Ministry
MAPP	Master of Arts in Public Policy
MAPS	Master of Arts in Pastoral Studies
	Master of Arts in Public Service
MAPT	Master of Practical Theology
MAPW	Master of Arts in Professional Writing
MAR	Master of Arts in Reading
	Master of Arts in Religion
Mar Eng	Marine Engineer
MARC	Master of Arts in Rehabilitation Counseling
MARE	Master of Arts in Religious Education
MARL	Master of Arts in Religious Leadership
MARS	Master of Arts in Religious Studies
MAS	Master of Accounting Science
	Master of Actuarial Science
	Master of Administrative Science
	Master of Advanced Study
	Master of Aeronautical Science
	Master of American Studies
	Master of Animal Science
	Master of Applied Science
	Master of Applied Statistics
	Master of Archival Studies
MASA	Master of Advanced Studies in Architecture
MASD	Master of Arts in Spiritual Direction
MASE	Master of Arts in Special Education
MASF	Master of Arts in Spiritual Formation
MASJ	Master of Arts in Systems of Justice
MASLA	Master of Advanced Studies in Landscape Architecture
MASM	Master of Aging Services Management
	Master of Arts in Specialized Ministries
MASP	Master of Applied Social Psychology
	Master of Arts in School Psychology
MASPAA	Master of Arts in Sports and Athletic Administration
MASS	Master of Applied Social Science
	Master of Arts in Social Science
MAST	Master of Arts in Science Teaching
MAT	Master of Arts in Teaching
	Master of Arts in Theology
	Master of Athletic Training

	Master's in Administration of Telecommunications
Mat E	Materials Engineer
MATCM	Master of Acupuncture and Traditional Chinese Medicine
MATDE	Master of Arts in Theology, Development, and Evangelism
MATDR	Master of Territorial Management and Regional Development
MATE	Master of Arts for the Teaching of English
MATESL	Master of Arts in Teaching English as a Second Language
MATESOL	Master of Arts in Teaching English to Speakers of Other Languages
MATF	Master of Arts in Teaching English as a Foreign Language/Intercultural Studies
MATFL	Master of Arts in Teaching Foreign Language
MATH	Master of Arts in Therapy
MATI	Master of Administration of Information Technology
MATL	Master of Arts in Teacher Leadership
	Master of Arts in Teaching of Languages
	Master of Arts in Transformational Leadership
MATM	Master of Arts in Teaching of Mathematics
MATS	Master of Arts in Theological Studies
	Master of Arts in Transforming Spirituality
MATSL	Master of Arts in Teaching a Second Language
MAUA	Master of Arts in Urban Affairs
MAUD	Master of Arts in Urban Design
MAURP	Master of Arts in Urban and Regional Planning
MAW	Master of Arts in Worship
MAWSHP	Master of Arts in Worship
MAYM	Master of Arts in Youth Ministry
MB	Master of Bioinformatics
MBA	Master of Business Administration
MBA-AM	Master of Business Administration in Aviation Management
MBA-EP	Master of Business Administration–Experienced Professionals
MBAA	Master of Business Administration in Aviation
MBAE	Master of Biological and Agricultural Engineering
	Master of Biosystems and Agricultural Engineering
MBAH	Master of Business Administration in Health
MBAi	Master of Business Administration–International
MBAICT	Master of Business Administration in Information and Communication Technology
MBATM	Master of Business Administration in Technology Management
MBC	Master of Building Construction
MBE	Master of Bilingual Education
	Master of Bioengineering
	Master of Bioethics
	Master of Biomedical Engineering
	Master of Business Economics
	Master of Business Education
MBEE	Master in Biotechnology Enterprise and Entrepreneurship
MBET	Master of Business, Entrepreneurship and Technology
MBID	Master of Biomedical Innovation and Development
MBIOT	Master of Biotechnology
MBiotech	Master of Biotechnology
MBL	Master of Business Law
	Master of Business Leadership
MBLE	Master in Business Logistics Engineering
MBME	Master's in Biomedical Engineering
MBMSE	Master of Business Management and Software Engineering

MBOE	Master of Business Operational Excellence
MBS	Master of Biblical Studies
	Master of Biological Science
	Master of Biomedical Sciences
	Master of Bioscience
	Master of Building Science
	Master of Business and Science
MBST	Master of Biostatistics
MBT	Master of Biomedical Technology
	Master of Biotechnology
	Master of Business Taxation
MBV	Master of Business for Veterans
MC	Master of Communication
	Master of Counseling
	Master of Cybersecurity
MC Ed	Master of Continuing Education
MC Sc	Master of Computer Science
MCA	Master in Collegiate Athletics
	Master of Commercial Aviation
	Master of Criminology (Applied)
MCAM	Master of Computational and Applied Mathematics
MCC	Master of Computer Science
MCD	Master of Communications Disorders
	Master of Community Development
MCE	Master in Electronic Commerce
	Master of Christian Education
	Master of Civil Engineering
	Master of Control Engineering
MCEM	Master of Construction Engineering Management
MCHE	Master of Chemical Engineering
MCIS	Master of Communication and Information Studies
	Master of Computer and Information Science
	Master of Computer Information Systems
MCIT	Master of Computer and Information Technology
MCJ	Master of Criminal Justice
MCL	Master in Communication Leadership
	Master of Canon Law
	Master of Comparative Law
MCM	Master of Christian Ministry
	Master of Church Music
	Master of City Management
	Master of Communication Management
	Master of Community Medicine
	Master of Construction Management
	Master of Contract Management
MCMin	Master of Christian Ministry
MCMP	Master of City and Metropolitan Planning
MCMS	Master of Clinical Medical Science
MCN	Master of Clinical Nutrition
MCOL	Master of Arts in Community and Organizational Leadership
MCP	Master of City Planning
	Master of Community Planning
	Master of Counseling Psychology
	Master of Cytopathology Practice
	Master of Science in Quality Systems and Productivity
MCPC	Master of Arts in Chaplaincy and Pastoral Care
MCPD	Master of Community Planning and Development
MCR	Master in Clinical Research
MCRP	Master of City and Regional Planning
	Master of Community and Regional Planning
MCRS	Master of City and Regional Studies
MCS	Master of Chemical Sciences
	Master of Christian Studies

	Master of Clinical Science
	Master of Combined Sciences
	Master of Communication Studies
	Master of Computer Science
	Master of Consumer Science
MCSE	Master of Computer Science and Engineering
MCSL	Master of Catholic School Leadership
MCSM	Master of Construction Science and Management
MCTM	Master of Clinical Translation Management
MCTP	Master of Communication Technology and Policy
MCTS	Master of Clinical and Translational Science
MCVS	Master of Cardiovascular Science
MD	Doctor of Medicine
MDA	Master of Dietetic Administration
MDB	Master of Design-Build
MDE	Master of Developmental Economics
	Master of Distance Education
	Master of the Education of the Deaf
MDH	Master of Dental Hygiene
MDM	Master of Design Methods
	Master of Digital Media
MDP	Master in Sustainable Development Practice
	Master of Development Practice
MDR	Master of Dispute Resolution
MDS	Master of Dental Surgery
	Master of Design Studies
	Master of Digital Sciences
ME	Master of Education
	Master of Engineering
	Master of Entrepreneurship
ME Sc	Master of Engineering Science
ME-PD	Master of Education–Professional Development
MEA	Master of Educational Administration
	Master of Engineering Administration
MEAE	Master of Entertainment Arts and Engineering
MEAP	Master of Environmental Administration and Planning
MEB	Master of Energy Business
MEBD	Master in Environmental Building Design
MEBT	Master in Electronic Business Technologies
MEC	Master of Electronic Commerce
Mech E	Mechanical Engineer
MED	Master of Education of the Deaf
MEDS	Master of Environmental Design Studies
MEE	Master in Education
	Master of Electrical Engineering
	Master of Energy Engineering
	Master of Environmental Engineering
MEEM	Master of Environmental Engineering and Management
MEENE	Master of Engineering in Environmental Engineering
MEEP	Master of Environmental and Energy Policy
MEERM	Master of Earth and Environmental Resource Management
MEH	Master in Humanistic Studies
	Master of Environmental Health
	Master of Environmental Horticulture
MEHS	Master of Environmental Health and Safety
MEIM	Master of Entertainment Industry Management
	Master of Equine Industry Management
MEL	Master of Educational Leadership
	Master of English Literature
MELP	Master of Environmental Law and Policy
MEM	Master of Engineering Management
	Master of Environmental Management
	Master of Marketing

MEME	Master of Engineering in Manufacturing Engineering
	Master of Engineering in Mechanical Engineering
MENR	Master of Environment and Natural Resources
MENVEGR	Master of Environmental Engineering
MEP	Master of Engineering Physics
MEPC	Master of Environmental Pollution Control
MEPD	Master of Environmental Planning and Design
MER	Master of Employment Relations
MERE	Master of Entrepreneurial Real Estate
MERL	Master of Energy Regulation and Law
MES	Master of Education and Science
	Master of Engineering Science
	Master of Environment and Sustainability
	Master of Environmental Science
	Master of Environmental Studies
	Master of Environmental Systems
	Master of Special Education
MESM	Master of Environmental Science and Management
MET	Master of Educational Technology
	Master of Engineering Technology
	Master of Entertainment Technology
	Master of Environmental Toxicology
METM	Master of Engineering and Technology Management
MEVE	Master of Environmental Engineering
MF	Master of Finance
	Master of Forestry
MFA	Master of Fine Arts
MFALP	Master of Food and Agriculture Law and Policy
MFAM	Master's of Food Animal Medicine
MFAS	Master of Fisheries and Aquatic Science
MFAW	Master of Fine Arts in Writing
MFC	Master of Forest Conservation
MFCS	Master of Family and Consumer Sciences
MFE	Master of Financial Economics
	Master of Financial Engineering
	Master of Forest Engineering
MFES	Master of Fire and Emergency Services
MFG	Master of Functional Genomics
MFHD	Master of Family and Human Development
MFM	Master of Financial Management
	Master of Financial Mathematics
MFPE	Master of Food Process Engineering
MFR	Master of Forest Resources
MFRC	Master of Forest Resources and Conservation
MFRE	Master of Food and Resource Economics
MFS	Master of Food Science
	Master of Forensic Sciences
	Master of Forest Science
	Master of Forest Studies
	Master of French Studies
MFST	Master of Food Safety and Technology
MFT	Master of Family Therapy
	Master of Food Technology
MFWB	Master of Fishery and Wildlife Biology
MFWCB	Master of Fish, Wildlife and Conservation Biology
MFWS	Master of Fisheries and Wildlife Sciences
MFYCS	Master of Family, Youth and Community Sciences
MG	Master of Genetics
MGA	Master of Global Affairs
	Master of Government Administration
	Master of Governmental Administration
MGC	Master of Genetic Counseling
MGD	Master of Graphic Design

MGE	Master of Geotechnical Engineering
MGEM	Master of Global Entrepreneurship and Management
MGIS	Master of Geographic Information Science
	Master of Geographic Information Systems
MGM	Master of Global Management
MGP	Master of Gestion de Projet
MGPS	Master of Global Policy Studies
MGREM	Master of Global Real Estate Management
MGS	Master of Gerontological Studies
	Master of Global Studies
MGsc	Master of Geoscience
MH	Master of Humanities
MH Sc	Master of Health Sciences
MHA	Master of Health Administration
	Master of Healthcare Administration
	Master of Hospital Administration
	Master of Hospitality Administration
MHB	Master of Human Behavior
MHC	Master of Mental Health Counseling
MHCA	Master of Health Care Administration
MHCD	Master of Health Care Design
MHCI	Master of Human-Computer Interaction
MHCL	Master of Health Care Leadership
MHE	Master of Health Education
	Master of Human Ecology
MHE Ed	Master of Home Economics Education
MHEA	Master of Higher Education Administration
MHHS	Master of Health and Human Services
MHI	Master of Health Informatics
	Master of Healthcare Innovation
MHIHIM	Master of Health Informatics and Health Information Management
MHIIM	Master of Health Informatics and Information Management
MHIS	Master of Health Information Systems
MHK	Master of Human Kinetics
MHM	Master of Healthcare Management
MHMS	Master of Health Management Systems
MHP	Master of Health Physics
	Master of Heritage Preservation
	Master of Historic Preservation
MHPA	Master of Heath Policy and Administration
MHPE	Master of Health Professions Education
MHR	Master of Human Resources
MHRD	Master in Human Resource Development
MHRIR	Master of Human Resources and Industrial Relations
MHRLR	Master of Human Resources and Labor Relations
MHRM	Master of Human Resources Management
MHS	Master of Health Science
	Master of Health Sciences
	Master of Health Studies
	Master of Hispanic Studies
	Master of Human Services
	Master of Humanistic Studies
MHSA	Master of Health Services Administration
MHSE	Master of Health Science Education
MHSM	Master of Health Systems Management
MI	Master of Information
	Master of Instruction
MI Arch	Master of Interior Architecture
MIA	Master of Interior Architecture
	Master of International Affairs
MIAA	Master of International Affairs and Administration
MIAM	Master of International Agribusiness Management

MIAPD	Master of Interior Architecture and Product Design
MIB	Master of International Business
MIBA	Master of International Business Administration
MICM	Master of International Construction Management
MID	Master of Industrial Design
	Master of Industrial Distribution
	Master of Interior Design
	Master of International Development
MIDA	Master of International Development Administration
MIDC	Master of Integrated Design and Construction
MIDP	Master of International Development Policy
MIE	Master of Industrial Engineering
MIHTM	Master of International Hospitality and Tourism Management
MIJ	Master of International Journalism
MILR	Master of Industrial and Labor Relations
MIM	Master in Ministry
	Master of Information Management
	Master of International Management
MIMLAE	Master of International Management for Latin American Executives
MIMS	Master of Information Management and Systems
	Master of Integrated Manufacturing Systems
MIP	Master of Infrastructure Planning
	Master of Intellectual Property
	Master of International Policy
MIPA	Master of International Public Affairs
MIPD	Master of Integrated Product Design
MIPM	Master of International Policy Management
MIPP	Master of International Policy and Practice
	Master of International Public Policy
MIPS	Master of International Planning Studies
MIR	Master of Industrial Relations
	Master of International Relations
MIRHR	Master of Industrial Relations and Human Resources
MIS	Master of Imaging Science
	Master of Industrial Statistics
	Master of Information Science
	Master of Information Systems
	Master of Integrated Science
	Master of Interdisciplinary Studies
	Master of International Service
	Master of International Studies
MISE	Master of Industrial and Systems Engineering
MISKM	Master of Information Sciences and Knowledge Management
MISM	Master of Information Systems Management
MISW	Master of Indigenous Social Work
MIT	Master in Teaching
	Master of Industrial Technology
	Master of Information Technology
	Master of Initial Teaching
	Master of International Trade
	Master of Internet Technology
MITA	Master of Information Technology Administration
MITM	Master of Information Technology and Management
MJ	Master of Journalism
	Master of Jurisprudence
MJ Ed	Master of Jewish Education
MJA	Master of Justice Administration
MJM	Master of Justice Management
MJS	Master of Judicial Studies

	Master of Juridical Studies
MK	Master of Kinesiology
MKM	Master of Knowledge Management
ML	Master of Latin
ML Arch	Master of Landscape Architecture
MLA	Master of Landscape Architecture
	Master of Liberal Arts
MLAS	Master of Laboratory Animal Science
	Master of Liberal Arts and Sciences
MLAUD	Master of Landscape Architecture in Urban Development
MLD	Master of Leadership Development
	Master of Leadership Studies
MLE	Master of Applied Linguistics and Exegesis
MLER	Master of Labor and Employment Relations
MLI Sc	Master of Library and Information Science
MLIS	Master of Library and Information Science
	Master of Library and Information Studies
MLM	Master of Leadership in Ministry
MLPD	Master of Land and Property Development
MLRHR	Master of Labor Relations and Human Resources
MLS	Master of Leadership Studies
	Master of Legal Studies
	Master of Liberal Studies
	Master of Library Science
	Master of Life Sciences
MLSCM	Master of Logistics and Supply Chain Management
MLSP	Master of Law and Social Policy
MLT	Master of Language Technologies
MLTCA	Master of Long Term Care Administration
MLW	Master of Studies in Law
MLWS	Master of Land and Water Systems
MM	Master of Management
	Master of Ministry
	Master of Missiology
	Master of Music
MM Ed	Master of Music Education
MM Sc	Master of Medical Science
MM St	Master of Museum Studies
MMA	Master of Marine Affairs
	Master of Media Arts
	Master of Ministry Administration
	Master of Musical Arts
MMAL	Master of Maritime Administration and Logistics
MMAS	Master of Military Art and Science
MMB	Master of Microbial Biotechnology
MMC	Master of Manufacturing Competitiveness
	Master of Mass Communications
	Master of Music Conducting
MMCM	Master of Music in Church Music
MMCSS	Master of Mathematical Computational and Statistical Sciences
MME	Master of Manufacturing Engineering
	Master of Mathematics Education
	Master of Mathematics for Educators
	Master of Mechanical Engineering
	Master of Mining Engineering
	Master of Music Education
MMF	Master of Mathematical Finance
MMFT	Master of Marriage and Family Therapy
MMH	Master of Management in Hospitality
	Master of Medical Humanities
MMI	Master of Management of Innovation
MMIS	Master of Management Information Systems
MML	Master of Managerial Logistics
MMM	Master of Manufacturing Management

	Master of Marine Management		Master of Physician Assistant
	Master of Medical Management		Master of Professional Accountancy
MMP	Master of Management Practice		Master of Professional Accounting
	Master of Marine Policy		Master of Public Administration
	Master of Medical Physics		Master of Public Affairs
	Master of Music Performance	MPAC	Master of Professional Accounting
MMPA	Master of Management and Professional Accounting	MPAID	Master of Public Administration and International Development
MMQM	Master of Manufacturing Quality Management	MPAP	Master of Physician Assistant Practice
MMR	Master of Marketing Research		Master of Public Administration and Policy
MMRM	Master of Marine Resources Management		Master of Public Affairs and Politics
MMS	Master of Management Science	MPAS	Master of Physician Assistant Science
	Master of Management Studies		Master of Physician Assistant Studies
	Master of Manufacturing Systems	MPC	Master of Professional Communication
	Master of Marine Studies		Master of Professional Counseling
	Master of Materials Science	MPD	Master of Product Development
	Master of Mathematical Sciences		Master of Public Diplomacy
	Master of Medical Science	MPDS	Master of Planning and Development Studies
	Master of Medieval Studies	MPE	Master of Physical Education
MMSE	Master of Manufacturing Systems Engineering	MPEM	Master of Project Engineering and Management
MMSM	Master of Music in Sacred Music	MPH	Master of Public Health
MMT	Master in Marketing	MPHE	Master of Public Health Education
	Master of Music Teaching	MPHM	Master in Plant Health Management
	Master of Music Therapy	MPHS	Master of Population Health Sciences
	Master's in Marketing Technology	MPHTM	Master of Public Health and Tropical Medicine
MMus	Master of Music	MPI	Master of Product Innovation
MN	Master of Nursing	MPIA	Master of Public and International Affairs
	Master of Nutrition	MPM	Master of Pastoral Ministry
MN NP	Master of Nursing in Nurse Practitioner		Master of Pest Management
MNA	Master of Nonprofit Administration		Master of Policy Management
	Master of Nurse Anesthesia		Master of Practical Ministries
MNAL	Master of Nonprofit Administration and Leadership		Master of Project Management
MNAS	Master of Natural and Applied Science		Master of Public Management
MNCM	Master of Network and Communications Management	MPNA	Master of Public and Nonprofit Administration
MNE	Master of Nuclear Engineering	MPNL	Master of Philanthropy and Nonprofit Leadership
MNL	Master in International Business for Latin America	MPO	Master of Prosthetics and Orthotics
MNM	Master of Nonprofit Management	MPOD	Master of Positive Organizational Development
MNO	Master of Nonprofit Organization	MPP	Master of Public Policy
MNPL	Master of Not-for-Profit Leadership	MPPA	Master of Public Policy Administration
MNpS	Master of Nonprofit Studies		Master of Public Policy and Administration
MNR	Master of Natural Resources	MPPAL	Master of Public Policy, Administration and Law
MNRD	Master of Natural Resources Development	MPPM	Master of Public and Private Management
MNRES	Master of Natural Resources and Environmental Studies		Master of Public Policy and Management
MNRM	Master of Natural Resource Management	MPPPM	Master of Plant Protection and Pest Management
MNRMG	Master of Natural Resource Management and Geography	MPRTM	Master of Parks, Recreation, and Tourism Management
MNRS	Master of Natural Resource Stewardship	MPS	Master of Pastoral Studies
MNS	Master of Natural Science		Master of Perfusion Science
MO	Master of Oceanography		Master of Planning Studies
MOD	Master of Organizational Development		Master of Political Science
MOGS	Master of Oil and Gas Studies		Master of Preservation Studies
MOL	Master of Organizational Leadership		Master of Prevention Science
MOM	Master of Organizational Management		Master of Professional Studies
	Master of Oriental Medicine		Master of Public Service
MOR	Master of Operations Research	MPSA	Master of Public Service Administration
MOT	Master of Occupational Therapy	MPSG	Master of Population and Social Gerontology
MP	Master of Physiology	MPSIA	Master of Political Science and International Affairs
	Master of Planning	MPSL	Master of Public Safety Leadership
MP Ac	Master of Professional Accountancy	MPSRE	Master of Professional Studies in Real Estate
MP Acc	Master of Professional Accountancy	MPT	Master of Pastoral Theology
	Master of Professional Accounting		Master of Physical Therapy
	Master of Public Accounting		Master of Practical Theology
MP Aff	Master of Public Affairs	MPVM	Master of Preventive Veterinary Medicine
MP Th	Master of Pastoral Theology	MPW	Master of Professional Writing
MPA	Master of Performing Arts		Master of Public Works

MQM	Master of Quality Management		Master of Science in Agriculture
MQS	Master of Quality Systems		Master of Science in Analytics
MR	Master of Recreation		Master of Science in Anesthesia
	Master of Retailing		Master of Science in Architecture
MRA	Master in Research Administration		Master of Science in Aviation
MRC	Master of Rehabilitation Counseling		Master of Sports Administration
MRCP	Master of Regional and City Planning		Master of Surgical Assisting
	Master of Regional and Community Planning	MSAA	Master of Science in Astronautics and Aeronautics
MRD	Master of Rural Development	MSAAE	Master of Science in Aeronautical and Astronautical Engineering
MRE	Master of Real Estate		
	Master of Religious Education	MSABE	Master of Science in Agricultural and Biological Engineering
MRED	Master of Real Estate Development		
MREM	Master of Resource and Environmental Management	MSAC	Master of Science in Acupuncture
		MSACC	Master of Science in Accounting
MRLS	Master of Resources Law Studies	MSACS	Master of Science in Applied Computer Science
MRM	Master of Resources Management	MSAE	Master of Science in Aeronautical Engineering
MRP	Master of Regional Planning		Master of Science in Aerospace Engineering
MRRD	Master in Recreation Resource Development		Master of Science in Applied Economics
MRS	Master of Religious Studies		Master of Science in Applied Engineering
MRSc	Master of Rehabilitation Science		Master of Science in Architectural Engineering
MRTP	Master of Rural and Town Planning	MSAEM	Master of Science in Aerospace Engineering and Mechanics
MS	Master of Science		
MS Cmp E	Master of Science in Computer Engineering	MSAF	Master of Science in Aviation Finance
MS Kin	Master of Science in Kinesiology	MSAG	Master of Science in Applied Geosciences
MS Acct	Master of Science in Accounting	MSAH	Master of Science in Allied Health
MS Accy	Master of Science in Accountancy	MSAL	Master of Sport Administration and Leadership
MS Aero E	Master of Science in Aerospace Engineering	MSAM	Master of Science in Applied Mathematics
MS Ag	Master of Science in Agriculture	MSANR	Master of Science in Agriculture and Natural Resources
MS Arch	Master of Science in Architecture		
MS Arch St	Master of Science in Architectural Studies	MSAPM	Master of Security Analysis and Portfolio Management
MS Bio E	Master of Science in Bioengineering		
MS Bm E	Master of Science in Biomedical Engineering	MSAS	Master of Science in Applied Statistics
MS Ch E	Master of Science in Chemical Engineering		Master of Science in Architectural Studies
MS Cp E	Master of Science in Computer Engineering	MSAT	Master of Science in Accounting and Taxation
MS Eco	Master of Science in Economics		Master of Science in Advanced Technology
MS Econ	Master of Science in Economics		Master of Science in Athletic Training
MS Ed	Master of Science in Education	MSB	Master of Science in Biotechnology
MS El	Master of Science in Educational Leadership and Administration		Master of Sustainable Business
		MSBA	Master of Science in Business Administration
MS En E	Master of Science in Environmental Engineering		Master of Science in Business Analysis
		MSBAE	Master of Science in Biological and Agricultural Engineering
MS Eng	Master of Science in Engineering		
MS Engr	Master of Science in Engineering		Master of Science in Biosystems and Agricultural Engineering
MS Env E	Master of Science in Environmental Engineering		
		MSBC	Master of Science in Building Construction
MS Exp Surg	Master of Science in Experimental Surgery		Master of Science in Business Communication
MS Mat E	Master of Science in Materials Engineering	MSBCB	Master's in Bioinformatics and Computational Biology
MS Mat SE	Master of Science in Material Science and Engineering		
		MSBE	Master of Science in Biological Engineering
MS Met E	Master of Science in Metallurgical Engineering		Master of Science in Biomedical Engineering
MS Mgt	Master of Science in Management	MSBENG	Master of Science in Bioengineering
MS Min	Master of Science in Mining	MSBH	Master of Science in Behavioral Health
MS Min E	Master of Science in Mining Engineering	MSBIT	Master of Science in Business Information Technology
MS Mt E	Master of Science in Materials Engineering		
MS Otol	Master of Science in Otolaryngology	MSBM	Master of Sport Business Management
MS Pet E	Master of Science in Petroleum Engineering	MSBME	Master of Science in Biomedical Engineering
MS Sc	Master of Social Science	MSBMS	Master of Science in Basic Medical Science
MS Sp Ed	Master of Science in Special Education	MSBS	Master of Science in Biomedical Sciences
MS Stat	Master of Science in Statistics	MSBTM	Master of Science in Biotechnology and Management
MS Surg	Master of Science in Surgery		
MS Tax	Master of Science in Taxation	MSC	Master of Science in Commerce
MS Tc E	Master of Science in Telecommunications Engineering		Master of Science in Communication
			Master of Science in Computers
MS-R	Master of Science (Research)		Master of Science in Counseling
MSA	Master of School Administration		Master of Science in Criminology
	Master of Science in Accountancy		Master of Strategic Communication
	Master of Science in Accounting	MSCC	Master of Science in Community Counseling
	Master of Science in Administration	MSCD	Master of Science in Communication Disorders
	Master of Science in Aeronautics		Master of Science in Community Development

MSCE	Master of Science in Civil Engineering
	Master of Science in Clinical Epidemiology
	Master of Science in Computer Engineering
	Master of Science in Continuing Education
MSCEE	Master of Science in Civil and Environmental Engineering
MSCF	Master of Science in Computational Finance
MSCH	Master of Science in Chemical Engineering
MSChE	Master of Science in Chemical Engineering
MSCI	Master of Science in Clinical Investigation
MSCIS	Master of Science in Computer and Information Science
	Master of Science in Computer and Information Systems
	Master of Science in Computer Information Science
	Master of Science in Computer Information Systems
MSCIT	Master of Science in Computer Information Technology
MSCJ	Master of Science in Criminal Justice
MSCJA	Master of Science in Criminal Justice Administration
MSCJS	Master of Science in Crime and Justice Studies
MSCLS	Master of Science in Clinical Laboratory Studies
MSCM	Master of Science in Church Management
	Master of Science in Conflict Management
	Master of Science in Construction Management
	Master of Supply Chain Management
MSCNU	Master of Science in Clinical Nutrition
MSCP	Master of Science in Clinical Psychology
	Master of Science in Community Psychology
	Master of Science in Computer Engineering
	Master of Science in Counseling Psychology
MSCPE	Master of Science in Computer Engineering
MSCPharm	Master of Science in Pharmacy
MSCR	Master of Science in Clinical Research
MSCRP	Master of Science in City and Regional Planning
	Master of Science in Community and Regional Planning
MSCS	Master of Science in Clinical Science
	Master of Science in Computer Science
	Master of Science in Cyber Security
MSCSD	Master of Science in Communication Sciences and Disorders
MSCSE	Master of Science in Computer Science and Engineering
MSCTE	Master of Science in Career and Technical Education
MSD	Master of Science in Dentistry
	Master of Science in Design
	Master of Science in Dietetics
MSE	Master of Science Education
	Master of Science in Economics
	Master of Science in Education
	Master of Science in Engineering
	Master of Science in Engineering Management
	Master of Software Engineering
	Master of Special Education
	Master of Structural Engineering
MSECE	Master of Science in Electrical and Computer Engineering
MSED	Master of Sustainable Economic Development
MSEE	Master of Science in Electrical Engineering
	Master of Science in Environmental Engineering
MSEH	Master of Science in Environmental Health
MSEL	Master of Science in Educational Leadership
MSEM	Master of Science in Engineering Management
	Master of Science in Engineering Mechanics

	Master of Science in Environmental Management
MSENE	Master of Science in Environmental Engineering
MSEO	Master of Science in Electro-Optics
MSEP	Master of Science in Economic Policy
MSES	Master of Science in Embedded Software Engineering
	Master of Science in Engineering Science
	Master of Science in Environmental Science
	Master of Science in Environmental Studies
	Master of Science in Exercise Science
MSET	Master of Science in Educational Technology
	Master of Science in Engineering Technology
MSEV	Master of Science in Environmental Engineering
MSF	Master of Science in Finance
	Master of Science in Forestry
	Master of Spiritual Formation
MSFA	Master of Science in Financial Analysis
MSFCS	Master of Science in Family and Consumer Science
MSFE	Master of Science in Financial Engineering
MSFM	Master of Sustainable Forest Management
MSFOR	Master of Science in Forestry
MSFP	Master of Science in Financial Planning
MSFS	Master of Science in Financial Sciences
	Master of Science in Forensic Science
MSFSB	Master of Science in Financial Services and Banking
MSFT	Master of Science in Family Therapy
MSGC	Master of Science in Genetic Counseling
MSH	Master of Science in Health
	Master of Science in Hospice
MSHA	Master of Science in Health Administration
MSHCA	Master of Science in Health Care Administration
MSHCI	Master of Science in Human Computer Interaction
MSHCPM	Master of Science in Health Care Policy and Management
MSHE	Master of Science in Health Education
MSHES	Master of Science in Human Environmental Sciences
MSHFID	Master of Science in Human Factors in Information Design
MSHFS	Master of Science in Human Factors and Systems
MSHI	Master of Science in Health Informatics
MSHP	Master of Science in Health Professions
	Master of Science in Health Promotion
MSHR	Master of Science in Human Resources
MSHRL	Master of Science in Human Resource Leadership
MSHRM	Master of Science in Human Resource Management
MSHROD	Master of Science in Human Resources and Organizational Development
MSHS	Master of Science in Health Science
	Master of Science in Health Services
	Master of Science in Homeland Security
MSI	Master of Science in Information
	Master of Science in Instruction
	Master of System Integration
MSIA	Master of Science in Industrial Administration
	Master of Science in Information Assurance
MSIB	Master of Science in International Business
MSIDM	Master of Science in Interior Design and Merchandising
MSIE	Master of Science in Industrial Engineering
	Master of Science in International Economics

MSIEM	Master of Science in Information Engineering and Management
MSIID	Master of Science in Information and Instructional Design
MSIM	Master of Science in Information Management
	Master of Science in International Management
MSIMC	Master of Science in Integrated Marketing Communications
MSIR	Master of Science in Industrial Relations
MSIS	Master of Science in Information Science
	Master of Science in Information Studies
	Master of Science in Information Systems
	Master of Science in Interdisciplinary Studies
MSISE	Master of Science in Infrastructure Systems Engineering
MSISM	Master of Science in Information Systems Management
MSISPM	Master of Science in Information Security Policy and Management
MSIST	Master of Science in Information Systems Technology
MSIT	Master of Science in Industrial Technology
	Master of Science in Information Technology
	Master of Science in Instructional Technology
MSITM	Master of Science in Information Technology Management
MSJ	Master of Science in Journalism
	Master of Science in Jurisprudence
MSJC	Master of Social Justice and Criminology
MSJE	Master of Science in Jewish Education
MSJFP	Master of Science in Juvenile Forensic Psychology
MSJJ	Master of Science in Juvenile Justice
MSJPS	Master of Science in Justice and Public Safety
MSJS	Master of Science in Jewish Studies
MSL	Master of School Leadership
	Master of Science in Leadership
	Master of Science in Limnology
	Master of Strategic Leadership
	Master of Studies in Law
MSLA	Master of Science in Legal Administration
MSLFS	Master of Science in Life Sciences
MSLP	Master of Speech-Language Pathology
MSLS	Master of Science in Library Science
MSLSCM	Master of Science in Logistics and Supply Chain Management
MSLT	Master of Second Language Teaching
MSM	Master of Sacred Ministry
	Master of Sacred Music
	Master of School Mathematics
	Master of Science in Management
	Master of Science in Medicine
	Master of Science in Organization Management
	Master of Security Management
MSMA	Master of Science in Marketing Analysis
MSMAE	Master of Science in Materials Engineering
MSMC	Master of Science in Mass Communications
MSME	Master of Science in Mathematics Education
	Master of Science in Mechanical Engineering
MSMFT	Master of Science in Marriage and Family Therapy
MSMHC	Master of Science in Mental Health Counseling
MSMIS	Master of Science in Management Information Systems
MSMIT	Master of Science in Management and Information Technology
MSMLS	Master of Science in Medical Laboratory Science
MSMOT	Master of Science in Management of Technology
MSMP	Master of Science in Medical Physics
MSMS	Master of Science in Management Science
	Master of Science in Marine Science
	Master of Science in Medical Sciences
MSMSE	Master of Science in Manufacturing Systems Engineering
	Master of Science in Material Science and Engineering
	Master of Science in Mathematics and Science Education
MSMT	Master of Science in Management and Technology
MSMus	Master of Sacred Music
MSN	Master of Science in Nursing
MSNA	Master of Science in Nurse Anesthesia
MSNE	Master of Science in Nuclear Engineering
MSNED	Master of Science in Nurse Education
MSNM	Master of Science in Nonprofit Management
MSNS	Master of Science in Natural Science
	Master of Science in Nutritional Science
MSOD	Master of Science in Organization Development
	Master of Science in Organizational Development
MSOEE	Master of Science in Outdoor and Environmental Education
MSOES	Master of Science in Occupational Ergonomics and Safety
MSOH	Master of Science in Occupational Health
MSOL	Master of Science in Organizational Leadership
MSOM	Master of Science in Operations Management
	Master of Science in Oriental Medicine
MSOR	Master of Science in Operations Research
MSOT	Master of Science in Occupational Technology
	Master of Science in Occupational Therapy
MSP	Master of Science in Pharmacy
	Master of Science in Planning
	Master of Speech Pathology
MSPA	Master of Science in Physician Assistant
	Master of Science in Professional Accountancy
MSPAS	Master of Science in Physician Assistant Studies
MSPC	Master of Science in Professional Communications
MSPE	Master of Science in Petroleum Engineering
MSPH	Master of Science in Public Health
MSPHR	Master of Science in Pharmacy
MSPM	Master of Science in Professional Management
	Master of Science in Project Management
MSPNGE	Master of Science in Petroleum and Natural Gas Engineering
MSPO	Master of Science in Prosthetics and Orthotics
MSPPM	Master of Science in Public Policy and Management
MSPS	Master of Science in Pharmaceutical Science
	Master of Science in Political Science
	Master of Science in Psychological Services
MSPT	Master of Science in Physical Therapy
MSpVM	Master of Specialized Veterinary Medicine
MSR	Master of Science in Radiology
	Master of Science in Reading
MSRA	Master of Science in Recreation Administration
MSRE	Master of Science in Real Estate
	Master of Science in Religious Education
MSRED	Master of Science in Real Estate Development
	Master of Sustainable Real Estate Development
MSRLS	Master of Science in Recreation and Leisure Studies
MSRM	Master of Science in Risk Management
MSRMP	Master of Science in Radiological Medical Physics
MSRS	Master of Science in Radiological Sciences
	Master of Science in Rehabilitation Science

MSS	Master of Security Studies	MTHM	Master of Tourism and Hospitality Management
	Master of Social Science	MTI	Master of Information Technology
	Master of Social Services	MTID	Master of Tangible Interaction Design
	Master of Software Systems	MTL	Master of Talmudic Law
	Master of Sports Science	MTM	Master of Technology Management
	Master of Strategic Studies		Master of Telecommunications Management
	Master's in Statistical Science		Master of the Teaching of Mathematics
MSSA	Master of Science in Social Administration	MTMH	Master of Tropical Medicine and Hygiene
MSSCM	Master of Science in Supply Chain Management	MTMS	Master in Teaching Mathematics and Science
MSSD	Master of Arts in Software Driven Systems Design	MTOM	Master of Traditional Oriental Medicine
	Master of Science in Sustainable Design	MTPC	Master of Technical and Professional Communication
MSSE	Master of Science in Software Engineering	MTR	Master of Translational Research
	Master of Science in Special Education	MTS	Master of Theatre Studies
MSSEM	Master of Science in Systems and Engineering Management		Master of Theological Studies
MSSI	Master of Science in Security Informatics	MTWM	Master of Trust and Wealth Management
	Master of Science in Strategic Intelligence	MTX	Master of Taxation
MSSL	Master of Science in School Leadership	MUA	Master of Urban Affairs
	Master of Science in Strategic Leadership	MUCD	Master of Urban and Community Design
MSSLP	Master of Science in Speech-Language Pathology	MUD	Master of Urban Design
MSSM	Master of Science in Sports Medicine	MUDS	Master of Urban Design Studies
MSSP	Master of Science in Social Policy	MUEP	Master of Urban and Environmental Planning
MSSPA	Master of Science in Student Personnel Administration	MUP	Master of Urban Planning
MSSS	Master of Science in Safety Science	MUPDD	Master of Urban Planning, Design, and Development
	Master of Science in Systems Science	MUPP	Master of Urban Planning and Policy
MSST	Master of Science in Security Technologies	MUPRED	Master of Urban Planning and Real Estate Development
MSSW	Master of Science in Social Work	MURP	Master of Urban and Regional Planning
MSSWE	Master of Science in Software Engineering		Master of Urban and Rural Planning
MST	Master of Science and Technology	MUS	Master of Urban Studies
	Master of Science in Taxation	MUSA	Master of Urban Spatial Analytics
	Master of Science in Teaching	MVP	Master of Voice Pedagogy
	Master of Science in Technology	MVPH	Master of Veterinary Public Health
	Master of Science in Telecommunications	MVS	Master of Visual Studies
	Master of Science Teaching	MWC	Master of Wildlife Conservation
MSTC	Master of Science in Technical Communication	MWM	Master of Water Management
	Master of Science in Telecommunications	MWPS	Master of Wood and Paper Science
MSTCM	Master of Science in Traditional Chinese Medicine	MWR	Master of Water Resources
MSTE	Master of Science in Telecommunications Engineering	MWS	Master of Women's Studies
	Master of Science in Transportation Engineering		Master of Worship Studies
MSTL	Master of Science in Teacher Leadership	MWSc	Master of Wildlife Science
MSTM	Master of Science in Technology Management	MZS	Master of Zoological Science
	Master of Science in Transfusion Medicine	Nav Arch	Naval Architecture
MSTOM	Master of Science in Traditional Oriental Medicine	Naval E	Naval Engineer
MSUASE	Master of Science in Unmanned and Autonomous Systems Engineering	ND	Doctor of Naturopathic Medicine
MSUD	Master of Science in Urban Design	NE	Nuclear Engineer
MSUS	Master of Science in Urban Studies	Nuc E	Nuclear Engineer
MSW	Master of Social Work	OD	Doctor of Optometry
MSWE	Master of Software Engineering	OTD	Doctor of Occupational Therapy
MSWREE	Master of Science in Water Resources and Environmental Engineering	PBME	Professional Master of Biomedical Engineering
MT	Master of Taxation	PC	Performer's Certificate
	Master of Teaching	PD	Professional Diploma
	Master of Technology	PGC	Post-Graduate Certificate
	Master of Textiles	PGD	Postgraduate Diploma
MTA	Master of Tax Accounting	Ph L	Licentiate of Philosophy
	Master of Teaching Arts	Pharm D	Doctor of Pharmacy
	Master of Tourism Administration	PhD	Doctor of Philosophy
MTCM	Master of Traditional Chinese Medicine	PhD Otol	Doctor of Philosophy in Otolaryngology
MTD	Master of Training and Development	PhD Surg	Doctor of Philosophy in Surgery
MTE	Master in Educational Technology	PhDEE	Doctor of Philosophy in Electrical Engineering
MTESOL	Master in Teaching English to Speakers of Other Languages	PMBA	Professional Master of Business Administration
		PMC	Post Master Certificate
		PMD	Post-Master's Diploma
		PMS	Professional Master of Science
			Professional Master's
		Post-Doctoral MS	Post-Doctoral Master of Science
		Post-MSN Certificate	Post-Master of Science in Nursing Certificate
		PPDPT	Postprofessional Doctor of Physical Therapy

Pro-MS	Professional Science Master's
Professional MA	Professional Master of Arts
Professional MBA	Professional Master of Business Administration
Professional MS	Professional Master of Science
PSM	Professional Master of Science
	Professional Science Master's
Psy D	Doctor of Psychology
Psy M	Master of Psychology
Psy S	Specialist in Psychology
Psya D	Doctor of Psychoanalysis
S Psy S	Specialist in Psychological Services
Sc D	Doctor of Science
Sc M	Master of Science
SCCT	Specialist in Community College Teaching
ScDPT	Doctor of Physical Therapy Science
SD	Doctor of Science
	Specialist Degree
SJD	Doctor of Juridical Sciences
SLPD	Doctor of Speech-Language Pathology
SM	Master of Science
SM Arch S	Master of Science in Architectural Studies

SMACT	Master of Science in Art, Culture and Technology
SMBT	Master of Science in Building Technology
SP	Specialist Degree
Sp Ed	Specialist in Education
Sp LIS	Specialist in Library and Information Science
SPA	Specialist in Arts
Spec	Specialist's Certificate
Spec M	Specialist in Music
Spt	Specialist Degree
SSP	Specialist in School Psychology
STB	Bachelor of Sacred Theology
STD	Doctor of Sacred Theology
STL	Licentiate of Sacred Theology
STM	Master of Sacred Theology
TDPT	Transitional Doctor of Physical Therapy
Th D	Doctor of Theology
Th M	Master of Theology
TOTD	Transitional Doctor of Occupational Therapy
VMD	Doctor of Veterinary Medicine
WEMBA	Weekend Executive Master of Business Administration
XMA	Executive Master of Arts

INDEXES

Displays and Close-Ups

Directories and Subject Areas

Following is an alphabetical listing of directories and subject areas. Also listed are cross-references for subject area names not used in the directory structure of the guides, for example, "City and Regional Planning (see Urban and Regional Planning)"

Graduate Programs in the Humanities, Arts & Social Sciences

Addictions/Substance Abuse Counseling
Administration (see Arts Administration; Public Administration)
African-American Studies
African Languages and Literatures (see African Studies)
African Studies
Agribusiness (see Agricultural Economics and Agribusiness)
Agricultural Economics and Agribusiness
Alcohol Abuse Counseling (see Addictions/Substance Abuse Counseling)
American Indian/Native American Studies
American Studies
Anthropology
Applied Arts and Design—General
Applied Behavior Analysis
Applied Economics
Applied History (see Public History)
Applied Psychology
Applied Social Research
Arabic (see Near and Middle Eastern Languages)
Arab Studies (see Near and Middle Eastern Studies)
Archaeology
Architectural History
Architecture
Archives Administration (see Public History)
Area and Cultural Studies (see African-American Studies; African Studies; American Indian/Native American Studies; American Studies; Asian-American Studies; Asian Studies; Canadian Studies; Cultural Studies; East European and Russian Studies; Ethnic Studies; Folklore; Gender Studies; Hispanic Studies; Holocaust Studies; Jewish Studies; Latin American Studies; Near and Middle Eastern Studies; Northern Studies; Pacific Area/Pacific Rim Studies; Western European Studies; Women's Studies)
Art/Fine Arts
Art History
Arts Administration
Arts Journalism
Art Therapy
Asian-American Studies
Asian Languages
Asian Studies
Behavioral Sciences (see Psychology)
Bible Studies (see Religion; Theology)
Biological Anthropology
Black Studies (see African-American Studies)
Broadcasting (see Communication; Film, Television, and Video Production)
Broadcast Journalism
Building Science
Canadian Studies
Celtic Languages
Ceramics (see Art/Fine Arts)
Child and Family Studies
Child Development
Chinese
Chinese Studies (see Asian Languages; Asian Studies)
Christian Studies (see Missions and Missiology; Religion; Theology)
Cinema (see Film, Television, and Video Production)
City and Regional Planning (see Urban and Regional Planning)
Classical Languages and Literatures (see Classics)
Classics

Clinical Psychology
Clothing and Textiles
Cognitive Psychology (see Psychology—General; Cognitive Sciences)
Cognitive Sciences
Communication—General
Community Affairs (see Urban and Regional Planning; Urban Studies)
Community Planning (see Architecture; Environmental Design; Urban and Regional Planning; Urban Design; Urban Studies)
Community Psychology (see Social Psychology)
Comparative and Interdisciplinary Arts
Comparative Literature
Composition (see Music)
Computer Art and Design
Conflict Resolution and Mediation/Peace Studies
Consumer Economics
Corporate and Organizational Communication
Corrections (see Criminal Justice and Criminology)
Counseling (see Counseling Psychology; Pastoral Ministry and Counseling)
Counseling Psychology
Crafts (see Art/Fine Arts)
Creative Arts Therapies (see Art Therapy; Therapies—Dance, Drama, and Music)
Criminal Justice and Criminology
Cultural Anthropology
Cultural Studies
Dance
Decorative Arts
Demography and Population Studies
Design (see Applied Arts and Design; Architecture; Art/Fine Arts; Environmental Design; Graphic Design; Industrial Design; Interior Design; Textile Design; Urban Design)
Developmental Psychology
Diplomacy (see International Affairs)
Disability Studies
Drama Therapy (see Therapies—Dance, Drama, and Music)
Dramatic Arts (see Theater)
Drawing (see Art/Fine Arts)
Drug Abuse Counseling (see Addictions/Substance Abuse Counseling)
Drug and Alcohol Abuse Counseling (see Addictions/Substance Abuse Counseling)
East Asian Studies (see Asian Studies)
East European and Russian Studies
Economic Development
Economics
Educational Theater (see Theater; Therapies—Dance, Drama, and Music)
Emergency Management
English
Environmental Design
Ethics
Ethnic Studies
Ethnomusicology (see Music)
Experimental Psychology
Family and Consumer Sciences—General
Family Studies (see Child and Family Studies)
Family Therapy (see Child and Family Studies; Clinical Psychology; Counseling Psychology; Marriage and Family Therapy)
Filmmaking (see Film, Television, and Video Production)
Film Studies (see Film, Television, and Video Production)
Film, Television, and Video Production
Film, Television, and Video Theory and Criticism
Fine Arts (see Art/Fine Arts)
Folklore
Foreign Languages (see specific language)
Foreign Service (see International Affairs; International Development)
Forensic Psychology
Forensic Sciences
Forensics (see Speech and Interpersonal Communication)
French

Gender Studies
General Studies (*see* Liberal Studies)
Genetic Counseling
Geographic Information Systems
Geography
German
Gerontology
Graphic Design
Greek (*see* Classics)
Health Communication
Health Psychology
Hebrew (*see* Near and Middle Eastern Languages)
Hebrew Studies (*see* Jewish Studies)
Hispanic and Latin American Languages
Hispanic Studies
Historic Preservation
History
History of Art (*see* Art History)
History of Medicine
History of Science and Technology
Holocaust and Genocide Studies
Home Economics (*see* Family and Consumer Sciences—General)
Homeland Security
Household Economics, Sciences, and Management (*see* Family and Consumer Sciences—General)
Human Development
Humanities
Illustration
Industrial and Labor Relations
Industrial and Organizational Psychology
Industrial Design
Interdisciplinary Studies
Interior Design
International Affairs
International Development
International Economics
International Service (*see* International Affairs; International Development)
International Trade Policy
Internet and Interactive Multimedia
Interpersonal Communication (*see* Speech and Interpersonal Communication)
Interpretation (*see* Translation and Interpretation)
Islamic Studies (*see* Near and Middle Eastern Studies; Religion)
Italian
Japanese
Japanese Studies (*see* Asian Languages; Asian Studies; Japanese)
Jewelry (*see* Art/Fine Arts)
Jewish Studies
Journalism
Judaic Studies (*see* Jewish Studies; Religion)
Labor Relations (*see* Industrial and Labor Relations)
Landscape Architecture
Latin American Studies
Latin (*see* Classics)
Law Enforcement (*see* Criminal Justice and Criminology)
Liberal Studies
Lighting Design
Linguistics
Literature (*see* Classics; Comparative Literature; specific language)
Marriage and Family Therapy
Mass Communication
Media Studies
Medical Illustration
Medieval and Renaissance Studies
Metalsmithing (*see* Art/Fine Arts)
Middle Eastern Studies (*see* Near and Middle Eastern Studies)
Military and Defense Studies
Mineral Economics
Ministry (*see* Pastoral Ministry and Counseling; Theology)
Missions and Missiology
Motion Pictures (*see* Film, Television, and Video Production)
Museum Studies
Music
Musicology (*see* Music)
Music Therapy (*see* Therapies—Dance, Drama, and Music)

National Security
Native American Studies (*see* American Indian/Native American Studies)
Near and Middle Eastern Languages
Near and Middle Eastern Studies
Near Environment (*see* Family and Consumer Sciences)
Northern Studies
Organizational Psychology (*see* Industrial and Organizational Psychology)
Oriental Languages (*see* Asian Languages)
Oriental Studies (*see* Asian Studies)
Pacific Area/Pacific Rim Studies
Painting (*see* Art/Fine Arts)
Pastoral Ministry and Counseling
Philanthropic Studies
Philosophy
Photography
Playwriting (*see* Theater; Writing)
Policy Studies (*see* Public Policy)
Political Science
Population Studies (*see* Demography and Population Studies)
Portuguese
Printmaking (*see* Art/Fine Arts)
Product Design (*see* Industrial Design)
Psychoanalysis and Psychotherapy
Psychology—General
Public Administration
Public Affairs
Public History
Public Policy
Public Speaking (*see* Mass Communication; Rhetoric; Speech and Interpersonal Communication)
Publishing
Regional Planning (*see* Architecture; Urban and Regional Planning; Urban Design; Urban Studies)
Rehabilitation Counseling
Religion
Renaissance Studies (*see* Medieval and Renaissance Studies)
Rhetoric
Romance Languages
Romance Literatures (*see* Romance Languages)
Rural Planning and Studies
Rural Sociology
Russian
Scandinavian Languages
School Psychology
Sculpture (*see* Art/Fine Arts)
Security Administration (*see* Criminal Justice and Criminology)
Slavic Languages
Slavic Studies (*see* East European and Russian Studies; Slavic Languages)
Social Psychology
Social Sciences
Sociology
Southeast Asian Studies (*see* Asian Studies)
Soviet Studies (*see* East European and Russian Studies; Russian)
Spanish
Speech and Interpersonal Communication
Sport Psychology
Studio Art (*see* Art/Fine Arts)
Substance Abuse Counseling (*see* Addictions/Substance Abuse Counseling)
Survey Methodology
Sustainable Development
Technical Communication
Technical Writing
Telecommunications (*see* Film, Television, and Video Production)
Television (*see* Film, Television, and Video Production)
Textile Design
Textiles (*see* Clothing and Textiles; Textile Design)
Thanatology
Theater
Theater Arts (*see* Theater)
Theology
Therapies—Dance, Drama, and Music
Translation and Interpretation

Transpersonal and Humanistic Psychology
Urban and Regional Planning
Urban Design
Urban Planning (*see* Architecture; Urban and Regional Planning; Urban Design; Urban Studies)
Urban Studies
Video (*see* Film, Television, and Video Production)
Visual Arts (*see* Applied Arts and Design; Art/Fine Arts; Film, Television, and Video Production; Graphic Design; Illustration; Photography)
Western European Studies
Women's Studies
World Wide Web (*see* Internet and Interactive Multimedia)
Writing

Graduate Programs in the Biological/ Biomedical Sciences & Health-Related Medical Professions

Acupuncture and Oriental Medicine
Acute Care/Critical Care Nursing Administration (*see* Health Services Management and Hospital Administration; Nursing and Healthcare Administration; Pharmaceutical Administration)
Adult Nursing
Advanced Practice Nursing (*see* Family Nurse Practitioner Studies)
Allied Health—General
Allied Health Professions (*see* Clinical Laboratory Sciences/Medical Technology; Clinical Research; Communication Disorders; Dental Hygiene; Emergency Medical Services; Occupational Therapy; Physical Therapy; Physician Assistant Studies; Rehabilitation Sciences)
Allopathic Medicine
Anatomy
Anesthesiologist Assistant Studies
Animal Behavior
Bacteriology
Behavioral Sciences (*see* Biopsychology; Neuroscience; Zoology)
Biochemistry
Bioethics
Biological and Biomedical Sciences—General Biological Chemistry (*see* Biochemistry)
Biological Oceanography (*see* Marine Biology)
Biophysics
Biopsychology
Botany
Breeding (*see* Botany; Plant Biology; Genetics)
Cancer Biology/Oncology
Cardiovascular Sciences
Cell Biology
Cellular Physiology (*see* Cell Biology; Physiology)
Child-Care Nursing (*see* Maternal and Child/Neonatal Nursing)
Chiropractic
Clinical Laboratory Sciences/Medical Technology
Clinical Research
Community Health
Community Health Nursing
Computational Biology
Conservation (*see* Conservation Biology; Environmental Biology)
Conservation Biology
Crop Sciences (*see* Botany; Plant Biology)
Cytology (*see* Cell Biology)
Dental and Oral Surgery (*see* Oral and Dental Sciences)
Dental Assistant Studies (*see* Dental Hygiene)
Dental Hygiene
Dental Services (*see* Dental Hygiene)
Dentistry
Developmental Biology Dietetics (*see* Nutrition)
Ecology
Embryology (*see* Developmental Biology)
Emergency Medical Services
Endocrinology (*see* Physiology)
Entomology

Environmental Biology
Environmental and Occupational Health
Epidemiology
Evolutionary Biology
Family Nurse Practitioner Studies
Foods (*see* Nutrition)
Forensic Nursing
Genetics
Genomic Sciences
Gerontological Nursing
Health Physics/Radiological Health
Health Promotion
Health-Related Professions (*see* individual allied health professions)
Health Services Management and Hospital Administration
Health Services Research
Histology (*see* Anatomy; Cell Biology)
HIV/AIDS Nursing
Hospice Nursing
Hospital Administration (*see* Health Services Management and Hospital Administration)
Human Genetics
Immunology
Industrial Hygiene
Infectious Diseases
International Health
Laboratory Medicine (*see* Clinical Laboratory Sciences/Medical Technology; Immunology; Microbiology; Pathology)
Life Sciences (*see* Biological and Biomedical Sciences)
Marine Biology
Maternal and Child Health
Maternal and Child/Neonatal Nursing
Medical Imaging
Medical Microbiology
Medical Nursing (*see* Medical/Surgical Nursing)
Medical Physics
Medical/Surgical Nursing
Medical Technology (*see* Clinical Laboratory Sciences/Medical Technology)
Medical Sciences (*see* Biological and Biomedical Sciences)
Medical Science Training Programs (*see* Biological and Biomedical Sciences)
Medicinal and Pharmaceutical Chemistry
Medicinal Chemistry (*see* Medicinal and Pharmaceutical Chemistry)
Medicine (*see* Allopathic Medicine; Naturopathic Medicine; Osteopathic Medicine; Podiatric Medicine)
Microbiology
Midwifery (*see* Nurse Midwifery)
Molecular Biology
Molecular Biophysics
Molecular Genetics
Molecular Medicine
Molecular Pathogenesis
Molecular Pathology
Molecular Pharmacology
Molecular Physiology
Molecular Toxicology
Naturopathic Medicine
Neural Sciences (*see* Biopsychology; Neurobiology; Neuroscience)
Neurobiology
Neuroendocrinology (*see* Biopsychology; Neurobiology; Neuroscience; Physiology)
Neuropharmacology (*see* Biopsychology; Neurobiology; Neuroscience; Pharmacology)
Neurophysiology (*see* Biopsychology; Neurobiology; Neuroscience; Physiology)
Neuroscience
Nuclear Medical Technology (*see* Clinical Laboratory Sciences/ Medical Technology)
Nurse Anesthesia
Nurse Midwifery
Nurse Practitioner Studies (*see* Family Nurse Practitioner Studies)
Nursing Administration (*see* Nursing and Healthcare Administration)
Nursing and Healthcare Administration
Nursing Education
Nursing—General
Nursing Informatics

Nutrition
Occupational Health (*see* Environmental and Occupational Health; Occupational Health Nursing)
Occupational Health Nursing
Occupational Therapy
Oncology (*see* Cancer Biology/Oncology)
Oncology Nursing
Optometry
Oral and Dental Sciences
Oral Biology (*see* Oral and Dental Sciences)
Oral Pathology (*see* Oral and Dental Sciences)
Organismal Biology (*see* Biological and Biomedical Sciences; Zoology)
Oriental Medicine and Acupuncture (*see* Acupuncture and Oriental Medicine)
Orthodontics (*see* Oral and Dental Sciences)
Osteopathic Medicine
Parasitology
Pathobiology
Pathology
Pediatric Nursing
Pedontics (*see* Oral and Dental Sciences)
Perfusion
Pharmaceutical Administration
Pharmaceutical Chemistry (*see* Medicinal and Pharmaceutical Chemistry)
Pharmaceutical Sciences
Pharmacology
Pharmacy
Photobiology of Cells and Organelles (*see* Botany; Cell Biology; Plant Biology)
Physical Therapy
Physician Assistant Studies
Physiological Optics (*see* Vision Sciences)
Podiatric Medicine
Preventive Medicine (*see* Community Health and Public Health)
Physiological Optics (*see* Physiology)
Physiology
Plant Biology
Plant Molecular Biology
Plant Pathology
Plant Physiology
Pomology (*see* Botany; Plant Biology)
Psychiatric Nursing
Public Health—General
Public Health Nursing (*see* Community Health Nursing)
Psychiatric Nursing
Psychobiology (*see* Biopsychology)
Psychopharmacology (*see* Biopsychology; Neuroscience; Pharmacology)
Radiation Biology
Radiological Health (*see* Health Physics/Radiological Health)
Rehabilitation Nursing
Rehabilitation Sciences
Rehabilitation Therapy (*see* Physical Therapy)
Reproductive Biology
School Nursing
Sociobiology (*see* Evolutionary Biology)
Structural Biology
Surgical Nursing (*see* Medical/Surgical Nursing)
Systems Biology
Teratology
Therapeutics
Theoretical Biology (*see* Biological and Biomedical Sciences)
Therapeutics (*see* Pharmaceutical Sciences; Pharmacology; Pharmacy)
Toxicology
Transcultural Nursing
Translational Biology
Tropical Medicine (*see* Parasitology)
Veterinary Medicine
Veterinary Sciences
Virology
Vision Sciences
Wildlife Biology (*see* Zoology)
Women's Health Nursing
Zoology

Graduate Programs in the Physical Sciences, Mathematics, Agricultural Sciences, the Environment & Natural Resources

Acoustics
Agricultural Sciences
Agronomy and Soil Sciences
Analytical Chemistry
Animal Sciences
Applied Mathematics
Applied Physics
Applied Statistics
Aquaculture
Astronomy
Astrophysical Sciences (*see* Astrophysics; Atmospheric Sciences; Meteorology; Planetary and Space Sciences)
Astrophysics
Atmospheric Sciences
Biological Oceanography (*see* Marine Affairs; Marine Sciences; Oceanography)
Biomathematics
Biometry
Biostatistics
Chemical Physics
Chemistry
Computational Sciences
Condensed Matter Physics
Dairy Science (*see* Animal Sciences)
Earth Sciences (*see* Geosciences)
Environmental Management and Policy
Environmental Sciences
Environmental Studies (*see* Environmental Management and Policy)
Experimental Statistics (*see* Statistics)
Fish, Game, and Wildlife Management
Food Science and Technology
Forestry
General Science (*see* specific topics)
Geochemistry
Geodetic Sciences
Geological Engineering (*see* Geology)
Geological Sciences (*see* Geology)
Geology
Geophysical Fluid Dynamics (*see* Geophysics)
Geophysics
Geosciences
Horticulture
Hydrogeology
Hydrology
Inorganic Chemistry
Limnology
Marine Affairs
Marine Geology
Marine Sciences
Marine Studies (*see* Marine Affairs; Marine Geology; Marine Sciences; Oceanography)
Mathematical and Computational Finance
Mathematical Physics
Mathematical Statistics (*see* Applied Statistics; Statistics)
Mathematics
Meteorology
Mineralogy
Natural Resource Management (*see* Environmental Management and Policy; Natural Resources)
Natural Resources
Nuclear Physics (*see* Physics)
Ocean Engineering (*see* Marine Affairs; Marine Geology; Marine Sciences; Oceanography)
Oceanography
Optical Sciences
Optical Technologies (*see* Optical Sciences)
Optics (*see* Applied Physics; Optical Sciences; Physics)
Organic Chemistry

Paleontology
Paper Chemistry (*see* Chemistry)
Photonics
Physical Chemistry
Physics
Planetary and Space Sciences
Plant Sciences
Plasma Physics
Poultry Science (*see* Animal Sciences)
Radiological Physics (*see* Physics)
Range Management (*see* Range Science)
Range Science
Resource Management (*see* Environmental Management and Policy; Natural Resources)
Solid-Earth Sciences (*see* Geosciences)
Space Sciences (*see* Planetary and Space Sciences)
Statistics
Theoretical Chemistry
Theoretical Physics
Viticulture and Enology
Water Resources

Graduate Programs in Engineering & Applied Sciences

Aeronautical Engineering (*see* Aerospace/Aeronautical Engineering)
Aerospace/Aeronautical Engineering
Aerospace Studies (*see* Aerospace/Aeronautical Engineering)
Agricultural Engineering
Applied Mechanics (*see* Mechanics)
Applied Science and Technology
Architectural Engineering
Artificial Intelligence/Robotics
Astronautical Engineering (*see* Aerospace/Aeronautical Engineering)
Automotive Engineering
Aviation
Biochemical Engineering
Bioengineering
Bioinformatics
Biological Engineering (*see* Bioengineering)
Biomedical Engineering
Biosystems Engineering
Biotechnology
Ceramic Engineering (*see* Ceramic Sciences and Engineering)
Ceramic Sciences and Engineering
Ceramics (*see* Ceramic Sciences and Engineering)
Chemical Engineering
Civil Engineering
Computer and Information Systems Security
Computer Engineering
Computer Science
Computing Technology (*see* Computer Science)
Construction Engineering
Construction Management
Database Systems
Electrical Engineering
Electronic Materials
Electronics Engineering (*see* Electrical Engineering)
Energy and Power Engineering
Energy Management and Policy
Engineering and Applied Sciences
Engineering and Public Affairs (*see* Technology and Public Policy)
Engineering and Public Policy (*see* Energy Management and Policy; Technology and Public Policy)
Engineering Design
Engineering Management
Engineering Mechanics (*see* Mechanics)
Engineering Metallurgy (*see* Metallurgical Engineering and Metallurgy)
Engineering Physics
Environmental Design (*see* Environmental Engineering)
Environmental Engineering
Ergonomics and Human Factors

Financial Engineering
Fire Protection Engineering
Food Engineering (*see* Agricultural Engineering)
Game Design and Development
Gas Engineering (*see* Petroleum Engineering)
Geological Engineering
Geophysics Engineering (*see* Geological Engineering)
Geotechnical Engineering
Hazardous Materials Management
Health Informatics
Health Systems (*see* Safety Engineering; Systems Engineering)
Highway Engineering (*see* Transportation and Highway Engineering)
Human-Computer Interaction
Human Factors (*see* Ergonomics and Human Factors)
Hydraulics
Hydrology (*see* Water Resources Engineering)
Industrial Engineering (*see* Industrial/Management Engineering)
Industrial/Management Engineering
Information Science
Internet Engineering
Macromolecular Science (*see* Polymer Science and Engineering)
Management Engineering (*see* Engineering Management; Industrial/Management Engineering)
Management of Technology
Manufacturing Engineering
Marine Engineering (*see* Civil Engineering)
Materials Engineering
Materials Sciences
Mechanical Engineering
Mechanics
Medical Informatics
Metallurgical Engineering and Metallurgy
Metallurgy (*see* Metallurgical Engineering and Metallurgy)
Mineral/Mining Engineering
Modeling and Simulation
Nanotechnology
Nuclear Engineering
Ocean Engineering
Operations Research
Paper and Pulp Engineering
Petroleum Engineering
Pharmaceutical Engineering
Plastics Engineering (*see* Polymer Science and Engineering)
Polymer Science and Engineering
Public Policy (*see* Energy Management and Policy; Technology and Public Policy)
Reliability Engineering
Robotics (*see* Artificial Intelligence/Robotics)
Safety Engineering
Software Engineering
Solid-State Sciences (*see* Materials Sciences)
Structural Engineering
Surveying Science and Engineering
Systems Analysis (*see* Systems Engineering)
Systems Engineering
Systems Science
Technology and Public Policy
Telecommunications
Telecommunications Management
Textile Sciences and Engineering
Textiles (*see* Textile Sciences and Engineering)
Transportation and Highway Engineering
Urban Systems Engineering (*see* Systems Engineering)
Waste Management (*see* Hazardous Materials Management)
Water Resources Engineering

Graduate Programs in Business, Education, Information Studies, Law & Social Work

Accounting
Actuarial Science

Adult Education
Advertising and Public Relations
Agricultural Education
Alcohol Abuse Counseling (*see* Counselor Education)
Archival Management and Studies
Art Education
Athletics Administration (*see* Kinesiology and Movement Studies)
Athletic Training and Sports Medicine
Audiology (*see* Communication Disorders)
Aviation Management
Banking (*see* Finance and Banking)
Business Administration and Management—General
Business Education
Communication Disorders
Community College Education
Computer Education
Continuing Education (*see* Adult Education)
Counseling (*see* Counselor Education)
Counselor Education
Curriculum and Instruction
Developmental Education
Distance Education Development
Drug Abuse Counseling (*see* Counselor Education)
Early Childhood Education
Educational Leadership and Administration
Educational Measurement and Evaluation
Educational Media/Instructional Technology
Educational Policy
Educational Psychology
Education—General
Education of the Blind (*see* Special Education)
Education of the Deaf (*see* Special Education)
Education of the Gifted
Education of the Hearing Impaired (*see* Special Education)
Education of the Learning Disabled (*see* Special Education)
Education of the Mentally Retarded (*see* Special Education)
Education of the Physically Handicapped (*see* Special Education)
Education of Students with Severe/Multiple Disabilities
Education of the Visually Handicapped (*see* Special Education)
Electronic Commerce
Elementary Education
English as a Second Language
English Education
Entertainment Management
Entrepreneurship
Environmental Education
Environmental Law
Exercise and Sports Science
Exercise Physiology (*see* Kinesiology and Movement Studies)
Facilities and Entertainment Management
Finance and Banking
Food Services Management (*see* Hospitality Management)
Foreign Languages Education
Foundations and Philosophy of Education
Guidance and Counseling (*see* Counselor Education)
Health Education
Health Law
Hearing Sciences (*see* Communication Disorders)
Higher Education
Home Economics Education
Hospitality Management
Hotel Management (*see* Travel and Tourism)
Human Resources Development
Human Resources Management
Human Services
Industrial Administration (*see* Industrial and Manufacturing Management)
Industrial and Manufacturing Management
Industrial Education (*see* Vocational and Technical Education)
Information Studies
Instructional Technology (*see* Educational Media/Instructional Technology)
Insurance
Intellectual Property Law
International and Comparative Education
International Business

International Commerce (*see* International Business)
International Economics (*see* International Business)
International Trade (*see* International Business)
Investment and Securities (*see* Business Administration and Management; Finance and Banking; Investment Management)
Investment Management
Junior College Education (*see* Community College Education)
Kinesiology and Movement Studies
Law
Legal and Justice Studies
Leisure Services (*see* Recreation and Park Management)
Leisure Studies
Library Science
Logistics
Management (*see* Business Administration and Management)
Management Information Systems
Management Strategy and Policy
Marketing
Marketing Research
Mathematics Education
Middle School Education
Movement Studies (*see* Kinesiology and Movement Studies)
Multilingual and Multicultural Education
Museum Education
Music Education
Nonprofit Management
Nursery School Education (*see* Early Childhood Education)
Occupational Education (*see* Vocational and Technical Education)
Organizational Behavior
Organizational Management
Parks Administration (*see* Recreation and Park Management)
Personnel (*see* Human Resources Development; Human Resources Management; Organizational Behavior; Organizational Management; Student Affairs)
Philosophy of Education (*see* Foundations and Philosophy of Education)
Physical Education
Project Management
Public Relations (*see* Advertising and Public Relations)
Quality Management
Quantitative Analysis
Reading Education
Real Estate
Recreation and Park Management
Recreation Therapy (*see* Recreation and Park Management)
Religious Education
Remedial Education (*see* Special Education)
Restaurant Administration (*see* Hospitality Management)
Science Education
Secondary Education
Social Sciences Education
Social Studies Education (*see* Social Sciences Education)
Social Work
Special Education
Speech-Language Pathology and Audiology (*see* Communication Disorders)
Sports Management
Sports Medicine (*see* Athletic Training and Sports Medicine)
Sports Psychology and Sociology (*see* Kinesiology and Movement Studies)
Student Affairs
Substance Abuse Counseling (*see* Counselor Education)
Supply Chain Management
Sustainability Management
Systems Management (*see* Management Information Systems)
Taxation
Teacher Education (*see* specific subject areas)
Teaching English as a Second Language (*see* English as a Second Language)
Technical Education (*see* Vocational and Technical Education)
Transportation Management
Travel and Tourism
Urban Education
Vocational and Technical Education
Vocational Counseling (*see* Counselor Education)

Directories and Subject Areas in this Book

NOTES

NOTES

NOTES

NOTES